HALLIWELL'S FILM & VIDEO GUIDE

Also edited by John Walker

HALLIWELL'S FILM QUIZ BOOK
HALLIWELL'S WHO'S WHO IN THE MOVIES

HALLIWELL'S FILM & VIDEO GUIDE 2004

LESLIE HALLIWELL

19th EDITION
Revised and Updated

Edited by
JOHN WALKER

HarperCollins*Entertainment*
An Imprint of HarperCollins*Publishers*

HarperCollins*Entertainment*
An Imprint of HarperCollins*Publishers*
77–85 Fulham Palace Road,
Hammersmith, London W6 8JB

www.harpercollins.co.uk

2004/Nineteenth edition published by HarperCollins*Publishers* 2003
1 3 5 7 9 8 6 4 2

First published by Granada 1977
Second edition 1979
Third edition 1981
Fourth edition 1983
Fifth edition 1985
Sixth edition published by Grafton Books 1987
Seventh edition 1989
Eighth edition 1991
Ninth edition published by HarperCollins*Publishers* 1993
Tenth edition 1994
Eleventh edition 1995
Twelfth edition 1996
Thirteenth edition 1997
Fourteenth edition 1998
Fifteenth edition 1999
Sixteenth edition 2000
Seventeenth edition 2001
Eighteenth edition 2002

A catalogue record for this book is
available from the British Library

ISBN 0 00 716712 1

Set in Goudy and Frutiger

Printed and bound by Legoprint Spa, Italy

Contents

Introduction

Welcome to the new edition of *Halliwell's Film, Video and DVD Guide*. As ever, packed into its many pages is as much information and detail as will fit about most of the films you are likely to encounter.

The *Guide* concentrates on movies made to be seen in the cinema, that temple of mass entertainment; it does also include films that, for one reason or another, failed to obtain a cinema release but which are available on video, DVD or can be seen on the often inadequate medium of television, which still treats them with contempt: butchering them to remove what it deems offensive, and chopping them up between distracting advertisements or even lengthy news bulletins. The *Guide* does not, however, include movies made for television, because, with very few exceptions, they are never more than time-wasters.

It has been another mixed year for movie enthusiasts, with Hollywood suffering from a failure of imagination, the British film industry in its usual state of disarray, and far too few foreign movies getting distribution here.

The highpoints included Roman Polanski's *The Pianist*, which deservedly won him an Oscar as director and Adrien Brody one as best actor; two very different but equally effective films from Philip Noyce – *Rabbit Proof Fence* and the timely *The Quiet American*; Michael Moore's *Bowling for Columbine*, which helped raise the profile of documentaries; the continuing collaboration of director Spike Jonze and screenwriter Charlie Kaufman with their wildly inventive *Adaptation*; Stephen Daldry's *The Hours*; and John Sayles' *Sunshine State*.

Unfortunately, Hollywood movies are becoming longer rather than better, turning into bloated monsters in which narrative and characterization are subordinated to special effects. Computer-generated effects have given modern directors the ability to show us brave new worlds and images never seen before, and all they can think of doing with this power is to compete with one another in staging ever-bigger and noisier car chases and crashes.

There was a telling correction in a recent edition of the film magazine *Premiere*, after stating that a new movie was to be made about the Roman emperor Constantine – 'it is, in fact, based on the DC comic-book character, John Constantine.' Indeed, it did seem improbable that Hollywood would consider making a movie about Constantine the Great, a man who played a pivotal role in history, ensuring the survival of Christianity throughout the Roman Empire, when there is still a comic-book character ripe for exploitation.

Just as every major Hollywood movie in the summer of 2003 was either a sequel or based on a comic-book, or both (with one exception, and that was inspired by a theme-park ride), so the future is equally uninspiring. There are currently a dozen comic-book movies in production and even more sequels and re-makes on the way.

Mouldering TV shows from the '70s are still being transformed into equally lacklustre big-budget movies. One studio recently had staff going through all its old movies to discover which could be re-made. Even past classics such as *Kind Hearts and Coronets* are not safe from meddling hands. The good news is that adventurous directors are becoming excited by the possibilities of shooting in digital video, perhaps inspired by the example of Iranian filmmakers who have shown that engrossing movies can be made on minimal budgets. The results so far have been patchy, but it gives hope for future originality and perhaps offers them and us a means of escape from the major studios' current stultifying attitudes.

I owe thanks to the many readers who have written to me with suggestions and criticisms. I'm grateful for the editorial skills of Monica Chakraverty and the technical expertise of Alan Trewartha at HarperCollins; and to the support of my agents Rivers Scott and Gloria Ferris. My love, as ever, goes to my wife Barbara, who lights my way out of the darkness in which I spend my working days.

John Walker

Explanatory Notes

Alphabetical Order

Unlike some books which take the complete title into account, as though there were no gaps between words, we have always persevered with the old-fashioned word-at-a-time arrangement. Thus, all titles starting with *In*, including *In Which We Serve*, are used up before one goes on to titles beginning *Incredible*, *Inspector*, *Intolerance*. Hyphenated or apostrophized words are counted as one word. Compressions such as *Dr* and *St* are treated as though they had been spelled out, as *Doctor* and *Saint*. *Mac* and *Mc* are regarded as interchangeable under *Mac*. Titles consisting of initials, such as *C. C. and Company* or *D.O.A.* are dealt with at the beginning of each alphabetical section, except where they have become acronyms (i.e. pronounceable as one word, e.g. AWOL). In all cases the complete title is given as billed, though the definite and indefinite articles are not counted in the alphabetical arrangement where they occur as the first word of a title. The spelling of the country of origin is used, e.g. *My Favorite Blonde* and not *My Favourite Blonde*.

Individual Entries

All entries follow the same format and the notes are set out below in the order in which they will be encountered.

Publicity tags These were used in the promotion of the film and, in the manner of trailers, precede the entry.

Ratings These range from none to four stars. Four stars indicate a film outstanding in many ways, a milestone in cinema history, remarkable for acting, direction, writing, photography or some other aspect of technique. Three stars indicate a very high standard of professional excellence or great historical interest. Or, if you like, three strong reasons for admiring it. Two stars indicate a good level of competence and a generally entertaining film. One star indicates a film not very satisfactory as a whole; it could be a failed giant or a second feature with a few interesting ideas among the dross. No stars at all indicates a totally routine production or worse; such films may be watchable but are at least equally missable.

Country of origin This is the first item on the second line.

Year of release This comes after the country of origin and is intended to indicate the year when the film was first shown, which is not necessarily the year that it was made. Dating is sometimes an onerous task, and the result debatable.

Running time This is given in minutes, signified by 'm'. So far as possible, this is the original release time. Very many films are cut as they appear in different countries, sometimes by twenty minutes or more. An engineering function of British television results in an imperceptible speeding-up of projection and a consequent loss of one minute in every twenty-five. A hundred-minute film, therefore, will run only ninety-six minutes on the box.

Colour This is indicated by 'bw' for black and white films and 'colour' for the others. The colour process used, such as Technicolor, is given when known.

Other notable points These are given at the end of the second line, indicating the use of a special process, such as Panavision.

Production credit This is the central credit on the third line. To the left comes the name of the distributor, which is followed by the production company if different. To the right comes the name or names of the actual producer – in brackets, unless he has a stake in the production, in which case he follows an oblique. These days, many films tend to have more producers of one kind or another than actors. The credit here refers to the person bearing the title of producer rather than to the executive producer, associate producer, production executive and so on.

Family viewing 👪 indicates that the film is suitable for family viewing, i.e. by parents together with young film-goers aged from four to fourteen.

Video ▪ indicates that the film has been released on VHS video-cassette for the British PAL system. ▪ indicates that the film has been released on VHS video-cassette for the British PAL system in wide-screen format. ✪ indicates that the film has been released on VHS video-cassette in a computer-colourized version. ▪ indicates that the film has been released in the American NTSC format (which is not compatible with the British PAL system). ◉ indicates that the film is available on laser disc in either American NTSC format or British PAL format. ◉ indicates that the film is available on Video CD. ♫ indicates that the film's soundtrack music has been released on compact disc. Video and record releases come and go with great rapidity these days; all that it is possible to indicate is whether a title has been available at some time. If a film or soundtrack has been available in the past, then it is very likely to become available again in the future. If you are desperate to acquire a particular film or soundtrack album, then it would be worthwhile checking film magazines for advertisements from companies that specialize in tracking down deleted titles. ◉ indicates DVD (Digital Video Disc) releases in Region 1 and ◉ indicates DVD releases in Region 2.

Alternative title This is given on a separate line, usually with a note of the country in which it was used. If no such distinction exists, the formula aka (also known as) is used. Alternative titles are also listed individually, cross-referenced to the main entry for the film to which they belong.

Synopsis This is a brief description of the film's plot.

Assessment Again, this is brief and to the point.

Writer credit (*w*) This appears first since the script precedes direction and is therefore, at least sometimes, more important than the director credit. The author of the screenplay is given; if this derives from a novel, play, musical, or story, this is given next, together with the original author.

Director credit (*d*) This follows next. If the director is also the writer, then there will be a combined *wd* credit.

Photography credit (*ph*) This indicates the cinematographer or lighting cameraman, otherwise known as the director of photography, rather than the actual camera operator.

Music credit (*m*) This means the composer of the background music score. Sometimes there is only a music director (*md*) who orchestrates library or classical music. When noteworthy songs are performed in a film, or are specially written for it, those responsible are indicated by a credit for music and lyrics (*m/ly*) or simply *songs*.

Other credits These include art director (*ad*), choreographer (*ch*), costume designer (*costume*), film editor (*ed*), production designer (*pd*) and special effects (*sp*). They are given when they seem important and when they can be found. In some cases it has not been possible to track down all the credits one would wish.

Cast ☆ A list of the principal actors is given, roughly in order of importance.

Italics These denote a contribution of a particularly high standard.

Critical comments Brief quotes from well-known professional critics are appended to many entries, sometimes because they wittily confirm the assessments and some times because they provide alternative opinions. The absence of a quote casts no reflection whatever on the film, only on the difficulty of finding an opinion worth quoting.

Additional notes Any points of interest about the film are given after the symbol †. The symbol ♫ indicates notable songs which appear in the film.

Academy Awards Awards ♟ and nominations ♙ are listed for all principal categories, including best picture, acting, direction, photography, music score and songs, and some minor ones, such as sound and make-up, when they seem of interest. British Academy of Film and Television Arts awards follow the symbol ☺.

A Bout de Souffle ****
France 1960 90m bw
SNC (Georges de Beauregard)
aka: *Breathless*
A young car thief kills a policeman and goes on the run with his American girlfriend.
Casual, influential, New Wave reminiscence of both Quai des Brumes and innumerable American gangster thrillers. (The film is dedicated to Monogram.) One of the first and most influential films of the French New Wave.
w Jean-Luc Godard *story* *François Truffaut*
d Jean-Luc Godard *ph* Raoul Coutard *m* Martial Solal *ed* Cécile Decugis
☆ *Jean-Paul Belmondo*, Jean Seberg, Daniel Boulanger, Jean-Pierre Melville, Jean-Luc Godard
'A film all dressed up for rebellion but with no real tangible territory on which to stand and fight.' – *Peter John Dyer*
† See also *Breathless* (1983), American remake.

A Double Tour
France/Italy 1959 110m Eastmancolor
Paris/Panitalia (Robert and Raymond Hakim)
aka: *Web of Passion*
A wealthy wine grower has trouble with his wife, his children, his best friend, and his mistress across the way, who is murdered.
Talented but irritating mixture of Hitchcock and Les Parents Terribles; rather an undergraduatish romp.
w Paul Gégauff *novel La Clé de la Rue Saint-Nicolas* *d* Claude Chabrol *ph* Henri Decaë *m* Paul Misraki
☆ Jacques Dacqmine, Madeleine Robinson, Jean-Paul Belmondo, Bernadette Lafont, Antonella Lualdi, André Jocelyn

'Journey To A World Where Robots Dream And Desire.'
A.I. Artificial Intelligence *
US 2001 145m
Warner/DreamWork/Amblin/Stanley Kubrick (Kathleen Kennedy, Steven Spielberg, Bonnie Curtis)
The first robot child to have emotions searches for the mother who abandons him so that she may love him.
Overlong, often spectacular, but fuzzy updating of the story of Pinocchio. Beneath its surface gloss, and sentimental whimsy, there is a darker theme of the end of humankind: the narrative equates love with biological imprinting and prefers mechanical fantasy to messier humanity.
wd Steven Spielberg *screen story* Ian Watson *story* *Supertoys Last All Summer Long* by Brian Aldiss *ph* Janusz Kaminski *m* John Williams *pd* Rick Carter *ed* Michael Kahn *cos* Bob Ringwood
☆ Haley Joel Osment (David), Jude Law (Gigolo Joe), Frances O'Connor (Monica Swinton), Brendan Gleeson (Lord Johnson-Johnson), Sam Robards (Henry Swinton), William Hurt (Professor Hobby), Jake Thomas (Martin Swinton), Ken Leung (Syatyoo-Sama), Michael Mantell (Dr Frazier), Michael Berresse (Stage Manager), Kathryn Morris (Teenage Honey), Adrian Grenier (Teen in Van)
'A dark, demanding piece of entertainment that's well worth seeing.' – *Cosmo Landesman, Sunday Times*
'Any movie buff worth his salt will want to sift through this fascinating wreck of a movie.' – *Peter Travers, Rolling Stone*
'Those gagging on the glut of cinematic junk food should welcome this brilliantly made visionary work that's bursting with provocative ideas.' – *Todd McCarthy, Variety*
† The film cost $90m and took $78m at the US box-office.
John Williams; visual effects (Dennis Muren, Scott Farrar, Stan Winston, Michael Lantieri)

AKA *
GB 2002 123m colour
City Screen/Julian Thunderock (Richard West)
In the 1970s, a working-class youth goes to Paris and, claiming to be the son of an aristocrat, mixes in the camper circles of high society.
Clever semi-autobiographical drama of class and identity, given a certain novelty by having the action shown on a screen split three ways.
d Duncan Roy *ph* Scott Taylor, Steve Smith, Claire Vinson, Ingrid Domeij *m* Matt Rowe *pd* Philip Robinson *ed* Lawrence Catford, Jackie Ophire, John Cross
☆ Matthew Leitch (Dean Page), George Asprey (David), Lindsey Coulson (Georgie), Diana Quick (Lady Tryffoyn), Peter Youngblood Hills (Benjamin)
'Deeply felt and consistently entertaining.' – *Anthony Quinn, Independent*

A la Folie: see *Six Days, Six Nights*

À La Folie... Pas Du Tout: see *He Love Me... He Loves Me Not*

A la Place du Coeur *
France 1998 112m colour
Artificial Eye/Agat/Diaphana/La Seot/France2/Canal+ (Gilles Sandoz, Michel Saint-Jean, Robert Guédiguian)
In Marseille, a pregnant 16-year-old white girl struggles to defend the black father of her expected child, who is accused of raping a Bosnian refugee.
An often clumsy French version of Baldwin's angry novel, which was set in Harlem; the change in locale has not affected the racial tension at the heart of the drama.
w Jean-Louis Milesi, Robert Guédiguian *novel If Beale Street Could Talk* by James Baldwin *d* Robert Guédiguian *ph* Bernard Cavalié *ad* Michel Vandestien *ed* Bernard Sasia
☆ Ariane Ascaride (Marianne Patché), Christine Brücher (Francine Lopez), Jean-Pierre Darroussin (Joel Patché), Gérard Meylan (Franck Lopez), Alexandre Ogou (François Lopez), Laure Raoust (Clémentine Patché), Véronique Ballme (Sophie Patché), Pierre Banderet (Mr d'Assas)
'A highly individual and personal piece of work. It's one that deserves a place in everyone's heart.' – *James Mottram, Film Review*

À L'attaque! *
France 2000 90m colour
Gala/Agat/Diaphana/TF1 (Gilles Sandoz, Michel Saint-Jean, Robert Guediguian)
US title: *Charge!*
Two screenwriters work on a movie set in Marseille, where the family who run a small garage kidnap the capitalist who forced them into bankruptcy.
Entertaining film within a film, as two writers quarrel over scenes, and the variations are immediately acted out, though they don't seem as real as the family they create.
w Robert Guédiguian, Jean Louis Milesi *d* Robert Guédiguian *ph* Bernard Cavalie *m* Jacques Menichetti *ad* Michel Vandestien *ed* Bernard Sasia
☆ Ariane Ascaride, Pierre Banderet, Frederique Bonnal, Patrick Bonnel, Jacques Boudet, Christine Brucher, Jean-Pierre Darroussin
'A funny, lively, lightweight film, but there's a serious centre to it.' – *Philip French, Observer*

À Ma Soeur! *
France/Italy 2001 86m colour
Metro Tartan/Flach/CB/Arte/Immagine/Urania (Jean-François Lepetit)
US title: *Fat Girl*
aka: *For My Sister*
An overweight 12-year-old girl observes her pretty, 15-year-old sister's sexual initiation on a summer holiday.
An often observant study of adolescent sexuality and sibling relationships vitiated by its violent ending.
d Catherine Breillat *ph* Yorgos Arvanitis *pd* François Renaud Labarthe *ed* Pascale Chavance *cos* Anne Dunsford Varenne
☆ Anais Reboux (Anais), Roxane Mesquida (Elena), Libero de Rienzo (Fernando), Arsinee Khanjian (Mother), Romain Goupil (Father), Laura Betti (Fernando's Mother), Albert Goldberg (Killer)
'Turns out to be more painful and shocking than we anticipate. It is like life, which has a way of interrupting our plans with its tragic priorities.' – *Roger Ebert, Chicago Sun-Times*

A Nos Amours: see *To Our Loves*

A Nous Deux **
France/Canada 1979 109m Eastmancolor
Films 13/Cinévidéo (Claude Lelouch, Denis Heroux, Joseph Beaubien)
aka: *An Adventure for Two*
aka: *The Two of Us*
A thief escapes from prison and goes on the run, becoming involved along the way with a man-hating prostitute who is also wanted by the police.
Clever, witty thriller, full of little visual surprises, and one that plays games with an audience's expectations.
wd Claude Lelouch *ph* Bernard Zitzermann *m* Francis Lai *ad* Jean-Louis Poveda *ed* Sophie Bhaud, Hugues Darmois
☆ Catherine Deneuve, Jacques Dutronc, Jacques Villeret, Paul Préboist, Bernard Lecoq, Gilberte Geniat, Monique Melinand, Jacques Godin, Daniel Auteuil

A Nous la Liberté ****
France 1931 95m bw
Tobis
US title: *Freedom for Us*
A factory owner is blackmailed about his past, and helped by an old prison friend, with whom he finally takes to the road.
Operetta-style satirical comedy with leftish attitudes and several famous sequences later borrowed by Chaplin for Modern Times. In terms of sheer film flair, a revelation, though the plot has its tedious turns.
wd René Clair *ph Georges Périnal* *m* Georges Auric *pd Lazare Meerson*
☆ Raymond Cordy, Henri Marchand, Rolla France, Paul Olivier
'Different from the usual run … easily understandable even to those who do not know French.' – *Variety*
'He demonstrates that sound pictures can be as fluid as silents were, and the picture is rightly considered a classic.' – *Pauline Kael, 1970s*
'I was close to the extreme left … I wanted to attack the Machine, which led men into starvation instead of adding to their happiness.' – *René Clair*

A Propos de Nice *
France 1930 30m bw
A satirical documentary on the millionaire's paradise of the French Riviera.
Cheaply made and rather naïve-looking after sixty years, this amusingly belligerent lampoon still has its striking moments.
wd Jean Vigo *ph* Boris Kaufman

A Toute Vitesse
France 1996 85m colour
Dangerous to Know/Magouric/Téléma/France2/Rhône-Alpes (Laurent Bénégui)
A young French writer befriends a homosexual Algerian in order to obtain material for his next novel.
An effective drama of racial, sexual and class prejudice, though it has nothing new to say about them.
wd Gaël Morel *ph* Jeanne Lapoirie *ad* Frédérique Hurpeau *ed* Catherine Schwartz
☆ Élodie Bouchez, Pascal Cerve, Stéphane Rideau, Meziane Bardadi, Romain Auger, Salim Kechiouche, Mohammed Dib
'Gives the impression of being less than the sum of its parts.' – *Sight and Sound*

AWOL
US 1990 108m colour
Guild/Wrong Bet Productions/Imperial Entertainment (Ash R. Shah, Eric Karson)
US title: *Lionheart*
aka: *The Wrong Bet*
A deserter from the Foreign Legion becomes a bare-knuckle fighter in America.
Musclebound action movie, sentimental when it is not violent.
w Sheldon Lettich, Jean-Claude Van Damme *d* Sheldon Lettich *ph* Robert C. New *m* John Scott *pd* Gregory Pickrell *ed* Mark Conte
☆ Jean-Claude Van Damme, Harrison Page, Deborah Rennard, Lisa Pelikan, Ashley Johnson, Brian Thompson

A-Haunting We Will Go *
US 1942 68m bw
TCF (Sol M. Wurtzel)
Gangsters dupe Laurel and Hardy into escorting a coffin, which is accidentally switched with one used in a magic act.
Nothing whatever to do with haunting: a poor comedy with no typical material for the stars, but interesting as a record of the touring show of Dante the Magician.
w Lou Breslow *d* Alfred Werker *ph* Glen MacWilliams *m* Emil Newman
☆ Stan Laurel, Oliver Hardy, *Dante*, Sheila Ryan, John Shelton, Elisha Cook Jnr
'The comedians' lack of enthusiasm for their material is rather evident.' – *William K. Everson, 1967*

Aan *
India 1952 190m approx Technicolor
All India Film Corporation/Mehboob Productions
aka: *Savage Princess*
A usurping young prince and his sister are tamed by an athletic peasant and his girlfriend.
One of the few examples to reach the West of Indian costume melodrama with music, spectacle and swashbuckling. Distinctly intriguing, if overpowering.
w Chaudary, Ali Raza *d* Mehboob *ph* Faredoon A. Irani *m* Naushad Dilip
☆ Kumar, Nimmi, Premnath, Nadira
'Disarmingly enthusiastic … exotic and yet charmingly naïve.' – *MFB*
† English version runs to 130 minutes.

De Aanslag: see *The Assault*

Aaron Slick from Punkin Crick *
US 1952 95m Technicolor
Paramount (William Perlberg, George Seaton)
GB title: *Marshmallow Moon*
A small-town girl is tricked into selling her farm and moving to the city, but eventually marries the simple farmer who rescues her.
Homespun entertainment based on a staple success of the American provincial theatre, with pleasant songs added.

wd Claude Binyon *play* Walter Benjamin Hare *ph* Charles B. Lang Jnr *m/ly* Jay Livingston, Ray Evans *ch* Charles O'Curran
☆ Alan Young, Dinah Shore, Robert Merrill, Adele Jergens, Minerva Urecal

Abandon Ship: see *Seven Waves Away*

Abbot and Costello in Society: see *In Society*

'They're too wild for one world!'
Abbott and Costello Go to Mars
US 1953 76m bw
U-I (Howard Christie)

Two incompetents accidentally launch a space ship and land first in Louisiana, then on Venus.
Dismal knockabout, badly made.
w John Grant, D. D. Beauchamp *d* Charles Lamont *ph* Clifford Stine *m* Joseph Gershenson
☆ Bud Abbott, Lou Costello, Mari Blanchard, Robert Paige, Martha Hyer

Abbott and Costello in Hollywood *
US 1945 85m bw
MGM (Martin Gosch)

Two agents have hectic adventures in a film studio.
Tolerable star romp on one of their biggest budgets, climaxing in a roller coaster ride.
w Nat Perrin, Lou Breslow *d* S. Sylvan Simon *ph* Charles Schoenbaum *m* George Bassman
☆ Bud Abbott, Lou Costello, Frances Rafferty, Warner Anderson, Robert Z. Leonard

Abbott and Costello in the Foreign Legion
US 1950 80m bw
U-I (Robert Arthur)

Incompetent legionnaires become heroes to the fury of their sergeant.
Dull star vehicle on ramshackle sets, with no memorable routines.
w John Grant, Leonard Stern, Martin Ragaway *d* Charles Lamont *ph* George Robinson *m* Joseph Gershenson
☆ Bud Abbott, Lou Costello, Patricia Medina, Walter Slezak, Douglass Dumbrille

Abbott and Costello in the Navy: see *In the Navy*

Abbott and Costello Lost in Alaska
US 1952 76m bw
U-I (Howard Christie)

Two San Francisco firemen take a melancholy prospector back to Alaska to find a gold mine.
Sub-standard comedy vehicle with poor production.
w Martin Ragaway, Leonard Stern *d* Jean Yarbrough *ph* George Robinson *m* Joseph Gershenson
☆ Bud Abbott, Lou Costello, *Tom Ewell*, Mitzi Green, Bruce Cabot

Abbott and Costello Meet Captain Kidd *
US 1952 70m Supercinecolor
Warner/Woodley (Alex Gottlieb)

Two servants have a treasure map, and a fearsome pirate wants it.
Crude knockabout: the stars are way below their best, and a famous actor is embarrassed.
w Howard Dimsdale, John Grant *d* Charles Lamont *ph* Stanley Cortez *m* Raoul Kraushaar
☆ Bud Abbott, Lou Costello, Charles Laughton, Hillary Brooke, Leif Erickson

Abbott and Costello Meet Dr Jekyll and Mr Hyde *
US 1953 77m bw
U-I (Howard Christie)

In Victorian London, two rookie policemen catch a monster.
Quite a lively spoof with some well-paced comedy sequences.
w John Grant, Lee Loeb *d* Charles Lamont *ph* George Robinson *m* Hans Salter
☆ Bud Abbott, Lou Costello, Boris Karloff, Reginald Denny, Craig Stevens, Helen Westcott, John Dierkes

'Gracious Boris Karloff is superior to his surroundings.' – *MFB (Though it is doubtful whether he ever got behind the Hyde make-up.)*
† In Britain, the film was given an 'X' certificate, though it later played on children's television.

'Jeepers! the creepers are after somebody – and guess who! More howls than you can shake a shiver at!!!'
Abbott and Costello Meet Frankenstein **
US 1948 83m bw
U-I (Robert Arthur)

GB title: *Abbott and Costello Meet the Ghosts*
Two railway porters deliver crates containing the Frankenstein monster, Dracula, and the Wolf Man.
Fairly lively spoof which put an end to Universal's monsters for a while. Good typical sequences for the stars, a few thrills, and some good lines. Dracula to Costello, lovingly: 'What we need is young blood ... and brains...'
w Robert Lees, Frederic I. Rinaldo, John Grant *d* Charles Barton *ph* Charles van Enger *m* Frank Skinner
☆ *Bud Abbott, Lou Costello, Bela Lugosi, Lon Chaney Jnr*, Glenn Strange, Lenore Aubert, Jane Randolph

WOLF MAN: 'You don't understand. Every night when the moon is full, I turn into a wolf.'
COSTELLO: 'You and twenty million other guys!'
† Probably the Abbott and Costello film which survives best.

Abbott and Costello Meet the Ghosts: see *Abbott and Costello Meet Frankenstein*

Abbott and Costello Meet the Invisible Man *
US 1951 82m bw
U-I (Howard Christie)

A boxer accused of murder makes himself invisible while two detectives clear him.
Quite a bright comedy with good trick effects.
w Robert Lees, Frederic I. Rinaldo, John Grant *d* Charles Lamont *ph* George Robinson *m* Hans Salter
☆ Bud Abbott, Lou Costello, Arthur Franz, Nancy Guild, Adele Jergens, Sheldon Leonard

'When every face wore a custard pie, and vamps broke hearts with a winking eye!'
Abbott and Costello Meet the Keystone Kops *
US 1954 79m bw
U-I (Howard Christie)

In pioneer film days, two incompetents are sold a dud studio by a con man, but succeed as stunt men.
Flabby comedy which never seems to get going until the chase finale; notable chiefly for a guest appearance by Mack Sennett.
w John Grant *d* Charles Lamont *ph* Reggie Lanning *m* Joseph Gershenson
☆ Bud Abbott, Lou Costello, Lynn Bari, Fred Clark, Frank Wilcox, Maxie Rosenbloom

'More ghoulish glee than when they met Frankenstein!'
Abbott and Costello Meet the Killer, Boris Karloff *
US 1948 84m bw
U-I (Robert Arthur)

Two bellboys help to solve mysterious murders in a remote hotel.
This clumsily titled comedy really does not work until the last sequence in a cavern. Boris Karloff is not the killer and appears very little.
w Hugh Wedlock Jnr, Howard Snyder, John Grant *d* Charles Barton *ph* Charles van Enger *md* Milton Schwarzwald
☆ Bud Abbott, Lou Costello, Boris Karloff, Gar Moore, Lenore Aubert, Alan Mowbray

'It has been said that a man's best friend is his mummy...'
Abbott and Costello Meet the Mummy *
US 1955 77m bw
U-I (Howard Christie)

A missing medallion leads to a lost tomb and a living mummy.
The comedians show their age in this one, but there is some typical if predictable humour and a thrill or two.
w John Grant *d* Charles Lamont *ph* George Robinson *m* Hans Salter
☆ Bud Abbott, Lou Costello, Kurt Katch, Marie Windsor, Michael Ansara, Dan Seymour

COSTELLO: 'How stupid can you get?'
ABBOTT: 'How stupid do you want me to be?'

The Abdication
GB 1974 102m Technicolor
Warner (Robert Fryer, James Cresson)
17th-century Queen Christina of Sweden journeys to Rome to embrace the Catholic church and falls in love with a cardinal.
Sombre historical fantasia, more irritating than interesting.
w Ruth Wolff *play* Ruth Wolff *d* Anthony Harvey *ph* Geoffrey Unsworth *m* Nino Rota
☆ Liv Ullmann, Peter Finch, Cyril Cusack, Paul Rogers, Graham Crowden, Michael Dunn, Lewis Fiander, Harold Goldblatt

'Dainty debauchery and titillating tease straight from twenties women's pulp magazines.' – *Variety*
'Embalmed in such reverence for its own cultural elevation that it loses all contact with the audience.' – *Pauline Kael*

'It'll steal your heart.'
The Abduction Club
GB/France/Ireland 2002 95m colour
'Scope
Pathé/Film Council/Canal+/Gruber/UGC/Samson (Neil Peplow, Yves Marmion, Richard Holmes, David Collins)

In the late 18th century, aristocratic younger sons kindap heiresses in the hope of persuading them into marriage.
Tiresome period romp, in the style of a raucous fancydress party.
w Bill Britten, Richard Crawford *d* Stefan Schwartz *ph* Howard Atherton *m* Shaun Davey *pd* Sarah Greenwood *ed* Pamela Power *cos* Consolata Boyle
☆ Alice Evans (Catherine Kennedy), Daniel Lapaine (Byrne), Sophia Myles (Anne Kennedy), Matthew Rhys (Strang), Liam Cunningham (John Power), Edward Woodward (Lord Fermoy), Patrick Malahide (Sir Myles), John Arthur (Robert Kennedy), Tom Murphy (Knox)

'Hardly likely to hold the attention of the young audience for whom a 12 certificate has been thoughtfully secured' – *Ryan Gilbey, Observer*
† Bill Britten was replaced as director by Stefan Schwartz.

The Abductors *
US 1957 80m bw Regalscope
TCF/Regal (Ray Wander)
Around 1870, criminals steal Lincoln's body as ransom to effect a convict's release.
Interesting minor melodrama, but not sufficiently well made.
w Ray Wander *d* Andrew V. McLaglen *ph* Joseph LaShelle *m* Paul Glass
☆ Victor McLaglen, Gavin Muir, George Macready

Abdul the Damned *
GB 1935 111m bw
BIP/Capitol (Max Schach)
In 1900 Turkey, an opera star gives herself to a villainous sultan to protect her fiancé.
Thoroughgoing hokum, well produced, which pleased some people in its day.
w Ashley Dukes, Warren Chetham Strode, Robert Burford *d* Karl Grune *ph* Otto Kanturek
☆ *Fritz Kortner*, Adrienne Ames, Nils Asther, John Stuart, Esme Percy, Walter Rilla, Patric Knowles, Eric Portman

Abe Lincoln in Illinois **
US 1940 110m bw
RKO (Max Gordon)

GB title: *Spirit of the People*
Episodes in the political and domestic life of Abraham Lincoln.
Pleasant, muted, careful film based on a Broadway success: generally informative and interesting.
w Grover Jones *play* Robert E. Sherwood *d* John Cromwell *ph James Wong Howe* *m* Roy Webb
☆ *Raymond Massey*, Ruth Gordon, Gene Lockhart, Mary Howard, Dorothy Tree, Minor Watson, Howard da Silva

'If you want attitudes, a five gallon hat, famous incidents, and One Nation Indivisible, they're all here. As a picture and as a whole, it just doesn't stick.' – *Otis Ferguson*
Raymond Massey, James Wong Howe

Abel **
Netherlands 1985 96m colour
First Floor Features (Laurens Geels, Dick Maas, Rob Swaab)
A 31-year-old mother's boy, thrown out of home, moves in with his father's mistress.
Witty, neatly plotted black farce of family life.
wd Alex Van Warmerdam *ph* Marc Felperlaan *ad* Harry Ammerlaan *ed* Hans Van Dongen
☆ Alex Van Warmerdam, Henri Garcin, Olga Zuiderhoek, Annet Malherbe, Loes Luca

Abendland
Germany/Portugal 1999 140m colour
Artificial Eye/Mediopolis/Filmes do Tejo/WDR (Alexander Ris)
aka: *Nightfall*
An unemployed couple in a hostile city spend a day and a night facing desolation and death.
Miserablist film suffused with urban despair, cruelty and pessimism about the human condition; its use of grainy video for close-ups of hopeless faces makes it hard to watch.
wd Fred Kelemen *ph* Fred Kelemen *m* Rainer Kirchmann *pd* Ralf Küfner, Anette Kuhn *ed* Fred Kelemen, Anja Nerall, Nicola Undritz Cope
☆ Verena Jasch (Leni), Wolfgang Michae (Anton), Adolfo Assor (Bell founder), Isa Hochgerner (Nina), Urs Remond (Paul), Thomas Baumann (Man in leather coat), Daniela Roque-Magalhaes (Little girl)

'There is evident artistry in the desolate tableaux and bizarre visual metaphors that Kelemen conjures up, but these are pretty measly rewards for enduring such a long, bludgeoning film.' – *Ed Porter, Sunday Times*

Abgeschminkt!: see *Making Up*

Abie's Irish Rose
US 1946 96m bw
UA/Bing Crosby Productions (Edward A. Sutherland)
An Irish girl marries a Jewish boy, leading to a clash of families.
Flat filming of the twenties Broadway play.
w Anne Nichols *play* Anne Nichols *d* A. Edward Sutherland *ph* William Mellor *m* John Scott Trotter
☆ Joanne Dru, Richard Norris, Michael Chekhov, Eric Blore, Art Baker
† There had been a silent version in 1928, and the plot was borrowed, to say the least, for the 1972 TV series *Bridget Loves Bernie*.

Abilene Town *
US 1946 89m bw
UA (Jules Levey)

An upright marshal routs crooked cattlemen.
Vigorous, enjoyable Western programmer.
w Harold Shumate *d* Edwin L. Marin
☆ Randolph Scott, Ann Dvorak, Rhonda Fleming, Edgar Buchanan, Lloyd Bridges

'Love means never having to say you're ugly!'
The Abominable Dr Phibes *
GB 1971 94m Movielab
AIP (Louis M. Heyward, Ron Dunas)

A disfigured musical genius devises a series of horrible murders, based on the ten curses of Pharaoh, for the surgeons who failed to save his wife.
Brisk but uninspired treatment of a promising theme, with more unintended nastiness than intended laughs. Some good moments and interesting low-budget thirties sets.
w James Whiton, William Goldstein *d* Robert Fuest *ph* Norman Warwick *m* Basil Kirchen, Jack Nathan *pd* Brian Eatwell
☆ Vincent Price, Joseph Cotten, Hugh Griffith, Terry-Thomas, Peter Jeffrey, Virginia North, Aubrey Woods

'The sets are awful, the plot ludicrous and the dialogue inane – what more could a horror freak desire?' – *Motion Picture Guide*

† Sequel: *Dr Phibes Rises Again* (1973).

'See it with someone brave!'

The Abominable Snowman *

GB 1957 91m bw RegalScope

Warner/Hammer/Clarion (Aubrey Baring)

US title: *The Abominable Snowman of the Himalayas*

Himalayan explorers are attacked one by one by the Yeti and their own fear.

A thin horror film with intelligent scripting: more philosophizing and characterization than suspense. The briefly glimpsed Yeti are disappointing creations.

w Nigel Kneale *TV play* Nigel Kneale *d* Val Guest *ph* Arthur Grant *m* Humphrey Searle *md* John Hollingsworth *pd* Bernard Robinson *ed* Bill Lenny

☆ *Peter Cushing*, Forrest Tucker, Maureen Connell, Richard Wattis, Robert Brown, *Arnold Marle*

'Growing up has nothing to do with age.'

About a Boy **

GB/US/Germany/France 2002 101m colour 'Scope

UIP/Universal/Tribeca/Working Title/Kalima (Jane Rosenthal, Robert De Niro, Brad Epstein, Tim Bevan, Eric Fellner)

An idle playboy, who exploits single mothers, learns about commitment when he is forced to befriend an unhappy 12-year-old boy.

Amusing comedy about the beginnings of masculine maturity, at its best when not taking itself too seriously.

w Peter Hedges, Chris Weitz, Paul Weitz *novel* Nick Hornby *d* Paul and Chris Weitz *ph* Remi Adefarasin *m* Badly Drawn Boy *pd* Jim Clay *ed* Nick Moore

☆ Hugh Grant (Will), Toni Collette (Fiona), Rachel Weisz (Rachel), Nicholas Hoult (Marcus), Isabel Brook (Angie), Sharon Small (Christine), Victoria Smurfit (Susie), Augustus Prew (Ali)

'The timing and cutting of the film are terrific, the build-up to an absurdly hilarious climax is just right, and the performances are near perfect.' – *Shawn Levy, Oregonian*

Peter Hedges, Chris Weitz, Paul Weitz

'They Were The Apple Of His Eye. All Three Of Them.'

About Adam *

Ireland/GB/US 2000 105m colour

Metrodome/BBC/Miramax/HAL/IFB/Venus (Anna Devlin, Marina Hughes)

A waitress in a Dublin restaurant brings home a young man she fancies, only to discover that he is a voracious sexual predator prepared to seduce her two sisters.

Often lively romantic comedy that skates over the central matter of betrayal in favour of the pleasures to be gained from seeing events from various perspectives.

wd Gerard Stembridge *ph* Bruno De Keyser *m* Adrian Johnston *pd* Fiona Daly *ed* Mary Finlay *cos* Eimear Ni Mhaoldomhnaigh

☆ Stuart Townsend (Adam), Kate Hudson (Lucy), Frances O'Connor (Laura), Charlotte Bradley (Alice), Rosaleen Linehan (Peggy), Tommy Tiernan (Simon), Alan Maher (David), Brendan Dempsey (Martin), Cathleen Bradley (Karen), Roger Gregg (Prof McCormick)

'Has the structure of a sex comedy, but the comedy seems to have gone missing.' – *Adam Mars-Jones, Times*

About Face

US 1952 96m Technicolor

Warner (William Jacobs)

Moronic remake of *Brother Rat* (qv), shorn of all wit, pace and style.

w Peter Milne *d* Roy del Ruth *ph* Bert Glennon *m/ly* Charles Tobias, Peter de Rose

☆ Eddie Bracken, Gordon MacRae, Dick Wesson, Virginia Gibson, Phyllis Kirk, Joel Grey

About Last Night

US 1986 113m MGM Color

Tri-Star (Jason Brett, Stuart Oken)

The ups and downs of an unmarried relationship.

Smart, slick, up-to-the-minute account of human coupling and uncoupling in the eighties ... but no plot.

w Tim Kazurinsky, Denise DeClue *play Sexual Perversity in Chicago* by David Mamet *d* Edward Zwick *ph* Andrew Dintenfass *m* Miles Goodman *pd* Ida Random

☆ Rob Lowe, Demi Moore, Jim Belushi, Elizabeth Perkins, George DiCenzo

'Savvy enough to recognize points of conflict but not daring enough to look beneath the surface.' – *Variety*

About Mrs Leslie *

US 1954 104m bw

Paramount (Hal B. Wallis)

An ageing nightclub singer has a platonic affair with a mysterious wealthy man, who leaves her enough money to buy a boarding house.

Odd, likeable romantic drama tailored for an unusual star; but its plot is too thin and its direction too drab for real success.

w Ketti Frings, Hal Kanter *novel* Vina Delmar *d* Daniel Mann *ph* Ernest Laszlo *m* Victor Young

☆ *Shirley Booth, Robert Ryan*, Alex Nicol, Marjie Millar, Eilene Janssen

'This quiet and curious film has an unexpectedly gentle, civilized flavour.' – *Gavin Lambert*

'It's all sunny disposition and sweet sadness for Miss Booth.' – *Judith Crist*

'One is reminded alternately of Chekhov and of *Back Street*.' – *Sight and Sound*

About Schmidt ***

US 2002 125m DeLuxe

Entertainment/New Line (Michael Gittes, Harry Besman)

A retired and suddenly-widowed actuary experiences a late-life crisis.

At once affecting and funny, slyly observant and celebratory, this dark, comic look at old age gains immeasurably from Nicholson's contained performance; he restrains his usual mannerisms to suggest the confusions and decencies of a man who has lost his place in the world.

w Alexander Payne, Jim Taylor *novel* Louis Begley *d* Alexander Payne *ph* James Glennon *m* Rolfe Kent *pd* Jane Ann Stewart *ed* Kevin Tent

☆ *Jack Nicholson* (Warren Schmidt), Hope Davis (Jeannie), Dermot Mulroney (Randall Hertzel), Kathy Bates (Roberta Hertzel), Len Cariou (Ray), Howard Hesseman (Larry), June Squibb (Helen Schmidt)

'The power of this great movie – part comedy, part tragedy, part satire, mostly masterpiece – is in the details.' – *Lisa Schwarzbaum, Entertainment Weekly*

'Sublimely funny and exquisitely sad, this might just turn out to be an American classic.' – *Peter Bradshaw, Guardian*

'Doesn't bring us deeply into the lives of its people because it's too busy trying to feel superior to them.' – *Peter Rainer, New York*

Jack Nicholson; Kathy Bates

'The love story behind the billion dollar secret!'

Above and Beyond *

US 1952 122m bw

MGM (Melvin Frank, Norman Panama)

The training of Colonel Paul Tibbets, who dropped the first atomic bomb on Japan.

Overstretched flagwaver with laborious domestic interludes. Of little real interest then or now.

w Melvin Frank, Norman Panama *story* Beirne Lay Jnr *d* Melvin Frank, Norman Panama *ph* Ray June *m* Hugo Friedhofer

☆ Robert Taylor, Eleanor Parker, James Whitmore, Larry Keating, Larry Gates

Beirne Lay Jnr, Hugo Friedhofer

Above Suspicion *

US 1943 91m bw

MGM (Victor Saville)

Just before World War II, an Oxford professor on a continental honeymoon is asked to track down a missing agent.

Patchy, studio-bound spy comedy-drama with a couple of good sequences. Notable also for Mr MacMurray's impersonation of a professor who hails a Nazi as 'Hiya, dope!'

w Keith Winter, Melville Baker, Patricia Coleman *novel* Helen MacInnes *d* Richard Thorpe *ph* Robert Planck *m* Bronislau Kaper

☆ Fred MacMurray, Joan Crawford, Conrad Veidt, *Basil Rathbone*, Reginald Owen, Felix Bressart, Richard Ainley

'Will need more than strong support for passable biz.' – *Variety*

Above the Law

US 1988 99m Technicolor

Warner (Steven Seagal, Andrew Davis)

aka: *Nico*

A cop, who is also a martial arts expert, uncovers dirty work in the CIA.

Woodenly acted, violent action movie with an unusual anti-establishment slant.

w Steven Pressfield, Ronald Shusett, Andrew Davis *story* Andrew Davis, Steven Seagal *d* Andrew Davis *ph* Robert Steadman *m* David M. Frank *pd* Maher Ahmad *ed* Michael Brown *sp* Art Brewer, Lee Solis

☆ Steven Seagal, Pam Grier, Henry Silva, Daniel Faraldo, Sharon Stone, Nicholas Kusenko

'The hardest part of winning is choosing sides.'

Above the Rim

US 1994 93m DeLuxe

First Independent/New Line (Jeff Pollack, Ben Medina)

A troubled, talented basketball player, who refuses to play for his high school team, becomes involved with a drug dealer and his brother, a former star player now working as a school security guard.

An attempt to combine the usual sports movie plot, with victory being snatched at the last minute, with the street credibility of the usual drug movie, with death for the bad guys and redemption for the good in the last reel; two sets of clichés do not make a classic.

w Barry Michael Cooper, Jeff Pollack, Ben Medina *d* Jeff Pollack *ph* Tom Priestley Jnr *m* Marcus Miller *pd* Ina Mayhew *ed* Michael Ripps, James Mitchell

☆ Duane Martin, Tupac Shakur, Leon, David Bailey, Tonya Pinkins, Marlon Wayans, Bernie Mac

'A fine cast and the movie's general energy can't overcome that mix of clichés and technical flaws, which should conspire to prevent any high flying at the box-office.' – *Brian Lowry, Variety*

'A story of impudent gallantry!'

Above Us the Waves

GB 1955 99m bw

Rank/London Independent Producers (William Macquitty)

In World War II, midget submarines attack a German battleship in a Norwegian fjord.

Archetypal stiff-upper-lip war drama with disappointing action sequences and jumbled continuity.

w Robin Estridge *d* Ralph Thomas *ph* Ernest Steward *m* Arthur Benjamin

☆ John Mills, John Gregson, Donald Sinden, James Robertson Justice, Michael Medwin, Lee Patterson, Lyndon Brook

'It tells a heroic story without any flowery effects at all.' – *Manchester Guardian*

'The wonder film of the century, about the most romantic figure who ever lived!'

Abraham Lincoln **

US 1930 97m bw

UA/Art Cinema Corporation/D. W. Griffith

An account of Lincoln's entry into politics and his years of power.

Rather boring even at the time, this straightforward biopic has the virtues of sincerity and comparative fidelity to the facts.

w Stephen Vincent Benet, Gerrit Lloyd *d D. W. Griffith* *ph* Karl Struss *m* Hugo Riesenfeld *pd* William Cameron Menzies

☆ *Walter Huston*, Una Merkel, Edgar Dearing, Russell Simpson, Henry B. Walthall

'A startlingly superlative accomplishment, one rejuvenating a greatest Griffith ... one smooth roll of literally pulsating passion, pathos, laughter ... it should be his greatest contribution to the exhibitor.' – *Variety*

'It brings to us – with a curious finality of disappointment, a sentimental sense of the closing of a chapter – the impression of a director who has nowhere made a valid contact with the condition of the screen today.' – *C. A. Lejeune*

'A treasure trove of magnificent moments.' – *MFB, 1973*

'Dull, episodic, overlong ... it is difficult to understand why contemporary critics were so impressed.' – *Anthony Slide, 70s*

† There was a silent biopic in 1924 starring George A. Billings, but it lacked cinematic interest. Written by Frances Marion and directed by Phil Rosen, for Rocket/Lincoln/AFN.

Abraham Valley

Portugal/France/Switzerland 1993 189m colour

Artificial Eye/Mandragoa/Gemini/Light Night (Paulo Branco)

original title: *Vale Abraao*

A lame and glamorous woman with romantic inclinations is frustrated both by her marriage and her affairs.

A deft variation of Flaubert's Madame Bovary (qv), in which the husband encourages his wife's infidelity without making her any more contented, but one that lacks heart.

wd Manoel de Oliviera *novel* Augustina Bessa-Luis *ph* Mário Barroso *ad* Maria José Branco *ed* Manoel de Oliviera, Valérie Loiseleux

☆ Leonor Silveira, Cecile Sanz de Alba, Luis Miguel Cintra, Rui de Carvalho, Luis Lima Barreto, Mário Barroso (narrator)

'Sometimes you can't wake from a nightmare, even if you do...'

Abre Los Ojos **

Spain/France/Italy 1997 119m colour

Redbus/Sogetel/El Escorpion/Alain Sarde/Lucky Red

aka: *Open Your Eyes*

Explaining to a prison psychiatrist how he came to be accused of murder, a wealthy young man, hideously disfigured in a road crash that killed his companion, realises that he is trapped in a unreal life.

Clever, tricksy, games-playing thriller that deals with the confusions of reality and illusion, and the limits of personality.

w Alejandro Amenábar, Matteo Gil *d* Alejandro Amenábar *ph* Hans Burmann *m* Alejandro Amenábar, Mariano Marin *ad* Wolfgang Burmann *ed* Maria Elena Sainz de Rojas

☆ Eduardo Noriega (Cesar), Penelope Cruz (Sofia), Chete Lera (Antonio), Fele Martinez (Pelayo), Najwa Nimri (Nuria), Gérard Barray (Duvernois), Jorge de Juan (Department head)

'Ambitiously complex, disturbing and terrific-looking thriller.' – *Jonathan Holland, Variety*

Abril Despedaçado *

Brazil/France/Switzerland 2001 105m colour 'Scope

Buena Vista/VideoFilmes/Haut et Court/Bac/Dan Valley (Arthur Cohn)

aka: *Behind the Sun*

A young boy recalls the blood feud over land between his and the neighbouring family, and its effect on his surviving brother.

An enjoyable fable that teeters on whimsy, with its artfully assembled ingredients in a dusty, golden-brown landscape: appealing boy, a soulful youth who falls for a fire-eating circus performer, and a feud in which killing is confused with honour.

w Walter Salles, Sergio Machado, Karim Ainouz *novel Broken April* by Ismail Kadare *d* Walter Salles *ph* Walter Carvalho *m* Antonio Pinto, Ed Cortes, Beto Villares *pd* Cassio Amarante *ed* Isabelle Rathery

☆ José Dumont (Father), Rodrigo Santoro (Tonho), Rita Assemany (Mother), Luiz Carlos Vasconcelos (Salustiano), Ravi Ramos Lacerda (Pacu), Flavia Marco Antonio (Clara), Othon Bastos (Mr Lourenco)

'You're always aware that you're watching a quaintly middle-class, museum-poster notion of an "elemental" peasant fable.' – *Owen Gleiberman, Entertainment Weekly*

† The British release ran for 92 minutes.

'Two roaring Romeos who thought even the dames were on lend lease!'

Abroad with Two Yanks *
US 1944 80m bw
Edward Small

Adventures around the Pacific with two woman-chasing sailors.
This simple-minded farce with its punny title was a great success in its day, and still generates a laugh or two.
w Charles Rogers, Wilkie Mahoney, Ted Sills *d* Allan Dwan *ph* Charles Lawton *m* Lud Gluskin
☆ Dennis O'Keefe, William Bendix, Helen Walker, John Abbott, John Loder

Abschied aus Buckow *
Germany 2000 93m colour
Artificial Eye/Novoskop/WDR/ORB/SWR/Arte/Studio Babelsberg/Arthur Hofer (Gesche Carstens, Henryk Romanowski, Jan Schütte)

GB title: *The Farewell: Brecht's Last Summer*
In August 1956, on the last day of a summer holiday, a dying Bertolt Brecht attempts to come to terms with his wife and mistresses, while secret police wait nearby to arrest a friend.
An engaging, melancholy drama of love and betrayal, anguish, and guilt; it provides a portrait of a writer who put artistic survival above all other commitments.
w Klaus Pohl *d* Jan Schütte *ph* Edward Klosinski *m* John Cale *ad* Katharina Woppermann *ed* Renate Merck
☆ Josef Bierbichler (Bertolt Brecht), Helene Weigel (Monica Bleibtreu), Margit Rogall (Ruth Berlau), Jeanette Hain (Kathe Reichel), Samuel Fintzi (Wolfgang Harich), Elfriede Irrall (Elisabeth Hauptmann)
'A brilliantly contrived study of Brechtian alienation.' – *Alexander Walker*
'An engrossing visit to the bizarre household of a sly yet candid master.' – *Stanley Kaufmann*

Abschied von Gestern *
West Germany 1966 90m bw
Kairos Film/Independent/Alexander Kluge
aka: *Yesterday Girl*
A Jewish girl escapes from East to West Germany but is disillusioned and gives herself up.
Witty and remarkably light-hearted satirical comedy which can be fully understood only by those living in Germany in the sixties.
wd Alexander Kluge *ph* Edgar Reitz, Thomas Mauch *ed* Beata Mainka
☆ Alexandra Kluge, Günther Mack, Hans Korte, Eva Marie Meinecke

Absence of Malice *
US 1981 116m DeLuxe
Columbia/Mirage (Sydney Pollack)

When a longshoremen's union leader disappears, a lady journalist throws an unfair spotlight on an innocent suspect.
Well-meaning but overwritten attack on journalistic abuses, hampered by unsuitable leading performances.
w Kurt Luedtke *d* Sydney Pollack *ph* Owen Roizman *m* Dave Grusin *pd* Terence Marsh
☆ Paul Newman, Sally Field, Bob Balaban, Melinda Dillon, Luther Adler, Barry Primus
'Pollack seems to be carving out a new niche for himself as an updater of Hollywood's most tried and true methods of sugaring a message.' – *Richard Combs, MFB*
'A thoroughly craftsmanlike movie that never quite delivers on the commercial or the artistic front.' – *Guardian*
'The story is perfunctory and disappointing in a movie that promises but does not deliver.' – *Motion Picture Guide*
screenplay; Paul Newman; Melinda Dillon

Absent without Leave
New Zealand 1993 96m Eastmancolor
Meridian/NZFC/Avalon/NFU (Robin Laing)
In New Zealand in 1942, a soldier, who is about to be sent overseas, goes absent so that he can take home to her parents his young wife, who has had a miscarriage.
Amiable, meandering domestic drama of no particular interest.
w James Edwards, Graeme Tetley *d* John Laing *ph* Allen Guilford *m* Don McGlashan, David Long, Mark Austin *pd* Rick Kofoed *ed* Paul Sutorius
☆ Craig McLachlan, Katrina Hobbs, Judie Douglass, Tony Barry, Ken Blackburn, Tony Burton

'It's all about a wacky prof who invents an anti-gravity goo that flew!'

The Absent-Minded Professor *
US 1961 97m bw
Walt Disney (Bill Walsh)

A lighter-than-air substance called flubber enables its inventor to drive his Model-T through the sky and catch some spies.
Foolishly engaging fantasy comedy with goodish trick effects.
w Bill Walsh *d* Robert Stevenson *ph* Edward Colman *m* George Bruns *sp* Robert A. Mattey, Peter Ellenshaw, Eustace Lycett
☆ Fred MacMurray, Tommy Kirk, Keenan Wynn, Nancy Olson, Leon Ames, Ed Wynn, Edward Andrews
† Sequel: *Son of Flubber* (1963) (qv).
†† Remake: *Flubber* (1997) (qv).
Edward Colman

Absinthe: see *Madame X (1929)*

'Welcome to the world of your dreams!'

Absolute Beginners
GB 1986 107m Super Techniscope
Virgin/Goldcrest/Palace (Stephen Woolley, Chris Brown)

Teen life and pop fashion in 1958 London.
Deafening, mindless, musical, multi-screen pot-pourri of teen culture which sadly needs narrative links not to mention better music and firmer control.
w Richard Burridge, Christopher Wicking, Don MacPherson *novel* Colin MacInnes *d* Julien Temple *ph* Oliver Stapleton *m* *David Bowie, Ray Davies, et al.* *pd* John Beard
☆ Eddie O'Connell, Patsy Kensit, David Bowie, Ray Davies, James Fox, Lionel Blair, Steven Berkoff, Mandy Rice Davies
'All that noise, all that energy, so little governing thought.' – *Time Out*

Absolute Power *
US 1997 120m Technicolor Panavision
Columbia/Castle Rock/Malpaso (Clint Eastwood, Karen Spiegel)

A thief attempts to prove that the US President was an accomplice in the murder of a woman.
Old-fashioned, lacklustre thriller with an implausible plot, though it does occasionally crank up the suspense.
w William Goldman *novel* David Baldacci *d* Clint Eastwood *ph* Jack N. Green *m* Lennie Niehaus *pd* Henry Bumstead *ed* Joel Cox
☆ Clint Eastwood (Luther Whitney), Gene Hackman (President Richmond), Ed Harris (Seth Frank), Laura Linney (Kate Whitney), Judy Davis (Gloria Russell), Scott Glenn (Bill Burton), Dennis Haysbert (Tim Collin), E. G. Marshall (Walter Sullivan), Melora Hardin (Christy Sullivan)
'Glum and depersonalized, as if Eastwood couldn't muster the energy to guide us through this maze of improbable twists.' – *Owen Gleiberman, Entertainment Weekly*

Absolute Quiet *
US 1936 71m bw
MGM (John Considine Jnr)
A planeload of strangers is forced down on a financier's ranch.
Interestingly-cast programmer, efficiently directed.
w Harry Clork *d* George B. Seitz
☆ Lionel Atwill, Louis Hayward, Raymond Walburn, Stuart Erwin, Wallace Ford, J. Carrol Naish

Absolution *
GB 1978 95m Technicolor
Bulldog (Danny O'Donovan, Elliott Kastner)

TV title: *Murder by Confession*
A schoolmaster priest at a Roman Catholic boarding school is taunted by a malicious pupil into committing murder.
Interesting and suspenseful, though finally too complicated compromise between a thriller of the Sleuth type and a downbeat character study.
w Anthony Shaffer *d* Anthony Page *ph* John Coquillon *m* Stanley Myers
☆ *Richard Burton*, Dominic Guard, Dai Bradley, Billy Connolly, Andrew Keir
'A dire slice of clever-clever narrative trickery.' – *Paul Taylor, MFB*
'You can't make real bricks from this kind of straw, since a potentially interesting study of character and environment is gradually weakened by the constraints of a second-rate murder mystery.' – *Guardian*

Abwärts: see *Out of Order*

'A place on earth more awesome than anywhere in space.'

The Abyss
US 1989 140m DeLuxe Super 35
Fox (Gale Anne Hurd)

Attempting to rescue a nuclear submarine, divers working on underwater drilling encounter aliens.
Despite some clever special effects, a tedious, overlong fantasy that is more excited by machinery than people.
wd James Cameron *ph* Mikael Salomon *m* Alan Silvestri *pd* Leslie Dilley *ed* Joel Goodman *sp* Laura Buff, John Bruno, ILM, Dennis Muren
☆ Ed Harris, Mary Elizabeth Mastrantonio, Michael Biehn, Leo Burmester, Todd Graff, John Bedford Lloyd, J. C. Quinn, Kimberly Scott
'For the most part, as exciting an undersea drama as one could imagine.' – *MFB*
† *The Abyss Special Edition* released on video and Laserdisc contained an extra 27m cut from the original cinema release.
visual effects
cinematography; art direction

Accattone *
Italy 1961 120m bw
Cino del Duca/Arco (Alfredo Bini)

A Roman pimp and thief is beset by troubles, and is finally killed escaping from the police.
Sordid and rough-edged but vividly realistic melodrama.
wd Pier Paolo Pasolini *ph* Tonino delli Colli *md* Carlo Rustichelli *ad* Bernardo Bertolucci
☆ Franco Citti, Franca Pasut, Silvana Corsini, Paola Giudi, Roberto Scaringella, Adele Cambria
'Discontinuous, lackadaisical, sometimes improbable, almost always superficial.' – *John Simon*

Accent on Love
US 1941 61m bw
TCF
A real estate executive walks out to become spokesman for his former underprivileged tenants.
Thin Capraesque romantic comedy.
w John Larkin *story* Dalton Trumbo *d* Ray McCarey
☆ George Montgomery, Osa Massen, J. Carrol Naish, Cobina Wright Jnr, Stanley Clements, Thurston Hall, Minerva Urecal

Accent on Youth *
US 1935 77m bw
Paramount (Douglas Maclean)
A secretary falls in love with her middle-aged playwright employer.
Reasonably sparkling comedy from a popular play, later remade as Mr Music and But Not for Me.
w Herbert Fields, Claude Binyon *play* Samson Raphaelson *d* Wesley Ruggles *ph* Leon Shamroy
☆ Herbert Marshall, Sylvia Sidney, Philip Reed, Astrid Allwyn, Holmes Herbert
'Well adapted, presented and produced for box office satisfaction.' – *Variety*

Accident **
GB 1967 105m Eastmancolor
London Independent Producers (Joseph Losey, Norman Priggen)

An Oxford undergraduate is killed in a car crash; his tutor looks back over the tangle of personal relationships that contributed to his death.
Ascetic drama in which the audience is too often left to observe at length and draw its own conclusions; good characterizations nevertheless.
w Harold Pinter *novel* Nicholas Mosley *d* Joseph Losey *ph* Gerry Fisher *m* John Dankworth
☆ Dirk Bogarde, Stanley Baker, Jacqueline Sassard, Vivien Merchant, Michael York
'The whole thing is such a teapot tempest, and it is so assiduously underplayed that it is neither strong drama nor stinging satire. It is just a sad little story of a wistful don.' – *Bosley Crowther*
'Everything is calm, unruffled, lacquered in a veneer of civilization, yet underneath it all, one gradually begins to realize, the characters are tearing each other emotionally to shreds.' – *MFB*
'Uneven, unsatisfying, but with virtuoso passages of calculated meanness.' – *New Yorker, 1977*

Accidental Hero: see *Hero*

The Accidental Tourist ***
US 1988 121m Technicolor Panavision
Warner (Lawrence Kasdan, Charles Okun, Michael Grillo)

Left by his wife, an uptight travel writer falls in love with an exuberant dog-trainer.
A liberating domestic drama, notable for some excellent acting.
w Frank Galati, Lawrence Kasdan *novel* Anne Tyler *d* *Lawrence Kasdan* *ph* John Bailey *m* John Williams *pd* Bo Welch *ed* Carol Littleton
☆ *William Hurt, Kathleen Turner, Geena Davis*, Amy Wright, Bill Pullman, Robert Gorman, David Ogden Stiers, Ed Begley Jnr
Geena Davis
picture; adapted screenplay; John Williams

Accidents Will Happen
US 1938 62m bw
Warner (Bryan Foy)
An insurance claims adjuster takes to crime.
Slack little programmer.
w George Bricker, Anthony Coldeway *d* William Clemens
☆ Ronald Reagan, Dick Purcell, Gloria Blondell, Addison Richards, Hugh O'Connell

Acción Mutante
Spain 1993 94m Fujicolour Cinemascope
Feature Film/El Deseo/CIBY 2000 (Agustin Almodóvar, Pedro Almodóvar)

In 2012, a disfigured man leads a group of disabled in a terrorist war against the healthy and perfectly formed for his own advantage.
Bizarre horror that can be taken as a black or sick joke, depending on your attitude to a movie with such characters as a half-dead, half-alive Siamese twin. Whatever, after a brisk beginning, it soon palls and even appals, with its emphasis on the gruesome.
w Jorge Guerricaechevarria, Alex de la Iglesia *d* Alex de la Iglesia *ph* Carles Gusi *m* Juan Carlos Cuello *ad* José Luis Arrizabalaga *ed* Pablo Blanco *sp* Oliver Gleyze, Yves Domenjoud, Jean-Bapiste Bonetto, Bernard-André le Boetti
☆ Antonio Resines, Frédérique Feder, Alex Angulo, Juan Viades, Karra Elejalde, Saturnino Garcia, Fernando Guillén, Jaime Blanch
'Officially a promising first film, this feels more like a disappointing second one.' – *Empire*

L'Accompagnatrice: see *The Accompanist*

The Accompanist
France 1992 111m colour
Gala/Film Par Film/De la Boissière Orly/Sedif France/3 Cinema (Jean-Louis Livi)

original title: *L'Accompagnatrice*
In occupied Paris of the early 1940s, a young star-struck woman becomes the accompanist to a fashionable French singer and her rich husband, a reluctant collaborator with the Germans.
The wartime setting is presumably intended to give resonance to this otherwise trite, but charming, tale of self-sacrifice; instead it makes the soul-searching of the central characters seem a luxury and an irrelevance.
w Claude Miller, Luc Béraud *novel* Nina Berberova *d* Claude Miller *ph* Yves Angelo *m* Alain Jomy *pd* Jean-Pierre Kohut Svelko *ed* Albert Jurgenson
☆ Richard Bohringer, Elena Safonova, Romane Bohringer, Bernard Verley, Samuel Labarthe, Nelly Borgeaud, Julien Rassam, Jean-Pierre Kohut Svelko
'Dramatically, the movie doesn't cover much ground ... all he ends up with is the thin old story of a supporting artist who lives by proxy.' – *Michael Sragow, New Yorker*
'The film's uniform visual and narrative dullness does act as a perfectly effective anaesthetic. And it also fits a certain, rather unpleasant way of

looking at French history in which these stories and images that we've seen a thousand times take on a mythical quality.' – *Martin Bright, Sight and Sound*

According to Mrs Hoyle
US 1951 60m bw
Monogram
A retired schoolteacher lives in a hotel run by criminals, and becomes involved.
Uninspired sentimental comedy providing a rare star part for a well-liked character actress.
w W. Scott Darling, Barney Gerard *d* Jean Yarbrough
☆ Spring Byington, Anthony Caruso, Brett King, Tanis Chandler

Account Rendered
GB 1957 60m bw
Rank/Major Productions (John Temple-Smith)
A detective inspector tracks down the killer of a banker's flirtatious wife.
Indifferent thriller lacking any distinguishing features.
w Barbara S. Harper *novel* Pamela Barrington *d* Peter Graham Scott *ph* Walter J. Harvey *ad* Norman Arnold *ed* Tom Simpson
☆ Honor Blackman, Griffith Jones, Ursula Howells, Ewen Solon, Robert Raikes, John Van Eyssen

'The standout suspense triumph of the year!'
The Accused *
US 1948 101m bw
Paramount (Hal B. Wallis)
aka: *Strange Deception*
In self-defence a lady professor kills a student who has sexually attacked her.
Dullish suspenser with the outcome never in doubt, though the production values are beyond reproach.
w Ketti Frings *d* William Dieterle *ph* Milton Krasner *m* Victor Young
☆ Loretta Young, Robert Cummings, Wendell Corey, Sam Jaffe, Douglas Dick

The Accused *
US 1988 110m Technicolor
UIP/Paramount (Stanley R. Jaffe, Sherry Lansing)
A provocatively-dressed woman is raped after performing a sexy dance at a seedy bar.
Unconvincing problem picture that fails to explore the issues it raises.
w Tom Topor *d* Jonathan Kaplan *ph* Ralf Bode *m* Brad Fiedel *pd* Richard Kent Wilcox *ed* Jerry Greenberg, O. Nicholas Brown
☆ Kelly McGillis, Jodie Foster, Bernie Coulson, Ann Hearn, Steve Antin, Tom O'Brien
'Another box-office winner which once again negotiates a fine line between social concern, feminism and exploitation.' – *MFB*
Jodie Foster

Ace in the Hole ***
US 1951 111m bw
Paramount (Billy Wilder)
aka: *The Big Carnival*
In order to prolong the sensation and boost newspaper sales, a self-seeking journalist delays the rescue of a man trapped in a cave.
An incisive, compelling melodrama taking a sour look at the American scene; one of its director's masterworks.
w Billy Wilder, Lesser Samuels, Walter Newman d Billy Wilder ph Charles B. Lang Jnr *m* Hugo Friedhofer
☆ *Kirk Douglas* (Chuck Tatum), Jan Sterling (Lorraine), *Porter Hall* (Boot), Bob Arthur (Herbie), Richard Benedict (Leo), Ray Teal (Sheriff), Frank Cady (Federber)
LORRAINE TO TATUM: 'I've met some hard-boiled eggs, but you – you're twenty minutes!'
LORRAINE: 'I don't go to church. Kneeling bags my nylons.'
TATUM TO EDITOR: 'I've done a lot of lying in my time. I've lied to men who wear belts. I've lied to men who wear suspenders. But I'd never be so stupid as to lie to a man who wears both belt and suspenders.'
TATUM, DYING, TO EDITOR: 'How'd you like to make a thousand dollars a day, Mr Boot? I'm a thousand-dollar-a-day newspaperman. You can have me for nothing.'
'Few of the opportunities for irony, cruelty and horror are missed.' – *Gavin Lambert*
'Style and purpose achieve for the most part a fusion even more remarkable than in *Sunset Boulevard*.' – *Penelope Houston*
'As stimulating as black coffee.' – *Richard Mallett, Punch*
'Americans expected a cocktail and felt I was giving them a shot of vinegar instead.' – *Billy Wilder*
'Some people have tried to claim some sort of satirical brilliance for it, but it's really rather nasty, in a sociologically pushy way.' – *New Yorker, 1980*
'A brilliant arrangement of cause and effect … unique as a mirror of the morbid psychology of crowds … revolting but incontrovertibly true.' – *New York Times*
† Locations were at Gallup, New Mexico.
script

Ace of Aces *
US 1933 76m bw
RKO
On the outbreak of World War I an American sculptor is branded a coward when he does not immediately enlist; but he disappears and turns up in France a hero, though with a sour taste in his mouth.
Melodrama of disillusion, dated in many respects but interesting to compare with The Dawn Patrol and The Last Flight.
w John Monk Saunders, H. W. Hanemann *story Bird of Prey* by John Monk Saunders *d* J. Walter Ruben *ph* Henry Cronjager *m* Max Steiner
☆ Richard Dix, Elizabeth Allan, Theodore Newton, Ralph Bellamy, Joseph Sawyer, Frank Conroy, William Cagney
'It's the fine photography and crashes that provide the thrills.' – *Variety*

'He's the best there is! (Actually, he's the only one there is.)'
Ace Ventura, Pet Detective
US 1994 93m colour
Warner/Morgan Creek (James G. Robinson)
A private eye who recovers missing pets is hired to recover the Miami Dolphins' dolphin mascot.
Featuring a relentlessly mugging comedian who makes Jerry Lewis seem as restrained as Buster Keaton, this is an extraordinarily inept comedy, with feeble jokes parodying other movies, feebler slapstick and much homophobia and misogyny; it also provides Sean Young with the most demeaning role of her career.
w Jack Bernstein, Tom Shadyac, Jim Carrey *d* Tom Shadyac *ph* Julio Macat *m* Ira Newborn *pd* William Elliott *ed* Don Zimmerman
☆ Jim Carrey, Courteney Cox, Sean Young, Dan Marino, Noble Willingham, Troy Evans, Udo Kier, Tone Loc
'Doesn't display the comic pedigree needed for the rubber-faced-and-limbed comedian to collar breakthrough dollars. That said, dumb good times still wield a strong lure for the Saturday night date crowd.' – *Variety*
† The film was an unexpected hit in America, earning more than $65m at the box-office and raising Jim Carrey's price per picture from $350,000 to a reported $7m.

Ace Ventura: When Nature Calls
US 1995 92m Technicolor Super 35
Warner/Morgan Creek (James G. Robinson)
A pet detective goes to Africa to find a sacred white bat, a creature he dislikes.
Carrey extends his range of lavatorial humour to include spit and vomit, and an exit from the anus of a mechanical rhinoceros. The bad-taste episodic narrative, resembling a very old version of King Solomon's Mines, has no other function than to give him plenty of scope for his unrestrained mugging.
wd Steve Oedekerk *ph* Donald E. Thorin *m* Robert Folk *pd* Stephen J. Lineweaver *ed* Malcolm Campbell
☆ Jim Carrey, Ian McNeice, Simon Callow, Maynard Eziashi, Bob Gunton, Sophie Okonedo, Tommy Davidson, Adewalé, Andrew Steel, Bruce Spence
'As fresh, brash and outrageous as the original' – *Variety*
† Director Tom DeCerchio left after shooting began, to be replaced by writer Steve Oedekerk. The film took $37.8m on its opening weekend in the United States, the highest figure so far for a comedy, and went on to gross more than $104m at the US box-office and another $37m elsewhere during 1995.

Aces High *
GB 1976 114m Technicolor
EMI/S. Benjamin Fisz/Jacques Roitfeld
In the air force during World War I, young pilots are needlessly sacrificed.
Spirited if rather unnecessary remake of Journey's End transposed to the air war, which makes it almost identical to The Dawn Patrol.
w Howard Barker *d* Jack Gold *ph* Gerry Fisher, Peter Allwork *m* Richard Hartley
☆ Malcolm McDowell, Christopher Plummer, Simon Ward, Peter Firth, John Gielgud, Trevor Howard, Richard Johnson, Ray Milland

'Their best and final mission.'
Aces: Iron Eagle III
US 1992 98m CFI color
New Line/7 Arts (Ron Samuels)
Veteran fighter pilots battle against South American drug barons.
Energetic but mindless action, with a little slapstick thrown in, and featuring muscle-woman Rachel McLish.
w Kevin Elders *d* John Glen *ph* Alec Mills *m* Harry Manfredini *pd* Robb Wilson King *ed* Bernard Gribble *sp* John Richardson
☆ Louis Gossett Jnr, Rachel McLish, Paul Freeman, Horst Buchholz, Christopher Cazenove, Sonny Chiba, Fred Dalton Thompson, Mitchell Ryan

Acid House
GB 1998 118m colour
Film Four/Picture Palace North/Umbrella/Channel 4 (David Muir, Alex Usborne)
Three stories about life in Scotland: 'The Granton Star Cause', in which God turns a failure into a fly; 'The Soft Touch', in which a man takes back his unfaithful wife; 'The Acid House', in which a drug-taking youth switches personalities with a baby.
Unsubtle portmanteau movie, in which anarchic wit struggles against a browbeating style and loses; the overall effect is dispiriting.
w Irvine Welsh *stories* Irvine Welsh *d* Paul McGuigan *ph* Alasdair Walker *m Primal Scream, Nick Cave et al. pd* Richard Bridgland, Mike Gunn *ed* Andrew Hulme
☆ 'The Granton Star Cause': Stephen McCole, Maurice Roeves, Garry Sweeney, Jenny McCrindle, Irvine Welsh, 'A Soft Touch': Kevin McKidd, Michelle Gomez, Tam Dean Burn, Gary McCormack, 'The Acid House': Ewen Bremner, Martin Clunes, Jemma Redgrave, Arlene Cockburn, Jane Stabler
'The acting throughout is broad, the direction has a sledgehammer coarseness, and the lack of compassion, though this cannot be intentional, seems absolute.' – *Philip French, Observer*

Across 110th Street ***
US 1972 102m DeLuxe
UA/Film Guarantors (Fouad Said, Ralph Serpe)
Police and the Mafia go after three blacks disguised as cops who rob a Harlem numbers bank and kill its operators.
Tough, clever thriller, set within a well-observed society of violence and deprivation.
w Luther Davis *novel* Wally Ferris *d* Barry Shear *ph* Jack Priestley *m* J. J. Johnson *ad* Perry Watkins *ed* Bryan Brandt
☆ Anthony Quinn, Yaphet Kotto, Anthony Franciosa, Paul Benjamin, Ed Barnard, Richard Ward, Antonio Fargas
† The film was cut to 99m on its British release.

'Once A Master Of Millions … Now A Fugitive In Flight!'
Across the Bridge *
GB 1957 103m bw
Rank/IPF (John Stafford)
A fugitive financier kills his pursuer, finds he was a murderer, and tries to hide out across the Mexican border.
This star tour de force is unconvincing in detail and rather unattractive to watch (British films never could cope with American settings), but the early sequences have suspense.
w Guy Elmes, Denis Freeman *novel* Graham Greene *d* Ken Annakin *ph* Reg Wyer *m* James Bernard
☆ Rod Steiger, David Knight, Marla Landi, Noel Willman, Bernard Lee

Across the Pacific ***
US 1942 99m bw
Warner (Hal B. Wallis)
Just before Pearl Harbor, an army officer is cashiered by arrangement in order to contact pro-Japanese sympathizers.
Hasty, easy-going and very enjoyable hokum, partly ship-set and successfully reteaming three stars of The Maltese Falcon.
w Richard Macaulay *serial Aloha Means Goodbye* by *Robert Carson d* John Huston *ph* Arthur Edeson *m* Adolph Deutsch
☆ *Humphrey Bogart* (Rick Leland), *Mary Astor* (Alberta Marlow), *Sydney Greenstreet* (Dr Lorenz), *Sen Yung* (Joe Totsuiko), Monte Blue, Richard Loo, Chester Gan, Kam Tong
'A spy picture which tingles with fearful uncertainties and glints with the sheen of blue steel.' – *Bosley Crowther*
† Huston was called up before the film was completed, and allegedly reshaped the script before leaving in order to put the hero in an impossible situation. Direction was eventually completed by Vincent Sherman
†† Monte Blue, who has a tiny last-reel part as the heroine's drunken father, starred in a 1926 silent film with the same title but a totally different plot. He played an army officer fighting Philippine guerrillas. Darryl F. Zanuck wrote the script, and Roy del Ruth directed, for Warner.

Across the Road: see *En Face*

Across the Tracks
US 1991 100m CFI color
Desert Productions (Dale Rosenbloom)
Two athletic brothers of differing temperaments become rivals.
A well-intentioned movie about teenage problems that may appeal to adolescents but not to adults.
wd Sandy Tung *ph* Michael Delahoussaye *m* Joel Goldsmith *pd* Thomas Meleck *ed* Farrel Levy
☆ Rick Schroder, Brad Pitt, Carrie Snodgress, David Anthony Marshall, Thomas Mikal Ford, John Linton

Across the Wide Missouri *
US 1951 77m Technicolor
MGM (Robert Sisk)
In the 1820s, a trapper marries an Indian girl and lives with her people.
Promising credits produce an unsatisfactory Western: despite honest efforts, the elements do not jell into a convincing whole.
w Talbot Jennings *d* William Wellman *ph* William C. Mellor *m* David Raksin
☆ Clark Gable, Ricardo Montalban, John Hodiak, Adolphe Menjou, Maria Elena Marques, J. Carrol Naish, Jack Holt, Alan Napier, Howard Keel (narrator)

Act of Love *
US 1954 104m bw
UA/Benagoss (Anatole Litvak)
In Paris in 1944, an American with the liberation army falls in love with a French girl, who commits suicide when he is posted and cannot make their rendezvous.
Cheerless romantic drama, rather thin and unmemorable despite the efforts of all concerned.
w Irwin Shaw *novel The Girl on the Via Flaminia* by Alfred Hayes *d* Anatole Litvak *ph* Armand Thirard *m* Michael Emer, Joe Hajos *pd* Alexander Trauner
☆ Kirk Douglas, Dany Robin, Barbara Laage, Robert Stauss, Gabrielle Dorziat, Gregoire Aslan, Fernand Ledoux, Serge Reggiani, Brigitte Bardot
† Made in France, an early Hollywood foreign location film.

An Act of Murder *
US 1948 90m bw
U-I (Jerry Bresler)
aka: *Live Today for Tomorrow*
A judge insists on being tried for the mercy killing of his incurably ill wife.
Earnest social drama which despite excellent acting can only reach an inconclusive ending.
w Michael Blankfort, Robert Thoeren *novel The Mills of God* by Ernst Lothar *d* Michael Gordon *ph* Hal Mohr *m* Daniele Amfitheatrof *ad* Robert Boyle, Bernard Herzbrun *ed* Ralph Dawson
☆ *Fredric March* (Judge Calvin Cooke), Florence Eldridge (Catherine Cooke), Edmond O'Brien (David Douglas), Geraldine Brooks (Ellie Cooke), Stanley Ridges (Dr Walter Morrison), John McIntire (Judge Ogden)

Act of Murder **
GB 1964 62m bw
Merton Park (Jack Greenwood)
A couple arrange a holiday by swapping houses with strangers, and a complex plot ensues.
Slick, superior example of the Edgar Wallace second feature series.
w Lewis Davidson *d Alan Bridges ph* James Wilson *m* Bernard Ebbinghouse *ed* Derek Holding
☆ John Carson (Tim Ford), Anthony Bate (Ralph Longman), Justine Lord (Ann Longman), Duncan Lewis (Will Peterson), Dandy Nichols (Maud Peterson), Richard Burrell (John Quick), Sheena Marshe (Pauline)
'This uncommonly intelligent little thriller is just the sort of film which is likely to arouse critical sneers for reaching too high on a low budget.' – *Tom Milne*

Act of Violence **
US 1948 82m bw
MGM (William Wright)
After the war, an ex-GI tracks down a prison camp informer.
Moody, glossy melodrama with tension well sustained, though the sentimental ending is a cop-out.
w Robert L. Richards *story* Collier Young *d Fred Zinnemann ph Robert Surtees m* Bronislau Kaper
☆ *Van Heflin, Robert Ryan*, Janet Leigh, Mary Astor
'Strong characterization, fine direction and good photography combine to put this film high among its kind.' – *MFB*
'An effortless narrative control and a real power to maintain tension.' – *Richard Winnington*

Act One *
US 1963 110m bw
Warner (Dore Schary)
Poor Brooklyn boy Moss Hart rises to Broadway eminence via his writing partnership with George S. Kaufman.
Incredibly stilted film version of an excellent autobiography, notable only for fragments of acting and the fact that a film so totally uncommercial was made at all.
wd Dore Schary *ph* Arthur J. Ornitz *m* Skitch Henderson
☆ George Hamilton (Hart), Jason Robards Jnr (Kaufman), Jack Klugman, Sam Levene, George Segal, Ruth Ford, Eli Wallach
'From the moment young Hart takes pencil in hand, we have nowhere to go except to that happy ending; and despite all the painstaking detail, we don't believe a word of it.' – *Judith Crist*

Action for Slander *
GB 1937 83m bw
London Films/Saville (Victor Saville)
A bankrupt officer, accused of cheating at cards, defends his honour with a writ.
Lively melodrama of the old school.
w Ian Dalrymple, Miles Malleson *novel* Mary Borden *d* Tim Whelan *ph* Harry Stradling *md* Muir Mathieson
☆ Clive Brook, Ann Todd, Margaretta Scott, Arthur Margetson, Ronald Squire, Athole Stewart, Percy Marmont, Frank Cellier, Morton Selten
'Hollywood in its most lavish spurt of extravagance never went to such pains to assemble a cast … general run of patrons however will chafe under the lack of physical movement.' – *Variety*

Action in the North Atlantic *
US 1943 127m bw
Warner (Jerry Wald)
[NTSC] [colourised]
An American convoy bound for Russia comes under U-boat attack.
Efficient propaganda potboiler; studio bound, but still works as a war actioner.
w John Howard Lawson *story* Guy Gilpatric *d* Lloyd Bacon *ph* Ted McCord *m* Adolph Deutsch
☆ Humphrey Bogart, Raymond Massey, Alan Hale, Julie Bishop, Ruth Gordon, Sam Levene, Dane Clark
'The production has interludes of tremendous power. What is lacking is dramatic cohesion.' – *Howard Barnes*
'Directly in line of descent from *The Perils of Pauline*.' – *Time*
'The American equivalent of our war documentaries … tough, exciting, with no concession to flim flam.' – *New Statesman*
'I cannot think I have ever seen such realistic battles, or lived so intimately with the characters who comprise the crew.' – *Evening Standard*
Ꮨ Guy Gilpatric

Action Jackson
US 1988 96m Metrocolor
Guild/Lorimar (Joel Silver)
[NTSC] [laser disc] [DVD]
A maverick cop is framed for a murder while investigating the killings of union officials.
Violent action movie, with spectacular deaths and car chases, a ludicrous plot and a hissable villain.
w Robert Reneau *d* Craig R. Baxley *ph* Matthew F. Leonetti *m* Herbie Hancock, Michael Kamen *ad* Virginia Randolph *ed* Mark Helfrich
☆ Carl Weathers, Craig T. Nelson, Vanity, Sharon Stone, Thomas F. Wilson, Bill Duke, Robert Davi

Actors and Sin *
US 1952 91m bw
UA/Sid Kuller (Ben Hecht)
[NTSC]
Two short stories. When an unsuccessful actress commits suicide, her father makes it look like murder so that for once she shall get attention. The authoress of a romantic script bought by Hollywood is discovered to be a horrid little 9-year-old.
Interesting but incompetent compendium which descends almost to the home movie level and leaves the actors struggling.
wd Ben Hecht *ph* Lee Garmes *m* George Antheil
☆ Edward G. Robinson, Marsha Hunt, Dan O'Herlihy, Rudolph Anders, Eddie Albert, Alan Reed, Jenny Hecht
'A depressing double bill.' – *Lindsay Anderson*

An Actor's Revenge **
Japan 1963 113m Daieicolor Daieiscope
Daiei (Masaichi Nagata)
[VHS] [NTSC] [DVD]
original title: *Yukinojo Henge*
In the early 19th century, a touring actor comes upon the rich merchant who had ruined his parents, and his revenge involves several deaths.
Complex, fascinating period melodrama, both rich and strange, with strong echoes of Jacobean melodrama.
w Daisuke Ito, Teinosuke Kinugasa, Natto Wada *novel* Otokichi Mikami *d Kon Ichikawa* *ph* Setsuo Kobayashi *m* Yasushi Akutagawa
☆ *Kazuo Hasegawa*, Fujiko Yamamoto, Ayako Wakao, Ganjiro Nakamura

The Actress *
US 1928 90m approx (24 fps) bw silent
MGM
GB title: *Trelawny of the 'Wells'*
A young Victorian actress marries a rich admirer.
Pleasing, well-cast version of a celebrated play.
w Albert Lewin, Richard Schayer *play* Sir Arthur Wing Pinero *d* Sidney Franklin *ph* William Daniels
☆ Norma Shearer, Ralph Forbes, O. P. Heggie, Owen Moore, Roy D'Arcy
'A thoughtful, rounded and provocative entertainment.' – *New York Times*
† Opening attraction at London's Empire Theatre, Leicester Square.

The Actress
US 1953 91m bw
MGM (Lawrence Weingarten)
Ruth Jones becomes an actress against the wishes of her stubborn seafaring father.
Episodes from Ruth Gordon's early life, based on her Broadway play Years Ago, make a pleasant though scarcely engrossing film: it is all a shade too discreet and wanly winning, and the few key events take place offscreen.
w Ruth Gordon *d* George Cukor *ph* Harold Rosson *m* Bronislau Kaper *ad* Cedric Gibbons, Arthur Lonergan
☆ Jean Simmons, Spencer Tracy, Teresa Wright, Anthony Perkins, Ian Wolfe, Mary Wickes

Actresses
Spain 1996 88m colour
Downtown/Els Films de la Rambla (Ventura Pons)
original title: *Actrius*
Before auditioning for the role of a legendary actress, a drama student interviews three of her former pupils.
This leisurely examination of the influence of past events on present lives reveals its theatrical origins by its static style; it also provides little opportunity for its cast to revel in the pleasures of acting.
w Ventura Pons, J. M. Benet I Jornet *play E.R.* by J. M. Benet I Jornet *d* Ventura Pons *ph* Tomás Pladevall *m* Carles Cases *pd* Rosa Ros *ed* Pere Abadal
☆ Nuria Espert, Rosa Maria Sardà, Anna Lizaran, Mercè Pons
'I can't think of anyone this film could possibly interest. It has the dramatic momentum of a slug.' – *James Christopher, The Times*

Acts of Love: see *Carried Away*

Ad Ogni Costo: see *Grand Slam*

Ada *
US 1961 109m Metrocolor Cinemascope
MGM/Avon/Chalmar (Lawrence Weingarten)
A political candidate marries a call girl who becomes his strong right arm and weathers a threat to reveal her past.
Indecisive romantic drama which pulls too many punches but has interesting background detail.
w Arthur Sheekman, William Driskill *novel Ada Dallas* by Wirt Williams *d* Daniel Mann *ph* Joseph Ruttenberg *m* Bronislau Kaper
☆ Susan Hayward, Dean Martin, Wilfrid Hyde-White, Ralph Meeker, Martin Balsam
'A bonanza for connoisseurs of perfectly awful movies.' – *Judith Crist*
'Its characterizations are sketchy, its political setting routine and symbolic.' – *New York Herald Tribune*

Adalen 31 **
Sweden 1969 115m Technicolor Techniscope
Svensk Filmindustri
A prolonged strike at a small-town paper mill ends in tragedy when the troops move in.
Effective period piece which emphasizes the idyllic qualities of the backgrounds rather than the foreground terrors.
wd Bo Widerberg ph Jorgen Persson
☆ Peter Schildt, Kerstin Tidelius, Roland Hedlund, Stefan Feierbach, Anita Bjork
Ꮨ foreign film

Adam *
GB 1991 7m colour
Aardman Animations (Christopher Moll)
[VHS]
A solitary figure living on a small world becomes excited when his creator decides to make him a companion.
Amusing cartoon of the beginning of the sex wars.
wd Peter Lord *ph* David Sproxton *m* Stuart Gordon *ed* Nigel Bell
Ꮨ animated film

Adam and Eva *
US 1923 83m approx bw silent
Paramount/Cosmopolitan
An extravagant girl reforms when her father goes bust.
Moral comedy with a happy ending: a hit of its day.
w Luther Reed *play* Guy Bolton and George Middleton *d* Robert G. Vignola
☆ Marion Davies, T. Roy Barnes, Tom Lewis, William Norris, Percy Ames

Adam and Evelyne
GB 1949 92m bw
Rank/Two Cities (Harold French)
A society playboy adopts his dead friend's daughter, and falls in love with her.
Undernourished romantic drama, a mild variation on Daddy Longlegs.
w Noel Langley, Lesley Storm, George Barraud, Nicholas Phipps *d* Harold French *ph* Guy Green *m* Mischa Spoliansky
☆ Stewart Granger, Jean Simmons, Helen Cherry, Edwin Styles, Beatrice Varley, Wilfrid Hyde-White

Adam at 6 A.M. *
US 1970 100m colour
National General (Robert Christiansen, Rick Rosenberg)
[VHS] [NTSC]
A disillusioned Californian university professor returns to Missouri and takes a labouring job.
Interesting and unconventional drama of a liberal kind.
w Stephen Karpf, Elinor Karpf *d* Robert Scheerer *ph* Charles Rosher *ad* Dale Hennessey *ed* Jack McSweeney
☆ Michael Douglas, Lee Purcell, Joe Don Baker, Grayson Hall, Charles Aidman, Louise Latham, Meg Foster

Adam Had Four Sons *
US 1941 81m bw
Columbia (Robert Sherwood)
[NTSC]
A widower's family is cared for by a governess.
Modest magazine fiction which established Ingrid Bergman as an American star.
w Michael Blankfort, William Hurlbut *novel Legacy* by Charles Bonner *d* Gregory Ratoff *ph* Peverell Marley *m* W. Franke Harling
☆ Warner Baxter, *Ingrid Bergman*, Susan Hayward, Richard Denning, Fay Wray

'It's naughty. It's nice. It's animated.'
Adam Sandler's Eight Crazy Nights
US 2002 76m DeLuxe
Columbia/Happy Madison (Adam Sandler, Jack Giarraputo, Allen Covert)
[DVD]
Sentenced to community service as an assistant to a baseball referee, a small town drunk learns the error of his ways.
A gruesome experience, with Sandler's gross, slapstick humour and sentimentality married to some unexceptional animation.
w Brooks Arthur, Allen Covert, Brad Isaacs, Adam Sandler *d* Seth Kearsley *m* Ray Ellis, Marc Ellis, Teddy Castellucci *pd* Perry Andelin Blake *ed* Amy Budden
☆ voices of: Adam Sandler (Davey/Whitey/Eleanore/Deer), Jackie Titone (Jennifer), Austin Stout (Benjamin), Kevin Nealon (Mayor), Rob Schneider (Chinese Waiter/Narrator), Norm Crosby (Judge), Jon Lovitz (Tom Baltezor)
'The usual Sandler mush of bad taste gags and schmaltz.' – *Nicholas Barber, Independent*
'A dark, vulgar, brooding turnoff of a movie, minus the steady laugh quotient needed to appease Sandler's core constituency.' – *Scott Foundas, Variety*

Adam's Rib *
US 1922 86m bw silent
Paramount (Cecil B. de Mille)
By offering herself in her stead, an American girl tries to prevent her mother's adultery with a European ex-monarch.
One of its director's 'sin in high life' melodramas, which packed 'em in at the time, this has nothing but decoration to offer to a modern audience.
w Jeanie MacPherson *d* Cecil B. de Mille
☆ Milton Sills, Elliott Dexter, Theodore Kosloff, Anna Q. Nilsson, Pauline Garon, Julia Faye

Adam's Rib **
US 1949 101m bw
MGM (Lawrence Weingarten)
[VHS] [NTSC] [laser disc] [DVD]
Husband and wife lawyers are on opposite sides of an attempted murder case.
A superior star vehicle which also managed to introduce four promising personalities; slangily written and

smartly directed, but perhaps a shade less funny than it once seemed.
w Ruth Gordon, Garson Kanin *d* George Cukor *ph* George J. Folsey *m* Miklos Rozsa
☆ *Spencer Tracy, Katharine Hepburn, David Wayne, Tom Ewell, Judy Holliday, Jean Hagen,* Hope Emerson, Clarence Kolb

'Hepburn and Tracy are again presented as the ideal US Mr and Mrs of upper-middle income. This time, as well as being wittily urbane, both are lawyers.' – *Time*

'It isn't solid food but it certainly is meaty and juicy and comically nourishing.' – *Bosley Crowther*

† A 1972 TV series of the same title provided a boring imitation, with Ken Howard and Blythe Danner.
Ruth Gordon and Garson Kanin

Adamson of Africa: see *The Killers of Kilimanjaro*

Adaptation ***
US 2002 115m DeLuxe
Columbia/Intermedia/Magnet/Clinica Estetico (Edward Saxon, Vincent Landay, Jonathan Demme)

A neurotic screenwriter has problems adapting a non-fiction book about a Florida orchid breeder, while his twin brother happily churns out a script about a serial killer.
Witty, inventive, playful movie about a blocked writer trying out various approaches to intractable material before relying on Hollywood clichés to get him through to the end; it's much funnier than it sounds, aided by some stylish direction and expertly comic performances.
w Charlie Kaufman, Donald Kaufman *book* The Orchid Thief by Susan Orlean *d* Spike Jonze *ph* Lance Acord *m* Carter Burwell *pd* KK Barrett *ed* Eric Zumbrunnen *cos* Ann Roth
☆ *Nicolas Cage* (Charlie Kaufman/Donald Kaufman), *Meryl Streep* (Susan Orlean), *Chris Cooper* (John Laroche), Tilda Swinton (Valerie), Cara Seymour (Amelia), Brian Cox (Robert McKee), Judy Greer (Alice the Waitress), Maggie Gyllenhaal (Caroline)

'Screenwriting this smart, inventive, passionate and rip-roaringly funny is a rare species. It's magic.' – *Peter Travers, Rolling Stone*

'The trouble with experimental comedies is that it's often impossible to figure out how to end them. But at least this one is intricate fun before it blows itself up.' – *David Denby, New Yorker*

Chris Cooper
Nicolas Cage; Meryl Streep; Charlie Kaufman, Donald Kaufman
Charlie Kaufman, Donald Kaufman

'Creepy. Kooky. Spooky. Ooky.'
The Addams Family *
US 1991 99m DeLuxe
Columbia TriStar/Paramount/Orion (Scott Rudin)

An impostor turns up at the Addams family mansion, claiming to be a long-lost elder brother.
Owing more to the TV series of the 1960s than to the macabre wit of the original New Yorker cartoons, an ill-conceived, coarse-grained comedy that nevertheless was a success at the box-office.
w Caroline Thompson, Larry Wilson *characters created by* Charles Addams *d* Barry Sonnenfeld *ph* Owen Roizman *m* Marc Shaiman *pd* Richard MacDonald *ed* Dede Allen, Jim Miller *sp* visual effects supervisor Alan Munro, Chuck Comisky
☆ Anjelica Huston, Raul Julia, Christopher Lloyd, Dan Hedaya, Elizabeth Wilson, Judith Malina, Carel Struycken, Dana Ivey, Christina Ricci, Paul Benedict, Christopher Hart (whose hand appears as The Thing)

'Plays like a collection of sitcom one-liners augmented by feature-film special effects – a combination that is stretched well beyond its limits.' – *Variety*

'Misguided graveyard slapstick.' – *New Yorker*

'Motherhood just got a little stranger.'
Addams Family Values *
US 1993 94m colour
UIP/Paramount (Scott Rudin)

The Addams children try to kill the new baby, but he is damage-proof; while their parents hire a nanny who is also a serial killer.
This is less a movie and more a sequence of gags set in an elongated sit-com, of which few are inspired and most too ordinary to amuse, but it has its moments.
w Paul Rudnick *d* Barry Sonnenfeld *ph* Donald Peterman *m* Marc Shaiman *pd* Ken Adam *ed* Arthur Schmidt, Jim Miller
☆ Anjelica Huston (Morticia Addams), Raul Julia (Gomez Addams), Christopher Lloyd (Uncle Fester), Joan Cusack (Debbie Jellinsky), *Christina Ricci* (Wednesday Addams), Carol Kane (Granny), Jimmy Workman (Pugsley Addams), Carel Struycken (Lurch), David Krumholtz (Joe Glicker), Christopher Hart (Thing), Kristin Hooper (Pubert Addams), Dana Ivey (Margaret), Peter MacNicol (Gary Granger), Christine Baranski (Becky Granger)

'It's the kind of wicked delicious comedy one can savor without adding the proviso of guilty pleasure.' – *Variety*

'The film does not know when to stop, has little idea of how to begin, and moves forward by a process of "Quick, who's got the next gimmick" jolts and nudges.' – *Nigel Andrews, Financial Times*

'The storyline is almost too slim to recall and the cast simply earn their bread and butter doing revue turns.' – *Derek Malcolm, Guardian*

Ken Adam

Addicted to Love *
US 1997 100m Technicolor
Warner/Outlaw/Miramax (Jeffrey Silver, Bobby Newmyer)

When his girlfriend leaves him for a French restaurateur, an astronomer joins with the man's jilted fiancée to break up their romance.
A romantic comedy with a cutting edge, as people behave badly to one another in the name of fidelity.
w Robert Gordon *d* Griffin Dunne *ph* Andrew Dunn *m* Rachel Portman *pd* Robin Standefer *ed* Elizabeth Kling
☆ Meg Ryan, Matthew Broderick, Kelly Preston, Tcheky Karyo, Maureen Stapleton, Nesbitt Blaisdell, Remak Ramsay, Dominick Dunne

'This odd juxtaposition of light drama and outrageous antics is apt to confuse more than charm audience.' – *Leonard Klady, Variety*

The Addiction
US 1995 82m bw
Guild/Fast Films (Denis Hann, Fernando Sulichin)

A philosophy student turns vampire and is turned on by the writings of Nietzsche.
Ferrara bites off more than he can chew in this horror movie, using images of massacres and concentration camp victims to emphasize his depiction of power-crazed bloodlust let loose on society; but his fiction shrivels in the light of these actual horrors.
w Nicholas St John *d* Abel Ferrara *ph* Ken Kelsch *m* Joe Delia *pd* Charlie Lagola *ed* Mayin Lo
☆ Lili Taylor, Christoper Walken, Annabella Sciorra, Edie Falco, Paul Calderon, Fredro Star, Kathryn Erbe, Michael Imperioli

'Dramatically surprising, stylishly made in black-and-white and very well acted.' – *Variety*

'Offensively pretentious.' – *Sunday Times*

The Adding Machine *
GB 1968 99m Technicolor
Universal/Associated London (Jerome Epstein)
Downtrodden clerk Mr Zero rebels against society by murdering his boss. Tried and executed, he spends thirty years in heaven before being 'laundered' and sent back to start again as another nonentity.
Elmer Rice's satirical fantasy of the twenties is here robbed of its expressionist staging and presented naturalistically, a fatal error from which the film never for one moment recovers.
wd Jerome Epstein *ph* Walter Lassally *m* Mike Leander, Lambert Williamson
☆ Phyllis Diller, Milo O'Shea, Billie Whitelaw, Sydney Chaplin, Julian Glover, Raymond Huntley, Phil Brown, Libby Morris

Addio, Fratello Crudele: see *'Tis Pity She's a Whore*

Address Unknown **
US 1944 72m bw
Columbia (William Cameron Menzies)
A German-American becomes a Nazi and is incriminated by false letters from his one-time friend.
Reasonably engrossing, cheaply-made adaptation of a slim little thriller which was widely read during World War II.
w Kressman Taylor, Herbert Dalmas *novel* Kressman Taylor *d* William Cameron Menzies *ph* Rudolph Maté *m* Ernst Toch *ad* Lionel Banks, Walter Holscher
☆ *Paul Lukas, Carl Esmond,* Peter Van Eyck, Mady Christians, Emory Parnell
Ernst Toch; art direction

Adieu Philippine *
France/Italy 1962 106m bw
Unitec/Alpha/Rome-Paris (Georges de Beauregard)
A young TV cameraman is torn between two girls.
Flimsy but attractive romantic comedy, slightly marred by New Wave improvisation with consequent rough edges.
w Michèle O'Glor, Jacques Rozier *d* Jacques Rozier *ph* René Mathelin *m* various
☆ Jean-Claude Aimini, Yveline Céry, Stefania Sabatini, Vittorio Caprioli

Adios, Sabata: see *The Bounty Hunters*

Adj Kiraly Katonat: see *The Princess*

'Sex ... Power ... Obsession.'
The Adjuster *
Canada 1991 102m colour Panavision
Metro/Ego Film Arts/Téléfilm Canada/Ontario Film Development Corp. (Atom Egoyan)

An insurance loss adjuster becomes involved in the sexual activities of his clients.
Offbeat movie that takes an oblique approach to the relationship between cinema and voyeurism.
wd Atom Egoyan *ph* Paul Sarossy *m* Mychael Danna *pd* Linda Del Rosario, Richard Paris *ed* Susan Shipton
☆ Elias Koteas, Arsinée Khanjian, Maury Chaykin, Gabrielle Rose, Jennifer Dale, David Hemblen, Rose Sarkisyan, Armen Kokorian

'Utterly compelling, a visual treat and, above all, a fiercely intelligent piece of work.' – *Empire*

The Admirable Crichton *
GB 1957 93m Technicolor Vistavision
Columbia/Modern Screenplays (Ian Dalrymple)
US title: *Paradise Lagoon*
Lord Loam and his family are shipwrecked on a desert island, where his manservant proves the undisputed leader.
Few laughs are to be had from this blunt, sentimental version of a famous play, but the photography and decor are excellent.
w Vernon Harris *play* J. M. Barrie *d* Lewis Gilbert *ph* Wilkie Cooper *m* Douglas Gamley, Richard Addinsell *ad* William Kellner *cos* Bernard Nevill *devices* Emmett
☆ Kenneth More, Cecil Parker, Sally Ann Howes, Diane Cilento, Martita Hunt, Jack Watling, Peter Graves, Gerald Harper

'Barrie's play now seems more remote than *Gammer Gurton*.' – *David Robinson*

The Admiral Was a Lady
US 1950 87m bw
Roxbury (Albert S. Rogell, Jack M. Warner)

Four ex-airmen and an ex-Wac try to live on their wits.
Unappealing comedy which gives the impression that it has tried to find a new style, and failed.
w Sidney Salkow, John O'Dea *d* Albert S. Rogell *ph* Stanley Cortez
☆ Edmond O'Brien, Wanda Hendrix, Rudy Vallee, Johnny Sands, Steve Brodie, Richard Erdman, Hillary Brooke, Richard Lane

The Adolescent
France/West Germany 1979 93m colour
Janus (Phillipe Dussart)
original title: *L'Adolescente*
In France in 1939, a 12-year-old girl is infatuated with a young Jewish doctor.
A solidly acted but otherwise uninspired account of the stirrings of adolescent angst.
w Henriette Jelinek, Jeanne Moreau *d* Jeanne Moreau *ph* Pierre Gautard *m* Philippe Sarde *ed* Albert Jurgenson
☆ Simone Signoret, Laetitia Chauveau, Edith Clever, Jacques Weber, Francis Huster

Adolf Hitler – My Part in His Downfall *
GB 1972 102m Technicolor
UA/Norcon (Gregory Smith, Norman Cohen)
Episodes in the life of a conscript at the beginning of World War II.
*Lumbering anarchic comedy based on Spike Milligan's own sidesplitting memoirs; an enfeebled British M*A*S*H.*
w Johnny Byrne *d* Norman Cohen *ph* Terry Maher *m* Wilfred Burns
☆ Jim Dale, Spike Milligan (as his own father), Arthur Lowe, Bill Maynard, Windsor Davies, Pat Coombs, Tony Selby, Geoffrey Hughes

'A convincing period shabbiness and sleaziness which are endearing when they're not being overstated.' – *MFB*

Adorable *
US 1933 85m bw
Fox
A Ruritanian princess falls in love with a naval officer.
Charming, lightweight romance of the old school.
w George Marion Jnr, Jane Storm *story* Paul Frank, Billy Wilder *d* William Dieterle *ph* John Seitz *m/ly* Werner Richard Heymann, George Marion, Richard Whiting
☆ Janet Gaynor, Henri Garat, C. Aubrey Smith, Herbert Mundin, Blanche Friderici, Hans von Twardowski
† The film was remade from German-French originals under a title which translated as *Her Majesty Commands*. The German version starred Kaethe von Nagy and Willy Fritsch, the French Lillian Harvey and Henri Garat.

Adorable Creatures
France 1952 105m bw
Sirius/Jacques Roitfeld
A Paris fashion executive recalls his love affairs.
A collection of four short sex comedies which did well on the heels of La Ronde.
w Charles Spaak, Jacques Companeez
d Christian-Jaque *ph* Christian Matras
m Georges Van Parys
☆ Daniel Gélin, *Danielle Darrieux*, Edwige Feuillère, Antonella Lualdi, Martine Carol, Marilyn Buferd

Adorable Julia
Austria/France 1962 97m bw
Wiener Mundus/Etoile

GB title: *The Seduction of Julia*
A middle-aged actress takes on a lover.
Moderately pleasing sex comedy, rather more heavily directed than Maugham would have liked.
w Johanna Sibelius, Eberhard Keindorff *novel* Theatre by Somerset Maugham *d* Alfred Weidenmann
☆ Lilli Palmer, Charles Boyer, Jean Sorel, Jeanne Valerie

Adorable Lies **
Cuba 1991 100m colour
ICAIC (Evelio Delgado)
original title: *Adorables Mentiras*
A married, unsuccessful scriptwriter pretends to be a film director in his efforts to seduce a woman he fancies, who turns out to be a frustrated actress married to a corrupt government official.
A deft and witty farce of false identities that makes fun of marriage, desire and ideologically correct cinema. Not surprisingly, it ran into censorship problems in Cuba and was hardly seen there.
w Senel Paz *d* Gerardo Chijona *ph* Julio Valdes *m* Edesio Alejandro, Gerardo Garcia *pd* Onelio Larralde *ed* Jorge Abello
☆ Isabel Santos, Luis Alberto Garcia, Mirtha Ibarra, Thais Valdes, Carlos Cruz, Silvia Planas, Santiago Alvarez

'Combines comedy and melodrama with uneven results. At times it seems to be a tongue-in-cheek soap opera, but in other scenes its tone becomes too dark. While there are some funny moments, this Cuban sudser goes on too long and eventually grows tiring.' – *Variety*

Adorables Mentiras: see *Adorable Lies*

Adrenalin: Fear the Rush
US 1996 77m colour Clairmont Scope
Columbia TriStar/Largo/Toga (Tom Karnowski, Gary Schmoeller)

In Boston in 2007, two cops try to track down a mad killer, who has escaped from a quarantine camp and is infected with a plague that depopulated Europe.
Daft and strikingly unoriginal action movie, which leaves its characters and its audience in the dark for much of the time.
wd Albert Pyun *ph* George Mooradian *m* Tony Riparetti *pd* Nenad Pecur *ed* Ken Morrisey *sp* John McLeod; Kevin Marks
☆ Christophe Lambert, Natasha Henstridge, Norbert Weisser, Elizabeth Barondes, Craig Davis, Xavier Declie, Nicholas Guest, Andrew Divoff
† Despite being set in Boston, the film was shot in Bratislava, which accounts for the police cars being marked *Policia*.

Adua e le Compagne
Italy 1960 150m bw
Zebra Film
GB title: *Hungry for Love*
When brothels in Italy are officially closed, four of the old girls open a restaurant.
Immensely overlong comedy drama whose rewards come entirely from the actors.
w Ruggero Maccari, Ettore Scola, Antonio Pietrangeli, Tullio Pinelli *d* Antonio Pietrangeli
☆ Simone Signoret, Marcello Mastroianni, Sandra Milo, Emmanuelle Riva, Gina Rovere
'The script becomes increasingly episodic, and clichés abound.' – *MFB*

Advance to the Rear *
US 1964 97m bw Panavision
MGM/Ted Richmond
GB title: *Company of Cowards?*
After the Civil War, a troop of misfits is sent west out of harm's way, but manages to capture a rebel spy and save a gold shipment.
Semi-satirical Western action comedy with a farcical climax; quite sharply made.
w Samuel A. Peeples, William Bowers *story* Jack Schaefer *d* George Marshall *ph* Milton Krasner *m* Randy Sparks
☆ Glenn Ford, *Melvyn Douglas*, Stella Stevens, Jim Backus, Joan Blondell, Andrew Prine, Alan Hale, James Griffith, Preston Foster

'In Space, *Everyone* Can Hear You Laugh!'
The Adventuires of Pluto Nash
US/Australia 2002 94m Technicolor
Warner/Castle Rock/Village Roadshow/NPV (Martin Bregman, Michael Bregman, Louis A. Stroller)
GB title: *Pluto Nash*
In the 2080s, the owner of the Moon colony's most popular club clashes with a gambler who wants to buy him out.
Woefully weak comedy with Eddie Murphy coasting on his past successes.
w Neil Cuthbert *d* Ron Underwood *ph* Oliver Wood *m* John Powell *pd* Bill Brzeski *ed* Paul Hirsch, Alan Heim
☆ Eddie Murphy (Pluto Nash), Randy Quaid (Bruno), Rosario Dawson (Dina Lake), Joe Pantoliano (Mogan), Jay Mohr (Tony Francis), Luis Guzman (Felix Laranga), James Rebhorn (Belcher), Peter Boyle (Rowland), Burt Young (Gino), Pam Grier (Flura Nash), John Cleese (James), Illeana Douglas (Dr Mona Zimmer)
'The comedy is thin stuff that doesn't remotely make up for the low-budget shoddiness of the action.' – *Edward Porter, Sunday Times*

'Gable's back and Garson's got him!'
Adventure *
US 1945 126m bw
MGM (Sam Zimbalist)

A roughneck sailor marries a librarian, but only settles down to love her when their child is born.
Uniquely embarrassing (and fascinating) mishmash of pretentious dialogue and cardboard characters.
w Frederick Hazlitt Brennan, Vincent Lawrence *novel* Clyde Brion Davis *d* Victor Fleming *ph* Joseph Ruttenberg *m* Herbert Stothart
☆ Clark Gable, Greer Garson, Thomas Mitchell, Joan Blondell, John Qualen, Richard Haydn
'MGM proudly announce *Adventure* as the meeting of a red-blooded man with a blue-blooded woman. Its impact on the bloodstream of your critic was a chilling one. Fifty years of the cinema, he thought, and this is where we've landed.' – *Richard Winnington*

Adventure for Two: see *The Demi-Paradise*

An Adventure for Two: see *A Nous Deux*

Adventure in Baltimore
US 1949 89m bw
RKO (Richard H. Berger)
GB title: *Bachelor Bait*
In 1905, a young society girl becomes a suffragette.
Inconsequential period comedy which did nothing for its young star's fading career.
w Lionel Houser *story* Christopher Isherwood, Lesser Samuels *d* Richard Wallace *ph* Robert de Grasse *m* Frederick Hollander
☆ Shirley Temple, Robert Young, John Agar, Albert Sharpe, Josephine Hutchinson, Johnny Sands, John Miljan, Norma Varden

Adventure in Manhattan
US 1936 73m bw
Columbia
GB title: *Manhattan Madness*
An actress helps an ace reporter to foil a bank robbery by a master criminal.
Flat romantic mystery comedy which wastes a good cast.
w Sidney Buchman, Harry Sauber, Jack Kirkland *d* Edward Ludwig *ph* Henry Freulich
☆ Jean Arthur, Joel McCrea, Thomas Mitchell, Reginald Owen, Herman Bing

Adventure Island
US 1947 67m Cinecolor
Paramount

Seafarers chance on an uncharted island, ruled by a deadly fanatic.
Hokum rehash of Stevenson's Ebb Tide, with Paul Kelly as the madman.
w Maxwell Shane *d* Peter Stewart (Sam Newfield)
☆ Paul Kelly, Rory Calhoun, Rhonda Fleming

The Adventure of Sherlock Holmes' Smarter Brother
GB 1975 91m DeLuxe
TCF/Jouer (Richard A. Roth)

More by good luck than good management, Sherlock's younger brother solves one of his cases.
Infuriating parody with little sense of the original and a hit-or-miss style all of its own. Amusing moments fail to atone for the general waste of opportunity.
wd Gene Wilder *ph* Gerry Fisher *m* John Morris *pd* Terry Marsh
☆ Gene Wilder, Marty Feldman, Madeline Kahn, Leo McKern, Dom DeLuise, Roy Kinnear, John Le Mesurier, Douglas Wilmer, Thorley Walters
'Like a compilation of the kind of numbers actors like to do at parties.' – *Howard Kissel*
'He has bitten off more than he can chew or I can swallow.' – *John Simon*
'A few stray chuckles but nothing more.' – *Sight and Sound*
'There's no mystery, and since you can't have a parody of a mystery without a mystery, there's no comic suspense.' – *New Yorker, 1980*

The Adventurer ***
US 1917 21m approx (24 fps) bw silent
Mutual
An escaped convict rescues two wealthy women from drowning and is invited to their home.
Hilarious early Chaplin knockabout, with his physical gags at their most streamlined.
wd Charles Chaplin ph William C. Foster, Rollie Totheroh
☆ Charles Chaplin, Edna Purviance, Eric Campbell, Henry Bergman

The Adventurers
GB 1950 86m bw
Rank/Mayflower (Maxwell Setton, Aubrey Baring)

US title: *The Great Adventure*
aka: *Fortune in Diamonds*
In 1902, two Boers and a cashiered English officer set out to recover stolen diamonds.
Lethargic South African Western in the wake of Treasure of the Sierra Madre; clumsy and unconvincing, with cardboard characters.
w Robert Westerby *d* David MacDonald *ph* Oswald Morris *m* Cedric Thorpe Davie
☆ Dennis Price, Jack Hawkins, Siobhan McKenna, Peter Hammond, Bernard Lee, Grégoire Aslan

The Adventurers *
US 1970 170m Technicolor Panavision
Paramount/Avco Embassy/Adventurers Film (Lewis Gilbert)

A sensualist brought up amid Europe's luxuries returns to his Central American homeland to take vengeance on the brutal security chief who raped and murdered his mother.
Sprawling, sexy, bloodstained extravaganza from a Harold Robbins novel. Expensive to look at and riddled with sensation, but that's about all.
w Michael Hastings, Lewis Gilbert *d* Lewis Gilbert *ph* Claude Renoir *m* Antonio Carlos Jobim *pd* Tony Masters
☆ Bekim Fehmiu, Alan Badel, Candice Bergen, Ernest Borgnine, Olivia de Havilland, Rossano Brazzi, Charles Aznavour, Sydney Tafler, Fernando Rey, Leigh Taylor-Young, Thommy Berggren, John Ireland
'A three-hour slog through every imaginable cliché of writing and direction … in addition to an abundance of flaccid sex and violence, it offers drugs, sadism, orchids, fireworks, orgies, lesbianism, a miscarriage, a private torture chamber, and the hell of several fashion shows with loud pop music accompaniment. This might well be described as the film with everything; trouble is, it is difficult to imagine anybody wanting any of it.' – *MFB*
'Lovers of rotten movies and close-up violence can revel in it.' – *Judith Crist*

Adventures in Babysitting: see *Night On the Town*

'Ladies...if you can't do-it-yourself call a plumber!'
Adventures of a Plumber's Mate
GB 1978 88m Eastmancolor
Salon (Stanley Long)
A plumber with debts is chased by crooks and by lustful women.
Tired sexploitation farce with little narrative, merely a succession of episodes in which women lose their clothes.
w Stephen D. Frances, Aubrey Cash *d* Stanley Long *ph* Peter Sinclair *m* Christopher Neil *ad* Carlotta Barrow *ed* Jo Gannon
☆ Christopher Neil (Sid South), Arthur Mullard (Blackie), Stephen Lewis (Crapper), Nina West (Sally), Anna Quayle (Loretta), Prudence Drage (Janice), Elaine Paige (Susie), William Rushton (Dodger)
'A glum essay in blue-nosed British farce.' – *Tim Pulleine, MFB*

Adventures of a Private Eye
GB 1977 90m Gevacolor
Alpha/Salon (Peter & Stanley Long)
An apprentice private detective investigates a woman being blackmailed over some compromising photographs.
Dreary slapstick comedy, crudely done and wasting the talents of many skilled character actors.
w Michael Armstrong *d* Stanley Long *ph* Peter Sinclair *m* De Wolfe *ad* Carlotta Barrow *ed* Jo Gannon
☆ Christopher Neil (Bob West), Suzy Kendal (Laura Sutton), Harry H. Corbett (Sydney), Fred Emney (Sir Basil Lemmington), Liz Fraser (Violet), Irene Handl (Miss Friggen), Ian Lavender (Derek), Julian Orchard (Police motorcyclist), Jon Pertwee (Judd Blake), Adrienne Posta (Lisa Moroni), Anna Quayle (Medea), William Rushton (Wilfred), Diana Dors (Mrs Horne)
'The script's incoherent lurchings and botched attempts at parody at least provide a kind of entertainment.' – *Geoff Brown, MFB*
† The film was a sort of sequel to the profitable *Adventures of a Taxi Driver*, although Barry Evans, the star of that film, refused to appear and was replaced by Christopher Neil.

Adventures of a Taxi Driver
GB 1975 89m Eastmancolor
Alpha/Salon (Peter Long, Stanley Long)

A taxi driver finds that his sex life is both busy and confusing.
Lamentable British comedy, in which a cast of reliable performers are allowed to embarrass themselves and their audience.
w Suzanne Mercer *d* Stanley Long *ph* Peter Sinclair *ed* Jo Gannon
☆ Barry Evans, Judy Geeson, Adrienne Posta, Diana Dors, Liz Fraser, Ian Lavender, Stephen Lewis, Robert Lindsay, Henry McGee, Brian Wilde
'A crass, lobotomised production, with no discernible style, humour or purpose.' – *MFB*

Adventures of a Young Man: see *Hemingway's Adventures of a Young Man*

The Adventures of Arsène Lupin *
France/Italy 1956 103m Eastmancolor
Chavane-SNE-Gaumont/Lambor-Costellazione (Robert Sussfeld)
In 1912, the famous jewel thief conducts several successful robberies and outwits the Kaiser.
The most stylish Lupin film, though not based on the original stories.
w Jacques Becker, Albert Simonin, based on the character created by Maurice Leblanc *d Jacques Becker ph Edmond Séchan ad* Rino Mondellini
☆ Robert Lamoureux, Liselotte Pulver, Otto Hasse, Henri Rollan

The Adventures of Baron Munchausen: see *Münchausen (1943)*

Adventures of Baron Munchausen **
GB/West Germany 1989 126m Eastmancolor
Prominent Features/Laura Film/Columbia-Tri Star (Thomas Schühly)

A German soldier tells tall stories of his escapades.
Ambitious, extravagant fantasy in which some of the parts are better than the whole.
w Charles McKeown, Terry Gilliam *story* Rudolph Erich Raspe *d* Terry Gilliam *ph* Giuseppe Rotunno *m* Michael Kamen *pd Dante Ferretti ed* Peter Hollywood *sp* Richard Conway
☆ John Neville, Eric Idle, Sarah Polley, Oliver Reed, Charles McKeown, Winston Dennis, Jack Purvis, Valentina Cortese, Jonathan Pryce, Bill Paterson, Peter Jeffrey, Uma Thurman
'Munchausen's inability to get into gear rather defeats what would seem the point of the picture: whereas the source is adroit at slipping between fantasy and reality, Gilliam's fiction can't even handle a flashback.' – *MFB*
art direction; costume design; makeup
Dante Ferretti

The Adventures of Barry Mackenzie *
Australia 1972 114m Eastmancolor
Columbia/Longford (Philip Adams)

A sex-hungry Australian gets into all kinds of trouble on a visit to the Old Country.
Occasionally funny, defiantly crude and tasteless, but poorly produced comedy-misadventure from the Private Eye comic strip. Australian slang combines with bad sound recording to make much of the film unintelligible.
w Barry Humphries, Bruce Beresford *d* Bruce Beresford *ph* Don McAlpine *m* Peter Best
☆ Barry Crocker (Barry Mackenzie), Barry Humphries (Dame Edna Everage), Peter Cook, Spike Milligan, Dennis Price, Avice Landone, Dick Bentley, Joan Bakewell, William Rushton
'A wildly uneven concoction of antipodean bad taste, probably only fully appreciated by Earls Court exiles.' – *Sight and Sound*
† Sequel 1974: *Barry Mackenzie Holds His Own*

'The shameless saga of a young Aussie in Pommyland!'
The Adventures of Barry McKenzie
Australia 1972
Columbia-Warner/Longford (Phillip Adams)

The escapades, usually involving sex and/or vomit, of a naive young Australian in London.
Coarse, deliberately tasteless comedy, based on a comic-strip from Private Eye magazine; it works better in print.

w Barry Humphries, Bruce Beresford *d* Bruce Beresford *ph* Donald McAlpine *m* Peter Best *pd* John Stoddart *ed* John Scott
☆ Barry Crocker (Barry McKenzie), Barry Humphries (Aunt Edna Everage/Hoot), Spike Milligan (Landlord), Peter Cook (Dominic), Paul Bertram (Curly), Dennis Price (Mr Gort), Avice Landone (Mrs Gort), Dick Bentley (Detective)
'May – because of the concreteness of film that inevitably puts a damper on Humphries' wild imaginings – puzzle, if not actually revolt, newcomers to the idiom.' – *Sylvia Millar, MFB*
† It was followed by *Barry McKenzie Holds His Own (qv)*, 1974.

The Adventures of Buckaroo Banzai Across the Eighth Dimension *
US 1984 102m colour Panavision
Sherwood (Neil Canton/W. D. Richter)
A Renaissance man – physicist, surgeon and rock star – crashes into the eighth dimension and releases evil aliens.
Genial spoof of science fiction and other movie genres.
w Earl MacRauch *d* W. D. Richter *ph* Fred J. Koenekamp *m* Michael Boddicker *pd* J. M. Riva *ed* Richard Marks, George Bowers
☆ Peter Weller, John Lithgow, Ellen Barkin, Jeff Goldblum, Christopher Lloyd

The Adventures of Bullwhip Griffin *
US 1965 110m Technicolor
Walt Disney (Bill Anderson)
In the 1849 California Gold Rush, two aristocrats and their butler head west.
Rather splendid spoof Western with careful attention to detail and comedy pointing, well above the average Disney standard.
w Lowell S. Hawley *novel* By the Great Horn Spoon by Sid Fleischman *d* James Neilson *ph* Edward Colman *m* George Bruns *titles* Ward Kimball
☆ Roddy McDowall, Suzanne Pleshette, Bryan Russell, Karl Malden, Harry Guardino, Richard Haydn, Mike Mazurki, Hermione Baddeley, Cecil Kellaway

The Adventures of Captain Fabian
US 1951 100m bw
Republic/Silver (William Marshall)
A sea captain returns to New Orleans to revenge himself on the family which had defrauded his father.
Stilted, old-fashioned Monte Cristoish melodrama with some curiosity value but little verve in the playing or production. An awful warning to independent producers.
w Errol Flynn *novel* Fabulous Ann Medlock by Robert Shannon *d* William Marshall *ph* Marcel Grignon *m* René Cloerec
☆ Errol Flynn, Micheline Presle, Agnes Moorehead, Vincent Price, Victor Francen, Jim Gerald
† Made in France.

Adventures of Captain Marvel *
US 1941 bw serial: 12 eps
Republic
When a scientific expedition goes to Siam, the assistant radio operator is endowed by the mysterious Shazam with the power to transform himself into Captain Marvel, and to defeat the evil Scorpion.
Modest classic serial, good for more than a few laughs.
d William Witney, John English
☆ Tom Tyler, Frank Coghlan Jnr, William Benedict, Louise Currie

Adventures of Casanova
US 1948 83m bw
Eagle-Lion
Casanova returns to Sicily and helps overthrow the tyrannical rule of the King of Naples.
Robin Hood transplanted, with a few amorous asides; but this is a totally stilted production which fails to entertain.
w Crane Wilbur, Walter Bullock, Ken de Wolf *d* Roberto Gavaldon
☆ Arturo de Cordova, Lucille Bremer, Turhan Bey

The Adventures of Don Juan **
US 1949 110m Technicolor
Warner (Jerry Wald)
GB title: *The New Adventures of Don Juan*
A reformed 17th-century rake saves his queen from the machinations of her first minister.
Expensive, slightly uneasy, but generally very entertaining swashbuckler with elements of self-spoofery. Flynn's last big-budget extravaganza.
w George Oppenheimer, Harry Kurnitz *d* Vincent Sherman *ph* Elwood Bredell *m* Max Steiner *ad* Edward Carrere
☆ *Errol Flynn*, Viveca Lindfors, Romney Brent, Robert Douglas, Alan Hale, Ann Rutherford, Robert Warwick, Jerry Austin, Douglas Kennedy, Una O'Connor, Aubrey Mather, Raymond Burr
'A lavish film on a truly magnificent scale.' – *The Times*
art direction

Adventures of Ford Fairlane
US 1990 104m DeLuxe Panavision
TCF (Joel Silver, Steve Perry)
A conceited rock 'n' roll detective solves the murder of a Los Angeles disc jockey.
Drearily vulgar comedy, featuring one of the more obnoxious stand-up comedians of the 90s and about as entertaining as stepping in something nasty in the street. It was a flop at the box-office, resulting in Fox's decision not to release Clay's concert film Dice Rules (qv).
w Daniel Waters, James Cappe, David Arnott *based on characters created by* Rex Weiner *d* Renny Harlin *ph* Oliver Wood *m* Yello *pd* John Vallone *ed* Michael Tronick
☆ Andrew Dice Clay, Wayne Newton, Priscilla Presley, Morris Day, Lauren Holly, Maddie Corman, Robert Englund, Ed O'Neill
'Surprisingly funny and expectedly rude.' – *Variety*
'What can you say about a movie whose comic highlight is the hanging of a koala bear?' – *Empire*

The Adventures of Gallant Bess
US 1948 71m Cinecolor
Eagle Lion
The master of a trained rodeo horse becomes a range wanderer.
Easy-going animal interest saga with a pleasant ending.
w Matthew Rapf *d* Lew Landers
☆ Cameron Mitchell, Audrey Long, Fuzzy Knight, James Millican, Ed Gargan

The Adventures of Gerard *
GB 1970 91m DeLuxe Panavision
UA/Sir Nigel Films (Henry Lester, Gene Gutowski)
A hussar of Napoleon becomes involved in a double spy game but comes out trumps and wins a fair lady.
A lighthearted historical spoof of military pomp, with plenty of attractive elements which unfortunately fail to jell into a satisfying film.
w H. A. L. Craig and others *stories* Arthur Conan Doyle *d* Jerzy Skolimowski *ph* Witold Sobocinski *m* Riz Ortolani
☆ Peter McEnery, Claudia Cardinale, Eli Wallach, Jack Hawkins, Mark Burns, Norman Rossington, John Neville
'Enormously graceful and witty ... picks its way with amazing delicacy through the reefs of facetiousness.' – *Tom Milne*

The Adventures of Hajji Baba *
US 1954 93m DeLuxe Cinemascope
Allied Artists/Walter Wanger
In ancient Arabia, a barber helps and falls in love with an escaping princess.
A reasonably dashing sword and sandal romp which no one takes very seriously.
w Richard Collins *d* Don Weis *ph* Harold Lipstein *m* Dimitri Tiomkin *pd* Gene Allen
☆ John Derek, Elaine Stewart, Thomas Gomez, Amanda Blake, Paul Picerni, Rosemarie Bowe

The Adventures of Huck Finn
US 1993 108m Technicolor
Buena Vista/Walt Disney/Mighty Miss/Steve White (Laurence Mark)
Huck Finn, escaping from his brutal father, goes on the run with Jim, an escaped slave, and takes to the river.
Bland and fussy remake of the familiar story, one that ignores the vigour of the original in favour of cuteness.
wd Stephen Sommers *novel* The Adventures of Huckleberry Finn by Mark Twain *ph* Janusz Kaminski *m* Bill Conti *pd* Richard Sherman *ed* Bob Ducsay
☆ Elijah Wood, Courtney B. Vance, Robbie Coltrane, Jason Robards, Ron Perlman, Dana Ivey, James Gammon, Anne Heche, Paxton Whitehead
'Wholesome family entertainment with a worthy anti-slavery message.' – *Empire*

The Adventures of Huckleberry Finn: see *Huckleberry Finn (1960)*

The Adventures of Ichabod and Mr Toad: see *Ichabod and Mr Toad*

The Adventures of Marco Polo *
US 1938 100m bw
Samuel Goldwyn
The medieval Italian explorer discovers China, fireworks, and a beautiful maiden.
One gets the impression that this began as a standard adventure and that during production it switched to comedy; whatever the cause, lively and amusing scenes fail to add up to more than a thinly scripted pantomime.
w Robert E. Sherwood *d* Archie Mayo *ph* Rudolph Maté *m* Hugo Friedhofer *md* Alfred Newman *ad* Richard Day
☆ Gary Cooper, Sigrid Gurie, Basil Rathbone, Ernest Truex, Binnie Barnes, Alan Hale, George Barbier
'In spite of its elaborate settings and the presence of Gary Cooper, it never quite lives up to its promises.' – *New York Sun*
'Goldwyn's most ambitious endeavour ... deserves and will get enthusiastic exhibitor plugging. Sherwood's more concerned with entertainment than with history.' – *Variety*
† Release prints were in sepiatone.

The Adventures of Mark Twain **
US 1944 130m bw
Warner (Jesse L. Lasky)
The life of America's foremost humorous writer, from a Mississippi riverboat to his becoming an honorary fellow of Oxford University.
Conventional biopic, quite watchable and with unusual side turnings, but eventually lacking the zest of the subject.
w Harold M. Sherman, Alan le May, Harry Chandler *d* Irving Rapper *ph* Sol Polito *m* Max Steiner *ad* John J. Hughes
☆ *Fredric March*, Alexis Smith, Donald Crisp, Alan Hale, C. Aubrey Smith, John Carradine, William Henry, Robert Barrat, Walter Hampden
'It's not that it's much worse than most cinematized biographies, because it does have its good moments. It's just that once more biographical inaccuracy is rampant, and once more the best dramatic possibilities have been overlooked, so it's hard to think of anything new, in the line of protest, to say.' – *David Lardner, New Yorker*
Max Steiner; John J. Hughes

The Adventures of Martin Eden
US 1942 87m bw
Columbia (B. P. Schulberg)
An American seaman fights a brutal captain and wins better conditions for his comrades.
Routine actioner based on what are virtually the author's memoirs.
w W. L. River *story* Jack London *d* Sidney Salkow
☆ Glenn Ford, Evelyn Keyes, Claire Trevor, Stuart Erwin, Dickie Moore

Adventures of Milo and Otis (dubbed) *
Japan 1986 75m Eastmancolor Panavision
Virgin/Fuji (Hisashi Hieda)
original title: *Koneko Monogatari*
A puppy leaves a farm to search for his friend, a kitten, who has floated downriver in a box.
Innocuous adventure, using real animals, that may appeal to the very young.
w Mark Saltzman *story* Masanori Hata *d* Masanori Hata *ph* Hideo Fuji, Shinji Tomita *m* Michael Boddicker *ad* Takeharu Sakahuchi *ed* Chizuko Osada
☆ Dudley Moore (narrator)
'Youngsters and pet lovers will adore this film. Grown-ups with a less positive attitude to the animal kingdom are well advised to stay away.' – *Empire*
† The film was the second most popular ever made in Japan.

The Adventures of Pinocchio *
GB/US/France/Germany 1996 96m DeLuxe Panavision
New Line/Savoy/Pangaea/Twin Continental (Raju Patel, Jeffrey M. Sneller)
The adventures of a wooden puppet who comes to life after he has been made by a lonely wood-carver.
A live-action account, with an animatronic puppet, of a story most familiar from Disney's version; it does not match up to the animated feature, but manages a certain charm.
w Sherry Mills, Steve Barron, Tom Benedek, Barry Berman *novel* Carlo Collodi *d* Steve Barron *ph* Juan Ruiz-Anchia *m* Rachel Portman *pd* Allan Cameron *ed* Sean Barton *sp* Jim Henson's Creature Shop
☆ Martin Landau, Jonathan Taylor Thomas, Geneviève Bujold, Udo Kier, Bebe Neuwirth, Rob Schneider, Griff Rhys Jones, Dawn French, John Sessions
'Well-crafted and gently charming.' – *Variety*

'Finally, a comedy that will change the way you think, the way you feel and, most importantly, the way you dress.'
The Adventures of Priscilla Queen of the Desert **
Australia 1994 103m colour Arriscope
Rank/Polygram/AFFC/Latent Image/Specific Films (Al Clark, Michael Hamlyn)
Two transvestites and a transsexual drive a bus from Sydney to Alice Springs for a cabaret engagement at a hotel run by a former wife of one of them.
A bright and brittle road movie, gaudy and fun and refusing to take seriously even the occasional glimpse of genuine emotion.
wd *Stephan Elliott* *ph* Brian J. Breheny *m* Guy Gross *pd* Owen Paterson *ed* Sue Blainey
☆ *Terence Stamp*, Hugo Weaving, Guy Pearce, Bill Hunter, Sarah Chadwick, Mark Holmes, Julia Cortez
'A cheerfully vulgar and bitchy, but essentially warmhearted, road movie with a difference.' – *David Stratton, Variety*
'A slick, shrewdly ingratiating entertainment that jumps from highlight to highlight and lives on sparkle.' – *David Denby, New York*
† Al Clark's book *The Lavender Bus* (1999) tells the story of the production of the film.
costume design (Lizzy Gardiner, Tim Chappell)

The Adventures of Quentin Durward: see *Quentin Durward*

'Only the rainbow can duplicate its brilliance!'
The Adventures of Robin Hood ****
US 1938 102m Technicolor
Warner (Hal B. Wallis)
Rebel outlaw Robin Hood outwits Guy of Gisbourne and the Sheriff of Nottingham, and saves the throne for the absent King Richard.
A splendid adventure story, rousingly operatic in treatment, with dashing action highlights, fine comedy balance, and incisive acting all round. Historically notable for its use of early three-colour Technicolor; also for convincingly recreating Britain in California.
w *Seton I. Miller, Norman Reilly Raine* *d* *William Keighley, Michael Curtiz* *ph* *Tony Gaudio, Sol*

Polito, W. Howard Greene m *Erich Wolfgang Korngold* ad *Carl Jules Weyl* ed Ralph Dawson
☆ *Errol Flynn* (Sir Robin of Locksley), *Basil Rathbone* (Sir Guy of Gisbourne), *Claude Rains* (Prince John), Olivia de Havilland (Maid Marian), *Alan Hale* (Little John), Patric Knowles (Will Scarlet), *Eugene Pallette* (Friar Tuck), *Ian Hunter* (King Richard), *Melville Cooper* (Sheriff of Nottingham), Una O'Connor (Bess), Herbert Mundin (Much the Miller's Son), Montagu Love (Bishop of Black Canons), Howard Hill (Captain of Archers)

PRINCE JOHN: 'Any objections to the new tax, from our Saxon friends?'

ROBIN TO GISBOURNE DURING DUEL: 'Did I upset your plans?'

GISBOURNE: 'You've come to Nottingham once too often!'

ROBIN: 'When this is over, my friend, there'll be no need for me to come again!'

PRINCE JOHN: 'Ho, varlets, bring Sir Robin food! Such insolence must support a healthy appetite!'

ROBIN: 'It's injustice I hate, not the Normans!'

'Magnificent, unsurpassable ... the film is lavish, brilliantly photographed, and has a great Korngold score.' – *NFT, 1974*

'Mostly the picture is full of movement, some of it dashing in fine romantic costume style, some of it just sprightly. The excitement comes from fast action – galloping steeds, men swinging Tarzan-like from the trees, hurling tables and chairs, rapid running swordplay, the sudden whiz of Robin's arrows coming from nowhere to startle his enemies – more than from any fear that Robin might be worsted. Somehow the whole thing has the air of being a costume party, a jolly and rather athletic one, with a lot of well-bred Englishmen playing at being in the greenwood.' – *James Shelley Hamilton, National Board of Review*

† At the time of its release this was Warner's most expensive film, costing more than two million dollars. Chico, California, stood in for Sherwood Forest; the archery contest was shot at Busch Gardens, Pasadena. Curtiz took over direction when it was felt that the action lacked impact.

Erich Wolfgang Korngold; Carl Jules Weyl; Ralph Dawson

picture

The Adventures of Robinson Crusoe ***

Mexico 1953 89m Pathécolor
Tepeyac (Oscar Dancigers, Henry F. Ehrlich)

A 17th-century mariner is shipwrecked on an uninhabited tropical island.

Fascinating version of a famous story, with only one character on screen until the belated arrival of Friday and the escape to civilization. Subtle and compelling, with only the colour unsatisfactory.

w *Luis Buñuel, Phillip Ansell Roll (Hugo Butler)* novel Daniel Defoe d *Luis Buñuel* ph Alex Phillips m Anthony Collins
☆ *Dan O'Herlihy*, Jaime Fernandez

'A film of which the purity, the tense poetic style, evokes a kind of wonder.' – *Gavin Lambert*

'Free of that deadly solicitude which usually kills off classics.' – *New Yorker, 1977*

† Hugo Butler used the pseudonym of Roll because he was blacklisted at the time.

Dan O'Herlihy

The Adventures of Rocky and Bullwinkle

US 2000 DeLuxe
Universal/Capella/KC Medien/Tribeca (Jane Rosenthal, Robert De Niro)

Rocky and Bullwinkle are brought out of retirement to prevent their old adversary Fearless Leader from taking over the world.

A feeble comedy, mixing live action and animation, that never catches the anarchic spirit of the original TV series.

w Kenneth Lonergan *characters developed by* Jay Ward d Des McAnuff ph Thomas Ackerman m Mark Mothersbaugh pd Gavin Bocquet ed Dennis Virkler cos Marlene Stewart
☆ Rene Russo (Natasha), Jason Alexander (Boris), Piper Perabo (Karen Sympathy), Randy Quaid (Cappy Von Trapment), Robert De Niro (Fearless Leader), June Foray (Voice of Rocky), Keith Scott (Voice of Bullwinkle/ Narrator), Janeane Garofalo (Minnie Mogul), Carl Reiner (P. G. Biggershot), Jonathan Winters (Whoppa Chopper Pilot/Ohio Cop/Jeb), John Goodman (Oklahoma Cop), Kenan Thompson (Lewis), Kel Mitchell (Martin), James Rebhorn (President Signoff), David Alan Grier (Measures)

'Scarcely seems worth the expenditure of time, money and talent.' – *Joe Leydon. Variety*

The Adventures of Sadie: see *Our Girl Friday*

The Adventures of Sherlock Holmes **

US 1939 83m bw
TCF (Gene Markey)

GB title: *Sherlock Holmes*

Moriarty sends Holmes on a false trail while he plots to steal the Crown jewels.

An engaging piece of pseudo-Victoriana: all elements smooth save an unconvincing plot.

w Edwin Blum, William Drake d Alfred Werker ph *Leon Shamroy* m Cyril Mockridge
☆ *Basil Rathbone* (Holmes), *Nigel Bruce* (Dr Watson), *George Zucco* (Moriarty), Ida Lupino (Ann Brandon), Alan Marshal (Jerrold Hunter), Terry Kilburn (Billy), E. E. Clive (Inspector Bristol), Henry Stephenson (Sir Ronald Ramsgate), Mary Gordon (Mrs Hudson)

'The "elementary my dear Watson" type of dialogue is soft-pedalled for more modern phrases or understandable patter.' – *Variety*

'Told with more movie art per foot than seven reels of anything the intellectual men have been finding good this whole year or more.' – *Otis Ferguson*

† This was the second and last of Rathbone's costume outings as Holmes, and the one in which he sang a comic song in disguise.

The Adventures of Tartu *

GB 1943 103m bw
MGM (Irving Asher)

US title: *Tartu*

During World War II, a British spy goes to Czechoslovakia to dismantle a poison gas factory.

Halting and artificial comedy-thriller, saved only by a graceful star performance.

w Howard Emmett Rogers, John Lee Mahin, Miles Malleson d Harold S. Bucquet ph John J. Cox m Hubert Bath md Louis Levy
☆ *Robert Donat*, Valerie Hobson, Walter Rilla, Glynis Johns, Martin Miller

'You are seeing all it has, and bald spots as well, first time around, whereas with a good Hitchcock or even a good Carol Reed, the pleasures visible at a first seeing stand up, or intensify, at a third or a fifth.' – *James Agee*

Adventures of the Wilderness Family

US 1975 101m colour
Pacific International

An urban family runs into trouble when it takes to the wilds.

Naïve little four-wall family movie in which the pretty scenery (Utah and the Canadian Rockies) and the animals compensate for the dramatic inadequacies.

wd Stewart Raffill
☆ Robert Logan, Susan Damante Shaw

† *Further Adventures of the Wilderness Family* appeared in 1977.

The Adventures of Tom Sawyer ***

US 1938 91m Technicolor
David O. Selznick (William H. Wright)

Small-town Mississippi boy tracks down a murderer, Injun Joe.

Set-bound but excellent version of the children's classic by Mark Twain.

w *John Weaver* d Norman Taurog ph James Wong Howe, Wilfrid Cline m Max Steiner ad *Lyle Wheeler*
☆ *Tommy Kelly* (Tom), *May Robson* (Aunt Polly), Walter Brennan (Muff Potter), Victor Jory (Injun Joe), Victor Kilian (Sheriff), Jackie Moran (Huckleberry Finn), Ann Gillis (Becky Thatcher), Donald Meek (Sunday School Superintendent), Margaret Hamilton (Mrs Sawyer), Marcia Mae Jones (Mary Sawyer)

'The familiar characters emerge in all their old amiability, the atmosphere is there and so is the excitement.' – *MFB*

'Should make Mark Twain circulate in his grave like a trout in a creel.' – *Otis Ferguson*

'Another Selznick International box office clean-up ... that there exists a broad audience for films whose essential appeal is to the family trade has always been true. *Snow White* touched a source of almost unlimited audience draw: *Tom Sawyer* follows to the same customers.' – *Variety*

Lyle Wheeler

The Adventuress: see *I See a Dark Stranger*

Advice to the Lovelorn *

US 1933 62m bw
TCF/Darryl F. Zanuck

A reporter is demoted to the lonelyhearts column and becomes absorbed in it.

Springy vehicle for Lee Tracy.

w Leonard Praskins novel *Miss Lonelyhearts* by Nathanael West d Alfred Werker
☆ *Lee Tracy*, Sally Blane, Sterling Holloway, Isabel Jewell, Jean Adair

† Compare the Paul Muni vehicle *Hi Nellie*. It was remade in 1958 as *Lonelyhearts* (qv).

'Are the men and women of Washington really like this?'

Advise and Consent **

US 1962 139m bw Panavision
Columbia/Alpha-Alpina/Otto Preminger

The President's choice of an unpopular secretary of state leads to divisions in the Senate and the blackmail and suicide of a senator.

Absorbing political melodrama from a novel which aimed to lift the lid off Washington. Many character actors make their mark, but the harsh-contrast photography seems misjudged.

w Wendell Mayes novel Allen Drury d Otto Preminger ph Sam Leavitt m Jerry Fielding titles Saul Bass
☆ Don Murray, *Charles Laughton*, Henry Fonda, Walter Pidgeon, Lew Ayres, Edward Andrews, Burgess Meredith, Gene Tierney, Franchot Tone, George Grizzard, Paul Ford, Peter Lawford, Inga Swenson, Will Geer

'The result is supremely ambivalent, a battle between fascinatingly real props and procedures and melodramatically unreal characters and situations.' – *Peter John Dyer*

'The parade of people helps to take one's mind off the overwrought melodrama.' – *New Yorker, 1980*

Aelita *

USSR 1924 70m approx bw silent
Mezhrabpom

Two Russian rocket pioneers land on Mars and start a revolution against the planet's queen.

Notable early space fiction, with footage of twenties Moscow as well as interesting set designs.

w Fedor Ozep, Alexei Faiko novel Alexei Tolstoy d Yakov Protazanov ph Yuri Zhelabuzhsky pd Sergei Kozlovsky
☆ Yulia Solntseva, Nikolai Batalov, Igor Ilinsky

Aerial Gunner

US 1943 78m bw
Paramount (William H. Pine, William G. Thomas)

A US air force pilot in hospital thinks back to his training and his young brother's problems.

A watered-down Wings (with process footage to match) which also starred Arlen.

w Maxwell Shane d William H. Pine
☆ Richard Arlen, Chester Morris, Jimmy Lydon, Lita Ward, Dick Purcell

Aerograd **

USSR 1935 81m bw
Mosfilm/Ukrainfilm

aka: *Frontier*

Guards keep Japanese spies out of Siberia, where an airport is being built.

An action film with style and pretensions.

wd *Alexander Dovzhenko* ph Edouard Tissé, Mikhail Gindin m Dmitri Kabalevsky
☆ Semyon Shagaida, Stepan Shkurat, Sergei Stolyarov

Affair at the Villa Fiorita: see *The Battle of the Villa Fiorita*

Affair in Monte Carlo: see *Twenty-Four Hours of a Woman's Life*

Affair in Trinidad *

US 1952 98m bw
Columbia/Beckworth (Vincent Sherman)

A nightclub singer whose husband is killed by gangsters works undercover for the police and routs the gang with the help of her husband's brother.

A tired tropical melodrama intended to follow up the success of Gilda, but without the verve. Some routine pleasures, though.

w Oscar Saul, James Gunn d Vincent Sherman ph Joseph Walker m Morris Stoloff, George Duning
☆ Rita Hayworth, Glenn Ford, Alexander Scourby, Torin Thatcher, Valerie Bettis, Steve Geray, Karel Stepanek, George Voskovec

'Improbable, foolish, but glossy.' – *Penelope Houston*

'Deception Was The Only Option.'

The Affair of the Necklace

US 2001 120m Technicolor Super 35
Warner/Alcon (Andrew A. Kosove, Broderick Johnson, Charles Shyer, Redmond Morris)

In the early 1780s, an aristocratic woman intrigues at the French court to steal a valuable necklace in order to regain the confiscated family estates.

Vapid and confusing period drama, based on actual events that contributed to the French Revolution, though it's impossible from this account to understand why.

w John Sweet d Charles Shyer ph Ashley Rowe m David Newman pd Alex McDowell ed David Moritz cos Milena Canonero
☆ Hilary Swank (Jeanne St Remy de Valois), Jonathan Pryce (Cardinal Louis de Rohan), Simon Baker (Retaux de Vilette), Adrien Brody (Nicolas De La Motte), Brian Cox (Minister Breteuil), Joely Richardson (Marie Antoinette), Christopher Walken (Cagliostro), Paul Brooke (Monsieur Bohmer), Peter Eyre (Monsieur Bassenge)

'A pageant of historical silliness.' – *Peter Bradshaw, Guardian*

'An endless illustrated Harlequin paperback of mawkish backstory and corset-popping purple prose.' – *Jessica Winter, Village Voice*

Milena Canonero

An Affair to Remember **

US 1957 114m Eastmancolor Cinemascope
TCF (Jerry Wald)

An ex-nightclub singer falls in love with a wealthy bachelor on a transatlantic liner, but an accident prevents her from attending their subsequent rendezvous.

Remake of Love Affair, a surprisingly successful mixture of smart lines, sentiment and tears, all applied with style and assurance.

w Delmer Daves, Leo McCarey d Leo McCarey ph Milton Krasner m Hugo Friedhofer
☆ *Cary Grant, Deborah Kerr, Cathleen Nesbitt*, Richard Denning, Neva Patterson

'A lush slice of Hollywood romanticism.' – *MFB*

'90 masterly minutes of entrancing light comedy and 25 beastly minutes of beastly, melodramatic, pseudo-tragic guff.' – *Paul Dehn*

† Donald Ogden Stewart, one of the writers of the original *Love Affair*, was excluded from the credits of this remake because he was blacklisted.

Milton Krasner; Hugo Friedhofer; title song (m Harry Warren, ly Harold Adamson, Leo McCarey)

Affair with a Stranger *

US 1953 87m bw
RKO (Robert Sparks)

Five friends reminisce about a marriage which seems about to break up.

This would-be-smart comedy has a good idea unsatisfactorily worked out, and could have used a more sparkling cast.

w Richard Flournoy d Roy Rowland ph Harry J. Wild m Roy Webb
☆ Jean Simmons, Victor Mature, Mary Jo Tarola, Monica Lewis, Jane Darwell, Nicholas Joy, Wally Vernon, Dabbs Greer

L'Affaire est dans le Sac *
France 1932 47m bw
Pathé/Nathan
aka: *It's in the Bag*
Two would-be kidnappers end up (a) married to and (b) employed by their intended victims.
Semi-professional nonsense comedy with political jokes.
w Jacques Prévert d Pierre Prévert ph A. Giboury, Eli Lotar m Maurice Jaubert
☆ J.-P. Le Chanois, Jacques Brunius, Etienne Decroux, Lucien Raimbourg, Julien Carette, Lora Hays

Affairs of a Rogue: see *The First Gentleman*

The Affairs of Anatol *
US 1921 95m approx (24 fps) bw silent
Famous Players-Lasky/de Mille-Paramount
A socialite interrupts his honeymoon to go looking for romance.
Dated but historically very interesting sophisticated farce from a time when Hollywood was aping Viennese naughtiness.
w *Jeanie MacPherson, Beulah Marie Dix, Lorna Moon, Elmer Harris from Granville Barker's paraphrase of the play Anatol by Arthur Schnitzler*
d Cecil B. de Mille ph Alvin Wyckoff, Karl Struss ed Anne Bauchens
☆ Wallace Reid, Gloria Swanson, Bebe Daniels, Elliott Dexter, Monte Blue, Wanda Hawley, Theodore Roberts
'Should be enormously popular, especially with those who think Schnitzler is a cheese.' – *Robert E. Sherwood*
'The man who doesn't sell out for every performance of a double run should turn his show shop into a Quaker meeting house.' – *Motion Picture Herald*

The Affairs of Annabel *
US 1938 69m bw
RKO (Lee Marcus, Lou Lusty)
A crackpot Hollywood press agent sends his star to jail as a publicity stunt.
An amusing frenetic comedy of its time, successful enough to warrant a sequel, Annabel Takes a Tour, in the same year.
w Bert Granet, Paul Yawitz d Ben Stoloff ph Russell Metty m Roy Webb
☆ Lucille Ball, Jack Oakie, Ruth Donnelly, Bradley Page, Fritz Feld, Thurston Hall, Elisabeth Risdon, Granville Bates, James Burke

The Affairs of Cellini *
US 1934 90m bw
Twentieth Century (Darryl F. Zanuck)
The complex amours of a 16th-century Florentine rake.
Lively period bedroom farce somewhat hampered by censorship.
w Bess Meredyth play *The Firebrand* by Edwin Justus Mayer d Gregory La Cava ph Charles Rosher m Alfred Newman ad Richard Day
☆ Fredric March, Constance Bennett, *Frank Morgan*, Fay Wray, Vince Barnett, Louis Calhern, Jessie Ralph
'Gay and entertaining though whipped up synthetically like circus ice cream.' – *Variety*
Charles Rosher; Frank Morgan; Richard Day

The Affairs of Dobie Gillis
US 1953 74m bw
MGM (Arthur M. Loew Jnr)
Adventures of an indolent and accident-prone university student.
Scatty comedy with good talent and musical numbers encased in a tatty production.
w Max Shulman d Don Weis ph William Mellor md Jeff Alexander
☆ Bobby Van, Debbie Reynolds, Hans Conried, Barbara Ruick, Bob Fosse

Affairs of Sally: see *The Fuller Brush Girl*

'She's so romantic she drives four men frantic!'
The Affairs of Susan **
US 1945 110m bw
Paramount (Hal B. Wallis)
Four men in Susan's life see her differently.
Occasionally witty comedy designed as a champagne vehicle for its star. It seemed quite good at the time.
w Richard Flournoy story Laszlo Gorog, T. Monroe d William A. Seiter ph David Abel m Frederick Hollander
☆ *Joan Fontaine, George Brent, Walter Abel*, Don Defore, Dennis O'Keefe
'The cast enters into the irresponsibilities with gusto.' – *MFB*
'A bright thing, a bit too long.' – *Richard Mallett, Punch*
Laszlo Gorog, T. Monroe

Affliction **
US 1997 113m DeLuxe
Largo (Linda Reisman)
In a small snowbound town, the local sheriff finally breaks under life's many humiliations.
A stolid drama of a cycle of childhood abuse spanning the generations; the excellent performances seem somehow stranded by the austere directorial approach.
wd Paul Schrader novel Russell Banks ph Paul Sarossy m Michael Brook pd Anne Pritchard ed Jay Rabinowitz
☆ *Nick Nolte*, Sissy Spacek, *James Coburn*, Willem Dafoe, Mary Beth Hurt, Jim True, Marian Seldes, Homes Osborne, Brigid Tierney, Sean McCann, Wayne Robson
'This is a powerhouse picture which comes to grips with some horrific home truths.' – *Kim Newman, Empire*
James Coburn
Nick Nolte

Afraid of the Dark *
GB/France 1992 91m colour
Rank/Sovereign/Telescope/Les Films Ariane/Cine Cinq (Simon Bosanquet)
A near-sighted 11-year-old boy with a blind mother worries about the identity of the slasher who is attacking blind women.
A thriller that turns out to be not what it seems, but the twist is ultimately an uninteresting one, though the film does work up a degree of terror.
wd Mark Peploe ph Bruno de Keyzer m Richard Hartley pd Caroline Ames ed Scott Thomas
☆ James Fox, Fanny Ardant, Paul McGann, Clare Holman, Ben Keyworth
'A rather stiff and self-conscious film, not without its pretensions, but also informed by considerable intelligence.' – *Derek Malcolm, Guardian*

Africa Screams
US 1949 79m bw
UA (Edward Nassour)
Two dumbbells go on safari with a treasure map.
Lower-case comedy.
w Earl Baldwin d Charles Barton ph Charles Van Enger
☆ Bud Abbott, Lou Costello, Hillary Brooke, Max Baer, Shemp Howard

Africa Texas Style *
GB 1967 109m Eastmancolor
Paramount/Vantors (Andrew Marton)
A Kenyan settler hires two Texas cowboys to help in his scheme of wild game ranching.
Excellent location sequences are dragged down by a very boring script, but it's a good family film nevertheless.
w Andy White d Andrew Marton ph Paul Beeson m Malcolm Arnold
☆ John Mills, Hugh O'Brian, Nigel Green, Tom Nardini, Adrienne Corri, Ronald Howard
† Forerunner of TV series, *Cowboy in Africa.*

African Fury: see *Cry the Beloved Country*

'They never dreamed of being in each other's arms, yet the mystic spell of the jungle swept them to primitive, hungry embrace! The greatest adventure a man ever had ... with a woman!'
The African Queen ***
GB 1951 103m Technicolor
IFD/Romulus-Horizon (Sam Spiegel)
In 1915, a gin-drinking river trader and a prim missionary make odd companions for a boat trip down a dangerous river, culminating in an attack on a German gunboat.
Despite some unfortunate studio sets mixed in with real African footage achieved through great hardship by all concerned, this is one of those surprising films that really work, a splendidly successful mixture of comedy, character and adventure.
w *James Agee* novel C. S. Forester d *John Huston* ph *Jack Cardiff* m Allan Gray
☆ *Humphrey Bogart* (Charlie Allnutt), *Katharine Hepburn* (Rose Sayer), Robert Morley (The Rev. Samuel Sayer), Peter Bull (Captain), Theodore Bikel (2nd Officer)
ROSE: 'I never dreamed that any experience could be so stimulating!'
'Entertaining but not entirely plausible or original.' – *Robert Hatch*
'The movie is not great art but it is great fun, essentially one long, exciting, old-fashioned movie chase.' – *Time*
'A Technicolor Cook's Tour of jungle wonders, enriched by performances unmatched by anything Hepburn or Bogart have yet contributed to the screen.' – *Cue*
† Peter Viertel's book, *White Hunter Black Heart*, filmed by Clint Eastwood, is basically about Huston during the making of this film. In 1987 Katharine Hepburn wrote a book about her experiences, entitled *The Making Of The African Queen, or How I went to Africa with Bogart, Bacall and Huston and almost lost my mind.*
Humphrey Bogart
James Agee; John Huston; Katharine Hepburn

Afrodite Dea Dell'Amore: see *Aphrodite, Goddess of Love*

'Seduced Beyond The Limits Of Deception. Betrayed Beyond The Limits Of Desire.'
After Dark, My Sweet
US 1990 111m colour Super 35
Virgin/Avenue (Ric Kidney, Bob Redlin)
A disturbed young drifter becomes involved with an alcoholic widow and a former policeman in a plan to kidnap a child.
Wildly melodramatic thriller with dull performances.
w Bob Redlin novel Jim Thompson d James Foley ph Mark Plummer m Maurice Jarre ad Kenneth A. Hardy ed Howard Smith
☆ Jason Patric, Rachel Ward, Bruce Dern, George Dickerson, James Cotton

After Eight Hours: see *Society Doctor*

'When it's after midnight in New York City, you don't have to look for love, laughter and trouble. They'll all find you!'
After Hours **
US 1985 97m DuArt
Warner/Geffen/Double Play (Amy Robinson, Griffin Dunne, Robert F. Colesberry)
Through a chapter of accidents, a mild-mannered computer programmer has a bad time in the night streets of New York.
An unsettling kind of black comedy with moments of malaise: nobody denies its touches of brilliance, but few people want to see it again.
w Joseph Minion d *Martin Scorsese* ph Michael Ballhaus m Howard Shore pd *Jeffrey Townsend* ed *Thelma Schoonmaker*
☆ Griffin Dunne, Rosanna Arquette, Verna Bloom, Thomas Chong, Teri Garr, Cheech Marin, Linda Fiorentino, John Heard
'The cinema of paranoia and persecution reaches an apogee ... would have been pretty funny if it didn't play like a confirmation of everyone's worst fears about contemporary urban life.' – *Variety*
'A film so original, so particular, that one is uncertain from moment to moment exactly how to respond to it. Interesting.' – *Roger Ebert*

'What Is The One Memory You Would Take With You?'
After Life ****
Japan 1998 118m colour
ICA/TV Man Union/Engine (Shiho Sato, Masayuki Akieda)
aka: *Wonderful Life*
original title: *Wandafuru Raifu*
After they die, people are processed by bureaucrats who allow them to take one memory of their life, in the form of a film re-creation, into eternity.
Simple, straightforward drama, mixing actual memories with imagined ones, that manages to touch deep emotions; it is both witty and moving in its depiction of the newly dead and the stranded officials who attempt to deal both with their lives and those fleeting moments that gave them meaning.
wd Hirokazu Kore-Eda ph Yamazaki Hiroshi m Yasuhiro Kasamatsu ad Toshihiro Isomi, Hideo Gunji ed Hirokazu Kore-Eda
☆ Arata (Takashi Mochizuki), Erika Oda (Shiori Satonaka), Susumu Terajima (Satoru Kawashima), Tsuyoshi Naito (Ichiro Watanabe), Kyoko Kagawa (Kyoko Watanabe), Kei Tani (Ken-nosuke Nakamura), Takashi Naito (Takuro Sugie), Sadao Abe (Ichiro Watanabe, as student)
'A profound meditation on life's meaning and value and the relationship of movies, memories and dreams.' – *Stephen Holden, New York Times*

After Midnight: see *Captain Carey USA (1950)*

After Midnight
US 1989 90m colour
MGM/High Bar (Richard Arlook, Peter Greene, Ken and Jim Wheat)
A lecturer on the psychology of fear invites his students to scare each other by telling frightening stories.
Portmanteau horror that relies on violent shocks for its effect.
wd Ken and Jim Wheat ph Phedon Papamichael m Marc Donahue pd Paul Chadwick ed Phillip Linson, Quinnie Martin Jnr
☆ Judie Aronson, Marg Helgenberger, Marc McClure, Ed Monaghan, Alan Rosenberg, Monique Salcido, Tracy Wells, Jillian McWhirter

After Midnight
Ireland 1990 100m colour
Lazer/Channel 4/Dublin Cinema Group (Maxine Julius)
An alcoholic nightwatchman in a Dublin hotel redeems himself with the help of a new assistant.
Despite the valiant efforts of Jaffrey, a broad farce that fails to amuse and sticks instead to clichéd characters and situations.
wd Shanis Grewal ph Jack Conroy m Mickey Gallagher pd Brien Vahey ed Carl Thomson
☆ Saeed Jaffrey, Hayley Mills, Ian Dury, Dhirendra, Vladek Sheybal

After Office Hours *
US 1935 75m bw
MGM (Bernard H. Hyman)
A newspaperman and his socialite reporter solve a murder mystery.
Crisply-written, fast-moving comedy melodrama; good stuff of its time and type.
w *Herman J. Mankiewicz* d Robert Z. Leonard ph Charles Rosher
☆ *Clark Gable, Constance Bennett*, Stuart Erwin, Billie Burke, Harvey Stephens, Katherine Alexander, Henry Travers, Henry Armetta
'One of the best balanced pix of the season; it has practically everything.' – *Film Daily*
'Mildly satisfactory entertainment ... story deficiencies are surprising ... Gable and Bennett will have to carry this one.' – *Variety*

After the Ball *
GB 1957 89m Eastmancolor
IFD/Beaconsfield (Peter Rogers)
The life and loves of music-hall singer Vesta Tilley, who married into the nobility.
Adequate if uninspired biopic with entertaining detail and songs.
w Hubert Gregg d Compton Bennett ph Jack Asher md Muir Mathieson ad Norman Arnold
☆ Pat Kirkwood, Laurence Harvey, Clive Morton, Jerry Verno, June Clyde

After the Fox *
US/Italy 1966 103m Technicolor Panavision
UA/Nancy/CCM (John Bryan)
The Fox escapes from jail to execute a gold bullion caper and save his young sister from the streets.
Unlikeable and unfunny farce which sets its star among excitable Italians and hopes for the best, adding a few wild stabs at satire on movie-making styles. Mature agreeably sends up his old image.
w Neil Simon, Cesare Zavattini d Vittorio de Sica ph Leonida Barboni m Burt Bacharach
☆ Peter Sellers, *Victor Mature*, Britt Ekland, Lidia Brazzi, Paolo Stoppa, Akim Tamiroff, Martin Balsam
'Never even begins to get off the ground.' – *MFB*

After the Rehearsal **

Sweden 1984 72m colour
Svenskfilmindustri/SV2

After a rehearsal for Strindberg's *Dream Play*, the director sits and remembers the circumstances surrounding an earlier production.

Typical but satisfyingly unpretentious Bergman piece of the second rank.

wd Ingmar Bergman
☆ Erland Josephson, Ingrid Thulin, Lena Olin

'What we are left with is the very strong sense of an artist who has sacrificed many lives for the sake of his art, and now wonders if perhaps one of those lives was his own.' – *Roger Ebert*

After the Thin Man **

US 1936 113m bw
MGM (Hunt Stromberg)

Nick and Nora Charles, not forgetting Asta, solve another murder.

Overlong but well-carpentered sequel to The Thin Man, developing the thesis that a married couple, even if they are detectives and drink too much, can be interesting and lovable.

w Frances Goodrich, Albert Hackett *d* W. S. Van Dyke II *ph* Oliver T. Marsh *m* Herbert Stothart, Edward Ward
☆ William Powell, Myrna Loy, James Stewart, Elissa Landi, Joseph Calleia, Jessie Ralph, Alan Marshal, Sam Levene

'It is evident that it was almost impossible to make a better mystery comedy than *The Thin Man*. Early speed would have helped, but ... few films this season have contained more risibles.' – *Variety*

Frances Goodrich; Albert Hackett

After Tomorrow

US 1932 70m bw
Fox

Family troubles and small salaries prevent a young couple from getting married.

Rather curious drama which was sold on the fact that it retained the sex discussion from its stage original.

w Sonya Levien *play* John Golden, Hugh Stange *d* Frank Borzage
☆ Charles Farrell, Marian Nixon, Minna Gombell, Josephine Hull, William Collier Snr, William Pawley

'In several sequences it pioneers for the picture business. That financial success is doubtful is rather unfortunate.' – *Variety*

After Tonight

US 1933 71m bw
RKO
GB title: *Sealed Lips*

During World War I a Russian lady spy falls for an Austrian officer.

Tediously talky romantic vehicle which barely gets started before it bogs down.

w Jane Murfin *d* George Archainbaud
☆ Constance Bennett, Gilbert Roland, Edward Ellis, Mischa Auer

Afterglow *

US 1997 113m DeLuxe
Entertainment/Moonstone/Sandcastle 5/Elysian Dreams (Robert Altman)

A middle-aged handyman, who is married to a washed-up 'B'-movie actress, begins an affair with a wealthy young woman; in retaliation, his wife spends a weekend with the woman's husband.

Glossy romantic drama that takes a great deal of time to say very little about relationships; the performances don't help.

wd Alan Rudolph *ph* Toyomichi Kurita *m* Mark Isham *pd* François Séguin *ed* Suzy Elmiger
☆ Julie Christie, Nick Nolte, Lara Flynn Boyle, Jonny Lee Miller

'Serious and comic, frivolous and substantial, giddy and lyrical all at once.' – *Emanuel Levy, Variety*

Julie Christie

Agaguk: see *Shadow of the Wolf*

Against a Crooked Sky

US 1975 89m colour Todd-AO 35
Doty/Dayton

Two Westerners set out to find the sister of one of them, who has been kidnapped by Indians.

Very ordinary variation on The Searchers, which in itself was a bit tedious at times.

w Douglas G. Stewart, Eleanor Lamb *d* Earl Bellamy
☆ Richard Boone, Stewart Petersen, Geoffrey Land, Jewel Blanch, Henry Wilcoxon

Against All Flags *

US 1952 83m Technicolor
U-I (Howard Christie)

A daring British seaman routs Spanish ships at the request of the king.

Standard pirate yarn, almost Flynn's last swashbuckler; production below par.

w Aeneas Mackenzie, Joseph Hoffman *d* George Sherman *ph* Russell Metty *m* Hans Salter
☆ Errol Flynn, Maureen O'Hara, Anthony Quinn, Mildred Natwick

† Remade as *The King's Pirate* (qv)
†† Though Flynn did most of his own stunts for this picture, he balked at the one involving sliding down through a sail on a rapier blade, which was originated by Douglas Fairbanks in *The Black Pirate*; it was performed by a stunt double.

Against All Odds

US 1984 121m Metrocolor
Columbia/Delphi (Jerry Bick)

An unemployed football player is hired by a bookmaker to find his missing wife.

Complex and lugubrious remake of Out of the Past (qv), which long outstays its welcome.

w Eric Hughes *d* Taylor Hackford *ph* Donald Thorin, E. Pershing Flynn *m* Michel Colombier, Larry Carlton *ad* Richard James Lawrence
☆ Jeff Bridges, Rachel Ward, James Woods, Richard Widmark, Jane Greer (from the original cast), Alex Karras, Dorian Harewood, Swoosie Kurtz

'It has so many convoluted double crosses that each time you are told what was really going on behind the scene you just witnessed, you care less.' – *Time Out*

'A tedious concatenation of narrative twists.' – *MFB*

'The best thing to do is accept the plot, then disregard it, and pay attention to the scenes of passion.' – *Roger Ebert*

title song (Phil Collins)

Against the Wind *

GB 1947 96m bw
Ealing (Sidney Cole)

In London during World War II, men and women are trained as saboteurs, and one of them is a traitor.

Thoughtful, well-made spy thriller with good performances; but a bit dour.

w T. E. B. Clarke, Michael Pertwee *d* Charles Crichton *ph* Lionel Banes *m* Leslie Bridgewater *ad* J. Elder-Wills *ed* Alan Osbiston
☆ Simone Signoret, Robert Beatty, Jack Warner, Gordon Jackson, Paul Dupuis, Gisele Preville, John Slater, Peter Illing, James Robertson Justice

Agantuk **

India/France 1991 120m colour
Artificial Eye/National Film Development Corporation of India/Erato/DD/Soprofilms/Canal (Satyajit Ray)
aka: *The Stranger*

A Calcutta family suspect that a long-lost uncle who comes to stay may be an impostor.

A charming and humorous examination of cultural differences and ingrained prejudices.

wd Satyajit Ray *ph* Barun Raha *m* Satyajit Ray *ed* Dulal Dutt
☆ Dipankar De, Mamata Shankar, Bikram Bhattacharya, Utpal Dutt, Dhritiman Chatterjee, Rabi Ghosh, Subrata Chatterjee

'A wise, witty and benevolent work, a worthy sign-off from a great film-maker.' – *Philip Kemp, Sight and Sound*

'Mitra, in Utpal Dutt's performance, combines, as Ray himself did, a powerful intellect and an unsentimental insight into human behaviour with a generosity of spirit and genuine humility.' – *Philip French, Observer*

† It was Ray's last film.

Agatha *

GB 1979 105m Technicolor
Warner/First Artists/Sweetwall/Casablanca (Jarvis Astaire, Gavrik Losey)

In 1926, Agatha Christie disappears after marital difficulties and tries to commit suicide in a Harrogate hotel under a pseudonym.

Lushly recreated but still imaginary and unconvincing solution to a real-life disappearance, complete with romantic encounter with an American newspaperman.

w Kathleen Tynan, Arthur Hopcraft *d* Michael Apted *ph Vittorio Storaro* *m* Johnny Mandel *pd Shirley Russell*
☆ Vanessa Redgrave, Dustin Hoffman, Timothy Dalton, Helen Morse, Timothy West, Tony Britton, Alan Badel

'With its shadowy characters, paucity of plot, and an abundance of stylistic red herrings, one doubts whether *Agatha* would have met Mrs Christie's own requirements for a thriller, though she may well have enjoyed its sumptuous recreation of hotel interiors in the 1920s.' – *Geoff Brown, MFB*

'It has a general air of knowingness, but seems to be missing the scenes which would explain why it was made.' – *New Yorker*

L'Age d'Or **

France 1930 63m bw
Vicomte de Noailles

A collection of strange events satirizing religion and the social order.

Deliberately shocking and possibly quite meaningless, this truly surrealist film is chiefly interesting now for its flashforwards to Buñuel's later work.

w Luis Buñuel, Salvador Dali *d Luis Buñuel* *ph* Albert Dubergen *m* Georges van Parys *ed* Luis Buñuel
☆ Gaston Modot, Lya Lys, Max Ernst, Pierre Prévert, Jacques Brunius

'In some way the juxtaposition of images causes in almost every spectator a train of reactions of unprecedented violence.' – *Basil Wright, 1972*

'The story is also a sequence of moral and surrealist aesthetic. The sexual instinct and the sense of death form its substance.' – *Luis Buñuel*

'It retains its outrageous anarchic vitality, as though unwilling to admit its age.' – *Observer 1980*

The Age for Love

US 1931 81m bw
UA/Howard Hughes

A wife does not want children; her husband leaves her and marries a woman who does.

Shapeless and would-be shocking, this forgotten film was written off as soon as it was made.

w Robert E. Sherwood, Frank Lloyd, Ernest Pascal *novel* Ernest Pascal *d* Frank Lloyd *m* Alfred Newman
☆ Billie Dove, Adrian Morris, Charles Starrett, Lois Wilson, Edward Everett Horton, Mary Duncan

'Everybody makes mistakes, and this is one by Howard Hughes.' – *Variety*

Age of Consent *

Australia 1969 103m Technicolor
Columbia/Nautilus (James Mason, Michael Powell)

An artist seduces the granddaughter of a drunken harridan with whom he shares a Barrier Reef island.

Mildly likeable but self-conscious and overlong South Pacific idyll.

w Peter Yeldham *novel* Norman Lindsay *d* Michael Powell *ph* Hannes Staudinger *m* Stanley Myers
☆ James Mason, Helen Mirren, Jack MacGowran, Neva Carr-Glyn, Frank Thring

Age of Innocence

US 1934 71m bw
RKO

In the 1870s, a young attorney's career is threatened when he falls in love with a divorcee.

Dated romantic drama, rather thinly performed and presented.

w Sarah Y. Mason, Victor Heerman *novel* Edith Wharton *d* Philip Moeller
☆ Irene Dunne, John Boles, Lionel Atwill, Laura Hope Crews, Helen Westley, Julie Haydon

'It will take smart selling to protect it at the box office, especially away from the social registers of the land.' – *Variety*

Age of Innocence

Canada/GB 1977 101m Eastmancolor
Judson/Willoughby (Henning Jacobsen)

After World War I, an English teacher in Canada develops pacifist views which stir up local resentment and lead to violence.

Rather uninteresting melodrama which never really comes to the boil despite care all round.

w Ratch Wallace *d* Alan Bridges *ph* Brian West *m* Lucio Agostini
☆ David Warner, Honor Blackman, Trudy Young, Cec Linder, Tim Henry, Lois Maxwell, Robert Hawkins

The Age of Innocence **

US 1993 138m Technicolor Super 35mm
Columbia (Barbara de Fina)

In New York in the 1870s, a wealthy and conventional lawyer falls in love with his wife's cousin, a woman of dubious reputation.

A deft study of a repressed society with some effective set-pieces, let down by an insufficiently dramatized narrative; the emotional weight of the film is carried not by the actors, but by the voice-over, which severely limits its impact.

w Jay Cocks, Martin Scorsese *novel* Edith Wharton *d* Martin Scorsese *ph* Michael Ballhaus *m* Elmer Bernstein *pd Dante Ferretti* *ed* Thelma Schoonmaker
☆ Daniel Day-Lewis, *Michelle Pfeiffer*, Winona Ryder, Richard E. Grant, Alec McCowen, Geraldine Chaplin, Mary Beth Hurt, Stuart Wilson, Miriam Margolyes, Sian Phillips, Michael Gough, Alexis Smith, Jonathan Pryce, Robert Sean Leonard

'Scorsese has met most of the challenges inherent in tackling such a formidable period piece, but the material remains cloaked by the very propriety, stiff manners and emotional starchiness the picture delineates in such copious detail.' – *Variety*

'The great virtue of the film is that it takes the past seriously and sets about the task of bringing it to life detail by detail, without false immediacy.' – *Adam Mars-Jones*

'For those whose idea of bliss is watching handsome people in a well-told story of love and denial, this is ecstasy from scene one.' – *Angie Errigo, Empire*

Winona Ryder; Jay Cocks, Martin Scorsese; Elmer Bernstein; Dante Ferretti; costume design (Gabriella Pescucci)

Miriam Margolyes

Agency

Canada 1981 94m colour
Farley

An advertising agency gets into political hands which send out messages through special TV packs.

Faded melodrama which did nothing for anyone involved in it.

w Noel Hynd *novel* Paul Gottlieb *d* George Kaczender
☆ Robert Mitchum, Lee Majors, Valerie Perrine, Saul Rubinek, Alexandra Stewart

Agent 8¾: see *Hot Enough for June*

Agent for Harm

US 1966 84m colour
Universal (Joseph F. Robertson)

A Washington agency prevents the Russians from abducting a scientist.

Spy spoof somewhat below the level of the TV UNCLE films.

w Blair Robertson *d* Gerd Oswald
☆ Wendell Corey, Mark Richman, Martin Kosleck, Carl Esmond, Barbara Bouchet

The Ages of Lulu *

Spain 1990 95m Eastmancolor
Iberoamericana/Apricot (Andrés Vicente Gomez)
original title: *Las Edades de Lulu*

After a young woman marries and leaves the man whom she allowed to seduce her, she explores the

darker side of sexuality in order to satisfy her desires.
An intriguing melodrama of the sexual education of a woman, in which males are the exploiters, though its overall point seems to be that female sexuality needs restraints.
w Almudena Grandes, Bigas Luna
novel Almudena Grandes *d* Bigas Luna
ph Fernando Arribas *m* Carlos Segarra *pd* Miguel Chicharro *ed* Pablo Gonzalez Del Amo
☆ Francesca Neri (Lulu), Oscar Ladoire (Pablo), María Barranco (Ely), Fernando Guillén Cuervo (Marcelo), Rosana Pastor, Javier Bardem, Juan Graell, Rodrigo Valverde, Pilar Bardem

The Agitator *
GB 1944 98m bw
British National (Louis H. Jackson)
An embittered mechanic becomes a loud-mouthed union spokesman, but fate eventually takes him into management.
Fairly absorbing, modest narrative of the flaws of socialism.
w Edward Dryhurst *novel Peter Pettinger* by William Riley *d* John Harlow *ph* James Wilson
☆ William Hartnell, Mary Morris, John Laurie, Moore Marriott, George Carney, Edward Rigby, Elliot Mason, Frederick Leister, Cathleen Nesbitt, Moira Lister

'When Agnes Brown's husband died she discovered something amazing... Herself.'
Agnes Browne
Ireland 1999 92m Technicolor
UIP/October/Hell's Kitchen
In Dublin in the mid 60s, a widow with seven children struggles to stay solvent.
Maudlin domestic drama of a plucky, warm-hearted woman battling against the odds that leaves no cliché of Irish life at all unfilmed or unspoken.
w John Goldsmith, Brendan O'Carroll *novel The Mammy* by Brendan O'Carroll *d* Anjelica Huston *ph* Anthony B. Richmond *m* Paddy Moloney *pd* David Brockhurst *ed* Eva Gardos
☆ Anjelica Huston (Agnes Browne), Marion O'Dwyer (Marion Monks), Ray Winstone (Mr Billy), Arno Chevrier (Pierre), Gerard McSorley (Mr Aherne), Niall O'Shea (Mark Browne), Ciaran Owens (Frankie Browne), Roxana Williams (Cathy Browne), Carl Power (Simon Browne), Mark Power (Dermot Browne), Tom Jones (Himself)

'Huston is no stranger to the comic tics of Dublin life, so frankly she should be lynched for directing a theme park ride as appalling as this.' – *James Christopher, Times*

'Hopelessly silly and sentimental.' – *Edward Porter, Sunday Times*

Agnes of God *
US 1985 98m Metrocolor
Columbia/Delphi IV (Patrick Palmer, Norman Jewison)
A young nun is accused of giving birth and then killing her baby.
Heavy hysterical weather with no clear solution, but a field day for three actresses.
w John Pielmeier *play* John Pielmeier *d* Norman Jewison *ph* Sven Nykvist *m* Georges Delerue *pd* Ken Adam *ed* Antony Gibbs
☆ *Jane Fonda, Anne Bancroft,* Meg Tilly

'Predictably, religion and reason play to something like a draw.' – *Variety*

Anne Bancroft; Meg Tilly (supporting actress); music

Agonia: see *Agony*

Agony **
USSR 1975 148m colour/bw Sovscope
Mosfilm/Second Film Group
original title: *Agonia*
aka: *Rasputin*
As discontent at the rule of the Tsar increases, and revolution looms in Russia, the monk Rasputin becomes the power behind the throne.
A gripping account of the downfall of the Romanovs and the extraordinary life and death of Rasputin, mixing drama and contemporary newsreels; at times it comes near to being a history lesson, but it fascinates for all that. Nine years in the making, it was banned for ten years by the Soviet authorities.
w Semyon Lungin, Ilya Nusinov *d* Elem Klimov *ph* Leonid Kalashnikov *m* Alfred Schittke *md* Eri Klas
☆ Alexei Petrenko, Anatoly Romashin, Velta Linne, Alisa Freindlikh
† The film also exists in a version that runs for 107m.

The Agony and the Ecstasy *
US 1965 140m DeLuxe Todd-AO
TCF/International Classics Inc (Carol Reed)
Pope Julius II persuades Michelangelo to leave his sculptures and paint the ceiling of the Sistine Chapel.
Dully reverent comic strip approach to art and history; generally heavy going, but good looking.
w Philip Dunne *novel* Irving Stone *d* Carol Reed *ph* Leon Shamroy *m* Alex North *pd* John DeCuir
☆ Charlton Heston, Rex Harrison, Diane Cilento, Harry Andrews, Alberto Lupo, Adolfo Celi

JULIUS: 'You dare to dicker with your pontiff?'

'The vulgarity of the whole concept has none of the joyfully enthusiastic philistinism of a de Mille; rather its tone is a dry, almost cynical, condescension.' – *Brenda Davies*

'All agony, no ecstasy.' – *Judith Crist*

'Not a strong and soaring drama but an illustrated lecture of a slow artist at work.' – *Bosley Crowther*

'Heston hits the ceiling.' – *New York Times*

† The film is said to have cost 12 million dollars and earned 4.
†† Michelangelo was apparently both a dwarf and a homosexual. He is played by Charlton Heston.
Leon Shamroy; Alex North

Aguirre, Wrath of God ****
West Germany 1972 95m colour
Hessicher Rundfunk/Werner Herzog
In 1560, one of Pizarro's lieutenants takes a party of forty down river by raft, and succumbs to megalomania.
Absorbing conquistador melodrama, vividly assembled and impossible to forget.
wd Werner Herzog ph Thomas Mauch *m* Popol Vuh
☆ *Klaus Kinski,* Ruy Guerra, Helena Rojo, Cecilia Rivera

'It ingeniously combines Herzog's gift for deep irony, his strong social awareness, and his worthy ambition to fashion a whole new visual perspective on the world around us via mystical, evocative, yet oddly direct imagery. It is a brilliant cinematic achievement.' – *David Skerritt, Christian Science Monitor*

Ah! Les Belles Bacchantes: see *Femmes de Paris*

'The play that startled the nation!'
Ah, Wilderness **
US 1935 101m bw
MGM (Hunt Stromberg)
Problems of a small-town family at the turn of the century.
Well-acted, affectionately remembered version of a play later musicalized as Summer Holiday. The commercial success of this film led to the Hardy family series.
w Albert Hackett, Frances Goodrich *play* Eugene O'Neill *d* Clarence Brown *ph* Clyde de Vinna *m* Herbert Stothart
☆ Wallace Beery, Lionel Barrymore, Eric Linden, Spring Byington, Mickey Rooney, Aline MacMahon, Charley Grapewin, Cecilia Parker, Frank Albertson, Bonita Granville

'A job of picture making, in craftsmanship and feeling, that is wonderful to see.' – *Otis Ferguson*

'That it is a fine artistic effort will not be denied anywhere, but for the public at large it will need all the boosting it can get.' – *Variety*

Ahfei Zhenjuang: see *Days of Being Wild*

Ai No Borei *
Japan/France 1978 105m Eastmancolor
Argos/Oshima (Anatole Dauman)
aka: *Empire of Passion*
aka: *Phantom Love; In the Realm of Passion*
In the 1890s, an adulterous wife and her young lover kill her husband and are haunted by his ghost.
A drama of lust, love and guilt set in a small, close-knit community; its formal quality distances the audience from the action so that it remains for the most part uninvolving.
wd Nagisa Oshima *story* Itoko Nakamura
ph Yoshio Miyajima *m* Toru Takemitsu *ad* Josho Toda *ed* Keiichi Uraoka
☆ Tatsuya Fuji, Kazuko Yoshiyuki, Takahiro Tamura, Takuzo Kawatani, Akiko Koyama, Taiji Tonoyama
† Oshima won the award for best director at the Cannes Film Festival in 1978 with this film, a companion piece to *Ai No Corrida* (qv).

Ai No Corrida **
France/Japan 1976 105m Eastmancolor
Argos/Oshima/Shibata (Anatole Dauman)
French title: *L'Empire des Sens*
aka: *Empire of the Passions; Empire of the Senses*
A sexually complicated servant girl has an intense affair with the master of the house, and finally murders and mutilates him.
Strong but stylish stuff, a kind of Japanese Last Tango in Paris. Those who like this kind of thing will like it a lot.
wd Nagisa Oshima *ph* Hideo Ito *m* Minoru Miki
☆ Tatsuya Fuji, Eiko Matsuda, Aoi Nakajima, Meika Seri

'By the final sequence, we are all implicated in the continuing social system which makes such love impossible. It is not Sade, but the censor in all of us who ultimately wields the knife.' – *Jan Dawson, MFB*

† The film was not given a certificate by the BBFC or a cinema release in Britain until 1991, although it had been shown in cinema clubs.

Aida
Italy 1953 95m Ferrania colour
Oscar Film (Ferrucio de Martino, Federico Teti)
A young Egyptian army officer loves the captive princess of the Ethiopians.
Stuffy, over-dressed, pantomimish version of the opera, with some pretension to cinematic vitality.
w various *opera* Verdi *d* Clemente Fracassi *ph* Piero Portalupi *ad* Flavio Mogherini
☆ Sophia Loren (sung by Renata Tebaldi), Lois Maxwell, Luciano della Marra

Aimée & Jaguar *
Germany 1998 126m colour
Optimum/Senator (Günter Rohrbach, Hanno Huth)
In Berlin in 1943, a mother of four, whose husband is away in the German army, begins an affair with another woman, a Jewish resistance worker.
Based on a true story, this is a flatly-told account of a passionate, short-lived love affair that is never as affecting as it ought to be, despite some accomplished acting.
w Max Färberböck, Rona Munro *novel* Erica Fischer *d* Max Färberböck *ph* Tony Imi *m* Jan A. P. Kaczmarek *pd* Albrecht Konrad *ed* Barbara Hennings
☆ Maria Schrader (Felice Schragenheim (Jaguar)), Juliane Köhler (Lilly Wust (Aimée)), Johanna Wokalek (Ilse), Heike Makatsch (Klärchen), Elisabeth Degen (Lotte), Detlev Buck (Günther Wust), Inge Keller (Lilly Wust, 1997), Kyra Mladeck (Ilse, 1997)

'With key scenes so vivid they barely feel scripted, this is more than a same-sex success, it's a most affecting, most sensual on-screen love affair, period.' – *Kenneth Turan, Los Angeles Times*

Aimez-Vous les Femmes?: see *Do You Like Women?*

Ain't Misbehavin' *
US 1955 81m Technicolor
U-I (Samuel Marx)
A young millionaire marries a cabaret girl, who determines to improve her mind and manners.
Lively American version of Pygmalion, with musical numbers and some bright lines.
w Edward Buzzell, Philip Rapp, Devery Freeman *d* Edward Buzzell *ph* Wilfrid Cline *m* Joseph Gershenson *ch* Kenny Williams, Lee Scott
☆ Rory Calhoun, *Piper Laurie, Reginald Gardiner,* Jack Carson, Barbara Britton, Mamie Van Doren

'The Few. The Proud. The Totally Insane.'
Air America
US 1990 118m DeLuxe Super 35
Guild/Indieprod/Carolco (Daniel Melnick)
CIA pilots indulge in illicit activities in Laos.
Frenetic mix of action and comedy – and unsuccessful at both.
w John Eskow, Richard Rush *book* Christopher Robbins *d* Roger Spottiswoode *ph* Roger Deakins *m* Charles Gross *pd* Allan Cameron *ed* John Bloom, Lois Freeman-Fox
☆ Mel Gibson, Robert Downey Jnr, Nancy Travis, Ken Jenkins, David Marshall Grant, Lane Smith, Art La Fleur, Ned Eisenberg, Marshall Bell

Air Bud
US 1997 97m Technicolor
Buena Vista/Walt Disney/Keystone (Robert Vince, William Vince)
A lonely young boy befriends a basketball-playing dog.
An enjoyable piece of whimsy that should appeal to the young.
w Paul Tamasy, Aaron Mendelsohn *character created by* Kevin DiCicco *d* Charles Martin Smith *ph* Mike Southon *m* Brahm Wenger *pd* Elizabeth Wilcox *ed* Alison Grace
☆ Michael Jeter, Kevin Zegers, Wendy Makkena, Bill Cobbs, Eric Christmas, Brendan Fletcher, Norman Browning, Buddy

'An old-fashioned heart-tugger in the tradition of *Old Yeller.*' – *Variety*

† Buddy, the golden retriever, was found to be suffering from cancer and had a leg amputated soon after filming finished; he died at the age of 10 in 1998.

'For one typical family, this Friday is to be like no other.'
Un Air de Famille **
France 1996 119m colour Panavision
Metro/Tartan/Téléma/Canal/France2 (Charles Gassot)
aka: *Family Resemblances*
A special family gathering in a café is marked by rifts and reconciliations.
A familiar setting – a celebratory occasion at which family members settle old scores and open fresh wounds – is made fresh by excellent acting and sparkling dialogue.
w Agnès Jaoui, Jean-Pierre Bacri, Cédric Klapisch *play* Agnès Jaoui, Jean-Pierre Bacri *d* Cédric Klapisch *ph* Benoît Delhomme *pd* François Emmanuelli *ed* Francine Sandberg
☆ Jean-Pierre Bacri, Jean-Pierre Darroussin, Catherine Frot, Agnès Jaoui, Claire Maurier, Wladimir Yordanoff

'A barbed but finally affectionate group portrait, all the more entertaining if your French is good enough to keep up with the argy-bargy.' – *Alexander Walker, London Evening Standard*

Air Force *
US 1943 124m bw
Warner (Hal B. Wallis)
A Flying Fortress and its crew see action in Manila, Pearl Harbor and the Coral Sea.
Propaganda piece concentrating on the characters of the crew members, with action set-pieces largely provided by newsreel; but skilled direction still conveys plenty of punch.
w Dudley Nichols *d Howard Hawks ph* James Wong Howe, Elmer Dyer, Charles Marshall *m* Franz Waxman *ed* George Amy
☆ John Garfield, Gig Young, Arthur Kennedy, Charles Drake, John Ridgely, Harry Carey, George Tobias, Stanley Ridgely, Moroni Olsen, Edward Brophy

'Maybe the story is high-flown, maybe it overdraws a recorded fact a bit. We'd hate to think it couldn't happen – or didn't – because it leaves you feeling awfully good.' – *Bosley Crowther*

'The film is one crisis after another, and the director stages the air battles handsomely, but for the rest it helps if you're interested in the factors involved in getting a bomber somewhere and back.' – *Pauline Kael, 70s*
George Amy
Dudley Nichols; James Wong Howe, Elmer Dyer, Charles Marshall

'Five miles up, The President of the United States is waging war on terrorism. Face to face.'
'Harrison Ford *is* the President.'

Air Force One
US 1997 124m Technicolor Super 35
Columbia/Beacon/Radiant (Armyan Bernstein, Wolfgang Petersen, Gail Katz, Jon Shestack)
The US President shows he is a man of action when, with the aid of a US agent, Russians hijack the presidential jet and hold his wife and daughter hostage.
Silly, implausible jingoistic thriller of surprising banality.
w Andrew W. Marlowe *d* Wolfgang Petersen *ph* Michael Ballhaus *m* Jerry Goldsmith *pd* William Sandell *ed* Richard Francis-Bruce
☆ Harrison Ford (President James Marshall), Gary Oldman (Ivan Korshunov), Glenn Close (Vice-President Kathryn Bennett), Wendy Crewson (Grace Marshall), Paul Guilfoyle (Chief of Staff Lloyd Shepherd), William H. Macy (Major Caldwell), Liesel Matthews (Alice Marshall), Dean Stockwell (Defense Secretary Walter Dean), Jürgen Prochnow (General Alexander Radek)
'Think of it as *Fly Hard* and you'll be in the right ballpark.' – *Jay Carr, Boston Globe*
'So preposterous that it begins to seem like a science-fiction artefact in its own right, the product of a parallel-universe 1990s which somehow bypassed the decades since the 1950s, in every area except technology ... utterly unreal in terms of story and character.' – *Adam Mars-Jones, Independent*
† The director rejected Randy Newman's original score for the film
†† The film grossed $172m at the US box-office and another $126m around the world.
Richard Francis-Bruce; sound

Air Mail *
US 1932 84m bw
Universal
Brash young pilot effects a daring rescue and gets the mail through.
Moderate actioner of its time.
w Dale Van Every, Frank Wead *d* John Ford
☆ Pat O'Brien, Ralph Bellamy, Russell Hopton, Gloria Stuart, Lillian Bond, Slim Summerville
'Far short of a smash ... it has no sock name, it is weak on the romantic side and the story material is directed at men.' – *Variety*
† There was also a good silent version in 1925, with Warner Baxter and Douglas Fairbanks Jnr, written by James Shelley Hamilton and directed by Irvin Willat; both had remarkable similarities to *Only Angels Have Wings* (1938).

Air Raid Wardens
US 1943 67m bw
MGM (B. F. Zeidman)
Rejected by the armed services, two incompetent air raid wardens accidentally round up Nazi spies.
Well below par star comedy: their incomparable dignity has disappeared.
w Jack Jevne, Martin Rackin, Charles Rogers, Harry Crane *d* Edward Sedgwick *ph* Walter Lundin *m* Nathaniel Shilkret
☆ Stan Laurel, Oliver Hardy, Edgar Kennedy, Jacqueline White, Stephen McNally, Nella Walker, Donald Meek

The Air Up There *
US 1994 108m Technicolor
Buena Vista/Hollywood/Interscope/Polygram (Ted Field, Rosalie Swedling, Robert W. Cort)
An American basketball coach has to train an African team to win a game in order to settle a tribal dispute, recruit a new star and save his job.
Amiable drama of a man discovering that sport is not all that matters in life.
w Max Apple *d* Paul M. Glaser *ph* Dick Pope *m* David Newman *pd* Roger Hall *ed* Michael E. Polakow
☆ Kevin Bacon, Charles Gitonga Maina, Yolanda Vasquez, Winston Ntshona, Mabutho 'Kid' Sithole, Sean McCann, Dennis Patrick, Nigel Miguel, Ilo Mitumbo
'Mildly entertaining ... isn't quite as stale as the numerous clichés it launches.' – *Brian Lowry, Variety*

Airborne
US 1993 90m Technicolor
Warner/Icon (Bruce Davey, Stephen McEveety)
An unhappy surfer, forced to move to Cincinnati, becomes a rollerblade champion.
A movie aimed at young 'teens, who may not mind the way it sticks to tried and test formulae, but who will appreciate its spectacular rollerblade sequences.
w Bill Apablasa, Stephen McEveety *d* Rob Bowman *ph* Daryn Okada *m* Stewart Copeland *pd* John Myhre *ed* Harry B. Miller III
☆ Shane McDermott, Seth Green, Brittney Powell, Chris Conrad, Edie McClurg, Patrick O'Brien, Jack Black

Airborne
Canada 1997 90m DeLuxe
Le Monde/C3 (John Gillespie)
An elite team of agents attempt to recover a deadly virus stolen from a germ warfare laboratory.
Risible thriller with moments of meaningless slow-motion; despite the permanent scowl, designer stubble and scars, Guttenberg makes an unconvincing action hero.
w Tony Johnston, Julian Grant *d* Julian Grant *ph* Russell Goozee *m* Christophe Beck *pd* Oleg Savytskyiy *ed* Paul Day
☆ Steve Guttenberg, Kim Coates, Torri Higginson, Colm Feore, Sean Bean, Philip Akin, David Fraser

Airheads
US 1994 92m DeLuxe
TCF/Island World (Robert Simonds, Mark Burg)
An unsuccessful rock band hold up a radio station and demand that their demo tape is played on the air.
A dim comedy of dimmer characters which simply keeps repeating its single joke.
w Rich Wilkes *d* Michael Lehmann *ph* John Schwartzman *m* Carter Burwell *pd* David Nichols *ed* Stephen Semel
☆ Brendan Fraser, Steve Buscemi, Chris Farley, Adam Sandler, Michael McKean, Judd Nelson, Ernie Hudson, Amy Locane, David Arquette, Joe Mantegna
'An anarchic screwball comedy for the Beavis and Butthead generation.' – *Nigel Robinson, Film Review*
'Unspeakable.' – *Observer*

Airplane **
US 1980 88m Metrocolor
Paramount/Howard W. Koch (Jon Davison)
A former pilot gets his nerve back when called upon to land a passenger plane because the crew all have food poisoning.
Arthur Hailey's play Flight into Danger and the film Zero Hour which was made from it get the zany parody treatment in this popular movie which is often funny but sometimes merely crude. It rang the box-office bell more loudly than most expensive epics of its year.
wd Jim Abrahams, David and Jerry Zucker *ph* Joseph Biroc *m* Elmer Bernstein *pd* Ward Preston
☆ Robert Stack, Lloyd Bridges, Robert Hays, Julie Hagerty, Peter Graves, Leslie Nielsen, Lorna Patterson, Ethel Merman, Kareem Abdul-Jabbar
'Parody may be the lowest form of humour, but few comedies in ages have rocked the laugh meter this hard.' – *Variety*
'It keeps going, like a dervish with skids on.' – *Derek Malcolm, Guardian*
'Proof that the cinema is alive and well and bursting with ingenuity.' – *David Hughes, Sunday Times*
'It's compiled like a jokebook and has the kind of pacing that goes with a laugh track.' – *Pauline Kael*
'All pretty juvenile really, though the relentless pace and sheer poor taste make up for a lack of originality.' – *Time Out, 1984*
'Practically a satirical anthology of movie clichés ... it compensates for its lack of original comic invention by its utter willingness to steal, beg, borrow and rewrite from anywhere.' – *Roger Ebert*

'Just when you thought it safe to go back into the departure lounge'

Airplane II: The Sequel
US 1982 85m Metrocolor
Paramount (Howard W. Koch)
A space shuttle gets into trouble but is rescued in the nick of time.
Palsied sequel to a funny film, with some of the same cast and some of the same jokes.
wd Ken Finkleman *ph* Joe Biroc *m* Elmer Bernstein *pd* William Sandell *ed* Dennis Virkler
☆ Robert Hays, Julie Hagerty, Lloyd Bridges, Peter Graves, William Shatner, Chad Everett, Steven Stucker, Sonny Bono, Raymond Burr, Chuck Connors, Rip Torn, John Dehner, Kent McCord, John Vernon
'All the pleasure lies in the humour's weakness.' – *Observer*

Airport ***
US 1970 136m Technicolor Todd-AO
Universal/Ross Hunter (Jacque Mapes)
Events of one snowy night at a midwestern international airport, culminating in airborne melodrama when a mad bomber is killed and the damaged plane has to be talked down.
Glossy, undeniably entertaining, all-star version of a popular novel, with cardboard characters skilfully deployed in Hollywood's very best style.
wd George Seaton *novel* Arthur Hailey *ph* Ernest Laszlo *m* Alfred Newman *ed* Stuart Gilmore
☆ Burt Lancaster, Dean Martin, Jean Seberg, *Helen Hayes*, Van Heflin, Jacqueline Bisset, George Kennedy, Maureen Stapleton, Barry Nelson, Dana Wynter, Lloyd Nolan, Barbara Hale, Gary Collins, Jessie Royce Landis
'The best film of 1944.' – *Judith Crist*
'For sheer contentment there is nothing to beat the sight of constant catastrophe happening to others.' – *Alexander Walker*
'A *Grand Hotel* in the sky ... every few years or so some more show-biz types would crowd onto a plane that would threaten to crash, collide with another, meet with terrorists, or otherwise be subjected to the perils of Pauline.' – *Les Keyser, Hollywood in the Seventies*
† The film cost 10 million dollars and earned 45.
Helen Hayes
best picture; George Seaton (as writer); Ernest Laszlo; Alfred Newman; Maureen Stapleton; editing; costumes (Edith Head)

'Something hit us ... the crew is dead ... help us, please, please help us!'

Airport 1975
US 1974 105m Technicolor Panavision
Universal (Jennings Lang, William Frye)
A private aircraft collides with a jet plane and kills or immobilizes its crew, so a stewardess has to manoeuvre the jumbo to safety.
Inept airborne suspenser loaded with stars who do nothing and marred by continuity lapses and boring dialogue.
w Don Ingalls *d* Jack Smight *ph* Philip Lathrop *m* John Cacavas
☆ Charlton Heston, *Karen Black*, George Kennedy, Helen Reddy, Efrem Zimbalist Jnr, Susan Clark, Myrna Loy, Gloria Swanson, Linda Blair, Dana Andrews, Roy Thinnes, Sid Caesar, Ed Nelson, Nancy Olson, Martha Scott
'Aimed squarely for the yahoo trade.' – *Variety*
'Processed schlock. One can have a fairly good time laughing at it, but it doesn't sit too well as a joke, because the people on the screen are being humiliated.' – *Pauline Kael, New Yorker*
'Good exciting corny escapism, and the kind of movie you would not want to watch as an inflight film.' – *Roger Ebert*

Airport '77
US 1977 114m Technicolor Panavision
Universal (William Frye)
A private airliner loaded with guests and art treasures hits an oil rig and settles underwater on a sandbank.
Hysteria, rescue, and guest stars with nothing to do; the mixture as before.
w Michael Scheff, David Spector *story* H. A. L. Craig, Charles Kuenstle *d* Jerry Jameson *ph* Philip Lathrop *m* John Cacavas *pd* George C. Webb
☆ Jack Lemmon, James Stewart, Brenda Vaccaro, Joseph Cotten, Olivia de Havilland, Lee Grant, Darren McGavin, Christopher Lee, Robert Foxworth, Robert Hooks, Monte Markham, Kathleen Quinlan, James Booth, George Kennedy
'Neither as riveting as it should be, nor as much fun as its absurd plotline would suggest.' – *Verina Glaessner, MFB*
† See also: *The Concorde – Airport '79*.

Airport '80: The Concorde: see *The Concorde: Airport '79*

Akahige: see *Redbeard*

Akai Hashi Noshitano Nurui Mizu *
Japan/France 2001 120m colour
Metro Tartan/Nikkatsu/Imamura/Bap/Eisei Gekijo/Maru/Comme Des Cinemas/Dussart (Hisa Iino)
aka: *Warm Water Under The Red Bridge*
An unemployed man visits a seaside town in search of treasure and begins a relationship with a woman whose orgasms are accompanied by floods of water.
Odd little fable that has some endearing moments, if you can go with the flow.
w Motofumi Tomikawa, Daisuke Tengan, Shohei Imamura *novel* Henmi Yo *d* Shohei Imamura *ph* Shigeru Komatsubara *m* Shinichiro Ikebe *pd* Hisao Inagaki *ed* Hajime Okayasu
☆ Koji Yakusho (Yosuke Sasano), Misa Shimizu (Saeko Aizawa), Mitsuko Baisho (Mitsu Aizawa), Mansaku Fuwa (Gen), Kazuo Kitramura (Taro), Isao Natsuyagi (Masayuki Uomi), Yukiya Kitamara (Shintaro Uomi), Hijiri Kojima (Miki Tagami)
'Too long and too whimsical.' – *Observer*

Akasen Chitai: see *Street of Shame*

Ake and His World *
Sweden 1984 103m colour
Sandrew/Svenska Film Institute/Scentext
original title: *Ake Och Hans Värld*
In the 1930s the six-year-old son of a Swedish country doctor observes the lives and deaths of his father's patients.
Charming, episodic, gently nostalgic account of childhood.
wd Allan Edwall *ph* Jörgen Persson *m* Thomas Lindahl *ad* Anna Asp *ed* Lars Hagström
☆ Martin Lindstrom, Loa Falkman, Gunnel Fred, Katja Blomquist, Ulla Sjöblom, Suzanne Ernrup, Björn Gustafson, Allan Edwall

Akenfield *
GB 1974 98m Techniscope
Angle Films/LWT (Peter Hall, Rex Pyke)
Semi-dramatized film version of a book which documented a Suffolk village by interviewing its older inhabitants.
An interesting venture ruined by imprecision, misty photography, lack of narrative drive or any compensating detail, and the appalling error of using a cheap wide screen process.
w Ronald Blythe *book* Ronald Blythe *d* Peter Hall *ph* Ivan Strasberg *m* Michael Tippett *ad* Ian Whittaker, Roger Christian
☆ Garrow Shand, Peggy Cole, Barbara Tilney, Lyn Brooks, Ida Page, Ted Dedman, Peter Tuddenham
'One of the best films – certainly the most unusual – made in England and about England.' – *Alexander Walker*
'A parochial drama-documentary, commercially dubious but otherwise an impressive achievement.' – *Variety*
'About the impact of the leading players, the beauty of the Edwardian scenes and the triumphantly enhancing use of music, there need be no reservations at all.' – *Michael Ratcliffe*

Akira (dubbed) **
Japan 1987 124m colour
ICA/Akira Committee (Ryohei Suzuki, Shunzo Kato)

In a future neo-Tokyo, filled with revolutionaries, terrorists and warring government factions, a young biker becomes the subject of experiments to create a super-being.
Brilliantly animated film, based on a comic-book, that eschews cartoon violence for the more realistic style of action movies. The narrative, which begins as fantasy and shifts into mysticism, is less enthralling.
w Katsuhiro Otomo, Izo Hashimoto *comic* Katsuhiro Otomo *d* Katsuhiro Otomo *ph* Katsuji Misawa *m* Shoji Yamashiro *ad* Toshiharu Mizutani *ed* Takeshi Seyama
'Probably the first animated feature with a genuinely novelistic density of incident and character.' – *Tony Rayns, MFB*

Akira Kurosawa's Dreams *
US 1990 119m colour
Warner/Akira Kurosawa USA (Hisao Kurosawa, Mike Y. Inoue)

Eight dream sequences, concerning animals, ghosts, spirits and nuclear destruction, the most successful of which involves entering the paintings of Van Gogh.
A lesser work of a master: visually fascinating, though too often trite in content.
wd Akira Kurosawa *ph* Takao Saito, Masaharu Ueda *m* Shinichiro Ikebe *ad* Yoshiro Muraki, Akira Sakuragi *ed* Tome Minami
☆ Mitsuko Baisho, Toshihiko Nakano, Mitsunori Isaki, Mie Suzuki, Akira Terao, Mieko Harada, Yoshitaka Zushi, Martin Scorsese, Chosuke Ikariya, Chishu Ryu
'His is not to shock us into surrendering to his visions but to seduce our consent to them. And this he does in one of the most lucid dreamworks ever placed on film.' – *Richard Schickel, Time*

'Fearlessly Told! Authentic! True!'
'He built a vicious crime syndicate of illegal liquor, vice and gambling that we are still fighting today!'
Al Capone **
US 1959 105m bw
Allied Artists (John H. Burrows, Leonard J. Ackerman)

An account of Chicago's most famous gangster, up to his arrest for income tax evasion.
Only slightly overplayed, semi-documentary retelling of a larger-than-life true story. Steiger gives a clever impersonation on the border of caricature.
w Malvin Wald, Henry Greenberg *d* Richard Wilson *ph* Lucien Ballard *m* David Raksin
☆ *Rod Steiger*, Fay Spain, Murvyn Vye, Nehemiah Persoff, Martin Balsam, James Gregory, Joe de Santis
'The most remarkable thing about it is its truth.' – *Daily Telegraph*
'This powerful production may turn out to be the definitive gangster film of all time.' – *Film Daily*

'Imagine if you had three wishes, three hopes, three dreams and they all could come true.'
Aladdin ****
US 1992 90m Technicolor
Buena Vista/Walt Disney (John Musker, Ron Clements)

An urchin with a magic lamp falls in love with a runaway princess.
Another brilliant return to classic form from Disney, notable for its quick-change genie to match the exuberance of Robin Williams' characterization, and some innovative computer animation.
w John Musker, Ron Clements, Ted Elliott, Terry Rossio *d* John Musker, Ron Clements *m* Alan Menken *m/ly* Alan Menken, Howard Ashman, Tim Rice *pd* R. S. Vander Wende *ed* H. Lee Peterson
☆ Featuring the voices of Scott Weinger, Brad Kane (Aladdin's singing), Robin Williams, Linda Larkin, Lea Salonga (Jasmine's singing), Jonathan Freeman, Frank Welker, Gilbert Gottfried, Douglas Seale
'Floridly beautiful, shamelessly derivative and infused with an irreverent, sophisticated comic flair.' – *Variety*
'A rollicking, bodaciously choreographed fantasy right out of Busby Berkeley.' – *Washington Post*
† It was followed by two sequels released direct to video: *Return of Jafar*, edited from an animated TV series, and *Aladdin and the King of Thieves*.
Academy Award: Alan Menken (score); song: 'Whole New World' (*m* Alan Menken, *ly* Tim Rice)
Academy Award nomination: song: 'Friends like Me' (*m* Alan Menken, *ly* Howard Ashman); sound; sound effects editing

Alakazam the Great *
Japan 1960 88m Eastmancolor Toeiscope
Toei (Hiroshi Okawa)

original title: *Saiyu-ki*
The arrogant monkey king of the animals is sent by his human master on a pilgrimage; he defeats evil King Gruesome and returns a hero.
Smartly animated, Disney-inspired cartoon based on the same legend as Monkey, translated by Arthur Waley.
w Osamu Tezuka, Keinosuke Uekusa *d* Taiji Yabushita

'The Mission That Became A Fortress ... The Fortress That Became A Shrine...'
The Alamo *
US 1960 193m Technicolor Todd-AO
UA/Batjac/John Wayne

In 1836 a small southern fort becomes the centre of Texas' fight for independence, but it is suddenly annihilated by a Mexican raid, and all its defenders killed.
Sprawling historical epic with many irrelevant episodes and distracting changes of mood.
w James Edward Grant *d* John Wayne *ph* William H. Clothier *m* Dimitri Tiomkin *ed* Stuart Gilmore
☆ John Wayne (Davy Crockett), Richard Widmark (Jim Bowie), Laurence Harvey (Travis), Richard Boone (Sam Houston), Frankie Avalon, Patrick Wayne, Linda Cristal, Chill Wills, Joseph Calleia
CROCKETT: 'Republic. I like the sound of the word. It means people can live free, talk free, go or come, buy or sell, be drunk or sober, however they choose. Some words give you a feeling. Republic is one of those words that makes me tight in the throat – the same tightness a man gets when his baby takes his first step or his first baby shaves and makes his first sound like a man. Some words can give you a feeling that makes your heart warm. Republic is one of those words.'
'Its sole redeeming feature lies in one of those crushing climaxes of total massacre which Hollywood can still pull off thunderingly well.' – *Peter John Dyer*
Academy Award nomination: picture; William H. Clothier; Dimitri Tiomkin; Chill Wills; song 'The Green Leaves of Summer' (*m* Dimitri Tiomkin, *ly* Paul Francis Webster); editing

Alamo Bay
US 1985 98m Metrocolor
Tri-Star/Delphi III (Louis and Vincent Malle)

Fisherfolk in Galveston Bay resent the intrusion of refugee Vietnamese.
Unsympathetic, slow-paced melodrama which ends up seeming pointless despite a Ku Klux Klan confrontation.
w Alice Arlen *d* Louis Malle *ph* Curtis Clark *m* Ry Cooder *pd* Trevor Williams *ed* James Bruce
☆ Amy Madigan, Ed Harris, Donald Moffat, Rudy Young, Ho Nguyen
'A failed piece of social consciousness.' – *Variety*

An Alan Smithee Film: Burn, Hollywood, Burn!
US 1997 86m colour
Buena Vista/Hollywood/Cinergi (Ben Myron)

After he loses control of his blockbuster film, a director steals the negative; those involved in its making explain what went wrong.
A lamentable, heavy-handed, ham-fisted attempt at a satire on Hollywood, in which all the jokes misfire.
w Joe Eszterhas *d* Alan Smithee (Arthur Hiller) *ph* Reynaldo Villalobos *m* Gary G-Wiz, Chuck D *pd* David L. Snyder *ed* Jim Langlois
☆ Ryan O'Neal, Coolio Leon, Chuck D, Richard Jeni, Eric Idle, Leslie Stefanson, Sandra Bernhard, Cheri Lunghi, Harvey Weinstein, Gavin Polone, MC Lite, Marcello Thedford, Nicole Nagel, Stephen Tobolowsky
'It becomes obvious well before the end that there wasn't really a movie here after all, at least not one that will be terribly edifying for general audiences.' – *Todd McCarthy, Variety*
† Those appearing as themselves include: Sylvester Stallone, Whoopi Goldberg, Jackie Chan, Billy Bob Thornton, Joe Eszterhas, Robert Evans and Shane Black
†† Alan Smithee is the pseudonym used by a director when he wants his name removed from the film's credits. In this instance Arthur Hiller, who asked for his name to be removed after a dispute with Joe Eszterhas
††† It was voted the worst film of 1998 in the Golden Raspberry Awards.

'Don't Be Alarmed...They're Professionals.'
The Alarmist
US 1997 91m FotoKem
Columbia TriStar/Life During Wartme (Dan Stone, Lisa Zimble)

A security system salesman suspects his boss of murdering one of his clients in order to increase sales.
Dim social comedy with misjudged performances and a sense of increasing desperation about its narrative twists.
wd Evan Dunsky *play* *Life During Wartime* by Keith Reddin *ph* Alex Nepomniaschy *m* Christopher Beck *pd* Amy B. Ancona *ed* Norman Buckley
☆ David Arquette (Tommy Hudler), Stanley Tucci (Heinrich Grigoris), Mary McCormack (Sally Brown), Kate Capshaw (Gale Ancona), Tricia Vessey (April), Ryan Reynolds (Howard Ancona), Hoke Howell (Henry Fielding), Ruth Miller (Mrs Fielding), Michael Learned (Beth Hudler), Lewis Arquette (Bruce Hudler), Richmond Arquette (Andrew Hudler)
'A cinematic experience not unlike being savaged by a sheep.' – *Kieron Corless, Sight and Sound*

Alaska
US 1995 109m Technicolor Suoer 35
Columbia/Castle Rock (Carol Fuchs, Andy Burg)

Two children go in search of their father after he crashes his plane in Alaska.
Uninspired adventure movie, demonstrating that children and animals (a bear cub this time around) are not infallible scene-stealers.
w Andy Burg, Scott Myers *d* Fraser Heston *ph* Tony Westman *m* Reg Powell *pd* Douglas Higgins *ed* Rob Kobrin
☆ Thora Birch, Vincent Kartheiser, Dirk Benedict, Charlton Heston, Duncan Fraser, Gordon Tootoosis

The Alaskan *
US 1924 80m approx bw
Famous Players/Paramount
An Alaskan defies robber barons intent on corrupting the new state.
Tough, effective and straightforward action drama, one of its star's best roles.
w Willis Goldbeck *novel* James Oliver Curwood *d* Herbert Brenon
☆ *Thomas Meighan*, Estelle Taylor, John Sainpolis, Anna May Wong

L'Albatross (dubbed)
France 1971 90m Eastmancolor
Antony Balch/Balzac/Profilm/Belstar (Jean-Pierre Mocky, Jacques Dorfmann, Frédérick Dorfmann)
GB title: *Love Hat*
After escaping from prison, a man accused of murder goes on the run, taking as hostage the daughter of a left-wing politician.
Complex romantic and political thriller, with an atmosphere ruined by its insensitive dubbing.
w Jean-Pierre Mocky, Claude Veillot, Raphael Delpard *d* Jean-Pierre Mocky *ph* Marcel Weiss *m* Léo Ferré *ad* Jacques Flamand, Jacques Dor *ed* Marguerite Renoir
☆ Jean-Pierre Mocky, Marion Game, André Le Gall, Paul Muller, Francis Terzian

Albert RN **
GB 1953 88m bw
Dial (Daniel M. Angel)
US title: *Break to Freedom*
Prisoners of war construct a lifelike dummy to cover the absence of escaping prisoners.
Competent, entertaining version of a successful play: an archetypal POW comedy drama.
w Guy Morgan, Vernon Harris *play* Guy Morgan, Edward Sammis *d* Lewis Gilbert *ph* Jack Asher *m* Malcolm Arnold
☆ Jack Warner, Anthony Steel, Robert Beatty, William Sylvester, Anton Diffring, Eddie Byrne, Guy Middleton, Paul Carpenter, Frederick Valk
† The film was based on fact. The prisoner-of-war who created the original dummy, artist John Worsley (1919-2000), also made the dummy used in the film, which is preserved at the Royal Naval Museum, Portsmouth.

Albino Alligator *
US 1996 97m colour 'Scope
Miramax/UGC DA/Motion Picture Corp (Brad Krevoy, Steve Stabler)

Three incompetent robbers take refuge in a basement bar, which is surrounded by armed police.
An efficient, claustrophobic suspense movie of a familiar kind.
w Christian Forte *d* Kevin Spacey *ph* Mark Plummer *m* Michael Brook *pd* Nelson Coates *ed* Jay Cassidy
☆ Matt Dillon (Dova), Faye Dunaway (Janet), Gary Sinise (Milo), William Fichtner (Law), Viggo Mortensen (Guy), John Spencer (Jack), Skeet Ulrich (Danny), M. Emmet Walsh (Dino), Joe Mantegna (G.D. Browning)
'Pro cast and muscular lensing aren't quite enough to overcome a script that isn't nearly as ingenious as it would like to seem.' – *Lisa Nesselson, Variety*

Albuquerque
US 1947 89m Cinecolor
Pine-Thomas/Paramount
GB title: *Silver City*
The nephew of a town tyrant steps in to save an independent wagon line.
Formula Western with adequate action.
w Gene Lewis and Clarence Upson Young *novel* Luke Short *d* Ray Enright
☆ Randolph Scott, Barbara Britton, George 'Gabby' Hayes, George Cleveland, Lon Chaney Jnr, Russell Hayden

Alcatraz Island
US 1937 64m bw
Warner/Cosmopolitan
The federal government decides to build a top-security prison on a rock in San Francisco Bay.
Cheap routine treatment of what might have been an interesting subject.
w Crane Wilbur *d* William McGann
☆ Ann Sheridan, Mary Maguire, Dick Purcell, Addison Richards, *George E. Stone*, Doris Lloyd, John Litel
'Should about complete the Warner file on prisons.' – *Variety*

The Alchemist
US 1981 84m DeLuxe
Video Form/Ideal Films (Lawrence Applebaum)

A beautiful woman cures a man of his century-old curse.
Low-budget amalgam of horror movie clichés, inexpertly combined.
w Alan J. Adler *d* Charles Band *ph* Andrew W. Friend *m* Richard H. Band *pd* Dale A. Pelton *ad* Pam Warner *ed* Ted Nicolaou
☆ Robert Ginty, Lucinda Dooling, John Sanderford, Viola Kate Stimpson, Robert Glaudini

Alex *
New Zealand/Australia 1992 92m colour
Isambard/Total/NZFC/NZOA/AFFC (Tom Parkinson, Phil Gerlach)

A 15-year-old New Zealand swimmer overcomes personal and professional difficulties to win a place in the 1960 Olympic Games.
Pleasant, sentimental account of a strong-willed girl succeeding against the odds.

w Ken Katran *book* Tessa Duder *d* Megan Simpson *ph* Donald Duncan *m* Todd Hunter, Johanna Pigott *pd* Kim Sinclair *ed* Tony Kavanagh
☆ Chris Haywood, Lauren Jackson, Josh Picker, Catherine Godbold, Elizabeth Hawthorn

Alex and the Gypsy
US 1976 99m DeLuxe
TCF (Richard Shepherd)
A cynical California bailbondsman involved in illicit activities chooses romantic freedom with a gypsy girl.
Incoherent hardbitten romance with an unconvincing set of characters.
w Lawrence B. Marcus *novel* The Bailbondsman by Stanley Elkin *d* John Korty *ph* Bill Butler *m* Henry Mancini
☆ Jack Lemmon, Geneviève Bujold, James Woods, Gino Ardito, Robert Emhardt
'Even if it were well done (which it is not) it would be banal, predictable and cloying.' – *Frank Rich*
'Off the beaten track, but that's just about the only thing you can give it points for.' – *Pauline Kael*

Alex in Wonderland
US 1970 109m colour
MGM (Larry Tucker)
A Hollywood director finds life tedious.
So did the small paying audiences who saw this pale imitation of Fellini. (Some wags called it One and a Half.)
w Paul Mazursky, Larry Tucker *d* Paul Mazursky *ph* Laszlo Kovacs *m* Tom O'Horgan *pd* Pato Guzman *ed* Stuart H. Pappe
☆ Donald Sutherland, Jeanne Moreau, Ellen Burstyn, Federico Fellini
'The Fellini elements are laid onto the film and don't quite sink in ... but the human story does work, remarkably well.' – *Roger Ebert*

Alexander Hamilton *
US 1931 73m bw
Warner
The life of America's 18th-century financier.
Star biopic, highly satisfying in its day.
w Julien Josephson, Maude Howell, George Arliss *d* John G. Adolfi *ph* James Van Trees
☆ George Arliss, Doris Kenyon, Montagu Love, Dudley Digges, Lionel Belmore, Ralf Harolde, Alan Mowbray

Alexander Nevsky ****
USSR 1938 112m bw
Mosfilm
In 1242, Prince Alexander Nevsky defeats the invading Teutonic Knights in a battle on the ice of Lake Peipus.
A splendid historical pageant which shows the director at his most inventively pictorial and climaxes in a superb battle sequence using music instead of natural sound.
w Pyotr Pavlenko, Sergei Eisenstein *d Sergei Eisenstein ph Edouard Tissé m Prokofiev ad* I. Shpinel, N. Soloviov, K. Yeliseyev
☆ *Nikolai Cherkassov*, Nikolai Okhlopkov, Andrei Abrikosov, Dmitri Orlov
'The picture will meet with good results wherever its political sentiments find established adherents. Otherwise it's almost nil for general appeal.' – *Variety*
'Superb sequences of cinematic opera that pass from pastoral to lamentation and end in a triumphal cantata.' – *Georges Sadoul*

'The colossus who conquered the world! The most colossal motion picture of all time!'
Alexander the Great *
US 1956 135m Technicolor Cinemascope
UA/Robert Rossen
The life and early death at 33 of the Macedonian warrior who conquered the entire known world.
Dour impassive epic which despite good intelligent stretches makes one long for Hollywood's usual more ruthless view of history.
wd Robert Rossen *ph* Robert Krasker *m* Mario Nascimbene *ad* Andrei Andreiev
☆ Richard Burton, Fredric March, Danielle Darrieux, Claire Bloom, Barry Jones, Harry Andrews, Peter Cushing, Stanley Baker, Michael Hordern, Niall MacGinnis
'Not a scene is held for a second longer than it is worth; greatness is pictured in constant dissolve.' – *Alexander Walker*
'Rossen has aimed for greatness and lost honourably.' – *Andrew Sarris*

Alexander's Ragtime Band ***
US 1938 106m bw
TCF (Darryl F. Zanuck, Harry Joe Brown)
Between 1911 and 1939, two songwriters vie for the affections of a rising musical comedy star.
Archetypal chronicle musical with 26 songs: well-paced, smartly made, and bursting with talent.
w Kathryn Scola, Lamar Trotti, Richard Sherman *d Henry King ph Peverell Marley m/ly Irving Berlin md Alfred Newman ad Bernard Herzbrun, Boris Leven ed* Barbara McLean
☆ Tyrone Power, *Alice Faye*, Don Ameche, *Ethel Merman, Jack Haley*, Jean Hersholt, Helen Westley, John Carradine, Paul Hurst, Wally Vernon, Ruth Terry, Eddie Collins, Douglas Fowley, Chick Chandler
'A grand filmusical which stirs and thrills, finding response in the American heart to memories of the exciting, sentimental and patriotic moments of the past quarter of a century.' – *Variety*
♫ 'Alexander's Ragtime Band'; 'Everybody's Doin' It'; 'When the Midnight Choo-Choo Leaves for Alabam'; 'Oh, How I Hate to Get Up in the Morning'; 'Say It with Music'; 'A Pretty Girl Is Like a Melody'; 'Blue Skies'; 'What'll I Do'; 'Easter Parade'; 'Heat Wave'.
Alfred Newman
picture; Irving Berlin (for original story); Irving Berlin (for song, 'Now It Can Be Told'); art direction; editing

Alf, Bill and Fred *
GB 1964 8m Eastmancolor
Biographic 4 (Bob Godfrey)
A man, a duck and a dog enjoy bouncing together.
Bittersweet cartoon fable which pleases much more than its synopsis might suggest.
w Stan Hayward *d Bob Godfrey*
† Animation by Bob Godfrey.

The Alf Garnett Saga
GB 1972 90m colour
Columbia/Associated London Films (Ned Sherrin, Terry Glinwood)
Bigoted Alf is exasperated by his council flat, his son-in-law, and the possibility that his daughter is pregnant by a black man.
Second inflation of the TV series, Till Death Us Do Part, even cruder and less funny than the first; listlessly written and developed.
w Johnny Speight *d* Bob Kellett *ph* Nic Knowland *m* Georgie Fame
☆ Warren Mitchell, Dandy Nichols, Adrienne Posta, Paul Angelis, John Le Mesurier, Joan Sims, John Bird, Roy Kinnear
'One long, repetitive and unfunny diatribe.' – MFB

Alfie **
GB 1966 114m Techniscope
Paramount/Sheldrake (Lewis Gilbert)
A Cockney Lothario is proud of his amorous conquests, but near-tragedy finally makes him more mature.
Garish sex comedy, an immense box-office success because of its frankness and an immaculate performance from its star.
w Bill Naughton play Bill Naughton *d* Lewis Gilbert *ph* Otto Heller *m* Sonny Rollins
☆ *Michael Caine*, Vivien Merchant, Shirley Anne Field, Millicent Martin, Jane Asher, Julia Foster, Shelley Winters, Eleanor Bron, Denholm Elliott
'A film exceptionally well made; never boring; composed of remarkable performances, scenes sharply observed and music neatly attuned.' – *Dilys Powell*
'Paramount thought it was a good bet because it was going to be made for 500,000 dollars, normally the sort of money spent on executives' cigar bills.' – *Lewis Gilbert*
picture; Bill Naughton; Michael Caine; Vivien Merchant; title song (*m* Burt Bacharach, *ly* Hal David)
Vivien Merchant

Alfie Darling
GB 1975 102m Technicolor
EMI/Signal (Dugald Rankin)
Further repetitive amorous exploits of the Cockney Lothario, now a continental truck driver.
Soft porn adventures quite unworthy of the writer-director, and tedious to sit through; the touch of tragedy at the end only makes matters worse.
wd Ken Hughes *ph* Ousama Rawi *m* Alan Price
☆ Alan Price, Jill Townsend, Paul Copley, Joan Collins, Sheila White, Annie Ross, Hannah Gordon, Rula Lenska

Alfred the Great *
GB 1969 122m Metrocolor Panavision
MGM/Bernard Smith
In AD 871 Alfred takes over kingship from his weak elder brother.
A 'realistic' youth-oriented view of history: blood and four-letter words alternate with cliché to make a dispiriting, disunified whole, though the background detail is interesting and the battle scenes vivid.
w Ken Taylor, James R. Webb *d* Clive Donner *ph* Alex Thomson *m* Ray Leppard *pd* Michael Stringer
☆ David Hemmings (Alfred), Michael York (Guthrum), Prunella Ransome (Aelhswith), Colin Blakely (Asher), Julian Glover (Athelstan), Ian McKellen (Roger), Alan Dobie (Ethelred), Christopher Timothy (Cedric)

Alfredo Alfredo
Italy/France 1971 110m Technicolor
CIC/RPA/Rizzoli/Francoriz (Pietro Germi)
A bank clerk, determined to divorce his sexually insatiable wife, recalls his courtship and their difficult marriage.
A laboured and inane comedy of marital misunderstanding; it's possible that you need to be Italian to find it at all interesting.
w Leo Benvenuti, Piero de Bernardi, Tullio Pinelli, Pietro Germi *d* Pietro Germi *ph* Aiace Parolin *m* Carlo Rustichelli *ad* Carlo Egidi *ed* Sergio Montanari
☆ Dustin Hoffman, Stefania Sandrelli, Carla Gravina, Clara Colosimo, Daniele Patella
'It simply limps on and on and on to no point or purpose.' – *Tom Milne, MFB*
† The version released in Britain ran for 98m.

Alf's Button
GB 1930 96m bw/colour
Gaumont
A soldier has a button, which, when rubbed, summons an all-powerful genie.
Not the first version (there was one in 1920 with Leslie Henson) but the first in sound of a lively knockabout comedy. It even had a colour sequence.
w L'Estrange Fawcett *play* W. A. Darlington *d* W. P. Kellino *ph* Percy Strong, William Shenton *ad* A. L. Mazzei
☆ Jimmy Nervo, Teddy Knox, Tubby Edlin, Alf Goddard, Nora Swinburne, Polly Ward, Anton Dolin

Alf's Button Afloat **
GB 1938 89m bw
Gainsborough (Edward Black)
Six itinerants encounter a genie, whose granting of their wishes brings riches and embarrassment.
Archetypal music hall farce descending at moments into surrealism (the lovers are eaten by a bear). It starred the six original members of the Crazy Gang, and all concerned are on top form.
w Marriott Edgar, Val Guest, Ralph Smart novel Alf's Button by W. A. Darlington *d Marcel Varnel ph* Arthur Crabtree *md* Louis Levy *ad* Vetchinsky *ed* R. E. Dearing, Alfred Roome
☆ Bud Flanagan, Chesney Allen, Jimmy Nervo, Teddy Knox, Charles Naughton, Jimmy Gold, *Alastair Sim*, Wally Patch, Peter Gawthorne

Algiers **
US 1938 95m bw
Walter Wanger
A romantic Casbah thief makes the mistake of falling in love.
Seminal Hollywood romantic drama based closely on a French original, Pepe le Moko; laughed at for years because of the alleged line 'Come with me to the Casbah' (which is never actually said), it holds up remarkably well in its fashion.
w John Howard Lawson, James M. Cain *d John Cromwell ph James Wong Howe m* Vincent Scotto, Mohammed Igorbouchen
☆ *Charles Boyer, Hedy Lamarr, Sigrid Gurie, Gene Lockhart, Joseph Calleia*, Alan Hale, Johnny Downs
'A quality of sustained suspense and excitement ... there is nothing makeshift about the production.' – *Variety*
'Few films this season, or any other, have sustained their mood more brilliantly.' – *New York Times*
'The general tone is that of the decent artistry we must demand and enjoy in pictures, which should someday be as respectable as books, only more near and vivid.' – *Otis Ferguson*
'This version is pure Hollywood, sacrificing everything to glamour, and the heavy make-up and studio lighting make it seem so artificial one can get giggly.' – *New Yorker, 1977*
† Remake: *Casbah* (qv).
James Wong Howe; Charles Boyer; Gene Lockhart

'He Shook Up The World'
Ali *
US 2001 158m DeLuxe Panavision
Columbia/Initial/Peters Entertainment/Forward Pass/Lee Caplin/Picture Entertainment/Overbrook (Jon Peters, James Lassiter, Paul Ardaji, Michael Mann, A. Kitman Ho)
Biopic of Muhammad Ali who, as Cassius Clay, became the world heavyweight boxing champion in 1964, before being stripped of his title for refusing to be drafted into the army; ten years later, he regains the title in a fight against George Foreman.
A dynamic performance from Will Smith holds together a somewhat diffuse account of the ten most significant years in Ali's boxing career, but there's too much pussy-footing around his life outside the ring.
w Stephen J. Rivele, Christopher Wilkinson, Eric Roth, Michael Mann *story* Gregory Allen Howard *d* Michael Mann *ph* Emmanuel Lubezki *m* Lisa Gerrard, Pieter Bourke *pd* John Myhre *ed* William Goldenberg, Stephen Rivkin, Lynzee Klingman *sp* makeup fx: Greg Cannom
☆ Will Smith (Cassius Clay/Muhammad Ali), Jamie Foxx (Drew 'Bundini' Brown), Jon Voight (Howard Cosell), Mario Van Peebles (Malcolm X), Angelo Dundee (Ron Silver), Jeffrey Wright (Howard Bingham), Mykelti Williamson (Don King), Jada Pinkett Smith (Sonji), Nona Gaye (Belinda), Michael Michele (Veronica), Joe Morton (Chancy Eskridge), Giancarlo Esposito (Cassius Clay Sr), LeVar Burton (Martin Luther King Jr), Albert Hall (Elijah Muhammad)
'Possesses an informed, intelligent perspective and is never uninteresting to watch.' – *Todd McCarthy, Variety*
Will Smith; Jon Voight

'Wild nights of sheer delights! Burning days of bold adventure! When beauty was the booty and the prize of all was love!'
Ali Baba and the Forty Thieves *
US 1944 87m Technicolor
Universal (Paul Malvern)
A deposed prince pretending to be a bandit regains his rightful throne.
Absurd but likeable wartime pantomime without much humour: a typical big-budget production of its studio and period.
w Edmund L. Hartmann *d* Arthur Lubin *ph* George Robinson *m* Edward Ward
☆ Jon Hall, Maria Montez, Scotty Beckett, Turhan Bey, Frank Puglia, Andy Devine, Kurt Katch
† Remake: *Sword of Ali Baba*, which over twenty years later used much of the same footage.

Ali Baba and the Forty Thieves *
France 1954 90m Eastmancolor
Films du Cyclope
Ali Baba is sent to buy a new wife for his master, and accidentally finds a thieves' treasure cave...
Sporadically amusing but finally disappointing version of the Arabian Nights (qv) story; it looks hasty.
w Jacques Becker, Marc Maurette, Maurice Griffe *d* Jacques Becker *ph* Robert Le Fèbvre *m* Paul Misraki

☆ Fernandel, Samia Gamal, Dieter Borsche, Henri Vilbert

Ali Baba Goes to Town *
US 1937 81m bw
TCF (Lawrence Schwab)
A hobo falls off a train into a film set and thinks he is back in the Arabian Nights (qv).
Rather flat star vehicle with a few compensations.
w Harry Tugend, Jack Yellen *d* David Butler *ph* Ernest Palmer *m* Louis Silvers *m/ly* Mack Gordon, Harry Revel *ch* Sammy Lee
☆ Eddie Cantor, Tony Martin, Roland Young, John Carradine, June Lang
'An elaborately produced filmusical which satirizes the New Deal policies, politicians and politics.' – *Variety*
Sammy Lee

'Cleaning Da Filth From Da PM's Hood.'
Ali G Indahouse
GB/US/Germany/France 2002 88m Technicolor
UIP/Working Title/Universal/StudioCanal/WT2 (Tim Bevan, Eric Fellner, Dan Mazer)
A racially confused rapper becomes a national hero after he is persuaded to become a Member of Parliament.
Occasionally amusing comedy, though closer in manner to the last Carry On movies or Benny Hill than the satirical TV outings that made Ali G a cult figure in Britain.
w Sacha Baron Cohen, Dan Mazer *d* Mark Mylod *ph* Ashley Rowe *md* Nick Angel *pd* Grenville Horner *ed* Paul Knight
☆ Sacha Baron Cohen (Ali G), Michael Gambon (Prime Minister), Charles Dance (David Carlton), Kellie Bright (Me Julie), Martin Freeman (Ricky C), Rhona Mitra (Kate Hedges), Barbara New (Nan), Ray Panthaki (Hassan B)
'A crude, shoddy affair.' – *Observer*
'An extremely silly, grossly scatological but often amusing picture.' – *Derek Elley, Variety*

Ali Zaoua *
France/Morocco/Belgium 2000 colour
Millennium/Playtime/TF1/Ali'N/Alexis (Jean Cottin, Etienne Comar, Antoine Voituriez)
Three boys who live on the streets of Casablanca try to give a burial at sea to a friend, who was killed in a fight.
Tough, unsparing drama about life on the margins of existence that uses, for the most part, a cast of actual street children.
w Nathalie Saugeon, Nabil Ayouch *d* Nabil Ayouch *ph* Vincent Mathias *m* Krishna Levy *ad* Said Rais *ed* Jean-Robert Thomann
☆ Mounim Kbab (Kwita), Mustapha Hansali (Omar), Hicham Moussoune (Boubker), Abdelhak Zhayra (Ali Zaoua), Saïd Taghmaoui (Dib), Amal Ayouch (Ali Zaoua's mother), Mohamed Majd (Fisherman)
'Nabil Ayouch's film, though indulging an occasional weakness for whimsy, is an engaging and powerful piece of work.' – *Peter Bradshaw, Guardian*

Alias Betty: see *Betty Fisher et Autres Histoires*

Alias Bulldog Drummond: see *Bulldog Jack*

Alias Jesse James *
US 1959 92m DeLuxe
Hope Enterprises (Jack Hope)
An incompetent insurance salesman sells a policy to Jesse James and has to protect his client until he can get it back.
Ho-hum star comedy saved by a climax in which Hope is protected by every cowboy star in Hollywood.
w William Bowers, D. D. Beauchamp *d* Norman Z. McLeod *ph* Lionel Lindon *m* Joseph J. Lilley
☆ Bob Hope, Rhonda Fleming, Wendell Corey, Jim Davis, Will Wright

Alias Jimmy Valentine
US 1928 75m bw
MGM
Crook comedy drama previously made in 1920.
This version is notable only as the first MGM sound film.
w Sarah Y. Mason, A. P. Younger *d* Jack Conway
☆ William Haines, Karl Dane, Lionel Barrymore

Alias 'La Gringa' *
Peru/Spain 1991 100m colour
Perfo/TV Española/Channel 4 (Andres Malatesta, Emilio Salomon)
A criminal returns to jail to rescue the university professor who, in the middle of a riot by terrorists, saved his life.
Harsh exposé of prison life, inspired by a true story, and providing a little insight into Peruvian life and politics.
w Alberto Durant, José Watanabé, José María Salcedo *d* Alberto Durant *ph* Mario García Joya *m* Pochi Marambio *pd* Matanabé *ed* Gianfranco Annichini
☆ Germano Gonzales, Elsa Oliveros, Orlando Sacha, Juan Manuel Ochoa, Enrique Victoria, Gonzalo de Miguel
'Basically action for undemanding Latino auds, but on its own terms it's efficiently and briskly handled.' – *Variety*

Alias Mary Dow
US 1935 65m bw
Universal
A millionaire persuades a chorus girl to pose as his long-lost kidnapped daughter, to satisfy his wife.
Obvious audience-pleaser of its time.
w Gladys Unger, Rose Franken, Arthur Caesar *d* Kurt Neumann
☆ Ray Milland, Sally Eilers, Henry O'Neill, Katherine Alexander
'Not a bad picture ... small towns should like it best.' – *Variety*

'No man ever held more terrible power over women than this tall dark handsome stranger from nowhere! The shock-filled story of a man whose love was more dangerous than a loaded gun!'
Alias Nick Beal ***
US 1949 93m bw
Paramount (Endre Bohem)
GB title: *The Contact Man*
A politician is nearly corrupted by a mysterious stranger offering wealth and power.
Highly satisfactory modern version of Faust, done in gangster terms but not eschewing a supernatural explanation. Acting, photography and direction all in the right key.
w Jonathan Latimer story Mindret Lord *d John Farrow ph Lionel Lindon m* Franz Waxman
☆ *Ray Milland, Thomas Mitchell*, Audrey Totter, George Macready, Fred Clark

Alibi *
US 1929 90m bw
Roland West
An ex-convict marries a policeman's daughter and uses her in his plan for the perfect murder.
Early talkie drama, mostly risible now but with interesting fragments of technique and imagination.
w Roland West, C. Gardner Sullivan *play Nightstick* by Elaine Sterne Carrington, John Wray, J. C. Nugent *d Roland West ph* Ray June *m* Hugo Riesenfeld *ad William Cameron Menzies*
☆ *Chester Morris*, Eleanor Griffith, Regis Toomey, Mae Busch, Harry Stubbs
picture; Chester Morris; William Cameron Menzies

Alibi
GB 1931 75m bw
Twickenham
Hercule Poirot proves that an apparent suicide was murder.
Tame adaptation, without the narrative gimmick of Agatha Christie's The Murder of Roger Ackroyd.
w H. Fowler Mear *d* Leslie Hiscott
☆ Austin Trevor, Franklin Dyall, Elizabeth Allan, J. H. Roberts, Mary Jerrold

Alibi *
GB 1942 82m bw
Corona (Josef Somlo)
A nightclub mindreader forces the lady owner to give him a murder alibi.
Interesting but disappointing minor suspenser copied from a sharper French original.
w uncredited *novel* Marcel Achard *d* Brian Desmond Hurst *ph* Otto Heller *m* Jack Beaver
☆ Margaret Lockwood, Hugh Sinclair, James Mason, *Raymond Lovell*, Enid Stamp-Taylor, Hartley Power, Jane Carr, Rodney Ackland, Edana Romney, Elizabeth Welch, Olga Lindo, Muriel George
† The French film, *L'Alibi*, was made in 1939 by B-N Films. The girl was Jany Holt, with Erich von Stroheim as the villain and Louis Jouvet as the inspector. Pierre Chenal directed.

Alibi Ike *
US 1935 73m bw
Warner (Edward Chodorov)
A baseball pitcher gets involved in all kinds of trouble.
Above average star comedy vehicle.
w William Wister Haines *story* Ring Lardner *d* Ray Enright *ph* Arthur Todd *md* Leo F. Forbstein
☆ *Joe E. Brown*, Olivia de Havilland, Ruth Donnelly, Roscoe Karns, William Frawley

Alice ***
GB/Switzerland/West Germany 1988 85m Eastmancolor
Condor-Hessisches/SRG/Film Four (Peter-Christian Fueter)
original title: *Neco z Alenky*
A young girl follows a rabbit through a broken glass case into Wonderland.
A free, sometimes disturbing interpretation with surrealist overtones, of Lewis Carroll's masterpiece by a great animator that, with its mix of live actors and animation, comes closer than any other to conjuring the curious atmosphere of the original.
wd Jan Svankmajer novel Alice in Wonderland by Lewis Carroll *ph* Svatoluk Maly *ad* Eva Svankmerova, Jiri Blaha *ed* Marie Drvotova
☆ Kristyna Kohoutova
'A film for children of a certain kind, for the quiet solitary ones who spend hours in conversation with their dolls; who invest the smallest cast-off objects with secret significance.' – *Terrence Rafferty, New Yorker*

Alice *
US 1990 106m DuArt
Orion/Jack Rollins, Charles H. Joffe
A bored housewife indulges in a fantasy life.
Moderately amusing comedy of a search for individuality.
wd Woody Allen *ph* Carlo di Palma *pd* Santo Loquasto *ad* Speed Hopkins
☆ Mia Farrow, Joe Mantegna, Alec Baldwin, Blythe Danner, Judy Davis, William Hurt, Keye Luke, Bernadette Peters, Cybill Shepherd, Gwen Verdon
'A likable little pic that will please his fans.' – *Variety*
original screenplay

Alice Adams **
US 1935 99m bw
RKO (Pandro S. Berman)
A social-climbing small-town girl falls in love.
Dated but interesting star vehicle with good production values.
w Dorothy Yost, Mortimer Offner, Jane Murfin *novel* Booth Tarkington *d George Stevens ph* Robert de Grasse *m* Max Steiner, Roy Webb
☆ *Katharine Hepburn, Fred MacMurray*, Evelyn Venable, Frank Albertson, Fred Stone, Ann Shoemaker, Charles Grapewin, Grady Sutton, Hedda Hopper
'Sturdy cinematic substance, virtually audience proof.' – *Variety*
'A nice middle-class film, as trivial as a schoolgirl's diary, and just about as pathetically true.' – *C. A. Lejeune*
'What was in 1922 a biting and observant novel emerges in 1935 as a bitingly satiric portrait of an era.' – *Time*
picture; Katharine Hepburn

Alice au Pays de Merveilles: see *Alice in Wonderland (1951)*

'A picture for anyone who has ever dreamed of a second chance'
Alice Doesn't Live Here Any More ***
US 1974 112m Technicolor
Warner (David Susskind, Audrey Maas)
A widow sets off with her young son for Monterey and a singing career.
Realistically squalid and foul-mouthed but endearing look at a slice of America today, with firm handling and excellent performances in a surprisingly old-fashioned theme.
w Robert Getchell d Martin Scorsese ph Kent L. Wakeford *m* various *md* Richard La Salle *pd* Toby Carr Rafelson
☆ *Ellen Burstyn, Alfred Lutter*, Kris Kristofferson, Billy Green Bush, *Diane Ladd*, Lelia Goldoni, Jodie Foster
'What Scorsese has done is to rescue an American cliché from the bland, flat but much more portentous naturalism of such as *Harry and Tonto* and restore it to an emotional and intellectual complexity through his particular brand of baroque realism.' – *Richard Combs*
'Full of funny malice and breakneck vitality.' – *New Yorker*
'A tough weepie, redeemed by its picturesque locations and its eye for social detail.' – *Michael Billington, Illustrated London News*
† The film inspired the TV sitcom *Alice* (1976–85).
Ellen Burstyn
Robert Getchell; Diane Ladd
picture; Robert Getchell; Ellen Burstyn; Diane Ladd

Alice et Martin *
France 1998 124m colour
Artificial Eye/France2/France3/Vertigo/Alain Sarde
A disturbed youth moves to Paris after his father's sudden death and begins an affair with a violinist who shares a flat with his gay brother, an actor.
An Oedipal drama of frustration and redemption, insightful on the dynamic of family relationships, but not helped by the difficulty in understanding why Binoche's down-to-earth musician should be attracted to the beautiful, wimpish blank portrayed by Alexis Loret. The revelation of the reason for his psychological problems comes as no surprise.
w André Téchiné,Gilles Taurand,Olivier Assayas *d* André Téchiné *ph* Caroline Champetier, Germain Desmoulins *m* Philippe Sarde *pd* Ze Branco *ed* Martine Giordano *cos* Elisabeth Tavernier
☆ Juliette Binoche (Alice), Alexis Loret (Martin Sauvagnac), Mathieu Amalric (Benjamin Sauvagnac), Carmen Maura (Jeanine Sauvagnac), Jean-Pierre Lorit (Frederic), Marthe Villalonga (Lucie), Roschdy Zem (Robert), Pierre Maguelon (Victor Sauvagnac), Eric Kreikenmayer (François Sauvagnac)
'A richly populated, observant film that suffers, forgivably, from an excess of curiosity about the world it depicts — a surfeit of generosity, intelligence and art.' – *A. O. Scott, New York Times*

Alice in the Cities
West Germany 1974 110m bw
Filmverlag der Autoren
original title: *Alice in den Städten*
A German journalist in America reluctantly escorts a small girl back to Germany.
Interesting but overlong collection of modern metaphors, occasionally reminiscent of Paper Moon.
wd Wim Wenders *ph* Robby Müller, Martin Schäfer *m* Irmin Schmid, Can *ed* Peter Przygodda
☆ Rüdiger Vogler, Yella Röttlander, Lisa Kreuzer, Edda Köchel

Alice in Wonderland **
US 1933 75m bw
Paramount (Louis D. Lighton)
Intriguing but disappointing version of the nonsense classic, keeping to the Tenniel drawings by dressing an all-star cast in masks, thereby rendering them ineffective.
w Joseph L. Mankiewicz, William Cameron Menzies *novel* Lewis Carroll *d* Norman Z. McLeod *ph* Henry Sharp, Bert Glennon *m* Dimitri Tiomkin
☆ Charlotte Henry (Alice), W. C. Fields (Humpty Dumpty), Cary Grant (Mock Turtle), Gary Cooper (White Knight), Edward Everett Horton (Mad Hatter), Edna May Oliver (Red Queen), Jack Oakie (Tweedledum), Leon Errol (Uncle), Charles Ruggles (March Hare), May Robson (Queen of Hearts), Louise Fazenda (White Queen), Ned Sparks (Caterpillar), Alison Skipworth (Duchess)

'Nothing grows out of anything else in this phantasmagoria. It's like reading a whole volume of separate four-line gags.' – *Variety*
'Lavishly produced, with great care given to costumes and settings and make-up, but the spirit is missing.' – *New Yorker, 1977*
† Ida Lupino was brought from the UK for the title role, but not used.

Alice in Wonderland *
US 1951 75m Technicolor
Walt Disney
Fully animated cartoon version which has good moments but modernizes and Americanizes the familiar characters.
w various *d* Clyde Geronimi, Hamilton Luske, Wilfred Jackson *m* Oliver Wallace *supervisor* Ben Sharpsteen
☆ Featuring the voices of Kathryn Beaumont, Ed Wynn, Richard Haydn, Sterling Holloway, Jerry Colonna, Verna Felton, Bill Thompson
Oliver Wallace

Alice in Wonderland *
USA/France/Great Britain 1951 83m Anscocolor
UGC/Rank/Lou Bunin
aka: *Alice au Pays de Merveilles*
Often interesting if sometimes crude version with Bunin's puppets, filmed in Nice; the simultaneous Disney cartoon version effectively kept it off the world's screens.
☆ Carol Marsh, Stephen Murray (Lewis Carroll), Pamela Brown (Queen Victoria), Felix Aylmer (Dr Liddell)

Alice, Sweet Alice: see *Communion (1978)*

Alice's Adventures in Wonderland *
GB 1972 101m Eastmancolor Todd-AO
TCF/Josef Shaftel (Derek Horne)
Live-action version which starts amiably enough but soon becomes flat and uninventive, with a star cast all at sea and tedium replacing the wit of the original.
wd William Sterling *ph* Geoffrey Unsworth *m* John Barry *pd* Michael Stringer
☆ Fiona Fullerton (Alice), Michael Crawford (White Rabbit), Robert Helpmann (Mad Hatter), Dudley Moore (Dormouse), Spike Milligan (Gryphon), Peter Sellers (March Hare), Dennis Price (King of Hearts), Flora Robson (Queen of Hearts), Rodney Bewes (Knave of Hearts), Peter Bull (Duchess), Michael Hordern (Mock Turtle), Ralph Richardson (Caterpillar)
Geoffrey Unsworth

Alice's Restaurant *
US 1969 110m DeLuxe
UA/Florin (Harold Leventhal)
Folk singer Arlo Guthrie, on the verge of being drafted, gets some varied experience of life among the drop-outs of Montana, Massachusetts and New York.
Typical of the freakish, anti-Vietnam, do-as-you-please movies which splurged from Hollywood in the wake of Easy Rider, this has the minor benefits of good production values and a few jokes.
w Venable Herndon, Arthur Penn *d* Arthur Penn *ph* Michael Nebbia *m/songs* Arlo Guthrie
☆ Arlo Guthrie, Pat Quinn, James Broderick, Michael McClanathan, Geoff Outlaw
'A subtle, funny, tender and original movie that may not perhaps increase Arthur Penn's present high standing but will certainly do nothing to diminish it.' – *Philip French, Sight and Sound*
Arthur Penn

'In space, no one can hear you scream!'
Alien ****
GB 1979 117m Eastmancolor Panavision
TCF/Brandywine (Walter Hill, Gordon Carroll, David Giler)
Astronauts returning to Earth visit an apparently dead planet and are infected by a violent being which has unexpected behaviour patterns and eliminates them one by one.
Deliberately scarifying and highly commercial shocker. On its own terms, a classic of suspense – and art direction.
w Dan O'Bannon *d Ridley Scott ph Derek Vanlint, Denys Ayling m* Jerry Goldsmith *chief designer H. R. Giger*
☆ Tom Skerritt, Sigourney Weaver, John Hurt, Veronica Cartwright, Harry Dean Stanton, Ian Holm, Yaphet Kotto
'A sort of inverse relationship to *The Thing* invites unfavourable comparisons.' – *Sight and Sound*
'Empty bag of tricks whose production values and expensive trickery cannot disguise imaginative poverty.' – *Time Out*
'It was not, as its co-author admitted, a think piece. The message he intended was simple: Don't close your eyes or it will get ya.' – *Les Keyser, Hollywood in the Seventies*
† It was followed by three sequels, *Aliens, Alien3* and *Alien Resurrection.*
visual effects (H. R. Giger, Carlo Rambaldi and others)
production design (Michael Seymour)

Alien Nation
US 1988 94m DeLuxe Super 35
Fox (Gale Anne Hurd, Richard Kobritz)
A detective, one of a despised minority of aliens stranded on Earth, is partnered with a bigoted human cop to solve a murder.
What begins as an interestingly oblique look at the problems of racism soon turns into a lacklustre action movie.
w Rockne S. O'Bannon *d* Graham Baker *ph* Adam Greenberg *m* Curt Sobel *pd* Jack T. Collis
☆ James Caan, Mandy Patinkin, Terence Stamp

Alien Resurrection *
US 1997 108m DeLuxe Panavision
TCF/Brandywine (Bill Badalato, Gordon Carroll, David Giler, Walter Hill)
Two hundred years after being impregnated with an alien queen and killing herself to save the world, Ripley is cloned as part of an experiment to bring the creatures back to life.
Stylish, occasionally impressive movie that all too soon settles into familiar routine.
w Joss Whedon *d* Jean-Pierre Jeunet *ph* Darius Khondji *m* John Frizzell *pd* Nigel Phelps *ed* Herve Schneid
☆ Sigourney Weaver, Winona Ryder, Ron Perlman, Dominique Pinon, Michael Wincott, Dan Hedaya, Gary Dourdan, Kim Flowers, J. E. Freeman, Brad Dourif
'It's a shame that this effort – though far more coherent, entertaining and exciting than Alien3 – should be the first film in the series to be almost anonymous.' – *Kim Newman, Sight and Sound*
† Sigourney Weaver was reportedly paid $11m for her role. The film cost $80m and took around $48m at the US box-office and more than $75m elsewhere.

'The Bitch Is Back.'
Alien³
US 1992 115m Rank Colour Panavision
TCF/Brandywine (Gordon Carroll, David Giler, Walter Hill)
Ripley crash-lands on a mining planet inhabited by convicts and discovers that she has brought an alien with her.
Grim, grey sequel that struggles, and fails, to add something new to the now familiar story.
w David Giler, Walter Hill, Larry Ferguson *story* Vincent Ward *d* David Fincher *ph* Alex Thomson *m* Elliot Goldenthal *pd* Norman Reynolds *ed* Terry Rawlings *sp* George Gibbs, Richard Edlund
☆ Sigourney Weaver, Charles S. Dutton, Charles Dance, Paul McGann, Brian Glover, Ralph Brown, Danny Webb, Christopher John Fields, Lance Henriksen
'A muddled effort offering little more than visual splendor to recommend it.' – *Variety*
'In space, no one can hear you snore.' – *Andy Klein, Los Angeles Reader*
'A lot of people hated *Alien³*. But no one hated it more than I did.' – *David Fincher*
visual effects

The Alienator
US 1989 92m colour
Amazing/American Independent/Majestic (Jeffrey C. Hogue)
An alien outlaw escapes to Earth, pursued by an indestructible android.
Any resemblance to Predator and The Terminator is presumably deliberate, and merely points up the general ineptitude on display.
w Paul Garson *d* Fred Olen Ray *ph* Gary Graver *m* Chuck Cirino *ad* Lindah Lauderbaugh *ed* Chris Roth
☆ Jan-Michael Vincent, John Phillip Law, Ross Hagen, Dyana Ortelli, Dawn Wildsmith, P. J. Soles, Jesse Dabson

Aliens *
US 1986 137m DeLuxe
TCF/Brandywine (Gale Anne Hurd)
The sole survivor of the space team in *Alien* goes back with another team to the mystery planet, and finds more monsters.
Frightening but mechanical sequel with none of the half-assed poetry of the original.
w James Cameron, Walter Hill, David Giler *d* James Cameron *ph* Adrian Biddle *m* James Horner *pd* Peter Lamont *ed* Ray Lovejoy
☆ Sigourney Weaver, Carrie Henn, Michael Biehn, Paul Reiser
'Audiences will be riveted to their seats with drooling dread in anticipation of the next horrifying attack.' – *Variety*
'I'm giving the movie a high rating for its skill and professionalism, and because it does the job it says it will do. I am also advising you not to eat before you see it.' – *Roger Ebert*
† A special edition was released on video running for 154m.
special visual effects (Robert Skotak, Stan Winston, John Richardson, Suzanne Benson)
music; production design; Ray Lovejoy; Sigourney Weaver

Alive
US 1992 127m Technicolor
UIP/Paramount (Robert Watts, Kathleen Kennedy)
Members of a South American rugby team whose plane crash-lands on an inaccessible mountain-top are forced to eat their dead in order to survive.
Efficient re-telling of a true story, but one that adds little to the sum of human knowledge or happiness.
w John Patrick Shanley *book* Piers Paul Read *d* Frank Marshall *ph* Peter James *m* James Newton Howard *pd* Norman Reynolds *ed* Michael Kahn, William Goldenberg
☆ Ethan Hawke, Vincent Spano, Josh Hamilton, Bruce Ramsay, John Haymes Newton, David Kriegel, Kevin Breznahan, Sam Behrens
'Neither the exploitative gross-out teens might be looking for nor quite the rousing adventure it needs to be.' – *Variety*
† In 1976 the story was filmed in Mexico by director Rene Cardona as *Survive!* (qv).

Alive and Kicking *
GB 1958 94m bw
ABP (Victor Skutezky)
Three old ladies escape from a home to an Irish island.
Agreeable minor comedy, a showcase for its elderly but vigorous stars.
w Denis Cannan *d* Cyril Frankel *ph* Gilbert Taylor *m* Philip Green
☆ *Sybil Thorndike, Kathleen Harrison, Estelle Winwood, Stanley Holloway,* Joyce Carey, Eric Pohlmann, Colin Gordon

Alive and Kicking: see *Indian Summer (1993)*

Alive and Kicking *
GB 1996 99m Rank Colour
Film Four/Channel 4 (Martin Pope)
An HIV-positive ballet dancer, in a dance troupe whose numbers are dwindling because of AIDS, has problems at work and at home, in his relationship with an older man.
A sometimes witty and engaging movie about loss and love, though its feel-good ending is unconvincing.
w Martin Sherman *d* Nancy Meckler *ph* Chris Seager *m* Peter Salem *pd* Cecelia Brereton *ed* Rodney Holland
☆ Jason Flemyng, Anthony Sher, Dorothy Tutin, Anthony Higgins, Bill Nighy, Philip Voss, Diane Parish, Aiden Waters, Natalie Roles
'Both watchable and moving, even if it falls into the by now well-worn category of gay suffering.' – *Derek Malcolm, Guardian*

'The most provocative picture of the year!'
All About Eve ***
US 1950 138m bw
TCF (Darryl F. Zanuck)
An ageing Broadway star suffers from the hidden menace of a self-effacing but secretly ruthless and ambitious young actress.
A basically unconvincing story with thin characters is transformed by a screenplay scintillating with savage wit and a couple of waspish performances into a movie experience to treasure.
wd Joseph L. Mankiewicz ph Milton Krasner m Alfred Newman *ad* Lyle Wheeler, George Davis *ed* Barbara McLean
☆ *Bette Davis* (Margo Channing), *George Sanders* (Addison de Witt), Anne Baxter (Eve), Celeste Holm (Karen Richards), Thelma Ritter (Birdie), Gary Merrill (Bill Sampson), Hugh Marlowe (Lloyd Richards), Gregory Ratoff (Max Fabian), Marilyn Monroe (Miss Caswell), Barbara Bates (Phoebe), Walter Hampden (Speaker at dinner)
MARGO: 'Fasten your seat belts, it's going to be a bumpy night!'
ADDISON: 'That I should want you at all suddenly strikes me as the height of improbability ... you're an improbable person, Eve, but so am I. We have that in common. Also a contempt for humanity, an inability to love or be loved, insatiable ambition – and talent. We deserve each other.'
BIRDIE: 'The bed looks like a dead animal act.'
ADDISON: 'That's all television is, dear – just auditions.'
BIRDIE: 'What a story! Everything but the bloodhounds snappin' at her rear end!'
ADDISON: 'I have lived in the theatre as a Trappist monk lives in his faith. In it I toil not, neither do I spin. I am a critic and a commentator. I am essential to the theatre – as ants to a picnic, as the boll weevil to a cotton field.'
'The wittiest, the most devastating, the most adult and literate motion picture ever made that had anything to do with the New York Stage.' – *Leo Mishkin*
'The dialogue and atmosphere are so peculiarly remote from life that they have sometimes been mistaken for art.' – *Pauline Kael, 1968*
'Plenty of surface cynicism, but no detachment, no edge and no satire. Boiled down it is a plush backstage drama.' – *Richard Winnington*
'Long, but continuously, wonderfully entertaining in a way I had almost forgotten was possible for films.' – *Richard Mallett, Punch*
'Someone remarked of this witty, exaggerated, cruel and yet wildly funny film that the secret of its success was the extreme bad taste shown throughout by all concerned (though I hope they didn't mean to include Milton Krasner's tactful camerawork in this).' – *Basil Wright, 1972*
'The picture seemed long – though it was not by today's standards of length – and the crispness of the dialogue was not matched by equally crisp editing.' – *Hollis Alpert, 1962*
† The idea for the film came from a short story, 'The Wisdom of Eve', by Mary Orr.
picture; Joseph L. Mankiewicz (as writer); Joseph L. Mankiewicz (as director); George Sanders
Milton Krasner; Alfred Newman; Bette Davis; Anne Baxter; Celeste Holm; Thelma Ritter; art direction; editing
picture

All About Lily Chou-Chou
Japan 2001 146m colour
ICA/Rockwell Eyes (Naoki Hashimoto)
A teenager escapes from his school life of being bullied by becoming an obsessive fan of a pop singer.
Over-long, fuzzily-shot movie that meanders along, taking in teenage rape and prostitution along the way.
wd Shunji Iwai *ph* Noboru Shinoda *m* Takeshi Kobayashi *ad* Noboru Ishida *ed* Shunji Iwai
☆ Hayato Ichihara (Yuichi Hasumi), Shugo Oshinari (Shusuke Hoshino), Ayumi Ito (Yoko Kuno), Yu Aoi (Shiori Tsuda)

'it's so enigmatic, oblique and meandering that it's like coded religious texts that requires monks to decipher.' – *Roger Ebert, Chicago Sun-Times*
'Mesmerizing: some of its plaintiveness could make you weep.' – *Elvis Mitchell, New York Times*

All About My Mother: see *Todo Sobre Mi Madre*

All Ashore
US 1952 80m Technicolor
Columbia (Jonie Taps)
Three sailors on shore leave work their passage to Catalina.
Very lightweight musical, no rival for On the Town.
w Blake Edwards, Richard Quine *d* Richard Quine *ph* Charles Lawton Jnr *m* Morris Stoloff, George Duning *ly* Robert Wells
☆ Mickey Rooney, Dick Haymes, Ray McDonald, Peggy Ryan, Barbara Bates, Jody Lawrance

All at Sea: see *Barnacle Bill*

All Coppers Are...
GB 1972 87m colour
Rank/Peter Rogers (George H. Brown)
A crook and a cop both fancy the same girl.
Pointlessly titled lowlife melodrama with no style whatever; any episode of Z Cars would be vastly preferable.
w Allan Prior *d* Sidney Hayers
☆ Nicky Henson, Martin Potter, Julia Foster, Ian Hendry

All Creatures Great and Small *
GB 1974 92m Eastmancolor
EMI/Venedon (David Susskind, Duane Bogie)
The pre-war Yorkshire life of a country vet.
Simple-minded popular entertainment of a long-forgotten kind, oddly sponsored by American TV in the shape of Readers' Digest and the Hallmark Hall of Fame.
w Hugh Whitemore *novel* James Herriot *d* Claude Whatham *ph* Peter Suschitzky *m* Wilfred Josephs
☆ Anthony Hopkins, Simon Ward, Lisa Harrow, Freddie Jones, Brian Stirner, T. P. McKenna, Brenda Bruce, John Collin
† 1976 sequel: *It Shouldn't Happen to a Vet.*

All Dogs Go to Heaven
Eire 1989 85m Technicolor
Rank/Sullivan Bluth/Goldcrest/Don Bluth, Gary Goldman, John Pomeroy
A dead dog returns to Earth to seek revenge on the vicious gangster dog who had him killed.
Skilful animation goes to waste in a confused and confusing narrative.
w David N. Weiss *d* Dan Kuenster, Gary Goldman *m* Ralph Burns *m/ly* Charles Strouse, T. J. Kuenster, Al Kasha/Joel Hirschhorn/Michael Lloyd *pd* Don Bluth, Larry Leker
☆ Featuring the voices of Burt Reynolds, Vic Tayback, Judith Barsi, Dom DeLuise, Loni Anderson, Melba Moore, Charles Nelson Reilly

All Dogs Go to Heaven 2
US 1996 82m colour
MGM (Paul Sabella, Jonathan Dern, Kelly Ward, Mark Young)
Two dogs are despatched from heaven to rescue Gabriel's trumpet.
Tame sequel, slow-moving, unexciting and unlikely to set any tails wagging.
w Arne Olsen, Kelly Ward, Mark Young *d* Paul Sabella, Larry Leker *m* Mark Watters *m/ly* Barry Mann, Cynthia Weil *ad* Deane Taylor *ed* Tony Garber
☆ Featuring the voices of: Ernest Borgnine, Sheena Easton, Bebe Neuwirth, Charlie Sheen, George Hearn, Dom DeLuise, Wallace Shawn, Adam Wylie
'Won't be bow-wowing them at the box-office.' – *Variety*

All Fall Down *
US 1962 111m bw Panavision
MGM (John Houseman)
A young man reveres his ne'er-do-well elder brother but determines to shoot him when he causes a girl's death.
Another gallery of middle American failures, competently portrayed by a writer and actors very practised at this sort of thing.
w William Inge *novel* James Leo Herlihy *d* John Frankenheimer *ph* Lionel Lindon *m* Alex North
☆ Warren Beatty, Brandon de Wilde, Angela Lansbury, Karl Malden, Eva Marie Saint
'That strange area of nostalgic Americana where the familiar is the Freudian grotesque.' – *New Yorker, 1982*

All for Mary *
GB 1955 82m Eastmancolor
Rank/Paul Soskin
Two rivals for the hand of the pretty daughter of a Swiss hotelier are struck down by chicken pox and cared for by the old nanny of one of them.
Simple-minded farce in which two grown men quail like children before a forceful old lady; on the strength of the latter characterization and a few funny lines the original play was a considerable West End success.
w Peter Blackmore, Paul Soskin *play* Harold Brooke, Kay Bannerman *d* Wendy Toye *ph* Reg Wyer *m* Robert Farnon
☆ *Kathleen Harrison*, Nigel Patrick, David Tomlinson, Jill Day, David Hurst, Leo McKern

All Good Citizens: see *All My Good Countrymen*

All Hands on Deck
US 1961 98m DeLuxe Cinemascope
TCF (Oscar Brodney)
Romantic and farcical adventures of sailors on leave.
Tired musical comedy romp with a second team cast.
w Jay Sommars *novel* Donald R. Morris *d* Norman Taurog *ph* Leo Tover *m* Cyril Mockridge *m/ly* Jay Livingston, Ray Evans
☆ Pat Boone, Buddy Hackett, Dennis O'Keefe, Barbara Eden, Warren Berlinger, Gale Gordon, Joe E. Ross

All I Desire
US 1953 79m bw
U-I (Ross Hunter)
A woman who had deserted her husband and family for a life on the stage returns for her daughter's graduation and is reconciled.
Resilient star melodrama with all stops out.
w James Gunn, Robert Blees *d* Douglas Sirk *ph* Carl Guthrie *md* Joseph Gershenson *ad* Alexander Golitzen, Bernard Herzbrun *ed* Milton Carruth
☆ *Barbara Stanwyck*, Richard Carlson, Lyle Bettger, Maureen O'Sullivan, Richard Long, Lori Nelson

'How Far Would You Go To Make A Wish Come True?'
All I Want For Christmas
US 1991 92m Technicolor
Paramount (Marykay Powell)
The Christmas wish of two children is that their divorced parents should get together again.
Dim comedy that even the season of good-will cannot make palatable.
w Thom Eberhardt, Richard Kramer *d* Robert Lieberman *ph* Robbie Greenberg *m* Bruce Broughton *pd* Herman Zimmerman *ed* Richard Berger, Dean Goodhill
☆ Ethan Randall, Thora Birch, Harley Jane Kozak, Jamey Sheridan, Lillian Brooks, Lauren Bacall

All in a Night's Work
US 1961 94m Technicolor
Paramount/Hal B. Wallis-Joseph Hazen
A publishing heir falls for a girl he suspects of having been his uncle's mistress.
Unpolished and not very amusing comedy which falters after an intriguing start.
w Edmund Beloin, Maurice Richlin, Sidney Sheldon *d* Joseph Anthony *ph* Joseph LaShelle *m* André Previn
☆ Shirley MacLaine, Dean Martin, Charles Ruggles, Cliff Robertson, Norma Crane, Gale Gordon, Jerome Cowan, Jack Weston
'Tame and aimless sex-and-big-business comedy.' – *MFB*

'She Longed To Be Remembered ... By A Man Who Wanted To Forget'
All Men Are Mortal
GB/Netherlands/France 1995 90m colour
Warner/Nova/Sigma/Rio (Rudolph Wichmann, Matthias Van Heijningen)
A successful actress ambitious for immortality begins an affair with a 700-year-old prince who cannot die.
A depressingly dull fantasy, with a cast that appears understandably unhappy and lost amid the trappings of existentialist Paris.
w Olwen Wymark, Ate de Jong, Stephen Gaydos *novel* Simone de Beauvoir *d* Ate de Jong *ph* Bruno de Keyzer *m* Michael Gibbs, Simon Fisher Turner *pd* Ben van Os *ed* Nicolas Gaster
☆ Stephen Rea, Irène Jacob, Marianne Sägebrecht, Colin Salmon, Derek de Lint, John Nettles, Maggie O'Neill, Chiara Mastroianni
'It has, and unerringly combines, all the ingredients for disaster.' – *Sheila Johnston, Independent*

All Mine To Give *
US 1956 102m Technicolor RKOscope
RKO (Sam Wiesenthal)
GB title: *The Day They Gave Babies Away*
In 1856, a pioneer couple in Wisconsin train their children to carry on the family after their own deaths.
Weird sentimental sob story, even odder under its English title. Surprisingly, some of it works quite well.
w Dale and Katherine Eunson (apparently about their own ancestors) *d* Allen Reisner *ph* William Skall *m* Max Steiner
☆ Glynis Johns, Cameron Mitchell, Patty McCormack, Rex Thompson, Ernest Truex, Hope Emerson, Alan Hale
'A strong mood of folksy western reminiscence.' – *MFB*

All My Good Countrymen **
Czechoslovakia 1968 126m colour
Filmove Studio Barrandov (Jaroslav Jilovec)
original title: *Všichni Dobři Rodáci*
aka: *All Good Citizens*
Life and death among seven friends caught in the turmoil following the Second World War and the rise of the Communist party.
Lyrical and moving account of political expediency and corruption and the human sacrifice it entails. Awarded the best director prize at the Cannes Film Festival in 1969, it was then banned by the Czech government and its director went into exile.
wd Vojtěch Jasný *ph* Jaroslav Kučera *m* Svatoplick Havelka *ed* Oldřich Mach
☆ Vlastimil Brodský, Radoslav Brzobohatý, Vladimir Mensik, Waldemar Matuška, Drahomira Hofmanová, Pavel Pavlovský

All My Sons *
US 1948 94m bw
U-I (Chester Erskine)
A young man establishes that his father sold defective airplanes during the war.
Heady family melodrama from a taut and topical stage play. The film is well-meaning but artificial and unconvincing.
w Chester Erskine *play* Arthur Miller *d* Irving Reis *ph* Russell Metty *m* Leith Stevens
☆ Edward G. Robinson, Burt Lancaster, Mady Christians, Howard Duff

All Neat in Black Stockings
GB 1969 99m Eastmancolor
Anglo Amalgamated/Miton (Leon Clore)
Sex adventures of an amorous window cleaner.
Modish comedy drama with surface entertainment of a sort, but no depth.
w Jane Gaskell, Hugh Whitemore *d* Christopher Morahan *ph* Larry Pizer *m* Robert Cornford
☆ Victor Henry, Susan George, Jack Shepherd, Anna Cropper, Clare Kelly, Terence de Marney

All Night *
US 1918 57m approx bw silent
Bluebird Films
A bright young entrepreneur throws a dinner for would-be investors.
Theatrical farce, with most characters pretending to be what they're not, this must have worked better on the stage but by all accounts did pretty well on film.
w Fred Myton *d* Paul Powell
☆ *Rudolph Valentino*, Carmel Myers, Charles Dorian, Mary Warren

All Night Long *
GB 1961 95m bw
Rank/Bob Roberts (Michael Relph, Basil Dearden)
Because of rumour set about by a jealous rival, a jazz trumpeter at an all-night party tries to strangle his wife.
Cheeky updating of Othello with jazz accompaniment, played a shade too grimly by an excellent cast. An interesting misfire. The soundtrack features jazz musicians Dave Brubeck, Tubby Hayes and John Dankworth.
w Nel King, Paul Jarrico *d* Basil Dearden *ph* Ted Scaife *m* Philip Green
☆ Patrick McGoohan, Richard Attenborough, Keith Michell, Betsy Blair, Marti Stevens, Paul Harris, Bernard Braden
† Because Paul Jarrico was a blacklisted writer, the film's credited writers Nel King and Peter Achilles.

All Night Long
US 1981 87m Technicolor
Universal (Leonard Goldberg, Jerry Weintraub)
The wife of the night manager of a supermarket has a hyperactive sex life.
Curiously misjudged and outdated farce which offers very few laughs.
w W. D. Richter *d* Jean-Claude Tramont *ph* Philip Lathrop *m* Ira Newborn, Richard Hazard *pd* Peter Jamison
☆ Barbra Streisand, Gene Hackman, Diane Ladd, Dennis Quaid, Kevin Dobson, William Daniels, Ann Doran
'Neither screenplay nor direction seem very clear what they're trying to say, and large chunks of it make no sense at all.' – *Daily Mail*

'There are two kinds of women, but only one kind of love!'
All of Me
US 1934 70m bw
Paramount (Louis Lighton)
An engineering professor on his way to Boulder Dam finds his life affected by the problems of a criminal.
Confused and uninteresting romantic melodrama with a good cast all at sea.
w Sidney Buchman, Thomas Mitchell *play* *Chrysalis* by Rose Porter *d* James Flood *ph* Victor Milner *m/ly* Ralph Rainger, Leo Robin
☆ Fredric March, Miriam Hopkins, George Raft, Helen Mack, Nella Walker, William Collier Jnr, Gilbert Emery, Blanche Friderici, Edgar Kennedy
'The most startling glorification of criminals that even the movies have ever dared.' – *New York Sun*
'The gags aren't thought out visually in terms of the L.A. locations, and the film has the bland ugliness of sitcoms.' – *Pauline Kael, New Yorker*

All of Me
US 1984 91m Technicolor
Thorn-EMI/Kings Road/Universal (Stephen Friedman)
A guru accidentally transfers a woman's soul after death into her lawyer's body.
Curiously vulgar sitcom with a familiar team trying and failing to go one better on The Man With Two Brains.
w Phil Alden Robinson *novel* Me Two by Ed Davis *d* Carl Reiner *ph* Richard H. Kline *m* Patrick Williams *pd* Edward Carfagno *ed* Bud Molin
☆ Steve Martin, Lily Tomlin, Victoria Tennant, Madolyn Smith, Dana Elcar

All or Nothing **
GB/France 2002 128m colour
UGC/Thin Man (Simon Channing Williams, Alain Sarde)
Couples living on a poor, South London housing estate have problems with their children and each other.
Glum portrait of people with an absence of love in their lives. The performaces capture the downtrodden humanity of the characters.
wd Mike Leigh *ph* Dick Pope *m* Andrew Dickson *pd* Eve Stewart *ed* Lesley Walker
☆ Timothy Spall (Phil Bassett), Lesley Manville (Penny Bassett), Alison Garland (Rachel Bassett), James Corden (Rory Bassett), Ruth Sheen

(Maureen), Marion Bailey (Carol), Paul Jesson (Ron), Sally Hawkins (Samantha)

'Just as the movie begins to break free of its sorrow-swamped moorings, the scenes grow longer, more maudlin, and more stage-bound.' – *David Edlestein, Slate*

'An exhilarating movie about sadness and renewal.' – *Michael Sragow, Baltimore Sun*

All Over Me

US 1997 90m colour

Medusa/Slam/Baldini (Dolly Hall)

Two teenage girls begin to explore their sexuality and their emergence into an adult world of confusion and violence.

A drab little adolescent drama, one of those movies that keeps nudging its audience in the ribs to emphasize its own sensitivity.

w Sylvia Sichel *d* Alex Sichel *ph* Joe DeSalvo *m* Miki Navazio *pd* Amy Beth Silver *ed* Sabine Hoffman

☆ Alison Folland (Claude), Tara Subkoff (Ellen), Cole Hauser (Mark), Wilson Cruz (Jesse), Ann Dowd (Anne), Shawn Hatosy (Gus)

'This gritty drama is so rich in ideas that it goes beyond being a coming-out or even a lesbian-themed story ... a gem. It is rare for an American film to portray with such delicacy, subtlety and candor the complex processes of coming of age.' – *Emanuel Levy, Variety*

All Over the Town *

GB 1949 88m bw

Rank/Wessex (Ian Dalrymple)

Two reporters revivify a West of England local newspaper, and expose local corruption.

Fresh, agreeable romantic comedy on sub-Ealing lines.

w Derek Twist and others *d* Derek Twist *ph* C. Pennington-Richards *m* Temple Abady

☆ Norman Wooland, Sarah Churchill, Fabia Drake, Cyril Cusack, James Hayter

All Over Town

US 1937 62m bw

Republic

A pair of vaudevillians with a trained seal save a theatre on the skids.

Routine knockabout comedy.

w Jack Townley, Jerome Chodorov *d* James Horne

☆ Ole Olsen, Chic Johnson, Mary Howard, Harry Stockwell, James Finlayson, Franklin Pangborn

All Quiet on the Western Front ****

US 1930 130m approx bw

Universal (Carl Laemmle Jnr)

In 1914, a group of German teenagers volunteer for action on the Western Front, but they become disillusioned, and none of them survives.

A landmark of American cinema and Universal's biggest and most serious undertaking until the sixties, this highly emotive war film with its occasional outbursts of bravura direction fixed in millions of minds the popular image of what it was like in the trenches, even more so than Journey's End which had shown the Allied viewpoint. Despite dated moments, it retains its overall power and remains a great pacifist work. Milestone's direction is reminiscent of Eisenstein and Lang.

w Lewis Milestone, Maxwell Anderson, Del Andrews, George Abbott *novel* Erich Maria Remarque *d Lewis Milestone ph Arthur Edeson* *m* David Broekman *ad* Charles D. Hall, William R. Schmidt *ed* Milton Carruth, Edgar Adams

☆ Lew Ayres (Paul Baumer), Louis Wolheim (Katczinsky), Slim Summerville (Tjaden), John Wray (Himmelstoss), Raymond Griffith (Gerard Duval), Russell Gleason (Muller), Ben Alexander (Kemmerick), Beryl Mercer (Mrs Baumer)

TJADEN: 'Me and the Kaiser, we are both fighting. The only difference is, the Kaiser isn't here.'

KATCZINSKY: 'At the next war let all the Kaisers, Presidents and Generals and diplomats go into a big field and fight it out first among themselves. That will satisfy us and keep us at home.'

PAUL: 'We live in the trenches out there. We fight. We try not to be killed, but sometimes we are. That's all.'

'A magnificent cinematic equivalent of the book ... to Mr Milestone goes the credit of effecting the similitude in united and dynamic picture terms. The sound and image mediums blend as one, as a form of artistic expression that only the motion screen can give.' – *National Board of Review*

'Nothing passed up for the niceties; nothing glossed over for the women. Here exhibited is war as it is, butchery. The League of Nations could make no better investment than to buy up the master-print, reproduce it in every language to be shown to every nation every year until the word war is taken out of the dictionaries.' – *Variety*

'A trenchant and imaginative audible picture ... most of the time the audience was held to silence by its realistic scenes.' – *New York Times*

† ZaSu Pitts originally played the role of Mrs Baumer in the film. When preview audiences, used to seeing her in comedies, were confused by her performance, her scenes were reshot with Beryl Mercer in the part.

picture; Lewis Milestone (as director)

Lewis Milestone, Maxwell Anderson, Del Andrews, George Abbott; Arthur Edeson

'Together again ... surpassing their performances in "Magnificent Obsession"'

All that Heaven Allows

US 1955 89m Technicolor

U-I (Ross Hunter)

A sad widow falls in love with the gardener at her winter home, and marries him despite local prejudice.

Standard tearjerker in the tradition of Magnificent Obsession, reuniting the same stars, producer and director in the same rich musical and photographic sauce.

w Peg Fenwick *d* Douglas Sirk *ph* Russell Metty *m* Frank Skinner

☆ Jane Wyman, Rock Hudson, Agnes Moorehead, Conrad Nagel, Virginia Grey, Charles Drake

'As laboriously predictable as it is fatuously unreal.' – *MFB*

All That Jazz ***

US 1979 123m Technicolor

COL/TCF (Robert Alan Aurthur, Daniel Melnick)

A stage musical director pushes himself too hard, and dies of a surfeit of wine, women and work.

Self-indulgent, semi-autobiographical tragi-comic extravaganza complete with heart operations and a recurring angel of death. Flashes of brilliant talent make it a must for Fosse fans.

w Robert Alan Aurthur, Bob Fosse *d Bob Fosse* *ph* Giuseppe Rotunno *m* Ralph Burns *pd* Philip Rosenberg, Tony Walton *ed* Alan Heim

☆ *Roy Scheider*, Jessica Lange, Ann Reinking, Leland Palmer, Ben Vereen, Cliff Gorman

'Egomaniacal, wonderfully choreographed, often compelling ... more an art item than a broad commercial prospect.' – *Variety*

'An improbable mixture of crass gags, song 'n' dance routines and open heart surgery. Not for the squeamish.' – *Time Out*

'By the end I felt I'd learned more about Fosse than I actually cared to know.' – *Daily Mail*

'High cholesterol hokum. Enjoyable, but probably not good for you.' – *Pauline Kael, New Yorker*

art direction; editing; musical adaptation; costume design (Albert Wolsky)

picture; Bob Fosse; Roy Scheider; Giuseppe Rotunno; script

cinematography; editing; sound

All that Money Can Buy ****

US 1941 106m bw

RKO/William Dieterle (Charles L. Glett)

aka: *The Devil and Daniel Webster*

aka: *Daniel and the Devil; Here Is a Man*

A hard-pressed farmer gives in to the Devil's tempting, but is saved from the pit by a famous lawyer's pleading at his 'trial'.

A brilliant Germanic Faust set in 19th-century New Hampshire and using historical figures, alienation effects, comedy asides and the whole cinematic box of tricks which Hollywood had just learned again through Citizen Kane. A magic act in more ways than one.

w Dan Totheroh story The Devil and Daniel Webster by Stephen Vincent Benet *d William Dieterle* *ph Joseph August m Bernard Herrmann ad Van Nest Polglase sp Vernon L. Walker*

☆ *Walter Huston* (Mr Scratch), James Craig, Anne Shirley, Simone Simon, *Edward Arnold* (Daniel Webster), Jane Darwell, Gene Lockhart, John Qualen. H. B. Warner

MR SCRATCH: 'A soul. A soul is nothing. Can you see it, smell it, touch it? No. Think of it – this soul – your soul – a nothing, against seven whole years of good luck! You will have money and all that money can buy.'

'Some of those in the movie industry who saw it restively called it a dog; but some of them cried it was another catapult hurling the cinema up to its glorious destiny.' – *Cecilia Ager*

Bernard Herrmann

Walter Huston

All the Brothers Were Valiant *

US 1953 94m Technicolor

MGM (Pandro S. Berman)

Rivalry between brothers on a whaling schooner.

Remake of a silent melodrama with predictable vengefulness and formula heroism, capably but unmemorably portrayed.

w Harry Brown *novel* Ben Ames Williams *d* Richard Thorpe *ph* George Folsey *m* Miklos Rozsa

☆ Stewart Granger, Robert Taylor, Ann Blyth, Betta St John, Keenan Wynn, James Whitmore, Kurt Kasznar, Lewis Stone

George Folsey

All the Fine Young Cannibals

US 1960 122m Metrocolor Cinemascope

MGM/Avon (Pandro S. Berman)

The son of a country clergyman loves the daughter of another clergyman; they both find the realities of life in New York a horrid shock.

The glum joys of sex and dope in the big city are revealed in this boring rather than daring farrago which is not even unintentionally funny.

w Robert Thom *novel The Bixby Girls* by Rosamond Marshall *d* Michael Anderson *ph* William H. Daniels *m* Jeff Alexander

☆ Robert Wagner, Natalie Wood, Pearl Bailey, Susan Kohner, George Hamilton, Jack Mullaney, Onslow Stevens, Anne Seymour

All the King's Horses

US 1935 87m bw

Paramount

A Hollywood star revisiting his native Langenstein turns out to be a double of the king, and finds himself romancing the queen.

Operetta-style entertainment grafted onto the plot of The Prisoner of Zenda; by no means unacceptable even now.

w Frank Tuttle, Frederick Stephani *play* Lawrence Clark, Max Giersberg *d* Frank Tuttle *ch* LeRoy Prinz

☆ Carl Brisson, Mary Ellis, Edward Everett Horton, Eugene Pallette, Katherine de Mille

LeRoy Prinz

'He thought he had the world by the tail – till it exploded in his face, with a bullet attached!'

All the King's Men ***

US 1949 109m bw

Columbia (Robert Rossen)

An honest man from a small town is elected mayor and then governor, but power corrupts him absolutely and he ruins his own life and those of his friends before being assassinated.

Archetypal American political melodrama based on the life of southern senator Huey Long. The background is well sketched in and there are excellent performances, but the overall narrative is rather flabby.

w Robert Rossen *novel* Robert Penn Warren *d Robert Rossen* *ph* Burnett Guffey *m* Louis Gruenberg *ad* Sturges Carne *ed* Robert Parrish, Al Clark

☆ *Broderick Crawford, John Ireland, Mercedes McCambridge, Joanne Dru*, John Derek, Anne Seymour, Shepperd Strudwick

'More conspicuous for scope and worthiness of intention than for inspiration.' – *Gavin Lambert*

'The film is like one of those lifeless digests, designed for people who cannot spare the time to read whole books. Perhaps that accounts for its popularity.' – *Lindsay Anderson*

'A superb pictorialism which perpetually crackles and explodes.' – *Bosley Crowther*

'Realism comes from within as well as without and the core of meaning that might have made this film a step forward from *Boomerang* does not exist amid all the courageous camera-work.' – *Richard Winnington*

'Broderick Crawford's Willie Stark might just make you feel better about the President you've got ... By no means a great film, but it moves along.' – *Pauline Kael, New Yorker*

picture; Broderick Crawford; Mercedes McCambridge

Robert Rossen (as writer); Robert Rossen (as director); John Ireland; editing

'Of all God's creatures... man is the cruellest.'

All The Little Animals

GB 1998 111m Technicolor 'Scope

Entertainment/Recorded Pictures/British Screen, J&M/IofMFC/BBC (Jeremy Thomas)

A brain-damaged adolescent, running away from his unhappy home, is befriended by an eccentric old man who protects wild animals from harm.

An unsatisfactory fable of the superiority of the natural world, yoked to a melodramatic tale of a usurping, wicked stepfather.

w Eski Thomas *novel* Walker Hamilton *d* Jeremy Thomas *ph* Mike Molloy *m* Richard Hartley *pd* Andrew Sanders *ed* John Victor Smith

☆ John Hurt (Mr Summers), Christian Bale (Bobby), Daniel Benzali (De Winter), James Faulkner (Mr Whiteside), John O'Toole (Lorry driver)

'Modest in ambition and accomplishment.' – *Variety*

All the Marbles...

US 1981 113m Metrocolor

MGM/Aldrich Company (William Aldrich)

GB title: *The California Dolls*

Problems of a women's wrestling team in the midwest.

Tasteless and tedious exploitation comedy with just a few flashes of the director's old flair.

w Mel Frohman *d* Robert Aldrich *ph* Joseph Biroc *m* Frank de Vol *pd* Carl Anderson *ed* Irving C. Rosenblum, Richard Lane

☆ Peter Falk, Vicki Frederick, Laurene Landon, Burt Young, Tracy Reed

'The most devastating detective story of the century!'

All the President's Men ****

US 1976 138m Technicolor

Warner/Wildwood (Robert Redford, Walter Coblenz)

A reconstruction of the discovery of the White House link with the Watergate affair by two young reporters from the *Washington Post*.

An absorbing drama from the headlines which despite its many excellences would have been better with a more audible dialogue track, less murky photography and a clearer introduction of the characters concerned. The acting however is a treat.

w William Goldman *book* Carl Bernstein, Bob Woodward *d* Alan J. Pakula *ph* Gordon Willis *m* David Shire *pd* George Jenkins

☆ *Robert Redford, Dustin Hoffman*, Jason Robards Jnr, Martin Balsam, Hal Holbrook, Jack Warden, Jane Alexander, Meredith Baxter

'It works as a detective thriller (even though everyone knows the ending), as a credible (if occasionally romanticized) primer on the prosaic fundamentals of big league investigative journalism, and best of all, as a chilling tone poem that conveys the texture of the terror in our nation's capital during that long night when an aspiring fascist regime held our democracy under siege.' – *Frank Rich, New York Post*

William Goldman; Jason Robards Jnr

picture; Alan J. Pakula; Jane Alexander

'Some passions can never be tamed.'

All The Pretty Horses *

US 2000 117m colour Panavision

Columbia (Robert Salerno, Billy Bob Thornton)

In 1949, a dispossessed young Texan and his best friend ride to Mexico to become cowboys, where they are confronted by matters of love and death.

A uneven attempt at an elegiac Western, combining nostalgia for a vanishing way of life with a coming-of-age narrative; but the central romance has no life to it, and it ends up as just another love story between two men and their horses.

w Ted Tally *novel* Cormac McCarthy *d* Billy Bob Thornton *ph* Barry Markowitz *m* Marty Stuart *pd* Clark Hunter *ed* Sally Menke

☆ Matt Damon (John Grady Cole), Henry Thomas (Lacey Rawlins), Lucas Black (Jimmy Blevins), Penélope Cruz (Alejandra), Ruben Blades (Rocha), Robert Patrick (Cole), Julio Oscar

Mechoso (Captain), Miriam Colon (Alfonsa), Bruce Dern (Judge), Sam Shepard (J. C. Franklin)

'Manages to be shallow and portentous at the same time…slick and superficial as a Marlboro advertisement on the back of a glossy magazine.' – *A. O. Scott, New York Times*

All the Right Moves
US 1983 91m colour
Fox (Stephen Deutsch)

An ambitious high school football star is helped to get an athletics scholarship.
Rather dislikeable melodrama with specifically American atmosphere.
w Michael Kane *d* Michael Chapman *ph* Jan de Bont *m* David Campbell *ad* Mary Ann Biddle *ed* David Garfield
☆ Tom Cruise, Craig T. Nelson, Lea Thompson, Charles Cioffi, Christopher Penn

All the Right Noises *
GB 1969 91m Eastmancolor
(TCF) Trigon (Anthony Hope)
The electrician of a touring company has an affair with a 15-year-old actress, but finally returns to his wife.
Sharp, sensible treatment of a cliché situation, as watchable as a superior television play.
wd Gerry O'Hara *ph* Gerry Fisher *m* John Cameron
☆ Tom Bell, Judy Carne, Olivia Hussey, John Standing
'Built on a solid framework of disciplined direction and animated performances.' – *MFB*

All the Vermeers in New York
US 1990 87m TVC Color
Complex Corporation (Henry S. Rosenthal)

A Wall Street trader begins a relationship with a French woman he meets at the Metropolitan Museum of Art.
A desultory, minimalist film that proceeds in a haphazard fashion, picking up and then dropping the threads of the story.
wd Jon Jost *ph* Jon Jost *m* Jon A. English *ed* Jon Jost
☆ Emmanuelle Chaulet, Stephen Lack, Grace Phillips, Laurel Kiefer, Gordon Joseph Weiss, Katherine Bean, Gracie Mansion, Roger Ruffin

'Love is not a thing that grows only in the dark!'
All the Way Home **
US 1963 107m bw
Paramount/Talent Associates (David Susskind)
In 1916 Tennessee, the beloved father of a family is killed in a car crash, and after the trauma wears off, mother helps the children to rebuild their lives.
Tactful, charming though finally depressing slice of small town period Americana, with generally eloquent performances.
w Philip Reisman Jnr *play* Tad Mosel *novel* A Death in the Family by James Agee *d* Alex Segal *ph* Boris Kaufman *m* Bernard Green
☆ Robert Preston, Jean Simmons, Aline MacMahon, Pat Hingle, Michael Kearney
'A heart-wrenching blend of nostalgia and sorrow.' – *Judith Crist*
'Terribly earnest, pictorial, and well intentioned. And a terrible mistake.' – *Pauline Kael, New Yorker*

All the Way Up *
GB 1970 97m Technicolor
Granada/EMI (Philip Mackie)
Social-climbing Dad makes his way by treachery and blackmail, but gets his come-uppance when his son takes after him.
Crudely farcical adaptation of a thoughtful comedy of its time; the treatment works in fits and starts but leaves one in no mood for the talkative finale.
w Philip Mackie *play* Semi Detached by David Turner *d* James MacTaggart *ph* Dick Bush *m* Howard Blake
☆ Warren Mitchell, Pat Heywood, Elaine Taylor, Kenneth Cranham, Vanessa Howard, Richard Briers, Adrienne Posta, Bill Fraser

All the Young Men
US 1960 87m bw
Columbia (Hall Bartlett/Jaguar)

A marine patrol in Korea is commanded by a black man, and racial tensions take precedence over fighting the enemy.
Simple-minded, parsimoniously-budgeted war melodrama.
wd Hall Bartlett *ph* Daniel Fapp *m* George Duning
☆ Alan Ladd, Sidney Poitier, Ingemar Johansson, Glenn Corbett, James Darren, Mort Sahl
'Strenuously engaged in exploiting the entertainment values of nostalgia, fear, suspense, hatred and sex.' – *MFB*

All the Youthful Days: see *The Boys from Fengkuei*

All These Women: see *Now About All These Women…*

All This and Glamour Too: see *Vogues of 1938*

All This and Heaven Too **
US 1940 143m bw
Warner (Jack L. Warner, Hal B. Wallis)

A 19th-century French nobleman falls in love with his governess and murders his wife.
Romantic, melodramatic soap opera from a mammoth best seller; well made for those who can stomach it, with excellent acting and production values.
w Casey Robinson *novel* Rachel Field *d* Anatole Litvak *ph* Ernest Haller *m* Max Steiner
☆ Charles Boyer, Bette Davis, Barbara O'Neil, Virginia Weidler, Jeffrey Lynn, Helen Westley, Henry Daniell, Harry Davenport, Walter Hampden, George Coulouris, Janet Beecher, Montagu Love
'Deserves extended runs and upped admissions … completely shorn of spectacle, but replete with finely drawn characters in absorbingly dramatic situations.' – *Variety*
'Litvak had it all on paper: he planned every move. There is not the spontaneity or flexibility.' – *Bette Davis*
picture; Ernest Haller; Barbara O'Neil

All This and Money Too: see *Love is a Ball*

All This and World War Two *
US 1977 88m bw/DeLuxe
Fox/Lou Reizner Productions
Wartime newsreels are interwoven with pop songs and clips from feature films.
A messy mélange with obvious items of interest, but totally confusing and uninformative for the young historian.
d Susan Winslow
'Desperately straining to make any kind of sense, it is reduced to making parallels that are either glib or facetious.' – *MFB*

'Killer Bogart takes the Gestapo for a ride!'
All Through the Night *
US 1942 107m bw
Warner (Jerry Wald)

Gangsters help to track down fifth columnists in World War II New York.
Highly entertaining muddle of several styles which somehow works well and allows several favourites to do their thing.
w Leonard Spigelgass, Edwin Gilbert *d* Vincent Sherman *ph* Sid Hickox *m* Adolph Deutsch
☆ Humphrey Bogart, Conrad Veidt, Peter Lorre, Karen Verne, Judith Anderson, Jane Darwell, Frank McHugh, Jackie Gleason, William Demarest, Phil Silvers
'Exciting slaphappy stuff.' – *Kine Weekly*
'The thrills and the jokes have both been sharpened to a pin point.' – *New Statesman*

The All-American
US 1932 73m bw
Universal
GB title: *Sport of a Nation*
A college football star finds his fame of little use to him in the outside world.
Lively drama of its day, but with little permanent interest.
w Frank Wead, Ferdinand Reyher, Richard Schayer, Dale Van Every *d* Russell Mack
☆ Richard Arlen, Andy Devine, Gloria Stuart, James Gleason, Preston Foster
'A pleaser for all audiences, having more than the football stuff to recommend it.' – *Variety*

The All-American
US 1952 83m bw
U-I (Aaron Rosenberg)
GB title: *The Winning Way*
When his parents are killed on the way to a match, a college football hero rejects sport for the groves of *academe*.
Very modest formula drama.
w D. D. Beauchamp *d* Jesse Hibbs *ph* Maury Gertsman *m* Joseph Gershenson
☆ Tony Curtis, Mamie Van Doren, Lori Nelson, Gregg Palmer, Richard Long, Paul Cavanagh

The All-American Boy
US 1973 118m colour Panavision
Warner
A young boxer has got to the top too fast, and is depressed by the future.
Uninteresting character study.
wd Charles Eastman
☆ Jon Voight, Carol Androsky, Anne Archer

Allan Quatermain and the Lost City of Gold
US 1987 99m colour JDC
Cannon (Menahem Golan, Yoram Globus)

A mysterious old gold piece sends Quatermain looking for his brother, missing in Africa after seeking a lost white race.
Abysmal follow-up to 1985's ghastly King Solomon's Mines.
w Gene Quintano *d* Gary Nelson *ph* Alex Phillips, Frederick Elmes *m* Michael Linn *pd* Trevor Williams, Leslie Dilley *ed* Alain Jakubowicz
☆ Richard Chamberlain, Sharon Stone, James Earl Jones, Henry Silva, Robert Donner
'The embarrassing screenplay jettisons Haggard's enduring fantasy and myth-making in favour of a back-of-the-envelope plotline and anachronistic jokes about Cleveland.' – *Daily Variety*

Allegheny Uprising
US 1939 98m bw
RKO (P. J. Wolfson)

GB title: *The First Rebel*
A young frontiersman smashes liquor traffic with the Indians.
Modestly efficient Western with an impressive cast.
w P. J. Wolfson *story* Neil Swanson *d* William A. Seiter *ph* Nicholas Musuraca
☆ John Wayne, Claire Trevor, Brian Donlevy, George Sanders, Wilfrid Lawson, Robert Barrat, Moroni Olsen, Eddie Quillan, Chill Wills
'Long on horsemanship and action, short on romance and suspense.' – *Variety*

Allegro Ma Troppo *
France 1963 16m Eastmancolor
Films Je Vois Tout
One night in Paris viewed through accelerated motion.
An amusing if not original conceit, smartly executed.
m François de Roubaix *ed* Robert Enrico
w/d/ph Paul de Roubaix

Allegro Non Troppo *
Italy 1977 74m colour/bw
Essential/Bruno Bozzetto

A mix of live action and animation to create a modernistic version of *Fantasia*, e.g. Ravel's 'Bolero' is danced by a Coca-Cola bottle.
Fast-paced feature with often dazzling use of colour, though the imagination sometimes flags, especially in the crude live-action slapstick routines.
w Bruno Bozzetto, Guido Manuli, Maurizio Nichetti *d* Bruno Bozzetto *ph* Mario Masini *m* Debussy, Dvorak, Ravel, Sibelius, Vivaldi, Stravinsky *md* Herbert von Karajan, Hans Stadlmair, Lorin Maazel
☆ Maurizio Nichetti, Nestor Garay, Maurizio Micheli, Maria Luisa Giovanni

Alley of Nightmares: see *She Freak*

Alligator *
US 1980 91m DeLuxe
Group 1/Alligator Associates (Brandon Chase)

A pet baby alligator is flushed down the toilet and later, grown to enormous size, goes on the rampage.
Jaws-type monster movie made tolerable by occasional flashes of humour but not otherwise remarkable.
w John Sayles *d* Lewis Teague *ph* Joseph Mangine *m* Craig Hundley *sp* Richard O. Helmer
☆ Robert Forster, Robin Ryker, Michael Gazzo, Dean Jagger, Jack Carter, Henry Silva
'Hair raising, funny, shrewdly scripted and politically telling.' – *Margaret Hinxman, Daily Mail*

Alligator Eyes *
US 1990 101m DuArt
Castle Hill/Laughing Man (John Feldman, Ken Schwenker)

Three friends from New York, driving off on holiday, pick up a beautiful hitchhiker, not realizing that she is blind and has her own sinister agenda.
Intriguing and suspenseful road movie for the most part, though its resolution disappoints.
wd John Feldman *ph* Todd Crockett *m* Sheila Silver *ed* Cynthia Rogers
☆ Annabelle Larsen, Roger Kabler, Mary McLain, Allen McCullough, John Mackay
'As a road movie, this one's unusually well-written, directed and acted.' – *Variety*

Alligator II: The Mutation
US 1991 90m DeLuxe Panavision
Golden Hawk (Brandon Chase)

After an unscrupulous property developer dumps toxic waste in the city sewers, a monstrous man-eating alligator emerges to terrorize the town.
Uninvolving sequel that follows a familiar and predictable pattern and lacks the wit and pace of the original.
w Curt Allen *d* Jon Hess *ph* Joseph Mangine *m* Jack Tillar *pd* George Costello *ed* Marshall Harvey, Chris Ellis
☆ Joseph Bologna, Dee Wallace Stone, Richard Lynch, Woody Brown, Holly Gagnier, Bill Dailey, Steve Railsback, Brock Peters

An Alligator Named Daisy
GB 1955 88m Technicolor
Vistavision
Rank (Raymond Stross)
A young songwriter finds himself saddled with a pet alligator.
The ultimate in silly animal comedies, this does score a few laughs.
w Jack Davies *novel* Charles Terrot *d* J. Lee-Thompson *ph* Reg Wyer *m* Stanley Black
☆ Donald Sinden, Diana Dors, Jean Carson, James Robertson Justice, Stanley Holloway, Roland Culver, Margaret Rutherford, Avice Landone, Richard Wattis, Frankie Howerd, Jimmy Edwards, Gilbert Harding
'Apart from a fairly Kafkaesque scene in which Daisy is discovered in an upright piano, the situation is treated with little wit or comic invention.' – *MFB*

'Nerve-Shattering Terror'
'Her Honeymoon Turned Into A Nightmare Of Horror!'
The Alligator People
US 1959 73m bw Cinemascope
TCF (Jerry Wald)
A doctor uses a revolutionary serum which unfortunately turns patients into the alligators from which it was derived.
Moderately inventive 'B' chiller.
w Orville H. Hampton *d* Roy del Ruth *ph* Karl Struss *m* Irving Gertz
☆ George Macready, Frieda Inescort, Beverly Garland, Bruce Bennett, Lon Chaney Jnr

The Allnighter
US 1987 94m CFI color
Universal/Aurora (Tamar Simon Hoffs)

Three girls party during their final days at college.

Unbelievably crass teen pic that is enough to put an entire generation off higher education – or sex, for that matter.
w M. I. Kessler, Tamar Simon Hoffs d Tamar Simon Hoffs ph Joseph Urbanczyk m Charles Bernstein pd Cynthia Sowder ed Dan M. Rich
☆ Susanna Hoffs, Dedee Pfeiffer, Joan Cusack, Michael Ontkean, Pam Grier, James Anthony Shanta, John Terlesky

All's Fair...
US 1989 90m colour
Midwood (John Gordon)
A marker for a VHS PAL video, and an American NTSC video.
Working for a firm run on macho-military lines, the female executives challenge their bosses to a weekend war game.
Coarse, loud, dispiriting one-joke comedy, in which shouting and over-acting substitute for humour.
w Randee Russell, John Finnegan, Tom Rondinella, William Pace d Rocky Lang ph Peter Lyons Collister m Bill Meyers pd Cynthia Charette ed Maryann Brandon
☆ Sally Kellerman, George Segal, Jane Kaczmarek, Jennifer Edwards, John Kapelos, Lou Ferrigno, Robert Carradine

Almonds and Raisins *
GB 1983 90m bw
Willowgold/Brook Productions and the National Center for Jewish Film
The story of the Yiddish cinema in thirties New York.
Interesting documentary compilation majoring in the work of Edgar G. Ulmer.
w Wolf Mankowitz d Russ Karel

Almost: see *Wendy Cracked a Walnut*

Almost a Bride: see *A Kiss for Corliss*

Almost an Angel
US 1990 95m DeLuxe
UIP/Paramount (John Cornell)
A petty crook returns to Earth as a good angel.
Trite comedy with little substance and fewer laughs.
w Paul Hogan d John Cornell ph Russell Boyd m Maurice Jarre pd Henry Bumstead ad Bernie Cutler ed David Stiven
☆ Paul Hogan, Elias Koteas, Linda Kozlowski, Doreen Lang, Robert Sutton, Travis Venable, Douglas Seale, Ruth Warshawsky

Almost Angels
US 1962 93m colour
Buena Vista
A boy joins the Vienna Boys' Choir.
The singing outweighs the story in this overlong but often pleasing filler.
w Vernon Harris story R. A. Stemmle d Steve Previn
☆ Vincent Winter, Peter Weck, Sean Scully, Hans Holt

'Experience it. Enjoy it. Just don't fall for it.'
Almost Famous **
US 2000 122m Technicolor
DreamWorks/Vinyl (Cameron Crowe, Ian Bryce)
A rock-obsessed teenager becomes a journalist so that he can get close to the musicians he admires.
Semi-autobiographical account of the director's start as a writer for Rolling Stone: he recreates the past with affection and wry amusement, but overdoses on blandness.
wd Cameron Crowe ph John Toll m Nancy Wilson ad Clay A. Griffith, Clayton R. Hartley, Virginia Randolph-Weaver ed Joe Hutshing, Saar Klein
☆ Billy Crudup (Russell Hammond), Frances McDormand (Elaine Miller), Kate Hudson (Penny Lane), Jason Lee (Jeff Bebe), Patrick Fugit (William Miller), Anna Paquin (Polexia Aphrodisia), Fairuza Balk (Sapphire), Noah Taylor (Dick Roswell), Zooey Deschanel (Anita Miller), John Fedevich (Ed Vallencourt), Bijou Phillips (Estrella Starr), Philip Seymour Hoffman (Lester Bangs), Eion Bailey (Jann Wenner), Terry Chen (Ben Fong-Torres)
'If this solemn and disconcertingly reactionary film gets Academy awards it will be very depressing.' – *Peter Bradshaw, Guardian*
'More gentle and modestly insightful than it is exhilarating or revelatory.' – *Todd McCarthy, Variety*
Cameron Crowe (script)
Kate Hudson; Frances McDormand; Joe Hutshing, Saar Klein
Cameron Crowe (script); sound (Jeff Wexler, D. M. Hemphill, Rick Kline, Paul Massey, Mike Wilhoit)

Almost Married
US 1932 50m bw
TCF
An insane Bolshevik breaks out of hospital when he hears of his wife's bigamous marriage.
Oddly-titled melodrama with flashes of interest, previously filmed by MGM in 1919.
w Wallace Smith novel *Devil's Triangle* by Andrew Soutar d William Cameron Menzies
☆ Violet Heming, Ralph Bellamy, Alexander Kirkland, Alan Dinehart

An Almost Perfect Affair *
US 1979 93m DeLuxe
Paramount/Terry Carr
A young film producer at the Cannes Festival falls for the wife of an Italian impresario.
Lively detail lifts many scenes of this eccentric romance, but the routine plot is a downer.
w Walter Bernstein, Don Petersen d Michael Ritchie ph Henri Decae m Georges Delerue
☆ Keith Carradine, Monica Vitti, Raf Vallone, Christian de Sica

Almost Summer
US 1978 88m colour
Universal (Rob Cohen)
High-school students hold an election for their new president.
Mercifully short farcical comedy, aimed at a teenage audience.
w Judith Berg, Sandra Berg, Martin Davidson, Marc Reid Rubel d Martin Davidson ph Stevan Larner m Ron Altbach, Charles Lloyd ad William F. Hiney ed Lynzee Klingman
☆ John Friedrich, Bruno Kirby, Lee Purcell, Didi Conn, Thomas Carter, Tim Matheson, Patronia Paley

Almost You
US 1984 96m DuArt
TCF/Wescom (Mark Lipson)
After his wife dislocates her hip, her wealthy and bored husband is attracted to the live-in nurse he hires to look after her.
A tedious romantic comedy that overstates the obvious.
w Mark Horowitz story Adam Brooks d Adam Brooks ph Alexander Gruszynski m Jonathan Elias ad Nora Chavoosian ed Mark Burns
☆ Brooke Adams, Griffin Dunne, Karen Young, Marty Watt, Laura Dean, Josh Mostel, Christine Estabrook, Spalding Gray

Aloha Bobby and Rose
US 1975 89m Metrocolor
Warner/Cine Artists International (Fouad Said)
A Los Angeles motor mechanic becomes unwittingly involved in crime and finds himself fleeing for the Mexican border with a girlfriend.
Warmed-over retread of They Live By Night, not badly done but of no abiding interest.
wd Floyd Mutrux ph William A. Fraker
☆ Paul Le Mat, Dianne Hull, Tim McIntire, Leigh French, Noble Willingham, Robert Carradine
'As accurate a picture of Southern California as I've yet seen.' – *Guardian*

Aloha Summer
US 1988 97m CFI color
Hanauma Bay (Mike Greco)
An American teenager holidaying in Hawaii learns about racial prejudice, sex and violence.
Typical teen picture, directed with a heavy hand.
w Mike Greco d Tommy Lee Wallace ph Steven Poster m Jesse Frederick, Bennet Salvay ad Donald Harris ed James Coblentz, Jack Hofstra, Jay Cassidy
☆ Chris Makepeace, Yuji Okumoto, Don Michael Paul, Tia Carrere, Sho Kosugi, Lorie Griffin

'Pagan love – in an exotic, exciting tropic paradise!'
Aloma of the South Seas
US 1941 77m Technicolor
Paramount (Monta Bell)
A young Polynesian chieftain returns to quell trouble on his island after being educated in the US.
Hoary goings-on in gory colour, a remake of a silent epic devised to display the star's sarong and the backlot's expensive volcano.
w Frank Butler, Seena Owen, Lillie Hayward d Alfred Santell ph Karl Struss, Wilfrid M. Cline, William Snyder m Victor Young sp Gordon Jennings
☆ Dorothy Lamour, Jon Hall, Lynne Overman, Philip Reed, Katherine de Mille, Fritz Leiber, Dona Drake, Esther Dale
'The mountain has the privilege of belching when it is dissatisfied, which is something no well-bred critic should do.' – *C. A. Lejeune*
† A silent version in 1926 had starred Gilda Gray. Directed by Maurice Tourneur, it adhered more closely to the original play (by John B. Hymer and Leroy Clemens).
Karl Struss, Wilfrid M. Cline, William Snyder

Alone: see *Solas*

Alone in the Dark
US 1982 93m Cineffects
New Line/Masada
Maximum-security prisoners in a mental hospital are liberated by a power failure.
Pretentious but incompetent horror flick of the Halloween school with a plot partly borrowed from Spellbound.
wd Jack Sholder
☆ Jack Palance, Donald Pleasence, Martin Landau, Dwight Schultz, Deborah Hedwall

Alone on the Pacific **
Japan 1963 104m Eastmancolor
Cinemascope
Ishihara-Nikkatsu (Akira Nakai)
original title: *Taiheiyo Hitoribochi*
A young man crosses from Osaka to San Francisco in a small yacht.
Fascinating Robinson-Crusoe-like exercise, with flashbacks to life on dry land.
w Natto Wada, based on the experiences of Kenichi Horie d Kon Ichikawa ph Yoshihiro Yamazaki m Yasushi Akatagawa, Tohru Takemitsu
☆ Yujiro Ishihara, Masayuki Mori, Kinuyo Tanaka, Ruriko Asaoko
'Wonderfully comic moments emerge, but they never overshadow the film's sheer pictorial value.' – *Brenda Davies, MFB*

Alone With a Stranger
US 1999 90m FotoKem
WIN (Pierre David, Noël A. Zanitsch, Ken Sanders)
When a man discovers that he has a wealthy and successful twin brother, he decides to take over his life and family.
Trivial and unconvincing thriller with a script that makes little sense.
w Peter Liapis, Richard Dana Smith d Peter Liapis ph M. David Mullen m Alan Howarth pd Helen Harwell ed Bernard Gribble
☆ William R. Moses (James/Max Kennington), Barbara Niven (Sandy Kennington), Priscilla Barnes (Claire), Scotty Cox (David Kennington), Aleksandra Vujcic (Lena), Mindy Cohn (Toni), Nia Peeples (Beth)

'The game is far from over.'
Along Came A Spider
US 2001 104m DeLuxe Panavision
Paramount/David Brown/Phase I/Revelations
A detective investigates the kidnapping of a senator's daughter from school by a media-obsessed teacher.
Involved, but uninvolving, thriller with a predictable paranoid twist to it.
w Marc Moss novel James Patterson d Lee Tamahori ph Matthew F. Leonetti m Jerry Goldsmith pd Ida Random ed Neil Travis cos Sanja Milkovic Hays
☆ Morgan Freeman (Alex Cross), Monica Potter (Jezzie Flannigan), Michael Wincott (Gary Soneji), Dylan Baker (Ollie McArthur), Mika Boorem (Megan Rose), Dimitri Starodubov (Anton Yelchin), Kim Hawthorne (Agent Hickley), Jay O. Sanders (Kyle Craig), Billy Burke (Ben Devine), Michael Moriarty (Senator Hank Rose), Penelope Ann Miller (Elizabeth Rose)
'Weaves a humdrum plot that's never ahead of the audience until three-quarters through.' – *Robert Koehler, Variety*
† Morgan Freeman also played the role of detective Alex Cross in the 1997 movie *Kiss the Girls* (qv).

Along Came Jones *
US 1945 90m bw
UA/Cinema Artists Corporation (Gary Cooper)
Two cowboys are mistaken for killers.
Very mild Western comedy melodrama, with the star at his most self-effacing and production only mediocre.
w Nunnally Johnson novel Alan le May d Stuart Heisler ph Milton Krasner m Charles Maxwell, Arthur Lange, Hugo Friedhofer
☆ Gary Cooper, Loretta Young, William Demarest, Dan Duryea, Russell Simpson

Along the Great Divide
US 1950 88m bw
Warner (Anthony Veiller)
A marshal prevents an old man from being hanged for murder, and eventually discovers the real culprit.
Adequate, modest Western with an unusual detective element.
w Walter Doniger, Lewis Meltzer d Raoul Walsh ph Sid Hickox m David Buttolph
☆ Kirk Douglas, Virginia Mayo, Walter Brennan, John Agar, Ray Teal
'It was awful. I hated the whole picture.' – *Kirk Douglas*

Along the Rio Grande
US 1941 64m bw
RKO (Bert Gilroy)
A cowboy and his two friends claim to be bank robbers to bring to justice a cattle rustler and outlaw.
Cheerful but unexceptional Western.
w Arthur V. Jones, Morton Grant story Stuart Anthony d Edward Killy ph Frank Redman m Paul Sawtell ad Van Nest Polglase ed Frederic Knudtson
☆ Tim Holt, Ray Whitley, Betty Jane Rhodes, Emmett Lynn, Robert Fiske, Hal Taliaferro

Alphabet City
US 1984 85m colour
Atlantic (Andrew Braunsberg)
A New York drug dealer decides it is time to go straight, providing he can pay his debts and stay alive.
Introspective, atmospheric low-life drama that is short on action.
w Amos Poe, Gregory Heller d Amos Poe ph Oliver Wood m Nile Rogers ad Stephen Lineweaver ed Grahame Weinbren
☆ Vincent Spano, Michael Winslow, Kate Vernon, Jami Gertz, Zohra Lampert, Raymond Serra, Kenny Marino

The Alphabet Murders
GB 1965 90m bw
MGM (Ben Arbeid)
Hercule Poirot solves a series of murders by an apparent lunatic choosing his victims in alphabetical order.
Ruination of a classic whodunnit novel, misguided both in its attempt to mix slapstick with detection and in its terrible central performance.
w David Pursall, Jack Seddon novel *The ABC Murders* by Agatha Christie d Frank Tashlin ph Desmond Dickinson m Ron Goodwin ed John Victor Smith
☆ Tony Randall (Hercule Poirot), Robert Morley (Hastings), Anita Ekberg (Amanda Beatrice Cross), Maurice Denham (Japp), Guy Rolfe (Duncan Doncaster), James Villiers (Franklin), Clive Morton (X), Sheila Allen (Lady Diane), Margaret Rutherford (Miss Marple)

Alphaville *
France/Italy 1965 98m bw
Chaumiane/Filmstudio (André Michelin)

A special agent travels across space to find out what happened to his predecessor, and finds himself in a loveless society.
A rather chill futuristic fantasy on the lines of 1984 but with an outer space background and a hero borrowed from Peter Cheyney. Interesting but not endearing.
wd Jean-Luc Godard *ph* Raoul Coutard *m* Paul Misraki
☆ Eddie Constantine, Anna Karina, Akim Tamiroff, Howard Vernon, Laszlo Szabo
'One surrenders to an experience which is the more disturbing for being so near the recognisable normal.' – *Dilys Powell*

Alpine Fire **
Switzerland 1985 117m colour
Electric/SRG/WDR/Rex/Bernard Lang
original title: *Höhenfeuer*
A sister and her deaf-mute brother, isolated on an Alpine farm, embark on an incestuous relationship.
Unsensational and austere, it creates an atmosphere all its own.
wd Fredi M. Murer *novel* Fredi M. Murer *ph* Pio Corradi *m* Mario Beretta *ed* Helena Gerber
☆ Thomas Nock, Johanna Lier, Dorothea Moritz, Rolf Illig, Tilli Breidenbach, Joerg Odermatt

Älskande Par: see *Loving Couples*

Altered States *
US 1980 102m Technicolor
Warner/Howard Gottfried, Daniel Melnick

A psychophysiologist uses a sensory deprivation tank to hallucinate himself back into primitive states of human evolution, in which guise he emerges to kill…
Amusing elaboration of Jekyll and Hyde (qv), not to mention the Karloff mad doctor second features of the forties. All very po-faced now, and certainly impeccably done.
w Sidney Aaron (Paddy Chayefsky) *novel* Paddy Chayefsky *d* *Ken Russell* *ph* Jordan Cronenweth *m* John Corigliano *pd* Richard McDonald
☆ William Hurt, Blair Brown, Bob Balaban, Charles Haid
'Russell clomps from one scene to the next, the psychedelic visions come at you like choppy slide shows, and the picture has a dismal, tired, humanistic ending.' – *Pauline Kael, New Yorker*
'A feast for special effects lovers and drugged philosophy majors only.' – *Roger Ebert*
John Corigliano

'A herd of cattle against a herd of cannon!'
Alvarez Kelly
US 1966 116m Technicolor Panavision
Columbia/Ray David (Sol C. Siegel)

The owner of a herd of 2500 cattle finds himself between two sides in the American Civil War.
Unusual if rather tepid Western which balances historical interest against social conscience and throws in a variety of other elements.
w Franklin Coen *d* Edward Dmytryk *ph* Joseph MacDonald *m* John Green
☆ William Holden, Richard Widmark, Janice Rule, Patrick O'Neal, Victoria Shaw, Roger C. Carmel, Richard Rust
'One of the soppiest and sloppiest of Civil War cow-operas to have come our way in years.' – *Judith Crist*

Alvin Purple
Australia 1973 97m colour
Hexagon (Tim Burstall)
A young man who finds himself irresistible to women finally lands a job … as gardener in a convent.
Dismal sex farce which nevertheless helped to start the present world-wide popularity of Australian cinema. It took over a million dollars at the Australian box-office.
w Alan Hopgood *d* Tim Burstall
☆ Graeme Blundell, Abigail, Lynette Curran, Christine Amor, Dina Mann
† A sequel *Alvin Rides Again* (qv) followed.

Alvin Rides Again
Australia 1974 89m colour
Hexagon (Tim Burstall)
Alvin continues to be irresistible to women.
Dire sequel to dim comedy, but one that failed to find an appreciative audience.
w Alan Hopgood *d* David Bilcock, Robin Copping
☆ Graeme Blundell, Alan Finney, Frank Thring, Chantal Contouri, Abigail

Always *
US 1989 123m DeLuxe
UIP/Amblin/Steven Spielberg, Frank Marshall, Kathleen Kennedy

A dead pilot returns as a ghost to aid a romance between another flyer and his girl-friend.
Sentimental remake of the 1944 movie A Guy Named Joe (qv).
w Jerry Belson, Diane Thomas *d* Steven Spielberg *ph* Mikael Salomon *m* John Williams *pd* James Bissell *ed* Michael Kahn
☆ Richard Dreyfuss, Holly Hunter, Brad Johnson, John Goodman, Audrey Hepburn, Roberts Blossom, Keith David, Ed Van Nuys

Always Goodbye
US 1938 75m bw
TCF (Raymond Griffith)
An unwed mother gives up her baby and later wants it back.
Tired sentimental warhorse, a remake of Gallant Lady (qv).
w Kathryn Scola, Edith Skouras *d* Sidney Lanfield *ph* Robert Planck *md* Louis Silvers
☆ Barbara Stanwyck, Herbert Marshall, Ian Hunter, Cesar Romero, Lynn Bari, Binnie Barnes
'A fair summer attraction … should do satisfactorily on the strength of its cast.' – *Variety*

Always in My Heart *
US 1942 92m bw
Warner (Walter McEwen, William Jacobs)
A convict returns home to find his daughter a stranger and his wife about to marry again.
Well acted sentimental drama.
w Adele Commandini *play* *Fly Away Home* by Dorothy Bennett, Irving White *d* Jo Graham *ph* Sid Hickox *m* Heinz Roemheld
☆ Walter Huston, Kay Francis, Gloria Warren, Frankie Thomas, Sidney Blackmer, Una O'Connor
title song (*m* Ernest Lecuona, *ly* Kim Gannon)

Always Leave Them Laughing *
US 1949 116m bw
Warner (Jerry Wald)
A vaudeville comedian craves the spotlight at the expense of his private life.
Raucous backstage vehicle, crammed with sentimental and melodramatic cliché but affording tantalizing glimpses of the stage acts of its two stars.
w Jack Rose, Mel Shavelson *d* Roy del Ruth *ph* Ernest Haller *md* Ray Heindorf *ed* Clarence Kolster *ly* Sammy Cahn
☆ Milton Berle, Bert Lahr, Virginia Mayo, Ruth Roman, Alan Hale, Jerome Cowan

Always Together *
US 1947 78m bw
Warner
Dying millionaire bequeaths his all to a working girl, then recovers and tries to retrieve it.
Oddball comedy about a girl who has film fantasies, killed by dull title.
w Henry and Phoebe Ephron, I. A. L. Diamond *d* Frederick de Cordova
☆ Joyce Reynolds, Robert Hutton, Cecil Kellaway, Ernest Truex, Errol Flynn (cameo), Humphrey Bogart (cameo)

Ama
GB 1991 100m colour
Artificial Eye/Efiri Tete (Kwesi Owusu, Kwate Nee-Owoo)
A young girl, who learns by means of a computer disk that she is an ancestral messenger of the Asante, is warned that disaster will overtake her brother and father unless they change their plans.
Confused story, overloaded with fantasy, of Africans living unhappily in London.
w Kwesi Owusu *d* Kwesi Owusu, Kwate Nee-Owoo *ph* Jonathan Collinson, Roy Cornwall *m* Kwesi Owusu, Vico Mensah *ad* Ruhi Chaudry, Nigel Ashby, Keith Khan *ed* Justin Hrish
☆ Thomas Baptiste, Anima Misa, Roger Griffiths, Nii Oma Hunter, Joy Elias Rilwan, Georgina Ackerman
'The film's nostalgia for the past, like all forms of sentimentality, implies an unwillingness to engage in reality.' – *Sight and Sound*

'The Man … The Music … The Madness … The Murder … The Motion Picture … Everything you've heard is true.'
Amadeus ***
US 1984 160m Technicolor Panavision
Saul Zaentz

Dying in 1823, the jealous composer Salieri claims to have murdered Mozart.
A musical legend performed with success and economy on stage now becomes an exciting baroque film, like an opera in high-pitched dialogue. Great to look at, and only the American accents jar the ear.
w *Peter Shaffer* *play* Peter Shaffer *d* *Milos Forman* *ph* *Miroslav Ondricek* *md* Neville Marriner *pd* *Patrizia Van Brandenstein* *ed* Nena Danevic, Michael Chandler
☆ F. Murray Abraham, Tom Hulce, Elizabeth Berridge, Simon Callow, Roy Dotrice, Christine Ebersole
picture; direction; F. Murray Abraham; adapted screenplay; make-up
Tom Hulce; photography; editing; art direction
Miroslav Ondricek

'She gave her innocence, her passion, her body. The one thing she couldn't give was her love.'
L'Amant *
GB/France 1992 115m colour
Guild/A2/Burrill/Giai Phong Film (Claude Berri, Timothy Burrill)

aka: *The Lover*
A 15-year-old French girl in Vietnam begins an obsessive affair with a wealthy Chinese man.
Lushly romantic drama that exerts a certain charm.
w Gérard Brach, Jean-Jacques Annaud *novel* Marguerite Duras *d* Jean-Jacques Annaud *ph* Robert Fraisse *m* Gabriel Yared *ad* Thanh At Hoang *ed* Noëlle Boisson
☆ Jane March, Tony Leung, Frédérique Meininger, Arnaud Giovaninetti, Melvil Poupaud, Lisa Faulkner, Jeanne Moreau (narrator)
'Lacks the distinctive voice and ambiance of the book, but the abundant sex – soft-core and tasteful – and the splendid sets make up for the film's banal style.' – *Variety*
'Duras's subtle portrait of festering colonialism is brought to the screen with some resource by Annaud … But neither Leung nor March, given a difficult role in her first film and certainly looking more fetching than she sounds, can provide a truly holding centre.' – *Derek Malcolm, Guardian*
'Touching, clear-eyed, utterly unsentimental, produced lavishly but with such discipline that the exotic locale never gets in the way of the minutely detailed drama at the center.' – *Vincent Canby, New York Times*
Robert Fraisse

Amantes: see *Lovers*

Amanti d'Oltretomba: see *Night of the Doomed*

Les Amants **
France 1958 88m bw Dyaliscope
Nouvelles Editions (Louis Malle)

aka: *The Lovers*
A rich provincial wife has a secret life in Paris, but finds real satisfaction in an affair with a young man.
A passionate romance which had some censorship difficulties at the time, this rather gloomy film never quite whirls one away as it should, and it doesn't have the eye for detail of Brief Encounter.
w Louis Malle, Louise de Vilmorin *novel* *Point de Lendemain* by Dominique Vivant *d* Louis Malle *ph* Henri Decaë *m* Brahms *ad* Jacques Saulnier, Bernard Evein *ed* Léonide Azar
☆ Jeanne Moreau, Alain Cuny, Jean-Marc Bory, Judith Magre

Les Amants de Montparnasse: see *The Lovers of Montparnasse*

Les Amants de Vérone *
France 1948 110m bw
CICC (Raymond Borderie)
aka: *The Lovers of Verona*
In modern Venice a film is being made of *Romeo and Juliet*, and the stand-ins for the stars feel they are re-enacting the old story.
A superbly stylish if rather empty piece, the dazzling detail being much more interesting than the main story.
w André Cayatte, Jacques Prévert *d* *André Cayatte* *ph* Henri Alekan *m* Joseph Kosma *ad* Moulaert
☆ *Pierre Brasseur*, Serge Reggiani, Anouk Aimée, Louis Salou, Marcel Dalio
'Visually exciting, immaculately made.' – *Penelope Houston*

Les Amants du Pont-Neuf
France 1991 125m colour
Artificial Eye/Christian Fechner

aka: *Lovers on the Pont-Neuf*
An artist, who fears she is going blind, takes to the streets and ends up on the Pont-Neuf, inhabited by an old tramp and a young fire-eating drop-out, with whom she has an affair.
An anti-romantic love story: grim, grey and ultimately boring with its uninteresting characters upstaged by the locations.
wd Leos Carax *ph* Jean-Yves Escoffier *m* Benjamin Britten, Johann Strauss and others *ad* Michael Vandestien *ed* Nelly Quettier
☆ Juliette Binoche, Denis Lavant, Klaus-Michael Gruber
'Neo-Godardian new wave: lazy in script, crazy in characterisation, wilfully disjunctive but undeniably powerful in performance and visual panache.' – *Ian Johnstone, Sunday Times*
'One of the most visually exhilarating and surprising films of recent years, a true "cinema of attractions" with music, colour, dazzling camerawork, melodramatic coincidences and tour de force performances.' – *Ginette Vincendeau, Sight and Sound*
'One has to admire the audacity, even if the result could be considered mere flim-flam.' – *Derek Malcolm, Guardian*
† The film, originally budgeted at 32 million francs (£3.2 million), became one of the most expensive of French films; its cost soared to between 100–160 million francs (£10–16 million) owing to building an elaborate set recreating the Pont-Neuf and its environs.

Les Amants du Tage: see *The Lovers of Lisbon*

Amarcord **
Italy/France 1973 123m Technicolor
FC Produzione/PECF (Franco Cristaldi)

Memories of a small Italian town during the fascist period.
A bizarre, intriguing mixture of fact, fantasy and obscurity, generally pleasing to watch though hardly satisfying. The title means 'I remember'.
w Federico Fellini, Tonino Guerra *d* *Federico Fellini* *ph* Giuseppe Rotunno *m* *Nino Rota* *ad* Danilo Donati
☆ Pupella Maggio, Magali Noel, Armando Brancia, Ciccio Ingrassia
'A rich surface texture and a sense of exuberant melancholia.' – *Michael Billington, Illustrated London News*
'Peaks of invention separated by raucous valleys of low comedy.' – *Sight and Sound*
'Some idea of attitudes within the film business may be conveyed by the fact that this witty, tender, humane, marvellously photographed picture has been booked into a cinema with 132 seats.' – *Benny Green, Punch*
'Hitchcock once said that he wanted to play his audiences like a piano. Fellini requires the entire orchestra.' – *Roger Ebert*
foreign film
script; direction

The Amateur
US 1981 111m Technicolor
TCF/Joel B. Michaels, Garth B. Drabinsky

A computer expert goes into action on his own account when his girlfriend is killed in the Munich consulate and the CIA takes no reprisals.

Ho-hum espionage adventure which has its moments but barely got released.
w Robert Littell, Diana Maddox *novel* Robert Littell *d* Charles Jarrott *ph* John Coquillon *m* Ken Wannberg
☆ John Savage, Christopher Plummer, Marthe Keller, Arthur Hill, Ed Lauter
'Ill constructed and largely implausible, with occasional atmospheric touches.' – *Guardian*

Amateur **
US/France 1994 105m colour
UGC/Zenith/True Fiction (Ted Hope, Hal Hartley)
A former nun turned pornographer helps an amnesiac crook discover who he really is, a search that involves sex, violence and death.
Enjoyably downbeat thriller that prefers philosophical asides to shoot-outs, though it manages to encompass both.
wd Hal Hartley ph Michael Spiller *m* Ned Rifle, Jeffrey Taylor *pd* Steve Rosenzweig *ed* Steven Hamilton
☆ Isabelle Huppert, Martin Donovan, Elina Lowensohn, Damian Young, Pamela Stewart, David Simmonds, Chuck Montgomery
'He's an acquired taste, but the new film has a warmth, humour and humanity that might please even hostile palates.' – *Sheila Johnston, Independent*

Amateur Daddy
US 1932 71m bw
Fox
A promise to a dying friend leaves a construction engineer with four orphans to look after.
Sentimental drama of the Daddy Longlegs school, with backwoods atmosphere which makes it seem even more dated than it is.
w William Conselman, Doris Malloy and Frank Dolan *novel Scotch Valley* by Mildred Cram *d* John Blystone
☆ Warner Baxter, Marian Nixon, Rita LaRoy, William Pawley, David Landau
'Strikes a strong human interest note ... more than often very agreeable entertainment.' – *Variety*

The Amateur Gentleman *
GB 1936 102m bw
Criterion (Marcel Hellman, Douglas Fairbanks Jnr)
A Regency innkeeper's son poses as a travelling pugilist in order to clear his father's name of theft.
Dated but rather fascinating period adventure, quite a lively production of its time.
w Clemence Dane, Edward Knoblock, Sergei Nolbandov *novel* Jeffrey Farnol *d* Thornton Freeland *ph* Gunther Krampf *m* Richard Addinsell
☆ Douglas Fairbanks Jnr, Elissa Landi, Gordon Harker, Basil Sydney, Hugh Williams, Irene Browne, Margaret Lockwood, Coral Browne, Frank Pettingell, Athole Stewart, Esmé Percy

Amator: see *Camera Buff*

Amazing Adventure: see *The Amazing Quest of Ernest Bliss*

The Amazing Captain Nemo
US 1978 103m colour
Warner
Underwater explosions in 1978 release Captain Nemo and his submarine from a hundred years of suspended animation; he continues his search for the lost continent of Atlantis while helping US naval intelligence agents deal with a mad scientist.
Moderate adventure story that may keep the young quiet for a time, though it lacks any big thrills.
w Norman Katkov, Preston Wood, Robert C. Dennis, William Keys, Mann Rubin, Robert Bloch, Larry Alexander *d* Alex March *ph* Lamar Boren *m* Richard LaSalle *ad* Eugene Lourie, Duane Alt *ed* Bill Brame
☆ José Ferrer, Burgess Meredith, Tom Hallick, Burr Debenning, Lynda Day George, Mel Ferrer, Richard Angarola, Horst Buchholz

'Growing! growing! growing! When will it stop?'
The Amazing Colossal Man *
US 1957 80m bw
AIP/Malibu (Bert I. Gordon)
GB title: *The Terror Strikes*
A plutonium explosion causes an army colonel to grow at the rate of ten feet a day.
Modest, quite well written sci-fi let down by shaky trick work.
w Bert I. Gordon, Mark Hanna *d* Bert I. Gordon *ph* Joe Biroc *m* Albert Glasser
☆ Glenn Langan, Cathy Downs, William Hudson, James Seay
† Sequel: *War of the Colossal Beast* (qv).

The Amazing Dobermans
US 1977 96m colour
Golden (David Chudnow)
A con man with five trained dogs helps a treasury agent get the better of a gangster.
So-so doggedly doggy comedy.
w Michael Kraike, William Goldstein, Richard Chapman *d* Byron Chudnow *ph* Gregory Sandor *m* Alan Silvestri *ed* James Potter
☆ Fred Astaire, James Franciscus, Barbara Eden, Jack Carter, Billy Barty, Parley Baer

The Amazing Dr Clitterhouse **
US 1938 87m bw
Warner (Robert Lord)
A criminologist researcher joins a gangster's mob and becomes addicted to crime.
Amusing, suspenseful, well acted comedy-melodrama.
w John Huston, John Wexley *play* Barre Lyndon *d* Anatole Litvak *ph* Tony Gaudio *m* Max Steiner
☆ *Edward G. Robinson*, Humphrey Bogart, Claire Trevor, Allen Jenkins, Gale Page, Donald Crisp, Maxie Rosenbloom
'An unquestionable winner ... the picture inculcates a bit of the sherlocking theme and modified romance.' – *Variety*
'The story is ingenious, but Anatole Litvak and his producing-acting crew have so thoroughly kept the larky mood of it while setting up the necessary mood of interest and suspense that it is hard to see where conception leaves off and the shaping of it into motion begins.' – *Otis Ferguson*

The Amazing Dr X
US 1948 78m bw
Eagle-Lion (Ben Stoloff)
GB title: *The Spiritualist*
A widow seeks comfort from a fraudulent medium.
An interesting subject for a thriller is muffed by naïve handling.
w Muriel Roy Bolton, Ian McLellan Hunter *story* Crane Wilbur *d* Bernard Vorhaus *ph* John Alton *m* Alexander Laszlo
☆ Lynn Bari, Richard Carlson, Turhan Bey, Cathy O'Donnell

Amazing Grace and Chuck
US 1987 115m colour
Tri-Star/Rastar (David Field)
GB title: *Silent Voice*
On both sides of the Iron Curtain, a weird selection of public personalities stand up in favour of the elimination of nuclear weapons.
Expensive but inept propaganda apparently motivated by Ted Turner.
w David Field *d* Mike Newell *ph* Robert Elswit *m* Elmer Bernstein *pd* Dena Roth *ed* Peter Hollywood
☆ Jamie Lee Curtis, Alex English, Gregory Peck, William L. Petersen, Joshua Zuehike
'As amazingly bad as it is audacious.' – *Daily Variety*

The Amazing Mr Beecham: see *The Chiltern Hundreds*

The Amazing Mr Blunden **
GB 1972 99m Eastmancolor
Hemdale/Hemisphere (Barry Levinson)
In 1918, a widow and her two children meet a kindly gentleman who offers them work in his old mansion. Here they meet two ghost children, discover that he is a ghost too, and travel a hundred years back in time to right a wicked wrong.
Involved ghost story for intellectual children, made generally palatable by oodles of period charm and good acting.
wd Lionel Jeffries story The Ghosts by Antonia Baker *ph* Gerry Fisher *m* Elmer Bernstein *pd* Wilfrid Shingleton
☆ Laurence Naismith, Diana Dors, James Villiers, David Lodge, Lynne Frederick, Dorothy Alison, Rosalyn Lander, Marc Granger
'Easy period charm ... fills every crevice.' – *Clyde Jeavons*

The Amazing Mr Forrest: see *The Gang's All Here (1939)*

The Amazing Mr Williams *
US 1939 86m bw
Columbia (Everett Riskin)
About-to-be-marrieds investigate a murder.
Brisk comedy-thriller on Thin Man lines.
w Dwight Taylor, Sy Bartlett, Richard Maibaum *d* Alexander Hall *ph* Arthur Todd *md* Morris Stoloff
☆ Melvyn Douglas, Joan Blondell, Ruth Donnelly, Clarence Kolb, Ed Brophy, Donald MacBride, Don Beddoe

The Amazing Mrs Holliday
US 1943 98m bw
Universal (Bruce Manning, Frank Shaw)
Torpedoed in mid-Pacific, a missionary's daughter arrives in San Francisco with eight Chinese orphans.
Unusual sentimental vehicle for its star; of no particular interest or merit in itself, but with the usual interludes for song.
w Frank Ryan, John Jacoby *d* Bruce Manning *ph* Elwood Bredell *m* Hans Salter, Frank Skinner *md* Charles Previn *ed* Ted J. Kent
☆ Deanna Durbin, Edmond O'Brien, Frieda Inescort, Barry Fitzgerald, Arthur Treacher, Harry Davenport, Grant Mitchell
'Timely drama with human interest angles.' – *Variety*
Hans Salter, Frank Skinner

The Amazing Panda Adventure
US 1995 84m Technicolor Panavision
Warner (Lee Rich, John Wilcox, Gary Foster, Dylan Sellers)
An American boy and a Chinese girl help save a baby panda and its nature reserve in China.
Inoffensively bland entertainment that may appeal to those who still take a teddy bear to bed with them.
w Jeff Rothberg, Laurice Elehwany *story* John Wilcox, Steven Allredge *d* Christopher Cain *ph* Jack N. Green *m* William Ross *pd* John Willett *ed* Jack Hofstra *sp* panda effects: Rick Baker
☆ Stephen Lang, Ryan Slater, Yi Ding, Huang Fei
'Harmless family fare might be deemed politically correct for its concern for endangered species, but whitewashing of Chinese regime will strike adults aware of current events as somewhat bizarre.' – *Variety*

The Amazing Quest of Ernest Bliss
GB 1936 63m bw
UA/Garrett-Klement (Alfred Zeisler)
aka: *The Amazing Adventure*
aka: *Romance and Riches*
A millionaire bets that he can rise to the top from his job as a chauffeur without using his wealth.
Mild comedy that depends on Cary Grant's charm to carry it through.
w John L. Balderston *novel* E. Phillips Oppenheim *d* Alfred Zeisler *ph* Otto Heller *ad* David Rawnsley *ed* Merrill White
☆ Cary Grant, Mary Brian, Henry Kendall, Leon M. Lion, Ralph Richardson

Amazon Women on the Moon
US 1987 85m colour
Universal (Robert K. Weiss)
A parody of a 1950s low-budget science fiction movie is interrupted by a series of supposedly comic sketches.
While the parody is precise and amusing, the surrounding material, which occupies the majority of the film, is weak and silly.
w Michael Barrie, Jim Mulholland *d* Joe Dante, Carl Gottlieb, Peter Horton, John Landis, Robert K. Weiss *ph* Daniel Pearl *ed* Bert Lovitt, Marshall Harvey, Malcolm Campbell
☆ Rosanna Arquette, Ralph Bellamy, Carrie Fisher, Griffin Dunne, Steve Guttenberg, Michelle Pfeiffer

The Ambassador
US 1984 95m TVC Color
Cannon/Northbrook (Isaac Kol)
An American ambassador to Israel gets in the line of fire with the Arabs; meanwhile his wife is having an affair with a man who is secretly a leader of the PLO.
Aged stars go gloomily through some tasteless paces in this politically unwise pseudo-thriller.
w Max Jack *novel 52 Pick Up* by Elmore Leonard *d* J. Lee Thompson *ph* Avi Karpik, Ofer Yanov, Rami Siman Tov *m* Dov Seltzer
☆ Robert Mitchum, Ellen Burstyn, Rock Hudson, Fabio Testi, Donald Pleasence
'Not wild enough to be funny.' – *Sight and Sound*
† Not much more than a year later, the original novel was filmed under its own title in its original setting (qv).

Ambassador Bill
US 1931 68m bw
Fox
An Oklahoma cattle man is appointed US ambassador to a foreign country ruled by a regency.
Poorly tailored star vehicle.
w Guy Bolton *story* Vincent Sheean *d* Sam Taylor
☆ Will Rogers, Marguerite Churchill, Greta Nissen, Gustav von Seyffertitz, Ray Milland
'Wilting yarn, illogical hoke.' – *Variety*

The Ambassador's Daughter *
US 1956 102m Technicolor Cinemascope
UA/Norman Krasna
An American senator in Paris decides that the presence of US forces in Paris constitutes a moral danger. The ambassador's daughter decides to investigate.
Thin comedy of the old-fashioned type: smart lines and intimate playing not helped by the vast screen.
wd Norman Krasna *ph* Miche Kelber *m* Jacques Metehen
☆ Olivia de Havilland, John Forsythe, Edward Arnold, Adolphe Menjou, Myrna Loy, Francis Lederer, Tommy Noonan, Minor Watson
'An experienced cast approach the story's frivolities with poise and style.' – *MFB*

The Ambulance
US 1990 95m DeLuxe Panavision
Epic/Sarlui/Diamant (Moctesuma Esparza, Robert Katz)
Aided by an old reporter, a photographer investigates the disappearance of people from the streets of New York.
Absurd thriller, with rather better acting than it deserves.
wd Larry Cohen *ph* Jacques Haitkin *m* Jay Chattaway *pd* Lester Cohen *ed* Arnold Lebowitz, Claudia Finkle
☆ Eric Roberts, James Earl Jones, Megan Gallagher, Richard Bright, Janine Turner, Eric Braeden, Red Buttons
'A seamless thriller with top-notch thrills.' – *Empire*

Ambush *
US 1938 62m bw
Paramount
A girl proves her brother innocent and brings gangsters to book.
Brisk second feature with an unexpected writing credit.
w S. J. and Laura Perelman *d* Kurt Neumann
☆ Gladys Swarthout, Lloyd Nolan, Ernest Truex
'Hard hitting, fast moving and at all times plausible.' – *Variety*

Ambush *
US 1949 89m bw
MGM (Armand Deutsch)
An army scout leads a posse to capture an Indian chief who is holding a white woman hostage.

Good, clean, robust Western, well produced and acted.
w Marguerite Roberts *d* Sam Wood *ph* Harold Lipstein *m* Rudolph Kopp
☆ Robert Taylor, John Hodiak, Arlene Dahl, Don Taylor, Jean Hagen, Leon Ames

'One man against the west!'
Ambush at Tomahawk Gap
US 1953 73m Technicolor
Columbia (Wallace MacDonald)

Four ex-convicts seek hidden loot in a ghost town.
Standard co-feature Western with rather more violence than usual for its date.
w David Lang *d* Fred F. Sears *ph* Henry Freulich *m* Ross Di Maggio
☆ John Hodiak, John Derek, David Brian, Maria Elena Marques, Ray Teal, John Qualen

Ambush Bay
US 1966 109m DeLuxe
UA/Aubrey Schenck
In 1944, nine Marines try to escape from a Japanese-held island.
Routine, lengthy, sub-standard heroics for action addicts.
w Marve Feinberg, Ib Melchior *d* Ron Winston *ph* Emanuel Rojas *m* Richard La Salle
☆ Hugh O'Brian, Mickey Rooney, James Mitchum, Tisa Chang, Harry Lauter

The Ambushers
US 1967 102m Technicolor
Columbia/Meadway/Claude (Irving Allen)

An experimental flying disc disappears on a test run, and the trail leads Matt Helm to the Mexican jungle.
The third Matt Helm adventure had such a stupid script that all concerned decided to send it up, unfortunately with too obvious a tendency to smirk at their own bravado.
w Herbert Baker *d* Henry Levin *ph* Burnett Guffey, Edward Colman *m* Hugo Montenegro
☆ Dean Martin, Senta Berger, Janice Rule, Kurt Kasznar, James Gregory, Albert Salmi
'Plot, jokes and gadgets all well below par.' – *MFB*

Amélie: see *Le Fabuleux Destin d'Amélie Poulain*

Amen *
France/Germany 2002 132m colour
Pathé/Katharina/Renn/TF1/Canal+/KC Medien (Claude Berri)
A Catholic priest attemps to help a Nazi officer inform the Pope about the extermination of Jews in concentration camps.
Mixing fact – the efforts of the real-life SS officer Kurt Gerstein to stop the Nazi death-camps – and fiction, in the person of the eager priest with access to the Pope, this is a slick, flawed thriller that might have been better had it stuck to the facts; but at least it raises some important questions.
w Costa-Gavras, Jean Claude- Grumberg *play The Representative* by Rolf Hochhuth *d* Costa-Gavras *ph* Patrick Blossier *m* Armand Amar *pd* Ari Hantke *ed* Yannick Kergoat
☆ Ulrich Tukur (Kurt Gerstein), Mathieu Kassovitz (Riccardo Fontana), Ulrich Muhe (The Doctor), Michel Duchaussoy (The Cardinal), Ion Caramitru (Count Fontana), Marcel Iures (The Pope), Friedrich von Thun (Gerstein's Father), Antje Schmidt (Mrs Gerstein)
'Repetitious, crudely dramatized, and awkwardly acted—in English, which seems to be the second or third language of everyone involved.' – *David Edelstein, Slate*
† Kurt Gerstein was arrested by the Allies and died, either by his own hand or at the hands of others, while in custody. His name was cleared in 1965, when it was acknowledged that he had done much to document Nazi atrocities and to try to prevent them.

'Love of tender girlhood! Passionate deeds of heroes! A rushing, leaping drama of charm and excitement!'
America *
US 1924 122m (24 fps) bw silent (UA)

Various characters experience the Revolutionary War.
The Birth of a Nation, one war back. Much of interest, but nothing new; Griffith was basically repeating himself.
w John Pell *d D. W. Griffith ph* Billy Bitzer, Hendrick Sartow, Marcel le Picard, Hal Sintzenich
☆ Neil Hamilton, Carol Dempster, Lionel Barrymore, Erville Alderson
'Here is the romance of one hundred million people, told in heartthrobs!' – *D. W. Griffith*
† As the English were the villains, the film was banned in Britain, but later released under the title *Love and Sacrifice.*

America, America *
US 1963 177m bw
Warner/Athena Enterprises (Elia Kazan)

GB title: *The Anatolian Smile*
In 1896 Turkey, a young Greek dreams of emigrating to America, and finally does so.
A massive piece of self-indulgence by a one-man band, fascinating for his family circle but so poorly constructed as to be of very limited interest elsewhere.
wd Elia Kazan *ph* Haskell Wexler *m* Manos Hadjidakis
☆ Stathis Giallelis, Frank Wolff, Harry Davis, Elena Karam, Estelle Hemsley, Lou Antonio
'Kazan has failed to film the adventure implicit in his material, and a potentially exciting story has gone to waste.' – *MFB*
'If he sinks his teeth in a scene or a sequence that he enjoys, the audience can just sit around and be damned.' – *Stanley Kauffmann*
'Every episode, almost every shot, has its own beginning, middle and end, and the numberless playlets are cemented together into a strip which after the first two hours threatens to stretch grimly into eternity.' – *Robert Hatch, The Nation*
picture; Elia Kazan (as writer); Elia Kazan (as director)

The American Beauty: see *La Belle Américaine*

'...look closer'
American Beauty ****
US 1999 122m Technicolor Panavision
DreamWorks (Bruce Cohen, Dan Jinks)

A dying suburban husband and father reviews his life and the events that led to his murder.
A terrific, biting comedy of a man dealing, in an adolescent way, with a midlife crisis and the aridities of the life he and those around him are living; it manages not only to expose the inanities of a conformist society, but also to suggest an alternative, in the small pleasures that existence affords. There is not a false note in either the acting or the direction.
w Alan Ball d Sam Mendes ph Conrad L. Hall m Thomas Newman *pd* Naomi Shohan *ed* Tariq Anwar, Christopher Greenbury
☆ *Kevin Spacey* (Lester Burnham), *Annette Bening* (Carolyn Burnham), Thora Birch (Jane Burnham), Wes Bentley (Ricky Fitts), Mena Suvari (Angela Hayes), Peter Gallagher (Buddy Kane), Allison Janney (Barbara Fitts), Scott Bakula (Jim Olmeyer), Sam Robards (Jim Berkley), Chris Cooper (Colonel Fitts)
'A film of incredible flair and formal, compositional brilliance.' – *Peter Bradshaw, Guardian*
'An acerbic, darkly comic critique of how social conventions can lead people into false, sterile and emotionally stunted lives.' – *Todd McCarthy, Variety*
'The picture is a con. Can't educated liberals see that it sucks up to them at every plot turn?' – *Pauline Kael*
† The film cost $15m to make and took $277m at the box office world wide.
picture; Kevin Spacey; Sam Mendes; Alan Ball; Conrad L. Hall
Annette Bening; Thomas Newman; Tariq Anwar, Christopher Greenbury
picture; Annette Bening; Kevin Spacey; Conrad L. Hall; Tariq Anwar, Christopher Greenbury; Thomas Newman

American Blue Note *
US 1989 97m Technicolor
Vested Interests/Fakebook (Ralph Toporoff)

aka: *Fakebook*
In the 1960s the leader of a jazz quintet struggles to find an audience for his music.
Gentle, well-observed off-beat film with a sense of humour.
w Gilbert Girion *d* Ralph Toporoff *ph* Joey Forsyte *m* Larry Schanker *pd* Charles Lagola *ed* Jack Haigis
☆ Peter MacNicol, Carl Capotorto, Tim Guinee, Bill Christopher-Myers, Jonathan Walker, Charlotte D'Amboise, Trini Alvarado

American Boyfriends
Canada 1989 90m Alpha Cine
Alliance/First Choice/Backseat (Steve Denure)

Three Canadian girls go across the border to attend a wedding and see California.
Dull sequel to My American Cousin, in which aimless talk and movement substitute for character and action.
wd Sandy Wilson *ph* Brenton Spencer *m* Terry Frewer *pd* Philip Schmidt *ed* Lara Mazur
☆ Margaret Langrick, John Wildman, Jason Blicker, Lisa Repo-Martell, Michele Bardeaux, Delia Brett

American Buffalo **
US, GB 1996 88m colour
Film Four/Capitol/Samuel Goldwyn/Channel 4/Punch (Gregory Mosher)

A junkshop owner discusses robbing the home of a coin collector with his teenage helper and a petty thief.
A conversation piece that shows its theatrical origins, but survives the transition to the screen thanks to Mamet's demotic dialogue and the expert performances it receives.
w David Mamet *play* David Mamet *d* Michael Corrente *ph* Richard Crudo *m* Thomas Newman *pd* Daniel Talpers *ed* Kate Sanford
☆ *Dustin Hoffman, Dennis Franz,* Sean Nelson

An American Dream
US 1966 103m Technicolor
Warner (William Conrad)
GB title: *See You in Hell, Darling*
A TV commentator is goaded into murdering his wife, becomes involved with gangsters and, tortured by guilt, allows them to kill him for shielding the girlfriend of one of them.
Ludicrously heavy-handed version of a semi-surrealist book which presumably had something to say about modern America, at least in its author's mind. Nothing comes through but relentless boredom at watching sordid and unlikely events, and sympathy for those involved. Eleanor Parker's one-scene role of screaming bitchery has to be seen to be believed.
w Mann Rubin *novel* Norman Mailer *d* Robert Gist *ph* Sam Leavitt *m* Johnny Mandel
☆ Stuart Whitman, Janet Leigh, Eleanor Parker, J. D. Cannon, Lloyd Nolan, Barry Sullivan, Murray Hamilton
'An idiotic melodrama laced with the salacious syndromes and little-boy nastiness that are the hall-mark of today's "mature film".' – *Judith Crist*
song, 'A Time for Love' (*m*Johnny Mandel, *ly* Paul Francis Webster)

American Dreamer
US 1984 105m Technicolor
Warner/Rank/CBS (Doug Chapin)

An Ohio housewife writes a novel, wins a trip to Paris, and finds her romantic dreams coming true.
A kind of lower-case reprise of Romancing the Stone, this modest comedy works only in fits and starts.
w Jim Kouf, David Greenwalt *story* Ann Biderman *d* Rick Rosenthal *ph* Giuseppe Rotunno *m* Lewis Furey *pd* Brian Eatwell *ed* Anne Goursaud
☆ JoBeth Williams, Tom Conti, Giancarlo Giannini, Coral Browne, James Staley
'A pleasant throwback to earlier forms of Hollywood farce.' – *Variety*

'The nation-blazing epic of America's westward march!'
American Empire
US 1942 82m bw
Harry Sherman/UA

GB title: *My Son Alone*
Brothers fall out over management of their Texas ranch.
Reasonable but forgettable semi-Western.
w Ben Grauman Kohn, Gladys Atwater, Robert Bren *d* William McGann
☆ Richard Dix, Preston Foster, Frances Gifford, Leo Carrillo

American Flyers
US 1985 114m Technicolor Panavision
Warner/Gareth Wigan, Paula Weinstein

Two brothers compete in a gruelling bicycle race.
Ambitious but ineffective drama with too much effort to explore personal dramas instead of getting on with the action.
w Steve Tesich *d* John Badham *ph* Don Peterman *m* Lee Ritenour, Greg Mathieson *pd* Lawrence G. Paull *ed* Frank Morriss
☆ Kevin Costner, David Grant, Rae Dawn Chong, Alexandra Paull, Janice Rule
'Overblown production just pumps hot air in too many directions and comes up limp.' – *Variety*

The American Friend *
West Germany 1977 127m colour
Road Movies/WDR/Wim Wenders

original title: *Der amerikanische Freund*
A Hamburg picture-framer thinks he is dying and is persuaded to become a Mafia hitman.
Strange melodrama which got the ear of the cognoscenti.
w Wim Wenders, Fritz Müller-Scherz *novel Ripley's Game* by Patricia Highsmith *d Wim Wenders ph* Robby Müller *m* Jürgen Knieper
☆ Dennis Hopper, Bruno Ganz, Lisa Kreuzer, Gerard Blain, Nicholas Ray, Samuel Fuller

American Friends *
GB 1991 95m Eastmancolor
Virgin/British Screen/Millennium/Mayday/Prominent Features (Patrick Cassavetti, Steve Abbott)

In Victorian England, a middle-aged Oxford academic, who is about to be elected president of his college, a post for a bachelor, falls in love with an American woman.
Gentle, quirky tale of romantic and academic intrigue that yields small pleasures.
w Michael Palin, Tristram Powell *d* Tristram Powell *ph* Philip Bonham-Carter *m* Georges Delerue *pd* Andrew McAlpine *ed* Dennis McTaggart
☆ Michael Palin, Trini Alvarado, Connie Booth, Bryan Pringle, Fred Pearson, Alfred Molina, Susan Denaker, Robert Eddison
'Not really the stuff of the big screen, but rather a perfectly acceptable, reasonably touching TV drama.' – *Empire*

'He's the highest paid lover in Beverly Hills!'
American Gigolo
US 1980 117m Metrocolor
Paramount/Pierre Associates (Freddie Fields)

A male prostitute finds that a client won't clear him when he is falsely charged with murder.
Thoroughly unattractive wallow on the seamy side of Los Angeles, with none of Midnight Cowboy's compassion.
wd Paul Schrader *ph* John Bailey *m* Giorgio Moroder
☆ Richard Gere, Lauren Hutton, Hector Elizondo, Nina Van Pallandt
'A hot subject, cool style and overly contrived plotting don't all mesh.' – *Variety*
'A perverse film devoted to perversity, typical of Schrader's apparently sadistic intent to pillory his audience with every kind of degenerate act he can manufacture.' – *Motion Picture Guide*
† Christopher Reeve allegedly refused one million dollars to play the lead. John Travolta also turned down the role.

American Gothic
GB/Canada 1988 90m colour
Manor Ground/Vidmark (John Quested/Christopher Harrop)

A murderous family, living in an old house on an otherwise deserted island, invites some stranded travellers to stay.
Ludicrous, hammily acted horror.
w Burt Wetanson, Michael Vines *d* John Hough *ph* Harvey Harrison *m* Alan Parker *pd* David Hiscox *ed* John Victor Smith *sp* Allen Benjamin

☆ Rod Steiger, Yvonne de Carlo, Sarah Torgov, Michael J. Pollard, Fiona Hutchinson, William Hootkins

'Where were you in '62?'
American Graffiti ***
US 1973 110m Techniscope
Universal/Lucasfilm/Coppola Company (Francis Ford Coppola, Gary Kurtz)

In 1962 California, four young men about to leave for college gather for a night's girl-chasing and police-baiting.
Nostalgic comedy recalling many sights and sounds of the previous generation and carefully crystallizing a particular time and place. Successful in itself, it led to many imitations.
wd George Lucas *ph* Ron Eveslage, Jan D'Alquen *m* popular songs
☆ *Richard Dreyfuss*, Ronny Howard, Paul le Mat, Charlie Martin Smith, Cindy Williams, Candy Clark, Mackenzie Phillips
† The film cost 750,000 dollars, and grossed 55 million.
picture; George Lucas (as writer); George Lucas (as director); Candy Clark

An American Guerilla in the Philippines
US 1950 104m colour
TCF (Lamar Trotti)
aka: *I Shall Return*
A stranded American naval officer forms a guerrilla band to fight the Japanese after the fall of the Philippines.
Muddled war story with a weak script; both its director and star disliked making the movie, and it shows.
w Lamar Trotti *novel* Ira Wolfert *d* Fritz Lang *ph* Harry Jackson *m* Cyril J. Mockridge *md* Lionel Newman *ad* Lyle Wheeler *ed* Robert Simpson
☆ Tyrone Power, Micheline Presle, Tom Ewell, Bob Patten, Tommy Cook, Juan Torena, Jack Elam, Carleton Young

'Jack Kelson is going straight. And his son's breaking the law to help him.'
American Heart *
US 1992 114m colour
Entertainment/Avenue/World Films (Rosilyn Heller, Jeff Bridges)

Out on parole, a former prisoner tries to go straight and also look after his teenage son.
An interesting attempt to deal with the lower reaches of American life in a realistic manner, but one that is only partly successful.
w Peter Silverman *story* Martin Bell, Mary Ellen Mark, Peter Silverman *d* Martin Bell *ph* James R. Bagdonas *m* James Newton Howard *pd* Joel Schiller *ed* Nancy Baker
☆ Jeff Bridges, Edward Furlong, Lucinda Jenney, Don Harvey, Tracey Tyla Kapisky, John Boylan

'Has plenty of passion and commitment but is rather too straightforward and disappointingly resolved to qualify as a total success.' – *Variety*

'The film tries now and then to be upbeat in the familiar American manner but doesn't press it and is rarely sentimental. Bell goes for the jugular when he can.' – *Derek Malcolm, Guardian*

American History X *
US 1998 118m DeLuxe
Entertainmnet/New Line (John Morrissey)

The leader of a neo-Nazi gang undergoes a reform in prison.
Tense melodrama of racism that looks a great deal better than it sounds; along the way, though, it invests its skinhead thugs with a kind of glamour.
w David McKenna *d* Tony Kaye *ph* Tony Kaye *m* Anne Dudley *pd* Jon Gary Steele *ed* Jerry Greenberg, Alan Heim
☆ *Edward Norton*, Edward Furlong, Fairuza Balk, Stacy Keach, Elliott Gould, Avery Brooks, Beverly D'Angelo, Paul Le Mat

'Norton's performance lets the film retain its primal power. But it doesn't redeem the overall concern such a film must cause us. You don't construct an anti-Nazi polemic that gratifies an audience's taste for brutality, nor end it so nihilistically that resistance to fascism seems futile.' – *Alexander Walker, London Evening Standard*

† Tony Kaye disowned the released version of his film. At the Berlin Film Festival in 1999, he issued a statement which said, in part: 'My vision of the film never made it to the screen. Edward Norton was permitted by the producers to edit and alter the film, which he did by increasing his role while decreasing the integrity of the film. The producers denied me the opportunity to present a black voice to provide depth and balance to the film. They denied me the opportunity to let a thousand voices be heard, if need be, so that a person watching the film might make an intelligent and informed decision about the compelling questions of our time.' Norton later commented, 'Let's not make any mistake: Tony Kaye is a victim of his own spiritual and creative immaturity.'
Edward Norton

American Hot Wax
US 1978 91m Metrocolor
Paramount (Art Linson)

The early days of rock and roll as seen by a prominent disc jockey of the time.
Mildly entertaining ragbag of semi-historical facts and authentic music, strictly for the youth market.
w John Kaye, Art Linson *d* Floyd Mutrux *ph* William A. Fraker *md* Kenny Vance
☆ Tim McIntire (Alan Freed), Fran Drescher, Jay Leno, Laraine Newman, Chuck Berry, Jerry Lee Lewis, Screamin' Jay Hawkins

An American in Paris ****
US 1951 113m Technicolor
MGM (*Arthur Freed*)

A carefree young artist scorns a rich woman's patronage and wins the love of a gamine.
Altogether delightful musical holiday, one of the highspots of the Hollywood genre, with infectious enthusiasm and an unexpected sense of the Paris that was.
w Alan Jay Lerner d Vincente Minnelli ph Al Gilks, John Alton m George Gershwin ch Gene Kelly ad Cedric Gibbons, Preston Ames ed Adrienne Fazan ly Ira Gershwin
☆ *Gene Kelly, Oscar Levant, Nina Foch, Leslie Caron, Georges Guetary*

'Too fancy and overblown, but the principal performers are in fine form and the Gershwin music keeps everything good-spirited.' – *New Yorker, 1977*

† Chevalier was originally paged for the Georges Guetary role, but turned it down because he lost the girl. The production cost $2,723,903, of which $542,000 went on the final ballet
♫ 'I Got Rhythm'; 'Embraceable You'; 'By Strauss'; 'Swonderful'; 'Tra La La'; 'Our Love Is Here to Stay'; 'Stairway to Paradise'; 'Concerto in F' (instrumental); 'An American in Paris' (ballet)
picture; Alan Jay Lerner; Al Gilks, John Alton; musical arrangement (Saul Chaplin, Johnny Green); art direction; costumes (Walter Plunkett, Irene Sharaff)
Vincente Minnelli; editing

American Madness **
US 1932 80m bw
Columbia

When a bank failure threatens, hundreds of small savers increase their deposits to save the situation.
Vivid, overstressed topical melodrama with crowd scenes typical of its director's later output.
w Robert Riskin *d* Frank Capra *ph* Joseph Walker
☆ Walter Huston, Pat O'Brien, Kay Johnson, Constance Cummings, Gavin Gordon, Berton Churchill

'It's a money picture. That goes both ways. It's about money and banks and spells dough for the box office. It's timely, topical, human, dramatic, punchy and good entertainment at one and the same time.' – *Variety*

'The sequence of the mounting panic and the storming of the bank are effectively staged, but the resolution is the usual Capra/Riskin populist hokum.' – *New Yorker, 1977*

American Me **
US 1992 125m DeLuxe
Y.O.Y. (Sean Daniel, Robert M. Young, Edward James Olmos)

A young Hispanic hoodlum serves an 18-year jail sentence and tries to make sense of his life on his release.
Grim, forceful and engrossing depiction of a savage world, inside and outside prison, where violence, crime and drugs are the shaping influences.
w Floyd Mutrux, Desmond Nakano *d Edward James Olmos* *ph* Reynaldo Villalobos *m* Dennis Lambert, Claude Gaudette *pd* Joe Aubel *ed* Arthur R. Coburn, Richard Candib
☆ *Edward James Olmos*, William Forsythe, Pepe Serna, Danny de La Paz, Evelina Fernandez, Cary-Hiroyuki Tagawa, Daniel Villareal, Sal Lopez

'Represents a massive downer by any conventional audience standards, and also runs the risk of attracting the type of crowd that will groove on the violence and ignore the message.' – *Variety*

'True tragedy; there are moments of Shakespearean power as well as graphic violence.' – *John Anderson, Newsday*

American Ninja
US 1986 95m TVC Color
Cannon/Menahem Golan/Yoram Globus

GB title: *American Warrior*
Two GIs use extreme violence to thwart gun-runners and other enemies in the Philippines.
Flaccid martial arts movie.
w Paul de Mielche *story* Avi Kleinberger, Gideon Amir *d* Sam Firstenberg *ph* Hanania Baer *m* Michael Linn *pd* Adrian H. Gorton *ed* Andrew Horvitch
☆ Michael Dudikoff, Steve James, Judie Aronson, Guich Koock

American Ninja 2: The Confrontation
US 1987 100m TVC Color
Cannon/Menahem Golan/Yoram Globus

Two US Army Rangers are sent to a small Caribbean island to investigate a mystery of disappearing marines.
Non-stop action, leavened with a touch of humour.
w Gary Conway, James Booth *d* Sam Firstenberg *ph* Gideon Porath *m* George S. Clinton *pd* Holger Gross *ed* Michael J. Duthie
☆ Michael Dudikoff, Steve James, Larry Poindexter, Gary Conway, Jeff Weston

American Ninja 3: Blood Hunt
US 1989 93m Rank Colour
Cannon/Breton (Harry Alan Towers)

The toughest man in the world takes his revenge after he is infected with a deadly disease by the men who murdered his father.
Dreary action movie, full of ineptly-staged fights.
wd Cedric Sundstrom *story* Gary Conway *ph* George Bartels *m* George S. Clinton *pd* Ruth Strimling *ed* Michael J. Duthie
☆ David Bradley, Steve James, Marjoe Gortner, Michele Chan, Yehuda Efroni, Calvin Jung

American Ninja 4: The Annihilation
US 1991 95m colour
Cannon (Christopher Pearce)

A teacher reverts to his martial arts training to rescue friends taken prisoner by an evil sheikh.
Dim and unexciting sequel, with little sign of life or interest from the participants.
w David Geeves *d* Cedric Sundstrom *ph* Joseph Wein *m* Nicolas Tenbroek *pd* Ruth Strimling *ed* Claudio Yrtuc
☆ Michael Dudikoff, David Bradley, James Booth, Dwayne Alexandre, Robin Stille, Ken Gampu

'Low-budget, no-talent programmer ... Even the genre's most devoted fans will be disappointed by the lack of imagination and energy in the fight scenes.' – *Variety*

'Bad is good again.'
American Outlaws
US 2001 93m FotoKem
Warner/Morgan Creek (James G. Robinson)

Angered by the underhand behaviour of the railroad, Frank and Jesse James form a gang of bank-robbers.
This is no more than another failed attempt, in the manner of the dire Young Guns movies, to find a young audience for Westerns by portraying its characters as rock star protoypes.
w Roderick Taylor, John Rogers *d* Les Mayfield *ph* Russell Boyd *m* Trevor Rabin *pd* Cary White, John Frick *ed* Michael Tronick
☆ Colin Farrell (Jesse James), Scott Caan (Cole Younger), Ali Larter (Zee Mimms), Gabriel Macht (Frank James), Gregory Smit (Jim Younger), Harris Yulin (Thaddeus Rains), Kathy Bates (Ma James), Timothy Dalton (Allan Pinkerton), Will McCormack (Bob Younger), Ronny Cox (Doc Mimms), Terry O'Quinn (Rollin Parker), Nathaniel Arcand (Comanche Tom)

'This is the 36th retelling of the James Younger gang's exploits, and by some way the most feeble.' – *Derek Malcolm, Guardian*

'There is no escape from destiny.'
American Perfekt
US 1997 99m Foto-Kem
Blue Dolphin/Nu Image (Irvin Kershner)

A serial killer, who leads his life according to the throw of a coin, gets his come-uppance.
The unexpected never happens in this predictable movie of women in peril from a madman; it's best to take a chance and avoid it.
wd Paul Chart *ph* William Wages *m* Simon Boswell *pd* Katherine Vallin *ed* Michael Russo
☆ Fairuza Balk (Alice), Robert Forster (Jake), Amanda Plummer (Sandra), Paul Sorvino (Frank), David Thewlis (Santini), Geoffrey Lewis (Willy), Chris Sarandon (Sammy), Joanna Gleason (Shirley)

'Within the arthousey road movie formula, it seems, sometimes there is no escape from predictability.' – *Tom Doyle, Empire*

'Have you had that loving filling?'
'There's something about your first piece.'
American Pie *
US 1999 96m DeLuxe
Universal (Warren Zide, Craig Perry, Chris Moore, Chris Weitz)

Four high school youths are determined to lose their virginity before they graduate.
The 90s equivalent of Porky's, a gross comedy of crude jokes about adolescent sexuality; its success was due to the fact that it went further than its predecessors.
w Adam Herz *d* Paul Weitz *ph* Richard Crudo *m* David Lawrence *pd* Paul Peters *ed* Priscilla Nedd-Friendly
☆ Jason Biggs (Jim), Shannon Elizabeth (Nadia), Alyson Hannigan (Michelle), Chris Klein (Oz), Natasha Lyonne (Jessica), Thomas Ian Nicholas (Kevin), Tara Reid (Vicky), Seann W. Scott (Stifler), Mena Suvari (Heather), Eddie Kaye Thomas (Finch), Eugene Levy

'Crude in more ways than one, this cheesy homage to a level of horniness Austin Powers could only imagine will be a dream movie for many a teenage boy.' – *Todd McCarthy*

'Marks a major shift in contemporary teen culture by making the girls as hip to sex as the boys.' – *Owen Gleiberman, Entertainment Weekly*

'The movie industry is dominated by 12-year-olds. I mean, I'm not trying to sound snobbish, but *American Pie*? Sticking your dick in a pie? That's a movie? Come on.' – *Spike Lee*

† It grossed around $102m at the US box office.

'This Summer It's All About Sticking Together.'
American Pie 2
US 2001 105m DeLuxe Panavision
Universal (Warren Zide, Craig Perry, Chris Moore)

Holidaying college students rent a beach house so that they can continue their sexual education.
The recipe is unchanging from the first Pie, with its below the belt humour among charmless young.
w Adam Herz; *d* J. B. Rogers *ph* Mark Irwin *m* David Lawrence *pd* Richard Toyon *ed* Larry Madaras, Stuart Pappe

☆ Jason Biggs (Jim), Shannon Elizabeth (Nadia), Alyson Hannigan (Michelle), Chris Klein (Oz), Natasha Lyonne (Jessica), Thomas Ian Nicholas (Kevin), Tara Reid (Vicky), Seann William Scott (Stifler), Mena Suvari (Heather), Eddie Kaye Thomas (Finch), Eugene Levy (Jim's Dad), Casey Affleck (Kevin's Brother)

'A genuinely depressing experience.' – *Steve Grant, Sunday Times*

The American President *

US 1995 113m Technicolor Panavision
Columbia/Castle Rock/Wildwood (Rob Reiner)

A US president who lacks a wife decides to date an attractive lobbyist, with the result that his popularity with his party and the public begins to slide.

This is a clever idea for a romantic comedy, as the most important man in America tries to behave like the boy next door, but it is one that is soon reduced to blandness by a refusal to take risks; playing safe may be good political practice but it does not make for more general hilarity.

w Aaron Sorkin *d* Rob Reiner *ph* John Seale *m* Marc Shaiman *pd* Lilly Kilvert *ed* Robert Leighton

☆ Michael Douglas, Annette Bening, Martin Sheen, Michael J. Fox, David Paymer, Samantha Mathis, Richard Dreyfuss

'Genial middlebrow fare that coasts a long way on the charm of its two stars.' – *Todd McCarthy, Variety*

'Its success will be a sign that movie-goers have scaled down their expectations for romantic comedy.' – *Terrence Rafferty, New Yorker*

† Robert Redford was to have starred, but was replaced after a disagreement with Reiner.

Marc Shaiman

'Killer looks.'
'No introductions necessary.'

American Psycho **

US/Canada 2000 101m DeLuxe Panavision
Entertainment/Lions gate/MUSE (Edward R. Pressman, Chris Hanley, Christian Halsey Solomon)

A successful, promiscuous Wall Street broker fantasizes about becoming a serial killer.

A deft, elegant portrait of a self-obsessed, fashionable, design-conscious man descending into psychosis as a result of his obsessions.

w Mary Harron, Guinevere Turner *novel* Bret Easton Ellis *d* Mary Harron *ph* Andrzej Sekula *m* John Cale *pd* Gideon Ponte *ed* Andrew Marcus

☆ Christian Bale (Patrick Bateman), Willem Dafoe (Donald Kimball), Jared Leto (Paul Allen), Reese Witherspoon (Evelyn Williams), Samantha Mathis (Courtney Rawlinson), Chloe Sevigny (Jean), Justin Theroux (Timothy Bryce), Josh Lucas (Craig McDermott), Guinevere Turner (Elizabeth), Matt Ross (Luis Carruthers), Bill Sage (David Van Patten), Cara Seymour (Christie)

'A stylish, disquieting, unexpectedly witty piece of cinema.' – *Peter Bradshaw, Guardian*

'The idea that a culture of rapacious consumerism breeds killers like Bateman is just too facile to take seriously. This is a satire with no roots in reality.' – *Cosmo Landesman, Sunday Times*

† Christian Bale bowed out of the film when Leonardo DiCaprio announced his interest in playing Bateman, and a new director was also sought. Bale and Harron returned when DiCaprio changed his mind.

††† An uninteresting sequel *American Psycho II: All American Girl* was released direct to video in 2002, directed by Morgan J. Freeman and starring Mila Kunis and Geraint Wyn Davies.

An American Romance *

US 1944 151m Technicolor
MGM (King Vidor)

The life of a European immigrant who becomes a master of industry.

Mind-boggling pageant of the American dream, coldly presented and totally humourless. Its saving grace is its smooth physical presentation.

w Herbert Dalmas, William Ludwig *d* King Vidor *ph* Harold Rosson *m* Louis Gruenberg

☆ Brian Donlevy, Ann Richards, John Qualen, Walter Abel, Stephen McNally

'A thousand chances to inform, excite or even interest have been flung away.' – *Richard Winnington*

'The whole aim of it is to boost The American Way.' – *Richard Mallett, Punch*

American Samurai

US 1992 87m colour
Cannon/Global (Allan Greenblatt)

An American journalist investigating a murder using a samurai sword is forced to enter a fight to the death.

Mundane action film, offering little that cannot be found in a dozen similar movies of equal banality.

w John Corcoran *d* Sam Firstenberg *ph* David Gurfinkel *m* Robbie Patton *pd* Kuly Sander *ed* Sebastian Serrell-Watts, Shlomo Chazan

☆ David Bradley, Mark Dacascos, Valarie Trapp, Rex Ryon, Melissa Hellman, John Fujioka

'Cheap and trite, this is yet another hymn to the ability of a handsome white guy to beat up ethnic opponents.' – *Empire*

The American Success Company *

US 1980 94m colour
Columbia (Edgar J. Scherick and Daniel H. Blatt)

The inexperienced son of a credit card tycoon becomes a tough guy.

Tilts at the American myth: not a notable success.

w William Richert, Larry Cohen *d* William Richert

☆ Jeff Bridges, Belinda Bauer, Ned Beatty, Steven Keats, Bianca Jagger

An American Tail *

US 1986 80m DeLuxe
Universal/Steven Spielberg (Don Bluth, John Pomeroy, Gary Goldman)

Russian mice encounter all kinds of trouble when in the 1880s they emigrate to the United States.

Expensive cartoon feature with old-fashioned full animation but not much in the way of narrative interest or indeed humour.

w Judy Freudberg, Tony Geiss *d* Don Bluth (also designer)

☆ voices: Cathianne Blore, Christopher Plummer, Dom DeLuise, Madeline Kahn

'Every character and every situation have been presented a thousand times before … anyone over the age of 12 will likely experience more boredom than pleasure.' – *Variety*

song, 'Somewhere Out There' (James Horner, Barry Mann, Cynthia Weil)

'Look Out Pardeners, There's A New Mouse In Town!'

An American Tail: Fievel Goes West **

US 1991 75m colour
UIP/Universal/Amblin (Steven Spielberg, Robert Watts)

A confidence trickster of a cat persuades a family of mice to move to the West.

Enjoyable and high-spirited animated film that borrows plot and attitudes from classic Westerns.

w Flint Dille *story* Charles Swenson *d* Phil Nibbelink, Simon Wells *m* James Horner

☆ Featuring the voices of Phillip Glasser, James Stewart, Erica Yohn, Cathy Cavadini, Nehemiah Persoff, Dom DeLuise, Amy Irving, John Cleese, Jon Lovitz

'Drama that happens around you every day – when the wild life of impetuous youth burns away age-old barriers!'

An American Tragedy **

US 1931 95m bw
Paramount

An ambitious young man murders his pregnant fiancée when he has a chance to marry a rich girl.

Dated but solidly satisfying adaptation of a weighty novel, more compelling than the 1951 remake A Place in the Sun.

wd Josef von Sternberg novel Theodore Dreiser *ph* Lee Garmes *ad* Hans Dreier

☆ Phillips Holmes, *Sylvia Sidney*, Frances Dee, Irving Pichel, Frederick Burton, Claire McDowell

'It unreels as an ordinary programme effort with an unhappy ending … as Sternberg has seen fit to present it the celluloid structure is slow, heavy and not always interesting drama. Its box office success is very doubtful.' – *Variety*

'It is the first time, I believe, that the subjects of sex, birth control and murder have been put into a picture with sense, taste and reality.' – *Pare Lorentz*

'An aimless, lugubrious mess. The fireworks may dazzle to schoolboys of criticism, but they will add no permanent color to the motion picture.' – *Harry Alan Potamkin*

American Warrior: see *American Ninja*

An American Werewolf in London ***

GB 1981 97m Technicolor
Polygram/Lycanthrope (Peter Guber, Jon Peters)

Two American tourists are bitten by a werewolf.

Curious but oddly endearing mixture of horror film and spoof, of comedy and shock, with everything grist to its mill including tourist Britain and the wedding of Prince Charles. The special effects are notable, and signalled new developments in this field.

wd John Landis *ph* Robert Paynter *m* Elmer Bernstein *sp Effects Associates, Rick Baker*

☆ David Naughton, Jenny Agutter, Griffin Dunne, John Woodvine

'The gear changes of tone and pace make for a very jerkily driven vehicle.' – *Sunday Times*

'Seems curiously unfinished, as though Landis spent all his energy on spectacular set-pieces and then didn't want to bother with things like transitions, character development, or an ending.' – *Roger Ebert*

'Things Are Going to Get A Little Hairy.'

An American Werewolf in Paris *

US/GB/France/Luxembourg 1997 98m colour
Entertainment/Stonewood/Hollywood/Cometstone/J&M (Richard Claus)

An American tourist in Paris is seduced and bitten by a female werewolf.

A sequel to An American Werewolf in London which often resembles a remake of the original, though it lacks that film's engaging mix of horror and black humour.

w Tim Burns, Tom Stern, Anthony Waller *based on characters created by* John Landis *d* Anthony Waller *ph* Egon Werdin *m* Wilbert Hirsch *pd* Matthias Kammermeier *ed* Peter R. Adam *sp* Santa Barbara Studios; Peter Lloyd; Magicon & Crawley Creatures

☆ Tom Everett Scott, Julie Delpy, Vince Vieluf, Phil Buckman, Julie Bowen, Pierre Cosso, Tom Novembre, Thierry Lhermitte

'Not funny enough, not scary enough, and deeply in need of a silver bullet.' – *Darren Bignell, Empire*

American Women: see *The Closer You Get*

American Yakuza

US/Japan 1993 91m Foto-Kem
Overseas Filmgroup/First Look/Ozla/Neo (Michael Leahy, Aki Komine)

An FBI agent infiltrates Japanese gangsters trying to muscle in on the Mafia.

Slick, moderately engaging action film that makes all the expected and customary moves of the genre.

w Max Strom, John Allen Nelson *story* Taka Ichise *d* Frank Cappello *ph* Richard Clabaugh *m* David C. Williams *pd* Shay Austin *ed* Sonny Baskin

☆ Viggo Mortensen, Ryo Ishibashi, Michael Nouri, Franklyn Ajaye, Cristina Lawson, Yuji Okumoto, Robert Forster

'A stylish action-thriller directed with flair.' – *Sight and Sound*

American Yakuza 2: Back to Back

US/Japan 1996 87m Foto-Kem
Overseas Filmgroup/Ozla/Neo (W. K. Border, Aki Komine)

In Los Angeles, a bad-tempered ex-detective with family problems is forced to help a Japanese gangster wage war on the Mafia and a corrupt cop.

Slick, violent, tongue-in-cheek, over-the-top action movie that takes delight in the excesses of the genre.

w Roger Nygard, Lloyd Keith *d* Roger Nygard *ph* Mark W. Gray *m* Walter Werzowa *pd* Anthony Stabley *ed* Roger Nygard

☆ Michael Rooker, Ryo Ishibashi, Danielle Harris, John Laughlin, Koh Takasugi, Tim Thomerson, Stephen Furst, Vincent Schiavella, Frank D'Amico, Bobcat Goldthwait

'A stylishly packaged combo of black humour, violence and well-staged action.' – *Film Review*

The Americanization of Emily *

US 1964 115m bw
MGM/Filmways (John Calley)

World War II: just before the Normandy landings, a war widow driver falls for an American commander who is a self-confessed coward.

Bizarre comedy full of eccentric characters, an uneasy choice for its female star but otherwise successful in patches in its random distillation of black comedy, sex and the tumbling of old-fashioned virtues.

w Paddy Chayefsky *novel* William Bradford Huie *d* Arthur Hiller *ph Philip Lathrop, Chris Challis* *m* Johnny Mandel

☆ Julie Andrews, James Garner, *Melvyn Douglas*, James Coburn, Liz Fraser, Joyce Grenfell, Edward Binns, Keenan Wynn, William Windom

'Out of it all there comes the definite feeling that Hitler's war is incidental to Paddy Chayevsky's war of ideas … no plot synopsis could begin to suggest how much the characters talk.' – *MFB*

Philip Lathrop

The Americano

US 1916 60m approx (24 fps) bw silent
Triangle (D. W. Griffith)

A young American engineer becomes involved in a revolution in Patagonia.

Early star adventure vehicle, an immense popular success; the last film Fairbanks made for Griffith.

w Anita Loos, John Emerson *novel Blaze Derringer* by Eugene P. Lyle Jnr *d* John Emerson *ph* Victor Fleming

☆ *Douglas Fairbanks*, Alma Rubens, Spottiswoode Aitken, Lillian Langdon

The Americano

US 1955 85m Technicolor
RKO (Robert Stillman)

A Westerner takes three prize bulls to Brazil, but finds the buyer has been murdered.

A Western with a twist, but otherwise extremely dull, with poor pace, colour and use of settings.

w Guy Trosper *d* William Castle *ph* William Snyder *m* Roy Webb

☆ Glenn Ford, Frank Lovejoy, Abbe Lane, Cesar Romero, Ursula Thiess

'A comedy about celebrity, family and other forms of insanity.'

America's Sweethearts

US 2001 102m DeLuxe Panavision
Columbia/Revolution (Billy Crystal, Susan Arnold, Donna Arkoff Roth)

An insecure PR attempts to persuade two feuding film stars to get together to promote their latest movie.

Narcissistic comedy of Hollywood that is too inbred to interest anyone in the real world; it tends to take celebrity at face value.

w Billy Crystal, Peter Tolan *d* Joe Roth *ph* Phedon Papamichael *m* James Newton Howard *pd* Garreth Stover *ed* Stephen A. Rotter *cos* Ellen Mirojnick, Jeffrey Kurland

☆ Julia Roberts (Kiki Harrison), Billy Crystal (Lee Phillips), Catherine Zeta-Jones (Gwen Harrison), John Cusack (Eddie Thomas), Hank Azaria (Hector), Stanley Tucci (Dave Kingman), Christopher Walken (Hal Weidmann), Alan Arkin (Wellness Guide), Seth Green (Danny Wax), Scot Zeller (Davis)

'Begins as a smartly promising, gently farcical comedy of manners and ends as sourly and haphazardly as the lives it is poking fun at.' – *Robert Koehler, Variety*

L'Amérique des autres: see *Someone Else's America*

L'Ami de Mon Amie: see *My Girlfriend's Boyfriend*

L'Ami Retrouvé: see *Reunion*

Un Ami Viendra ce Soir

France 1946 111m bw
CGC (R. Artus)

During World War II a French patriot uses a lunatic asylum as a resistance headquarters.

Rather glum wartime melodrama, lacking in tension.

w Jacques Companeez, Raymond Bernard *d* Raymond Bernard *ph* Robert Le Febvre *m* Arthur Honegger
☆ Michel Simon, Louis Salou, Saturnin Fabre, Paul Bernard, Madeleine Sologne, Marcel André

Le Amiche *
Italy 1955 90m bw
Trionfalcine (Giovanni Addessi)
aka: *The Girl Friends*
The interaction of five girls living together in Turin.
Highbrow lending library stuff, quite watchable but equally forgettable.
w Suso Cecchi d'Amico, Alba de Cespedes *story* *Tra Donne Sole* by Cesare Pavese *d* Michelangelo Antonioni *ph* Gianni di Venanzo *m* Giovanni Fusco
☆ Eleonora Rossi Drago, Valentina Cortese, Yvonne Furneaux, Gabriele Ferzetti, Franco Fabrizi, Madeleine Fischer

La Amiga
Argentina/West Germany 1988 108m colour
Journal/Alma/Jorge Estrada Mora (Jorge Estrada, Klaus Volkenberg)
aka: *The Girlfriend*
Stages in the life of two women in Buenos Aires: one a Jewish actress, the other a mother who becomes politically involved after her son is taken away by security officers and never seen alive again.
Involved and somewhat sentimental drama of survival in a hostile world.
w Jeanine Meerapfel, Alcides Chiesa *d* Jeanine Meerapfel *ph* Axel Block *pd* Jorge Marchegiano, Rainer Schaper *ed* Juliane Lorenz
☆ Liv Ullmann, Cipe Lincovsky, Federico Luppi, Victor Laplace, Harry Baer, Lito Cruz, Greger Hansen, Nicolas Frei

Amistad **
US 1997 152m Technicolor 'Scope
DreamWorks/HBO (Steven Spielberg, Debbie Allen, Colin Wilson)
African slaves who escape their chains and kill the crew of a slave ship are tried in America for murder, while the ship's owners, the salvagers and the Spanish Queen claim them as their property.
Earnest and dogged, well meaning but too often dramatically inert, this tells a true story from a white viewpoint, in which the slaves remain exotic accessories to the real conflict, which takes place in courtrooms.
w David Franzoni *d* Steven Spielberg *ph* Janusz Kaminski *m* John Williams *pd* Rick Carter *ed* Michael Kahn
☆ Matthew McConaughey, Anthony Hopkins, Morgan Freeman, Nigel Hawthorne, Djimoun Hounsou, David Paymer, Pete Postlethwaite, Stellan Skarsgård, Anna Paquin, Tomas Milian, Austin Pendleton
'Artistically solid, if not always dramatically exciting.' – *Variety*
Anthony Hopkins; Janusz Kaminski; John Williams; Ruth E. Carter (costumes)

Amityville 3: The Demon: see *Amityville 3-D*

Amityville 3-D
US 1984 93m colour ArriVision 3-D
EMI/Universal/Dino de Laurentiis/Orion (Stephen F. Kesten)
aka: *Amityville 3: The Demon*
A sceptical journalist moves into the haunted house but is jolted out of his complacency.
Ragbag of supernatural incident with neither cohesion nor plausibility, but good 3-D.
w William Wales *d* Richard Fleischer *ph* Fred Schuler *m* Howard Blake *ad* Giorgio Postiglione, Justin Scoppa *ed* Frank J. Urioste
☆ Tony Roberts, Tess Harper, Robert Joy, Candy Clark, John Beal, Leora Dana
'An assortment of unrelated happenings precedes the final appearance of a crude bug-eyed monster.' – *MFB*

'Evil never dies.'
Amityville Dollhouse
US 1996 93m colour
Promark/Spectacor/Zeta (Zane W. Levitt, Mark Yellen, Steve White)
A family move into a new home, which includes a dollhouse that carries the curse of the Amityville horror.
A dull horror movie that begins by locating horrors at the heart of normal family life, but soon abandons this promising approach for the usual predictable shocks.
w Joshua Michael Stern *d* Steve White *ph* Tom Callaway *m* Ray Colcord *pd* Jerry Fleming *ed* Kert VanderMeulen
☆ Robin Thomas, Starr Andreeff, Clayton Murray, Lenore Kasdorf, Allen Cutler, Rachel Duncan, Franc Ross, Lisa Robin Kelly, Jarrett Lennon

The Amityville Horror
US 1979 118m Movielab
AIP/Cinema 77 (Ronald Saland, Elliot Geisinger)
Newlyweds move into a house where a murder was committed, and experience strange manifestations which drive them away.
Sub-Exorcist goings on, a shameless exaggeration of some of the alleged facts retailed in the best-selling book. A shocker for the uncritical.
w Sandor Stern *book* Jay Anson *d* Stuart Rosenberg *ph* Fred J. Koenekamp *m* Lalo Schifrin
☆ James Brolin, Margot Kidder, Rod Steiger, Don Stroud, Murray Hamilton
Lalo Schifrin

Amityville II: The Possession
US 1982 104m DeLuxe
Dino de Laurentiis/Orion (Ira N. Smith, Stephen R. Greenwald)
The sequel turns out to be a prequel, dealing with the events that led to the house at Amityville becoming haunted.
Everything but the kitchen sink is thrown into this ghoulish brew, and most of it is red; but the script is hopeless from the start.
w Tommy Lee Wallace *book* *Murder in Amityville* by Hans Holzer *d* Damiano Damiani *ph* Franco Di Giacomo *m* Lalo Schifrin *pd* Pierluigi Basile *ed* Sam O'Steen
☆ Burt Young, Rutanya Alda, James Olson, Jack Magner, Andrew Prine
'There probably isn't a more unsympathetic bunch on screen this year. They're sure to make audiences root for the house.' – *Variety*

Amnesia *
Chile 1994 90m Eastmancolor
Arca/Cine Chile/Fondart
After a civil war, a soldier and a survivor of a prison camp take revenge on a brutal sergeant.
A tense and gripping drama concerned with individual responsibility which also touches on the theme of national amnesia about atrocities committed on behalf of the state.
w Gustavo Frias, Gonzalo Justiniano *d* Gonzalo Justiniano *ph* Hans Burmann *m* José Miguel Tobar, Miguel Miranda *ad* Carlos Garrido *ed* Danielle Fillios
☆ Julio Jung, Pedro Vicuña, Nelson Villagra, José Secall, Marcela Osorio, Carla Cristi
'An offbeat, sometimes nightmarish black comedy.' – *Variety*

Amok: see *Schizo*

'Some heights can only be reached by the heart.'
Among Giants *
GB 1998 96m colour
Kudos/British Screen/Capitol/Arts Council/YMPA/BBC
An Australian backpacker becomes the only female member of a group of climbers who earn their living painting electricity pylons.
A working-class romantic tragi-comedy that does not scale the heights.
w Simon Beaufoy *d* Sam Miller *ph* Witold Stok *m* Tim Atack *pd* Luana Hanson *ed* Paul Green, Elen Pierce Lewis
☆ Pete Postlethwaite, Rachel Griffiths, James Thornton, Rob Jarvis, Andy Serkis, Lennie James, Alan Williams, Emma Cunniffe
'This small-scale, bittersweet film has many fine qualities, but it lacks the crucial dramatic spark that would have made it truly memorable.' – *Stephen Farber, Movieline*

Among the Living *
US 1941 68m bw
Paramount (Sol C. Siegel)
In a small town live twin brothers, one of whom is a murderer.
Offbeat suspenser with effective performances.
w Lester Cole, Garrett Fort *d* Stuart Heisler *ph* Theodor Sparkuhl
☆ Albert Dekker, Susan Hayward, Frances Farmer, Harry Carey, Gordon Jones
'Head and shoulders above all the filler shows ground out by Hollywood to perpetuate the double feature system.' – *Howard Barnes, New York Herald Tribune*

'Born With Everything They Had To Have More.'
Amongst Friends
US 1993 87m Technicolor
Rank/Last Outlaw/Island World (Matthew Blumberg)
Three boyhood friends from the wealthy middle class fall out when they try to become gangsters.
Heavily influenced by Martin Scorsese's Mean Streets, this lacks any sense of observable reality, relying instead on fast talking and undistinguished songs to carry the action, which disintegrates into violence to compensate for its lack of anything better to show.
wd Rob Weiss *ph* Michael Bonvillain *m* Mick Jones *pd* Terrence Foster *ed* Leo Trombetta
☆ Steve Parlavecchio, Joseph Lindsey, Patrick McGaw, Mira Sorvino, Chris Santos, Brett Lambson, Michael Artura, Frank Medrano, Louis Lombardi
'A truly numbskulled use of violence.' – *Nigel Andrews, Financial Times*
'The whole structure is a mess and there's a strong sense of been-here-before about the project.' – *Derek Malcolm, Guardian*

El Amor Brujo: see *A Love Bewitched*

L'Amore *
Italy 1948 79m bw
Tevere Film (Roberto Rossellini)
Two short films. *The Human Voice:* a woman talks on the phone to the man who has forsaken her. *The Miracle:* a peasant woman is seduced and is convinced she will give birth to a new Messiah.
A tour de force by an actress to be reckoned with; but hardly compulsive as cinema.
w Tullio Pinelli, Roberto Rossellini, Federico Fellini *play* Jean Cocteau *d* Roberto Rossellini *ph* Robert Juillard, Aldo Tonti *m* Renzo Rossellini
☆ *Anna Magnani*, Federico Fellini
† *The Miracle* was separately released in some countries.

'She searched for the truth but found only lies...'
L'Amore Molesto *
Italy 1995 103m Technicolor
Arrow/Kucky Red/Teatri Uniti (Angelo Curti, Andrea Occhipinti, Kermit Smith)
aka: *Wounded Love*
A middle-aged comic-book artist investigates her mother's mysterious death.
Complex thriller, structured around flashbacks that may, or may not, be accurate memories of the past; it does not entirely reward the effort required to understand its somewhat sleazy subject matter.
wd Mario Martone *novel* Elena Ferrante *ph* Luca Bigazzi *ad* Giancarlo Muselli *ed* Jacopo Quadri
☆ Anna Bonaiuto, Angela Luce, Gianni Cajafa, Peppe Lanzetta, Licia Maglietta, Anna Calato, Italo Celero
'A moody rather than an event-filled thriller which holds the viewer with its eccentric charm and quite nasty after-taste.' – *Marianne Gray, Film Review*

Amores Perros ***
Mexico 2000 154m colour
Optimum/Zeta Film/AltaVista (Alejandro Gonzalez Inarritu)
aka: *Love's a Bitch*
In Mexico city, a car crash alters the lives of a teenager in love with his brother's wife, a model, who is disfigured in the accident, and a bored hitman.
Dazzling, brutal movie of love and death, in which three stories intertwine, all involving dogs, from a pampered pet to a Rottweiler, a vicious champion dogfighter.
w Guillermo Arriaga Jordan *d* Alejandro Gonzalez Inarritu *ph* Rodrigo Prieto *m* Gustavo Santaolatta *pd* Brigitte Broch *ed* Alejandro Gonzalez Inarritu, Luis Carballar, Fernando Perez Unda
☆ Emilio Echevarria (El Chivo), Gael Garcia Bernal (Octavio), Goya Toledo (Valeria), Alvaro Guerrero (Daniel), Vanessa Bauche (Susana), Jorge Salinas (Luis), Marco Pérez (Ramiro)
'Feels like the first classic of the new decade, with sequences that will probably make their way into history.' – *Elvis Mitchell, New York Times*
'The individual stories, which weave in and out of each other with true-life untidiness, are so gripping you'll go along with them until everything becomes clear.' – *Kim Newman, Empire*
foreign language film
foreign film

'The rollicking story of a ribald century that should have been ashamed of itself!'
The Amorous Adventures of Moll Flanders
GB 1965 125m Technicolor Panavision
Paramount/Winchester (Marcel Hellman)
An ambitious servant girl loses her virtue to a succession of rich gentlemen but finally settles for a highwayman.
The aim was to make a female Tom Jones, but this bawdy romp never achieves the freewheeling fluency of that surprise success, and a vacuous central performance makes the constant couplings more boring than exciting.
w Denis Cannan, Roland Kibbee *novel* Daniel Defoe *d* Terence Young *ph* Ted Moore *m* John Addison *pd* Syd Cain
☆ Kim Novak, Richard Johnson, George Sanders, Lilli Palmer, Angela Lansbury, Leo McKern, Vittorio de Sica, Cecil Parker, Daniel Massey
'Further from Defoe than *Tom Jones* was from Fielding, but with much the same combination of crude table manners and clean sets to stand in for period flavour.' – *MFB*

The Amorous Milkman
GB 1975 94m colour
Variety/Lanka (Derren Nesbitt)
A young milkman becomes engaged to two women at the same time.
Trivial and heavy-handed comedy, in which the hero is the victim of rapacious women; intended to titillate, it fails miserably.
wd Derren Nesbitt *novel* Derren Nesbitt *ph* Jim Allen *m* Roger Webb *ad* Tony Curtis *ed* Russell Lloyd
☆ Julie Ege, Diana Dors, Brendan Price, Donna Reading, Nancie Wait, Alan Lake, Bill Fraser, Fred Emney, Patrick Holt, Roy Kinnear, Ray Barrett, Anthony Sharp, Megs Jenkins, Arnold Ridley, Sam Kydd
'All in all, this is British graffiti at its worst.' – *MFB*

The Amorous Prawn *
GB 1962 89m bw
BL/Covent Garden (Leslie Gilliat)
US title: *The Playgirl and the War Minister (an attempt to cash in on the Profumo case)*
A hard-up general's wife invites American paying guests to their official highland home.
This film version of a stage success seems very mild, but the cast is eager to please: the result is a frantic high-class farce.
w Anthony Kimmins, Nicholas Phipps *play* Anthony Kimmins *d* Anthony Kimmins *ph* Wilkie Cooper *m* John Barry
☆ Joan Greenwood, Ian Carmichael, Cecil Parker, Dennis Price, Robert Beatty, Finlay Currie, Liz Fraser, Derek Nimmo

Amos & Andrew
US 1993 94m Technicolor
Columbia/Castle Rock/New Line (Gary Goetzman)
A black writer moves into an exclusive neighbourhood and finds himself taken for a

burglar, befriended by a petty crook and involved in a shoot-out with police.
A crass farce of mistaken identity, a would-be satire of racial attitudes that neither illumines nor entertains.
wd E. Max Frye *ph* Walt Lloyd *m* Richard Gibbs *pd* Patricia Norris *ed* Jane Kurson
☆ Nicolas Cage, Samuel L. Jackson, Dabney Coleman, Michael Lerner, Margaret Colin, Brad Dourif, Giancarlo Esposito, Bob Balaban
'Raises the question: "How did this film ever get made?" Few audience members will sit through its entirety to ponder the issue.' – *Lawrence Cohn, Variety*

L'Amour à Mort *
France 1984 90m colour
Dussart/Ariane/A2 (Philippe Dussart)
An archaeologist and his mistress come to the conclusion that their love will reach its fullest expression in death.
Chilly symbolic drama, a continuation of the same team's preoccupations with the meaning of life which were previously explored (via the same four actors) in Mon Oncle d'Amérique and La Vie est un Roman. Interesting but not especially rewarding.
w Jean Gruault *d* Alain Resnais *ph* Sacha Vierny *m* Hans Werner Henze
☆ Sabine Azema, Fanny Ardant, Pierre Arditi, André Dussolier

Un Amour de Pluie: see *Loving in the Rain*

Un Amour de Swann: see *Swann in Love*

L'Amour, L'Après-midi *
France 1972 97m colour
Les Films du Losange/Barbet Schroeder (Pierre Cottrell)
US title: *Chloë in the Afternoon*
aka: *Love in the Afternoon*
A married man's flirtation with an old flame leads him to a greater appreciation of his wife.
The last of Rohmer's six moral tales and the least interesting.
wd Eric Rohmer *ph* Nestor Almendros *m* Arié Dzierlatka *ad* Nicole Rachline *ed* Cécile Decugis, Martine Kalfon
☆ Bernard Verley, Zouzou, Françoise Verley, Daniel Ceccaldi, Malvina Penne, Babette Ferrier
'The director shows life going on realistically enough. But the elegance with which he presents it, the wit – and the film doesn't merely sound witty, it looks witty – remove it from the tedium of the realistic.' – *Dilys Powell*

Les Amours de la Reine Elisabeth: see *Queen Elizabeth*

Amsterdam Affair
GB 1968 91m Eastmancolor
LIP/Trio/Group W (Gerry Willoughby)
Inspector Van der Valk investigates when a writer is accused of murdering his mistress.
Tolerable roman policier.
w Edmund Ward *novel* Love in Amsterdam by Nicolas Freeling *d* Gerry O'Hara *ph* Gerry Fisher *m* Patrick John Scott
☆ Wolfgang Kieling, William Marlowe, Catherina von Schell

The Amsterdam Kill
Hong Kong 1977 93m Technicolor Panasonic
Golden Harvest/Fantastic Films/Raymond Chow
An American ex-Drug Enforcement Agency officer tries to protect an old friend caught in the Hong Kong drug wars.
Roughly made and uninventive thriller in which the Hong Kong film makers fail to consolidate the international ground they gained with kung fu films.
w Robert Clouse, Gregory Teifer *d* Robert Clouse *ph* Alan Hume *m* Hal Schaffer
☆ Robert Mitchum, Bradford Dillman, Richard Egan, Leslie Nielsen, Keye Luke

'Be glad you're afraid. It means you're still alive'
Amsterdamned *
Netherlands 1988 113m colour
Vestron/First Floor Features (Laurens Geels, Dick Maas)
A cop is assigned to discover the murderer of a prostitute found floating in a canal.
Deft action picture that makes the most of its waterfront setting.
wd Dick Maas *ph* Marc Felperlaan *m* Dick Maas *pd* Dick Schillemans *ed* Hans Van Dongen
☆ Huub Stapel, Monique Van de Ven, Serge-Henri Valcke, Tanneke Hartsuiker, Wim Zomer, Hidde Maas

Amy
US 1981 100m Technicolor
Walt Disney
A spinster is taught a little about life and love.
Unmemorable family comedy drama.
w Noreen Stone *d* Vincent McEveety
☆ Jenny Agutter, Barry Newman, Kathleen Nolan, Chris Robinson, Margaret O'Brien, Nanette Fabray

'In the heart of an outcast He found his destiny. In the passion of an outsider She found her home.'
Amy Foster
GB/US/France 1997 113m Technicolor Panavision
Columbia TriStar (Polly Tapson, Charles Steel, Beeban Kidron)
US title: *Swept from the Sea*
In Cornwall, a shipwrecked Russian marries a local servant girl, but the course of true love is far from smooth.
A period story of love blossoming in an inward-looking and isolated community, this good-looking movie is curiously short of felt emotion; it may look more at home on video or TV.
w Tim Willocks *story* Joseph Conrad *d* Beeban Kidron *ph* Dick Pope *m* John Barry *pd* Simon Holland *ed* Alex Mackie, Andrew Mondshein
☆ Vincent Perez, Rachel Weisz, Ian McKellen, Joss Ackland, Kathy Bates, Tom Bell, Zoë Wanamaker, Tony Haygarth
'Almost exemplary of present Hollywood practice in that prodigious amounts of touch, care and technical skill have succeeded in turning Conrad's hard nugget of a yarn into a piece of sumptuous mush.' – *Peter Matthews, Sight and Sound*

'When you can't breathe, you can't scream.'
'It will take your breath away.'
Anaconda
US 1997 89m colour Panavision
Columbia/CL Cinema Line (Verna Harrah, Leonard Rabinowitz, Carole Little)
An anthropologist goes looking for a tribe of Indians in the rainforest and finds a gigantic killer snake instead.
A bungled rip-off of Jaws, with Voight, who seems to relish his role as an expert snake-hunter, providing what sounds like a parody of Brando at his most excessive; otherwise the action is decidedly tame.
w Hans Bauer, Jim Cash, Jack Epps Jnr *d* Luis Llosa *ph* Bill Butler *m* Randy Edelman *pd* Kirk M. Petruccelli *ed* Michael R. Miller *sp* Walt Conti, John Nelson
☆ Jennifer Lopez, Ice Cube, Jon Voight, Eric Stoltz, Jonathan Hyde, Owen Wilson, Kari Wuhrer, Vincent Castellanos, Danny Trejo
'The big, bad anaconda never really develops any personality – menacing or otherwise – and remains nothing more than a jack-in-the-box gimmick.' – *Joe Leydon, Variety*
† Like Congo the year before, it was a bad adventure film that found an audience, grossing $66m in the US, and another $70m elsewhere.

'Back in therapy.'
Analyze That
US/Australia 2002 96m Technicolor
Warner/Village Roadshow/NPV/Baltimore Spring Creek/Face/Tribeca (Paula Weinstein, Jane Rosenthal)
An imprisoned gangster fakes a breakdown so he can be released into the custody of his neurotic psychiatrist.
Unnecessary sequel; the second time around the jokes fall flat.
w Peter Steinfeld, Harold Ramis, Peter Tolan *d* Harold Ramis *ph* Ellen Kuras *m* David Holmes *pd* Wynn Thomas *ed* Andrew Mondshein
☆ Robert De Niro (Paul Vitti), Billy Crystal (Ben Sobel), Lisa Kudrow (Laura Sobel), Joe Viterelli (Jelly), Reg Rogers (Raoul Berman), Cathy Moriarty-Gentile (Patti LoPresti), John Finn (Richard Chapin), Kyle Sabihy (Michael Sobel)
'Somewhat lacking any genuine spark. However, this doesn't stop it being surprisingly funny at points.' – *Empire*
'Some of the jokes work, some don't; the best you can say is that the time passes pleasantly.' – *Andrew Pulver, Guardian*

'You try telling him his 50 minutes are up.'
Analyze This **
US 1999 103m Technicolor
Warner/Village Roadshow/NPV/Baltimore/Spring Creek/Face/Tribeca (Paula Weinstein, Jane Rosenthal)
An ageing Mafia gangster consults a psychiatrist about his anxiety attacks.
A witty comedy that lets De Niro play to good effect against his more familiar Mafia roles and which also has fun at the excesses of psychobabble.
w Peter Tolan, Kenneth Lonergan *d* Harold Ramis *ph* Stuart Dryburgh *m* Howard Shore *pd* Wynn Thomas *ed* Christopher Tellefsen
☆ Robert De Niro, Billy Crystal, Lisa Kudrow, Joe Viterelli, Chazz Palminteri, Bill Macy, Leo Rossi, Kyle Sabihy, Rebecca Schull, Molly Shannon, Max Casella, Pat Cooper
'Has a funny title, an even funnier premise and inspired odd-couple casting that's enough to prompt laughter just on the basis of its two-shots in the ad campaign. Think of it as an offer you can't refuse.' – *Janet Maslin, New Yorker*
† It was followed by a sequel *Analyze That* (*qv*).

'The most amazing conspiracy the world has ever known, and love as it never happened to a man and woman before!'
Anastasia **
GB 1956 105m Eastmancolor Cinemascope
TCF (Buddy Adler)
In 1928 Paris, a group of exiled White Russians claim to have found the living daughter of the Tsar, presumed executed in 1918; but the claimant is a fake schooled by a general, with whom she falls in love.
Slick, highly theatrical entertainment for the upper classes; it dazzles and satisfies without throwing any light on history. The film marked Bergman's Hollywood comeback after some years in Europe under a cloud for her 'immoral' behaviour.
w Arthur Laurents *play* Marcelle Maurette, Guy Bolton *d* Anatole Litvak *ph* Jack Hildyard *m* Alfred Newman *ad* Andrei Andreiev, Bill Andrews
☆ *Ingrid Bergman*, Yul Brynner, *Helen Hayes*, Martita Hunt, Akim Tamiroff, Felix Aylmer, Ivan Desny
'Little weight but considerable and urbane charm.' – *John Cutts*
Ingrid Bergman
Alfred Newman

'Discover the Adventure Behind the Greatest Mystery of Our Time.'
Anastasia
US 1997 94m Technicolor Cinemascope
TCF (Don Bluth, Gary Goldman)
A young girl travels from Russia to Paris, claiming to be the long-lost Anastasia, the daughter of Tsar Nicholas.
An extraordinarily misguided attempt to make a Disney-styled animated feature from events that do not fit the formula: the villains here are a dead Rasputin and his pet bat.
w Susan Gautheir, Bruce Graham, Bob Tzudiker, Noni White *play* Marcelle Maurette, adapted by Guy Bolton *screenplay* Arthur Laurents, adapted by Eric Tuchman *d* Don Bluth, Gary Goldman *m* David Newman *m/ly* Lynn Ahrens, Stephen Flaherty *ed* Fiona Trayler
☆ Featuring the voices of: Meg Ryan, John Cusack, Kelsey Grammer, Christopher Lloyd, Hank Azaria, Bernadette Peters, Kirsten Dunst; singers: Liz Callaway, Lacey Chabert, Jim Cummings, Jonathan Dokuchitz
'An ambitious, serious but not particularly stimulating musical feature that unconvincingly attempts to graft warm and cuddly family fare onto turbulent aspects of modern history and mythology.' – *Todd McCarthy, Variety*
Stephen Flaherty, Lynn Ahrens, David Newman; song 'Journey to the Past' (*m* Stephen Flaherty, *ly* Lynn Ahrens)

Anatahan
Japan 1953 92m bw
Daiwa (K. Takimura)
aka: *The Saga of Anatahan*
During World War II, Japanese seamen are shipwrecked on the same deserted island as a man and a woman; the latter causes jealousy and murder.
Downright peculiar studio-set melodrama, based on true events and its creator through interpreters, with results far from happy.
m A. Ifukube *wd/ph* Josef von Sternberg
☆ Akemi Negishi, T. Sugunuma, K. Onoe, T. Bandoh
'The main impression is of tedium relieved by moments of far from intentional humour.' – *Penelope Houston*

The Anatolian Smile: see *America, America*

'Last year's number one best seller. This year's (we hope) number one motion picture!'
Anatomy of a Murder **
US 1959 161m bw
Columbia/Carlyle/Otto Preminger
A small-town lawyer successfully defends an army officer accused of murdering a bartender who had assaulted his wife.
Overlong and over-faithful version of a highly detailed courtroom bestseller. The plot is necessarily equivocal, the characterizations overblown, but the trial commands some interest, and the use of 'daring' words in evidence caused controversy at the time. It was Scott's first notable role, as the prosecutor.
w Wendell Mayes *novel* Robert Traver *d* Otto Preminger *ph* Sam Leavitt *m* Duke Ellington *pd* Boris Leven *ed* Louis R. Loeffler
☆ James Stewart (Paul Biegler), Ben Gazzara (Lt Frederick Manion), Lee Remick (Laura Manion), Eve Arden (Maida), Arthur O'Connell (Parnell McCarthy), George C. Scott (Claude Dancer), Kathryn Grant (Mary Pilant), Orson Bean (Dr Smith), Murray Hamilton (Alphonse Paquette)
† The trial judge was played by Joseph N. Welch, a real-life judge who had gained fame in 1954 by representing the army against Senator McCarthy.
picture; Wendell Mayes; Sam Leavitt; James Stewart; Arthur O'Connell; George C. Scott; editing

Anchor Zone
Canada 1994 82m colour
Norstar/Red Ochre (Ken Pittman)
In 2010, at a seaport controlled by a ruthless corporation, a trainee and a young boy, the subject of an experiment to increase his intelligence, join young runaways in a hostile society.
Dreary low-budget science-fiction, with the usual mad scientists in an apocalyptic setting.
w T. H. Hatte *d* Andrée Pelletier *ph* Michael Jones *m* Sandy Morris *pd* Pam Hall *ed* Hélène Girard, Mike Munn
☆ Michael Luke (Ved), Henry Czerny (Lawson Hughes), Nicole Stoffman (Robin), Phelim Martin (Dogface), Andrew Younghusband (Brogan), Mark Critch (Radd), Ron Hynes (Colonel Bob), Janis Spence (Coral), Sebastian Spence (Duke), John Ryan (Sam)

Anchoress
GB/Belgium 1993 108m bw
BFI/Corsan (Paul Breuls, Ben Gibson)
In 14th-century England, a young woman obsessed by the Virgin Mary is walled up in a small cell in the village church and then decides she wants to leave.
Grimly downbeat account of medieval life, hovering on the edge of parody and lacking narrative drive.
w Judith Stanley-Smith, Catherine Vandeleene *d* Chris Newby *ph* Michel Baudour *pd* Niek Kortekaas *ed* Brand Thumin
☆ Natalie Morse, Eugene Bervoets, Toyah Wilcox, Peter Postlethwaite, Christopher Eccleston, Michael Pas, Brenda Bertin
'Evocatively designed period pic creates a long ago world yet remains relevant on such issues as what recourse women have in a man's world and

how faith grounded in nature fares against faith dictated by the clergy.' – *Variety*

Anchors Aweigh **
US 1945 139m Technicolor
MGM (Joe Pasternak)
Two sailors on leave in Los Angeles get involved with a small boy who wants to join the navy.
Rather droopy musical most notable as a forerunner of On the Town, though on much more conventional lines. Amiable performances, and a brilliant dance with a cartoon mouse, save the day.
w Isobel Lennart d George Sidney ph Robert Planck, Charles Boyle m George Stoll m/ly Jule Styne, Sammy Cahn pd Cedric Gibbons
☆ Frank Sinatra, Gene Kelly, Kathryn Grayson, Jose Iturbi, Sharon McManus, Carlos Ramirez, Dean Stockwell, Pamela Britton
♫ 'We Hate to Leave'; 'What Makes the Sun Set?'; 'The Charm of You'; 'I Begged Her'; 'I Fall in Love Too Easily'; 'The Worry Song'
George Stoll
picture; Robert Planck; Gene Kelly; song 'I Fall in Love Too Easily' (m Jule Styne, ly Sammy Cahn)

And Baby Makes Three
US 1950 83m bw
Columbia (Robert Lord)
A wife divorces her compromised husband before discovering that she is pregnant.
Thin marital comedy with minor compensations.
w Lou Breslow, Joseph Hoffman d Henry Levin ph Burnett Guffey m George Duning
☆ Robert Young, Barbara Hale, Billie Burke, Robert Hutton, Janis Carter, Nicholas Joy, Lloyd Corrigan
'It has everything but a story that hangs together.' – *New York Herald Tribune*

'And God created woman. But the Devil created Brigitte Bardot'
And God Created Woman
France 1957 90m Eastmancolor
Cinemascope
Iéna-Hodu/UCIL/Cocinor (Raoul Lévy)
original title: *Et Dieu Créa la Femme*
aka: *And Woman ... Was Created*
An 18-year-old finds herself fatally attracted towards men.
Rather a feeble excuse for its star to strip on the St Tropez beach, but one that made her an international star.
w Roger Vadim, Raoul Lévy d Roger Vadim ph Armand Thirard m Paul Misraki ad Jean André
☆ Brigitte Bardot, Curt Jurgens, Jean-Louis Trintignant, Christian Marquand, Georges Poujouly, Jane Marken, Paul Faivre
'An open violation of conventional morality.' – *Catholic Legion of Decency*
'I'm prepared to bet an overcoat to a bikini that this film will make its star Miss Sex of the Universe.' – *Sketch*
'One of the most genuine, youthful and original works produced in France since 1945.' – *Louis Marcorelles, Sight and Sound*
† Vadim made a second film with this title (US 1987), see below.

And God Created Woman
US 1987 100m DeLuxe
Crow/Vestron (George P. Braunstein/Ron Hamady)
A woman marries so that she can get parole from prison and pursue her ambition to become a rock star.
Silly raucous remake that has nothing in common with Vadim's original but the title. This time the stripping is done by Rebecca de Mornay.
w R. J. Stewart d Roger Vadim ph Stephen M. Katz m Tom Chase, Steve Rucker pd Victor Kempster ed Suzanne Pettit
☆ Rebecca de Mornay, Vincent Spano, Frank Langella, Donovan Leitch

And Hope to Die
US/France/Canada 1972 104m bw
Serge Silberman/TCF
original title: *La Course du lièvre à travers les champs*
A fugitive Frenchman in Canada runs foul of criminals and gypsies and causes several deaths.
Muddled melodrama of the worst 'international' kind.
w Sebastien Japrisot d René Clément
☆ Jean-Louis Trintignant, Robert Ryan, Aldo Ray, Tisa Farrow, Lea Massari

And Justice for All
US 1979 119m Metrocolor
Columbia/Malton (Joe Wizan)
An American lawyer gets into all kinds of trouble, including the defence of a judge on a rape charge.
Not so much a satire as a series of random pot-shots at the legal system, sometimes funny but cumulatively stultifying.
w Valerie Curtin, Barry Levinson d Norman Jewison ph Frank Holgate m Dave Grusin
☆ Al Pacino, Jack Warden, John Forsythe, Lee Strasberg, Christine Lahti, Sam Levene, Jeffrey Taybor
'Most incriminating is its own hysterical imprecision and sentimental pleading.' – *Sight and Sound*
Al Pacino; screenplay

And Life Goes On... **
Iran 1992 108m colour
ICA/I.I.D.C.Y.A. (Ali Reza Zarrin)
original title: *Zendegi Va Digar Hich...*
A film director and his son visit part of Iran hit by an earthquake to discover if a boy who starred in his recent film is still alive.
An austere road movie composed of small episodes, in which, despite their tragedies, the survivors continue with the mundane matter of getting through the day.
wd Abbas Kiarostami ph Homayun Payvar m Vivaldi ed Abbas Kiarostami
☆ Ferhed Kherdamend, Buba Bayour

...and millions will die!
Australia 1973 96m Eastmancolor
Allied Artists/Apa (Mende Brown)
A scientist tracks down a hidden store of nerve gas, secreted by a Nazi war criminal, that threatens the population of Hong Kong.
Muddled thriller with irrelevant and undeveloped subplots; it lacks suspense, probably because the bad guys are killed off early in the film.
w Michael Fisher d Leslie H. Martinson ph Paul Onorato m Laurie Lewis ed Richard Hindley
☆ Richard Basehart, Susan Strasberg, Leslie Nielsen, Peter Sumner, Joseph Furst, Alwyn Kurts, Tony Wager

And Now for Something Completely Different **
GB 1971 88m colour
Columbia/Kettledrum/Python (Patricia Casey)
Monty Python's Flying Circus perform again a selection of sketches from the BBC television series.
The first Monty Python film, intended to introduce the team's humour to an American audience. It lacks any overall coherence, but many of the individual sketches are a joy.
w Graham Chapman, John Cleese, Terry Gilliam, Eric Idle, Terry Jones, Michael Palin d Ian MacNaughton ph David Muir ad Colin Grimes ed Thom Noble
☆ Graham Chapman, John Cleese, Terry Gilliam, Eric Idle, Terry Jones, Michael Palin, Carol Cleveland
'Very funny.' – *MFB*

And Now Miguel *
US 1965 95m Technicolor
Universal/Robert B. Radnitz
A 10-year-old Mexican boy proves himself worthy to work on the mountain with the sheep.
A children's film typical of its producer: good to look at, documentarily convincing, but too slight and too slow.
w Ted Sherdeman, Jane Klove novel Joseph Krumgold d James B. Clark ph Clifford Stine m Phillip Lambro
☆ Pat Cardi, Guy Stockwell, Clu Gulager, Michael Ansara, Joe de Santis

And Now My Love **
France/Italy 1974 121m Technicolor
Avco Embassy/Films 13/Rizzoli (Pierre Pardon)
original title: *Toute une Vie*
The love stories of three generations, from 1900 to 1974: a son is born to the wife of a soldier who dies in the First World War; he marries a woman who dies in childbirth; their daughter finds happiness with a film director.
An enjoyably romantic, if somewhat bland, panorama of the 20th century, taking in on the way most of the major events, seen as a background to individual relationships; the passage of time is paralleled by the development of cinema, the story beginning with grainy black and white photography and moving through the silent period to colour.
w Claude Lelouch, Pierre Uytterhoeven d Claude Lelouch ph Jean Collomb m Francis Lai ad François de Lamothe ed George Klotz
☆ Marthe Keller, André Dussolier, Charles Denner, Carla Gravina, Charles Gerard, Gilbert Bécaud, Alain Basnir, Daniel Boulanger
'No amount of technical wizardry can fully disguise the naivety of Lelouch's basic concept.' – *Geoff Brown, MFB*
† The version released in France ran for 150m and included a sequence set in the future.
screenplay

And Now The Screaming Starts
GB 1973 91m colour
Amicus (Max J. Rosenberg, Milton Subotsky)
A new bride in a country house is haunted by hallucinations of the past.
Grisly ghost story which overplays its hand and outstays its welcome.
w Roger Marshall novel Fengriffen by David Case d Roy Ward Baker ph Denys Coop m Douglas Gamley
☆ Peter Cushing, Stephanie Beacham, Herbert Lom, Patrick Magee, Ian Ogilvy, Geoffrey Whitehead, Guy Rolfe, Rosalie Crutchley

'Who are you that a man can't make love to you?'
And Now Tomorrow *
US 1944 86m bw
Paramount (Fred Kohlmar)
A rich girl goes deaf, loses her fiancé, but wins the poor doctor who cares for her.
Bestselling slush turned into a routine star romance. It was Ladd's first film in confirmed top-star status after a meteoric rise interrupted by war service.
w Frank Partos, Raymond Chandler (!) novel Rachel Field d Irving Pichel ph Daniel L. Fapp m Victor Young
☆ Loretta Young, Alan Ladd, Susan Hayward, Beulah Bondi, Cecil Kellaway, Barry Sullivan
'A vernal sign of the boys getting back to one of their favourite legends after the wintry days of war.' – *Richard Winnington*

And One Was Beautiful
US 1940 68m bw
MGM (Frederick Stephani)
A girl sets a trap for a playboy, who falls for her sister.
Cinderella-style second feature, quite unremarkable.
w Harry Clork story Alice Duer Miller d Robert Sinclair
☆ Robert Cummings, Laraine Day, Jean Muir, Billie Burke, Esther Dale

And So They Were Married
US 1935 74m bw
Columbia (B. P. Schulberg)
A widow and a widower try to get married despite the ill-feeling of their children.
Predictable romantic farce.
w Doris Anderson, Joseph Anthony d Elliott Nugent ph Henry Freulich m Howard Jackson
☆ Melvyn Douglas, Mary Astor, Edith Fellows, Jackie Moran, Donald Meek, Dorothy Stickney

And Soon the Darkness *
GB 1970 99m Technicolor
Associated British (Albert Fennell, Brian Clemens)
Of two young nurses on a cycling holiday in France, one is murdered by a local sex maniac and the other almost shares her fate.
Slow, overstretched, often risible suspenser on vanishing lady lines; long on red herrings and short on humour, but with some pretension to style. The action all takes place along a mile or two of sunlit country road.
w Brian Clemens, Terry Nation d Robert Fuest ph Ian Wilson m Laurie Johnson
☆ Pamela Franklin, Michele Dotrice, Sandor Eles, John Nettleton

'There's nothing but trouble in Paradise when the bandleader tries to make love to a whole sister act – simultaneously!'
And the Angels Sing *
US 1943 95m bw
Paramount (E. D. Leshin)
Four singing sisters have hectic adventures with a bandleader.
Mildly disarming romantic comedy with music, more firmly set in a recognizable social milieu than the usual fan product from this studio.
w Melvin Frank, Norman Panama, Claude Binyon d George Marshall ph Karl Struss m Victor Young m/ly Johnny Burke, Jimmy Van Heusen
☆ Dorothy Lamour, Diana Lynn, Betty Hutton, Mimi Chandler, Fred MacMurray, Raymond Walburn, Eddie Foy Jnr, Frank Albertson, Mikhail Rasumny
'Slapstick sophistication in a sub-Sturges manner.' – *MFB*
'Cruel, soggily professional, over-elaborate, and inclined towards snobbish whimsy.' – *James Agee*

And the Band Played On *
US 1993 141m colour
ITC/Odyssey/HBO (Midge Sanford, Sarah Pillsbury)
Doctors investigating a disease affecting homosexual men in America discover that it is sexually transmitted and first name it GRID (Gay Related Immune Deficiency) and then, when it is discovered that the virus is no respecter of sexuality, call it AIDS.
A confusing dramatization of Shilts's angry book on the first years of AIDS and the inactivity of the government and other organizations in dealing with it; it leaves one little wiser, though sadder, than before.
w Arnold Schulman book Randy Shilts d Roger Spottiswoode ph Paul Elliott, Paul Ryan m Carter Burwell pd Victoria Paul ed Lois Freeman-Fox
☆ Matthew Modine, Alan Alda, Richard Gere, Patrick Bauchau, Nathalie Baye, Christian Clemenson, Phil Collins, Bud Cort, Alex Courtney, David Dukes, David Clennon, Anjelica Huston, Steve Martin, Ian McKellen, Lily Tomlin
'Spottiswoode's engrossing, powerful work still accomplishes its mission: Shilts' book, with all its shock, sorrow and anger, has been transferred decisively to the screen.' – *Variety*
'The result is sometimes both informative and moving but also in places a little dull and unfocused, as if those who made the film were too conscientious to leave anything out and too scared to make a proper fiction out of history.' – *Derek Malcolm, Guardian*
† The film, made for American television, was given a cinema release in Britain. The book was originally optioned in 1989 but twice plans to film it fell through. This version had a troubled production, with two directors quitting and Spottiswoode leaving during the post-production process, and it was criticized by Shilts himself shortly before his death in February 1994.

And the Ship Sails On *
Italy/France 1983 132m Technicolor
Panavision
RAI/Vides/Gaumont (Franco Cristaldi)
original title: *E la Nave Va*
From Naples in 1914 a luxurious liner sets forth to scatter the ashes of an opera singer.
Less a Ship of Fools than a theatre of the absurd, with familiar Fellini caricatures going through their paces against studio sets. Fascination alternates with boredom.
w Federico Fellini, Tonino Guerra d Federico Fellini ph Giuseppe Rotunno m Gianfranco Plenizio ad Dante Ferretti ed Ruggero Mastroianni
☆ Freddie Jones, Barbara Jefford, Victor Poletti, Peter Cellier, Elisa Mainardi, Norma West
'A genial movie, although a bit discontinuous.' – *Alberto Moravia*
'A vessel that is chock-full of his best gags, visual fun and love of cinema as artful technique.' – *Variety*
'Too much a work of the pure imagination with the result that the audience is cast adrift on a styrofoam sea without a lifeline to any kind of recognizable reality.' – *Andrew Sarris, Village Voice*

And Then There Were None ****

US 1945 97m bw
Popular Pictures/Harry M. Popkin (René Clair)

GB title: *Ten Little Niggers*

Ten people are invited to a house party on a lonely island, and murdered one by one.

A classic mystery novel is here adapted and directed with the utmost care to provide playful black comedy, stylish puzzlement, and some splendid acting cameos.

w Dudley Nichols *novel* Agatha Christie (aka: Ten Little Niggers) *d* René Clair *ph* Lucien Andriot *m* Mario Castelnuovo-Tedesco

☆ Walter Huston, Barry Fitzgerald, Louis Hayward, June Duprez, Roland Young, Richard Haydn, C. Aubrey Smith, Judith Anderson, Queenie Leonard, Mischa Auer

MISS BRENT: 'Very stupid to kill the only servant in the house. Now we don't even know where to find the marmalade.'

JUDGE QUINCANNON: 'Mr Owen could only come to the island in one way. It's perfectly clear. Mr Owen is one of us.'

ROGERS: 'Never in my life have I been accused of any crime, sir – and if that's what you think of me, I shan't serve any dinner.'

'Rich in the elements which have made mystery melodramas popular, yet not in the precise form of any previously made.' – *Hollywood Reporter*

'The efforts at sprightly, stylish comedy don't gain much momentum.' – *Pauline Kael, New Yorker, 70s*

And Then There Were None

GB 1974 98m Technicolor
EMI/Filibuster (Harry Alan Towers)
US title: *Ten Little Indians*

Ten people are lured to an isolated Persian hotel and murdered one by one.

Listless remake, often so inept you could scream.

w Peter Welbeck (Harry Alan Towers) *d* Peter Collinson *ph* Fernando Arribas *m* Bruno Nicolai

☆ Oliver Reed, Richard Attenborough, Elke Sommer, Herbert Lom, Gert Frobe, Stéphane Audran, Charles Aznavour, Adolfo Celi, Alberto de Mendoza, Maria Rohm

And There Was Jazz *

Poland 1981 90m bw
Zespoly Filmowe (Andrzej Soltysik)
aka: *Byl Jazz*

In Poland of the 1950s, a group of students playing classic jazz become a symbol of opposition in a conformist society.

Like its subject matter, a small but engaging gesture of revolt. It was banned by the Polish authorities.

wd Feliks Falk *ph* Witold Sobocinski *m* Jerzy Matula *ad* Teresa Smus-Barska *ed* Miroslawa Garlicka

☆ Bozena Adamkowna, Michal Bajor, Andrzej Grabarczyk, Kazimierz Wysota, Jerzy Gudejko, Adrzej Chichlowski, Jacek Strzemzalski, Jacek Sass-Uhrynowski

And Woman ... Was Created: see *And God Created Woman*

And You Thought Your Parents Were Weird

US 1991 92m CFI color
Trimark/Panorama/Just Betzer

Two young inventors create a robot which is then possessed by the spirit and voice of their dead father.

Dull, sickly family comedy, which also exhibits some dubious attitudes to deception and death.

wd Tony Cookson *ph* Paul Elliot *m* Randy Miller *pd* Alexandra Kicenik *ed* Michael Ornstein

☆ Marcia Strassman, Joshua Miller, Edan Gross, John Quade, Sam Behrens, Alan Thicke (voice), Susan Gibney, A. J. Langer

'Cookson lays on the sentiment with a spatula towards the end. Still, story has plenty of heart, cast is enjoyable and Cookson has an instinct for the material that makes this humble outing uncalculated and even a bit soulful.' – *Variety*

† The film was released direct to video in Britain.

And Your Mother Too: see *Y Tu Mamá También*

The Anderson Tapes *

US 1971 98m Technicolor Panavision
Columbia/Robert M. Weitman

An ex-con forms a gang to rob a building, not knowing that police and others, for various purposes, are making tape recordings of his conversations.

Superficially slick and fashionable crime thriller, marred by unnecessarily flashy direction, a failure to explain enough about the tapes, and a climax which oddly mixes bloodshed and farce.

w Frank R. Pierson *novel* Lawrence Sanders *d* Sidney Lumet *ph* Arthur J. Ornitz *m* Quincy Jones

☆ Sean Connery, Martin Balsam, Dyan Cannon, Alan King, Ralph Meeker

'Out of the sea and into your heart.'

Andre *

US 1994 94m Eastmancolor
Clairmont Scope
Rank/Kushner-Locke (Annette Handley, Adam Shapiro)

A seven-year-old girl befriends a baby seal and protects it from the locals who regard it as a pest.

A film, based on a true story, to delight most children and which for the most part successfully skirts sentimentality; it gains immeasurably from the exuberant personality of its animal star.

w Dana Baratta *novel* A Seal Called Andre by Harry Goodridge, Lew Dietz *d* George Miller *ph* Thomas Burstyn *m* Bruce Rowland *pd* William Elliot *ed* Harry Hitner, Patrick Kennedy

☆ Keith Carradine, Tina Majorino, Chelsea Field, Aidan Pendleton, Shane Meier, Keith Szarabajka, Joshua Jackson, Tory

'For people who like to see animals put through their paces in the world's Marinelands without getting their own feet wet.' – *Alexander Walker, London Evening Standard*

'Call me heartless, but somehow I can't warm to a hero who resembles a giant garden slug in a false moustache.' – *Jonathan Romney, Guardian*

† Andre is played not by a seal but by a sea lion.

Andrei Rublev ****

USSR 1966 181m bw/colour Cinemascope
Mosfilm

Imaginary episodes from the life of a 15th-century icon painter.

A superb recreation of medieval life dramatizes the eternal problem of the artist, whether to take part in the life around him or merely comment on it.

w Andrei Mikhalkov-Konchalovsky, Andrei Tarkovsky *d* Andrei Tarkovsky *ph* Vadim Yusov *m* Vyacheslav Tcherniaiev

☆ Anatoly Solonitsin, Ivan Lapikov, Nikolai Grinko, Nikolai Sergeyev

'The one indisputable Russian masterpiece of the last decade.' – *Nigel Andrews, MFB, 1973*

'With the exception of the great Eisenstein, I can't think of any film which has conveyed a feeling of the remote past with such utter conviction ... a durable and unmistakable masterpiece.' – *Michael Billington, Illustrated London News*

† The film was later released in a "director's cut" running for 205m.

Androcles and the Lion **

US 1952 96m bw
RKO (Gabriel Pascal)

A slave takes a thorn from the paw of a lion which later, in the arena, refuses to eat him.

Shavian drollery, with interpolated discussions on faith, is scarcely ideal cinema material, but gusto in the performances keeps it going despite stolid direction.

w Chester Erskine *play* Bernard Shaw *d* Chester Erskine *ph* Harry Stradling *m* Frederick Hollander *ad* Harry Horner

☆ Alan Young, Jean Simmons, Robert Newton, Victor Mature, Maurice Evans (Caesar), Reginald Gardiner, Elsa Lanchester, Alan Mowbray, Gene Lockhart

† Production had previously begun with Harpo Marx as Androcles and Rex Harrison as Caesar.

Android *

US 1982 80m DeLuxe
New World/Android (Mary Ann Fisher)

In 2036, a police transport vehicle is hijacked in space, and the scientists on board, some of them androids, react in unexpected ways.

Cheaply made, but a bobby dazzler for science fiction addicts.

w James Reigle, Don Opper *d* Aaron Lipstadt *ph* Tim Suhrstedt *m* Don Preston

☆ Klaus Kinski, Brie Howard, Norbert Weisser, Crofton Hardester, Kendra Kirchner, Don Opper

'The best first feature since *Dark Star*.' – *Tom Milne, MFB*

The Andromeda Strain **

US 1970 131m Technicolor Panavision
Universal/Robert Wise

Scientists work frantically to neutralize an infected village, knowing that the least infection will cause their laboratory to self-destruct.

Solemn and over-detailed but generally suspenseful thriller, with a sense of allegory about man's inhumanity to man.

w Nelson Gidding *novel* Michael Crichton *d* Robert Wise *ph* Richard H. Kline *m* Gil Melle *ad* Boris Leven

☆ Arthur Hill, David Wayne, James Olson, Kate Reid, Paula Kelly

Andy Hardy Comes Home *

US 1958 81m bw
MGM (Red Doff)

Fortyish Andy returns to Carvel, his home town, to negotiate a land deal.

Rather dismal sequel to the celebrated series of Hardy family comedies which were enormously popular in the early forties: a thirteen-year gap is too long, and although most of the family is reunited the old Judge is sadly missed.

w Edward Everett Hutshing, Robert Morris Donley *d* Howard W. Koch *ph* William W. Spencer, Harold E. Wellman *m* Van Alexander

☆ Mickey Rooney, Fay Holden, Cecilia Parker, Patricia Breslin, Sara Haden, Jerry Colonna

† See also under *Hardy Family*.

Andy Warhol's Bad

US 1976 109m Technicolor
EMI/Andy Warhol (Jeff Tornberg)

A housewife, who runs an assassination bureau using young female killers, employs a man – with fatal results.

A tedious, sloppily made horror movie.

w Pat Hackett, George Abagnalo *d* Jed Johnson *ph* Alan Metzger *m* Mike Bloomfield *ad* Eugene Rudolf *ed* David McKenna

☆ Carroll Baker, Perry King, Gordon Oas-Heim, Cyrinda Fox, Matthew Anton, Cathy Roskam, Susan Tyrrell, Brigid Polk, Lawrence Tierney

† The film was cut to 104m on its British release.

Andy Warhol's Dracula: see *Dracula*

Andy Warhol's Flesh: see *Flesh*

Andy Warhol's Heat: see *Heat*

Andy Warhol's Lonesome Cowboys: see *Lonesome Cowboys*

Andy Warhol's Trash: see *Trash*

'I want love – and I'm going to get it!'

Angel *

US 1937 98m bw
Paramount (Ernst Lubitsch)

The wife of an English diplomat finds herself neglected and almost has an affair with his old friend.

A curious romantic comedy in many ways typical of its time, yet with very few laughs, showing none of its director's usual cinematic sense, and compromised by the censor's refusal to let a spade be called a spade. Underplaying, and a sense that we watch a way of life about to be swept away, just about save it.

w Samson Raphaelson *play* Melchior Lengyel *d* Ernst Lubitsch *ph* Charles Lang *m* Frederick Hollander

☆ Marlene Dietrich, Herbert Marshall, Melvyn Douglas, Edward Everett Horton, Laura Hope Crews, Ernest Cossart

MARIA: 'What's the matter, darling? Is it France?'
SIR FREDERICK: 'No, no. Jugoslavia.'
MARIA: 'Oh, I see.'

'A rich Hollywood dish that copies foreign recipes. It's a good picture and in the keys, especially for the carriage trade, it can't miss.' – *Variety*

'Very sophisticated, very subtle, very chic, vastly polished and entertaining.' – *Literary Digest*

'The production is performed with studied deliberation.' – *New York Times*

'This movie isn't essentially different from the best of Lubitsch, but it's attenuated. It's the sort of cultivated triangular love affair in which each of the three has a turn at the piano.' – *Pauline Kael, 70s*

Angel *

Eire 1982 92m Technicolor
Motion Picture Company of Ireland/Irish Film Board/Channel 4 (John Boorman)
US title: *Danny Boy*

Against a background of the Irish troubles, a saxophonist is drawn into a maze of violence when he attempts to avenge the murder of a mute girl.

Glumly Irish thriller with metaphysical overtones as well as references to the state of Ireland. Keen narrative style is dissipated by overkill.

wd Neil Jordan *ph* Chris Menges *m* Verdi

☆ Stephen Rea, Veronica Quilligan, Alan Devlin, Peter Caffrey

'The film's style might be called flamboyant or baroque – or damned as pretentious – but it's a genuine style, a way of speaking. No one else speaks quite this way.' – *Michael Wilmington, Los Angeles Times*

'Honor student by day – hooker by night!'
'You're young, attractive and healthy – and swimming in a toilet bowl!'

Angel

US 1983 93m CFI color
New World/Adam's Apple/Angel (Sandy Howard)

A 15-year-old student doubles as a Hollywood hooker and takes on a psychopathic killer.

Yucky melodrama with no holds barred, not even moments of humour.

w Robert Vincent O'Neil, Joseph M. Cala *d* Robert Vincent O'Neil *ph* Andrew Davis *m* Craig Safan

☆ Cliff Gorman, Donna Wilkes, Rory Calhoun, Susan Tyrrell, Dick Shawn, John Diehl, Elaine Giftos

'A tasteless blend of realism and farce.' – *Sunday Times*

† A sequel appeared in 1985 under the title *Avenging Angel*. Betsy Russell was the girl, now hunting down her mentor.

Angel and the Badman *

US 1946 100m bw
Republic (John Wayne)

The love of a Quaker girl converts a wounded gunslinger to an honourable life.

Thoughtful Western with good background detail and a fair measure of action.

wd James Edward Grant *ph* Archie Stout *m* Richard Hageman *pd* Ernst Fegte

☆ John Wayne, Gail Russell, Harry Carey, Bruce Cabot, Irene Rich, Tom Powers

'Unpretentious, sweet-tempered and quite likeable.' – *James Agee*

Angel, Angel, Down We Go

US 1969 93m colour
AIP (Jerome F. Katzman)

Decadence in Hollywood: rock and rollers invade the lives of a rich family.

Unpleasant blather with a star well past her prime.

wd Robert Thom

☆ Jennifer Jones, Jordan Christopher, Roddy McDowall, Lou Rawls, Holly Near, Charles Aidman

An Angel at My Table **
New Zealand/Australia 1990 160m colour
Hibiscus Films/N.Z. Film Commission/TV New Zealand/ABC (Bridget Ikin)

A shy and introverted writer is wrongly diagnosed as a schizophrenic.
The biography of a notable poet, edited from a three-hour television miniseries.
w Laura Jones *book* Janet Frame's autobiographies *d* Jane Campion *ph* Stuart Dryburgh *m* Don McGlashan *pd* Grant Major *ed* Veronica Haussler
☆ Kerry Fox, Alexia Keogh, Karen Fergusson, Iris Churn, K. J. Wilson, Melina Bernecker, Glynis Angell, Sarah Smuts-Kennedy, Colin McColl
'A potentially painful and harrowing film is imbued with gentle humor and great compassion, which makes every character (even the unappealing ones) come vividly to life.' – *Variety*

Angel Baby *
US 1960 97m bw
Madera (Thomas F. Woods)

A mute girl is cured by an evangelist, and renounces her sins.
Strident, vigorous low-budget melodrama.
w Oris Borstem, Samuel Roeca, Paul Mason *novel* Jenny Angel by Elsie Oaks Barbour *d* Paul Wendkos *ph* Haskell Wexler, Jack Marta *m* Wayne Shanklin
☆ Salome Jens, George Hamilton, Joan Blondell, Mercedes McCambridge, Henry Jones, Burt Reynolds

'In Love. In Deep. In Danger.'
Angel Baby *
Australia 1995 103m colour
AFFC/Stamen/Meridian (Timothy White, Jonathan Shteinman)

After they meet at a clinic, two psychiatric patients fall in love and decide to set up home together.
A grim and harrowing tale of a doomed love, a relationship between damaged people in a world that fails to understand them; its tragic protagonists lack depth, and are characterized mainly by their sickness.
wd Michael Rymer *ph* Ellery Ryan *m* John Clifford White, Gavin Friday, Maurice Seezer *pd* Chris Kennedy *ed* Danny Cooper
☆ John Lynch, *Jacqueline McKenzie*, Colin Friels, Deborra-Lee Furness, Robyn Nevin, David Argue, Jane Menelaus
'Should click with young auds who'll connect with the radiant but deeply troubled lovers.' – *Variety*

Angel Dust *
France 1987 95m colour
UGC/President Films/Top No 1/FR3/Films de La Saga/La Sofica (Jacques-Eric Strauss)

aka: *Poussière d'Ange*
A detective, whose life begins to fall to pieces after his wife leaves him, becomes involved with a young girl and a series of strange murders.
Acerbic thriller about the corrupting influence of sexual desire.
w Edouard Niermans, Jacques Audiard, Alain le Henry *d* Edouard Niermans *ph* Bernard Lutic *m* Leon Senza, Vincent-Marie Bouvot *pd* Dominique Maleret *ed* Yves Deschamps, Jacques Witta
☆ Bernard Giraudeau, Fanny Bastien, Fanny Cottencon, Michel Aumont, Jean-Pierre Sentier, Gérard Blain, Luc Lavandier

El Angel Exterminador: see *The Exterminating Angel*

'The Deeper You Look, The More You Will Find.'
Angel Eyes
US 2001 104m DeLuxe
Warner/Morgan Creek/Franchise (Mark Canton, Elie Samaha)

A tough, streetwise female cop begins an affair with a mysterious, sensitive man after he saves her life.
Slick, glutinous, melodramatic soap opera of a mismatched couple.
w Gerald DiPego *d* Luis Mandoki *ph* Piotr Sobocinski *m* Marco Beltrami *pd* Dean Tavoularis *ed* Jerry Greenberg
☆ Jennifer Lopez (Sharon Pogue), Jim Caviezel (Catch), Sonia Braga (Josephine Pogue), Terrence Howard (Robby), Jeremy Sisto (Larry), Victor Argo (Carl Pogue), Monet Mazur (Kathy Pogue), Shirley Knight (Elanora), Daniel Magder (Larry Jnr)
'Takes an offensively simple, sentimental view of the way a little love and forgiveness can solve problems of abusive relationships.' – *Philip French, Observer*
'A riveting drama about wounded hearts and second chances.' – *Joe Leydon, San Francisco Examiner*

Angel Face *
US 1952 91m bw
RKO (Otto Preminger)
A demented girl murders her father and stepmother, involving her chauffeur, whom she finally kills, and commits suicide.
Outrageous melodrama, so absurd as to be almost endearing.
w Frank Nugent, Oscar Millard *d* Otto Preminger *ph* Harry Stradling *m* Dimitri Tiomkin
☆ Jean Simmons, Robert Mitchum, Herbert Marshall, Barbara O'Neil, Leon Ames, Mona Freeman, Kenneth Tobey, Raymond Greenleaf
'The one lyrical nightmare in the cinema.' – *Ian Cameron*

An Angel from Texas *
US 1940 69m bw
Warner (Robert Fellows)
Misadventures of a country boy in New York.
Modest revamping of a much filmed farce, also made as The Tenderfoot (1928) and Dance Charlie Dance (1937).
w Fred Niblo Jnr, Bertram Millhauser *play* *The Butter and Egg Man* by George F. Kaufman *d* Ray Enright *ph* Arthur L. Todd *m* Howard Jackson *ed* Clarence Kolster
☆ Eddie Albert, Rosemary Lane, Wayne Morris, Ronald Reagan, Milburn Stone

Angel Heart *
US 1987 113m Technicolor
Tri-Star/Kassar-Vajna/Carolco/Winkast-Union (Alan Marshall, Elliott Kastner)

In 1955, a New York private eye descends into Hell.
He does, literally, in pursuit of a missing person who's opted out of a pact with the devil. Thoroughly unpleasant in detail, this wallow in the private eye cult constantly takes the eye with its pictorial qualities, even at its most nauseating.
wd Alan Parker novel Falling Angel by William Hjortsberg *ph* Michael Seresin *m* Trevor Jones *pd* Brian Morris
☆ Mickey Rourke, Robert De Niro, Lisa Bonet, Charlotte Rampling, Stocker Fontelieu, Brownie McGhee
'Faustian theme, heavy bloodletting and pervasive grimness may represent barriers too great for general audiences to surmount.' – *Daily Variety*

Angel in Exile
US 1948 90m bw
Republic
An ex-con heads for an abandoned Arizona mine to recover stolen gold.
Modest, effective Western about a baddie who reforms.
w Charles Larson *d* Allan Dwan, Philip Ford *ph* Reggie Lanning *m* Nathan Scott
☆ John Carroll, Adele Mara, Thomas Gomez

Angel in My Pocket
US 1969 105m Technicolor Techniscope
Universal (Ed Montagne)
A minister and his family arrive in a small town.
Simplistic comedy-drama with nothing to distinguish it from a dozen others in similar vein.
w Jim Fritzell, Everett Greenbaum *d* Alan Rafkin
☆ Andy Griffith, Jerry Van Dyke, Kay Medford, Edgar Buchanan, Margaret Hamilton, Gary Collins, Lee Meriwether, Henry Jones

The Angel Levine *
US 1970 105m DeLuxe
UA/Belafonte Enterprises (Chiz Schultz)
An elderly Jewish tailor complains to God of his bad luck; a black angel appears and seems to help him for a while.
Muddled and seemingly pointless parable with occasional felicities.
w Bill Gunn, Ronald Ribman *story* Bernard Malamud *d* Jan Kadar *ph* Richard Kratina *m* Zdenek Linka *pd* George Jenkins
☆ Zero Mostel, Harry Belafonte, Ida Kaminska, Milo O'Shea, Eli Wallach, Anne Jackson, Gloria Foster
'A prolonged variation on the theme that faith can produce miracles, but only if there is enough of it.' – *John Gillett*

The Angel of Broadway *
US 1927 82m approx bw silent
DeMille/Pathé
A night-club entertainer haunts Salvation Army missions in search of material, but ultimately joins the cause.
Fairly impressive propaganda piece of its time.
w Lenore J. Coffee *d* Lois Weber
☆ Leatrice Joy, Victor Varconi, May Robson, Alice Lake

Angel on My Shoulder **
US 1946 101m bw
UA/Charles R. Rogers

The devil promises leniency to a dead gangster if he will return to Earth and take over the body of a judge who is stamping out evil.
Crude but lively fantasy on the tail-end of the Here Comes Mr Jordan cycle, and by the same author.
w Harry Segall, Roland Kibbee *d* Archie Mayo *ph* James Van Trees *m* Dimitri Tiomkin
☆ *Paul Muni, Claude Rains*, Anne Baxter, Erskine Sanford, Hardie Albright
'The story is so imitative that it's hard to feel any more towards it than a mildly nostalgic regard.' – *Bosley Crowther*
'Witty, caustic and exciting.' – *Motion Picture Guide*

Angel on the Amazon
US 1948 86m bw
Republic (John H. Auer)
GB title: *Drums Along the Amazon*
An elderly white lady resident of the Amazon jungle looks only 25 after being scared by a panther...
Ludicrous melodrama which the actors take seriously.
w Lawrence Kimble *d* John H. Auer *ph* Reggie Lanning *m* Nathan Scott
☆ George Brent, Constance Bennett, Vera Hruba Ralston, Brian Aherne, Fortunio Bonanova, Alfonso Bedoya, Gus Schilling

Angel Sharks *
France 1997 93m colour 'Scope
Blue Light/Les Films de la Suane/Studio Image 2/La Sept/Lelia (Philippe Rousselet)
original title: *Marie Baie des Anges*
In a coastal area where teenage gangs roam, two outsiders come together for a brief moment of happiness.
Episodic low-life drama of petty crimes and promiscuity among doomed youth, directed with a sometimes haphazard energy.
wd Manuel Pradal *ph* Christopher Pollock *m* Carlo Crivelli *pd* Javier Po, Véronique Mellery *ed* Valerie Deseine
☆ Nicolas Welbers, Amira Casar, Swan Carpio, Jamie Harris, Frédéric Malgras, Vahina Giocante, Andrew Clover
'The plot simply isn't coherent or interesting enough to stop boredom setting in about halfway through and winds up really testing the outer regions of patience.' – *Jessica Mellor, Empire*

Angel Square *
Canada 1990 106m colour
Rendez-Vous/Wheeler-Hendren/Western International/Arvi Liimatainen

During Christmas in the late 1940s, a dreamy youth solves the mystery of who attacked the father of his Jewish friend.
Genial account of boyhood fantasies, complete with excursions into cartoon-like parodies of comic-strip adventures.
w James Defelice, Anne Wheeler *novel* Brian Doyle *d* Anne Wheeler *ph* Tobias Schliesller *m* George Blondheim *pd* John Blackie *ed* Peter Svab, Lenka Svab
☆ Ned Beatty, Jeremy Radick, Guillaume Lemay Thivierge, Marie Stefane Gaudry, Sarah Meyette, Nicola Cavendish, Brian Dooley, Michel Barrette

Angel Street: see *Gaslight (1939)*

The Angel Who Pawned Her Harp *
GB 1954 76m bw
Group Three (Sidney Cole)
A real angel arrives on a goodwill visit to seamy Islington, and manages to right a few wrongs.
Simple-minded whimsy, spottily effective, with good performances.
w Charles Terrot, Sidney Cole *d* Alan Bromly *ph* Arthur Grant *m* Antony Hopkins
☆ Diane Cilento, Felix Aylmer, Robert Eddison, Jerry Desmonde, Sheila Sweet, Alfie Bass

The Angel with the Trumpet
GB 1949 98m bw
British Lion/London Films (Karl Hartl)
An Austrian lady has an affair with a crown prince but marries for security and dies in defiance of the Nazis.
Curious European cavalcade, dully directed to keep the budget down and accommodate long stretches of an Austrian original. An eccentricity.
w Karl Hartl, Franz Tassie *novel* Ernst Lothar *d* Anthony Bushell *ph* Robert Krasker *m* Willy Schmidt-Gentner
☆ Eileen Herlie, Basil Sydney, Norman Wooland, Anthony Bushell, Maria Schell, John Justin, Oskar Werner, Andrew Cruickshank

The Angel Wore Red
US 1960 105m bw
MGM/Titanus/Spectator (Gottfredo Lombardo)
The love story of a priest and a prostitute in the Spanish Civil War.
Turgid farrago, unsatisfactory both romantically and politically.
wd Nunnally Johnson *ph* Giuseppe Rotunno *m* Bronislau Kaper
☆ Ava Gardner, Dirk Bogarde, Joseph Cotten, Vittorio de Sica, Aldo Fabrizi, Finlay Currie
'The stars show no apparent surprise that a film so empty of reward should take itself so seriously.' – *Peter John Dyer*

Angela
US 1955 81m bw
TCF/Patricia/Telecinema (Steven Pallos)
A former American racing driver working as a salesman in Italy finds himself involved in murder when he falls in love with a secretary.
Moody, unoriginal thriller in the film noir tradition, given a slight twist by being set in Rome.
w Jonathan Rix, Eduardo Anton *story* Steve Carruthers *d* Dennis O'Keefe *ph* Leonida Barboni *m* Mario Nascimbene *ad* Alfredo Montori *ed* Giancarlo Cappelli
☆ Dennis O'Keefe, Mara Lane, Rossano Brazzi, Arnoldo Foa, Galeazzo Benti, Nino Crisman, Enzo Fiermonte, John Fostini, Aldo Pini, Maria Teresa Paliani

Angela's Ashes **
US 1999 145m Technicolor
Universal/Paramount/Dirty Hands (Scott Rudin/David Brown/Alan Parker)

An Irish writer remembers his miserable Catholic childhood in Limerick, before he left to live in the United States.
Based on a best-selling memoir, this puts a Hollywood gloss on the rain-soaked poverty it depicts which, coupled with miscasting of the leading role, mutes its impact; it sputters only sporadically to life.
w Laura Jones, Alan Parker *book* Frank McCourt *d* Alan Parker *ph* Michael Seresin *m* John Williams *pd* Geoffrey Kirkland *ed* Gerry Hambling
☆ Emily Watson (Angela), Robert Carlyle (Dad), Joe Breen (Young Frank), Ciaran Owens (Middle Frank), Michael Legge (Older Frank), Ronnie Masterson (Grandma Sheehan), Pauline McLynn (Aunt Aggie), Liam Carney (Uncle Pa Keating),

Eanna Macliam (Uncle Pat), Andrew Bennett (Narrator)

'This is the kind of film about hardship in which nobody has indoor plumbing, but everyone has clean hair.' – *Janet Maslin, New York Times*

'The resilience of McCourt is admirable, but the film doesn't manage to enlist one's sympathies for his hard lot so much as eventually sow the suspicion that he's working it off on us.' – *Alexander Walker, London Evening Standard*

John Williams

The Angelic Conversation
GB 1985 80m colour
BFI/Derek Jarman (James Mackay)

Readings from Shakespeare's sonnets by Judi Dench are accompanied by a film of young men striking Christ-like poses or caressing each other.
Moody, grainy photography, much of it in jerky slow-motion, fails to illuminate the text.
d Derek Jarman *ph* Derek Jarman *m* Coil
ed Cerith Wyn Evans, Peter Cartwright
☆ Paul Reynolds, Philip Williamson

Angelina *
Italy 1947 98m bw
Lux-Ora (Paulo Frasca)
An impoverished housewife becomes the spokeswoman for her community on flooding, housing and other slum problems.
Reasonably rewarding star vehicle in the neo-realist tradition, this time angled for comedy.
w Suso Cecchi d'Amico, Piero Tellini, Luigi Zampa *d* Luigi Zampa *ph* Mario Craveri *m* Enzio Masetti
☆ Anna Magnani, Nando Bruno, Gianni Glori, Franco Zeffirelli

'At once kindly and fierce, witty and humorous, sad and richly gay. It warms your heart and breaks it, and has you laughing almost continuously.' – *Fred Majdalany*

'Behind the bubble and the chatter, the shouting and the running, the crowd and corteges that the Italians have always adored in their cinema, there is a genuine spring of fun that can only rise from a hopeful attitude towards God, and the right sort of optimism about one's neighbour.' – *C. A. Lejeune*

Angélique
France/West Germany/Italy 1964 116m
Eastmancolor Dyaliscope
Francos/CICC/Gloria/Fona Roma (Francis Cosne)

original title: *Angélique Marquise des Anges*
Adventures of a nobleman's daughter at the court of Louis XIV.
Watchable swashbuckling nonsense, a kind of French Forever Amber. Several sequels were made.
w Claude Brûlé, Bernard Borderie, Francis Cosne
novel Serge and Anne Golon *d* Bernard Borderie
ph Henri Persin *m* Michel Magne
☆ Michèle Mercier, Robert Hossein, Giuliano Gemma, Jean Rochefort, François Maistre, Jacques Toja

Angelo My Love
US 1982 116m colour
Lorton

Adventures of an eight-year-old gypsy boy in Manhattan.
Angelo is a precocious little rogue, but two hours is a long haul for this kind of ethnic medley.
wd Robert Duvall
☆ Angelo Evans, Michael Evans, Ruthie Evans, Steve Tsigonoff

'Duvall has done wonders with his actors and then robbed them of their glory by mishandling the tempo of the piece.' – *Sunday Times*

Angels: see *Angels in the Outfield (1994)*

'An elegant seduction. An erotic deception. A stunning revelation.'
Angels & Insects *
GB/US 1995 117m Technicolor
Film Four/Samuel Goldwyn/Playhouse (Joyce Herlihy, Belinda Haas)

A naturalist from a working-class background, who goes to work for an aristocrat, is attracted by his patron's eldest daughter and marries her, with unexpected results.
A dry, austere and sometimes stilted period drama, emphasizing the resemblance between the human and the insect world that obsesses the hero, though the final revelation seems more anagrammatic than anything else.
w Belinda Haas, Philip Haas *novel Morpho Eugenia* by A. S. Byatt *d* Philip Haas *ph* Bernard Zitzerman *m* Alexander Balanescu *pd* Jennifer Kernke *ed* Belinda Haas
☆ Mark Rylance, Kristin Scott-Thomas, Patsy Kensit, Jeremy Kemp, Douglas Henshall, Annette Badland, Chris Larkin, Anna Massey, Saskia Wickham

'It's not the usual period piece, but its literary origins are too evident and the passion for insect metaphors soon begins to pall.' – *Tom Shone, Sunday Times*

Paul Brown (costumes)

Angels and the Pirates: see *Angels in the Outfield (1952)*

Angel's Dance
US 1999 102m FotoKem
Promark/Videal (David Bixler)

A hitman and his apprentice are stalked by the woman they tried to use for target practice.
Tacky thriller, given to cheap sentimentality and risible situations.
wd David L. Corley *ph* Michael G. Wojciechowski *m* Tim Truman *pd* Patti Podesta
ed Sean Albertson
☆ James Belushi (Steve Rossellini), Sheryl Lee (Angelica Chaste), Kyle Chandler (Tony), Frank John Hughes (Nick), Ned Bellamy (Police Detective), Mark Carlton (Bob), Mac Davis (Norman), Jon Polito (Uncle Vinnie)

Angels Hard as They Come
US 1971 90m Metrocolor
New Realm/New World (Jonathan Demme)

Three bikers run into trouble in a ghost town inhabited by hippies but controlled by another gang of bikers.
Ponderous action movie, with a plot that seems to have been wrenched from some spaghetti Western, in which violence is seen as a force for good.
w Jonathan Demme, Joe Viola *d* Joe Viola
ph Steve Katz *m* Richard Hieronymous, Carp
ad Jack Fisk *ed* Joe Ravetz
☆ Scott Glenn, Charles Dierkop, Gilda Texter, James Iglehart, Garry Littlejohn, Gary Busey, Janet Wood, Don Carerra, Brendan Kelly, Larry Tucker

'The film's strivings for social and political significance are effectively smothered by the obligatory overlay of sex and violence.' – *John Raisbeck, MFB*

† The film was cut to 82m on its British release.

Angel's Holiday
US 1937 74m bw
John Stone/TCF
The niece of a newspaper editor rounds up a gang of racketeers.
Smart comedy vehicle for Shirley Temple's only rival.
w Frank Fenton, Lynn Root *d* James Tinling
☆ Jane Withers, Robert Kent, Joan Davis, Sally Blane, Harold Huber, Frank Jenks, John Qualen, Lon Chaney Jnr

Angels in the Outfield
US 1952 99m bw
MGM (Clarence Brown)

GB title: *Angels and the Pirates*
The profane and bad-tempered manager of an unsuccessful baseball team gets help from an angel.
Unamusing, saccharine whimsy which does not deserve its excellent production values.
w Dorothy Kingsley, George Wells *d* Clarence Brown *ph* Paul C. Vogel *m* Daniele Amfitheatrof
☆ Paul Douglas, Janet Leigh, Keenan Wynn, Lewis Stone, Donna Corcoran, Spring Byington, Bruce Bennett

'Ya Gotta Believe! It Could Happen.'
Angels in the Outfield
US 1994 102m Technicolor
Buena Vista/Walt Disney/Caravan (Irby Smith, Joe Roth, Roger Birnbaum)

GB title: *Angels*
A boy enlists the aid of angels so that a baseball team can be transformed from losers to winners, enabling him to be reunited with his father.
A remake that has made many alterations to the original story and added fancy special effects so that the angels are now visible; it is also far sweeter and no more successful as entertainment.
w Dorothy Kingsley, George Wells, Holly Goldberg Sloan *d* William Dear *ph* Matthew F. Leonetti *m* Randy Edelman *pd* Dennis Washington *ed* Bruce Green *sp* Giedra Rackauskas
☆ Danny Glover, Tony Danza, Brenda Fricker, Christopher Lloyd, Ben Johnson, Taylor Negron, Jay O. Sanders, Milton Davis Jnr

'Serves up its corn so unabashedly it's hard to take offence at its sappiness.' – *Variety*

Angels One Five *
GB 1952 98m bw
Templar (John W. Gossage)

A slice of life in an RAF fighter station during the Battle of Britain.
Underplayed semi-documentary drama with stiff upper lips all round and the emphasis on characterization rather than action. A huge commercial success in Britain.
w Derek Twist *d* George More O'Ferrall
ph Christopher Challis, Stanley Grant (air scenes)
m John Wooldridge
☆ Jack Hawkins, John Gregson, Michael Denison, Andrew Osborn, Cyril Raymond, Humphrey Lestocq, Dulcie Gray, Veronica Hurst

Angels Over Broadway
US 1940 80m bw
Columbia/Ben Hecht

During one rainy New York night, three of life's failures have one last stab at success.
Would-be poetic, moralizing melodrama very typical of its author; interesting but not a success.
w Ben Hecht *d* Ben Hecht, Lee Garmes *ph* Lee Garmes *m* George Antheil
☆ Douglas Fairbanks Jnr, Rita Hayworth, Thomas Mitchell, John Qualen, George Watts, Ralph Theodore

'There's a genial, original spirit to it.' – *New Yorker, 1978*

'It has excitement, fast talk, some knowable people, cynicism and sentiment.' – *Otis Ferguson*

† Sample dialogue: 'This town's a giant dice game ... come on, seven!'

Ben Hecht (as writer)

The Angels Wash Their Faces *
US 1939 86m bw
Warner (Max Siegel)
original title: *The Battle of City Hall*
A bad boy joins the Dead End Kids, but they all reform in the end.
Routine programmer, hastily concocted after the success of Angels with Dirty Faces.
w Michael Fessier, Niven Busch, Robert Buckner
d Ray Enright *ph* Arthur Todd *m* Adolph Deutsch
☆ Ann Sheridan, Ronald Reagan, the Dead End Kids, Bonita Granville, Frankie Thomas, Henry O'Neill, Berton Churchill, Eduardo Ciannelli

'Ray Enright's terrific meller pace makes it the sort of fare the average audience will eat up ... he has an eye for the spectacular, including a thrilling fire sequence and a dramatic courtroom scene.' – *Variety*

Angels with Dirty Faces ****
US 1938 97m bw
Warner (Sam Bischoff)

A Brooklyn gangster is admired by slum boys, but for their sake pretends to be a coward when he goes to the electric chair.
A shrewd, slick entertainment package and a seminal movie for all kinds of reasons. It combined gangster action with fashionable social conscience; it confirmed the Dead End Kids as stars; it provided archetypal roles for its three leading players and catapulted the female lead into stardom. It also showed the Warner style of film-making, all cheap sets and shadows, at its most effective.
w John Wexley, Warren Duff *story* Rowland Brown *d Michael Curtiz ph Sol Polito m* Max Steiner
☆ *James Cagney, Pat O'Brien, Humphrey Bogart, The Dead End Kids, Ann Sheridan*, George Bancroft, Edward Pawley

'Should do fair business, but the picture itself is no bonfire.' – *Variety*

'A rousing, bloody, brutal melodrama.' – *New York Mirror*

Rowland Brown; Michael Curtiz; James Cagney

'Let the Healing Begin.'
Anger Management *
US 2003 106m Technicolor Panavision
Columbia-TriStar/Revolution/Happy Madison (Jack Giarraputo, Barry Bernardi)
After an incident on an aeroplane, a mild-mannered man is sentenced to undergo treatment with a confrontational therapist.
Sporadically amusing comedy for as long as Sandler's propensity for playing an aggressive man-child is held in check.
w David Dorfman *d* Peter Segal *ph* Donald M. McAlpine *m* Teddy Castellucci *pd* Alan Au
ed Jeff Gourson
☆ Adam Sandler (Dave Buznik), Jack Nicholson (Dr Buddy Rydell), Marisa Tomei (Linda), Luis Guzman (Lou), Allen Covert (Andrew), Lynne Thigpen (Judge Daniels), Kurt Fuller (Frank Head), Woody Harrelson (Guard), John Turturro (Chuck), John C, Reilly (uncredited) (Arnie Shankman)

'A couple of brakes-off set pieces to the side, the antics here are strained, graceless and tiresomely crude.' – *Todd McCarthy, Variety*

'Unless you're 15 at heart, you may need anger management yourself after sitting through this aggressively crass comedy, which alternates between mean-spirited slapstick and arbitrary uplift.' – *David Ansen, Newsweek*

Les Anges du Péché *
France 1943 73m bw
Synops/Robert Paul
A novice nun has trouble with the mother superior because of her obsessive interest in a rebellious delinquent girl, and dies before taking her vows.
Interesting study of an enclosed society, notable as its director's first film.
w R. P. Bruckberger, Jean Giraudoux, Robert Bresson
d Robert Bresson *ph* Philippe Agostini *m* Jean-Jacques Grunenwald
☆ Renée Faure, Jany Holt, Sylvie, Mila Parély, Marie-Hélène Dasté

Angi Vera ***
Hungary 1978 93m Eastmancolor
Mafilm/Objektiv

English title: *The Education of Vera*
In the late 40s, an idealistic 18-year-old girl becomes a dedicated Communist Party worker and learns that betrayal is part of the system.
A deft and moving examination of the totalitarian mind-set, expressed in human terms; at the time, it was a courageous film to make.
w Pál Gábor story Endre Vészi *ph* Lajos Koltai
m György Selmeczi *ed* Éva Karmentö
☆ *Veronika Papp*, Erzsi Pásztor, Eva Szabó, Tamás Dunai, László Horváth

'Angie wants to stay single, have a baby, and fall in love. But she's willing to negotiate.'
Angie *
US 1994 108m Technicolor Panavision
Buena Vista/Hollywood Pictures/Caravan/Morra-Brezner-Steinberg-Tenenbaum (Larry Brezner, Patrick McCormick)

A Brooklyn girl grows up and decides that life should have more to offer than her pregnancy by a plumber she's known since her schooldays.
Drama of a woman searching for some meaning to her life, enjoyable mainly for the performances of Geena Davis and Stephen Rea as her casual lover; it falls away towards the end to a neat and sentimental resolution that falsifies what has gone before.
w Todd Graff *novel Angie, I Says* by Avra Wing
d Martha Coolidge *ph* Johnny E. Jensen *m* Jerry Goldsmith *pd* Mel Bourne *ed* Steven Cohen

☆ Geena Davis, James Gandolfini, Aida Turturro, Stephen Rea, Philip Bosco, Jenny O'Hara, Michael Rispoli

'One of the year's dampest celluloid squibs.' – *James Keen, Film Review*

† The role of Angie was originally written for Madonna.

Anglagärd: see *House of Angels*

L'Anglaise et Le Duc **
France/Germany 2001 129m colour
Pathé/Compagnie Eric Rohmer, Pathe Image (Françoise Etchegaray)

aka: *The Lady and the Duke*
A Scots woman, a former royal mistress, is in danger of losing her life during the French Revolution for saving an aristocrat from the guillotine.
Delberately artificial historical drama, using painted backgrounds, that conjures up the period as well as telling a timeless tale of courage and loss.
wd Eric Rohmer *memoir Journal of My Life During the French Revolution* by Grace Elliott *ph* Diane Baratier *pd* Antoine Fontaine *ed* Mary Stephen *background paintings* Jean-Baptiste Marot
☆ Lucy Russell (Grace Elliott), Jean-Claude Dreyfus (Philippe, Duke d'Orleans), Francois Marthouret (Dumourier), Leonard Cobiant (Champcenetz), Caroline Morin (Nanon), Alain Libolt (Duke de Biron), Helena Dubeil (Madame Meyler), Daniel Tarrare (Justin, the porter), Francois Marie Banier (Robespierre)

'History comes alive with verve and cold-sweat suspense.' – *Lisa Nesselson, Variety*

Angora Love **
US 1929 20m bw silent
Hal Roach

Laurel and Hardy keep a goat in their lodgings.
Lively comedy, even funnier when remade two years later as Laughing Gravy.
w Leo McCarey and H. M. Walker *d* Lewis R. Foster
☆ Laurel and Hardy, Edgar Kennedy, Charlie Hall

The Angry Dragon
Hong Kong 1974 80m Eastmancolor Scope
Mark Associates/Oriental Film (Mah Jam Sheng)
A police inspector defeats a local gangster with the aid of martial arts students.
The usual high-kicking kung-fu mayhem, with an uninteresting narrative and unattractive leads.
wd Chiang Hung
☆ Cheng Lei, Christine Hui, Lee Wan Chung

'Possibly the least prepossessing of all independent Hong Kong features.' – *Tony Rayns, MFB*

Angry Harvest: see *Bittere Ernte*

The Angry Hills
GB 1959 105m bw
MGM/Raymond Stross
In 1940, an American war correspondent is helped by Greek freedom fighters.
Laboured war melodrama with pretentious dialogue but little characterization.
w A. I. Bezzerides *novel* Leon Uris *d* Robert Aldrich *ph* Stephen Dade *m* Richard Rodney Bennett *ad* Ken Adam
☆ Robert Mitchum, Gia Scala, Elisabeth Mueller, Stanley Baker, Donald Wolfit, Kieron Moore, Theodore Bikel, Sebastian Cabot, Peter Illing, Marius Goring, Leslie Phillips

The Angry Red Planet *
US 1959 83m colour Cinemagic
Sino (Sid Pink, Norman Maurer)

Four astronauts who land on Mars fight for their lives against a variety of monsters and giant Martians.
Enjoyably quaint science fiction, filmed in a process that gives a pink tinge to the action.
w Ib Melchior, Sid Pink *d* Ib Melchior
ph Stanley Cortez *ad* Herman Townsley, Michael Sternlight, Art Wasson
☆ Gerald Mohr, Nora Hayden, Les Tremayne, Jack Kruschen

The Angry Silence **
GB 1960 94m bw
British Lion/Beaver (Richard Attenborough, Bryan Forbes)

A worker who refuses to join an unofficial strike is 'sent to Coventry' by his mates; the matter hits national headlines, and the communists use it to their own advantage.
Irresistibly reminding one of a po-faced I'm All Right Jack, this remains a fresh and urgent film which unfortunately lost excitement in its domestic scenes.
w Bryan Forbes *story* Michael Craig, Richard Gregson *d* Guy Green *ph* Arthur Ibbetson *m* Malcolm Arnold
☆ *Richard Attenborough*, Michael Craig, Pier Angeli, Bernard Lee, Alfred Burke, Laurence Naismith, Geoffrey Keen

'Vastly entertaining as well as thought-provoking. Matter and manner are for once wholly in harmony.' – *Daily Mail*

'A film made by people who care about the screen and care what they are saying on it.' – *Dilys Powell*

Bryan Forbes, Richard Gregson, Michael Craig
Bryan Forbes

Die Angst des Tormanns beim Elfmeter: see *The Goalkeeper's Fear of the Penalty Kick*

Angus *
US 1995 90m colour
Entertainment/Atlas/BBC/Syalis/Tele München/Quality/Turner (Dawn Steel, Charles Roven)

An overweight teenager, who is mocked at school, finds the courage to fight back.
Pleasant, old-fashioned, though unexceptional comedy of an outsider who insists on being part of a community.
w Jill Gordon *story* Chris Crutcher *d* Patrick Read Johnson *ph* Alexander Grusynski *m* David Russo *pd* Larry Miller *ed* Janice Hampton
☆ Kathy Bates, George C. Scott, Charlie Talbert, Ariana Richards, James Van Der Beek, Chris Owen, Lawrence Pressman, Rita Moreno

'Fat kids deserve a better deal from this movie that merely manages to re-establish American college students as the most obnoxiously cruel species since the Hitler Youth went out of fashion. Angus gets his moment of triumph, but it's the sour taste of juvenile hostility that lasts a lot longer.' – *Tom Hutchinson, Film Review*

'He wasn't much of a man… Now he's not much of an animal.'
The Animal
US 2001 83m DeLuxe
Columbia TriStar/Revolution/Happy Madison (Barry Bernardi, Carr D'Angelo, Todd Garner)

A feeble clerk develops unusual powers after he has transplants of animal organs.
Crude slapstick comedy that deserves to be put down.
w Tom Brady, Rob Schneider *d* Luke Greenfield *ph* Peter Lyons Collister *m* Teddy Castellucci *pd* Alan Au *ed* Jeff Gourson, Peck Prior
☆ Rob Schneider (Marvin), Colleen Haskell (Rianna), John C. McGinley (Sgt Sisk), Edward Asner (Chief Wilson), Michael Caton (Dr Wilder), Louis Lombardi (Fatty), Guy Torry (Miles)

'This abysmal film: a dull sub-gross-out non-comedy.' – *Peter Bradshaw, Guardian*

'Just a sweethearted trifle.' – *Variety*

Animal Attraction: see *Someone Like You*

Animal Behavior
US 1989 89m DeLuxe
Millimeter (Kjehl Rasmussen)

A university music teacher is attracted to an animal behavourist, who is teaching a chimpanzee sign language, but finds it difficult to communicate her own feelings.
A would-be romantic comedy that is ambitious in its scope, trying to cram in several plot strands while examining the odd behaviour of humans, but fatally flawed in its execution, and with an unhappily mannered performance from Karen Allen.
w Susan Rice *d* H. Anne Riley *ph* David Spellvin *m* Cliff Eidelman *pd* Jeannine Oppewall *ed* Joseph Weintraub
☆ Karen Allen, Armand Assante, Holly Hunter, Josh Mostel, Richard Libertini, Alexa Kenin, Jon Matthews, Nan Martin
† H. Anne Riley is a name that hides the real identity of director Jenny Bowen, who began making the film in 1984, and its producer, who completed it much later; after that, it sat on the shelf before being released in the US, and was not seen in Britain until 1997, when the new TV station Channel 5 inflicted it upon its viewers.

Animal Crackers ***
US 1930 98m bw
Paramount

Thieves covet a valuable oil painting unveiled at a swank party.
An excuse for the Marx Brothers, and a lively one in patches, though sedate and stagebound in treatment. The boys are all in top form, and many of the dialogue exchanges are classics.
w Morrie Ryskind *musical play* Morrie Ryskind, George S. Kaufman *d* Victor Heerman *ph* George Folsey *m/ly* Bert Kalmar, Harry Ruby
☆ *Groucho, Chico, Harpo, Zeppo, Margaret Dumont*, Lillian Roth, Louis Sorin, Robert Greig, Hal Thompson

GROUCHO: 'You're the most beautiful woman I've ever seen, which doesn't say much for you.'

GROUCHO: 'One morning I shot an elephant in my pajamas. How he got into my pajamas I'll never know.'

GUESTS: 'Hooray for Captain Spaulding, the African explorer!'

GROUCHO: 'Did someone call me schnorrer?'

GUESTS: 'Hooray, hooray, hooray!'

ZEPPO: 'He went into the jungle, where all the monkeys *throw* nuts.'

GROUCHO: 'If I stay here, I'll *go* nuts.'

GUESTS: 'Hooray, hooray, hooray!
He put all his reliance
In courage and defiance
And risked his life for science.'

GROUCHO: 'Hey, hey!'

MRS RITTENHOUSE: 'He is the only white man who covered every acre…'

GROUCHO: 'I think I'll try and make her…'

GUESTS: 'Hooray, hooray, hooray!'

'A hit on the screen before it opened, and in the money plenty.' – *Variety*

Animal Farm **
GB 1955 75m Technicolor
Louis de Rochemont/Halas and Batchelor

Oppressed by the cruelty and inefficiency of their master, the animals take over a farm but find fresh tyrants among themselves.
George Orwell's political fable – 'all animals are equal but some animals are more equal than others' – is faithfully followed in this ambitious but rather disappointingly flat cartoon version.
m Matyas Seiber *w/p/d* John Halas, Joy Batchelor
☆ Featuring voices: Maurice Denham

'A melodramatic fantasy that is mordant, tender and quixotic, shot with ironic humour.' – *New York Times*

The Animal Kingdom *
US 1932 95m bw
RKO (David O. Selznick)

GB title: *The Woman in His House*
An intellectual publisher tries to justify keeping both a wife and a mistress.
Smart comedy-drama from a Broadway success, later bowdlerized as One More Tomorrow (qv).
w Horace Jackson *play* Philip Barry *d* Edward H. Griffith *ph* Lucien Andriot *m* Max Steiner
☆ Leslie Howard, Ann Harding, Myrna Loy, Neil Hamilton, William Gargan, Henry Stephenson, Ilka Chase

'A wise and engaging picture addressed to the upper levels of fandom.' – *Variety*

'Two billion years in the making!'
The Animal World *
US 1956 80m Technicolor
Warner/Windsor (Irwin Allen)
The evolution of animals from their primitive beginnings.
Ambitious documentary with a popular science approach; very variable, with poorish model work.
wd Irwin Allen *ph* Harold Wellman *m* Paul Sawtell *sp* Willis O'Brien, Ray Harryhausen

The Animals
US 1970 86m Technicolor Techniscope
MGM-EMI/XYZ (Richard Bakalyan)
aka: *Five Savage Men*
A schoolteacher, raped by a sadistic killer and his gang, takes her revenge with the aid of an Indian who saves her life.
Notably grim and violent Western, made with no sense of style or period and overweighted by the heavy irony of its climax.
w Richard Bakalyan *d* Ron Joy *ph* Keith Smith *m* Rupert Holmes *ed* Pier Laskey
☆ Henry Silva, Keenan Wynn, Michele Carey, John Anderson, Joseph Turkel, Pepper Martin, Bobby Hall, Peter Hellmann

'As with other forms of pornography, the possibilities of originality within the pornography of violence are distinctly finite.' – *James D. White, MFB*

The Animals Film *
GB/US 1981 136m colour/bw
Slick Pix
A hard-hitting documentary recording human ill-treatment of animals, with obvious hints that humans themselves will be next. Narrated by Julie Christie.
Not for the squeamish.
wd Victor Schonfeld

Animalympics
US 1979 80m Technicolor
Lisburger (Steven Lisburger, Donald Kushner)

Wild animals from around the world compete in athletic events.
A lively, though inconsequential, animated spoof of the Olympics, with a US bias; its hyperactive style, though, seems tame alongside the hysteria of TV coverage of the actual event.
w Michael Fremer, Steven Lisburger *story* Steven Lisburger, Roger Allers, John Norton *d* Steven Lisburger, Bill Kroyer *m* Graham Gouldman *ad* Roger Allers, John Norton, Peter Mueller *ed* Matt Cope
☆ Featuring the voices of: Gilda Radner, Billy Crystal, Harry Shearer, Michael Fremer

Animated Genesis *
GB 1952 22m Technicolor (blown up from 16mm)
Korda/British Lion
Greed and the machine enslave mankind.
Ambitious and decorative cartoon conceived and drawn by Joan and Peter Foldes from whom little was subsequently heard.
m Thomas Henderson

Anita and Me
GB 2002 92m colour
Icon/Portman//Film Council/BBC/EMMI/Starfield (Paul Raphael)
In a small Midlands town in the early 70s, a 12 year-old Punjabi girl becomes friends with her new neighbour, a delinquent English teenager.
Haphazardly plotted movie that tries to take in a great deal of good and bad cross-cultural experience, but somehow loses its way.
w Meera Syal *novel* Meera Syal *d* Metin Huseyin *ph* Cinders Forshaw *m* Nitin Sawhney *pd* Caroline Hanania *ed* Annie Kocur
☆ Chandeep Uppal (Meena Kumar), Anna Brewster (Anita Rutter), Sanjeev Bhaskar (Meena's father), Ayesha Dharker (Meena's mother), Kathy Burke (Anita's mother), Lynn Redgrave (Shopkeeper), Max Beesley (Rocker), Meera Syal (Meena's aunt)

'Just an extended sit-com staged in a sentimentalised community of caricatures who are held together less by a common humanity than by a shared propensity for over-acting.' – *Philip French, Observer*

Ann Vickers *
US 1933 72m bw
RKO (Pandro S. Berman)

A feminist social worker is taught a thing or two by life and settles down with a corrupt judge.
Reasonably effective version of a popular though heavy-going novel of the time.

w Jane Murfin *novel* Sinclair Lewis *d* John Cromwell *ph* David Abel, Edward Cronjager *m* Max Steiner
☆ Irene Dunne, Walter Huston, Conrad Nagel, Bruce Cabot, Edna May Oliver, Mitchell Lewis, Murray Kinnell
'Her sufferings are bearable and her ultimate happiness is assured, so this is vicarious enjoyment for any woman. Lovely romance, moderate penance, final respectability. All of which suggests that *Ann Vickers* should do moderately good biz.' – *Variety*

Anna
Italy 1951 100m bw
Lux (Ponti/de Laurentiis)
A novice nun recalls her former life and almost gives up her vocation.
Soupy woman's picture of no particular merit.
w Giuseppe Berto, Dino Risi, Ivo Perilli, Franco Brusati, Rodolfo Sonego *d* Alberto Lattuada *ph* Otello Martelli *m* Nino Rota
☆ Silvana Mangano, Raf Vallone, Vittorio Gassman, Gaby Morlay, Jacques Dumesnil

Anna
US 1987 100m TVC Color
Magnus (Zanne Devine, Yurek Bogayevicz)
A Czech-born actress in the New York fringe theatre is betrayed by a young female admirer.
Echoes of All About Eve seem less important than the political asides, and the whole thing is a bit of a muddle.
w Agnieszka Holland *d* Yurek Bogayevicz *ph* Bobby Bukowski *m* Greg Hawkes
☆ *Sally Kirkland*, Robert Fields, Paulina Porizkova
Sally Kirkland

Anna and the King *
US 1999 148m DeLuxe Panavision
TCF (Lawrence Bender, Ed Albert)
In the 1860s an Englishwoman becomes tutor to the children of the embattled King of Siam.
A lavish production, often gorgeous to look at, is laced with sentimentality and a simple approach to history; Foster adds a little frosty femininity to the role of Anna, which chills the romantic interludes.
w Steve Meerson, Peter Krikes *diaries* Anna Leonowens *d* Andy Tennant *ph* *Caleb Deschanel* *m* George Fenton *pd* *Luciana Arrighi* *cos* *Jenny Beavan*
☆ Jodie Foster (Anna), Chow Yun-Fat (King Mongkut), Bai Ling (Tuptim), Tom Felton (Louis), Syed Alwi (The Kralahome), Randall Duk Kim (General Alak), Lim Kay Siu (Prince Chowfa), Melissa Campbell (Princess Fa-Ying), Deanna Yusoff (Lady Thiang)
'A schmaltzy, ultra-elaborate, overly long production, all too consciously conceived as an old-fashioned family entertainment.' – *Emanuel Levy, Variety*
'Picturesque but stodgy… unfolds like an exotic historical diorama with dramatic vignettes thrown in for spice.' – *Stephen Holden, New York Times*
Luciana Arrighi; Jenny Beavan

Anna and the King of Siam **
US 1946 128m bw
TCF (Louis D. Lighton)
In 1862 an English governess arrives in Bangkok to teach the 67 children of the king.
Unusual and lavish drama, tastefully handled and generally absorbing despite miscasting and several slow passages.
w Talbot Jennings, Sally Benson *book* Margaret Landon *d* John Cromwell *ph* *Arthur Miller* *m* Bernard Herrmann *ad* *Lyle Wheeler, William Darling*
☆ Irene Dunne, Rex Harrison, Linda Darnell, Gale Sondergaard, Lee J. Cobb, Mikhail Rasumny
'A film that never touches the imagination, a film that leaves the mind uninformed and the memory unburdened.' – *Richard Winnington*
'It's pitifully unauthentic, and not a very good movie either, but the story itself holds considerable interest.' – *Pauline Kael, 70s*
Arthur Miller
Talbot Jennings, Sally Benson; Bernard Herrmann; Gale Sondergaard

'Garbo talks!'
Anna Christie **
US 1930 86m bw
MGM
A waterfront prostitute falls in love with a young seaman.
Primitive sound version of an earthy theatrical warhorse: it has a niche in history as the film in which Garbo first talked.
w Frances Marion *play* Eugene O'Neill *d* Clarence Brown *ph* William Daniels
☆ *Greta Garbo*, Charles Bickford, *Marie Dressler*, James T. Mack, Lee Phelps
'Great artistically and tremendous commercially … in all respects a wow picture.' – *Variety*
'A very talkie, uncinematic affair, more old-fashioned than the silent movies. If it were not so well acted it would be pretty tiresome.' – *National Board of Review*
† A 1923 silent version starred Blanche Sweet and was directed by John Wray.
Clarence Brown; William Daniels; Greta Garbo

Anna Karenina **
US 1935 95m bw
MGM (David O. Selznick)
The wife of a Russian aristocrat falls for a dashing cavalry officer.
Well-staged but finally exasperating romantic tragedy, sparked by good performances and production.
w Clemence Dane, Salka Viertel *novel* Leo Tolstoy *d* *Clarence Brown* *ph* *William Daniels* *m* Herbert Stothart
☆ *Greta Garbo* (Anna), Fredric March (Vronsky), *Basil Rathbone* (Karenin), Freddie Bartholomew (Sergei), Maureen O'Sullivan (Kitty), May Robson (Countess), Reginald Owen (Silva), Reginald Denny (Yashvin)
'Cinch b.o. anywhere. In the foreign markets it should come close to establishing modern-day highs.' – *Variety*
'A dignified and effective drama which becomes significant because of that tragic, lonely and glamorous blend which is the Garbo personality.' – *André Sennwald*
'It reaches no great heights of tragedy or drama but rather moves forward relentlessly and a little coldly.' – *The Times*
† Previously filmed as a 1928 silent called *Love*, with Garbo and John Gilbert.

Anna Karenina *
GB 1948 139m bw
London Films (Alexander Korda)
Tiresomely overlong but very handsomely staged remake marred by central miscasting.
w Jean Anouilh, Guy Morgan, Julien Duvivier *d* Julien Duvivier *ph* *Henri Alekan* *m* Constant Lambert *ad* André Andrejew *ed* Russell Lloyd
☆ Vivien Leigh, Kieron Moore, *Ralph Richardson*, Marie Lohr, Sally Ann Howes, Niall MacGinnis, Michael Gough, Helen Haye, Mary Kerridge
'Vivien Leigh is lashed about by the tremendous role of Anna like a pussy cat with a tigress by the tail. She is not helped by a script which insists on sentimentally ennobling one of fiction's most vehemently average women.' – *James Agee*

Anna Karenina: see *Leo Tolstoy's Anna Karenina (1997)*

Anna Lucasta *
US 1949 86m bw
Columbia/Security (Philip Yordan)
The bad girl of a farming family comes home to marry, but her past catches up with her.
Polish immigrant melodrama, a touring company staple, adequately transferred to the screen.
w Philip Yordan, Arthur Laurents *play* Philip Yordan *d* Irving Rapper *ph* Sol Polito *m* David Diamond
☆ Paulette Goddard, Oscar Homolka, Broderick Crawford, William Bishop, Gale Page, Mary Wickes

Anna Lucasta *
US 1958 97m bw
(UA) Longridge Enterprises (Sidney Harmon)
Black version of the long-running play; performances standard.
w Philip Yordan *d* Arnold Laven *ph* Lucien Ballard *m* Elmer Bernstein
☆ Eartha Kitt, Frederick O'Neal, Sammy Davis Jnr, Henry Scott, Rex Ingram, James Edwards

Anna of Brooklyn
Italy/France/US 1958 106m colour Technirama
Circeo Cinematografica/France Cinema/RKO (Milko Skofic)
An attractive widow returns from New York to her native Italian village in search of a husband.
Footling romantic drama which wastes its cast and budget.
w Ettore Margadonna, Dino Risi *d* Reginald Denham, Carlo Lasticati *ph* Giuseppe Rotunno *m* Alessandro Cicognini, Vittorio de Sica
☆ Gina Lollobrigida, Dale Robertson, Vittorio de Sica, Amedeo Nazzari, Peppino de Felippo, Gabriella Palotta

Annabel Takes a Tour
US 1939 69m bw
RKO
A star on a publicity tour balks at the stunts she is expected to perform.
Thinnish sequel to The Affairs of Annabel (qv).
w Bert Granet and Olive Cooper *d* Lew Landers
☆ Lucille Ball, Jack Oakie, Ruth Donnelly, Bradley Page, Ralph Forbes

Annabelle Partagée
France 1990 80m colour
Gala/ça Films (Sophie Delochée, Anne Fieschl)
A student dancer ditches her middle-aged boyfriend for someone younger.
Dull film, in which little happens and nothing of any consequence.
wd Francesca Comencini *ph* Michel Abramowicz *m* Les Valentins, Etienne Daho *ad* Valérie Grall *ed* Yves Deschamps
☆ Delphine Zingg, François Marthouret, Jean-Claude Adelin
'A French film about l'amour in which l'ennui takes over early on.' – *Nigel Andrews, Financial Times*
'The one notable moment of Francesca Comencini's mildly feminist debut is an erect penis, slightly out of focus and looking rather like a toadstool, seen in the foreground of the opening shot. This might be a small milestone, so to speak, in popular French cinema.' – *Philip French, Observer*

Annabelle's Affairs
US 1931 74m bw
Fox
When her husband disappears, a young bride becomes head cook at his rival's home. Then the husband turns up.
Standard farce which worked pretty well in its day.
w Leon Gordon *play* *Good Gracious Annabelle* by Clare Kummer *d* Alfred Werker
☆ Jeanette MacDonald, Victor McLaglen, Roland Young, Sam Hardy, William Collier Snr

An Annapolis Story
US 1953 81m colour
Allied Artists/Walter Mirisch
GB title: *The Blue and the Gold*
Two cadets at the naval academy love the same girl.
Artless recruiting poster heroics.
w Dan Ullman *d* Don Siegel *ph* Sam Leavitt *m* Marlin Skiles
☆ Diana Lynn, John Derek, Kevin McCarthy, Pat Dooley, L. Q. Jones
'Seldom have so many scrubbed, wholesome-looking young people thronged any picture.' – *New York Times*

Anne and Muriel ***
France 1971 108m Eastmancolor
Gala/Les Films du Carrosse/Cinetel (Marcel Berbert)
original title: *Les Deux Anglaises et le Continent*
A French writer falls in love with two English sisters.
Elegant variation on the eternal triangle.
w François Truffaut, Jean Grualt *novel* Henri-Pierre Roche *d* François Truffaut *ph* Nestor Almendros *m* Georges Delerue *ad* Michel de Broin *ed* Yann Dedet
☆ Jean-Pierre Léaud, Kika Markham, Stacey Tendeter, Sylvia Marriott, Marie Mansart, Philippe Léotard, Irene Tunc

Anne of Green Gables *
US 1934 79m bw
RKO (Kenneth MacGowan)
An orphan girl goes to the country to live with her aunt.
Standard version of the classic for young girls. Anne Shirley had been known as Dawn O'Day and legally adopted the name of her character in this, her first starring role.
w Sam Mintz *novel* L. M. Montgomery *d* George Nicholls Jnr *ph* Lucien Andriot *m* Max Steiner
☆ *Anne Shirley*, Tom Brown, O. P. Heggie, Helen Westley, Sara Haden, Charley Grapewin
'Made up and monotonous – tragedy having its breakfast in bed.' – *Otis Ferguson*
† *Anne of Windy Poplars* (qv), with the same stars and production team, followed in 1940.

Anne of the Indies *
US 1951 87m Technicolor
TCF (George Jessel)
Lady pirate Anne Bonney, the terror of the Caribbean, is at odds with her former master Blackbeard.
Routine swashbuckler, generally well handled.
w Philip Dunne, Arthur Caesar *d* Jacques Tourneur *ph* Harry Jackson *m* Franz Waxman
☆ Jean Peters, Louis Jourdan, Debra Paget, Herbert Marshall, Thomas Gomez, James Robertson Justice, Sean McClory, Francis Pierlot

Anne of the Thousand Days *
GB 1969 146m Technicolor Panavision
Universal/Hal B. Wallis
Henry VIII divorces his wife to marry Anne Boleyn, but soon finds evidence of adultery.
A somewhat unlikely view of history, rather boringly presented on a woman's magazine level, but with occasional good moments from a cast of British notables.
w John Hale, Bridget Boland *play* Maxwell Anderson *d* Charles Jarrott *ph* Arthur Ibbetson *m* Georges Delerue *pd* Maurice Carter *cos* Margaret Furse
☆ *Richard Burton, Geneviève Bujold, John Colicos* (Cromwell), Irene Papas, Anthony Quayle, Michael Hordern, Katharine Blake, Peter Jeffrey, William Squire, Esmond Knight, Nora Swinburne
'The costumes, beautiful in themselves, have that unconvincing air of having come straight off the rack at Nathan's.' – *Brenda Davies*
'A decent dullness is, alas, the keynote.' – *Michael Billington, Illustrated London News*
'The quintessential work of art for people who haven't the foggiest notion of what art is.' – *John Simon*
'Intelligent from line to line, but the emotions supplied seem hypocritical, and the conception lacks authority … Burton's performance is colourless. It's as though he *remembered* how to act but couldn't work up much enthusiasm or involvement.' – *Pauline Kael*
Margaret Furse
picture; John Hale, Bridget Boland; Arthur Ibbetson; Georges Delerue; Richard Burton; Geneviève Bujold; Anthony Quayle

Anne of Windy Poplars
US 1940 88m bw
RKO (Cliff Reid)
The newly appointed vice-principal of a small-town school charms her way out of a neighbourhood feud.
Pleasant family drama in a minor key, but all very forgettable.
w Michael Kanin, Jerry Cady *novel* L. M. Montgomery *d* Jack Hively *ph* Frank Redman *md* Roy Webb *ad* Van Nest Polglase *ed* George Hively
☆ Anne Shirley, James Ellison, Henry Travers, Patric Knowles, Slim Summerville, Elizabeth Patterson, Louise Campbell, Joan Carroll
† It was a sequel to *Anne of Green Gables* (qv).

Anne Trister
Canada 1986 100m colour
Vision 4 (Roger Frappier, Claude Bonin)
After the death of her father, a young Jewish artist leaves her boyfriend and moves from her Swiss home to Quebec to make sense of her life; there she falls in love with a woman friend.
Sombre, slow-paced study of a woman seeking her true identity; there is a great deal of heart-searching but not much action.
w Marcel Beaulieu, Léa Pool *d* Léa Pool *ph* Pierre Mignot *m* René Dupéré *ad* Vianney Gauthier *ed* Michel Arcand
☆ Albane Guilhe, Louise Marleau, Hugues Quester, Lucie Laurier, Nuvit Ozdogru, Guy Thauvette, Kim Yaroshevskaya

L'Année Dernière à Marienbad: see *Last Year at Marienbad*

Annie
US 1982 128m Metrocolor
Panavision
Columbia/Ray Stark (Joe Layton)
In 1933 an orphan waif charms a munitions millionaire and is adopted by him.
Misguided opening-out of a charming stage musical based on the comic strip which is basically a reversal of Oliver Twist. Some of the best numbers have been discarded, the dancing is ponderous, the acting distinctly uneasy, and the choice of director stupefying. None of it works at all.
w Carol Sobieski, from the stage play *book* Thomas Meehan *comic strip* Harold Gray *d* John Huston *ph* Richard Moore *m* Ralph Burns *pd* Dale Hennesy *ly* Martin Charnin
☆ Albert Finney, Carol Burnett, Aileen Quinn, Ann Reinking, Bernadette Peters, Tim Curry, Geoffrey Holder, Edward Herrmann (Franklin D. Roosevelt)
'Whatever indefinable charm the stage show had is completely lost in this lumbering and largely uninteresting and uninvolving exercise, where the obvious waste reaches almost Pentagonian proportions.' – *Variety*
'The whole thing has the air of a vast, hollow Christmas tree bauble intended not so much for children as for the infantile-minded middle-aged.' – *Sunday Times*
'This is the film I want on my tombstone.' – *Ray Stark*
'Funeral services may be held starting this week at a theatre near you.' – *Time*
† The cost of *Annie*, starting with $9,000,000 for the rights, rose to $42,000,000. It was not recovered.
art direction; original song score

Annie Get Your Gun *
US 1950 107m Technicolor
MGM (Arthur Freed)
A young female hillbilly joins Frank Butler's sharpshooting act, and is sophisticated by her love for him.
Gaudy, stagey, generally uninspired screen version of the famous musical show based remotely on a historical character of post-wild-west days. There is a lack of dancing, the direction is stodgy, and in general flair the production falls disappointingly below MGM's usual standard.
w Sidney Sheldon *musical play* Herbert and Dorothy Fields *d* George Sidney *ph* Charles Rosher *m/ly* Irving Berlin *md* Adolph Deutsch, Roger Edens *ch* Robert Alton *ad* Cedric Gibbons, Paul Groesse
☆ Betty Hutton, *Howard Keel*, Edward Arnold, J. Carroll Naish, Louis Calhern
† The real Annie Oakley was born Phoebe Ann Oakley Mozie in 1860, and died in 1926. The role was to have been played by Judy Garland, who was fired after displays of temperament; also considered were Doris Day, Judy Canova and Betty Garrett.
†† Louis Calhern replaced Frank Morgan, who died during production.
♫ 'Colonel Buffalo Bill'; 'Doing What Comes Naturally'; 'The Girl That I Marry'; 'You Can't Get a Man with a Gun'; 'There's No Business Like Show Business'; 'My Defenses Are Down'; 'I'm an Indian Too'; 'I Got the Sun in the Morning'; 'Anything You Can Do'; 'They Say It's Wonderful'
music direction
Charles Rosher

Annie Hall ****
US 1977 93m DeLuxe
UA/Jack Rollins-Charles H. Joffe (Fred T. Gallo)
Sub-title: *A Nervous Romance*
Against the neuroses of New York and Los Angeles, a Jewish comedian has an affair with a midwestern girl.
Semi-serious collage of jokes and bits of technique, some of the former very funny and some of the latter very successful. For no very good reason it hit the box-office spot and turned its creator, of whom it is very typical, from a minority performer to a superstar.
w Woody Allen, Marshall Brickman *d* Woody Allen *ph* Gordon Willis *m* various
☆ *Woody Allen*, Diane Keaton, Tony Roberts, Carol Kane, Paul Simon, Shelley Duvall
ALLEN: 'Hey, don't knock masturbation. It's sex with someone I love.'
'The film's priceless vignettes about the difficulties in chitchatting with strangers, the awkward moments in family visits, and the frequent breakdowns in intimacy, its reminiscences about the palpable horrors of growing up in Brooklyn, and its comic encounters with lobsters in the kitchen or spiders in the bathroom, all seem like snapshots from Allen and Keaton's own romance.' – *Les Keyser, Hollywood in the Seventies*
† The narrative supposedly mirrors the real-life affair of the stars, who separated before the film came out. (Diane Keaton's family name is Hall.)
picture; script; direction; Diane Keaton
Woody Allen (as actor)
picture; script; Woody Allen (as director); Diane Keaton

Annie Oakley *
US 1935 90m bw
RKO (Cliff Reid)
The historical story, more or less, of the lady later immortalized in *Annie Get Your Gun*.
Lively semi-Western with good dialogue but gluey plot development.
w Joel Sayre, John Twist *d* *George Stevens* *ph* J. Roy Hunt *md* Alberto Colombo *ad* Van Nest Polglase
☆ Barbara Stanwyck, Preston Foster, Melvyn Douglas, Moroni Olsen, Pert Kelton, Andy Clyde, Chief Thunderbird
'A swell idea that doesn't quite come through.' – *Variety*

Annie's Coming Out *
Australia 1984 93m Eastmancolor
Film Australia (Don Murray)
A physically handicapped child, wrongly characterized as mentally retarded also, is brought out by a devoted teacher.
Fictionalized version of a true story: predictably well intentioned, shocking, and consistently watchable.
w John Patterson, Chris Borthwick *book* Rosemary Crossley *d* Gil Brealey *ph* Mick Van Borneman *m* Simon Walker
☆ Angela Punch-McGregor, Drew Forsythe, Tina Arhondis, Liddy Clark, Monica Maughan

The Annihilators
US 1985 84m colour
New World (Allan C. Pedersen, Tom Chapman)
Vietnam veterans are hired as small-town vigilantes.
Violent action film of no visible merit.
w Brian Russell *d* Charles E. Sellier Jnr *ph* Henning Schellerup *m* Bob Summers *ad* Simon Gittins *ed* Dan Gross
☆ Christopher Stone, Andy Wood, Lawrence Hilton-Jacobs, Gerrit Graham, Dennis Redfield, Paul Koslo

The Anniversary *
GB 1968 95m Technicolor
Warner/Hammer (Jimmy Sangster)
A malevolent one-eyed widow will stop at nothing to prevent her grown sons from leaving the family orbit, and they meet each year to mourn the death of the husband she really hated.
Agreeable but over-talkative black comedy with a splendid role for its star and some good scattered moments, marred by a general lack of style.
w Jimmy Sangster *play* Bill MacIlwraith *d* Roy Ward Baker *ph* Harry Waxman *m* Philip Martell *ad* Reece Pemberton *ed* James Needs, Peter Weatherley
☆ *Bette Davis*, Jack Hedley, *James Cossins*, Sheila Hancock, Elaine Taylor, Christian Roberts, Timothy Bateson
'It all reminds one of a love scene in a funeral parlour.' – *Variety*
'Magisterially grotesque in elegantly tailored eye-patch and exotic gown, she snaps out her bitchy insults with all 57 varieties of relish.' – *MFB*
† Alvin Rakoff was replaced as director during filming.

Ano Natsu, Ichiban Shizukana Umi: see *A Scene at the Sea*

El Anonimo
Spain 1990 87m Eastmancolor
Sagutxo (Alfonso Arandia)
Four students try to recover an incriminating letter addressed to one of their professors.
Amiable, lackadaisical comedy.
w Alfonso Arandia, Jose Antonio Gomez *d* Alfonso Arandia *ph* Gonzalo F. Berridi *m* Mikel Erentxum *ed* Juan I. Sanmateo
☆ Miguel Molina, Jorge de Juan, Martxelo Rudio, Carlos Zabala, Nacho Martinez, Rosa Maria Sarda, Alejandra Greppi

The Anonymous Letter: see *El Anonimo*

'The Boys Are Back In Town.'
Another 48 Hrs
US 1990 95m Technicolor
Paramount/Eddie Murphy Productions (Lawrence Gordon, Robert D. Wachs)
A cop enters into a partnership with a criminal to catch a drug dealer.
A virtual remake of 48 Hours (qv), but lacking in energy or interest.
w John Fasano, Jeb Stuart, Larry Gross *story* Fred Braughton *d* Walter Hill *ph* Matthew F. Leonetti *m* James Horner *pd* Joseph C. Nemec III *ad* Gary Wissner *ed* Freeman Davies, Carmel Davies, Donn Aron
☆ Eddie Murphy, Nick Nolte, Brion James, Kevin Tighe, Ed O'Ross, David Anthony Marshall, Andrew Divoff, Bernie Casey, Brent Jennings, Ted Markland, Tisha Campbell
'Disappoints in its failure, after eight years, to introduce even the faintest wrinkle of something new.' – *Variety*

'Convention outraged ... a class abandoned ... a country betrayed!'
Another Country *
GB 1984 90m colour
TCF/Virgin/Goldcrest (Alan Marshall)
A homosexual defector to Russia reflects on the public school pressures which influenced him.
Upper-crust militarism, arrogance, sadism and homosexuality rolled up in a package which pleased the West End theatre crowds but seems faintly absurd on film. Not much of a recruiting poster for Eton.
w Julian Mitchell *play* Julian Mitchell *d* Marek Kanievska *ph* Peter Biziou *m* Michael Storey *pd* Brian Morris
☆ Rupert Everett, Colin Firth, Michael Jenn, Robert Addie, Anna Massey, Rupert Wainwright, Betsy Brantley
'Inevitably it went down well at the Cannes Film Festival, where movies critical of their own country's shortcomings are always favoured.' – *Margaret Hinxman, Daily Mail*

Another Dawn
US 1937 73m bw
Warner (Harry Joe Brown)
In a British army post in Africa, a wife is torn between duty and romance.
Absurdly sudsy melodrama, a potboiler for stars between more important assignments.
w Laird Doyle *d* William Dieterle *ph* Tony Gaudio *m* Erich Wolfgang Korngold
☆ Errol Flynn, Kay Francis, Ian Hunter, Frieda Inescort, Herbert Mundin
† In every Warner film where a cinema canopy was shown, the title advertised was *Another Dawn*, so its use here as an actual title is presumably a piece of cynicism.

Another Day in Paradise **
US 1998 100m CFI
Metrodome/Chinese Bookie (Stephen Chin, Larry Clark, James Woods)
In the 1970s, a middle-aged drug dealer and his girlfriend career across Oklahoma with a young junkie and his girlfriend.
Hectic road movie, set in sleazy motels and featuring various varieties of low-life, given an extra jolt by the nervy authenticity of the performances of Woods and Griffith.
w Christopher Landon, Stephen Chin *book* Eddie Little *d* Larry Clark *ph* Eric Edwards *pd* Aaron Osborne *ed* Luis Colina
☆ *James Woods* (Mel), *Melanie Griffith* (Sid), Vincent Kartheiser (Bobbie), Natasha Gregson Wagner (Rosie), James Otis (Reverend), Peter Sarsgaard (Ty), Paul Hipp (Richard Johnson), Brent Briscoe (Clem), Branden Williams (Danny), Kim Flowers (Bonnie Johnson)
'This imperfect but compelling outlaw drama may be too raw and unflinching to make a wide splash, but should find an audience ready to respond to its gritty aesthetic.' – *David Rooney, Variety*
† Lou Diamond Phillips appears uncredited as Jewels.

Another Face
US 1935 72m bw
RKO
GB title: *It Happened in Hollywood*
A gangster has his face lifted and becomes a film star.
Rather heavy comedy with some good laughs.
w Garrett Graham, John Twist, Ray Mayer, Thomas Dugan *d* Christy Cabanne
☆ *Brian Donlevy*, Wallace Ford, Phyllis Brooks, Erik Rhodes, Molly Lamont, Alan Hale

Another Fine Mess **
US 1930 30m bw
Hal Roach
On the run from a cop, Stan and Ollie masquerade as master and maid.
Elaborate star comedy with spoken introduction instead of titles; very satisfying but not quite vintage.
w H. M. Walker, from a sketch by Stan Laurel's father *d* James Parrott
☆ Laurel and Hardy, James Finlayson, Thelma Todd, Charles Gerrard

Another Girl, Another Planet
US 1992 56m bw Pixelvision
ICA/Michael Almereyda, Robin O'Hara, Bob Gosse
A man attempts to seduce women passing through his apartment by showing them old cartoon films, while his married neighbour looks on or discusses the meaning of life.
Depression as an art form: a minimalist film shot with a toy camera that renders everything slightly out of focus and provides at best a murky image of shadows and fog, turning human life into a grey smear on the wall.
wd Michael Almereyda *ph* Jim Denault *ed* David Leonard
☆ Nic Ratner, Barry Sherman, Mary Ward, Lisa Perisot, Maggie Rush
'An elegantly-crafted chamber piece that effortlessly belies its no-budget origins.' – *Steve Bode, London Film Festival*
'We're so often up to the director's pretensions in angst that despair starts to creep almost palpably off the screen and into the auditorium. Joyful it ain't.' – *Tom Hutchinson, Film Review*
† The film was shot using a Fisher-Price PXL 2000 child's camcorder, made of moulded plastic, with a fixed lens, and recording on standard audio cassettes. The images it produces fade rapidly and are composed of easily visible pixels, like an over-enlarged computer image. The camera, which was made as a toy for Christmas 1987 and discontinued soon after, has become a favourite of a group of experimental film-makers because of its technical limitations.

Another Language
US 1933 75m bw
MGM (Walter Wanger)
A young wife does not fit in with her husband's snobby family and falls in love with his nephew.
Flat treatment of a dated play.

w Herman J. Mankiewicz, Gertrude Purcell, Donald Ogden Stewart *play* Rose Franken *d* Edward H. Griffith *ph* Ray June
☆ Helen Hayes, Robert Montgomery, John Beal, Louise Closser Hale, Henry Travers, Margaret Hamilton

'A very good picture that will get more than average box office attention … everything is handled with intellect and due restraint.' – *Variety*

Another Life
GB 2001 101m DeLuxe
Winchester/Lucida/Boxer/Alibi/Arts Council (Angela Hart)
In the 1920s, a middle-class wife begins an affair with a sailor; when her husband is stabbed to death, both are accused of killing him.
A confused re-telling of a once notorious English murder, with little period feel and much almost unspeakable dialogue.
wd Philip Goodhew *ph* Simon Archer *m* James McConnel *pd* James Merifield *ed* Jamie Trevill
☆ Natasha Little (Edith Thompson), Nick Moran (Percy Thompson), Ioan Gruffudd (Freddy Bywaters), Imelda Staunton (Ethel Graydon), Rachael Stirling (Avis Graydon), Tom Wilkinson (Mr Carlton), Diana Coupland (Mrs Lester)

'Suffers from a wavering tone in script and direction but when all its gears are clicking has a distinctive appeal.' – *Derek Elley, Variety*

Another Man, Another Chance
France/US 1977 132m Eastmancolor
UA/Films 13/Ariane (Alexandre Mnouchkine, George Dancigers)
French title: *Un Autre Homme, une Autre Chance*
aka: *Another Man, Another Woman*
A Yank vet and a French widow meet and fall in love in the old west.
Pretty, overlong, rather enervating romance with an unusual and not entirely convincing setting.
wd Claude Lelouch *ph* Jacques Lefrançois *m* Francis Lai
☆ James Caan, Geneviève Bujold, Francis Huster, Susan Tyrrell

Another Man's Poison *
GB 1951 89m bw
Douglas Fairbanks Jnr/Daniel M. Angel
A lady novelist poisons her husband and lover, then unwittingly takes a fatal dose herself.
Hysterical vehicle for a fading Hollywood star reduced to repeating her tantrums in an English studio on a low budget; she should have stayed home, as should her director.
w Val Guest *play* *Deadlock* by Leslie Sands *d* Irving Rapper *ph* Robert Krasker *m* John Greenwood
☆ Bette Davis, Anthony Steel, Gary Merrill, Emlyn Williams, Barbara Murray, Reginald Beckwith, Edna Morris

'Barnstormers as rich and improbable as this are rare … the general atmosphere takes one back to 1935.' – *Gavin Lambert*
'Like reading Ethel M. Dell by flashes of lightning.' – *Frank Hauser*
'The melodramatic gamut has seldom experienced such a workout.' – *Hollywood Reporter*

Another Part of the Forest *
US 1948 108m bw
U-I (Jerry Bresler)
In the post-Civil War years, Marcus Hubbard leads his family to worldly success by cheating and the misuse of power: he lives to regret it, as the children learn their lessons all too well.
This backwards sequel to The Little Foxes (qv), showing how the characters of that play got to be their nasty selves, is quite absorbingly acted but stagily presented, with plenty of care but no style.
w Vladimir Pozner *play* *Lillian Hellman* *d* Michael Gordon *ph* Hal Mohr *m* Daniele Amfitheatrof *ad* Robert Boyle, Bernard Herzbrun *ed* Milton Carruth
☆ *Fredric March, Florence Eldridge, Ann Blyth, Dan Duryea, Edmond O'Brien*, John Dall

'The Hubbards are the greatest collection of ghouls since *The Old Dark House*.' – *Pauline Kael, 70s*

Another Shore *
GB 1948 77m bw
Ealing (Ivor Montagu)
A young Irishman dreams of life in the South Seas but gives up his fancies for love.
Curiously whimsical, artificial and unconvincing comedy drama from a famous studio, but not without its moments of interest.
w Walter Meade *novel* Kenneth Reddin *d* Charles Crichton *ph* Douglas Slocombe *m* Georges Auric
☆ Robert Beatty, Stanley Holloway, Moira Lister, Michael Medwin, Dermot Kelly, Wilfrid Brambell, Irene Worth

'The Perfect Family Has Just Moved Into The Neighbourhood.'
Another Stakeout
US 1993 108m Technicolor Scope
Buena Vista/Touchstone (Jim Kouf, Cathleen Summers, Lynn Bigelow)
Two cops and a lawyer pretend to be a family when they stake out a house for the witness to a murder.
Slight and ineffectual flop that substitutes poor gags for thrills.
w Jim Kouf *d* John Badham *ph* Roy H. Wagner *m* Arthur B. Rubinstein *pd* Lawrence G. Paull *ed* Frank Morris, Kevin Stitt
☆ Richard Dreyfuss, Emilio Estevez, Rosie O'Donnell, Dennis Farina, Marcia Strassman, Cathy Moriarty, Madeleine Stowe, John Rubinstein, Miguel Ferrer

'The "another" … is a declaration by the makers of *Stakeout*, a successful 1987 comedy-thriller, that this follow-up is a reprise rather than a sequel, and an indication that they suspect the targeted audience might have trouble reading roman numerals.' – *Philip French, Observer*
'It's one of those sequels that, though reasonably entertaining, go in one eye and out the other.' – *Derek Malcolm, Guardian*

'It's a blessed event!'
Another Thin Man
US 1939 102m bw
MGM (Hunt Stromberg)
Nick Charles solves a murder on a Long Island weekend.
Overwritten and distinctly tedious star sequel to The Thin Man and After the Thin Man (qqv). The title refers (erroneously) to Nick and Nora's baby.
w Frances Goodrich, Albert Hackett *d* W. S. Van Dyke II *ph* Oliver T. Marsh, William Daniels *m* Edward Ward
☆ William Powell, Myrna Loy, Otto Kruger, C. Aubrey Smith, Virginia Grey, Nat Pendleton, Tom Neal, Ruth Hussey, Sheldon Leonard

'The screenplay tosses shootings and skulduggery and repartee at us before we're ready, and then Nick Charles takes an unconscionable amount of time sorting things out.' – *Pauline Kael, 70s*

Another Time, Another Place
GB 1958 98m bw Vistavision
Paramount/Kaydor (Lewis Allen, Smedley Aston)
During World War II an American newspaperwoman has an affair with a British war correspondent; when he is killed in action, she consoles his widow.
Drippy romance, unsympathetically played and artificially set in a Cornish village.
w Stanley Mann *novel* Lenore Coffee *d* Lewis Allen *ph* Jack Hildyard *m* Douglas Gamley
☆ Lana Turner, Barry Sullivan, Glynis Johns, Sean Connery, Sidney James

Another Time, Another Place **
GB 1983 102m Eastmancolor
Cinegate/Umbrella/Rediffusion/Channel 4/Scottish Arts Council (Simon Perry)
In the late 40s, a Scottish farmer's wife falls in love with an Italian prisoner-of-war working on her husband's isolated farm.
The puritan north meets the sensual south in an emotional encounter, in which overheated passions contrast with a bleak landscape.
wd Michael Radford *novel* Jessie Kesson *ph* Roger Deakins *m* John McLeod *ad* Hayden Pearce *ed* Tom Priestley
☆ *Phyllis Logan*, Giovanni Mauriello, Denise Coffey, Gian Luca Favilla, Tom Watson, Gregor Fisher, Paul Young, Claudio Rosini

'More than adequately fills the big screen with bold imagery and emotions.' – *Film Yearbook*

† The film was made for television, but was given a cinema release.
BAFTA: Phyllis Logan

Another Way **
Hungary 1982 109m colour
Mafilm/Dialog Filmstudio
original title: *Egymásra Nézve*
In 1958, a married journalist recalls her love affair with an uncompromising lesbian colleague which led to attempted murder, death and misery.
A passionate, timely and excellently acted examination of the state of the nation through the individual experience of those seeking freedom from repression.
w Károly Makk, Erzsébet Galgóczi *novel* Erzsébet Galgóczi *d* *Károly Makk* *ph* Tamás Andor *m* László Dés, János Másik *ed* György Sivó
☆ *Jadwiga Jankowska*, Grazyna Szapolowska, *Jozef Kroner*, Adám Szirtes, Judit Pogány, Gábor Reviczky

† Jadwiga Jankowska won the best actress award at the Cannes Film Festival in 1982 for her performance.

Another Woman *
US 1988 84m colour
Rank/Orion/Jack Rollins, Charles H. Joffe (Robert Greenhut)
An unemotional academic discovers her inner self.
Woody Allen at his most gloomy and introspective.
wd Woody Allen *ph* Sven Nykvist *pd* Santo Loquasto *ed* Susan E. Morse
☆ Gena Rowlands, Mia Farrow, Ian Holm, Blythe Danner, Gene Hackman, Betty Buckley, Martha Plimpton, John Houseman

'Not only Allen's most wholly personal movie since *Stardust Memories* but arguably the most substantial achievement of his career.' – *Tim Pulleine, MFB*

Ansiktet: see *The Face*

Antefatto: see *A Bay of Blood*

Anthony Adverse *
US 1936 141m bw
Warner (Henry Blanke)
Adventures of an ambitious young man in early 19th-century America.
A rousing spectacle of its day, from a bestselling novel, this award-winning movie quickly dated and now seems very thin and shadowy despite the interesting talents involved.
w Sheridan Gibney *novel* Hervey Allen *d* Mervyn Le Roy *ph* *Tony Gaudio* *m* *Erich Wolfgang Korngold* *ad* *Anton Grot* *ed* Ralph Dawson
☆ Fredric March, Olivia de Havilland, Gale Sondergaard, Edmund Gwenn, Claude Rains, Anita Louise, Louis Hayward, Steffi Duna, Donald Woods, Akim Tamiroff, Ralph Morgan, Henry O'Neill

'A bulky, rambling and indecisive photoplay which has not merely taken liberties with the letter of the original but with its spirit.' – *Frank S. Nugent, New York Times*
'In the dramatizing there is shown no relish or conviction, only a retentive memory for all the old clothes of show business.' – *Otis Ferguson*
'A lavish gold-leaf from Hervey Allen's book, an earnest cinema endeavour, taxing alike its studio's purse and artistry.' – *Douglas Gilbert, New York World Telegraph*
'The show is fairly glutted with plot and counter-plot and is apt to make one feel that one is witnessing a serial run off continuously at a single performance.' – *Howard Barnes, New York Herald Tribune*
'It goes on too long, otherwise it might have been the funniest film since *The Crusades*.' – *Graham Greene*

Academy Award: Tony Gaudio; Erich Wolfgang Korngold; Gale Sondergaard; Ralph Dawson
Academy Award nomination: picture; Anton Grot

Anti-Extortion Woman: see *Minbo No Onna*

'Trust is not an option.'
Antitrust
US 2001 110m DeLuxe Panavision
TCF/MGM/Hyde Park/Industry Entertainment (Nick Wechsler, Keith Addis, David Nicksay)
A young computer expert discovers that his new boss, head of a leading software company, is behaving unethically in order to control the market.
Moderately clever and topical movie, despite its reliance on the over-familiar ploy of making the FBI the bad guys; it can be enjoyed for Tim Robbins' quirky physical impersonation of Bill Gates of Microsoft.
w Howard Franklin *d* Peter Howitt *ph* John Bailey *m* Don Davis *pd* Catherine Hardwicke *ed* Zach Staenberg
☆ Ryan Phillippe (Milo Hoffman), Rachael Leigh Cook (Lisa Calighan), Claire Forlani (Alice Poulson), Tim Robbins (Gary Winston), Douglas McFerran (Bob Shrot), Richard Roundtree (Lyle Barton), Tygh Runyan (Larry Banks), Yee Jee Tso (Teddy Chin)

'Strikes an uneasy balance between topicality and tradition, trendy techno jargon and musty thriller clichés.' – *Joe Leydon, Variety*

Antoine et Antoinette *
France 1947 87m bw
SNEG/Gaumont
A young married couple find they have won a lottery but lost the ticket.
A bubbly soufflé, most expertly served but leaving one still a little hungry; not quite in the Clair class.
w Françoise Giroud, M. Griffe, Jacques Becker *d* *Jacques Becker* *ph* Pierre Montazel *m* *Jean-Jacques Grunenwald*
☆ Roger Pigaut, Clair Maffei

Antonia's Line ***
Netherlands/Belgium/GB 1995 102m Fujicolour
Guild/Antonia's Line/Bergen/Prime Time/Bard/NPS (Hans de Weers)
On her deathbed, an elderly woman recalls the events of her life and of those she gave a home to over a period of 40 years.
A celebration of domestic and feminine virtues, a vivid, sprawling account that mixes fantasy and reality to heighten the story of love and survival.
wd *Marleen Gorris* *ph* Willy Stassen *m* Ilona Sekacz *ad* Harry Ammerlaan *ed* Michiel Reichwein, Wim Louwrier
☆ Willeke van Ammelrooy, Els Dottemans, Jan Decleir, Mil Seghers, Marina de Graaf, Jan Steen, Veerle van Overloop, Dora van der Groen

'A delightful, enjoyable and generous film.' – *Film Review*

Academy Award: foreign language film

Antonio (dubbed)
Chile 1973 82m colour
Saga/Claudio Guzmán
A poor village potter, given an expensive car by an indulgent American millionaire, drives to Santiago so that he can return the gift.
A confused and innocuous little fable about the corruption of urban life, aimed at a family audience.
w Mervin Walkenstein, Claudio Guzmán *d* Claudio Guzmán *ph* Andres Martorell *m* Ralph Ferraro *pd* Pato Guzmán
☆ Trini Lopez, Larry Hagman, Naomi Guerrero, Mervin Walkenstein

Antonio das Mortes **
Brazil 1969 95m Eastmancolor
Connoisseur/Produções Cinematograficas Mapa/Glauber Rocha (Claude-Antoine Mapa, Glauber Rocha)
original title: *O Dragao da Maldade contra o Santo Guerreiro*
A mercenary, hired by a rich landowner to kill an outlaw and his poor followers, realizes that he is supporting the wrong side.
Vivid, exotic South American Western with political overtones, a sequel of sorts to Black God, White Devil (qv).
wd Glauber Rocha *ph* Alfonso Beato *m* Marlos Nobre, Walter Queiroz, Sergio Ricardo *ad* Glauber Rocha *ed* Eduardo Escorel
☆ Mauricio Do Valle, Odete Lara, Hugo Carvana, Othon Bastos, Joffre Soares, Lorival Pariz

'Rocha's magnificent film is in fact firmly tied to the present-day political and social reality of his underdeveloped homeland.' – *Konstantin Bazarov, MFB*

Antony and Cleopatra *

GB/Spain/Switzerland 1972 170m
Technicolor Todd-AO 35
Transac/Izaro/Folio Films (Peter Snell)

A Roman general loses everything for the love of Cleopatra.
Well-meaning, well-mounted, but quite uninspired rendering.
wd Charlton Heston *play* William Shakespeare *ph* Rafael Pacheco *m* John Scott *pd* Maurice Pelling
☆ Charlton Heston, Hildegarde Neil, Eric Porter, *John Castle* (Octavius), Fernando Rey, Freddie Jones, Peter Arne, Roger Delgado
† Olivier and Orson Welles were both sought for the lead.

'See the world from a whole new perspective.'
Antz **

US 1998 83m Technicolor
DreamWorks/PDI (Brad Lewis, Aron Warner, Patty Wooton)

A worker ant, who falls in love with a princess ant, prevents a coup by her soldier-ant fiancé.
Enjoyable computer-animated feature with a verbal wit that may well appeal more to adults than children; the narrative follows a familiar outline, but the animation itself is brilliantly done.
w Todd Alcott, Chris Weitz, Paul Weitz *d* Eric Darnell, Tim Johnson *m* Harry Gregson-Williams, John Powell *pd* John Bell *ed* Stan Webb
☆ Featuring the voices of: Woody Allen, Dan Aykroyd, Anne Bancroft, Jane Curtin, Danny Glover, Gene Hackman, Jennifer Lopez, John Mahoney, Paul Mazursky, Sylvester Stallone, Sharon Stone, Christopher Walken

'Winds up overplotted in bizarrely grandiose ways. Must every child-friendly adventure film boil down to a struggle for world domination? And did this one really need to invoke genocide in its final reel?' – *Janet Maslin, New York Times*

'Life Is A Contact Sport. Play. Or Be Played.'
Any Given Sunday *

US 1999 162m Technicolor Panavision
Warner/Ixtlan/The Donners' Co (Lauren Shuler Donner, Clayton Townsend, Dan Halsted)

A veteran coach and a commercially-minded owner of a football team clash over attitudes and tactics, while the players undergo crises of their own.
Stone has said the film was intended as a homage to Robert Aldrich, and it has as its subject the same aggressive, amoral masculinity and bonding of the two movies, The Dirty Dozen and The Longest Yard, that inspired it: the problem for many non-US audiences will be trying to summon up some interest in American football.
w John Logan, Oliver Stone, Daniel Pyne *d* Oliver Stone *ph* Salvatore Totino *m* Robbie Robertson, Paul Kelly, Richard Horowitz *pd* Victor Kempster *ed* Tom Nordberg, Keith Salmon, Stuart Waks, Stuart Levy
☆ Al Pacino (Tony D'Amato), Cameron Diaz (Christina Pagniacci), Dennis Quaid (Jack 'Cap' Rooney), James Woods (Dr Harvey Mandrake), Jamie Foxx (Willie Beamen), LL Cool J (Julian Washington), Dr Ollie Powers (Matthew Modine), Jim Brown (Montezuma Monroe), Charlton Heston (AFFA Commissioner), Ann-Margret (Margaret Pagniacci), Aaron Eckhart (Nick Crozier), John C. McGinley (Jack Rose), Lauren Holly (Cindy Rooney)

'A rambunctious, hyperkinetic, testosterone-and-adrenaline-drenched look at that American obsession known as professional football.' – *Todd Mccarthy, Variety*

'Delivers a credible, action-charged vision of the frenzied world of professional sports as a metaphor for the volatility of American culture.' – *Stephen Holden, New York Times*

† Oliver Stone cut 12 minutes from the film for its European version.

Any Number Can Play *

US 1949 103m bw
MGM (Arthur Freed)

A gambling casino owner has health problems, is reconciled with his son and retires from the game.
Rather boring drama redeemed by slightly offbeat dialogue and excellent star acting, albeit in routine roles.
w Richard Brooks *novel* E. H. Heth *d* Mervyn Le Roy *ph* Harold Rosson *m* Lennie Hayton
☆ Clark Gable, Alexis Smith, Mary Astor, Wendell Corey, Audrey Totter, Lewis Stone, Frank Morgan, *Marjorie Rambeau*, Barry Sullivan

Any Old Port *

US 1932 20m bw
Hal Roach

Stan and Ollie are sailors on leave, and Ollie enters Stan for a boxing match.
Minor star comedy with good moments but a weak finish.
w H. M. Walker *d* James W. Horne
☆ Stan Laurel, Oliver Hardy, Walter Long

Any Wednesday *

US 1966 109m Technicolor
Warner (Julius J. Epstein)

GB title: *Bachelor Girl Apartment*

A millionaire businessman spends every Wednesday with his mistress, but complications arise when his young associate is accidentally sent to use the company flat.
Overlong screen version of a thinly scripted Broadway success in which yawns gradually overtake laughs. Rosemary Murphy is a breath of fresh air as the deceived wife who doesn't mind.
w Julius J. Epstein *play* Muriel Resnik *d* Robert Ellis Miller *ph* Harold Lipstein *m* George Duning
☆ Jane Fonda, Dean Jones, Jason Robards Jnr, Rosemary Murphy, Ann Prentiss, King Moody

Any Which Way You Can

US 1980 116m DeLuxe
Malpaso/Warner (Fritz Manes)

The hero of *Every Which Way But Loose* (qv) becomes involved in further brawls and car crashes, with the help of his friendly orang-utan.
A sequel designed entirely for the box-office, its tone set by the scene in which the villains on motorcycles are covered in tar.
w Stanford Sherman *d* Buddy Van Horn *ph* David Worth *md* Steve Dorf *pd* William J. Creber *ed* Ferris Webster, Ron Spang
☆ Clint Eastwood, Ruth Gordon, Sondra Locke, Geoffrey Lewis, William Smith, Harry Guardino

'This kind of thing is clearly beyond or beneath criticism.' – *Variety*

'Where the previous comedy set up a zany situation, this one ploughs it into the ground.' – *Daily Mail*

Anything Can Happen *

US 1952 93m bw
Paramount/William Perlberg, George Seaton

Adventures of a Russian immigrant family in New York.
A standard Hollywood product based on a sentimental best-seller.
w George Seaton, George Oppenheimer *book* George and Helen Papashvily *d* George Seaton *ph* Daniel L. Fapp *m* Victor Young
☆ José Ferrer, Kim Hunter, Kurt Kasznar, Alex Danaroff, Oscar Beregi

'Exploits to the hilt the somewhat limited possibilities of quaintness and whimsicality with a broken accent.' – *Penelope Houston*

Anything Goes **

US 1936 92m bw
Paramount (Benjamin Glazer)

TV title: *Tops is the Limit*

Romantic adventures on board a transatlantic liner.
Amiably batty musical comedy, zestfully directed and blithely performed.
w Guy Bolton, P. G. Wodehouse, Howard Lindsay, Russel Crouse, from their Broadway show *d* Lewis Milestone *ph* Karl Struss *m/ly* Cole Porter *md* Victor Young *ad* Hans Dreier
☆ *Bing Crosby, Ethel Merman, Charles Ruggles*, Grace Bradley, Ida Lupino, Chill Wills, the Avalon Boys, Arthur Treacher
† Only three of Cole Porter's songs were retained from the Broadway show: 'Anything Goes', 'You're the Top' and 'I Get a Kick out of You'. Others by various hands include 'Moonburn', 'Sailor Beware', 'My Heart and I', 'Am I Awake?', 'Hopelessly in Love'.

Anything Goes *

US 1956 106m Technicolor Vistavision
Paramount (Robert Emmett Dolan)

The male stars of a musical comedy each sign a girl to play the female lead; resulting complications are ironed out during a transatlantic voyage.
Below-par reworking of the 1936 film in which technical gloss and dull sets virtually reduce the characters to puppets. A few good moments transcend the general lack of imagination.
w Sidney Sheldon, from show as credited in 1936 version *d* Robert Lewis *ph* John F. Warren *m/ly* Cole Porter *md* Joseph J. Lilley *ch* Nick Castle, Roland Petit *ad* Hal Pereira, Joseph M. Johnson
☆ Bing Crosby, Donald O'Connor, Zizi Jeanmaire, Mitzi Gaynor, Phil Harris, Kurt Kasznar

'The story of a mother who knows best... and a daughter who knows better.'
Anywhere But Here

US 1999 114m DeLuxe 'Scope
TCF/Fox 2000 (Laurence Mark)

A mother and her 14 year-old daughter find it hard to cope with one another when they move from Wisconsin to Los Angeles.
A domestic drama skewed in favour of the younger of two women, who is presented as more mature than her childlike mother, possibly in the hope of appealing to a highschool audience; adults may find it harder going.
w Alvin Sargent *novel* Mona Simpson *d* Wayne Wang *ph* Roger Deakins *m* Danny Elfman *pd* Donald Graham Burt *ed* Nicholas C. Smith
☆ Susan Sarandon (Adele August), Natalie Portman (Ann August), Eileen Ryan (Lillian), Ray Baker (Ted), John Diehl (Jimmy), Shawn Hatosy (Benny), Bonnie Bedelia (Carol), Caroline Aaron (Gail), Hart Bochner (Josh Spritzer)

'A sumptuously crafted but extremely old-fashioned comedy-drama, made in the manner of Hollywood weepies of yesteryear.' – *Emanuel Levy, Variety*

† Contemporary with the movie was *Tumbleweeds* (qv),on a very similar mother-daughter conflict.

Anzio

Italy 1968 117m Technicolor Panavision
Columbia/Dino de Laurentiis (Marcel Bebert)

GB title: *The Battle for Anzio*

A war correspondent joins American and British troops preparing for the 1944 landing in Italy.
Threadbare war film which wastes an all-star American cast.
w H. A. L. Craig *book* Wynford Vaughan Thomas *d* Edward Dmytryk *ph* Giuseppe Rotunno *m* Riz Ortolani
☆ Robert Mitchum, Peter Falk, Arthur Kennedy, Robert Ryan, Earl Holliman, Mark Damon, Reni Santoni, Anthony Steel, Patrick Magee

'It must be a long time since a script managed to pack in so many crassly portentous statements about why men fight wars.' – *MFB*

Apache *

US 1954 91m Technicolor
UA/Hecht-Lancaster (Harold Hecht)

After the surrender of Geronimo, one Apache leader is unconquered; after creating much havoc, he settles for domesticity, and the white men let him go unharmed.
Sober Western in the wake of Broken Arrow (qv), with a predictably sympathetic star performance and a surprising happy ending. More decency than excitement along the way.
w James R. Webb *novel* *Bronco Apache* by Paul I. Wellman *d* Robert Aldrich *ph* Ernest Laszlo *m* David Raksin
☆ Burt Lancaster, Jean Peters, John McIntire, Charles Bronson, John Dehner, Paul Guilfoyle, Walter Sande, Monte Blue

'The picture was seriously compromised. You make a picture about one thing, the inevitability of Massai's death. His courage is measured against the inevitable. The whole previous two hours becomes reduced if at the end he can just walk away.' – *Robert Aldrich*

Apache Drums

US 1951 75m Technicolor
U-I (Val Lewton)

A gambler helps a town under Indian attack.
Standard co-feature Western, perfectly adequate but showing no sign of its producer's former tastes and skills.
w David Chandler *d* Hugo Fregonese *ph* Charles Boyle *m* Hans Salter *ad* Robert Clatworthy, Bernard Herzbrun *ed* Milton Carruth
☆ Stephen McNally, Willard Parker, Coleen Gray, Arthur Shields, James Griffith

Apache Rifles

US 1964 92m DeLuxe
Admiral Pictures/TCF

In 1879 Arizona, an Indian-hating officer falls for a half-caste.
Tolerable mid-budget Western.
w Charles B. Smith *d* William H. Witney
☆ Audie Murphy, Michael Dante, Linda Lawson, L. Q. Jones

Apache Uprising

US 1965 90m Techniscope
Paramount/A. C. Lyles

Assorted passengers in a stagecoach survive an Indian attack at a way station.
It sounds like a remake, and almost is, but the handling is lively enough and the producer's usual cast of nostalgic stars is in evidence.
w Harry Sanford, Max Lamb *d* R. G. Springsteen *ph* W. Wallace Kelley *m* Jimmie Haskell
☆ Rory Calhoun, Corinne Calvet, John Russell, Lon Chaney Jnr, Gene Evans, DeForest Kelley, Arthur Hunnicutt, Richard Arlen, Johnny Mack Brown, Jean Parker

Apache War Smoke

US 1952 67m bw
MGM

An Indian killer is among those sheltering in a desert outpost before an Apache raid.
Talkative but tense lower-berth Western.
w Jerry Davis *story* Ernest Haycox *d* Harold Kress
☆ Gilbert Roland, Robert Horton, Glenda Farrell, Barbara Ruick, Henry Morgan

Apache Woman

US 1955 82m Pathecolor
AIP/Golden State (Roger Corman)

A government agent discovers that a series of killings blamed on Apaches are caused by a gang led by a half-breed.
Routine Western, to which Corman added a subplot about racial prejudice, which may have improved its liberal credentials but does little for it as a movie.
w Lou Rusoff *d* Roger Corman *ph* Floyd Crosby *m* Ronald Stein *ed* Ronald Sinclair
☆ Lloyd Bridges, Joan Taylor, Lance Fuller, Morgan Jones, Paul Birch, Lou Place, Paul Dubov, Dick Miller, Chester Conklin
† The film was shot in under two weeks at a cost of around $80,000. Dick Miller played both a cowboy and an Apache in the film.

Aparajito ****

India 1956 113m bw
Epic Films Private Ltd (Satyajit Ray)

aka: *The Unvanquished*

After his father's death, a poor country boy is helped by his mother to study for the university.
A detailed and moving study of two characters who are universally familiar despite an unusual background.
wd Satyajit Ray *ph* Subrata Mitra *m* Ravi Shankar
☆ Pinaki Sen Gupta, Karuna Banerjee, Kanu Banerjee
† This was the sequel to *Pather Panchali*, and was itself followed by *The World of Apu* (qv).

'Movie-wise, there has never been anything like it – laugh-wise, love-wise, or otherwise-wise!'
The Apartment **

US 1960 125m bw Panavision
UA/Mirisch (Billy Wilder)

A lonely, ambitious clerk rents out his apartment to philandering executives and finds that one of them is after his own girl.

film suitable for family viewing | VHS video-cassette for the British PAL system | VHS video-cassette for the British PAL system in wide screen-format | Video cassette in a computer-colourised version | American NTSC video-cassette | Laser disc

Overlong and patchy but agreeably mordant and cynical comedy with a sparkling view of city office life and some deftly handled individual sequences.
w Billy Wilder, I. A. L. Diamond *d* Billy Wilder *ph* Joseph LaShelle *m* Adolph Deutsch *ad* Alexander Trauner *ed* Daniel Mandell
☆ *Jack Lemmon* (C. C. Baxter), *Shirley MacLaine* (Miss Kubelik), *Fred MacMurray* (Jeff D. Sheldrake), Ray Walston (Joe Dobisch), Jack Kruschen (Dr Dreyfuss), Joan Shawlee (Sylvia), Edie Adams (Miss Olsen), David Lewis (Al Kirkeby)

BAXTER'S OPENING NARRATION: 'On November 1st, 1959, the population of New York City was 8,042,753. If you laid all these people end to end, figuring an average height of five feet six and a half inches, they would reach from Times Square to the outskirts of Karachi, Pakistan. I know facts like this because I work for an insurance company – Consolidated Life of New York. We are one of the top five companies in the country. Last year we wrote nine point three billion dollars worth of policies. Our home office has 31,259 employees, which is more than the entire population of Natchez, Mississippi, or Gallup, New Mexico. I work on the 19th floor – Ordinary Policy department – Premium Accounting division – Section W – desk number 861.'

BAXTER: 'Miss Kubelik, one doesn't get to be a second administrative assistant around here unless he's a pretty good judge of character, and as far as I'm concerned you're tops. I mean, decency-wise and otherwise-wise.'

BAXTER: 'You know, I used to live like Robinson Crusoe – shipwrecked among eight million people. Then one day I saw a footprint in the sand and there you were. It's a wonderful thing, dinner for two.'

MISS KUBELIK (LAST LINE OF FILM): 'Shut up and deal.'

'Without either style or taste, shifting gears between pathos and slapstick without any transition.' – *Dwight MacDonald*

'Billy Wilder directed this acrid story as if it were a comedy, which is a cheat, considering that it involves pimping and a suicide attempt and many shades of craven ethics.' – *New Yorker, 1980*

🏆 picture; Billy Wilder, I. A. L. Diamond (as writers); Billy Wilder (as director)
🎗 Joseph LaShelle; Jack Lemmon; Shirley MacLaine; Jack Kruschen; art direction; editing
BAFTA picture; Jack Lemmon; Shirley MacLaine

Apartment for Peggy *

US 1948 98m Technicolor
TCF (William Perlberg)

A retired professor finds a new lease of life through caring for the homeless family of an ex-GI.
Sentimental comedy with serious undertones (the professor twice attempts suicide). Signs of enterprise are smothered by regulation charm.
wd George Seaton *story* Faith Baldwin *ph* Harry Jackson *m* David Raksin
☆ Edmund Gwenn, Jeanne Crain, William Holden, Gene Lockhart, Henri Letondal, Charles Lane, Houseley Stevenson

'A first rate experience for observers with comprehending minds.' – *Bosley Crowther, New York Times*

The Apartment on the 13th Floor: see *Cannibal Man*

Apartment Zero

GB 1988 125m colour
Mainline/The Summit Company (Martin Donovan, David Koepp)

In Buenos Aires, a repressed crypto-Englishman takes as a lodger a mysterious American.
Unpleasant psychological thriller about unlovely people.
w Martin Donovan, David Koepp *d* Martin Donovan *ph* Miguel Rodriguez *m* Elia Cmiral *pd* Miguel Angel Lumaldo *ed* Conrad M. Gonzalez
☆ Colin Firth, Hart Bochner, Dora Bryan, Liz Smith, Cipe Lincovsky

The Ape

US 1940 61m bw
Monogram (Scott R. Dunlap)

Dr Adrian seeks to cure polio by means of a serum which can only be obtained from the spinal fluid of a human being. He kills an escaped ape and dresses in its skin to seek victims.
Silly and rather boring addition to the mad doctor cycle.
w Curt Siodmak, Richard Carroll *play* Adam Shirk *d* William Nigh *ph* Harry Neumann *m* Edward Kay
☆ Boris Karloff, Maris Wrixon, Gertrude Hoffman, Henry Hall

Ape and Super Ape

Netherlands/USA 1972 103m Technicolor
Unicorn (Bert Haanstra Films)
original title: *Bij de Beesten Af*

An alleged documentary comparing human and animal behaviour seems regrettably to turn into a series of episodes depicting animal savagery in close-up.
wd Bert Haanstra *ph* Anton Van Munster *ed* Bert Haanstra

'It lacks even associational interest for the wild-life enthusiast, and is best written off as an inconclusive, unoriginal and often repellent exercise unworthy of its maker.' – *John Baxter, MFB*

🎗 documentary

The Ape Man

US 1943 64m bw
Monogram (Sam Katzman, Jack Dietz)
GB title: *Lock Your Doors*

A scientist injects himself with spinal fluid which turns him into an ape creature.
Cheap rubbish shot in a couple of corners and offering no thrill whatever.
w Barney A. Sarecky *story* *They Creep in the Dark* by Karl Brown *d* William Beaudine *ph* Mack Stengler *m* Edward Kay
☆ Bela Lugosi, Wallace Ford, Louise Currie, Minerva Urecal

'Bela Lugosi, rigged out in a shaggy beard and formal morning attire, ambling like an ape and sharing a cage with a gorilla, scares nobody. It's strictly a dual support.' – *Variety*

† A supposed sequel the following year, *Return of the Ape Man*, had in fact no plot connection. In this Lugosi thawed out a neanderthal man, inserted John Carradine's brain, and the composite turned into George Zucco!

APEX

US 1994 103m Foto-Kem
Republic/Green Communications (Talaat Captan)

A time-traveller, sent back a hundred years to 1973 to find a malfunctioning robot, catches a virus that alters the future, turning it into a disease-ridden epoch, alive with killer robots.
Enjoyable low-budget variation on a familiar science-fiction theme of man versus machines, which borrows from bigger-budget successes such as The Terminator, among others. The title is an acronym for Advanced Prototype Extermination Unit.
w Phillip J. Roth, Ronald Schmidt *d* Phillip J. Roth *ph* Mark W. Gray *m* Jim Goodwin *ed* Daniel Lawrence *sp* Ultra Matrix; make-up: Altered Anatomy FX
☆ Richard Keats, Mitchell Cox, Lisa Russell, Marcus Aurelius, Adam Lawson, Brian Richard Peck

'Made with more imagination than skill, and more resourcefulness than polish, pic makes the absolute most of an obviously limited budget.' – *Variety*

Der Apfel ist ab **

West Germany 1949 105m bw
Camera Film/Helmut Beck-Herzog
Translated title: *The Apple Fell*

Adam and Eve have marital problems in Paradise, and consult a psychiatrist.
Lively sophisticated fantasy, perhaps a bit arch for general consumption, but almost as interesting in post-war Nazi Germany as Caligari was in 1919.
w Kurd E. Heyne, Helmut Kautner, Bobby Todd, from their musical comedy *d* *Helmut Kautner* *ph* Igor Oberberg *m* Bernhard Eichhorn
☆ Bobby Todd, Bettina Moissi, Joana Maria Gorvin

'Hollywood should look over this Kautner. He has a Lubitsch touch that runs all over this picture.' – *Variety*

Aphrodite, Goddess of Love

Italy 1958 90m Ferrania colour
Schermi (Adriano Merkel)
original title: *Afrodite Dea Dell'Amore*
aka: *Slave Women of Corinth*

The governor of Corinth has to cope with the Emperor Nero, his infatuation with a prostitute, plague, Christians and revolting locals.
Better-than-average example of its genre, mixing power politics and romance to some effect.
w Ugo Moretti, Mario Bonnard, Sergio Leone, Mario Di Nardo *d* Mario Bonnard *ph* Tino Santoni *m* Giovanni Fusco *pd* Saverio D'Eugenio *ed* Nella Nannuzzi
☆ Isabelle Corey, Antonio de Teffe, Irene Tunc, Ivo Garrani, Giulio Donnini, Carlo Tamberlani

Apo Tin Akri Tis Polis *

Greece 1998 93m colour
Millivres/Mythos/Rosebud/Hot Shot (Dionysis Samioris, Anastasios Vasilou)
aka: *From the Edge of the City*

In Athens, a young Russian-Greek immigrant, who scrapes a living as a thief and and rent boy, falls in love with a prostitute belonging to the local pimp.
A drama of urban low-life, semi-documentary in style, that uses a cast of street boys and professional actors for its narrative of rootless, displaced and deprived young searching for an identity in a hostile environment.
wd Constantine Giannaris *ph* Giorgos Argyroiliopoulos *m* Akis Daoutis *pd* Roula Nicolaou *ed* Ioanna Spillopoulou
☆ Stathis Papadopoulos (Sasha), Kostas Kotsianidis (Kotsian), Panagiotis Chartomtsidis (Panagiotis), Dimitris Papoulidis (Giorgos), Theodora Tzimou (Natasha), Anestis Polychronidis (Anestis), Nikos Kamontos (Philippos), Stelios Tsemboglidis (Stelios), Panagiota Vlachosotirou (Elenitsa)

'It captures a gritty urban reality without moralizing or sentimentalizing its hapless young protagonist.' – *Stephen Holden, New York Times*

Apocalypse Now **

US 1979 153m Technicolor Technovision
Omni Zoetrope (Francis Coppola)

A Vietnam captain is instructed to eliminate a colonel who has retired to the hills and is fighting his own war.
Pretentious war movie, made even more hollow-sounding by the incomprehensible performance of Brando as the mad martinet. Some vivid scenes along the way, and some interesting parallels with Conrad's Heart of Darkness, but these hardly atone for the director's delusion that prodigal expenditure of time and money will result in great art. (The movie took so long to complete that it was dubbed Apocalypse Later.)
w John Milius, Francis Coppola *d* Francis Coppola *ph* *Vittorio Storaro* *m* Carmine Coppola, Francis Coppola *pd* Dean Tavoularis *ed* Richard Marks, Walter Murch, Gerald B. Greenberg, Lisa Fruchtman
☆ Martin Sheen, Robert Duvall, Frederic Forrest, Marlon Brando, Sam Bottoms, Dennis Hopper

'The characters are living through Vietnam as pulp adventure fantasy, as movie, as stoned humour.' – *New Yorker*

'Emotionally obtuse and intellectually empty.' – *Time*

† Coppola admitted the following at the Cannes Film Festival: 'It's more of an experience than a movie. At the beginning there's a story. Along the river the story becomes less important and the experience more important.'

†† Apocalypse Now Redux, a version running at 202m, was released in 2001.

🏆 Vittorio Storaro; sound (Walter Murch, Mark Berger, Richard Beggs, Nat Boxer)
🎗 picture; John Milius, Francis Coppola (script); Francis Coppola (as director); Robert Duvall; art direction; editing
BAFTA Francis Coppola; Robert Duvall

'Houston, we have a problem.'

Apollo 13 **

US 1995 140m colour Super 35
Imagine (Brian Grazer)

In 1970 NASA Mission Control works feverishly to bring back three astronauts alive when there is an explosion aboard the Apollo 13 spacecraft to the moon.
A gripping documentary-style recreation of an averted tragedy, excellently done but one that is an uncritical celebration of the American way and which makes no attempt to put the mission into a wider historical context; it settles for simple patriotism.
w William Broyles Jnr, Al Reinert *book* *Lost Moon* by Jim Lovell, Jeffrey Kluger *d* Ron Howard *ph* Dean Cundey *m* James Horner *pd* Michael Corenblith *ed* Mike Hill, Dan Hanley
☆ Tom Hanks, Bill Paxton, Kevin Bacon, Ed Harris, Gary Sinise, Kathleen Quinlan, Mary Kate Schellhardt, Emily Ann Lloyd

'Makes all the right moves, but lacks inspiration.' – *Sight and Sound*

'Plays boringly safe ... The drama proceeds in a narrow line that leaves no room for poetry, surprise or true excitement.' – *Geoff Brown, The Times*

† The film took more than $331m at the box-office worldwide.

🏆 Mike Hill, Dan Hanley; sound effects
🎗 picture; Ed Harris; Kathleen Quinlan; James Horner; Michael Corenblith; William Broyles Jnr, Al Reinert; visual effects

The Apostle **

US 1997 134m CFI color
Universal/October/Butchers Run (Rob Carliner)

After he loses his church and beats his wife's lover unconscious with a baseball bat, a middle-aged preacher leaves Texas and goes to a small Louisiana town, where he starts a new church.
Engrossing portrait of a man driven by the need to communicate his religion, though it is not always easy to empathize with a preacher whose approach is wholly emotional, and never rational.
wd Robert Duvall *ph* Barry Markowitz *m* David Mansfield *pd* Linda Burton *ed* Stephen Mack
☆ *Robert Duvall* (Euliss Dewey), Farrah Fawcett (Jessie Dewey), Todd Allen (Horace), John Beasley (Brother Blackwell), June Carter Cash (Mrs Dewey), Walton Goggins (Sam), Billy Joe Shaver (Joe), Billy Bob Thornton (Troublemaker), Miranda Richardson (Toosie)

'A triumph on every level but one: its excessive running time.' – *Emanuel Levy, Variety*

† Robert Duvall put up $5m of his own money to make the film.

🎗 Robert Duvall

The Appaloosa *

US 1966 99m Techniscope
Universal (Alan Miller)
GB title: *Southwest to Sonora*

A cowboy's plan to start a stud farm with his magnificent horse is interrupted by badmen who think he has molested their girl.
Mannered, slow Western set on the Mexican border, with star and director apparently striving to upstage each other.
w James Bridges, Roland Kibbee *novel* Robert MacLeod *d* Sidney J. Furie *ph* *Russell Metty* *m* Frank Skinner *ad* Alexander Golitzen, Alfred Sweeney *ed* Ted J. Kent
☆ Marlon Brando, Anjanette Comer, John Saxon, Rafael Campos, Frank Silvera, Emilio Fernandez, Alex Montoya, Miriam Colon

'Seems intent less on telling a story than in carving out the incidental details.' – *MFB*

'The camerawork concentrates on beady eyes, sweaty foreheads, spurred boots and anonymous midriffs being studied through a variety of frames, ranging from tequila bottles to cook fires to grillwork to fingers to feet.' – *Judith Crist*

'A dog of a movie about a horse.' – *Pauline Kael*

L'Appartement **

France/Spain/Italy 1996 102m colour
Artificial Eye/Ima/UGC/La Sept/M6/Mate/Cecchi Gori (Georges Benayoun)

In Paris, a young executive neglects his job because of his involvement with three women – his fiancée, a former lover he tracks down, and an

actress he saves from suicide – who also lead complex lives.
Intriguing, complex tragi-comedy of tangled love affairs, in which the audience is led on a quest as baffling and rewarding as that of its protagonist; it acknowledges its debt to Shakespeare's A Midsummer Night's Dream.
wd Gilles Mimouni *ph* Thierry Arbogast *m* Peter Chase *ad* Philippe Chiffre *ed* Caroline Biggerstaff, Françoise Bonnot
☆ Romane Bohringer, Vincent Cassel, Jean-Philippe Ecoffey, Monica Bellucci, Sandrine Kiberlain, Olivier Granier
'The kind of movie that you'll want to actively consume rather than passively watch ... thoroughly engaging cinema.' – *Helen Van Kruyssen, Film Review*
foreign film

L'Appât: see *The Bait*

'Is Kitty a mother?'
Applause **
US 1929 78m bw
Paramount (Jesse L. Lasky, Walter Wanger)
A vaudeville star gradually loses the love of her daughter.
Absorbing treatment of a has-been tearjerking theme, full of cinematic touches and with unusual use of New York locations.
w Garrett Fort *novel* Beth Brown *d* Rouben Mamoulian *ph* George Folsey
☆ *Helen Morgan*, Joan Peers, Henry Wadsworth, Fuller Mellish Jnr
'An oasis of filmic sophistication in a desert of stage-bound early talkies.' – *William Everson, 1966*
'A cohesive, well integrated series of pictures. Its intensity, its sharp projection of tragedy, emerge from the eye of the camera; an omniscient, omnipresent eye that slides easily over the links of the story and emphasizes only the true and the relevant.' – *Thornton Delehanty, The Arts*

The Apple **
Iran/France 1997 85m colour
Artificial Eye/MK2
original title: *Sib*
Two 12-year-old twin girls, who have been kept locked away in their home by their unemployed father and blind mother, experience the outside world for the first time.
An extraordinary film, based on an actual event, with the cast playing themselves; it occupies an unusual space between documentary and drama, but is in no way exploitative.
w Mohsen Makhmalbaf *d* Samirah Makhmalbaf *ph* Ebrahim Ghafouri *ed* Mohsen Makhmalbaf
☆ Massoumeh Naderi, Za Naderi, Ghorban Ali-Naderi, Azizeh Mohamadi, Zahra Sagharisaz, Amir Hossein Khosrojerdi
'A remarkable achievement, proving poignant, funny and very human.' – *James Mottram, Film Review*

The Apple Dumpling Gang
US 1974 100m Technicolor
Walt Disney (Bill Anderson)
Three orphan children strike gold in 1878 California.
Better-than-average Disney romp.
w Don Tait *novel* Jack M. Bickham *d* Norman Tokar *ph* Frank Phillips *m* Buddy Baker
☆ Bill Bixby, Susan Clark, David Wayne, Don Knotts, Tim Conway, Slim Pickens, Harry Morgan, John McGiver, Marie Windsor, Iris Adrian

The Apple Dumpling Gang Rides Again
US 1979 88m Technicolor
Walt Disney (Ron Miller)
Two incompetent bank robbers trying to go straight find themselves in trouble with a sheriff, the cavalry, Indians and a rival gang.
Limp, slow-paced comedy Western that is a dull sequel to an ordinary original.
w Don Tait *d* Vincent McEveety *ph* Frank Phillips *m* Buddy Baker *ad* John B. Mansbridge, Frank T. Smith *ed* Gordon D. Brenner
☆ Tim Conway, Don Knotts, Tim Matheson, Kenneth Mars, Elyssa Davalos, Jack Elam, Robert Pine, Harry Morgan, Ruth Buzzi

The Apple Fell: see *Der Apfel ist ab*

Appleseed (dubbed)
Japan 1991 71m colour
Manga/Gainax/AIC/Centre Studio/Tohokushinsha/Bandai/Movie (Taro Maki, Atsushi Sugita, Masaki Sawanobori, Tohru Miura)
Power struggles in Olympus, a haven built after World War III, between humans, terrorist outlaws, cyborgs and biodroids, half-human, half-robot creatures developed to protect the city, who wish to control it as well.
Poorly animated science-fiction thriller with a predictable narrative, dubbed with too many expletives. The stories on which the film is based were highly regarded in Japan, so something must have been lost in their translation to the screen.
wd Kazuyoshi Katayama *stories* Appleseed by Masumune Shirow *m* Norimasa Yamanaka *ad* Hiroaki Ogura
☆ Featuring the voices of Larissa Murray, Bill Roberts, David Reynolds, Lorelei King, Vincent Marzello, Julia Brahms

The Appointment *
US 1969 100m colour
MGM (Martin Poll)
A businessman suspects his wife of spare time prostitution.
Unusual sophisticated fable, dressed to kill but rather stretched out for its substance. Shades of El and The Chinese Room.
w James Salter *d* Sidney Lumet *m* John Barry, Don Walker
☆ Omar Sharif, Anouk Aimée, Lotte Lenya

Appointment for Love *
US 1941 89m bw
Universal (Bruce Manning)
A doctor and a playwright agree to marry 'without love'.
A familiar theme quite amusingly explored by a practised cast.
w Bruce Manning, Felix Jackson *d* William A. Seiter *ph* Joseph Valentine *m* Frank Skinner *md* Charles Previn *ad* Jack Otterson *ed* Ted J. Kent
☆ Charles Boyer, Margaret Sullavan, Eugene Pallette, Rita Johnson, Gus Schilling, Reginald Denny, Ruth Terry
sound (Bob R. Brown)

Appointment in Honduras
US 1953 79m Technicolor
RKO/Benedict Bogeaus
Three assorted types and four criminals escape through the jungle from a revolution.
Predictable adventure drama sabotaged by poor colour.
w Karen de Wolf *d* Jacques Tourneur *ph* Joseph Biroc *m* Louis Forbes
☆ Glenn Ford, Ann Sheridan, Zachary Scott, Rodolfo Acosta, Jack Elam

Appointment in London *
GB 1952 96m bw
Mayflower (Aubrey Baring, Maxwell Setton)
The exploits of a squadron of Bomber Command during one month in 1943.
Dullish war film with standard credits.
w John Wooldridge, Robert Westerby *d* Philip Leacock *ph* Stephen Dade *m* John Wooldridge
☆ Dirk Bogarde, Ian Hunter, Dinah Sheridan, Bill Kerr, Bryan Forbes, William Sylvester, Charles Victor

Appointment with a Shadow
US 1957 72m bw Cinemascope
Universal-International
GB title: *The Big Story*
An alcoholic reporter redeems himself by capturing a criminal single-handed.
Maudlin melodrama which takes itself too seriously.
w Alec Coppel, Norman Jolley *d* Richard Carlson
☆ George Nader, Joanna Moore, Brian Keith, Virginia Field

Appointment with Crime
GB 1945 97m bw
British National
Ex-convict revenges himself on the former friends who shopped him.
Stodgy melodrama which seemed about to make a big star of William Hartnell.
wd John Harlow
☆ William Hartnell, Robert Beatty, Joyce Howard, Raymond Lovell, Herbert Lom

Appointment with Danger *
US 1949 89m bw
Paramount (Robert Fellows)
A nun becomes the government's chief witness in identifying the murderers of a US postal inspector.
Routine but entertaining star thick ear.
w Richard Breen, Warren Duff *d* Lewis Allen *ph* John Seitz *m* Victor Young
☆ Alan Ladd, Phyllis Calvert, Paul Stewart, Jan Sterling, Jack Webb, Henry Morgan

Appointment with Death
GB 1988 108m colour
Cannon (Michael Winner)
A domineering step-mother, who cheats her husbands' children out of their rightful inheritance, is found murdered.
Another starry Hercule Poirot tale, this time in 30s Palestine.
w Anthony Shaffer, Peter Buckman, Michael Winner *novel* Agatha Christie *d* Michael Winner *ph* David Gurfinkel *m* Pino Donaggio *pd* John Blezard *ed* Arnold Crust Jnr (Michael Winner)
☆ Peter Ustinov (Hercule Poirot), Lauren Bacall, Carrie Fisher, John Gielgud, Piper Laurie

'They came home with the milk!'
Appointment with Venus **
GB 1951 89m bw
GFD/British Film Makers (Betty E. Box)
US title: *Island Rescue*
During World War II, a pedigree cow is rescued from the German-occupied Channel Islands.
Curious but generally agreeable mixture of comedy and war adventure, pleasantly shot on Sark.
w Nicholas Phipps *novel* Jerrard Tickell *d* Ralph Thomas *ph* Ernest Steward *m* Benjamin Frankel
☆ David Niven, Glynis Johns, George Coulouris, Barry Jones, Kenneth More, Noel Purcell, Bernard Lee, Jeremy Spenser

Apprentice to Murder
Norway 1988 94m colour
New World (Howard K. Grossman)
In Pennsylvania in the 1920s, a teenaged boy comes under the influence of a faith healer who is cursed by the devil.
Odd little thriller that relies too heavily on special effects to hold an audience's attention.
w Allan Scott, Wesley Moore *d* R. L. Thomas *ph* Kelvin Pike *m* Charles Gross *pd* Gregory Bolton *ed* Patrick McMahon *sp* Derek Meddings, Mark Meddings, Roy Spencer
☆ Donald Sutherland, Chad Lowe, Mia Sara, Knut Husebo, Rutanya Alda, Eddie Jones, Mark Burton, Adrian Sparks

The Apprenticeship of Duddy Kravitz *
Canada 1974 121m Bellevue-Pathé Panavision
Duddy Kravitz Syndicate (Gerald Schneider)
An ambitious young Jew finds that it is best to be liked.
Amusing adventures of an anti-hero; good scenes but rather patchy technique.
w Mordecai Richler *novel* Mordecai Richler *d* Ted Kotcheff *ph* Miklos Lente *m* Stanley Myers
☆ *Richard Dreyfuss*, Micheline Lanctot, Jack Warden, Randy Quaid, Denholm Elliott, Joseph Wiseman
Mordecai Richler

Les Apprentis *
France 1995 98m colour
Gala/Péléas/Glem (Philippe Martin)
A would-be photographer makes and loses a friend when he moves into a flat with an older writer.
Desultory but amusing comedy of an odd couple who share no more than a desire for love and an inability to find employment.
w Pierre Salvadori, Philippe Harel, Marc Syrigas, Nicolas Cuche, Franck Bauchard *d* Pierre Salvadori *ph* Gilles Henry *m* Philippe Eidel *ad* François Emmanuelli *ed* Hélène Viard
☆ François Cluzet, Guillaume Depardieu, Judith Henry, Claire Laroche, Philippe Girard, Barnard Yerles, Marie Trintignant
'Feels as if it was written from day to day and heavily dependent on how its stars were feeling when they got up. Might have been better to stay in bed.' – *Alexander Walker*

Après l'Amour *
France 1992 105m colour
Mayfair/Alexandre/TF1/Prodeve (Jean-Bernard Fetoux)
aka: *Love After Love*
Love and desire among the thirty-somethings of Parisian glitterati.
A complex story of sexual relationships over a period of a year, enjoyable enough if you can keep track of all the shifting couplings, but not particularly insightful.
w Diane Kurys, Antoine Lacomblez *d* Diane Kurys *ph* Fabio Conversi *m* Yves Simon, Serge Parathoner, Jannick Top *ad* Tony Egry *ed* Hervé Schneid
☆ Isabelle Huppert, Bernard Giraudeau, Hippolyte Girardot, Lio, Yvan Attal, Judith Reval, Ingrid Held, Laure Killing, Mehdi Iossen, Florian Billon
'It copes with agony, bluster, lies and voyeurism in a cynically relaxed spirit that places it firmly in the French "relationship movie" genre; though with the difference, outdated as it may seem anywhere except France, that it is a woman through whose eyes we look.' – *Amanda Lipman, Sight and Sound*

'He has a wife. She has a husband. With so much in common they just have to fall in love.'
The April Fools *
US 1969 95m Technicolor Panavision
Cinema Center/Jalem (Gordon Carroll)
An unhappy New York husband elopes to Paris with an unhappy wife.
Whimsical romantic comedy which rather strains its resources without giving full value for money in romance, humour or simple charm. Good moments, though.
w Hal Dresner *d* Stuart Rosenberg *ph* Michel Hugo *m* Marvin Hamlisch *pd* Richard Sylbert
☆ Jack Lemmon, Catherine Deneuve, Myrna Loy, Charles Boyer, Peter Lawford, Jack Weston, Harvey Korman, Sally Kellerman
'Painfully modish, from the opening party in an apartment filled with fashionable objets d'art to the final mad dash to the airport in an expensive sports car.' – *MFB*

April Fool's Day
US 1986 88m Metrocolor Panavision
Paramount/Hometown (Frank Mancuso Jnr)
College friends go to spend a weekend in an isolated house with a wealthy practical joker, who has a taste for murderous pranks.
A teenage slasher movie with an original twist, but one that does not alter the usual tedium of the genre.
w Danilo Bach *d* Fred Walton *ph* Charles Minsky *m* Charles Bernstein *ad* Stewart Campbell *ed* Bruce Green
☆ Jay Baker, Deborah Foreman, Deborah Goodrich, Ken Olandt, Griffin O'Neal, Leah King Pinsent, Clayton Rohner

April in Paris *
US 1952 100m Technicolor
Warner (William Jacobs)
A chorus girl is mistakenly invited to a US Arts Festival in Paris, and bewitches the bureaucrat in charge.
Poorly produced star musical with a thin plot and a few redeeming wisps of wit.
w Jack Rose, Melville Shavelson *d* David Butler *ph* Wilfrid Cline *m/ly* Sammy Cahn, Vernon Duke, E. Y. Harburg *md* Ray Heindorf *ch* Le Roy Prinz
☆ Doris Day, *Ray Bolger*, Claude Dauphin, Eve Miller, George Givot

April Love
US 1957 99m Eastmancolor Cinemascope
TCF (David Weisbart)
For stealing a car, a teenager is sent on probation to his uncle's stud farm, where circumstances seem once again to put him in trouble with the law.
Easygoing star vehicle with little to recommend it to adults.
w Winston Miller *novel* George Agnew Chamberlain *d* Henry Levin *ph* Wilfrid Cline *m/ly* Sammy Fain, Paul Francis Webster
☆ Pat Boone, Shirley Jones, Dolores Michaels, Arthur O'Connell, Jeanette Nolan
† A remake of *Home in Indiana* (qv).
title song (*m* Sammy Fain, *ly* Paul Francis Webster)

April One
Canada 1993 85m colour
Astral/April One (Julia Sereny)
In Ottawa, a diplomat becomes protective towards the confused ex-convict who takes her hostage.
Based on a true story, a suspenseless thriller that leaves its audience no wiser than before, or any more understanding of the motives of those involved.
wd Murray Battle *ph* Mark Irwin *m* Jonathan Goldsmith *ad* Ian Brock *ed* Roger Mattiussi
☆ Stephen Shellen, Djanet Sears, David Strathairn, Wayne Robson, Gordon Clapp, Pierre Curzi, Martin Julien

April Romance: see *Blossom Time*

April Showers *
US 1948 94m bw
Warner (William Jacobs)
In a family vaudeville act, Dad takes to drink.
Hoary musical melodrama enlivened by occasional acts.
w Peter Milne *musical adaptation* Max Steiner *d* James V. Kern *ph* Carl Guthrie *md* Ray Heindorf *songs* various
☆ Jack Carson, Robert Alda, Ann Sothern, Robert Ellis, S. Z. Sakall

Aprile *
Italy/France 1998 78m Technicolor
Metro Tartan/Sacher/BAC (Angelo Barbagallo, Nanni Moretti)
A film director begins and abandons a musical, starts a political documentary, wishes he were making a musical and is distracted by the birth of his son and the sense that time is running out.
Moretti managed to transform his life into art with his charming Dear Diary (qv). This time around his autobiographical concerns are so personal that the result is too inward-looking to fully engage the interest of others.
wd Nanni Moretti *ph* Giuseppe Lanci *ad* Marta Maffucci *ed* Angelo Nicolin
☆ Nanni Moretti, Silvio Orlando, Silvia Nono, Pietro Moretti, Agata Apicella Moretti, Nuria Schoenberg, Angelo Barbagallo, Silvia Bonucci, Quentin de Fouchecour, Renato De Maria, Daniele Luchetti, Andrea Molaioli, Nicola Piepoli, Corrado Stajano
'The film is a delight to watch (even more so if you know anything about Italy). It is also a cinematic masterpiece.' – *Chris Wagstaff, Sight and Sound*

Apt Pupil **
US/France 1997 111m Technicolor Panavision
Columbia TriStar/Phoenix/Bad Hat Harry/Canal+ (Jane Hamsher, Don Murphy, Bryan Singer)
In California, a schoolboy threatens a former Nazi with disclosure unless he tells him about the Holocaust.
An effective drama about the corruption caused by contact with evil, though it descends into horror-movie clichés towards the end.
w Brandon Boyce *novella* Stephen King *d* Bryan Singer *ph* Newton Thomas Sigel *m* John Ottman *pd* Richard Hoover *ed* John Ottman
☆ Ian McKellen, Brad Renfro, Bruce Davison, Elias Koteas, Joe Morton, Jan Triska, Michael Byrne, Heather McComb, David Schwimmer
'Has more than enough chilling dramatic scenes to rivet the attention but suffers from some hokey contrivances and underlying insufficiencies of motivation.' – *Todd McCarthy, Variety*
'I didn't like my character. He didn't seem very deep. He just seemed a representative of evil.' – *Ian McKellen*

Aquila Nera: see *Black Eagle*

The Arab: see *The Barbarian*

Arabella
US/Italy 1969 91m Technicolor
Cram Film/Universal
A female confidence trickster needs the money to pay her grandmother's back taxes.
Floppy, tedious comedy adventure with an international cast all at sea.
w Adriano Barocco *d* Mauro Bolognini
☆ Virna Lisi, James Fox, Terry-Thomas, Margaret Rutherford

'The real excitement begins when they run out of bullets!'
Arabesque **
US 1966 118m Technicolor Panavision
Universal (Stanley Donen)
An Oxford professor is asked by Middle Eastern oil magnates to decipher a hieroglyphic, and finds afterwards that he is marked for assassination.
The ultimate in sixties spy kaleidoscopes, in which the working out of the plot matters much less than the stars, the jokes and the lavish backgrounds. Fast moving, amusing and utterly forgettable.
w Julian Mitchell, Stanley Price, Pierre Marton *novel* The Cipher by Gordon Cotler *d* Stanley Donen *ph* Christopher Challis *m* Henry Mancini *ad* Reece Pemberton *ed* Frederick Wilson
☆ Gregory Peck, Sophia Loren, *Alan Badel*, Kieron Moore, Carl Duering, John Merivale, Duncan Lamont, George Coulouris, Ernest Clark
'Nothing could look more "with it", or somehow matter less.' – *MFB*
'A strikingly visual chase and intrigue yarn.' – *Robert Windeler*
'All rather too flashy for comfort.' – *Sight and Sound*
† Pierre Marton was a pen name for Peter Stone.
Christopher Challis

Arabian Adventure
GB 1979 98m colour
Badger Films/John Dark
The dictator of Jadur promises his daughter's hand in marriage if a young prince will seek and find a magic rose.
Artless juggling of elements from The Thief of Baghdad, including magic carpets, monsters and a bottle djinn.
w Brian Hayles *d* Kevin Connor *ph* Alan Hume *m* Ken Thorne *pd* Elliot Scott
☆ Christopher Lee, Oliver Tobias, Mickey Rooney, Milo O'Shea, Elizabeth Welch, Peter Cushing, Capucine
'Resolutely well mounted, but somehow lacking that necessary fillip of Hollywood vulgarity or exuberance.' – *John Pym, MFB*

Arabian Nights *
US 1942 86m Technicolor
Universal (Walter Wanger)
The Caliph of Baghdad is deposed by his half-brother but wins back his throne with the help of a dancer and an acrobat.
Well presented oriental adventure which has nothing to do with its source material but entertained multitudes in search of relief from total war and was followed by several vaguely similar slices of hokum with the same stars.
w Michael Hogan *d John Rawlins* *ph* Milton Krasner, William V. Skall, W. Howard Greene *m* Frank Skinner *ad* Alexander Golitzen, Jack Otterson
☆ Jon Hall, Maria Montez, Sabu, Leif Erickson, Thomas Gomez, Turhan Bey, John Qualen, Billy Gilbert, Shemp Howard
Milton Krasner, William V. Skall, W. Howard Greene; Frank Skinner; art direction

Arabian Nights: see *Il Fiore delle Mille e una Notte (1974)*

'They Have Come From Another World...To Stay!'
Arachnid
Spain 2001 93m colour
Fantastic Factory/Castelao/Via Digital/TVC/TVG (Julio Fernandez, Brian Yuzna)
In the South Pacific, a expedition who are searching for the survivor of a plane crash encounter giant alien spiders.
Old-fashioned B movie horror played straight which, given the weak script, was a mistake.
w Mark Sevi *d* Jack Sholder *ph* Carlos Gonzalez *m* Frances Giner *ad* Enrique Echeverria *ed* Jaume Vilalta
☆ Alex Reid (Mercer), Chris Potter (Valentine), Pepe Sancho (Dr Samuel Leon), Neus Asensi (Susana), Ravil Isyanov (Henry Capri), Roqueford Allen (Bear)

'Eight legs. Two fangs. And an attitude.'
Arachnophobia **
US 1990 109m DeLuxe
Hollywood Pictures/Amblin/Tangled Web (Kathleen Kennedy, Richard Vane)
A doctor moves with his family from the town to the country to find himself confronting local hostility and a plague of killer spiders.
Executive producer Steven Spielberg's influence is evident in this effectively scary movie set in a small town threatened by a menace it doesn't understand.
w Don Jacoby, Wesley Strick *story* Don Jacoby, Al Williams *d* Frank Marshall *ph* Mikael Salomon *m* Trevor Jones *pd* James Bissell *ad* Christopher Burian-Mohr *ed* Michael Kahn *sp* Chris Walas (creatures effects)
☆ Jeff Daniels, Harley Jane Kozak, John Goodman, Julian Sands, Stuart Pankin, Brian McNamara, Mark L. Taylor, Henry Jones
'Not since *Jaws* has a film come along to make audiences jump in their seats so regularly and enjoyably.' – *Variety*

Aranyer Din Ratri ***
India 1969 115m bw
Contemporary/Priya (Nepal Dutta, Ashim Dutta)
GB and US title: *Days and Nights in the Forest*
A group of friends leave Calcutta to spend a few days in the country.
Episodic drama of four middle-class idlers forced to re-examine their lives in an unfamiliar environment, comic in tone, with an underlying seriousness.
wd Satyajit Ray *novel* Sunil Ganguli *ph* Soumendu Roy, Purnendu Bose *m* Satyajit Ray *ad* Bansi Chandragupta *ed* Dulal Dutta
☆ Soumitra Chatterjee, Subhendu Chatterjee, Samit Bhanja, Rabi Ghose, Pahari Sanyal, Sarmila Tagore, Kaveri Bose, Simi Garewal, Aparna Sen
'One would rate this lucid, ironic and superlatively graceful film among the very best of his work.' – *Penelope Huston, MFB*
'A major film by one of the great film artists.' – *Pauline Kael*
'Pretentious, short on plot but striving to be long on character, stylistically awkward as a sign of sincere emotions, and all of it held together by a title that is more poetic than anything in the movie itself.' – *William Paul, Village Voice*

The Arc
US 1991 95m colour
Cinema Parallel/Film Four (J. K. Eareckson)
A welder, who loses his job, his house, his friends and his wife, decides to take the first bus out of Baltimore.
An episodic, eccentric, low-budget road movie of occasional sharp humour, but more often given over to windy philosophizing.
wd Rob Tregenza *ph* Rob Tregenza *pd* Dolores Deluxe
☆ Jason Adams, Kathryn Kelley, Catherine Fogarty, Jennifer Mendenhall

'The story of an outcast and a killer!'
Arch of Triumph *
US 1948 120m bw
Enterprise (David Lewis)
In postwar Paris, an embittered refugee seeks his former Nazi tormentor and has a tragic romance with a would-be suicide.
Doleful, set-bound melodrama knee-deep in misery and artificial melodramatics. An expensive, ambitious failure, both commercially and artistically, but an interesting one.
w Lewis Milestone, Harry Brown *novel* Erich Maria Remarque *d* Lewis Milestone *ph* Russell Metty *m* Leonard Gruenberg *md* Morris Stoloff
☆ Ingrid Bergman, Charles Boyer, Charles Laughton, Louis Calhern
'Cutting *Arch of Triumph* improved it considerably. It was terrible for four hours, but now it is only terrible for two hours.' – *Charles Boyer*
† The film cost 5 million dollars and grossed 1.5 million. The story was remade for TV in 1984.

La Ardilla Roja: see *The Red Squirrel*

Are We All Murderers?: see *Nous Sommes Tous les Assassins*

Are You Being Served?
GB 1977 95m Technicolor
EMI (Andrew Mitchell)
The staff of the clothing section of a department store go on holiday to the Costa Plonka.
Feeble enlargement of an old-fashioned but very popular TV series relying heavily on sexual badinage and ancient jokes.
w Jeremy Lloyd, David Croft *d* Bob Kellett *ph* Jack Archeler *m* various
☆ John Inman, Frank Thornton, Mollie Sugden, Trevor Bannister, Wendy Richard, Arthur Brough, Nicholas Smith, Arthur English, Harold Bennett, Glyn Houston
'A withering selection of patent British puns.' – *John Pym, MFB*

Are You With It? *
US 1948 90m bw
Universal-International (Robert Arthur)
An insurance executive with doubts joins a fun fair and has a whale of a time.
Pleasantly lively low-budget musical.
w Oscar Brodney *musical comedy* Sam Perrin, George Balzer *d* Jack Hively *ph* Maury Gertsman *m/ly* Sidney Miller, Inez James *md* Walter Scharf
☆ Donald O'Connor, Olga San Juan, Martha Stewart, Lew Parker

'Men And Women Who Live Dangerously!'
Arena
US 1953 83m Anscocolor 3-D
MGM (Arthur M. Loew Jnr)
A rodeo rider regains his wife and his sense when his best friend is killed.
Routine actioner, distinguished by 3-D camerawork.
w Harold Jack Bloom *story* Arthur Loew Jnr *d* Richard Fleischer *ph* Paul C. Vogel *m* Rudolph G. Kopp *ad* Cedric Gibbons, Merrill Pye *ed* Irvine 'Cotton' Warburton
☆ Gig Young (Bob Dawson), Jean Hagen (Meg Hutchins), Polly Bergen (Ruth Danvers), Henry Morgan (Lew Hutchins), Barbara Lawrence (Sylvia Morgan), Robert Horton (Jackie Roach), Lee Van Cleef (Smitty), Lee Aaker (Teddy Hutchins)

The Arena
US 1973 83m Technicolor Techniscope
EMI/New World (Mark Damon)
aka: *Naked Warriors*
Female slaves, who have been forced to fight one another as gladiators, rebel against their small-town owner.
Standard exploitation picture, ringing a slight change on the genre's usual women's prison dramas but employing many of the same clichés.
w John William Corrington, Joyce Hooper Corrington *d* Steve Carver *ph* Aristide Massacessi *m* Francesco de Masi *ad* Mimmo Scavia *ed* Joe Dante, Piera Bruni
☆ Pam Grier, Margaret Markov, Lucretia Love, Paul Muller, Daniel Vargas, Marie Louise, Mary Count

L'Argent *
Switzerland/France 1983 84m colour
EOS/Marion's Films/FR3 (Jean-Marc Henchoz)
A tragic chain of events is started when a forged note is passed in a photographer's shop.
A bleak Bressonian study of conscience, fate and atonement.
wd Robert Bresson *story* The False Note by Leo Tolstoy *ph* Emmanuel Machuel, Pasqualino de Santis *m* Bach

☆ Christian Patey, Sylvie Van Den Elsen, Michel Briguet, Caroline Lang

L'Argent de Poche: see *Small Change*

Aria *
GB/US 1988 98m colour
Virgin Vision/Warner (Don Boyd)

A man wanders through Italian streets and buildings, a journey interrupted as operatic arias are combined with glossy visuals.
Ten directors, given freedom to illustrate the music in any manner they wanted, display a paucity of imagination.
w Nicolas Roeg, Charles Sturridge, Jean-Luc Godard, Julien Temple, Bruce Beresford, Robert Altman, Franc Roddam, Ken Russell, Derek Jarman, Bill Bryden, Don Boyd *d* Nicolas Roeg, Charles Sturridge, Jean-Luc Godard, Julien Temple, Bruce Beresford, Robert Altman, Franc Roddam, Ken Russell, Derek Jarman, Bill Bryden *ph* Harvey Harrison, Gale Tattersall, Carolyn Champetier, Oliver Stapleton, Dante Spinotti, Pierre Mignot, Frederick Elmes, Gabriel Beristain, Mike Southon, Christopher Hughes *m* Verdi, Lully, Korngold, Rameau, Wagner, Puccini, Charpentier, Leoncavallo *md* Ralph Mace *pd* Diana Johnstone, Andrew McAlpine, Stephen Altman, Piers Plowden, Scott Bushnell, John Hay, Matthew Jacobs, Paul Dufficey, Christopher Hobbs *ed* Marie Therese Boiche, Mike Cragg, Tony Lawson, Matthew Longfellow, Neil Abrahamson, Jennifer Auge, Rich Elgood, Michael Bradsell, Peter Cartwright, Angus Cook
☆ Theresa Russell, Nicola Swain, Jack Kyle, Marion Peters, Valerie Allain, Buck Henry, Anita Morris, Beverly D'Angelo, Elizabeth Hurley, Peter Birch, Bertrand Bonvoison, Julie Hagerty, Bridget Fonda, James Mathers, Linzi Drew and also Andreas Wisniewski, Tilda Swinton, Spencer Leigh, John Hurt, Sophie Ward

Ariane
Germany 1931 78m bw
Nerofilm
An innocent young girl falls for a man of the world and makes him think she is a cocotte.
Sophisticated comedy later remade as Love in the Afternoon (qv); this version is interesting chiefly for its presentation of a new star.
w Paul Czinner, Carl Mayer *novel* Claude Anet *d* Paul Czinner
☆ *Elisabeth Bergner*, Rudolf Forster, Annemarie Steinsieck, Hertha Guthmar

Ariel *
Finland 1988 72m colour
Electric/Villealfa (Aki Kaurismäki)

A redundant miner is forced by circumstances to take to a life of crime.
Episodic movie with not much sense of reality.
wd Aki Kaurismäki *ph* Timo Salminen *pd* Risto Karhula *ed* Raija Talvio
☆ Turo Pajala, Susanna Haavisto, Matti Pellonpää, Eetu Hilkamo, Erkki Pajala, Matti Jaaranen, Hannu Viholainen
'It's a documentation of the destruction of Finland.' – *Aki Kaurismäki*

'Here's the gay, glorious story of a war correspondent and a war ace ... a romance that could happen only in 1940!'
Arise My Love ***
US 1940 113m bw
Paramount (Arthur Hornblow Jnr)
American reporters in Europe and in love survive the Spanish Civil War, a wrathful editor in Paris and the sinking of the *Athenia*.
Unique sophisticated entertainment gleaned from the century's grimmest headlines, ending with a plea against American isolationism. A significant and stylish comedy melodrama.
w Charles Brackett, Billy Wilder d Mitchell Leisen *ph* Charles Lang *m* Victor Young *ad* Hans Dreier, Robert Usher
☆ *Claudette Colbert* (Augusta Nash), *Ray Milland* (Tom Martin), *Walter Abel* (Mr Phillips), Dennis O'Keefe (Joe Shepard), George Zucco (Prison Governor), Dick Purcell (Pinky O'Connor), Frank Puglia (Fr. Jacinto), Esther Dale (Secretary)
WALTER ABEL (MR PHILLIPS): "I'm not happy. I'm not happy at all…"
'Against the background of European fisticuffs, Paramount brings forth a film of absorbing romantic interest, proving that love will find a way through the hazards of air raids, torpedo attacks and enemy invasions.' – *Variety*
† Joel McCrea was originally cast for the Milland role.
original story (Benjamin Glazer, John S. Toldy)
Charles Lang; Victor Young; art direction

The Aristocats **
US 1970 78m Technicolor
Walt Disney (Wolfgang Reiterman, Winston Hibler)

Two cats are deliberately lost by a butler who fears they will inherit his mistress's wealth; but a variety of animal friends restore them to their rightful place.
Cartoon feature, a moderate example of the studio's work after Disney's death, with rather too few felicitous moments.
w Larry Clemmons and others *d* Wolfgang Reitherman
☆ Featuring the voices of Phil Harris, Eva Gabor, Sterling Holloway, Scatman Crothers, Paul Winchell, Hermione Baddeley, Roddy Maude-Roxby

Arizona
US 1940 125m bw
Columbia (Wesley Ruggles)

A Tucson wildcat meets her match in a travelling Missourian who helps her outwit villains who are sabotaging her wagon trains.
Loosely built, deliberately paced Western which for all its pretensions makes very little impact.
w Claude Binyon *d* Wesley Ruggles *ph* Joseph Walker, Harry Hollenberger, Fayte Brown *m* Victor Young *ad* Lionel Banks, Robert Peterson
☆ Jean Arthur, William Holden, Warren William, Porter Hall, Paul Harvey, George Chandler, Byron Foulger, Regis Toomey, Edgar Buchanan
'Lacks the sweep and dramatic impulse that would have made it a great picture.' – *Variety*
Victor Young; art direction

Arizona Dream **
US/France 1991 142m colour
Electric/Constellation/UGC/Hachette (Claudie Ossard, Yves Marmion)

A young New York fish counter visits his uncle in Arizona and falls in love with an older woman.
A quirky fantasy, sometimes engaging, sometimes maddening in its deliberate oddness, but always original and often surprising.
w David Atkins *d* Emir Kusturica *ph* Vilko Filac *m* Goran Bregovic *pd* Miljen Kljakovic *ed* Andrija Zafranovic
☆ Johnny Depp, Faye Dunaway, Jerry Lewis, Lili Taylor, Paulina Porizkova, Vincent Gallo, Candyce Mason
'A marathon, self-indulgent, often profoundly tedious sprawl which you go with, part of the time at least, for its sudden flashes of visionary splendour.' – *Sheila Johnston, Independent*
† The film was cut to 119m for its British and US releases. Kusturica walked off the film at one point following a dispute with his producers, and only returned when he was allowed to continue without interference.

Arizona Raiders
US 1965 88m Techniscope
Admiral/Columbia

Two of Quantrell's Raiders are offered a pardon if they will round up renegades.
Stereotyped Western, poorly processed.
w Alex Gottlieb, Mary and Willard Willingham *d* William Witney
☆ Audie Murphy, Michael Dante, Ben Cooper, Buster Crabbe, Gloria Talbott

Arizona to Broadway
US 1933 66m bw
Fox
A small-town girl in the big city is changed by a con man.
Fast-moving support which has its moments.
w William Conselman, Henry Johnson *d* James Tinling
☆ James Dunn, Joan Bennett, Herbert Mundin, Sammy Cohen, Theodore von Eltz, J. Carrol Naish, Walter Catlett

The Arizonian
US 1935 72m bw
RKO
Lawless Silver City gets a reform marshal.
Adequate first-feature Western, but not a spectacular.
w Dudley Nichols *d* Charles Vidor
☆ Richard Dix, Margot Grahame, Preston Foster, Louis Calhern
'Through the names it can slip into the keys where westerns rarely treat, and where, therefore, horse operas are regarded as refreshing novelties.' – *Variety*

'How Well Do You Know Your Neighbour?'
Arlington Road **
US 1999 DeLuxe Panavision
Sony/Screen Gems/Lakeshore Entertainment (Peter Samuelson, Tom Gorai, Marc Samuelson)

A history professor suspects that his suburban neighbour is a terrorist.
Clever psychological thriller, in which the paranoia is justified.
w Ehren Kruger *d* Mark Pellington *ph* Bobby Bukowski *m* Angelo Badalamenti *pd* Therese Deprez *ed* Conrad Buff
☆ Jeff Bridges, Tim Robbins, Joan Cusack, Hope Davis, Robert Gossett, Mason Gamble, Spencer Treat Clark, Stanley Anderson
'An intelligent, insidiously plotted Hitchcockian thriller directed in souped-up, modern expressionistic style.' – *Todd McCarthy, Variety*

Armageddon
Canada/Netherlands 1997 93m colour
Nu Image (Brian Irving)

In an authoritarian Russia of the future, a former CIA agent, murdered in Moscow by his partner-in-crime, is brought back to life to take revenge on his killer.
Turgid and violent action movie that offers no surprises, due to its reliance on the usual clichés of the genre; it is, however, sillier than most of its kind.
w Tibor Takacs, Brian Irving *d* Tibor Takacs *ph* Zoltan David *m* Guy Zerafa *pd* Istvan Ocztos *ed* Neil Grieve
☆ Rutger Hauer, Mark Dacascos, Yvonne Scio, Patrick Dreihauss, Randall William Cook
'Eye-catching production values, some nicely atmospheric lighting and a winning line in throwaway humour buoy up this classy action fodder.' – *Sight and Sound*

Armageddon
US 1998 150m Technicolor Panavision
Buena Vista/Touchstone/Valhalla (Jerry Bruckheimer, Gale Anne Hurd, Michael Bay)

A maverick gang of oil-drillers go into space to put a nuclear bomb on an asteroid that threatens to destroy the Earth.
Loud and brainless action movie that was among the top box-office successes of 1998.
w Jonathan Hensleigh, J. J. Abrams, Robert Roy Pool, Tony Gilroy, Shane Salerno *d* Michael Bay *ph* John Schwartzman *m* Trevor Rabin *pd* Michael White *ed* Mark Goldblatt, Chris Lebenzon, Glen Scantlebury *sp* Pat McClung, Richard Hoover; Dream Quest Images
☆ Bruce Willis (Harry S. Stamper), Billy Bob Thornton (Dan Truman), Liv Tyler (Grace Stamper), Ben Affleck (A.J. Frost), Will Patton (Charles Chapple), Peter Stormare (Lev Andropov), Keith David (General Kimsey), Steve Buscemi (Rockhound), Owen Wilson (Oscar Choi), William Fichtner (Col William Sharp), Jessica Steen (Jennifer Watts), Jason Isaacs (Ronald Quincy), Grace Zabriskie (Dottie), Udo Kier (Psychologist), Michael Clarke Duncan (Jayotis Kurleenbear) and also Charlton Heston (narrator)
'Effects-obsessed and dramatically be-numbed.' – *Variety*
† The film cost $150m and took more than $464m at the box-office worldwide. It was preceded by *Deep Impact* (qv), a film with an identical theme.
song 'I Don't Want to Miss a Thing (m/ly Diane Warren); sound; sound effects editing; visual effects

Armed and Dangerous
US 1985 85m DeLuxe
Columbia (Brian Grazer, James Keach)

An ex-cop and a former lawyer uncover criminal activities at a private security company.
Comedy in which most of the humour depends on high-speed car crashes.
w Harold Ramis, Peter Torokvei *story* Brian Grazer, Harold Ramis, James Keach *d* Mark L. Lester *ph* Fred Schuler *pd* David L.Snyder *ed* Michael Hill, Daniel Hanley, Gregory Prange
☆ John Candy, Eugene Levy, Robert Loggia, Kenneth McMillan, Meg Ryan, Brion James, Jonathan Banks, Don Stroud, Larry Hankin
'In a way, this is a highly immoral film. It is made for the very young and will undoubtedly give them the idea that they can drive as recklessly and the like without doing anyone serious damage. Not a pint of blood is spilled. Victims climb unscathed out of cars that have been reduced to so much abstract sculpture. This is bad propaganda, but, like so much that is immoral, it is highly entertaining.' – *Quentin Crisp*

Armed Response
US 1986 85m United Color
Cinetel (Paul Hertzberg)

A private eye retrieves a jade antique for a Japanese gangster.
Violent low budgeter with allusions for film buffs.
w T. L. Lankford *d* Fred Olen Ray
☆ David Carradine, Lee Van Cleef, Mako, Lois Hamilton, Ross Hagen

L'Armée Des Ombres: see *The Army in the Shadows*

Armored Attack: see *North Star*

Armored Car Robbery *
US 1950 67m bw
RKO (Herman Schlom)

A police lieutenant leads the recovery of half a million dollars stolen by gangsters.
Good competent second feature with Los Angeles locations and detailed observation of police methods.
w Earl Felton, Gerald Drayson Adams *d* Richard Fleischer *ph* Guy Roe *m* Constantin Bakaleinikoff
☆ Charles McGraw, Adele Jergens, William Talman, Douglas Fowley, Steve Brodie

Armored Command
US 1961 105m bw
Allied Artists (Ron W. Alcorn)

During the Battle of the Bulge, a ravishing Nazi spy is infiltrated into an American army outpost.
Incredible Mata Hari melodrama posing as a war film, nicely shot in bleak snowscapes. Not exactly rewarding, but unusual.
w Ron W. Alcorn *d* Byron Haskin *ph* Ernest Haller *m* Bert Grund
☆ Howard Keel, Tina Louise, Burt Reynolds, Earl Holliman, Warner Anderson, Carleton Young, Marty Ingels

The Armour of God
Hong Kong 1987 90m colour
Golden Harvest (L. K. C. Ho, Chua Lam)

original title: *Long Xiong Hu Di*
A martial arts expert goes in search of a valuable suit of armour.
Standard kung-fu adventure.
w Edward Tang *story* Barry Wong *d* Jackie Chan *ph* Bob Thompson *m* Michael Rai *ad* William Cheung *ed* Cheung Yiu Chung
☆ Jackie Chan, Alan Tam, Rosamund Kwan, Lola Forner

Armour of God II: see *Operation Condor*

Arms and the Girl: see *Red Salute*

Arms and the Man
GB 1932 85m bw
BIP/Wardour
A soldier who finds discretion the better part of valour hides in a girl's bedroom.
Faithful but uninspired version of Bernard Shaw's play.

wd Cecil Lewis *play* George Bernard Shaw *ad* John Mead *ed* Walter Stokvis
☆ Barry Jones, Anne Grey, Angela Baddeley

The Army in the Shadows ***
France/Italy 1969 143m colour
Films Corona/Fono Roma (Jacques Dorfman)
original title: *L'Armée Des Ombres*
A group of Resistance fighters in Lyon try to discover the traitors in their midst.
Moving, harrowing and, in its depiction of a bungled execution, horrific account of the French Resistance at work, notable for the excellence of the direction and acting.
wd Jean-Pierre Melville *novel* Joseph Kessel *ph* Pierre L'homme *m* Eric de Marsan *ad* Théobald Meurisse *ed* Françoise Bonnot
☆ Lino Ventura, Simone Signoret, Jean-Pierre Cassel, Paul Meurisse, Claude Mann, Paul Crauchet, Christian Barbier

Army of Darkness
US 1992 109m DeLuxe
Guild/Renaissance/Introvision (Robert Tapert)
aka: *Evil Dead III*
aka: *Army of Darkness: The Medieval Dead*
Thrust back in time to medieval England, a supermarket assistant searches for a spell to return him to his own time and instead causes the dead to rise from their graves.
Comic horror of uncertain tone, which occasionally raises a smile, but is much influenced for the worse by the work of the Three Stooges.
w Sam Raimi, Ivan Raimi *d* Sam Raimi *ph* Bill Pope *m* Joseph LoDuca *pd* Tony Tremblay *ed* Bob Murawski, R. O. C. Sandstorm
☆ Bruce Campbell, Embeth Davidtz, Marcus Gilbert, Ian Abercrombie, Richard Grove, Michael Earl Reid, Bridget Fonda
'Preoccupied with repetitive and clumsy battle scenes and mild, bloodless effects, *Army of Darkness* falls off the knife-edge between humour and horror.' – *Kim Newman*
'Neither fantastic nor funny enough, despite its plethora of special effects and artful jokiness, to pass muster as anything much.' – *Derek Malcolm, Guardian*
† It was the third film in Raimi's sequence, following *The Evil Dead* and *The Evil Dead II* (qqv).

Army of One: see *Joshua Tree*

Arnold
US 1973 95m DeLuxe
Avco/Fenady (Charles A. Pratt, Andrew Fenady)
Via cassette recordings, a dead man toys with his would-be heirs, and several are murdered.
Unpleasant and very laboured black comedy on the lines of And Then There Were None and a hundred others, all better than this.
w Jameson Brewer, John Fenton Murray *d* George Fenady *ph* William Jurgenson *m* George Duning
☆ Stella Stevens, Roddy McDowall, Elsa Lanchester, Shani Wallis, Farley Granger, Victor Buono, John McGiver, Bernard Fox, Patric Knowles
† Apparently made back to back with *Terror in the Wax Museum* (qv), which has very similar credits.

Around the World
US 1943 81m bw
RKO (Allan Dwan)
Kay Kyser's band goes on a world tour to entertain troops overseas.
Typical wartime patriotic musical, now of sociological interest.
w Ralph Spence *d* Allan Dwan *ph* Russell Metty *m* George Duning *m/ly* Jimmy McHugh, Harold Adamson *md* Constantin Bakaleinikoff
☆ Kay Kyser, Ish Kabibble, Ginny Simms, Joan Davis, Mischa Auer

'It's a wonderful world, if you'll only take the time to go around it!'
Around the World in Eighty Days ***
US 1956 178m Technicolor Todd-AO
UA (*Michael Todd*)
A Victorian gentleman and his valet win a bet that they can go round the world in eighty days.
Amiable large-scale pageant resolving itself into a number of sketches, which could have been much sharper, separated by wide screen spectacle. What was breathtaking at the time seems generally slow and blunted in retrospect, but the fascination of recognizing 44 cameo stars remains. The film is less an exercise in traditional skills than a tribute to its producer's energy.
w James Poe, John Farrow, S. J. Perelman *novel* Jules Verne *d* Michael Anderson, Kevin McClory *ph Lionel Lindon m Victor Young* *ad* James W. Sullivan, Ken Adams *ed* Gene Ruggiero, Paul Weatherwax *titles Saul Bass*
☆ *David Niven, Cantinflas, Robert Newton*, Shirley MacLaine, Charles Boyer, Joe E. Brown, Martine Carol, John Carradine, Charles Coburn, *Ronald Colman*, Melville Cooper, *Noël Coward*, Finlay Currie, Reginald Denny, Andy Devine and also Marlene Dietrich, Luis Dominguin, Fernandel, *John Gielgud*, Hermione Gingold, Jose Greco, Cedric Hardwicke, Trevor Howard, Glynis Johns, *Buster Keaton*, Evelyn Keyes, Beatrice Lillie, Peter Lorre, Edmund Lowe, A. E. Matthews, Mike Mazurki, Tim McCoy, Victor McLaglen, John Mills, Alan Mowbray, Robert Morley, Jack Oakie, George Raft, Gilbert Roland, Cesar Romero, Frank Sinatra, *Red Skelton*, Ronald Squire, Basil Sidney, *Harcourt Williams*, Ed Murrow
'Michael Todd's "show", shorn of the ballyhoo and to critics not mollified by parties and sweetmeats, is a film like any other, only twice as long as most ... the shots of trains and boats seem endless.' – *David Robinson*
picture; James Poe, John Farrow, S. J. Perelman; Lionel Lindon; Victor Young
Michael Anderson; art direction; editing

Around the World under the Sea
US 1966 110m Metrocolor Panavision
MGM/Ivan Tors (Andrew Marton)
An ultra-modern underwater craft travels around the seabed fixing sensors to give early warning of volcanoes.
Earnest, dullish, elementary sci-fi with cardboard characters providing routine five men-one woman skirmishes.
w Arthur Weiss, Art Arthur *d* Andrew Marton, Ricou Browning *ph* Clifford Poland, Lamar Boren *m* Harry Sukman
☆ Lloyd Bridges, Shirley Eaton, Brian Kelly, David McCallum, Keenan Wynn, Marshall Thompson, Gary Merrill

Arouse and Beware: see *The Man from Dakota*

The Arrangement **
US 1969 127m Technicolor Panavision
Warner/Athena (Elia Kazan)
A wealthy advertising man fails in a suicide attempt and spends his convalescence reflecting on his unsatisfactory emotional life.
A lush, all-American melodrama, rich in technique but peopled by characters who have nothing to say; the film makes no discernible point except as a well-acted tirade against the compromises of modern urban living.
wd Elia Kazan *novel* Elia Kazan *ph Robert Surtees* *m* David Amram *pd* Malcolm C. Bert
☆ Kirk Douglas, Faye Dunaway, Deborah Kerr, Richard Boone, Hume Cronyn
'The sort of collage that won't fit together, no matter where you stand.' – *PS*
'As dead as a flower arrangement in an undertaker's parlour ... all possible cinematic clevernesses – usually yesterday's – are dragged out in an endless parade, to illustrate a senseless and banal story that reels from platitude to platitude.' – *John Simon*

Arrest Bulldog Drummond: see *Bulldog Drummond*

The Arrival *
US 1996 115m Technicolor
Entertainment/Live/Steelwork (Thomas G. Smith, James Steel)
An astronomer realizes that aliens are among us.
Conspiratorial science fiction exhibiting some interesting ideas and managing to incorporate them into a sometimes suspenseful story.
wd David Twohy *ph* Hiro Narita *m* Arthur Kempel *pd* Michael Novotny *ed* Martin Hunter *sp* Pacific Data Images
☆ Charlie Sheen, Ron Silver, Lindsay Crouse, Teri Polo, Richard Schiff, Leon Rippy, Tony T. Johnson
'Confusing and incoherent, implausible even by SF standards.' – *Sight and Sound*

Arrivederci Baby: see *Drop Dead Darling*

Arrow in the Dust
US 1954 80m Technicolor
Allied Artists (Hayes Goetz)
An army deserter assumes the identity of a cavalry captain to help defend a wagon-train from marauding Indians.
Effective minor Western, gaining from its redemptive, reluctant hero, forced to act against his own best interests.
w Don Martin *novel* L.L. Foreman *d* Lesley Selander *ph* Ellis W. Carter *m* Marlin Skiles *ad* David Milton *ed* William Austin
☆ Sterling Hayden, Coleen Gray, Keith Larsen, Tom Tully, Jimmy Wakely, Tudor Owen, Lee Van Cleef, John Pickard, Carleton Young

Arrowhead
US 1953 105m Technicolor 3D
Paramount (Nat Holt)
Enmity between an army scout and an Indian chief is resolved by single combat.
Standard Western, good-looking but rather lifeless.
wd Charles Marquis Warren *novel* W. R. Burnett *ph* Ray Rennahan *m* Paul Sawtell
☆ Charlton Heston, Jack Palance, Katy Jurado, Brian Keith, Milburn Stone

Arrowsmith *
US 1931 108m bw
Samuel Goldwyn
The self-sacrificing career of a doctor.
Emotionally satisfactory, dramatically slow and unsurprising variation on a theme which has since been treated far too often.
w Sidney Howard *novel* Sinclair Lewis *d* John Ford *ph* Ray June *m* Alfred Newman *ad* Richard Day
☆ Ronald Colman, Helen Hayes, Richard Bennett, Myrna Loy, Charlotte Henry, Beulah Bondi, A. E. Anson
'Pictures would do better to stay clear of these elaborately biographical novels with their wealth of actionless detail ... That portion of the citizenry which read the Sinclair Lewis novel will probably be in sympathy with the film, those who didn't will not be prone to deem this macabre tale entertainment.' – *Variety*
† The negative was later cut to about 89m for reissue, and this version, virtually eliminating Myrna Loy, is the only one now available.
best picture; Sidney Howard; Ray June; Richard Day

Arsenal **
USSR 1929 99m (16 fps) bw silent
VUFKU
The 1914 war is made worse by strikes at home.
Patchy propagandist drama with brilliant sequences.
wd Alexander Dovzhenko *ph* Danylo Demutsky
☆ S. Svashenko, A. Buchma, M. Nademsky
'A romantic and lyrical masterpiece.' – *Georges Sadoul*

The Arsenal Stadium Mystery
GB 1939 85m bw
G&S/GFD
A footballer is poisoned during a match.
Brisk little mystery, with an amiable star performance.
w Thorold Dickinson, Donald Bull *novel* Leonard Gribble *d* Thorold Dickinson
☆ *Leslie Banks*, Greta Gynt, Esmond Knight, Brian Worth
'This picture is as good to watch as either of the *Thin Man* films, and Dickinson gives us wit instead of facetiousness – wit of cutting and wit of angle.' – *Graham Greene*

Arsène Lupin **
US 1932 75m bw
MGM
The Parisian gentleman thief accomplishes some daring robberies and is almost caught stealing the Mona Lisa.
Amusing crook comedy with a few flat passages but much sparkle in between, and a lively finale.
w Carey Wilson, Lenore Coffee, Bayard Veiller *play* Maurice Le Blanc, Francis de Croisset *d* Jack Conway *ph* Oliver Marsh *ad* Cedric Gibbons *ed* Hugh Wynn
☆ *John Barrymore*, Lionel Barrymore, Karen Morley, Tully Marshall, John Miljan
'First screen appearance of John and Lionel together and their acting of this old standard detective story ensures its box office in spite of the absence of other qualities that make for notable screen successes ... At least it addresses itself to a higher class of fans than the lurid type of dime novel subject.' – *Variety*

Arsène Lupin Returns
US 1938 81m bw
MGM (John W. Considine Jnr)
The reformed jewel thief helps an American detective to track down a French criminal.
Smooth but disappointingly scripted sequel which never quite rises to a climax despite sympathetic casting.
w James Kevin McGuinness, Howard Emmett Rogers, George Harmon Coxe *d* George Fitzmaurice *ph* George Folsey *m* Franz Waxman
☆ Melvyn Douglas, Warren William, Virginia Bruce, John Halliday, Nat Pendleton, Monty Woolley, George Zucco, E. E. Clive
'A first-class mystery jewel theft combo ... for the top side of the marquee pairing, missing A classification quite a little, but still being okay.' – *Variety*

Arsenic and Old Lace ***
US 1944 118m bw
Warner (Frank Capra)
Two dear, well-meaning old ladies invite lonely old men to their Brooklyn home, poison them with elderberry wine, and have their mad brother, who believes the corpses are yellow fever victims, bury them in the cellar. A homicidal nephew then turns up with bodies of his own.
A model for stage play adaptations, this famous black farce provided a frenzy of hilarious activity, and its flippant attitude to death was better received in wartime than would have been the case earlier or later. The director coaxed some perfect if overstated performances from his star cast, and added his own flair for perpetuating a hubbub.
w Julius J. and Philip G. Epstein, with help from Howard Lindsay, Russel Crouse *play* Joseph Kesselring *d Frank Capra ph Sol Polito* *m* Max Steiner
☆ *Cary Grant* (Mortimer Brewster), *Josephine Hull* (Abby Brewster), *Jean Adair* (Martha Brewster), Priscilla Lane (Elaine Harper), Raymond Massey (Jonathan Brewster), *John Alexander* (Teddy Brewster), Peter Lorre (Dr Einstein), James Gleason (Lt Rooney), Jack Carson (Officer O'Hara), Edward Everett Horton (Mr Witherspoon), Grant Mitchell (Reverend Harper)
MORTIMER: 'Insanity runs in my family. It practically gallops.'
MARTHA: 'One of our gentlemen found time to say "How delicious!" before he died...'
† Made in 1942 but not released immediately.

The Art of Dying
US 1991 93m Foto-Kem
PM (Richard Pepin, Joseph Merhi)
A maverick cop tracks down a pornographer who films and kills his victims while re-enacting famous murders from the movies.
Slow, unpleasant homophobic thriller about a cut-rate Dirty Harry; the emphasis is on atmosphere and the hero's uninteresting love-life rather than on action.
w Joseph Merhi *d* Wings Hauser *ph* Richard Pepin *m* John Gonzalez *pd* Greg Martin *ed* Geraint Bell, Paul Volk
☆ Wings Hauser, Kathleen Kinmont, Michael J. Pollard, Gary Werntz, Mitch Hara, Sarah Douglas, Sydney Lassick

The Art of Love
US 1965 99m Technicolor
Universal/Cherokee/Ross Hunter
To stimulate interest in his work, a penniless artist fakes suicide, subsequently becoming so famous that he finds it difficult to reappear.
A pleasant black comedy idea is buried under lush production, dull direction and a host of unattractive Parisian sets.
w Carl Reiner *d* Norman Jewison *ph* Russell Metty *m* Cy Coleman *ed* Milton Carruth
☆ James Garner, Dick Van Dyke, Angie Dickinson, Elke Sommer, Ethel Merman, Pierre Olaf

The Art of Love (dubbed)
France/Italy 1983 87m colour
ZT/Distributione/Nija/Oitra Impex/Man International (Ugo Tucci)
In Rome, Ovid lectures on the subject of love, while some of his pupils practise his teachings.
Soft-core eroticism with a little twist at the end, done with slightly more style than usual.
wd Walerian Borowczyk *m* Luis Bacalov
ed Walerian Borowczyk
☆ Marina Pierro, Massimo Girotti, Laura Betti, Milena Vukotic, Philippe Lemaire, Michele Placido

'Do you know who your enemy is?'
The Art of War
US/Canada 2000 117m DeLuxe
Warner/Morgan Creek/Franchise/Amen Ra/Filmline (Nicolas Clermont)
An agent for the United Nations finds himself on the run from the FBI and Triad gangs after being framed for the murder of the Chinese UN ambassador.
Luridly ridiculous thriller that juggles all the usual stereotypes and situations to little effect.
w Wayne Beach, Simon Davis Barry *d* Christian Duguay *ph* Pierre Gill *m* Normand Corbeil
pd Anne Pritchard *ed* Michel Arcand *cos* Odette Gadoury
☆ Wesley Snipes (Neil Shaw), Anne Archer (Eleanor Hooks), Maury Chaykin (Capella), Cary-Hiroyuki Tagawa (David Chan), Donald Sutherland (Douglas Thomas), Michael Biehn (Bly), Marie Matiko (Julia), Liliana Kmorowska (Novak), James Hong (Ambassador Wu)
'Ludicrous, impenetrable and headache-inducing.' – *Stephen Holden, New York Times*
'It is an understatement to say that this ugly, strident, boring film leaves a nasty taste in the mouth.' – *Peter Bradshaw, Guardian*

'Sexy. Defiant. Provocative. Her passion for art changed the face of history.'
Artemisia *
France/Germany/Italy 1997 102m Technicolor
Premiere Heure/France3/Schlemmer/3 Emme (Patrice Haddad)
In 17th-century Italy, a female artist comes to grief when she ignores the social and sexual barriers of her time and class.
Engrossing period drama, richly photographed, though it is romance, rather than art, that is at the centre oif the action.
w Agnes Merlet, Christine Miller, Patrick Amos
d Agnes Merlet *ph* Benoit Delhomme *m* Krishna Levy *pd* Antonello Geleng *ed* Guy Lecorne
cos Dominique Borg
☆ Michel Serrault (Orazio Gentileschi), Valentina Cervi (Artemisia Gentileschi), Miki Manojlovic (Agostino Tassi), Luca Zingaretti (Cosimo Quorli), Brigitte Catillon (Tuzia), Frederic Pierrot (Roberto), Maurice Garrel (The Judge), Emmanuelle Devos (Costanza)
'When all is said and done, *Artemisia* is still essentially a bodice-ripper. But it is one that also happens to have a brain.' – *Stephen Holden, New York Times*

'I race cars, I play tennis, I fondle women, but I have weekends off and I am my own boss!'
Arthur *
US 1981 97m Technicolor
Warner/Orion (Robert Greenhut)
A rich New York layabout is forced to moderate his life style in order to qualify for his inheritance.
An unattractive excuse for the star to do his drunk act. In effect his thunder was stolen by Gielgud as the valet who is not above a few choice four-letter words; but over the whole enterprise hung a pall of desperation. It is a sign of its times that it made a lot of money.
wd Steve Gordon *ph* Fred Schuler *m* Burt Bacharach *pd* Stephen Hendrikson
☆ Dudley Moore, *John Gielgud*, Liza Minnelli, Geraldine Fitzgerald, Jill Eikenberry, Stephen Elliott
'It comes as no surprise to find the funniest sequences packed into the first half-hour.' – *Martyn Auty, MFB*
'Gielgud may be the most poised and confident funnyman you'll ever see.' – *New Yorker*
'Arthur may be the surprise hit of 1981, but to me he's a pain in the neck.' – *Margaret Hinxman, Daily Mail*
John Gielgud (supporting actor); song 'Best That You Can Do' (Burt Bacharach, Carole Bayer Sager, Christopher Cross, Peter Allen)
screenplay; Dudley Moore

Arthur 2: On the Rocks
US 1988 113m colour
Warner (Robert Shapiro)
Arthur's fortune is threatened by his former fiancée's father, bent on revenge, while his wife wants to adopt a baby.
Moore and friends are much less funny the second time around, and much more sentimental; it's just a sloppy would-be comedy.
w Andy Breckman *d* Bud Yorkin *ph* Stephen H. Burum *m* Burt Bacharach *pd* Gene Callahan
ed Michael Kahn *cos* Anna Hill Johnston
☆ Dudley Moore, Liza Minnelli, John Gielgud, Geraldine Fitzgerald, Stephen Elliott, Paul Benedict, Cynthia Sikes, Kathy Bates, Jack Gilford, Barney Martin
'Still manages to be an amusing romp.' – *Variety*

'When the heroes are forgotten. When the stakes are life and death. There's one stand you've got to take. There's one rule you've got to break.'
Article 99
US 1992 100m DeLuxe
Orion/Gruskoff/Levy (Michael Gruskoff, Michael I. Levy)
Doctors and surgeons at a Veterans' Administration hospital ignore red tape in order to treat their patients.
A frenetic movie with more than a touch of hysteria in its treatment of an emotive subject.
w Ron Cutler *d* Howard Deutch *ph* Richard Bowen *m* Danny Elfman *pd* Virginia L. Randolph *ed* Richard Halsey
☆ Ray Liotta, Kiefer Sutherland, Forest Whitaker, Lea Thompson, John Mahoney, John C. McGinley, Keith David, Kathy Baker, Eli Wallach
'Is ultimately more successful in awakening the viewer to a desperate situation than in providing a good time.' – *Variety*

An Artist with Ladies: see *Coiffeur pour Dames*

Artistes at the Top of the Big Top: Disorientated **
West Germany 1968 103m bw/colour
Kairos Film
The daughter of a dead trapezist dreams of creating the ideal circus with a moral for mankind but step by step gives up her ambition.
A melancholy satire, told in fragmented fashion with some brilliant tricks and memorable sequences.
wd *Alexander Kluge* *ph* Gunther Hörmann, Thomas Mauch
☆ Hannelore Hoger, Siegfried Graue, Alfred Edel, Bernd Höltz
'Those who interpret it simply as an allegory of German politics or of the present crisis in film-making narrow it unnecessarily.' – *Jan Dawson, MFB*

Artists and Models *
US 1937 97m bw
Paramount (Lewis E. Gensler)
An advertising man has to find the right girl as symbol for a silverware company.
Fairly stylish comedy musical with many elements typical of its studio.
w Walter de Leon, Francis Martin *d* Raoul Walsh *ph* Victor Milner *m* Victor Young *songs* various
☆ Jack Benny, Ida Lupino, Richard Arlen, Gail Patrick, Ben Blue, Judy Canova, Martha Raye, Donald Meek, Hedda Hopper, André Kostelanetz and his Orchestra, Louis Armstrong and his Orchestra
'Should be a box-office bonanza for exhibitors. It holds enough variety, comedy, colour, spectacle, flash, dash and novelty for a couple of pictures.' – *Variety*
song 'Whispers in the Dark' (*m*Frederick Hollander, *ly* Leo Robin)

Artists and Models *
US 1955 109m Technicolor Vistavision
Paramount/Hal B. Wallis
A goonish young man receives telepathic top secret information in his nightmares, which are used by his artist friend in comic strips; foreign agents and the CIA get interested.
A good zany idea is worked into an overlong dyspeptic comedy which neither the stars nor frantic treatment can hope to save.
w Frank Tashlin, Don McGuire *d* Frank Tashlin *ph* Daniel Fapp *m* Walter Scharf
☆ Dean Martin, Jerry Lewis, Shirley MacLaine, Dorothy Malone, Eddie Mayehoff, Eva Gabor, Anita Ekberg, George 'Foghorn' Winslow, Jack Elam

'It's an ooh-la-lalapalooza!'
Artists and Models Abroad *
US 1938 90m bw Paramount (Arthur Hornblow Jnr)
GB title: *Stranded in Paris*
Stranded in Paris, a troupe of girls and their manager are helped by a Texas oil millionaire.
Generally agreeable comedy musical with emphasis on fashion.
w Howard Lindsay, Russel Crouse, Ken Englund
d *Mitchell Leisen* *ph* Ted Tetzlaff *md* Boris Morros
ad *Hans Dreier, Ernst Fegte* *songs* various
☆ Jack Benny, Joan Bennett, Mary Boland, Charley Grapewin, Joyce Compton, the Yacht Club Boys, Fritz Feld, G. P. Huntley, Monty Woolley
'Straight farce comedy. The models are in a fashion show and the artists are missing entirely.' – *Variety*

The Aryan *
US 1916 75m (16 fps) bw silent
Triangle (Thomas Ince)
A gold prospector is cheated by a woman and becomes an outlaw.
Striking early star Western.
w C. Gardner Sullivan *d* William S. Hart, Cliff Smith *ph* Joseph August, Clyde de Vinna
☆ *William S. Hart*, Bessie Love, Louise Glaum, Herschel Mayall

'A comedy from the heart that goes for the throat.'
As Good as It Gets ***
US 1997 138m Technicolor
Columbia TriStar/Gracie (James L. Brooks, Bridget Johnson, Kristi Zea)
A misanthropic writer suffering from a compulsive-obsessive disorder learns to love again when he reluctantly involves himself in the lives of a neighbour and a waitress.
A sour-toned comedy about damaged people that, for all its occasional glibness and the ease with which its problems are solved, somehow works; it convinces as long as the movie lasts.
w Mark Andrus, James L. Brooks *d* *James L. Brooks* *ph* John Bailey *m* Hans Zimmer *pd* Bill Brzeski *ed* Richard Marks
☆ *Jack Nicholson* (Melvin Udall), *Helen Hunt* (Carol Connelly), *Greg Kinnear* (Simon Bishop), Cuba Gooding Jnr (Frank Sachs), Skeet Ulrich (Vincent), Shirley Knight (Beverly), Yeardley Smith (Jackie), Lupe Ontiveros (Nora)
'A sporadically funny romantic comedy with all the dramatic plausibility and tonal consistency of a TV variety show.' – *Todd McCarthy, Variety*
Jack Nicholson; Helen Hunt
Best picture; Greg Kinnear; Mark Andrus, James L. Brooks; Richard Marks; Hans Zimmer

As Long as They're Happy *
GB 1955 91m Eastmancolor
Rank/Regroup (Raymond Stross)
The suburban home of a London stockbroker is invaded by an American sob singer.
Frantic farce expanded from a stage satire of the Johnnie Ray cult; a patchy but sometimes funny star vehicle.
w Alan Melville *play* Vernon Sylvaine *d* J. Lee-Thompson *ph* Gilbert Taylor *m* Stanley Black
☆ *Jack Buchanan*, Brenda de Banzie, Diana Dors, Jean Carson, Janette Scott, Susan Stephen, Jerry Wayne, Hugh McDermott

As Long as You're Near Me
West Germany 1954 94m colour
Warner/NDF
original title: *Solange Du da bist*
A film director almost ruins a small-part actress's life by insisting on making her a star.
Reasonably absorbing drama chiefly remarkable for being a great hit in the US when dubbed.
w Jochen Huth *d* Harold Braun
☆ O. W. Fischer, Hardy Kruger, Maria Schell

As Tears Go By **
Hong Kong 1988 94m colour
In-Gear (Rover Tang)
original title: *Mongkok Kamun*
An aggressive debt collector, living on the edge, finds himself drawn back by his loyalties into a world of urban gangsters when he tries to escape to a quieter life with his country cousin.
Tough thriller, in which the violent fight scenes have a disturbing reality; the direction occasionally strains after effect in an otherwise tense movie of thugs who come to believe in their own publicity.
wd *Wong Kar-Wai* *ad* William Cheung
☆ Andy Lau, Maggie Cheung, Jacky Cheung
'A superbly gritty debut, let down by Wong's tendency to go for the big scene – complete with MTV-style music – every five minutes.' – *Sight and Sound*

As Time Goes By
Australia 1987 94m colour
Valhalla/Monroe Stahr (Chris Kiely)
A man travels into the outback to keep a rendezvous made by his mother 25 years earlier, and finds an interplanetary traveller waiting for him.
Oddball comedy that runs out of steam at the halfway mark, though it tries hard; the alien, who talks in dialogue culled from old movies, may interest film buffs (and the credits include, along with Best Boy, Worst Boy).
wd Barry Peak *ph* John Ogden *m* Peter Sullivan *pd* Paddy Reardon *ed* Ralph Strasser
☆ Bruno Lawrence, Nique Needles, Ray Barrett, Marcelle Schmitz, Mitchell Faircloth, Max Gillies

'You don't need us to tell you not to miss this film. You couldn't be kept away!'
As You Desire Me *
US 1931 71m bw
MGM (George Fitzmaurice)
The amnesiac mistress of a novelist rediscovers her real husband and falls in love with him again.
Interesting star vehicle with good cast and production.
w Gene Markey *play* Luigi Pirandello *d* George Fitzmaurice *ph* William Daniels
☆ *Greta Garbo*, Melvyn Douglas, Erich von Stroheim, Owen Moore, Hedda Hopper, Rafaela Ottiano
'Pretty subtle for the generality of fans. It was more of a courageous gesture towards production ideals than good business judgement that dictated its choice for filming in the first place.' – *Variety*

As You Like It *
GB 1936 96m bw
TCF/Inter-Allied (Joseph M. Schenck, Paul Czinner)
The fortunes of an exiled king take a turn in the Forest of Arden.
Stylized, rather effete but often amusing version of Shakespeare's pastoral comedy.
w J. M. Barrie, Robert Cullen *play* William Shakespeare *d* Paul Czinner *ph* Harold Rosson *m* William Walton

☆ Elisabeth Bergner, Laurence Olivier, Sophie Stewart, Leon Quartermaine, Henry Ainley, Richard Ainley, Felix Aylmer, Mackenzie Ward, Aubrey Mather, John Laurie, Peter Bull

'Rather too respectably lighthearted, but by no means a contemptible production.' – *New Yorker, 1978*

'There are far too many dull middle-length shots from a fixed camera, so that we might just as well be seated in the circle above the deep wide stage at Drury Lane.' – *Graham Greene*

As You Like It
GB 1992 117m colour
Squirrel/Sands Films (Richard Goodwin)

Banished from City of London splendour to a grimy slum where locals live in cardboard boxes, Orlando falls in love with the banished and disguised Rosalind.
Modern-dress version of the play, with the Forest of Arden becoming an urban wasteland inhabited by the homeless. It sounds as ugly as it looks, with some wretched speaking of the verse.
play William Shakespeare *d* Christine Edzard *ph* Robin Vidgeon *m* Michel Sanvoisin *ed* Christine Edzard
☆ James Fox, Emma Croft, Cyril Cusack, Griff Rhys Jones, Andrew Tiernan, Miriam Margolyes, Don Henderson, Celia Bannerman, Murray Melvin

'We feel like victims of a mobile theatre experiment, moving our camp stools from one daft venue to the next as we follow a bunch of under-rehearsed actors belting it out into the void.' – *Nigel Andrews, Financial Times*

'In this misguided and also perversely endearing version, Christine Edzard ultimately proves the Bard's resilience, but she proves it the hard way.' – *Adam Mars-Jones, Independent*

'Edzard restores to filmed Shakespeare the means and immediacy of cinema, daring to present, as the theatre has been doing since the nineteenth century, Shakespearean text in a modern context.' – *Ilona Halberstadt, Sight and Sound*

As Young as You Feel *
US 1951 77m bw
TCF (Lamar Trotti)

An elderly employee, forced to retire, impersonates the company president, saves the firm from bankruptcy, and proves his continued worth.
Good-natured comedy, ably presented.
w Lamar Trotti *story* Paddy Chayefsky *d* Harmon Jones *ph* Joe MacDonald *m* Cyril Mockridge
☆ *Monty Woolley*, Constance Bennett, Thelma Ritter, David Wayne, Jean Peters, Marilyn Monroe, Allyn Joslyn, Albert Dekker

Ascendancy *
GB 1982 85m colour
British Film Institute Production Board (Penny Clark, Ian Elsey)

In 1920 Belfast a shipyard owner's daughter, shocked by the death of her brother in the war, cannot come to terms with the sectarian slaughter around her.
Unilluminatingly argumentative character study which fails to make its purpose very clear despite a stunning central performance.
w Edward Bennett, Nigel Gearing *d* Edward Bennett *ph* Clive Tickner *m* Ronnie Leahy
☆ *Julie Covington*, Ian Charleson, John Phillips, Susan Engel, Philip Locke

Ascenseur pour l'Echafaud: see *Lift to the Scaffold*

Ash Wednesday
US 1973 99m Technicolor
Sagittarius (Dominick Dunne)

An ageing American beauty rejuvenates herself via plastic surgery, leads a vivid sex life, and leaves her stolid husband.
The bloodthirsty operation scenes are revolting, yet this joyless saga seems meant as a celebration of the wonders of cosmetic surgery and Sex for the Aged. Hypnotic but hardly rewarding.
w Jean Claude Tramont *d* Larry Peerce *ph* Ennio Guarnieri *m* Maurice Jarre
☆ Elizabeth Taylor, Henry Fonda, Helmut Berger, Keith Baxter, Maurice Teynac

'Endless shots of Elizabeth Taylor expensively attired against the plush background of Cortina.' – *Michael Billington, Illustrated London News*

'A long-drawn-out ghoulish commercial for cosmetic surgery – made apparently for people who can't think of anything to do with their lives but go backwards.' – *Pauline Kael*

Ashanti
Switzerland 1979 117m Technicolor Panavision
Columbia/Beverly (Luciano Sacripanti)

In West Africa, the wife of a member of the World Health Organization is seized by slave traders.
Absurd and rather unattractively brutal adventure story, decked out with appearances by guest stars.
w Stephen Geller *novel* Ebano by Alberto Vasquez-Figueroa *d* Richard Fleischer *ph* Aldo Tonti *m* Michael Melvoin
☆ Michael Caine, Omar Sharif, Peter Ustinov, Rex Harrison, Kabir Bedi, William Holden, Zia Mohyeddin, Beverly Johnson

Ashes and Diamonds ****
Poland 1958 104m bw
Film Polski

original title: *Popiol y Diament*
A Polish partisan is confused by the apparent need to continue killing after the war is over.
A chilling account of the intellectual contradictions to which war leads, and a moving and sensitive film in its own right.
wd Andrzej Wajda novel Jerzy Andrzejewski *ph* Jerzy Wojcik
☆ *Zbigniew Cybulski*, Ewa Krzyzanowska, Adam Pawlikowski

Ashik Kerib **
USSR 1988 78m colour
Georgia Film Studio

aka: *The Lovelorn Minstrel*
A poor minstrel goes to seek his fortune so that he can marry the daughter of a rich Turkish merchant.
Richly coloured, episodic fable, told in the artful and artless manner of silent cinema.
w Giya Badridze *story* Mikhail Lermontov *d Sergei Paradjanov, David Abashidze ph* Albert Yavuryan *m* Zhavanshir Kuliev *pd* G. Meskhishvili, Shota Gogolashvili, Nikolai Zandukeli, K. Davidov
☆ Yuri Mgoyan, Veronique Matonidze, Levan Natroshvili, Solico Chaureli

'The film chronicles a spiritual journey in profane, worldly terms, and it is the earthy vulgarity of the detail that gives the spirituality its edge.' – *Tony Rayns, MFB*

Ask a Policeman **
GB 1938 82m bw
Gainsborough (Edward Black)

In a small coastal village, incompetent policemen accidentally expose smugglers who are scaring the locals with a headless horseman legend.
One of the best comedies of an incomparable team, with smart dialogue, good situations and a measure of suspense.
w Marriott Edgar, Val Guest, J. O. C. Orton d Marcel Varnel ph Derek Williams *md* Louis Levy
☆ *Will Hay, Moore Marriott, Graham Moffatt*, Glennis Lorimer, *Peter Gawthorne, Herbert Lomas*, Charles Oliver

'A good laugh getter and safe second feature on any programme.' – *Variety*

Ask Any Girl *
US 1959 98m Metrocolor Cinemascope
MGM/Euterpe (Joe Pasternak)

A husband-hunting receptionist in New York catches the eye of a wealthy playboy but finally settles for his elder brother.
Predictable Cinderella story with a lively but forgettable script and actors going through familiar paces.
w George Wells *novel* Winifred Wolfe *d* Charles Walters *ph* Robert Bronner *m* Jeff Alexander
☆ David Niven, Shirley MacLaine, Gig Young, Rod Taylor, Jim Backus, Claire Kelly

'Like a comic strip transposed to the glossy pages of *Vogue*.' – *MFB*

Shirley MacLaine

Asking for Trouble *
GB 1941 81m bw
British National

A bookie poses as a big game hunter.
The last opportunity to see a great music hall comic on film, his style admittedly bowdlerized.
w Oswald Mitchell, Con West *d* Oswald Mitchell
☆ Max Miller, Carole Lynne, Wilfrid Hyde-White, Mark Lester

Asoka *
India 2001 158m colour
Enzo/Miracle/Arclightz/Filmz India

Adventures in love and war of an emperor of Magadha, who, after beginning his reign in slaughter, became a Buddhist in the third century BC.
Epic account of a famous Indian historical figure that sticks close to the standard Bollywood treatment, mixing action, melodrama and slapstick comedy with song and dance.
w Saket Chaudhary, Santosh Sivan, Abbas Tyrewala *d* Santosh Sivan *ph* Santosh Sivan *m* Sandeep Chowta *md* Anu Malik *ch* Farha Khan, Brinda, Geeta Kapoor *ad* Sabu Cyril *ed* Shreekar Prasad
☆ Shah Rukh Khan (Asoka), Kareena Kapoor (Kaurwaki), Danny Denzongpa (Virat), Ajit (Susima), Rahul Dev (Bheema), Hrishitaa Bhatt (Devi)

'This movie's narrative gusto, its intricate, indirect eroticism – no sex, or even kissing – its lavish musical numbers and its sheer self-belief are a treat.' – *Peter Bradshaw, Guardian*

Aspern *
Portugal 1981 96m colour
VO/Oxala (Paulo Branco)

The French biographer of a deceased poet goes to Venice to get unpublished papers from his aged mistress.
This very well-known story (see also The Lost Moment and various theatrical versions) is styled with exceeding solemnity in this well-acted but boring version.
w Michael Graham *story* Henry James *d* Eduardo de Grigorio *ph* Acacio de Almeida *m* mainly from Mozart
☆ Alida Valli, Jean Sorel, Bulle Ogier, Ana Marta

Asphalt *
Germany 1929 101m bw
UFA

A young policeman accidentally kills his rival for a worthless girl.
Heavily expressionist melodrama, overlong but good to watch.
w Rolf Vanloo, Fred Majo, Hans Szekely *d Joe May ph* Günther Rittau
☆ Gustav Fröhlich, Betty Amann, Else Heller, Albert Steinruck, Hans Albers

'So well produced that it is good entertainment in spite of itself.' – *Variety*

The Asphalt Jungle ***
US 1950 112m bw
MGM (Arthur Hornblow Jnr)

An elderly crook comes out of prison and assembles a gang for one last robbery.
Probably the very first film to show a 'caper' from the criminals' viewpoint (a genre which has since been done to death several times over), this is a clever character study rather than a thriller, extremely well executed and indeed generally irreproachable yet somehow not a film likely to appear on many top ten lists; perhaps the writer-director stands too far back from everybody, or perhaps he just needed Humphrey Bogart.
w Ben Maddow, John Huston *novel* W. R. Burnett *d John Huston ph* Harold Rosson *m* Miklos Rozsa
☆ *Sterling Hayden* (Dix Handley), Louis Calhern (Alonzo D Emmerich), *Sam Jaffe* (Doc Erwin Riedenschneider), Jean Hagen (Doll Conovan), James Whitmore (Gus Minissi), John McIntire (Police Commissioner Hardy), Marc Lawrence (Cobby), Marilyn Monroe (Angela Phinlay), Barry Kelley (Lt Ditrich)

RIEDENSCHNEIDER: 'Crime is a left-handed form of human endeavour.'

'Where this film excels is in the fluency of its narration, the sharpness of its observation of character and the excitement of its human groupings.' – *Dilys Powell*

'That Asphalt Pavement thing is full of nasty, ugly people doing nasty things. I wouldn't walk across the room to see a thing like that.' – *Louis B. Mayer (who was head of the studio which made it)*

† Apart from imitations, the film has been directly remade as *The Badlanders, Cairo* and *A Cool Breeze* (qqv).
Ben Maddow, John Huston (writers); John Huston (as director); Harold Rosson; Sam Jaffe

The Asphyx
GB 1972 99m Eastmancolor Todd-AO 35
Glendale (John Brittany)

A Victorian aims to become immortal by separating the spirit of death from his body.
Interminable hocus pocus with a plethora of talk, seldom exciting but watchable because of its remarkable cast and other credits.
w Brian Comport *d* Peter Newbrook *ph* Freddie Young *m* Bill McGuffie *sp* Ted Samuels
☆ Robert Stephens, Robert Powell, Jane Lapotaire

The Assam Garden
GB 1985 90m colour
Contemporary/Moving Picture Company (Nigel Stafford-Clark)

A widow returns from Assam to the English house where many years previously her husband had created a garden full of eastern plants, and where events now help her to free herself of the past.
Muted and somewhat ineffective treatment of a familiar television theme. Not unpleasant to watch despite obvious economies, but instantly forgettable.
w Elisabeth Bond *d* Mary McMurray *ph* Bryan Loftus *m* Richard Harvey
☆ Deborah Kerr, Madhur Jaffrey, Alec McCowen, Zia Mohyeddin, Iain Cuthbertson

The Assassin: see *Gunfighters (1947)*

The Assassin: see *Venetian Bird (1952)*

The Assassin **
Italy/France 1961 105m bw
Titanus-Vides-SGC (Franco Cristaldi)

A prosperous antique dealer is accused of murder and his unsavoury past is revealed; but when he is freed, he prides himself on his new personality.
A careful, detailed and wholly enjoyable character study, somewhere between comedy and drama.
w Elio Petri and others *d Elio Petri ph* Carlo di Palma *m* Piero Piccioni
☆ *Marcello Mastroianni*, Salvo Randone, Micheline Presle, Andrea Checci

Assassin
GB 1973 83m Technicolor
Pemini (David M. Jackson)

MI5 arranges the liquidation of an Air Ministry spy.
Old hat espionage melodrama, top heavy with artiness which makes it look like an endless TV commercial.
w Michael Sloan *d* Peter Crane *ph* Brian Jonson *m* Zack Lawrence
☆ Ian Hendry, Edward Judd, Frank Windsor, Ray Brooks, John Hart Dyke

Assassin: see *Point of No Return (1993)*

Assassin for Hire *
GB 1951 67m bw
Merton Park (Julian Wintle/Anglo Amalgamated)

A professional killer is trapped into admitting a murder he didn't do.
Taut little suspenser, quite watchable.
w Rex Rienits *d Michael McCarthy*
☆ Sydney Tafler, Ronald Howard, John Hewer, Martin Benson

L'Assassin habite au 21 **
France 1947 83m bw
Mage/Liote

aka: *The Murderer Lives at 21*
A police detective assumes the guise of a clergyman to investigate mass killings which seem to centre on a boarding house.
Agreeable, straight-faced but tongue-in-cheek comedy thriller which was probably even funnier in French.
wd Henri-Georges Clouzot novel S. A. Steerman *ph* Armand Thirard

☆ Pierre Fresnay, Suzy Delair, Pierre Larquey, Noel Roquevert

Assassin of the Tsar (dubbed)
Russia/GB 1991 104m Eastmancolor
Blue Dolphin/Mosfilm/Spectator/Courier (Christopher Gawor, Erik Vaisberg, Anthony Sloman)

Russian title: *Tsareubiitsa*
A doctor decides on a dangerous plan to cure a patient in a Russian psychiatric ward who believes he is both the killer of Tsar Alexander II in 1881 and one of the murderers of Tsar Nicholas and his family in 1918.
An odd movie that is unsuccessful in its attempt to frame the demise of the Russian royal family within a modern-day story; the result is confusing and unconvincing.
w Aleksandr Borodianski, Karen Shakhnazarov *d* Karen Shakhnazarov *ph* Nikolai Nemoliaev *m* John Altman, Vladislav Shut *ad* Liudmila Kusakova *ed* Lidiia Miliotti
☆ Malcolm McDowell, Oleg Yankovsky, Armen Dzhigarkhanyan, Iurii Sherstnev, Angela Ptashuk, Viktor Seferov
'Both a compelling modern pyschodrama and a powerful recreation of one of the pivotal events of modern history, addressing Russian history and the current turbulent state of the country in an effective and compelling manner.' – *Kim Newman, Empire*
'Unsatisfactory psychology and unsatisfactory historiography.' – *Sight and Sound*

Assassination
US 1986 88m TVC Color
Cannon (Pancho Kohner)
A White House secret service man finds himself on the run with the first lady.
Mildly diverting but over-mysterious chase movie, less violent than the Bronson norm.
w Richard Sale *d* Peter Hunt
☆ Charles Bronson, Jill Ireland, Stephen Elliott, Jan Gan Boyd, Randy Brooks, Michael Ansara

The Assassination Bureau *
GB 1968 110m Technicolor
Paramount/Heathfield (Michael Relph)
In 1906 a lady journalist breaks up an international gang of professional killers by falling in love with their leader.
Black comedy period pastiche which resolves itself into a series of sketches leading up to a spectacular zeppelin climax. Plenty going on, but the level of wit is not high.
w Michael Relph, Wolf Mankowitz *d* Basil Dearden *ph* Geoffrey Unsworth *m* Ron Grainer
☆ Oliver Reed, Diana Rigg, Telly Savalas, Curt Jurgens, Philippe Noiret, Warren Mitchell, Clive Revill, Beryl Reid, Kenneth Griffith

The Assassination of the Duc de Guise *
France 1908 15m (16 fps) bw silent
Film d'Art
Henry III arranges the killing of the Duc de Guise when he comes to court.
Influential early story film.
w Henri Lavedan *d* Charles le Bargy *m* Saint-Saëns
☆ Charles le Bargy, Albert Lambert, Gabrielle Lavinne

'For one moment, they hold history in their hands. With one terrible blow, they make it'
The Assassination of Trotsky
Italy/GB/France 1972 103m Technicolor
Dino de Laurentiis/Josef Shaftel/Cinetel (Norman Priggen, Joseph Losey)
In 1940, Trotsky is hiding out in Mexico; a Stalinist infiltrates his presence and kills him with an ice pick.
Glum historical reconstruction with much fictitious padding; basically undramatic.
w Nicholas Mosley, Masolino d'Amico *d* Joseph Losey *ph* Pasquale de Santis *m* Egisto Macchi
☆ Richard Burton, Alain Delon, Romy Schneider, Valentina Cortese, Jean Desailly
'Not for anyone who knows, or cares, anything about Leon Trotsky.' – *New Yorker, 1977*

Assassino ... è al telefono: see *The Killer Is on the Phone*

Assassins
US 1995 132m Technicolor
Warner/Silver Pictures (Richard Donner, Joel Silver, Bruce Evans, Raynold Gideon, Andrew Lazar, Jim Van Wyck)
A top hitman, who has decided that it is time to quit, is menaced by a younger rival.
Even by the standards of some other of Stallone's movies, this is relentlessly silly stuff about extremely nasty characters; you may keep watching just to discover what illogicality happens next, in which case the ending will not disappoint you.
w Andy Wachowski, Larry Wachowski, Brian Helgeland *d* Richard Donner *ph* Vilmos Zsigmond *m* Mark Mancina *pd* Tom Sanders *ed* Richard Marks
☆ Sylvester Stallone, Antonio Banderas, Julianne Moore, Anatoly Davydow, Muse Watson, Stephen Kahan
'Has a few suspenseful confrontations, but to get to them you have to wade through countless scenes of monosyllabic brooding, all shot in the kind of elegantly sterile beige and slate tones that suggest someone's half-baked idea of a "minimalist" thriller.' – *Entertainment Weekly*

Les Assassins du Dimanche
France 1956 94m bw Cinepanoramic
EDIC
aka: *Every Second Counts*
Dozens of people help to track down a holiday car which has been driven away from a garage in a dangerous condition.
Watchable but artificial suspenser.
w Alex Joffé, Gabriel Arout *d* Alex Joffé *ph* Jean Bourgoin
☆ Barbara Laage, Jean-Marc Thibault, Dominique Wilms, Paul Frankeur

Assault
GB 1970 91m Eastmancolor
Rank/Peter Rogers (George H. Brown)
An art mistress helps police to solve a case of multiple rape in an English village.
Old-fashioned police mystery with new-fangled shock treatment. Routine excitements.
w John Kruse *novel* Kendal Young *d* Sidney Hayers *ph* Ken Hodges *m* Eric Rogers
☆ Frank Finlay, Suzy Kendall, James Laurenson, Lesley-Anne Down, Freddie Jones, Tony Beckley, Anthony Ainley, Dilys Hamlett
'All right for that wet afternoon.' – *Michael Billington, Illustrated London News*

The Assault ***
Netherlands 1986 148m colour
Cannon (Fons Rademakers)
original title: *De Aanslag*
An adult is forced to recall the traumatic events of his childhood, when he saw his family murdered by the Nazis.
Part gripping thriller, part indictment of those who would forget the past, and wholly watchable.
w Gerard Soeteman *novel* Harry Mulisch *d* Fons Rademakers *ph* Their Van Der Sande *m* Jurriaan Andriessen *ed* Kees Linthorst
☆ Derek de Lint, Marc Van Uchelen, Monique Van de Ven, John Kraaykamp, Huub Van Der Lubbe, Elly Weller, Ina Van Der Molen
best foreign film

Assault on a Queen
US 1966 106m Technicolor Panavision
Paramount/Seven Arts/Sinatra Enterprises (William Goetz)
Crooks dredge up a submarine and use it to hi-jack the *Queen Mary*.
Strained caper film which remains uncertain whether to play for drama or thrills, and achieves neither. Special effects unconvincing.
w Rod Serling *novel* Jack Finney *d* Jack Donohue *ph* William Daniels *m* Duke Ellington
☆ Frank Sinatra, Virna Lisi, Tony Franciosa, Alf Kjellin, Errol John, Richard Conte, Murray Matheson, Reginald Denny
'Just about as enthralling as plastic boats in the bath.' – *MFB*

Assault on Precinct 13 ***
US 1976 91m Metrocolor Panavision
CKK (Joseph Kaufman)
Gang members on a vendetta attack a police station.
Violent but basically efficient and old-fashioned programmer which shows that not all the expertise of the forties in this then-familiar field has been lost.
ph Douglas Knapp *wd/m* John Carpenter
☆ Austin Stoker, Darwin Joston, Laurie Zimmer, Martin West
'One of the most effective exploitation movies of the last ten years ... Carpenter scrupulously avoids any overt socio-political pretensions, playing instead for laughs and suspense in perfectly balanced proportions.' – *Time Out*

The Assignment
Canada/US 1997 115m colour
Columbia TriStar/Triumph/Allegro (Tom Berry, Franco Battista)
An American naval officer, who is the double of Carlos 'The Jackal' Sanchez, is persuaded by the CIA to impersonate the terrorist.
Tepid spy thriller, which seems more like propaganda than entertainment; despite its use of fact, it never suggests a convincing reality.
w Dan Gordon, Sabi H. Shabtai *d* Christian Duguay *ph* David Franco *m* Normand Corbeil *pd* Michael Joy *ed* Yves Langlois
☆ Aidan Quinn, Donald Sutherland, Ben Kingsley, Claudia Ferri, Celine Bonnier, Vlasta Vrana, Liliana Komorowska
'Visually proceedings veer between made-for-television stodge and inexpert gimmickry.' – *Danny Leigh, Sight and Sound*

Assignment in Brittany
US 1943 96m bw
MGM (J. Walter Ruben)
A Free French soldier stays in occupied France to fight the Nazis.
Routine propagandist actioner, totally unbelievable.
w Anthony Veiller, William Wright, Howard Emmett Rogers *novel* Helen MacInnes *d* Jack Conway *ph* Charles Rosher *m* Lennie Hayton
☆ Jean Pierre Aumont, Signe Hasso, Susan Peters, Reginald Owen, Richard Whorf, Margaret Wycherly, John Emery, Miles Mander, George Coulouris

Assignment Paris
US 1952 85m bw
Columbia (Sam Marx, Jerry Bresler)
A reporter on the Paris staff of the *New York Herald-Tribune* goes to Yugoslavia, is arrested as a spy, and has to be exchanged.
Dim cold war melodrama with occasional entertaining moments.
w William Bowers *novel* *Trial by Terror* by Paul Gallico *d* Robert Parrish *ph* Burnett Guffey, Ray Cory *m* George Duning
☆ George Sanders, Dana Andrews, Sandro Giglio, Marta Toren, Audrey Totter, Herbert Berghof

Assignment to Kill
US 1967 99m Technicolor Panavision
Warner Seven Arts (William Conrad)
A New York insurance company hires a private eye to investigate a dubious European financier.
Routine international intrigue with muddled plot and unusual cast. A nice production wasted.
wd Sheldon Reynolds *ph* Harold Lipstein *m* William Lava
☆ Patrick O'Neal, John Gielgud, Peter Van Eyck, Joan Hackett, Herbert Lom, Eric Portman, Oscar Homolka, Leon Greene

The Assisi Underground
Italy/US 1985 178m colour
Cannon (Menahem Golan, Yoram Globus)
During World War II, Assisi monasteries hide Jewish refugees.
Expansive but generally abysmal war adventure which was released in various forms, including a television miniseries. No amount of re-editing can disguise an empty script and incompetent direction.
wd Alexander Ramati *novel* Alexander Ramati *ph* Giuseppe Rotunno *m* Dov Seltzer *pd* Luciano Spadoni

☆ Ben Cross, James Mason, Irene Papas, Maximilian Schell, Simon Ward, Giancarlo Giannini
'There is simply not enough story to fill three hours, so the scenery upstages the actors.' – *Variety*

The Associate
US 1996 113m Technicolor
Polygram/Interscope (Frédérick Golchan, Patrick Markey, Adam Leipzig)
Faced with the problems of succeeding in a man's world, a female financial analyst invents a male partner, and then discovers she needs to impersonate him.
Perhaps it was time for a male impersonation, after an overdose of other drag acts in mainstream films, but this vehicle is too ramshackle and lacking in humour to make the effort seem worthwhile.
w Nick Thiel *novel* *El socio* by Jenaro Prieto *d* Donald Petrie *ph* Alex Nepomniaschy *m* Christopher Tyng *pd* Andrew Jackness *ed* Bonnie Koehler *film* L'Associé
☆ Whoopi Goldberg, Dianne Wiest, Tim Daly, Bebe Neuwirth, Eli Wallach, Austin Pendleton, Lainie Kazan, George Martin, Kenny Kerr
'Shallow cut-and-paste Hollywood formula.' – *Sight and Sound*

Asterix & Obelix: Mission Cleopatra *
France/Germany 2002 108m colour
Pathé/Katharina/RennTF1Chez Wam/CP Medien/KC Medien/KG Munich (Claude Berri)
In 52 BC, Gauls travel to Egypt to help Cleopatra win a bet with Julius Caesar that she can build a palace in three months.
Jolly slapstick romp through Roman history with some good gags along the way.
wd Alain Chabat *comic book* Rene Goscinny, Albert Uderzo *ph* Laurent Dailland *m* Philippe Chany *pd* At Hoang *ed* Stephane Pereira
☆ Gérard Depardieu (Obelix), Christian Clavier (Asterix), Jamel Debbouze (Numerobis), Monica Bellucci (Cleopatra), Claude Rich (Panoramix), Gerard Darmon (Amonbofis), Alain Chabat (Cesar), Dieudonne (Casius Ceplus)
'It's silly, it's funny, the whole family can go.' – *Variety*
† It was the most expensive French film yet made, costing $47m.

Asterix & Obelix Take on Caesar (dubbed) *
France/Germany/Italy 1999 110m colour Super 35
Pathé/Katharina/Renn/TF1/Bavaria/Melampo (Claude Berri)
original title: *Astérix & Obélix contre Caesar*
In Gaul, a small village, where the men are made strong by their druid's magic potion, holds out against Julius Caesar's invading army.
Lavish live-action version of the much-loved comic books, well-cast but suffering in the English-language version from the dubbing, which loses much of the humour.
w Claude Zidi, Gérard Lauzier (English version: Terry Jones) *characters created by* Albert Uderzo, René Goscinny *d* Claude Zidi *ph* Tony Pierce-Roberts *pd* Jean Rabasse *ed* Nicole Saunier, Hervé de Luze
☆ Christian Clavier (Asterix), Gérard Depardieu (Obelix), Roberto Benigni (Detritus), Michel Galabru (Vitalstatistix), Claude Piéplu (Panoramix), Daniel Prévost (Prolix), Pierre Palmade (Cacofonix), Laetitia Casta (Panacea), Arielle Dombasle (Mrs Jerry Atrix), Sim (Agecanonix), Marianne Sagebrecht (Benamenture), Gottfried John (Caesar), Jean-Pierre Castaldi (Caius Bonus), Jean-Jacques Devaux (Unhygenix), Jean-Roger Milo (Fulliautomatix)
'Trades in suitably lively slapstick but perhaps without ever doing the cool Gaul total justice.' – *William Thomas, Empire*
† One of the most expensive films ever made in France, it was also a smash hit at the French box-office.

Asterix and the Big Fight
France/West Germany 1989 81m
Eastmancolor
Palace/Gaumont/Extrafilm (Nicolas Pesques)
original title: *Le Coup de Menhir*
Asterix attempts to restore the village soothsayer's memory in order to make a potion to defeat the invading Romans.
Dull adaptation of a far wittier comic-book original.
w George Roubicek *novel* *Asterix and the Big Fight* by Rene Goscinny and Alberto Uderzo *d* Philippe Grimond *ph* Craig Simpson *m* Michel Colombier *pd* Nicolas Pesques *ed* Jean Goudier
☆ Featuring the voices of Bill Oddie, Bernard Bresslaw, Ron Moody, Sheila Hancock, Peter Hawkins, Brian Blessed, Michael Elphick, Andrew Sachs, Tim Brooke-Taylor, Douglas Blackwell

Asterix Conquers America
Germany 1994 85m colour
TCF/Extrafilm (Jürgen Wohlrabe)
Asterix and friends end up accidentally in America, where they spend some time with an Indian tribe before returning home to fight the Romans once more.
Uninventive animated cartoon, making mild and inoffensive fun of national characteristics.
w Thomas Platt, Rhett Rooster, Robin Lyons, Andrew Offiler *d* Gerhard Hahn *m* Harold Faltermayer *ed* Ulrich Steinvorth
☆ Featuring the voices of John Rye, Craig Charles, Howard Lewis, Henry McGee, Geoffrey Bayldon, Christopher Biggins
'Pretty weary stuff, suitable only for avid fans.' – *Guardian*

Asterix in Britain
Denmark/France 1986 74m
Eastmancolor
Gaumont Dargaud (Yannik Piel)
Asterix and friends go to Britain to help the locals repel the Roman invasion.
Amiable animated version of the comic-book characters, poking good-natured fun at national stereotypes.
w Pierre Tchernia *comic* Goscinny and Uderzo *d* Pino Van Lamsweerde *m* Vladimir Cosma
☆ Featuring the voices of Jack Beaver, Bill Kearns, Graham Bushnell, Herbert Baskind, Ed Marcus

The Asthenic Syndrome ***
Russia 1989 153m bw/Fujicolor
Odessa Film Studio
original title: *Asteniceskij Sindrom*
A bleak tale of a woman who cannot come to terms with her bereavement turns out to be a film within the film; the real story is of modern-day Moscow and events centring around a narcoleptic teacher.
The film opens with a chorus of three old ladies chanting, 'In my childhood and youth I thought that if everybody read Leo Tolstoy carefully they would understand absolutely everything and would become very kind and wise.' What follows in this witty, episodic, structurally bold, harshly ironic account is the obverse: a society of uncaring and hostile people who will not wake up to their condition.
w Kira Muratova, Sergei Popov, Alexander Tschernych *d* Kira Muratova *ph* Vladimir Pankov *ed* Vladimir Olinik
☆ Olga Antonova, Sergei Popov, Galina Zakhrudayeva
† The film was banned on its release, and was only seen in Russia after it won the Special Jury Prize at the Berlin Film Festival in 1990.

The Astonished Heart *
GB 1949 89m bw
Gainsborough/Sydney Box (Anthony Darnborough)
A psychiatrist is permitted by his wife to fall in love with another woman but finds the situation intolerable and kills himself.
The star, looking like a Chinese mandarin, reached his nadir in this unwise screen adaptation, inelegantly directed, of one of his slightest short plays about boring and effete people. It sank without trace.
w Noël Coward *play* Noël Coward *d* Terence Fisher, Anthony Darnborough *ph* Jack Asher *m* Noël Coward
☆ Noël Coward, Margaret Leighton, Celia Johnson, Graham Payn, Joyce Carey, Ralph Michael, Michael Hordern

The Astounding She-Monster
US 1957 59m bw
Hollywood International (Ronnie Ashcroft)
GB title: *Mysterious Invader*
In a remote spot, some crooks and a scientist combat a female space visitor with remarkable powers.
An early sub-Corman pot-boiler with only its camp qualities to recommend it.
w Frank Hall *d* Ronnie Ashcroft
☆ Robert Clarke, Kenne Duncan, Marilyn Harvey

'Imagine the face of terror is the one you love.'
The Astronaut's Wife
US 1999 109m DeLuxe
Entertainment/New Line/Mad Chance (Andrew Lazar)
An astronaut's wife comes to believe that, while in space, her husband was taken over by an alien entity; then she becomes pregnant.
A sort of science-fiction variation on Rosemary's Baby, but much less effective and interesting.
wd Rand Ravich *ph* Allen Daviau *pd* Jan Roelfs *ed* Steve Mirkovich, Tim Alverson
☆ Johnny Depp (Spencer Armacost), Charlize Theron (Jillian Armacost), Joe Morton (Sherman Reese), Clea DuVall (Nan), Donna Murphy (Natalie Streck), Samantha Eggar (Doctor), Gary Grubbs (NASA Director), Blair Brown (Shelly McLaren), Tom Noonan (Jackson McLaren)
'The abiding atmosphere is one of tedium and unreality.' – *James Christopher, Times*

Asya's Happiness **
USSR 1967 94m bw
Artificial Eye/Mosfilm (M. Zarzhitskaya)
original title: *Istoria Asi Klyachinoi, kotoraya lyubila, da nie vshla zamuzh*
The film's epigraph is 'The story of a woman who loved but did not marry', but it is more a loving account of a rural community at work and play.
A candid portrait of Soviet life, using amateur actors, that was banned for more than 20 years for reasons only the Russians will understand.
w Yuri Klepikov *d* Andrei Konchalovsky *ph* Georgy Rerberg *pd* Mikhail Romadin *ed* L. Pokrovskoi
☆ Iya Savvina, Lyubov Sokolova, Alexander Surin, Gennady Yegorychev, Ivan Petrov
'A major film in its own right, a worthy addition to that great agrarian cinema of Vidor and Ford.' – *Ian Christie, MFB*

'You have nothing to lose but your mind!'
Asylum *
GB 1972 88m Eastmancolor
Amicus (Max J. Rosenberg, Milton Subotsky)
aka: *House of Crazies*
A doctor applies for a job at an asylum, hears weird stories from four patients, and finds himself in the middle of a weirder one.
Lively horror compilation with echoes of Caligari and Dead of Night. Gruesomeness sometimes overdone.
w Robert Bloch *d* Roy Ward Baker *ph* Denys Coop *m* Douglas Gamley
☆ Patrick Magee, Robert Powell, Geoffrey Bayldon, Barbara Parkins, Sylvia Syms, Richard Todd, Peter Cushing, Barry Morse, Britt Ekland, Charlotte Rampling, James Villiers, Megs Jenkins, Herbert Lom

At Close Range
US 1986 111m CFI color Panavision
Orion/Hemdale (Elliott Lewitt, Don Guest)
In Pennsylvania, a gang of young robbers is picked off one by one by the father of one of them, who feels they know too much about his own criminal activities.
Relentlessly brutal, dispiriting and quite pointless melodrama, even with the saving grace of a factual basis.
w Nicholas Kazan *d* James Foley *ph* Juan Ruiz-Anchia *m* Patrick Leonard
☆ Sean Penn, Christopher Walken, Mary Stuart Masterson, Christopher Penn, Millie Perkins, Eileen Ryan, Candy Clark
'A very tough picture ... runs the risk of being an audience turnoff.' – *Variety*

At Dawn We Die: see *Tomorrow We Live*

'Seeing is believing.'
At First Sight
US 1999 128m DeLuxe Panavision
MGM (Irwin Winkler, Rob Cowan)
A blind masseur is encouraged by his girlfriend to have an operation that may restore his sight.
A sentimental romantic drama that should be neither seen nor heard.
w Steve Levitt *story* *To See and Not See* by Oliver Sacks *d* Irwin Winkler *ph* John Seale *m* Mark Isham *pd* Jane Musky *ed* Julie Monroe
☆ Val Kilmer, Mira Sorvino, Kelly McGillis, Steven Weber, Bruce Davison, Nathan Lane, Ken Howard
'Fluffy, oversweet and not particularly nourishing.' – *Lael Loewenstein, Variety*
'The film itself could have done with an eye-test, since it apparently can't see its story except in soft-focus.' – *Alexander Walker, London Evening Standard*

At Gunpoint
US 1955 80m Technicolor Cinemascope
Allied Artists
GB title: *Gunpoint*
A Western storekeeper accidentally kills a bank robber, whose brothers seek revenge; will the townsfolk come to his aid?
Fair Western on the lines of High Noon.
w Dan Ullman *d* Alfred Werker
☆ Fred MacMurray, Dorothy Malone, Walter Brennan, John Qualen, Skip Homeier

'A new kind of musical!'
At Long Last Love
US 1975 114m Technicolor
TCF/Copa de Oro (Peter Bogdanovich)
The 1935 romance of a New York millionaire and a musical star.
An attempt to recapture the simple pleasures of an Astaire-Rogers musical; unfortunately true professionalism is lacking and the wrong kind of talent is used. The result is awful to contemplate.
wd Peter Bogdanovich *ph* Laszlo Kovacs *m* Cole Porter *pd* Gene Allen
☆ Burt Reynolds, Cybill Shepherd, Eileen Brennan, Madeline Kahn, Duilio del Prete, John Hillerman, Mildred Natwick
'He works hard at reducing all his sets and costumes to variations of black against silver or white on white, and uncovers in his most oft-repeated visual motif – the elegant mirrors before which his cast seem at all times to be posed – the perfect metaphor for this endlessly narcissistic, thoroughly calcified enterprise.' – *Richard Combs*
'It just lies there, and it dies there.' – *Variety*
'Studios bury more films than the public or the critics. Fox gave up on *At Long Last Love* instantly. A six million dollar film was written off while it was doing well because their lawyers told them they could make more money that way.' – *Peter Bogdanovich*
'It is justly included on most lists of the ten worst films ever made.' – *Les Keyser, Hollywood in the Seventies*
'Stillborn ... a relentlessly vapid pastiche.' – *Pauline Kael*

At Play in the Fields of the Lord *
US 1991 186m Technicolor
Entertainment/Saul Zaentz
American mercenaries become embroiled in a battle for the land and souls of an Indian tribe in the Amazon.
Over-long and over-earnest treatment of a fashionable theme, though it does have its moments.
w Jean-Claude Carrière, Hector Babenco *novel* Peter Mathiessen *d* Hector Babenco *ph* Lauro Escorel *m* Zbigniew Preisner *pd* Clovis Bueno *ed* William Anderson, Aremn Minasian, Louise Innes
☆ Tom Berenger, John Lithgow, Daryl Hannah, Aidan Quinn, Tom Waits, Kathy Bates, Stenio Garcia, Nelson Xavier
'The Amazonian tragedy is surely not best served by three hours of tedium.' – *Empire*

At Sword's Point *
US 1952 81m Technicolor
RKO (Jerrold T. Brandt)
GB title: *Sons of the Musketeers*
The sons of the three musketeers rally around their ageing queen to prevent her daughter's marriage to a villain.
Adequate swashbuckler with plenty of pace and a sound cast.
w Walter Ferris, Joseph Hoffman *d* Lewis Allen *ph* Ray Rennahan *m* Roy Webb
☆ Cornel Wilde, Maureen O'Hara, Gladys Cooper, Robert Douglas, Dan O'Herlihy, Alan Hale Jnr, Blanche Yurka, Nancy Gates

At the Circus **
US 1939 87m bw
MGM (Mervyn Le Roy)
aka: *The Marx Brothers at the Circus*
A shyster lawyer and two incompetents save a circus from bankruptcy.
This film began the decline of the Marx Brothers; in it nothing is ill done but nothing is very fresh either apart from the rousing finale which shows just what professionalism meant in the old Hollywood. Highlights include Groucho singing about Lydia the Tattooed Lady, his seduction of Mrs Dukesbury, and the big society party.
w Irving Brecher *d* Edward Buzzell *ph* Leonard M. Smith *m* Franz Waxman *m/ly* Harold Arlen, E. Y. Harburg
☆ Groucho, Chico, Harpo, Margaret Dumont, Florence Rice, Kenny Baker, Eve Arden, Nat Pendleton, Fritz Feld
GROUCHO: 'I don't know what I'm doing here when I could be at home in bed with a hot toddy. That's a drink.'
'Rousing physical comedy and staccato gag dialogue ... geared for fine b.o. and general audience appeal.' – *Variety*
'We must regretfully accept the fact that, thanks to the Metro millions, the Marx Brothers are finally imprisoned in the Hollywood world.' – *Graham Greene*
♫ 'Lydia the Tattooed Lady', 'Two Blind Loves', 'Step up and Take a Bow'

At the Earth's Core
GB 1976 90m Technicolor
Amicus (John Dark)
Scientists testing a geological excavator are carried by it to the centre of the Earth, and find a prehistoric land inhabited by feuding tribes.
Mainly feeble science fiction for kids, with occasional amusing moments.
w Milton Subotsky *novel* Edgar Rice Burroughs *d* Kevin Connor *ph* Alan Hume *m* Mike Vickers *pd* Maurice Carter *sp* Ian Wingrove
☆ Doug McClure, Peter Cushing, Caroline Munro, Cy Grant, Godfrey James, Keith Barron
'Papier mâché people-eaters, idiotic situations, and a frequent sense of confusion as to what is going on.' – *David Stewart, Christian Science Monitor*

At The Height of Summer: see *Mua He Chieu Thang Dung*

At the Stroke of Nine
GB 1957 72m bw
Tower/Grand National
A mad concert pianist plots to murder a young girl reporter.
Absurd and rather endearing melodrama of the very old school.
w Tony O'Grady, Harry Booth, Jon Pennington, Michael Deeley *d* Lance Comfort
☆ Stephen Murray, Patricia Dainton, Patrick Barr, Dermot Walsh

At the Villa Rose
This murder mystery by A. E. W. Mason has had three British filmings: in 1920 with Teddy Arundell as Inspector Hanaud; in 1930 with Austin Trevor; in 1939 with Keneth Kent. All were adequate to their time. The story concerns a medium framed for the murder of a rich widow.

At War with the Army
US 1951 93m bw
Paramount/Fred K. Finklehoffe
A couple of song and dance men have trouble as army recruits.
American service farce, based on a play and confined largely to one set; rather untypical of Martin and Lewis, yet oddly enough the film which sealed their success.
w Fred Finklehoffe *play* James Allardice *d* Hal Walker *ph* Stuart Thompson *m* Joseph Lilley
☆ Dean Martin, Jerry Lewis, Mike Kellin, Polly Bergen, Jimmie Dundee

L'Atalante *
France 1934 89m bw
J. L. Nounez-Gaumont
A barge captain takes his new wife down river.
One of those classics which no longer provide the authentic thrill; its lack of incident and plot leads quickly to boredom.
w Jean Guinée, Jean Vigo, Albert Riera *d* Jean Vigo *ph* Boris Kaufman, Louis Berger *m* Maurice Jaubert
☆ Jean Dasté, Dita Parlo, *Michel Simon*, Giles Margarites
'The singular talent – for once I think I may say genius – of the film lies in its translation into visual images of the mysterious and terrible and piteous undertones of even the simplest human life.' – *Dilys Powell*

¡Atame!: see *Tie Me Up! Tie Me Down!*

Atanarjuat The Fast Runner **
Canada 2001 168m colour
ICA/Igoolik Isuma/NFBC (Paul Apak Angilirq, Norman Cohn, Zacharias Kunuk)
In the Arctic two thousand years ago, a struggle for leadership develops between two Inuit families.
A film like no other: based on an Inuit legend, it depicts a way of life, full of strange rituals and magic, that seems other-worldly; the desire for power, family betrayals, and the survival of the wiliest, though, connect with modern life.
w Paul Apak Angilirq *d* Zacharias Kunuk *ph* Norman Cohn *ad* James Ungalaaq *ed* Zacharias Kunuk, Norman Cohn, Marie-Christine Sarda
☆ Natar Ungalaaq (Atanarjuat), Sylvia Ivalu (Atuat), Peter Henry Arnatsiaq (Oki), Lucy Tulugarjuk (Puja), Pakkak Innushuk (Amaqjuaq), Madeline Ivalu (Panikpak), Paul Qulitalik (Qulitalik)
'Mysterious, bawdy, emotionally intense, and replete with virtuoso throat singing, this three-hour movie is engrossing from first image to last, so devoid of stereotype and cosmic in its vision it could suggest the rebirth of cinema.' – *J. Hoberman, Village Voice*

El Ataque de los Muertos sin Ojo: see *The Return of the Evil Dead*

Athena
US 1954 96m Eastmancolor
MGM (Joe Pasternak)
A young lawyer falls in love with the eldest of seven sisters brought up to high standards of moral conduct and physical fitness.
Promising but unfulfilling light musical which smothers a good idea in routine treatment.
w William Ludwig, Leonard Spigelgass *d* Richard Thorpe *ph* Robert Planck *m/ly* Hugh Martin, Ralph Blane *md* George Stoll
☆ Edmund Purdom, Jane Powell, Debbie Reynolds, Louis Calhern, Evelyn Varden, Vic Damone, Linda Christian, Ray Collins

'The Leviathan of Talkies'
'A thunderbolt of drama impossible to describe'
Atlantic
GB 1929 90m bw
BIP
A passenger liner sinks in mid-Atlantic.
Veiled retelling of the Titanic story, here in a clumsy Anglo-German version with extremely primitive sound and a plethora of pregnant silences.
w Victor Kendall *play* The Berg by Ernest Raymond *d* E. A. Dupont
☆ Franklin Dyall, Madeleine Carroll, Monty Banks, John Stuart, John Longden, Ellaline Terriss
'If you want to be mentally shipwrecked or lost at sea, see *Atlantic* ... It's something unnecessary to see; something no one wants to see; something horrible to even think of.
'...It will draw to and drive away from the box office. Draw to because it holds horror, thrills and suspense; drive away through children not being permitted to see it and the suggested gruesomeness too strong for many, not only women.
'...A faint try at comedy with a valet was like a ghoul in a cemetery ... but Franklin Dyall excelled as an aged invalid with John Longden as a ship's officer, making a splendid appearance.' – *Variety*

Atlantic City *
US 1944 87m bw
Republic (Albert J. Cohen)
aka: *Atlantic City, U.S.A.*
Before World War I, a young showman aims to make Atlantic City the entertainment centre of the world.
Simple-minded romantic musical, quite pacy and effectively staged for a Republic product.
w Doris Gilbert, Frank Gill Jnr, George Carleton Brown *d* Ray McCarey *ph* John Alton *m/ly* various
☆ Constance Moore, Brad Taylor, Jerry Colonna, Charley Grapewin

Atlantic City ***
Canada/France 1981 105m colour
Cine-Neighbour/Selta Films (Denis Heroux)
Small-time crooks congregate round Atlantic City's new casinos.
Elegiac character drama which often achieves the mood it seeks but on the whole remains too understated for its own good.
w John Guare *d* *Louis Malle* *ph* Richard Ciupka *m* Michel Legrand *pd* Anne Pritchard
☆ *Burt Lancaster*, Susan Sarandon, Kate Reid, Michel Piccoli, Hollis McLaren
best picture; John Guare; Burt Lancaster; Susan Sarandon; Louis Malle
best direction; Burt Lancaster

L'Atlantide *
France 19[illegible] 125m approx (16 fps) bw
silent
Thalman
Two explorers find the lost continent of Atlantis and fall in love with its queen.
Highly commercial adventure fantasy of its day; it cost two million francs and ran in Paris for a year. Some scenes still sustain, and the desert scenes are impressive.
Other versions include:
1932 *Queen of Atlantis*, Germany, *d* G. W. Pabst, with Brigitte Helm
1948 *Siren of Atlantis*, US, *d* Gregg Tallas, with Maria Montez
1961 *L'Atlantide*, France/Italy, *d* Edgar G. Ulmer
wd Jacques Feyder *novel* Pierre Benoît *ph* Georges Specht, Victor Morin
☆ Jean Angelo, Stacia Napierkowska, Georges Melchior

Atlantis **
France 1991 75m colour
Warner/Gaumont/Cecchi Gori
An episodic documentary, with musical accompaniment, on life under the sea.
A fascinating attempt at what its director defined as an 'underwater opera', full of quirky detail and showing various species that may soon die out.
d Luc Besson *ph* Christian Petron *m* Eric Serra *ed* Luc Besson

Atlantis, the Lost Continent
US 1961 91m Metrocolor
MGM/Galaxy/George Pal
A Greek fisherman is imprisoned when he returns a maiden he has rescued to her island home of Atlantis, but escapes just before volcanic eruption overtakes the decadent nation.
Penny-pinching fantasy spectacle with very little entertainment value.
w Daniel Mainwaring *play* Sir Gerald Hargreaves *d* George Pal *ph* Harold E. Wellman *m* Russell Garcia
☆ Anthony Hall, Joyce Taylor, John Dall, Edward Platt, Frank de Kova, Jay Novello

Atlantis: The Lost Empire *
US 2001 95m Technicolor
CinemaScope
Buena Vista/Walt Disney (Don Hahn)
In 1914, a linguist leads an expedition to discover the underwater city of Atlantis.
Interesting attempt to revitalise Disney's approach to traditional animation, abandoning songs and cute animals and using the style of comic-book artist Mike Mignola; a less hackneyed story, without mushy mysticism at its centre, would have been an even greater improvement.
w Tab Murphy, Gary Trousdale, Kirk Wise, Joss Whedon, Bryce Zabel, Jackie Zabel *d* Gary Trousdale, Kirk Wise *m* James Newton Howard *ed* Ellen Keneshea
☆ voices of: Michael J. Fox (Milo Thatch), James Garner (Commander Rourke), Cree Summer (Princess Kida), Leonard Nimoy (King of Atlantis), Vinny Santorini (Don Novello), Claudia Christian (Helga Sinclair), Jacqueline Obradors (Audrey Ramirez), John Mahoney (Preston B. Whitmore), Corey Burton (Mole), David Ogden Stiers (Fenton Q. Harcourt), Jim Varney (Cookie)
'An outstanding creative and artistic achievemenr...a masterpiece of the storyteller's craft.' – *Ben Woodhams, Film Review*
'Recycles familiar adventure and cartoon devices with minimal wit and flair.' – *Todd McCarthy, Variety*

Atoll K: see *Robinson Crusoeland*

Atolladero
Spain 1995 99m colour Panavision
FDG/Canal+ (Arturo Duque)
In 2048 in Texas, where despots rule over desert regions, an epileptic cop tries to escape from the small community in which he lives.
Curious pulp science fiction which mixes comic-book characters with the style of a slightly surreal spaghetti Western; most of the action takes place off-screen.
wd Oscar Aibar *ph* Carles Gusi *m* Javier Navarrete *ad* Llorenç Miquel *ed* Anastasi Rinos, Xavier Cabrera
☆ Pere Ponce, Joaquin Hinojosa, Iggy Pop, Félix Rotaeta, Carlos Lucas, Pep Molina, Oriol Tramvia, Ion Gabella, Xevi Collelmir
'Strong on atmosphere and character, but let down by flimsy plotting.' – *Sight and Sound*

The Atomic City *
US 1952 85m bw
Paramount (Joseph Sistrom)
The young son of a leading atomic scientist is kidnapped but his father and the FBI rescue him.
Routine but well-paced thriller with a documentary background of research at Los Alamos.
w Sydney Boehm *d* Jerry Hopper *ph* Charles B. Lang Jnr *m* Leith Stevens
☆ Gene Barry, Lydia Clarke, Lee Aaker, Nancy Gates, Milburn Stone
Sydney Boehm

The Atomic Kid
US 1954 86m bw
Republic/Mickey Rooney (Maurice Duke)
After an atomic blast, a prospector accidentally left in the area proves immune to uranium, and after various adventures rounds up some communist spies.
Inane romp which raises a few laughs.
w Benedict Freeman, John Fenton Murray *story* Blake Edwards *d* Leslie H. Martinson *ph* John L. Russell Jnr *m* Van Alexander
☆ Mickey Rooney, Robert Strauss, Elaine Davis, Bill Goodwin, Whit Bissell

Atomic Submarine
US 1959 72m bw
Allied Artists (Alex Gordon)
The crew of an atomic submarine save the world from an alien invasion under the North Pole.
Engaging nonsense of the period.
w Orville H. Hampton *d* Spencer Gordon Bennet *ph* Gilbert Warrenton *m* Alexander Laszlo *ad* Dan Haller, Dan Ament *ed* William Austin
☆ Arthur Franz, Dick Foran, Brett Halsey, Tom Conway, Paul Dubov, Bob Steele, Victor Varconi, Selmer Jackson

The Atonement of Gösta Berling **
Sweden 1924 200m approx (16 fps) bw
silent
Svensk Filmindustri
original title: *Gösta Berlings Saga*
A pastor is defrocked for drinking, becomes a tutor, and has various love affairs.
Lumpy but often engrossing picturization of a famous novel, veering mostly into melodrama but finding its way to a happy ending.
w Mauritz Stiller, Ragnar Hylten-Cavallius *novel* Selma Lagerlof *d* Mauritz Stiller *ph* Julius Jaenzon
☆ Lars Hanson, Gerda Lundeqvist, Ellen Cederstrom, Mona Martensson, Jenny Hasselqvist, Otto Elg-Lundberg, Greta Garbo
'Stiller was a master at unifying visual beauty and emotional effect; the complicated narrative is blurry, but there are sequences as lovely and expressive as any on film.' – *New Yorker, 1980*
† It was her small role in this film which led directly to Greta Garbo's American stardom.

Attack! **
US 1956 104m bw
UA/Associates and Aldrich
In 1944 Belgium, an American infantry command is led by a coward.
High-pitched, slick, violent and very effective war melodrama, even though by the end we seem to be in the company of raving lunatics rather than soldiers.
w *James Poe* *play* *Fragile Fox* by Norman Brooks *d* *Robert Aldrich* *ph* *Joseph Biroc* *m* Frank de Vol
☆ *Jack Palance, Eddie Albert*, Lee Marvin, Buddy Ebsen, Robert Strauss, Richard Jaeckel, William Smithers, Peter Van Eyck
'The film does not so much tackle a subject as hammer it down.' – *Penelope Houston*

Attack Force Z
Australia 1981 110m colour
John McCallum/Central Motion Picture Corp (Lee Robinson)
A secret commando group attempts to rescue survivors of a plane crash in Japanese-held territory during the Second World War.
Downbeat adventure, which was intended as a tribute to Australasian special operations, but conveys instead the waste of humanity that war entails.
w Roger Marshall *d* Tim Burstall *ph* Lin Hun-Chung *m* Eric Jupp *ed* David Stiven
☆ John Phillip Law, Mel Gibson, Sam Neill, Chris Haywood, John Waters, Koo Chuan-Hsiung, Sylvia Chang, O Ti

Attack of the 50 Ft. Woman
US 1993 90m colour
Entertainment/HBO/Bartleby (Debra Hill)
After an encounter with a UFO a woman grows to enormous size and deals with her philandering husband.
A feminist remake that adds nothing of interest to the original, merely seeming a story yanked out of its time.
w Joseph Dougherty *d* Christopher Guest *ph* Russell Carpenter *m* Nicholas Pike *pd* Joseph T. Garrity *ed* Harry Keramidas *sp* Fantasy II Film Effects
☆ Daryl Hannah, Daniel Baldwin, William Windom, Frances Fisher, Paul Benedict, O'Neal Compton, Cristi Conaway
† Made for cable TV, the film had a brief cinema showing in Britain.

The Attack of the 50-Foot Woman
US 1958 72m bw
Allied Artists (Bernard Woolner)
A neurotic woman is lured inside a space ship, becomes radio-active, and grows to alarming proportions.
Hilarious tailpiece to the fifties monster cycle, a dismal movie worth remembering only for its title.
w Mark Hanna *d* Nathan Hertz (Nathan Juran) *ph* Jacques Marquette *m* Ronald Stein *ed* Edward Mann
☆ Allison Hayes, William Hudson, Roy Gordon

'From the depths of the sea ... A Tidal Wave of Terror!'

Attack of the Crab Monsters
US 1956 62m bw
Allied Artists (Roger Corman)

25-foot mutant crabs cause landslides on a Pacific island.
Bottom-of-the-barrel monster mayhem from this tongue-in-cheek producer; now a cult.
w Charles B. Griffith *d* Roger Corman *ph* Floyd Crosby *m* Ronald Stein *ed* Charles Gross Jnr
☆ Richard Garland, Pamela Duncan, Russell Johnson

Attack of the Giant Leeches
US 1959 62m bw
Corman/AIP

aka: *Demons of the Swamp*
A bar owner forces his wife and her lover into a swamp to be eaten by monsters.
The bottom of the Corman/AIP barrel, good only for a few unintentional laughs.
w Leo Gordon *d* Bernard Kowalski *ph* John M. Nickolaus Jnr
☆ Ken Clark, Michael Emmet, Yvette Vickers, Bruno Ve Sota

Attack of the Killer Tomatoes
US 1978 87m colour
Four Square/NAI

Vegetables go berserk in the big city.
Apparently a cult film made deliberately as such, which is a contradiction in terms. Nothing for the ordinary audience, anyway.
w Costa Dillon, Steve Peace, John de Bello
d John de Bello
☆ David Miller, George Wilson, Sharon Taylor, Jack Riley
'Though the idea sounds funny, actually sitting through nearly 90 minutes of it is enough to make anyone long for *Attack of the Fifty Foot Woman*.' – *Motion Picture Guide*

Attack of the Puppet People
US 1957 79m bw
Alta Vista (Bert I. Gordon)
GB title: *Six Inches Tall*
A doll-maker has also learned to shrink people.
Inferior entry in the Dr Cyclops mould; mildly amusing moments are sandwiched between chunks of tedium.
w George Worthing Yates *d* Bert I. Gordon
☆ John Hoyt, John Agar, June Kenny

Attack on the Iron Coast
GB 1967 90m DeLuxe
UA/Mirisch (John Champion)
In World War II, a Canadian commando unit destroys a German installation on the French coast.
Stagey low-budgeter with modest action sequences.
w Herman Hoffman *d* Paul Wendkos *ph* Paul Beeson *m* Gerard Schurmann
☆ Lloyd Bridges, Andrew Keir, Mark Eden, Sue Lloyd

Attila the Hun
Italy/France 1954 79m Technicolor
Lux Ponti de Laurentiis/LCCF (Georgio Andriani)

original title: *Attilo Flagello di Dio*
The barbarian chief attacks the forces of the Emperor Valentinian and marches on Rome.
Predictably violent adventures after de Mille; a bit slow to start.
w Ennio de Concini, Primo Zeglio *d* Pietro Francisci *ph* Aldo Tonti *m* Enzo Masetti
☆ Anthony Quinn, Sophia Loren, Henri Vidal, Irene Papas, Ettore Manni, Claude Laydu

Attilo Flagello di Dio: see *Attila the Hun*

Attorney for the Defense
US 1932 70m bw
Columbia
A prosecutor's wiles result in an innocent man being executed, so he turns crusader and takes on defence cases.
Punchy if unconvincing courtroom melodrama which would certainly satisfy at the time.
w Jo Swerling, J. K. McGuinness *d* Irving Cummings
☆ Edmund Lowe, Evelyn Brent, Constance Cummings, Donald Dillaway, Dorothy Peterson, Dwight Frye, Nat Pendleton, Clarence Muse

Au Coeur Du Mensonge **
France 1999 113m colour
Cinéfrance/MK2/France 3/Canal+ (Marin Karmitz)

GB title: *The Colour of Lies*
When one of his pupils is raped and murdered, an art teacher is thought by many to be the killer, but he suspects a local celebrity, a novelist who is attempting to seduce his wife.
Complex, intriguing drama of jealousy, guilt and suspicion that is not to be taken too seriously; it has fun at the expense of celebrity.
w Odile Barski, Claude Chabrol *d* Claude Chabrol *ph* Eduardo Serra *m* Matthieu Chabrol *ad* Françoise Benoit-Fresco *ed* Monique Fardoulis *cos* Corinne Jorry
☆ Sandrine Bonnaire (Viviane Sterne), Jacques Gamblin (Rene Sterne), Valeria Bruni-Tedeschi (Frederique Lesage), Antoine de Caunes (Germain-Roland Desmot), Bernard Verley (Detective Loudun), Bulle Ogier (Yvelyne Bordier), Pierre Martot (Regis Marchal), Noel Simsolo (M Bordier), Adrienne Pauly (Anna)
'A delicious sense of suspense haunts Claude Chabrol's latest character-study-cum-whodunit' – *Lisa Nesselson, Variety*

Au delà des Grilles
Italy/France 1949 90m bw
Italia Produzione/Francinex (Alfredo Guarini)
Italian title: *La mura de Malapaga*
aka: *Beyond the Gates; The Walls of Malapaga*
A murderer on the run in Genoa falls in love with a waitress and loses his chance of escape.
Quai des Brumes reworked against an Italian neo-realist setting; dramatic values less interesting now than historical ones.
w Jean Aurenche, Pierre Bost, Cesare Zavattini, Suso Cecchi d'Amico *d* René Clément *ph* Louis Page *m* Roman Vlad
☆ Jean Gabin, *Isa Miranda*, Vera Talchi, Andrea Checci
best foreign film

Au Hasard, Balthazar: see *Balthazar*

Au Pair Girls
GB 1972 86m Eastmancolor
LMG/Kenneth Shipman (Guido Coen)

The adventures of four au pair girls in London.
Dire comedy in the depressing cycle of British sexploitation films of the 70s, one that wasted some excellent talents.
w Val Guest, David Adnopoz *story* David Grant *d* Val Guest *ph* John Wilcox *m* Roger Webb *ad* Roy Smith *ed* John Colville
☆ Gabrielle Drake, Astrid Frank, Nancie Wait, Me Me Lay, Richard O'Sullivan, John Le Mesurier, Geoffrey Bayldon, Rosalie Crutchley, Ferdy Mayne, John Standing, Johnny Briggs
'Val Guest hits rock bottom with this humourless attempt at a sex comedy.' – *Derek Elley, MFB*

Au Revoir Les Enfants ****
France 1988 107m Eastmancolor
Nouvelles éditions de Films/MK2/Stella Films (Louis Malle)

During the German occupation of France, a boy at a Catholic school inadvertently betrays his Jewish schoolfriend to the Nazis.
A coolly-understated, intensely personal, semi-autobiographical movie much admired by the French and winner of the Golden Lion at the Venice Film Festival.
wd Louis Malle *ph* Renato Berta *ad* Willy Holt *ed* Emmanuelle Castro
☆ Gaspard Manesse, Raphaël Fejtö, Francine Racette, Stanlislas Carre de Malberg, Philippe Morier-Genoud, François Berleand
'Malle has said of *Au Revoir*, "I reinvented the past in the pursuit of a haunting and timeless truth." Maybe that's why I felt as if I were watching a faded French classic, something I dimly recalled.' – *Pauline Kael, New Yorker*
best foreign film; Louis Malle (as writer)
Louis Malle (as director)

Au Royaume des Cieux
France 1949 108m bw
Regina (Julien Duvivier)
aka: *Woman Hunt*
An 18-year-old girl suffers at a reform school.
Shoddy melodrama, more sensational than Hollywood ever dared to be.
wd Julien Duvivier *ph* Victor Armenise
☆ Suzanne Cloutier, Serge Reggiani, Monique Mélinand, Suzy Prim, Jean Davy, Juliette Greco
'A depressing exhibit from a director who once had a serious reputation.' – *Gavin Lambert*

L'Auberge Rouge: see *The Red Inn*

Auch Zwerge Haben Klein Angefangen: see *Even Dwarfs Started Small*

Audition: see *Odishon*

Audrey Rose *
US 1977 113m DeLuxe Panavision
United Artists (Joe Wizan, Frank de Felitta)

A man believes that a 12-year-old girl is the reincarnation of his dead daughter.
Rather painful and not very persuasive spiritualist thriller in the wake of The Exorcist; only moments of dramaturgy survive.
w Frank de Felitta *novel* Frank de Felitta
d Robert Wise *ph* Victor J. Kemper *m* Michael Small *pd* Harry Horner
☆ Anthony Hopkins, Marsha Mason, John Beck, Susan Swift, Norman Lloyd, John Hillerman, Robert Walden

'You can live a whole lifetime in a single weekend...'

August **
GB 1995 94m colour
Film Four/Majestic/Newcomm/Granada (June Wyndham Davies, Pippa Cross)

A visit by the head of the family and his much younger wife to the estate managed by his brother-in-law precipitates a crisis which leads its members to examine the disappointments of their lives.
An elegant, civilized version, though lacking in urgency, of Chekhov's play, which translates well to the Wales of the 1890s, with a narrative that gives some sense of life outside the stifled family at its centre.
w Julian Mitchell *play* *Uncle Vanya* by Anton Chekhov *d* Anthony Hopkins *ph* Robin Vidgeon *m* Anthony Hopkins *pd* Eileen Diss *ed* Edward Mansell
☆ Anthony Hopkins, Leslie Phillips, Kate Burton, Gawn Grainger, Hugh Lloyd, Rhoda Lewis, Menna Trussler, Rhian Morgan
'It is very much an actor's piece. Lines are delivered rather than spoken, and the cast frequently freezes into a tableau, everyone staring rigidly into the distance.' – *George Perry*

Aunt Julia and The Scriptwriter: see *Tune In Tomorrow*

Auntie Mame *
US 1958 144m Technirama
Warner (Morton da Costa)

An orphan boy is adopted by his volatile extravagant aunt, whose giddy escapades fill his memory of the twenties and thirties.
A rather unsatisfactory star revue from a book and play later turned into a musical, Mame (qv). A few splendid moments, otherwise rather dull and irritating.
w Betty Comden, Adolph Green *play* Jerome Lawrence, Robert E. Lee *novel* *Patrick Dennis*
d Morton da Costa *ph* Harry Stradling
m Bronislau Kaper *ad* Malcolm Bert *ed* William Ziegler
☆ *Rosalind Russell*, Forrest Tucker, *Coral Browne*, Fred Clark, Roger Smith, Patric Knowles, Peggy Cass, Lee Patrick, Joanna Barnes
best picture; Harry Stradling; Rosalind Russell; Peggy Cass; art direction; editing

The Aurora Encounter
US 1985 90m colour
New World (Jim McCullough)

In the 1890s, an alien visits a small Texas town in a flying saucer.
Unexciting, soft-centred family fare, featuring Elam in his later incarnation as an avuncular buffoon.
w Jim McCullough Jnr *d* Jim McCullough *ph* Joseph Wilcots *m* Ron F. Dilulio *pd* Drew E. Hunter *ed* Sheri Galloway
☆ Jack Elam, Peter Brown, Carol Bagdasarian, Dottie West, Mickey Hays, Spanky McFarland

Aus Dem Leben Der Marionetten *
West Germany 1980 104m colour/bw
ITC/Personafilm (Horts Wendlandt, Ingrid Bergman, Richard Brick)

aka: *From the Life of Marionettes*
An inquiry into the killing of a prostitute by a rich businessman.
A film somehow very typical of its director, but far from his most interesting work.
wd Ingmar Bergman *ph* *Sven Nykvist* *m* Rols Wilhelm *pd* Rolf Zehetbauer *ed* Petra von Oelffen, Geri Ashur
☆ Robert Atzorn, Christine Buchegger, Martin Benrath
'In its unalloyed pessimism, its complete negation of hope, the film, stripped of the incidents, the excitements which have illumined the director's earlier work, is the purest of Bergman. He can go no farther.' – *Dilys Powell, Punch*

Aus Einem Deutschen Leben: see *Death Is My Trade*

Une Aussi Longue Absence *
France/Italy 1961 96m bw Dyaliscope
Procinex/Lyre/Galatea (Jacques Nahum)
aka: *The Long Absence*
A widow who owns a Paris café meets an amnesiac tramp who may be her long-lost husband.
Romantic character study which just about comes off thanks to good acting.
w Marguerite Duras, Gérald Jarlot *d* *Henri Colpi* *ph* Marcel Weiss *m* Georges Delerue
☆ *Alida Valli*, Georges Wilson, Jacques Harden

Austerlitz
France/Italy/Liechtenstein/Yugoslavia 1959 166m Eastmancolor Dyaliscope
CFPI/SCLF/Galatea/Michael Arthur/Dubrava (Alexander and Michael Salkind)
aka: *The Battle of Austerlitz*
Napoleon defeats the Austro-Russian army.
Elaborate pageant with a hopelessly cluttered narrative line arranged to take in a roster of guest stars who merely distract from the central theme.
wd Abel Gance *ph* Henri Alekan, Robert Juillard *m* Jean Ledrut
☆ *Pierre Mondy*, Jean Mercure, Jack Palance, Orson Welles, Michel Simon, Jean-Louis Trintignant, Martine Carol, Leslie Caron, Claudia Cardinale, Rossano Brazzi, Ettore Manni, Jean Marais, Vittorio de Sica
'Strictly for connoisseurs of Gance's brand of hyperbolic history.' – *Peter John Dyer, MFB*

'What do you call a swinger old enough to be your father? Daddy!'

Austin Powers in Goldmember
US 2002 94m Foto-Kem Panavision
Entertainment/New Line/Gratitude/Team Todd/Moving Pictures (Suzanne Todd, Jennifer Todd, Demi Moore, Eric McLeod, John Lyons, Mike Myers)

A swinging secret agent travels in time to prevent Dr Evil from swamping the world.
Amiable spy spoof, though most of the jokes are of a rude and rudimentary kind; in the end, though, its childish glee wears you down.
w Mike Myers, Michael McCullers *d* Jay Roach *ph* Peter Deming *m* George S. Clinton *pd* Rusty Smith *ed* Jon Poll, Greg Hayden *cos* Deena Appel
☆ Mike Myers (Austin Powers/Dr Evil/Goldmember/Fat Bastard), Beyonce Knowles (Foxxy Cleopatra), Seth Green (Scott Evil), Michael York (Basil Exposition), Robert Wagner (Number Two), Mindy Sterling (Frau Farbissina), Verne Troyer (Mini Me), Michael Caine (Nigel Powers)
'An absolute treasure trove of laughs.' – *Neil Roberts, Sun*
'An aimless, scatological pastiche.' – *Philip French, Observer*

'"Shall we shag now, or shall we shag later?" – Austin Powers'

Austin Powers: International Man of Mystery **

US 1997 89m CFI color Panavision
Guild/New Line/Capella/KC Medien/Eric's Boy (Suzanne Todd, Demi Moore, Jennifer Todd, Mike Myers)

A cryogenically frozen spy from the 60s is thawed out to deal with a master criminal who threatens the peace of the world.

Very late in the day comes a spoof of James Bond and films of swinging London that manages to be engaging, mainly by contrasting the fashions of yesterday with those of today.

w Mike Myers *d* Jay Roach *ph* Peter Deming *m* George S. Clinton *pd* Cynthia Charette *ed* Debra Neil-Fisher

☆ Mike Myers (Austin Powers/ Dr Evil), Elizabeth Hurley (Vanessa Kensington), Michael York (Basil Exposition), Mimi Rogers (Mrs Kensington), Robert Wagner (Number Two), Seth Green (Scott Evil), Fabiana Udenio (Alotta Fagina), Charles Napier

'For noise, enthusiasm and silliness, Austin Powers is a bit of a gas.' – *Richard Williams, Guardian*

† The film cost $17m and took $54m at the US box-office.

make-up (Michele Burke, Mike Smithson)

'First he fought for the Crown. Now he's fighting for the Family Jewels.'

Austin Powers: The Spy Who Shagged Me *

US 1999 95m DeLuxe Super 35
New Line/Eric's Boy/Moving Pictures/Team Todd (Suzanne Todd, Jennifer Todd, Demi Moore, Eric McLeod, John Lyons, Mike Myers)

A secret agent goes back in time to recover his lost mojo.

The mixture is much as before, though with a greater preponderance of fart jokes, and a few engagingly silly moments. This time around, audiences who had stayed away from the first Powers film flocked to see this one.

w Mike Myers, Michael McCullers *d* Jay Roach *ph* Ueli Steiger *m* George S. Clinton *pd* Rusty Smith *ed* Jon Poll, Debra Neil-Fisher

☆ Mike Myers (Austin Powers/ Dr Evil/ Fat Bastard), Heather Graham (Felicity Shagwell), Michael York (Basil Exposition), Robert Wagner (Number Two), Rob Lowe (Young Number Two), Seth Green (Scott Evil), Mindy Sterling (Frau Farbissina), Verne J. Troyer (Mini-Me), Elizabeth Hurley (Vanessa), Kristen Johnston (Ivana Humpalot), Gia Carides (Robin Swallows)

'Tickles the funny bone ably enough for 95 minutes, yet feels like a quickie where it ultimately counts most: in the writing.' – *Dennis Harvey, Variety*

† The film also includes cameos by Burt Bacharach, Elvis Costello, Woody Harrelson, Charles Napier, Willie Nelson, Tim Robbins, and Jerry Springer.

†† It was the fourth most successful movie of 1999, grossing more than $250m at the box-office.

Australia

France/Belgium/Switzerland 1989 124m colour
Christian Bourgois/AO/Les Films de La Dreve/CAB/RTBF/Cine 5 (Marie Pascale Osterrieth)

A Belgium wool merchant, returning home from Australia to sort out a family problem, falls in love with a married woman.

Superior soap opera.

w Jean Gruault, Jacques Audiard, Jean-Jacques Andrien *d* Jean-Jacques Andrien *ph* Yorgos Arvanitis *m* Nicola Piovani *pd* Herbert Westbrook *ed* Ludo Troch

☆ Jeremy Irons, Fanny Ardant, Tcheky Karyo, Agnes Soral, Danielle Lyttleton, Helene Surgere

Austria 1700: see *Mark of the Devil*

Author, Author! *

US 1982 109m TVC Color
TCF (Irwin Winkler)

A Broadway playwright has worries about his wife's fidelity.

Like a sixties update of All About Eve, *this thin but sometimes witty sex-behind-the-footlights comedy had nothing to offer the general audience of the eighties, and one can only speculate as to why it was made. The acting does help, but it's a long haul.*

w Israel Horovitz *d* Arthur Hiller *ph* Victor J. Kemper *m* Dave Grusin *pd* Gene Rudolf *ed* William Reynolds

☆ Al Pacino, Dyan Cannon, Tuesday Weld, Bob Dishy, Bob Elliott

'In trying to dig a little deeper than the average Neil Simon comedy, it only prepares its own grave.' – *Observer*

'A day without sex is a day wasted.'

Auto Focus *

US 2002 105m DeLuxe
Columbia TriStar/Good MachinePropaganda (Scott Alexander, Larry Karaszewski, Todd Rosken, Pat Dollard, Alicia Allain)

A happily married actor becomes a star in a TV sitcom and, under the influence of a video technician, turns to promiscuity and pornography.

Based on the life and murder of Bob Crane, star of Hogan's Heroes, this cautionary tale of sleazy, voyeuristic masculinity lacks resonance outside the US, where Crane was unknown, and never quite manages to convey a wider significance.

w Michael Gerbosi *book* The Murder of Bob Crane by Robert Graysmith *d* Paul Schrader *ph* Fred Murphy *m* Angelo Badalamenti *pd* James Chinlund *ed* Kristina Boden

☆ Greg Kinnear (Bob Crane), Willem Dafoe (John Carpenter), Rita Wilson (Anne Crane), Maria Bello (Patricia Crane), Ron Leibman (Lenny), Kurt Fuller (Werner Klemperer/Klink), Ed Begley Jnr (Mel Rosen)

'Ranks as a shrewd expose of recent Hollywood's slimy underside.' – *Todd McCarthy, Variety*

'Schrader's objectification of sad and stupid material is neither tragic nor transgressive. It is just undramatic and uninvolving.' – *Richard Corliss, Time*

† Crane played Colonel Robert Hogan in *Hogan's Heroes*, a TV sitcom set in a Nazi prisoner of war camp that ran on CBS from 1965-71.

Autobiography of a Princess **

GB 1975 59m colour
Contemporary/Merchant-Ivory (Ismail Merchant)

In London, the exiled daughter of a maharajah and her father's former English secretary watch ancient home movies and swap barbed reminiscences about India in the days of Empire.

A gently bitter look back in regret and disappointment, as two elderly people reinterpret the past to suit their own concerns.

w Ruth Prawer Jhabvala *d* James Ivory *ph* Walter Lassally *m* Vic Flick *ad* Jaquemine Charrot-Lodwidge *ed* Humphrey Dixon

☆ James Mason, Madhur Jaffrey, Keith Varnier, Diane Fletcher, Timothy Bateson, Johnny Stuart, Nazrul Rahman

'Undoubtedly Ivory's best film to date.' – *MFB*

Autobus ***

France 1991 98m colour
Artificial Eye/Les Productions Lazennec/FR3/SGGC/La Générale d'Images/Canal (Alain Rocca)

French title: *Aux yeux du monde*

A frustrated and unemployed youth hijacks a bus full of schoolchildren so that he can go to visit his girlfriend.

An unexpected and uplifting exploration of a familiar theme which manages to avoid all the conventional routes.

wd Eric Rochant *ph* Pierre Novion *m* Gérard Torikian *pd* Pascale Fenouillet *ed* Catherine Quesemand

☆ Yvan Attal, Kristin Scott-Thomas, Marc Berman, Charlotte Gainsbourg, Renan Mazeas

'Slight and well-meaning, and less incisive than it could be. But it is also much more appealing than its rather whimsical premise would suggest.' – *Verina Glaessner, Sight and Sound*

Automania 2000 **

GB 1963 10m Eastmancolor
Halas and Batchelor

New cars have the ability to reproduce themselves: city dwellers of the future consequently live in stationary vehicles piled on top of each other.

Amusing cartoon fantasy, neatly executed.

w Joy Batchelor *d* John Halas

Un Autre Homme, une Autre Chance: see *Another Man, Another Chance*

An Autumn Afternoon ***

Japan 1962 113m Agfa-Shochikucolor
Shochiku

original title: *Samma no Aji*

A widower, horrified by the thought of his daughter becoming an old maid by looking after him, is encouraged by his friends to find her a husband.

Ozu's last film, in which form matters as much as content, is an elegiac account of the disintegration of family life and the prospect of lonely old age.

w Kogo Noda, Yasujiro Ozu *d* *Yasujiro Ozu* *ph* Yuharu Atsuta *m* Kojun Saito *ad* Tatsuo Hamada *ed* Yoshiyasu Hamamura

☆ Shima Iwashita, Chishu Ryu, Keiji Sada, Mariko Okada, Shinichiro Mikami, Teruo Yoshida, Noriko Maki, Nobuo Nakamura, Eijiro Tono

Autumn Crocus

GB 1934 86m bw
ATP

A British schoolmistress on holiday falls for her Tyrolean innkeeper.

Difficult now to conceive the popularity in its day of this novelettish romance, which seems frozen in amber.

wd Basil Dean *play* C. L. Anthony

☆ Ivor Novello, Fay Compton, Jack Hawkins, Diana Beaumont, Muriel Aked, George Zucco

'He fell in love for the first time... she fell in love forever.'

Autumn in New York

US 2000 103m DeLuxe
MGM/Lakeshore (Amy Robinson, Gary Lucchesi, Tom Rosenberg)

A middle-aged playboy-restaurateur falls for a 22-year-old woman with a fatal illness.

Glutinous romantic drama that trivialises everything it touches.

w Allison Burnett *d* Joan Chen *ph* Changwei Gu *m* Gabriel Yared *pd* Mark Friedberg *ed* Ruby Yang *cos* Carol Oditz

☆ Richard Gere (Will Keane), Winona Ryder (Charlotte Fielding), Anthony LaPaglia (John), Elaine Stritch (Dolly), Vera Farmiga (Lisa), Sherry Stringfield (Sarah), Jill Hennessy (Lynn)

'An all-stops-out love story with uncommon intelligence and honesty.' – *Kevin Thomas, Los Angeles Times*

'Not a bad picture, just utterly banal.' – *Emanuel Levy, Variety*

† The film cost $40m and took $38m at the US box office.

'In the dark, when I feel his heart pounding against mine – is it love? or frenzy? or terror?'

Autumn Leaves *

US 1956 108m bw
Columbia/William Goetz

A middle-aged spinster marries a young man who turns out to be a pathological liar and tries to murder her.

Skilfully tailored star vehicle for female audiences.

w Jack Jevne (Jean Rouveral), Lewis Meltzer, Robert Blees *d* Robert Aldrich *ph* Charles Lang *m* Hans Salter

☆ *Joan Crawford*, Cliff Robertson, Lorne Greene, Vera Miles, Ruth Donnelly, Shepperd Strudwick

† Screenwriter Hugo Butler was excluded from the credits because he was blacklisted at the time.

Autumn Moon **

Hong Kong/Japan 1992 108m colour
ICA/Trix (Clara Law/Fong Ling Ching)

original title: *Qiuyue*

A Japanese youth in Hong Kong forms a friendship with a young girl, soon to emigrate to Canada to be with her family, and her grandmother who has to remain behind.

Charming, understated exploration of uprooted lives and uncertain futures.

w Fong Ling Ching *d* *Clara Law* *ph* Tony Cheung *m* Lau Lee Tat *ad* Timmy Yip *ed* Fong Ling Ching

☆ Masatoshi Nagase, Li Pui Wei, Maki Kiuchi, Choi Siu Wan, Suen Ching Hung, Sung Lap Yeung

'A way of life is seen to be tragically on the wane. Clara Law's fascinating movie catches its dying glow with engrossing sensitivity.' – *Tom Hutchinson, Film Review*

Autumn Sonata *

Sweden/West Germany/GB 1978 97m colour
ITC/Personafilm (Ingmar Bergman)

When her lover dies, a concert pianist visits the daughter she has not seen for many years.

Typically Bergmanesque, understated conversation piece with no obvious happy ending for anybody.

wd Ingmar Bergman *ph* Sven Nykvist *m* Chopin, Handel, Bach

☆ *Ingrid Bergman*, Liv Ullmann, Halvar Bjork

'Professional gloom.' – *Time*

'It fills these middle-class rooms with the deep music of conflict and reconciliation that must strike home to any audiences in any culture or society.' – *Jack Kroll, Newsweek*

script; Ingrid Bergman

An Autumn Tale: see *Conte D'Automne*

Aux yeux du monde: see *Autobus*

'Six million tons of icy terror!'

Avalanche

US 1978 91m Metrocolor
New World (Roger Corman)

Snow threatens holidaymakers at a ski lodge.

A disaster movie which, while quite competent in most ways, is no better than TV movies of this kind, especially as it resorts for its climaxes to scratched old stock film.

w Claude Pola, Corey Allen *d* Corey Allen *ph* Pierre-William Glenn *m* William Kraft

☆ Rock Hudson, Mia Farrow, Robert Forster, Jeanette Nolan, Rick Moses, Steve Franken, Barry Primus

'The Fast Track For All-Star Adventure.'

Avalanche Express

Eire 1979 88m DeLuxe Panavision
TCF/Lorimar (Mark Robson)

Spies of all nations converge on a train from Milan to Rotterdam.

Fitfully amusing hodgepodge which had to be finished off in a hurry following the death of its star and director in mid-production.

w Abraham Polonsky *novel* Colin Forbes *d* Mark Robson *ph* Jack Cardiff *m* Allyn Ferguson

☆ Robert Shaw, Lee Marvin, Linda Evans, Maximilian Schell, Mike Connors, Joe Namath, Horst Buchholz

'The most impressive work of montage to emerge from a big-budget adventure movie.' – *Richard Combs, MFB*

'Pell-mell direction and editing perform a precarious, oddly suspenseful balancing act.' – *Sight and Sound*

Les Avaleuses: see *Female Vampire*

Avalon **

US 1990 128m Technicolor
Columbia TriStar/Baltimore Pictures (Mark Johnson, Barry Levinson)

The lives and good times over half-a-century of an immigrant family in Baltimore.

Sprawling, episodic and too stolid for its ambitions, but with enjoyable moments from the ensemble cast.

wd Barry Levinson *ph* Allen Daviau *m* Randy Newman *pd* Norman Reynolds *ed* Stu Linder

☆ Armin Mueller-Stahl, Elizabeth Perkins, Joan Plowright, Kevin Pollak, Aidan Quinn, Leo Fuchs, Eve Gordon, Lou Jacobi

'A lifeless experience devoid of a central conflict or purpose ... The film is mostly a celebration of the mundane, and, while watching grandma and grandpa bicker at the dinner table may spur a fond glimmer of recognition, it's a wispy premise on which to hang this sort of lavish undertaking.' – *Variety*

'This movie is an elegy to a mythical past. That's probably why people emerge from the theatre sniffling.' – *Pauline Kael, New Yorker*

Barry Levinson (as writer); Allen Daviau; Randy Newman; costume design (Gloria Gresham)

'When someone knocks at your door and says "Permesso?", be careful before you say...'

Avanti! **

US 1972 144m DeLuxe
UA/Mirisch/Phalanx/Jalem (Billy Wilder)

A young American goes to Ischia to collect the body of his father who has died on holiday. He finds that the fatal accident had also killed his father's mistress, and amid overwhelming bureaucratic problems proceeds to fall in love with her daughter.

Absurdly overlong black comedy, with compensations in the shape of a generally witty script and some fine breakneck sequences of culminating confusion.

w Billy Wilder, I. A. L. Diamond play Samuel Taylor *d Billy Wilder ph* Luigi Kuveiller *m* Carlo Rustichelli

☆ Jack Lemmon, Juliet Mills, Clive Revill, Edward Andrews, Gianfranco Barra

'A movie flatter than a pizza.' – *Donald J. Mayerson, Cue*

Avanti-Popolo

Israel 1986 88m colour
TTG/Kastel Communications (Rafi Bukaee)

In the final hours of the Six Day War between Israel and Egypt in 1967, two Egyptian conscripts flee towards the safety of the Suez Canal.

Drama on the futility of war that lacks the performances to compensate for its snail-like pace, or the style to accommodate its mix of comedy and death.

wd Rafi Bukaee *ph* Yoav Kosh *m* Uri Ofir *ad* Ariel Glazer *ed* Zohar Sela

☆ Salim Daw, Suheil Haddad, Dani Roth, Dani Segev, Tuvya Gelber

The Avenger: see *Texas Addio*

The Avengers: see *The Day Will Dawn (1942)*

'She's Peel. He's Steed. Their world is a dangerous place. And they love it.'
'Saving The World In Style.'
'Two Amazing Secret Agents. One Diabolical Madman. Conditions Are Dark. The Forecast Is Deadly. Tea, Anyone?'

The Avengers

US 1998 89m Technicolor
Warner (Jerry Weintraub)

A secret agent foils a mad meteorologist's plans to hold the world to ransom by controlling its weather.

A complete dud, a direly boring thriller: miscast, mishandled and miserable. Nothing about it works, from its over-insistent score and over-elaborate plot to its unsophisticated attempt at urbanity.

w Don Macpherson *d* Jeremy Chechik *ph* Roger Pratt *m* Joel McNeely *pd* Stuart Craig *ed* Mick Audsley

☆ Ralph Fiennes, Uma Thurman, Sean Connery, Patrick MacNee, Jim Broadbent, Fiona Shaw, Eddie Izzard, Eileen Atkins, John Wood, Carmen Ejogo, Keeley Hawes

'About as inviting as a cement soufflé.' – *Philip French, Observer*

'An abomination. As the awful movie version of the brilliant TV classic of the Swinging '60s, it is worse than anyone ever imagined it might be.' – *Bruce Kirland, Toronto Sun*

'I heard actual cries of "Ugh!" on the way out of the door.' – *New York Times*

† The film, which cost some $60m, opened simultaneously in the UK and the US without being given a press show or a première. Of the 32 leading British and American critics who reviewed the film, only one liked it.

†† *The Avengers* was one of the most successful British TV series, starring Patrick MacNee as the bowler-hatted secret agent John Steed; his various female sidekicks included Diana Rigg as Emma Peel. It ran from 1961 to 1969.

'May God Have Mercy On His Enemies!'

The Avenging Boxer (dubbed)

Hong Kong 1973 90m colour
Alpha Motion Picture Co. (Jimmy Shaw)
US title: *Fearless Young Boxer*

A son learns kung fu so that he can avenge his father's death at the hands of a hired killer.

Standard martial-arts mayhem consisting of acrobatic fights interspersed with broad comedy, although it does manage a spectacular finale.

wd Jimmy Shaw *m* Chang Fang Gi *ad* David Wong *ed* W. C. Leung

☆ Peter Chang, Ca Sa Fa, Lee Lo Ling, Lee Kwun, Chan Wai Lau, Lung Fee

The Avenging Conscience *

US 1914 58m (24 fps) bw silent
Mutual

An elaboration of Poe's *The Tell Tale Heart* in which Griffith first shows his ability to control a feature-length movie, with many cinematic devices.

wd D. W. Griffith *ph* Billy Bitzer

☆ Henry B. Walthall, Blanche Sweet, Spottiswoode Aitken, Mae Marsh

L'Avenir d'Emilie: see *The Future of Emily*

Les Aventures de Rabbi Jacob

France/Italy 1973 94m Eastmancolor
Fox-Rank/Films Pomereu/Horse Film (Bernard Javal)
GB title: *The Mad Adventures of 'Rabbi' Jacob*

A French businessman with anti-Semitic views is forced by an Arab agitator on the run to impersonate a rabbi presiding at a Bar Mitzvah in Paris.

Broad comedy that raises a few laughs at the expense of xenophobia.

w Gérard Oury, Daniele Thompson, Josy Eisenberg *d* Gérard Oury *ph* Henri Decae *m* Vladimir Cosma *ad* Théo Meurisse *ed* Albert Jurgenson

☆ Louis de Funès, Suzy Delair, Marcel Dalio, Claude Giraud, Claude Piéplu, Renzo Montagnani

'Much loved in France, this comedy of errors has not travelled well and turns up in Britain looking painfully unfunny.' – *David McGillivray*

L'Aveu: see *The Confession*

The Aviator

US 1985 96m Metrocolor
MGM-UA/Mace Neufeld

In 1928, a spoiled rich girl is cared for by a sullen pilot when they crashland in the Sierras.

Drawn-out, actionless adventure concerning unattractive characters; it has been seen before in at least two TV movies.

w Marc Norman *novel* Ernest Gann *d* George Miller *ph* David Connell *m* Dominic Frontiere *pd* Brenton Swift *ed* Duane Hartzell

☆ Christopher Reeve, Rosanna Arquette, Jack Warden, Sam Wanamaker, Scott Wilson, Tyne Daly

'Doesn't fly.' – *Variety*

The Aviator's Wife *

France 1980 106m Eastmancolor (blown up from 16mm)
Les Films du Losange (Margaret Menegoz)
original title: *La Femme de L'Aviateur*

Anne and François are having an affair, but each has other entanglements.

Meticulously arranged conversations in this director's best style, but this time not seeming to amount to very much.

wd Eric Rohmer *ph* Bernard Lutic *m* Jean-Louis Valero

☆ Philippe Marlaud, Marie Rivière, Anne-Laure Maeury, Mathieu Carrière

'Does the aviator Christian's wife exist? It really does not matter: she is a formal device in a play of formalist devices.' – *Jill Forbes, MFB*

De Avonden: see *Evenings*

L'Avventura **

Italy/France 1960 145m bw
Cino del Duca/PCE/Lyre (Amato Pennasilico)

Young people on a yachting holiday go ashore on a volcanic island. One of them disappears; this affects the lives of the others, but she is never found.

Aimless, overlong parable with lots of vague significance; rather less entertaining than the later Picnic at Hanging Rock (qv), it made its director a hero of the highbrows.

w Michelangelo Antonioni, Elio Bartolini, Tonino Guerra *d Michelangelo Antonioni ph* Aldo Scavarda *m* Giovanni Fusco

☆ *Monica Vitti*, Lea Massari, Gabriele Ferzetti, Dominique Blanchar, James Addams, Lelio Luttazi

'A film of complete maturity, sincerity and creative intuition.' – *Peter John Dyer, MFB*

The Awakening

GB 1980 105m Technicolor
EMI/Orion (Robert Solo)

An obsessed archaeologist believes that the spirit of a long-dead Egyptian queen has entered into the soul of his daughter.

Unpersuasive and humourless mumbo jumbo from the same intractably complex novel that provided the basis for Blood from the Mummy's Tomb (qv).

w Allan Scott, Chris Bryant, Clive Exton *novel Jewel of the Seven Stars* by Bram Stoker *d* Mike Newell *ph* Jack Cardiff *m* Claude Bolling *pd* Michael Stringer

☆ Charlton Heston, Susannah York, Jill Townsend, Stephanie Zimbalist, Patrick Drury, Bruce Myers

'An almost total waste of the talents involved.' – *Sunday Times*

'It is difficult to imagine a film more likely to put you to sleep.' – *Guardian*

Awakening of the Beast: see *Ritual dos Sadicos*

Awakenings *

US 1990 121m Technicolor Panavision
Columbia TriStar (Walter F. Parkes, Lawrence Lasker)

A young doctor discovers a treatment that temporarily revives sufferers from encephalitis who have been in a state of suspended animation for 30 years or more.

Over-sentimentalized treatment of a fascinating subject, too insistent on leaving its audience feeling good.

w Steven Zaillian *book* Oliver Sacks *d* Penny Marshall *ph* Miroslav Ondricek *m* Randy Newman *pd* Anton Furst *ed* Jerry Greenberg, Battle Davis

☆ Robert De Niro, Robin Williams, Julie Kavner, Ruth Nelson, John Heard, Penelope Ann Miller, Alice Drummond, Judith Malina, Barton Heyman, Max von Sydow

'The movie douses everything fiery. Everything is shaped for you to root for the resurrections, and then nothing much happens ... the humanism is so pallid that the awakened patients don't seem very different from the way they were in their comatose states.' – *Pauline Kael, New Yorker*

Academy Award nomination: best picture; Robert De Niro; Steven Zaillian

Away All Boats

US 1956 114m Technicolor Vistavision
U-I (Howard Christie)

Adventures of a small transport boat during the Pacific War.

Competent drum-beating war heroics with expensive action sequences.

w Ted Sherdeman *novel* Kenneth M. Dodson *d* Joseph Pevney *ph* William Daniels, Clifford Stine *m* Frank Skinner *ed* Ted J. Kent

☆ Jeff Chandler, George Nader, Julie Adams, Lex Barker, Keith Andes, Richard Boone, Frank Faylen

The Awful Dr Orloff

Spain 1962 88m bw
Hispamer (Serge Newman, Leo Lax)
original title: *Gritos en la Noche*

A mad doctor tries to restore his disfigured daughter to beauty by kidnapping and skinning young women.

Sleazy ill-made horror, notable only for being the first of a sequence of films featuring the awful doctor.

wd Jesús Franco *novel* David Kuhne *ph* Godofredo Pacheco

☆ Howard Vernon, Conrado Sanmartin, Perla Cristal, Diana Lorys, Ricardo Valle

'An utterly dreadful movie.' – *The Dark Side*

The Awful Truth ***

US 1937 90m bw
Columbia (Leo McCarey)

A divorcing couple endure various adventures which lead to reconciliation.

Classic crazy comedy of the thirties, marked by a mixture of sophistication and farce and an irreverent approach to plot.

w Vina Delmar *play* Arthur Richman *d Leo McCarey ph* Joseph Walker *md* Morris Stoloff *ed* Al Clark

☆ *Irene Dunne, Cary Grant, Ralph Bellamy*, Alexander D'Arcy, Cecil Cunningham, Molly Lamont, Esther Dale, Joyce Compton

IRENE DUNNE: 'You've come back and caught me in the truth, and there's nothing less logical than the truth.'

CARY GRANT: 'In the spring a young man's fancy lightly turns to what he's been thinking about all winter.'

'Fast, smart comedy that will please everywhere and do strong general biz.' – *Variety*

'The funniest picture of the season.' – *Otis Ferguson*

'Among the ingredients the raising powder is the important thing and out of the oven comes a frothy bit of stuff that leaves no taste in the mouth and is easy on the stomach.' – *Marion Fraser, World Film News*

'Delightfully effective entertainment.' – *Time Out, 1985*

† Remade 1953 as *Let's Do It Again* (qv).

Academy Award: Leo McCarey

Academy Award nomination: best picture; script; Irene Dunne; Ralph Bellamy; Al Clark

'In A World Of Make Believe Stella Is About To Discover The Difference Between True Love ... And Real Life.'

An Awfully Big Adventure *

GB 1994 112m Metrocolor
TCF/Portman/British Screen/BBC/Wolfhound (Hilary Heath, Philip Hinchcliffe)

In 1947, a gullible 15-year-old girl joins a rundown Liverpool repertory theatre, where she falls in love with its manipulative director and begins an affair with its flamboyant leading actor.

Good on atmospherics and the detail of backstage bitchery and theatrical ambition, but flawed in its wider ambitions of a girl growing to maturity in circumstances of betrayal, this is a broken-backed melodrama: the first half belongs to Grant's ambiguous director, the second to Rickman's reckless leading man, but the innocent girl at its centre is not a strong enough character to hold it together as a satisfying whole.

w Charles Wood *novel* Beryl Bainbridge *d* Mike Newell *ph* Dick Pope *m* Richard Hartley *pd* Mark Geraghty *ed* Jon Gregory

☆ Georgina Cates, Hugh Grant, Alan Rickman, *Peter Firth*, Alun Armstrong, Prunella Scales, Rita Tushingham, Edward Petherbridge, Nicola Pagett, Alan Cox, Carol Drinkwater, Clive Merrison, Gerard McSorley

'The unsympathetic characters and oblique storytelling make large demands on the audience, limiting the film's appeal essentially to art-house aficionados.' – *Colin Brown, Screen International*

Ay, Carmela! **

Spain/Italy 1990 103m colour
Iberoamericana/Ellepi/Television Espanola (Andres Vicente Gomez)

During the Spanish Civil War a trio of vaudeville performers entertaining the Republican troops are taken prisoner by the Nationalist army.

Very watchable but flawed political film with a bungled ending.

w Rafael Azcona, Carlos Saura *play* José Sanchis Sinisterra *d* Carlos Saura *ph* José Luis Alcaine *m* Alejandro Masso *ad* Rafael Palmero *ed* Pablo G. Del Amo

☆ Carmen Maura, Andres Pajares, Gabino Diego, Maurizio de Razza, José Sancho, Mario de Candia

B.F.'s Daughter *
US 1948 106m bw
MGM (Edwin A. Knopf)
GB title: *Polly Fulton*
The wife of a penniless lecturer secures her husband's rise to fame without his knowing that she is the daughter of a millionaire.
Solid upper-class romantic drama with a touch of Peg's Paper.
w Luther Davis *novel* John P. Marquand *d* Robert Z. Leonard *ph* Joseph Ruttenberg *m* Bronislau Kaper
☆ Barbara Stanwyck, Van Heflin, Charles Coburn, Richard Hart, Keenan Wynn, Margaret Lindsay, Spring Byington, Marshall Thompson

BMX Bandits
Australia 1984 90m colour
Panavision
Rank/BMX/Nilsen (Tom Broadbridge, Paul Davies)
Bike enthusiasts become unpopular when they cause havoc in the streets, but become heroes when they capture bank robbers.
Lively action piece with unacceptable behaviour followed by reformation and an old-fashioned moral for early teenagers.
w Patrick Edgeworth *story* Russell Hagg *d* Brian Trenchard-Smith *ph* John Seale *m* Colin Stead, Frank Strangio *pd* Ross Major *ed* Alan Lake
☆ David Argue, John Ley, Nicole Kidman, Bryan Marshall, Angelo d'Angelo

'Trouble never looked so good.'
B. Monkey
GB/US 1998 90m Technicolor
Buena Vista/Miramax/Scala/Synchronistic (Colin Vaines, Stephen Woolley)
A staid London infant schoolteacher begins an affair with an impulsive Italian jewel thief, who wants a different life.
A bit of a mess: a romantic thriller of unremitting unreality, cut to the bone, with no spark between its two unlikely lovers; lacking any emotional centre, it tries for irony and misses.
w Michael Thomas, Michael Radford, Carole King *novel* Andrew Davies *d* Michael Radford *ph* Ashley Rowe *m* Jennie Muskett *pd* Sophie Becker *ed* Joelle Hache
☆ Asia Argento (Beatrice), Jared Harris (Alan), Rupert Everett (Paul), Jonathan Rhys Meyers (Bruno), Tim Woodward (Frank), Ian Hart (Steve), Julie T. Wallace (Mrs Sturge), Bryan Pringle (Goodchild), Clare Higgins (Cherry)
'As an offbeat time-filler, with one's critical faculties on hold, the picture is an entertaining enough ride.' – *Derek Elley, Variety*
† The film was made in 1996 and not shown until the London Film Festival in 1998 in a version that ran for 115m. The current version was released direct to video in the UK.

B.S. I Love You
US 1971 98m DeLuxe
Motion Pictures International/Fox (A. M. Broidy)
A director of TV commercials is beset by passionate women.
Tiresomely trendy sex comedy with a visual style that never lets up.
wd Steven Hilliard Stern *ph* David Dans *m* Jimmy Dale, Mark Shekter
☆ Peter Kastner, Joanna Cameron, Louise Sorel, Gary Burghoff, Joanna Barnes, Richard B. Shull
† The initials in the title are short for bullshit.

Ba Mua: see *Three Seasons*

Ba Wang Bie Ji: see *Farewell My Concubine*

Baara
Mali 1979 93m colour
Souleymanne Cissé Productions
A factory owner orders the killing of his manager for calling a meeting of workers to improve their conditions.
A slice of African industrial life, contrasting the lives of the rich and corrupt with the poor and exploited.
wd Souleymane Cissé *ph* Etienne Carton de Grammont *m* Lamine Konté
☆ Balla Moussa Keita, Baba Niaré, Bubakar Keita, Umu Diarra, Ismaila Sarr, Umir Kone

Bab El Hadid: see *Cairo Station*

Bab el-Oued City *
Algeria/France 1994 93m colour
Les Matins/Flash Back/La Sept/ZDF/Thelma (Tahar Harhoura)
A carefree young baker finds himself driven from his home and the woman he loves by a gang of Moslem fundamentalists.
Well-made, low-key and topical drama of the current political unrest in Algiers, with a wider theme of bigotry and intolerance; its general appeal, though, is likely to be limited.
wd Merzak Allouache *ph* Jean-Jacques Mréjen *m* Rachid Bahri *ed* Marie Colonna
☆ Nadia Kaci, Mohamed Ourdache, Hassan Abdou, Mabrouk Ait Amara, Messaoud Hattou, Mourad Khen, Djamilia, Nadia Samir, Simone Vignote, Michel Such
'To date the most lucid depiction on film of the rise of Islamic fundamentalism in Algeria and its perils. It's essential viewing for anyone interested in getting insight into the people's reaction to this broad political change.' – *Deborah Young, Variety*
† The film won the International Critics' Prize at the 1994 Cannes Film Festival.

Babar: The Movie
Canada/France 1989 76m colour
Winstone/Nelvana/Ellipse (Patrick Loubert, Michael Hirsch, Clive A. Smith)
King Babar tells his children of his adventures as a young elephant.
Lacklustre story, with simple animation.
w Peter Sauder, J. D. Smith, John de Klein, Raymond Jaffelice, Alan Bunce *story* Peter Sauder, Patrick Loubert, Michael Hirsch *based on characters created by* Jean de Brunhoff, Laurent de Brunhoff *d* Alan Bunce *m* Milan Kymlicka *m/ly* Maribeth Solomon *pd* Ted Bastien *ad* Clive Powsey, Carol Bradbury *ed* Evan Landis
☆ Featuring the voices of Gordon Pinsent, Elizabeth Hanna, Lisa Yamanaka, Marsha Moreau, Bobby Beckon, Amos Crawley, Gavin Magrath, Sarah Polley

Babbitt *
US 1934 74m bw
Warner (Sam Bischoff)
Problems of a middle-aged man in a small American town.
A minor attempt to film a major novel: quite tolerable but lacking density.
w Mary McCall Jnr *novel* Sinclair Lewis *d* William Keighley *ph* Arthur Todd
☆ *Guy Kibbee, Aline MacMahon,* Claire Dodd, Maxine Doyle, Minor Watson, Minna Gombell, Alan Hale, Berton Churchill, Russell Hicks, Nan Grey
'Smooth, pleasant but trite.' – *Variety*
† Previously filmed in 1924 with Willard Louis.

The Babe
US 1992 115m DeLuxe
Universal (John Fusco)
Biopic of the life of the baseball player Babe Ruth.
An undistinguished film with little appeal outside America, although Goodman brings some individuality to his portrayal of the flawed hero.
w John Fusco *d* Arthur Hiller *ph* Haskell Wexler *m* Elmer Bernstein *pd* James D. Vance *ed* Robert C. Jones
☆ John Goodman, Kelly McGillis, Trini Alvarado, Bruce Boxleitner, James Cromwell, Peter Donat, Bernard Kates, Michael McGrady
'The thinly dramatised, overly episodic Babe Ruth biopic resembles a telepic that has lost its way to the big screen.' – *Variety*
† The film was released direct to video in Britain.

'A Little Pig Goes a Long Way.'
Babe ***
Australia 1995 94m colour
Universal/Kennedy Miller (George Miller, Doug Mitchell, Bill Miller)
An orphaned piglet is adopted by a sheepdog and decides that he wants to grow up and follow in his mother's pawprints.
Delightful, witty, clever and almost irresistible children's film with a wide appeal; the mid-Atlantic voices given the animals take a little getting used to, but otherwise it's a pleasure all the way.
w George Miller, Chris Noonan *novel* The Sheep-Pig by Dick King-Smith *d* Chris Noonan *ph* Andrew Lesnie *m* Nigel Westlake *pd* Roger Ford *ed* Marcus D'Arcy, Jay Friedkin
☆ James Cromwell, Magda Szubanski, Roscoe Lee Browne (narrator) and also the voices of Christine Cavanaugh, Miriam Margolyes, Danny Mann, Hugo Weaving
'A dazzling family entertainment with enormous charm and utilizing breathtaking technical innovation.' – *Leonard Klady, Variety*
visual effects
best picture; Chris Noonan; George Miller, Chris Noonan (screenplay adaptation); James Cromwell; Marcus D'Arcy, Jay Friedkin; Roger Ford

'In the heart of the city, a pig with heart.'
Babe: Pig in the City *
Australia 1998 97m Atlab
Universal (George Miller, Doug Mitchell, Bill Miller)
A hero for winning the sheepdog trials, a pig visits the city and rescues a motley collection of animals impounded by the authorities.
A muddled sequel that lacks the charm of the original; its approach to humour is laborious and overelaborate.
w George Miller, Judy Morris, Mark Lamprell *characters created by* Dick King-Smith *d* George Miller *ph* Andrew Lesnie *m* Nigel Westlake *pd* Roger Ford *ed* Jay Friedkin, Margaret Sixel *sp* Rhythm & Hues, Mill Film, Animal Logic Film, Neal Scanlan Studio
☆ Magda Szubanski, James Cromwell, Mary Stein, Mickey Rooney, Julie Godfrey and also the voices of: E. G. Daily, Danny Mann, Glenne Headly, Steven Wright, James Cosmo, Roscoe Lee Browne
'There is plenty of fun in this cinematic menagerie, consummate screen magic and a series of well-intentioned messages that sidestep the cloying and saccharine.' – *Leonard Klady, Variety*
† The film cost around $100m to make and market. Its failure at the box-office led to the departure of several top executives from Universal.
song 'That'll Do' (*m/ly* Randy Newman)

The Babe Ruth Story
US 1948 107m bw
Allied Artists (Roy del Ruth)
The biography of a baseball player who was thought of as something of a saint.
Dim, sentimental and faintly mystical biopic, throughout which the star presents his familiar image.
w Bob Considine, George Callahan *d* Roy del Ruth *ph* Philip Tannura, James Van Trees *m* Edward Ward
☆ William Bendix, Claire Trevor, Charles Bickford

Babes in Arms **
US 1939 96m bw
MGM (Arthur Freed)
The teenage sons and daughters of retired vaudevillians put on a big show.
Simple-minded backstage musical which marked the first enormously successful teaming of its two young stars.
w Jack McGowan, Kay Van Riper *Broadway show* Rodgers and Hart *ph* Ray June *m* Roger Edens, George Stoll *m/ly* Rodgers and Hart and others *d/ch* Busby Berkeley
☆ *Judy Garland, Mickey Rooney,* Charles Winninger, Douglas Macphail, Leni Lynn, June Preisser
'A topflight filmusical entertainment. It will click mightily in the key deluxers, and roll up hefty profits for exhibits in the subsequent runs and smaller situations.' – *Variety*
♫ 'Where or When'; 'Babes in Arms'; 'I Cried for You'; 'God's Country'; 'Good Morning'; 'You Are My Lucky Star'
Roger Edens, George Stoll; Mickey Rooney

Babes in Baghdad
US 1952 77m Exotic Color
UA (Danziger Brothers)
Harem ladies go on strike.
Embarrassing attempt at satire by stars who are over the hill and not helped by abysmal technique.
w Felix E. Feist, Joe Anson *d* Edgar G. Ulmer
☆ Paulette Goddard, Gypsy Rose Lee, Richard Ney, John Boles, Sebastian Cabot

Babes in Toyland **
US 1934 77m bw
Hal Roach
aka: *Wooden Soldiers*
aka: *March of the Wooden Soldiers; Laurel and Hardy in Toyland*
Santa Claus's incompetent assistants accidentally make some giant wooden soldiers, which come in useful when a villain tries to take over Toyland.
Comedy operetta in which the stars have pleasant but not outstanding material; the style and decor are however sufficient to preserve the film as an eccentric minor classic.
w Nick Grinde, Frank Butler *original book* Glen MacDonough *d* Gus Meins, Charles Rogers *ph* Art Lloyd, Francis Corby *m* Victor Herbert
☆ Stan Laurel, Oliver Hardy, Charlotte Henry, Henry Brandon, Felix Knight, Florence Roberts, Johnny Downs, Marie Wilson
'It is amusing enough to entertain older persons who remember when they were young.' – *Variety*

Babes in Toyland
US 1961 105m Technicolor
Walt Disney
The wicked Barnaby is foiled in his plans to get rid of Tom Piper so that he can marry Mary Contrary.
A misfiring remake, all charm and no talent apart from some excellent special effects at the climax. Bolger is miscast as the villain, and Sheldon and Calvin imitate Laurel and Hardy.
w Ward Kimball, Joe Rinaldi, Lowell S. Hawley *operetta* Victor Young, Glenn McDonough *d* Jack Donohue *ph* Edward Colman *m/ly* Victor Young; George Bruns, Mel Leven *md* George Bruns *ch* Tommy Mahoney *ad* Carroll Clark, Marvin Aubrey Davis *ed* Robert Stafford *sp* Eustace Lycett, Robert A. Mattey, Bill Justice, Xavier Atencio, Yale Gracey

film suitable for family viewing | VHS video-cassette for the British PAL system | VHS video-cassette for the British PAL system in wide screen-format | Video cassette in a computer-colourised version | American NTSC video-cassette | Laser disc

☆ Ray Bolger (Barnaby), Tommy Sands (Tom Piper), Annette Funicello (Mary Contrary), Tommy Kirk (Grumio), Gene Sheldon (Roderigo), Henry Calvin (Gonzorgo), Ed Wynn (The Toymaker), Kevin Corcoran (Boy Blue), Mary McCarty (Mother Goose)
♫ I Can't Do the Sum, Just a Toy, Floretta, Castle in Spain, We Won't Be Happy Till We Get It, Lemonade, Just a Whisper Away, March of the Toys, Toyland, The Workshop Song, Slowly He Sank into the Sea.
Academy Award nomination: George Bruns

Babes on Broadway **
US 1941 118m bw
MGM (Arthur Freed)
A sequel to *Babes in Arms*, in which the kids get to Broadway and share some disillusion.
Inflated and less effective than the original, but with good numbers.
w Fred Finklehoffe, Elaine Ryan *ph* Lester White *m/ly* Burton Lane, Ralph Freed *d/ch* Busby Berkeley
☆ Judy Garland, Mickey Rooney, Virginia Weidler, Ray Macdonald, Richard Quine, Fay Bainter
'Enough energy and enthusiasm to make older people wish they were young, and young people glad that they are.' – *MFB*
† The Virginia Weidler role was originally intended for Shirley Temple, but TCF wouldn't loan her.
♫ 'Babes on Broadway'; 'Anything Can Happen in New York'; 'How About You?'; 'Bombshell from Brazil'; 'Minstrel Show'; 'Blackout over Broadway'; 'FDR Jones'
Academy Award nomination: song 'How About You' (*m* Burton Lane, *ly* Ralph Freed)

Babette Goes to War
France 1959 103m Eastmancolor
Cinemascope
Iéna (Raoul Lévy)
original title: *Babette S'en Va-t-en Guerre*
In 1940 a French refugee girl is sent by British intelligence from London to Paris as bait in a plot to kidnap a German general and delay the Nazi invasion of England.
Witless war farce which goes on for ever.
w Raoul Lévy, Gérard Oury *d* Christian-Jaque *ph* Armand Thirard *m* Gilbert Bécaud
☆ Brigitte Bardot, Jacques Charrier, Hannes Messemer, Yves Vincent, Ronald Howard, Francis Blanche
'A kind of *Private's Progress* without comedians.' – *MFB*

Babette S'en Va-t-en Guerre: see *Babette Goes to War*

Babette's Feast **
Denmark 1987 103m Eastmancolor
Panorama/Nordisk/Danish Film Institute
A French refugee in 19th-century Norway wins 10,000 francs in a lottery and spends it all on preparing a sumptuous banquet for her Lutheran employers and their friends.
Ironic and elegant fable juxtaposing bacchanalian extravagance with narrow piety.
wd Gabriel Axel *story* Isak Dinesen *ph* Henning Kristiansen *m* Per Norgard *ad* Sven Wichman
☆ Stéphane Audran, Jean-Philippe Lafont, Jarl Kulle, Bibi Andersson, Bodil Kjer, Birgitte Federspiel
Academy Award: best foreign film
BAFTA: best foreign film

'Torture ... Terror ... It's A Nightmare You'll Never Forget!'
The Baby
US 1973 102m colour
Quintet (Milton Polsky, Abe Polsky)
A social worker becomes obsessed by one of her charges: a mentally retarded man who behaves like a one-year-old in a household dominated by his mad mother and two disturbed sisters.
Unpleasant low-budget shocker, with over-the-top performances and general grotesqueness.
w Abe Polsky *d* Ted Post *ph* Michael Margulies *m* Gerald Fried *ad* Michael Devine *ed* Dick Wormell, Bob Crawford Snr
☆ Anjanette Comer, Ruth Roman, Marianna Hill, Suzanne Zenor, Tod Andrews, Michael Pataki, Beatrice Manley Blau, David Manzy
'Ultimately, it seems a long walk round a very small sick joke.' – *Tom Milne, MFB*

The Baby and the Battleship
GB 1956 96m Eastmancolor
British Lion/Jay Lewis
Two sailors hide an Italian baby on their battleship.
Simple-minded lower decks farce, with lots of confusion and cooing over the baby, but not much to laugh at.
w Jay Lewis, Gilbert Hackforth-Jones, Bryan Forbes *d* Jay Lewis *ph* Harry Waxman *m* James Stevens
☆ John Mills, Richard Attenborough, André Morell, Bryan Forbes, Michael Howard, Lisa Gastoni, Ernest Clark, Lionel Jeffries, Thorley Walters
'In this British film the predicament is made splendidly funny.' – *Dilys Powell*

Baby Be Good: see *Brother Rat and a Baby*

Baby Blue Marine *
US 1976 90m Metrocolor
Columbia/Spelling-Goldberg (Robert LaVigne)
In 1943, a failed marine returns home and pretends to be a war hero.
Careful small-town drama with good period feel but not much dramatic punch: Hail the Conquering Hero *did it better.*
w Stanford Whitmore *d* John Hancock *ph* Laszlo Kovacs *m* Fred Karlin
☆ Jan-Michael Vincent, Glynnis O'Connor, Katherine Helmond, Dana Elcar, Bert Remsen, Richard Gere
'A rickety structure of strange events.' – *New York Post*

Baby Boom
US 1987 110m colour
UIP/MGM
The life of a busy executive changes when she acquires a small baby.
Moderately enjoyable comedy, though it lacks any particular distinction.
w Nancy Meyers, Charles Shyer *d* Charles Shyer *ph* William A. Fraker *m* Bill Conti *pd* Jeffrey Howard *ed* Lynzee Klingman
☆ Diane Keaton, Harold Ramis, Sam Wanamaker, Sam Shepard, James Spader, Pat Hingle, Britt Leach
'If there were justice in the world of entertainment, *Baby Boom* would be unwatchable. But Diane Keaton gives a smashing, glamorous performance that rides over many of the inanities.' – *Pauline Kael, New Yorker*

Baby Boy
US 2001 129m DeLuxe
Columbia/New Deal (John Singleton)
Tales of unmarried required love in South Central Los Angeles.
A drama that confronts the problems of masculine identity, single mothers and fatherless children in a black community; heavy-handed contrivance, though, robs it of much of its intended power.
wd John Singleton *ph* Charles E. Mills *m* David Arnold *pd* Keith Brian Burns *ed* Bruce Cannon
☆ Tyrese Gibson (Jody), Omar Gooding (Sweetpea), A.J. Johnson (Juanita), Taraji P. Henson (Yvette), Snoop Dogg (Rodney), Tamara LaSeon Bass (Peanut), Ving Rhames (Melvin)
'An amusing, engaging, well thought out and impressive picture.' – *Jim Smith, Film Review*

'19 years old and married ... but not really!'
Baby Doll **
US 1956 116m bw
Warner/Elia Kazan
In the deep South, the child wife of a broken-down cotton miller is seduced by her husband's revenge-seeking rival.
An incisive, cleverly-worked-out study of moral and physical decay; whether it was worth doing is another question, for it's a film difficult to remember with affection.
w Tennessee Williams *play 27 Wagonloads of Cotton* by Tennessee Williams *d* Elia Kazan *ph Boris Kaufman* *m* Kenyon Hopkins *ad* Richard Sylbert
☆ *Karl Malden, Eli Wallach, Carroll Baker*, Mildred Dunnock, Lonny Chapman
'Just possibly the dirtiest American-made motion picture that has ever been legally exhibited, with Priapean detail that might well have embarrassed Boccaccio.' – *Time*
'He views southern pretensions with sardonic humor, and builds an essentially minor story into a magnificently humorous study of the grotesque and the decadent.' – *Hollis Alpert*
'A droll and engrossing carnal comedy.' – *Pauline Kael, 1968*
'A film in which everything works: narration, casting, tempo, rhythm, dramatic tension.' – *Basil Wright, 1972*
† Another publicity tag read: 'Condemned by Cardinal Spellman!'
Academy Award nomination: script; Boris Kaufman; Carroll Baker; Mildred Dunnock
BAFTA: Eli Wallach (newcomer)

'She climbed the ladder of success – wrong by wrong!'
Baby Face **
US 1933 70m bw
Warner (Ray Griffith)
Amorous adventures of an ambitious working girl.
Sharp melodrama very typical of its time, with fast pace and good performances.
w Gene Markey, Kathryn Scola *story* Mark Canfield (Darryl F. Zanuck) *d* Alfred E. Green *ph* James Van Trees *ad* Anton Grot
☆ Barbara Stanwyck, George Brent, Donald Cook, Margaret Lindsay, Arthur Hohl, John Wayne, Henry Kolker, Douglass Dumbrille
'Blue and nothing else. It possesses no merit for general or popular appeal, is liable to offend the family trade and can't count on any juve attendance.
'...This is reputed to be a remake on the first print, which was considered too hot. Anything hotter than this for public showing would call for an asbestos audience blanket.' – *Variety*

Baby Face Harrington
US 1935 63m bw
MGM
A timid man is mistakenly identified as a public enemy, and chased by both cops and rival gangsters.
Thin but appealing comedy.
w Nunnally Johnson, Edwin Knopf *d* Raoul Walsh
☆ Charles Butterworth, Una Merkel, Nat Pendleton, Eugene Pallette, Donald Meek
'Weak satire, grievously overacted.' – *Variety*

Baby Face Morgan
US 1942 60m bw
Jack Schwartz/PRC
The son of a racketeer is made a figurehead by his father's old mob.
Curious comedy of non-violent crime; also non-entertaining.
w Edward Dein, Jack Rubin, Oscar Brodney *d* Arthur Dreifuss
☆ Richard Cromwell, Mary Carlisle, Robert Armstrong, Chick Chandler, Warren Hymer, Vince Barnett

'Don't see it unless your nerves are bullet proof!'
Baby Face Nelson *
US 1957 85m bw
UA/Fryman-ZS (Al Zimbalist)
Fragmentary account of the life of a thirties public enemy, with the star over the top and the technicians doing what they can on an obviously low budget.
w Irving Shulman, Daniel Mainwaring *d* Don Siegel *ph* Hal Mohr *m* Van Alexander
☆ Mickey Rooney, Cedric Hardwicke, Carolyn Jones, Chris Dark, Ted de Corsia, Leo Gordon, John Hoyt, Anthony Caruso, Jack Elam

Baby It's You *
US 1982 104m colour
Paramount/Double Play (Griffin Dunne, Amy Robinson)
In the sixties, a well-heeled high school girl is wooed and won by a greasy street sheikh with ambitions.
Curious sweet-and-sour romance with a determination to be modern; agreeable in parts but basically empty, and rather undermined by a torrent of rock music on the sound track.
wd John Sayles *story* Amy Robinson *ph* Michael Ballhaus *md* Joel Dorn *pd* Jeffrey Townsend
☆ Rosanna Arquette, Vincent Spano, Joanna Merlin, Jack Davidson, Nick Ferrari, Leora Dana

Baby Love
GB 1968 93m Eastmancolor
Avco/Avton/Michael Klinger (Guido Coen)
An orphaned nymphet causes trouble among the men in her foster home.
Ludicrous sexploiter which embarrasses a good cast and descends into bathos.
w Alastair Reid, Guido Coen, Michael Klinger *novel* Tina Chad Christian *d* Alastair Reid *ph* Desmond Dickinson *m* Max Harris
☆ Linda Hayden, Ann Lynn, Keith Barron, Derek Lamden, Diana Dors, Patience Collier, Dick Emery

The Baby Maker
US 1970 109m Technicolor
Robert Wise/National General (Richard Goldstone)
A freewheeling girl agrees to have a baby for a childless couple.
Stretched-out fable for our time which refrains from pointing a moral and is generally tastefully done but nevertheless outstays its welcome.
wd James Bridges *m* Fred Karlin, Tylwyth Kymry
☆ Barbara Hershey, Collin Wilcox-Horne, Sam Groom, Scott Glenn, Jeannie Berlin
Academy Award nomination: Fred Karlin, Tylwyth Kymry

The Baby of Macon **
GB/Netherlands/France/Germany 1993 122m colour Panavision
Allarts/UGC/La Sept/Cine Electra II/Channel 4/Filmstiftung/Canal (Kees Kasander)
In the 1650s, encouraged by a naïve and sadistic prince, a play about a miraculous child, exploited by his sister and the church, becomes all too real, and rape, death and dismemberment follow.
A puzzling and audacious work, visually sumptuous and frequently confusing in its mix of artifice and actuality, but original and intriguing as it explores the themes of art and its influence, the translation of experience into consumerism, alienation and voyeurism. Audiences are likely to love or hate the film, though at Cannes and elsewhere it mostly met with a hostile reception.
wd Peter Greenaway *ph* Sacha Vierny *m* Henry Purcell, Matthew Locke and others *pd* Jan Roelfs, Ben van Os *ed* Chris Wyatt
☆ Julia Ormond, Ralph Fiennes, Philip Stone, Jonathan Lacey, Don Henderson, Celia Gregory, Jeff Nuttall, Kathryn Hunter, Gabrielle Reidy, Jessica Stevenson, Frank Egerton
'An uneven film which, for all its formal excellence, is a major let-down.' – *Geoffrey Macnab, Sight and Sound*
'All fluff and no filling.' – *Variety*

Baby on Board
Canada 1992 90m colour
Rose & Ruby/WEN/Sandy Howard/ABC/Prism (Damian Lee)
A taxi driver's life becomes complicated after he finds in his cab the small daughter of a Mafia widow, who is on the run for accidentally shooting the hitman who mistakenly killed her husband.
A comedy that tries too hard to be amusing to be amusing.
w Damian Lee *story* Doug Moore *d* Francis A. Schaeffer *ph* Curtis Petersen *m* Ronald J. Weiss *ed* Douglas Caron, Allan Mestel
☆ Judge Reinhold, Carol Kane, Geza Kovacs, Alex & Holly Stapley, Conrad Bergschneider, Lou Pitoscias, Errol Slue

Baby – Secret of the Lost Legend
US 1985 95m Technicolor Supertechnirama
Touchstone (Jonathan T. Taplin)
Palaeontologists in the African jungle discover a family of living dinosaurs.
Technically and dramatically less than effective, this latter-day King Kong demonstrates yet again the Disney company's difficulties in hitting the right note for the modern family audience.
w Clifford and Ellen Green *d* B. W. L. Norton *ph* John Alcott *m* Jerry Goldsmith *sp* Philip Meador, Peter Anderson
☆ William Katt, Sean Young, Patrick McGoohan, Julian Fellowes

Baby Take a Bow *
US 1934 76m bw
Fox
An ex-convict is accused of theft, but his small daughter unmasks the real culprit.
Shirley Temple's first star vehicle was a solid enough commercial property to take her right to the top.
w Philip Klein, E. E. Paramore Jnr *d* Harry Lachman
☆ *Shirley Temple*, James Dunn, Claire Trevor, Alan Dinehart
'A pretty obvious and silly melodrama, but it has Shirley Temple, so it can go down in the books as a neat and sure b.o. hit.' – *Variety*

'The more he gets into trouble, the more he gets under her skin!'
Baby, the Rain Must Fall
US 1964 100m bw
Columbia/Pakula-Mulligan (Alan Pakula)
A parolee rejoins his wife and daughter in a Southern town, but his outbursts of violence separate them again.
Hard work by all concerned scarcely produces absorbing interest in this filmed play of the Tennessee Williams school.
w Horton Foote *play The Travelling Lady* by Horton Foote *d* Robert Mulligan *ph* Ernest Laszlo *m* Elmer Bernstein
☆ Steve McQueen, Lee Remick, Don Murray, Paul Fix, Josephine Hutchinson, Ruth White, Charles Watts

The Baby Vanishes: see *Broadway Limited*

'Friends 4-Ever.'
The Baby-Sitters Club
US 1995 94m colour
Columbia/Beacon/Scholastic (Jane Startz, Peter O. Almond)
A group of 11 year-old girls organise a summer day-camp.
Bland, slow-moving drama of small-town life, seen through rose-coloured lenses, the sort of cute movie that gives respectability a bad name.
w Dalene Young *books* Ann M. Martin *d* Melanie Mayron *ph* Willy Kurant *m* David Michael Frank *pd* Larry Fulton *ed* Christopher Greenbury
☆ Schuyler Fisk (Kristy), Bre Blair (Stacey), Rachael Leigh Cook (Mary Anne), Larisa Oleynik (Dawn), Tricia Joe (Claudia), Stacey Linn Ramsower (Mallory), Zelda Harris (Jessi), Vanessa Zima (Rosie Wilder), Brooke Adams (Elizabeth Thomas Brewer), Bruce Davison (Watson), Ellen Burstyn (Mrs Haberman), Peter Horton (Patrick)
'A warm, cuddly and earnest tale of modern youth.' – *Variety*
'The film's nature and even its title peg it as an ensemble work, and Mayron's group footage looks like crude camcording of a ninth-grade picnic.' – *Mike Clark, USA Today*

'When The Big City Called He Had To Answer.'
'Born To Go Wild!'
Baby's Day Out
US 1994 98m DeLuxe
TCF (John Hughes, Richard Vane)
A baby escapes from his kidnappers and leads them a chase across the city, using methods taken from his favourite book.
The Home Alone *formula, of cute kid, dim crooks and violent slapstick topped with sentimentality, fails to raise a laugh this time around.*
w John Hughes *d* Patrick Read Johnson *ph* Thomas Ackerman *m* Bruce Broughton *pd* Doug Kraner *ed* David Rawlins
☆ Joe Mantegna, Lara Flynn Boyle, Joe Pantoliano, Brian Haley, Cynthia Nixon, Fred Dalton Thompson, John Neville, Matthew Glave, Eddie Bracken
'A tired retread of past comic formulas played a pitch higher, a rhythm faster. It tries too hard to please and fails miserably.' – *Leonard Klady, Variety*

The Bacchantes
Italy/France 1961 96m colour 'Scope
Cino Del Duca/Vic Film/Lyre Film (Gian Paolo Bigazzi)
original title: *Le Baccanti*
Dionysius takes his revenge after King Pentheus bans his worship in his home city of Thebes.
Enjoyably silly mythological romp, with bacchantes looking as if they had stepped out of the pages of pin-up magazines.
w Giorgio Stegani, Giorgio Ferroni *play The Bacchae* by Euripides *d* Giorgio Ferroni *ph* Pier Ludovico Pavoni *m* Mario Nascimbene *ch* Herbert Ross *ad* Arrigo Equini
☆ Taina Elg, Pierre Brice, Alberto Lupo, Alessandro Panaro, Raf Mattioli, Akim Tamiroff

'One thousand brides. One hundred million dollars. Jimmie Shannon is about to discover the true value of love.'
The Bachelor
US 1999 101m DeLuxe Panavision
Entertainment/New Line/George Street
A bachelor, who must marry on his 30th birthday in order to inherit $100m, is pursued by hundreds of prospective brides.
A re-make of Buster Keaton's Seven Chances *(qv), but one singularly lacking in humour, romance and charm.*
w Steve Cohen *play Seven Chances* by Roi Copper Megrue *screenplay* Clyde Bruckman, Jean Havez, Joseph Mitchell *d* Gary Sinyor *ph* Simon Archer *m* David A. Hughes, John Murphy *pd* Craig Stearns *ed* Robert Reitano *cos* Terry Dresbach
☆ Chris O'Donnell (Jimmy Shannon), Renée Zellweger (Anne), Hal Holbrook (O'Dell), James Cromwell (Priest), Artie Lange (Marco), Edward Asner (Gluckman), Marley Shelton (Natalie), Sarah Silverman (Carolyn), Stacy Edwards (Zoe), Rebecca Cross (Stacey), Jennifer Esposito (Daphne), Katharine Towne (Monique), Peter Ustinov (Grandad), Mariah Carey (Ilana), Brooke Shields (Buckley)
'Crude, frantic yuppie farce.' – *New York Times*

The Bachelor and the Bobbysoxer ***
US 1947 95m bw
RKO (Dore Schary)
GB title: *Bachelor Knight*
A lady judge allows her impressionable young sister to get over her crush on an errant playboy by forcing them together.
Simple but unexpectedly delightful vehicle for top comedy talents, entirely pleasant and with several memorable moments.
w Sidney Sheldon *d* Irving Reis *ph* Robert de Grasse, Nicholas Musuraca *m* Leigh Harline
☆ *Cary Grant, Myrna Loy,* Shirley Temple, *Ray Collins,* Rudy Vallee, *Harry Davenport,* Johnny Sands, Don Beddoe
'Sure-fire stuff guaranteed to do no conceivable harm ... the audience laughed so loud I missed some of the lines.' – *Shirley O'Hara, New Republic*
Sidney Sheldon

Bachelor Apartment
US 1931 77m bw
RKO (William Le Baron)
A virtuous working girl in New York falls for a rich woman-chasing bachelor.
Mildly agreeable early talking romantic comedy.
w J. Walter Ruben, John Howard Lawson *d* Lowell Sherman *ph* Leo Tover
☆ Irene Dunne, Lowell Sherman, Mae Murray, Norman Kerry, Claudia Dell, Ivan Lebedeff
'It oversteps the reasonable limits of sophisticated art ... thus the film is doubtful for small towns.' – *Variety*

Bachelor Bait: see *Adventure in Baltimore*

Bachelor Father
US 1931 90m bw
MGM (B. P. Fineman)
A much-married elderly man visits his grown children.
Unremarkable star comedy of its day.
w Laurence E. Johnson *play* Edward Childs Carpenter *d* Robert Z. Leonard *ph* Oliver T. Marsh
☆ Marion Davies, C. *Aubrey Smith,* Ray Milland, Ralph Forbes, Halliwell Hobbes, Guinn Williams, David Torrence
'Where they have used the old hoke they have masked it with commendable skill.' – *Variety*

Bachelor Flat
US 1961 91m DeLuxe Cinemascope
TCF/Jack Cummings
An English professor at an American university is unrelentingly pursued by girls.
Flat one-joke comedy which simply hasn't the style to sustain itself.
w Frank Tashlin, Budd Grossman *play* Budd Grossman *d* Frank Tashlin *ph* Daniel L. Fapp *m* Johnny Williams
☆ Terry-Thomas, Richard Beymer, Tuesday Weld, Celeste Holm, Francesca Bellini, Howard McNear

Bachelor Girl Apartment: see *Any Wednesday*

Bachelor Girls: see *The Bachelor's Daughters*

Bachelor in Paradise
US 1961 109m Metrocolor Cinemascope
MGM/Ted Richmond
A famous writer of advice to the lovelorn settles incognito in a well-heeled Californian community to observe its social habits.
Mildly amusing satire is too frequently interrupted by unsuitable romantic interludes in this rather ill-considered star comedy.
w Valentine Davies, Hal Kanter *d* Jack Arnold *ph* Joseph Ruttenberg *m* Henry Mancini
☆ Bob Hope, Lana Turner, Janis Paige, Don Porter, Paula Prentiss, Jim Hutton, Virginia Grey, Reta Shaw, John McGiver, Agnes Moorehead
title song (*m*Henry Mancini, *ly* Mack David)

Bachelor Knight: see *The Bachelor and the Bobbysoxer*

'Just ten tiny fingers and ten tiny toes ... Trouble? Scandal? Gosh, nobody knows!'
Bachelor Mother ***
US 1939 82m bw
RKO (B. G. de Sylva)
A shopgirl finds an abandoned baby and is thought to be its mother; the department store owner's son is then thought to be the father.
Blithely-scripted comedy which stands the test of time and provided several excellent roles.
w Norman Krasna story Felix Jackson *d Garson Kanin ph* Robert de Grasse *m* Roy Webb
☆ *Ginger Rogers, David Niven, Charles Coburn,* Frank Albertson, E. E. Clive, Ernest Truex
'Carries some rather spicy lines aimed at the adult trade, but broad enough in implication to catch the fancy of general audiences ... a surprise laugh hit that will do biz generally and overcome hot weather box office lethargy.' – *Variety*
'An excellent comedy, beautifully done.' – *Richard Mallett, Punch*
'This is the way farce should be handled, with just enough conviction to season its extravagances.' – *New York Times*
† Remade as *Bundle of Joy* (qv).
Felix Jackson

Bachelor of Hearts
GB 1958 94m Technicolor
Rank/Independent Artists (Vivian A. Cox)
Adventures of a German student at Cambridge University.
Sometimes agreeable, sometimes annoying, especially when romance gets in the way of the possibilities for fun.
w Leslie Bricusse, Frederic Raphael *d* Wolf Rilla *ph* Geoffrey Unsworth *m* Hubert Clifford
☆ Hardy Kruger, Sylvia Syms, Ronald Lewis, Eric Barker, Newton Blick

The Bachelor Party ***
US 1957 93m bw
UA/Norma (Harold Hecht)
New York book-keepers throw a wedding eve party for one of their fellows, but drink only brings to the fore their own private despairs.
Though the last half-hour lets it down, most of this is a brilliantly observed social study of New York life at its less attractive, and the acting matches the incisiveness of the script.
w Paddy Chayefsky TV play Paddy Chayefsky *d* Delbert Mann *ph* Joseph LaShelle *m* Alex North
☆ *Don Murray, E. G. Marshall, Jack Warden,* Philip Abbott, Larry Blyden, Patricia Smith, Carolyn Jones
Carolyn Jones

Bachelor Party
US 1984 105m DeLuxe
Fox/Aspect Ratio/Twin Continental (Ron Moler, Bob Israel)
A bachelor party is beset by a series of disasters.
Crude, exploitative farce full of physical mess and tending to get most of its humour from the destruction of order and some teetering on the brink of pornography.
w Neal Israel, Pat Proft *story* Bob Israel *d* Neal Israel *ph* Hal Trussell *m* Robert Folk *ad* Kevin Conlin, Martin Price *ed* Tom Walls
☆ Tom Hanks, Tawny Kitaen, Adrian Zmed, George Grizzard, Barbara Stuart, Robert Prescott

The Bachelor's Daughters *
US 1946 90m bw
UA/Andrew Stone
GB title: *Bachelor Girls*
Four shopgirls and a floorwalker rent a Long Island house and pass themselves off as a wealthy family in order to lure suitable husbands for the girls.
Mildly amusing comedy with good performances.
wd Andrew Stone *ph* Theodor Sparkuhl *m* Heinz Roemheld
☆ Adolphe Menjou, Gail Russell, Claire Trevor, Billie Burke

Back Door to Heaven
US 1939 81m bw
Odessco/Paramount (William K. Howard)
A boy born on the wrong side of the tracks is prevented from going straight, and, having escaped execution for murder, is bumped off by gangsters.
Heavy-going indictment of society; too glum to work, it seems to have finished off the career of its talented director.
w John Bright, Robert Tasker *story William K. Howard d* William K. Howard
☆ Wallace Ford, Aline MacMahon, Stuart Erwin, Jimmy Lydon, William Harrigan, Bert Frohman
'Artistic drama, too heavy and slow-tempoed for general b.o.' – *Variety*
† William K. Howard also appears as the prosecuting attorney.

'Lost Together ... Locked Together In The Jungle.'
'As the Jivaro drums grew louder, love changed to fear, selfishness to tenderness, passion to pity.'
Back from Eternity
US 1956 97m bw
RKO (John Farrow)
An airliner is forced to crashland in headhunter country, and when repairs are made only five of the eight survivors can be carried.
Remake by the same producer-director of his own 1939 'B', Five Came Back, *this time to considerably less effect despite superior production.*
w Jonathan Latimer *d* John Farrow *ph* William Mellor *m* Franz Waxman
☆ Robert Ryan, Anita Ekberg, Rod Steiger, Phyllis Kirk, Gene Barry, Keith Andes, Beulah Bondi, Fred Clark, Cameron Prud'homme, Jesse White

Back from the Dead
US 1957 78m bw Regalscope
TCF/Regal (Robert Stabler)
A girl on honeymoon becomes possessed by the spirit of her husband's first wife.
Blithe Spirit played for real but getting just as many laughs, unintentional this time.

w Catherine Turney *novel The Other One* by Catherine Turney *d* Charles Marquis Warren *ph* Ernest Haller *m* Raoul Kraushaar
☆ Peggie Castle, Arthur Franz, Marsha Hunt, Don Haggerty

Back in Circulation
US 1937 80m bw
Warner
Girl news reporter wins her editor's attention by solving a murder.
Sub-Front Page melodrama, of no intrinsic interest.
w Warren Duff *story* Adela Rogers St. Johns *d* Ray Enright *ph* Arthur Todd *md* Leo F. Forbstein *ad* Hugh Reticker *ed* Clarence Kolster
☆ Pat O'Brien, Joan Blondell, Margaret Lindsay
'The newspaper boys, the goofy photographers and the hysterical city are on the murder trail, relentlessly pursuing the accused, telling coroners, district attorneys and defence counsel how to conduct their business.' – *Variety*

Back in the USSR
US 1991 87m DeLuxe
Warner/Largo/JVC/Mosfilm (Lindsay Smith, Ilmar Taska)
In Moscow, an American tourist becomes involved in murder and the theft of a priceless icon from a country church.
Involved and unconvincing thriller with enough twists and turns in the narrative to confuse anyone patient enough to watch it until the end.
w Lindsay Smith *d* Deran Sarafian *ph* Yuri Neyman *m* Les Hooper *pd* Vladimir Philippov *ed* Ian Crafford
☆ Frank Whaley, Roman Polanski, Natalya Negoda, Dey Young, Andrew Divoff, Brian Blessed, Ravil Issyanov
'The plot is contrived and lacklustre and the performances, with a few exceptions, profoundly lacking in presence. The only laughs are unintentional, and the thrills negligible.' – *James Keen, Film Review*

Back of Beyond
Australia 1995 85m colour
Imagine/AFFC/Back of Beyond/Peter Szabo/Tourist/ John Sexton
A diamond thief and his girlfriend are stranded in the desert, near a derelict garage, where a mechanic mourns the death of his sister.
An odd little ghost story about loss and love, lacking in much substance.
w Paul Leadon, A. M. Brooksbank, Richard J. Sawyer *original treatment* Michael Robertson *d* Michael Robertson *ph* Stephen Dobson *m* Mark Moffatt, Wayne Goodwin *pd* Ross Major *ed* Timothy Wellburn
☆ Paul Mercurio, Colin Friels, John Polson, Dee Smart, Bob Mazza

Back Roads
US 1981 95m DeLuxe Panavision
CBS Theatrical/Meta Films (Ronald Shedlo)
A hooker and an ex-boxer hitch-hike to California.
Tiresomely with-it update of It Happened One Night *(qv); the humour and romance of the original are preferable to this dollop of bad language, boring people and bed-hopping.*
w Gary DeVore *d* Martin Ritt *ph* John A. Alonzo *m* Henry Mancini
☆ Sally Field, Tommy Lee Jones, David Keith, Miriam Colon, Michael Gazzo
'Decidedly sticky, and instantly forgettable.' – *Guardian*

Back Room Boy *
GB 1942 82m bw
GFD/Gainsborough (Edward Black)
A timid meteorologist is sent to an Orkney lighthouse and unmasks a bunch of spies.
Fairly spirited star comedy of interest as a shameless rip-off of The Ghost Train *and* Oh Mr Porter, *whose plotlines are milked but not improved: note also that Askey took over Will Hay's discarded stooges.*
w Val Guest, Marriott Edgar *d* Herbert Mason *ph* Jack Cox
☆ Arthur Askey, Moore Marriott, Graham Moffatt, Googie Withers, Vera Frances, John Salew

Back Street *
US 1932 93m bw
Universal (Carl Laemmle Jnr)
A married man has a sweet-tempered mistress who effaces herself for twenty years.
Popular version of a sudsy bestselling novel.
w Gladys Lehman, Lynn Starling *novel* Fannie Hurst *d* John M. Stahl *ph* Karl Freund
☆ Irene Dunne, John Boles, June Clyde, George Meeker, ZaSu Pitts, Doris Lloyd
'Swell romance, a little tear-jerking, and a woman's picture – which means a money production.' – *Variety*

Back Street *
US 1941 89m bw
Universal (Bruce Manning)
Competent remake.
w Bruce Manning, Felix Jackson *d* Robert Stevenson *ph* William Daniels *m* Frank Skinner *ad* Seward Webb *ed* Ted J. Kent
☆ Margaret Sullavan, Charles Boyer, Richard Carlson, Frank McHugh, Tim Holt, Frank Jenks, Esther Dale, Samuel S. Hinds
Frank Skinner

Back Street *
US 1961 107m Technicolor
U-I/Ross Hunter/Carrollton
Glossy remake typical of its producer: unfortunately it fails to work because the heroine suffers too luxuriously.
w Eleanore Griffin, William Ludwig *d* David Miller *ph* Stanley Cortez *m* Frank Skinner *ad* Alexander Golitzen *ed* Milton Carruth
☆ Susan Hayward, John Gavin, Vera Miles, Virginia Grey, Charles Drake, Reginald Gardiner
'Though there is a lot to be said for this new version's thesis that one can be just as lonely in a series of apartments and lovers' nests apparently never less than a hundred yards wide, the illusion is quickly shattered the moment one gets the impression that the lovers prefer to keep much the same distance during their moments of passion.' – *Peter John Dyer*
'Ross Hunter has updated this old faithful and given it a contemporary lack of significance.' – *Hollis Alpert, Saturday Review*
'The bathrooms look like the lobby of the Beverly Hilton ... the fallen woman falls, not into the pit of shame, but into the lap of luxury.' – *Time*

Back to Bataan
US 1945 97m bw
RKO (Robert Fellows)
When Bataan is cut off, a Marine colonel organizes guerrilla resistance.
Modestly made and rather dislikeable flagwaver.
w Ben Barzman, Richard Landau *d* Edward Dmytryk *ph* Nicholas Musuraca *m* Roy Webb
☆ John Wayne, Anthony Quinn, Beulah Bondi, Fely Franquelli, Leonard Strong, Richard Loo, Philip Ahn, Lawrence Tierney, Paul Fix

Back to School
US 1986 94m DeLuxe
Orion/Paper Clip (Chuck Russell)
A millionaire enrols in university as a freshman so as to teach his son the ropes.
Crass and ineptly made comedy vehicle for a star with distinct limitations.
w Steven Kampmann, Harold Ramis, Will Porter, Peter Torokvei *d* Alan Metter *ph* Thomas E. Ackerman *m* Danny Elfman *pd* David Snyder *ed* David Rawlins
☆ Rodney Dangerfield, Sally Kellerman, Burt Young, Keith Gordon, Paxton Whitehead

Back to the Beach
US 1987 92m colour
Paramount (Frank Mancuso Jnr)
Former teenage surfers return to the beach in middle age and help kids with problems.
Not so bad as it sounds, but for cultists only.
w Peter Krikes, Steve Meerson, Christopher Thompson *d* Lyndall Hobbs *ph* Bruce Surtees *m* Steve Dorff *pd* Michael Helmy *ed* David Finfer
☆ Annette Funicello, Frankie Avalon, Connie Stevens, Lori Loughlin, Tommy Hinkley, Bob Denver, Jerry Mathers, Pee-wee Herman, Don Adams
'A wonderfully campy trip down pop culture's trash-filled memory lane.' – *Daily Variety*

Back to the Future ***
US 1985 116m Technicolor
Universal/Steven Spielberg (Bob Gale, Neil Canton)
With the help of a not-so-crazy scientist, a teenager goes back thirty years to make a man out of his dimwit father.
Lighthearted Twilight Zone *(qv) fantasy which certainly pleased the international multitudes.*
w Robert Zemeckis, Bob Gale d Robert Zemeckis *ph* Dean Cundey *m* Alan Silvestri *pd* Lawrence G. Paull *ed* Arthur Schmidt, Harry Keramidas
☆ *Michael J. Fox*, Christopher Lloyd, Crispin Glover, Lea Thompson, Claudia Wells
'Accelerates with wit, ideas, and infectious, wide-eyed wonder.' – *Variety*
original screenplay; song ('The Power of Love'); sound

Back to the Future II
US 1989 108m DeLuxe
UIP/Amblin Entertainment (Bob Gale, Neil Canton)
A scientist and his young friend discover, on their return from a trip to the future, that the present has been altered for the worse.
Extraordinarily raucous, confusingly plotted, poorly performed (rarely have actors aged so unconvincingly) sequel that amounts to little more than a trailer for the third part of the series.
w Bob Gale *story* Bob Gale, Robert Zemeckis *d* Robert Zemeckis *ph* Dean Cundey *m* Alan Silvestri *pd* Rick Carter *ad* Margie Stone McShirley *ed* Arthur Schimdt, Harry Keramidas
☆ Michael J. Fox, Christopher Lloyd, Lea Thompson, Thomas F. Wilson, Harry Waters Jnr, Charles Fleischer, Joe Flaherty

'They've saved the best trip to the last. But this time they may have gone too far.'

Back to the Future III **
US 1990 118m DeLuxe
UIP/Amblin (Bob Gale, Neil Canton)
A teenager travels back in time to rescue his friend, a scientist stranded in the Wild West.
Good-natured fun at the expense of classic Western movies.
w Bob Gale *story* Robert Zemeckis *d Robert Zemeckis* *ph* Dean Cundey *m* Alan Silvestri *pd* Rick Carter *ed* Arthur Schmidt, Harry Keramidas
☆ Michael J. Fox, Christopher Lloyd, Mary Steenburgen, Thomas F. Wilson, Lea Thompson, Elisabeth Shue, Matt Clark, Richard Dysart, James Tolkan
'Has a joyousness seldom seen on the screen these days, a sense of exuberance in the breaking of boundaries of time, space and genre.' – *Variety*

Backbeat *
GB 1993 100m Eastmancolor Panavision
Rank/Polygram/Scala/Channel 4 Films/Royal (Finola Dwyer, Stephen Woolley)
Stuart Sutcliffe, a promising young painter, plays with the Beatles in Hamburg, where he falls for a German photographer and decides his future is with art not rock.
A deft and enjoyable movie about the birth of the 60s and the Beatles, concentrating on the tragically short life of Sutcliffe, who died of a brain tumour in 1962.
w Iain Softley, Michael Thomas, Stephen Ward *d* Iain Softley *ph* Ian Wilson *m* Don Was *pd* Joseph Bennett *ed* Martin Walsh
☆ Sheryl Lee, Stephen Dorff, Ian Hart, Gary Bakewell, Chris O'Neill, Scot Williams, Kai Wiesinger, Jennifer Ehle
'Shrewd rather than clever, lively rather than memorable and possessed of just enough wit and heart to convince that it is essentially more than a nostalgia-stirring package.' – *Derek Malcolm, Guardian*
'Has quite a bit going for it in the way of cultural and musical history but lacks a crucial, heightened artistic quality and point of view that would have given it real distinction.' – *Variety*
music

Backdraft *
US 1991 136m DeLuxe Super 35
UIP/Trilogy/Imagine (Richard B. Lewis, Pen Densham, John Watson)
Two brothers track down an arsonist and expose corruption in the fire department.
Overheated, muddled melodrama saved from tedium by its fiery special effects.
w Gregory Widen *d* Ron Howard *ph* Mikael Salomon *m* Hans Zimmer *pd* Albert Brenner *ed* Daniel Hanley, Michael Hill *sp* Visual effects: Industrial Light and Magic. Pyrotechnics: Allen Hall
☆ Kurt Russell, William Baldwin, Robert De Niro, Donald Sutherland, Jennifer Jason Leigh, Scott Glenn, Rebecca DeMornay, Jason Gedrick, J. T. Walsh
'Visually, pic is often exhilarating, but it's shapeless and dragged down by corny, melodramatic characters and situations.' – *Variety*

Backfire
US 1949 90m bw
Warner (Anthony Veiller)
A war veteran solves the murder of which his best friend is accused.
Confusing murder mystery of a very familiar kind, adequately made but with no particular style. Flashbacks don't help.
w Larry Marcus, Ivan Goff, Ben Roberts *d* Vincent Sherman *ph* Carl Guthrie *m* Ray Heindorf *ad* Anton Grot
☆ Gordon MacRae, Virginia Mayo, Edmond O'Brien, Dane Clark, Viveca Lindfors, Ed Begley

Backfire
US 1987 91m colour
Virgin/ITC (Danton Rissner)
A Vietnam veteran with nightmares seems to be in the middle of a murder plot.
Too-murky thriller which takes an awful long time to come clean.
w Larry Brand, Rebecca Reynolds *d* Gilbert Cates *ph* Tak Fujimoto *m* David Shire *pd* Daniel Lomino *ed* Melvin Shapiro
☆ Karen Allen, Keith Carradine, Jeff Fahey, Bernie Casey, Dean Paul Martin

Background *
GB 1953 82m bw
Group Three (Herbert Mason)
US title: *Edge of Divorce*
Two people decide on divorce, but thoughts of their children bring them together again.
Low-budget, stiff-upper-lip marriage guidance tract, well acted but more well-intentioned than memorable.
w Warren Chetham Strode, Don Sharp *play* Warren Chetham Strode *d* Daniel Birt *ph* Arthur Grant
☆ Valerie Hobson, Philip Friend, Norman Wooland, Janette Scott, Mandy Miller, Jeremy Spenser, Richard Wattis

Background to Danger
US 1943 80m bw
Warner (Jerry Wald)
An adventurer thwarts Nazi intrigue in Turkey.
Flat, studio-bound wartime potboiler with a good cast all at sea.
w W. R. Burnett *novel* Uncommon Danger by Eric Ambler *d* Raoul Walsh *ph* Tony Gaudio *m* Frederick Hollander
☆ George Raft, Brenda Marshall, Sydney Greenstreet, Peter Lorre, Osa Massen, Turhan Bey, Kurt Katch
'You could use this film for one kind of measurement of the unconquerable difference between a good job by Hitchcock and a good job of the Hitchcock type.' – *James Agee*
'There's nothing for the cast to do other than concentrate on the display of melodramatics.' – *Variety*

Backlash *
US 1956 84m Technicolor
U-I (Aaron Rosenberg)
A gunman seeks the father he has never met, who turns out to be a villain who sold his partners for gold to attacking Indians.
Rather unusual suspense Western, very watchable for its mystery elements.
w *Borden Chase* *d* *John Sturges* *ph* Irving Glassberg *m* Herman Stein
☆ Richard Widmark, Donna Reed, John McIntire, William Campbell, Barton MacLane

Backlash
Australia 1986 110m colour
Mermaid Beach/Multifilms (Bill Bennett)
An antagonistic pair of cops – one male, one female – are stranded in the outback with an Aborigine woman accused of the castration and murder of her employer.
Glum melodrama: its heart may be in the right place, but its mind is elsewhere.
wd Bill Bennett *ph* Tony Wilson *m* Michael Atkinson, Michael Spicer *ed* Denise Hunter
☆ David Argue, Gia Carides, Lydia Miller, Brian Syron

Backsliding
Australia/GB 1991 88m colour
Film4/Itel/AFFC/Charles and Simon Target (Sue Wild)
An incompetent engineer is stranded in the outback with a born-again Christian, who has a violent past and believes that he is being tempted by the devil.
Creepy little psychological drama, but one that lacks much in the way of suspense or character development.
w Simon Target, Ross Wilson *d* Simon Target *ph* Tom Cowan *m* Nigel Westlake *pd* Ross Major *ed* Nicolas Holmes
☆ Tim Roth, Jim Holt, Odile Le Clezio, Ross McGregor, Michelle Fillery, Patrick Duggan, Jim Morlock, Adrian Shirley

Backstreet Dreams
US 1990 104m DeLuxe
Trimark (Jason O'Malley, Lance H. Robbins)
A petty gangster decides to go straight to care for his autistic son.
Lurid melodrama, alternately mawkish and violent, but never bearing any resemblance to an observable reality.
w Jason O'Malley *d* Rupert Hitzig *ph* Stephen M. Katz *m* Bill Conti *ed* Robert Gordon
☆ Jason O'Malley, Brooke Shields, Sherilyn Fenn, Tony Fields, Nick Cassavetes, Ray Mancini, Burt Young, Anthony Franciosa, Joe Pantoliano (uncredited)
'A vanity production unsuccessfully mixing exploitation film clichés with fake uplift of a tv disease-of-the-week pic.' – *Variety*

The Bacon Grabbers *
US 1929 20m bw silent
Hal Roach
Bailiffs fail to recover a radio on which the instalments are overdue.
Modestly pleasing star comedy on the lines of Big Business *(qv).*
w Leo McCarey, H. M. Walker *d* Lewis R. Foster
☆ Stan Laurel, Oliver Hardy, Edgar Kennedy, Jean Harlow, Charlie Hall

'The story of a blonde who wanted to go places, and a brute who got her there – the hard way!'
The Bad and the Beautiful **
US 1952 118m bw
MGM (John Houseman)
A director, a star, a screenwriter and an executive recall their experiences at the hands of a go-getting Hollywood producer.
Very much a Hollywood 'in' picture, this rather obvious flashback melodrama offers good acting chances and a couple of intriguing situations; never quite finding the style it seeks, it offers good bitchy entertainment along the way, and there are references back to it in Two Weeks in Another Town *(qv), made ten years later.*
w Charles Schnee *d* Vincente Minnelli *ph* Robert Surtees *m* David Raksin *ad* Cedric Gibbons, Edward Carfagno
☆ Kirk Douglas (Jonathan Shields), Lana Turner (Georgia Lorrison), Walter Pidgeon (Harry Pebbel), Dick Powell (James Lee Bartlow), Barry Sullivan (Fred Amiel), Gloria Grahame (Rosemary Bartlow), Gilbert Roland (Victor Ribera), Leo G. Carroll (Henry Whitfield), Vanessa Brown (Kay Amiel), Paul Stewart (Syd Murphy)
'For all the cleverness of the apparatus, it lacks a central point of focus.' – *Penelope Houston*
'Clever, sharply observed little scenes reflect the Hollywood surface: the egotistic babble at a party, the affectations of European directors, the sneak preview, the trying on of suits for catmen in a B picture.' – *MFB*
'It is a crowded and colourful picture, but it is choppy, episodic and vague. There does not emerge a clear picture of exactly how movies are made.' – *Bosley Crowther*
† The relationship between Jonathan Shields and Georgia Lorrison is modelled on that between producer David Selznick and actress Jennifer Jones.
Charles Schnee; Robert Surtees; art direction; Gloria Grahame
Kirk Douglas

Bad Bascomb *
US 1946 110m bw
MGM (Orville Dull)
A sentimental bank robber becomes the hero of a group of travelling Mormons.
Pleasing though overlong star Western, with good production values.
w William Lipman, Grant Garrett *d* S. Sylvan Simon *ph* Charles Schoenbaum *m* David Snell
☆ *Wallace Beery, Margaret O'Brien, Marjorie Main,* J. Carrol Naish, Russell Simpson, Sara Haden

'The Mother, The Planner And The Gobshite.'
Bad Behaviour
GB 1993 104m colour
First Independent/Channel 4/British Screen/Parallax (Sarah Curtis)
An Irish couple living in North London with their two young sons muddle through life, not helped by the attentions of a neighbour, an unscrupulous landlord and his slapdash friends in the building trade.
A small-scale improvised comedy that concerns itself with the details of everyday existence to the detriment of drama; it may be realistic, but it is often uninteresting, despite the best efforts of its cast.
d Les Blair *ph* Witold Stok *m* John Altman *pd* Jim Grant *ed* Martin Walsh
☆ Stephen Rea, Sinead Cusack, Philip Jackson, Clare Higgins, Phil Daniels, Saira Todd, Mary Jo Randle
'A delightful comedy of manners ... The pic is character, not knockabout, comedy, but this is a group of mild eccentrics you want to follow to the end.' – *Variety*

Bad Blood *
New Zealand/GB 1981 105m colour
Southern (Andrew Brown)
A paranoid farmer kills seven people and goes on the run.
Based on a true story, a grim, tense thriller that maintains its excitement.
w Andrew Brown *book* *Manhunt: The Story of Stanley Graham* by Howard Willis *d* Mike Newell *ph* Gary Hansen *m* Richard Hartley *ad* Kai Hawkins *ed* Peter Hollywood
☆ Jack Thompson, Carol Burns, Dennis Lill, Donna Akersten, Martyn Sanderson, Marshall Napier

Bad Blood: see *The Night Is Young (1986)*

Bad Boy Bubby **
Australia/Italy 1993 114m colour Super 35
Entertainment/Fandango/Bubby (Domenico Procacci, Giorgio Draskovic, Rolf de Heer)
A retarded 35-year-old, who has never been allowed out of his home, murders his parents and experiences the wider world.
An odd and disturbing black comedy of a man who replays everything said and done to him; many may find it repugnant, but it offers a skewed and satirical perspective on everyday life and communication.
wd *Rolf de Heer* *ph* Ian Jones *m* Graham Tardiff *pd* Mark Abbott *ed* Suresh Ayyar
☆ *Nicholas Hope,* Claire Benito, Ralph Cotterill, Sid Brisbane, Norman Kaye, Carmel Johnson, Bridget Walters
'Provocative, stylistically daring and inventive.' – *Variety*
† Apart from its director of photography, the film used 30 other cinematographers, one for each location. The film won awards for best director, best actor, best original screenplay and best editing at the 1994 Australian Film Institute awards.

Bad Boys
US 1983 123m Astrocolor
EMI/Robert Solo
Delinquents get out of control in a Juvenile Correctional Facility.
Ugly but yawnworthy saga of up-to-date Dead End Kids.
w Richard di Lello *d* Rick Rosenthal *ph* Bruce Surtees, Don Thorin *m* Bill Conti
☆ Sean Penn, Reni Santoni, Jim Moody, Eric Gurry, Esai Morales, Ally Sheedy
'It has been made in a brutal, realistic neo-Warners style ... Even when episodes are powerful, they're banal.' – *New Yorker*

'Watcha Gonna Do?'
Bad Boys *
US 1995 118m Technicolor
Columbia (Don Simpson, Jerry Bruckheimer)
Two Miami cops go after the gang that stole a fortune in heroin from their station-house.
High-octane entertainment in which smart dialogue alternates with frenetic action and large-scale destruction.
w Michael Barrie, Jim Mulholland, Doug Richardson *story* George Gallo *d* Michael Bay *ph* Howard Atherton *m* Mark Mancina *pd* John Vallone *ed* Christian Wagner
☆ Martin Lawrence, Will Smith, Téa Leoni, Tcheky Karyo, Theresa Randle, Marg Helgenberger, Joe Pantoliano
'Ultra-slick combination of expensive action, rude attitude, sassy humor, trendy locations, fast cars, heavy soundtrack and decorous violence.' – *Variety*
'A wholly unambitious reworking of a stock formula.' – *Sheila Johnston, Independent*

Bad Company ***
US 1972 92m Technicolor
Paramount (Stanley R. Jaffe)
During the Civil War, two youths on the run team up and become outlaws.
A successful attempt to recreate the feeling of past time, by the writers of another criminal myth, Bonnie and Clyde.
w *David Newman, Robert Benton* *d* Robert Benton *ph* Gordon Willis *m* Harvey Schmidt
☆ Jeff Bridges, Barry Brown, Jim Davis, David Huddleston, John Savage

Bad Company
Canada 1994 108m Technicolor
Panavision
Buena Vista/Touchstone (Amedeo Ursini, Jeffrey Chernov)
A former CIA agent becomes involved in industrial espionage and murder.
Lacklustre thriller about uninteresting characters being unpleasant to one another; it lives up to its title.
w Ross Thomas *d* Damian Harris *ph* Jack N. Green *m* Carter Burwell *pd* Andrew McAlpine *ed* Stuart Pappe
☆ Ellen Barkin, Laurence Fishburne, Frank Langella, Michael Beach, Gia Carides, David Ogden Stiers, Spalding Gray
'With its uninvolving story, listless delivery and the unsympathetic characters ... would-be suspenser fails even on the erotic level.' – *Godfrey Cheshire, Variety*
† It was released direct to video in Britain.

Bad Day at Black Rock ****
US 1955 81m Eastmancolor Cinemascope
MGM (Dore Schary)
A one-armed stranger gets off the train at a sleepy desert hamlet and is greeted with hostility by the townsfolk, who have something to hide.
Seminal suspense thriller – the guilty town motif became a cliché – with a terse script and professional presentation. The moments of violence, long awaited, are electrifying.
w *Millard Kaufman* *story* *Bad Time at Hondo* by Howard Briskin *d* *John Sturges* *ph* *William C. Mellor* *m* André Previn
☆ *Spencer Tracy, Robert Ryan,* Dean Jagger, Walter Brennan, Ernest Borgnine, Lee Marvin, Anne Francis, John Ericson, Russell Collins
'A very superior example of motion picture craftsmanship.' – *Pauline Kael*
'The movie takes place within twenty-four hours. It has a dramatic unity, an economy of word and action, that is admirable in an age of flabby Hollywood epics that maunder on forever.' – *William K. Zinsser, New York Herald Tribune*
'The skill of some sequences, the mood and symbiosis between man and nature makes this film sometimes superior to *High Noon*.' – *G. N. Fenin*
Millard Kaufman; John Sturges; Spencer Tracy

Bad Dreams
US 1988 84m DeLuxe
TCF (Gale Anne Hurd)
After 13 years in a coma, a woman who survived a mass suicide discovers that the murderous spirit of her cult leader is still active.
Unsuccessful horror movie, too imitative of others of the genre and too feeble in its own right to be effective.
w Andrew Fleming, Steven E. de Souza *d* Andrew Fleming *ph* Alexander Gruszynski *m* Jay Michael Ferguson *pd* Ivo Crisante *ed* Jeff Freeman
☆ Jennifer Rubin, Bruce Abbott, Richard Lynch, Harris Yulin, Dean Cameron, Susan Barnes

Bad for Each Other
US 1954 83m bw
Columbia (William Fadiman)
A doctor back from the army scorns his home town for high society, but a mine disaster reverses his decision.
Misleadingly titled cliché drama, patterned after The Citadel *(qv). Actors ill at ease, handling competent but routine.*
w Irving Wallace, Horace McCoy *novel* Horace McCoy *d* Irving Rapper *ph* Franz Planer *md* Mischa Bakaleinikoff
☆ Charlton Heston, Lizabeth Scott, Dianne Foster, Mildred Dunnock, Arthur Franz, Ray Collins, Marjorie Rambeau

Bad Girl *
US 1931 90m bw
Fox
Two New York youngsters have to get married and find life bewildering.
Typical Borzage sentiment which was well received at the time.
w Edwin Burke *novel* Vina Delmar *d* *Frank Borzage* *ph* Chester Lyons
☆ Sally Eilers, James Dunn, Minna Gombell, William Pawley, Frank Darien
Frank Borzage; Edwin Burke
best picture

'It was a dangerous time to be a woman. And a good time to have friends.'
Bad Girls
US 1994 99m DeLuxe
TCF (Albert S. Ruddy, André E. Morgan, Charles Finch)
Four prostitutes flee town after a killing and head for the wide open spaces to become outlaws.
Comic and unconvincing Western romp, impossible to take seriously and too silly to be amusing.
w Ken Friedman, Yolande Finch *story* Albert S. Ruddy, Charles Finch, Gray Frederickson *d* Jonathan Kaplan *ph* Ralf Bode *m* Jerry Goldsmith *pd* Guy Barnes *ed* Jane Kurson
☆ Madeleine Stowe, Mary Stuart Masterson, Andie MacDowell, Drew Barrymore, James Russo, Robert Loggia, Dermot Mulroney
'Drinks from an empty trough of wit and style.' – *Variety*
† Tamra Davis was the original director, but left soon after shooting began.

Bad Influence *
US 1990 99m DeLuxe
Entertainment/Epic/Sarlui/Diamant (Steve Tisch)
A mysterious stranger manipulates the life of a disgruntled office worker.

Thriller requiring a more-than-usual suspension of disbelief.
w David Koepp *d* Curtis Hanson *ph* Robert Elswit *m* Trevor Jones *ed* Bonnie Koehler
☆ Rob Lowe, James Spader, Lisa Zane, Christian Clemenson, Kathleen Wilhoite, Tony Maggio, Marcia Cross
'A reasonably taut, suspenseful thriller that provides its share of twists before straying into silliness during its final third.' – *Variety*

Bad Jim
US 1990 90m Rank Colour
21st Century (Joseph Wouk)
A cowboy buys Billy the Kid's horse and turns bank robber, riding across the country with his gang, doing a few good turns.
Amiable, unmemorable Western that goes through familiar routines without much enthusiasm.
wd Clyde Ware *ph* David Golia *m* Jaime Sheriff *pd* Michael E. Forrell *ed* Glenn Garland
☆ James Brolin, Richard Roundtree, John Clark Gable, Harry Carey Jnr, Rory Calhoun, Pepe Serna, Ty Hardin

Bad Lieutenant
US 1992 96m colour
Guild/Pressman (Edward R. Pressman, Mary Kane)
A corrupt cop goes from bad to worse.
A lurid and exploitative melange of drugs, sex, masturbation, rape and religiosity, hardly justified by the suggestion of redemption tacked on to its end. What does save it, even if it doesn't justify it, is the force of Harvey Keitel's performance.
w Zoe Lund, Abel Ferrara *d* Abel Ferrara *ph* Ken Kelsch *m* Joe Delia *pd* Charles Logola *ed* Anthony Redman
☆ *Harvey Keitel*, Frankie Thorn, Zoe Lund, Anthony Ruggiero, Eddie Daniels, Bianca Bakija
'Film's frank treatment of drug addiction, obsessive sexuality and loss of religious faith spells instant controversy.' – *Variety*
'Not exactly comfortable viewing, of course, but this is disturbing, raw filmmaking and award-winning acting.' – *Kim Newman, Empire*

Bad Little Angel
US 1939 72m bw
MGM
A sad little girl flees an orphanage and brightens up several lives in a small town.
Pollyanna-type period drama, definitely for small-town audiences but well enough done.
w Dorothy Yost *novel* *Looking after Sandy* by Margaret Turnbull *d* William Thiele
☆ Virginia Weidler, Gene Reynolds, Guy Kibbee, Ian Hunter, Elizabeth Patterson, Reginald Owen, Henry Hull, Lois Wilson
'Homespunner for the nabes.' – *Variety*

The Bad Lord Byron *
GB 1949 85m bw
Triton (Aubrey Baring)
Byron lies dying, and imagines his life and loves under review in a heavenly court.
Thought risible at the time, this historical romance in flashback now seems no worse and even a little more stylish than most, though the script suffers from too many cooks.
w Terence Young, Anthony Thorne, Peter Quennell, Laurence Kitchin, Paul Holt *d* David MacDonald *ph* Stephen Dade *m* Cedric Thorpe Davie
☆ *Dennis Price*, Mai Zetterling, Linden Travers, *Joan Greenwood*, Sonia Holm, Raymond Lovell, Leslie Dwyer
† The end of the British costume cycle which began with *The Man in Grey* (qv).

The Bad Man
US 1940 70m sepia
MGM (J. Walter Ruben)
GB title: *Two Gun Cupid*
A Mexican outlaw helps a former friend and unites two lovers.
Forgettable Western comedy drama with a sterling cast.
w Wells Root *play* Porter Emerson Browne *d* Richard Thorpe *ph* Clyde de Vinna *m* Franz Waxman
☆ Wallace Beery, Lionel Barrymore, Laraine Day, Ronald Reagan, Henry Travers

Bad Man of Brimstone
US 1937 89m bw
MGM
An old bandit discovers his long-lost son and sees the light.
Hilariously predictable but enjoyable star vehicle, quite palatable when it isn't too lachrymose.
w Richard Maibaum, Cyril Hume *d* J. Walter Ruben
☆ Wallace Beery, Virginia Bruce, Noah Beery, Dennis O'Keefe, Lewis Stone, Guy Kibbee, Joseph Calleia

Bad Man of Wyoming: see *Wyoming (1940)*

Bad Man's River
Spain/Italy/France 1972 90m Eastmancolor Franscope
Zurbano/Apollo/Roitfeld (Bernard Gordon)
Four outlaws accept the job of blowing up a government arsenal in Mexico.
Lurid Western with comedy leanings and a somewhat eccentric cast.
w Philip Yordan, Eugenio Martin *d* Eugenio Martin *ph* Alexander Ulloa *m* Waldo de Los Rios
☆ Lee Van Cleef, James Mason, Gina Lollobrigida, Simon Andreu, Diana Lorys
'When shooting a western in Spain one should not say to oneself, "Never mind, no one is going to see it," because that will be just the film which the Rank Organization will choose to release in England.' – *James Mason*

Bad Medicine
US 1985 96m DeLuxe
TCF/Lantana (Alex Winitsky, Arlene Sellers)
A student goes to medical school in Mexico.
Condescending farce which the Mexicans certainly won't like. Nothing much in it for general audiences either.
wd Harvey Miller *novel* Steven Horowitz *ph* Kelvin Pike *m* Lalo Schifrin *pd* Les Dilley
☆ Steve Guttenberg, Alan Arkin, Julie Hagerty, Bill Macy
'With the tone shifting constantly from realistic to slapstick, the film has no center and just sprawls on.' – *Variety*

Bad Men of Missouri
US 1941 72m bw
Warner
The Younger brothers become outlaws when they fight the influence of carpetbaggers.
Whitewashing of a family of Western criminals; good double-bill entertainment.
w Charles Grayson *d* Ray Enright *ph* Arthur Todd *ed* Clarence Kolster
☆ Dennis Morgan, Arthur Kennedy, Wayne Morris, Jane Wyman, Victor Jory, Walter Catlett

Bad Moon
US 1996 79m colour Clairmont Scope
Warner/Morgan Creek (James G. Robinson)
An American photojournalist turns werewolf after being attacked by a creature in Nepal.
Dull horror movie that sticks to familiar clichés, lacking any sense of conviction.
wd Eric Red *novel* *Thor* by Wayne Smith *ph* Jan Kiesser *m* Daniel Licht *pd* Richard Paris, Linda Del Rosario *ed* C. Timothy O'Meara *sp* make-up fx: Steve Johnson
☆ Mariel Hemingway, Michael Paré, Mason Gamble, Primo
'Too silly to be suspenseful, yet not quite awful enough – or unintentionally funny enough – to qualify as camp.' – *Variety*

The Bad News Bears
US 1976 103m Movielab
Paramount (Stanley Jaffe)
An ex-baseball professional coaches a team of tough kids.
Rough-tongued, sentimental star comedy.
w Bill Lancaster *d* Michael Ritchie *ph* John A. Alonzo *m* Jerry Fielding (after Bizet)
☆ Walter Matthau, Tatum O'Neal, Vic Morrow, Joyce Van Patten

The Bad News Bears Go to Japan
US 1978 91m Movielab
Paramount (Michael Ritchie)
Yet another unnecessary sequel with a self-explanatory title.
w Bill Lancaster *d* John Berry *ph* Gene Polito *m* Paul Chihara
☆ Tony Curtis, Jackie Earle Haley, Tomisaburo Wayakama, George Wyner

The Bad News Bears in Breaking Training
US 1977 100m Movielab
Paramount/Leonard Goldberg (Fred T. Gallo)
The Bears are invited to play in the Houston Astrodome but have trouble finding a coach.
Dimwitted and alarmingly sentimental sequel to a raucously vulgar oncer which should have been left alone.
w Paul Brickman *d* Michael Pressman *ph* Fred J. Koenekamp *m* Craig Safan from Tchaikovsky's 1812 Overture *ed* John W. Wheeler
☆ William Devane, Clifton James, Jackie Earle Haley, Jimmy Baio, Chris Barnes

The Bad Seed *
US 1956 129m bw
Warner (Mervyn Le Roy)
A sweet-looking 8-year-old girl is a liar and a murderess; her mother finds out and attempts to kill her and commit suicide.
A real curiosity from an unexpected stage hit: absurd melodrama treated with astonishing high literary style and some censor-induced levity; at the end, after the little villainess has been struck by lightning, a curtain call shows her being soundly spanked. Nancy Kelly rather uneasily recreates her stage role as the mother.
w John Lee Mahin *play* Maxwell Anderson *novel* William March *d* Mervyn Le Roy *ph* Harold Rosson *m* Alex North
☆ *Nancy Kelly, Patty McCormack*, Henry Jones, Eileen Heckart, Evelyn Varden, William Hopper, Paul Fix, Jesse White
Academy Award nomination: Harold Rosson; Nancy Kelly; Patty McCormack; Eileen Heckart

Bad Sister
US 1931 71m bw
Universal (Carl Laemmle Jnr)
A small-town coquette falls for a city slicker, and her quiet sister gets her steady boyfriend.
A teenager potboiler of its day, remarkable only for its cast.
w Raymond L. Schrock, Tom Reed *story* *The Flirt* by Booth Tarkington *d* Hobart Henley *ph* Karl Freund *ed* Ted J. Kent
☆ Conrad Nagel, Sidney Fox, Bette Davis, Humphrey Bogart, ZaSu Pitts, Slim Summerville, Emma Dunn, Bert Roach

Bad Sister: see *The White Unicorn (1947)*

The Bad Sleep Well **
Japan 1960 151m bw Tohoscope
Toho (Tomoyuki Tanaka, Akira Kurosawa)
original title: *Warui Yatsu Yoku Nemuru*
As part of his plan for revenge, a man marries the daughter of the businessman responsible for his father's death.
Moody thriller, in the style of American gangster movies of the 40s, but with an ending that Hollywood would have rejected as too downbeat.
w Akira Kurosawa, Hideo Oguni, Eijiro Kusaka, Ryuzo Kikushima, Shinobu Hashimoto *novel* Ed McBain *d* Akira Kurosawa *ph* Yazuru Aizawa *m* Sasuru Sato
☆ Toshiro Mifune, Masayuki Mori, Kyoko Kagawa, Tatsuya Mihashi, Takashi Shimura, Akira Nishimura, Takeshi Kato
'It's a strangely mixed movie – an attempt at social significance but with several borrowings from *Hamlet* that take bizarre forms.' – *Pauline Kael*

Bad Taste
New Zealand 1987 92m colour
Blue Dolphin/Wing Nut Films/Peter Jackson
Alien fast-food restaurateurs add humans to their menu.
A deliberately gross low-budget movie, mixing gore and comedy, that gained a cult following among those with strong stomachs. Chacun à son goût.
w Peter Jackson, Tony Hiles, Ken Hammon *m* Michelle Scullion *ed* Peter Jackson, Jamie Selkirk *sp* Peter Jackson *d/ph* Peter Jackson
☆ Terry Potter, Pete O'Herne, Craig Smith, Mike Minett, Peter Jackson, Doug Wren
'Some kind of triumph in its horror-comic verve.' – *MFB*

Bad Timing
GB 1980 123m colour Technovision
Rank/Recorded Picture Company (Jeremy Thomas)
In Vienna, an American divorcee has a strange and unhappy affair with a psychoanalyst.
Weird and unsympathetic sex melodrama, presented with the disconnected style expected from this director as a series of flashbacks from the heroine's near-deathbed.
w Yale Udoff *d* Nicolas Roeg *ph* Anthony Richmond *m* Richard Hartley
☆ Art Garfunkel, Theresa Russell, Harvey Keitel, Denholm Elliott, Daniel Massey
'An enervating experience. Technically flashy, and teeming with degenerate chic, the downbeat tale is unrelieved by its tacked-on thriller ending, and deals purely in despair.' – *Variety*

Badge 373
US 1973 116m Technicolor
Paramount (Howard W. Koch)
A police detective is enraged by the murder of his partner and his own suspension after the death of a suspect.
'Realistic' (i.e. violent and foul-mouthed) cop thriller in the wake of The French Connection, *tolerable only for action highlights.*
w Pete Hamill, from the exploits of Eddie Egan *d* Howard W. Koch *ph* Arthur J. Ornitz *m* J. J. Johnson
☆ Robert Duvall, Verna Bloom, Henry Darrow, Eddie Egan, Felipe Luciano, Tina Christiana, Marina Durell
'A deeply divided and scarcely reassuring addition to the movies' composite portrait of the American police force.' – *John Gillett*
'Nasty, violent and humourless.' – *Sight and Sound*
'A movie well worth protesting about.' – *Michael Billington, Illustrated London News*

The Badge of Marshal Brennan
US 1957 75m bw
Allied Artists
A man on the run takes on the identity of a dying marshal, and cleans up a corrupt town.
Satisfying lower-case Western.
w Thomas G. Hubbard *d* Albert C. Gannaway
☆ Jim Davis, Arleen Whelan, Louis Jean Heydt, Lee Van Cleef

Badkonake Sefid: see *The White Balloon*

The Badlanders *
US 1958 83m Metrocolor Cinemascope
MGM/Arcola (Aaron Rosenberg)
Crooked Westerners plan to rob a goldmine.
Rather sloppy Western remake of The Asphalt Jungle.
w Richard Collins *d* Delmer Daves *ph* John Seitz
☆ Alan Ladd, Ernest Borgnine, Katy Jurado, Claire Kelly, Kent Smith, *Nehemiah Persoff*, Robert Emhardt

Badlands ****
US 1973 94m CFI color
Warner/Pressman/Williams/Badlands (Terrence Malick)
A teenage girl and a young garbage collector wander across America leaving a trail of murder behind them.
A violent folk tale for moderns; very well put together, it quickly became a cult film. It has proved to be a seminal film in its depiction of aimless anger as a means of attempting to connect with the world.
wd Terrence Malick *ph* Brian Probyn, Tak Fujimoto, Stevan Larner *m* George Tipton
☆ Martin Sheen, Sissy Spacek, Warren Oates, Ramon Bieri
'One of the finest literate examples of narrated cinema since the early days of Welles and Polonsky.' – *Jonathan Rosenbaum*

'So preconceived that there's nothing left to respond to.' – *New Yorker*

Badman's Country
US 1958 72m bw
Warner
Pat Garrett, Wyatt Earp, Buffalo Bill Cody and Bat Masterson have a showdown with Butch Cassidy.
Wildly unhistorical Western.
w Orville H. Hampton *d* Fred F. Sears
☆ George Montgomery, Buster Crabbe, Malcolm Atterbury, Gregory Walcott, Neville Brand

'The west's worst killers strike again!'
Badman's Territory
US 1946 97m bw
RKO
The brutality of the Texas state police forces a sheriff to seek help from outlaws.
Unconvincing Western with good moments.
w Jack Natteford, Luci Ward *d* Tim Whelan
☆ Randolph Scott, Steve Brodie, Gabby Hayes, Ann Richards

Bagdad Café ***
West Germany 1988 91m Eastmancolor
Mainline/Pelemele/Pro-Ject (Percy and Eleonore Adlon)
aka: *Out of Rosenheim*
A middle-aged Bavarian woman, left stranded in the Mojave desert by her husband, transforms a seedy motel she stumbles across.
High-spirited comedy, full of gentle wit and charm.
w Percy and Eleonore Adlon, Christopher Doherty *d* *Percy Adlon* *ph* Bernd Heinl *m* Bob Telson *ad* Bernt Amadeus Capra *ed* Norbert Herzner
☆ *Marianne Sägebrecht*, Jack Palance, C. C. H. Pounder, Christine Kaufmann, Monica Calhoun, Darron Flagg
† The success of the film resulted in an American TV series starring Whoopi Goldberg.
song 'Calling You' (*m/ly* Bob Telson)

Baghdad
US 1949 81m Technicolor
U-I (Robert Arthur)
A chieftain's daughter seeks revenge for her father's death.
Thinly-conceived Arabian Nights *modernization, unsure whether to take itself seriously.*
w Robert Hardy Andrews *d* Charles Lamont *ph* Russell Metty *m* Frank Skinner, Jack Brooks
☆ Maureen O'Hara, Vincent Price, Paul Christian, John Sutton, Jeff Corey, Frank Puglia
'Silly, but not in the least muddle-headed. The producers are fully aware that all the customers want to see of Baghdad is Maureen O'Hara, with a touch of leopard-skin at the throat to warm up a generous décolletage.' – *C. A. Lejeune*

La Baie des Anges **
France 1962 85m bw CinemaScope
Sud-Pacifique (Paul-Edmond Decharme)
GB title: *Bay of Angels*
A bank clerk who has had unexpected winnings at the Nice Casino falls in love with a compulsive gambler.
Good-looking romantic drama utilizing many of the cinema's most dazzling resources.
wd Jacques Demy ph Jean Rabier m Michel Legrand
☆ *Jeanne Moreau*, Claude Mann, Paul Guers, Henri Nassiet
'Immense lightness, speed and gaiety … stunning visual texture.' – *Tom Milne, MFB*
'It's like a French attempt to purify, to get to the essence of, a Warner's movie of the 30s.' – *Pauline Kael*

Baise-Moi
France 2000 76m colour
Toute Premiere Fois/Canal+ (Philippe Godeau)
US title: *Rape Me*
A prostitute and her friend, who is angry after being raped, go on a sex and killing spree.
Crudely filmed, and with cruder content, this provides little intellectual justification for its levels of violence and hatred; it caused great controversy in France, where it was hailed by some as a feminist masterpiece.
wd Virginie Despentes, Coralie Trinh Thi *novel* Virginie Despentes *ph* Benoit Chamaillard *m* Varou Jan *ad* Irene Galitzine *ed* Ailo Auguste, Francine Lemaitre
☆ Raffaela Anderson (Manu), Karen Bach (Nadine), Delphine McCarty (Severine), Lisa Marshall (Karla), Estelle Issac (Alice), Hervé P. Gustave (Martin), Marc Rioufol (Architect), Ouassini Embarek (Radouan)
'A half-baked, punk-inflected porn odyssey masquerading as a movie worth seeing and talking about.' – *Lisa Nesselson, Variety*
'A numbing alternation of pornographic scenarios and brutal killings. The result is like something you'd see momentarily unscrambled on a hotel television set, but with better music and a little more of a story line.' – *A. O. Scott, New York Times*
'Gives power to women; or, rather, it is about women taking power, though not, to be sure, in a politically correct manner.' – *Ginette Vincendeau, Sight and Sound*

Baisers Volés: see *Stolen Kisses*

Bait
US 1954 79m bw
Columbia (Hugo Haas)
Gold prospectors fall out over a mine and a woman.
Antediluvian melodrama typical of this director, made more risible than usual by Cedric Hardwicke's introduction in the shape of Satan.
w Samuel W. Taylor *d* Hugo Haas *ph* Edward P. Fitzgerald *m* Vaclav Divina
☆ Hugo Haas, Cleo Moore, John Agar, Emmett Lynn

'They are young. They want results. She is…'
The Bait *
France 1995 117m colour
Artificial Eye/Mayfair/Hachette/Little Bear/France 2/ M6 (René Cleitman, Frederic Bourboulon)
original title: *L'Appât*
Two layabouts use an 18-year-old shop assistant to flirt with wealthy men and gain access to their apartments so that they can be robbed.
Grim little parable of the acquisitive society, but one that offers little in the way of fresh insights.
w Colo Tavernier O'Hagan, Bertrand Tavernier *book* Morgan Sportès *d* Bertrand Tavernier *ph* Alain Choquart *m* Philippe Haim *ad* Emile Ghico *ed* Luce Grunenwaldt
☆ Marie Gillain, Olivier Sitruk, Bruno Putzulu, Richard Berry, Philippe Duclos, Marie Ravel
'It simply trundles out shock horror with very little interpretation.' – *Derek Malcolm, Guardian*
† It was winner of the Golden Bear award for best film at the 1995 Berlin Film Festival.

The Baited Trap: see *The Trap*

Baker's Hawk *
US 1976 96m colour
Doty-Dayton
A reclusive Westerner becomes the victim of hoodlum vigilantes and is helped by a boy and his father.
Refreshingly simple-minded Western for the family audience.
w Dan Greer, Hal Harrison Jnr *novel* Jack Bickham *d* Lyman D. Dayton
☆ Clint Walker, Burl Ives, Diane Baker, Lee H. Montgomery, Alan Young

The Baker's Wife: see *La Femme du Boulanger*

Bakushu: see *Early Summer*

Le Bal **
France/Italy/Algeria 1982 112m Fujicolour
S.A./A2/Massfil/Oncic (Giorgio Silvagni)
Scenes from the history of a small Paris ballroom between 1936 and 1983.
Striking if overlong attempt at a totally speechless drama, with handling very nearly good enough to meet the challenge, though the result will not be to everyone's taste, and one's reaction in any case will depend very much on mood.
w Jean-Claude Penchenat, Ruggero Maccari, Furio Scarpelli, Ettore Scola, from an idea by the first-named and the stage production by the Théâtre du Campagnol *d Ettore Scola ph* Ricardo Aranovich *m Vladimir Cosma*
☆ Jean-Claude Penchenat, Chantal Capron, Etienne Guichard

Balalaika *
US 1939 102m bw
MGM (Lawrence Weingarten)
Russian exiles gather in Paris.
Mildly pleasing star musical.
w Jacques Deval, Leon Gordon *play* Eric Maschwitz *d* Reinhold Schunzel *ph* Joseph Ruttenberg, Karl Freund *m* Herbert Stothart
☆ Nelson Eddy, Ilona Massey, Charles Ruggles, Frank Morgan, C. Aubrey Smith, Lionel Atwill, Walter Woolf King, Joyce Compton
'A sumptuously produced operetta in the opulent MGM tradition.' – *Variety*
† Only the title song was retained from the original score
♫ 'At the Balalaika'; 'Tanya'; 'Ride, Cossack, Ride'; 'Shadows on the Sand'; 'Tale of the Tailors'; 'Beneath the Winter's Snows'; 'In a Heart as Brave as Your Own'; 'Soldiers of the Czar'; 'How Many Miles to Go'; 'The Magic of Your Love'; 'My Heart Is a Gypsy'

La Balance ***
France 1982 102m colour
Les Films Ariane/Films A2 (Georges Dancigers, Alexandre Mnouchkine)
A pimp and his girlfriend are pressured by the police into becoming informers.
Tough thriller in which the only difference between the cops and the crooks is that the police are the more violent. A box-office success in France, where it was voted the best film of the year.
w M. Fabiani, Bob Swaim *d* Bob Swaim *ph* Bernard Zitzermann *m* Roland Bocquet *pd* Eric Moulard *ed* Françoise Javet
☆ Nathalie Baye, Philipe Léotard, Richard Berry, Maurice Ronet

Balboa
US 1983 91m DeLuxe
Entertainment/Production Associates (James Polakof)
Plans by a crooked Californian entrepreneur to set up a casino are opposed by the daughter of the man he ruined.
A glossy and confused soap opera of plot and counter-plot, cut from from a TV mini-series that, understandably, was never broadcast.
w James Polakof, Gail Willumsen, Nicki Lewis *d* James Polakof *ph* Christopher Lynch *m* Richard Hieronymus *pd* Charles D. Tomlinson *ed* Millie Paul
☆ Tony Curtis, Carol Lynley, Chuck Connors, Sonny Bono, Steve Kanaly, Jennifer Chase, Martine Beswick

The Balcony *
US 1963 86m bw
Walter Reade/Sterling/Allen Hodgdon/City Film (Joseph Strick, Ben Maddow)
In a war-torn world, a brothel continues to attract customers of every variety.
Low-budget adaptation of a rather confused allegorical play: vivid moments hardly atone for reels of surrealist groping.
w Ben Maddow *play* Jean Genet *d* Joseph Strick *ph* George Folsey *m* Igor Stravinsky
☆ Shelley Winters, Peter Falk, Lee Grant, Peter Brocco, Kent Smith, Ruby Dee, Jeff Corey, Leonard Nimoy
'Relentlessly funny, shaggy, shocking.' – *The Times*
'Unfit for exhibition to man, woman or child.' – *People*
George Folsey

Ball of Fire *
US 1941 111m bw
Samuel Goldwyn
working title: *The Professor and the Burlesque Queen*
Seven professors compiling a dictionary give shelter to a stripteaser on the run from gangsters.
Rather overstretched but fitfully amusing romp inspired by Snow White and the Seven Dwarfs*.*
w Charles Brackett, Billy Wilder d Howard Hawks *ph* Gregg Toland *m* Alfred Newman
☆ Barbara Stanwyck, Gary Cooper, Oscar Homolka, Henry Travers, S. Z. Sakall, Tully Marshall, Leonid Kinskey, Richard Haydn, Aubrey Mather, Allen Jenkins, Dana Andrews, Dan Duryea
'It's played as if it were terribly bright, but it's rather shrill and tiresome.' – *New Yorker, 1982*
† Ginger Rogers was first choice for the Stanwyck role.
original story (Thomas Monroe, Billy Wilder); Alfred Newman; Barbara Stanwyck

Ballad in Blue
GB 1964 88m bw
(Warner) Alexander and Miguel Salkind (Herman Blaser)
US title: *Blues for Lovers*
A famous pianist becomes friendly with a blind boy and helps reconcile his parents.
Curious sentimental drama with the star playing himself; competent but hardly rousing.
w Burton Wohl *d* Paul Henreid *ph* Ron Taylor *m* Ray Charles, Stanley Black
☆ Ray Charles, Mary Peach, Dawn Addams, Tom Bell, Piers Bishop, Betty McDowall

Ballad of a Soldier **
USSR 1959 89m bw
Mosfilm
original title: *Ballada o Soldate*
A soldier is granted four days' home leave before returning to be killed at the front.
Lyrical tear-jerker most notable for its impeccably photographed detail of Russian domestic and everyday life.
w Valentin Yoshov, Grigori Chukrai *d Grigori Chukrai ph Vladimir Nikolayev, Era Saveleva* *m* Mikhail Ziv
☆ Vladimir Ivashev, Sharma Prokhorenko, Antonina Maximova
'In an epoch when the entertainment in most entertainment films is little more than offensive, its persuasive charm is particularly welcome.' – *MFB*
Valentin Yoshov, Grigori Chukrai
best picture

The Ballad of Berlin: see *Berliner Ballade*

The Ballad of Cable Hogue *
US 1970 121m Technicolor
Warner/Phil Feldman (Sam Peckinpah)
A gold prospector takes a lengthy and ineffectual revenge on men who robbed him, and dies trying to be a hero.
Curious peripatetic Western with the director in uncharacteristically experimental and comparatively non-violent mood. All concerned seem to be enjoying themselves, but the fun is not always communicated.
w John Crawford, Edmund Penney *d Sam Peckinpah ph Lucien Ballard m* Jerry Goldsmith
☆ Jason Robards, David Warner, Strother Martin, Slim Pickens, L. Q. Jones, Peter Whitney, R. G. Armstrong, Gene Evans, Stella Stevens
'A curiously compelling film. Like a child's playhouse, we come to love it not for its perfect symmetry but for the open way it expressed the feelings of its creator.' – *Richard Schickel*

The Ballad of Joe Hill **
Sweden 1971 115m Eastmancolor
Bo Widerberg Film (Waldemar Bergendahl)
aka: *Joe Hill*
In 1902, a Swedish immigrant in New York becomes a revolutionary and is executed for the murder of a grocer.
Romantic propaganda which incidentally gives a delightfully detailed outsider's view of period America.
wd Bo Widerberg *ph* Peter Davidson, Jorgen Persson *m* Stefan Grossman *ad* Ulf Axen
☆ Thommy Berggren, Anja Schmidt, Evert Anderson, Cathy Smith

The Ballad of Josie
US 1967 102m Techniscope
Universal (Marty Melcher)
Cleared of the manslaughter of her husband, a Western widow renovates a derelict ranch and sets up as a sheep farmer.

Tediously whimsical, unsuitably cast women's lib comedy with so few laughs that it may require to be taken seriously.
w Harold Swanton *d* Andrew V. McLaglen
ph Milton Krasner *m* Frank de Vol
☆ Doris Day, Peter Graves, George Kennedy, William Talman, Andy Devine, Audrey Christie

'In 1866, A Woman Had Two Choices ... She Could Be A Wife Or She Could Be A Whore. Josephine Monaghan Made The Boldest Choice Of All. She Chose To Be A Man.'

The Ballad of Little Jo
US 1993 121m Technicolor Panavision
Rank/Fine Line/Polygram/Joco (Fred Berner, Brenda Goodman)
A New York woman disguises herself as a man and becomes a cowboy and rancher.
Based on a true story, this becomes a feminist tract about the impossibility of being free and female in the West, which may also be true but here makes for a dull movie.
wd Maggie Greenwald *ph* Declan Quinn
m David Mansfield *pd* Mark Friedberg *ed* Keith Reamer
☆ Suzy Amis, Bo Hopkins, Ian McKellen, David Chung, Carrie Snodgress, Rene Auberjonois, Heather Graham, Sam Robards, Tom Bower
'This well-intentioned, revisionist frontier saga is too solemn and dramatically unexciting to generate wild appeal beyond a core of female viewers and ardent followers of indie pics.' – *Variety*
'It has a nice feeling for the smallness of man and his or her tenuous presence on the Western landscape.' – *Philip French, Observer*

The Ballad of Narayama *
Japan 1983 130m colour
Cannon/Toei
original title: *Narayama Bushi-Ko*
An old woman prepares to die in a community where the elderly are exposed on a mountainside when they reach the age of 70.
Often ponderous, though gripping, remake of Keisuke Kinoshita's more restrained movie, made in 1958. It won the prize for the best film at the Cannes Film Festival in 1983.
wd Shohei Imamura *novel Narayama Bushi-Ko* by Shichiro Fukazawa *ph* Masao Tochizawa
m Shinichiro Ikebe *pd* Toshio Inagaki *ed* Hajime Okayasu
☆ Ken Ogata, Sumiko Sakamoto, Tonpei Hidari, Takejo Aki, Shoichi Ozawa, Mitsuaki Fukamizu
'One of the most intense portraits of personal fulfilment in all cinema.' – *Tony Rayns, MFB*

The Ballad of Tam-Lin: see *Tam-Lin*

The Ballad of the Sad Café
US/GB 1990 101m Technicolor
Hobo/Merchant Ivory (Ismail Merchant)
On his release from prison, a rejected husband takes his revenge on his wife, a small-town store-owner.
A Southern Gothic fairy-tale transferred poorly to the screen.
w Michael Hirst *play* Edward Albee
novel Carson McCullers *d* Simon Callow
ph Walter Lassally *m* Richard Robbins *pd* Bruno Santini *ed* Andrew Marcus
☆ Vanessa Redgrave, Keith Carradine, Cork Hubbert, Rod Steiger, Austin Pendleton, Beth Dixon, Lanny Flaherty, Mert Hatfield, Earl Hindman, Anne Pitoniak
'A film of quite exceptional gracelessness.' – *Tom Milne, Sight and Sound*
'Difficult to respond to and probably will not engage mainstream audiences.' – *Variety*

Ballada o Soldate: see *Ballad of a Soldier*

Ballet Mécanique *
France 1924 10m bw silent
Fernand Léger, Dudley Murphy
Famous experimental short in which everyday images form abstract patterns.
A key to all subsequent surrealist experiments in the cinema.
wd Fernand Léger, Dudley Murphy m Georges Antheil

Balthazar *
France/Sweden 1966 95m bw
Parc/Ardos/Athos/Svenska Filminstitutet (Philippe Dussart)
original title: *Au Hasard, Balthazar*
The life of a talented donkey, born in the Swiss alps and eventually killed during a smuggling escapade.
Something between Black Beauty *and a Christian parable, this quiet, episodic film is counted by some as its director's best work.*
wd Robert Bresson ph Ghislain Cloquet *m* Jean Wiener (and Schubert) *ad* Pierre Charbonnier
ed Raymond Lamy
☆ Anne Wiazemsky, François Lafarge, Walter Green

Baltic Deputy *
USSR 1937 100m bw Lenfilm
An old professor is finally reconciled to the 1917 revolution.
Propagandist biography (of scientist K. A. Timiriazev) with interesting scenes and a strong central performance.
w the directors and others *d* Alexander Zharki, Josef Heifits *ph* M. Kaplan *m* M. Timofeyev
☆ *Nikolai Cherkassov, M. Damasheva*, A. Melnikov

The Baltimore Bullet
US 1980 103m Eastmancolor
Avco Embassy/Filmfair (John F. Brescia)
Adventures of a pair of pool sharks.
Flabby comedy attempting a lighthearted version of The Hustler *(qv). The rewards are meagre.*
w John F. Brescia, Robert Vincent O'Neill
d Robert Ellis Miller *ph* James A. Crabe
m Johnny Mandel
☆ James Coburn, Omar Sharif, Bruce Boxleitner, Ronee Blakley, Calvin Lockhart
'It manages to be stupidly macho and hopelessly incompetent at one and the same time.' – *Guardian*

Balto
US/GB 1995 77m DeLuxe
Universal/Amblin (Steve Hickner)
A woman explains to her granddaughter how a statue in New York's Central Park commemorates Balto, a half-wolf, half-dog which led a sled team that brought antitoxins to the town of Nome, Alaska, during an epidemic of diphtheria in 1925.
Bland family entertainment that begins as live action and then becomes a rather dull animated film that attempts to make some point about miscegenation.
w Cliff Ruby, Elana Lesser, David Steven Cohen, Roger S. H. Schulman *d* Simon Wells *ph* Jan Richter-Friis *m* James Horner *pd* Hans Bacher
ed Nick Fletcher, Sim Evan-Jones
☆ Miriam Margolyes, Lola Bates-Campbell and also the voices of: Kevin Bacon, Bob Hoskins, Bridget Fonda, Jim Cummings, Phil Collins, Donald Sinden
'Grossly sentimentalised as the triumph of an unwanted mongrel, but it won't do much harm to small children.' – *Derek Malcolm, Guardian*
† Balto and the other dogs in his sled team starred in a silent movie, *Balto's Race to Nome*, before becoming sideshow attractions, from which they were rescued and moved to Cleveland Zoo, where Balto lived until his death at the age of 11 in 1933.

La Bamba: see *La Bamba (under L)*

Bambi ****
US 1942 72m Technicolor
Walt Disney
The story of a forest deer, from the book by Felix Salten.
Anthropomorphic cartoon feature, one of Disney's most memorable and brilliant achievements, with a great comic character in Thumper the rabbit and a climactic forest fire sequence which is genuinely thrilling. A triumph of the animator's art.
m Frank Churchill, Edward Plumb
supervisor David Hand
☆ Featuring the voices of Peter Behn, Paula Winslowe
'The ultimate stag movie.' – *anon*
'The film, charming and touching as it can be, belongs more to the Disney of whimsy and sentiment than it does to the creative artist; and those who remember the Schubert in *Fantasia* will know what I mean when I say that a good deal of this tale of a forest deer is in Disney's Ave Maria manner.' – *Dilys Powell*
'Sheer enchantment.' – *C. A. Lejeune*
Frank Churchill, Edward Plumb; song 'Love Is a Song' (*m*Frank Churchill, *ly* Larry Morey)

Bamboozled *
US 2000 135m colour
Entertainment/New Line/40 Acres and a Mule
A lone black executive at a TV network dreams up a blackface minstrel show to shame his boss, only to discover that it becomes a hit.
Provocative, fierce and angry polemic about race that might have been more effective as a documentary: its dramatic purpose is often blunted, and is not helped by the muddy quality of the transfer from digital video.
wd Spike Lee *ph* Ellen Kuras *m* Terence Blanchard *pd* Victor Kempster *ed* Sam Pollard
cos Ruth Carter
☆ Damon Wayans (Pierre Delacroix), Savion Glover (Manray/Mantan), Jada Pinkett-Smith (Sloan Hopkins), Tommy Davidson (Womack/Sleep 'N Eat), Dunwitty (Michael Rapaport), Thomas Jefferson Byrd (Honeycutt), Paul Mooney (Junebug), Sarah Jones (Dot), Gillian Iliana Waters (Verna), Susan Batson (Orchid Dothan), Mos Def (Big Black)
'Basically sloppy, all-over-the-map filmmaking with few hints of self-criticism and few genuine laughs.' – *Jonathan Rosenbaum, Chicago Reader*
'The historical reality of all the racially insulting movies and stage acts which Lee lampoons is far more shocking than anything his film extrapolates from them.' – *Alexander Walker*

Banana Ridge
GB 1941 87m bw
ABPC
A business man's old flame presents him with an alleged son.
Stagey farce salvaged by star performances.
w Walter C. Mycroft, Lesley Storm, Ben Travers
play Ben Travers *d* Walter C. Mycroft
☆ Robertson Hare, Alfred Drayton, Isabel Jeans, Nova Pilbeam, Adele Dixon, Stewart Rome

Bananas *
US 1971 81m DeLuxe
UA/Rollins and Joffe (Jack Grossberg)
A meek and mild product tester for a New York corporation accidentally becomes a South American rebel hero.
Disjointed anarchic comedy with a few good jokes typical of their author.
w Woody Allen, Mickey Rose *d* Woody Allen
ph Andrew M. Costikyan *m* Marvin Hamlisch
☆ Woody Allen, Louise Lasser, Carlos Montalban, Jacobo Morales
'Full of hilarious comic ideas and lines, supplied by Allen and his collaborator; then Allen, the director and actor, murders them.' – *Stanley Kauffmann*
† Asked why his film was called *Bananas*, Allen replied: 'Because there are no bananas in it.'

The Bananas Boat: see *What Changed Charley Farthing?*

'You're no blue blood any more, honey. The master bought you ... and now he's waitin'!'

Band of Angels
US 1957 127m Warnercolor
Warner (no producer credited)
In 1865, a Kentucky girl learns that her mother was black and is sold as a slave, but quickly becomes her owner's mistress.
Long-winded romantic adventure, rather lamely scripted and developed. The star's presence reinforces the impression of sitting through the ghost of Gone with the Wind.
w John Twist, Ivan Goff, Ben Roberts
novel Robert Penn Warren *d* Raoul Walsh
ph Lucien Ballard *m* Max Steiner
☆ Clark Gable, Yvonne de Carlo, Sidney Poitier, Efrem Zimbalist Jnr, Patric Knowles, Rex Reason, Torin Thatcher, Andrea King
'Too absurd to be dislikeable.' – *MFB*

The Band Plays On
US 1934 87m bw
MGM
Four street kids are saved by football and eventually become national stars.
Ho-hum sentimental melodrama with plot trouble.
w Bernard Schubert, Ralph Spence, Harvey Gates
d Russell Mack
☆ Robert Young, Stuart Erwin, Leo Carrillo, Betty Furness, Ted Healy, Preston Foster, Russell Hardie, William Tannen
'Slow, long, and weak on cast names.' – *Variety*

Band Waggon *
GB 1939 85m bw
GFD/Gainsborough (Edward Black)
Comedians running a pirate TV station in a ghostly castle round up a gang of spies.
Film version of a long-running radio comedy series; quite a serviceable record of a phenomenon.
w Marriott Edgar, Val Guest *d* Marcel Varnel
ph Henry Harris
☆ *Arthur Askey, Richard Murdoch*, Jack Hylton and his band, Pat Kirkwood, Moore Marriott, Peter Gawthorne, Wally Patch, Donald Calthrop

The Band Wagon ****
US 1953 112m Technicolor
MGM (Arthur Freed)
A has-been Hollywood dancer joins forces with a temperamental stage producer to put on a Broadway musical.
Simple but sophisticated musical with the bare minimum of plot, told mostly in jokes, and the maximum of music and song. Numbers include those listed below, as well as a spoof Mickey Spillane ballet finale. Level of technical accomplishment very high.
w Adolph Green, Betty Comden d Vincente Minnelli
ph Harry Jackson *m* Adolph Deutsch
m/ly Howard Dietz, Arthur Schwartz ad Cedric Gibbons, Preston Ames
☆ *Fred Astaire, Jack Buchanan, Oscar Levant*, Cyd Charisse, Nanette Fabray
'The best musical of the month, the year, the decade, or for all I know of all time.' – *Archer Winsten*
† The Jack Buchanan character, Jeffrey Cordova, was first offered to Clifton Webb. It was loosely based on José Ferrer, who in the early fifties produced four Broadway shows all running at the same time, and acted in a fifth
♫ 'A Shine on Your Shoes', 'By Myself', 'That's Entertainment', 'Dancing in the Dark', 'Triplets', 'New Sun in the Sky', 'I Guess I'll Have to Change My Plan', 'Louisiana Hayride', 'I Love Louisa', 'Girl Hunt' ballet.
Adolph Green, Betty Comden; Adolph Deutsch

Bande à Part
France 1964 95m bw
Anouchka/Orsay (Philippe Dussart)
aka: *The Outsiders*
Aimless young people plan a robbery which ends in murder.
Despite the plot, the emphasis is on fragments of lyricism, and the film is not among its director's greatest successes.
wd Jean-Luc Godard *novel Fool's Gold* by Dolores Hitchens *ph* Raoul Coutard *m* Michel Legrand
ed Agnes Guillemot
☆ Anna Karina (Odile), Claude Brasseur (Arthur), Sami Frey (Franz), Louisa Colpeyn (Mme Victoria), Daniele Girard (English teacher)
'In a sense, the whole film is a metaphor illustrating this glancing collision, when fantasy and reality merge but one may still remain unsure which is which.' – *Tom Milne, MFB*

Bandido
US 1956 92m DeLuxe Cinemascope
UA/Robert L. Jacks
Mexico 1916: an American adventurer helps a rebel leader to defeat a gun runner.
Standard action fare, rather slackly handled.
w Earl Felton *d* Richard Fleischer *ph* Ernest Laszlo *m* Max Steiner
☆ Robert Mitchum, Gilbert Roland, Zachary Scott, Ursula Thiess

The Bandit *
Brazil 1953 119m bw
Companhia Cinematographica (Cid Leite da Silva)
original title: *O'Cangaceiro*
The leader of a gang of outlaws comes to grief after falling out with his second in command over a woman.
One of the few Brazilian films to achieve international popularity, mainly because of its memorable theme tune. The film itself looks attractive but becomes a bit of a bore.
wd Lima Barreto *ph* Chick Fowle *m* Gabriel Migliori
☆ Alberto Ruschel, Milton Ribeiro, Marisa Prado

The Bandit of Sherwood Forest *
US 1946 87m Technicolor
Columbia (Leonard S. Picker, Clifford Sanforth)
Robin Hood frustrates the Regent who plans to usurp the throne from the boy king.
A lively romp through Sherwood Forest with a capable cast.
w Wilfrid H. Pettitt, Melvin Levy *novel* Son of Robin Hood by Paul A. Castleton *d* George Sherman, Henry Levin *ph* Tony Gaudio, William Snyder, George Meehan *m* Hugo Friedhofer
☆ Cornel Wilde, Anita Louise, Edgar Buchanan, Jill Esmond, Henry Daniell, George Macready, Russell Hicks, John Abbott, Lloyd Corrigan

The Bandit of Zhobe
GB 1959 81m Technicolor Cinemascope
Warwick/Columbia
An Indian chieftain kidnaps a British major's daughter in retaliation for the death of his wife.
Tinpot action melodrama in the wake of the rather better Zarak *(qv).*
wd John Gilling
☆ Victor Mature, Anthony Newley, Anne Aubrey, Norman Wooland

The Bandit Queen
US 1950 69m bw
Lippert (William Berke)
The daughter of murdered Spaniards in California takes revenge against violent settlers from the east.
Predictable Western adventure on a low budget.
w Victor West and Budd Lesser *d* William Berke
☆ Barbara Britton, Willard Parker, Barton MacLane, Philip Reed, Victor Kilian, Thurston Hall

Bandit Queen *
GB/India 1994 120m colour
Mainline/Kaleidoscope/Channel 4 (Sundeep Singh Bedi)
Phoolan Devi, an illiterate, low-caste, much-abused woman, becomes a feared leader of outlaws and takes her revenge on her tormentors before surrendering to the authorities.
An Indian movie made for the West, often stirring and always interesting but raising more questions than it answers in its treatment of its real-life heroine, who is alternately presented as a victim and a victimizer.
w Mala Sen, Ranjit Kapoor *d* Sheka Kapur *ph* Ashok Mehta *m* Nusrat Fateh Ali Khan *pd* Eve Mavrakis *ed* Renu Saluja
☆ Seema Biswas, Nirmal Pandey, Manjoj Bajpai, Rajesh Vivek, Raghuvir Yadav, Saurabh Shukla, Govind Namdeo
'This makes a welcome breather from all the usual air-brushed Raj epics and dotty Bollywood excesses, presenting an India which is dirty, unglamorous but still so mysterious.' – *Steve Beard, Empire*
'Essentially *Bandit Queen* just transforms Phoolan Devi from being India's best-known bandit into history's most famous victim of rape.' – *Arundhati Roy, Independent*
† The film's Indian release was delayed after Phoolan Devi sued Channel 4 and the makers of the film for invasion of her privacy by depicting her rape and for prejudicing her forthcoming trial by implicating her in a mass murder that she denies.

Bandit Ranger
US 1942 60m bw
RKO (Bert Gilroy)
A rancher, attempting to expose a phoney Texas Ranger and a gang of cattle-rustlers, finds himself framed for murder.
Second-feature Western with a better than average narrative, though otherwise it's the usual mix of action, romance, a song or two, and a little comedy.
w Bennett R. Cohen, Morton Grant *d* Lesley Selander *ph* Nicholas Musuraca *m* Paul Sawtell *m/ly* Fred Rose, Ray Whitley *ad* Albert S. D'Agostino, Walter E. Keller *ed* Les Millbrook
☆ Tim Holt, Cliff Edwards, Joan Barclay, Kenneth Harlan, Glenn Strange, Leroy Mason

Banditi a Orgosolo: see *Bandits of Orgosolo*

'Two's Company, Three's A Crime.'
Bandits
US 2001 122m DeLuxe Panavision
TCF/Hyde Park/Empire/Lotus/Baltimore/Spring Creek/Cheyenne (Michael Birnbaum, Michele Berk, Barry Levinson, Paula Weinstein, Ashok Amritraj, David Hoberman, Arnold Rifkin)
Two bankrobbers both fall for a frustrated housewife who joins their gang.
Wise-cracking buddy movie, too slapdash to be more than occasionally amusing.
w Harley Peyton *d* Barry Levinson *ph* Dante Spinotti *m* Christopher Young *pd* Victor Kempster *ed* Stu Linder *cos* Gloria Gresham
☆ Bruce Willis (Joe Blake), Billy Bob Thornton (Terry Collins), Cate Blanchett (Kate Wheeler), Troy Garity (Harvey Pollard), Brian F. O'Byrne (Darill Miller), Stacey Travis (Cloe Miller), Bobby Slayton (Darren Head), January Jones (Claire), William Converse-Roberts (Charles Wheeler)
'A comedy that might have made Butch and Sundance jump off a cliff.' – *Liza Schwarzbaum, Entertainment Weekly*

Bandits of Corsica *
US 1951 83m bw
Global/UA
GB title: *The Return of the Corsican Brothers*
Mario and his gypsy twin get together to unseat a tyrant.
Rather muffled actioner with adequate highlights.
w Richard Schayer *d* Ray Nazarro
☆ Richard Greene, Paula Raymond, Raymond Burr, Dona Drake, Raymond Greenleaf, Lee Van Cleef
† See also: *The Corsican Brothers.*

Bandits of Orgosolo
Italy 1961 98m bw
Vittorio de Seta/Titanus
A Sardinian shepherd shelters some bandits and becomes one of them.
Rather slow character adventure which achieved some international reputation on its first release.
w Vittorio de Seta, Vera Gherarducci *m* Valentino Bucci *d/ph* Vittorio de Seta
☆ Michele Cossu, Peppeddu Cuccu, and amateur cast

Bandolero! *
US 1968 108m DeLuxe Panavision
Fox (Robert L. Jacks)
In Texas, fugitive outlaw brothers run into trouble with their Mexican counterparts.
Dour and downbeat but well-staged Western with emphasis on hanging and rape; an unusual mixture but smoothly assembled.
w James Lee Barrett *d* Andrew V. McLaglen *ph* William H. Clothier *m* Jerry Goldsmith
☆ James Stewart, Dean Martin, Raquel Welch, George Kennedy, Will Geer, Andrew Prine

Bang: see *The Big Bang Theory (1995)*

Bang *
US 1996 110m colour
Polygram/Eagle Eye (Daniel M. Berger, Ladd Vance)
Thrown out of her apartment for non-payment of rent and humiliated by everyone she meets, a Los Angeles actress steals a cop's uniform, motorbike and gun after he propositions her for sex, and discovers how empowering her appearance becomes.
Energetic, low-budget, independent movie that shows signs of haste in its making, but also of a quirky and individual talent.
wd Ash *ph* David Gasperik *pd* Daniel M. Berger *ed* Ash, Daniel M. Berger
☆ Darling Narita, Peter Greene, Michael Newland, David Allan Graff, Stanley Herman, Noble James, Art Cruz, Luis Guizar
† The film was made at a cost of $20,000.

Bang the Drum Slowly
US 1973 96m Movielab
Paramount (Maurice and Lois Rosenfield)
A baseball star finds that he is dying of leukemia.
Cliché-ridden tearjerker in the modern style.
w Mark Harris *novel* Mark Harris *d* John Hancock *ph* Richard Shore *m* Stephen Lawrence
☆ Michael Moriarty, Robert De Niro, Vincent Gardenia, Phil Foster
Vincent Gardenia

Bang, You're Dead
GB 1954 88m bw
British Lion/Wellington (Lance Comfort)
US title: *Game of Danger*
A small boy accidentally shoots a local villain, and another man is arrested.
Singularly pointless and unattractive melodrama, a long way behind The Window *and* The Yellow Balloon *(qqv).*
w Guy Elmes, Ernest Borneman *d* Lance Comfort *ph* Brendan J. Stafford *m* Eric Spear
☆ Jack Warner, Derek Farr, Veronica Hurst, Gordon Harker, Michael Medwin, Anthony Richmond, Philip Saville

Bangkok: Dangerous
Thailand 2000 106m colour
Metro Tartan/Film Bangkok (Nonzee Nimibutr)
A deaf-mute hitman develops some remorse for his killings.
Flashy, brutal thriller that aims for fashionable gloss and a high body count; it achieves the latter.
wd Oxide Pang, Danny Pang *ph* Decha Srimantra *m* Orange Music *pd* Wut Chaosilp *ed* Oxide Pang, Danny Pang
☆ Pawalit Mongkolpisit (Kong), Premsinee Ratanasopha (Fon), Patharawarin Timkul (Aom), Pisek Intrakanchit (Joe), Korkiate Limpapat, Piya Boonnak
'A violent, hyperkinetic film noir overpainted in broad sentimental strokes.' – *David Kehr, New York Times*
'The narrative is repeatedly lost in a blizzard of subliminal editing and stylishly angled shots: I counted 35 separate "cuts" inside a minute. It's like watching an entire film in fast-forward mode.' – *Alexander Walker, London Evening Standard*

Banjo on my Knee **
US 1936 95m bw
TCF (Nunnally Johnson)
In a Mississippi riverboat shanty town, a wedding night is interrupted when the groom is arrested during a brawl.
Unusual, easy-going comedy in which the stars sing and dance as well as fool around.
w Nunnally Johnson novel Harry Hamilton *d John Cromwell ph* Ernest Palmer *m* Arthur Lange *m/ly* Jimmy McHugh, Harold Adamson
☆ Barbara Stanwyck, Joel McCrea, Buddy Ebsen, Walter Brennan, Helen Westley, Walter Catlett, Tony Martin, Katherine de Mille
'Too complicated for any better than moderate reception.' – *Variety*

The Bank Breaker: see *Kaleidoscope*

The Bank Detective: see *The Bank Dick*

The Bank Dick ***
US 1940 73m bw
Universal
GB title: *The Bank Detective*
In Lompoc, California, a ne'er-do-well accidentally stops a hold-up, is made a bank detective, acquires deeds to a worthless mine and interferes in the production of a film.
Imperfect, but probably the best Fields vehicle there is: the jokes sometimes end in mid-air, but there are delicious moments and very little padding. The character names are sometimes funnier than the script: they include Egbert Sousè (accent grave over the 'e'), J. Pinkerton Snoopington, Ogg Oggilbie and Filthy McNasty.
w Mahatma Kane Jeeves (W. C. Fields) *d* Eddie Cline *ph* Milton Krasner *md* Charles Previn
☆ *W. C. Fields*, Franklin Pangborn, Una Merkel, Shemp Howard, Jack Norton, Grady Sutton, Cora Witherspoon
'One of the great classics of American comedy.' – *Robert Lewis Taylor*
'When the man is funny he is terrific ... but the story is makeshift, the other characters are stock types, the only pace discernible is the distance between drinks or the rhythm of the fleeting seconds it takes Fields to size up trouble coming and duck the hell out.' – *Otis Ferguson*
'Individualistic display of broad comedy ... adequate program supporter.' – *Variety*
† Fields's writing nom-de-plume was allegedly borrowed from noble characters in old English plays he squirmed through as a youth. They kept saying: 'M'hat, m'cane, Jeeves.'

Bank Holiday *
GB 1938 86m bw
GFD/Gainsborough (Edward Black)
US title: *Three on a Weekend*
The lives of various people intertwine during a day out in Brighton.
Simple but effective slice-of-life comedy-drama, establishing several actors and a director. Still quite refreshing.
w Hans Wilhelm, Rodney Ackland, Roger Burford *d Carol Reed ph* Arthur Crabtree *md* Louis Levy *ad* Vetchinsky *ed* R. E. Dearing, Alfred Roome
☆ Margaret Lockwood, Hugh Williams, John Lodge, Kathleen Harrison, Wally Patch, Rene Ray, Linden Travers, Garry Marsh, Wilfrid Lawson
'Ranges from pathos to farce with a nice avoidance of overstatement.' – *Daily Telegraph*

Bank Robber
US 1993 91m Foto-Kem
IRS/Initial (Lisa Cazés)
A bank robber hides in a seedy hotel where every guest recognizes him and demands a share of the loot in return for keeping quiet about it.
Vacuous comedy that lacks jokes and tries to compensate by putting the emphasis on sex.
wd Nick Mead *ph* Andrzej Sekula *m* Stewart Copeland
☆ Patrick Dempsey, Lisa Bonet, Judge Reinhold, Forest Whitaker, Olivia D'Abo, Mariska Hargitay, Michael Jeter
'File under misfire.' – *Film Review*

The Bank Shot *
US 1974 83m DeLuxe
UA/Hal Landers, Bobby Roberts
Using house-moving equipment, an escaped convict steals a whole bank.
Extended chase comedy with scenes of gleeful destruction. Acceptable for those in the mood, but a shade overdone.
w Wendell Mayes *novel* Donald E. Westlake *d* Gower Champion *ph* Harry Stradling Jnr *m* John Morris
☆ George C. Scott, Joanna Cassidy, Sorrell Booke, G. Wood, Clifton James

Bannerline *
US 1951 87m bw
MGM (Henry Berman)
To comfort a dying old man, a young reporter prints a fake newspaper showing the indictment of the old man's gangster enemy. By an odd chain of events, the story becomes true.
Worthy but rather dull MGM 'B', typical of the regime of Dore Schary, boasting a pleasing small-town atmosphere and a remarkable cast of old actors.
w Charles Schnee *story* Samson Raphaelson *d* Don Weis *ph* Harold Lipstein *m* Rudolph Kopp
☆ Lionel Barrymore, Keefe Brasselle, Sally Forrest, Lewis Stone, Elisabeth Risdon, J. Carrol Naish, Spring Byington, Larry Keating

Banning
US 1967 102m Techniscope
Universal (Dick Berg)
A golf pro has sporting and amorous adventures at a country club.
Tedious, complexly plotted melodrama of life among the idle rich; handling generally laboured. A showcase for the studio's young contract talent.

w James Lee *d* Ron Winston *ph* Loyal Griggs *m* Quincy Jones

☆ Robert Wagner, Anjanette Comer, Jill St John, Guy Stockwell, James Farentino, Susan Clark, Howard St John, Mike Kellin, Sean Garrison, Gene Hackman

song 'The Eyes of Love' (*m*Quincy Jones, *ly* Bob Russell)

BAPS

US 1997 92m DeLuxe

Entertainment/New Line/Island (Mark Burg, Loretha Jones)

A waitress is offered a small fortune to impersonate the lost granddaughter of a dying millionaire's old love.

Exceptionally dreary and raucous comedy, feebly plotted.

w Troy Beyer *d* Robert Townsend *ph* Bill Dill *m* Stanley Clarke *pd* Keith Brian Burns *ed* Patrick Kennedy

☆ Halle Berry, Martin Landau, Ian Richardson, Natalie Desselle, Troy Beyer, Luigi Amodeo, Jonathan Fried

'Words cannot convey the multi-hued frightfulness of this film.' – *Derek Malcolm, Guardian*

† The title is an acronym for Black American Princesses.

'Finally ... a romantic comedy without men.'

Bar Girls

US 1994 94m Foto-Kem

Lavender Hill Mob (Lauren Hoffman, Marita Giovanni)

A lesbian begins a relationship with a married actress whom she picks up at her local bar.

A slick, somewhat theatrical low-budget movie that isn't likely to have much appeal outside its target audience; its emphasis on courtship rituals among its youngish lesbians has an earnestness that precludes both romance and wit.

w Lauren Hoffman *play* Lauren Hoffman *d* Marita Giovanni *ph* Michael Ferris *m* Lenny Meyers *ad* Darryl Fong, Keith Brunsmann *ed* Carter De Haven

☆ Nancy Allison Wolfe, Liza D'Agostino, Camila Griggs, Lisa Parker, Justine Slater, Paula Sorge, Michael Harris

The Bar Sinister

US 1955 87m Eastmancolor Cinemascope

MGM (Henry Berman)

GB title: *It's a Dog's Life*

The rise in lifestyle of a Bowery bull terrier, as told by himself.

Tolerable whimsy, in MGM's best family manner; ten years earlier it might have been a hit.

w John Michael Hayes *story* Richard Harding Davis *d* Herman Hoffman *ph* Paul Vogel *m* Elmer Bernstein

☆ Edmund Gwenn, Jeff Richards, Jarma Lewis, Dean Jagger

Barabbas *

Italy/US 1962 144m Technirama

Columbia/Dino de Laurentiis

Pardoned instead of Christ, Barabbas is sentenced to the silver mines, turns Christian, and becomes a gladiator.

Overblown epic which starts with a genuine eclipse of the sun and has nowhere to go but down. The cast sparks a few moments, but it is generally a gaudy display of carnage.

w Christopher Fry, Nigel Balchin, Diego Fabbri, Ivo Perilli *novel* Pär Lagerkvist *d* Richard Fleischer *ph* Aldo Tonti *m* Mario Nascimbene *ad* Mario Chiari

☆ Anthony Quinn, Silvana Mangano, Vittorio Gassman, Ernest Borgnine, Jack Palance, Arthur Kennedy, Norman Wooland, Valentina Cortese, Harry Andrews, Katy Jurado, Michael Gwynn

'Unacceptable in its pain-preoccupation and its religiosity.' – *Peter John Dyer*

† The eclipse of the sun at the beginning is a real one, photographed at Nice.

'A world beyond words.'

Baraka *

US 1992 97m colour Todd-AO

Mayfair/Magidson (Mark Magidson)

Scenes of nature are followed by those of religious celebrations around the world, of human life and work, of death in war and funeral rituals.

A film made by the cinematographer of Koyaanisqatsi *(qv), and similar in style, though less coherent in its selection of images, stunning though they often are.*

w Ron Fricke, Mark Magidson, Bob Green *d* Ron Fricke *ph* Ron Fricke *m* Michael Stearns *ed* Ron Fricke, Mark Magidson, David E. Aubrey, Alton Walpole

'Comes over as an animated *National Geographic*.' – *Sight and Sound*

'Perhaps one needs to see it on a psychedelic substance to discern a pattern or coherent structure.' – *Empire*

'In A World Gone To Hell Even Angels Carry Guns.'

Barb Wire

US 1996 99m Technicolor

Polygram/Propaganda/Dark Horse (Mike Richardson, Todd Moyer, Brad Wyman)

In 2017, while civil war rages in the States, a club-owner and bounty hunter, who favours tight black leather and high heels, goes in search of some contact lenses that can save the world.

A film that renders criticism superfluous: a comic-book adventure that seems even more cartoon-like than the original.

w Chuck Pfarrer, Ilene Chaiken *d* David Hogan *ph* Rick Bota *m* Michel Colombier *pd* Jean-Philippe Carp *ed* Peter Schink

☆ Pamela Anderson Lee, Temuera Morrison, Victoria Rowell, Jack Noseworthy, Xander Berkeley, Udo Kier, Steve Railsback, Clint Howard

'Resembles *Mad Max* with brassieres and deserves to be mocked.' – *Guardian*

'A slow, dim-witted, second-rate rock video that is devoid of energy, excitement or imagination.' – *Sunday Times*

'See her do her thing!'

Barbarella *

France/Italy 1967 98m Technicolor Panavision

Marianne/Dino de Laurentiis

A beautiful young 40th-century astronaut prevents the positronic ray from getting into the wrong hands.

Campy and slightly sick adventures with angels and other space people, from a highly censorable comic strip; some ingenious gadgetry and design, but not much of interest in the foreground.

w Terry Southern *book* Jean-Claude Forest *d* Roger Vadim *ph* Claude Renoir *m* Bob Crewe, Charles Fox *pd* Mario Garbuglia

☆ Jane Fonda, John Phillip Law, Anita Pallenberg, Milo O'Shea, David Hemmings, Marcel Marceau, Ugo Tognazzi, Claude Dauphin

'A leading science fiction authority has claimed that if Lewis Carroll were alive today he would inevitably have written not *Alice's Adventures in Wonderland* but *Lolita*. He might perhaps equally well have written *Barbarella*.' – *Jack Ibberson*

'A flaccid, jaded appeal to our baser appetites, always liberally doused with essence of cop-out, resulting in elucubrated, anaemic pornography.' – *John Simon*

The Barbarian

US 1933 82m approx bw

MGM

GB title: *A Night in Cairo*

An American lady travelling in the Middle East falls for a local potentate.

Shades of The Sheik *(qv). Actually this version was first filmed in 1915 by Edgar Selwyn from his own play, then again in 1924. Any version would seem fairly hysterical now.*

w Anita Loos, Elmer Harris *play* Edgar Selwyn *d* Sam Wood *ph* Harold Rosson

☆ Ramon Novarro, Myrna Loy, Reginald Denny, C. Aubrey Smith, Louise Closser Hale, Edward Arnold

'An abrupt switch to melodrama at the halfway mark makes this a maudlin, doubtful desert melodrama.' – *Variety*

The Barbarian and the Geisha *

US 1958 105m Eastmancolor Cinemascope

TCF (Eugene Frenke)

In 1856 the first US diplomat to visit Japan meets local opposition but is helped by a geisha.

Episodic semi-historical romance which scarcely suits the talents of those involved.

w Charles Grayson *d* John Huston *ph* Charles G. Clarke *m* Hugo Friedhofer

☆ John Wayne, Eiko Ando, Sam Jaffe, So Yamamura

'It is saddening to think that the director of *The Asphalt Jungle* has gained professional freedom and international celebrity to become, at 51, yet another taskmaster who goes out in the midday sun.' – *Arlene Croce*

Barbarian Queen

US 1985 82m colour

Concorde/Rodeo (Frank Isaac, Alex Sessa)

When their men are kidnapped, women warriors go on the warpath.

One of the reasons that the fad for films of the sword and sorcery genre was so short-lived – muscle-bound men and scantily clad women of minimal acting ability are not enough to attract an audience.

d Hector Olivera *ph* Rudy Donovan *m* Chris Young, Jamie Horner *pd* Julia Bertram *ed* Sylvia Roberts, Leslie Rosenthal *sp* Willy Smith, Arny Alfieri

☆ Lana Clarkson, Katt Shea, Frank Zagarino, Dawn Dunlap, Susana Traverso, Victor Bo, Arman Chapman, Andrea Barbizon

† A sequel of even less interest, *Barbarian Queen 2*, directed by Joe Finley, followed in 1988.

The Barbarians

US/Italy 1987 88m colour

Cannon (John Thompson)

In a primitive world, twin musclemen take on warring tribes and wizards to rescue their queen.

Dim-witted sword and sorcery movie that never rises above the risible.

w James R. Silke *d* Ruggero Deodato *ph* Lorenzo Battaglia *m* Pino Donaggio *pd* Giuseppe Mangano *ed* Eugene Alabiso

☆ David Paul, Peter Paul, Richard Lynch, Eva La Rue, Virginia Bryant, Sheeba Alahani, Michael Berryman, Nanni Bernini

Barbarosa *

US 1981 90m Eastmancolor Panavision

ITC/Wittliff-Nelson-Busey (Paul N. Lazarus III)

An outlaw's legend grows along with his enemies.

Undercast but interestingly directed Western, with more than enough elegiac qualities mixed with some nods to the old enjoyable style.

w William D. Wittliff *d* Fred Schepisi *ph* Ian Baker *m* Bruce Smeaton

☆ Willie Nelson, Gary Busey, Isela Vega, Gilbert Roland, George Voskovec

'The most spirited and satisfying new western epic in several years.' – *New Yorker*

'More than its share of artistic merit.' – *Variety*

Barbary Coast **

US 1935 91m bw

Samuel Goldwyn

During San Francisco's gold rush days a ruthless club owner builds a lonely girl into a star attraction but cannot win her love.

Juicy melodrama tailored for its stars, but with excellent background detail, sets and lighting.

w Ben Hecht, Charles MacArthur *d* Howard Hawks *ph* Ray June *m* Alfred Newman

☆ Edward G. Robinson, Miriam Hopkins, Joel McCrea, Walter Brennan, Frank Craven, Brian Donlevy, Donald Meek

'More than a year ago Sam Goldwyn picked Barbary Coast as a title and called in Hecht and MacArthur to write a story to fit. Result is a picture that has all it takes to get along in thoroughbred company.' – *Variety*

† David Niven made his first screen appearance as an extra.

Ray June

Barbary Coast Gent

US 1944 87m bw

MGM (Orville Dull)

A bandit from the Californian goldfields tries to go straight in San Francisco.

Star comedy drama, somewhat below par despite attractive settings and good production.

w William Lipman, Grant Garrett, Harry Ruskin *d* Roy del Ruth *ph* Charles Salerno Jnr *m* David Snell

☆ Wallace Beery, Binnie Barnes, Frances Rafferty, Chill Wills, Ray Collins, John Carradine, Noah Beery, Morris Ankrum, Henry O'Neill, Donald Meek, Paul Hurst, Louise Beavers

Barbed Wire *

US 1927 85m approx bw silent

Paramount

A French girl falls for a German prisoner of war.

Almost forgotten war film which seems at least worthy of comparison with All Quiet on the Western Front *(qv), which was made three years later.*

w Jules Furthman and Rowland V. Lee *novel The Woman of Knockaloe* by Hall Caine *d* Rowland V. Lee *ph* Bert Glennon

☆ Pola Negri, Clive Brook, Einar Hanson, Claude Gillingwater, Gustav von Seyffertitz

The Barber of Siberia

Russia/France/Italy/Czech 1999 176m colour Panavision

Intermedia/Three T/Camera One/France 2/MedusaBarrandov Biografia (Michel Seydoux)

original title: *Sibirski Tsiriulnik*

An American woman remembers her visit to Russia and romantic involvements with a jealous cadet and a general.

Heavy-handed comedy and an unconvincing romance wreck this good-looking but over-extended drama.

w Nikita Mikhalkov, Rustam Ibragimbekov, Rospo Pallenberg *d* Nikita Mikhalkov *ph* Pavel Lebeshev *m* Edward Nicolai Artemyev *pd* Vladimir Aronin *ed* Enzo Meniconi *cos* Natasha Ivanova, Sergei Struchev

☆ Julia Ormond (Jane Callahan), Oleg Menshikov (Andrei Tolstoy), Richard Harris (Douglas McCracken), Alexei Petrenko (Gen Radlov), Vladimir Ilyin (Capt Mokin), Alexander Yakovlev (Maximich), Marat Basharov (Polievsky), Daniel Olbrychski (Kopnovsky), Anna Mikhalkova (Dunvasha), Robert Hardy (Forsten), Nikita Mikhalkov (Czar Alexander III), Isabelle Renauld (Czarina), Evgeny Steblov (Grand Duke), Mac MacDonald (Sgt 'Mad Dog' O'Leary)

'Surely a contender for the Most Boring film of All Time award.' – *Peter Bradshaw, Guardian*

'Americans. Anti-Americans. In love.'

Barcelona *

US 1994 101m Technicolor

Rank/Castle Rock//Westerly (Whit Stillman)

In the mid-1980s, two American cousins find that life and love in the Spanish city are fraught with problems.

A leisurely exploration of cultural and racial differences that is intermittently interesting but not always convincing; it consists of a great deal of talk about not very much.

wd Whit Stillman *ph* John Thomas *m* Mark Suozzo *pd* José Mareia Botines *ed* Christopher Tellefsen

☆ Taylor Nichols, Chris Eigeman, Tushka Bergen, Mira Sorvino, Hellena Schmied, Pep Munne, Nuria Badia, Francis Creighton

'Although the picture begins promisingly, its charm peters out fast. Every scene seems to make the same not very interesting point: that Americans get a bum rap from foreigners.' – *Terrence Rafferty, New Yorker*

'The city of Barcelona looks beautiful, but everything in the movie is negligent, underdeveloped, unfelt.' – *David Denby, New York*

Bardelys the Magnificent

US 1926 88m (24 fps) bw silent

MGM

A 16th-century French adventurer finally wins his fair lady.

Laboured swashbuckler.

w Dorothy Farnum *novel* Rafael Sabatini *d* King Vidor

☆ John Gilbert, Eleanor Boardman, George K. Arthur

The Bare Breasted Countess: see *Female Vampire*

Barefaced Flatfoot ***

US 1952 7m Technicolor

UPA (Stephen Bosustow)

Mr Magoo battles shortsightedly to save his nephew from the underworld.

Archetypal Magoo cartoon. ('Didn't we meet in Heidelberg?' he murmurs to the dummy he is duelling with his umbrella.) The title is a spoof on a contemporary Columbia movie, The Barefoot Mailman *(qv).*

pd John Hubley

'The world's most beautiful animal!'

The Barefoot Contessa *

US 1954 128m Technicolor

UA/Figaro (Forrest E. Johnston)

A glamorous barefoot dancer in a Spanish cabaret is turned into a Hollywood star, but her sexual frustrations lead to a tragic end.

A fascinating farrago of addled philosophy and lame wisecracks, very typical of a writer-director here not at his best, decorated by a splendid gallery of actors and some attractive settings.

wd Joseph L. Mankiewicz ph Jack Cardiff m Mario Nascimbene

☆ Humphrey Bogart (Harry Dawes), Ava Gardner (Maria Vargas), Edmond O'Brien (Oscar Muldoon), Marius Goring (Alberto Bravano), Valentina Cortesa (Eleonora Torlato-Favrini), Rossano Brazzi (Vincenzo Torlato-Favrini), Elizabeth Sellars (Jerry), Warren Stevens (Kirk Edwards), Franco Interlenghi (Pedro), Mari Aldon (Myrna)

HARRY: 'Life, every now and then, behaves as though it had seen too many bad movies, when everything fits too well – the beginning, the middle, the end – from fade-in to fade-out.'

'This example of the Higher Lunacy must vie with *Johnny Guitar* for the silliest film of the year.' – *Gavin Lambert*

'A trash masterpiece: a Cinderella story in which the prince turns out to be impotent.' – *Pauline Kael, 1968*

Edmond O'Brien

Joseph L. Mankiewicz (as writer)

The Barefoot Executive *

US 1970 96m Technicolor

Walt Disney (Bill Anderson)

A TV network discovers that its most infallible average viewer is a chimpanzee.

Quite a beguiling little farcical comedy with mild doses of satire.

w Joseph L. McEveety *d* Robert Butler *ph* Charles F. Wheeler *m* Robert F. Brunner

☆ Kurt Russell, Harry Morgan, Joe Flynn, Wally Cox, Heather North, Alan Hewitt, Hayden Rorke

'Break the rules! Make love! Fall over laughing!'

Barefoot in the Park **

US 1967 109m Technicolor

Paramount/Hal B. Wallis

A pair of New York newlyweds rent a cold water flat at the top of a liftless building, and manage to marry the bride's mother to an eccentric neighbour.

Breezy but overlong adaptation of a stage play which succeeded through audience response to its one-liners, which on the screen sometimes fall flat. The people are nice, though.

w Neil Simon play Neil Simon *d* Gene Saks *ph* Joseph LaShelle *m* Neal Hefti

☆ Robert Redford (Paul Bratter), Jane Fonda (Corie Bratter), *Mildred Natwick* (Ethel Banks), *Charles Boyer* (Victor Velasco), Herb Edelman (Harry Pepper), Mabel Albertson (Aunt Harriet), Fritz Feld (restaurant owner)

ETHEL: 'Make him feel important. If you do that, you'll have a happy and wonderful marriage – like two out of every ten couples.'

ETHEL: 'I feel like we've died and gone to heaven – only we had to climb up.'

Mildred Natwick

The Barefoot Mailman

US 1951 82m Supercinecolor

Columbia (Robert Cohn)

In 19th-century Florida, the mailman is joined by a confidence trickster who later has a change of heart.

Inept comedy adventure which never really gets started.

w James Gunn, Francis Swann *novel* Theodore Pratt *d* Earl McEvoy *ph* Ellis W. Carter *m* George Duning

☆ Robert Cummings, Jerome Courtland, Terry Moore, John Russell, Will Geer, Arthur Shields, Trevor Bardette

† This is the title parodied by the Mr Magoo cartoon *Barefaced Flatfoot* (qv).

Barfly *

US 1987 99m TVC Color

Cannon/Barbet Schroeder, Fred Roos, Tom Luddy

A self-styled poet of the bottle lords it over a Los Angeles bar.

Unrelieved serio-comic wallow in the underside of American life. For connoisseurs and idiots as well as star fans.

w Charles Bukowski *d* Barbet Schroeder *ph* Robby Muller *m* none *pd* Bob Ziembicki

☆ Mickey Rourke, Faye Dunaway, Alice Krige, Jack Nance

The Bargee *

GB 1964 106m Techniscope

AB/Galton-Simpson (W. A. Whitaker)

A canal barge Casanova is trapped into marriage.

The long-awaited comedy which was supposed to make a film star out of TV's Young Steptoe turned out to be rough and vulgar but not very funny.

w Ray Galton, Alan Simpson *d* Duncan Wood *ph* Harry Waxman *m* Frank Cordell

☆ Harry H. Corbett (Hemel), Ronnie Barker (Ronnie), Hugh Griffith (Joe), Eric Sykes (Mariner), Julia Foster (Christine), Miriam Karlin (Nellie), Eric Barker (Foreman), Derek Nimmo (Dr Scott), Norman Bird, Richard Briers (Tomkins)

Baritone **

Poland 1984 96m colour

PRF Zespoly Filmowe/Zespol Perspektywa (Barbara Pec-Slesicka)

original title: *Baryton*

In the early 1930s a famous Polish opera singer returns home after 25 years, only to lose his voice before a celebratory concert.

Zestful satiric portrayal of egomania and doublecross, set against the rise of Nazism.

w Feliks Falk *d* Janusz Zaorski *ph* Witold Adamek *m* Jerzy Satanowski *ad* Allan Starski *ed* Halina Pruga-Ketling

☆ Zbigniew Zapasiewicz, Piotr Fronczewski, Janusz Blyczyński, Marcin Troński, Malgorzata Pieczyńska, Zofia Saretok

The Barkleys of Broadway *

US 1949 109m Technicolor

MGM (Arthur Freed)

A quarrelling couple of musical comedy stars split up, and she becomes a serious actress.

A rather flat and unattractive reunion for a famous pair, with a witless script, poorish numbers and very little style. The compensations are minor.

w Adolph Green, Betty Comden *d* Charles Walters *ph* Harry Stradling *m/ly* Harry Warren, Ira Gershwin *md* Lennie Hayton

☆ Fred Astaire, Ginger Rogers, Oscar Levant, Jacques François, Billie Burke

† Ginger Rogers was in fact second choice; Judy Garland was cast but withdrew through illness.

Harry Stradling

Barnabo of the Mountains

France/Italy/Switzerland 1994 124m colour

Artificial Eye/Nautilus/Number One/Flach/RAI-1 (Tommaso Dazzi, Gabriella Lazzoni)

original title: *Barnabo della Montagne*

In the early 20s, a mountain ranger with pacifist tendencies is sacked for failing to shoot at some murderous poachers and, after much wandering, returns to the mountains.

More a celebration of the Dolomites than an exploration of character, this is a film where little happens, very slowly; its mainly amateur cast are required only to register rock-like characteristics and to blend with the magnificence of the landscape.

w Angelo Pasquini, Mario Brenta, Francesco Alberti, Enrico Soci *novel* Dino Buzzati *d* Mario Brenta *ph* Vincenzo Marano *m* Stefano Caprioli *ad* Giorgio Bertolini *ed* Roberto Missiroli

☆ Marco Pauletti, Alessandra Milan, Marco Tonin, Duilo Fontana, Carlo Caserotti, Antonio Vecellio, Angelo Chiesura

'This sort of art movie is easy to mock. And hardly for the likes of those who enjoy the familiar narrative drive and special effects driven melodramas that cram the cinemas.' – *Derek Malcolm, Guardian*

'Like watching three coats of paint dry.' – *Independent*

Barnaby and Me

Australia 1977 90m colour

ABC/Force Ten/Transatlantic (Matthew N. Herman)

A koala recalls how an American con man disrupted the lives of an Australian family.

Affable but silly family comedy that relies too heavily on the skills of Caesar to provide some amusement and features a koala with a heavy American accent.

w James Henderson *d* Norman Panama *ph* Peter Hendry *m* Brian May *ad* George Liddle *ed* Tim Wellburn

☆ Sid Caesar, Juliet Mills, Sally Boyden, Hugh Keays-Byrne, Rangi Nicholls, James Condon, Kenneth Laird, Bruce Spence, Daws Butler (voice)

Barnacle Bill

US 1941 90m bw

MGM (Milton Bren)

A fishing boat skipper gets romantic in the hope of financing his enterprises.

Adequate waterfront comedy on Min and Bill *lines, consolidating a popular star teaming.*

w Jack Jevne, Hugo Butler *d* Richard Thorpe *ph* Clyde de Vinna *m* Bronislau Kaper

☆ *Wallace Beery, Marjorie Main,* Leo Carrillo, Virginia Weidler, Donald Meek, Barton MacLane, Connie Gilchrist, Sara Haden

♫ 'They Can't Take That Away from Me', 'Shoes with Wings On', 'My One and Only Highland Fling', 'Swing Trot', 'Manhattan Downbeat', 'You'd Be So Hard to Replace', 'A Weekend in the Country', 'Sabre Dance'

Barnacle Bill *

GB 1957 87m bw

Ealing (Michael Balcon)

US title: *All at Sea*

The last of a long line of sailors suffers from seasickness, and takes command of a decaying Victorian pier at an English seaside resort.

Quite an amusing comedy which had the misfortune to come at the tag-end of the Ealing classics and so seemed too mild and predictable. Perhaps it was a little staid.

w T. E. B. Clarke *d* Charles Frend *ph* Douglas Slocombe *m* John Addison

☆ Alec Guinness, Irene Browne, Percy Herbert, Harold Goodwin, Maurice Denham, George Rose, Lionel Jeffries, Victor Maddern

Barney's Great Adventure

US 1998 75m DeLuxe

Polygram/Lyrick (Sheryl Leach, Dennis DeShazer)

With the aid of a toy that turns into a lifesize dinosaur, two children hunt for a special egg.

A tacky film for children about an irrepressibly cheerful purple dinosaur, whose appeal is less than universal.

w Stephen White *d* Steve Gomer *ph* Sandi Sissel *ch* Debra Brown *pd* Vincent Jefferds *ed* Richard Halsey *sp* Cinemotion Pictures

☆ George Hearn, Shirley Douglas, Trevor Morgan, Kyla Pratt, Diana Rice, David Joyner (Barney's body), Bob West (Barney's voice)

'No film could have a higher must-see rating among the 2-to-5-year-old target audience.' – *Variety*

Barocco *

France 1976 105m Eastmancolor

La Boétie/Sara (André Génovès, Alain Sarde)

A woman manipulates the killer of her boyfriend, murdered for his part in a political scandal, into becoming the double of the dead man.

A stylized, stylish thriller that hovers on the edge of parody, it is enjoyable to watch, even though its narrative is sometimes difficult to follow.

w André Téchiné, Marilyn Goldin *d* André Téchiné *ph* Bruno Nuytten *m* Philippe Sarde *ad* Ferdinando Scarfiotti *ed* Claudine Merlin

☆ Isabelle Adjani, Gérard Depardieu, Marie-France Pisier, Hélène Surgère, Jean-François Stevenin, Julien Guiomar, Claude Brasseur, Jean-Claude Brialy

Baron Blood (dubbed)

Italy/West Germany 1972 92m Technicolor

Leone International/Cinevision (Alfred Leone)

original title: *Gli Orrori del Castello di Norimberga*

aka: *Chamber of Tortures; The Thirst of Baron Blood; The Torture Chamber of Baron Blood*

In Austria, an American student brings back to life his sadistic 300-year-old ancestor, who resumes his old pastime of torturing the locals.

Dull, unimaginative and lurid horror, in which the director's penchant for pointless zooms detracts from his attempts at atmosphere; an occasional chase sequence reveals what might have been, if those involved had been more committed or if its stars had bothered to act.

w Vincent Fotre, William A. Bairn *d* Mario Bava *ph* Antonio Rinaldi *m* Stelvio Cipriani *ad* Enzo Bulgarelli *ed* Carlo Reali *sp* Franco Tocci

☆ Joseph Cotten, Elke Sommer, Massimo Girotti, Rada Rassimov, Antonio Cantafora, Humi Raho, Alan Collins, Dieter Tressler

Le Baron Fantôme *

France 1943 100m bw

Consortium de Productions de Films (Robert Florat)

GB title: *The Phantom Baron*

In the early 19th century, the disappearance of a nobleman causes problems for his heirs.

Macabre fairy tale with effective scenes which seem to relate to Cocteau's later fantasies; the film as a whole is less effective.

wd Serge de Poligny *ph* Roger Hubert *m* Louis Beydts *narrator* Jean Cocteau

☆ Jany Holt, Odette Joyeux, Alain Cuny, Gabrielle Dorziat

Baron Münchhausen *

Czechoslovakia 1962 81m Agfacolor

Ceskoslovensky Film

original title: *Baron Prasil*

An astronaut finds on the moon the famous liar Baron Münchhausen, who takes him back to Earth and a variety of exaggerated adventures.

Amusing variation on the old stories, using live action against deliberately artificial backgrounds.

wd Karel Zeman novel Gottfried Burger (illustrations by Gustave Doré) *ph* Jiri Tarantik *m* Zdenek Liska

☆ Milos Kopecky, Rudolf Jelinek, Jana Becjchova

The Baron of Arizona

US 1950 85m bw

Lippert (Carl Hittleman)

In the 19th century a clerk tries to claim the whole of Arizona by false land grants.

Initially appealing but basically rather feeble tall tale, ineffectively worked out and decidedly undernourished as a production.

wd Samuel Fuller *ph* James Wong Howe *m* Paul Dunlap

☆ Vincent Price, Ellen Drew, Beulah Bondi, Vladimir Sokoloff, Reed Hadley, Robert Barrat

Baron Prasil: see *Baron Münchhausen*

The Baroness and the Butler

US 1938 75m bw

TCF (Raymond Griffith)

The Hungarian prime minister's butler is loved by a princess.

Thin mittel-European romantic star whimsy.

w Sam Hellman, Lamar Trotti, Kathryn Scola *play The Lady Has a Heart* by Ladislaus Bus-Fekete *d* Walter Lang *ph* Arthur Miller *md* Louis Silvers

☆ William Powell, Annabella, Henry Stephenson, Nigel Bruce, Helen Westley, Joseph Schildkraut, J. Edward Bromberg, Lynn Bari

Barquero!

US 1970 114m DeLuxe

Aubrey Schenck (Hal Klein)

A Western ferryman is taken prisoner by bandits but turns the tables.

Long, violent, rather uninteresting Western in the Spanish manner.

w George Schenck, William Marks *d* Gordon Douglas *ph* Jerry Finnerman *m* Dominic Frontiere
☆ Lee Van Cleef, Forrest Tucker, Warren Oates, Kerwin Mathews, Mariette Hartley, Brad Weston, John Davis Chandler

'When poets love, heaven and earth fall back to watch!'
The Barretts of Wimpole Street **
US 1934 109m bw
MGM (Irving Thalberg)
TV title: *Forbidden Alliance*
Invalid Elizabeth Barrett plans to marry poet Robert Browning, against her tyrannical father's wishes.
Claustrophobic but well-acted adaptation of a stage play which has become more forceful than history. Stilted now, but still better than the remake.
w Ernst Vajda, Claudine West, Donald Ogden Stewart *play* Rudolf Besier *d* Sidney Franklin *ph* William Daniels *m* Herbert Stothart
☆ Norma Shearer (Elizabeth Barrett), Fredric March (Robert Browning), *Charles Laughton* (Edward Moulton-Barrett), Maureen O'Sullivan (Henrietta), Katherine Alexander (Arabel), Una O'Connor (Wilson), Ralph Forbes (Captain Surtees-Cook), Ian Wolfe (Harry Bevan)
'Box office for all its celluloid lethargy … truly an actor's picture, with long speeches and verbose philosophical observations.' – *Variety*
best picture; Norma Shearer

The Barretts of Wimpole Street
GB 1956 105m Metrocolor Cinemascope
MGM (Sam Zimbalist)
Dreadful, miscast remake of the above, with emphasis on the Freudian father-daughter relationship.
An unattractive and boring film.
w John Dighton *d* Sidney Franklin *ph* Frederick A. Young *m* Bronislau Kaper
☆ Jennifer Jones, Bill Travers, John Gielgud, Virginia McKenna
'That rarity – a remake of an established Hollywood classic that is exceptionally fine in every respect.' – *New York Times*

Barricade
US 1939 71m bw
TCF (Edward Kaufman)
A newsman and a girl with a past fight Mongolian bandits in North China.
A bagful of clichés which does not quite add up to entertainment.
w Granville Walker *d* Gregory Ratoff *ph* Karl Freund *m* David Buttolph
☆ Warner Baxter, Alice Faye, Charles Winninger, Arthur Treacher, Keye Luke, Willie Fung, Doris Lloyd
'Inadequate and confusing … it was launched as an A, but winds up as a B that will have to groove generally in the supporting spots.' – *Variety*

Barricade
US 1949 75m Technicolor
Warner (Saul Elkins)
A tough mine-owner who runs a camp miles from civilization meets his come-uppance when three strangers are forced to accept his hospitality.
Rough Western only notable as an (almost) scene-for-scene steal from The Sea Wolf *(qv): a text-book adaptation.*
w William Sackheim *d* Peter Godfrey *ph* Carl Guthrie *m* William Lava *ed* Clarence Kolster
☆ Raymond Massey, Dane Clark, Ruth Roman, Robert Douglas, Morgan Farley

The Barrier
US 1926 79m (24 fps) bw silent
MGM
A brutal sea captain tries to prevent his protégé's marriage.
Brooding melodrama climaxing in an Alaskan storm. It was Barrymore's first film for the studio where he spent the rest of his career.
w Rex Beach *d* George Hill
☆ Lionel Barrymore, Henry B. Walthall, Marceline Day, Norman Kerry

The Barrier
US 1937 90m bw
Paramount/Harry Sherman
A gold rush prospector kidnaps a child and brings her up in the belief that she is a half-breed.
Lyceum-like melodrama against spectacular natural settings; somehow not of interest.
w Bernard Schubert, Mordaunt Shairp, Harrison Jacobs *novel* Rex Beach *d* Lesley Selander
☆ Leo Carrillo, Jean Parker, Robert Barrat, James Ellison, Otto Kruger, Andy Clyde, Addison Richards, Sara Haden

Barry Lyndon **
GB 1975 187m Eastmancolor
Warner/Hawk/Peregrine (Stanley Kubrick)
Adventures of an 18th-century Irish gentleman of fortune.
A curiously cold-hearted enterprise, like an art gallery in which the backgrounds are sketched in loving detail and the human figures totally neglected; there is much to enjoy, but script and acting are variable to say the least, and the point of it all is obscure, as it certainly does not tell a rattling good story.
wd Stanley Kubrick *novel* W. M. Thackeray *ph* John Alcott *md* Leonard Rosenman *pd* Ken Adam
☆ Ryan O'Neal, Marisa Berenson, Patrick Magee, Hardy Kruger, Steven Berkoff, Gay Hamilton, Marie Kean, Murray Melvin, André Morell, Leonard Rossiter, Philip Stone, Michael Hordern
'The motion picture equivalent of one of these very large, very expensive, very elegant and very dull books that exist solely to be seen on coffee tables.' – *Charles Champlin*
'Watching the movie is like looking at illustrations for a work that has not been supplied.' – *John Simon*
'All art and no matter: a series of still pictures which will please the retina while denying our hunger for drama. And far from re-creating another century, it more accurately embalms it.' – *Michael Billington, Illustrated London News*
John Alcott; Leonard Rosenman; Ken Adam; costumes (Britt Soderlund, Milena Canonero)
best picture; Stanley Kubrick (as writer); Stanley Kubrick (as director)
Stanley Kubrick (as director); John Alcott

Barry McKenzie Holds His Own
Australia 1974 98m Eastmancolor Panavision
EMI/Reg Grundy (Bruce Beresford)
The twin nephews of Edna Everage, an Australian housewife, go to her rescue when she is mistaken for the Queen and kidnapped by Transylvanians.
Coarse slapstick comedy of a deliberately tasteless kind.
w Barry Humphries, Bruce Beresford *d* Bruce Beresford *ph* Don McAlpine *m* Peter Best *pd* John Stoddart *ed* William Anderson
☆ Barry Crocker, Barry Humphries, Donald Pleasence, Dick Bentley, Ed Devereaux, Tommy Trinder, Frank Windsor, Deryck Guyler, Arthur English, Roy Kinnear, John Le Mesurier

Bartleby *
GB 1970 79m Eastmancolor
Pantheon (Rodney Carr-Smith)
A young clerk gradually refuses to take part in life.
A non-action film from an independent source, praiseworthy but overlong and fairly lacking in any kind of appeal except to literary connoisseurs.
w Anthony Friedmann, Rodney Carr-Smith *story* Herman Melville *d* Anthony Friedmann *ph* Ian Wilson *m* Roger Webb
☆ Paul Scofield, John McEnery, Thorley Walters, Colin Jeavons

'There's Only One Thing Stranger Than What's Going On Inside His Head. What's Going On Outside.'
'Between Heaven and Hell there's always Hollywood.'
Barton Fink ***
US 1991 116m colour
Rank/Circle (Ethan Coen)
In the 1940s an intellectual left-wing playwright goes to work in Hollywood, where he is told to write a wrestling picture for Wallace Beery.
What begins as a satire on the film industry, with a central character owing much to Clifford Odets, turns halfway through into something darker and more disturbing, a dizzying trip inside two disturbed minds.
w Ethan and Joel Coen *d* Joel Coen *m* Carter Burwell *pd* Dennis Gassner *ed* Roderick Jaynes
☆ John Turturro, John Goodman, Judy Davis, Michael Lerner, John Mahoney, Tony Shalhoub, Jon Polito, Steve Buscemi
'Scene after scene is filled with a ferocious strength and humour.' – *Variety*
† The film took an unprecedented three prizes at the 1991 Cannes Film Festival: Palme d'Or for best film, best actor (John Turturro) and best director.
Michael Lerner; Dennis Gassner

Baryton: see *Baritone*

Bas Ya Bahar: see *La Mer Cruelle*

Les Bas-fonds *
France 1936 92m bw
Albatros (Alexander Kamenka)
aka: *The Lower Depths*
A clash of temperaments flares up between derelicts in a dosshouse.
Uneven transposition of a famous work, with patches of good acting.
w Jean Renoir, Charles Spaak and others *play* Maxim Gorky *d Jean Renoir* *ph* Jean Bachelet *m* Jean Wiener
☆ *Jean Gabin, Louis Jouvet*, Vladimir Sokoloff, Robert Le Vigan, Suzy Prim

BASEketball
US 1998 103m DeLuxe
Universal (David Zucker, Robert LoCash, Gil Netter)
Two basketball players invent a new variation on the game, in which teams can insult one another and try to unsettle opposing players.
Broad comedy which sends up the clichés of sports movies without managing to be particularly amusing.
w David Zucker, Robert LoCash, Lewis Friedman, Jeff Wright *d* David Zucker *ph* Steve Mason *m* James Ira Newborn *pd* Steven Jordan *ed* Jeffrey Reiner
☆ Trey Parker, Matt Stone, Yasmine Bleeth, Jenny McCarthy, Robert Vaughn, Ernest Borgnine, Dian Bachar
'The broad, bawdy antics onscreen will be a slam-dunk at the box office.' – *Leonard Klady, Variety*

'Flesh seduces. Passion kills.'
Basic Instinct *
US 1991 128m Technicolor Panavision
Guild/Carolco/Canal (Alan Marshall)
A violent, suspended detective falls in love with the chief suspect in a murder investigation, a bisexual millionairess whose latest novel contains a detailed description of a similar killing.
Overheated, overlong melodramatic thriller with an implausible plot that requires its audience to accept that Michael Douglas is irresistibly attractive to bisexual women. But the skill and pace of the direction makes one regret that they were not exercised on better material.
w Joe Eszterhas *d* Paul Verhoeven *ph* Jan de Bont *m* Jerry Goldsmith *pd* Terence Marsh *ed* Frank J. Urioste *sp* Rob Bottin
☆ Michael Douglas, Sharon Stone, George Dzundza, Jeanne Tripplehorn, Denis Arndt, Leilani Sarelle, Dorothy Malone
'Saddled with extremely unattractive characters, vile dialogue and sex that appeals only to your baser instincts.' – *Jami Bernard, New York Post*
'The film falls down simply because its three-million-dollar script is just a gimmick, an unfeeling house of cards which falls apart when the loopholes and logical flaws that sustain the ambiguous resolution come to light.' – *Kim Newman, Sight and Sound*
'An outrageous film, a great big rubbishy sort of popcorn Saturday night movie with bags of sex and violence, blokes being blokes and ice-cool blondes being just that, and even a couple of quite stupendous car chases thrown in just for old times' sake.' – *Empire*
Jerry Goldsmith; editing

Basil, The Great Mouse Detective: see *The Great Mouse Detective*

'The Tenant In Room Seven Is Very Small, Very Twisted And Very Mad.'
Basket Case
US 1982 93m TVC Color
Alpha (Edgar Ievins)
Siamese twins, one a tiny, deformed creature, take revenge on the doctors who separated them.
Grisly, jokey, low-budget horror that gained a cult following.
wd Frank Henenlotter *ph* Bruce Torbet *m* Gus Russo *ad* Frederick Loren *ed* Frank Henenlotter
☆ Kevin Van Hentenryck, Terri Susan Smith, Beverly Bonner, Robert Vogel, Diana Browne, Lloyd Pace

Basket Case 2
US 1990 90m TVC Color
Medusa/Shapiro, Glickenhaus Entertainment/Ievins-Henenlotter (Edgar Ievins)
Twins, one of them a deformed creature in a basket, take refuge in a community of freaks.
Tediously grotesque comedy.
wd Frank Henenlotter *ph* Robert M. Baldwin *m* Joe Renzetti *pd* Michael P. Moran *ad* Daniel Ouellette *ed* Kevin Tent
☆ Kevin Van Hentenryck, Judy Grafe, Annie Ross, Heather Rattray, Chad Brown, Beverly Bonner, Leonard Jackson, Alexandra Auder
'Henenlotter seems unsure whether to play his outré offerings for laughs, shocks or sympathy, and this remains an uncertain (and somewhat unnecessary) sequel to a sure-footed original.' – *MFB*

'It's Time To Build A Bigger Basket!'
Basket Case 3: The Progeny
US 1992 90m TVC Color
Shapiro, Glickenhaus (Edgar Ievins)
A deformed twin becomes a father of monsters, but has to battle to protect them from the forces of law and order.
The mixture much as before, only of interest to fans of cheap horror.
w Frank Henenlotter, Robert Martin *d* Frank Henenlotter *ph* Bob Paone *m* Joe Renzetti *pd* William Barclay *ed* Greg Sheldon *sp* creature effects: Gabe Bartalos, David Kindlon
☆ Annie Ross, Kevin Van Hentenryck, Dan Biggers, Gil Roper, Tina Louise Hilbert, James O'Doherty
'The flick's fast pace, perverse tone, clever dialog and suitably grotesque cartoon-styled gore make it a legit treat for frightcom fans.' – *New York Daily News*
'Henenlotter's mix of wild over-acting, cartoon color scheme and heavy-handed message regarding tolerance is tough to take for the uninitiated.' – *Variety*

'The true story of the death of innocence and the birth of an artist…'
The Basketball Diaries *
US 1995 102m Technicolor
New Line/Island (Liz Heller)
A rebellious teenager at a Catholic school becomes a heroin addict, prostitute and thief.
The precocious Carroll's diaries might have once caused a minor sensation, but their attitudinizing romanticism has palled, and there is little of value to be found in the lower depths as depicted here, in a bio-pic that gives little indication of a specific time or place for its action.
w Brian Goluboff *book* Jim Carroll *d* Scott Kalvert *ph* David Phillips *m* Graeme Revell *pd* Christopher Nowak *ed* Dana Congdon
☆ Leonardo DiCaprio, Bruno Kirby, Lorraine Bracco, Ernie Hudson, Patrick McGaw, James Madio, Mark Wahlberg, Michael Rapaport
'It has lost its uniquely disturbing quality by being relocated by director Scott Kalvert in present-day New York, where the incidents are now simply a string of junkie clichés.' – *Alexander Walker*
† DiCaprio took over the leading role after River Phoenix died of a drug overdose.

Basquiat *
US 1996 106m DuArt
Guild/Eleventh Street/Miramax (Jon Kilik, Randy Ostrow, Sigurjon Sighvatsson)

A graffiti artist gains a mainstream reputation, but succumbs to drug addiction.
Biopic of Jean-Michel Basquiat, who died in 1988 at the age of 27; it has its moments, yet the story is told in a cautious manner, and displays little insight into his extraordinary career and the environment which nurtured and, possibly, destroyed him.
wd Julian Schnabel *story* Lech Majewski, John Bowe *ph* Ron Fortunato *m* John Cale *pd* Dan Leigh *ed* Michael Berenbaum
☆ Jeffrey Wright, David Bowie (Andy Warhol), Dennis Hopper, Gary Oldman, Claire Forlani, Michael Wincott, Parker Posey, Elina Löwensohn, Willem Dafoe, Tatum O'Neal, Benicio Del Toro, Christopher Walken, Courtney Love, Paul Bartel
'Decently modest, though decidedly unexciting.' – *Variety*
† Basquiat's estate refused permission for his paintings to be used in the film. Those shown were painted by Schnabel.

'When it flies, someone dies!'
The Bat
US 1959 78m bw
AA/Liberty (C. J. Tevlin)

A lady mystery writer rents a spooky old house and finds herself and her guests at the mercy of a maniac in search of hidden loot.
Poor remake of a standard twenties stage thriller; everyone chews the scenery.
wd Crane Wilbur *play* Mary Roberts Rinehart *ph* Joseph Biroc *m* Louis Forbes
☆ Vincent Price, Agnes Moorehead, Gavin Gordon, John Sutton, Lenita Lane, Darla Hood

Bat 21 **
US 1988 105m DeLuxe
Tri-Star/Vision/Eagle (David Fisher, Gary A. Neill, Michael Balson)

In Vietnam an American pilot attempts to rescue a 53-year-old Air Force missile intelligence expert when he is shot down behind enemy lines.
Effective and suspenseful drama of the muddle and moral expediencies of war, based on a true story.
w William C. Anderson, George Gordon *book* William C. Anderson *d* Peter Markle *ph* Mark Irwin *m* Christopher Young *pd* Vincent Cresciman *ed* Stephen E. Rivkin
☆ Gene Hackman, Danny Glover, Jerry Reed, David Marshall Grant, Clayton Rohner, Erich Anderson, Joe Dorsey

'Greatest all talking thriller!'
The Bat Whispers **
US 1930 82m bw Magnifilm
UA (Roland West)

Classic early sound version of *The Bat* (qv) by the director of the 1926 silent version.
Excellent use of camera, sets, and unusual models.
wd Roland West ph Ray June, Robert Planck
☆ Chester Morris, Una Merkel, Chance Ward, Grayce Hampton, Maude Eburne, Spencer Charters, Gustav von Seyffertitz
† Originally released in a 'wide screen' process.

'The story America will never forget!'
Bataan *
US 1943 114m bw
MGM (Irving Starr)

Thirteen soldiers holding a bridge against the Japanese die one by one.
Uncredited remake of The Lost Patrol *(qv) transposed to the Pacific war, with stereotyped characters and much flagwaving. Very dated, but a big box-office film of its time, despite its studio jungles.*
w Robert D. Andrews *d* Tay Garnett *ph* Sidney Wagner *m* Bronislau Kaper
☆ Robert Taylor, George Murphy, Thomas Mitchell, Lloyd Nolan, Lee Bowman, Robert Walker, Desi Arnaz, Barry Nelson, Philip Terry
'Naïve, coarse-grained, primitive, honest, accomplished and true.' – *James Agee*
'One of the most convincing attempts I have ever seen to show a bit of hell on the screen.' – *Observer*

La Bataille du Rail **
France 1945 87m bw
CGCF
Reconstructions of heroic resistance work by the French railwaymen during World War II.
Reasonably compulsive documentary fiction which was plainly more inspiring at the time than it seems now.
wd René Clément ph Henri Alekan *m* Yves Baudrier
☆ Salina, Daurand, Lozach, Tony Laurent
'There is no lingering, no declaiming, no attempt to hide a certain volatile small boy's enjoyment of sabotage (an aspect of resistance never before touched upon), there is a natural unescapable dramatic tension and speed and perfect unostentatious playing by everybody.' – *Richard Winnington*

Bathing Beauty
US 1944 101m Technicolor
MGM (Jack Cummings)

A songwriter plans to retire and settle down, but his publisher schemes to set his fiancée against him.
Witless, artificial aqua-musical, with plenty of unpersuasive high jinks but no real style despite a capable cast.
w Dorothy Kingsley, Allen Boretz, Frank Waldman *d* George Sidney *ph* Harry Stradling *m* Johnny Green *ch* John Murray Anderson
☆ Esther Williams, Red Skelton, Basil Rathbone, Keenan Wynn, Ethel Smith, Xavier Cugat, Bill Goodwin
'I could not resist the wish that MGM had topped its aquatic climax – a huge pool full of girls, fountains and spouts of flame – by suddenly draining the tank and ending the show with the entire company writhing like goldfish on a rug.' – *James Agee*
♫ 'Faculty Row'; 'Tico Tico'; 'Echo of a Serenade'; 'I Cried for You'; 'Bim Bam Boom'; 'By the Waters of Minnetonka'; 'I've Got a Problem'; 'I'll Take the High Note'

Batman
US 1943 bw serial: 15 eps
Columbia
With the help of the Boy Wonder, the Caped Crusader battles an enemy underground ring led by Dr Daka.
Reasonably spirited romp marred by the usual tinpot sets.
d Lambert Hillyer
☆ Lewis Wilson, Douglas Croft, J. Carrol Naish, William Austin
† *Batman and Robin* (15 eps) followed in 1948, directed by Spencer Bennet. The leads were played by Robert Lowery and John Duncan: they combated The Wizard with the help of Lyle Talbot as the police commissioner.

Batman *
US 1966 105m DeLuxe
TCF/Greenlawn/National Periodical Publications (William Dozier)

The cloaked avenger saves an important executive from the clutches of four of the world's most notorious criminals.
Glossy feature version of the old and new serials about the comic strip hero who scurries around in his Batmobile making sure that justice is done. The scriptwriter's invention unfortunately flags halfway, so that despite a fairly sharp production the result is more childish than camp.
w Lorenzo Semple Jnr *d* Leslie Martinson *ph* Howard Schwartz *m* Nelson Riddle
☆ Adam West, Burt Ward, Cesar Romero, Frank Gorshin, Burgess Meredith, Lee Meriwether, Alan Napier, Neil Hamilton

Batman **
US 1989 126m Technicolor
Warner (Jon Peters, Peter Guber)

A young boy who witnesses his parents' murder grows up to become Batman, a masked and emotionally disturbed vigilante who battles against an arch-criminal known as The Joker.
The campness of earlier versions of the comic-book hero gives way to a gloomier psychological interpretation that loses much of the fun of the original, while the brilliant production design, of a grim, grey Metropolis, overshadows all. Narrative is reduced to a succession of set-pieces.
w Sam Hamm, Warren Skaaren *d* Tim Burton *ph* Roger Pratt *m* Danny Elfman *m/ly* Prince, John L. Nelson *pd Anton Furst ed* Ray Lovejoy *sp* John Evans
☆ Michael Keaton, Jack Nicholson, Kim Basinger, Robert Wuhl, Pat Hingle, Billy Dee Williams, Michael Gough, Jack Palance, Jerry Hall
'A moderately entertaining fantasy, with good design, some strong performances and a desperate need of a script doctor.' – *Adam Mars-Jones, Independent*
best art direction

Batman & Robin
US 1997 130m Technicolor
Warner (Peter Macgregor-Scott)

Batman thwarts the ambitions of Mr Freeze, a deformed scientist who has to acquire diamonds to survive.
The dullest of the series so far, gaudy but empty of emotional or narrative interest, and the action soon palls.
w Akiva Goldsman *d* Joel Schumacher *ph* Stephen Goldblatt *m* Elliot Goldenthal *pd* Barbara Ling *ed* Dennis Virkler *sp* John Dykstra
☆ George Clooney (Bruce Wayne/Batman), Arnold Schwarzenegger (Dr Victor Fries/Mr Freeze), Chris O'Donnell (Dick Grayson/Robin), Uma Thurman (Dr Pamela Isley/Poison Ivy), Alicia Silverstone (Barbara Wilson/Batgirl), Michael Gough (Alfred Pennyworth), Pat Hingle (Commissioner Gordon), John Glover (Dr Jason Woods), Elle Macpherson (Julie Madison), Vivica A. Fox (Ms B. Haven)
'A film which tries hard but seldom manages to be anything more than moderately entertaining.' – *Derek Malcolm, Guardian*
'It's a pretty horrendous film.' – *George Clooney*
† The film grossed some $107m in the US and another $126m elsewhere.

Batman Forever *
US 1995 121m Technicolor
Warner (Tim Burton, Peter MacGregor-Scott)

With the aid of Robin, Batman battles against criminals Two Face and The Riddler while resisting the temptations of a female psychologist.
A high-camp sequel, with the tone set by the redesigned, ever-more fetishistic Batman costume, the arrival of Robin, and the unrestrained antics of The Riddler; it's fun for much of the time.
w Lee Batchler, Janet Scott Batchler, Akiva Goldsman *d* Joel Schumacher *ph* Stephen Goldblatt *m* Elliot Goldenthal *pd* Barbara Ling *ed* Dennis Virkler
☆ Val Kilmer (Batman), Tommy Lee Jones (Harvey Two-Face), *Jim Carrey* (The Riddler), Chris O'Donnell (Robin), Nicole Kidman, Michael Gough, Pat Hingle, Drew Barrymore, Rene Auberjonois
'It doesn't have much on its mind except emptying yours for two hours.' – *Tom Shone, Sunday Times*
† The film took more than $333m at the box-office worldwide.
Stephen Goldblatt; sound; sound effect editing

Batman Returns **
US 1992 126m Technicolor
Warner (Denise Di Novi, Tim Burton)

Batman does battle with Catwoman and The Penguin.
More comic-strip story-telling, done as a succession of set pieces, with the towering design of the city and its sewers overshadowing the performances.
w Daniel Waters *story* Daniel Waters, Sam Hamm *d* Tim Burton *ph* Stefan Czapsky *m* Danny Elfman *pd Bo Welch ed* Chris Lebenzon, Bob Badami
☆ Michael Keaton, Danny DeVito, Michelle Pfeiffer, Christopher Walken, Michael Gough, Michael Murphy, Cristi Conaway, Pat Hingle
'Resembles nothing so much as a blacker, spikier but less focused version of a Disney animation feature made flesh.' – *Derek Malcolm, Guardian*
'A blend of playful novelty and reassuring familiarity – a difficult mixture to get right.' – *New Yorker*
Visual effects; make-up

'They Will Suck You Dry!'
Bats
US 1999 91m Technicolor
Columbia TriStar/Destination (Brad Jenkel, Louise Rosner)

In Texas, Asian flying foxes escape from an experimental laboratory and turn local bats into clever, vicious killers.
Predictable monster movie that incorporates many of the usual clichés of the genre; efficiently made, the movie takes itself very seriously, apart from one squelching joke at the end.
w John Logan *d* Louis Morneau *ph* George Mooradian *m* Graeme Revell *pd* Philip J.C. Duffin *ed* Glenn Garland *sp* animatronics: KNB EFX; visual effects: Netter Digital *cos* Alexis Scott
☆ Lou Diamond Phillips (Emmett Kimsey), Dina Meyer (Dr Sheila Casper), Bob Gunton (Dr Alexander McCabe), Leon (Jimmy Sands), Carlos Jacott (Dr Tobe Hodge), David Shawn McConnell (Deputy Munn), Marcia Dangerfield (Mayor Branson), Oscar Rowland (Dr Swanbeck), Tim Whitaker (Quint)
'An unabashedly retrograde horror opus.' – *Variety*

La Battaglia di Algeri: see *The Battle of Algiers*

La Battaglia di El Alamein: see *The Battle of El Alamein*

La Battaglia di Maratona: see *The Giant of Marathon*

I Battellieri del Volga: see *Prisoner of the Volga*

Battement de Coeur **
France 1940 100m bw
Ciné Alliance/Osso
A poor Parisienne joins a school for pickpockets but falls for the ambassador she robs.
Amusing romance later remade in the US as Heartbeat *(qv).*
w Jean Villeme, Max Colpet, Michel Duran *d* Henri Decoin
☆ Danielle Darrieux, André Luguet, Claude Dauphin, Julien Carette, Saturnin Fabre
'Dauphin fails to rate in hero roles ... he lacks personality, is short of stature, and dresses like a bank clerk.' – *Variety*

Batteries Not Included
US 1987 106m DeLuxe
UIP/Universal (Ronald L. Schwary)

A Manhattan neighbourhood where everyone has problems is helped out by miniature flying saucers with angelic intentions.
Frank Capra would have done it much better.
w Matthew Robbins, Brad Bird, Brent Maddock, S. S. Wilson *story* Mick Garris *d* Matthew Robbins *ph* John McPherson *m* James Horner *pd* Ted Haworth *ed* Cynthia Scheider
☆ Hume Cronyn, Jessica Tandy, Frank McRae, Elizabeth Pena, Michael Carmine

'Forced by her husband to love another man ... to exchange her kisses for naval secrets!'
The Battle *
France 1934 85m bw
Lionofilm (Leon Garganoff)
English language version aka: *Thunder in the East, Hara Kiri*
A Japanese aristocrat urges his wife to befriend an English naval attaché and steal secrets from him; she does, and falls in love.
Stagey but discreet melodrama of the old school, quite well made and acted.
w Nicolas Farkas, Bernard Zimmer, Robert Stevenson *novel* Claude Farrère *d* Nicolas Farkas *ph* Roger Hubert
☆ Charles Boyer, Merle Oberon, John Loder, Betty Stockfeld, Miles Mander

Battle Beneath the Earth *
GB 1967 92m Technicolor
MGM/Reynolds/Vetter (Charles Reynolds)

US title: *Battle Beneath the Sea*
Enemy agents burrow under the US by means of a giant laser.

Agreeable schoolboy science fiction with fair special effects.
w L. Z. Hargreaves *d* Montgomery Tully
ph Kenneth Talbot *m* Ken Jones *sp* Tom Howard
☆ Kerwin Mathews, Viviane Ventura, Robert Ayres, Peter Arne, Martin Benson

Battle Beneath the Sea: see *Battle Beneath the Earth*

Battle Beyond the Stars *
US 1980 104m Metrocolor
New World/Roger Corman (Ed Carlin)
A small planet hires help to repel invaders.
Impertinent and sometimes amusing space fiction rip-off of Seven Samurai *(qv), with plenty of in-jokes and quite pleasant special effects.*
w John Sayles *d* Jimmy T. Murakami *ph* Daniel Lacambre *m* James Horner *ad* Jim Cameron, Charles Breen
☆ Richard Thomas, Robert Vaughn, John Saxon, George Peppard, Sam Jaffe, Morgan Woodward, Darlanne Fluegel, Sybil Danning

Battle Circus
US 1952 90m bw
MGM (Pandro S. Berman)
A patriotic nurse and a disillusioned major fall in love at a mobile army hospital in Korea.
A flat, studio-bound potboiler with miscast stars, bound to provoke hilarity now as a serious version of M*A*S*H.
wd Richard Brooks *ph* John Alton *m* Lennie Hayton
☆ Humphrey Bogart, June Allyson, Keenan Wynn, Robert Keith, William Campbell
'It is disappointing that Brooks, whose early work … suggested considerable promise, should have descended to such a glib, uninteresting piece of film-making.' – *MFB*

'The men who fought … The women who waited. And the stolen moments they shared.'
Battle Cry
US 1955 148m Warnercolor Cinemascope
Warner (producer not credited)
During World War II, marines endure tough training before combat in Saipan; their sex lives come a close second to the war.
Interminable cheapie epic with both eyes on the box-office: the cast salvages an odd moment or two, but violence of all kinds is the key to the entertainment.
w Leon Uris *novel* Leon Uris *d* Raoul Walsh
ph Sid Hickox *m* Max Steiner *ad* John Beckman
ed William Ziegler
☆ Van Heflin, Aldo Ray, Mona Freeman, Dorothy Malone, Raymond Massey, Nancy Olson, James Whitmore, Tab Hunter, Anne Francis, William Campbell
Max Steiner

The Battle Cry of Peace *
US 1915 120m approx bw silent
Blackton/VIT
Lost film in which New York was invaded by forces of apparently German origin.
It caused great political unrest and was followed by Thomas Ince's Civilisation *which took the pacifist point of view.*
w J. Stuart Blackton *book* Defenceless America by Hudson Maxim *d* Wilfred North
☆ Charles Richman, L. Rogers Lytton, Charles Kent, James Morrison

The Battle for Anzio: see *Anzio*

Battle for Music *
GB 1943 87m bw
Strand Films (Donald Taylor)
The story of the wartime ups and downs of the London Philharmonic Orchestra.
Not many films feature a classical orchestra, and this simple tribute, a mediocre production at best, has considerable historical interest.
w St John L. Clowes *d* Donald Taylor
☆ Hay Petrie, Joss Ambler, Charles Carson, Jack Hylton, J. B. Priestley, Eileen Joyce, Moiseiwitch, Sir Adrian Boult, Sir Malcolm Sargent

Battle for Russia ***
US 1943 80m bw
US Army Signal Corps (Anatole Litvak)
Fifth of Frank Capra's Why We Fight documentaries, and like the others a brilliant compilation of carefully selected footage.
m Dimitri Tiomkin *commentary* Anthony Veiller

Battle for the Planet of the Apes
US 1973 86m DeLuxe Panavision
TCF/APJAC (Frank Capra Jnr)
Following a nuclear war, apes are the only surviving leaders of society, but begin to fight among themselves.
Fifth and last in an increasingly confusing chronology, this is at least more thoughtful than violent.
w John William Corrington, Joyce Hooper Corrington *d* J. Lee-Thompson *ph* Richard H. Kline *m* Leonard Rosenman *make-up* John Chambers
☆ Roddy McDowall, Claude Akins, John Huston, Natalie Trundy, Severn Darden, Lew Ayres, Paul Williams
† See *Planet of the Apes*.

Battle Hell: see *Yangtse Incident*

Battle Hymn
US 1957 108m Technicolor Cinemascope
U-I (Ross Hunter)
An American preacher with a guilt complex volunteers to help the South Koreans and after many adventures founds an orphanage.
Earnest, somnolent biopic of one Dean Hess; its mixture of drama, comedy, religion and war heroics is indigestible despite professional handling.
w Charles Grayson, Vincent B. Evans *d* Douglas Sirk *ph* Russell Metty *m* Frank Skinner
☆ Rock Hudson, Anna Kashfi, Dan Duryea, Don Defore, Martha Hyer, Jock Mahoney, James Edwards, Carl Benton Reid
'The film seems to infer that heroic self-sacrifice, a little homely Eastern philosophy and a capacity for combining battle experience with an awareness of spiritual values are enough to overcome all emergencies.' – *John Gillett*

'The Revolt That Stirred The World!'
The Battle of Algiers ****
Algeria/Italy 1965 135m bw
Casbah/Igor (Antonio Musi, Yacef Saadi)
original title: *La Battaglia di Algeri*
In 1954 Algiers, an ex-convict joins the terrorists in rebellion against the French government.
Politically oriented reconstruction of a bitter period of French colonial history, made better propaganda by its wealth of effective detail.
w Franco Solinas *d* Gillo Pontecorvo
ph Marcello Gatti *m* Ennio Morricone, Gillo Pontecorvo
☆ Brahim Haggiag, Jean Martin, Yacef Saadi, Tommaso Neri
'An astonishing piece of work in directorial technique processing to achieve not merely a newsreel tempo but a grainy realism unmatched by the average news film and all too rarely approached by even the better ventures into cinema verité. What is equally noteworthy is Pontecorvo's objectivity in showing both the exhilaration and the heart-break of a fight for liberation, with neither the oppressed nor the oppressor able to survive at ease with his conscience.' – *Judith Crist*
best foreign film; Franco Solinas; Gillo Pontecorvo (as director)

The Battle of Austerlitz: see *Austerlitz*

Battle of Britain ***
US 1943 52m bw
Fourth of the Why We Fight series. (See *Battle for Russia*.)
'It will emerge as one of the vital documents depicting a people's courage when the torch of freedom flickered at its lowest.' – *Variety*

Battle of Britain *
GB 1969 131m Technicolor Panavision
UA/Spitfire (Harry Saltzman, Ben Fisz)
Summer 1940: England defends itself against aerial onslaught.
Plodding attempt to cover an historic event from too many angles and with too many guest stars, all indistinguishable from each other when masked in the cockpit during the repetitive and interminable dogfight sequences. On the ground, things are even duller.
w James Kennaway, Wilfred Greatorex *d* Guy Hamilton *ph* Frederick A. Young *m* William Walton, Ron Goodwin
☆ Laurence Olivier (Dowding), Robert Shaw, Michael Caine, Christopher Plummer, Kenneth More, Susannah York, Trevor Howard, Ralph Richardson, Patrick Wymark, Curt Jurgens, Michael Redgrave, Nigel Patrick, Robert Flemyng, Edward Fox
† The film lost ten million dollars worldwide.

Battle of Broadway
US 1938 84m bw
TCF
Two American legionnaires at a New York convention try to break up the infatuation of their boss's son with a showgirl.
Amiably rowdy Flagg-and-Quirt imitation.
w Lou Breslow, John Patrick *d* George Marshall
☆ Victor McLaglen, Brian Donlevy, Gypsy Rose Lee, Raymond Walburn, Lynn Bari, Jane Darwell, Hattie McDaniel
'Flagg and Quirt shenanigans … rowdy, good-natured fun.' – *Variety*

The Battle of City Hall: see *The Angels Wash Their Faces*

The Battle of El Alamein
Italy/France 1968 105m Eastmancolor Cromoscope
Zenith Cinematografica/Les Films Corona (Mino Loy, Luciano Martino)
original title: *La Battaglia di El Alamein*
aka: *Desert Tanks*
In June 1942 Italian troops, who have been ordered to beat their German allies to Alexandria, run into British resistance.
The North African campaign as seen from an Italian viewpoint: the Italian troops are gallant and courageous, the British foolish and treacherous, and the Germans coldly inhumane and equally treacherous.
w Ernesto Gastaldi, Remigio Del Grosso *d* Calvin Jackson Padget (Giorgio Ferroni) *ph* Sergio D'Offizi *m* Carlo Rustichelli *ed* Eugenio Alabiso
☆ Frederick Stafford, George Hilton, Michael Rennie (Field Marshal Montgomery), Robert Hossein (Rommel), Marco Guglielmi, Ettore Manni, Gérard Herter, Ira Furstenberg, Enrico Maria Salerno
'An ingenious attempt to whitewash Italy's military record in the last war and to justify her alliance with Germany as part of that lovable Mediterranean characteristic of being "too trusting".' – *Jan Dawson, MFB*

The Battle of Gallipoli: see *Tell England*

The Battle of Midway: see *Midway*

The Battle of Neretva
Yugoslavia/US/Italy/W. Germany 1969 106m colour Cinemascope
Jadran-Bosna
In 1943, Yugoslav partisans resist German and Italian invaders.
War spectacular with international cast; despite brilliant handling of the climaxes it didn't travel.
w Ugo Pirro and others *d* Veljko Bulajic
☆ Yul Brynner, Curt Jurgens, Sylva Koscina, Orson Welles, Hardy Kruger, Franco Nero
best foreign film

Battle of Powder River: see *Tomahawk*

Battle of the Bulge **
US 1965 167m Technicolor Ultra Panavision
Warner/United States Pictures (Sidney Harmon, Milton Sperling, Philip Yordan)
In December 1944, the Allies take longer than expected to win a land battle in the Ardennes because of a crack Nazi Panzer commander.
Bloody and unbowed war spectacle, quite literate and handsome but deafeningly noisy and with emphasis on strategy rather than character.
w Philip Yordan, Milton Sperling, John Melson
d Ken Annakin *ph* Jack Hildyard *m* Benjamin Frankel
☆ Henry Fonda, Robert Shaw, Robert Ryan, Telly Savalas, Dana Andrews, George Montgomery, Ty Hardin, Pier Angeli, Barbara Werle, Charles Bronson, James MacArthur, Werner Peters

The Battle of the Century **
US 1927 20m bw silent
Hal Roach
The manager of an unsuccessful boxer accidentally starts a marathon pie fight.
The first reel is lost, but the pie sequence is what matters, being one of the most celebrated pieces of slapstick in cinema history.
w Hal Roach, H. M. Walker *d* Clyde Bruckman
☆ Stan Laurel, Oliver Hardy, Eugene Pallette

Battle of the Coral Sea
US 1959 85m bw
Columbia (Charles H. Schneer)
During World War II a submarine commander, sent to photograph the Japanese fleet, is captured but escapes.
Routine, unconvincing war heroics.
w Dan Ullman, Stephen Kandel *d* Paul Wendkos
☆ Cliff Robertson, Gia Scala, Patricia Cutts

The Battle of the River Plate *
GB 1956 119m Technicolor Vistavision
Rank/Powell and Pressburger
US title: *Pursuit of the Graf Spee*
Semi-documentary account of the 1939 trapping of the German pocket battleship *Graf Spee* in Montevideo Harbour, and of her subsequent scuttling.
A sympathetic view of a German hero, Commander Langsdorff (not unexpected from these producers), is the most notable feature of this disappointingly patchy and studio-bound war epic, with too many actors in ill-defined bit parts, too undisciplined a storyline, and too confusing scenes of battle.
wd Michael Powell, Emeric Pressburger
ph Christopher Challis *m* Brian Easdale
☆ John Gregson, Anthony Quayle, Peter Finch, Bernard Lee, Ian Hunter, Jack Gwillim, Lionel Murton, Anthony Bushell, Peter Illing
'It is difficult to understand how English film-makers can have done thus badly with material so apt to their gifts.' – *Stanley Kauffmann*

The Battle of the Sexes
US 1914 60m approx bw silent
Mutual/Reliance-Majestic
A wealthy middle-aged man is taken in by a fortune-hunting couple.
A commercial potboiler, made on the cheap but enormously successful.
wd D. W. Griffith *play* The Single Standard by Daniel Carson Goodman *ph* G. W. Bitzer
☆ Lillian Gish, Owen Moore, Mary Alden, Fay Tincher, Robert Harron
† In 1928 Griffith remade the property with Phyllis Haver, Jean Hersholt, Belle Bennett, Sally O'Neil and Don Alvarado.

The Battle of the Sexes *
GB 1960 83m bw
Prometheus (Monja Danischewsky)
A lady efficiency expert upsets the even tenor of life at an Edinburgh tweed manufactory, and the chief accountant plans to eliminate her.
Sub-Ealing black comedy which tends to misfire despite effort all round.
w Monja Danischewsky *story* The Catbird Seat by James Thurber *d* Charles Crichton *ph* Freddie Francis *m* Stanley Black
☆ Peter Sellers, Constance Cummings, Robert Morley, Jameson Clark, Moultrie Kelsall, Alex Mackenzie, Roddy McMillan, Donald Pleasence, Ernest Thesiger

The Battle of the V1
GB 1958 109m bw
Criterion (George Maynard)
US titles: *Unseen Heroes*
aka: *Missiles from Hell*
Polish patriots sabotage the German rocket installation at Peenemünde.

Effective though schoolboyish war adventure shot on a low budget: story development reasonably brisk though predictable.
w Jack Hanley, Eryk Wlodek *book* Bernard Newman *d* Vernon Sewell *ph* Basil Emmott *m* Robert Sharples
☆ Michael Rennie, Patricia Medina, Milly Vitale, David Knight, Esmond Knight, Christopher Lee

The Battle of the Villa Fiorita
GB 1964 111m Technicolor Panavision
Warner (Delmer Daves)
US title: *Affair at the Villa Fiorita*
Two children aim to break up their mother's romance with an Italian concert pianist.
Quite lively, old-fashioned romantic comedy-drama largely set in a splendid Mediterranean villa; happy ending never in doubt.
wd Delmer Daves *novel* Rumer Godden *ph* Oswald Morris *m* Mischa Spoliansky
☆ Maureen O'Hara, Rossano Brazzi, Richard Todd, Phyllis Calvert, Olivia Hussey, Martin Stephens, Elizabeth Dear

'The Kids Definitely Aren't Alright!'
'Could You Kill Your Best Friend?'
Battle Royale **
Japan 2001 114m colour
Metro Tartan/Toei/Battle Royale (Masao Sato, Masumi Okada, Teruo Kamaya, Tetsu Kayama)
In the near future, a class of teenagers is chosen by lottery to be stranded on a remote island and given three days in which to kill one another until only one survives.
Bracing, violent, blackly humorous satire on the bleaker aspects of modern society that manages to be more than merely an excuse for a killing spree.
w Kenta Fukasaku *novel* Koshun Takami *d* Kinji Fukasaku *ph* Katsumi Yanagijima *m* Masamichi Amano *pd* Kyoko Heya *ed* Hirohide Abe
☆ Tatsuya Fujiwara (Shuya), Aki Maeda (Noriko), Taro Yamamoto (Kawada), Masanobu Ando (Kiriyama), Kou Shibasaki (Mitsuko), Chiaki Kuriyama (Chigusa), Beat Takeshi (Kitano)
'At heart a cruel, gripping gore-fest that offers sadistic entertainment.' – *Cosmo Landesman, Sunday Times*
'A film put together with remarkable confidence and flair. Its steely candour, and weird, passionate urgency make it compelling.' – *Peter Bradshaw, Guardian*

Battle Stations
US 1956 81m bw
Columbia
Life on an aircraft carrier as seen by the padre.
Cliché-strewn, mini-budgeted war thriller.
w Crane Wilbur *d* Lewis Seiler
☆ John Lund, William Bendix, Keefe Brasselle, Richard Boone

Battle Stripe: see *The Men*

Battle Taxi
US 1954 82m bw
UA (Ivan Tors)
A newcomer to the helicopter rescue service in Korea resents his non-combatant status, but becomes a hero.
The story takes second place to one damned rescue after another in this lively but overlong second feature.
w Malvin Wald *d* Herbert L. Strock
☆ Sterling Hayden, Arthur Franz, Marshall Thompson

'Prepare To Go Psychlo'
Battlefield Earth
US 2000 117m colour
Warner/Morgan Creek/Franchise/JPT (Elie Samaha, Jonathan D. Krane, John Travolta)
A thousand years in the future, a human rebels against a race of giant aliens who control the Earth.
Asinine pulp science-fiction is treated with the utmost respect: the result is never less than ridicuous, from the aliens' appearance to the juvenile narrative.
w Corey Mandell, J. D. Shapiro *novel* L. Ron Hubbard *d* Roger Christian *ph* Giles Nuttgens *m* Elia Cmiral *pd* Patrick Tatopoulos *ed* Robin Russell *cos* Patrick Tatopoulos
☆ John Travolta (Terl), Barry Pepper (Jonnie Goodboy Tyler), Forest Whitaker (Ker), Kim Coates (Carlo), Richard Tyson (Robert the Fox), Sabine Karsenti (Chrissie), Michael Byrne (Parson Staffer), Sean Hewitt (Heywood), Michel Perron (Rock), Shaun Austin-Olsen (Planetship), Christian Tessler (Mickey), Kelly Preston (Chirk), Jim Meskimen (Blythe)
'Haplessly cliched dialogue, cardboard characters and dunderheaded plot logic...This may be the loudest actioner yet, challenging viewer tolerance with incessant sonic-boom footfalls, detonations, gunplay and screamed dialogue.' – *Dennis Harvey, Variety*
'Utterly, utterly dreadful.' – *Edward Porter, Sunday Times*
† The film cost $73m to make, and took $21.5m at the US box office.

'The guts! The girls! The glory! of a lot of wonderful guys!'
Battleground *
US 1949 118m bw
MGM (Dore Schary)
How a group of American soldiers in 1944 endured the Battle of the Bulge.
Enormously successful at the box-office, this studio-bound production now seems stilted and unpersuasive, despite some good writing and direction.
w Robert Pirosh *d* William Wellman *ph* Paul C. Vogel *m* Lennie Hayton *ed* John Dunning
☆ Van Johnson (Holley), John Hodiak (Jarvess), Ricardo Montalban (Roderigues), George Murphy (Pop Stazak), Marshall Thompson (Jim Layton), Jerome Courtland (Abner Spudler), Don Taylor (Standiferd), Bruce Cowling (Wolowicz), James Whitmore (Kinnie), Douglas Fowley ('Kipp' Kippton), Guy Anderson (Hansan), Richard Jaeckel (Bettis)
'Engrossingly well done.' – *Richard Mallett, Punch*
Robert Pirosh; Paul C. Vogel
best picture; William Wellman; James Whitmore; editing

Battles of Chief Pontiac
US 1953 75m bw
Jack Broder
In the mid-18th century, peace talks with the Detroit Indians are sabotaged.
Slightly unusual but undistinguished slice of Western history.
w Jack de Witt *d* Felix E. Feist
☆ Lon Chaney Jnr, Lex Barker, Helen Westcott, Berry Kroeger, Roy Roberts

The Battleship Potemkin ****
USSR 1925 75m approx (16 fps) bw silent; sound version 65m
Goskino
original title: *Bronenosets Potemkin*
A partly fictitious account of the mutiny at Odessa, an episode in the 1905 revolution. (The film was made as part of the 20th anniversary celebrations.)
A textbook cinema classic, and masterpiece of creative editing, especially in the famous Odessa Steps sequence in which innocent civilians are mown down in the bloodshed; the happenings of a minute are drawn into five by frenzied cross-cutting. The film contains 1,300 separate shots, and was judged the best film ever made in 1948 and 1958 by a panel of international judges.
wd Sergei Eisenstein ph Edouard Tissé, V. Popov
☆ A. Antonov, Grigori Alexandrov, Vladimir Barsky, Levshin

Battlestar Galactica
US 1979 125m colour
Universal (John Dykstra)
A spaceship crew battles its way back towards Earth.
Cobbled together from episodes of an unsuccessful TV series, the movie resembles a space version of another TV series, Bonanza, and borrows heavily from Star Wars to little effect.
w Glen A. Larson *d* Richard A. Colla *ph* Ben Coleman *m* Stu Phillips, John E. Chilberg II *ed* Robert L. Kimble, Leon Ortiz-Gil, Larry Strong *sp* Apogee
☆ Richard Hatch, Dirk Benedict, Lorne Greene, Ray Milland, Lew Ayres, Jane Seymour, Wilfrid Hyde-White, John Colicos, Patrick Macnee

Battletruck
New Zealand 1981 94m colour
Battletruck Films (Lloyd Phillips, Rob Whitehouse)
aka: *Warlords of the 21st Century*
In the future, when civilization has been reduced to a few isolated communities, a lone hero on a motorbike battles a ruthless gang leader and his armoured truck.
A latter-day Western, full of gratuitous sadism, and no more than a pale shadow of Mad Max *(qv).*
w Irving Austin, Harley Cokliss, John Beech *d* Harley Cokliss *ph* Chris Menges *m* Kevin Peek *pd* Gary Hansen *ed* Michael Horton
☆ Michael Beck, Annie McEnroe, James Wainwright, Bruno Lawrence, John Bach, John Ratzenberger, Randolph Powell

Battling Bellhop: see *Kid Galahad (1937)*

Battling Butler *
US 1926 68m approx (24 fps) bw silent
MGM (Joseph M. Schenck)
A young millionaire pretends to be a boxer in order to win a sweetheart.
Middling star comedy.
w Al Boasberg, Charles Smith, Paul Gerard Smith, Lex Neal *d* Buster Keaton *ph* J. Devereux Jennings, Bert Haines
☆ Buster Keaton, Sally O'Neil

The Bawdy Adventures of Tom Jones
GB 1976 94m Technicolor
Universal/Robert Sadoff
See *Tom Jones*, of which this is a musical version.
Not quite as bad as one would expect, but not up to the original.
w Jeremy Lloyd *play* Don McPherson *d* Cliff Owen *ph* Douglas Slocombe *m* Ron Grainer *m/ly* Paul Holden
☆ Nicky Henson, Trevor Howard, Terry-Thomas, Arthur Lowe, Georgia Brown, Joan Collins, William Mervyn, Murray Melvin, Geraldine McEwan, Michael Bates, James Hayter, Isabel Dean, Gladys Henson
'A cheap, crude, sexed-up rehash with only three actual musical numbers ... more boring than bawdy.' – *Kevin Thomas, Los Angeles Times*

Baxter *
GB 1972 100m Technicolor
EMI/Performing Arts (Arthur Lewis)
An American son of divorced parents comes to London with his mother, meets tragedy in the shape of a friend's death, and responds to treatment for a speech defect.
Slight, appealing case history of a maladjusted 12-year-old; a rather unnecessarily uncommercial slice of life with no easy solution offered.
w Reginald Rose *d* Lionel Jeffries *ph* Geoffrey Unsworth *m* Michael J. Lewis *ad* Anthony Pratt *ed* Teddy Darvas
☆ Patricia Neal (Dr Clemm), Scott Jacoby (Robert Baxter), Britt Ekland (Chris Bentley), Jean-Pierre Cassel (Roger Tunnell), Lynn Carlin (Mrs Baxter), Paul Eddington (Mr Rawling), Sally Thomsett (Nemo), Paul Maxwell (Mr Baxter)

The Bay Boy
Canada/France 1984 101m colour
Rank/Hachette Fox/Antenne 2/A2/CTV/HBO/Orion (John Kemeny, Denis Héroux)
In 1937 Nova Scotia, a 16-year-old boy is distracted by real-life problems from his supposed vocation as a priest.
Doleful, weatherbeaten slice of autobiography which remains of interest only to those who know the country and the people.
wd Daniel Petrie *ph* Claude Agostini *m* Claude Bolling *pd* Wolf Kroeger *ed* Susan Shanks
☆ Liv Ullmann, Kiefer Sutherland, Peter Donat, Alan Scarfe, Chris Wiggins

Bay of Angels: see *La Baie des Anges*

'The first motion picture to require a face-to-face warning. May be the last shock film you will ever want to see!'
A Bay of Blood (dubbed)
Italy 1971 90m colour
Nuovo Linea (Giuseppe Zaccariello)
original title: *Ecologia del Delitto*
aka: *Antefatto; Bloodbath Bay of Blood; Carnage; Last House on the Left Part II; Twitch of the Death Nerve*
In a struggle to gain control of a beautiful bay ripe for development, thirteen people are murdered.
There's not much narrative in this movie, which is more an exercise in thinking up inventive ways for people to die, with each victim killed by a different means. It is original, in that there are multiple killers at work, as each murderer becomes a victim in turn, and it is done with some style and a heavy irony.
w Mario Bava, Joseph McLee (Giuseppe Zaccariello), Filippo Ottoni *story* Dardano Sacchetti, Franco Barberi *d* Mario Bava *ph* Mario Bava *m* Stelvio Cipriani *ad* Sergio Canevari *ed* Carlo Realy
☆ Claudine Auger, Luigi Pistilli, Claudio Volonte, Anna M. Rosati, Chris Avram, Leopoldo Trieste, Laura Betti, Brigitte Skay, Isa Miranda
† The British video release runs for 81m. When it was first shown in America, as a gimmick ticket-holders had to pass through a 'final warning station' before being allowed to see the film.

Be Big *
US 1931 20m bw
Hal Roach
Ollie feigns illness to avoid a trip with his wife, but Stan's help proves disastrous.
Comedy warm-up for Sons of the Desert *(qv); Ollie spends most of the second reel trying to rid himself of a tight boot.*
w H. M. Walker *d* James Parrott
☆ Stan Laurel, Oliver Hardy, Anita Garvin, Isabelle Keith

'Somewhere on this planet it must exist.'
The Beach *
US 2000 120m Technicolor 'Scope
TCF/Figment (Andrew Macdonald)
An American backpacker discovers that the rumour is true of a hippy community living by a perfect beach on a remote Thailand island.
Fitfully engaging tale of an expulsion from paradise, hampered by being too obviously fitted around the requirements of its star.
w John Hodge *novel* Alex Garland *d* Danny Boyle *ph* Darius Khondji *m* Angelo Badalamenti *pd* Andrew McAlpine *ed* Masahiro Hirakubo
☆ Leonardo DiCaprio (Richard), Tilda Swinton (Sal), Virginie Ledoyen (Francoise), Guillaume Canet (Etienne), Paterson Joseph (Keaty), Robert Carlyle (Daffy), Peter Youngblood Hills (Zeph), Jerry Swindall (Sammy), Lars Arentz Hansen (Bugs)
'Not a terrible movie. just an insubstantial one. All of Mr DiCaprio's charisma and the director's savvy are used to divert us from the fact that there's not much going on.' – *Elvis Mitchell, New York Times*

Beach Blanket Bingo
US 1965 98m Pathécolor Panavision
Orion/AIP (James H. Nicholson, Samuel Z. Arkoff)
Teenage surfers become involved with a publicity man organizing a series of stunts to make a star of a new singer.
It has sea, surf, sand, slapstick, sky-diving, a mermaid and a little cynicism, making fun of youth-oriented pop while at the same time celebrating it; possibly the best of its imperturbably bland genre.
w William Asher, Leo Townsend *d* William Asher *ph* Floyd Crosby *m* Les Baxter *ch* Jack Baker *ad* Howard Campbell *ed* Fred Feitshans, Eve Newman
☆ Frankie Avalon, Annette Funicello, Deborah Walley, Harvey Lembeck, John Ashley, Jody McCrea, Donna Loren, Marta Kristen, Linda Evans, Timothy Carey, Paul Lynde, Don Rickles, Buster Keaton, Earl Wilson
† The fifth in AIP's beach movies, it was followed by *How to Stuff a Wild Bikini* (qv).

The Beach Girls and the Monster
US 1966 70m bw
Edward Janis/Films
An oceanographer finds something very strange emerging from the waters of Waikiki Beach.
Elementary horror flick which fails to scare and is only notable for the re-emergence of its star.
w Joan Gardner *d* Jon Hall
☆ Jon Hall, Sue Casey, Walker Edmiston, Arnold Lessing

Beach House
US 1982 76m TVC Color
New Line/Galaxy Industries (Marino Amoruso)
Teenagers congregate in Ocean City to indulge in banal dialogue, stupid pranks, dull sex and duller rock.
Garish, jejune, indifferently acted and directed attempt at a comedy that even the youth of its participants cannot excuse.
d John Gallagher *ph* Peter Stein *m* C. P. Roth *m/ly* Adam Roth *ed* Victor Kanefsky, John Bloomgarden
☆ Ileana Seidel, Richard Duggan, Kathy McNeil, John Cosola, Marino Amoruso, Spence Waugh, Paul Anderson, Adam Roth

The Beach of Lost Children
Mali 1991 88m colour
Paris Plage/Herakles (Mohamed Abderrahman Tazi)
aka: *La Plage des Enfants Perdus*
A father hides away his simple-minded daughter when he discovers that she is pregnant by a local taxi driver.
Leaden and curiously inert treatment of a dramatic story.
wd Jillali Ferhati *ph* Gilberto Azevedo, Jacques Besse *m* Djamel Allam *ad* Abdelkrim Akkelach *ed* Natalie Perrey
☆ Souad Ferhati, Mohamed Timod, Fatima Loukili, Larbi El Yacoubi, Nezha Zakaria, Mohamed Larbi Khazzan, Safia Ziani

Beach Party *
US 1963 104m Pathécolor Panavision
AIP/Alta Vista (James H. Nicholson, Lou Rusoff)
An anthropologist sets up house on a California beach to study the mating habits of young people but becomes personally involved when one of them falls for him.
Vaguely satirical pop musical with relaxed performances; quite tolerable in itself, it started an excruciating trend.
w Lou Rusoff *d* William Asher *ph* Kay Norton *m* Les Baxter *ad* Daniel Haller *ed* Homer Powell
☆ Bob Cummings, Dorothy Malone, Annette Funicello, Frankie Avalon, Vincent Price, Harvey Lembeck, Morey Amsterdam, Jody McCrea

Beach Red *
US 1967 105m Technicolor
UA/Theodora (Cornel Wilde)
In 1943, American assault craft take a Japanese-held Pacific island.
Brutal, pacifist war film, simply and clearly portrayed but not exactly entertaining.
w Clint Johnston, Donald A. Peters, Jefferson Pascal *d* Cornel Wilde *ph* Cecil R. Cooney *m* Antonio Buenaventura
☆ Cornel Wilde, Rip Torn, Burr de Benning, Jean Wallace

The Beachcomber: see *Vessel of Wrath (1938)*

The Beachcomber *
GB 1954 90m Technicolor
GFD/London Independent (William MacQuitty)
An alcoholic ne'er-do-well in the Dutch East Indies reforms after an unexpected adventure with a lady missionary.
Styleless remake of Vessel of Wrath *(qv); the acting just about holds the interest, but all other contributions are flat.*
w Sydney Box *story* Somerset Maugham *d* Muriel Box *ph* Reg Wyer *m* Francis Chagrin
☆ *Robert Newton*, Glynis Johns, Donald Sinden, Paul Rogers, Donald Pleasence, Walter Crisham, Michael Hordern, Ronald Lewis

Beaches *
US 1988 123m Metrocolor
Warner/Touchstone/An All Girl Production (Bonnie Bruckheimer-Martell, Bette Midler, Margaret Jennings South)
A singer visits her dying friend, a lawyer, and recalls their long and volatile friendship.
In another age, this sentimental feminist weepie would have been classified as a woman's picture, though Midler's singing gives it a wider appeal.
w Mary Agnes Donoghue *novel* Iris Rainer Dart *d* Garry Marshall *ph* Dante Spinotti *m* Georges Delerue *pd* Albert Brenner *ad* Garrett Lewis *ed* Richard Halsey
☆ Bette Midler, Barbara Hershey, John Heard, Spalding Gray, Lainie Kazan, James Read, Grace Johnston, Mayim Bialik, Marcie Leeds
best art direction

The Beads of One Rosary *
Poland 1979 116m colour
Cinegate/PRF-Zespol Filmowy
original title: *Paciorki Jednego Różańca*
A retired miner and his wife defy attempts by property developers to demolish their cottage.
There is something of the charm of an Ealing comedy in this tale of a little man standing up to bureaucratic pressures.
wd Kazimierz Kutz *ph* Wieslaw Zdort *m* Wojciech Kilar *ad* Andrzej Plocki, Miroslaw Krelik *ed* Jozef Bartczak
☆ Augustyn Halotta, Marta Straszna, Ewa Wiśniewska, Franciszek Pieczka

'The Ultimate Disaster Movie'
Bean *
GB 1997 90m colour
Polygram/Working Title/Tiger Aspect (Tim Bevan, Eric Fellner, Peter Bennett-Jones)
An accident-prone attendant at London's Royal National Gallery accompanies *Whistler's Mother* to America.
Slapstick farce of embarrassment, based on a highly successful television series; it features one of the least likeable and most mean-spirited of comic creations.
w Richard Curtis, Robin Driscoll, Rowan Atkinson *d* Mel Smith *ph* Francis Kenny *m* Howard Goodall *pd* Peter Larkin *ed* Chris Blunden
☆ Rowan Atkinson, Peter MacNicol, Pamela Reed, Harris Yulin, Burt Reynolds, John Mills, Richard Gant, Tricia Vessey, Andrew Lawrence, Peter Egan, Peter Capaldi
'Not only consistently entertaining, but frequently laugh-out-loud funny.' – *Caroline Westbrook, Empire*
'The ultimate movie disaster.' – *Mike Higgins, Independent*
† The film cost £17m and grossed around $45m in the US, and another $172m elsewhere.

The Bear **
France 1989 98m Eastmancolor Panavision
Tri-Star/Renn/Price Entertainment (Claude Berri)
An orphaned bear cub tries to cope with life in the wild.
Charming film, told from the bear's point of view, with natural sounds substituting for dialogue.
w Gérard Brach *novel* *The Grizzly King* by James Oliver Curwood *d* Jean-Jacques Annaud *ph* Philippe Rousselot *m* Philippe Sarde *pd* Toni Ludi *ed* Noelle Boisson
☆ Bart, Youk, Jack Wallace, Tcheky Karyo, André Lacombe
best film editing

Bear Country: see *The Living Desert*

'Below freezing and beyond fear ... will anyone survive its terror?'
Bear Island
GB/Canada 1979 118m colour Panavision
Columbia/Bear Island/Selkirk (Peter Snell)
Meteorological experts on an Arctic island are menaced by neo-Nazis.
Highly implausible adventure yarn, indifferently presented.
w David Butler, Don Sharp, Murray Smith *novel* Alistair MacLean *d* Don Sharp *ph* Alan Hume *m* Robert Farnon *pd* Harry Pottle *ed* Eric Boyd Perkins
☆ Vanessa Redgrave (Heddi Lindquest), Donald Sutherland (Frank Lansing), Richard Widmark (Otto Gerran), Christopher Lee (Lechinski), Barbara Parkins (Judith Rubin), Lloyd Bridges (Smithy), Lawrence Dane (Paul Hartman), Patricia Collins (Inge Van Zipper), Michael Reynolds (Heyter), Nicholas Courtland (Jungbeck)

The Bears and I
US 1974 89m Technicolor
Walt Disney (Winston Hibler)
An army veteran goes to live near an Indian settlement and adopts three bear cubs, later becoming a Park Ranger.
Simple, pleasing outdoor family film.
w John Whedon *novel* Robert Franklin Leslie *d* Bernard McEveety *ph* Ted D. Landon *m* Buddy Baker
☆ Patrick Wayne, Chief Dan George, Andrew Duggan, Michael Ansara

'War brings out the beast in every man.'
The Beast
US 1988 109m colour
Columbia/A&M (John Fiedler)
aka: *The Beast of War*
In 1981 in Afghanistan a Russian soldier turns rebel after he is left to die by his brutal comrades, who are trying to reach safety with their tank while being attacked by Afghan guerrillas.
Dull, violent, unilluminating war movie, conducted on a pitch of hysteria.
w William Mastrosimone *play* *Nanawatai* by William Mastrosimone *d* Kevin Reynolds *ph* Douglas Milsome *m* Mark Isham *ad* Richard James
☆ George Dzundza, Jason Patric, Steven Bauer, Stephen Baldwin, Don Harvey, Erick Avari, Kabir Bedi
'This superior war movie effortlessly fuses the moral complexity of scriptwriter William Mastrosimone's original stage play with the visual spectacle and narrative drive of a full-blown cinema feature.' – *Time Out*

'A Thrill-Story Beyond All Imagining!'
'King of Prehistoric Sea Giants ... Raging Up From The Bottom of Time!'
The Beast from Twenty Thousand Fathoms
US 1953 80m bw
Warner (Hal Chester, Jack Dietz)
Heat generated by an atomic bomb test in the Arctic thaws out a prehistoric rhedosaurus which travels down the American coast to cause havoc in New York until cornered and destroyed on Coney Island.
Flat-footed, though influential, addition to the monster cycle, with an interminable wait for the beast's appearance and inferior trick work when he goes on the rampage.
w Lou Morheim, Fred Freiberger *d* Eugène Lourié *ph* Jack Russell *m* David Buttolph *sp* Ray Harryhausen
☆ Paul Christian, Paula Raymond, Cecil Kellaway, Kenneth Tobey, Donald Woods, Lee Van Cleef

The Beast in the Cellar
GB 1970 87m Eastmancolor
Tigon-Leander (Tony Tenser, Graham Harris)
A rampaging killer in the Lancashire woods turns out to be the deranged ex-soldier brother of two elderly spinsters who have kept him locked up for thirty years.
Idiotically boring farrago, totally lacking in suspense and wasting good talent.
wd James Kelly *ph* Harry Waxman, Desmond Dickinson *m* Tony Macaulay
☆ Flora Robson, Beryl Reid, Tessa Wyatt, John Hamill, T. P. McKenna

The Beast Must Die: see *Que la Bête Meure (1969)*

The Beast Must Die *
GB 1974 93m Technicolor
BL/Amicus (Milton Subotsky)
aka: *Black Werewolf*
A millionaire big game hunter holds a weekend party to track down a werewolf, but his guest list rapidly gets smaller...
A savage variation on Ten Little Indians *(qv), not badly done, with such gimmicks as a 'guess who' break near the end.*
w Michael Winder *story* James Blish *d* Paul Annett *ph* Jack Hildyard *m* Douglas Gamley
☆ Calvin Lockhart, Peter Cushing, Charles Gray, Anton Diffring, Marlene Clark, Ciaran Madden, Michael Gambon

The Beast of Hollow Mountain
US/Mexico 1956 78m DeLuxe
Cinemascope/Regiscope
UA/Peliculas Rodriguez (William and Edward Nassour)
An American rancher in Mexico has to deal with a jealous rival and a rampaging tyrannosaurus rex.
Uneasy mix of routine cowboy movie and substandard science fiction.
w Robert Hill, Jack DeWitt *story* Willis O'Brien *d* Edward Nassour, Ismael Rodriguez *ph* Jorge Stahl Jnr *m* Raul Lavista *ed* Holbrook Todd, Maury Wright
☆ Guy Madison, Patricia Medina, Carlos Rivas, Edward Noriega, Julio Villareal, Mario Novarro
'It should rack up handsome returns for its producers and provide moppet audiences particularly with edge-of-the-seat entertainment during its fantasy sequences.' – *Variety*
† The Regiscope system promised 'animation in depth', but its stop motion effects with fuzzy back projection are comic rather than horrific. The central notion of this first science-fiction Western turned up again in *Valley of Gwangi* (qv).

Beast of Morocco: see *The Hand of Night*

Beast of the City
US 1932 80m bw
MGM
A police captain is determined to get a ruthless racketeer by fair means or foul.
Curiously dour little crime melodrama with a high death rate; the cast does not quite save it.
w John Lee Mahin *story* W. R. Burnett *d* Charles Brabin *ph* Barney McGill
☆ Walter Huston, Jean Harlow, Wallace Ford, Jean Hersholt, Dorothy Peterson, Tully Marshall, John Miljan
'A gang story for rural and home circle consumption, preaching the gospel of civic righteousness and the glory of steadfast purpose. Aiming at domestic patronage, they even make Miss Harlow keep her skirts down.' – *Variety*
'Endowed with vitality and realism.' – *New York Times*

The Beast of War: see *The Beast*

The Beast with a Million Eyes
US 1955 84m bw
San Matteo/AIP
A malicious space creature lands in the desert but is defeated by human love.
Semi-professional would-be horror story, on a level with the Corman horrors of the period.
w Tom Filer *d* David Karmansky
☆ Paul Birch, Lorna Thayer, Dick Sargent

The Beast with Five Fingers *
US 1946 88m bw
Warner (William Jacobs)
A famous pianist dies and his severed hand returns to commit murder.
Slow-moving, Italian-set horror thriller which wastes an excellent original; a superb central performance and clever trick effects can hardly redeem the stodgy script or the ending which reveals the hauntings as a hallucination.
w Curt Siodmak *story* W. F. Harvey *d* Robert Florey *ph* Wesley Anderson *m* Max Steiner
☆ *Peter Lorre*, Andrea King, Robert Alda, J. Carrol Naish, Victor Francen, Charles Dingle

Beastcops

Hong Kong 1998 108m colour
Media Asia/People's Production (F.K. Ma, John Chong)
original title: *Yeshou Xingling*
Two mismatched cops become involved with girls and gangsters when the Triad boss leaves town.
Violent thriller with some bloody fight scenes and a lot of desultory action as the two cops become buddies.
w Chan Hing-kai, Gordon Chan *d* Gordon Chan *ph* Tony Cheung *m* T2 *ad* Alfred Yau *ed* Chan Ki-hop
☆ Michael Fitzgerald Wong (Michael Cheung), Anthony Wong (Tung), Kathy Chau (Yoyo), Roy Cheung (Big Brother), Sam Lee (Sam)
'High on testosterone, but short on lyricism or humour.' – *Sight and Sound*
† It was voted Best Film at the Hong Kong Film Awards in 1999.

The Beastmaster

US 1982 118m colour
EMI/Ecta/Leisure Investments (Paul Pepperman, Sylvio Tabet)
A royal child, stolen at birth by a witch, is rescued by a peasant who brings him up skilled in the martial arts.
Comic strip sword and sorcery: fairly high budget but very low intelligence.
w Don Coscarelli, Paul Pepperman *d* Don Coscarelli *ph* John Alcott *m* Lee Holdridge *pd* Conrad E. Angone *ed* Roy Watts
☆ Marc Singer, Tanya Roberts, Rip Torn, John Amos, Rod Loomis

Beastmaster II: Through the Portals of Time

US 1991 107m CFI color
Republic/Films 21 (Sylvio Tabet)
A mythical warrior and his animal friends are transported through time to present-day Los Angeles to battle against his evil brother.
More comic-strip sword and sorcery: very low budget, even lower intelligence.
w R. J. Robertson, Jim Wynorski, Sylvio Tabet, Ken Hauser, Doug Miles *novel* The Beastmaster by André Norton *d* Sylvio Tabet *ph* Ronn Schmid *m* Robert Folk *pd* Allen Jones *ed* Adam Bernardi
☆ Marc Singer, Kari Wuhrer, Wings Hauser, Sarah Douglas, Charles Young

'A legendary hero. A battle beyond imagination.'

Beastmaster III: The Eye of Braxus

US 1995 92m colour
MCA (Stu Segall, Sylvio Tabet, David Wise)
The Beastmaster battles against an evil tyrant who plans to rule the world by summoning an ancient god.
Feeble low-budget fantasy with a risible demon and more bad acting, even from the animals, than any dozen other B movies.
w David Wise *d* Gabrielle Beaumont *ph* Michael J. Davis *m* Jan Hammer *pd* Nigel Clinker *ed* Ken Bornstein
☆ Marc Singer (Dar), David Warner (Lord Agon), Lesley-Anne Down (Morgana), Tony Todd (Seth), Casper Van Dien (King Tal), Keith Coulouris (Bey), Sandra Hess (Shada), Patrick Kilpatrick (Jaggart)
'Ineptly directed but that's part of its charm.' – *Sight and Sound*

The Beat Generation

US 1959 95m bw Cinemascope
Albert Zugsmith
aka: *This Rebel Age*
A vicious rapist joins the beatniks.
Bankrupt exploitation melodrama, not easy to sit through.
w Richard Matheson, Lewis Meltzer *d* Charles Haas *ph* Walter H. Castle *m* Albert Glasser
☆ Ray Danton, Steve Cochran, Fay Spain, Mamie Van Doren, Jackie Coogan, Louis Armstrong, Maggie Hayes, Jim Mitchum, Irish McCalla, Maxie Rosenbloom
'An enervating mixture of slapstick, religiosity, psychological hokum and grubby sensationalism.' – *MFB*

'Beat' Girl

GB 1960 85m bw
Renown
US title: *Wild for Kicks*
An architect's teenage daughter goes to the dogs.
Risible exposé-style melodrama.
w Dail Ambler *d* Edmond T. Gréville *ph* Walter Lassally *m* John Barry
☆ David Farrar, Noelle Adam, Christopher Lee, Gillian Hills, Adam Faith, Peter McEnery, Nigel Green

Beat Street

US 1984 106m DeLuxe Movielab
Orion (David V. Picker, Harry Belafonte)
An aspiring DJ from South Bronx has trouble getting into showbiz.
For teenagers only; a rehash of Saturday Night Fever *(qv) applied to the new fad of break-dancing.*
w Andy Davis, David Gilbert, Paul Golding *d* Stan Lathan *ph* Tom Priestley *m* Harry Belafonte *pd* Patrizia von Brandenstein *ed* Dov Hoenig
☆ Rae Dawn Chong, Guy Davis, Jon Chardiet, Leon W. Grant, Saundra Santiago

'Adventure at its boldest! Bogart at his best!'

Beat the Devil *

GB 1953 100m bw
Romulus/Santana (Jack Clayton)
In a small Mediterranean port, and subsequently on a boat bound for the African coast, oddly assorted travellers plan to acquire land known to contain uranium deposits. Unsatisfactory, over-talkative and inconsequential burlesque of the director's own *The Maltese Falcon* and *Across the Pacific* (qqv).
Good fun was obviously had by the cast, but audiences were mostly baffled by the in-jokes, the extra-strange characters, and the lack of attention to pace, suspense and plot development.
w Truman Capote, John Huston *novel* James Helvick *d* John Huston *ph* Oswald Morris *m* Franco Mannino
☆ Humphrey Bogart (Billy Dannreuther), *Jennifer Jones* (Gwendolen Chelm), Gina Lollobrigida (Maria Dannreuther), *Edward Underdown* (Harry Chelm), Peter Lorre (O'Hara), Robert Morley (Petersen), *Ivor Barnard* (Major Ross), Bernard Lee (Inspector), Marco Tulli (Ravello)
GWENDOLEN: 'Harry, we must beware of these men. They're desperate characters. Not one of them looked at my legs.'
DANNREUTHER: 'Trouble with England, it's all pomp and no circumstance. You're very wise to get out of it, escape while you can.'
O'HARA: 'Time! Time! What is time? The Swiss manufacture it. The French hoard it. Italians want it. Americans say it is money. Hindus say it does not exist. Do you know what I say? I say time is a crook.'
'A potential treat emerged as a wet firecracker … the incidents remain on a naggingly arch and lagging verbal keel.' – *New York Times*
'Each of its cinematic clichés appears to be placed in the very faintest of mocking quotation marks.' – *Time*
'Only the phonies liked it. It's a mess!' – *Humphrey Bogart*
'The formula of *Beat the Devil* is that everyone is slightly absurd.' – *John Huston*
† James Helvick was the pseudonym of Claud Cockburn.

Beau Brummell *

US 1924 104m approx (24 fps) bw silent
Warner
A Regency dandy becomes the right-hand man of the Prince of Wales, but falters through his own arrogance.
Elegant period romance which marked the beginning of its star's great movie decade.
w Dorothy Farnum *d* Harry Beaumont
☆ *John Barrymore*, Mary Astor, Carmel Myers, Willard Louis

Beau Brummell *

GB 1954 111m Eastmancolor
MGM (Sam Zimbalist)
A Regency dandy enjoys a close relationship with the Prince of Wales, and when this is eventually withdrawn he dies in penury.
Stodgy historical romance with entertaining patches; the main story is too graceful and conventional to be believed.
w Karl Tunberg *play* Clyde Fitch *d* Curtis Bernhardt *ph* Oswald Morris *m* Richard Addinsell *ad* Alfred Junge
☆ Stewart Granger, Elizabeth Taylor, *Peter Ustinov* (Prince Regent), *Robert Morley* (George III), James Donald, James Hayter, Rosemary Harris, Paul Rogers, Noel Willman, Peter Bull, Peter Dyneley

Beau Chumps: see *Beau Hunks*

'Hard lives, quick deaths, undying love!'

Beau Geste **

US 1926 120m approx (24 fps) bw (colour sequences) silent
Paramount (Herbert Brenon)
Three English brothers join the Foreign Legion, suffer under a brutal sergeant, and die fighting the Arabs.
Although outmoded even when first filmed, this tale of derring-do and self sacrifice usually works, and in this case it gave its star a fresh image. One of the best remembered silents of the twenties.
w Paul Schofield *novel* P. C. Wren *d Herbert Brenon ph* Roy Hunt *ad* Julian Boone Fleming
☆ *Ronald Colman*, Neil Hamilton, Ralph Forbes, Alice Joyce, Mary Brian, *Noah Beery*, William Powell, Victor McLaglen
† Remade 1939 and 1966; sequel, *Beau Ideal*, 1931.

'Three against the world! Brothers and soldiers all!'

Beau Geste **

US 1939 120m bw
Paramount (William Wellman)
Three aristocratic brothers join the Foreign Legion to hide a family scandal.
Spirited remake, with a famous flashback opening of the desert fort defended by corpses. Style and acting generally satisfactory.
w Robert Carson *d* William Wellman *ph* Theodor Sparkuhl, Archie Stout *m* Alfred Newman *ad* Hans Dreier, Robert Odell
☆ Gary Cooper, Ray Milland, Robert Preston, *Brian Donlevy*, *J. Carrol Naish*, Susan Hayward, Heather Thatcher, James Stephenson, Donald O'Connor, G. P. Huntley Jnr, Albert Dekker, Broderick Crawford
FOREWORD: 'The love of a man for a woman waxes and wanes like the moon, but the love of brother for brother is steadfast as the stars and endures like the word of the prophet…' Arabian proverb'
MARKOFF: "Keep shooting, you scum! You'll get a chance yet to die with your boots on!'
'Its melodrama is sometimes grim but never harrowing, its pace is close to hectic and its suspense is constant.' – *Herbert Cohn, Brooklyn Daily Eagle*
'A morbid picture, but I doubt whether any morality council will take action, the whole story being so wrapped up in the school colours – in comradeship and loyalty and breeding, and the pure girl left behind; morbid because the brutality has no relation whatever to the real world; it is uncriticized daydreaming.' – *Graham Greene*
'A handsome treatment of a well-loved adventure tale.' – *New York Daily Mirror*
'Will do nominal biz, but lacks punch for smash proportions.' – *Variety*
† Shot in Buttercup Valley, west of Yuma
†† The nasty sergeant, originally Lejeune, became Markoff to avoid offending the French.
Brian Donlevy; Hans Dreier, Robert Odell

Beau Geste

US 1966 105m Techniscope
Universal (Walter Seltzer)
Three brothers join the Foreign Legion, where they face a sadistic sergeant and marauding Arabs.
A cheap leery melodrama is what results from the jettisoning of all the romantic portions of the original. Savalas is rampant as the sergeant. The central desert section of the story is here augmented, with violence stressed, and Beau allowed to survive at the end.
wd Douglas Heyes *ph* Bud Thackery *m* Hans Salter
☆ Telly Savalas, Guy Stockwell, Doug McClure, Leslie Nielsen, Leo Gordon, Michael Constantine

Beau Hunks **

US 1931 40m bw
Hal Roach
GB title: *Beau Chumps*
A fool and his friend join the Foreign Legion to forget.
Patchy but amiable star comedy with memorable high spots. In-joke: the woman the whole legion wants to forget is Jean Harlow.
w H. M. Walker *d* James W. Horne
☆ Stan Laurel, Oliver Hardy, Charles Middleton

Beau Ideal

US 1931 75m bw
RKO (William Le Baron)
John Geste and a new legionnaire friend become involved in a religious war started by a rascally emir.
Lame sequel to Beau Geste *(qv), fettered by primitive dialogue.*
w Paul Schofield *novel* P. C. Wren *d* Herbert Brenon *ph* J. Roy Hunt *m* Max Steiner
☆ Lester Vail, Ralph Forbes, Don Alvarado, Loretta Young, Irene Rich
'Ordinary programme picture with slight romance. Doubtful draw for women.' – *Variety*

'He took New York for its wildest joy ride!'

Beau James *

US 1957 107m Technicolor Vistavision
Paramount/Hope Enterprises (Jack Rose)
The vaguely crooked career of Jimmy Walker, mayor of New York in the twenties.
Romanticized biopic with few funny moments: Hope cannot cope with the drama, and the result is a creaking vehicle apart from a well-recreated twenties atmosphere and excellent production values.
w Jack Rose, Melville Shavelson *book* Gene Fowler *d* Melville Shavelson *ph* John F. Warren *m* Joseph J. Lilley
☆ Bob Hope, Paul Douglas, Vera Miles, Alexis Smith, Darren McGavin, Joe Mantell, Walter Catlett

Le Beau Mariage *

France 1981 97m colour
Les Films du Losange/Les Films du Carrosse (Margaret Menegoz)
GB title: *A Good Marriage*
An art student abandons her many affairs and announces her intention of getting married, but her intended proves reluctant …
Quietly amusing conversation piece in the style expected of this director; an after-dinner entertainment for the Sunday Times set.
wd Eric Rohmer *ph* Bernard Lutic *m* Ronan Girre, Simon des Innocents
☆ Beatrice Ronand, André Dussollier, Feodor Atkine, Arielle Dombasle

Le Beau Serge *

France 1958 97m bw
AYJM (Jean Cotet)
A student returns to his home town and tries to redeem his old friend who has become a drunkard.
Enjoyable character drama with well observed village backgrounds. Credited with being the spearhead of the 'new wave'.
wd Claude Chabrol ph Henri Decaë m Emile Delpierre
☆ Gérard Blain, Jean-Claude Brialy, Michèle Meritz, Bernadette Lafont

Beau Travail *

France 1999 93m colour
Artificial Eye/La Sept Arte/Pathé/SM (Jerome Minet)
A former sergeant in the French Foreign Legion recalls the events in Africa that led to his downfall, when he feared that the arrival of a popular new recruit would threaten his relationship with his commandant.
This is Billy Budd with sand: a glumly repressed drama that is closer to ballet than narrative cinema, with

much slow homoerotic posturing but little tension; it found an appreciative audience at film festivals.
w Jean-Pol Fargeau, Claire Denis *novella* Billy Budd, Sailor by Herman Melville *d* Claire Denis *ph* Agnes Godard *m* Eran Tzur *pd* Arnaud de Moleron *ed* Nelly Quettier
☆ Denis Lavant (Galoup), Michel Subor (Commandant Bruno Forestier), Grégoire Colin (Sentain), Richard Courcet (Legionnaire)
'Beautiful, brutal and utterly hypnotic.' – *Scotsman*
'A majestic work, in terms of both its cinematography and its grand musical score.' – *Film Review*

Beau-Père *
France 1981 120m colour
Antenne 2/Sara
aka: *Stepfather*
After the death of her mother, an adolescent girl decides to seduce her stepfather.
A drama of innocence and experience that is played mainly for comedy, though there is also an underlying tenderness.
wd Bertrand Blier *novel* Bertrand Blier *ph* Sacha Vierny *m* Philippe Sarde *ad* Theobald Meurisse *ed* Claudine Merlin
☆ Patrick Dewaere, Ariel Besse, Maurice Ronet, Nicole Garcia, Nathalie Baye, Maurice Risch, Genevieve, Macha Meril

Beaumarchais *
France 1996 100m colour Panavision
Artificial Eye/Téléma/Canal+/France 2/France 3 (Charles Gossot)
original title: *Beaumarchais l'Insolent*
The playwright Beaumarchais overcomes imprisonment and adversity to support revolution in America and France.
Enjoyable and episodic period romp, stronger on decor than narrative.
w Edouard Molinaro, Jean-Claude Brisville *play* Sacha Guitry *d* Edouard Molinaro *ph* Michaêl Epp *m* Jean-Claude Petit *ad* Jean-Marc Kerdelhue, Jamie Leonard *ed* Véronique Parnet
☆ Fabrice Luchini, Manuel Blanc, Sandrine Kiberlain, Michael Serrault, Jacques Weber, Michel Piccoli, Jean-Claude Brialy, Murray Head, Jean Yanne, Claire Nebout
'This gorgeous film is witty, intelligent and consistently thought-provoking.' – *Marianne Gray, Film Review*

La Beauté du Diable ***
Italy/France 1949 96m bw
AYJM
The Faust story with the protagonists agreeing to change places.
Dazzling plot twists and cinematic virtuosity make this a richly enjoyable fantasy, though perhaps not among Clair's greatest works.
w René Clair, Armand Salacrou *d René Clair* *ph* Michel Kelber *m* Roman Vlad *ad* Léon Barsacq
☆ *Michel Simon, Gérard Philipe*, Raymond Cordy, Nicole Besnard, Gaston Modot, Paolo Stoppa

The Beautician and the Beast
US 1997 105m DeLuxe
Paramount/Koch/High School Sweethearts (Howard W. Koch Jnr, Todd Graff)
An ambitious beautician, mistakenly hired as a tutor to the children of an eastern European dictator, falls for her boss.
An attempt at a romantic frivolity, relying on a clash between New York Jewish humour and communist rigidity for its humour; its appeal is likely to be limited to New Yorkers.
w Todd Graff *d* Ken Kwapis *ph* Peter Lyons Collister *m* Cliff Eidelman *pd* Rusty Smith *ed* Jon Poll
☆ Fran Drescher, Timothy Dalton, Ian McNeice, Patrick Malahide, Lisa Jakub, Michael Lerner, Phyllis Newman
'The cinematic equivalent of a cheesy, multi-accented and self-consciously naïve college production.' – *Emanuel Levy, Variety*

'She's got the biggest six-shooters in the west!'
The Beautiful Blonde from Bashful Bend *
US 1949 77m Technicolor
TCF (Preston Sturges)
A temperamental saloon entertainer accidentally shoots the sheriff and takes refuge as a schoolmistress.
A dishevelled Western farce unworthy of its creator, but with the advantage of appearances by many of his usual repertory of players.
wd Preston Sturges *ph* Harry Jackson *m* Cyril Mockridge
☆ Betty Grable, Cesar Romero, El Brendel, Hugh Herbert, Rudy Vallee, Olga San Juan, Sterling Holloway, Porter Hall, Esther Howard, Margaret Hamilton
'It erects a fabric of roaring slapstick on a conventional western foundation, and from time to time it succeeds in being very funny.' – *Richard Mallett, Punch*
'Somehow the ramshackle air of Bashful Bend itself seems to have permeated the whole film.' – *MFB*

Beautiful but Broke
US 1944 74m bw
Columbia (Irving Briskin)
An agent and a girls' band get romantically marooned on the way to a date in Cleveland.
Haphazard comedy with music; just an occasional smile amid the tedium.
w Monte Brice, Manny Seff *story* Arthur Housman *d* Charles Barton
☆ Joan Davis, Jane Frazee, John Hubbard, Judy Clark, Bob Haymes, Danny Mummert, Byron Foulger
'Commonplace B entry.' – *Variety*

Beautiful but Dangerous: see *She Couldn't Say No (1952)*

Beautiful but Dangerous (dubbed)
Italy/France 1955 115m Eastmancolor
GESI/SEDIF (Maleno Malenotti)
original title: *La Piu Bella Donna del Mondo*
An orphaned Italian singer falls in love with a Russian prince.
A lively piece of kitsch, which at one moment has Lollobrigida imitating Botticelli's Venus as part of a music-hall act.
w Cesare Cavagna, Liana Ferri, Luciano Martino, Mario Monicelli, Piero Pierotti, Franco Solinas, Giovanna Soria *d* Robert Z. Leonard *ph* Mario Bava *m* Renzo Rossellini *ch* Margherita Wallman *ad* Alberto Boccianti *ed* Eraldo da Roma
☆ Gina Lollobrigida, Vittorio Gassman, Robert Alda, Anne Vernon, Tamara Lees, Gino Sinimberghi, Enzo Biliotti, Peter Trent, Mario del Monaco

The Beautiful Cheat: see *What a Woman*

'Dorothy & Petula Have A Body To Die For.'
Beautiful Creatures
GB 2000 86m Technicolor
Universal/DNA/Snakeman/Arts Council (Alan J. Wands, Simon Donald)
A woman with a violent, drug-addicted boyfriend helps another woman dispose of the body of her abusive lover.
An incoherent black comedy about death and friendship, one of the more significant failures of Lottery funding of British films.
w Simon Donald *d* Bill Eagles *ph* James Welland *m* Murray Gold *pd* Andy Harris *ed* Jon Gregory *cos* Trisha Biggar
☆ Rachel Weisz (Petula), Susan Lynch (Dorothy), Alex Norton (Det Insp George Hepburn), Iain Glen (Tony), Maurice Roeves (Ronnie McMinn), Tom Mannion (Brian McMinn), Robin Laing (Kiosk Guy)
'Misfires on so many levels it's hard even to guess at the filmmakers' original intentions.' – *Derek Elley, Variety*

Beautiful Dreamers
Canada 1990 105m colour
Blue Dolphin/Starway/National Film Board of Canada (Michael MacLear, Martin Walters, Sally Bochner)
The poet Walt Whitman forms a friendship with the liberal superintendent of a Canadian mental asylum.
Hokum, disguised as a life-enhancing drama.
wd John Kent Harrison *ph* François Protat *m* Lawrence Shragge *pd* Seamus Flannery *ed* Ron Wisman
☆ Colm Feore, Rip Torn, Wendel Meldrum, Sheila McCarthy, Colin Fox, David Gardner, Barbara Gordon, Marsha Moreau, Albert Schultz

The Beautiful End of This World
West Germany 1983 95m colour
Pentagramma (Rainer Erler)
Sent to Australia to establish a pesticide factory, a German chemical engineer is persuaded that the project would be an ecological disaster.
Dull, if well-meaning, demonstrating that, in movies, good intentions are never enough.
wd Rainer Erler *ph* Wolfgang Grasshoff *m* Eugen Thomass *ad* Chris Harrison, Michael Pilz *ed* Ulrike Pahl
☆ Robert Atzorn, Claire Oberman, Judy Winter, Gotz George

'Good times never seemed so good.'
Beautiful Girls *
US 1996 107m DeLuxe
Buena Vista/Miramax (Cary Woods)
Returning home from New York for a high-school reunion, a bar-room pianist meets his old friends, now in dead-end jobs, to talk about their problems with women.
A single-minded ensemble piece, in which sex is relentlessly discussed; its cast is rather young for the prevalent repining for the recent past.
w Scott Rosenberg *d* Ted Demme *ph* Adam Kimmel *m* David A. Stewart *pd* Dan Davis *ed* Jeffrey Wolf
☆ Matt Dillon, Noah Emmerich, Tim Hutton, Natalie Portman, Annabeth Gish, Lauren Holly, Rosie O'Donnell, Max Perlich, Mira Sorvino, Uma Thurman, Martha Plimpton
'A great title in search of a movie to live up to, this startlingly uneventful compendium of thick-headed boy-talk and female tolerance squanders a fine cast on incredibly ordinary characters and situations.' – *Todd McCarthy, Variety*

'He Saw The World In A Way No One Could Have Imagined.'
A Beautiful Mind **
US 2001 134m DeLuxe
Universal/DreamWorks, Imagine (Brian Grazer, Ron Howard)
Biopic of the brilliant mathematician John Nash, whose schizophrenia caused him to develop paranoid obsessions; after years of treatment, he returned to work at Princeton and was awarded a Nobel Prize.
A throwback in style to Warner's biopics of the 30s on Louis Pasteur and others, with Crowe standing in for Paul Muni: a messy life is rendered in simple, bright colours and given the standard narrative trajectory of triumph over adversity.
w Akiva Goldsman *book* Sylvia Nasar *d* Ron Howard *ph* Roger Deakins *m* James Horner *pd* Wynn Thomas *ed* Mike Hill, Dan Hanley
☆ *Russell Crowe* (John Nash), Ed Harris (William Parcher), *Jennifer Connelly* (Alicia Larde Nash), Paul Bettany (Charles Herman), Adam Goldberg (Sol), Judd Hirsch (Helinger), Josh Lucas (Hansen), Anthony Rapp (Bender), Christopher Plummer (Dr Rosen), Austin Pendleton (Thomas King)
'Consistently engrossing as an unusual character study and as a trip to the mysterious border-crossing between rarified brilliance and madness.' – *Todd McCarthy, Variety*
'The governing dynamic of *A Beautiful Mind* is sentimentality of a familiar and not altogether unwelcome kind. The movie can — indeed, should — be intellectually rejected, but you can't quite banish it from your mind.' – *A. O. Scott, New York Times*
'A glossy example of how a troubled and troublesome life can be sanitized into a Movieland saga.' – *Stanley Kaufmann, New Republic*
Academy Award: picture; Akiva Goldsman; Ron Howard; Jennifer Connelly
Academy Award nomination: Russell Crowe; Mike Hill, Dan Hanley; best make-up (Greg Cannom, Colleen Callaghan); James Horner
BAFTA: Russell Crowe; Jennifer Connelly

Beautiful People **
GB 1999 109m colour
Warner/Channel Four/Tall Stories (Ben Woolford)
In London, in 1993, Serbian and Croatian refugees from Bosnia attempt to carry on their dispute, which widens to involve locals.
An often contrived and ramshackle drama-cum-romantic comedy, but one that is also lively and convincing in its depiction of the confusions of life (not for nothing is a new baby, conceived as the result of a rape, called Chaos); its upbeat ending is tempered by its final image of a clenched fist.
wd Jasmin Dizdar *ph* Barry Ackroyd *m* Garry Bell *pd* Jon Henson *ed* Justin Krish
☆ Charlotte Coleman (Portia Thornton), Charles Kay (George Thornton), Rosalind Ayres (Nora Thornton), Roger Sloman (Roger Midge), Heather Tobias (Felicity Midge), Danny Nussbaum (Griffin Midge), Siobhan Redmond (Kate Higgins), Gilbert Martin (Jerry Higgins), Steve Sweeney (Jim), Linda Bassett (Sister), Nicholas Farrell (Dr Mouldy), Edin Dzandzanovic (Pero Guzina)
'Derives a dramatic charge from dark and intractable issues, only to suggest that warm-hearted comedy is their solvent.' – *Peter Bradshaw, Guardian*
'There's basically nothing going on here beyond pantomime of the lamest kind.' – *Derek Elley, Variety*

The Beautiful Rebel: see *Janice Meredith*

Beautiful Stranger
GB 1954 89m bw
Marksman (Maxwell Setton, John R. Sloan)
US title: *Twist of Fate*
On the Riviera, an actress discovers that her fiancé is a criminal.
Tawdry star melodrama of virtually no interest.
w Robert Westerby, Carl Nystrom *d* David Miller *ph* Robert Day, Ted Scaife *m* Malcolm Arnold
☆ Ginger Rogers, Jacques Bergerac, Herbert Lom, Stanley Baker, Margaret Rawlings, Eddie Byrne, Coral Browne

Beautiful Thing *
GB 1995 91m colour
Film Four/World (Tony Garnett, Bill Shapter)
Two teenage schoolboys on a South London housing estate fall in love with each other.
A reticent, feelgood summer romance, to the music of the Mamas and the Papas; it deals more in nostalgic fantasy than reality, despite its gritty, urban setting.
w Jonathan Harvey *play* Jonathan Harvey *d* Hettie Macdonald *ph* Chris Seager *m* John Altman *pd* Mark Stevenson *ed* Don Fairservice
☆ Linda Henry, Glen Berry, Scott Neal, Ben Daniels, Tameka Empson
'If *Beautiful Thing* was any more desperate to be liked, it would be following the audience home, wagging its tail and wanting to be thrown choc drops.' – *Adam Mars-Jones, Independent*

Beauty and the Beast: see *La Belle et la Bête (1946)*

'The most beautiful love story ever told.'
Beauty and the Beast ***
US 1991 85m Technicolor
Buena Vista/Walt Disney/Silver Screen Partners IV (Don Hahn)
A prince, turned into a beast by enchantment, is rescued by the love of a beautiful girl.
A return to top form by Disney, with excellent animation and a singable score. The picture has been credited with starting a new Hollywood fashion for animated musicals.
w Linda Woolverton *d* Gary Trousdale, Kirk Wise *m/ly* Alan Menken, Howard Ashman *ad* Brian McEntee *ed* John Carnochan
☆ Featuring the voices of Paige O'Hara, Robby Benson, Jerry Orbach, Angela Lansbury, Richard

White, David Ogden Stiers, Jesse Corti, Rex Everhart, Bradley Michael Pierce, Jo Anne Worley, Kimmy Robertson

'A lovely film that ranks with the best of Disney's animated classics.' – *Variety*

'It's got storytelling vigour and clarity, bright eclectic animation, and a frisky musical wit.' – *New Yorker*

Alan Menken; song 'Beauty and the Beast' (*m* Alan Menken, *ly* Howard Ashman)

film; song 'Belle'; song 'Be Our Guest'; sound

Beauty and the Boss

US 1932 75m bw

Warner

A girl down on her luck becomes secretary to an amorous banker and eventually becomes his wife.

Artless Cinderella story in an uneasy Viennese setting.

w Joseph Jackson *play* The Church Mouse by Ladislas Fodor, Paul Frank *d* Roy del Ruth

☆ Warren William, Marian Marsh, Charles Butterworth, Frederick Kerr, Lillian Bond

'Elementary stuff for the B houses, titularly phrased for flap appeal.' – *Variety*

Beauty for Sale

US 1933 85m bw

MGM

aka: *Beauty!*

An innocent girl snares a rich man while working in a beauty parlour.

Well-mounted romantic comedy-drama with most of the elements the 1933 public wanted.

w Zelda Sears and Eve Greene *novel* Beauty by Faith Baldwin *d* Richard Boleslawski

☆ Madge Evans, Alice Brady, Una Merkel, Otto Kruger, May Robson, Phillips Holmes, Eddie Nugent, Hedda Hopper

'Pulp magazine fiction made for subway-riding stenographers ... romantic hoke skilfully dressed up.' – *Variety*

Beauty for the Asking

US 1939 68m bw

RKO

Jealousies flourish among the women in a cosmetics showroom.

Average supporting drama for female audiences.

w Doris Anderson, Paul Jarrico *d* Glenn Tryon

☆ Lucille Ball, Frieda Inescort, Patric Knowles, Donald Woods, Inez Courtney

The Beauty Jungle *

GB 1964 114m Eastmancolor Cinemascope

Rank/Val Guest

US title: *Contest Girl*

A typist enters a beauty contest and step by step becomes Miss Globe; but her descent is equally rapid.

Wicked show biz and the road to ruin in one glossy package, predictable, but not badly done; always something going on, and performed with gusto.

w Robert Muller, Val Guest *d* Val Guest *ph* Arthur Grant *m* Laurie Johnson

☆ Janette Scott, Ian Hendry, Ronald Fraser, Edmund Purdom, Kay Walsh, Norman Bird, Janina Faye, Tommy Trinder, Francis Matthews

Beavis and Butthead Do America *

US 1996 80m DeLuxe

Paramount/Geffen/MTV (Abby Terkuhle)

Two simple- and dirty-minded teenagers travel from Las Vegas to Washington for the wrong reasons.

Crudely, if effectively, animated lowbrow comedy, most likely to be enjoyed by those familiar with the dim-witted duo's appearances on MTV.

w Mike Judge, Joe Stillman *d* Mike Judge *m* John Frizzell *ed* Terry Kelley, Gunter Glinka, Neil Lawrence

☆ Featuring the voices of: Mike Judge, Cloris Leachman, Robert Stack, David Spade, Eric Bogosian, Richard Linklater, Bruce Willis (uncredited), Demi Moore (uncredited)

'Has some genuinely amusing moments of dumb and dumber silliness. But it arrives too late in the day to fully exploit the popularity of the once-trendy MTV series.' – *Joe Leydon, Variety*

Because of Him *

US 1945 88m bw

Universal (Felix Jackson)

A waitress pesters a Broadway author and actor for a leading role in their new show.

Moderately sprightly star vehicle with bonuses in the leading men; handling disappointingly routine.

w Edmund Beloin *d* Richard Wallace *ph* Hal Mohr *m* Miklos Rozsa *ed* Ted J. Kent

☆ Deanna Durbin, Charles Laughton, Franchot Tone, Helen Broderick, Stanley Ridges, Donald Meek

'Even in the first wild joy of his arms, she realized that she would be ... an unfit mother!'

Because of You

US 1952 95m bw

U-I (Albert J. Cohen)

A female ex-convict marries on parole but does not tell her husband of her past. Her old associates involve her innocently in another crime, and her husband divorces her; but years later she gets him and their child back.

Soap opera of the stickiest kind, made quite tolerable by good production.

w Ketti Frings *d* Joseph Pevney *ph* Russell Metty *m* Frank Skinner

☆ Loretta Young, Jeff Chandler, Alex Nicol, Frances Dee, Lynne Roberts, Alexander Scourby, Mae Clarke

'Shows the most whole-hearted devotion to woman's magazine conventions.' – *MFB*

'Whoever you are, you're in this picture! Because this tells of youth's challenge to grown-ups who can't understand!'

Because They're Young

US 1960 98m bw

Columbia/Drexel (Jerry Bresler)

A high school teacher helps one of his tougher pupils not to slip into crime.

Routine sentimental melodrama, slightly redeemed by directorial expertise.

w James Gunn *novel* Harrison High by John Farris *d* Paul Wendkos *ph* Wilfrid Cline *m* Johnny Williams

☆ Dick Clark, Michael Callan, Tuesday Weld, Victoria Shaw, Warren Berlinger, Doug McClure

Because You're Mine

US 1952 103m Technicolor

MGM (Joe Pasternak)

An opera singer becomes a GI and wins the sergeant's sister.

Lumberingly inept star vehicle, giving the impression of nothing at all happening between the songs.

w Leonard Spigelgass, Karl Tunberg *d* Alexander Hall *ph* Joseph Ruttenberg *md* Johnny Green

☆ Mario Lanza, Doretta Morrow, James Whitmore, Dean Miller, Paula Corday, Jeff Donnell, Spring Byington

'On a dull day in Manchester it will bring colour to the greyness of life.' – *Sunday Express*

title song (*m* Nicholas Brodszky, *ly* Sammy Cahn)

'The screen explodes with rage and passion and greatness!'

Becket **

GB 1964 149m Technicolor Panavision

Paramount/Hal B. Wallis

Henry II leans on his boisterous Saxon friend Thomas à Becket, but when the latter is made first chancellor and then archbishop a rift between them widens and ends in Becket's assassination by Henry's over-eager knights.

Jean Anouilh's bitter stage comedy is filmed literally and soberly as a rather anaemic epic, so that the point is lost and the edge blunted. The paucity of physical action causes good scenes to alternate with long stretches of tedium.

w Edward Anhalt *d* Peter Glenville *ph* Geoffrey Unsworth *m* Laurence Rosenthal *pd* John Bryan

☆ Richard Burton, Peter O'Toole, Donald Wolfit, John Gielgud, Martita Hunt, Pamela Brown, Sian Phillips, Paolo Stoppa

'Handsome, respectable and boring.' – *John Simon*

'The power of the film is in the close-up, the concentration on the two protagonists. And what is so fascinating is that Burton and O'Toole provide no ultimate answers for each other or for us.' – *Judith Crist*

Edward Anhalt

best picture; Peter Glenville; Geoffrey Unsworth; Laurence Rosenthal; Richard Burton; Peter O'Toole; John Gielgud

John Bryan; Geoffrey Unsworth

Becky Sharp **

US 1935 83m Technicolor

RKO (Kenneth MacGowan)

An ambitious girl makes her way into Regency society.

Chiefly notable as the first feature in three-colour Technicolor, this rather theatrical piece has its civilized enjoyments and the director made a few predictable cinematic experiments; the overall effect, however, is patchy.

w Francis Edward Faragoh *play* Landon Mitchell *novel* Vanity Fair by W. M. Thackeray *d* Rouben Mamoulian *ph* Ray Rennahan *m* Roy Webb *pd* Robert Edmond Jones

☆ Miriam Hopkins, Cedric Hardwicke, Frances Dee, Billie Burke, Alison Skipworth, Nigel Bruce, Alan Mowbray, Colin Tapley, G. P. Huntley Jnr

'Beautiful cinematographically but weak on story. No cinch, and should be sold on colour angle.' – *Variety*

'As pleasing to the eye as a fresh fruit sundae, but not much more.' – *Otis Ferguson*

'If colour is to be of permanent importance a way must be found to use it realistically, not only as a beautiful decoration. It must be made to contribute to our sense of truth. The machine gun, the cheap striped tie, the battered Buick and the shabby bar will need a subtler colour sense than the Duchess of Richmond's ball, the girls of Miss Pinkerton's Academy, the Marquess of Steyne's dinner for two. Can Technicolor reproduce with the necessary accuracy the suit that has been worn too long, the oily hat?' – *Graham Greene*

Miriam Hopkins

Bed and Board **

France/Italy 1970 97m Eastmancolor

Columbia/Les Films du Carrosse/Valoria/Fida Cinematografica (Marcel Berbert)

original title: *Domicile Conjugal*

Antoine Doinel, the hero of three previous films, becomes a husband, father, writer and adulterer.

The fourth, and least rewarding, of the series of five films, although it has some amusing moments.

w François Truffaut, Claude de Givray, Bernard Revon *d* François Truffaut *ph* Nestor Almendros *m* Antoine Duhamel *ad* Jean Mandaroux *ed* Agnes Guillemot

☆ Jean-Pierre Léaud, Claude Jade, Hiroko Berghauer, Daniel Ceccaldi, Claire Duhamel, Barbara Laage

'It's nice to have a man around the house.'

Bed and Breakfast

US 1992 98m DuArt

Hemdale (Jack Schwartzman)

A widow running a seaside boarding house falls for an affable con man.

Mundane romantic drama that trundles along on familiar lines.

w Cindy Myers *d* Robert Ellis Miller *ph* Peter Sova *m* David Shire *pd* Suzanne Cavedon *ed* John F. Burnett

☆ Roger Moore, Talia Shire, Colleen Dewhurst, Nina Siemaszko, Ford Rainey, Stephen Root, Jamie Walters, Cameron Arnett

'Pic is so predictable and sentimental that it will be quickly forgotten at the box office.' – *Variety*

† The film was released direct to video in Britain.

Bed of Roses

US 1995 88m DeLuxe

Entertainment (Allan Mindel, Denise Shaw)

A florist, whose wife died in childbirth, falls for a lonely workaholic banker who had an abusive stepfather.

An attempt to update the type of romantic movie made in the 40s by adding a dash of dysfunction and a little New Age back-to-nature dressing; the result is as remote from reality as ever and poor escapism as well.

wd Michael Goldenberg *ph* Adam Kimmel *m* Michael Convertino *pd* Stephen McCabe *ed* Jane Kurson

☆ Christian Slater, Mary Stuart Masterson, Pamela Segall, Josh Brolin, Ally Walker, Debra Monk

'One of those acutely sensitive American movies about love and loss that manage to be, despite their sincerity, incredibly dull.' – *Derek Malcolm, Guardian*

The Bed Sitting Room *

GB 1969 91m DeLuxe

UA/Oscar Lewenstein (Richard Lester)

Surrealist romance; after a nuclear war, motley survivors in the waste lands turn into bed sitting rooms, cupboards and parakeets.

Arrogantly obscure fantasy, a commercial flop which kept its director in the wilderness for four years. Fans of Monty Python may salvage a joke or two.

w John Antrobus *play* John Antrobus, Spike Milligan *d* Richard Lester *ph* David Watkin *m* Ken Thorne *pd* Assheton Gorton

☆ Ralph Richardson, Rita Tushingham, Michael Hordern, Arthur Lowe, Mona Washbourne, Peter Cook, Dudley Moore, Spike Milligan, Harry Secombe, Marty Feldman, Jimmy Edwards

Bedazzled *

GB 1967 96m DeLuxe Panavision

TCF/Stanley Donen

A short order cook is saved from suicide by Mr Spiggott, who offers him seven wishes in exchange for his soul.

A camped-up version of Faust which resolves itself into a series of threadbare sketches for the stars. All rather desperate apart from the leaping nuns.

w Peter Cook *d* Stanley Donen *ph* Austin Dempster *m* Dudley Moore

☆ Peter Cook, Dudley Moore, Michael Bates, Raquel Welch, Eleanor Bron

Bedazzled

US/Germany 2000 93m DeLuxe Panavision

TCF/Regency (Trevor Albert, Harold Ramis)

The devil in the form of a woman offers an office worker seven wishes in exchange for his soul; but the wishes go wrong.

An episodic series of jokey sketches which soon become lacklustre; temptation has rarely seemed so uninviting.

w Harold Ramis, Larry Gelbart, Peter Tolan *screenplay* Peter Cook, Dudley Moore *ph* Bill Pope *m* David Newman *pd* Rick Heinrichs *ed* Craig P. Herring *sp* Rhythm & Hues Studios *cos* Deena Appel

☆ Brendan Fraser (Elliot Richards), Elizabeth Hurley (The Devil), Frances O'Connor (Alison/Nicole), Miriam Shor (Carol/ Penthouse Hostess), Orlando Jones (Dan/Esteban/Beach Jock/Sportscaster/Party Guest), Paul Adelstein (Bob/Roberto/Beach Jock/Sportscaster/Lincoln Aide), Toby Huss (Jerry/Alejandro/Beach Jock/Sportscaster/Lance), Gabriel Casseus (Elliot's Cellmate), Brian Doyle-Murray (Priest), Jeff Doucette (Desk Sergeant)

'As mainstream entertainment, this scores a bull's eye. It's cute and instantly forgettable.' – *Ian Spelling, Film Review*

Bedelia

GB 1946 90m bw

John Corfield (Isadore Goldsmith)

A psychotic woman is discovered to have poisoned three husbands.

Dreary upper-class British murder drama, totally devoid of style or suspense but a big star hit of the time.

w Vera Caspary, Moie Charles, Herbert Victor, Roy Ridley, Isadore Goldsmith *novel* Vera Caspary *d* Lance Comfort *ph* F. A. Young

☆ Margaret Lockwood, Ian Hunter, Barry K. Barnes, Anne Crawford, Jill Esmond, Ellen Pollock

Bedevilled

US 1955 86m Eastmancolor Cinemascope

MGM (Henry Berman)

In Paris, a novice priest befriends a girl on the run from gangsters, who turns out to be a murderess.

Absurd high-flown bosh, unsuitably cinemascoped in ugly colour, and surprisingly badly handled by old professionals.

w Jo Eisinger *d* Mitchell Leisen *ph* Frederick A. Young *m* William Alwyn

☆ Anne Baxter, Steve Forrest, Simone Renant, Victor Francen, Maurice Teynac, Joseph Tomelty
'This mixture of melodrama and religion provides a most unedifying entertainment.' – *MFB*

The Bedford Incident ***
GB 1965 102m bw
Columbia/Bedford Productions (James B. Harris)

A ruthlessly efficient US destroyer captain in the Arctic chases a Russian submarine and accidentally fires an atomic weapon.
Gripping mixture of themes from Dr Strangelove *and* The Caine Mutiny *(qqv), very tense and forceful, with excellent acting. It was Poitier's first role with no reference to his colour.*
w James Poe novel Mark Rascovich *d James B. Harris ph* Gilbert Taylor *m* Gerard Schurmann
☆ *Richard Widmark, Sidney Poitier*, James MacArthur, Eric Portman, Wally Cox, Martin Balsam, Phil Brown, Michael Kane, Gary Cockrell, Donald Sutherland
'Strong on virtues of a rather negative kind.' – *Penelope Houston*

Bedknobs and Broomsticks
US 1971 117m Technicolor
Walt Disney (Bill Walsh)

In 1940 three evacuee children and a kindly witch ride on a magic bedstead and defeat the invasion of England.
Extraordinarily dishevelled and incompetent Disney follow-up to Mary Poppins *(qv), a very muddled narrative with few high points and evidence of much cutting. Redeemed occasionally by camera trickery.*
w Bill Walsh, Don DaGradi *d* Robert Stevenson *ph* Frank Phillips *m/ly* Richard M. Sherman, Robert B. Sherman *sp* Eustace Lycett, Alan Maley, Danny Lee
☆ Angela Lansbury, David Tomlinson, Roy Snart, Cindy O'Callaghan, Sam Jaffe, Roddy McDowall, Bruce Forsyth, Tessie O'Shea, Reginald Owen
special visual effects (Alan Maley, Eustace Lycett, Danny Lee)
Richard M. Sherman, Robert B. Sherman; song 'The Age of Not Believing' by the Shermans

Bedlam **
US 1946 80m bw
RKO (*Val Lewton*)

In 18th-century London, a sane girl is confined by the malevolent asylum master.
Interesting but rather flatly handled addition to the Val Lewton gallery of horrors, perhaps too carefully and discreetly done for pace or suspense.
w Mark Robson, Carlos Keith *d* Mark Robson *ph* Nicholas Musuraca *m* Roy Webb
☆ Boris Karloff, Anna Lee, Billy House, Richard Fraser, Glenn Vernon
† Carlos Keith was Val Lewton's pseudonym
†† *Bedlam* was never granted a certificate in Britain.

The Bedroom
Japan 1992 63m colour
Kokuei (Daisuke Asakura)

A woman becomes unable to distinguish between fantasy and reality after her sister dies in a club where men act out their fantasies on drugged women.
Odd, unpleasant, voyeuristic, poorly subtitled Japanese erotica, given a modish treatment; its images of inert, passive women are most likely to appeal to necrophiliacs.
w Yumeno Shiro *d* Sato Hisayasu *ph* Masashi Inayashi *ed* Shoji Sakai
☆ Ito Kiyomi, Asano Mamori, Nakamura Kyoko, Sagawa Issei
'Inventively shot in a sub-David Lynch sort of way, but pretty repugnant all the same.' – *Sight and Sound*

Bedroom Eyes
Canada 1984 90m Medallion
Alliance/RSL (Robert Lantos, Stephen J. Roth)

A stockbroker, who is a Peeping Tom by night, is accused of murder when the woman he spies on is killed.
Dull and risible psychological thriller, which uses sex as a substitute for narrative interest and excitement.
w Michael Alan Eddy *d* William Fruet *ph* Miklos Lente *m* John Tucker *pd* Lindsey Goddard *ed* Tony Lower
☆ Kenneth Gilman, Dayle Haddon, Christine Cattell, Lawrence K. Philips, Jayne Catling, Barbara Law

The Bedroom Window
US 1986 115m colour JDC Widescreen
De Laurentiis (Robert Towne, Martha Schumacher)

From her boyfriend's apartment window, an adulterous wife witnesses an assault, and sends her boyfriend to the police in her place.
Sub-Hitchcock thriller, almost as creaky as it sounds.
wd Curtis Hanson *ph* Gil Taylor *m* Michael Shrieve, Patrick Gleeson *ed* Scott Conrad
☆ Steve Guttenberg, Elizabeth McGovern, Isabelle Huppert, Paul Shenar, Frederick Coffin, Wallace Shawn
'Less than riveting entertainment.' – *Daily Variety*

'Re-Model Your Love Life.'
Bedrooms & Hallways
GB/France/Germany 1998 96m Rank Colour
Alliance/ARP/Pandora/BBC (Ceci Dempsey, Dorothy Berwin)

A group of friends enjoy varied sexual relationships with one another.
A slight comedy of bisexuality and serial partners.
w Robert Farrar *d* Rose Troche *ph* Ashley Rowe *m* Alfredo D. Troche, Ian MacPherson *pd* Richard Bridgland *ed* Christopher Blunden
☆ Kevin McKidd, Hugo Weaving, James Purefoy, Tom Hollander, Christopher Fulford, Julie Graham, Con O'Neill, Paul Higgins, Jennifer Ehle, Simon Callow, Harriet Walter
'Watching B&H is a bit like sitting in a luke-warm bath, waiting for someone to turn the hot water back on. The longer you wait, the colder it gets.' – *Charlotte O'Sullivan, Independent*

Bedtime for Bonzo
US 1951 83m bw
U-I (Michel Kraike)

To prove that environment determines character, a chimpanzee is brought up as a human baby.
Very moderate fun and games which proved successful enough for a sequel, Bonzo Goes to College.
w Val Burton, Lou Breslow *d* Frederick de Cordova *ph* Carl Guthrie *m* Frank Skinner *ed* Ted J. Kent
☆ Ronald Reagan, Diana Lynn, Walter Slezak, Lucille Barkley, Herbert Heyes

Bedtime Story *
US 1942 85m bw
Columbia (B. P. Schulberg)
A playwright's wife wants to retire instead of acting in his next play.
Pleasantly sparkling comedy with good performances.
w Horace Jackson, Grant Garrett, Richard Flournoy *d* Alexander Hall *ph* Joseph Walker *m* Werner Heymann
☆ *Fredric March, Loretta Young*, Robert Benchley, Allyn Joslyn, Eve Arden, Helen Westley, Joyce Compton, Tim Ryan

Bedtime Story *
US 1964 99m Eastmancolor
U-I/Lankershim/Pennebaker (Stanley Shapiro)

Two Riviera confidence tricksters outwit each other.
A fairly lively script is defeated by dull handling, but performances and backgrounds are attractive.
w Stanley Shapiro, Paul Henning *d* Ralph Levy *ph* Clifford Stine *m* Hans Salter
☆ David Niven, Marlon Brando, Shirley Jones, Dody Goodman, Aram Stephan, Marie Windsor
'The most vulgar and embarrassing film of the year.' – *Daily Express*
† It was remade as *Dirty Rotten Scoundrels* (qv).

A Bee in the Rain
Portugal 1968 74m bw
Media (Fernando Matos Silva)
original title: *Uma Abelha na Chuva*
A farmer's unhappy marriage to an aristocratic wife brings tragedy in its wake.
Slow-moving, doom-laden tale of marital discord, not helped by the self-consciously arty direction, with freeze frames and lingering, inconsequential close-ups.
wd Fernando Lopes *novel* Carlos de Oliveira *ph* Manuel Costa e Silva *m* Manuel Jorge Veloso *ed* Fernando Lopes
☆ Laura Soveral, João Guedes, Zita Duarte, Ruy Furtado, Carlos Ferreiro, Adriano Reys

The Beekeeper **
Greece/France 1986 122m colour
Greek Film Centre/ERTI/MK2/Theodoros Angelopoulos

original title: *O Melissokomos*
A retired schoolmaster, visiting the sites of beehives around Greece, picks up a teenage hitchhiker, an act which is to drive him to desperation.
Melancholy but moving film, with a finely judged performance from Mastroianni.
w Theodoros Angelopoulos, Dimitris Nollas *d Theodoros Angelopoulos ph* Giorgos Arvantis *m* Helen Karaindrou *ad* Mikes Karapiperis *ed* Takis Yannopoulos
☆ *Marcello Mastroianni*, Nadia Mourouzi, Serge Reggiani, Jenny Roussea, Dinos Iliopoulos, Vassia Panagopolou, Dimitris Poulikakos

Beer
US 1985 82m DeLuxe
Orion (Robert Chartoff)

original title: *The Selling of America*
A lady executive on Madison Avenue promotes a brand of beer by promoting three honest Joes from the street and turning them into macho media figures.
Another shred of proof that satire is what closes Saturday night. A few smiles, but no release.
w Allan Weisbecker *d* Patrick Kelly *ph* Bill Butler *m* Bill Conti *pd* Bill Brodie *ed* Alan Heim
☆ Loretta Swit, Rip Torn, Kenneth Mars, David Alan Grier, William Russ, Dick Shawn

Bees in Paradise
GB 1943 75m bw
Gainsborough
Four airmen find themselves on a South Sea island ruled by women who kill their spouses after the honeymoon.
Saucy farce, too talkative to be very interesting even in the dark days of war.
w Val Guest, Marriott Edgar *d* Val Guest
☆ Arthur Askey, Peter Graves, Max Bacon, Anne Shelton, Jean Kent

'The head of the family is the one with the tail.'
Beethoven
US 1992 87m DeLuxe
UIP/Universal (Joe Medjuck, Michael C. Gross)

A St Bernard dog causes havoc in a family household to the delight of the children and the annoyance of their father.
Predictable comedy of the dreariest kind.
w Edmond Dantes, Amy Holden Jones *d* Brian Levant *ph* Victor J. Kemper *m* Randy Edelman *pd* Alex Tavoularis *ed* Sheldon Kahn, William D. Gordean
☆ Charles Grodin, Bonnie Hunt, Dean Jones, Oliver Platt, Stanley Tucci, David Duchovny, Patricia Heaton, Laurel Cronin, O-Lan Jones
'Could be called harmless if it wasn't so badly made and blandly characterised.' – *Derek Malcolm, Guardian*
'Laugh? We wait like locked-in dogs whose noses are pressed to the window for the first sign of life or human interest coming up the driveway. Wit we have already despaired of in reel one.' – *Nigel Andrews, Financial Times*

Beethoven's 2nd
US 1993 89m DeLuxe
Universal (Michael C. Gross, Joe Medjuck)

Beethoven becomes the father of pups, which are promptly kidnapped.
A sentimental sequel that will be enjoyed by fans of large, slobbering dogs and obvious jokes.
w Len Blum *d* Rod Daniel *ph* Bill Butler *m* Randy Edelman *pd* Lawrence Miller *ed* Sheldon Kahn, William D. Gordean
☆ Charles Grodin, Bonnie Hunt, Nicholle Tom, Christopher Castile, Sarah Rose Karr, Debi Mazar, Chris Penn, Ashley Hamilton, Maury Chaykin
'Universal unleashes what should be a big, slobbering hit with this reasonably entertaining sequel, certainly a more pleasing tale than the one that sired it.' – *Variety*
'It's so insubstantial that it flies from the mind's eye almost as soon as the lights go up.' – *Derek Malcolm, Guardian*
'All the wit and spontaneity of a suet pudding.' – *Sight and Sound*
song 'The Day I Fall In Love' (*m/ly* Carole Bayer Sager, James Ingram, Cliff Magness)

Beetlejuice *
US 1988 92m Technicolor
Warner Bros/Geffen (Michael Bender)

The newly dead at a New England barn try to scare off objectionable new buyers.
Mainly unpleasant and seldom funny fantasy.
w Michael McDowell, Warren Skaaren *d* Tim Burton *ph* Thomas Ackerman *m* Danny Elfman *pd* Bo Welch
☆ Alec Baldwin, Geena Davis, Michael Keaton, Catherine O'Hara, Glenn Shadix

'A murder. A suspect. A shadow of a doubt.'
Before and After
US 1996 108m Technicolor
Buena Vista/Hollywood/Caravan (Barbet Schroeder, Susan Hoffman)

When their teenage son is accused of murdering his girlfriend, his parents take differing attitudes on how best to deal with the situation.
Indifferent and windy drama that avoids any proper conflict or confrontation of the issues; it doesn't even hold the interest of its participants.
w Ted Tally *novel* Rosellen Brown *d* Barbet Schroeder *ph* Luciano Tovoli *m* Howard Shore *pd* Stuart Wurtzel *ed* Lee Percy
☆ Meryl Streep, Liam Neeson, Edward Furlong, Alfred Molina, Julia Weldon, Daniel von Bargen, John Heard
'A wan, flat little anecdote, implausible to a preposterous degree.' – *Alexander Walker*

Before Dawn *
US 1933 60m bw
RKO
Three murders take place in a mysterious mansion.
Lively comedy-thriller which won't bore anybody: good in its class.
w Garrett Fort, Marion Dix, Ralph Block *story* Edgar Wallace *d Irving Pichel m* Max Steiner
☆ Warner Oland, Stuart Erwin, Dorothy Wilson, Dudley Digges, Oscar Apfel

Before Hindsight **
GB 1977 78m Eastmancolor
Elizabeth Taylor-Mead
Interviews and clips show how inadequately cinema newsreels covered world events in the 1930s.
Hard tack for entertainment seekers, but a clear exposition of a proven case of importance to film-makers and politicians.
w Elizabeth Taylor-Mead *d* Jonathan Lewis
'Certainly not the kind of picture people will pay money to see.' – *Variety*

'Beware! When Karloff Stops The Clock ... Your Hour Has Come!'
Before I Hang *
US 1940 71m bw
Columbia (Wallace MacDonald)

A research scientist experiments with a new serum which turns him into a murderer.
Archetypal Karloff mad doctor flick, Jekyll and Hyde model: still quite tolerable.
w Robert D. Andrews *d* Nick Grinde *ph* Benjamin Kline *md* Morris Stoloff
☆ *Boris Karloff*, Evelyn Keyes, Bruce Bennett, Pedro de Cordoba, Edward Van Sloan, Don Beddoe
'Karloff is so good he makes you believe this nonsense.' – *The Dark Side*

Before Night Falls *
US 2000 132m Technicolor
TCF/Fine Line/Grandview/El Mar (Jon Kilik)
The life of Chilean poet Reinaldo Arenas, whose homosexuality brought him into conflict with the Cuban regime in the 1960s.
Episodic account of a hectic existence, often requiring an audience to work harder than it should to make sense of events.
w Cunningham O'Keefe, Lazaro Gomez Carriles, Julian Schnabel *book* Reinaldo Arenas *d* Julian Schnabel *ph* Xavier Perez Grobet, Guillermo Rosas *m* Carter Burwell, Lou Reed, Laurie Anderson *pd* Salvador Parra *ed* Michael Berenbaum
☆ Javier Bardem (Reinaldo Arenas), Olivier Martinez (Lazaro Gomez Carilles), Andrea Di Stefano (Pepe Malas), Johnny Depp (Bon Bon/Lieutenant Victor), Sean Penn (Cuco Sanchez), Michael Wincott (Herberto Zorilla Ochoa), Najwa Nimri (Fina Correa), Hector Babenco (Virgilio Pinera), Olatz Lopez Garmendia (Reinaldo's mother), Vito Maria Schnabel (Teenage Reinaldo), Jerzy Skolimowski (Professor)
'A masterpiece and Bardem's crowning glory.' – *Alan Jones, Film Review*
Javier Bardem

Before Sunrise *
US 1995 101m Technicolor
Rank/Castle Rock/Detour/Filmhaus (Anne Walker-McBay)
A young American meets a French woman on a train and persuades her to spend the night talking and walking around Vienna.
A conversation piece that has a certain inconsequential charm but cannot sustain itself for the length of the film; the talk is simply not interesting enough.
w Richard Linklater, Kim Krizan *d* Richard Linklater *ph* Lee Daniel *pd* Florian Reichmann *ed* Sandra Adair
☆ Ethan Hawke, Julie Delpy
'This two character talkfest wins points for daring to be a love story – how defiantly unhip is that? – and is presumably meant as sensitivity training for 20-year-olds. But in reaching for winsome charm, the film falls flat. This meeting of bright minds often plays like desperate showing off.' – *Richard Corliss, Time*
'While pic remains sympathetic and appealing, the endless dialogue and repetitive settings become wearing through the couple's one long night together, and the artifice of the premise may contribute to the difficulty the film has in coming to romantic life.' – *Todd McCarthy, Variety*

Before the Nickelodeon **
US 1982 60m bw/colour
Film for Thought
The life, times and films of the pioneer Edwin S. Porter.
Valuable documentary on a little-known figure, with films ranging from 1896 to 1907.
w Warren D. Leight, Charles Musser *d* Charles Musser

Before the Night: see *One Night Stand (1995)*

Before the Rain ***
GB/France/Macedonia 1994 113m Eastmancolor
Electric/Aim/Noe/Vardar (Judy Counihan, Cedomir Kolar, Sam Taylor, Cat Villiers)
original title: *Pred Dozdot*
An expatriate Macedonian photographer leaves his pregnant English lover in London and returns to his homeland, caught in the conflict that has destroyed Yugoslavia, to witness the effects of the civil war on the village where he grew up.
Three separate stories intertwine in a gripping drama, although the connections between them, and the way each leads forward and back to the other, is not evident until the final moments; the construction mirrors the circle of violence the film depicts, with its characters mired in unthinking hate.
wd Milcho Manchevski *ph* Manuel Teran *m* Anastasia *pd* Sharon Lamofsky, David Munns *ed* Nicolas Gaster
☆ Katrin Cartlidge, Rade Serbedzija, Gregoire Colin, Labina Mitevska, Jay Villiers, Silvija Stojanovska, Phyllida Law
'Dense with threat and tense with the possibility of its release.' – *Tom Shone, Sunday Times*
best foreign film

Before the Revolution *
Italy 1964 115m bw
Cineriz/Iride
original title: *Prima della Rivoluzione*
The suicide of a friend leads a middle-class youth living in Parma to consider his own life and attitudes before opting for safe conformity.
A talented but confused debate on politics, which upset Catholic authorities at the time, but leaves an audience only a little wiser.
wd Bernardo Bertolucci *m* Gino Paoli, Ennio Morricone *md* Aldo Scavarda *ad* Romano Pampaloni *ed* Roberto Perpignani
☆ Francesco Barilli, Adriana Asti, Alain Midgette, Morando Morandini
'He captures what has rarely been seen on the screen – the extravagance and poetry of youthful ardour.' – *Pauline Kael, New Yorker*

Before Winter Comes *
GB 1968 107m Technicolor
Columbia/Windward (Robert Emmett Ginna)
Austria 1945: a British major in charge of displaced persons is helped and hindered by a cheerful Yugoslav refugee who turns out to be a Russian deserter.
Likeable, well-produced drama hampered by a plot which becomes unnecessarily schematic, coincidental and downbeat in its attempts to tug at the heartstrings.
w Andrew Sinclair *novel* *The Interpreter* by Frederick L. Keefe *d* J. Lee-Thompson *ph* Gilbert Taylor *m* Ron Grainer
☆ *David Niven, Topol,* Ori Levi, Anna Karina, John Hurt, Anthony Quayle
'One of those films with a message on every page of its script.' – *MFB*

Beg, Borrow or Steal
US 1937 70m bw
MGM
An American expatriate lives by his wits in Paris.
Flabby comedy which misses on all cylinders.
w Leonard Lee, Harry Ruskin, Marion Parsonnet *d* William Thiele
☆ Frank Morgan, Florence Rice, John Beal, Janet Beecher, Herman Bing, Erik Rhodes, E. E. Clive, Reginald Denny, George Givot
'Nothing quite so incredible as this story has been tossed to the double bills since the major studios started competing among themselves to turn out low-grade entertainment for the filler-in spots.' – *Variety*

Beggars of Life *
US 1928 80m bw part-talkie
Paramount
Adventures of a hobo.
Curious melodramatic farrago notable chiefly for technical advances but far from boring to watch for its own sake.
w Benjamin Glazer, Jim Tully *d* William Wellman
☆ Richard Arlen, Wallace Beery, Louise Brooks, Edgar Blue Washington, H. A. Morgan, Roscoe Karns

The Beggar's Opera *
GB 1952 94m Technicolor
British Lion/Imperadio (Herbert Wilcox, Laurence Olivier)
A highwayman in Newgate jail devises an opera based on his own exploits.
Exuberant potted version of the 1728 low opera, generally likeable but lacking a strong coherent approach and marred by violent colour and raggedly theatrical presentation. It nearly but not quite comes off.
w Denis Cannan, Christopher Fry *opera* John Gay *d* Peter Brook *ph* Guy Green *ad* George Wakhevitch, William C. Andrews *musical arrangement and additions* Arthur Bliss
☆ Laurence Olivier, Stanley Holloway, Dorothy Tutin, Daphne Anderson, Mary Clare, George Devine, Athene Seyler, Hugh Griffith, Margot Grahame, Sandra Dorne, Laurence Naismith
'The failure is equalled only by the ambition.' – *Gavin Lambert*

'New Thrills! New Shocks! New Terror!'
The Beginning of the End
US 1957 73m bw
ABPT/Republic (Bert I. Gordon)
Radiation breeds giant grasshoppers which are only stopped when they can't withstand the waters of Lake Michigan.
Bottom-of-the-sci-fi-barrel rubbish, very boring to watch.
w Fred Freiberger, Lester Corn *d* Bert I. Gordon
☆ Peggie Castle, Peter Graves, Morris Ankrum, James Seay, Richard Benedict, Pierre Watkin

The Beginning or the End
US 1947 112m bw
MGM (Samuel Marx)
During World War II American scientists continue to perfect the atom bomb despite their own misgivings, and one dies in an explosion.
Semi-documentary marred by sentimental personal asides and of very little continuing interest.
w Robert Considine *d* Norman Taurog *ph* Ray June *m* Daniele Amfitheatrof
☆ Brian Donlevy, Robert Walker, Tom Drake, Beverly Tyler, Hume Cronyn, Audrey Totter, *Godfrey Tearle* (Roosevelt)
'The documentary value is so offset by sickly sentiment that it is practically just another love story.' – *W. A. Wilcox, Sunday Dispatch*

Begone Dull Care ****
Canada 1953 9m colour
National Film Board (Norman McLaren)
Abstract images drawn directly onto the film are accompanied by three pieces of jazz performed by the Oscar Peterson Trio.
The central movement is a little too slow, but the first piece is witty and the climax is an irresistible frenzy of sound and image. Undeniably a classic short, and probably McLaren's best.
conceived and made by Norman McLaren

'One man ... seven women ... in a strange house!'
The Beguiled *
US 1971 109m Technicolor
Universal/Malpaso (Don Siegel)
A wounded Unionist soldier hides out in a Confederate ladies' school; the teachers fend for him until he causes trouble among the sexually frustrated women, who eventually kill him.
Eccentric melodrama which does not really work despite its credentials and patient work all round.
w John B. Sherry, Grimes Grice *novel* Thomas Cullinan *d* Don Siegel *ph* Bruce Surtees *m* Lalo Schifrin *pd* Ted Haworth
☆ Clint Eastwood, Geraldine Page, Elizabeth Hartman, Jo Ann Harris, Darleen Carr, Mae Mercer
'A must for sadists and woman-haters.' – *Judith Crist*

Behave Yourself *
US 1951 81m bw
RKO (Jerry Wald, Norman Krasna)
A young married couple and their dog get mixed up in a chain of murders.
Zany black comedy in the wake of A Slight Case of Murder *and* The Thin Man *(qqv). The humour is spread too thin for success.*
wd George Beck *ph* James Wong Howe *m* Leigh Harline
☆ Farley Granger, Shelley Winters, William Demarest, Francis L. Sullivan, Margalo Gillmore, Lon Chaney, Hans Conried, Elisha Cook Jnr

Behemoth the Sea Monster: see *The Giant Behemoth*

Behind Convent Walls (dubbed)
Italy 1977 95m Telecolor
Trust International (Giuseppe Vezzani)
original title: *Interno d'un Convento*
US title: *Sex Life in a Convent; aka: Within a Cloister*
A mother superior finds that her sisters are more interested in carnal knowledge than religious faith.
A staple of soft-core porn – nuns behaving badly – is given a little visual distinction in an otherwise dull and predictable offering.
wd Walerian Borowczyk *stories* *Promenades Romanes* by Stendhal *ph* Luciano Tovolli *m* Sergio Montori *ad* Luciano Spadoni
☆ Ligia Branice, Howard Ross, Marina Pierro, Gabriella Giaccobe, Rodolfo Dal Pra', Loredana Martinez, Mario Maranzana

'One Rule: Evade And Survive.'
Behind Enemy Lines
US 2001 106m DeLuxe Panavision
TCF (John Davis)
Sometime in the future, an American naval pilot is shot down in Bosnia and hunted by Serbian troops.
Old-fashioned war movie propaganda, of the type one might have hoped that Hollywood had outgrown, filmed in an obtrusively ostentatious style that owes more to video games than any reality.
w David Veloz, Zak Penn *d* John Moore *ph* Brendan Galvin *m* Don Davis *pd* Nathan Crawley *ed* Paul Martin Smith
☆ Owen Wilson (Burnett), Gene Hackman (Reigart), Gabriel Macht (Stackhouse), Charles Malik Whitfield (Rodway), Joaquim de Almeida (Piquet), David Keith (O'Malley), Olek Krupa (Lokar), Vladimir Mashkov (Tracker), Marko Ogonda (Bazda)
'A live-action recruiting poster for today's military, the film shows how some time under fire turns undisciplined wiseacres into men Uncle Sam can be proud to call his own.' – *Kenneth Turan, Los Angeles Times*
† Although apparently set 'the day after tomorrow', the film's inspiration seems to be the ordeal in 1995 of Scott O'Grady, an Air Force captain who was shot down by a Bosnian-Serb missile and survived for six days before he was rescued.

Behind Prison Gates
US 1939 63m bw
Columbia
A secret agent follows bank robbers into prison.
Standard undercover crime support.
w Arthur T. Horman, Leslie T. White *d* Charles Barton
☆ Brian Donlevy, Jacqueline Wells, Joseph Crehan, Paul Fix

Behind Prison Walls
US 1943 64m bw
PRC (Arthur Ripley)
GB title: *Youth Takes a Hand*
Too-honest son gets his tycoon father sent to prison, but ends up there himself.
Curious moral comedy drama which can't work on a low budget.
w Van Norcross, W. A. Ulman Jnr *d* Steve Sekely
☆ Alan Baxter, Tully Marshall, Gertrude Michael, Edwin Maxwell, Matt Willis

Behind That Curtain
US 1929 91m bw
Fox
Murder follows when a ne'er-do-well aspires to marry an heiress.
Nominally the third Charlie Chan film, but Chan, played by E. L. Park, is whittled down to a tiny role. As it stands, a clumsy effort, but could be worth remaking.
w Sonya Levien, Clarke Silvernail *novel* Earl Derr Biggers *d* Irving Cummings
☆ Warner Baxter, Lois Moran, Gilbert Emery, Claude King, Philip Strange, Boris Karloff

Behind the Door: see *The Man with Nine Lives*

Behind the High Wall
US 1956 85m bw
U-I (Stanley Rubin)
A prison warder, taken as hostage by escaping convicts, steals some of the money they have taken.
Glum melodrama, capably presented.
w Harold Jack Bloom *d* Abner Biberman *ph* Maury Gertsman *m* Joseph Gershenson *ed* Ted J. Kent
☆ Tom Tully, Sylvia Sidney, John Gavin, Betty Lynn, John Larch, Barney Phillips, Don Beddoe

Behind the Iron Mask: see *The Fifth Musketeer*

'Who is the murdering monster?'
Behind the Mask
US 1932 68m bw
Columbia
A crazy doctor operates fatally on those who know too much.
Semi-horror mystery using two members of the Frankenstein cast.
w Jo Swerling *d* John Francis Dillon
☆ Jack Holt, Constance Cummings, Edward Van Sloan, Boris Karloff
'Exploited as another horror picture, this doesn't horrify sufficiently to class with preceding baby-scarers. But its virtues are a not-so-bad Secret Service story, well-acted by a cast of veterans.' – *Variety*

Behind the Mask *
GB 1958 99m Eastmancolor
BL/GW Films (Sergei Nolbandov, Josef Somlo)
Political infighting causes tension on the board of a local hospital.
Oddly titled social drama with interesting detail but not much tension or conclusion.
w John Hunter *novel* The Pack by John Rowan Wilson *d* Brian Desmond Hurst *ph* Robert Krasker *m* Geoffrey Wright
☆ Michael Redgrave, Tony Britton, Carl Mohner, Niall MacGinnis, Vanessa Redgrave, Ian Bannen, Brenda Bruce, Lionel Jeffries, Miles Malleson, John Welsh, Ann Firbank

Behind the Rising Sun *
US 1943 88m bw
RKO
An American-educated Japanese goes home in the thirties, comes under the influence of war-mongers, and causes his father to commit hara-kiri.
Outrageous wartime flagwaver designed to vilify 'Uncle Tojo's dogs', from the writer and director of the similar Hitler's Children *(qv).*
w Emmet Lavery *novel* James R. Young *d* Edward Dmytryk *ph* Russell Metty *m* Roy Webb
☆ J. Carrol Naish, Tom Neal, Margo, Robert Ryan, Gloria Holden, Don Douglas, Adeline de Walt Reynolds

Behind the Sun: see *Abril Despedaçado*

Behold a Pale Horse *
US 1964 121m bw
Columbia/Highland/Brentwood (Fred Zinnemann, Alexander Trauner)
A Spanish guerrilla goes into exile at the end of the Civil War. Twenty years later he is persuaded to return and kill a brutal police chief.
An action film which unfortunately insists on saying something significant about morality, destiny and death. Impeccably made, but somehow not very interesting apart from the action sequences.
w J. P. Miller *novel* Killing a Mouse on Sunday by Emeric Pressburger *d* Fred Zinnemann *ph* Jean Badal *m* Maurice Jarre *ad* Alexander Trauner
☆ Gregory Peck, Omar Sharif, Anthony Quinn, Raymond Pellegrin, Paolo Stoppa, Mildred Dunnock, Daniela Rocca, Christian Marquand
'A fine example of a high class failure.' – *Judith Crist*

Beijing Bastards *
China/Hong Kong 1993 95m colour
Beijing Bastards (Cui Jian, Zhang Yuan, Shu Qi, Du Kefeng)
original title: *Beijing Zazhong*
Groups of friends with artistic aspirations drink, fight, talk, drink, play music and complain about their aimless lives.
A disjointed look at the disaffected young, in which the slight narrative is disrupted by rock performances; interesting mainly for its portrait of a shiftless generation not usually seen on film.
w Zhang Yuan, Tang Danian, Cui Jian *d* Zhang Yuan *ph* Zhang Jian *m* Cui Jian, Dou Wei, Ha Yong *ad* Liu Xiaodong *ed* Feng Shuangyuan
☆ Cui Jian, Li Wei, Wu Gang, Bian Tianshuo, Tang Danian, Bian Wing
'The first film to tackle the anger and frustration of today's youth in China ... communicates a strong sense of squalor and brutishness, a depressing lack of purpose and lack of contact between people. All told, pic is quite a downer.' – *Deborah Young, Variety*
† The film was banned by the Chinese authorities, who also tried to prevent it being shown at the Locarno Festival in 1993.

Beijing Zazhong: see *Beijing Bastards*

'Suddenly one Summer...'
Being at Home with Claude
Canada 1993 85m colour/bw
Out on a Limb/Les Productions du Cerf (Louise Gendron)
A young hustler explains to a policeman why he murdered his lover, a shy intellectual.
This small-scale play transferred to the screen retains its theatrical air, being all talk and no action; the talk, though, and the interaction between the two protagonists retain one's interest for the most part.
wd Jean Beaudin *play* René-Daniel Dubois *ph* Thomas Vamos *m* Richard Grégoire *ed* André Corriveau
☆ Roy Dupuis, Jacques Godin, Jean-François Pichette, Gaston Lepage
'It's hard not to respect something so extreme in its stylisation, emotional intensity and naked romanticism, but it's also hard to cosy up to a film which combines such posiness with hidebound theatre conventions. Beautifully crafted but entirely resistible.' – *Kim Newman, Empire*

'From the dawn of time man has struggled for just four things. Food. Safety. Someone to Love. And a pair of shoes that fit.'
Being Human *
US/GB 1994 122m Technicolor
Warner/Enigma/Fujisankei/BSB/NatWest Ventures (Robert F. Colesberry, David Puttnam)
In five historical eras, from the Bronze Age to modern-day America, a father fails to provide for his family and ends alone and in near-despair.
Bleak variations on the theme of man's inability to make sense of the world, of people inventing stories to comfort themselves in impossible situations. There are moments of wry amusement, but despite its originality, it has too little variation in pace, and the episodes are too inconclusive to provide much satisfaction.
wd Bill Forsyth *ph* Michael Coulter *m* Michael Gibbs *pd* Norman Garwood *ed* Michael Ellis
☆ Robin Williams, John Turturro, Anna Galiena, Vincent D'Onofrio, Hector Elizondo, Lorraine Bracco, Lindsay Crouse, Jonathan Hyde, Bill Nighy, Theresa Russell (narrator)
'An affecting piece that follows its own path against the odds, and certainly does not need any excuses made for it.' – *Jonathan Romney, Guardian*
'This still-born series of little fables is so flat and ill-conceived that it could convince the uninitiated that neither Robin Williams nor the highly idiosyncratic Scottish writer/director Bill Forsyth had any talent.' – *Todd McCarthy, Variety*
† After being left on the shelf for a year, the film, which cost $20m to make, flopped at the US box-office, taking $2m, and was released direct to video in Britain.

Being John Malkovich ***
US/GB 1999 112m colour
Universal/Gramercy/Propaganda/Single Cell (Michael Stipe, Sandy Stern, Steve Golin, Vincent Landay)
Having discovered a portal that allows him to spend time inside the brain of John Malkovich, an unhappily married, unsuccessful puppeteer decides to exploit the situation.
A witty, highly original comedy that manages to be both surreal and ordinary in its depiction of the world and the everyday oddballs that inhabit it, though it does disappear up its own inventiveness towards the end.
w Charlie Kaufman d Spike Jonze ph Lance Acord *m* Carter Burwell *pd* K. K. Barrett *ed* Eric Zumbrunnen
☆ John Cusack (Craig Schwartz), Cameron Diaz (Lotte Schwartz), Catherine Keener (Maxine), Orson Bean (Dr Lester), Mary Kay Place (Floris), John Malkovich (John Horatio Malkovich), Charlie Sheen (Charlie)
'Touches on questions of love, identity, sex, gender and penetration with a playful perverseness few other semi-mainstream productions would ever dare to dabble in. Devilishly inventive and so far out there it's almost off the scale.' – *David Rooney, Variety*
'Manages any number of resourceful riffs on the cult of success without losing its own sweetness.' – *Adam Mars-Jones, Times*
† Sean Penn, Brad Pitt and Christopher Bing appear uncredited as themselves.
Catherine Keener; Spike Jonze; Charlie Kaufman
Charlie Kaufman

'Getting there is half the fun; being there is all of it!'
Being There **
US 1979 130m Metrocolor
Lorimar/North Star/CIP (Andrew Braunsberg)
An illiterate gardener is taken for a homespun philosopher and becomes a national celebrity.
Overlong serio-comic parable hinging on a somewhat dubious star performance. Chance made it a popular urban success, but few who saw it were enthused.
w Jerzy Kosinski *novel* Jerzy Kosinski *d* Hal Ashby *ph* Caleb Deschanel *m* John Mandel *pd* Michael Haller
☆ Peter Sellers, Shirley MacLaine, *Melvyn Douglas*, Jack Warden, Richard Dysart, Richard Basehart
'It pulls off its long shot and is a confoundingly provocative movie.' – *Roger Ebert*
Melvyn Douglas
Peter Sellers
screenplay

Beiqing Chengshi *
Taiwan 1989 160m colour
Artificial Eye/3-H/Era International (Qui Fusheng)
aka: *A City of Sadness*
During the 1940s, from the end of the Japanese occupation of Taiwan to the communist takeover of the Chinese mainland, a family, headed by a local gangster, undergoes domestic upheavals.
Winner of the Golden Lion at the Venice Film Festival in 1989, it nevertheless remains fairly impenetrable to Western audiences not familiar with the political intricacies of the period.
w Wu Nianzhen, Zhu Tianwen *d* Hou Hsiao-Hsien *ph* Chen Huai'en *m* Tachikawa Naoki, Zhang Hongyi *pd* Liu Zhihua, Lin Chongwen *ed* Liao Qingsong
☆ Li Tianlu, Chen Songyong, Gao Jie, Tony Leung, Wu Yifang, Xin Shufen, Chen Shufang, Ke Suyun, Lin Liqing, He Aiyun
'Its balance between the personal and the political is spectacular and exemplary, as if a brilliant miniaturist had miraculously filled a huge canvas.' – *Tony Rayns, MFB*

Bela Lugosi Meets a Brooklyn Gorilla
US 1952 74m bw
Jack Broder
GB title: *The Monster Meets the Gorilla*
A tropical island scientist turns one half of a stranded comedy team into a gorilla.
Stupid farce which never rises to the occasion.
w Tim Ryan *d* William Beaudine
☆ Bela Lugosi, Duke Mitchell, Sammy Petrillo, Ray 'Crash' Corrigan, Muriel Landers
'Neighbourhood and small-town audiences will get some laughs.' – *Box Office*

Believe in Me
US 1971 90m colour
MGM (Irwin Winkler, Robert Chartoff)
Two young marrieds take to drugs.
Tedious and unenlightening modern drama which seems to think it's saying something new.
w Israel Horovitz *d* Stuart Hagmann *ph* Dick Kratina, Richard C. Brooks *m* Fred Karlin
☆ Michael Sarrazin, Jacqueline Bisset, Jon Cypher, Allen Garfield

The Believer *
US 2001 98m DuArt
Pathé/Fuller (Christopher Roberts, Susan Hoffman)
A brilliant Jewish student becomes the leader of an anti-Semitic gang.
Intriguing exploration of belief and identity, bouyed by an intensely convincing performance from Gosling.
wd Henry Bean *ph* Jim Denault *m* Joel Diamond *pd* Susan Block *ed* Mayin Lo, Lee Percy
☆ *Ryan Gosling* (Danny Balint), Summer Phoenix (Carla Moebius), Glenn Fitzgerald (Drake), Theresa Russell (Lina Moebius), Billy Zane (Curtis Zampf), Garret Dillahunt (Billings), Kris Eivers (Carleton), Joel Garland (O. L)
'A fireball of contradictory ideas that will pin you to your seat.' – *Peter Travers, Rolling Stone*

The Believers *
US 1987 114m DeLuxe
Orion/John Schlesinger, Michael Childers, Beverly Camhe
New York's occult underworld is permeated by a sinister Catholic ritual.
Most of the time it's hard to say what's going on in this intensely melodramatic thriller, but there are the odd rewards along the way. Not too many, actually.
w Mark Frost *book* The Religion by Nicholas Conde *d* John Schlesinger *ph* Robby Müller *m* J. Peter Robinson *pd* Simon Holland *ed* Peter Honess
☆ Martin Sheen, Helen Shaver, Harley Cross, Robert Loggia, Elizabeth Wilson, Harris Yulin
'If nothing else, Schlesinger knows how to produce a film where pain and horror are beautiful to watch.' – *Daily Variety*

'A bewitching comedy about an enchanting subject!'
Bell, Book and Candle *
US 1958 103m Technicolor
Columbia/Phoenix (Julian Blaustein)
A publisher slowly becomes aware that his new girlfriend is a witch.
A gossamer stage comedy has been fatally flattened in translation; most of the actors are miscast, and sentiment soaks the script. But it remains a civilized entertainment.
w Daniel Taradash *play* John Van Druten *d* Richard Quine *ph* James Wong Howe *m* George Duning *ad* Cary Odell
☆ James Stewart, Kim Novak, Jack Lemmon, Ernie Kovacs, *Hermione Gingold*, Elsa Lanchester, Janice Rule
'Rarely has so much cinematic talent been expended so successfully on so little.' – *Films in Review*
art direction

Bell Bottom George
GB 1943 97m bw
Columbia
A medically exempt waiter dons uniform and catches a ring of spies.
Formula star comedy, too long and too familiar.
w Peter Fraser, Edward Dryhurst *d* Marcel Varnel
☆ George Formby, Anne Firth, Reginald Purdell, Peter Murray Hill

A Bell for Adano *
US 1945 104m bw
TCF (Louis D. Lighton, Lamar Trotti)
An American major takes over an Italian town and wins affection by replacing the local bell.
Slight end-of-war mood piece, still quite pleasant but without the undercurrents of feeling it had at the time.
w Lamar Trotti, Norman Reilly Raine *novel* John Hersey *d* Henry King *ph* Joseph LaShelle *m* Alfred Newman
☆ John Hodiak, Gene Tierney, William Bendix, Glenn Langan, Richard Conte, Stanley Prager, Henry Morgan

The Bell Jar
US 1979 107m colour
Peerce-Goldston/Avco
A teenage girl becomes mentally ill when her father dies.
Numbingly tedious case history without much apparent point.
w Marjorie Kellogg *novel* Sylvia Plath *d* Larry Peerce
☆ Marilyn Hassett, Julie Harris, Anne Jackson, Barbara Barrie

Belladonna
GB 1934 91m bw
Twickenham (Julius Hagen)
A selfish woman tries to poison her husband for love of an Egyptian.
Intriguingly-cast version of a story that was later filmed in Hollywood as Temptation *(qv).*
w H. Fowler Mear *play* J. B. Fagan *novel Robert Hichens d* Robert Milton *ph* Sydney Blythe, William Luff *ad* James Carter

☆ Mary Ellis, Conrad Veidt, Cedric Hardwicke, John Stuart, Michael Shepley

Il Bell'Antonio *
Italy/France 1960 105m bw
Cina del Duca-Arco/Lyre Cinématographique (Alfredo Bini)
GB title: *Handsome Antonio*
A youngish man returns to his native town with the reputation of a lady-killer, but when married turns out to be impotent.
Amusing but finally exhausting Sicilian comedy with all the expected exaggeration of speech and gesture.
w Pier Paolo Pasolini, Gino Visentini *novel* Vitaliano Brancati *d* Piero Piccioni
☆ Marcello Mastroianni, Claudia Cardinale, Pierre Brasseur, Rina Morelli, Tomas Milian

The Bellboy *
US 1960 72m bw
Paramount/Jerry Lewis Productions (Jerry Lewis)
An incompetent bellboy causes havoc in a Miami hotel.
Plotless essence of a comedian who divides opinion and will never be better than variable. This ragbag of old gags at least prevents his usual sentimental excesses, and is mercifully short.
wd Jerry Lewis *ph* Haskell Boggs *m* Walter Scharf
☆ *Jerry Lewis*, Alex Gerry, Bob Clayton, Herkie Styles, Milton Berle

La Belle Américaine *
France 1961 101m bw (colour finale)
CCFC/Film d'Art/Panorama/Corflor (Henri Diamant-Berger, Arthur Lesser)
GB and US titles: *What a Chassis*
aka: *The American Beauty*
A Parisian factory worker gets into all kinds of trouble when he buys an American supercar for a ridiculously low price.
Some brilliant gags are separated by long dull spots of unnecessary storytelling.
w Robert Dhéry, Pierre Tchernia, Alfred Adam *d* Robert Dhéry *ph* Ghislain Cloquet *m* Gérard Calvi
☆ *Robert Dhéry*, Louis de Funes, Colette Brosset, Alfred Adam, Bernard Lavalette, Annie Ducaux

Belle de Jour ****
France/Italy 1967 100m Eastmancolor
Paris Film/Five Film (Robert and Raymond Hakim)
A surgeon's wife finds herself drawn to afternoon work in a brothel.
Fascinating Buñuel mixture of fact and fantasy, impeccably woven into a rich fabric.
w Luis Buñuel, Jean-Claude Carrière novel Joseph Kessel *d Luis Buñuel ph Sacha Vierny m* none *ad* Robert Clavel *ed* Louisette Hautecoeur, Walter Spohr
☆ *Catherine Deneuve*, Jean Sorel, Michel Piccoli, Genevieve Page, Pierre Clémenti
'Oppressively powerful. Like being buried alive in Sarah Bernhardt's dressing room.' – *Wilfred Sheed*
'The rhythm of the writing, the color changes, acting tempos, camera angles, the whole editing – all this is perfect. There is not one extraneous shot, nor one that is missing. Disparate elements are embraced in a self-possessed, lucidly enchanting flow.' – *John Simon*

Belle Epoque *
Spain 1992 109m Eastmancolor
Cinemascope
Mayfair/Lola/Animatografo/French Production/
Fernando Trueba
In Spain in the early 30s, a deserter from the army hides in the house of a widower with four attractive daughters, who teach him the pleasures of life.
A leisurely, enjoyable film of the past, as seen through rose-coloured spectacles; it is inoffensive and amusing without being particularly memorable.
w Rafael Azcona *story* Rafael Azcona, José Luis Garcia Sanchez, Fernando Trueba *d* Fernando Trueba *ph* José Luis Alcaine *m* Antoine Duhamel *ad* Juan Botella *ed* Carmen Frias
☆ Fernando Fernán Gómez, Jorge Sanz, Maribel Verdú, Ariadna Gil, Miriam Diaz-Aroca, Penélope Cruz, Gabino Diego, Michel Galabru
'The tone is merry as well as erotic, but generally takes the easy way out, suggesting there is more than one country in Europe that sees the benefit of making warmly pleasurable period films that will attract nostalgic audiences.' – *Derek Malcolm, Guardian*
best foreign film

La Belle Equipe *
France 1936 74m bw
Ciné Arts
Five unemployed Parisians win the lottery and open a restaurant, but things do not go smoothly.
Interesting but rather lumpy star drama which finally descends into melodrama; alternative tragic and happy endings were originally offered.
w Charles Spaak, Julien Duvivier *d* Julien Duvivier *ph* Jules Kruger, Marc Fessard *m* Maurice Yvain
☆ Jean Gabin, Charles Vanel, Viviane Romance, Raymond Aimos, Robert Lynen, Raymond Cordy, Raphael Medina

La Belle et la Bête **
France 1946 96m bw
Discina (André Paulvé)
aka: *Beauty and the Beast*
Beauty gives herself to the Beast who has kidnapped her father; through love the monster turns into a handsome prince.
Slightly heavy-handed though usually stunning-looking adaptation of the fairy tale.
wd Jean Cocteau *story* Madame LePrince de Beaumont *ph* Henri Alekan *m* Georges Auric *ad Christian Bérard ed* Claude Ibéria
☆ Jean Marais (Avenant/The Beast/The Prince), Josette Day (Beauty), Mila Parély (Adelaide), Marcel André (Merchant), Nane Germon (Felice), Michel Auclair (Ludovic)
'Perhaps the most sumptuously elegant of all filmed fairy tales.' – *New Yorker, 1980*
'Absolute magic: diamond cold and lunar bright.' – *CBS*
'A sensuously fascinating film, a fanciful poem in movement given full articulation on the screen.' – *Bosley Crowther, New York Times*

Une Belle Fille Comme Moi
France 1972 98m colour
Columbia/Les Films du Carrosse (Marcel Berbert, Claude Ganz)
US title: *Such a Gorgeous Kid Like Me*
A gullible sociologist hears the confession of a promiscuous murderess.
Moderately interesting black comedy.
w Jean-Loup Dabadie, François Truffaut *novel* Henry Farrell *d* François Truffaut *ph* Pierre-William Glenn *m* Georges Delerue *ad* Jean-Pierre Kohut *ed* Yann Dedet, Martine Barraque
☆ Bernadette Lafont, Claude Brasseur, Charles Denner, Guy Marchand, André Dussollier, Anne Kreis, Philippe Léotard

La Belle Noiseuse ***
France 1991 240m colour
Artificial Eye/Pierre Grise
The beautiful young mistress of a friend inspires a famous artist to finish a painting, for which his wife modelled, that he put aside ten years before.
A gripping and penetrating movie on the themes of obsession, art and love, although it offers little in the way of conventional narrative.
w Pascal Bonitzer, Christine Laurent, Jacques Rivette story Le Chef d'Oeuvre Inconnu (The Unknown Masterpiece) by Honoré de Balzac *d Jacques Rivette ph William Lubtchansky m* Stravinsky *ad* Emmanuel de Chauvigny *ed* Nicole Lubtchansky
☆ Michel Piccoli, Jane Birkin, *Emmanuelle Béart*, Marianne Denicourt, David Bursztein, Gilles Arbona
'Perhaps the most meticulous and seductive depiction in movies of the hard work of making art.' – *Richard Corliss, Time*
† Artist Bernard Dufour, whose hand is the only part of him to be seen, did the painting
†† *La Belle Noiseuse: Divertimento*, a two-hour version of the film using different takes, was produced for French TV and also given a cinema and video release.

The Belle of New York *
US 1952 82m Technicolor
MGM (Arthur Freed)
An 1890s playboy falls for a Salvation Army girl.
A rather dreary version of the old musical, with undistinguished additions.
w Robert O'Brien, Irving Elinson *play* Hugh Morton *d* Charles Walters *ph* Robert Planck *m/ly* Johnny Mercer, Harry Warren *md* Adolph Deutsch *ad Jack Martin Smith*
☆ Fred Astaire, Vera-Ellen, Marjorie Main, Keenan Wynn, Alice Pearce, Clinton Sundberg, Gale Robbins
† Vera-Ellen's singing was dubbed by Anita Ellis
♫ 'When I'm Out with the Belle of New York'; 'Oops'; 'Baby Doll'; 'Naughty but Nice'; 'Seeing's Believing'; 'Thank You Mr Currier, Thank You Mr Ives'; 'I Love to Beat a Big Bass Drum'; 'I Wanna Be a Dancing Man'; 'Let a Little Love Come In'

Belle of the Nineties *
US 1934 75m bw
Paramount (William Le Baron)
A saloon entertainer loves two men, one of whom is a crook.
Much-laundered star vehicle which despite superior production seems a pale shadow of the star's better pieces.
w Mae West d Leo McCarey *ph* Karl Struss *m/ly* Arthur Johnston, Sam Coslow
☆ *Mae West*, Roger Pryor, John Miljan, John Mack Brown, Katherine de Mille, Duke Ellington and his Orchestra
'It's been sufficiently denatured from within, yet not completely emasculated.' – *Variety*

Belle of the Yukon *
US 1945 84m Technicolor
International
A troupe of saloon entertainers in the Yukon become involved with a bank robbery.
Threads of plot support comedy, dancing and songs in this thin but reasonably fresh musical imitation of The Spoilers *(qv).*
w James Edward Grant *d* William A. Seiter *ph* Ray Rennahan *md* Arthur Lange
☆ Gypsy Rose Lee, Randolph Scott, Dinah Shore, Charles Winninger, Bob Burns
Arthur Lange; song 'Sleigh Ride in July' (*m* Jimmy Van Heusen, *ly* Johnny Burke)

Belle Starr
US 1941 87m Technicolor
TCF (Kenneth MacGowan)
Angry at losing her lands to the Yankees in the Civil War, Belle Starr marries a Confederate guerilla leader and continues to battle on.
Absurdly laundered version of the life of the west's most notorious female outlaw, with the star laughably miscast.
w Lamar Trotti *d* Irving Cummings *ph* Ernest Palmer, Ray Rennahan *m* Alfred Newman
☆ Gene Tierney, Randolph Scott, Dana Andrews, Shepperd Strudwick, Elizabeth Patterson, Chill Wills, Louise Beavers

Belle Starr's Daughter
US 1947 86m bw
TCF/Alson (Edward L. Alperson)
After the truce between outlaw Belle Starr and the town of Antoich breaks down, her daughter seeks revenge for the death of her mother.
Lacklustre western, perfunctorily plotted and composed of most of the clichés of the genre, with an unlikely romance at its centre; its only novelty lies in its musical score, which is often elegiac in tone and more complex than those usually accompanying B features.
w W.R. Burnett *d* Lesley Selander *ph* William Sickner *m* Dr Edward Kilenyi *ad* Lucius Croxton *ed* Jason Bernie
☆ George Montgomery, Rod Cameron, Ruth Roman, Wallace Ford, Charles Kemper, William Phipps, Edith King, Jack Lambert, Fred Libby, Isabel Jewell

Les Belles de Nuit **
France/Italy 1952 89m bw
Franco London/Rizzoli
A discontented music teacher dreams of beautiful women through the ages.
Charming but very slight dream fantasy with many of the master's touches. (He claims to have intended a comic Intolerance.*)*
wd René Clair ph Armand Thirard, Robert Juilliard, Louise Née *m Georges Van Parys* *ad* Léon Barsacq
☆ Gérard Philipe, Gina Lollobrigida, Martine Carol, Magali Vendeuil, Paolo Stoppa, Raymond Bussières, Raymond Cordy

The Belles of St Trinian's *
GB 1954 91m bw
BL/London Films/Launder and Gilliat
At an unruly and bankrupt school for girls, more time is spent backing horses than studying subjects, and the headmistress's bookmaker brother has a scheme or two of his own.
Fairly successful film version of Ronald Searle's awful schoolgirl cartoons, the emphasis shifted to a groiesque older generation with the star in drag. An enormous commercial success, but the three sequels Blue Murder at St Trinian's, The Pure Hell of St Trinian's, The Great St Trinian's Train Robbery *(qqv), went from bad to awful.*
w Frank Launder, Sidney Gilliat, Val Valentine *d* Frank Launder *ph* Stan Pavey *m* Malcolm Arnold
☆ *Alastair Sim*, George Cole, Joyce Grenfell, Hermione Baddeley, Betty Ann Davies, Renée Houston, Beryl Reid, Irene Handl, Mary Merrall, Joan Sims, Sidney James
'Not so much a film as an entertainment on celluloid, a huge charade, a rich pile of idiotic and splendidly senseless images.' – *David Robinson*

Belles on Their Toes
US 1952 89m Technicolor
TCF (Samuel G. Engel)
Further adventures in the growing up of the twelve Gilbreth children.
Flat sequel to Cheaper by the Dozen *(qv) with sentimentality instead of Clifton Webb. Period atmosphere attractive.*
w Phoebe and Henry Ephron *book* Frank B. Gilbreth Jnr and Ernestine Gilbreth Carey *d* Henry Levin *ph* Arthur E. Arling *m* Cyril Mockridge
☆ Myrna Loy, Jeanne Crain, Debra Paget, Jeffrey Hunter, Edward Arnold, Hoagy Carmichael, Barbara Bates, Robert Arthur

Bellissima *
Italy 1951 100m bw
Bellissima Films (Salvo d'Angelo)
A mother struggles to get a part in a film for her 7-year-old daughter.
Highly detailed, very noisy star vehicle with neo-realist working-class backgrounds. Exhausting.
w Suso Cecchi d'Amico, Francesco Rosi, Luchino Visconti, Cesare Zavattini *d* Luchino Visconti *ph* Piero Portalupi *m* Franco Mannino
☆ Anna Magnani, Walter Chiari, Tina Apicella, Gastone Renzelli, Alessandro Blasetti

Bellman and True *
GB 1987 122m Technicolor
Handmade/Euston (Michael Wearing, Christopher Neame)
A young burglar in a heist is protected by an older crook's computer skills.
Good crime drama with television derivation.
w Desmond Lowder, Richard Loncraine, Michael Wearing *novel* Desmond Lowder *d* Richard Loncraine *ph* Ken Westbury *m* Colin Towns *pd* Jon Bunker *ed* Paul Green
☆ Bernard Hill, Derek Newark, Kieran O'Brien, Richard Hope, Frances Tomelty

The Bells
GB 1931 75m bw
PDC/BSFP (Sergei Nolbandov)
An Alsatian burgomaster is forced by conscience to confess to the killing of a Jew.
Only sound version of a famous melodrama first played on stage by Henry Irving in 1871.
w C. H. Dand *play Le Juif Polonais* by Erckmann and Chatrian *d* Oscar M. Werndorff, Harcourt Templeman (in three language versions) *ph* Gunther Krampf, Eric Cross *m* Gustav Holst *ad* Oscar Werndorff *ed* Lars Moen, Michael Hankinson

☆ Donald Calthrop, Jane Welsh, Edward Sinclair
† In a 1926 silent version Lionel Barrymore played the murderer and Boris Karloff the mesmerist.

Bells Are Ringing *
US 1960 126m Metrocolor Cinemascope
MGM (Arthur Freed)

A telephone answering service operator becomes passionately involved in the lives of her clients.
Dull, rather ugly and boring transcription of a Broadway musical, with all talents below par, not enough dancing and too much plot.
w Betty Comden, Adolph Green *play* Betty Comden, Adolph Green *d* Vincente Minnelli *ph* Milton Krasner *m* Jule Styne *md* André Previn *ch* Charles O'Curran *ad* George W. Davis, Preston Ames *ly* Betty Comden, Adolph Green
☆ Judy Holliday, Dean Martin, Fred Clark, Eddie Foy Jnr, Jean Stapleton, Ruth Storey, Frank Gorshin
André Previn

The Bells Go Down *
GB 1943 89m bw
Ealing (S. C. Balcon)
The exploits of a London firefighting unit during World War II.
Tragi-comedy with lively scenes, a good record of the historical background of the blitz.
w Roger Macdougall, Stephen Black *d* Basil Dearden *ph* Ernest Palmer *m* Roy Douglas
☆ Tommy Trinder (Tommy), James Mason, Mervyn Johns (Sam), Philippa Hiatt (Nan), Finlay Currie (D.O. MacFarlane), Philip Friend, Meriel Forbes (Susie), Beatrice Varley (Ma Turk), Billy Hartnell (Brookes), Norman Pierce (Pa Robbins), Muriel George (Ma Robbins), Julien Vedey (Lou Freeman), Johnnie Schofield (Milkman)

Bells of St Angelo
US 1947 78m Trucolor
Republic (Edward J. White)
In between songs, Roy Rogers foils smugglers who are taking silver across the Mexican border.
A tougher movie than usual for Rogers, but still a curious mixture of comedy, songs, fist-fights and death.
w Sloan Nibley *story* Paul Gangelin *d* William Witney *ph* Jack Marta *md* Morton Scott *ad* Gano Chittenden *ed* Les Orlebeck
☆ Roy Rogers, Dale Evans, Andy Devine, Bob Nolan and the Sons of the Pioneers

'Your heart will be wearing a smile!'
The Bells of St Mary's **
US 1945 126m bw
RKO/Rainbow (Leo McCarey)

At a big city Catholic school, Father O'Malley and Sister Benedict indulge in friendly rivalry, and succeed in extending the school through the gift of a building.
Sentimental and very commercial sequel to Going My Way *(qv), with the stars at their peak and the handling as cosy and well-paced as might be expected.*
w Dudley Nichols *d* Leo McCarey *ph* George Barnes *m* Robert Emmett Dolan *ed* Harry Marker
☆ *Bing Crosby, Ingrid Bergman*, Henry Travers, William Gargan, Ruth Donnelly, Rhys Williams, Una O'Connor, Eva Novak

'The picture is full of shrewd and pleasant flashes. It is also fascinating to watch as a talented, desperate effort to repeat the unrepeatable. But on the whole it is an unhappy film.' – *James Agee*

best picture; Leo McCarey; Robert Emmett Dolan; Bing Crosby; Ingrid Bergman; song 'Aren't You Glad You're You' (*m* Jimmy Van Heusen, *ly* Johnny Burke); Harry Marker

Belly
US 1998 96m DeLuxe
Alliance/Artisan/Big Dog (Ron Rotholz, Hype Williams, Robert Salerno, Larry Meistrich)

Two successful young black gangsters face an uncertain future.
A first feature from a director of music-videos, which has flash and style but little characterisation; you could say it suffers from substance abuse: there's not enough of it beneath the slick surface and raucous hiphop soundtrack.
w Hype Williams, Anthony Bodden, Nas *d* Hype Williams *ph* Malik Sayeed *m* Stephen Cullo *pd* Regan Jackson *ed* David Leonard
☆ Nas (Sincere), DMX (Tommy Brown), Taral Hicks (Kisha), Tionne 'T-Boz' Watkins (Tionne), Method Man (Shameek), Hassan Johnson (Mark), Power (Knowledge), Louie Rankin (Lennox), Tyrin Turner (Big), Minister Benjamin F. Muhammed (Rev Saviour)

'Shackled to a threadbare plot and guided by primary school philosophy, unfortunately *Belly* fails in every department.' – *Ben Falk, Empire*

The Belly of an Architect
GB/Italy 1987 118m Technicolor
Recorded Releasing/Mondial/Tangram/Film Four International/British Screen (Colin Callender, Walter Donohue)

An American architect in Rome discovers he is terminally ill, is deserted by his wife, and commits suicide.
Ravishing evocation of 18th-century Roman architecture is no compensation for the multi-layered psychological complexity.
wd Peter Greenaway *ph* Sacha Vierny *m* Wim Mertens *ad* Luciana Vedovelli *ed* John Wilson
☆ Brian Dennehy, Chloe Webb, Lambert Wilson

Beloved
US 1933 80m bw
Universal (Bennie F. Zeidman)
A composer ages from 10 to 90 while trying to place his symphony; he dies happy.
Curious fictional biopic with plenty of incident but no plot.
w Paul Gangelin, George O'Neil *d* Victor Schertzinger
☆ John Boles, Gloria Stuart, Albert Conti, Dorothy Peterson, Morgan Farley

'Too hopelessly muddled in conception to reach the important money class.' – *Variety*

The Beloved
US/Greece 1972 94m Technicolor
Filmex Curtwel/Pageant (Patrick Curtis, Yorgo (George) Pan Cosmatos)

aka: *Sin*
aka: *Restless*
Returning from London to his Greek island home, a man begins an affair with the wife of a friend and connives in his death.
Glossy, folksy, and very dull domestic drama, as unconvincing as you would expect from a production that casts Raquel Welch in the role of a Greek peasant.
wd Yorgo (George) Pan Cosmatos *ph* Mercello Gatti *m* Yannis Markopoulos *pd* John Corbidge *ed* Terry Williams
☆ Raquel Welch, Richard Johnson, Jack Hawkins, Flora Robson, Renato Romano, Frank Wolff

Beloved *
US 1998 172m Technicolor
Buena Vista/Touchstone/Harpo/Clinica Estetico (Edward Saxon, Jonathan Demme, Gary Goetzman, Oprah Winfrey, Kate Forte)

In Ohio in the 1870s, a former slave gives a home to a strange young woman, who seems to be the ghost of her dead daughter.
Meticulous version of a novel dealing with the effects and aftermath of slavery; it is, though, both too earnest and too long to be entirely satisfactory.
w Akosua Busia, Richard LaGravenese, Adam Brooks *novel* Toni Morrison *d* Jonathan Demme *ph* Tak Fujimoto *m* Rachel Portman *pd* Kristi Zea *ed* Carol Littleton, Andy Keir
☆ Oprah Winfrey, Danny Glover, Thandie Newton, Kimberly Elise, Beah Richards, Lisa Gay Hamilton, Albert Hall, Irma P. Hall, Carol Jean Lewis, Kessia Kordelle, Jason Robards

'They should have called it Belaboured.' – *Tom Shone, Sunday Times*

Colleen Atwood (costumes)

The Beloved Bachelor
US 1931 72m bw
Paramount
A man falls in love with his adopted daughter.
Innocuous tearjerker made with some style.
w Sidney Buchman, Raymond Griffith, Agnes Brand Leahy, Edward H. Peple *d* Lloyd Corrigan
☆ Paul Lukas, Dorothy Jordan, Betty Van Allen, Charles Ruggles, Vivienne Osborne

'A particularly femme appealing yarn with apt dialogue and natural continuity.' – *Variety*

'There she sat ... Tense ... Silent ... Watching!'
Beloved Enemy *
US 1936 90m bw
Samuel Goldwyn (George Haight)

During the 1921 Irish rebellion, the fiancée of a British army officer falls in love with the leading revolutionary.
Dreamy-eyed romance with little relevance to the real situation; not badly done of its kind.
w John Balderston, Rose Franken, William Brown Meloney, David Hart *d* H. C. Potter *ph* Gregg Toland *m* Alfred Newman
☆ *Brian Aherne*, Merle Oberon, David Niven, Karen Morley, Jerome Cowan, Henry Stephenson, Donald Crisp

'One of the most incredible screen yarns which has been shown in many a day ... If when the film is shown in Dublin a tidal wave engulfs Hollywood, it will be caused by the Emerald Isle turning somersaults.' – *Variety*

Beloved Infidel *
US 1959 123m DeLuxe Cinemascope
TCF/Company of Artists (Jerry Wald)

Sheilah Graham, a British chorus girl turned Hollywood columnist, lives with Scott Fitzgerald but fails to cure him of alcoholism.
A bitter and even sordid true story becomes a slice of Hollywood romance, with stars unsuitably cast. On all levels it falls between two stools, satisfying nobody.
w Sy Bartlett *book* Sheilah Graham, Gerold Frank *d* Henry King *ph* Leon Shamroy *m* Franz Waxman
☆ Gregory Peck, Deborah Kerr, Eddie Albert, Philip Ober, Herbert Rudley, Karin Booth, Ken Scott

'Catastrophically misguided.' – *Penelope Houston*

The Beloved Rogue *
US 1927 99m (24 fps) bw silent
Art Cinema Corporation

15th-century poet and thief François Villon becomes a friend of the king, but is banished when he falls for a lady of the court.
Stylish star vehicle remade as If I Were King *(qv).*
w Paul Bern *d* Alan Crosland *pd* William Cameron Menzies
☆ John Barrymore, Conrad Veidt, Marceline Day, Mack Swain, Slim Summerville

'He kissed many but loved one!'
The Beloved Vagabond *
GB 1936 78m bw
ABFD/Ludovico Toeplitz
At the turn of the century, a jilted French artist becomes a vagabond and falls in love with an orphan girl.
Mildly amusing bi-lingual production from a bestselling picaresque novel; production quite lively.
w Wells Root, Arthur Wimperis, Hugh Mills, Walter Creighton *novel* W. J. Locke *d* Curtis Bernhardt *ph* Franz Planer *m* Darius Milhaud *md* Leslie Bridgewater *ad* Andrei Andreiev *ed* Dug Myers
☆ Maurice Chevalier, Margaret Lockwood, Betty Stockfeld, Desmond Tester, Austin Trevor, Peter Haddon, Cathleen Nesbitt

'A weak sister, mostly for the duals.' – *Variety*

Below Zero **
US 1930 20m bw
Hal Roach
Street musicians treat a policeman to lunch on the contents of a found wallet which turns out to be his.
Slow-paced but likeable star comedy from their best period.
w H. M. Walker *d* James Parrott
☆ Laurel and Hardy, Frank Holliday, Tiny Sandford

The Belstone Fox *
GB 1973 103m Eastmancolor Todd-AO 35
Rank/Independent Artists (Sally Shuter)

A fox and a hound grow up together but the fox leads to tragedy for its masters.
Good animal and countryside photography barely compensate for a fragmentary story with unpleasant moments or for a muddled attitude towards humans and animals; one is not clear what audience the result is supposed to appeal to.
wd James Hill *novel The Ballad of the Belstone Fox* by David Rook *ph* John Wilcox, James Allen *m* Laurie Johnson
☆ Eric Porter, Rachel Roberts, Jeremy Kemp, Bill Travers, Dennis Waterman

Beltenebros
Spain 1991 114m Eastmancolor Panavision
Metro/Iberoamerican/Floradora (Andrés Vicente Gómez)

aka: *Prince of Shadows*
In the early 1960s, a Spanish political exile is sent to kill a traitor to the anti-fascist cause.
Good-looking but dull and disastrously miscast drama of betrayal.
w Pilar Miró, Mario Camus, Juan Antonio Porto *novel Beltenebros* by Antonio Muñoz Molina *d* Pilar Miró *ph* Javier Aguirresarobe *m* José Nieto *pd* Fernando Saénz, Luis Vallés, Ewa Braun *ed* José Luis Matesanz
☆ Terence Stamp, Patsy Kensit, José Luis Gómez, John McEnery, Geraldine James, Simón Andreu, Aleksander Bardini, Bernice Stegers

Ben
US 1972 92m DeLuxe
Cinerama/Bing Crosby (Mort Briskin)

A sickly boy inherits an army of trained rats.
Boring reprise of Willard *(qv) in which the audience knows only too well what to expect. Production and development quite routine.*
w Gilbert A. Ralston *d* Phil Karlson *ph* Russell Metty *m* Walter Scharf
☆ Lee Harcourt Montgomery, Arthur O'Connell, Rosemary Murphy, Meredith Baxter, Kaz Garas, Paul Carr, Kenneth Tobey, Joseph Campanella
title song (*m* Walter Scharf, *ly* Don Black)

'The great decade (1915–25) of the progress of motion picture art reaches its summit! A cast of 125,000!'
'The inspired love of the prince of Hur for the gentle lovely Esther!'
Ben-Hur ***
US 1925 170m approx (16 fps) bw (colour sequence) silent
MGM

In the time of Christ, a Jew suffers mightily under the Romans.
The American silent screen's biggest epic; the sea battle and the chariot race are its most famous sequences.
w Bess Meredyth, Carey Wilson *novel* Lew Wallace *d Fred Niblo ph* Karl Struss, Clyde de Vinna, and others *ad* Horace Jackson, Ferdinand Pinney Earle
☆ *Ramon Novarro, Francis X. Bushman*, Carmel Myers, May McAvoy, Betty Bronson

'Masterpiece of study and patience, a photodrama filled with artistry.' – *New York Times*

† To begin with, the film was directed by Charles Brabin and starred George Walsh. Both were replaced after Louis Mayer saw the first rushes. Previously filmed in 1907.

Ben-Hur **
US 1959 217m Technicolor Camera 65
MGM (Sam Zimbalist)

At the time of Christ, a Palestinian Jew battles against the might of the Roman Empire.
Solid, expensive, surprisingly unimaginative remake; generally less sprightly than the silent version, with the chariot race being its high spot.
w Karl Tunberg *d William Wyler, Andrew Marton ph* Robert L. Surtees *m* Miklos Rozsa *ad* William A. Horning, Edward Carfagno *ed* Ralph E. Winters, John D. Dunning *cos* Elizabeth Haffenden
☆ Charlton Heston (Judah Ben Hur), Haya Harareet (Esther), Jack Hawkins (Quintus Arrius), Stephen Boyd (Messala), Hugh Griffith (Sheik Ilderim), Martha Scott (Miriam), Sam Jaffe (Simonides), Cathy O'Donnell (Tirzah), Finlay Currie (Balthasar), Frank Thring (Pontius Pilate),

Terence Longdon (Drusus), André Morell (Sextus), George Relph (Tiberius)

'Watching it is like waiting at a railroad crossing while an interminable freight train lumbers by, sometimes stopping altogether.' – *Dwight MacDonald*

'A Griffith can make a hundred into a crowd while a Wyler can reduce a thousand to a confused cocktail party.' – *Ibid.*

'The most tasteful and visually exciting film spectacle yet produced by an American company.' – *Albert Johnson, Film Quarterly*

'Spectacular without being a spectacle ... not only is it not simple-minded, it is downright literate.' – *Saturday Review*

'A major motion picture phenomenon.' – *Films in Review*

† The production cost four million dollars, twice the maximum at the time. Rock Hudson, Marlon Brando and Burt Lancaster were all sought in vain for the lead before Heston was selected.

†† This version was subtitled 'A Tale of the Christ'.

picture; William Wyler; Robert L. Surtees; Miklos Rozsa; Charlton Heston; Hugh Griffith; art direction; costumes; editing; special effects (Arnold Gillespie, Robert MacDonald, Milo Lory); sound (Franklin Milton)

Karl Tunberg

film

Benchley

The one-reel shorts in which Robert Benchley, sitting behind a desk, delivered nonsensical lectures on aspects of modern life were very popular with better-class audiences, and launched Benchley onto his movie career as a light actor. Here is a list of them:

1928 The Treasurer's Report, The Sex Life of the Polyp, The Spellbinder

1929 Lesson Number One (2 reels), Furnace Trouble (2 reels), Stewed, Fried and Boiled (2 reels)

1933 Your Technocracy and Mine (2 reels)

1935 How to Break 90 at Croquet, How to Sleep

1936 How to Behave, How to Train a Dog, How to Vote, How to Be a Detective

1937 The Romance of Digestion, How to Start the Day, A Night at the Movies

1938 How to Figure Income Tax, Music Made Simple, An Evening Alone, How to Raise a Baby, The Courtship of the Newt, How to Read, How to Watch Football, Opening Day, Mental Poise, How to Sublet

1939 An Hour for Lunch, Dark Magic, Home Early, How to Eat, The Day of Rest, See Your Doctor

1940 That Inferior Feeling, Home Movies, The Trouble with Husbands

1941 Waiting for Baby, Crime Control, The Forgotten Man, How to Take a Vacation

1942 Nothing but Nerves, The Witness, Keeping in Shape, The Man's Angle

1943 My Tomato, No News Is Good News

1944 Important Business, Why, Daddy?

1945 Boogie Woogie (2 reels), I'm a Civilian Here Myself

† In the late seventies a feature compilation was made under the title *Those Marvellous Benchley Shorts*.

'Who wants to cook Aloo Gobi when you can bend a ball like Beckham?'

Bend It Like Beckham

US/GB/Germany 2002 112m DeLuxe

Helkon SK/Kintop/Film Council/Filmfoerderung (Deepak Nayar, Gurinder Chadha)

An 18-year-old London girl wants to become a professional footballer, in defiance of her Punjabi Sikh parents, who want her to study law and marry.

Broad comedy of cultural differences with no surprises but a few laughs along the way.

w Gurinder Chadha, Guljit Bindra, Paul Mayeda Berges *d* Gurinder Chadha *ph* Jong Lin *m* Craig Pruess *pd* Nick Ellis *ed* Justin Krish

☆ Parminder Nagra (Jess Bhamra), Keira Knightley (Jules Paxton), Jonathan Rhys Meyers (Joe), Anupam Kher (Mr Bhamra), Archie Panjabi (Pinky Bhamra), Shaznay Lewis (Mel), Frank Harper (Alan Paxton), Juliet Stevenson (Paula Paxton)

'A feel-good comedy that promotes, with total political correctness, the cultural equivalence between two tribal religions – English football and Indian weddings.' – *Alexander Walker, London Evening Standard*

Bend of the River *

US 1952 91m Technicolor

U-I (Aaron Rosenberg)

GB title: *Where the River Bends*

1880 wagon trains arrive in Oregon, and the pioneers have trouble with the local bad man.

Good standard Western with pace and period feeling but not much plot sense.

w Borden Chase *novel Bend of the Snake* by William Gulick *d* Anthony Mann *ph* Irving Glassberg *m* Hans Salter *ad* Bernard Herzbrun, Nathan Juran *ed* Russell Schoengarth

☆ James Stewart, Arthur Kennedy, Rock Hudson, Julia Adams, Lori Nelson, Jay C. Flippen, Henry Morgan, Royal Dano, Stepin Fetchit

Beneath the Planet of the Apes *

US 1969 94m DeLuxe Panavision

TCF/APJAC (Mort Abrahams)

Astronauts on the ape planet discover that it is really Earth and that subterranean human mutants are nursing a live atom bomb.

Violence replaces the thoughtfulness of the original, but this is not at all a bad sequel as sequels go.

w Paul Dehn, Mort Abrahams *d* Ted Post *ph* Milton Krasner *m* Leonard Rosenman

☆ James Franciscus, Charlton Heston, Linda Harrison, Kim Hunter, Maurice Evans, Paul Richards, Victor Buono, Jeff Corey, James Gregory, Thomas Gomez

† See *Planet of the Apes*.

Beneath the Twelve Mile Reef

US 1953 102m Technicolor Cinemascope

TCF (Robert Bassler)

Jealousy, tragedy and romance among the Florida sponge fishers.

Fox's early Cinemascope production involved much underwater shooting, a trick octopus, and predictable plot devices.

w A. I. Bezzerides *d* Robert D. Webb *ph* Edward Cronjager *m* Bernard Herrmann

☆ Robert Wagner, Terry Moore, Gilbert Roland, Peter Graves, J. Carrol Naish, Richard Boone, Angela Clarke, Jay Novello

'The dead weight of a melodramatic script overtaxes the gallant attempts at conviction.' – *MFB*

Edward Cronjager

Benefit of the Doubt

US/Germany 1993 91m DeLuxe

Warner/Benefit/Cine Vox/Monument (Michael Spielberg, Brad M. Gilbert)

Out on parole after more than 20 years in prison for the murder of his wife, a man goes to live near his daughter, persuading her that he is innocent of the crime.

A dull thriller that warms over familar plot devices to little purpose.

w Jeffrey Polman, Christopher Keyser *story* Michael Lieber *d* Jonathan Heap *ph* Johnny E. Jensen *m* Hummie Mann *pd* Marina Kieser *ed* Sharyn L. Ross

☆ Donald Sutherland, Amy Irving, Rider Strong, Christopher McDonald, Graham Greene, Theodore Bikel, Gisela Kovach, Ferdinand Mayne

'The result is pretty silly and demeaning.' – *Derek Malcolm, Guardian*

Bengal Brigade

US 1954 87m Technicolor

U-I (Ted Richmond)

GB title: *Bengal Rifles*

In 19th-century India, an officer is cashiered through false evidence, and becomes an undercover man with the wicked local rajah.

Routine Hollywood heroics with a few unintended laughs.

w Richard Alan Simmons *novel Bengal Tiger* by Hall Hunter *d* Laslo Benedek *ph* Maury Gertsman *m* Hans Salter

☆ Rock Hudson, Arlene Dahl, Dan O'Herlihy, Ursula Thiess, Torin Thatcher, Michael Ansara, Arnold Moss

Bengal Rifles: see *Bengal Brigade*

Benjamin, or The Diary of an Innocent Young Man

France 1966 104m Eastmancolor

Paramount/Parc/Marianne (Mag Bodard)

In the 18th century, a 17-year-old orphan is taken in hand by his wealthy aunt and initiated into the mysteries of sex.

Imitation Tom Jones *(qv), quite good to look at but rather boring.*

w Nina Companeez *d* Michel Déville *ph* Ghislain Cloquet

☆ Pierre Clémenti, Michèle Morgan, Catherine Deneuve, Michel Piccoli, Francine Bergé, Anna Gaël, Odile Versois

'Heavy with Gallic naughtiness rather than airy charm ... a plethora of colourful costumes, foliage and fireworks.' – *MFB*

'A marathon tease ... an unending series of interrupted coitions ... a gorgeously wrapped and beribboned Christmas package containing an empty box.' – *John Simon*

Benji *

US 1974 86m CFI color

Mulberry Square (Joe Camp)

A stray mongrel dog saves two kidnapped children.

Family film par excellence which rang the box-office bell in a big way in the US. Its modest merits are rather beside the point.

wd Joe Camp *ph* Don Reddy *m* Euel Box

☆ Peter Breck, Edgar Buchanan, Terry Carter, Christopher Connelly

† A sequel, *For the Love of Benji* (qv), followed in 1977. In 1980 came the curious *Oh Heavenly Dog* (qv). Then in 1987 the same team presented a quirky movie of a different kind: *Benji the Hunted* (qv).

song 'I Feel Love' (*m* Euel Box, *ly* Betty Box)

Benji the Hunted

US 1987 88m CFI color

Mulberry Square/Embark/Buena Vista (Ben Vaughn)

A mongrel dog is shipwrecked and fosters a pack of cougar cubs.

Freaky fable about a dog with a high IQ; but the training is remarkable.

wd Joe Camp *ph* Don Reddy *m* Euel Box, Betty Box *sp* Bryan L. Renfro, Frank and Juanita Inn (Benji's trainers)

☆ Benji, Frank Inn (trainer), Red Steagall

'Benny's breaking up his sister Joon's romance. Isn't that what big brothers are for?'

'A romance on the brink of reality.'

Benny and Joon

US 1993 99m DeLuxe

MGM (Susan Arnold, Donna Roth)

A mentally disturbed painter falls for a fey mime, to the displeasure of her uptight brother.

A romantic comedy about mental illness, by turns whimsical and sentimental and never less than saccharine.

w Barry Berman, Leslie McNeil *d* Jeremiah Chechik *ph* John Schwartzman *m* Rachel Portman *pd* Neil Spisak *ed* Carol Littleton

☆ Johnny Depp, Mary Stuart Masterson, Aidan Quinn, Julianne Moore, Oliver Platt, C. C. H. Pounder, Dan Hedaya, Joe Grifasi

'Embarrassingly, relentlessly cute.' – *Observer*

The Benny Goodman Story *

US 1955 117m Technicolor

U-I (Aaron Rosenberg)

A clarinettist from the Jewish section of Chicago becomes internationally famous.

Sentimental biopic of a familiar figure which comes to life when the sound track is given its head (and the real Goodman's clarinet).

wd Valentine Davies *ph* William Daniels *md* Joseph Gershenson

☆ *Steve Allen*, Donna Reed, *Berta Gersten*, Herbert Anderson, Robert F. Simon, Sammy Davis Snr, Harry James, Martha Tilton, Gene Krupa

'The customary fictional liberties appear to have been taken.' – *MFB*

Benny's Video *

Austria/Switzerland 1992 105m colour

ICA/Wega/Bernard Lang

A bored, middle-class, video-obsessed teenager picks up a girl at a video-rental store, takes her home and kills her on camera.

A low-budget movie of alienation that creates unease and questions the role of video violence in society.

wd Michael Haneke *ph* Christian Berger *pd* Christoph Kanter *ed* Marie Homolkova

☆ Arno Frisch, Angela Winkler, Ulrich Mühe, Ingrid Stassner

'Neatly states its case against the anesthetizing properties of too much violent imagery too soon. Urban terror story plays like an icy thriller, but the message runs deeper, lending an intellectual edge.' – *Variety*

† The director has said that the film is a statement 'about the American sensational cinema and its power to rob viewers of their ability to form their own opinions'.

Bent

GB/US/Japan 1996 116m colour

Film Four/NDF/Ask Kodansha/Channel 4/Nippon (Michael Solinger, Dixie Linder)

A homosexual man, sent to a German concentration camp, forms an intense relationship with another prisoner.

A briefly controversial play of the 70s, in which love flourished under appalling conditions, transfers to the screen and just lies there.

w Martin Sherman *play* Martin Sherman *d* Sean Mathias *ph* Yorgos Arvanitis *m* Philip Glass *pd* Stephen Brimson Lewis *ed* Isabel Lorente

☆ Lothaire Bluteau, Clive Owen, Brian Webber, Ian McKellen, Mick Jagger, Nikolaj Waldau, Jude Law, Suzanne Bertish

'Makes all the right motions on screen. But it's hard to feel for its argument the way that people did in a theatre.' – *Alexander Walker, London Evening Standard*

Benvenuta *

Belgium 1983 106m Eastmancolor

Artificial Eye/La Nouvelle Imageries/UGC/Europe 1/FR3/Opera Film (Jean-Claude Batz)

A screenwriter meets a reclusive novelist to write a treatment of her once-famous semi-autobiographical book.

Constantly shifting between fiction and reality, between appearance and fantasy, it soon wears out its welcome.

wd André Delvaux *novel La Confession Anonyme* by Suzanne Lilar *ph* Charlie Van Damme *m* Frédérick Devreese *ad* Claude Pignot *ed* Jean Goudier

☆ Fanny Ardant, Vittorio Gassman, Françoise Fabian, Mathieu Carrière, Claire Wauthion, Philippe Geluck

'Unleash your dark side.'

Beowulf

US 1998 89m DeLuxe

Threshold/European/Kushner-Locke/Capitol (Lawrence Kasanoff)

In some neo-Gothic future, a warrior fights a monster that is killing the inhabitants of a beseiged border castle.

Banal, boring and risible 'B' sword-and-sorcery movie, set in an unimaginable and unimagined period, which is heavily indebted to spaghetti westerns and comicbook simplicities; it has only the vaguest connection to the Anglo-Saxon poem from which it takes its title.

w Mark Leahy, David Chappe *d* Graham Baker *ph* Christopher Faloona *m* Ben Watkins *pd* Jonathan Carlson *ed* Roy Watts

☆ Christopher Lambert (Beowulf), Rhona Mitra (Kyra), Oliver Cotton (Hrothgar), Götz Otto (Roland), Charlie Robinson (Weapons Master), Layla Roberts (Grendel's Mother), Vincent Hammond (Grendel), Roger Sloman (Karl), Brent Jefferson Lowe (Will), Robert Willcox (Chief Officer)

Bequest to the Nation *

GB 1973 116m Technicolor

Universal/Hal B. Wallis

US title: *The Nelson Affair*

The story of Nelson's long affair with the tempestuous Lady Hamilton.

Undistinguished historical drama from a thin play which despite hard work all round makes very ordinary

screen entertainment. Glenda Jackson's performance is way over the top.
w Terence Rattigan *play* Terence Rattigan *d* James Cellan Jones *ph* Gerry Fisher *m* Michel Legrand *pd* Carmen Dillon
☆ Peter Finch, Glenda Jackson, Michael Jayston, Anthony Quayle, Margaret Leighton, Dominic Guard, Nigel Stock, Roland Culver
'As empty as an out-of-town matinee.' – *MFB*

Berkeley Square **
US 1933 87m bw
Fox (Jesse L. Lasky)
A London house reincarnates its owner as his 18th-century ancestor.
Romantic fantasy on a time lapse theme, the first of many and perhaps the most stylish and self-assured.
w Sonya Levien, John Balderston *play* John Balderston *d* Frank Lloyd *ph* Ernest Palmer *m* Louis de Francesco *ad* William Darling
☆ Leslie Howard, Heather Angel, Valerie Taylor, Irene Browne, Beryl Mercer, Colin Keith-Johnston, Alan Mowbray
'Too far above the heads of ordinary theatergoers and too British in tempo and execution to break any box office records.' – *Variety*
† Remade as *The House in the Square* (qv).
Leslie Howard

Berlin Correspondent
US 1942 70m bw
TCF (Bryan Foy)
In pre-war Germany an American reporter is kidnapped by the Nazis and replaced by a double…
Preposterous melodrama, so silly as to be often quite funny.
w Steve Fisher, Jack Andrews *d* Eugene Forde *ph* Virgil Miller *md* Emil Newman
☆ Dana Andrews, Virginia Gilmore, Mona Maris, Martin Kosleck, Sig Rumann, Kurt Katch, Torben Meyer

Berlin, die Symphonie einer Grosstadt: see *Berlin, Symphony of a Great City*

Berlin Express *
US 1948 87m bw
RKO (Bert Granet)
Police of four nations guard a German VIP on a crack train to Berlin.
Rather muddled suspenser with attempts at political moralizing; the cast provides some good moments.
w Harold Medford *story* Curt Siodmak *d* Jacques Tourneur *ph* Lucien Ballard *m* Frederick Hollander
☆ Merle Oberon, Robert Ryan, Charles Korvin, Paul Lukas, Robert Coote

Berlin, Symphony of a Great City ***
Germany 1927 78m bw silent
Fox-Europa
original title: *Berlin, die Symphonie einer Grosstadt*
An impression of the life of a city from dawn to midnight, expressed by cinematic montages, angles, sequences, etc, and set to music.
*A leader in the field of 'impressionistic' documentaries which are now so familiar (*Rien que les Heures *did a similar job for Paris at around the same time), this still has moments of poetry which have seldom been equalled.*
w Walter Ruttman, Karl Freund, Carl Mayer d Walter Ruttman ph Reimar Kuntze, Robert Baberske, Laszlo Schäffer m Edmund Meisel *ed* Walter Ruttman

Berliner Ballade *
Germany 1948 77m bw
Comedia Film (Alf Teichs)
aka: *The Ballad of Berlin*
Otto Nobody, an unwilling soldier, returns home to find himself at the mercy of bureaucrats and black marketeers.
Melancholy satire presented as a series of sketches, almost a forerunner of That Was the Week That Was.
w Gunter Neumann *d* Robert Stemmle *ph* Georg Krause *m/ly* Gunter Neumann, Werner Eisbrenner
☆ *Gert Fröbe*, Anton Zeithammer, Tatjana Sais, O. E. Hasse
'Very much the film of a defeated people.' – *Penelope Houston*

Bernadette
France 1988 105m colour
Cannon/Films de L'Etoile D'Or/Bernadette Association International (Jacques Quintard)
A peasant girl sees visions of the Virgin Mary at Lourdes and invokes the hostility of the authorities.
Ponderously reverent treatment of a saintly girl, providing no more than moments of piety.
w Jean Delannoy, Robert Arnaut *d* Jean Delannoy *ph* Jean-Bertrand Penzer *m* Francis Lai *ad* Alain Paroutaud *ed* Annick Charvein
☆ Sydney Penney, Jean-Marc Bory, Michèle Simonnet, Roland Lesaffre, Bernard Dhéran, François Dalout, Stephan Garcin

Bernardine *
US 1957 95m Eastmancolor Cinemascope
TCF (Samuel G. Engel)
A college student forced to swot for exams asks a friend's elder brother to look after his girl.
Henry Aldrich-style high school comedy, showing the lighter side of Rebel without a Cause *(qv). Notable for the clean-living hero played by a clean-living singing star, and the reappearance of Janet Gaynor for the only time since 1939, in a routine mother role.*
w Theodore Reeves *play* Mary Chase *d* Henry Levin *ph* Paul Vogel *m* Lionel Newman
☆ *Pat Boone*, Richard Sargent, Terry Moore, *Janet Gaynor*, Walter Abel, Dean Jagger, Natalie Schafer, James Drury

Berry Gordy's The Last Dragon: see *The Last Dragon*

Berserk!
GB 1967 96m Technicolor
Columbia (Herman Cohen)
A lady circus owner revels in the publicity brought about by a series of murders.
Grisly and unattractive thriller with an ageing star in a series of unsuitably abbreviated costumes; the script is beyond redemption.
w Herman Cohen, Aben Kandel *d* Jim O'Connolly *ph* Desmond Dickinson *m* Patrick John Scott
☆ *Joan Crawford*, Diana Dors, Ty Hardin, Judy Geeson, Michael Gough, Robert Hardy, Geoffrey Keen, Sydney Tafler, Philip Madoc

Bert Rigby, You're a Fool
USA 1989 94m Metrocolor
Warner/Lorimar/A Clear Production (George Shapiro)
A former miner becomes a mostly unsuccessful song-and-dance man in Hollywood.
Dim comedy, intended as a showcase for the slight charm of Robert Lindsay.
wd Carl Reiner *ph* Jan de Bont *m* Ralph Burns *pd* Terence Marsh *ad* Dianne Wager, Michael Seirton *ed* Bud Molin, Stephen Myers
☆ Robert Lindsay, Anne Bancroft, Corbin Bernsen, Robbie Coltrane, Cathryn Bradshaw, Jackie Gayle, Bruno Kirby, Liz Smith, Lila Kaye
'Mixes sentimentality with vulgarity and reckless abandon.' – *John Pym, MFB*

Berth Marks
US 1929 20m bw silent
Hal Roach
Stan and Ollie, on a train, have to share an upper berth.
Overstretched single-situation comedy, one of the team's poorest.
w Leo McCarey, H. M. Walker *d* Lewis R. Foster
☆ Stan Laurel, Oliver Hardy

Die Berührte: see *No Mercy No Future*

Besieged
Italy 1998 94m Technicolor
Fiction/Navert/Mediaset (Massimo Cortesi)
In Rome, a British pianist falls in love with his African maid and agrees to help her husband, who is being held as a political prisoner.
Turgid drama of obsessive love that fails to engage emotionally or intellectually.
w Clare Peploe, Bernardo Bertolucci *story* James Lasdun *d* Bernardo Bertolucci *ph* Fabio Cianchetti *m* Alessio Vlad *pd* Gianni Silvestri *ed* Jacopo Quadri
☆ Thandie Newton, David Thewlis, Claudio Santamaria
'A dull, simple-minded, almost deliberately clumsy affair.' – *Philip French, Observer*

The Bespoke Overcoat **
GB 1956 33m bw
Romulus (Jack Clayton)
A clerk in a clothing warehouse is refused a coat and asks a tailor friend to make him one. But he dies of cold and his ghost persuades the tailor to steal the coat he deserved.
The story seems stiff, but the production has a rich Dickensian feel and may be the best short drama filmed in Britain.
w Wolf Mankowitz *story* Gogol *d Jack Clayton ph Wolfgang Suschitzky* *m* Georges Auric
☆ *Alfie Bass, David Kossoff*
'A triumph of talent, small means and originality.' – *New Statesman*
best short

Best
GB/Ireland 2000 106m Metrocolor bw/Technicolor
Optimum/IAC/Sky/IoMFC/Smoke & Mirrors/Pembridge (Mary McGuckian, Chris Roff, Elvira Bolz)
Biopic of the self-destructive Manchester United footballer of the 50s, the most gifted of his generation, who drank his talent away.
A narrative that sticks to the facts, following Best from his early days to his later incarnation as an after-dinner entertainer in the 90s, but offering very little insight into the man or his problems.
w John Lynch, Mary McGuckian *d* Mary McGuckian *ph* Witold Stok *m* Mark Stevens *pd* Max Gottlieb *ed* Kant Pan
☆ John Lynch (George Best), Ian Bannen (Matt Busby), Jerome Flynn (Bobby Charlton), Ian Hart (Nobby Stiles), Patsy Kensit (Anna), Cal MacAninch (Paddy Crerand), Linus Roache (Denis Law), Adrian Lester (Rocky), David Hayman (Tommy Docherty/barman), James Ellis (Dickie Best), Roger Daltrey (Rodney Marsh), Clive Anderson (Interviewer), Sophie Dahl (Eva Haraldsted), Stephen Fry (Frazer Crane)
'Simply the worst.' – *Variety*

Best Boy ***
US 1979 111m colour 16mm
Ira Wohl
A documentary, shot by his cousin, of the problems of a mentally retarded 53-year-old man whose elderly parents are ailing.
A film with very moving elements, though they would have been even sharper at half the length.
wd Ira Wohl
best documentary

Best Defense
US 1984 94m Movielab
Paramount (Gloria Katz)
A US tank goes hopelessly out of control in Kuwait; intercut with this are some of the problems which confronted its designer two years earlier.
Weird, unappetizing and disjointed farce, composed mainly of irrelevancies.
w Gloria Katz, Willard Huyck *novel Easy and Hard Ways Out* by Robert Grossbach *d* Willard Huyck *ph* Don Peterman *m* Patrick Williams *pd* Peter Jamison
☆ Dudley Moore, Eddie Murphy, Kate Capshaw, George Dzundza, Helen Shaver
'As bereft of charm and spontaneity as it is overburdened with tedious gesticulation.' – *Tim Pulleine, MFB*
'About as funny as getting hi-jacked by a group of kamikaze terrorists.' – *Derek Malcolm, Guardian*
'How did I get involved? The door opened, and four men came in carrying a cheque.' – *Eddie Murphy*

Best Foot Forward
US 1943 94m Technicolor
MGM (Arthur Freed)
A glamorous publicity-seeking film star accepts an invitation to a military college ball.
Old-fashioned formula musical based on a lightweight Broadway success.
w Irving Brecher, Fred Finklehoffe *play* John Cecil Holmes *d* Edward Buzzell *ph* Leonard Smith *m/ly* Hugh Martin, Ralph Blane *md* Lennie Hayton *ch* Charles Walters
☆ Lucille Ball, William Gaxton, Virginia Weidler, Harry James and his Orchestra, June Allyson, Gloria de Haven
† Lucille Ball's singing was dubbed by Martha Mears.

Best Friends *
US 1982 116m Technicolor
Warner/Joe Wizan/Norman Jewison
Two writers who have enjoyed a peaceful professional relationship find problems when they get married and visit their respective families.
Rather a heavy comedy which seems to have no real point, this gets by on enjoyable sequences and star performances.
w Valerie Curtin, Barry Levinson *d* Norman Jewison *ph* Jordan Cronenweth *m* Michel Legrand *ad* Joe Russo *ed* Don Zimmerman
☆ Burt Reynolds, Goldie Hawn, Jessica Tandy, Barnard Hughes, Audra Lindley, Keenan Wynn
'A print-out of a script conference at which everyone collapsed at everyone else's contributory sally.' – *Sunday Times*
song 'How Do You Keep the Music Playing?' (Michel Legrand, Alan and Marilyn Bergman)

The Best House in London *
GB 1968 96m Eastmancolor
MGM/Bridge/Carlo Ponti (Philip Breen, Kurt Unger)
A Victorian publicity agent tries to organize a government-sponsored brothel.
Cheerful slam-bang historical send-up with as many dull thuds of banality as pleasant witticisms.
w Denis Norden *d* Philip Saville *ph* Alex Thomson *m* Mischa Spoliansky *pd* Wilfrid Shingleton
☆ David Hemmings, George Sanders, Joanna Pettet, Warren Mitchell, Dany Robin, William Rushton

'Some pets deserve a little more respect than others.'
Best in Show **
US 2000 90m Technicolor
Warner/Castle Rock (Karen Murphy)
Contestants and their pets gather in Philadelphia to compete in a leading dog show.
Witty documentary-style comedy that derives its fun from its parade of ill-assorted, competitive couples and their obsessions.
w Christopher Guest, Eugene Levy *d* Christopher Guest *ph* Robert Schaefer *m* Jeffery CJ Vanston *pd* Joseph T. Garrity; *ed* Robert Leighton
☆ Bob Balaban (Dr Theodore W. Millbank III), Jennifer Coolidge (Sherri Ann Ward Cabot), Christopher Guest (Harlan Pepper), John Michael Higgins (Scott Donlan), Michael Hitchcock (Hamilton Swan), Eugene Levy (Gerry Fleck), Jane Lynch (Christy Cummings), Michael McKean (Stefan Vanderhoof), Catherine O'Hara (Cookie Fleck), Parker Posey (Meg Swan), Fred Willard (Buck Laughlin), Patrick Cranshaw (Leslie Cabot), Don Lake (Graham Chissolm), Jim Piddick (Trevor Beckwith), Ed Begley Jnr (Hotel Manager)
'Consistently just plain funny and sometimes ascends to a kind of crazed genius.' – *Roger Ebert, Chicago Sun-Times*
'Essentially a well-organized, exquisitely nuanced skit comedy.' – *Stephen Holden, New York Times*

The Best Intentions ***
Sweden 1992 181m colour
Artificial Eye/STV1/ZDF/Channel 4/RAIDU/La Sept/DR/YLE 2/NRK/RUV (Lars Bjälkeskog)
original title: *Den Goda Viljan*
In Sweden in the early 1900s, a priest overcomes parental objections to marry a nurse, but their union is a troubled one.
A sharply observed, fascinating semi-biographical account by a son of the early years of his parents' marriage, ending just before his birth.
w Ingmar Bergman *d* Bille August *ph* Jörgen Persson *m* Stefan Nilsson *pd* Anna Asp *ed* Janus Billeskov Jansen
☆ Samuel Fröler, *Pernilla August*, Max von Sydow, Ghita Norby, Lennart Hjulström, Mona Malm, Lena Endre, Keve Hjelm
'The picture is uniformly well acted, has a wonderful feeling for the distinct Scandinavian seasons, and re-creates social occasions with an acute moral edge.' – *Philip French, Observer*

'Ingmar Bergman may have officially retired from film direction, but his genius marches on.' – *Geoff Brown, The Times*

† At the 1992 Cannes Film Festival, the film won the Palme D'Or for best film and Pernilla August the award for best actress.

Best Laid Plans *

US 1999 93m Technicolor

TCF/Fox 2000/Dogstar (Alan Greenspan, Betsy Beers, Chris Moore, Sean Bailey)

Robberies go wrong for a man trying to raise money to escape his dreary life and pay off a local hoodlum.

Quirky thriller that begins well but ends with a whimper, never exploring the increasingly unlikely motivations needed to keep the narrative moving.

w Ted Griffin *d* Mike Barker *ph* Ben Seresin *m* Craig Armstrong *pd* Sophie Becher *ed* Sloane Klevin

☆ Alessandro Nivola, Reese Witherspoon, Josh Brolin, Rocky Carroll, Michael G. Hagerty, Terence Howard, Jimmy Marsh, Gene Wolande

'Fundamentally, it's a small pleasure rather than a fully-blown triumph.' – *Peter Bradshaw, Guardian*

The Best Little Whorehouse in Texas

US 1982 114m Technicolor Panavision

Universal/RKO (Thomas L. Miller, Edward K. Milkis, Robert L. Boyett)

A long-established Texas whorehouse becomes the object of a clean-up campaign.

Flat and feeble screen version of a limp and tuneless musical which astonishingly was a Broadway hit, perhaps because people thought it was naughty. Onscreen the acting is too easy-going and the script too coy for anybody to have a good time.

w Larry L. King, Peter Masterson *play* Larry L. King, Peter Masterson *d* Colin Higgins *ph* William A. Fraker *m* Patrick Williams *m/ly* Carol Hall *pd* Robert F. Boyle

☆ Burt Reynolds, Dolly Parton, Charles Durning, Dom DeLuise, Jim Nabors, Robert Mandan, Lois Nettleton, Noah Beery Jnr

'Rancid, self-deceiving, hypocritical stuff.' – *Observer*

'A sanitized, coyly predictable piece of brothel creeping, set to musak by a poorly programmed computer.' – *Guardian*

'Almost everything about it is misjudged.' – *Daily Mail*

'High on jollity, low on country and western, and very uncertainly directed.' – *Sight and Sound*

'Never gets beyond the concept stage.' – *Roger Ebert*

Charles Durning

The Best Man ***

US 1964 104m bw

UA/Stuart Millar, Lawrence Turman

Two contenders for a presidential nomination seek the support of the dying ex-president.

Brilliant political melodrama, ingeniously adapted on a low budget from an incisive play, with splendid dramatic scenes, memorable performances and good convention detail.

w Gore Vidal play Gore Vidal *d Franklin Schaffner ph* Haskell Wexler *m* Mort Lindsey

☆ *Henry Fonda*, Cliff Robertson, Lee Tracy, Margaret Leighton, Edie Adams, Kevin McCarthy, *Shelley Berman*, Ann Sothern, Gene Raymond, Mahalia Jackson

'A fine opportunity to watch pros at work in a hard-hitting and cogent drama that seems to become more topical and have more relevance with each showing.' – *Judith Crist*

'Some of the wittiest lines since *Strangelove* ... the acting fairly crackled with authenticity.' – *Isabel Quigly*

'You are left gasping at its sheer professionalism.' – *Evening News*

Lee Tracy

The Best Man

US 1999 120m DeLuxe

Universal/40 Acres and a Mule Filmworks (Spike Lee, Sam Kitt, Bill Carraro)

An author nearly wrecks his friend's forthcoming marriage by writing a semi-autobiographical novel that suggests he had an affair with the bride-to-be.

Bland romantic comedy among the upwardly mobile, in which women come off as second best to the men.

wd Malcolm D. Lee *ph* Frank Prinzi *m* Stanley Clarke *pd* Kalina Ivanov *ed* Kara Silverman

☆ Taye Diggs (Harper), Nia Long (Jordan), Morris Chestnut (Lance), Harold Perrineau (Murch), Terrence Howard (Quentin), Sanaa Lathan (Robin), Monica Calhoun (Mia), Melissa De Sousa (Shelby), Victoria Dillard (Anita)

'This smooth, glossy, enjoyable film showcases an impressive new authorial voice.' – *Emanuel Levy, Variety*

'A really horrible film, at once boorish and sentimental, and riddled with smug and repulsive misogyny.' – *Peter Bradshaw, Guardian*

Best Men *

US/GB 1997 89m DeLuxe Panavision

Film Four/Orion/Rank (Brad Krevoy, Steve Stabler, Brad Jenkel, Deborah Ridpath)

When a bank robbery on the way to a wedding goes wrong, five friends are trapped with their hostage inside a bank, surrounded by the police and FBI.

Talky confessional thriller, in which everyone blames society for their particular failings; despite its sometimes desperate contrivances, it has a slight charm.

w Art Edler Brown, Tracy Fraim *d* Tamra Davis *ph* James Glennon *m* Mark Mothersbaugh *pd* Tony Corbett *ed* Paul Trejo

☆ Dean Cain, Andy Dick, Sean Patrick Flanery, Mitchell Whitfield, Luke Wilson, Fred Ward, Raymond J. Barry, Drew Barrymore, Brad Dourif

'It's the sheer *joie de vivre* and good timing that enables this tragi-comedy about a group of misfits to succeed.' – *Nina Caplan, Sight and Sound*

The Best of Enemies

US/Italy 1961 104m colour Technirama

Columbia/Dino de Laurentiis

During the Abyssinian campaign of 1941, an Italian and a British officer learn mutual respect.

Mild satirical comedy drama with a few points to make about war; the elements blend rather obviously and dispiritingly.

w Jack Pulman *d* Guy Hamilton *ph Giuseppe Rotunno m* Nino Rota

☆ David Niven, Alberto Sordi, Michael Wilding, Amedeo Nazzari, Harry Andrews, David Opatoshu, Kenneth Fortescue, Duncan Macrae

The Best of Everything *

US 1959 121m DeLuxe Cinemascope

TCF (Jerry Wald)

Personal problems of a New York publisher's female staff.

Slick novelette on the lines of a naughty Peg's Paper; pure Hollywood gossamer.

w Edith Sommer, Mann Rubin *novel* Rona Jaffe *d* Jean Negulesco *ph* William C. Mellor *m* Alfred Newman

☆ Hope Lange, Stephen Boyd, Joan Crawford, Louis Jourdan, Suzy Parker, Martha Hyer, Diane Baker, Brian Aherne, Robert Evans, Brett Halsey, Donald Harron

'A cautionary tale sensationally told.' – *Alexander Walker*

title song (*m*Alfred Newman, *ly*Sammy Cahn)

Best of the Badmen *

US 1951 84m Technicolor

RKO (Herman Schlom)

At the end of the Civil War Jeff Clanton organizes the break-up of Quantrell's Raiders, but is himself arrested on a trumped-up charge and needs the Raiders' help.

Standard Western notable for a good cast and for bringing in a remarkable number of historical outlaws, doing rather unhistorical things.

w Robert Hardy Andrews, John Twist *d* William D. Russell *ph* Edward Cronjager *m* Paul Sawtell

☆ Robert Ryan, Claire Trevor, Jack Buetel, Robert Preston, Walter Brennan, Bruce Cabot, John Archer, Lawrence Tierney

'Apart, They're Tough. Together, They're Awesome.'

Best of the Best

US 1989 97m CFI color

Entertainment/Best of the Best/Kuys (Phillip Rhee, Peter E. Strauss)

An American Tae-kwon-do team prepares to compete against the Korean champions.

Plodding, sentimental and over-familiar variation on The Karate Kid *and* Rocky *(qqv).*

w Paul Levine *story* Phillip Rhee, Paul Levine *d* Bob Radler *ph* Doug Ryna *pd* Kim Rees *ed* William Hoy

☆ Eric Roberts, James Earl Jones, Sally Kirkland, John P. Ryan, John Dye, David Agresta, Tom Everett, Louise Fletcher, Simon Rhee

Best of the Best II

US 1992 100m DeLuxe

Entertainment/Picture Securities (Peter E. Strauss, Phillip Rhee)

Members of the US karate team avenge a friend's death at the hands of a ruthless champion who wants them killed.

The stock plot of virtually every martial arts movie is wheeled out yet again, together with the obligatory violence and the chest-thumping moral that might is right; it is no more convincing this time around.

w Max Strom, John Allen Nelson *d* Robert Radler *ph* Fred Tammes *m* David Michael Frank *pd* Gary Frutkoff *ed* Bert Lovitt

☆ Eric Roberts, Phillip Rhee, Edan Gross, Ralph Moeller, Christopher Penn, Sonny Landham, Wayne Newton, Meg Foster

'Film looks and plays like a drive-in picture of 20 years ago, only less fun.' – *Variety*

The Best of Times

US 1985 104m Technicolor

Universal/Kings Road (Gordon Carroll)

A small-town loser determines to have one more shot at the big time.

Curious, almost plotless comedy drama with nothing to draw the punters.

w Ron Shelton *d* Roger Spottiswoode *ph* Charles F. Wheeler *m* Arthur B. Rubinstein *ad* Anthony Brockliss *ed* Garth Craven

☆ Robin Williams, Kurt Russell, Pamela Reed, Holly Palance, Donald Moffat, M. Emmet Walsh

'Required magic is in too short supply and box office returns should be also.' – *Variety*

The Best Pair of Legs in the Business *

GB 1972 97m Technicolor

Sunny (Andrew Mitchell, Johnny Goodman)

An ageing comedian, reduced to working at a caravan holiday camp, is forced to face up to his own inadequacies and his wife's adultery.

A sad story of a seedy, miserable comic that provides Varney with an opportunity to display some acting skill, but which overstays its welcome.

w Kevin Laffan *d* Christopher Hodson *ph* Jimmy Allen *m* Harry Robinson *ad* Robert Jones *ed* Richard Best

☆ Reg Varney, Diana Coupland, Lee Montague, Jean Harvey, Johnny Briggs, Geoffrey Chater, Michael Hadley, Clare Kelly, Jane Seymour

Best Revenge

Canada 1983 94m colour

John Watson, Pen Densham (Michael M. Lebowitz)

Two American friends become involved in a drug deal in Morocco that goes wrong.

A dull thriller that never commands attention, thanks to an ill-constructed script and uninspired direction.

w David Rothberg, Rick Rosenthal, Logan N. Danforth *d* John Trent *ph* John Coquillon *m* Keith Emerson *pd* William Beeton *ed* James Symons

☆ John Heard, Levon Helm, Alberta Watson, Stephen McHattie, Moses Znaimer, John Rhys-Davies, Benjamin Gordon

Best Seller *

US 1987 110m CFI color

Orion/Hemdale (Carter de Haven)

A former hit-man helps an ex-cop write a book based on an old unsolved case.

Tortuous but generally lively and interesting melodrama which at least tries to be different.

w Larry Cohen *d* John Flynn *ph* Fred Murphy *m* Jay Ferguson *pd* Gene Rudolf *ed* David Rosenbloom

☆ James Woods, Brian Dennehy, Victoria Tennant, Allison Balson, Paul Shenar, George Coe

Best Shot: see *Hoosiers*

The Best Things in Life Are Free *

US 1956 103m Eastmancolor Cinemascope

TCF (Henry Ephron)

From Broadway to Hollywood in the twenties, the story of songwriting team de Sylva, Brown and Henderson.

Gangsters, movie studios and the writing of 'Sonny Boy' for Al Jolson all figure in this amiable musical which spends more time on jokes than romance; the numbers are disappointing despite good tunes.

w William Bowers, Phoebe Ephron *d* Michael Curtiz *ph* Leon Shamroy *md* Lionel Newman

☆ Ernest Borgnine, Gordon MacRae, Dan Dailey, Sheree North, Jacques d'Amboise, Norman Brooks, Murvyn Vye

Lionel Newman

'Three wonderful loves in the best picture of the year!'

The Best Years of Our Lives ****

US 1946 182m bw

Samuel Goldwyn

Three men come home from war to a small middle-American community, and find it variously difficult to pick up where they left off.

The situations and even some of the characters now seem a little obvious, but this was a superb example of high-quality film-making in the forties, with smiles and tears cunningly spaced, and a film which said what was needed on a vital subject.

w Robert Sherwood novel Glory for Me by Mackinlay Kantor *d William Wyler ph Gregg Toland m* Hugo Friedhofer *ed* Daniel Mandell

☆ Fredric March, Myrna Loy, Teresa Wright, Dana Andrews, Virginia Mayo, Cathy O'Donnell, *Hoagy Carmichael, Harold Russell*, Gladys George, Roman Bohnen, Ray Collins

'One of the best pictures of our lives!' – *Variety*

'The result is a work of provocative and moving insistence and beauty.' – *Howard Barnes*

'One recognizes everything and in the end this recognition is all the excitement, for what is on the screen becomes finally as accustomed and undramatic as the shabby decor of the theatre itself.' – *Robert Warshow, The Immediate Experience*

'One of the very few American studio-made movies in years that seem to me profoundly pleasing, moving and encouraging.' – *James Agee*

'Easily the best film from Hollywood on the warrior's return.' – *Sunday Graphic*

† In 1977 came a TV remake *Returning Home* but it did not lead to the expected series.

†† Harold Russell was a handless veteran, with no training as an actor, whose only film this was until Inside Moves in 1980.

picture; Robert Sherwood; William Wyler; Hugo Friedhofer; Fredric March; Harold Russell; Daniel Mandell

picture

La Bête Humaine **

France 1938 99m bw

Paris Films (Robert Hakim)

aka: *The Human Beast*

aka: *Judas Was a Woman*

A psychopathic train driver falls for a married woman, plans with her to kill her husband, but finally strangles her instead.

Curious melodrama with strong visual sequences, flawed by its ambivalent attitude to its hero-villain.

wd Jean Renoir novel Emile Zola *ph Curt Courant m Joseph Kosma*

☆ Jean Gabin, Simone Simon, Julien Carette, Fernand Ledoux, Jean Renoir

'French production at its best.' – *Variety*

'Marvellous atmosphere and a fine cast, but the material turns oppressive.' – *New Yorker, 1978*

'What is most deft is the way Renoir works the depot and the man's job into every scene – conversations on platforms, in washrooms and canteens, views from the station master's window over the steaming metal waste: the short sharp lust worked out in a wooden platelayer's shed among shunted trucks under the steaming rain.' – *Graham Greene*

† Remade in Hollywood as *Human Desire* (qv).

Betrayal *
GB 1982 95m colour
Horizon/Sam Spiegel (Eric Rattray)
The story of a publisher, his wife and her lover is told in scenes that go backwards in time.
Sharply acted stuff very typical of its author, for audiences with wideawake minds; but more theatrical than cinematic.
w Harold Pinter *play* Harold Pinter *d* David Jones *ph* Mike Fash *m* Dominic Muldowney
☆ Jeremy Irons, Ben Kingsley, Patricia Hodge, Avril Elgar
'Occasionally I pined for a little zest – perhaps a nude lesbian chariot race on ice.' – *Quentin Crisp*
screenplay adaptation

Betrayal from the East
US 1945 83m bw
RKO (Herman Schlom)
Japanese out to sabotage the Panama Canal are thwarted by a carnival showman.
Extravagant but penny-pinching flagwaver.
w Kenneth Gamet, Aubrey Wisberg *novel* Alan Hynd *d* William Berke *ph* Russell Metty *m* Roy Webb
☆ Lee Tracy, Nancy Kelly, Richard Loo, Abner Biberman, Regis Toomey, Philip Ahn, Addison Richards, Sen Yung, Drew Pearson

Betrayed: see *When Strangers Marry (1944) (1944)*

Betrayed
US 1954 108m Eastmancolor
MGM (Gottfried Reinhardt)
In 1943 a Dutch intelligence officer works with a resistance leader who turns out to be a traitor.
Slow-moving, studio-set romantic melodrama of the old school; not very lively.
w Ronald Millar, George Froeschel *d* Gottfried Reinhardt *ph* Frederick A. Young *m* Walter Goehr
☆ Clark Gable, Victor Mature, Lana Turner, Louis Calhern, O. E. Hasse, Wilfrid Hyde-White, Ian Carmichael, Niall MacGinnis, Nora Swinburne

Betrayed *
US 1988 128m Alpha/Astro
MGM/UA/Irwin Winkler (Joe Eszterhas)
Following the murder of a radio talk show hostess, a couple on the run find themselves in a web of political intrigue.
Heavygoing piece with Something to Say, but not much to watch.
w Joe Eszterhas *d* Costa-Gavras *ph* Patrick Blossier *m* Bill Conti *pd* Patrizia von Brandenstein
☆ Debra Winger, Tom Berenger, John Heard, Betsy Blair, John Mahoney

Betrogen bis zum Jungsten Tag: see *Duped Till Doomsday*

'The Harold Robbins people: what you dream, they do!'
The Betsy
US 1977 125m Technicolor
Allied Artists/Harold Robbins International (Robert R. Weston)
Jockeying for power in the boardroom and the family life of an aged car manufacturer.
Rather tame and obvious melodrama enlivened by its star performance.
w William Bast, Walter Bernstein *novel* Harold Robbins *d* Daniel Petrie *ph* Mario Tosi *m* John Barry
☆ *Laurence Olivier*, Robert Duvall, Tommy Lee Jones, Katharine Ross, Jane Alexander, Lesley-Anne Down, Joseph Wiseman, Edward Herrmann
'Almost compulsively dreadful.' – *Derek Malcolm, Guardian*

Betsy's Wedding *
US 1990 94m Technicolor
Warner/Touchstone/Silver Screen Partners IV (Martin Bregman, Louis A. Stroller)
A father gives his daughter a no-expense-spared wedding.
Intermittently amusing comedy of domestic mishaps.
wd Alan Alda *ph* Kelvin Pike *m* Bruce Broughton *pd* John Jay Moore *ed* Michael Polakow
☆ Alan Alda, Joey Bishop, Madeline Kahn, Anthony LaPaglia, Catherine O'Hara, Joe Pesci, Molly Ringwald, Ally Sheedy, Burt Young
'Surges ahead with tart one-liners, absurd spectacle, and ebullient side turns.' – *MFB*

Better Late Than Never
US 1983 87m colour
Warner (Jack Haley Jnr, David Niven Jnr)
From two possibilities, an heiress selects her true grandfather. (Her grandmother wasn't sure.)
Would-be risqué comedy which fails to spark despite the talents involved.
wd Bryan Forbes *m* Henry Mancini
☆ David Niven, Art Carney, Maggie Smith, Kimberley Partridge, Catherine Hicks, Lionel Jeffries
'As predictable as a rumbling stomach after a bowl of chilli.' – *Motion Picture Guide*

Better Off Dead
US 1985 98m Technicolor
Warner/A&M (Michael Jaffe)
When his fickle girlfriend leaves him, a lonely teenager becomes despondent, but the sun shines when another girl shows interest.
Plotless, almost legless comedy drama with no direction whatever.
wd Savage Steve Holland *ph* Isidore Mankovsky *m* Rupert Hine *pd* Herman Zimmerman
☆ John Cusack, David Ogden Stiers, Kim Darby, Demian Slade, Scooter Stevens, Diane Franklin
'Kids deserve better than this.' – *Variety*

The Better 'Ole
US 1926 97m (24 fps) bw silent
Warner
A British sergeant in Flanders proves that his major is actually a German spy.
Comedy-drama based on the cartoons of Old Bill by Bruce Bairnsfather. (The title comes from one in which Old Bill, in the trenches, is saying to a disgruntled soldier: 'If yer knows of a better 'ole, go to it.'). Criticism is irrelevant now, but the piece has historical interest.
w Charles Reisner, Darryl F. Zanuck *d* Charles Reisner *ph* Ed Du Par, Walter Robinson
☆ Syd Chaplin, Doris Hill, Harold Goodwin, Edgar Kennedy

A Better Tomorrow *
Hong Kong 1987 95m colour
Atlas/Cinema City/Film Workshop (Tsui Hark)
original title: *Yingxiong Bense*
Two gangsters fall on hard times when they attempt to go straight, and the younger brother of one, a naïve but ambitious cop, finds that he cannot get promotion because of their relationship.
Sentimental tale of male bonding and sibling relationships, intercut with action set-pieces and culminating in a violent dockside shoot-out.
w Chan Hing Kai, Leung Suk Wah *d* John Woo *ph* Wong Wing Hang
☆ Chow Yun-Fat, Ti Lung, Leslie Cheung, Emily Chu
† The film was released on video in a dubbed and a wide-screen subtitled version.

A Better Tomorrow II
Hong Kong 1987 100m colour
Golden Princess/Cinema City (Tsui Hark)
Two brothers, one a cop and the other a convicted criminal, go undercover as rivals to expose a counterfeiting racket, while an American-based restaurateur seeks revenge on local protection racketeers and the gangsters who drove his friend mad.
An unconvincing and, for those who have not seen the original film, confusing action melodrama, particularly in its New York scenes, partly redeemed by the final half-hour of balletic violence. The subtitling uses somewhat erratic English.
wd John Woo (action director: Ching Siu Tung) *story* Tsui Hark *ph* Wong Wing Hang *m* Joseph Koo *ad* Andy Lee
☆ Chow Yun-Fat, Leslie Cheung, Dean Shek, Ti Lung, Emily Chu, Kwan San, Kent Tsang, Regina Kent
'The mesmerising shoot-out at the conclusion makes up for any shortcomings in the plot.' – *Sight and Sound*

'The Making of a Killer.'
A Better Tomorrow III *
Hong Kong 1989 107m colour
Golden Princess/Film Workshop (Tsui Hark)
In the confusion of the fall of Saigon, a Hong Kong mechanic takes revenge against the crime boss who was responsible for the death of his uncle and falls in love with the boss's gun-toting mistress.
A prequel to John Woo's original film, alternating violence and romance and with an over-the-top melodramatic finale combining both, done with a certain panache.
d Tsui Hark
☆ Chow Yun-Fat, Tony Leung, Anita Mui, Saburo Tokito

Betty Blue *
France 1986 120m Fujicolour
Gaumont/Constellation/Cargofilms (Claudie Ossard)
original title: *37.2 au matin*
A waitress indulges her animal attraction for an odd job man but discovers him to be a literary genius.
What virtues this film has are more in style than content, but most people will find it over the top anyway.
wd Jean-Jacques Beineix *novel* Philippe Dijan *ph* Jean-François Robin *m* Gabriel Yared *ed* Monique Prim
☆ Béatrice Dalle, Jean-Hugues Anglade, Consuelo de Haviland

Between Heaven and Hell
US 1956 94m Eastmancolor Cinemascope
TCF (David Weisbart)
After Pearl Harbor a young Southern landowner is called up and finds himself on active service with mixed racial types.
Vaguely anti-war, pro-understanding action thriller which ends up going through predictable heroics in a professional but not too sympathetic manner.
w Harry Brown *novel The Day the Century Ended* by Francis Gwaltney *d* Richard Fleischer *ph* Leo Tover *m* Hugo Friedhofer
☆ Robert Wagner, Buddy Ebsen, Broderick Crawford, Brad Dexter, Mark Damon, Robert Keith, Ken Clark, Skip Homeier, Harvey Lembeck
Hugo Friedhofer

Between Midnight and Dawn
US 1950 89m bw
Columbia (Hunt Stromberg)
Radio policemen track down a racketeer.
Competent, undistinguished programmer.
w Eugene Ling *d* Gordon Douglas *ph* George E. Diskant *m* George Duning
☆ Mark Stevens, Edmond O'Brien, Gale Storm, Donald Buka, Gale Robbins, Roland Winters

Between the Lines *
US 1977 101m TVC Color
Essential/Midwest Film Productions (Raphael Silver)
Workers on a Boston underground newspaper are worried by rumours of an impending sale.
Sharply observed but slackly structured slice of provincial life.
w Fred Barron *d* Joan Micklin Silver *ph* K. V. Sickle *pd* Stuart Wurtzel *ed* John Carter
☆ John Heard, Lindsay Crouse, Jeff Goldblum, Jill Eikenberry, Bruno Kirby, Stephen Collins, Michael J. Pollard

Between Two Women
US 1937 88m bw
MGM
Romance between doctor and nurse is interrupted by her alcoholic husband and his infatuation with a patient.
Incident-packed men-in-white melodrama.
w Carey Wilson *story* Erich von Stroheim *d* George B. Seitz
☆ Franchot Tone, Maureen O'Sullivan, Virginia Bruce, Edward Norris, Cliff Edwards, Janet Beecher
'Class B that almost grew up. Eternal triangle in a hospital; okay dualler for nabes.' – *Variety*
† Title later changed to *Surrounded by Women* to avoid confusion with a *Dr Kildare* episode.

Between Two Worlds *
US 1944 112m bw
Warner (Mark Hellinger)
A number of air-raid victims, and two lovers who have committed suicide, find themselves on a luxury ship en route to the next world.
Nice-looking but slow and turgid remake of Outward Bound *(qv), largely sunk in its own misery but redeemed by two performances.*
w Daniel Fuchs *play* Sutton Vane *d* Edward A. Blatt *ph* Carl Guthrie *m* Erich Wolfgang Korngold
☆ John Garfield, *Edmund Gwenn*, Eleanor Parker, Paul Henreid, *Sydney Greenstreet*, Sara Allgood, George Tobias, Faye Emerson, George Coulouris, Dennis King, Isobel Elsom
'For ferry service from a world so saturated with death, the ship seems strangely empty – a fact that was not obtrusive in a day when death was not intrusive.' – *James Agee*

Between Us Girls
US 1942 89m bw
Universal (Henry Koster, Phil Karlson)
A mother and daughter are both involved in romances which tend to cross.
Mild comedy, a disappointing bid for stardom for a disappointing young star.
w Myles Connolly, True Boardman *play Le Fruit Vert* by Regis Gignoux, Jacques Thery *d* Henry Koster *ph* Joseph Valentine *m* Frank Skinner
☆ Diana Barrymore, Kay Francis, Robert Cummings, John Boles, Scotty Beckett, Ethel Griffies

The Beverly Hillbillies
US 1993 93m DeLuxe
TCF (Ian Bryce, Penelope Spheeris)
A hillbilly family strikes oil and moves to live in a Beverly Hills mansion.
Based on the mouldering television sit-com, this is a wearisome concoction of old jokes about country folk trying to cope with city ways; its unsophisticated appeal is limited.
w Lawrence Konner, Mark Rosenthal, Jim Fisher, Jim Staahl *d* Penelope Spheeris *ph* Robert Brinkmann *m* Lalo Schifrin *pd* Peter Jamison *ed* Ross Albert
☆ Diedrich Bader, Dabney Coleman, Erika Eleniak, Cloris Leachman, Rob Schneider, Lea Thompson, Lily Tomlin, Jim Varney, Buddy Ebsen, Zsa Zsa Gabor, Dolly Parton
'Just as corny and stupid as the long-running series, pic version has been cleverly cast and shrewdly skewed to appeal jointly to original fans of the show and younger viewers only vaguely familiar with it.' – *Variety*
† The TV series ran from 1962 to 1971 and starred Buddy Ebsen in Jim Varney's role as Jed Clampett, Irene Ryan in Cloris Leachman's role as Granny, Donna Douglas in Erika Eleniak's role as the nubile Elly May, and Max Baer Jnr in Diedrich Bader's role of the dim Jethro. Created by Paul Henning, in its early years it was the most popular programme on American television, with a weekly audience of around 60 million.

Beverly Hills Brats
US 1989 91m Technicolor
Taurus (Terry Moore, Jerry Rivers)
The teenage son of wealthy, preoccupied parents decides to arrange his own kidnapping in order to remind them of his existence.
Tedious and unsubtle comedy, ploddingly directed and shrilly acted.
w Linda Silverthorn *story* Terry Moore, Jerry Rivers *d* Dimitri Sotirakis *ph* Harry Mathias *m* Barry Goldberg *pd* George Costello *ed* Jerry Frizell
☆ Burt Young, Martin Sheen, Terry Moore, Peter Billingsley, Natalie Schafer, Ramon Sheen, Cathy Podewell

Beverly Hills Cop ★★
US 1984 105m Technicolor
Paramount/Don Simpson/Jerry Bruckheimer
A Detroit cop races to Los Angeles to track down the killers of his best friend.
Filled with foul language and frenetic action, this rough-edged action comedy became one of the top box-office grossers of its year. So much for its year.
w Daniel Petrie Jnr *d* Martin Brest *ph* Bruce Surtees *m* Harold Faltermeyer *pd* Angelo Graham *ed* Billy Weber, Arthur O. Coburn
☆ Eddie Murphy, Judge Reinhold, Lisa Eilbacher, John Ashton, Ronny Cox, Steven Berkoff
'The film's only function is to provide Murphy with the opportunity to work a dozen or so variations on his familiar and oddly endearing routine.' – *Time*
† The role was originally tailored for Sylvester Stallone.
original screenplay

'Axel Foley Is Back. Back Where He Doesn't Belong.'
Beverly Hills Cop 2
US 1987 102m Technicolor Panavision
UIP/Paramount/Don Simpson-Jerry Bruckheimer/Eddie Murphy
A cop returns to Beverly Hills to solve a series of crimes.
Further helpings from the same bowl. In no respect is the second film an improvement on the first.
w Larry Ferguson, Warren Skaaren, David Giler, Dennis Klein *story* Eddie Murphy, Robert D. Wachs *d* Tony Scott *ph* Jeffrey L. Kimball *m* Harold Faltermeyer *pd* Ken Davis *ed* Billy Weber, Chris Lebenzon, Michael Tronick
☆ Eddie Murphy, Judge Reinhold, Jurgen Prochnow, Ronny Cox, Allen Garfield, Brigitte Nielsen, Dean Stockwell, Paul Guilfoyle
'A noisy, numbing, unimaginative, heartless remake ... all has gone sour and cold.' – *Daily Variety*

'In For The Ride Of His Life.'
Beverly Hills Cop 3
US 1994 104m DeLuxe
UIP/Paramount
A cop discovers that the head of security at a Los Angeles theme park is a murderer and counterfeiter.
The law of diminishing returns features yet again in this violent, noisy and predictable thriller that trades on past success but offers nothing for the future.
w Steven E. de Souza *d* John Landis *ph* Mac Ahlberg *m* Nile Rodgers *pd* Michael Seymour *ed* Dale Beldin
☆ Eddie Murphy, Judge Reinhold, Hector Elizondo, Timothy Carhart, Stephen McHattie, Theresa Randle, John Saxon, Alan Young, Bronson Pinchot
'A soulless, faceless, worthless dud.' – *Kim Newman, Empire*
song 'Shakedown' (*m* Harold Faltermeyer; Keith Forsey; *ly* Harold Faltermeyer; Keith Forsey; Bob Seger)

'Kung Fool!'
Beverly Hills Ninja
US 1997 88m Foto-Kem
TriStar/Motion Picture Corp (Brad Krevoy, Steve Stabler, Brad Jenkel)
A woman wanting a martial arts expert to track down her missing boyfriend gets an overweight incompetent instead.
Dim-witted, ponderously performed slapstick featuring a comedian of very limited appeal.
w Mark Feldberg, Mitch Klebenoff *d* Dennis Dugan *ph* Arthur Albert *m* George S. Clinton *pd* Ninkey Dalton *ed* Jeff Gourson
☆ Chris Farley (Haru), Nicolette Sheridan (Alison Page), Robin Shou (Gobei), Nathaniel Parker (Martin Tanley), Chris Rock (Joey), Soon-Tek Oh (Sensei)
'By no means a black belt in comedy or action choreography. Still, you have to give it high marks for tenacity and the ability to get the job done.' – *Leonard Klady, Variety*

Beware My Lovely
US 1952 77m bw
RKO/Filmmakers (Collier Young)
A handyman employed by a widow turns out to be a mental defective who imprisons and threatens to rape and murder her.
Dismal suspenser with a lot of screaming and running around but very little flair.
w Mel Dinelli *play* The Man by Mel Dinelli *d* Harry Horner *ph* George E. Diskant *m* Leith Stevens
☆ Ida Lupino, Robert Ryan, Taylor Holmes, Barbara Whiting
'Inept characterization and ludicrously repetitive situations will surely rank this among the silliest films of the year.' – *MFB*

Beware of Pity ★
GB 1946 106m bw
Two Cities (W. P. Lipscomb)
An officer courts a crippled girl out of pity. She finds out and kills herself.
Ambitious but rather artificial and dreary drama, a shade too pleased with its own literariness; performances straitjacketed by production.
w W. P. Lipscomb, Elizabeth Baron, Marguerite Steen *novel* Stefan Zweig *d* Maurice Elvey *ph* Derick Williams
☆ Lilli Palmer, Albert Lieven, Cedric Hardwicke, Gladys Cooper, Linden Travers, Ernest Thesiger, Emrys Jones

Beware Spooks!
US 1939 65m bw
Columbia (Robert Sparks)
A nervous policeman routs crooks operating from a fairground.
Standard star comedy with some funny moments.
w Richard Flournoy, Albert Duffy, Brian Marlow *d* Edward Sedgwick
☆ Joe E. Brown, Mary Carlisle, Clarence Kolb, Marc Lawrence, Don Beddoe

Beware! The Blob
US 1971 88m DeLuxe
Jack H. Harris
GB title: *Son of Blob*
A mysterious jelly from outer space consumes most of the population of a small town.
Spoofy sequel to one of the original space monster movies of the fifties. It's all too laboured to raise a thrill or a smile.
w Jack Woods, Anthony Harris *d* Larry Hagman *ph* Al Hamm *m* Mort Garson *sp* Tim Baar
☆ Robert Walker, Gwynne Gilford, Godfrey Cambridge, Richard Webb, Shelley Berman, Carol Lynley, Burgess Meredith, Gerrit Graham, Larry Hagman

Der Bewegte Man: see *The Most Desired Man*

Bewitched
US 1945 65m bw
MGM (Jerry Bresler)
A girl with twin personalities has her murderous element exorcized by a spiritualist.
Hilarious nonsense, ancestor of the Eve and Lizzie schizos of the fifties.
wd Arch Oboler *story* Alter Ego by Arch Oboler *ph* Charles Salerno Jnr *m* Bronislau Kaper
☆ Phyllis Thaxter, Edmund Gwenn, Addison Richards, Kathleen Lockhart
'Oboler manages the first persuasive imitations of stream of consciousness I know of in a movie. Much more often, he bores to desperation with the vulgarity and mere violence of his effects.' – *James Agee*

Beyond a Reasonable Doubt ★
US 1956 80m bw
RKO (Bert Friedlob)
A novelist is persuaded by a crusading newspaper proprietor to fake circumstantial evidence incriminating himself in a murder, thus proving the uselessness of such evidence.
Ingenious but rather cheerless and mechanical thriller. The actors extract what they can from a script intent on sleight of hand, but the distinguished director is at his most flatulent.
w Douglas Morrow *d* Fritz Lang *ph* William Snyder *m* Herschel Burke Gilbert
☆ Dana Andrews, Joan Fontaine, Sidney Blackmer, Philip Bourneuf, Shepperd Strudwick, Arthur Franz, Edward Binns

Beyond Bedlam
GB 1994 89m Technicolor
Feature Film/Metrodome (Paul Brooks)
A detective's murder investigations lead him to a psychiatrist experimenting with mind-altering drugs on a serial killer.
Convoluted and unengrossing thriller, lacking any credibility and relying on most of the stereotypes of this kind of fiction: aggressive cop, insane killer, glamorous psychiatrist.
w Rob Walker, Vadim Jean *novel* Harry Adam Knight *d* Vadim Jean *ph* Gavin Finney *m* David A. Hughes, John Murphy *pd* James Helps *ed* Liz Webber
☆ Craig Fairbrass, Elizabeth Hurley, Keith Allen, Anita Dobson, Craig Kelly, Jesse Birdsall, Georgina Hale
'A profound failure.' – *Sight and Sound*
'More than a bit of a mess, combining fantasy and reality in such a way that it is difficult to decide which is which.' – *Derek Malcolm, Guardian*

'An adventure which cowards quit early and weaklings never finish at all!'
Beyond Glory
US 1948 82m bw
Paramount (Robert Fellows)
The honour of a West Point cadet is vindicated.
Proficient but dramatically turgid vehicle for an absurdly over-age star.
w Jonathan Latimer, Charles Marquis Warren, William Wister Haines *d* John Farrow *ph* John F. Seitz *m* Victor Young
☆ Alan Ladd, Donna Reed, George Coulouris, George Macready, Audie Murphy

Beyond Mombasa
GB 1955 90m Technicolor
Columbia/Hemisphere (Adrian Worker)
In East Africa, an American avenges his brother's death at the hands of the Mau Mau (here called the Leopard Men and revealed to be run by a mad English missionary).
Tasteless and rather humdrum jungle adventure using real-life problems purely as a backdrop.
w Richard English, Gene Levitt *novel* Mark of the Leopard by James Eastwood *d* George Marshall *ph* Frederick A. Young *m* Humphrey Searle *ed* Ernest Walter
☆ Cornel Wilde, Donna Reed, Leo Genn, Ron Randell, Christopher Lee

'Truth has a witness...'
Beyond Rangoon ★★
US 1995 97m Technicolor Panavision
Columbia/Castle Rock (Barry Spikings, Eric Pleskow)
aka: *Rangoon*
In 1988, an American doctor visits Burma and becomes aware of the country's political situation, with a repressive dictatorship crushing any moves towards democracy.
An earnest and slightly uneasy attempt to combine a narrative of an innocent in peril with a polemic exposing an unlovely regime; it works better on the level of a suspense drama than as a political one.
w Alex Lasker, Bill Rubenstein *d* John Boorman *ph* John Seale *m* Hans Zimmer *pd* Anthony Pratt *ed* Ron Davis
☆ Patricia Arquette, Frances McDormand, Spalding Gray, U Aung Ko, Victor Slezak, Adelle Lutz
'A remarkably well-judged attempt to educate an audience's consciousness without altogether abandoning the function of entertainment.' – *Adam Mars-Jones*
'At the heart of *Beyond Rangoon* is an embarrassing contradiction. The heroine is presumably there to be the audience's representative. But since the focus is entirely on her naïveté, her struggle, her growth, the film effectively reduces the Burmese quagmire to a vacation from hell.' – *Entertainment Weekly*

Beyond Reasonable Doubt ★
New Zealand 1980 127m colour
Endeavour/Fay, Richwhite/Brierley/Bob Jones/BRD (John Barnett)
In 1970, a police inspector frames a farmer for the murder of a couple from a neighbouring farm.
Based on a true story, this intriguing and disturbing exposé of official corruption and suppression of evidence is given a somewhat stolid treatment.
w David Yallop *book* David Yallop *d* John Laing *ph* Alun Bollinger *m* Dave Fraser
☆ David Hemmings, John Hargreaves, Tony Barry, Martyn Sanderson, Grant Tilly, Diana Rowan, Ian Watkin, Terence Cooper, Bruno Lawrence

'The queen of the tropics finds a new jungle man!'
Beyond the Blue Horizon ★
US 1942 76m Technicolor
Paramount (Monta Bell)
An orphan white girl grows up on a tropical island with a chimpanzee and a swimming tiger; when rescued and her story doubted, she leads an expedition back to prove it.
The most tongue-in-cheek of the Lamour jungle extravaganzas, with plenty of simple fun.
w Frank Butler *d* Alfred Santell *ph* Charles Boyle *m* Victor Young
☆ Dorothy Lamour, Richard Denning, Jack Haley, Patricia Morison, Walter Abel, Helen Gilbert, Elizabeth Patterson

Beyond the Clouds ★★
France/Italy/Germany 1995 109m Eastmancolor
Artificial Eye/Sunshine/Cine B/France 3/Cecchi Gori/Road Movies (Stéphane Tchal Gadjieff, Arlette Danys, Philippe Carcassonne)
A film director imagines or remembers four stories involving partings between a man and a woman.
A slight but enjoyable postscript to Antonioni's career, with pared-down anecdotes of the disabling power of love.
w Wim Wenders, Michelangelo Antonioni, Tonino Guerra *stories* Quel Bowling sul Tevere by Michelangelo Antonioni *d* Michelangelo Antonioni, Wim Wenders *ph* Alfio Contini, Robby Müller *m* Lucio Dalla, Laurent Petitgang, Van Morrison, U2 *ad* Thierry Flamand *ed* Claudio di Mauro, Michelangelo Antonioni, Peter Przygodda, Luciano Segura
☆ Sophie Marceau, Vincent Perez, Irène Jacob, Marcello Mastroianni, Fanny Ardant, John Malkovich, Kim Rossi Stuart, Chiara Caselli, Jean Reno, Peter Weller, Jeanne Moreau, Ines Sastre
'Might be the most intimate, personal film Michelangelo Antonioni has ever made, but it may also be his least significant.' – *Deborah Young, Variety*

Beyond the Door: see *Devil within Her*

'A twelve o'clock girl in a nine o'clock town!'
'Nobody's as good as Bette when she's bad!'
Beyond the Forest
US 1949 96m bw
Warner (Henry Blanke)
The discontented wife of a small-town doctor has an affair with a wealthy Chicagoan, murders a witness, attempts suicide, and dies of fever.
The star caricatures herself in this overblown melodrama which marked the unhappy end of her association with the studio. The rest of the cast suffer more dumbly from the script's unintentional hilarities.
w Lenore Coffee *novel* Stuart Engstrand *d* King Vidor *ph* Robert Burks *m* Max Steiner
☆ Bette Davis (Rosa Moline), Joseph Cotten (Dr Lewis Moline), David Brian (Neil Latimer), Minor Watson, Dona Drake, Regis Toomey
ROSA: 'What a dump!'
ROSA: 'If I don't get out of here, I'll just die! Living here is like waiting for the funeral to begin.'
'This peerless piece of camp.' – *New Yorker, 1978*
'Miss Davis makes a regrettably melodramatic mess of what is undoubtedly one of the most unfortunate stories she has ever tackled.' – *Newsweek*
Max Steiner

Beyond the Gates: see *Au delà des Grilles*

Beyond the Limit: see *The Honorary Consul*

Beyond the Poseidon Adventure
US 1979 114m Technicolor Panavision
Warner/Irwin Allen

When rescuers reach the topsy-turvy passenger liner, one of them is intent on plunder.
Dreary alternative ending to The Poseidon Adventure *(qv), with cardboard character studies, cut-price action, and tenth-rate technicalities.*
w Nelson Gidding *d* Irwin Allen *ph* Joseph Biroc *m* Jerry Fielding *pd* Preston Ames
☆ Michael Caine, Telly Savalas, Karl Malden, Sally Field, Peter Boyle, Jack Warden, Shirley Knight, Shirley Jones, Slim Pickens

Beyond the River: see *The Bottom of the Bottle*

Beyond the Stars
US 1989 94m TVC Color
Five Star Entertainment (Joseph Perez)

aka: *Personal Choice*
A mixed-up adolescent, determined to walk on the moon, strikes up a friendship with a former astronaut who has become a reclusive alcoholic after a strange incident on his last mission.
Meandering and sentimental account of a youth's coming of age, overweighted with messages about the environment.
wd David Saperstein *ph* John Bartley *m* Geoff Levin, Chris Many *pd* John J. Moore *ed* Frank Irvine, Stanley Warnow, Judith Blume
☆ Martin Sheen, Christian Slater, Robert Foxworth, Sharon Stone, Olivia d'Abo, F. Murray Abraham

'Trapped! ... in the incredible cosmic world that moves 100 years beyond time!'
'Adam and Eve of the year 2024! Only they could repopulate the world!'

Beyond the Time Barrier
US 1959 75m bw
AIP/Pacific International/Miller-Consolidated (Robert Clarke)

A test pilot crosses the fifth dimension and finds himself in 2024 when civilization has gone underground to avoid nuclear contamination.
Crude science fiction, roughly on the level of Flash Gordon *but less entertaining.*
w Arthur C. Pierce *d* Edgar G. Ulmer *ph* Meredith Nicholson *m* Darrell Calker
☆ Robert Clarke, Darlene Tompkins, Arianne Arden, Vladimir Sokoloff, Stephen Bekassy

Beyond the Universe
US 1981 90m colour/bw
Gold Key
A hundred years after a nuclear holocaust, a scientist trying to save a dying Earth uncovers a plot to exterminate all the sick and elderly.
Earnest, deadly dull ecological fable. Fortunately the entire cast is sucked into a black hole; unfortunately, they survive.
w uncredited *d* Robert Emenegger *ph* José Luis Mignone *ad* Michael Scheffe *ed* Brian Varaday
☆ David Ladd, Jacqueline Ray, Christopher Cary, John Dewey-Carter, Frank A. Miller, Stephanie Faulkner, Henry Darrow

Beyond the Valley of the Dolls
US 1970 109m DeLuxe Panavision
TCF (Russ Meyer)

Three girls in Hollywood enjoy the wilder reaches of show biz high life.
The skinflick director's first film for a major studio, with positively no connection with Valley of the Dolls, *is not explicitly pornographic but pussyfoots around with as many general excesses as can be crammed into two hours. If taken as high camp it provides a laugh or two, but is chiefly notable as marking a major studio's deepest dip into muddy waters.*
w Roger Ebert *d* Russ Meyer *ph* Fred J. Koenekamp *m* Stu Phillips, William Loose
☆ Dolly Read, Cynthia Myers, Marcia McBroom, John La Zar, Michael Blodgett, Edy Williams
'If one can resist walking out, the last half hour is quite manic.' – *MFB*
'A film whose total, idiotic, monstrous badness raises it to the pitch of near-irresistible entertainment.' – *Alexander Walker*
'Awful, stupid and preposterous ... also weirdly funny and a real curio, rather like a Grandma Moses illustration for a work by the Marquis de Sade.' – *John Simon*

Beyond Therapy
US 1986 93m colour
Entertainment/Sandcastle 5/New World (Steven M. Haft)
Psychiatrists become personally involved in the hang-ups of young New Yorkers.
Unfunny film version of a play which may have had something.
w Robert Altman, Christopher Durang *play* Christopher Durang *d* Robert Altman *ph* Pierre Mignot *m* Gabriel Yared *pd* Stephen Altman *ed* Jennifer Agué
☆ Glenda Jackson, Tom Conti, Julie Hagerty, Jeff Goldblum, Christopher Guest, Genevieve Page

Beyond This Place *
GB 1959 90m bw
Renown/Georgefield (Maxwell Setton, John R. Sloan)
US title: *Web of Evidence*
An American visiting London finds his supposedly dead father in prison serving a life sentence for murder; he delves into history and finds the real culprit.
Spiritless murder mystery with less serious intent than the original novel; tolerable entertainment.
w Kenneth Taylor *novel* A. J. Cronin *d* Jack Cardiff *ph* Wilkie Cooper *m* Douglas Gamley *ad* Ken Adam
☆ Van Johnson, Vera Miles, Bernard Lee, Emlyn Williams, Jean Kent, Moultrie Kelsall, Leo McKern, Ralph Truman

Beyond Tomorrow
US 1940 84m bw
RKO

Two elderly ghosts return at Christmas to help young lovers.
An amiably modest example of the kind they don't do any more.
w Adele Commandini *story* Mildred Cram *d* Edward Sutherland
☆ Richard Carlson, Jean Parker, C. Aubrey Smith, Charles Winninger

Bez Konca: see *No End*

Bez Svidetelei: see *A Private Conversation*

Bezhin Lug: see *Bezhin Meadow*

Bezhin Meadow **
USSR 1937 31m bw
Mosfilm

original title: *Bezhin Lug*
Fragments from an incomplete Eisenstein film are held together by freeze frames.
Even this collection of bits and pieces shows the power of the master.
w Alexander Rozhdestvenski *story* Ivan Turgenev *d* Sergei Eisenstein *ph* Edouard Tissé
☆ Vitya Kartashov, Boris Zakhava, Igor Pavlenko
† The film was reconstructed in 1966.

Bezness **
Tunisia/France 1992 100m colour
CTF/Flach/TMP/Canal (Ahmed Baha Eddine Attia, Jean-François Lepetit)
A young Tunisian offering sexual and other services to tourists is torn between Islamic and Western ways of life and confused by his own double standards.
Absorbing account of cultural conflict, of exploitation and corruption told through the interlocking lives of a gigolo, the girl he wishes to marry, and a French photographer.
wd Nouri Bouzid *ph* Alain Levent *m* Anouar Braham *ad* Khaled Joulak *ed* Kahena Attia
☆ Abdel Kechiche, Jacques Penot, Ghalia Lacroix, Ahmed Ragoubi

'A Day To Set Yourself Free!'

Bhaji on the Beach *
GB 1993 101m colour
First Independent/Umbi/Channel 4 (Nadine Marsh-Edwards)

A group of Asian women living in Birmingham go on a day trip to the seaside at Blackpool.
An enjoyable slice of life, covering not only racism and culture clashes, but the generational differences between the young and the old women as well as problems of gender.
w Meera Syal *d* Gurinder Chadha *ph* John Kenway *m* Craig Pruess, John Altman, Kuljit Bhamra *pd* Derek Brown *ed* Oral Norrie Otley
☆ Kim Vithana, Jimmi Harkishin, Sarita Khajuria, Mo Sesay, Lalita Ahmed, Shaheen Khan, Zohra Segal, Amer Chadha-Patel, Nisha Nayar
'As a look at the Afro-Asian community in Britain, it's everything one could ask for: funny and serious at the same time, good-tempered but not afraid of giving offence.' – *Alexander Walker*

Bhowani Junction *
GB 1956 110m Eastmancolor
Cinemascope
MGM (Pandro S. Berman)

Adventures of an Anglo-Indian girl during the last years of British India.
Disappointingly anaemic semi-epic from a gutsy novel, variably handled by all concerned.
w Sonya Levien, Ivan Moffat *novel* John Masters *d* George Cukor *ph* Frederick A. Young *m* Miklos Rozsa
☆ Ava Gardner, Stewart Granger, *Francis Matthews*, Bill Travers, Abraham Sofaer, Marne Maitland, Peter Illing, Freda Jackson, Edward Chapman
'An unwieldy, flatly-conceived charade.' – *MFB*
'One may believe with Henry Ford that history is bunk; if so, be assured that the labour pains of India are not half as much bunk as the romance of Victoria Jones, daughter of a Hindu lady, and a Welsh engine driver.' – *Alexander Walker*

Bian Zhou Bian Chang: see *Life on a String*

The Bible *
US/Italy 1966 174m DeLuxe Dimension 150 (70mm)
TCF/Dino de Laurentiis (Luigi Luraschi)

Through the Old Testament from Adam to Isaac.
A portentous creation with whispered commentary gives way to a dull misty Eden with decorous nudes, a sprightly Noah's Ark, a spectacular Babel, a brooding Sodom and a turgid Abraham. The pace is killingly slow and the script has little religious sense, but the pictures are often pretty.
w Christopher Fry and others *d* John Huston *ph* *Giuseppe Rotunno* *m* Toshiro Mayuzumi *ad* Mario Chiari
☆ Michael Parks (Adam), Ulla Bergryd (Eve), Richard Harris (Cain), *John Huston* (Noah), Stephen Boyd (Nimrod), George C. Scott (Abraham), Ava Gardner (Sarah), Peter O'Toole (the three angels)
'An Old Testament spectacular like any other.' – *David Robinson*
'At a time when religion needs all the help it can get, John Huston may have set its cause back a couple of thousand years.' – *Rex Reed*
Toshiro Mayuzumi

'One robot's 200 year journey to become an ordinary man.'

Bicentennial Man
US 1999 140m Technicolor
Buena Vista/Columbia/Touchstone/1492/Radiant (Wolfgang Petersen, Gail Katz, Neal Miller, Laurence Mark, Chris Columbus, Mark Radcliffe, Michael Barnathan)

A domestic android gradually achieves his ambition to become fully human
This is a movie that covers a span of 200 years in which nothing very interesting happens, although the time does provide scope for one of Williams's more simpering performances.
w Nicholas Kazan *story* Isaac Asimov *novel* *The Positronic Man* by Isaac Asimov, Robert Silverberg *d* Chris Columbus *ph* Phil Meheux *m* James Horner *pd* Norman Reynolds *ed* Neil Travis
☆ Robin Williams (Andrew), Sam Neill (Sir), Wendy Crewson (Ma'am), Embeth Davidtz (Little Miss/Portia), Oliver Platt (Rupert Burns), Hallie Kate Eisenberg (Little Miss), Stephen Root (Dennis Mansky), Lynne Thigpen (Female President), Bradley Whitford (Lloyd), Kiersten Warren (Galatea Robotic/Human)
'Perhaps, one day, there will be robot film reviewers. And if they beg not to be sent to Robin Williams movies, we'll know they are developing human feelings.' – *Edward Porter, Sunday Times*
'An ambitious tale handled in a dawdling, sentimental way.' – *Todd McCarthy, Variety*
make-up (Greg Cannom)

Les Biches **
France/Italy 1968 99m Eastmancolor
La Boétie/Alexandra (André Génovès)

aka: *The Does*
Two lesbians form an uneasy *ménage à trois* with a young architect, who loves both of them.
Fascinating and well-detailed character study with more depth than at first appears.
w *Paul Gégauff*, *Claude Chabrol* *d* *Claude Chabrol* *ph* *Jean Rabier* *m* Pierre Jansen
☆ *Stéphane Audran*, Jacqueline Sassard, Jean-Louis Trintignant
'You can almost see tubes attached to the heels of all the characters, through which the meaning has been sucked out of them and Chabrol pumped in.' – *John Simon*

Bicycle Thieves ***
Italy 1948 90m bw
PDS-ENIC (Umberto Scarparelli)

original title: *Ladri di Biciclette*
US title: *Bicycle Thief*
An Italian workman, long unemployed, is robbed of the bicycle he needs for his new job, and he and his small son search Rome for it.
The epitome of Italian neo-realism, the slight human drama is developed so that it has all the force of King Lear, and both the acting and the backgrounds are vividly compelling.
w *Cesare Zavattini* *d* *Vittorio de Sica* *ph* Carlo Montuori *m* Alessandro Cicognini
☆ *Lamberto Maggiorani*, *Enzo Staiola*
'A film of rare humanity and sensibility.' – *Gavin Lambert*
'A memorable work of art with the true flavour of reality. To see it is an experience worth having.' – *Richard Mallett, Punch*
'My idea is to de-romanticize the cinema.' – *Vittorio de Sica*
foreign film
Cesare Zavattini
picture

Les Bicyclettes de Belsize *
GB 1969 29m Eastmancolor
Delmore/Ullustria (Jacques de Lane Lea)
The way to true love for a Hampstead shop owner is found through his bicycle.
Mildly attractive whimsy, obviously patterned after Les Parapluies de Cherbourg *but not quite hitting the spot.*
w Michael Newling *d* Douglas Hickox *ph* Wolfgang Suschitzky *m/ly* Les Reed, Barry Mason
☆ Anthony May, Judy Huxtable

Il Bidone **
Italy/France 1955 109m bw
Titanus/SGC

aka: *The Swindlers*
A group of petty swindlers fails to move into the higher criminal bracket.
Sharply observed but rather sentimental melodrama with tragic pretensions.
w Federico Fellini, Ennio Flaiano, Tullio Pinelli *d* *Federico Fellini* *ph* Otello Martelli *m* Nino Rota *ad* Dario Cecchi *cos* Dario Cecchi
☆ *Broderick Crawford* (Augusto), Richard Basehart (Picasso), Franco Fabrizi (Roberto), Giulietta Masina (Iris), Sue Ellen Blake (Crippled girl)

Big **
US 1988 102m DuArt/DeLuxe
TCF (James L. Brooks, Robert Greenhut)

A 13-year-old boy has his wish to grow 'big' granted by a carnival wishing machine.
Magic fun, better done than it has been since Turnabout *(qv) in 1940.*
w Gary Ross, Anne Spielberg *d* *Penny Marshall* *ph* Barry Sonnenfeld *m* Howard Shore *pd* Santo Loquasto
☆ *Tom Hanks*, Elizabeth Perkins, John Heard, Jared Rushton, Robert Loggia, David Moscow
Tom Hanks; best original screenplay

The Big and the Bad (dubbed)
Italy/France/Spain 1971 84m Technicolor
MGM-EMI/Sancrosiap-Terzafilm/Jacques Roitfeld/Atlantida (Alfonso Sansone, Enrico Chroscicki)
original title: *Si Può Fare ... Amigo*
A gunfighter hunts for the man who seduced his sister so that he can force him to marry her before he kills him.
Comic, slapstick spaghetti Western, with heavy-handed jokes.
w Rafael Azcona *story* Ernesto Gastaldi *d* Maurizio Lucidi *ph* Aldo Tonti *m* Luis Enriquez Bacalov *ad* Eduardo Torre della Fuentes *ed* Renzo Lucidi
☆ Jack Palance, Bud Spencer (Carlo Pedersoli), Francisco Rabal, Renato Cestiè, Dany Saval

'Men, money and moonshine ... when it comes to vice, Mama knows best!'
Big Bad Mama
US 1974 85m Metrocolor
Santa Cruz (Roger Corman)
In 1932 Texas, a desirable widow becomes a bank robber.
Fast moving, violent nonsense, like a caricature of Bonnie and Clyde *(qv), which was itself a caricature.*
w William Norton, Frances Doel *d* Steve Carver *ph* Bruce Logan *m* David Grisman
☆ Angie Dickinson, William Shatner, Tom Skerritt, Susan Sennett, Robbie Lee

Big Bad Mama II
US 1987 83m colour
Concorde (Roger Corman)
A mother and her daughters rob banks as a revenge for her husband's death.
A sequel that is more like a re-run of the original movie, and it is less interesting and stylish the second time around.
w R. J. Robertson, Jim Wynorski *d* Jim Wynorski *ad* Billie Breenbaum
☆ Angie Dickinson, Robert Culp, Danielle Brisebois, Julie McCullough, Jeff Yagher, Bruce Glover, Ebbe Roe Smith, Charles Cyphers

The Big Bang *
US 1989 81m colour
Kanter/Toback (Joseph H. Kanter)
A documentary in which people, from a nun to a gangster, a restaurant owner to a basketball player, are asked about the meaning of life.
Engaging conversational piece, cutting quickly from one person to another, that holds one's interest.
d James Toback *ad* Nicole C. Nicola *ed* Stephanie Kempf, Keith Robinson
☆ Emma Astner, Missy Boyd, Max Brockman, Darryl Dawkins, Eugene Fodor, Polly Frost, Veronica Geng, Julius Hemphill, Fred Hess, Elaine Kaufman, Sheila Kennedy, Anne Marie Keyes, Charles Lassiter, Marcia Oakley, Jack Richardson and also Don Simpson, Tony Sirico, José Torres, Barbara Traub

The Big Bang Theory *
US 1995 100m colour
Polygram/Renegade/Eagle Eye/Asylum (Daniel M. Bergers, Ladd Vance)
GB title: *Bang*
In Los Angeles, a young woman discovers the power a uniform and a gun give her when she takes them from a cop who tried to sexually assault her.
Offbeat, episodic, independent movie that deals sympathetically with the dispossessed, and treats with disdain those that abuse their authority.
wd Ash *ph* Dave Gasperik *pd* Daniel M. Berger *ed* Ash, Daniel M. Berger
☆ Darling Narita, Peter Greene, Everlast, Michael Arturo, James Sharpe, Luis Guizar
'A powerful sleeper, convincing, provocative and exciting – an adventure in "guerrilla filmmaking" that uses an unexpected story device to hold up a mirror to a big US city.' – *Roger Ebert, Chicago Sun-Times*

The Big Bankroll: see *King of the Roaring Twenties*

The Big Blockade *
GB 1941 73m bw
Ealing (Alberto Cavalcanti)
A semi-documentary showing the importance of blockading Germany in winning the war.
A curious all-star propaganda revue with some sketches more effective than others. It was Will Hay's only serious role.
w Charles Frend, Angus Macphail *d* Charles Frend *ph* Wilkie Cooper *m* Richard Addinsell
☆ Leslie Banks, Michael Redgrave, John Mills, Will Hay, Frank Cellier, Robert Morley, Alfred Drayton, Michael Rennie, Marius Goring, Bernard Miles
'Topical subject matter, graphic descriptive work, pungent commentary, thrilling spectacle, clever characterisation.' – *Kine Weekly*

The Big Blue
US 1988 119m Eastmancolor
Cinemascope
TCF (Patrice Ledoux)
Two competitive deep-sea divers combine to rescue a dolphin.
Bizarre, over-long fantasy, much of it filmed murkily underwater.
w Luc Besson, Robert Garland, Marilyn Goldin, Jacques Mayol, Marc Perrier *d* Luc Besson *ph* Carlo Varini, Luc Besson, Christian Petron *m* Eric Serra, Bill Conti *pd* Dan Weil *ed* Olivier Mauffroy
☆ Rosanna Arquette, Jean-Marc Barr, Jean Reno
'The director's future as a significant cinematic navigator looks, on this evidence, rather less than watertight.' – *Philip Strick, MFB*
† The film was cut by nine minutes for its US release. It was released on video in two versions, one running for the same length of time as the cinema release, and the other, a special edition, running for 168m.

The Big Boodle
US 1957 83m bw
UA/Monteflor (Lewis F. Blumberg)
GB title: *Night in Havana*
A croupier in a Havana gambling casino is suspected of knowing where counterfeited plates are hidden...
An undistinguished chase film with the star very tired and a long way from home.
w Jo Eisinger *novel* Robert Sylvester *d* Richard Wilson *ph* Lee Garmes *m* Raul Lavista
☆ Errol Flynn, Pedro Armendariz, Gia Scala, Rossana Rory

The Big Boss (dubbed) **
Hong Kong 1971 98m Eastmancolor
Dyaliscope
Cathay/Golden Harvest (Raymond Chow)
aka: *Fists of Fury*
A worker in an ice factory takes revenge on a gang of heroin smugglers led by his crooked and murderous boss.
Possibly Bruce Lee's best film; certainly it is the one that shows his skills to best advantage.
wd Lo Wei *ph* Chen Ching Cheh *m* Wang Fu Ling *ed* Fan Chia Kun
☆ Bruce Lee (Chen Chao-an), Maria Yi Yi (Lin Hau-mei), James Tien (Hsu Chien), Nora Miao (Prostitute)

The Big Bounce
US 1969 102m Technicolor Panavision
Warner/Greenway (William Dozier)
An ex-GI with a criminal record gets into sexual and criminal trouble while working at a Californian motel.
Unattractive melodrama with no discernible point, certainly not to entertain.
w Robert Dozier *novel* Elmore Leonard *d* Alex March *ph* Howard R. Schwartz *m* Michael Curb
☆ Ryan O'Neal, Leigh Taylor Young, Van Heflin, James Daly, Robert Webber, Lee Grant

Big Boy
US 1930 68m approx bw
Warner
A jockey wins a big race.
Star musical from a Broadway original; routine except that Jolson plays in blackface, then comes on as himself for the finale.
w William K. Wells, Perry Vekroff *d* Alan Crosland
☆ Al Jolson, Louise Closser Hale, Noah Beery
'Comedy entertaining in hoke way, but production inferior to previous Jolson pictures.' – *Variety*

The Big Brawl
US 1980 95m Technicolor Panavision
Warner Brothers/Golden Harvest (Raymond Chow)
The son of a Chinese restaurateur in Chicago outwits gangsters.
Silly but quite entertaining chopsocky melodrama laced with comedy.
wd Robert Clouse *ph* Robert Jessup *m* Lalo Schifrin
☆ Jackie Chan, José Ferrer, Kristine de Bell, Mako, David Sheiner

The Big Broadcast **
US 1932 78m bw
Paramount
A failing radio station is saved by an all-star show.
Revue-style show with a minimum of plot, valuable as archive material covering many stars of the time.
w George Marion Jnr *novel* Wild Waves by William Ford Manley *d* Frank Tuttle *ph* George Folsey
☆ Bing Crosby, Kate Smith, George Burns, Gracie Allen, Stuart Erwin, Leila Hyams, Cab Calloway, the Mills Brothers, the Boswell Sisters
'Flock of radio names ensures b.o. interest, especially in hinterland.' – *Variety*
♫ 'Please'; 'Here Lies Love'; 'Hot Toddy'; 'Where the Blue of the Night Meets the Gold of the Day'; 'Tiger Rag'; 'Crazy People'; 'It Was So Beautiful'; 'Kicking the Gong Around'

'A musical meteor of songs, comedy and romance!'
The Big Broadcast of 1936 *
US 1935 97m bw
Paramount (Ben Glazer)
The 'radio lover' of a small radio station is kidnapped by a man-hungry countess.
Zany comedy with interpolated variety acts and a totally Marxian climax.
w Walter de Leon, Francis Martin, Ralph Spence *d* Norman Taurog *ph* Leo Tover *ch* LeRoy Prinz
☆ Jack Oakie, George Burns, Gracie Allen, Henry Wadsworth, Wendy Barrie, Lyda Roberti, C. Henry Gordon, Benny Baker, Bing Crosby, Ethel Merman, Richard Tauber, Amos 'n Andy, Mary Boland, Charles Ruggles, Virginia Weidler and also Guy Standing, Gail Patrick, Bill Robinson, the Nicholas Brothers, the Vienna Boys Choir, Akim Tamiroff
'Names are in and out as fast and as often as a firefly's tail light.' – *Variety*
'It hasn't much story, but the lack won't bother.' – *Variety*
♫ 'Miss Brown to You'; 'Through the Doorway of Dreams'; 'Double Trouble'; 'Why Dream?'; 'Amargura'; 'I Wished on the Moon'; 'Crooner's Lullaby'; 'Why Stars Come Out at Night'
LeRoy Prinz

The Big Broadcast of 1937 **
US 1936 100m bw
Paramount (Lewis Gensler)
A radio station manager has trouble with his sponsors.
More recorded acts separated by a measure of plot.
w Erwin Gelsey, Arthur Kober, Barry Travers, Walter de Leon, Francis Martin *d* Mitchell Leisen *ph* Theodor Sparkuhl *songs* various
☆ Jack Benny, George Burns, Gracie Allen, Bob Burns, Martha Raye, Shirley Ross, Ray Milland, Benny Fields, Benny Goodman and his Orchestra, Leopold Stokowski and the Philadelphia Orchestra, Eleanore Whitney, Larry Adler, Louis da Pron
'It isn't a comedy and it isn't a musical, but it has a lot of laughs, the best in several types of music, and I don't know where in the world you will see anything like it.' – *Otis Ferguson*

The Big Broadcast of 1938 **
US 1937 90m bw
Paramount (Harlan Thompson)
A steamship owner engaged in a transatlantic race is hampered by his practical joking twin brother.
Glamorous, empty-headed all-star nonsense with the expected bevy of interpolated acts.
w Walter de Leon, Francis Martin, Ken Englund, Frederick Hazlitt Brennan *d* Mitchell Leisen *ph* Harry Fischbeck *m/ly* Ralph Rainger, Leo Robin
☆ W. C. Fields, Bob Hope, Martha Raye, Dorothy Lamour, Shirley Ross, Lynne Overman, Ben Blue, Leif Erickson, Kirsten Flagstad, Tito Guizar, Shep Fields and his Rippling Rhythm Orchestra
'Pictorially original and alluring, with the rejuvenated W. C. Fields at his inimitable best.' – *Variety*
♫ 'Thanks for the Memory'; 'Don't Tell a Secret to a Rose'; 'You Took the Words Right Out of My Heart'; 'Mama That Moon Is Here Again'; 'This Little Ripple Has Rhythm'; 'The Waltz Lives On'; 'Zuni Zuni'; 'Sawing a Woman in Half'
song 'Thanks for the Memory' (*m* Ralph Rainger, *ly* Leo Robin)

Big Brown Eyes
US 1936 76m bw
Paramount (Walter Wanger)
A private detective and his wisecracking girlfriend catch a jewel thief.
Minor league Thin Man *stuff, quite acceptably done.*
w Raoul Walsh, Bert Hanlon *d* Raoul Walsh *ph* George Clemens *m* Gerard Carbonara *md* Morris Stoloff
☆ Cary Grant, Joan Bennett, Walter Pidgeon, Lloyd Nolan, Alan Baxter, Marjorie Gateson, Isabel Jewell, Douglas Fowley
'A fast, well-directed and quite unsentimental gangster film, pleasantly free from emotion – for emotion on the screen is nearly always false emotion.' – *Graham Greene*

'A comedy for the kid in all of us.'
Big Bully
US 1996 93m colour
Warner/Morgan Creek (Lee Rich, Gary Foster)
A former schoolboy bully reverts to his old ways when, 25 years later, his victim returns to their old school as a teacher.
Raucous slapstick comedy of minimal interest.
w Mark Steven Johnson *d* Steve Miner *ph* Daryn Okada *m* David Newman *pd* Ian Thomas *ed* Marshall Harvey
☆ Rick Moranis, Tom Arnold, Julianne Phillips, Carol Kane, Jeffrey Tambor, Curtis Armstrong, Faith Prince, Tony Pierce, Don Knotts
'This moronic, half-arsed and desperately obvious comedy has about the same level of entertainment as toothache.' – *Empire*

The Big Bus
US 1976 88m Movielab Panavision
Paramount (Fred Freeman, Lawrence J. Cohen)
Misadventures of a giant atomic-powered bus on its first cross-country trip.
Rather feeble spoof on disaster pictures, with some good moments.
w Fred Freeman, Lawrence J. Cohen *d* James Frawley *ph* Harry Stradling Jnr *m* David Shire *pd* Joel Schiller
☆ Joseph Bologna, Stockard Channing, John Beck, René Auberjonois, Ned Beatty, Bob Dishy, José Ferrer, Ruth Gordon, Harold Gould, Larry Hagman, Sally Kellerman, Richard Mulligan, Lynn Redgrave
'It's all fast, bright, surface stuff, almost obsessively intent on never letting a laugh get away, misfiring, backfiring, skidding and crashing gears gaily all the way, often quite as thrilling, if not always as ludicrous, as some of the films it mocks.' – *Alan Brien, Sunday Times*
'It has been produced with such consummate bad taste, schlock acting and feeble attempts at verbal and visual humour that whatever laughs are engendered are at it rather than with it.' – *Dave Pomeroy, Film Information*

Big Business ****
US 1929 20m bw silent
Hal Roach
Stan and Ollie fail to sell a Christmas tree to a belligerent householder.
Classic silent comedy consisting largely of a brilliant tit-for-tat routine of reciprocal destruction, to which scripting, acting and editing equally combine.

w Leo McCarey, H. M. Walker *d* James W. Horne *ed* Richard Currier
☆ Stan Laurel, Oliver Hardy, James Finlayson

Big Business
US 1988 97m Metrocolor
Buena Vista/Touchstone/Silver Screen Partners III (Steve Tisch, Michael Peyser)
Big business complexities are made more so by the fact that the principals are discovered to have been exchanged at birth.
Loud-shouting farce which just about gets by on star value.
w Dori Pierson, Marc Rubel *d* Jim Abrahams *ph* Dean Cundey *m* Lee Holdridge
☆ Bette Midler, Lily Tomlin, Fred Ward, Edward Herrmann

The Big Carnival: see *Ace in the Hole*

The Big Cat
US 1949 75m Technicolor
Eagle-Lion
Feuding mountain families combine to track a marauding lion.
Standard outdoor melodrama, almost a straight version of Track of the Cat *(qv).*
w Morton Grant, Dorothy Yost *d* Phil Karlson
☆ Peggy Ann Garner, Lon McCallister, Preston Foster, Forrest Tucker, Skip Homeier, Sara Haden

'How much love, sex, fun and friendship can a person take?'
'In a cold world, you need your friends to keep you warm!'
The Big Chill **
US 1983 105m Metrocolor
Columbia/Carson Productions (Michael Shamberg)
University contemporaries try to comfort each other after the death of a friend.
Wry satirical comedy which seems to be nostalgic for the sixties, but is funny anyway.
w Lawrence Kasdan, Barbara Benedek d Lawrence Kasdan ph John Bailey *m* various *pd* Ida Random *ed* Carol Littleton
☆ Tom Berenger, Glenn Close, Jeff Goldblum, William Hurt, Kevin Kline, Mary Kay Place, Meg Tilly, JoBeth Williams, Don Galloway
'The final impression left is of a collage of small relishable moments.' – *Kim Newman, MFB*
'An entertainment in which humour and sentiment are finely balanced and profundities are artfully skirted.' – *Sight and Sound*
'A splendid technical exercise ... but there's no pay-off and it doesn't lead anywhere.' – *Roger Ebert*
♔ best picture; Glenn Close; screenplay

The Big Circus *
US 1959 109m Technicolor Cinemascope
AA (Irwin Allen)
A bankrupt circus owner tries to get his show back on the road despite the murderous schemes of his ex-partners.
Fast-paced melodrama which makes little sense but generally provides the expected thrills.
w Irwin Allen, Charles Bennett, Irving Wallace *d* Joseph Newman *ph* Winton C. Hoch *m* Paul Sawtell, Bert Shefter
☆ Victor Mature, Red Buttons, Rhonda Fleming, Kathryn Grant, Vincent Price, Peter Lorre, *Gilbert Roland*, David Nelson, Adele Mara, Steve Allen

The Big City *
US 1937 80m bw
MGM (Norman Krasna)
An honest cab driver and his wife hold out against corruption.
Sentimental realism of the type expected of its director. Smooth and syrupy.
w Dore Schary, Hugo Butler *d* Frank Borzage *ph* Joseph Ruttenberg *m* William Axt
☆ Spencer Tracy, Luise Rainer, Charley Grapewin, Janet Beecher, Irving Bacon, William Demarest, Eddie Quillan
'Domesticity and tenderness are heavily laid on: people in this film are *too* happy before disaster: no one is as happy as all that, no one so little prepared for what life is bound to do sooner or later.' – *Graham Greene*

Big City
US 1948 103m bw
MGM (Joe Pasternak)
In New York's East Side, a little girl is the adopted daughter of three bachelors, but trouble looms when they all get ideas of romance.
Latter-day star vehicle for which the young star is really too old and all else is excessively sentimental and sprawling.
w Whitfield Cook, Anne Chapin *d* Norman Taurog *ph* Robert Surtees
☆ Margaret O'Brien, Robert Preston, Danny Thomas, George Murphy, Karin Booth, Jackie Butch Jenkins, Betty Garrett, Lotte Lehmann, Edward Arnold
† Margaret O'Brien's singing was dubbed by Marni Nixon.

The Big City **
India 1963 131m bw
R. D. Bansal
original title: *Mahanagar*
A poverty-stricken Calcutta bank accountant sends his wife out to work; then the bank crashes, and she becomes the sole breadwinner.
Immensely detailed, overlong, but mainly fascinating account of modern urban India and its attitudes.
wd Satyajit Ray novel Narendra Nath Mitra *ph* Subrata Mitra *m* Satyajit Ray
☆ Madhabi Mukherjee, Anil Chatterjee, Haren Chatterjee, Haradhan Banerjee

Big City Blues
US 1932 65m bw
Warner
A country boy gets into trouble on his first trip to New York.
Predictable comedy drama which seems to have no point other than the obvious one.
w Ward Morehouse, Lillie Hayward *d* Mervyn Le Roy
☆ Joan Blondell, Eric Linden, Inez Courtney, Evalyn Knapp, Guy Kibbee, Walter Catlett, Humphrey Bogart, Ned Sparks

'The strangest and most savage manhunt in history!'
The Big Clock *
US 1947 95m bw
Paramount (John Farrow)
A publishing magnate murders his mistress and assigns one of his editors to solve the crime.
Slick but rather empty thriller with judicious use of adequate talent.
w Jonathan Latimer *novel* Kenneth Fearing *d* John Farrow *ph* John Seitz *m* Victor Young
☆ Charles Laughton, Ray Milland, Maureen O'Sullivan, Rita Johnson, Elsa Lanchester
† Remade as *No Way Out* (1987) (qv).

The Big Combo *
US 1955 80m bw
Allied Artists/Security-Theodora (Sidney Harmon)
The police crush a crime syndicate.
An otherwise uninspired thriller memorable for starting the new violence, with some ugly scenes of torture which suffered at the time from the censor.
w Philip Yordan *d* Joseph H. Lewis *ph* John Alton *m* David Raksin
☆ Cornel Wilde, Richard Conte, Jean Wallace, Brian Donlevy, Robert Middleton, Lee Van Cleef, Ted de Corsia, Helen Walker, John Hoyt

The Big Country ***
US 1958 165m Technicolor Technirama
UA/Anthony/Worldwide (William Wyler, Gregory Peck)
The Terrills and the Hannesseys feud over water rights, and peace is brought about only with the deaths of the family heads.
Big-scale Western with a few pretensions to say something about the Cold War. All very fluent, star-laden and easy to watch.
w James R. Webb, Sy Bartlett, Robert Wilder *novel* Donald Hamilton *d William Wyler ph Franz Planer m Jerome Moross*
☆ *Gregory Peck*, Jean Simmons, Charlton Heston, Carroll Baker, *Burl Ives, Charles Bickford*, Alfonso Bedoya, Chuck Connors
'Has, in fact, most of the elements one asks for in the Western. Especially it has a feeling of size and space ... Yet something, I think, is missing: the romantic heart.' – *Dilys Powell*
♛ Burl Ives
♔ Jerome Moross

'Once you adopt a kid, you've got to keep him.'
Big Daddy
US 1999 93m Technicolor
Columbia/Out of the Blue (Sid Ganis, Jack Giarraputo)
A thirties-something playboy adopts a five-year-old in the hope of impressing his girlfriend.
Sandler's familiar persona of a dim but charming manchild wears ever thinner here, in a heavy-handed, predictable and sentimental comedy.
w Steve Franks, Tim Herlihy, Adam Sandler *d* Dennis Dugan *ph* Theo Van de Sande *m* Teddy Castellucci *pd* Perry Andelin Blake *ed* Jeff Gourson
☆ Adam Sandler (Sonny Koufax), Joey Lauren Adams (Layla), Jon Stewart (Kevin), Cole Sprouse (Julian), Dylan Sprouse (Julian), Josh Mostel (Mr Brooks), Leslie Mann (Corinne), Allen Covert (Phil), Rob Schneider (Delivery Guy), Kristy Swanson (Vanessa), Joe Bologna (Mr Koufax), Steve Buscemi (Homeless guy)
'Easily the laziest, most slapdash and altogether crummiest picture Sandler's done to date.' – *New York Post*
'Sandler's goofy, infantile act, profoundly unattractive when juxtaposed with an actual infant, is about as amusing as a broken collar-bone.' – *Peter Bradshaw, Guardian*
† The film was among the box-office successes of the year, grossing more than $163m in the USA.

Big Deal at Dodge City: see *A Big Hand for the Little Lady*

Big Deal on Madonna Street: see *Persons Unknown*

The Big Doll House
US 1971 93m colour
MGM/New World (Jane Schaffer)
Tough new revolutionary inmates plan an escape from a woman's prison run by a sadistic wardress.
Dull, cheap exploitation movie, concentrating on nudity and violence; it is indifferently acted, and perfunctorily written and directed.
w Don Spencer *d* Jack Hill *ph* Fred Conde *m* Hall Daniels *pd* Ben Otico *ed* Cliff Fenneman
☆ Judy Brown, Roberta Collins, Pam Grier, Brooke Mills, Pat Woodell, Sid Haig, Christiane Schmidtmer

The Big Easy *
US 1986 108m DeLuxe
Kings Road (Stephen Friedman)
A New Orleans homicide detective is persuaded by a lady investigator from the DA's office to look into irregularities in the department.
Sassy, easy-going melodrama with comedy asides.
w Dan Petrie Jnr *d* Jim McBride *ph* Affonso Beato *m* Brad Fiedel *pd* Jeannine Claudia Oppewall
☆ Dennis Quaid, Ellen Barkin, Ned Beatty, John Goodman, Ebbe Roe Smith
'The cooks did the best they could with ingredients that tasted good but were a little tough to chew.' – *Daily Variety*

Big Fella *
GB 1937 73m bw
British Lion/Fortune (H. Fraser Passmore)
In Marseilles, a black man returns a lost child to his English parents.
Pleasant light vehicle with the star in typical easy form.
w Fenn Sherie, Ingram d'Abbes *novel Banjo* by Claude McKay *d* J. Elder Wills *ph* Cyril Bristow *m* Eric Ansell
☆ *Paul Robeson*, Elizabeth Welch, Roy Emerton, Marcelle Rogez
'A very unpretentious vehicle.' – *Variety*

The Big Fisherman
US 1959 166m Technicolor Panavision
Centurion (Rowland V. Lee)
An Arab princess meets disciple Simon Peter, who dissuades her from her plan to assassinate her stepfather Herod.
Well-meaning but leaden adaptation of a bestselling novel which followed on from The Robe *(qv). Too reverent by half, and in many respects surprisingly incompetent.*
w Howard Estabrook, Rowland V. Lee *novel* Lloyd C. Douglas *d* Frank Borzage *ph* Lee Garmes *m* Albert Hay Malotte *pd* John DeCuir
☆ Howard Keel, Alexander Scourby, Susan Kohner, John Saxon, Martha Hyer, Herbert Lom, Ray Stricklyn, Beulah Bondi
'Its overall flatness of conception and execution is a stiff price to pay for the lack of spectacular sensationalism characterizing its fellow-epics.' – MFB
'The picture is three hours long, and, except for those who can be dazzled by big gatherings of props, horses and camels, it is hard to find three minutes of entertainment in it.' – *Hollywood Reporter*
♔ Lee Garmes; John DeCuir

The Big Fix
US 1978 108m Technicolor
Universal (Carl Borack, Richard Dreyfuss)
An industrial investigator fancies himself as a private eye and gets involved in a political corruption case.
Hard to follow and harder still to care about, this rather sloppy, with-it movie is a little too pleased with itself from the word go.
w Roger L. Simon *novel* Roger L. Simon *d* Jeremy Paul Kagan *ph* Frank Stanley *m* Bill Conti *pd* Robert F. Boyle
☆ Richard Dreyfuss, Susan Anspach, Bonnie Bedelia, John Lithgow
'The strength of this film lies in the cool, meandering discretion with which its central theme is fleshed out: regret for lost illusions as the protest generation of the sixties finds its arteries hardening.' – *Tom Milne, MFB*

The Big Gamble *
US 1960 100m DeLuxe Cinemascope
TCF/Darryl F. Zanuck
Three people drive an ailing truck to a remote African township where they hope to start a haulage business.
Curious comedy-drama-adventure which starts off with family matters in Dublin and gradually develops into a lighter-hearted Wages of Fear *(qv). It has its moments.*
w Irwin Shaw *d* Richard Fleischer, Elmo Williams *ph* William Mellor, Henri Persin *m* Maurice Jarre
☆ Stephen Boyd, Juliette Greco, David Wayne, *Gregory Ratoff*, Sybil Thorndike, Fernand Ledoux

Big Girls Don't Cry ... They Get Even
US 1992 104m CFI color
Rank/New Line/Perlman/MG Entertainment (Laurie Perlman, Gerald T. Olson)
GB title: *Stepkids*
A 13-year-old girl runs away from home, unhappy at the lack of attention she is getting from her mother and her new family, and from her father who has started another family of his own.
Sentimental domestic drama that is no more than a soap opera screened large.
w Frank Mugavero *story* Mark Goddard, Melissa Goddard *d* Joan Micklin Silver *ph* Theo Van de Sande *m* Patrick Williams *pd* Victoria Paul *ed* Janice Hampton
☆ Griffin Dunne, Dan Futterman, Patricia Kalember, Jenny Lewis, Ben Savage, Adrienne Shelly, David Strathairn, Trenton Teigen, Margaret Whitton, Hillary Wolf
'Promises much, delivers little.' – *Kim Newman, Empire*

'Mr Ugly comes to town!...'
'Big action and big excitement!'
The Big Gundown
Italy/Spain 1966 105m Techniscope
PEA/PC (Alberto Grimaldi)
Italian title: *La Resa dei Conti*
A Texas lawman is hired to catch a Mexican outlaw, who repeatedly escapes and finally proves his innocence.
Violent but moderately enjoyable spaghetti Western.
w Sergio Donati, Sergio Sollima *d* Sergio Sollima *ph* Carlo Carlini *m* Ennio Morricone
☆ Lee Van Cleef, Tomas Milian, Walter Barnes, Luisa Rivelli

'All the action you can take ... all the adventure you can wish for!'

A Big Hand for the Little Lady **

US 1966 96m Technicolor
Warner/Eden (Fielder Cook)
GB title: *Big Deal at Dodge City* (though the action clearly takes place in Laredo)

Five rich poker players are outwitted by a family of confidence tricksters.

Diverting but thinly stretched acting-piece from a much shorter TV original; still, suspense builds nicely until the disappointingly handled revelation.

w Sidney Carroll *TV play* Sidney Carroll *d* Fielder Cook *ph* Lee Garmes *m* David Raksin

☆ Henry Fonda, *Joanne Woodward*, Jason Robards, Paul Ford, Kevin McCarthy, *Charles Bickford*, Robert Middleton, *Burgess Meredith*, John Qualen

The Big Hangover

US 1950 82m bw
MGM (Norman Krasna)

A lawyer struggling to mingle with the mighty finds he is allergic to strong drink.

Woefully unfunny comedy with virtually no plot.

wd Norman Krasna *ph* George Folsey *m* Adolph Deutsch

☆ Van Johnson, Elizabeth Taylor, Percy Waram, Fay Holden, Leon Ames, Edgar Buchanan, Rosemary de Camp, Gene Lockhart, Selena Royle

The Big Heart: see *Miracle on 34th Street*

'A hard cop and a soft dame!'

The Big Heat **

US 1953 90m bw
Columbia (Robert Arthur)

A police detective's wife is killed by a bomb meant for himself; he quits his job to track down the gangsters responsible.

Considered at the time to reach a new low in violence (boiling coffee in the face), this dour little thriller also struck a new note of realism in crime films and produced one of Glenn Ford's most typical performances.

w Sydney Boehm *novel* William P. McGivern *d* Fritz Lang *ph* Charles Lang *m* Arthur Morton *md* Mischa Bakaleinikoff

☆ Glenn Ford, Gloria Grahame, Alexander Scourby, Jocelyn Brando, Lee Marvin, Jeanette Nolan, Peter Whitney

'The main impression is of violence employed arbitrarily, mechanically and in the long run pointlessly.' – *Penelope Houston*

'Executed with style.'

The Big Hit *

US 1998 91m DeLuxe
TriStar/Amen Ra Films/Zide-Perry/Lion Rock (Warren Zide, Wesley Snipes)

A hitman who begins to fall for the girl he has kidnapped is betrayed by his confederate in the crime.

All the hallmarks of Hong Kong action films, with their gun-battles and intricately choreographed mayhem, are here translated to an American setting, with the addition of wisecracking gangsters and sick jokes.

w Ben Ramsey *d* Che-Kirk Wong *ph* Danny Nowak *m* Graeme Revell *pd* Taavo Soodor *ed* Robin Russell, Pietro Scalia

☆ Mark Wahlberg (Melvin Smiley), Lou Diamond Phillips (Cisco), Christina Applegate (Pam Shulman), Avery Brooks (Paris), Bokeem Woodbine (Crunch), China Chow (Keiko Nishi), Antonio Sabato Jnr (Vince), Lainie Kazan (Jeanne Shulman), Elliott Gould (Morton Shulman), Sab Shimono (Jiri Nishi)

'A fleet piece of sock-'em entertainment, its kinetic force plows through myriad plot holes and inconsistencies with game abandon.' – *Leonard Klady, Variety*

The Big House **

US 1930 88m bw
MGM (Irving Thalberg)

Tensions in prison lead to an attempted breakout and a massacre.

Archetypal prison melodrama and a significant advance in form for early talkies.

w Frances Marion d George Hill ph Harold Wenstrom

☆ Chester Morris, Wallace Beery, Robert Montgomery, Lewis Stone, Leila Hyams, George F. Marion, J. C. Nugent, Karl Dane

'Not a two-dollar talker, but virile, realistic melodrama, a cinch for any week-stand and hold-overable generally.' – *Variety*

'We all gave our roles the best that was in us, and the virility and truthfulness of the picture were more satisfying than anything else I've done.' – *Chester Morris, 1953*

† The role played by Wallace Beery had been intended for Lon Chaney, who died during preparation.

Frances Marion

best picture; Wallace Beery

Big House USA

US 1954 82m bw
UA/Bel Air (Aubrey Schenck)

Convicts stage a break-out to get at hidden loot.

Though less explicit in its violence than many later films, this is a singularly unpleasant melodrama with not one attractive character.

w John C. Higgins *d* Howard W. Koch *ph* Gordon Avil *m* Paul Dunlap

☆ Broderick Crawford, Ralph Meeker, Lon Chaney, Charles Bronson, William Talman, Reed Hadley

Big Jake *

US 1971 110m Technicolor Panavision
Batjac/Cinema Center (Michael A. Wayne)

An elderly Texas cattleman swings into action when his grandson is kidnapped.

Satisfactory example of the star's later vehicles, with efficient production and familiar cast and brawling.

w Harry Julian Fink, R. M. Fink *d* George Sherman *ph* William Clothier *m* Elmer Bernstein

☆ *John Wayne*, Richard Boone, Maureen O'Hara, Patrick Wayne, Chris Mitchum, Bobby Vinton, Bruce Cabot, Glenn Corbett, Harry Carey Jnr, John Agar

'Another genial celebration of Big John's ability to carry a film practically single-handed.' – *MFB*

Big Jim McLain

US 1952 90m bw
Wayne/Fellows (Robert Fellows)

A special agent for the House of UnAmerican Activities Committee routs communists in Hawaii.

Curious and rather offensive star vehicle in which the right-wing political shading interferes seriously with the entertainment value.

w James Edward Grant *d* Edward Ludwig *ph* Archie Stout *m* Paul Dunlap *md* Emil Newman

☆ John Wayne, Nancy Olson, James Arness, Alan Napier, Veda Ann Borg, Hans Conried, Gayne Whitman

'Brings to the screen all the unattractively hysterical mentality of the witch hunt.' – *Penelope Houston*

The Big Job

GB 1965 88m bw
Allied Artists/Adder (Peter Rogers)

After 15 years in prison, a gang of inept bank robbers discover that the hollow tree in which they hid their loot now stands in the yard of a new police station.

Broad slapstick comedy, involving many of the Carry On team, that has some occasional amusing moments, though the best joke, when the gang make their getaway in a hearse, comes at the beginning.

w Talbot Rothwell *story* John Antrobus *d* Gerald Thomas *ph* Alan Hume *m* Eric Rogers *ad* Bert Davey *ed* Rod Keys

☆ Sidney James, Sylvia Syms, Dick Emery, Lance Percival, Joan Sims, Jim Dale, Edina Ronay, Deryck Guyler, Reginald Beckwith, Wanda Ventham

'The Hottest Hunk Of Film Hollywood Ever Shot!'

The Big Knife *

US 1955 111m bw
UA/Aldrich and Associates

A depressed Hollywood star who wants better things for himself is blackmailed into signing a new contract.

Overheated argument between Art and Mammon, with rather disagreeable people shouting at each other, for too long a time. Limited interest is provided by the acting.

w James Poe *play* Clifford Odets *d* Robert Aldrich *ph* Ernest Laszlo *m* Frank de Vol

☆ Jack Palance, Ida Lupino, *Rod Steiger*, Everett Sloane, Jean Hagen, Shelley Winters, Wendell Corey, Ilka Chase, Wesley Addy

'Everything in it is garish and overdone: it's paced too fast and pitched too high, immorality is attacked with almost obscene relish, the knife turns into a buzz saw.' – *Pauline Kael, 1968*

The Big Land

US 1957 92m Warnercolor
Warner/Jaguar (George C. Bertholon)
GB title: *Stampeded*

Cattlemen encourage the building of a rail link for Texas.

Undistinguished star Western.

w David Dortort, Martin Rackin *novel Buffalo Grass* by Frank Gruber *d* Gordon Douglas *ph* John F. Seitz *m* David Buttolph

☆ Alan Ladd, Virginia Mayo, Edmond O'Brien, Anthony Caruso, Julie Bishop, John Qualen

'Hackneyed, humdrum western.' – *Howard Thompson*

'Her Life Was In Their Hands. Now Her Toe Is In The Mail.'

The Big Lebowski **

US 1998 127m Technicolor
Polygram/Working Title (Ethan Coen)

A middle-aged nobody is attacked having been mistaken for his namesake, a millionaire whose wife, an actress in pornographic films, has apparently been kidnapped.

A meandering thriller that provides a great deal of incidental pleasures on a journey to nowhere in particular.

w Joel and Ethan Coen *d* Joel Coen *ph* Roger Deakins *m* Carter Burwell *pd* Rick Heinrichs *ed* Roderick Jaynes, Tricia Cooke

☆ Jeff Bridges, John Goodman, Julianne Moore, Steve Buscemi, Peter Stormare, David Huddleston, Sam Elliott, John Turturro, David Thewlis, Ben Gazzara

'A pseudo-mystery thriller with a keen eye and ear for societal mores and modern figures of speech, nonetheless adds up to considerably less than the sum of its often scintillating parts, simply because the film does not seem to be about anything other than its own cleverness.' – *Todd McCarthy, Variety*

'A shaggy dog story out for a constitutional.' – *Alexander Walker, London Evening Standard*

The Big Lift *

US 1950 119m bw
TCF (William Perlberg)

When the Russians blockade Berlin, British and American airmen get supplies there via a massive airlift; two men on one plane hold opposite views of the matter, and both have chastening experiences.

Rather heavy-going fiction based on fact, with earnest performances and good production.

wd George Seaton *ph* Charles G. Clarke *m* Alfred Newman

☆ Montgomery Clift, Paul Douglas, Cornell Borchers, O. E. Hasse, Bruni Lobel

'There are some acute touches ... just enough to make the slick evasions of the rest all the more regrettable.' – *Gavin Lambert*

The Big Man

GB 1990 116m colour
Palace/Miramax/BSB/British STV Film Enterprises (Stephen Woolley)
US title: *Crossing the Line*

An unemployed miner becomes a bare-knuckle fighter.

What begins as social realism, at its most powerful in a brutal fight sequence, ends as a mess of sentimental cinematic clichés.

w Don MacPherson *novel* William McIlvanney *d* David Leland *ph* Ian Wilson *m* Ennio Morricone *pd* Carol Amies *ed* George Akers

☆ Liam Neeson, Joanne Whalley-Kilmer, Billy Connolly, Ian Bannen, Maurice Roeves, Kenny Ireland, John Beattie, Amanda Walker

'Rarely plausible, frequently risible, occasionally embarrassing, this morally confused melodrama falls with a dull thud between social realism and mythic fable.' – *Philip French, Observer*

'This FBI Agent Is Going Undercover... And He's concealing More Than A Weapon.'

Big Momma's House

US 2000 98m DeLuxe
TCF/Regency/David T. Friendly/Runteldat/Taurus

An FBI agent disguises himself as an obese grandmother in order to track down an escaped bank robber.

Trite and flatulent lowbrow comedy that lacks character and charm, with Martin Lawrence once more content to be a unfunny clone of Eddie Murphy.

w Darryl Quarles, Don Rhymer *d* Raja Gosnell *ph* Michael D. O'Shea *m* Richard Gibbs *pd* Craig Stearns *ed* Bruce Green, Kent Beyda *sp* makeup fx: Greg Cannom *cos* Francine Jamison-Tanchuck

☆ Martin Lawrence (Malcolm Turner), Nia Long (Sherry), Paul Giamatti (John), Terrence Howard (Lester), Anthony Anderson (Nolan), Ella Mitchell (Big Momma), Jascha Washington (Trent), Carl Wright (Ben), Phyllis Applegate (Sadie), Starletta DuPois (Miss Patterson), Octavia L. Spencer (Twila)

'Filled with sketchlike comic set pieces, only a few of which come near fulfilling their humorous potential.' – *Todd McCarthy, Variety*

'If you think comedy based on farting, lechery, drag and the huge bottom and bowel movements of a large black woman is funny, then this one is for you.' – *Cosmo Landesman, Sunday Times*

† The film was a hit in the US, taking more than $117.5m at the box office.

The Big Money

GB 1956 86m Technicolor Vistavision
Rank (Joseph Janni)

A family of petty crooks is ashamed of its eldest son, who is an incompetent thief.

A would-be high-spirited lark in which none of the jokes comes off, and a note of forced artificiality hangs over the whole production.

w John Baines *d* John Paddy Carstairs *ph* Jack Cox *m* Van Phillips

☆ Ian Carmichael, Belinda Lee, Kathleen Harrison, Robert Helpmann, James Hayter, George Coulouris, Jill Ireland, Renée Houston, Leslie Phillips

The Big Mouth

US 1967 107m Pathécolor
Columbia (Jerry Lewis)

A meek bank auditor finds he is the double of a dying gangster and is put on the trail of stolen diamonds.

The comedian at his worst, most repetitive and long drawn out.

w Jerry Lewis, Bill Richmond *d* Jerry Lewis *ph* W. Wallace Kelley, Ernest Laszlo *m* Harry Betts

☆ Jerry Lewis, Harold J. Stone, Susan Bay, Buddy Lester, Del Moore

The Big Night

US 1951 75m bw
UA/Philip A. Waxman

A 17-year-old youth goes on the rampage in the underworld to avenge the beating up of his father by gangsters.

Hysterical melodrama presenting a rather false and dismal view of the world. Amazingly typical of its director's later output.

w Stanley Ellin, Joseph Losey *novel Dreadful Summit* by Stanley Ellin *d* Joseph Losey *ph* Hal Mohr *m* Lyn Murray

☆ John Barrymore Jnr, Preston Foster, Howard St John, Philip Bourneuf, Howland Chamberlin, Emile Meyer, Dorothy Comingore, Joan Lorring

'We are in that familiar underworld of the American cinema: dark streets gleaming with rain, sleazy apartments, garish night clubs, with Negro singers, drunks who spout philosophy, discontented blondes and fierce pock-marked thugs.' – *Gavin Lambert*

† The script was written by Ring Lardner Jnr and Hugo Butler, who did not receive a screen credit as they were blacklisted at the time.

'Comedy with Taste.'

Big Night **

US 1996 108m DeLuxe
Rysher/Timpano (Jonathan Filley)

In New Jersey in the late 50s, two brothers, who run an authentic but failing Italian restaurant, prepare a feast in the belief that entertainer Louis Prima will be coming for a meal.

Charming small-scale comedy of brotherly rivalry and love, immaculately done.

w Stanley Tucci, Joseph Tropiano *d* Stanley Tucci, Campbell Scott *ph* Ken Kelsch *m* Gary DeMichele *pd* Andrew Jackness *ed* Suzy Elmiger

☆ Minnie Driver, Ian Holm, Isabella Rossellini, Tony Shalhoub, Stanley Tucci, Caroline Aaron, Marc Anthony, Allison Janney

'A smartly made, delightfully acted period piece whose sensibility neatly straddles art films and the mainstream.' – *Todd McCarthy, Variety*

The Big Noise

US 1944 74m bw
TCF (Sol M. Wurtzel)

Two incompetent detectives accidentally round up a spy gang.

Very thin star vehicle consisting largely of poorly staged and warmed up versions of a few old routines.

w Scott Darling *d* Mal St Clair *ph* Joe MacDonald *m* Cyril Mockridge

☆ Stan Laurel, Oliver Hardy, Doris Merrick, Arthur Space, Jack Norton

The Big Operator

US 1959 91m bw Cinemascope
MGM/Albert Zugsmith-Fryman (Red Doff)

The racketeer head of a labour union goes berserk when the government has him investigated.

Unpleasant gangster exploitation melodrama from the bottom of the barrel.

w Robert Smith, Allen Rivkin *d* Charles Haas *ph* Walter H. Castle *m* Van Alexander

☆ Mickey Rooney, Steve Cochran, Mamie Van Doren, Mel Tormé, Ray Danton, Jim Backus, Jackie Coogan, Ray Anthony, Charles Chaplin Jnr

'The epic of the American doughboy!'

The Big Parade ***

US 1925 115m approx (24 fps) bw silent
MGM

A young American enlists in 1917, learns the realities of war, is wounded but survives.

Enormously successful commercially, this 'anti-war' film survives best as a thrilling spectacle and a well-considered piece of film-making.

w Laurence Stallings, Harry Behn *d King Vidor ph John Arnold m* William Axt, David Mendoza

☆ John Gilbert, Renee Adoree, Hobart Bosworth, Karl Dane, George K. Arthur

'The human comedy emerges from a terrifying tragedy.' – *King Vidor*

'A cinegraphically visualized result of a cinegraphically imagined thing … something conceived in terms of a medium and expressed by that medium as only that medium could properly express it.' – *National Board of Review*

'The extraordinary impression of the rush of lorries, the queer terror of the woods … it was amazing how much fear could be felt in the mere continuous pace of movement.' – *Bryher, Close Up*

† The biggest grossing silent film of all.

The Big Parade **

China 1986 103m colour Scope
ICA/Guangxi Film Studio (Chen Liguo)
original title: *Da Yuebing*

Four hundred volunteers from the Airborne Division of the People's Liberation Army train for the National Day Parade in Beijing's Tiananmen Square.

Well-made film that concentrates on the relationship between individuals and the institution they serve. Changes to the movie were forced on the director by the People's Army, including the final scenes of the parade itself.

w Gao Lili *d* Chen Kaige *ph* Zhang Yimou *m* Qu Xiasong, Zhao Jiping *ad* He Qun *ed* Zhou Xinxia

☆ Wang Xueqi, Sun Chun, Lu Lei, Wu Ruofu, Guan Qiang, Kang Hua

The Big Parade of Comedy **

US 1964 90m approx bw
MGM (Robert Youngson)
aka: *MGM's Big Parade of Comedy*

A compilation by Robert Youngson, including material as diverse as *Ninotchka*, Laurel and Hardy and the Marx Brothers.

One is grateful for the excerpts but the assembly of them is somewhat graceless.

The Big Picture **

US 1988 101m DeLuxe
Hobo/Columbia (Michael Varhol)

A student film maker goes to Hollywood.

Amusing satire of the movie business.

w Michael Varhol, Christopher Guest, Michael McKean *d* Christopher Guest *ph* Jeff Jur *m* David Nichtern *pd* Joseph T. Garrity *ad* Patrick Tagliaferro *ed* Martin Nicholson

☆ Kevin Bacon, Emily Longstreth, J. T. Walsh, Jennifer Jason Leigh, Martin Short, Michael McKean, Kim Miyori, Teri Hatcher

The Big Pond *

US 1930 79m bw
Paramount (Monta Bell)

The son of an important French family acts as a tourist guide in Venice.

Reasonably lively, semi-satirical early musical with Americans the butt of the jokes.

w Robert Presnell, Garrett Fort, Preston Sturges *play* George Middleton, A. E. Thomas *d* Hobart Henley *ph* George Folsey *m* arranged by John Green *songs* various

☆ Maurice Chevalier, Claudette Colbert, George Barbier, Nat Pendleton, Marion Ballou

'An amiable and ingratiating comedy that will give the Chevalier momentum another good shove.' – *Variety*

Maurice Chevalier

Big Red

US 1962 89m Technicolor
Walt Disney (Winston Hibler)

An orphan boy protects a dog which later saves him from a mountain lion.

Simple boy-and-dog yarn with impressive Canadian settings.

w Louis Pelletier *d* Norman Tokar *ph* Edward Colman *m* Oliver Wallace

☆ Walter Pidgeon, Gilles Payant, Emile Genest

The Big Red One **

US 1980 111m colour
UA/Lorimar (Gene Corman)

Five foot-soldiers survive action in several theatres of war between 1940 and 1945.

Symbolic action drama, very well made but finally lacking a cumulative impact.

wd Samuel Fuller ph Adam Greenberg *m* Dana Kaproff

☆ Lee Marvin, Mark Hamill, Robert Carradine, Bobby DiCicco, Kelly Ward, Stéphane Audran, Serge Marquand

'A picture of palpable raw power which manages both intense intimacy and great scope at the same time.' – *Variety*

'Like all Fuller movies, about an inch from cliché all the way.' – *Guardian*

The Big Shakedown

US 1934 64m bw
Warner (Sam Bischoff)

A racketeer finds a new gimmick: cut-price medicine.

Action programmer with emphasis on the young couple forced into helping the racket.

w Niven Busch, Rian James *d* John Francis Dillon *ph* Sid Hickox

☆ Bette Davis, Ricardo Cortez, Charles Farrell, Glenda Farrell, Allen Jenkins, Henry O'Neill, Samuel S. Hinds

'A routine assortment of gang-film impedimenta.' – *New York Times*

The Big Shave **

US 1967 6m colour 16mm
Contemporary/McGraw-Hill

To the soundtrack accompaniment of Bunny Berigan's 'I Can't Get Started', a man shaves in a white bathroom, imperturbably cutting himself almost with every stroke until his face runs with blood.

A short, gruesome, macabre joke, intended by Scorsese as an angry comment on the process of self-mutilation that was the war in Vietnam.

wd Martin Scorsese *ph* Ares Demertzis

☆ Peter Bernuth

† The film carries the credit 'Whiteness Herman Melville' as well as the line 'Viet '67'. It was released on video with three other shorts under the title *Scorsese x 4*.

The Big Shot *

US 1942 82m bw
Warner (Walter MacEwen)

An ill-fated criminal has trouble with women and his former companions.

Dullish star vehicle.

w Bertram Millhauser, Abem Finkel, Daniel Fuchs *d* Lewis Seiler *ph* Sid Hickox *m* Adolph Deutsch

☆ Humphrey Bogart, Irene Manning, Richard Travis, Donald Crisp, Stanley Ridges, Henry Hull, Susan Peters, Howard da Silva

The Big Show

US 1961 113m DeLuxe Cinemascope
TCF/API (Ted Sherdeman)

A circus proprietor dominates his sons; after his death they fight for supremacy.

Another remake of House of Strangers, *which was also remodelled as* Broken Lance *(qqv). Not too bad as circus melodramas go.*

w Ted Sherdeman *d* James B. Clark *ph* Otto Heller *m* Paul Sawtell, Bert Shefter

☆ Esther Williams, Cliff Robertson, *Nehemiah Persoff*, Robert Vaughn, Carol Christensen, Margia Dean, David Nelson

The Big Silence

France/Italy 1969 115m Eastmancolor
Adelphia/Corona
original title: *Il Grande Silencio*

A mute gunfighter comes to a small lawless town to kill a ruthless bounty hunter.

Brutal Western in which the bad guys win, but one with a genuine feeling for the genre and the snowbound landscape.

wd Sergio Corbucci *ph* Silvano Ippoliti *m* Ennio Morricone

☆ Jean-Louis Trintignant, Klaus Kinski, Vonetta McGee

The Big Sky *

US 1952 122m bw
RKO/Winchester (Howard Hawks)

In 1830 two Kentucky mountain men join an exploration up the Missouri and become preoccupied with Indian trouble.

A large-scale adventure, loaded with talent, which becomes oddly tedious.

w Dudley Nichols *novel* A. B. Guthrie Jnr *d* Howard Hawks *ph* Russell Harlan *m* Dimitri Tiomkin

☆ Kirk Douglas, Arthur Hunnicutt, Elizabeth Threatt, Dewey Martin, Buddy Baer, Steve Geray, Jim Davis

'It has the timeless, relentless quality of the long American historical novel.' – *Penelope Houston*

Russell Harlan; Arthur Hunnicutt

The Big Sleep ***

US 1946 114m bw
Warner (Howard Hawks)

Private eye Philip Marlowe is hired to protect General Sternwood's wild young daughter from her own indiscretions, and finds several murders later that he has fallen in love with her elder sister.

Inextricably complicated, moody thriller from a novel whose author claimed that even he did not know 'who done it'. The film is nevertheless vastly enjoyable along the way for its slangy script, star performances and outbursts of violence, suspense and sheer fun.

w William Faulkner, Leigh Brackett, Jules Furthman novel Raymond Chandler d Howard Hawks ph Sid Hickox *m Max Steiner*

☆ *Humphrey Bogart* (Philip Marlowe), *Lauren Bacall* (Vivian Sternwood Rutledge), John Ridgely (Eddie Mars), Martha Vickers (Carmen Sternwood), Dorothy Malone (Proprietress), Regis Toomey (Bernie Ohls), Charles Waldron (General Sternwood), Charles D. Brown (Norris), Elisha Cook Jnr (Harry Jones), Louis Jean Heydt (Joe Brody), Bob Steele (Canino), Peggy Knudsen (Mona Mars), Sonia Darrin (Agnes)

MARLOWE: 'My, my, my. Such a lot of guns around town and so few brains.'

GENERAL: 'You may smoke, too. I can still enjoy the smell of it. Nice thing when a man has to indulge his vices by proxy.'

VIVIAN: 'So you're a private detective. I didn't know they existed, except in books – or else they were greasy little men snooping around hotel corridors. My, you're a mess, aren't you?'

MARLOWE: 'I don't mind if you don't like my manners. I don't like 'em myself. They're pretty bad. I grieve over 'em on long winter evenings.'

GENERAL: 'If I seem a bit sinister as a parent, Mr Marlowe, it's because my hold on life is too slight to include any Victorian hypocrisy. I need hardly add that any man who has lived as I have and indulges for the first time in parenthood at the age of 55 deserves all he gets.'

MARLOWE: 'Speaking of horses … you've got a touch of class, but I don't know how far you can go.'

VIVIAN: 'A lot depends on who's in the saddle. Go ahead Marlowe. I like the way you work. In case you don't know it, you're doing all right.'

'A sullen atmosphere of sex saturates the film, which is so fast and complicated you can hardly catch it.' – *Richard Winnington*

'A violent, smoky cocktail shaken together from most of the printable misdemeanours and some that aren't.' – *James Agee*

'Harder, faster, tougher, funnier and more laconic than any thriller since.' – *NFT, 1974*

'Wit, excitement and glamour in generous doses.' – *Francis Wyndham*

'Some days business is good – and some days it's murder!'

The Big Sleep

GB 1977 99m DeLuxe
Winkast (Elliott Kastner, Michael Winner)

An American private eye is hired by a crippled General to protect his uncontrolled younger daughter.

Straight remake of the 1946 film, curiously and ineffectively set in London.

wd Michael Winner *ph* Robert Paynter *m* Jerry Fielding

☆ Robert Mitchum, Sarah Miles, Richard Boone, Candy Clark, Edward Fox, Joan Collins, John Mills, James Stewart, Oliver Reed, Harry Andrews, Richard Todd, James Donald, Colin Blakely

'The 1946 film takes on even more stature in light of this. For a Winner film, however, it's quite good.' – *Variety*

The Big Stampede

US 1932 54m bw
Warner

A deputy sheriff cleans up Arizona, gets the girl and defeats a cattle rustler.

Pleasant undemanding Western with Wayne working on his taciturn screen presence while remaking Ken Maynard's silent oaters, in this instance, Land beyond the Law.

w Kurt Kempler *story* Marion Jackson *d* Tenny Wright *ph* Ted McCord *ed* Frank Ware

☆ John Wayne, Noah Beery, Mae Madison, Berton Churchill, Paul Hurst, Sherwood Bailey, Luis Alberni, Lafe McKee, Paul Hurst

The Big Steal **

US 1949 72m bw
RKO (Jack J. Gross)

An army officer is framed for the theft of a payroll, and sets off across Mexico in hectic pursuit of the real culprit.

Unexpectedly enjoyable comedy melodrama with a plethora of twists and a pace that never lets up. Routine Hollywood at a level seldom achieved, and short enough to leave one asking for more.

w Gerald Drayson Adams, Geoffrey Homes story The Road to Carmichael's by Richard Wormser *d Don Siegel ph* Harry J. Wild *m* Leigh Harline

☆ Robert Mitchum, Jane Greer, William Bendix, Ramon Novarro, Patric Knowles, Don Alvarado, John Qualen

'Vigour and excellent craftsmanship.' – *Gavin Lambert*

'He Wants The Key To Her Heart. They Want The Key To His Car.'
The Big Steal *
Australia 1990 100m colour
Hobo/Cascade/Film Victoria/Australia Film Finance Corp. (David Parker, Nadia Tass)

An 18-year-old boy plots revenge against the car salesman who sold him a faulty Jaguar with which he had hoped to impress his new girl-friend.
Mildly amusing comedy of the eccentricity underlying suburban life.
w David Parker, Max Dunn *d* Nadia Tass *ph* David Parker *m* Philip Judd *pd* Paddy Reardon *ed* Peter Carrodus
☆ Ben Mendelsohn, Claudia Karvan, Steve Bisley, Marshall Napier, Damon Herriman, Angelo D'Angelo, Tim Robertson, Maggie King
'Has a low-key charm that's appealing, and a couple of riotously funny scenes.' – *Variety*

The Big Store *
US 1941 83m bw
MGM (Louis K. Sidney)

An eccentric private eye saves a department store from the hands of crooks.
Reckoned to be the Marx Brothers' weakest MGM vehicle, but it has its moments, especially the first reel and the bedding department scene, also Groucho's rendering of 'Sing While You Sell'.
w Sid Kuller, Hal Fimberg, Ray Golden *d* Charles Reisner *ph* Charles Lawton *m* George Stoll
☆ *Groucho, Chico, Harpo, Margaret Dumont, Douglass Dumbrille*, Tony Martin, Virginia Grey, Virginia O'Brien, Henry Armetta

The Big Story: see *Appointment with a Shadow (1957)*

The Big Story *
GB 1995 2m bw
Screwball Films

A reporter demands to be given a big story to cover.
Witty compendium of newspaper movie clichés, in which all the animated characters resemble Kirk Douglas.
wd Tim Watts, David Stoten *ph* Tristan Oliver
☆ Featuring voices: Frank Gorshin
animated short

The Big Street *
US 1942 88m bw
RKO (Damon Runyon)

A Broadway night-club waiter falls in love with a crippled singer who selfishly accepts his help without loving him in return.
Unusual but mawkish material from an author who never really suited the screen; a mixture of laughs, tears and sentimentality, with a comic gangster background.
w Leonard Spigelgass *story* Little Pinks by Damon Runyon *d* Irving Reis *ph* Russell Metty *m* Roy Webb
☆ Henry Fonda, Lucille Ball, Eugene Pallette, Virginia Weidler, Agnes Moorehead, Barton MacLane, Ozzie Nelson and his Orchestra, Sam Levene, Ray Collins, Marion Martin

'Five Couples. With One Big Idea.'
The Big Swap
GB 1997 122m colour
Film Four/Mayfair/Moonlit (Niall Johnson)

Five couples who are old friends decide to swap partners for a night, and find their lives are changed.
An earnest, low-budget movie about relationships; but the group of thirtysomethings involved are an unsympathetic bunch, and the concentration on their behaviour in bed becomes claustrophobic.
wd Niall Johnson *ph* Gordon Hickie *m* Jason Flinter, Craig Johnson *pd* Craig Johnson *ed* David Thrasher
☆ Mark Adams, Sorcha Brooks, Mark Caven, Alison Egan, Richard Cherry, Julie-Ann Gillitt, Antony Edridge, Clarke Hayes, Thierry Harcourt, Jackie Sawiris, Kevin Howarth
'In attempting to deliver a slight, soft-porn comedy for the upwardly mobile, Johnson gives all he's got in the first hour.' – *Jessica Mellor, Empire*

'He Saw. He Combed. He Conquered.'
The Big Tease *
US 1999 86m DeLuxe
Warner/Crawford P./I Should Coco (Philip Rose)

A Glaswegian hairdresser goes to Los Angeles in the expectation of competing in the World Freestyle Hairdressing Championship.
A fitfully amusing comedy, done in documentary style but lacking bite, and relying on Ferguson's performance to maintain any comic momentum.
w Sacha Gervasi, Craig Ferguson *d* Kevin Allen *ph* Seamus McGarvey *m* Mark Thomas *pd* Joseph Hodges *ed* Chris Peppe
☆ Craig Ferguson (Crawford Mackenzie), Frances Fisher (Candy Harper), Chris Langham (Martin Samuels), Mary McCormack (Monique), Donal Logue (Eamonn), Larry Miller (Dunstan Cactus), David Rasche (Stig Ludwigssen), Kevin Allen (Gareth Pritchard), Charles Napier (Warren Crockett), Isabella Aitken (Beasie Mackenzie)
'A silly, often funny and finally engaging mocku-comedy that's the *This Is Spinal Tap* of the Hollywood crimping scene.' – *Derek Elley, Variety*
'It overstays its limited welcome by nearly an hour, freewheeling uphill to an embarrassing climax.' – *Philip French, Observer*

Big Time Operators: see *The Smallest Show on Earth*

Big Town
US 1947 59m bw
Paramount/Pine-Thomas

Adventures of the crusading editor of a city newspaper.
Anaemic support which surprisingly started a series.
w Geoffrey Homes from radio scripts *d* William Thomas
☆ Philip Reed, Hillary Brooke, Robert Lowery, Byron Barr, Veda Ann Borg

The Big Town
US 1987 110m colour
Rank/Columbia (Martin Ransohoff, Don Carmody)

A crapshooter on a winning streak goes to the big city to make good.
Ineffectual drama of a youth learning about life from his elders, drably directed.
w Robert Roy Pool *novel* The Arm by Clark Howard *d* Ben Bolt *ph* Ralf D. Bode *m* Michael Melvoin *pd* Bill Kenney *ed* Stuart Pappe
☆ Matt Dillon, Diane Lane, Tommy Lee Jones, Bruce Dern, Tom Skerritt, Lee Grant, David Marshall Grant, Don Francks

Big Town Girl
US 1937 66m bw
TCF (Milton H. Feld)
A night-club singer adopts a disguise to elude her escaped convict husband.
Satisfactory supporting comedy-melodrama.
w Lou Breslow, John Patrick, Robert Ellis, Helen Logan *d* Alfred Werker
☆ Claire Trevor, Donald Woods, Alan Dinehart, Alan Baxter, Murray Alper, Spencer Charters
'First-class dualler which should please everywhere.' – *Variety*

The Big Trail *
US 1930 125m bw Grandeur
Fox

A wagon train struggles along the Oregon trail.
Simple-minded early talkie Western spectacular with a new young star who took another nine years to make it big. Originally shown on a giant 70mm gauge and intended for big screens.
w Jack Peabody, Marie Boyle, Florence Postal *d* Raoul Walsh *ph* Lucien Andriot, Arthur Edeson
☆ John Wayne, Marguerite Churchill, El Brendel, Tully Marshall, Tyrone Power Snr, David Rollins, Ward Bond, Helen Parrish
'Failing to own a kick or a punch, other than scenically, and with no outstanding cast names, it remains only a western of the pioneering sort, so thoroughly made familiar by those pioneering epics preceding it.' – *Variety*
'Printed upon the new wide film and projected upon the vastly large Grandeur screen, the landscapes, wagon trains, vistas and camp scenes achieve an incredibly greater sweep [than *The Covered Wagon*]. *The Big Trail* is often stagey, melodramatic, ranty.' – *Theatre Magazine*

The Big Trees **
US 1952 89m Technicolor
Warner (Louis F. Edelman)

An unscrupulous lumberman tries to exploit California's giant redwood forests but is won over by the local Quakers who hold the trees in awe.
Pleasing, old-fashioned outdoor drama with a plot which allows the star much opportunity for derring-do.
w John Twist, James R. Webb *d* Felix Feist *ph* Bert Glennon *m* Heinz Roemheld *ed* Clarence Kolster
☆ Kirk Douglas, Eve Miller, Patrice Wymore, Edgar Buchanan, John Archer, Alan Hale Jnr
'It was a bad movie.' – *Kirk Douglas*
† A remake of *Valley of the Giants* (qv).
†† Douglas did the film for nothing in order to get out of his contract with Warners.

Big Trouble
US 1984 93m Metrocolor
Columbia/Delphi III (Michael Lobell)

Two incompetent con men try to swindle an insurance company.
Witless comic farrago apparently designed to cash in on the success of The In-Laws *by utilizing the plot of* Double Indemnity *(qqv). Not a goer.*
w Warren Bogle (Andrew Bergman) *d* John Cassavetes *ph* Bill Butler *m* Bill Conti
☆ Peter Falk, Alan Arkin, Beverly D'Angelo, Charles Durning, Paul Dooley, Robert Stack, Valerie Curtin

Big Trouble in Little China
US 1986 99m DeLuxe Panavision
TCF/Paul Monash, Keith Barish (Larry J. Franco)

A philosophizing truck driver in San Francisco finds himself combating an ancient, evil Chinese magician.
Misfiring attempt to equal the nonsense of the Indiana Jones sagas; occasional effective action moments don't stop the whole from being tiresome.
w W. D. Richter, Gary Goldman, David Z. Weinstein *d* John Carpenter *ph* Dean Cundey *m* John Carpenter *pd* John J. Lloyd
☆ Kurt Russell (Jack Burton), Kim Cattrall (Gracie Law), Dennis Dun (Wang Chi), James Hong (David Lo Pan), Victor Wong (Egg Shen), Kate Burton (Margo)
'Glitzy sets, vacuous characters, limping fantasy.' – *Sight and Sound*

Big Wednesday *
US 1978 119m Metrocolor Panavision
Warner/A-Team (Alex Rose, Tamara Asseyev)

Three California surfing friends of the early sixties get back together after the Vietnam war.
It isn't clear whether the intent is to extol or deride the mystical camaraderie of surfing, but for those who can stand rumbustious beach behaviour this curious movie may have at least as much to say as The Deer Hunter *(qv).*
w John Milius, Dennis Aaberg *d* John Milius *ph* Bruce Surtees *m* Basil Poledouris *surfing photography* Greg MacGillivray
☆ Jan-Michael Vincent, William Katt, Gary Busey, Darrell Fetty

The Big Wheel
US 1949 92m bw
UA/Popkin/Stiefel/Dempsey (Samuel H. Stiefel)

The son of a racing driver is determined to follow in father's footsteps.
Grubby star actioner.
w Robert Smith *d* Edward Ludwig *ph* Ernest Laszlo *m* Nat W. Finston
☆ Mickey Rooney, Spring Byington, Thomas Mitchell, Mary Hatcher, Allen Jenkins

Big Zapper
GB 1973 90m Technicolor Techniscope
Miracle/Lindsay Shonteff

aka: *The Sex Life of a Female Private Eye*
A tough female detective with a masochistic boyfriend, Rock Hard, is hired to discover the fate of a brother and sister, who have been murdered by a pimp.
Dreary and sniggering would-be erotic thriller, concerned solely and ineptly with sex and violence.
w Hugh Brody *d* Lindsay Shonteff *ph* John C. Taylor *m* Colin Pearson *ed* Spencer Reeve
☆ Linda Marlowe, Richard Monette, Gary Hope, Sean Hewitt, Michael O'Malley
'A paltry and nasty sexual fantasy which looks as though it has been dreamed up for the entertainment of impotent sadists.' – *Sylvia Miller, MFB*

'Wanted by two women!'
The Bigamist *
US 1953 80m bw
Filmmakers (Collier Young)

A travelling salesman has two wives.
Minor melodrama which took its subject seriously but failed to make absorbing drama of it. Very much a family affair, starring the producer's present and past wives, the latter also directing.
w Collier Young *d* Ida Lupino *ph* George Diskant *m* Leith Stevens
☆ Edmond O'Brien, Joan Fontaine, Ida Lupino, Edmund Gwenn, Jane Darwell
'The film seems to have summoned all its energy to shout defiantly that bigamous marriages exist and, finding no one to defy, retires deflated.' – *MFB*

The Bigamist *
Italy/France 1956 97m bw
Royal/Filmel/Alba
An innocent young salesman is accused of bigamy and dragged into court.
Noisy comedy of mistaken identity; some laughs, but the talents are not at their best.
w Sergio Amidei, Age Scarpelli, Francesco Rosi, Elio Talarico *d* Luciano Emmer *ph* Mario Montuori *m* Alessandro Cicognini
☆ Marcello Mastroianni, Vittorio de Sica, Franca Valeri, Giovanna Ralli

Bigfoot and the Hendersons: see *Harry and the Hendersons*

Bigger than Life *
US 1956 95m Eastmancolor Cinemascope
TCF/James Mason
A small-town schoolteacher is prescribed cortisone for arthritis; it gradually turns him into a bullying megalomaniac full of grandiose schemes.
Exaggerated and sensationalized but still not very dramatic expansion of a genuine case history. A curious choice for all concerned.
w Cyril Hume, Richard Maibaum *d* Nicholas Ray *ph* Joe MacDonald *m* David Raksin
☆ James Mason, Barbara Rush, Walter Matthau, Robert Simon, Roland Winters

'This is the world's sexiest robbery!'
The Biggest Bundle of Them All
US 1967 110m Metrocolor Panavision
MGM/Shaftel-Stewart
A retired gangster is kidnapped by other gangsters and shows them how to steal five million dollars worth of platinum.
Very moderately amusing international comedy caper.
w Josef Shaftel, Sy Salkowitz *d* Ken Annakin *ph* Piero Portalupi *m* Riz Ortolani
☆ Raquel Welch, Robert Wagner, Vittorio de Sica, Edward G. Robinson, Godfrey Cambridge, Davy Kaye
'It begins like one of these really bad movies that are unintentionally funny. Then it becomes clear that it intends to be funny, and it isn't.' – *Renata Adler*

Biggles
GB 1986 92m Technicolor
UIP/Compact Yellowbill/Tambarle (Kent Walwin, Pom Oliver)

US title: *Biggles: Adventures in Time*
A young New York businessman is transported back in time to 1917, and his help solicited by a daredevil airman.
The bookends set a spoofy tone, but most of the movie is the same old teenage gunge.
w John Groves, Kent Walwin, characters created by Captain W. E. Johns *d* John Hough *ph* Ernest Vincze *m* Stanislas *pd* Terry Pritchard

☆ Neil Dickson, Alex Hyde-White, Peter Cushing, Fiona Hutchison, Marcus Gilbert, William Hootkins

'If you're in the right undemanding mood it's just daft enough to be enjoyable.' – *The Dark Side*

Bij de Beesten Af: see *Ape and Super Ape*

Les Bijoutiers du Clair de Lune: see *Heaven Fell That Night*

Bike Boy *
US 1967 96m Eastmancolor
Vaughan/Factory Films (Andy Warhol)

A motorcyclist from the West Coast visiting New York has encounters with various women, one of whom seduces him.

Leisurely and occasionally witty exploration of low life, enlivened by the casually commanding presence of Viva.

w Andy Warhol and cast *d* Andy Warhol *ph* Paul Morrissey

☆ Joe Spencer, Viva, Brigid Polk, Ingrid Superstar, Ed Hood

'A strikingly pure exposition of Warhol's belief that the actor is the most important element in a film, and that the film-maker's job is simply to situate the actor to his best advantage.' – *Tony Rayns, MFB*

Bikini Beach
US 1964 100m Pathécolor Panavision
American International

A California beach is disputed by surfers, motor bikers, and a businessman who wants to build a retirement community.

Mindless youth nonsense with flashes of satire.

w William Asher, Leo Townsend, Robert Diller *d* William Asher

☆ Frankie Avalon, Annette Funicello, Martha Hyer, Don Rickles, Harvey Lembeck, Keenan Wynn, John Ashley, Boris Karloff (cameo)

Bill and Coo
US 1947 61m colour
Republic

Trials and tribulations of the inhabitants of Chirpendale are enacted entirely by birds, mostly wearing hats and neckties.

An eccentricity which won its creator, Ken Murray, a special Academy Award.

'By conservative estimate, the goddamnedest thing ever seen.' – *James Agee*

'Once ... they made history. Now ... they are history.'

Bill & Ted's Bogus Journey
US 1991 93m DeLuxe
Columbia TriStar/Orion/Nelson Entertainment (Scott Kroopf)

Killed by robots designed to resemble them, two inept college boys trick Death, enlist the help of God and become heavy-metal heroes.

A sequel that, like the original, has attracted a cult following, though the joke, depending on the slang spoken by its dim heroes, remains a thin one.

w Ed Solomon, Chris Matheson *d* Peter Hewitt *ph* Oliver Wood *m* David Newman *ed* David Finfer

☆ Alex Winter, Keanu Reeves, Jeff Miller, David Carrera, George Carlin, Joss Ackland, William Sadler

'A sequel that contrives another elaborate but non-excellent adventure.' – *Variety*

Bill and Ted's Excellent Adventure
US 1988 89m Technicolor Panavision
Castle Premier/Interscope Communications/Soisson-Murphey Productions/De Laurentiis Film Partners (Scott Kroopf, Michael S. Murphey, Joel Soisson)

In order to improve their essays, two high-school students, with the aid of a time machine, abduct famous historical figures and take them to modern-day America.

Mild comedy depending for its effect on an understanding of teenage Californian mores.

w Chris Matheson, Ed Solomon *d* Stephen Herek *ph* Timothy Suhrstedt *m* David Newman *pd* Roy Forge Smith, Lynda Paradise *ad* Gordon White, Pierluigi Basile *ed* Larry Bock, Patrick Rand

☆ Keanu Reeves, Alex Winter, Robert V. Barron, Terry Camilleri, Clifford David, Al Leong, Rod Loomis, Dan Shor, Tony Steedman, Jane Wiedlin

A Bill of Divorcement **
US 1932 76m bw
RKO/David O. Selznick

A middle-aged man, released from a mental institution, comes home and meets his strong-willed daughter.

Pattern play which became a celebrated star vehicle; now very dated but the performances survive. It was Hepburn's first film.

w Howard Estabrook, Harry Wagstaff Gribble *play* Clemence Dane *d* George Cukor *ph* Sid Hickox *m* Max Steiner, W. Franke Harling

☆ *John Barrymore, Katharine Hepburn,* Billie Burke, David Manners, Paul Cavanagh, Henry Stephenson, Elizabeth Patterson

'A money picture for all classes of houses ... the most potent tear jerker in many a moon.' – *Variety*

'A very good picture, tender, emotional and intensely gripping.' – *Picturegoer*

A Bill of Divorcement *
US 1940 69m bw
RKO
GB title: *Never To Love*

Virtually a scene-for-scene remake of the above.

Again the acting holds the material together.

w Dalton Trumbo *d* John Farrow *ph* Nicholas Musuraca *m* Roy Webb

☆ *Adolphe Menjou, Maureen O'Hara,* Patric Knowles, Herbert Marshall, C. Aubrey Smith, Dame May Whitty

Billie
US 1965 87m Technicolor Techniscope
UA/Peter Lawford (Don Weis)

A teenage tomboy runs into trouble because she is better at sport than her boyfriends.

Routine American college/domestic comedy with a young star and good comedy support.

w Ronald Alexander *play* *Time Out for Ginger* by Ronald Alexander *d* Don Weis *ph* John Russell *m* Dominic Frontière

☆ *Patty Duke,* Jim Backus, Jane Greer, Warren Berlinger, Billy de Wolfe, Charles Lane, Dick Sargent, Richard Deacon

Billion Dollar Brain
GB 1967 111m Technicolor Panavision
UA/Lowndes (Harry Saltzman)

Ex-secret agent Harry Palmer agrees to take a mysterious canister to Finland and becomes involved in an American megalomaniac's bid to take over the world.

Incomprehensible spy story smothered in the kind of top dressing now expected from this director, but which almost killed his career at the time. Occasional pictorial pleasures, but the total kaleidoscopic effect is enough to drive most audiences to the exit.

w John McGrath *novel* Len Deighton *d* Ken Russell *ph* Billy Williams *m* Richard Rodney Bennett *pd* Syd Cain

☆ Michael Caine, *Oscar Homolka,* Françoise Dorléac, Karl Malden, Ed Begley

Billion Dollar Scandal
US 1932 81m bw
Paramount

Ex-convicts are involved by a millionaire in a shady oil deal.

Competent but complex and talky melodrama 'from the headlines'.

w Gene Towne, Graham Baker *d* Harry Joe Brown

☆ Robert Armstrong, Constance Cummings, Frank Morgan, Olga Baclanova, James Gleason, Irving Pichel

A Billion for Boris
US 1990 89m TVC Color
Comworld Pictures (Sandy Russell Gartin, Ned Kandel)

An adolescent boy, who has problems with his mother, tries to get rich quick after he discovers that his old TV set shows the next day's programmes.

Predictable, soft-centred, slow-moving, lacklustre comedy.

w Sandy Russell Gartin *novel* Mary Rodgers *d* Alex Grasshoff *ph* Peter Stein *m* Robert Christianson *pd* Dan Leigh *ed* Sheila Bakerman

☆ Scott Tiler, Mary Tanner, Seth Green, Tim Kazurinsky, Lee Grant

Billy Bathgate
US 1991 106m DuArt
Warner/Touchstone (Arlene Donovan, Robert F. Colesbury)

A teenager becomes an assistant to gangster Dutch Schultz.

Curiously uninvolving and tepid thriller, with a lacklustre central performance.

w Tom Stoppard *novel* E. L. Doctorow *d* Robert Benton *ph* Nestor Almendros *m* Mark Isham *pd* Patrizia von Brandenstein *ed* Alan Heim, Robert Reitano

☆ Dustin Hoffman, Nicole Kidman, Loren Dean, Bruce Willis, Steven Hill, Steve Buscemi, Billy Jaye

'This refined, intelligent drama about thugs appeals considerably to the head but has little impact in the gut, which is not exactly how it should be with gangster films.' – *Variety*

'A film of minor virtues and major faults.' – *Sight and Sound*

'It has a grace and gravity rare just now in American films.' – *Richard Corliss, Time*

Billy Budd *
GB 1962 125m bw Cinemascope
Anglo-Allied (A. Ronald Lubin, Peter Ustinov)

In 1797 the sadistic master at arms of a British warship terrorizes the crew and is killed by young Billy Budd, who must hang for his unpremeditated crime.

Handsomely photographed but obtusely scripted and variously acted attempt at the impossible, an allegory of good and evil more suited to opera or the printed page than film: in any case, a hopelessly and defiantly uncommercial enterprise. Some actors bore, others chew the scenery.

w Peter Ustinov, Robert Rossen *novel* Herman Melville *play* *Louis O. Coxe, Robert H. Chapman* *d* Peter Ustinov *ph* Robert Krasker *m* Antony Hopkins *pd* Don Ashton *ed* Jack Harris *cos* Anthony Mendleson

☆ Peter Ustinov (Capt Edward Fairfax Vere), Robert Ryan (Master-at-Arms Claggart), Terence Stamp (Billy Budd), Melvyn Douglas (The Dansker), Paul Rogers (Lt Seymour), John Neville (Lt John Ratcliffe), Ronald Lewis (Jenkins), David McCallum (Lt Wyatt), Lee Montague (Squeak), John Meillon (Kincaid), Thomas Heathcote (Payne), Niall MacGinnis (Capt Graveling), Cyril Luckham (Hallam), Ray McAnally (O'Daniel)

'A beautiful, terrifying and heartbreaking film.' – *Time*

Academy Award nomination: Terence Stamp

Billy Elliot ***
GB 2000 111m colour
UIP/Working Title/BBC/Arts Council/Tiger Aspect/WT2 (Greg Brenman, Jon Finn)

In a Durham village during a year-long strike in 1984, an eleven-year-old miner's son defies his father by learning ballet rather than boxing.

Ingratiating, uplifting drama, deftly directed and with strong performances that disguise until later how manipulative the narrative is; its feel-good ending, though, is a cheat.

w Lee Hall *d* *Stephen Daldry* *ph* Brian Tufano *m* Stephen Warbeck *pd* Maria Djurkovic *ed* John Wilson *ch* Peter Darling

☆ *Julie Walters* (Mrs Wilkinson), *Gary Lewis* (Dad), *Jamie Bell* (Billy), Jamie Draven (Tony), Jean Heywood (Grandmother), Stuart Wells (Michael), Nicola Blackwell (Debbie)

'Has a feel-good factor that registers off the scale.' – *Allan Hunter, Screen International*

'The first genuinely exhilarating Brit flick of the new millennium, a no-holds-barred triumph.' – *Caroline Westbrook, Empire*

Academy Award nomination: Stephen Daldry; Lee Hall; Julie Walters

BAFTA: British film; Jamie Bell; Julie Walters

Billy Galvin *
US 1986 94m colour
American Playhouse/Vestron (Sue Jett, Tony Mark)

Frictions develop between father and son in blue collar Boston.

Old-fashioned family drama, quite rewarding for old-fashioned audiences.

wd John Gray *ph* Eugene Shlugleit *pd* Shay Austin *ed* Lou Kleinman

☆ Karl Malden, Lenny von Dohlen, Joyce Van Patten, Toni Kalem, Paul Guilfoyle

Billy Jack *
US 1971 113m Technicolor
Warner/National Student Film Corporation (Mary Rose Solti)

A half-breed Vietnam veteran roams the Arizona desert protecting wild mustangs and a runaway teenager.

A trendy radical drama, virtually a one-man show which had an enormous success in the US and led to a sequel, The Trial of Billy Jack.

w Tom Laughlin, Delores Taylor *d* Tom Laughlin (T. C. Frank) *ph* Fred Koenekamp, John Stephens *m* Mundell Lowe

☆ Tom Laughlin, Delores Taylor, Bert Freed, Clark Howat, Julie Webb, Ken Tobey, Victor Izay

'A plea for the alternative society with a format of the crudest melodrama.' – *MFB*

Billy Liar ***
GB 1963 98m bw Cinemascope
Vic Films (Joe Janni)

In a drab North Country town, an undertaker's clerk lives in a world of fantasy.

Flawed only by its unsuitable Cinemascope ratio, this is a brilliant urban comedy of its time, seminal in acting, theme, direction and permissiveness.

w *Keith Waterhouse, Willis Hall* *play* Keith Waterhouse, Willis Hall *novel* *Keith Waterhouse inspired by Thurber's Walter Mitty* *d* *John Schlesinger* *ph* Denys Coop *m* Richard Rodney Bennett

☆ *Tom Courtenay, Julie Christie,* Wilfred Pickles, Mona Washbourne, *Ethel Griffies,* Finlay Currie, Rodney Bewes, Leonard Rossiter

'John Schlesinger's direction, I am delighted to say, is rich in wit.' – *Dilys Powell*

† It was later turned into a TV series and a successful stage musical, making Billy a universal figure of the period.

Billy Madison
US 1995 90m DeLuxe
Universal (Robert Simonds)

A rich slacker vows to work his way through a different grade of school every two weeks to prove himself to his father so that he can inherit the family business.

Dim and coarse-toned comedy that does not travel well, featuring a performer of slight appeal outside the US, and material that might have sufficed for a funny five minutes.

w Tim Herlihy, Adam Sandler *d* Tamra Davis *ph* Victor Hammer *m* Randy Edelman *pd* Perry Blake *ed* Jeffrey Wolf

☆ Adam Sandler, Darren McGavin, Bridgette Wilson, Bradley Whitford, Josh Mostel, Norm MacDonald

'As derivative a compound as the dross left over from a particularly noxious junior school chemistry experiment.' – *Leslie Felperin, Sight and Sound*

† Steve Buscemi appears uncredited.

Billy Rose's Diamond Horseshoe: see *Diamond Horseshoe*

Billy Rose's Jumbo: see *Jumbo*

Billy the Kid *
US 1930 90m bw
MGM

A young Western outlaw is relentlessly pursued by Sheriff Pat Garrett.

Mildly interesting early talkie Western with the usual romanticized view of Billy. Originally made and shown in 70mm.

w Wanda Tuchock, Laurence Stallings, Charles MacArthur *d* King Vidor *ph* Gordon Avil

☆ Johnny Mack Brown, Wallace Beery, Kay Johnson, Karl Dane, Roscoe Ates

'Should stand up for slightly better than average business where shown on Realife. Otherwise just an ordinary western.' – *Variety*

Billy the Kid *

US 1941 95m Technicolor

MGM (Irving Asher)

Remake of the above, equally false and rather less well acted, but a striking outdoor colour film of its period.

w Gene Fowler *d* David Miller *ph* Leonard Smith, William V. Skall *m* David Snell

☆ Robert Taylor, Brian Donlevy, Ian Hunter, Mary Howard, Gene Lockhart, Henry O'Neill, Frank Puglia, Cy Kendall, Ethel Griffies

Leonard Smith, William V. Skall

Billy the Kid and the Green Baize Vampire

GB 1985 93m colour

ITC/Zenith (Simon Mallin)

A hustling young snooker player takes on a formidable opponent.

Predictable sporting melodrama with curious supernatural overtones; not a coherent whole.

w Trevor Preston *d* Alan Clarke *ph* Clive Tickner *m* George Fenton *pd* Jamie Leonard

☆ Phil Daniels, Alun Armstrong, Bruce Payne, Louise Gold, Eve Ferret

'Weird, not to say downright perverse.' – *Sight and Sound*

Billy the Kid vs Dracula

US 1965 89m Pathécolor

Avco Embassy/Circle/Embassy (Carroll Case)

Billy the Kid rescues his fiancée from the clutches of Dracula.

Comic treatment of horror and Westerns, with Billy as a clean-cut hero, that may appeal to fans of bad movies.

w Carl K. Hittleman *d* William Beaudine *ph* Lothrop Worth *m* Raoul Kraushaar *ad* Paul Sylos, Harry Reif *ed* Roy Livingston

☆ Chuck Courtney, John Carradine, Melinda Plowman, Virginia Christine, Walter Janovitz, Olive Carey, Harry Carey Jnr

'Great fun, pleasingly economical, and by no means an unworthy conclusion to Beaudine's career' – *David McGillivray, MFB*

Billy Two Hats

US 1973 99m Technicolor

UA/Algonquin (Norman Jewison, Patrick Palmer, Mitchell Lifton)

aka: *The Lady and the Outlaw*

The friendship of an old Scottish outlaw and a young half-breed is broken only by the old man's death.

Curiously miscast Western shot in Israel; it makes no discernible point and is not very entertaining.

w Alan Sharp *d* Ted Kotcheff *ph* Brian West *m* John Scott

☆ Gregory Peck, Desi Arnaz Jnr, Jack Warden, Sian Barbara Allen, David Huddleston

'Lights... Camera... Attraction!'

Billy's Hollywood Screen Kiss

US 1998 92m colour Panavision

Revolutionary Eye LLC (David Moseley)

A gay photographer desires his male model, who claims to be heterosexual.

Trivial romantic comedy, so insubstantial as to hardly register at all.

wd Tommy O'Haver *ph* Mark Mervis *m* Alan Ari Lazar *ch* Michele Spears, Joseph McKee *pd* Franco-Giacomo Carbone *ed* Jeff Betancourt

☆ Sean P. Hayes (Sean P. Hayes), Brad Rowe (Gabriel), Richard Ganoung (Perry), Meredith Scott Lynn (Georgiana), Matthew Ashford (Whitey), Armando Valdes-Kennedy (Fernando), Paul Bartel (Rex Webster), Carmine D. Giovinazzo (Gundy), Holly Woodlawn (Holly), Christopher Bradley (Andrew)

'I felt like I'd seen it many, many times before.' – *Peter Bradshaw, Guardian*

Biloxi Blues *

US 1988 106m colour Panavision

Universal/Rastar (Ray Stark)

Standard, quite pleasing version of a Broadway comedy about a conscript called up in 1945 when World War Two was ending.

w Neil Simon *play* Neil Simon *d* Mike Nichols *ph* Bill Butler *m* Georges Delerue *pd* Paul Sylbert *ed* Sam O'Steen

☆ Matthew Broderick, Christopher Walken, Matt Mulhern, Corey Parker

Bingo

US 1991 90m Technicolor

Tri-Star (Thomas Baer)

A runaway circus dog follows across country the boy who befriended him, when his family moves home.

Dully dogged comedy in which the animals behave like humans; it may amuse small children given to anthropomorphism, but I doubt it.

w Jim Strain *d* Matthew Robbins *ph* John McPherson *m* Richard Gibbs *pd* Mark Freeborn *ed* Maryann Brandon

☆ Cindy Williams, David Rasche, Robert J. Steinmiller Jnr, David French, Kurt Fuller, Joe Guzaldo, Glenn Shadix

The Bingo Long Traveling All-Stars and Motor Kings

US 1976 111m Technicolor

Universal (Rob Cohen)

Adventures of a black baseball team in the 1940s.

High-spirited japes and exhibitions of athleticism which dramatically do not add up to very much.

w Hal Barwood, Matthew Robbins *novel* William Brashler *d* John Badham *ph* Bill Butler *m* William Goldstein

☆ Billy Dee Williams, James Earl Jones, Richard Pryor, Rico Dawson

'Modest pleasures and dull stretches co-exist in equal abundance.' – *Frank Rich, New York Times*

Bio-Dome

US 1996 95m colour

MGM/Motion Picture Corp/Weasel/3 Arts (Brad Krevoy, Steve Stabler, Brad Jenkel)

Two dim students are inadvertently trapped for a year in a sealed dome where scientists are carrying out environmental experiments.

Yet another in the 90s cycle of dumb comedies involving stupid heroes and their bodily functions; this, though, may be the dumbest so far.

w Kip Koenig, Scott Marcano *story* Adam Leff, Mitchell Peck, Jason Blumenthal *d* Jason Bloom *ph* Phedon Papamichael *m* Andrew Gross *pd* Michael Johnston *ed* Christopher Greenbury

☆ Pauly Shore, Stephen Baldwin, William Atherton, Joey Lauren Adams, Teresa Hill, Henry Gibson, Kevin West, Kylie Minogue

'Definitely a dome of doom, the "Bio" pic is likely to leapfrog the endangered list for deserved extinction.' – *Leonard Klady, Variety*

Biography (of a Bachelor Girl) *

US 1935 84m bw

MGM (Irving Thalberg)

The biography of a sophisticated lady portrait painter reveals surprising details of her love life.

Leaden, bowdlerized screen version of a sparkling Broadway play, fragments of which do however survive. It isn't helped by the miscasting of Ann Harding.

w Anita Loos *play* S. N. Behrman *d* Edward H. Griffith *ph* James Wong Howe *m* Herbert Stothart

☆ Ann Harding, Robert Montgomery, Edward Everett Horton, Edward Arnold, Una Merkel, Charles Richman, Donald Meek

'Smart entertainment for top houses. Possibly too smart for the other end.' – *Variety*

Birch Interval

US 1976 105m colour

Gamma III (Robert B. Radnitz)

A twelve-year-old girl goes to live with her Amish relations in the country.

Simple-minded moral tale which needed some old-fashioned style to bring it off.

w Joanna Crawford *novel* Joanna Crawford *d* Delbert Mann

☆ Eddie Albert, Rip Torn, Susan McClung, Ann Wedgeworth, Bill Lucking

Bird *

US 1988 161m Technicolor

Warner/Malpaso (Clint Eastwood)

The life of Charlie Parker.

Long, downbeat, heavygoing treatment of America's greatest black alto saxophonist; but not a popular choice.

w Joel Oliansky *d* Clint Eastwood *ph* Jack N. Green *m* Lennie Niehaus

☆ Forest Whitaker, Diane Venora, Michael Zelniker

Bird of Paradise

US 1932 80m bw

RKO (David O. Selznick)

An adventurer on a South Sea island marries a native girl and causes trouble.

Never-never romance which remains stilted despite care obviously taken.

w Wells Root *d* King Vidor *ph* Clyde de Vinna *m* Max Steiner

☆ Joel McCrea, John Halliday, *Dolores del Rio*, Skeets Gallagher

'The old tropical romance nicely done. OK for the main stem stands.' – *Variety*

Bird of Paradise

US 1951 100m Technicolor

TCF (Harmon Jones)

Opulent remake of the above; the trappings make it even more absurd, and the ritual sacrifice of the heroine seems misplaced in what is otherwise a pantomime.

wd Delmer Daves *ph* Winton Hoch *m* Daniele Amfitheatrof

☆ Louis Jourdan, Jeff Chandler, Debra Paget, Maurice Schwartz, Everett Sloane, Jack Elam

'The Kahuna is a naively grotesque figure, with a Central European accent and carrying what appears to be an outsize radish: he personifies the film's dubious approach to Polynesian myth and culture.' – *Gavin Lambert*

Bird of Prey

US/Bulgaria 1995 101m Foto-Kem

BM5/Sneak Preview/First Private Bank (Boyan Milushev, Jonathan Debin)

A policeman's son takes revenge on an American drug and arms dealer who murdered his father, beginning with the seduction of the man's daughter.

The Bulgarian setting is the only novelty in an otherwise unremarkable movie, full of the usual confrontations, gun battles and explosions of the genre.

w Boyan Milushev, James J. Mellon, Tracy Hall Adams, Lynette Prucha *d* Temistocles Lopez *ph* David Knaus *m* Brian Clifton *pd* Robert Harbour *ed* Ila von Hasperg, Tracy Hall Adams

☆ Jennifer Tilly, Boyan Milushev, Richard Chamberlain, Lesley Ann Warren, Robert Carradine, Lenny von Dohlen

'A conventional thriller that hasn't quite got the extra punch needed to elevate it above video fare.' – *Variety*

Bird on a Wire

US 1990 111m DeLuxe Super 35

UIP/Universal/Badham-Cohen-Interscope Communications (Ron Cohen)

A lawyer and her former lover run from their would-be assassins.

Chase comedy, too frenetic to be funny.

w David Seltzer, Louis Venosta, Eric Lerner *d* John Badham *ph* Robert Primes *m* Hans Zimmer *pd* Philip Harrison *ad* Richard Hudolin *ed* Frank Morriss, Dallas Puett

☆ Mel Gibson, Goldie Hawn, David Carradine, Bill Duke, Stephen Tobolowsky, Joan Severance, Harry Caesar, Jeff Corey

'One of those star vehicles from deepest Hollywood for which there seems no adequate reason other than to pay someone's mortgage.' – *Derek Malcolm, Guardian*

The Bird with the Crystal Plumage

Italy 1969 98m colour Cromosscope

Salvatore Argento

GB title: *The Gallery Murders*

A supposed murderer is vindicated when his alleged next victim turns out to be a psychopath.

Tolerable shocker which was popular in dubbed version.

wd Dario Argento

☆ Suzy Kendall, Tony Musante

'What could possibly come between a match made in heaven? The parents. Dinner. And a nightclub called..'

The Birdcage *

US 1996 119m Technicolor Panavision

United Artists (Mike Nichols)

The son of a homosexual club-owner persuades his father to act the heterosexual at a dinner with his future in-laws, a right-wing senator and his wife, but his father's lover, a drag artiste, insists on appearing as his mother.

An American version of a 20-year-old French farce; it has some funny moments, but, despite the best efforts of all concerned, seems resolutely old-fashioned and adds nothing to the original; the jokes at the expense of effeminacy begin to wear after a while.

w Elaine May *script* *La Cage aux Folles* by *Francis Veber, Edouard Molinaro, Marcello Danon, Jean Poiret* *d* Mike Nichols *ph* Emmanuel Lubezki *m* Jonathan Tunick, Steven Goldstein *pd* Bo Welch *ed* Arthur Schmidt

☆ Robin Williams, Nathan Lane, Gene Hackman, Dianne Wiest, Christine Baranski, Hank Azaria, Dan Futterman, Calista Flockhart

'This is a copy of an old success which doesn't bother much about reality, and ends more like a pantomime than a proper dramatic entity.' – *Derek Malcolm, Guardian*

'Performed with matchless aplomb and made with a plush professionalism, pic serves up pure pleasure from beginning to end.' – *Todd McCarthy, Variety*

† The film is a remake of the French hit *La Cage aux Folles* (qv). It was a hit, taking more than $110m at the US box-office.

Bo Welch

Birdman of Alcatraz *

US 1962 148m bw

UA/Hecht-Lancaster (Stuart Millar, Guy Trosper)

An imprisoned murderer makes a name for himself as an ornithologist.

Overlong and rather weary biopic of Robert Stroud, who spent nearly sixty years in prison and became a cause célèbre. One cannot deny many effective moments, notably of direction, but it's a long haul.

w Guy Trosper *book* Thomas E. Gaddis *d* *John Frankenheimer* *ph* Burnett Guffey *m* Elmer Bernstein

☆ Burt Lancaster, Karl Malden, Thelma Ritter, Edmond O'Brien, Betty Field, Neville Brand, Hugh Marlowe, Telly Savalas, James Westerfield

Burnett Guffey; Burt Lancaster; Thelma Ritter; Telly Savalas

Burt Lancaster

'Suspense and shock beyond anything you have ever seen or imagined!'

The Birds ***

US 1963 119m Technicolor

Universal/Alfred Hitchcock

In a Californian coastal area, flocks of birds unaccountably make deadly attacks on human beings.

A curiously absorbing work which begins as light comedy and ends as apocalyptic allegory, this piece of Hitchcockery has no visible point except to tease the audience and provide plenty of opportunity for shock, offbeat humour and special effects (which despite the drumbeating are not quite as good as might be expected). The actors are pawns in the master's hand.

w Evan Hunter *story* Daphne du Maurier *d* *Alfred Hitchcock* *ph* *Robert Burks* *m* Bernard Herrmann *pd* Robert Boyle *ed* George Tomasini *sp* Lawrence A. Hampton, Ub Iwerks *sound consultant* Bernard Herrmann *cos* Edith Head

☆ Rod Taylor (Mitch Brenner), Tippi Hedren (Melanie Daniels), Jessica Tandy (Lydia Brenner), Suzanne Pleshette (Annie Hayworth), Ethel Griffies (Mrs Bundy), Charles McGraw (Sebastian

Sholes), Ruth McDevitt (Mrs MacGruder), Doodles Weaver (Fisherman)

'Enough to make you kick the next pigeon you come across.' – *Judith Crist*

'The dialogue is stupid, the characters insufficiently developed to rank as clichés, the story incohesive.' – *Stanley Kauffmann*

'We must sit through half an hour of pachydermous flirtation between Rod and Tippi before the seagull attacks, and another fifteen minutes of tedium ... before the birds attack again. If one adds later interrelations between mother, girlfriend and a particularly repulsive child actress, about two-thirds of the film is devoted to extraneous matters. Poe would have been appalled.' – *Dwight MacDonald*

The Birds and the Bees: see *Three Daring Daughters (1948) (1948)*

The Birds and the Bees
US 1956 94m Technicolor Vistavision
Paramount (Paul Jones)

On a transatlantic voyage a wealthy simpleton is fleeced by a card sharp and his daughter; but the latter falls in love with her victim.
Competent but uninspired reworking of The Lady Eve *(qv) as a vehicle for a rather charmless comic. Lacking Preston Sturges at the helm, the mixture of slapstick and sentiment fails to jell.*
w Sidney Sheldon after Preston Sturges
d Norman Taurog *ph* Daniel Fapp *m* Walter Scharf
☆ George Gobel, David Niven, Mitzi Gaynor, Fred Clark, Reginald Gardiner, Harry Bellaver, Hans Conried

'Beneath her icy composure lay a deep desire to love!'
Birds Come to Die in Peru
France 1968 98m Technicolor Franscope
Universal France (Jacques Natteau)
On a Peruvian beach a tormented nymphomaniac makes love to several men and attempts suicide, but is rescued by her true love.
Elaborate high-flown bosh, quite fun to watch.
wd Romain Gary *ph* Christian Matras *m* Kenton Coe
☆ Jean Seberg, Maurice Ronet, Danielle Darrieux, Pierre Brasseur

Birds of a Feather: see *La Cage aux Folles*

The Birds, the Bees and the Italians
Italy/France 1965 98m colour
Dear Film/Films du Siècle (Robert Haggiag, Pietro Germi)
original title: *Signore e Signori*
Stories of adultery in an Italian provincial town.
Mainly tedious sex comedy full of gesticulating actors.
w Furio Scarpelli, Luciano Vincenzoni, Pietro Germi *d* Pietro Germi *ph* Aiace Parolin
m Carlo Rustichelli
☆ Gastone Moschin, Virna Lisi, Alberto Lionello, Gigi Ballista, Beba Loncar, Franco Fabrizi

The Birdwatcher *
Estonia 1987 84m colour
Palinfilm
A young man studying seagulls on a remote island nature reserve has a stormy relationship with a grouchy middle-aged widow.
Enjoyable account of a clash of temperaments – town against country, idealism versus pragmatism, masculine and feminine – with an unexpectedly harsh ending.
w Marina Sheptunova *d* Arvo Ikho *ph* Tatyana Loginova *m* Lepo Sumera
☆ Svetlana Tormakhova, Eric Ruus

Birdy
US 1984 120m Metrocolor
Tri-Star (Alan Marshall)
A psychologically disturbed war veteran thinks he can fly like a bird.
A case history which somewhat lacks plot advancement. Too self-indulgent even to earn marks for trying.
w Sandy Kroopf, Jack Behr *novel* William Wharton *d* Alan Parker *ph* Michael Seresin
m Peter Gabriel *pd* Geoffrey Kirkland
☆ Matthew Modine, Nicolas Cage, John Harkins, Sandy Baron

'Likely will fall short of taking full flight at the box office.' – *Variety*

Birth of a Legend *
US 1966 26m bw
Mary Pickford Corporation
Sprightly compilation of clips from the films of Mary Pickford and Douglas Fairbanks; the treatment is cursory but sympathetic.
wd Matty Kemp

'The dawn of a new art!'
The Birth of a Nation ****
US 1915 185m approx (16 fps) bw silent
Epoch (D. W. Griffith, Harry E. Aitken)
Northern and Southern families are caught up in the Civil War.
The cinema's first and still most famous epic, many sequences of which retain their mastery despite negro villains, Ku Klux Klan heroes, and white actors in blackface. Originally shown as The Clansman*; a shorter version with orchestral track was released in 1931.*
w D. W. Griffith, Frank E. Woods *novel The Klansman* by Thomas Dixon Jnr *d D. W. Griffith ph* G. W. Bitzer
☆ Henry B. Walthall, Mae Marsh, Miriam Cooper, Lillian Gish, Robert Harron, Wallace Reid, Donald Crisp, Joseph Henabery, Raoul Walsh, Eugene Pallette, Walter Long

'A film version of some of the melodramatic and inflammatory material contained in *The Clansman* ... a great deal might be said concerning the sorry service rendered by its plucking at old wounds. But of the film as a film, it may be reported simply that it is an impressive new illustration of the scope of the motion picture camera.' – *New York Times*

'Griffith was, in his prime, a nineteenth-century humanist working in a twentieth-century medium. And, speaking for myself, I should welcome today some infusion of that unashamed humane sentiment into the smart machine-made films I see every week.' – *Dilys Powell, 1945*

† The soundtrack album features a recording of the score written by Joseph Carl Breil to accompany the film in 1915.

The Birth of the Blues *
US 1941 85m bw
Paramount (B. G. de Sylva, Monta Bell)
Trials and tribulations of a jazz band in New Orleans.
Thin fiction on which is strung a multitude of jazz-influenced musical entertainment. Not bad, even now.
w Harry Tugend, Walter de Leon *d* Victor Schertzinger *ph* William C. Mellor *md* Robert Emmett Dolan
☆ Bing Crosby, Mary Martin, Brian Donlevy, Jack Teagarden, Eddie 'Rochester' Anderson, Carolyn Lee
♫ 'The Birth of the Blues'; 'By the Light of the Silvery Moon'; 'Wait 'til the Sun Shines, Nellie'; 'My Melancholy Baby'; 'The Waiter and the Porter and the Upstairs Maid'; 'St Louis Blues'.
Robert Emmett Dolan

The Birthday Party *
GB 1968 126m Technicolor
Palomar (Max Rosenberg, Milton Subotsky)
The down-at-heel lodger in a seaside boarding house is menaced by two mysterious strangers, who eventually take him away.
Overlong but otherwise satisfactory film record of an entertaining if infuriating play, first of the black absurdities which proliferated in the sixties to general disadvantage, presenting structure without plot and intelligence without meaning.
w Harold Pinter *play* Harold Pinter *d* William Friedkin *ph* Denys Coop *m* none *pd* Edward Marshall
☆ Sydney Tafler, Patrick Magee, Robert Shaw, *Dandy Nichols*, Moultrie Kelsall

The Birthday Present *
GB 1957 100m bw
BL/Jack Whittingham
A toy salesman's life is changed when he is charged with smuggling a watch through the customs.
Downcast, prolonged and rather uninteresting domestic drama; attention is held by generally good acting.
w Jack Whittingham *d* Pat Jackson *ph* Ted Scaife *m* Clifton Parker
☆ *Tony Britton*, Sylvia Syms, Jack Watling, Walter Fitzgerald, Geoffrey Keen, Howard Marion Crawford, John Welsh

Biruma no Tategoto: see *The Burmese Harp*

Bis ans Ende der Welt: see *Until the End of the World*

The Biscuit Eater
GB title, 1940 version: *God Gave Him a Dog*
Two versions exist of this story by James Street about a white and a black boy who turn a stray into a crack hunting dog. The first was by Stuart Heisler for Paramount in 1940; it starred Billy Lee and made quite a box-office impact. The second was by Vincent McEveety for Disney in 1972, with Johnny Whittaker; despite the presence of Earl Holliman and Lew Ayres it made no impact at all.

The Bishop Misbehaves *
US 1935 87m bw
MGM
GB title: *The Bishop's Misadventures*
A bishop gets on the wrong side of the law when he helps a young girl to see justice done.
Amusing trifle with strong cast.
w Leon Gordon, George Auerbach *play* Frederick Jackson *d* E. A. Dupont
☆ Edmund Gwenn, Maureen O'Sullivan, Lucile Watson, Reginald Owen, Robert Greig, Dudley Digges, Melville Cooper, Lillian Bond

'Reaches a grade above the average programmer, but points mainly to sophisticated patronage.' – *Variety*

The Bishop Murder Case
US 1930 91m bw
MGM
Philo Vance unmasks a killer who sends warning notes in rhyme.
Mildly interesting early talkie detection which moves at too stately a pace.
w Lenore Coffee *novel* S. S. Van Dine *d* Nick Grinde, David Burton *ph* Roy Overbaugh
ad Cedric Gibbons *ed* William Le Vanway
☆ Basil Rathbone, Leila Hyams, Alec B. Francis, Roland Young, George Marion

The Bishop's Misadventures: see *The Bishop Misbehaves*

The Bishop's Wife **
US 1947 108m bw
Samuel Goldwyn
An angel is sent down to mend the ways of a bishop whose absorption with cathedral buildings has put him out of touch with his wife and parishioners.
Whimsical, stolid and protracted light comedy saved by its actors and its old-fashioned Hollywood style.
w Robert E. Sherwood, Leonardo Bercovici
novel Robert Nathan *d* Henry Koster *ph* Gregg Toland *m* Hugo Friedhofer *ed* Monica Collingwood
☆ Cary Grant, Loretta Young, David Niven, Monty Woolley, James Gleason, Gladys Cooper, Elsa Lanchester, Sara Haden, Regis Toomey

'It is the Protestant comeback to the deadly successful RC propaganda of *Going My Way* and *The Bells of St Mary's*. It surpasses in tastelessness, equals in whimsy and in technique falls well below those crooning parables. It is really quite a monstrous film.' – *Richard Winnington, News Chronicle*

'When a film undertakes to bring audiences a spiritual message, we wonder whether the director doesn't owe it to us to clothe such messages in less muddled characterizations and to dispense with caricature.' – *Scholastic Magazine*

'A sophisticated *Christmas Carol*.' – *Philip Hartung*

'As cheerful an invasion of the realm of conscience as we have seen.' – *New York Times*

† Director William A. Seiter was replaced when the film was half complete; this caused nearly one million dollars to be wasted.
best picture; Henry Koster; Hugo Friedhofer; editing

A Bit of Scarlet
GB 1996 75m colour
BFI/Channel 4/Maya Vision (Rebecca Dobbs)
Documentary on the way homosexuality has been treated or ignored by the British cinema, with clips to illustrate various rules of representation.
Irritating approach to an interesting subject, cutting from one unidentified film clip to another in a specious but ultimately unconvincing manner.
d Andrea Weiss *m* John Eacott *ed* Andrea Weiss
☆ Ian McKellen (narrator)

The Bit Player: see *Salut l'Artiste*

The Bitch
GB 1979 94m colour
Brent Walker (John Quested)
A woman of much influence in London's underworld has a temporary liaison with a young gangster wanted by the Mafia.
Intolerable sexed-up sequel to The Stud *(qv), hard on both eyes and ears.*
wd Gerry O'Hara *story* Jackie Collins *ph* Denis Lewiston *m* Biddu *ad* Malcolm Middleton *ed* Ed Joseph
☆ Joan Collins, Kenneth Haigh, Michael Coby, Ian Hendry, Carolyn Seymour, Sue Lloyd, Mark Burns

'Appropriately enough for a film whose sole rationale seems to be its chic consumerist decoration (and of course its disco soundtrack), *The Bitch* ruthlessly pares away any other elements of interest.' – *Richard Combs, MFB.*

The Bitch
France 1984 100m colour
Sara Films/FR3 (Alain Sarde)
French title: *La Garce*
After serving a six-year sentence for rape, a former cop finds work as a private detective and finds himself investigating the girl he assaulted.
Routine thriller of double-crossed lovers.
w Pierre Fabre, Laurent Heynemann, Christine Pascal, A. M. Delocque Fourcaud *d* Christine Pascal *ph* Raoul Coutard *m* Philippe Sarde
ed Jacques Comets
☆ Isabelle Huppert, Richard Berry, Vittorio Mezzogiorno, Jean Benguigui, Jean-Claude Legay, Jean-Pierre Moulin, Clement Harrari

Bite the Bullet *
US 1975 131m Metrocolor Panavision
Columbia/Persky-Bright/Vista (Richard Brooks)
Several cowboys compete in a 700-mile endurance horse race.
Episodic adventure story with too much muddled chat and a very thin connecting story line; good to look at, though.
wd Richard Brooks *ph* Harry Stradling Jnr
m Alex North
☆ Gene Hackman, Candice Bergen, James Coburn, Ben Johnson, Ian Bannen, Jan-Michael Vincent, Paul Stewart
Alex North

Bits and Pieces *
Italy 1995 109m Technicolor
Electric/Fandango/Colorado (Domenico Procacci, Maurizio Totti)
original title: *Il cielo è sempre più blu*
As a jogger takes his exercise, events involving theft, desire, deception and death happen in Rome.
An episodic account of a day in the life of an urban jungle, full of casual betrayals, curious happenings and cruelty; but there is a sense of randomness about the events, which fail to come together to form a bigger picture.
w Daniele Cesarano, Paolo Marchesini
d Antonella Grimaldi *ph* Alessandro Pesci
m Enzo Favata, Jana Project *ad* Giada Calabria
ed Angelo Nicolini
☆ Asia Argento, Luca Barbareschi, Margherita Buy, Roberto Citran, Enrico Lo Verso, Ivano Marescotti, Dario Argento

'I want something good to happen to me before I die!'
Bitter Harvest
GB 1963 96m Eastmancolor
Rank/Independent Artists (Albert Fennell)
An innocent Welsh girl comes to London, is deflowered, and sets off in search of wealth and luxury at any price.

Naïve 60s version of the road to ruin, quite well done if you like that kind of thing.
w Ted Willis *d* Peter Graham Scott *ph* Ernest Steward *m* Laurie Johnson
☆ Janet Munro, John Stride, Anne Cunningham, Alan Badel, Thora Hird, Vanda Godsell, Terence Alexander

'Some lovers never know when to stop...'
Bitter Moon
GB/France 1992 139m colour
Columbia Tristar/Les Films Alain Sarde/Canal/R.P. Productions/Timothy Burrill Productions (Roman Polanski)
original title: *Lunes de Fiel*
On board a liner an English couple are drawn into the sadistic sexual fantasies of a crippled American writer and his French wife.
Incoherent melodrama of the corruption of innocence; but we've all been here too many times before for this treatment to carry any appeal.
w Roman Polanski, Gérard Brach, John Brownjohn *novel* Pascal Bruckner *d* Roman Polanski *ph* Tonino Delli Colli *m* Vangelis *pd* Willy Holt, Gérard Viard *ed* Hervé de Luze
☆ Peter Coyote, Emmanuelle Seigner, Hugh Grant, Kristin Scott-Thomas, Victor Banerjee, Sophie Patel, Stockard Channing
'A slick psycho-drama ... the work of a perverse, exhausted talent narrated by a perverse, exhausted, talentless writer to trap a dim-witted listener.' – *Philip French, Observer*

Bitter Rice *
Italy 1949 108m bw
Lux Films
original title: *Riso Amaro*
In the rice fields of the Po valley, a thief on the run meets a girl who tries to steal his loot.
Well-made exploitation melodrama which made a star of the well-endowed Mangano but is not otherwise more memorable than its innumerable American counterparts.
w Carlo Lizzani, Carlo Musso, Gianni Puccini, Corrado Alvaro, Ivo Perilli, Giuseppe de Santis *d* Giuseppe de Santis *ph* Otello Martelli *m* Goffredo Petrassi
☆ *Silvana Mangano*, Raf Vallone, Doris Dowling, Vittorio Gassman
† Its scene of peasant women in the mud of the paddy fields is said to have inspired one of William de Kooning's best-known paintings, *Excavation* (1950).
original story

Bitter Springs *
GB 1950 89m bw
Ealing (Leslie Norman)
A pioneer family in Australia buys a patch of ground but has trouble with aborigines.
Thinnest of the Ealing attempts to make movies down under, suffering from a lack of pace and sharpness as well as obvious studio settings.
w Monja Danischewsky, W. P. Lipscomb *d* Ralph Smart *ph* George Heath *m* Vaughan Williams
☆ Chips Rafferty, Tommy Trinder, Gordon Jackson, Jean Blue, Charles Tingwell

Bitter Sweet
GB 1933 93m bw
UA/British and Dominion (Herbert Wilcox)
In 1875 Vienna, a violinist marries a girl dancer and is later killed by a gambler.
Rather feeble filming of Noël Coward's operetta: it pleased a lot of people at the time.
w Lydia Hayward, Herbert Wilcox, Monckton Hoffe *d* Herbert Wilcox *ph* Freddie Young *m* Noël Coward *md* Lew Stone *ad* L. P. Williams
☆ Anna Neagle, Fernand Gravet, Ivy St Helier, Miles Mander, Esmé Percy, Hugh Williams, Pat Paterson, Kay Hammond

Bitter Sweet
US 1940 94m Technicolor
MGM (Victor Saville)
Remake of the above, retailored for unsuitable leads and with the story and music unattractively rearranged.
w Lesser Samuels *d* W. S. Van Dyke II *ph* Oliver T. Marsh, Allen Davey *m* Noël Coward *ad* Cedric Gibbons, John S. Detlie
☆ Jeanette Macdonald, Nelson Eddy, George Sanders, Felix Bressart, Ian Hunter, Fay Holden, Sig Rumann, Herman Bing, Curt Bois
'It's now chiefly eye-and-ear entertainment, with the original sentimental charm and romance missing.' – *Variety*
Oliver T. Marsh, Allen Davey; art direction

The Bitter Tea of General Yen **
US 1932 89m bw
Columbia (Walter Wanger)
An American lady missionary in Shanghai is captured by a Chinese warlord and falls in love with him.
Arty miscegenation story which bids fair to become a cult film and certainly has a number of interesting sequences.
w Edward Paramore *story* Grace Zaring Stone *d Frank Capra* *ph* Joseph Walker *m* W. Franke Harling
☆ Barbara Stanwyck, Nils Asther, Toshia Mori, Walter Connolly, Gavin Gordon, Lucien Littlefield
'It is doubtful whether this picture can make the grade without support ... photographic advantages cannot overcome the queer story.' – *Variety*
† The film chosen to open Radio City Music Hall.

The Bitter Tears of Petra von Kant
West Germany 1972 124m colour
Tango/Rainer Werner Fassbinder, Michael Fengler
original title: *Die bitteren Tränen der Petra von Kant*
Lesbian jealousies in the fashion world.
Interesting but exhausting hothouse confection, no more likeable than the Hollywood kind for being more intelligent about its perversions.
wd Rainer Werner Fassbinder *ph* Michael Ballhaus *m* The Platters and others *ed* Thea Eymèsz
☆ Margit Carstensen, Irm Hermann, Hanna Schygulla, Eva Mattes
'Dazzling in the brittle brilliance of its execution, the precision of its structure and movement, the total hermetic self-containment of the little world it creates.' – *David Robinson, The Times*

Bittere Ernte **
West Germany 1985 102m colour
Filmkunst (Artur Brauner)
GB title: *Angry Harvest*
An inhibited farmer shelters a Jewish woman from the authorities, with tragic results.
Intermittently moving, though heavy going at times.
w Paul Hengge, Agnieszka Holland *d* Agnieszka Holland *ph* Josef Ort-Snep *m* Jorg Strass Burger *ed* Barbara Kunze
☆ Armin Muller-Stahl, Elisabeth Trissenaar, Kathe Jaenicke, Hans Beerhenke, Isla Haller, Margit Carstensen
best foreign film

Bittersweet Love
US 1976 92m colour
Zappala-Slott
Newlyweds discover that they both had the same father.
Old-fashioned family shocker which needed a lot more zip if it was going to shock anybody.
w Adrian Morrall, D. A. Kellogg *d* David Miller
☆ Lana Turner, Robert Alda, Celeste Holm, Robert Lansing, Scott Hylands, Denise DeMirjian
'Performances and settings are all very high class. I mean, when you have all that money and those great surroundings you can still suffer, but you do have multiple choices.' – *Archer Winsten, New York Post*

Bizarre, Bizarre: see *Drôle de Drame*

Black and White **
US 1999 99m colour
Columbia TriStar/Palm (Michael Mailer, Daniel Bigel, Ron Rotholz)
A black gangster who decides to become a rap artist attracts a white following, but is unable to escape his violent past.
Hectic study of racial politics, partly improvised and homing in on white appropriation and corruption of other cultures.
wd James Toback *ph* David Ferrara *m* American Cream Team *pd* Anne Ross *ed* Myron Kerstein *cos* Jacki Roach
☆ Scott Caan (Scotty), Robert Downey Jnr (Terry), Stacy Edwards (Sheila King), Allan Houston (Dean), Gaby Hoffman (Raven), Kidada Jones (Jesse), Jared Leto (Casey), Marla Maples (Muffy), Joe Pantoliano (Bill King), Bijou Phillips (Charlie), Power (Rich Bower), Raekwon (Cigar), Claudia Schiffer (Greta), Brooke Shields (Sam), William Lee Scott (Will King) and also Ben Stiller, Mike Tyson
'As lively and amusing as the film is in some ways, it does set up expectations at the outset that are never really delivered upon.' – *Todd McCarthy, Variety*

Black and White in Colour *
France/Switzerland/Ivory Coast 1976 100m Eastmancolor
Reggance/SFP/Artco/Société Ivorienne de Production (Arthur Cohn, Jacques Perrin, Giorgio Silvagni)
original title: *La Victoire en Chantant*
In French West Africa in 1915, easy-going colonials learn of the outbreak of war and prepare to attack a neighbouring German garrison.
Curious mixture of Ealing-style comedy and mordant satire; interesting without being wholly engaging.
w Georges Conchon, Jean-Jacques Annaud *d* Jean-Jacques Annaud *ph* Claude Agostini, Eduardo Serra, Nanamoudou Magassouda *m* Pierre Bachelet, Mat Camison
☆ Jean Carmet, Jacques Dufilho, Catherine Rouvel, Jacques Spiesser, Dora Doll
best foreign film

Black Angel *
US 1946 80m bw
U-I (Roy William Neill, Tom McKnight)
A drunk sets out to find the murderer of his wife, and finds it was himself.
Stylish but empty version of a tired theme, interesting for performances and atmosphere.
w Roy Chanslor *novel* William Irish *d* Roy William Neill *ph* Paul Ivano *m* Frank Skinner
☆ Dan Duryea, Peter Lorre, Broderick Crawford, June Vincent, Wallace Ford, Hobart Cavanaugh, Constance Dowling

The Black Arrow
US 1948 76m bw
Columbia
GB title: *The Black Arrow Strikes*
During the Wars of the Roses, an English knight seeks the murderer of his father.
Pennypinching swashbuckler which contrives to entertain despite total disregard of probability.
w Richard Schayer, David P. Sheppard, Thomas Seller *novel* R. L. Stevenson *d* Gordon Douglas *ph* Charles Lawton Jnr
☆ Louis Hayward, Janet Blair, George Macready, Edgar Buchanan, Paul Cavanagh

The Black Arrow Strikes: see *The Black Arrow*

Black Bart
US 1948 80m Technicolor
U-I (Leonard Goldstein)
GB title: *Black Bart, Highwayman*
Lola Montez, on an American tour, falls for an American bandit.
Acceptable Western programmer with historical trimmings and some evidence of tongue-in-cheek attitudes.
w Luci Ward, Jack Natteford, William Bowers *d* George Sherman *ph* Irving Glassberg *m* Frank Skinner
☆ Yvonne de Carlo, Dan Duryea, Jeffrey Lynn, Percy Kilbride, Lloyd Gough, Frank Lovejoy, John McIntire, Don Beddoe

Black Bart, Highwayman: see *Black Bart*

Black Beauty
US 1946 74m bw
TCF (Edward L. Alperson)
In Victorian England, a girl searches for her lost colt.
Stilted children's film with little relation to the book.
w Lillie Hayward, Agnes Christine Johnston *novel* Anna Sewell *d* Max Nosseck *ph* J. Roy Hunt *m* Dimitri Tiomkin
☆ Mona Freeman, Richard Denning, Evelyn Ankers, J. M. Kerrigan, Terry Kilburn

Black Beauty *
GB 1971 106m colour
Tigon/Chilton (Tony Tenser)
A luckless horse passes from hand to hand but is finally restored to its original young master and has a happy retirement.
Pleasant, episodic animal story which stays pretty close to the book. A shade yawn-inducing for adults, but fine for children.
w Wolf Mankowitz *novel* Anna Sewell *d* James Hill *ph* Chris Menges *m* Lionel Bart, John Cameron
☆ Mark Lester, Walter Slezak, Peter Lee Lawrence, Patrick Mower, John Nettleton, Maria Rohm

Black Beauty
GB/US 1994 88m Technicolor
Warner (Robert Shapiro, Peter MacGregor-Scott)
An old horse put out to pasture tells the story of his life, from pampered pet and heroic coach-horse to broken-down cart-horse.
Sadly inert version of the classic tale, narrated by the horse itself, a device that robs the story of any dramatic quality, since the events tend to be described before they are shown, and which also plays down any human interest.
wd Caroline Thompson *novel* Anna Sewell *ph* Alex Thomson *m* Danny Elfman *pd John Box* *ed* Claire Simpson
☆ Alan Cumming (voice), Sean Bean, David Thewlis, Jim Carter, Peter Davison, Eleanor Bron, Alun Armstrong, John McEnery, Peter Cook
'Certainly beautiful in both the equine and cinematic senses, but its penchant for lengthy montages could leave its young viewers squirming in their seats.' – *Denis Seguin, Screen International*

The Black Bird
US 1975 98m colour
Columbia/Rastar (Michael Levee, Lou Lombardo)
Sam Spade's son finds himself beset by crooks still after the Maltese falcon.
Dismal, witless, boring parody of a classic crime film, with none of the humour of the original.
wd David Giler *ph* Philip Lathrop *m* Jerry Fielding
☆ George Segal, Stéphane Audran, *Lee Patrick*, Elisha Cook Jnr, Lionel Stander, John Abbott, Signe Hasso, Felix Silla
'A dumb comedy with an insecure tone and some good ideas mixed up with some terrible ones.' – *Variety*
'It doesn't work because it has nothing to say.' – *Michael Billington, Illustrated London News*

The Black Book *
US 1949 88m bw
Eagle-Lion
GB title: *Reign of Terror*
A member of a secret organization which plans to replace Robespierre with a moderate goes undercover with the French Revolutionaries.
Moderate period melodrama with an attractive though artificial look.
w Philip Yordan, Aeneas Mackenzie *d* Anthony Mann *ph* John Alton *m* Sol Kaplan
☆ Robert Cummings, Arlene Dahl, Richard Basehart, Richard Hart, Arnold Moss

Black Caesar
US 1973 87m DeLuxe
Gala/Larco (Larry Cohen)
GB title: *The Godfather of Harlem*
A black hoodlum takes over Mafia territory to become a Harlem big-shot.
Slapdash movie that attempts to update the style of Warner's 30s gangster movies.
wd Larry Cohen *ph* Fenton Hamilton, James Signorelli *m* James Brown *pd* Larry Lurin *ed* George Folsey Jnr
☆ Fred Williamson, D'Urville Martin, Julius W. Harris, Gloria Hendry, Art Lund, Val Avery, Minnie Gentry

'A welcome attempt to move black films off the beaten track.' – *David McGillivray, MFB*
† The film was cut to 84m on its British release. It was followed by a sequel, *Hell up in Harlem*.

The Black Camel
US 1931 67m bw
Fox
Charlie Chan solves the murder of a film starlet in Honolulu.
Second in the Oland series (see under Charlie Chan), not easy to see these days.
w Barry Conners, Philip Klein *d* Hamilton McFadden
☆ Warner Oland, Dorothy Revier, Bela Lugosi, Sally Eilers, Victor Varconi, Robert Young

Black Candles (dubbed)
Spain 1981 82m colour
Films Around The World
original title: *Los Ritos Sexuales del Diablo*
A woman investigates the sudden death of her brother and discovers that he was a victim of black magic.
Cheaply made soft-core porn that combines devil worship, blasphemy, lesbianism, interminable scenes of love-making and tedium.
wd Joseph Braunstein (José Ramón Larraz)
ph Alan Clarke *m* Cam *ad* John Hanford
ed Harold Wallmann
☆ Martha Belton, Vanesa Ashley, Jeffrey Healey, Betty Webster, Christopher Bright, John McGrat
'No-one in that film could act. So what do you do with them? You put them in bed and have them jump on each other.' – *José Ramón Larraz*

The Black Cannon Incident *
China 1985 99m colour
ICA/Xi'an Film Studio (Wu Tiangming, Manfred Durniok)
An engineer and interpreter involved in a project with the Germans is replaced by an incompetent after Party members suspect him of spying.
A satire on bureaucratic bungling, one of the few to have emerged from China.
w Li Wei *story* *Langman de Heipao* by Zhang Xianliang *d* Huang Jianxin *ph* Wang Xinsheng, Feng Wei *m* Zhu Shirui *ad* Liu Yichuan
ed Chen Dali
☆ Liu Zifeng, Gerhard Olschewski, Gao Ming, Wang Yi, Yang Yazhou, Ge Hui

The Black Castle
US 1952 80m bw
Universal-International (William Alland)
An 18th-century knight avenges the deaths of two friends who have attended a hunting party at the castle of a sadistic Viennese count.
A variation on The Most Dangerous Game *(qv), and not a good one: the pace is far too plodding and the atmosphere unpleasant.*
w Jerry Sackheim *d* Nathan Juran *ph* Irving Glassberg *m* Hans Salter *md* Joseph Gershenson
☆ Richard Greene, Stephen McNally, Boris Karloff, Lon Chaney Jnr, Paula Corday, John Hoyt, Michael Pate

'It's tremonstrous! The absolute apex of the super-shivery!'
The Black Cat *
US 1934 65m bw
Universal (Carl Laemmle Jnr)
GB title: *House of Doom*
A revengeful doctor seeks out the Austrian architect and devil-worshipper who betrayed his country in World War I.
Absurd and dense farrago set in a modernistic but crumbling castle which is eventually blown to bits just as its owner is skinned alive. Mostly rather dull despite the extraordinary plot, but the thing has moments of style, a delightful cod devil worship sequence (especially for audiences with a rudimentary knowledge of Latin) and nothing at all to do with the title or Edgar Allan Poe.
w Peter Ruric *d* Edgar G. Ulmer *ph* John Mescall *md* Heinz Roemheld *ad* Charles D. Hall
☆ Boris Karloff, *Bela Lugosi*, David Manners, Jacqueline Wells, Egon Brecher
'On the counts of story, novelty, thrills and distinction, the picture is sub-normal.' – *Variety*

'A truly bizarre concoction of mayhem, necrophilia, sadism and satanism.' – *Clive Hirschhorn, 1980s*

The Black Cat *
US 1941 70m bw
Universal (Burt Kelly)
Murder follows the summoning of the family to the spooky house of a cat-loving recluse.
Disappointing mystery which squanders a splendid cast on a script full of non-sequiturs and makes heavy weather of its light relief.
w Robert Lees, Fred Rinaldo, Eric Taylor, Robert Neville *d* Albert S. Rogell *ph* Stanley Cortez
ed Ted J. Kent
☆ Basil Rathbone, Gladys Cooper, Broderick Crawford, Hugh Herbert, Gale Sondergaard, Anne Gwynne, Alan Ladd, Cecilia Loftus, Bela Lugosi
HUGH HERBERT (READING INSCRIPTION): 'That house is doubly blest, Which to our feline friends gives rest.'
BRODERICK CRAWFORD (NOT IMPRESSED): 'Her hats are full of bats, For spending all her dough on cats.'

Black Cat: see *Kuroneko (1968)*

The Black Cat (dubbed)
Italy 1981 91m Technicolor Technovision
Selenia (Giulio Sbarigia)
original title: *Il Gatto Nero*
A black cat and its owner, an eccentric medium, are locked in a battle of wills, one that results in many deaths in an English village.
A ghoulish and moderately stylish modern-day variation on Poe's story; hampered by its low budget, it is nevertheless an effective little shocker.
w Biagio Proietti, Lucio Fulci *story* Edgar Allan Poe *d* Lucio Fulci *ph* Sergio Salvati *m* Pino Donaggio *pd* Francesco Calabrese *ed* Vincenzo Tomassi
☆ Patrick Magee, Mimsy Farmer, David Warbeck, Al Cliver, Dagmar Lassander, Bruno Corazzari, Geoffrey Copleston, Daniela Dorio
'Aims for a more psychological approach, even if it is for the most part bogged down by Fulci's usual muddled style.' – *Shivers*

Black Cat, White Cat *
France/Germany/Yugoslavia 1998 129m colour
October/Ciby 2000/Pandora/Komuna (Karl Baumgartner)
When a robbery goes wrong, a Yugoslavian crook can only extricate himself by agreeing to marry his son to the unattractive daughter of a scheming gypsy godfather.
Sprawling, exuberant, messy comedy that finally outstays its welcome.
w Gordan Mihic, Emir Kusturica *d* Emir Kusturica *ph* Thierry Arbogast, Michel Amathieu *m* D. Nele Karajilic, Vajislav Aralica, Dejo Sparavalo *pd* Milenko Jeremic *ed* Svetolik Mica Zajc
☆ Bajram Severdzan, Florijan Ajdini, Salija Ibraimova, Branka Katic, Srdan Todorovic, Zabit Memedov, Sabri Sulejman, Jasar Destani, Ljubica Adzovic
'A colorful, frenetic mixture of slapstick and folklore that stands a good chance of delighting arthouse audiences the world over.' – *David Stratton, Variety*

The Black Cauldron *
US 1985 80m Technicolor Super Technirama 70
Walt Disney Productions (Joe Hale)
A medieval hero combats magic swords, wicked witches and skeletal tyrants.
Assured but somehow quite forgettable Disney cartoon feature.
w David Jonas, Vance Gerry, Ted Berman, Richard Rich, Al Wilson, Roy Morita, Peter Young, Art Stevens, Joe Hale, from The Chronicles of Prydain by Lloyd Alexander *d* Ted Berman, Richard Rich
m Elmer Bernstein *key animator* Walt Stanchfield
☆ Featuring the voices of Freddie Jones, Nigel Hawthorne, John Hurt, John Huston, John Byner, Arthur Malet
† Production allegedly took ten years and cost 25 million dollars.

'If this doesn't make your skin crawl ... it's on too tight!'
Black Christmas
Canada 1974 97m Technicolor
EMI/Film Funding/Vision IV (Robert Clark)
aka: *Silent Night, Evil Night*
Girls in a college sorority house are attacked by a lurking psychopath.
Moderate suspense chiller.
w Roy Moore *d* Bob Clark
☆ Olivia Hussey, Keir Dullea, Margot Kidder, Andrea Martin, John Saxon, Marian Waldman, Art Hindle

Black Diamond Rush
US 1993 100m colour
Black Diamond (Kurt Miller, Peter Speek)
A documentary on the pleasures of skiing.
A celebration of skiers as exemplars of personal freedom, filmed to a rock soundtrack; it is likely to appeal only to the initiated.
w Warren Miller *d* Kurt Miller, Peter Speek
ph Don Brolin *m* Middleman *ed* Paul Burack, Kim Schneider
☆ Warren Miller (narrator:)

Black Dog
US 1998 88m DeLuxe Super 35
Universal/Mutual/Prelude (Raffaella de Laurentiis, Peter Saphier, Mark W. Koch)
An ex-convict, tricked into driving a truck that contains guns from Georgia to New Jersey, is harassed by hijackers.
Predictable action fare, done with energy but no originality.
w William Mickelberry, Dan Vining *d* Kevin Hooks *ph* Buzz Feitshans IV *m* George S. Clinton *pd* Victoria Paul *ed* Debra Neil Fisher, Sabrina Plisco Morris
☆ Patrick Swayze, Meat Loaf, Randy Travis, Gabriel Casseus, Brian Vincent, Brenda Strong, Stephen Tobolowsky, Charles S. Dutton
'Overly familiar but fitfully exciting.' – *Variety*

Black Eagle
US 1988 93m colour
Rotecon/Magus (Shimon Arama)
Americans hire a top agent to foil a Russian attempt to recover a US plane fitted with top-secret equipment that crashed into the Mediterranean.
An action picture full of meaningless and irrelevant action; it seems to have been made in the belief that innumerable gun and fist fights will compensate for the lack of characterization and engrossing narrative, and also to disguise the fact that few of its leading characters speak comprehensible English.
w A. E. Peters, Michael Gonzales *story* Shimon Arama *d* Eric Karson *ph* George Koblasa
m Terry Plumeri *ed* Michael Kelly
☆ Sho Kosugi, Jean-Claude Van Damme, Doran Clark, Bruce French, Vladimir Skomarovsky, Kane Kosugi, Shane Kosugi

Black Eyes
GB 1939 72m bw
Associated British (Walter Mycroft)
A Moscow head waiter has raised his daughter to believe he's a big wheel in the business world.
Well-made comedy drama from a French original, Les Yeux Noirs.
w Dudley Leslie *d* Herbert Brenon *ph* Gunther Krampf *m* Walford Hyden, Bela Bizoni *ad* Ian White
☆ Otto Kruger, Mary Maguire, Walter Rilla, John Wood

Black Eyes **
Italy 1987 117m colour
Excelsior/RAI (Silvia D'Amico Bendico)
original title: *Oci Ciornie*
GB title: *Dark Eyes*
At the turn of the century, an aged Italian recounts his lapses.
Highly amusing star vehicle based on stories by Chekhov.
w Nikita Mikhalkov, Alexander Adabachian, Suso Cecchi d'Amico *d* *Nikita Mikhalkov* *ph* Franco di Giacomo *m* Francis Lai *pd* Mario Garbuglia, Alexander Adabachian

☆ *Marcello Mastroianni*, Silvana Mangano, Marthe Keller, Elena Sofonova
'The film effortlessly swings from farce to tenderness, love to betrayal, exuberance to poignancy without missing a beat.' – *Daily Variety*
Marcello Mastroianni

Black Flowers
Argentina/Mexico 1993 106m colour
Aleph/IMDC/Channel 4
original title: *Un Muro de Silencio*
aka: *A Wall of Silence*
A British film director, visiting Buenos Aires in 1990 to make a feature about the repressive regime of the mid-70s, discovers that many Argentinians prefer to forget their recent past.
Confusing drama, switching back and forth in time and between a film within a film and the actual lives of its protagonists; the result is sometimes interesting, but never gripping.
w Lita Stantic, Graciela Maglie, Gabriela Massuh
d Lita Stantic *ph* Félix Monti *m* Néstor Marconi
ad Margarita Jusid *ed* Juan Carlos Macias
☆ Vanessa Redgrave, Ofelia Medina, Lautaro Murúa, Lorenzo Quinteros, Soledad Villamil, André Melançon, Alberto Segado, Julio Chávez
'Pic's awkward structure, slow pacing and unexciting direction result in a moderately absorbing drama that will appeal mainly to viewers interested in political cinema.' – *Emanuel Levy, Variety*

Black Flowers for the Bride: see *Something for Everyone*

Black Fox
US 1962 89m bw
Jack Le Vien
Slick documentary on the rise of Hitler, using the expected newsreels reinforced not too artfully by references to art and to the medieval folk tale of Reynard the Fox.
wd Louis Clyde Stoumen
☆ Marlene Dietrich (narrator)
best documentary

Black Friday *
US 1940 70m bw
Universal (Burt Kelly)
After an accident, a college professor is given a gangster's brain, and the surgeon encourages him to believe that he is the gangster so as to find hidden loot.
Plot-packed melodrama which fails to provide the chills suggested by the cast, but passes the time agreeably enough.
w Curt Siodmak, Eric Taylor *d* Arthur Lubin
ph Woody Bredell *m* Hans Salter
☆ Boris Karloff, Bela Lugosi, *Stanley Ridges*, Anne Nagel, Anne Gwynne, Virginia Brissac, Paul Fix
† Lugosi was originally cast as the professor, but proved wrong for the part; Stanley Ridges replaced him and walked off with the movie.

Black Fury *
US 1934 95m bw
Warner (Robert Lord)
A coal miner comes up against union problems, unsafe conditions and corruption.
Typical Warner social drama, good for its time but now very obvious.
w Abem Finkel, Carl Erickson *play* *Bohunk* by Harry R. Irving *d* Michael Curtiz *ph* Byron Haskin *md* Leo Forbstein
☆ Paul Muni, Karen Morley, William Gargan, Barton MacLane, John Qualen, J. Carrol Naish, Vince Barnett, Tully Marshall, Henry O'Neill
'Basic box office, packed with promotional potentialities.' – *Variety*
'The most powerful strike picture that has yet been made, and I am aware of the better-known Soviet jobs in the field.' – *Otis Ferguson*

The Black Glove: see *Face the Music*

Black God, White Devil **

Brazil 1964 110m bw

New Cinema/Luiz Augosto Mendes/Copacabana (Glauber Rocha)

original title: *Deus e o Diabo na Terra do Sol*

A peasant follows the teachings of a fanatical prophet who preaches a gospel of suffering and death and becomes an outlaw.

Grim and violent tale of striving humanity at the mercy of a desolate landscape which established the reputation of its director as a new and disquieting voice in international cinema.

wd Glauber Rocha *ph* Waldemar Lima *m* Villa-Lobos *ad* Glauber Rocha *ed* L. Ririra

☆ Yona Magalhaes, Geraldo Del Rey, Othon Bastos, Mauricio Do Valle, Lidio Silva

'One is left wondering what a film so locked in its own oppressive landscape can really communicate to a European audience – other than the seduction of alien violence and alien despair.' – *Penelope Houston, Sight and Sound*

† The hired killer Antonio das Mortes became the eponymous hero of a film Rocha made in 1969 (qv).

Black Gold

US 1947 90m Cinecolor

Allied Artists

An Indian couple on the reservation adopt a Chinese boy who becomes a famous jockey.

Tears all round in this enterprising if rather muddled B picture with a social conscience.

w Agnes Christine Johnston *story* Caryl Coleman *d* Phil Karlson

☆ Anthony Quinn, Katherine de Mille, Elyse Knox, Kane Richmond, Ducky Louie, Raymond Hatton, Thurston Hall, Alan Bridge

Black Gold

US 1963 98m bw

Warner

Novice wildcatter makes it rich in Oklahoma despite villains on every side.

Absolutely predictable actioner which unspools like a remake even if it isn't.

w Bob and Wanda Duncan *d* Leslie H. Martinson

☆ Philip Carey, Diane McBain, Claude Akins, Iron Eyes Cody, James Best

Black Gunn

US 1972 95m Eastmancolor

Columbia-Warner/Champion (John Heyman, Norman Priggen)

With the aid of a group of black militants, an LA club owner takes revenge on gangsters who killed his brother.

Mundane action film, with nothing to distinguish it from a hundred others.

w Franklin Coen, Robert Shearer *d* Robert Hartford-Davis *ph* Richard H. Kline *m* Tony Osborne *ad* Jack DeShields *ed* Pat Somerset

☆ Jim Brown, Martin Landau, Brenda Sykes, Luciana Paluzzi, Vida Blue, Stephen McNally, Keefe Brasselle

Black Hand *

US 1949 92m bw

MGM (William H. Wright)

In New York at the turn of the century, an Italian boy avenges his father's death at the hands of the Mafia.

Neatly produced, studio-set melodrama, unusual in subject but very stereotyped and artificial in treatment.

w Luther Davis *d* Richard Thorpe *ph* Paul C. Vogel *m* Alberto Colombo

☆ Gene Kelly, J. Carrol Naish, Teresa Celli, Marc Lawrence, Frank Puglia, Barry Kelley

'Leave No Man Behind.'

Black Hawk Down *

US 2001 144m Technicolor

Columbia/Revolution/Scott Free/Jerry Bruckheimer

In 1993, elite American troops, who are dropped into Mogadishu to seize the aides of a local warlord, find themselves outnumbered and engaged in a fierce fight for survival.

A success in re-creating the experience of battle in all its violence and immediacy, this fails in any wider aim: there is no attempt to explain what the US mission hoped to achieve, or why they met with such resistance from the Somalis.

w Ken Nolan, Steve Zaillian *book* Mark Bowden *d* Ridley Scott *ph* Slawomir Idziak *m* Hans Zimmer *pd* Arthur Max *ed* Pietro Scalia

☆ Josh Hartnett (Ranger Staff Sgt Matt Eversmann), Ewan McGregor (Ranger Spec Grimes), Tom Sizemore (Ranger Lt Col Danny McKnight), Eric Bana (Delta Sgt First Class 'Hoot' Gibson), William Fichtner (Delta Sgt First Class Jeff Sanderson), Ewen Bremner (Specs Sgt Shawn Nelson), Sam Shepard (Maj Gen William F. Garrison), Gabriel Casseus (Ranger Spec Mike Kurth), Ron Eldard (Chief Warrant Officer Mike Durant), Ioan Gruffudd (Ranger Beales), Jeremy Piven (Chief Warrant Officer Cliff Wolcott), Kim Coates (Delta Master Sgt Chris Wexler), Hugh Dancy (Ranger Sgt First Class Kurt Schmid)

'One of the most vacuous, banal and tedious war films ever made.' – *Cosmo Landesman, Sunday Times*

'Macho obtuse posturing, puffed up with ersatz valour.' – *Peter Bradshaw, Guardian*

'A relentless immersion in combat strikingly realized but none too pleasurable to sit through.' – *Todd McCarthy, Variety*

Pietro Scalia; sound (Mike Minkler, Myron Nettinga, Chris Munro)

Ridley Scott; Slawomir Idziak

'A journey that begins where everything ends!'

The Black Hole *

US 1979 98m Technicolor Technovision

Walt Disney (Ron Miller)

A research team in space is welcomed aboard a mysterious survey ship poised on the edge of a black hole.

The special effects are superb, though achieved through a general gloom which is barely acceptable. But the story is an ill-worked-out remake of Twenty Thousand Leagues under the Sea *(qv), the characterization is ridiculously inept, and the final disclosure that black holes are doorways to hell sends one home rather bemused.*

w Jeb Rosebrook, Gerry Day *d* Gary Nelson *ph* Frank Phillips *m* John Barry *pd* Peter Ellenshaw

☆ Maximilian Schell, Robert Forster, Anthony Perkins, Joseph Bottoms, Yvette Mimieux, Ernest Borgnine

'As pastiche, it sounds promising; as drama, encumbered with references to Cicero and Goethe, it is merely tedious.' – *John Halford, MFB*

'Rated PG, but the only danger to children is that it may make them think that outer space is not much fun any more.' – *New Yorker*

Frank Phillips

Black Horse Canyon

US 1954 81m Technicolor

Universal-International

Two cowpunchers help a lady rancher to capture and train a wild black stallion.

Slight but agreeable outdoor programmer.

w Geoffrey Homes *d* Jesse Hibbs

☆ Joel McCrea, Mari Blanchard, Race Gentry, Murvyn Vye, Irving Bacon

Black Ice: see *A Passion for Murder*

Black Jack

GB 1979 110m colour

Enterprise/Kestrel (Tony Garnett)

In 1750 Yorkshire, a rascally French sailor recovers from a hanging and has adventures on the road with a young apprentice.

The purpose of this costume adventure, from these creators, is obscure, but the execution of it is muddled and amateurish.

w none credited *novel* Leon Garfield *d* Ken Loach *ph* Chris Menges *m* Bob Pegg *ad* Martin Johnson *ed* Bill Shapter

☆ Jean Franval, Stephen Hirst, Louise Cooper

'Ploddingly unpersuasive. Not only narrative clarity but simple credibility is lacking.' – *Tim Pulleine, MFB*

Black Joy *

GB 1977 109m Eastmancolor

Winkast/West One (Elliott Kastner, Martin Campbell)

A Guyanan immigrant in Brixton is tricked by a Jamaican good-for-nothing but later goes into partnership with him and learns to stand up for his rights.

Vivid but eventually wearying ethnic comedy-melodrama.

w Anthony Simmons, Jamal Ali *play* Dark Days and Light Nights by Jamal Ali *d* Anthony Simmons *ph* Philip Meheux *md* Lou Reizner from reggae songs

☆ Norman Beaton, Trevor Thomas, Floella Benjamin, Dawn Hope

'I wanted to show the reality of life in an immigrant area, angry and frustrated like so many parts of Britain – but full of hope and humour.' – *Anthony Simmons*

The Black Knight

GB 1954 85m Technicolor

Warwick (Irving Allen, Albert R. Broccoli)

A humble swordmaker reveals a traitor to King Arthur.

Hilarious travesty of English historical legend, meant seriously for Anglo-American consumption. Shades of Zorro, Babes in the Wood *and* 1066 and All That.

w Alec Coppel *d* Tay Garnett *ph* John Wilcox *m* John Addison

☆ Alan Ladd (John), Peter Cushing (Sir Palamides), Patricia Medina (Linet), Harry Andrews (Earl of Yeovil), André Morell (Sir Ontzlake), Anthony Bushell (King Arthur), Patrick Troughton (King Mark), Laurence Naismith (Majordomo), John Laurie (James), Ronald Adam (The Abbot), Elton Hayes

'Alan Ladd galahads with wild west *gentillesse* in this Technicolored rampage through British history.' – *MFB*

'Unmasking America's brotherhood of butchery!'

Black Legion **

US 1937 83m bw

Warner (Robert Lord)

A factory worker becomes involved with the Ku Klux Klan.

Social melodrama typical of its studio, and good of its kind.

w Robert Lord, Abem Finkel, William Wister Haines *d* Archie Mayo *ph* George Barnes

☆ Humphrey Bogart, Erin O'Brien Moore, Dick Foran, Ann Sheridan, Robert Barrat, John Litel, Charles Halton

'Powerful story of the horror spread by the hooded order; Surefire man's picture.' – *Variety*

'An honest job of film work, and one of the most direct social pieces released from Hollywood.' – *Otis Ferguson*

Robert Lord (original story)

Black Limelight *

GB 1938 70m bw

ABPC (Walter C. Mycroft)

The wife of a man convicted of killing his mistress proves that a 'moon murderer' did it.

Naïve but effective little chiller.

w Dudley Leslie, Walter Summers *play* Gordon Sherry *d* Paul Stein *ph* Claude Friese-Greene *ad* Cedric Dawe

☆ Raymond Massey, Joan Marion, Walter Hudd, Henry Oscar, Coral Browne

Black Lucia: see *The Premonition*

'The biggest picture in ten years! The greatest cavalcade of intrigue, spectacle, adventure and excitement you'll ever see on the screen'

Black Magic *

US 1949 105m bw

Edward Small (Gregory Ratoff)

Cagliostro the magician becomes involved in a plot to supply a double for Marie Antoinette.

Deliriously complicated historical romp which unfortunately suffers from a stolid script and production which kill all the flights of fancy.

w Charles Bennett *d* Gregory Ratoff *ph* Ubaldo Arata, Anchise Brizzi *m* Paul Sawtell

☆ Orson Welles, Nancy Guild, Akim Tamiroff, Valentina Cortese, Margot Grahame, Charles Goldner, Frank Latimore, Stephen Bekassy

'At times a grotesque, and at others a melancholy spectacle; including one scene of humiliating burlesque at the expense of physical disability that is as vile as anything I have witnessed in a cinema. But on the whole, absurdity predominates, and one must grin if one is to bear it. Whether Mr Welles deliberately enhanced the joke by adding bad acting to bad material is between him and his own soul.' – *C. A. Lejeune*

Black Mama, White Mama

US 1972 85m Movielab

New Realm/Four Associates (Eddie Romero, John Ashley)

aka: *Hot, Hard and Mean*

In Latin America, a black prostitute and a white guerrilla leader escape from a women's prison chained together.

Cheap and uninteresting exploitation movie, much in the manner of The Hot Box *(qv), from the same writers.*

w H. R. Christian *story* Jonathan Demme, Joseph Viola *d* Eddie Romero *ph* Justo Paulino *m* Harry Betts *ad* berto Formoso *ed* Asagni V. Pastor

☆ Pam Grier, Margaret Markov, Sid Haig, Lynn Borden, Zaldy Zshornack, Laurie Burton

'Despite Eddie Romero's years of experience in filming in the Philippines, the location possibilities are consistently thrown away; and no one has made any attempt to integrate the crude sexploitation sequences.' – *Tony Rayns, MFB*

The Black Marble

US 1980 113m DeLuxe Panavision

Avco/Frank Capra Jnr

A drunken cop redeems himself when teamed with a policewoman who is less cynical about the work.

Curious cop show with emphasis on child murders and dog torturing. An unhappy film with a garbled message.

w Joseph Wambaugh *novel* Joseph Wambaugh *d* Harold Becker *ph* Owen Roizman *m* Maurice Jarre

☆ Robert Foxworth, Paula Prentiss, Harry Dean Stanton, Barbara Babcock, John Hancock

Black Mask (dubbed) *

Hong Kong 1996 96m colour

Film Workshop/Wins Entertainment (Tsui Hark)

original title: *Hak Hap*

A former member of an elite squad of killers, who have been surgically altered to feel no pain, discovers that his comrades are killing drug dealers in order to take over the trade.

Extravagently absurd and violent martial arts movie, which is often visually inventive, with fights that prefigure some of the action in The Matrix, on which Yuen Wo-Ping also worked.

w Tsui Hark, Koan Hui, Teddy Chen, Joe Ma *d* Daniel Lee *ph* Cheung Tung Leung *m* Teddy Robin, Ben Vaughn *ad* Eddie Ma, Bill Lui *ed* Cheung Ka Tai, Ettie Feldman *martial art director* Yeun Wo-Ping

☆ Jet Li, Lau Ching Wan, Karen Mol, Francoise C.J. Yip, Patrick Lung, Anthony Wong

Black Moon Rising

US 1985 100m CFI color

Thorn EMI/New World (Joel B. Michaels, Douglas Curtiss)

An adventurer in the pay of the US government hides much-wanted evidence in the back of a super-high-powered car.

Absurd, almost impenetrable action shenanigans with more than enough violent action.

w John Carpenter, Desmond Nakano, William Gray *d* Harley Cokliss *ph* Mischa Suslov *m* Lalo Schifrin *pd* Bryan Ryman *ed* Todd Ramsay

☆ Tommy Lee Jones, Linda Hamilton, Robert Vaughn, Richard Jaeckel, Keenan Wynn

Black Narcissus ***

GB 1947 100m Technicolor

GFD/The Archers (Michael Powell, Emeric Pressburger)

Anglo-Catholic nuns in the Himalayas have trouble with climate, morale, and one of their number who goes mad with sexual frustration.

An unlikely theme produces one of the cinema's most beautiful films, a visual and emotional stunner despite some narrative uncertainty.

wd Michael Powell, Emeric Pressburger *novel* Rumer Godden *ph* Jack Cardiff *m* Brian Easdale *pd* Alfred Junge *ed* Reginald Mills *cos* Hein Heckroth

☆ Deborah Kerr (Sister Clodagh), David Farrar (Mr Dean), Sabu (Young General), Jean Simmons (Kanchi), Kathleen Byron (Sister Ruth), Flora Robson (Sister Philipaa), Esmond Knight (Old General), Jenny Laird (Sister Honey), May Hallatt (Angu Ayah), Judith Furse (Sister Briony), Nancy Roberts (Mother Dorothea), Eddie Whaley Jnr (Joseph Anthony), Shaun Noble (Con)
Jack Cardiff

The Black Orchid *
US 1958 95m bw Vistavision
Paramount (Carlo Ponti, Marcello Girosi)
A widower incurs hostility from his daughter when he plans to marry a gangster's widow.
Rather solemn New York/Italian romantic melodrama, with much gesticulation all round.
w Joseph Stefano *d* Martin Ritt *ph* Robert Burks *m* Alessandro Cicognini
☆ Sophia Loren, Anthony Quinn, Ina Balin, Jimmy Baird, Mark Richman

Black Orpheus *
France/Italy/Brazil 1958 106m Eastmancolor Cinemascope
Dispatfilm/Gemma/Tupan (Sacha Gordine)
original title: *Orfeu Negro*
Against a background of the Rio carnival, a black tram driver accidentally kills his girlfriend, and kills himself to be with her.
Rather irritating and noisy attempt to update a legend, without showing very much reason for doing so.
w Vinitius de Moraes *d* Marcel Camus *ph* Jean Bourgoin *m* Luis Bonfa, Antonio Carlos Jobim
☆ Breno Mello, Marpessa Dawn, Ademar da Silva, Lourdes de Oliviera
best foreign film

Black Patch
US 1957 84m bw
Warner/Montgomery
A marshal is wrongly suspected of murder.
Dour, dark Western, occasionally worth looking at.
w Leo Gordon *wd* Allen H. Miner *ph* Edward Colman *m* Jerry Goldsmith *ad* Nicolai Remisoff *ed* Jerry Young
☆ George Montgomery, Diane Brewster, Tom Pittman, Leo Gordon

The Black Pirate ***
US 1926 76m approx (24 fps) Technicolor silent
Douglas Fairbanks
A shipwrecked mariner swears revenge on the pirates who blew up his father's ship.
Cheerful swashbuckler with the star in top form.
w Douglas Fairbanks, Jack Cunningham *d* Albert Parker *ph Henry Sharp ad* Oscar Borg, Dwight Franklin
☆ *Douglas Fairbanks*, Billie Dove, Donald Crisp, Sam de Grasse

Black Rain *
Japan 1988 123m bw
Artificial Eye/Imamura Productions/ Hayashibara/ Tohokushinsha (Hisa Iino)
original title: *Kuroi Ame*
Caught in the destruction of Hiroshima, a Japanese family copes with the onset of radiation sickness in the ensuing years.
Intermittently moving, despite its uncertainties of tone.
w Toshiro Ishido, Shohei Imamura *novel* Masuji Ibuse *d* Shohei Imamura *ph* Takashi Kawamata *m* Toru Takemitsu *ad* Hiasao Inagaki *ed* Hajime Okayasu
☆ Yoshiko Tanaka, Kazuo Kitamura, Etsuko Ichihara, Shoichi Ozawa, Norihei Miki
'When Imamura conjures a string of imagery out of next to nothing, he achieves results as disquieting and resonant as anything he has ever done.' – *Tony Rayns, MFB*

Black Rain
US 1989 125m Technicolor Super 35
UIP/Paramount/Stanley R. Jaffe, Sherry Lansing
A rebellious and corrupt New York cop tracks down an escaped killer in Tokyo.
Effective thriller, though many may find unappetising its theme of redemption through revenge and violence.
w Craig Bolotin, Warren Lewis *d* Ridley Scott *ph* Jan de Bont *m* Hans Zimmer *pd* Norris Spencer *ad* John J. Moore, Herman F. Zimmerman, Kazuo Takenaka *ed* Tom Rolf
☆ Michael Douglas, Andy Garcia, Ken Takakura, Kate Capshaw, Yusaku Matsuda, Shigeru Koyama, John Spencer

Black Rainbow
GB 1989 103m colour
Palace/Goldcrest (John Quested, Geoffrey Helman)
A medium foretells the violent death of members of her audience, including her father.
Unconvincing story of the supernatural.
wd Mike Hodges *ph* Gerry Fisher *m* John Scott *pd* Voytek *ad* Patty Klawonn *ed* Malcolm Cooke
☆ Rosanna Arquette, Jason Robards, Tom Hulce, Mark Joy, Ron Rosenthal, John Bennes, Linda Pierce

The Black Rider
GB 1954 66m bw
Butcher's/Balblair (A. R. Rawlinson)
A journalist investigating the legend of a haunted castle exposes a gang of foreign saboteurs.
Plodding thriller that begins promisingly, but soon settles for genteel tedium.
w A. R. Rawlinson *d* Wolf Rilla *ph* Geoffrey Faithfull *m* Wilfred Burns *ad* John Stoll *ed* John Trumper
☆ Jimmy Hanley, Rona Anderson, Leslie Dwyer, Lionel Jeffries, Beatrice Varley, Michael Golden, Valerie Hanson, Vincent Ball, Edwin Richfield, Kenneth Connor, Robert Rietty

Black Robe ***
Canada/Australia 1991 100m Eastmancolor
Samuel Goldwyn/Alliance/Samson/Telefilm Canada (Robert Lantos, Stephane Reichel, Sue Milliken)
In the 17th century, a Jesuit priest travels through Quebec to convert the Indians.
Tough-minded, compassionate, excellently acted account of inadvertent tragedy.
w Brian Moore novel Brian Moore *d Bruce Beresford ph* Peter James *m* Georges Delerue *pd* Herbert Pinter *ed* Tim Wellburn
☆ Lothaire Bluteau, Aden Young, Sandrine Holt, August Schellenberg, Tantoo Cardinal, Frank Wilson
'A magnificently staged combination of top talents delivering a gripping and tragic story.' – *Variety*
'An adventure story in the truest sense: the filmmakers lead us into unknown territory, and keep pushing us farther and farther on, until, by the end, we find ourselves deep in the wilderness of the seventeenth-century consciousness.' – *Terrence Rafferty, New Yorker*

The Black Room *
US 1935 70m bw
Columbia
A nobleman's power is claimed by his evil twin brother.
Rather splendid old barnstormer with touches of horror, a neatly produced star vehicle.
w Henry Myers, from the writings of Arthur Strawn *d Roy William Neill ph* Al Siegler
☆ *Boris Karloff*, Marian Marsh, Katherine de Mille, Thurston Hall
'Eerie affair, dull and destined for negative results. Its best qualities are scenic investiture and photography, which do not excite dollars to elope from people's pokes.' – *Variety*
'Mrs Radcliffe would not have been ashamed of this wild and exciting film, of the bones in the oubliette, the scene at the altar when the dog leaps and the paralysed arm comes to life in self-defence, of the Count's wild drive back to the castle, of the rearing horses, the rocketing coach, the strange valley of rocks with its leaning cross and neglected Christ, the graveyard with its owls and ivy.' – *Graham Greene*

The Black Rose *
GB 1950 120m Technicolor
TCF (Louis D. Lighton)
A 13th-century English scholar journeys to the land of the Mongols, and after many adventures returns to a knighthood for his scientific discoveries.
Portentous and slow-moving adventure with good things along the way.
w Talbot Jennings *novel* Thomas B. Costain *d* Henry Hathaway *ph Jack Cardiff m* Richard Addinsell *ad* Paul Sheriff
☆ Tyrone Power, Orson Welles, Cecile Aubry, Jack Hawkins, Finlay Currie, Henry Oscar, Michael Rennie

'This is the night of the nightmare ... when a headless corpse rides the cold night wind, when a woman's soul inhabits the body of a buzzing fly.'
Black Sabbath
Italy 1963 99m Pathécolor
American International
Three supernatural stories introduced by Boris Karloff. *The Drop of Water* (Jacqueline Pierreux); *The Telephone* (Michele Mercier); *The Wurdelak* (Boris Karloff, Mark Damon).
Tolerable horror portmanteau.
stories Anton Chekhov, Howard Snyder, Leo Tolstoy *d* Mario Bava

'The management reserves the right to put up the lights any time the audience becomes too emotionally disturbed. We urge you not to panic or bolt from your seats.'
'From the earth's depths comes the deadliest sting of all!'
The Black Scorpion
US 1957 88m bw
Warner (Frank Melford, Jack Dietz)
Volcanic explosions uncover a nest of prehistoric giant scorpions near a Mexican village.
Apart from a genuinely terrifying sequence in the scorpion's lair, this is a poor monster movie in which excessively dark photography seems intended to cover up very variable trick work.
w David Duncan, Robert Blees *d* Edward Ludwig *ph* Lionel Lindon *m* Paul Sawtell *sp* Willis O'Brien
☆ Richard Denning, Mara Corday, Carlos Rivas, Mario Navarro

Black Shack Alley: see *Rue Cases Nègres*

'He's Bad...He's Mean...He's A Lovin' Machine!'
Black Shampoo
US 1975 83m Movielab
Transit/World Amusement (Alvin L. Fast)
A hairdresser fights back when a rival sends thugs to wreck his salon.
Presumably intended as an attempt to cash in on the success of Shampoo *(qv), it develops instead into a dull gangster movie; or maybe it was always a dull gangster movie, and was given a catch-penny title.*
w Alvin L. Fast, Greydon Clark *d* Greydon Clark *ph* Dean Cundey, Michael J. Mileham *m* Gerald Lee *ed* Earl Watson Jnr
☆ John Daniels, Tanya Boyd, Joe Ortiz, Skip Lowe, Gary Allen, Bruce Kerley, Jack Mehoff
'Script and performances are strictly make-and-mend; the direction, which contrives several flashily irrelevant optical effects, and finally sacrifices all for a blood bath involving a fashionable chain-saw, is audacious.' – *David McGillivray, MFB*

'There's one in every family.'
Black Sheep
US 1996 87m DeLuxe
Paramount (Lorne Michaels)
A politician's aide is detailed to see that the candidate's accident-prone brother stays out of trouble.
Crass and coarse comedy, relying for laughs on uninspired slapstick.
w Fred Wolf *d* Penelope Spheeris *ph* Daryn Okada *m* William Ross *pd* Peter Jamison *ed* Ross Albert
☆ Chris Farley, David Spade, Tim Matheson, Christine Ebersole, Gary Busey, Grant Heslov, Timothy Carhart
'Not only is the film sickeningly unfunny, it is crassly sentimental and predictable as well.' – *James Cameron-Wilson, Film Review*

The Black Sheep of Whitehall *
GB 1941 80m bw
Ealing (S. C. Balcon)
An incompetent teacher is mistaken for an economics expert and saves the real expert from spies who run a nursing home.
Pretty good wartime star comedy, with a succession of briskly timed gags.
w Angus Macphail, John Dighton *d* Basil Dearden, Will Hay *ph* Gunther Krampf
☆ *Will Hay*, John Mills, Basil Sydney, Frank Cellier, Felix Aylmer

The Black Shield of Falworth *
US 1954 99m Technicolor Cinemascope
U-I (Robert Arthur, Melville Tucker)
The son of a disgraced knight prevents an attempt against the throne of King Henry IV.
An amiable romp which alternates between comic strip dialogue and a surprisingly convincing sense of medieval custom. The training scenes are as sharp as the romantic asides are pallid.
w Oscar Brodney *novel Men of Iron* by Howard Pyle *d* Rudolph Maté *ph* Irving Glassberg *m* Herman Stein, Hans Salter *md* Joseph Gershenson *ad* Alexander Golitzen, Richard H. Riedel *ed* Ted J. Kent *cos* Rosemary Odell
☆ Tony Curtis (Myles Falworth), Janet Leigh (Lady Anne), David Farrar (Earl of Alban), Barbara Rush (Meg Falworth), Herbert Marshall (Earl of Mackworth), Rhys Williams (Diccon Bowman), Daniel O'Herlihy (Prince Hal), Torin Thatcher (Sir James), Ian Keith (Henry IV), Patrick O'Neal (Walter Blunt), Craig Hill (Francis Gascoyne)
'A straightforward piece of hokum with no pretensions, and spoken in a variety of accents that only Hollywood could muster.' – *John Gillett*

'A horror horde of monster mutants walk the earth!'
The Black Sleep
US 1956 81m bw
UA/Bel Air (Howard W. Koch)
A Victorian brain surgeon experiments on human beings and produces freaks who eventually turn on him.
Gruesome and humourless horror film notable only for its gallery of wasted talent.
w John C. Higgins *d* Reginald Le Borg *ph* Gordon Avil *m* Les Baxter
☆ Basil Rathbone, Bela Lugosi, Lon Chaney Jnr, John Carradine, Akim Tamiroff, Tor Johnson, Herbert Rudley, Patricia Blake

The Black Stallion *
US 1980 117m Technicolor
UA/Omni Zoetrope (Fred Ross, Tom Sternberg)
After a 1946 shipwreck, a boy and a stallion are cast up on the African shore; many years later, he rides the horse to victory at Santa Anita.
1980 seems a bit late for boy-and-horse pictures, but this one is so beautifully directed and photographed, if drastically overlong, that most adults thought their children should see it.
w Melissa Mathison, Jeanne Rosenberg, William D. Witliff *novel* Walter Farley *d Carroll Ballard ph Caleb Deschanel m* Carmine Coppola
☆ Kelly Reno, Mickey Rooney, Teri Garr, Clarence Muse, Hoyt Axton
'A perfect gem – the beautiful craftsmanship alone makes it a joy to behold.' – *Variety*
Mickey Rooney

The Black Stallion Returns
US 1983 93m Technicolor
MGM-UA/Coppola/Zoetrope (Tom Sternberg)
Rather desperate sequel in which a teenager loses his horse in Morocco and gets him back after various daredevil adventures.
Tame, predictable and boring.
w Richard Kletter, Jerome Kass *novel* Walter Farley *d* Robert Dalva *ph* Carlo DiPalma *m* Georges Delerue *ad* Aurelio Crugnolo *ed* Paul Hirsch
☆ Kelly Reno, Ferdy Mayne, Woody Strode, Vincent Spano, Allen Goorwitz
'Well-intentioned, but overall it doesn't look like a winner.' – *Variety*

Black Sunday: see *Mask of Satan*

'The undead demons of hell terrorize the world!'

Black Sunday *

Italy 1960 83m bw

Galatra/Jolly

aka: *Mask of the Demon*

A beautiful witch is put to death in an iron maiden but rises from the dead to wreak vengeance.

Stylish horror comic which started the Italian cult for such things.

wd Mario Bava *story* Gogol

☆ Barbara Steele, John Richardson, Ivo Garrani

Black Sunday *

US 1977 143m Movielab Panavision

Paramount (Robert Evans)

The Black September movement threatens a football game to be held in Miami's Superbowl.

Spectacular, heavily detailed, but somehow unexciting disaster melodrama.

w Ernest Lehman, Kenneth Ross, Ivan Moffat *novel* Thomas Harris *d* John Frankenheimer *ph* John A. Alonzo *m* John Williams

☆ Robert Shaw, Marthe Keller, Bruce Dern, Fritz Weaver, Steven Keats, Bekim Fehmiu, Michael V. Gazzo, William Daniels, Walter Gotell

'There's only one real motivation for this movie, and that's the desire to make money. Why else would anyone make an ostensibly anti-terrorist film that in actuality could end up promoting terrorism?' – *Frank Rich, New York Post*

The Black Swan ***

US 1942 85m Technicolor

TCF (Robert Bassler)

Morgan the pirate is made governor of Jamaica and enlists the help of his old friends to rid the Caribbean of buccaneers.

Rousing adventure story with comic asides: just what action hokum always aimed to be, with a spirited gallery of heroes and villains and an entertaining narrative taken at a spanking pace.

w Ben Hecht, Seton I. Miller novel Rafael Sabatini *d Henry King ph Leon Shamroy m* Alfred Newman

☆ Tyrone Power, Maureen O'Hara, *Laird Cregar, Thomas Mitchell, George Sanders,* Anthony Quinn, George Zucco, Edward Ashley

'Performed by actors as though to the hokum born.' – *Time*

'Battles between sailing ships, realistic sword fights, assaults, abductions, tortures and love making.' – *CEA Report*

Leon Shamroy

Alfred Newman

The Black Tent

GB 1956 93m Technicolor Vistavision

Rank/William MacQuitty

During a Libyan battle a wounded army captain is cared for by Arabs and marries the sheikh's daughter. Ten years later, after his death, his son elects to live with the tribe.

Pleasantly shot but otherwise dull, formless and interminable romantic drama, all very stiff upper lip.

w Robin Maugham, Bryan Forbes *d* Brian Desmond Hurst *ph Desmond Dickinson m* William Alwyn

☆ Anthony Steel, Donald Sinden, *André Morell,* Anna Maria Sandri, Ralph Truman, Donald Pleasence, Anthony Bushell, Michael Craig

'What was the deadly power that desired and devoured the women of Fordyke?'

The Black Torment *

GB 1964 85m Eastmancolor

Compton-Tekli (Robert Hartford-Davis)

The second wife of an 18th-century baronet investigates the hauntings which have followed the apparent suicide of his first.

Agreeably unpretentious period ghost story (with a rational explanation). Not exactly good, but better than one might expect.

w Donald and Derek Ford *d* Robert Hartford-Davis *ph* Peter Newbrook *m* Robert Richards

☆ John Turner, Heather Sears, Ann Lynn, Joseph Tomelty, Peter Arne, Raymond Huntley

Black Tuesday *

US 1954 80m bw

UA/Leonard Goldstein (Robert Goldstein)

A killer escapes from Death Row and hides out with hostages in a disused warehouse.

Starkly melodramatic gangster vehicle with the star up to his oldest tricks. Good tension, but generally rather unpleasant.

w Sydney Boehm *d* Hugo Fregonese *ph* Stanley Cortez *m* Paul Dunlap

☆ Edward G. Robinson, Jean Parker, Peter Graves, Milburn Stone, Warren Stevens, Jack Kelly, James Bell

'An electrifying drama about a predatory female! All the suspense your system can take!'

Black Widow *

US 1954 95m DeLuxe Cinemascope

TCF (Nunnally Johnson)

A Broadway producer is suspected of the murder of an ambitious young girl.

Reasonably classy whodunnit with glamorous settings and an able cast, but a little lacking in wit and pace.

wd Nunnally Johnson *novel Fatal Woman* by Patrick Quentin *ph* Charles G. Clarke *m* Leigh Harline

☆ Ginger Rogers, Van Heflin, George Raft, Gene Tierney, Peggy Ann Garner, Reginald Gardiner, Virginia Leith, Otto Kruger, Hilda Simms, Cathleen Nesbitt

Black Widow *

US 1987 103m colour

TCF/Laurence Mark (Harold Schneider)

A lady cop tracks down a lady murderer in Hawaii.

Watchable but overlong cop show with nothing very surprising about it once the plot is clear: TV movies have done just as well.

w Ronald Bass *d* Bob Rafelson *ph* Conrad Hall *m* Michael Small *pd* Gene Callahan

☆ Debra Winger, Theresa Russell, Sami Frey, Dennis Hopper, Nicol Williamson, Lois Smith

'A moderately interesting tale of one woman's obsession for another's glamorous and criminal lifestyle.' – *Daily Variety*

The Black Windmill *

GB 1974 106m Technicolor Panavision

Universal/Zanuck-Brown (Don Siegel)

A secret service agent has to fight a lone battle when his young son is kidnapped by spies.

Unconvincing variant on The Man Who Knew Too Much *(qv), with an unwieldy and incoherent plot and more borrowings from Hitchcock than you can count. It ends up as fair predictable fun despite its jaded air.*

w Leigh Vance *novel Seven Days to a Killing* by Clive Egleton *d* Don Siegel *ph* Ousama Rawi *m* Roy Budd

☆ Michael Caine, Janet Suzman, Joseph O'Conor, Donald Pleasence, Delphine Seyrig, John Vernon, Joss Ackland

'A flaccid spy thriller, vaguely reminiscent of Hitchcock and *Foreign Correspondent*, with direction as blank as the expression on Michael Caine's face throughout.' – *Sight and Sound*

Blackbeard the Pirate *

US 1952 99m Technicolor

RKO (Edmund Grainger)

In the 17th century, reformed pirate Sir Henry Morgan is commissioned to rid the Caribbean of the rascally Blackbeard.

A farrago of action clichés with the star giving his eye-rolling all. The romantic element is dreary and the whole a shade bloodthirsty for family fare.

w Alan le May *d* Raoul Walsh *ph* William E. Snyder *m* Victor Young

☆ Robert Newton, Linda Darnell, Keith Andes, William Bendix, Torin Thatcher, Irene Ryan, Alan Mowbray, Richard Egan

Blackbeard's Ghost

US 1967 107m Technicolor

Walt Disney (Bill Walsh)

The famous pirate returns as a ghost to help the old ladies who own a hotel he loved.

Ponderous and lengthy comedy, partially salvaged by performances.

w Bill Walsh, Don Da Gradi *d* Robert Stevenson *ph* Edward Colman *m* Robert F. Brunner

☆ Peter Ustinov, Dean Jones, Suzanne Pleshette, Elsa Lanchester, Richard Deacon

The Blackbird

US 1925 70m (24 fps) bw silent

MGM

A Limehouse thief pretends to be a cripple, and after committing a murder finds that he is.

Standard star vehicle with recollections of several others.

wd Tod Browning *ph* Percy Hilburn *ad* Cedric Gibbons, Arnold Gillespie *ed* Errol Taggart

☆ Lon Chaney, Renee Adoree, Owen Moore, Doris Lloyd

'I'm a teacher. My pupils are the kind you don't turn your back on, even in class!'

The Blackboard Jungle *

US 1955 101m bw

MGM (Pandro S. Berman)

In a slum school, a teacher finally gains the respect of his class of young hooligans.

Seminal fifties melodrama more notable for its introduction of 'Rock Around the Clock' behind the credits than for any intrinsic interest.

wd Richard Brooks *novel* Evan Hunter *ph* Russell Harlan *m Bill Haley and the Comets ad* Cedric Gibbons, Randall Duell *ed* Ferris Webster

☆ Glenn Ford, Anne Francis, Louis Calhern, Margaret Hayes, John Hoyt, Richard Kiley, Emile Meyer, Warner Anderson, Basil Ruysdael, *Sidney Poitier, Vic Morrow,* Rafael Campos

'It could just as well have been the first good film of this kind. Actually, it will be remembered chiefly for its timely production and release.' – G. N. Fenin, *Film Culture*

Richard Brooks (as writer); Russell Harlan; art direction; editing

Blackboards *

Iran/Italy/Japan 2000 84m colour

Artificial Eye/Makhmalbaf Film House/Fabrica (Mohsen Makmalbaf, Marco Muller)

original title: *Takhte Siah*

On the Iraq-Iranian border, two itinerant teachers, each carrying a blackboard, go their separate ways: one follows children being used to smuggle goods, while the other attempts to join a group of elderly refugees.

A film as elusive and allusive as a dream, where the meaning is carried by often ambiguous images: the society depicted is one where knowledge and understanding are rejected as irrelevant to existence.

w Mohsen Makmalbaf, Samira Makmalbaf *d* Samira Makmalbaf *ph* Ebrahim Ghafori *m* Monamed Reza Darvishi *ed* Mohsen Makmalbaf

☆ Bahman Ghobadi (Reeboir), Said Mohamadi (Said), Behnaz Jafari (Halaleh)

'A bold and provocative look at the plight of refugees and other outsiders struggling to survive on the dangerous Iran-Iraq border.' – *David Stratton, Variety*

Blackjack: see *Captain Blackjack*

Blackjack Ketchum, Desperado

US 1956 76m bw

Columbia (Sam Katzman)

A former gunslinger turns sheriff and defeats the local badman.

Standard lower-case Western with predictable excitements.

w Luci Ward, Jack Natteford *novel* Louis L'Amour *d* Earl Bellamy

☆ Howard Duff, Victor Jory, Maggie Mahoney, Angela Stevens

Blackmail ***

GB 1929 78m bw

BIP (John Maxwell)

A Scotland Yard inspector finds that his girl is involved in a murder; he conceals the fact and is blackmailed.

Hitchcock's first talkie is now a very hesitant entertainment but fully bears the director's stamp and will reward patient audiences in several excitingly staged sequences.

w Alfred Hitchcock, Benn W. Levy, Charles Bennett *play* Charles Bennett *d Alfred Hitchcock ph* Jack Cox *m* Campbell and Connelly, arranged Hubert Bath, Henry Stafford *md* John Reynders *ad* Wilfred and Norman Arnold *ed* Emile de Ruelle

☆ Anny Ondra, Sara Allgood, John Longden, Charles Paton, Donald Calthrop, Cyril Ritchard

'Hitchcock's ending was to have been ironic, the detective seeing the cell door shut on the arrested girl, going home and then being asked if he was going out with his girlfriend that evening. His answer: "Not tonight." This was unacceptable commercially and a happy ending was substituted.' – *George Perry*

Blackmail

US 1939 81m bw

MGM (John Considine Jnr)

A man is released from prison after serving a sentence for a crime he did not commit. Immediately a blackmailer pounces…

Co-feature drama for a star marking time; not bad in its way.

w David Hertz, William Ludwig *d* H. C. Potter *ph* Clyde de Vinna *m* David Snell, Edward Ward

☆ Edward G. Robinson, Ruth Hussey, Gene Lockhart, Guinn Williams, Esther Dale

'The family circuit will accept it as sufficient entertainment for a suspenseful evening.' – *Variety*

Blackmailed

GB 1950 85m bw

GFD/Harold Huth

Several victims of a blackmailer are involved in his murder.

Interestingly plotted and well cast melodrama which suffers from a flat script and production.

w Hugh Mills, Roger Vadim *novel Mrs Christopher* by Elizabeth Myers *d* Marc Allégret *ph* George Stretton *m* John Wooldridge

☆ Dirk Bogarde, Mai Zetterling, Fay Compton, Robert Flemyng, Michael Gough, James Robertson Justice, Joan Rice, Wilfrid Hyde-White, Harold Huth

Blackout: see *Contraband (1940)*

'Sex+Drugs+Alcohol+'

The Blackout

US 1997 94m Technicolor

Feature/Films Number One/CIPA/MDP (Edward R. Pressman, Clayton Townsend)

A self-destructive Hollywood star hastens along the primrose path before deciding to clean up his act.

Drearily self-indulgent stuff, in which the only pleasure is the cruel one of watching its actors slowly drown in its pretensions.

w Marla Hanson, Chris Zois, Abel Ferrara *d* Abel Ferrara *ph* Ken Kelsch *m* Joe Delia *pd* Richard Hoover *ed* Anthony Redman

☆ Matthew Modine, Claudia Schiffer, Dennis Hopper, Béatrice Dalle, Sarah Lassez

'It's doubtful that even Ferrara's hard-core fans will like this sleazy, borderline exploitation movie that is burdened by psychological and therapeutic concerns.' – *Emanuel Levy, Variety*

'Imbecilic piffle.' – *Empire*

Blackwell's Island

US 1939 71m bw

Warner (Bryan Foy)

A reporter goes to jail to get the goods on a smart gangster.

Forgettable exposé of the lighter kind.

w Crane Wilbur *d* William McGann *ph* Sid Hickox

☆ John Garfield, Rosemary Lane, Dick Purcell, Victor Jory, Stanley Fields

'An exploitation natural … a portrayal of incredible events taken from real life.' – *Variety*

Blacula

US 1972 93m Movielab

AIP (Joseph T. Naar)

In 1815 in Transylvania, an African prince falls victim to Dracula. A hundred and fifty years later, his body is shipped to Los Angeles and accidentally revivified.

Jaded semi-spoof notable chiefly as the first black horror film. The star's performance is as stately as could be wished in the circumstances.

w Joan Torres, Raymond Koenig *d* William Crain *ph* John Stevens *m* Gene Page

☆ *William Marshall,* Vonetta McGee, Denise Nicholas, Gordon Pinsent, Charles Macaulay

The Blade *
Hong Kong 1995 104m colour
Golden Harvest/Film Workshop/Paragon (Tsui Hark)
original title: *Dou*
An orphaned sword-maker goes to revenge the death of his father at the hands of a tatooed savage, but first he must overcome the obstacle of losing his forearm in a mantrap.
A remake of The One-Armed Swordsman, *notable for abandoning the usual graceful martial arts choreography for a much more expressionistic style, using quick cutting, red and blue filters, handheld cameras and expressive sound to achieve a more visceral and brutal approach.*
w Tsui Hark, So Man-Sing, Koan Hui *d* Tsui Hark *ph* Keung Kwok-Man *m* Wu Wai-Lap, Raymond Wong Ying-Wa *pd* William Chang, Yau Wai-Ming, Bill Lui *ed* Tsui Hark, Kam Ma
☆ Wing Zhao (Ding On), Xiong Xin-Xin (Falcon), Su Tsui-Yu (Siu Ling), Moses Chan (Ti Tau), Wai Tin-Chi (Master), Valerie Chow Ka-Ling (Whore), Chung Bik-Ha (Orphan), Chan Wing-Chung (Eye Patch), Ngai Sing (Fast Saber)

'The power of an immortal. The soul of a human. The heart of a hero.'
Blade *
US 1998 121m colour 'Scope
New Line/Amen Ra/Imaginary Forces (Peter Frankfurt, Wesley Snipes, Robert Engleman)
A half-human, half-vampire hero battles to prevent vampires from ruling the world.
Comic-book hokum done with some style and a great deal of noisy action; its nonsense is taken more seriously than it deserves.
w David S. Goyer *characters created by* Marv Wolfman, Gene Colan *d* Stephen Norrington *ph* Theo Van de Sande *m* Mark Isham *pd* Kirk M. Petruccelli *ed* Paul Rubell *sp* make-up fx: Greg Cannom
☆ Wesley Snipes, Stephen Dorff, Kris Kristofferson, N'Bushe Wright, Donal Logue, Udo Kier, Arly Jover, Traci Lords, Kevin Patrick Walls, Tim Guinee, Sanaa Lathan, Eric Edwards
'Though slick and diverting in some aspects, increasingly silly pic has trouble meshing disparate elements – horror, superhero fantasy, straight-up action – into a workable whole.' – *Dennis Harvey, Variety*

'One Man Still Has The Edge.'
Blade II *
US/Germany 2002 117m DeLuxe
Entertainment/New LineAmen RaImaginary Forces (Peter Frankfurt, Wesley Snipes, Patrick Palmer)
Blade, a half-human, half vampire hero, joins with hia old enemies in a battle against a new breed of vampire.
Slickly directed mayhem, full of loud and fast-paced action that gives little time to contemplate the ridiculousness of it all.
w David S. Goyer *based on the Marvel Comics character created by* Marv Wolfman, Gene Colan *d* Guillermo del Toro *ph* Gabriel Beristain *m* Marco Beltrami, Danny Saber *pd* Carol Spier *ed* Peter Amundson
☆ Wesley Snipes (Blade), Kris Kristofferson (Whistler), Ron Perlman (Reinhardt), Leonor Varela (Nyssa), Norman Reedus (Scud), Thomas Kretschmann (Damaskinos), Luke Goss (Nomak), Donnie Yen (Snowman)
'Enjoyable tosh.' – *Sunday Times*
'The new film seems equally influenced by videogames and open-heart surgery.' – *Owen Gleiberman, Entertainment Weekly*

'A chilling, bold, mesmerizing, futuristic detective thriller.'
Blade Runner **
US 1982 117m Technicolor Panavision
Warner/Ladd/Blade Runner Partnership (Michael Deeley, Ridley Scott)
Los Angeles, AD 2019; a licensed-to-kill policeman tracks down and destroys a group of intelligent robots who have hijacked a space shuttle and returned to Earth.
Gloomy futuristic thriller, looking like a firework display seen through thick fog, and for all the tiring tricks and expense adding up to little more than an updated Philip Marlowe case.
w Hampton Fancher, David Peoples *novel Do Androids Dream of Electric Sheep?* by Philip K. Dick *d* Ridley Scott *ph* Jordan Cronenweth *m* Vangelis *pd* Lawrence G. Paull
☆ Harrison Ford, Rutger Hauer, Sean Young, Edward James Olmos, M. Emmet Walsh, Daryl Hannah
'The sets are indeed impressive, but they are no compensation for a narrative so lame that it seems in need of a wheelchair.' – *Tom Milne, MFB*
'A richly detailed and visually overwhelming trip to 2019 which sticks with you like a recurrent nightmare.' – *Sunday Times*
'A massive assault on the senses which seems to have been launched from a madhouse equipped with all computerized mod cons.' – *Daily Mail*
'Glitteringly and atmospherically designed; but ultimately mechanics win out over philosophizing.' – *Sight and Sound*
† Ridley Scott's original cut of the film, which dispenses for the most part with the voice-over narration and has a different ending, was shown to general critical approval in 1991 and also released on video and DVD.
art direction; visual effects (Douglas Trumbull, Richard Yuricich, David Dryer)
Jordan Cronenweth; Lawrence G. Paull

The Blair Witch Project ***
US 1998 81m bw/colour
Pathé/Haxan (Gregg Hale, Robin Cowie)
Three students set out to film a documentary about a local legend of a witch; they are never heard of again, but the footage they shot is found a year later.
A extraordinary box-office success, this looks and sounds like the amateur movie it's meant to be, yet somehow, with its horrors never quite seen, scared audiences the world over, so well-faked was its feeling of reality.
wd Daniel Myrick, Eduardo Sanchez *ed* Daniel Myrick, Eduardo Sanchez
☆ Heather Donahue, Michael Williams, Joshua Leonard, Bob Griffith, Jim King, Sandra Sanchez, Ed Swanson, Patricia Decou
'An intensely imaginative piece of conceptual filmmaking that also delivers the goods as a dread-drenched horror movie.' – *Todd McCarthy, Variety*
'The sort of film that gets its best effects by creeping up on you unawares and whispering scary things in the dark.' – *Kim Newman, Empire*
† The film's three actors were shown how to use a video and a 16mm camera and then sent out into the woods for eight days, with the directors leaving messages for them at pre-established points. Within these limits, the film was improvised, with the cast not knowing what would happen next.
†† The original film was made at a cost of $25,000, though more was spent later on improving its quality. It took more than $140.5m at the US box-office, making it probably the most profitable film so far released.
††† It was followed by a sequel: *Book of Shadows: Blair Witch 2.*

'She's the hottest thing on the beach. She's also his best friend's daughter!'
Blame It on Rio
US 1983 100m Metrocolor
Sherwood (Stanley Donen)
A businessman is enlisted by his best friend to find his daughter's seducer, who is in fact himself.
Totally joyless and witless comedy with a South American background which is supposedly presumed to take away the bad taste.
w Charlie Peters, Larry Gelbart, from Claude Berri's 1977 film Un Moment d'Egarement d Stanley Donen *ph* Reynaldo Villalobos *md* Ken Wannberg
☆ Michael Caine, Joseph Bologna, Valerie Harper, Michelle Johnson, Demi Moore

'Murder, mistresses, madness and mayhem ... It's all part of the service.'
Blame It on the Bellboy
GB 1992 78m Technicolor
Warner/Bellboy/Hollywood Pictures (Jennifer Howarth)
At a hotel in Venice, a bellboy confuses the identities of a hitman, a timid estate agent and a mayor who has arranged a romantic assignation.
Tired and tepid farce, given the performances it deserves.
wd Mark Herman *ph* Andrew Dunn *md* Guy Dagel *pd* Gemma Jackson *ed* Mike Ellis
☆ Dudley Moore, Bryan Brown, Richard Griffiths, Andreas Katsulas, Patsy Kensit, Alison Steadman, Penelope Wilton, Bronson Pinchot, Lindsay Anderson
'A lightweight ensemble comedy that should check out fast from most hospices. Ingenious plotting is let down by weak dialog and stop-go direction that largely squanders the talent involved.' – *Variety*

Blame It on the Night
US 1984 85m Technicolor
Tri-Star (Gene Taft)
A rock star tries to make friends with the 13-year-old son he's only just met.
Resolutely uninteresting pattern play which slouches its way to a predictable ending.
w Len Jenkin *d* Gene Taft *ph* Alex Phillips *m* Ted Whitfield *pd* Ted Haworth *ed* Tony Lombardo
☆ Nick Mancuso, Byron Thames, Leslie Ackerman, Dick Bakalyan

Blanche *
France 1971 92m Eastmancolor
Telepresse/Abel et Charton (Dominique Duvergé, Philippe d'Argila)
In 13th-century France, a baron's beautiful young wife excites dark passions in her stepson and in the king.
An adult fairy tale full of symbols for those who seek them; but its main virtue is its highly decorative pictorialism.
wd Walerian Borowczyk novel Mazepa by Juliusz Slowacki *ph* Guy Durban *m* 13th-century music
☆ Ligia Branice, Michel Simon, Lawrence Trimble, Jacques Perrin
'Live-action *Jeux des Anges*, a brilliant, terrifying ballad of imprisonment.' – *Philip Strick, MFB*

Blanche Fury
GB 1948 95m Technicolor
GFD/Cineguild (Anthony Havelock-Allan)
A governess marries a wealthy heir, then with a steward connives at his murder.
Chilly Victorian melodrama without much interest outside the decor: the actors have unplayable roles and the handling is very flat.
w Audrey Erskine Lindop, Hugh Mills, Cecil McGivern *novel* Joseph Shearing *d* Marc Allégret *ph* Guy Green, Geoffrey Unsworth *m* Clifton Parker
☆ Valerie Hobson, Stewart Granger, Walter Fitzgerald, Michael Gough, Maurice Denham, Sybilla Binder
'This is all about murder, mayhem and seduction among the Furys in 1860. Our interest in them is not enhanced by the necessity of watching Miss Hobson pose against fulsome backgrounds for long stretches, though she is very beautifully coloured and they are very beautifully decorated.' – *Richard Winnington*

'He knew what to do with a million dollars.'
'Every kid's dream ... every parent's nightmare!'
Blank Check
US 1994 93m Technicolor
Buena Vista/Walt Disney (Craig Baumgarten, Gary Adelson)
GB title: *Blank Cheque*
An 11-year-old boy is mistakenly given a blank cheque by a crook and cashes it for one million dollars.
A greed-is-good movie for young teens.
w Blake Snyder, Colby Carr *d* Rupert Wainwright *ph* Bill Pope *m* Nicholas Pike *pd* Nelson Coates *ed* Hubert C. de La Bouillerie, Jill Savitt
☆ Brian Bonsall, Karen Duffy, Miguel Ferrer, James Rebhorn, Tone Loc, Rick Ducommun, Jayne Atkinson, Debbie Allen, Michael Lerner
'Charmless tripe.' – *Film Review*

Blankman
US 1994 92m Technicolor
Columbia/Wife'N'Kids (Eric L. Gold, C. O. Erickson)
An inventor, worried by the amount of crime in his neighbourhood, makes himself a cloak out of his grandmother's housecoat and becomes a masked avenger of evil.
Rough slapstick parody of Superman *and* Batman *(qqv) that manages high spirits but not much actual humour; its likely audience is the young.*
w Damon Wayans, J. F. Lawton *d* Mike Binder *ph* Tom Sigel *m* Miles Goodman *pd* James Spencer *ed* Adam Weiss
☆ Damon Wayans, David Alan Grier, Robin Givens, Christopher Lawford, Lynne Thigpen, Jon Polito, Jason Alexander
'Young viewers will rejoice at a comic-book fable that celebrates a self-appointed neighborhood crime fighter in the "Superman" mold. Adults, however, may find the film too goofy, too loud and vastly uneven in humor and execution.' – *Emanuel Levy, Variety*

Blast from the Past *
US 1999 111m colour 'Scope
New Line/Midnight Sun (Renny Harlin, Hugh Wilson)
A family emerges from a nuclear fallout shelter after 35 years.
Amiable comedy of a culture clash, with Fraser perfecting his standard role as an innocent exposed to experience.
w Bill Kelly, Hugh Wilson *d* Hugh Wilson *ph* Jose Luis Alcaine *m* Steve Dorff *pd* Robert Ziembicki *ed* Don Brochu
☆ Brendan Fraser, Alicia Silverstone, Christopher Walken, Sissy Spacek, Dave Foley, Joey Slotnick, Dale Raoul
'Expends scant imagination or style on a fun premise that seems an open invitation to both.' – *Dennis Harvey, Variety*

Blast Off: see *Jules Verne's Rocket to the Moon*

Blaze *
US 1989 117m DuArt
Warner/Touchstone/Silver Screen Partners IV/A&M (Gil Friesen, Dale Pollock)
Earl Long, the governor of Louisiana, enjoys an affair with a stripper.
Warmed-over political scandal from the 1950s.
w Ron Shelton *book Blaze Starr* by Blaze Starr, Huey Perry *d* Ron Shelton *ph* Haskell Wexler *m* Bennie Wallace *pd* Armin Ganz *ad* Edward Richardson *ed* Robert Leighton, Adam Weiss
☆ Paul Newman, Lolita Davidovich, Jerry Hardin, Gailard Sartain, Jeffrey DeMunn, Garland Bunting
'The combination of sex and political intrigue would probably be enough to make *Blaze* a winner, but Shelton's characteristically quirky perspective and surreal ear for dialogue propels the film into a higher league.' – *MFB*
best cinematography

'She kept her love for one – by sharing it with all!'
Blaze of Noon
US 1947 91m bw
Paramount (John Farrow)
Three stunt-flyer brothers in the 20s leave their circus to start a commercial airline.
Predictable romantic drama with little flying: tragic pretensions, routine performances.
w Frank Wead, Arthur Sheekman *d* John Farrow *ph* William C. Mellor *m* Adolph Deutsch
☆ William Holden, Anne Baxter, Sonny Tufts, Sterling Hayden, William Bendix, Howard da Silva
'So long as it sticks to stunt flying and mild comedy it is pleasant enough, but the last half, during which the obsessed brothers come one by one to grief and the little woman waits it out, gets pretty monotonous.' – *James Agee*

Blazing Magnum
Canada 1976 99m colour Panavision
Security Investment Trust Inc
A tough cop solves his sister's murder.
Tired rehash of the Dirty Harry formula, with plenty of violent action.
w Vincent Mann, Frank Clark *d* Martin Herbert
☆ Stuart Whitman, John Saxon, Martin Landau, Tisa Farrow, Gayle Hunnicutt, Carole Laure
'The stunts are well-managed and staged; the script, performances and direction make it unlikely that any viewer will care who survives them.' – *Scott Meek, MFB*

Blazing Saddles *
US 1974 93m Technicolor Panavision
Warner/Crossbow (Michael Herzberg)
A black railroad worker and an alcoholic ex-gunfighter foil a crooked attorney and his henchmen.
Wild Western parody in which the action eventually shifts to the Warner backlot, after which the actors repair to Grauman's Chinese Theater to find out what happened at the end of the story. At least as many misses as hits, and all aimed squarely at film buffs.
w Norman Steinberg, Mel Brooks, Andrew Bergman, Richard Pryor, Alan Unger *d* Mel Brooks *ph* Joseph Biroc *m* John Morris
☆ Cleavon Little, Gene Wilder, Slim Pickens, Harvey Korman, Madeline Kahn, Mel Brooks, Burton Gilliam, Alex Karras
'One suspects that the film's gradual disintegration derives not from the makers' inability to end it, so much as from their inability to stop laughing at their own jokes.' – *Jan Dawson*
'A surfeit of chaos and a scarcity of comedy.' – *Judith Crist*
'"I just about got everything out of me," said Brooks, "all my furor, my frenzy, my insanity, my love of life and hatred of death." Audiences flocked to this insane affirmation of dancing girls, Hollywood production numbers, stomach gas around the campfire, and gallows humor. Brooks had found the perfect vehicle for the age.' – *Les Keyser, Hollywood in the Seventies*
Madeline Kahn; title song (*m* John Morris, *ly* Mel Brooks)

Bleak Moments *
GB 1971 110m Eastmancolor
Autumn/Memorial/BFI (Leslie Blair)
Scenes from drab lives in a south London suburb.
Clearly not likely to appeal to the entertainment-seeking masses, and undeniably overlong, this small movie nevertheless has plenty of telling and even amusing detail about life as most of us recognize it.
wd Mike Leigh ph Bahram Manoochehri
songs: Mike Bradwell
☆ Anne Raitt, Sarah Stephenson, Eric Allan, Mike Bradwell
'A prolonged poem to inhibitions, speechlessness, and social unease.' – *John Coleman, New Statesman*

Die Blechtrommel: see *The Tin Drum*

Bleeder **
Denmark 1999 97m colour
Metrodome/Kamikaze/Scanbox/TV2/Zentropa/Tempo (Henrik Danstrup, Thomas Falck, Nicolas Winding Refn)
In Copenhagen, an evening watching B movies turns nasty for a video-shop worker, his abusive friend, his friend's pregnant girlfriend and her violent, criminal brother.
Disturbing drama of urban life at its lower levels among the inarticulate, dispossessed and plain nasty.
wd Nicolas Winding Refn *ph* Morten Syborg *m* Peter Peter *pd* Peter De Neergaard *ed* Anne Osterud
☆ Kim Bodnia (Leo), Mads Mikkelsen (Lenny), Rikke Louise Andersson (Louise), Liv Corfixen (Lea), Levino Jensen (Louis), Zlatko Buric (Kitjo), Claus Flygare (Joe), Ole Abildgaard (Video shop customer)
'A hard-boiled slice of Danish menace, and an extremely playful and unsettling account of cinema violence.' – *James Christopher, Times*

Die Bleierne Zeit: see *The German Sisters*

Bless the Beasts and Children *
US 1971 110m colour
Columbia/Stanley Kramer
Six boys on an adventure holiday try to free a herd of buffalo earmarked for destruction.
Rather obviously pointed melodrama, well enough done but not very interesting.
w Mac Benoff *novel* Glendon Swarthout *d* Stanley Kramer
☆ Bill Mumy, Barry Robins, Miles Chapin, Jesse White, Ken Swofford
title song (*m/ly* Barry de Vorzon, Perry Botkin Jnr)

'Mankind's Last Hope Just Turned Six.'
Bless the Child
2000 107m DeLuxe Panavision
Paramount/Icon (Mace Neufeld)
A Satanic cult kidnaps a child with miraculous powers.
Dim-witted horror movie with a feeble, derivative narrative and risible angelic interventions whenever inspiration reaches rock-bottom.
w Tom Rickman, Clifford Green, Ellen Green *novel* Cathy Cash Spellman *d* Chuck Russell *ph* Peter Menzies *m* Christopher Young *pd* Carol Spier *ed* Alan Heim *sp* makeup and creature fx: Keith Vanderlaan's Captive Audience Prods *cos* Denise Cronenberg
☆ Kim Basinger (Maggie O'Connor), Jimmy Smits (John Travis), Holliston Coleman (Cody), Rufus Sewell (Eric Stark), Angela Bettis (Jenna), Christina Ricci (Cheri), Michael Gaston (Bugatti), Lumi Cavazos (Sister Rosa), Dimitra Arlys (Dahnya), Eugene Lipinski (Stuart), Anne Betancourt (Maria), Ian Holm (Reverend Grissom)
'Combines the most rudimentary of Catholic-inspired good vs evil plots with visual effects that would barely pass muster in episodic TV.' – *Robert Koehler, Variety*

Bless This House
GB 1972 89m Eastmancolor
Rank/Peter Rogers
A suburbanite's multifarious frustrations culminate in preparations for his son's wedding.
This tedious spin-off from a TV sitcom virtually abandons plot in favour of an endless series of slapstick gags which could have been better presented.
w Dave Freeman *d* Gerald Thomas
☆ Sid James, Diana Coupland, Terry Scott, June Whitfield, Peter Butterworth, Sally Geeson, Robin Askwith, Bill Maynard

Blessed Event **
US 1932 84m bw
Warner (Ray Griffith)
A gossip columnist gets himself into hot water.
Amusing vehicle for a fast-talking star, and quite an interesting historical document.
w Howard Green *play* Manuel Seff, Forest Wilson *d* Roy del Ruth *ph* Sol Polito
☆ *Lee Tracy*, Ned Sparks, Mary Brian, Dick Powell, Ruth Donnelly, Frank McHugh, Allen Jenkins
'A potential clean-up … a sustained hour and a half or so of smart entertainment.' – *Variety*
'Quick and pacy and very likeable.' – *Pauline Kael, 70s*
† A historically interesting note was small-part actress Emma Dunn's use of the expression 'Well I'll be damned', which was technically forbidden at the time.

Blighty *
GB 1926 93m (24 fps) bw silent
Gainsborough–Piccadilly (Michael Balcon, Carlyle Blackwell)
A chauffeur becomes an officer and after the war finds himself looking after the master's family.
Fairly unwatchable in a normal sense, but of historical interest as one of the key British films of the twenties to make a comment about the war.
w Elliot Stannard, Charles McEvoy, Ivor Montagu *d* Adrian Brunel
☆ Jameson Thomas, Ellaline Terriss, Lilian Hall Davis, Godfrey Winn, Wally Patch, Seymour Hicks
'It was, quietly, an anti-war picture rather than a pro-war picture.' – *Adrian Brunel*

Blind Alley **
US 1939 68m bw
Columbia
An escaped killer takes refuge in the home of a psychiatrist, who explores his subconscious and tames him.
Unusual lowercase thriller with effective dream sequences; it was much imitated.
w Michael Blankfort, Albert Duffy *play* James Warwick *d Charles Vidor ph* Lucien Ballard *m* Morris Stoloff
☆ *Chester Morris, Ralph Bellamy*, Ann Dvorak, Melville Cooper, Rose Stradner, Marc Lawrence
'Psychoanalysis of a criminal provides a new twist to what would otherwise be another crime picture of general trend.' – *Variety*
'As un-Hollywood as anything that has come from France this year.' – *New York Daily News*
'Survive a sticky ten minutes and you have a thriller of quite unusual merit.' – *Graham Greene*
† Remake: *The Dark Past* (qv).

Blind Alley
US 1984 91m colour
Hemdale (Paul Kurta)
aka: *Perfect Strangers*
A three-year-old witnesses a murder, and the hitman responsible begins a relationship with the boy's mother.
Lacklustre thriller, lacking in any tension or suspense.
wd Larry Cohen *ph* Paul Glickman *m* Dwight Dixon *ed* Armond Lebowitz
☆ Anne Carlisle, Brad Rijn, John Woehrle, Matthew Stockley, Stephen Lack
'Abandon everything – even sex – to watch it … its real power lies not in what we are shown but in what we fear may happen. Interest never flags from the grim beginning of this tale to its appalling climax.' – *Quentin Crisp*

A Blind Bargain *
US 1922 60m approx bw silent
Goldwyn
A demented scientist creates an ape monster.
Interesting star vehicle, a precursor of many hokum thrillers.
w J. G. Hawks *novel The Octave of Claudius* by Barry Pain *d* Wallace Worsley
☆ Lon Chaney, Jacqueline Logan, Raymond McKee, Virginia True Boardman

Blind Date *
GB 1959 95m bw
Rank/Sydney Box/Independent Artists (David Deutsch)
US title: *Chance Meeting*
A young Dutch painter in London discovers his mistress's body and finds himself in a web of deceit.
Tolerable, comparatively sophisticated murder puzzle; rather glum looking, but the plot holds the interest.
w Ben Barzman, Millard Lampell *novel* Leigh Howard *d* Joseph Losey *ph* Christopher Challis *m* Richard Rodney Bennett
☆ Hardy Kruger, Stanley Baker, Micheline Presle, Robert Flemyng, Gordon Jackson, John Van Eyssen

Blind Date *
US 1987 93m Metrocolor Panavision
Tri-Star/Blake Edwards (Tony Adams)
A company executive needs a date for a company function, and takes a remote relative who turns out to be an easy drunk.
One-note gag movie which spurs some laughs but wears out its welcome.
w Dale Launer *d* Blake Edwards *ph* Harry Stradling Jnr *m* Henry Mancini
☆ Kim Basinger, Bruce Willis, John Larroquette, William Daniels, Phil Hartman, Alice Hirson
'In short, hokey and hip – which in this case is a foolproof formula.' – *Daily Variety*

The Blind Dead: see *Tombs of the Blind Dead*

Blind Fury
US 1989 86m Technicolor
Columbia TriStar (Daniel Grodnik, Tim Matheson)
A blind martial arts expert takes on a drug dealer and his gang.
Violent American variation on a Japanese samurai series of the 1960s featuring Zatoichi the blind swordsman, which gains nothing from being transferred from the 1800s to present-day Los Angeles.
w Charles Robert Carner *screenplay* Ryozo Kasahara *d* Phillip Noyce *ph* Don Burgess *m* J. Peter Robinson *pd* Peter Murton *ad* John Myhre *ed* David Simmons
☆ Rutger Hauer, Terrance O'Quinn, Brandon Call, Noble Willingham, Lisa Blount, Nick Cassavetes, Rick Overton, Randall 'Tex' Cobb

The Blind Goddess
GB 1947 88m bw
Gainsborough (Betty Box)
The private secretary to a public figure finds that his idol has feet of clay, and suffers in court for his discovery.
Courtroom drama from an old-fashioned stage play: surefire for addicts, but routine as a film.
w Muriel and Sydney Box *play Patrick Hastings d* Harold French *ph* Ray Elton *ad* Norman Arnold *ed* Gordon Hales
☆ Eric Portman, Anne Crawford, Hugh Williams, Michael Denison, Nora Swinburne, Claire Bloom, Raymond Lovell, Frank Cellier

Blind Husbands **
US 1919 90m approx (24 fps) bw silent
Universal (Erich von Stroheim)
An Austrian officer, on holiday in the Alps, seduces the wife of a rich American.
Stroheim's first comedy of sexual manners, now of mainly archival interest.
wd Erich von Stroheim ph Ben Reynolds *ad* Erich von Stroheim
☆ Erich von Stroheim, Sam de Grasse, Gibson Gowland, Francella Billington

Blind Man's Bluff: see *Cauldron of Blood (1968)*

'No Witness, No Evidence, No Way Out.'
Blind Side
US 1993 CFI color
HBO (Jay Roewe)
Returning from Mexico, a couple run over a cop and leave his apparently dead body by the roadside; later, a stranger who claims to have witnessed the accident turns up to blackmail them.
A non-too-serious variation on the familiar theme of the psychopath who comes to call, with over-the-top performances and a parody of a spaghetti Western to add a little novelty.
w Stewart Lindh, Solomon Weingarten, John Carlen *d* Geoff Murphy *ph* Paul Elliott *m* Brian May *pd* Nina Ruscio *ed* Rick Shaine
☆ Rutger Hauer, Rebecca DeMornay, Ron Silver, Jonathan Banks, Mariska Hargitay, Tamara Clatterbuck
'A cracking thriller combining an ingenious script, effective direction and good acting.' – *Sight and Sound*

Blind Terror
GB 1971 89m colour
Columbia/Filmways/Genesis (Leslie Linder)
US title: *See No Evil*
A blind girl is the sole, hunted survivor of a maniac's rampage on a lonely estate.
Shocks, screams and starts fill a cliché-ridden but still effective script which is faithfully turned into a competent but routine heart-stopper.
w Brian Clemens *d* Richard Fleischer *ph* Gerry Fisher *m* Elmer Bernstein
☆ *Mia Farrow*, Robin Bailey, Dorothy Alison, Diane Grayson, Norman Eshley, Brian Rawlinson
'For those who like to watch folks pull the wings off flies.' – *Judith Crist*

Blind Vision
US 1990 92m DeLuxe
Saban/Vertigo (Jonathon Braun)
A repressed, mother-dominated amateur photographer is suspected of murdering the boyfriend of a woman on whom he spies obsessively from his flat opposite.
Dreary, fourth-rate, risible thriller, not helped by being told mainly from the viewpoint of its unsympathetic protagonist, a voyeuristic nerd.
w Shuki Levy, Winston Richard *d* Shuki Levy *ph* Frank Byers *m* Shuki Levy, Hiram Titus *ad* Jayne Asman *ed* Jon Braun, Shuki Levy

☆ Lenny von Dohlen, Deborah Shelton, Stoney Jackson, Robert Vaughn, Ned Beatty, Louise Fletcher

Blindfold **

US 1965 102m Technicolor Panavision
Universal (Marvin Schwartz)

A society psychiatrist is enlisted by the CIA to make regular blindfold journeys to a secret destination where he treats a neurotic physicist. Discovering that his contacts are really enemy agents, he tracks down the destination by sound and guesswork, and routs the villains.

Lively spy spoof with rather too much knockabout between the Hitchcockian suspense sequences; it has indeed the air of a script which Hitchcock rejected, but provides reliable entertainment.

w Philip Dunne, W. H. Menger *novel* Lucille Fletcher *d* Philip Dunne *ph* Joseph MacDonald *m* Lalo Schifrin *ed* Ted J. Kent

☆ Rock Hudson, Claudia Cardinale, Jack Warden, Guy Stockwell, Brad Dexter, Anne Seymour, Alejandro Rey

Blindman (dubbed)

US/Italy 1971 96m Technicolor
Techniscope
Fox-Rank/ABKCO/Primex (Tony Anthony, Saul Swimmer)

A blind man goes in search of 50 mail-order brides who have been stolen by a bandit and his gang.

Comic spaghetti Western in which the only point of interest, apart from its bizarre hero, lies in seeing a former Beatle in the role of a Mexican outlaw.

w Tony Anthony, Piero Anchisi, Vincenzo Cerami *story* Tony Anthony *d* Ferdinando Baldi *ph* Riccardo Pallottino *m* Stelvio Cipriani *ad* Gastone Garsetti *ed* Reberto Perpignani

☆ Tony Anthony, Ringo Starr, Agneta Eckemyr, Lloyd Batista, Magda Konopka, Raf Baldassare

'Indistinguishable from the ruck in its crude direction, garbled plot, obsessive violence, variable technical achievements, and pot-pourri cast and acting styles.' – *Tom Milne, MFB*

† The original version of the film ran for 105m.

'Illusion. Deception. Murder.'
'In the blink of an eye things are not what they seem.'

Blink

US 1994 106m DeLuxe Super 35
Guild/New Line (David Blocker)

A cop investigating a murder is attracted by the only witness, a formerly blind woman who has just regained her sight but is not sure of what she sees.

Dumb woman-in-peril thriller that relies on cliché to see it through to its unexciting end.

w Dana Stevens *d* Michael Apted *ph* Dante Spinotti *m* Brad Fiedel *pd* Dan Bishop *ed* Rick Shaine

☆ Madeleine Stowe, Aidan Quinn, Laurie Metcalf, Peter Friedman, James Remar, Bruce A. Young, Paul Dillon, Matt Roth

'So numbingly banal and predictable it might as well have been called *Wink*, of which you need 40 to get through it.' – *Leslie Felperin Sharman, Sight and Sound*

Bliss *

Australia 1985 111m colour
Entertainment (Anthony Buckley)

After a heart attack, an advertising executive realizes the rottenness of his wife and children and seeks happiness elsewhere.

Energetic black comedy, intermittently entertaining, that won awards in its home country.

w Ray Lawrence, Peter Carey *novel* Peter Carey *d* Ray Lawrence *ph* Paul Murphy *m* Peter Best *ad* Owen Paterson *ed* Wayne Leclos

☆ Barry Otto, Lynette Curran, Helen Jones, Miles Buchanan, Gia Carides, Tim Robertson, Jeff Truman, Bryan Marshall

'Love is only the beginning.'

Bliss

US 1997 103m colour
Triumph (Allyn Stewart)

A newly married wife seeks the advice of a therapist, who has sexual relationships with his patients.

Bizarre and risible would-be erotic drama that frequently resembles an instructional video for the unenlightened.

wd Lance Young *ph* Michael Molloy *m* Jan A. P. Kaczmarek *pd* John Willett, David Lloyd Fischer *ed* Allan Lee

☆ Craig Sheffer, Sheryl Lee, Terence Stamp, Casey Siemaszko, Spalding Gray, Leigh Taylor Young, Lois Chiles

'Tone of the film is too smug, the earnestness of its lesson creating the off-putting impression of the recently converted trying to preach newly acquired wisdom to the masses.' – *Todd McCarthy, Variety*

The Bliss of Mrs Blossom

GB 1968 93m Technicolor
Paramount (Josef Shaftel)

The wife of a bra manufacturer keeps her lover in the attic.

Silly, wild-eyed sex comedy decorated with the flashy tinsel of swinging London's dying fall.

w Alec Coppel, Denis Norden *d* Joe McGrath *ph* Geoffrey Unsworth *m* Riz Ortolani *pd* Assheton Gorton

☆ Richard Attenborough, Shirley MacLaine, James Booth, Freddie Jones, William Rushton, Bob Monkhouse, Patricia Routledge

Blithe Spirit ***

GB 1945 96m Technicolor
Two Cities/Cineguild (Anthony Havelock-Allan)

A cynical novelist's second marriage is disturbed when the playful ghost of his first wife materializes during a séance.

Direction and acting carefully preserve a comedy which on its first West End appearance in 1941 achieved instant classic status. The repartee scarcely dates, and altogether this is a most polished job of film-making.

w Noël Coward play Noël Coward *scenario David Lean, Anthony Havelock-Allan, Ronald Neame* *d* David Lean *ph* Ronald Neame *m* Richard Addinsell

☆ *Rex Harrison, Kay Hammond, Constance Cummings, Margaret Rutherford,* Hugh Wakefield, Joyce Carey, Jacqueline Clark

'Ninety minutes of concentrated, cultivated fun.' – *C. A. Lejeune*

† After seeing this, Noël Coward reputedly told Rex Harrison: 'After me you're the best light comedian in the world.'

Blitz on Britain *

GB 1960 71m bw
Anglo-Continental/British Lion

A very acceptable record of the Battle of Britain as it affected the home front, narrated by Alistair Cooke.

w Patrick Brawn *d/ed* Harry Booth

'Indescribable ... Indestructible! Nothing Can Stop It!'

The Blob

US 1958 83m DeLuxe
Tonylyn/Jack H. Harris

A small town combats a slimy space invader.

Padded hokum for drive-ins, with a few effective moments.

w Theodore Simonson, Kate Phillips *d* Irvin S. Yeaworth Jnr *ph* Thomas Spalding *m* Ralph Carmichael

☆ Steve McQueen, Aneta Corseaut, Olin Howlin, Earl Rowe

'Classic teen horror which really sums up the spirit of 50s drive-in movies.' – *The Dark Side*

† Sequel 1971: *Beware! The Blob* (aka *Son of Blob*).

The Blob

US 1988 92m Technicolor
Tri-Star (Jack H. Harris/Elliott Kastner)

A small town is threatened by alien goo.

Fifties sci-fi horror dressed up for the 80s, no better than it was the first or second time around.

w Chuck Russell, Frank Darabont *d* Chuck Russell *ph* Mark Irwin *m* Michael Hoenig *pd* Craig Stearns *ed* Terry Stokes, Tod Feuerman

☆ Shawnee Smith, Kevin Dillon, Donovan Leitch, Jeffrey de Munn, Candy Clark, Joe Seneca

'A great B-movie with an A-pic budget.' – *Variety*

Block Busters

US 1944 60m bw
Monogram/Banner (Sam Katzman, Jack Dietz)

The East Side Kids are upset when a rich French boy moves into the neighbourhood.

Lacklustre programmer, although jazz fans may enjoy a rare, if brief, glimpse of the great clarinettist Jimmy Noone in action.

w Houston Branch *d* Wallace Fox *ph* Marcel LePicard *md* Edward Kay *ad* David Milton *ed* Carl Pierson

☆ Leo Gorcey, Huntz Hall, Gabriel Dell, Billy Benedict, Frederick Pressel, Noah Beery, Harry Langdon, Bernard Gorcey

Blockade *

US 1938 84m bw
Walter Wanger

During the Spanish Civil War, a peace-loving young farmer has to take up arms to defend his land.

Much touted as Hollywood's first serious contribution to international affairs, this dogged drama was in fact so bland that audiences had difficulty ascertaining which side it was on, especially as neither Franco nor the Fascists were mentioned. As a romantic action drama, however, it passed muster.

w John Howard Lawson *d* William Dieterle *ph* Rudolf Maté *m* Werner Janssen

☆ Henry Fonda, Madeleine Carroll, Leo Carrillo, John Halliday, Vladimir Sokoloff, Robert Warwick, Reginald Denny

'It misses any claim to greatness because it pulls its punches ... and it's going to be tough to sell.' – *Variety*

'The film has a curious unreality considering the grim reality behind it.' – *Frank S. Nugent*

'There is achieved a deadly numb level of shameless hokum out of which anything true or decent rises only for a second to confound itself.' – *Otis Ferguson*

† Original publicity carried this disclaimer: NOTE: Care has been taken to prevent any costume of the production from being accurately that of either side in the Spanish Civil War. The story does not attempt to favour any cause in the present conflict.

John Howard Lawson; Werner Janssen

Blockheads ***

US 1938 60m bw
Hal Roach/Stan Laurel

Twenty years after World War I, Stan is still guarding a trench because nobody told him to stop. Ollie takes him home to meet the wife, with disastrous consequences.

The last first-class Laurel and Hardy comedy is shapeless but hilarious, a fragmented reworking of earlier ideas, all of which work beautifully. Gags include encounters with a tip-up truck and an automatic garage, and a brilliantly worked out sequence up and down several flights of stairs.

w James Parrott, Harry Langdon, Felix Adler, Charles Rogers, Arnold Belgard *d* John G. Blystone *ph* Art Lloyd *m* Marvin Hatley

☆ *Stan Laurel, Oliver Hardy,* Billy Gilbert, Patricia Ellis, Minna Gombell, James Finlayson

'Hodge-podge of old-fashioned slapstick and hoke.' – *Variety*

Marvin Hatley

Den Blodiga Tiden: see *Mein Kampf*

Blonde Bombshell: see *Bombshell*

Blonde Crazy *

US 1931 74m bw
Warner

GB title: *Larceny Lane*

A bellhop and a chambermaid set out to fleece all-comers.

Smart con man comedy with the star in excellent form.

w Kubec Glasmon, John Bright *d* Roy del Ruth *ph* Sid Hickox

☆ *James Cagney,* Joan Blondell, Ray Milland, Louis Calhern, Guy Kibbee, Polly Walters, Charles Lane, Maude Eburne

'Naughty cracks galore, and one says "Nuts". But he doesn't push a grapefruit in the girlfriend's face, though they expect it any time.' – *Variety*

'A chipper, hard-boiled, amusing essay in petty thieving.' – *Time*

Blonde Fever

US 1944 69m bw
MGM

A middle-aged husband falls for a blonde waitress.

Very ho-hum comedy on familiar lines.

w Patricia Coleman *play* Ferenc Molnar *d* Richard Whorf

☆ Philip Dorn, Mary Astor, Gloria Grahame, Felix Bressart, Marshall Thompson, Curt Bois

Blonde Fist

GB 1991 102m colour
Blue Dolphin/Film Four (Christopher Figg, Joseph D'Morais)

The fighting daughter of a bare-knuckle boxer goes in search of her father and of a new life.

Brain-damaged knockabout comedy.

wd Frank Clarke *ph* Bruce McGowan *m* Alan Gill *pd* Colin Pocock *ed* Brian Peachey

☆ Margi Clarke, Carroll Baker, Ken Hutchinson, Sharon Power, Angela Clarke, Lewis Bester

A Blonde in Love: see *Loves of a Blonde*

Blonde Sinner: see *Yield to the Night*

'What could she do but flee from love? She loved two men at once!'

Blonde Venus *

US 1932 97m bw
Paramount

A German café singer marries an English research chemist, but their marriage doesn't run smoothly.

Rather dreary, fragmented star vehicle with good moments, notably the star's opening appearance as a gorilla.

w Jules Furthman, S. K. Lauren *d* Josef von Sternberg *ph* Bert Glennon *m* Oscar Potoker

☆ Marlene Dietrich, Herbert Marshall, Cary Grant, Dickie Moore

'Weak story, inept direction and generally sluggish total count heavily against it ... it'll require plenty of bally.' – *Variety*

'The story has all the dramatic integrity of a sashweight murderer's tabloid autobiography.' – *Pare Lorentz*

'There is more pleasure for the eye in *Blonde Venus* than in a hundred of its fellows. But what does beauty ornament? The story of a wife who becomes a kept woman for the sake of her husband, and a prostitute for the sake of her child.' – *Forsyth Hardy, Cinema Quarterly*

Blondes for Danger

GB 1938 68m bw
British Lion/Herbert Wilcox

A Cockney taxi driver takes an unwanted fare and becomes involved in a deep dark plot.

Modest but effective star vehicle.

w Gerald Elliott *novel Red for Danger* by Evadne Price *d* Jack Raymond

☆ Gordon Harker, Enid Stamp-Taylor, Ivan Brandt

Blondie *

US 1938 68m bw
Columbia

Misadventures of a harassed suburban family man.

Dagwood Bumstead and his wife Blondie were Mr and Mrs Small Town America throughout the thirties and forties, and received their perfect screen incarnations in this unambitious but quite watchable series, which provided familiar and often quite observant fun.

Other episodes were as follows:
1939 Blondie Meets the Boss, Blondie Takes a Vacation, Blondie Brings Up Baby
1940 Blondie on a Budget, Blondie Has Servant Trouble, Blondie Plays Cupid
1941 Blondie Goes Latin, Blondie in Society
1942 Blondie Goes to College, Blondie's Blessed Event, Blondie for Victory
1943 It's a Great Life, Footlight Glamour
1945 Leave It to Blondie
1946 Blondie Knows Best, Life with Blondie, Blondie's Lucky Day
1947 Blondie's Big Moment, Blondie's Holiday, Blondie in the Dough, Blondie's Anniversary
1948 Blondie's Reward
1949 Blondie's Secret, Blondie's Big Deal, Blondie Hits the Jackpot
1950 Blondie's Hero, Beware of Blondie

w Richard Flournoy *comic strip* Chic Young *d* Frank R. Strayer *ph* Henry Freulich

☆ Arthur Lake, Penny Singleton, Larry Simms, Daisy the Dog, Jonathan Hale (Mr Dithers), Gene Lockhart, Ann Doran, Irving Bacon (the mailman)

'Light fare, but universal in appeal ... could be clicko series.' – *Variety*

† TV series were started in the fifties and sixties, but both failed.

Blondie Johnson

US 1933 67m bw

Warner

The career of a female larcenist who eventually takes her medicine.

Competent programmer very typical of its studio and year.

w Earl Baldwin *d* Ray Enright

☆ Joan Blondell, Chester Morris, Allen Jenkins, Claire Dodd

'After she departs for the pen, she lets the public in on the fact that crime doesn't pay. Neither will the picture.' – *Variety*

Blondie of the Follies *

US 1932 97m bw

MGM (Marion Davies)

Two New York showgirls graduate from tenements to luxury.

Adequate comedy-melodrama with an interesting cast and good dialogue.

w Frances Marion, Anita Loos *d* Edmund Goulding *ph* George Barnes *m* William Axt

☆ Marion Davies, Jimmy Durante, Robert Montgomery, Billie Dove, James Gleason, ZaSu Pitts, Sidney Toler, Douglass Dumbrille

'Not bad, but not very good, with chances that it will just get by. Length and slow pace the drawbacks ... It isn't padded out, it's just flatfooted.' – *Variety*

'An unjustly forgotten film.' – *New Yorker, 1979*

Blood Alley

US 1955 115m Warnercolor Cinemascope

Warner/Batjac (no producer credited)

An American sailor is helped by local people to escape from a Chinese jail; he then escorts them to Hong Kong.

Rudimentary anti-Red heroics with expensive spectacle punctuating a tacky script.

w A. S. Fleischman *novel* A. S. Fleischman *d* William Wellman *ph* William H. Clothier *m* Roy Webb *pd* Alfred Ybarra

☆ John Wayne, Lauren Bacall, Paul Fix, Joy Kim, Berry Kroeger, Mike Mazurki, Anita Ekberg

'Becomes A Terror House Of Blood!!'
'Guaranteed! The 8 Greatest Shocks Ever Filmed!'

Blood and Black Lace

Italy 1964 90m Eastmancolor

Emmepi

original title: *Sei Donne per l'Assassino*

Six women are nastily murdered in a fashion house.

Vaguely necrophiliac but trendy suspense-horror flick in the wake of Psycho *(qv).*

w Marcello Fondato, Giuseppe Barilla, Mario Bava *d* Mario Bava

☆ Cameron Mitchell, Thomas Reiner, Mary Arden

'The wooden nature of the script and performances makes it hard to get into the complicated narrative. Don't bother. Just settle back and enjoy the sex and violence.' – *The Dark Side*

Blood and Roses

France/Italy 1960 87m colour Technirama

Eger/Documento (Raymond Eger)

original title: *Et Mourir de Plaisir*

Carmilla takes on the vampiric personality of her ancestress Millarca, whom she closely resembles.

A rather half-hearted attempt to make an elegant horror story; boring rather than charming or frightening.

w Claude Brûlé, Claude Martin, Roger Vadim *d* Roger Vadim *ph* Claude Renoir *m* Jean Prodromidès

☆ Mel Ferrer, Elsa Martinelli, Annette Vadim, Marc Allégret

Blood and Sand *

US 1922 80m (24 fps) bw silent

Paramount

A matador falls under the spell of an aristocratic woman.

Elegant star vehicle which established his image.

w June Mathis *novel* Vicente Blasco Ibanez *d* Fred Niblo

☆ Rudolph Valentino, Nita Naldi, Lila Lee, Walter Long

'Love flamed in the shadow of death!'

Blood and Sand *

US 1941 123m Technicolor

TCF (Darryl F. Zanuck, Robert T. Kane)

A matador's life goes wrong when he is torn between the love of his wife and the attractions of a vamp.

Rather boring version, fine to look at but dramatically deadly.

w Jo Swerling *novel* Vicente Blasco Ibanez *d* Rouben Mamoulian *ph* Ernest Palmer, Ray Rennahan *m* Alfred Newman *ad* Richard Day, Joseph C. Wright

☆ Tyrone Power, Rita Hayworth, Linda Darnell, Nazimova, Anthony Quinn, J. Carrol Naish, John Carradine, Lynn Bari, Laird Cregar, Monty Banks

† Carole Landis turned down the role that made a star of Rita Hayworth because she refused to change her hair colour from blonde to red.

Ernest Palmer, Ray Rennahan

Richard Day, Joseph C. Wright

'There is no honor amongst thieves.'

Blood & Wine *

US 1996 98m DeLuxe

TCF/Blood & Wine/Marmont/Recorded Picture/Majestic (Jeremy Thomas)

A wine merchant steals a valuable necklace, but loses it to his wife and stepson.

A grim and violent thriller with some effective performances; but its portrait of a greedy and dysfunctional family leaves little lasting impression.

w Nick Villiers, Alison Cross *d* Bob Rafelson *ph* Newton Thomas Sigel *m* Michel Lorenc *pd* Richard Sylbert *ed* Steven Cohen

☆ Jack Nicholson, Michael Caine, Stephen Dorff, Jennifer Lopez, Judy Davis, Harold Perrineau Jnr

'The film doesn't seem very significant. Everyone's good, but it's less than the sum of its watchable parts.' – *Derek Malcolm, Guardian*

Blood Beach

US 1980 90m colour

Miracle/Empress (Steven Nalevansky)

A monster, lurking beneath the sand of a beach, swallows passers-by.

Dull, lethargic, low-budget variation on Jaws *(qv); not only could they not afford much of a monster, they also skimped on the script and actors.*

w Jeffrey Bloom *story* Jeffrey Bloom, Steven Nalevansky *d* Jeffrey Bloom *ph* Steve Poster *m* Gil Mellé *ad* William Sandell *ed* Gary Griffen

☆ David Huffman, Marianna Hill, John Saxon, Otis Young, Stefan Gierasch, Burt Young

'It's so slow and boring, just like a bad television movie.' – *The Dark Side*

Blood Beast from Outer Space: see *The Night Caller*

The Blood Beast Terror

GB 1967 88m Eastmancolor

Tigon (Arnold L. Miller)

A Victorian entomologist creates human beings who can change themselves into monster death's-head moths.

Unpersuasive and totally idiotic cheapjack horror fare.

w Peter Bryan *d* Vernon Sewell *ph* Stanley A. Long *m* Paul Ferris

☆ Robert Flemyng, Peter Cushing, Wanda Ventham, Vanessa Howard, David Griffin, John Paul, Kevin Stoney, Roy Hudd

The Blood Demon

West Germany 1967 76m colour

Techniscope

New Realm/Constantin (Wolfgang Kuehnlenz)

original title: *Die Schlangengrube und das Pendel*

aka: *The Torture Chamber of Dr Sadism*

An aristocrat dismembered after killing 12 virgins returns from the dead to kill a 13th and achieve immortality.

An extremely free adaptation of Poe, given over to narrative incoherence and startling images.

w Manfred R. Koehler *story* *The Pit and the Pendulum* by Edgar Allan Poe *d* Harald Reinl *ph* Ernst W. Kalinke

☆ Christopher Lee, Lex Barker, Karin Dor, Carl Lange, Vladimir Medar, Christiane Rucker, Dieter Eppler

'A perfectly dreadful composite of *The House of Legends, Eternal Life, The Hunchback of Notre Dame* and *The Pit and the Pendulum*.' – *Christopher Lee*

'Nothing So Appalling In The Annals of Horror!'

Blood Feast

US 1963 67m colour

Box Office Spectaculars (David F. Friedman, Stanford S. Kohlberg, Herschell Gordon Lewis)

A caterer commits multiple murders in worship of a bloodthirsty Egyptian goddess.

A truly terrible movie, in which the bad acting, incompetent direction and brain-dead narrative are the true horrors, rather than its body parts and gallons of gore; yet its influence is with us still, as it inspired a seemingly endless succession of slasher movies.

w Louise Downe *d* Herschell Gordon Lewis *ph* Herschell Gordon Lewis *m* Herschell Gordon Lewis *ed* Frank Romolo, Robert Sinise *sp* Gordon Lewis

☆ Thomas Wood (Pete Thornton), Mal Arnold (Ramses), Connie Mason (Suzette), Scott H. Hall (Police Captain), Lyn Bolton (Mrs Fremon), Toni Calvert (Trudy), Gene Courtier (Tony)

'Offensive, nasty, shabby, and revolting, but also great fun, if you can stand the sight of guts (of course ya' can, you wimp).' – *Jerry Renshaw, Austin Chronicle*

Blood Feud

Italy 1979 112m Technospes

ITC/Liberty Films (Harry Columbo)

aka: *Revenge*

In Sicily, as the fascists come to power, a rich socialist lawyer and a small-time crook court the same vengeful woman.

Unsatisfactory, melodramatic mix of romance and politics.

wd Lina Wertmuller *ph* Tonino Delli Colli *m* Dangio-Nando de Luca *ad* Enrico Job *ed* Franco Fraticelli

☆ Sophia Loren, Marcello Mastroianni, Giancarlo Giannini, Mario Scarpetta

Blood for Dracula: see *Dracula (1974)*

'A severed hand beckons from an open grave!'

Blood from the Mummy's Tomb *

GB 1971 94m Technicolor

MGM-EMI/Hammer (Howard Brandy)

Twenty years after a female mummy is brought back to England, members of the expedition are killed one by one, and their leader's daughter is possessed by the spirit of the dead princess.

Interesting but over-complicated and hard-to-enjoy attempt to maintain the mummy saga without an actual marauding mummy. Intelligently handled but sadly lacking in a sense of humour.

w Christopher Wicking *novel* *Jewel of the Seven Stars* by Bram Stoker *d* Seth Holt, Michael Carreras *ph* Arthur Grant *m* Tristram Cary *ad* Scott MacGregor *ed* Peter Weatherley

☆ Andrew Keir, Valerie Leon, James Villiers, Hugh Burden, George Coulouris, Mark Edwards, Rosalie Crutchley, Aubrey Morris, David Markham

'Makes the genre seem like new.' – *Tony Rayns*

† Seth Holt died while the shooting was still incomplete, and Michael Carreras took over for the last few days.

'Two Cats... One Car... And A World Of Hurt'

Blood Guts Bullets & Octane *

US 1997 86m colour

Downtown/Short Fuse/Next Wave (Dan Leis, Leon Corcos, Patrick Lynn)

Two car dealers, given money to look after a Pontiac Le Mans, decide to steal the car instead, not knowing that the FBI believe it contains drugs and was used by a serial killer.

A low-budget movie, made with enough verve and energy to overcome its familiar, low-life narrative.

wd Joe Carnahan *ph* John Alexander Jimenez *m* Mark Priolo, Martin Birke *ad* Eric Lutes *ed* Joe Carnahan

☆ Joe Carnahan (Sid French), Dan Leis (Bob Melba), Ken Rudulph (FBI Agent Jared), Dan Harlan (Danny Woo), Hugh McChord (Mr Reich), Kurt Johnson (Hillbilly Sniper), Mark S. Allen (FBI Agent Franks), Kellee Benedic (FBI Agent Littel)

Blood In, Blood Out **

US 1992 180m Technicolor

Buena Vista/Hollywood Pictures/Touchstone Pacific Partners I (Taylor Hackford, Jerry Gershwin)

A decade in the life of three Chicanos, two half-brothers and their half-white cousin, caught up in gang warfare on the streets and in prison.

Tough, violent, gripping drama of oppression and redemption in the East Los Angeles barrio, depicting an aspect of America not often seen on-screen; its length is justified not only by its narrative drive but by the fleshing out of individual lives caught in a destructive system.

w Jimmy Santiago Baca, Jeremy Iacone, Floyd Mutrux *story* Ross Thomas *d* Taylor Hackford *ph* Gabriel Beristain *m* Bill Conti *pd* Bruno Rubeo *ed* Fredric Steinkamp, Karl F. Steinkamp

☆ Jesse Borrego, Benjamin Bratt, Enrique Castillo, Damian Chapa, Delroy Lindo, Tom Wilson, Karmin Murcelo, Ving Rhames, Jenny Gago

'Triumphs over cliché to sustain its vast length and space. The key to this success lies in its epic size, a mood and a scale more akin to a mini-series than grandiose cinema.' – *Olly Blackburn, Sight and Sound*

'Seems compelled to say something profound but too often stands on a soapbox to do it.' – *Variety*

Blood Is My Heritage: see *Blood of Dracula*

Blood Money *

US 1933 66m bw

Fox/Darryl F. Zanuck

The decline of a bail-bond racketeer.

Smartly made melodrama with good work all round.

wd Rowland Brown

☆ George Bancroft, Judith Anderson, Chick Chandler, Frances Dee, Blossom Seeley

Blood Money: see *Requiem for a Heavyweight (1962)*

Blood Oath

Australia 1990 108m Eastmancolor

Rank/Sovereign/Village Roadshow/Siege (Graham Burke, Greg Coote, John Tarnoff)

In 1946, an Australian Army captain prosecutes the Japanese commandant of a camp where the bodies of more than 300 prisoners were discovered in a mass grave.

A routine courtroom drama of no particular interest, despite its factual basis.

w Denis Whitburn, Brian A. Williams *d* Stephen Wallace *ph* Russell Boyd *m* David McHugh *ad* Virginia Bieneman *ed* Nicholas Beauman, Bernard Hides

☆ Bryan Brown, George Takei, Terry O'Quinn, John Bach, Toshi Shioya, John Clarke, Deborah Unger, Jason Donovan

'Reduces the moral complexities of war to the simplest Boy's Own level.' – *Sight and Sound*

The Blood of a Poet **

France 1931 58m bw

Vicomte de Noailles

original title: *Le Sang d'un Poète*

Aspects of a poet's vision, taking place while a chimney is falling down.

An indescribable film full of striking imagery which may, or may not, be meaningful. Its author claims that

it is not surrealist, but that label for most people will do as well as any other.
wd Jean Cocteau *ph* Georges Périnal *m* Georges Auric *ad* Jean Gabriel d'Aubonne
☆ Lee Miller, Enrique Rivero, Pauline Carton, Feral Benga, Jean Desbordes, Barbette, Odette Talazac
'It must be placed among the classic masterpieces of the seventh art.' – *Revue du Cinéma*

'In her eyes Desire! In her veins the blood of a ... Monster!'
Blood of Dracula
US 1957 68m bw
Anglo Amalgamated/Carmel/AIP (Herman Cohen)
GB title: *Blood Is My Heritage*
aka: *Blood of the Demon*
A feminist high-school chemistry teacher hypnotizes an unhappy student into becoming a vampire to prove that men control, and will destroy, the world.
Risible mix of horror and teenage rebellion movies that does not miss a cliché of either genre.
w Ralph Thornton *d* Herbert L. Strock *ph* Monroe Askins *m* Paul Dunlap *ad* Leslie Thomas *ed* Robert Moore *sp* Philip Scheer
☆ Sandra Harrison, Louise Lewis, Gail Ganley, Jerry Blaine, Heather Ames, Malcolm Atterbury, Mary Adams
† With a change in gender for the leading characters and a different monster, the script was recycled by Thornton as *I Was a Teenage Werewolf* (qv).

Blood of the Demon: see *Blood of Dracula*

Blood of the Dragon
Japan 1974 88m Eastmancolor Toeiscope
Eural/Toei-Kyoto Eiga/Titan (Norimichi Matsudaira)
original title: *Satsujinken 2*
Double-crossed by his employers, who front for the Mafia, an assassin goes on the rampage.
Convoluted martial arts mayhem that makes little narrative sense; but then all that matters is its fights.
w Hajime Takaiwa, Shigehiro Ozawa *story* Koji Yakada *d* Sonny Chiba, Gerald Yamada, Doris Nakajima, Tony Cetera, Tatsuro Endo, Masashi Ishibashi *m* Tony Tsushima *ad* Tokumichi Igawa *ed* Kozo Horiike
☆ Sonny Chiba, Yoko Ichiji, Masafumi Suzuki, Kaoru Nakajima, Naoki Shima, Masashi Ishibashi

Blood of the Undead: see *Schizo*

Blood of the Vampire
GB 1958 85m Eastmancolor
Baker-Berman/Artistes Alliance
A doctor, raised from the dead, takes over an asylum and experiments on the inmates.
Heavy-handed, crudely made horror comic.
w Jimmy Sangster *d* Henry Cass *ph* Monty Berman *m* Stanley Black *ad* John Elphick *ed* Douglas Myers
☆ Donald Wolfit, Barbara Shelley, Vincent Ball, Victor Maddern, Andrew Faulds, John Le Mesurier, Bernard Bresslaw

Blood of the Virgins: see *Sangre de Virgenes*

Blood on His Lips: see *The Hideous Sun Demon*

Blood on My Hands: see *Kiss the Blood Off My Hands*

Blood on Satan's Claw
GB 1970 93m Eastmancolor
Tigon-Chilton (Tony Tenser, Malcolm B. Heyworth, Peter L. Andrews)
aka: *Satan's Skin*
A devil's claw wreaks havoc among children in a 17th-century English village.
Moderately frightening, rather silly but at least original period horror comic.
w Robert Wynne-Simmons *d* Piers Haggard *ph* Dick Bush *m* Marc Wilkinson
☆ Patrick Wymark, Linda Hayden, Barry Andrews, Avice Landon, Simon Williams, Tamara Ustinov, Anthony Ainley

Blood on the Arrow
US 1964 91m DeLuxe
Leon Fromkess/Allied Artists
An outlaw is the only survivor of an Indian raid, and later becomes a hero when the Indians attack again.
Unremarkable Western, with every turn of plot to order.
w Robert E. Kent *d* Sidney Salkow
☆ Dale Robertson, Martha Hyer, Wendell Corey, Paul Mantee, Ted de Corsia

Blood on the Moon *
US 1948 88m bw
RKO (Sid Rogell, Theron Warth)
A homesteader finds that his best friend is the villainous leader of a group of cattlemen.
Good-looking but rather pedestrian Western, generally well handled.
w Lillie Hayward *novel* *Gunman's Choice* by Luke Short *d* Robert Wise *ph* Nicholas Musuraca *m* Roy Webb
☆ Robert Mitchum, Barbara Bel Geddes, Robert Preston, Walter Brennan

Blood on the Streets: see *Borsalino & Co*

Blood on the Sun *
US 1945 94m bw
Cagney Productions (William Cagney)
In the twenties, the American editor of a Tokyo newspaper reveals a Japanese militarist plan for world conquest.
Satisfactory star actioner with good production and exciting highlights.
w Lester Cole *d* Frank Lloyd *ph* Theodor Sparkuhl *m* Miklos Rozsa *ad* Wiard Ihnen
☆ James Cagney, Sylvia Sidney, Wallace Ford, Rosemary de Camp, Robert Armstrong, John Emery, Leonard Strong, Frank Puglia
'It ought to be fine for those who enjoy a good ninety-minute massacre.' – *New Yorker*
'Tough, hard-hitting and explosive, with just enough rudimentary suspense.' – *Bosley Crowther*
'Pure unadulterated melodrama has a safe niche in cinematic offerings, but this folderol is more pretentious than persuasive.' – *Howard Barnes*
Academy Award: Wiard Ihnen

Blood Relatives
Canada/France 1977 100m colour Panavision
Classic/Cinevideo/Filmel (Denis Heroux, Eugene Lepecier)
aka: *Les Liens du Sang*
A 15-year-old girl accuses her brother of murdering their 17-year-old cousin.
Dull psychological thriller, with stock characters and showing none of the flair that Chabrol has exhibited when examining the French middle classes under pressure.
w Claude Chabrol, Sydney Banks *novel* Ed McBain *d* Claude Chabrol *ph* Jean Rabier *m* Howard Blake *pd* Anne Pritchard *ed* Yves Langlois
☆ Donald Sutherland, Stéphane Audran, Micheline Lanctot, Aude Landry, Lisa Langlois, Laurent Malet, Donald Pleasence, David Hemmings

Blood Simple *
US 1983 99m DuArt
Palace/River Road (Ethan Coen)
A saloon owner hires a hit man to kill his unfaithful wife and her lover, but the plot rebounds on him.
Yet another variation on The Postman Always Rings Twice *(qv), and one with strong moments.*
w Joel and Ethan Coen *d* Joel Coen *ph* Barry Sonnenfeld *m* Carter Burwell *pd* Jane Musky *ed* Roderick Jaynes, Don Wiegmann, Peggy Connolly
☆ John Getz, Frances McDormand, Dan Hedaya, M. Emmet Walsh

Blood Sisters: see *Sisters*

The Blood Spattered Bride: see *La Novia Ensangrentada*

Blood Suckers: see *Incense of the Damned*

The Blood Virgin: see *Symptoms*

Blood Wedding **
Spain 1981 72m Eastmancolor
Artificial Eye/Emiliano Piedra
Dancers of the Antonio Gades company first prepare for, and then rehearse in a bare room, their flamenco-ballet treatment of Lorca's play of passion, jealousy and death.
An exhilarating treatment of both Lorca and the dancers, moving from a documentary style to one more involved in the commitment, energy and techniques on display.
play Federico Garcí Lorca *d* Carlos Saura *ph* Teo Escamilla *m* Emilion de Diego *ch* Antonio Gades *ad* Rafael Lammero *ed* Pablo del Amo
☆ Antonio Gades, Cristina Hoyos, Juan Antonio, Pilar Cardenas, Carmen Villena, Marisol, Pepe Blanco, El Guito, Lario Diaz
'A feast for dance lovers.' – *Sight and Sound*

Bloodbath at the House of Death
GB 1983 92m colour
EMI/Wildwood (Ray Cameron)
Scientists investigate a haunted house.
Spoof tailored to the requirements of a zany television comedian who never knows when enough is enough. Too much gore and far too much smut.
w Ray Cameron, Barry Cryer *d* Ray Cameron *ph* Brian West, Dusty Miller *m* Mike Moran, Mark London
☆ Kenny Everett, Pamela Stephenson, Vincent Price, Gareth Hunt, Don Warrington, John Fortune, Sheila Steafel, Graham Stark
'Presumably intended as high camp; looks like low-grade *Carry On*.' – *Martyn Auty, MFB*

Bloodbath Bay of Death: see *A Bay of Blood*

Bloodbrothers
US 1978 116m Technicolor
Warner/Stephen Friedman/Kings Road
The disintegration through failure and inadequacy of a noisy Italian-American family.
The kind of self-indulgence that has one seeking the exit before it's half over.
w Walter Newman *novel* Richard Price *d* Robert Mulligan *ph* Robert Surtees *m* Elmer Bernstein *pd* Gene Callahan
☆ Paul Sorvino, Tony Lo Bianco, Richard Gere, Lelia Goldoni
'The director is trying for something crude, powerful, volatile ... but it goes terribly wrong. People laugh with hysterical heartiness, or say things like: "Life can hurt. It's made me feel close to all those doing the hurting dance."' – *Pauline Kael, New Yorker*
Academy Award nomination: Walter Newman

Bloodfist
US 1989 85m colour
Concorde (Roger Corman)
A kick-boxer seeks to avenge his brother's death.
Unexciting and turgid action movie.
w Robert King *d* Terence H. Winkless *ph* Ricardo Jacques Gale *m* Sasha Matson *ed* Karen Horn
☆ Don 'The Dragon' Wilson, Joe Marie Avellana, Michael Shaner, Riley Bowman, Rob Kamen, Billy Blanks, Kris Aguilar

Bloodfist II
US 1990 88m colour
Concorde (Roger Corman)
A kick-boxer attempts to infiltrate an island fortress.
A cheap re-run of Enter the Dragon *(qv) with a far less charismatic hero.*
w Catherine Cyran *d* Andy Blumenthal *ph* Bruce Dorfman *m* Nigel Holton *ed* Karen Joseph
☆ Don 'The Dragon' Wilson, Rina Reyes, Joe Marie Avellana, Robert Marius, Maurice Smith, Tim Baker, James Warring

Bloodfist III
US 1992 88m Foto-Kem
Concorde (Roger Corman)
A wrongly imprisoned kick-boxer goes to the aid of a friend attacked by fellow convicts.
Fast action movie, with some fierce fights, which should satisfy fans of the genre.
w Allison Burnett, Charles Mattera *d* Oley Sassone *ph* Rick Bota *m* Nigel Holton *pd* James Shumaker *ed* Eric L. Beason
☆ Don 'The Dragon' Wilson, Richard Roundtree, Gregory McKinney, Rick Dean, Richard Paul, Charles Boswell, John Cardone

Bloodhounds of Broadway *
US 1952 90m Technicolor
TCF (George Jessel)
With the help of a gangster, an orphan girl and her pet bloodhounds make a big hit in cabaret.
Absurd but sporadically amusing gangster burlesque, typical of its author. Lively production values.
w Sy Gomberg *story* Damon Runyon *d* Harmon Jones *ph* Edward Cronjager *m* David Raksin *md* Lionel Newman
☆ Mitzi Gaynor, Scott Brady, Mitzi Green, Marguerite Chapman, Michael O'Shea, Wally Vernon, George E. Stone

Bloodhounds of Broadway
US 1989 90m DeLuxe
Columbia (Howard Brookner)
Interwoven stories of the escapades of gangsters, guys and dolls on New Year's Eve, 1928.
Bland and forgettable and lacking the particular flavour of the original tales.
wd Howard Brookner *short stories* Damon Runyon *ph* Elliot Davis *m* Jonathan Sheffer *pd* Linda Conway-Parsole *ed* Camilla Toniolo
☆ Josef Sommer, Madonna, Tony Azito, Jennifer Grey, Tony Longo, Rutger Hauer, Matt Dillon, Julie Hagerty, Randy Quaid, William Burroughs

Bloodline
US 1979 117m Movielab
Paramount/Geria (David V. Picker, Sidney Beckerman)
A pharmaceutical tycoon is murdered and his daughter seems likely to be the next victim.
Involved all-star suspense shocker which seems constantly about to be better than it ever is.
w Laird Koenig *novel* Sidney Sheldon *d* Terence Young *ph* Freddie Young *m* Ennio Morricone *pd* Ted Haworth
☆ Audrey Hepburn, Ben Gazzara, James Mason, Claudia Mori, Omar Sharif, Irene Papas, Maurice Ronet, Romy Schneider, Beatrice Straight, Gert Frobe, Michelle Phillips
'Unutterably chic, inexpressibly absurd, and saved from being painfully tedious only by a personable cast doing their damnedest.' – *Tom Milne, MFB*

Bloodsport
US 1988 92m TVC Color
Cannon (Mark DiSalle)
An American commando goes to Hong Kong to take part in the Kumite, a clandestine martial arts competition.
Despite being based on the true story of Frank Dux (who supervised the fight sequences), the movie emerges as pulp fiction that will be of interest only to martial arts enthusiasts, who may not wonder why an American should speak with a heavy Belgian accent.
w Sheldon Lettich, Christopher Crosby, Mel Friedman *d* Newt Arnold *ph* David Worth *m* Paul Hertzog *pd* David Searl *ed* Carl Kress
☆ Jean-Claude Van Damme, Donald Gibb, Leah Ayres, Norman Burton, Forest Whitaker, Roy Chiao, Philip Chan, Pierre Rafini, Bolo Yeung

The Bloodstained Shadow (dubbed)
Italy 1978 107m Technospes
PAC (Teodoro Agrimi)
original title: *Solamente Nero*
The visit of an overworked university lecturer to his brother, a priest, coincides with a series of murders.
Dull and slow-moving thriller, with an explanation of the crimes that makes very little sense, although a similar and equally unlikely plot turns up in Dario Argento's Creepers *(qv).*
w Antonio Bido, Marisa Andalo, Domenico Malan *d* Antonio Bido *ph* Mario Vulpiani *m* Stelvio Cipriani *ad* Carlo Leva *ed* Amedeo Giomini

☆ Lino Capolicchio, Stefania Casini, Craig Hill, Massimo Serato, Juliette Mayniel, Laura Nucci, Attilio Duse

Bloodstream
US 1993 90m CFI color
HBO Showcase (John Bard Manulis)

In the near, grim future, a woman falls in love with the leader of a resistance movement against government policy, in which people suffering from an AIDS-like disease are imprisoned while order is maintained by gangs of young vigilantes.
Moderately effective science-fiction drama of an era when individual liberty is subordinated to the interests of the state, though making only a perfunctory attempt to explore the concept in any depth.
wd Stephen Tolkin *play* Beirut by Alan Bowne *ph* Tom Sigel *m* Michel Colombier *pd* Leslie Pope *ed* Brunilda Torres
☆ Cuba Gooding Jnr, Moira Kelly, Omar Epps, Martha Plimpton, Alice Drummond, David Eigenberg, Jon Seda, Nick Chinlund
'Maintains a delicate balance between fantasy and reality, enveloping its political message in an easy-to-swallow dramatic capsule ... a real find.' – *Sight and Sound*
† The film was made for cable TV.

Bloodsucking Freaks
US 1977 93m colour Ghoulovision
Troma (Alan Margolin)

aka: *The Incredible Torture Show*
Nasty things happen during a Grand Guignol-style stage show given over to sadism and the white slave trade.
Extraordinarily unpleasant farrago, in which one of the pleasanter moments has someone's brain being sucked out with a straw. According to Troma's Lloyd Kaufman, it is 'only for the demented'; but it won't do them any good.
wd Joel M. Reed *ph* Gerry Toll *m* Michael Sahl *ed* Victor Kanevsky
☆ Seamus O'Brien, Niles McMaster, Luis de Jesus, Viju Krim, Alan Dellay

Bloody Angels: see *1732 Høtten*

The Bloody Bushido Blade: see *The Bushido Blade*

'The family that stays together slays together!'
Bloody Mama *
US 1969 90m Movielab
AIP (Roger Corman)

In the thirties, outlaw Kate Barker and her four sons conduct a reign of terror until what's left of the gang is riddled with machine gun bullets.
Violent gangster story with a star on the rampage; the attempt to philosophize is more than the facts will bear, but the production moves smartly enough.
w Robert Thom *d* Roger Corman *ph* John Alonzo *m* Don Randi
☆ Shelley Winters, Pat Hingle, Don Stroud, Diane Varsi, Bruce Dern, Clint Kimbrough, Robert De Niro, Robert Walden, Alex Nicol

Bloody Sunday **
GB/Ireland 2002 110m colour
Portman/Hell's Kitchen/FC/IFC (Mark Redhead)
In 1972, in the town of Derry in Northern Ireland, British paratroopers, claiming to be under fire, shoot dead 13 demonstrators during a civil rights march that turned into a riot.
Engrossing documentary-style reconstruction of a still controversial event; the truth of what happened is still under investigation, but this probably gets as close as we are ever likely to know.
wd Paul Greengrass *book* Eyewitness Bloody Sunday by Don Mullan *ph* Ivan Strasburg *m* Dominic Muldoon *pd* John Paul Kelly *ed* Clare Douglas *cos* Dinah Collin
☆ James Nesbitt (Ivan Cooper), Tim Pigott-Smith (Major General Ford), Nicholas Farrell (Brigadier Maclellan), Gerard McSorley (Chief Supt Lagan), Kathy Kiera Clarke (Frances), Allan Gildea (Kevin McCorry), Gerard Crossan (Eamonn McCann), Mary Moulds (Bernadette Devlin), Carmel McCallion (Bridget Bond), Declan Duddy (Gerry Donaghy)
'A stunning work, revisiting controversial events with journalistic objectivity and a meticulous eye for detail.' – *Scott Foundas, Variety*

Blossom Time
GB 1934 90m bw
BIP (Walter Mycroft)

US title: *April Romance*
In old Vienna, a composer stands by while the girl he loves weds a dragoon.
Stilted musical romance redeemed by its star's singing presence.
w John Drinkwater, Walter Burford, Paul Perez, G. H. Clutsam *story* Franz Schulz *d* Paul Stein *ph* Otto Kanturek, Bryan Langley *m* Schubert *md* Idris Lewis *ad* David Rawnsley, Clarence Elder *ed* Leslie Norman
☆ Richard Tauber, Jane Baxter, Carl Esmond, Athene Seyler

Blossoms in the Dust **
US 1941 99m Technicolor
MGM (Irving Asher)

A woman who loses her husband and child founds a state orphanage.
Archetypal tearjerker of the forties, a glossy 'woman's picture' which distorts the facts into a star vehicle. Excellent colour helped to make it an enormous success.
w Anita Loos, based on the life of Edna Gladney *d* Mervyn Le Roy *ph* Karl Freund, W. Howard Greene *m* Herbert Stothart *ad* Cedric Gibbons, Urie McCleary
☆ *Greer Garson*, Walter Pidgeon, Felix Bressart, Marsha Hunt, Fay Holden, Samuel S. Hinds
art direction
best picture; Karl Freund, W. Howard Greene; Greer Garson

'Heading for the laff round-up!'
Blossoms on Broadway
US 1937 88m bw
Paramount (B. P. Schulberg)
A girl who owns a Death Valley gold mine comes to New York and is hounded by confidence men.
Tolerably fast-moving comedy.
w Theodore Reeves *d* Richard Wallace
☆ Edward Arnold, Shirley Ross, John Trent, Weber and Fields, Frank Craven, Rufe Davis, William Frawley
'Won't do much b.o. blossoming. Good songs, but story stumbles badly.' – *Variety*

Blotto *
US 1930 20m bw
Hal Roach

Ollie helps Stan escape his wife for a night on the town, but the lady takes revenge.
Palatable star comedy with a strained second half following a splendidly typical opening.
w Leo McCarey, H. M. Walker *d* James Parrott
☆ Stan Laurel, Oliver Hardy, Anita Garvin

Blow *
US 2001 123m DeLuxe Panavision
Entertainment/New Line/Spanky/Apostle (Ted Demme, Joel Stillerman, Denis Leary)

A Boston boy grows up to become America's biggest smuggler of cocaine from Colombia in the 1970s.
Fitfully interesting drama, based on a true story, that sets a hectic pace its cast can hardly keep up with; it's a mad dash through pop culture, bland in texture before it stumbles to a halt.
w David McKenna, Nick Cassavetes *book* Bruce Porter *d* Ted Demme *ph* Ellen Kuras *m* Graeme Revell *pd* Michael Hanan *ed* Kevin Tent
☆ Johnny Depp (George Jung), Penelope Cruz (Mirtha Jung), Jordi Molla (Diego Delgado), Franka Potente (Barbara Buckley), Rachel Griffiths (Ermine Jung), Ray Liotta (Fred Jung), Ethan Suplee (Tuna), Paul Reubens (Derek Foreal), Max Perlich (Kevin Dulli), Cliff Curtis (Pablo Escobar), Bobcat Goldthwait (Mr T)
'Like most movie drug experiences and illicit substance-themed films, this delivers an hour of 'up' entertainment, then inevitably plunges into a compensatory hour of misery and moralising.' – *Kim Newman, Empire*

'Love is in the hair.'
Blow Dry
GB/Germany/US 2001 90m colour
Buena Vista/Intermedia/Miramax/West Eleven/Mirage/IMF (Ruth Jackson, William Horberg, David Rubin)

In the Yorshire town of Keighley, a barber teams up with his former wife and her girlfriend to compete against the reigning champion in a British Hairdressing contest.
Mild sub-Ealing comedy with a cast seemingly not at ease with their roles.
w Simon Beaufoy *based on screenplay* Never Better by Simon Beaufoy *d* Paddy Breathnach *ph* Cian De Buitlear *m* Patrick Doyle *pd* Sophie Becher *ed* Tony Lawson *cos* Rosie Hackett
☆ Alan Rickman (Phil), Natasha Richardson (Shelly), Rachel Griffiths (Sandra), Rachael Leigh Cook (Christina), Josh Hartnett (Brian), Bill Nighy (Ray), Warren Clarke (Tony), Rosemary Harris (Daisy), Hugh Bonneville (Louis), Heidi Klum (Jasmine), Peter McDonald (Vincent), Michael McElhatton (Robert)
'It's not a good hair day.' – *Variety*

'Murder has a sound all of its own!'
Blow Out
US 1981 108m Technicolor Panavision
Filmways/Cinema 77/Geria (George Litto)

A sound effects man accidentally captures on film what turns out to be a murder.
Showily unpleasant thriller concocted of equal parts of The Conversation, Blow Up, *and* Kennedy at Chappaquiddick; *the work of a copycat talent operating below par.*
wd Brian de Palma *ph* Vilmos Zsigmond *m* Pino Donaggio *pd* Paul Sylbert *ed* Paul Hirsch
☆ John Travolta, Nancy Allen, John Lithgow, Dennis Franz, John McMartin, John Aquino, Curt May
'The camera is better deployed than the script.' – *Guardian*

Blow to the Heart
Italy 1982 105m colour
Other Cinema/RAI/Antea Cinematografica (Enzo Porcelli)
original title: *Colpire Al Cuore*
A conformist son suspects his radical father of terrorist sympathies.
Moderately gripping, though it suffers from indecision over whether its subject matter is politics or family relationships.
w Gianni Amelio, Vincenzo Cerami *d* Gianni Amelio *ph* Tonino Nardi *m* Franco Piersanti *ad* Marco Dentici *ed* Anna Napoli
☆ Jean-Louis Trintignant, Laura Morante, Fausto Rossi, Sonia Gessner, Vanni Corbellini

Blow-Out **
France/Italy 1973 133m Eastmancolor Panavision
Gala/Mara/Les Films 66/Capitolina (Jean-Pierre Rassam)

original title: *La Grande Bouffe*
A master chef, a television personality, a pilot and a judge get together for a prolonged orgy of gourmandizing and sex that ends with their deaths.
Grotesque celebration of, or satire on, the consumer society in which amusement gradually turns to disgust.
w Marco Ferreri, Rafael Azcona, Francis Blanche *d* Marco Ferreri *ph* Mario Vulpiani *m* Philippe Sarde *ad* Michel de Broin *ed* Claudine Merlin, Gina Pignier
☆ Marcello Mastroianni, Ugo Tognazzi, Michel Piccoli, Philippe Noiret, Andréa Ferreol, Solange Florence, Blondeau Giorgetti, Michele Alexandre, Monique Chaumette
'The film is never negligible thanks to Ferreri's consistently inventive use of detail; and whatever else, it stands as an overdue riposte to the contemporary cinema's ubiquitous hymns to male camaraderie.' – *Tony Rayns, MFB*

Blow-Up **
GB 1966 110m Eastmancolor
MGM/Carlo Ponti

A London fashion photographer thinks he sees a murder, but the evidence disappears.
Not a mystery but a fashionable think-in on the difference (if any) between fantasy and reality. Agreeable to look at for those who can stifle their irritation at the non-plot and non-characters; a huge audience was lured by flashes of nudity and the trendy 'swinging London' setting.
wd Michelangelo Antonioni *ph* Carlo di Palma *m* Herbert Hancock *ad* Assheton Gorton
☆ David Hemmings, Sarah Miles, Vanessa Redgrave
'A beautiful and startling film, startling because if the credits didn't say it was coauthored and directed by Michelangelo Antonioni you'd never believe it on the basis of the movie itself, and beautiful because in his first made-in-England English-language film the Italian director proves himself a master of the use of color, both literally and figuratively.' – *Judith Crist*
Michelangelo Antonioni (as writer and director)

Blowing Wild *
US 1953 88m bw
Warner/United States (Milton Sperling)

A Mexican oil driller becomes involved with the psychotic wife of an old friend; the triangle leads to murder and retribution.
Pot-boiling star vehicle with adequate melodramatic interest, full of reminiscences of other movies, with a wicked lady to end them all.
w Philip Yordan *d* Hugo Fregonese *ph* Sid Hickox *m* Dimitri Tiomkin
☆ Gary Cooper, Barbara Stanwyck, Anthony Quinn, Ruth Roman, Ward Bond

'Trusting Someone Can Be Deadly.'
Blown Away
Canada 1992 92m colour
Norstar (Peter R. Simpson)

A young resort worker becomes involved with the spoilt, self-destructive 17-year-old daughter of his violent boss.
Tawdry tale of thwarted teenage sex that is both trivial and tedious, shot in the style of an unimaginative promotional video for a pop song.
w Robert Cooper *d* Brenton Spencer *ph* Perci Young *m* Paul J. Zaza *ad* Ian Brock *ed* Bill Towgood
☆ Corey Haim, Corey Feldman, Nicole Eggert, Gary Farmer, Kathleen Robertson, Jean LeClerc
'Daft "erotic" thriller.' – *Sight and Sound*

'5-4-3-2-1-Time's Up.'
Blown Away
US 1994 121m DeLuxe Panavision
MGM/Trilogy (John Watson, Richard Lewis, Pen Densham)

A Boston bomb disposal expert hunts down an escaped Irish bomber who knows his guilty secret and is killing his friends.
An action movie with more holes in its plot than there are in some of its mad bomber's victims; the cast give the impression that they were anxious to be somewhere else, but it is enjoyable enough in a mindless way, as long as you do not expect it to make any sense.
w Joe Batteer, John Rice *d* Stephen Hopkins *ph* Peter Levy *m* Alan Silvestri *pd* John Graysmark *ed* Timothy Wellburn
☆ Jeff Bridges, Tommy Lee Jones, Lloyd Bridges, Forest Whitaker, Suzy Amis
'Diehard action seekers may be drawn into its technical bag of tricks, but those in search of a gripping, emotional genre pic will be disappointed.' – *Leonard Klady, Variety*

Blue
US 1968 113m Technicolor Panavision
Paramount/Kettledrum (Judd Bernard, Irwin Winkler)

The white adopted son of a Mexican bandit prevents his cohorts from raping a white girl, and falls in love with her.
Pretentious, self-conscious, literary Western without much zest.
w Meade Roberts, Ronald M. Cohen *d* Silvio Narizzano *ph* *Stanley Cortez* *m* Manos Hadjidakis
☆ Terence Stamp, Joanna Pettet, Karl Malden, Ricardo Montalban
'I don't know which is worse – bad cowboy movies or bad arty cowboy movies. *Blue* is both.' – *Rex Reed*

Blue **

GB 1993 76m Technicolor

Basilisk/Uplink (James Mackay, Takashi Asai)

A meditation on AIDS and the colour blue; the screen is suffused with a blue light as the director muses on the death of friends and his own illness and deteriorating sight.

Jarman's valediction to the cinema is more a radio play than a film, but is nevertheless a superior piece of radio.

wd Derek Jarman *m* Simon Fisher Turner

☆ Featuring the voices of John Quentin, Derek Jarman, Nigel Terry, Tilda Swinton

'Given the choice between art and socially oriented moviemaking, he has opted for art.' – *Robert Horton, Film Comment*

† *Blue* was given a simultaneous first broadcast on British television and stereo radio. Jarman himself said of it, 'I think it's quite nice to have that visual silence in the cinema.'

The Blue and the Gold: see *An Annapolis Story*

The Blue Angel ****

Germany 1930 98m bw

UFA (Erich Pommer)

A fuddy-duddy professor is infatuated with a tawdry night-club singer. She marries him but is soon bored and contemptuous; humiliated, he leaves her and dies in his old classroom.

A masterwork of late twenties German grotesquerie, and after a slowish beginning an emotional powerhouse, set in a dark nightmare world which could be created only in the studio. Shot also in English, it was highly popular and influential in Britain and America. It instantly catapulted Dietrich to international stardom.

w Robert Liebmann, Carl Zuckmayer, Karl Vollmoeller *novel* *Professor Unrath* by Heinrich Mann *d* Josef von Sternberg *ph* Günther Rittau, Hans Schneeberger *m* Frederick Hollander (inc 'Falling in Love Again', 'They Call Me Wicked Lola') *ad* Otto Hunte, Emil Hasler

☆ *Emil Jannings, Marlene Dietrich,* Kurt Gerron, Hans Albers

'It will undoubtedly do splendidly in the whole of Europe and should also appeal strongly in the States ... only fault is a certain ponderousness of tempo which tends to tire.' – *Variety*

'At the time I thought the film was awful and vulgar and I was shocked by the whole thing. Remember, I was a well brought up German girl.' – *Marlene Dietrich*

The Blue Angel

US 1959 107m DeLuxe Cinemascope

TCF (Jack Cummings)

An academic falls for a nightclub singer.

Ill-advised attempt at a 'realistic', updated remake of the Germnan original; the result is a total travesty, with the actors aware that stylized melodrama is turning before their eyes into unintentional farce.

w Nigel Balchin *d* Edward Dmytryk *ph* Leon Shamroy *m* Hugo Friedhofer

☆ Curt Jurgens, May Britt, Theodore Bikel, John Banner

'It totally lacks the stifling atmosphere of sordid and oppressive sexuality which is essential to give conviction to the German sadism of the story.' – *Brenda Davies*

The Blue Bird ***

US 1940 98m Technicolor (bw prologue)

TCF (Gene Markey)

In a Grimm's Fairy Tale setting, the two children of a poor woodcutter seek the bluebird of happiness in the past, the future and the Land of Luxury, but eventually discover it in their own back yard.

An imaginative and often chilling script clarifies Maurice Maeterlinck's fairy play, and the art direction is outstanding, but the children are necessarily unsympathetic and the expensive production paled beside the success of the more upbeat Wizard of Oz *(qv), which was released almost simultaneously. Slashed for re-release, the only existing prints now open with confusing abruptness and no scene-setting before the adventures begin.*

w Ernest Pascal d Walter Lang ph Arthur Miller, Ray Rennahan m Alfred Newman *ad Richard Day, Wiard B. Ihnen*

☆ Shirley Temple, Johnny Russell, *Gale Sondergaard* (Cat), *Eddie Collins* (Dog), Nigel Bruce, Jessie Ralph, Spring Byington, Sybil Jason, Helen Ericson, Russell Hicks, Al Shean, Cecilia Loftus

'One of the most deliciously lovely productions to be brought to the screen.' – *MFB*

Academy Award nomination: Arthur Miller, Ray Rennahan

The Blue Bird

US/USSR 1976 83m Technicolor Panavision

TCF/Edward Lewis/Lenfilm

Two children seek the bluebird of happiness.

Abortive remake, widely touted as the first Russian–American co-production, but sabotaged by a flabby script, unsuitable casting and unresolved production problems.

w Hugh Whitemore, Alfred Hayes *d* George Cukor *ph* Freddie Young, Ionas Gritzus *m* Irwin Kostal, Andrei Petrov

☆ Elizabeth Taylor (Mother, Maternal Love, Light and the Witch), Ava Gardner, Cicely Tyson, Jane Fonda, Harry Andrews, Will Geer, Mona Washbourne, George Cole

'It works so hard at making history that it forgets to make sense.' – *David Sterritt, Christian Science Monitor*

'If you have any naughty children you want to punish, take them to *The Blue Bird* and make them sit all the way through it.' – *William Wolf, Cue*

'It turns a work for adults that children can enjoy into a charade for children that must sicken adults.' – *John Simon, New Yorker*

'Senile and interminable.' – *Stephen Farber, New West*

'Lavishly done; limited box office.' – *Variety*

Blue Black Permanent

GB 1992 86m colour

BFI/Channel 4/Viz Permanent (Barbara Grigor)

An Edinburgh photographer remembers her childhood in the Orkneys and returns there with her lover to sort out the problems that plague her.

A shifting and complex narrative explores feminine identity across two generations.

wd Margaret Tait *ph* Alex Scott *m* John Gray *pd* Andrew Semple *ed* John MacDonnell

☆ Celia Imrie, Jack Shepherd, Gerda Stevenson, James Fleet, Sean Scanlan, Hilary Maclean, Walter Leask, Sheena Mar

'Tait's achievement is to suggest the processes that lie behind our ways of seeing, our declarations, and to find a style that enacts, or at least simulates, those very processes.' – *Robert Yates, Sight and Sound*

Blue Blood

GB 1973 86m Technicolor

Mallard-Impact Quadrant (Kent Walwin, John Trent)

A German governess arrives at an English stately home and finds the malevolent butler plotting to show his supremacy over his effete master.

An extremely unattractive, would-be satirical melodrama which plays like a Grand Guignol version of The Servant *(qv).*

wd Andrew Sinclair *novel* *The Carry-Cot* by Alexander Thynne *ph* Harry Waxman *m* Brian Gascoigne

☆ Oliver Reed, Derek Jacobi, Fiona Lewis, Anna Gael, Meg Wynn Owen

Blue Canadian Rockies

US 1952 60m bw

Columbia/Gene Autry (Armand Schaefer)

A ranch foreman goes to Canada to stop the boss's daughter from marrying the wrong man.

Uninteresting Western with a flimsy plot and minimal action, interrupted by some indifferent songs.

w Gerald Geraghty *d* George Archainbaud *ph* William Bradford *md* Mischa Bakaleinikoff *ad* George Brooks *ed* James Sweeney

☆ Gene Autry, Champion, Pat Buttram, Gail Davis, Carolina Cotton, Ross Ford, Tom London, Mauritz Hugo, Cass County Boys

Blue Chips *

US 1994 108m Technicolor

Paramount (Michele Rappaport)

A college basketball coach, in trouble with a losing streak, condones bribery to get the talent he needs for his team.

A loud and frenetic melodrama of endemic corruption with an appeal likely to be limited to fans of the sport.

w Ron Shelton *d* William Friedkin *ph* Tom Priestley Jnr *m* Nile Rodgers, Jeff Beck, Jed Leiber *pd* James Bissell *ed* Robert K. Lambert, David Rosenbloom

☆ Nick Nolte, Mary McDonnell, J. T. Walsh, Ed O'Neill, Alfre Woodard, Bob Cousy, Shaquille O'Neal, Matt Nover, Louis Gossett Jnr, Robert Wuhl, Anfernee 'Penny' Hardaway

'A riveting, intelligent work.' – *Independent*

'A deafness-inducing but otherwise ho-hum would-be exposé of shady recruiting practices by college basketball programs.' – *Todd McCarthy, Variety*

Blue City

US 1986 83m Technicolor

Paramount (William Hayward, Walter Hill)

A drifter returns home to discover that his father has been murdered and his step-mother is living with the probable killer.

Dull, predictable and unpleasantly amoral thriller in which the hero's investigative methods into the killing consist of beating up most people he meets while waging a criminal war against his enemies.

w Lukas Heller, Walter Hill *novel* Ross MacDonald *d* Michelle Manning *ph* Steven Poster *m* Ry Cooder *ad* Richard Lawrence *ed* Ross Albert

☆ Judd Nelson, Ally Sheedy, David Caruso, Paul Winfield, Scott Wilson, Anita Morris, Julie Carmen, Luis Contreras

Blue Collar ***

US 1978 114m Technicolor

Universal/TAT (Don Guest)

Three car factory workers try to improve their lot by unionization and robbery.

Salty, rough, downbeat but impressively realistic modern drama, a belated American equivalent of Saturday Night and Sunday Morning *(qv).*

w Paul Schrader, Leonard Schrader *d* Paul Schrader *ph* Bobby Byrne *m* Jack Nitzsche

☆ Richard Pryor (Zeke Brown), Harvey Keitel (Jerry Bartowski), Yaphet Kotto (Smokey), Ed Begley Jnr (Bobby Joe), Harry Bellaver (Eddie Johnson), George Memmoli (Jenkins), Lucy Saroyan (Arlene Bartowski), Lane Smith (Clarence Hill)

'This is Schrader's first directing job and the best elements in the script fit his ability like a role tailored for an actor. His work is easy and quick, imaginative but not ostentatious.' – *Stanley Kauffmann*

'Tamed by a brunette – framed by a blonde – blamed by the cops!'

The Blue Dahlia **

US 1946 99m bw

Paramount (John Houseman)

A returning war veteran finds his faithless wife murdered and himself suspected.

Hailed on its first release as sharper than average, this mystery suspenser is now only moderately compelling despite the screenplay credit; direction and editing lack urgency and the acting lacks bounce.

w Raymond Chandler d George Marshall *ph* Lionel Lindon *m* Victor Young

☆ Alan Ladd, Veronica Lake, William Bendix, Howard da Silva, Doris Dowling, Tom Powers, Hugh Beaumont, Howard Freeman, Will Wright

'It threatens to turn into something, but it never does.' – *New Yorker, 1978*

'The picture is as neatly stylized and synchronized, and as uninterested in moral excitement, as a good ballet; it knows its own weight and size perfectly and carries them gracefully and without self-importance; it is, barring occasional victories and noble accidents, about as good a movie as can be expected from the big factories.' – *James Agee*

Academy Award nomination: Raymond Chandler

Blue Denim *

US 1959 89m bw Cinemascope

TCF (Charles Brackett)

GB title: *Blue Jeans*

Teenagers confronted with the prospect of illegitimate parenthood consult an abortionist, but all ends with wedding bells.

First of its rather dreary kind but better than most, this only slightly mawkish domestic drama has its heart in the right place and steers surprisingly towards a nick-of-time chase climax.

w Edith Sommer, Philip Dunne *play* James Leo Herlihy, William Noble *d* Philip Dunne *ph* Leo Tover *m* Bernard Herrmann

☆ Carol Lynley, Brandon de Wilde, Macdonald Carey, Marsha Hunt, Nina Shipman, Warren Berlinger

Blue Fire Lady

Australia 1978 95m Eastmancolor

AIFC (Anthony Ginnane)

A young girl defies her father's opposition to work with horses.

A soft-centred romance between a girl and a horse which follows the usual pattern – girl meets horse, girl loses horse, girl gets horse – and which will appeal to other horse-lovers.

w Bob Maumill *d* Ross Dimsey

☆ Cathryn Harrison, Mark Holden, Peter Cummins, Marion Edward, Lloyd Cunnington, Syd Conabere, Philip Barnard-Brown, Gary Waddell

The Blue Gardenia

US 1953 90m bw

Warner/Gloria/Blue Gardenia (Alex Gottlieb)

A girl gets drunk and wakes up in a strange apartment with a dead man by her side.

Totally undistinguished mystery which leaves egg on the actors' faces.

w Charles Hoffman *d* Fritz Lang *ph* Nicholas Musuraca *m* Raoul Kraushaar

☆ Anne Baxter, Richard Conte, Ann Sothern, Raymond Burr, Jeff Donnell, Richard Erdman, Nat King Cole

Blue Hawaii

US 1961 101m Technicolor Panavision

Hal B. Wallis

A GI comes home to Honolulu and becomes a beachcomber.

Lifeless star vehicle shot on glamorous locations.

w Hal Kanter *d* Norman Taurog *ph* Charles Lang Jnr *m* Joseph J. Lilley

☆ Elvis Presley, Joan Blackman, Nancy Walters, Roland Winters, Angela Lansbury, John Archer, Howard McNear

Blue Heat

US 1990 106m colour

Rank/Orion/Davis (John A. Davis)

US title: *The Last of the Finest*

An ex-cop goes after the drugs and arms dealer who caused his resignation from the force.

Standard cops 'n' robbers mayhem.

w Jere Cunningham, Thomas Lee Wright, George Armitage *d* John MacKenzie *ph* Juan Ruiz-Anchia *m* Jack Nitzsche, Michael Hoenig *pd* Lawrence G. Paull *ed* Graham Walker, Gregory Mark Gerlich, Albert Coleman, Karen Dale Greene

☆ Brian Dennehy, Joe Pantoliano, Jeff Fahey, Bill Paxton, Michael C. Gwynne

'If Harry's past ever catches up with him, he won't live long enough to regret it.'

Blue Ice

US 1992 105m colour

Guild/M&M (Martin Bregman, Michael Caine)

A jazz-club owner, a former secret agent, is asked by his mistress to find an old boyfriend and becomes embroiled in murder and arms smuggling.

Dreary thriller, lacking in surprise and suspense, with a cast that gives the impression that its attention is understandably elsewhere.

w Ron Hutchinson *novel* Ted Allbeury *d* Russell Mulcahy *ph* Denis Crossan *m* Michael Kamen *pd* Grant Hicks *ed* Seth Flaum

☆ Michael Caine, Sean Young, Ian Holm, Bobby Short, Alun Armstrong, Sam Kelly, Jack Shepherd,

Philip Davis, Patricia Hayes, Alan MacNaughton, Bob Hoskins

'Belongs to that familiar genre, the bad British thriller, with Michael Caine playing a version of Harry Palmer depoliticised for the Nineties and Sean Young giving the non-performance of her career.' – *Sheila Johnston, Independent*

'A resolutely old-fashioned thriller which, in its quaint view of London (all Tower Bridge and Soho dives), seems like an inflated 50s quota quickie.' – *Kim Newman, Sight and Sound*

The Blue Iguana

US 1988 88m CFI color

TCF/Polgram/Propaganda (Sigurjon Sighvatsson, Steven Colin)

An incompetent and down-at-heel bounty hunter is forced by inland revenue agents to undertake a suicidal mission in Mexico.

A comic take on the clichés of tough-guy thrillers that suffers from overstatement, with jokes being repeated three or four times in case you missed the point first time around.

wd John Lafia *ph* Rodolfo Sanchez *m* Ethan James *pd* Cynthia Sowder *ed* Scott Chestnut

☆ Dylan McDermott, Jessica Harper, James Russo, Tovah Feldshuh, Dean Stockwell, Pamela Gidley, Yano Anaya, Flea

'Just Over The Bridge, Around The Corner From Reality Is A Place That's Out Of This World. Welcome To Planet Brooklyn.'

Blue in the Face

US 1995 89m DuArt

Miramax (Greg Johnson, Peter Newman, Diana Phillips)

Customers drop in to a Brooklyn cigar store, presided over by an affable manager, while residents talk about life in the locality.

A semi-improvised piece that grew out of rehearsals for Smoke *(qv), its more structured companion piece; it may well be rewarding for those who enjoyed that film, but is otherwise of limited interest.*

wd Wayne Wang, Paul Auster *ph* Adam Holender *m* John Lurie *pd* Kalina Ivanov *ed* Christopher Tellefsen

☆ Harvey Keitel, Lou Reed, Roseanne, Michael J. Fox, Jim Jarmusch, Lily Tomlin, Mel Gorham, Jared Harris, Giancarlo Esposito, Victor Argo, Madonna, Keith David, Mira Sorvino

'The pointlessness would be vastly more appealing if Wang and Auster didn't make such a point of it.' – *Terrence Rafferty, New Yorker*

Blue Jean Cop

US 1988 105m colour

Universal/Shapiro-Glickenhaus Entertainment (J. Boyce Harman Jnr)

US title: *Shakedown*

A lawyer defending a drug dealer uncovers corruption in the police force.

Over-the-top car chases and gun battles mar what might have been a good action thriller.

wd James Glickenhaus *ph* John Lindley *m* Jonathan Ellis *pd* Charles Bennett *ed* Paul Fried

☆ Peter Weller, Sam Elliott, Patricia Charbonneau, Antonio Fargas, William Prince, Blanche Baker

Blue Jeans: see *Blue Denim*

'On the waves, he's the king. On land, he's in trouble.'

'One Life. Use It.'

Blue Juice *

GB 1995 98m colour

Film Four/Pandora/Skreba (Peter Salmi, Simon Relph)

Surfers gather in Cornwall for one last fling before they succumb to life's responsibilities.

Pleasing small-scale movie of people searching for something to commit to, and finding, for the most part, only stormy weather.

w Carl Prechezer, Peter Salmi *d* Carl Prechezer *ph* Richard Greatrex *m* Simon Davison *pd* Mark Tildesley *ed* Michael Ellis

☆ Sean Pertwee, Catherine Zeta Jones, Steven Mackintosh, Ewan McGregor, Peter Gunn, Heathcote Williams, Keith Allen, Jenny Agutter

'Absolutely charming, unabashedly offbeat.' – *Variety*

The Blue Kite **

China/Japan 1993 138m colour

Longwick/Beijing Film Studio

original title: *Lan Fengzheng*

A boy recalls his mother's three marriages and the troubles that beset his family life during the 1950s and 60s, a time of political upheaval during China's Great Leap Forward and the Cultural Revolution inspired by the Red Guards.

A gripping, though often depressing, domestic drama seen against the ideological upheavals that made a hero of one period a villain of the next; there is warmth and humour in the telling, but the story is one of personal tragedy.

w Xiao Mao *d* Tian Zhuangzhuang *ph* Hou Yong *m* Yoshihide Otomo *ad* Zhang Xiande *ed* Qian Lengleng

☆ Zhang Wenyao, Chen Xiaoman, Lu Piping, Pu Quanxin, Li Xuejian, Guo Baochang, Zhong Ping, Chu Qhuangzhong, Song Xiaoying, Zhang Hong

'Major surprise of the movie is that, despite a story and multi-character cast that looks more fitted to a mini-series, it works on a simple emotional level as a feature film. Characters emerge as real people rather than political stereotypes.' – *Variety*

'Vividly and touchingly conveys the insecurity, fear and confusion of the family.' – *Sheila Johnston, Independent*

† The film had a troubled production with interference from Chinese officials, who forbade a print to leave the country for post-production work. The film was finished from the director's script and notes after a print was smuggled out of the country. In a statement made at the 1993 Cannes Film Festival the director said, 'The stories in the film are real, and they are related with total sincerity. What worries me is that it is precisely a fear of reality that has led to the ban on such stories being told.' It has not been shown in China, and in April 1994 Tian Zhuangzhuang was one of seven film directors banned from making films in mainland China.

The Blue Lagoon *

GB 1949 103m Technicolor

GFD/Individual (Frank Launder, Sidney Gilliat)

A shipwrecked boy and girl grow up on a desert island, ward off smugglers, have a baby, and eventually sail away in search of civilization.

Rather lifeless, though pretty, treatment of a famous novel: the story never becomes vivid despite splendid Fijian locations.

w Frank Launder, John Baines, Michael Hogan *novel* H. de Vere Stacpoole *d* Frank Launder *ph Geoffrey Unsworth* *m* Clifton Parker

☆ Jean Simmons, Donald Houston, Noel Purcell, Cyril Cusack, James Hayter

The Blue Lagoon

US 1980 102m Colorfilm

Columbia/Randal Kleiser

A boy and a girl grow up after being shipwrecked on a desert island.

Remake with poor narrative balance and a great deal of nudity and adolescent frankness about sex. Adolescents are probably its only audience.

w Douglas Day Stewart *d* Randal Kleiser *ph* Nestor Almendros *m* Basil Poledouris

☆ Brooke Shields, Christopher Atkins, Leo McKern, William Daniels

'At best a damp dream, a Sunday school fairy tale which makes the story of Adam and Eve seem like hard porn, as hygienically sanitized as a Hilton Hotel lavatory seat.' – *Sunday Times*

'A total fraud from beginning to end.' – *Guardian*

'The film has an inevitable, built-in prurience. All we have to look forward to is: when are these two going to discover fornication?' – *Pauline Kael, New Yorker*

'This movie made me itch.' – *Roger Ebert*

Nestor Almendros

The Blue Lamp ***

GB 1949 84m bw

Ealing (Michael Relph)

A young man joins London's police force. The elderly copper who trains him is killed in a shootout, but the killer is apprehended.

Seminal British police film which spawned not only a long line of semi-documentary imitations but also the twenty-year TV series Dixon of Dock Green *for which the shot PC was happily revived. As an entertainment, pacy but dated; more important, it burnished the image of the British copper for generations.*

w T. E. B. Clarke *d Basil Dearden* *ph* Gordon Dines *md* Ernest Irving

☆ *Jack Warner*, Jimmy Hanley, Dirk Bogarde, Meredith Edwards, Robert Flemyng, Bernard Lee, Patric Doonan, Peggy Evans, Gladys Henson, Dora Bryan

'The mixture of coyness, patronage and naive theatricality which has vitiated British films for the last ten years.' – *Gavin Lambert*

'A soundly made crime thriller which would not be creating much of a stir if it were American.' – *Richard Mallett, Punch*

'It is not only foreigners who find the English policeman wonderful, and, in composing this tribute to him, the Ealing Studios are giving conscious expression to a general sentiment.' – *The Times Film Correspondent*

British picture

The Blue Light *

Germany 1932 68m bw

H. R. Sokal/Leni Riefenstahl

In the early 19th century, a painter defies a local legend to climb a Dolomite mountain.

Romantic fairy tale with a story more suited to a ballet. It still takes the eye, and is recognizable as the work of its director.

wd Leni Riefenstahl *ph* Hans Schneeberger, Henry Jaworsky *m* Giuseppe Becce

☆ *Leni Riefenstahl*, Matthias Wieman, Max Holsboer

† This version was put together in 1950 after the original negative had been lost; among other things, a flashback frame was removed.

'There was no quiet on the western front for the heroes and cowards who flew to their rendezvous with hell!'

The Blue Max *

US 1966 156m DeLuxe Cinemascope

TCF (Christian Ferry)

In Germany after World War I an ambitious and skilful pilot causes the death of his comrades and steals the wife of his High Command superior, who eventually finds a means of revenge.

For once, an action spectacular not too badly let down by its connecting threads of plot, apart from some hilarious and unnecessary bedroom scenes in which the female star's bath towel seems to become conveniently adhesive.

w David Pursall, Jack Seddon, Gerald Hanley *novel* Jack Hunter *d John Guillermin* *ph* Douglas Slocombe *m* Jerry Goldsmith *pd* Wilfred Shingleton

☆ George Peppard, *James Mason*, Ursula Andress, Jeremy Kemp, Karl Michael Vogler, Anton Diffring, Derren Nesbitt

'Addicts of flying movies swear by this one, but for others, the monoplanes and biplanes can't smash or burn fast enough.' – *Pauline Kael*

Wilfred Shingleton

Blue Murder at St Trinians *

GB 1957 86m bw

British Lion/John Marvel (Launder and Gilliat)

The awful schoolgirls win a UNESCO prize trip which takes them to Rome where they become involved with a jewel thief.

Possibly the best of this series, which isn't saying much. See The Belles of St Trinians.

w Frank Launder, Val Valentine, Sidney Gilliat *d* Frank Launder *ph* Gerald Gibbs *m* Malcolm Arnold *ed* Geoffrey Foot

☆ Terry-Thomas, George Cole, Joyce Grenfell, Alastair Sim, Judith Furse, Sabrina, Lionel Jeffries, Lloyd Lamble, Thorley Walters, Kenneth Griffith, Eric Barker, Richard Wattis

Blue Parrot

GB 1953 69m bw

ACT (Stanley Haynes)

An American detective helps Scotland Yard solve a murder mystery.

Uninteresting thriller, no more than a programme-filler.

w Allan MacKinnon *story* Percy Hoskins *d* John Harlow *ph* Bob Navarro *ad* Don Russell *ed* Robert Hill

☆ Dermot Walsh, Jacqueline Hill, Ballard Berkeley, June Ashley, Victor Lucas, John Le Mesurier, Arthur Rigby, Ferdy Mayne, Richard Pearson, Edwin Richfield

The Blue Peter

GB 1955 93m Eastmancolor

British Lion/Beaconsfield (Herbert Mason)

US title: *Navy Heroes*

A confused war hero becomes a trainer at an Outward Bound school for boys.

Pleasant but uninspired open air adventure for young people.

w Don Sharp, John Pudney *d* Wolf Rilla *ph* Arthur Grant *m* Antony Hopkins

☆ Kieron Moore, Greta Gynt, Sarah Lawson, Mervyn Johns, Ram Gopal, Edwin Richfield, Harry Fowler, John Charlesworth

'It's the nearest thing to heaven!'

Blue Skies *

US 1946 104m Technicolor

Paramount (Sol C. Siegel)

A dancing star and a night-club owner fight for years over the same girl.

Thin musical with splendid Irving Berlin tunes and lively individual numbers, including Astaire dancing 'Puttin' on the Ritz'.

w Arthur Sheekman *d* Stuart Heisler *ph* Charles Lang Jnr, William Snyder *md* Robert Emmett Dolan *ad* Hans Dreier, Hal Pereira *ed* LeRoy Stone

☆ *Fred Astaire*, Bing Crosby, Joan Caulfield, Billy de Wolfe, Olga San Juan, Robert Benchley, Frank Faylen, Victoria Horne, Jack Norton

♫ A Couple of Song and Dance Men; Getting Nowhere; I'll Dance Rings Around You; It's A Lovely Day for a Walk; Puttin' on the Ritz; Heat Wave; How Deep is the Ocean?; A Pretty Girl is Like a Melody; All By Myself; Blue Skies; I've Got My Captain Working For Me Now; Russian Lullaby; White Christmas

Robert Emmett Dolan; song 'You Keep Coming Back Like a Song' (*m/ly* Irving Berlin)

'In a world of secrets, love is the most powerful weapon.'

Blue Sky **

US 1994 101m DeLuxe

Orion (Robert H. Solo)

In the early 60s, an army scientist involved in dubious nuclear experiments has problems with his work and his marriage.

An old-fashioned melodrama that gains from some good performances, though its resolution is unconvincing.

w Rama Laurie Stagner, Arlene Sarner, Jerry Leichtling *d Tony Richardson* *ph* Steve Yaconelli *m* Jack Nitzsche *pd* Timian Alsaker *ed* Robert K. Lambert

☆ *Jessica Lange, Tommy Lee Jones*, Powers Boothe, Carrie Snodgress, Amy Locane, Chris O'Donnell, Mitchell Ryan, Annie Ross

† Made in 1991.

Jessica Lange

Blue Steel

US 1934 54m bw

Lone Star (Paul Malvern)

A sheriff goes undercover to expose a gang of crooks attempting to swindle a town out of its riches.

Lacklustre Western enlivened by a few stunts.

wd Robert N. Bradbury *ph* Archie Stout *ed* Carl Pierson

☆ John Wayne, Eleanor Hunt, George Hayes, Edward Peil, Yakima Canutt, George Cleveland

'For a rookie cop, there's one thing more dangerous than uncovering a killer's fantasy. Becoming it.'

Blue Steel

US 1990 102m Technicolor

Vestron/Lightning Pictures/Precision Films/Mack-Taylor Productions (Edward R. Pressman, Oliver Stone)

A new cop, hunting a serial killer, falls for the chief suspect.

Lurid and ludicrous melodrama.

w Kathryn Bigelow, Eric Red *d* Kathryn Bigelow *ph* Amir Mokri *m* Brad Fiedel *pd* Tony Corbett *ed* Hal Levinsohn
☆ Jamie Lee Curtis, Ron Silver, Clancy Brown, Elizabeth Pena, Louise Fletcher, Philip Bosco

'He's A Cop That's Not. Believe That!'
Blue Streak
US 1999 95m DeLuxe
Columbia/Global (Toby Jaffe, Neal H. Moritz)
After serving his prison sentence, a jewel thief discovers that his hiding place for his loot is now a police station.
A corny excuse for a comedy is given occasional life by the vigorous performance of its star, but even he cannot salvage such hand-me-down material.
w Michael Berry, John Blumenthal, Steve Carpenter *d* Les Mayfield *ph* David Eggby *m* Edward Shearmur *pd* Bill Brzeski *ed* Michael Tronick
☆ Martin Lawrence (Miles Logan), Luke Wilson (Carlson), Peter Greene (Deacon), Dave Chappelle (Tulley), William Forsythe (Hardcastle), Nicole Ari Parker (Melissa Green), Graham Beckel (Rizzo), Robert Miranda (Glenfiddish), Olek Krupa (LaFleur), Saverio Guerra (Benny)
'Though unevenly devised as an homage to the whole range of '70s crime pics from blaxploitation to buddie cop comedies, modest production plays closer to a made-for-TV project than anything worthy of the big screen.' – *Robert Koehler, Variety*

Blue Thunder *
US 1983 110m Technicolor Panavision
Columbia/Rastar/Gordon Carroll
A policeman in Los Angeles' Astro Division is haunted by memories of Vietnam and goes berserk when using his new ultra-sophisticated helicopter to wage war against crime.
Slick but hollow thriller most remarkable for its helicopter stunting between city skyscrapers. Otherwise, it is too often fashionably inaudible and almost invisible.
w Dan O'Bannon, Don Jakoby *d* John Badham *ph* John A. Alonzo *m* Arthur B. Rubinstein *ed* Frank Morriss, Edward Abroms *aerial photography* Frank Holgate
☆ Roy Scheider, Warren Oates, Candy Clark, Daniel Stern, Malcolm McDowell
† A watered-down TV version was quickly assembled, but its comic-strip dialogue grounded it after 13 episodes.
film editing

Blue Tiger
US 1994 87m colour
NEO/Ozla (Michael Leahy, Aki Komine)
After her young son is accidentally shot by a Japanese gangster, his mother searches for his killer, a man with a distinctive tattoo of a blue tiger.
On its own undemanding level, an enjoyable and well-made thriller.
w Joel Soisson *d* Norberto Barba *ph* Christopher Walling *md* Larry Scharf *ed* Caroline Ross
☆ Virginia Madsen, Harry Dean Stanton, Toru Nakamura, Ryo Ishibashi, Dean Hallo, Sal Lopez, Lewis Arquette, Henry Mortensen
'Handsome photography, slick direction and a fun script make this a top quality B-movie.' – *Sight and Sound*

The Blue Veil *
US 1951 114m bw
RKO/Wald-Krasna (Raymond Hakim)
The vocational career of a children's nurse who descends into poverty but is rescued by one of her own charges, now grown up.
*Sober American remake of a French tearjerker (*Le Voile bleu*) with the star suffering nobly but being upstaged by the cameo players.*
w Norman Corwin, from the original by François Campaux *d* Curtis Bernhardt *ph* Franz Planer *m* Franz Waxman
☆ Jane Wyman, Charles Laughton, Richard Carlson, Joan Blondell, Agnes Moorehead, Don Taylor, Audrey Totter, Everett Sloane, Cyril Cusack, Natalie Wood, Warner Anderson
Jane Wyman; Joan Blondell

Blue Velvet **
US 1986 120m colour J-D-C Scope
De Laurentiis (Richard Roth)
Murder, mutilation and sexual perversion in Middle America.
Bizarrely stylish exercise by the director of The Elephant Man *(qv), popular at the box-office.*
wd David Lynch *ph* Frederick Elmes *m* Angelo Badalamenti *pd* Patricia Norris
☆ Kyle MacLachlan, Isabella Rossellini, Dennis Hopper, Laura Dern, Hope Lange, Dean Stockwell
'Horrifying in ways that genre horror movies never are ... Lynch's nightmare has a sort of irregular, homemade quality, as if it had been cooked up with familiar but not entirely wholesome ingredients – a fresh apple pie with a couple of worms poking through the crust.' – *Terrence Rafferty, Nation*
David Lynch

Blue Water, White Death *
US 1971 99m Techniscope
Blue Water Films/Cinema Center
A skilful and quite frightening documentary about the habits of the Great White Shark, with a lead-up showing events on the expedition which set out in search of it.
wd Peter Gimbel *ph* James Lipscomb

Bluebeard *
US 1944 73m bw
PRC
A strangler of young girls is at large in Paris.
Poverty Row chiller with effective moments; possibly the most interesting film ever to come from PRC (which isn't saying very much).
w Pierre Gendron *d Edgar G. Ulmer* *ph* Jockey Feindel
☆ John Carradine, Jean Parker, Ludwig Stossel, Nils Asther, Iris Adrian

Bluebeard: see *Landru (1962)*

Bluebeard
France/Italy/Germany 1972 124m Technicolor
Barnabé/Gloria/Geiselgasteig (Alexander Salkind)
The lady-killer in this case is an Austrian aristocrat who has been driven to desperation and murder by a long line of mistresses whose bodies he keeps frozen in his cellar.
Would-be macabre comedy which becomes totally off-putting by its emphasis on close-up death agonies.
w Ennio de Concini, Edward Dmytryk, Maria Pia Fusco *d* Edward Dmytryk *ph* Gabor Pogany *m* Ennio Morricone
☆ Richard Burton, Raquel Welch, Joey Heatherton, Virna Lisi, Nathalie Delon, Marilu Tolo
'Somewhere between (and a long way behind) *Kind Hearts and Coronets* and *The Abominable Dr Phibes*.' – *Clyde Jeavons, MFB*

Bluebeard's Eighth Wife *
US 1938 85m bw
Paramount (Ernst Lubitsch)
The daughter of an impoverished French aristocrat marries for money a millionaire who has had seven previous wives, and determines to teach him a lesson.
Very thin sophisticated comedy with unsympathetic characters and little wit after the first scene; a disappointment from the talent involved.
w Charles Brackett, Billy Wilder *play* Alfred Savoir *d* Ernst Lubitsch *ph* Leo Tover *m* Werner Heymann, Frederick Hollander
☆ Claudette Colbert, Gary Cooper, David Niven, Edward Everett Horton, Elizabeth Patterson, Herman Bing, Warren Hymer, Franklin Pangborn
'Light and sometimes bright, but it gets a bit tiresome.' – *Variety*
'In these days it is bad enough to have to admire millionaires in any circumstances; but a millionaire with a harem complex simply can't help starting the bristles on the back of a sensitive neck.' – *New York Times*
† A previous version, released by Paramount in 1923 and directed by Sam Wood, starred Gloria Swanson and Huntley Gordon.

Bluebeard's Seven Wives *
US 1926 94m approx bw silent
First National
A bank teller becomes a film star and is transformed, notably by seven imaginary marriages.
Amusing spoof on the film industry that was.
w Blanche Merrill, Paul Scofield *d* Alfred Santell
☆ Ben Lyon, Lois Wilson, Blanche Sweet, Dorothy Sebastian, Sam Hardy

Bluebeard's Ten Honeymoons
GB 1960 93m bw
Anglo-Allied (Roy Parkinson)
Another version of the story of Landru, alternating wildly between fantasy, farce and melodrama.
Not a success in any of its moods.
w Myles Wilder *d* W. Lee Wilder *ph* Stephen Dade *m* Albert Elms
☆ George Sanders, Corinne Calvet, Patricia Roc, Ingrid Hafner, Jean Kent, Greta Gynt, Maxine Audley, Selma Vaz Diaz, George Coulouris
'The unedifying narrative is developed along the most obvious lines imaginable.' – *MFB*

Blueberry Hill
US 1988 93m colour
MGM/Mediacom/Prism/MVA-1/Tricoast (Mark Michaels)
In an isolated logging community, a mother tries to conceal from her daughter the truth about her dead father.
Unoriginal domestic drama of young rebellion, set in the 50s, which provides the excuse for its soundtrack of rock 'n' roll hits.
w Lonon Smith *d* Strathford Hamilton *ph* David Lewis *m* Ira Ingber *pd* John Sperry Wade *ed* Marcy Hamilton
☆ Carrie Snodgress, Margaret Avery, Jennifer Rubin, Matt Lattanzi, Tommy Swerdlow

The Bluebird: see *The Blue Bird*

A Blueprint for Murder *
US 1953 77m bw
TCF (Michael Abel)
After the death of his brother and niece, a man proves that his sister-in-law is a murderess.
Unpleasant but efficient murder story with enough twists to keep one watching.
wd Andrew Stone *ph* Leo Tover *m* David Raksin *md* Lionel Newman
☆ Jean Peters, Joseph Cotten, Gary Merrill, Catherine McLeod, Jack Kruschen, Barney Phillips, Joyce McCluskey, Mae Marsh

Blueprint for Robbery *
US 1960 87m bw
Paramount (Bryan Foy)
Crooks plan and execute a robbery, agreeing not to touch the proceeds for two and a half years. But some get tired of waiting...
Minor but effective crime melodrama in semi-documentary vein.
w Irwin Winehouse, A. Sanford Wolf *d* Jerry Hopper *ph* Loyal Griggs *m* Van Cleave
☆ J. Pat O'Malley, Robert Gist, Romo Vincent, Marion Ross, Tom Duggan
'A not uninteresting entry in the screen log-book on crime.' – *MFB*

The Blues Brothers *
US 1980 133m Technicolor
Universal (Robert K. Weiss)
A massive car chase develops when two brothers collect money for their old orphanage without too much regard for law and order.
Fashionable chase comedy with so many stunts that its cost ran up to 33,000,000 dollars. The public stayed away, though it has gained a cult following since.
w Dan Aykroyd, John Landis *d* John Landis *ph* Stephen M. Katz *md* Ira Newborn *pd* John Lloyd
☆ John Belushi, Dan Aykroyd, Kathleen Freeman, James Brown, Henry Gibson, Cab Calloway, Carrie Fisher
'It meanders expensively like some pedigreed shaggy dog through 70s/80s American cinema and 50s/60s American rock, cocking its leg happily at every popular landmark on the way.' – *Paul Taylor, MFB*
'There's not a *soupçon* of wit or ingenuity in this brainless exercise in overspending.' – *Daily Mail*
'There's even room, in the midst of the carnage and mayhem, for a surprising amount of grace, humor and whimsy.' – *Roger Ebert*

Blues Brothers 2000
US 1998 123m DeLuxe
Universal (John Landis, Dan Aykroyd, Leslie Belzberg)
Chased by cops, gangsters and militia, an ex-jailbird and singer tries to reassemble his old band.
Virtually a remake of The Blues Brothers*; even those who enjoyed its conspicuous destruction and ersatz rhythm and blues the first time around may find that more is worse.*
w Dan Aykroyd, John Landis *d* John Landis *ph* David Herrington *m* Paul Shaffer *pd* Bill Brodie *ed* Dale Beldin
☆ Dan Aykroyd, John Goodman, Joe Morton, J. Evan Bonifant, Nia Peeples, Frank Oz, Steve Lawrence, Aretha Franklin, James Brown, B. B. King
'A warmed-up corpse of a movie, having neither the courage to do anything new or the wit to make a joke out of its own unoriginality.' – *Adam Smith, Empire*

Blues for Lovers: see *Ballad in Blue*

Blues in the Night *
US 1941 88m bw
Warner (Henry Blanke)
Career and romantic problems for the members of a travelling jazz band.
Atmospheric little melodrama with good score and smart dialogue.
w Robert Rossen *play* Hot Nocturne by Edwin Gilbert *d* Anatole Litvak *ph* Ernest Haller *m/ly* Harold Arlen, Johnny Mercer
☆ Priscilla Lane, Richard Whorf, Lloyd Nolan, Betty Field, Jack Carson, Elia Kazan, Wallace Ford, Billy Halop, Peter Whitney
title song (*m* Harold Arlen, *ly* Johnny Mercer)

Blume in Love *
US 1973 116m Technicolor
Warner (Paul Mazursky)
A divorced American lawyer in Venice reminisces about his love life.
Shapeless but enjoyable 'serious comedy' with star and director in good form.
wd Paul Mazursky *ph* Bruce Surtees *m* various
☆ George Segal, Susan Anspach, Kris Kristofferson, Marsha Mason, Shelley Winters

Boardwalk
US 1979 100m Eastmancolor
ITC/Stratford (Gerald T. Herrod)
An old couple in Coney Island are affected by escalating violence.
Well-meaning but somewhat absurd moral tale for our times, in which the harassed septuagenarian finally chokes the young punk leader to death.
w Stephen Verona, Leigh Chapman *d* Stephen Verona *ph* Billy Williams *m* various
☆ Ruth Gordon, Lee Strasberg, Janet Leigh, Joe Silver, Eddie Barth
'One would probably have to reach as far back as *The Birth of a Nation* to find a more direct incitement to racial hatred.' – *Richard Combs, MFB*

The Boat **
West Germany 1981 149m Fujicolour
Columbia/Bavaria Atelier/Radiant Film (Gunter Röhrbach)
original and US title: *Das Boot*
Adventures of a German U-boat during World War II.
Well-crafted but totally unsurprising saga of heroism and self-sacrifice; a decent view of war from the German side, designed to impress world markets. It did so only moderately.
wd Wolfgang Petersen *ph Jost Vacano* *m* Klaus Doldinger *pd* Rolf Zehetbauer
☆ Jürgen Prochnow, Herbert Grönemeyer, Klaus Wennemann, Hubertus Bengsch, Martin Semmelrogge
† A director's cut, running for 209m, was released in 1997.
direction; screenplay (adaptation); cinematography; editing; sound; sound editing

The Boatmen: see *Prisoner of the Volga*

The Boatniks *
US 1970 100m Technicolor
Walt Disney (Ron Miller)
An accident-prone coastguard officer creates havoc at a yachting marina but is acclaimed a hero after catching three jewel thieves.
Simple fresh-air farce for the family, pleasantly set but flatly directed.
w Arthur Julian *d* Norman Tokar *ph* William Snyder *m* Robert F. Brunner
☆ *Phil Silvers*, Robert Morse, Stefanie Powers, Norman Fell, Mickey Shaughnessy, Wally Cox, Don Ameche, Joey Forman

Bob & Carol & Ted & Alice **
US 1969 105m Technicolor
Columbia/M. J. Frankovich (Larry Tucker)
Two California couples, influenced by a group therapy session advocating natural spontaneous behaviour, decide to admit their extra-marital affairs and narrowly avoid a wife-swapping party.
Fashionable comedy without the courage of its convictions: it starts and finishes very bashfully, but there are bright scenes in the middle. An attempt to extend it into a TV series was a failure.
w Paul Mazursky, Larry Tucker *d* Paul Mazursky *ph* Charles E. Lang *m* Quincy Jones
☆ Natalie Wood, Robert Culp, Elliott Gould, Dyan Cannon, Horst Ebersberg
'An old-fashioned romantic comedy disguised as a blue picture.' – *Arthur Schlesinger Jnr*
Paul Mazursky, Larry Tucker; Charles E. Lang; Elliott Gould; Dyan Cannon

Bob Roberts **
US 1992 104m Technicolor
Rank/Polygram/Working Title/Live Entertainment (Forrest Murray)
An American folk singer and right-wing politician makes a record that goes to the top of the hit parade and wins a seat in the Senate.
Clever satire on politics, done as a documentary film, that has the message that it is appearance and the manipulation of the media that counts, not reality.
wd Tim Robbins *ph* Jean Lépine *m* David Robbins *pd* Richard Hoover *ed* Lisa Churgin
☆ Tim Robbins, Giancarlo Esposito, Alan Rickman, Ray Wise, Brian Murray, Gore Vidal, Rebecca Jenkins, Harry J. Lennix, Susan Sarandon, John Cusack, Bob Balaban
'Both a stimulating social satire and a depressing commentary on the devolution of the US political system.' – *Variety*

Bob, Son of Battle
US 1947 110m Technicolor
TCF (Robert Bassler)
aka: *Thunder in the Valley*
A surly old shepherd discovers that his sheepdog, which he loves above his son, is a killer.
Soft-centred family drama that relies overmuch on Gwenn's roguish charm and sudden redemption.
w Jerome Cady *novel* Alfred Ollivant *d* Louis King *ph* Charles Clarke *m* Cyril Mockridge
☆ Edmund Gwenn, Lon McCallister, Peggy Ann Garner, Reginald Owen, Charles Irwin, Dave Thursby, John Rogers, Leyland Hodgson

Bobbikins
GB 1959 90m bw Cinemascope
TCF (Oscar Brodney, Bob McNaught)
A downtrodden variety artist finds that his baby can not only talk but also give him tips on the stock exchange.
Not at all a good idea, and feebly executed.
w Oscar Brodney *d* Robert Day *ph* Geoffrey Faithfull *m* Philip Green
☆ Max Bygraves, Shirley Jones, Billie Whitelaw, Barbara Shelley, Colin Gordon, Charles Tingwell, Lionel Jeffries, Rupert Davies

'He had to meet her – to find himself!'
Bobby Deerfield
US 1977 123m Metrocolor Panavision
Warner/First Artists (Sydney Pollack)
A depressive motor racing driver falls for a girl with an incurable illness.
A kind of understated Love Story *(qv) for intellectuals; nicely made, but nothing that anybody will be wildly concerned about.*
w Alvin Sargent *novel* *Heaven Has No Favourites* by Erich Maria Remarque *d* Sydney Pollack *ph* Henri Decaë *m* Dave Grusin *pd* Stephen Grimes
☆ Al Pacino, Marthe Keller, Anny Duperey, Walter McGinn, Romolo Valli, Jaime Sanchez

The Bobo
US 1967 105m Technicolor
Warner/Gina (Elliott Kastner, Jerry Gershwin) (David R. Schwartz)
An unsuccessful and timid bullfighter is offered a contract if within three days he can seduce the local belle.
Stylized, silly and boring comedy from an obviously dated play; Chaplinesque pathos was not this star's strong suit.
w David R. Schwartz *play* David R. Schwartz *novel* *Olimpia* by Burt Cole *d* Robert Parrish *ph* Gerry Turpin *m* Francis Lai
☆ Peter Sellers, Britt Ekland, Rossano Brazzi, Adolfo Celi, Hattie Jacques, Ferdy Mayne, Kenneth Griffith, John Wells

Bob's Birthday **
GB 1993 11m colour
Snowden Fine Animation/Channel 4/NFBC (Alison Snowden, David Fine)
A dentist is unhappy about celebrating his 40th birthday, while his wife prepares a surprise party for him.
Witty animated cartoon about middle-aged angst and embarrassment.
wd Alison Snowden, David Fine *m* Patrick Godfrey
☆ Featuring the voices of: Andy Hamilton, Harry Enfield, Alison Snowden
animated short

La Boca del Lobo **
Peru/Spain 1988 116m Agfacolor
New People's Cinema/Twinray/Inca Films/Tornasol Films (Gerardo Herrero, Francisco J. Lombardi)
English title: *The Lion's Den*
A tough and embittered lieutenant orders his troops to massacre villagers sympathetic to the Communists.
Gripping investigation of the morality of war, based on a true incident.
w Augusto Cabada, Giovanni Pollarolo, Gerardo Herrero *d* Francisco J. Lombardi *ph* Jose Luis Lopez Linares *m* Bernardo Bonezzi *pd* Marta Mendez *ed* Juan San Mateo
☆ Gustavo Bueno, Tono Vega, Joe Tejada, Gilberto Torres, Antero Sanchez, Aristoteles Picho, Fernando Vasquez, Luis Saavedra, Bertha Pagaza

Boccaccio '70 *
Italy/France 1962 210m Eastmancolor
TCF/CCC/Cineriz/Francinex/Gray Films (Antonio Cervi, Carlo Ponti)
Four modern stories which Boccaccio might have written (on an off day).
Overlong portmanteau with inevitable bright moments but many more longueurs. The fourth episode was dropped when the film was released in the States and elsewhere.
The Temptation of Dr Antonio
w Federico Fellini, Tullio Pinelli, Ennio Flaiano *d* Federico Fellini *ph* Otello Martelli; with Anita Ekberg
The Job
w Suso Cecchi d'Amico, Luchino Visconti *d* Luchino Visconti *ph* Giuseppe Rotunno; with Romy Schneider, Tomas Milian
The Raffle
w Cesare Zavattini *d* Vittorio de Sica *ph* Otello Martelli; with Sophia Loren
Renzo and Luciana
d Mario Monicelli

Boda Secreta: see *Secret Wedding*

Bodies, Rest and Motion
US 1993 94m DeLuxe
Electric/Fine Line/August (Allan Mindel, Denise Shaw, Eric Stoltz)
A couple split up: he goes in search of his parents with a stolen television set, she begins a casual affair with a decorator.
An aimless movie about feckless people, the sort of film you'd continue watching on television if the remote control was not to hand.
w Roger Hedden *d* Michael Steinberg *ph* Bernd Heinl *m* Michael Convertino *pd* Stephen McCabe *ed* Jay Cassidy
☆ Phoebe Cates, Bridget Fonda, Tim Roth, Eric Stoltz, Alicia Witt, Sandra Lafferty, Peter Fonda
'Uncompelling but moderately engaging throughout.' – *Variety*
'Billed as a comedy, it's mighty short on laughs.' – *Sheila Johnston, Independent*

The Body
US 2001 109m Technicolor Panavision
Metrodome/Avalanche/Helkon/Green Moon (Rudy Cohen)
An archeologist discovers in a tomb in Jerusalem a crucified body that may be that of Jesus.
Melodramatic hokum served up with portentous solemnity.
wd Jonas McCord *novel* Richard Ben Sapir *ph* Vilmos Zsigmond *m* Serge Colbert *pd* Allan Starski *ed* Alain Jakubowicz *cos* Caroline Harris
☆ Antonio Banderas (Father Matt Gutierrez), Olivia Williams (Sharon Golban), John Shrapnel (Moshe Cohen), Derek Jacobi (Father Lavelle), Jason Flemyng (Father Walter Winstead), John Wood (Cardinal Pesci), Makhram J. Khoury (Nasir Hamid), Vernon Dobtcheff (Monsignor), Ian McNeice (Dr. Sproul), Muhamed Bakri (Aby Yusef)
'Less a serious religious-themed film than a moth-eaten tapestry of foreign intrigue and badly miscast international stars to rival the Cannon Films productions of the 1980s.' – *Scott Foundas, Variety*
'The sluggishness of "The Body" may remind viewers of a joke David Letterman used to make: if the film were a fight, they'd have stopped it.' – *Elvis Mitchell, New York Times*

Body and Soul *
US 1947 104m bw
Enterprise (Bob Roberts)
A young boxer fights his way unscrupulously to the top.
Melodramatic but absorbing study of prizefighting's seamy side. (Is there any other?) Inventively studio-bound and almost impressionist in treatment.
w *Abraham Polonsky* *d* *Robert Rossen* *ph* *James Wong Howe* *m* Hugo Friedhofer *md* Rudolph Polk *ed* Francis Lyon, Robert Parrish
☆ *John Garfield*, Lilli Palmer, Hazel Brooks, Anne Revere, William Conrad, Joseph Pevney, Canada Lee
'Here are the gin and tinsel, squalor and sables of the depression era, less daring than when first revealed in *Dead End* or *Golden Boy* but more valid and mature because shown without sentiment or blur.' – *National Board of Review*
Francis Lyon, Robert Parrish
Abraham Polonsky; John Garfield

Body and Soul
US 1981 122m colour
Cannon/Golan-Globus (Cliff Roquemore)
An amateur boxer turns professional to earn money for medical treatment for his kid sister.
Blood in the ring, sentimentality on the sidelines. Despite the credit, this repellent movie has virtually no connection with the previous 'version'.
w Leon Isaac Kennedy *screenplay* Abraham Polonsky *d* George Bowers *ph* James Forrest *m* Webster Lewis
☆ Leon Isaac Kennedy, Jayne Kennedy, Muhammad Ali, Michael Gazzo, Perry Lang, Kim Hamilton, Peter Lawford

Body Count
GB/US 1997 84m DeLuxe
Polygram/Island/Main Line (Mark Burg, Doug McHenry, George Jackson)
Four quarrelling art thieves, on the run from cops, pick up a double-crossing woman along the way.
Slick but uninvolving thriller, with an unhelpful style in flashbacks.
w Theodore Witcher *d* Robert Patton-Spruill *ph* Charles Mills *m* Curt Sobel *pd* Tim Eckel *ed* Richard Nord
☆ David Caruso, Linda Fiorentino, John Leguizamo, Ving Rhames, Donnie Wahlberg, Forest Whitaker

The Body Disappears
US 1941 72m bw
Warner (Ben Stoloff)
A professor invents an invisibility formula.
Uninspired comedy switch on a familiar theme.
w Scott Darling, Erna Lazarus *d* D. Ross Lederman *ph* Allen G. Seigler *m* Howard Jackson
☆ Edward Everett Horton, Jeffrey Lynn, Jane Wyman, Herbert Anderson, Marguerite Chapman, Craig Stevens, David Bruce, Willie Best

Body Double
US 1984 114m Metrocolor
Columbia/Delphi II (Brian de Palma)
An out-of-work actor finds himself drawn into a nightmare when he spies on a lady stripteaser across the street.
Semi-porno melodrama with many echoes of Hitchcock overlaid with fashionable extremes of violence.
w Robert J. Avrech, Brian de Palma *d* Brian de Palma *ph* Stephen H. Burum *m* Pino Donaggio *pd* Ida Random *ed* Jerry Greenberg, Bill Pankow
☆ Craig Wasson, Gregg Henry, Melanie Griffith
'De Palma lets all his obsessions hang out.' – *Variety*

'She taught him everything he knew – about passion and murder!'
Body Heat **
US 1981 113m Technicolor
Warner/Ladd (Fred T. Gallo)
A Florida lawyer becomes involved with a married woman and they plot to kill her businessman husband.
Oversexed and superfluous, not to mention uncredited, revamp of Double Indemnity *(qv). Some evidence of flair does not relieve that 'I have been here before' feeling.*
wd *Lawrence Kasdan* *ph* Richard H. Kline *m* John Barry *pd* Bill Kenney *ed* Carol Littleton
☆ William Hurt, *Kathleen Turner*, Richard Crenna, Ted Danson
'Film noir, if it is to be successfully reworked, needs to be approached with a sense of analysis, rather than simple excess.' – *Steve Jenkins, MFB*

Body Melt
Australia 1993 84m colour
Dumb Films/Australian Film Commission/Film Victoria (Rod Bishop, Daniel Scharf)
A mad scientist invents a vitamin supplement that has an appalling side-effect: it causes people to explode or disintegrate.
A gruesomely visceral horror with stomach-turning effects; beneath all the gore there are signs of a certain wit and intelligence at work.
w Philip Brophy, Rod Bishop *d* Philip Brophy *ph* Ray Argall *m* Philip Brophy *pd* Maria Kozic *ed* Bill Murphy *sp* Bob McCarron
☆ Gerard Kennedy, Andrew Daddo, Ian Smith, Vince Gil, Regina Gaigalas, Maurie Annese, Nick Polites, William McInnes
'A schlocky, tongue-in-cheek gore pic … cheerfully sick humor.' – *Variety*
† The film's credits include the unusual lines: 'Testicles Philip Brophy, Buttocks Maria Kozic'.

Body of Evidence
US 1992 99m DeLuxe
UIP/Dino de Laurentiis
A woman, who is accused of killing by too much sexual activity the elderly man who left her a fortune in his will, begins an affair with her defence counsel.
Almost silly enough to be enjoyable, in its calculated mix of kinky sex and courtroom scenes, but finally it is just too silly for words.
w Brad Mirman *d* Uli Edel *ph* Doug Milsome *m* Graeme Revell *pd* Victoria Paul *ed* Thom Noble
☆ Madonna, Willem Dafoe, Joe Mantegna, Anne Archer, Julianne Moore, Jurgen Prochnow, Frank Langella, Stan Shaw
'This showcase for the singer-thesp as femme fatale is titillating enough to lure an initially

curious public and follow up as a good video title, but its theatrical endurance would seem closer to that of her victim than to Madonna's.' – *Variety*

'The transplant was a success. Then the donor came to take it back.'

Body Parts

US 1991 88m Technicolor Panavision
Paramount (Frank Mancuso Jnr)

A psychiatrist, injured in a car crash, is one of several patients to have body parts transplanted from a homicidal maniac, with predictable results.

Dull horror movie that tries to revive an old, familiar plot by injecting plenty of gore.

w Eric Red, Norman Snider *novel* Choice Cuts by Boileau-Narcejac *story* Patricia Herskovic, Joyce Taylor *d* Eric Red *ph* Theo Van de Sande *m* Loek Dikker *pd* Bill Brodie *ed* Anthony Redman

☆ Jeff Fahey, Lindsay Duncan, Zakes Mokae, Kim Delaney, Peter Murnik, Paul Benvictor, Brad Dourif

'There are movies that define every decade... One night will change eight lives forever.'

Body Shots

US 1999 106m DeLuxe Panavision
Entertainment/New Line (Jennifer Keohane, Harry Colomby)

The sexual misadventures of four young men and women in Los Angeles.

A drama of casual coupling, centred around the accusation of rape from one participant; what begins as comedy ends as a more earnest investigation of varying sexual attitudes, but it never strikes the right note in either part.

w David McKenna *d* Michael Cristofer *ph* Rodrigo Garcia *m* Mark Isham *pd* David J. Bomba *ed* Eric Sears

☆ Sean Patrick Flanery (Rick Hamilton), Jerry O'Connell (Michael Penorisi), Amanda Peet (Jane Bannister), Tara Reid (Sara Olswang), Ron Livingston (Trent Barber), Emily Procter (Whitney Bryant), Brad Rowe (Shawn Denigan), Sybil Temchen (Emma Cooper)

'Essentially an exercise in adult TV framed for widescreen. The project exudes a lush look entombed in a self-important manner that's culturally tone-deaf.' – *Robert Koehler, Variety*

Body Slam

US 1987 89m CFI color
Musifilm/Hemdale (Shel Lytton, Mike Curb)

A promoter on the skids accidentally creates the rock 'n' wrestling craze.

Easy-going comedy which would have benefited from more confident production.

w Shel Lytton, Steve Burkow *d* Hal Needham *ph* Mike Shea *m* Michael Lloyd, John D'Andrea *ad* Pamela Warner *ed* Randy Thornton

☆ Dirk Benedict, Tanya Roberts, Roddy Piper, Lou Albano, Charles Nelson Reilly, Billy Barty, Barry Gordon, John Astin

'Shriek And Shudder.'
'Graves Raided! Coffins Robbed! Corpses Carved! Midnight Murder! Body Blackmail! Stalking Ghouls! Mad Thrills Of Terror And Macabre Mystery!'

The Body Snatcher ***

US 1945 77m bw
RKO (Val Lewton)

In 19th-century Edinburgh a doctor obtains 'specimens' from grave-robbers, and murder results when supplies run short.

A familiar theme very imaginatively handled, and well acted, though the beginning is slow. The best of the Lewton thrillers.

w Philip MacDonald, Carlos Keith (Val Lewton) story R. L. Stevenson *d Robert Wise ph Robert de Grasse m* Roy Webb

☆ *Henry Daniell, Boris Karloff,* Bela Lugosi, Edith Atwater, Russell Wade

'A humane sincerity and a devotion to good cinema ... However, most of the picture is more literary than lively.' – *Time*

'Imagine ... You're Gone And Someone Else Is Living Inside Your Body.'

Body Snatchers **

US 1993 90m Technicolor Arriscope
Warner (Robert H. Solo)

Aliens replicate and replace the inhabitants of military camps.

An effective and suspenseful retelling of the classic of conformity and paranoia, given a modern gloss with its teenage heroine and its concerns about toxic waste and environmental damage.

w Stuart Gordon, Dennis Paoli, Nicholas St John *novel* Jack Finney *story* Raymond Cistheri, Larry Cohen *d* Abel Ferrara *ph* Bojan Bazelli *m* Joe Delia *pd* Peter Jamison *ed* Anthony Redman

☆ Gabrielle Anwar, Terry Kinney, Billy Wirth, Meg Tilly, Christine Elise, R. Lee Ermey, G. Elvis Phillips, Reilly Murphy, Kathleen Doyle, Forest Whitaker

'A tremendously exciting thriller that compares favourably with Don Siegel's classic.' – *Variety*

'A gem which seduces the eye, captures the imagination and makes the adrenalin race.' – *Sight and Sound*

† The film was released direct to video in Britain. Jack Finney's novel was filmed in 1956 by Don Siegel and remade in 1978 by Philip Kaufman under the title *Invasion of the Body Snatchers* (qqv), the later version also being produced by Robert H. Solo.

Body Stealers

GB 1969 91m colour
Tigon (Tony Tenser)
US title: *Thin Air*

A NATO general calls for an investigation when parachutists training for space disappear in mid-air.

Conventional low-budget science fiction, predictable from the first moment to the last.

w Mike St Clair, Peter Marcus *d* Gerry Levy *ph* Johnny Coquillon *m* Reg Tilsey *ad* Wilfred Arnold *ed* Howard Lanning

☆ George Sanders, Maurice Evans, Patrick Allen, Hilary Dwyer, Lorna Wilde, Neil Connery, Robert Flemyng, Allan Cuthbertson

The Bodyguard: see *Yojimbo (1961)*

'Never let her out of your sight. Never let your guard down. Never fall in love.'

The Bodyguard

US 1992 129m Technicolor
Warner/Tig/Kasdan Pictures (Lawrence Kasdan, Jim Wilson, Kevin Costner)

A former CIA agent is hired as a bodyguard by a singer who has received threats on her life.

Predictable mix of song, romance and action that found surprising favour at the box-office.

w Lawrence Kasdan *d* Mick Jackson *ph* Andrew Dunn *m* Alan Silvestri *pd* Jeffrey Beecroft *ed* Richard A. Harris

☆ Kevin Costner, Whitney Houston, Gary Kemp, Bill Cobbs, Ralph Waite, Tomas Arana, Michele Lamar Richards, Mike Starr

'A jumbled mess with a few enjoyable moments but little continuity or flow.' – *Variety*

'The film is highly professional and perfectly watchable. But there's nothing memorable in it at all.' – *Derek Malcolm, Guardian*

Song: 'I Have Nothing' (*m* Jud Friedmann, *ly* Allan Rich); song: 'Run to You'

'Drive carefully, live dangerously.'

Bodywork

GB 1998 93m colour
Guerilla/Wolfmoon (Richard McGill)

Second-hand car dealers frame a complaining customer for murdering a prostitute.

Tepid gangster movie about unlovely people, feebly scripted and totally predictable.

wd Gareth Rhys Jones *ph* Thomas Wüthrich *m* Srdjan Kurpjel, Black Tooth *pd* Jeremy Bear *ed* Susan Spivey

☆ Hans Matheson (Virgil Guppy), Charlotte Coleman (Tiffany Shades), Peter Ferdinando (Alex Gordon), Beth Winslet (Fiona Money), Lynda Bellingham (Poppy Fields), Clive Russell (Billy Hunch), Michael Attwell (David Leer), Peter Moreton (Buddy Lear)

'While one can only assume there are some Brit underworld scripts that are actually rejected by film companies, it seems very difficult to believe while watching this dog-eared tale of murder and mayhem.' – *Clark Collis, Empire*

'The big comedy of nineteen sexty-sex!'

Boeing-Boeing

US 1965 102m Technicolor
Paramount/Hal B. Wallis

By successfully juggling with plane schedules, a Paris journalist manages to live with three air hostesses at the same time.

Frenetic, paper-thin sex comedy from a one-joke play; film style generally undistinguished. It was Jerry Lewis's first 'straight' role.

w Edward Anhalt *play* Marc Camoletti *d* John Rich *ph* Lucien Ballard *m* Neal Hefti

☆ Tony Curtis, Jerry Lewis, Dany Saval, Christiane Schmidtmer, Suzanna Leigh, *Thelma Ritter*

'A sort of jet-age French farce.' – *Judith Crist*

'The hardest part of love...is surviving it.'

Boesman & Lena *

France/South Africa 1999 88m colour
Pathé/Primedia (François Ivernel, Pierre Rissient)

In South Africa during apartheid, a homeless, childless, unhappy mixed-race couple set up a temporary camp and recall how they have reached their present desperate condition.

Effective screen version of Athol Fugard's existentialist play of the late 60s, though the work has lost a little of its resonance since.

wd John Berry *play* Athol Fugard *ph* Alain Choquart *m* Wally Badarou *pd* Max Berto *ed* Claudine Bouché, Jeanne Moutard

☆ Danny Glover (Boesman), Angela Bassett (Lena), Willie Jonah (Old Man)

'Sensitive, often affecting, and mesmerizing...the power of the performances, characters, and direction takes over, and one gets a profound, nuanced feeling for what it means to be poor and disenfranchised.' – *Jonathan Rosenbaum, Chicago Reader*

The Bofors Gun *

GB 1968 105m Technicolor
Rank/Everglades (Robert A. Goldston, Otto Plaschkes)

In 1954 Germany a British army unit runs into trouble when a violent and unstable Irish private picks on a weakly National Service corporal.

Keen, fascinating, but often crude and eventually rather silly expansion of a TV play chiefly notable for the excellent acting opportunities provided by its unattractive but recognizable characters.

w John McGrath *play* Events While Guarding the Bofors Gun by John McGrath *d* Jack Gold *ph* Alan Hume *m* Carl Davis

☆ *Nicol Williamson,* John Thaw, *David Warner,* Ian Holm

Ian Holm

'A comedy about losing your heart, finding your inner child and meeting the one friend you've always tried to avoid.'

Bogus

US 1996 110m DeLuxe Panavision
Warner/Regency/Yorktown/New Regency (Arnon Milchan, Norman Jewison, Jeff Rothberg)

An orphan who goes to live with his child-hating aunt invents an imaginary friend.

Slight and sentimental fantasy that depends too much on the slender charms of its stars, who are at their most smug.

w Alvin Sargent *story* Jeff Rothberg, Francis X. McCarthy *d* Norman Jewison *ph* David Watkin *m* Marc Shaiman *pd* Ken Adam *ed* Stephen Rivkin

☆ Whoopi Goldberg, Gérard Depardieu, Haley Joel Osment, Nancy Travis, Denis Mercier, Ute Lemper, Sheryl Lee Ralph

'Sweetly sentimental and anachronistically whimsical.' – *Variety*

La Bohème

US 1926 75m approx (24 fps) bw silent
MGM

Mimi starves to death in a Paris garret.

Overacted straight version of the opera, with two passionate star performances.

w Harry Behn, Ray Doyle, after Murger *d* King Vidor

☆ Lillian Gish, John Gilbert, Renee Adoree, Edward Everett Horton

La Bohème *

France/Italy 1988 107m Eastmancolor
Electric Pictures/Erato Films/La Sept/SFPC/Generale d'Images, Travelling Productions/Video-Schermo (Jean-Claude Borlat)

A penniless bohemian loves and loses a poor seamstress.

Uncinematic treatment of Puccini's opera, though well-enough sung.

w Giuseppe Giacosa, Luigi Illica *novel* Scènes de la vie de Bohème by Henri Murger *d* Luigi Comencini *ph* Armando Nannuzzi *m* Giacomo Puccini *md* James Conlon *ad* Paolo Comencini *ed* Sergio Buzi, Reine Wekstein

☆ Barbara Hendricks, Luca Canonici, Jose Carreras (voice only), Angela Maria Blasi, Gino Quilico

The Bohemian Girl *

US 1936 74m bw
MGM/Hal Roach

Gypsies kidnap a nobleman's daughter and bring her up as their own.

One of several operettas reworked for Laurel and Hardy, this is an inoffensive entertainment which devotes too little care to their need for slowly built-up gag structure; their sequences tend to fizzle out and the singing is a bore.

operetta Michael W. Balfe *d* James Horne, Charles Rogers *ph* Art Lloyd, Francis Corby *md* Nathaniel Shilkret *ed* Bert Jordan, Louis McManus

☆ Stan Laurel, Oliver Hardy, Mae Busch, Antonio Moreno, Jacqueline Wells, Darla Hood, Zeffie Tilbury, James Finlayson, Thelma Todd (for one song, apparently dubbed: presumably before her sudden death she had been cast as the heroine)

† There was in 1922 a British silent version with a splendid cast including Ivor Novello, Gladys Cooper, C. Aubrey Smith, Ellen Terry and Constance Collier.

Il Boia di Venezia: see *Executioner of Venice*

'Welcome to the New American Dream'

Boiler Room *

US 2000 120m DeLuxe
Entertainment/New Line (Suzanne Todd, Jennifer Todd)

A college drop-out joins a brokerage firm that makes its money by selling dubious stocks to gullible clients.

A study in high pressure salesmanship that updates Wall Street *and* Glengarry Glenn Ross *without quite matching the verve or guilty fascination of either.*

wd Ben Younger *ph* Enrique Chediak *m* The Angel *pd* Anne Stuhler *ed* Chris Peppe

☆ Giovanni Ribisi (Seth), Vin Diesel (Chris), Nia Long (Abby), Nicky Katt (Greg), Scott Caan (Richie), Ron Rifkin (Seth's Father), Jamie Kennedy (Adam), Taylor Nichols (Harry Reynard), Tom Everett Scott (Michael), Ben Affleck (Jim Young)

'Portrays the testosterone-flavoured soup of the trading floor superbly.' – *James White, Total Film*

'Seductive and disturbing...a dynamic piece of film-making.' – *James Cameron-Wilson, Film Review*

Boiling Point *

Japan 1990 96m colour
ICA/Bandai/Shochiku/Fuji (Hisao Nabeshima, Takio Yoshida, Masayuki Mori)
original title: *3-4x Jugatsu*

An ineffectual garage worker discovers that passivity gets you nowhere when he becomes embroiled in a violent vendetta after punching a bullying local gangster.

An offbeat mix of deadpan comedy and deader-pan thriller with a disjointed narrative style, enlivened by quirky directorial touches and a visual wit.

wd Takeshi Kitano *ph* Katsumi Yanagishima *ad* Osumu Sasaki *ed* Toshio Taniguchi

☆ 'Beat' Takeshi (Takeshi Kitano), Masahiko Ono, Yuriko Ishida, Takahito Iguchi, Minoru Iizuka, Hisashi Igawa, Bengal, Katsuo Tokashiki

'Formally inventive, profligate with visual and dramatic ideas, and always giving the sense that it has more creative horsepower under its bonnet than it needs to use, this film is a delight.' – *Tony Rayns, Sight and Sound*

'As an absurdist gangster melodrama it has enough insight in its brutality to make Scorsese look to his Oriental laurels.' – *Tom Hutchinson, Film Review*

Boiling Point *
US/France 1993 92m Technicolor
Guild/Warner/Hexagon (Marc Frydman, Leonardo de la Fuente)
Two men have a week to solve their problems: a Treasury agent, obsessed with avenging the murder of his partner, and the con man whose partner is responsible for the killing.
Although promoted as an action film, this is more an engaging character study that hovers on the edge of cliché but manages to maintain its balance.
wd James B. Harris *novel* Money Men by Gerald Petievich *ph* King Baggot *m* Cory Lerois, John D'Andrea *pd* Ron Foreman *ed* Jerry Brady
☆ Wesley Snipes, Dennis Weaver, Lolita Davidovich, Viggo Mortensen, Dan Hedaya, Seymour Cassel, Jonathan Banks, Christine Elise, Tony Lo Bianco, Valerie Perrine
'Low-key and bland in the extreme, it's strictly for film buffs.' – *Variety*
'Hardly substantial, but it's also consistently entertaining.' – *Sight and Sound*

The Bold and the Brave
US 1956 87m bw Superscope
RKO/Hal E. Chester
An assortment of American types come together in the Italian campaign of 1944.
Routine war heroics chiefly remembered (if at all) for a crap game sequence.
w Robert Lewin *d* Lewis Foster *ph* Sam Leavitt *m* Herschel Burke Gilbert
☆ Wendell Corey, *Mickey Rooney*, Nicole Maurey, Don Taylor
Robert Lewin; Mickey Rooney

Bolei Cheun: see *Gorgeous*

'He rose to fame on a ladder of dancing ladies!'
Bolero *
US 1934 85m bw Paramount
A New York dancer neglects his personal life to become king of the European night-club circuit.
Lively romantic drama which performed remarkably at the box-office and led to a kind of sequel, Rumba *(qv). Sally Rand performs the fan dance, for which she was famous.*
w Carey Wilson, Kubec Glasmon, Ruth Ridenour, Horace Jackson *d* Wesley Ruggles *ph* Leo Tover
☆ *George Raft, Carole Lombard*, Sally Rand, Frances Drake, William Frawley, Ray Milland, Gertrude Michael
'A studio conference product: lots of surefire elements. On screen it's a little enervating ... depends on Raft's popularity with the women.' – *Variety*

Bolero
US 1984 104m colour
Cannon/City (Bo Derek)
In 1926, a wealthy romantic girl travels the world in search of a man worthy of the sacrifice of her virginity.
Ludicrous sexual charade with unpleasant overtones resulting from the fact that the star's husband wrote and photographed this embarrassing piece of near-pornography.
wd John Derek *ph* John Derek *m* Peter Bernstein *pd* Alan Roderick-Jones
☆ Bo Derek, George Kennedy, Andrea Occhipinti, Greg Bensen, Ana Obregon
'The only ecstatic moment a filmgoer might derive will be at the discovery that it's over.' – *Philip Strick, MFB*

Bomba the Jungle Boy
US 1949 71m bw or sepia
Monogram (Walter Mirisch)
Photographers in Africa meet a junior Tarzan who rescues their girlfriend.
Cut-rate hokum starring the lad who had played Johnny Weissmuller's 'son' in earlier Tarzan movies; it led to several tedious sequels.
Sequels were as follows:
1948 Bomba on Panther Island (76m, with Allene Roberts)
1949 Bomba and the Lost Volcano (76m, with Donald Woods), Bomba and the Hidden City (71m, with Paul Guilfoyle)
1950 Bomba and the Elephant Stampede (71m, with Myron Healey)
1951 Bomba and the African Treasure (70m, with Lyle Talbot), Bomba and the Jungle Girl (70m, with Karen Sharpe), Bomba and the Lion Hunters (75m, with Morris Ankrum)
1953 Safari Drums (71m, with Douglas Kennedy)
1954 The Golden Idol (71m, with Paul Guilfoyle), Killer Leopard (70m, with Beverly Garland)
1955 Lord of the Jungle (69m, with Wayne Morris)
w Jack de Witt, from the comic strip by Roy Rockwell *d* Ford Beebe *ph* William Sickner *m* Edward Kay
☆ Johnny Sheffield, Peggy Ann Garner, Onslow Stevens, Charles Irwin

Bombardier
US 1943 99m bw
RKO (Robert Fellows)
Cadet bombardiers learn the realities of war on raids over Japan.
Totally routine recruiting poster heroics.
w John Twist *d* Richard Wallace *ph* Nicholas Musuraca *m* Roy Webb
☆ Pat O'Brien, Randolph Scott, Anne Shirley, Eddie Albert, Walter Reed, Robert Ryan, Barton MacLane

Bombay Talkie *
India 1970 105m Eastmancolor
Merchant-Ivory (Ismail Merchant)
A sophisticated American woman comes to Bombay and falls for two men involved in film-making.
Interesting but unsatisfactory romantic drama, rather pointlessly set against film studio backgrounds.
w Ruth Prawer Jhabvala, James Ivory *d* James Ivory *ph* Subrata Mitra *m* Shankar Jaikishan
☆ Jennifer Kendal, Shashi Kapoor, Zia Mohyeddin

Bombers B-52
US 1957 106m Warnercolor Cinemascope
Warner (Richard Whorf)
GB title: *No Sleep till Dawn*
A USAF sergeant considers applying for a discharge so that he can earn more money in civilian life.
Glossy domestic melodrama punctuated by aircraft shots.
w Irving Wallace *d* Gordon Douglas *ph* William Clothier *m* Leonard Rosenman
☆ Karl Malden, Marsha Hunt, Natalie Wood, Efrem Zimbalist Jnr, Don Kelly
'No one questions the basic assumption – that the good life consists of servicing bigger and better bombers.' – *MFB*

Bomber's Moon
US 1943 70m bw
TCF
An American pilot crashlands into Germany and makes for the coast.
Modestly budgeted war adventure with conventional thrills.
w Kenneth Gamet *d* 'Charles Fuhr' (Edward Ludwig and Harold Schuster)
☆ George Montgomery, Annabella, Kent Taylor, Walter Kingsford, Martin Kosleck

Bombshell ***
US 1933 91m bw
MGM (Hunt Stromberg)
GB title and aka: *Blonde Bombshell*
A glamorous film star yearns for a new image.
Crackpot farce which even by today's standards moves at a fair clip and enabled the star to give her best comedy performance.
w Jules Furthman, John Lee Mahin play Caroline Francke, Mack Crane *d Victor Fleming* *ph* Chester Lyons, Hal Rosson
☆ Jean Harlow, Lee Tracy, Frank Morgan, Franchot Tone, Pat O'Brien, Ivan Lebedeff, Una Merkel, Ted Healy, Isabel Jewell, C. Aubrey Smith, Louise Beavers, Leonard Carey, Mary Forbes
'Bound to click and the best legitimate comedy in a long time.' – *Variety*

Bombsight Stolen: see *Cottage to Let*

Bon Voyage *
US 1962 133m Technicolor
Walt Disney (Bill Walsh, Ron Miller)
An American family spends a holiday in Paris.
Simple-minded, overlong comedy of mishaps, with Daddy finally trapped in the sewer. Smoothly done of its kind.
w Bill Walsh *novel* Marrijane and Joseph Hayes *d* James Neilson *ph* William Snyder *m* Paul Smith
☆ Fred MacMurray, Jane Wyman, Michael Callan, Deborah Walley, Jessie Royce Landis, Tommy Kirk, Ivan Desny

Bonaventure: see *Thunder on the Hill*

Bond Street
GB 1948 107m bw
ABP/World Screenplays (Anatole de Grunwald)
Four stories, each concerning an item of an expensive wedding trousseau.
Mild and laboured short story compendium.
w Anatole de Grunwald *d* Gordon Parry *ph* Otto Heller *m* Benjamin Frankel
☆ *Roland Young*, Jean Kent, Paula Valenska, Kathleen Harrison, Derek Farr, *Kenneth Griffith*, Hazel Court, Ronald Howard
'Even a glimpse of actual Bond Street makes little contact with reality.' – *MFB*

'Two cops on the trail of a serial killer. They must see as one...They must act as one... They must think as one... Before another victim falls.'
The Bone Collector
US 1999 118m DeLuxe Super 35
Universal/Columbia (Martin Bregman, Louis A. Stroller, Michael Bregman)
A paralysed former detective and forensic expert works with an inexperienced female cop to catch a serial killer.
A wearying, downbeat thriller of a familiar kind, dragged down by a script that makes little narrative sense and leaves too many questions unanswered.
w Jeremy Iacone *novel* Jeffery Deaver *d* Phillip Noyce *ph* Dean Semler *m* Craig Armstrong *pd* Nigel Phelps *ed* William Hoy
☆ Denzel Washington (Lincoln Rhyme), Angelina Jolie (Amelia Donaghy), Queen Latifah (Thelma), Michael Rooker (Capt Howard Cheney), Mike McGlone (Detective Kenny Solomon), Leland Orser (Richard Thompson), Luis Guzman (Eddie Ortiz), John Benjamin Hickey (Dr Barry Lehman)
'One of the year's most gruesome movies... ingenious but preposterous.' – *Stephen Holden, New York Times*

Bone Daddy
Canada 1998 87m DeLuxe
Kushner-Locke (Lewis B. Chesler, Jean Desormeaux)
After a former medical examiner writes a bestselling novel based on unsolved serial murders that happened seven years earlier, the killings begin again.
Gruesome and predictable thriller of no particular interest.
w Tom Szollosi *d* Mario Azzopardi *ph* Danny Nowak *m* Christophe Beck *pd* Jeff Ginn *ed* Dean Balser
☆ Rutger Hauer, Barbara Williams, R. H. Thomson, Joseph Kell, Robin Gammell, Blu Mankuma, Mimi Kuzyk

'Take one Wall Street tycoon, his Fifth Avenue mistress, a reporter hungry for fame, and make the wrong turn in The Bronx ... then sit back and watch the sparks fly'
The Bonfire of the Vanities
US 1990 125m Technicolor
Warner (Brian de Palma)
The successful life of a New York bond dealer crumbles when he is arrested for injuring a black youth in a street accident.
Strained attempt at social satire, miscast and missing all its targets.
w Michael Cristofer *novel* Tom Wolfe *d* Brian de Palma *ph* Vilmos Zsigmond *m* Dave Grusin *pd* Richard Sylbert *ad* Peter Lansdown Smith *ed* David Ray, Bill Pankow
☆ Tom Hanks, Bruce Willis, Melanie Griffith, Kim Cattrall, Saul Rubinek, Morgan Freeman, F. Murray Abraham, John Hancock, Kevin Dunn, Clifton James
'A misfire of inanities.' – *Variety*
† Julie Salamon's book *The Devil's Candy: The Bonfire of the Vanities Goes to Hollywood* follows the production from its inception to its release.

Le Bonheur *
France 1965 79m Eastmancolor
Parc/Mag Bodard
A young carpenter is happy with his wife and family, happier still when he finds a mistress, whom he marries when his wife is found drowned.
Slight, good looking, ambivalent little fable which finally expires in a surfeit of style.
wd Agnès Varda *ph* Jean Rabier, Claude Beausoleil *m* Mozart
☆ Jean-Claude Drouot, Claire Drouot, Marie-France Boyer

Le Bonheur Est dans le Pré *
France 1995 106m colour
Guild/Téléma/Canal+/Champ Poirier/France 2/France 3 (Charles Gassot)
An unhappy factory owner leaves home to start a new life with a Spanish woman whose missing husband he resembles.
Undemanding comedy of sexual mishap, lacking the bite of its director's earlier movies.
w Florence Quentin *d* Etienne Chatiliez *ph* Philippe Welt *m* Pascal Andreacchio *ad* Stéphane Makedonshy *ed* Ann Lafarge
☆ Michel Serrault, Eddy Mitchell, Sabine Azéma, Carmen Maura, François Morel, Guillaine Londez, Virginie Darmon, Eric Cantona
'A feel-good movie first and foremost, in which only the occasional force-fed duck or woman clipped round the ear is likely to dissent from the bucolic chorus of bliss.' – *Keith Reader, Sight and Sound*

Bonjour Tristesse *
GB 1957 93m Technicolor Cinemascope
Columbia/Wheel Films (Otto Preminger)
A teenage girl becomes involved with her sophisticated father's amours and causes the death of his would-be mistress.
The novel's rather repellent characters are here played like royal personages against a background of Riviera opulence. The result is very odd but often entertaining, especially when it slips into self-parody.
w Arthur Laurents *novel* Françoise Sagan *d* Otto Preminger *ph Georges Périnal* *m* Georges Auric *pd* Roger Furse
☆ David Niven, Deborah Kerr, Jean Seberg, Mylene Demongeot, Geoffrey Horne, Juliette Greco, Martita Hunt, Walter Chiari, Jean Kent, Roland Culver
'An elegant, ice-cold charade of emotions.' – *Judith Crist*
'Sagan not so much translated as traduced – opened out, smartened up, the sickness overlaid with Riviera suntan.' – *Alexander Walker*
'Long, untidy, muddled and mushy.' – *Financial Times*
† Shot in monochrome for Paris, colour for the Riviera.

La Bonne Année: see *Happy New Year*

Bonne Chance
France 1935 75m bw
Sacha Guitry
An artist who wins a lottery takes on holiday with him, on a purely platonic basis, the girl who gave him half her ticket.
Modest star comedy which pleased at the time.
wd Sacha Guitry
☆ Sacha Guitry, Jacqueline Delubac, Robert Darthez

La Bonne Soupe
France/Italy 1963 97m bw CinemaScope
Belstar/Du Siècle/Dear Film (André Hakim)
A high-class prostitute tells her life story.
A saucy frolic complete with three-in-a-bed and rapidly closing doors; quite enjoyable of its kind.
wd Robert Thomas *play* Félicien Marceau *ph* Roger Hubert *m* Raymond le Sénéchal

☆ Annie Girardot, Marie Bell, Gérard Blain, Bernard Blier, Jean-Claude Brialy, Claude Dauphin, Sacha Distel, Daniel Gélin, Blanchette Brunoy, Jane Marken, Raymond Péllégrin, Franchot Tone

Les Bonnes Femmes **
France 1960 102m bw
Paris/Panitalia (Robert and Raymond Hakim)
aka: *The Girls*
Four shop assistants dream of getting away from the boredom and mediocrity of their lives.
Tough and compassionate study of women trapped in a second-rate world, from which death offers the only real escape.
w Paul Gégauff, Claude Chabrol *d* Claude Chabrol *ph* Henri Decae *m* Paul Misraki, Pierre Jansen *ed* Jacques Gaillard
☆ Bernadette Lafont, Clotilde Joano, Stéphane Audran, Lucile Saint-Simon, Pierre Bertin, Jean-Louis Maury, Claude Berri, Mario David
'Uneven and, in parts, somewhat tedious and tawdry, yet it has more tenderness and is more emotionally compelling than much of Chabrol's more refined work.' – *Pauline Kael*

'They're young ... they're in love ... and they kill people!'
Bonnie and Clyde ****
US 1967 111m Technicolor
Warner/Seven Arts/Tatira/Hiller (*Warren Beatty*)
In the early thirties, a car thief and the daughter of his intended victim team up to become America's most feared and ruthless bank robbers.
Technically brilliant evocation of sleepy mid-America at the time of the public enemies, using every kind of cinematic trick including fake snapshots, farcical interludes, dreamy soft-focus and a jazzy score. For all kinds of reasons a very influential film which even made extreme violence quite fashionable (and very bloody it is).
w David Newman, Robert Benton d Arthur Penn ph Burnett Guffey m Charles Strouse, using 'Foggy Mountain Breakdown' by Flatt and Scruggs
☆ *Warren Beatty, Faye Dunaway*, Gene Hackman, Estelle Parsons, *Michael J. Pollard*, Dub Taylor, Denver Pyle, Gene Wilder
'It is a long time since we have seen an American film so perfectly judged.' – *MFB*
'...all to the rickety twang of a banjo and a saturation in time and place.' – *Judith Crist*
'The formula is hayseed comedy bursting sporadically into pyrotechnical bloodshed and laced with sentimental pop-Freudianism.' – *John Simon*
'A film from which we shall date reputations and innovations in the American cinema.' – *Alexander Walker*
'It works as comedy, as tragedy, as entertainment, as a meditation on the place of guns and violence in American society.' – *Roger Ebert*
Burnett Guffey; Estelle Parsons
best picture; David Newman, Robert Benton; Arthur Penn; Warren Beatty; Faye Dunaway; Gene Hackman; Michael J. Pollard
Faye Dunaway

The Bonnie Parker Story
US 1958 80m bw Superama
James H. Nicholson, Sam Arkoff
A waitress joins up with a cheap crook in a series of bank raids.
Tinpot 'B' gangster film chiefly notable for comparison with the later Bonnie and Clyde *(qv). All it really has is a certain exuberance in the action sequences.*
w Stan Shpetner *d* William Witney *ph* Jack Marta *m* Ronald Stein
☆ Dorothy Provine, Jack Hogan, Richard Bakalyan, Joseph Turkel

Bonnie Prince Charlie
GB 1948 140m approx Technicolor
British Lion/London Films (Edward Black)
The hope of the Stuarts returns from exile but is eventually forced to flee again.
Good highland photography combines with appalling studio sets, an initially confused narrative, a draggy script and uneasy performances to produce an ill-fated attempt at a British historical epic. Alexander Korda, who masterminded it, sulked in public at the critical roasting, but on this occasion the critics were right.
w Clemence Dane *d* Anthony Kimmins *ph* Robert Krasker *m* Ian Whyte
☆ David Niven, Margaret Leighton, Jack Hawkins, Judy Campbell, Morland Graham, Finlay Currie, John Laurie
'I have a sense of wonder about this film, beside which *The Swordsman* seems like a dazzling work of veracity and art. It is that London Films, having surveyed the finished thing, should not have quietly scrapped it.' – *Richard Winnington*
'The picture is not lacking in moments of unconscious levity, what with David Niven rallying his hardy Highlanders to his standard in a voice hardly large enough to summon a waiter.' – *New Yorker*
'Time has made it the film industry's biggest joke. But the joke turns a little sour when one reflects how extravagance, recklessness and sheer bungling administration during the fat and prosperous years left the British film industry so poor and vulnerable when the hard times came along.' – *Gerald Garret, 1975*
† Running time was later cut to 118 minutes.

Bonnie Scotland *
US 1935 80m bw
MGM/Hal Roach
Two Americans journey to Scotland to collect a non-existent inheritance, then follow their friend in the army and wind up in India.
Generally disappointing star comedy which still contains excellent sequences when it is not vainly trying to preserve interest in a boring plot. An obvious parody on Lives of a Bengal Lancer *(qv), released earlier that year; Scotland has almost nothing to do with it.*
w Frank Butler, Jeff Moffitt *d* James Horne *ph* Art Lloyd, Walter Lundin *ed* Bert Jordan
☆ *Stan Laurel, Oliver Hardy*, James Finlayson, Daphne Pollard, William Janney, June Lang
'Packed with Laurel and Hardy hokum and good for plenty of laughs' – *Boxoffice*

Bonnie's Kids
US 1972 105m Eastmancolor
Variety/Tommy J. Productions (Charles Stroud)
After killing their lecherous stepfather, two young women take to a life of sex and crime.
Cut-rate exploitation picture, celebrating amorality, that attempts to cash in on the success of Bonnie and Clyde *(qv).*
wd Arthur Marks *ph* Robert Charles Wilson *m* Carson Whitsett *ed* Richard Greer
☆ Tiffany Bolling, Robin Mattson, Leo Gordon, Steve Sandor, Scott Brady, Leonore Stevens, Alex Rocco, Timothy Brown

'You'll be tickled to death over this gay chiller diller!'
The Boogie Man Will Get You
US 1944 66m bw
Columbia (Colbert Clark)
Bodies accumulate when mad doctors get to work creating supermen in a small village.
Desperately unfunny spoof notable only for the fact that it was attempted with these players and at that time.
w Edwin Blum *d* Lew Landers *ph* Henry Freulich *md* Morris Stoloff
☆ Boris Karloff, Peter Lorre, Maxie Rosenbloom, Jeff Donnell, Larry Parks, Maude Eburne, Don Beddoe

'The life of a dreamer, the days of a business and the nights in between.'
Boogie Nights **
US 1997 156m DeLuxe Panavision
Entertainment/New Line/Ghoulardi/Lawrence Gordon (Lloyd Levin, Paul Thomas Anderson, John Lyons, Joanne Sellar)
The rise and fall of a well-endowed youth who becomes a star of pornographic movies in the 70s.
An entertaining and sometimes savage account of the last moments of hard-core films, just before the industry switched to video; witty and satiric for much of the time, it is spoilt by its use of gratuitous violence to overcome its narrative flaws.
wd Paul Thomas Anderson *ph* Robert Elswit *m* Toby Emmerich *pd* Bob Ziembicki *ed* Dylan Tichenor
☆ Mark Wahlberg, Burt Reynolds, Julianne Moore, John C. Reilly, Don Cheadle, Heather Graham, Luis Guzman, Philip Seymour Hoffman, William H. Macy, Alfred Molina
'Darkly comic, vastly entertaining and utterly original.' – *Variety*
Burt Reynolds; Julianne Moore; Paul Thomas Anderson (as writer)

'A controversial retelling of the Apocalypse.'
The Book of Life
US/France 1998 63m colour
La Sept Arte/Haut et Court/True Fiction (Thierry Cagianut, Matthew Myers)
On the last day of 1999, Jesus arrives in New York, reluctant to carry out his mission to bring the world to an end.
Disjointed, aimless movie in which the jerky, blurred handheld camera-work is a distraction, though the loquacious script is no aid to enjoyment, either.
wd Hal Hartley *ph* Jim Denault *ad* Andy Biscontini *ed* Steve Hamilton
☆ Martin Donovan (Jesus Christ), Anna Köhler (Hotel clerk), Martin Pfeffercorn (Martyr), Olga Alexandrova (Waitress), Michael Ornstein (Computer wizard), Paul Albe (Mormon Thug), Don Creech (Mormon Thug), Joseph McKenna (Man at Airport), Abby Royle (Woman at Airport), P.J. Harvey (Magdalena)

Book of Love *
US 1990 87m CFI color
Entertainment/New Line
A successful writer remembers when he was 16 and was too shy to ask the girl he loved to go to the prom.
Pleasantly done, nostalgic rites-of-passage movie. It travels over familiar ground, but with a light tread.
w William Kotzwinkle *novel Jack in the Box* by William Kotzwinkle *d* Robert Shaye *ph* Peter Deming *m* Stanley Clarke *pd* C. J. Strawn *ed* Terry Stokes
☆ Chris Young, Keith Coogan, Aeryk Egan, Josie Bissett, Tricia Leigh Fisher, Danny Nucci, John Cameron Mitchell, Beau Dremann

Book of Numbers *
US 1973 80m colour
Brut (Raymond St Jacques)
Black waiters set up a numbers racket in a small Arkansas town during the Depression, to the annoyance of white gangsters.
Enjoyable blaxploitation movie, energetic and driven by a genuine anger, perception and humour – the high spot is a courtroom scene – which overcomes many of its low-budget inadequacies.
w Larry Spiegel *novel* Robert Deane Pharr *d* Raymond St Jacques *ph* Gayne Rescher *m* Al Schackman, Sonny Terry, Brownie McGhee *ad* Robert D. Shepherd, Edward Burbridge *ed* Irving G. Rosenblum
☆ Raymond St Jacques, Philip M. Thomas, Freda Payne, Hope Clarke, D'Urville Martin, Gilbert Green

Book of Shadows: Blair Witch 2
US 2000 90m DeLuxe
Momentum/Artisan/Haxan (Bill Carraro)
After success of *The Blair Witch Project* brings tourists to Burkittsville, Maryland, a local youth takes four people on a tour of the sites connected with the deaths.
Just another haunted house horror; lightning has not struck twice.
w Dick Beebe, Joe Berlinger *d* Joe Berlinger *ph* Nancy Schreiber *m* Carter Burwell *pd* Vince Peranio *ed* Sarah Flack *cos* Melissa Toth
☆ Kim Director (Kim), Jeffrey Donovan (Jeff), Erica Leerhsen (Erica), Tristen Skyler (Tristen), Stephen Turner (Stephen)
'Disappointing in every aspect.' – *Variety*
'Spectacularly bad.' – *Guardian*

'She outlived six rich men!'
Boom!
GB 1968 113m Technicolor Panavision
Universal/World Film Services/Moon Lake Productions (John Heyman, Norman Priggen)
On the volcanic Mediterranean island which she owns, a dying millionairess plans to take as her last lover a wandering poet who is the angel of death.
Pretentious, boring nonsense, showing that when talent goes awry it certainly goes boom.
w Tennessee Williams *play The Milk Train Doesn't Stop Here Any More* by Tennessee Williams *d* Joseph Losey *ph* Douglas Slocombe *m* John Barry
☆ Elizabeth Taylor, Richard Burton, *Noël Coward*, Michael Dunn, Joanna Shimkus
'It's a beautiful picture, the best ever made of one of my plays.' – *Tennessee Williams*
'A pointless, pompous nightmare.' – *Paul D. Zimmermann, Newsweek*
'An ordeal in tedium.' – *Hollywood Reporter*
'Outright junk.' – *Saturday Review*
'The title could not be more apt: it is precisely the sound of a bomb exploding.' – *Richard Schickel, Life*
'*Boom!* isn't doing little business; it's doing no business at all.' – *Universal executive*

Boom in the Moon (dubbed)
Mexico 1946 90m bw
Alsa (Alexander Salkind)
original title: *El Moderno Barba Azul*
A shipwrecked sailor is mistaken for a mass murderer and sent on the first expedition to the moon.
Embarrassingly bad, feebly scripted and cheaply made comedy in which Keaton displays none of his skill or invention, but sleepwalks through his role.
w Victor Trivas, Jaime Salvador *d* Jaime Salvador *m* George Tzipine
☆ Buster Keaton, Angel Garasa, Virginia Seret, Luis Bareiro, Fernando Sotto
† The film was never released in American cinemas and was hardly seen outside Mexico until its video release; it surfaces occasionally on television in a version that runs for 70m.

Boom Town **
US 1940 120m bw
MGM (Sam Zimbalist)
Two friendly oil drillers strike it rich.
Enjoyable four-star, big-studio product of its time: world-wide entertainment of assured success, with a proven mix of romance, action, drama and comedy.
w John Lee Mahin *story* James Edward Grant *d Jack Conway ph* Harold Rosson *m* Franz Waxman *ad* Cedric Gibbons
☆ *Clark Gable, Spencer Tracy*, Claudette Colbert, Hedy Lamarr, *Frank Morgan*, Lionel Atwill, Chill Wills
'Western high jinks, a wee child, and courtroom speeches about individual enterprise constitute the various come-ons in a scrambled and inept picture.' – *New York Herald Tribune*
'More colourful action in the oil fields and less agitation indoors might have made it a great picture.' – *Bosley Crowther*
Harold Rosson

Boomerang! ***
US 1947 88m bw
TCF (Louis de Rochemont)
In a New England town, a clergyman is shot dead on the street. The DA prevents an innocent man from being convicted, but cannot track down the guilty party.
Incisive real life thriller: based on a true case, it was shot in an innovative documentary style which was much copied, and justice is not seen to be done, though the murderer is known to the audience. A milestone movie of its kind.
w Richard Murphy d Elia Kazan ph Norbert Brodine *m* David Buttolph
☆ *Dana Andrews*, Jane Wyatt, Lee J. Cobb, Cara Williams, Arthur Kennedy, Sam Levene, Taylor Holmes, Robert Keith, Ed Begley
'A study of integrity, beautifully developed by Dana Andrews against a background of political corruption and chicanery that is doubly shocking because of its documentary understatement.' – *Richard Winnington*
'For the first time in many a moon we are treated to a picture that gives a good example of a typical small American city – the people, their way of living, their mode of government, the petty politics practised, the power of the press.' – *Frank Ward, National Board of Review*
Richard Murphy

'A Player Who's About To Be Played.'
Boomerang
US 1992 117m Technicolor
UIP/Paramount (Brian Grazer, Warrington Hudlin)
An executive in a cosmetics firm has an unsuccessful affair with his boss before finding true love.
Dim comedy that substitutes gloss for wit and deprives its star of everything except uncritical adulation.
w Barry W. Blaustein, David Sheffield *d* Reginald Hudlin *ph* Woody Omens *m* Marcus Miller *pd* Jane Musky *ed* Earl Watson, John Carter, Michael Jablow
☆ Eddie Murphy, Robin Givens, Halle Berry, David Alan Grier, Martin Lawrence, Grace Jones, Geoffrey Holder, Eartha Kitt, Melvin Van Peebles
'This Eddie Murphy vehicle tries hard to be positive. It's a pity that the movie isn't any good.' – *Michael Sragow, New Yorker*
'An ill-fitting comedy vehicle that's desperately in need of a reality check.' – *Variety*

The Boost *
US 1988 95m colour
Hemdale/Becker-Blatt-Ponicsan (Daniel H. Blatt)
A fast-talking salesman and his wife are ruined by their addiction to cocaine.
Cautionary tale of an acquisitive society, coolly told.
w Darryl Ponicsan *novel* Ludes by Benjamin Stein *d* Harold Becker *ph* Howard Atherton *m* Stanley Myers *ad* Ken Hardy *ed* Maury Winetrobe
☆ James Woods, Sean Young, John Kapelos, Steven Hill, Kelle Kerr, John Rothman, Amanda Blake, Grace Zabriskie

Das Boot: see *The Boat*

'When you don't know your next step... improvise.'
Bootmen *
Australia/US 2000 95m DeLuxe
Fox Searchlight/AFFC/Bootmen (Hilary Linstead, Dein Perry)
In the Australian steel town of Newcastle, a young, impulsive tap-dancing machinist recruits his mates to form a macho dance troupe that reflects their industrial background.
Formulaic drama enlivened by the vitality of its thunderous tap dancing.
w Steve Worland *d* Dein Perry *ph* Steve Mason *m* Cezary Skubiszewski *ch* Dein Perry *pd* Murray Picknett *ed* Jane Moran *cos* Tess Schofield
☆ Adam Garcia (Sean Okden), Sophie Lee (Linda), Sam Worthington (Mitch Okden), William Zappa (Walter), Richard Carter (Gary Okden), Susie Porter (Sara), Anthony Hayes (Huey)
'A vigorous re-working of the puttin'-on-a-show formula... great fun.' – *David Stratton, Variety*
† The film's director Dein Perry was founder of the Australian dance troupe Tap Dogs.

Boots! Boots!
GB 1934 80m bw
Blakeley/John E. Blakeley
A simple hotel employee turns entertainer with the scullery maid.
Formby's first film, based on a stage show, and filmed cheaply and with little imagination: the camera remains static as if the proceedings are being viewed from the stalls. It retains some slight interest as an example of popular entertainment of the period.
w Jack Cottrill, George Formby *d* Bert Tracey *ph* James S. Hodgson *md* Harry Hudson *ad* Thomas Fleetwood
☆ George Formby, Beryl Formby, Arthur Kingsley, Tonie Forde, Lillian Keyes, Donald Reid, Constance Fletcher, Wallace Boscoe, Betty Driver

Boots Hill (dubbed) *
Italy 1969 106m Technicolor Techniscope
San Marco/Crono
original title: *La Collina degli Stivali*
A man wounded and hunted by a gang of killers takes refuge with a travelling circus.
Lively spaghetti Western that threatens to be more original than most, with its chase narrative concerned with greed and exploitation, but which finally settles, with the arrival of Bud Spencer at the halfway mark, for broad comedy, gunfights and pub brawls.
wd Giuseppe Colizzi *ph* Marcello Masciocchi *m* Carlo Rustichelli *ad* Gastone Carsetti *ed* Tatiana Morigi Casini
☆ Terence Hill (Mario Girotti), Woody Strode, Bud Spencer (Carlo Pedersoli), Victor Buono, Lionel Stander, Edward Ciannelli, Luca Montefiori, Glauca Onorato

Boots Malone
US 1952 103m bw
Columbia (Milton Holmes)
A would-be jockey tags along with a down-at-heel agent who gets him work and finally persuades him not to throw a crooked race.
Dullish racetrack melodrama bogged down by repetitive and unsympathetic plot twists.
w Milton Holmes *d* William Dieterle *ph* Charles Lawton *m* Elmer Bernstein
☆ William Holden, Johnny Stewart, Stanley Clements, Basil Ruysdael, Carl Benton Reid, Ed Begley, Henry Morgan
† Screenwriter Harold Buchman was excluded from the credits of the film because he was blacklisted at the time.

'Some guys will do anything for a little something.'
Booty Call
US 1997 79m DeLuxe
Columbia (John Morrissey)
Two couples decide to indulge in intercourse providing the men equip themselves with condoms.
A prolonged, comic commercial for safe sex that detumesces quickly.
w Takashi Bufford *d* Jeff Pollack *ph* Ron Orieux *m* Robert Folk *pd* Sandra Kybartas *ed* Christopher Greenbury
☆ Jamie Foxx, Tommy Davidson, Vivica A. Fox, Tamala Jones, Scott LaRose, Gedde Watanabe
'An oddly effective comic mix of the politically correct and outré stereotyping.' – *Variety*
† Art Malik appears uncredited.

Bopha! *
US 1993 121m DeLuxe
Paramount/Arsenio Hall/Taubman
In South Africa in 1980, a black policeman, living in a turbulent township, finds himself torn between supporting his repressive white boss or approving the actions of his outspoken son, who believes in revolution.
A sincere, well-acted movie about apartheid and its consequences, but over-simplistic and too conventional in its approach.
w Brian Bird, John Wierick *play* Percy Mtwa *d* Morgan Freeman *ph* David Watkin *m* James Horner *pd* Michael Philips *ed* Neil Travis
☆ Danny Glover (Micah Mangena), Malcolm McDowell (De Villiers), Rosie Mangena (Alfre Woodard), Marius Weyers (Van Tonder), Maynard Eziashi (Zweli Mangena), Malick Bowens (Pule Rampa), Michael Chinyamurindi (Solomon), Christopher John Hall (Naledi Machikano)
'A handsomely crafted, potently played drama that brings the issue of apartheid down to a visceral human dimension.' – *Leonard Klady, Variety*

The Border
US 1982 108m Technicolor Panavision
Universal/RKO (Neil Hartley)
A Los Angeles cop joins the border patrol in El Paso and becomes involved in squalor, violence and double-dealing.
A rather solemn elaboration on a well-worn theme, with nothing very memorable except its excesses.
w Deric Washburn, Walon Green, David Freeman *d* Tony Richardson *ph* Ric Waite *m* Ry Cooder *pd* Toby Rafelson *ed* Robert K. Lambert
☆ Jack Nicholson, Harvey Keitel, Valerie Perrine, Warren Oates, Elpidia Carrillo

Border Incident
US 1949 93m bw
MGM (Nicholas Nayfack)
Police stop the illegal immigration of labourers from Mexico.
Routine semi-documentary cops and robbers, well enough made.
w John C. Higgins *d* Anthony Mann *ph* John Alton *m* André Previn
☆ Ricardo Montalban, George Murphy, Howard da Silva, James Mitchell, Alfonso Bedoya

Border Radio
US 1987 84m bw
Coyote/Marcus de Leon
A punk rock musician goes on the run to Mexico after stealing money from a promoter who failed to pay him.
Probably a learning experience for those involved: the jerky narrative (one title reads '2 or 6 months later'), abrupt editing, deliberately inconsequential, improvised dialogue and amateurish acting suggest that its participants were determined to make a film but were uncertain of precisely how to do it.
wd Allison Anders, Dean Lent, Kurt Voss *ph* Dean Lent *m* Dave Alvin
☆ Chris D., Luana Anders, Chris Shearer, John Doe, Dave Alvin, Iris Berry, Devon Anders, Texacala Jones
† The credits include: 'Many curses on: Those Who Tried To Thwart Us'.

Border River
US 1953 80m Technicolor
Universal-International (Albert J. Cohen)
In 1865, after stealing $2m in gold from the Union to buy supplies for the South, a Confederate Major takes refuge in Zona Libre, a Mexican town controlled by a powerful outlaw, where others are determined to relieve him of the treasure.
Western programmer that mixes action and romance in an unusual setting.
w William Sackheim, Louis Stevens *d* George Sherman *ph* Irving Glassberg *m* Joseph Gershenson *ad* Bernard Herzbrun, Richard H. Riedel *ed* Frank Fross
☆ Joel McCrea (Clete Mattson), Yvonne de Carlo (Carmelita Carrias), Pedro Armendariz (General Calleja), Ivan Triesault (Baron Von Hollden), Alfonso Bedoya (Capt Vargas), Howard Petrie (Newlund), Erika Nordin (Annina Strasser), George J. Lewis (Sanchez), Nacho Galindo (Lopez), George Wallace (Fletcher), Lane Chandler (Anderson), Martin Garralaga (Guzman), Joe Bassett (Stanton), Salvador Baguez (General Robles), Felipe Turice (Pablo)

Border Shootout
US 1990 110m colour
Turner/Phoenix
A naïve rancher becomes the sheriff of a town in thrall to the crooked son of its largest landowner.
Inept Western, in which the various strands of the narrative never quite come together; the acting is variable – from acceptable to bad – and the direction clumsy. Despite his star billing, Ford, whose mind seems to be on other things, plays a secondary role.
wd C. T. McIntyre *novel* The Law at Randado by Elmore Leonard *ph* Dennis Dalzell *m* Coley Music Group *pd* Craig B. Stein *ed* Grant Johnson
☆ Glenn Ford, Charlene Tilton, Jeff Kaake, Michael Horse, Russell Todd, Cody Glenn, Sergio Calderon, Michael Ansara

Borderline
US 1980 97m colour
ITC (Martin Starger)
A Mexican border patrolman chases illegal immigrants and the big time crooks making money out of them.
Routine, quite effective action programmer.
w Steve Kline, Jerrold Freedman *d* Jerrold Freedman *ph* Tak Fujimoto *m* Gil Melle
☆ Charles Bronson, Bruno Kirby, Karmin Murcelo, Michael Lerner, Ed Harris

Borderlines: see *The Caretakers*

Bordertown *
US 1934 80m bw
Warner (Robert Lord)
In a North Mexican town, a shabby lawyer becomes infatuated with the neurotic wife of a businessman.
Satisfying melodrama whose plot climax was later borrowed for They Drive by Night (qv).
w Laird Doyle, Wallace Smith *novel* Carroll Graham *d* Archie Mayo *ph* Tony Gaudio *md* Leo Forbstein
☆ Paul Muni, Bette Davis, Margaret Lindsay, Eugene Pallette, Robert Barrat, Henry O'Neill, Hobart Cavanaugh
'A strictly box office film, well written and paced.' – *Variety*
† *Blowing Wild* (qv) was also a partial uncredited remake.

Bordertown Cafe
Canada 1991 95m colour
Cinexus/Flat City/NFBC (Norma Bailey)
A woman running a small-town café has problems with her mother, son and truck-driving former husband.
Fraught and talkative soap opera of regrets and disappointments.
w Kelly Rebar *d* Norma Bailey *ph* Ian Elkin *m* Ben Mink *pd* John Blackie *ed* Lara Mazur
☆ Susan Hogan, Janet Wright, Gordon Michael Woolvett, Sean McCann, Nicholas Campbell

Born Again
US 1978 110m Technicolor
Robert L. Munger/Frank Capra Jnr
Charles Colson, sent to prison after Watergate, becomes a devout Christian.
Part evangelism, part reconstruction through rose-tinted spectacles; not particularly entertaining or instructive as either.
w Walter Block *d* Irving Rapper *ph* Harry Stradling Jnr *m* Les Baxter
☆ Dean Jones, Anne Francis, Jay Robinson, Dana Andrews, Raymond St Jacques, George Brent, Harry Spillman (Richard Nixon)

Born for Glory: see *Brown on Resolution*

Born for Trouble: see *Murder in the Big House*

Born Free **
GB 1966 95m Technicolor
Panavision
Columbia/Open Road (Carl Foreman)/High Road/Atlas (Sam Jaffe, Paul Radin)
A Kenyan game warden and his wife rear three lion cubs, one of which eventually presents them with a family.
Irresistible animal shots salvage this rather flabbily put together version of a bestselling book. An enormous commercial success, it was followed by the even thinner Living Free and To Walk With Lions (qv), by a TV series, and by several semi-professional documentaries.
w Gerald L. C. Copley (Lester Cole) *book* Joy Adamson *d* James Hill *ph* Kenneth Talbot *m* John Barry
☆ Virginia McKenna, Bill Travers, Geoffrey Keen
† Screenwriter Cole wrote under a pseudonym because he was blacklisted at the time.
John Barry; title song (*m* John Barry, *ly* Don Black)

Born in East L.A.
US 1987 87m colour
Universal (Peter Macgregor-Scott)
An American Mexican is mistaken for an illegal immigrant and deported to Tijuana.
Mercifully short brain-dead comedy.
wd Cheech Marin *ph* Alex Phillips *m* Lee Holdridge *ed* Don Brochu
☆ Cheech Marin, Daniel Stern, Paul Rodriguez, Jan Michael Vincent, Kamala Lopez, Tony Plana

Born Losers
US 1967 112m colour
AIP (Delores Taylor)
California teeny-boppers claim to have been gang-raped by wandering motorcyclists.
Teenage shocker, only notable for its credits, and for being the first Billy Jack film.
wd Tom Laughlin *ph* Gregory Sandor *m* Mike Curb
☆ Tom Laughlin, Jane Russell, Elizabeth James, Jeremy Slate, William Wellman Jnr
'It's so pokey and crudely obvious that it seems almost guileless – helplessly inept.' – *Pauline Kael*

'A true story of innocence lost and courage found'
Born on the Fourth of July **
US 1989 144m DeLuxe Panavision
UIP/Ixtlan (A Kitman Ho, Oliver Stone)
A crippled Vietnam veteran joins the anti-war movement.
Rousing drama, based on fact.

w Oliver Stone, Ron Kovic *book* Ron Kovic *d* Oliver Stone *ph* Robert Richardson *m* John Williams *pd* Bruno Rubeo *ad* Victor Kempster, Richard L. Johnson *ed* David Brenner, Joe Hutshing
☆ Tom Cruise, Bryan Larkin, Raymond J. Barry, Caroline Kava, Josh Evans, Seth Allan, Jamie Talisman, Sean Stone, Anne Bobby, Jenna von Oy
Oliver Stone; best film editing
Tom Cruise; John Williams; best picture; best adapted screenplay; best cinematography

Born Reckless
US 1937 60m bw
TCF
Big-town taxi drivers start a war among themselves.
Second-feature actioner, well enough done.
w John Patrick, Helen Logan, Robert Ellis *d* Malcolm St Clair
☆ Brian Donlevy, Rochelle Hudson, Barton MacLane, Robert Kent, Harry Carey, Pauline Moore, Chick Chandler
'Houses in the knuckle districts will give it its best play.' – *Variety*

'Romance isn't dead... it's just not very well.'
Born Romantic
GB 2000 97m DeLuxe
Optimum/BBC/Harvest/Kismet (Michele Camarda)
In London three young men pursue three women at a salsa club.
Episodic romantic comedy that is enjoyable in fits and starts, though its over-schematic structure dampens the fun.
wd David Kane *ph* Robert Alazraki *m* Simon Boswell *pd* Sarah Greenwood *ed* Michael Parker
☆ Craig Ferguson (Frankie), Ian Hart (Second Cab Driver), Jane Horrocks (Mo), Adrian Lester (Jimmy), Catherine McCormack (Jocelyn), Jimi Mistry (Eddie), David Morrissey (Fergus), Olivia Williams (Eleanor), Kenneth Cranham (Barney), John Thomson (First Cab Driver), Paddy Considine (Ray)
'Highly enjoyable when all its gears are clicking, but rarely as good as it should be.' – *Derek Elley, Variety*

Born to Be Bad
US 1934 70m bw
Twentieth Century (William Goetz, Raymond Griffith)
A girl schemes to seduce the man who has adopted her illegitimate son.
Batty mother-love melodrama.
w Ralph Graves *d* Lowell Sherman *ph* Barney McGill *m* Alfred Newman
☆ Loretta Young, Cary Grant, Jackie Kelk, Henry Travers, Russell Hopton, Andrew Tombes, Harry Green

Born to Be Bad
US 1950 70m bw
RKO (Robert Sparks)
An ambitious girl marries a millionaire but continues her affair with a novelist; finally both men discover her true character.
Tentative bad girl novelette, just about passable.
w Edith Sommer *novel All Kneeling* by Anne Parrish *d* Nicholas Ray *ph* Nicholas Musuraca *m* Frederick Hollander
☆ Joan Fontaine, Robert Ryan, Zachary Scott, Joan Leslie, Mel Ferrer
'Trash story too much for cast and director to live down.' – *Variety*

Born to Be Wild
US 1995 100m Technicolor
Warner/Fuji/Outlaw (Robert Newmyer, Jeffrey Silver)
A teenage delinquent makes a friend of a gorilla in a research laboratory who can communicate by sign language; when she is reclaimed by her unpleasant owner, he runs off with her.
Pleasant, undemanding entertainment; when attention flags, you can try to decide whether or not the ape is real or a large, electronically controlled puppet.
w John Bunzel, Paul Young *d* John Gray *ph* Donald M. Morgan *m* Mark Snow *pd* Roy Forge Smith *ed* Maryann Brandon
☆ Wil Horneff, Helen Shaver, Peter Boyle, Jean Marie Barnwell, John McGinley, Marvin J. McIntyre
'Contains all the requisite charms and values of a feel-good, politically correct child-animal story.' – *Variety*

Born to Dance *
US 1936 108m bw
MGM (Jack Cummings)
A sailor meets a girl in New York.
Well remembered musical with good numbers but a rather lame look.
w Jack McGowan, Sid Silvers, B. G. de Sylva *d* Roy del Ruth *ph* Ray June *m/ly* Cole Porter *md* Alfred Newman *ch* Dave Gould *ad* Cedric Gibbons *ed* Blanche Sewell
☆ *Eleanor Powell*, James Stewart, Virginia Bruce, Una Merkel, Sid Silvers, Frances Langford, Raymond Walburn, *Reginald Gardiner*, Buddy Ebsen
'Corking entertainment ... Cast is youthful, sight stuff is lavish, the specialities are meritorious, and as for songs, the picture is positively filthy with them.' – *Variety*
'The plot is a half-hearted reprise of *42nd Street* ... this time Eleanor Powell is the understudy who replaces the star ... and by the time she finishes the finale, you're overpowered and feel you should cheer.' – *Pauline Kael, 70s*
♫ 'I've Got You Under My Skin'; 'Easy to Love'; 'Rap Tap on Wood'; 'Swinging the Jinx Away'; 'Rolling Home'; 'Hey Babe Hey'; 'Love Me Love My Pekinese'
song 'I've Got You Under My Skin'; Dave Gould

Born to Kill *
US 1947 92m bw
RKO (Herman Schlom)
GB title: *Lady of Deceit*
A psychotic involves his new wife in his criminal pursuits.
Unusual, heavy-going, well acted melodrama.
w Eve Greene, Richard Macaulay *novel* James Gunn *d* Robert Wise *ph* Robert de Grasse *m* Paul Sawtell *md* C. Bakaleinikoff *ad* Albert D'Agostino, Walter E. Keller *ed* Les Millbrook *cos* Edward Stevenson
☆ Lawrence Tierney (Sam), Claire Trevor (Helen), Walter Slezak (Arnett), Phillip Terry (Fred), Elisha Cook Jnr (Marty), Audrey Long (Georgia), Isabell Jewell (Laury Palmer), Esther Howard (Mrs Kraft), Kathryn Card (Grace), Tony Barrett (Danny), Grandon Rhodes (Inspector Wilson)

Born to Kill: see *Cockfighter (1974)*

Born to Love
US 1931 84m bw
RKO
During World War I a nurse bears the child of an army pilot who is reported missing; but he turns up after she has married an English milord.
A useful compendium of thirties romantic clichés, quite attractively packaged.
w Ernest Pascal *d* Paul Stein *ph* John Mescall
☆ Constance Bennett, Joel McCrea, Paul Cavanagh, Frederick Kerr, Anthony Bushell, Louise Closser Hale, Edmund Breon, Mary Forbes

Born to Ride
US 1991 88m Technicolor
Warner/Inconvent (Fred Weintraub, Sandra Weintraub)
In 1939, a biker is hired by the army to teach the cavalry to switch from horses to motorbikes and rescue an American scientist from fascist kidnappers.
A curious attempt to combine the style of a 60s biker movie with a period war film; it very quickly runs out of gas.
w Michael Pardridge, Janice Hickey *d* Graham Baker *ph* Frank Gell *m* Shirley Walker *pd* Francis J. Pezza *ed* Alan Balsam
☆ John Stamos, John Stockwell, Teri Polo, Sandy McPeak, Kriss Kamm, Keith Cooke

Born to Run
US 1977 90m Technicolor
Walt Disney (Jerome Courtland)
In Australia at the turn of the century, a boy and his colt win a race to save the family farm.
Pleasant if unmemorable film that will appeal to young horse-lovers.
w Ed Jurist *novel* Walter D. Edmonds *d* Don Chaffey *ph* Geoff Burton *m* Ron Goodwin *ad* David Copping *ed* Peter Boita
☆ Tom Farley, Robert Bettles, Andrew McFarlane, Mary Ward, Julieanne Newbould, John Meillon

Born to Sing
US 1941 82m bw
Frederick Stephani/MGM
Kids put together a patriotic show.
Curiously undernourished family musical in the wake of Babes in Arms: *(qv) lots of talent but no star.*
w Franz Spencer, Harry Clork *d* Edward Ludwig
☆ Virginia Weidler, Douglas McPhail, Leo Gorcey, Ray McDonald, Rags Ragland, Sheldon Leonard, Margaret Dumont, Larry Nunn, Henry O'Neill

'A perfectly swell motion picture!'
Born Yesterday **
US 1950 103m bw
Columbia (S. Sylvan Simon)
The ignorant ex-chorus girl mistress of a scrap iron tycoon takes English lessons, falls for her tutor, and politically outmanoeuvres her bewildered lover.
Pleasant film version of a cast-iron box-office play, subtle and intelligent in all departments yet with a regrettable tendency to wave the flag.
w Albert Mannheimer *play* Garson Kanin *d George Cukor* *ph* Joseph Walker *m* Frederick Hollander
☆ *Judy Holliday, Broderick Crawford*, William Holden, Howard St John
† The original choices for the Judy Holliday role were Rita Hayworth and Jean Parker (who had played it on tour).
Judy Holliday
best picture; Albert Mannheimer; George Cukor

Born Yesterday
US 1993 100m Technicolor
Warner/Hollywood/Touchwood Pacific Partners I (D. Constantine Conte)
A journalist turns a millionaire's seemingly dumb chorus-girl mistress into a bright and intelligent woman, falling in love with her in the process.
A remake that does nothing but point up the superiority of the original and, in particular, Judy Holliday's priceless gift for comedy; the jokes are mistimed here and the romance is hardly in evidence.
w Douglas McGrath *play* Garson Kanin *d* Luis Mandoki *ph* Lajos Koltai *m* George Fenton *pd* Lawrence G. Paull *ed* Lesley Walker
☆ Melanie Griffith, John Goodman, Don Johnson, Edward Herrmann, Max Perlich, Benjamin C. Bradlee, Sally Quinn, William Frankfather, Fred Dalton Thompson
'This version has great casting, canny scripting and only fair direction, but still jollies along nicely.' – *Kim Newman, Empire*

The Borrower
US 1989 88m colour
Cannon/Vision (R. P. Sekon, Steven A. Jones)
An alien murderer is 'genetically devolved' and marooned on Earth; but his head keeps exploding so he replaces it by ripping off fresh human ones.
Hysterical gore-filled horror – so ineptly made that the body of the alien also changes whenever he gains a new head (since he is played by a different actor each time).
w Mason Nage, Richard Fire *d* John McNaughton *ph* Julio Macat, Robert New *m* Robert McNaughton, Ken Hale, Steven A. Jones *pd* Robert Henderson *ed* Elena Maganini
☆ Rae Dawn Chong, Don Gordon, Antonio Fargas, Tom Towles

'Small Is Awesome.'
The Borrowers **
GB 1997 83m Technicolor
Polygram/Working Title (Tim Bevan, Eric Fellner, Rachel Talalay)
The future of a family of tiny people, who live under the floorboards of a house, is threatened by an unscrupulous lawyer.
Clever, if hectic and noisy, children's film; it doesn't have the quiet humour of the original books, but nevertheless creates an odd, fanciful world that mixes English and American influences.
w Gavin Scott, John Camps *novels Mary Norton* *d* Peter Hewitt *ph* John Fenner, Trevor Brooker *m* Harry Gregson-Williams *pd* Gemma Jackson *ed* David Freeman, Annie Kocur
☆ John Goodman, Jim Broadbent, Mark Williams, Hugh Laurie, Bradley Pierce, Flora Newbigin, Tom Felton, Raymond Pickard, Celia Imrie
'A top-notch family film that welds English quaintness and eccentricity with high-tech effects.' – *Derek Elley, Variety*
'It blends old with new, irony with sincerity, and plain with fancy in such a way as to give post-modernism a good name and to entertain an audience of all ages.' – *Richard Williams, Guardian*

Borsalino *
France/Italy 1970 126m Eastmancolor
Adel-Marianne-Mars (Alain Delon)
In the thirties two Marseilles gangsters become firm friends and join forces.
Semi-spoof, but with 'real' blood, and period atmosphere laid on thick. The stars just about keep it ticking over.
w Jean-Claude Carrière, Claude Sautet, Jacques Deray, Jean Cau *d* Jacques Deray *ph* Jean-Jacques Tarbès *m* Claude Bolling
☆ Jean-Paul Belmondo, Alain Delon, Michel Bouquet, Catherine Rouvel, Corinne Marchand
'Rather like a Hollywood musical where someone has forgotten to insert the production numbers.' – *MFB*

Borsalino & Co (dubbed)
France/Italy/West Germany 1974 91m Eastmancolor
Adel/Comacico/Medusa/TIT (Maurice Jacquin, Alain Delon)
aka: *Blood on the Streets*
A fascist gangleader runs into trouble when he tries to take over Marseilles.
A violent thriller, a sequel to Borsalino *but lacking wit and substance. It was among the top ten box-office successes of the year in France.*
w Pascal Jardin *d* Jacques Deray *ph* Jean-Jacques Tarbès *m* Claude Bolling *ad* François de Lamothe *ed* Henri Lanoë
☆ Alain Delon, Catherine Rouvel, Riccardo Cucciolla, Daniel Ivernel

Bosambo: see *Sanders of the River*

The Boss *
US 1956 89m bw
UA/Frank N. Seltzer
After World War I, a ne'er-do-well becomes a corrupt small town political boss.
Low budgeted, complexly plotted, occasionally quite powerful and efficient crime melodrama.
w Ben L. Parry *d* Byron Haskin *ph* Hal Mohr *m* Albert Glasser
☆ *John Payne*, William Bishop, Gloria McGhee, Doe Avedon, Joe Flynn

Le Bossu **
France/Italy 1997 128m colour Panavision
Aliceleo/TFI/CGG Tiger/Gemini
aka: *On Guard!*
In the early 18th century, a swordsman rescues a baby girl from a murderous nobleman, and promises revenge.
Enjoyable period romp, a romantic swashbuckler performed with great panache.
w Jean Cosmos, Jerome Tonnerre, Philippe de Broca *novel* Paul Feval *d* Philippe de Broca *ph* Jean-François Robin *m* Philippe Sarde *ad* Bernard Vezat *ed* Henri Lanoë
☆ Daniel Auteuil, Fabrice Luchini, Vincent Perez, Marie Gillain, Yann Collette, Jean-François Stevenin, Didier Pain, Philippe Noiret
'Has an energy and a thrill that restore the swashbuckler to its rightful place in screen society.' – *Gaby Wood, Guardian*
† Paul Feval's novel has been filmed in France at least six times since 1914; notably starring Jean Marais in 1959.

Boston Blackie
An American second feature series made by Columbia between 1941 and 1949. There had been silent films about the character, a reformed crook and con man who has to solve crimes because he is suspected by the law.
Cheap but sometimes vigorous productions, they had a loyal following and starred Chester Morris with George E. Stone as his assistant The Runt.
The titles were:
1941 Meet Boston Blackie, Confessions of Boston Blackie
1942 Alias Boston Blackie, Boston Blackie Goes to Hollywood
1943 After Midnight with Boston Blackie
1944 One Mysterious Night
1945 Boston Blackie Booked on Suspicion, Boston Blackie's Rendezvous
1946 A Close Call for Boston Blackie, The Phantom Thief
1947 Boston Blackie and the Law
1948 Trapped By Boston Blackie
1949 Boston Blackie's Chinese Venture
† A television series starring Kent Taylor followed in 1951.

'Going mad ... going places ... going straight ... going nowhere...'
Boston Kickout *
GB 1996 105m colour
First Independent/Boston/Aramanth/Trijbits Worrell (Paul Hills, Danny Cannon)
A teenager manages to free himself from the delinquency and despair that motivate his unemployed friends.
Disaffection in the concrete wilderness of Stevenage makes for less than revelatory viewing, despite energetic performances from its talented cast.
w Paul Hills, Diane Whitley, Roberto Troni *d* Paul Hills *ph* Roger Bonnici *m* Robert Hartshorne *pd* Simon Elliott *ed* Melanie Adams
☆ John Simm, Emer McCourt, Marc Warren, Andrew Lincoln, Richard Hanson, Nathan Valente, Derek Martin, Vincent Phillips
'One of the best recent British films.' – *Danny Boyle*

The Boston Strangler **
US 1968 118m DeLuxe Panavision
TCF (Robert Fryer)
A semi-factual account of the sex maniac who terrified Boston in the mid-sixties.
Ambitious policier rendered less effective by pretentious writing and flashy treatment, including multi-image sequences; the investigation is more interesting than the psychoanalysis.
w Edward Anhalt *book* Gerold Frank *d* Richard Fleischer *ph* Richard Kline *m* Lionel Newman
☆ Henry Fonda, *Tony Curtis*, George Kennedy, Mike Kellin, Hurd Hatfield, Murray Hamilton, Sally Kellerman, Jeff Corey, George Voskovec

The Bostonians
GB 1984 122m colour
Merchant Ivory/WGBH/Rediffusion/Almi (Ismail Merchant)
In 1876 Boston, the cause of female emancipation wrecks Verena Tarrant's relationship with the determined Basil Ransome.
Another sluggish literary adaptation from the heavily meaningful Merchant Ivory team: the material, one feels, would have worked better as a TV bestseller.
w Ruth Prawer Jhabvala *novel* Henry James *d* James Ivory *ph* Walter Lassally *m* Richard Robbins *pd* Leo Austin
☆ Christopher Reeve, Vanessa Redgrave, Madeleine Potter, Jessica Tandy, Nancy Marchand, Linda Hunt, Wesley Addy
'Although it's not so limp as some of their other collaborations, they don't dramatize the material, and Ivory doesn't shape the performances.' – *Pauline Kael, New Yorker*
Vanessa Redgrave

Botany Bay
US 1952 94m Technicolor
Paramount (Joseph Sistrom)
On a convict ship in 1787 an American student unjustly accused of robbery clashes with the brutal captain for the favours of the only woman aboard.
Cramped and brutal action melodrama, a let-down considering the talent involved.
w Jonathan Latimer *novel* Charles Nordhoff and James Hall *d* John Farrow *ph* John Seitz *m* Franz Waxman
☆ James Mason, Alan Ladd, Patricia Medina, Cedric Hardwicke, Murray Matheson, Jonathan Harris

Both Ends of the Candle: see *The Helen Morgan Story*

Both Sides of the Law: see *Street Corner*

'They're not really criminals, but everybody's got to have a dream.'
Bottle Rocket *
US 1996 95m Technicolor
Columbia/Gracie/Boyle-Taylor (Polly Platt, Cynthia Hargrave)
Three young incompetents decide to embark on a life of crime.
Enjoyable and witty small-scale independent film that manages some original variations on a familiar theme.
w Owen C. Wilson, Wes Anderson *d* Wes Anderson *ph* Robert Yeoman *m* Mark Mothersbaugh *pd* David Wasco *ed* David Moritz
☆ Luke Wilson, Owen C. Wilson, Robert Musgrave, Andrew Wilson, Lumi Cavazos, James Caan, Teddy Wilson, Jim Ponds
'Full of surprising warmth and charm, unexpected plot turns and droll characters that bounce off each other in refreshing ways.' – *David Rooney, Variety*

The Bottom of the Bottle
US 1956 86m Eastmancolor Cinemascope
TCF (Buddy Adler)
GB title: *Beyond the River*
A wealthy attorney is visited by his drunken brother, on the run from the police and needing help to escape into Mexico.
Dreary drama in muddy colour, a clearly misguided enterprise.
w Sydney Boehm *novel* Georges Simenon *d* Henry Hathaway *ph* Lee Garmes *m* Leigh Harline
☆ Joseph Cotten, Van Johnson, Ruth Roman, Jack Carson

Bottoms Up
GB 1959 89m bw
ABPC (Mario Zampi)
A seedy schoolmaster passes off his bookie's son as an eastern prince.
Rambling film version of a successful TV series Whacko!, *written by Frank Muir and Denis Norden.*
w Michael Pertwee *d* Mario Zampi *ph* Gilbert Taylor *m* Stanley Black *ad* Ivan King *ed* Richard Best
☆ Jimmy Edwards, Arthur Howard, Martita Hunt, Sydney Tafler, Raymond Huntley, Reginald Beckwith, Vanda Hudson, Richard Briers

Le Boucher ***
France/Italy 1969 94m Eastmancolor
La Boétie/Euro International (André Génoves)
aka: *The Butcher*
Murders in a small French town are traced to the inoffensive-seeming young butcher who is courting the local schoolmistress.
Curious, mainly charming film which can't make up its mind whether to be an eccentric character study or a Hitchcock thriller, but has its moments as each.
wd Claude Chabrol ph Jean Rabier m Pierre Jansen
☆ Stéphane Audran, Jean Yanne, Antonio Passalia, Mario Beccaria
'A thriller, but a superlative example of the genre.' – *Times*

Boudu Sauvé des Eaux ***
France 1932 87m bw
Michel Simon/Jean Gehret
aka: *Boudu Saved from Drowning*
A scruffy tramp is not grateful for being rescued from suicide, and plagues the family who invite him to stay.
A minor classic of black comedy, interesting equally for its characterizations, its acting, and its film technique.
wd Jean Renoir play René Fauchois *ph* Marcel Lucien *m* from Raphael and Johann Strauss
☆ *Michel Simon, Charles Granval*, Marcelle Hainia, Séverine Lerczinska, Jean Dasté, Jacques Becker
'A beautifully rhythmed film that makes one nostalgic for the period when it was made.' – *New Yorker, 1977*
† Remade 1985, more or less, as *Down and Out in Beverly Hills* (qv).

Boudu Saved from Drowning: see *Boudu Sauvé des Eaux*

Bought
US 1931 70m bw
Warner
An ambitious working girl rebels against her slum existence and seeks a rich man.
Typical star vehicle of its time, with a predictable and unlikely change of heart for a finale.
w Charles Kenyon, Raymond Griffith *novel Jackdaw's Strut* by Harriet Henry *d* Archie Mayo *ph* Ray June
☆ Constance Bennett, Ben Lyon, Richard Bennett, Dorothy Peterson, Ray Milland, Doris Lloyd, Maude Eburne
'It's an entertainment in itself to be seated among women auditors during a Constance Bennett picture. They love that girl and she mustn't be worsted by men.' – *Variety*

Boulder Dam
US 1936 70m bw
Sam Bischoff/Warner
A mechanic accidentally kills a man and seeks anonymity among the crews building Boulder Dam.
Routine melo with an unusual setting.
w Sy Bartlett, Ralph Block *d* Frank McDonald
☆ Ross Alexander, Patricia Ellis, Lyle Talbot, Eddie Acuff, Henry O'Neill

Boulevard
US 1994 96m colour
Norstar (Peter Simpson, Ray Sager)
An abused wife becomes a prostitute and is victimized by a ruthless pimp.
Brutal thriller of little merit which makes the most of its frequent bouts of violence.
w Rae Dawn Chong *d* Penelope Buitenhuis *ph* David Frazee *m* Ian Thomas *pd* Jasna Stefanovic *ed* Bernadette Kelly
☆ Rae Dawn Chong, Lou Diamond Phillips, Lance Henriksen, Kari Wuhrer, Joel Bissonnette
'Suggests the importance of female camaraderie, but ultimately the violence against women is so excessive and exploitational that it's shocking to realise pic was written and directed by women.' – *Emanuel Levy, Variety*

Boulevard Nights
US 1979 102m colour
Warner (Bill Benenson)
Two Mexican-American brothers become involved with a street gang.
Well-meaning but uninvolving account of life lived at an inescapably violent level.
w Desmond Nakano *d* Michael Pressman *ph* John Bailey *m* Lalo Schifrin *pd* Jackson DeGovia *ed* Richard Halsey
☆ Richard Yniguez, Danny de La Paz, Marta Du Bois, James Victor, Betty Carvalho
'Earnest, uninspired.' – *Pauline Kael*

'Two strangers fall in love. One knew it wasn't by chance.'
Bounce *
US 2000 106m DeLuxe
Buena Vista/Miramax (Steve Golin, Michael Besman)
An advertising executive falls for the widow of a writer, whose death he inadvertently caused.
Sentimental romantic comedy that touches on the themes of guilt and sadness.
wd Don Roos *ph* Robert Elswit *m* Mychael Danna *pd* David Wasco *ed* David Codron *cos* Peter Mitchell
☆ Ben Affleck (Buddy Amaral), Gwyneth Paltrow (Abby Janello), Joe Morton (Jim Weller), Natasha Henstridge (Mimi), Tony Goldwyn (Greg Janello), Johnny Galecki (Seth), Alex D. Linz (Scott Janello), David Dorfman (Joey Janello), Jennifer Grey (Janice Guerrero), Caroline Aaron (Donna Heisen)
'Bounce is enjoyable. It could not be more predictable, but it could be a lot less pleasant.' – *Stanley Kauffmann*

'A Trust So Deep It Cuts Both Ways.'
'Stealing's a lot like sex. You've got two people who want the same thing.'
Bound **
US 1996 108m DeLuxe
Guild/Dino de Laurentiis/Summit/Newmarket (Andrew Lazar, Stuart Boros)
In Chicago, a lesbian thief falls for a gangster's mistress, and the pair decide to make a new life with the Mob's millions.
A lesbian twist on a familiar film noir narrative, delivered with a campily violent knowingness and much twirling of the camera.
wd Andy Wachowski, Larry Wachowski *ph* Bill Pope *m* Don Davis *pd* Eve Cauley *ed* Zach Staenberg
☆ Jennifer Tilly, Gina Gershon, Joe Pantoliano, John P. Ryan, Christopher Meloni, Richard C. Sarafian, Barry Kivel
'Who needs good taste when you can have this much fun? It's a blast.' – *Neil Norman, London Evening Standard*

Bound and Gagged – A Love Story
US 1992 94m colour
Metro Tartan/Cinescope (Dennis J. Mahoney)
A woman, married to a violent husband, is abducted by her female lover and her friend, a suicidal, unhappily married man who has lost the ability to speak.
A doggedly well-meaning movie about abusive and dependent behaviour that is also virtually unwatchable.
wd Daniel B. Appleby *ph* Dean Lent *m* William Murphy *pd* Dane Pizzuti Krogman *ed* Kaye Davis
☆ Ginger Lynn Allen, Karen Black, Chris Denton, Elizabeth Saltarrelli, Mary Ella Ross, Chris Mulkey
'This is not a good film. In fact, it is a pretty bad one – unevenly acted, scripted without much real wit and directed with the kind of careless abandon that sometimes passes for imagination when one's had too much of Hollywood's professional vacuity.' – *Derek Malcolm, Guardian*
'Resolutely unengaging, almost repugnant. It is muddily photographed and poorly scripted.' – *Caren Myers, Sight and Sound*
† The film has been described by its director, who is noted for his documentaries on similar subject-matter, as a labour of love, taking two and a half years to make.

Bound for Glory *
US 1976 148m DeLuxe Panavision
UA/Robert F. Blumhofe, Harold Leventhal
In 1936 Woody Guthrie leaves the Texas dust bowl for California, and after various hardships his musical talent is recognized.
Care and occasional beauty in the photography do not obscure memories of The Grapes of Wrath *(qv), which told much the same story more dramatically and succinctly, and with less earnestness and self-pity.*
w Robert Getchell *autobiography* Woody Guthrie *d* Hal Ashby *ph Haskell Wexler m* Leonard Rosenman *pd* Michael Haller *songs* Woody Guthrie
☆ David Carradine, Ronny Cox, Melinda Dillon, Gail Strickland, John Lehne
'The movie spends two-and-a-half hours and seven million dollars gazing wistfully at a little man and a big country, and it ends up prettily embalming them both.' – *Janet Maslin, Newsweek*
Haskell Wexler; Leonard Rosenman
best picture; Robert Getchell

Boundaries of the Heart *
Australia 1988 100m colour
IFM/Tra La La/FGH (Patrick Juillet)
In a dying desert town, where only 49 people remain, two unexpected visitors disrupt the life of a hotel owner and his unhappy daughter.
Intense, claustrophobic, domestic drama, of disappointments in life and love.
w Peter Yeldham *d* Lex Marinos *ph* David Sanderson, Geoff Simpson *m* Sharon Calcraft *pd* Melody Cooper *ed* Philip Howe

☆ Wendy Hughes, John Hargreaves, Norman Kaye, Max Cullen, Julie Nihill, Michael Siberry, John Clayton

The Bounty *
GB 1984 133m Technicolor Panavision
Dino de Laurentiis (Bernard Williams)

William Bligh is summoned before a court martial to explain the events leading up to the famous mutiny.
Rather independent version of the twice-told movie tale, and the least compelling of all. Despite the emphasis on character, only occasionally interesting.
w Robert Bolt *book Captain Bligh and Mr Christian* by Richard Hough *d* Roger Donaldson *ph* Arthur Ibbetson *m* Vangelis *pd* John Graysmark
☆ Anthony Hopkins (Bligh), Mel Gibson (Fletcher Christian), Laurence Olivier (Admiral Hood), Edward Fox (Captain Greetham), Daniel Day-Lewis (John Fryer), Bernard Hill (Cole), Liam Neeson (Churchill)
'A long voyage to nowhere.' – *Nick Roddick, MFB*
'This misshapen movie doesn't work as an epic – it doesn't have the scope or the emotional surge.' – *Pauline Kael, New Yorker*
'A great adventure, a lush romance, and a good movie.' – *Roger Ebert*

The Bounty Hunter
US 1954 79m WarnerColor
Warner (Samuel Bischoff)
Three respectable citizens are unmasked as masterminds behind a series of train robberies.
Predictable but enjoyable star action fare.
w Winston Miller *d* André de Toth *ph* Edwin DuPar *m* David Buttolph *ed* Clarence Kolster
☆ Randolph Scott (Jim Kipp), Dolores Dorn (Julie Spencer), Marie Windsor (Alice), Ernest Borgnine (Rachin), Howard Petrie (Sheriff Brand), Harry Antrim (Dr Spencer), Robert Keys (George Williams), Dub Taylor (Danvers), Phil Chambers (Ed), Tyler MacDuff (Vance), Paul Picerni (Jud), Archie Twitchell (Harrison)

The Bounty Hunters (dubbed) *
Italy 1970 106m Technicolor Techniscope
UA/PEA (Alberto Grimaldi)
original title: *Indio Black, Sai che ti Dico: Sei un Gran Figlio di…*
aka: *Adios, Sabata*
In Mexico in the 1860s, a time of revolution, a bounty hunter leads an expedition to steal a shipment of Austrian gold.
Dubbing turned the central character from Indio Black into Sabata, a role played by Lee Van Cleef in a successful movie made by the same director a year earlier; this time around, the result was more conventional and less enjoyable.
w Renato Izzo, Gianfranco Parolini *d* Frank Kramer (Gianfranco Parolini) *ph* Sandro Mancori *m* Bruno Nicolai *ad* Pierluigi Basile *ed* Gianfranco Parolini, Salvatore Avantario
☆ Yul Brynner, Dean Reed, Pedro Sanchez (Ignazio Spalla), Gerard Herter, Sal Borgese, Franco Fantasia, Gianni Rizzo
'Since the characterisations are quite lively and the message agreeably cynical … it is a pity that so much of the action is clogged up by that old stand-by of the Italian Western – extras falling off roofs in graceful death-falls.' – *Tom Milne, MFB*
† *Return of Sabata* (qqv), a sequel to the original *Sabata* (qqv), appeared in 1972.

The Bowery ***
US 1933 92m bw
Twentieth Century (Darryl F. Zanuck) (Raymond Griffith, William Goetz)
In 1890s New York, two boisterous rivals settle their differences after one has jumped off the Brooklyn Bridge for a bet.
Roistering saga of cross and double cross on the seamy side, splendidly vigorous in acting and treatment.
w Howard Estabrook, James Gleason
novel Michael L. Simmons, Bessie Roth Solomon *d Raoul Walsh ph* Barney McGill *m* Alfred Newman *ad Richard Day*
☆ Wallace Beery, George Raft, Pert Kelton, Jackie Cooper, Fay Wray, Herman Bing
'It delivers as entertainment. It should draw by itself, while the cast will be a considerable help.' – *Variety*
'A model of skilful reconstruction and ingenious research.' – *Times*
'Fairly reeking with authentic, rowdy, hurdy-gurdy atmosphere … a grand evening of fun for everybody.' – *Photoplay*
† *The Bowery* was the first production of Twentieth Century
†† Gable was sought for the Raft role, but proved unavailable.

Bowery at Midnight
US 1942 61m bw
Monogram
A criminal by night doubles as a mission proprietor by day.
Star horror cheapie with echoes of Lugosi's previous Dark Eyes of London *(qv).*
w Gerald Schnitzer *d* Wallace Fox
☆ Bela Lugosi, John Archer, Wanda McKay, Tom Neal, Dave O'Brien, Vince Barnett

The Bowery Boys
A cheap and cheerful series of American second features, immensely popular between 1946 and 1958, these adventures of a group of ageing Brooklyn layabouts had their origin in the 1937 film *Dead End*, from which the Dead End Kids graduated to other features at Warner: *Crime School, They Made Me a Criminal, Angels with Dirty Faces, Angels Wash their Faces* (qqv), etc. A couple of the 'boys' then defected to Universal and made *Little Tough Guy* (qv) and a series of half a dozen subsequent pictures; while in 1940 Monogram took a couple more and built up another group called the East Side Kids. In 1946 a formal merger of talent at Monogram consolidated the remaining members into the Bowery Boys. The members were Leo Gorcey, Huntz Hall, Bobby Jordan, Gabriel Dell (all from the Dead End Kids), Bernard Gorcey, David Gorcey, Billy Benedict, and Bennie Bartlett. The films are:
1946 In Fast Company, Bowery Bombshell, Live Wires, Spook Busters, Mr Hex
1947 Bowery Buckaroos, Hard Boiled Mahoney, News Hounds, Angels' Alley
1948 Jinx Money, Smuggler's Cove, Trouble Makers
1949 Angels in Disguise, Fighting Fools, Hold That Baby, Master Minds
1950 Blonde Dynamite, Blues Busters, Lucky Losers, Triple Trouble
1951 Bowery Battalion, Crazy over Horses, Ghost Chasers, Let's Go Navy
1952 Feudin' Fools, Here Come the Marines, Hold That Line, No Holds Barred
1953 Clipped Wings, Jalopy, Loose in London, Private Eyes
1954 The Bowery Boys Meet the Monsters, Jungle Gents, Paris Playboys
1955 Bowery to Bagdad, High Society, Jail Busters, Spy Chasers
1956 Dig That Uranium, Crashing Las Vegas, Fighting Trouble, Hot Shots
1957 Spook Chasers, Hold That Hypnotist, Looking for Danger
1958 Up in Smoke, In the Money

Bowery to Broadway
US 1944 94m bw
Universal (John Grant)
In the 1890s, a Bowery songstress makes it to the big time.
Simple-minded musical in which the drama has no drive and the guest stars are given inferior material.
w Joseph Lytton, Arthur T. Horman *d* Charles Lamont *ph* Charles Van Enger *md* Edward Ward
☆ Maria Montez, Turhan Bey, Susanna Foster, Jack Oakie, Donald Cook, Louise Allbritton, Andy Devine, Rosemary de Camp, Ann Blyth, Donald O'Connor, Peggy Ryan, Frank McHugh, Leo Carrillo, Evelyn Ankers, Mantan Moreland
♫ 'The Love Waltz'; 'There'll Always Be a Moon'; 'My Song of Romance'; 'Montevideo'; 'Coney Island Waltz' (plus standards)

'They're going to lie, cheat and steal—but in a nice way.'
Bowfinger *
US 1998 97m DeLuxe
Universal/Imagine (Brian Grazer)
An unsuccessful producer decides to use a superstar in his new film without the actor being aware of what's happening.
Mildly amusing comedy of Hollywood wheeling and dealing, with a few good jokes but rather more poor ones.
w Steve Martin *d* Frank Oz *ph* Ueli Steiger *m* David Newman *pd* Jackson DeGovia *ed* Richard Pearson
☆ Steve Martin (Bobby Bowfinger), Eddie Murphy (Kit Ramsey/Jiff Ramsey), Heather Graham (Daisy), Christine Baranski (Carol), Jamie Kennedy (Dave), Adam Alexi-Malle (Afrim), Kohl Sudduth (Slater), Barry Newman (Kit's Agent), Robert Downey Jnr (Jerry Renfro), Terence Stamp (Terry Stricter)
'A splendidly funny piece of work.' – *Empire*

'Some people have a hard time unwinding.'
Box of Moonlight *
US 1996 112m Technicolor
First Independent/Lakeshore/Largo/JVC/Lemon Sky (Marcus Viscidi, Thomas A. Bliss)
A boring construction foreman gives a lift to a young drop-out, who teaches him to relax and enjoy life moment by moment.
A somewhat unconvincing paean to spontaneity, as opposed to the mundane realities of life, but given a little boost by Turturro's performance as an uptight family man; it is less an example of carpe diem, though, and more caveat emptor.
wd Tom DiCillo *ph* Paul Ryan *m* Jim Farmer *pd* Thérèse DePrez *ed* Camilla Toniolo
☆ *John Turturro* (Al Fountain), Sam Rockwell (Kid), Catherine Keener (Floatie Dupre), Lisa Blount (Purlene Dupre), Annie Corley (Deb Fountain), Rica Martens (Doris), Ray Aranha (Soapy), Alexander Goodwin (Bobby Fountain), Dermot Mulroney (Wick)

Boxcar Bertha *
US 1972 88m DeLuxe
AIP (Roger Corman)
In early thirties Arkansas, an unhappy girl falls in with gangsters and train robbers.
Competent imitation of Bonnie and Clyde *(qv).*
w Joyce H. and John W. Corrington *d Martin Scorsese ph* John Stephens *m* Gib Guilbeau, Thad Maxwell
☆ Barbara Hershey, David Carradine, Barry Primus, Bernie Casey, John Carradine

'Love is always worth fighting for.'
The Boxer **
GB/Ireland/US 1997 113m Technicolor
Universal/Hell's Kitchen (Jim Sheridan, Arthur Lappin)
A former IRA prisoner takes up his old profession of boxing and opens a gym for young hopefuls with the aid of an alcoholic trainer.
A tough and gritty drama about controlled violence as redemption. The fight sequences have an authentic, sweaty feel about them; the rest is too schematic in its condemnation of bigotry to convince.
w Jim Sheridan, Terry George *d* Jim Sheridan *ph* Chris Menges *m* Gavin Friday, Maurice Seezer *pd* Brian Morris *ed* Gerry Hambling
☆ Daniel Day-Lewis, Emily Watson, Brian Cox, Ken Stott, Gerard McSorley, Eleanor Methven, Ciaran Fitzgerald, Kenneth Cranham
'An involving but rather prosaic report from the Belfast front with a melancholy undertow of romantic yearning.' – *Todd McCarthy, Variety*
† Daniel Day-Lewis spent several years in preparation for his role, and was trained by former world champion boxer, and Irish hero, Barry McGuigan.

'A Deep Dark Obsession That Bares A Woman's Body And A Man's Soul.'
Boxing Helena
US 1993 105m Technicolor Panavision
Entertainment/Main Line (Carl Mazzocone)
A surgeon seemingly takes advantage of an accident to amputate the legs and arms of the woman who rejected his love.
A tedious, neurotic tale that would have benefited from hefty cuts; it is unable to sustain interest in either its minimal plot or its unsympathetic characters.
wd Jennifer Chambers Lynch *story* Philippe Caland *ph* Frank Byers *m* Graeme Revell *ad* Paul Huggins *ed* David Finfer
☆ Julian Sands, Sherilyn Fenn, Bill Paxton, Art Garfunkel, Betsy Clark, Kurtwood Smith
'Not only is the script unbelievably bad – packed with clumsy, forced and often banal dialogue – but some of the acting has to be seen to be believed.' – *Amanda Lipman, Sight and Sound*
'Just might have passed muster as a 15-minute film school gag. With performances as inept as the script, the self-parody cannot be passed off as intentional.' – *David Robinson, The Times*
'Simply cannot be taken seriously, in a large part because it takes itself so seriously that we can only respond to it with gales of derisive crowing.' – *Michael Atkinson, Movieline*
† The film was most memorable for what happened off-screen, when Kim Basinger was sued for changing her mind over her agreement to star in it, and ordered to pay some $8 million in damages. In a settlement reached in 1995, she agreed to pay around $3 million.

A Boy a Girl and a Bike
GB 1949 92m bw
Gainsborough (Ralph Keene)
Romantic jealousies arise between members of a Yorkshire cycling club.
Mild comedy drama with the advantage of fresh air locations.
w Ted Willis *d* Ralph Smart *ph* Ray Elton *m* Kenneth Pakeman
☆ John McCallum, Honor Blackman, Patrick Holt, Diana Dors, Leslie Dwyer, Thora Hird, Anthony Newley, Megs Jenkins, Maurice Denham

'A rather kinky tale of survival.'
A Boy and His Dog *
US 1975 89m colour Techniscope
LG Jaf (Alvy Moore)
While searching for food in an apocalyptic future, a young man and his more intelligent telepathic dog find an apparently Utopian community that needs masculine input.
Quirky science fiction, not to be taken too seriously, and managing a surprise ending.
wd L. Q. Jones *story* Harlan Ellison *ph* John Arthur Morrill *m* Tim McIntire *pd* Ray Boyle *ed* Scott Conrad
☆ Don Johnson, Susanne Benton, Jason Robards, Ron Feinberg, Tim McIntire, Charles McGraw

The Boy and the Bridge
GB 1959 91m bw
Xanadu (Kevin McClory)
A boy who believes he has committed a murder hides in the ramparts of Tower Bridge.
This tiny fable adds up to very weak entertainment, despite inventive photography, because it has virtually no plot development.
w Geoffrey Orme, Kevin McClory, Desmond O'Donovan *d* Kevin McClory *ph Ted Scaife* *m* Malcolm Arnold
☆ Ian MacLaine, Liam Redmond, James Hayter, Norman MacOwan, Geoffrey Keen, Jack MacGowran, Royal Dano, Rita Webb

The Boy and the Pirates
US 1960 84m Eastmancolor
Perceptovision
United Artists
A small boy finds an old bottle on the seashore, wishes he could live in pirate days, and hey presto…
Modest juvenile fantasy on the lines of The Wizard of Oz *(qv) but without the talent.*
w Lillie Hayward, Jerry Sackheim *d* Bert I. Gordon
☆ Charles Herbert, Susan Gordon, Murvyn Vye, Paul Guilfoyle

A Boy Called Hate
US 1995 98m CFI color
Pacific/J&M
A young biker rescues a girl from rape by shooting her assailant, and is soon being sought by the police for murder.
Trashy story of two young killers on the run, featuring a great deal of moody teenage posturing, in a sub-

James Dean manner, and lacking any moral or wider social dimension.
wd Mitch Marcus *ph* Paul Holahan *m* Pray for Rain
☆ Scott Caan, Missy Crider, Elliott Gould, Adam Beach, James Caan

'No more bubble bath, she screamed!'
Boy, Did I Get a Wrong Number
US 1966 99m DeLuxe
UA/Edward Small (George Beck)
Trying to phone his wife, an estate agent gets involved with a runaway actress.
Lifeless and generally resistible star comedy, the first of several hard and unfunny vehicles for an ageing Bob Hope seeming to hark back to the least attractive aspects of burlesque rather than the sympathetic wisecracking which suits him best.
w Burt Styler, Albert E. Lewin, George Kennett *d* George Marshall *ph* Lionel Lindon *m* Richard Lasalle *ly* By Dunham
☆ Bob Hope, Elke Sommer, Phyllis Diller, Marjorie Lord, Cesare Danova, Benny Baker

The Boy Friend *
GB 1971 125m Metrocolor Panavision
MGM/Russflix (Ken Russell)
On a wet Wednesday afternoon in Portsmouth in the late twenties, a tatty company with backstage problems puts on an empty-headed musical.
Russell the mastermind effectively destroys Sandy Wilson's charming period pastiche, sending up all the numbers (via badly staged dream sequences on the wrong shape screen) in a Busby Berkeley manner which had not yet been invented. Moments do work, but a non-star doesn't help, and the whole thing is an artistic disaster of some significance both to Russell's career and to the cinema of the early seventies.
wd Ken Russell *musical play* Sandy Wilson *ph* David Watkin *md* Ian Whittaker, Peter Greenwell, Peter Maxwell Davies *pd* Tony Walton
☆ Twiggy, Christopher Gable, *Max Adrian*, Tommy Tune, Barbara Windsor, Moyra Fraser, Bryan Pringle, Vladek Sheybal, *Antonia Ellis*, *Glenda Jackson*
'The glittering, joyless numbers keep coming at you: you never get any relief from Russell's supposed virtuosity.' – *New Yorker, 1977*
'The acting was too broad, the gags too laboured and the pacing too slow.' – *Ken Russell*
Ian Whittaker, Peter Greenwell, Peter Maxwell Davies

The Boy from Barnardo's: see *Lord Jeff*

The Boy from Mercury *
GB/France 1996 87m colour
Blue Dolphin/Mercurian/Blue Dahlia/Blue Rose/Jo Manuel (Marina Hughes)
In Ireland in the late 50s, a young boy fantasizes that he is from the planet Mercury and has been sent to investigate the Earth.
Nostalgic, gently humorous account of childhood, in which small events assume large proportions.
wd Martin Duffy *ph* Seamus Deasy *m* Stephen McKeon *pd* Tom Conroy *ed* John Victor Smith
☆ Rita Tushingham, Tom Courtenay, Hugh O'Conor, James Hickey, Ian McElhinney, Joanne Gerard

The Boy from Oklahoma *
US 1953 88m Warnercolor
Warner (David Weisbart)
A genial plainsman studying law becomes sheriff of a small town and uncovers its mayor as a killer.
Modest, pleasing Western with the star imitating his father.
w Frank Davis, Winston Miller *d* Michael Curtiz *ph* Robert Burks *m* Max Steiner
☆ Will Rogers Jnr, Nancy Olson, Lon Chaney Jnr, Anthony Caruso, Wallace Ford, Clem Bevans, Merv Griffin

The Boy in Blue
Canada 1986 97m DeLuxe
TCF/ICC/Denis Heroux/John Kemeny
In the 1870s, a young ne'er-do-well Canadian oarsman becomes a world champion.
The true story of Ned Hanlan, straightforwardly and unremarkably told.
w Douglas Bowie *idea* John Trent *d* Charles Jarrott *ph* Pierre Mignot *m* Roger Webb *pd* William Beeton *ed* Rit Wallis
☆ Nicolas Cage, Christopher Plummer, Cynthia Dale, David Naughton, Sean Sullivan, Melody Anderson

Boy Meets Girl *
US 1938 86m bw
Warner (George Abbott)
Two crazy Hollywood scenario writers make a star of an infant yet unborn.
Freewheeling film version of a hilarious play: fine crazy comedy and excellent Hollywood satire.
w Bella and Sam Spewack play Bella and Sam Spewack *d* Lloyd Bacon *ph* Sol Polito *m* Leo Forbstein
☆ *James Cagney, Pat O'Brien*, Marie Wilson, Ralph Bellamy, Frank McHugh, Dick Foran, Bruce Lester, Ronald Reagan, James Stephenson
'Satisfactory, but not socko.' – *Variety*
'It bounces from one hilarious absurdity to another with all the resilience of a rubber ball.' – *MFB*

Boy Meets Girl: see *A Lover and His Lass (1975)*

Boy Meets Girl *
France 1984 100m bw
Other Cinema/Abilene (Patricia Moraz)
An aimless youth ends his romance with one girl and starts a new one with another.
A low-budget movie, made by its writer-director at the age of 22, of interest mainly for its photography of Paris by night.
wd Leos Carax *ph* Jean-Yves Escoffier *m* Jacques Pinault *ad* Serge Marzolff, Jean Bauer *ed* Nelly Meunier, Francine Sandberg
☆ Denis Lavant, Mireille Périer, Carroll Brooks, Elie Poicard, Anna Baldaccini

Boy of the Streets
US 1937 75m bw
Monogram
A city youngster falls in with racketeers.
Ho-hum Dead End melodrama.
w Scott Darling, Gilson Brown *d* William Nigh
☆ Jackie Cooper, Maureen O'Connor, Kathleen Burke, Marjorie Main, Robert Emmett O'Connor
'Will do biz for independents … easily Monogram's most ambitious production effort to date.' – *Variety*

Boy on a Dolphin *
US 1957 111m Eastmancolor Cinemascope
TCF (Samuel G. Engel)
A Greek girl diver discovers a sunken artifact of great value and the news spreads to an American archaeologist and an unscrupulous collector.
Likeable, sunswept Mediterranean adventure romance marred by the miscasting of the male lead.
w Ivan Moffat, Dwight Taylor *novel* David Divine *d* Jean Negulesco *ph Milton Krasner* *m* Hugo Friedhofer *md* Lionel Newman
☆ Alan Ladd, Sophia Loren, *Clifton Webb*, Laurence Naismith, Alexis Minotis, Jorge Mistral
Hugo Friedhofer

Boy Slaves
US 1938 70m bw
RKO
A boy leaves home and ends up in a forced labour camp.
Topical preachment drama which kicked up a bit of dust at the time.
w Albert Bein, Ben Orkow *d* P. J. Wolfson
☆ Anne Shirley, Roger Daniel, James McCallion, Alan Baxter.
'Devoid of essential entertainment factors for general theatre showings.' – *Variety*

A Boy Ten Feet Tall: see *Sammy Going South*

Boy Trouble
US 1939 75m bw
Paramount
A small-towner finds his life upset when his wife adopts two orphans.
Sentimental comedy which caused a few tears to trickle.
w Laura and S. J. Perelman *story* Lloyd Corrigan, Monte Brice *d* George Archainbaud
☆ *Charles Ruggles*, Mary Boland, Donald O'Connor, Joyce Matthews, Billy Lee, Andrew Tombes
'Good old hokum with an emotional wallop … Exhibitors can use more pictures of this type.' – *Variety*

The Boy Who Could Fly
US 1986 114m DeLuxe Panavision
TCF/Lorimar (Gary Adelson)
After the death of their father, two children move with their mother to a new home and make friends with the boy next door, who believes that he can fly.
A family drama, about the problems of coping with loss, that moves into fantasy without altogether losing its slight charm and effectiveness.
wd Nick Castle *ph* Steven Poster, Adam Holender *m* Bruce Broughton *pd* Jim Bissell *ed* Patrick Kennedy
☆ Lucy Deakins, Jay Underwood, Bonnie Bedelia, Fred Savage, Colleen Dewhurst, Fred Gwynne, Mindy Cohen, Janet MacLachlan, Jason Priestley

'Those who don't believe – are dead!'
The Boy Who Cried Werewolf
US 1973 93m Technicolor
Universal/RFK
On a camping trip, a boy and his father are attacked by a werewolf, and later on Dad starts acting mighty strange…
Disappointingly straight rewrite of the old hokum.
w Bob Homel *d* Nathan Juran *ph* Michael P. Joyce *m* Ted Stovall *ed* Barton Hayes
☆ Kerwin Mathews (Robert Bridgestone), Elaine Devry (Sandy Bridgestone), Scott Sealey (Richie Bridgestone), Robert J. Wilke (Sheriff), Susan Foster (Jenny), Jack Lucas (Harry), Bob Homel (Bother Christopher), George Gaynes (Dr Marderosian)
'Pretty much a matter of stilted dialogue and thumping shocks.' – *Tom Milne, MFB*

The Boy Who Had Everything
Australia 1985 94m colour
Multi Films/Alfred Roads (Richard Mason, Julia Overton)
In 1965, as Australian troops are about to be sent to Vietnam a university freshman submits to initiation rites but renounces his mother and his future.
Angry, rather muddled character study which seems to be drawn from life but doesn't know what moral to point.
wd Stephen Wallace *ph* Geoff Burton *m* Ralph Schneider
☆ Jason Connery, Diane Cilento, Laura Williams, Lewis Fitz-Gerald

The Boy Who Stole a Million
GB 1960 81m bw
British Lion/Fanfare/George H. Brown
A young page in a Spanish bank 'borrows' some money to help his father but finds Dad, police and crooks all after him.
Half-hearted attempt at a British Bicycle Thieves (qv), oddly set in Spain and never quite managing to convince or interest us.
w John Eldridge, Charles Crichton *story* Neils West Larsen, Antonio de Leon *d* Charles Crichton *ph* Douglas Slocombe *m* Tristram Cary *ad* Maurice Carter *ed* Peter Bezencenet
☆ Maurice Reyna (Paco), Virgilio Teixeira (Miguel), Harold Kasket (Luis), George Coulouris (Bank Manager), Edwin Richfield (Commissionaire), Curt Christian (Currito), Bill Nagy (Police Chief), Marianne Benet (Maria), Cyril Shaps (Bank Clerk), Warren Mitchell (Pedro)

The Boy with Green Hair
US 1948 82m Technicolor
RKO (Stephen Ames)
When he hears that his parents were killed in an air raid, a boy's hair turns green; other war orphans encourage him to parade himself publicly as an image of the horror and futility of war.
Muddled, pretentious and unpersuasive fantasy, typical of this producer's do-goodery. One of those oddities which make Hollywood endearing, but not very entertaining apart from Pat O'Brien's garrulous grandpa.
w Ben Barzman, Alfred Lewis Levitt *story* Betsy Beaton *d* Joseph Losey *ph* George Barnes *m* Leigh Harline
☆ Dean Stockwell, Pat O'Brien, Robert Ryan, Barbara Hale

The Boyars' Plot: see *Ivan the Terrible*

The Boys
GB 1962 123m bw Cinemascope
Gala/Columbia (Sidney J. Furie)
Four boys are on trial for killing a garage attendant.
Elaborate courtroom drama with flashbacks, stars for counsel, a tricksy director, and about forty minutes too much footage.
w Stuart Douglass *d* Sidney J. Furie *ph* Gerald Gibbs *m* The Shadows
☆ Richard Todd, Robert Morley, Felix Aylmer, Dudley Sutton, Ronald Lacey, Tony Garnett, Jess Conrad, Wilfrid Brambell, Allan Cuthbertson, Colin Gordon

Boys
US 1996 89m Technicolor
Polygram/Interscope (Peter Frankfurt, Paul Feldsher, Erica Huggins)
A frustrated high-school student discovers a mysterious young woman, who is unconscious after a fall from her horse, and takes her back to his room.
Thin and vapid tale of a mixed-up teenager, almost totally lacking in either content or interest; clumsily structured, it fails to reach a satisfactory or acceptable conclusion.
wd Stacy Cochran *story Twenty Minutes* by James Salter *ph* Robert Elswit *m* Stewart Copeland *pd* Dan Bishop *ed* Camilla Toniolo
☆ Winona Ryder, Lukas Haas, John C. Reilly, James LeGros, Skeet Ulrich, Spencer Vrooman, Charlie Hofheimer, Bill Sage, Jessica Harper
'Never advances beyond banality, and the cop-out ending is both glib and unreal.' – *George Perry, Sunday Times*

The Boys *
Australia 1998 84m Movielab
Globe/Arenafilm/AFC (Robert Connolly, John Maynard)
Released from prison, a violent man returns home to disrupt family life.
Chilling portrait of a manipulative and aggressive psychopath; by the end we are no wiser, though more appalled, than we were at the beginning.
w Stephen Sewell *play* Gordon Graham *d* Rowan Woods *ph* Tristan Milani *m* The Necks *pd* Luigi Pittorino *ed* Nick Meyers
☆ David Wenham, Toni Collette, Lynette Curran, John Polson, Anthony Hayes, Jeanette Cronin, Anna Lise, Pete Smith

'A True Story About Finding The Courage To Be Yourself.'
Boys Don't Cry ***
US 1999 118m DeLuxe
TCF/Killer Films (Jeffrey Sharp, John Hart, Eva Kolodner, Christine Vachon)
In Nebraska in the early 90s, a girl decides to live as a boy.
Abrasive, jolting drama of shock and outrage, more disturbing than the grisliest horror movie because, based on fact, it exposes a desperation at the heart of America.
w Kimberly Peirce, Andy Bienen *d Kimberly Peirce* *ph* Jim Denault *m* Nathan Larson *pd* Michael Shaw *ed* Lee Percy, Tracy Granger
☆ *Hilary Swank* (Brandon Teena), *Chloe Sevigny* (Lana), Peter Sarsgaard (John), Brendan Sexton III (Tom), Alison Folland (Kate), Alicia Goranson (Candace), Matt McGrath (Lonny), Rob Campbell (Brian), Jeannetta Arnette (Lana's Mom)
'Audacious, accomplished pic should play well with open minded viewers seeking edgy, mature fare.' – *Emanuel Levy, Variety*
'A delicately conceived, fearless movie.' – *David Denby, New Yorker*
'Scorches the screen like a prairie fire.' – *J. Hoberman, Village Voice*
Hilary Swank
Chloe Sevigny

'94 men must die to keep alive a dream – or a nightmare!'

The Boys from Brazil *

US/GB 1978 124m DeLuxe
ITC/Producer Circle (Martin Richards, Stanley O'Toole)

A renegade Nazi in hiding has a sinister plot to reconquer the world.
Suspense fantasy firmly based on a gripping book; excellent performances, but a shade too long.
w Heywood Gould *novel* Ira Levin *d* Franklin Schaffner *ph* Henri Decaë *m* Jerry Goldsmith *pd* Gil Parrando
☆ *Gregory Peck, Laurence Olivier*, James Mason, Lilli Palmer, Uta Hagen, Steve Guttenberg, Denholm Elliott, Rosemary Harris, John Dehner, John Rubinstein, Anne Meara, David Hurst, Michael Gough
Jerry Goldsmith; Laurence Olivier

The Boys from Fengkuei **

Taiwan 1983 104m colour
Evergreen
original title: *Feng-Kuei-Lai-Te Jen*
aka: *All the Youthful Days*
In search of excitement, three youths move to the city from the fishing village where they were born.
Absorbingly detailed drama of the young coming to terms with the pleasures and problems of adult life.
w Chu T'ien-wen *d* Hou Hsiao-hsien *ph* Ch'en K'un'hou
☆ Niu Cheng-tse, Lin Xiuling, To Tsung-hua, Chang Shih

The Boys from Syracuse *

US 1940 74m bw
Universal (Jules Levey)
The Comedy of Errors with modern wisecracks, and a few songs.
Predictable well-drilled confusion arises from master and slave having identical twins, but the general tone is a bit flat for an adaptation from a hilarious Broadway success. Still, the songs are lively and the chariot race finale shows spirit.
w Leonard Spigelgass, Charles Grayson, Paul Gerard Smith *play* George Abbott, William Shakespeare *d* A. Edward Sutherland *ph* Joseph Valentine *m* Frank Skinner *m/ly* Richard Rodgers, Lorenz Hart *md* Charles Previn *ad* Jack Otterson *ed* Milton Carruth
☆ Allan Jones, Joe Penner, Charles Butterworth, Rosemary Lane, Irene Hervey, Martha Raye, Alan Mowbray
† The writing credit on screen ends: 'After a play by William Shakespeare ... long, long after!
♫ 'Who Are You?'; 'This Can't be Love'; 'Falling in Love with Love'; 'The Greeks Have No Word for It'; 'Sing for Your Supper'; 'He and She'
John Otterson; special effects (John P. Fulton), sound (Bernard B. Brown, Joseph Lapis)

The Boys in Blue

GB 1983 91m colour
Elstree/Rank
Village policemen catch art thieves.
Horribly incompetent remake of Ask a Policeman *(qv), with a totally untalented star team.*
wd Val Guest
☆ Tommy Cannon, Bobby Ball, Suzanne Danielle, Roy Kinnear, Eric Sykes, Jack Douglas, Edward Judd, Jon Pertwee, Arthur English
'The perfect antidote to sweeping claims about the British renaissance.' – *Geoff Brown, MFB*

Boys in Brown

GB 1949 84m bw
Gainsborough (Anthony Darnborough)
Life in a Borstal institution.
The stars make elderly boys, but Jack Warner is a cuddly governor. Boring and unpersuasive non-documentary fiction in Britain's most tiresome style.
wd Montgomery Tully *play* Reginald Beckwith *ph* Gordon Lang, Cyril Bristow *m* Doreen Carwithen
☆ Jack Warner, Dirk Bogarde, Michael Medwin, Jimmy Hanley, Richard Attenborough, Alfie Bass, Barbara Murray, Thora Hird
† Made by the Independent Frame method, which blended real backgrounds with studio sets.

The Boys in Company C

Hong Kong 1977 125m Technicolor Panavision
Golden Harvest (Andre Morgan)

Five marines find their lives changed by the Vietnam war.
Crude action melodrama.
w Rick Natkin, Sidney J. Furie *d* Sidney J. Furie *ph* Godfrey Godar *m* Jaime Mendoza-Nava
☆ Stan Shaw, Andrew Stevens, James Canning, Michael Lembeck, Craig Wasson, James Whitmore Jnr
'Laden with barrack room dialogue and played at the enlisted man's level.' – *Variety*
'An exploitation war movie, like dirty TV.' – *New Yorker*

The Boys in the Band *

US 1970 120m Technicolor
Cinema Center/Leo (Mart Crowley, Kenneth Utt)

Tempers fray and true selves are revealed when a heterosexual is accidentally invited to a homosexual party.
Careful but claustrophobic filming of a Broadway play, which at the screen's closer quarters becomes overpowering well before the end.
w Mart Crowley *play* Mart Crowley *d* William Friedkin *ph* Arthur J. Ornitz *m* none
☆ Leonard Frey, Kenneth Nelson, Cliff Gorman, Frederick Combs, Reuben Greene, Robert La Tourneaux, Laurence Luckinbill, Keith Prentice, Peter White
'They crack jokes while their hearts are breaking.' – *New Yorker*

Boys' Night Out

US 1962 115m Metrocolor Cinemascope
MGM/Filmways (Martin Ransohoff)
Three married men and their bachelor friend share a flat and a 'mistress'.
Would-be saucy comedy in which nothing sexy ever happens and the helpless players are as witless as the script.
w Ira Wallach *d* Michael Gordon *ph* Arthur E. Arling *m* Frank de Vol
☆ James Garner, Kim Novak, Tony Randall, Howard Duff, Howard Morris, Oscar Homolka, Janet Blair, Patti Page, Jessie Royce Landis

Boys on the Beach: see *Le Ciel, Les Oiseaux... Et Ta Mere!*

Boys on the Side

US 1995 117m Technicolor Super 35
Warner/Canal/Regency/Alcor (Arnon Milchan, Steven Reuther, Herbert Ross)

Three women – a lesbian musician, a heterosexual with AIDS and the pregnant, confused girlfriend of a drug dealer – go on the road together.
Manipulative twaddle, mired in sentimentality and remote from reality, a modern version of a woman's picture, all female-bonding and buddies together, and extremely old-fashioned under its slick, hip surface.
w Don Roos *d* Herbert Ross *ph* Donald E. Thorin *m* David Newman *pd* Ken Adam *ed* Michael R. Miller
☆ Whoopi Goldberg, Mary Louise Parker, Drew Barrymore, Matthew McConaughey, James Remar, Billy Wirth, Anita Gillette
'Lush, weepy, topically correct, emotional button pusher – a chick flick for women who sing "We Are Family" too much.' – *Lisa Schwarzbaum, Entertainment Weekly*

'More laughs than Laurel and Hardy! More thrills than *Test Pilot!* More tears than *Captains Courageous!*'

Boys Town *

US 1938 93m bw
MGM (John W. Considine Jnr)

The story of Father Flanagan and his school for juvenile delinquents.
Well-made, highly successful, but sentimental crowd pleaser.
w John Meehan, Dore Schary *story* Eleanore Griffin, Dore Schary *d* Norman Taurog *ph* Sidney Wagner *m* Edward Ward
☆ *Spencer Tracy, Mickey Rooney*, Henry Hull, Gene Reynolds, Sidney Miller, Frankie Thomas, Bobs Watson, Tommy Noonan
'A production that should build goodwill for the whole industry.' – *Variety*
Eleanore Griffin, Dore Schary; Spencer Tracy
best picture; John Meehan, Dore Schary; Norman Taurog

Boys Will Be Boys **

GB 1935 75m bw
Gaumont/Gainsborough (Michael Balcon)

An incompetent headmaster thwarts a jewel robber.
The first recognizable Will Hay vehicle, based in part on J. B. Morton's Narkover sketches.
w Will Hay, Robert Edmunds *d* William Beaudine *ph* Charles Van Enger *m* Louis Levy
☆ *Will Hay*, Gordon Harker, Jimmy Hanley, Davy Burnaby, Norma Varden, Claude Dampier, Charles Farrell, Percy Walsh
'It is hard to see how his distinctive sketch writing could have found a satisfactory screen equivalent. Nevertheless, a good augury of the films to come.' – *Ray Seaton and Roy Martin, 1978*

'Increase The Peace.'

Boyz N The Hood **

US 1991 112m DeLuxe
Columbia TriStar (Steve Nicolaides)

Young blacks try to survive in the hostile urban world of Los Angeles gangs.
Episodic in form and over-schematic in its depiction of social difficulties, particularly those caused by absentee fathers, but it holds one's interest throughout.
wd John Singleton *ph* Charles Mills *m* Stanley Clarke *ad* Bruce Bellamy *ed* Bruce Cannon
☆ Ice Cube, Cuba Gooding Jnr, Morris Chestnut, Larry Fishburne, Nia Long, Tyra Ferrell
'An absorbing, smartly made dramatic encyclopedia of problems and ethics in the black community, 1991.' – *Variety*
'Conveys a vivid sense of the dangers, both physical and emotional, of day-to-day existence in this ravaged urban environment.' – *New Yorker*
John Singleton (as director); John Singleton (screenplay)

The Brady Bunch Movie *

US 1995 88m DeLuxe
Paramount (Sherwood Schwartz, Lloyd Schwartz, David Kirkpatrick)

In a troubled modern-day Los Angeles, the Brady family behave as if they were still living in the mid-70s, displaying sweetness and good behaviour on every possible occasion.
Pleasantly amusing comedy that exploits the gap between the fantasy of family relationships and the reality, though it will mean most to viewers of the original TV sitcom.
w Laurice Elehwany, Rick Copp, Bonnie Turner, Terry Turner *d* Betty Thomas *ph* Mac Ahlberg *m* Guy Moon *pd* Steven Jordan *ed* Peter Teschner
☆ Shelley Long, Gary Cole, Michael McKean, Jean Smart, Henriette Mantel, Christopher Daniel Barnes, Christine Taylor, Jennifer Elise Cox, Jesse Lee, Olivia Hack, RuPaul
'It's a very good-humoured, unspiteful movie, and mounted with great energy. Everyone acts in that manic, twitchy, over-emphatic manner of bad US sitcoms, while Betty Thomas directs with speed and wit.' – *Sheila Johnston, Independent*
'This is not a very good film, being less well-written than it might have been and directed as if we are all as moronic as the people in the movie.' – *Derek Malcolm, Guardian*
† *The Brady Bunch*, created by Sherwood Schwartz, was a clean-cut television sitcom that ran from 1969 to 1974 and was followed by an animated version, *The Brady Kids* (1972–74). The family returned for *The Brady Bunch Hour* in 1977 and *The Bradys* in 1990 and also made several TV movies. None of TV's Brady Bunch appeared in the film.

The Brain: see *Vengeance (1962)*

The Brain

France/US 1969 115m colour Franscope
Paramount (Alain Poire)
original title: *Le Cerveau*
A British colonel leads an international crew in an attempt to rob NATO.
Exhausting and generally misfiring international crook comedy.
w Gérard Oury, Marcel Julian, Daniele Thompson *d* Gérard Oury *ph* Vladimir Ivanov, Armand Thirard *m* Georges Delerue
☆ David Niven, Jean-Paul Belmondo, Bourvil, Eli Wallach, Silvia Monti

Brain Damage

US 1988 90m colour
Palace/Frank Henenlotter (Edgar Levins)

A man is provided with hallucinatory pleasures in return for helping a brain-eating parasite.
Low-budget nastiness intended to amuse rather than shock.
wd Frank Henenlotter *ph* Bruce Torbet *m* Gus Russo, Clutch Reiser *ad* Ivy Rosovsky *ed* James Y. Kwei, Frank Henenlotter
☆ Rick Herbst, Jennifer Lowry, Gordon Macdonald, Theo Barnes, Lucille Saint-Peter, Vicki Darnell

Brain Donors

US 1992 79m colour
Paramount/Zucker (Gil Netter, James D. Brubaker)

A trio of idiots attempt to part a widow from her wealth by running a ballet company for her.
A misfiring farce and a leaden attempt to revive the Marx Brothers' style of comedy. Inspired by A Night at the Opera, *it doesn't even approach the low level of* Love Happy *(qqv).*
w Pat Proft *d* Dennis Dugan *ph* David M. Walsh *m* Ira Newborn *pd* William J. Cassidy *ed* Malcolm Campbell
☆ John Turturro, Bob Nelson, Mel Smith, Nancy Marchand, John Savident, George de La Pena
'Sounds like a horror film and for those expecting a comedy, it is.' – *Variety*

'Crawling, Slimy Things Terror-Bent On Destroying The World!'

The Brain Eaters

US 1958 60m bw
AIP/Corinthian (Edwin Nelson)

Parasites from the Earth's core isolate a small town and begin to take over its citizens.
Low-budget imitation of Invasion of The Body Snatchers *(qv), but with little evidence of intelligence in its making.*
w Gordon Urquhart *d* Bruno Ve Sota *ph* Larry Raimond *m* Tom Jonson *ad* Burt Shonberg *ed* Carlo Lodato
☆ Edwin Nelson, Alan Frost, Jack Hill, Joanna Lee, Jody Fair, David Hughes, Leonard Nimoy
† Leonard Nimoy is credited as Nemoy and plays a bearded ancient.

'Science-fiction's most astounding story!'

The Brain from Planet Arous

US 1957 70m bw
Howco International (Jacques Marquette)

A criminal alien, consisting of a disembodied brain, takes possession of the body of a nuclear scientist.
Laughably inept science fiction that leaves few clichés unspoken.
w Ray Buffum *d* Nathan Hertz (Nathan Juran) *ph* Jacques Marquette *m* Walter Greene *ed* Irving Schoenberg
☆ John Agar, Joyce Meadows, Robert Fuller, Thomas B. Henry, Henry Travis
'It's not actually as hilariously awful as you might think, but bad movie buffs will still get a kick out of it.' – *The Dark Side*

The Brain Machine *

GB 1954 83m bw
Alec Snowden/Merton Park
Through an electroencephalograph, a hospital psychiatrist recognizes a patient as a dangerous psychopath.
Very tolerable crime thriller with a fresh angle.
wd Ken Hughes
☆ Elizabeth Allan, Patrick Barr, Maxwell Reed, Russell Napier, Vanda Godsell, Gibb McLaughlin

Brain Waves
US 1982 80m colour
CinAmerica Pictures (Ulli Lommel)
A brain-dead accident victim is brought back to life through the electronic transfer of the brain patterns of a murder victim, with disastrous results.
Ponderous and sentimental fantasy, a high-tech variation on Frankenstein.
wd Ulli Lommel *ph* Jon Kranhouse *m* Robert O. Ragland *ed* Richard Brummer
☆ Tony Curtis, Keir Dullea, Suzanne Love, Vera Miles, Percy Rodrigues, Paul Willson

'A romantic comedy about a boy, a girl and their power tools.'
Braindead
New Zealand 1992 104m colour
Polygram/Wingnut Films (Jim Booth)
US title: *Dead Alive*
A bite from a rat monkey turns a woman into a zombie; soon her cellar is full of other zombies.
Grossly gory horror, played for sick laughs, with a climactic massacre of the zombies by lawnmower that must rank as one of the bloodiest twenty minutes on film. It is difficult to understand why the British censors are happy to let us watch such jejune and tiresome stuff uncut while refusing a video release for such films as Straw Dogs *and* Reservoir Dogs *(qqv).*
w Stephen Sinclair, Frances Walsh, Peter Jackson *d* Peter Jackson *ph* Murray Milne *pd* Kenneth Leonard-Jones *ed* Jamie Selkirk
☆ Timothy Balme, Diana Penalver, Elizabeth Moody, Ian Watkin, Brenda Kendal, Stuart Devenie, Jed Brophy
'Soon jettisons characterisations and story development in favour of an orgy of tasteless effects.' – *Kim Newman*
'It's impossible to imagine anyone out-grossing the New Zealander's effort, or wanting to.' – *Sight and Sound*

Brainscan
US 1994 95m colour
Guild/Coral (Michael Roy)
A youth finds that the deaths in a computer game he is playing are happening in the real world.
A tasteless dose of teenage fantasy, just another failed attempt to bridge the gap between cinema and computer games.
w Andrew Kevin Walker *story* Brian Owens *d* John Flynn *ph* François Protat *pd* Paola Ridolfi *ed* Jay Cassidy *visual effects and character design* René Daalder
☆ Edward Furlong, Frank Langella, T. Ryder Smith, Amy Hargreaves, Jamie Marsh, Victor Ertmanis, David Hemblen
'May be too tame for the creature-feature fans and slasher devotees who will be drawn by its ad campaign.' – *Variety*

Brainstorm
US 1965 110m bw Panavision
Warner/Kodima (William Conrad)
A passer-by saves a married woman from suicide, has an affair with her, and conspires to murder her husband. This accomplished, she leaves him and he goes insane.
Overlong thriller which starts off agreeably in the Double Indemnity *vein; but goes slow and solemn around the half way mark.*
w Mann Rubin *d* William Conrad *ph* Sam Leavitt *m* George Duning
☆ Jeffrey Hunter, Anne Francis, Dana Andrews, Viveca Lindfors, Stacy Harris
'A sub-B potboiler for those who find comic books too intellectual.' – *Judith Crist*

'Open the doors to your mind...'
Brainstorm
US 1983 106m Metrocolor Super Panavision
MGM/UA/JF (Douglas Trumbull)
A technological device records emotions so faithfully as to make other people feel them through each of the five senses. The enemy is discovered to be using it for brainwashing purposes; but it has recorded the experience of death...
Scientific mumbo jumbo which went far too far as an attack on the audience's senses, and was jinxed by the death of its star during production.
w Robert Stitzel, Philip Frank Messina, Bruce Joel Rubin *d* Douglas Trumbull *ph* Richard Yuricich *m* James Horner *pd* John Vallone
☆ Natalie Wood, Christopher Walken, Louise Fletcher, Cliff Robertson, Jordan Christopher, Alan Fudge
'A monstrous bore, with uninteresting characters buried beneath a mass of even less interesting technology.' – *Tom Milne, MFB*

Brainwashed
France/Italy 1972 Eastmancolor
Lira/Fox Europa/Pegaso (Roland Girard, Jean Bolvary)
original title: *Le Droit d'Aimer*
aka: *The Right to Love*
After a two-year wait, a woman visits her lover, a political prisoner held on a grim island jail, and discovers that their relationship has changed.
A glum fable of requited love.
w Jean-Claude Carrière, Françoise Xenakis, Jean Bolvary, Eric Le Hung *novel Elle Lui Dirait dans l'Ile* by Françoise Xenakis *d* Eric Le Hung *ph* Henri Decaë *m* Philippe Sarde *ed* Jacqueline Thiédot
☆ Omar Sharif, Florinda Bolkan, Pierre Michael, Gilles Ségal

Bram Stoker's Count Dracula
Spain/Italy/West Germany/Liechtenstein 1970 98m Eastmancolor Panavision
Hemdale/Fénix/Corona/Filmar/Towers of London (Harry Alan Towers)
original title: *El Conde Dracula*
aka: *Count Dracula, Dracula 71*
An English solicitor, Jonathan Harker, tracks Dracula to his castle after the Count kills his wife's friend, and destroys him by burning his coffin.
A feeble effort, in which a good cast is wasted by directorial incompetence. It was claimed, wrongly, that it was the first film to stick closely to the original story.
w Peter Welbeck (Harry Alan Towers), Carlo Fadda, Milo C. Cuccia, Dietmar Behnke *novel Dracula* by Bram Stoker *d* Jess (Jesús) Franco *ph* Manuel Merino *m* Bruno Nicolai *sp* Sergio Pagoni
☆ Christopher Lee, Herbert Lom, Klaus Kinski, Frederick Williams, Maria Rohm, Soledad Miranda, Jack Taylor
'Disappointingly unimaginative in treatment ... the evidently low budget reveals day-for-night shots for what they are, also permitting a cardboard rock clearly to be seen bouncing off a horse's head before "crushing" a peasant.' – *John Raisbeck, MFB*

'Love Never Dies.'
Bram Stoker's Dracula
US 1992 128m Technicolor
Columbia TriStar/American Zoetrope/Osiris (Francis Ford Coppola, Fred Fuchs, Charles Mulvehill)
In the 1480s Dracula curses God and becomes a vampire after his wife, thinking that he has died in battle, commits suicide; 400 or so years later in London he falls in love with a woman who seems to be her reincarnation.
A lush, over-dressed Gothic romance that plays down the menace and dread of the original, with performances that range from the inadequate to the over-ripe.
w James V. Hart *d* Francis Ford Coppola *ph* Michael Ballhaus *m* Wojciech Kilar *pd* Thomas Sanders *ed* Nicholas C. Smith, Glen Scantlebury, Anne Goursaud *sp* Roman Coppola
☆ Gary Oldman, Winona Ryder, Anthony Hopkins, Keanu Reeves
'Remains in essentials a fairly comprehensive and often vulgar mess ... The whole somehow seems to sum up what people want from cinema nowadays: style hinting at content but gradually drowning it out with pyrotechnics.' – *Derek Malcolm, Guardian*
'You emerge from the vampire's feast hungry and disappointed.' – *Geoff Brown, The Times*
'Everybody knows that Dracula has a heart; Coppola knows that it is more than an organ to drive a stake into. To the director, the count is a restless spirit who has been condemned for too many years to interment in cruddy movies. This luscious film restores the creature's nobility and gives him peace.' – *Richard Corliss, Time*
Eiko Ishioka (costumes); make-up; sound effects editing
Thomas Sanders

Bram Stoker's Legend of the Mummy
US 1997 93m colour
Goldbar/Unapix (Harel Goldstein, Bill Barnett)
aka: *Bram Stoker's The Mummy*
An archaeologist summons to life the preserved body of an ancient queen of Egypt.
A horror movie shocking only in its cheapness and incompetence: it has several scenes of people fighting off an invisible assailant, no doubt to save the cost of providing a mobile mummy, who is otherwise impersonated by a set of false teeth and some bandages.
wd Jeffrey Obrow *novel The Jewel of Seven Stars* by Bram Stoker *ph* Antonio Soriano *m* Rick Cox *pd* Ken Larson *ed* Gary Meyers
☆ Louis Gossett Jnr, Amy Locane, Eric Lutes, Mark Lindsay-Chapman, Richard Karn, Lloyd Bochner, Victoria Tennant, Aubrey Morris

The Bramble Bush
US 1960 105m Technicolor
Warner/United States (Milton Sperling)
A doctor returns to his home town and finds himself involved in old tragedies including the mercy killing of his friend.
Sordid small-town melodrama in the Peyton Place *vein, with adequate production values but dispiriting treatment.*
w Milton Sperling, Philip Yordan *novel* Charles Mergendahl *d* Daniel Petrie *ph* Lucien Ballard *m* Leonard Rosenman
☆ Richard Burton, Barbara Rush, Jack Carson, Angie Dickinson, James Dunn, Tom Drake, Henry Jones, Frank Conroy, Carl Benton Reid, William Hansen

The Branches of the Tree **
India 1990 120m colour
Erato/DD/Soproffilms
When their famous father is taken ill, his three successful sons and their wives and children return home to visit him.
A rigorous examination of family relationships and values.
wd Satyajit Ray *ph* Sandip Ray *m* Satyajit Ray
☆ Ajit Banerjee, Soumitra Chatterjee, Maradan Banerjee, Lily Charraborty, Deepankar De, Mamata Shankar, Ranjit Malik
'An honest, thoughtful, compassionate film.' – *Philip French, Observer*

Branded
US 1950 104m Technicolor
Paramount (Mel Epstein)
A gunman poses as a rancher's lost heir, but redeems himself by finding the real one.
Competent, brisk Western.
w Sydney Boehm, Cyril Hume *d* Rudolph Maté *ph* Charles Lang Jnr *m* Roy Webb
☆ Alan Ladd, Charles Bickford, Mona Freeman, Robert Keith, Joseph Calleia, Peter Hansen, Selena Royle, Tom Tully

Branded to Kill: see *Koroshi No Rakuin*

Brandy for the Parson *
GB 1951 79m bw
Group Three (Alfred Shaughnessy)
A couple on a yachting holiday find themselves unwittingly smuggling brandy into Britain.
Pleasant little sub-Ealing comedy with agreeable locations but not much drive.
w John Dighton, Walter Meade *story* Geoffrey Household *d* John Eldridge *ph* Martin Curtis *m* John Addison
☆ James Donald, Kenneth More, Jean Lodge, Frederick Piper, Charles Hawtrey, Michael Trubshawe, Alfie Bass, Reginald Beckwith

'Detective-Lieutenant Brannigan is in London ... God Save the Queen!'
Brannigan *
GB 1975 111m DeLuxe Panavision
UA/Wellborn (Jules Levy, Arthur Gardner)
A Chicago policeman is sent to London to pick up a gangster.
Cheerful crime pastiche and tour of London, quite an agreeable entertainment despite its obviously over-age star.
w Christopher Trumbo, Michael Butler, William P. McGivern, William Norton *d* Douglas Hickox *ph* Gerry Fisher *m* Dominic Frontière
☆ John Wayne, Richard Attenborough, Judy Geeson, Mel Ferrer, John Vernon, Daniel Pilon, John Stride, James Booth, Barry Dennen

The Brasher Doubloon *
US 1946 72m bw
TCF
GB title: *The High Window*
Philip Marlowe investigates the theft of a rare coin and finds himself involved in a series of murders.
The poorest of the Chandler adaptations, previously filmed as Time to Kill, *still contains good moments, though the star is lightweight and the production low-budget.*
w Dorothy Bennett *novel The High Window* by Raymond Chandler *d* John Brahm *ph* Lloyd Ahern *m* David Buttolph
☆ George Montgomery, Nancy Guild, Florence Bates, Conrad Janis, Fritz Kortner

The Brass Bottle
US 1964 89m Eastmancolor
U-I/Scarus (Robert Arthur)
A young architect finds an old brass bottle which contains a troublesome genie.
Simple-minded farce with little invention and poor trickwork.
w Oscar Brodney *novel* F. Anstey *d* Harry Keller *ph* Clifford Stine *m* Bernard Green *ed* Ted J. Kent *sp* Roswell Hoffman
☆ Tony Randall, Burl Ives, Barbara Eden, Edward Andrews, Ann Doran, Kamala Devi, Richard Erdman

The Brass Legend
US 1956 79m bw
UA (Herman Cohen/Bob Goldstein)
A sheriff finds himself in trouble when he tries to protect his fiancée's young brother.
Stolid programmer of the High Noon *school, but without the flair.*
w Don Martin *d* Gerd Oswald
☆ Hugh O'Brian, Nancy Gates, Raymond Burr, Reba Tassell

The Brass Monkey
GB 1948 84m bw
Diadem/Alliance/UA (N. A. Bronsten)
aka: *Lucky Mascot*
A radio singer thwarts the theft of a Buddhist idol.
Flat thriller based round a radio 'discovery' programme.
w Alec Coppel, Thornton Freeland *d* Thornton Freeland *ph* Basil Emmott
☆ Carole Landis, Carroll Levis, Herbert Lom, Avril Angers, Ernest Thesiger

Brass Target
US 1978 111m Metrocolor Panavision
MGM (Berle Adams)
The alleged story behind the death of General Patton, who according to these sources was eliminated because he had discovered a bullion robbery attempt.
Good-looking but interminably complex and talkative, with nothing much for its star cast to do.
w Alvin Boretz *novel The Algonquin Project* by Frederick Nolan *d* John Hough *ph* Tony Imi *m* Laurence Rosenthal
☆ Sophia Loren, George Kennedy, Max von Sydow, John Cassavetes, Patrick McGoohan, Robert Vaughn, Bruce Davison, Edward Herrmann, Ed Bishop

Brassed Off *
GB 1996 107m Rank Colour
Film Four/Miramax/Prominent Features (Steve Abbott)
A mining community, facing the closure of its pit, struggles to keep its brass band going so that it may play in a national competition.
Sentimental comedy mixed with political preaching, saved from bathos by some good character acting.
wd Mark Herman *ph* Andy Collins *m* Trevor Jones *pd* Don Taylor *ed* Michael Ellis
☆ Pete Postlethwaite (Danny), Tara Fitzgerald (Gloria), Ewan McGregor (Andy), Jim Carter (Harry), *Stephen Tompkinson* (Phil), Ken Colley (Greasely), Stephen Moore (Mackenzie), Peter Gunn (Simmo), Mary Healey (Ida), Melanie Hill

(Sandra), Philip Jackson (Jim), Sue Johnston (Vera)

'Full to the brim with lazy effects, grabbing at a sentimentality it hasn't earned and a seriousness of tone for which it hasn't put in an inch of work.' – *Tom Shone, Sunday Times*

Brat
Russia 1997 99m colour
Kino Kino/STW/Roskomkino (Sergei Selianov)
aka: *Brother*
A former soldier becomes involved in the criminal underworld in St Petersburg.
A hectic picture of modern Russia with the young (at whom this movie seems aimed) floundering in moral and social uncertainties.
wd Alexei Balabanov *ph* Sergei Astakhov *m* Viacheslav Butusov *pd* Vladimir Kartakov *ed* Marina Lipartiy
☆ Sergei Bodrov (Danila Bragov), Viktor Suhorukov (Viktor Bragov), Svetlana Pismichenko (Sveta), Maria Joukova (Kat), Yuri Kuznetsov (The German), Viacheslav Butusov (Butusov)
'Terrifically stylish gangster film.' – *New York Times*

Brats *
US 1930 20m bw
Hal Roach
Stan and Ollie have trouble baby-sitting their own mischievous kids.
Fairly ambitious star comedy with trick sets and photography enabling Laurel and Hardy to play their own sons. About half the gags come off.
w Leo McCarey, H. M. Walker, Hal Roach *d* James Parrott *ph* George Stevens *ed* Richard Currier
☆ Stan Laurel, Oliver Hardy

The Bravados *
US 1958 98m Eastmancolor Cinemascope
TCF (Herbert B. Swope)
A widower chases four killers who, he believes, raped and murdered his wife.
Dour Western with a downbeat ending; production good, but entertainment uneasy.
w Philip Yordan *novel* Frank O'Rourke *d* Henry King *ph* Leon Shamroy *m* Hugo Friedhofer *md* Emil Newman
☆ Gregory Peck, Stephen Boyd, Joan Collins, Albert Salmi, Henry Silva, George Voskovec, Barry Coe, Lee Van Cleef

The Brave and the Beautiful: see *The Magnificent Matador*

The Brave Bulls
US 1951 108m bw
Columbia (Robert Rossen)
A Mexican matador regains his courage but loses his girl in a car crash.
Muddled narrative with dollops of bull-fighting mystique; a rather miserable movie despite effort all round.
w John Bright *novel* Tom Lea *d* Robert Rossen *ph* James Wong Howe, Floyd Crosby
☆ Mel Ferrer, Miroslava, Anthony Quinn, Eugene Iglesias

The Brave Don't Cry *
GB 1952 90m bw
Group Three (John Baxter)
Over a hundred men are rescued in a Scottish mine disaster.
Semi-documentary based on a real incident well done on a small budget, but hardly memorable.
w Montagu Slater *d* Philip Leacock *ph* Arthur Grant *m* none
☆ John Gregson, Meg Buchanan, John Rae, Fulton Mackay, Andrew Keir, Russell Waters, Jameson Clark, Jean Anderson, Eric Woodburn

The Brave Little Toaster
US 1987 90m DeLuxe
Castle Premier/Hyperion/Kushner-Locke/Wang Film/Global Communications (Donald Kushner, Thomas L. Wilhite)
Domestic appliances go in search of their owner.
Odd fantasy of pots and pans with no more than adequate animation.
w Jerry Rees, Joe Ranft *novel* Thomas M. Disch *d* Jerry Rees *m* David Newman
☆ Featuring the voices of Jon Lovitz, Tim Stack, Timothy E. Day, Thurl Ravenscroft, Deanna Oliver, Phil Hartman, Joe Ranft

The Brave One *
US 1956 100m Technicolor Cinemascope
King Brothers
A small boy saves the life of his pet bull when it is sent into the ring.
Mildly beguiling minor drama for those who adore small boys and bulls.
w Harry Franklin, Merrill G. White *story* Robert Rich (Dalton Trumbo) *d* Irving Rapper *ph* Jack Cardiff *m* Victor Young *ed* Merrill G. White
☆ Michel Ray, Rodolfo Hoyos, Elsa Cardenas, Joi Lansing, Carlos Navarro
† Dalton Trumbo was not credited at the time of the film's release because he had been blacklisted.
Robert Rich. (There was much confusion when the mysterious Rich turned out to be Dalton Trumbo, who was blacklisted at the time.)
editing

'His passion captivated a woman. His courage inspired a country. His heart defied a king.'
Braveheart ***
US 1995 177m DeLuxe Panavision
TCF/Icon/Ladd (Mel Gibson, Alan Ladd Jnr, Bruce Davey)
William Wallace leads a Scottish rebellion against the claims of the English king, Edward I.
A stirring nationalistic epic, acted and directed with great verve; some of the history may be suspect, but the film creates a sense of myth with its sweep and passion.
w Randall Wallace *d* Mel Gibson *ph* John Toll *m* James Horner *pd* Tom Sanders *ed* Steven Rosenblum
☆ Mel Gibson, Sophie Marceau, Patrick McGoohan, Catherine McCormack, Brendan Gleeson, James Cosmo, Alun Armstrong, Angus Macfadyen, Ian Bannen
'At last: a costume drama that wears its costumes with pride, a period drama that has the courage of its convictions.' – *Tom Shone, Sunday Times*
† The film took $168.5m at the box-office worldwide, according to *Variety*'s figures.
best film; Mel Gibson (as director); John Toll; makeup; sound effects editing
Randall Wallace; James Horner; Steven Rosenblum; costume design (Charles Knode); sound

Brazil
US 1944 91m bw
Republic (Robert North)
A lady novelist goes to Brazil for material; a local composer poses as her guide in order to pay her back for her previous remarks about his country.
Acceptable lower case musical with pleasant tunes and humour.
w Frank Gill Jnr, Laura Kerr *d* Joseph Santley *ph* Jack Marta *m* Walter Scharf *songs* Bob Russell and others
☆ Virginia Bruce, Tito Guizar, Edward Everett Horton, Roy Rogers
song 'Rio de Janeiro' (*m* Ary Barrosa, *ly* Ned Washington); Walter Scharf

Brazil *
GB 1985 142m colour
Embassy (Arnon Milchan)
A comically pessimistic view of the future, seen through the eyes of a dutiful civil servant who is eventually crushed by the system.
An expensive, wild, overlong, hit-or-miss Orwellian satire: enough good jabs to please the intelligentsia, but a turnoff for patrons at the local Odeon.
w Terry Gilliam, Tom Stoppard, Charles McKeown *d* Terry Gilliam *ph* Roger Pratt *m* Michael Kamen *pd* Norman Garwood *ed* Julian Doyle
☆ Jonathan Pryce, Robert De Niro, Michael Palin, Kim Greist, Katherine Helmond, Ian Holm, Ian Richardson, Peter Vaughan, Bob Hoskins
'It will not be everybody's cup of poisoned tea.' – *Variety*
'Exuberantly violent, cruelly funny and sometimes sickeningly scatological ... the whole is wrapped up in a melancholy wistfulness.' – *Sight and Sound*
original screenplay, art direction
production design

Breach of Promise
GB 1941 79m bw
British Mercury/MGM
US title: *Adventure in Blackmail*
A girl chases the man she wants by filing a breach of promise suit against him.
Dated but lively comedy with agreeable playing.
w Roland Pertwee *d* Harold Huth, Roland Pertwee
☆ Clive Brook, Judy Campbell, C. V. France, Marguerite Allan, Percy Walsh

Bread and Chocolate *
Italy 1973 112m Eastmancolor
Verona Cinematografica (Maurizio Lodo-Fe)
An Italian waiter in Switzerland is accused of murder and indecent exposure.
Amusing and often pathetic account of an inveterate loser, its flavour impossible to define.
w Franco Brusati, Iaia Fiastri, Nino Manfredi *d* Franco Brusati *ph* Luciano Tovoli *md* Daniele Patrucchi
☆ Nino Manfredi, Anna Karina, Johnny Dorelli, Paolo Turco

'The Balance Of Power Is About To Change.'
Bread and Roses **
GB/Germany/Spain 2000 110m colour
Parallax/Road Movies/Tornasol/Alta (Rebecca O'Brien)
A Mexican woman is smuggled into Los Angeles to live with her sister, join other immigrants working as office cleaners, and protest about their exploitation.
Engrossing, heartfelt movie about the underside of LA, and those invisible workers busy executives step over on their way to the elevators; it suffers from an often clumsy script, but is worth seeing just for Elpidia Carrillo's electrifying outburst explaining her seemingly indefensible betrayal of fellow workers.
w Paul Laverty *d* Ken Loach *ph* Barry Ackroyd, Haskell Wexler *m* George Fenton *pd* Martin Johnson *ed* Jonathan Morris
☆ Pilar Padilla (Maya), Adrien Brody (Sam), Elpidia Carrillo (Rosa), Jack McGee (Bert), George Lopez (Perez), Alonso Chave (Ruben), Monica Rivas (Simona), Frank Davila (Luis)
'A genuine consciousness-raiser, but it's less a social-realist narrative than a high-volume rally. Which might be exactly what the director intended.' – *Jessica Winter, Village Voice*
'A minor piece of agitprop drama.' – *Variety*

Bread, Love and Dreams *
Italy 1953 90m bw
Titanus (Marcello Girosi)
The new sergeant of police in a small rural village comes looking for a wife.
Pleasant rather than exciting rural comedy which spun off a number of vaguely related sequels (Bread, Love and Jealousy, *etc).*
w Luigi Comencini *story* Ettore Margadonna *d* Luigi Comencini *ph* Arturo Gallea *m* Alessandro Cicognini
☆ Vittorio de Sica, Gina Lollobrigida, Marisa Merlini, Roberto Risso
Ettore Margadonna

Break in the Circle
GB 1955 91m Eastmancolor (bw in US)
Exclusive/Hammer (Michael Carreras)
The owner of a cabin cruiser is hired to smuggle a scientist out of Germany.
Routine action yarn of cross and double-cross, tolerably staged.
wd Val Guest *novel* Philip Lorraine *ph* Walter Harvey *m* Doreen Carwithen *ad* J. Elder Wills *ed* Bill Lenny
☆ Forrest Tucker, Eva Bartok, Marius Goring, Eric Pohlmann, Guy Middleton, Arnold Marlé

Break of Hearts
US 1935 80m bw
RKO (Pandro S. Berman)
A girl composer falls in love with a distinguished conductor who becomes a dipsomaniac.
Well acted soap opera, not really worthy of its stars.
w Sarah Y. Mason, Victor Heerman, Anthony Veiller *d* Philip Moeller *ph* Robert de Grasse *m* Max Steiner
☆ Katharine Hepburn, Charles Boyer, Jean Hersholt, John Beal, Sam Hardy
'A stale turnip story that relies entirely upon characterization to hide the basic dullness.' – *Variety*
'In spite of some capable acting, it lacks a certain compelling warmth. The audience's heart never breaks.' – *Eileen Creelman, New York Sun*

Break the News *
GB 1938 78m bw
GFD/Jack Buchanan
A dancer arranges his partner's 'death' for publicity reasons but is sent to jail when the partner disappears.
Thin but lively comedy with a remarkable couple of song and dance men. Negative apparently lost.
w Geoffrey Kerr *novel* *La Mort en Fuite* by Loic de Gouriadec *d* René Clair *ph* Phil Tannura *m* Theo Mackeben *m/ly* Cole Porter *md* Van Phillips *ad* Lazare Meerson *ed* Francis Lyon, Fred Wilson
☆ *Jack Buchanan, Maurice Chevalier*, June Knight, Marta Labarr, Garry Marsh, Felix Aylmer, Robb Wilton
† Various remakes include *The Art of Love* (qv).

Break to Freedom: see *Albert RN*

'Silent Betrayal. Deadly Passion. Sweet Revenge.'
Break Up
US 1999 101m colour
Millennium/Nu Image (Jonas Goodman, Harvey Kahn, Elie Samaha)
A woman, who is suspected of having murdered her abusive husband, fears that he is still alive and dangerous.
Routine thriller that follows in the footsteps of better films; the acting seems unengaged.
w Anne Amanda Opotowsky *d* Paul Marcus *ph* Hubert Taczanowski *m* Laura Karpman *pd* Clark Hunter *ed* Arthur Coburn
☆ Bridget Fonda (Jimmy Dade), Kiefer Sutherland (John Box), Hart Bochner (Frankie Dade), Steven Weber (Ramsey), Penelope Ann Miller (Grace), Tippi Hedren (Mom), Leslie Stefanson (Shelly)

Breakdance: see *Breakin'*

Breakdance 2: Electric Boogaloo: see *Breakin' 2: Electric Boogaloo*

Breakdown **
US 1997 93m DeLuxe Super 35
TCF/Dino de Laurentiis/Spelling
After his car breaks down, a man finds that his wife has disappeared and that a gang of roughnecks want to steal all his money.
Slick, unpretentious action thriller that effectively exploits urban fears of wide-open spaces.
w Jonathan Mostow, Sam Montgomery *d* Jonathan Mostow *ph* Doug Milsome *m* Basil Poledouris *pd* Victoria Paul *ed* Derek Brechin, Kevin Stitt
☆ Kurt Russell, J. T. Walsh, Kathleen Quinlan, M. C. Gainey, Jack Noseworthy, Rex Linn, Ritch Brinkley, Moira Harris
'A tremendously tense thriller that expertly keeps tightening the screws throughout its taut running time.' – *Variety*
'A rough-hewn thriller, enjoyable in its simplicity and occasional silliness.' – *Edward Porter, Sunday Times*

Breaker Morant ***
Australia 1980 107m Eastmancolor Panavision
South Australian Film Corporation (Matthew Carroll)
During the Boer War three Australian officers are courtmartialled for murdering prisoners.
Careful, moving military drama which gives a more sympathetic view of the facts than history does.
w Jonathan Hardy, Bruce Beresford, David Stevens *play* Kenneth Ross *d* Bruce Beresford *ph* Donald McAlpine *md* Phil Cuneen
☆ Edward Woodward, Jack Thompson, John Waters, Charles Tingwell, Terence Donovan, Vincent Ball

'It is impossible to suppress a feeling that the spirit of Stanley Kramer is abroad on the veldt.' – *Tim Pulleine, MFB*
screenplay

Breakfast at Tiffany's *
US 1961 115m Technicolor
Paramount (Martin Jurow, Richard Shepherd)

A young New York writer has as neighbour the volatile Holly Golightly, a slightly crazy call girl with an exotic social and emotional life.
Impossibly cleaned up and asexual version of a light novel which tried to be the American I Am a Camera *(qv). Wild parties, amusing scenes and good cameos, but the pace is slow, the atmosphere is unconvincingly clean and luxurious, and the sentimentality kills it.*
w George Axelrod novel Truman Capote *d* Blake Edwards *ph* Franz Planer *m Henry Mancini ad* Hal Pereira, Roland Anderson *ed* Howard Smith *cos* Edith Head
☆ Audrey Hepburn (Holly Golightly), George Peppard (Paul Varjak), Patricia Neal (2-E), Buddy Ebsen (Doc Golightly), Martin Balsam (O.J. Berman), *John McGiver* (Tiffany salesman), Mickey Rooney (Mr Yunioshi)
Henry Mancini; song 'Moon River' (*m* Henry Mancini, *ly* Johnny Mercer)
George Axelrod; Audrey Hepburn; art direction

The Breakfast Club
US 1985 97m Technicolor
A&M/Universal (Ned Tanen, John Hughes)

Five rebellious students at Shermer High blame their parents for their misfortunes.
Abysmal apologia for loutish teenage behaviour.
wd John Hughes *ph* Thomas Del Ruth, George Bouillet *m* Keith Forsey *ed* Dede Allen
☆ Emilio Estevez, Judd Nelson, Molly Ringwald, Anthony Michael Hall, Ally Sheedy

Breakfast for Two *
US 1937 65m bw
RKO (Edward Kaufman)
A Texas heiress turns a playboy into a businessman.
Star crazy comedy with some wildly funny scenes.
w Charles Kaufman, Paul Yawitz, Viola Brothers Shore *d* Alfred Santell *ph* J. Roy Hunt
☆ Barbara Stanwyck, Herbert Marshall, Donald Meek, Glenda Farrell, Eric Blore, Etienne Girardot
'Heaps of laughs in a breezily-paced farce.' – *Variety*

Breakfast in Hollywood
US 1945 90m bw
Golden Pictures/United Artists

GB title: *The Mad Hatter*
A day in the life of a radio breakfast show host.
Topical programme filler, more interesting historically than entertaining.
w Earl W. Baldwin *d* Harold Schuster
☆ Tom Breneman, Bonita Granville, Beulah Bondi, Eddie Ryan, Raymond Walburn, Billie Burke, ZaSu Pitts, Spike Jones and his City Slickers, Andy Russell, Hedda Hopper

'In a world gone mad you can trust Dwayne Hoover.'
Breakfast of Champions
US 1999 110m
Summit/Flying Heart/Sugar Creek (David Blocker, David Willis)

A successful car dealer finds that his life is disappointing, and wants to know why.
Muddled and meandering satire on the American dream that misses most of its targets.
wd Alan Rudolph *novel* Kurt Vonnegut Jnr *ph* Elliot Davis *m* Mark Isham *pd* Nina Ruscio *ed* Suzy Elmiger *cos* Rudy Dillon
☆ Bruce Willis (Dwayne Hoover), Albert Finney (Kilgore Trout), Nick Nolte (Harry Le Sabre), Barbara Hershey (Celia Hoover), Glenne Headly (Francine Pefko), Lukas Haas (Bunny Hoover), Omar Epps (Wayne Hoobler), Buck Henry (Fred T. Barry), Vicki Lewis (Grace Le Sabre), Ken Campbell (Eliot Rosewater), Jake Johannsen (Bill Bailey), Will Patton (Moe), Owen Wilson (Monte Rapid), Commercials Director (Kurt Vonnegut Jnr)
'A hearty meal that starts off tickling the taste buds but ends up smothering them.' – *Derek Elley, Variety*

Breakheart Pass *
US 1975 94m DeLuxe
UA/Elliott Kastner (Jerry Gershwin)

Various mysterious passengers on an 1873 train across the frozen west to Fort Humboldt turn out to have smuggling and murder in mind.
Botched murder mystery on wheels: there are some exciting scenes, but the plot makes little sense and the 'action finale' is muddled.
w Alistair MacLean *novel* Alistair MacLean *d* Tom Gries *ph* Lucien Ballard *m* Jerry Goldsmith
☆ Charles Bronson, Ben Johnson, Richard Crenna, Jill Ireland, Charles Durning, Archie Moore, Ed Lauter

Breakin'
US 1984 87m Metrocolor
MGM-UA/Cannon (Allen DeBevoise, David Zito)

GB title: *Breakdance*
Youngsters promote a new form of dancing.
Minor exploitation item, the form little improved on Rock around the Clock *(qv) thirty years earlier.*
w Charles Parker, Allen DeBevoise, Gerald Scaife *d* Joel Silberg *ph* Hanania Baer *m* Gary Remal, Michael Boyd *pd* Ivo Cristante *ed* Mark Helfrich
☆ Lucinda Dickey, Adolfo 'Shabba-Doo' Quinones, Michael 'Boogaloo-Shrimp' Chambers, Ben Lokey, Phineas Newborn III, Tracey 'Ice T' Marrow

Breakin' 2: Electric Boogaloo
US 1984 94m TVC Color
Cannon

GB title: *Breakdance 2: Electric Boogaloo*
Youngsters raise 200,000 dollars to save their local community centre; a dance show does it.
Hurried sequel of no interest apart from the briefly popular musical gyrations.
w Jan Ventura, Julie Reichert *d* Sam Firstenberg
☆ Lucinda Dickey, Adolfo Quinones, Michael Chambers, Susie Bono

Breaking Away *
US 1979 101m DeLuxe
TCF (Peter Yates)

An imaginative teenager has trouble adjusting to adult life after high school.
Andy Hardy would have felt at home in this fragmented comedy of the American hinterland; 1979 audiences found it a welcome relief from the stronger brews to which they had become accustomed.
w Steve Tesich d Peter Yates *ph* Matthew F. Leonetti *m* Patrick Williams *md* Lionel Newman
☆ Dennis Christopher, Dennis Quaid, Daniel Stern, Jackie Earle Haley, Barbara Barrie, Paul Dooley
'Affection for the middle classes, the landscapes of Indiana, and bicycle racing.' – *New Yorker*
'It is not devoid of pleasures ... but it fatally lacks a clear purpose and identity.' – *Geoff Brown, MFB*
'Here's a sunny, goofy, intelligent little film about coming of age in Bloomington, Indiana.' – *Roger Ebert*
† An unsuccessful TV series followed in 1980.
Steve Tesich
best picture; Peter Yates; Patrick Williams; Barbara Barrie
Dennis Christopher

'The experience is shattering!'
Breaking Glass
GB 1980 104m Technicolor Panavision
GTO/Film and General (Dodi Fayed)

Vicissitudes of a pop band and of its singer who can't stand the pace.
Garish, freakish musical with unattractive characters strung along an oft-told tale. Some commendable vigour in the presentation, but it won't appeal to anybody over 21.
wd Brian Gibson *ph* Stephen Goldblatt *md* Tony Visconti
☆ Hazel O'Connor, Phil Daniels, Jon Finch, Jonathan Pryce

Breaking In *
US 1989 94m colour
Castle Premier/Breaking In Productions/Sam Goldwyn Company (Harry Gittes)

A veteran safe-breaker teaches a teenager the tricks of the trade.
Mildly rewarding comedy of crooked manners.
w John Sayles *d* Bill Forsyth *ph* Michael Coulter *pd* Adrienne Atkinson, John Willett *ed* Michael Ellis
☆ Burt Reynolds, Casey Siemaszko, Sheila Kelley, Lorraine Toussaint, Albert Salmi, Harry Carey, Maury Chaykin
'Less a barrel of laughs than elliptically funny in its observation of the unconscious discrepancy between word and deed.' – *Tom Milne, MFB*

The Breaking of Bumbo
GB 1970 90m colour
Associated British (Jeffrey Selznick)
A misfit of a Guards officer goes to pieces thanks to his own, and his fellow officers', shortcomings.
A misfiring comedy which, like its hero, falls flat on its face.
wd Andrew Sinclair *novel* Andrew Sinclair
☆ Richard Warwick, Joanna Lumley, Natasha Pyne, Jeremy Child, John Bird, Donald Pickering
† The film was never given a general release and was shown briefly in one London cinema, although it is occasionally seen on television.

'There's nothing more deadly than a gentle man pushed too far!'
The Breaking Point *
US 1950 97m bw
Warner (Jerry Wald)
A charterboat owner becomes involved with crooks but turns them in when they have killed his friend.
Adequate if slightly humdrum attempt by Warner to atone for what they had done to a Hemingway novel, the infidelity of To Have and Have Not *and the unauthorized variation of* Key Largo. *(See also:* The Gun Runners*) qqv.*
w Ranald MacDougall *novel To Have and Have Not* by Ernest Hemingway *d* Michael Curtiz *ph* Ted McCord *m* (uncredited) William Lava, Max Steiner
☆ John Garfield, Patricia Neal, Phyllis Thaxter, Juano Hernandez, Wallace Ford, Edmon Ryan, William Campbell
'All the character, color, and cynicism of Mr Hemingway's lean and hungry tale are wrapped up in this realistic picture.' – *New York Times*

'Innocence and fury don't mix – they explode!'
Breaking Point
Canada 1976 92m colour Panavision
TCF/Astral Belle Vue (Harold Greenberg, Harold Pariser)

An innocent witness against the Mafia takes off against them vigilante style when his partner is murdered and his own life threatened.
Comic strip thuggery with performances to match; plenty of excitement for toughies.
w Roger E. Swaybill, Stanley Mann *d* Bob Clark *ph* Marc Champion *m* David McLey
☆ Bo Svenson, Robert Culp, John Colicos, Belinda J. Montgomery, Stephen Young

Breaking the Ice
US 1938 80m bw
RKO/Sol Lesser
A Pennsylvania Dutch boy runs away to the city so that his mother can afford her own farm.
Slim star musical which had its pleasing moments.
w Mary McCall Jnr, Manuel Seff, Bernard Schubert *d* Edward F. Cline *ph* Jack MacKenzie *m* Victor Young
☆ Bobby Breen, Charles Ruggles, Dolores Costello, Robert Barrat, Dorothy Peterson, John King, Billy Gilbert, Margaret Hamilton
'Moderately engrossing, combination folk drama and musical.' – *Variety*
Victor Young

Breaking the Sound Barrier: see *The Sound Barrier*

'Love is a mighty power.'
Breaking the Waves ****
Denmark/Sweden/France/Netherlands 1996
159m colour Super 35
Guild/Zentropa/Trust/Liberator/Argus/Northern Lights (Vibeke Windelöv, Peter Aalbaek Jensen)

In a remote part of Scotland, a young woman humiliates herself in the hope of saving the life of her husband, paralysed in an accident on an oil rig.
A remarkable and striking film, though in some ways a dislikeable one. It has a raw, emotional power rarely encountered on film, owing to its soulful and guileless central performance and the restlessly casual, close-up camerawork; but its theme, an apparent celebration of self-sacrifice through sexual degradation, is often unlovely and hard to take.
w Lars von Trier, Peter Asmussen d Lars von Trier ph Robby Müller *m* Joachim Holbek *ad* Karl Juliusson *ed Anders Refn*
☆ *Emily Watson*, Stellan Skarsgård, *Katrin Cartlidge*, Jean-Marc Barr, Udo Kier, Adrian Rawlins, Jonathan Hackett, Sandra Voe
'An astonishing film, so well thought-out and passionately executed that it's only afterwards, if then, that audiences will wonder exactly what they have been persuaded to think and feel.' – *Adam Mars-Jones, Independent*
'Acted with a conviction you rarely find, it's one of those movies that affects you in such a profound way. Believe me, this one's a life-altering experience.' – *Alan Jones, Film Review*
† The film won the Grand Jury Prize at the Cannes Film Festival in 1996.
Emily Watson

Breaking Up
US 1996 90m colour
Warner/Regency (Robert Greenwald, George Moffly)

A married couple recount their on-and-off relationship.
A small-scale film in which two people bicker and make up without seeming of any interest to anyone else.
w Michael Cristofer *d* Robert Greenwald *ph* Mauro Fiore *m* Mark Mothersbaugh *pd* Terence Foster *ed* Suzanne Hines
☆ Russell Crowe, Salma Hayek, Abraham Alvarez
'An exercise in tedium that has you looking at your watch wondering why time is passing so slowly.' – *George Perry, Sunday Times*
'The sort of picture that can sap your will to live.' – *Ryan Gilbey, Independent*

Breakout: see *Danger Within (1958)*

'No Prison Is Strong Enough To Hold Bronson!'
Breakout
US 1975 96m colour Panavision
Columbia/Persky-Bright (Robert Chartoff, Irwin Winkler)

A professional rescuer gets an innocent man out of a Mexican jail.
Rough and ready adventure thriller which starts slowly and confusingly but later works up a fair head of steam.
w Howard B. Kreitsek, Frank Kowalski *novel Ten Second Jailbreak* by Howard B. Kreitsek, Frank Kowalski *d* Tom Gries *ph* Lucien Ballard *m* Jerry Goldsmith *ad* Alfred Sweeney *ed* Bud S. Isaacs
☆ Charles Bronson (Nick Colton), Robert Duvall (Jay Wagner), John Huston (Harris Wagner), Jill Ireland (Ann Wagner), Randy Quaid (Hawk Hawkins), Sheree North (Myrna)

Breakthrough
US 1950 91m bw
Warner (Bryan Foy)

Adventures of a US army unit in Normandy after D-Day.
Routine low-budgeter which improves after a slow start.
w Bernard Girard, Ted Sherdeman, Joseph I. Breen Jnr *d* Lewis Seiler *ph* Edwin DuPar *m* William Lava
☆ David Brian, John Agar, Frank Lovejoy, William Campbell, Paul Picerni, Greg McClure, Edward Norris, Matt Willis, Dick Wesson

Breakthrough: see *Sergeant Steiner (1978)*

The Breakup: see *La Rupture*

Breath of Scandal: see *His Glorious Night (1929)*

A Breath of Scandal
US 1960 98m Technicolor
Paramount/Titanus/Ponti-Girosi (Carlo Ponti, Marcello Girosi)

A spirited Ruritanian princess falls for an American industrialist.
Exceedingly flat-footed and boring international co-production of an old Molnar play; if anyone concerned had bright ideas, they don't show.
w Walter Bernstein *play* *Olimpia* by Ferenc Molnar *d* Michael Curtiz, Mario Russo *ph* Mario Montuori *m* Alessandro Cicognini
☆ Sophia Loren, Maurice Chevalier, John Gavin, Isabel Jeans, Angela Lansbury, Roberto Risso, Friedrich Ledebur, Tullio Carminati, Milly Vitale
† A remake of *His Glorious Night* (qv), filmed by MGM in 1929.

Breathless: see *A Bout de Souffle (1959)*

Breathless
US 1983 101m DeLuxe
Miko/Breathless Associates/Greenberg Brothers (Martin Erlichman)

A street-smart hustler steals a car in Las Vegas and heads for the coast.
Fashionable amalgam of sex and violence, borrowed from A Bout de Souffle *(qv) but far too long after the event.*
w L. M. Kit Carson, Jim McBride *d* Jim McBride *ph* Richard H. Kline *m* Jack Nitzsche *pd* Richard Sylbert
☆ Richard Gere, Valerie Kaprisky, William Tepper, John P. Ryan, Art Metrano
'Not much more than an ego trip for a bankable star.' – *Daily Mail*

'Vampires live amongst us.'
The Breed
US 2001 91m colour
Columbia TriStar/MPCA/Starz! (Jim Burke, Kelli Konop, Brad Krevoy, Adam Richman)

In a future world, a cop on the trail of a serial killer discovers that the government is attempting to integrate vampires into normal society.
Cheap horror that goes awry in attempting to use vampirism as a metaphor for racial persecution.
w Ruth C. Fletcher, Christos N. Gage *d* Michael Oblowitz *ph* Chris Squires *m* Steve Gurevitch, Roy Hay *pd* Trae King *ed* Emma E. Hickox *sp* make up fx: Sean Anderson, Ivan Poharnok; visual: Catalyst FX
☆ Adrian Paul (Aaron Gray), Bokeem Woodbine (Steve Grant), Bai Ling (Lucy Westenra), Peter Halasz (Cross), James Booth (Fleming), Ming Lo (Seward), Paul Collins (Calmet), Debbie Javor (Section Chief)

A Breed Apart
US 1984 101m colour Panavision
Hemdale/Sagittarius (John Daly, Derek Gibson)

A rich collector hires a mountaineer to rob the almost inaccessible nest of a rare bald eagle, guarded by a militant conservationist.
Ecological propaganda given the sugar coating of a sentimental love story with a little action thrown in.
w Paul Wheeler *d* Philippe Mora *ph* Geoffrey Stephenson *m* Maurice Gibb *pd* William Barclay *ed* Christopher Lebenzon
☆ Rutger Hauer, Powers Boothe, Kathleen Turner, Brion James, Donald Pleasence

'It's Time To Prey.'
Breeders
GB 1997 98m colour
Peakviewing/Apix/IoMFC (Elizabeth Matthews)

In Boston, a falling meteor brings with it an alien monster and a woman clad in tight black rubber.
Terrible low-grade movie, with dire script, cardboard characters and wooden acting; the monster is as unconvinving as the American setting, and the ludicrous narrative is the true horror.
wd Paul Matthews *ph* Peter Thornton *m* Ben Heneghan, Ian Lawson *pd* Edward Thomas *ed* Peter H. Matthews
☆ Todd Jensen (Ashley), Samantha Janus (Louise), Kadamba Simmons (Space Girl), Nigel Harrison (Horace), Oliver Tobias (Moore), Clifton Lloyd-Bryan (Alien), Melanie Walters (Roper), Myra (Katy Lawrence)

Breezy
US 1973 107m Technicolor
Universal/Malpaso (Robert Daley)
A divorced 50-year-old real estate agent is rejuvenated by an affair with a young girl hippy.
An abrasive veneer covers the most stereotyped of January/May love stories. Technically an attractive piece of work.
w Jo Heims *d* Clint Eastwood *ph* Frank Stanley *m* Michel Legrand
☆ William Holden, Kay Lenz, Roger C. Carmel, Marj Dusay, Joan Hotchkis

Brenda Starr
US 1992 87m CFI
New World/AM/PM (Myron A. Hyman)

An artist drawing a comic-strip becomes trapped within it, as reporter Brenda Starr goes to South America to find a mad scientist who has invented a cheap fuel that threatens the security of the world
Brightly coloured atttempt at cartoon-like action, let down by its limp script and limper performance from Shields.
w Noreen Stone, James David Buchanan, Jenny Wolkind *comic strip* Dale Messick *d* Robert Ellis Miller *ph* Freddie Francis *m* Johnny Mandel *pd* John J. Lloyd *ed* Mark Melnick *cos* Bob Mackie, Peggy Farrell
☆ Brooke Shields (Brenda Starr), Timothy Dalton (Basil St John), Tony Peck (Mike Randall), Diana Scarwid (Libby 'Lips' Lipscomb), Jeffrey Tambor (Vladimir), June Gable (Luba), Tom Aldredge (Fake Captain Borg), Matthew Cowles (Real Captain Borg), Nestor Serrano (José), Kathleen Wilhoite (Hank O'Hare), John Short (Pesky Miller), Charles Durning (Francis J. Livright), Eddie Albert (Police Chief Maloney), Henry Gibson (Professor von Kreutzer)
† The film was made in 1986.

Brewster McCloud
US 1970 105m Metrocolor Panavision
MGM/Adler-Phillips/Lion's Gate (Lou Adler)

A man hides out under the roof of the Houston Astrodrome, prepares to learn to fly with man-made wings, and refuses all offers of help; when he launches himself, he falls to his death.
Anarchic, allegorical fantasy, a delight no doubt for connoisseurs of way-out humour. Everyone else, forget it.
w Doran William Cannon *d* Robert Altman *ph* Lamar Boren, Jordan Cronenweth *m* Gene Page
☆ Bud Cort, Sally Kellerman, Michael Murphy, William Windom, Shelley Duvall, René Auberjonois, Stacy Keach, John Schuck, Margaret Hamilton
'Amorphous and rather silly ... the idea seems to be left over from a Victorian fable, but the style is like a Road Runner cartoon.' – *New Yorker, 1974*

Brewster's Millions *
GB 1935 84m bw
British and Dominion (Herbert Wilcox)
If he can spend a million pounds within two months, a playboy will inherit many millions more.
Artless but lively version of a famous comedy which provided a good role for its star.
w Arthur Wimperis, Paul Gangelin, Douglas Furber, Clifford Grey, Donovan Pedelty, Wolfgang Wilhelm *play* George Barr McCutcheon, Winchell Smith *novel* *George Barr McCutcheon* *d* Thornton Freeland *ph* Henry Harris, Barney McGill *m* Ray Noble *ad* L. P. Williams *ed* Merrill White
☆ *Jack Buchanan*, Lili Damita, Nancy O'Neil, Amy Veness, Sydney Fairbrother, Fred Emney, Sebastian Shaw
'As near 100% film entertainment as can be expected.' – *Variety*
† There had been silent versions in 1916 (with Edward Abeles) and 1921 (with Roscoe Arbuckle).

Brewster's Millions *
US 1945 79m bw
Edward Small

A G.I. is given a month to spend a million dollars in order to inherit millions more.
Competent American remake of a familiar story.
w Sig Herzig, Charles Rogers *d* Allan Dwan *ph* Charles Lawton Jnr *m* Hugo Friedhofer
☆ Dennis O'Keefe, Eddie 'Rochester' Anderson, Helen Walker, Gail Patrick, Mischa Auer, June Havoc, Joe Sawyer, Nana Bryant, John Litel, Thurston Hall, Byron Foulger
† Remade as *Three on a Spree* (GB 1961).
Academy Award nomination: Lou Forbes (music scoring)

Brewster's Millions
US 1985 97m Technicolor
Universal (Lawrence Gordon, Joel Silver)

A baseball player learns that in order to inherit 30 million dollars he must spend one million a day for 30 days.
Frantically noisy remake of an old chestnut.
w Herschel Weingrod, Timothy Harris *d* Walter Hill *ph* Ric Waite *m* Ry Cooder *pd* John Vallone *ed* Freeman Davis, Michael Ripps
☆ Richard Pryor, John Candy, Lonette McKee, Stephen Collins, Jerry Orbach, Pat Hingle, Tovah Feldshuh

The Bribe *
US 1949 98m bw
MGM (Pandro S. Berman)
A US agent tracks down a group of criminals in Central America.
Steamy melodrama with pretensions but only moderate entertainment value despite high gloss. The rogues' gallery, however, is impressive.
w Marguerite Roberts *d* Robert Z. Leonard *ph* Joseph Ruttenberg *m* Miklos Rozsa
☆ Robert Taylor, Ava Gardner, Charles Laughton, Vincent Price, John Hodiak

The Bridal Path *
GB 1959 95m Technicolor
Vale/British Lion (Sidney Gilliat, Frank Launder)
A stalwart Hebridean islander journeys to the mainland in search of a wife.
Mild, episodic, very pleasant open-air comedy set amid splendid locations.
w Frank Launder, Geoffrey Willans *novel* Nigel Tranter *d* Frank Launder *ph* Arthur Ibbetson *m* Cedric Thorpe Davie *md* Muir Mathieson *ad* Wilfred Shingleton *ed* Geoffrey Foot
☆ Bill Travers, Fiona Clyne, George Cole, Duncan Macrae, Gordon Jackson, Dilys Laye, Bernadette O'Farrell, Alex MacKenzie, Eddie Byrne, Patricia Bredin, Terry Scott, Gordon Jackson, Roddy McMillan

'A woman born of electricity ... a man driven by passion!'
The Bride
US 1985 118m Rank Colour
Columbia/Victor Drai

Frankenstein creates a bride for his monster, but she falls for him instead, and the monster goes off with a garrulous dwarf.
Insane romantic-feminist remake of The Bride of Frankenstein *(qv), extremely dull and aimless after an arresting start.*
w Lloyd Fonvielle *d* Franc Roddam *ph* Stephen H. Burum *m* Maurice Jarre *pd* Michael Seymour *ed* Michael Ellis
☆ Sting, Jennifer Beals, Clancy Brown, David Rappaport, Geraldine Page, Anthony Higgins, Quentin Crisp
'A misbegotten exercise.' – *Sight and Sound*

The Bride Came C.O.D. *
US 1941 92m bw
Warner (Hal B. Wallis)

A charter pilot agrees to kidnap a temperamental heiress, but is stuck with her when they crashland in the desert.
Feeble comedy with a script totally unworthy of its stars. The mass of talent does however provide a smile or two towards the end.
w Julius J. and Philip G. Epstein *d* William Keighley *ph* Ernest Haller *m* Max Steiner
☆ Bette Davis, James Cagney, Harry Davenport, Stuart Erwin, Eugene Pallette, Jack Carson, George Tobias, William Frawley, Edward Brophy, Chick Chandler
'Neither the funniest comedy ever made, nor the shortest distance between two points, but for the most part a serviceable romp.' – *Theodore Strauss*
'Both of them mug good-naturedly, and it's pleasantly fast.' – *New Yorker, 1977*

The Bride Goes Wild
US 1948 98m bw
MGM (William H. Wright)
As his lady illustrator finds out, a writer of children's books is not quite the sober uncle she expected, especially when he has to pretend to adopt an unruly orphan.
Scatty comedy with farcical interludes, quite pleasantly played but lacking style.
w Albert Beich *d* Norman Taurog *ph* Ray June *m* Rudolf Kopp
☆ June Allyson, Van Johnson, Jackie 'Butch' Jenkins, Hume Cronyn, Richard Derr

The Bride Is Much Too Beautiful (dubbed)
France 1956 90m bw
Leo Lax/Production Générale/Pathé-Cinéma (Fred Surin)

original title: *La Mariée Est Trop Belle*
A village girl becomes a top magazine model and falls for her editor.
Routine film, made just before Bardot's stardom, which even she admitted to finding silly.
w Philippe Agostini, Juliette Saint-Giniez *novel* Odette Joyeux *d* Pierre Gaspard-Huit *ph* Louis Page *m* Norbert Glanzberg *pd* Pierre Duquesne, Marc Frederix, Jean d'Eaubonne *ed* Louisette Hautcoeur
☆ Louis Jourdan, Brigitte Bardot, Micheline Presle, Marcel Amont, Marcelle Arnold, Roger Dumas, Jean-François Calvé

'The Honeymoon's Gonna Be Killer.'
Bride of Chucky *
US 1998 89m DeLuxe
Universal (David Kirschner, David Gilroy)

The girlfriend of a dead serial killer resurrects his spirit in the body of a doll; she then becomes a living doll herself.
Horror movie done with some panache, and a nod or two in the direction of The Bride of Frankenstein.
w Don Mancini *d* Ronnie Yu *ph* Peter Pau *m* Graeme Revell *pd* Alicia Keywan *ed* David Wu, Randolph K. Bricker *sp* puppet fx: Kevin Yagher
☆ Jennifer Tilly (Tiffany), Katherine Heigl (Jade), Nick Stabile (Jesse), John Ritter (Chief Warren Kincaid), Alexis Arquette (Howard Fitzwater), Gordon Michael Woolvett (David), Lawrence Dane (Det Preston), Michael Johnson (Officer Norton), James Gallanders (Russ), Janet Kidder (Diane), Kathy Najimy (Motel maid), Brad Dourif (voice of Chucky)
'Emerges with recharged batteries and a mordantly funny edge that's attuned to the dawning millennium. A relatively straightforward genre piece, it has flair and a dash of wit.' – *Leonard Klady, Variety*
† The film was a sequel to the *Child's Play* series (qv).

'The monster demands a mate!'
The Bride of Frankenstein ****
US 1935 90m bw
Universal (Carl Laemmle Jnr)

Baron Frankenstein is blackmailed by Dr Praetorious into reviving his monster and building a mate for it.
Frankenstein *was startlingly good in a primitive way; this sequel is the screen's sophisticated masterpiece of black comedy, with all the talents working deftly to one end. Every scene has its own delights, and they are woven together into a superb if wilful cinematic narrative which, of its gentle mocking kind, has never been surpassed.*
w John L. Balderston, William Hurlbut d James Whale ph John Mescall m Franz Waxman
☆ *Boris Karloff* (The Monster), Colin Clive (Henry Frankenstein), *Ernest Thesiger* (Dr Septimus Pretorius), Valerie Hobson (Elizabeth Frankenstein), *E. E. Clive* (Burgomaster), Dwight

Frye, O. P. Heggie (Hermit), Una O'Connor (Minnie), *Elsa Lanchester* (Mary Shelley and the monster's mate), Gavin Gordon (Byron), Douglas Walton

FRANKENSTEIN: 'I've been cursed for delving into the mysteries of life!'

'It is perhaps because Whale was by now master of the horror film that this production is the best of them all.' – *John Baxter, 1968*

'An extraordinary film, with sharp humour, macabre extravagance, and a narrative that proceeds at a fast, efficient pace.' – *Gavin Lambert, 1948*

'A great deal of art has gone into it, but it is the kind of art that gives the healthy feeling of men with their sleeves rolled up and working, worrying only about how to put the thing over in the best manner of the medium – no time for nonsense and attitudes and long hair.' – *Otis Ferguson*

† The regular release version runs 75m, having dropped part of the Mary Shelley prologue and a sequence in which the monster becomes unsympathetic by murdering the burgomaster

†† The title was originally to have been *The Return of Frankenstein.*

Bride of the Gorilla

US 1951 65m bw
Jack Broder Productions

The manager of a rubber plantation is poisoned by a native woman and turns into a gorilla.
Incredibly inane two-bit shocker, a strong contender for any list of the worst films of all time.
wd Curt Siodmak
☆ Barbara Payton, Lon Chaney Jnr, Raymond Burr, Tom Conway, Paul Cavanagh

'The screen's master of the weird … In his newest and most daring shocker!'

Bride of the Monster

US 1953 69m bw
Rolling M (Edward D. Wood)

Dr Vornoff has an atomic machine which will convert people into beings of superhuman strength; it is turned on himself, but a giant octopus, also with superoctopus strength, gets him.
A perfectly terrible movie, on a par with this director's other works.
w Edward D. Wood Jnr, Alex Gordon *d* Edward D. Wood Jnr
☆ Bela Lugosi, Tor Johnson, Tony McCoy, Loretta King, Harvey Dunne

Bride of the Re-Animator: see *Re-Animator 2*

Bride of Vengeance *

US 1948 91m bw
Paramount (Richard Maibaum)
The story of the Borgias (whitewashing Lucretia) and the Duke of Ferrara.
Superb looking but appallingly acted and rather stodgily directed piece of historical melodrama. Totally studio-bound, but one of these days it could find a sympathetic audience.
w Cyril Hume, Michael Hogan *d* Mitchell Leisen *ph* Daniel L. Fapp *m* Hugo Friedhofer *ad* Hans Dreier, Roland Anderson, Albert Nozaki
☆ Paulette Goddard, John Lund, Macdonald Carey, Albert Dekker, Raymond Burr

'A dud … it just couldn't be that bad by accident.' – *Los Angeles Times*

The Bride Walks Out

US 1936 81m bw
RKO (Edward Small)

A successful mannequin tries to manage on her engineer husband's lowly salary.
Thin, pleasant marital comedy with no surprises.
w P. J. Wolfson, Philip G. Epstein *d* Leigh Jason *ph* J. Roy Hunt *m* Roy Webb
☆ Barbara Stanwyck, Gene Raymond, Robert Young, Ned Sparks, Helen Broderick, Willie Best, Robert Warwick, Billy Gilbert, Hattie McDaniel, Irving Bacon

The Bride Wasn't Willing: see *Frontier Gal*

The Bride Wore Black *

France/Italy 1968 107m Eastmancolor
UA/Films du Carrosse/Artistes Associés/Dino de Laurentiis (Marcel Bébert)

original title: *La Mariée Était en Noir*
A melancholy lady traces and kills the five men responsible for her fiancé's death.
Uncertain and not very entertaining attempt to turn a Hitchcock situation into a character study.
w François Truffaut, Jean-Louis Richard *novel* William Irish *d* François Truffaut *ph* Raoul Coutard *m* Bernard Herrmann *ad* Pierre Guffroy *ed* Claudine Bouché
☆ Jeanne Moreau, Jean-Claude Brialy, Michel Bouquet, Charles Denner, Claude Rich, Michel Lonsdale

'Truffaut has called the film a love story; others have taken it as a tribute to his master, a Hitchcockian thriller. In fact it is neither; it is a piece of junk.' – *John Simon*

The Bride Wore Boots

US 1946 86m bw
Paramount (Seton I. Miller)
A woman who loves horses is married to a man who does not.
Flimsy, silly, but mainly quite tolerable light comedy sustained by its stars.
w Dwight Mitchell Wiley *d* Irving Pichel *ph* Stuart Thompson *m* Frederick Hollander
☆ Barbara Stanwyck, Robert Cummings, Diana Lynn, Patric Knowles, Peggy Wood, Robert Benchley, Willie Best, Natalie Wood

The Bride Wore Red *

US 1937 103m bw
MGM (Joseph L. Mankiewicz)

A whimsical count arranges for a chorus girl to spend two weeks at an aristocratic Tyrol resort, where she is pursued by two rich men.
Cinderella *retold in fancy dress; a typically unreal but quite entertaining star confection of its day.*
w Tess Slesinger, Bradbury Foote *play* *The Girl from Trieste* by Ferenc Molnar *d* Dorothy Arzner *ph* George Folsey *m* Franz Waxman
☆ Joan Crawford, Robert Young, Franchot Tone, Billie Burke, Reginald Owen, George Zucco, Lynne Carver, Mary Philips, Paul Porcasi

'Marquee values will have to bolster this one.' – *Variety*

'In the privacy of a girls' school he sought his prey – turning innocent beauty into a thing of unspeakable horror!'

The Brides of Dracula **

GB 1960 85m Technicolor
U-I/Hammer/Hotspur (Anthony Hinds)

Baron Meinster, a disciple of Dracula, is locked up by his mother; but a servant lets him out and he goes on the rampage in a girls' school.
The best of the Hammer Draculas, with plenty of inventive action, some classy acting and a good sense of place and period.
w Jimmy Sangster, Peter Bryan, Edward Percy *d* *Terence Fisher* *ph* Jack Asher *m* Malcolm Williamson *ed* James Needs, Alfred Cox
☆ *David Peel* (Meinster), *Peter Cushing*, Freda Jackson, *Martita Hunt*, Yvonne Monlaur, Andrée Melly, Mona Washbourne, Henry Oscar, Miles Malleson

The Brides of Fu Manchu *

GB 1966 94m Eastmancolor
Anglo Amalgamated

The yellow peril kidnaps twelve young women in order to blackmail their influential boyfriends.
Very adequate sequel to The Face of Fu Manchu *(qv for details of series), after which Fu Manchu went rapidly downhill.*
w Peter Welbeck (Harry Alan Towers) *d* Don Sharp
☆ Christopher Lee, Douglas Wilmer, Howard Marion Crawford, Marie Versini, Tsai Chin, Rupert Davies

The Bridge *

West Germany 1959 106m bw
Fono/Jochen Severin (Hermann Schwerin)
In 1945, only a handful of 16-year-old schoolboys is left to defend the bridge of a small German town.
Painful but memorable war vignette, almost an updating of All Quiet on the Western Front.
w Michael Mansfield, Karl-Wilhelm Vivier *novel* Manfred Gregor *d* *Bernhard Wicki* *ph* Gerd von Bonen *m* Hans-Martin Majewski
☆ Vokler Bohnet, Fritz Wepper, Michael Hinz, Frank Glaubrecht, Karl Michael Balzer, Gunther Hoffman
foreign film

The Bridge

GB 1991 99m Fujicolour
Moonlight/British Screen/Film Four (Lyn Goleby)

A young artist and a bored wife, who is on holiday with her young daughters, fall in love.
Genteel period drama, lacking in any dramatic impetus.
w Adrian Hodges *d* Sydney MacCartney *ph* David Tattersall *m* Richard G. Mitchell *pd* Terry Pritchard *ed* Michael Ellis
☆ Saskia Reeves, David O'Hara, Joss Ackland, Anthony Higgins, Rosemary Harris, Geraldine James

'Beautiful but inert … firmly belongs to the Laura Ashley school of genteel British cinema.' – *Variety*

'Frozen with timidity. This British costume drama sits on the screen like little Miss Muffet, spinning the trite tale of a summer's dalliance.' – *Geoff Brown, The Times*

The Bridge at Remagen *

US 1968 116m DeLuxe Panavision
UA/Wolper (David L. Wolper)

February 1945: Germans and Americans fight over a Rhine bridge.
Disenchanted, violent war film in which incessant bang-bang, adroitly staged, is all that matters.
w Richard Yates, William Roberts *d* John Guillermin *ph* Stanley Cortez *m* Elmer Bernstein
☆ George Segal, Robert Vaughn, Ben Gazzara, Bradford Dillman, E. G. Marshall, Peter Van Eyck

'Viable viewing if explosions and clichés are your shtick and exciting if you're not sure who won that war.' – *Judith Crist*

The Bridge of San Luis Rey *

US 1944 85m bw
UA/Benedict Bogeaus

Five people die when a Peruvian rope bridge collapses; the film investigates why they were each on the bridge at the time.
An intriguing novel is turned into tedious film drama, with actors, director, scenarist and production designer all making heavy weather.
w Howard Estabrook *novel* Thornton Wilder *d* Rowland V. Lee *ph* John Boyle *m* Dimitri Tiomkin
☆ Lynn Bari, Francis Lederer, Nazimova, Louis Calhern, Akim Tamiroff, Blanche Yurka, Donald Woods

'As a remake for present-day audiences, up to their ears in war news, this picture will be a welcome divertissement.' – *Variety*

† A silent version, with a few minutes of hasty talk, was made in 1929 by Charles Brabin for MGM, from a script by Alice Duer Miller, Ruth Cummings and Marian Ainslee. The cast included Lili Damita, Ernest Torrence, Don Alvarado, Raquel Torres, and Henry B. Walthall.
Dimitri Tiomkin

'It spans a whole new world of entertainment!'

The Bridge on the River Kwai ****

GB 1957 161m Technicolor Cinemascope
Columbia/Sam Spiegel

British POWs in Burma are employed by the Japs to build a bridge; meanwhile British agents seek to destroy it.
Ironic adventure epic with many fine moments but too many centres of interest and an unforgivably confusing climax. It is distinguished by Guinness's portrait of the English CO who is heroic in his initial stand against the Japs but finally cannot bear to see his bridge blown up: and the physical detail of the production is beyond criticism.
w Carl Foreman, Michael Wilson *novel* Pierre Boulle *d* *David Lean* *ph* Jack Hildyard *m* Malcolm Arnold *ed* Peter Taylor
☆ *Alec Guinness* (Colonel Nicholson), William Holden (Shears), Jack Hawkins (Major Warden), Sessue Hayakawa (Colonel Saito), James Donald (Major Clipton), Geoffrey Horne (Lieut. Joyce), Andre Morell (Col. Green), Percy Herbert (Grogan)

'It may rank as the most rousing adventure film inspired by the last World War.' – *Alton Cook, New York World Telegram*

† Cary Grant was originally sought for the William Holden role
†† Michael Wilson should also have been credited for the script, but he was blacklisted at the time.
picture; adaptation (now credited to Carl Foreman, Michael Wilson and Pierre Boulle); David Lean; Jack Hildyard; Malcolm Arnold; Alec Guinness; editing
Sessue Hayakawa
film; British film; Alec Guinness; Pierre Boulle

Bridge to the Sun *

France/US 1961 112m bw
MGM/Cité Films (Jacques Bar)
Just before Pearl Harbor, an American girl marries a Japanese diplomat and goes to live in Tokyo.
Romantic drama which oddly sides with the Japanese and shows America in a poor light. Interesting if not very compelling, with some unfamiliar views of Japan.
w Charles Kaufman *autobiography* Gwendolen Terasaki *d* Etienne Périer *ph* Marcel Weiss, Seiichi Kizuka, Bill Kelly *m* Georges Auric
☆ Carroll Baker, James Shigeta, James Yagi, Tetsuro Tamba

'In yet another burst of national flagellation, Hollywood turns on itself and unthinking Americans for being so beastly about the wartime Japanese.' – *MFB*

A Bridge Too Far **

US/GB 1977 175m Technicolor Panavision
UA/Joseph E. Levine (John Palmer)

The story of the Allied defeat at Arnhem in 1944.
Like all large-scale military films, this one fails to make its tactics clear, and its sober intent conflicts with its roster of guest stars. For all that, there are impressive moments of acting and production.
w William Goldman *book* Cornelius Ryan *d* Richard Attenborough (and Sidney Hayers) *ph* *Geoffrey Unsworth, Harry Waxman, Robin Browne* *m* John Addison *pd* Terence Marsh
☆ Dirk Bogarde, James Caan, Michael Caine, Sean Connery, Edward Fox, Elliott Gould, Gene Hackman, Anthony Hopkins, Hardy Kruger, *Laurence Olivier*, Ryan O'Neal, Robert Redford, Maximilian Schell, Liv Ullmann, Arthur Hill and also Wolfgang Preiss

'A film too long.' – *Anon*

'So wearily, expensively predictable that by the end the viewer will in all likelihood be too enervated to notice Attenborough's prosaic moral epilogue.' – *John Pym, MFB*

Geoffrey Unsworth; Edward Fox; John Addison

The Bridges at Toko-Ri *

US 1954 104m Technicolor
Paramount/Perlberg-Seaton

The comradeship and death of two jet pilots during the Korean War.
Ambitiously staged action thriller with points to make about war, death and politics: a well-worn American formula pitched very hard.
w Valentine Davies *novel* James A. Michener *d* Mark Robson *ph* Loyal Griggs *m* Lyn Murray *ed* Alma Macrorie
☆ William Holden, Mickey Rooney, Grace Kelly, Fredric March, Robert Strauss, Charles McGraw, Earl Holliman, Willis Bouchey

'A taut, thrilling, top flight documentary drama of men, war, ships and planes.' – *Cue*

editing

The Bridges of Madison County **

US 1995 135m Technicolor
Warner/Amblin/Malpaso (Clint Eastwood, Kathleen Kennedy)

An Italian-born farmer's wife in Iowa has a passionate four-day affair with a photographer.

Eastwood's restraint, both as actor and director, adds a little rigour to a swooningly sentimental best-seller, and Meryl Streep surprisingly finds some truth in her character; but for all their efforts, it is a thin thing.
w Richard LaGravenese *d* Clint Eastwood
ph Jack N. Green *m* Lennie Niehaus
pd Jeannine Oppewall *ed* Joel Cox
☆ Clint Eastwood, Meryl Streep, Annie Corley, Victor Slezak, Jim Haynie

'A handsomely crafted, beautifully acted adult love story.' – *Variety*

'Dull, dull, dull.' – *Pauline Kael*

† The film took more than $172m at the box-office worldwide.
Meryl Streep

'For anyone who's ever been set up, stood up or felt up.'

Bridget Jones's Diary **
US 2001 92m Technicolor
Universal/StudioCanal/MiramaxWorking Title (Tim Bevan, Eric Fellner, Jonathan Cavendish)

An over-anxious, overweight single woman in her 30s looks for love in the wrong places.
Enjoyable romantic comedy, based on a best-selling column and book, though some clumsy directorial flourishes hamper the fun.
w Helen Fielding, Andrew Davies, Richard Curtis *novel* Helen Fielding *d* Sharon Maguire
ph Stuart Dryburgh *m* Patrick Doyle *pd* Gemma Jackson *ed* Martin Walsh *cos* Rachael Fleming
☆ Renée Zellweger (Bridget Jones), Colin Firth (Mark Darcy), Hugh Grant (Daniel Cleaver), Gemma Jones (Bridget's Mum), Jim Broadbent (Bridget's Dad), Embeth Davidtz (Natasha), Shirley Henderson (Jude), Sally Phillips (Shazza), James Callis (Tom)

'Despite being edited down to a bare-bones 90-odd minutes, forcing the elimination of key characters and scenes and the underdevelopment of others, pic manages to feel, paradoxically, as dramatically flabby as the 10 pounds Bridget cannot seem to shed.' – *Lael Loewenstein, Variety*

'Not big, clever or remotely grown-up – but it is tremendous fun.' – *Nina Caplan, London Evening Standard*

Renée Zellweger

Brief Encounter ****
GB 1945 86m bw
Eagle-Lion/Cineguild (Anthony Havelock-Allan, Ronald Neame)

A suburban housewife on her weekly shopping visits develops a love affair with a local doctor; but he gets a job abroad and they agree not to see each other again.
An outstanding example of good middle-class cinema turned by sheer professional craft into a masterpiece; even those bored by the theme must be riveted by the treatment, especially the use of a dismal railway station and its trains.
w Noël Coward, David Lean, Ronald Neame, Anthony Havelock-Allan play Still Life by Noël Coward *d David Lean ph Robert Krasker*
m Rachmaninov *md* Muir Mathieson *ad* L. P. Williams *ed* Jack Harris
☆ *Celia Johnson, Trevor Howard,* Stanley Holloway, Joyce Carey, Cyril Raymond

'Both a pleasure to watch as a well-controlled piece of work, and deeply touching.' – *James Agee*

'Polished as is this film, its strength does not lie in movie technique, of which there is plenty, so much as in the tight realism of its detail.' – *Richard Winnington*

'A celebrated, craftsmanlike tearjerker, and incredibly neat. There's not a breath of air in it.' – *Pauline Kael, 70s*

† A TV film version was made in 1975 by ITC, starring Richard Burton and Sophia Loren and directed by Alan Bridges. It was an unqualified disaster.
Anthony Havelock-Allan, Ronald Neame, David Lean (script); David Lean (director); Celia Johnson

A Brief History of Time **
GB/US 1992 84m Technicolor
(David Hickman)

A documentary on the theories of Stephen Hawking concerning the origins and likely fate of the universe.
A more accessible but less complex approach to Hawking's views than his bestselling, if seldom finished, book. It includes interviews with Hawking himself.
wd Errol Morris *book* Stephen Hawking *ph* John Bailey *m* Philip Glass *pd* Ted Bafaloukos
ed Brad Fuller

Brigadoon *
US 1954 108m Anscocolor Cinemascope
MGM (Arthur Freed)

Two Americans in Scotland find a ghost village which awakens only once every hundred years.
Likeable but disappointing adaptation of a Lost Horizon*ish Broadway musical, marred by artificial sets and jaded direction.*
w Alan Jay Lerner *play* Alan Jay Lerner
d Vincente Minnelli *ph* Joseph Ruttenberg
m/ly Frederick Loewe, Alan Jay Lerner
md Johnny Green *ad* Cedric Gibbons, Preston Ames
☆ Gene Kelly, Cyd Charisse, Van Johnson, Jimmy Thompson, Elaine Stewart, Barry Jones, Eddie Quillan

'The whimsical dream world it creates holds no compelling attractions.' – *Penelope Houston*

† Cyd Charisse's singing was dubbed by Carole Richards.
art direction

The Brigand *
US 1952 93m Technicolor
Columbia
A Moroccan adventurer looks like the king and is reprieved from execution if he will impersonate the latter and root out his enemies.
Cheeky revamp of The Prisoner of Zenda *(qv), quite acceptably done.*
w Jesse Lasky Jnr *d* Phil Karlson *ph* W. Howard Greene *m* Mario Castelnuovo-Tedesco
☆ Anthony Dexter, Jody Lawrance, Gale Robbins, Anthony Quinn, Carl Benton Reid, Ron Randell

Brigham Young *
US 1940 112m bw
TCF (Kenneth MacGowan)
The story of the Mormon trek to Utah.
Ambitious but rather dull interpretation of history, seen as a Western with romantic fictional trimmings.
w Lamar Trotti *story* Louis Bromfield *d* Henry Hathaway *ph Arthur Miller m* Alfred Newman
☆ *Dean Jagger,* Tyrone Power, Linda Darnell, Brian Donlevy, Jane Darwell, John Carradine, Mary Astor, Vincent Price, Moroni Olsen

'A big picture in every respect.' – *Variety*

'One of the year's outstanding films.' – *Newsweek*

† The production had a 133-day schedule, and cost 2,700,000 dollars.

Bright Eyes *
US 1934 84m bw
Fox (Sol M. Wurtzell)

An orphan finds herself torn between foster-parents.
The first of Shirley Temple's genuine star vehicles has a liveliness and cheerfulness hard to find today. As a production, however, it is decidedly economical.
w William Conselman *d* David Butler *ph* Arthur Miller *m* Samuel Kaylin
☆ *Shirley Temple, James Dunn,* Lois Wilson, *Jane Withers,* Judith Allen

'It seems a cinch to please generally, the family and sentimental strata particularly.' – *Variety*

Bright Leaf
US 1950 110m bw
Warner (Henry Blanke)
A 19th-century tobacco farmer builds a cigarette empire.
Quite agreeable but disjointed fictional biopic, more about love than tobacco.
w Ranald MacDougall *novel* Robert Wilder
d Michael Curtiz *ph* Karl Freund *m* Victor Young
☆ Gary Cooper, Lauren Bacall, Patricia Neal, Jack Carson, Donald Crisp, Gladys George, Elizabeth Patterson, Jeff Corey, Taylor Holmes

Bright Lights *
US 1935 86m bw
Warner
GB title: *Funny Face*
A vaudevillian lets success go to his head.
The plot served for a score or more of thirties musicals, but this had Busby Berkeley routines and an unusual star role for Joe E. Brown.
w Bert Kalmar, Harry Ruby *d* Busby Berkeley
☆ Joe E. Brown, Ann Dvorak, Patricia Ellis, William Gargan

'Practically an 86-minute monologue, with the star doing everything but taking tickets.' – *Variety*

† The same title covered a 1925 MGM silent with Charles Ray as a country boy in love with a Broadway star, also a 1930 Warner film with Frank Fay.

Bright Lights, Big City
US 1988 107m colour
UIP/United Artists (Mark Rosenberg, Sydney Pollack)

A cocaine-snorting magazine researcher goes to pieces in New York.
Some good performances compensate for the unsympathetic central character of a lightweight drama.
w Jay McInerney *novel* Jay McInerney *d* James Bridges *ph* Gordon Willis *m* Donald Fagen
pd Santo Loquasto *ed* John Bloom
☆ Michael J. Fox, Kiefer Sutherland, Phoebe Cates, Frances Sternhagen, Dianne Wiest, Swoosie Kurtz, John Houseman, Jason Robards, Tracy Pollan

'The banality comes down on you like drizzle.' – *Pauline Kael, New Yorker*

Bright Road *
US 1953 69m bw
MGM (Sol Baer Fielding)
In an all-black school, a problem child finds himself when he helps to rid the school of a swarm of bees.
Slight but attractive second feature, unostentatiously set in a black community.
w Emmet Lavery *d* Gerald Mayer *ph* Alfred Gilks *m* David Rose
☆ Dorothy Dandridge, Harry Belafonte, Robert Horton, Philip Hepburn, Barbara Ann Sanders

Bright Victory *
US 1951 97m bw
Universal (Robert Buckner)
GB title: *Lights Out*
A blinded soldier adjusts to civilian life.
Well-meaning if rather slow and sticky, this drama is more sentimental than realistic but has good performances.
w Robert Buckner *novel* Baynard Kendrick
d Mark Robson *ph* William Daniels *m* Frank Skinner
☆ Arthur Kennedy, Peggy Dow, Julie Adams, James Edwards, Will Geer, Minor Watson, Jim Backus
Arthur Kennedy

A Brighter Summer Day ***
Taiwan 1991 237m colour
ICA/Yang and His Gang (Yu Welyan)
original title: *Guling Jie Shaonian Sha Ren Shijan*
In the early 1960s, a 14-year-old boy falls in love with the girlfriend of a young gang leader.
A long but engrossing film, set against troubled times and the fear of Communist China, which provides a detailed examination of the society of the time.
w Edward Yang, Yan Hongya, Yang Shunqing, Lai Mingtang *d Edward Yang ph* Zhang Hulgong, Li Longyu *pd* Yu Welyan, Edward Yang *ed* Chen Bowen
☆ Lisa Yang, Zhang Zhen, Zhang Guozhu, Elaine Jin, Wang Juan, Zhang Han

'One of the major feats of non-American cinema of its time ... Gathers an extraordinary momentum, showing that you really can delineate the lives of ordinary people in an extraordinary way without either flashiness or pretension.' – *Derek Malcolm, Guardian*

† The film also exists in a version that is 50m shorter. The longer version is the director's preferred cut.

Brightness: see *Yeelen*

Brighton Beach Memoirs *
US 1986 108m colour
Universal/Rastar (David Chasman)

In 1937 Brooklyn, a lower-middle-class Jewish family has assorted crises.
Standard picturization of a Neil Simon play, somewhat flattened out in the process but with funny moments.
w Neil Simon *play* Neil Simon *d* Gene Saks
ph John Bailey *m* Michael Small
☆ Blythe Danner, Bob Dishy, Brian Drillinger, Stacey Glick, Judith Ivey, Lisa Waltz

'Simon instinctively makes things easy and palatable, and there's a penalty: it's the retrograde, pepless snooziness of the picture. You come out feeling half dead.' – *New Yorker*

Brighton Rock ***
GB 1947 92m bw
Associated British/Charter Films (Roy Boulting)

US title: *Young Scarface*
The teenage leader of a racetrack gang uses a waitress as alibi to cover a murder, and marries her. He later decides to be rid of her, but fate takes a hand in his murder plot.
A properly 'seedy' version of Graham Greene's 'entertainment', very flashily done for the most part but with a trick ending which allows the heroine to keep her illusions.
w Graham Greene, Terence Rattigan
novel Graham Greene *d* John Boulting *ph* Harry Waxman *m* Hans May *ad* John Howell *ed* Peter Scott
☆ Richard Attenborough, Hermione Baddeley, *Harcourt Williams,* William Hartnell, Alan Wheatley, Carol Marsh, Nigel Stock

'The film is slower, much less compelling, and, if you get me, less cinematic than the book, as a child's guide to which I hereby offer it.' – *Richard Winnington*

'It proceeds with the efficiency, the precision and the anxiety to please of a circular saw.' – *Dilys Powell*

The Brighton Strangler
US 1945 67m bw
RKO (Herman Schlom)

An actor takes over in real life the part he is playing – of a murderer.
This hoary plot had seen better days even in 1945, and was not helped by an establishing shot which put Parliament on the wrong side of the Thames.
w Arnold Phillips, Max Nosseck *d* Max Nosseck
ph J. Roy Hunt *m* Leigh Harline
☆ John Loder, June Duprez, Miles Mander

Brimstone
US 1949 90m Trucolor
Republic

A US Marshal tracks down Public Outlaw Number One.
High-spirited Western co-feature.
w Thames Williamson *d* Joseph Kane
☆ Rod Cameron, Walter Brennan, Adrian Booth, Forrest Tucker, Jack Holt, Jim Davis, James Brown, Guinn Williams

Brimstone and Treacle *
GB 1982 87m Technicolor
Namara/Alan E. Salke/Herbert Solow

A strange young man has a sinister effect on the family of a middle-aged writer of doggerel, whose crippled daughter he finally rapes.
Similar in mood to Pennies from Heaven *(qv), this is basically a television play very typical of its author. (Some years ago it was taped and then banned by the BBC.) In substance no more than a reversal of* The Passing of the Third Floor Back *(qv), its points of interest are mainly technical.*
w Dennis Potter *play* Dennis Potter *d* Richard Loncraine *ph* Peter Hannan *m* Sting *pd* Milly Burns
☆ Sting, Denholm Elliott, Joan Plowright, Suzanna Hamilton, Benjamin Whitrow, Dudley Sutton

Bring 'Em Back Alive
US 1932 65m bw
RKO/Van Beuren
A documentary showing how an animal hunter scoured Malayan jungles for specimens to stock the world's zoos.
Very dated now, but quite an attraction in its day. The title was used again in 1982 for a TV series in which Bruce Boxleitner played Buck; the emphasis now, however, was on serial-like intrigue.
d Clyde Elliott
☆ Frank Buck
'Will get money but needs alert exploitation.' – *Variety*

'May the best moves win.'
Bring It On
US 2000 98m colour
Universal/Beacon (Marc Abraham, Thomas A. Bliss, John Ketcham)
A new girl who joins a prize-winning squad of cheerleaders helps them to recover their self-respect in time for the national championships.
Pleasant teen comedy that fortunately doesn't take its subject-matter too seriously.
w Jessica Bendinger *d* Peyton Reed *ph* Shawn Maurer *m* Christophe Beck *pd* Sharon Lomofsky *ed* Larry Bock *cos* Mary Jane Fort *ch* Anne Fletcher
☆ Kirsten Dunst (Torrance Shipman), Eliza Dushku (Missy Pantone), Jesse Bradford (Cliff Pantone), Gabrielle Union (Isis), Clare Kramer (Courtney), Nicole Bilderback (Whitney), Tsianina Joelson (Darcy), Rini Bell (Kasey), Ian Roberts (Sparky Polastri), Richard Hillman (Aaron), Lindsay Sloane (Big Red), Cody McMains (Justin Shipman)
'As pure a bubble gum movie as can be imagined in this cynical age.' – *Robert Koehler, Variety*

'It's got guts!'
Bring Me the Head of Alfredo Garcia
US 1974 112m DeLuxe
UA/Optimus/Churubusco (Martin Baum)
A wealthy Mexican offers a million dollars for the head of a man who seduced his daughter, and claimants find that grave robbing is involved.
Gruesome, sickly action melodrama with revolting detail; the nadir of a director obsessed by violence.
w Gordon Dawson, Sam Peckinpah *d* Sam Peckinpah *ph* Alex Phillips Jnr *m* Jerry Fielding
☆ Warren Oates, Gig Young, Isela Vega, Robert Webber, Helmut Dantine, Emilio Fernandez, Kris Kristofferson
'Few movies are as tedious. Bring me the head of the studio that released this one.' – *Gene Shalit*
'The only kind of analysis it really invites is psychoanalysis.' – *Wall Street Journal*
'Peckinpah clearly doesn't lack talent – what he lacks is brains.' – *John Simon*

Bring Me the Head of Mavis Davis
GB 1997 99m Technicolor
Feature/Goldcrest/BBC/Mission (Stephen Colegrave, Joanne Reay)
A record producer hires a hitman when he suddenly realizes that his star singer would be worth more to him dead than alive.
Some slick performances fail to save this would-be black comedy from being unpleasant and unamusing.
w Craig Strachan *idea* Joanne Reay *d* John Henderson *ph* Clive Tickner *m* Christopher Tyng *pd* Michael Carlin *ed* Paul Endacott
☆ Rik Mayall, Jane Horrocks, Danny Aiello, Ronald Pickup, Philip Martin-Brown, Jaclyn Mendoza, Ross Boatman, Paul Shearer
'A TV-style effort decapitated by a lame script and often clumsy direction.' – *Derek Elley, Variety*

Bringing Out the Dead ***
US 1999 120m DeLuxe Panavision
Buena Vista/Paramount/Touchstone (Scott Rudin, Barbara De Fina)
In New York City, an overworked ambulance driver careers towards a breakdown over the unremitting horrors of his night shift.
Scorsese revisits familiar territory for him and his audience: hellish streets inhabited by low-life predators and victims; but his perspective has shifted from his customary petty gangsters and psychopaths to the good guys, however unbalanced they may seem. Despair is here tempered with humanity.
w Paul Schrader *novel* Joe Connelly *d* Martin Scorsese *ph* Robert Richardson *m* Elmer Bernstein *pd* Dante Ferretti *ed* Thelma Schoonmaker *sp* Industrial Light & Magic
☆ Nicolas Cage (Frank Pierce), Patricia Arquette (Mary Burke), John Goodman (Larry), Ving Rhames (Marcus), Tom Sizemore (Tom Wolls), Marc Anthony (Noel), Mary Beth Hurt (Nurse Constance), Cliff Curtis (Cy Coates), Nestor Serrano (Dr Hazmat), Aida Turturro (Nurse Crupp)
'An intense, volatile movie full of sorrow and wild, mordant humor.' – *Janet Maslin, New York Times*
'This is a work of bad imitation from an immature talent who thinks he's Martin Scorsese.' – *Cosmo Landesman, Sunday Times*

Bringing Up Baby ***
US 1938 102m bw
RKO (Howard Hawks)
A zany girl causes a zoology professor to lose a dinosaur bone and a pet leopard in the same evening.
Outstanding crazy comedy which barely pauses for romance and ends up with the whole splendid cast in jail.
w Dudley Nichols, Hagar Wilde d Howard Hawks *ph* Russell Metty *m* Roy Webb
☆ *Katharine Hepburn, Cary Grant, May Robson, Charles Ruggles, Walter Catlett, Fritz Feld,* Jonathan Hale, Barry Fitzgerald
'Harum-scarum farce comedy ... definite box-office.' – *Variety*
'I am happy to report that it is funny from the word go, that it has no other meaning to recommend it ... and that I wouldn't swap it for practically any three things of the current season.' – *Otis Ferguson*
'It may be the American movies' closest equivalent to Restoration comedy.' – *Pauline Kael*
'Crazy comedies continue to become crazier, and there will soon be few actors and actresses left who have no straw in their hair.' – *Basil Wright*
† The dog George was played by Asta from *The Thin Man* movies.

Bringing Up Father
US 1928 70m approx (24 fps) bw silent
MGM
Mild domestic comedy about a henpecked husband, from the famous comic strip.
It marked the successful comeback of Marie Dressler (as the maid).
w Frances Marion *d* Jack Conway
☆ J. Farrell MacDonald, Marie Dressler, Polly Moran, Gertrude Olmsted, Grant Withers
† Two or three second features about Jiggs and Maggie, featuring Renie Riano and Joe Yule, appeared in the late forties.

Brink of Hell: see *Toward the Unknown*

Brink of Life: see *So Close to Life*

The Brinks Job
US 1978 103m Technicolor
Universal/Dino de Laurentiis (Ralph Serpe)
In 1944, amateur criminals bring off a raid on the vaults of a Boston security company.
Farcical variation of a much-told true tale. Despite much mugging by the stars and a frantic narrative style, it does not come off.
w Walon Green *book* *Big Stick-Up at Brinks* by Noel Behn *d* William Friedkin *ph* Norman Leigh *m* Richard Rodney Bennett *pd* Dean Tavoularis
☆ Peter Falk, Warren Oates, Peter Boyle, Allen Goorwitz, Gena Rowlands, Paul Sorvino, Sheldon Leonard

Britannia Hospital
GB 1982 116m colour
EMI/Film and General/NFFC (Davina Belling, Clive Parsons)
Problems besetting a British hospital celebrating its 500th anniversary include strikes, demonstrators, and a mad doctor who transplants heads.
Looking as crummy as a Carry On at the end of its tether, this intended lampoon of the state of the nation never warms up and can only fire off stale jokes in all directions while repelling the eye with its Frankenstein scenes.
w David Sherwin *d* Lindsay Anderson *ph* Mike Fash *m* Alan Price *pd* Norris Spencer
☆ Malcolm McDowell, Leonard Rossiter, Graham Crowden, Fulton Mackay, Vivian Pickles, Joan Plowright, Peter Jeffrey, Robin Askwith, Dandy Nichols, Valentine Dyall, Roland Culver, Alan Bates, Arthur Lowe, Marsha Hunt
'It has all the intensity, along with the flailing incoherence, of a soapbox jeremiah.' – *Richard Combs, MFB*
'Having once created a general shambles, the film is at a loss to clean it up.' – *Margaret Hinxman, Daily Mail*
'Inexplicably muddled and inconclusive.' – *Guardian*
'It mentholates the tubes and oxygenates the brain.' – *Sunday Telegraph*

Britannia Mews
GB 1948 91m bw
TCF (William Perlberg)
US title: *The Forbidden Street*
In Victorian times, the widow of a puppetmaster eventually marries his lookalike who rebuilds their puppet theatre.
Curious and uncertain comedy drama set among yesterday's high society, with poorly played leads but an interesting supporting cast and technical assurance.
w Ring Lardner Jnr *novel* Margery Sharp *d* Jean Negulesco *ph* Georges Périnal *m* Malcolm Arnold *ad* Andrei Andreiev
☆ Dana Andrews, Maureen O'Hara, Sybil Thorndike, Wilfrid Hyde-White, Fay Compton, A. E. Matthews

British Agent *
US 1934 75m bw
Warner (Henry Blanke)
In 1910 Russia, a Britisher falls in love with a lady spy.
Sluggish and dated romantic melodrama, notable only for Howard's performance and some directional felicities.
w Laird Doyle *novel* H. Bruce Lockhart *d* Michael Curtiz *ph* Ernest Haller *ad* Anton Grot
☆ *Leslie Howard,* Kay Francis, William Gargan, *Irving Pichel,* Philip Reed, Walter Byron, J. Carrol Naish, Halliwell Hobbes
'One of those rare cases of a film both artistically and cinematically good entertainment ... an exciting story well told, excellent acting, draw names and production value.' – *Variety*

British Intelligence
US 1940 63m bw
Warner (Bryan Foy)
GB title: *Enemy Agent*
During World War I a German lady spy becomes a guest in the house of a British war official, the butler of which is the leader of a German spy ring.
Second feature remake of Three Faces East *(qv); still quite an entertaining melodrama.*
w Lee Katz *play* Anthony Paul Kelly *d* Terry Morse *ph* Sid Hickox *m* Heinz Roemheld
☆ Boris Karloff, Margaret Lindsay, Maris Wrixon, Bruce Lester, Leonard Mudie, Holmes Herbert

Broadcast News *
US 1987 31m DeLuxe
UKFD/Fox/Gracie Films (James L. Brooks)
An ambitious TV news reader with personality but little talent gets to the top.
Mildly satirical look at the world of television journalism that slips into romantic comedy.
wd James L. Brooks *ph* Michael Ballhaus *m* Bill Conti *pd* Charles Rosen *ed* Richard Marks
☆ William Hurt, Albert Brooks, *Holly Hunter,* Robert Prosky, Lois Chiles, Joan Cusack, Jack Nicholson (uncredited cameo)
best picture; William Hurt; Holly Hunter; Albert Brooks; best original screenplay; best cinematography; best film editing

Broadminded *
US 1931 65m bw
First National
A bashful swain leaves town after a misunderstanding and becomes involved in an intercontinental chase.
Modest star farce with some hilarious moments.
w Bert Kalmar, Harry Ruby *d* Mervyn Le Roy
☆ *Joe E. Brown,* Ona Munson, William Collier Jnr, Marjorie White, Holmes Herbert, Bela Lugosi
'Best he has ever done ... any audience will enjoy it.' – *Variety*

Broadway
US 1942 90m bw
Universal (Bruce Manning)
George Raft recalls his days as a hoofer in a New York speakeasy, and in particular a murder involving gangsters and chorus girls.
Minor crime melodrama which after interminable scene-setting paints an effective picture of the twenties but has too slack a grip on narrative.
w Felix Jackson, John Bright *play* Philip Dunning, George Abbott *d* William A. Seiter *ph* George Barnes *md* Charles Previn *ed* Ted J. Kent
☆ George Raft, Pat O'Brien, S. Z. Sakall, Janet Blair, Broderick Crawford, Marjorie Rambeau

Broadway Bill **
US 1934 104m bw
Columbia (Frank Capra)
GB title: *Strictly Confidential*
A cheerful horse trainer finds he has a winner.
Easygoing romantic comedy with the energetic Capra style in fairly full bloom.
w Robert Riskin *story* Mark Hellinger *d Frank Capra* *ph* Joseph Walker
☆ Warner Baxter, Myrna Loy, Walter Connolly, Helen Vinson, Douglass Dumbrille, Raymond Walburn, Lynne Overman, Clarence Muse, Margaret Hamilton, Paul Harvey, Claude Gillingwater, Charles Lane, Ward Bond
'The effect of capable direction is discernible in every foot.' – *Variety*
'It will be a long day before we see so little made into so much: it is gay and charming and will make you happy, and I am sorry to say I do not know recommendations much higher.' – *Otis Ferguson*
† Remade as *Riding High* (qv).

Broadway Bound *
US 1991 94m colour
Blue Dolphin/ABC Productions (Terry Nelson)
In the 40s, two brothers struggle to become writers and move away from home, where their father and mother quarrel and their grandfather grumbles.
An autobiographical slice of life, delivered with a gently effective humour.
w Neil Simon *play* Neil Simon *d* Paul Bogart *ph* Isidore Mankofsky *m* David Shire *pd* Ben Edwards *ed* Andy Zall
☆ Anne Bancroft, Hume Cronyn, Corey Parker, Jonathan Silverman, Jerry Orbach, Michele Lee
'Certain to delight those with a taste for the theatrical.' – *Empire*

Broadway Danny Rose *
US 1984 84m DeLuxe
Orion (Robert Greenhut)
An artists' agent and former comic falls foul of the Mafia while promoting a client.
Generally appealing comedy-melodrama with rather less self-examination than has latterly been typical of its star.
wd Woody Allen *ph* Gordon Willis *md* Dick Hyman *pd* Mel Bourne *ed* Susan E. Morse
☆ Woody Allen, Mia Farrow, Nick Apollo Forte, Craig Vandenburgh, Herb Reynolds
direction, original screenplay
original screenplay

Broadway Hostess
US 1935 69m bw
Warner
A small-town girl becomes a night-club singer.
Modest musical which failed to create a new star.
w George Bricker *d* Frank McDonald *ch* Bobby Connolly

☆ Wini Shaw, Genevieve Tobin, Lyle Talbot, Allen Jenkins, Phil Regan, Marie Wilson, Spring Byington

'Adequate for family audience consumption.' – *Variety*

Bobby Connolly

Broadway Limited *

US 1941 75m bw

Hal Roach

GB title: *The Baby Vanishes*

On an express train, a Hollywood publicity stunt backfires.

Wild farce which is not very funny as a whole but has entertaining comic performances.

w Rian James *d* Gordon Douglas *ph* Henry Sharp *m* Charles Previn

☆ *Victor McLaglen*, Patsy Kelly, *Leonid Kinskey*, Marjorie Woodworth, Dennis O'Keefe, ZaSu Pitts, George E. Stone

'The pulsating drama of Broadway's bared heart speaks and sings with a voice to stir your soul!'

'The new wonder of the screen!'

The Broadway Melody *

US 1929 110m bw (Technicolor scenes)

MGM (Lawrence Weingarten)

Chorus girls try to make it big on Broadway.

The screen's very first musical, exceedingly primitive by the standards of even a year later, but rather endearing and with a splendid score.

w James Gleason, Norman Houston, Edmund Goulding *d* Harry Beaumont *ph* John Arnold *m/ly* *Nacio Herb Brown, Arthur Freed* *ad* Cedric Gibbons

☆ Charles King, Anita Page, Bessie Love, Jed Prouty, Kenneth Thomson, Mary Doran, Eddie Kane

'A basic story with some sense to it, action, excellent direction, laughs, a tear, a couple of great performances and plenty of sex.' – *Variety*

† The plot resurfaced in *Two Girls On Broadway* (qv), made by MGM in 1940.

best picture

Harry Beaumont, Bessie Love

'You have waited seven years for this!'

Broadway Melody of 1936 **

US 1935 103m bw

MGM (John W. Considine Jnr)

A Broadway producer is at loggerheads with a columnist.

Fairly lively musical with lavish numbers.

w Jack McGowan, Sid Silvers, Harry Conn *story* Moss Hart *d* Roy del Ruth *ph* Charles Rosher *m/ly* *Nacio Herb Brown, Arthur Freed* *md* Alfred Newman *ch* Dave Gould *ed* Blanche Sewell

☆ Jack Benny, Robert Taylor, Una Merkel, *Eleanor Powell*, June Knight, Vilma and Buddy Ebsen, Nick Long Jnr

'Smash musical with strong dancing and comedy framework.' – *Variety*

♫ 'You Are My Lucky Star'; 'I've Gotta Feelin' You're Foolin''; 'Broadway Rhythm'; 'On a Sunday Afternoon'; 'Sing Before Breakfast'; 'All I Do Is Dream Of You'

Dave Gould

best picture; Moss Hart

'So Big It Tops Them All. So New It's A Year Ahead!'

Broadway Melody of 1938 *

US 1937 110m bw

MGM (Jack Cummings)

Backstage problems threaten the opening of a musical show.

Lavish but fairly forgettable musical with top talent.

w Jack McGowan, Sid Silvers *d* Roy del Ruth *ph* William Daniels *m/ly* Nacio Herb Brown, Arthur Freed *md* George Stoll *ed* Blanche Sewell

☆ Eleanor Powell, George Murphy, *Sophie Tucker*, Judy Garland, Robert Taylor, Buddy Ebsen, Sid Silvers, Billy Gilbert, Raymond Walburn

'Explosion in the cash drawers ... will do smash business everywhere.' – *Variety*

♫ 'Some of These Days'; 'Your Broadway and My Broadway'; 'Yours and Mine'; 'I'm Feelin' Like a Million'; 'Dear Mr Gable'

Broadway Melody of 1940 *

US 1939 102m bw

MGM (Jack Cummings)

A dance team gets to the top.

Splendidly produced but thinly plotted extravaganza with good numbers.

w Leon Gordon, George Oppenheimer *story* Jack McGowan, Dore Schary *d* Norman Taurog *ph* Oliver T. Marsh, Joseph Ruttenberg *m/ly* Cole Porter *md* Alfred Newman *ad* Cedric Gibbons *ed* Blanche Sewell

☆ *Fred Astaire, Eleanor Powell*, George Murphy, Douglas Macphail, Florence Rice, Frank Morgan, Ian Hunter

♫ 'I Concentrate on You'; 'Begin the Beguine'; 'Between You and Me'

Broadway Rhythm *

US 1943 113m Technicolor

MGM (Jack Cummings)

A Broadway producer looks in the wrong places for talent for his new show.

Originally intended as Broadway Melody of 1944, *this putting-on-a-show extravaganza had only the numbers to commend it.*

w Dorothy Kingsley, Harry Clork *operetta* *Very Warm for May* *by Jerome Kern and Oscar Hammerstein* *d* Roy del Ruth *ph* Leonard Smith *m/ly* various *md* John Green

☆ George Murphy, Ginny Simms, Charles Winninger, Gloria de Haven, Lena Horne, Nancy Walker, Hazel Scott, Eddie Anderson, Ben Blue, Tommy Dorsey and his Orchestra

'It contains perhaps three minutes of good acrobatic dancing and lasts nearly two hours.' – *James Agee*

Broadway Serenade

US 1939 114m bw

MGM (Robert Z. Leonard)

GB title: *Serenade*

Career problems split the marriage of a songwriter and his singing wife.

Lavish but rather dull romantic drama with music.

w Charles Lederer, Lew Lipton, John T. Foote, Hans Kraly *d* Robert Z. Leonard *ph* Oliver T. Marsh *md* Herbert Stothart

☆ Jeanette Macdonald, Lew Ayres, Frank Morgan, Ian Hunter, Rita Johnson, Virginia Grey, William Gargan, Katherine Alexander

'With all its lavishness, it impresses as only mild box office material.' – *Variety*

♫ 'No Time to Argue'; 'Time Changes Everything but Love'; 'For Every Lonely Heart'; 'Broadway Serenade'; 'High Flyin''; 'One Look at You'

Broadway Singer: see *Torch Singer*

Broadway thru a Keyhole *

US 1933 90m bw

UA/Twentieth Century (William Goetz, Raymond Griffith)

A tough New York gangster falls for a singer in his night-club.

Reputed acid observation of the New York scene distinguishes this low-budget gangster drama.

w Gene Towne, Graham Baker *story* Walter Winchell *d* Lowell Sherman *ph* Barney McGill *m/ly* Mack Gordon, Harry Revel

☆ Constance Cummings, Russ Columbo, Paul Kelly, *Blossom Seeley*, Gregory Ratoff, *Texas Guinan*, Hobart Cavanaugh, C. Henry Gordon

'Not a big picture, but good entertainment.' – *Variety*

† The film was based on Ruby Keeler's relationships with gangster Johnny Costello and Al Jolson.

Broadway to Hollywood

US 1933 90m bw

MGM

GB title: *Ring Up the Curtain*

A vaudeville family makes it in movies.

Cliché-strewn rags-to-riches saga with songs; good moments.

wd Willard Mack

☆ Frank Morgan, Alice Brady, Jackie Cooper, Madge Evans, Jimmy Durante, Nelson Eddy, May Robson, Una Merkel, Mickey Rooney

'A saga of the theatre that will please.' – *Variety*

† Some material was salvaged from an abandoned MGM musical of 1929, *The March of Time*.

'For just a little while, it was all so perfect.'

'How far would you go to protect a friend?'

Brokedown Palace *

US 1999 100m DeLuxe Panavision

TCF/Fox 2000 (Adam Fields)

Two teenage girls are jailed in Thailand after being tricked into carrying heroin through customs.

Mundane drama with nothing to lift it out of the ordinary.

w David Arata, Adam Fields *d* Jonathan Kaplan *ph* Newton Thomas Sigel *m* David Newman *pd* James Newport *ed* Curtiss Clayton

☆ Claire Danes (Alice Marano), Kate Beckinsale (Darlene Davis), Bill Pullman (Hank Greene), Jacqueline Kim (Yon Greene), Lou Diamond Phillips (Roy Knox), Daniel Lapaine (Nick Parks), Tom Amandes (Doug Davis), Aimee Graham (Beth Ann Gardener), John Doe (Bill Marano), Kay Tong Lim (Chief Detective Jagkrit)

'Utterly indistinguishable from the heap of Third World prison movies involving gullible Westerners.' – *James Christoper, Times*

Broken Arrow *

US 1950 92m Technicolor

TCF (Julian Blaustein)

A US army scout brings about peace between white man and Apache.

Solemn Western which at the time was acclaimed for giving the Indian's point of view (something which had scarcely happened since silent days). As entertainment it was not exciting, but it set Jeff Chandler off on a career playing Cochise with variations, and a TV series of the same name surfaced in 1956.

w Albert Maltz *novel* *Blood Brother* by Elliott Arnold *d* Delmer Daves *ph* Ernest Palmer *m* Hugo Friedhofer *md* Alfred Newman

☆ James Stewart, Jeff Chandler, Debra Paget, Basil Ruysdael, Will Geer, Arthur Hunnicutt, Jay Silverheels

'It has probably done more to soften racial hostilities than most movies designed to instruct, indict and inspire.' – *Pauline Kael*

† Screenwriter Albert Maltz did not receive a credit when the film was released because he was blacklisted. Instead, the script was credited to Michael Blankfort.

Michael Blankfort; Ernest Palmer; Jeff Chandler

'Prepare To Go Ballistic!'

Broken Arrow

US 1996 86m DeLuxe Panavision

TCF/WCG (Mark Gordon, Bill Badalato, Terence Chang)

A pilot chases a rival who has stolen a Stealth bomber containing live nuclear bombs.

An object lesson in how to make violence aesthetically interesting, but it is a pity the director cannot do the same with the plot or the characters; the narrative is implausible and the people little more than automatons equipped with a couple of vaguely human characteristics.

w Graham Yost *d* John Woo *ph* Peter Levy *m* Hans Zimmer *pd* Holger Gross *ed* John Wright, Steve Mirkovich, Joe Hutshing

☆ John Travolta, Christian Slater, Samantha Mathis, Delroy Lindo, Bob Gunton, Frank Whaley, Howie Long, Vondie Curtis-Hall, Jack Thompson

'Highly proficient and almost totally empty.' – *Derek Malcolm, Guardian*

'For explosion nerds only.' – *Tom Shone, Sunday Times*

Broken Blossoms **

US 1919 105m (16 fps) bw silent

UA/D. W. Griffith

In slummy Limehouse, a young Chinaman loves the daughter of a brute, who kills her; the Chinaman then kills him and commits suicide.

Victorian-style melodrama presented by Griffith with all the stops out; sometimes striking, but very dated even on its first appearance.

wd D. W. Griffith *story* *Limehouse Nights* (The Chink and the Child) by Thomas Burke *ph* G. W. Bitzer, Hendrik Sartov, Karl Brown

☆ Lillian Gish, Donald Crisp, Richard Barthelmess

'This is a Limehouse which neither Mr Burke nor anybody else who knows his East End of London will be able to recognize ... but *Broken Blossoms* is a genuine attempt to bring real tragedy onto the screen as opposed to machine-made drama, and for that Mr Griffith deserves the thanks of all who are convinced of the potentialities of the film.' – *The Times*

'I know of no other picture in which so much screen beauty is obtained ... attributable to the Whistlerian fogs and shadows, with that dock in Limehouse recurring like some pedal point.' – *James Agate, 1928*

† The film was made for $88,000, but Adolph Zukor regarded it as uncommercial and sold it to United Artists for $250,000. It went on to make a profit of $700,000. Leslie Henson appeared in a parody, *Broken Bottles*, in 1920.

Broken Blossoms *

GB 1936 84m bw

Twickenham (Julius Hagen)

A Chinese man becomes involved in a tragic love affair.

A remake originally intended to be directed by Griffith; quite stylish, and in some ways more interesting than its predecessor.

w Emlyn Williams *d* John Brahm *ph* Curt Courant

☆ Dolly Haas, Arthur Margetson, Emlyn Williams, Donald Calthrop, Ernest Sefton, Kathleen Harrison, Basil Radford

'There isn't much reason for this one.' – *Variety*

'The language of love, honour and betrayal.'

Broken English **

New Zealand 1996 92m colour

First Independent/Communicado/Village Roadshow (Robin Scholes)

In New Zealand, a young Croatian woman, eager to escape her domineering father, falls in love with the Maori chef at the Chinese restaurant where she works.

Tough, compelling account of immigrant life, and of love, of fears of the future on the part of those locked in their past, of culture clashes and misunderstandings.

w Gregor Nicholas, Johanna Pigott, Jim Salter *d* Gregor Nicholas *ph* John Toon *m* Murray Grindlay, Murray McNabb *pd* Michael Kane *ed* David Coulson

☆ Rade Serbedzija, Aleksandra Vujcic, Julian Arahanga, Marton Csokas, Madeline McNamara, Zhoa Jing, Yang Li, Temuera Morrison

'Well-intentioned but overly harrowing viewing which will leave its audience craving a shot of escapism.' – *Rob Driscoll, Empire*

'The shortest distance between friends isn't always a straight line.'

The Broken Hearts Club: A Romantic Comedy

US 2000 95m colour 'scope

Columbia TriStar/Banner (Mickey Liddell, Joseph Middleton)

In West Hollywood, a group of gay men gather to play softball, gossip and look for love.

Slick, feel-good comedy of startling superficiality.

wd Greg Berlanti *ph* Thomas Bango *pd* Charlie Daboub *ed* Todd Busch

☆ Timothy Olyphant (Dennis), Andrew Keegan (Kevin), John Mahoney (Jack), Dean Cain (Cole), Matt McGrath (Howie), Zach Braff (Benji), Ben Weber (Patrick), Billy Porter (Taylor)

'At its best, it is funny and feelgood; at its mildest, a PR primer for newly "out" men.' – *Alexander Walker, London Evening Standard*

The Broken Horseshoe

GB 1953 79m bw

Butchers/Nettlefold (Ernest G. Roy)

A doctor becomes implicated in the murder of a patient when he falls for a mysterious woman.

A thriller with an over-reliance on plot to maintain an audience's interest, which it soon dissipates with its implausibility.

w A. R. Rawlinson *TV serial* Francis Durbridge *d* Martyn C. Webster *ph* Gerald Gibbs *m* Wilfred Burns *ad* Bernard Robinson *ed* Joseph Sterling

☆ Robert Beatty, Elizabeth Sellars, Peter Coke, Hugh Kelly, Vida Hope, Janet Butler, Ferdy Mayne, George Benson, Roger Delgado

Broken Journey
GB 1948 89m bw
Gainsborough (Sydney Box)
A plane crashes in the Alps, and the survivors take different attitudes to their situation.
Unpersuasive and stagey melodrama which wastes some good talent.
w Robert Westerby *d* Ken Annakin *ph* Jack Cox *m* John Greenwood
☆ Phyllis Calvert, James Donald, Margot Grahame, Francis L. Sullivan, Raymond Huntley, Derek Bond, Guy Rolfe, David Tomlinson

Broken Lance *
US 1954 96m DeLuxe Cinemascope
TCF (Sol C. Siegel)
An autocratic cattle baron causes dissension among his sons.
Western remake of House of Strangers *(qv), quite well done.*
w Richard Murphy *story* Philip Yordan *d* Edward Dmytryk *ph* Joe MacDonald *m* Leigh Harline
☆ Spencer Tracy, Richard Widmark, Robert Wagner, Jean Peters, Katy Jurado, Earl Holliman, Hugh O'Brian, Eduard Franz, E. G. Marshall
Philip Yordan
Katy Jurado

Broken Lullaby *
US 1931 77m bw Paramount
GB and original title: *The Man I Killed*
A young Frenchman goes to Germany to seek out the family of the man he killed in the war, and is accepted by them as a friend.
This most untypical Lubitsch film now seems very dated but was deeply felt at the time and has plenty of cinematic grip.
w Ernest Vajda, Samson Raphaelson *play* *L'Homme que J'ai Tué* by Maurice Rostand *d* *Ernst Lubitsch* *ph* Victor Milner *m* W. Franke Harling *ad* Hans Dreier
☆ Lionel Barrymore, Phillips Holmes, Nancy Carroll, Tom Douglas, ZaSu Pitts, Lucien Littlefield, Louise Carter, Emma Dunn
'Well made, but heavy themes and actionless … hardly attuned to film patronage as a whole.' – *Variety*
'The best talking picture that has yet been seen and heard.' – *Robert E. Sherwood*
'I cannot remember a film so beautifully made, so completely fine in its execution.' – *John Grierson*
'Lubitsch can't entirely escape his own talent, and the film is beautifully crafted, but he mistook drab, sentimental hokum for ironic, poetic tragedy.' – *Pauline Kael, 70s*

Broken Mirrors
Holland 1984 116m Eastmancolor
Sigma (Matthijs van Heijningen)
Brothel girls consider the worthlessness of their lives.
Would-be symbolic melodrama with feminist overtones. Hard to take from beginning to end.
wd Marleen Gorris *ph* Frans Bromet *m* Lodewijk de Boer
☆ Lineke Rijxman, Henriette Tol, Edda Barends, Coby Stunnenberg

Broken Noses *
US 1987 77m bw/colour
Mainline/Kira Films (Emie Amemiya)
Documentary of a young boxer training younger boys.
Ambivalent account of a violent sport, chicly photographed.
d Bruce Weber *ph* Julio Macat *md* Cherry Vanilla *ed* Phyllis Famiglietti, Howie Weisbrot
☆ Andy Minsker, The Mount Scott Boxing Club
'This is not so much a sporting profile as a poetic essay on American masculinity using boxing as a metaphor for the transformations involved in acquiring male identity.' – *MFB*

Broken Vessels **
US 1998 92m DeLuxe
Feature/Unapix/Zeitgeist (Roxana Zal, Scott Ziehl)
In Los Angeles, a newcomer to an ambulance service lives on the edge, under the influence of the veteran paramedic with whom he is teamed.
An engaging, low-budget, drug-fuelled movie with a dark sense of humour, a tragic projectory and a disregard for propriety.
w David Baer, John McMahon, Scott Ziehl *d* Scott Ziehl *ph* Antonio Calvache *m* Bill Laswell, Martin Blasick, Brent David Fraser *pd* Rodrigo Castillo *ed* David Moritz, Chris Figler
☆ *Todd Field* (Jimmy Warzniak), Jason London (Tom Meyer), Roxana Zal (Elizabeth Capalino), Susan Traylor (Susy), James Hong (Mr Chen), Patrick Cranshaw (Gramps), Brent David Fraser (Jed), Stephanie Feury (Jill), David Nelson (Rick), William Smith (Bo), David Baer (Bob)
'Is powered by a contagious headlong energy and is often outrageously funny.' – *Philip Kemp, Sight and Sound*

Bronco Billy **
US 1980 116m DeLuxe Panavision
Warner/Second Street (Neal Dobrofsky, Dennis Hackin)
A New Jersey shoe salesman takes over a rundown wild west show.
Enjoyable, sentimental, satirical comedy which unaccountably let down its star's box-office record.
w Dennis Hackin *d* Clint Eastwood *ph* David Worth *md* Snuff Garrett, Steve Dorff *ad* Eugene Lourie
☆ Clint Eastwood, Sondra Locke, Geoffrey Lewis, Scatman Crothers, Bill McKinney, Sam Bottoms
'Eastwood seems to have most enjoyed toying with some distinctly old-fashioned materials: a runaway heiress, a murder plot that isn't, some consequent punning on points of identity, and the most mischievously brittle set of greedy Eastern sophisticates since Frank Capra.' – *Richard Combs, MFB*

Bronenosets Potemkin: see *The Battleship Potemkin*

'One Man Lives In The Neighborhood. Another Man Owns It.'
A Bronx Tale *
US 1993 121m Technicolor
Rank/Price/Tribeca (Jane Rosenthal, Jon Kilik, Robert De Niro)
In the 1960s, in the Italian neighbourhood of the Bronx, a boy grows up, torn between affection for his father, a bus driver, and admiration for the local gang boss, and caught in the growing struggle for control between blacks and whites.
An enjoyable stroll through familiar territory, which at least shows the ordinary life of the time, even if it, too, is seduced by the glamour of the gangsters.
w Chazz Palminteri *play* Chazz Palminteri *d* Robert De Niro *ph* Reynaldo Villalobos *m* Butch Barbella *pd* Wynn Thomas *ed* David Ray, R. Q. Lovett
☆ Robert De Niro, Chazz Palminteri, Lillo Brancato, Francis Capra, Taral Hicks, Katherine Narducci, Clem Caserta, Joe Pesci, Alfred Sauchelli Jnr
'A wonderfully vivid snapshot of a colorful place and time, as well as a very satisfactory directorial debut.' – *Variety*

'The Ultimate Experience Of Inner Terror.'
The Brood
Canada 1979 91m colour
Mutual/Elgin (Claude Heroux)
The rage of a mentally disturbed woman produces homicidal 'babies'.
Idiotic and repellent shocker.
wd David Cronenberg *ph* Mark Irwin *m* Howard Shore *ad* Carol Spier *ed* Allan Collins
☆ Oliver Reed, Samantha Eggar, Art Hindle, Cindy Hinds
'In Cronenberg's hands, horror is no longer a disreputable bastard genre but a new avenue of expression, glistening with possibility … Horror is his native language. He dreams in it.' – *Stephen Schiff*

'Family First. Friends Second. The Mob Above All.'
A Brooklyn State of Mind
Canada 1997 87m colour
Norstar/Storm (Peter R. Simpson)
A gangster discovers the truth about the killing of his father 20 years earlier, and decides to avenge his death.
Mundane gangster drama, containing nothing that has not been better done before.
w Frank Rainone, Frederick Stroppel *d* Frank Rainone *ph* Ken Kelsch *m* Paul J. Zaza *pd* William Barclay *ed* Nick Rotundo
☆ Danny Aiello, Vincent Spano, Maria Grazia Cucinotta, Abe Vigoda, Tony Danza, Morgana King
'Dramatically functional but has little to add to the well-trodden genre.' – *Variety*

Brother: see *Brat*

Brother *
Japan/GB/US/France 2000 112m colour
Film Four/Recorded Picture/Office Kitano/BAC (Jeremy Thomas, Masayuki Mori)
A Japanese yakuza avoids a gang-war in Tokyo by going to Los Angeles to reorganise his half-brother's unsuccessful attempt at drug dealing.
Kitano's familiar tough-guy persona gains from being in an unfamiliar American setting, but his difficulties with the English language lead to a narrative clumsiness that the violent action cannot disguise.
wd Takeshi Kitano *ph* Katsumi Yanagijima *m* Joe Hisaishi *pd* Norihiro Isoda *ed* Takeshi Kitano *cos* Yohji Yamamoto
☆ Beat Takeshi (Yamamoto), Claude Maki (Ken), Omar Epps (Shirase), Ren Ohsugi (Harada), Susumu Terajima (Kato), Ryo Ishibashi (Ishibashi), James Shigeta (Susimoto), Tetsuya Watari (Jinseikai Boss)
'His style of close-to-the-vest brutality travels extremely well.' – *Elvis Mitchell, New York Times*
'This poorly constructed gangster thriller shows the director not entirely at home in a new environment.' – *David Rooney, Variety*

Brother Can You Spare a Dime?
GB 1975 109m bw
VPS/Goodtimes
A 'documentary' picture of America in the thirties, attempted by an apparently random collage of newsreel and feature film extracts, sometimes difficult to tell one from the other.
Sometimes entertaining but mainly unpardonable.
wd Philippe Mora

The Brother from Another Planet
US 1984 108m Movielab
A-Train Films
An alien lands in Harlem and is protected by locals from the horrors he finds there.
Moderately amusing combination of science fiction, farce and satire, which outstays its welcome by at least half an hour.
wd John Sayles
☆ Joe Morton, Tom Wright, Caroline Aaron, Randy Sue Carter

Brother John *
US 1970 94m Eastmancolor
Columbia/E and R (Joel Glickman)
A mysterious black man comes to town for a family funeral and is suspected by the townsfolk of various sinister motives, but when they imprison him he is freed by a sympathizer.
The humans are all mean-minded, the saintly visitor is either Christ or an emissary from another planet. Either way, we have been here before, but although this little fantasy has nothing clear to say it is quite enjoyable on the surface.
w Ernest Kinoy *d* James Goldstone *ph* Gerald Perry Finnerman *m* Quincy Jones
☆ Sidney Poitier, Bradford Dillman, Will Geer, Beverly Todd, Ramon Bieri, Warren J. Kemmerling, Paul Winfield, Lincoln Kilpatrick
'It starts out as an engaging mystery with sociological overtones but ends up as a muddle-headed doomsday parable.' – *Judith Crist, 1977*

Brother Orchid *
US 1940 91m bw
Warner (Hal B. Wallis)
A gangster, 'taken for a ride' by his former friends, escapes and becomes a monk.
Rather uneasy blend of comedy, drama and religion, with some good scenes.
w Earl Baldwin *story* Richard Connell *d* Lloyd Bacon *ph* Tony Gaudio *m* Heinz Roemheld
☆ Edward G. Robinson, Humphrey Bogart, Donald Crisp, Ann Sothern, Ralph Bellamy, Allen Jenkins, Cecil Kellaway

Brother Rat *
US 1938 89m bw
Warner (Robert Lord)
Fun and games with the cadets at a military academy.
Brisk but dated farce from a highly successful Broadway original; remade as About Face *(qv).*
w Richard Macaulay, Jerry Wald *play* Fred Finklehoffe, John Monks Jnr *d* William Keighley *ph* Ernest Haller
☆ Wayne Morris, Eddie Albert, Ronald Reagan, Priscilla Lane, Jane Bryan, Jane Wyman, Johnnie Davis, Henry O'Neill
'Exhibs who dig into exploitation fields will hit paydirt.' – *Variety*

Brother Rat and a Baby
US 1939 87m bw
Warner (Robert Lord)
GB title: *Baby Be Good*
Scatty follow-up to *Brother Rat*, with the cadets graduating.
w Jerry Wald, Richard Macaulay *d* Ray Enright *ph* Charles Rosher *m* Heinz Roemheld
☆ Wayne Morris, Eddie Albert, Ronald Reagan, Priscilla Lane, Jane Wyman, Jane Bryan, Arthur Treacher, Moroni Olsen

Brother Sun, Sister Moon
GB/Italy 1972 122m Technicolor Panavision
Paramount/Vic Films/Euro International (Luciano Perugia)
The life of Francis of Assisi.
Good-looking but relentlessly boring view of a medieval saint as a kind of early flower person.
w Suso Cecchi d'Amico, Kenneth Ross, Lina Wertmuller, Franco Zeffirelli *d* Franco Zeffirelli *ph* Ennio Guarnieri *m* Donovan, Riz Ortolani *pd* Lorenzo Mongiardino *ed* Reginald Hills, John Ruston
☆ Graham Faulkner (Francesco), Judi Bowker (Clare), Alec Guinness (Pope Innocent III), Leigh Lawson (Bernardo), Kenneth Cranham (Paolo), Lee Montague (Father), Valentina Cortese (Mother), Michael Feast (Silvestro), Nicholas Willatt (Giocondo), John Sharp (Bishop)
'If I were Pope, I would burn it.' – *Stanley Kauffmann*

The Brotherhood *
US 1968 96m Technicolor
Paramount/Brotherhood Company (Kirk Douglas)
A Mafia executive welcomes his younger brother into the syndicate, but is finally executed by him.
Dour melodrama with tragic pretensions: well made but rather tedious and violent.
w Lewis John Carlino *d* Martin Ritt *ph* Boris Kaufman *m* Lalo Schifrin
☆ Kirk Douglas, Alex Cord, *Luther Adler*, Irene Papas, Susan Strasberg, Murray Hamilton, Eduardo Ciannelli

The Brotherhood of Satan *
US 1970 93m Techniscope
Columbia/LQJAF/Four Star Excelsior (L. Q. Jones, Alvy Moore)
A village is isolated by an outbreak of diabolism.
Fresh and intriguing minor horror film with imaginative touches.
w William Welch *d* *Bernard McEveety* *ph* John Arthur Morril *m* Jaime Mendoza-Nava
☆ Strother Martin, L. Q. Jones, Charles Bateman, Ahna Capri, Charles Robinson, Alvy Moore, Geri Reischl

Brotherhood of the Wolf: see *Le Pacte des Loups*

Brotherly Love: see *Country Dance*

The Brothers **
GB 1947 98m bw
Triton (Sydney Box)
An orphan girl comes to a Skye fishing family at the turn of the century, and causes superstition, sexual jealousy and tragedy.

Wildly melodramatic but good-looking open-air melodrama, a surprising and striking British film of its time. Macrae gives a splendidly malevolent performance.
w Muriel and Sydney Box *novel* L. A. G. Strong *d* *David Macdonald* *ph* *Stephen Dade* *m* Cedric Thorpe Davie *ad* George Provis *ed* Vladimir Sagovsky
☆ Patricia Roc (Mary), Maxwell Reed (Fergus Macrae), *Duncan Macrae* (John Macrae), Will Fyffe (Aeneas Macrae), Andrew Crawford (Willie McFarish), Finlay Currie (Hector Macrae), John Laurie (Dugald), James Woodburn (Priest), Megs Jenkins (Angusina), Morland Graham (Angus McFarish)
'Heavy breathing, heavier dialect, and any number of quaint folk customs ... the island and its actual inhabitants are all right; the rest is Mary Webb with hair on her chest.' – *James Agee*

Brothers
GB 1999 98m colour
Paradise/Brothers (Martin Dunkerton, Joanna Garvin)
Seven young English men pursue women and pleasure during a week's holiday on a Greek island.
Episodic tale of lager loutish behaviour that is no more attractive on the screen than it is in reality.
w Martin Dunkerton, Nick Valentine *d* Martin Dunkerton *ph* Richard Terry *m* Julian Stewart Lindsey *pd* Conrad Butlin *ed* John Grover
☆ Justin Brett (Matt), Daren Jacobs (Chris), Daniel Fredenburgh (Julian), Rebecca Cardinale (Anna), Nick Valentine (Alec), Fin Wild (Victor), Leigh Tapper (Joseph), Stephen Maggio (Ben), Crystal Shepherd Cross (Juliette)
'Badly misconceived fiasco.' – *Empire*
† The credits list 62 associate producers.

The Brothers
US 2001 101m DeLuxe
Columbia TriStar/Screen Gems (Darin Scott, Paddy Cullen)
The romantic adventures of four male friends in search of the right woman.
Glossy romantic drama with too much talk and too little characterisation.
wd Gary Hardwick *ph* Alexander Gruszynski *pd* Amy Ancona *ed* Earl Watson
☆ Morris Chestnut (Jackson Smith), D. L. Hughley (Derrick West), Bill Bellamy (Brian Palmer), Shemar Moore (Terry White), Gabrielle Union (Denise Johnson), Tatyana Ali (Cherie Smith), Jenifer Lewis (Louise Smith), Tamala Jones (Sheila West)
'Nothing special, but it's amiable enough.' – *Alan Jones, Film Review*

Brothers in Arms (dubbed)
France 1989 125m Eastmancolor
Alexandre/SGGC/FR3 (Alexandre Arcady)
In Paris, a Jewish cop and an Algerian-born undercover agent form an uneasy partnership to combat Islamic fundamentalists who are planning a terrorist campaign using drugs and violence.
Tough and topical, though otherwise unremarkable, thriller.
w Daniel Saint-Hamont, Alexandre Arcady, Pierre Aknine *d* Alexandre Arcady *ph* Robert Alazraki *m* Jean-Jacques Goldman, Roland Romanelli *pd* Gerard Daoudal, Tony Egry *ed* Joële Van Effenterre, Anne-Marie Leduc
☆ Richard Berry, Patrick Bruel, Bruno Cremer, Claude Brasseur, Marthe Villalonga, Saïd Amadis, Corinne Dacla, Amidou

Brothers in Law *
GB 1957 97m bw
British Lion/The Boultings (John Boulting)
A young barrister has comic misdemeanours in and out of court.
The lighter side of the law, from a bestseller by a judge; mechanically amusing and not in the same street as its predecessor Private's Progress *(qv), though it seemed hilarious at the time.*
w Roy Boulting, Frank Harvey, Jeffrey Dell *novel* *Henry Cecil* *d* Roy Boulting *ph* Max Greene *m* Benjamin Frankel
☆ *Ian Carmichael*, Terry-Thomas, Richard Attenborough, *Miles Malleson*, *Eric Barker*, Irene Handl, John Le Mesurier, Olive Sloane, Kynaston Reeves
FOREWORD: IF ALL THE CHARACTERS IN THIS FILM WERE NOT FICTITIOUS – IT WOULD BE ALARMING!
CLERK: 'You start with a blue robing bag, sir. Then if you do good work for counsel, he'll give you a red one. If at the end of seven years you haven't been given a red bag – use a suitcase.'
Eric Barker (newcomer)

'A story of survival and belonging.'
Brothers in Trouble *
GB 1996 103m colour
BFI/BBC/Renegade/Kinowelt/Mikado (Robert Buckler)
In the 60s, a Pakistani arrives in Britain as an illegal immigrant and eventually prospers, despite the fear in which he at first lives with other immigrants.
Revealing look at English life from an unusual viewpoint.
w Robert Buckler *novel* *Return Journey* by Abdullah Hussein *d* Udayan Prasad *ph* Alan Almond *m* Stephen Warbeck *pd* Chris Townsend *ed* Barrie Vince
☆ Om Puri, Pavan Malhotra, Angeline Ball, Ahsen Bhatti, Bhasker, Pravesh Kumar, Badi Uzzaman
'A touching, optimistic fable about friendship and survival.' – *Empire*

The Brothers Karamazov *
US 1958 146m Metrocolor
MGM/Avon (Pandro S. Berman)
In 19th-century Russia, the father of three sons is murdered and the wrong brother is found guilty.
Decent but decidedly unenthralling Hollywood compression of a classic, faithful to the letter but not the spirit of the book, and with few memorable moments or performances.
w Richard Brooks *novel* Fyodor Dostoyevsky *d* Richard Brooks *ph* John Alton *m* Bronislau Kaper *ad* William A. Horning, Paul Groesse
☆ Yul Brynner, Maria Schell, Richard Basehart, Claire Bloom, Lee J. Cobb, Albert Salmi, William Shatner, Judith Evelyn
'A picture full of ferocity and passion, with streaks of genius in the lighting, mounting and music.' – *News of the World*
† In 1968 came Ivan Pyryev's massive 220m Russian version, little seen in the west.
Lee J. Cobb

'Jack is Trying to Save His Marriage. Patrick is in a Hopeless Relationship. But Their Biggest Problem is Barry's Brotherly Advice.'
'Sometimes the Best Friends Are the Ones You've Known Your Whole Life.'
The Brothers McMullen **
US 1995 118m DuArt
TCF/Marlboro Road Gang/Videography/Good Machine (Edward Burns, Dick Fisher)
Three Irish-American brothers are having trouble with their relationships.
A character-driven, low-budget film that is observant in its examination of the dynamics of interaction between the brothers and the women in their lives; for most of the time, it steers clear of mawkishness.
wd Edward Burns *ph* Dick Fisher *m* Seamus Egan *ed* Dick Fisher
☆ Jack Mulcahy, Mike McGlone, Edward Burns, Connie Britton, Maxine Bahns, Elizabeth P. McKay, Shari Albert, Jennifer Jostyn
'Straightforward and disarming in its utter disregard for trendiness and current fashion.' – *Todd McCarthy, Variety*

The Brothers Rico
US 1957 91m bw
Columbia/William Goetz (Lewis J. Rachmil)
An accountant fails to retrieve his brothers from a life of crime.
Moderate gangster fare with good credentials but more talk than action.
w Lewis Meltzer, Ben Perry *novel* Georges Simenon *d* Phil Karlson *ph* Burnett Guffey *m* George Duning
☆ Richard Conte, James Darren, Dianne Foster, Kathryn Grant, Larry Gates, Lamont Johnson, Harry Bellaver

Brown of Harvard
US 1926 70m approx (24 fps) bw silent
MGM
Two college students, one academic and one sporty, love the same girl.
Best-known version of a 1909 play first filmed in 1917: archetypal campus drama.
w Donald Ogden Stewart, A. P. Younger *play* Rida Johnson Young *d* Jack Conway
☆ William Haines, Jack Pickford, Mary Brian

Brown on Resolution *
GB 1935 80m bw
Gaumont (Michael Balcon)
Later retitled: *Forever England*
US title: *Born for Glory*
In the 1914 war in the Mediterranean, a seaman holds a German warship at bay with a rifle.
Uneasy amalgam of adventure heroics and character study, interesting for its effort.
w Michael Hogan, Gerard Fairlie, J. O. C. Orton *novel* C. S. Forester *d* Walter Forde *ph* Bernard Knowles
☆ John Mills, Betty Balfour, Barry Mackay, Jimmy Hanley, Howard Marion Crawford, H. G. Stoker
'A milestone in British pictures ... an attractive and interesting feature anywhere.' – *Variety*

The Browning Version *
GB 1951 90m bw
GFD/Javelin (Teddy Baird)
Retiring through ill health, a classics master finds that he is hated by his unfaithful wife, his headmaster and his pupils. An unexpected act of kindness gives him courage to face the future.
A rather thin extension of a one-act play, capped by a thank-you speech which is wildly out of character. Dialogue and settings are smooth, but the actors are not really happy with their roles.
w Terence Rattigan *play* Terence Rattigan *d* Anthony Asquith *ph* Desmond Dickinson *ad* Carmen Dillon *ed* John D. Guthridge
☆ Michael Redgrave, Jean Kent, Nigel Patrick, Wilfrid Hyde-White, Bill Travers, Ronald Howard
'If the sustained anguish of the role does not allow Redgrave a great deal of room to move around in, it does give him a chance to show what he can do in tight quarters, and that, it turns out, is considerable.' – *Pauline Kael, 70s*

The Browning Version *
GB 1994 97m colour Panavision
UPI/Percy Main (Ridley Scott, Mimi Polk)
As he retires, a repressed and disliked schoolteacher, treated badly by his headmaster and adulterous wife, comes to terms with himself.
A remake of no particular distinction or point, cut adrift from its original period setting and losing in credibility because of it.
w Ronald Harwood *play* Terence Rattigan *d* Mike Figgis *ph* Jean-François Robin *m* Mark Isham *pd* John Beard *ed* Hervé Schneid
☆ Albert Finney, Greta Scacchi, Matthew Modine, Julian Sands, Michael Gambon, Ben Silverstone, James Sturgess, Joe Beattie, Mark Bolton, Heathcote Williams
'Strong and affecting – perhaps because neither the director nor the star has worked with this sort of material before.' – *Terrence Rafferty, New Yorker*
'One can't help returning to the question of why the film was made if neither director, scriptwriter nor star had anything new to add to the innumerable *Browning Versions* that have gone before it.' – *Geoffrey McNab, Sight and Sound*
'The play is done all the time but who under the age of 30 knows it? Doing it in period would have no bearing on younger audiences and I wanted to attract them.' – *Mike Figgis*

Brown's Requiem *
US 1998 104m DeLuxe
J&T/Savvy Lad (Tim Youd, David Scott Rubin)
In Los Angeles, an alcoholic ex-cop turned private eye runs into trouble when he is hired to investigate a young girl's relationship with an elderly, wealthy crook.
A thriller stuck in a sub-Chandler mode, with a world-weary hero in a situation he doesn't comprehend; the clichés are neatly shuffled, but overfamiliarity leads to ennui before the end.
wd Jason Freeland *novel* James Ellroy *ph* Seo Mutarevic *m* Cynthia Millar *pd* Marc Rizzo *ed* Toby Yates
☆ Michael Rooker (Fritz Brown), Tobin Bell (Stan the Man), Selma Blair (Jane Baker), Jack Conley (Richard Ralston), Kevin Corrigan (Walter), Brad Dourif (Wilson Edwards), Harold Gould (Solly K), Brion James (Haywood Cathcart), Barry Newman (Jack Skolnick), Valerie Perrine (Marguerita Hansen), William Sasso

'One Man Against A Cruel System.'
Brubaker *
US 1980 130m DeLuxe
TCF (Ron Silverman)
A new governor fails to make much headway with his reform plan at Wakefield Prison Farm.
Fairly brutal but unsurprising prison drama which takes itself somewhat too seriously.
w W. D. Richter *d* Stuart Rosenberg *ph* Bruno Nuytten *m* Lalo Schifrin
☆ Robert Redford, Yaphet Kotto, Jane Alexander, Murray Hamilton, David Keith, Morgan Freeman
'It's hard to imagine a broad audience wanting to share the two hours of agony.' – *Variety*
screenplay

The Brute *
Mexico 1952 83m bw
International Cinematografica
original title: *El Bruto*
Victimized slum tenants call for help to a slow-witted giant, who kills the landlord and falls in love with his daughter.
Eccentric melodrama which doesn't quite seem to make its point.
wd Luis Buñuel *ph* Augustin Jiminez *m* Raul Lavista
☆ Pedro Armendariz, *Katy Jurado*, Rosita Arenas, Andres Soler

Brute Force **
US 1947 96m bw
U-I (Mark Hellinger)
Six violent convicts revolt against a sadistic warden and try to escape.
Vivid and rather repellent prison melodrama leading up to an explosive climax; its savagery seemed at the time to break fresh ground.
w Richard Brooks *d* Jules Dassin *ph* William Daniels *m* Miklos Rozsa
☆ Burt Lancaster, Charles Bickford, Hume Cronyn, Ella Raines, Yvonne de Carlo

'Towering new terror! No woman safe from his crushing arms...'
The Brute Man
US 1946 60m bw
Universal
A disfigured paranoic is helped by a blind pianist and kills again to help her.
Schlock horror programmer.
w George Bricker, M. Coates Webster *d* Jean Yarbrough
☆ Rondo Hatton, Tom Neal, Jane Adams
† Universal were so ashamed of it that they farmed it out to PRC

El Bruto: see *The Brute*

'They were enemies in war and rivals in love.'
The Brylcreem Boys
GB 1996 105m Rank Colour
Rough Magic (Alan Latham, Bernie Stampfer, Terence Ryan, Paul Madigan)
During the Second World War, English and German prisoners of war share the same camp in Ireland.
Apparently based on a real-life situation, this stumbles from romantic comedy to drama with no sense of direction or style.
w Terence Ryan, Jamie Brown, Susan Morrall *d* Terence Ryan *ph* Gerry Lively *m* Richard Hartley *pd* Steve Hardie *ed* Emma E. Hickox
☆ Bill Campbell, William McNamara, Angus MacFadyen, Gabriel Byrne, Jean Butler, John Gordon Sinclair, Oliver Tobias
'A toe-curlingly terrible film.' – *Peter Bradshaw, Guardian*
'It gets on the list of the 10 worst films about the war.' – *Philip French, Observer*

'A Spaced Odyssey'
The Bubble *
US 1966 112m Eastmancolor Spacevision (aka Stereovision 3D)
Arch Oboler
aka: *Fantastic Invasion of Planet Earth*
Three people find themselves trapped in a small town that is surrounded by an invisible bubble of energy.
Originally made in 3D, the film was a good advertisement for that process but not, with its indifferent acting and talky, slow-moving narrative, for any other reason.
wd Midwestern Magic-Vuers (Arch Oboler) *ph* Charles F. Wheeler *m* Paul Sawtell, Bert Shefter *ad* Marvin Chomsky *ed* Igo Kanter
☆ Michael Cole, Deborah Walley, Johnny Desmond, Virginia Gregg, Chester Jones
† The film was cut to 94m and re-released in 1972 as *Fantastic Invasion of Planet Earth*, though no invasion occurs during the film. It has been released on video in its 3D version.

The Buccaneer *
US 1938 125m bw
Paramount (Cecil B. de Mille)
During the 1812 war, pirate Jean Lafitte helps general Andrew Jackson to repel the British.
Sprightly adventure romance with generally good production and acting.
w Jeanie Macpherson, Edwin Justus Mayer, Harold Lamb, C. Gardner Sullivan *d* Cecil B. de Mille *ph* Victor Milner *m* Georges Antheil *md* Boris Morros
☆ Fredric March, Franciska Gaal, *Akim Tamiroff*, Margot Grahame, Walter Brennan, Ian Keith, Spring Byington, Douglass Dumbrille, Robert Barrat, Hugh Sothern, Beulah Bondi, Anthony Quinn, Montagu Love
'A cinch for big box-office returns around the world.' – *Variety*
'From de Mille's skilled craftsmanship have come other pictures quite as ambitious, none more adroitly fabricated, skilfully adjusted to the norm of appeal to the world audience that such imposing and costly productions must command.' – *Terry Ramsaye*
Victor Milner

The Buccaneer
US 1958 121m Technicolor Vistavision
Paramount/Cecil B. de Mille (Henry Wilcoxon)
As the British fleet sails for New Orleans, defended by General Andrew Jackson and a handful of troops, pirate Jean Lafitte has to decide which side to support.
Slow, slack and stolid remake of the 1938 film, with practically no excitement or interest and very obvious studio sets.
w Jesse L. Lasky Jnr, Bernice Mosk, from the earlier screenplay *d* Anthony Quinn *ph* Loyal Griggs *m* Elmer Bernstein
☆ Yul Brynner, Claire Bloom, Charles Boyer, Inger Stevens, Henry Hull, Charlton Heston, E. G. Marshall, Douglass Dumbrille, Lorne Greene, Ted de Corsia, Robert F. Simon

Buchanan Rides Alone
US 1958 78m colour
Columbia (Harry Joe Brown)
A wandering Texan helps a young Mexican accused of murder.
Very moderate star Western.
w Charles Lang *novel* *The Name is Buchanan* by Jonas Ward *d* Budd Boetticher *ph* Lucien Ballard
☆ Randolph Scott, Craig Stevens, Barry Kelley, Peter Whitney

Die Büchse der Pandora: see *Pandora's Box*

Buck and the Preacher
US 1971 103m colour
Columbia/E & R/Belafonte (Joel Glickman)
Nightriders chasing escaped slaves are outwitted by a wagon train guide and a con man.
Lively, easygoing Western with a largely black cast, and a message of militancy sugar-coated by Hollywood hokum.
w Ernest Kinoy *d* Sidney Poitier *ph* Alex Phillips *m* Benny Carter *pd* Sydney Z. Litwack *ed* Pembroke J. Herring
☆ Sidney Poitier (Buck), Harry Belafonte (Preacher), Ruby Dee (Ruth), Cameron Mitchell (Deshay), Denny Miller (Floyd), Nita Talbot (Madame Esther), John Kelly (Sheriff)
'Quite an agreeable entertainment.' – *MFB*

Buck Benny Rides Again *
US 1940 82m bw
Paramount (Mark Sandrich)
A radio comedian goes west but finds he's no cowboy.
Moderate filming of episodes and characters from the star's weekly radio show.
w William Morrow, Edmund Beloin *d* Mark Sandrich
☆ Jack Benny, Ellen Drew, Eddie Anderson, Andy Devine, Phil Harris, Dennis Day
'Swell mass entertainment.' – *Variety*

Buck Privates *
US 1941 84m bw
Universal (Alex Gottlieb)
GB title: *Rookies*
Two incompetents accidentally enlist in the army.
Abbott and Costello's first starring vehicle is a tired bundle of army jokes and old routines separated by plot and romance, but it sent the comedians right to the top, where they stayed for ten years.
w Arthur T. Horman *d* Arthur Lubin *ph* Milton Krasner *md* Charles Previn
☆ *Bud Abbott, Lou Costello*, Lee Bowman, Alan Curtis, Jane Frazee, *The Andrews Sisters, Nat Pendleton*, Samuel S. Hinds, Shemp Howard
Charles Previn; song 'The Boogie Woogie Bugle Boy of Company B' (*m* Hugh Prince, *ly* Don Raye)

Buck Privates Come Home
US 1946 77m bw
U-I (Robert Arthur)
GB title: *Rookies Come Home*
Incompetent war veterans are demobilized and find civilian life tough.
Thin star comedy with a good final chase.
w John Grant, Frederic I. Rinaldo, Robert Lees *d* Charles T. Barton *ph* Charles Van Enger
☆ Bud Abbott, Lou Costello, Beverly Simmons, Tom Brown, Nat Pendleton

Buck Rogers
US 1939 bw serial: 12 eps
Universal
After crashing in the Arctic and being preserved by gas for five hundred years, Buck discovers that the world has been conquered by gangsters led by Killer Kane.
Acceptable science fiction hokum with moments of ingenuity.
d Ford Beebe, Saul Goodkind
☆ Buster Crabbe, Constance Moore, Jackie Moran, Jack Mulhall, Anthony Warde

Buck Rogers in the 25th Century
US 1979 89m colour
Universal (Richard Coffey)
Launched 500 years into the future, an astronaut helps save civilization.
Dull and bland version of comic strip heroics, originally made for television, which lacks even the low-budget charm of the 30s serial.
w Glen A. Larson, Leslie Stevens *d* Daniel Haller *ph* Frank Beascoechea *m* Stu Phillips *ad* Paul Peters *ed* John J. Dumas
☆ Gil Gerard, Pamela Hensley, Erin Gray, Henry Silva, Tim O'Connor, Joseph Wiseman, Duke Butler, Felix Silla, Mel Blanc (voice)

'You'll be sick – from laughing!'
A Bucket of Blood
US 1959 65m bw
Alta Vista (Roger Corman)
A waiter becomes a renowned sculptor when he hits on the idea of moulding clay round corpses.
Heavy-handed spoof with a few choice if bloody moments.
w Charles B. Griffith *d* Roger Corman *ph* Jack Marquette *m* Fred Katz *ad* Daniel Haller *ed* Anthony Carras
☆ Dick Miller, Barboura Morris, Antony Carbone, Ed Nelson

Buckskin
US 1968 97m Pathécolor
Paramount/A. C. Lyles
In the frontier town of Gloryhole a gambler is routed by the new marshal.
Routine old-fashioned Western with this producer's predictable gallery of weatherbeaten familiar faces.
w Michael Fisher *d* Michael Moore *ph* W. Wallace Kelley *m* Jimmie Haskell
☆ Barry Sullivan, Joan Caulfield, Lon Chaney Jnr, John Russell, Richard Arlen, Barbara Hale, Bill Williams, Barton MacLane

Budbringeren: see *Junk Mail*

Buddies
Australia 1983 95m colour Panavision
J. D. Productions/John Dingwall
Two sapphire miners outwit an attempt by an unscrupulous rival to grab their claim.
Comic celebration of what an Australian premier once described as 'mateship'.
w John Dingwall *d* Arch Nicholson *ph* David Eggby *m* Chris Neal *pd* Philip Warner *ad* Ron Highfield *ed* Martyn Down
☆ Colin Friels, Harold Hopkins, Kris McQuade, Norman Kaye, Dennis Miller, Bruce Spence

'Welcome to a family that will make yours seem tame.'
Buddy
US 1997 84m Technicolor Panavision
Columbia/Jim Henson/American Zoetrope (Steve Nicolaides, Fred Fuchs)
In the 20s, a wealthy Brooklyn woman saves a baby gorilla and raises him as a member of her animal-filled household.
One of those movies where you cannot quite imagine why it was ever made, though it has a slight, cutesy animal appeal.
wd Caroline Thompson *book* *Animals are My Hobby* by Gertrude Davies Linz *ph* Steve Mason *m* Elmer Bernstein *pd* David Nichols, Daniel Lomino *ed* Jonathan Shaw *sp* Jim Henson's Creature Shop
☆ René Russo, Robbie Coltrane, Alan Cumming, Irma P. Hall, Peter Elliott, Paul Reubens
'I watched this movie with steadily mounting incredulity. I was trying to find the category for it, and there isn't one ... It could be a study in undiagnosed mental illness, if it weren't shot on perky 1930s sets, scored with upbeat music and played by the actors like a *Thin Man* movie with Nick and Nora on Prozac.' – *Roger Ebert, Chicago Sun-Times*

Buddy Buddy
US 1981 96m Metrocolor Panavision
MGM (Jay Weston)
A hit man on a job is hampered by a woebegone fellow intent on committing suicide.
Painful remake of the French L'Emmerdeur (A Pain in the A ...) (qv). Lugubriously funny at times, but generally much less attractive than the original.
w Billy Wilder, I. A. L. Diamond *play* Francis Veber *d* Billy Wilder *ph* Harry Stradling Jnr *m* Lalo Schifrin *pd* Daniel A. Lomino
☆ Walter Matthau, Jack Lemmon, Paula Prentiss, Klaus Kinski, Dana Elcar
'The saddest episode in Wilder's career.' – *Richard Combs, MFB*

'Music Never Felt This Good.'
The Buddy Holly Story
US 1978 113m colour
Columbia/Innovisions/ECA (Fred Bauer)
The life of a fifties rock-and-roller who died young in an accident.
Solidly carpentered showbiz biopic for the youth market.
w Robert Gittler *d* Steve Rash *ph* Stevan Larner *md* Joe Renzetti
☆ Gary Busey, Don Stroud, Charles Martin Smith, William Jordan, Maria Richwine
'A B movie leavened by grade-A talent.' – *Les Keyser, Hollywood in the Seventies*
Joe Renzetti
Gary Busey

Buddy's Song
GB 1990 106m Eastmancolor
Castle Premier/Buddy/Bill Curbishley, Roy Baird, Roger Daltrey
A rock 'n' roll father becomes manager of his son's more modern band, with mixed results.
Dreary attempt at a generation gap musical, unlikely to appeal to any age-group.
w Nigel Hinton *novel* Nigel Hinton *d* Claude Whatham *ph* John Hooper *m* Roger Daltrey *pd* Grant Hicks *ed* John Grover
☆ Roger Daltrey, Chesney Hawkes, Sharon Duce, Michael Elphick, Douglas Hodge, Paul McKenzie
'Breezy, anodyne fare better suited to the tube.' – *Variety*

'In Havana, music isn't a pastime... it's a way of life.'
Buena Vista Social Club ***
Germany 1998 105m colour
Film Four/Road Movies/Kintop/Arte/ICAIC (Ulrich Felsberg, Deepak Nayar)
A documentary on a forgotten generation of now elderly Cuban musicians, brought back into the limelight by guitarist Ry Cooder for a best-selling record album.
Charming account of some exceptional musicians enjoying a late flowering; their enjoyment of life and the style of music they developed is evident, with the energetic, 90-year-old Compay Segundo slyly stealing the show with his reminiscences and vocals.
d Wim Wenders *ph* Joerg Widmer, Robby Mueller, Lisa Renzler *ed* Brian Johnson
☆ Ry Cooder, Compay Segundo, Ruben Gonzalez, Ibrahim Ferrer, Eliades Ochoa, Omara Portuondo, Manuel 'Guajiro' Mirabal, Orlando 'Cachaito' Lopez, Barbarito Torres, Manuel 'Puntillita' Licea, Raul Planes, Felix Valoy, Maceo Rodriguez, Richard Eques, Joaquim Cooder
'A film of ineffable sweetness and glorious music, which puts the shallow, affectless popular culture of our prosperous west to shame.' – *Peter Bradshaw, Guardian*
documentary

Buffalo '66 *
US 1998 112m colour
Lions Gate/Cinepix/Muse (Chris Hanley)
In order to impress his parents, who believe him to have been on government work, a newly released convict kidnaps a dancer and persuades her to pretend to be his wife.
An oddity: this has the look and style of a gritty low-life drama about one of life's unloveliest losers, but the content is closer to absurdist drama with its close-up study of a comically dysfunctional family.
w Vincent Gallo, Alison Bagnall *d* Vincent Gallo *ph* Lance Acord *m* Vincent Gallo *pd* Gideon Ponte *ed* Curtiss Clayton
☆ Vincent Gallo, Christina Ricci, Anjelica Huston, Ben Gazzara, Kevin Corrigan, Mickey Rourke, Rosanna Arquette, Jan-Michael Vincent
'A small but almost perfectly formed film.' – *Guardian*
'A sustained and dolorous hymn to male self-pity.' – *Sunday Times*

Buffalo Bill *
US 1944 89m Technicolor
TCF (Harry Sherman)
A moderately fictitious account of the life of William Cody, from buffalo hunter to wild west showman.
Easygoing entertainment which turns from Western excitements to domestic drama. Generally watchable.
w Aeneas Mackenzie, Clements Ripley, Cecile Kramer *d* William Wellman *ph* Leon Shamroy *m* David Buttolph
☆ Joel McCrea, Maureen O'Hara, Linda Darnell, Thomas Mitchell, Edgar Buchanan, Anthony Quinn, Moroni Olsen

Buffalo Bill and the Indians, or Sitting Bull's History Lesson
US 1976 118m colour Panavision
EMI/Dino de Laurentiis (Robert Altman)
During winter camp for his wild west show, Buffalo Bill Cody and his friends discuss life and his own myth.
Anti-action, alienation-effect talk piece which has some points of interest for sophisticates but is likely to set Western addicts asking for their money back.

w Alan Rudolph, Robert Altman *play Indians* by Arthur Kopit *d* Robert Altman *ph* Paul Lohmann *m* Richard Baskin
☆ Paul Newman, Burt Lancaster, Joel Grey, Kevin McCarthy, Geraldine Chaplin, Harvey Keitel, John Considine, Denver Pyle
'The western is an enormously resilient form, but never has that resilience been tested quite so much as in this movie ... it isn't really a movie, it's a happening.' – *Arthur Knight*
'Whereas Kopit's play offered a hallucinatory mosaic, Altman's script has the one-dimensional clarity of a cartoon.' – *Michael Billington, Illustrated London News*
'That American history is the creation of flamboyant lies and showmanship strikes us at first as an amusing trifle and then quickly becomes an epigram shaggy-dogging its way across two hours of eccentric Altmanship.' – *Will Aitken, Take One*

Buffalo Bill – Hero of the Far West
France/Italy/West Germany 1964 90m
Technicolor Techniscope
Gloria/Corona/Cinematografica
Buffalo Bill thwarts a gang of gun-runners selling rifles to renegade Indians.
Standard Western, slavishly imitating its Hollywood models.
w Nino Stresa, Luciano Martino *d* J. W. Fordson (Mario Costa) *ph* Jack Dalmas
☆ Gordon Scott, Jan Hendricks, Mirko Ellis, Mario Brega, Roldano Lupi, Hans von Borsody, Peter Lull

Buffet Froid **
France 1979 93m Eastmancolor
Sara Films/Antenna 2 (Alain Sarde)
US title: *Cold Cuts*
A police inspector joins up with two new acquaintances: they discover that they all like killing people.
Satirical black comedy which goes on a little too long for its own good; invention gives way to glumness.
wd Bertrand Blier *ph* Jean Penzer *m* classical extracts
☆ Gérard Depardieu, Bernard Blier, Jean Carmet, Geneviève Page

'Sometimes it takes more than just good looks to kill.'
Buffy the Vampire Slayer
US 1992 94m DeLuxe
TCF/Sandollar/Kuzui (Kaz Kazui, Howard Rosenman)
A Californian bimbo learns that her destiny is to be a killer of vampires.
Curiously ineffectual teen comedy.
w Joss Whedon *d* Fran Rubel Kuzui *ph* James Hayman *m* Carter Burwell *pd* Lawrence Miller *ed* Camilla Toniolo, Jill Savitt, Richard Candib
☆ Kristy Swanson, Donald Sutherland, Paul Reubens, Rutger Hauer, Luke Perry, Michele Abrams, Hilary Swank, Paris Vaughan, David Arquette, Natasha Gregson Wagner
'A bloodless comic resurrection of the undead that goes serious just when it should get wild and woolly.' – *Variety*
'To enjoy this moronic rubbish, you need to put your IQ into total unconsciousness.' – *Alexander Walker, Evening Standard*
† The film was the basis of a successful TV series in 1997, created by Joss Whedon and starring Sarah Michelle Gellar.

The Bug
US 1975 101m Movielab
Paramount/William Castle
Large rocklike insects appear after an earthquake and set fire to themselves and their victims.
Absurd, overlong and rather nasty horror film with no visible redeeming features.
w William Castle, Thomas Page *novel The Hephaestus Plague* by Thomas Page *d* Jeannot Szwarc *ph* Michel Hugo, Ken Middleham *m* Charles Fox
☆ Bradford Dillman, Joanna Miles, Richard Gilliland, Jamie Smith Jackson, Alan Fudge, Patty McCormack
'The finer scientific points are to say the least elusive.' – *David Robinson*

The Bugle Sounds
US 1941 101m bw
MGM (J. Walter Ruben)
An old cavalry sergeant, discharged for insubordination, rounds up fifth columnists and is reinstated.
Ho-hum star vehicle on familiar lines but at undue length.
w Cyril Hume *d* S. Sylvan Simon *ph* Clyde de Vinna *m* Lennie Hayton
☆ Wallace Beery, Marjorie Main, Lewis Stone, George Bancroft, William Lundigan, Henry O'Neill, Donna Reed, Chill Wills, Roman Bohnen, Jerome Cowan, Tom Dugan, Guinn Williams, Jonathan Hale

Bugles in the Afternoon
US 1952 85m Technicolor
Warner/Cagney Productions (William Cagney)
In the US army at the time of Custer's last stand, a young officer is victimized by a jealous rival.
Modest, adequate Western with nice scenery but no surprises.
w Geoffrey Homes, Harry Brown *novel* Ernest Haycox *d* Roy Rowland *ph* Wilfrid Cline *m* Dimitri Tiomkin
☆ Ray Milland, Hugh Marlowe, Helena Carter, Forrest Tucker, Barton MacLane, George Reeves, James Millican, Gertrude Michael

A Bug's Life **
US 1998 96m Technicolor Cinemascope
Buena Vista/Walt Disney/Pixar (Darla K. Anderson, Kevin Reher)
A worker ant enlists the help of some circus bugs in defeating a threatening gang of grasshoppers.
Enjoyable computer-animated feature, though pleasure in its technical qualities – the play of light and shade – outweighs its narrative virtues and its lack of outstanding characterization.
w Andrew Stanton, Donald McEnery, Bob Shaw, John Lasseter, Joe Ranft *d* John Lasseter *ph* Sharon Calahan *m* Randy Newman *pd* William Cone *ed* Lee Unkrich
☆ Featuring the voices of: Dave Foley, Kevin Spacey, Julia Louis-Dreyfus, Hayden Panettiere, Phyllis Diller, Richard Kind, David Hyde Pierce, Joe Ranft, Denis Leary, Jonathan Harris, Madeline Kahn, Bonnie Hunt, Michael McShane, John Ratzenberger, Roddy McDowall
'Makes jaunty, imaginative use of both extraordinary technology and bold storytelling possibilities within the insect world.' – *Janet Maslin, New York Times*
'A pale imitation of Disney's best.' – *Derek Malcolm, Guardian*
† *Antz* (qv) is another computer-animated film on a similar theme.
Randy Newman

Bugsy **
US 1991 135m Technicolor
Columbia TriStar/Mulholland/Baltimore (Mark Johnson, Barry Levinson, Warren Beatty)
A starstruck gangster goes to Las Vegas and transforms the place into a gambler's paradise.
Romanticized account of the life and violent death of Bugsy Siegel, done with charm and style.
w James Toback *d* Barry Levinson *ph* Allen Daviau *m* Ennio Morricone *pd* Dennis Gassner *ed* Stu Linder
☆ *Warren Beatty*, Annette Bening, Harvey Keitel, Ben Kingsley, Elliott Gould, Joe Mantegna, Bebe Neuwirth, Wendy Phillips, Richard Sarafian, Bill Graham
'Elegantly made, wickedly perverse and very smart.' – *Richard Schickel, Time*
'An absorbing narrative flow and a parade of colourful underworld characters vie for screen time with an unsatisfactory central romance.' – *Variety*
Dennis Gassner; costume (Albert Wolsky)
film; Barry Levinson; Warren Beatty; Harvey Keitel; Ben Kingsley; James Toback; Allen Daviau; Ennio Morricone

Bugsy Malone **
GB 1976 93m Eastmancolor
Rank/Bugsy Malone Productions (David Puttnam, Allan Marshall)
New York 1929: gangster Fat Sam fights it out with Dandy Dan, and the best man wins the girl.
Extremely curious musical gangster spoof with all the parts played by children and the guns shooting ice cream. Very professionally done, but one wonders to whom it is supposed to appeal.
wd Alan Parker ph Michael Seresin, Peter Biziou *pd* Geoffrey Kirkland *m/songs* Paul Williams
☆ Scott Baio, Jodie Foster, Florrie Dugger, John Cassisi
'If for nothing else, you would have to admire it for the sheer doggedness of its eccentricity.' – *David Robinson, The Times*
'All the pizazz in the world couldn't lift it above the level of empty camp.' – *Frank Rich, New York Post*
'I only wish the British could make adult movies as intelligent as this one.' – *Michael Billington, Illustrated London News*
'In an uncanny way the movie works as a gangster movie and we remember that the old Bogart and Cagney classics had a childlike innocence too. The world was simpler then. Now it's so complicated maybe only a kid can understand the Bogart role.' – *Roger Ebert*
Paul Williams
Alan Parker (script); Geoffrey Kirkland; Jodie Foster

Build My Gallows High: see *Out of the Past*

Bull Durham *
US 1988 108m colour
Rank/Orion/Mount Company (Thom Mount, Mark Burg)
An English teacher prevaricates between choosing a rookie or an experienced baseball player as her latest lover.
Odd-ball movie, more in love with the game than its characters.
wd Ron Shelton *ph* Bobby Byrne *m* Michael Convertino *pd* Armin Ganz *ad* David Lubin *ed* Robert Leighton, Adam Weiss
☆ Kevin Costner, Susan Sarandon, Tim Robbins, Trey Wilson, Robert Wuhl, William O'Leary, David Neidorf, Danny Gans
best original screenplay

The Bulldog Breed
GB 1960 97m bw
Rank (Hugh Stewart)
A grocer joins the navy.
Elementary raw recruit comedy with many familiar ruses.
w Jack Davies, Henry Blyth, Norman Wisdom *d* Robert Asher
☆ Norman Wisdom, Edward Chapman, Ian Hunter, David Lodge, Robert Urquhart, Eddie Byrne, Peter Jones
'A farce which ought never to have put to sea.' – *MFB*

Bulldog Drummond *
US 1929 90m bw
Samuel Goldwyn
After advertising for adventure, ex-war hero Drummond is approached by an American girl whose uncle is being held prisoner in a fake nursing home by villainous Carl Petersen.
This is the closest the screen ever came to the original Drummond character, debonair yet taking personal and unnecessary vengeance on the chief villain. A fairly primitive talkie with little movement, yet consistently interesting.
w Sidney Howard *play Sapper* by H. C. McNeile *d* F. Richard Jones *ph* George Barnes, Gregg Toland *ad William Cameron Menzies*
☆ *Ronald Colman*, Joan Bennett, *Claud Allister* (Algy), Lilyan Tashman, Montagu Love, Lawrence Grant
Ronald Colman; William Cameron Menzies

Bulldog Drummond at Bay
GB 1937 78m bw
BIP/ABPC (Walter Mycroft)
Foreign spies use a peace club as a front, but are routed by Drummond the adventurer.
A very poor entry in this occasional series: production, directing and acting are as bad as the dialogue.
w Patrick Kirwan, James Parrish *novel Sapper* by H. C. McNeile *d* Norman Lee *ph* Walter Harvey *ad* John Mead *ed* J. Corbett
☆ John Lodge, Dorothy Mackaill, Victor Jory, Claud Allister, Richard Bird

Bulldog Drummond Strikes Back *
US 1934 83m bw
UA/Twentieth Century (Darryl F. Zanuck)
Drummond gets married, but delays his honeymoon to investigate a mysterious London house with a disappearing body.
Slow-starting, then intriguing light mystery which becomes repetitive and silly. Performances and production enjoyable.
The full complement of Drummond films is as follows:
1922 Bulldog Drummond (GB, silent with Carlyle Blackwell)
1925 The Third Round (GB, silent with Jack Buchanan)
1929 Bulldog Drummond (US, see above)
1930 Temple Tower (US, lost Fox film with Kenneth MacKenna)
1934 The Return of Bulldog Drummond (GB, perhaps the most Fascist of the series, with Ralph Richardson)
1934 Bulldog Jack (GB, amiable spoof with Jack Hulbert and Richardson as the Moriarty-like villain; finale in an Underground tunnel)
1934 Bulldog Drummond Strikes Back (US, see above)
1936 Bulldog Drummond at Bay (GB, see above)
1937 Bulldog Drummond Escapes (US, start of minor series with Ray Milland, later replaced by John Howard, and Guy Standing as Colonel Neilson)
1937 Bulldog Drummond Comes Back (US, John Howard takes over from Milland, John Barrymore from Standing)
1938 Bulldog Drummond's Revenge (US, Howard and Barrymore)
1938 Bulldog Drummond's Peril (US, ditto)
1938 Bulldog Drummond in Africa (US, Howard and H. B. Warner)
1938 Arrest Bulldog Drummond (US, ditto)
1939 Bulldog Drummond's Secret Police (US, ditto)
1939 Bulldog Drummond's Bride (US, ditto)
1939 Bulldog Sees It Through (GB, imitation with Jack Buchanan)
1947 Bulldog Drummond at Bay (US, second feature with Ron Randell)
1947 Bulldog Drummond Strikes Back (US, see above)
1948 The Challenge (US, with Tom Conway)
1948 Thirteen Lead Soldiers (US, ditto)
1951 Calling Bulldog Drummond (GB, with Walter Pidgeon)
1967 Deadlier than the Male (GB, Richard Johnson as a Bond-like Drummond)
1970 Some Girls Do (GB, Johnson again in a feeble sequel)
w Nunnally Johnson *d* Roy del Ruth *ph* Peverell Marley *m* Alfred Newman
☆ *Ronald Colman*, Loretta Young, C. Aubrey Smith, Charles Butterworth (Algy), Warner Oland, Mischa Auer, Una Merkel
'Zippy, snappy comedy melodrama with a swashbuckling flavour. Packed with what it takes.' – *Variety*

Bulldog Jack *
GB 1934 72m bw
Gaumont (Michael Balcon)
US title: *Alias Bulldog Drummond*
A playboy poses as Bulldog Drummond when the real man is injured, and manages to foil the thieves and save the girl.
After a slowish start, this comedy thriller works up into a fine frenzy with exciting scenes on the London Underground and in the British Museum.
w Gerard Fairlie, J. O. C. Orton, Sidney Gilliat, Jack Hulbert *novel Sapper d Walter Forde ph* Mutz Greenbaum (Max Greene) *md* Louis Levy *ad* Alfred Junge *ed* Otto Ludwig

☆ *Jack Hulbert, Ralph Richardson, Claude Hulbert,* Fay Wray, Athole Fleming, Paul Graetz

'There is … a mad train ride towards the terminus and destruction, as good as anything in screen melodrama.' – *Peter John Dyer, 1965*

'A sense of showmanship that is rewarded in a full quota of thrills and laughs.' – *Kine Weekly*

'You only get one shot at revenge.'

Bullet

US 1995 90m CFI color

Village Roadshow-Clipsal/Red Ruby (John Flock)

A self-destructive drug addict gets out of prison and returns to his old thieving and violent ways in Brooklyn.

Brutal and uninteresting drama of street life, with a subtext of bad feeling between Jews and blacks; the movie provides Rourke with an opportunity to punch people and walls and wear several silly hats.

w Bruce Rubenstein, Sir Eddie Cook *d* Julien Temple *ph* Crescenzo G. P. Notarile *pd* Christopher Nowak *ed* Niven Howie

☆ Mickey Rourke, Tupac Shakur, Ted Levine, Adrien Brody, John Enos III, Suzanne Shepherd, Jerry Grayson

'The sundry ultra-violent confrontations play like an action-movie parody.' – *Sight and Sound*

Bullet for a Badman

US 1964 80m Technicolor

Universal-International

An ex-Texas Ranger escapes from prison to prove his innocence of murder.

Lively Western programmer.

w Mary and Willard Willingham *d* R. G. Springsteen

☆ Audie Murphy, Darren McGavin, Ruta Lee, Skip Homeier, George Tobias

A Bullet for Joey

US 1955 85m bw

UA/Sam Bischoff, David Diamond

A Canadian policeman prevents the murder of an atomic scientist.

Listless low-budgeter with familiar stars below par.

w Geoffrey Homes, A. I. Bezzerides *d* Lewis Allen *ph* Harry Neumann *m* Harry Sukman

☆ Edward G. Robinson, George Raft, Audrey Totter, George Dolenz, Peter Hanson, Peter Van Eyck

A Bullet for the General (dubbed) *

Italy 1966 126m colour Scope

MCM (Bianco Manini)

original title: *El Chucho, Quién Sabe?*

An American mercenary joins a gang of bandits in order to assassinate a Mexican revolutionary leader.

Slow-paced, interesting spaghetti Western concerned with matters of life and death and the making of moral choices.

w Salvatore Laurani, Franco Solinas *d* Damiano Damiani *ph* Tony Secchi *m* Luis Bacalov *md* Ennio Morricone *ad* Sergio Canevari *ed* Renato Cinquini

☆ Gian-Maria Volontè, Klaus Kinski, Martine Beswick, Lou Castel, Jaime Fernandez

† The film exists in several versions, ranging in length from 77 to 135 minutes, with the shorter concentrating on its moments of violence.

Bullet in the Head

Hong Kong 1990 100m colour

Milestone/John Woo

Three young tough Chinese gangsters continue their criminal activities in Saigon during the Vietnamese war.

Blood-soaked adventure with an individual, frenetic style.

w John Woo, Patrick Leung, Janet Chun *d* John Woo *ph* Ardy Lam, Wilson Chan, Somchai Kittikun, Wong Wing-Hang *m* James Wong, Romeo Diaz *ad* James Leung *ed* John Woo

☆ Tony Leung, Jacky Cheung, Waise Lee, Simon Yam, Yolinda Yan

'Graphically violent, vile and thoroughly disturbing depiction of war.' – *Variety*

Bullet to Beijing

GB/Canada/Russia 1995 122m colour

Quebec 3099-3081/Lenfilm/Harry Palmer (Alexander Goloutva, John Dunning, André Link)

Retired on a reduced pension, a British secret agent is hired by a mysterious Russian to recover a deadly biological weapon that has gone missing.

Caine returns to the role of Harry Palmer, the unconventional agent he first played in the 60s, but the reunion is not a happy one; the problem is the dull script that defeats everyone.

w Peter Welbeck (Harry Alan Towers) *novel* Len Deighton *d* George Mihalka *ph* Peter Benison, Terence Cole *m* Rick Wakeman *pd* Yuri Pashigorie *ed* François Gill

☆ Michael Caine, Jason Connery, Mia Sara, Michael Gambon, Michael Sarrazin, Lev Prygunov, Anatoly Davidov, Sue Lloyd, Burt Kwouk, Patrick Allen

Bulletproof

US 1987 94m colour

Virgin/Bulletproof Productions (Paul Hertzberg, N. C. Lundell)

A Los Angeles cop undertakes a dangerous mission against terrorists in Mexico.

Absurd action picture.

w T. L. Lankford, Steve Carver *d* Steve Carver *ph* Francis Grumman *m* Tom Chase, Steve Rucker *pd* Adrian H. Gorton *ed* Jeff Freeman

☆ Gary Busey, Darlanne Fluegel, Henry Silva, Thalmus Rasulala, L. Q. Jones, Rene Enriquez, Mills Watson, James Andronica

'Their friendship could survive anything…except each other!'

Bulletproof

US 1996 85m DeLuxe Super 35

Universal (Robert Simonds)

A car thief discovers that his partner is actually an undercover cop.

Frenetic action movie that tries no new variations on the plot of an ill-assorted, bickering couple trying to straighten out a confused situation with as much shooting and noise as possible.

w Joe Gayton, Lewis Colick *d* Ernest Dickerson *ph* Steven Bernstein *m* Elmer Bernstein *ad* Perry Andelin Blake, William F. Matthews *ed* George Folsey Jnr

☆ Damon Wayans, Adam Sandler, James Caan, Jeep Swenson, James Farentino, Kristen Wilson, Bill Nunn

'Industrial-strength action comedy.' – *Time*

'Murder was his game, until she changed the rules.'

Bulletproof Heart

US 1994 98m colour

First Independent/Keystone/Worldvision (Robert Vince, William Vince)

GB title: *Killer*

A burned-out hitman is hired to kill a woman who wants to die, but also wants to talk about it, after first seducing him.

A killer who needs a psychiatrist meets a woman whose shrink has a drinking problem. The result is a great deal of psycho-babble in a thriller with pretensions above its genre; the action is divided into chapters, for no perceptible reason.

w Gordon Melbourne *story* Mark Malone *d* Mark Malone *ph* Tobias Schliessler *m* Graeme Coleman *pd* Lynne Stopkewich *ed* Robin Russell

☆ Anthony LaPaglia, Mimi Rogers, Matt Craven, Peter Boyle, Monika Schnarre, Joseph Maher

'What the film lacks is suspense and a pinch of human credibility. It would have made a good short, though.' – *Film Review*

Bullets for O'Hara

US 1941 50m bw

Warner

A gangster's wife helps an FBI man to trap her husband.

Fast-moving filler with action scenes lifted from its original, Public Enemy's Wife *(qv).*

w Raymond L. Schrock *d* William K. Howard

☆ Roger Pryor, Anthony Quinn, Joan Perry, Maris Wrixon, Dick Purcell

'Every real citizen should see it!'

Bullets or Ballots *

US 1936 81m bw

Warner (Lou Edelman)

A city cop goes undercover to break the mob.

Vivid routine gangster thriller, not quite of the top flight, but nearly.

w Seton I. Miller *d* William Keighley *ph* Hal Mohr *m* Heinz Roemheld

☆ Edward G. Robinson, Joan Blondell, Humphrey Bogart, Barton MacLane, Frank McHugh, Dick Purcell, George E. Stone

'A good gangster film of the second class … all the old chivalrous situations of *Chums* and the *Boy's Own Paper* are agreeably translated into sub-machine gun terms.' – *Graham Greene*

Bullets over Broadway **

US 1994 99m Technicolor

Buena Vista/Magnolia/Sweetland (Robert Greenhut)

In 1920s New York, a writer agrees to hire an untalented actress so that her lover, a gangster, will back his new play; but her bodyguard has other ideas when he realizes she is ruining the production.

Witty and entertaining backstage comedy on the theme of artistic integrity, performed and directed in a sprightly manner.

w Woody Allen, Douglas McGrath *d* Woody Allen *ph* Carlo Di Palma *pd* Santo Loquasto *ed* Susan E. Morse

☆ John Cusack, Jack Warden, *Chazz Palminteri,* Joe Viterelli, Jennifer Tilly, Rob Reiner, Mary-Louise Parker, *Dianne Wiest,* Harvey Fierstein, Jim Broadbent, Tracey Ullman

'Allen bathes his fable in a seductive, rosy light, grants everyone in the wonderful ensemble cast a comic high point, and gives us a film that combines impeccable craftsmanship and a basic exuberance that's been missing from his work for years.' – *Richard Schickel, Time*

'What's fatally missing from the movie is any love for the way of life being mocked. There's too much contempt – contempt joined strangely with self-exculpation.' – *New York*

Dianne Wiest

Woody Allen (as director); Woody Allen, Douglas McGrath (screenplay); Chazz Palminteri; Jennifer Tilly; art direction; costume design

The Bullfighter and the Lady

US 1951 87m bw

Republic/John Wayne (Budd Boetticher)

A young American in Mexico is fascinated by bullfighting but during training accidentally causes the death of a great matador.

Predictable, rather boring plot given routine treatment: for aficionados only.

w James Edward Grant *d* Budd Boetticher *ph* Jack Draper *m* Victor Young

☆ Robert Stack, Gilbert Roland, Joy Page, Katy Jurado, Virginia Grey, John Hubbard

original story (Budd Boetticher, Ray Nazarro)

The Bullfighters *

US 1945 60m bw

TCF (William Girard)

Two detectives in Mexico find that one of them resembles a famous matador.

Laurel and Hardy's last American feature is poor enough as a whole, but at least has a few sequences in their earlier style.

w Scott Darling *d* Mal St Clair *ph* Norbert Brodine *m* David Buttolph *ad* Lyle Wheeler, Chester Gore *ed* Stanley Rabjohn

☆ Stan Laurel, Oliver Hardy, Richard Lane, Margo Woode, Carol Andrews

Bullitt **

US 1968 113m Technicolor

Warner/Solar (Philip D'Antoni)

A San Francisco police detective conceals the death of an underground witness in his charge, and goes after the killers himself.

Routine cop thriller with undoubted charisma, distinguished by a splendid car chase which takes one's mind off the tedious plot. Technical credits first class.

w Harry Kleiner, Alan R. Trustman *novel* Mute *Witness* by Robert L. Pike *d* Peter Yates *ph William A. Fraker* *m* Lalo Schifrin *ed* Frank P. Keller

☆ *Steve McQueen,* Jacqueline Bisset, Robert Vaughn, Don Gordon, Robert Duvall, Simon Oakland

'It has energy, drive, impact, and above all, style.' – *Hollis Alpert*

Frank P. Keller

Bullseye!

US 1990 92m colour

Castle Premier/21st Century (Michael Winner)

Two con-men impersonate crooked nuclear scientists.

Tedious comedy with few laughs.

w Leslie Bricusse, Laurence Marks, Maurice Gran *story* Leslie Bricusse, Michael Winner, Nick Mead *d* Michael Winner *ph* Alan Jones *pd* John Blezard *ad* Alan Cassie *ed* Arnold Crust

☆ Michael Caine, Roger Moore, Sally Kirkland, Deborah Barrymore, Lee Patterson, Mark Burns, Derren Nesbitt

'Wallowing in its excremental humour, *Bullseye!* is content to reinforce the crudest of racial and sexual stereotypes.' – *MFB*

Bullshot

GB 1983 88m Technicolor

HandMade (Ian La Frenais)

In the twenties, Bullshot Crummond is pitted against his arch enemy Count Otto von Bruno.

Very flat-footed spoof which belies the talents involved.

w Ron House, Diz White, Alan Shearman *d* Dick Clement *ph* Alex Thomson *m* John Du Prez *pd* Norman Garwood

☆ Alan Shearman, Diz White, Ron House, Frances Tomelty, Michael Aldridge, Ron Pember, Mel Smith, Billy Connolly, Geoffrey Bayldon, Bryan Pringle

'Unrelievedly ghastly … even canned laughter would be hard pressed to raise a titter.' – *Gilbert Adair, MFB*

'Behind every mannered line you can hear technicians laughing the fun to death on the studio floor.' – *Sunday Times*

'It's 4 a.m… do you know where your kids are?'

Bully *

US 2001 112m colour

Film4/Studio Canal/Lions Gate/Muse/Blacklist/Gravity (Chris Hanley, Don Murphy, Fernando Sulichin)

In Florida, teenage friends and lovers decide to kill the most unpleasant and aggressive member of their group.

Based on a true story, this unlovely but memorable movie offers little in the way of explanation and nothing in condemnation; it is content to observe, and even admire.

w Zachary Long, Roger Pullis *d* Larry Clark *ph* Steve Gainer *m* Dillinger & Young Gotti et al *pd* Linda Burton *ed* Andrew Hafitz

☆ Brad Renfro (Marty Puccio), Rachel Miner (Lisa Connelly), Nick Stahl (Bobby Kent), Bijou Phillips (Ali Willis), Michael Pitt (Donny Semenec), Kelli Garner (Heather Swaller), Daniel Franzese (Derek Dzvirko), Leo Fitzpatrick (Hitman)

'Likely to elicit just a passing belch from more discerning/jaded viewers… By turns turgid, embarrassing and plain off-putting.' – *Dennis Harvey, Variety*

'A magnificent, coldly brilliant movie conveyed to us in an amoral neon glare, in which the director's only compelling value judgment is a swooning reverie at the beauty of his teen stars.' – *Peter Bradshaw, Guardian*

Bulworth *

US 1998 107m Technicolor

TCF (Warren Beatty, Pieter Jan Brugge)

Having arranged his assassination in order to provide wealth for his family, a Democratic senator decides to tell the unvarnished truth during his election campaign.

A satire on the corporate control of political parties that, however accurate, lacks bite; Beatty's embrace of urban black culture, as his senator breaks into rap, seems self-indulgent rather than revolutionary.

w Warren Beatty, Jeremy Pikser *d* Warren Beatty *ph* Vittorio Storaro *m* Ennio Morricone *pd* Dean Tavoularis *ed* Robert C. Jones, Billy Weber

☆ Warren Beatty, Halle Berry, Don Cheadle, Oliver Platt, Paul Sorvino, Jack Warden, Isaiah Washington, Joshua Malina, Christine Baranski, Richard Sarafian, Amiri Baraka, Sean Astin, Laurie Metcalf, Wendell Pierce

'One of the best films to emerge from a Hollywood studio in the 90s.' – *Richard Kelly, Sight and Sound*

Warren Beatty, Jeremy Pikser (script)

Bun Ngo Tsong Tinngai: see *Wild Search*

Bundle of Joy
US 1956 98m Technicolor RKOscope
RKO/Edmund Grainger

A shopgirl finds an abandoned baby and everyone thinks it is hers.
Tame musical remake of Bachelor Mother *(qv); some laughs, but poor numbers.*
w Norman Krasna, Arthur Sheekman, Robert Carson *d* Norman Taurog *ph* William Snyder *m* Josef Myrow
☆ Debbie Reynolds, Eddie Fisher, Adolphe Menjou, Melville Cooper, Tommy Noonan, Nita Talbot, Una Merkel, Robert H. Harris

'As bad as I was, the picture was worse.' – *Eddie Fisher*

Bunker Bean
US 1936 67m bw
RKO
aka: *His Majesty Bunker Bean*
A meek office clerk rises to power after a personality course.
Old-fashioned comedy previously filmed in 1917 and 1924.
w Edmund North, James Gow and Dorothy Yost *novel* Harry Leon Wilson *d* William Hamilton, Edward Killy
☆ Owen Davis Jnr, Lucille Ball, Berton Churchill, Louise Latimer, Jessie Ralph, Hedda Hopper

Bunny Lake Is Missing **
GB 1965 107m bw Panavision
Columbia/Wheel (Otto Preminger)
The 4-year-old illegitimate daughter of an American girl in London disappears, and no one can be found to admit that she ever existed.
A nightmarish gimmick story, with more gimmicks superimposed along the way to say nothing of a Psychoish ending; some of the decoration works and makes even the unconvincing story compelling, while the cast alone is worth the price of admission.
w John and Penelope Mortimer *novel* Evelyn Piper *d* Otto Preminger *ph* Denys Coop *m* Paul Glass *pd* Don Ashton *titles* Saul Bass
☆ *Laurence Olivier*, Carol Lynley, Keir Dullea, Noël Coward, Martita Hunt, Finlay Currie, Clive Revill, Anna Massey, Lucie Mannheim

'It has the enjoyable hallmarks of really high calibre professionalism.' – *Penelope Houston*

Bunny O'Hare
US 1971 92m Movielab
AIP (Gerd Oswald, Norman T. Herman)
A middle-aged widow and an ex-con plumber become bank robbers, dressed as hippies and escaping on a motor cycle.
Unappealing, ill-thought-out comedy with pretensions to satire, an unhappy venture for both stars.
w Stanley Z. Cherry, Coslough Johnson *d* Gerd Oswald *ph* Loyal Griggs, John Stephens *m* Billy Strange
☆ Bette Davis, Ernest Borgnine, Jack Cassidy, Joan Delaney, Jay Robinson, John Astin

Buona Sera Mrs Campbell *
US 1968 113m Technicolor
UA/Connaught (Melvin Frank)

Wartime USAF comrades reassemble twenty years later in an Italian village, and three find that they have been paying paternity money to the same local glamour girl.
Agreeably cast, pleasantly set and photographed, quite funny in parts, this comedy of middle age unfortunately outstays its welcome and lets its invention peter out.
w Melvin Frank, Denis Norden, Sheldon Keller *d* Melvin Frank *ph* Gabor Pogany *m* Riz Ortolani
☆ Gina Lollobrigida, Telly Savalas, Phil Silvers, Peter Lawford, Lee Grant, Marian Moses, Shelley Winters

Il Buono, il Brutto, il Cattivo: see *The Good, the Bad and the Ugly*

The 'burbs **
US 1988 102m DeLuxe
UIP/Imagine (Michael Finnell, Larry Brezner)

Neighbours decide that there is something sinister about a new family on the block.
One-joke black comedy that has its moments.
w Dana Olsen *d* Joe Dante *ph* Robert Stevens *m* Jerry Goldsmith *pd* James Spencer *ed* Marshall Harvey
☆ Tom Hanks, Bruce Dern, Carrie Fisher, Rick Ducommun, Corey Feldman, Wendy Schaal, Henry Gibson, Brother Theodore, Courtney Gains, Gale Gordon

'For the most part, this is one of the most extraordinary major studio films of the late 80s.' – *Kim Newman, MFB*

Bureau of Missing Persons *
US 1933 73m bw
Warner

Police chief helps a girl find her husband, who turns out to have been murdered.
Fast-moving potboiler typical of its studio.
w Robert Presnell *story Missing Men* by John H. Ayers, Carol Bird *d* Roy del Ruth
☆ Pat O'Brien, Bette Davis, Lewis Stone, Glenda Farrell, Allen Jenkins, Hugh Herbert

'Pretty fair entertainment. Nothing socko, but it will please.' – *Variety*

The Burglar *
US 1957 80m bw
Columbia (Louis W. Kellerman)
A burglar is shadowed by a policeman who is also after the loot.
Slightly pretentious but watchable low-budgeter.
w David Goodis *novel* David Goodis *ph* Don Malkames *m* Sol Kaplan *d/ed* Paul Wendkos
☆ Dan Duryea, Jayne Mansfield, Martha Vickers, Peter Capell

Burglar
US 1987 102m Technicolor
Warner/Nelvana (Kevin McCormick, Michael Hirsch)

An ex-con turns tec to avoid arrest as a cat burglar.
Strained comedy which is too goofy to sustain its mystery elements.
w Joseph Loeb III, Matthew Weisman, Hugh Wilson *books* Lawrence Block *d* Hugh Wilson *ph* William A. Fraker *m* Sylvester Levay
☆ Whoopi Goldberg, Bob Goldthwait, G. W. Bailey, Lesley Ann Warren, James Handy, Anne de Salvo

The Burglar
Russia 1987 89m colour
First Film Group/Lenfilm
original title: *Vzlomshchik*
A youth steals a synthesiser in order to prevent his elder brother, a rock musician, from committing the crime.
Teenage alienation among Soviet punk rockers.
w Valeri Priyomkhov *d* Valery Ogorodnikov *ph* Valery Mironov *m* Viktor Kisin *ad* Irakli Kvirikadze
☆ Oleg Elykomov, Konstantin Kirchev, Yuri Tsapnik, Svetlana Gaitan, Polina Petrenko, Mikhail Parfonov, Pyotr Semak, Oleg Garkusha, Valdimir Dyatlov

The Burglars
France/Italy 1971 120m Eastmancolor Panavision
Columbia/Vides (Henri Verneuil)
original title: *La Casse*
A determined policeman chases three burglars and their girl accomplice.
Expensive, camped-up version of The Burglar, *with plenty going on, most of it borrowed from other films.*
w Vahe Katcha, Henri Verneuil *novel The Burglar* by David Goodis *d* Henri Verneuil *ph* Claude Renoir *m* Ennio Morricone
☆ Omar Sharif, Jean-Paul Belmondo, Dyan Cannon, Robert Hossein, Nicole Calfan, Renato Salvatori

'Electronic equipment, wild action, exotic locales and bland villainy.' – *Tom Milne, MFB*

Buried Alive
US 1991 91m colour
21st Century/Breton (Harry Alan Towers)

A psychiatrist, made mad by his father's experiments, turns a former asylum into a school for disturbed girls.
Dim and gory exploitation movie that borrows ideas from several of Poe's stories but has little notion of what to do with them.
w Jake Clesi, Stuart Lee *story* Edgar Allan Poe *d* Gérard Kikoine *ph* Gérard Loubeau *m* Frederic Targorn *pd* Leonardo Coen Calgi *ed* Gilbert Kikoine
☆ Robert Vaughn, Donald Pleasence, Karen Witter, John Carradine, Nia Long, Ginger Lynn Allen, Bill Butler
† It was John Carradine's last film.

Burke and Hare
GB 1971 91m DeLuxe
UA/Kenneth Shipman/Armitage (Guido Coen)
The story of anatomist Dr Knox and his body snatchers, retold with emphasis on the local brothel.
Depressing in its childish attempts to be gruesome and perverted.
w Ernie Bradford *d* Vernon Sewell *ph* Desmond Dickinson *m* Roger Webb
☆ Harry Andrews, Derren Nesbitt, Glynn Edwards, Yootha Joyce, Dee Sjendery, Alan Tucker

Burke and Wills *
Australia 1985 140m Eastmancolor Panavision
Hoyts Edgley (Graeme Clifford, John Sexton)

An account of the 1860 expedition across Australia.
Downbeat epic with interesting highlights; but the length is against it.
w Michael Thomas *d* Graeme Clifford *ph* Russell Boyd *m* Peter Sculthorpe *pd* Ross Major
☆ Jack Thompson, Nigel Havers, Greta Scacchi, Matthew Fargher
† A parody film, *Wills and Burke*, appeared simultaneously.

The Burmese Harp ***
Japan 1956 116m bw
Nikkatsu (Masayuki Takagi)

original title: *Biruma no tategoto*
A shell-shocked Japanese soldier stays in the Burmese jungle to bury the unknown dead.
Deeply impressive and horrifying war film with an epic, folk-tale quality, emphasized by superbly controlled direction.
w Natto Wada novel Michio Takeyama *d Kon Ichikawa ph Minoru Yokoyama m* Akira Ifukube
☆ Shoji Yasui, Rentaro Mikuni, Tatsuya Mihashi
best foreign film

Burn!: see *Queimada!*

Burn 'Em Up O'Connor
US 1938 70m bw
MGM
The life and loves of a speedway ace.
Modestly effective second from the time when the studios were trying to make a star of Dennis O'Keefe.
w Milton Merlin, Byron Morgan *novel Salute to the Gods* by Sir Malcolm Campbell *d* Edward Sedgwick
☆ Dennis O'Keefe, Harry Carey, Cecilia Parker, Nat Pendleton, Charley Grapewin

'Will fill better half of duals for good b.o.' – *Variety*

Burn, Witch, Burn: see *Night of the Eagle*

'Don't look he'll see you. Don't breathe he'll hear you. Don't move you're dead.'

The Burning
US 1981 91m colour
HandMade/Miramax (Harvey Weinstein)

An incinerated caretaker takes his revenge on teenagers at a summer camp.
Dire, totally predictable, uninventive low-budget horror.
w Peter Lawrence, Bob Weinstein *story* Harvey Weinstein, Tony Maylam, Brad Grey *d* Tony Maylam *ph* Harvey Harrison *m* Rick Wakeman *ad* Peter Politanoff *ed* Jack Sholder
☆ Brian Matthews, Leah Ayres, Brian Backer, Larry Joshua, Jason Alexander, Ned Eisenberg, Holly Hunter

Burning an Illusion
GB 1981 111m Eastmancolor
BFI (Vivien Pottersman)
A black secretary in London, reluctantly intrigued by the activities of her political boyfriend, becomes a political militant.
Most people would sigh at the thought of sitting through this decently made but rather earnest document which preaches only to the converted.
wd Menelik Shabazz *ph* Roy Cornwall *songs* various
☆ Cassie McFarlane, Victor Romero, Beverley Martin, Angela Wynter

The Burning Hills
US 1956 92m Warnercolor Cinemascope
Warner (Richard Whorf)
A young rancher gets even with a cattle baron who had his brother killed.
Reasonable but unexciting star vehicle.
w Irving Wallace *novel* Louis L'Amour *d* Stuart Heisler *ph* Ted McCord *m* David Buttolph *ed* Clarence Kolster
☆ Natalie Wood, Tab Hunter, Skip Homeier, Eduard Franz, Earl Holliman

The Burning Question: see *Reefer Madness*

Burning Rubber
West Germany 1980 84m colour
Ocean Films/Safe Productions (Stefan Abendroth, Barrie Saint Clair)
A car mechanic becomes a drag-racer with the aid of a rich girlfriend.
An attempt to combine the appeals of pop music and motor-racing, to the detriment of both.
w Dale Cutts, Bill Flynn *d* Norman Cohen *ph* Keith Jones *m* Bay City Rollers *ed* Wayne Lines
☆ Olivia Pascal, Alan Longmuir, Sascha Hehn, Stuart 'Woody' Wood, Derek Longmuir, Duncan Faure

Burning Secret *
GB/US 1988 105m colour
Vestron/NFH/CLG Films (Norma Heyman, Eberhard Junkersdoft, Carol Lynn Greene)

An asthmatic boy on the edge of adolescence interferes in a holiday romance between his mother and a stranger.
Constantly promising more than it delivers, though with some interesting stops on an unsatisfying journey.
wd Andrew Birkin *story Brennendes Geheimnis* by Stefan Zweig *ph* Ernest Day *m* Hans Zimmer *pd* Bernd Lepel *ed* Paul Green
☆ Faye Dunaway, David Eberts, Klaus Maria Brandauer, Ian Richardson

'Stately, elegant, and stiflingly old-fashioned, producing many exquisite coils of smoke but nothing resembling a real fire.' – *Philip Strick, MFB*

Burnt by the Sun ***
Russia/France 1994 134m colour
Studio Trite/Camera One (Nikita Mikhalkov, Michel Seydoux)

original title: *Utomlennye Solntsem*
In rural Russia in the Stalinist mid-30s, an ageing military hero of the Revolution is betrayed by a former acquaintance, his wife's old boyfriend, who is a turncoat White Russian now working for the secret police.
Complex and tragic, at times almost Chekhovian, evocation of an ambiguous time, of unthinking brutality darkening a summer landscape.
w Nikita Mikhalkov, Rustam Ibragimbekov *d* Nikita Mikhalkov *ph* Vilen Kaliuta *m* Eduard Artemiev *ad* Aleksandr Samuelekin, Vladimir Aronin *ed* Enzo Meniconi, Joëlle Hache
☆ Nikita Mikhalkov, Oleg Menchikov, Ingeborga Dapkunaité, Nadya Mikhalkov, Viacheslav Tikhonov, Svetlana Kriuchkova, Vladimir Ilyin

'The acting is excellent and the direction sympathetic to it, so that the whole glimmers in the mind's eye in a totally different way to anything the American cinema seems capable of at the moment.' – *Derek Malcolm, Guardian*

'Surely the most charming movie about the horrors of totalitarianism ever made.' – *Tom Shone, Sunday Times*

† The film shared the Grand Prix at the Cannes Film Festival in 1995. It is dedicated to 'everyone who was burnt by the sun of Revolution'.

best foreign film

Burnt Offerings

US 1976 115m DeLuxe

UA/PEA-Dan Curtis (Robert Singer)

An evil house restores itself by feeding on its tenants.

An agreeably macabre idea for a five-page story is dragged out to interminable length, and seizes the attention only by a few shock moments. The title is mysteriously irrelevant.

w William F. Nolan, Dan Curtis *novel* Robert Marasco *d* Dan Curtis *ph* Jacques Marquette *m* Robert Colbert *pd* Eugene Lourie

☆ Oliver Reed, Karen Black, Bette Davis, Lee Montgomery, Burgess Meredith, Eileen Heckart, Dub Taylor

'Before the ludicrous dénouement, the movie merely piles on one special effect after another – none of them too special – and stalls for time.' – *Janet Maslin, Newsweek*

Bury Me Dead *

US 1947 68m bw

Charles F. Reisner/Eagle Lion

A girl reappears on the day of her 'funeral', and determines to discover who is being buried in her name.

Complex mystery which might have been worthy of a Grade A production.

w Karen de Wolf, Dwight V. Babcock *story* Irene Winston *d* Bernard Vorhaus

☆ Cathy O'Donnell, June Lockhart, Hugh Beaumont, Mark Daniels, Greg McClure

Bus Riley's Back in Town *

US 1965 93m Eastmancolor

U-I (Elliott Kastner)

An ex-sailor wants to settle back into small-town life but finds that his girlfriend has married.

Watchable, middling, routine small-town drama in the style of Picnic *(qv).*

w Walter Gage (William Inge) *d* Harvey Hart *ph* Russell Metty *m* Richard Markowitz

☆ Michael Parks, Ann-Margret, Jocelyn Brando, Janet Margolin, Kim Darby, Brad Dexter, Larry Storch, Crahan Denton, Mimsy Farmer, David Carradine

Bus Stop **

US 1956 96m Eastmancolor Cinemascope

TCF (Buddy Adler)

TV title: *The Wrong Kind of Girl*

In a rodeo town, a simple-thinking cowboy meets a café singer and asks her to marry him.

Sex comedy-drama, a modest entertainment in familiar American vein, very well done but rather over-inflated by its star.

w George Axelrod *play* William Inge *d* Joshua Logan *ph* Milton Krasner *m* Alfred Newman, Cyril Mockridge

☆ Marilyn Monroe, Don Murray, Betty Field, Arthur O'Connell, Eileen Heckart, Robert Bray, Hope Lange, Hans Conried, Casey Adams

'The film demands of its principal performers a purely physical display of their bodies viewed as sexual machinery.' – *David Robinson*

Don Murray

Bush Christmas

GB 1947 77m bw

ABFD/Children's Entertainment Films (Ralph Smart)

Australian children on holiday help catch horse thieves.

Rather stolid family feature which got a reputation it hardly deserved.

wd Ralph Smart

☆ Chips Rafferty, John Fernside, Stan Tolshurst, Pat Penny, Thelma Grigg, John McCallum

The Bushido Blade

GB/US 1978 92m colour

Trident/Rankin-Bass (Arthur Rankin Jnr)

aka: *The Bloody Bushido Blade*

Yokohama 1854; a US-Japanese treaty is in jeopardy because the Shogun's gift of a ceremonial sword has been stolen.

Unappealing hybrid with much beheading and other random action, but little sense.

w William Overgard *d* Tom Kotani *ph* Shoji Uedo *m* Maury Laws

☆ Richard Boone, Frank Converse, Laura Gemser, Toshiro Mifune, Sonny Chiba, James Earl Jones, Mako

Bushwhacked

US 1995 90m DeLuxe

TCF (Charles B. Wessler, Paul Schiff)

Framed for murder, a dim-witted van driver heads for the mountains to prove his innocence and is forced to impersonate a Ranger Scout leader who is taking a troop on an overnight jaunt.

Crude, brash, loud would-be comedy, with a manic central performance; its intended audience of children is likely to find it as unamusing as any adults unfortunate enough to watch it.

w John Jordan, Danny Byers, Tommy Swerdlow, Michael Goldberg *d* Greg Beeman *ph* Theo Van de Sande *m* Bill Conti *pd* Mark W. Mansbridge, Sandy Veneziano *ed* Ross Albert

☆ Daniel Stern, Jon Polito, Brad Sullivan, Ann Dowd, Anthony Heald, Tom Wood, Blake Bashoff, Corey Carrier, Michael Galeota

A Business Affair

GB/France/Germany/Spain 1993 102m colour

Entertainment/Film and General/Osby/Connexion (Clive Parsons, Davina Belling, Xavier Larere)

An author with writer's block is annoyed by his wife's success as a novelist and her decision to leave him for his agent.

Slick, forgettable romantic nonsense, through which its talented cast dispiritedly flounders.

w William Stadiem, Lucy Flannery *novel Tears before Bedtime, Weep No More* by Barbara Skelton *d* Charlotte Brandstorm *ph* Willy Kurant *m* Didier Vasseur *pd* Sophie Becher *ed* Laurence Méry-Clark

☆ Christopher Walken, Jonathan Pryce, Carole Bouquet, Sheila Hancock, Anna Manahan, Tom Wilkinson

'A whimsical love-triangle saga with the production values of a mineral water commercial.' – *Geoffrey Macnab, Sight and Sound*

Business and Pleasure

US 1931 76m bw

Fox

A down-to-earth husband is tempted by a *femme fatale.*

Mild star comedy for his regular fans.

w Gene Towne, William Conselman *novel The Plutocrat* by Booth Tarkington *d* David Butler

☆ Will Rogers, Jetta Goudal, Joel McCrea, Dorothy Peterson, Jed Prouty

'West of Albany, perhaps, it will see some good business.' – *Variety*

Business As Usual

GB 1987 90m colour

Cannon (Sara Geater)

The manageress of a shop, sacked for objecting to her boss's sexual harassment of his staff, fights back.

Agit-prop drama with some forceful performances.

wd Lezli-An Barrett *ph* Ernie Vincze *ad* Hildegarde Betchler *ed* Henry Richardson

☆ *Glenda Jackson*, John Thaw, Cathy Tyson, Mark McGann, Buki Armstrong, Stephen McGann, Philip Foster, Natalie Duffy, James Hazeldine, Mel Martin

Buster

GB 1988 102m colour

Vestron/The Movie Group (Norma Heyman)

True story of Great Train Robber, actually a small-time thief, on the run.

Uneasy combination of romantic comedy and chase thriller.

w Colin Schindler *d* David Green *ph* Tony Imi *m* Anne Dudley *pd* Simon Holland *ed* Lesley Walker

☆ Phil Collins, Julie Walters, Larry Lamb, Stephanie Lawrence, Martin Jarvis, Sheila Hancock, Anthony Quayle

best song 'Two Hearts' (*m/ly* Lamont Dozier, Phil Collins)

Buster and Billie

US 1973 99m CFI color

Black Creek Billie/Columbia

A sensitive high school senior elects to marry the school's derided 'easy lay', with tragic results.

Unattractive reminiscences of rural Georgia with a rather desperate appeal to oversexed teenagers.

w Ron Turbeville *d* Daniel Petrie *ph* Mario Tosi

☆ Jan-Michael Vincent, Pamela Sue Martin, Joan Goodfellow, Clifton James

Buster Keaton: A Hard Act to Follow ***

GB 1987 156m colour/bw

Thames TV (Kevin Brownlow, David Gill)

A three-part investigation of the art and life of Keaton, including many clips from his films as well as interviews with him and those who worked with him.

An exemplary and fascinating documentary on one of the greatest of cinematic clowns.

w Kevin Brownlow, David Gill *m* Carl Davis

☆ Lindsay Anderson (narrator)

The Buster Keaton Story *

US 1957 91m bw Vistavision

Paramount (Sidney Sheldon, Robert Smith)

A biopic of the great silent comedian, with the emphasis on his years of downfall through drink.

An interesting recreation of Hollywood in the twenties and thirties is the main asset of this otherwise dismal tribute to a man whose greatness the star is unable to suggest apart from a few acrobatic moments.

w Robert Smith, Sidney Sheldon *d* Sidney Sheldon *ph* Loyal Griggs *m* Victor Young

☆ Donald O'Connor, Rhonda Fleming, Ann Blyth, Peter Lorre, Larry Keating, Richard Anderson, Dave Willock

Bustin' Loose

US 1981 94m Technicolor

Universal/Richard Pryor (William Greaves)

A thief on parole learns to look after a school for maladjusted children en route to a mountain retreat.

A fairly nauseous compendium of pratfalls and sentiment, not too bad while it keeps on the move.

w Roger L. Simon *d* Oz Scott *ph* Dennis Dalzell *m* Mark Davis, Roberta Flack

☆ Richard Pryor, Cicely Tyson, Angel Ramirez, Jimmy Hughes

'The sort of forties-style warm experience I could well do without.' – *Derek Malcolm, Guardian*

Busting

US 1973 92m DeLuxe

UA/Chartoff-Winkler (Henry Gellis)

Two Los Angeles vice squad officers fight corruption inside and outside the force.

Violent, exhausting, but totally routine police caper of the seventies.

wd Peter Hyams *ph* Earl Rath *m* Billy Goldenberg

☆ Elliott Gould, Robert Blake, Allen Garfield, Antonio Fargas

'The farcical version of *Serpico*.' – *Michael Billington, Illustrated London News*

Busy Bodies **

US 1933 20m bw

MGM/Hal Roach

Stan and Ollie are involved in various disasters in a sawmill.

Though not among their most sympathetic comedies, this is a sustained and brilliantly contrived slapstick sequence.

w Anon (and Stan Laurel) *d* Lloyd French *ph* Art Lloyd *ed* Bert Jordan

☆ Laurel and Hardy, Tiny Sandford, Charlie Hall

The Busy Body

US 1966 102m Technicolor Techniscope

Paramount/William Castle

A gangster is buried in a suit with a million dollar lining which various people are out to get.

Unfunny black comedy; laboured handling makes it a joke in poor taste.

w Ben Starr *novel* Donald E. Westlake *d* William Castle *ph* Hal Stine *m* Vic Mizzy

☆ Robert Ryan, Sid Caesar, Arlene Golonka, Anne Baxter, Kay Medford, Charles McGraw

'A Comedy Of Sexual Disorientation.'

But I'm A Cheerleader

US 1999 81m colour

Fine Line/Ignite/Kushner-Locke/HKM (Andrea Sperling, Leanna Creel)

A cheerleader, who is suspected of lesbian tendencies by her uptight parents, is sent to a rehabiliation camp to change her sexual orientation.

Camp camp comedy likely to enjoy a cult following among gays, but too obvious to provide more than a few laughs.

w Brian Wayne Peterson *d* Jamie Babbit *ph* Jules LaBarthe *m* Pat Irwin *pd* Rachel Kamerman *ed* Cecily Rhett

☆ Natasha Lyonne (Megan), Clea DuVall (Graham), Cathy Moriarty (Mary Brown), Bud Cort (Peter), Mink Stole (Nancy), RuPaul Charles (Mike), Eddie Cibrian (Rock), Julie Delpy (Lipstick Lesbian)

'A shallow, only mildly entertaining satire.' – *Variety*

But Not for Me

US 1959 105m bw

Paramount (William Perlberg, George Seaton)

An ageing, washed-up Broadway producer is loved by his young drama student secretary.

Rather heavy-going remake of Accent on Youth *(qv), efficiently performed but lacking the original gaiety.*

w John Michael Hayes *d* Walter Lang *ph* Robert Burks *m* Leith Stevens

☆ Clark Gable, Carroll Baker, Lilli Palmer, Lee J. Cobb, Barry Coe, Thomas Gomez

But the Flesh Is Weak

US 1932 82m bw

MGM

A widower and his son both decide to marry wealthy widows.

Amusing high society comedy from Ivor Novello's The Truth Game.

w Ivor Novello *d* Jack Conway

☆ Robert Montgomery, C. Aubrey Smith, Heather Thatcher, Edward Everett Horton, Nils Asther

Butch and Sundance: The Early Days *

US 1979 112m DeLuxe

TCF (Gabriel Katzka, Stephen Bach)

Early episodes in the careers of the famous outlaws, culminating in a train robbery.

'Prequel' to a more celebrated but not a fresher or more lyrical Western.

w Allan Burns *d* Richard Lester *ph* Laszlo Kovacs *m* Patrick Williams *pd* Brian Eatwell

☆ Tom Berenger, William Katt, Jeff Corey, John Schuck, Michael C. Gwynne, Brian Dennehy, Peter Weller

'Not that it matters, but most of it is true!'

Butch Cassidy and the Sundance Kid ****

US 1969 110m DeLuxe Panavision

TCF/Campanile (John Foreman)

A hundred years ago, two Western train robbers keep one step ahead of the law until finally tracked down to Bolivia.

Humorous, cheerful, poetic, cinematic account of two semi-legendary outlaws, winningly acted and directed. One of the decade's great commercial successes, not least because of the song 'Raindrops Keep Fallin' on My Head'.

w William Goldman d George Roy Hill ph Conrad Hall m Burt Bacharach

☆ *Paul Newman, Robert Redford,* Katharine Ross, Strother Martin, Henry Jones, Jeff Corey, Cloris Leachman, Ted Cassidy, Kenneth Mars

'A mere exercise in smart-alecky device-mongering, chock-full of out of place and out of period one-upmanship, a battle of wits at a freshman smoker.' – *John Simon*

'The film does wonderful things with mood and atmosphere. The touches are fleeting, but they are there.' – *Hollis Alpert, Saturday Review*

🏆 William Goldman; Conrad Hall; Burt Bacharach; song 'Raindrops Keep Fallin' on My Head' (*m* Burt Bacharach, *ly* Hal David)

Academy Award nomination: best picture; George Roy Hill

BAFTA: best picture; George Roy Hill; Conrad Hall; Burt Bacharach; William Goldman; Robert Redford; Katharine Ross

The Butcher: see *Le Boucher*

Butcher Boy ***

Ireland/US 1997 110m Technicolor
Warner/Geffen (Redmond Morris, Stephen Woolley)

In the early 60s, an Irish boy with an alcoholic father and suicidal mother grows up to be a murderer.

Sustained by a superb performance in the title role, this is a bleak, dark drama of alienation and despair, shot through with a gallows humour.

w Neil Jordan, Patrick McCabe *novel* Patrick McCabe *d* Neil Jordan *ph* Adrian Biddle *m* Elliot Goldenthal *pd* Anthony Pratt *ed* Tony Lawson

☆ Stephen Rea, Fiona Shaw, *Eamonn Owens*, Alan Boyle, Brendan Gleeson, Milo O'Shea, Ian Hart, Sinead O'Connor, Patrick McCabe

'A heart-wrenching black comedy.' – *Paddy Barrett, Screen International*

'Grips like *The 400 Blows* crossed with *A Clockwork Orange*.' – *Alexander Walker*

'It's not about meat, it's about magic.'

The Butcher's Wife

US 1991 105m Technicolor
Blue Dolphin/Paramount (Wallis Nicita, Lauren Lloyd)

A clairvoyant marries a butcher and tells customers of her premonitions concerning them.

Whimsical romantic comedy that sank without a trace.

w Ezra Litwak, Marjorie Schwartz *d* Terry Hughes *ph* Frank Tidy *m* Michael Gore *pd* Charles Rosen *ed* Donn Cambern

☆ Demi Moore, Jeff Daniels, George Dzundza, Mary Steenburgen, Frances McDormand, Margaret Colin, Max Perlich, Miriam Margolyes

'The jokes and folksy apothegms are the sort that fill out the pages of *Reader's Digest*, the over-acting is the kind of thing good performers resort to in long-running Broadway plays.' – *Philip French, Observer*

The Butler's Dilemma

GB 1943 83m bw
British National/Shaftesbury (Elizabeth Hiscott)

A jewel thief has to pose as his fiancée's butler.

Predictable comedy of pretence and mistaken identity; a tolerable co-feature of its day.

w Michael Barringer *d* Leslie Hiscott *ph* James Wilson *m* John Blore

☆ Richard Hearne, Francis L. Sullivan, Judy Kelly, Hermione Gingold, Henry Kendall, Wally Patch

Butley *

US/GB 1973 130m Eastmancolor
American Express/Ely Landau/Cinevision

Personal problems assail an English lecturer at a university college.

Adequate but not outstanding transcription (for the American Film Theater) of a successful and percipient play.

w Simon Gray *play* Simon Gray *d* Harold Pinter *ph* Gerry Fisher *m* none *ad* Carmen Dillon

☆ *Alan Bates*, Jessica Tandy, Richard O'Callaghan, Susan Engel, Michael Byrne

The Butter and Egg Man

This pleasant George S. Kaufman comedy about a cowboy in New York was filmed as a silent in 1928, with Jack Mulhall; in 1932 as *The Tenderfoot* (qv) with Joe E. Brown; in 1937 as *Dance Charlie Dance* with Stuart Erwin; and in 1940 as *An Angel from Texas* (qv) with Eddie Albert.

The Buttercup Chain *

GB 1970 95m Technicolor Panavision
Columbia (Leslie Gilliat, John Whitney, Philip Waddilove)

A hothouse sex quartet changes partners with bewildering rapidity against a background of European splendour.

Chi-chi romance with a fashionably disillusioned and tragic ending. As watchable as the best TV commercials, but totally empty.

w Peter Draper *novel* Janice Elliott *d* Robert Ellis Miller *ph* Douglas Slocombe *m* Richard Rodney Bennett

☆ Hywel Bennett, Leigh Taylor-Young, Jane Asher, Sven-Bertil Taube, Clive Revill, Roy Dotrice

'British bathos about the unhappy overprivileged.' – *Variety*

'The most desirable woman in town, and the easiest to find!'

Butterfield Eight

US 1960 108m Metrocolor Cinemascope
MGM/Afton/Linebrook (Pandro S. Berman)

A society call girl has a complex love life.

This coy sex drama seemed mildly daring in 1960, but has since been well outclassed in that field and certainly has nothing else going for it except good production values.

w Charles Schnee, John Michael Hayes *novel* John O'Hara *d* Daniel Mann *ph* Joseph Ruttenberg, Charles Harten *m* Bronislau Kaper

☆ Elizabeth Taylor, Laurence Harvey, Eddie Fisher, Dina Merrill, Mildred Dunnock, Betty Field, Jeffrey Lynn, Kay Medford, Susan Oliver

'The mixture resolutely refuses to come to the boil.' – *John Gillett*

🏆 Elizabeth Taylor

Academy Award nomination: Joseph Ruttenberg, Charles Harten

Butterflies Are Free

US 1972 109m Eastmancolor
Columbia/M. J. Frankovich

An aspiring actress falls for a blind neighbour but is handicapped by his possessive mother.

Three-character comedy-drama from a slight, sentimental but successful Broadway play.

w Leonard Gershe *play* Leonard Gershe *d* Milton Katselas *ph* Charles B. Lang *m* Bob Alcivar

☆ Goldie Hawn, Edward Albert, Eileen Heckart

🏆 Eileen Heckart

Academy Award nomination: Charles B. Lang

Butterfly

US 1981 108m Metrocolor
Par Par (Matt Cimber)

A 17-year-old sexpot reappears in her father's life, commits incest with him, and sets in train a grotesque series of plot developments.

Risible concatenation of murders, repentances, illegitimate sex and various kinds of lust, all revolving round butterfly marks and set in 1937 backwoods Arizona. Tobacco Road *it ain't, though.*

w John Goff, Matt Cimber *novel* *The Butterfly* by James M. Cain *d* Matt Cimber *ph* Eddy Van Der Enden *m* Ennio Morricone

☆ Stacy Keach, Pia Zadora, Orson Welles, Lois Nettleton, Edward Albert, Stuart Whitman, Ed MacMahon, June Lockhart, James Franciscus

The Butterfly Effect

Spain/France/GB 1995 109m colour
Blue Dolphin/Fernando Colomo/Mainstream/Portman/Oceandeep (Beatriz de la Gindara)

The tangled love life of a student and his family in London brings down the Spanish government.

Chaos theory, in which minor happenings can have major effects, is meant to underpin this camp comedy; those who watch it may be put off international co-productions for life.

w Joaquin Oristrell, Fernando Colomo *d* Fernando Colomo *ph* Jean-François Robin *m* Ketama *ad* John Roberts *ed* Miguel Angel Santamaria

☆ Maria Barranco, Coque Malla, Rosa Maria Sarda, James Fleet, Peter Sullivan, Cécile Pallas, John Faal

'A delightful comedy of manners. Its cross-cultural observations on Spanish and British cultural mores are perceptively written.' – *José Arroyo, Sight and Sound*

'This one's entire cast should be garrotted. You thought there couldn't be a worse director in Spain than the punk cartoonist Almodovar. Wrong: his name is Fernando Colomo.' – *Alexander Walker, London Evening Standard*

Butterfly Kiss *

GB 1995 88m colour/bw
Electric/Dan/British Screen (Julie Baines)

An assistant at a motorway services shop takes in a suicidal young wanderer and the couple begin a lesbian affair; they travel the roads together, killing those they meet.

A grim and downbeat tale of obsessive love and despair, displaying an undeniable, though depressing, talent.

w Frank Cottrell Boyce *d* Michael Winterbottom *ph* Seamus McGarvey *m* John Harle *ad* Rupert Miles *ed* Trevor Waite

☆ Amanda Plummer, Saskia Reeves, Kathy Jamieson, Des McAleer, Freda Dowie, Lisa Jane Riley, Ricky Tomlinson

'The film's quiet sense of style, its sensibly short length, expert editing and sure touch … proclaim an exceptional new director for the cinema.' – *Derek Malcolm, Guardian*

'Resembles nothing so much as a trawl through dirt-cheap, one dimensional thrilleramics. A film unlikely to do much for either the serial killer genre or motorway services tourist trade.' – *Clark Collis, Empire*

Butterfly Legend

US 1999 80m Technicolor
3 Sirens/Gun For Hire (Ronnie Shapiro)

video title: *The Stranger*

After the death of her young daughter, the wife of a wealthy businessman is haunted by dreams of a childhood trauma, and of making love to a stranger.

Interminably boring, would-be sophisticated psychological drama, which tries to impress with glossy setting and windy platitudes.

w Elliot Geisinger, Bruce David Klein *d* Bruce David Klein *ph* Wolfgang Held *m* Evan Lurie *pd* Roshelle Berliner *ed* Merril Stern

☆ William Atherton (Arthur), Roxana Zal (Juliet), Robert Cuccioli (Man), Allison Mackie (Kate), Thom Christopher (Steve), Jenifer Krater (Bridgette), Philippe Mao (Anton)

The Butterfly Murders ***

Hong Kong 1979 colour 'Scope
Ng See Yuen (Ng See Kin)

A wandering scholar, at a time of warring factions, solves the mystery of an aristocratic family apparently plagued by killer butterflies.

A visually splendid martial arts fantasy with elaborately choreographed fight sequences, done with immense melodramatic style.

w Lam Fan *d* *Tsui Hark* *ph* Fun Chin Yu

☆ Lau Siu Ming, Wong Shee Tong, Michelle, Chan Chi Chi, Cheong Kwok Chu, Kuo Hung, Wong Cheong, Kiu Fung

Butterfly's Tongue **

Spain 1998 96m colour Panavision
Metrodome/Sogetel/Grupo Voz/Canal+/TVG/TVE

original title: *La Lengua de las Mariposas*

In 1936, a small boy in Catalonia observes the everday life around him, and the growing hostility between Republicans and Nationalists that signaled the beginning of the Spanish Civil War.

An elegiac drama, full of charm and humanity, with its nostalgia of a child's eye view of events undercut by an awareness of the betrayals to come.

w Rafael Azcona, José Luis Cuerda, Manuel Rivas *d* José Luis Cuerda *ph* Javier G. Salmones *m* Alejandro Amenabar *ad* Josep Rosell *ed* Ignacio Cayetano Rodriguez, Nacho Ruiz Capillas *cos* Sonia Grande

☆ Fernando Fernan Gomez (Don Gregorio), Manuel Lozano (Moncho), Uxía Blanco (Rosa), Gonzalo Uriarte (Ramon), Alexis de los Santos (Andres), Jesus Castejon (Don Avelino), Guillermo Toledo (O'lis), Elena Fernandez (Carmina), Tamar Novas (Roque), Tatan (Roque Padre), Roberto Vidal (Boal)

'A modest and unassuming picture that offers all the pleasures of the period genre.' – *Paul Julian Smith, Sight and Sound*

Buy & Cell

US 1989 95m colour
Empire/Altar (Frank Yablans)

Framed for embezzlement, a stockbroker runs a successful investment company from inside prison.

Dire comedy on the theme that greed makes brothers of us all; every scene goes on too long and unsubtle performances are encouraged.

w Ken Krauss, Merrin Holt *story* Leonard Montana, Louis Peraino *d* Robert Boris *ph* Daniele Nannuzzi *m* Mark Shreeve *pd* Giovanni Natalucci *ed* Bert Glatstein

☆ Robert Carradine, Michael Winslow, Ben Vereen, Malcolm McDowell, Randall 'Tex' Cobb, Imogene Coca, Fred Travalena, Roddy Piper, Lise Cutter, Tony Plana, Michael Goodwin

Buy Me That Town *

US 1941 70m bw
Paramount (Sol C. Siegel)

Gangsters take over a small town and pull the community out of bankruptcy.

Unusual comedy-drama, quite well done for a second feature.

w Gordon Kahn *d* Eugene Forde *ph* Theodor Sparkuhl

☆ Lloyd Nolan, Albert Dekker, Constance Moore, Sheldon Leonard, Vera Vague, Edward Brophy, Horace MacMahon, Warren Hymer

Bwana Devil

US 1952 79m Anscocolor 3D
(UA)

At the turn of the century, two man-eating lions threaten an African railroad.

Inept actioner notable only as the first film in 3-D ('Natural Vision'), advertised with the famous slogan 'A lion in your lap'.

wd Arch Oboler *ph* Joseph Biroc *m* Gordon Jenkins

☆ Robert Stack, Barbara Britton, Nigel Bruce, Ramsay Hill

By Candlelight *

US 1933 70m bw
Universal (Carl Laemmle Jnr)

On a transcontinental train a woman meets a butler and takes him for a prince; he does not disillusion her.

Moderately pleasing romantic comedy of the old school.

w Hans Kraly, F. Hugh Herbert, Karen de Wolf, Ruth Cummings *play* Siegfried Geyer *d* *James Whale*

☆ Elissa Landi, *Paul Lukas*, Nils Asther

'A nice little class picture that should make money all round.' – *Variety*

'A dazzling display of romantic confidence trickery which takes on Lubitsch in his own territory.' – *Tom Milne, 1978*

By Hook or by Crook: see *I Dood It*

By Love Possessed *

US 1961 116m DeLuxe Panavision
UA/Mirisch/Seven Arts (Walter Mirisch)

A Massachusetts lawyer reflects on the outlandish sexual mores of himself, his family and friends.

Peyton Place moved up in the social scale; a reasonably absorbing melodrama but hardly memorable.

w John Dennis *novel* James Gould Cozzens *d* John Sturges *ph* Russell Metty *m* Elmer Bernstein

☆ Lana Turner, Efrem Zimbalist Jnr, Jason Robards Jnr, Barbara Bel Geddes, George Hamilton, Susan Kohner, Thomas Mitchell, Yvonne Craig, Everett Sloane

'A talky succession of soap opera situations.' – *Robert Windeler*

'The most warm-hearted musical under the sun!'

By the Light of the Silvery Moon *

US 1953 101m Technicolor
Warner (William Jacobs)

In a small American town in 1918, the Winfield family has several problems arising from the return of daughter Marjorie's soldier boyfriend.

A sequel to On Moonlight Bay *(qv), presenting further situations from the Penrod stories retailored for Doris Day. Inoffensive, well-made, old-fashioned entertainment with nostalgic songs and an archetypal family.*
w Robert O'Brien, Irving Elinson *stories* Booth Tarkington *d* David Butler *ph* Wilfrid M. Cline *m* Max Steiner *md* Ray Heindorf *ch* Donald Saddler *ad* John Beckman *ed* Irene Morra
☆ Doris Day (Marjorie), Gordon MacRae (William Sherman), *Leon Ames* (George Winfield), *Rosemary de Camp* (Mrs Winfield), *Mary Wickes* (Stella), Billy Gray (Wesley), Russell Arms (Chester Finley), Maria Palmer (Miss LaRue), Howard Wendell (John Harris), Walter Flannery (Pee Wee)
William Goldman

By Your Leave
US 1934 81m bw
RKO
A restless husband tries to be a Don Juan.
Very mild domestic comedy.
w Allan Scott *play* Gladys Hurlbut, Emma B. C. Wells *d* Lloyd Corrigan
☆ Frank Morgan, Genevieve Tobin, Neil Hamilton, Marian Nixon, Glenn Anders, Gene Lockhart, Margaret Hamilton, Betty Grable, Charles Ray
'Once the customers are in they'll get some laughs, but they're not going to be easy to entice.' – *Variety*

Bye Bye Birdie
US 1963 112m Eastmancolor Panavision
Columbia/Fred Kohlmar/George Sidney
Havoc suffuses the last TV show of a pop star before he goes into the army.
Noisy, frenetic musical, hard to follow and even harder to like, with all the satire of the stage original subtracted. For young audiences who enjoy incoherence.
w Irving Brecher *musical* Michael Stewart *d* George Sidney *ph* Joseph Biroc *m/ly* Charles Strouse, Lee Adams *md* Johnny Green
☆ Janet Leigh, Dick Van Dyke, Maureen Stapleton, Ann-Margret, Bobby Rydell, Jesse Pearson, Ed Sullivan, Paul Lynde, Robert Paige
Johnny Green

Bye Bye Blues
Canada 1989 117m colour
Artificial Eye/True Blue Films/Allarcom/Telefilm Canada/CFCN TV/CITV (Anne Wheeler, Arvi Liimatainen, Jerry Krepakevich)
A mother with two young children awaits the return of her soldier husband.
Uninteresting throwback to women's movies of the 1940s.
wd Anne Wheeler *ph* Vic Sarin *m* George Blondheim *pd* John Blackie *ad* Scott Dobbie, Jayoo Patwarchan, Chinu Patwarchan *ed* Christopher Tate
☆ Michael Ontkean, Rebecca Jenkins, Luke Reilly, Stuart Margolin, Wayne Robson, Robyn Stevan
'A film which, without exactly bowling one over, will probably remain in the memory longer than most.' – *Derek Malcolm, Guardian*

Bye Bye Braverman *
US 1968 92m Technicolor
Warner/Sidney Lumet
New Yorkers get drunk and disillusioned on their way home from the funeral of a friend.
Witty, downbeat Jewish comedy which does not quite come off and would in any case be caviare to the general.
w Herbert Sargent *novel* *To an Early Grave* by Wallace Markfield *d* Sidney Lumet *ph* Boris Kaufman *m* Peter Matz
☆ George Segal, Jack Warden, Joseph Wiseman, Sorrell Booke, Jessica Walter, Phyllis Newman, Zohra Lampert, Alan King, Godfrey Cambridge
'You don't have to be Jewish to love it, but it helps a lot to be a New Yorker.' – *Robert Hatch, The Nation*

Bye Bye Love
US 1995 106m DeLuxe
TCF/UBU (Gary David Goldberg, Brad Hall, Sam Weisman)
Three divorced fathers spend the weekend with their kids in various ways.
Bland and innocuous comedy in favour of family values and McDonald's hamburgers, though not necessarily in that order.
w Gary David Goldberg, Brad Hall *d* Sam Weisman *ph* Kenneth Zunder *m* J. A. C. Redford *pd* Linda DeScenna *ed* Roger Bondelli
☆ Matthew Modine, Randy Quaid, Paul Reiser, Janeane Garofalo, Rob Reiner, Amy Brenneman, Eliza Dushku, Ed Flanders, Maria Pitillo, Lindsay Crouse
'Funny and poignant, with the good-natured effort and its affable cast elevating a sometimes schematic story.' – *Leonard Klady, Variety*

Bye Bye Monkey
Italy/France 1977 114m Eastmancolor
18 Dicembre/Prospectacle/Action Film (Giorgio Nocella, Maurice Bernart)
original title: *Ciao Maschio*
A Frenchman, dividing his time between a wax museum and a theatre group run by women, finds a chimpanzee and adopts it as his son.
Desultory drama of misfits drifting through New York that is never sharp or observant enough to be either amusing or interesting; and the deaths at the end do not make it tragic.
w Marco Ferreri, Gérard Brach, Rafael Azcona *d* Marco Ferreri *ph* Luciano Tovoli *m* Philippe Sarde *ad* Dante Ferretti *ed* Ruggero Mastroianni
☆ Gérard Depardieu, James Coco, Marcello Mastroianni, Geraldine Fitzgerald, Gail Lawrence, Stefania Casini, Francesca de Sapio, Mimsy Farmer

'A rap-to-riches comedy.'

CB4
US 1993 88m DeLuxe
Universal (Nelson George)

Clean-living middle-class youths form a gangsta rap group called Cell Block 4 and pretend to be tough.

Brief appearances from Ice T, Ice Cube, Flavour Flav and others add a little authenticity to a slight but amusing satire at the expense of the macho posturing of rappers. It will be most enjoyed by those attuned to the phenomenon of hip hop.

w Chris Rock, Nelson George, Robert LoCash *d* Tamra Davis *ph* Karl Walter Lindenlaub *m* John Barnes *pd* Nelson Coates *ed* Earl Watson

☆ Chris Rock, Allen Payne, Deezer D, Phil Hartman, Arthur Evans, Theresa Randle, Willard E. Pugh, Richard Gant, Charlie Murphy, Chris Elliott

'Lively is the word for its better parts. Terminally disorganised would be the best one for the rest.' – *Derek Malcolm, Guardian*

'The satire is feeble, the pastiche documentary botched. Stereotypes are peeled away to reveal stereotypes beneath.' – *Philip French, Observer*

C.C. and Company
US 1971 84m colour
Allan Carr-Roger Smith/Avco Embassy

Adventures of a motorcycle gang.

Bottom of the barrel programme-filler.

w Roger Smith *d* Seymour Robbie

☆ Joe Namath, Ann-Margret, William Smith, Jennifer Billingsley, Don Chastain

C.H.O.M.P.S.: see *Chomps*

Ca Commence Aujourd'hui: see *It All Starts Today*

Ça Peut Pas être L'Hiver, On N'a Même Pas Eu Été: see *It Can't Be Winter, We Haven't Had Summer Yet*

'A divinely decadent experience!'

Cabaret ****
US 1972 123m Technicolor
ABC Pictures/Allied Artists (Cy Feuer)

In the early thirties, Berlin is a hot-bed of vice and anti-Semitism. In the Kit Kat Klub, singer Sally Bowles shares her English lover with a homosexual German baron, and her Jewish friend Natasha has troubles of her own.

This version of Isherwood's Berlin stories regrettably follows the plot line of the play I Am a Camera *rather than the Broadway musical on which it is allegedly based, and it lacks the incisive remarks of the MC, but the very smart direction creates a near-masterpiece of its own, and most of the songs are intact.*

w Jay Presson Allen *novel* Goodbye to Berlin by Christopher Isherwood *ph Geoffrey Unsworth* *m/ly John Kander, Fred Ebb* *md* Ralph Burns *pd* Rolf Zehetbauer *d/ch Bob Fosse*

☆ *Liza Minnelli, Joel Grey, Michael York*, Helmut Griem, Fritz Wepper, Marisa Berenson

'A stylish, sophisticated entertainment for grown-up people.' – *John Russell Taylor*

'Film journals will feast for years on shots from this picture; as it rolled along, I saw page after illustrated page from a not-too-distant book called *The Cinema of Bob Fosse*.' – *Stanley Kauffmann*

Bob Fosse (as director); Geoffrey Unsworth; Ralph Burns; Liza Minnelli; Joel Grey

picture; Jay Presson Allen

film; Rolf Zehetbauer; Geoffrey Unsworth; Bob Fosse; Liza Minnelli; Joel Grey

Cabaret Balkan ***
France/Greece/Macedonia/Turkey /Yugoslavia 1998 102m colour
Macht/Ticket/Vans/Stefi/Mine/Gradski/Canal+ (Antoine De Clermont-Tonnerre, Goran Paskaljevic)

original title: *Bure Baruta*

The lives of many people intersect during one night in Belgrade, with tragic and comic results.

An entertaining, powerful, blackly ironic account of the life of ordinary people in a city of casual violence and desperation.

w Dejan Dukovski, Goran Paskaljevic, Filip David, Zoran Andric *play Bure Baruta* by Dejan Dukovski *d* Goran Paskaljevic *ph* Milan Spasic *m* Zoran Simjanovic *ad* Milenko Jeremic *ed* Petar Putnikovic *cos* Zora Mojsilovic-Popovic

☆ Aleksandar Bercek (Dimitri), Vojislav Brajovic (Topi), Bogdan Diklic (Jovan), Nebojsa Glogovac (Taxi Driver), Mirjana Jokovic (Ana), Mirjana Karanovic (Natalia), Miki Manojlovic (Michael), Toni Mihajlovski (George), Nebojsa Milovanovic (Bosnian Serb Son), Dragan Nikolic, Lazar Ristovski (Boxer), Nikola Ristanovski, Ana Sofrenovic, Sergej Trifunovic (Young Man)

'Presents a devastating vision of a war-torn country in which the basic laws of civilized behavior have eroded in a climate of all-consuming suspicion, hatred and vengeance.' – *Stephen Holden, New York Times*

Cabeza de Vaca *
Mexico/Spain 1990 111m Eastmancolor
Iguana Productions (Rafael Cruz, Jorge Sánchez, Julio Solórzano Foppa, Bertha Navarro)

In the 1520s, the leader of a group of Spanish conquistadores, shipwrecked off the coast of Florida, survives ambush, torture and privation by learning to live with the natives.

An ambitious, overlong, often mystic and sometimes violent epic, taken from a contemporary account, which is on the side of the native Americans.

w Guillermo Sheridan, Nicolás Echevarria *book Naufragios* by Alvar Nunez Cabeza de Vaca *d* Nicolás Echevarria *ph* Guillermo Navarro *m* Mario Lavista *ad* José Luis Aguilar Gil *ed* Rafael Castanedo

☆ Juan Diego, Daniel Gimenez Cacho, Roberto Sosa, Carlos Castañón, Gerardo Villarreal, Roberto Cobo, José Flores

'It's a demanding pic for audiences, but they will be well rewarded with a film that's exotic, mysterious, bizarre (shades of Alexandro Jodorowsky) and dramatic.' – *Variety*

'He's setting sail on the high seas. Without a rudder, a compass or a clue!'

Cabin Boy
US 1994 80m Foto-Kem
Hollywood (Tim Burton, Denise di Novi)

A rich and snobbish youth boards the wrong boat and finds himself in rough and fantastic company.

Coarse and unattractive comedy that veers into a spoof of Sinbad's adventures with some ill-chosen fantasy.

wd Adam Resnick *ph* Steve Yaconelli *m* Steve Bartek *pd* Steven Legler *ed* Jon Poll

☆ Chris Elliott, Richard Brinkley, James Gammon, Brian Doyle-Murray, Brion James, Russ Tamblyn, Ricki Lake

'Obnoxious, snide and pointless, this ill-fated spoof carries the bonus of being as crude and gamy as the hold of an old fishing barge.' – *Brian Lowry, Variety*

† Made in 1992.

The Cabin in the Cotton *
US 1932 79m bw
Warner (Hal B. Wallis)

A sharecropper is almost ruined by a Southern belle.

Dated melodrama with interesting style and performances.

w Paul Green *novel* Harry Harrison Kroll *d* Michael Curtiz *ph* Barney McGill

☆ Richard Barthelmess, Dorothy Jordan, Bette Davis, David Landau, Tully Marshall, Henry B. Walthall, Hardie Albright

'Not well done … less than a moderate grosser all round.' – *Variety*

† The film in which Bette Davis drawled: 'Ah'd love to kiss yuh, but Ah just washed mah hair.'

'Broadway's big, fun-jammed music show is on the screen at last – crowded with stars and songs and spectacle in the famed MGM manner!'

Cabin in the Sky **
US 1943 99m bw
MGM (Arthur Freed)

An idle, gambling husband is reformed by a dream of his own death, with God and Satan battling for his soul.

Consistently interesting, often lively, but generally rather stilted all-black musical which must have seemed a whole lot fresher on the stage. Still, a good try.

w Joseph Schrank *musical play* *Lynn Root* *d* Vincente Minnelli *ph* Sidney Wagner *m/ly* Harold Arlen, E. Y. Harburg, Vernon Duke, John Latouche, Ted Fetter *md* George Stoll *ad* Cedric Gibbons, Leonid Vasian

☆ *Eddie 'Rochester' Anderson* (Little Joe), Ethel Waters (Petunia Jackson), Lena Horne (Georgia Brown), Louis Armstrong (Trumpeter), Rex Ingram (Lucius, Lucifer Jnr), Kenneth Spencer (Rev Green, the General), John W. Sublett ('Bubbles') (Domino), Ford L. Washington ('Buck'), Mantan Moreland (First Idea Man), Willie Best (Second Idea Man)

'Whatever its box office fate, a worthwhile picture for Metro to have made, if only as a step toward Hollywood recognition of the place of the colored man in American life.' – *Variety*

♫ 'Li'l Black Sheep'; 'Ain't It De Truth'; 'Life's Full Of Consequence'; 'Honey in the Honeycomb'; 'Taking a Chance on Love'; 'Going Up'; 'I Got A Song'; 'Shine'

song 'Happiness Is Just a Thing Called Joe' (*m* Harold Arlen, *ly* E. Y. Harburg)

'No one permitted out or in during the last thirteen nerve-shattering minutes!'

The Cabinet of Caligari
US 1962 105m bw Cinemascope
TCF/Lippert (Roger Kay)

A young woman whose car breaks down near a country house is held prisoner by the sinister Caligari. Eventually it transpires that the mystery is all in her imagination: he is a psychiatrist and she an old lady whose sexual fantasies he has been curing.

Interminably talkative and frequently (unintentionally) funny trick film with the odd moment of effective suspense. The original ending, which cast some doubt on who was mad and who sane, is no longer available. The actors do not entirely escape absurdity.

w Robert Bloch *d* Roger Kay *ph* John Russell *m* Gerald Fried

☆ Glynis Johns, Dan O'Herlihy, Constance Ford, Dick Davalos, Lawrence Dobkin

'It is impossible to be grateful for the film on any of its levels.' – *MFB*

'The most complete essay in the décor of delirium.' – *New Yorker, 1979*

† The fact that the story is told through the eyes of a mad person is the only link with the 1919 classic.

'See the sleepwalker, floating down the street, ripped from some nightmare! A street of misshapen houses with brooding windows, streaked by dagger strokes of light and darkened by blots of shadow! You will immediately feel the terror in the movements of that floating grotesque!'

The Cabinet of Dr Caligari ****
Germany 1919 90m approx (16 fps) bw silent
Decla-Bioscop (Erich Pommer)

A fairground showman uses a somnambulist for purposes of murder and is finally revealed to be the director of a lunatic asylum; but the whole story is only the dream of a madman.

Faded now, but a film of immense influence on the dramatic art of cinema, with its odd angles, stylized sets and hypnotic acting, not to mention the sting in the tail of its story (added by the producer).

w Carl Mayer, Hans Janowitz d Robert Wiene ph Willy Hameister ad Hermann Warm, Walter Röhrig, Walter Reiman

☆ *Werner Krauss, Conrad Veidt*, Lil Dagover, Friedrich Feher, Hans von Twardowski

'The first hundred shocks are the hardest.' – *New York Evening Post, 1924*

† The film cost 18,000 dollars to make.

Cabiria ***
Italy/France 1957 110m bw
Dino de Laurentiis/Les Films Marceau

original title: *Le Notti di Cabiria*
aka: *Nights of Cabiria*

A Roman prostitute has dreams of romance and respectability.

A bitter Cinderella story which was later turned into the Broadway musical Sweet Charity. *Much of interest, but the leading lady is too Chaplinesque.*

w Federico Fellini, Ennio Flaiano, Tullio Pinelli *d* Federico Fellini *ph* Aldo Tonti *m* Nino Rota

☆ Giulietta Masina, François Périer, Amedeo Nazzari, Franca Marzi, Dorian Gray

'Any nobility in the original conception slowly suffocates in an atmosphere of subjective indulgence bordering dangerously on self-pity.' – *Peter John Dyer*

'Stylistically the whole film with its dejected setting and its riotously fluent movement is brilliant. And the acting is superb.' – *Dilys Powell*

best foreign film

'Are You Ready To Get Wired?'

The Cable Guy
US 1996 96m Technicolor Super 35
Columbia (Andrew Licht, Jeffrey A. Mueller, Judd Apatow)

A yuppie businessman is at first befriended and then terrorized by a cable TV installation man.

Carrey's frenetic mugging here sits oddly with the naturalistic style of the rest of the cast; some satire at the expense of a television-fixated generation is no doubt intended, but is too heavy-handed to be effective.

w Lou Holtz Jnr *d* Ben Stiller *ph* Robert Brinkman *m* John Ottman *pd* Sharon Seymour *ed* Steven Weisberg

☆ Jim Carrey, Matthew Broderick, Leslie Mann, George Segal, Diane Baker, Jack Black, Ben Stiller, Janeane Garofalo, Eric Roberts (himself), Charles Napier

'This fuzzy-focus outing is hopelessly disconnected and ultimately unsatisfying.' – *Variety*

† Carrey was paid $20m for his role, which had originally been intended for Chris Farley. The

movie took around $60m at the US box-office and another $42m worldwide.

'An Epic Adventure That Explodes At The Edge Of The World'
Caboblanco
US 1981 87m colour Panavision
Avco/Martin V. Smith
A café proprietor in the Caribbean dodges various groups of criminals.
Witless spoof of Casablanca *which seems to have been cobbled together from a half-finished negative.*
w Mort Fine, Milton Gelman *d* J. Lee Thompson *ph* Alex Phillips Jnr *m* Jerry Goldsmith
☆ Charles Bronson, Jason Robards Jnr, Dominique Sanda, Fernando Rey, Simon MacCorkindale, Camilla Sparv, Denny Miller, Gilbert Roland

Cactus *
Australia 1986 96m colour
Dofine/Film Victoria/AFC (Jane Ballantyne, Paul Cox)
A Frenchwoman, whose eyesight begins to deteriorate after a car crash, falls in love with a blind man.
Austere and sensitive drama about a woman finding herself, but too underplayed to be entirely effective.
w Paul Cox, Bob Ellis, Norman Kaye, Morris Lurie *d* Paul Cox *ph* Yuri Sokol *pd* Asher Bilu *ed* Tim Lewis
☆ Isabelle Huppert, Robert Menzies, Norman Kaye, Monica Maughan, Banduk Marika, Sheila Florance

Cactus Flower *
US 1969 103m Technicolor
Columbia/M. J. Frankovich
To deceive his mistress, a dentist employs his starchy secretary to pose as his wife, and falls for her when she loosens up.
Amusing sophisticated comedy, generally well handled.
w I. A. L. Diamond *play* Abe Burrows, French original by Pierre Barillet, Jean Pierre Gredy *d* Gene Saks *ph* Charles E. Lang *m* Quincy Jones *pd* Robert Clatworthy
☆ Ingrid Bergman, Walter Matthau, Goldie Hawn, Jack Weston, Rick Lenz, Vito Scotti, Irene Hervey
Goldie Hawn

Cactus in the Snow: see *You Can't Have Everything*

Cactus Jack: see *The Villain*

Cadaveri Eccellenti: see *Illustrious Corpses*

Caddie *
Australia 1976 106m Eastmancolor
Roadshow/Anthony Buckley
A deceived wife takes off with her two children and becomes a barmaid.
Desultory account of aimless low life to which Caddie brings a spark of sunshine. Watchable but forgettable.
w Joan Long, from the autobiography by 'Caddie' *d* Donald Crombie *ph* Peter James *m* Peter Flynn
☆ Helen Morse, Takis Emmanuel, Kirrily Nolan, Jacki Weaver, Jack Thompson

The Caddy
US 1953 95m bw
Paramount (Paul Jones)
A music hall comedy act recall how they got together.
Less a feature than a series of short sketches, this ragbag has its choice moments, but they are few.
w Edmund Hartmann, Danny Arnold *d* Norman Taurog *ph* Daniel L. Fapp *m* Joseph L. Lilley
☆ Dean Martin, Jerry Lewis, Donna Reed, Barbara Bates, Joseph Calleia, Fred Clark, Clinton Sundberg, Marshall Thompson
song 'That's Amore' (*m* Harry Warren, *ly* Jack Brooks)

'The Snobs Against The Slobs!'
Caddyshack
US 1980 98m Technicolor
Warner/Orion (Douglas Kenney)
Misadventures at a golf club.
A relentlessly crude and lumbering series of farcical incidents which mainly fail to raise laughs.
w Brian Doyle-Murray, Harold Ramis, Douglas Kenney *d* Harold Ramis *ph* Stevan Larner *m* Johnny Mandel *pd* Stan Jolley *ed* William Carruth
☆ Chevy Chase, Rodney Dangerfield, Ted Knight, Michael O'Keefe
'There are jests about vomiting and nose-picking, while the most elaborate gag sequence involves a chocolate bar falling into a swimming pool and being mistaken for a turd … a sustained exercise in tiresomeness.' – *Tim Pulleine, MFB*

'The shack is back!'
Caddyshack II
US 1988 99m colour
Warner (Neil Canton, Jon Peters, Peter Guber)
A self-made millionaire is persuaded by his upwardly mobile daughter to apply for membership of an exclusive golf club.
Dim sequel that reprises the central situation of the original without even managing its crude humour; this one is just crude.
w Harold Ramis, Peter Torokvei *d* Allan Arkush *ph* Harry Stradling Jnr *m* Ira Newborn *pd* Bill Matthews *ed* Bernard Gribble
☆ Jackie Mason, Robert Stack, Dina Merrill, Dyan Cannon, Jonathan Silverman, Randy Quaid, Chevy Chase, Dan Aykroyd

'If You Can't trust A Car Salesman–Who Can You Trust?'
Cadillac Man
US 1990 97m colour
Rank/Orion (Charles Roven, Roger Donaldson)
A car salesman is held hostage by a jealous husband.
Frenetic farce that is rarely funny.
w Ken Friedman *d* Roger Donaldson *ph* David Gribble *m* J. Peter Robinson *pd* Gene Rudolf *ed* Richard Francis-Bruce
☆ Robin Williams, Tim Robbins, Pamela Reed, Fran Drescher, Zack Norman, Annabella Sciorra, Lori Petty, Paul Guilfoyle, Bill Nelson, Eddie Jones
'A rarity among recent films – a comedy that is in touch with a recognizable reality.' – *Richard Schickel, Time*

'Days of magnificent adventure … nights of maddest revelry … a temptation in Technicolor!'
Caesar and Cleopatra **
GB 1945 135m Technicolor
Rank/Gabriel Pascal
An elaborate screen treatment of Bernard Shaw's comedy about Caesar's years in Alexandria.
Britain's most expensive film is an absurd extravaganza for which the producer actually took sand to Egypt to get the right colour. It has compensations however in the sets, the colour, the performances and the witty lines, though all its virtues are theatrical rather than cinematic and the play is certainly not a major work.
w Bernard Shaw *d* Gabriel Pascal *ph* F. A. Young, Robert Krasker, Jack Hildyard, Jack Cardiff *m* Georges Auric *decor/costumes* Oliver Messel *sets* John Bryan
☆ *Claude Rains*, Vivien Leigh, Cecil Parker, Stewart Granger, Flora Robson, Francis L. Sullivan, Raymond Lovell, Anthony Harvey, Anthony Eustrel, Basil Sydney, Ernest Thesiger, Stanley Holloway, Leo Genn, Jean Simmons, Esmé Percy and also Michael Rennie
'It cost over a million and a quarter pounds, took two and a half years to make, and well and truly bored one spectator for two and a quarter hours.' – *Richard Winnington*
'It is so wonderful as to make my other films look naive.' – *Bernard Shaw*
'When Rains played a small part he sometimes gave the impression that he was carrying the movie, but here his impish grin and his equanimity aren't enough.' – *Pauline Kael, 70s*
John Bryan

Café Metropole
US 1937 83m bw
TCF (Nunnally Johnson)
An heiress in Paris romances a Russian nobleman who is actually a penniless American.
Lighter-than-air romance which passed the time at the time.
w Jacques Duval *d* Edward H. Griffith *ph* Lucien Andriot *md* Louis Silvers
☆ Loretta Young, Adolphe Menjou, Tyrone Power, Charles Winninger, Gregory Ratoff, Christian Rub, Helen Westley
'It's smart, sophisticated (not too much so), has the proper romantic ingredients, and will pull 'em in almost anywhere.' – *Variety*
'Here is a very amusing script, admirable acting … all thrown away by inferior direction. The camera is planked down four-square before the characters like a plain, honest, inexpressibly dull guest at a light and loony party.' – *Graham Greene*

Café of Seven Sinners: see *Seven Sinners*

La Cage aux Folles *
France/Italy 1978 91m Eastmancolor
UA/PAA/Da Ma (Marcello Danon)
aka: *Birds of a Feather*
A homosexual night-club owner is persuaded by his straight son to behave properly in front of his girlfriend's parents, but chaos comes on the night of the party.
Internationally popular near-the-knuckle farce with excellent moments and some longueurs.
w Francis Veber, Edouard Molinaro, Marcello Danon, Jean Poiret *play* Jean Poiret *d* Edouard Molinaro *ph* Armando Nannuzzi *m* Ennio Morricone
☆ Ugo Tognazzi, Michel Serrault, Michel Galabru, Claire Maurier, Remi Laurent
Edouard Molinaro (as director); script

La Cage aux Folles II
France/Italy 1980 99m Technicolor
UA/PAA/Da Ma (Marcello Danon)
An ageing homosexual tells his partner he is too old to be an effective female impersonator. Trying to prove the opposite, the partner becomes involved in a spy search for hidden microfilm.
Rather dimwitted sequel to a comedy which though deliberately 'naughty' showed some restraint; here, all is noise and excess.
w Jean Poiret, Francis Veber, Marcello Danon *d* Edouard Molinaro *ph* Armando Nannuzzi *m* Ennio Morricone
☆ Ugo Tognazzi, Michel Serrault, Marcel Bozzuffi, Paola Borboni
'The juxtaposition of campy histrionics with the dreariest kind of espionage comedy offers quickly diminishing returns.' – *Gilbert Adair, MFB*

La Cage aux Folles III
France/Italy 1985 87m Eastmancolor
Da Ma/Columbia (Marcello Danon)
In order to inherit a fortune, Albin must marry and produce an heir.
Yawnworthy attempt to milk more gags out of a formula which exhausted itself with number one.
w Philippe Nicaud, Christine Carere, Marcello Danon, Jacques Audiard, Michel Audiard, Georges Lautner, Gerald Lamballe *d* Georges Lautner *ph* Luciano Tavoli *m* Ennio Morricone *pd* Mario Garbuglia *ed* Michelle David, Elisabeth Guido, Lidia Pascolini
☆ Ugo Tognazzi, Michel Serrault, Michel Galabru, Antonella Interlenghi
'Lots of cooks but not much broth.' – *Variety*

Cage of Doom: see *Terror from the Year 5000*

Cage of Gold *
GB 1950 83m bw
Ealing (Michael Relph)
A girl's philandering ex-husband comes back into her life and is murdered.
Mild mystery melodrama in which the puzzle comes too late.
w Jack Whittingham *d* Basil Dearden *ph* Douglas Slocombe *m* Georges Auric
☆ Jean Simmons, David Farrar, James Donald, Madeleine Lebeau, Maria Mauban, Herbert Lom, Bernard Lee, Gladys Henson, Harcourt Williams, Grégoire Aslan

'Will she come out woman or wildcat?'
Caged *
US 1949 96m bw
Warner (Jerry Wald)
After being involved in a robbery a 19-year-old girl is sent to prison, and finds the staff more terrifying than the inmates.
Slick, superficial, hysterically harrowing women-in-prison melodrama; predictably overblown but also effective and powerful.
w Virginia Kellogg, Bernard Schoenfeld *d* John Cromwell *ph* Carl Guthrie *m* Max Steiner
☆ *Eleanor Parker*, Agnes Moorehead, Ellen Corby, *Hope Emerson*, Betty Garde, Jan Sterling, Lee Patrick, Olive Deering, Jane Darwell, Gertrude Michael, Joan Miller
† Remade in 1962 as *House of Women*, directed by Walter Doniger, with Shirley Knight.
Virginia Kellogg, Bernard Schoenfeld; Eleanor Parker; Hope Emerson

'White Hot Desires Melting Cold Prison Steel!'
Caged Heat *
US 1974 83m DeLuxe
Target/Artists Entertainment Complex/Renegade Women (Samuel Gelfman)
A new convict is horrified by the way a crippled governess runs a women's prison.
Quirky, individual, anti-authoritarian take on the standard ingredients of an exploitation picture set among female prisoners.
wd Jonathan Demme *ph* Tak Fujimoto *m* John Cale *ad* Eric Thierman *ed* Johanna Demetrakis, Carolyn Hicks
☆ Juanita Brown, Roberta Collina, Erica Gavin, Ella Reid, Lynda Gold, Warren Miller, Barbara Steele, Toby Carr
'A distinctly exceptional exploitation movie.' – *Tony Rayns, MFB*
† The British release was cut to 79m.

Caged Virgins: see *Requiem for a Vampire*

'Break the law and he's the last man you'll want to see. And the last man you ever will!'
Cahill, US Marshal
US 1973 103m Technicolor Panavision
Warner/Batjac (Michael A. Wayne)
A stalwart Western marshal finds that his own young sons are involved in a robbery he is investigating.
Satisfactory but sentimental John Wayne vehicle with the star too often yielding place to the rather boring young folk.
w Harry Julian Fink, Rita M. Fink *d* Andrew V. McLaglen *ph* Joseph Biroc *m* Elmer Bernstein
☆ John Wayne, George Kennedy, Gary Grimes, Neville Brand, Clay O'Brien, Marie Windsor, Royal Dano, Denver Pyle, Jackie Coogan

La Caida: see *The Fall*

'It's unlike any musical you've ever seen before – Timed to the Tantalizing Tempo of Today!'
Cain and Mabel *
US 1936 90m bw
Warner (Sam Bischoff)
Tribulations of a prizefighter in love with a showgirl.
Generously produced but weakly written comedy drama with rather unexpected musical numbers; not a successful whole, but interesting.
w Laird Doyle, H. C. Witwer *d* Lloyd Bacon *ph* George Barnes *m/ly* Harry Warren, Al Dubin *ch* Bobby Connolly
☆ Clark Gable, Marion Davies, Allen Jenkins, Roscoe Karns, Walter Catlett, Hobart Cavanaugh, Pert Kelton, Ruth Donnelly, E. E. Clive
Bobby Connolly

'As big as the ocean!'
The Caine Mutiny **
US 1954 125m Technicolor
Columbia/Stanley Kramer
Jealousies and frustrations among the officers of a peacetime destroyer come to a head when the neurotic captain panics during a typhoon and is relieved of his post. At the resulting trial the officers learn about themselves.
Decent if lamely paced version of a bestseller which also made a successful play; the film skates too lightly over

the characterizations and even skimps the courtroom scene, but there are effective scenes and performances.
w Stanley Roberts *novel* Herman Wouk
d Edward Dmytryk *ph* Franz Planer *m* Max Steiner *ed* William A. Lyon, Henry Batista
☆ *Humphrey Bogart* (Captain Queeg), José Ferrer (Lt Barney Greenwald), Van Johnson (Lt Steve Maryk), Fred MacMurray (Lt Tom Keefer), Robert Francis (Ensign Willie Keith), May Wynn (May), Tom Tully (Captain DeVriess), E. G. Marshall (Lt Cdr Challee), Lee Marvin (Meatball), Claude Akins (Horrible)

QUEEG: 'There are four ways of doing things on board my ship. The right way, the wrong way, the navy way, and my way. If they do things my way, we'll get along.'

QUEEG: 'Ah, but the strawberries! That's where I had them. They laughed and made jokes, but I proved beyond the shadow of a doubt, and with geometric logic, that a duplicate key to the wardroom icebox did exist. And I'd have produced that key if they hadn't pulled the *Caine* out of action. I know now they were out to protect some fellow officer.'

KEEFER: 'There is no escape from the *Caine*, save death. We're all doing penance, sentenced to an outcast ship, manned by outcasts, and named after the greatest outcast of them all.'

best picture; Stanley Roberts; Max Steiner; Humphrey Bogart; Tom Tully; editing

Cairo *
US 1942 100m bw
MGM (Joseph L. Mankiewicz)
An American war reporter in Egypt meets a screen star and thinks she is a spy.
Mildly pleasing light comedy-drama with self-spoofing elements.
w John McClain *d* W. S. Van Dyke II *ph* Ray June *md* Herbert Stothart
☆ Jeanette MacDonald, Robert Young, Ethel Waters, Reginald Owen, Lionel Atwill, Mona Barrie, Eduardo Ciannelli, Dennis Hoey, Dooley Wilson
'Confusing if not amusing.' – *Variety*

Cairo
GB 1963 91m bw
MGM (Ronald Kinnoch)
Crooks plan to steal Tutankhamun's jewels from the Cairo Museum.
Spiritless remake of The Asphalt Jungle *(qv).*
w Joanne Court (Joan Scott) *d* Wolf Rilla *ph* Desmond Dickinson *m* Kenneth V. Jones
☆ George Sanders, Richard Johnson, Faten Hamama, John Meillon, Eric Pohlmann, Walter Rilla
† Joan Scott wrote the script under a pseudonym because she was blacklisted at the time.

Cairo Station
Egypt 1958 95m bw
Gabriel Talhami
original title: *Bab El Hadid*
A crippled newspaper seller goes mad through thwarted love.
Popular melodrama, acted with verve.
d Youssef Chahine *ph* Alvise *m* Fouad El Zahiry *ad* Gabriel Karraze *ed* Kamal Abul Ela
☆ Farid Chawki, Hind Rostom, Youssef Chahine, Safia Sarwat, Assaad Kellam, Sherine

Cal *
GB 1984 102m colour
Warner/Goldcrest/Enigma (Stuart Craig, David Puttnam)
A young Catholic in Ulster falls for the widow of the policeman in whose murder he has been an accomplice.
More clichés about the troubles: the film belies its publicity as 'a love story which happens to take place in Northern Ireland'. But it has style.
w Bernard MacLaverty *novel* Bernard MacLaverty *d* Pat O'Connor *ph* Jerzy Zielinski *m* Mark Knopfler *pd* Stuart Craig
☆ Helen Mirren, John Lynch, Donal McCann, John Kavanagh, Ray McAnally

Calabuch *
Spain/Italy 1956 93m bw
Aguila/Constellaxione (José Luis Jerez)
An atomic scientist settles delightedly in a peaceful Spanish village, but sacrifices his own privacy when he invents a sky rocket.
Semi-satirical Ealing-type comedy which starts engagingly but runs out of steam.
w Leonardo Martin, Ennio Flaiano, Florentino Soria, Luis Berlanga *d* Luis Berlanga *ph* Francisco Sempere *m* Francesco Lavagnino
☆ *Edmund Gwenn*, Valentina Cortese, Franco Fabrizi

Calamity Jane **
US 1953 101m Technicolor
Warner (William Jacobs)
Calamity helps a saloon owner friend find a star attraction, and wins the heart of Wild Bill Hickok.
Agreeable, cleaned-up, studio-set Western musical patterned after Annie Get Your Gun, *but a much friendlier film, helped by an excellent score.*
w James O'Hanlon *d* David Butler *ph* Wilfrid Cline *m/ly Sammy Fain, Paul Francis Webster* *md* Ray Heindorf *ch* Jack Donohue
☆ *Doris Day, Howard Keel*, Allyn McLerie, Phil Carey, Dick Wesson, Paul Harvey
song 'Secret Love'
Ray Heindorf

Calamity Jane and Sam Bass
US 1949 85m Technicolor
Universal-International
Sam Bass murders the man who poisoned his horse, becomes an outlaw, and tangles with Jane Carraway.
Routine Western programmer from this stable.
w Maurice Geraghty, Melvin Levy *d* George Sherman
☆ Yvonne de Carlo, Howard Duff, Dorothy Hart, Willard Parker, Houseley Stevenson, Ann Doran, Norman Lloyd

Calcutta
US 1946 83m bw
Paramount (Seton I. Miller)
Two flyers seek the murderer of their friend in the hotels and bazaars of Calcutta.
Studio-bound action potboiler, simple-minded but quite good fun.
w Seton I. Miller *d* John Farrow *ph* John F. Seitz *m* Victor Young
☆ Alan Ladd, Gail Russell, William Bendix, June Duprez, Lowell Gilmore

Calendar
Canada/Germany 1993 75m colour
ZDF/Ego Film Arts
A Canadian photographer of Armenian descent recalls how his wife left him for his guide while they were on assignment to photograph Armenian churches for a calendar.
A meditation on what it means to be Armenian and on photography and its limitations. It is so personal to its maker as to be somewhat impenetrable to anyone else; at the least, it requires tolerance from the viewer.
wd Atom Egoyan *ph* Norayr Kasper *m* Duduk *ed* Atom Egoyan
☆ Arsinée Khanjian, Ashot Adamian, Atom Egoyan
'The photographer has been freed from his assimilation assignment, but at what cost? Given the self-referential and revisionist subtext of the film, this open-ended question evokes a sense of genuine anticipatory excitement for Egoyan's next venture.' – *Farrah Anwar, Sight and Sound*

Calendar Girl
US 1993 90m colour
Columbia/Parkway (Debbie Robins, Gary Marsh)
Three 60s students go to Los Angeles in the hope of meeting Marilyn Monroe.
Uninteresting drama of teenage wish-fufilment that may please fans of its star but few others.
w Paul W. Shapiro *d* John Whitesell *ph* Tom Priestley *m* Hans Zimmer *pd* Bill Groom *ed* Wendy Greene Bricmont
☆ Jason Priestley, Gabriel Olds, Jerry O'Connell, Joe Pantoliano, Steve Railsback, Kurt Fuller, Stephen Tobolowsky, Chubby Checker
'A dull, sanctimonious morality tale about the meaning of friendship and manhood.' – *Variety*

'No town would have her! No man could tame her!'
California
US 1946 97m Technicolor
Paramount (Seton I. Miller)
An army deserter joins the 1848 California gold rush.
Standard glamorized star Western; not bad if you accept the conventions.
w Frank Butler, Theodore Strauss *d* John Farrow *ph* Ray Rennahan *m* Victor Young
☆ Ray Milland, Barbara Stanwyck, Barry Fitzgerald, Albert Dekker, George Coulouris, Anthony Quinn
'It quickly loses its stirrups and ends up caught by the chaps in a bed of cactus.' – *Newsweek*

The California Dolls: see *All the Marbles*

California Holiday: see *Spinout*

California Man: see *Encino Man*

California Split *
US 1974 109m Metrocolor Panavision
Columbia/Persky-Bright/Reno (Robert Altman, Joseph Walsh)
Two cheerful gamblers get drunk, laid, cheated and happy.
Sporadically entertaining character comedy sunk in a sea of chatter.
w Joseph Walsh *d* Robert Altman *ph* Paul Lohmann *m* Phyllis Shotwell
☆ Elliott Gould, George Segal, Gwen Welles, Ann Prentiss, Joseph Walsh
'The film seems to be being improvised ... we catch at events and personalities by the ends of threads.' – *New Yorker*
† An end title reads: FOR BARBARA, 1933–1973. This was Barbara Ruick, who played the barmaid and died on location.

California Straight Ahead *
US 1937 57m bw
Universal (Trem Carr)
A nationwide race is held between a special train and a convoy of high-powered trucks.
Unusual and quite lively second feature shot on location.
w Scott Darling *story* Herman Boxer *d* Arthur Lubin *ph* Harry Neumann *m* Charles Previn
☆ John Wayne, Louise Latimer, Robert McWade, Tully Marshall
'Everything happens as the audience expects and wishes, so in its field it will do okay.' – *Variety*

'The best two-hour vacation in town!'
California Suite *
US 1978 103m colour
Columbia//Ray Stark
Misadventures of four groups of guests at the Beverly Hills Hotel.
Two hits, two misses; closer intercutting might have helped. No doubt that Maggie Smith and Michael Caine come off best, with bitcheries about the Academy Awards.
w Neil Simon *play* Neil Simon *d* Herbert Ross *ph* David M. Walsh *m* Claude Bolling *pd* Albert Brenner
☆ Michael Caine, Maggie Smith, Walter Matthau, Elaine May, Alan Alda, Jane Fonda, Richard Pryor, Bill Cosby
'By turns silly and thoughtful, tedious and charming, broad and delicate.' – *Frank Rich*
Maggie Smith
Neil Simon; art direction

'What would you have done if you had been given absolute power of life and death over everyone else in the whole wide world?'
Caligula
Italy/US 1979 150m Eastmancolor
GTO/Felix/Penthouse Films (Bob Guccione, Franco Rossellini)
The violent life and times of a decadent Roman emperor.
What would have been a dull and worthless pseudo-epic has been perked up by violence and hardcore sex. The result is a vile curiosity of interest chiefly to sado-masochists.
w Bob Guccione *screenplay* Gore Vidal *d* Tinto Brass, Giancarlo Lui, Bob Guccione *ph* Danilo Donati *m* Paul Clemente *ed* Nino Bragli
☆ Malcolm McDowell, John Gielgud, Peter O'Toole, Helen Mirren, Teresa Ann Savoy, John Steiner
'An anthology of sexual aberrations in which incest is the only face-saving relationship ... far more Gore than Vidal.' – *Variety*
'It just keeps rolling along at inordinate length, suggesting de Mille grinding slowly to a frequent stoppage for a display of bums, breasts and pubic hair.' – *Time Out*

Call a Messenger
US 1939 65m bw
Universal
Working as telegraph messengers, the Little Tough Guys prevent a hold-up.
Second-feature offshoot of the Dead End Kids, some of whom had now departed to become the East Side Kids (who later blossomed forth as the Bowery Boys).
w Arthur T. Horman *d* Arthur Lubin
☆ Billy Halop, Huntz Hall, Billy Benedict, David Gorcey, Robert Armstrong, Mary Carlisle, Anne Nagel, Victor Jory, El Brendel, Larry 'Buster' Crabbe
'A rowdy, gripping production patterned as heavy bolstering in dual set-ups.' – *Variety*

Call Harry Crown: see *99 and 44/100 Per Cent Dead*

Call Her Savage
US 1932 88m bw
Paramount (Sam E. Rork)
Trials and tribulations of a half-breed Indian girl who marries a cad and later takes to the streets.
Rough and ready melodrama for female audiences; the penultimate appearance of a star who did not take to talkies.
w Edwin Burke *novel* Tiffany Thayer *d* John Francis Dillon *ph* Lee Garmes
☆ Clara Bow, Gilbert Roland, Monroe Owsley, Thelma Todd, Estelle Taylor
'The return of Clara Bow in a madcap role makes a natural ... the result is bound to be money.' – *Variety*

Call Him Mr Shatter: see *Shatter*

Call Him Savage
France/Italy 1975 103m colour
Lira/Produzioni Artistiche Internazionali (Raymond Danon)
aka: *Lovers Like Us*
A French *parfumier*, trying to escape from his business, meets a woman on the run from her Venezuelan fiancé.
Dim attempt at a romantic comedy.
w Jean-Paul Rappeneau, Elizabeth Rappeneau, Jean-Loup Dabadie *d* Jean-Paul Rappeneau *ph* Pierre Lhomme *m* Michel Legrand *ed* Marie-Joseph Yoyotte
☆ Yves Montand, Catherine Deneuve, Tony Roberts, Luigi Vannucchi, Dana Wynter

Call It a Day *
US 1937 89m bw
Warner (Henry Blanke)
An upper-class British family has problems during a single day.
Surprising, and not very effective, Hollywood treatment of a very British comedy.
w Casey Robinson *play* Dodie Smith *d* Archie Mayo *ph* Ernest Haller
☆ Olivia de Havilland, Ian Hunter, Anita Louise, Alice Brady, Roland Young, Frieda Inescort, Bonita Granville, Peggy Wood, Walter Woolf King, Una O'Connor, Beryl Mercer
'A fine cast rowing a very thin boat ... charm, many a giggle but nary a sock laugh.' – *Variety*

Call It Murder: see *Midnight*

Call Me Bwana *
GB 1962 93m Eastmancolor
Rank/Eon (Harry Saltzman, Albert R. Broccoli)
A fake African explorer is sent to the jungle to recover a space capsule.
Moderate star farce with occasional bright moments.
w Nate Monaster, Johanna Harwood *d* Gordon Douglas *ph* Ted Moore *m* Monty Norman

☆ Bob Hope, Anita Ekberg, Edie Adams, Lionel Jeffries, Percy Herbert, Paul Carpenter, Orlando Martins

Call Me Genius: see *The Rebel*

Call Me Madam ***
US 1953 114m Technicolor
TCF (Sol C. Siegel)
A Washington hostess is appointed Ambassador to Lichtenberg and marries the foreign minister.
Studio-bound but thoroughly lively transcription of Irving Berlin's last big success, with most of the performers at their peak and some topical gags which may now be mystifying.
w Arthur Sheekman *play* Howard Lindsay, Russel Crouse *d* Walter Lang *ph* Leon Shamroy *m/ly* *Irving Berlin* *md* Alfred Newman *ch* Robert Alton
☆ *Ethel Merman*, *Donald O'Connor*, *George Sanders*, *Vera-Ellen*, Billy de Wolfe, Helmut Dantine, Walter Slezak, Steve Geray, Ludwig Stossel
'Good-tempered, warm, generous and about as quiet as a massed brass band festival.' – *Dilys Powell*
† Vera-Ellen's singing was dubbed by Carole Richards
♫ 'The Hostess with the Mostes''; 'Can You Use Any Money Today?'; 'Marrying for Love'; 'It's a Lovely Day Today'; 'That International Rag'; 'The Ocarina'; 'What Chance Have I with Love?'; 'The Best Thing for You'; 'Something to Dance About'; 'You're Just in Love'.
🏆 Alfred Newman

Call Me Mister
US 1951 95m Technicolor
TCF (Fred Kohlmar)
A husband-and-wife dance team entertain the troops in Japan and after the war.
Passable musical of a very predictable kind.
w Albert E. Lewin, Burt Styler *book* Arnold Auerbach, Arnold B. Horwitt *d* Lloyd Bacon *ph* Arthur E. Arling *m* Harold Rome *m/ly* various *ch* Busby Berkeley
☆ Betty Grable, Dan Dailey, Danny Thomas, Dale Robertson, Richard Boone

Call Northside 777 **
US 1948 111m bw
TCF (Otto Lang)
[NTSC]
A Chicago reporter helps a washerwoman prove her son not guilty of murdering a policeman.
Overlong semi-documentary crime thriller based on a real case. Acting and detail excellent, but the sharp edge of Boomerang is missing.
w Jerome Cady, Jay Dratler *d* Henry Hathaway *ph* *Joe MacDonald* *m* Alfred Newman
☆ James Stewart, Lee J. Cobb, Helen Walker, *Kasia Orzazewski*, Betty Garde, Richard Conte
'A most satisfying thriller, generously streaked with class.' – *Daily Mail*
'Absorbing, exciting, realistic.' – *Star*

Call of the Wild *
[family] US 1935 81m bw
Twentieth Century (Darryl F. Zanuck)
A young widow falls in love with a wild Yukon prospector.
Inaccurate but pleasing adaptation of an adventure novel with dog interest.
w Gene Fowler, Leonard Praskins *novel* Jack London *d* William Wellman *ph* Charles Rosher *m* Alfred Newman
☆ Clark Gable, Loretta Young, Jack Oakie, Reginald Owen, Frank Conroy
'The lion-hearted dog emerges as a stooge for a rather conventional pair of human lovebirds ... looks like box office.' – *Variety*

Call of the Wild
[family] GB/W. Germany/Spain/Italy/France 1972 105m Eastmancolor
Massfilms/CCC/Izaro/Oceania/UPF (Harry Alan Towers)
[NTSC] [colourised]
During the Klondike gold rush, a stolen dog becomes a miner's best friend before joining the wolf-pack.
Closer to the book than the previous version, but curiously scrappy and unsatisfactory.
w Harry Alan Towers, Wyn Wells, Peter Yeldham *d* Ken Annakin *ph* John Cabrera, Dudley Lovell *m* Carlo Rustichelli
☆ Charlton Heston, Michèle Mercier, Raimund Harmstorf, George Eastman

Call the Cops!: see *Find the Lady*

Callan *
GB 1974 106m Eastmancolor
EMI/Magnum (Derek Horne)
[NTSC]
aka: *The Neutralizer*
A former secret agent is seconded to a government section devoted to the elimination of undesirables.
Expanded rewrite of the first episode of a long-running TV series, quite fresh and vivid in the circumstances, especially as it comes at the tail end of ten years of similar bouts of blood and thunder.
w James Mitchell *novel* *A Magnum for Schneider* by James Mitchell *d* *Don Sharp* *ph* Ernest Steward *m* Wilfred Josephs
☆ *Edward Woodward*, Eric Porter, Carl Mohner, Catherine Schell, Peter Egan, Russell Hunter, Kenneth Griffith

Callaway Went Thataway *
US 1951 81m bw
MGM (Melvin Frank, Norman Panama)
GB title: *The Star Said No*
The old movies of a Hollywood cowboy become popular on TV, but the star has become a hopeless drunk and an actor is hired to pose as him for public appearances.
Reasonably engaging comedy using charm rather than acid.
wd Melvin Frank, Norman Panama *ph* Ray June *m* Marlin Skiles
☆ Dorothy McGuire, Fred MacMurray, Howard Keel, Jesse White, Natalie Schafer

Calle Mayor *
Spain/France 1956 95m bw
Play Art Iberia/Cesareo Gonzales
aka: *Grande Rue*
In a small Spanish town, a young stud pretends for a bet to be in love with a plain spinster.
Interesting but rather unattractive and certainly unconvincing little comedy-drama, rather too obviously styled for its American star after her success in Marty.
wd Juan Antonio Bardem *ph* Michel Kelber *m* Joseph Kosma
☆ Betsy Blair, Yves Massard, René Blancard, Lila Kedrova

Calling Bulldog Drummond
GB 1951 80m bw
MGM (Hayes Goetz)
Drummond goes undercover to catch a gang of thieves.
Minor-league quota quickie addition to the exploits of a long-running character (see Bulldog Drummond*).*
w Howard Emmett Rogers, Gerard Fairlie, Arthur Wimperis *d* Victor Saville *ph* F. A. Young *m* Rudolph Kopp
☆ Walter Pidgeon, Margaret Leighton, Robert Beatty, David Tomlinson, Peggy Evans, Charles Victor, Bernard Lee, James Hayter

'Terror strikes as a madman rules!'
Calling Doctor Death
US 1943 63m bw
Universal
A doctor's wife is murdered; her lover is arrested; but did the doctor himself do it?
Probably not, as the tendency of the tinpot Inner Sanctum *series, of which this was the first, was to make its star look anguished for six reels and then show him to be as innocent as the film was (mercifully) short.*
w Edward Dein *d* Reginald Le Borg
☆ Lon Chaney, Patricia Morison, Fay Helm, David Bruce, Ramsay Ames, J. Carrol Naish

Calling Dr Gillespie *
US 1942 84m bw
MGM
A deranged ex-patient breaks into Blair Hospital for the purpose of killing Dr Gillespie.
The point at which cranky old wheelchair-bound Dr Gillespie took over the Kildare series, its star (Lew Ayres) having effectually abdicated from acting by declaring himself a conscientious objector. Production values up to par.
w Kubec Glasmon, Willis Goldbeck, Harry Ruskin *d* Harold S. Bucquet
☆ Lionel Barrymore, Philip Dorn, Phil Brown, Donna Reed, Nat Pendleton, Mary Nash, Alma Kruger, Walter Kingsford
† See *Dr Kildare* for titles in series.

Calling Dr Kildare *
US 1939 86m bw
MGM
Kildare becomes innocently involved in murder and needs Dr Gillespie's help.
The second in the Kildare series had the confidence that comes of box-office approval.
w Harry Ruskin, Willis Goldbeck *d* Harold S. Bucquet
☆ Lew Ayres, Lionel Barrymore, Lana Turner, Nat Pendleton, Samuel S. Hinds, Laraine Day, Alma Kruger

Calling Philo Vance
US 1939 62m bw
Warner
A manufacturer is murdered and foreign agents are discovered among his servants.
Essentially a remake of The Kennel Murder Case*; inferior as a whole, but with an excellent new Vance.*
w Tom Reed *d* William Clemens
☆ James Stephenson, Margot Stevenson, Henry O'Neill, Ed Brophy, Ralph Forbes, Martin Kosleck

Calm Yourself
US 1935 70m bw
MGM
An advertising man helps solve a kidnapping.
Spoofy comedy-drama which simply doesn't work.
w Edward Hope, Arthur Kober *d* George B. Seitz
☆ Robert Young, Madge Evans, Betty Furness, Nat Pendleton, Hardie Albright, Ralph Morgan
'Strictly for the not too particular nabe clientele.' – *Variety*

Caluga o Menta
Chile 1991 90m colour
Arca/TVE/Filmocentro (Patricia Navarrete)
aka: *Candy or Mint*
In Santiago, a gang of disaffected youngsters turn to crime and drug-running to relieve the everyday monotony of their lives.
A downbeat study of no-hopers, filmed with a partly non-professional cast, which is mainly of sociological interest.
w Gonzalo Justiniano, Gustavo Frias, Jose Andres Peña *d* Gonzalo Justiniano *ph* Gaston Roca *m* Jaime de Aguirre *ed* Claudio Martinez
☆ Mauricio Vega, Patricia Rivadeneira, Aldo Parodi, Myriam Palacios

Camelot **
[family] US 1967 181m Technicolor
Panavision 70
Warner (Jack L. Warner)
[VHS] [NTSC] [laser] [colourised] [colourised] [audio]
King Arthur marries Guinevere, loses her to Lancelot, and is forced into war.
A film version of a long-running Broadway show with many excellent moments. Unfortunately the director cannot make up his mind whether to go for style or realism, and has chosen actors who cannot sing. The result is cluttered and overlong, with no real sense of period or sustained imagination, but the photography and the music linger in the mind.
w Alan Jay Lerner *novel* The Once And Future King by T. H. White *d* Joshua Logan *ph* *Richard H. Kline* *m/ly* *Frederick Loewe, Alan Jay Lerner* *md* Ken Darby, Alfred Newman *ad* *Edward Carrere* *pd/costumes* *John Truscott*
☆ Richard Harris, Vanessa Redgrave, David Hemmings, Lionel Jeffries, Laurence Naismith, Franco Nero
'One wonders whether the fashion for musicals in which only the chorus can actually sing may be reaching its final stage.' – *MFB*
'Three hours of unrelieved glossiness, meticulous inanity, desperate and charmless striving for charm.' – *John Simon*
'The sets and costumes and people seem to be sitting there on the screen, waiting for the unifying magic that never happens.' – *New Yorker, 1977*
† Franco Nero's singing was dubbed by Gene Merlina
♫ 'The Merry Month of May'; 'Camelot'; 'If Ever I Would Leave You'; 'Take Me to the Fair'; 'C'est Moi'
🏆 art direction; costumes; music direction
🏅 cinematography

The Camels are Coming
GB 1934 80m bw
Gainsborough (Michael Balcon)
An officer in the camel corps catches Egyptian drug smugglers.
Light, bouncy star vehicle.
w Jack Hulbert, Guy Bolton, W. P. Lipscomb *d* Tim Whelan *ph* Glen MacWilliams, Bernard Knowles *m* Ray Noble, Max Kester, Noel Gay *md* Louis Levy *ad* Oscar Werndorff *ed* Frederick Y. Smith
☆ Jack Hulbert, Anna Lee, Hartley Power, Harold Huth, Allan Jeayes

Camera Buff *
Poland 1979 112m colour
Cinegate/Zespoly Filmowe/Film Polski
original title: *Amator*
A factory worker finds himself in conflict with his bosses when he becomes obsessed with making films at work.
Lively political allegory.
wd Krzysztof Kieslowski *ph* Jacek Petrycki *m* Krzysztof Knittel *ad* Rafal Waltenberger *ed* Halina Nawrocka
☆ Jerzy Stuhr, Malgorzata Zabkowska, Ewa Pokas, Stefan Czyzewski, Jerzy Nowak, Tadeusz Bradecki, Krzysztof Zanussi

The Cameraman ***
US 1928 78m approx (24 fps) bw silent
MGM (Lawrence Weingarten)
[NTSC] [laser]
In order to woo a film star, a street photographer becomes a newsreel cameraman.
Highly regarded chapter of farcical errors, among the star's top features.
w Clyde Bruckman, Lex Lipton, Richard Schayer *d* Edward Sedgwick *ph* Elgin Lessley, Reggie Manning
☆ Buster Keaton, Marceline Day, Harry Gribbon, Harold Goodwin
† The film was remade in 1948 for Red Skelton as *Watch the Birdie*, with Keaton supervising the gags but sadly getting no credit.

The Cameraman's Revenge **
Russia 1912 11m bw/tinted
Ladislaw Starewicz
[VHS]
Two beetles, a brother and a sister, try to conceal their marriages from one another so that they may inherit the family fortune of a pot of beer.
An early and still impressive example of stop-motion animation.
wd Ladislaw Starewicz *m* Roger White
† The film has been released on video with the feature-length *The Tale of the Fox* (qv) and four other shorts under the title *Ladislaw Starewicz: Selected Films.*

'A new place to look for terror.'
'Don't ever open the door.'
Cameron's Closet
US 1987 87m colour
Medusa/Smart Egg (Luigi Cingolani)
[VHS] [NTSC] [laser]
Subjected by his father to experiments in psychokinesis, a boy summons up a demon.
Ineffectual horror, with a boring monster.
w Gary Brandner *novel* Gary Brandner *d* Armand Mastroianni *ph* Russell Carpenter *m* Harry Manfredini *pd* Michael Bingham *ed* Frank de Palma
☆ Cotter Smith, Mel Harris, Scott Curtis, Chuck McCann, Leigh McCloskey, Kim Lankford
'The contents of this particular closet are decidedly shop-worn and second-hand.' – *MFB*

Camila **
Argentina/Spain 1984 97m colour
GEA Cinematografica/Impala (Lila Stanic)
In Argentina in the 1840s the strong-willed daughter of an upper-class family scandalizes Church and government by eloping with a priest.
A powerful drama that manages to say much about present-day repression despite its period setting.
w Maria Luisa Bemberg, Beda Docampo Feijoo, Juan Bautista Stagnaro *d* Maria Luisa Bemberg *ph* Fernando Arribas *m* Luis Maria Serra *ad* Miguel Rodriguez *ed* Luis Cesar D'Angiolillo

☆ Susu Pecoraro, Imanol Arias, Hector Alterio, Carlos Muñoz, Hector Pelligrini, Juan Levrado, Cecilio Madanes, Mona Maris, Elena Tasisto

Camilla
GB/Canada 1994 95m Colour
Entertainment/Shaftesbury/Skreba (Christina Jennings, Simon Relph)
An unhappily married woman, a frustrated musician, abandons her husband and goes on the road with an elderly former concert violinist, anxious to get away from her son.
Jessica Tandy, in her last role, provides the watchable moments in an otherwise undernourished and meandering movie that covers a lot of ground without getting anywhere very interesting.
w Paul Quarrington *story* Ali Jennings *d* Deepa Mehta *ph* Guy Dufeau *m* Daniel Lanois
pd Sandra Kybartas *ed* Barry Farrell
☆ *Jessica Tandy*, Bridget Fonda, Elias Koteas, Maury Chaykin, Hume Cronyn, Graham Greene
'Endless drollery and treacle, with amiable eccentrics lurking at every pit-stop.' – *Jonathan Romney, Guardian*

'You who are so young – where can you have learned all you know about women like me?'
'Their lips meet for the first time ... a superb thrill seared in your memory forever!'
Camille **
US 1937 108m bw
MGM (Irving Thalberg, Bernard Hyman)
A dying courtesan falls for an innocent young man who loves her, and dies in his arms.
This old warhorse is an unsuitable vehicle for Garbo but magically she carries it off, and the production is elegant and pleasing.
w Frances Marion, James Hilton, Zoe Akins
novel Alexandre Dumas *d* *George Cukor*
ph William Daniels *m* Herbert Stothart
☆ *Greta Garbo*, Robert Taylor, Lionel Barrymore, *Henry Daniell*, Elizabeth Allan, Lenore Ulric, Laura Hope Crews, Rex O'Malley, Jessie Ralph, E. E. Clive
'Pretty close to the top mark in showmanship, direction, photography and box office names.' – *Variety*
'The slow, solemn production is luxuriant in its vulgarity: it achieves that glamor which MGM traditionally mistook for style.' – *Pauline Kael, 1968*
'The surprise is to find a story that should by rights be old hat coming to such insistent life on the screen.' – *Otis Ferguson*
'It steadily builds up an impression of being a spectacle of manners and fashions, a socially true background for its characters to move against.' – *National Board of Review*
'This is not death as mortals know it. This is but the conclusion of a romantic ritual.' – *Bosley Crowther*
† A 1927 silent version starred Norma Talmadge with Gilbert Roland.
Greta Garbo

Camille Claudel **
France 1988 174m colour Panavision
Cannon/Films Christian Fechner/Lilith Films/Gaumont/A2 TV France/Films A2/DD Productions (Bernard Artigues)
A talented sculptress becomes Rodin's pupil and mistress with tragic results.
Overlong, and lacking a visual flair to match its subject, but nevertheless engrossing for the most part.
w Bruno Nuytten, Marilyn Goldin *book* Reine-Marie Paris *d* Bruno Nuytten *ph* Pierre Lhomme
m Gabriel Yared *ad* Bernard Vezat *ed* Joëlle Hache, Jeanne Kef
☆ Isabelle Adjani, Gérard Depardieu, Laurent Grevill, Alain Cuny, Philippe Clevenot, Katrine Boorman, Danielle Lebrun, Maxime Leroux
'As a cultural coffee-table artefact, it has everything.' – *Tom Milne, MFB*
Isabelle Adjani; best foreign film

El Camino del Sur: see *Journey to the South*

Il Cammino della Speranza *
Italy 1950 105m bw
Lux (Luigi Rovere)
aka: *The Road to Hope*
Unemployed Sicilian miners travel to France in search of work.
Episodic location melodrama with a social conscience, a kind of Italian Grapes of Wrath. *Very watchable, but not moving.*
w Federico Fellini, Tullio Pinelli *d* Pietro Germi
ph Leonido Barboni *m* Carlo Rustichelli
☆ Raf Vallone, Elena Varzi, Saro Urzi, Franco Navarra

Camorra: the Naples Connection
Italy 1985 106m colour
Cannon/Italian International (Menahem Golan, Yoram Globus)
original title: *Un complicato intrigo di donne, vicoli e delitto*
Mothers take revenge on the drug dealers who have killed their children.
Highly charged, full of sound and fury and signifying very little.
w Lina Wertmüller, Elvio Porta *d* Lina Wertmüller *ph* Giuseppe Lanci *m* Tony Esposito
ad Enrico Job *ed* Luigi Zita
☆ Angela Molina, Francisco Rabal, Harvey Keitel, Daniel Ezralow

Camp de Thiaroye **
Senegal/Algeria/Tunisia 1988 152m colour
Metro/SNPC/ENAPROC/SATPEC (Mamadou Mbengue)
African soldiers, returning home after fighting in the Second World War, are massacred in a dispute over pay.
Powerful indictment of colonialism.
wd Ousmane Sembène, Thierno Faty Sow
ph Ismail Lakhdar Hamina *m* Ismaila Lo *ad* El hadj Abdoulaye Diouf *ed* Kahena Attia-Riveill
☆ Ibrahima Sane, Sigiri Bakara, Hamed Camara, Ismaila Cissé, Ababacar Sy Cissé

Camp Nowhere
US 1994 96m Technicolor
Buena Vista/Hollywood (Michael Peyser)
A group of disaffected kids decide to create their own summer camp to escape from their parents' expectations.
Moderate comedy that pretends to be rebellious before settling for an affirmation of family values.
w Andrew Kurtzman, Eliot Wald *d* Jonathan Prince *ph* Sandi Sissel *m* David Lawrence
pd Rusty Smith *ed* Jon Poll, David Street
☆ Christopher Lloyd, Wendy Makkena, M. Emmet Walsh, Jonathan Jackson, Andrew Keegan, Melody Kay, Ray Baker, Kate Mulgrew, Burgess Meredith
'Interesting premise needed more than the so-so treatment delivered here.' – *Variety*

The Camp on Blood Island
GB 1958 81m bw MegaScope
Columbia/Hammer (Anthony Hinds)
The sadistic commandant of a Japanese POW camp swears to kill all the inmates. Japan surrenders, and a great effort is made to prevent the news from reaching him.
Dubious melodrama parading sadism and brutality as entertainment.
w Jon Manchip White, Val Guest *d* Val Guest
ph Jack Asher *m* Gerard Schurmann *ad* John Stoll *ed* James Needs, Bill Lenny
☆ André Morell, Carl Mohner, Edward Underdown, Michael Goodliffe, Ronald Radd, Walter Fitzgerald, Phil Brown, Barbara Shelley, Michael Gwynn, Richard Wordsworth, Marne Maitland, Mary Merrall

Campbell's Kingdom *
GB 1957 102m Eastmancolor
Rank (Betty E. Box)
A young man who thinks he is dying arrives in the Canadian Rockies to take over his father's oil valley, but a scheming contractor opposes him.
Competent and entertaining romantic thick ear.
w Robin Estridge *novel* Hammond Innes
d Ralph Thomas *ph* Ernest Steward *m* Clifton Parker
☆ Dirk Bogarde, Michael Craig, Stanley Baker, Barbara Murray, Athene Seyler, Mary Merrall, James Robertson Justice
'Yet another large budget British film doggedly maintaining a B-picture standard' – *John Osborne, London Evening Standard*

Campfire Tales
US 1996 83m Foto-Kem/bw
Vault/Kunert/Manes (Eric Manes, Lori Miller, Larry Weinberg)
After crashing their car on a remote road at night, four teenagers shelter in a ruined church and tell each other horror stories.
A compendium of three stories, each favouring a slow build-up to moments of shock and content, for the most part to retread over-familiar ways.
w Martin Kunert, Eric Manes, Matt Cooper
d David Semel, Martin Kunert, Matt Cooper
ph John Peters *m* Andrew Rose *pd* Shay Austin
ed Luis Colina, Steve Nevius, Richard H. Fields
☆ Jay R. Ferguson, Christine Taylor, Christopher Kennedy Masterson, Kim Murphy, Ron Livingston, Jennifer MacDonald, Hawthorne James, Alex McKenna, Devon Odessa, Jonathan Fuller
'A superior horror compendium.' – *Sight and Sound*

Can Can
US 1960 131m DeLuxe Todd-AO
TCF/Suffolk-Cummings (Jack Cummings)
A Parisian night-club dancer in the 90s is sued for performing the Can Can.
Flat film of a dull musical, with just a few plums in the pudding.
w Dorothy Kingsley, Charles Lederer *play* Abe Burrows *d* Walter Lang *ph* William Daniels
m/ly Cole Porter *md* Nelson Riddle *ch* Hermes Pan
☆ Frank Sinatra, Shirley MacLaine, Maurice Chevalier, Louis Jourdan, Juliet Prowse, Marcel Dalio, Leon Belasco
Nelson Riddle

Can Hieronymus Merkin Ever Forget Mercy Humppe and Find True Happiness?
GB 1969 117m Technicolor
Universal/Taralex (Anthony Newley)
A performer on a beach assembles a huge pile of personal bric-à-brac and reminisces about his life in the style of a variety show.
Obscure and pointless personal fantasy, financed at great expense by a major film company as a rather seedy monument to Anthony Newley's totally uninteresting sex life, and to the talent which he obviously thinks he possesses. The few mildly amusing moments are not provided by him.
w Herman Raucher, Anthony Newley *d* Anthony Newley *ph* Otto Heller *m* Anthony Newley
☆ Anthony Newley, Joan Collins, George Jessel, Milton Berle, Bruce Forsyth, Stubby Kaye, Patricia Hayes, Victor Spinetti
'If I'd been Anthony Newley I would have opened it in Siberia during Christmas week and called it a day.' – *Rex Reed*
'The kindest thing for all concerned would be that every available copy should be quietly and decently buried.' – *Michael Billington, Illustrated London News*

Can She Bake a Cherry Pie?
US 1983 90m DuArt
Jagfilm/International Rainbow
An abandoned wife has an experimental affair with a hypochondriac divorcé.
What the writer-director calls 'a bitter-sweet comedy about loneliness and love' has more to say to him than to an audience; but there are wryly amusing moments.
wd Henry Jaglom *ph* Robert Fiore
☆ Karen Black, Michael Emil, Michael Margotta, Frances Fisher

Can This Be Dixie?
US 1936 68m bw
TCF (Sol M. Wurtzel)
In the old South, a medicine showman and his daughter help a bankrupt Kentucky colonel.
Agreeable supporting material, with elements of satire, spoof and musical comedy.
w Lamar Trotti *d* George Marshall
☆ Jane Withers, Slim Summerville, Claude Gillingwater, Helen Wood, Thomas Beck, Sara Haden, Donald Cook, Hattie McDaniel
'Plenty of ingredients were thrown into the soup ... it will hold its own in the duals.' – *Variety*

Can You Keep It Up For A Week?
GB 1974 94m Technicolor
Pyramid (Elton Hawke)
A woman tells her accident-prone lover that she will marry him only if he can hold down a job for seven days.
Little more than a succession of archly delivered double entendres, it enjoyed a surprising success at the time of its original release, though now it is merely indicative of the banality of the British film industry of the period.
w Robin Gough *d* Jim Atkinson *ph* Ricky Briggs
m Dave Quincy *md* Harry South *ad* Jacquemine Charrott-Lodwige *ed* David Docker
☆ Jeremy Bulloch, Neil Hallett, Sue Longhurst, Jill Damas, Richard O'Sullivan, Jenny Cox, Joy Harrington, Valerie Leon
'Dreary sexual encounters, rudimentary direction and 94 minutes of witless Old English puns.' – *David McGillivray, MFB*
† The producer's name was a pseudonym for Hazel Adair, best known as co-creator of the TV soap opera *Crossroads*, and TV wrestling commentator Kent Walton.

Canadian Bacon
US 1995 90m DeLuxe/bw
Polygram/Propaganda/Maverick (Michael Moore, David Brown, Ron Rotholz, Steve Golin)
The American President, needing to boost his popularity by belligerence, decides that Canada is a threat to the free world.
A one-joke movie that will mean little outside North America, and not a great deal more inside it.
wd Michael Moore *ph* Haskell Wexler *m* Elmer Bernstein, Peter Bernstein *pd* Carol Spier
ed Wendy Stanzler, Michael Berenbaum
☆ Alan Alda, John Candy, Rhea Perlman, Kevin Pollak, Rip Torn, Bill Nunn, Kevin J. O'Connor, G. D. Spradlin, Carlton Watson, James Belushi, Dan Aykroyd
'An amusing outing for a sophisticated crowd. More hip and flip than broadly humorous, pic is too much of an in-joke to translate to the mainstream.' – *Variety*

'The blazing saga of untamed men and a savage wilderness!'
Canadian Pacific
US 1949 95m Cinecolor
TCF (Nat Holt)
A surveyor discovers the vital pass through the Rockies, and chooses between a lady doctor and a wilful half-breed.
Fairly unhistorical Western; watchable, though.
w Jack de Witt, Kenneth Gamet *d* Edwin L. Marin
☆ Randolph Scott, Jane Wyatt, Nancy Olson, J. Carrol Naish, Victor Jory, Robert Barrat

The Canadians
GB/Canada 1961 85m DeLuxe Cinemascope
TCF (Herman E. Webber)
After Custer's defeat at Little Big Horn, 6,000 Sioux flee north and are victimized by villainous Canadians; but the Mounties come to the rescue.
Dreary, stumbling semi-Western which set back Canadian production by a year or two. The blame seems to be equally shared by all concerned.
wd Burt Kennedy *ph* Arthur Ibbetson *m* none
☆ Robert Ryan, John Dehner, Torin Thatcher, Burt Metcalfe, Teresa Stratas, Michael Pate, John Sutton

Cancel My Reservation
US 1972 99m Technicolor
Naho Enterprises
A TV talk show host retreats to his ranch and finds himself mixed up with murder.
Bob Hope's last film, though it reverted to farce and his bumbling coward persona, proved a sorry affair with egg on the face of everybody concerned.
w Arthur Marx, Robert Fisher *novel* *The Broken Gun* by Louis L'Amour *d* Paul Bogart
☆ Bob Hope, Eva Marie Saint, Ralph Bellamy, Forrest Tucker, Anne Archer, Keenan Wynn, Doodles Weaver

The Candidate ***
US 1972 110m Technicolor
Warner/Redford-Ritchie (Walter Coblenz)

A young Californian lawyer is persuaded to run for senator; in succeeding, he alienates his wife and obscures his real opinions.
Put together in a slightly scrappy but finally persuasive style, this joins a select band of rousing, doubting American political films.
w Jeremy Larner *d* Michael Ritchie *ph* Victor J. Kemper *m* John Rubinstein
☆ *Robert Redford*, Peter Boyle, *Don Porter*, Allen Garfield, Karen Carlson, Quinn Redeker, Morgan Upton, *Melvyn Douglas*
'Decent entertainment … it is never boring, but it is never enlarging, informationally or emotionally or thematically.' – *Stanley Kauffmann*
Jeremy Larner

Candles at Nine
GB 1944 86m bw
British National
A young heiress in her benefactor's old mansion is menaced by his housekeeper.
Elementary Cat and the Canary *reprise; cast understandably uneasy.*
w John Harlow, Basil Mason *novel* Anthony Gilbert *d* John Harlow
☆ Jessie Matthews, John Stuart, Beatrix Lehmann, Winifred Shotter, Reginald Purdell

Candleshoe
GB 1977 101m Technicolor
Walt Disney Productions (Hugh Attwooll)

An attempt to pass off a fake heiress to an English stately home is prevented by the resourceful butler.
Slackly handled comedy adventure full of easy targets and predictable incidents.
w David Swift, Rosemary Anne Sisson *novel* *Christmas at Candleshoe* by Michael Innes *d* Norman Tokar *ph* Paul Beeson *m* Ron Goodwin
☆ David Niven, Helen Hayes, Jodie Foster, Leo McKern, Veronica Quilligan, Ian Sharrock, Vivian Pickles
'It might have been conceived by a computer called upon to produce the definitive pastiche of a Disney film of the 1970s.' – *Financial Times*

Candy
US/France/Italy 1968 124m Technicolor
Selmur/Dear/Corona (Robert Haggiag)

An innocent girl defends herself from a fate worse than death in a variety of international situations.
Witless and charmless perversion of a sex satire in which the point (if any) was that the nymphet gladly surrendered herself to all the gentlemen for their own good. A star cast flounders helplessly in a morass of bad taste, bad film-making, and boredom.
w Buck Henry *novel* Terry Southern *d* Christian Marquand *ph* Giuseppe Rotunno *m* Dave Grusin
☆ Ewa Aulin, Richard Burton, Marlon Brando, James Coburn, Walter Matthau, Charles Aznavour, John Huston, Elsa Martinelli, Ringo Starr, John Astin
'Hippy psychedelics are laid on with the self-destroying effect of an overdose of garlic.' – *MFB*
'As an emetic, liquor is dandy, but Candy is quicker.' – *John Simon*

Candy Mountain *
Switzerland/France/Canada 1987 92m Eastmancolor
Oasis/Xanadu/Films Plant Chant/Films Vision 4 (Ruth Waldburger)

An enterprising musician goes in search of a reclusive guitar-maker.
An occasionally engaging road movie, accompanied by many songs, of an innocent being taken for a ride, literally and metaphorically.
w Rudy Wurlitzer *d* Robert Frank, Rudy Wurlitzer *ph* Pio Corradi *m* Dr John, David Johansen, Leon Redbone and others *ed* Jennifer Auge
☆ Kevin J. O'Connor, Harris Yulin, Tom Waits, Bulle Ogier, Roberts Blossom, Leon Redbone, Dr John, Rita McNeil, Joe Strummer, Laurie Metcalf

Candy or Mint: see *Caluga o Menta*

Candyman *
US 1992 93m DeLuxe
Columbia TriStar/Polygram/Propaganda (Steve Golin, Sigurjon Sighvatsson, Alan Poul)

An anthropology student becomes convinced of the reality of a mythical hook-handed serial killer, the son of a murdered slave.
Effective horror that manages not only to be scary but also delivers a parable on contemporary attitudes to race and sex.
wd Bernard Rose *story* *The Forbidden* by Clive Barker *ph* Anthony B. Richmond *m* Philip Glass *pd* Jane Ann Stewart *ed* Dan Rae *sp* Image Animation
☆ Virginia Madsen, Tony Todd, Xander Berkeley, Kasi Lemmons, Vanessa Williams, DeJuan Guy, Michael Culkin, Stanley DeSantis, Gilbert Lewis
'An upper-register horror item that delivers the requisite shocks and gore but doesn't cheat or cop out.' – *Variety*

Candyman: Farewell to the Flesh
US 1995 94m DeLuxe
Polygram/Propaganda (Sigurjon Sighvatsson, Gregg D. Fienberg)

A teacher discovers that the Candyman has been conjured into life once again, after her brother is accused of murdering an expert on the legend.
At its second outing, the urban myth of a hook-handed victim of injustice has deteriorated into just another slasher movie.
w Rand Ravich, Mark Kruger *story* Clive Barker *d* Bill Condon *ph* Tobias Schliessler *m* Philip Glass *pd* Barry Robison *ed* Virginia Katz *cos* Bruce Finlayson
☆ Tony Todd, Kelly Rowan, Timothy Carhart, Veronica Cartwright (Octavia), William O'Leary, Fay Hauser, Bill Nunn, Joshua Gibran Mayweather
'Still delivers a requisite number of shocks to satisfy the core cult that propelled the original to hitdom.' – *Variety*
'Eleven dead bodies. One dead cat. No breasts. Hand hacked off. One bar-room brawl, with head through mirror. Multiple hooks through the breast, with spurtin' gouts. Multiple killer-bee attacks, with facial goo … Four stars. Joe Bob says check it out.' – *Joe Bob Briggs*

O'Cangaceiro: see *The Bandit*

Cannery Row
US 1982 120m Metrocolor
MGM/Michael Philips

Incidents in the life of a 1940s marine biologist who lives on the waterfront with bums and floozies.
Badly out of its time, this curious attempt at sentimental realism was long in the works but emerged as a bloodless, stultifying entertainment.
wd David S. Ward *novel* John Steinbeck *ph* Sven Nykvist *m* Jack Nitzsche *pd* Richard MacDonald *ed* David Bretherton
☆ Nick Nolte, Debra Winger, Audra Lindley, Frank McRae, M. Emmet Walsh, John Huston (narrator)
'Another MGM item in which the entertainment values are difficult to locate.' – *Variety*
† Raquel Welch, originally cast for the Winger role, was fired in mid-production.

Cannibal Girls
Canada 1972 84m Eastmancolor
Target/Scary Pictures (Daniel Goldberg)
A couple whose car breaks down check into a motel in a small town where the inhabitants are cannibals.
Standard undistinguished and improvised horror fare, influenced by George Romero's Night of the Living Dead *and itself an influence on* The Texas Chainsaw Massacre. *The film is not helped by the gimmick of a buzzer that sounds just before shock scenes and a bell that signals when the horror is over.*
w Robert Sandler *d* Ivan Reitman *ph* Robert Saad *m* Doug Riley *ed* Daniel Goldberg *sp* Richard Whyte, Michael Lotosky
☆ Eugene Levy, Andrea Martin, Ronald Ulrich, Randall Carpenter, Bonnie Neilson, Mira Pawluk
'Aggravatingly hammy and corny.' – *MFB*

Cannibal Man (dubbed)
Spain 1972 120m colour
Atlas (Joe Truchado)

original title: *La Semana del Asesino*
aka: *The Apartment on the 13th Floor; Week of the Killer*
A slaughterhouse worker embarks on a killing spree to cover up his murder of a taxi driver during an argument over the fare.
An unconvincing psychological thriller. Cannibalism plays no part in the movie, other than indirectly, when human remains are fed with other meat into a machine for making soup.
w Eloy de la Iglesia, Anthony Fos, Robert H. Oliver *d* Eloy de la Iglesia *ph* Raul Artigot *m* Fernando G. Morcillo *ed* Joe Louis Martinez *sp* Baquero
☆ Vincent Parra, Emma Cohen, Eusebio Poncela, Vicky Lagos, Lola Herrera
† The English video release was cut to 92m.

Cannibal! The Musical
US 1996 105m colour
Troma/Avenging Conscience/Cannibal (Ian Hardin, Alexandra Kelly, Jason McHugh, Trey Parker, Matthew Stone)

In the 1880s, an imprisoned goldminer tells a female reporter how he was accused of cannibalism in Colorado.
Claiming to be a restoration of a 1954 film with violent scenes 'edited out for your viewing pleasure', this deliberately amateurish movie begins and ends with an excess of gore played for comedy; in between there are moments of the ghoulish humour better known from Stone and Parker's TV series South Park.
wd Trey Parker *ph* Robert Muratore, Chris Graves *m* Trey Parker, Rich Sanders *m/ly* Trey Parker *pd* David Hedge *ed* Ian Hardin
☆ Juan Schwartz, Ian Hardin, Matt Stone, Jon Hegel, Jason McHugh, Dian Bachar, Toddy Walters, Robert Muratore, Stan Brakhage

Cannon for Cordoba
US 1970 104m DeLuxe Panavision
UA/Mirisch (Stephen Kandel, Vincent Fennelly)
In 1912, the Mexican bandit Cordoba is outgunned and outwitted by a US army captain.
Fast-moving but rather uninteresting action adventure.
w Stephen Kandel *d* Paul Wendkos *ph* Antonio Macasoli *m* Elmer Bernstein *ad* José Maria Tapiador *ed* Walter Hanneman
☆ George Peppard (Capt. Rod Douglas), Raf Vallone (Cordoba), Giovanna Ralli (Leonora Cristobal), Pete Duel (Andy Rice), Don Gordon (Sgt Jackson Harkness), Nico Minardos (Peter Andros), John Russell (Brig. Gen. John J. Pershing), Francine York (Sophia)
'It remains a B film, but an unusually watchable one.' – *Tom Milne, MFB*

'A free-wheeling, stunt-studded, dented and demented story of a road racer without rules.'
Cannonball
US/Hong Kong 1976 93m Metrocolor
Harbor/Shaw Brothers (Samuel W. Gelfman)

GB title: *Carquake*
Aggressive drivers compete in the Trans-American Grand Prix.
The plot is a thin excuse for multiple pile-ups and other road disasters. Moments amuse, but the violence quickly palls.
w Paul Bartel, Donald C. Simpson *d* Paul Bartel *ph* Tak Fujimoto *m* David A. Axelrod
☆ David Carradine, Bill McKinney, Veronica Hamel, Gerrit Graham, Judy Canova

Cannonball Fever: see *Speed Zone*

The Cannonball Run
US 1980 95m Technicolor
Golden Harvest (Albert S. Ruddy)

The adventures of ill-assorted contestants in the illegal Cannonball coast-to-coast race.
Well-known stars are all at sea in this comedy/disaster extravaganza, which seems to have begun as a joke rather than a script.
w Brock Yates *d* Hal Needham *ph* Michael Butler *md* Al Capps
☆ Burt Reynolds, Roger Moore, Farrah Fawcett, Dom DeLuise, Dean Martin, Sammy Davis Jnr, Adrienne Barbeau, Jack Elam, Bert Convy, Jamie Farr, Peter Fonda, Molly Picon, Bianca Jagger
'Lacking any recognizable plot or characterization, or indeed incidental invention, it merely offers a parade of inept whimsy and lame intra-mural reference.' – *Tim Pulleine, MFB*
'Moviegoers who relish the screech of tyres taking a fast turn on a narrow bend should have a whale of a time.' – *Daily Mail*

Cannonball Run II
US 1983 108m Technicolor
Golden Harvest/Warner (Albert S. Ruddy)

An Arab sheik puts up a million-dollar prize for the Cannonball Run.
Dispirited rehash of number one, with poor technique and non-performances by stars who should have known better than to get involved.
w Hal Needham, Albert S. Ruddy, Harvey Miller *d* Hal Needham *ph* Nick McLean *m* Al Capps *ad* Thomas E. Azzari *ed* William Gordean, Carl Kress
☆ Burt Reynolds, Dom DeLuise, Sammy Davis Jnr, Dean Martin, Jamie Farr, Telly Savalas, Shirley MacLaine, Frank Sinatra, Susan Anton, Catherine Bach, Richard Kiel, Tim Conway, Sid Caesar, Don Knotts, Ricardo Montalban and also Jim Nabors, Henry Silva

Canon City *
US 1948 82m bw
Eagle Lion/Bryan Foy (Robert T. Kane)
Convicts break out of the Colorado State Prison.
Minor semi-documentary melodrama, quite effectively presented.
wd Crane Wilbur *ph* John Alton
☆ Scott Brady, Jeff Corey, Whit Bissell, Stanley Clements, DeForest Kelley

Can't Buy Me Love
US 1987 94m colour
Warner/Touchstone (Thom Mount)

A wimp hires a popular cheerleader to be his girlfriend for a month to improve his social standing.
Predictable comedy aimed at a teenage audience, and they are welcome to it.
w Michael Swerdlick *d* James Foley *ph* Peter Lyons Collister *m* Robert Folk *pd* Donald Light-Harris *ed* Jeff Gourson
☆ Patrick Dempsey, Amanda Peterson, Courtney Gains, Seth Green, Tina Caspary, Devin Devasquez, Darcy de Moss, Eric Bruskotter

'Yesterday's history. Tomorrow's the future. Tonight's the party.'
Can't Hardly Wait
US 1998 98m Technicolor
Columbia/Tall Trees

At a wild party to celebrate graduation from high school, a shy youth approaches the girl he loves, who has just broken up with her boyfriend.
Noisy lowbrow comedy of American school life, unlikely to interest anyone who's not an adolescent of limited horizons.
wd Harry Elfton, Deborah Kaplan *ph* Lloyd Ahern *m* David Kitay, Matthew Sweet *pd* Marcia Hinds-Johnson *ed* Michael Jablow
☆ Jennifer Love Hewitt, Ethan Embry, Charlie Korsmo, Lauren Ambrose, Seth Green, Peter Facinelli, Adam Hann-Byrd
'A mediocre attempt to recapture the exuberance and candid portraiture of such high school movie classics as *American Graffiti*.' – *Emanuel Levy, Variety*

Can't Help Singing *
US 1944 90m Technicolor
Universal (Frank Ross)
A Washington heiress chases her army lieutenant lover across the Wild West to California.
Lively star musical which could have used a little more wit in its lighthearted script.
w Lewis Foster, Frank Ryan *d* Frank Ryan *ph* Woody Bredell, W. Howard Greene *m/ly* Jerome Kern, E. Y. Harburg *md* Jerome Kern, Hans Salter *ed* Ted J. Kent
☆ *Deanna Durbin*, David Bruce, Robert Paige, *Akim Tamiroff, Leonid Kinskey*, Ray Collins, Thomas Gomez

'This could have been a beautiful and gay picture, but it is made without much feeling for beauty or gaiety.' – *James Agee*

'She can carry a simple part charmingly; she looks very well; her manners are impeccable; and she can sing a role just short of grand opera better than any actress on the screen.' – *Observer*

♫ 'Elbow Room'; 'Any Moment Now'; 'Californ-i-ay'; 'Swing Your Sweetheart round the Fire'; 'Finale Ultimo'

Jerome Kern, Hans Salter; song 'More and More'

Can't Stop the Music

US 1980 124m Metrocolor Panavision

EMI/Allan Carr

A Greenwich Village pop group hits the bigtime.

Curiously old-fashioned youth musical, unwisely touted as something special, which it wasn't.

w Bronte Woodward, Allan Carr *d* Nancy Walker *ph* Bill Butler *m* Jacques Morali

☆ The Village People, Valerie Perrine, Paul Sand, Bruce Jenner, Tammy Grimes, June Havoc, Barbara Rush, Jack Weston

'The hype disaster of the 80s, a grisly rehash of the let's-start-a-group-of-our-own plot, peopled with butch gay stereotypes of both sexes pretending to be straight. The pervasive tackiness is unrelieved.' – *Time Out*

'Desperately knowing about the eighties but fixed remorselessly in a time warp of fifties hokum.' – *Guardian*

'All noise, lights, slogans, movement and dazzle, like a 124m commercial devoted to selling you a product you can't use.' – *Sunday Times*

'One doesn't watch it, one is attacked by it.' – *New England Entertainment Digest*

'Considering the low level of wit, perhaps the Village People should consider renaming themselves the Village Idiots.' – *Los Angeles Magazine*

'This shamefully tacky musical extravaganza fails on every aesthetic level.' – *Los Angeles Herald Examiner*

'A forced marriage between the worst of sitcom plotting and the highest of high camp production numbers.' – *New West*

Cantata de Chile *

Cuba 1976 119m colour

ICAIC (Orlando de La Huerta, Camilo Vives)

Revolutionary history of Cuba, told from a Marxist viewpoint.

An ambitious, epic mix of realism, symbolic action, songs and poems, intermixed with scenes of appalling violence, and filmed with exuberance and panache. But two hours in the company of excessively noble peasants is too much.

wd Humberto Solas *ph* Jorge Herrera *m* Leo Brouwer *pd* Fedora Robles *ed* Nelson L. Rodriguez

☆ Nelson Villagra, Shenda Roman, Eric Heresmann

A Canterbury Tale **

GB 1944 124m bw

Rank/Archers (Michael Powell, Emeric Pressburger)

A batty magistrate is unmasked by a land girl, an army sergeant and a GI.

Curious would-be propaganda piece with Old England bathed in a roseate wartime glow, but the plot seems to have little to do with Chaucer. Indeed, quite what Powell and Pressburger thought they were up to is hard to fathom, but the detail is interesting.

wd Michael Powell, Emeric Pressburger *ph* Erwin Hillier

☆ Eric Portman, Sheila Sim, John Sweet, Dennis Price, Esmond Knight, Charles Hawtrey, Hay Petrie, George Merritt, Edward Rigby

'To most people the intentions of the filmmakers remained highly mysterious; nor did this picture of the British administration of justice commend itself to the authorities, who showed some reluctance to encourage its export to our allies.' – *Basil Wright, 1972*

The Canterbury Tales

Italy/France 1971 109m Technicolor

UA/PEA/PAA (Alberto Grimaldi)

Medieval pilgrims amuse each other by telling stories on the way to Canterbury.

A sweaty selection of the tales in their more prurient aspects; even (or especially) with a Chaplinesque interlude, it soon becomes obvious that Pasolini has no understanding of English humour.

wd Pier Paolo Pasolini, after Chaucer *ph* Tonino Delli Colli *m* Ennio Morricone

☆ Pier Paolo Pasolini (Chaucer), Hugh Griffith, Laura Betti, Tom Baker, Ninetto Davoli, Franco Citti, Robin Askwith

'Caricature Chaucer, with pilgrims losing the way to Canterbury amid a forest of male genitalia.' – *Sight and Sound*

'The vivid depiction of taboo subjects emerges less as an affirmation of the Chaucerian belief that all human activity lies within the artist's scope, than as a bludgeoning over-emphasis on physical appetite as man's primal motive for action.' – *Nigel Andrews, MFB*

The Canterville Ghost *

US 1944 95m bw

MGM (Arthur Field)

The young girl heiress of an English castle introduces GIs to the resident ghost.

Leaden comedy a long way after Oscar Wilde, sunk by slow script and direction, but partly salvaged by the respective roguishness and infant charm of its stars.

w Edwin Blum *d* Jules Dassin *ph* Robert Planck *m* George Bassman

☆ *Charles Laughton, Margaret O'Brien*, Robert Young, William Gargan, Rags Ragland, Peter Lawford, Una O'Connor, Mike Mazurki

† In the mid 1970s, a television version starring David Niven was made by HTV. Another TV version followed in 1996, starring Patrick Stewart and Neve Campbell.

Canyon Pass: see *Raton Pass*

Canyon Passage *

US 1946 99m Technicolor

Universal (Walter Wanger)

In the 1850s along the pioneering tracks the west's first towns were being built...

Simple, scrappy but generally pleasing film which gives a vivid picture of pioneering life while minimizing its hardships.

w Ernest Pascal, William Fosche *d* Jacques Tourneur *ph* Edward Cronjager *m* Frank Skinner *m/ly* Jack Brooks, Hoagy Carmichael *ad* John B. Goodman, Richard H. Riedel *ed* Milton Carruth

☆ Dana Andrews, Patricia Roc, Hoagy Carmichael, Brian Donlevy, Susan Hayward, Ward Bond, Andy Devine, Lloyd Bridges

'Miles of beautiful scenery, lavishly punctuated with rough-and-tumble episodes, moments of tender romance and a smattering of folk customs.' – *New York Times*

song 'Ole Buttermilk Sky' (*m/ly* Hoagy Carmichael, Jack Brooks)

Cape Fear

US 1961 106m bw

U-I/Melville-Talbot (Sy Bartlett)

An ex-convict blames a lawyer for his sentence and threatens to rape the lawyer's wife.

Unpleasant and drawn out suspenser with characters of cardboard and situations from stock.

w James R. Webb *novel The Executioners* by John D. MacDonald *d* J. Lee-Thompson *ph* Sam Leavitt *m* Bernard Herrmann *ad* Robert Boyle, Alexander Golitzen *ed* George Tomasini

☆ Gregory Peck (Sam Bowden), Robert Mitchum (Max Cady), Polly Bergen (Peggy Bowden), Martin Balsam (Mark Dutton), Lori Martin (Nancy Bowden), Jack Kruschen (Dave Grafton), Telly Savalas (Charles Sievers), Barrie Chase (Diane Taylor)

'There is nothing in the dark that isn't there in the light. Except fear.'

Cape Fear ***

US 1991 128m Technicolor Panavision

Universal/Amblin/Cappa/Tribeca (Barbara de Fina)

A psychopathic ex-convict returns to threaten the family of the lawyer who unsuccessfully defended him on a charge of rape.

A remake superior to the original, a grimly effective thriller, filled with a sense of brooding menace.

w Wesley Strick *novel The Executioners* by John D. MacDonald *screenplay James R. Webb* *d Martin Scorsese* *ph* Freddie Francis *m* Bernard Herrmann *md* Elmer Bernstein *pd* Henry Bumstead *ed* Thelma Schoonmaker

☆ *Robert DeNiro* (Max Cady), Nick Nolte (Sam Bowden), Jessica Lange (Leigh Bowden), *Juliette Lewis* (Danielle Bowden), Joe Don Baker (Claude Kersek), Robert Mitchum (Lieutenant Elgart), Gregory Peck (Lee Heller), Martin Balsam (Judge), Illeana Douglas (Lori Davis)

'A highly potent thriller that will strike fear into the hearts of a sizable public.' – *Variety*

'The film begins as it goes on; undeviatingly and unrelievedly brutal. This said, I must admit I mistrust myself for admiring it so much. For more than two hours it puts one's moral conscience under assault, not just one's nerves.' – *Alexander Walker, London Evening Standard*

'A picture whose sole aim is to give its audience huge, bowel-loosening shocks; the veneer of moral seriousness and psychological complexity that Scorsese brings to the enterprise feels like an attempt to convince himself that he's not doing what he's doing ... This is Scorsese's worst picture – an ugly, incoherent piece of work.' – *New Yorker*

'Have our lives truly become so hollow that this kind of unapologetic bludgeoning of our sensibilities passes for jolly weekend entertainment?' – *Kenneth Turan, Los Angeles Times*

'I'm glad I saw the film. I found it as gripping and offensive as Scorsese intended. But, apart from de Niro's transcendent performance, I'm not sure I'd want to see it again.' – *Ian Johnstone, Sunday Times*

† Gregory Peck, Robert Mitchum and Martin Balsam all featured in the 1962 version, as did Bernard Herrmann's score.

Robert DeNiro, Juliette Lewis

The Caper of the Golden Bulls

US 1966 104m Pathécolor

Embassy (Clarence Greene)

GB title: *Carnival of Thieves*

Ex-air-aces rob banks in order to pay for the restoration of a French cathedral they had to bomb; to avoid incrimination they are blackmailed into doing one last job in Pamplona.

Ingeniously plotted, flatly executed suspenser set in Pamplona during the bull run.

w Ed Waters, William Moessinger *novel* William P. McGivern *d* Russel Rouse *ph* Hal Stine *m* Vic Mizzy

☆ Stephen Boyd, Giovanna Ralli, Yvette Mimieux, Walter Slezak, Vito Scotti

Capetown Affair

US/South Africa 1967 100m DeLuxe

TCF/Killarney (Robert D. Webb)

A pickpocket on a South African bus steals a purse containing secret microfilm.

Flatulent remake of Pickup on South Street *with nothing but the unfamiliar locale to recommend it.*

w Harold Medford, Samuel Fuller *d* Robert D. Webb *ph* David Millin *m* Bob Adams

☆ James Brolin, Jacqueline Bisset, Claire Trevor, Bob Courtney, Jon Whiteley

'The man who made the twenties roar! Now, after 45 years, his true story can be told!'

Capone

US 1975 101m DeLuxe

TCF/Santa Fe (Roger Corman)

The rise and fall of Chicago's most famous gangster.

Exploitation version of the Capone story, with the emphasis on unpleasant violence.

w Howard Browne *d* Steve Carver *ph* Vilis Lapenieks *m* David Grisman

☆ Ben Gazzara, Sylvester Stallone, Susan Blakely, Harry Guardino, John Cassavetes, John Davis Chandler, Peter Maloney, Royal Dano

† See also: Al Capone.

Le Caporal Epinglé: see *The Vanishing Corporal*

Caprice *

US 1967 98m DeLuxe Cinemascope

TCF/Aaron Rosenberg, Marty Melcher

A career girl investigating the death of her boss discovers that a cosmetics empire is the front for international drug smuggling.

Incoherent kaleidoscope which switches from farce to suspense and Bond-style action, scattering in-jokes along the way. Bits of it however are funny, and it looks good.

w Jay Jayson, Frank Tashlin *d* Frank Tashlin *ph* Leon Shamroy (who also appears) *m* Frank de Vol

☆ Doris Day, Richard Harris, Edward Mulhare, Ray Walston, Jack Kruschen, Lilia Skala, Irene Tsu, Michael Romanoff, Michael J. Pollard

Capricious Summer *

Czechoslovakia 1968 75m Eastmancolor

Ceskoslovensky Film (Jan Libora)

The beautiful assistant of a wandering tightrope walker sets up sexual tensions when they stop at a sleepy riverside town.

Amusing little period comedy in a period setting.

wd Jiri Menzel *ph* Jaromir Sofr *m* Jiri Sust

☆ Rudolf Hrusinsky, Vlastimil Brodsky, Frantisek Rehak, Jana Drchalova, Jiri Menzel

'The mission was a sham. The murders were real.'

Capricorn One

US 1978 128m CFI color Panavision

Associated General/Lew Grade (Paul N. Lazarus III)

A reporter discovers that the first manned space flight to Mars was a hoax.

Smartly packaged topical adventure thriller rather marred by its all star cast.

wd Peter Hyams *ph* Bill Butler *m* Jerry Goldsmith *pd* Albert Brenner

☆ Elliott Gould, James Brolin, Brenda Vaccaro, Sam Waterston, O. J. Simpson, Hal Holbrook, Telly Savalas, Karen Black, David Huddleston

'After weighing in with some Watergate/Bernstein pretensions, the makers then opt for boring, Bondish derring-do.' – *Sight and Sound*

Captain America

US 1989 97m Eastmancolor

Castle/21st Century/Marvel/Jadran Film (Menahem Golan)

Frozen in the ice for decades, Captain America is freed to battle against an arch-criminal The Red Skull.

Comic-book nonsense, half-heartedly presented.

w Stephen Tolkin *d* Albert Pyun *ph* Philip Alan Waters *m* Barry Goldberg *ed* David Reale

☆ Matt Salinger, Ronny Cox, Ned Beatty, Darren McGavin, Michael Nouri, Melinda Dillon, Francesca Neri, Bill Mumy, Kim Gillingham

'It comprises reams of tedious exposition interlarded with out-dated heroics.' – *MFB*

Captain Apache

US/Spain 1971 94m Technicolor 'Scope

Benmar (Milton Sperling, Philip Yordan, Irving Lerner)

An Indian serving with US army intelligence tracks down a gun runner.

An old formula tarted up with the new violence. Very ho-hum.

w Philip Yordan, Milton Sperling *novel* S. E. Whitman *d* Alexander Singer *ph* John Cabrera *m* Dolores Claman

☆ Lee Van Cleef, Carroll Baker, Stuart Whitman, Percy Herbert, Tony Vogel

Captain Applejack

US 1931 70m bw

Warner

A timid man turns the tables on crooks who plan to find treasure beneath his ancestral home.

Early talkie version of a well-worn play previously filmed in 1923.

w Maude Fulton *novel Ambrose Applejohn's Adventure* by Walter Hackett *d* Hobart Henley

☆ John Halliday, Kay Strozzi, Arthur Edmund Carewe, Mary Brian, Louise Closser Hale

Captain Bill
GB 1935 81m bw
Leslie Fuller (Joe Rock)
A bargee saves a schoolmistress from trouble with crooks.
By reputation the best of its star's modest comedies, which have not yet been rediscovered.
w Val Valentine, Syd Courtenay and George Harris *d* Ralph Ceder
☆ Leslie Fuller, Georgie Harris, Judy Kelly, Hal Gordon, O. B. Clarence

Captain Blackjack
US/France 1952 90m bw
Alsa/Jungla (Julien Duvivier)
aka: *Blackjack*
A Riviera socialite pretends to be an undercover agent but is really a smuggler; she is unmasked by a doctor who is really a detective.
Trashy hodgepodge with a remarkable cast of ageing stars.
w Julien Duvivier, Charles Spaak, Michael Pertwee *story* Robert Gaillard *d* Julien Duvivier *ph* André Thomas *m* Joseph Kosma
☆ George Sanders, Agnes Moorehead, Herbert Marshall, Patricia Roc, Marcel Dalio, Howard Vernon, Dennis Wyndham
† The film was meant to take eight weeks to shoot; instead, it took seven months, which is why Sanders, who ate too much out of boredom, is thin in some scenes and fat in others. The stars were to be paid out of the film's receipts and, as a result, earned no money from the picture.

'A million dollars worth of adventure! To do justice in words to its fascination is impossible!'
'His sword carved his name across the continents – and his glory across the seas!'

Captain Blood **
US 1935 119m bw
Warner (Harry Joe Brown)
A young British surgeon, wrongly condemned by Judge Jeffreys for helping rebels, escapes and becomes a Caribbean pirate.
Modestly produced but quite exhilarating pirate adventure notable for making a star of Errol Flynn. Direction makes the most of very limited production values.
w Casey Robinson *novel* Rafael Sabatini *d Michael Curtiz ph Hal Mohr m Erich Wolfgang Korngold ad Anton Grot*
☆ *Errol Flynn*, Olivia de Havilland, *Basil Rathbone*, Lionel Atwill, Guy Kibbee, Ross Alexander, Henry Stephenson, Forrester Harvey, Hobart Cavanaugh, Donald Meek

'A lavish, swashbuckling saga of the Spanish Main … it can't fail at the wickets.' – *Variety*
'Here is a fine spirited mix-up with clothes and wigs which sometimes hark back to the sixteenth century and sometimes forward to the period of Wolfe … one is quite prepared for the culminating moment when the Union Jack breaks proudly, anachronistically forth at Peter Blood's masthead.' – *Graham Greene*
'Magnificently photographed, lavishly produced, and directed with consummate skill.' – *Picturegoer*

best picture

Captain Blood, Fugitive: see *Captain Pirate*

Captain Boycott *
GB 1947 93m bw
GFD/Individual (Frank Launder, Sidney Gilliat)
In 1880, poor Irish farmers rebel against their tyrannical English landlords.
Modest historical drama in which a splendid cast is rather subdued.
w Wolfgang Wilhelm, Frank Launder, Paul Vincent Carroll, Patrick Campbell *novel* Philip Rooney *d* Frank Launder *ph* Wilkie Cooper *m* William Alwyn *ad* Edward Carrick *ed* Thelma Myers *cos* Sophie Harris
☆ Stewart Granger (Hugh Davin), Kathleen Ryan (Anne Killain), Alastair Sim (Father McKeogh), Robert Donat (cameo) (Parnell), Cecil Parker (Captain Boycott), Mervyn Johns (Watty Connell), Noel Purcell (Daniel McGinty), Niall MacGinnis (Mark Killain), Maureen Delany (Mrs Davin), Eddie Byrne (Sean Kerin), Liam Redmond (Martin Egan), Maurice Denham (Lt-Col Strickland), Bernadette O'Farrell (Mrs Fagan)

'It is said that no actor can survive playing opposite a child or a dog. Let me add here that it is just as lethal playing with the Abbey Players. Apart from being able to act you off the stage, they can also drink you under the table.' – *Sidney Gilliat, 1982*

Captain Carey USA
US 1950 83m bw
Paramount (Richard Maibaum)
GB title: *After Midnight*
After the war, a military officer returns to an Italian village to expose the informer who betrayed his comrades.
Muddled and rather boring melodrama with a labyrinthine plot which seems to have stultified all concerned. It did produce a hit song, 'Mona Lisa'.
w Robert Thoeren *novel Dishonoured* by Martha Albrand *d* Mitchell Leisen *ph* John F. Seitz *m* Hugo Friedhofer
☆ Alan Ladd, Francis Lederer, Wanda Hendrix, Joseph Calleia, Celia Lovsky, Angela Clarke, Jane Nigh, Frank Puglia, Luis Alberni
song 'Mona Lisa' (*m/ly* Ray Evans, Jay Livingston)

Captain Caution
US 1940 84m bw
Hal Roach
In 1812, a girl takes over her dead father's ship and fights the British.
Lively though unconvincing adventure with emphasis on comedy.
w Grover Jones *novel* Kenneth Roberts *d* Richard Wallace *ph* Norbert Brodine *m* Phil Ohman
☆ Victor Mature, Louise Platt, Bruce Cabot, Leo Carrillo, Robert Barrat, Vivienne Osborne, Alan Ladd

Captain Clegg *
GB 1962 82m Technicolor
Universal/Hammer (John Temple-Smith)
US title: *Night Creatures*
The vicar of an 18th-century village in Romney Marsh is really a retired pirate, now doing a little smuggling on the side.
Mild remake of Dr Syn with a few moments of violence added; watchable for those who like totally predictable plot development.
w John Elder (Anthony Hinds) *d* Peter Graham Scott *ph* Arthur Grant *m* Don Banks *ad* Bernard Robinson, Don Mingaye *ed* James Needs, Eric Boyd-Perkins
☆ Peter Cushing, Patrick Allen, Michael Ripper, Oliver Reed, Derek Francis, Milton Reid, Martin Benson, David Lodge, Yvonne Romain

Captain Corelli's Mandolin
US/France/GB 2001 131m DeLuxe Panavision
UIP/Miramax Films/Universal Working Title/ StudioCanal/Free Range (Tim Bevan, Eric Fellner, Kevin Loader, Mark Huffam)
During the Second World War on the island of Cephalonia, a Greek woman is torn between her love for a fisherman and an opera-loving Italian soldier.
Unsatisfactory adaptation of a best-selling novel, with a clash of accents among the multi-national cast and an unconvincing performance from Cage as the gentle Italian officer.
w Shawn Slovo *wd* John Madden *novel* Louis de Bernières *ph* John Toll *m* Stephen Warbeck *pd* Jim Clay *ed* Mick Audsley *cos* Alexandra Byrne
☆ Nicolas Cage (Capt Antonio Corelli), Penelope Cruz (Pelagia), John Hurt (Dr Iannis), Christian Bale (Mandras), David Morrissey (Capt Gunter Weber), Irene Pappas (Drosoula), Piero Maggio (Carlo), Patrick Malahide (Col Barge), Stamatis (Gerasimos Skiadaresis)

'A holiday romance with silly voices… What a droopy, disappointing film this is.' – *Peter Bradshaw, Guardian*
'A cinematic box of chocolates. It looks good and has yummy moments, but leaves you wanting something more substantial.' – *Angie Errigo, Empire*

Captain Eddie
US 1945 107m bw
TCF/Eureka
Eddie Rickenbacker, adrift on a life raft after a plane crash in the Pacific, thinks back on his adventurous life in aviation.
Flat and surprisingly poorly made biopic with little to hold the attention.
w John Tucker Battle *d* Lloyd Bacon *ph* Joe MacDonald *m* Cyril Mockridge
☆ Fred MacMurray, Lynn Bari, Thomas Mitchell, Lloyd Nolan, Charles Bickford

Captain from Castile
US 1947 140m Technicolor
TCF (Lamar Trotti)
A young 15th-century Spaniard hopes for fame and fortune in the New World.
Rather empty and boring adventure epic from a bestseller; high production values produce moments of interest.
w Lamar Trotti *novel* Samuel Shellabarger *d* Henry King *ph* Charles Clarke, Arthur E. Arling *m* Alfred Newman *ad* Richard Day, James Basevi
☆ Tyrone Power, Jean Peters, Lee J. Cobb, Cesar Romero, John Sutton, Antonio Moreno, Thomas Gomez, Alan Mowbray, Barbara Lawrence, George Zucco, Roy Roberts, Marc Lawrence

'The first few reels have flow and a kind of boy's-book splendour; the rest is locomotor ataxia.' – *James Agee*

Alfred Newman

The Captain Hates the Sea *
US 1934 92m bw
Columbia
Crime and comedy on an ocean voyage.
Zany, rather endearing comedy which gave the star his last role.
w Wallace Smith *d* Lewis Milestone *ph* Joseph August
☆ John Gilbert, Victor McLaglen, Walter Connolly, Alison Skipworth, Wynne Gibson, Helen Vinson, Leon Errol, Walter Catlett, Donald Meek, Arthur Treacher, Akim Tamiroff

'A fine cast, excellent comedy relief and expert direction.'–*Variety*
'The best neglected picture in two years.' – *Otis Ferguson, 1936*

Captain Horatio Hornblower RN
GB 1951 117m Technicolor
Warner (Raoul Walsh)
Events from the adventure novels about a 19th-century sailor who outwits the Spaniards and the French and marries his admiral's widow.
Sprawling, plotless sea saga with the cast ill at ease in highly unconvincing sets: no air seems to blow across the decks of the Lydia.
w Ivan Goff, Ben Roberts, Aeneas Mackenzie *novels C. S. Forester d* Raoul Walsh *ph* Guy Green *m* Robert Farnon *ad* Tom Morahan
☆ Gregory Peck, Virginia Mayo, Robert Beatty, James Robertson Justice, Terence Morgan, Moultrie Kelsall, Richard Hearne, Denis O'Dea

'No point makes a strong enough impression to suggest a main line of criticism.' – *Richard Mallett, Punch*

The Captain Is a Lady *
US 1940 63m bw
MGM
A sea captain is forced by ill-fortune to send his wife to an old ladies' home, but he dresses as a woman to be with her.
Absurd-sounding comedy not without a certain lunatic charm.
w Harry Clork *play* Rachel Crothers *d* Robert Sinclair
☆ Charles Coburn, Billie Burke, Beulah Bondi, Dan Dailey, Virginia Grey, Helen Broderick, Helen Westley

Captain Jack
GB 1998 100m colour
Feature Film/Captain Jack (John Goldschmidt)
A sailor sets out on an unseaworthy vessel with an amateur crew to commemorate the 200th anniversary of a voyage from Whitby to the Arctic.
Ramshackle drama, based on a real incident, that unsuccessfully attempts to revive the style of Ealing comedies.
w Jack Rosenthal *article* Nick Davies *d* Robert Young *ph* John McGlashan *m* Richard Harvey *pd* Simon Holland *ed* Edward Mansell
☆ Bob Hoskins, Sadie Frost, Gemma Jones, Anna Massey, Peter McDonald, David Troughton, Maureen Lipman, Patrick Malahide, Michelle Dotrice

'The result is ham-fisted and more than a little irritating.' – *Empire*

Captain January *
US 1936 74m bw
TCF (Darryl F. Zanuck)
A little girl is rescued from a shipwreck by a lighthouse keeper.
Standard Shirley Temple vehicle with pleasing dialogue and numbers.
w Sam Hellman, Gladys Lehman, Harry Tugend *novel* Laura E. Richards *d* David Butler *ph* John F. Seitz *m* Louis Silvers *m/ly* Lew Pollack, Sidney Mitchell, Jack Yellen
☆ *Shirley Temple, Guy Kibbee, Buddy Ebsen*, Slim Summerville, June Lang, Sara Haden, Jane Darwell

'Sentimental, a little depraved, with an appeal interestingly decadent.' – *Graham Greene*

Captain Kidd
US 1945 90m bw
Benedict Bogeaus
A pirate tricks King William III into giving him royal orders, but enemies he believes dead return to see him hanged.
Rather poorly produced vehicle for a star who however rants and raves to some effect.
w Norman Reilly Raine *d* Rowland V. Lee *ph* Archie Stout *m* Werner Janssen
☆ *Charles Laughton*, Randolph Scott, Barbara Britton, Reginald Owen, John Carradine, Gilbert Roland, Sheldon Leonard

Werner Janssen

Captain Kidd and the Slave Girl
US 1954 82m CFI color
Reliance/UA
A scheming earl reprieves Captain Kidd so that he can steal his treasure.
Cut-price swashbuckler with more vigour than some.
w Aubrey Wisberg, Jack Pollexfen *d* Lew Landers
☆ Anthony Dexter, Eva Gabor, Alan Hale Jnr, James Seay

Captain Kronos, Vampire Hunter *
GB 1973 91m colour
Hammer (Albert Fennell, Brian Clemens)
The title explains almost all; in this case he tackles an old vampire crone who becomes young when she sucks blood.
Lively horror yarn with amusing asides.
wd Brian Clemens *ph* Ian Wilson *m* Laurie Johnson *pd* Robert Jones *ed* James Needs
☆ Horst Janson, John Carson, Shane Briant, Caroline Munro, John Cater, Wanda Ventham

Captain Lightfoot
US 1955 92m Technicolor Cinemascope
U-I (Ross Hunter)
Adventures of a 19th-century Irish rebel.
Dullish adventure story with the star ill at ease.
w W. R. Burnett, Oscar Brodney *d* Douglas Sirk *ph* Irving Glassberg *m* Hans Salter
☆ Rock Hudson, Barbara Rush, Jeff Morrow, Kathleen Ryan, Finlay Currie, Denis O'Dea, Geoffrey Toone

Captain Moonlight: see *D'Ye Ken John Peel?*

Captain Nemo and the Underwater City
GB 1969 106m Metrocolor Panavision
MGM/Omnia (Steven Pallos, Bertram Ostrer)
Six survivors from an Atlantic shipwreck are picked up by a mysterious submarine and have adventures in a spectacular underwater city.
Further adventures of Jules Verne's engaging Victorian character from Twenty Thousand Leagues under the Sea. *Here however the general production values are stolid rather than solid, and the script makes heavy weather.*

w Pip Baker, Jane Baker, R. Wright Campbell *d* James Hill *ph* Alan Hume, Egil Woxholt *m* Walter Stott *ad* Bill Andrews
☆ Robert Ryan, Chuck Connors, Bill Fraser, Kenneth Connor, Nanette Newman, John Turner, Luciana Paluzzi, Allan Cuthbertson

Captain Newman MD *
US 1963 126m Eastmancolor
Universal-Brentwood-Reynard (Robert Arthur)

At an army air base during World War II, a psychiatrist has varied success with his patients.
A decidedly curious comedy drama on the fringe of bad taste; it should have turned out better than it does, but will entertain those who like hospital heroics drenched in bitter-sweet sentimentality.
w Richard L. Breen, Phoebe and Henry Ephron *novel* Leo Rosten *d* David Miller *ph* Russell Metty *m* Joseph Gershenson
☆ Gregory Peck, Tony Curtis, Angie Dickinson, Eddie Albert, Bobby Darin, James Gregory, Jane Withers, Bethel Leslie, Robert Duvall, Larry Storch, Robert F. Simon, Dick Sargent
script; Bobby Darin

'Passions run hot and blood runs cold!'
Captain Pirate
US 1952 85m Technicolor
Columbia (Harry Joe Brown)
GB title: *Captain Blood, Fugitive*
A reformed pirate, accused of sacking Cartagena, returns to piracy to discover the perpetrators.
Lively buccaneering programmer with an adequate budget and plenty of high spirits.
w Robert Libbott, Frank Burt, John Meredyth Lucas *novel* *Captain Blood Returns* by Rafael Sabatini *d* Ralph Murphy *ph* Charles Lawton Jnr *m* George Duning
☆ Louis Hayward, Patricia Medina, John Sutton, George Givot, Rex Evans, Ted de Corsia, Charles Irwin

'The only thing Martin wanted was a nice, quiet family vacation. Instead, he got ... Captain Ron.'
Captain Ron
US 1992 100m Technicolor
Touchstone/Touchwood Pacific Partners I (David Permut, Paige Simpson)

An American family inherits an ancient yacht in the Caribbean and hire a dubious one-eyed captain to help them sail it back to the States.
Tedious and indifferently acted comedy, in which the jokes consist of people either falling over or falling into the water.
w John Dwyer, Thom Eberhardt *d* Thom Eberhardt *ph* Daryn Okada *m* Nicholas Pike *pd* William F. Matthews *ed* Tina Hirsch
☆ Kurt Russell, Martin Short, Mary Kay Place, Benjamin Salisbury, Meadow Sisto, Paul Anka
'Inoffensive but unexciting.' – *Variety*
† The film was released direct to video in Britain.

Captain Scarlett
US 1952 75m Technicolor
UA/Craftsman (Howard Dimsdale)
After the Napoleonic wars, southern France is in need of a protector against the villainous Duke of Corlaine. Captain Scarlett rides into action…
Robin Hood in all but name, an old tale retold without much flair.
w Howard Dimsdale *d* Thomas Carr *ph* Charles Carbajal *m* Elias Breeskin
☆ Richard Greene, Leonora Amar, Nedrick Young, Eduardo Noriega

Captain Sinbad *
US/Germany 1963 88m Eastmancolor Wonderscope
King Brothers

Sinbad returns to Baristan and by means of magic deposes a sultan.
Rather splendid adventure fantasy with a European flavour, good trick effects and full-blooded performances.
w Samuel B. West, Harry Relis (Ian McLellan Hunter, Guy Endore) *d* Byron Haskin *ph* Gunther Senftleben, Eugen Shuftan *m* Michel Michelet *ad* Werner and Isabell Schlicting *sp* Tom Howard
☆ Guy Williams, Pedro Armendariz, Heidi Bruhl, Abraham Sofaer

† The script was written under psuedonyms because of the blacklist.

Captains Courageous **
US 1937 116m bw
MGM (Louis D. Lighton)

A spoiled rich boy falls off a cruise liner and lives for a while among fisherfolk who teach him how to live.
Semi-classic Hollywood family film which is not all that enjoyable while it's on but is certainly a good example of the prestige picture of the thirties. (It also happened to be good box-office.)
w John Lee Mahin, Marc Connelly, Dale Van Every *novel* Rudyard Kipling *d* Victor Fleming *ph* Harold Rosson *m* Franz Waxman *ed* Elmo Veron
☆ Spencer Tracy, Lionel Barrymore, Freddie Bartholomew, Mickey Rooney, Melvyn Douglas, Charley Grapewin, Christian Rub, John Carradine, Walter Kingsford, Leo G. Carroll, Charles Trowbridge
'Will not have to go begging for patronage … one of the best pictures of the sea ever made.' – *Variety*
'Another of those grand jobs of movie-making we have come to expect from Hollywood's most profligate studio.' – *Frank S. Nugent, New York Times*
† 1977 brought a TV movie remake, as did 1995, both inferior to the movie.
Spencer Tracy
best picture; script; editing

Captains of the Clouds
US 1942 113m Technicolor
Warner (Hal B. Wallis, William Cagney)
A flippant Canadian Air Force pilot proves his worth under fire.
Recruiting poster heroics, reasonably well done but lacking the vital spark.
w Arthur T. Horman, Richard Macaulay, Norman Reilly Raine *d* Michael Curtiz *ph* Sol Polito, Wilfrid M. Cline *m* Max Steiner *ad* Ted Smith
☆ *James Cagney*, Dennis Morgan, Brenda Marshall, George Tobias, Alan Hale, Reginald Gardiner, Reginald Denny, Paul Cavanagh, Clem Bevans, J. M. Kerrigan
'Pure tribute to the unchanging forcefulness of James Cagney.' – *New York Post*
Sol Polito, Wilfrid M. Cline; Ted Smith

The Captain's Paradise *
GB 1953 89m bw
BL/London (Anthony Kimmins)

The captain of a steamer plying between Gibraltar and Tangier has a wife in each port, one to suit each of his personalities.
Over-dry comedy in which the idea is much funnier than the script. One is left with the memory of a pleasant star performance.
w Alec Coppel, Nicholas Phipps *d* Anthony Kimmins *ph* Ted Scaife *m* Malcolm Arnold
☆ *Alec Guinness*, Celia Johnson, Yvonne de Carlo, Charles Goldner, Miles Malleson, Bill Fraser, Nicholas Phipps, Ferdy Mayne, George Benson
original story (Alec Coppel)

The Captain's Table *
GB 1958 89m Eastmancolor
Rank (Joseph Janni)

A cargo skipper is given command of a luxury liner and has to watch his manners.
Lively adaptation of a frivolous book of obvious jokes, most of which come up quite funny amid the luxurious surroundings.
w John Whiting, Bryan Forbes, Nicholas Phipps *novel* Richard Gordon *d* Jack Lee *ph* Christopher Challis *m* Frank Cordell
☆ *John Gregson*, Peggy Cummins, *Donald Sinden*, *Reginald Beckwith*, Nadia Gray, Richard Wattis, Maurice Denham, Nicholas Phipps, Joan Sims, Miles Malleson

La Captive
France/Belgium 2000 112m colour
Artificial Eye/GeminiArte France/Paradise (Paulo Branco)

aka: *The Captive*
A rich, young, asthmatic man stalks his girlfriend to ensure that she remains faithful to him.
Stiflingly claustrophobic study of an obsessionally possessive person that becomes a trial to watch.
w Chantal Akerman, Eric de Kuyper *inspired by* *La Prisonnière* by Marcel Proust *d* Chantal Akerman *ph* Sabine Lancelin *ad* Christian Marti *ed* Claire Atherton *cos* Nathalie du Roscoat
☆ Stanislas Merhar (Simon), Sylvie Testud (Ariane), Olivia Bonamy (Andrée), Liliane Rovere (Françoise), Françoise Bertin (Grandmother), Aurore Clément (Lea)
'Feels like an authentic art-house movie brought out of the 1960s deep freeze and only partially thawed' – *Alexander Walker*

The Captive City **
US 1951 91m bw
UA/Aspen (Theron Warth)
Small-town corruption imposed by the Mafia is revealed by a crusading editor who defies threats to his wife and family and tells all to the Kefauver Commission.
Excellent documentary melodrama made in a style then original, also notable for use of the Hoge deep focus lens.
w *Karl Lamb, Alvin Josephy Jnr* *d* *Robert Wise* *ph* *Lee Garmes* *m* Jerome Moross
☆ John Forsythe, Joan Camden, Harold J. Kennedy, Marjorie Crossland, Victor Sutherland, Ray Teal, Martin Milner, Hal K. Dawson

The Captive City
Italy 1963 110m bw
Paramount
Italian title: *La Città Prigionera*
Rebels keep an assorted group of people captive in an Athens hotel.
Dim would-be thriller which rambles on far too long.
w Guy Elmes, Eric Bercovici, Marc Brandel *novel* John Appleby *d* Joseph Anthony
☆ David Niven, Lea Massari, Ben Gazzara, Daniela Rocca, Martin Balsam, Michael Craig, Percy Herbert

La Captive du Desert
France 1990 101m colour
Artificial Eye/La Sept/Roger Diamantis/St-André-des-Arts/Jean-Bernard Fetoux/SGGC/Jean-Luc Larguler/Titane (Pascale Dauman, Jean-Luc Ormires)
A Frenchwoman is held captive in the desert by nomadic tribesmen.
A minimalist movie, based on a true story, with little dialogue or action but a great deal of sand.
wd Raymond Depardon *ph* Raymond Depardon *m* Jean-Jacques Lemtre *ed* Roger Ikhief, Camille Cotte, Pascale Charolais
☆ Sandrine Bonnaire, Dobi Kor, Fadi Taha, Dobi Wachink, Badei Barka
'Half the audience with whom I watched the film left before the end while the other half remained, fascinated by the vividness of the photography and the highly personal nature of the film. It is one of those in which nothing, and everything, happens.' – *Derek Malcolm, Guardian*

The Captive Heart **
GB 1946 108m bw
Ealing (Michael Relph)

Stories of life among British officers in a German POW camp, especially of a Czech who has stolen the papers of a dead Britisher.
Archetypal POW drama lacing an almost poetic treatment with humour and melodrama.
w Angus MacPhail, Guy Morgan *story* Patrick Kirwan *d* *Basil Dearden* *ph* Douglas Slocombe *m* Alan Rawsthorne *ad* Michael Relph
☆ Michael Redgrave, *Jack Warner*, Basil Radford, Mervyn Johns, Jimmy Hanley, Gordon Jackson, Ralph Michael, Derek Bond, Karel Stepanek, Guy Middleton, Jack Lambert, Gladys Henson, Rachel Kempson, Meriel Forbes
'A warm, emotional, intensely human document, entitled to rate among the best twenty films of the last ten years.' – *News of the World*

Captive Hearts: see *Fire with Fire (1986)*

Captive Hearts
US 1987 97m Metrocolor
MGM/Kurissama (John A. Kuri)

Rescued from instant execution and put to work by the headman of a remote village after being shot down over Japan in 1944, an American soldier falls in love with a local woman
Simple-minded romance that lacks dramatic impetus or interest.
w Patrick N. Morita, John A. Kuri *story* *The Hawk* by Sargon Tamimi *d* Paul Almond *ph* Thomas Vamos *m* Osamu Kitajima *pd* François de Lucy, Steve Sardanis *ed* Yurij Luhovy
☆ Noriyuki (Pat) Morita, Chris Makepeace, Michael Sarrazin, Mari Sato, Seth Sakai, Denis Akiyama

'A human form with animal instincts!'
Captive Wild Woman
US 1943 60m bw
Universal
A doctor finds a way of developing the glands of an ape and turning it into a beautiful girl.
Lamebrain horror item which amazingly spawned two sequels, Jungle Woman *(1944) and* Jungle Captive *(1945).*
w Griffin Jay, Henry Sucher *d* Edward Dmytryk *ed* Milton Carruth
☆ Evelyn Ankers, Acquanetta, John Carradine, Martha Vickers, Milburn Stone

Captives
GB 1994 100m Rank Colour
Entertainment/BBC/Distant Horizon (David M. Thompson)

A female dentist is blackmailed after she begins an affair with a convicted murderer.
An oddly unconvincing melodrama, in which the contrivances of the plot prevent the development of character.
w Frank Deasy *d* Angela Pope *ph* Remi Adefarasin *m* Colin Towns *pd* Stuart Walker *ed* Dave King
☆ Julia Ormond, Tim Roth, Richard Hawley, Jeff Nuttall, Kenneth Cope, Keith Allen, Bill Moody, Peter Capaldi
'A botched job, with many an unfilled plot cavity.' – *Guardian*

The Capture
US 1950 91m bw
RKO/Showtime (Niven Busch)
On the run from the police, a former oil company field boss explains to a priest how he, by accident, came to be a fugitive.
Run-of-the-mill melodrama, all talk and no action.
w Niven Busch *d* John Sturges *ph* Edward Cronjager *m* Daniele Amfitheatrof *pd* William E. Flannery
☆ Lew Ayres, Teresa Wright, Victor Jory, Jacqueline White, Victor Hunt, Edwin Rand, Duncan Renaldo

Captured
US 1933 72m bw
Warner
A prisoner-of-war discovers that his best friend was his wife's lover.
Turgid and heavy-going early variation on a theme which would become very familiar indeed; the stars couldn't save it.
w Edward Chodorov *novel* Sir Philip Gibbs *d* Roy Del Ruth
☆ Leslie Howard, Paul Lukas, Douglas Fairbanks Jnr, Margaret Lindsay, J. Carrol Naish, Arthur Hohl
'Too many obviously adverse ingredients, chiefly story, to chalk this one up as a winner … at best its earnings shape up as spotty.' – *Variety*

'Is it a phantom, a demon, or the devil himself?'
The Car
US 1977 98m Technicolor Panavision
Universal (Marvin Birdt, Elliot Silverstein)

A small south-western town is terrorized by a driverless car which may be a creation of the devil.
Silly suspenser with a draggy midsection.
w Dennis Shryack, Michael Butler, Lane Slate *d* Elliot Silverstein *ph* Gerald Hirschfeld *m* Leonard Rosenman

☆ James Brolin, Kathleen Lloyd, John Marley, John Rubinstein, R.G. Armstrong

Car of Dreams
GB 1935 72m bw
Gaumont British (Michael Balcon)
A rich man's son buys a car for one of his father's factory girls.
Silly comedy with sillier music, remade from a German original.
w Austin Melford *d* Austin Melford, Graham Cutts *ph* Mutz Greenbaum *m* Mischa Spoliansky *ad* Alfred Junge
☆ John Mills, Grete Mosheim, Mark Lester, Robertson Hare, Norah Howard

Car Trouble
GB 1986 93m colour
Thorn EMI/GTO/Goldfarb (Howard Malin, Gregory J. DeSantis)
A woman having an affair with a car salesman finds herself sexually locked to him in her husband's new vehicle.
This weird premise for a comedy rings up remarkably few laughs.
w James Whaley, A. J. Tipping *d* David Green *ph* Michael Garfath
☆ Julie Walters, Ian Charleson, Stratford Johns, Vincenzo Ricotta

Car Wash
US 1976 96m Technicolor
Universal
Various eccentrics congregate around the Dee Luxe Car Wash.
Zany ethnic (black) comedy with little rhyme or reason in its development but a certain vigour in some of its sketches. A subsequent TV series didn't last.
w Joel Schumacher *d* Michael Schultz
☆ Franklyn Ajaye, Sully Boyar, Richard Pryor, Ivan Dixon, Antonio Fargas, Tracy Reed
'Its specialty is yanking laughs by having blacks do dirtier versions of the standard pranks that naughty kids used to do in comedies.' – *Pauline Kael*

Caravaggio *
GB 1986 89m Technicolor
BFI/Channel 4/Nicholas Ward-Jackson (Sarah Radclyffe)
An imaginary biopic of the Italian painter who died in 1610, with emphasis on homosexual models, a variety of scandals, and jokey anachronisms.
A classic for the gay crowd; something of a mystery for everyone else.
wd Derek Jarman *ph* Gabriel Beristain *m* Simon Fisher Turner *pd* Christopher Hobbs
☆ Nigel Terry, Sean Bean, Garry Cooper, Spencer Leigh
'It rises above its financial restrictions to prove that less can be a lot more.' – *Variety*

Caravan
GB 1946 122m bw
Gainsborough (Harold Huth)
A young man on a mission in Spain is left for dead by emissaries of his rival in love; he is nursed back to health by a gypsy girl who falls in love with him.
Artificial, romantic, high-flown period tosh without the courage of its lack of convictions. At the time, an exhibitor's dream.
w Roland Pertwee *novel* Lady Eleanor Smith *d* Arthur Crabtree *ph* Stephen Dade
☆ Stewart Granger, Jean Kent, Anne Crawford, *Robert Helpmann*, Dennis Price, Gerard Heinz, Enid Stamp-Taylor, David Horne, John Salew

Caravan: see *Himalaya (1999)*

Caravan to Vaccares
GB/France 1974 98m Eastmancolor Panavision
Crowndale (Geoffrey Reeve)
An American drifter on the Riviera is employed to escort a mysterious Hungarian to New York.
Lumpy Alistair MacLean action thriller, all a bit déjà vu.
w Paul Wheeler *d* Geoffrey Reeve *ph* Frederic Tammes *m* Stanley Myers
☆ David Birney, Charlotte Rampling, Michel Lonsdale, Marcel Bozzuffi, Michael Bryant
'An undernourished plot advanced only by a series of venerable clichés.' – *MFB*
'The biggest load of schoolboy hokum since Boy's Own Paper ceased circulation.' – *Michael Billington, Illustrated London News*

Caravans
US/Iran 1978 123m Technicolor Panavision
Ibex/FIDCI (Elmo Williams)
In the Middle East in 1948, a junior diplomat is sent to bring back the daughter of a US politician, who has married an Arab, left him, and joined a Bedouin caravan.
Curiously halting succession of pretty pictures and not much plot; what there is tends to take second place to philosophy and eastern promise.
w Nancy Voyles Crawford, Thomas A. MacMahon, Lorraine Williams *novel* James Michener *d* James Fargo *ph* Douglas Slocombe *m* Mike Batt
☆ Anthony Quinn, Michael Sarrazin, Jennifer O'Neill, Christopher Lee, Joseph Cotten, Barry Sullivan, Jeremy Kemp
'A tiresome exercise in anti-climax.' – *Tim Pulleine, MFB*
† The film cost 14 million dollars and is said to have been financed by the Shah of Iran.

Carbine Williams
US 1952 93m bw
MGM (Armand Deutsch)
An imprisoned bootlegger perfects a new gun and is pardoned.
Flat fictionalization of a true story, with the star miscast.
w Art Cohn *d* Richard Thorpe *ph* William Mellor *m* Conrad Salinger
☆ James Stewart, Jean Hagen, Wendell Corey, Carl Benton Reid, Paul Stewart, Otto Hulett, James Arness

Carbon Copy
US 1981 91m Metrocolor Panavision
Hemdale/RKO (Stanley Shapiro, Carter de Haven)
An executive is shocked when his long-lost son turns out to be black.
Stale comedy. The producers clearly think the basic idea worth ramming home a score of times; the characterization is thin and the production undernourished.
w Stanley Shapiro *d* Michael Schultz *ph* Fred J. Koenekamp *m* Bill Conti
☆ George Segal, Susan Saint James, Jack Warden, Dick Martin, Denzel Washington, Paul Winfield
'It makes *Guess Who's Coming to Dinner?* look like a tract for the nineties.' – *Derek Malcolm, Guardian*

'He's the cheekiest man in town!'
The Card **
GB 1952 91m bw
Rank/British Film Makers (John Bryan)
US title: *The Promoter*
A bright young clerk from the potteries finds many ingenious ways of improving his bank account and his place in society.
Pleasing period comedy with the star in a made-to-measure role and excellent production values.
w Eric Ambler *novel* Arnold Bennett *d Ronald Neame ph* Oswald Morris *m* William Alwyn *ad T. Hopwell Ash*
☆ *Alec Guinness, Glynis Johns*, Petula Clark, *Valerie Hobson*, Edward Chapman, Veronica Turleigh, Gibb McLaughlin, Frank Pettingell

Card of Fate: see *Le Grand Jeu*

Cardboard Cavalier *
GB 1949 96m bw
Rank/Two Cities (Walter Forde)
In Cromwellian England, royalists commission a barrow boy to carry a secret letter. Helped by Nell Gwynn, he succeeds after encounters with a castle ghost and custard pies.
A pantomime crossed with an Aldwych farce in a period setting. It failed at the time but now seems a brave try, with nice judgment all round.
w Noel Langley *d Walter Forde ph* Jack Hildyard *m* Lambert Williamson
☆ *Sid Field, Margaret Lockwood*, Mary Clare, Jerry Desmonde, Claude Hulbert, Irene Handl, Brian Worth, Edmund Willard (Cromwell)

Cardiac Arrest
US 1980 80m DeLuxe
Film Ventures (Richard Helzberg)
A murderer in San Francisco cuts out the hearts of his victims.
Trivial slasher movie.
☆ Gerry Goodrow, Mike Chan, Max Gail, Susan O'Connell, Ray Reinhardt

Cardigan's Last Case: see *State's Attorney*

The Cardinal *
US 1963 175m Technicolor Panavision 70
Gamma/Otto Preminger
A 1917 ordinand becomes a Boston curate, a fighter of the Ku Klux Klan, a Rome diplomat, and finally gets a cardinal's hat.
Heavy-going documentary melodrama with many interesting sequences marred by lack of cohesion, too much grabbing at world problems, and over-sensational personal asides.
w Robert Dozier *novel* Henry Morton Robinson *d Otto Preminger ph* Leon Shamroy *m* Jerome Moross *pd* Lyle Wheeler *titles* Saul Bass
☆ Tom Tryon, *Carol Lynley*, Dorothy Gish, Maggie MacNamara, Cecil Kellaway, John Saxon, *John Huston*, Robert Morse, Burgess Meredith, Jill Haworth, Raf Vallone, Tullio Carminati, Ossie Davis, Chill Wills, Arthur Hunnicutt and also Murray Hamilton, Patrick O'Neal, Romy Schneider
'Very probably the last word in glossy dishonesty posturing as serious art.' – *John Simon*
'Mere and sheer wide screen Technicolor movie.' – *Stanley Kauffmann*
Otto Preminger; Leon Shamroy; John Huston

'To thwart a king's passion, he gambled the fate of a nation!'
Cardinal Richelieu *
US 1935 83m bw
Twentieth Century (Darryl F. Zanuck)
Fictionalized biography of the unscrupulous cardinal who was the grey eminence behind Louis XIII.
One of George Arliss's better star vehicles, with not much conviction but excellent production values.
w Maude Howell, Cameron Rogers, W. P. Lipscomb *d* Rowland V. Lee *ph* Peverell Marley *m* Alfred Newman
☆ George Arliss, Maureen O'Sullivan, Edward Arnold, Cesar Romero
'In selecting the churchly cardinal of Bulwer-Lytton rather than the cavalier-cardinal beloved of Dumas, they have lost romance and dash but gained compensating dignity ... a fine technical production.' – *Variety*
† Nunnally Johnson, who wrote the original script, asked for his name to be removed from the credits because he objected to the way Arliss rewrote his lines.

The Care Bears' Adventure In Wonderland!
Canada 1987 75m colour
Fox/Nelvana Productions (Michael Hirsch, Patrick Loubert, Clive A. Smith)
The Care Bears go through the looking glass with Alice.
Undemanding and uninteresting whimsy for the under-sixes.
w Susi Snooks, John DeKlein *story* Peter Sauder *d* Raymond Jafelice *m* Trish Cullen, John Sebastian
☆ Featuring the voices of Colin Fox, Bob Dermer, Eva Almos, Dan Hennessy, Jim Henshaw

The Care Bears Movie
US 1985 75m colour
Nelvana (Michael Hirsch, Patrick Loubert, Clive Smith)
Magical bears combat an evil spirit who aims to make everybody miserable.
Cartoon feature, sluggishly animated and narrated, with appeal to nobody over five years old. Produced as a back-up to a range of toys.
w Peter Sauder *d* Arna Selznick *m* John Sebastian
☆ Featuring the voices of Mickey Rooney, Georgia Engel, Harry Dean Stanton

Care of the Spitfire Grill: see *The Spitfire Grill*

Career *
US 1959 105m bw
Paramount/Hal B. Wallis (Paul Nathan)
An actor from the midwest finally gets his chance in New York.
A location melodrama with the feel of a documentary, well played but slow and rather indeterminate.
w James Lee *play* James Lee *d* Joseph Anthony *ph* Joseph LaShelle *m* Franz Waxman
☆ Anthony Franciosa, Dean Martin, Shirley MacLaine, Carolyn Jones, Joan Blackman, Robert Middleton, Frank McHugh, Donna Douglas
Joseph LaShelle

Career Girls *
GB 1997 87m Metrocolor
Film Four/Thin Man/Matrix (Simon Channing-Williams)
Two flatmates who studied at the North London Polytechnic meet again 10 years later to recall their past times together.
With a cast twitching away like contestants at a St Vitus's dance marathon, this is an intensely caricatured, unenlightening account of student life and its aftermath.
wd Mike Leigh *ph* Dick Pope *m* Marianne Jean-Baptiste, Tony Remy *pd* Eve Stewart *ed* Robin Sales
☆ Katrin Cartlidge, Lynda Steadman, Kate Byers, Mark Benton, Andy Serkis, Joe Tucker, Margot Stanley, Michael Hay
'A masterly observation of the foibles of the human condition, rendered with an incisive bite and delivered with a boisterous wit.' – *Christopher Hemblade, Empire*
'Manages to be bleak, lightweight and histrionic at the same time. Even Leigh aficionados might balk at such relentless toothlessness.' – *John Diamond, New Statesman*

Career Opportunities
US 1991 85m DeLuxe Panavision
Universal/Hughes Entertainment (John Hughes, A. Hunt Lowry)
A young nightwatchman outwits thieves trying to rob a department store.
Tired teen comedy that runs out of jokes long before the end.
w John Hughes *d* Bryan Gordon *ph* Don McAlpine *m* Thomas Newman *pd* Paul Sylbert *ed* Glenn Farr, Peck Prior
☆ Frank Whaley, Jennifer Connelly, Dermot Mulroney, Kieran Mulroney, John M. Jackson, Jenny O'Hara, Noble Willingham, Barry Corbin, John Candy (uncredited)
'Plenty of absorbing characters, smart, snappy dialog and delightful stretches of comic foolery.' – *Variety*

Carefree *
US 1938 85m bw
RKO (Pandro S. Berman)
A humourless lawyer sends his undecided girlfriend to an alienist, with whom she falls in love.
Slight, frothy comedy musical; quite palatable, but it signalled the end of the Astaire-Rogers series.
w Allan Scott, Ernest Pagano *d* Mark Sandrich *ph* Robert de Grasse *m/ly* Irving Berlin *md* Victor Baravalle *ch* Hermes Pan *ad* Van Nest Polglase
☆ Fred Astaire, Ginger Rogers, Ralph Bellamy, Luella Gear, Clarence Kolb, Jack Carson, Franklin Pangborn, Walter Kingsford, Hattie McDaniel
'Perhaps their poorest musical ... a disappointing story and the stars alone may save it.' – *Variety*
♫ 'I Used to Be Colour Blind'; 'The Yam'; 'The Night Is Filled with Music'
Victor Baravalle; Van Nest Polglase; song 'Change Partners'

Careful
Canada 1992 100m colour
ICA/Greg and Tracy Film Ministry (Greg Klymkiw, Tracy Traeger)
Sex and death engulf two families living in constant danger of being killed by Alpine avalanches.
A deliberately over-the-top melodramatic concoction, a heady stew of rape, incest, requited and unrequited love, a deformed child kept hidden in an attic and ghosts bringing warnings of doom. It's a low-budget camp extravaganza that can amuse, but can as easily infuriate by its knowing air.
w George Toles, Guy Maddin *d* Guy Maddin *ph* Guy Maddin *m* John McCulloch *pd* Guy Maddin *ed* Guy Maddin
☆ Kyle McCulloch, Gosia Dobrowolska, Sarah Neville, Brent Neale, Paul Cox, Victor Cowie, Jackie Burroughs
'In a film which can afford real animals but not real mountains, a couple of goats running up a slope – swathed in dry ice, shot in purple or blue monochrome and captioned to tell us the altitude – stand in for the Alps.' – *Claire Monk, Sight and Sound*

Careful, Soft Shoulder *
US 1942 69m bw
TCF (Walter Morosco)
A Washington socialite becomes a spy for both sides.
Modest, slightly unusual second feature which over the years has gathered for itself more reputation than it really deserves.
wd Oliver H. P. Garrett *ph* Charles Clarke *m* Leigh Harline, Emil Newman
☆ Virginia Bruce, James Ellison, Aubrey Mather, Sheila Ryan, Ralph Byrd

Careless Lady
US 1932 76m bw
Fox
A young girl from the country pretends to be a married society woman and finds herself with a husband she doesn't want.
It was the scriptwriter who was careless: the story doesn't make much sense.
w Guy Bolton *story* Reita Lambert *d* Kenneth MacKenna
☆ Joan Bennett, John Boles, Minna Gombell, Weldon Heyburn, Raul Roulien, Fortunio Bonanova, Josephine Hull
'Reaching house averages will be beyond expectations regardless of campaign.' – *Variety*

The Caretaker *
GB 1964 105m bw
Caretaker Films (Michael Birkett)
US title: *The Guest*
Two brothers invite a revolting tramp to share their attic.
Rather doleful filming of the fashionable play with its non-plot, irregular conceits and interesting interplay of character. It remains a theatrical experience.
w Harold Pinter *d* Clive Donner *ph* Nicolas Roeg *m* Ron Grainer
☆ Alan Bates, Robert Shaw, Donald Pleasence

'Now the screen tells what makes a woman – and what breaks her!'
The Caretakers *
US 1963 97m bw
UA/Hall Bartlett
GB title: *Borderlines*
The interrelationship of several cases in a state mental hospital.
Rather hysterical melodrama, lacking in the stature required for its subject, but sometimes perversely entertaining.
w Henry F. Greenberg *novel* Daniel Telfer *d* Hall Bartlett *ph* *Lucien Ballard* *m* Elmer Bernstein
☆ Polly Bergen, Robert Stack, Joan Crawford, Diane McBain, Janis Paige, Van Williams, Robert Vaughn, Herbert Marshall, Constance Ford
Academy Award nomination: Lucien Ballard

The Carey Treatment *
US 1972 101m Metrocolor Panavision
MGM (William Belasco)
A Boston pathologist investigating the death of an abortion victim becomes the potential murder victim of a father turned killer.
Pretentious thriller with a tendency to make moral points among the bloodshed; vigorously but variably made.
w James P. Bonner (Irving Ravetch, Harriet Frank Jnr, John D. F. Black) *novel* *A Case of Need* by Jeffrey Hudson (Michael Crichton) *d* Blake Edwards *ph* Frank Stanley *m* Roy Budd
☆ James Coburn, Jennifer O'Neill, Skye Aubrey, Pat Hingle, Dan O'Herlihy, Elizabeth Allen, Alex Dreier, Regis Toomey

Cargo of Innocents: see *Stand By for Action*

Cargo to Capetown
US 1950 84m bw
Columbia
A merchant ship captain shanghais his friend on a long voyage.
Routine, competently staged thick ear.
w Lionel Houser *d* Earl McEvoy
☆ Broderick Crawford, John Ireland, Ellen Drew, Edgar Buchanan, Ted de Corsia

Caribbean
US 1952 94m Technicolor
Paramount/Pine-Thomas (William H. Pine, William C. Thomas)
GB title: *Caribbean Gold*
An 18th-century pirate captures the nephew of his old enemy.
Adequate but not very exciting swashbuckler with fair production values.
w Frank L. Moss, Edward Ludwig *d* Edward Ludwig *ph* Lionel Lindon *m* Lucien Cailliet
☆ John Payne, Arlene Dahl, Cedric Hardwicke, Francis L. Sullivan, Dennis Hoey

Caribbean Gold: see *Caribbean*

The Caribbean Mystery
US 1945 65m bw
William Girard/TCF
A retired cop investigates the disappearance of several geologists on an oil company payroll.
Modest mystery, previously filmed as Murder in Trinidad.
w W. Scott Darling *novel* John W. Vandercook *d* Robert Webb
☆ James Dunn, Sheila Ryan, Edward Ryan, Jackie Paley, Reed Hadley

The Cariboo Trail
US 1950 80m Cinecolor
TCF (Nat Holt)
A cattle rancher from Montana takes his cows along when he goes prospecting for gold in British Columbia.
In its brief length, it manages to cram just about every standard Western ingredient – cowboys and Indians, fist and gun fights, cows and gold, a wicked town boss and a glamorous saloon owner – without displaying any originality; its underlying theme, the appropriation of Indian lands, no longer seems as heroic as it once did.
w Frank Gruber *story* John Rhodes Sturdy *d* Edwin L. Marin *ph* Fred Jackman *m* Paul Sawtell *ad* Arthur Lonergan *ed* Philip Martin
☆ Randolph Scott, George 'Gabby' Hayes, Bill Williams, Victor Jory, Karin Booth, Dale Robertson

'A dream called freedom. A nightmare called Nicaragua.'
Carla's Song *
GB/Germany/Spain 1996 125m Metrocolor
Polygram/Channel 4/GFF/Parallax/Road Movies/Tornasol (Sally Hibbin)
In the mid-80s, a Glaswegian bus driver falls in love with a Nicaraguan woman and returns with her to her homeland in search of her missing boyfriend.
A political and personal drama played out against the civil war in Nicaragua, it too often lapses into confused agitprop to convince an audience of its relevance or point.
w Paul Laverty *d* Ken Loach *ph* Barry Ackroyd *m* George Fenton *pd* Martin Johnson *ed* Jonathan Morris
☆ Robert Carlyle, Oyanka Cabezas, Scott Glenn, Salvador Espinoza, Louise Goodall, Richard Loza, Gary Lewis
'What the film clearly intends is a lest-we-forget drama, and this is an angry film, understandably so. But, strangely, the angrier it gets, the less effective it becomes.' – *Derek Malcolm*

Carlito's Way *
US 1993 145m DeLuxe Panavision
Universal (Martin Bregman, Willi Baer, Michael A. Bregman)
A drug dealer finds it tough when he tries to go straight.
A good, if unoriginal, gangster movie with some action sequences that add a little distinction; it would benefit, though, from being shorter.
w David Koepp *novels* *Carlito's Way, After Hours* by *Edwin Torres* *d* Brian de Palma *ph* Stephen H. Burum *m* Patrick Doyle *pd* Richard Sylbert *ed* Bill Pankow, Kristina Boden
☆ Al Pacino, Sean Penn, Penelope Ann Miller, John Leguizamo, Ingrid Rogers, Luis Guzman, James Rebhorn, Viggo Mortensen
'Handsomely made, expertly directed and colorfully acted, it should satisfy action buffs and slightly more sophisticated audiences.' – *Variety*
'An old-style gangster movie with some neat contemporary knobs on.' – *Derek Malcolm*

Carlton-Browne of the FO
GB 1958 88m bw
British Lion/Charter Films (John Boulting)
US title: *Man in a Cocked Hat*
When valuable mineral deposits are found in a small British colony, the diplomat sent to cement good relations does quite the reverse.
Hit-or-miss farcical comedy several rungs below the Ealing style, with all concerned in poor form.
wd Jeffrey Dell, Roy Boulting *ph* Max Greene *m* John Addison
☆ Terry-Thomas, Peter Sellers, Ian Bannen, Thorley Walters, Raymond Huntley, John Le Mesurier, Luciana Paluzzi, Miles Malleson, Kynaston Reeves, Marie Lohr

Carmen **
Spain 1983 101m Eastmancolor
Emiliano Piedra Productions/Television Española (Emiliano Piedra)
A rehearsal for the ballet *Carmen* finds dancers playing out in reality the parts of the drama.
Enjoyable but exhausting melodrama with elements of The Red Shoes; *meticulous choreography and direction are its chief assets.*
w Carlos Saura, Antonio Gades *novel* Prosper Mérimée *d* *Carlos Saura* *ph* Teo Escamilla *m* Paco de Lucia *ad* Felix Murcia *ed* Pedro del Rey
☆ Antonio Gades, Laura del Sol, Paco de Lucia, Cristina Hoyos
'Extremely enjoyable, but lacks the edge that would make it in any way compelling.' – *Jill Forbes, MFB*
Academy Award nomination: best foreign film
BAFTA: best foreign film

Carmen **
Italy/France 1984 152m Eastmancolor Panavision
Opera/Gaumont (Patrice Ledoux)
A luxuriantly filmed version of Bizet's opera, generally received with critical rapture.
d Francesco Rosi ph Pasqualino de Santis pd Enrico Job
☆ Julia Migenes-Johnson, Placido Domingo, Ruggero Raimondi
† Silent versions stretch back to 1915 – that one starred Geraldine Farrar the opera singer (in a silent movie, by producer Cecil B. de Mille's whim).

Carmen Jones *
US 1954 105m DeLuxe Cinemascope
TCF (Otto Preminger)
A factory girl marries a soldier, and is strangled by him for infidelity.
Black American updating of Bizet's opera, not really satisfactory but given full marks for trying, though the main singing is dubbed and the effect remains doggedly theatrical.
w Harry Kleiner *d* Otto Preminger *ph* Sam Leavitt *md* Herschel Burke Gilbert *ly* Oscar Hammerstein II *titles* *Saul Bass*
☆ *Dorothy Dandridge*, Harry Belafonte, *Pearl Bailey*, Olga James, Joe Adams, Roy Glenn, Nick Stewart, Diahann Carroll, Brock Peters
'All one regrets is that the director has been unable to impose a unifying style on this promising material.' – *Gavin Lambert*
† Joe Adams's vocals were dubbed by Marvin Hayes, Harry Belafonte's by LeVerne Hutcherson, Diahann Carroll's by Bernice Peterson, and Dorothy Dandridge's by Marilyn Horne.
Academy Award nomination: Herschel Burke Gilbert; Dorothy Dandridge

Carmin Profond: see *Deep Crimson*

Carnage: see *A Bay of Blood*

Carnal Knowledge *
US 1971 97m Technicolor Panavision
Avco Embassy/Icarus (Mike Nichols)
A college student embarks on an enthusiastic and varied sex life but by middle age is bored and empty.
Hampered by an unsuitable wide screen, this pretentious but fragmented comedy drama is embarrassingly conscious of its own daring in subject and language, and good performances are weighed down by an unsubtle script and tricksy direction.
w Jules Feiffer *d* Mike Nichols *ph* Giuseppe Rotunno *m* various songs *pd* Richard Sylbert
☆ Jack Nicholson, *Arthur Garfunkel*, Candice Bergen, *Ann-Margret*, Rita Moreno
Academy Award nomination: Ann-Margret

Carne Tremula: see *Live Flesh*

Carnegie Hall
US 1947 134m bw
Federal Films (Boris Morros, William Le Baron)
The story of New York's music centre, based on a fiction about a cleaner who finally becomes a concert organizer when her son is a famous pianist.
Slim and risible excuse for a classical concert, featuring among others Bruno Walter, Leopold Stokowski, Artur Rubinstein, Jascha Heifetz, Lily Pons, Rise Stevens, Ezio Pinza, Jan Peerce, Harry James, Vaughn Monroe and the New York Philharmonic Symphony Orchestra.
w Karl Kamb *d* Edgar G. Ulmer *ph* William Miller
☆ Marsha Hunt, William Prince, Frank McHugh, Martha O'Driscoll
'The thickest and sourest mess of musical mulligatawny I have yet had to sit down to.' – *James Agee*

Un Carnet de Bal **
France 1937 135m bw
Lévy/Strauss/Sigma
aka: *Life Dances On*
A rich widow seeks her partners at a ball she remembers from her youth, finding that they are all failures and the ball a village hop.
Considering its fame, this is a lumpy porridge of a picture, good in parts but often slow, pretentious and banal. Its gallery of actors is, however, unique.
w Jean Sarment, Pierre Wolff, Bernard Zimmer, Henri Jeanson, Julien Duvivier *d* Julien Duvivier *ph* Michel Kelber, Philippe Agostini *m* Maurice Jaubert
☆ Marie Bell, Françoise Rosay, *Louis Jouvet*, *Raimu*, *Harry Baur*, *Fernandel*, *Pierre Blanchar*
'Recent winner of the Mussolini Cup is loaded with top names, but it is not the film of the year ... it tries to take in too much and takes too long to put across.' – *Variety*
† The film's international success took Duvivier to Hollywood, where he half-remade it as *Lydia* and went on to other multi-story films such as *Tales of Manhattan* and *Flesh and Fantasy*.

Les Carnets de Major Thompson: see *The Diary of Major Thompson*

Carnival
US 1934 77m bw
Columbia
A widowed puppeteer takes custody of his child, which is sought by the maternal grandfather, and seeks anonymity in a circus.
Curious sentimental melodrama with the stars shown in an unusual light.
w Robert Riskin *d* Walter Lang

☆ Lee Tracy, Jimmy Durante, Sally Eilers, Dickie Walters, Thomas Jackson, Florence Rice, Lucille Ball

'This should hold its own, though it probably will not climb to big grosses.' – *Variety*

Carnival
GB 1946 93m bw
Rank/Two Cities (John Sutro, William Sassoon)
In the 1890s, a ballet dancer marries a dour Cornish farmer, who shoots her when her erstwhile lover comes after her.
Flimsy screen version of a solidly old-fashioned romantic drama.
w Eric Maschwitz *novel* Compton Mackenzie *d* Stanley Haynes *ph* Guy Green
☆ Sally Gray, Michael Wilding, Bernard Miles, Cathleen Nesbitt, Stanley Holloway, Jean Kent, Nancy Price, Hazel Court, Brenda Bruce, Catherine Lacey
† The story was previously filmed in 1931, as *Dance Pretty Lady*, with Ann Casson and Carl Harbord. The 1931 film *Carnival*, with Matheson Lang, is based on a story identical to *Men Are Not Gods* and *A Double Life*: an actor becomes obsessed with the part of Othello and strangles his wife.

Carnival in Costa Rica
US 1947 97m Technicolor
TCF (William A. Bacher)
A young Costa Rican, engaged to an American singer, returns home to find that his parents expect him to marry his childhood sweetheart.
Decidedly rundown musical in which incessant carnival largely supplants the wispy plot.
w John Larkin, Samuel Hoffenstein, Elizabeth Reinhardt *d* Gregory Ratoff *ph* Harry Jackson *m/ly* Harry Ruby, Ernesto Lecuona *ch* Leonid Massine
☆ Dick Haymes, Vera-Ellen, Celeste Holm, J. Carrol Naish, Cesar Romero

Carnival in Flanders: see *La Kermesse Héroïque*

'Is there death after life?'
Carnival of Souls
US 1962 80m bw
Herts-Lion (Herk Harvey)
After an accident, a lady ghost emerges to become the new church organist.
Absurd but occasionally compelling independently made horror film which would have been better in half-hour form.
w John Clifford *d* Herk Harvey *ph* Maurice Prather *m* Gene Moore *ed* Dan Palmquist, Bill de Jarnette
☆ Candace Hilligoss, Herk Harvey, Francis Feist, Sidney Berger

'Has the power to detach you from your surroundings and put you in the middle of its own distinctive nowhere.' – *Terrence Rafferty, New Yorker*

† Made in Kansas, allegedly for less than 100,000 dollars.

Carnival of Terror: see *The Funhouse*

Carnival of Thieves: see *The Caper of the Golden Bulls*

Carnival Story
US/Germany 1954 95m Technicolor
The King Brothers
A starving girl becomes a trapezist at a German circus and stirs up jealousy among her partners.
Bleak reworking of The Three Maxims *(qv), reworked again with more expertise in* Trapeze *(qv); this version is a cheap and unattractive co-production.*
w Kurt Neumann, Hans Jacoby *d* Kurt Neumann *ph* Ernest Haller *m* Willy Schmidt-Gentner
☆ Anne Baxter, Steve Cochran, Lyle Bettger, George Nader, Jay C. Flippen

'63 million years ago they ruled the Earth. They're back, and it's no theme park!'
Carnosaur
US 1993 83m Foto-Kem
New Horizons (Mike Elliott)
A scientist breeds giant meat-eating mutant chickens in an attempt to recreate dinosaurs and replace humans by a kinder species.
Cheap attempt to cash in on the Jurassic Park *craze from Roger Corman's outfit, recast as a conventional, gory, monster-on-the-loose, mad-scientist horror pic: nasty, brutish and, fortunately, short.*
wd Adam Simon *novel* Harry Adam Knight (John Brosnan) *ph* Keith Holland *m* Nigel Holton *pd* Aaron Osborne *ed* Richard Genter *sp* John Buechler, Magical Media Industries, Alan Lasky
☆ Diane Ladd, Raphael Sbarge, Jennifer Runyon, Harrison Page, Ned Bellamy, Clint Howard

'This breezy outing is a not-very-filling popcorn treat. Predictably plotted with bargain-basement effects, it's a serviceable programmer.' – *Variety*

Carny
US 1980 105m Technicolor
Lorimar/Jonathan Taplin (Robbie Robertson)
Three wacky characters join a travelling carnival.
Sordid, sexy melodrama which seems to be doing a Jules and Jim with no holds barred. Not badly made, but full of people one would cross the road to avoid.
w Thomas Baum *story* Phoebe Kaylor, Robert Kaylor, Robbie Robertson *d* Robert Kaylor *ph* Harry Stradling Jnr *m* Alex North
☆ Gary Busey, Jodie Foster, Robbie Robertson, Kenneth McMillan, Meg Foster, Elisha Cook Jnr, Fred Ward

'Too dark and turbulent a vision to be palatable to a large public.' – *Variety*

Caro Diario: see *Dear Diary*

Carolina
US 1934 85m bw
Fox (Darryl F. Zanuck)
GB title: *House of Connelly*
A Yankee farmer's daughter falls in love with a Southern plantation owner.
Mildly pleasing period piece.
w Reginald Berkeley *play* *The House of Connelly* by Paul Green *d* Henry King *ph* Hal Mohr *m* Louis de Francesco
☆ Janet Gaynor, Lionel Barrymore, Robert Young, Henrietta Crosman, Mona Barrie, Richard Cromwell, Stepin Fetchit

'An arresting saga of a proud old southern family that starts out threateningly strong but peters to the point where it misses being another *State Fair*.' – *Variety*

Caroline Chérie
France 1951 115m approx bw
SNEG/Cinéphonie
Adventures of an attractive and willing young French girl in the days of the revolution.
A cheerful French imitation of Forever Amber; *witless and not very entertaining despite good period sense and a certain amount of self-mockery.*
w Jean Anouilh *novel* Cécil Saint-Laurent *d* Richard Poitier *ph* Maurice Barry *m* Georges Auric
☆ Martine Carol, Jacques Dacqmine, Marie Déa, Paul Bernard, Pierre Cressoy
† After several sequels, a colour remake appeared in 1967.

'More than your eyes have ever seen!'
Carousel *
US 1956 128m Eastmancolor
Cinemascope 55
TCF (Henry Ephron)
A ne'er-do-well dies while committing a holdup. Fifteen years later he returns from heaven to set his family's affairs in order.
Based on a fantasy play with an honourable history, this super-wide-screen version of an effective stage musical is hollow and boring, a humourless whimsy in which even the songs seem an intrusion.
w *Phoebe and Henry Ephron, from the musical based on Ferenc Molnar's play Liliom* *d* Henry King *ph* Charles G. Clarke *m/ly* Rodgers and Hammerstein *ch* Rod Alexander, Agnes de Mille
☆ Gordon MacRae, Shirley Jones, Cameron Mitchell, Gene Lockhart, Barbara Ruick, Robert Rounseville

'This is adult entertainment!'
The Carpetbaggers **
US 1964 150m Technicolor Panavision
Paramount/Embassy (Joseph E. Levine)
A young playboy inherits an aircraft business, becomes a megalomaniac tycoon, and moves to Hollywood in his search for power.
Enjoyable pulp fiction clearly suggested by the career of Howard Hughes. Lashings of old-fashioned melodrama, quite well pointed by all concerned.
w John Michael Hayes *novel* Harold Robbins *d* *Edward Dmytryk* *ph* Joseph MacDonald *m* Elmer Bernstein *ad* Hal Pereira, Walter Tyler
☆ *George Peppard*, Carroll Baker, *Alan Ladd*, *Martin Balsam*, Bob Cummings, Martha Hyer, Elizabeth Ashley, Lew Ayres, Ralph Taeger, Archie Moore, Leif Erickson, Audrey Totter

'One of those elaborate conjuring tricks in which yards and yards of coloured ribbon are spread all over the stage merely to prove that the conjuror has nothing up his sleeve.' – *Tom Milne*

† It was Ladd's last film.

'A dad in a hurry. A man on the run. And five kids with an attitude.'
Carpool
US 1996 119m Technicolor
Warner/Regency (Arnon Milchan, Michael Nathanson)
A harassed businessman, together with a car load of children is taken hostage by an incompetent armed robber.
Dumb, ramshackle comedy, of infantile adults and precocious children, that is a pain to sit through.
w Don Rhymer *d* Arthur Hiller *ph* David M. Walsh *m* John Debney *pd* James D. Vance *ed* William Reynolds, L. James Langlois
☆ Tom Arnold (Franklin Laszlo), David Paymer (David Paymer), Rhea Perlman (Martha), Kim Coates (Det Erdman), Obba Babatundé (Jeffery), Rachel Leigh Cook (Kayla), Micah Gardener (Bucky Miller), Jordan Blake Warkol (Travis), Rod Steiger (Mr Hammerman)
† Tom Arnold was awarded a Golden Raspberry as worst actor of the year for his performance.

Carquake: see *Cannonball*

Carrefour *
France 1938 75m bw
BUP Tuscherer
A French manufacturer, wounded during the war, finds himself the centre of blackmail plots.
Intriguing melodrama which was later rather flatly remade in Hollywood as Crossroads.
w Hans Kofka *d* Curtis Bernhardt
☆ Charles Vanel, Jules Berry, Suzy Prim, Tania Fedor

'One of the best French films of the late season, and worthy of American attention.' – *Variety*

Carrie **
US 1952 122m bw
Paramount (William Wyler)
In the early 1900s a country girl comes to Chicago, loses her innocence and goes on the stage, meanwhile reducing a wealthy restaurant manager to penury through love for her.
A famous satirical novel is softened into an unwieldy narrative with scarcely enough dramatic power to sustain interest despite splendid production values. Heavy pre-release cuts remain obvious, and the general effect is depressing; but it is very good to look at.
w Ruth and Augustus Goetz *novel* *Sister Carrie* by Theodore Dreiser *d* *William Wyler* *ph* *Victor Milner* *m* David Raksin *ad* *Hal Pereira, Roland Anderson*
☆ *Laurence Olivier*, Jennifer Jones, Miriam Hopkins, Eddie Albert, Basil Ruysdael, Ray Teal, Barry Kelley, Mary Murphy

'Olivier is so impassioned and so painfully touching that everything else in the movie, including the girl whose story it's meant to be, fades into insignificance.' – *Variety*

'They shot the later episodes for the strongest dramatic effect only, despite the fact that the story had stopped following a melodramatic line and become a sociological study ... each additional episode exploits the audience's hope that things will be brought to a satisfactory conclusion, but they never are.' – *Films in Review*

art direction

Carrie *
US 1976 98m MGM-DeLuxe
UA/Red Bank (Paul Monash)
A repressed teenager with remarkable mental powers takes a macabre revenge on classmates who taunt and persecute her.
Stylish but unattractive shocker which works its way up to a fine climax of gore and frenzy, and takes care to provide a final frisson just when the audience thinks it can safely go home.
w Lawrence D. Cohen *novel* Stephen King *d* *Brian de Palma* *ph* Mario Tosi *m* Pino Donaggio *ad* Jack Fisk *ed* Paul Hirsch
☆ Sissy Spacek, *Piper Laurie*, Amy Irving, William Katt, John Travolta, Betty Buckley, Nancy Allen, P. J. Soles

'Combining Gothic horror, offhand misogyny and an air of studied triviality, *Carrie* is de Palma's most enjoyable movie in a long while, and also his silliest.' – *Janet Maslin, Newsweek*

'The horror is effective only once, and the attempts at humour are never very successful and come almost when one is inclined to be moved by somebody's plight, so that the non-jokes yield authentic bad taste.' – *John Simon, New York*

Sissy Spacek; Piper Laurie

'No man is safe from temptation...'
Carried Away *
US 1995 108m Alpha Cine
First Independent/Cinetel (Lisa Hansen, Paul Hertzberg)
GB title: *Acts of Love*
In a small Texan town, a middle-aged schoolteacher is seduced by a teenaged schoolgirl.
Slow-paced story of restricted lives, carrying some convincing emotion owing to Hopper's performance as a downtrodden man discovering a renewed enthusiasm for life.
w Ed Jones *novel* *Farmer* by Jim Harrison *d* Bruno Barreto *ph* Declan Quinn *m* Bruce Broughton *pd* Peter Paul Raubertas *ed* Bruce Cannon
☆ *Dennis Hopper*, Amy Irving, Amy Locane, Julie Harris, Gary Busey, Hal Holbrook, Christopher Pettiet

'The film wins out through refreshing performances and a vibrant irresistible charm.' – *Empire*

The Carriers Are Waiting: see *Les Convoyeurs Attendent*

'A Love Story So Unusual It Has To Be True'
Carrington *
GB/France 1995 120m Technicolor
Polygram/Freeway/Shedlo/Dora (Ronald Shedlo, John McGrath)
A woman artist falls in love with the writer Lytton Strachey, a homosexual, and he with her.
The tangled love-life of the Bloomsbury group is exhibited in one of its more curious relationships, for the couple's love survived Carrington's marriage and she ended her life following Strachey's death; despite the film's title, it is Strachey who dominates the film, partly owing to a miscast and querulous Emma Thompson, but also because Carrington remains a cipher throughout, seen only in relationship to the men in her life.
wd Christopher Hampton *book* *Lytton Strachey* by Michael Holroyd *ph* Denis Lenoir *m* Michael Nyman *pd* Caroline Amies *ed* George Akers
☆ Emma Thompson (Carrington), *Jonathan Pryce* (Lytton Strachey), Steven Waddington (Ralph Partridge), Samuel West (Gerald Brenan), Rufus Sewell (Mark Gertler), Penelope Wilton (Lady Ottoline Morrell), Janet McTeer (Vanessa Bell), Peter Blythe (Philip Morrell)

'Prettily dressed, but cinematically stilted, and makes its characters' anguish and chatter seem ultimately of little consequence.' – *Geoff Brown, The Times*

'Emerges as an unsentimental salute to unselfish love and friendship.' – *Stephen Farber, Movieline*

'What the film wants to pass off as a dangerous liaison looks more like the ultimate in safe sex.' – *Entertainment Weekly*

† The film won the Special Jury Prize and Jonathan Pryce the Best Actor award at the 1995 Cannes Film Festival. It was originally to have been directed by Herbert Ross, and then by Mike Newell. Hampton wrote his original script in the mid-70s.

Carrington VC *
GB 1954 106m bw
British Lion/Romulus (Teddy Baird)

US title: *Court Martial*
An army major is courtmartialled for embezzling mess funds.
Good courtroom drama with a few plot surprises, convincing characters, and very serviceable acting and direction.
w John Hunter *play* Dorothy and Campbell Christie *d* Anthony Asquith *ph* Desmond Dickinson
☆ *David Niven*, Margaret Leighton, Noelle Middleton, Laurence Naismith, Clive Morton, Mark Dignam, Allan Cuthbertson, Victor Maddern, John Glyn-Jones, Raymond Francis, Newton Blick, John Chandos

Le Carrosse d'Or: see *The Golden Coach*

Carry Me Back
New Zealand 1982 90m colour
Kiwi Films/New Zealand Film Commission (Graeme Cowley)
Two sons attempt to smuggle their father's corpse from the city to their farm in order to benefit from his will.
Blackish comedy of mishaps and misfits that occasionally amuses.
w Derek Morton, Keith Aberdein, John Reid *story* Joy Cowley *d* John Reid *ph* Graeme Cowley *m* Tim Bridgewater, James Hall *ad* Jim Barr *ed* Simon Reece, Michael Horton
☆ Grant Tilley, Kelly Johnson, Dorothy McKegg, Derek Hardwick, Joanne Mildenhall

Carry On Abroad *
GB 1972 88m Eastmancolor
Fox-Rank/Peter Rogers

A couple who go on a package holiday to Spain find that their hotel is still being built and there is a staff of no more than three.
Every opportunity for bathroom jokes is relished in what is otherwise an average effort.
w Talbot Rothwell *d* Gerald Thomas *ph* Alan Hume *m* Eric Rogers *ad* Lionel Couch *ed* Alfred Roome
☆ Sidney James, Kenneth Williams, Charles Hawtrey, Joan Sims, Bernard Bresslaw, Barbara Windsor, Kenneth Connor, Peter Butterworth, Jimmy Logan, June Whitfield, Hattie Jacques
'Travelling well-trodden paths of slapstick, *double entendre* and nudging innuendo.' – *Nigel Andrews*

Carry On Admiral
GB 1957 83m bw Spectascope
George Minter

aka: *The Ship Was Loaded*
In a drunken moment, an MP changes clothes with a naval officer and is forced to adopt his friend's identity aboard ship.
Bland and undemanding farce, taken at a too-leisurely pace.
wd Val Guest *play Off the Record* by Ian Hay, Stephen King-Hall *ph* Arthur Grant *m* Philip Green
☆ David Tomlinson, Peggy Cummins, Ronald Shiner, Brian Reece, A. E. Matthews, Joan Sims, Ronald Adam, Alfie Bass
† The film has no connection with the long-running *Carry On* series.

Carry On Again Doctor
GB 1969 89m Eastmancolor
Rank/Adder (Peter Rogers)

A doctor, exiled to a tropical island, returns to Britain with a special slimming cure.
A slight air of desperation hangs over the often-used setting of a hospital, and most of the jokes remain in intensive care.
w Talbot Rothwell *d* Gerald Thomas *ph* Ernest Steward *m* Eric Rogers *pd* Jack Blezard *ed* Alfred Roome
☆ Sidney James, Kenneth Williams, Jim Dale, Charles Hawtrey, Joan Sims, Barbara Windsor, Hattie Jacques, Patsy Rowlands, Peter Butterworth, Pat Coombs
'Perhaps the team go that much further than ever before. Their fans will be delighted; those who aren't won't care.' – *Richard Davis, Films and Filming*

Carry On at Your Convenience
GB 1971 90m Eastmancolor
Rank/Peter Rogers

A union leader at the firm of W. A. Boggs, makers of fine toiletware, keeps ordering the workers to come out on strike.
No toilet joke is left unplumbed here, and the result is dire.
w Talbot Rothwell *d* Gerald Thomas *ph* Ernest Steward *m* Eric Rogers *ed* Alfred Roome
☆ Sidney James, Kenneth Williams, Charles Hawtrey, Joan Sims, Bernard Bresslaw, Hattie Jacques, Kenneth Cope, Patsy Rowlands, Jacki Piper, Richard O'Callaghan
'One of the least funny of this staggeringly successful series.' – *Eric Braun*
'Even more scrappily assembled than usual and, with the exception of a fairly amusing parody of sex education films, the level of humour, though noticeably cleaner than of late, is still rock bottom.' – *David McGillivray*

Carry On Behind **
GB 1975 90m Eastmancolor
Fox-Rank/Peter Rogers

Archaeologists arrive to search for Roman remains at a caravan site full of holiday-makers.
One of the best of the series and certainly the last watchable film the team produced.
w Dave Freeman *d* Gerald Thomas *ph* Ernest Steward *m* Eric Rogers *ed* Alfred Roome
☆ Elke Sommer, Kenneth Williams, Joan Sims, Bernard Bresslaw, Kenneth Connor, Peter Butterworth, Jack Douglas, Windsor Davies, Liz Fraser, Patsy Rowlands
'Emerges as the most consistently funny *Carry On* in many years … a strong vein of comedy is mined from the simple situation of campsite overcrowding, with some of the best sight gags involving a lugubrious Irish wolf-hound and a foul-mouthed mynah bird.' – *Verina Glaessner, MFB*

Carry On Cabby *
GB 1963 91m bw
Anglo Amalgamated/Peter Rogers

The neglected wife of the owner of a taxi firm sets up a rival firm with women drivers.
A deft farcical battle of the sexes.
w Talbot Rothwell *d* Gerald Thomas *ph* Alan Hume *m* Eric Rogers *ed* Archie Ludski
☆ Sidney James, Charles Hawtrey, Kenneth Connor, Hattie Jacques, Esma Cannon, Liz Fraser, Bill Owen, Milo O'Shea, Jim Dale
'The golden formula of the *Carry On* series is back with a bang.' – *Variety*

Carry On Camping *
GB 1969 88m Eastmancolor
Rank/Peter Rogers

Two men take their girlfriends on holiday to a nudist camp in the hope that it will make them less inhibited.
A partly successful attempt to provide the characters with fewer sexual repressions than usual.
w Talbot Rothwell *d* Gerald Thomas *ph* Ernest Steward *m* Eric Rogers *ad* Lionel Couch *ed* Alfred Roome
☆ Sidney James, Kenneth Williams, Joan Sims, Charles Hawtrey, Terry Scott, Barbara Windsor
'Suffers somewhat in comparison to some of its predecessors in that it lacks a storyline, however slim.' – *Variety*

Carry On Cleo *
GB 1964 92m Eastmancolor
Anglo Amalgamated/Peter Rogers

Ancient Britons are captured by the Romans while Mark Antony carries on with Cleopatra.
Sporadically amusing parody of the Elizabeth Taylor epic, though it should have been much funnier.
w Talbot Rothwell *d* Gerald Thomas *ph* Alan Hume *m* Eric Rogers *ad* Bert Davey *ed* Archie Ludski
☆ Sidney James, Kenneth Williams, Charles Hawtrey, Joan Sims, Kenneth Connor, Jim Dale, Amanda Barrie, E. V. H. Emmett, Sheila Hancock, Jon Pertwee
'Gags, both verbal and visual, suffer from repetition.' – *Variety*
† As a result of a court case for breach of copyright brought by Twentieth Century-Fox, the film's poster, which parodied the advertising for *Cleopatra*, had to be withdrawn.

'Up your anchor for a well crewed voyage!!'
Carry On Columbus
GB 1992 91m colour
Island World/Comedy House/Peter Rogers (John Goldstone)

Columbus's voyage to find a route to the East is sabotaged by spies in the pay of the Sultan of Turkey.
Ill-starred attempt, with a succession of single entendres and some inept performances, to revive a tired old formula.
w Dave Freeman *d* Gerald Thomas *ph* Alan Hume *m* John Du Prez *pd* Harry Pottle *ed* Chris Blunden
☆ Jim Dale, Bernard Cribbins, Maureen Lipman, Peter Richardson, Rik Mayall, Alexei Sayle, Charles Fleischer, Larry Miller, Leslie Phillips, Julian Clary, Sara Crowe, Rebecca Lacey, Nigel Planer, June Whitfield, Richard Wilson
'Painfully unfunny, lacking imagination and energy.' – *Philip French, Observer*

Carry On Constable *
GB 1960 86m bw
Anglo Amalgamated/Peter Rogers

Four new and inept constables report for duty at their local police station.
In part a parody of the popular TV series Dixon of Dock Green *and moderately amusing despite the absence of a plot.*
w Norman Hudis *story* Brock Williams *d* Gerald Thomas *ph* Ted Scaife *m* Bruce Montgomery *ad* Carmen Dillon *ed* John
☆ Sidney James, Kenneth Williams, Charles Hawtrey, Joan Sims, Kenneth Connor, Eric Barker, Leslie Phillips, Hattie Jacques, Shirley Eaton, Cyril Chamberlain, Irene Handl, Esma Cannon, Freddie Mills
'Simply an anthology of police gags and situations.' – *Variety*

'How The West Was Lost!!'
Carry On Cowboy **
GB 1965 95m Eastmancolor
Anglo Amalgamated/Peter Rogers

A sanitary engineer is given the task of cleaning up a town being terrorized by outlaws.
Amusing parody of High Noon *and other classic Westerns.*
w Talbot Rothwell *d* Gerald Thomas *ph* Alan Hume *m* Eric Rogers *ad* Bert Davey *ed* Rod Keys
☆ Sidney James, Kenneth Williams, Charles Hawtrey, Joan Sims, Jim Dale, Percy Herbert, Angela Douglas, Bernard Bresslaw, Peter Butterworth, Jon Pertwee
'Less a string of irrelevant situations than usual, giving the team more opportunity for comedy thesping.' – *Variety*

Carry On Cruising
GB 1962 89m Eastmancolor
Anglo Amalgamated/Peter Rogers

The captain of a cruise liner finds his peace of mind threatened by new crew members and tourists.
Weak comedy that doesn't seem to know where it's going.
w Norman Hudis *story* Eric Barker *d* Gerald Thomas *ph* Alan Hume *m* Bruce Montgomery, Douglas Gamley *ad* Carmen Dillon *ed* John Shirley
☆ Sidney James, Kenneth Williams, Kenneth Connor, Liz Fraser, Dilys Laye, Esma Cannon, Lance Percival, Ronnie Stevens, Cyril Chamberlain, Anton Rodgers
'Direction by Gerald Thomas is boisterously effective.' – *Variety*

Carry On Dick
GB 1974 91m Eastmancolor
Rank/Peter Rogers

Bow Street Runners ask a village clergyman to help them catch the highwayman Dick Turpin, better known as Big Dick.
Inspiration flags in a comedy where both cast and director seem hardly interested in what they were doing, probably because they had been doing it for too long.
w Talbot Rothwell *story* Lawrie Wyman, George Evans *d* Gerald Thomas *ph* Ernest Steward *m* Eric Rogers *ed* Alfred Roome
☆ Sidney James, Kenneth Williams, Kenneth Connor, Barbara Windsor, Hattie Jacques, Bernard Bresslaw, Joan Sims, Peter Butterworth, Jack Douglas, Patsy Rowlands, Bill Maynard
'These tireless upholders of the "saucy" postcard tradition soldier on with their perennial rib-poking, elbow-nudging, albeit scarcely jaw-breaking esprit … Maybe their continuing appeal is beyond criticism – or according to taste, beneath it.' – *Nigel Gearing, MFB*
'The script is utterly banal. It is incredible that human minds can put such muck on to paper.' – *Kenneth Williams*

Carry On Doctor *
GB 1968 94m Eastmancolor
Rank/Peter Rogers

Hospital patients revolt against a tyrannical matron when their favourite doctor is sacked.
Occasionally amusing farce.
w Talbot Rothwell *d* Gerald Thomas *ph* Alan Hume *m* Eric Rogers *ed* Alfred Roome
☆ Frankie Howerd, Sidney James, Kenneth Williams, Jim Dale, Charles Hawtrey, Joan Sims, Barbara Windsor, Hattie Jacques, Anita Harris, Bernard Bresslaw, Peter Butterworth
'Usual unabashed mixture of double-meanings, down-to-earth vulgarity, blue jokes.' – *Variety*

Carry On – Don't Lose Your Head
GB 1966 90m Eastmancolor
Rank/Peter Rogers

aka: *Don't Lose Your Head*
A foppish Briton, the Black Fingernail, rescues French aristocrats from the guillotine during the French Revolution.
A limp parody of The Scarlet Pimpernel *causes no more than a few chuckles.*
w Talbot Rothwell *d* Gerald Thomas *ph* Alan Hume *m* Eric Rogers *ed* Rod Keys
☆ Sidney James, Kenneth Williams, Jim Dale, Charles Hawtrey, Joan Sims, Peter Butterworth, Dany Robin, Peter Gilmore
'A crazy debauch of duelling, doublecrossing and disaster. The troupers jump through their well-known hoops with agility.' – *Variety*

Carry On Emmannuelle
GB 1978 88m Technicolor
Hemdale/Peter Rogers

The wife of an impotent French ambassador to England seduces every man she meets.
A doomed attempt to update the formula for more sexually permissive times that resulted in the worst of the series, and the last for fourteen years, until it was revived in 1992.
w Lance Peters *d* Gerald Thomas *ph* Alan Hume *m* Eric Rogers *ad* Jack Shampan *ed* Peter Boita
☆ Suzanne Danielle, Kenneth Williams, Kenneth Connor, Jack Douglas, Joan Sims, Peter Butterworth, Larry Dann, Beryl Reid, Eric Barker
'This one is rude, certainly, but the relentless phallic innuendo is as labored as makers' determination to show nothing to worry the censor. Leaden comic timing…' – *Variety*
'It's rather like watching endearing elderly relatives disgracing themselves at a party.' – *Andy Medhurst, Sight and Sound*

Carry On England
GB 1976 89m colour
Rank/Peter Rogers

In 1940 the men and women who form an experimental anti-aircraft battery prefer to make love rather than war, to the annoyance of their new commanding officer.
One of the weakest of the series and a sign that the series was running out of energy, unable to find suitable replacements for its usual team and handicapped more than usual by a weak script.
w Jack Seddon, David Pursall *d* Gerald Thomas *ph* Ernest Steward *m* Max Harris *ad* Lionel Couch *ed* Richard Marden
☆ Kenneth Connor, Windsor Davies, Patrick Mower, Judy Geeson, Jack Douglas, Diane Langton, Melvyn Hayes, Joan Sims, Peter Jones, Peter Butterworth, David Lodge
'Suffers from a particularly unfortunate hangup. It's not funny.' – *Variety*
'The laboured puns and overacting are as tiresome as ever.' – *MFB*

Carry On – Follow That Camel
GB 1966 90m Eastmancolor
Rank/Peter Rogers

aka: *Follow That Camel*
An English gentleman, accused of behaving badly at cricket, joins the Foreign Legion to regain his honour.
An ill-match between American and English styles of vaudeville and music-hall humour results in a direly unamusing movie.
w Talbot Rothwell *d* Gerald Thomas *ph* Alan Hume *m* Eric Rogers *ed* Alfred Roome
☆ Phil Silvers, Kenneth Williams, Jim Dale, Charles Hawtrey, Joan Sims, Peter Butterworth, Anita Harris, Bernard Bresslaw, Angela Douglas, Peter Gilmore
'It all works with considerable bounce, with elements of parody of Beau Geste-style movies for those alert to them. All the regular comics are on first-rate form.' – *Variety*

Carry On Girls
GB 1973 88m Eastmancolor
Fox-Rank/Peter Rogers

The organizer of a seaside beauty contest annoys the local members of the Women's Liberation movement.
Below average romp.
w Talbot Rothwell *d* Gerald Thomas *ph* Alan Hume *m* Eric Rogers *ad* Robert Jones *ed* Alfred Roome
☆ Sidney James (Sidney Fiddler), Kenneth Connor (Frederick Bumble), Joan Sims (Connie Philpotts), Barbara Windsor (Hope Springs), Bernard Bresslaw (Peter Potter), Peter Butterworth (Admiral), June Whitfield (Augusta Prodworthy), Jack Douglas (William), Patsy Rowlands (Mildred Bumble), Valerie Leon (Paula Perkins), Joan Hickson (Mrs Dukes), David Lodge (Police Inspector), Sally Geeson (Debra), Robin Askwith (Larry), Jimmy Logan (Cecil Gaybody)
'Herculean efforts on the part of the entire cast do eventually pull off (in the context, I must insist this is not meant as a *double entendre*) some fairly effective slapstick.' – *Eric Braun*
'Thriving as ever on the sexual repression of its audience, Talbot Rothwell's windy, radio-style script ... turns out the routine quota of puns on such words as bang, boob, bed, bust, bristol and bash, and makes such weary labour of it that every joke can be heard creaking into place long before the arrival of the punch-line.' – *Gareth Jones, MFB*

'A Great Guy With His Chopper!'
Carry On Henry **
GB 1971 89m Eastmancolor
Rank/Adder (Peter Rogers)

US title: *Carry On Henry VIII*
King Henry tries to get rid of his wife when he discovers she smells of garlic.
A coarsely successful parody of Anne of the Thousand Days *and other period films.*
w Talbot Rothwell *d* Gerald Thomas *ph* Alan Hume *m* Eric Rogers *ed* Alfred Roome
☆ Sidney James, Kenneth Williams, Charles Hawtrey, Joan Sims, Terry Scott, Barbara Windsor, Kenneth Connor, Peter Butterworth, Peter Gilmore, Patsy Rowlands
'They have managed to come up with a bit of a winner ... there is a delicious send up of that most boring and perennial line of cinematic yawns, the historical romance.' – *Peter Buckley*
'The cast is the familiar stock company at full force; the script is from Talbot Rothwell at his most characteristic; and the film is at any rate better looking than most of its shoe-string predecessors.' – *John Pidgeon, MFB*
'I read the script of *Carry On Henry* and I think it's abysmal.' – *Kenneth Williams, 1970*
'We saw the TV and it was *Carry On Henry* ... amazing how well this was made! Everyone in it was competent and the sheer *look* of the thing was very professional.' – *Kenneth Williams, 1979*
'ITV showed *Carry On Henry*. Oh dear! It was so bad in places ... truly chronic dialogue ... dreadful acting. Sid James had never been quite as bad as this. A collection of such rubbish you're amazed it could ever have been stuck together. Only an audience of illiterates could ever have found this tripe amusing.' – *Kenneth Williams, 1988*

Carry On Jack
GB 1964 91m Eastmancolor
Anglo Amalgamated/Peter Rogers

US title: *Carry On Venus*
A midshipman finds himself at the mercy of a bullying captain and they are both put overboard after a mutiny.
Salty but unamusing parody of Mutiny on The Bounty *and other sea-faring sagas.*
w Talbot Rothwell *d* Gerald Thomas *ph* Alan Hume *m* Eric Rogers *ad* Jack Shampan *ed* Archie Ludski
☆ Bernard Cribbins, Kenneth Williams, Charles Hawtrey, Juliet Mills, Donald Houston, Percy Herbert, Peter Gilmore, Jim Dale, Anton Rodgers, Cecil Parker, Patrick Cargill
'Gerald Thomas steers his cast through a maze of mixups and misadventures.' – *Variety*

Carry On Loving
GB 1970 88m Eastmancolor
Rank/Adder (Peter Rogers)

Assorted misfits try their luck at a computer dating agency.
Limp comedy for which the regulars show little enthusiasm.
w Talbot Rothwell *d* Gerald Thomas *ph* Ernest Steward *m* Eric Rogers *ad* Lionel Couch *ed* Alfred Roome
☆ Sidney James, Kenneth Williams, Charles Hawtrey, Joan Sims, Terry Scott, Hattie Jacques, Richard O'Callaghan, Bernard Bresslaw, Jacki Piper, Imogen Hassall, Patsy Rowlands, Bill Maynard
'Full of tired jokes, obvious situations and ludicrous performances, we have all been here at least three times before, but the crew have a way of working over the old material.' – *Peter Buckley, Films and Filming*
'Scrapings from the bottom of Talbot Rothwell's barrel of well-worn double entendre, delivered with mechanical efficiency by an equally well-worn cast.' – *MFB*

Carry On Matron *
GB 1972 87m Eastmancolor
Rank/Peter Rogers

A con man persuades his son to dress as a nurse in order to infiltrate a maternity hospital to steal contraceptive pills.
Intermittently amusing comedy.
w Talbot Rothwell *d* Gerald Thomas *ph* Ernest Steward *m* Eric Rogers *ad* Lionel Couch *ed* Alfred Roome
☆ Sidney James, Kenneth Williams, Charles Hawtrey, Joan Sims, Hattie Jacques, Bernard Bresslaw, Terry Scott, Kenneth Cope, Barbara Windsor, Kenneth Connor, Jacki Piper, Patsy Rowlands, Jack Douglas
'A largely successful if slightly patchy addition to the series; its comic highlight involves Sid James, required to assume a medical alias, introducing himself as "Dr Zhivago".' – *Kenneth Thompson, MFB*

Carry On Nurse **
GB 1959 86m bw
Anglo Amalgamated/Peter Rogers

Male patients in a hospital rebel against the dictatorial matron.
The first true Carry On, *done when the whole notion was still fresh and the cast responded with glee to its crudities.*
w Norman Hudis *story* Patrick Cargill, Jack Searle *d* Gerald Thomas *ph* Reg Wyer *m* Bruce Montgomery *ad* Alex Vetchinsky *ed* John Shirley
☆ Shirley Eaton, Kenneth Williams, Charles Hawtrey, Hattie Jacques, Joan Sims, Kenneth Connor, Terence Longdon, Bill Owen, Leslie Phillips, Wilfrid Hyde-White, Irene Handl
'The yocks come thick and fast.' – *Variety*
'A seaside postcard come to life, a shameless procession of vulgarities. Utterly irresistible.' – *Andy Medhurst, Sight and Sound*
† The film topped the box-office in Britain and was surprisingly successful in the US where it ran for two-and-a-half years.

Carry On Regardless
GB 1961 90m bw
Anglo Amalgamated/Peter Rogers

A group of incompetent unemployed join an odd-job agency.
Less a film than a series of sketches, which are very variable in quality.
w Norman Hudis *d* Gerald Thomas *ph* Alan Hume *m* Bruce Montgomery *ed* John Shirley
☆ Sidney James, Kenneth Williams, Charles Hawtrey, Joan Sims, Kenneth Connor, Bill Owen, Liz Fraser, Terence Longdon, Esma Cannon, Hattie Jacques, Fenella Fielding
'Ingenuity of scriptwriter Norman Hudis is sometimes a bit strained, but he has come up with some sound comedy situations.' – *Variety*

Carry On Screaming *
GB 1966 97m Eastmancolor
Anglo Amalgamated/Peter Rogers

Police investigate a mad doctor and his sister, who are turning young women into mannequins.
A send-up of Hammer horrors that manages to emulate the garishness of the originals.
w Talbot Rothwell *d* Gerald Thomas *ph* Alan Hume *m* Eric Rogers *ed* Rod Keys
☆ Harry H. Corbett, Kenneth Williams, Jim Dale, Charles Hawtrey, Fenella Fielding, Joan Sims, Angela Douglas, Bernard Bresslaw, Peter Butterworth, Jon Pertwee
'Puts the skids under horror pix. Snag is that most horror films themselves teeter on the edge of parody and it is rather tough trying to burlesque a parody.' – *Variety*

Carry On Sergeant
GB 1958 83m bw
Anglo Amalgamated/Insignia (Peter Rogers)

An army training sergeant accepts a bet that his last platoon of raw recruits will win the Star Squad award.
Shabby farce with humdrum script and slack direction, saved by energetic performances.
w Norman Hudis *play* The Bull Boys by R. F. Delderfield *d* Gerald Thomas *ph* Peter Hennessy *m* Bruce Montgomery
☆ Bob Monkhouse, William Hartnell, Kenneth Williams, Charles Hawtrey, Shirley Eaton, Eric Barker, Dora Bryan, Bill Owen, Kenneth Connor

'They're At It Again – O.O.O.H!'
Carry On Spying
GB 1964 87m bw
Anglo Amalgamated/Peter Rogers

British spies are sent to recapture a secret formula stolen by the Society for the Total Extinction of Non-Conforming Humans, otherwise known as Stench.
A feeble parody of the Bond films.
w Talbot Rothwell, Sid Colin *d* Gerald Thomas *ph* Alan Hume *m* Eric Rogers *ed* Archie Ludski
☆ Kenneth Williams, Bernard Cribbins, Charles Hawtrey, Barbara Windsor, Eric Pohlmann, Eric Barker, Dilys Laye, Jim Dale, Richard Wattis
'A dazzling return to form, milking every last drop from the ripe targets of espionage in general and Bond in particular.' – *Andy Medhurst, Sight and Sound*

Carry On Teacher *
GB 1959 86m bw
Anglo Amalgamated/Peter Rogers

Pupils at a school sabotage the headmaster's attempts to get another job because they don't want to lose him.
Amiable comedy that is less frenetic than many in the series, and all the better for it.
w Norman Hudis *d* Gerald Thomas *ph* Reginald Wyer *m* Bruce Montgomery *ed* John Shirley
☆ Ted Ray, Kenneth Williams, Charles Hawtrey, Leslie Phillips, Joan Sims, Kenneth Connor, Hattie Jacques, Rosalind Knight, Cyril Chamberlain
'The laughs come readily.' – *Variety*

Carry On up the Jungle
GB 1970 89m Eastmancolor
Rank/Peter Rogers

An ornithologist journeys to Africa in search of the rare Oozulum bird.
A tired parody of Tarzan and jungle films; the jokes get lost in the undergrowth.
w Talbot Rothwell *d* Gerald Thomas *ph* Ernest Steward *m* Eric Rogers *ad* Alex Vetchinsky *ed* Alfred Roome
☆ Frankie Howerd, Sidney James, Charles Hawtrey, Joan Sims, Terry Scott, Kenneth Connor, Bernard Bresslaw, Jacki Piper
'The film is an assured success.' – *Films and Filming*

Carry On up the Khyber ***
GB 1968 88m Eastmancolor
Rank/Adder (Peter Rogers)

A Scots regiment, the Third Foot and Mouth, fails to defend British interests in India.
The best of the series, a wonderfully vulgar and ripe low comedy on an imperial theme.
w Talbot Rothwell *d* Gerald Thomas *ph* Alan Hume *m* Eric Rogers *ad* Alex Vetchinsky *ed* Alfred Roome
☆ Sidney James, Kenneth Williams, Charles Hawtrey, Joan Sims, Roy Castle, Bernard Bresslaw, Peter Butterworth, Terry Scott, Angela Douglas, Cardew Robinson, Julian Holloway, Peter Gilmore
'Continues to rely primarily on low-comedy visual and verbal gag situations for its yocks.' – *Variety*
† The movie was filmed in Wales.

Carry On Venus: see *Carry On Jack*

The Cars that Ate Paris *
Australia 1974 88m Eastmancolor
Panavision
Saltpan/AFDC/Royce Smeal (Jim and Howard McElroy)

Car travellers become victims of a small town whose youthful inhabitants live on the pickings of engineered road accidents.
Another small town with a guilty secret, in this case more suitable to a half-hour than a feature, but with rewarding attention to detail.
wd Peter Weir *ph* John McLean *m* Bruce Smeaton
☆ Terry Camilleri, John Meillon, Melissa Jaffa, Kevin Miles

Carson City *
US 1952 87m Warnercolor
Warner (David Weisbart)
A stagecoach service suffers from bandit raids, so a local banker finances a railroad.
Agreeably conventional Western with plenty of reliable plot and a satisfactory outcome for the goodies.
w Sloan Nibley, Winston Miller *d* André de Toth *ph* John Boyle *m* David Buttolph
☆ Randolph Scott, Raymond Massey, Lucille Norman, Richard Webb, James Millican, Larry Keating, George Cleveland

Cartouche
Italy/US 1954 85m approx bw
Venturini/RKO (John Nasht)
A French prince clears himself of a murder charge and brings the villain to book.
Flat costume drama.

w Louis Stevens, Tullio Pinelli *d* Steve Sekely, Gianni Vernuccio *ph* Massimo Dallamano *m* Bruce Montgomery
☆ Richard Basehart, Patricia Roc, Massimo Serato, Akim Tamiroff

Cartouche **
France/Italy 1961 114m Eastmancolor Dyaliscope
Ariane/Filmsonor/Vides (Georges Danciger)
aka: *Swords of Blood*
An 18th-century cooper's son becomes a quick-witted and gallant thief.
Slightly bitter fairy tale based on a French legend, vigorously encompassing tragedy, farce, violence and high-flown adventure.
w Daniel Boulanger, Philippe de Broca *d* *Philippe de Broca* *ph* Christian Matras *m* Georges Delerue
☆ *Jean-Paul Belmondo*, Claudia Cardinale, Odile Versois, Marcel Dalio, Philippe Lemaire, Jean Rochefort
'A tour de force of virtuosity.' – *Peter John Dyer, MFB*

Carve Her Name with Pride *
GB 1958 119m bw
Rank/Keyboard (Daniel M. Angel)
In 1940, the young British widow of a French officer is enlisted as a spy, and after various adventures dies before a German firing squad.
Slightly muddled if ultimately moving biopic in which initial light comedy gives way to romance, documentary, character study, blazing war action and finally tragedy. Generally well made.
w Vernon Harris, Lewis Gilbert *book* R. J. Minney *d* *Lewis Gilbert* *ph* John Wilcox *m* William Alwyn
☆ *Virginia McKenna* (Violette Szabo), *Paul Scofield*, Jack Warner, Sydney Tafler, Denise Grey, Alain Saury, Maurice Ronet, Nicole Stéphane, Noel Willman, Bill Owen, William Mervyn, Anne Leon
'What is missing is the deeply charged passion which would have gone beyond the quietly decent statement intermittently achieved.' – *John Gillett*

La Casa del Angel: see *The House of the Angel*

'As big and timely a picture as ever you've seen! You can tell by the cast it's important! gripping! big!'
Casablanca ****
US 1942 102m bw
Warner (Hal B. Wallis)
Rick's Café in Casablanca is a centre for war refugees awaiting visas for America. Rick abandons his cynicism to help an old love escape the Nazis with her underground leader husband.
Cinema par excellence: a studio-bound Hollywood melodrama which after various chances just fell together impeccably into one of the outstanding entertainment experiences of cinema history, with romance, intrigue, excitement, suspense and humour cunningly deployed by master technicians and a perfect cast.
w Julius J. Epstein, Philip G. Epstein, Howard Koch play Everybody Comes to Rick's by Murray Burnett, Joan Alison *d Michael Curtiz ph Arthur Edeson m Max Steiner ed Owen Marks*
☆ *Humphrey Bogart* (Rick Blaine), *Ingrid Bergman* (Ilse Lund), Paul Henreid (Victor Laszlo), *Claude Rains* (Captain Louis Renault), Sydney Greenstreet (Ferrari), Peter Lorre (Ugarte), S. Z. Sakall (Carl), *Conrad Veidt* (Major Strasser), *Dooley Wilson* (Sam), *Marcel Dalio* (Croupier), Joy Page, John Qualen, Ludwig Stossel, Leonid Kinskey, Helmut Dantine and also Ilka Gruning
RICK: 'I stick out my neck for nobody. I'm the only cause I'm interested in.'
LOUIS: 'How extravagant you are, throwing away women like that. Someday they may be scarce.'
RICK: 'Ilse, I'm no good at being noble, but it doesn't take much to see that the problems of three little people don't amount to a hill of beans in this crazy world. Someday you'll understand that. Not now. Here's looking at you, kid.'
RICK: 'I came to Casablanca for the waters.'
LOUIS: 'What waters? We're in the desert.'
RICK: 'I was misinformed.'
RICK: 'Louis, I think this is the beginning of a beautiful friendship.'
'A picture which makes the spine tingle and the heart take a leap ... they have so combined sentiment, humour and pathos with taut melodrama and bristling intrigue that the result is a highly entertaining and even inspiring film.' – *New York Times*
'Its humour is what really saves it, being a mixture of Central European irony of attack and racy Broadway-Hollywood Boulevard cynicism.' – *Herman G. Weinberg*
'The happiest of happy accidents, and the most decisive exception to the *auteur* theory.' – *Andrew Sarris, 1968*
'A film which seems to have been frozen in time ... the sum of its many marvellous parts far exceeds the whole.' – *NFT, 1974*
'It's far from a great film, but it has an appealingly schlocky romanticism, and you're never really pressed to take its melodramatic twists and turns seriously.' – *Pauline Kael, 70s*
† Originally named for the leads were Ronald Reagan, Ann Sheridan and Dennis Morgan
♫ 'As Time Goes By', 'Knock on Wood'
Academy Award: best picture; Julius J. and Philip G. Epstein, Howard Koch; Michael Curtiz
Academy Award nomination: Arthur Edeson; Max Steiner; Humphrey Bogart; Claude Rains; Owen Marks

Casanova
Italy 1976 163m Technicolor Scope
TCF/PEA (Alberto Grimaldi)
aka: *Fellini's Casanova*
Episodes from the life of the 18th-century libertine, in the course of which he seduces, among others, a nun, a mechanical doll, and a hunchbacked nymphomaniac.
A curiously rarefied spectacle which seldom comes to anything like life and despite its vast expense seems more likely to provoke yawns than lust.
w Federico Fellini, Bernardino Zapponi *d* Federico Fellini *ph* Giuseppe Rotunno *m* Nino Rota *pd* Danilo Donati, Federico Fellini
☆ Donald Sutherland, Tina Aumont, Cicely Browne, Carmen Scarpitta
'It may well be the most ponderous specimen of imaginative vacuity ever devised.' – *John Simon, New York*
'I distinctly remember walking out of *Casanova* well before the end.' – *Luis Buñuel*
Academy Award nomination: script
BAFTA: Danilo Donati

Casanova Brown
US 1944 99m bw
International/Christie (Nunnally Johnson)
Just as his divorce comes through, a man discovers that his wife is pregnant.
Very mild star comedy which tiptoes round its subject.
w Nunnally Johnson *play Bachelor Father* by Floyd Dell, Thomas Mitchell *d* Sam Wood *ph* John F. Seitz *m* Arthur Lange *ad* Perry Ferguson
☆ Gary Cooper, Teresa Wright, Frank Morgan, Anita Louise, Patricia Collinge, Edmund Breon, Jill Esmond, Isobel Elsom, Mary Treen, Halliwell Hobbes
'There is so much clowning with so little subject that one is exposed to the impression that anything went for a laugh.' – *Bosley Crowther, New York Times*
† A remake of *Little Accident* (qv).
Academy Award nomination: Arthur Lange; Perry Ferguson

Casanova in Burlesque
US 1944 74m bw
Republic
A professor has a secret summer life as a burlesque performer.
Unusual, amiable comedy.
w Frank Gill *d* Leslie Goodwins
☆ Joe E. Brown, June Havoc

Casanova's Big Night
US 1954 86m Technicolor
Paramount (Paul Jones)
In old Italy, the great lover is fleeing from his creditors and changes places with a tailor's apprentice.
The last of Bob Hope's big-budget, big-studio burlesques is a lumbering vehicle which wastes its star cast and mistimes its laughs. Joan Fontaine is an unhappy comedy foil.
w Hal Kanter, Edmund Hartmann *d* Norman Z. McLeod *ph* Lionel Lindon *m* Lyn Murray
☆ Bob Hope, Joan Fontaine, Basil Rathbone, Vincent Price, Audrey Dalton, Hugh Marlowe, John Carradine, Primo Carnera, Arnold Moss, Lon Chaney Jnr

Casbah
US 1948 94m bw
Universal (Erik Charell)
Remake of *Algiers* (qv) with songs added.
Not too bad in the circumstances, but a wholly artificial exercise, and another version was really not needed. The sets seem overlit and claustrophobic.
w Ladislaus Bus-Fekete, Arnold Manoff *novel* Detective Ashelbe *musical* *Erik Charell* *d* John Berry *ph* Irving Glassberg *m/ly* Harold Arlen, Leo Robin
☆ *Tony Martin*, Yvonne de Carlo, Marta Toren, *Peter Lorre*, Hugo Haas
Academy Award nomination: song 'For Every Man There's a Woman'

The Case against Brooklyn
US 1958 81m bw
Charles H. Schneer/Columbia
An undercover cop smashes a gambling syndicate.
Competent second feature treatment of a story we have heard somewhere before.
w Raymond T. Marcus (Bernard Gordon, Julian Zimet) *story* Daniel B. Ullman *d* Paul Wendkos
☆ Darren McGavin, Maggie Hayes, Warren Stevens, Emile Meyer, Nestor Paiva
† Gordon and Zimet wrote the script under a pseudonym because they were blacklisted at the time.

The Case of Charles Peace
GB 1949 88m bw
John Argyle
The story of a burglar and murderer of the 1870s whose career caught the public fancy.
Antediluvian and largely fictitious treatment of a Victorian cause célèbre.
w Doris Davison, Norman Lee *d* Norman Lee
☆ Michael Martin Harvey, Chili Bouchier, Valentine Dyall, Bruce Belfrage, Ronald Adam

The Case of Mrs Pembroke: see *Two Against the World*

The Case of the Black Cat
US 1936 66m bw
Warner
An old man is murdered after changing his will: Perry Mason investigates.
One of the better tales of the lawyer sleuth.
w F. Hugh Herbert *d* William McGann
☆ Ricardo Cortez, Harry Davenport, June Travis, Jane Bryan

The Case of the Curious Bride
US 1935 80m bw
Warner
Perry Mason helps a woman who is being blackmailed by her 'dead' husband.
Smoothish mystery.
w Tom Reed *story* Erle Stanley Gardner *d* Michael Curtiz
☆ Warren William, Margaret Lindsay, Donald Woods, Claire Dodd, Allen Jenkins, Errol Flynn

The Case of the Frightened Lady
GB 1940 81m bw
Pennant
A dowager knows that her son is mad and tries to prevent him from strangling his cousin.
Quite a lively suspenser of its time.
w Edward Dryhurst *novel* Edgar Wallace *d* George King
☆ Marius Goring, Penelope Dudley Ward, Helen Haye, Patrick Barr, Felix Aylmer
† A previous version was released in 1932 as *The Frightened Lady* (qv).

The Case of the Howling Dog
US 1934 75m bw
Warner
Two men claim the same woman as their wife.
Adequate Perry Mason mystery.
w Ben Markson *story* Erle Stanley Gardner *d* Alan Crosland
☆ Warren William, Mary Astor, Allen Jenkins, Grant Mitchell, Helen Trenholme, Dorothy Tree

The Case of the Lucky Legs
US 1935 77m bw
Warner
Perry Mason chases a beauty contest promoter who skips town with the winnings.
Fair lighthearted mystery, with a somewhat dissipated sleuth.
w Ben Markson, Brown Holmes *story* Erle Stanley Gardner *d* Archie Mayo
☆ Warren William, Genevieve Tobin, Allen Jenkins, Patricia Ellis, Lyle Talbot, Barton MacLane
'An admirable film.' – *Graham Greene*

The Case of the Missing Blonde: see *Lady in the Morgue*

The Case of the Stuttering Bishop
US 1937 70m bw
Warner
Perry Mason investigates an heiress who may be an impostor.
Thin mystery with another different star in the lead.
w Don Ryan, Kenneth Gamet *story* Erle Stanley Gardner *d* William Clemens
☆ Donald Woods, Ann Dvorak, Anne Nagel, Linda Perry

The Case of the Velvet Claws
US 1936 63m bw
Warner
Perry Mason's honeymoon is postponed when he finds himself on a murder charge.
Moderate light-hearted mystery, but they should have awarded prizes to anyone who could explain the title.
w Tom Reed *story* Erle Stanley Gardner *d* William Clemens
☆ Warren William, Claire Dodd, Wini Shaw, Gordon Elliott, Addison Richards

Casey's Shadow
US 1978 116m Metrocolor Panavision
Columbia/Ray Stark (Michael Levee)
A Cajun family in New Mexico breeds a champion horse which wins the annual race.
Shades of Maryland: an old-fashioned movie of the kind which absolutely nobody should want to revive, at least not so ineptly or at such length.
w Carol Sobieski *story Ruidoso* by John McPhee *d* Martin Ritt *ph* John A. Alonzo *m* Patrick Williams
☆ Walter Matthau, Alexis Smith, Robert Webber, Murray Hamilton, Andrew A. Rubin, Stephan Burns, Michael Hershewe

C.A.S.H.: see *W.H.I.F.F.S.*

Cash and Carry: see *Ringside Maisie*

Cash McCall
US 1960 102m Technicolor
Warner (Henry Blanke)
A Napoleon of the stock market gets into trouble for the first time when love interferes with business.
Slightly unusual comedy drama, quite sharply made and played, but not adding up to much.
w Lenore Coffee, Marion Hargrove *novel* Cameron Hawley *d* Joseph Pevney *ph* George Folsey *m* Max Steiner
☆ James Garner, Natalie Wood, Nina Foch, Dean Jagger, E. G. Marshall, Henry Jones, Otto Kruger, Roland Winters

Cash on Demand *
GB 1963 86m bw
Columbia/Woodpecker/Hammer (Michael Carreras)
A fussy bank manager outwits a classy robber.
Quietly effective suspenser with an admirable middle-aged cast and no love interest.
w Lewis Greifer, David T. Chantler *TV play* Jacques Gillies *d* Quentin Lawrence *ph* Arthur Grant *m* Wilfred Josephs
☆ *Peter Cushing, André Morell, Richard Vernon*, Norman Bird, Edith Sharpe

Casino ***
US 1995 178m Technicolor Super 35
Universal/Syalis/Legende/De Fina/Cappa (Barbara de Fina)
A gambler who is put in charge of a Las Vegas casino by the Mafia runs into trouble when he tries

to run the business honestly and falls in love with a call-girl.
Deft, involving and intriguing depiction of the inescapable corruption of the spirit, in a city built on greed. It begins in a leisurely, documentary style before focusing on individuals as flawed as the system they operate and as expendable as the chips they bet.
w Nicholas Pileggi, Martin Scorsese
book Nicholas Pileggi *d* Martin Scorsese
ph Robert Richardson *pd* Dante Ferretti
ed Thelma Schoonmaker
☆ Robert DeNiro, Sharon Stone, Joe Pesci, James Woods, Don Rickles, Alan King, Kevin Pollak, L. Q. Jones, Dick Smothers

'I simply can't see any urgent reason for *Casino* to exist. Scorsese has always been a master of camera movement, but here the camera is just going through the motions.' – *Tom Shone, Sunday Times*

'It doesn't seem too much to ask, in exchange for three hours of our lives, to be offered an emotion less tainted than watching nasty people fall foul of one another.' – *Adam Mars-Jones, Independent*

'A must-see for cinema-savvy audiences.' – *Variety*

Sharon Stone

Casino de Paree: see *Go Into Your Dance*

The Casino Murder Case

US 1935 85m bw
MGM
Philo Vance solves a murder in a family of neurotics.
Rather heavy-going detection.
w Florence Ryerson, Edgar Allan Woolf *story* S. A. Van Dine *d* Edwin Marin *ph* Charles Clarke *ed* Conrad A. Nervig
☆ Paul Lukas, Rosalind Russell, Eric Blore, Donald Cook, Louise Fazenda, Ted Healy, Isabel Jewell, Leo G. Carroll

Casino Royale

GB 1967 130m Technicolor Panavision
Columbia/Famous Artists (Charles K. Feldman, Jerry Bresler)
The heads of the allied spy forces call Sir James Bond out of retirement to fight the power of SMERSH.
Woeful all-star kaleidoscope, a way-out spoof which generates far fewer laughs than the original. One of the most shameless wastes of time and talent in screen history.
w Wolf Mankowitz, John Law, Michael Sayers *novel* Ian Fleming *d* John Huston, Ken Hughes, Val Guest, Robert Parrish, Joe McGrath, Richard Talmadge *ph* Jack Hildyard, John Wilcox, Nicolas Roeg *m* Burt Bacharach *pd* Michael Stringer *ed* Bill Lenny *cos* Julie Harris
☆ David Niven (Sir James Bond), Deborah Kerr (Agent Mimi), Orson Welles (Le Chiffre), Peter Sellers (Evelyn Tremble), Ursula Andress (Vesper Lynd), Woody Allen (Jimmy Bond), William Holden (Ransome), Charles Boyer (Le Grand), John Huston (McTarry), Joanna Pettet (Mata Bond), Daliah Lavi (The Detainer), Kurt Kasznar (Smernov), Jacqueline Bisset (Miss Goodthighs), Derek Nimmo (Hadley), George Raft (Himself) and also Terence Cooper (James Bond), Ronnie Corbett (Polo), Peter O'Toole, Jean-Paul Belmondo (French Legionnaire, Geoffrey Bayldon (Q), Duncan Macrae (Inspector Mathis), Barbara Bouchet (Moneypenny)

'One of those wild wacky extravaganzas in which the audience is expected to have a great time because everybody making the film did. It seldom works out that way, and certainly doesn't here.' – *John Russell Taylor*

'The dialogue is witless and unhampered by taste, and the interminable finale is a collection of clichés in a brawl involving the cavalry, parachuted Indians, split-second appearances by George Raft and Jean-Paul Belmondo, every variety of mayhem, and Woody Allen burping radiation as a walking atom bomb.' – *Judith Crist*

'The worst film I ever enjoyed.' – *Donald Zec*

song 'The Look of Love' (*m* Burt Bacharach, *ly* Hal David)

'No Such Things As Ghosts?'

Casper

US 1995 100m DeLuxe
UIP/Amblin/Harvey (Colin Wilson)
A greedy woman searches for treasure in a haunted house, with the aid of an expert in ghosts and his teenage daughter.
An unpleasant attempt to revive a comic-book character, both sickly with sentiment and tasteless in its attitudes to life and death; the special effects are spectacular, though.
w Sherri Stoner, Deanna Oliver *story* Casper the Friendly Ghost by Joseph Oriolo, Seymour Rait *d* Brad Silberling *ph* Dean Cundey *m* James Horner *pd* Leslie Dilley *ed* Michael Kahn *sp* Michael Lantieri
☆ Christina Ricci, Bill Pullman, Cathy Moriarty, Eric Idle and also the voices of Malachi Pearson, Joe Nipote, Joe Alaskey, Brad Garrett

'Attempts, with a host of clever special effects, to be both wise and innocent as well as funny and scary. But it is outrageously sentimental; half of the fun of the piece is buried in buttery popcorn covering.' – *Derek Malcolm, Guardian*

'Purest ectoplasmic slush.' – *Sunday Times*

† The film took more than $277m at the box-office worldwide

†† In 1997 came a prequel, *Casper, a Spirited Beginning*, which was released direct to video and aimed at a young audience.

Casque d'Or ***

France 1952 96m bw
Speva/Paris (Robert Hakim)
aka: *Golden Marie*
1898. In the Paris slums, an Apache finds passionate love but is executed for murder.
A tragic romance which on its first release seemed bathed in a golden glow and is certainly an impeccable piece of film-making.
w Jacques Becker, Jacques Companeez *d* Jacques Becker *ph* Robert Le Fèbvre *m* Georges Van Parys
☆ *Simone Signoret, Serge Reggiani*, Claude Dauphin, Raymond Bussières, Gaston Modot

'Takes its place alongside *Le Jour Se Lève* among the masterpieces of the French cinema.' – *Karel Reisz*

'A screen alive with sensuousness and luminous figures.' – *Dilys Powell*

Simone Signoret

Cass Timberlane *

US 1947 119m bw
MGM (Arthur Hornblow Jnr)
A judge marries a working-class girl, who is unsettled at first but finally comes to realize her good fortune.
Solid drama with an understanding star performance and good production values.
w Donald Ogden Stewart *novel* Sinclair Lewis *d* George Sidney *ph* Robert Planck *m* Roy Webb
☆ *Spencer Tracy*, Lana Turner, Zachary Scott, Tom Drake, Mary Astor, Albert Dekker, Selena Royle, Josephine Hutchinson, Margaret Lindsay

Cassandra

Australia 1987 93m colour
Parallel (Trevor Lucas)
A young woman's nightmares of murder begin to turn into reality.
Spooky little chiller with a certain amount of suspense but not much substance.
w Colin Eggleston, John Ruane, Chris Fitchett *d* Colin Eggleston *ph* Garry Wapshott *m* Trevor Lucas, Ian Mason *pd* Stewart Burnside *ed* Josephine Cook
☆ Shane Briant, Briony Behets, Kit Taylor, Lee James, Susan Barling, Tim Burns, Tessa Humphries

The Cassandra Crossing

GB/Italy/West Germany 1976 129m Technicolor Panavision
AGF/CCC/International Cine (Lew Grade, Carlo Ponti)
A terrorist carrying a deadly plague virus boards a transcontinental train.
Disaster spectacular with a number of fashionable interests but no observable filmmaking technique.
w Tom Mankiewicz, Robert Katz, George Pan Cosmatos *d* George Pan Cosmatos *ph* Ennio Guarnieri *m* Jerry Goldsmith *pd* Aurelio Crugnola
☆ Sophia Loren, Richard Harris, Ava Gardner, Burt Lancaster, Martin Sheen, Ingrid Thulin, Lee Strasberg, John Phillip Law, Lionel Stander, Ann Turkel, O. J. Simpson, Alida Valli

La Casse: see *The Burglars*

Cast a Dark Shadow *

GB 1955 82m bw
Frobisher/Daniel M. Angel (Herbert Mason)
A wife-murderer marries an ex-barmaid and tries again.
Unambitious but enjoyable melodrama, well acted though with directorial opportunities missed.
w John Cresswell *play* Murder Mistaken by Janet Green *d* Lewis Gilbert *ph* Jack Asher *m* Antony Hopkins
☆ Dirk Bogarde, *Margaret Lockwood*, Kay Walsh, Kathleen Harrison, Robert Flemyng, Mona Washbourne, Walter Hudd

'Outnumbered – unarmed – unprepared – they hurled back their answer in flesh and flame!'

Cast a Giant Shadow *

US 1966 141m DeLuxe Panavision
UA/Mirisch/Llenroc/Batjac (Melville Shavelson)
An American military lawyer and ex-colonel goes to Israel in 1947 to help in the fight against the Arabs.
Spectacular war biopic with all concerned in good form but lacking the clarity and narrative control of a real smash.
w Melville Shavelson, from Ted Berkman's biography of Col. David Marcus *d* Melville Shavelson *ph* *Aldo Tonti* *m* Elmer Bernstein *pd* Michael Stringer
☆ *Kirk Douglas*, Angie Dickinson, Senta Berger, Luther Adler, Stathis Giallelis, Chaim Topol, John Wayne, Frank Sinatra, Yul Brynner, James Donald, Gordon Jackson, Michael Hordern, Gary Merrill, Allan Cuthbertson, Jeremy Kemp

Cast a Long Shadow

US 1959 82m bw
Mirisch/UA
A hard-drinking drifter thinks he may be the illegitimate son of a dead cattle baron.
Would-be psychological Western with not enough going for it.
w Martin M. Goldsmith, John McGreevey *novel* Wayne D. Overholser *d* Thomas Carr
☆ Audie Murphy, John Dehner, Terry Moore, James Best, Denver Pyle

'At the edge of the world, his journey begins.'

Cast Away **

US 2000 144m DeLuxe
TCF/Dreamworks (Steve Starkey, Tom Hanks, Robert Zemeckis, Jack Rapke)
Marooned on an uninhabited tropical island, a FedEx executive discovers that delivering parcels on time is not the sole purpose of life.
A movie that is less interested in exploring the consequences of the isolation of a hyperactive manager than in demonstrating the ability of its star to hold an audience on his own, with no more than a charismatic volleyball for company; Hanks manages it well, even though the movie cheats by dealing with despair only in retrospect.
w William Broyles Jnr *d* Robert Zemeckis *ph* Don Burgess *m* Alan Silvestri *pd* Rick Carter *ed* Arthur Schmidt
☆ Tom Hanks (Chuck Noland), Helen Hunt (Kelly Frears), Nick Searcy (Stan), Lari White (Bettina Peterson), Michael Forest (Pilot Jack), Viveka Davis (Pilot Gwen)

'As compelling a cinematic adventure as any Hollywood has produced… awes us with its sheer oceanic sweep and its cosmic apprehension of human insignificance.' – *Stephen Holden, New York Times*

'This is just deeply silly.' – *Peter Bradshaw, Guardian*

Tom Hanks; sound (Randy Thom, Tom Johnson, Dennis Sands, William B. Kaplan)

Cast Iron: see *The Virtuous Sin*

Castaway

GB 1986 118m Fujicolour
Cannon/United British Artists (Rick McCallum)
A bored London girl answers an ad placed by a man who wants a wife to take to a tropical island for a year; but he expects sex and she doesn't.
Extended absurdity uncharacteristic of its director.
w Allan Scott *book* Lucy Irvine *d* Nicolas Roeg *ph* Harvey Harrison *m* Stanley Myers *pd* Andrew Sanders *ed* Tony Lawson
☆ Oliver Reed, Amanda Donohoe, Georgina Hale

'Prospects are good for those interested in beautiful scenery and naked bodies.' – *Daily Variety*

The Castaway Cowboy *

US 1974 91m Technicolor
Walt Disney (Ron Miller, Winston Hibler)
In 1850, a Shanghaied sailor on Hawaii helps a lady potato farmer to turn her land into a cattle ranch.
Unexciting and unexceptional family fare.
w Don Tait *d* Vincent McEveety *ph* Andrew Jackson *m* Robert F. Brunner
☆ James Garner, Vera Miles, Robert Culp, Eric Shea, Elizabeth Smith

The Castle

West Germany 1969 93m colour
Maximilian Schell/Alfa/Glarus/Rudolf Noelte
A surveyor is summoned to a remote castle but prevented by the villagers from getting there.
Attempt, partly successful, to film an unfinished Kafka obscurity. Marks all round for trying.
wd Rudolf Noelte
☆ Maximilian Schell, Cordula Trantow, Trudik Daniel, Franz Misar

The Castle *

Australia 1997 85m Cinevex
UIP/Village Roadshow/Working Dog/Frontline TV (Debra Choate)
A dim-witted family, living happily at the edge of an airport, fights the government's plan to extend the runways by demolishing its home.
Low-budget comedy of victory for the little man, enjoyable in its ramshackle way.
w Rob Sitch, Santo Cilauro, Tom Gleisner, Jane Kennedy *d* Rob Sitch *ph* Miriana Marusic *m* Craig Harnath *pd* Carrie Kennedy *ed* Wayne Hyett
☆ Michael Caton, Anne Tenney, Sophie Lee, Anthony Simcoe, Stephen Curry, Wayne Hope, Eric Bana, Tiriel Mora, Charles (Bud) Tingwell, Robyn Nevin, Costas Kilias

'Inanity elevated to a jubilantly funny and optimistic fable, beautifully acted with unflagging sincerity.' – *Angie Errigo, Empire*

Castle Freak

US/Italy 1994 95m colour
Full Moon (Maurizio Maggi)
An American family inherit an Italian castle with a grisly secret.
Ineffectual horror that fails to generate much suspense.
w Dennis Paoli *d* Stuart Gordon *ph* Mario Vulpiani *m* Richard Band *ad* Frank Vanorio *ed* Bert Glastein
☆ Jeffrey Combs, Barbara Crampton, Jonathan Fuller, Jessica Dollarhide, Massimo Sarchielli, Elizabeth Kaza, Luca Zingaretti, Helen Stirling

Castle in the Air

GB 1952 90m bw
Hallmark/ABP
A nobleman fails to turn his castle into a hotel but hopes to sell it to the Coal Board.
Topical comedy which sparkled rather more on the stage.
w Alan Melville, Edward Dryhurst *play* Alan Melville *d* Henry Cass
☆ David Tomlinson, Helen Cherry, Margaret Rutherford, Barbara Kelly, A. E. Matthews, Pat Dainton, Brian Oulton, Ewan Roberts

Castle in the Desert *
US 1942 62m bw
TCF

Murders take place at the remote castle of an eccentric millionaire.
One of the sharpest Charlie Chan mysteries, with a lively plot and some good lines.
w John Larkin *d* Harry Lachman
☆ Sidney Toler, Arleen Whelan, Richard Derr, Douglass Dumbrille, Henry Daniell, Steve Geray, Sen Yung, Ethel Griffies, Milton Parsons

'A one-eyed major and his oddball heroes fight a twentieth-century war in a tenth-century castle!'
Castle Keep *
US 1969 107m Technicolor Panavision
Columbia/Filmways (Martin Ransohoff, John Calley)
During World War II seven battle-weary American soldiers occupy a 10th-century castle filled with art treasures, then die defending it. Or are they dead all the time?
The film version of this fantastic novel never seems quite sure, and the uncertainty finally deadens it despite careful work all round.
w Daniel Taradash, David Rayfiel *novel* William Eastlake *d* Sydney Pollack *ph* Henri Decaë *m* Michel Legrand
☆ Burt Lancaster, Peter Falk, Jean Pierre Aumont, Patrick O'Neal, Al Freeman Jnr, Scott Wilson, Tony Bill, Bruce Dern, Astrid Heeren

Castle of Evil
US 1966 81m Eastmancolor
NTA

A disfigured industrialist summons six people to a remote Caribbean island for the reading of his will.
Tedious variation on Ten Little Niggers *and* The Cat and the Canary, *with horror asides and the lowest of budgets.*
w Charles A. Wallace *d* Francis D. Lyon
☆ Virginia Mayo, Scott Brady, David Brian, Lisa Gaye, Hugh Marlowe

Castle of Fu Manchu
West Germany/Spain/Italy/GB 1968 92m Eastmancolor
Terra Filmkunst/Balcazar/Italian International/Towers of London

The yellow peril wrecks an ocean-going liner by turning water into ice, and keeps the inventor a prisoner.
Extraordinarily tatty entry in a series which started off well. (See Fu Manchu *for list.)*
w Harry Alan Towers *d* Jesús Franco *ph* Manuel Merino *m* Carlo Camilleri
☆ Christopher Lee, Richard Greene, Howard Marion Crawford, Gunther Stoll, Maria Perschy

Castle of the Doomed: see *Kiss Me Monster*

Castle on the Hudson *
US 1940 77m bw
Warner (Sam Bischoff)
GB title: *Years without Days*
A hardened criminal is not helped by his years in prison.
Adequate, gloomy remake of Twenty Thousand Years in Sing Sing.
w Seton I. Miller, Brown Holmes, Courteney Terrett *d* Anatole Litvak *ph* Arthur Edeson *m* Adolph Deutsch
☆ John Garfield, Pat O'Brien, Ann Sheridan, Burgess Meredith, Jerome Cowan, Henry O'Neill, Guinn Williams, John Litel

Casual Sex?
US 1988 97m colour
Universal/Jascat (Ilona Herzberg, Sheldon Kahn)

Two women, one promiscuous, the other prim, who are both scared of being single, find true love at a health resort.
Based on a stage musical and transferred to the screen without songs, it is an inconsequential jejune look at sexual relationships, full of direct-to-camera monologues that are at best coy and often embarrassing.
w Wendy Goldman, Judy Toll *play* book and lyrics Wendy Goldman, Judy Toll, music Alan Axelrod *d* Genevieve Robert *ph* Rolf Kestermann *m* Van Dyke Parks *pd* Randy Ser *ed* Sheldon Kahn, Donn Cambern
☆ Lea Thompson, Victoria Jackson, Stephen Shellen, Jerry Levine, Mary Gross, Peter Dvorsky, Andrew Dice Clay

'Even in war... murder is murder.'
Casualties of War *
US 1989 113m DeLuxe Panavision
Columbia TriStar (Art Linson)

In Vietnam, a soldier is horrified when others kidnap and rape a village girl.
Simple minded, melodramatic account of a true incident.
w David Rabe *book* Daniel Lang *d* Brian de Palma *ph* Stephen H. Burum *m* Ennio Morricone *pd* Wolf Kroeger *ed* Bill Pankow
☆ Michael J. Fox, Sean Penn, Don Harvey, John C. Reilly, John Leguizamo, Thuy Thu Le, Erik King, Jack Gwaltney
'This new film is the kind that makes you feel protective. When you leave the theatre, you'll probably find that you're not ready to talk about it. You may also find it hard to talk lightly about anything.' – *Pauline Kael*

The Cat *
France 1973 88m colour
Raymond Danon
After twenty-five years of marriage an embittered trapeze star and her husband simply don't talk to each other.
Absorbing drama for two characters, brilliantly acted, but with a somewhat unsatisfactory conclusion.
w Pascal Jardin *d* Pierre Granier-Deferre
☆ Jean Gabin, Simone Signoret

Cat and Mouse *
GB 1958 79m bw
Eros/Anvil (Paul Rotha)
The daughter of a man executed for murder is threatened by criminals seeking hidden loot.
Interesting rather than exciting second feature thriller directed by a documentary maker.
wd Paul Rotha *novel* Michael Halliday *ph* Wolfgang Suschitzky
☆ Lee Patterson, Ann Sears, Hilton Edwards, Victor Maddern, George Rose, Roddy McMillan

The Cat and the Canary ***
US 1927 84m (24 fps) bw silent
Universal

Greedy relatives assemble in an old house to hear an eccentric's will, and a young girl's sanity is threatened.
Archetypal spooky house comedy horror, here given an immensely stylish production which influenced Hollywood through the thirties and was spoofed in The Old Dark House.
w Alfred Cohn, Robert F. Hill play John Willard d Paul Leni ph Gilbert Warrenton ad Charles D. Hall
☆ Creighton Hale, Laura La Plante, Forrest Stanley, Tully Marshall, Flora Finch, Gertrude Astor, Arthur Carewe

The Cat and the Canary ***
US 1939 72m bw
Paramount (Arthur Hornblow Jnr)
Ten years after the death of an eccentric millionaire, relatives gather at his home for the reading of his will.
The comedy-thriller par excellence, *with Bob Hope fresh and sympathetic in his first big star part. A superbly staged remake, briskly paced, perfectly cast and lusciously photographed.*
w Walter de Leon, Lynn Starling d Elliott Nugent ph Charles Lang m Dr Ernst Toch ad Hans Dreier, Robert Usher *ed* Archie Marshek
☆ *Bob Hope* (Wally Campbell), *Paulette Goddard* (Joyce Norman), *Gale Sondergaard* (Miss Lu), Douglass Montgomery (Charlie Wilder), John Beal (Fred Blythe), *George Zucco* (Lawyer Crosby), *Nydia Westman* (Cicily), *Elizabeth Patterson* (Aunt Susan), John Wray (Hendricks)
CICILY: 'Do you believe people come back from the dead?'
WALLY: 'You mean like Republicans?'
CICILY: 'Don't these big empty houses scare you?'
WALLY: 'Not me, I was in vaudeville.'
WALLY: 'I get goose pimples. Even my goose pimples have goose pimples.'
'The objective is carried out briskly and to our complete satisfaction.' – *New York Times*
'A top programmer for upper-bracket bookings in the keys, and will hit a consistent stride down the line in the subsequents.' – *Variety*
'Beautifully shot, intelligently constructed.' – *Peter John Dyer, 1966*

The Cat and the Canary
GB 1979 98m Technicolor
Gala/Grenadier (Richard Gordon)

Relatives gather at a haunted house to hear the tape-recorded will of an eccentric millionaire.
An overpoweringly cast but half-heartedly scripted remake, which after a spirited beginning bores more than it thrills.
wd Radley Metzger *ph* Alex Thomson *m* Steven Cagan
☆ Honor Blackman, Michael Callan, Edward Fox, Wendy Hiller, Beatrix Lehmann, Olivia Hussey, Daniel Massey, Carol Lynley, Peter McEnery, Wilfrid Hyde-White
'So mechanically are characters shunted through the indistinguishable rooms and corridors that one is surprised not to see the parquet marked off in neat little squares, as on a Cluedo board.' – *Gilbert Adair, MFB*

The Cat and the Fiddle
US 1933 90m bw (colour sequence)
MGM (William K. Howard)

In a taxi in Brussels, a leading lady of Broadway musicals meets a European composer.
Very lightweight musical comedy.
w Sam and Bella Spewack *stageshow* Jerome Kern, Otto Harbach *d* William K. Howard *ph* Harold Rosson, Charles Clarke *md* Herbert Stothart *ad* Alexander Toluboff *ed* Frank Hull
☆ Jeanette MacDonald, Ramon Novarro, Charles Butterworth, Frank Morgan, Jean Hersholt, Vivienne Segal, Henry Armetta
'The only thing remaining of merit is the music.' – *Variety*

Cat Ballou **
US 1965 96m Technicolor
Columbia (Harold Hecht)

Young Catherine Ballou hires a drunken gunfighter to protect her father from a vicious gunman, but despite her efforts he is shot, so she turns outlaw.
Sometimes lively, sometimes somnolent Western spoof which considering the talent involved should have been funnier than it is. The linking ballad helps.
w Walter Newman, Frank R. Pierson *novel* Roy Chanslor *d* Elliot Silverstein *ph* Jack Marta *m* Frank de Vol
☆ Jane Fonda, *Lee Marvin*, Michael Callan, Dwayne Hickman, Nat King Cole, Stubby Kaye, Tom Nardini, John Marley, Reginald Denny
'Uneven, lumpy, coy and obvious.' – *Pauline Kael*
'The ultimate American spoof of the American Western, done with a judicious restraint and sly satire and, above all, a consistency all too rarely found in Hollywood.' – *Judith Crist*
Lee Marvin
Walter Newman, Frank R. Pierson; Frank de Vol; song 'The Ballad of Cat Ballou' (*m* Jerry Livingston, *ly* Mack David)
Lee Marvin

Cat Chaser
US 1988 98m Technicolor
Whiskers Productions (Peter A. Davis, William Panzer)

A motel owner becomes involved with an old girlfriend, who is now married to an exiled Dominican thug who keeps a fortune in banknotes in a secret hiding place.
Another botched attempt to find the cinematic equivalent to Leonard's tense, witty novels, not helped by an obtrusive voice-over.
w James Borelli, Elmore Leonard *novel* Elmore Leonard *d* Abel Ferrara *ph* Anthony B. Richmond *m* Chick Corea *pd* Dan Leigh *ed* Anthony Redman
☆ Peter Weller, Kelly McGillis, Charles Durning, Frederic Forrest, Tomas Milian, Juan Fernandez, Phil Leeds, Kelly Jo Minter, Tony Bolano

The Cat Creeps *
US 1930 71m bw
Universal
After relatives gather for the reading of a millionaire's will, attempts are made to send mad the girl who stands to inherit everything.
A sound remake of the 1927 Cat and the Canary. *Not too bad on its own account.*
w Gladys Lehman, William Hurlbut *d* Rupert Julian
☆ Helen Twelvetrees, Raymond Hackett, Neil Hamilton, Jean Hersholt, Montagu Love, Blanche Friderici, Elizabeth Patterson, Theodore von Eltz, Lilyan Tashman, Lawrence Grant

The Cat Creeps
US 1946 58m bw
Universal
A reporter and photographer solve a murder and uncover missing millions.
Terrible programme filler, nothing to do with the earlier movie of the same name that was a version of The Cat and the Canary.
w Edward Dein, Jerry Warner *d* Erle C. Kenton
☆ Noah Beery Jnr, Lois Collier, Paul Kelly, Douglass Dumbrille, Rose Hobart, Jonathan Hale

The Cat from Outer Space
US 1978 103m Technicolor
Walt Disney Productions (Ron Miller)

A superintelligent extraterrestrial cat is forced to land on Earth for running repairs.
Fairly modest studio offering which pleased its intended market but could have been sharper.
w Ted Key *d* Norman Tokar *ph* Charles F. Wheeler *m* Lalo Schifrin *sp* Eustace Lycett, Art Cruickshank, Danny Dee
☆ Ken Berry, Roddy McDowall, Sandy Duncan, Harry Morgan, McLean Stevenson, Jesse White, Alan Young, Hans Conried

Cat o' Nine Tails
Italy/France/Germany 1971 112m Technicolor Techniscope
Spettacoli/Mondial/Terra/Labrador (Salvatore Argento)
A blind reporter overhears an industrial espionage plot that turns into murder.
Smart surface mechanics camouflage poor storytelling.
wd Dario Argento *story* Dario Argento, Luigi Collo, Dardano Sacchetti *ph* Enrico Menczer *m* Ennio Morricone *ad* Carlo Leva *ed* Franco Fraticelli
☆ Karl Malden, James Franciscus, Catherine Spaak
'The sort of thriller where professional expertise and a certain visual elegance struggle to give "tone" and "style" to blandly undistinguished material.' – *Richard Combs, MFB*

'All the sultry drama of Tennessee Williams' Pulitzer Prize winning play is now on the screen!'
Cat on a Hot Tin Roof **
US 1958 108m Metrocolor
MGM/Avon (Lawrence Weingarten)

A rich plantation owner, dying of cancer, finds his two sons unsatisfactory: one is a conniver, the other a neurotic who refuses to sleep with his wife.
Slightly bowdlerized version of Tennessee Williams's most straightforward melodrama, watchable for the acting but still basically a theatrical experience.
w Richard Brooks, James Poe *play* Tennessee Williams *d* Richard Brooks *ph* William Daniels *m* uncredited
☆ *Paul Newman, Burl Ives*, Elizabeth Taylor, Jack Carson, Judith Anderson, Madeleine Sherwood, Larry Gates
BIG DADDY: 'Truth is pain and sweat and paying bills and making love to a woman that you don't love any more. Truth is dreams that don't come true and nobody prints your name in the paper until you die.'
MAGGIE: 'Win what? What is the victory of a cat on a hot tin roof?'
BRICK: 'Just staying on it, I guess.'
best picture; Richard Brooks, James Poe; Richard Brooks (as director); William Daniels; Paul Newman; Elizabeth Taylor

'Kiss me and I'll claw you to death!'

Cat People **

US 1942 73m bw

RKO (Val Lewton)

A beautiful Yugoslavian girl believes she can turn into a panther; before she is found mysteriously dead, several of her acquaintances are attacked by such a beast.

The first of Lewton's famous horror series for RKO is a slow starter but has some notable suspense sequences. It was also the first monster film to refrain from showing its monster.

w De Witt Bodeen *d* Jacques Tourneur *ph* Nicholas Musuraca *m* Roy Webb

☆ Simone Simon, Kent Smith, Tom Conway, Jane Randolph, Jack Holt

'(Lewton) revolutionized scare movies with suggestion, imaginative sound effects and camera angles, leaving everything to the fear-filled imagination.' – *Pauline Kael, 1968*

† *Curse of the Cat People* (qv) was a very unrelated sequel.

'An Erotic Fantasy For The Animal In Us All.'

Cat People

US 1982 118m Technicolor

Universal (Charles Fries)

A kinky version of the 1942 horrorpic. The feline lady now has an incestuous relationship with her brother, only changes after sex, and then must kill to become human again. (It is therefore safe to mate only with relatives.)

One presumes that among the eroticism and bloodlust a statement is being made, but it is never evident.

w Alan Ormsby *d* Paul Schrader *ph* John Bailey *m* Giorgio Moroder *ed* Jacqueline Cambas *sp* Tom Burman, Albert Whitlock *visual consultant* Ferdinando Scarfiotti

☆ Nastassja Kinski, Malcolm McDowell, John Heard, Annette O'Toole, Ruby Dee, Ed Begley Jnr

'The final impression is of a phantasmagoric indulgence in sound and vision by a filmmaker who fears sex and is excited by violence.' – *Sunday Times*

'The hobgoblins of an actual horror movie aren't easily translatable into the demons that haunt a Schrader hero on his way to a religious transcendence that is also a renunciation.' – *Richard Combs, MFB*

The Cat that Hated People **

US 1948 7m Technicolor

MGM

A weary Manhattan cat rockets to the moon but finds it even noisier and is glad to come home.

Violent but dazzlingly inventive cartoon from this madcap director; a little classic of its kind.

w Heck Allen *d* Tex Avery

'See: The Lost City Of Love-Starved Cat-Women!'

Cat Women of the Moon

US 1953 63m bw 3D

Three Dimensional Pictures

aka: *Rocket to the Moon*

Five American astronauts find the moon inhabited solely by ravenous cat women.

One of the top claimants to film history's booby prize, along with such other space fiction entrants as Fire Maidens from Outer Space, Plan 9 from Outer Space *and* Santa Claus Conquers the Martians. *It has more than a chance.*

w Roy Hamilton *d* Arthur Hilton

☆ Sonny Tufts, Victor Jory, Marie Windsor, William Phipps, Douglas Fowley

'The special effects look like they came free with a cornflakes packet.' – *The Dark Side*

Catch 22 *

US 1970 122m Technicolor Panavision

Paramount/Filmways (John Calley, Martin Ransohoff)

At a US Air Force base in the Mediterranean during World War II, one by one the officers are distressingly killed; a survivor paddles towards neutral Sweden.

Intensely black comedy, more so than M*A*S*H *and less funny, effectively mordant in places but too grisly and missing several tricks.*

w Buck Henry *novel* Joseph Heller *d* Mike Nichols *ph* David Watkin *m* none *pd* Richard Sylbert

☆ *Alan Arkin*, Martin Balsam, Richard Benjamin, Art Garfunkel, Jack Gilford, Buck Henry, Bob Newhart, Anthony Perkins, Paula Prentiss, Jon Voight, Martin Sheen, Orson Welles

'There are startling effects and good revue touches here and there, but the picture keeps going on and on, as if it were determined to impress us.' – *New Yorker, 1977*

'As hot and heavy as the original was cool and light.' – *Richard Schickel*

'It goes on so long that it cancels itself out, even out of people's memories; it was long awaited and then forgotten almost instantly.' – *Pauline Kael*

'Dr Strangelove out of Alice in Wonderland.' – *Daily Mail*

Catch Me a Spy

GB 1971 94m Technicolor

Rank/Ludgate/Capitol/Films de la Pleiade (Steven Pallos)

A British agent smuggling Russian manuscripts into England falls for the wife of a Russian spy and finally gets his money as well.

Complex, patchy comedy thriller with dispirited action scenes in Bucharest and Scotland. Technical credits rather dim.

w Dick Clement, Ian La Frenais *novel* George Marton, Tibor Meray *d* Dick Clement *ph* Christopher Challis *m* Claude Bolling *ad* Carmen Dillon *ed* John Bloom

☆ Kirk Douglas, Trevor Howard, Tom Courtenay, Marlene Jobert, Patrick Mower, Bernadette Lafont, Bernard Blier

Catch Me If You Can

US 1989 105m Foto-Kem

Medusa/Management Company Entertainment Group/Sterling Entertainment (Jonathan D. Krane)

A high-school student becomes a champion drag-racer to prevent his school from closing through lack of funds.

A drive-in movie for undemanding adolescents.

wd Stephen Sommers *ph* Ronn Schmidt *m* Tangerine Dream *ad* Stuart Blatt *ed* Bob Ducsay

☆ Matt Lattanzi, Loryn Locklin, Grant Heslov, Billy Morrissette, M. Emmet Walsh

'The true story of a real fake.'

Catch Me If You Can **

US 2002 141m Technicolor

DreamWorks/Amblin/Kemp/Splendid (Steven Spielberg, Walter F. Parkes)

A young con-man lives a lkife of fraud as a pilot, doctor, lawyer and forger, while keeping one step ahead of an FBI agent.

Based on a true story, an entertaining comedy about as teenager trying on different identities to see which one fits; at half-an-hour shorter, it would have been a better movie, but it will still leave you smiling.

w Jeff Nathanson *book* Frank W. Abagnale with Stan Redding *d* Steven Spielberg *ph* Janusz Kaminski *m* John Williams *pd* Jeannine Oppewall *ed* Michael Kahn

☆ Leonardo DiCaprio (Frank Abagnale Jnr), Tom Hanks (Carl Hanratty), *Christopher Walken* (Frank Abagnale), Martin Sheen (Roger Strong), Nathalie Baye (Paula Abagnale), Amy Adams (Brenda Strong), James Brolin (Jack Barnes)

'Deeply moving, quite wonderfully acted coming-of-age black comedy, packed with equal measures of pathos and plain fun.' – *Mark Dinning, Empire*

'Gently funny, sweetly adventurous film that makes you feel genuinely good, that is to say, entirely unconned by false sentiment or sharp, overmanipulative Hollywood practices.' – *Richard Shickel, Time*

Christopher Walken; John Williams

Christopher Walken

Catch My Soul

US 1973 95m DeLuxe

Fox-Rank/Metromedia (Richard Rosenbloom, Jack Good)

A black evangelist, led astray by a member of his congregation possessed by a demon, becomes jealous of his wife and murders her.

A rock and country musical version of Othello, *in which the tragic original is trivialized to the point of boredom.*

w Jack Good *musical play Jack Good from Shakespeare's Othello d* Patrick McGoohan *ph* Conrad Hall *m* Paul Glass *m/ly* Tony Joe White, Jack Good *md* Delaney Bramlett *pd* Tex Reed *ed* Sid Levin

☆ Richie Havens (Othello), Lance LeGault (Iago), Season Hubley (Desdemona), Tony Joe White (Cassio), Susan Tyrrell (Emilia)

'A sort of comic strip travesty of the play.' – *Tom Milne, MFB*

♫ Othello; Wash Us Clean; Catch My Soul; Working on a Building; Open Our Eyes; Looking Back; Eat the Bread, Drink the Wine; That's What God Said; Chug a Lug; I Found Jesus; Run Shaker Life; Book of Prophecy; Lust of the Blood; Tickle His Fancy; Put Out the Light

Catch Us If You Can

GB 1965 91m bw

Anglo Amalgamated/Bruton (David Deutsch)

US title: *Having a Wild Weekend*

Freelance stuntmen have various adventures in the west of England.

The first film of a pretentious director is a bright but wearisomely high-spirited imitation of A Hard Day's Night.

w Peter Nichols *d* John Boorman *ph* Manny Wynn *m* Dave Clark

☆ The Dave Clark Five, Barbara Ferris, David Lodge, Robin Bailey, Yootha Joyce

'An uneven script, rather uncertainly making its point about disillusionment and capitulation to the sham; but – like Mr Boorman's direction – at its best well worth your attention.' – *Dilys Powell*

'When murder is your business, you'd better not fall in love with your work.'

Catchfire

US 1989 99m CFI color

Vestron/Precision Films/Mack-Taylor Productions (Dick Clark, Dan Paulson)

A female artist who witnessed a Mafia killing falls in love with the man sent to murder her.

Unbelievable, though occasionally enjoyable, thriller.

w Rachel Kronstadt Mann, Ann Louise Bardach *d* Alan Smithee (Dennis Hopper) *ph* Ed Lachman *m* Curt Sobel *pd* Ron Foreman *ed* David Rawlins

☆ Dennis Hopper, Jodie Foster, Dean Stockwell, Vincent Price, John Turturro, Joe Pesci, Fred Ward, Julie Adams, G. Anthony Sirico

The Catered Affair *

US 1956 93m bw

MGM (Sam Zimbalist)

GB title: *Wedding Breakfast*

When the daughter of a New York taxi driver gets married, her mother insists on a bigger function than they can afford.

Rather heavy-going comedy with amusing dialogue, from the period when Hollywood was seizing on TV plays like Marty *and* Twelve Angry Men.

w Gore Vidal *TV play* Paddy Chayefsky *d* Richard Brooks *ph* John Alton *m* André Previn

☆ *Bette Davis*, Ernest Borgnine, Debbie Reynolds, Barry Fitzgerald, Rod Taylor, Robert Simon, Madge Kennedy, Dorothy Stickney

Catherine the Great *

GB 1934 93m bw

London Films/Alexander Korda

aka: *The Rise of Catherine the Great*

How Catherine married the mad prince and slowly conquered the Russian court.

Dated but well acted and written account, sober by comparison with The Scarlet Empress *which came out at the same time.*

w Lajos Biro, Arthur Wimperis, Marjorie Deans *play The Czarina* by Melchior Lengyel, Lajos Biro *d* Paul Czinner *ph* Georges Périnal, Robert Lapresle *m* Ernest Toch *md* Muir Mathieson *ad* Vincent Korda *ed* Harold Young

☆ Elisabeth Bergner, Douglas Fairbanks Jnr, Flora Robson, Gerald du Maurier, Irene Vanbrugh, Griffith Jones, Joan Gardner, Diana Napier

'It rates no raves but is a good piece of merchandise.' – *Variety*

† The style is typified by a speech given to Grand Duke Peter: 'If she wasn't on the throne she'd be on the street.'

Catholic Boys: see *Heaven Help Us*

Cathy Tippel: see *Keetje Tippel*

Catlow *

GB 1971 101m Metrocolor

MGM/Euan Lloyd

A likeable outlaw tries to avoid problems while recovering his hidden gold.

Light-hearted, cheerfully cast, fast-moving, Spanish-located Western.

w Scot Finch, J. J. Griffith *novel* Louis L'Amour *d* Sam Wanamaker *ph* Ted Scaife *m* Roy Budd

☆ Yul Brynner, Leonard Nimoy, Richard Crenna, Daliah Lavi, Jo Ann Pflug, Jeff Corey, Bessie Love, David Ladd

Catman of Paris

US 1946 63m bw

Republic (Marek M. Libkov)

An amnesia victim may be the mad killer who prowls the boulevards.

Poverty Row thriller with a few sharp moments.

w Sherman Lowe *d* Lesley Selander

☆ Carl Esmond, Lenore Aubert, Adele Mara, Douglass Dumbrille, Gerald Mohr, Fritz Feld

'Settings have solid mahogany look but the script has only a literate veneer.' – *Variety*

'Things Are Gonna Get Hairy.'

Cats & Dogs

US 2001 87m Technicolor

Warner/Village Roadshow/NPV/Mad Chance/Zide/Perry

A Persian cat's plans to take over the world are foiled by a puppy.

Dull and dogged movie, eager to please but unable to inspire affection, and fatally hampered by a silly script.

w John Requa, Glenn Ficarra *d* Lawrence Guterman *ph* Julio Macat *m* John Debney *pd* James Bissell *ed* Michael A. Stevenson, Rick W. Finney *sp* Jim Henson's Creature Shop; Rhythm & Hues; Tippett Studio

☆ Jeff Goldblum (Professor Brody), Elizabeth Perkins (Mrs Brody), Miriam Margolyes (Sophie), Alexander Pollock (Scott Brody), voices of: Tobey Maguire (Lou), Alec Baldwin (Butch), Sean Hayes (Mr Tinkles), Susan Sarandon (Ivy), Joe Pantoliano (Peek), Michael Clarke Duncan (Sam), Jon Lovitz (Calico), Charlton Heston (The Mastiff)

'An exhausting experience for anyone over 10.' – *Rob Mackie. Guardian*

'A half-digested hairball of a movie.' – *Leslie Felperin, Sight and Sound*

Cat's Eye

US 1985 93m Technicolor J-D-C Scope

Famous Films/Dino de Laurentiis (Martha J. Schumacher)

Three semi-horror stories linked by a cat.

This omnibus is weak in every department.

w Stephen King *d* Lewis Teague *ph* Jack Cardiff *m* Alan Silvestri *pd* Giorgio Postiglione

☆ Drew Barrymore, James Woods, Alan King, Kenneth McMillan, Robert Hays, Candy Clark, James Naughton

'It creeps in on foggy feet.' – *Variety*

The Cat's Paw *

US 1936 101m bw

Harold Lloyd

The son of a Chinese missionary returns home and finds himself in the middle of a Tong war.

Very moderate star comedy from the time when he was considering himself a character comedian rather than a slapstick ace.

w Harold Lloyd, Sam Taylor *story* Clarence Budington Kelland *d* Sam Taylor

☆ Harold Lloyd, George Barbier, Una Merkel, Nat Pendleton, Grant Mitchell, Vince Barnett

'The picture gets its laughs all right, but it approaches them at a crawl.' – *Variety*

Cattle Annie and Little Britches

US 1980 98m CFI color

Hemdale/UATC (Rupert Hitzig, Alan King)

In 1893, two girls head west in search of adventure.

Rather winsome family Western, with too little real action and too much romping about.

w Robert Ward, David Eyre *novel* Robert Ward *d* Lamont Johnson *ph* Larry Pizer *m* Sanh Berti, Tom Slocum
☆ Burt Lancaster, John Savage, Rod Steiger, Diane Lane, Amanda Plummer, Scott Glenn, Steven Ford
'Its storyline meanders and it never clinches any central conflict. But it has qualities of feeling that grab-'em movies can't approach.' – *Peter Rainer, Los Angeles Herald Examiner*

Cattle Drive
US 1951 78m Technicolor
Universal-International (Aaron Rosenberg)
The spoiled teenage son of a magnate finds humanity and friendship with a cowhand during a cattle drive.
Captains Courageous *out west, not badly done.*
w Jack Natteford, Lillie Hayward *d* Kurt Neumann
☆ Joel McCrea, Dean Stockwell, Chill Wills, Leon Ames, Bob Steele

Cattle Empire
US 1958 82m DeLuxe Cinemascope
TCF (Robert Stabler)
A trail boss out of prison gets a new assignment and signs up helpers who had previously made life difficult for him.
Fair general Western, entirely dependent on its star.
w Endre Bohem, Eric Norden *d* Charles Marquis Warren *ph* Brydon Baker *m* Paul Sawtell, Bert Shefter
☆ Joel McCrea, Gloria Talbott, Don Haggerty, Phyllis Coates, Paul Brinegar

Cattle King
US 1963 90m Metrocolor
MGM/Missouri (Nat Holt)
GB title: *Guns of Wyoming*
A big rancher opposes a cattle trail and starts a range war.
Moderately expert but very familiar star Western.
w Thomas Thompson *d* Tay Garnett *ph* William E. Snyder *m* Paul Sawtell
☆ Robert Taylor, Joan Caulfield, Robert Middleton, Robert Loggia, Larry Gates, Malcolm Atterbury

Cattle Queen of Montana
US 1954 88m Technicolor
RKO/Benedict Bogeaus
A tough woman inherits her father's rangeland and resists cattle rustlers.
A Western which runs in predictable grooves, and could have done with more vigour.
w Robert Blees, Howard Estabrook *story* Robert Blackburn *d* Allan Dwan *ph* John Alton *md* Louis Forbes
☆ Barbara Stanwyck, Ronald Reagan, Gene Evans, Lance Fuller, Anthony Caruso, Jack Elam

Caught!
US 1931 71m bw
Paramount
A US cavalry officer discovers that Calamity Jane is his mother.
Curious mother-love Western.
w Agnes Brand Leahy, Keene Thompson, Sam and Bella Spewack *d* Edward Sloman
☆ Richard Arlen, Louise Dresser, Frances Dee

Caught *
US 1948 88m bw
Enterprise (Wolfgang Reinhardt)
The ill-treated wife of a vicious millionaire leaves him for a doctor, but finds she is to have the millionaire's baby.
Pretentious film noir, *rather typical of its time, with much talent squandered on a very boring plot.*
w Arthur Laurents *novel Wild Calendar* by Libbie Block *d Max Ophüls ph Lee Garmes m* Frederick Hollander *ed* Robert Parrish
☆ James Mason (the doctor), Robert Ryan (the millionaire), Barbara Bel Geddes, Natalie Schafer, Curt Bois
'Ophuls had suffered at Hughes' hands … had wasted time on worthless projects … and had been referred to as "the oaf". Laurents built the script on stories which Ophuls told him about Hughes, and on the accounts given by one of Hughes' girls.' – *Pauline Kael*

Caught
US 1995 109m DuArt
Cinehaus/DuArt/Circle Films (Richard Brick, Irwin Young)
Tensions within a Hispanic family explode after an Irish drifter moves in.
A thriller that works a few variations on a familiar theme, but lacks the style to capture and maintain an audience's interest.
w Edward Pomerantz *novel Into It* by Edward Pomerantz *d* Robert M. Young *ph* Michael Barrow *m* Chris Botti *pd* Hilary Rosenfeld *ed* Norman Buckley
☆ Edward James Olmos, Maria Conchita Alonso, Arie Verveen, Steven Schub, Bitty Schram, Shawn Elliott

Caught in the Act
GB 1996 97m colour
Midsummer (Christopher Milburn)
Smitten by a theatrical agent, a young woman persuades her two equally unmusical friends to form a singing group to perform on his talent show.
Feeble comedy that never rises above sitcom predictability.
w Caroline Hill, Mark Greenstreet *d* Mark Greenstreet *ph* David Evans *m* Simon May *pd* James Hendy *ed* Nick Arthurs
☆ Sara Crowe (Lucinda), Annette Badland (Katherine), Nadia Sawalha (Amanda), Paul Shelley (Neville Goodenough), Leslie Phillips (Sydney Fisher), Guy Henry (Algie), Tim McMullan (Pip), Gerard Kelly (Ronnie Rich), Nickolas Grace (Melvin), Gaye Brown (Maureen Riley)

Caught in the Draft **
US 1941 82m bw
Paramount (B. G. de Sylva)
A nervous film star cannot avoid being drafted into the army.
Sprightly comedy from the star's best period, with gags and supporting cast well up to form.
w Harry Tugend *d* David Butler *ph* Karl Struss *m* Victor Young
☆ *Bob Hope, Lynne Overman,* Dorothy Lamour, Clarence Kolb, Eddie Bracken, Paul Hurst, Irving Bacon

Caught Plastered
US 1931 68m bw
RKO
In helping an old lady save her drug store, two hams get mixed up with bootleggers.
Tedious star farce.
w Ralph Spence, Douglas MacLean *d* William Seiter
☆ Bert Wheeler, Robert Woolsey, Dorothy Lee, Lucy Beaumont, Jason Robards
'Best for combo and three-dayers.' – *Variety*

Caught Short
US 1930 75m approx bw
Cosmopolitan/MGM
Feuding boarding house landladies play the stock market – and win.
Lumbering comedy which marked the first big success for the team of Dressler and Moran.
w Willard Mack, Robert Hopkins *d* Charles Reisner
☆ Marie Dressler, Polly Moran, Charles Morton, Anita Page
'A gold mine … the apex of the career of this pair of sublimated film-makers … a box office smash for all classes anywhere.' – *Variety*
† A credit reads: Story suggested by Eddie Cantor's gag book.

Caught Up *
US 1998 97m DeLuxe
Heller Highwater/Live/Mediaworks
A former convict forms a relationship with a duplicitous woman when a hitman opens fire on them both.
Enjoyable, slickly directed modern excursion into film noir, *set among the black community of South Central Los Angeles.*
wd Darin Scott *ph* Thomas Callaway *m* Marc Bonilla *pd* Terrence Foster *ed* Charles Bornstein
☆ Cynda Williams, Bokeem Woodbine, Joseph Lindsey, Clifton Powell, Basil Wallace, Tony Todd, LL Cool J, Snoop Doggy Dog, Jeffrey Combs
'An engrossing, skillful yarn that takes its protag on a twisted path of murder, deceit, treachery and passion.' – *Leonard Klady, Variety*

Cauldron of Blood
Spain/US 1968 97m Eastmancolor Panoramica
Tigon/Hispamer/Robert D. Weinbach
aka: *Blind Man's Bluff*
A sculptor, blinded in a car crash, is unaware that his wife has turned killer to keep him supplied with the skeletons he uses in his work.
Dreary horror movie that is interesting only for the presence of Karloff, and even he seems to wish himself elsewhere.
w John Melson, Edward Mann, José Luis Bayonas *d* Edward Mann (Santos Alcocer) *ph* Francisco Sempere *m* Ray Ellis *ad* Gil Parrondo *ed* J. Antonio Rojo *sp* Thierre Pathé
☆ Boris Karloff, Viveca Lindfors, Jean-Pierre Aumont, Jacqui Speed
'Its heavy Freudian symbolism becomes almost laughable in conjunction with the wooden dialogue and ludicrous situations.' – *David Pirie, MFB*
† The film was cut to 87m for its British release.

Cause for Alarm *
US 1951 74m bw
MGM (Tom Lewis)
A housewife tries frantically to retrieve a posted letter containing manufactured evidence which may put her on a murder charge.
Minor-league suspenser, watchable but disappointingly handled.
w Mel Dinelli, Tom Lewis *d* Tay Garnett *ph* Joe Ruttenberg *m* André Previn
☆ Loretta Young, Barry Sullivan, Bruce Cowling, Margalo Gillmore, Irving Bacon

'A love that suffered and rose triumphant above the crushing events of this modern age! The march of time measured by a mother's heart!'
Cavalcade **
US 1933 109m bw
Fox (Winfield Sheehan)
The story of an upper-class English family between the Boer War and World War I.
Rather static version of the famous stage spectacular, very similar in setting and style to TV's later Upstairs Downstairs. *Good performances, flat handling.*
w Reginald Berkeley *play* Noël Coward *d* Frank Lloyd *ph* Ernest Palmer *m* Louis de Francesco *ad* William Darling *war scenes* William Cameron Menzies
☆ Clive Brook, Diana Wynyard, Ursula Jeans, Herbert Mundin, Una O'Connor, Irene Browne, Merle Tottenham, Beryl Mercer, Frank Lawton, Billy Bevan
'Dignified and beautiful spectacle that will demand respect.' – *Variety*
'If there is anything that moves the ordinary American to uncontrollable tears, it is the plight – the constant plight – of dear old England … a superlative newsreel, forcibly strengthened by factual scenes, good music, and wonderful photography.' – *Pare Lorentz*
'Greater even than *Birth of a Nation!*' – *Louella Parsons*
'An orgy of British self-congratulation.' – *Pauline Kael, 70s*
best picture; Frank Lloyd; William Darling
Diana Wynyard

The Cave Dwellers: see *One Million BC*

Cave of Outlaws
US 1951 76m Technicolor
Universal-International (Leonard Goldstein)
After 15 years in prison, a bandit finds that locals are determined to relieve him of the fortune in gold he is alleged to have stolen and hidden in a cave.
Modest Western with an interesting view on celebrity and small town greed; it gains novelty value from scenes shot in the Carlsbad Caverns in New Mexico.
w Elizabeth Wilson *d* William Castle *ph* Irving Glassberg *md* Joseph Gershenson *ad* Bernard Herzbrun, Nathan Juran *ed* Edward Curtiss
☆ Macdonald Carey (Pete Carver), Alexis Smith (Liz Trent), Edgar Buchanan (Dobbs), Victor Jory (Ben Cross), Hugh O'Brian (Garth), Houseley Stevenson (Cooley), Hugh Sanders, Raymond Bond, Robert Osterloh

Caveman
US 1981 91m Technicolor
UA (Lawrence Turman, David Foster)
Adventures of a prehistoric man.
Witless farrago of puns and farts on a lower level than Mel Brooks, if such a thing were possible.
w Rudy de Luca, Carl Gottlieb *d* Carl Gottlieb *ph* Alan Hume *m* Lalo Schifrin *pd* Philip M. Jefferies *ed* Gene Fowler
☆ Ringo Starr, Dennis Quaid, Jack Gilford, Barbara Bach, Avery Schreiber
'Too gross and leery for children and not nearly sprightly or sly enough for adults.' – *Daily Mail*
'Worth about half an hour of anybody's time. Unfortunately it runs 97 minutes.' – *Guardian*

El Cazador de la Muerte: see *Deathstalker*

Cease Fire
US 1985 97m Continental Color
Double Helix/Cineworld (William Grefe)
Ex-Vietnam vets in Miami have trouble getting work and forgetting the past.
Honest but predictable drama from behind the headlines.
w George Fernandez *play Vietnam Trilogy* by George Fernandez *d* David Nutter *ph* Henning Schellerup *m* Gary Fry *ad* Alan Avchen *ed* Julio Chaves
☆ Don Johnson, Lisa Blount, Robert F. Lyons, Richard Chaves, Rick Richards

'Long Live Guerilla Film Making!'
'Punish Bad Cinema!'
Cecil B. Demented *
US 2000 88m colour
Artisan/Canal+/Polar (John Fielder, Joe Caracciolo Jr, Mark Tarlov)
A guerilla filmmaker kidnaps a Hollywood star and forces her to appear in his subversive picture.
A movie that is really no better than the flicks it satirises, but some fun can be had along the way.
d John Waters *ph* Robert Stevens *m* Basil Poledouris, Zoe Poledouris *pd* Vincent Peranio *ed* Jeffrey Wolf
☆ Melanie Griffith (Honey Whitlock), Stephen Dorff (Cecil B. Demented), Alicia Witt (Cherish), Larry Giliard Jnr (Lewis), Maggie Gyllenhaal (Petie), Eric M. Barry (Fidget), Zenzele Uzoma (Chardonnay), Erika Lynn Rupli (Pam), Harriet Dodge (Dinah), Adrian Grenier (Lyle), Jack Noseworthy (Rodney), Mink Stole (Mrs Mallory), Ricki Lake (Libby), Patricia Hearst (Fidget's Mom), Eric Roberts (Honey's Ex-husband)
'You don't have to be the kind of middle-aged gay film buff who lives in Brighton with a poodle called Baby Jane to love this movie, but it would help.' – *Cosmo Landesman, Sunday Times*
'A strange air of pointlessness pervades this film, mostly aiming pseudo-satire at non-targets.' – *Peter Bradshaw, Guardian*

Ceiling Zero *
US 1935 95m bw
Warner/Cosmopolitan (Harry Joe Brown)
Amorous and airborne adventures of an irresponsible but brilliant civil airlines pilot.
Splendid star vehicle which turns maudlin in the last reel but until then provides crackling entertainment.
w Frank 'Spig' Wead *play* Frank Wead *d Howard Hawks ph* Arthur Edeson
☆ *James Cagney,* Pat O'Brien, June Travis, Stuart Erwin, Henry Wadsworth, Isabel Jewell, Barton MacLane
'An entertainment wallop of extraordinary power.' – *Variety*
'The best of all airplane pictures.' – *Otis Ferguson, 1939*
'Directed at a breakneck pace which emphasizes its lean fibre and its concentration on the essentials of its theme.' – *Andrew Sarris, 1963*
† Remade in 1939 as *International Squadron.*

Cela s'appelle l'Aurore *
France/Italy 1955 108m bw
Marceau/Laetitia
A Corsican company doctor falls for a young widow while his wife is on holiday, and events lead to tragedy.
Efficient melodrama, given an extra dimension by its auteur.
w Luis Buñuel, Jean Ferry *novel* Emmanuel Robles *d* Luis Buñuel *ph* Robert Le Fèbvre *m* Joseph Kosma
☆ Georges Marchal, Lucia Bose, Gianni Esposito, Julien Bertheau, *Henri Nassiet*

The Celebration: see *Festen*

'A new comedy about people who will do anything to get famous ... or stay famous.'
Celebrity *
US 1998 113m bw
Buena Vista/Sweetland (Jean Doumanian)
After a marital break-up, a promiscuous journalist and his insecure former wife look for love.
With the neurotic centre of energy being occupied by both Branagh and Davis, Allen's on-screen presence is much missed here, while on the other side of the camera he recycles his usual attitudes to relationships without much apparent enthusiasm but with the occasional good joke.
wd Woody Allen *ph* Sven Nykvist *pd* Santo Loquasto *ed* Susan E. Morse
☆ Hank Azaria, Kenneth Branagh, Judy Davis, Leonardo DiCaprio, Melanie Griffith, Famke Janssen, Michael Lerner, Joe Mantegna, Bebe Neuwirth, Winona Ryder, Charlize Theron
'Annoyingly mannered in performance as well as tiresomely familiar in the way it trots out its angst-ridden urban characters' problems.' – *Todd McCarthy, Variety*

Céleste
West Germany 1981 106m Eastmancolor
Artificial Eye/Pelemele/Bayerische Rundfunk (Eleonore Adlon)
Proust's housekeeper recalls their life together.
Stifling, slow-moving account, likely to interest only admirers of the author.
wd Percy Adlon *book* *Monsieur Proust* by Céleste Albaret *ph* Jürgen Martin, Horst Becker, Helmo Sahliger, Hermann Ramelow *m* Cesar Franck *ad* Hans Gailling *ed* Clara Fabry
☆ *Eva Mattes, Jürgen Arndt*, Norbert Wartha, Wolf Euba, Joseph Manoth, Leo Bardischewski

Celia
GB 1949 67m bw
Exclusive/Hammer (Anthony Hinds)
An impecunious actress becomes a temporary private eye investigating the case of a rich aunt who marries a man young enough to be her son and refuses to meet her relatives.
Mildly amusing, cheaply made comedy thriller, based on a BBC radio serial by Mason.
w A. R. Rawlinson, Edward J. Mason, Francis Searle, Roy Plomley *d* Francis Searle *ph* Cedric Williams *md* Frank Spencer, Rupert Grayson *ad* Denis Wreford *ed* R. C. Cox
☆ Hy Hazell, Bruce Lester, John Bailey, Joan Hickson, Elsie Wagstaff

Celia *
Australia 1988 103m colour
BCB/Seon (Timothy White, Gordon Glenn)
Grieving over the death of her grandmother and caught up in political and sexual acrimony that she doesn't understand, a nine-year old girl retreats into a fantasy world of childish violence.
Unconvincing tale of a child's development, warped by the red-baiting, rabbit-hating suburban Australian society of the 1950s.
wd Ann Turner *ph* Geoffrey Simpson *m* Chris Neal *pd* Peta Lawson *ed* Ken Sallows
☆ Rebecca Smart, Nicholas Eadie, Victoria Longley, Mary-Anne Fahey

Celine and Julie Go Boating *
France 1974 192m Eastmancolor
Les Films du Losange (Barbet Schroeder)
Two girls change the outcome of a drama played daily in a haunted house.
Odd, dreamlike, absurdly long and semi-improvisational mood piece, with reverberations from Alice in Wonderland *and* Orphée. *Not an unpleasant experience, but sometimes a tiresome one.*
w Eduardo de Gregorio, Juliet Berto, Dominique Labourier, Bulle Ogier, Marie-France Pisier, Jacques Rivette, partly suggested by two stories by Henry James *d* Jacques Rivette *ph* Jacques Renard *m* Jean-Marie Senia
☆ Juliet Berto, Dominique Labourier, Bulle Ogier, Marie-France Pisier, Barbet Schroeder
'Rivette uncannily combines slapstick, suspense and tears in his most watchable assault on the narrative form.' – *Jan Dawson*
† Shot in 16mm.

'Enter the mind of a killer.'
The Cell *
US 2000 107m DeLuxe
New Line/Radical Media (Julio Caro, Eric McLeod)
A child psychotherapist goes inside the mind of a comatose serial killer to discover where he has hidden his latest victim.
Deliriously daft thriller that uses its minimal narrative as an excuse for over-indulgence in digital imagery that ransacks the furthest reaches of psychedelia before subsiding into banality; it is ideal viewing for those with short attention spans.
w Mark Protosevich *d* Tarsem *ph* Paul Laufer *m* Howard Shore *pd* Tom Foden *ed* Paul Rubell, Robert Duffy *cos* Eiko Ishioka, April Napier
☆ Jennifer Lopez (Catherine Deane), Vince Vaughn (Peter Novak), Vincent D'Onofrio (Carl Stargher), Jake Weber (Gordon Ramsey), Dylan Baker (Henry West), Marianne Jean-Baptiste (Dr Miriam Kent), James Gammon (Teddy Lee), Tara Subkoff (Julia Hickson), Colton James (Edward Baines), Patrick Bauchau (Lucien Baines), Gareth Williams (Stargher's Father)
'So cool to the touch that it could be kept in your grocer's freezer' – *Elvis Mitchell, New York Times*
'Contains images the likes of which you won't have seen before–and, unless Tarsem learns a little self-control and improves his story-telling skills, you probably won't see again.' – *Empire*
🏆 make-up (Michele Burke, Edouard Henriques)

Cell 2455 Death Row
US 1955 77m bw
Columbia (Wallace MacDonald)
A convicted murderer staves off execution with appeal after appeal.
Cheap run-off of the case of Caryl Chessman, who was executed ten years after his trial for rape and murder. Retold in a 1977 TV movie, Kill Me If You Can.
w Jack de Witt *book* Caryl Chessman *d* Fred F. Sears *ph* Fred Jackman Jnr *md* Mischa Bakaleinikoff
☆ William Campbell, Kathryn Grant, Harvey Stephens, Marian Carr, Vince Edwards

The Celluloid Closet **
US 1995 101m colour
Electric/Reflective/Telling Pictures/HBO/Channel 4/ZD (Rob Epstein, Jeffrey Friedman)
A documentary, illustrated with interviews and excerpts from films, about the way homosexuals have been presented in Hollywood movies.
An interesting and provocative examination of Hollywood attitudes towards sexuality, though it never quite gets to grips with how far movies reflect and influence the attitudes of a wider society.
w Rob Epstein, Jeffrey Friedman, Sharon Wood, Armistead Maupin *book* Vito Russo *d* Rob Epstein, Jeffrey Friedman *ph* Nancy Schreiber *m* Carter Burwell *ad* Scott Chambliss *ed* Jeffrey Friedman, Arnold Glassman
☆ Tony Curtis, Armistead Maupin, Susie Bright, Whoopi Goldberg, Quentin Crisp, Harvey Fierstein, Arthur Laurents, Gore Vidal, Farley Granger, Paul Rudnick, Shirley MacLaine, Tom Hanks, John Schlesinger, Lily Tomlin (narrator)
'Fascinating, insightful, often funny.' – *George Perry*

Celtic Pride
US 1996 91m Technicolor
Buena Vista/Hollywood/Caravan (Roger Birnbaum)
Two basketball fans kidnap the star player from a rival team so that their own team can win an important game.
A comedy, of working-class passion for sporting heroes, which does not travel well.
w Judd Apatow *d* Tom De Cerchio *ph* Oliver Wood *m* Basil Poledouris *pd* Stephen Marsh *ed* Hubert de la Bouillerie
☆ Damon Wayans, Daniel Stern, Dan Aykroyd, Gail O'Grady, Adam Hendershott, Paul Guilfoyle
'An uneven but largely likeable basketball-themed comedy.' – *Variety*

Celui Qui Doit Mourir: see *He Who Must Die*

'Love Knows No Limits.'
The Cement Garden *
GB/Germany/France 1993 105m colour
Metro Tartan/Constantin/Torii/Sylvia Montalti/Laurentic (Bee Gilbert, Ene Vanaveski)
After their parents die, a teenage boy and girl, while trying to look after their younger brothers and sisters, begin an incestuous affair.
A cool, distanced and unsettling account of adolescent angst and sexuality, notable for some excellent acting.
wd Andrew Birkin *novel* Ian McEwan *ph* Stephen Blackman *m* Edward Shearmur *pd* Bernd Lepel *ed* Toby Tremlett
☆ *Andrew Robertson, Charlotte Gainsbourg*, Alice Coulthard, Ned Birkin, Sinead Cusack, Hanns Zischler, Jochen Horst, Gareth Brown, William Hootkins
'Neither a black comedy nor a horror story, but a delicate and beautifully filmed and performed account of the innocence and confusions of youth, within an adult world, unlikely to be mature enough to comprehend it.' – *Derek Malcolm, Guardian*
† Birkin won the award for best director at the Berlin Film Festival.

Cemetery Man *
France/Italy 1994 100m Eastmancolor Technovision
KG/Canal+/Audifilm/Urania (Tilde Corsi, Gianni Romoli, Michele Soavi)
original title: *Dellamorte Dellamore*
The watchman at a cemetery where the dead rise from their graves after seven days begins an affair with a beautiful young widow when she visits her newly buried husband.
A horror film that is more original than most, as it veers between elegance and extreme goriness, eroticism and necrophilia, camp humour and sudden shock, coarseness and mysticism. It is not, however, for the squeamish.
w Gianni Romoli *novel* Tiziano Sclavi *d* Michele Soavi *ph* Mauro Marchetti *m* Manuel de Sica *pd* Antonello Geleng *ed* Franco Fraticelli *sp* Sergio Stivaletti
☆ Rupert Everett, François Hadji-Lazaro, Anna Falci, Mickey Knox, Fabiana Formica, Clive Riche, Katja Anton, Stefano Masciarelli
'A hip, offbeat horror item floating on a bed of dark philosophy.' – *Variety*

Centennial Summer **
US 1946 102m Technicolor
TCF (Otto Preminger)
A Philadelphia family responds to the Great Exposition of 1876.
Pleasing family comedy with music, the kind of harmless competence Hollywood used to throw off with ease but can no longer manage.
w Michael Kanin *novel* Albert E. Idell *d* Otto Preminger *ph* Ernest Palmer *m* Alfred Newman *m/ly* Jerome Kern, Oscar Hammerstein II, E. Y. Harburg, Leo Robin
☆ Jeanne Crain, Cornel Wilde, Linda Darnell, William Eythe, Walter Brennan, *Constance Bennett*, Dorothy Gish
† Jeanne Crain's songs were dubbed by Louanne Hogan.
🏆 Alfred Newman; song 'All Through the Day' (*m* Jerome Kern, *ly* Oscar Hammerstein II)

The Center of the World
US 2001 88m colour
Momentum/Redeemable Features (Peter Newman, Wayne Wang)
GB title: *The Centre of the World*
An internet millionaire and a stripper spend a dirty weekend in Las Vegas.
Filmed in muddy digital video, this murky study of the commercialisation of relationships irritates more than it enlightens.
w Ellen Benjamin Wong *d* Wayne Wang *ph* Mauro Fiore *pd* Donald Graham Burt *ed* Lee Percy
☆ Peter Sarsgaard (Richard Longman), Molly Parker (Florence), Carla Gugino (Jerri), Balthazar Getty (Brian Pivano)
'A movie that illustrates what I've already noted... Namely how the sewage of pornographic movies is now infiltrating mainstream cinema.' – *Alexander Walker, London Evening Standard*
'Even at their sweatiest and most naked, the characters never exhale the humidity of real life. Instead they breathe the thin, parched air of an abstract, literary point of view that can only touch life by condescending to it.' – *A. O. Scott, New York Times*

'Life Doesn't Hold Tryouts.'
Center Stage
US/Germany 2000 116m DeLuxe Panavision
Columbia (Laurence Mark)
The trials, tribulations and triumphs of students at the American Ballet Academy in New York.
Even non-dancers will find this offstage and backstage story familiar from A Chorus Line, The Turning Point *and dozens of other movies: all the old clichés are dusted off and given another glamorous outing.*
w Carol Heikkinen *d* Nicholas Hytner *ph* Geoffrey Simpson *m* George Fenton *ch* Susan Stroman, Christopher Wheeldon *pd* David Gropman *ed* Tariq Anwar *cos* Ruth Myers
☆ Amanda Schull (Jody), Zoe Saldana (Eva), Susan May Pratt (Maureen), Peter Gallagher (Jonathan), Donna Murphy (Juliette), Debra Monk (Nancy), Ethan Stiefel (Cooper), Sascha Radetsky (Charlie), Julie Kent (Kathleen), Ilia Kulik (Sergei), Eion Bailey (Jim), Shakiem Evans (Erik), Elizabeth Hubbard (Joan Miller), Victor Anthony (Thomas)
'Terrible, yet it's such fun that its clichés and unintentional hilarity cease to matter after a while.' – *Empire*

Central Airport
US 1933 75m bw
Warner
After the war the only job an ace pilot can get is as 'chauffeur' to a lady parachutist.
Rather stiff romantic drama with aeronautics thrown in.
w Rian James, James Seymour *story* *Hawk's Mate* by Jack Moffitt *d* William A. Wellman *ph* Sid Hickox *md* Leo F. Forbstein *ad* Jack Okey *ed* James Morley
☆ Richard Barthelmess, Sally Eilers, Tom Brown, Glenda Farrell, Harold Huber
'The aerial excitement should bring sufficient response to bring it over to the right side of the box office.' – *Variety*

Central Do Brasil: see *Central Station*

Central Park
US 1932 57m bw
Warner
Stories of life in New York's park.
Nifty portmanteau which moves fast and does not bore.
w Ward Morehouse, Earl Baldwin *d* John Adolfi
☆ Joan Blondell, Guy Kibbee, Wallace Ford, Henry B. Walthall, Patricia Ellis, Spencer Charters

Central Station ***
Brazil/France 1998 110m colour 'Scope
MACT/Videofilms/Riofilme/Canal+ (Arthur Cohn, Martine de Clermont-Tonnerre)
original title: *Central Do Brasil*
A cynical elderly former schoolteacher accompanies a young boy across Brazil in search of his father.

A delight – a charming, but tough, study in loss and redemption, wise, witty and compassionate without losing touch with the harsher realities of life.
w João Emanuel Carneiro, Marcos Bernstein *idea* Walter Salles *d Walter Salles ph* Walter Carvalho *m* Antonio Pinto, Jaques Morelembaum *pd* Cassio Amarante, Carla Caffe *ed* Isabelle Rathery, Felipe Lacerda
☆ *Fernanda Montenegro*, Marilia Pera, Vinicius de Oliveira, Soia Lira, Othon Bastos, Otavio Augusto, Stela Freitas, Matheus Nachtergaele, Caio Junqueria
'A melancholy Brazilian road movie shot through with gently stressed cultural commentary.' – *Todd McCarthy, Variety*
'Shrewd, tough and big-hearted.' – *David Denby, New Yorker*
foreign-language film; Fernanda Montenegro
foreign-language film

Century *
GB 1994 112m colour
Electric/BBC/Beambright (Therese Pickard)
At the end of the 19th century, a Jewish doctor goes to work at a research institute where the doctor in charge is sterilizing poor women to prevent them breeding.
An interesting drama of the beginning of the 20th century, but one that often seems too diagrammatic in its concerns to be convincing.
wd Stephen Poliakoff *ph* Witold Stok *m* Michael Gibbs *pd* Michael Pickwoad *ed* Michael Parkinson
☆ Charles Dance, Clive Owen, Miranda Richardson, Robert Stephens, Joan Hickson, Lena Headey, Neil Stuke, Liza Walker
'Deserves to be celebrated for its effortless integration of contemporary issues – immigration, genetic engineering in the broadest sense of that phrase – with a convincing historical story.' – *Adam Mars-Jones, Independent*
'While rarely less than intelligent and provocative, *Century* is frequently implausible – dramatically, psychologically and historically.' – *Philip French, Observer*

Le Cercle Rouge: see *The Red Circle*

La Cérémonie **
France/Germany 1995 112m colour
Gala/MK2/France3/Prokino/Olga/ZDF (Marin Karmitz)
aka: *A Judgement in Stone*
Two women, an illiterate new housekeeper to a wealthy couple and the local postmistress, form a close friendship and begin to resent those in authority over them.
A deft psychological thriller, sympathetic towards its apparently servile rebels, and enjoying the way that its middle-class characters get their come-uppance.
w Claude Chabrol, Caroline Eliacheff *novel* A Judgement in Stone by Ruth Rendell *d* Claude Chabrol *ph* Bernard Zitzermann *m* Matthieu Chabrol *ad* Daniel Mercier *ed* Monique Fardoulis
☆ Sandrine Bonnaire, Isabelle Huppert, Jean-Pierre Cassel, Jacqueline Bisset, Virginie Ledoyen, Jean-François Perrier
'Deliriously nasty.' – *Sunday Times*

The Ceremony
US/Spain 1963 107m bw
UA/Magla (Laurence Harvey)
In a Tangier jail, a bank robber awaits the firing squad, but he and his brother have an escape plan.
Murky and pretentious melodrama with aspirations to high style and symbolism. A bore.
w Ben Barzman *novel* Frederic Grendel *d* Laurence Harvey *ph* Oswald Morris *m* Gerard Schurmann
☆ Laurence Harvey, Sarah Miles, Robert Walker, John Ireland, Ross Martin, Lee Patterson, Jack MacGowran, Murray Melvin, Fernando Rey

A Certain Smile *
US 1958 105m Eastmancolor Cinemascope
TCF (Henry Ephron)
A girl student falls in love with her philandering uncle.
Another sordid novella by Françoise Sagan (see Bonjour Tristesse*), transformed by Hollywood into a glowing romantic saga of life among the Riviera rich. On this level, very competent.*
w Frances Goodrich, Albert Hackett *d* Jean Negulesco *ph* Milton Krasner *m* Alfred Newman *ad* Lyle R. Wheeler, John DeCuir
☆ Christine Carere, Rossano Brazzi, Joan Fontaine, Bradford Dillman, Eduard Franz, Kathryn Givney, Steve Geray
title song (*m* Sammy Fain, *ly* Paul Francis Webster); art direction

Cervantes
Spain/Italy/France 1968 119m Eastmancolor Supertotalvision
Prisma/Protor/Procinex (Alexander Salkind)
US title: *The Young Rebel*
Cervantes, an assistant papal envoy, helps persuade Philip of Spain to join the Holy League, then turns soldier and has various adventures.
Rather boring spectacular with conventional set-pieces.
w Enrique Llovet, Enrico Bomba *novel* Bruno Frank *d* Vincent Sherman *ph* Edmond Richard *m* Jean Ledrut *ad* Enrique Alarcon, Luciano De Nardi *ed* Margarita Ochoa
☆ Horst Buchholz (Miguel de Cervantes), Gina Lollobrigida (Giulia), Louis Jourdan (Cardinal Acquaviva), José Ferrer (Hassam Bey), Fernando Rey (King Philip II of Spain), Francisco Rabal (Rodrigo de Cervantes), Soledad Miranda (Nessa), Maurice de Canonge (Antonio Casa)

César: see *Marius (1931)*

César ***
France 1936 117m bw
La Société des Films Marcel Pagnol
A son sets out to find his real father, who returns home after 20 years of unhappy exile.
The triumphant climax of Pagnol's trilogy, marked with the same wit, warmth and humanity as the previous episodes.
wd Marcel Pagnol ph Willy *m* Vincent Scotto *ed* Suzanne de Troeye, Jeanette Ginestet
☆ *Raimu*, Orane Demazis, Pierre Fresnay, Fernard Charpin, André Fouché, Alida Rouffe, Robert Vattier, Auguste Mouriès, Milly Mathis, Maupi, Edouard Delmont, Paul Dulac
† This was the third film in Pagnol's Marseilles trilogy, following *Marius* and *Fanny* (qqv).

César and Rosalie *
France/Italy/West Germany 1972 105m Eastmancolor
Fildebroc/UPS/Mega Paramount/Orion (Michèle de Broca)
A divorcee living with a rich merchant becomes attracted to a young artist. Unexpectedly, the two become friends…
Wryly amusing comedy for adults.
w Jean-Loup Dabadie, Claude Sautet *d* Claude Sautet *ph* Jean Boffety *m* Philippe Sarde
☆ *Yves Montand*, Romy Schneider, Sami Frey, Umberto Orsini

C'est arrivé près de chez vous: see *Man Bites Dog*

C'est la Vie *
France 1990 96m colour Panavision
Electric/Contemporary/Alexandre/SGGC/A2/CNC (Alexandre Arcady)
original title: *La Baule-les pins*
During a summer holiday, two sisters are onlookers at the end of their parents' marriage as their mother begins a romance with a younger man.
A slight domestic tale, but filmed with some charm and humour.
w Diane Kurys, Alain Le Henry *d* Diane Kurys *ph* Giuseppe Lanci *m* Philippe Sarde *ad* Tony Egry *ed* Raymonde Guyot
☆ Nathalie Baye, Richard Berry, Zabou, Jean-Pierre Bacri, Vincent Lindon, Valéria Bruni-Tedeschi, Didier Benureau, Julie Bataille, Candice Lefranc

Ceux Qui M'aiment Prendront le Train: see *Those Who Love Me Can Take the train*

Chacun cherche son chat: see *When the Cat's Away*

Chad Hanna *
US 1940 86m Technicolor
TCF (Darryl F. Zanuck, Nunnally Johnson)
Life in a New York state circus in the 1840s.
Mild romantic drama from a bestseller; local colour excellent, dramatic interest thin.
w Nunnally Johnson *novel* Red Wheels Rolling by Walter D. Edmonds *d* Henry King *ph* Ernest Palmer *m* David Buttolph
☆ Henry Fonda, Dorothy Lamour, Linda Darnell, Guy Kibbee, Jane Darwell, John Carradine, Ted North, Roscoe Ates

The Chain *
GB 1984 100m Eastmancolor
Quintet/County Bank/Channel 4 (Victor Glynn)
Seven groups of people, corresponding to the seven deadly sins, are involved in a house-moving chain.
Rather tedious and predictable 'all star' comedy with effective moments but no narrative command.
w Jack Rosenthal *d* Jack Gold *ph* Wolfgang Suschitzky *m* Stanley Myers
☆ Denis Lawson, Maurice Denham, Nigel Hawthorne, Billie Whitelaw, Judy Parfitt, Leo McKern, Warren Mitchell, Gary Waldhorn, Anna Massey

Chain Lightning
US 1950 94m bw
Warner (Anthony Veiller)
After World War II a bomber pilot learns how to control the new jets.
Absolutely routine romance and heroics.
w Liam O'Brien, Vincent Evans *story* J. Redmond Prior (Lester Cole) *d* Stuart Heisler *ph* Ernest Haller *m* David Buttolph
☆ Humphrey Bogart, Eleanor Parker, Raymond Massey, Richard Whorf, James Brown, Roy Roberts, Morris Ankrum
† Lester Cole used a pseudonym because he was blacklisted at the time.

Chain of Desire
US 1992 107m Technicolor
Distant Horizon/Anant Singh (Brian Cox)
Sexual permutations link a group of 14 people.
A bisexual updating of La Ronde *for the AIDS generation, among people given over to the kinkier forms of sex; for all that its treatment tends to the unsophisticated and lacks any sense of irony.*
wd Temistocles Lopez *ph* Nancy Schreiber *m* Nathan Birnbaum *pd* Scott Chambliss *ed* Suzanne Fenn
☆ Linda Fiorentino, Elias Koteas, Tim Guinee, Grace Zabriskie, Assumpta Serna, Patrick Bauchau, Seymour Cassel, Malcolm McDowell
'An uneven but alluringly sexy melodrama that gets better as it goes along.' – *Variety*
'Avoid.' – *Empire*

The Chain Reaction
Australia 1980 90m colour
Palm Beach (David Elfick)
aka: *Nuclear Run*
A scientist dying from a fatal dose of radiation in an accident at a nuclear plant attempts to warn the public of the danger they face from contaminated water.
Paranoid thriller that tries too hard to conjure up a sinister atmosphere of multinational conspiracies; with its mute assassin, amnesiac scientist and interminable car chases, it swiftly becomes absurd.
wd Ian Barry *ph* Russell Boyd *m* Andrew Thomas Wilson *ad* Graham Walker *ed* Tim Wellburn
☆ Steve Bisley, Arna-Maria Winchester, Ross Thompson, Ralph Cotterill, Hugh Keays-Byrne, Lorna Lesley, Richard Moir
† George Miller, director of *Mad Max*, was responsible for second-unit direction.

Chain Reaction
US 1996 106m colour Panavision
TCF/Zanuck Co./Chicago Pacific (Arne L. Schmidt, Andrew Davis)
After discovering how to make limitless energy from water, scientists go on the run from secret agents who plan to kill them.
In the tradition of recent action movies, the narrative is paranoid and impenetrable, and the action is spectacular; but it's a chase movie that leads nowhere interesting.
w Josh Friedman, J. F. Lawton, Michael Bortman *d* Andrew Davis *ph* Frank Tidy *m* Jerry Goldsmith *pd* Maher Ahmad *ed* Donald Brochu, Dov Hoenig, Arthur Schmidt *sp* Digital Domain
☆ Keanu Reeves, Morgan Freeman, Rachel Weisz, Fred Ward, Brian Cox, Kevin Dunn, Joanna Cassidy, Chelcie Ross
'One attends this sort of claptrap for the delights of overscaled technological barbarism; and indeed the exploding megatonnage in the opening and closing sequences is shot and edited to knock you out of your seat.' – *Peter Matthews, Sight and Sound*

Chaindance
Canada 1991 110m colour
R&R/Telefilm Canada/BC (Richard Davis)
An armed robber in a tough prison learns the error of his ways after being involved in a rehabilitation programme, working in a home for the handicapped.
Often brutal drama that, in trying to avoid sentimentality, ascends into heated melodrama and loses credibility.
w Alan Aylward, Michael Ironside *d* Allan A. Goldstein *ph* Tobias Schliessler *m* Graeme Coleman *pd* Phil Schmidt *ed* Allan Lee
☆ Michael Ironside, Rae Dawn Chong, Brad Dourif, Bruce Glover, Ken Pogue, Sheila Moore, Leslie Carlson

'When she's in his arms, it's the grandest thrill the screen can give!'
Chained *
US 1934 77m bw
MGM (Hunt Stromberg)
A devoted wife has a shipboard romance with another man.
Moderate star romantic drama.
w John Lee Mahin *d* Clarence Brown *ph* George Folsey *m* Herbert Stothart
☆ Joan Crawford, Clark Gable, Otto Kruger, Stuart Erwin, Una O'Connor, Akim Tamiroff
'Simple in story and unoriginal in idea, its weight is in words rather than action and dramatic potency.' – *Variety*

Chained for Life
US 1950 70m bw
Classic films
One of two girl Siamese twins is accused of murder.
Real life freak show starring the English Hilton twins (1908–64) who were joined at the hip. Hard to watch because of the subject but otherwise a routine lower-case effort.
w Nat Tanchuck *d* Harry Fraser
☆ Violet and Daisy Hilton, Allen Jenkins

Chained to Yesterday: see *Limbo*

The Chairman: see *The Most Dangerous Man in the World*

Chairman of the Board
US 1998 95m colour Panavision
Trimark/101st Street (Peter M. Lenkov, Rupert Harvey)
A mad inventor helps an old man and inherits a multimillion-dollar corporation, causing annoyance to the man's heirs and associates.
Broad comedy by a gadget-obsessed stand-up comedian, whose appeal does not travel well.
w Al Septien, Turi Meyer, Alex Zamm *d* Alex Zamm *ph* David Lewis *m* Chris Hajian *pd* Aaron Osborne *ed* Jim Hill
☆ Carrot Top, Courtney Thorne-Smith, Larry Miller, Raquel Welch, Mystro Clark, Jack Plotnick, Jack Warden, M. Emmet Walsh
'Peppered with the comic's signature gag inventions and enough fart jokes to keep your average 11-year-old in hysterics.' – *Glenn Lovell, Variety*

A Chairy Tale **
Canada 1957 10m bw
National Film Board of Canada
A young man finds that a kitchen chair is unwilling for him to sit on it, but they arrive at a compromise.
The simplest and most effective of fantasies is told at somewhat excessive length but remains among its director's more memorable creations.
wd Norman McLaren
☆ Claude Jutra

The Chalk Garden *
GB 1964 106m Technicolor
U-I/Quota Rentals (Ross Hunter)

The governess in a melancholy household has an effect on the lives of her aged employer and the young granddaughter.
Sub-Chekhovian drama in a house by the sea, flattened by routine handling into something much less interesting than it was on the stage.
w John Michael Hayes novel Enid Bagnold d Ronald Neame ph Arthur Ibbetson m Malcolm Arnold
☆ Edith Evans, Deborah Kerr, Hayley Mills, John Mills, Felix Aylmer, Elizabeth Sellars, Lally Bowers, Toke Townley
'Crashing symbolism, cracker-motto sententiousness.' – *MFB*
Edith Evans

The Challenge
US 1948 69m bw
Reliance (TCF)
Bulldog Drummond solves the mystery of a yacht which is stolen after its owner is murdered.
Modest addition to a long-running series.
w Frank Gruber, Irving Elman d Jean Yarbrough
☆ Tom Conway, June Vincent, Richard Stapley

The Challenge
GB 1960 89m bw
John Temple-Smith/Alexandra

US title: *It Takes a Thief*
In search of buried loot, a lady gangster kidnaps a convict's son.
Murky and unsympathetic melodrama.
wd John Gilling
☆ Jayne Mansfield, Anthony Quayle, Carl Mohner, Barbara Mullen, Peter Reynolds, Dermot Walsh

The Challenge
US 1982 112m Eastmancolor
CBS Theatrical Film Group (Lyle Poncher, Robert L. Rosen, Ron Beckman)

An American boxer in Japan becomes involved in a feud between two brothers.
Belated martial arts saga with a good deal of head-lopping and plenty of pretensions but no apparent message to spike its dismal entertainment values.
w Richard Maxwell, John Sayles d John Frankenheimer ph Kozo Okazaki m Jerry Goldsmith pd Yoshiyuki Ishida ed Jack Wheeler
☆ Scott Glenn, Toshiro Mifune, Donna Kei Benz, Atsuo Nakamura, Calvin Young, Clyde Kusatsu
'Ridiculous, demeaning stuff.' – *Guardian*

A Challenge for Robin Hood *
GB 1967 96m Technicolor
Hammer (Clifford Parkes)
A retelling of the original Robin Hood legend.
Unassuming, lively, predictable adventure hokum.
w Peter Bryan d C. Pennington-Richards ph Arthur Grant m Gary Hughes
☆ Barrie Ingham, James Hayter, Leon Greene, John Arnatt, Peter Blythe, Gay Hamilton, William Squire

'Daring! Dangerous! Death-Defying!'
Challenge to Lassie *
US 1949 76m Technicolor
MGM (Robert Sisk)

In Edinburgh in the 1860s, a sheepdog keeps vigil over the grave of its dead master.
Well-made sentimental tale, inspired by the story of Greyfriars Bobbie (which was later filmed), though it's possible that its winsome charm may no longer find a receptive audience.
w William Ludwig novel *Greyfriars Bobby* by Eleanor Atkinson d Richard Thorpe ph Charles Schoenbaum m André Previn ad Cedric Gibbons, Eddie Imazu ed George White
☆ Edmund Gwenn, Donald Crisp, Geraldine Brooks, Reginald Owen, Alan Webb, Ross Ford, Henry Stephenson, Alan Napier, Sara Allgood, Lassie
† Eleanor Atkinson's novel, originally about a Skye terrier, was also filmed in 1961 as *Greyfriars Bobby* (qv).

The Chamber *
US 1996 110m DeLuxe Panavision
Universal/Imagine/Brian Grazer/Davis Entertainment (John Davis, Brian Grazer, Ron Howard)

A young lawyer, whose father killed himself, tries to prevent his grandfather, convicted of a racist atrocity, from being executed.
Unconvincing and rather plodding drama, though Hackman's performance almost manages to keep one's interest alive.
w William Goldman, Chris Reese novel John Grisham d James Foley ph Ian Baker m Carter Burwell pd David Brisbin ed Mark Warner
☆ Chris O'Donnell, Gene Hackman, Faye Dunaway, Robert Prosky, Lela Rochon, Raymond Barry, Bo Jackson, David Marshall Grant, Nicholas Pryor, Harve Presnell
'An intelligently proficient thriller that works more effectively as a family drama than a legal thriller.' – *Emanuel Levy, Variety*
† Grisham was paid $3.7m for his story outline, before writing the novel. The film cost around $45m and took $14.5m at the US box-office.

Chamber of Horrors: see *The Door with Seven Locks (1940)*

'The unspeakable vengeance of the crazed Baltimore strangler!'
Chamber of Horrors
US 1966 99m Warnercolor
Warner (Hy Averback)
A maniacal murderer is finally trapped by two amateur criminologists who run a wax museum in Baltimore.
Zany horror thriller originally meant for TV; it turned out a shade too harrowing. Advertised as 'the picture with the Fear Flasher and the Horror Horn', shock gimmicks which proved much more startling than the crude events they heralded.
w Stephen Kandel d Hy Averback ph Richard Kline m William Lava
☆ Patrick O'Neal, Cesare Danova, Wilfrid Hyde-White, Laura Devon, Patrice Wymore, Suzy Parker, Jeanette Nolan, Tony Curtis

Chamber of Tortures: see *Baron Blood*

La Chambre des Officiers **
France 2001 134m colour
Optimum/ARP/France2/Canal+ (Michele and Laurent Petin)

GB title: *The Officers' Ward*
Disfigured by an exploding bomb during the First World War, a young officer spends five years in hospital and tries to come to terms with his scarred face.
Moving, understated account of the traumas of physical deformity and their effect on disfigured and the wider world.
wd François Dupeyron novel *La Chambre des officiers* by Marc Dugain ph Tetsuo Nagata m Arvo Part ad Patrick Durand ed Dominique Faysse sp make-up fx: Dominique Colladant
☆ Eric Caravaca (Adrien), Denis Podalydes (Henri), Gregori Derangere (Pierre), Sabine Azema (Anais), Andre Dussollier (The Surgeon), Marguerite (Isabelle Renauld), Geraldine Pailhas (Clemence), Jean-Michel Portal (Alain)
'A gem of a movie by any standards...superbly furnished, passionately acted, and exquisitely photographed and lit.' – *Peter Bradshaw, Guardian*

'Don't fail to get a ringside seat!'
'The knockout picture of the year!'
The Champ *
US 1931 87m bw
MGM (Harry Rapf)

A young boy has faith in a washed-up prizefighter.
Maudlin drama, highly commercial in its day and a box-office tonic for its two stars. Remade as The Clown *(qv).*
w Leonard Praskins, Frances Marion d King Vidor ph Gordon Avil
☆ Wallace Beery, Jackie Cooper, Irene Rich, Roscoe Ates, Edward Brophy
'This picture will hit 'em all, large or small, and that means lots of money.' – *Variety*
original story (Frances Marion); Wallace Beery
best picture; King Vidor

The Champ *
US 1979 122m Metrocolor
MGM (Dyson Lovell)

A remake of the 1931 movie of a boy's belief in a washed-up fighter, with Florida racetrack asides.
A lush version, so little updated in mood that its tearfulness seems to have strayed from another age.
w Walter Newman d Franco Zeffirelli ph Fred J. Koenekamp m Dave Grusin pd Herman A. Blumenthal
☆ Jon Voight, Faye Dunaway, *Ricky Schroder*, Jack Warden, Arthur Hill, Strother Martin, Joan Blondell, Elisha Cook
Dave Grusin

Champagne
GB 1928 90m (24 fps) bw silent
BIP (John Maxwell)

A millionaire pretends to be bankrupt so that his daughter won't marry.
Tedious comedy drama with very few of the master's touches.
w Eliot Stannard, Walter C. Mycroft, Alfred Hitchcock d Alfred Hitchcock ph Jack Cox
☆ Betty Balfour, Jean Bradin, Gordon Harker, Theodore von Alten
'Dreadful.' – *Alfred Hitchcock*

Champagne Charlie
US 1936 60m bw
TCF (Edward T. Lowe)
A gambler double-crosses the gangsters who financed him to seduce and marry an heiress.
Efficient, fast-moving 'B'-movie thriller.
w Allen Rivkin d James Tinling ph Daniel B. Clark md Samuel Kaylin ad Duncan Cramer, Lewis Creber ed Nick de Maggio
☆ Paul Cavanagh, Helen Wood, Thomas Beck, Minna Gombell, Herbert Mundin, Noel Madison

Champagne Charlie *
GB 1944 107m bw
Ealing (John Croydon)
The life of Victorian music hall singer George Leybourne and his rivalry with the Great Vance.
Careful period reconstruction and good songs and acting are somehow nullified by unsympathetic handling and photography.
w Austin Melford, Angus Macphail, John Dighton d Alberto Cavalcanti ph Wilkie Cooper md Ernest Irving ad Michael Relph
☆ *Tommy Trinder, Stanley Holloway*, Betty Warren, Austin Trevor, Jean Kent, Guy Middleton, Frederick Piper, Harry Fowler, James Robertson Justice
'Cavalcanti's taste for the bizarre and the vigour of the performances make it something more than a museum piece.' – *Time Out, 1984*

Champagne for Caesar *
US 1950 99m bw
Cardinal (George Moskov)

A self-confessed genius with a grudge against a soap company determines to win astronomical sums on its weekly radio quiz.
Agreeable, mildly satirical star comedy which tends to peter out halfway.
w Hans Jacoby, Fred Brady d Richard Whorf ph Paul Ivano m Dimitri Tiomkin
☆ Ronald Colman, Vincent Price, Celeste Holm, Barbara Britton, Art Linkletter

Champagne for Everybody: see *Here Come the Girls*

The Champagne Murders
France 1967 107m Techniscope
Universal (France) (Jacques Natteau)
original title: *Le Scandale*
A disturbed champagne millionaire thinks he may be a murderer.
Complex but uninvolving mystery story in which the director's eye seems to be more on satire than on narrative.
w Claude Brûlé, Derek Prouse, Paul Gégauff story William Benjamin d Claude Chabrol ph Jean Rabier m Pierre Jansen ad Rino Mondellini ed Jacques Gaillard
☆ Anthony Perkins, Maurice Ronet, Stéphane Audran, Yvonne Furneaux, Suzanne Lloyd

'As gay and sparkling as a champagne cocktail!'
Champagne Waltz
US 1937 90m bw
Paramount (Harlan Thompson)
A press agent takes a swing band to Vienna.
Rather tedious romantic comedy with music.
w Don Hartman, Frank Butler story Billy Wilder, H. S. Kraft d A. Edward Sutherland ph William Mellor ed Paul Weatherwax
☆ Fred MacMurray, Gladys Swarthout, Jack Oakie
'On the slow side, but should do fairly.' – *Variety*

'This is the only sport in the world where two guys get paid for doing something they'd be arrested for if they got drunk and did it for nothing.'
Champion **
US 1949 99m bw
Stanley Kramer

An ambitious prizefighter alienates his friends and family, and dies of injuries received in the ring.
Interesting exposé of the fight racket, presented in good cinematic style and acted with great bravura.
w Carl Foreman story Ring Lardner d Mark Robson ph Franz Planer m Dimitri Tiomkin ed Harry Gerstad
☆ *Kirk Douglas, Arthur Kennedy*, Marilyn Maxwell, Paul Stewart, Ruth Roman, Lola Albright, Luis Van Rooten
Harry Gerstad
Carl Foreman; Franz Planer; Dimitri Tiomkin; Kirk Douglas; Arthur Kennedy

Champions *
GB 1983 115m colour
Embassy/Archerwest/Ladbroke/United British Artists (Peter Shaw, Eva Monley)

A leading jockey develops cancer and his horse receives a leg injury, but both survive to win the Grand National.
Gruelling factual story which could have done with a little more drama, not to mention a more sympathetic hero.
w Evan Jones book Bob Champion, Jonathan Powell d John Irvin ph Ronnie Taylor m Carl Davis
☆ John Hurt, Edward Woodward, Ben Johnson, Jan Francis, Peter Barkworth, Ann Bell, Judy Parfitt
'It ignores any inner aspect, the better to concentrate on tearjerking externals.' – *Tom Milne, MFB*
'Told as an indecent tearjerker, directed with the discretion of a rampaging steamroller.' – *Sight and Sound*

Champions: see *The Mighty Ducks (1992)*

Chan Is Missing *
US 1981 80m bw
Wayne Wang Productions/Wayne Wang

In San Francisco, two Chinese-American cab drivers search for a friend who has disappeared with $4,000 of their money.
Rambling but engaging in its different perspective on America.
w Isaac Cronin, Wayne Wang, Terrel Seltzer d Wayne Wang ph Michael Chin m Robert Kikuchi-Yngojo
☆ Wood Moy, Marc Hayashi, Lauren Chew, Peter Wang, George Woo

Chance Meeting: see *The Young Lovers (1954)*

Chance Meeting: see *Blind Date (1959)*

Chance of a Lifetime *
GB 1950 93m bw
Pilgrim Pictures (Bernard Miles)
The owner of a small engineering works, impatient with the unionism of his men, gives them a chance to run the factory themselves.
Quiet comedy-drama on sub-Ealing lines; always interesting, it never quite catches fire despite a reliable cast.
w Walter Greenwood, Bernard Miles d Bernard Miles ph Eric Cross
☆ Bernard Miles, Basil Radford, Niall MacGinnis, Geoffrey Keen, Julien Mitchell, Josephine Wilson, Kenneth More, Hattie Jacques
'The film's triumph lies in the integrity with which it draws its picture of factory life and it is flawlessly acted.' – *The Times*

'It held me from beginning to end. I found it amusing, exciting and at times moving enough to raise some embarrassing and surreptitious tears.' – *Milton Shulman*

'British workmen are shown for the first time as characters, not comic caricatures. They are authentic, breezy and warm, sympathetically played by comparatively fresh actors.' – *Richard Winnington*

† The major circuits in Britain refused to give a showing to this independent movie, which was made at a cost of £150,000, on the grounds that it wasn't entertaining. They were forced to do so after its director appealed to the Film Selection Committee.

Chance or Coincidence *

France/Canada 1998 121m colour Panavision
Films13/TFI/SDA/UGC/Neuilly/FCC (Claude Lelouch)

original title: *Hasards ou Coincidences*

A man becomes infatuated with a ballerina he sees on some stolen video-tapes.

A melodramatic narrative, of loss and grief, betrayal and unexpected love, all hinging on unlikely accidents, is offset by some luxuriant scene-setting; the result is a feast for the eyes, but not the mind.

wd Claude Lelouch *ph* Pierre-William Glenn *m* Francis Lai, Claude Bolling *ch* Richard Wherlock *ed* Hélène du Luze

☆ Alessandra Martines (Myriam Lini), Pierre Arditi (Pierre Turi), Marc Hollonge (Marc Deschamps), Laurent Hilaire (Laurent), Véronique Moreau (Catherine Desvilles), Patrick Labbé (Michel Bonhomme), Geoffrey Holder (Gerry), Luigi Bonino (Mauro Lini)

'Full of staggering images as well as entrancing techniques to constantly engage the audience.' – *Alan Jones, Film Review*

Chances *

US 1931 72m bw
Warner

In wartime London, two soldiers on leave fall for the same girl.

Unexpectedly sensitive and pleasing romance, generally well handled.

w Waldemar Young *novel* Hamilton Gibbs *d* Allan Dwan

☆ Douglas Fairbanks Jnr, Anthony Bushell, Rose Hobart

'Enough contributing sidelights to keep the emphasis away from the combat ... should be pleasant b.o.' – *Variety*

Chances Are

US 1989 108m Metrocolor
Tri-Star (Mike Lobell)

A widow realizes that her daughter's boyfriend is the reincarnation of her dead husband.

Excessively contrived romantic comedy; we have all been here before and there is nothing noteworthy about this particular variation on a familiar theme.

w Perry Howze, Randy Howze *d* Emile Ardolino *ph* William A. Fraker *m* Maurice Jarre *pd* Dennis Washington *ed* Harry Keramidas

☆ Cybill Shepherd, Robert Downey Jnr, Ryan O'Neal, Mary Stewart Masterson, Christopher McDonald, Josef Sommer, Joe Grifasi, Henderson Forsythe

song 'Chances Are' (*m/l* Tom Snow, Dean Pitchford)

Chandler

US 1971 88m Metrocolor Panavision
MGM

An ex-private eye becomes a security guard and an alcoholic but even worse befalls when he agrees to keep an eye on a government witness.

Downbeat, generally unamusing and little seen piece of thick ear which harks back unsuccessfully to the forties.

w John Sacret Young *d* Paul Magwood

☆ Warren Oates, Leslie Caron, Alex Dreier, Mitchell Ryan, Gordon Pinsent, Charles McGraw, Richard Loo, Walter Burke, Gloria Grahame, Royal Dano, Scatman Crothers

Chandu the Magician *

US 1932 74m bw
Fox

A spiritualist battles against a madman with a death ray which could destroy the world.

Rather dim serial-like thriller, with interesting talent not at its best.

w Philip Klein, Barry Conners *d* Marcel Varnel, William Cameron Menzies *ph* James Wong Howe *m* Louis de Francesco

☆ Edmund Lowe, Bela Lugosi, Irene Ware, Herbert Mundin, Henry B. Walthall

† Sequels (whittled down from serials) include *The Return of Chandu* and *Chandu and the Magic Isle*.

Chanel Solitaire

France/GB 1981 124m colour
Gardenia/Todrest (Larry G. Spangler)

Fashion designer Coco Chanel thinks back on her long career.

Moderately elegant but frigid autobiopic with very little entertainment value.

w Julian More *novel* Claude Dulay *d* George Kaczender *ph* Ricardo Aronovich *m* Jean Musy

☆ Marie-France Pisier, Timothy Dalton, Rutger Hauer, Karen Black, Brigitte Fossey

'The producer says the film is devoted to providing what every woman wants – men, money, jewellery, castles, caviare, champagne and love, love, love. I never realized they could be so boring.' – *Sunday Times*

Chang **

US 1927 71m (24 fps) bw silent
Paramount

The life of a rice-grower in Thailand.

Influential but now rather boring documentary with animal interest.

wd/ph/ed Merian C. Cooper, Ernest B. Schoedsack

'I can remember no more terrible adventure in the kinema than the moment in the middle of Chang when suddenly the curtains divide, and the screen seems to swell and tremble and burst its bounds, and the great herd of elephants comes trampling out of the picture and bears down upon us in a multitude of tossing trunks and angry feet.' – C. A. *Lejeune*

Unique and Artistic Picture

Change of Habit

US 1969 97m colour
Universal

A young doctor working in a ghetto has his opinions changed by three nuns.

A notably unsuccessful attempt by a star to change his image.

w James Lee, S. S. Schweitzer, Eric Bercovici *d* William Graham *ph* Russell Metty *m* Billy Goldenberg *ad* Alexander Golitzen *ed* Douglas Stewart

☆ Elvis Presley, Mary Tyler Moore, Barbara McNair, Ed Asner, Leora Dana, Jane Elliot, Robert Emhardt

Change of Heart

US 1937 65m bw
TCF (Sol M. Wurtzel)

A bored man and wife go their separate ways but are eventually reconciled.

Bright little comedy on a tired old theme.

w Frances Hyland, Albert Ray *d* James Tinling

☆ Michael Whalen, Gloria Stuart, Lyle Talbot, Jane Darwell

'More originality, freshness of treatment and solid entertainment than in half the more expensive efforts from the Hollywood studios.' – *Variety*

Change of Heart: see *Hit Parade of 1943 (1943)*

Change of Mind

US 1969 98m Eastmancolor
Sagittarius (Seeleg Lester, Richard Wesson)

The life of a liberal white DA can only be 'saved' by transplanting his brain into the body of a dead black man.

Fantasy melodrama with a social conscience, about a half-and-half which is acceptable to neither whites nor blacks. Very obvious and rather boring.

w Seeleg Lester, Richard Wesson *d* Robert Stevens *ph* Arthur J. Ornitz *m* Duke Ellington

☆ Raymond St Jacques, Susan Oliver, Janet McLachlan, Leslie Nielsen

A Change of Seasons

US 1980 102m DeLuxe
TCF/Martin Ransohoff/Film Finance Group Ltd

A college professor takes a mistress and his wife retaliates.

Zestless and unhumorous rehash of Who's Afraid of Virginia Woolf? *and* Bob and Carol and Ted and Alice. *Not a new thought anywhere.*

w Erich Segal, Ronni Kern, Fred Segal *d* Richard Lang *ph* Philip Lathrop *m* Henry Mancini *pd* Bill Kenney

☆ Shirley MacLaine, Anthony Hopkins, Bo Derek, Michael Brandon, Mary Beth Hurt, Ed Winter

'A tired rehash of themes that might have been provocative a decade ago ... it would take a Lubitsch to do justice to the incredibly tangled relationships.' – *Variety*

'The situation soon melts into a gooey mess, like a Mars bar left too long in a trouser pocket.' – *Sunday Times*

The Changeling

Canada 1979 107m colour Panavision
Chessman Palk Productions (Joel B. Michaels, Garth H. Drabinsky)

A widowed academic takes on an old house haunted by the spirit of a murdered child.

Tedious and not very brief, this uninspired ghost story comes very late in the horror stakes and contains very little to make one care about its outcome.

w William Gray, Diana Maddox *d* Peter Medak *ph* John Coquillon *m* Rick Wilkins

☆ George C. Scott, Melvyn Douglas, Trish Van Devere, John Colicos, Jean Marsh, Barry Morse

'None of its most eerily untoward occurrences proceed from any spectral intervention, but from the worst abuses of Peter Medak's infuriatingly fidgety camera.' – *Gilbert Adair, MFB*

Changing Habits

US 1997 95m colour
Teagarden/Initial (Abra Edelman, James Dodson)

An unhappy, shoplifting artist is given a room at a convent, where she secretly paints a mural in an abandoned chapel.

A film about a woman's journey in search of her identity; only the very patient would wish to accompany her.

w Scott Davis Jones *d* Lynn Roth *ph* Michael Mayers *m* David McHugh *pd* Dena Roth, Gail Bennett *ed* Susan Godfrey, Clayton Halsey

☆ Moira Kelly, Christopher Lloyd, Dylan Walsh, Shelley Duvall, Bob Gunton, Marissa Ribisif, Anne Hanley, Frances Bay, Eileen Brennan, Teri Garr

'Never locates the charm and depth it hopes for, thanks largely to an unappealingly conceived protagonist.' – *Dennis Harvey, Variety*

'One Wrong Turn Deserves Another.'

Changing Lanes *

US 2002 99m DeLuxe Panavision
Paramount (Scott Rudin)

Two men – one an ambitious, high-flying lawyer, the other an insurance salesman and recovering alcoholic – become locked in an escalating battle to do the other down after they are involved in a traffic accident.

A story of urban rancour and impatience that begins by exploring moral dilemmas before declining into Hollywood-style saccharine redemption.

w Chap Taylor, Michael Tolkin *d* Roger Michell *ph* Salvatore Totino *m* David Arnold *pd* Kristi Zea *ed* Christopher Tellefsen *cos* Ann Roth

☆ Ben Affleck (Gavin Banek), Samuel L. Jackson (Doyle Gipson), Toni Collette (Michelle), Sydney Pollack (Delano), William Hurt (Sponsor), Amanda Peet (Cynthia Banek), Richard Jenkins (Walter Arnell), Kim Staunton (Valerie Gipson), John Benjamin Hickey (Carlyle), Jennifer Dundas Lowe (Mina Dunne), Dylan Baker (Finch), Matt Malloy (Ron Cabot)

'Combines a knack for storytelling with a rare instinct for exploring ideas within the framework of a major, star-driven Hollywood movie.' – *Robert Koehler, Variety*

'The final effect is like having two guys yelling in your face for two hours.' – *Peter Travers, Rolling Stone*

The Chant of Jimmie Blacksmith ****

Australia 1978 122m Eastmancolor Panavision
Film House (Fred Schepisi)

In 1900, a half-caste mingles with high-class whites, goes berserk, and slaughters several of them with an axe.

A powerful film on the tragedy of an outcast at home in no society, torn between the world he has lost and the one he cannot gain. The violence is shocking, as it is meant to be. It is one of the great achievements of Australian cinema.

wd Fred Schepisi *novel* Thomas Keneally *ph* Ian Baker *m* Bruce Smeaton *pd* Wendy Dickson *ed* Brian Cavanagh

☆ Tommy Lewis, Ray Barrett, Jack Thompson, Freddy Reynolds

'One of the greatest pieces of political film making I know, because it doesn't impose rhetorical nobility on its characters or twist their lives into social statement.' – *Stephen Schiff*

'This is a large scale film – a visually, impassioned epic.' – *Pauline Kael*

'A big film intended for a big audience. On its own terms, it is a powerful indictment of the insidious, pervasive canker of white racism.' – *David Wilson, Sight and Sound*

Chapayev *

USSR 1934 94m bw
Lenfilm

Exploits of a Red Army commander during the 1919 battles.

Moderately striking propaganda piece.

wd Sergei and Georgy Vasiliev *ph* Alexander Sigayev *m* Gavril Popov

☆ Boris Babochkin, B. Blinov, Leonid Kmit

'Easily the best film turned out in Russia since sound.' – *Variety*

Un Chapeau de Paille d'Italie: see *An Italian Straw Hat*

'He made the whole world laugh and cry. He will again.'

'Everyone has a wild side. Even a legend.'

Chaplin **

GB 1992 145m Technicolor
Guild/Lambeth/Carolco/Studio Canal (Richard Attenborough, Mario Kassar)

In old age, Charlie Chaplin tells the story of his life to a biographer – from his early childhood to his Hollywood triumphs, his exile from America and his honorary Oscar in 1972.

Somewhat stolid biopic that tries to cram in too much of a long life, but which has a fascinating story to tell and often tells it well; it might have been better had it been longer.

w William Boyd, Bryan Forbes, William Goldman *book* My Autobiography by Charles Chaplin; *Chaplin – His Life and Art* by David Robinson *story Diana Hawkins d* Richard Attenborough *ph* Sven Nykvist *m* John Barry *pd* Stuart Craig *ed* Anne V. Coates

☆ *Robert Downey Jnr*, Dan Aykroyd, Geraldine Chaplin, Kevin Dunn, Anthony Hopkins, Milla Jovovich, Kevin Kline, Diane Lane, Penelope Ann Miller, Paul Rhys, John Thaw, Marisa Tomei, Nancy Travis, James Woods

'Old-fashioned bio-pic does an inadequate job of getting beneath the skin of one of the most famous Englishmen of the century.' – *Iain Johnstone, Sunday Times*

Robert Downey Jnr; Stuart Craig; John Barry

Robert Downey Jnr

The Chapman Report

US 1962 125m Technicolor
Warner/Darryl F. Zanuck (Richard D. Zanuck)

Dr Chapman conducts a study of female sex behaviour in an American suburb.

Influenced by the Kinsey report, this melodramatic compendium takes itself far too seriously, and the director's smooth style is barely in evidence.

w Wyatt Cooper, Don M. Mankiewicz *novel* Irving Wallace *d* George Cukor *ph* Harold Lipstein *m* Leonard Rosenman

☆ Shelley Winters, Claire Bloom, *Glynis Johns*, Efrem Zimbalist Jnr, Jane Fonda, Ray Danton, Ty Hardin, Andrew Duggan, John Dehner, Henry Daniell, Corey Allen, Harold J. Stone

'We had a preview which went very well, and then it was sent over to Mr Zanuck, who did what I thought was a most horrendous job of cutting it up.' – *George Cukor*

Chapter Two
US 1979 127m Metrocolor
Columbia/Rastar (Margaret Booth)

A widowed novelist reluctantly embarks on an affair with a divorcee.
Simon in sad mood means that the wisecracks are still there but the pauses between them are longer. The thin but heavy-going plot finally militates against enthusiasm.
w Neil Simon *d* Robert Moore *ph* David M. Walsh, Richard Kratina *m* Marvin Hamlisch *pd* Gene Callahan
☆ James Caan, Marsha Mason, Joseph Bologna, Valerie Harper, Alan Fudge
'The regular Neil Simon Broadway takeaway for people who watch movies with their ears. Over two hours of theatrical smart talk and unfailing wit-under-pressure as Simon-surrogate Caan and the real Mrs Simon swap marital repartee in front of a reverent camera.' – *Time Out*
'All the couple have to do is swap wisecracks and nurse their rather pretty emotional bruises.' – *Observer*
'More than two hours of discussions, arguments, debates, reconciliations and accusations that quickly become tedious.' – *Roger Ebert*
Marsha Mason

Character **
Netherlands 1997 125m colour
Gala/Almerica/NPS Made (Laurens Geels)
original title: *Karakter*
A grasping bailiff persecutes his illegimate son, an unsuccessful businessman.
Powerful, downbeat, Oedipal drama of obsession in a period setting.
w Mike van Diem, Laurens Geels, Ruud van Megen *novel Karakter* by F. Bordewijk *d* Mike van Diem *ph* Rogier Stoffers *m* Het Paleis van Boem *pd* Jelier & Schaaf *ed* Jessica de Koning
☆ Jan Decleir, Fedja van Huêt, Betty Schuurman, Tamar van den Dop, Victor Löw, Hans Kesting
'Turgid, interminable … strong on atmosphere but surprisingly weak on variation in tone.' – *James Cameron-Wilson, Film Review*
foreign language film

Charade
US 1952 83m bw
Portland (James Mason)
Three stories conceived and produced by the stars.
Everything about this triptych is on the dull side, and Mason himself later regretted embarking on it.
w James and Pamela Mason *d* Roy Kellino
☆ James Mason, Pamela Mason, Scott Forbes, Paul Cavanagh, Bruce Lester
† Roy Kellino was Pamela Mason's first husband.

'You can expect the unexpected when they play...'
Charade **
US 1963 113m Technicolor
Universal/Stanley Donen

A Parisienne finds her husband murdered. Four strange men are after her, and she is helped by a handsome stranger … but is he hero, spy or murderer?
Smoothly satisfying sub-Hitchcock nonsense, effective both as black romantic comedy and macabre farce.
w Peter Stone *d* Stanley Donen *ph* Charles Lang Jnr *m* Henry Mancini
☆ Cary Grant, *Audrey Hepburn, Walter Matthau*, James Coburn, George Kennedy, Ned Glass, Jacques Marin
'One hesitates to be uncharitable to a film like *Charade*, which seeks only to provide a little innocent merriment and make a pot of money … Of itself, it is a stylish and amusing melodrama, but in the context of the bloodlust that seems unloosed in our land it is as sinister as the villains who stalk Miss Hepburn through the cobbled streets of Paris.' – *Arthur Knight*
† Cary Grant conceals his age of sixty by taking a shower fully clothed.
song 'Charade' (*m* Henry Mancini, *ly* Johnny Mercer)
Audrey Hepburn

Charge!: see *À L'attaque!*

The Charge at Feather River *
US 1953 96m Warnercolor
Warner (David Weisbart)
An army platoon composed of men from the guardhouse tries to rescue two women kidnapped by Indians.
Formula Western distinguished by 3-D photography, probably the best to be achieved in the brief life of the medium. Warnerphonic sound was less successfully added; the sum total would be trying for nervous people.
w James R. Webb *d* Gordon Douglas *ph* Peverell Marley *m* Max Steiner
☆ Guy Madison, Frank Lovejoy, Vera Miles, Helen Westcott, Dick Wesson, Onslow Stevens, Steve Brodie
'From the start we are involved in a whirl of frenzied activity: a cavalry charge, knife throwing, sabre practice, flaming arrows – not a trick missed.' – *MFB*

The Charge Is Murder: see *Twilight of Honor*

'The reckless lancers sweep on and on – so that a woman's heart might not be broken! You're not fighting a single legion – you're fighting the entire British army, Surat Khan!'
The Charge of the Light Brigade ***
US 1936 115m bw
Warner (Hal B. Wallis, Sam Bischoff)

An army officer deliberately starts the Balaclava charge to even an old score with Surat Khan, who's on the other side.
Though allegedly 'based on the poem by Alfred Lord Tennyson', this is no more than a travesty of history, most of it taking place in India. As pure entertainment however it is a most superior slice of Hollywood hokum and the film which set the seal on Errol Flynn's superstardom.
w Michel Jacoby, Rowland Leigh *d Michael Curtiz ph Sol Polito, Fred Jackman m Max Steiner md* Leo Forbstein *ad* John Hughes *ed* George Amy
☆ *Errol Flynn* (Major Geoffrey Vickers), Olivia de Havilland (Elsa Campbell), Patric Knowles (Capt. Perry Vickers), Donald Crisp (Col Campbell), David Niven (Capt. Randall), Henry Stephenson (Sir Charles Macefield), Nigel Bruce (Sir Benjamin Warrenton), C. *Henry Gordon* (Surat Kahn), Spring Byington (Lady Octavia Warrenton), E. E. Clive (Sir Humphrey Harcourt), Robert Barrat (Count Igor Volonoff), J. Carrol Naish (Subahdar-Major Puran Singh)
'When the noble six hundred, lances level and stirrups touching, pace, canter and, finally, charge down the mile-long valley, with the enemy guns tearing great holes in their ranks, you are a dead stock if your pulses don't thunder and your heart quicken perceptibly. This scene may be villainous history, but it is magnificent cinema, timed, shot, and cut with brilliance. It only cramps the patriotic effect a trifle that the Union Jack, nine times out of ten in the picture, is shown resolutely flying upside down.' – *C. A. Lejeune*
Max Steiner

The Charge of the Light Brigade *
GB 1968 141m DeLuxe Panavision
UA/Woodfall (Neil Hartley)

An historical fantasia with comic, sociological and cartoon embellishments.
This version for the swinging sixties has a few splendid moments but apes Tom Jones *all too obviously and leaves audiences with an even dimmer view of history than they started with.*
w Charles Wood *d* Tony Richardson *ph* David Watkin, Peter Suschitzky *m* John Addison *ad* Edward Marshall *animation Richard Williams*
☆ *Trevor Howard, John Gielgud*, David Hemmings, Vanessa Redgrave, Jill Bennett, Harry Andrews, Peter Bowles, Mark Burns
'Considering the lucid book on which it is largely based, it is almost as inexcusably muddled as the British commanders at Balaclava.' – *John Simon*
'The point of the film is to recreate mid-Victorian England in spirit and detail.' – *Stanley Kauffmann*
'Notions for at least three interesting films are on view … what seems signally lacking is a guiding hand, an overriding purpose.' – *John Coleman*
'This epic has so little feeling for the courage that went with the idiocies of the past that it diminishes itself along with its targets.' – *Pauline Kael*

'Two men chasing dreams of glory!'
Chariots of Fire ***
GB 1981 121m colour
TCF/Allied Stars/Enigma (David Puttnam)

In the 1924 Paris Olympics, a Jew and a Scotsman run for Britain.
A film of subtle qualities, rather like those of a BBC classic serial. Probably not quite worth the adulation it received, but full of pleasant romantic touches and sharp glimpses of the wider issues involved.
w Colin Welland d Hugh Hudson ph David Watkin m Vangelis *ad* Roger Hall, Jonathan Amberston, Len Huntingford, Andrew Sanders, Anna Ridley *ed* Terry Rawlings *cos* Milena Canonero
☆ *Ben Cross, Ian Charleson*, Nigel Havers, Nicholas Farrell, Daniel Gerroll, Cheryl Campbell, Alice Krige, John Gielgud, Lindsay Anderson, Nigel Davenport, *Ian Holm*, Patrick Magee
'The whole contradictory bundle is unexpectedly watchable.' – *Jo Imeson, MFB*
'A piece of technological lyricism held together by the glue of simple-minded heroic sentiment.' – *Pauline Kael*
'A hymn to the human spirit as if scored by Barry Manilow.' – *Richard Corliss, Film Comment*
best picture; Colin Welland; Vangelis; Milena Canonero
Hugh Hudson; Terry Rawlings; Ian Holm
best picture; Ian Holm; Milena Canonero

Charles and Lucie *
France 1979 97m colour
Avon/Cythere Films/Films de La Chouette/Antenne 2 (Claude Makovski)
original title: *Charles et Lucie*
An antique dealer and a singer, both down on their luck, are the victims of a confidence trick.
An enjoyable divertissement.
w Jean Chapot *d* Nelly Kaplan *ph* Gilbert Sandoz *m* Pierre Perret *ed* Nelly Kaplan, Jean Chapot
☆ Daniel Ceccaldi, Ginette Garcin, Jean-Marie Proslier, Samson Fainsilber, Georges Claisse, Guy Grosso

Charley and the Angel *
US 1974 93m Technicolor
Walt Disney (Bill Anderson)

A small-town sporting goods storekeeper in the thirties escapes death three times and finds an impatient angel waiting for him.
Mild sentimental whimsy on the lines of On Borrowed Time, *but with a happy ending and attractive period trappings.*
w Roswell Rogers *novel The Golden Evenings of Summer* by Will Stanton *d* Vincent McEveety *ph* Charles F. Wheeler *m* Buddy Baker *ad* John B. Mansbridge *ed* Ray de Leuw, Bob Bring
☆ Fred MacMurray, Cloris Leachman, Harry Morgan, Kurt Russell, Kathleen Cody, Edward Andrews, Barbara Nichols

Charley Moon *
GB 1956 92m Eastmancolor
Colin Lesslie, Aubrey Baring
A music hall comic becomes swollen-headed but returns to his home village and marries his childhood sweetheart.
Faltering musical lacking the gusto of its background, but providing a generally believable impression of life on the halls.
novel Reginald Arkell *d* Guy Hamilton *ph* Jack Hildyard *m* Francis Chagrin *w/songs* Leslie Bricusse
☆ Max Bygraves, Dennis Price, Michael Medwin, Florence Desmond, Shirley Eaton, Patricia Driscoll, Reginald Beckwith

'When he runs out of dumb luck he always has genius to fall back on!'
Charley Varrick ***
US 1973 111m Technicolor Panavision
Universal (Don Siegel)

A bank robber discovers he has stolen Mafia money, and devises a clever scheme to get himself off the hook.
Sharp, smart, well-observed but implausible thriller, astringently handled and agreeably set in Californian backlands. Accomplished, forgettable entertainment.
w Howard Rodman, Dean Riesner *novel The Looters* by John Reese *d* Don Siegel *ph* Michael Butler *m* Lalo Schifrin
☆ *Walter Matthau*, Joe Don Baker, Felicia Farr, Andy Robinson, John Vernon, Sheree North, Norman Fell
'It proves there is nothing wrong with an auteur director that a good script can't cure.' – *Stanley Kauffmann*
'The narrative line is clean and direct, the characterizations economical and functional, and the triumph of intelligence gloriously satisfying.' – *Andrew Sarris*
Walter Matthau

Charley's American Aunt: see *Charley's Aunt*

Charley's Aunt **
US 1941 81m bw
TCF (William Perlberg)
GB title: *Charley's American Aunt*
For complicated reasons, an Oxford undergraduate has to impersonate his friend's rich aunt from Brazil (where the nuts come from).
Very adequate version of the Victorian farce, with all concerned in excellent form.
w George Seaton *play* Brandon Thomas *d* Archie Mayo *ph* Peverell Marley *m* Alfred Newman *ad* Richard Day, Nathan Juran
☆ *Jack Benny*, Kay Francis, James Ellison, Anne Baxter, *Laird Cregar*, Edmund Gwenn, Reginald Owen, Richard Haydn, Arleen Whelan, Ernest Cossart
† See also: *Where's Charley?*

Charley's Big-Hearted Aunt
GB 1940 76m bw
Gainsborough (Edward Black)
A student is forced to impersonate his wealthy friend's Brazilian aunt.
Rather disappointing British version of the famous farce, dully assembled and rather unsuitably cast.
w Marriott Edgar, Val Guest *d* Walter Forde *ph* Jack Cox
☆ Arthur Askey, Phyllis Calvert, Moore Marriott, Graham Moffatt, Richard Murdoch, Jeanne de Casalis, J. H. Roberts, Felix Aylmer, Wally Patch

Charlie Bubbles ***
GB 1968 91m Technicolor
Universal/ Memorial (Michael Medwin, George Pitcher)
A successful novelist loathes the pointlessness of the good life and tries unsuccessfully to return to his northern working class background.
A little arid and slow in its early stages, and with a rather lame end (our hero escapes by air balloon), this is nevertheless a fascinating, fragmentary character study with a host of wry comedy touches and nimbly sketched characters; in its unassuming way it indicts many of the symbols people lived by in the sixties.
w Shelagh Delaney d Albert Finney ph Peter Suschitzky m Mischa Donat
☆ *Albert Finney*, Billie Whitelaw, Liza Minnelli, Colin Blakely, Timothy Garland, Diana Coupland, Alan Lake, Yootha Joyce, Joe Gladwin
'A modest thing, but like all good work in minor keys it has a way of haunting the memory.' – *Richard Schickel*
'The supreme deadweight is Liza Minnelli, whose screen debut proves easily the most inauspicious since Turhan Bey's.' – *John Simon*
Billie Whitelaw

Charlie Chan
The Oriental detective created by Earl Derr Biggers began his film career as a minor character (played by George Kuwa) in a 1926 serial called HOUSE WITHOUT A KEY. In 1928 Kamiyama Sojin had a bigger role in THE CHINESE PARROT, but in 1929 E. L. Park did almost nothing in BEHIND THAT CURTAIN. In 1931 however began the fully-fledged Chan movies,

which entertained a generation. Chan, based on a real-life Chinese detective named Chang Apana, became a citizen of Honolulu and was developed as a polite family man, aided by his impulsive number one or number two son (out of a family of fourteen), in solving murder puzzles. He had a treasury of aphorisms (a whole book of which has been published), and his technique was to gather all the suspects into one room before unmasking one as the murderer. The films built to a peak around 1936–9, but tailed off disastrously in the mid-forties. They were never noted for production values, but many retain interest for their scripts, their puzzles, and their casts of budding stars, as well as the central character. This is a complete list:
For Fox (later Twentieth Century Fox), with *Warner Oland* as Chan:
1931 Charlie Chan Carries On*, The Black Camel
1932 Charlie Chan's Chance
1933 Charlie Chan's Greatest Case
1934 Charlie Chan's Courage, Charlie Chan in London
1935 Charlie Chan in Paris*, Charlie Chan in Egypt, Charlie Chan in Shanghai
1936 Charlie Chan's Secret*, Charlie Chan at the Circus*, Charlie Chan at the Race Track, Charlie Chan at the Opera**
1937 Charlie Chan at the Olympics, Charlie Chan on Broadway*, Charlie Chan at Monte Carlo
For Twentieth Century Fox, with *Sidney Toler*:
1938 Charlie Chan in Honolulu
1939 Charlie Chan in Reno, Charlie Chan on Treasure Island**, City of Darkness
1940 Charlie Chan in Panama, Charlie Chan's Murder Cruise, Charlie Chan at the Wax Museum*, Murder over New York
1941 Dead Men Tell, Charlie Chan in Rio, Castle in the Desert*
For Monogram, with Sidney Toler:
1944 Charlie Chan in the Secret Service, The Chinese Cat, Black Magic
1945 The Scarlet Clue, The Jade Mask, Shanghai Cobra, Red Dragon
1946 Shadows over Chinatown, Dangerous Money
1947 The Trap
For Monogram, with *Roland Winters*:
1947 The Chinese Ring
1948 Docks of New Orleans, Shanghai Chest, The Golden Eye, The Feathered Serpent
1949 Sky Dragon
† In the late fifties J. Carrol Naish appeared in a half-hour TV series as Chan, but the episodes were dull. In 1971 Universal tried to revive the character in a 96-minute pilot film *Happiness is a Warm Clue*, but Ross Martin was woefully miscast. See also below.

Charlie Chan and the Curse of the Dragon Queen
US 1980 95m CFI color
UA/American Cinema/Jerry Sherlock
The villainous Dragon Queen puts a curse on Chan and his descendants, and works it out some years later in San Francisco.
The targets in this spoof are somewhat elementary (the sinister housekeeper is Mrs Danvers, the wheelchair-bound butler Gillespie) and almost all the jokes fall flat on their faces.
w Stan Burns, David Axelrod *d* Clive Donner *ph* Paul Lohmann *m* Patrick Williams
☆ Peter Ustinov, Angie Dickinson, Richard Hatch, Brian Keith, Roddy McDowall, Rachel Roberts, Johnny Sekka, Michelle Pfeiffer

Charlie McCarthy, Detective
US 1939 65m bw
Universal
Ventriloquist Edgar Bergen helps to solve a murder.
Slightly tiresome mystery comedy with no real place for the wisecracking dummy.
w Edward Eliscu *d* Frank Tuttle
☆ Edgar Bergen, Robert Cummings, Constance Moore, John Sutton, Louis Calhern, Edgar Kennedy, Samuel S. Hinds, Warren Hymer, Harold Huber
'Looks like a corner-cutter ... will have to struggle as top half of the duallers.' – *Variety*

Charlie the Lonesome Cougar *
US 1967 75m colour
Disney
The growing-up of a cougar.
Amiable true-life adventure.
w Jack Speirs *d* Winston Hibler

'Get some action.'
Charlie's Angels *
US 2000 98m DeLuxe Panavision
Columbia/Flower Films/Tall Trees (Leonard Goldberg, Drew Barrymore, Nancy Juvonen)
Three female crime fighter thwart an attempt to murder their boss.
Light-hearted, hyper-kinetic version of the 70s TV series, though its insistence on 'female empowerment' amounts to no more than its stars' ability to do high kicks on wires and look good in skin-tight clothing.
w Ryan Rowe, Ed Solomon, John August *TV series created by* Ivan Goff, Ben Roberts *d* McG *ph* Russell Carpenter *m* Edward Shearmur *pd* J. Michael Riva *ed* Wayne Wahrman, Peter Teschner *sp* martial fx: Cheung-Yan Yuen
☆ Cameron Diaz (Natalie), Drew Barrymore (Dylan), Lucy Liu (Alex), Bill Murray (Bosley), Sam Rockwell (Eric Knox), Tim Curry (Roger Corwin), Kelly Lynch (Vivian Wood), Crispin Glover (Thin Man), Matt LeBlanc (Jason), LL Cool J (Mr Jones), Tom Green (Chad), Luke Wilson (Pete), John Forsythe (Voice of Charlie)
'Its delight in the powerfulness of femininity does mark it out from all those action pictures where machismo is the governing religion.' – *Andy Medhurst, Sight and Sound*

Charlotte
France/Italy/West Germany 1974 103m Eastmancolor
New Realm/Claude Capra/Sedimo/Gerico/TIT (Roger Vadim)
original title: *La Jeune Fille Assassinée*
An author investigates the unsolved murder of a former lover, a police chief's promiscuous daughter, at the invitation of a rich German who claims to have killed her.
A glossy, essentially trivial mix of sex and murder.
wd Roger Vadim *ph* William Glenn *m* Mike Oldfield *ed* Victoria Mercanton
☆ Sirpa Lane, Michel Duchaussoy, Mathieu Carrière, Roger Vadim, Alexandre Astruc
† The film was cut to 99m on its British release.

'The story of an extraordinary woman in an extraordinary time.'
Charlotte Gray
GB/Australia 2001 121m Technicolor
Warner/FilmFour/Senator/Ecosse/Pod (Sarah Curtis, Douglas Rae. Executive producers, Paul Webster, Robert Bernstein, Hanno Huth)
During the Second World War, a young Scots woman volunteers to be a spy in France, where she becomes involved with a local resistance worker.
Curiously leaden adaptation of a best-selling novel, stressing Blanchett's glamour and with its cast speaking English with funny French accents, so emphasising the unreality of it all.
w Jeremy Brock *novel* Sebastian Faulks *d* Gillian Armstrong *ph* Dion Beebe *m* Stephen Warbeck *pd* Joseph Bennett *ed* Nicholas Beauman *cos* Janty Yates
☆ Cate Blanchett (Charlotte Gray), Billy Crudup (Julien Levade), Michael Gambon (Levade), Rupert Penry-Jones (Peter Gregory), Anton Lesser (Renech), James Fleet (Richard Cannerley), Ron Cook (Mirabel), Jack Shepherd (Pichon), Nicholas Farrell (Mr Jackson)
'A movie that looks great, is well-acted, and tells a story that you can't believe for a moment.' – *Roger Ebert, Chicago Sun-Times*
'The movie works so diligently to convey a spirit of heroic uplift and fails so completely that it feels like a tragic misfire.' – *Stephen Holden, New York Times*

Charlotte's Web
US 1972 96m Technicolor
Sagittarius/Hanna-Barbera
Farmyard animals who sense their fate are stimulated and encouraged by a resourceful spider.
Interesting but overlong and rather plodding version of a stylish book for children; the animation has no style at all.
w Earl Hamner Jnr *novel* E. B. White *d* Charles A. Nichols, Iwao Takamoto *m/ly* Richard and Robert Sherman *md* Irwin Kostal
☆ Featuring the voices of Debbie Reynolds, Henry Gibson, Paul Lynde, Martha Scott, Agnes Moorehead

Charly *
US 1968 106m Techniscope
Selmur/Robertson Associates (Ralph Nelson)
New methods of surgery cure a mentally retarded young man, who becomes a genius, but the effects wear off.
Smooth, unconvincing, rather pointless fantasy which ultimately leaves a bad taste in the mouth.
w Stirling Silliphant *novel Flowers for Algernon* by Daniel Keyes *d* Ralph Nelson *ph* Arthur J. Ornitz *m* Ravi Shankar
☆ *Cliff Robertson*, Claire Bloom, Leon Janney, Lilia Skala
'The most distressing thing about *Charly* is not its ticklish subject, nor yet its clumsily modish surface, but its insistent, persistent sentimentality.' – *Tom Milne*
Cliff Robertson

Charmant Garçons: see *Too Many Lovers*

Le Charme Discret de la Bourgeoisie: see *The Discreet Charm of the Bourgeoisie*

Charro
US 1969 98m Technicolor Panavision
National General (Charles Marquis Warren)
A reformed outlaw is framed for the theft of a cannon.
Dismal Western with a singing star playing straight. A bad experience.
wd Charles Marquis Warren *ph* Ellsworth Fredricks *m* Hugo Montenegro
☆ Elvis Presley, Ina Balin, Barbara Werle, Lynn Kellogg, Victor French, Solomon Sturges

Chartroose Caboose
US 1960 76m Eastmancolor Panavision
Red-Bill/U-I
A runaway couple take refuge with a retired train conductor in his converted rolling stock home.
Old-fashioned to the point of seeming half-witted, this comedy has little to offer but geniality.
w Rod Peterson *d* William Reynolds
☆ Molly Bee, Ben Cooper, Edgar Buchanan, O. Z. Whitehead, Slim Pickens

Charulata *
India 1964 117m bw
RDP (R. D. Bansal)
aka: *The Lonely Wife*
In Calcutta in the 1880s, the neglected wife of a wealthy newspaper editor turns to her husband's cousin for the love she craves.
A sombre story of repressed passion and domestic tragedy, but told at a too leisurely pace so that the tensions slacken and thin.
wd Satyajit Ray *novella Nastanirh* by *Rabindranath Tagore* *ph* Subrata Mitra *m* Satyajit Ray *ad* Bansi Chandragupta *ed* Dulal Dutta
☆ *Soumitra Chatterjee, Madhabi Mukherjee*, Sailen Mukherjee, Syamal Ghosal, Gitali Roy, Bholanath Koyal, Suku Mukherjee, Dilip Bose
'Ray's most nearly flawless film ... a flowing opulent tale that seems to be lit from the inside like a velvet-lined carriage with a lantern in it rocked by a hot monsoon wind.' – *Penelope Gilliat, New Yorker*
'Unutterably boring.' – *John Simon*
† Ray had to take care in photographing Madhabi Mukherjee in order to conceal the fact that her lower teeth were in poor condition and stained black.

The Chase *
US 1947 84m bw
Nero Pictures (Seymour Nebenzal)
A shell-shocked ex-serviceman foils a criminal and falls for his wife.
Weird Cuban-set film noir with a strange cast and stranger atmosphere. A genuine bomb, but worth a look for its pretensions, its cast, and its trick ending.
w Philip Yordan *novel The Black Path of Fear* by Cornell Woolrich *d Arthur Ripley* *ph* Franz Planer *m* Michel Michelet
☆ Robert Cummings, Michèle Morgan, Peter Lorre, Steve Cochran, Lloyd Corrigan, Jack Holt

The Chase *
US 1966 135m Technicolor Panavision
Columbia/Sam Spiegel
When a convict escapes and heads for his small Texas home town, almost all the inhabitants are affected in one way or another.
Expensive but shoddy essay in sex and violence, with Brando as a masochistic sheriff lording it over Peyton-Place-in-all-but-name. Literate moments do not atone for the general pretentiousness, and we have all been here once too often.
w Lillian Hellman *novel* Horton Foote *d* Arthur Penn *ph* Joseph LaShelle *m* John Barry *pd* Richard Day
☆ Marlon Brando, Jane Fonda, Robert Redford, Angie Dickinson, Janice Rule, James Fox, Robert Duvall, E. G. Marshall, Miriam Hopkins, Henry Hull
'The worst thing that has happened to movies since Lassie played a war veteran with amnesia.' – *Rex Reed*
'Considering all the talent connected with it, it is hard to imagine how *The Chase* went so haywire.' – *Philip T. Hartung*

'Life can be Hell loving in the fast lane...'
'A high-speed romance.'
The Chase
US 1994 88m colour
TCF/Hercules (Brad Wyman, Cassian Elwes)
An escaped prisoner kidnaps a glamorous heiress and heads for Mexico in her car chased by police and journalists.
This is a hectic, jokey journey to nowhere in particular, with nothing to engage the eye or mind along the way.
wd Adam Rifkin *ph* Alan Jones *m* Richard Gibbs *pd* Sherman Williams *ed* Peter Schink
☆ Charlie Sheen, Kristy Swanson, Henry Rollins, Josh Mostel, Ray Wise, Wayne Grace, Rocky Carroll, Miles Dougal
'A romantic road movie of acute banality. A film which relies more heavily on its music score and its stars to carry it through. I doubt if either will be enough.' – *Derek Malcolm, Guardian*

Chase a Crooked Shadow **
GB 1957 87m bw
ABP/Associated Dragon Films (Douglas Fairbanks Jnr)
An heiress finds her home invaded by a stranger posing as her dead brother.
Tricksy, lightly controlled suspense melodrama with a perfectly fair surprise ending. Handling equivocal but competent.
w David D. Osborn, Charles Sinclair *d Michael Anderson* *ph* Erwin Hillier *m* Matyas Seiber
☆ Richard Todd, Anne Baxter, Faith Brook, Herbert Lom, Alexander Knox, Alan Tilvern
'It'll lead the wisest guessers up the garden and give them the surprise of their life!' – *Kine Weekly*
† The plot was borrowed from an episode in *The Whistler* TV series, and later reversed for a 1975 TV film, *One of my Wives is Missing*.

'It was supposed to be a routine prison transfer. But this was no ordinary prisoner.'
Chasers
US 1994 101m Technicolor
Warner/Morgan Creek (James G. Robinson)
A glamorous woman uses her sex-appeal to outwit the two men who are escorting her to a naval prison.
Uninteresting comedy, with thinly realized characters, contrived situations, and only the occasional eccentric moment from its minor characters to give it any life.
w Joe Batteer, John Rice *d* Dennis Hopper *ph* Ueli Steiger *m* Dwight Yoakam, Peter Anderson *pd* Robert Pearson *ed* Christian A. Wagner
☆ Tom Berenger, William McNamara, Erika Eleniak, Crispin Glover, Dean Stockwell, Gary Busey, Seymour Cassel, Frederic Forrest, Matthew Glave, Marilu Henner, Dennis Hopper
'Mangy, dimwitted gender switch on *The Last Detail*.' – *Variety*

'Sex Is Easy. Love Is Hard.'

Chasing Amy **
US 1997 111m Technicolor
Metrodome/Miramax/View Askew (Scott Mosier)

A comic-book artist is attracted to a lesbian with wide sexual experience.
Enjoyable, often witty low-budget movie about the complexities of love and friendship.
wd Kevin Smith *ph* David Klein *m* David Pirner *pd* Robert 'Ratface' Holtzman *ed* Kevin Sith, Scott Mosier
☆ Ben Affleck, Joey Lauren Adams, Jason Lee, Dwight Ewell, Jason Mewes, Kevin Smith
'Fundamentally amusing and appealing.' – *Variety*
† The film was made for $250,000
†† The credits include the dedication: 'To the critics who hated our last flick – all is forgiven.'

Chasing Dreams
US 1982 105m CFI color
Nascent (Therese Conte, David G. Brown)

A shy youth with family problems and a handicapped brother discovers that he has a gift for playing baseball.
Sentimental family drama that is unlikely to stir any interest outside its home country.
w David G. Brown *d* Sean Roche *ph* Connie Holt *m* Gregory Conte *pd* Bobbi Peterson Himber *ed* Jerry Weldon, Robert Sinise
☆ David G. Brown, John Fife, Jim Shane, Matthew Clark, Lisa Kingston, Kevin Costner

Chasing the Deer
GB 1994 97m colour
Feature Film/Cromwell/La Mancha (Bob Carruthers)

A father and son find themselves, by force of circumstances, on opposite sides at the Battle of Culloden in 1746, when Bonnie Prince Charlie's Jacobite forces were defeated by the Duke of Cumberland.
Rather like the rebellion it celebrates, a gallant failure; it looks good but sadly lacks inspiration.
w Jerome Vincent, Bob Carruthers, Steve Gillham *d* Graham Holloway *ph* Alan M. Trow *m* John Wetton *ed* Patrick Moore
☆ Brian Blessed, Iain Cuthbertson, Fish, Matthew Zajax, Sandy Welch, Brian Donald, Peter Gordon, Lynn Ferguson
'You do need scale and a certain directorial flair. It's the lack of that which makes this properly sincere film into what is essentially a bit of a plod.' – *Derek Malcolm, Guardian*
† The producers raised much of the film's budget of £460,000 by offering roles as extras to those who invested in it.

Chasing Yesterday
US 1935 78m bw
RKO
An elderly archaeologist seeks to renew his lost youth through the daughter of the woman he once loved but lost.
Slow and old-fashioned melodrama.
w Francis E. Faragoh *novel The Crime of Sylvestre Bonnard* by Anatole France *d* George Nicholls Jnr
☆ O. P. Heggie, Anne Shirley, Elizabeth Patterson, Helen Westley, John Qualen, Etienne Girardot
'Prospects not bright.' – *Variety*

Chastnaya Zhizn: see *Private Life*

Le Château de Ma Mère *
France 1990 98m Eastmancolor
Gaumont/Gueville/TF1 (Marc Goldstaub, Guy Azzi)

aka: *My Mother's Castle*
A novelist and film-maker remembers his childhood holidays spent among the hills of Provence.
Slow-paced, soft-centred account of a blissful past; nostalgia is laid on with a trowel.
w Jérôme Tonnerre, Yves Robert *autobiography* Marcel Pagnol *d* Yves Robert *ph* Robert Alazraki *m* Vladimir Cosma *ad* Jacques Dugied *ed* Pierre Gillette
☆ Philippe Caubère, Nathalie Roussel, Didier Pain, Thérèse Liotard, Julien Ciamaca, Victorien Delamare, Joris Molinas, Julie Timmerman, Jean Carmet, Jean Rochefort, Georges Wilson, Jean-Pierre Darras (as narrator)
† A sequel to *La Gloire de Mon Papa* (qv).

Chato's Land
GB 1971 100m Technicolor
UA/Scimitar (Michael Winner)

An Apache half-breed kills a man in self-defence, subsequently eluding and destroying the sheriff's posse.
Exhaustingly violent Western in which the audience is spared no gory detail; efficiently put together for those who like this kind of fracas.
w Gerald Wilson *d* Michael Winner *ph* Robert Paynter *m* Jerry Fielding
☆ Charles Bronson, Jack Palance, Richard Basehart, James Whitmore, Simon Oakland, Richard Jordan, Ralph Waite, Victor French, Lee Patterson

Chattahoochee
US 1989 97m TVC Color
Hemdale (Aaron and Faye Schwab)

In the mid-1950s a veteran of the Korean War suffers a breakdown and is sent to a decaying, violent mental hospital.
Downbeat and depressing.
w James Hicks *d* Mick Jackson *ph* Andrew Dunn *m* John Keane *pd* Joseph T. Garrity *ed* Don Fairservice
☆ Gary Oldman, Dennis Hopper, Frances McDormand, Pamela Reed, Ned Beatty, M. Emmet Walsh

Chatterbox
US 1935 68m bw
RKO
A country maiden aspires to the stage.
Mildly likeable comedy for family audiences.
w Sam Mintz *play* David Carb *d* George Nicholls Jnr
☆ Anne Shirley, Phillips Holmes, Edward Ellis, Erik Rhodes, Margaret Hamilton, Granville Bates
'Discounting the nice job all around, the picture isn't there.' – *Variety*

Che?: see *What?*

'With a dream of justice, he created a nightmare of violence!'

Che!
US 1969 94m DeLuxe Panavision
TCF (Sy Bartlett)

Fidel Castro is helped in his subversion of Batista's Cuban regime by an Argentinian doctor named Che Guevara.
Fictionalized biography, and a dull one, of a man who became a myth.
w Michael Wilson, Sy Bartlett *d* Richard Fleischer *ph* Charles Wheeler *m* Lalo Schifrin
☆ Omar Sharif, Jack Palance (Castro), Cesare Danova, Robert Loggia, Woody Strode, Barbara Luna
'It goes at the pace of a drugged ox, and hasn't an ounce of political or historical sense in its nut.' – *New Yorker*

The Cheap Detective
US 1978 92m Metrocolor Panavision
Columbia/Ray Stark

Forties private eye Lou Peckinpaugh is involved in a complex case with echoes of *Casablanca*, *The Big Sleep*, *The Maltese Falcon* and *Farewell My Lovely*.
Lame spoof which might have seemed funnier on a small screen in black and white; as it is, the strain is evident and desperate.
w Neil Simon *d* Robert Moore *ph* John A. Alonzo *m* Patrick Williams
☆ Peter Falk (Lou Peckinpaugh/Humphrey Bogart), John Houseman (Jasper Blubber/Sydney Greenstreet), Nicol Williamson (Colonel Schlissel/Conrad Veidt), *Louise Fletcher* (Marlene Duchard/Ingrid Bergman), Fernando Lamas (Paul Duchard/Paul Henreid), Madeline Kahn (Mrs Montenegro/ Mary Astor), Dom DeLuise (Pepe Damascus/Peter Lorre), Paul Williams (Boy/Elisha Cook), Marsha Mason (Georgia Merke/Gladys George), Ann-Margret (Jezebel Dezire/Claire Trevor), Eileen Brennan (Betty DeBoop/Lauren Bacall), Stockard Channing (Bess/Lee Patrick), Sid Caesar (Ezra Dezire/Miles Mander), Scatman Crothers (Tinker/Dooley Wilson), Phil Silvers (Hoppy) and also Abe Vigoda, Vic Tayback, James Coco, James Cromwell
'Frankly they did this sort of thing just as well, and a lot more quickly, on *The Carol Burnett Show*.' – *Richard Schickel, Time*
'There is about enough talent around for a twenty-minute sketch at the Edinburgh fringe.' – *Derek Malcolm, Guardian*
† The film was a follow-up to the not much more effective but at least more controlled *Murder by Death*.

Cheaper by the Dozen **
US 1950 86m Technicolor
TCF (Lamar Trotti)
Efficiency expert Frank Gilbreth and his wife Lillian have twelve children, a fact which requires mathematical conduct of all their lives.
Amusing family comedy set in the twenties, unconvincing in detail though based on a book by two of the children. A great commercial success and a Hollywood myth-maker. Sequel: Belles on their Toes *(qv).*
w Lamar Trotti *book* Frank B. Gilbreth Jnr, Ernestine Gilbreth Carey *d Walter Lang ph* Leon Shamroy *m* Cyril Mockridge *md* Lionel Newman *ad* Lyle Wheeler, Leland Fuller
☆ *Clifton Webb, Myrna Loy*, Jeanne Crain, Edgar Buchanan, Barbara Bates, Betty Lynn, Mildred Natwick, Sara Allgood

The Cheat *
US 1915 95m (16 fps) bw silent
Famous Players Lasky/Paramount
A society lady borrows from a rich Japanese, and he brands her when she refuses to become his mistress.
Hoary melodrama which caused a sensation in its day.
w Hector Turnbull *d Cecil B. de Mille ph Alvin Wyckoff*
☆ Fanny Ward, Jack Dean, Sessue Hayakawa, James Neill
† Remade in 1923 by George Fitzmaurice, in 1931 by George Abbott, and in 1937 (in France, as *Forfaiture*) by Marcel L'Herbier.

The Cheaters *
US 1945 86m bw
Republic
A selfish and ostentatious family is reformed by the ministrations of a down-and-out actor.
Fairly engaging variation on The Passing of the Third Floor Back, *with sweetness and light brought into people's lives by a fireside recital of* A Christmas Carol.
w Frances Hyland *d* Joseph Kane *ph* Reggie Lanning *m* Walter Scharf
☆ Joseph Schildkraut, Billie Burke, Eugene Pallette, Ona Munson, Raymond Walburn

Check and Double Check
US 1930 71m bw
RKO

Comic adventures of a couple of black handymen.
Feeble comedy notable only for the film appearance of radio's immensely popular Amos 'n' Andy, *played by white actors in blackface.*
w Bert Kalmar, Harry Ruby, J. Walter Ruben *d* Melville Brown *ph* William Marshall *m* Max Steiner
☆ Freeman F. Gosden, Charles V. Correll, Sue Carol, Charles Morton, Irene Rich, Ralf Harolde, Duke Ellington and his Orchestra
'The best picture for children ever put on the screen ... as a freak talking picture it's in the money immediately.' – *Variety*

Checkers
US 1937 79m bw
TCF
The niece of a ne'er-do-well horse owner brings him success.
One of the most successful vehicles of Shirley Temple's arch rival.
w Lynn Root, Frank Fenton, Karen de Wolf *play* Rida Johnson Young *d* H. Bruce Humberstone
☆ Jane Withers, Stuart Erwin, Una Merkel, Marvin Stephens, Andrew Tombes, Minor Watson
'Will delight the moppet's following ... due for heavy dual booking.' – *Variety*

Checking Out
GB 1988 95m Technicolor Super 35
Virgin/Handmade (Ben Myron)

A successful advertising man becomes a hypochondriac after the sudden death of a friend.
Mildly amusing comedy.
w Joe Eszterhas *d* David Leland *ph* Ian Wilson *m* Carter Burwell *pd* Barbara Ling *ed* Lee Percy
☆ Jeff Daniels, Melanie Mayron, Michael Tucker, Kathleen York, Ann Magnuson, Allan Harvey, Jo Harvey Allen, Ian Wolfe

Checkpoint *
GB 1956 84m Eastmancolor
Rank (Betty Box)
A tycoon sends an industrial spy to Italy in search of new motor racing car designs.
Acceptable hokum, cleanly assembled, with motor race highlights.
w Robin Estridge *d* Ralph Thomas *ph* Ernest Steward *m* Bruce Montgomery
☆ Anthony Steel, Stanley Baker, James Robertson Justice, Odile Versois, Maurice Denham, Michael Medwin, Lee Patterson

Cheech and Chong: Still Smokin'
US 1983 92m colour
Paramount/Cheech & Chong's Comedy Film Festival Number One Inc (Peter MacGregor-Scott)
Two slobbish comedians attend a Burt Reynolds-Dolly Parton film festival in Amsterdam.
Dreary, plotless exercise in futility that reaches its nadir in excerpts from the duo's concert performance.
w Thomas Chong, Cheech Marin *d* Thomas Chong *ph* Harvey Harrison *m* George A. Clinton *ad* Ruud Van Dijk *ed* David Ramirez, James Coblenz
☆ Cheech Marin, Thomas Chong, Hans Man In't Veld, Carol Van Herwijnen, Shireen Strocker, Susan Hahn

Cheech and Chong's Next Movie
US 1980 95m Technicolor
Howard Brown/Universal

GB title: *High Encounters of the Ultimate Kind*
Two dopers have various rude adventures.
Totally repulsive comedy which gives a bad name to self-indulgence.
w Cheech Marin, Thomas Chong *d* Thomas Chong
☆ Cheech Marin, Thomas Chong, Evelyn Guerrero, Betty Kennedy, Sy Kramer

Cheech and Chong's The Corsican Brothers
US 1984 90m colour
Orion (Peter MacGregor-Scott)

Twin brothers run amuck during the French Revolution.
Coarse and unfunny parody of a swashbuckling adventure.
w Cheech Marin, Thomas Chong *d* Thomas Chong *ph* Harvey Harrison *m* GEO *ad* Daniel Budin *ed* Tom Avildsen
☆ Cheech Marin, Thomas Chong, Roy Dotrice, Shelby Fiddis, Rikki Marin, Edie McClurg, Rae Dawn Chong, Robbi Chong

Cheer Boys Cheer
GB 1939 84m bw
ATP (Michael Balcon)
Brewery owners hate each other but their children fall in love.
A highly predictable plot provides some incidental pleasures in this modest precursor of the Ealing comedies.
w Roger MacDougall, Allan MacKinnon *story* Ian Dalrymple, Donald Bull *d* Walter Forde *ph* Ronald Neame, Gordon Dines *md* Ernest Irving *ad* Wilfred Shingleton *ed* Ray Pitt
☆ Nova Pilbeam, Edmund Gwenn, Jimmy O'Dea, Moore Marriott, Graham Moffatt, C. V. France, Alexander Knox

Cheer Up!
GB 1936 72m bw
Associated British/Stanley Lupino
An unemployed actor is mistaken for a millionaire by an out-of-work actress.
Jolly though undistinguished musical, hampered by its low humour and lower budget.

w Michael Barringer *story* Stanley Lupino *d* Leo Mittler *ph* Curt Courant *m/ly* Billy Mayerl, Val Guest, Noel Gay, Frank Eyton, Stanley Lupino, Desmond Carter *md* Percy Mackey *ad* J. Elder Wills *ed* Sam Simmonds, Ronald Deeming
☆ Stanley Lupino, Sally Gray, Roddy Hughes, Wyn Weaver, Marjorie Chard, Ernest Sefton, Gerald Barry, Kenneth Kove, Doris Rogers, Arthur Rigby

Cheers for Miss Bishop *
US 1941 94m bw
UA (Richard A. Rowland)
The life of a schoolmistress in a small mid-western town.
Acceptable sentimental hokum, quite pleasantly done.
w Adelaide Heilbron *novel* Bess Streeter Aldrich *d* Tay Garnett *ph* Hal Mohr *m* Edward Ward
☆ Martha Scott, William Gargan, Edmund Gwenn, Sterling Holloway, Sidney Blackmer, Mary Anderson, Dorothy Peterson
Edward Ward

Cheetah
US 1984 84m Metrocolor
Buena Vista/Walt Disney (Robert Halmi)
Two American teenagers, who spend six months in Africa with their parents, rescue and rear a cheetah cub.
Bland and innocuous entertainment aimed at children, but too tame to hold their interest for long.
w Erik Tarloff, John Cotter, Griff du Rhone *book The Cheetahs* by Alan Caillou *d* Jeff Blyth *ph* Tom Burstyn *m* Bruce Rowland *pd* Jane Cavedon *ed* Eric Albertson
☆ Keith Coogan, Lucy Deakins, Timothy Landfield, Breon Gorman, Collin Mothupi

Chelovek sKinoapparatom: *see The Man with the Movie Camera*

The Chelsea Girls **
US 1966 255m bw/colour
Andy Warhol
Episodic look at life in a series of hotel rooms, consisting of unedited conversations between spaced-out individuals – the Pope of Greenwich Village hearing confessions and losing his temper, a drug dealer talking to a customer as she injects them both, a woman being reduced to tears by aggressive questioning, a mother chastising her son, a dancer stripping as he talks about his desires, and so on.
Shown on a double screen, with two different rooms visible at a time, but only one conversation audible, this was the film which, more than any other, brought the underground to public attention. It has worn less well than some of Morrissey and Warhol's other work but survives as a monument of sorts, exactly capturing the sights and sounds of a particular era despite its technical shortcomings.
d Paul Morrissey *ph* Andy Warhol *m* The Velvet Underground
☆ Marie Mencken, Mary Woronov, Gerard Malanga, International Velvet, Ingrid Superstar, Ondine, Mario Montez, Eric Emerson, Nico, Brigid Polk
'An epic movie-novel.' – *Jonas Mekas*
'Warhol's people are more real than real because the camera encourages their exhibitionism. They are all "performing" because their lives are one long performance and their party is never over.' – *Andrew Sarris, Village Voice*
'It has come time to wag a warning finger at Andy Warhol and his underground friends and tell them politely but firmly that they are pushing a reckless thing too far.' – *Bosley Crowther, New York Times*
'A three and a half hour cesspool of vulgarity and talentless confusion which is about as interesting as the inside of a toilet bowl.' – *Rex Reed*
† The film, which cost less than $3,000 to make, took more than $300,000 in its first six months.

Chère Inconnue: *see I Sent a Letter To My Love*

Cherry 2000
US 1988 93m DeLuxe
Orion (Edward R. Pressman, Caldecot Chubb)
In the year 2017 after his robotic sex-toy breaks down, a man discovers human romance when he hires a female mercenary to obtain the spare part he needs to repair it from a heavily guarded desert warehouse.
Post-apocalyptic fantasy of a familiar kind, silly but enjoyable if you are in a tolerant enough mood to accept Melanie Griffith as the female equivalent of Mad Max.
w Michael Almereyda *story* Lloyd Fonvielle *d* Steve de Jarnatt *ph* Jacques Haitkin *m* Basil Poledouris *pd* John J. Moore *ed* Edward Abroms, Duwayne Dunham
☆ Melanie Griffith, David Andrews, Ben Johnson, Brion James, Tim Thomerson, Harry Carey Jnr, Pamela Gidley
† The film was made in 1985.

'At Virgin High... it's put out or die...'
Cherry Falls
US 1999 92m DeLuxe
Entertainment/Rogue/Industry Entertainment/Fresh Produce (Marshall Persinger, Eli Selden)
In Cherry Falls, Virginia, a serial killer picks chaste adolescents as victims.
This reverses the usual slasher movie tradition of killing those who indulge in sex, but otherwise offers the traditional gore mixed in with a little obvious black humour.
w Ken Selden *d* Geoffrey Wright *ph* Anthony Richmond *m* Walter Wersowa *pd* Marek Dobrowolsky *ed* John F. Link, Russ DeNove *cos* Louise Frogley
☆ Michael Biehn (Sheriff Brent Marken), Brittany Murphy (Jody Marken), Jay Mohr (Leonard Marliston), Gabriel Mann (Kenny), Joe Inscoe (Tom Sisler), Keram Malicki-Sanchez (Timmy), Natalie Ramsey (Sandy), Candy Clark (Marge Marken), Amanda Anka (Mina), Clementine Ford (Annette)
'This is so-so, a watchable hark back to the slew of early '80s slasher fare.' – *Mark Dinning, Empire*

Cherry, Harry and Raquel!
US 1969 71m colour
Panamint/Eve (Russ Meyer)
A crooked sheriff gets his come-uppance.
Little more than a series of violent or sexual incidents, which only have a vague connection with each other; as with Meyer's other films, there's time to contemplate why his characters are always so angry with each other.
w Tom Wolfe, Russ Meyer *d* Russ Meyer *ph* Russ Meyer *m* William Loose *ed* Russ Meyer, Richard S. Brummer
☆ Larissa Ely, Linda Ashton, Charles Napier, Bert Santos, Franklin H. Bolger, Astrid Lillimor, John Milo

The Cherry Picker
GB 1972 92m Eastmancolor
Fox-Rank/Elsinore (Peter Curran, Derek Kavanagh)
The rich, hippy son of an American tycoon loses his appetite for the sybaritic life.
Typical British product of its time, a failed attempt to mix sex and satire; what we get instead is a cheap-looking movie with a confused narrative and an uncertain tone.
wd Peter Curran *novel Pick Up Sticks* by Mickey Phillips *ph* Billy Jordan *m* Bill McGuffie *pd* Frank White *ed* Jack Knight
☆ Lulu, Bob Sherman, Wilfrid Hyde-White, Spike Milligan, Patrick Cargill, Robert Hutton, Priscilla Morgan, Jack Hulbert, Terry-Thomas
'The film dithers over an inadequately scripted and crudely shot narrative that might be charitably described as "rambling" or "picaresque".' – *MFB*

Chess Fever *
USSR 1925 20m (24 fps) bw silent
Mezhrabpom-Russ
A chess fanatic is so absorbed that he misses his wedding.
Spirited visual comedy which still raises the intended laughs.
w Nikolai Shpikovsky *d* Nikolai Shpikovsky, Vsevolod Pudovkin
☆ Vladimir Fogel, Anna Zemtsova

The Chess Players *
India 1977 129m Eastmancolor
Devki Chitra (Suresh Jindal)
original title: *Shatranj Ke Khilari*
In 1856 Lucknow, two noblemen are more interested in playing chess than in their state's imminent annexation by the British.
Patchy but frequently charming historical piece with more specifically Indian elements than are usual from its director.
wd Satyajit Ray *story* Prem Chand *m* Satyajit Ray *ad* Bansi Chandragupta *ed* Dulal Dutta
☆ Sanjeev Kumar, Saeed Jaffrey, Richard Attenborough, Amjad Khan

Le Cheval d'Orgueil: *see The Proud Ones*

Cheyenne
US 1947 100m bw
Warner
later retitled: *The Wyoming Kid*
A gambler turns lawman, catches a robber and marries his wife.
Rather sluggish Western which later inspired a long-running TV series.
w Alan Le May, Thames Williamson *d* Raoul Walsh
☆ Dennis Morgan, Bruce Bennett, Jane Wyman, Arthur Kennedy, Janis Paige, Alan Hale

Cheyenne Autumn *
US 1964 170m Technicolor Panavision 70
Warner/Ford-Smith (Bernard Smith)
In the 1860s, Cheyenne Indians are moved to a new reservation 1500 miles away; wanting aid, they begin a trek back home, and various battles follow.
Dispirited, shapeless John Ford Western with little of the master's touch; good to look at, however, with effective cameos, notably an irrelevant and out-of-key comic one featuring James Stewart as Wyatt Earp.
w James R. Webb *novel* Mari Sandoz *d* John Ford *ph* *William H. Clothier* *m* Alex North *ad* Richard Day *ed* Otho Lovering
☆ Richard Widmark, Carroll Baker, Karl Malden, *Dolores del Rio*, Sal Mineo, Edward G. Robinson, *James Stewart*, Ricardo Montalban, Gilbert Roland, Arthur Kennedy, Patrick Wayne, Elizabeth Allen, Victor Jory, John Carradine, Mike Mazurki and also John Qualen, George O'Brien
'Although one would like to praise the film for its high-minded aims, it is hard to forget how ponderous and disjointed it is.' – *Moira Walsh*
'The acting is bad, the dialogue trite and predictable, the pace funereal, the structure fragmented and the climaxes puny.' – *Stanley Kauffmann*
William H. Clothier

The Cheyenne Social Club *
US 1970 102m Technicolor Panavision
National General (James Lee Barrett, Gene Kelly)
Two itinerant cowboys inherit a high-class brothel.
Disappointing star comedy Western with pleasing moments and a lively climactic shootout. Perhaps the girls are just a shade too winsome.
w James Lee Barrett *d* Gene Kelly *ph* William H. Clothier *m* Walter Scharf
☆ James Stewart, Henry Fonda, Shirley Jones, Sue Ane Langdon, Robert Middleton, Arch Johnson
'Co-starring Shirley Jones and Rigor Mortis, who enters early and stays through the very last scene.' – *Rex Reed*

Chi L'ha Vista Morire?: *see Who Saw Her Die?*

Chi sei?: *see Devil within Her*

'If you can't be famous...be infamous.'
Chicago **
US/Germany 2002 113m DeLuxe
Buena Vista/Miramax /Producer Circle (Martin Richards)
In Chicago of the 1920s a singer and a showgirl both enjoy a brief notoriety and rivalry when each is tried for murder.
A clever screenplay that treats the songs as moments of fantasy and wish fulfillment, and slick direction make for a diverting, cynical account of short-lived celebrity and the collusions between the media and its stars; it is let down by the singing and dancing, which rarely rise above the competent.
w *Bill Condon* *musical play* Bob Fosse, Fred Ebb *play* Maurine Dallas Watkins *d* *Rob Marshall* *ph* *Dion Beebe* *m* Danny Elfman *m/ly* John Kander, Fred Ebb *ch* Rob Marshall *pd* John Myhre *ed* *Martin Walsh* *cos* *Colleen Atwood*
☆ Catherine Zeta Jones (Velma Kelly), Renee Zellweger (Roxie Hart), Richard Gere (Billy Flynn), *Queen Latifah* (Matron 'Mama' Morton), John C. Reilly (Amos Hart), Christine Baranski (Mary Sunshine), Lucy Liu (Kitty), Taye Diggs (Bandleader), Colm Feore (Martin Harrison), Dominic West (Fred Casely)
'It's rare to find a picture as exuberant, as shallow — and as exuberant about its shallowness.' – *Elvis Mitchell, New York Times*
'A shallow work without a true moral framework, it sees the world as a posturing showbusiness arena, a stage for celebrities to briefly strut their stuff and go on their way.' – *Philip French, Observer*
'the net effect of the incessant dazzle is depressing.' – *Stanley Kaufmann, New Republic*
† Maurine Watkins' play was first filmed in 1927 with Phyllis Haver, and again in 1942 as *Roxie Hart*, starring Ginger Rogers.
♫ 'And All That Jazz'; 'When You're Good to Mama'; 'Cell Block Tango'; 'Roxie'; 'Me and My Baby'; 'Razzle Dazzle'; 'Funny Honey'; 'All I Care About Is Love'; 'We Both Reached For the Gun'; 'I Can't Do It Alone'; 'Mr Cellophane'; 'Nowadays'; 'I Move On'.
picture; Catherine Zeta-Jones; John Myhre (with Gordon Sim); Colleen Atwood; Martin Walsh; sound (Michael Minkler, Dominic Tavella, David Lee)
Bill Condon; Rob Marshall; Renée Zellweger; John C. Reilly; Queen Latifah; Dion Beebe; song 'I Move On' (*m* John Kander, *l* Fred Ebb)
Catherine Zeta-Jones; sound (Michael Minkler, Dominic Tavella, David Lee, Maurice Schell)

Chicago Calling *
US 1951 75m bw
UA/Arrowhead/Joseph Justman (Peter Berneis)
A drunk cannot pay his phone bill and is waiting for a vital call about his daughter's involvement in a car crash.
Moderate, location-shot minor melodrama with a few good ideas.
w John Reinhardt, Peter Berneis *d* John Reinhardt *ph* Robert de Grasse *m* Heinz Roemheld
☆ *Dan Duryea*, Mary Anderson, Gordon Gebert, Ross Elliott

Chicago, Chicago: *see Gaily, Gaily*

Chicago Confidential
US 1957 74m bw
Peerless/UA
A gambling syndicate takes over a labour union and frames its incorruptible president for murder.
Very routine gangster potboiler.
w Raymond T. Marcus (Bernard Gordon) *story* Hugh King *book* *Jack Lait, Lee Mortimer* *d* Sidney Salkow
☆ Brian Keith, Beverly Garland, Dick Foran, Elisha Cook Jnr
† Bernard Gordon wrote the script under a pseudonym because he was blacklisted at the time.

Chicago Deadline
US 1949 87m bw
Paramount (Robert Fellows)
A reporter researches the life of a lonely girl who died of tuberculosis.
Flat star vehicle consisting mainly of overplayed cameos.
w Warren Duff, Tiffany Thayer *d* Lewis Allen *ph* John F. Seitz *m* Victor Young
☆ Alan Ladd, Donna Reed, *June Havoc*, Berry Kroeger, Arthur Kennedy, Gavin Muir, Shepperd Strudwick
† Remade as the TV pilot of *The Name of the Game*.

'Where desire has no limits ... Fantasies become dangerous realities!'

Chicago Joe and the Showgirl
GB 1989 103m colour
Palace/New Line/Polygram/Working Title/BSB (Tim Bevan)
During the Second World War, an American deserter and his English girlfriend, a stripper, enhance their affair by committing a series of crimes.
Based on actual events, but a movie that rarely seems more than a laboured fantasy and one that the public ignored.
w David Yallop *d* Bernard Rose *ph* Mike Southon *m* Hans Zimmer, Shirley Walker *pd* Gemma Jackson *ed* Dan Rae
☆ Kiefer Sutherland, Emily Lloyd, Patsy Kensit

Chicago Masquerade: see *Little Egypt*

Chicago Syndicate
US 1955 86m bw
Clover/Columbia
A young accountant breaks up an outwardly respectable crime syndicate.
Formula racket-busting melodrama.
w Joseph Hoffman *d* Fred F. Sears
☆ Dennis O'Keefe, Abbe Lane, Paul Stewart, Xavier Cugat, Alison Haynes

The Chicken Chronicles
US 1977 94m CFI color
Chicken Enterprises/Avco Embassy
Problems of a teenager in an American small town.
Extremely boring comedy drama, obsessed with sex and lacking background detail.
w Paul Diamond *d* Francis Simon
☆ Phil Silvers, Ed Lauter, Steve Guttenberg, Meredith Baer, Lisa Reeves

Chicken Every Sunday *
US 1949 94m bw
TCF
The Hefferans have run a boarding house for twenty years, but dad's wild schemes run away with any possible profit.
Archetypal, folksy, American small-town chronicle, reasonably well made, for an audience that later watched The Waltons.
w George Seaton, Valentine Davies *d* George Seaton *ph* Harry Jackson *m* Alfred Newman
☆ Dan Dailey, Celeste Holm, Colleen Townsend, Alan Young, Natalie Wood

'This Ain't No Chick Flick'

Chicken Run ***
US/GB 2000 85m Technicolor
Pathé/DreamWorks, Aardman (Peter Lord, David Sproxton, Nick Park)
A circus rooster helps organise chickens to escape the jail-like farm where they face certain death in an automated pie-making machine.
In part a parody of prisoner-of-war films such as The Great Escape, *which will mean little to its intended audience, this gradually develops a comic momentum and absurdity all of its own, with a quaint handmade charm that proves irrestible.*
w Karey Kirkpatrick *story* Peter Lord, Nick Park *d* Peter Lord, Nick Park *ph* Dave Alex Riddett, Tristan Oliver, Frank Passingham *m* John Powell, Harry Gregson-Williams *pd* Phil Lewis
☆ voices of: Mel Gibson (Rocky), Julia Sawalha (Ginger), Miranda Richardson (Mrs Tweedy), Jane Horrocks (Babs), Lynn Ferguson (Mac), Imelda Staunton (Bunty), Benjamin Whitrow (Fowler), Tony Haygarth (Mr Tweedy), Timothy Spall (Nick), Phil Daniels (Fetcher)

'Always engaging, full of bright humor, marvelous stop-motion work with Plasticine figures, dramatic conflict and wonderfully nuanced characterizations.' – *Todd McCarthy, Variety*

'A smart mix of nostalgia, sweetness and flip modernity in design and dialogue.' – *Angie Errigo, Empire*

'Pretty modest fare, with nothing like the style and invention of the *Toy Story* films.' – *Peter Bradshaw, Guardian*

Chickens Come Home *
US 1931 30m bw
Hal Roach
Stan helps his boss Ollie to evade the attentions of an old flame.
Rather heavy and untypical, but mainly very enjoyable star comedy, a remake of Love 'Em and Weep *in which all three leading players had appeared four years earlier in different roles.*
w H. M. Walker *story* Hal Roach *d* James W. Horne *ph* Art Lloyd, Jack Stevens *ed* Richard Currier
☆ Stan Laurel, Oliver Hardy, James Finlayson, Mae Busch, Thelma Todd

The Chief
US 1933 80m bw
MGM
GB title: *My Old Man's a Fireman*
A fireman's son becomes a Bowery candidate for alderman.
Feeble comedy with the star ill at ease.
w Arthur Caesar, A. E. Hopkins *d* Charles F. Riesner
☆ Ed Wynn, Dorothy Mackaill, Charles 'Chic' Sale, William Boyd, George Givot, C. Henry Gordon

'With the radio draw angle discarded it is weak entertainment.' – *Variety*

Chief Crazy Horse
US 1954 86m Technicolor Cinemascope
U-I (William Alland)
GB title: *Valley of Fury*
The tribal problems of the Indian chief who defeated Custer at Little Big Horn.
Competent pro-Indian Western.
w Franklin Coen, Gerald Drayson Adams *d* George Sherman *ph* Harold Lipstein *m* Frank Skinner
☆ Victor Mature, Suzan Ball, John Lund, Ray Danton, Keith Larsen, Paul Guilfoyle, David Janssen

Un Chien Andalou *
France 1928 17m bw silent
Luis Buñuel
Famous surrealist short which includes dead donkeys on pianos and starts with a woman's eyeball being cut by a razor blade.
It had meaning for its makers, but very few other people saw anything in it but sensationalism.
w Luis Buñuel, Salvador Dali d Luis Buñuel ph Albert Dubergen ed Luis Buñuel
☆ Simone Mareuil, Pierre Batcheff, Jaime Miravilles, Salvador Dali, Luis Buñuel

La Chienne *
France 1931 85m bw
Braunberger-Richebé
A bank clerk falls for a prostitute and later kills her; her pimp is executed for the crime and the bank clerk becomes a tramp.
Heavy-going, old-fashioned melodrama with some interesting detail.
wd Jean Renoir novel Georges de la Fouchardière *ph* Theodor Sparkuhl, Roger Hubert
☆ *Michel Simon*, Janie Marèze, Georges Flament, Jean Gehret

'If the English translation of the title is unfit to print, the film's dialogue cannot be translated into English. Okay for sophisticated audiences that look for a taste of spice in a ritzy spot.' – *Variety*

† Remade as *Scarlet Street* (qv).

La Chiesa: see *The Church*

Child in the House
GB 1956 88m bw
Eros/Golden Era (Ben Fisz)
When her mother is ill and her father in hiding from the police, a 12-year-old girl goes to stay with her fussy uncle and aunt.
Modest family drama of the novelette type in which adult problems are put right by the wisdom of a child.
wd Cy Endfield *novel* Janet McNeill *ph* Otto Heller *m* Mario Nascimbene *ad* Ken Adam
☆ Eric Portman, Phyllis Calvert, Stanley Baker, Mandy Miller, Dora Bryan, Joan Hickson, Victor Maddern, Percy Herbert

A Child Is Born
US 1939 79m bw
Warner (Sam Bischoff)
A slice of life in the maternity ward.
Adequately dramatic sequence of cameos, with mothers-to-be including a gangster's moll: a remake of Life Begins *(qv).*
w Robert Rossen *play* Mary M. Axelson *d* Lloyd Bacon *ph* Charles Rosher *m* Heinz Roemheld
☆ Geraldine Fitzgerald, Jeffrey Lynn, Gladys George, Gale Page, Spring Byington, Henry O'Neill, John Litel, Gloria Holden, Eve Arden, Nanette Fabares, Hobart Cavanaugh, Johnny Downs, Johnnie Davis

A Child Is Waiting **
US 1963 104m bw
UA/Stanley Kramer
A mixed-up spinster joins the staff of a school for mentally handicapped children.
Worthy semi-documentary marred by having a normal boy play the central character (albeit very well). A little over-dramatized but cogent and unsentimental.
w Abby Mann *d* John Cassavetes *ph* Joseph LaShelle *m* Ernest Gold
☆ Burt Lancaster, *Judy Garland, Bruce Ritchey,* Steven Hill, Gena Rowlands, *Paul Stewart,* Lawrence Tierney

The Childhood of Maxim Gorky ***
USSR bw
Soyuzdetfilm
Orphan Gorky is raised by his grandparents, and becomes a ship's cook and a painter before going on to university.
This simple and direct story is told in three beautifully detailed if rather overlong films: 'The Childhood of Maxim Gorky' (1938, 101m), 'Out in the World' (1939, 98m), 'My Universities' (1940, 104m).
w Mark Donskoi, I. Grudzev *d* Mark Donskoi *ph* Pyotr Yermolov *m* Lev Schwartz *ad* I. Stepanov
☆ Alexei Lyarsky, Y. Valbert, M. Troyanovski, Valeria Massalitinova

'This is for grown-up minds. It is episodic and sprawling, the photography is by no means good – quite inferior to the polished camera work of the average Hollywood product – but it touches the mind and heart as no film within years has done.' – *Richard Winnington*

The Children *
GB/West Germany 1990 115m colour
Isolde/Arbo Film & Maran/Channel 4 (Andrew Montgomery)
Returning from Brazil to marry a rich widow, an engineer finds his plans disrupted when he becomes guardian to the boisterous children of an old friend.
A leisurely account of thwarted love, held together by Kingsley's strong central performance of repressed emotion.
w Timberlake Wertenbaker *novel* Edith Wharton *d* Tony Palmer *ph* Nic Knowland *m* Benjamin Britten, Samuel Barber, Vaughan Williams, Evelyn Glennie *pd* Chris Bradley, Paul Templeman
☆ *Ben Kingsley*, Kim Novak, Siri Neal, Geraldine Chaplin, Joe Don Baker, Britt Ekland, Karen Black, Donald Sinden, Robert Stephens, Rupert Graves, Rosemary Leach

Children of a Lesser God *
US 1986 110m Film Lab Color
Paramount (Burt Sugarman, Patrick Palmer)
A deaf woman falls in love with her speech therapist.
Sluggish adaptation of a play which meant more on the stage.
w Hesper Anderson, Mark Medoff *play* Mark Medoff *d* Randa Haines *ph* John Seale *m* Michael Convertino *pd* Gene Callahan *ed* Lisa Fruchtman
☆ William Hurt, Marlee Matlin, Piper Laurie, Philip Bosco
Marlee Matlin
best picture; William Hurt; Piper Laurie; screenplay

Children of Chance
GB/Italy 1949 99m bw
British Lion/Ortus/Lux (John Sutro, Ludovico Toeplitz)
At the end of the Second World War, a woman on the island of Ischia discovers that her savings, which she sent to her village priest for safe-keeping, have been spent on opening a home for the illegimate children of Allied soldiers.
A slow-moving, sentimental drama which, although based on a true story and filmed on location, lacks authenticity owing to the restrained performances of its impeccably English cast.
w Piero Tellini, Michael Medwin *d* Luigi Zampa *ph* Carlo Montuori *m* Nino Rota
☆ Patricia Medina, Manning Whiley, Yvonne Mitchell, Barbara Everest, Eliot Makeham, George Woodbridge, Frank Tickle, Eric Pohlmann

Children of Hiroshima **
Japan 1952 97m bw
Kendai Eiga Lyokai/Gekidan Mingei
A young teacher returns to Hiroshima seven years after the bomb.
Restrained yet harrowing social documentary in fiction form, with the most effective use of flashbacks to show the horror of the bomb and its aftermath.
wd Kaneto Shindo novel Arata Osada *ph Takeo Itoh m* Akira Ifukube
☆ Nobuko Otowa, Chikako Hoshawa, Niwa Saito

Children of Paradise: see *Les Enfants du Paradis*

The Children of Sanchez
US/Mexico 1978 126m colour
Hall Bartlett
A macho Mexican and one of his daughters have ideas above the semi-slum in which they live.
The star is still looking for another Zorba the Greek, *but this isn't it. Glum, glum, glum.*
w Cesare Zavattini, Hall Bartlett *novel* Oscar Lewis *d* Hall Bartlett *ph* Gabriel Figueroa *m* Chuck Mangione
☆ Anthony Quinn, Dolores del Rio, Lupita Ferrer, Katy Jurado, Stathis Giallelis

Children of the Corn
US 1984 92m CFI color
New World/Angeles/Cinema Group (Donald P. Borchers, Terence Kirby)
A doctor and his girlfriend run down a child, discover that his throat has been cut, and find themselves in a community of murderous adolescents.
Nightmarish modern fantasy with style but very little to like.
w George Goldsmith *story* Stephen King *d* Fritz Kiersch *ph* Raoul Lomas *m* Jonathan Elias
☆ Peter Horton, Linda Hamilton, R. G. Armstrong, John Franklin

'The aim seems to be to reassure rather than to disturb.' – *Robert Murphy, MFB*

Children of the Corn II: The Final Sacrifice
US 1992 Foto-Kem
Fifth Avenue Entertainment (Scott A. Stone, David G. Stanley)
Teenagers who have killed all the adults in a small town in the Bible Belt are moved to another small town, where they proceed to do the same.
Inept sequel, so predictable as to be almost unwatchable.
w A. L. Katz, Gilbert Adler *story Children of the Corn* by Stephen King *d* David F. Price *ph* Levie Isaacks *m* Daniel Licht *pd* Greg Melton *ed* Barry Zetlin *sp* Bob Keen
☆ Terence Knox, Paul Scherrer, Ryan Bollman, Christie Clark, Rosalind Allen, Ned Romero

'More effective on a shock and shriek level than the original but not a major contribution to anything.' – *Empire*

† *Children of the Corn III; Urban Harvest, Children of the Corn IV; The Gathering,* and *Children of the Corn V: Fields of Terror* followed, providing ever-diminishing returns.

'So young, so innocent, so deadly – they came to conquer the world!'

Children of the Damned *
GB 1964 90m bw
MGM (Ben Arbeid)
Six super-intelligent children of various nations are brought to London by UNESCO, and turn out to be invaders from another planet.
Moderate sequel to Village of the Damned, *well made but with no new twists.*
w John Briley *d* Anton M. Leader *ph* David Boulton *m* Ron Goodwin *ad* Elliot Scott *ed* Ernest Walter
☆ Ian Hendry, Alan Badel, Barbara Ferris, Alfred Burke, Sheila Allen, Ralph Michael, Martin Miller, Harold Goldblatt

Children of the Marshland: see *Les Enfants du Marais*

Children Shouldn't Play with Dead Things
US 1972 87m colour
Geneni (Bob Clark, Gary Goch)
A group of film-makers travel to an isolated island cemetery, where they try to raise the dead as a joke, and find they have created zombie cannibals.
A low-budget horror that begins slowly and then quickens to a gory finale, though those who have seen Night of the Living Dead *may experience a feeling of déjà vu.*
w Benjamin Clark (Bob Clark), Alan Ormsby *d* Benjamin Clark (Bob Clark) *ph* Jack McGowan
☆ Alan Ormsby, Anya Ormsby, Valerie Manches, Jane Daly, Jeff Gillen, Paul Cronin, Bruce Solomon, Seth Sklarey

The Children's Hour *
US 1962 108m bw
UA/Mirisch (William Wyler)
GB title: *The Loudest Whisper*
A spoilt schoolgirl spreads a rumour that her schoolmistresses are lesbians.
Frank sixties version of a play originally filmed in a much bowdlerized version as These Three. *Unfortunately frankness in this case leads to dullness, as nothing is done with the theme once it is stated, and the treatment is heavy-handed.*
w Lillian Hellman *play* Lillian Hellman *d* William Wyler *ph* Franz Planer *m* Alex North
☆ Audrey Hepburn, Shirley MacLaine, James Garner, Miriam Hopkins, Fay Bainter, Karen Balkin
'All very exquisite, and dead as mutton.' – *Tom Milne*
Franz Planer; Fay Bainter

The Children's Midsummer Night's Dream
GB 2001 118m colour
Squirrel/Sands (Olivier Stockman)
While watching a puppet version of Shakespeare's play, a group of children take over the play.
A cast of young children from London schools struggle to cope with Shakespeare's verse.
w William Shakespeare *wd* Christine Edzard *play* A Midsummer Night's Dream *ph* Joachim Bergamin *m* Michel Sanvoisin
☆ Jamie Peachey (Hermia), John Heyfron (Demetrius), Danny Bishop (Lysander), Jessica Fowler (Helena), Leane Lyson (Puck), Daniel Rouse (Quince), Oliver Szczypka (Bottom), Jack Nottage (Snout), Dominic Haywood-Benge (Oberon), Rajouana Zalal (Titania)

Child's Play *
GB 1952 68m bw
British Lion/Group 3 (Herbert Mason)
Village children find a way to create atomic energy and use the power to set up a flourishing popcorn business.
A lively children's feature that has now acquired a quaint charm in its attitude to nuclear energy.
w Peter Blackmore *story* Don Sharp, Margaret Thomson *d* Margaret Thomson *ph* Denny Densham *m* Anthony Hopkins *ad* Michael Stringer *ed* John Legard
☆ Mona Washbourne, Peter Martyn, Dorothy Alison, John Sharp, Peter Sallis, Christopher Beeny, Wendy Westcott
'A child's chief glories are its energy and its noise; and this picture very properly bombinates with both.' – *Paul Dehn*

Child's Play *
US 1972 100m colour Movielab
Paramount (David Merrick)
In a Catholic boarding school for boys, an unpopular master is hounded and discredited by another whose motives may be diabolic.
Enjoyable overblown melodrama with hints of many nasty goings on, rather spoiled by too much talk and too little local colour.
w Leon Prochnik *play* Robert Marasco *d* Sidney Lumet *ph* Gerald Hirschfeld *m* Michael Small *pd* Philip Rosenberg *ed* Edward Warschilka, Joanne Burke
☆ James Mason (Jerome Malley), *Robert Preston* (Joseph Dobbs), Beau Bridges (Paul Reis), Ronald Weyand (Father Mozian), Charles White (Father Griffin), David Rounds (Father Penny), Kate Harrington (Mrs Carter), Jamie Alexander (Sheppard)
† Marlon Brando, in the role of Joseph Dobbs, left the cast after rehearsing for three days.

Child's Play
US 1988 87m Astrocolor
UIP/United Artists (David Kirschner)
The personality of a serial killer is transferred to a young boy's doll.
Unexciting horror, too predictable to be frightening.
w Don Mancini, John Lafia, Tom Holland *d* Tom Holland *ph* Bill Butler *m* Joe Renzetti *pd* Daniel A. Lomino *ed* Edward Warschilka, Roy E. Peterson
☆ Catherine Hicks, Chris Sarandon, Alex Vincent, Brad Dourif, Dinah Manoff, Tommy Swerdlow

Child's Play 2
US 1990 85m DeLuxe
Universal (David Kirschner)
A doll possessed by the spirit of a mass murderer attempts to kill a small boy.
Tiresome and unpleasant.
w Don Mancini *d* John Lafia *ph* Stefan Czapsky *m* Graeme Revell *pd* Ivo Cristante *ad* Donald Maskovich *ed* Edward Warschilka
☆ Alex Vincent, Jenny Agutter, Gerrit Graham, Christine Elise, Brad Dourif, Grace Zabriskie
'Another case of rehashing the few novel elements of the original to the point of utter numbness.' – *Variety*

Child's Play 3
US 1991 89m DeLuxe
Universal/David Kirschner (Robert Latham Brown)
A killer doll infiltrates a military school in order to kill the students.
Mindless and unpleasant sequel, ever straining for effect.
w Don Mancini *d* Jack Bender *ph* John A. Leonetti *m* Cory Lerios, John D'Andrea *pd* Richard Sawyer *ed* Edward Warschilka
☆ Justin Whalin, Perrey Reeves, Jeremy Sylvers, Travis Fine, Dean Jacobson, Brad Dourif, Andrew Robinson
† It was followed in 1998 by a sequel, *Bride of Chucky* (qv).

'Two guys, one bomb, and a whole lot of ice cream.'

Chill Factor
US 1999 102m Technicolor Panavision
Warner/Morgan Creek (James G. Robinson)
Terrorists pursue an ice-cream delivery driver and his friend, who have stored in their refrigerated truck an explosive chemical weapon that has to be kept at a temperature below 50 degrees.
A feeble variant on Speed, *in which acting, direction and script combine to produce a flat and uninteresting experience.*
w Drew Gitlin, Mike Cheda *d* Hugh Johnson *ph* David Gribble *m* Hans Zimmer, John Powell *pd* Jeremy Conway *ed* Pamela Power *cos* Deborah Everton
☆ Cuba Gooding Jnr (Arlo), Skeet Ulrich (Tim Mason), Peter Firth (Capt Andrew Brynner), David Paymer (Dr Richard Long), Hudson Leick (Vaughn), Daniel Hugh Kelly (Col Leo Vitelli), Kevin J. O'Connor (Telstar), Judson Mills (Dennis), Jordan Mott (Carl), Dwayne Macopson (Burke), Jim Grimshaw (Deputy Pappas)
'Utterly lacking the drive and roller-coaster energy expected of top action pics.' – *Robert Koehler, Variety*
'Simply a very dull movie.' – *Edward Porter, Sunday Times*

Chilly Scenes of Winter: see *Head Over Heels (1980)*

The Chiltern Hundreds *
GB 1949 84m bw
Rank/Two Cities (George H. Brown)
US title: *The Amazing Mr Beecham*
An aged earl is bewildered when his son fails to be elected to parliament as a socialist but his butler gets in as a Tory.
Satisfactory filming of an amusing stage comedy, with the aged A. E. Matthews repeating his delightful if irrelevant act as the dotty earl.
w William Douglas Home, Patrick Kirwan *play William Douglas Home* *d* John Paddy Carstairs *ph* Jack Hildyard *m* Benjamin Frankel
☆ *A. E. Matthews, Cecil Parker, David Tomlinson, Marjorie Fielding,* Joyce Carey

Chimes at Midnight **
Spain/Switzerland 1966 119m bw
Internacional Films Española/Alpine (Alessandro Tasca)
aka: *Falstaff*
Prince Hal becomes King Henry V and rejects his old friend Falstaff.
Clumsy adaptation of Shakespeare with brilliant flashes and the usual Welles vices of hasty production, poor synchronization and recording, etc. One wonders why, if he wanted to make a telescoped version of the plays, he did not spare the time and patience to make it better.
wd Orson Welles *ph* Edmond Richard *m* Angelo Francesco Lavagnino *pd* Gustavo Quintano *ed* Fritz Mueller
☆ Orson Welles (Falstaff), Keith Baxter (Prince Hal), John Gielgud (Henry IV), Margaret Rutherford (Mistress Quickly), Jeanne Moreau (Doll Tearsheet), Norman Rodway (Henry Percy), Alan Webb (Justice Shallow), Marina Vlady, Tony Beckley, Fernando Rey, Michael Aldridge
'One of Orson Welles' best and least-seen movies … The film is a near-masterpiece.' – *New Yorker*
'Ridiculous is the word for the whole enterprise – not funny and certainly not moving.' – *John Simon*
'A testament to the enduring genius of Orson Welles as screenwriter, director and actor … does justice to Shakespeare, to cinema and to his own great talents.' – *Judith Crist*

The Chimp *
US 1932 30m bw
Hal Roach
Stan and Ollie try to get lodgings without revealing that their friend is a chimp, their share of a bankrupt circus.
The circus scenes are better than the rather tired farce which follows, especially as it is so similar to Laughing Gravy.
w H. M. Walker *d* James Parrott *ph* Walter Lundin *ed* Richard Currier
☆ Stan Laurel, Oliver Hardy, James Finlayson, Billy Gilbert, Tiny Sandford

'Alan Ladd and twenty girls – trapped by the rapacious Japs!'

China
US 1943 79m bw
Paramount (Richard Blumenthal)
An oil salesman joins a Chinese guerrilla force and sacrifices himself.
Solemnly hilarious propaganda piece tailored to its star, showing the immense superiority of one lone American to the entire Japanese army.
w Frank Butler *novel The Fourth Brother* by Reginald Forbes *d* John Farrow *ph* Leo Tover *m* Victor Young
☆ Alan Ladd, Loretta Young, William Bendix, Philip Ahn, Iris Wong, Sen Yung, Richard Loo, Tala Birell
'A most exciting, turbulent affair.' – *James Agate, Tatler*

China 9, Liberty 37 *
Spain/Italy 1978 109m Technicolor Technovision
Lorimar/Compagnia Europe Cinematografica/Aspa (Gianni Bozzacchi, Valerio de Paolis, Monte Hellman)
aka: *Gunfire*
Hired to shoot a retired killer, a gunfighter runs off with his wife instead and is pursued by the irate husband and his brothers.
Intriguing spaghetti Western, slow-paced, with a brooding atmosphere and some sharp dialogue.
w Jerry Harvey, Douglas Venturelli *d* Monte Hellman *ph* Giuseppe Rotunno *m* Pino Donaggio *ad* Luciano Spadoni *ed* Cesare D'Amico
☆ Warren Oates, Fabio Testi, Jenny Agutter, Sam Peckinpah, Isabel Mestres, Gianrico Tondivelli, Franco Interlenghi, Carlos Bravo
† The title refers to a signpost which a travelling hangman passes at the beginning of the film. He takes the road to China.

China Caravan: see *A Yank on the Burma Road*

China Clipper *
US 1936 89m bw
Warner (Sam Bischoff)
An aviator neglects his wife while building up a trans-Pacific civil aviation link.
Solid entertainment feature of its day, with adequate production and performance.
w Frank 'Spig' Wead *d* Ray Enright *ph* Arthur Edeson *m* Bernhard Kaun, W. Franke Harling
☆ Pat O'Brien, Beverly Roberts, Ross Alexander, Humphrey Bogart, Marie Wilson, Henry B. Walthall, Joseph Crehan, Addison Richards

China Cry
US 1991 107m CFI color
TBN/Parakletos (Don LeRoy Parker)
During Mao's revolution, a young middle-class woman, who is condemned to a labour camp for aiding her husband's escape from China, survives hardship to join him in Hong Kong.
An interesting story of a spoilt child maturing through the experience of war and injustice, but so flatly told that it makes little emotional impact.
wd James F. Collier *book* Nora Lam, Irene Burke *ph* David Worth *m* Al Kasha, Joel Hirschhorn *pd* Norman Baron *ed* Duane Hartzell
☆ Julia Nickson-Soul, Russell Wong, James Shigeta, France Nuyen, Philip Tan, Elizabeth Sung

China Doll
US 1958 99m bw
Romina/Batjac (Frank Borzage)
In 1943 an American air force officer accidentally buys the services of a young Chinese housekeeper. He marries her but they are both killed in action; years later their daughter is welcomed to America by members of his old air crew.
Incurably sentimental and icky romantic drama in the style of the director's silent films; something of a curiosity for historians.
w Kitty Buhler *d* Frank Borzage *ph* William H. Clothier *m* Henry Vars
☆ Victor Mature, Li Li Hua, Bob Mathias, Ward Bond, Stuart Whitman

'An American dynamiter love-locked in war-locked China!'

China Gate
US 1957 90m bw Cinemascope
TCF (Samuel Fuller)
A Eurasian girl guides her American husband to a communist arms dump.
Anti-Red thick ear, slick but undistinguished.
wd Samuel Fuller *ph* Joseph Biroc *m* Victor Young, Max Steiner
☆ Gene Barry, Angie Dickinson, Nat King Cole, Paul Dubov, Lee Van Cleef, George Givot

China Girl
US 1943 95m bw
TCF (Ben Hecht)
A newsreel cameraman in China falls in love with a Eurasian schoolteacher.
Routine adventure romance with splodges of love and self-sacrifice.
w Ben Hecht *d* Henry Hathaway *ph* Lee Garmes *m* Hugo Friedhofer

☆ Gene Tierney, George Montgomery, *Lynn Bari*, Victor McLaglen, Alan Baxter, Sig Rumann, Myron McCormick, Philip Ahn

China Girl
US 1987 90m colour
Vestron (Michael Nozik)
In New York an Italian youth with Mafia connections falls in love with a Chinese girl from a family involved with the Triads.
Romeo and Juliet updated to Little Italy and Chinatown and used as an occasion for blood-letting and much gang violence.
w Nicholas St John *d* Abel Ferrara *ph* Bojan Bazelli *m* Joe Delia *ed* Anthony Redman
☆ James Russo, Richard Panebianco, Sari Chang, David Caruso, Russell Wong, Joey Chin, Judith Malina, James Hong
'A masterfully directed, uncompromising drama and romance.' – *Variety*
'Even die-hard fans of New York urban violence movies will find this tough going.' – *Stefan Jaworzyn, Shock Xpress*

China Moon *
US 1994 99m DeLuxe Panavision
Orion (Barrie M. Osborne)
A seductive woman, married to an adulterous wife-beating banker, persuades a detective to forget about law and order.
Accomplished but sometimes predictable foray into film noir, an agreeable time-waster.
w Roy Carlson *d* John Bailey *ph* Willy Kurant *m* George Fenton *pd* Conrad Angone *ed* Carol Littleton, Jill Savitt
☆ Ed Harris, Madeleine Stowe, Charles Dance, Pruitt Taylor Vince, Patricia Healy, Benicio del Toro
'Avoids slick montage and the cheap thrills of shock cuts and instead aims for the eyes – and heart.' – *Emanuel Levy, Variety*
† The film was made in 1992.

China, My Sorrow: see *Niu-Peng*

China O'Brien
US 1988 90m Image Transform colour
Golden Harvest/Fred Weintraub
A former cop replaces her murdered father as sheriff of a small town.
The usual martial arts mayhem with the novelty of a high-kicking female hero.
wd Robert Clouse *story* Sandra Weintraub *ph* Kent Wakeford *m* David Wheatley, Paul Antonelli *ed* Mark Harrah
☆ Cynthia Rothrock, Richard Norton, Keith Cooke, Patrick Adamson, David Blackwell

China O'Brien II
US 1989 86m colour
Imperial/Golden Harvest (Fred Weintraub)
A female sheriff is threatened by an escaped drug pusher.
Routine high-kicking martial arts, with the usual rudimentary acting.
w James Hennessy, Craig Clyde *story* Sandra Weintraub *d* Kent Wakeford *m* David Wheatley, Paul F. Antonelli *ed* Mark Harrah
☆ Cynthia Rothrock, Richard Norton, Keith Cooke, Frank Magner, Harlow Marks, Tiffany Soter
'A haphazard affair, generating little interest.' – *Variety*

China Seas **
US 1935 89m bw
MGM (Albert Lewin)
Luxury cruise passengers find themselves involved with piracy.
Omnibus shipboard melodrama, tersely scripted and featuring a splendid cast all somewhere near their best; slightly dated but very entertaining.
w Jules Furthman, James Kevin McGuinness *novel* Crosbie Garstin *d Tay Garnett ph* Ray June *m* Herbert Stothart
☆ Clark Gable, Jean Harlow, Wallace Beery, Rosalind Russell, Lewis Stone, C. Aubrey Smith, Dudley Digges, Robert Benchley
'It will do double-barrelled duty, drawing business and providing ace entertainment.' – *Variety*
'The hell with art this time. I'm going to produce a picture that will make money.' – *Irving Thalberg*

The China Syndrome ***
US 1979 122m Metrocolor
Columbia/IPC (Michael Douglas)
The controller of a nuclear power plant discovers an operational flaw which could lead to disaster, but the unscrupulous authorities want to cover it up.
Topical thriller-with-a-moral, absorbingly done in the old style but perhaps in the end a shade too hysterical and self-congratulatory.
w Mike Gray, T. A. Cook, James Bridges *d James Bridges ph* James Crabe *m* various *pd* George Jenkins *ed* David Rawlins
☆ Jane Fonda, *Jack Lemmon*, Michael Douglas, Scott Brady, Peter Donat, James Hampton
'The performances are so good, and the screen so bombarded with both action and informative images ... that it's only with considerable hindsight that one recovers sufficient breath to reproach the script with the occasional glib symmetry.' – *Jan Dawson, MFB*
Jack Lemmon, Jane Fonda; script
Jack Lemmon; Jane Fonda

Chinatown ****
US 1974 131m Technicolor Panavision
Paramount/Long Road (Robert Evans)
In 1937, a Los Angeles private eye takes on a simple case and burrows into it until it leads to murder and a public scandal.
Teasing, complex mystery that uses the conventions of detective stories to explore civic and personal corruption, in the style of Raymond Chandler, but adding a more modern perspective. It is eminently watchable, with effective individual scenes and performances and photography which is lovingly composed though tending to suggest period by use of an orange filter.
w Robert Towne d Roman Polanski ph John A. Alonso m Jerry Goldsmith pd Richard Sylbert
☆ *Jack Nicholson*, Faye Dunaway, John Huston, Perry Lopez, John Hillerman, Roman Polanski, Darrell Zwerling, Diane Ladd
'You are swept along as helpless as any of the corpses so unaccountably drowned in empty lake-beds.' – *Dilys Powell*
'The success of *Chinatown* – with its beautifully structured script and draggy, overdeliberate direction – represents something dialectically new: nostalgia (for the thirties) openly turned to rot, and the *celebration of rot*.' – *Pauline Kael*
Robert Towne
best picture; Roman Polanski; John A. Alonso; Jerry Goldsmith; Jack Nicholson; Faye Dunaway
Roman Polanski; Robert Towne; Jack Nicholson

Chinese Box
US/France/Japan 1997 109m colour
Canal+/NDF/WW (Lydia Dean Pilcher, Jean-Louis Piel)
As the British prepare to hand over Hong Kong to the Chinese, a dying English journalist tries to make his own farewells through his relationship with two contrasting women.
Tepid topical drama that uses TV newscasts to provide an urgency that is otherwise lacking.
w Jean-Claude Carriere, Larry Gross *d* Wayne Wang *ph* Vilko Filac *m* Graeme Revell *pd* Chris Wong *ed* Christopher Tellefsen
☆ Jeremy Irons, Gong Li, Maggie Cheung, Ruben Blades, Michael Hui
'This tale of impossible cross-cultural love is rendered dreary by lukewarm chemistry between stars Jeremy Irons and Gong Li, and a script that provides no character depth.' – *David Rooney, Variety*

Chinese Boxes
GB 1984 87m colour
Palace/Road Movies (Chris Sievernich)
An American in Berlin discovers a dead 15-year-old girl in his apartment.
A thriller that resembles a jigsaw with some of the pieces missing. It is told in such an elliptical fashion as to leave the viewer not only confused but indifferent.
w L. M. Kit Carson, Christopher Petit *d* Christopher Petit *ph* Peter Harvey *m* Günter Fischer *ad* Edgar Hinz, Klaus Beiger *ed* Fred Srp
☆ Will Patton, Gottfried John, Adelheid Arndt, Robbie Coltrane, Beate Jensen, L. M. Kit Carson, Chris Sievernich, Christopher Petit

The Chinese Bungalow
GB 1939 72m bw
George King
US title: *Chinese Den*
A Chinese merchant plots to kill the lover of his English wife.
Stolid version of an old melodrama which can hardly fail; previously filmed in 1926 with Matheson Lang and Genevieve Townsend (directed by Sinclair Hill) and in 1930 with Matheson Lang and Anna Neagle (directed by J. B. Williams).
w A. R. Rawlinson, George Wellesley *play* Matheson Lang, Marian Osmond *d* George King *ph* Hone Glendinning
☆ Paul Lukas, Jane Baxter, Robert Douglas, Kay Walsh, Jerry Verno

The Chinese Connection: see *Fist of Fury*

Chinese Den: see *The Chinese Bungalow*

A Chinese Feast
Hong Kong 1995 107m colour 'Scope
Mandarin/Film Workshop
original title: *Gamyuk Muntong*
An inept chef seeks the help of a one-time master, now a derelict, to enter a contest to cook the Qing and Han Imperial Feast, an elaborate banquet of more than 100 dishes.
Broad slapstick comedy that is unlikely to be to Western tastes, any more than the main dishes prepared for the banquet: bear's paw, elephant's trunk and monkey's brains with shark's fin.
w Tsui Hark, Ng Man-fai, Tseng Tsung-tai *d* Tsui Hark *ph* Peter Pau *m* Lowell Lo *pd* William Chang *ed* Mak Tsi-sin
☆ Leslie Cheung, Anita Yuen, Kenny Bee, Ni Shu-chun, Lo Ka-ying, Zhao Wenzhuo, Hung Yan-yan
'A comic kung-food movie about dueling chefs that's funny, skillful and a heart-warmer to boot.' – *Derek Elley, Variety*
† Subtitles on the video are so small as to be almost unreadable, and even when they can be read they are frequently incomprehensible ('Make sure dismoral to the fish, not me').

A Chinese Ghost Story
Hong Kong 1988 98m colour
Film Workshop (Tsui Hark)
original title: *Qiannu Youhun*
A wandering tax collector falls in love with a ghost condemned to lure men to their death.
Fast-moving mix of horror, romance and martial arts; its narrative, involving reincarnation and a soul-sucking tree demon with a killer tongue, confuses as much as it entertains.
story Pu Songling *d* Ching Siu-tung *ph* Poon Hang-Seng *m* Romeo Diaz *pd* Xi Zhongwen *ed* David Wu
☆ Leslie Cheung, Joey Wong, Wu Ma, David Lam

A Chinese Ghost Story II
Hong Kong 1990 104m colour
Golden Princess (Tsui Hark)
original title: *Qiannu Youhun – Renjian Dao*
A wandering scholar falls for the reincarnation of his ghostly lover and rescues her father from evil spirits.
With its half-comic, half-horrific demon creeping up behind the hero, magic spells, broad humour and evil golden Buddha, this, in Western terms, resembles a lavish pantomime; on that level, it is moderately enjoyable.
d Ching Siu-tung *ph* Wong Ngok-Tai
☆ Leslie Cheung, Joey Wong, Jackie Cheung, Michelle Reis, Waise Lee, Wu Ma, Ku Feng

Chinese Roulette *
West Germany/France 1976 86m
Eastmancolor
Albatros/Losange (Rainer Werner Fassbinder)
Various related people, mainly adulterous, meet in a country château and play a truth game which ends in violence.
Interestingly enigmatic character melodrama reminiscent of Bergman at his prime, but concerning people who barely seem to matter.
wd Rainer Werner Fassbinder *ph* Michael Ballhaus *m* Peer Raben
☆ Margit Carstensen, Andrea Schober, Ulli Lommel, Anna Karina, Macha Meril
'Locked into their private hell ... this vicious octet form their own coherent and compelling universe.' – *Jan Dawson, MFB*

Chino: see *The Valdez Horses*

Chino
US/Italy 1973 98m colour
Dino de Laurentiis
A runaway boy helps a half-breed run a ranch in New Mexico.
Undistinguished Western.
w Clair Huffaker *novel* Lee Hoffman *d* John Sturges
☆ Charles Bronson, Jill Ireland, Vincent Van Patten

La Chinoise ***
France 1967 95m Eastmancolor
Fair Enterprises/Productions de la Guéville/Parc/Simar/Anouchka/Athos
In 1967, five Parisian Maoist revolutionaries debate the best ways of achieving the end of the capitalist system, from closing the universities to acting Brecht, and decide that terrorism is the way forward.
With hindsight, a prophetic movie of the student politics that shook Paris a year later, which is still a troubling and wittily intriguing film in its search for new means of cinematic expression.
wd Jean-Luc Godard *ph* Raoul Coutard *m* Karl-Heinz Stockhausen *ed* Agnès Guillemot, Delphine Desfons
☆ Anne Wiazemsky, Jean-Pierre Léaud, Michel Séméniako, Lex de Brujin, Juliet Berto, Omar Diop, Francis Jeanson
'The movie is like a speed-freak's anticipatory vision of the political horrors to come; it's amazing.' – *Pauline Kael*
'A piece of mitigated trash ... Godard, his material, his pretentiousness and undisciplined garrulity, are boring when not exasperating.' – *John Simon*

Chisum *
US 1970 110m Technicolor Panavision
Warner/Batjac (Michael Wayne, Andrew J. Fenady)
A corrupt businessman plots against the head of a vast cattle empire, who is saved by the intervention of numerous friends including Pat Garrett and Billy the Kid.
Desultory, overlong, friendly Western in the Ford manner. Easy to watch and easier to forget.
w Andrew J. Fenady *d* Andrew V. McLaglen *ph William H. Clothier m* Dominic Frontière
☆ John Wayne, Forrest Tucker, Christopher George, Ben Johnson, Glenn Corbett, Bruce Cabot, Andrew Prine, Patric Knowles, Richard Jaeckel, Lynda Day George, John Agar, Ray Teal, Glenn Langan, Alan Baxter, Abraham Sofaer
'A curious mixture of styles and myths.' – *John Gillett*

Chitty Chitty Bang Bang
GB 1968 145m Technicolor Super Panavision 70
UA/Warfield/DFI (Albert R. Broccoli)
An unsuccessful inventor rescues a derelict car and gives it magical properties, then helps the children who own it to overthrow the government of a country which hates children.
A bumpy ride. Sentiment, slapstick, whimsy and mild scares do not combine but are given equal shares of the limelight, while poor trickwork prevents the audience from being transported.

w Roald Dahl, Ken Hughes *d* Ken Hughes *ph* Christopher Challis *m* Irwin Kostal *m/ly* The Sherman Brothers *ad* Rowland Emmett
☆ Dick Van Dyke, Sally Ann Howes (Truly Scrumptious), Lionel Jeffries, Robert Helpmann, Gert Frobe, Benny Hill, James Robertson Justice
🏆 title song

Chloë in the Afternoon: see *L'Amour, L'Après-midi*

Le Choc: see *The Shock*

Chocolat **
France/Germany/Cameroon 1988 105m colour
Electric/Cinemanuel/MK2/Cerio/Wim Wenders Productktion/TF1/SEPT/Caroline/FODIC (Alain Belmondo, Gerard Crosnier)

A French woman recalls her colonial childhood in French West Africa and her relationship with the family servant.
Cool, distanced, semi-autobiographical account of racism and its effects.
w Claire Denis, Jean-Pol Fargeau *d* Claire Denis *ph* Robert Alazraki *m* Abdullah Ibrahim *pd* Thierry Flamand *ed* Claudine Merlin
☆ Isaach de Bankole, Giula Boschi, François Cluzet, Jean-Claude Adelin
'Undoubtedly over-generous, fictionalised and nostalgic, but it is also well paced, well observed and shot through with a dry sense of humour.' – *Jill Forbes, MFB*

'One taste is all it takes.'
Chocolat *
US 2000 121m Technicolor
(David Brown, Kit Golden, Leslie Holleran)

A single mother arrives in a small, dull French town ruled by an over-righteous mayor and opens a chocolate shop that changes the lives of the inhabitants.
A overly sweet confection that makes individuality seem the last refuge of the smug; it's not so much soft-centred as positively melting over Binoche's ever-tolerent heroine. Even on its fairy-tale level, there's no real tension or contest here between freedom and repression – it's Red Riding Hood without the wolf.
w Robert Nelson Jacobs *novel* Joanne Harris *d* Lasse Hallström *ph* Roger Pratt *m* Rachel Portman *pd* David Gropman *ed* Andrew Mondshein *cos* Renée Ehrlich Kalfus
☆ Juliette Binoche (Vianne Rocher), Lena Olin (Josephine Muscat), Johnny Depp (Roux), Judi Dench (Armande Voizin), Alfred Molina (Comte de Reynaud), Peter Stormare (Serge Muscat), Carrie-Anne Moss (Caroline Clairmont), Leslie Caron (Madame Audel), John Wood (Guillaume Blerot), Hugh O'Conor (Pere Henri), Victoire Thivisol (Anouk Rocher), Aurelien Parent Koenig (Luc Clairmont)
'This crowd-pleaser is the feature-film version of milk chocolate: an art house movie for people who don't like art house movies.' – *Elvis Mitchell, New York Times*
'A richly textured comic fable that blends Old World wisdom with a winking, timely commentary on the assumed moral superiority of the political right.' – *Lael Loewenstein, Variety*
'The sheer, unmitigated ickiness of the film is what gets you down in the end.' – *Peter Bradshaw, Guardian*
🏆 picture; Juliette Binoche; Judi Dench; Robert Nelson Jacobs; Rachel Portman

The Chocolate Soldier *
US 1941 102m bw
MGM (Victor Saville)

Married opera singers fall out backstage.
Talky musical remake of The Guardsman*: nearly comes off but not quite.*
w Keith Winter, Leonard Lee *d* Roy del Ruth *ph* Karl Freund *m* Herbert Stothart, Bronislau Kaper *m/ly* Oscar Straus
☆ Nelson Eddy, Rise Stevens, Nigel Bruce, Florence Bates, Nydia Westman
🏆 Karl Freund; Herbert Stothart, Bronislau Kaper

The Choice
Burkina Faso 1987 88m colour
Les Films de L'Avenir
original title: *Yam Daabo*
The pleasures and tribulations of African village life.
Rudimentary and episodic first feature, lacking the resonance of the director's later films such as Yaaba *and* Tilai *(qv).*
wd Idrissa Ouédraogo *ph* Jean Monsigny, Sekou Ouedraogo, Issaka Thiombiano *m* Francis Bebey *ed* Arnaud Blin
☆ Aoua Guiraud, Moussa Bologo, Ousmana Sawadogo, Fatima Ouedraogo

Choice of Arms *
France 1981 130m Fujicolour Panavision
Sara/Parafrance/Antenne 2/RMC (Daniel Deschamps)
original title: *Le Choix des Armes*
A successful, retired gangster is drawn back into a world of violence when, after a jail break, a seriously wounded friend seeks refuge at his stud farm together with a young, violent, reckless hoodlum.
Interesting but too-leisurely account of people unable to escape their past.
w Michel Grisolia, Alain Corneau *d* Alain Corneau *ph* Pierre William Glenn *m* Philippe Sarde *ad* Jean-Pierre Kohut Svelko *ed* Thierry Derocles
☆ Yves Montand, Gérard Depardieu, Catherine Deneuve, Michel Galabru, Gérard Lanvin, Jean-Claude Dauphin, Jean Rougerie, Christian Marquand, Richard Anconina

Choice of Weapons: see *Trial by Combat*

The Choirboys
US 1978 119m Technicolor
Lorimar/Airone (Lee Rich, Merv Adelson)

Members of a police department are if anything more delinquent, vicious and mentally retarded than their quarries.
A vulgar and repellent anti-establishment display, apparently intended as black comedy. Just the thing to put an end to the art of the movie once and for all.
w Christopher Knopf *novel* Joseph Wambaugh *d* Robert Aldrich *ph* Joseph Biroc *m* Frank de Vol
☆ Charles Durning, Lou Gossett Jnr, Perry King, Stephen Macht, Tim McIntire, Clyde Kusatsu, Randy Quaid, Don Stroud, Robert Webber, Blair Brown

Le Choix des Armes: see *Choice of Arms*

Chomps
👪 US 1979 89m Movielab
American International (Joseph Barbera)

A young inventor is successful with a robot dog (Canine Home Protection System).
Rather feeble family-oriented comedy.
w Dick Robbins, Duane Poole *story* Joseph Barbera *d* Don Chaffey *ph* Charles F. Wheeler *m* Hoyt Curtin *pd* Ted Shell *ed* Warner Leighton, Dick Darling
☆ Wesley Eure, Jim Backus, Valerie Bertinelli, Chuck McCann, Regis Toomey, Red Buttons, Hermione Baddeley

Choose Me
US 1984 106m Movielab
Island Alive/Tartan (Carolyn Pfeiffer, David Blocker)

Two lonely people in LA become a couple.
Even for those not irritated by the director's style and interests, this is an entertainment which goes around in circles and gets nowhere, except Las Vegas.
wd Alan Rudolph *ph* Jan Kiesser *m* Luther Vandross *pd* Steve Legler *ed* Mia Goldman
☆ Geneviève Bujold, Keith Carradine, Lesley Ann Warren, Patrick Bachau, Rae Dawn Chong
'An L.A. flower, a neon orchid – hip, outrageous, beautiful. It's a romance – music at its heart and farce around its edges – for those afraid to be in love.' – *Sheila Benson, Los Angeles Times*

Choose Your Partner: see *Two Girls on Broadway*

Chop Suey *
US 2000 98m bw/colour
Just Blue
Fashion photographer Bruce Weber details some of his friends and interests.
A smörgåsbord of assorted moments from the life of Weber, a photographer noted for his homoerotic images, which are reflected here in his obessive interest in a young wrestler.
wd Bruce Weber *ph* Lance Accord, Douglas Cooper, Jim Fealy *m* John Leftwich *ad* Dimitri Levas *ed* Angelo Corrao, Elizabeth Heeden
☆ Peter Johnson, Frances Faye, Rickson Gracie, Robert Mitchum, Jan Michael Vincent, Diana Vreeland, Sir Wilfred Thesiger
'"Spending time with Weber and hearing his stories makes you realize you might be listening to the secret of a happy life.' – *Jeffrey M. Anderson, San Francisco Examiner*

'The Truth, The Half Truth And Nothing Like The Truth.'
Chopper *
Australia 2000 94m colour
Metrodome/Mushroom/Pariah/AFFC (Michele Bennett)

A notorious Australian criminal, killer and best-selling author looks back over his life and crimes.
An engaging central performance enlivens this portrait, based on fact, of a frightening and brutal man, convincingly mixing violence and humour.
wd Andrew Dominik *ph* Geoffrey Hall, Kevin Hayward *m* Mick Harvey *pd* Paddy Reardon *ed* Ken Sallows
☆ *Eric Bana* (Mark 'Chopper' Read), Vince Colosimo (Neville Bartos), Simon Lyndon (Jimmy Loughnan), Kate Beahan (Tanya), David Field (Keithy George), Dan Wyllie (Bluey), Bill Young (Detective Downey), Kenny Graham (Keith Read), Gary Waddell (Kevin Darcy), Fred Barker (Governor Beasley)
'Unsettling and at times uneven, but always fascinating material for anyone prepared for a grim ride.' – *Mark Dinning, Empire*

Chopper Chicks in Zombietown
US 1989 89m Foto-Kem
Chelsea (Arthur Sarkissian)

A gang of female bikers ride into a small town where the funeral director is killing the locals and turning them into mine-working zombies.
Incoherent Z movie with unconvincing bikers and zombies; it is cheap and cheerless.
wd Dan Hoskins *ph* Tom Fraser *m* Daniel May *ad* Tim Baxter *ed* W.O. Garret
☆ Jamie Rose (Dede), Catherine Carlin (Rox), Lycia Naff (T.C.), Vicki Frederick (Jewel), Kristina Loggia (Jojo), Gretchen Palmer (Rusty), Nina Peterson (Tanya), Whitney Reis (Lucille), Ed Gale (Bob), Don Calfa (Ralph Willum), Billy Bob Thornton (Donny), Lewis Arquette (Sheriff Bugiere), Martha Quinn (Mae Clutter)

A Chorus Line
US 1985 111m Technicolor Panavision
Embassy/Polygram (Cy Feuer, Ernest Martin)

A Broadway musical chorus is selected.
Overpraised musical drama which took nine years to reach the screen because nobody could figure out how to 'open it up', despite Universal's payment of 5.5 million dollars for the rights. The present team has not solved the problem.
w Arnold Schulman *play* Nicholas Dante, James Kirkwood *d* Richard Attenborough *ph* Ronnie Taylor *m/ly* Marvin Hamlisch, Edward Kleban *pd* Patrizia von Brandenstein *ed* John Bloom
☆ Michael Douglas, Terrence Mann, Alyson Reed, Cameron English, Vicki Frederick
'Static and confined, rarely venturing beyond the immediate.' – *Variety*
'He makes his camera fly like a bird around the near-deserted theatre.' – *Shaun Usher, Daily Mail*
🏆 editing; song 'Surprise, Surprise' (*m* Marvin Hamlisch, *ly* Edward Kleban)

A Chorus of Disapproval *
GB 1988 99m colour
Hobo/Curzon/Palisades Entertainment (André Blay, Elliott Kastner)

A new tenor joins an amateur choir to find the sopranos lusting after him.
Ponderous direction almost ruins a witty comedy of suburban life.
w Michael Winner, Alan Ayckbourn *play* Alan Ayckbourn *d* Michael Winner *ph* Alan Jones *pd* John Du Prez *ed* Arnold Crust
☆ Anthony Hopkins, Jeremy Irons, Richard Briers, Gareth Hunt, Patsy Kensit, Alexandra Pigg, Prunella Scales, Jenny Seagrove, Peter Lee-Wilson, Barbara Ferris, Lionel Jeffries, Sylvia Syms, David King

The Chosen: see *Holocaust 2000 (1977)*

The Chosen
US 1981 108m Movielab
The Chosen Film Company (Edie and Ely Landau)

In New York in the early forties, a family feud between Zionist and Hassidic Jews interferes with a friendship between two boys.
A sentimental minority piece which does what it has to do quite effectively.
w Edwin Gordon *novel* Chaim Potok *d* Jeremy Paul Kagan *ph* Arthur Ornitz *m* Elmer Bernstein *pd* Stuart Wurtzel
☆ Maximilian Schell, Rod Steiger, Robby Benson, Barry Miller, Hildy Brooks, Kaethe Fine

Chosen Survivors
US 1974 98m colour
Alpine/Metromedia (Charles Fries)
Ten people with special skills are chosen to test human reaction to thermo-nuclear war, but find themselves at the mercy of vampire bats.
Another misfit group united by disaster; more shocks than suspense, and not much characterization, but for adventure/horror addicts it will pass the time.
w H. B. Cross, Joe Reb Moffly *d* Sutton Roley *ph* Gabriel Torres *m* Fred Karlin
☆ Jackie Cooper, Alex Cord, Richard Jaeckel, Diana Muldaur, Lincoln Kilpatrick, Bradford Dillman, Pedro Armendariz Jnr, Gwen Mitchell, Barbara Babcock, Christina Moreno

Les Choses de la Vie
France/Italy 1969 89m Eastmancolor
Lira/Fida (Raymond Danon)

aka: *These Things Happen*
aka: *The Things of Life*
An architect has his wife and mistress neatly balanced when an accident upsets his scheme of things.
*Nicely observed tragi-comedy in the best French manner; since it starts with the car crash, a mini-*Bridge of San Luis Rey.
w Paul Guimard, Claude Sautet, Jean-Loup Dabadie *novel* Paul Guimard *d* Claude Sautet *ph* Jean Boffety *m* Philippe Sarde
☆ Michel Piccoli, Romy Schneider, Lea Massari, Gérard Lartigau, Jean Bouise

Christ Stopped at Eboli ***
Italy/France 1979 155m Technospes
Cinematografica/RAI/Action Film/Gaumont/Vides (Franco Cristaldi, Nicola Carraro)

In 1935 an Italian doctor is exiled because of his political views to a remote southern part of the country.
An attractively faithful account of a book which was part personal statement, part symbolism, part political opinion and part local colour. Non-Italians will be unable to extract the full flavour.
w Francesco Rosi, Tonino Guerra, Raffaele La Capria *book* Carlo Levi *d* Francesco Rosi *ph* Pasqualino de Santis *m* Piero Piccioni
☆ Gian Maria Volonte, Alain Cuny, Paolo Bonacelli, Lea Massari, Irene Papas, François Simon
🏆 best foreign film

The Christian Licorice Store
US 1971 90m colour
National General
A Hollywood tennis player succumbs to corrupting influences.

Odd item with interesting credits but not much flesh on the bones.
w Floyd Mutrux d James Frawley
☆ Beau Bridges, Maud Adams, Gilbert Roland, Alan Arbus, Monte Hellman

Christiane F *
West Germany 1981 131m colour
Maran Film/Popular Film/Hans H. Kaden/TCF (Bernd Eichinger, Hans Weth)
A teenage girl becomes a drug addict.
Slick melodrama hoked up from 'true' confessions with excellent background detail.
w Herman Weigel d Ulrich Edel ph Justus Pankau, Jürgen Jürges m David Bowie ed Jane Seitz
☆ Natja Brunckhorst, Thomas Haustein, Jens Kuphal

'For Every Credit There Must Be A Debit'
Christie Malry's Own Double-Entry
GB/Netherlkands/Luxembourg 2000 95m colour
Ian Rattray/Movie Masters/Delux/Woodline (Kees Kasander)
A lowly clerk works out his own system of accounts, based on the humiliations he suffers, and tries to make the figures balance by commiting appalling crimes.
Dark, stylish comedy of a worm who turns, making his fantasies into a terrible reality; in the final analysis, though, there seems little point in its satire.
w Simon Bent novel B. S. Johnson d Paul Tickell ph Reinier van Brummelen m Luke Haines pd Wilbert Van Dorp ed Chris Wyatt
☆ Nick Moran (Christie Malry), Neil Stuke (Headlam), Kate Ashfield (Carol), Mattia Sbragia (Leonardo), Marcello Mazzarella (Pacioli), Salvatore Lazzaro (Giacomo), Sergio Albelli (Duke Ludovice), Francesco Giuffrida (Salai), Shirley Anne Field (Mary)
'If you don't like this, stop going to the cinema.' – *Steve Grant, Sunday Times*
'An engagingly truculent black comedy.' – *Philip Kemp, Sight and Sound*

Christina: see *Virgin among the Living Dead*

'How do you kill something that can't possibly be alive?'
'Hell hath no Fury...like Christine.'
Christine
US 1983 110m Technicolor Panavision
Columbia/Delphi (Richard Kobritz)
A diabolical car maims and kills its owner's girlfriends.
Thin and gruesomely extended horror flick which never begins to be convincing. For teenagers only.
w Bill Phillips novel Stephen King d John Carpenter ph Donald M. Morgan m John Carpenter pd Daniel Lomino ed Marion Rothman
☆ Keith Gordon, John Stockwell, Alexandra Paul, Robert Prosky, Harry Dean Stanton, Christine Belford

A Christmas Carol *
US 1938 69m bw
MGM (Joseph L. Mankiewicz)
Scrooge the miser is reformed when four ghosts visit him on Christmas Eve.
Standard Dickensian frolic, quite well mounted.
w Hugo Butler d Edwin L. Marin ph Sidney Wagner m Franz Waxman
☆ Reginald Owen, Gene Lockhart, Kathleen Lockhart, Terry Kilburn, Leo G. Carroll, Lynne Carver
'Top production, inspired direction, superb acting.' – *Variety*
† See also *Scrooge*.

Christmas Carol: The Movie
GB/Germany 2001 80m colour
Pathé/Film Consortium/Scala/MBP/Illuminated (Iain Harvey)
On Christmas Eve, a miser is redeemed by ghosts.
Bland animation and feeble humour supplied by two mice soon sink this version of Dickens's story.
w Piet Kroon, Robert Llewellyn novel Charles Dickens d Jimmy T. Murakami m Julian Nott ad Errol Bryant ed Taylor Grant
☆ Simon Callow (Charles Dickens), voices of: Simon Callow (Scrooge), Kate Winslet (Belle), Nicolas Cage (Jacob Marley), Michael Gambon (Ghost of Christmas Present), Jane Horrocks (Ghost of Christmas Past), Rhys Ifans (Bob Cratchit), Juliet Stevenson (Mrs Cratchit/Mother Gimlet)
'An unimaginatively drawn, boring and saccharine cartoon.' – *Alan Jones, Film Review*
'The images are dull, the figures verge on the characterless, and the vocal performances fall far short of what Radio 4 would find acceptable.' – *Philip French, Observer*

Christmas Eve *
US 1947 92m bw
Benedict Bogeaus
aka: *Sinners' Holiday*
An old lady needs the help of her three adopted sons to prevent herself from being swindled.
Basically three short stories sealed by a Christmas Eve reunion, this is old-fashioned sentimental stuff, but it works on its level and the cast is interesting.
w Laurence Stallings d Edwin L. Marin ph Gordon Avil m Heinz Roemheld
☆ Ann Harding, George Raft, Randolph Scott, George Brent, Joan Blondell, Virginia Field, Reginald Denny

Christmas Holiday
US 1944 93m bw
Universal (Felix Jackson)
A young girl marries a murderer, and later, as a shady songstress in a night-club, is forced to help him escape.
A weird change of pace for Deanna Durbin, whose forte had been sweetness and light, this relentlessly grim and boring melodrama was also a travesty of the novel on which it was based.
w Herman J. Mankiewicz novel Somerset Maugham d Robert Siodmak ph Elwood Bredell m Hans Salter ad Robert Clatworthy, John B. Goodman ed Ted J. Kent
☆ Deanna Durbin, Gene Kelly, Dean Harens, Gladys George, Richard Whorf, Gale Sondergaard
'A jolly title for a Deanna Durbin film, but it's the only jolly thing about it. Miss Durbin is an accomplished singer; so they cut her songs to two and make them blues numbers. She has a naturally modest and ingenuous manner, so they cast her as a hostess in a seedy night club.' – *C. A. Lejeune*
Hans Salter

Christmas in Connecticut *
US 1945 101m bw
Warner (William Jacobs)
GB title: *Indiscretion*
The spinster writer of a successful column about love and marriage has to conjure up a family for herself in the cause of publicity.
Predictable but fairly brisk comedy with excellent talent well deployed.
w Lionel Houser, Adele Commandini d Peter Godfrey ph Carl Guthrie m Frederick Hollander
☆ Barbara Stanwyck, Dennis Morgan, Sydney Greenstreet, Reginald Gardiner, S. Z. Sakall, Robert Shayne, Una O'Connor, Frank Jenks
† Arnold Schwarzenegger directed a remake for cable television in 1992 starring Dyan Cannon, Kris Kristofferson and Tony Curtis.

'If you can't sleep at night, it isn't the coffee – it's the bunk!'
Christmas in July **
US 1940 67m bw
Paramount
A young clerk and his girl win first prize in a big competition.
Slightly unsatisfactory as a whole, this Preston Sturges comedy has echoes of Clair and a dully predictable plot line, but is kept alive by inventive touches and a gallery of splendid character comedians.
wd Preston Sturges ph Victor Milner m Sigmund Krumgold
☆ Dick Powell, Ellen Drew, Ernest Truex, Al Bridge, Raymond Walburn, William Demarest
'The perfect restorative for battered humors and jangled nerves.' – *Bosley Crowther*
'Agreeable enough, but it lacks the full-fledged Sturges lunacy.' – *New Yorker, 1977*

Christmas Present *
Italy 1986 101m Telecolor Technovision
Duea/DMV/RAI Uno (Antonio Avati)
original title: *Regalo di Natale*
Four old friends, each needing money, get together on Christmas Eve to play poker in the hope of fleecing a rich industrialist.
Enjoyably sour little drama of masculine pride, obsession and betrayal.
wd Pupi Avati ph Pasquale Rachini m Riz Ortolani pd Giuseppe Pirrotta ed Amedeo Salfa
☆ Diego Abatantuono, Gianni Cavina, Alessandro Haber, Carlo delle Piane, George Eastman, Kristina Sevieri

A Christmas Story *
US 1983 93m colour
MGM/UA (René Dupont, Bob Clark)
In an Indiana suburb during the 1940s, a schoolboy hopes to get a rifle for Christmas.
Curious, almost plotless family comedy of the old school, with the difference that some grotesquerie and tastelessness is added. On the whole, however, an amusing entertainment for adults who don't mind their mood of sentimental nostalgia being tilted at by the director of Porky's.
w Jean Shepherd, Leigh Brown, Bob Clark novel *In God We Trust, All Others Pay Cash* by Jean Shepherd d Bob Clark ph Reginald H. Morris m Carl Zittrer, Paul Zaza pd Gavin Mitchell ed Stan Cole
☆ Peter Billingsley, Melinda Dillon, Darren McGavin, Ian Petrella

The Christmas Tree
France/Italy 1969 110m Eastmancolor
Corona/Jupiter (Robert Dorfmann)
The small son of a millionaire widower is fatally infected by radioactivity.
Painfully sentimental and overdrawn weepie, the most lachrymose film of the sixties.
wd Terence Young novel Michel Bataille ph Henri Alekan m Georges Auric
☆ William Holden, Virna Lisi, Brook Fuller, Bourvil
'Depending on your taste threshold, there may not be a dry eye – nor a full stomach – in the house.' – *Judith Crist*

Christopher Columbus
US 1949 104m Technicolor
Rank/Gainsborough/Sydney Box (Betty E. Box)
Columbus seeks and receives the patronage of the Spanish court for his voyage to the west.
An extraordinarily tediously paced historical account of basically undramatic events; interesting without being stimulating.
w Muriel and Sydney Box, Cyril Roberts d David MacDonald ph Stephen Dade m Arthur Bliss
☆ Fredric March, Florence Eldridge, Francis L. Sullivan, Linden Travers
'Even ten-year-olds will find it about as thrilling as an afternoon spent looking at Christmas cards.' – *Time*

Christopher Columbus: The Discovery
US 1992 121m Technicolor Panavision
Rank/Peel Enterprises (Alexander Salkind, Ilya Salkind)
Backed by Spain, Columbus sets sail to discover the New World on a disastrous voyage, but returns in triumph to be created Viceroy of the Indies.
Risible pageant with some notably poor performances and little to maintain one's interest.
w John Briley, Cary Bates, Mario Puzo d John Glen ph Alec Mills, Arthur Wooster m Cliff Eidelman pd Gil Parrondo ed Matthew Glen
☆ Marlon Brando, Tom Selleck, George Corraface, Rachel Ward, Robert Davi, Catherine Zeta Jones, Oliver Cotton, Benicio Del Toro, Mathieu Carrière, Nigel Terry
'Dead meat. It's the sort of film that makes you worry not about its characters but about the actors playing them ... The basic trouble is that the whole film is devised in cliché terms.' – *Derek Malcolm, Guardian*

'She gave herself to the great God speed, and tried to run away from the fires within her!'
'The personal story of a million daughters!'
Christopher Strong *
US 1933 72m bw
RKO (Pandro S. Berman)
A daring lady aviator has an affair with a married businessman and commits suicide when she finds herself pregnant.
A curious and unsatisfactory yarn for Hepburn's second film; well enough made, it died at the box-office.
w Zoe Akins novel Gilbert Frankau d Dorothy Arzner ph Bert Glennon m Max Steiner
☆ *Katharine Hepburn, Colin Clive, Billie Burke,* Helen Chandler, Ralph Forbes, Irene Browne, Jack La Rue
'Draggy society play with circusy aeroplane stunt incidentals ... interest in the star will outweigh other elements.' – *Variety*

Chronicle of a Death Foretold **
Italy/France 1987 110m Eastmancolor Panavision
Virgin/Italmedia/Soprafilms/Ariane/FR3/RAI (Frances von Buren, Yves Gasset)
original title: *Cronica di una Morte Annunciata*
After 27 years a doctor returns to his home-town to discover the truth about the death of his best friend.
Despite its stately rhythm, a powerful examination of the codes of masculine honour and female virtue.
w Francesco Rosi, Tonino Guerra novel Gabriel García Marquez d Francesco Rosi ph Pasqualino de Santis m Piero Piccioni pd Andrea Crisanti ed Ruggero Mastroianni
☆ Rupert Everett, Ornella Muti, Gian Maria Volonte, Irene Papas, Lucia Bose, Anthony Delon, Alain Cuny

Chronique d'un Été *
France 1961 90m bw
Argos
Parisians talk about their lives.
Curious but rather stimulating acted documentary, with two interviewers pontificating; saved by shrewd editing to keep interest at its maximum.
wd Jean Rouch, Edgar Morin ph various

Chu Chin Chow *
GB 1934 102m bw
Gaumont British/Gainsborough (Michael Balcon)
In old Arabia, a slave girl foils a robber posing as a dead mandarin.
Second screen version (the first was silent) of the old Arabian Nights stage musical. A curiosity.
w Edward Knoblock, L. DuGarde Peach, Sidney Gilliat play Oscar Asche, Frederick Norton d Walter Forde ph Max Greene m/ly Frederick Norton md Louis Levy ch Anton Dolin ad Ernö Metzner ed Derek Twist
☆ George Robey, Fritz Kortner, Anna May Wong, John Garrick, Pearl Argyle, Malcolm MacEachern, Dennis Hoey, Francis L. Sullivan, Sydney Fairbrother
'A colourful, extravagant costume film that makes its bid for attention purely on an extravaganza platform, and makes the grade.' – *Variety*
'Gaumont British have broken away for the first time from their careful refinement, and produced something that has guts as well as grace.' – *C. A. Lejeune*

Chu Chu and the Philly Flash
US 1981 100m colour
TCF (Jay Weston)
A one-woman band performer and a drunken ex-baseball player lay claim to the same lost briefcase.
Weird comedy which doesn't come off except at odd moments.
w Barbara Dana d David Lowell Rich
☆ Carol Burnett, Alan Arkin, Jack Warden, Danny Aiello, Adam Arkin, Ruth Buzzi

Chubasco
US 1967 100m Technicolor Panavision
Warner Seven Arts (William Conrad)
A wild beach boy takes a job on a tuna fishing boat.

Old-fashioned boy-makes-good melodrama à la Captains Courageous. *Excellent action sequences at sea.*
wd Allen H. Miner *ph* Louis Jennings, Paul Ivano *m* William Lava
☆ Chris Jones, Richard Egan, Susan Strasberg, Ann Sothern, Simon Oakland, Preston Foster, Audrey Totter, Peter Whitney

'When Does A Close Friend Become Too Close?'
Chuck & Buck **
US 2000 96m colour
Metrodome/Artisan/Blow Up/Flan De Coco (Matthew Greenfield)

A successful 27-year-old music executive in Los Angeles is stalked by a childhood friend who seems stuck in early adolescence and wants them to resume their boyish sexual games.
Clever blackish comedy, with a creepy undertone, that uses childhood to question adult attitudes.
w Mike White *d* Miguel Arteta *ph* Chuy Chavez *m* Joey Waronker, Tony Maxwell *pd* Renee Davenport *ed* Jeff Betancourt
☆ Mike White (Buck), Chris Weitz (Chuck), Lupe Ontiveros (Beverly), Beth Colt (Carlyn), Paul Weitz (Sam), Maya Rudolph (Jamila), Mary Wigmore (Diane), Paul Sand (Barry), Gino Buccola (Tommy)
'Whether you buy its creepsome Odd Couple seriocomedy as an audacious tale well told, or find the same a questionable one-joke conceit stretched to feature length, pic does go out on an intriguing limb.' – *Dennis Harvey, Variety*

Chuka
US 1967 105m Technicolor
Paramount/Rod Taylor

A wandering gunfighter defends the inhabitants of a fort against Indian attack.
Ill-assorted characters under stress is the theme of this rather pedestrian and slightly pretentious Western.
w Richard Jessup *d* Gordon Douglas *ph* Harold Stine *m* Leith Stevens
☆ Rod Taylor, Ernest Borgnine, John Mills, Luciana Paluzzi, James Whitmore, Louis Hayward, Angela Dorian

A Chump at Oxford **
US 1940 63m bw
Hal Roach

Two street cleaners foil a bank hold-up and are presented with an Oxford education.
Patchy but endearing Laurel and Hardy romp, starting with an irrelevant two reels about their playing butler and maid, but later including Stan's burlesque impersonation of Lord Paddington.
w Charles Rogers, Harry Langdon, Felix Adler *d* Alfred Goulding *ph* Art Lloyd *m* Marvin Hatley *ed* Bert Jordan
☆ *Stan Laurel, Oliver Hardy*, James Finlayson, Forrester Harvey, Wilfred Lucas, Peter Cushing
'Ranks with their best pictures – which, to one heretic, are more agreeable than Chaplin's. Their clowning is purer; they aren't out to better an unbetterable world; they've never wanted to play Hamlet.' – *Graham Greene*

Chung On Tsou: see *Crime Story*

Chunghing Samlam: see *Chungking Express*

Chungking Express **
Hong Kong 1994 103m colour
ICA/Jet Tone (Chan Yi-Kan)

original title: *Chunghing Samlam*
A film in two parts: in the first, a lonesome policeman, whose girlfriend has left him, becomes involved with a female drug dealer; in the second, another solitary cop is loved from afar by a woman working in a fast-food restaurant.
A mood of nostalgia-tinged melancholia pervades this enjoyable movie of young, urban workers caught in a web of disappointment and desire, but still hopelessly optimistic.
wd Wong Kar-Wai *ph* Christopher Doyle, Lau Wai-Keung *m* Frankie Chan, Roel A. Garcia *ad* William Chang *ed* William Chang, Hai Kit-Wai, Kwong Chi-Leung
☆ Brigitte Lin, Takeshi Kaneshiro, Tony Leung, Faye Wong, Valerie Chow, 'Piggy' Chan
'A curious mix of maudlin male romanticism … and impish absurdity.' – *Sheila Johnston, Independent*
'Not only the zingiest visit to Heartbreak Hotel in many years but also one of the first films of the 90s to feel genuinely fresh and original.' – *Tony Rayns, Sight and Sound*

'It Will Make You Squirm.'
The Church (dubbed)
Italy 1991 98m colour
ADC/Cecchi Gori/Tiger/Reteitalia (Dario Argento)

aka: *La Chiesa*
A group of worshippers are trapped in a cathedral where the new librarian has been possessed by the spirits of devil worshippers, massacred in medieval times and buried beneath the building.
Stylishly gruesome horror with a confused narrative, much influenced by the work of its producer and co-writer Dario Argento and likely to appeal to admirers of his work.
w Dario Argento, Franco Ferrini, Michele Soavi *d* Michele Soavi *ph* Renato Tafuri *m* Keith Emerson, The Goblins *ad* Antonello Geleng *ed* Franco Fraticelli
☆ Hugh Quarshie, Tomas Arana, Feodor Chaliapin, Barbara Cupisti, Antonella Vitale, Giovanni Lombardo Radice, Asia Argento
'Inventively gory deaths, lavish surreal set-pieces and lashings of religious hokum make this a treat which yields greater rewards on subsequent viewings.' – *Sight and Sound*
'Visually it's great, but don't bother trying to strain your brain figuring out the plot.' – *Dark Side*

Ciao Maschio: see *Bye Bye Monkey*

Cible Émouvante: see *Wild Target*

Cidade de Deus: see *City of God*

'A story about how far we must travel to find the place where we belong.'
The Cider House Rules **
US 1999 131m DeLuxe 'Scope
Miramax/FilmColony (Richard N. Gladstein)

A young man leaves the orphanage where he feels safe and needed to discover his destiny.
A leisurely drama, of a boy growing to manhood, that has an intensely nostalgic feel to it, so that even unpleasant moments have a warm glow to them; this is life seen through rose-coloured memories, given some touch of reality by its quality of acting.
w John Irving *novel* John Irving *d* Lasse Hallström *ph* Oliver Stapleton *m* Rachel Portman *pd* David Gropman *ed* Lisa Zeno Churgin
☆ *Tobey Maguire* (Homer Wells), Charlize Theron (Candy Kendall), Delroy Lindo (Mr Rose), Paul Rudd (Wally Worthington), *Michael Caine* (Dr Wilbur Larch), Jane Alexander (Nurse Edna), Kathy Baker (Nurse Angela), Erykah Badu (Rose Rose), Kieran Culkin (Buster), Kate Nelligan (Olive Worthington)
'A touching, old-fashioned charmer that ultimately satisfies.' – *David Rooney, Variety*
'Beautifully enacted literary cinema.' – *Angie Errigo, Empire*
Michael Caine; John Irving
picture; Lasse Hallstrom; Lisa Zeno Churgin; Rachel Portman; David Gropman

Le Ciel, Les Oiseaux... Et Ta Mere! *
France 1999 90m colour
Extravaganza/Orly/Sedif/France2/Sofica/Canal+ (Didier Creste, Yann Gilbert, Joel Leyendecker, Nicolas Vannier)

aka: *Boys on the Beach*
Four working-class youths from a Paris suburb win a seaside holiday in Biarritz.
Engaging comedy of a group of hapless teens out of their depth as they try to come to grips with life and girls; it was a box-office success in France.
w Djamal Bensalah, Gilles Laurent *d* Djamal Bensalah *ph* Martin Legrand *m* Enfaz *pd* Gérard Marcireau *ed* Fabrice Rouaud *cos* Thierry Delettre
☆ Jamel Debbouze (Youssef), Julien Courbey (Mike), Lorànt Deutsch (Christophe), Stéphane Soo Mongo (Stéphane), Olivia Bonamy (Lydie), Mariu Roversi, Jessica Beudaert (Dora), Julia Vaidis-Bogard (Léa), Sam Karmann (Le contrôleur)
'Basically an unpretentious teen comedy lightly flavoured with social conscience.' – *Chris Darke, Sight and Sound*

Il cielo è sempre più blu: see *Bits and Pieces*

La Ciénaga *
Argentina/US/Japan/France/Switzerland/Spain/Brazil 2001 100m colour
iCA/Cuatro Cabezas (Lita Stantic)
US title: *The Swamp*
In a hot summer in north-western Argentina, two accidents bring together a feckless family and their more successful cousin.
Stifling account of somnolent lives mired in indolence, sometimes difficult to follow but always interesting to watch.
wd Lucrecia Martel *ph* Hugo Colace *ad* Graciela Oderigo *ed* Santiago Ricci
☆ Mercedes Moran (Tali), Graciela Borges (Mecha), Martin Adjemian (Gregorio), Diego Baenas (Joaquin), Leonora Balcarce (Veronica), Silvia Bayle (Mercedes), Sofia Berolotto (Momi)
'By its end we are glad to see the last of most of its characters, but we will not quickly forget them.' – *Roger Ebert*

'Earth-shaking in its grandeur! A titanic canvas sprung to life!'
Cimarron *
US 1930 130m bw
RKO (Louis Sarecky)

The life of an Oklahoma homesteader from 1890 to 1915.
Sprawling Western family saga; a big early talkie, it dates badly.
w Howard Estabrook *novel* Edna Ferber *d* Wesley Ruggles *ph* Edward Cronjager *m* Max Steiner *ad* Max Ree
☆ Richard Dix, Irene Dunne, Estelle Taylor, Nance O'Neil, William Collier Jnr, Roscoe Ates, George E. Stone, Stanley Fields, Edna May Oliver
'An elegant example of super film-making … big money feature for all classes.' – *Variety*
best picture; Howard Estabrook
Wesley Ruggles; Edward Cronjager; Richard Dix; Irene Dunne; Max Ree

Cimarron *
US 1960 147m Metrocolor Cinemascope
MGM (Edmund Grainger)
A frontier family prosper in Oklahoma from the 1880s.
Flabby, relentlessly boring remake of the 1930 movie of Edna Ferber's sprawling novel.
w Arnold Schulman *d* Anthony Mann *ph* Robert L. Surtees *m* Franz Waxman *ad* George W. Davis, Addison Hehr
☆ Glenn Ford, Maria Schell, Anne Baxter, Lili Darvas, Russ Tamblyn, Henry Morgan, David Opatoshu, Charles McGraw, Aline MacMahon, Edgar Buchanan, Arthur O'Connell, Mercedes McCambridge, Vic Morrow, Robert Keith, Mary Wickes and also Royal Dano, Vladimir Sokoloff
art direction

The Cimarron Kid
US 1951 84m Technicolor
Universal-International (Ted Richmond)
A paroled convict is forced by circumstances to join the Dalton gang of outlaws.
Unusual western featuring a hero reluctantly on the wrong side, and with a somewhat downbeat ending.
w Louis Stevens, Kay Lenard *d* Budd Boetticher *ph* Charles P. Boyle *md* Joseph Gershenson *ad* Bernard Herzbrun, Emrich Nicholson *ed* Frank Gross
☆ Audie Murphy (Bill Doolin), Beverly Tyler (Carrie Roberts), James Best (Bittercreek), Yvette Dugay (Cimarron Rose), John Hudson (Dynamite Dick), Hugh O'Brian (Red Buck), Roy Roberts (Pat Roberts), David Wolfe (Swanson), Noah Beery (Bob Dalton), Leif Erickson (Marshal Sutton)

The Cincinnati Kid **
US 1965 113m Metrocolor
MGM/Filmways (Martin Ransohoff, John Calley)

In New Orleans in the late thirties, stud poker experts compete for supremacy.
This is to poker what The Hustler *was to pool, a fascinating suspense study of experts at work; as before, the romantic asides let down the effectiveness of the others.*
w Ring Lardner Jnr, Terry Southern *novel* Richard Jessup *d Norman Jewison ph* Philip Lathrop *m* Lalo Schifrin
☆ Steve McQueen, *Edward G. Robinson*, Karl Malden, Ann-Margret, Tuesday Weld, Joan Blondell, Rip Torn, Jack Weston, Cab Calloway, Jeff Corey
'I took out all the primaries. There are no reds, greens, whites or blues in the film outside of the red cards and the cockfight.' – *Norman Jewison*

Cinderella **
US 1950 75m Technicolor
Walt Disney

The Perrault fairy tale embroidered with animal characters.
A feature cartoon rather short on inspiration, though with all Disney's solid virtues. The mice are lively and the villainous cat the best character.
d Wilfred Jackson, Hamilton Luske, Clyde Geronimi *m* Oliver Wallace, Paul J. Smith *supervisor* Ben Sharpsteen
☆ Featuring the voices of Ilene Woods, William Phipps, Eleanor Audley, Rhoda Williams, Lucille Bliss, Verna Felton
Oliver Wallace, Paul J. Smith; song 'Bibbidy Bobbidy Boo' (*m/ly* Mack David, Al Hoffman, Jerry Livingston)

Cinderella Jones
US 1946 89m bw
Warner (Alex Gottlieb)
To collect an inheritance, a girl must marry a brainy man.
Witless comedy for the easily pleased.
w Charles Hoffman *story* Philip Wylie *d* Busby Berkeley *ph* Sol Polito *m* Frederick Hollander
☆ Joan Leslie, Robert Alda, S. Z. Sakall, Edward Everett Horton, Julie Bishop, William Prince, Charles Dingle, Ruth Donnelly, Elisha Cook Jnr, Hobart Cavanaugh, Chester Clute

'A movie for every woman who thinks she can never fall in love again!'
Cinderella Liberty
US 1974 117m DeLuxe Panavision
TCF/Sanford (Mark Rydell)

A sailor on shore leave picks up a prostitute and falls in love with her.
Assertively 'modern' yet glutinously sentimental love story in squalid settings. It presumably has an audience.
w Darryl Ponicsan *novel* Darryl Ponicsan *d* Mark Rydell *ph* Vilmos Zsigmond *m* John Williams
☆ James Caan, Marsha Mason, Eli Wallach, Kirk Calloway, Allyn Ann McLerie
'A sordid, messy affair which wants to jerk tears but just doesn't have the knack.' – *New Yorker*
John Williams; Marsha Mason; song 'You're So Nice To Be Around' (*m* John Williams, *ly* Paul Williams)

Cinderfella
US 1960 91m Technicolor
Paramount/Jerry Lewis

Luxury pantomime featuring a male Cinderella.
Annoyingly lavish and empty star vehicle with precious little to laugh at: Lewis's own jokes are strung out to snapping point and no one else gets a look in.
wd Frank Tashlin *ph* Haskell Boggs *m* Walter Scharf
☆ Jerry Lewis, Ed Wynn, Judith Anderson, Anna Maria Alberghetti, Henry Silva, Robert Hutton, Count Basie
'A drought of comic inspiration, followed by a flood of mawkish whimsy, gradually increases one's early misgivings to a degree which finally verges on revulsion.' – *Peter John Dyer*

Cinema Paradiso ****
Italy/France 1989 122m colour
Palace/Films Ariana/RAI TRE/Forum/Franco Cristaldi

original title: *Nuovo Cinema Paradiso*
A film director remembers his early life and his boyhood friendship with the projectionist at his local cinema.

Nostalgic in its celebration of the cinema, beautifully detailed in its enjoyment of the rituals of small-town life with, underneath it all, a toughness in its depiction of a child's growth to maturity.
wd Giuseppe Tornatore *ph* Blasco Giurato *m* Ennio Morricone, Andrea Morricone *pd* Andrea Crisanti *ed* Mario Morra
☆ Antonelli Attli, Enzo Cannavale, Isa Danieli, Leo Gullotta, Marco Leonardi, Pupella Maggio, Agnese Nano, Leopoldo Trieste, Salvatore Cascio, Jacques Perrin, *Philippe Noiret*
† A director's cut lasting 175m was released in 1994.
best foreign film
best foreign film; original screenplay; Philippe Noiret; Salvatore Cascio; Ennio and Andrea Morricone

Cinque Bambole per la Luna d'Agosto: see *Five Dolls for an August Moon*

Le Cinquième Elément: see *The Fifth Element*

La Ciociara: see *Two Women*

The Circle: see *Dayereh*

The Circle: see *The Vicious Circle (1957)*

Circle of Danger *

GB 1950 89m bw
Coronado/David Rose (Joan Harrison)
An American in England investigates the strange death some years earlier of his brother during a commando raid.
Individual scenes are well milked for suspense and dramatic emphasis, but the plot line has virtually no mystery and absolutely no danger. It all seems mildly reminiscent of several Hitchcock films.
w Philip MacDonald *d Jacques Tourneur* *ph* Oswald Morris *m* Robert Farnon
☆ Ray Milland, Patricia Roc, Marius Goring, Hugh Sinclair, Naunton Wayne, Marjorie Fielding, Edward Rigby, Colin Gordon, Dora Bryan

Circle of Deceit *

West Germany/France 1981 109m Eastmancolor
Bioskop/Artemis/Hessischer Rundfunk/Argos (Eberhard Junkersdorf)
original title: *Die Fälschung*
A German journalist has a crisis of conscience while covering the war in Beirut.
Fashionable self-scrutiny based on a published 'faction'. As a film, quite engrossing and occasionally hair-raising.
w Volker Schlöndorff, Jean-Claude Carrière, Margarethe von Trotta, Kai Hermann *novel* Nicolas Born *d* Volker Schlöndorff *ph* Igor Luther *m* Maurice Jarre
☆ Bruno Ganz, Hanna Schygulla, Jerzy Skolimowski, Gila von Weitershausen
'Rarely can a fiction film about war have had such a vividly authentic background, with real corpses and real destruction lending a bleak chill never captured by staged reconstructions.' – *Tom Milne, MFB*

Circle of Deception

GB 1960 100m bw Cinemascope
TCF (T. H. Morahan)
An officer is parachuted into Germany with the intention that he should crack under interrogation and reveal false information.
Depressing World War II tall tale, with suspense sacrificed by flashback structure.
w Nigel Balchin, Robert Musel *novel* Alec Waugh *d* Jack Lee *ph* Gordon Dines *m* Clifton Parker
☆ Bradford Dillman, Harry Andrews, Suzy Parker, Robert Stephens, John Welsh, Paul Rogers, Duncan Lamont, Michael Ripper

Circle of Friends *

Ireland/US 1995 96m colour
Rank/Price/Lantana (Arlene Sellers, Alex Winitsky, Frank Price)
Three young women from an Irish village go to Dublin University, where one falls in love with a handsome, rugby-playing medical student.
Pleasant, sugar-coated account of growing up, set in the 50s and much concerned with Catholic notions of sin; it is all neatly and glossily done, and the acting carries more conviction than might be expected from its conventional story.
w Andrew Davies *novel* Maeve Binchy *d* Pat O'Connor *ph* Ken MacMillan *m* Michael Kamen *pd* Jim Clay *ed* Jim Jympson
☆ *Chris O'Donnell, Minnie Driver*, Geraldine O'Rawe, Alan Cumming, Colin Firth, Ciaran Hinds, Saffron Burrows, Tony Doyle
'Sentimental, old-fashioned fare.' – *Variety*

Circle of Two

Canada 1980 105m colour
Film Consortium of Canada (Henk Van der Kolk)
A 60-year-old artist falls for a teenage student.
Dreary and uninteresting star drama which never really gets going.
w Thomas Hedley *novel A Lesson in Love* by Marie Terese Baird *d* Jules Dassin *ph* Lazlo George *m* Paul Hoffert
☆ Richard Burton, Tatum O'Neal, Nuala FitzGerald, Kate Reid, Robin Gammell, Patricia Collins

Circonstances Atténuantes *

France 1939 85m bw
CCFC
A retired magistrate becomes innocently involved with a gang of crooks.
Nimble farce, most skilfully acted.
w Jean-Pierre Feydeau *novel* Marcel Arnac *d* Jean Boyer
☆ Michel Simon, Arletty, Suzanne Dantes, Arnoux, Mila Parely

Circuitry Man

US 1990 93m Foto-Kem
IRS Media (Steven Reich, John Schouweiler)
In subterranean Los Angeles in the near future, a woman and an android go on the run with a suitcase containing contraband computer chips.
Drear science-fiction flick that sticks close to standard thriller conventions; it takes place in no convincing reality, or fantasy for that matter. The cast content themselves with attitudinizing, which is understandable considering the clichés they have been hired to enunciate.
w Steven Lovy, Robert Lovy *d* Steven Lovy *ph* Jamie Thompson *m* Deborah Holland *pd* Robert Lovy *ed* Jonas Thaler
☆ Jim Metzler, Dana Wheeler-Nicholson, Barbara Alyn Woods, Lu Leonard, Andy Goldberg, Vernon Wells, Dennis Christopher, Paul Willson
† A sequel, *Plughead Rewired: Circuitry Man II*, followed in 1994, directed by Steven and Robert Lovy.

The Circus *

US 1928 72m (24 fps) bw silent (UA)
A tramp on the run from the police takes refuge in a circus and falls for an equestrienne.
Pathos often descends to bathos in this self-constructed star vehicle which has far too few laughs.
wd Charles Chaplin *ph* Rollie Totheroh, Jack Wilson, Mark Marlott
☆ Charles Chaplin, Merna Kennedy, Allan Garcia, Harry Crocker
Special Award to Chaplin for acting, writing, directing and producing the film

'Don't Trust Any Of These Clowns.'

Circus

GB/US 2000 95m DeLuxe
Columbia/FDC (James Gibb, Alan Latham)
A conman and a crook attempt to outwit one another.
Complex, glossy thriller in which everyone tries too hard to be smart and cool; the double-, triple- and quadruple-crossing behaviour slows down the action to a funereal pace.
w David Logan *d* Rob Walker *ph* Ben Seresin *m* Simon Boswell *pd* James Merifield *ed* Oral Norrie Ottey
☆ John Hannah (Leo), Famke Janssen (Lily), Peter Stormare (Julius), Eddie Izzard (Troy), Fred Ward (Elmo), Brian Conley (Bruno), Tiny Lister (Moose), Amanda Donohoe (Gloria), Ian Burfield (Caspar), Neil Stuke (Roscoe), Michael Attwell (Magnus), Jason Watkins (Dom), Christopher Biggins (Arnie)
'Enjoyably awful… eccentric enough to qualify for cult status.' – *Geoffrey Macnab, Sight and Sound*

Circus Boys *

Japan 1989 106m bw
ICA/Eizo Tanteisha/CBS Sony (Mituhisa Hida, Yoichi Sakurai)
original title: *Ni ju-seiki Shonen Dokuhon*
A boy grows up to become a circus clown before leaving to work as an itinerant pedlar and falling in love with a gangster's concubine.
Strange and wayward film with a powerful poetic quality.
wd Kaizo Hayashi *ph* Yuichi Nagata *ad* Takeo Kimura, Hidemitsu Yamazaki *ed* Osamu Tanaka
☆ Hiroshi Mikami, Moe Kamura, Xia Jian, Michiru Akiyoshi, Yuki Asayama, Sanshi Katsura, Haruko Wanibuchi
'It isn't very often you see a film that understands so well that the cinema should be a place with some magic in it as well as simple story-telling ability.' – *Derek Malcolm, Guardian*

Circus of Fear

GB 1966 83m Eastmancolor
Circus Films (Harry Alan Towers)
aka: *Psycho-Circus*
A circus performer is the mastermind behind a daring daylight robbery on Tower Bridge.
Efficient B-movie thriller with a few traces of wit and a better cast than might have been expected.
w Peter Welbeck (Harry Alan Towers) *d* John Moxey *ph* Ernest Steward *m* Johnny Douglas *ad* Frank White *ed* John Trumper
☆ Christopher Lee, Leo Genn, Maurice Kaufmann, Anthony Newlands, Heinz Drache, Klaus Kinski, Eddi Arent, Margaret Lee, Suzy Kendall, Cecil Parker, Victor Maddern

'One man's lust turns men into beasts, strips women of their souls!'

Circus of Horrors

GB 1960 91m Eastmancolor
Anglo Amalgamated/Lynx/Independent Artists (Norman Priggen)
A plastic surgeon staffs a semi-derelict circus with criminals whose faces he has altered, and murders any who try to flee.
Stark horror comic; quite professionally made, but content-wise a crude concoction of sex and sadism.
w George Baxt *d* Sidney Hayers *ph* Douglas Slocombe *m* Franz Reizenstein, Muir Mathieson
☆ Anton Diffring, Erika Remberg, Yvonne Monlaur, Donald Pleasence, Jane Hylton, Kenneth Griffith, Conrad Phillips, Jack Gwillim

Circus World

US 1964 138m Technicolor Super Technirama 70
Bronston/Midway (Samuel Bronston)
GB title: *The Magnificent Showman*
An American circus owner tours Europe in search of his alcoholic ex-wife who left him when her lover fell to death from the trapeze.
Lethargic big-screen epic which exhausts its spectacle in the first hour and then settles down to a dreary will-daughter-guess-who-the-strange-lady-is plot, without even the plus of an exciting finale.
w Ben Hecht, Julian Halevy (Julian Zimet), James Edward Grant *story* Philip Yordan, Nicholas Ray *d* Henry Hathaway *ph* Jack Hildyard *m* Dimitri Tiomkin *pd* John DeCuir *ed* Dorothy Spencer
☆ John Wayne, *Rita Hayworth*, Claudia Cardinale, John Smith, Lloyd Nolan, Richard Conte, Wanda Rotha, Kay Walsh
'To sit through this film is something like holding an elephant on your lap for two hours and fifteen minutes.' – *Time*
† Screenwriter Julian Zimet wrote under a pseudonym because he was blacklisted at the time.

The Cisco Kid

The Cisco Kid, a ruthless Mexican bandit originally created by O. Henry in a short story, was turned by Hollywood into a dashing wild Western Robin Hood in twenty-three sound features (following a few silent ones) and a long-running TV series. In most of them he was accompanied by his fat side-kick Pancho.
For Fox:
1929 In Old Arizona (Warner Baxter)
1931 The Cisco Kid (Baxter)
For Twentieth Century Fox:
1939 The Return of the Cisco Kid (Baxter), The Cisco Kid and the Lady (Cesar Romero: who played the role in all the remaining TCF movies).
1940 Viva Cisco Kid, Lucky Cisco Kid, The Gay Caballero
1941 Romance of the Rio Grande, Ride On, Vaquero
For Monogram:
1945 The Cisco Kid Returns (Duncan Renaldo), The Cisco Kid in Old New Mexico (Renaldo), South of the Rio Grande (Renaldo)
1946 The Gay Cavalier (Gilbert Roland), South of Monterey (Roland), Beauty and the Bandit (Roland)
1947 Riding the California Trail (Roland), Robin Hood of Monterey (Roland), King of the Bandits (Roland)
For United Artists (all with Renaldo):
1949 The Valiant Hombre, The Gay Amigo, The Daring Caballero, Satan's Cradle
1950 The Girl from San Lorenzo
† The 50s TV series starred Renaldo with Leo Carrillo.

Cisco Kid and The Lady

US 1939 73m bw
TCF (John Stone)
The Cisco Kid accidentally acquires, and sensibly disposes of, a baby and a gold mine.
Lively 'B' feature, full of action, humour and narrative twists.
w Frances Hyland *story* Stanley Rauh *character created by William Sydney Porter (O. Henry)* *d* Herbert I. Leeds *ph* Barney McGill *md* Samuel Kaylin *ad* Richard Day, Chester Gore *ed* Nick de Maggio
☆ Cesar Romero, Marjorie Weaver, Chris-Pin Martin, George Montgomery, Robert Barrat, Virginia Field, Harry Green, Ward Bond

Cisco Pike

US 1971 94m Eastmancolor
Columbia/Acrobat (Gerald Ayres)
A former pop group leader and drug pusher is blackmailed by a cop into selling marijuana.
Low-key, would-be realistic study of a section of life in 70s LA. Flashy, boring and almost plotless.
wd Bill L. Norton *ph* Vilis Lapenieks *m* Sonny Terry, Sir Douglas Quintet, Lee Montgomery, Kris Kristofferson *pd* Rosanna White *ad* Alfred Sweeney
☆ Kris Kristofferson (Cisco Pike), Gene Hackman (Officer Leo Holland), Karen Black (Sue), Harry Dean Stanton (Jesse Dupre), Viva (Merna), Roscoe Lee Browne (Music Store Owner), Joy Bang (Lynn)
'A moody, melancholy little film whose strength lies in its evocation of the rootless, aimless, irresponsible life-style of the pop/drug culture.' – *Brenda Davies*

The Citadel: see *El Kalaa*

'Secrets of a doctor as told by a doctor!'

The Citadel **

GB 1938 113m bw
MGM (Victor Saville)
A young doctor has a hard time in the mining villages but is later swayed by the easy rewards of a Mayfair practice.
Solidly produced adaptation of a bestseller; the more recent deluge of doctors on television make it appear rather elementary, but many scenes work in a classical way. One of the first fruits of MGM's British studios which were closed by World War II.
w Elizabeth Hill, Ian Dalrymple, Emlyn Williams, Frank Wead *novel* A. J. Cronin *d* King Vidor *ph* Harry Stradling *m* Louis Levy *ad* Lazare Meerson, Alfred Junge *ed* Charles Frend
☆ *Robert Donat*, Rosalind Russell, Ralph Richardson, Emlyn Williams, Penelope Dudley Ward, Francis L. Sullivan, Rex Harrison
'General audience limited … strong for the Anglo market.' – *Variety*
'I think any doctor will agree that here is a medical picture with no Men in White hokum, no hysterical, incredible melodrama, but with an honest story, honestly told. And that's a rare picture.' – *Pare Lorentz*
'We are grateful that a worthy idea has been handled with intelligence and imagination, that Vidor has shown respect both for his talent and

for the sensibilities of the audience.' – *Robert Stebbins*

'Numerous passages shine brilliantly with those deft touches that first brought Vidor to prominence.' – *Variety*

'The pace of Hollywood, the honest characterization of England's best.' – *New York Times*

† The parts played by Russell and Richardson were originally intended for Elizabeth Allan and Spencer Tracy.

best picture; script; King Vidor; Robert Donat

Citizen Kane **

US 1941 119m bw

RKO (Orson Welles)

A newspaper tycoon dies, and a magazine reporter interviews his friends in an effort to discover the meaning of his last words.

A brilliant piece of Hollywood cinema using all the resources of the studio; despite lapses of characterization and gaps in the narrative, almost every shot and every line is utterly absorbing both as entertainment and as craft. See The Citizen Kane Book *by Pauline Kael, and innumerable other writings.*

w Herman J. Mankiewicz, Orson Welles d Orson Welles ph Gregg Toland m Bernard Herrmann ad Van Nest Polglase ed Robert Wise sp Vernon L. Walker

☆ *Orson Welles* (Kane), *Joseph Cotten* (Jedediah Leland), *Dorothy Comingore* (Susan Alexander), *Everett Sloane* (Bernstein), *Ray Collins* (Boss Jim Geddes), *Paul Stewart* (Raymond), *Ruth Warrick* (Emily Norton), *Erskine Sanford* (Herbert Carter), *Agnes Moorehead* (Kane's mother), *Harry Shannon* (Kane's father), *George Coulouris* (Walter Parks Thatcher), *William Alland* (Thompson), *Fortunio Bonanova* (music teacher)

NEWSREEL: 'Then, last week, as it must to all men, death came to Charles Foster Kane.'

BERNSTEIN: 'Old age ... it's the only disease you don't look forward to being cured of.'

THOMPSON: 'Mr Kane was a man who got everything he wanted, and then lost it. Maybe Rosebud was something he couldn't get, or something he lost. Anyway, I don't think it would have explained everything. I don't think any word can explain a man's life. No, I guess Rosebud is just a piece in a jigsaw puzzle ... a missing piece.'

SUSAN: 'Forty-nine acres of nothing but scenery and statues. I'm lonesome.'

KANE: 'You're right, Mr Thatcher, I did lose a million dollars last year. I expect to lose a million dollars this year. I expect to lose a million dollars next year. You know, Mr Thatcher, at the rate of a million dollars a year, I'll have to close this place – in sixty years.'

KANE: 'I run a couple of newspapers. What do you do?'

BERNSTEIN: 'One day back in 1896 I was crossing over to Jersey on the ferry, and as we pulled out, there was another ferry pulling in, and on it there was a girl waiting to get off. A white dress she had on. She was carrying a white parasol. I only saw her for one second. She didn't see me at all, but I'll bet a month hasn't gone by since that I haven't thought of that girl.'

'On seeing it for the first time, one got a conviction that if the cinema could do that, it could do anything.' – *Penelope Houston*

'What may distinguish *Citizen Kane* most of all is its extracting the mythic from under the humdrum surface of the American experience.' – *John Simon, 1968*

'Probably the most exciting film that has come out of Hollywood for twenty-five years. I am not sure it isn't the most exciting film that has ever come out of anywhere.' – *C. A. Lejeune*

'At any rate Orson Welles has landed in the movies, with a splash and a loud yell.' – *James Shelley Hamilton*

'More fun than any great movie I can think of.' – *Pauline Kael, 1968*

'It is a fascinating picture, but because of its congestion of technical stunts, it fails to move us.' – *Egon Larsen*

'A quite good film which tries to run the psychological essay in harness with the detective thriller, and doesn't quite succeed.' – *James Agate*

Herman J. Mankiewicz, Orson Welles (script)

best picture; Orson Welles (as director); Gregg Toland; Bernard Herrmann; Orson Welles (as actor); art direction; Robert Wise

Citizens' Band: see *FM*

Citizens Band: see *Handle with Care (1977)*

La Città delle Donne: see *City of Women*

La Città Si Difende

Italy 1951 90m bw

Cines (Carlo Civallero)

A gang is recruited to rob a football stadium.

Moderate forerunner of The Good Die Young, The Killing, *and a hundred other caper films.*

w Federico Fellini, Tullio Pinelli, Luigi Comencini *d* Pietro Germi *ph* Carlo Montuori *m* Carlo Rustichelli

☆ Fausto Tozzi, Gina Lollobrigida, Patrizia Manca, Enzo Maggio

'As anonymous as the average B picture.' – *Gavin Lambert*

The City *

US 1939 32m bw

American Institute of Planners

A historical, social and psychoanalytical study of urban living.

Slightly guarded but convention-breaking documentary which though of its time still fascinates mildly by its style.

w Henwar Rodakiewicz *book The Culture of Cities* by Lewis Mumford *d* Ralph Steiner, Willard Van Dyke *ph* Ralph Steiner, Willard Van Dyke

City across the River

US 1949 91m bw

U-I (Howard Christie)

Brooklyn delinquents get involved in murder.

Semi-documentary throwback to the Dead End Kids, with location shooting influenced by The Naked City. *Dull.*

w Maxwell Shane, Dennis Cooper *novel The Amboy Dukes* by Irving Shulman *d* Maxwell Shane *ph* Maury Gertsman *m* Walter Scharf *ad* Bernard Herzbrun, Emrich Nicholson *ed* Ted J. Kent

☆ Stephen McNally, Barbara Whiting, Peter Fernandez, Al Ramsen, Joshua Shelley, Anthony Curtis (Tony Curtis in his first film role)

City after Midnight: see *That Woman Opposite*

The City and the Dogs **

Peru 1985 135m colour

Inca Films (Francisco J. Lombardi)

original title: *La Ciudad Y Los Perros*

With the aid of an incorruptible officer, a cadet tries to expose the organized brutality at a miltary academy.

A passionate allegory of military dictatorship.

w José Watanabe *novel* Mario Vargas Llosa *d* Francisco J. Lombardi *ph* Pili Flores Guerra *m* Enrique Iturriaga *ad* Lloyd Moore *ed* Gianfranco Annichini, Augusto Tamayo San Roman

☆ Pablo Serra, Gustavo Bueno, Luis Alvarez, Jan Manuel Ochva, Eduardo Adrianzen

City beneath the Sea

US 1953 87m Technicolor

U-I (Albert J. Cohen)

Deep sea divers fall out over a sunken treasure.

Adequate double-biller with little to stir the interest.

w Jack Harvey, Ramon Romero *d* Budd Boetticher *ph* Charles P. Boyle *md* Joseph Gershenson

☆ Robert Ryan, Anthony Quinn, Mala Powers, Suzan Ball, George Mathews, Karel Stepanek, Lalo Rios

City beneath the Sea

US 1970 98m DeLuxe

Warner/Kent/Motion Pictures International (Irwin Allen)

GB theatrical release title: *One Hour to Doomsday*

An undersea city is threatened by an errant planetoid.

Futuristic adventure from a familiar stable; it will satisfy followers of Voyage to the Bottom of the Sea. *Originally made for TV.*

w John Meredyth Lucas *d* Irwin Allen *ph* Kenneth Peach *m* Richard La Salle *ad* Rodger E. Maus, Stan Jolley

☆ Stuart Whitman, Robert Wagner, Rosemary Forsyth, Robert Colbert, Burr de Benning, Richard Basehart, Joseph Cotten, James Darren, Sugar Ray Robinson, Paul Stewart

'When you're searching for a killer... the last suspect you want to see is your son.'

City by the Sea

US 2001 108m DeLuxe Panavision

Warner/Franchise (Brad Grey, Elie Samaha, Michael Caton-Jones, Matthew Baer)

A New York homicide detective discovers that the son he abandoned is the chief suspect in a murder investigation.

Despite being based on a true story, this talky, downbeat drama rarely rings true. The role of veteran cop fits De Niro like a well-worn overcoat, but there's nothing out of the ordinary for either star or audience.

w Ken Hixon *article Mark of a Murderer* by Michael McAlary *ph* Karl Walter Lindenlaub *m* John Murphy *pd* Jane Musky *ed* Jim Clark

☆ Robert De Niro (Vincent LaMarca), Frances McDormand (Michelle), James Franco (Joey), Eliza Dushku (Gina), William Forsythe (Spyder), George Dzundza (Reg Duffy), Patti Lupone (Maggie)

'In its workmanship it aspires not to be remarkable but to be well made, dependable, moving us because of the hurt in the hero's eyes.' – *Roger Ebert, Chicago Sun-Times*

'An overgrown – and quite mediocre – TV movie, despite the big names.' – *New York Post*

City for Conquest **

US 1940 106m bw

Warner (Anatole Litvak)

An East Side truck driver becomes a boxer but is blinded in a fight; meanwhile his composer brother gives up pop music for symphonies.

Phony but oddly persuasive melodrama set in a studio in New York and heavily influenced by the pretensions of the Group theatre.

w John Wexley *novel* Aben Kandel *d* Anatole Litvak *ph* Sol Polito, James Wong Howe *m* Max Steiner

☆ *James Cagney*, Ann Sheridan, Frank Craven, Donald Crisp, *Arthur Kennedy*, Frank McHugh, George Tobias, Anthony Quinn, Jerome Cowan, Lee Patrick, Blanche Yurka, Thurston Hall

'Sometimes we wonder whether it wasn't really the Warner brothers who got New York from the Indians, so diligent and devoted have they been in feeling the great city's pulse, picturing its myriad facets and recording with deep compassion the passing life of its seething population.' – *Bosley Crowther*

City Girl *

US 1930 77m bw

Fox

A city girl finds rural life has its own drama.

Rural drama distinguished by directorial touches.

w Berthold Viertel, Marion Orth *play The Mud Turtle* by Elliott Lester *d* F. W. Murnau *ph* Ernest Palmer *m* Arthur Kay

☆ Charles Farrell, Mary Duncan, David Torrence, Edith Yorke, Dawn O'Day (Anne Shirley)

'It Started With A Shootout On A Rainswept Street And Ended In A Scandal That Shattered New York.'

City Hall **

US 1996 111m Technicolor

Rank/Castle Rock (Edward R. Pressman, Ken Lipper, Charles Mulvehill, Harold Becker)

Investigation of a triple shooting in Brooklyn, involving a cop and a gangster, reveals high-level corruption among city officials.

An involving political thriller that is less interested in the guilt of its participants and more concerned with examining the compromises and short-cuts that are necessary to run a big city, and the dangers they involve.

w Ken Lipper, Paul Schrader, Nicholas Pileggi, Bo Goldman *d* Harold Becker *ph* Michael Seresin *m* Jerry Goldsmith *pd* Jane Musky *ed* Robert C. Jones, David Bretherton

☆ Al Pacino, John Cusack, Bridget Fonda, Danny Aiello, Martin Landau, David Paymer, Tony Franciosa, Lindsay Duncan

'A film that aims to tell the dark truth about a modern metropolis yet doesn't stint on fun.' – *Variety*

'If the message is ho-hum, so is the plot of this talky, convoluted, predictable tale. Despite the best efforts of an impressive cast, this wan thriller has virtually no thrills at all.' – *Stephen Farber, Movieline*

† Frank Pierson worked uncredited on the screenplay. Ken Lipper was deputy mayor of New York under Ed Koch.

City Heat

US 1984 97m Technicolor

Warner/Malpaso/Deliverance (Fritz Manes)

In the early thirties, a private eye's partner is bumped off, and he teams against the baddies with an old cop friend.

A tedious teaming for two tired stars who seem to imagine that all they have to do is show up.

w Sam O. Brown (Blake Edwards), Joseph C. Stinson *d* Richard Benjamin *ph* Nick McLean *m* Lennie Niehaus *pd* Edward Carfagno

☆ Clint Eastwood, Burt Reynolds, Jane Alexander, Madeline Kahn, Rip Torn, Irene Cara, Richard Roundtree, Tony Lo Bianco

'It evaporates from the mind instantly upon its conclusion.' – *Variety*

The City Is Dark: see *Crime Wave*

The City Jungle: see *The Young Philadelphians*

City Lights ***

US 1931 87m bw silent (with music and effects)

UA/Charles Chaplin

A tramp befriends a millionaire and falls in love with a blind girl.

Sentimental comedy with several delightful sequences in Chaplin's best manner.

ph Rollie Totheroh *md* Alfred Newman *wd/m* Charles Chaplin

☆ Charles Chaplin, Virginia Cherrill, Florence Lee, Harry Myers

'Chaplin has another good picture, but it gives indications of being short-winded, and may tire fast after a bombastic initial seven days ... he has sacrificed speed to pathos, and plenty of it.' – *Variety*

'Even while laughing, one is aware of a faint and uneasy feeling that Chaplin has been pondering with more than a bit of solemnity on conventional story values, and it has led him further than ever into the realms of what is often called pathetic.' – *National Board of Review*

'She Didn't Believe In Angels Until She Fell In Love With One.'

City of Angels

US/Germany 1998 117m Technicolor Panavision

Warner/Regency/Atlas (Charles Roven, Dawn Steel)

An angel, who watches over Los Angeles, decides to become human after he falls in love with a heart surgeon.

Slick romantic comedy with ambitions beyond its reach; it settles, finally, for heavy sentimentality.

w Dana Stevens *d* Brad Silberling *ph* John Seale *m* Gabriel Yared *pd* Lilly Kilvert *ed* Lynzee Klingman *sp* Sony Picture Imageworks *film Wings of Desire by Wim Wenders*

☆ Nicolas Cage, Meg Ryan, Andre Braugher, Dennis Franz, Colm Feore, Robin Bartlett, Joanna Merlin, Sarah Dampf

'The film is glossy and soft, and has none of the intelligence or bitter humour of Wenders' film.' – *Gaby Wood, Guardian*

City of Bad Men *

US 1953 82m Technicolor

TCF (Leonard Goldstein)

In Carson City during the Corbett/ Fitzsimmons boxing match, outlaws plan to rob the arena of its receipts.

Slightly unusual Western suspenser with generally accomplished handling.

w George W. George, George Slavin *d* Harmon Jones *ph* Charles G. Clarke *md* Lionel Newman

☆ Dale Robertson, Jeanne Crain, Richard Boone, Lloyd Bridges, Carl Betz, Carole Mathews, Whitfield Connor

City of Chance *

US 1939 57m bw

Sol M. Wurtzel/TCF

A girl reporter crusades against gangster gamblers.

Smart little second feature with no time to be boring.
w John Larkin, Barry Trivers *d* Ricardo Cortez
☆ Lynn Bari, C. Aubrey Smith, Donald Woods, Amanda Duff, June Gale, Richard Lane

'A half crazed man in a terror crazed town!'
City of Fear
US 1958 81m bw
Columbia/Orbit (Leon Chooluck)

A convict escapes with a canister of radioactive cobalt, which he believes to be heroin. After terrifying the city, he finally dies of exposure to it.
Rough-edged but occasionally gripping minor thriller from an independent company.
w Steven Ritch, Robert Dillon *d* Irving Lerner *ph* Lucien Ballard *m* Jerry Goldsmith
☆ Vince Edwards, John Archer, Patricia Blair, Steven Ritch, Lyle Talbot

'Fight and you'll never survive..... Run and you'll never escape.'
City of God **
Brazil/Germany/France 2002 130m colour
Panavision
Buena Vista/Studio Canal//02/VideoFilmes/Globo/Lumiere/ Wild Bunch (Andrea Barata Ribeiro, Mauricio Andrade Ramos)

original title: *Cidade de Deus*
In the slums of Rio de Janeiro, a poor boy who wants to escape to a better life watches his contemporaries turn to drugs and crime.
In essence, this resembles many slickly-made Hollywood gangland drug dramas: what sets it apart is the age of its swaggering, gun-toting street kids – many are barely teenagers – and the vitality of the acting from its non-professional cast.
w Braulio Mantovani *novel* Paulo Lins *d* Fernando Meirelles, Katia Lund *ph* Cesar Charlone *m* Antonio Pinto, Ed Cortes *ad* Tule Peake *ed* Daniel Rezende
☆ Matheus Nachtergaele (Sandro Cenoura), Seu Jorge (Mane Galinha), Buscape (Alexandre Rodrigues), Leandro Firmino da Hora (Ze Pequeno), Phelipe Haagensen (Bene), Jonathan Haagensen (Cabeleira), Douglas Silva (Dadinho), Roberta Rodriguez Silvia (Berenice)
'An exhilarating slap in the face, bracing and sexy, smart and visceral, stylish and raw – the advent of a fabulously exciting new moviemaking talent.' – *Shawn Levy, Oregonian*
'We are made to witness horrific acts of cruelty, and yet there is something unseemly in the way Meirelles glamorizes them with fancy effects: split screens, slo-mo, jump cuts. He's trying to turn us on.' – *Peter Rainer, New York*
Daniel Rezende

City of Gold **
Canada 1957 23m bw
National Film Board of Canada
The story of Dawson City, capital of the Klondike in 1897–8, is told by an accumulation of details from still photographs.
A film with much to answer for, being the first documentary exclusively using the rostrum camera, a technique later adopted extensively by television. The subject matter is fascinating.
w and narrated by Pierre Berton *d/ph* Colin Low, Wolf Koenig

City of Hope ***
US 1991 130m DuArt Panavision
Mainline/Esperanza

Corruption and crime in Hudson City, New Jersey touches the lives of locals, from building contractors and petty thieves to the mayor.
Complex and engrossing, with a narrative style that brings to busy life a whole community.
wd John Sayles *ph* Robert Richardson *m* Mason Daring *pd* Dan Bishop, Dianna Freas *ed* John Sayles
☆ Vincent Spano, Joe Morton, Tony Lo Bianco, Barbara Williams, Stephen Mendillo, Chris Cooper, Charlie Yanko, Jace Alexander, Todd Graff, Scott Tiler, John Sayles, Frankie Faison, Gloria Foster, Tom Wright
'A major film, suggesting that Sayles might become as significant a film-maker for the 90s as Altman was for the 70s.' – *Kim Newman, Sight and Sound*
'Epic, masterly, urgent, adult and unforgettable. Put simply – which is grossly unfair to its complexity – it is *Bonfire of the Vanities* without the vanities.' – *Alexander Walker, London Evening Standard*
'It plays as if it were still on the drawing board.' – *Michael Sragow, New Yorker*

'Wanting a man dead can be reason enough to live.'
City of Industry *
US 1996 97m DeLuxe
Largo (Evzen Kolar, Ken Solarz)

The surviving member of a gang of jewel robbers hunts down the person who double-crossed his friends and escaped with the loot.
Forceful, violent revenge thriller; the narrative is predictable, but the action is directed in an appropriately hard-hitting style, and Keitel – 'I'm my own police' – brings an angry intensity to his role as the implacable and indestructible avenger.
w Ken Solarz *d* John Irvin *ph* Thomas Burstyn *m* Stephen Endelman *pd* Michael Novotny *ed* Mark Conte
☆ Harvey Keitel, Stephen Dorff, Timothy Hutton, Famke Janssen, Wade Dominguez, Michael Jai White, Elliott Gould (uncredited)
'In its detached way, the film seems to be trying to get at the quintessence of revenge movies, free of all superfluity.' – *Rob White, Sight and Sound*

'He was a man who couldn't care less ... until he met a man who couldn't care more.'
City of Joy *
GB/France 1992 135m Eastmancolor
Warner/Lightmotive/Pricel (Jake Eberts, Roland Joffé)

In Calcutta an American doctor becomes involved in a clinic for the poor and helps them in their struggle against local gangsters.
Well-meaning movie that tends to talk about, rather than dramatize, its theme of the need for commitment.
w Mark Medoff *book* Dominic LaPierre *d* Roland Joffé *ph* Peter Biziou *m* Ennio Morricone *pd* Roy Walker *ed* Gerry Hambling
☆ Patrick Swayze, Pauline Collins, Om Puri, Shabana Azmi, Art Malik, Ayesha Dharker, Santu Chowdhury, Imran Badsah Khan
'Joffé's noble attempt to portray the tenacity and strength of the human spirit under the most trying conditions comes off as curiously ineffectual due to predictable plotting and character evolution.' – *Variety*
'Hopelessly fraudulent, with an uplifting finale that could make a strong man heave.' – *Stephen Farber, Movieline*

City of Lost Children *
France 1995 111m colour Technovision
Entertainment/Lumiere/Canal Plus/France 3 (Claudie Ossard)

original title: *La Cité des Enfants Perdus*
A circus strongman goes in search of his adopted child, kidnapped, like many others, by a madman who lives in mid-ocean and hopes to steal the children's dreams to make up for the loss of his own.
A bizarre, hyperactive fantasy that yields many incidental pleasures, although coherence is not among them.
w Gilles Adrien, Jean-Pierre Jeunet, Marc Caro *d* Jean-Pierre Jeunet, Marc Caro *ph* Darius Khondji *m* Angelo Badalamenti *ad* Marc Caro *ed* Hervé Schneid
☆ Ron Perlman, Daniel Emilfork, Judith Vittet, Dominique Pinon, Jean-Claude Dreyfus, Genevieve Brunet, Odile Mallet, Ticky Holgado, Jean-Louis Trintignant
'The film's obscure plot, its vast assemblage of weird characters and its refusal to centre any of them securely in the emotions make for a peculiarly imperfect general effect.' – *Derek Malcolm, Guardian*

City of Lost Souls: see *Hyôryuu-gai*

A City of Sadness: see *Beiqing Chengshi*

City of Silent Men
US 1942 64m bw
PRC (Dixon R. Harwin)
Two ex-convicts finally get work but are hounded by a newspaper publisher.
Decent second feature, a cut above the average for its source.
w Joseph Hoffman, Robert E. Kent *d* William Nigh
☆ Frank Albertson, June Lang, Jan Wiley, Richard Clarke

City of the Dead *
GB 1960 78m bw
Vulcan (Donald Taylor)

US title: *Horror Hotel*
In Massachusetts, a woman burned as a witch 250 years ago is still 'alive', running a local hotel and luring unwary strangers into becoming sacrificial victims.
A deadly first half gives way to splendid cinematic terror when the scene shifts to the village by night, all dry ice and limpid fog, and the heroine becomes a human sacrifice. A superior horror comic.
w George Baxt *story* Milton Subotsky *d* John Moxey *ph* Desmond Dickinson *m* Douglas Gamley, Ken Jones *ad* John Blezard
☆ *Patricia Jessel*, Betta St John, Christopher Lee, Dennis Lotis, Valentine Dyall, Venetia Stevenson, Norman MacOwan, Fred Johnson

'From The Bowels Of The Dead They Came To Collect The Living...'
City of the Living Dead (dubbed)
Italy 1980 93m colour
Dania/Medusa/National Cinematografia (Giovanni Masini)

original title: *Paura nella Città dei Morti Viventi*
aka: *Gates of Hell; Twilight of The Dead; The Fear*
In the Massachusetts town of Dunwich a priest hangs himself and opens a gateway to hell, through which stagger the living dead.
A slow-moving horror with little narrative and a great deal of gore. It was supposedly inspired by H. P. Lovecraft, although it bears little resemblance to his stories.
w Lucio Fulci, Dardano Sacchetti *d* Lucio Fulci *ph* Sergio Salvati *m* Fabio Frizzi *pd* Massimo Antonello Geleng *ed* Vincenzo Tomassi
☆ Christopher George, Katriona MacColl, Carlo de Mejo, Antonella Interlenghi, Giovanni Lombardo Radice, Daniela Doria, Janet Agren
'The ending is somewhat incomprehensible and acting and dialogue as usual leave a good deal to be desired. However, one doesn't really look to the "fantastique" for that kind of thing.' – *Julian Petley, Films and Filming*
† The film was cut to 92m on its British cinema release in 1982 and to 86m for its video release, removing the goriest episodes, including a youth having an electric drill pushed through his head, and making the narrative, like a few of its characters, somewhat disjointed.

City of the Walking Dead: see *Nightmare City*

City of Women *
Italy/France 1980 140m Eastmancolor
Opera Film-Gaumont (Renzo Rossellini)

original title: *La Città delle Donne*
A businessman finds himself trapped and threatened by women en masse.
Often leaden but sometimes spectacular fantasy in which the director spews out his views of the war between men and women. Fascinating in patches, but generally indigestible.
w Federico Fellini, Bernardino Zapponi *d* Federico Fellini *ph* Giuseppe Rotunno *m* Luis Bacalov
☆ Marcello Mastroianni, Anna Prucnal, Bernice Stegers, Ettore Manni, Donatella Damiani
'Another visual tour de force in an elaborate dream framework; narrative thin, overlong, and finally overweight.' – *Variety*

City on Fire
Canada/US 1979 106m colour
Rank/Astral Bellevue/Pathé/Sandy Howard/Harold Greenberg (Claude Héroux)

A slum fire threatens an entire city.
Shoddy disaster movie which does its cast no favour.
w Jack Hill, David P. Lewis, Celine La Frenière *d* Alvin Rakoff *ph* René Verzier *m* William and Matthew Macauley *pd* William McCrow *ed* Jean-Pol Passer, Jacques Clairoux *sp* Cliff Wenger, Carol Lynn
☆ Barry Newman, Susan Clark, Shelley Winters, Henry Fonda, Leslie Nielsen, James Franciscus, Ava Gardner

City on Fire *
Hong Kong 1987 101m colour
Cinema City (Ringo Lam)

An undercover cop reluctantly replaces a murdered colleague and infiltrates a ruthless gang planning a big jewel robbery.
Brutal action thriller that was one of the inspirations for Quentin Tarantino's Reservoir Dogs, though it concerns loyalty and rivalry between an elderly inspector and a brash new cop as much as dissension between gangsters.
w Tommy Sham *story* Ringo Lam *d* Ringo Lam *ph* Andrew Lau *m* Teddy Robin, Kwan *ad* Luk Tze Fung *ed* Wong Ming Lam
☆ Chow Yun-Fat, Sun Yeuh, Lee Sau Yin, Carrie Ng, Roy Cheung, Danny

'Three urban hombres heading west, seeking adventure, craving excitement ... and longing for room service.'
City Slickers ***
US 1991 114m CFI color
First Independent/Castle Rock/Nelson/Face (Irby Smith)

Three friends, all facing midlife crises, decide to spend their vacation on a cattle drive.
A witty and engaging comedy for the most part, with some affectionate parodies of moments from classic Westerns.
w Lowell Ganz, Babaloo Mandel *d* Ron Underwood *ph* Dean Semler *m* Marc Shaiman, Hummie Mann *pd* Lawrence G. Paull *ed* O. Nicholas Brown
☆ Billy Crystal, Daniel Stern, Bruno Kirby, Patricia Wettig, Helen Slater, Jack Palance, Josh Mostel, David Paymer, Noble Willingham
'A deft blend of wry humour and warmth (albeit with a little too much *thirty-something*-esque angst for its own good).' – *Variety*
Jack Palance

City Slickers II: The Legend of Curly's Gold
US 1994 116m Technicolor Panavision
Columbia TriStar/Face/Castle Rock (Billy Crystal)

Three city friends head west in search of treasure buried by a dead cowboy, helped and hindered by his tough twin brother.
Disappointing sequel that settles for tired comedy routines and slack jokes about old movies.
w Billy Crystal, Lowell Ganz, Babaloo Mandel *d* Paul Weiland *ph* Adrian Biddle, Craig Haagensen *m* Marc Shaiman *pd* Stephen J. Lineweaver *ed* William Anderson, Armen Minasian
☆ Billy Crystal, Daniel Stern, Jon Lovitz, Jack Palance, Patricia Wettig, Bill McKinney, Pruitt Taylor Vince, Beth Grant, Noble Willingham
'A sure-shootin' entertainment that shouldn't have much trouble rounding up an audience for the high jinks on the range.' – *Variety*
'A charmless, redundant sequel that replaces greed for character development and skimps on the laughs. Dull, dull, dull.' – *Movie Collector*

'Love and courage pitted against a ruthless hate!'
City Streets **
US 1931 86m bw
Paramount (Rouben Mamoulian)
A gangster's daughter is sent to jail for a murder she did not commit, and on release narrowly escapes being 'taken for a ride'.
Tense, dated gangland melodrama of primary interest because of its director's very cinematic treatment.
w Max Marcin, Oliver H. P. Garrett, Dashiell Hammett *story* Ladies of the Mob by Ernest Booth *d* Rouben Mamoulian *ph* Lee Garmes
☆ Sylvia Sidney, Gary Cooper, Paul Lukas, Guy Kibbee, William (Stage) Boyd, Stanley Fields, Wynne Gibson
'So many brilliant touches that anyone who sees it will have to predict for Mamoulian a brilliant career.' – *Film Spectator*
'Too much attempt to artify hurts though the sophisticated treatment and elegant settings will help.' – *Variety*

'A love story in a gangster setting which got carried away into so much fancy expressionism and symbolism that it seems stylized out of all relationship to the actual world.' – *Pauline Kael, 70s*

City that Never Sleeps
US 1953 90m bw
Republic (John H. Auer)
The work of the Chicago police force during one night.
Adequate minor semi-documentary police yarn.
w Steve Fisher *d* John H. Auer *ph* John I. Russell *m* R. Dale Butts
☆ Gig Young, Mala Powers, William Talman, Edward Arnold, Chill Wills, Paula Raymond, Marie Windsor

'They dared the most romantic journey that has ever challenged the imagination!'
City under the Sea
GB 1965 84m Eastmancolor Colorscope
Bruton/AIP (Daniel Haller)
US title: *War Gods of the Deep*
An American heiress in Cornwall meets Victorian smugglers who have lived a hundred years under the sea in Lyonesse.
Childlike, unpersuasive nonsense which wastes some good talent.
w Charles Bennett, Louis M. Heyward *d* Jacques Tourneur *ph* Stephen Dade *m* Stanley Black
☆ Vincent Price, David Tomlinson, Susan Hart, Tab Hunter, Henry Oscar, John Le Mesurier

City War
Hong Kong 1988 93m colour
Cinema City (Catherine Lau)
A drug dealer who gets out of jail after serving a 10-year sentence vows to kill the bad-tempered cop who put him away.
Violent, efficient thriller that also charts changes in the local landscape, with cops playing by the rules, or suffering the consequences, and gangsters going legitimate.
w Tung Lo, Leung Wai Ting, Chung Kai-Cheong *d* Sun Chung *ph* Li Hsin Yeh *m* Michael Lai *ad* Jason Mok, Eric Lam *ed* Wong Ming Lam
☆ Chow Yun-Fat, Ti Lung, Tien Niu, Chui Siu Kwung, Mary Hon, Michael Chow, Teresa Carpio

A City's Child
Australia 1971 80m Eastmancolor
Pleasant Pastures/Brian Kavanagh
A reclusive woman, who becomes obsessed with dolls after her mother's death, takes as a lover a young man who may not exist.
A daft excursion into experimental cinema which fails to hold the attention.
w Don Battye *story* Brian Kavanagh *d* Brian Kavanagh *ph* Bruce McNaughton *m* Peter Pinne *ad* Trevor Ling *ed* Brian Kavanagh
☆ Monica Maughan, Sean Scully, Moira Carleton, Vivean Gray, Marguerite Lofthouse

The City's Edge
Australia 1985 86m colour
Eastcaps (Pom Oliver, Errol Sullivan)
A troubled man takes a room in a Bondi boarding house and finds others worse off than himself.
Dreary mini-dramas, somewhat arbitrarily linked and without a shred of hope in sight for anybody.
w Robert J. Merritt, Ken Quinnell *novel* W. A. Harbinson *d* Ken Quinnell
☆ Hugo Weaving, Tommy Lewis, Shirley Cameron, Mark Lee, Ralph Cotterill

La Ciudad Y Los Perros: see *The City And The Dogs*

A Civil Action **
US 1998 112m DeLuxe
Buena Vista/Paramount/Touchstone (Scott Rudin, Robert Redford, Rachel Pfeffer)
A successful lawyer runs into difficulties when he sets out to prove that the dumping of toxic waste by a chemical company has caused the death of several children.
Engrossing, muted drama, taken from a true story, that is as much concerned with the cost of the awakening of an individual's social conscience as the case itself.
wd Steven Zaillian *book* Jonathan Harr *ph* Conrad L. Hall *m* Danny Elfman *pd* David Gropman *ed* Wayne Wahrman
☆ John Travolta, Robert Duvall, Tony Shalhoub, William H. Macy, Zeljko Ivanbeck, Bruce Norris, John Lithgow, Kathleen Quinlan, Peter Jacobson, Sydney Pollack
'A solid and intelligent legal thriller that may be too complex in its issues, and too low-key and unexciting in its style, for today's market demands.' – *Emanuel Levy, Variety*
Robert Duvall; Conrad L. Hall

Civilization ***
US 1916 68m bw silent
Triangle
A mythical country starts war, but one of the principals has a vision of Christ on the battlefields and the king is persuaded to sign a peace treaty.
Surprisingly impressive parable showing this early director at his best; intended as a pacifist tract in the middle of World War I.
w C. Gardner Sullivan *d Thomas Ince ph* Irvin Willat
☆ Enid Markey, Howard Hickman, J. Barney Sherry

'Everything has a price.'
The Claim *
GB/Canada 2000 120m DeLuxe
Revolution, Pathe, Arts Council, Canal+, BBC, Alliance Atlantis (Andrew Eaton)
The owner of a mining town in the Sierra Nevada finds his past has come back to haunt him, in the persons of his abandoned wife and child.
The snow-covered mountains and isolated community form an ideal backdrop for a chill family drama based on Thomas Hardy's The Mayor of Casterbridge; it lacks the moral dimension of Hardy's tale, settling for a more familiar Western story of a rubber baron undone by progress.
w Frank Cottrell Boyce *inspired by The Mayor of Casterbridge* by Thomas Hardy *d* Michael Winterbottom *ph* Alwin Kuchler *m* Michael Nyman *pd* Mark Tildesley, Ken Rempel *ed* Trevor Waite
☆ Peter Mullan (Dillon), Wes Bentley (Dalglish), Milla Jovovich (Lucia), Nastassja Kinski (Elena), Sarah Polley (Hope), Julian Richings (Bellinger), Sean McGinley (Sweetley)
'Boasts the physical scale and formal beauty of an epic Western, but it suffers from a slim and fractured narrative, unengaging mode of storytelling and yet another irritating performance from Milla Jovovich.' – *Emanuel Levy, Variety*
'The movie unfolds like a slow-motion dream of an endless long-ago winter illuminated with fiery portents of doom.' – *Stephen Holden, New York Times*

Claire Dolan *
France/US 1998 95m DuArt
ICA/MK2/Serene (Ann Ruark)
An introverted Irish prostitute in New York tries to start a new life.
A claustrophobic film about repressed emotions; its lack of overt passion and its restrained approach will deter many, but there are rewards for those who persevere with its enigmatic style.
wd Lodge Kerrigan *ph* Teodoro Maniaci *m* Ahrin Mishan, Simon Fisher Turner *pd* Sharon Lomofsky *ed* Kristina Boden
☆ Katrin Cartlidge (Claire Dolan), Vincent D'Onofrio (Elton Garrett), Colm Meaney (Roland Cain), John Doman (Cain's friend), Maryanne Plunkett (Mary Egan), Miranda Stuart-Rhyne (Angela), Kate Skinner (Madeline Garrett), David Little (Man in Chicago Cafe), Lola Pashalinski (Salon Client), Jim Frangione (Man in Bar), Ed Hodson (Driver)
'Of possible appeal only to the most intellectual critics and viewers, some of whom will be very taken with the film's cinematic discipline, this will fall in the watching-paint-dry category even for specialized audiences.' – *Todd McCarthy, Variety*

Claire of the Moon
US 1992 107m Foto-Kem
Demi-Monde (Pamela S. Kuri)
At a women writers' retreat, an untidy, promiscuous heterosexual novelist finds herself sharing an apartment with an introverted lesbian sexual behaviourist.
Humourless, slow-moving romance, given over to psycho-babble and caricature.
wd Nicole Conn *ph* Randolph Sellars *m* Michael Allen Harrison *ed* Michael Solinger
☆ Trisha Todd, Karen Trumbo, Faith McDevitt, Caren Graham, Sheila Dickinson
'A talky drama that plays like a lesbian version of *The Odd Couple*.' – *Variety*

Claire's Knee ***
France 1970 106m Eastmancolor
Gala/Les Films du Losange (Pierre Cottrell)
original title: *Genou de Claire*
A 35-year-old diplomat who is about to be married confides to a female friend that he is attracted to a 16-year-old girl and her 17-year-old half-sister.
Witty and perceptive conversation piece, probably the best of Rohmer's explorations of the ambiguities of love and desire.
wd Eric Rohmer ph Nestor Almendros ed Cécile Decugis
☆ Jean-Claude Brialy, Aurora Cornu, Béatrice Romand, Laurence de Monaghan, Michèle Montel, Gérard Falconetti, Fabrice Luchini
'Rohmer's quiet, complacent movie-novel game is pleasing.' – *Pauline Kael, New Yorker*

'Hexed By The Evil Eye. Ruled By A Female Svengali.'
The Clairvoyant *
GB 1934 80m bw
Gainsborough (Michael Balcon)
A fraudulent mindreader predicts a disaster which comes true.
Effective minor suspenser on predictable but enjoyable lines.
w Charles Bennett, Bryan Edgar Wallace, Robert Edmunds *novel* Ernst Lothar *d* Maurice Elvey *ph* Glen MacWilliams *ad* Alfred Junge
☆ Claude Rains, Fay Wray, Jane Baxter, Mary Clare, Athole Stewart, Ben Field, Felix Aylmer, Donald Calthrop

Clambake
US 1967 98m Technicolor Techniscope
UA/Rhodes (Laven-Gardner-Levy)
The son of an oil millionaire sets out to see life.
Painless, forgettable star vehicle.
w Arthur Browne Jnr *d* Arthur H. Nadel *ph* William Margulies *m* Jeff Alexander
☆ Elvis Presley, Shelley Fabares, Bill Bixby, James Gregory, Will Hutchins, Gary Merrill

Clan of the Cave Bear
US 1985 98m Technicolor Technovision
Warner/PSO/Guber-Peters/Jozak-Decade/Jonesfilm (Gerald I. Isenberg)
In Neanderthal days, a blonde outcast girl is adopted by a swarthy tribe who think her ugly.
Comic-strip prehistory: better revive One Million BC *or even the 1912 Griffith epic* Man's Genesis.
w John Sayles *novel* Jean M. Auel *d* Michael Chapman *ph* Jan de Bont *m* Alan Silvestri *pd* Anthony Masters
☆ Daryl Hannah, Pamela Reed, James Remar, Thomas G. Waites
make-up (Michael G. Westmore, Michele Burke)

Clancy Street Boys
US 1943 66m bw
Pathé/Monogram/Banner (Sam Katzman, Jack Dietz)
Muggs has to produce five brothers and a sister when a rich relation comes to call.
Ponderous comic outing for the East Side Kids, though it comes briefly to life when Huntz Hall pretends to be a girl.
w Harvey Gates *d* William Beaudine *ph* Mack Stengler *md* Edward Kay *ad* Dave Milton *ed* Carl Pierson
☆ Leo Gorcey, Huntz Hall, Bobby Jordan, Noah Beery, Lita Ward, Bennie Bartlett, Rick Vallin, Billy Benedict

'For Better...Or For Worse'
The Clandestine Marriage
GB 1999 90m Technicolor
UIP/Portman/BBC/British Screen/Milesian (Steve Clark-Hill, Rod Gunner, Johnathan B. Stables)
A nouveau riche, social-climbing landowner attempts to wed his daughter to a penniless aristocrat, unaware that she is already married.
Undistinguished period romp, with the emphasis on farce and notable for its clashing acting styles.
w Trevor Bentham *play* George Coleman the Elder, David Garrick *d* Christopher Miles *ph* Denis Crossan *m* Stanislas Syrewicz *pd* Martin Childs *ed* George Akers *cos* Deirdre Clancy
☆ Nigel Hawthorne (Lord Ogleby), Joan Collins (Mrs Heidelberg), Timothy Spall (Sterling), Tom Hollander (Sir John Ogleby), Paul Nicholls (Richard Lovewell), Natasha Little (Fanny), Emma Chambers (Betsy), Cyril Shaps (Canton)
'A likable and generally well-played costume comedy.' – *Derek Elley, Variety*

Clarence the Cross-Eyed Lion
US 1965 98m Metrocolor
MGM (Leonard Kaufman)
Adventures of animal farmers in Africa.
Amiable theatrical 'pilot' for the Daktari *TV series.*
w Alan Caillou, Marshall Thompson, Art Arthur *d* Andrew Marton *ph* Lamar Boren
☆ Marshall Thompson, Betsy Drake, Richard Haydn, Cheryl Miller

'Livin' in my house! Lovin' another man! Is that what you call honest? That's just givin' it a nice name!'
Clash by Night *
US 1952 105m bw
RKO (Harriet Parsons) (A Wald-Krasna Production)
In a northern fishing village, jealousy and near-tragedy are occasioned by the return home of a hardened girl from the big city.
Absurdly overblown melodrama of the Anna Christie school, burdened with significance and doggedly acted by a remarkable cast.
w Alfred Hayes *play* Clifford Odets *d* Fritz Lang *ph* Nicholas Musuraca *m* Roy Webb
☆ Barbara Stanwyck, Paul Douglas, Robert Ryan, Marilyn Monroe, J. Carrol Naish, Keith Andes
'When Stanwyck snarls into a pub and belts down a straight shot, we think we're watching a remake of *Anna Christie*; when she is shyly and ineptly courted by Douglas we think it's a remake of *Min and Bill*; a sub-plot involving Monroe and Andes plays like *Gidget Faces an Identity Crisis*.' – *Kit Parker catalogue*

Clash of the Titans
GB 1981 118m Metrocolor Dynarama
MGM/Charles H. Schneer, Ray Harryhausen
Perseus sets out to win Andromeda despite the impossible obstacles set for him by Thetis, which include a number of mythical monsters.
Star-packed but feebly imagined mythological spectacular, further hampered by gloomy photography which is presumably required to offset the jerkiness of the monsters. A very few moments provide the right kind of elation.
w Beverley Cross *d* Desmond Davis *ph* Ted Moore *m* Laurence Rosenthal *pd* Frank White *sp* Ray Harryhausen
☆ Laurence Olivier, Claire Bloom, Maggie Smith, Ursula Andress, Jack Gwillim, Harry Hamlin, Judi Bowker, Burgess Meredith, Siân Phillips, Flora Robson, Freda Jackson, Donald Houston
'There's a real possibility some audiences will be turned to stone before Medusa even appears.' – *Geoff Brown, MFB*
'Unspeakable dialogue, muddy photography and a motley, lacklustre cast.' – *Sight and Sound*

'The good news is, Jonathan's having his first affair. The bad news is, she's his roommate's mother!'
Class
US 1983 98m Astrocolor
Orion/Martin Ransohoff
A shy student has an affair with an older woman who turns out to be his best friend's mother.

Ghastly travesty of The Graduate *which aspires to every kind of sophistication it can think of but ends nowhere.*
w Jim Kouf, David Greenwalt *d* Lewis John Carlino *ph* Ric Waite *m* Elmer Bernstein *ad* Jack Poplin
☆ Jacqueline Bisset, Cliff Robertson, Rob Lowe, Andrew McCarthy, Stuart Margolin, John Cusack

'It is not often that one comes across a film of such muddled aspirations and widely divergent achievements.' – *Nick Roddick, MFB*

Class Act
US 1992 98m Technicolor
Warner/Wizan Black/Gordy de Passe (Todd Black, Maynell Thomas)
Two high-school students – one an intellectual, the other a delinquent – swop identities.
Dim-witted teen comedy.
w John Semper, Cynthia Friedlob *story* Michael Swerdlick, Wayne Rice, Richard Brenne *d* Randall Miller *ph* Francis Kenny *m* Vassal Benford *pd* David L. Snyder *ed* John F. Burnett
☆ Christopher Reid, Christopher Martin, Karyn Parsons, Alysia Rogers, Meshach Taylor, Doug E. Doug, Lamont Johnson

'Nothing Personal. It's Just Father vs Daughter in The Fight Of Their Lives.'
Class Action
US 1990 109m colour
TCF/Interscope (Ted Field, Scott Kroopf, Robert W. Cort)
A father and a daughter, both lawyers, find themselves on opposing sides in the courtroom.
Moderately engrossing, though predictable, drama.
w Carolyn Shelby, Christopher Ames, Samantha Shad *d* Michael Apted *ph* Conrad L. Hall *m* James Horner *pd* Todd Hallowell *ed* Ian Crafford
☆ Gene Hackman, Mary Elizabeth Mastrantonio, Colin Friels, Joanna Merlin, Larry Fishburne, Donald Moffat, Jan Rubes, Matt Clark

'A remarkably well-made and well-mannered film.' – *Sight and Sound*

'Pic's parameters may be worn, but Apted's keen focus on its emotional core helps it transcend the everyday.' – *Variety*

'It's 1999. School is a warzone. The latest in automatic weapons are the teachers.'
Class of 1999
US 1989 93m colour
Original Pictures (Mark L. Lester)
Three android teachers, hired to bring discipline to a lawless high school, go haywire.
A sort of robot Blackboard Jungle, *aimed at teenage audiences in love with violence.*
w C. Courtney Joyner *story* Mark L. Lester *d* Mark L. Lester *ph* Mark Irwin *m* Michael Hoenig *pd* Steven Legler *ed* Scott Conrad
☆ Bradley Gregg, Traci Lin, John P. Ryan, Pam Grier, Patrick Kilpatrick, Joshua Miller, Stacy Keach, Malcolm McDowell

Class of '44
US 1973 95m Technicolor Panavision
Warner (Paul Bogart)
Sex problems of college students during World War II.
Thin sequel to Summer of '42, *nostalgic to Americans over forty but not much of a trip for anyone else.*
w Herman Raucher *d* Paul Bogart *ph* Andrew Laszlo *m* David Shire
☆ Gary Grimes, Jerry Houser, Oliver Conant, William Atherton, Sam Bottoms, Deborah Winters

Class of 84
Canada 1981 98m colour
Columbia/Guerrilla (Arthur Kent)
A new teacher finds his students involved in drug and vice rackets.
The Blackboard Jungle *goes several steps further, to general indifference.*
w Mark Lester, John Saxton, Tom Holland *d* Mark Lester *ph* Albert Dunk *m* Lalo Schifrin *ad* no credit
☆ Perry King, Merrie Lynn Ross, Timothy Van Patten, Roddy McDowall

The Class of Miss McMichael
GB 1978 90m colour
Brut/Kettledrum (Judd Bernard)
A dedicated schoolmistress has no chance against her slum surroundings.
The Blackboard Jungle *lives on, very boringly.*
w Judd Bernard *novel* Sandy Hutson *d* Silvio Narizzano *ph* Alex Thomson *m* Stanley Myers
☆ Glenda Jackson, Oliver Reed, John Standing, Michael Murphy, Rosalind Cash

'Poorly mannered, simple minded, badly disciplined ... gives social science a bad name.' – *Variety*

Class of Nuke 'Em High
US 1986 92m colour
Troma/TNT (Lloyd Kaufman, Michael Hertz)
After nuclear waste contaminates the water supply, students who don't turn nasty are terrorized by a monster.
Cheap, over-the-top horror movie that makes fun of its lack of pretension.
w Richard W. Haines, Mark Rudnitsky, Lloyd Kaufman, Stuart Strutin *d* Richard W. Haines, Lloyd Kaufman *ph* Michael Mayers *m* Michael Lattanzi, Biohazard *ad* Art Skopinsky, Arthur Lorenz *ed* Richard Haines
☆ Janelle Brady, Gilbert Brenton, Robert Prichard, R. L. Ryan, James Nugent Vernon, Brad Dunker, Gary Schneider
† It was followed by two sequels, *Class of Nuke 'Em High 2: Subhumanoid Meltdown*, and *Class of Nuke 'Em High 3: The Good, the Bad and the Subhumanoid.*

Class Trip *
France 1998 96m colour
Warner/Films de La Boissiere/PECF/France3/Rhone-Alpes (Annie Miller)
original title: *La Classe de Neige*
The shy son of over-protective parents goes on a school skiiing holiday, where he indulges in dreams of death and destruction.
A chill little psychological thriller, designed to make the flesh creep; it hints at more than it delivers.
w Emmanuel Carrere, Claude Miller *novel* Emmanuel Carrere *d* Claude Miller *ph* Guillaume Schiffman *m* Henri Texier *pd* Jean-Pierre Kohut-Svelko *ed* Anne Lafarge *cos* Jacqueline and Catherine Bouchard
☆ Clement Van Den Bergh (Nicolas), Lokman Nalcakan (Hodkann), François Roy (The Father), Yves Verhoeven (Patrick), Emmanuelle Bercot (Mlle Grimm), Tina Sportolaro (The Mother), Chantal Banlier (Marie Ange), Benoit Herlin (Ribotton), Julien Le Mouel (Lucas)

'It sure says a lot of uncomfortable things about the tragedies that families sometimes wish upon themselves.' – *Alexander Walker*

La Classe de Neige: see *Class Trip*

Claudelle Inglish
US 1961 99m bw
Warner (Leonard Freeman)
GB title: *Young and Eager*
A poor farmer's daughter scorns a wealthy man for a succession of young studs.
Would-be sensational novelette from the author of Tobacco Road; *it does not begin to be interesting.*
w Leonard Freeman *novel* Erskine Caldwell *d* Gordon Douglas *ph* Ralph Woolsey *m* Howard Jackson
☆ Diane McBain, Arthur Kennedy, Constance Ford, Chad Everett, Claude Akins, Will Hutchins, Robert Colbert, Ford Rainey, James Bell

'My agent told me that the movie of my novel *Claudelle Inglish* was so poor that I shouldn't even bother to see it. So I didn't.' – *Erskine Caldwell*

Claudia **
US 1943 92m bw
TCF (William Perlberg)
A middle-class husband helps his child-wife to mature.
Typical of the best of Hollywood's 'woman's pictures' of the period, this is a pleasant domestic comedy-drama featuring recognizably human characters in an agreeable setting.
w Morrie Ryskind *novel and play* Rose Franken *d* Edmund Goulding *ph* Leon Shamroy *m* Alfred Newman
☆ *Dorothy McGuire, Robert Young, Ina Claire*, Reginald Gardiner, Olga Baclanova, Jean Howard, Elsa Janssen

'It won't leave a dry eye in the house.' – *Variety*
† Cary Grant was sought for the Robert Young part.

Claudia and David *
US 1946 78m bw
TCF (William Perlberg)
Claudia and her husband survive assorted crises including their son's illness and David's involvement in a car crash.
Patchwork sequel to Claudia, *quite pleasant but obviously contrived quickly from scraps.*
w Rose Franken, William Brown Meloney *d* Walter Lang *ph* Joseph LaShelle *m* Cyril Mockridge
☆ Dorothy McGuire, Robert Young, Mary Astor, John Sutton, Gail Patrick, Florence Bates

Claudine
US 1974 92m DeLuxe
Fox-Rank/Third World Cinema/Joyce Selznick, Tina Pine (Hannah Weinstein)
A garbage collector falls for a poor woman with six kids.
Sugar-coated account, with romantic overtones, of life at the bottom in New York.
w Tina and Lester Pine *d* John Berry *ph* Gayne Rescher *m* Curtis Mayfield *pd* Ted Haworth *ed* Luis San Andres
☆ Diahann Carroll, James Earl Jones, Lawrence Hilton-Jacobs, Tamu, David Kruger, Yvette Curtis, Eric Jones

'Substitute white actors for the black cast, tone down the fashionably outspoken situations a little, and it would be just like one of those perennial Disney movies about happy families and the difficulty of living and loving in this problematic world.' – *Tom Milne, MFB*

Diahann Carroll

Claws
US 1977 100m colour
Alaska Pictures (Chuck D. Keen)
A grizzly bear, wounded by hunters, turns maneater and begins to kill the inhabitants of a small Alaskan town.
Cheap and unimaginative Jaws *rip-off, displaying no creativity whatsoever, though the landscape is impressive.*
w Chuck D. Keen, Brian Russell *d* Richard Bansbach, Robert E. Pierson *ph* Chuck D. Keen *m* Gene Kaver, Douglas Lackey *ed* Richard Bansbach
☆ Jason Evers, Leon Ames, Anthony Caruso, Carla Layton, Glenn Sipes, Buck Young, Myron Healey

'Lester Long Never Forgets A Friend.'
Clay Pigeons
US 1998 104m colour
Gramercy/Scott Free (Ridley Scott, Chris Zarpas)
An affable, adulterous but guileless gas station attendant is suspected of being a serial killer.
A blackish comedy of escalating disaster that rarely strikes the requisite heartless tone; a little more wit might have helped.
w Matt Healy *d* David Dobkin *ph* Eric Edwards *m* John Lurie *pd* Clark Hunter *ed* Stan Salfas
☆ Vince Vaughn, Joaquin Pheonix, Janeane Garofalo, Georgina Cates, Scott Wilson, Phil Morris, Vince Vieluf, Nikki Arlyn

'Pic's air of jaunty (albeit somewhat flat) humor, plus its lack of genuine tension or character empathy, renders the serial-sadist aspect slightly distasteful, even irresponsible.' – *Dennis Harvey, Variety*

Clean and Sober **
US 1988 124m Technicolor
Warner/Imagine Entertainment (Tony Ganz, Deborah Blum)
An embezzler hides out in a rehabilitation clinic, refusing to admit to himself that he is an alcoholic and cocaine addict.
Unrelenting and powerful drama.
w Tod Carroll *d* Glenn Gordon Caron *ph* Jan Kiesser *m* Gabriel Yared *pd* Joel Schiller *ed* Richard Chew
☆ *Michael Keaton*, Kathy Baker, Morgan Freeman, Tate Donovan, Henry Judd Baker, Claudia Christian, M. Emmet Walsh, Luca Bercovici

'I only wish there were some honest way of describing this movie that would make everyone go and see it.' – *Philip French, Observer*

Clean, Shaven **
US 1993 77m DuArt
ICA/DSM III (Lodge Kerrigan)
A schizophrenic man goes looking for his daughter in Canada while being chased by a detective who believes he murdered a young girl.
A brilliant, but downbeat and difficult to watch, evocation of a shattered mind, full of pain and aggression and shot in a dislocated style.
wd Lodge Kerrigan *ph* Teodoro Maniaci *m* Hahn Rowe *pd* Tania Ferrier *ed* Jay Rabinowitz
☆ Peter Greene, Robert Albert, Megan Owen, Molly Castelloe, Jennifer MacDonald, Alice Levitt

'An almost unbearably intense, exceedingly concentrated study of schizophrenia by a clearly talented new filmmaker. Using a fragmented narrative and some avant-garde techniques, pic is so unsettling that many viewers won't be able to tolerate it.' – *Todd McCarthy, Variety*
† The film was made over a period of two years.

Clean Slate: see *Coup de Torchon (1981)*

Clean Slate
US 1994 107m DeLuxe
MGM (Richard D. Zanuck, Lili Fini Zanuck)
A private detective forgets everything whenever he falls asleep.
A shaggy dog comedy in which all the laughs are stolen by a one-eyed Jack Russell terrier; it is a pity he couldn't have been persuaded to write the script.
w Robert King *d* Mick Jackson *ph* Andrew Dunn *m* Alan Silvestri *pd* Norman Reynolds *ed* Priscilla Nedd-Friendly
☆ Dana Carvey, Valeria Golino, James Earl Jones, Kevin Pollak, Michael Gambon, Michael Murphy

'This convoluted comedy feels like a pale follow-up to *Groundhog Day*.' – *Variety*

'Truth needs a soldier.'
Clear and Present Danger *
US 1994 141m DeLuxe Panavision
Paramount (Mace Neufeld, Robert Rehme)
A leading CIA agent investigating the Colombian drug trade discovers that its corruption reaches the highest level of American government.
Fast-moving thriller of betrayal and the abuse of power, simple-minded but effective entertainment.
w Donald Stewart, Steven Zaillian, John Milius *novel* Tom Clancy *d* Phillip Noyce *ph* Donald McAlpine *m* James Horner *pd* Terence Marsh *ed* Neil Travis
☆ Harrison Ford, Willem Dafoe, Anne Archer, Henry Czerny, Joaquim de Almeida, Harris Yulin, Donald Moffat, Miguel Sandoval, James Earl Jones

'Long, uneven and sometimes downright tedious.' – *Screen International*

'The filmmakers haven't simply tamed the rogue elephant of Clancy's narrative; they've turned it into something that moves as gracefully and powerfully as a gazelle.' – *Terrence Rafferty, New Yorker*

sound; sound effects editing

Clearcut
Canada 1991 98m colour Panavision
Northern Arts/Cinexus (Stephen J. Roth, Ian McDougal)
After losing a court battle to save Native American lands from a logging company, an idealistic lawyer witnesses the kidnapping of the sawmill's manager by an enigmatic Native American who believes in primitive vengeance.
A flawed film that abandons thoughtfulness in favour of brutal action; it is almost worth watching for Greene's performance as a nightmare figure beyond the reach of reason.
w Rob Forsyth *novel A Dream Like Mine* by M. T. Kelly *d* Richard Bugajski *ph* François Protat *m* Shane Harvey *pd* Perri Gorrara *ed* Michael Rea
☆ Ron Lea, Graham Greene, Michael Hogan, Rebecca Jenkins, Floyd Red Crow Westerman

'Despite its surface blandness, and though it wobbles precariously on the brink of oversimplification, it's as radical in its message as any picture you're likely to see.' – *Hal Hinson, Washington Post*

Cleo from 5 to 7 *
France/Italy 1961 90m bw/colour
Rome/Paris (Bruno Drigo)
original title: *Cleo de 5 à 7*
A girl waiting for the result of a medical examination wanders around Paris thinking she has cancer.
Impressively handled character sketch with gratifying attention to detail.
wd Agnès Varda *ph* Jean Rabier *m* Michel Legrand
☆ Corinne Marchand, Antoine Bourseiller, Dorothée Blanck, Michel Legrand

'The love affair that shook the world!'
Cleopatra **
US 1934 101m bw
Paramount/Cecil B. de Mille
After Julius Caesar's death, Cleopatra turns her attention to Mark Antony.
More of the vices than the virtues of its producer are notable in this fustian epic, which is almost but not quite unwatchable because of its stolid pace and miscasting. Some of the action montages and the barge scene, however, are superb cinema.
w Waldemar Young, Vincent Lawrence *d* Cecil B. de Mille *ph* Victor Milner *m* Rudolph Kopp *ed* Anne Bauchens
☆ Claudette Colbert (Cleopatra), Henry Wilcoxon (Antony), Warren William (Caesar), Gertrude Michael (Calpurnia), Joseph Schildkraut (Herod), Ian Keith (Octavian), C. Aubrey Smith (Enobarbus), Leonard Mudie (Pothinos), Irving Pichel (Brutus), Arthur Hohl, Ian MacLaren

'He has certainly made the most sumptuous of Roman circuses out of Roman history ... a constant succession of banquets, dancers, triumphs, and a fleet set on fire.' – *The Times*

'Gorgeous optically but mentally weak ... a handpicked audience was polite but not over-enthusiastic.' – *Variety*

'A great cinematic achievement, a spectacle of breathtaking brilliance.' – *Daily Express*

'It is remarkable how Cecil B. de Mille can photograph so much on such a vast scale and still say nothing ... it reeks of so much pseudo-artistry, vulgarity, philistinism, sadism, that it can only be compared with the lowest form of contemporary culture: Hitlerism. This is the type of "culture" that will be fed to the audience of Fascist America.' – *Irving Lerner, 1968*

Academy Award: Victor Milner
Academy Award nomination: best picture; Anne Bauchens

'The motion picture the world has been waiting for!'
Cleopatra
US 1963 243m DeLuxe Todd-AO
TCF (Walter Wanger)
The unsurprising story is told at inordinate length and dullness in this ill-starred epic, one of the most heralded, and mismanaged, in film history. (Its story is best told in the producer's *My Life with Cleopatra*.)
The most expensive film made up to that date, for various reasons which do not appear on the screen.
w Joseph L. Mankiewicz, Ranald MacDougall, Sidney Buchman, and others *d* Joseph L. Mankiewicz (and others) *ph* Leon Shamroy *m* Alex North *ad* John DeCuir, Jack Martin Smith, and others
☆ Elizabeth Taylor (Cleopatra), Richard Burton (Mark Anthony), Rex Harrison (Julius Caesar), Pamela Brown (High Priestess), George Cole (Flavius), Hume Cronyn (Sosigenes), Cesare Danova (Apollodorus), Kenneth Haigh (Brutus), Andrew Keir (Agrippa), Martin Landau (Rufio), Roddy McDowall, Robert Stephens, Francesca Annis, Martin Benson, Herbert Berghof and also Grégoire Aslan, Richard O'Sullivan

'Whatever was interesting about it clearly ended up somewhere else: on the cutting room floor, in various hotel rooms, in the newspaper columns ... it lacks not only the intelligent spectacle of *Lawrence of Arabia* but the spectacular unintelligence of a Cecil B. de Mille product...' – *John Simon*

'The small screen does more than justice to this monumental mouse.' – *Judith Crist*

'I only came to see the asp.' – *Charles Addams*

'Surely the most bizarre piece of entertainment ever to be perpetrated.' – *Elizabeth Taylor*

† Archivists are attempting to restore a six-hour 'director's cut' of the film. After its opening, it was also shown in versions running for 227m and 192m.

Academy Award: Leon Shamroy; John DeCuir and others; costumes (Irene Sharaff, Vittorio Nino Novarese, Renie); special visual effects (Emil Kosa Jnr)
Academy Award nomination: best picture; Alex North; Rex Harrison

Cleopatra Jones
US 1973 89m Technicolor Panavision
Warner
A black female CIA agent eliminates a ring of dope peddlers.
Grotesque comic strip fantasy with a high mortality rate.
w Max Julien, Sheldon Keller *d* Jack Starrett
☆ Tamara Dobson, Shelley Winters, Bernie Casey, Brenda Sykes

'It hampers the cause of racial entente more effectively than any work since *Uncle Tom's Cabin*.' – *John Baxter, MFB*

Cleopatra Jones and the Casino of Gold
US/Hong Kong 1975 96m Technicolor Panavision
Warner/Shaw Bros (William Tennant, Run Run Shaw)
A tough female government agent goes to Hong Kong to smash a drugs ring.
Feeble sequel lacking the brashness of the original, but equally tasteless.
w William Tennant *d* Chuck Bail *ph* Alan Hume *m* Dominic Frontiere *ad* Johnson Tsao *ed* Willy Kemplen
☆ Tamara Dobson, Stella Stevens, Tanny, Norman Fell, Albert Popwell

'The film is cut together quite incoherently, and Chuck Bail's barely competent direction seizes up completely when called upon now and then for some large-scale action set-piece.' – *Verina Glaessner, MFB*

Clerks **
US 1994 103m bw
Artificial Eye/View Askew (Kevin Smith, Scott Mosier)
An unhappy clerk is forced to work in a grocery store on his day off, which turns out to be full of mishaps and laconic conversations with his friend, who runs the low-class neighbourhood video shop.
Witty, episodic, foul-mouthed account of the slacker generation doing what it does best: nothing in particular; it is often inventive, making the most of its low-budget restrictions, if too determinedly quirky.
wd Kevin Smith *ph* David Klein *m* Scott Angley *ed* Scott Mosier, Kevin Smith
☆ Brian O'Halloran, Jeff Anderson, Marilyn Ghigliotti, Lisa Spoonauer, Jason Mewes, Kevin Smith

'A randy, irreverent, slice-of-life no-budgeter that's played for laughs and gets them.' – *Todd McCarthy, Variety*

† The film was shot on 16mm for $27,000.

'A district attorney out for a conviction. A new lawyer out of her league. A young boy who knew too much.'
The Client *
US 1994 121m Technicolor Panavision
Warner/Regency/Alcor (Arnon Milchan, Steven Reuther)
A female lawyer is hired to protect an 11-year-old boy, being chased by the Mafia and hounded by the FBI because he knows where the body of a murder victim is buried.
Slick and enjoyable thriller that lacks subtlety but maintains a high level of tension.
w Akiva Goldsman, Robert Getchell *novel* John Grisham *d* Joel Schumacher *ph* Tony Pierce-Roberts *m* Howard Shore *pd* Bruno Rubeo *ed* Robert Brown
☆ *Susan Sarandon*, Tommy Lee Jones, Mary-Louise Parker, Anthony LaPaglia, J. T. Walsh, Anthony Edwards, Brad Renfro, Will Patton, Ossie Davis

'Safe-as-houses entertainment, directed with no particular finesse, but it's refreshingly straightforward and unpretentious.' – *Terrence Rafferty, New Yorker*

Academy Award nomination: Susan Sarandon
BAFTA: Susan Sarandon

'Hang on.'
Cliffhanger *
US 1993 112m Technicolor Panavision
Carolco/Canal/Pioneer/RCS Video (Alan Marshall, Renny Harlin)
A mountain rescue expert turns the tables on violent gangsters who crash in the Rocky Mountains with suitcases stuffed with money.
Enjoyably silly action adventure, with some spectacular, edgy stunts, although it never touches reality at any point and has one of the more ludicrous lip-smacking villains this side of melodrama.
w Michael France, Sylvester Stallone *story* Michael France *based on a premise by* John Long *d* Renny Harlin *ph* Alex Thomson *m* Trevor Jones *pd* John Vallone *ed* Frank J. Urioste *sp* Neil Krepela, John Richardson, John Bruno, Pamela Easley
☆ Sylvester Stallone, John Lithgow, Michael Rooker, Janine Turner, Rex Linn, Caroline Goodall, Leon, Craig Fairbrass, Gregory Scott Cummins, Paul Winfield, Ralph Waite

'Harlin displays perfect pitch, not just with the individual scenes of jaw-dropping stunt work, but in the way these episodes flow into each other with varying degrees of intensity.' – *Henry Sheehan, Sight and Sound*

'A two-hour roller-coaster ride that never stops from first minute to last. A high-octane action suspenser with thrilling vertiginous footage unlike anything seen before in a feature.' – *Variety*

Academy Award nomination: sound; sound effects editing; visual effects

A Climate for Killing
US 1991 103m Foto-Kem
Propaganda
aka: *A Row of Crows*
A new cop who goes by the book finds himself at odds with an old-style sheriff and in love with his daughter as they investigate the murder of a woman who apparently died 16 years earlier.
Competent but unexciting murder mystery.
wd J. S. Cardone *ph* Michael Cardone *m* Robert Folk
☆ John Beck, Steven Bauer, Mia Sara, Katharine Ross, John Diehl, Dedee Pfeiffer, Phil Brock, Tony Frank

'The screen's classic of suspense!'
The Climax *
US 1944 86m Technicolor
Universal (George Waggner)
A young opera singer is hypnotized by a mad doctor, who has kept his murdered mistress embalmed for ten years.
Gothic romantic melodrama invented to capitalize on the success – and the sets – of Phantom of the Opera. *Curiously endearing, with a good eye-rolling part for Karloff.*
w Curt Siodmak, Lynn Starling *play* Edward Cochran *d* George Waggner *ph* Hal Mohr, W. Howard Greene *m* Edward Ward *ad* John B. Goodman, Alexander Golitzen
☆ Boris Karloff, Susanna Foster, Gale Sondergaard, Turhan Bey, Thomas Gomez, Scotty Beckett

'All quite unalarming, which is a bit of a handicap.' – *New Yorker, 1978*

Academy Award nomination: art direction

Climbing High *
GB 1938 78m bw
Gaumont (Michael Balcon)
A rich man pretends to be a male model in order to win a girl.
Light-hearted romantic musical with interesting credits.
w Stephen Clarkson *story* Lesser Samuels, Marian Dix *d* Carol Reed *ph* Mutz Greenbaum (Max Greene) *ad* Alfred Junge *ed* Michael Gordon
☆ Jessie Matthews, Michael Redgrave, Noel Madison, Alastair Sim, Margaret Vyner, Mary Clare, Francis L. Sullivan

The Clinging Vine *
US 1926 71m (24 fps) bw silent
Cecil B. de Mille
The president's secretary is the real driving force of a paint company, but finds that love is more important than business.
Interesting silent predecessor of many career girl comedies of the thirties and forties.
w Jeannie Macpherson *d* Paul Sloane
☆ *Leatrice Joy*, Tom Moore, Toby Claude, Robert Edeson

'People are going to **** whether you like it or not – and this place is here to see that they enjoy it!'
The Clinic *
Australia 1982 92m colour
Film House/Generation Films (Bob Weis, Robert le Tet)
One day in the life of a clinic for venereal diseases.
Slightly dishevelled comedy-drama which will be generally remembered as a very naughty carry-on.
w Greg Millen *d* David Stevens
☆ Chris Haywood, Simon Burke, Gerda Nicolson, Rona McLeod, Suzanne Roylance

'Six words from a woman changed the map of Asia!'
Clive of India *
US 1934 90m bw
Twentieth Century (Darryl F. Zanuck, William Goetz, Raymond Griffith)
The life of the 18th-century empire builder, with special emphasis on his marriage.
A very tame and now faded epic, with more romance than adventure. The production relies more on stars than technique, but it works.
w W. P. Lipscomb, R. J. Minney *play* W. P. Lipscomb, R. J. Minney *d* Richard Boleslawski *ph* Peverell Marley *m* Alfred Newman
☆ Ronald Colman, Loretta Young, Colin Clive, Francis Lister, Montagu Love, Robert Greig, Leo G. Carroll, C. Aubrey Smith, Mischa Auer

'It may be spoken of as another of the best British pictures made in Hollywood ... Should be strong b.o.' – *Variety*

'Patriotic pageantry, undistorted by facts.' – *J. R. Parish*

Academy Award nomination: art direction

'The moment he fell in love was his moment of greatest danger!'
Cloak and Dagger *
US 1946 106m bw
United States Pictures (Milton Sperling)
A physics professor joins the secret service and is parachuted into Germany to interview a kidnapped scientist.
Supposedly authoritative espionage adventure which turned out dull and humourless; plot routine, direction absent-minded.
w Albert Maltz, Ring Lardner Jnr *d* Fritz Lang *ph* Sol Polito *m* Max Steiner
☆ Gary Cooper, Lilli Palmer, Robert Alda, Vladimir Sokoloff, J. Edward Bromberg, Ludwig Stossel, Helene Thimig, Marc Lawrence

'Just a B plot dressed up in A trimmings.' – *Newsweek*

Clochemerle
France 1948 93m bw
Cinéma Productions (Ralph Baum)
The progressive mayor of a French village erects a gentlemen's convenience in the main street and shocks the local reactionaries.
Most of the book's political satire was ironed out in this cheap and opportunist production which got a few easy laughs but failed to sustain itself.
w Gabriel Chevalier *novel* Gabriel Chevalier *d* Pierre Chénal *ph* Robert Le Fèbvre *m* Henri Sauguet
☆ Brochard, Maximilienne, Simone Michels, Jane Marken, Paul Demange, Felix Oudart, Saturnin Fabre

The Clock **
US 1945 90m bw
MGM (Arthur Freed)
GB title: *Under the Clock*
A girl meets a soldier at New York's Grand Central Station and marries him during his 24-hour leave.
Everyone now seems far too nice in this winsome romance full of comedy cameos and convincing New

York locations, but if you can relive the wartime mood it still works as a corrective to the Betty Grable glamour pieces.
w Robert Nathan, Joseph Schrank *story* Paul and Pauline Gallico *d* Vincente Minnelli *ph* George Folsey *m* George Bassman
☆ Judy Garland, Robert Walker, James Gleason, Lucille Gleason, Keenan Wynn, Marshall Thompson, Chester Clute

'Sweetly charming, if maybe too irresistible ... fortunately the director fills the edges with comic characters.' – *New Yorker, 1978*

'The emotion may have been honest, but the method was too rich for my eyes, and the writing as used on the screen too weak for my mind.' – *Stephen Longstreet*

'Strictly a romance ... safely told, disappointing and angering in the thought of the great film it might have been.' – *James Agee*

'Amazingly, it was all shot in the studio, using street sets and back projection; even the old Penn Station, where so much of the action takes place, is a set.' – *Pauline Kael, 70s*

Clockers **
US 1995 128m DeLuxe
UIP/Universal/40 Acres and a Mule (Martin Scorsese, Spike Lee, Jon Kilik)

After a drug pusher is shot, a Brooklyn detective suspects that the man who confesses to the crime is doing so to protect his younger brother who is a clocker, a small-time crack dealer working on the streets.
A harsh report from the urban front line, where drugs cause blacks to kill blacks and even those who reject that culture find themselves unable to escape it; it is a powerful and despairing film, but often tends to be more didactic than dramatic.
w Richard Price, Spike Lee *novel* Richard Price *d* Spike Lee *ph* Malik Hassan Sayeed *m* Terence Blanchard *pd* Andrew McAlpine *ed* Sam Pollard
☆ Harvey Keitel, John Turturro, Delroy Lindo, *Mekhi Phifer*, Isaiah Washington, Keith David, Pee Wee Love, Regina Taylor, Sticky Fingaz

'A kaleidoscopic vision of a community mired in betrayal, psychosis, and murder. The images are like something out of a nightmare newsreel, raw and grainy and pulsatingly alive.' – *Owen Gleiberman, Entertainment Weekly*

'Confirms Lee's position as the cinema's great surgeon-general, alternately taking the pulse of America and probing its open wounds. But it is still, in many ways, a bad film – so full of holes you can see right through it.' – *Tom Shone, Sunday Times*

† Originally, the film was to have been directed by Martin Scorsese. But he decided to make *Casino* instead, and Lee took over as director, rewriting the script to change its emphasis: in Price's novel, the protagonist is the Brooklyn detective played by Harvey Keitel.

'Freeze the future .'
Clockstoppers
US 2002 94m DeLuxe
Paramount/Nickelodeon/Valhalla (Gale Anne Hurd, Julia Pistor)

A teenager discovers a way to make time stand still.
When what it needed, when confronted by this dull concoction, is a way to make time move very much faster.
w Rob Hedden, J. David Stem, David N. Weiss *d* Jonathan Frakes *ph* Tim Suhrstedt *m* Jamshied Sharifi *pd* Marek Dobrowolski *ed* Peter E. Berger, Jeff W. Canavan
☆ Jesse Bradford (Zak), French Stewart (Dopler), Paula Garces (Francesca), Michael Biehn (Gates), Robin Thomas (Dad), Garikayi Mutambirwa (Meeker), Julia Sweeney (Mom), Lindze Letherman (Kelly)

'Blandly conceived youth adventure lacking zing or style.' – *Robert Koehler, Variety*

Clockwise *
GB 1986 97m Technicolor
EMI/Moment (Michael Codron)

A headmaster on his way to a conference is delayed by circumstance.
What was intended as an escalating climax of comic chaos falls away as the script runs out of steam, but the nation's need for comedy ensured box-office success.
w Michael Frayn *d* Christopher Morahan *ph* John Coquillon *m* George Fenton *pd* Roger Murray-Leach *ed* Peter Boyle
☆ John Cleese, Alison Steadman, Penelope Wilton, Stephen Moore, Joan Hickson, Charon Maiden

'Whichever way you point him, as soon as you let Conrad go ... He's off and over the edge.'
Clockwork Mice
GB 1995 99m colour
Feature Film/Metrodome

An idealistic young teacher attempts to encourage a young boy in cross-country running when he goes to work in a special school.
Confused and episodic drama that veers abruptly from actuality to fantasy before climaxing with an unconvincing finale and unlikely romance; quite what the point of it all is, is impossible to know.
w Rod Woodruff *d* Vadim Jean *ph* Gordon Hickie *m* John Murphy, David Hughes *pd* David Munns *ed* Liz Webber
☆ Ian Hart, *Ruaidhri Conroy*, Catherine Russell, Art Malik, John Alderton, Claire Skinner, James Bolam, Nigel Planer, Lilly Edwards, Frankie Bruno

'If you can keep your cynicism in check, this is that rarest of breeds, a stirring British movie with a mind of its own.' – *Empire*

'Being the adventures of a young man whose principal interests are rape, ultra-violence, and Beethoven!'
A Clockwork Orange *
GB 1971 136m colour
Warner/Polaris (Bernard Williams)

In a future Britain of desolation and violence, a young gangster guilty of rape and murder obtains a release from prison after being experimentally brainwashed: he finds society more violent than it was in his time.
A repulsive film in which intellectuals have found acres of social and political meaning; the average judgement is likely to remain that it is pretentious and nasty rubbish for sick minds who do not mind jazzed-up images and incoherent sound.
wd Stanley Kubrick *novel* Anthony Burgess *ph* John Alcott *m* Walter Carlos *pd* John Barry
☆ Malcolm McDowell, Michael Bates, Adrienne Corri, Patrick Magee, Warren Clarke

'Very early there are hints of triteness and insecurity, and before half an hour is over it begins to slip into tedium ... Inexplicably the script leaves out Burgess' reference to the title.' – *Stanley Kauffmann*

'It might be the work of a strict and exacting German professor who set out to make a porno violent sci-fi comedy.' – *New Yorker, 1980*

'Kubrick handles his medium with a confidence almost insolent. For the rest – the flashes of farce, the variations on distance and distortion and dream-imagery – he has given us the most audacious of horror-films. And the most inhuman.' – *Dilys Powell*

best picture; Stanley Kubrick (as writer and director)

'We are not alone...'
Close Encounters of the Third Kind *
US 1977 135m Metrocolor Panavision
Columbia/EMI (Julia and Michael Phillips)

A series of UFOs takes Indiana by surprise, and a workman is led by intuition and detection to the landing site which has been concealed from the public.
There's a lot of padding in this slender fantasy, which has less plot and much less suspense than It Came from Outer Space *which was made on a tiny budget in 1955; but the technical effects are masterly though their exposure is over-prolonged, and the benevolent mysticism filled a current requirement of popular taste, accounting for the enormous box-office success of a basically flawed film. Much of the dialogue is inaudible.*
wd Steven Spielberg *ph* Vilmos Zsigmond *m* John Williams *pd* Joe Alves *ed* Michael Kahn *sp* *Douglas Trumbull*
☆ Richard Dreyfuss, François Truffaut, Teri Garr, Melinda Dillon, Cary Guffey

'It somehow combines Disney and 1950s SF and junk food into the most persuasive (if arrested) version of the American dream yet.' – *Time Out*

'It has visionary magic and a childlike comic spirit, along with a love of surprises and a skeptical, let's-try-it-on spirit.' – *New Yorker*

† The cost of this film was estimated at 20,000,000 dollars

†† In 1980 a 'special edition' was released with some success: this pared down the idiotic middle section and extended the final scenes of the space ship, including some new interiors

††† This film used the largest set in film history: the inside of an old dirigible hangar. Of the special edition, Derek Malcolm in the *Guardian* wrote: 'One is inclined to feel that with all the money at his disposal, Spielberg might have got it right the first time.'

Vilmos Zsigmond

direction; John Williams; Melinda Dillon; visual effects (Douglas Trumbull and others)

Joe Alves

Close My Eyes
GB 1991 108m colour
Artificial Eye/Beambright/Film Four (Thérèse Pickard)

A long-separated brother and sister meet and fall in love.
Hysterical and dull, peopled by fashionable but inert characters given to boring introspection.
wd Stephen Poliakoff *ph* Witold Stok *m* Michael Gibbs *pd* Luciana Arrighi *ed* Michael Parkinson
☆ Alan Rickman, Saskia Reeves, Clive Owen, Karl Johnson, Lesley Sharp, Kate Gartside, Karen Knight, Niall Buggy

'Should have a solid career ahead of it and is a major plus for all concerned.' – *Variety*

'Drags itself across the screen. After much huffing and puffing, the script refuses to become the sum of its many, many scholarly observations about life, love, the universe. The lack of feeling is fatal.' – *John Lyttle, Independent*

A Close Shave **
GB 1995 30m colour
BBC/Aardman Animations (Carla Shelley, Michael Rose)

Wallace and Gromit defeat a sheep-rustling operation; in the process Wallace experiences the pangs of requited love and Gromit is accused of murder.
Enjoyable slapstick comedy of misapplied ingenuity, with nostalgic overtones, close in spirit to the British 'little man' comedies of the 50s with a few nods to more modern movies, such as The Terminator, *along the way.*
w Bob Baker, Nick Park *d* Nick Park *ph* David Alex Riddett *m* Julian Nott *ad* Phil Lewis *ed* Helen Garrard
☆ Featuring the voices of: Peter Sallis, Anne Reid

best animated short

Close to Eden: see *Urga (1991)*

Close to Eden
US 1992 111m colour
Rank/Propaganda/Sandollar/Isis (Steve Golin, Sigurjon Sighvatsson, Howard Rosenman)

aka: *A Stranger Among Us*
A female cop infiltrates the Hasidic community in New York to track down a murderer.
An odd and unconvincing thriller, ignoring the narrative for much of the time as it becomes almost a promotional film on behalf of the Hasidim.
w Robert J. Avrech *d* Sidney Lumet *ph* Andrzej Bartkowiak *m* Jerry Bock *pd* Philip Rosenberg *ed* Andrew Mondshein
☆ Melanie Griffith, Eric Thal, John Pankow, Tracy Pollan, Lee Richardson, Mia Sara, Jamey Sheridan, Jake Weber

'With its *Fiddler on the Roof* score and some sneakily hypocritical espousing of deeply conservative religious values, this is little more than a 111-minute love letter to Sidney Lumet's rabbi.' – *Kim Newman, Empire*

Close to My Heart
US 1951 90m bw
Warner (William Jacobs)
An adopted baby is discovered to have a murderer for a father; but environment is proved to be more important than heredity.
Routine sentimental drama.
wd William Keighley *story* *A Baby for Midge* by James R. Webb *ph* Robert Burks *m* Max Steiner *ed* Clarence Kolster
☆ Ray Milland, Gene Tierney, Fay Bainter, Howard St John, Mary Beth Hughes

Close-Up **
Iran 1989 93m colour
BFI/IIDCYA (Hassan Agha-Karimi)

original title: *Namayeh Nazdik*
A young man is tried for fraud after he persuades a family that he is the director Mohsen Makhmalbaf, and borrows money from them.
An oddity, and a fascinating one: a true story of a fantasist, part re-enacted, part actual, as the trial itself was filmed at the request of the accused.
wd Abbas Kiarostami *ph* Ali Reza Zarrin-Dast *ed* Abbas Kiarostami
☆ Hossain Sabzian, Mohsen Makhmalbaf, Abolfazi Ahankhah, Mehrdad Ahankhah, Manoochehr Ahankhah, Hossein Farazmand, Abbas Kiarostami

Closely Observed Trains **
Czechoslovakia 1966 92m bw
Ceskoslovensky Film (Zdenek Oves)

During World War II, an apprentice railway guard at a country station falls in love and becomes a saboteur.
Warm, amusingly detailed comedy with a disconcerting downbeat ending.
wd Jiri Menzel *novel* Bohumil Hrabal *ph* Jaromir Sofr *m* Jiri Pavlik
☆ Vaclav Neckar, Jitka Bendova, Vladimir Valenta, Josef Somr

'Like Forman, Menzel seems incapable of being unkind to anybody.' – *Tom Milne*

'The director has made extraordinarily effective use of the solitude which the characters share.' – *Dilys Powell*

best foreign film

'For five desperate Irishmen the perfect girl is abroad.'
The Closer You Get
GB/Ireland 2000 90m DeLuxe
Redwave (Uberto Pasolini)

US title: *American Women*
Bachelors in a small County Donegal town put an advertisement in a Miami paper inviting eligible young women to visit them.
Cute whimsical comedy that would have seemed old-fashioned forty years ago.
w William Ivory *story* Herbie Wave *d* Aileen Ritchie *ph* Robert Alazraki *m* Rachel Portman *pd* Tom McCullagh *ed* Sue Wyatt *cos* Kathy Strachan
☆ Ian Hart (Kieran), Sean McGinley (Ian), Niamh Cusack (Kate), Ruth McCabe (Mary), Ewan Stewart (Pat), Pat Shortt (Ollie), Cathleen Bradley (Siobhan), Sean McDonagh (Sean), Risteard Cooper (Father Hubert Mallone), Maureen O'Brien (Dollie), Pat Laffan (Giovanni), Britta Smith (Mrs Duncannon), Deborah Barnett (Ella), Frank Laverty (Brian), Dessie Gallagher (Mickey)

'Cute but oh-so-predictable stuff.' – *Nigel Cliff, Times*

The Closet: see *Le Placard*

Closet Land *
US 1991 89m DeLuxe
Universal/Imagine (Janet Meyers)

A children's writer is arrested, interrogated and tortured by a government official on a charge of subverting the young.
Intense psychological drama of a battle of wills, but lacking the required emotional impact through being set in no recognizable society; the acting almost carries it, but its heavy-handed symbolism sinks it before the end.
wd Radha Bharadwaj *ph* Bill Pope *m* Richard Einhorn *pd* Eiko Ishioka *ed* Lisa Churgin
☆ Madeleine Stowe, *Alan Rickman*

'Not an experience many filmgoers will want to put down money for.' – *Variety*

† Philip Glass was credited with 'creative musical supervision'.

The Cloud Capped Star **
India 1960 127m bw
BFI/Chitrakalpa (Ritwik Ghatak)
original title: *Meghe Dhaka Tara*
In Calcutta, the daughter of a refugee family struggling to survive sacrifices herself for the sake of her heedless parents and siblings.
A powerful and enraged account of suffering and waste, of exile and disappointment.
wd Ritwik Ghatak *story* Shaktipada Rajguru *ph* Dinen Gupta *m* Jyotirindra Moitra *ad* Ravi Chattopadhyay *ed* Ramesh Joshi
☆ Supriya Choudhury, Anil Chatterjee, Bijon Bhattacharya, Guita De, Gita Ghatak, Dwiju Bhawal, Niranjan Roy
'An underrated modern masterpiece.' – *Film Review*

Cloud Dancer
US 1977 108m colour
Melvin Simon
Episodes in the life of a stunt flyer.
Technically proficient, loosely assembled amble through the problems of a man with an obsession for danger; not a great crowd-puller.
w William Goodhart *d* Barry Brown
☆ David Carradine, Jennifer O'Neill, Joseph Bottoms, Albert Salmi, Salome Jens, Colleen Camp

Cloudburst
GB 1951 92m bw
Exclusive/Hammer (Anthony Hinds)
A vengeful code expert goes after the criminals who ran down his wife in making a getaway.
Watchable potboiler.
w Leo Marks, Francis Searle *d* Francis Searle *ph* Walter Harvey *m* Frank Spencer
☆ Robert Preston, Elizabeth Sellars, Colin Tapley, Sheila Burrell, Harold Lang
† The US version ran for 83m.

The Clouded Yellow *
GB 1950 96m bw
Sydney Box/Carillon (Betty Box)
A sacked secret service agent gets work tending a butterfly collection and finds that this involves him in a murder plot.
Implausible but quite engaging thriller in the Hitchcock style, involving a chase across the Lake District.
w Janet Green, Eric Ambler *d* Ralph Thomas *ph* Geoffrey Unsworth
☆ Trevor Howard, Jean Simmons, Barry Jones, Sonia Dresdel, Maxwell Reed, Kenneth More, André Morell

Clouds Over Europe: see *Q Planes*

The Clown
US 1952 91m bw
MGM (William H. Wright)
A drunken clown, once a great star, is idolized by his son who believes in a comeback.
Maudlin reworking of The Champ *(qv), with not a surprise in the plot and a star way over the top.*
w Martin Rackin *d* Robert Z. Leonard *ph* Paul C. Vogel *m* David Rose
☆ Red Skelton, Jane Greer, Tim Considine, Loring Smith, Philip Ober

A Clown Must Laugh: see *Pagliacci*

The Club **
Australia 1980 90m colour Panavision
South Australia Film Corp/New South Wales Film Corp (Matt Carroll)
aka: *Players*
The arrival of an expensive, university-educated player precipitates a crisis among management and players at a football club.
Incisive, excellently acted drama of boardroom manoeuvres and conflicting loyalties.
w David Williamson *play* David Williamson *d* Bruce Beresford *ph* Don McAlpine *pd* David Copping *ed* William Anderson
☆ Jack Thompson, Harold Hopkins, Graham Kennedy, John Howard, Frank Wilson, Alan Cassell

Club Extinction: see *Dr M*

Club Havana
US 1946 62m bw
PRC
Several stories come to a head in a night-club.
Slight musical multi-drama with moments of interest.
w Raymond L. Schrock, Fred Jackson *d* Edgar G. Ulmer
☆ Tom Neal, Margaret Lindsay, Don Douglas, Isabelita, Ernest Truex, Renie Riano, Paul Cavanagh, Marc Lawrence

Club Le Monde
GB 2002 79m Technicolor
ScreenProjex/SPA/2M (Piers Jackson, Simon Rumley)
In the early 90s, life becomes complicated for the staff and custoimers during one night at a London club.
Low budget movie that promises more than it delivers as it examines the intersecting lives of a group of clubbers, who turn out to be an unlovely and uninteresting lot.
wd Simon Rumley *ph* Simon Starling *m* Ed Butt *pd* Mark Larkin *ed* Eddie Hamilton
☆ Dawn Steele (Jacqui), Allison McKenzie (Ali), Brad Gorton (Mike), Daniel Ainsleigh (Steve), Tania Emery (Kelly), Emma Pike (Yaz), Frank Harper (Danny), Danny Nussbaum (Mr Sunglasses)
'Dated, boring paean to clubbing, with a duff script and lazy, 2-D characters.' – *Peter Bradshaw, Guardian*

Club Paradise
US 1986 104m Technicolor
Warner (Michael Shamberg)
A Chicago fireman retires to a Caribbean island to manage a rundown club.
Dismal waste of talent.
w Harold Ramis, Brian Doyle-Murray *story* Ed Roboto, Tom Leopold, Chris Miller, David Standish *d* Harold Ramis *ph* Peter Hannan *m* David Mansfield, Van Dyke Parks *pd* John Graysmark *ed* Marion Rothman
☆ Robin Williams, Peter O'Toole, Rick Moranis, Jimmy Cliff, Twiggy, Adolph Caesar, Eugene Levy, Joanna Cassidy
'Like one of those giddy, casual farces that Paramount turned out in the thirties ... Those pictures often got terrible reviews but kept audiences giggling cheerfully.' – *Pauline Kael, New Yorker*

Clubbed to Death
France/Portugal/Netherlands 1997 88m colour
Artificial Eye/Madar/La Sept/Grupo de Estudos/Meteor (Odile Gervais)
A young, middle-class woman is thrilled to discover rave culture and a drug-taking, impotent Arab boxer in the Parisian suburbs.
A slim narrative with little worthwhile dialogue, on which is hung the pounding music and pill-popping antics of the rave scene; for addicts only.
w Yolande Zauberman, Noémie Lvovsky *d* Yolande Zauberman *ph* Denis Lenoir *m* various *pd* Olivier Radot *ed* François Gédigier
☆ Elodie Bouchez, Roschdy Zem, Béatrice Dalle, Richard Courcet, Alex Descas
'Nothing other than a pretentious attempt to portray meaning to a culture that most of us couldn't care less about.' – *Helen Van Kruyssen, Film Review*

'It's not just a game...anymore.'
Clue
US 1985 87m Metrocolor
Paramount/Guber-Peters/Debra Hill/Polygram
A murder game becomes reality.
A rather arch attempt to film an internationally popular board game; those not in on the joke may tend to restlessness.
wd Jonathan Lynn *ph* Victor J. Kemper *m* John Morris *pd* John Lloyd
☆ Eileen Brennan, Tim Curry, Madeline Kahn, Christopher Lloyd, Michael McKean, Lesley Ann Warren
'Enough wit, neuroses and motive to intrigue even the most inept whodunnit solver.' – *Variety*
† Three alternative solutions were originally provided.

Clueless **
US 1995 97m DeLuxe
Paramount (Robert Lawrence, Scott Rudin)
A Beverly Hills teenager, the daughter of a successful lawyer, worries about losing her position as the most popular girl in the school and winning the boy she wants.
A surprisingly successful comedy about a girl who loves to shop, an activity that satisfies when all else fails. The dialogue is witty, the performances are smart and the tone is one of affectionate amusement touched with a little irony; the result is greatly enjoyable.
wd Amy Heckerling *ph* Bill Pope *m* David Kitay *pd* Steve Jordan *ed* Debra Chiate
☆ *Alicia Silverstone*, Stacey Dash, Brittany Murphy, Paul Rudd, Dan Hedaya, Donald Faison, Elisa Donovan, Wallace Shawn
'A highly satisfactory piece of work.' – *Adam Mars-Jones, Independent*
'The plot, a blend of *Heathers* and Sandra Dee, makes you feel as if you're biting into a tamale filled with Marshmallow Fluff.' – *Entertainment Weekly*
† The film is loosely based on Jane Austen's *Emma*.

Cluny Brown **
US 1946 100m bw
TCF (Ernst Lubitsch)
A plumber's niece goes into service and falls for a Czech refugee guest.
Romantic comedy in a never-never pre-war England; it does no more than poke casual fun at upper-class conventions, but the smooth direction and some excellent character comedy keep it well afloat.
w Samuel Hoffenstein, Elizabeth Reinhardt *novel* Margery Sharp *d Ernst Lubitsch* *ph* Joseph LaShelle *m* Cyril Mockridge, Emil Newman
☆ Jennifer Jones, Charles Boyer, *Richard Haydn, Una O'Connor*, Peter Lawford, Helen Walker, Reginald Gardiner, Reginald Owen, C. Aubrey Smith, Sara Allgood, Ernest Cossart, Florence Bates, Billy Bevan
'A lovely, easygoing comedy, full of small surprising touches.' – *Pauline Kael, 70s*

The Co-Optimists *
GB 1929 83m bw
New Era (Edwin Greenwood)
A revue by a popular pierrot troupe of the time.
Famous as Britain's first musical, this is a dated but valuable record of a stage performance of the kind long vanished.
w Melville Gideon, Laddie Cliff *d* Edwin Greenwood, Laddie Cliff *ph* Basil Emmott, Sydney Blythe
☆ Davy Burnaby, Stanley Holloway, Laddie Cliff, Phyllis Monkman, Melville Gideon, Gilbert Childs, Betty Chester, Elsa MacFarlane, Peggy Petronella, Harry S. Pepper

Coal Miner's Daughter ***
US 1980 124m Technicolor
Universal (Bob Larson)
The wife of a Kentucky hillbilly becomes a star of country music.
'With-it' version of the old show business story: gradual success, stardom, nervous breakdown, reconciliation. Based on the life of Loretta Lynn, but mainly notable for its depiction of backwoods Kentucky.
w Tom Rickman *d Michael Apted* *ph Ralf D. Bode* *md* Owen Bradley *pd* John W. Corso *ed* Arthur Schmidt
☆ *Sissy Spacek* (Loretta), Tommy Lee Jones (Doolittle Lynn), Levon Helm (Ted Webb), Jennifer Beasley (Peggy Lynn), Phyllis Boyens (Clara Webb)
Sissy Spacek
best picture; Tom Rickman; Ralf D. Bode; editing (Arthur Schmidt); art direction (John W. Corso, John M. Dwyer)

Coast of Terror: see *Summer City*

Coast to Coast
US 1980 94m Movielab
Paramount (Terry Carr)
A Los Angeles wife flees her husband and hitches a lift from a truck driver with problems.
Comedy for easy watching: pleasant characters are given very little of interest to do.
w Stanley Weiser *d* Joseph Sargent *ph* Joel King *m* Charles Bernstein
☆ Dyan Cannon, Robert Blake, Quinn Redeker, Michael Lerner, Bill Lucking, Maxine Stuart

Coastal Command **
GB 1942 69m bw
Crown Film Unit (Ian Dalrymple)
The RAF's Coastal Command at work, protecting a homeward-bound convoy of 42 merchant ships threatened by U-boats and a German raider.
Gripping documentary, full of exciting action, that has acquired additional historical worth with the passing of the years; it is also notable for Vaughan Williams's evocative score.
d J. B. Holmes *ph* Jonah Jones, F. Gamage *m Ralph Vaughan Williams* *md* Muir Mathieson *ed* Michael Gordon
'The whole piece is full of action, and yet it is somehow possible to watch it with imperturbability. A little more perturbation, and some humour, too, perhaps might not have hurt this picture.' – *C. A. Lejeune*

Cobb
US 1994 128m Technicolor Panavision
Warner/Regency/Alcor (David Lester)
A sports writer working on the official biography of Ty Cobb, the legendary American baseball player, discovers that the sporting hero is a thoroughly unpleasant person.
A revisionist biopic, with a larger-than-life performance in the title role; it is only likely to appeal to a dedicated sports fan.
wd Ron Shelton *book* *Cobb: A Biography* by Al Stump *ph* Russell Boyd *m* Elliot Goldenthal *pd* Armin Ganz, Scott Ritenour *ed* Paul Seydor, Kimberly Ray
☆ Tommy Lee Jones, Robert Wuhl, Lolita Davidovich, Stephen Mendillo, Lou Myers, J. Kenneth Campbell, William Utay, Rhoda Griffis
'It's neither character study nor historic drama. It's ambitious but oblique and unfocused, and only the most generous of viewers will forgive its numerous lapses and vagaries.' – *Leonard Klady, Variety*

Cobra
US 1925 85m approx bw silent
Ritz-Carlton
An impoverished Italian nobleman collects women as a hobby.
The star's first independent production won no plaudits and was thought to be a mistake conceived by his wife Natacha Rambova, who appeared in a dance act with him.
w Anthony Coldeway *d* Joseph Henabery
☆ Rudolph Valentino, Nita Naldi, Casson Ferguson, Gertrude Olmstead, Hector V. Sarno

'Crime is a disease. Meet the cure.'
'The strong arm of the law.'
Cobra
US 1986 87m Technicolor
Warner/Cannon (James D. Brubaker)
A tough LA cop tracks down a serial killer.
Relentless but unsurprising carbon of Dirty Harry, *a bit too tough for its own good.*
w Sylvester Stallone *novel* *Fair Game* by Paula Gosling *d* George Pan Cosmatos *ph* Ric Waite *m* Sylvester Levay *pd* Bill Kenney *ed* Don Zimmerman, James Symons
☆ Sylvester Stallone, Brigitte Nielsen, Reni Santoni, Andrew Robinson
† 2,131 prints were made for the launch
†† It was remade in 1995 as *Fair Game* (qv), starring Cindy Crawford.

Cobra Verde
West Germany 1988 111m colour
Palace/Concorde/Werner Herzog Film Production/ZDF/Ghana Film Industry Corp (Luigi Stipetic)
A Brazilian peasant-turned-bandit goes to West Africa to revive the slave trade.
Disjointed, episodic and uninteresting.
w Werner Herzog *novel* *The Viceroy of Ouidah* by Bruce Chatwin *d* Werner Herzog *ph* Viktor Ruzicka *m* Popol Vuh *pd* Ulrich Bergfelder *ed* Maximiliane Mainka
☆ Klaus Kinski, King Ampaw, Jose Lewgoy, Salvatore Basile

Cobra Woman
US 1944 71m Technicolor
U-I (George Waggner)
A South Seas girl is abducted by snake worshippers ruled by her evil twin.
A monument of undiluted hokum with some amusing sets and performances but not enough self-mockery in the script.
w Richard Brooks, Gene Lewis *d* Robert Siodmak *ph* George Robinson, W. Howard Greene
m Edward Ward
☆ Maria Montez, Jon Hall, Sabu, Lon Chaney Jnr, Mary Nash, Edgar Barrier, Lois Collier, Samuel S. Hinds, Moroni Olsen
'Among the exotic treats: a rumbling volcano, a pet chimp, ominous gong sounds, forest glade love scenes, human sacrifices, handmaidens in high-heeled pumps, Tollea's imperious writhing during a demonic dance, and the good Nadja's plea for the symbol of the power that is rightly hers: "Gif me the cobra jool."' – *Pauline Kael, 70s*

The Cobweb
US 1955 124m Eastmancolor
Cinemascope
MGM (John Houseman)
Tensions among the staff of a private mental clinic reach a new high over the purchase of curtains.
The patients seem saner than the doctors in this strained and verbose character drama which despite its cast and big studio look never begins to engage the interest.
w John Paxton *novel* William Gibson
d Vincente Minnelli *ph* George Folsey
m Leonard Rosenman
☆ Richard Widmark, Lauren Bacall, Charles Boyer, *Lillian Gish*, Gloria Grahame, John Kerr, Susan Strasberg, *Oscar Levant*, Tommy Rettig, Paul Stewart, Adèle Jergens
'An overwrought and elaborately artificial exercise, made scarcely more plausible by reliance on the basic jargon of psychiatry.' – *Penelope Houston*
'By the mid-50s, nobody was surprised that the new variant on *Grand Hotel* was an expensive, exclusive loony bin.' – *Pauline Kael, 70s*

The Coca-Cola Kid
Australia 1985 94m Eastmancolor
Palace/Cinema Enterprises/Film Gallery/Columbia (David Roe)
A Coca-Cola rep is sent to Australia to combat a remote land baron who brews and distributes his own brand.
Flaccid drama with an eventually mystifying superabundance of style.
w Frank Moorhouse *d* Dusan Makavejev
ph Dean Semler *m* William Motzing *pd* Graham (Grace) Walker *ed* John Scott
☆ Eric Roberts, Greta Scacchi, Bill Kerr, Max Gillies, Kris McQuade

Cockeyed Cavaliers
US 1934 72m bw
RKO
Two idiots have various adventures in medieval England.
Fairly tolerable slapstick from a team which never seemed quite at its best.
w Edward Kaufman, Ben Holmes *d* Mark Sandrich
☆ Bert Wheeler, Robert Woolsey, Thelma Todd, Noah Beery, Dorothy Lee, Franklin Pangborn, Robert Greig
'With a fair quota of laughs, it eclipses their previous releases.' – *Variety*

The Cockeyed Cowboys of Calico County
US 1969 99m Technicolor
Universal
A Western blacksmith stops working when his mail order bride doesn't arrive.
Styleless American rehash of La Femme du Boulanger, *with all concerned trying too hard.*
w Ranald MacDougall *d* Tony Leader
☆ Dan Blocker, Nanette Fabray, Mickey Rooney

The Cockeyed Miracle
US 1946 92m bw
MGM
GB title: *Mr Griggs Returns*
Family ghosts return to sort out domestic chaos.
Moderate 'Topper'-style comedy with amiable cast.
w Karen de Wolf *play* George Seaton *d* S. Sylvan Simon
☆ Frank Morgan, Cecil Kellaway, Gladys Cooper, Audrey Totter, Marshall Thompson, Leon Ames

The Cockeyed World *
US 1929 115m bw
Fox
Further adventures of Sergeants Flagg and Quirt, the boisterous heroes of *What Price Glory*.
Lively early talkie; the adventure comedy remains interesting, though the technique is badly faded.
w William K. Wells, Laurence Stallings, Maxwell Anderson, Wilson Mizner, Tom Barry *d* Raoul Walsh *ph* Arthur Edeson
☆ Victor McLaglen, Edmund Lowe, Lili Damita, Lelia Karnelly, El Brendel, Bob Burns, Stuart Erwin

Cockfighter
US 1974 83m Metrocolor
Rio Pinto/New World/Artists Entertainment Complex (Roger Corman)
aka: *Born to Kill*
A professional cockfighter ends a run of bad luck but loses his girl.
Not badly made but rather seedy film about appalling people.
w Charles Willeford *novel* Charles Willeford
d Monte Hellman *ph* Nestor Almendros
m Michael Franks
☆ Warren Oates, Richard B. Shull, Harry Dean Stanton, Ed Begley Jnr, Laurie Bird, Troy Donahue

Cockleshell Heroes
GB 1955 97m Technicolor Cinemascope
Columbia/Warwick (Phil C. Samuel)
During World War II, ten marines are trained to travel by canoe into Bordeaux harbour and attach limpet mines to German ships.
Absolutely predictable semi-documentary war heroics, with barrack-room humour turning eventually into tragedy. The familiar elements, including a display of stiff upper lips, ensured box-office success.
w Bryan Forbes, Richard Maibaum *d* José Ferrer
ph John Wilcox, Ted Moore *m* John Addison
☆ José Ferrer, *Trevor Howard*, Dora Bryan, Victor Maddern, Anthony Newley, Peter Arne, David Lodge, Walter Fitzgerald, Beatrice Campbell

Cocktail
US 1988 103m Metrocolor
Warner/Touchstone/Silver Screen Partners III/ Interscope Communications (Ted Field, Robert W. Cort)
A young man becomes a bartender in the belief he will meet rich and beautiful women.
Glossy nonsense.
w Heywood Gould *novel* Heywood Gould
d Roger Donaldson *ph* Dean Semler *m* Peter Robinson *pd* Mel Bourne *ad* Dan Davis *ed* Neil Travis, Barbara Dunning
☆ Tom Cruise, Bryan Brown, Elisabeth Shue, Lisa Banes, Laurence Luckinbill, Kelly Lynch, Gina Gershon, Ron Dean

The Cocoanuts **
US 1929 96m bw
Paramount (Walter Wanger, James R. Cowan)
A chiselling hotel manager tries to get in on the Florida land boom.
Considering its age and the dismal prints which remain, this is a remarkably lively if primitive first film by the Marxes, with some good routines among the excess footage.
w George S. Kaufman, Morrie Ryskind d Robert Florey, Joseph Santley *ph* George Folsey
m/ly Irving Berlin
☆ *The Four Marx Brothers, Margaret Dumont,* Oscar Shaw, Mary Eaton, Kay Francis, Basil Ruysdael
'The camerawork showed all the mobility of a concrete fire hydrant caught in a winter freeze.' – *Paul D. Zimmermann*

Cocoon **
US 1985 117m DeLuxe
TCF/Zanuck-Brown (Lili Zanuck)
Aliens from another galaxy leave pods in the pool of a Florida retirement home, whose bathers are rejuvenated.
Unusual, amusing and sentimentally effective movie of the kind which gets hearty word-of-mouth recommendation.
w Tom Benedek novel David Saperstein *d Ron Howard ph* Don Peterman *m* James Horner
pd Jack T. Collis *ed* Daniel Hanley, Michael J. Hill
☆ Don Ameche, Wilford Brimley, Hume Cronyn, Brian Dennehy, Jack Gilford, Steve Guttenberg, Maureen Stapleton, Jessica Tandy, Gwen Verdon
'A mesmerizing tale that's a certified audience pleaser.' – *Variety*
best supporting actor, Don Ameche

Cocoon: The Return
US 1988 116m DeLuxe
Fox/Richard D. Zanuck, David Brown, Lili Fini Zanuck
After a visit to another planet, three rejuvenated elderly couples return to Earth to rescue alien pods.
Lacklustre sequel, a concept in search of a script.
w Stephen McPherson *story* Stephen McPherson, Elizabeth Bradley *d* Daniel Petrie *ph* Tak Fujimoto *m* James Horner *pd* Lawrence Paull
ed Mark Warner
☆ Don Ameche, Wilford Brimley, Courteney Cox, Hume Cronyn, Jack Gilford, Steve Guttenberg, Barret Oliver, Maureen Stapleton, Elaine Stritch, Jessica Tandy, Gwen Verdon, Tahnee Welch
'Extraordinarily scrappy.' – *MFB*

'Toni wanted a crowd… he got the mob'
Cocozza's Way
GB 2001 97m Technicolor
UIP/DNA (Ruth Kenley-Letts)
In Glasgow, a Frank Sinatra impersonator becomes involved with local gangsters.
Momentarily interesting feature, in which small-time crooks attempt to ape Mafia styles in the same way that a pub crooner tries to emulate Sinatra, but it soon settles for low-life clichés.
wd Peter Capaldi *ph* Stephen Blackman
m Stanislas Syrewicz *pd* Martyn John *ed* Martin Walsh
☆ Ian Hart (Toni Cocozza), Kelly Macdonald (Irene), Alun Armstrong (Bill), Brian Cox (Chisolm), Tommy Flanagan (Michelangelo), Iain Cuthbertson (Connolly), Billy McColl (John the Watchman), Richard E. Grant (Himself)
'It turns it into a small, cliché-ridden telly entertainment. Its narrative cracks mightn't have shown up so damningly on the small screen and it has a few sound native virtues.' – *Alexander Walker*

Code Inconnu: Recit Incomplet De Divers Voyages *
France/Germany/Romania 2000 117m colour
Artificial Eye/MK2/Alain Sarde
aka: *Code Unknown*
In Paris, an illegal immigrant, a teacher, a photographer and a runaway all find themselves excluded from some aspect of society.
An intricate film of several loosely connected lives, all exhibiting distress with present day society; it has arresting moments but feels too much like a hellfire sermon to convince.
wd Michael Haneke *ph* Jurgen Jurges *m* Giba Gonçalves *pd* Manuel de Chauvigny *ed* Andreas Prochaska, Karin Hartusch, Nadine Muse
cos Françoise Clavel
☆ Juliette Binoche (Anne), Thierry Neuvic (Georges), Luminita Gheorghiu (Maria), Ona Lu Yenke (Amadou), Helene Diarra (Aminate), Sepp Bierbichler (Farmer), Alexandre Hamidi (Jean)
'A major achievement… the most intellectually stimulating and emotionally provocative piece of European cinema of recent times.' – *Richard Falcon, Sight & Sound*

Code Name: Emerald
US 1985 93m Metrocolor
NBC/MGM-UA
A double agent is sent to Paris in 1944 to make sure that a captured American officer doesn't talk about the D-Day plans.
Plodding, old hat war melodrama with no specific virtues.
w Ronald Bass *novel The Emerald Illusion* by Ronald Bass *d* Jonathan Sanger *ph* Freddie Francis
☆ Ed Harris, Max von Sydow, Horst Buchholz, Helmut Berger, Graham Crowden

Code Name: Trixie: see *The Crazies*

Code Name: Zebra
US 1985 96m Foto-Kem
Pac-West (Joseph Lucchese)
On his release from prison, a gangster takes his revenge against a gang of ex-Vietnam War veterans who put him inside.
Cheap and nasty exploitation film that rehashes in a ham-fisted manner all the usual shoot-outs, car crashes and casual violence; if it has any originality, it is that the good guys are even more unpleasant than the bad.
w Robert Leon *d* Joe Tornatore *ph* Bill Dickson, Tom Denove *m* Louis Febre, Peter Rotter *ed* Ed Hansen
☆ Jim Mitchum, Mike Lane, Timmy Brown, Joe Dante, Chuck Morrell, Deana Jurgens, Lindsey Crosby, Frank Sinatra Jnr

Code of Scotland Yard: see *The Shop at Sly Corner*

Code of Silence
US 1985 101m Astrocolor
Rank/Orion (Raymond Wagner)
A Chicago cop raids a drug den and sets off a gang war.
Routine tough stuff which just about avoids self-parody.
w Michael Butler, Dennis Shryack, Mike Gray
d Andrew Davis *ph* Frank Tidy *m* David Frank
pd Maher Ahmed *ed* Peter Parasheles, Christopher Holmes
☆ Chuck Norris (Eddie Cusack), Henry Silva (Luis Comacho), Bert Remsen (Commander Kates), Mike Genovese (Tony Luna), Nathan Davis (Felix Scalese), Ralph Foody (Cragie), Joseph Guzaldo (Nick Kopalas), Molly Hagan (Diana Luna), Dennis Farina (Dorato)

Code of the Secret Service
US 1939 58m bw
Warner
Agents track a gang who stole treasury banknote plates.
Serial-like adventures, one of several from the same stable, all featuring the future president of the US.
w Lee Katz, Dean Franklin *d* Noel Smith
☆ Ronald Reagan, Eddie Foy Jnr, Rosella Towne, Moroni Olsen, Edgar Edwards
'Filler fodder; a wild actioner for lower dual bookings.' – *Variety*

Code Unknown: see *Code Inconnu: Recit Incomplet De Divers Voyages*

Codename Wild Geese
Italy 1984 101m colour
Entertainment/Ascot/Gico Cinematografica (Erwin C. Dietrich)
Mercenaries are sent to destroy heavily guarded opium depots in Thailand.
Brisk but undistinguished action movie, with a large cast of expendable Orientals.
w Michael Lester *d* Anthony M. Dawson (Antonio Margheriti) *ph* Peter Baumgartner
m Jan Nemec
☆ Lewis Collins, Lee Van Cleef, Ernest Borgnine, Klaus Kinski, Manfred Lehmann, Mimsy Farmer, Thomas Dannenberg, Wolfgang Pampel, Harmut Neugubauer

Un Coeur en Hiver *
France 1991 104m colour
Artificial Eye/Film Par Film/Cinea/Orly/Sedif/Paravision/DA Films/FR 3 (Jean-Louis Livi, Philippe Carcassonne)
aka: *A Heart in Winter*
A young violinist, about to leave the home of her female manager to live with a violin maker, falls in love with his friend and partner.
A familiar story, impeccably acted but failing to touch the emotions, possibly because of its distanced direction and the rigid, symphonic structure which restricts its humanity.
w Claude Sautet, Jacques Fieschi, Jérôme Tonnerre *d* Claude Sautet *ph* Yves Angelo *m* Philippe Sarde *ad* Christian Marti *ed* Jacqueline Thiedot
☆ Daniel Auteuil, Emmanuelle Béart, André Dussollier, Elisabeth Bourgine, Brigitte Catillon, Maurice Garrel
'Extremely subtle and intensely enjoyable, impressive pic deserves international art house attention.' – *Variety*

Coffy
US 1973 91m Movielab
Focus/AIP (Robert A. Papazian)
A nurse pretends to be a drug addict in order to exact revenge on those responsible for destroying the life of her 11-year-old sister.
Lively, violent blaxploitation movie, in which Grier moves like an avenging angel through a corrupt society.
wd Jack Hill *ph* Paul Lohmann *m* Roy Ayers *ad* Perry Ferguson *ed* Charles McClelland
☆ Pam Grier, Booker Bradshaw, Robert DoQui, William Elliott, Allan Arbus, Sid Haig, Barry Cahill
'What distinguishes this superficially rough and routine effort from the run of the black sexploitation mill is its all-embracing grimness. Its moral blackness, in fact.' – *Verina Glaessner, MFB*
† Grier and director Hill followed it with *Foxy Brown*, (qv), which started out as a sequel and remains a similar movie.

Cohen and Tate
US 1988 86m DeLuxe
Guild/Nelson Films (Antony Rufus Isaacs, Jeff Young)
Two hit men kidnap a boy who witnessed a gangland murder.
A thriller lacking suspense.
wd Eric Red *ph* Victor J. Kemper *pd* David M. Haber *ed* Edward Abroms
☆ Roy Scheider, Adam Baldwin, Harley Cross, Cooper Huckabee, Suzanne Savoy, Marco Perella, Tom Campitelli, Andrew R. Gill

The Cohens and the Kellys
Seven comedies were made, all for Universal, about the friendly rivalry of Jewish and Irish neighbours. They were:
1926 The Cohens and Kellys
1928 The Cohens and Kellys in Paris
1929 The Cohens and Kellys in Atlantic City
1930 The Cohens and Kellys in Scotland
1931 The Cohens and Kellys in Africa
1932 The Cohens and Kellys in Hollywood
1933 The Cohens and Kellys in Trouble
George Sidney played Cohen in all of the series and Charlie Murray played Kelly in five films. He was replaced by J. Farrell MacDonald in *Paris* and by Mack Swain in *Atlantic City*.

Coiffeur pour Dames
France 1952 87m approx bw
Hoche (Jean Boyer)
GB title: *An Artist with Ladies*
A Provençal sheep shearer becomes a fashionable ladies' hairdresser with a Champs-élysées salon, and finds that his clients are all susceptible to his charms.
Obvious star comedy with a fair measure of laughs; more in fact than the much later Shampoo.
w Serge Véber, Jean Boyer *play* P. Armont, M. Gerbidon *d* Jean Boyer *ph* Charles Suin *m* Paul Misraki
☆ *Fernandel*, Blanchette Crunoy, Renée Devillers, Arlette Poirier

'Never trust the one you love.'
Cold around the Heart
US 1997 96m colour
TCF/Illusion/Baumgarten-Prophet/Kushner Locke (Dan Halsted, Craig Baumgarten, Adam J. Merims)
aka: *Cold Heart*
A jewel thief is double-crossed by his girlfriend and framed for the murders she has committed.
Tough thriller set among crooks to whom duplicity is as natural as breathing, and who like to discuss their attitudes to one another at length.
wd John Ridley *ph* Malik Hassan Sayeed *m* Mason Daring *pd* Kara Lindstrom, Missy Okum *ed* Eric L. Beason
☆ David Caruso, Kelly Lynch, Stacey Dash, Chris Noth, John Spencer, Pruitt Taylor Vince, Richard Kind
'A derivative but fitfully effective modern *film noir*.' – *Sight and Sound*

Cold Blood (dubbed)
West Germany 1975 76m colour
City/Televox
A teacher becomes involved with a pilot who is on the run after stealing a million dollars from gangsters.
Run-of-the-mill thriller, with an ending that attempts to be clever but is merely botched.
w Günter Vaessen *d* Ralf Gregan *ph* Michael Ballhaus *m* Rolg Bauer *pd* Herbert Kluver *ed* Christel Orthmann
☆ Rutger Hauer, Vera Tschechowa, Horst Frank, Walter Richter, Günther Stoll

Cold Comfort
Canada 1989 88m colour
Norstar/Telefilm (Lana Frank, Ray Sager)
A snowbound motorist is kidnapped by an unbalanced truck driver as a birthday present for his 18-year-old daughter.
Claustrophobic thriller that lacks suspense.
w Richard Beattie, Elliot L. Sims *play* James Garrard *d* Vic Sarin *ph* Vic Sarin *m* Jeff Dana *ad* Jo-Ann Chorney *ed* Nick Rotundo
☆ Maury Chaykin, Margaret Langrick, Paul Gross

'She discovered a new branch of her family tree...the one with all the nuts.'
Cold Comfort Farm *
GB 1995 95m colour
BBC/Thames TV (Alison Gilby)
A London cousin brings changes to the family who inhabit a decaying farm, ruled by an ageing matriarch who once saw something nasty in the woodshed.
Enjoyable comedy that doesn't quite capture the flavour of the original satire or the high and rural romanticism of Mary Webb's novels.
w Malcolm Bradbury *novel* Stella Gibbons *d* John Schlesinger *ph* Chris Seager *m* Robert Lockhart *pd* Malcolm Thornton *ed* Mark Day
☆ Eileen Atkins, Kate Beckinsale, Sheila Burrell, Stephen Fry, Freddie Jones, Joanna Lumley, Ian McKellen, Miriam Margolyes, Rufus Sewell
'A deliciously eccentric, fabulously acted comedy of manners.' – *Variety*
† Shown on television in Britain, it was given a cinema release in the US.

Cold Cuts: see *Buffet Froid*

Cold Dog Soup
US 1989 88m Technicolor
Palace/HandMade/Aspen (Richard G. Abramson, William E. McEuen)
Given a dead dog to bury by his new girlfriend, a man attempts to sell it to a furrier and a Chinese restaurateur.
Dismal attempt at a black comedy.
w Thomas Pope *book* Stephen Dobyns *d* Alan Metter *ph* Frederick Elmes *m* Michael Kamen, Mark Snow *pd* David L. Snyder *ed* Kaja Fehr
☆ Randy Quaid, Frank Whaley, Christine Harnos, Sheree North, Nancy Kwan
'Miserably unwatchable.' – *MFB*

Cold Eyes of Fear
Italy/Spain 1971 95m colour
Cinemar/Atlantida (José Frade)
A lawyer and a prostitute are held hostage by two convicts, one of whom is intent on killing the lawyer's uncle, a judge who wrongly condemned him to prison.
Low-budget thriller in which a battle of wits holds the attention for a time.
w Leo Anchoriz, Tito Carpi, Enzo G. Castellari *d* Enzo G. Castellari *ph* Antonio Ballesteros *m* Ennio Morricone *pd* Roman Calatayud *ed* Vincenzo Tomassi
☆ Giovanna Ralli, Frank Wolff, Fernando Rey, Julian Mateos, Gianni Garko, Karin Schubert, Leon Lenoir, Franco Marletta

Cold Feet *
US 1989 94m colour
Virgin/Avenue Pictures (Cassian Elwes)
Three petty crooks fall out after smuggling emeralds into America inside a horse.
Amusingly ramshackle semi-Western.
w Thomas McGuane, Jim Harrison *d* Robert Dornhelm *ph* Brian Duggan *m* Tom Bahler *pd* Bernt Capra
☆ Keith Carradine, Sally Kirkland, Tom Waits, Bill Pullman, Rip Torn, Kathleen York, Macon McCalman

Cold Fever *
US/Denmark/Germany/Iceland 1995 86m colour
Theatrical Experience/Icicle/IFC/Film Fonds/Sunrise/Pandora/Zentropa/Alta (Jim Stark)
A Japanese man travels by bus, car and horse to a remote part of Iceland to hold a memorial service for his parents, who died there.
A quirky road movie where different cultures don't so much clash as collide head-on.
w Jim Stark, Fridrik Thor Fridriksson *d* Fridrik Thor Fridriksson *ph* Ari Kristinsson *m* Hilmar Orn Hilmarsson *pd* Arni Poll Johansson *ed* Steingrimur Karlsson
☆ Masatoshi Nagase, Lili Taylor, Fisher Stevens, Gisli Halldorsson, Laura Hughes, Seijun Suzuki, Katrin Olafsdottir
'Drive-by surrealism with ice on top.' – *Tom Shone, Sunday Times*

'A cold-hearted killer. A hot-blooded cop. A blood-boiling thriller.'
Cold Front
Canada 1989 96m colour
Beacon Group (Ed Richardson, Sean Allan)
An American and a Canadian cop become entangled in dirty deals made by the KGB and the CIA when they investigate a killing.
Cheap, nasty and stupidly violent thriller with no redeeming qualities.
w Sean Allan, Stefan Arngrim *d* Paul Bnarbic (Allan Goldstein) *ph* Thomas Burstyn *m* Braun Farnon, Craig Zurba *pd* Sarina Rotstein-Cheikes *ed* Martin Hunter
☆ Martin Sheen, Michael Ontkean, Kim Coates, Beverly D'Angelo, Jan Rubes, Yvan Ponton, Miguel Fernandes

Cold Heart: see *Cold around the Heart*

Cold Heaven
US 1992 105m colour
(Allan Scott, Jonathan Crane)
An adulterous wife, a lapsed Catholic, has a vision of the Virgin Mary while on holiday in Mexico after she believes that her husband has been killed in a boating accident.
A flawed attempt to transfer to the screen a novel dealing with thought and feelings rather than action; it holds the attention without satisfying.
w Allan Scott *novel* Brian Moore *d* Nicolas Roeg *ph* Francis Kenny *m* Stanley Myers *pd* Steve Legler *ed* Tony Lawson
☆ Theresa Russell, Mark Harmon, James Russo, Talia Shire, Will Patton, Richard Bradford, Seymour Cassel
'Confused and confusing, dazzling and disturbing, fascinating and frustrating.' – *Film Review*

The Cold Light of Day
Netherlands 1995 96m colour
Polygram/Meteor/Capitol (Chris Brouwer, Haig Balian)
In Eastern Europe, an obsessional former police inspector determines to track down the killer of young children, after his chief, facing re-election, forces a drug addict to confess to the crimes.
Melodramatic and implausible drama, with occasional moments of suspense.
w Doug Magee *story Es geschah am hellichten Tag* by Friedrich Dürrenmatt *d* Rudolf Van Den Berg *ph* Igor Luther *m* Stefan Truyman, Yves Elegeert *ad* Zdenek Fleming *ed* Kant Pan
☆ Richard E. Grant, Lynsey Baxter, Simon Cadell, James Laurenson, Heathcote Williams, Thom Hoffman, Gerard Thoolen, Perdita Weeks
'This ludicrous thriller lacks atmosphere, while the cast's English accents are idiotically at odds with the locale.' – *Sight and Sound*

The Cold Summer of '53 **
USSR 1987 100m colour
Mosfilm
In the period after Stalin's death when criminals were freed, an exile in a remote part of Siberia is roused from his apathy to defend a small community when it is terrorized by a gang of thugs.
A tense and gripping, though slow-paced, thriller that can also be seen as a sharp comment on the changing politics of its time.
w Edgar Dubrovsky *d* Alexander Proshkin *ph* Boris Brozhovsky *m* V. Martynov *pd* Valery Filippov
☆ Valeri Priyomykhov, Anatoli Papanov, Victor Stepanov, Nina Usatova, Zoya Buryak, Yuri Kuznetsov, Vladimir Kashpur
† It was the second-highest grossing movie in the USSR in 1988.

'Revenge can be chilling...'
Cold Sweat
Italy/France 1970 94m colour
Corona/Fair (Robert Dorfmann)
aka: *The Man With Two Shadows*
An American living peaceably on the Riviera is forced into drug smuggling.
Reliable tough stuff for those who like that sort of thing.
w Shimon Wincelberg, Albert Simonin *novel Ride the Nightmare* by Richard Matheson *d* Terence Young *ph* Jean Rabier *m* Michel Magne
☆ Charles Bronson, James Mason, Liv Ullmann, Jill Ireland, Jean Topart

Cold Turkey *
US 1970 102m DeLuxe
UA/Tandem/DFI (Norman Lear)
A tobacco company offers 25 million dollars to any town which can give up smoking for thirty days.
Rather wild and strained but sporadically amusing satirical comedy, aggressively littered with unpleasant detail.
w Norman Lear *novel I'm Giving Them Up for Good* by Margaret and Neil Rau *d* Norman Lear *ph* Charles F. Wheeler *m* Randy Newman
☆ Dick Van Dyke, Pippa Scott, Tom Poston, Edward Everett Horton, Bob Newhart, Vincent Gardenia, Jean Stapleton
'An eager desire to debunk and shock at the same time.' – *David McGillivray*

Cold Water: see *L'Eau Froide*

A Cold Wind in August *
US 1960 77m bw
UA/Troy Films (Robert L. Ross, Philip Hazleton)
An ageing stripper seduces a 17-year-old janitor but the affair ends when he sees her do her act.
Roughly-made, well-acted sex drama which at the time seemed mildly shocking but can only survive for its central acting performance.
w Burton Wohl *novel* Burton Wohl *d* Alexander Singer *ph* Floyd Crosby *m* Gerald Fried
☆ *Lola Albright*, Scott Marlowe, Joe de Santis, Herschel Bernardi

'Cosmo's planning to get his life in order. He just has to kill a few people first.'

Coldblooded

US 1994 92m FotoKem
Polygram/Propaganda/MPCA/Snowback (Michael J. Fox, Matt Tolmach, Brad Krevoy, Steve Stabler, Brad Jenkel)

A dimwitted youth who works for a gangster is promoted to hitman and discovers that he has a talent for murder.
Lifeless, slow-paced black comedy with a blank at its centre; its attempt to marry romance and murder fails to bring a smile.
wd M. Wallace Wolodarsky *ph* Robert Yeoman *m* Steve Bartek *pd* Rae Fox *ed* Craig Bassett *cos* Matthew Jacobson
☆ Jason Priestley (Cosmo), Peter Riegert (Steve), Kimberly Williams (Jasmine), Janeane Garofalo (Honey), Robert Loggia (Gordon), Michael J. Fox (Tim Alexander), Josh Charles (Randy), Jay Kogen (John)
'This is a picture about nothing but its own style, and its style isn't good.' – *Mick LaSalle, San Francisco Chronicle*

The Colditz Story **

GB 1954 97m bw
British Lion/Ivan Foxwell

Adventures of British POWs in the German maximum security prison in Saxony's Colditz Castle during World War II.
Probably the most convincing of the British accounts of POW life, with a careful balance of tragedy and comedy against a background of humdrum, boring daily existence. A TV series followed in 1972.
w Guy Hamilton, Ivan Foxwell *book* P. R. Reid *d* Guy Hamilton *ph* Gordon Dines *m* Francis Chagrin
☆ John Mills, Eric Portman, Christopher Rhodes, Lionel Jeffries, Bryan Forbes, Ian Carmichael, Richard Wattis, Frederick Valk, Anton Diffring, Eugene Deckers, Theodore Bikel
'It has all the realism, dignity and courage of the men it commemorates.' – *News of the World*

'What Would You Do If You Lost Everything?'

Collateral Damage

US 2002 109m Technicolor
Warner/Bel-Air (David Foster, Steven Reuther)

A Los Angeles firefighter decides to take his revenge on a rebel leader who blows up the Colombian consulate, killing his wife and child.
Inadequate, simple-minded action picture featuring a star who is well past his sell-by date.
w David Griffiths, Peter Griffiths, Ronald Rose *d* Andrew Davis *ph* Adam Greenberg *m* Graeme Revell *pd* Philip Rosenberg *ed* Dennis Virkler, Dov Hoenig *sp* William Mesa; Flash Film Works
☆ Arnold Schwarzenegger (Gordy Brewer), Elias Koteas (Brandt), Francesca Neri (Selena), Cliff Curtis (Claudio (The Wolf)), Miguel Sandoval (Phipps), Harry Lennix (Dray), John Leguizamo (Felix), John Turturro (Armstrong)
'Its preposterous contrivances and ludicrous implausibilities make it look like the very definition of puerile Hollywood superstar fantasy in the present real-world context.' – *Todd McCarthy, Variety*

'You won't dare open your mouth, but you'll be screaming for her to escape!'

The Collector *

US 1965 119m Technicolor
Columbia (Jud Kinberg, John Kohn)

An inhibited young butterfly specialist kidnaps a girl to add to his collection.
Talkative and unrewarding suspenser with pretensions, sluggishly handled and not very interestingly acted.
w Stanley Mann, John Kohn *novel* John Fowles *d* William Wyler *ph* Robert L. Surtees, Robert Krasker *m* Maurice Jarre
☆ Terence Stamp, Samantha Eggar, Mona Washbourne
Stanley Mann, John Kohn; William Wyler; Samantha Eggar

Colleen *

US 1936 89m bw
Warner (Robert Lord)

Boy meets Irish girl in New York.
Typical light musical of the period with standard studio talent.
w Peter Milne, F. Hugh Herbert, Sig Herzig *d* Alfred E. Green *ph* Byron Haskin, Sol Polito *m/ly* Harry Warren, Al Dubin *ch* Bobby Connolly *gown* Orry-Kelly
☆ Dick Powell, Ruby Keeler, Jack Oakie, Joan Blondell, Hugh Herbert, Louise Fazenda, Paul Draper, Marie Wilson, Luis Alberni, Hobart Cavanaugh, Berton Churchill

'You'll graduate with a perpetual smile!'

College *

US 1927 65m (24 fps) bw silent
Buster Keaton Productions (Joseph M. Schenck)

A brainy high school student becomes a college football star.
Disappointing comedy from this great stone-faced clown: the plums are there, but few and far between.
w Carl Harbaugh, Bryan Foy *d* James W. Horne *ph* J. Devereux Jennings, Bert Haines
☆ Buster Keaton, Ann Cornwall, Harold Goodwin, Snitz Edwards, Florence Turner

College Coach

US 1933 75m bw
Warner

A tough football coach finds that his best star is a timid chemistry student.
Unremarkable studio programmer despite a strong cast.
w Niven Busch, Manuel Seff *d* William A. Wellman
☆ Dick Powell, Pat O'Brien, Ann Dvorak, Arthur Byron, Lyle Talbot, Hugh Herbert, Guinn Williams, Donald Meek
'Hasn't enough punch for real sock grosses.' – *Variety*

College Scandal

US 1935 75m bw
Paramount

A killer attacks three male students.
With stars, it could have been memorable.
w Frank Partos, Charles Brackett, Marguerite Roberts *d* Elliott Nugent
☆ Arline Judge, Kent Taylor, Wendy Barrie, Mary Nash, William Stack, William Frawley, Benny Baker, Johnny Downs
'Worthwhile summer fare for high-grade dual houses.' – *Variety*

College Swing

US 1938 86m bw
Paramount (Lewis Gensler)
GB title: *Swing, Teacher, Swing*

A dumb girl must graduate if a college is to inherit a fortune.
Mild comedy more notable for its cast than its script.
w Walter de Leon, Francis Martin *d* Raoul Walsh *ph* Victor Milner *m/ly* various
☆ George Burns, Gracie Allen, Martha Raye, Bob Hope, Edward Everett Horton, Florence George, Ben Blue, Betty Grable, Jackie Coogan, John Payne, Cecil Cunningham, Robert Cummings
'A medley of vaude specialties, bits and numbers strung together in not too happy a manner.' – *Variety*

La Collina degli Stivali: see *Boots Hill*

Colonel Blimp: see *The Life and Death of Colonel Blimp*

'Back from the dead ... To reclaim his life and the woman he loved.'

Le Colonel Chabert *

France 1994 111m colour Panavision
Guild/Film Par Film/DD/Paravision/Sidonie/Orly/Sedif/TF1 (Jean Louis-Livi)

Ten years after his supposed death in battle, an army officer returns to France to reclaim his identity, his fortune and his wife, now married to an ambitious politician.
Impressive moments, particularly the opening scenes of the aftermath of battle, do not quite compensate for the often stilted approach to a period drama of loss and betrayal.
w Jean Cosmos, Yves Angelo *novel* Honoré de Balzac *d* Yves Angelo *ph* Bernard Lutic *m* Beethoven, Mozart, Schubert *ad* Bernard Vezat *ed* Thierry Derocles
☆ Gérard Depardieu, Fanny Ardant, Fabrice Luchini, André Dussollier, Daniel Prévost, Claude Rich, Romane Bohringer, Maxime Leroux
'Predictable and uninspiring.' – *Sight and Sound*

Colonel Effingham's Raid

US 1946 70m bw
TCF (Lamar Trotti)
GB title: *Man of the Hour*

A retired Southern colonel tries to straighten out a corrupt Georgia town.
Competent, unsurprising programmer.
w Kathryn Scola *novel* Berry Fleming *d* Irving Pichel *ph* Edward Cronjager *m* Cyril Mockridge
☆ Charles Coburn, Joan Bennett, William Eythe, Allyn Joslyn, Elizabeth Patterson, Donald Meek, Frank Craven, Thurston Hall, Cora Witherspoon, Emory Parnell, Henry Armetta, Roy Roberts, Charles Trowbridge

Colonel Redl **

Hungary/West Germany/Austria 1984 149m Eastmancolor
Mafilm/Mokep/Manfred Durniok/ZDF/ORF
original title: *Oberst Redl*

The career of a railwayman's son who in the early years of the century rises high in the military but is condemned by his own insecurities and forced to commit suicide as a spy.
Whether or not one cares for the ironic parable (also treated by John Osborne in his play A Patriot for Me*) this is a handsome film full of brilliant visuals.*
w István Szabó, Peter Dobai *d* *István Szabó* *ph* *Lajos Koltai* *m* Zdenko Tamassy
☆ *Klaus Maria Brandauer*, Hans-Christian Blech, Armin Müller-Stahl, Gudrun Landgrebe, Jan Niklas
best picture
best foreign film

The Color of Money **

US 1986 119m DuArt
Touchstone (Irving Axelrod, Barbara de Fina)

Twenty-five years later, the hero of *The Hustler* teaches a young man his skills.
Slackly told but consistently enjoyable adventures of Fast Eddie Felson in his older age.
w Richard Price, based on characters created by Walter Tevis *d* *Martin Scorsese* *ph* Michael Ballhaus *m* Robbie Robertson
☆ *Paul Newman*, *Tom Cruise*, Mary Elizabeth Mastrantonio, Helen Shaver, Bill Cobbs, John Turturro
'Fast and absorbing and often thrillingly well made, but there's something impure about it: it's a streamlined, best-sellerish replay of Scorsese's work in the 1970s.' – *Terrence Rafferty, Nation*
Paul Newman
Michael Balhaus; Boris Leven (art direction); Kevin J. O'Hara (sound); Mary Elizabeth Mastrantonio; Richard Price

Color of Night

US 1994 123m colour
Guild/Cinergi/Hollywood Pictures (David Matalon, Buzz Feitshans)

A traumatized psychiatrist takes over a group of patients that includes the person who murdered his colleague.
A ludicrous thriller that reaches depths of absurdity rarely seen on screen, particularly in its risibly overblown finale. Willis acts in Die Hard *mode while the rest of the cast twitch uncontrollably around him.*
w Matthew Chapman, Billy Ray *d* Richard Rush *ph* Dietrich Lohmann *m* Dominic Frontiere *pd* James L. Schoppe *ed* Jack Hofstra
☆ Bruce Willis, Jane March, Ruben Blades, Lesley Ann Warren, Scott Bakula, Brad Dourif, Lance Henriksen, Shirley Knight
'A sure bet for many Worst of the Year lists, this wholly terrible movie is far more enjoyable and astonishing than many halfway good ones.' – *Kim Newman, Sight and Sound*
'It's hard not to regard this as another woeful addition to the ever-growing canon of Willis stinkers.' – *Empire*
'This trashy, over the top, often funny feature has sex, nudity, gore, *Vertigo* scenes and lots of nutty patients.' – *Psychotronic Video*
† The version shown in cinemas was recut by the production company. The director's cut, lasting six minutes longer, was released on video.

The Color Purple **

US 1985 152m DeLuxe
Warner/Amblin (Steven Spielberg, Kathleen Kennedy, Frank Marshall, Quincy Jones)

The growth of a Southern black family during the first half of the century.
Well-intentioned and gracious but not always dramatically cohesive generation saga from a director trying to prove he has depth.
w Menno Meyjes *novel* Alice Walker *d* *Steven Spielberg* *ph* *Allen Daviau* *m* Quincy Jones *pd* J. Michael Riva *ed* Michael Kahn
☆ Whoopi Goldberg, Danny Glover, Margaret Avery, Oprah Winfrey, Willard Pugh, Adolph Caesar
best picture; Whoopi Goldberg; Margaret Avery (supporting actress); Oprah Winfrey (supporting actress); adapted screenplay; photography; music; editing; costumes (Aggie Guerard Rodgers); song 'Miss Celie's Blues' (*m* Quincy Jones, Rod Tempeston, *ly* Lionel Richie)

Colorado Territory *

US 1949 93m bw
Warner (Anthony Veiller)

An outlaw escapes from prison planning one last robbery but is shot in the attempt.
Moderate Western remake of High Sierra.
w John Twist, Edmund H. North *d* Raoul Walsh *ph* Sid Hickox *m* David Buttolph
☆ Joel McCrea, Virginia Mayo, Dorothy Malone, Henry Hull, John Archer, James Mitchell, Morris Ankrum, Basil Ruysdael, Frank Puglia

Colors *

US 1988 120m Metrocolor
Rank/Orion (Robert H. Solo)

A veteran cop and his young and cocky partner try to keep the peace between rival Los Angeles street gangs.
A documentary-style look at street violence and its relationship to poverty and drugs. It works well for the first half-hour, but soon loses coherence as a narrative and goes on too long before the effective climax.
w Michael Schiffer *d* Dennis Hopper *ph* Haskell Wexler *m* Herbie Hancock *pd* Ron Foreman *ed* Robert Estrin
☆ Sean Penn, Robert Duvall, Maria Conchita Alonso, Randy Brooks, Grand Bush, Don Cheadle, Damon Wayans
'A solidly crafted depiction of some current big-city horrors.' – *Variety*

The Colossus of Rhodes

Italy 1961 129m Technicolor SuperTotalScope
MGM (Michele Scaglione)

In 300 BC, a huge statue doubles as a fortress to prevent the Phoenicians from invading.
Good-looking spectacle with the usual muddled script.
w Sergio Leone and seven others *d* Sergio Leone *ph* Emilio Foriscot, Antonio Lopez Ballesteros *m* Angelo Francesco Lavagnino
☆ Rory Calhoun, Lea Massari, Georges Marchal

Colossus, the Forbin Project: see *The Forbin Project*

The Colour of Lies: see *Au Coeur Du Mensonge*

The Colour of Paradise *

Iran 1999 81m colour
Varahonar (Mehdi Karimi)
original title: *Ranghe Khoda*

A widower wishes to marry again, but is embarrassed by his young, blind son, whom he sends away to become a carpenter.
A simple and sometimes affecting drama of a boy who overcomes his disabilities and an adult who is blind to his own faults.
wd Majid Majidi *ph* Mohammad Davudi, Hashem Attar *m* Ali Reza Kohandiri, Keyvan Jahanshahi *pd* Masood Madadi, Asghar Nezhadimani *ed* Hassan Hassandoost
☆ Mohsen Ramezani (Mohammad), Hossein Mahjub (Father), Salime Feizi (Grandma), Elham

Sharifi (Little Sister), Farahnaz Safari (Big Sister), Behzad Rafice (Village teacher)

'In artistic terms, it's pretty basic. But on a human level, it's an inspirational delight.' – *Empire*

The Colour of Pomegranates ***

USSR 1969 73m colour
Armenfilm

original title: *Tsvet Granata*

Biopic of the 18th-century Armenian poet Sayat Nova, as he rises from a child working as a wool dyer to courtier and monk, told in the manner of his poems.

Extraordinary lyrical film, full of richly coloured emblematic images, like a succession of animated icons.

wd Sergei Paradjanov *ph* Suren Shakhbazian *m* Tieran Mansurian *ad* Stepan Andranikan

☆ Sofiko Chiaureli, M. Alekian, V. Glastian, G. Gegechkori, O. Minasian

Colpire Al Cuore: see *Blow to the Heart*

Colt 45

US 1950 74m Technicolor
Warner (Saul Elkins)
US TV title: *Thundercloud*

A new kind of gun, intended to bring law and order to the west, gets into the wrong hands.

Routine, watchable Western which achieved a surprising popularity.

w Thomas Blackburn *d* Edwin L. Marin *ph* Wilfred M. Cline *m* William Lava

☆ Randolph Scott, Zachary Scott, Ruth Roman, Lloyd Bridges, Chief Thundercloud

'Has all the artistry of a picture-strip.' – C. A. Lejeune

Coma *

US 1978 113m Metrocolor
MGM (Martin Erlichman)

A lady doctor suspects that patients are being put deliberately into coma so that their organs can be sold, and finds herself in deadly peril.

Hitchcockian suspense thriller with nobody but the audience believing the heroine; the fact that there are more dead than living characters makes it slightly too ghoulish at times.

wd Michael Crichton *novel* Robin Cook *ph* Victor J. Kemper, Gerald Hirschfeld *m* Jerry Goldsmith *pd* Albert Brenner

☆ Geneviève Bujold, Michael Douglas, Richard Widmark, Elizabeth Ashley, Rip Torn, Lois Chiles, Hari Rhodes, Tom Selleck

'A stupid, silly mad-scientist thriller, with a plucky Girl-Surgeon out to solve the mysteries of some strange deaths.' – *Stanley Kauffmann*

Comanche

US 1955 87m DeLuxe Cinemascope
UA (Carl Krueger)

In 1875 New Mexico, a renegade Indian prevents peace between white and red man.

Cheerful action Western, satisfying to the easily pleased.

w Carl Krueger *d* George Sherman *m* Herschel Burke Gilbert

☆ Dana Andrews, Kent Smith, Nestor Paiva, Henry Brandon, John Litel, Lowell Gilmore, Mike Mazurki

Comanche Station

US 1960 74m Technicolor Cinemascope
Columbia (Budd Boetticher)

A man seeks his wife, taken prisoner by Indians.

Below-par star Western, indifferently plotted.

w Burt Kennedy *d* Budd Boetticher *ph* Charles Lawton Jnr *md* Mischa Bakaleinikoff

☆ Randolph Scott, Nancy Gates, Claude Akins, Skip Homeier

Comanche Territory

US 1950 76m Technicolor
Universal (Leonard Goldstein)

Jim Bowie prevents an Indian war by stopping settlers taking over the silver mines on Comanche land.

Routine Western, given more handsome treatment than it deserves.

w Oscar Brodney, Lewis Meltzer *d* George Sherman *ph* Maury Gertsman *m* Frank Skinner *ad* Bernard Herzbrun, Richard H. Riedel *ed* Frank Gross

☆ Maureen O'Hara, Macdonald Carey, Will Geer, Charles Drake, Pedro de Cordoba, Ian MacDonald, Edmond Cobb, Glenn Strange

The Comancheros **

US 1961 107m DeLuxe Cinemascope
TCF (George Sherman)

A Texas Ranger and his gambler prisoner join forces to clean up renegade gunmen operating from a remote armed compound.

Easy-going, cheerfully violent Western with lively roughhouse sequences.

w James Edward Grant, Clair Huffaker *d* Michael Curtiz *ph* William H. Clothier *m* Elmer Bernstein

☆ *John Wayne*, Stuart Whitman, Nehemiah Persoff, Lee Marvin, Ina Balin, Bruce Cabot

'A struggle for Power, Wealth and the Love of the Same Woman.'

Come and Get It *

US 1936 99m bw
Samuel Goldwyn (Merritt Hulburd)

The life and loves of a lumber tycoon in 19th-century Wisconsin.

Disappointingly conventional, mainly studio-bound action drama using top talent of the period.

w Jules Furthman, Jane Murfin *novel* Edna Ferber *d* Howard Hawks, William Wyler *ph* Gregg Toland, Rudolph Maté *m* Alfred Newman *ed* Edward Curtiss

☆ Edward Arnold, Joel McCrea, Frances Farmer, Walter Brennan, Andrea Leeds

Academy Award: Walter Brennan

Academy Award nomination: Edward Curtiss

Come Back Charleston Blue *

US 1972 101m Technicolor
Warner/Formosa (Samuel Goldwyn Jnr)

Harlem detectives Coffin Ed Johnson and Gravedigger Jones investigate the case of a long-dead gangster who seems to be still taking vengeance.

Occasionally funny but disturbingly violent crime kaleidoscope with a black ambience, more sophisticated and therefore more generally acceptable than its predecessor Cotton Comes to Harlem *(qv).*

w Bontche Schweig, Peggy Elliott *novel The Heat's On* by Chester Himes *d* Mark Warren *ph* Dick Kratina *m* Donny Hathaway

☆ Godfrey Cambridge, Raymond St Jacques, Peter de Anda, Jonelle Allen, Percy Rodrigues, Minnie Gentry

'That girl in their house spelled trouble!'

Come Back Little Sheba *

US 1952 99m bw
Paramount (Hal B. Wallis)

An ex-alcoholic is let down not only by his slovenly wife but by the young girl he idolizes.

Stagey but theatrically effective transcription of a popular domestic drama, with one outstanding performance.

w Ketti Frings *play William Inge* *d* Daniel Mann *ph* James Wong Howe *m* Franz Waxman *ed* Warren Low

☆ *Shirley Booth*, Burt Lancaster, Terry Moore, Richard Jaeckel

Academy Award: Shirley Booth

Academy Award nomination: Terry Moore; editing

Come Back Peter: see *Some Like It Sexy*

Come Back to Me: see *Doll Face*

Come Back to the Five and Dime, Jimmy Dean, Jimmy Dean

US 1983 110m DuArt
Sandcastle 5/Mark Goodman/Viacom

Misfits meet to celebrate the twentieth anniversary of the death of James Dean.

Filmed play which descends from cynicism through gloom to hysteria and is never very revealing.

w Ed Graczyk *play* Ed Graczyk *d* Robert Altman *ph* Pierre Mignot *m* various

☆ Sandy Dennis, Karen Black, Cher, Sudie Bond, Kathy Bates

'It may seem perverse to describe as Altman's masterpiece so self-contained and "alien" a work, with an existence pre-dating his own involvement and a thrusting (if perverse) biological life that owes nothing to the audience's willingness to participate. But the irony depends solely on which side of Altman's own two-way world one stands.' – *Richard Combs, MFB*

Come Blow Your Horn *

US 1963 112m Technicolor Panavision
Paramount/Lear and Yorkin

A country boy in New York is envious of his older brother's sophisticated life.

Amusing characters and funny lines permeate this stolid transcription of an early Neil Simon success; the big screen is not the place for them.

w Norman Lear *play Neil Simon* *d* Bud Yorkin *ph* William Daniels *m* Nelson Riddle

☆ Frank Sinatra, Tony Bill, Lee J. Cobb, Molly Picon, Jill St John, Barbara Rush, Dan Blocker

Come Clean **

US 1931 20m bw
Hal Roach

Two much-married men go out for ice-cream and bring back a woman of the streets they have saved from suicide.

Splendid star comedy with the famous characterizations fully rounded.

w H. M. Walker *d* James W. Horne *ph* Art Lloyd *ed* Richard Currier

☆ Stan Laurel, Oliver Hardy, Mae Busch, Charlie Hall, Gertrude Astor, Linda Loredo

† Remade in 1942 as *Brooklyn Orchid*, with William Bendix and Joe Sawyer.

Come Fill the Cup *

US 1951 113m bw
Warner (Henry Blanke)

An alcoholic newspaperman cures himself, then his boss's alcoholic son who is involved with gangsters.

Unlikely but solidly entertaining melodrama, powerfully cast.

w Ivan Goff, Ben Roberts *novel* Harlan Ware *d* Gordon Douglas *ph Robert Burks* *m* Ray Heindorf

☆ *James Cagney, Gig Young, Raymond Massey*, Phyllis Thaxter, James Gleason, Selena Royle, Larry Keating

Academy Award nomination: Gig Young

Come Fly with Me

US 1962 109m Metrocolor Panavision
MGM/Anatole de Grunwald

The romantic adventures of three air hostesses.

Good-looking girls and airplanes but little else make thin entertainment.

w William Roberts *d* Henry Levin *ph* Oswald Morris *m* Lyn Murray

☆ Hugh O'Brian, Dolores Hart, Karl Malden, Pamela Tiffin, Lois Nettleton, Karl Boehm

Come Live with Me *

US 1941 86m bw
MGM (Clarence Brown)

In order to stay in America, a girl refugee from Vienna arranges a strictly platonic marriage with a struggling author.

Hypnotically predictable comedy, quite well presented and performed.

w Patterson McNutt, Virginia Van Upp *d* Clarence Brown *ph* George Folsey *m* Herbert Stothart

☆ James Stewart, Hedy Lamarr, Ian Hunter, Verree Teasdale, Donald Meek, Barton MacLane, *Adeline de Walt Reynolds*

Come Next Spring *

US 1955 92m Trucolor Republic

A drunkard returns to his Arkansas farm family and wins the respect of them and the community.

D. W. Griffith-type pastoral melodrama which surprisingly works pretty well and leaves one with the intended warm glow.

w Montgomery Pittman *d* R. G. Springsteen *ph* Jack Marta *m* Max Steiner

☆ Ann Sheridan, Steve Cochran, Walter Brennan, Sherry Jackson, Richard Eyer, Edgar Buchanan, Sonny Tufts, Mae Clarke

'An unpretentious film with a good deal of charm.' – *MFB*

Come on George *

GB 1939 88m bw
ATP/Ealing (Jack Kitchin)

A stableboy calms a nervous racehorse and rides him to victory.

Standard comedy vehicle, well mounted, with the star at his box-office peak.

w Anthony Kimmins, Leslie Arliss, Val Valentine *d* Anthony Kimmins *ph* Ronald Neame, Gordon Dines *m* Ernest Irving *ad* Wilfred Shingleton *ed* Ray Pitt

☆ *George Formby*, Pat Kirkwood, Joss Ambler, Meriel Forbes, Cyril Raymond, George Carney, Ronald Shiner

Come Out Fighting

US 1945 62m bw
Monogram/Pathé/Banner (Sam Katzman, Jack Dietz)

The East Side Kids reform the naïve, ballet-dancing son of the police commissioner by saving him from crooked gamblers.

Dull programmer, with rough-and-ready direction and performances and lacking the series' usual boisterous humour.

w Earle Snell *d* William Beaudine *ph* Ira Morgan *md* Edward Kay *ad* David Milton *ed* William Austin

☆ Leo Gorcey, Huntz Hall, Billy Benedict, Gabriel Dell, June Carlson, Amelita Ward, Johnny Duncan

Come Out of the Pantry

GB 1935 73m bw
British and Dominions (Herbert Wilcox)

An English milord is forced by circumstance to take a job as his boss's footman.

Pleasing if obvious comedy, later remodelled as Spring in Park Lane.

w Austin Parker, Douglas Furber *story* Alice Duer Miller *d* Jack Raymond *ph* Freddie Young, Henry Harris *ad* L. P. Williams *ed* Frederick Wilson

☆ Jack Buchanan, Fay Wray, James Carew, Ronald Squire, Olive Blakeney, Fred Emney

Come See the Paradise *

US 1990 133m DeLuxe
Fox (Robert F. Colesberry)

After Pearl Harbor, a Japanese-American woman, married to an Irish-American soldier, is interned with her family.

A fascinating subject, of racism and culture clash, is submerged by a concentration on an ordinary romance.

wd Alan Parker *ph* Michael Seresin *m* Randy Edelman *pd* Geoffrey Kirkland *ed* Gerry Hambling

☆ Dennis Quaid, Tamlyn Tomita, Sab Shimono, Shizuko Hoshi, Stan Egi, Ronald Yamamoto, Akemi Nishino, Naomi Nakano, Brady Tsurutani, Elizabeth Gilliam

Come September

US 1961 112m Technicolor CinemaScope
Universal/7 Pictures Corporation/Raoul Walsh Enterprises (Robert Arthur)

A wealthy American discovers that his Italian villa is being used as a hotel by his once-a-year mistress, who is about to marry.

Clumsy sex farce with lush trimmings and generation gap asides; effort more noticeable than achievement.

w Stanley Shapiro, Maurice Richlin *d* Robert Mulligan *ph* William Daniels *m* Hans J. Salter

☆ Rock Hudson, Gina Lollobrigida, Sandra Dee, Bobby Darin, Walter Slezak, Brenda de Banzie, Joel Grey, Rossana Rory, Ronald Howard

Come to the Stable *

US 1949 94m bw
TCF (Samuel G. Engel)

Two French nuns arrive in New England to build a local hospital, and melt the hearts of the local grumps.

This old-time charmer simply brims with sweetness and light and is produced with high-class studio efficiency.

w Oscar Millard, Sally Benson *story* Clare Boothe Luce *d* Henry Koster *ph* Joseph LaShelle

m Cyril Mockridge *md* Lionel Newman *ad* Lyle Wheeler, Joseph C. Wright
☆ *Loretta Young, Celeste Holm*, Hugh Marlowe, Elsa Lanchester, Thomas Gomez, Dorothy Patrick, Basil Ruysdael, Dooley Wilson, Regis Toomey, Henri Letondal
Clare Boothe Luce; Joseph LaShelle; Loretta Young; Celeste Holm; Elsa Lanchester; song 'Through a Long and Sleepless Night' (*m* Alfred Newman, *ly* Mack Gordon); art direction

Come Undone: see *Presque Rien*

'Millions loved him, could someone hate him enough to kill and kill again?'

The Comeback

GB 1978 100m colour
Enterprise (Peter Walker)

aka: *The Day the Screaming Stopped*

An American singer in London deals with the murder of his wife – and with her ghost.
Dim mixture of mystery and horror, not at all persuasive.
w Murray Smith *d* Peter Walker *m* Stanley Myers
☆ Jack Jones, Sheila Keith, Pamela Stephenson, David Doyle, Bill Owen, Richard Johnson

The Comedians *

US/Bermuda/France 1967 160m Metrocolor Panavision
MGM/Maximilian/Trianon (Peter Glenville)

A variety of English-speaking eccentrics are caught up in the violent events of Haiti under Papa Doc Duvalier.
Clumsy and heavy-going compression of a too-topical novel, with most of the plot left in at the expense of character. Neither entertaining nor instructive, but bits of acting please.
w Graham Greene *novel* Graham Greene *d* Peter Glenville *ph* Henri Decaë *m* Laurence Rosenthal
☆ Richard Burton, Elizabeth Taylor, *Alec Guinness*, Peter Ustinov, Lillian Gish, Paul Ford, Roscoe Lee Browne, James Earl Jones, Raymond St Jacques, Cicely Tyson

'So thick and fast do the clichés come that one feels the script can only have been salvaged from some *New Statesman* competition.' – *Tom Milne*

'It's pleasant to spend two hours again in Greeneland, still well-stocked with bilious minor crucifixions, furtive fornication, cynical politics, and reluctant hope.' – *Stanley Kauffmann*

Comédie de L'Innocence

France 2000 103m colour
Artificial Eye/MACT/TF1/Camelia (Martine and Antoine de Clermont-Tonnerre)

aka: *Son of Two Mothers or the Comedy of Innocence*

A 9-year-old boy suddenly refuses to accept his mother and insists that she take him to live with his real mother.
A psychological thriller that creates a creepy atmosphere and then quickly dissipates it.
w Francoise Dumas, Raúl Ruiz *novel* Massimo Bontempelli *d* Raúl Ruiz *ph* Jacques Bouquin *m* Jorge Arriagada *ad* Bruno Beauge *ed* Mireille Hannon
☆ Isabelle Huppert (Ariane), Jeanne Balibar (Isabella), Charles Berling (Serge), Nils Hugon (Camille), Edith Scob (Laurence), Denis Podalydes (Pierre), Laure de Clermont-Tonnerre (Helene)

'No genre excuses the movie's bizarre, somnolent atmosphere. No believable emotions are displayed at any point.' – *Peter Bradshaw, Guardian*

'Mr Ruiz seems enchanted with his own coyness and the curlicues and indirections the story allows him.' – *A. O. Scott, New York Times*

The Comedy Man *

GB 1964 92m bw
British Lion-Gray-Consort (Jon Pennington)

A middle-aged actor on the skids desperately rounds up his contacts and becomes the star of a TV commercial.
Determinedly depressing satirical melodrama with engaging moments; comedy emphasis would have better suited the talents.
w Peter Yeldham *novel* Douglas Hayes *d* Alvin Rakoff *ph* Ken Hodges *m* Bill McGuffie
☆ Kenneth More, Cecil Parker, Dennis Price, Billie Whitelaw, Norman Rossington, Angela Douglas, Edmund Purdom, Frank Finlay, Alan Dobie

'Humour and intelligent irony.' – *Sunday Express*

'A merciless and accurate picture of the brave band of actors who live from hand to mouth and commute between the Salisbury Arms pub and the Poland Street Labour exchange.' – *Evening News*

'A grave case of greed gone too far!'

The Comedy of Terrors *

US 1963 88m Pathécolor Panavision
Alta Vista/AIP (Anthony Carras, Richard Matheson)

Two impecunious funeral directors decide to speed up the demise of their prospective clients.
Disappointingly slackly-handled and rather tiresome macabre frolic, notable for a few splendid moments and an imperishable cast.
w Richard Matheson *d* Jacques Tourneur *ph* Floyd Crosby *m* Les Baxter
☆ Vincent Price, Peter Lorre, Boris Karloff, Basil Rathbone, Joe E. Brown, Joyce Jameson

Comes a Horseman

US 1978 118m Technicolor Panavision
UA/Chartoff-Winkler (Robert Caan)

In the forties, Montana ranchers have a hard time holding onto their land against the pressures of progress and a villainous cattle baron.
Portentous and wholly unexciting modern Western, not helped by a loftily unexplained title and show-off photography.
w Dennis Lynton Clark *d* Alan J. Pakula *ph* Gordon Willis *m* Michael Small *pd* George Jenkins
☆ Jane Fonda, Jason Robards Jnr, James Caan, George Grizzard, Richard Farnsworth, Jim Davis

'It's a film of few words (and about a quarter of them mangled by the sound recording). The melodrama is smothered under sullen, overcast skies. How can you get involved in the conflict between the good guys and the bad guys if you can't even see them?' – *Pauline Kael*

Richard Farnsworth

Comet over Broadway

US 1938 65m bw
Warner

An actress, having been involved in a murder, is torn between burning ambition and mother love.
Arrant melodrama which overtaxes its star.
w Mark Hellinger, Robert Buckner *story* Faith Baldwin *d* Busby Berkeley
☆ Kay Francis, Ian Hunter, John Litel, Donald Crisp, Minna Gombell, Sybil Jason, Melville Cooper

'A backstage yarn that goes overboard on assorted heartbreaks.' – *Variety*

Comfort and Joy *

GB 1984 106m colour
Lake/EMI/STV (Davina Belling, Clive Parsons)

A Scottish radio disc jockey becomes involved in a war between two ice-cream firms.
Heavy comedy, short of laughs and sympathy; a distinct descent from Local Hero, *which was a comedown after* Gregory's Girl.
wd Bill Forsyth *ph* Chris Menges *m* Mark Knopfler
☆ Bill Paterson, Eleanor David, C. P. Grogan, Alex Norton

The Comfort of Strangers

Italy/GB 1990 104m Technicolor
Rank/Erre/Sovereign/Reteitalia (Angelo Rizzoli)

original title: *Cortesie per gli ospiti*

On holiday in Venice, a conventional husband and wife become involved with a sadomasochistic couple.
Bleak and icy tale that will induce a shiver, although the mannered performances aren't an attraction.
w Harold Pinter *novel* Ian McEwan *d* Paul Schrader *ph* Dante Spinotti *m* Angelo Badalamenti *pd* Gianni Quaranta *ed* Bill Pankow
☆ Christopher Walken, Rupert Everett, Natasha Richardson, Helen Mirren, Manfredi Aliquo

The Comic *

US 1969 95m Technicolor
Columbia (Carl Reiner)

The success, downfall and old age of a silent film comedian in Hollywood.
Remarkably bright and cinematic tragicomedy obviously based on Buster Keaton, with a Citizen Kane*-type framework. Not a commercial success, but a must for professionals.*
w Carl Reiner, Aaron Rubin *d* Carl Reiner *ph* W. Wallace Kelley *m* Jack Elliott
☆ Dick Van Dyke, Mickey Rooney, Cornel Wilde, Carl Reiner, Michele Lee, Pert Kelton

'Offers a variety of delights.' – *Judith Crist*

'A furious editorial about a business that treats its veterans like over-exposed celluloid.' – *Variety*

Comic Book Confidential **

US/Canada 1989 90m bw/colour
Sphinx/Don Haig/Martin Harbury/Charles Lippincott (Ron Mann)

A documentary on the evolution of the comic book in North America, from its beginnings in the 30s, with interviews with leading exponents.
Graphic account of comic books and the controversies and cults they have started, concentrating in particular on the 50s, when they were condemned as corrupters of the young, followed by a period of self-censorship and the return of the Superheroes in the 60s; it is accompanied by a well-chosen soundtrack of the more eccentric songs of each era.
d Ron Mann *ph* Robert Fresco, Joan Churchill *ad* Gerlinde Scharinger *ed* Robert Kennedy, Ron Mann
☆ Lynda Barry, Charles Burns, Sue Coe, Robert Crumb, Will Eisner, Al Feldstein, Shary Flenniken, William M. Gaines, Bill Griffith, Jaime Hernandez, Jack Kirby, Harvey Kurtzman, Stan Lee, Paul Mavrides, Frank Miller and also Victor Moscoso, Françoise Mouly, Dan O'Neill, Harvey Pekar, Gilbert Shelton, Spain, Art Spiegelman

Comic Strip Hero: see *Jeu de Massacre*

Comin' at Ya!

US 1981 101m Technicolor
Dimensionscope 3-D
GTO Films (Marshall Lupo, Stan Torchia)

An ex-outlaw goes in search of three outlaws who kidnapped his wife-to-be.
Determined three-dimensional attack on the sensibilities, with nothing to interest in story or acting.
w Wolf Lowenthal, Lloyd Battista, Gene Quintano *story* Tony Petitto *d* Ferdinando Baldi *ph* Fernando Arribas *m* Carlo Savina *ad* Luciano Spadoni *ed* Franco Fraticelli
☆ Tony Anthony, Gene Quintano, Victoria Abril, Ricardo Palacios

Comin' thro' the Rye

GB 1923 85m approx (24 fps) bw silent
Hepworth Picture Plays

In Victorian England, lovers meet periodically in a rye field, but events move against them.
Statuesque romantic drama whose reputation may be largely due to its accidental survival. (There was a previous version from the same producer in 1916, with the same leading actress.)
w Blanche McIntosh *novel* Helen Mathers *d* Cecil M. Hepworth *ph* Geoffrey Faithfull
☆ Alma Taylor, Shayle Gardner, Eileen Dennes, Ralph Forbes, Francis Lister

'My best and most important film.' – *Cecil M. Hepworth*

'Hepworth's directorial style matches his material in simplicity.' – *Geoff Brown, MFB, 1976*

'A man who believed in war! A man who believed in nothing! And a woman who believed in both of them!'

Coming Home *

US 1978 128m DeLuxe
UA/Jerome Hellman

An embittered Vietnam veteran falls for the wife of a serving soldier.
Self-pitying romantic wallow which must mean more to American audiences than to others. Goodish acting.
w Waldo Salt, Robert C. Jones *story* Nancy Dowd *d* Hal Ashby *ph* Haskell Wexler *m* various *pd* Mike Haller *ed* Don Zimmerman
☆ Jane Fonda, Jon Voight, Bruce Dern, Robert Carradine, Penelope Milford

'Just one more story about a wife who gets entangled with another man while her husband is away. Everything in the script that is contemporary is mere updating of that perennial story.' – *Stanley Kauffmann*

Jon Voight; Jane Fonda; best screenplay
best picture; Hal Ashby; Bruce Dern; Penelope Milford; editing

Coming to America

US 1988 116m Technicolor
UIP/Paramount (George Folsey Jnr, Robert D. Wachs)

A wealthy African prince poses as a poor student in New York so he can find a bride who will love him for himself.
Tired comedy that fails to exploit Murphy's strengths, despite his popping up heavily disguised in several minor roles.
w David Sheffield, Barry W. Blaustein *story* Eddie Murphy *d* John Landis *ph* Woody Omens *m* Nile Rodgers *ed* Malcolm Campbell, George Folsey Jnr *sp* make-up: Rick Baker
☆ Eddie Murphy, Arsenio Hall, John Amos, James Earl Jones, Shari Headley, Madge Sinclair

'A true test for loyal fans.' – *Variety*

Coming Up Roses *

GB 1986 93m Eastmancolor
Red Rooster/S4C
Welsh Title: *Rhosyn a Rhith*

When the local cinema closes down the local community takes it over for mushroom-growing.
Charming curiosity in Welsh with English subtitles, reminiscent of Ealing in its heyday.
w Ruth Carter *d* Stephen Bayley *ph* Dick Pope *m* Michael Story *pd* Hildegard Bechtler
☆ Dafydd Hywel, Iola Gregory, Olive Michael, Mari Emlyn

A Coming-Out Party: see *Very Important Person*

The Command

US 1954 94m Warnercolor Cinemascope
Warner (David Weisbart)

A cavalry troop escorts a wagon train through Indian country.
Competent but unsurprising 'second team' Western.
w Russell Hughes *novel* James Warner Bellah *d* David Butler *ph* Wilfrid M. Cline *m* Dimitri Tiomkin
☆ Guy Madison, Joan Weldon, James Whitmore, Carl Benton Reid, Harvey Lembeck, Ray Teal, Bob Nichols

'Heroes, cowards, fighters, braggarts, liars ... and what goes on in their hearts!'

Command Decision *

US 1949 111m bw
MGM (Sidney Franklin)

War among the back-room boys; a general, his staff and his peers debate the aerial bombardment of Germany.
Plainly reproduced version of a determinedly serious play, with a remarkable cast partly at sea.
w William R. Laidlaw, George Froeschel *play* William Wister Haines *d* Sam Wood *ph* Harold Rosson *m* Miklos Rozsa
☆ Clark Gable, Walter Pidgeon, Van Johnson, Brian Donlevy, John Hodiak, Charles Bickford, Edward Arnold, Marshall Thompson, Richard Quine, Cameron Mitchell, Clinton Sundberg, Ray Collins, Warner Anderson, John McIntire, Moroni Olsen

Command Performance

GB 1937 84m bw
Grosvenor (Harcourt Templeman)

Fearing a breakdown through overwork a singer takes to the open road and falls in love with a gypsy.
Innocuous musical, which is mainly a vehicle for Tracy to sing sentimental ballads and attempt an operatic aria.
w Stafford Dickens, George Pearson, Michael Hankinson *story* Sinclair Hill *d* Sinclair Hill *ph* Cyril Bristow *m/ly* Tolchard Evans, Stanley Damerell, Irwin Dash *md* Louis Levy *ad* C. Wilfred Arnold *ed* Michael Hankinson

☆ The Street Singer (Arthur Tracy), Lilli Palmer, Mark Daly, Finlay Currie, Jack Milford, Stafford Hilliard

'He's getting even ... by breaking all the rules.'
Commandments
US 1997 86m DeLuxe
Gramercy/Northern Lights (Michael Chinich, Daniel Goldberg, Joe Medjuck)

Having lost everything that makes his life worthwhile, a doctor decides to break every one of the Ten Commandments.
A blackish comedy with an uncertain tone and an often squeamish approach to its subject matter.
wd Daniel Taplitz *ph* Slavomir Idziak *m* Joseph Vitarelli *pd* Robin Standefer *ed* Michael Jablow
☆ Aidan Quinn, Courteney Cox, Anthony LaPaglia, Louis Zorich, Pamela Gray, Pat McNamara, Tom Aldredge
'Too glib and too oblique to break out of niche interest.' – *Variety*

Commando
US 1985 88m DeLuxe
TCF (Joel Silver)

Unlikely mates are thrown together in pursuit of a deadly Latin dictator.
Hard action nonsense with the saving grace of humour.
w Steven de Souza *d* Mark L. Lester *m* James Horner *pd* John Vallone *ed* Mark Goldblatt, John F. Link, Glenn Farr
☆ Arnold Schwarzenegger, Rae Dawn Chong, Dan Hedaya, Vernon Wells, David Patrick Kelly
'Palatable actioner, inoffensively silly.' – *Variety*

The Commandos Strike at Dawn *
US 1942 98m bw
Columbia (Lester Cowan)

Norwegian commandos outwit the Nazis with the help of the British navy.
Standard war adventure shot on Vancouver Island.
w Irwin Shaw *story* C. S. Forester *d* John Farrow *ph* William C. Mellor *m* Louis Gruenberg
☆ Paul Muni, Anna Lee, Lillian Gish, Cedric Hardwicke, Robert Coote, Ray Collins, Rosemary de Camp, Richard Derr, Alexander Knox, Rod Cameron
Ⓐ Louis Gruenberg

La Commare Secca: see *The Grim Reaper*

Comment J'Ai Tué Mon Pére **
France/Spain 2001 98m colour
Pathé/Cine B/Cinea/France 2/PHF

GB title: *The Way I Killed My Father*
A successful doctor's life starts to unravel when his elderly father, who abandoned him as a child, moves in with him and his wife.
Cool, insightful psychodrama of how a damaged child can grow up to be a damaged adult.
w Jacques Fieschi, Anne Fontaine. *d* Anne Fontaine *ph* Jean-Marc Fabre *m* Jocelyn Pook *ad* Sylvain Chauvelot *ed* Guy Lecorne
☆ Michel Bouquet (Maurice), Charles Berling (Jean-Luc), Natacha Regnier (Isa), Amira Casar (Myriem), Stephane Guillon (Patrick), Hubert Kounde (Jean-Toussaint)
'There is a palpable air of tension and suspense about this insightful film, a realization that the greatest and most provocative mystery of all is the human soul.' – *Kenneth Turan, Los Angeles Times*

The Commissar: see *Komissar*

'They Had Absolutely Nothing. But They Were Willing To Risk It All.'
The Commitments **
US 1991 118m Technicolor
TCF/Beacon/First Film/Dirty Hands (Roger Randall-Cutler, Lynda Myles)

Dublin youths, believing that the Irish are the blacks of Europe, form a soul band.
Lively and energetic account of backstage traumas, troubles and triumphs.
w Dick Clement, Ian La Frenais, Marc Abraham *novel* Roddy Doyle *d* Alan Parker *ph* Gale Tattersall *pd* Brian Morris *ed* Gerry Hambling
☆ Robert Arkins, Michael Aherne, Angeline Ball, Maria Doyle, Dave Finnegan, Bronagh Gallagher, Félim Gormley, Glen Hansard, Dick Massey, Johnny Murphy, Kenneth McCluskey, Andrew Strong
'Isn't likely to overwhelm at the box-office, any more than a band like this one devoted to covering classics would get much mileage in the music industry. Still, the pic is so fresh, well-executed and original that, properly handled, it should enjoy a long if modest run and inspire much hardcore devotion among music fans.' – *Variety*
'A hilariously funny, richly humane, consistently truthful story ... the movie pulsates with vitality, high spirits and the exhilarating feeling of people growing as they work together to transcend the seeming hopelessness of their surroundings.' – *Philip French, Observer*
Ⓐ editing
Ⓣ best picture; adapted screenplay; Alan Parker

'She'll get what she wants...no matter what it takes!'
Committed
US 2000 94m colour
Miramax (Marlen Hecht, Dean Silvers)

An abandoned wife goes to great lengths to get back her husband.
Thin and undernourished comedy that stays in the shallows.
wd Lisa Krueger *ph* Tom Krueger *m* Calexico *pd* Sharon Lomofsky *ed* Curtiss Clayton, Colleen Sharp
☆ Heather Graham (Joline), Casey Affleck (Jay), Luke Wilson (Carl), Goran Visnjic (Neil), Patricia Velasquez (Carmen), Alfonso Arau (Grampy), Clea DuVall (Mimi), Mark Ruffalo (T-Bo), Summer Phoenix (Meg)
'Relies heavily on voice-over narration and on comic situations that take forever to establish and then never really pay off.' – *A. O. Scott, New York Times*

Common-Law Cabin
US 1967 70m colour
Eve (Russ and Eve Mayer)

A group of tourists are stranded on an isolated pleasure beach on the Colorado River.
A typical Meyer product, which mixes sex and a little violence in a confused narrative of inadequate men, and willing women.
w John Moran *d* Russ Meyer *ph* Wady C. Medawar, Jack Lucas *ed* Russ Meyer
☆ Jack Moran, Babette Bardot, Adele Rein, Franklin Bolger, Alaina Capri, John Furlong, Ken Swofford, Andrew Hagara

Communion
US 1977 108m colour Super 35
Allied Artists (Richard K. Rosenberg)

aka: *Alice, Sweet Alice*
aka: *Holy Terror*
A young girl is suspected of killing several of her relatives.
Moderate low-budget thriller, mainly of interest for the brief appearances of Brooke Shields, in her first film, and of Roth as a pathologist.
w Rosemary Ritvo, Alfred Sole *d* Alfred Sole *ph* John Friberg, Chuck Hall *m* Stephen Lawrence *pd* John Lawless *ed* Edward Salier
☆ Paula Sheppard, Brooke Shields, Linda Miller, Jane Lowry, Alphonso DeNoble, Rudolph Willrich, Lillian Roth
'One of the most complex and satisfying American films in years.' – *Colin Pahlow, MFB*
'Strictly formulaic.' – *Sight and Sound*

'On December 25 1985 Whitley Strieber had a dream. Weeks later he discovered his family had the same dream. Months later he made the most shocking discovery of his life. Now, you will discover it.'
Communion
US 1990 101m DeLuxe
Vestron/Pheasantry Films/Allied Vision/Picture Property Co. (Philippe Mora, Whitley Strieber, Dan Allingham)

A writer recalls his meeting with extra-terrestrials and resolves to write a book about it.
Supposedly based on fact, the film has the style of an ill-conceived fantasy more rewarding to its author than to any audience.
w Whitley Strieber *book* Whitley Strieber *d* Philippe Mora *ph* Louis Irving *m* Eric Clapton *pd* Linda Pearl *ed* Lee Smith
☆ Christopher Walken, Lindsay Crouse, Joel Carlson, Frances Sternhagen, Andreas Katsulas, Terri Hanauer, Basil Hoffman

Como agua para chocolate: see *Like Water for Chocolate*

Compañeros *
Italy/Spain/West Germany 1970 118m
Technicolor Techniscope
TCF/Tritone/Atlantida/Terra

aka: *Vamos a Matar, Compañeros!*
A Swedish mercenary and a Mexican free a revolutionary being held by the Americans in order to get their hands on a fortune.
A baroque spaghetti Western, what with Nero as a straw-hatted Swede and Palance as a wooden-handed gunman, whose real hand was eaten by his pet hawk; underneath the extravagant action is buried a message about the exploitation of the poor.
w Sergio Corbucci, Dino Maiuri, Massimo de Rita, Fritz Ebert *d* Sergio Corbucci *ph* Alejandro Ulloa *m* Ennio Morricone *ad* Adolfo Cofiño *ed* Eugenio Alabiso
☆ Franco Nero, Tomas Milian, Jack Palance, Fernando Rey, Iris Berben, Karin Schubert, Francisco Bodalo
'Nasty, brutish and not particularly short.' – *Tom Milne, MFB*
'Tremendously entertaining.' – *Sight and Sound*
† It was a sequel to *The Mercenary* (qv).

Company Business
US 1991 98m Technicolor
MGM (Steven-Charles Jaffe)

An ageing agent is recalled by the CIA to make a covert spy swap with the KGB, only to discover it is a set-up, and he and his prisoner are to be killed.
Paranoid thriller that begins well but soon degenerates into a great deal of chasing around to little effect.
wd Nicholas Meyer *ph* Gerry Fisher *m* Michael Kamen *pd* Ken Adam *ed* Ronald Roose
☆ Gene Hackman, Mikhail Baryshnikov, Kurtwood Smith, Terry O'Quinn, Daniel von Bargen, Oleg Rudnick, Geraldine Danon
'This comedic thriller, which asks what spies do after the cold war, doesn't figure to have much company or do much business.' – *Variety*

Company Limited **
India 1971 112m bw
Chitranjali (Bharat Shamsher Rana)
original title: *Seemabaddha*
A sales manager uses underhand methods to gain promotion.
Long-winded drama of Calcutta life among westernized young executives where ambition stifles morality.
wd Satyajit Ray *novel* *Seemabaddha* by Shankar *ph* Soumendu Roy *m* Satyajit Ray *ad* Ashoke Bose *ed* Dulal Dutta
☆ Sharmila Tagore, Barun Chanda, Parumita Chowdhury

Company of Cowards: see *Advance to the Rear*

The Company of Strangers **
Canada 1990 101m colour
Electric/Contemporary/National Film Board of Canada (David Wilson)

aka: *Strangers In Good Company*
Seven old women are forced to camp out for several days in a derelict farmhouse after their bus breaks down.
A small gem of a movie, using a cast of non-actors to great effect.
w Gloria Demers, Cynthia Scott, David Wilson, Sally Bochner *d* Cynthia Scott *ph* David de Volpi *m* Marie Bernard *ed* David Wilson
☆ Alice Diabo, Constance Garneau, Winifred Holden, Cissy Meddings, Mary Meigs, Catherine Roche, Michelle Sweeney, Beth Webber
'In its quiet way this truthful, affecting, unsentimental movie tells us as much as any film I know about the female experience in this century.' – *Philip French, Observer*

The Company of Wolves **
GB 1984 95m colour
ITC/Palace (Chris Brown, Stephen Woolley)

A young girl dreams of wolves and werewolves.
Fragmentary adult fantasy which had an unexpected box-office success, chiefly because of its sexual allusiveness, its clever make-up and its pictorial qualities.
w Angela Carter, Neil Jordan *stories* Angela Carter *d* Neil Jordan *ph* Bryan Loftus *m* George Fenton *pd* Anton Furst *special make-up effects* Christopher Tucker
☆ Angela Lansbury, David Warner, Graham Crowden, Brian Glover, Sarah Patterson, Micha Bergese, Stephen Rea
'A horror film as literate as it is visionary, it's great fun – and that's not a cheap thrill.' – *J. Hoberman, Village Voice*

Compartiment Tueurs: see *The Sleeping Car Murders*

The Competition *
US 1980 129m Metrocolor
Columbia/Rastar/William Sackheim

An ageing piano prodigy has one last shot at fame in a San Francisco piano competition.
Slightly curious, old-fashioned but heavy-handed romance which aims to do for the piano what The Turning Point *did for ballet. It doesn't sustain its length but at least the milieu is interesting.*
wd Joel Oliansky *ph* Richard H. Kline *pd* Dale Hennesy *ed* David Blewitt *m/md* Lalo Schifrin
☆ Richard Dreyfuss, Lee Remick, Amy Irving, Sam Wanamaker, Joseph Cali
Ⓐ film editing; best song 'People Alone' (*m* Lalo Schifrin, *ly* Wilbur Jennings)

Un Complicato Intrigo di Donne, Vicoli e Delitto: see *Camorra: The Naples Connection*

Complicity *
GB 1999 99m DeLuxe
Entertainment/Carlton/J&M/Talisman (Richard Jackson, Neil Dunn)

While investigating the deaths of people involved in a top secret government project, a journalist finds himself suspected of being a serial killer.
Gritty thriller with a political subtext, set against a background of riots over nuclear waste, the predations of multinational corporations and the machinations of the arms trade.
w Bryan Elsley *novel* Iain Banks *d* Gavin Millar *ph* David Odd *m* Colin Towns *pd* Jamie Leonard *ed* Angus Newton *cos* Kate Carin
☆ Jonny Lee Miller (Cameron Colley), Brian Cox (DCI McDunn), Keeley Hawes (Yvonne), Paul Higgins (Andy Gould), Jason Hetherington (William), Bill Paterson (Wallace Byatt), Samuel West (Neil), Rachael Stirling (Claire Gould)

'You're About To Find Out Why The Women Of Shorehaven Would Kill Rather Than Miss An Appointment With Dr Bruce Fleckstein.'
Compromising Positions
US 1985 98m colour
Paramount (Frank Perry)

The murder of a philandering dentist has repercussions among his many mistresses.
Combination sex comedy and whodunnit which never seems to hit the right groove.
w Susan Isaacs *novel* Susan Isaacs *d* Frank Perry *ph* Barry Sonnenfeld *m* Brad Fiedel *pd* Peter Larkin *ed* Peter Frank
☆ Susan Sarandon, Raul Julia, Edward Herrmann, Judith Ivey, Mary Beth Hurt, Joe Mantegna

Compulsion *
US 1959 103m bw Cinemascope
TCF/Darryl F. Zanuck Productions (Richard F. Zanuck)

In the twenties, two Chicago students kidnap and murder a young boy for kicks.
Rather dogged but earnest fictionalization of the Leopold-Loeb case with solid performances and production.
w Richard Murphy *novel* Meyer Levin *d* Richard Fleischer *ph* William C. Mellor *m* Lionel Newman *ed* William Reynolds

☆ Dean Stockwell, Bradford Dillman, Orson Welles, Diane Varsi, E. G. Marshall, Martin Milner, Richard Anderson, Robert Simon
† Welles's cameo court appearance as a lawyer is based on Clarence Darrow.

The Computer Wore Tennis Shoes
US 1970 90m Technicolor
Disney
While mending a computer a college student gets an electric shock and becomes omniscient.
Ho-hum Disney comedy, eager to please but instantly forgotten.
w Joseph L. McEveety *d* Robert Butler
☆ Kurt Russell, Cesar Romero, Joe Flynn, William Schallert, Alan Hewitt

Comrade X *
US 1940 89m bw
MGM (Gottfried Reinhardt)
An American correspondent in Russia is blackmailed into smuggling a girl out of the country.
Lame satirical comedy in the wake of Ninotchka; *a few good moments, but generally heavy-handed.*
w Ben Hecht, Charles Lederer *story* Walter Reisch *d* King Vidor *ph* Joseph L. Ruttenberg *m* Bronislau Kaper
☆ Clark Gable, Hedy Lamarr, Felix Bressart, Oscar Homolka, Eve Arden, Sig Rumann
'Broadest comedic strokes and not-too-subtle satire ... a smacko entry for topflight biz.' – *Variety*
Walter Reisch

Comrades ***
GB 1987 180m colour
Curzon/Skreba/National Film Finance (Simon Relph)
In the 1830s six Dorset farm labourers who form a union to campaign against low wages are tried and transported to Australia as criminals.
Subtitled 'a lanternist's account', and based on the true story of the Tolpuddle Martyrs, it is a flawed masterpiece: too long and too preachy, yet its qualities outweigh these defects.
wd Bill Douglas *ph* Gale Tattersall *m* Hans Werner Henze, David Graham *pd* Michael Pickwood *ed* Mick Audsley
☆ Robin Soans, William Gammara, Stephen Bateman, Philip Davis, Jeremy Flynn, Keith Allen, Alex Norton, Michael Clark, Arthur Dignam, James Fox, John Hargreaves, Michael Hordern, Freddie Jones, Vanessa Redgrave, Robert Stephens and also Murray Melvin, Barbara Windsor, Imelda Staunton

Comradeship *
GB 1919 67m (24 fps) bw silent
Stoll
Two friends endure varying fortunes during World War I.
An early British 'A' feature which was highly popular in its day.
w Jeffrey Bernerd *d* Maurice Elvey
☆ Lily Elsie, Gerald Ames, Guy Newall, Peggy Carlisle

Comradeship: see *Kameradschaft (1931)*

La Comtesse aux Seins Nu: see *Female Vampire*

La Comtesse Noire: see *Female Vampire*

'Buckle up ... and hang on.'
Con Air *
US 1997 115m Technicolor Panavision
Buena Vista/Touchstone (Jerry Bruckheimer)
A tough parolee decides to support law and order when a violent criminal hijacks a convict transport plane.
Uproarious but enjoyable nonsense, marked by much gunfire, loud explosions, over-the-top acting and, when it can be heard, some witty dialogue.
w Scott Rosenberg *d* Simon West *ph* David Tattersall *m* Mark Mancina, Trevor Rabin *ad* Edward T. McAvoy *ed* Chris Lebenzon, Steve Mirkovich, Glen Scantlebury
☆ Nicolas Cage (Cameron Poe), John Cusack (Vince Larkin), John Malkovich (Cyrus Grissom), Steve Buscemi (Garland Greene), Ving Rhames (Diamond Dog), Colm Meaney (Duncan Malloy), Mykelti Williamson (Baby-O), Rachel Ticotin (Sally Bishop), Monica Potter (Tricia Poe), Dave Chappelle (Pinball), M. C. Gainey
'For a bit of dumb fun, the fun goes out of *Con Air* pretty quickly.' – *Sunday Times*
† The film was among the most commercially successful of the year, grossing some $101m in the US, and another $122m elsewhere.
song 'How Do I Live' (*m/ly* Dianne Warren); sound

'Thief. Warrior. Gladiator. King.'
Conan the Barbarian
US 1981 129m Technicolor Todd-AO
Dino de Laurentiis/Edward R. Pressman (Buzz Feitshans, Raffaella de Laurentiis)
In the Dark Ages, a young stalwart seeks out the barbarian tribe which murdered his parents.
Intolerably doomladen, slow-moving and mainly unintelligible rubbish which failed to put a lift into the long-announced sword-and-sorcery cycle.
w John Milius, Oliver Stone, from a character created by Robert E. Howard *d* John Milius *ph* Duke Callaghan *m* Basil Poledouris *pd* Ron Cobb *ed* C. Timothy O'Meara
☆ Arnold Schwarzenegger, James Earl Jones, Max von Sydow, Sandahl Bergman, Ben Davidson, Mako, Gerry Lopez
'A ragbag of half-witted kitsch, where even locations resemble a set, actors look like extras, violence like a stunt and life a bad dream.' – *Sunday Times*
'An indigestible blend of anti-liberal braggadocio, post-60s mysticism and echt-60s blockbusting.' – *Sight and Sound*

Conan the Destroyer
US 1984 101m Technicolor Scope
Dino de Laurentiis
An evil queen offers to bring Conan's last love back to life, if he will undertake a magical quest for her.
More heavy-handed and unpleasant nonsense, with a slightly better pace than before.
w Stanley Mann *d* Richard Fleischer *ph* Jack Cardiff
☆ Arnold Schwarzenegger, Grace Jones, Wilt Chamberlain, Mako, Tracey Walter, Sarah Douglas

Concealment: see *The Secret Bride*

Concerto: see *I've Always Loved You*

The Concierge: see *For Love or Money*

'At twice the speed of sound, can the Concorde evade attack?'
The Concorde: Airport '79
US 1979 113m Technicolor
Universal (Jennings Lang)
GB title: *Airport '80: The Concorde*
Various disasters befall the Concorde on its way from Washington to Paris.
Stultified final (one presumes) effort in the Airport series; it could hardly be funnier if it were intended as a comedy, but somehow it entertains.
w Eric Roth *d* David Lowell Rich *ph* Philip Lathrop *m* Lalo Schifrin
☆ Alain Delon, Susan Blakely, Robert Wagner, Sylvia Kristel, George Kennedy, Eddie Albert, Bibi Andersson, John Davidson, Martha Raye, Cicely Tyson, Mercedes McCambridge
'Larger-than-life characters are thrown together on a storyboard and must fend for themselves against attacks, chases and assorted escapades ... this would be soporific even as a transatlantic inflight movie.' – *Martyn Auty, MFB*

The Concrete Jungle: see *The Criminal*

El Conde Dracula: see *Bram Stoker's Count Dracula*

'A kiss that cannot be forgotten!'
Condemned *
US 1929 86m bw
Samuel Goldwyn
aka: *Condemned to Devil's Island*
A bank robber is sent to Devil's Island and falls in love with the wife of the brutal warden.
Slow-moving but pictorially attractive melodrama with old-style performances.
w Sidney Howard *novel Condemned to Devil's Island* by Blair Niles *d* Wesley Ruggles *ph* George Barnes, Gregg Toland *pd* William Cameron Menzies
☆ Ronald Colman, Ann Harding, Louis Wolheim, Dudley Digges, William Elmer
'A piece of nonsense from which it would appear that French convicts on Devil's Island live a life consisting entirely of hot-towel shaves and flirtations with the governor's wife.' – *James Agate*
Ronald Colman

The Condemned of Altona *
Italy/France 1962 113m bw
(TCF) Titanus/SGC (Carlo Ponti)
The head of a German shipping empire discovers he has only a few months to live and tries to bring his family to order.
Strident intellectual melodrama whose credits tell all. Watchable for the acting, but very glum.
w Abby Mann, Cesare Zavattini *play* Jean-Paul Sartre *d* Vittorio de Sica *ph* Roberto Gerardi *m* Dmitri Shostakovich
☆ Fredric March, Sophia Loren, Robert Wagner, Maximilian Schell, Françoise Prévost, Alfredo Franchi
'This film is such a hopeless mess that it is difficult to know where to begin criticizing it.' – *Tom Milne*

Condemned to Death *
GB 1932 75m bw
Twickenham (Julius Hagen)
A condemned killer hypnotizes a judge into murdering those who turned him in.
Irresistible nonsense of the old school, with spirited direction and a good cast.
w Bernard Merivale, Harry Fowler Mear, Brock Williams *play Jack O'Lantern* by George Goodchild, James Dawson *d Walter Forde* *ph* Sidney Blythe, William Luff
☆ Arthur Wontner, Gillian Lind, Edmund Gwenn, Gordon Harker, Jane Welsh, Cyril Raymond
'A weak daily changer with double-headed programming its merited rating.' – *Variety*
'It would be difficult to find a dull moment.' – *The Bioscope*

Condemned to Devil's Island: see *Condemned*

Condemned to Life: see *Life for Ruth*

Condorman
US 1981 90m Technicolor Panavision
Walt Disney (Jan Williams)
The author of a 'superman' comic tries to act like his hero in real life.
Very mildly amusing spy spoof with inadequate special effects.
w Marc Sturdivant, Glen Caron, Mickey Rose *novel The Game of X* by Robert Sheckley *d* Charles Jarrott *ph* Charles F. Wheeler *m* Henry Mancini *pd* Albert Witherick *sp* Art Cruickshank
☆ Michael Crawford, Oliver Reed, Barbara Carrera, James Hampton, Jean-Pierre Kalfon

Conduct Unbecoming
GB 1975 107m Technicolor
British Lion/Crown (Michael Deeley, Barry Spikings)
In an officers' mess in India in the 1890s, a cadet is accused of assault on a lady but the real culprit is a paranoic who has taken to pigsticking in quite the wrong way.
Disappointingly flatly-handled and quite unatmospheric picturization of an absorbing West End melodrama. The cast is largely wasted, but stretches of dialogue maintain their interest.
w Robert Enders *play* Barry England *d* Michael Anderson *ph* Bob Huke *m* Stanley Myers
☆ Michael York, Stacy Keach, Trevor Howard, Christopher Plummer, Richard Attenborough, Susannah York, James Faulkner, James Donald

The Conductor *
Poland 1979 102m Orwocolor
PRF/X Films of Poland
original title: *Dyrygent*
A Polish girl violinist finds her life affected when an elderly international conductor returns to her town.
Initially interesting but finally tedious and muddled allegory, further handicapped by stilted post-synching of the English version.
w Andrzej Kijowski *d* Andrzej Wajda *ph* Slawomir Idziak *m* from Beethoven
☆ John Gielgud, Krystyna Janda, Andrzej Seweryn

'Young ones! Parental units! We summon you!'
Coneheads
US 1993 83m DeLuxe
Paramount (Lorne Michaels)
An illegal pointy-headed alien crash-lands in the United States.
Dim one-joke comedy at the expense of suburbia.
w Tom Davis, Dan Aykroyd, Bonnie Turner, Terry Turner *d* Steve Barron *ph* Francis Kenny *m* David Newman *pd* Gregg Fonseca *ed* Paul Trejo
☆ Dan Aykroyd, Jane Curtin, Michael McKean, Laraine Newman, Jason Alexander, Lisa Jane Persky, Chris Farley, David Spade, Michelle Burke
'A sweet, funny, anarchic pastiche that should find broad-based popularity.' – *Variety*
'Quite extraordinarily bad ... worth renting only if you take a perverse pleasure in watching a very large amount of someone else's money going down the drain.' – *Jonathan Ross, Empire*
† The film was released direct to video in Britain.

Coney Island *
US 1943 96m Technicolor
TCF (William Perlberg)
Two fairground showmen vie for the affections of a songstress.
Brassy, simple-minded, entertaining musical. Very typical of its time; later remade as Wabash Avenue *(qv).*
w George Seaton *d Walter Lang* *ph* Ernest Palmer *m* Alfred Newman *m/ly* Leo Robin, Ralph Rainger *ch* Hermes Pan *ad* Richard Day, Joseph C. Wright
☆ *Betty Grable*, George Montgomery, Cesar Romero, Charles Winninger, Phil Silvers, Matt Briggs, Paul Hurst, Frank Orth, Andrew Tombes, Alec Craig, Hal K. Dawson
Alfred Newman

Confession
US 1937 90m bw
Warner (Henry Blanke)
An errant mother shoots her former lover to protect her daughter.
Stilted romantic melodrama copied scene for scene from a 1936 German film Mazurka.
w Julius J. Epstein, Margaret Le Vino *original screenplay* Hans Rameau *d* Joe May *ph* Sid Hickox *m* Peter Kreuder *md* Leo F. Forbstein *ad* Anton Grot
☆ Kay Francis, Ian Hunter, Basil Rathbone, Jane Bryan, Donald Crisp, Dorothy Peterson, Laura Hope Crews, Robert Barrat
'Distinctly in the upper bracket and made to order for important first runs.' – *Variety*

Confession
GB 1955 90m bw
Anglo Guild
US title: *The Deadliest Sin*
A murderer stalks the priest who knows his guilt through the confessional but may not reveal it.
So-so reworking of the theme that daunted Hitchcock in I Confess; *some pleasant touches are nullified by slow pacing.*
wd Ken Hughes
☆ Sydney Chaplin, Audrey Dalton, John Welsh, John Bentley, Peter Hammond

The Confession: see *Quick Let's Get Married (1965)*

The Confession *
France/Italy 1970 160m Eastmancolor
Films Corona/Films Pomereu/Selena Cinematografica (Robert Dorfmann)
original title: *L'Aveu*
In Prague in 1951, a minister is secretly imprisoned and interrogated, and finally confesses under duress to anti-communist activities.
Brutally long but frequently impressive anti-Soviet tract, extremely well acted but less exciting than Z. Based on a true account.
w Jorge Semprun *book* Lise and Artur London *d Costa-Gavras ph* Raoul Coutard *m* not credited
☆ *Yves Montand, Simone Signoret,* Gabriele Ferzetti, Michel Vitold

Le Confessional **
Canada/GB/France 1995 101m colour/bw
Artificial Eye/Téléfilm Canada/Cinémaginaire/Enigma/Cinéa (Denise Robert, David Puttnam, Philippe Carcassonne)
Returning home to Quebec for his father's funeral, an artist helps his adopted brother, now a homosexual prostitute, search for his real father, who they suspect may have been a priest.
Stylish, intelligent mystery story, full of echoes of Hitchcock, and moving between 1989 and 1952, where the tragedy that engulfs them had its roots. Set against Hitchcock's filming of I Confess, *it is told in a cool, distancing manner that is emotionally uninvolving; it is to be admired more than enjoyed.*
wd Robert Lepage *ph* Alain Dostie *m* Sacha Puttnam *ad* François Laplante *ed* Emmanuelle Castro
☆ Lothaire Bluteau, Patrick Goyette, Kristin Scott-Thomas, Jean-Louis Millette, Richard Fréchette, François Papineau, Marie Gignac, Ron Burrage (Alfred Hitchcock)
'A few moments of daftness aside, this is a superbly watchable and seamlessly structured film.' – *Nigel Robinson, Film Review*

Confessions from a Holiday Camp
GB 1977 88m colour
Columbia/Swiftdown (Greg Smith)
An entertainments officer at a holiday camp attempts to deal with the disciplinarian in charge while seducing every woman he meets.
Heavy-handed slapstick comedy intended to titillate, in the style of a lower-budget Carry On, with single entendres and no laughs.
w Christopher Wood *novel* Timothy Lea (Christopher Wood) *d* Norman Cohen *ph* Ken Hodges *m* Ed Welch *ad* Harry Pottle *ed* Geoffrey Foot
☆ Robin Askwith, Anthony Booth, Doris Hare, Bill Maynard, Sheila White, Colin Crompton, Liz Fraser, Linda Hayden, John Junkin, Lance Percival
'Strained and patronising low comedy.' – *MFB*

Confessions of a Counterspy: see *Man on a String*

'Some things are better left top secret.'
Confessions of a Dangerous Mind **
US/Germany/GB 2002 113m DeLuxe Panavision
Buena Vista/MiramaxMad ChanceSection Eight (Andrew Lazar)
An ambitious TV producer, who creates crass game-shows, combines his day job with working for the CIA as an assassin.
Lively and entertaining account of the life of Chuck Barris that does not question his claims to have been a hitman, but instead extracts the maximum amusement from them.
w Charlie Kaufman *autobiography* Chuck Barris *d* George Clooney *ph* Newton Thomas Sigel *m* Alex Wurman *pd* James O. Bissell *ed* Stephen Mirrione
☆ Sam Rockwell (Chuck Barris), Drew Barrymore (Penny), George Clooney (Jim Byrd), Julia Roberts (Patricia), Rutger Hauer (Keeler), Maggie Gyllenhaal (Debbie), Kristen Wilson (Loretta), Jennifer Hall (Georgia)
'A funny, strange, sad and wonderful picture, packed with delightful performances by Hollywood stars and made by a director with a startling facility for the form and an expansive cinematic imagination.' – *Andrew O'Hehir, Salon.com*
'The film is much more smug and pleased with itself than it has any reason to be.' – *Kenneth Turan, Los Angeles Times*

Confessions of a Driving Instructor
GB 1976 90m colour
Columbia-Warner/Swiftdown (Greg Smith)
A newly qualified driving instructor seduces his female pupils and all the other women he meets.
A tired farce that cannot even rise to the level of the Carry On series' double entendres.
w Christopher Wood *novel* Timothy Lea *d* Norman Cohen *ph* Ken Hodges *m* Ed Welch *ad* Albert Witherick *ed* Geoffrey Foot
☆ Robin Askwith, Anthony Booth, Sheila White, Doris Hare, Bill Maynard, Windsor Davies, Liz Fraser, Irene Handl, Lynda Bellingham, Avril Angers
'A fifth-rate potboiler of proven commercial value.' – *John Pym, MFB*

Confessions of a Nazi Spy ***
US 1939 110m bw
Warner (Robert Lord)
How G-men ferreted out Nazis in the United States.
Topical exposé with all concerned in top form; a semi-documentary very typical of Warner product throughout the thirties and forties, from G-Men *to* Mission to Moscow *and* I Was a Communist for the FBI*: well made, punchy, and smartly edited, with a loud moral at the end.*
w Milton Krims, John Wexley, from materials gathered by former FBI agent Leon G. Turrou *d Anatole Litvak ph Sol Polito m* Max Steiner
☆ *Edward G. Robinson, Paul Lukas,* George Sanders, Francis Lederer, Henry O'Neill, Lya Lys, James Stephenson, Sig Rumann, Dorothy Tree, Joe Sawyer
'Its social implications are far more important than the immediate question of how much money the release makes for Warner Brothers.' – *Variety*
'The Warner brothers have declared war on Germany with this one ... with this precedent there is no way any social or political theme on the grounds that he's afraid of domestic or foreign censorship. Everybody duck.' – *Pare Lorentz*
'Has a remarkable resemblance to a full-length *Crime Does Not Pay*.' – *David Wolff*
'One of the most sensational movie jobs on record, workmanlike in every respect and sprang across the headlines.' – *Otis Ferguson*

Confessions of a Pop Performer
GB 1975 91m colour
Columbia-Warner/Swiftdown
A window cleaner joins a rock group and enjoys the groupies.
A broad and unsubtle slapstick comedy.
w Christopher Wood *novel Confessions from the Pop Scene* by Timothy Lea *d* Norman Cohen *ph* Alan Hume *m* Bugatti Musker *pd* Robert Jones *ed* Geoffrey Foot
☆ Robin Askwith, Anthony Booth, Sheila White, Doris Hare, Bill Maynard, Bob Todd, Jill Gascoine, Peter Jones, Diane Langton, Ian Lavender
'Creaky gags, overly familiar slapstick routines, sniggering innuendo, grimly leaden mugging and a nervously regular injection of titillating sequences on the lines of the average German sex comedy.' – *Verina Glaessner, MFB*

Confessions of a Sex Maniac
GB 1974 81m Eastmancolor
Oppidan/Rothernorth (Alan Birkinshaw)
aka: *Design for Lust*
aka: *The Man Who Couldn't Get Enough*
An architect searches for the perfect breast so that he can use it as the design for a new building.
Tired farce, intended to titillate, but more likely to act as a soporific.
w Alan Paz *d* Alan Birkinshaw *ph* Arthur Lavis *m* Derek Warne, John Shakespeare *ad* Tessa Davis *ed* David White
☆ Roger Lloyd Pack, Vicki Hodge, Derek Royle, Stephanie Marrian, Louise Rush, Candy Baker
'A perilously weak plot premise is just about kept alive by the two appealing lead performances, before being smothered by a platitudinous ton of groping and grappling.' – *Richard Combs*

Confessions of a Trickbaby: see *Freeway II Confessions of a Trickbaby*

Confessions of a Window Cleaner
GB 1974 90m Eastmancolor
Columbia-Warner/Swiftdown (Greg Smith)
A window cleaner discovers many amorous housewives on his round.
A broad, but not bawdy, comedy for the sexually repressed. Despite its low level, it did well enough at the box-office to spawn several sequels.
w Christopher Wood, Val Guest *d* Val Guest *ph* Norman Warwick *m* Sam Sklair *pd* Robert Jones *ed* Bill Lenny
☆ Robin Askwith, Anthony Booth, Sheila White, Dandy Nichols, Bill Maynard, Linda Hayden, John Le Mesurier, Joan Hickson, Richard Wattis, Katya Wyeth, Sam Kydd
'The humour is of the sniggering, innuendo-squeezing variety and is aimed with unnerving mediocrity at a particular kind of embarrassed – and distinctly British – audience reaction.' – *Gareth Jones, MFB*
† The lead role was turned down by Nicky Henson, Dennis Waterman and Richard Beckinsale.

'Take One Daring Step Beyond The Threshold Of Your Own Imagination!'
Confessions of an Opium Eater
US 1962 85m bw
Albert Zugsmith
GB title: *Evils of Chinatown*
In San Francisco in the 1890s, a seaman falls into the clutches of a tong.
The hero is called de Quincey, but that is the only association with the famous book of the same title. This absurd melodrama is just about bad enough to be funny, but not very.
w Robert Hill *d* Albert Zugsmith *ph* Joseph Biroc *m* Albert Glasser *ad Eugene Lourié*
☆ Vincent Price, Linda Ho, Richard Loo, Philip Ahn, June Kim
'Has to be seen to be believed ... starved girls captive in cages, secret panels, sliding doors, sewer escape routes, opium dens and nightmares...' – *MFB*

Confidential
Canada 1987 88m colour
Brightstar (Anthony Kramreither)
A reporter goes missing on an assignment to track down a woman who killed her father with an axe years before.
Undistinguished, claustrophobic thriller, a low-budget pastiche of hard-boiled pulp fiction, tightly shot to try to hide the paucity of its sets.
wd Bruce Pittman *ph* John Herzog *m* Bruce Ley *ed* Bruce Pittman
☆ August Schellenberg, Chapelle Jaffe, Neil Munro, Tom Butler, Anthony Parr, Linda Goranson, Doris Petrie, Michael Fletcher

Confidential Agent **
US 1945 122m bw
Warner (Robert Buckner)
An emissary of Franco's Spain comes to England in the late thirties to make a munitions deal, and falls in love with the tycoon's daughter.
Heavy-going simplification of Graham Greene's lowering novel, with cast and (especially) set designers all at sea but nevertheless providing striking moments.
w Robert Buckner *d* Herman Shumlin *ph James Wong Howe m* Franz Waxman
☆ Charles Boyer, Lauren Bacall, Katina Paxinou, Peter Lorre, Victor Francen, George Coulouris, Wanda Hendrix, George Zucco, Miles Mander
'In some ways an exciting and good picture, the best attempt yet, though still inadequate, to make the best of a Greene novel.' – *James Agee*

Confidential Report
Spain 1955 99m bw
Sevilla Studios (Louis Dolivet, Orson Welles)
aka: *Mr Arkadin*
A wealthy and powerful financier employs a young American to seek out figures from his own past, who are soon found dead...
Silly melodrama which might have been suspenseful if done by Hitchcock, or even by Welles at his peak; as it is, weak writing and sloppy production remove most of the interest and reveal it as a very obvious bag of tricks.
wd Orson Welles *novel Mr Arkadin* by Orson Welles *ph* Jean Bourgoin *m* Paul Misraki *pd* Orson Welles *ed* Renzo Lucidi
☆ Orson Welles, Michael Redgrave, Katina Paxinou, Akim Tamiroff, Mischa Auer, Patricia Medina, Jack Watling, Peter Van Eyck, Paola Mori, Robert Arden, Grégoire Aslan, Suzanne Flon
'Tilted camera angles, heavy atmospheric shots, overlapping dialogue – all the trademarks are here, sometimes over-used to an almost hysterical degree, but they have little significance ... (the film) springs not from life but from the earlier cinematic world of Welles himself and from the kind of thriller written about thirty years ago by E. Philips Oppenheim.' – *Gavin Lambert*
'The quality of the soundtrack is quite disastrous, but there is a certain grandeur about the carelessness of the film's construction which makes one forget everything except the immediacy of the moment.' – *Basil Wright, 1972*

Confirm or Deny *
US 1941 78m bw
TCF (Len Hammond)
An American reporter falls for a wireless operator in wartime London.
Artificial but watchable minor romantic melodrama.
w Jo Swerling, Henry Wales, Samuel Fuller *d* Archie Mayo *ph* Leon Shamroy
☆ Don Ameche, Joan Bennett, Roddy McDowall, Arthur Shields, Raymond Walburn, John Loder
† Fritz Lang directed some scenes.

Conflict *
US 1945 86m bw
Warner (William Jacobs)
A man murders his wife and is apparently haunted by her; but the odd happenings have been arranged by a suspicious psychiatrist.
Leaden and artificial melodrama with both stars miscast; a few effective moments.
w Arthur T. Horman, Dwight Taylor *story* Robert Siodmak, Alfred Neumann *d* Curtis Bernhardt *ph* Merritt Gerstad *m* Frederick Hollander *md* Leo F. Forbstein *ad* Ted Smith *ed* David Weisbart *cos* Orry-Kelly
☆ Humphrey Bogart (Richard Mason), Sydney Greenstreet (Dr Mark Hamilton), Alexis Smith (Evelyn Turner), Rose Hobart (Katherine Mason), Charles Drake (Prof Norman Holdsworth), Grant Mitchell (Dr Grant), Patrick O'Moore (Detective Lt Egan)
† The film was completed in August 1943.

Conflict of Wings *
GB 1953 84m Eastmancolor
British Lion/Group Three (Herbert Mason)
US title: *Fuss over Feathers*
East Anglian villagers fight to save a bird sanctuary from being taken over by the RAF as a rocket range.
Sub-Ealing comedy-drama with a highly predictable outcome; generally pleasant but without much bite.
w Don Sharp, John Pudney *d* John Eldridge *ph* Arthur Grant *m* Philip Green *ed* Lito Carruthers
☆ John Gregson (Bill Morris), Muriel Pavlow (Sally), Kieron Moore (Squadron Leader Parsons), Niall MacGinnis (Harry Tilney), Sheila Sweet (Fanny Bates), Harry Fowler (Buster), Barbara Hicks (Mrs Thompson), Charles Lloyd Pack (Bookie)

The Conformist ***
Italy/France/West Germany 1969 108m Technicolor
Mars/Marianne/Maran (Giovanni Bertolucci)
original title: *Il Conformista*
In 1938 an inhibited young man tries to conform to the prevailing mood of Fascism, but gets out of his depth when he turns informer.
Psychologically confusing but brilliantly realized recreation of an age.
wd Bernardo Bertolucci novel Alberto Moravia *ph Vittorio Storaro m* Georges Delerue
☆ *Jean-Louis Trintignant,* Stefania Sandrelli, Gastone Moschin, Enzo Taroscio, Dominique Sanda, Pierre Clementi
'It's a triumph of feeling and of style – lyrical, flowing, velvety style, so operatic that you come

away with sequences in your head like arias.' – *New Yorker*

Bernardo Bertolucci (as writer)

Il Conformista: see *The Conformist*

'Where you are the endagered species.'

Congo

US 1995 108m DeLuxe

UIP/Paramount (Kathleen Kennedy, Sam Mercer)

A talking gorilla, a primatologist, a woman in search of rare blue diamonds, a mysterious Romanian and a great black hunter combine on an expedition to Africa where they find King Solomon's mines guarded by killer apes.

Heady nonsense, a throwback to those old movies based on Victorian adventure stories; it is hokum of a sort rarely seen since the days of Nyoka the Jungle Girl.

w John Patrick Shanley *novel* Michael Crichton *d* Frank Marshall *ph* Allen Daviau *m* Jerry Goldsmith *pd* J. Michael Riva *ed* Anne V. Coates *sp* Industrial Light and Magic; Stan Winston Studio

☆ Dylan Walsh, Laura Linney, Ernie Hudson, Tim Curry, Joe Don Baker, Grant Heslov

'A shamelessly inane confection.' – *Sight and Sound*

† The film took more than $151m worldwide at the box-office, $81m in the US.

Congo Crossing

US 1956 85m Technicolor

U-I (Howard Christie)

Assorted fugitives from justice gather at Congotanga, which has no extradition laws.

The poor man's Casablanca, *quite good looking but dully written and presented.*

w Richard Alan Simmons *d* Joseph Pevney *ph* Russell Metty *m* Joseph Gershenson

☆ George Nader, Virginia Mayo, *Peter Lorre*, Michael Pate, Rex Ingram

Congorilla *

US 1932 74m bw

Fox

A record of two years spent in the Belgian Congo by Mr and Mrs Martin Johnson.

Excellent exploration documentary of its time.

wd The Johnsons

'Replete with thrills, adventure and laughs, making withal for an excellent entertainment.' – *Variety*

Congress Dances *

Germany 1931 92m bw

UFA (Erich Pommer)

original title: *Der Kongress Tanzt*

At the Congress of Vienna, Metternich attempts to decoy the Tsar with a countess; but the Tsar has a double.

Lubitsch-like treatment of sexual dalliance in high places; no doubt a stunner in its time, but rather faded now.

w Norbert Falk, Robert Liebmann *d Erik Charell* *ph* Carl Hoffmann *m Werner Heymann* *ad* Robert Herlth, Walter Röhrig

☆ *Conrad Veidt* (Prince Metternich), Willy Fritsch (Czar Alexander), Lilian Harvey (Christel), Lil Dagover (Countess), Henry Garat (Czar Alexander/Uralsky), Gib McLaughlin (Bibikoff)

'A revue more than a story … grace, taste and a light hand.' – *Variety*

A Connecticut Yankee *

US 1931 96m bw

Fox

A man dreams himself back to the court of King Arthur, and teaches the Middle Ages a thing or two about modern living.

First sound version of Mark Twain's classic fantasy, also filmed in 1921 and 1949. Creaky now, but amiable.

w William Conselman *d* David Butler *ph* Ernest Palmer

☆ *Will Rogers*, Maureen O'Sullivan, Myrna Loy, Frank Albertson, William Farnum

'Good deluxe comedy … should draw substantial grosses.' – *Variety*

'Its laughter will ring through the centuries!'

A Connecticut Yankee in King Arthur's Court *

US 1949 106m Technicolor

Paramount (Robert Fellows)

GB title: *A Yankee in King Arthur's Court*

Gossamer musical version of the above with the emphasis on song and knockabout.

Palatable, with the 'Busy Doin' Nothin' ' sequence the most memorable.

w Edmund Beloin *d* Tay Garnett *ph* Ray Rennahan *m/ly* Johnny Burke, Jimmy Van Heusen *md* Victor Young

☆ *Bing Crosby*, Rhonda Fleming, William Bendix, *Cedric Hardwicke*, Murvyn Vye

'The tacky pageantry is more suited to the opening of a West Coast supermarket than to an English court in the 6th century.' – *Pauline Kael, 70s*

Connecting Rooms

GB 1969 103m Technicolor

Telstar/Franklin Gollings (Harry Field)

In a seedy Bayswater boarding house, a dismissed schoolmaster befriends a failed cellist whose protégé is a sponging songwriter.

Aggressively dismal melodrama which would be hilarious if it were not so sadly slow and naïve.

wd Franklin Gollings *play The Cellist* by Marion Hart *ph* John Wilcox *m* John Shakespeare

☆ Bette Davis, Michael Redgrave, Alexis Kanner, Kay Walsh, Gabrielle Drake, Leo Genn, Olga Georges-Picot, Richard Wyler, Brian Wilde

The Connection

US 1961 110m bw

Shirley Clarke/Lewis Allen

Junkies hang around waiting for a fix and are filmed by a documentary unit.

Unattractive low-budgeter with occasional impressive moments.

w Jack Gelber *play* Jack Gelber *d* Shirley Clarke *ph* Arthur J. Ornitz *m* Freddie Redd *ad* Richard Sylbert

☆ Warren Finnerty, Jerome Raphael, Jim Anderson, Carl Lee, Roscoe Browne

'Spectacular as its barbaric passions and savage conquests!'

The Conqueror

US 1955 112m Technicolor Cinemascope

Howard Hughes (Dick Powell)

A romance of the early life of Genghis Khan, who captures and is enamoured by the daughter of an enemy.

Solemn pantomime with a measure of bloodthirsty action and dancing girls, but featuring too many dull spots between, especially as the star is the most unlikely of eastern warriors and the production values careful but not too steady.

w Oscar Millard *d* Dick Powell *ph* Joseph LaShelle, Leo Tover, Harry J. Wild *m* Victor Young

☆ John Wayne, Susan Hayward, Pedro Armendariz, Agnes Moorehead, Thomas Gomez, John Hoyt, William Conrad, Ted de Corsia, Lee Van Cleef

GENGHIS KHAN: 'This tartar woman is for me, and my blood says, take her!'

'Simply an oriental western.' – *New York Times*

'History has not been well served and nor has the popcorn public.' – *Richard Hatch, Nation*

'It's all that its makers wanted it to be.' – *Manchester Guardian*

'John Wayne as Genghis Khan – history's most improbable piece of casting unless Mickey Rooney were to play Jesus in King of Kings.' – *Jack Smith, L.A. Times*

† The location was Utah's Escalante Desert, and three local mountains were renamed Mount Wayne, Mount Hughes and Mount Powell. The desert had been used for atom bomb tests, and twenty-five years after the production, questions were asked when several members of the cast died of cancer

†† Wayne asked for his role. 'The way the screenplay reads, this is a cowboy picture, and that's how I am going to play Genghis Khan. I see him as a gunfighter.'

The Conqueror Worm: see *Witchfinder General*

The Conquerors

US 1932 88m bw

RKO (David O. Selznick)

TV title: *Pioneer Builders*

Nebraska settlers in the 1870s set the seeds of a banking empire.

Routine family epic with the star playing himself and his own grandson.

w Robert Lord *story* Howard Estabrook *d* William Wellman *ph* Edward Cronjager *m* Max Steiner

☆ Richard Dix, Ann Harding, Edna May Oliver, Guy Kibbee, Donald Cook, Julie Haydon, Jed Prouty

'As good as a depression story can be, which isn't much box office.' – *Variety*

Conquest **

US 1937 115m bw

MGM (Bernard Hyman)

GB title: *Marie Walewska*

The life of Napoleon's most enduring mistress.

Measured, dignified, and often rather dull historical fiction, lightened by excellent performances and production.

w Samuel Hoffenstein, Salka Viertel, S. N. Behrman, from a Polish play dramatized by Helen Jerome *d* Clarence Brown *ph* Karl Freund *m* Herbert Stothart *ad* Cedric Gibbons

☆ Greta Garbo, *Charles Boyer*, Reginald Owen, Alan Marshal, Henry Stephenson, Dame May Whitty, Leif Erickson

'For special first-run openings – and then the clean up.' – *Variety*

'Ornate, unexpectedly tasteful, carefully detailed – and lifeless.' – *Pauline Kael, 70s*

Charles Boyer; Cedric Gibbons

The Conquest of Everest *

GB 1953 73m Technicolor

British Lion/Group 3/Countryman Films

Documentary on the successful 11th attempt on Everest, the expedition led by Colonel John Hunt.

A documentary with some fascinating footage of early expeditions, and of the detailed planning of the expedition, opening in a burst of patriotism as success followed the coronation of Queen Elizabeth II.

w Louis MacNeice *d* uncredited *ph Thomas Stobart, George Lowe, Captain J. B. L. Noel* *m* Arthur Benjamin *md* Muir Mathieson *ed* Adrian de Potier

☆ Meredith Edwards (narration)

'See how it will happen – in your lifetime!'

Conquest of Space

US 1954 80m Technicolor

Paramount (George Pal)

In 1980, the Americans have built a space station in the atmosphere, and plan a voyage to the moon but are sent to Mars instead.

So history catches up with science fiction. This sober prophecy looks good but very little happens and the result is as dull as it is bright and shiny.

w James O'Hanlon *book* Chesley Bonestell, Willy Ley *d* Byron Haskin *ph* Lionel Lindon *m* Van Cleeve *ad* Hal Pereira, James McMillan Johnson *sp* John P. Fulton, Irmin Roberts, Paul Lerpae, Ivyl Burks, Jan Domella

☆ Eric Fleming, Walter Brooke, Mickey Shaughnessy, William Hopper, Ross Martin

Conquest of the Air

GB 1940 71m bw

London Films/Alexander Korda

A history of man's discovery of the power of flight.

Curious schoolbook documentary, of historical interest.

w Hugh Gray, Peter Bezencenet *d* Zoltan Korda and others

☆ Laurence Olivier (Lunardi), Franklin Dyall, Henry Victor, Hay Petrie, John Turnbull

† Work began on the film in 1935, when it was planned as part of a series on land, sea and air transport through the ages. It was completed in 1937 but not released for another three years.

Conquest of the Planet of the Apes

US 1972 85m DeLuxe Todd-AO 35

TCF/APJAC (Arthur P. Jacobs)

In the 1990s, apes used as slaves revolt against their human masters.

Ragged science fiction in a series that was going rapidly downhill.

w Paul Dehn *d* J. Lee Thompson *ph* Bruce Surtees *m* Tom Scott *ad* Philip Jefferies *ed* Marjorie Fowler, Allan Jaggs

☆ Roddy McDowall, Don Murray, Ricardo Montalban, Natalie Trundy, Hari Rhodes, Severn Darden

'In spite of some crude allegorical pretensions, it can't really be considered seriously as more than another excuse for APJAC to get maximum wear out of an expensive set of costumes. Even on that score, the film falls down rather badly.' – *Clyde Jeavons, MFB*

† The film was fourth in the series that began with *The Planet of the Apes*, and continued with *Beneath the Planet of the Apes* and *Escape from the Planet of the Apes*. It was followed by *Battle for the Planet of the Apes* (qqv).

Conquest of the South Pole

GB 1989 95m colour

Jam Jar Films/Channel 4 (Gareth Wardell)

Five unemployed Glaswegian youths recreate Amundsen's expedition to Antarctica in a decaying urban landscape.

Awkward transfer to the screen of an impressionistic play.

w Gareth Wardell *play* Manfred Karge *d* Gillies Mackinnon *ph* Sean Van Hales *m* Guy Woolfenden *ad* Andy Harris *ed* Stephen Singleton

☆ Stefan Rimkus, Ewen Bremner, Leonard O'Malley, Laura Girling, Gordon Cameron, Alastair Galbraith, John Michie, Julie-Kate Olivier

Conrack *

US 1974 106m DeLuxe Panavision

TCF (Martin Ritt, Irving Ravetch)

A young white teacher is assigned to an all-black school in South Carolina, and after some difficulty makes friends with children and parents.

Nostalgically mellow happy-film, lit by bright smiles all around.

w Irving Ravetch, Harriet Frank Jnr *novel The Water Is Wide* by Pat Conroy *d* Martin Ritt *ph* John Alonzo *m* John Williams

☆ Jon Voight, Paul Winfield, Hume Cronyn, Madge Sinclair, Tina Andrews

'For all its craftsman-like virtues, it seems a conscious turning aside from the complexities of modern cinema to the simpler alternatives of yesteryear. Indeed, with underprivileged white children instead of black and Greer Garson substituting for Jon Voight, the film might have been made all of thirty years ago.' – *John Raisbeck*

'Thou Shalt Not Covet Thy Neighbor's Wife.'

Consenting Adults

US 1992 99m Technicolor

Buena Vista/Hollywood Pictures (Alan J. Pakula, David Permut)

A money-obsessed financial adviser accuses his friend of murdering his wife after a night in which they swopped partners.

A thriller that owes much to Hitchcock but is unable to maintain either interest or suspense.

w Matthew Chapman *d* Alan J. Pakula *ph* Stephen Goldblatt *m* Michael Small *pd* Carol Spier *ed* Sam O'Steen

☆ Kevin Kline, Mary Elizabeth Mastrantonio, Kevin Spacey, Rebecca Miller, E. G. Marshall, Forest Whitaker

'Initially seems a little brainier than its brethren but soon gives way to the same cavernous lapses in logic and formula ending.' – *Variety*

'Nobody can do anything much to enliven this ponderous telling of a barely credible story and the result is curiously flat and unholding.' – *Derek Malcolm, Guardian*

Consider Your Verdict

GB 1938 40m bw

Charter (John Boulting)

A juror proves an accused man not guilty by falsely confessing to the crime himself.

Fairly smart little entry into the feature film scene for the Boulting Brothers, from a popular radio play of the time.

w Francis Miller *play* Laurence Housman *d* Roy Boulting *ph* D. P. Cooper

☆ Marius Goring, Manning Whiley, Olive Sloane, Hay Petrie, George Carney

Consolation Marriage
US 1931 62m bw
RKO
A wife keeps a stiff upper lip when her husband strays.
Ho-hum domestic drama with attempts at comedy relief.
w Humphrey Pearson *d* Paul Sloane
☆ Irene Dunne, Pat O'Brien, John Halliday, Matt Moore, Myrna Loy
'Fair entertainment; will satisfy with good stage support.' – *Variety*

'What conflict in the heart of a nun would make her break her vows?'
Conspiracy of Hearts *
GB 1960 113m bw
Rank (Betty E. Box)
During World War II, Italian nuns smuggle Jewish children across the border from a nearby prison camp.
Highly commercial combination of exploitable sentimental elements: Germans, Jews, nuns, children, war, suspense. Remarkably, it gets by without causing nausea.
w Robert Presnell Jnr *story* Dale Pitt *d* Ralph Thomas *ph* Ernest Steward *m* Angelo Lavagnino
☆ Lilli Palmer, Sylvia Syms, Yvonne Mitchell, Albert Lieven, Ronald Lewis, Peter Arne, Nora Swinburne, Michael Goodliffe, Megs Jenkins, David Kossoff, Jenny Laird, George Coulouris, Phyllis Neilson-Terry
† The story was written by Adiran Scott. Because he was blacklisted at the time, Dale Pitt fronted for him.

'What You Know Could Kill You...'
Conspiracy Theory
US 1997 135m Technicolor Panavision
Warner (Joel Silver, Richard Donner)
A Manhattan taxi driver's obsessions, with government conspiracies and a beautiful lawyer, put his life in danger,
Ridiculously paranoid thriller that degenerates into an overlong chase movie.
w Brian Helgeland *d* Richard Donner *ph* John Schwartzman *m* Carter Burwell *pd* Paul Sylbert *ed* Frank J. Urioste, Kevin Stitt
☆ Mel Gibson (Jerry Fletcher), Julia Roberts (Alice Sutton), Patrick Stewart (Dr Jonas), Cylk Cozart (Agent Lowry), Stephen Kahan, Terry Alexander
'Sporadically amusing but listless thriller that wears its humorous, romantic and political components like mismatched articles of clothing.' – *Todd McCarthy, Variety*

Conspirator
GB 1949 87m bw
MGM (Arthur Hornblow Jnr)
A guards officer, unknown to his young wife, is a communist spy.
Singularly awful romantic melodrama which never convinces or entertains for a moment.
w Sally Benson, Gerard Fairlie *novel* Humphrey Slater *d* Victor Saville *ph* F. A. Young *m* John Wooldridge
☆ Robert Taylor, Elizabeth Taylor, Harold Warrender, Robert Flemyng, Marie Ney

The Conspirators *
US 1944 101m bw
Warner (Jack Chertok)
A Dutch underground leader escapes to Lisbon and clears up international intrigue.
Interestingly cast but often listless wartime melodrama, a doomed attempt to reprise Casablanca *without Humphrey Bogart.*
w Vladimir Pozner, Leo Rosten *novel City of Shadows* by Frederick Prokosch *d* Jean Negulesco *ph* Arthur Edeson *m* Max Steiner
☆ Hedy Lamarr, Paul Henreid, Sydney Greenstreet, Peter Lorre, *Victor Francen*, Carol Thurston, Vladimir Sokoloff, Joseph Calleia, Edward Ciannelli, Steve Geray, Kurt Katch, George Macready
SYDNEY GREENSTREET (AS QUINTANILLA): 'This may seem to you melodramatic, but indulge me, please, I like melodrama.'
'As exciting as baseball and almost as gentlemanly as cricket.' – *New Statesman*
'I enjoyed it as much as any Warner melodrama since *Casablanca*.' – *Observer*

Conspirators of Pleasure **
Czech Republic/Switzerland/GB 1996 75m colour
ICA/Athanor/Pierre Assouline/Delfilm/Keith Griffiths/Koninck (Jaromir Kallista)
original title: *Spiklenci slasti*
In Prague, various people indulge in solitary acts of love which have unexpected consequences.
Surreal film on the way perversity interacts with normal life, odd and intriguing in its own perverse way.
wd Jan Svankmajer *ph* Miloslav Spála
md Norbert Baxter *pd* Jan Svankmajer *ed* Marie Zemanová
☆ Petr Meissel, Gabriela Wilhelmová, Barbora Hrzánová, Anna Wetlinská
'A Freudian shaggy-dog story that is as hilarious, idiosyncratic and terrifying as the most unspeakable sexual fantasy you've ever entertained. Yes, that good.' – *Independent*

Constans: see *The Constant Factor*

The Constant Factor *
Poland 1980 91m Eastmancolor
Cinegate/PRF/Zespol Filmowy
original title: *Constans*
A precise idealist refuses to adjust to the petty corruptions of life.
Cool dissection of human fallibility.
wd Krzysztof Zanussi *ph* Slawomir Idziak
m Wojciech Kilar *ad* Tadeusz Wybult, Maciej Putowski *ed* Urszula Sliwinska, Ewa Smal
☆ Tadeusz Bradecki, Zofia Mrozowska, Malgorzata Zajaczkowska, Cezary Morawski, Witold Pyrkosz

The Constant Husband *
GB 1955 88m Technicolor
British Lion/London Films (Frank Launder, Sidney Gilliat)
An amnesiac discovers that he is a multiple bigamist, still wanted by each of his five wives.
Flimsy comedy which never really gets going despite an attractive cast.
w Sidney Gilliat, Val Valentine *d* Sidney Gilliat *ph* Ted Scaife *m* Malcolm Arnold
☆ Rex Harrison, Kay Kendall, Margaret Leighton, Cecil Parker, Nicole Maurey, George Cole, Raymond Huntley, Michael Hordern, Eric Pohlmann, Robert Coote

The Constant Nymph *
GB 1933 98m bw
Gaumont (Michael Balcon)
In the Tyrol, a composer leaves his rich wife for a schoolgirl suffering from a heart condition.
Archetypal romantic drama from Margaret Kennedy's book, first filmed in 1928 by the same producer (and then directed by Adrian Brunel, starring Ivor Novello and Mabel Poulton). A standard production of its time, which seems to have vanished with the literary copyright.
w Margaret Kennedy, Basil Dean, from their play based on her novel *d* Basil Dean *ph* Max Greene *m* John Greenwood
☆ Brian Aherne, Victoria Hopper, Leonora Corbett, Lyn Harding, Mary Clare, Jane Baxter
'Beautifully done artistic success from England, of doubtful box office for America.' – *Variety*
'One can say that it has a beginning, a middle and an end, but it lacks something vital.' – *E. V. Lucas, Punch*

The Constant Nymph *
US 1943 112m bw
Warner (Henry Blanke)
A composer marries a rich woman without appreciating a young girl's love for him.
Artificially well-produced, overlong Hollywood version of a once famous romantic novel and play.
w Kathryn Scola *d* Edmund Goulding *ph* Tony Gaudio *m* Erich Wolfgang Korngold
☆ Charles Boyer, *Joan Fontaine*, Alexis Smith, Brenda Marshall, Charles Coburn, Dame May Whitty, Peter Lorre, Joyce Reynolds, Jean Muir, Edward Ciannelli, Montagu Love, André Charlot
Joan Fontaine

Consuming Passions
GB/US 1988 100m colour
Samuel Goldwyn/Euston Films (William Cartlidge)
By adding a new ingredient to chocolate – human flesh – a young man rises to the top of his profession.
Dire attempt to revive the tradition of Ealing comedy.
w Paul D. Zimmerman, Andrew Davies
play Secrets by Michael Palin, Terry Jones *d* Giles Foster *ph* Roger Pratt *m* Richard Hartley
pd Peter Lamont *ed* John Grover
☆ Vanessa Redgrave, Freddie Jones, Jonathan Pryce, Tyler Butterworth, Sammi Davis, Thora Hird, Prunella Scales

'A message from deep space. Who will be the first to go? A journey to the heart of the universe.'
Contact *
US 1997 150m Technicolor Panavision
Warner/South Side Amusement
An astronomer picks up a signal from intelligent life on another planet.
After a brilliant beginning, an awe-inspiring journey through space, the film soon settles for sentimentality and psychobabble, being less interested in the consequences of the possibilities of alien contact than in self-help and exploring one's inner being.
w James V. Hart, Michael Goldenberg *novel* Carl Sagan *d* Robert Zemeckis *ph* Don Burgess
m Alan Silvestri *pd* Ed Verreaux *ed* Arthur Schmidt
☆ Jodie Foster (Ellie Arroway), Matthew McConaughey (Palmer Joss), James Woods (Michael Kitz), John Hurt (S.R. Hadden), Tom Skerritt (David Drumlin), Angela Bassett (Rachel Constantine)
'A serious and sober piece of speculative fiction, designed to play off of apprehensions about the forthcoming millennium in a positive and uplifting manner.' – *Variety*
sound

The Contact Man: see *Alias Nick Beal*

Conte D'Automne **
France 1998 112m colour
Artificial Eye/Films du Losange/La Sept (Margaret Ménégoz)
aka: *An Autumn Tale*
Friends of a lonely widow, who works as a wine grower in the Rhone valley, conspire to find her a new man.
Gently perceptive, witty drama, given a physical and spiritual autumnal setting, and one that is rooted in the realities of everyday life.
wd Eric Rohmer *ph* Diane Baratier *m* Claude Marti, Gérard Pansanel, Pierre Peyras, Antonello Salis *ed* Mary Stephen
☆ Marie Riviere (Isabelle), Béatrice Romand (Magali), Alain Libolt (Gérald), Didier Sandre (Etienne), Alexia Portal (Rosine), Stéphane Darmon (Léo), Aurélia Alcais (Emilia), Mathieu Davette (Grégoire), Yves Alcais (Jean-Jacques)
'Like Woody Allen, Rohmer may be remaking the same film again and again, but this time it's a great one.' – *Ian Freer, Empire*

Conte de Printemps **
France 1990 110m colour
Roissy Films/Films du Losange (Margaret Ménégoz)
aka: *A Spring Tale*
A teenage daughter, whose parents are separated, attempts to persuade her father to change girlfriends.
Witty, sophisticated comedy of manners.
wd Eric Rohmer *ph* Luc Pages *m* Beethoven, Schumann *ed* Lisa Garcia
☆ Anne Teyssedre, Hugues Quester, Florence Durrell, Eloise Bennett, Sophie Robin

Conte d'été *
France 1996 114m colour
Artificial Eye/Films du Losange/La Sept (Françoise Etchegaray)
aka: *A Summer's Tale*
A young musician on holiday toys with the affections of three women.
Slight and inconsequential tale of an indecisive protagonist drifting through life, given a certain charm by the performances.
wd Eric Rohmer *ph* Diane Baratier *m* Philippe Eidel, Sébastien Erms *ed* Mary Stephen
☆ Melvil Poupaud, Amanda Langlet, Gwenaëlle Simon, Aurélia Nolin, Aimé Lefèvre, Alain Guellaff
'Fans of French cinema should delight in its playful and leisurely insights into the teenage condition.' – *James Cameron-Wilson, Film Review*

Conte d'hiver **
France 1992 114m bw
Artificial Eye/Films du Losange (Margaret Ménégoz)
aka: *A Winter's Tale*
A French hairdresser, waiting in hope for the man who fathered her child to return to her, has unsatisfactory relationships with two other men.
An enjoyable variation on the themes of Shakespeare's play, complete with happy ending and as little concerned with reality.
wd Eric Rohmer *ph* Luc Pages, Maurice Giraud *m* Sebastian Erms *ed* Mary Stephen
☆ Charlotte Very, Frederic Van Den Driessche, Michel Voletti, Hervé Furic, Ava Loraschi, Christiane Desbois, Rosette, Jean-Luc Revol
'Fittingly, Rohmer's winter story has an affirmative inner glow.' – *Philip Strick, Sight and Sound*

Contempt **
France/Italy 1963 103m Technicolor Franscope
Rome-Paris/Concordia/CCC (Carlo Ponti, Joseph E. Levine)
original title: *Le Mépris*
In Rome, a screenwriter has troubles with his wife as he tries to set up a film of *The Odyssey* with a philistine American producer.
A clever and engrossing account of a marital crisis and of film-making; in both, none of the principals are able to communicate with the other.
wd Jean-Luc Godard *novel A Ghost at Noon* by Alberto Moravia *ph* Raoul Coutard *m* Georges Delerue *ed* Agnès Guillemot, Lila Lakshmanan
☆ Brigitte Bardot, Michel Piccoli, Jack Palance, Fritz Lang, Giorgia Moll, Jean-Luc Godard
'Portentous without having anything to say, improvisatory without imagination, full of esoteric references without relevance and in-group allusions without interest. Its puppets behave with meaningless meanness if not with sheer meaninglessness.' – *John Simon*
'We are still subjected to the banalities of film "in" jokes, the fake spontaneity that is supposed to cover up the plotless pointlessness of his work and the meandering literaliness of his camera.' – *Judith Crist*
† The disdain for producers shown in the film was mirrored by real events: Godard had his name removed from the Italian version owing to cuts imposed by the producers and other changes, which included redubbing to remove the different languages spoken by the participants, and a new musical score by Piero Piccioni.

'Sometimes you can assassinate a leader without firing a shot.'
The Contender *
US 2000 126m colour
DreamWorks/Cinerenta/Cinecontender/Battleground/SE8 (Marc Frydman, Douglas Urbanski, Willi Baer, James Spies)
A Republican congressman digs up the dirt on the US president's choice of a new vice-president.
Political thriller that holds the attention for most of the time, before succumbing to sentimentality that obviates all its insights into wheeling and dealing in the corridors of power.
wd Rod Lurie *ph* Denis Maloney *m* Larry Groupe *pd* Alexander Hammond *ed* Michael Jablow *cos* Matthew Jacobsen
☆ Joan Allen (Laine Hanson), Gary Oldman (Shelly Runyon), Jeff Bridges (President Jackson Evans), Sam Elliott (Kermit Newman), Christian Slater (Reginald Webster), William Petersen (Jack Hathaway), Philip Baker Hall (Oscar Billings), Saul Rubineck (Jerry Toliver)
'Engages in the cinematic equivalent of not inhaling. The result is only a contact high.' – *Lisa Schwarzbaum, Entertainment Weekly*
Joan Allen; Jeff Bridges

Contest Girl: see *The Beauty Jungle*

Continental Divide
US 1981 103m Technicolor
Universal/Amblin (Bob Larson)
A national columnist finds himself banished to the wilds with a lady ornithologist studying the bald eagle.
Old-fashioned comedy, a cross between Bringing Up Baby *and* Woman of the Year. *Not actually bad, but somewhat lacking in personality.*
w Lawrence Kasdan *d* Michael Apted *ph* John Bailey *m* Michael Small
☆ John Belushi, Blair Brown, Allen Goorwitz, Carlin Glynn

Continuavamo a Chiamarlo Trinity: see *Trinity Is Still My Name*

Contraband **
GB 1940 92m bw
British National (John Corfield)
US title: *Blackout*
A Danish merchant captain and a girl in wartime London expose a gang of spies using a cinema as headquarters.
Enjoyable lightweight comedy melodrama on Hitchcock lines, reuniting the unlikely star team from The Spy in Black.
w Emeric Pressburger, Michael Powell, Brock Williams *d* Michael Powell *ph* F. A. Young
☆ *Conrad Veidt, Valerie Hobson*, Esmond Knight, Hay Petrie, Raymond Lovell, Harold Warrender, Charles Victor, Manning Whiley
'A light romantic comedy with bondage overtones.' – *Ken Russell*

The Contract **
Poland 1980 111m colour
Cinegate/PRF/Zespol Filmowy
original title: *Kontrakt*
Despite the reluctance of a couple to marry, the groom's father celebrates with a lavish reception.
Comic and satirical look at Polish high life.
wd Krzysztof Zanussi *ph* Slawomir Idziak *m* Wojciech Kilar *ad* Tadeusz Wybult *ed* Urszula Sliwinska, Ewa Smal
☆ Maja Komorowska, Tadeusz Lomnicki, Magda Jaroszowna, Krzysztof Kilberger, Leslie Caron

The Convent
US 2000 84m colour
Alpine (Jed Nolan)
Highschool students break into a deserted convent where, according to legend, forty years earlier a girl had slaughtered everyone.
Lurid and risibly ludicrous horror, with an excess of gore, cheap effects and jokes, bad acting and demon nuns.
w Chaton Anderson *d* Mike Mendez *ph* Jason Lowe *m* Joey Bishara *pd* Robert E. Hummel *ed* John Rosenberg
☆ Adrienne Barbeau (Adult Christine), Joanna Canton (Clarissa), Coolio (Officer Starkey), Megahn Perry (Monica 'Mo'), Jason Dax Miller (Chad), Richard Trapp (Frijole), Liam Kyle Sullivan (Brant), Alison Dunbar (Davina), Kelly Mantle (Dickie-Boy), David Gunn (Saul), Jim Golden (Biff)

Convention City *
US 1933 78m bw
Warner (Henry Blanke)
Extra-marital fun and games at a Chicago convention.
Amusing and rather risqué comedy which helped to bring down on Hollywood the wrath of the Legion of Decency.
w Robert Lord *d* Archie Mayo *ph* William Reese
☆ Joan Blondell, Guy Kibbee, Adolphe Menjou, Dick Powell, Mary Astor, Frank McHugh, Ruth Donnelly, Hugh Herbert, Hobart Cavanaugh
'Not a dull foot … probably the fastest complex comedy of the year and a certain money picture.' – *Variety*

The Conversation ***
US 1974 113m Technicolor
Paramount/Francis Ford Coppola
A bugging device expert lives only for his work, but finally develops a conscience.
Absorbing but extremely difficult to follow in detail, this personal, timely (in view of Watergate), Kafkaesque suspense story centres almost entirely on director and leading actor, who have a field day.
wd Francis Ford Coppola *ph* Bill Butler *m* David Shire
☆ *Gene Hackman*, John Cazale, Allen Garfield, Frederic Forrest
'A private, hallucinatory study in technical expertise and lonely guilt.' – *Sight and Sound*
'A terrifying depiction of a ransacked spirit.' – *New Yorker, 1977*
'Alert, truthful, unarty and absolutely essential viewing.' – *Michael Billington, Illustrated London News*
best picture; Francis Ford Coppola (as writer)

Conversation Piece
Italy/France 1974 121m Technicolor Todd-AO 35
Rusconi/Gaumont (Giovanni Bertolucci)
original title: *Gruppo di Famiglia in un Interno*
When a reclusive professor is persuaded to let his top floor to a young couple he is brought face to face with his latent homosexuality and his approaching death.
Death in Venice *revisited, but with much less style and even more obscurity.*
w Luchino Visconti, Suso Cecchi d'Amico, Enrico Medioli *d* Luchino Visconti *ph* Pasqualino de Santis *m* Franco Mannino
☆ Burt Lancaster, Helmut Berger, Claudia Marsani, Silvana Mangano

Convict 99 *
GB 1938 91m bw
Gainsborough (Edward Black)
A seedy schoolmaster accidentally becomes a prison governor and lets the convicts run the place.
Patchily funny if overlong and in some ways rather serious Will Hay comedy, not quite typical of him.
w Marriott Edgar, Val Guest, Ralph Smart, Jack Davies *d* Marcel Varnel *ph* Arthur Crabtree *md* Louis Levy *ad* Vetchinsky *ed* R. E. Dearing
☆ Will Hay, Graham Moffatt, Moore Marriott, Googie Withers, Garry Marsh, Peter Gawthorne, Basil Radford, Kathleen Harrison

Convicts Four *
US 1962 106m bw
Allied Artists-Lubin-Kaufman (A. Ronald Lubin)
original and GB title: *Reprieve*
A convict reprieved from the electric chair spends eighteen years in prison, becomes a painter, and is rehabilitated.
Odd and unsatisfactory mixture of documentary, melodrama, sentimentality and character study, with stars unexpectedly popping in for cameo appearances. Something worthier was obviously intended.
wd Millard Kaufman *autobiography* John Resko *ph* Joseph Biroc *m* Leonard Rosenman
☆ *Ben Gazzara*, Vincent Price, Rod Steiger, Broderick Crawford, Stuart Whitman, Ray Walston, Jack Kruschen, Sammy Davis Jnr

Convoy *
GB 1940 90m bw
Ealing (Sergei Nolbandov)
A German pocket battleship menaces a British convoy, and a merchant ship sacrifices itself to prevent disaster.
Fluent British war film of the early days, the only substantial work of a much vaunted director who was subsequently killed.
w Pen Tennyson, Patrick Kirwan *d* *Pen Tennyson* *ph* Gunther Krampf, Roy Kellino *m* Ernest Irving
☆ Clive Brook, John Clements, Edward Chapman, Judy Campbell, Penelope Dudley Ward, Edward Rigby, Allan Jeayes, Albert Lieven

'Kristofferson and MacGraw…ain't nothin' gonna get in their way!'
Convoy *
US 1978 110m DeLuxe Panavision
UA/EMI (Robert M. Sherman)
A folk hero truck driver survives several crashes and his policeman nemesis.
A virtually plotless anthology of wanton destruction. Too noisy to sleep through.
w B. W. L. Norton, based on the song by C. W. McCall *d* Sam Peckinpah *ph* Harry Stradling Jnr *m* Chip Davis
☆ Kris Kristofferson, Ali MacGraw, Ernest Borgnine, Burt Young, Madge Sinclair
'There's a whole lot of nothing going on here … strictly a summer popcorn picture for the nondiscriminating.' – *Variety*
'Roughly as much fun as a ride on the New Jersey turnpike with the window open. It not only numbs the brain but pollutes the senses.' – *Richard Schickel, Time*

Les Convoyeurs Attendent **
France/Belgium/Switzerland 1999 94m bw
Entertainment/K-Star/K2/RTBF/CAB/SSR (Dominique Janne)
aka: *The Carriers Are Waiting*
Desperate to win a car in a competition, a moped-riding newspaper photographer forces his teenage son to attempt the world record for opening and closing a door for 24 hours.
Quirky, dark-tinged comedy of a dysfunctional father that still somehow manages to celebrate the pleasures of family life.
w Emmanuelle Bada, Benoit Mariage, Jean-Luc Seigle *d* Benoit Mariage *ph* Philippe Guilbert *m* Stéphane Huguenin, Yves Sanna *ad* Chris Cornil *ed* Philippe Bourgueil
☆ *Benoit Poelvoorde* (Roger), Morgane Simon (Luise), Bouli Lanners (Coach), Dominique Baeyens (Madeleine), Philippe Grand'Henry (Felix), Jean-Francois Devigne (Michel), Lisa LaCroix (Jocelyne), Philippe Nahon (Overseer), Edith Lemerdy (Edith), Patrick Audin (Patrick)
'As moving and as thought-provoking a film as you would hope to see, offering a unique and insightful sideways glance at the world we live in.' – *James Mottram, Film Review*

Coogan's Bluff **
US 1968 94m Technicolor
Universal (Don Siegel)
An Arizona sheriff takes an escaped killer back to New York, and when the man escapes uses Western methods to recapture him.
Violent, well-done police story which inspired the TV series McCloud.
w Herman Miller, Dean Riesner, Howard Rodman *d* *Don Siegel* *ph* Bud Thackery *m* Lalo Schifrin
☆ Clint Eastwood, Lee J. Cobb, Susan Clark, Don Stroud, Tisha Sterling, Betty Field, Tom Tully

The Cook, the Thief, His Wife & Her Lover **
GB/France 1989 124m colour Cinemascope
Palace/Allarts Cook/Erato Films (Kees Kasander)
A coarse gangster holds court in a fashionable restaurant while his wife conducts a passionate affair in the kitchens with a fellow diner.
Elegant, stylized, painterly and extremely brutal variation on a Jacobean revenge tragedy, though some have seen it as a political satire on our materialistic times.
wd *Peter Greenaway* *ph* Sacha Vierny *m* Michael Nyman *pd* Ben Van Os, Jan Roelfs *ed* John Wilson
☆ Richard Bohringer, Michael Gambon, Helen Mirren, Alan Howard, Tim Roth, Ciaran Hinds, Gary Olsen, Ewan Stewart, Roger Ashton Griffiths, Ron Cook, Liz Smith
'Watching this picture is like being trapped in a nightmare art-history seminar: we sit there, cowed and miserable, as the teacher spews high-toned abstractions and dares us, smirkingly, to raise a common-sense objection – we know we'll be ridiculed if we do.' – *Terrence Rafferty, New Yorker*

Cookie
US 1989 93m DuArt
Warner/Lorimar (Laurence Mark)
A gangster's daughter shows that she has her father's dubious skills.
Lame drama of family relationships in gangland setting.
w Nora Ephron, Alice Arlen *d* Susan Seidelman *ph* Oliver Stapleton *m* Thomas Newman *pd* Michael Haller *ad* Bill Groom *ed* Andrew Mondshein
☆ Peter Falk, Dianne Wiest, Emily Lloyd, Michael V. Gazzo, Brenda Vaccaro, Adrian Pasdar, Lionel Stander, Jerry Lewis, Bob Gunton, Ben Rayson, Ricki Lake
'Cookie has the feel of a worn-out vehicle grinding to a halt.' – *Pam Cook, MFB*

'Where there's a will, there's a way.'
Cookie's Fortune **
US 1999 159m DeLuxe
Alliance/October/Sandcastle 5/Elysian Dreams (Robert Altman, Etchie Stroh)
Fearing scandal in a small Southern town, a woman attempts to cover up the suicide of her wealthy aunt, which leads to a black oddjob man being accused of murder.
Enjoyable, lesiurely, ramshackle social comedy that gives its characters room to blossom and reveal their humanity.
w Anne Rapp *d* Robert Altman *ph* Toyomichi Kurita *m* David A. Stewart *pd* Stephen Altman *ed* Abraham Lim
☆ Glenn Close (Camille Orcutt), Julianne Moore (Cora Duvall), Liv Tyler (Emma Duvall), Chris O'Donnell (Jason Brown), *Charles S. Dutton* (Willis Richland), Patricia Neal (Jewel Mae 'Cookie' Orcutt), Ned Beatty (Lester Boyle), Courtney B. Vance (Otis Tucker), Donald Moffat (Jack Palmer), Lyle Lovett (Manny Hood), Danny Darst (Billy Cox), Ruby Wilson (Josie Martin)
'May or not be Robert Altman's best film in years, but it is certainly his most pleasurable.' – *Todd McCarthy, Variety*

Cool and Crazy: see *Heftig og Begeistret*

'Seven savage punks on a binge of violence.'
The Cool and the Crazy
US 1958 78m bw
AIP/Imperial Productions (E. C. Rhoden Jnr)
A rebellious high-school student causes havoc after he persuades his fellow students to smoke marijuana.
Typical teen drive-in drama of its time, never less than hysterical and acted by a cast who look as if they've left puberty far behind.
w Richard C. Sarafian *d* William Witney *ph* Harry Birch *m* Raoul Kraushaar *ed* Helene Turner
☆ Scott Marlowe, Gigi Perreau, Dick Bakalyan, Dick Jones

'When a girl has a heart of stone, there's only one way to melt it. Just add Ice.'
Cool as Ice
US 1991 93m DeLuxe
Universal/Alive (Carolyn Pfieffer, Lionel Wigram)
A new biker in town helps save the parents of the girl he fancies when they are threatened by gangsters.
A failed attempt to make a film star out of a white rapper.
w David Stenn *d* David Kellogg *ph* Janusz Kaminski *m* Stanley Clarke *pd* Nina Ruscio *ed* Debra Goldfield, Caroline Biggerstaff
☆ Vanilla Ice, Kristin Minter, Michael Gross, Sydney Lassick, Dody Goodman, Naomi Campbell, Candy Clark
'Universal's hopes of springing another Elvis Presley on the screen are, at best, laughable.' – *Variety*

Cool Breeze
US 1972 102m Metrocolor
MGM/Penelope (Gene Corman)
A miscellaneous gang of crooks is rounded up to commit a robbery, which ultimately fails.
Third, all-black remake of The Asphalt Jungle *(the others being* The Badlanders *and* Cairo*). Fashionable violence against a Los Angeles backdrop, but not at all memorable.*
wd Barry Pollack *ph* Andy Davis *m* Solomon Burke
☆ Thalmus Rasulala, Judy Pace, Jim Watkins, Raymond St Jacques, Lincoln Kilpatrick

'What we've got here is a failure to communicate.'
Cool Hand Luke **
US 1967 126m Technicolor Panavision
Warner/Jalem (Gordon Carroll)
Sentenced to two years' hard labour with the chain gang, a convict becomes a legend of invulnerability but is eventually shot during an escape.

Allegedly a Christ-allegory, this well-made and good-looking film is only partially successful as an entertainment; slow stretches of soul-searching alternate with brutality, and not much acting is possible.
w Donn Pearce, Frank R. Pierson *novel* Donn Pearce *d Stuart Rosenberg ph Conrad Hall m* Lalo Schifrin
☆ Paul Newman, George Kennedy, Jo Van Fleet, J. D. Cannon, Lou Antonio, Robert Drivas, Strother Martin, Clifton James
'May be the best American film of 1967.' – *John Simon*
George Kennedy
Donn Pearce, Frank R. Pierson; Lalo Schifrin; Paul Newman

Cool Mikado
GB 1963 81m colour
UA/Gilbert and Sullivan Operas (Harold Baim)
In Japan, the son of an American judge is kidnapped when he falls in love with a girl engaged to a gangster.
An updated and unsuccessful version of the Gilbert and Sullivan operetta, one that allows little scope for its cast of comedians.
w Michael Winner, Maurice Browning, Lew Schwartz *operetta The Mikado by W. S. Gilbert and Arthur Sullivan d* Michael Winner *ph* Denys Ayling, Martin Curtis *md* John Barry *pd* Derek Barrington *ed* Frank Galvin
☆ Frankie Howerd, Stubby Kaye, Tommy Cooper, Dennis Price, Mike Winters, Bernie Winters, Lionel Blair, Tsai Chin, Kevin Scott, Glen Mason, Peter Murray, Dermot Walsh, The John Barry Seven

The Cool Ones
US 1967 96m Technicolor Panavision
Warner (William Conrad)
Former pop singer makes a comeback.
Zazzy showbiz saga with ear-splitting track, quite professionally assembled.
w Joyce Geller *d* Gene Nelson *ph* Floyd Crosby *m* Ernie Freeman
☆ Roddy McDowall, Debbie Watson, Robert Coote, Phil Harris, Nita Talbot

Cool Runnings *
US 1993 97m Technicolor
Buena Vista/Walt Disney (Dawn Steel)
A Jamaican athlete who fails to qualify for the Olympics decides to compete by forming a bobsled team with the aid of a white coach living on the island.
Based on the true story of the Jamaican bobsled team in the 1988 Olympics, an amiable, good-natured comedy of some charm.
w Lynn Siefert, Tommy Swerdlow, Michael Goldberg *story* Lynn Siefert, Michael Ritchie *d* Jon Turteltaub *ph* Phedon Papamichael *m* Hans Zimmer *pd* Stephen Marsh *ed* Bruce Green
☆ John Candy, Leon, Doug E. Doug, Malik Yoba, Rawle D. Lewis, Raymond Barry, Larry Gilman, Peter Outerbridge, Paul Coeur
'The offbeat, fact-based saga is enlivened by the perfect balance of humor, emotion and insight.' – *Variety*

Cool World
US 1992 102m Technicolor
Blue Dolphin/Paramount (Frank Mancuso Jnr)
A cartoonist and his creations flit in and out of the real world and the Cool World of his imagination.
Dreary attempt to marry live action and cartoon characters, with a plot obsessed by the possibility of sex between the two, which seems nothing to get excited about.
w Michael Grais, Mark Victor *d* Ralph Bakshi *ph* John A. Alonzo *m* Mark Isham, John Dixon *pd* Michael Corenblith *ed* Steve Mirkovich, Annamaria Szanto
☆ Kim Basinger, Gabriel Byrne, Brad Pitt, Michele Abrams, Deirdre O'Connell, Janni Brenn-Lowen
'A combination funhouse ride/acid trip that will prove an ordeal for most visitors in the form of trial by animation. Visually dazzling but utterly soulless.' – *Variety*

Cooley High
US 1975 107m Movielab
Brent Walker/AIP (Steve Krantz)
The adventures of high-school students in Chicago of the mid-60s.
A lively first feature, full of energy but lacking in focus.
w Eric Monte *d* Michael Schultz *ph* Paul von Brack *m* Freddie Perren *ad* William B. Fosser *ed* Christopher Holmes
☆ Glynn Turman, Lawrence-Hilton Jacobs, Garrett Morris, Cynthia Davis, Corin Rogers, Maurice Leon Havis
'The promising debut of a very talented director, intermittently doing what he can with an uneven and somewhat routine script.' – *Jonathan Rosenbaum, MFB*
† The film was the basis of a US TV sitcom, *What's Happening* (1976–79).

Le Cop *
France 1985 107m Eastmancolor Panavision
Cannon/Films 7/Editions 23
original title: *Les Ripoux*
A corrupt veteran cop is teamed with an incorruptible recruit.
Enjoyably comic exposé, much admired by the French.
w Claude Zidi *story* Simon Michael *d* Claude Zidi *ph* Jean-Jacques Tarbes *m* Francis Lai *ad* Françoise de Leu *ed* Nicole Saunier
☆ Philippe Noiret, Thierry Lhermitte, Regine, Grace de Capitani, Claude Brosset, Albert Simono

Cop
US 1987 110m colour
Entertainment/Atlantic (James B. Harris)
A cop tracks down a serial killer to the detriment of his marriage and his relationship with his colleagues.
Tough, violent but not particularly memorable thriller.
wd James B. Harris *novel Blood on the Moon* by James Ellroy *ph* Steve Dubin *m* Michel Colombier *pd* Gene Rudolf *ed* Anthony Spano
☆ James Woods, Lesley Ann Warren, Charles Durning, Charles Haid, Raymond J. Barry, Randi Brooks, Steven Lambert, Christopher Wynne, Jan McGill

Le Cop 2
France 1989 108m Eastmancolor
Gala/Films 7/Orly/Sedif/TF1 (Pierre Gauchet)
original title: *Ripoux contre ripoux*
Two corrupt policemen, suspended from duty, turn the tables on the crooks and cops who try to put them out of the force.
Weak sequel, with a complicated but uninteresting plot and nowhere to go for its central characters.
w Simon Michael, Claude Zidi, Didier Kaminka *d* Claude Zidi *ph* Jean-Jacques Tarbes *m* Francis Lai *ad* Françoise Deleu *ed* Nicole Saunier
☆ Philippe Noiret, Thierry Lhermitte, Guy Marchand, Line Renaud, Grace de Capitani, Michel Aumont, Jean-Pierre Castaldi, Jean-Claude Brialy

'One kid's fantasy. One cop's nightmare.'
Cop and a Half
US 1993 97m DeLuxe
Universal/Imagine (Paul Maslansky)
An eight-year-old boy, witness to a murder, gets to be a cop for a day.
Ghastly, sentimental comedy aimed at the lowest common demoninator.
w Arne Olsen *d* Henry Winkler *ph* Bill Butler *m* Alan Silvestri *pd* Maria Caso *ed* Daniel Hanley, Roger Tweten, C. Timothy O'Meara
☆ Burt Reynolds, Norman D. Golden II, Ruby Dee, Holland Taylor, Ray Sharkey, Sammy Hernandez, Frank Sivero
'Unashamedly caters to children's crudest fantasies and leaves the rest of the world at a loss. There are few adult pleasures to be had.' – *Sight and Sound*

Cop au Vin *
France 1984 110m Eastmancolor Panavision
Virgin/MK2/Marin Karmitz
original title: *Poulet au Vinaigre*
An unorthodox police inspector investigates two deaths in a small provincial town.
Glossy thriller exposing the pettiness of the bourgoisie.
w Dominique Roulet, Claude Chabrol *novel Un Mort En Trop* by Dominique Roulet *d* Claude Chabrol *ph* Jean Rabier *m* Matthieu Chabrol *ad* Françoise Benoît-Fresco *ed* Monique Fardoulis
☆ Jean Poiret, Stéphane Audran, Michel Bouquet, Jean Topart, Lucas Blevaux, Pauline Lafont, Caroline Cellier, Josephine Chaplin

'No One Is Above The Law.'
Cop Land **
US 1997 105m DeLuxe
Buena Vista/Woods Entertainment (Cary Woods, Cathy Konrad, Ezra Swerdlow)
A sheriff in a small New Jersey town that is home to many policemen investigates the deaths of two youths at the hands of a cop.
A thriller interesting mainly for Stallone's attempt to get away from his usual macho roles by playing an overweight, deaf sheriff, though it is never less than enjoyable.
wd James Mangold *ph* Eric Edwards *m* Howard Shore *pd* Lester Cohen *ed* Craig McKay
☆ Sylvester Stallone (Freddy Heflin), Harvey Keitel (Ray Donlan), Ray Liotta (Gary Figgis), Robert de Niro (Moe Tilden), Peter Berg (Joey Randone), Janeane Garofalo (Deputy Cindy Betts), Robert Patrick (Jack Rucker), Michael Rapaport (Murray Babitch), Annabella Sciorra (Liz Randone), Noah Emmerich (Deputy Bill Geisler), Cathy Moriarty
'Has the feel of a classic frontier Western in which the amiable sheriff is forced to wake up to the dastardly doings of the community's most prominent citizens.' – *Todd McCarthy, Variety*

Copacabana
US 1947 91m bw
UA/Sam Coslow
A quick-thinking agent forms two acts out of one client, which makes things awkward when both are needed at once.
Thinly produced comedy with both stars doing what is expected of them in surroundings less glamorous than those to which they were previously accustomed.
w Allen Boretz, Howard Harris *story* Laslo Vadnay *d* Alfred E. Green *ph* Bert Glennon *m* Edward Ward *ch* Larry Ceballos *ed* Philip Cahn
☆ *Groucho Marx*, Carmen Miranda, Steve Cochran, Gloria Jean, Andy Russell

Copper Canyon
US 1949 84m Technicolor
Paramount
After the Civil War, Southern veterans trying to rebuild their homes are helped by a gunslinger.
Shiny unpersuasive Western with stars ill at ease.
w Jonathan Latimer *d* John Farrow
☆ Ray Milland, Hedy Lamarr, Macdonald Carey, Mona Freeman, Harry Carey Jnr

Cops ***
US 1922 20m (24 fps) bw silent
First National/Comique Film (Joseph M. Schenck)
An innocent disrupts a parade and is pursued by a horde of policemen.
The perfect Keaton short, a careful assembly of perfectly timed gags.
wd Buster Keaton ph Elgin Lessley
☆ *Buster Keaton*, Virginia Fox

'Will these cops measure up as crooks?'
Cops and Robbers *
US 1973 89m DeLuxe
UA/EK Corp (Elliott Kastner)
Two New York cops turn crook and pull off a job for the Mafia.
Trendily anti-establishment comedy, quite snappy and smart when you can follow it.
w Donald E. Westlake *d* Aram Avakian *ph* David L. Quaid *m* Michel Legrand
☆ Cliff Gorman, Joe Bologna, Dick Ward, Shepperd Strudwick, Ellen Holly, John P. Ryan

Cops and Robbersons
US 1994 93m Technicolor
TriStar/Channel (Ned Tanen, Nancy Graham Tanen, Ronald L. Schwary)
Two cops move in with a suburban family to keep watch on a forger who lives next door.
Tame, formulaic comedy that pulls its punches in its depiction of the conventionalities of middle-class life, although Palance, as a cop who eats his food with a cigarette stuck in the corner of his mouth, provides moments of pleasure.
w Bernie Somers *d* Michael Ritchie *ph* Gerry Fisher *m* William Ross *pd* Stephen J. Lineweaver *ed* Stephen A. Rotter, William S. Scharf
☆ Chevy Chase, Jack Palance, Dianne Wiest, Robert Davi, David Barry Gray, Jason James Richter, Fay Masterson, Miko Hughes
'Best suited to a juvenile crowd who will thrive on the obvious nature of the proceedings.' – *Variety*

Copycat *
US 1995 123m Technicolor Panavision
Warner/New Regency/Monarchy (Arnon Milchan, Mark Tarlov)
A female detective and an agoraphobic psychologist team up to track down a serial killer who copies the style of murders carried out by other serial killers
A well-acted thriller on over-familiar themes; the performances do not compensate for its sense of staleness.
w Ann Biderman, David Madsen *d* Jon Amiel *ph* Laszlo Kovacs *m* Christopher Young *pd* Jim Clay *ed* Alan Heim, Jim Clark
☆ Sigourney Weaver, Holly Hunter, Dermot Mulroney, William McNamara, Harry Connick Jnr, J. E. Freeman, Will Patton, John Rothman
'An upscale suspenser by virtue of its classy cast, its extremely bright characters and the chillingly intellectual approach of the murderer, this shrewdly devised pulse-pounder may actually be too refined to click in a big way with mass audiences.' – *Todd McCarthy, Variety*
'This all-too-aptly titled film suggests it is time to find another dead horse to flog.' – *Kim Newman, Empire*

Coquette
US 1929 75m bw
Mary Pickford
A Southern belle has a flirtatious nature.
Disappointing talkie start for a first lady of the silents; she did not recover from it, despite her Oscar.
w John Grey, Allen McNeil, Sam Taylor *play* George Abbott, Anne Preston *d* Sam Taylor
☆ Mary Pickford, Johnny Mack Brown, Matt Moore, William Janney
Mary Pickford

Le Corbeau **
France 1943 92m bw
L'Atelier Français
US title: *The Raven*
Poison pen letters disturb a small provincial town.
Impressively characterized whodunnit with the usual French qualities of detail and discretion. Remade in Hollywood to less effect as The Thirteenth Letter *(qv).*
w Louis Chavance *d Henri-Georges Clouzot ph* Nicholas Hayer *m* Tony Aubain
☆ Pierre Fresnay, Pierre Larquey, Ginette Leclerc, Hélène Manson
'By no means as malign or as brilliant as it's cracked up to be, but a sour, clever, amusing job.' – *James Agee*

Coriolanus – Hero without a Country
(dubbed)
Italy/France 1965 100m Eastmancolor Euroscope
Dorica/Explorer/CFFP (Diego Alchimede)
original title: *Coriolano, Eroe senza Patria*
aka: *Thunder of Battle*
In a Rome riven by class conflict, its greatest general, Coriolanus, is exiled by the popular leaders.
Above-average Italian historical epic.
w Remigio Del Grosso *d* Giorgio Ferroni *ph* Augusto Tiezzi *m* Carlo Rustichelli *ad* Arrigo Equini *ed* Antonietta Zita

☆ Gordon Scott, Alberto Lupo, Lilla Brignone, Philippe Hersent, Rosalba Neri

The Corn Is Green *
US 1945 118m bw
Warner (Jack Chertok)

In 1895 Miss Moffat starts a village school for Welsh miners, and after some tribulations sees one of them off to Oxford.
A very theatrical production with unconvincing sets and mannered acting, but the original play has its felicities.
w Casey Robinson, Frank Cavett *play* Emlyn Williams *d* Irving Rapper *ph* Sol Polito *m* Max Steiner *ad* Carl Jules Weyl
☆ Bette Davis, John Dall, Nigel Bruce, Joan Lorring, Rhys Williams, Rosalind Ivan, Mildred Dunnock, Arthur Shields
'It's very apparent that Hollywood isn't Wales ... but the film lingers in the memory anyway.' – *New Yorker, 1978*
† Remade as a TV movie in 1978, with Katharine Hepburn.
John Dall; Joan Lorring

Cornered *
US 1945 102m bw
RKO

After demobilization, a French-Canadian pilot tracks down the collaborationist responsible for the death of his wife.
Well-made but humourless revenge thriller.
w John Paxton *story* John Wexley *d* Edward Dmytryk *ph* Harry J. Wild *m* Roy Webb
☆ Dick Powell, Micheline Cheirel, Walter Slezak, Morris Carnovsky

Coroner Creek
US 1948 89m Cinecolor
Columbia (Harry Joe Brown)

A Western crusader tracks down the man behind a stagecoach raid.
Solid action Western between the A and B categories.
w Kenneth Gamet *novel* Luke Short *d* Ray Enright
☆ Randolph Scott, Marguerite Chapman, George Macready, Sally Eilers, Edgar Buchanan, Barbara Reed, Wallace Ford, Forrest Tucker, Douglas Fowley

Corps Profond *
France 1963 21m Technicolor
Delpire
A tour inside the human body by courtesy of micro-photography.
Spellbinding and educative documentary of a new kind, and just the right length; the later British imitation, The Body, *outstayed its welcome.*
wd Igor Barrière, Etienne Lalou

'Horror to make your hair stand on end!'
The Corpse Vanishes
US 1942 70m bw
Monogram (Sam Katzman)

A botanist kidnaps young brides for their body fluids, in the hope of reviving his dead wife.
An especially dreary example of Poverty Row horror.
w Harvey Gates *d* Wallace Fox
☆ Bela Lugosi, Frank Moran, Minerva Urecal, Luana Walters

Corridor of Mirrors
GB 1948 105m bw
Cartier-Romney-Apollo (Rudolph Cartier)

An eccentric art collector believes that he and his mistress are reincarnations of 400-year-old lovers in a painting; but they are separated by murder.
Pretentious melodrama of no urgent narrative interest, with all concerned sadly at sea.
w Rudolph Cartier, Edana Romney *novel* Chris Massie *d* Terence Young *ph* André Thomas *m* Georges Auric *ad* Terence Verity *ed* Douglas Myers
☆ Eric Portman, Edana Romney, Barbara Mullen, Hugh Sinclair
'It has aimed at Art. It is, in fact, Effect. Some members of the cast wander in and out of the scenes as if they are not quite sure what has happened to them. Their confusion is not beyond comprehension.' – *MFB*

'Tops In Terror!'
Corridors of Blood *
GB 1958 86m bw
Producers' Associates (John Croydon)

original title: *Doctor from Seven Dials*
Seeking to discover anaesthetics, a Victorian doctor falls a prey to resurrection men.
Unpleasant but well-mounted semi-horror backed by strong cast and art direction.
w Jean Scott Rogers *d* Robert Day *ph* Geoffrey Faithfull *m* Buxton Orr *ad* Anthony Masters
☆ Boris Karloff, Christopher Lee, Finlay Currie, Frank Pettingell, Betta St John, Francis Matthews, Adrienne Corri, Marian Spencer
† Not released until 1964.

'An enchanting comedy comedy.'
Corrina, Corrina
US 1994 114m colour
Guild/New Line (Paula Mazur, Steve Tisch, Jessie Nelson)

In the late 1950s, a new housekeeper forms a motherly relationship with a nine-year-old girl, struck dumb by the death of her mother, and also becomes close to the girl's father.
A sentimental movie movie, which seems to have been mainly designed to sell its soundtrack album of the songs of the period.
wd Jessie Nelson *ph* Bruce Surtees *m* Rick Cox *pd* Jeannine Claudia Oppewall *ed* Lee Percy
☆ Ray Liotta, Whoopi Goldberg, Tina Majorino, Wendy Crewson, Larry Miller, Jenifer Lewis, Erica Yohn, Joan Cusack, Don Ameche
'Hopelessly pedantic – chock full of lessons about grief, racism, and, so help us, God.' – *Michael Sragow, New Yorker*
'Like *The Sound of Music* remade as an AT & T commercial.' – *Entertainment Weekly*

'Cross the line... pay the price.'
Corrupt
US 1999 70m colour
Filmwerks/Ice-T/Imperial/Detonator (Tom Karnowski, Gary Schmoeller)

A gangster forces a rival's lover to sleep with him in order to save the life of her brother.
Atrocious, cheap-looking, foul-mouthed thriller, worse than you can possibly imagine, with clichéd gangsta-rap dialogue ("some day you gonna be proud to call y'self my bitch") and much tough-guy posturing by its cast. It doesn't end so much as stop, as if everyone, understandably, lost interest.
w Andrew Markell *story* Hannah Blue *d* Albert Pyun *ph* Philip Alan Waters *m* Ice-T, Tony Riparetti *pd* Nenad Pecur *ed* Errin Vasquez
☆ Silkk the Shocker (M. J.), Ice-T (Corrupt), Tarsha Nicole Jones (Margo), Ernie Hudson Jnr (Miles), Karen Dyer (Jodi), T. J. Storm (Cinque), Tahitia (Lisa), Taylor Scott (Pammi), Jahi J. J. Zuri (Yazu), Romany Malco (Snackbar Dude), Vince Klyn (The Sayer)

The Corrupt Ones: see *The Peking Medallion*

Corruption
GB 1967 91m Technicolor
Columbia/Titan (Peter Newbrook)
A surgeon kills for pituitary gland fluid to restore his fiancée's beauty.
Highly derivative shocker with no inspiration of its own except an accumulation of gory detail.
w Donald and Derek Ford *d* Robert Hartford Davis *ph* Peter Newbrook *m* Bill McGuffie
☆ Peter Cushing, Sue Lloyd, Noel Trevarthen, Kate O'Mara, David Lodge

'You can't play by the rules when there aren't any.'
The Corruptor *
US 1999 110m DeLuxe Panavision
New Line/Illusion (Dan Halsted)

A young New York cop whose beat is Chinatown discovers that his new Asian-American partner has links to the Triads.
Tough, street-smart thriller on familiar themes of integrity and betrayal, given a fresh twist by its setting and its subject-matter of illegal immigration.
w Robert Pucci *d* James Foley *ph* Juan Ruiz-Anchia *m* Carter Burwell *pd* David Brisbin *ed* Howard E. Smith
☆ Chow Yun-Fat, Mark Wahlberg, Ric Young, Paul Ben-Victor, Jon Kit Lee, Andrew Pang, Brian Cox, Elizabeth Lindsey, Byron Mann, Kim Chan, Bill Macdonald, Susie Trinh, Tovah Feldshuh
'The movie may be a conventional story of police corruption, temptation and conflicting loyalties, but it never loses its smarts.' – *Stephen Holden, New York Times*

Corsa dell'Innocente: see *Flight of the Innocent*

The Corsican Brothers *
US 1941 111m bw
UA/Edward Small

Siamese twins are separated but remain spiritually tied through various adventures.
Adequately exciting picturization of the Dumas swashbuckler.
w George Bruce, Howard Estabrook *d* Gregory Ratoff *ph* Harry Stradling *m* Dimitri Tiomkin
☆ Douglas Fairbanks Jnr, Akim Tamiroff, Ruth Warrick, J. Carrol Naish, H. B. Warner, Henry Wilcoxon
† In 1953 came an undistinguished sequel, *Bandits of Corsica* (GB: *The Return of the Corsican Brothers*), with Richard Greene, Paula Raymond, Raymond Burr and Dona Drake. Written by Richard Schayer; directed by Ray Nazarro; for Global/UA. A comic version, *Cheech and Chong's Corsican Brothers* (qv), was released in 1984.
Dimitri Tiomkin

Cortesie per gli ospiti: see *The Comfort of Strangers*

Corvette K 225 *
US 1943 97m bw
Universal (Howard Hawks)
GB title: *The Nelson Touch*
A Canadian corvette commander encounters submarines and bombers in mid-Atlantic.
Good war film of its period, marred by romantic interest.
w Lt John Sturdy *d* Richard Rosson *ph* Tony Gaudio *m* David Buttolph
☆ Randolph Scott, James Brown, Ella Raines, Barry Fitzgerald, Andy Devine, Richard Lane
Tony Gaudio

Corvette Summer
US 1979 104m Metrocolor
MGM/Plotto (Hal Barwood)

GB title: *The Hot One*
A Los Angeles student spends the summer looking for his stolen customized car, and has various adventures around Las Vegas.
There are a few choice moments in this disconnected comedy drama, but the appeal is almost entirely to moonstruck teenagers.
w Hal Barwood, Matthew Robbins *d* Matthew Robbins *ph* Frank Stanley *m* Craig Safan
☆ Mark Hamill, Annie Potts, Eugene Roche, Kim Milford, Richard McKenzie

Cosh Boy
GB 1952 75m bw
Romulus (Daniel M. Angel)
US title: *The Slasher*
A young thug resists all attempts to reform him.
A competent social drama of its time; it has not worn well, though it remains of interest for what it reveals about the attitudes of the period.
w Lewis Gilbert, Vernon Harris *play* Master Crook by Bruce Walker *d* Lewis Gilbert *ph* Jack Asher *m* Lambert Williamson *ad* Bernard Robinson *ed* Charles Hasse
☆ James Kenney, Joan Collins, Hermione Baddeley, Hermione Gingold, Betty Ann Davies, Robert Ayres, Nancy Roberts, Laurence Naismith, Ian Whittaker
'There is something about this film which goes beyond the sordid nature of the subject and leaves a peculiarly distasteful impression. Whether by design or accident, there is a feeling about the piece that this sort of behaviour is not a deadly public menace, but a half-humorous escapade of youth.' – *C. A. Lejeune*
† The film, which was an early recipient of a British 'X' certificate, opens with an on-screen message: 'By itself, the "Cosh" is the cowardly implement of a contemporary evil; in association with "Boy", it marks a post-war tragedy – the juvenile delinquent. "Cosh Boy" portrays starkly the development of a young criminal, an enemy of society at sixteen. Our Judges and Magistrates, and the Police, whose stern duty it is to resolve the problem, agree that its origins lie mainly in the lack of parental control and early discipline. The problem exists – and we cannot escape it by closing our eyes. This film is presented in the hope that it will contribute towards stamping out this social evil.'

'His Hypnotic Eyes See All!'
The Cosmic Man
US 1958 72m bw
Futura (Robert A. Terry)

An alien is met with hostility when he visits Earth preaching peace.
Typical low-budget sci-fi movie of its time that offers nothing out of the ordinary.
w Arthur C. Pierce *d* Herbert Greene *ph* John F. Warren *m* Paul Sawtell, Bert Shefter *ed* Helene Turner
☆ Bruce Bennett, John Carradine, Angela Greene, Paul Langton, Scotty Morrow, Lyn Osborn, Walter Maslow

Cosmic Monsters: see *Strange World of Planet X*

Costa Brava *
Spain 1994 92m colour
DTK/Marta Balletbò-Coll

A female engineer falls in love with a lesbian writer.
Slight, pleasant romantic comedy set in Barcelona, with its Spanish cast speaking English.
w Marta Balletbò-Coll, Ana Simón Cerezo, Steven Winchell, Marel Malaret, Desi del Valle *d* Marta Balletbò-Coll *ph* Teo López Garcia *m* Emili Remolins Casas, Xavier Martorell, Miquel Amor *pd* Gloria Marti-Palanques *ed* Ignacio Pérez de Olaguer Córdoba
☆ Desi del Valle, Marta Balletbò-Coll, Montserrat Gausachs, Josep Maria Brugués, Ramon Mari, Sergi Schaaff
'A lesbian fairy tale with the lightest of touches, a fragile but charming confection.' – *Sight and Sound*

Cottage to Let *
GB 1941 90m bw
Gainsborough (Edward Black)

US title: *Bombsight Stolen*
Evacuated to Scotland, a Cockney helps prevent spies from kidnapping his inventor foster-father.
Stagey but often amusing comedy-thriller which after a shaky start becomes agreeably Hitchcockian.
w Anatole de Grunwald, J. O. C. Orton *play* Geoffrey Kerr *d* Anthony Asquith *ph* Jack Cox *md* Louis Levy
☆ Leslie Banks, *Alastair Sim, John Mills,* Jeanne de Casalis, George Cole, Carla Lehmann, Michael Wilding, Frank Cellier, Wally Patch, Muriel Aked, Muriel George, Catherine Lacey, Hay Petrie

'Where crime lords rub elbows with the rich and famous!'
The Cotton Club
US 1984 127m Technicolor Panavision
Zoetrope (Robert Evans)

The story of Harlem's famous night-club and the gangsters who frequented it.
A lumpy vehicle, eventually costing fifty million dollars, for some of the talents who made The Godfather *ten years earlier. Despite a few effective moments, a prime example of the careless extravagance which all but killed the film business.*
w William Kennedy, Francis Coppola *d* Francis Coppola *ph* Stephen Goldblatt *m* John Barry *pd* Richard Sylbert *ed* Barry Malkin, Robert Lovett
☆ Richard Gere, Gregory Hines, Diane Lane, Lonette McKee, Bob Hoskins, James Remar, Nicolas Cage, Allen Garfield, Fred Gwynne, Gwen Verdon
'The narrative is a mess, and keeps interrupting the heartstopping hoofing.' – *Time Out*
editing, art direction

Cotton Comes to Harlem
US 1970 97m DeLuxe
Formosa/UA

Two black detectives try to beat the police to a bale of cotton containing a fortune in stolen dollars.
Rickety vehicle for two amiable black characters presented rather more surely in Come Back Charleston Blue *(qv).*
w Arnold Perl, Ossie Davis, Chester Himes *novel* Chester Himes *d* Ossie Davis
☆ Godfrey Cambridge, Raymond St Jacques, Calvin Lockhart, Judy Pace, Redd Foxx

Cotton Mary *
GB 1999 123m Technicolor
UIP/Merchant Ivory (Nayeem Hafizka, Richard Hawley)

An Anglo-Indian nurse in a white household in India in the 1950s imagines that she can supplant her mistress.
An effective drama of colonialism and racial identity, fought out within a family that is losing its cohesion.
w Alexandra Viets *play* Alexandra Viets *d* Ismail Merchant *ph* Pierre Lhomme *m* Richard Robbins *pd* Alison Riva *ed* John David Allen
☆ Greta Scacchi (Lily Macintosh), Madhur Jaffrey (Cotton Mary), James Wilby (John Macintosh), Sarah Badel (Mrs Evans), Riju Bajaj (Mugs), Gerson Da Cunha (Dr Correa), Joanna David (Mrs Smythe), Neena Gupta (Blossom), Sakina Jaffrey (Rosie), Gemma Jones (Mrs Freda Davids), Firdausi Jussawalla (Mr Panamal)
'An enjoyable, sturdy little film that is uniformly well-acted and beautifully shot.' – *Clayton Hickman, Film Review*

The Couch Trip *
US 1988 98m colour
Rank/Orion (Lawrence Gordon)

A mental patient escapes to Los Angeles where he becomes a success as a radio doctor.
Sporadically amusing comedy that mocks obvious targets.
w Steven Kampmann, Will Port, Sean Stein *novel* Ken Kolb *d* Michael Ritchie *ph* Donald E. Thorin *m* Michel Colombier *pd* Jimmy Bly *ed* Richard A. Harris
☆ Dan Aykroyd, Walter Matthau, Charles Grodin, Donna Dixon, Richard Romanus, Mary Gross, David Clennon

Council of the Gods *
Germany 1950 106m bw
DEFA (Adolf Fischer)
A research chemist working for a big chemical company denounces them after the war when he finds they have been producing poison gas for the concentration camps.
Self-flagellatory expiation of war crimes encased in an absorbing drama.
w Friedrich Wolff, Philipp Gebb *d* Kurt Maetzig *ph* Friedl Behn-Grund *m* Hanns Eisler, Erwin Lehn
☆ Paul Bildt, Agnes Windeck, Yvonne Merin, Fritz Tillman

Counsellor at Law *
US 1933 78m bw
Universal (Henry Henigson)
Life in the New York office of a successful Jewish lawyer.
Practised film-making from a Broadway hit.
w Elmer Rice *play* Elmer Rice *d William Wyler* *ph* Norbert Brodine
☆ John Barrymore, Bebe Daniels, Melvyn Douglas, Doris Kenyon, Onslow Stevens, Isabel Jewell, Thelma Todd, Mayo Methot
'Good drama, well produced and with strong b.o. potentialities.' – *Variety*
† Paul Muni was the first choice for the lead, but refused to play a Jewish role.

Counsel's Opinion
GB 1933 76m bw
London Films (Alexander Korda)
A widow wins a barrister by pretending to be a flighty socialite.
Semi-sophisticated comedy; this rather thin quickie version was done over four years later and became The Divorce of Lady X *(qv).*
w Dorothy Greenhill, Arthur Wimperis *play* Gilbert Wakefield *d* Allan Dwan *ph* Bernard Browne *ad* Holmes Paul *ed* Harold Young
☆ Henry Kendall, Binnie Barnes, Cyril Maude, Lawrence Grossmith
'There is perhaps more naivety than usual about this comedy of a divorce counsel who imagines himself mixed up in his own case. The director is an American, Allan Dwan, who must either have come or gone away with odd ideas of British humour.' – *Observer*

Count A Lonely Cadence: see *Stockade*

Count Dracula: see *Bram Stoker's Count Dracula*

Count Five and Die *
GB 1957 92m bw Cinemascope
TCF/Zonic (Ernest Gartside)
British intelligence seeks to give the Nazis false information about the 1944 invasion, but conviction grows that a double agent is among them.
Terse, downbeat war suspenser, gripping in parts but quite forgettable.
w Jack Seddon, David Pursall *d* Victor Vicas *ph* Arthur Grant *m* John Wooldridge
☆ *Nigel Patrick*, Jeffrey Hunter, Anne-Marie Duringer, David Kossoff

The Count of Monte Cristo ***
US 1934 114m bw
Reliance (Edward Small)

After spending years in prison, Edmond Dantes escapes and avenges himself on those who framed him.
Classic swashbuckler, extremely well done with due attention to dialogue as well as action; a model of its kind and period.
w Philip Dunne, Dan Totheroh, Rowland V. Lee *novel* Alexandre Dumas *d Rowland V. Lee* *ph* Peverell Marley *m* Alfred Newman
☆ *Robert Donat*, Elissa Landi, Louis Calhern, Sidney Blackmer, Raymond Walburn, O. P. Heggie, William Farnum
'A near-perfect blend of thrilling action and grand dialogue.' – *Variety*

'Prepare for adventure. Count on revenge.'
The Count of Monte Cristo *
US/GB/Ireland 2002 131m Technicolor
Buena Vista/Touchstone/Spyglass (Roger Birnbaum, Gary Barber, Jonathan Glickman)

In France in the 1800s, a man escapes from 13 years of wrongful imprisonment to take revenge on those who betrayed him.
Old fashioned swashbuckler that provides simple pleasures even though it lacks the requisite panache.
w Jay Wolpert *novel* Alexandre Dumas *d* Kevin Reynolds *ph* Andrew Dunn *m* Edward Shearmur *pd* Mark Geraghty *ed* Stephen Semel, Chris Womack *cos* Tom Rand
☆ Jim Caviezel (Edmond Dantes), Guy Pearce (Fernand Mondego), Dagmara Dominczyk (Mercedes), Richard Harris (Abbe Faria), Luis Guzman (Jacopo), James Frain (Villefort), Henry Cavill (Albert), Albie Woodington (Danglars), Michael Wincott (Dorleac), Alex Norton (Napoleon Bonaparte), Freddie Jones (Col Villefort)
'In its forthright, sincere attempt to harness the narrative drive and emotional sweep of the Dumas novel, the film is close in spirit (though not in style) to the 1934 version.' – *A. O. Scott, New York Times*

The Count of the Old Town
Sweden 1935 75m bw
Svensk Filmindustri/AB Fribergs Filmbyra
original title: *Munkbrogreven*
A mysterious stranger moves into a hotel frequented by some elderly work-shy drinkers, and begins a romance with the maid.
A broad and episodic comedy of clever crooks and dim cops, dominant women and henpecked men, with enough absurd impetus to its set-pieces to still raise a smile or two.
w Gösta Stevens *play Greven Av Gamla Sta'n* by Siegfried and Arthur Fischer *d* Edvin Adolphson *ph* Åke Dahlquist *m* Eric Bengtson *ed* Rolf Husberg
☆ Waldemar Dalquist, Julia Caesar, Sigurd Wallén, Tollie Zellman, Edvin Adolphson, Ingrid Bergman, Eric Abrahamson, Weyler Hildebrand
† It was Ingrid Bergman's first film.

Count Three and Pray
US 1955 92m Technicolor Cinemascope
Columbia/Copa (Ted Richmond)
After the Civil War a roistering Southerner comes home to rebuild his town and become its parson.
Moderate semi-Western, fresh and pleasing but not memorable.
w Herb Meadow *d* George Sherman *ph* Burnett Guffey *m* George Duning
☆ Van Heflin, Joanne Woodward, Phil Carey, Raymond Burr, Allison Hayes, Myron Healey, Nancy Kulp, James Griffiths

'Don't dare come alone!'
Count Yorga Vampire
US 1970 90m Movielab
Erica/AIP (Michael Macready)

aka: *The Loves of Count Iorga, Vampire*
Inquisitive Los Angeles teenagers are vampirized by a suave foreign visitor.
A semi-professional film that looks it but amid the longueurs provides one or two nasty frissons.
wd Bob Kelljan *ph* Arch Archambault *m* William Marx
☆ Robert Quarry, Roger Perry, Michael Murphy, Michael Macready, Donna Anders, Judith Lang
† *The Return of Count Yorga* followed a year later.

Count Your Blessings
US 1959 102m Metrocolor Cinemascope
MGM (Karl Tunberg)
An English girl marries an aristocratic Frenchman, but the war and other considerations make them virtual strangers until their son is nine years old, when it becomes clear that daddy is a philanderer.
Slight upper-crust comedy, basically rather tedious but kept buoyant by Chevalier as commentator.
w Karl Tunberg *novel The Blessing* by Nancy Mitford *d* Jean Negulesco *ph* Milton Krasner, George Folsey *m* Franz Waxman
☆ Deborah Kerr, *Maurice Chevalier*, Rossano Brazzi, Martin Stephens, Tom Helmore, Ronald Squire, Patricia Medina, Mona Washbourne
'Negulesco's aspirations to elegance are now familiar ... this is far too absurd an example of Hollywood's infatuation with Old Europe to arouse much interest.' – *MFB*

Countdown *
US 1967 101m Technicolor Panavision
Warner (William Conrad)

Russian and American spaceships race for the moon.
Earnest, simply-plotted science-fiction in which technology is the centre of interest.
w Loring Mandel *d* Robert Altman *ph* William W. Spencer *m* Leonard Rosenman *ad* Jack Poplin
☆ James Caan, Robert Duvall, Barbara Baxley, Joanna Moore, Charles Aidman, Steve Ihnat

Counterattack
US 1945 89m bw
Columbia
GB title: *One against Seven*
Resistance fighters go behind enemy lines for purposes of sabotage.
Standard World War II actioner, the star appearing above his surroundings.
w John Howard Lawson *play* Janet and Philip Stevenson *d* Zoltan Korda *ph* James Wong Howe *m* Louis Gruenberg
☆ Paul Muni, Marguerite Chapman, Larry Parks, George Macready, Roman Bohnen

Counterblast
GB 1948 99m bw
British National
An escaped Nazi poses as a British scientist in a research laboratory.
Overlong espionage thick ear with some compensations.
w Jack Whittingham *story* Guy Morgan *d* Paul Stein
☆ Robert Beatty, Mervyn Johns, Nova Pilbeam, Margaretta Scott, Marie Lohr, Karel Stepanek, Alan Wheatley

The Counterfeit Traitor *
US 1962 140m Technicolor
Paramount/Perlberg-Seaton

An oil importer, a naturalized Swede born in America, is blackmailed by the Allies into becoming a spy.
Heavy-going espionage drama which divides its time between action and moralizing. Excellent production does not quite make it exciting.
wd George Seaton *book* Alexander Klein *ph* Jean Bourgoin *m* Alfred Newman
☆ William Holden, Lilli Palmer, Hugh Griffith, Werner Peters, Eva Dahlbeck
'The picture is too long, it is also incessantly exciting, occasionally witty ... and in its expression of organized sadism comparatively subtle.' – *Time*

The Counterfeiters
US 1948 73m bw
TVF/Reliance (Maurice H. Conn)
A Scotland Yard detective and a US Treasury agent team up to track down a gang of forgers who are flooding Europe with fake twenty-dollar bills and five-pound notes.
Undemanding and undistinguished time-filler with a reliance on stereotype – the Englishman cop smokes a pipe, the American cigarettes – and with Chaney doing the dim hulk routine that he perfected in Of Mice and Men.
w Fred Myton, Barbara Worth *story* Maurice H. Conn *d* Peter Stewart (Sam Newfield) *ph* James S. Brown *m* Irving Gertz *ad* Frank Dexter *ed* Martin G. Cohn
☆ John Sutton, Doris Merrick, Hugh Beaumont, Lon Chaney, George O'Hanlon, Douglas Blackley, Herbert Rawlinson

Counterforce: see *Rogue Force*

Counterpoint *
US 1967 107m Technicolor Techniscope
Universal (Dick Berg)
In 1944, an American symphony orchestra is captured by the Germans and threatened with execution.
Bizarre war suspenser, quite unconvincing but with effectively suspenseful moments and an old-fashioned portrayal of the Nazis as sadistic music-loving Huns.
w James Lee, Joel Oliansky *novel The General* by Alan Sillitoe *d* Ralph Nelson *ph* Russell Metty *m* Bronislau Kaper
☆ *Charlton Heston*, Maximilian Schell, Anton Diffring, Kathryn Hays, Leslie Nielsen

Countess Dracula
GB 1971 93m Eastmancolor
Rank/Hammer (Alexander Paal)

A Hungarian noblewoman restores her youth by bathing in the blood of young virgins.
Risibly sub-Freudian addition to a grotesque Hammer gallery of monsters, indistinguishable from the others once it gets going.
w Jeremy Paul *story* Alexander Paal, Peter Sasdy, Gabriel Ronay *d* Peter Sasdy *ph* Ken Talbot *m* Harry Robinson *ad* Philip Harrison *ed* Henry Richardson
☆ *Ingrid Pitt*, Nigel Green, Sandor Eles, Maurice Denham, Patience Collier, Peter Jeffrey, Lesley-Anne Down
'At its best the film employs the kind of romantic imagery one associates with Keats; and if it doesn't quite live up to that comparison, it is at least a worthy companion to Corman's *Bloody Mama*.' – *David Pirie, MFB*
† Ingrid Pitt's performance was dubbed because the director found her accent caused problems in some key scenes.

A Countess from Hong Kong
GB 1967 120m Technicolor
Universal (Jerome Epstein)
An American millionaire diplomat is followed from Hong Kong by his Russian émigrée girlfriend, and complications mount when his wife boards the ship at Hawaii.
Flatulent comedy with neither the sparkle of champagne nor even the fizz of lemonade: Chaplin's writing, direction and music are alike soporific, and commiserations are due to the cast.
ph Arthur Ibbetson *pd* Don Ashton *wd/m* Charles Chaplin

☆ Marlon Brando, Sophia Loren, *Patrick Cargill*, Margaret Rutherford, Charles Chaplin, Sydney Chaplin, Oliver Johnston, John Paul

'An unfunny, mindless mess.' – *Robert Windeler*

'So old-fashioned and dull that one can hardly believe it was made now.' – *Philip T. Hartung*

Countess of Monte Cristo
US 1948 76m bw
Universal International/Westwood
Two Norwegian barmaids visit a smart resort, pretending to be a countess and her maidservant.
Lacklustre musical comedy that brought Henie's US career to an end.
w William Bowers *story* Walter Reisch *d* Frederick De Cordova *ph* Edward Cronjager *m* Walter Scharf *m/ly* Saul Chaplin, Jack Brooks *ch* Louis Da Pron *ad* Bernard Herzbrun, Emrich Nicholson *ed* Edward Curtiss
☆ Sonja Henie, Michael Kirby, Olga San Juan, Dorothy Hart, Arthur Treacher, Hugh French, Ransom Sherman, Freddie Trenkler
† The film was a musical remake of a 1934 movie of the same name.
♫ Friendly Polka, Count Your Blessings, Who Believes in Santa Claus?

'In This Country, When The Land Is Your Life... You Fight For Your Life.'
Country *
US 1984 109m Technicolor Panavision
Touchstone/Far West/Pangaea (William D. Wittliff, Jessica Lange)
Iowa farmers, on the breadline after a tornado, face foreclosure.
Deeply felt modern variation on The Grapes of Wrath, *not particularly dramatic for those who have not felt the pressure.*
w William D. Wittliff *d* Richard Pearce *ph* David M. Walsh *m* Charles Gross *pd* Ron Hobbs *ed* Bill Yahraus
☆ Jessica Lange, Sam Shepard, Wilford Brimley, Matt Clark, Therese Graham
Jessica Lange

Country Dance
GB 1969 112m Metrocolor
MGM/Keep-Windward (Robert Emmett Ginna)
aka: *Brotherly Love*
An eccentric baronet's incestuous love for his sister finally breaks up her marriage.
Rambling melodrama with O'Toole going mad in squire's tweeds; tediously fashionable but too pallid for general success, it was barely released.
w James Kennaway *novel* *Household Ghosts* by James Kennaway *d* J. Lee-Thompson *ph* Ted Moore *m* John Addison
☆ Peter O'Toole, Susannah York, Michael Craig, Harry Andrews, Cyril Cusack, Judy Cornwell, Brian Blessed

The Country Doctor *
US 1936 94m bw
TCF (Darryl F. Zanuck)
A rural physician becomes famous when quintuplets are born to one of his patients.
Fictionalization of the birth of the Dionne Quintuplets; pleasantly nostalgic even sixty years after its raison d'être.
w Sonya Levien *d* Henry King *ph* John F. Seitz, Daniel B. Clark
☆ Jean Hersholt, the Dionne Quins, Dorothy Peterson, June Lang, Slim Summerville, Michael Whalen, Robert Barrat

'Admirably genuine: the camera – rare occasion in the cinema – doesn't lie, and Mr Jean Hersholt gives one of the most sympathetic performances I have seen this year.' – *Graham Greene*

† Sequels: *Reunion* (1936), *Five of a Kind* (1938).

Country Gentlemen
US 1936 66m bw
Republic
A couple of con men help a widow who runs a small-town hotel.
Strained comedy in which the gag men misguidedly try to play straight.
w Milton Raison, Jack Harvey, Jo Graham *d* Ralph Staub
☆ Ole Olsen, Chic Johnson, Joyce Compton, Lila Lee, Pierre Watkin

'Missing is the rapidfire buffoonery with which they have been identified in vaudeville.' – *Variety*

'How far should a woman go to redeem the man she loves?'
The Country Girl *
US 1954 104m bw
Paramount (William Perlberg)
The wife of an alcoholic singer blossoms when he is stimulated into a comeback.
Theatrically effective but highly unconvincing, this rather glum stage success made a cold film, miscast with an eye on the box-office.
w Stanley Roberts *play* Clifford Odets *d* George Seaton *ph* John F. Warren *m* Victor Young *m/ly* Ira Gershwin, Harold Arlen *ad* Hal Pereira, Roland Anderson
☆ Bing Crosby, Grace Kelly, William Holden, Anthony Ross, Gene Reynolds

'The dramatic development is not really interesting enough to sustain a film of the intensity for which it strives.' – *Karel Reisz*

'Rather inexplicably, this sado-masochist morass was one of the biggest box office hits of its year.' – *Pauline Kael, 70s*

Grace Kelly
best picture; John F. Warren; Bing Crosby; George Seaton; Stanley Roberts; art direction

Country Life **
Australia 1994 117m colour
Metro Tartan/AFFC/Robin Dalton
Just after the end of the First World War, a snobbish, failed literary critic returns from London with his young wife to the Australian sheep farm run by his brother-in-law.
Gentle, well-observed comedy of unfulfilled lives and broken dreams.
wd Michael Blakemore *play* *Uncle Vanya* by Anton Chekhov *ph* Stephen Windon *m* Peter Best *pd* Laurence Eastwood *ed* Nicholas Beauman
☆ Greta Scacchi, Sam Neill, John Hargreaves, Kerry Fox, Michael Blakemore, Googie Withers, Patricia Kennedy, Ron Blanchard, Maurie Fields

'A very funny film with a rippling undercurrent of imminent melancholy. It does more than entertain, with an observant view of humanity's pardonable frailties.' – *Alexander Walker, London Evening Standard*

County Hospital **
US 1932 20m bw
Hal Roach
Ollie is in hospital; Stan brings him some hardboiled eggs and some nuts, and nearly wrecks the place.
Archetypal star comedy with brilliant character and slapstick sequences, let down by a badly processed car ride home.
w H. M. Walker *d* James Parrott *ph* Art Lloyd *ed* Bert Jordan, Richard Currier
☆ Stan Laurel, Oliver Hardy, Billy Gilbert, William Austin, May Wallace

Coup de Foudre *
France 1983 111m colour Cinemascope
Gala/Partners Productions/Alexandre Films/Hachette Première/A2/SFPC (Ariel Zeitoun)
US title: *Entre Nous*
Two women leave their husbands to live and work together.
Charm predominates in this nostalgic piece, based on the life of the director's mother.
w Olivier Cohen, Diane Kurys *book* Diane Kurys *d* Diane Kurys *ph* Bernard Lutic *m* Luis Bacalov *pd* Jacques Bufnoir *ed* Joele Van Effenterre
☆ Miou-Miou, Isabelle Huppert, Guy Marchand, Jean-Pierre Bacri, Robin Renucci, Patrick Bauchau, Jacques Alric
best foreign film

Coup de Torchon
France 1981 128m colour
Les Films de la Tour/Les Films A2/Little Bear (Adolphe Viezzi)
GB title: *Clean Slate*
In French West Africa in 1938, an apparently easy-going police officer is inspired to commit a series of murders.
Well-made, heavy-going study of mania.
w Jean Aurenche, Bertrand Tavernier *novel* *POP. 1280* by Jim Thompson *d* Bertrand Tavernier *ph* Pierre William Glenn *m* Philippe Sarde
☆ Philippe Noiret, Isabelle Huppert, Jean-Pierre Marielle, Stéphane Audran, Eddy Mitchell
best foreign film

'A movie for everyone who's ever struggled to love a brother ... Or strangle one.'
Coupe de Ville **
US 1990 97m DeLuxe Super 35
Warner/Morgan Creek (Larry Brezner, Paul Schiff)
In the early 1960s, a father asks his three sons to drive a 1950s Cadillac Coupe de Ville from Michigan to Miami for their mother's birthday.
Engaging and amusing low-key road movie centring on family relationships.
w Mike Binder *d* Joe Roth *ph* Reynaldo Villalobos *m* James Newton Howard *pd* Angelo Graham *ed* Paul Hirsch
☆ Patrick Dempsey, Arye Gross, Daniel Stern, Annabeth Gish, Rita Taggart, Joseph Bologna, Alan Arkin

'A road movie with a difference, this one has heart and quality.' – *Shaun Usher, Daily Mail*

'For the most part a very shrewd, well-made and well-acted film.' – *Derek Malcolm, Guardian*

Courage: see *Raw Courage (1985)*

Courage Fuyons *
France 1979 98m Eastmancolor
Gaumont/Gueville (Yves Robert)
A middle-aged man embarks on a series of surprising romantic adventures.
A mainly enjoyable exercise in wish-fulfilment, sharply written and acted.
w Jean-Loup Dabadie, Yves Robert *d* Yves Robert *ph* Yves Lafaye *m* Vladimir Cosma
☆ Jean Rochefort, Catherine Deneuve, Robert Webber, Philippe Leroy-Beaulieu

Courage Mountain
US 1989 98m CFI color
Entertainment/Epic/Stone Group (Stephen Ujlaki)
A Swiss schoolgirl, stranded in Italy with some friends, makes her way back home.
A new adventure, told in an old-fashioned way, of that one-time children's favourite Heidi.
w Weaver Webb *story* Fred Brogger, Mark Brogger *d* Christopher Leitch *ph* Jacques Steyn *m* Sylvester Levay *pd* Robb Wilson King *ed* Martin Walsh
☆ Juliette Caton, Charlie Sheen, Leslie Caron, Yorgo Voyagis, Laura Betti, Jan Rubes, Joanna Clarke

Courage Under Fire *
US 1996 115m DeLuxe
TCF/Fox 2000/Davis Entertainment (Joseph M. Singer, David T. Friendly)
A colonel investigates the suitability of awarding a posthumous Medal of Honor to a female helicopter pilot killed in the Gulf War.
A film that begins as a complex investigation into behaviour in wartime but ends as a straightforward flag-waving exercise.
w Patrick Sheane Duncan *d* Edward Zwick *ph* Roger Deakins *m* James Horner *pd* John Graysmark *ed* Steven Rosenblum
☆ Denzel Washington, Meg Ryan, Lou Diamond Phillips, Michael Moriarty, Matt Damon, Bronson Pinchot, Scott Glenn, Sean Astin

'An intelligent well-crafted film that pays few concessions to Hollywood melodrama.' – *James Cameron-Wilson, Film Review*

The Courageous Mr Penn: see *Penn of Pennsylvania*

The Courier
Ireland 1987 85m
Palace/City Vision (Hilary McLoughlin)
A motorcycle messenger becomes an unknowing carrier of drugs.
Violent, low-budget thriller with no redeeming qualities.
w Frank Deasy *d* Joe Lee, Frank Deasy *ph* Gabriel Beristain *m* Declan MacManus *pd* David Wilson *ed* Derek Trigg, Annette D'Alton
☆ Gabriel Byrne, Ian Bannen, Cait O'Riordan, Padraig O'Loingsigh, Patrick Bergin, Andrew Connolly

Cours du Soir
France 1967 25m colour
Telecip/Specta (Bernard Maurice)
An evening-class lecturer demonstrates the various ways people smoke, walk and play sport.
Tati goes through some of his familiar routines, but the setting is not a sympathetic one and he looks tired and unenthusiastic about what he is doing.
w Jacques Tati *d* Nicolas Rybowski *ph* Jean Badal *m* Léo Petit *ed* Nicole Cauduchon
☆ Jacques Tati

The Court Jester ***
US 1955 101m Technicolor Vistavision
Paramount/Dena (Melvin Frank, Norman Panama)
Opposition to a tyrannical king is provided by the Fox, but it is one of the rebel's meekest men who, posing as a jester, defeats the usurper.
One of the star's most delightful vehicles, this medieval romp has good tunes and lively action, not to mention an exceptional cast and the memorable 'chalice from the palace' routine.
wd Norman Panama, Melvin Frank *ph* Ray June *m/ly* Sylvia Fine, Sammy Cahn *ad* Hal Pereira, Roland Anderson
☆ *Danny Kaye*, Glynis Johns, *Basil Rathbone*, Cecil Parker, *Mildred Natwick*, Angela Lansbury, Edward Ashley, Robert Middleton, Michael Pate, Alan Napier

Court Martial: see *Carrington VC*

The Court Martial of Billy Mitchell *
US 1955 100m Warnercolor Cinemascope
United States Pictures (Milton Sperling)
GB title: *One Man Mutiny*
In the early twenties, an American general of the Army Air Service is court-martialled for accusing the war department of criminal negligence.
Adequate recreation of a historical incident, with a cast of excellent actors converging for a courtroom scene of some effectiveness.
w Milton Sperling, Emmet Lavery *d* Otto Preminger *ph* Sam Leavitt *m* Dimitri Tiomkin
☆ Gary Cooper, *Rod Steiger*, Ralph Bellamy, Charles Bickford, Elizabeth Montgomery, Fred Clark, Darren McGavin, James Daly
Milton Sperling, Emmet Lavery

The Courtney Affair: see *The Courtneys of Curzon Street*

The Courtneys of Curzon Street *
GB 1947 120m bw
Imperadio (Herbert Wilcox)
US title: *The Courtney Affair*
In Victorian times, a baronet's son marries a lady's maid ... and many years later, their grandson marries a factory worker.
Unbelievable upstairs-downstairs romantic drama spanning three generations; all to be taken with a gigantic pinch of salt, but a huge success when released.
w Nicholas Phipps *novel* Florence Tranter *d* Herbert Wilcox *ph* Max Greene *m* Anthony Collins *ad* William C. Andrews *ed* Flora Newton, Vera Campbell
☆ Anna Neagle (Catherine O'Halloran), Michael Wilding (Sir Edward Courtney), Gladys Young (Lady Courtney), Coral Browne (Valerie), Michael Medwin (Edward Courtney), Daphne Slater (Cynthia), Jack Watling (Teddy Courtney), Helen Cherry (Mary Courtney), Bernard Lee (Colonel Gascoyne), Ethel O'Shea (Mrs O'Halloran), Thora Hird (Kate)

'The dignity of Curzon Street is Hollywoodized, and it is rare in 1945 that people in their sixties look as though they have one foot in the grave.' – *MFB*
'If my livelihood depended on booking the right film into the average cinema, this is one I would not dare to miss.' – *Observer*

The Courtship of Eddie's Father *
US 1962 117m Metrocolor Panavision
MGM/Joe Pasternak
The small son of a widower tries to interest Dad in another woman.
Fairly icky American-style sentimental comedy with most of the stops pulled out; way over-length and too self-indulgently solemn in the last part, but with professional touches.
w John Gay *novel* Muriel Toby *d* Vincente Minnelli *ph* Milton Krasner *m* George Stoll
☆ Glenn Ford, Ronny Howard, Shirley Jones, Stella Stevens, Dina Merrill
† A TV series starring Bill Bixby followed in 1971.

'Who Knew Deception, Treachery And Revenge Could Be This Much Fun...'
'A Delicious Tale Of Revenge.'
Cousin Bette *
US 1998 107m colour Panavision
Fox Searchlight (Sarah Radclyffe)
A hard-up seamstress plots revenge against her wealthy cousins.
Slight but enjoyable version of a more complex novel, a period romp with a hissable villainess.
w Lynn Siefert, Susan Tarr *novel* Honoré de Balzac *d* Des McAnuff *ph* Andrzej Sekula *m* Simon Boswell *ch* Jane Gibson *pd* Hugo Luczyc-Wyhowksi *ed* Tariq Anwar, Barry Alexander Brown
☆ Jessica Lange, Elisabeth Shue, Bob Hoskins, Hugh Laurie, Kelly Macdonald, Aden Young, Geraldine Chaplin, Toby Stephens, John Sessions
'As a frothy confection it can't be faulted.' – *Ryan Gilbey, Independent*

Cousin Bobby *
US 1992 69m colour
Electric/Tesauro
A documentary on the life and work of the Rev. Robert Castle, an outspoken Episcopalian priest working in Harlem, made by his film director cousin.
Well-made and interesting account of a dedicated priest that cuts from the public life to the private man.
d Jonathan Demme *ph* Ernest Dickerson, Craig Haagensen, Tony Jannelli, Jacek Laskus, Declan Quinn *m* Anton Sanko *ed* David Greenwald
'A low-key, occasionally touching documentary ... essentially a home movie, but one with broad appeal.' – *Variety*

Cousin, Cousine ***
France 1975 95m Eastmancolor
Pomereu/Gaumont (Bertrand Javal)
Various furtive love affairs centre on a family wedding.
Sprightly satirical comedy full of pleasing touches, mostly jibes at French bourgeois standards.
wd Jean Charles Tacchella ph Georges Lendi *m* Gerard Anfosso
☆ Marie-France Pisier, Marie-Christine Barrault, Victor Lanoux, Guy Marchand, Ginette Garcin
'One of those rare delights you want to see again and again just to share the sheer joy of living, zest for love, genuine affection, all-too-human absurdity, and pure happiness of all those delicious people on screen.' – *Judith Crist, Saturday Review*
best foreign film; script; Marie-Christine Barrault

Les Cousins *
France 1959 110m bw
AJYM (Claude Chabrol)
A law student stays with his sophisticated cousin in Paris, and his life is altered.
The country cousin fable filled with undramatic detail and given a rather perverse ending without any apparent point.
wd Claude Chabrol ph Henri Decaë *m* Paul Misraki *ad* Jacques Saulnier, Bernard Evein *ed* Jacques Gaillard
☆ Jean-Claude Brialy, Gérard Blain, Juliette Mayniel, Claude Cerval

'They already have a lot in common. Her husband is sleeping with his wife.'
Cousins
US 1989 113m Technicolor
UIP/Paramount (William Allyn)
Two couples, who meet at a relative's wedding, swop partners.
An adaptation of the French film Cousin, Cousine *without the exuberant charm of the original.*
w Stephen Metcalfe *d* Joel Schumacher *ph* Ralf Bode *m* Angelo Badalamenti *pd* Mark S. Freeborn *ed* Robert Brown
☆ Ted Danson, Isabella Rossellini, Sean Young, William Petersen, Lloyd Bridges, Norma Aleandro, Keith Coogan, Gina DeAngelis, George Coe
'Combines satire, near-farce, and incipient fantasy with great dexterity.' – *Tim Pulleine, MFB*

A Covenant with Death
US 1966 97m Technicolor
Warner (William Conrad)
A half-Mexican judge in a border town convicts a man who accidentally kills the hangman just as the real murderer confesses.
Dreary moral melodrama with accents, nicely photographed but cold, remote and drawn out.
w Larry Marcus, Saul Levitt *novel* Stephen Becker *d* Lamont Johnson *ph Robert Burks* *m* Leonard Rosenman
☆ George Maharis, Katy Jurado, Earl Holliman, Sidney Blackmer, Laura Devon, Gene Hackman

'Too thrilling for words, so they set it to music!'
Cover Girl **
US 1944 107m Technicolor
Columbia (Arthur Schwartz)
The road to success for magazine cover models.
Wartime glamour musical with a stronger reputation than it really deserves apart from Kelly's solos; it does however manage a certain joie de vivre *which should not be despised.*
w Virginia Van Upp *d* Charles Vidor *ph* Rudolph Maté *m/ly* Jerome Kern, Ira Gershwin *md* Morris Stoloff, Carmen Dragon *ad* Lionel Banks, Cary Odell
☆ *Rita Hayworth, Gene Kelly, Phil Silvers,* Lee Bowman, Jinx Falkenburg, Otto Kruger, Eve Arden, Ed Brophy
'Kelly and Silvers are better than Kelly and Hayworth, though she does look sumptuous, and her big smile could be the emblem of the period.' – *New Yorker, 1977*
'Much of it is not as fresh as it may seem; but its second-handedness and its occasional failures cannot obliterate the pleasure of seeing the work of a production company which obviously knows, cares about and enjoys what it is doing.' – *James Agee*
† Rita Hayworth's singing was dubbed by Martha Mears.
Morris Stoloff, Carmen Dragon
Rudolph Maté; song 'Long Ago and Far Away'; art direction

Cover Up
US 1948 82m bw
Strand/UA
An insurance investigator finds senior officials conspiring to obscure the facts of a small-town murder.
Modest mystery, initially intriguing but finally unsatisfying.
w Jerome Odlum, Jonathan Ritz *d* Alfred E. Green
☆ Dennis O'Keefe, William Bendix, Barbara Britton, Art Smith

The Covered Wagon *
US 1923 103m (24 fps) bw silent
Paramount/Famous Players-Lasky
Pioneer settlers travel west by wagon train.
A classic Western which now seems painfully undernourished in terms of plot and character but still retains moments of epic sweep.
w Jack Cunningham *novel* Emerson Hough *d* James Cruze *ph Karl Brown*
☆ Ernest Torrence, Tully Marshall, J. Warren Kerrigan, Lois Wilson, Alan Hale
'There wasn't a false whisker in the film.' – *James Cruze*
'Forthright, impressive and vigorous, it brought a breath of fresh air into the jazz-ridden film world.' – *Lewis Jacobs*

The Cow and I
France 1959 119m bw
Cyclope/Omnia (Walter Rupp)
original title: *La Vache et le Prisonnier*
A French soldier escapes from a prison camp and takes a farm cow as cover.
Curiously overlong war adventure which hovers uncertainly between comedy and suspense.
w Henri Verneuil, Henri Jeanson, Jean Manse *d* Henri Verneuil *ph Roger Hubert* *m* Paul Durand
☆ Fernandel, René Havard, Albert Remy, Bernard Musson

'Authentic Greatness!'
Cowboy *
US 1958 92m Technicolor
Columbia/Phoenix (Julian Blaustein)
Frank Harris becomes a cattle herder for love of a lady but is quickly disillusioned with the outdoor life.
Fashioned from a lively autobiography, this has interesting moments but is never as fascinating as one would expect.
w Edmund H. North *book On the Trail* by Frank Harris *d* Delmer Daves *ph* Charles Lawton Jnr *m* George Duning *ed* William A. Lyon, Al Clark
☆ Jack Lemmon, Glenn Ford, Brian Donlevy, Anna Kashfi, Dick York, Richard Jaeckel, King Donovan
'Describes with an engaging mixture of saddlesore truth and reach-for-leather fiction what a cowboy's life was like in the Old West.' – *Time*
editing

The Cowboy and the Girl: see *A Lady Takes a Chance*

The Cowboy and the Lady
US 1938 91m bw
Samuel Goldwyn
The daughter of a presidential candidate becomes infatuated with a rodeo cowboy.
Insubstantial and witless romantic comedy which suffered many sea changes from script to screen.
w Leo McCarey, S. N. Behrman, Sonya Levien *d* H. C. Potter *ph* Gregg Toland *m* Alfred Newman
☆ Gary Cooper, Merle Oberon, Patsy Kelly, Walter Brennan, Fuzzy Knight, Henry Kolker, Harry Davenport
'By and large only mildly diverting ... the interest and promise of the early reels is not sustained in the latter half.' – *Variety*
'Just a lot of chestnuts pulled out of other people's dead fires.' – *Otis Ferguson*
Alfred Newman; title song (*m* Lionel Newman, *ly* Arthur Quenzer)

Cowboy from Brooklyn
US 1938 80m bw
Warner
A supposed cowboy crooner is taken out west and proves to be terrified of animals.
Genial but witless spoof of a trend of the times.
w Earl Baldwin *play Howdy Stranger* by Robert Sloane, Louis Pelletier Jnr *d* Lloyd Bacon
☆ Pat O'Brien, Dick Powell, Priscilla Lane, Dick Foran, Ann Sheridan, Ronald Reagan, Johnnie Davis, James Stephenson
† Remade as *Two Guys from Texas.*

'How the East was won.'
The Cowboy Way
US 1994 105m DeLuxe
Universal/Imagine/Brian Grazer
Two rodeo stars go to New York in search of a kidnapped daughter of a Cuban friend.
Smug and unlikeable lead performances sink this comedy from the start, though it would have sunk anyway, whoever had played the roles.
w Joe Gayton, William Wittliff *d* Gregg Champion *ph* Dean Semler *m* David Newman *ed* Michael Tronick
☆ Woody Harrelson, Kiefer Sutherland, Ernie Hudson, Dylan McDermott, Cara Buono, Marg Helgenberger, Tomas Milian
'The action sequences are lacklustre and the bickering and bonding between the likeable leads is drearily predictable.' – *Film Review*

The Cowboys *
US 1972 128m Technicolor Panavision 70
Sanford/Warner (Mark Rydell)
Deserted by his ranch hands, a cattle drover on a long trail enlists the help of eleven schoolboys, who later avenge his death.
Ambling, climactically violent, extremely unlikely Western with good scenes along the way.
w Irving Ravetch, Harriet Frank Jnr *novel* William Dale Jennings *d* Mark Rydell *ph Robert Surtees* *m* John Williams
☆ *John Wayne* (Wil Andersen), *Roscoe Lee Browne* (Jebediah Nightlinger), Bruce Dern (Long Hair), Colleen Dewhurst (Kate), Slim Pickens (Anse), Sarah Cunningham (Annie Andersen), A. Martinez (Cimarron), Robert Carradine (Slim Honeycutt), Alfred Barker Jnr (Fats), Nicolas Beauvy (Dan), Steve Benedict, Norman Howell Jnr, Stephen Hudis (Charlie Schwartz), Sean Kelly (Stuttering Bob), Clay O'Brien and also Sam O'Brien, Mike Pyeatt
† A TV series followed in 1974 but was shortlived.

Coyote (dubbed)
Canada 1993 99m colour
Alliance/Stock International/Molecule/Canal+ (Richard Sadler, Henry Lange)
A student film-maker falls in love with a free-thinking woman.
Turgid 'teen romance, visually and dramatically undistinguished, and unconvincing in its moments of joy and misery.
w Michel Michaud, Richard Sadler, Richard Ciupka, Louise Anne Bouchard *novel* Michel Michaud *d* Richard Ciupka *ph* Steve Danyluk *m* Reinhardt Wagner *ad* Jean-Baptiste Tard *ed* Jean-Guy Monpetit
☆ Mitsou, Patrick Labbé, Thierry Magnier, Claude Legault, François Massicotte, Jean-Claude Dreyfus

Coyote Moon: see *Desert Heat*

'Tonight, they're calling the shots.'
Coyote Ugly
US 2000 100m Technicolor Panavision
Buena Vista/Touchstone (Jerry Bruckheimer)
Facing hard times in New York, a songwriter from the suburbs falls in love with a hamburger cook and gets a job working in a rowdy club where the waitresses are expected to dance on the bar.
One of those romantic, innocent-makes-good, rags-to-riches plots that Hollywood has never been able to resist, though the audience may find it easier to do so.
w Gina Wendkos *d* David McNally *ph* Amir Mokri *m* Trevor Horn *pd* Jon Hutman *ed* William Goldenberg *cos* Marlene Stewart *ch* Travis Payne
☆ Piper Perabo (Violet Sanford), Adam Garcia (Kevin O'Donnell), Maria Bello (Lil), John Goodman (Bill), Melanie Lynskey (Gloria), Izabella Miko (Cammie), Bridget Moynahan (Rachel), Tyra Banks (Zoe), Del Pentacost (Lou), Michael Weston (Danny), LeAnn Rimes (Herself)
'More laughably misguided than outright offensive.' – *Sight and Sound*
'Almost bad enough to be good.' – *Empire*
† Piper Perabo's singing was dubbed by LeAnn Rimes.

Crack in the Mirror
US 1960 97m bw Cinemascope
TCF/Darryl F. Zanuck
A young lawyer and his ageing mentor are at opposite sides of a murder case.
Pointless Paris-set melodrama in which for no obvious reason each of the three stars plays two roles. Relentlessly boring.
w Mark Canfield (Darryl F. Zanuck) *d* Richard Fleischer *ph* William C. Mellor *m Maurice Jarre*
☆ Orson Welles, Bradford Dillman, Juliette Greco, William Lucas, Alexander Knox, Catherine Lacey

Crack in the Mirror
US 1988 94m colour
Blue Dolphin/Jubran Group (Fred Berner, Jubran Jubran)

A drug-dealer, on the run from a rival gangster, asks a friend to look after his business.
Convoluted tale of killers and addicts, full of heavy-handed anti-drugs polemic.
w Robert Madero *d* Robby Benson *ph* Neil Smith *m* Nile Rodgers *ed* Alan Miller, Craig McKay
☆ Robby Benson, Tawny Kitaen, Danny Aiello, Kevin Gray, Cliff Bemis, Tony Gillan, Paul Herman, Tony Sirico, Mark Ornstein

'Thank God it's only a motion picture!'
Crack in the World
US 1965 96m Technicolor
Paramount/Security (Philip Yordan, Bernard Glasser, Lester A. Sansom)
A dying scientist fires a missile into the Earth's centre, and nearly blows the planet apart.
Jaded science-fiction melodrama, overburdened with initial chat but waking up when the special effects take over.
w Jon Manchip White, Julian Halevy (Julian Zimet) *d* Andrew Marton *ph* Manuel Berenguer *m* John Douglas *ad Eugene Lourié sp John Douglas*
☆ Dana Andrews, Janette Scott, Kieron Moore, Alexander Knox, Peter Damon, Gary Lasdun
† Screenwriter Zimet used a pseudonym because he was blacklisted at the time.

Crack Up *
US 1946 93m bw
RKO

A museum curator with an eye for forgery is discredited by crooks who make him appear drunk or half-crazed when he recounts a set of strange events which have happened to him…
The intriguing mystery of the opening reels, when solved, is replaced by rather dull detection, but this remains a thriller with a difference, generally well presented.
w John Paxton *d* Irving Reis *ph* Robert de Grasse *m* Leigh Harline
☆ Pat O'Brien, Claire Trevor, Herbert Marshall, Ray Collins

Cracked Nuts
US 1931 65m bw
RKO
Two Americans get mixed up in a revolution in a mythical country.
Padded farce vehicle for a comedy team.
w Al Boasberg, Ralph Spence *d* Edward F. Cline *ph* Charles Van Enger *ad* Jack Otterson *ed* Milton Carruth
☆ Bert Wheeler, Robert Woolsey, Ben Turpin, Edna May Oliver, Dorothy Lee
'As a two-reeler it would be fair entertainment.' – *Variety*

Crackerjack *
GB 1938 79m bw
Gainsborough (Edward Black)
US title: *The Man with a Hundred Faces*
A gentleman thief poses as butler at a stately home.
Fairly smart sardonic star vehicle.
w A. R. Rawlinson, Michael Pertwee, Basil Mason *novel* W. B. Ferguson *d* Albert de Courville *ph* J. J. Cox
☆ *Tom Walls*, Lilli Palmer, Noel Madison, Leon M. Lion, Edmund Breon, Charles Heslop
'Carelessly made but fairly engrossing.' – *Variety*

Crackers
US 1984 92m Technicolor
Universal/Edward Lewis

Incompetent crooks run a pawnshop.
Insufficiently rethought, San Francisco set, updating of Monicelli's 1956 comedy Big Deal on Madonna Street/I Soliti Ignoti. *No longer at all funny.*
w Jeffrey Fiskin *d* Louis Malle *ph* Laszlo Kovacs *m* Paul Chihara *pd* John L. Lloyd
☆ Donald Sutherland, Jack Warden, Sean Penn, Wallace Shawn, Larry Riley, Trinidad Silva, Charlaine Woodard, Irwin Corey
'One can sense that it would all sound much funnier in Italian.' – *Variety*

The Cracksman
GB 1963 112m Technicolor Cinemascope
ABPC

A master locksmith becomes the unwitting dupe of a gang of safecrackers.
The most elaborate vehicle devised for this diminutive star; despite bright moments, conventional mounting and over-generous length finally defeat it.
w Lew Schwartz, Charlie Drake *d* Peter Graham Scott
☆ Charlie Drake, George Sanders, Dennis Price, Nyree Dawn Porter, Eddie Byrne, Finlay Currie, Percy Herbert

Cradle Song *
US 1933 78m bw
Paramount (E. Lloyd Sheldon)
A nun adopts a foundling.
Stately transcription of a once-fashionable play, too concerned with its own artistic background and handicapped by a star who didn't travel well, except to those partial to Jewish nuns.
w Marc Connelly *play* G. M. Martinez Sierra *d Mitchell Leisen ph* Charles Lang *m* W. Franke Harling
☆ Dorothea Wieck, Evelyn Venable, Sir Guy Standing, Louise Dresser, Kent Taylor, Gertrude Michael, Nydia Westman, Eleanor Wesselhoeft
'It moves slowly, laboriously … as a commercial entry decidedly dubious.' – *Variety*

The Cradle Will Rock **
US 1999 135m Technicolor Super 35
Buena Vista/Touchstone/Havoc (Jon Kilik, Lydia Dean Pilcher, Tim Robbins)

When, in New York in 1936, the authorities prevent the opening of Marc Blitzstein's musical play *The Cradle Will Rock*, the cast march to another theatre and, forbidden to act on stage, play it from the auditorium.
A true story, and a fascinating and important one, is given a rousing treatment, providing a panoramic view of the artistic ferment of the time, when passions ran high, and art and politics could be united in a common cause.
wd Tim Robbins *ph* Jean Yves Escoffier *m* David Robbins *m/ly* Marc Blitzstein *pd* Richard Hoover *ed* Geraldine Peron *cos* Ruth Myers
☆ Hank Azaria (Marc Blitzstein), Ruben Blades (Diego Rivera), Joan Cusack (Hazel Huffman), John Cusack (Nelson Rockefeller), Cary Elwes (John Houseman), Philip Baker Hall (Gray Mathers), Cherry Jones (Hallie Flanagan), Angus Macfadyen (Orson Welles), Bill Murray (Tommy Crickshaw), Vanessa Redgrave (Comtesse LaGrange), Susan Sarandon (Margherita Sarfatti), Jamey Sheridan (John Adair), John Turturro (Aldo Silvano), Emily Watson (Olive Stanton), Bob Balaban (Harry Hopkins) and also Barnard Hughes, Barbara Sukowa, John Carpenter, Gretchen Mol, Harris Yulin
'What Robbins also achieves here is an astonishingly moving tribute to the power of theatre… but you have to actually be *interested* in the subject matter to appreciate it.' – *Lorien Haynes, Film Review*

'Exorcise Your Rites.'
The Craft
US 1996 100m Technicolor
Columbia (Douglas Wick)

A new girl at school joins forces with three others who practise witchcraft.
Tiresome and unoriginal teenage horror, notably lacking in any imaginative use of the powers its protagonists summon up.
w Peter Filardi, Andrew Fleming *d* Andrew Fleming *ph* Alexander Gruszynski *m* Graeme Revell *pd* Marek Dobrowolski *ed* Jeff Freeman
☆ Robin Tunney, Fairuza Balk, Neve Campbell, Rachel True, Skeet Ulrich, Christine Taylor, Breckin Meyer, Nathaniel Marston, Cliff de Young, Helen Shaver, Assumpta Serna
'Full of gorgeous young actresses – high school girls have rarely been given such an appealing lustre – but it also has great visuals, sure drama and applied intelligence; a rare combination in horror movies.' – *Chris Savage King, Sight and Sound*

Craig's Wife *
US 1936 77m bw
Columbia

A middle-class wife lets her house take precedence over her husband.
Capable picturization of a Broadway success, later remade as Harriet Craig *(qv).*
w Mary McCall Jnr, George Kelly *play* George Kelly *d* Dorothy Arzner *ph* Lucien Ballard *md* Morris Stoloff
☆ Rosalind Russell, John Boles, Billie Burke, Jane Darwell, Dorothy Wilson, Alma Kruger, Thomas Mitchell, Elizabeth Risdon, Raymond Walburn

Crainquebille *
France 1922 70m approx (16 fps) bw silent
Trarieux Films
A street trader is unjustly accused and imprisoned, afterwards finding happiness as a tramp.
Somewhere between Chaplin and Kafka, this fable was long admired for its style.
wd Jacques Feyder story Anatole France *ph* Léonce Burel
☆ *Maurice de Féraudy*, Françoise Rosay, Felix Oudart
† Remade 1933 by Jacques de Baroncelli with Maurice Tramel; 1954 by Ralph Habib with Yves Deniaud.

The Cranes Are Flying **
USSR 1957 94m bw
Mosfilm

original title: *Letyat Zhuravli*
When her lover goes to war, a girl refuses to believe later reports of his death even though she has suffered much, including marriage to a bully, in the interim.
Sleek, moving love story with most of the Hollywood production virtues plus an attention to detail and a realism which are wholly Russian.
w Victor Rosov d Mikhail Kalatozov ph Sergei Urusevski
☆ *Tatiana Samoilova*, Alexei Batalov, Vasili Merkuriev

Crash!
US 1977 85m DeLuxe Panavision
Group One/Charles Band
A crippled husband sets out to murder his wife, but she is protected by a good-luck charm with magic powers.
Ineffably silly occult thriller, consisting mainly of unspectacular car crashes which are all reprised towards the end of the film to ensure total tedium.
w Marc Marais *d* Charles Band *ph* Andrew Davis, Bill Williams *m* Andrew Belling *ad* Patrick McFadden *ed* Harry Keramidas
☆ José Ferrer, Sue Lyon, John Ericson, Leslie Parrish, John Carradine, Jerome Guardino, Reggie Nalder

Crash **
Canada 1996 98m DeLuxe
Columbia TriStar/Alliance (David Cronenberg)

After being injured in a car crash, a man and a woman are initiated into a group that is sexually aroused by such occurrences.
A compelling, not very likeable movie that gives new meaning to auto-eroticism, in an account of technological fetishism that is stylishly made and seriously intended.
wd David Cronenberg *novel* J. G. Ballard *ph* Peter Suschitzky *m* Howard Shore *pd* Carol Spier *ed* Ronald Sanders
☆ James Spader (James Ballard), Holly Hunter (Helen Remington), Elias Koteas (Vaughan), Deborah Unger (Catherine Ballard), Rosanna Arquette (Gabrielle), Peter MacNeill (Colin Seagrave)
'A forbiddingly frigid piece of esoteric erotica.' – *Todd McCarthy, Variety*
† After much controversy, the film was passed uncut in Britain; the British Board of Film Classification consulted a forensic psychologist, an audience of the disabled and a QC, who concluded that 'rather than sympathising or identifying with the attitudes or tastes of the characters in this film, the average viewer would in the end be repelled by them, and would reject the values and sexual proclivities displayed.' The *Daily Mail* condemned the BBFC's decision, commenting, 'All the pyscho-babble in the world cannot refute the simple fact: The film is sick. It should not be shown.'

Crash Dive *
US 1943 105m Technicolor
TCF (Milton Sperling)
A submarine lieutenant and his commander love the same girl.
Well-staged war thrills in the final reels are prefaced by a long romantic comedy build-up, which probably seemed good propaganda at the time.
w Jo Swerling *story* W. R. Burnett *d* Archie Mayo *ph* Leon Shamroy *m* David Buttolph *md* Emil Newman *sp Fred Sersen*
☆ Tyrone Power, Anne Baxter, Dana Andrews, James Gleason, Dame May Whitty, Henry Morgan, Frank Conroy, Minor Watson
'One of those films which have no more sense of reality about this war than a popular song.' – *Bosley Crowther*

The Crash of Silence: see *Mandy*

Crashout
US 1955 83m bw
Hal E. Chester/Standard

Six convicts escape from prison, but most of them die en route.
Watchable melodrama, fairly savage for its day.
w Hal E. Chester, Lewis R. Foster *d* Lewis R. Foster
☆ William Bendix, Arthur Kennedy, Luther Adler, William Talman, Gene Evans, Marshall Thompson, Beverly Michaels

The Crawling Eye: see *The Trollenberg Terror*

Craze
GB 1973 95m Technicolor
EMI/Harbour (Herman Cohen)

An African idol accidentally causes a death which brings money to its owner, who kills again and again in the hope of more loot.
Crude shocker from the bottom of even this producer's barrel, notable for the star cast which was surprisingly roped in.
w Aben Kandel, Herman Cohen *novel Infernal Idol* by Henry Seymour *d* Freddie Francis *ph* John Wilcox *m* John Scott
☆ Jack Palance, Diana Dors, Julie Ege, Edith Evans, Hugh Griffith, Trevor Howard, Michael Jayston, Suzy Kendall, Martin Potter, Percy Herbert, Kathleen Byron

'Why Are The Good People Dying?'
The Crazies *
US 1973 102m
Pittsburgh Films/Cambist/Lee Hessel (A. C. Croft)

aka: *Code Name: Trixie*
The army seals off a small town when its inhabitants become mad and violent following the crash of a plane carrying a deadly virus; but the locals object to martial law.
Fast-moving, low-budget horror movie that also attempts to be a satire on rigid, military attitudes; it does achieve a certain frisson by its driving relentlessness and copious killing.
wd George A. Romero *story* Paul McCollough *ph* S. William Hinzman *m* Bruce Roberts *ed* George A. Romero *sp* Regis Survinski, Tony Pantanello
☆ Lane Carroll, W. G. McMillan, Harold Wayne Jones, Lloyd Hollar, Lynn Lowry, Richard Liberty, Richard France, Harry Spillman
'Average paranoia movie … Romero is better at maintaining a high body count than being profound.' – *Sight and Sound*

Crazy/Beautiful
US 2001 99m colour
Buena Vista/Touchstone (Mary Jane Ufland, Harry J. Ufland, Rachel Pfeffer)

A spoilt rich girl disrupts the life of a hardworking Latino student.
Convincing performances make this an occasionally insightful teen romance, though its predictability soon swamps its attempts to portray any reality about relationships.

w Phil Hay, Matt Manfredi *d* John Stockwell *ph* Shane Hurlbut *m* Paul Haslinger *pd* Maia Javan *ed* Melissa Kent *cos* Susan Matheson
☆ Kirsten Dunst (Nicole Oakley), Jay Hernandez (Carlos Nunez), Bruce Davison (Tom Oakley), Lucinda Jenney (Courtney), Taryn Manning (Maddy), Rolando Molina (Hector)

'An unusually observant film about adolescence.' – *Roger Ebert, Chicago Sun-Times*

'There is much to grate on your nerves in this TV Afterschool Special trying to pass as a real movie.' – *Peter Travers, Rolling Stone*

Crazy Desires of a Murderer
Italy 1977 95m Eastmancolor Vistavision
GI.BA.SI. (Salvatore Siciliano)

original title: *I Vizi Morbosi di una Governante*
A limping inspector investigates murders at a castle inhabited by a senile baron whose mad son is incarcerated in the cellars, his promiscuous daughter, her decadent friends, an alcoholic doctor, and criminal servants.
An unpalatable mix of old-fashioned detective mystery, melodrama, gruesome horror and irrelevant couplings; the solution to the mystery leaves much unexplained.
w Ambrogio Molteni *d* Peter Rush (Filippo Ratti) *ph* Gino Santini *m* Piero Piccioni *ad* Gino Tonni *ed* Sergio Muzzi
☆ Corrado Gaipa, Roberto Zattin, Isabelle Marchal, Anie Edel, Gaetano Russo, Beppe Colombo, Sergio Orsi, Claudio Peticchio, Patrizia Gori
† The British video release runs for 85m.

Crazy House
US 1943 80m bw
Universal (Erle C. Kenton)
Olsen and Johnson go to Hollywood to make a film.
Lame sequel to Hellzapoppin; *after an explosively well edited first reel of panic in the studio, it degenerates into a slew of below-par variety turns.*
w Robert Lees, Frederic I. Rinaldo *d* Edward F. Cline *ph* Charles Van Enger *md* George Hale, Milt Rosen
☆ Ole Olsen, Chic Johnson, Martha O'Driscoll, Patric Knowles, Percy Kilbride, Cass Daley, Thomas Gomez, Edgar Kennedy
† Sherlock Holmes fans may or may not wish to record a two-line comic bit by Basil Rathbone and Nigel Bruce in character.

Crazy House: see *The House in Nightmare Park (1973)*

'Sometimes you have to lose your mind to find your freedom.'
Crazy in Alabama *
US 1999 111m DeLuxe 'Scope
Columbia/Green Moon (Meir Teper, Linda Goldstein Knowlton, Debra Hill, Diane Sillan Isaacs)

In the mid-60s a young Southern boy combats racism in his community, while his aunt abandons her seven children and heads for Hollywood, carrying with her the severed head of her husband.
An odd movie: on the one hand, a serious look at bigotry and the struggle against segregation, as seen through the eyes of a 13-year-old white youth; on the other, the comic odyssey of a naive woman who will do anything to become a star; the two stories hardly cohere, and the sudden shifts in tone are unsettling, but it is at least out of the ordinary.
w Mark Childress *novel* Mark Childress *d* Antonio Banderas *ph* Julio Macat *m* Mark Snow *pd* Cecilia Montiel *ed* Maysie Hoy, Robert C. Jones *cos* Graciela Mazon
☆ Melanie Griffith (Lucille), David Morse (Dove), Lucas Black (Peejoe), Cathy Moriarty (Earlene), Meat Loaf Aday (Sheriff John Doggett), Rod Steiger (Judge Mead), Richard Schiff (Norman), John Beasley (Nehemiah), Robert Wagner (Harry Hall), Noah Emmerich (Sheriff Raymond), Sandra Seacat (Meemaw), Paul Ben-Victor (Mackie), Brad Beyer (Jack), Fannie Flagg (Sally), Elizabeth Perkins (Joan Blake) and also Paul Mazursky (Walter Schwegmann)

'An ungainly fit of three stories that have no business being shoehorned into the same movie.' – *Roger Ebert, Chicago Sun-Times*

† It was released direct to video in Britain.

Crazy Joe
US/Italy 1973 99m Technicolor
Bright-Persky/De Laurentiis

The rise and fall of a Mafia hood in New York.
Noisy, violent, reasonably proficient gangster movie which seems to have some pretensions to play against stereotype.
w Lewis John Carlino *d* Carlo Lizzani
☆ Peter Boyle, Paula Prentiss, Fred Williamson, Charles Cioffi, Rip Torn, Luther Adler, Eli Wallach, Henry Winkler

Crazy Love *
Belgium 1987 87m Eastmancolor
Mainline/Multimedia (Erwin Provoost, Alain Keytsman)

US title: *Love Is a Dog from Hell*
A frustrated boy, full of romantic longings, grows up to be a necrophiliac.
Episodic and squalid story of a journey from innocence to drug-addicted desperation, told with style.
w Marc Didden, Dominique Deruddere *story* The Copulating Mermaid of Venice, California and other works by Charles Bukowski *d* Dominique Deruddere *ph* Willy Stassen *m* Raymond Van Het Groenewoud *pd* Hubert Pouille, Erik Van Belleghem *ed* Ludo Troch, Guido Henderickx
☆ Josse de Pauw, Geert Hunaerts, Michael Pas, Gene Bervoets, Amid Chakir, François Beukelaers, Florence Beliard, Carmela Locantore

'A movie for people with a perverse sense of humor or a persistent sexual acne – a low-keyed sexual reverie.' – *Pauline Kael, New Yorker*

Crazy Mama **
US 1975 80m colour
New World (Julie Corman)

In 1958 Arkansas, mother and daughter set off on a series of robberies and kidnaps which end in violence.
Exploitation crime movie with no apparent basis in fact; as such, occasionally exciting for those who can tolerate this kind of thing.
w Robert Thom *d* Jonathan Demme *ph* Bruce Logan *m* Snotty Scotty and the Hankies
☆ Cloris Leachman, Ann Sothern, Stuart Whitman, Jim Backus, Linda Purl, Brian Englund

Crazy Moon
Canada 1987 90m colour
Miramax/Tom Berry, Stefan Wodoslawsky

A rich, clever, miserable and inhibited youth falls for a tough-minded, deaf shop assistant.
While the couple may have enjoyed a moment's happiness, it is doubtful whether an audience will; a dull drama of teenage traumas, acted and directed without much conviction.
w Tom Berry, Stefan Wodoslawsky *d* Allan Eastman *ph* Savas Kalogeras *m* Lou Forestieri *ad* Guy Lalande *ed* Franco Battista
☆ Kiefer Sutherland, Vanessa Vaughan, Peter Spence, Sean McCann, Bronwen Mantel, Eve Napier, Ken Pogue

'A comedy about truth in advertising.'
Crazy People
US 1990 92m Technicolor
UIP/Paramount (Thomas Barad)

An ad-man runs his business from a rest home for mental patients.
Unsatisfactory would-be satire.
w Mitch Markowitz *d* Tony Bill *ph* Victor J. Kemper *m* Cliff Eidelman *ad* Steven Schwartz *ed* Mia Goldman
☆ Dudley Moore, Daryl Hannah, Paul Reiser, J. T. Walsh, Bill Smitrovich, Alan North, David Paymer

'Damp, indulgent squib of a film.' – *Geoff Brown, MFB*

† Markowitz began as director, with John Malkovich in the leading role. When Markowitz was replaced, Malkovich left, to be replaced by Dudley Moore.

The Crazy Ray: see *Paris Qui Dort*

Crazy Streets: see *Forever Lulu*

Crazy to Kill: see *Dr Gillespie's Criminal Case*

The Crazy World of Julius Vrooder
US 1974 98m colour
TCF
A Vietnam veteran withdraws from the world.
Well-meaning but tiresome problem pic which gets nowhere.
w Daryl Henry *d* Arthur Hiller
☆ Timothy Bottoms, Barbara Seagull, Lawrence Pressman, Albert Salmi

The Crazy World of Laurel and Hardy **
US 1964 83m bw
Hal Roach/Jay Ward
A compilation of Laurel and Hardy extracts from their classic period.
Although the material is in itself excellent and some of the build-up sequences well done, the clips are all too short to achieve maximum impact, and virtually none is identified.
w Bill Scott *m* Jerry Fielding *narrator* Garry Moore

Creator
US 1985 107m Technicolor
Entertainment/Universal/Kings Road (Stephen Friedman)

A research scientist tries to clone his dead wife.
Sentimental and eccentric comedy of little interest.
w Jeremy Leven *novel* Jeremy Leven *d* Ivan Passer *ph* Robbie Greenberg *m* Sylvester Levay *ad* Josan F. Russo *ed* Richard Chew
☆ Peter O'Toole, Mariel Hemingway, Vincent Spano, Virginia Madsen, David Ogden Stiers, John Dehner

Creature Comforts ***
GB 1989 5m colour
Aardman Animations/Channel 4 (Sara Mullock)

Animals discuss the pleasures and disadvantages of living in a zoo.
A clever and witty marrying of stop-motion animation with vox-pop interviews; it was successful enough to spawn a series of similar TV commercials and product merchandising.
d Nick Park *ed* William Ennals
animated short

'Not since the beginning of time has the world beheld terror like this!'
The Creature from the Black Lagoon
US 1954 79m bw 3-D
U-I (William Alland)

Up the Amazon, scientists encounter a fearful fanged creature who is half man, half fish.
Unpersuasive and unsuspenseful horror hokum from the bottom drawer of imagination: it did, however, coin enough pennies to generate two even worse sequels, Revenge of the Creature *(1955) and* The Creature Walks Among Us *(1956). And the underwater photography is super.*
w Harry Essex, Arthur Ross *d* Jack Arnold *ph* William E. Snyder *m* Herman Stein, Hans Salter *md* Joseph Gershenson *ed* Ted J. Kent
☆ Richard Carlson (Dr David Reed), Julie Adams (Kay Lawrence), Richard Denning (Mark Williams), Antonio Moreno (Dr Carl Maia), Nestor Paiva (Lucas), Ben Chapman (Gill Man), Whit Bissell (Dr Thompson)
† Ricou Browning played the Gill Man in the underwater scenes, as he did in its two lesser sequels.

'He Comes From Beyond The Grave!'
'Based On Scientific Facts!'
The Creature with the Atom Brain
US 1955 80m bw
Columbia (Sam Katzman)
A scientist creates super-strong robot men, who go on the rampage.
Comic strip style chiller, not too bad to sit through.
w Curt Siodmak *d* Edward L. Cahn
☆ Richard Denning, Angela Stevens, Gregory Gaye, Tristram Coffin

Creatures the World Forgot
GB 1971 95m Technicolor
Columbia/Hammer (Michael Carreras)

Quarrels break out between rival tribes of Stone Age men.
Feeble follow-up to One Million Years BC *and* When Dinosaurs Ruled the Earth: *someone forgot to order any monsters.*
w Michael Carreras *d* Don Chaffey *ph* Vincent Cox *m* Mario Nascimbene *pd* John Stoll *ed* Chris Barnes
☆ Julie Ege, Brian O'Shaughnessy, Robert John, Marcia Fox, Rosalie Crutchley

The Creeper
US 1948 63m bw
TCF

Scientists disagree over a serum which changes humans into cats.
Nonsense horror item with stalwart cast.
w Maurice Tombragel *d* Jean Yarbrough
☆ Ralph Morgan, Eduardo Ciannelli, Onslow Stevens, June Vincent, Richard Lane

Creepers
Italy 1984 110m Eastmancolor
Palace/Dacfilm (Dario Argento)

aka: *Phenomena*
In Switzerland, a sleep-walking schoolgirl with the ability to communicate with insects is helped by a wheelchair-bound entomologist and his chimpanzee to track down a serial killer who murders girls and keeps their bodies.
Daft and gruesome horror that lacks style and sense; it has a plethora of murderers, it is never fully explained who did what to whom, its intention is to disgust rather than shock, and its heavy-metal soundtrack is a frequent distraction.
w Dario Argento, Franco Ferrini *d* Dario Argento *ph* Romano Albani *m* Goblin, Bill Wyman, Iron Maiden, Motorhead, Andy Sex Gang and others *pd* Maurizio Garrone, Nello Giorgetti, Luciano Spadoni, Umberto Turco *ed* Franco Fraticelli
☆ Jennifer Connelly, Daria Nicolodi, Dalila di Lazzaro, Donald Pleasence, Patrick Bauchau, Fiore Argento, Federica Mastroianni, Fiorenza Tessari, Michele Soavi

'The saddest aspect of this farrago is the way that, even in this toned-down version, Argento goes for sickness after the manner of Lucio Fulci.' – *Kim Newman, MFB*

'Argento is the rock Toscanini of the hack-em-up.' – *David Edelstein, Village Voice*

† The version released in Britain runs for 83m. It was Argento's first English-language film.

The Creeping Flesh *
GB 1972 91m Eastmancolor
Tigon/World Film Services (Michael Redbourn)

A Victorian scientist discovers that water causes the recomposing of tissue on the skeleton of a Neanderthal man.
Absurd but persuasive horror film, quite well done in all departments.
w Peter Spenceley, Jonathan Rumbold *d* Freddie Francis *ph* Norman Warwick *m* Paul Ferris
☆ Peter Cushing, Christopher Lee, Lorna Heilbron, George Benson, Kenneth J. Warren, Duncan Lamont, Michael Ripper

'The theme of the different attempts to locate and hence control evil is interestingly and sensitively worked out.' – *Robin Wood, MFB*

The Creeping Unknown: see *The Quatermass Experiment*

'The most fun you'll ever have being scared!'
Creepshow
US 1982 120m colour
United Film Distribution/Laurel Show (Richard P. Rubenstein)

A boy reads five gruesome stories from a horror comic.
Supposedly funny but mainly rather nasty recreation of a famous 'comic' style; far too extended for its own good.
w Stephen King *d* George A. Romero *ph* Michael Gornick *m* John Harrison *pd* Tom Savini
☆ Carrie Nye, Viveca Lindfors, Stephen King, Leslie Nielsen, Hal Holbrook, Adrienne Barbeau, E. G. Marshall

'Robert Bloch and Freddie Francis did it all so much better in *Torture Garden*.' – *Tom Milne, MFB*

Creepshow 2
US 1987 89m colour
Laurel/New World (David Ball)
Horror anthology of three gory pulp stories.
Cheapjack sequel, of no interest whatsoever.
w George A. Romero *stories* Stephen King *d* Michael Gornick *ph* Dick Hart, Tom Hurwitz *m* Les Reed *ed* Peter Weatherly
☆ Lois Chiles, George Kennedy, Dorothy Lamour, Tom Savini, Page Hannah

Crest of the Wave: see *Seagulls over Sorrento*

'It may be artificial, but it's still their turf.'
The Crew *
US 2000 87m Technicolor
Buena Vista/Touchstone/George Litto (Barry Sonnenfeld, Barry Josephson)
Aged gangsters living in a rundown retirement hotel decide to stage a murder in order to scare away the wealthy young who are moving into the area and putting up the cost of living.
Mildly amusing comedy, where the pleasure derives from seeing professionals enjoying their work.
w Barry Fanaro *d* Michael Dinner *ph* Juan Ruiz-Anchia *m* Steve Bartek *pd* Peter Larkin *ed* Nicholas C. Smith *cos* Betsy Cox
☆ Burt Reynolds (Joey 'Bats' Pistella), Richard Dreyfuss (Bobby Bartellemeo), Dan Hedaya (Mike 'The Brick' Donatelli), Seymour Cassel (Tony 'Mouth' Donato), Carrie-Anne Moss (Det Olivia Neal), Jennifer Tilly (Ferris Lowenstein), Lainie Kazan Raul (Pepper Lowenstein), Miguel Sandoval (Ventana), Jeremy Piven (Det Steve Menteer), Casey Siemaszko (Young Bobby), Matt Borlenghi (Young Joey), Billy Jayne (Young Tony), Jeremy Ratchford (Young Mike)
'Lightweight but surprisingly likable comedy.' – *Variety*

Le Cri de Hibou **
France/Italy 1987 102m colour
Italfrance Films/TF1 (Gerard Croce)
aka: *The Cry of the Owl*
As his divorce to his vindictive wife becomes absolute, a depressed commercial artist introduces himself to a young woman on whose apparently happy life he has been spying; before long, he finds himself accused of murder and the target of a killer.
An intriguing, downbeat psychological thriller, a study of a man who seems to carry death with him, and of jealousy, revenge and love, observed with a dispassionate eye.
w Odile Barski, Claude Chabrol *novel* Patricia Highsmith *d* Claude Chabrol *ph* Jean Rabier *m* Matthieu Chabrol *md* Michel Ganot *ed* Monique Fardoulis
☆ Christophe Malavoy, Mathilda May, Jacques Penot, Jean-Pierre Kalfon, Virginie Thevenet
'For the most part shows Chabrol at his best.' – *Sight and Sound*

Le Cri du Coeur *
France 1994 86m colour
Les Films de la Plaine/De L'Avenir/CEC Rhône-Alpes (Bernard Granger)
An 11-year-old boy, who travels with his mother from his African village to join his father in Paris, is haunted by visions of a hyena roaming the city streets.
Interesting drama of assimilation into a foreign land and culture, as seen through the eyes of a child, but lacking in dramatic impetus.
w Idrissa Ouédraogo, Robert Gardner, Jacques Akchoti, Olivier Douyère *d* Idrissa Ouédraogo *ph* Jean Monsigny, Jean-Paul Meurisse *m* Henri Texler *ad* Olivier Paultre, Alain Poirot *ed* Luc Barnier
☆ Richard Bohringer, Said Diarra, Félicité Wouassi, Alex Descas, Clémentine Célarié, Jean-Yves Gautier
'Well-made, dignified ... though pic's main audience will be viewers interested in African cinema.' – *Variety*

Cria!: see *Raise Ravens*

Cria Cuervos: see *Raise Ravens*

Cries and Whispers: see *Visskningar och Rop*

Crime and Punishment *
US 1935 88m bw
Columbia
A student kills a pawnbroker and is tortured by remorse.
Heavy-going rendering of Dostoievsky with some pictorial interest.
w S. K. Lauren, Joseph Anthony *novel* Dostoievsky *d Josef von Sternberg ph* Lucien Ballard *m* Arthur Honegger *md* Louis Silvers
☆ *Peter Lorre*, Edward Arnold, Tala Birell, Marian Marsh, Elizabeth Risdon, Mrs Patrick Campbell
'Will have to be sold, but should average fair takings.' – *Variety*

Crime and Punishment *
France 1935 110m bw
A murderer is overcome with remorse for his crime.
Incisive, well-acted French version of Dostoievsky's novel.
w Marcel Aymé *novel* Dostoievsky *d* Pierre Chenal *m* Arthur Honegger
☆ *Pierre Blanchar, Harry Baur*, Marcelle Geniat, Madeleine Ozeray
'There's a real picture in this Dostoievsky book, and the French have proved it.' – *Variety*

Crime and Punishment USA
US 1958 96m bw
Allied Artists/Sanders Associates (Terry Sanders)
A student murders an old pawnbroker and is driven mad by guilt.
Pointless updating of Dostoievsky by two young film-makers who seemed for years to be on the brink of a masterpiece but never actually produced it. Some points of interest, but the low budget is cramping.
w Walter Newman *d* Denis Sanders *ph* Floyd Crosby *m* Herschel Burke Gilbert
☆ George Hamilton, Frank Silvera, Mary Murphy, John Harding, Marian Seldes
'There is about it a strange quality of aimlessness which nullifies much of its effect.' – *MFB*

Crime by Night *
US 1944 72m bw
Warner (William Jacobs)
A private detective reluctantly solves a small-town murder, and finds a spy.
Second feature which was thought at the time to have established a new pair of married detectives in the tradition of The Thin Man. *However, one poor sequel,* Find the Blackmailer, *put paid to the idea.*
w Richard Weil, Joel Malone *novel Forty Whacks* by Geoffrey Homes *d* William Clemens *ph* Henry Sharpe
☆ *Jerome Cowan, Jane Wyman*, Faye Emerson, Charles Lang, Eleanor Parker, Cy Kendall, Creighton Hale

Crime Doctor *
US 1943 66m bw
Columbia
An amnesiac becomes a successful psychiatrist, then discovers that he was once a wanted gangster.
Time-passing second feature from a popular radio series. Ten Crime Doctor films were made between 1943 and 1949, all starring Warner Baxter, all except the first being locked room mysteries which seldom played fair with the audience.
The sequels:
1943 Crime Doctor's Strangest Case
1944 Shadows in the Night, Crime Doctor's Courage
1945 Crime Doctor's Warning
1946 Crime Doctor's Manhunt, Just before Dawn
1947 The Millerson Case
1948 Crime Doctor's Gamble
1949 Crime Doctor's Diary
w Graham Baker, Louise Lantz *d* Michael Gordon *m* Louis Silvers
☆ Warner Baxter, Margaret Lindsay, John Litel, Ray Collins, Harold Huber, Leon Ames, Don Costello

Crime Does Not Pay
A celebrated series of two-reel shorts made by MGM between 1935 and 1947.
In a hard-driving, tensely commentated manner more reminiscent of Warner filmmaking, they gave ample scope to trainee actors and directors in allegedly truthful re-enactments of contemporary crimes, often introduced by the state governor or police commissioner. The titles were as follows:
The titles were as follows:
1935 Buried Loot, *d* George B. Seitz; with Robert Taylor, Robert Livingston
1935 Racket, *d* George B. Seitz
1935 Desert Death, *d* George B. Seitz; with Raymond Hatton, Harvey Stephens
1935 A Thrill for Thelma, *d* Edward Cahn; with Irene Hervey, Robert Warwick
1935 Hit and Run Driver, *d* Edward Cahn; with Morgan Wallace, Jonathan Hale
1935 Perfect Set-up, *d* Edward Cahn
1936 Foolproof, *d* Edward Cahn; with Niles Welch, Alonzo Price
1936 The Public Pays, *d* Errol Taggart; with Paul Stanton, Cy Kendall
1936 Torture Money, *d* Harold S. Bucquet
1937 It May Happen to You, *d* Harold S. Bucquet
1937 Soak the Poor, *d* Harold S. Bucquet
1937 Give Till it Hurts, *d* Felix Feist; with Janet Beecher, Howard Hickman
1937 Behind the Criminal, *d* Harold S. Bucquet; with Edward Emerson, Walter Kingsford
1938 What Price Safety, *d* Harold S. Bucquet; with John Wray, George Houston
1938 Miracle Money, *d* Leslie Fenton; with John Miljan, Claire DuBrey
1938 Come Across, *d* Harold S. Bucquet; with Bernard Nedell, Donald Douglas
1938 A Criminal is Born, *d* Leslie Fenton; with George Breakston, David Durand
1938 They're Always Caught, *d* Harold S. Bucquet; with Stanley Ridges, John Eldredge
1938 Think it Over, *d* Jacques Tourneur; with Lester Matthews, Dwight Frye
1938 The Wrong Way Out, *d* Gustav Machaty; with Linda Terry, Kenneth Howell
1939 Money to Loan, *d* Joe Newman; with Alan Dinehart, Paul Guilfoyle
1939While America Sleeps, *d* Fred Zinnemann; with Dick Purcell, Roland Varno
1939 Help Wanted, *d* Fred Zinnemann; with Tom Neal, Jo Ann Sayers
1939 Think First, *d* Roy Rowland; with Laraine Day, Marc Lawrence, Sara Haden
1939 Drunk Driving, *d* David Miller; with Dick Purcell, Jo Ann Sayers
1940 Pound Foolish, *d* Felix Feist; with Neil Hamilton, Lynne Carver
1940 Know Your Money, *d* Joe Newman; with Dennis Moore, Noel Madison
1940 Jackpot, *d* Roy Rowland; with Tom Neal, Ann Morriss
1940 Women in Hiding, *d* Joe Newman; with Marsha Hunt, C. Henry Gordon
1940 Buyer Beware, *d* Joe Newman; with Charles Arnt
1940 Soak the Old, *d* Sammy Lee; with Ralph Morgan, Kenneth Christy
1940 You the People, *d* Roy Rowland; with C. Henry Gordon, Paul Everton
1941 Respect the Law, *d* Joe Newman.
1941 Forbidden Passage, *d* Fred Zinnemann; with Harry Woods
1941 Coffins on Wheels, *d* Joe Newman; with Cy Kendall, Darryl Hickman
1941 Sucker List, *d* Roy Rowland; with Lynne Carver, John Archer
1942 For the Common Defense, *d* Allen Kenward; with Van Johnson, Douglas Fowley
1942 Keep 'em Sailing, *d* Basil Wrangell; with Jim Davis, Lou Smith
1943 Plan for Destruction, *d* Edward Cahn; with Lewis Stone
1944 Patrolling the Ether, *d* Paul Burnford
1944 Easy Life, *d* Walter Hart; with Bernard Thomas, Steve Geray
1944 Dark Shadows, *d* Paul Burnford; with Arthur Space, Henry O'Neill
1945 Fall Guy, *d* Paul Burnford; with Leon Ames
1945 The Last Instalment, *d* Walter Hart; with Cameron Mitchell, Walter Sande
1945 Phantoms Inc., *d* Harold Young; with Frank Reicher, Ann Shoemaker
1945 A Gun in His Hand, *d* Joseph Losey; with Anthony Caruso, Richard Gaines
1945 Purity Squad, *d* Harold Kress; with Byron Foulger, Dick Elliott
1947 Luckiest Guy in the World, *d* Joe Newman; with Barry Nelson, Eloise Hardt

Crime in the Streets *
US 1956 91m bw
Allied Artists (Vincent M. Fennelly)
Rival knife gangs bring havoc to tenement dwellers.
Lively semi-documentary low-life melodrama; routine subject, excellent credits.
w Reginald Rose TV play Reginald Rose *d Don Siegel ph* Sam Leavitt *m* Franz Waxman
☆ John Cassavetes, James Whitmore, Sal Mineo, Mark Rydell

The Crime of Dr Crespi
US 1935 64m bw
Republic
A surgeon induces suspended animation in a hated rival, and has him buried.
Crude and tasteless variation on Poe's 'The Premature Burial'.
w Lewis Graham, Edward Olmstead *d* John H. Auer
☆ Erich von Stroheim, Dwight Frye, Paul Guilfoyle, Harriet Russell
'As a baby scarer it's a weak entry.' – *Variety*

The Crime of Monsieur Lange **
France 1936 85m bw
Obéron (André Halley des Fontaines)
When the hated boss of a publishing house is believed killed, the workers turn it into a successful co-operative. When he reappears, he is killed.
The political elements of this fable now seem unimportant, but it still shows its original charm and cinematic skill.
w Jacques Prévert d Jean Renoir ph Jean Bachelet *m* Jean Wiener
☆ René Lefèbvre, Jules Berry, Florelle, Sylvia Bataille, Henri Guisol

Crime of Passion
US 1956 86m bw
UA/Bob Goldstein (Herman Cohen)
An executive's wife sleeps her way to the top, but when the boss does not come through with promotion she shoots him.
Old-fashioned star melodrama on a low budget.
w Jo Eisinger *d* Gerd Oswald *ph* Joseph LaShelle *m* Paul Dunlap
☆ *Barbara Stanwyck*, Sterling Hayden, Raymond Burr, Fay Wray, Royal Dano, Virginia Grey

The Crime of the Century: see *Walk East on Beacon (1952)*

'Some kids have lots of time to kill.'
Crime + Punishment in Suburbia
US 2000 100m DeLuxe
United Artists/Killer (Pamela Koffler, Larry Gross, Christine Vachon)
A teenage girl asks her boyfriend to help her kill her drunken stepfather, who is making sexual advances to her.
An edgy and flawed work, with arthouse intentions (the narrative is divided into eight chapters and the visual style is blurry) at odds with the often derivative characters, who are rarely sharply defined.
w Larry Gross *d* Rob Schmidt *ph* Bobby Bukowski *m* Michael Brook *pd* Ruth Ammon *ed* Gabriel Wrye *cos* Sophie de Rakoff Carbonell
☆ Monica Keena (Roseanne Skolnik), Vincent Kartheiser (Vincent), Ellen Barkin (Maggie Skolnik), Jeffrey Wright (Chris), James DeBello (Jimmy), Michael Ironside (Fred Skolnik), Christian Payne (Dean), Conchata Ferrell (Bella), Marshall Teague (Coach), Nicki Aycox (Cecil), Brad Greenquist (Calvin Berry), Lucinda Jenney (Vincent's Mom)
'Summons up a been-there-seen-that reaction at nearly every turn.' – *Variety*
'A remarkable, haunting work.' – *Kim Newman*

Crime School *
US 1938 86m bw
Warner (Bryan Foy)
Problems of the warden of a reform school.
Predictable vehicle for the Dead End Kids; watchable at the time.
w Crane Wilbur, Vincent Sherman *d* Lewis Seiler *ph* Arthur Todd *m* Max Steiner

☆ Humphrey Bogart, Gale Page, Billy Halop, Huntz Hall, Leo Gorcey, Bobby Jordan, Gabriel Dell, Bernard Punsley, Paul Porcasi, Al Bridge

'A rough entertainment, sometimes brutal ... should do well where audiences like 'em tough.' – *Variety*

Crime Story *

Hong Kong 1993 100m colour

Golden Harvest (Leonard K. C. Ho)

original title: *Chung On Tsou*

A cop hunts down the ruthless kidnappers who have grabbed the millionaire he was assigned to guard.

There is less action and more acting than usual from its star in a tough and tense thriller, which builds to a satisfactory climax.

w Cheun Tin-nam, Chan Man-keung, Cheung Lai-ling *d* Kirk Wong *ph* Leu Wai-keung *m* James Wong *ad* Tony Au, Lui Cho-hung, Luk Tsi-leung *ed* Peter Cheung

☆ Jackie Chang, Kent Cheng, K'o Shou-liang, Ng Wing-mei, Poon Ling-ling

'Action set pieces and firepower are both high caliber, with a simmering tension that holds the whole together.' – *Variety*

'He had tired of her – and for that he was sorry! He was tied to her – and for that he hated her!'

Crime without Passion **

US 1934 82m bw

Paramount (Ben Hecht, Charles MacArthur)

A lawyer is driven to commit murder.

Effective melodrama notable for then-new techniques which were blended into the mainstream of movie-making, and for the first appearance in Hollywood of a smart new writer-producer-director team.

wd Ben Hecht, Charles MacArthur story Caballero of the Law by Ben Hecht, Charles MacArthur *ph Lee Garmes m* Oscar Levant *sp* Slavko Vorkapich

☆ Claude Rains, Margo, Whitney Bourne, Stanley Ridges

'It turns a lot of established motion picture conventions topsy-turvy ... shouldn't have much trouble at the box office, and inside the theatre it is safe.' – *Variety*

'The whole venture seems to take a long stride forward for the movies.' – *Otis Ferguson*

'A flamboyant, undisciplined, but compulsively fascinating film classic.' – *Peter John Dyer, 1966*

Crimes and Misdemeanors ***

US 1989 104m DeLuxe

Rank/Orion (Robert Greenhut)

Brothers-in-law deal with marital crises.

Two interlinked stories, one comic, the other tragic, form a winning combination.

wd Woody Allen ph Sven Nykvist *md* Joe Malin *pd* Santo Loquasto *ed* Susan E. Morse

☆ Caroline Aaron, Alan Alda, Woody Allen, Claire Bloom, Mia Farrow, Joanna Gleason, Anjelica Huston, Martin Landau, Jenny Nichols, Jerry Orbach

♘ best director; best original screenplay; Martin Landau

Crimes at the Dark House

GB 1939 69m bw

Pennant (George King)

A Victorian landowner kills his wife and conceals the fact by using a lunatic as her double.

Cheeky adaptation of a classic to make one of the star's most lip-smacking barnstormers.

w Edward Dryhurst, Frederick Hayward, H. F. Maltby *novel The Woman in White* by Wilkie Collins *d* George King *ph* Hone Glendinning

☆ *Tod Slaughter*, Hilary Eaves, Sylvia Marriott, Hay Petrie, David Horne

Crimes of Passion

US 1984 104m colour

New World (Barry Sandler)

A prostitute tells her story at a group therapy session.

Predictably from this director, a hysterically overheated stew of sex and murder; one to walk away from.

w Barry Sandler *d* Ken Russell *ph* Dick Bush *m* Rick Wakeman

☆ Kathleen Turner, Anthony Perkins, John Laughlin, Annie Potts

'Film walks an uneasy line at times between comedy and drama, but is entertaining in the manner of a great B picture all about sex.' – *Variety*

'One of the silliest movies in a long time.' – *Roger Ebert*

Crimes of the Heart *

US 1986 105m Technicolor

De Laurentiis/Freddie Fields-Burt Sugarman

Three sisters try to reconcile themselves with their family past.

Somewhat overwrought but generally compelling Southern comedy-drama.

w Beth Henley *play* Beth Henley *d* Bruce Beresford *ph* Dante Spinotti *m* Georges Delerue *pd* Ken Adam

☆ *Diane Keaton, Jessica Lange, Sissy Spacek*, Sam Shepard, Tess Harper, David Carpenter, Hurd Hatfield

♘ Sissy Spacek, Tess Harper; Beth Henley

'To be seen is to exist.'

Crimetime *

GB/US/Germany 1996 118m colour

First Independent/Focus/Channel 4/Pandora/Trimark (David Pupkewitz)

An actor begins to identify with a serial killer after he plays the murderer on a television show recreating the crimes as they occur.

A thriller that promises more than it finally delivers, raising intriguing questions about TV and identity which it then ignores.

w Brendan Somers *d* George Sluizer *ph* Jules van den Steenhoven *m* David A. Stewart *pd* Bernd Lepel *ed* Fabienne Rawley

☆ Stephen Baldwin, Pete Postlethwaite, Sadie Frost, Geraldine Chaplin, Karen Black, James Faulkner, Philip Davis, Marianne Faithfull

'Not helped by a succession of unappealing performances, nor the faintly surreal atmosphere, the mishmash of styles, accents and performances, or a host of dramatic short cuts that do no favours for credibility.' – *Anwar Brett, Film Review*

Crimewave

US 1986 83m Technicolor

Embassy/Pressman/Renaissance (Robert Tapert)

Two psychopaths are hired by a timid security man to murder his double-crossing partner.

Broad black farcical horror that is very noisy, but never funny.

w Ethan Coen, Joel Coen, Sam Raimi *d* Sam Raimi *ph* Robert Primes *m* Arlon Ober *ad* Gary Papierski *ed* Michael Kelly, Kathie Weaver

☆ Louise Lasser, Paul L. Smith, Brion James, Sheree J. Wilson, Edward R. Pressman, Bruce Campbell, Reed Birney

'A fiasco.' – *Bruce Campbell*

The Criminal *

GB 1960 97m bw

Merton Park (Jack Greenwood)

US title: *The Concrete Jungle*

Sent to jail for a racecourse snatch, a gangster comes out fifteen years later to regain the loot and is followed by other criminals who kill him.

Relentlessly grim saga of prison life, with a few sensational trimmings.

w Alun Owen, Jimmy Sangster *d* Joseph Losey *ph Robert Krasker m* Johnny Dankworth

☆ Stanley Baker, Sam Wanamaker, Margit Saad, *Patrick Magee*, Noel Willman, Grégoire Aslan, Jill Bennett, Kenneth J. Warren, Nigel Green, Patrick Wymark, Murray Melvin

'A savage, almost expressionistic picture of English underworld life.' – *NFT, 1973*

'Innocence Is No Protection.'

The Criminal *

GB/US 1999 100m DeLuxe

Downtown/Storm/Palm (Christopher Johnson, Mark Aarons, David Chapman)

After a girl he picks up is killed, a musician is suspected of her murder and goes on the run.

Tense, paranoid thriller that almost manages to persuade its audience of the plausibility of its increasingly unlikely narrative.

wd Julian Simpson *ph* Nic Morris *m* Music Sculptors *pd* Martyn John *ed* Mark Aarons

☆ Steven Mackintosh (Jasper Rawlins), Bernard Hill (Detective-Inspector Walker), Eddie Izzard (Peter Hume), Natasha Little (Sarah Maitland), Yvan Attal (Mason), Holly Aird (Det-Sgt Rebecca White), Jana Carpenter (Grace), Barry Stearn (Noble), Norman Lovett (Clive), Lisa Jacobs (Lucy), Georgia Mackenzie (Maggie), Daniel Brocklebank (Jonny)

'An above-average mystery-thriller.' – *Variety*

The Criminal Code *

US 1930 97m bw

Columbia (Harry Cohn)

A young man kills in self-defence, is railroaded into jail and becomes involved in another murder.

Impressive melodrama with good performances and sharp handling.

w Seton I. Miller, Fred Niblo Jnr *play* Martin Flavin *d Howard Hawks ph* James Wong Howe, Ted Tetzlaff

☆ Walter Huston, Phillips Holmes, Constance Cummings, Mary Doran, De Witt Jennings, John Sheehan, Boris Karloff

† Remade as *Penitentiary* (1938) with Walter Connolly and *Convicted* (1950) with Broderick Crawford.

♘ Seton I. Miller, Fred Niblo Jnr

'Whoever fights monsters should see to it that in the process he does not become a monster.' Nietzsch'

Criminal Law

US 1989 118m colour Panavision

Hemdale/Northwood (Robert MacClean, Hilary Heath)

A successful lawyer decides that his client is a murderer.

Hysterical thriller that never convinces on any level.

w Mark Kasdan *d* Martin Campbell *ph* Philip Meheux *m* Jerry Goldsmith *ed* Chris Wimble

☆ Gary Oldman, Kevin Bacon, Karen Young, Joe Don Baker, Tess Harper, Ron Lea, Karen Woolridge, Terence Labrosse, Jennie Walker

'It dares to elaborate on its unbelievable central relationship between a driven yuppie lawyer and a charming old-money psychopath with hokey devices more redolent of some 40s old-dark-house movie than of a supposedly "serious" modern thriller.' – *Kim Newman, MFB*

Criminal Lawyer

US 1937 72m bw

RKO

A smart lawyer who has devoted his career to getting criminals off the hook has a change of heart when appointed district attorney.

Standard programmer with a first-rate star performance.

w G. V. Atwater, Thomas Lennon *story* Louis Stevenson *d* Christy Cabanne

☆ *Lee Tracy*, Margot Grahame, Eduardo Ciannelli, Erik Rhodes

'Strong fronter for a dual, but can go solo where Tracy's name will draw.' – *Variety*

The Criminal Life of Archibaldo de la Cruz *

Mexico 1955 91m bw

Alianza Cinematografica (Roberto Figueroa)

original title: *Ensayo de un Crimen*

A fantasist determines to kill all women who cross his path, but fate intervenes.

Cheaply made macabre joke, one of its director's throwaway oddities: not too smooth, but often amusing.

w Luis Buñuel, E. Ugarte *d Luis Buñuel ph* Augusto Jimenez *md* Jorge Perez

☆ Ernesto Alonso, Ariadna Welter, Miroslava Stern, Rita Macedo

'Buñuel has not only given a frightful reality to melodramatic obsessions; he has created, in place of the grimaces, by now laughable, of the conventional madman of the screen, a whole repertory of erotic and deathly gestures which chill the flesh.' – *Dilys Powell*

The Crimson Blade: see *The Scarlet Blade*

The Crimson Canary

US 1945 64m bw

Universal (Bob Faber)

A jazz band vocalist is murdered.

Routine murder mystery with appearances by Coleman Hawkins, Oscar Pettiford and Josh White.

w Henry Blankfort, Peggy Phillips *d* John Hoffman

☆ Noah Beery Jnr, Lois Collier, Danny Morton, John Litel, Steve Geray

The Crimson Code: see *Red Team*

The Crimson Cult: see *Curse of the Crimson Altar*

The Crimson Curtain *

France 1952 43m bw

Argos

original title: *Le Rideau Cramoisi*

An officer billeted with a bourgeois family is visited at night by the beautiful daughter, who finally dies in his arms.

A curious polished fragment with narration replacing spoken dialogue. For those in the mood, it works.

wd Alexandre Astruc *story* Barbey d'Aurevilly *ph* Eugene Schufftan *m* Jean-Jacques Grunenwald

☆ Jean-Claude Pascal, Anouk Aimée, Madeleine Garcia, Jim Gerald

'In its limited time, with the greatest economy of means, it evokes an authentic sense of the past, as well as telling a story movingly and dramatically.' – *Richard Roud*

The Crimson Kimono *

US 1959 82m bw

Columbia/Globe (Samuel Fuller)

Detectives seeking the murderer of a stripper in Los Angeles' Little Tokyo both fall in love with a witness.

Self-conscious local colour, though quite freshly observed and well photographed, finally overwhelms an ordinary little murder mystery.

wd Samuel Fuller *ph* Sam Leavitt *m* Harry Sukman

☆ Glenn Corbett, James Shigeta, Victoria Shaw, Anna Lee, Paul Dubov

'Ask me no questions: believe only what you see!'

The Crimson Pirate *

GB 1952 104m Technicolor

Warner/Norma (Harold Hecht)

An 18th-century pirate and an eccentric inventor lead an island's people in rebellion against a tyrant.

One suspects that this started off as a straight adventure and was turned halfway through production into a spoof; at any rate, the effect is patchy but with spirited highlights, and the star's acrobatic training is put to good use.

w Roland Kibbee *d* Robert Siodmak *ph* Otto Heller *m* William Alwyn

☆ *Burt Lancaster, Nick Cravat*, Eva Bartok, Torin Thatcher, James Hayter, Margot Grahame, Noel Purcell, Frank Pettingell

The Crimson Rivers: see *Les Rivières Pourpres*

Crimson Tide **

US 1995 116m Technicolor Panavision

Buena Vista/Hollywood (Don Simpson, Jerry Bruckheimer)

The veteran captain of a US submarine and his Harvard-educated executive officer clash over what action should be taken after Russian rebels seize a nuclear missile base and they are under attack.

A thriller that grips and entertains despite its predictability and the familiarity of its doomsday scenario.

w Michael Schiffer *d* Tony Scott *ph* Dariusz Wolsky *m* Hans Zimmer *pd* Michael White *ed* Chris Lebenzon

☆ Denzel Washington, Gene Hackman, George Dzundza, Viggo Mortensen, James Gandolfini, Matt Craven, Rick Schroder, Jason Robards (uncredited)

'*The Caine Mutiny* on steroids.' – *Tom Shone, Sunday Times*

'A boy's movie all the way, with enough expensive military hardware and tough-guy power plays to appeal to teenagers of all ages.' – *Todd McCarthy, Variety*

† Quentin Tarantino, Robert Towne and Steve Zaillian worked uncredited on the script.

♘ Chris Lebenzon; sound; sound effects editing

Crin Blanc **
France 1953 47m bw
Albert Lamorisse
aka: *Wild Stallion*
A small boy befriends and rides a wild horse in the Camargue.
A favourite short film of great beauty, but a shade overlong for its content.
wd Albert Lamorisse *ph* Edmond Séchan
m Maurice Le Roux
☆ Alain Emery, Pascal Lamorisse

'For every man who struck gold – a hundred tried to take it away from him!'
Cripple Creek
US 1952 78m colour
Columbia (Edward Small)
A federal agent uncovers smugglers during a gold rush.
Adequate co-feature Western in murky colour.
w Richard Schayer *d* Ray Nazarro
☆ George Montgomery, Karin Booth, Jerome Courtland, William Bishop, Richard Egan, Don Porter

La Crise *
France 1992 95m colour Panavision
Electric/TFI/Leader/Raidue/Canal/Alain Sarde
A man loses his wife and his job on the same day and cannot find anyone, apart from a drunk, to sympathize with his predicament.
An amusing, if slightly mechanical comedy, of a workaholic discovering that life has more to offer than work.
wd Coline Serreau *ph* Robert Alazraki *m* Sonia Wieder-Atherton *pd* Guy-Claude François
ed Catherine Renault
☆ Vincent Lindon, Patrick Timsit, Annik Alane, Valerie Alane, Gilles Privat, Nanou Garcia, Christian Benedetti, Didier Flamand
'Amiable, crowd-pleasing entertainment with more than its fair share of good jokes.' – *Sight and Sound*

Crisis *
US 1950 96m bw
MGM (Arthur Freed)
A brain surgeon is forced to operate secretly on a South American dictator, and his wife is kidnapped by revolutionaries.
Dour intellectual suspense piece, in key with the genteel enlightenment of the Dore Schary regime at MGM. Well made but cold.
wd Richard Brooks *story* George Tabori *ph* Ray June *m* Miklos Rozsa
☆ Cary Grant, José Ferrer, Signe Hasso, Paula Raymond, Ramon Navarro, Antonio Moreno, Leon Ames, Gilbert Roland
'Original, arresting and considered ... so far the most striking example of Dore Schary's policy of encouraging the development of new talents.' – *Gavin Lambert*
'A bold piece of movie adventuring.' – *L.A. Mirror*

Criss Cross *
US 1948 87m bw
U-I (Michel Kraike)
An armoured car guard and his double-crossing ex-wife get mixed up with vicious gangsters.
Sordid film noir with a poor plot but suspenseful sequences.
w Daniel Fuchs *novel* Don Tracy *d* Robert Siodmak *ph* Franz Planer *m* Miklos Rozsa
ad Bernard Herzbrun, Boris Leven *ed* Ted J. Kent
☆ Burt Lancaster, Yvonne de Carlo, Dan Duryea, Stephen McNally, Richard Long, Tom Pedi, Alan Napier
'Siodmak's talent for brooding violence and the sombre urban setting gives the film a relentlessly mounting tension.' – *Peter John Dyer*

CrissCross
US 1992 100m colour
MGM/Hawn-Sylbert (Anthea Sylbert)
A 12-year-old boy turns to crime to help his mother who works as a waitress and a stripper in order to support them.
Slow-moving domestic drama that fails to sustain one's interest.
w Scott Sommer *novel* Scott Sommer *d* Chris Menges *ph* Ivan Strasburg *m* Trevor Jones
pd Crispian Sallis *ed* Tony Lawson
☆ Goldie Hawn, Arliss Howard, James Gammon, David Arnott, Keith Carradine, J. C. Quinn, Steve Buscemi

'At Memorial Hospital no one ever dies ... until their insurance runs out.'
Critical Care
US 1997 105m DeLuxe
Live Entertainment/Mediaworks (Steven S. Schwartz, Sidney Lumet)
An ambitious young hospital doctor is drawn into a battle between two sisters over the fate of their comatose father and his money.
Ailing satire on the medical profession, a heavy-handed melodrama with occasional pleasures.
w Steven S. Schwartz *book* Richard Dooling
d Sidney Lumet *ph* David Watkin *m* Michael Convertino *pd* Philip Rosenberg *ed* Tom Swartwout
☆ James Spader, Kyra Sedgwick, Helen Mirren, Margo Martindale, Jeffrey Wright, Wallace Shawn, Anne Bancroft, Albert Brooks, Philip Bosco, Edward Herrmann, Colm Feore
'A sadly anemic and uncharacteristically unenergetic addition to Sidney Lumet's career.' – *Todd McCarthy, Variety*

'A comedy of epidemic proportions.'
Critical Condition
US 1986 100m Technicolor
Paramount (Ted Field, Robert Cort)
Pretending to be mad in order to escape the Mafia, our hero is instead mistaken for a doctor.
Zany, hepped-up comedy which fails on all counts.
w Denis and John Hamill *d* Michael Apted
ph Ralf D. Bode *m* Alan Silvestri *pd* John Lloyd
ed Robert K. Lambert
☆ Richard Pryor, Rachel Ticotin, Ruben Blades, Joe Mantegna, Bob Dishy
'Fans will find little to cheer about.' – *Daily Variety*

Critic's Choice
US 1963 100m Technicolor Panavision
Warner/Frank P. Rosenberg
A ruthless Broadway critic is forced by his scruples to write a bad review of his wife's play.
Unsuitable vehicle for stars who have shorn a good comedy of wit and strive vainly for sentiment, wisecracks and pratfalls.
w Jack Sher *play* Ira Levin *d* Don Weis
ph Charles Lang *m* George Duning
☆ Bob Hope, Lucille Ball, Marilyn Maxwell, Rip Torn, Jessie Royce Landis, John Dehner, Jim Backus, Marie Windsor
'For instant stultification.' – *Judith Crist*

Critters
US 1986 86m DeLuxe
Sho Films/Smart Egg/New Line (Rupert Harvey)
Hair-ball-like creatures arrive from an asteroid and devastate Kansas.
Childish horror spoof which makes Gremlins *look like* War and Peace.
w Stephen Herek, Domonic Muir *d* Stephen Herek *ph* Tim Suhrstedt, Chris Tufty *m* David Newman *pd* Gregg Fonseca *ed* Larry Bock
☆ Dee Wallace Stone, M. Emmet Walsh, Billy Green Bush, Scott Grimes
'Irritatingly insipid and lightweight.' – *Variety*

Critters 2
US 1988 86m colour
Palace/New Line/Sho films (Barry Opper)
original title: *Critters 2: The Main Course*
Killer aliens terrorise a town.
Even judged by the standards of the original, a dull and boring movie.
w D. T. Twohy, Mick Garris *d* Mick Garris
ph Russell Carpenter *m* Nicholas Pike *pd* Philip Dean Foreman *ed* Charles Bornstein
☆ Terrence Mann, Don Opper, Cynthia Garris, Scott Grimes, Al Stevenson, Tom Hodges, Douglas Rowe, Liane Curtis
'A soft-centred remake of its amiable but unremarkable original.' – *MFB*

Critters 3
US 1992 86m colour
Newline/OH Films (Barry Opper, Rupert Harvey)
Furry man-eating aliens invade an apartment block in Los Angeles.
A mixture of gore and comedy that borrows from Die Hard.
w David J. Schow *story* Barry Opper, Rupert Harvey *d* Kristine Peterson *ph* Tom Callaway
m David C. Williams *pd* Philip Dean Foreman
ed Terry Stokes
☆ Aimee Brooks, John Calvin, Katherine Cortez, Leonardo DiCaprio, Geoffrey Blake, Don Opper, Diana Bellamy, Terrence Mann

Critters 4
US 1992 90m colour
New Line/OH Films (Barry Opper, Rupert Harvey)
A space salvage crew is trapped on a space station between the last surviving Krites and ruthless killers who want the creatures for biological warfare.
Almost a standard low-budget space parody of Alien, *with a couple of jokes and the Critters reduced to occasional roll-on, roll-off roles.*
w Joseph Lyle, David J. Schow *story* Barry Opper, Rupert Harvey *d* Rupert Harvey *ph* Tom Callaway *m* Peter Manning Robinson *pd* Philip Dean Foreman *ed* Terry Stokes
☆ Don Opper, Paul Whitthorne, Angela Bassett, Anders Hove, Eric DaRe, Brad Dourif

'Crocodile' Dundee *
Australia 1986 102m Kodak Color
Panavision
Paramount/Hoyts/Rimfire (John Cornell)
An outback hero goes to Manhattan and puts New Yorkers in their place.
Easygoing comedy with no real style, which astounded the industry by becoming one of America's most popular films in 1986.
w Paul Hogan, Ken Shadie *d* Peter Faiman
ph Russell Boyd *m* Peter Best
☆ Paul Hogan, Linda Koslowski, John Meillon, Mark Blum
*'*Romancing the Stone *combined with* Tarzan's New York Adventure.*' – Sight and Sound*
'A movie doggedly designed to make you feel good.' – *Vincent Canby, New York Times*
best original screenplay

'Crocodile' Dundee II
Australia 1988 111m DuArt Panavision
Paramount/Rimfire (John Cornell, Jane Scott)
Hunted in New York by drug dealers seeking the return of an incriminating photograph, 'Crocodile' Dundee returns to the Australian bush where his superior skills can outwit them.
Ineffectual sequel that offers nothing new for its central character to do and merely recycles episodes from the first hit.
w Paul Hogan, Brett Hogan *d* John Cornell
ph Russell Boyd *m* Peter Best *pd* Lawrence Eastwood *ed* David Stiven
☆ Paul Hogan, Linda Kozlowski, John Meillon, Ernie Dingo, Steve Rackman, Charles Dutton, Juan Fernandez, Hechter Ubarry
'A wasted opportunity if ever there was one.' – *MFB*

'He heard there was wildlife in L.A. He didn't know how wild.'
Crocodile Dundee in Los Angeles
US 2001 105m DeLuxe Panavision
Paramount/Silver Lion/Bangalow (Lance Hool, Paul Hogan)
An unemployed Australian crocodile hunter follows his journalist girlfriend to Los Angeles, where she is investigating a shady film producer.
The joke has worn very thin in this second sequel to a ramshackle hit of the mid-80s, and invention appears to have given out completely.
w Matthew Berry, Eric Abrams *d* Simon Wincer
ph David Burr *m* Basil Poledouris *pd* Leslie Binns *ed* Terry Blythe
☆ Paul Hogan (Mick Dundee), Linda Kozlowski (Sue Charleton), Jere Burns (Arnan Rothman), Jonathan Banks (Milos Drubnik), Alec Wilson (Jacko), Paul Rodriguez (Diego), Serge Cockburn (Mikey Dundee), Mike Tyson (Himself)
'Nostalgia and comedy are run through a food processor until they become a flavorless paste. There must be somebody who gets a chuckle out of being led by the hand down memory lane, where the best surprise is no surprise.' – *Elvis Mitchell, New York Times*

'Crickey!'
The Crocodile Hunter: Collision Course
US/Australia 2002 90m DeLuxe
Panavision
TCF/MGM/Best/Cheyenne
In Australia, CIA agents and a wildlife expert try to find a crocodile that has swallowed a surveillance device containing sensitive information.
A curious mix of croc-doc and childish thriller, featuring a popular, intrepid collector of dangerous animals and insects. The thriller elements are an irritating distraction, and the remainder is a re-run of Irwin's hyper-active television performances.
w Holly Goldberg Sloan *d* John Stainton
ph David Burr *m* Mark McDuff *pd* Jon Dowding
ed Suresh Ayyar , Bob Blasall
☆ Steve Irwin (Himself), Terri Irwin (Herself), Magda Szubanski (Brozzie Drewitt), David Wenham (Sam Flynn), Lachy Hulme (Robert Wheeler), Aden Young (Ron Buckwhiler), Kenneth Ransom (Vaughan Archer)
'One of the most purely pointless films you will ever see.' – *Peter Bradshaw, Guardian*

Cromwell *
GB 1970 141m Technicolor Panavision
Columbia/Irving Allen (Andrew Donally)
An account of the rise of Cromwell to power, the execution of Charles I, and the Civil War.
Disappointingly dull schoolbook history, with good production values but glum handling..
wd Ken Hughes *ph Geoffrey Unsworth* *m* Frank Cordell *pd John Stoll*
☆ Richard Harris, Alec Guinness, Robert Morley, Dorothy Tutin, Frank Finlay, Timothy Dalton, Patrick Wymark, Patrick Magee, Nigel Stock, Charles Gray, Michael Jayston, Anna Cropper, Michael Goodliffe
'It tries to combine serious intentions with the widest kind of popular appeal and falls unhappily between the two. It will offend the purists and bore the kiddies.' – *Brenda Davies*
'Shakespeare spoiled us for this sort of thing. We wait for great speeches and witty remarks, for rage and poetry, and we get dedicated stodginess.' – *Pauline Kael*
costumes (Nino Novarese)
Frank Cordell

Cronica di una Morte Annunciata: see *Chronicle of a Death Foretold*

Cronos **
Mexico 1992 92m Foto-Kem
October Films/Iguana/Ventana (Arthur H. Gorson)
An antique dealer finds a 400-year-old clockwork device containing a blood-sucking insect that confers immortality upon its user; but a rich, ruthless, dying industrialist is determined to obtain it for himself.
Deft, imaginative, original and gruesome variation on the vampire myth, stylishly directed and conjuring an atmosphere of genuine horror.
wd Guillermo del Toro *ph* Guillermo Navarro
pd Tolita Figueroa *ed* Raul Davalos
☆ Federico Luppi, Ron Perlman, Claudio Brook, Margarita Isabel, Tamara Shanath
'With spot-on pulp dialogue, simple, poetic imagery and gothic sound-effects, this is nothing short of a near-masterpiece.' – *Steve Beard, Empire*
'Audaciously reinvents the vampire legend in order to deliver a completely satisfying film that is both entertaining and intelligent in a manner that few contemporary horror films are.' – *Michael Lucas, Guardian*

The Crook: see *Le Voyou*

The Crooked Road

GB/Yugoslavia 1964 92m bw
Agro/Triglav

An American journalist plans to expose as a crook the dictator of a small Balkan state, but finds himself framed for murder.
Lugubrious and too-talkative melodrama of political intrigue.
w J. Garrison, Don Chaffey *novel* *The Big Story* by Morris West *d* Don Chaffey
☆ Robert Ryan, Stewart Granger, Marius Goring, Nadia Gray, Catherine Woodville, George Coulouris

The Crooked Way

US 1949 87m bw
Benedict Bogeaus

An amnesiac ex-veteran finds that he was once a minor gangster.
Predictable thick ear with film noir *aspirations.*
w Richard Landau *play* *No Blade Too Sharp* by Robert Monroe *d* Robert Florey *ph* John Alton
☆ John Payne, Sonny Tufts, Ellen Drew, Rhys Williams

The Crooked Web

US 1955 77m bw
Columbia (Sam Katzman)

A restaurant owner is lured into a scheme to recover buried Nazi gold from Germany, but finds it is a means of arresting him on an old murder charge.
Ingenious but somehow uninteresting puzzle melodrama.
w Lou Breslow *d* Nathan Juran
☆ Frank Lovejoy, Richard Denning, Mari Blanchard

'A sweet concoction of 70's soul and fun, fun, fun!'

Crooklyn *

US 1994 114m colour
Electric Triangle/40 Acres and a Mule/Child Hoods (Spike Lee)

In Harlem during the 1970s, an out-of-work jazz musician and his wife, a teacher, struggle to bring up their five unruly children.
A semi-autobiographical film, which may explain why it is as undisciplined as the family at its centre, as if the director were too close to his material to control it; much of the action is seen through the eyes of a 10-year-old girl, including a long sequence, shown in squeezed images, in which she is sent away to relatives; it has moments of vitality in which all the elements cohere.
w Joie Susannah Lee, Cinqué Lee, Spike Lee *d* Spike Lee *ph* Arthur Jafa *m* Terence Blanchard *pd* Wynn Thomas *ed* Barry Alexander Brown
☆ Alfre Woodard, Delroy Lindo, Spike Lee, Zelda Harris, Carlton Williams, Sharif Rashed

'The juke-box principle of film-making was never applied so enthusiastically, with practically every scene anchored by a song. But it's all too tempting to shut your eyes and pretend you're listening to The Best Soul Album Ever, since the film's dramatic content is so confused.' – *Jonathan Romney, Guardian*

Crooks and Coronets

GB 1969 106m Technicolor
Warner Seven Arts/Herman Cohen

US title: *Sophie's Place*

American gangsters plan to rob a stately home but are taken over by the dowager in charge.
Overlong and mainly flatulent comedy, with a good climax involving a vintage plane.
wd Jim O'Connolly *ph* Desmond Dickinson *m* Patrick John Scott
☆ Telly Savalas, Edith Evans, Warren Oates, Nicky Henson, Cesar Romero, Harry H. Corbett

Crooks Anonymous *

GB 1962 87m bw
Anglo Amalgamated (Nat Cohen)

A pretty thief joins an organization for reforming criminals, but is tempted again ... and so are they.
Amusingly devised and plotted minor comedy with an exceptional cast.
w Jack Davies, Henry Blyth *d* Ken Annakin *ph* Ernest Steward *m* Muir Mathieson, Henry Martin
☆ Leslie Phillips, Stanley Baxter, Wilfrid Hyde-White, Julie Christie, James Robertson Justice, Robertson Hare, Charles Lloyd Pack

Crooks in Cloisters

GB 1963 97m Technicolor Scope
ABPC

Forgers pose as monks but are reformed by the country life.
Busy comedy full of familiar faces; perhaps a small cut above the Carry Ons.
w Mike Watts *d* Jeremy Summers
☆ Ronald Fraser, Barbara Windsor, Grégoire Aslan, Bernard Cribbins, Davy Kaye, Wilfrid Brambell

Crooks in Clover: see *Penthouse*

Crooks' Tour *

GB 1940 84m bw
British National (John Corfield)

English tourists are mistaken for spies by Nazis in Baghdad.
Amusing vehicle for two comic actors who excelled at portraying the English abroad.
w John Watt, Max Kester *radio serial* Sidney Gilliat, Frank Launder *d* John Baxter *ph* James Wilson *m* Kennedy Russell
☆ *Basil Radford, Naunton Wayne*, Greta Gynt, Abraham Sofaer, Gordon McLeod

'Their bland imperturbability in the face of extraordinary circumstances provides no little fun.' – *Picture Show*

The Cross and the Switchblade

US 1970 106m colour
Fox/Dick Ross Associates

A minister sets out to rid his New York streets of delinquents.
Arrant but alas unconvincing do-goodery.
w Don Murray, James Bonnet *d* Don Murray
☆ Pat Boone, Erik Estrada, Jackie Giroux, Jo-Ann Robinson

Cross Country

Canada 1983 104m colour
Filmline/Yellowbill

The boyfriend of a murdered girl finds himself being driven west at gunpoint by a mad nymphomaniac and her protector.
No-holds-barred 'adult' thriller whose excesses become risible.
w Logan N. Danforth (John Hunter) *d* Paul Lynch
☆ Richard Beymer, Nina Axelrod, Michael Ironside, Brent Carver

'The true story about the woman who wrote *The Yearling*'

Cross Creek *

US 1983 122m Technicolor
EMI/Radnitz/Ritt (Robert B. Radnitz)

In 1928 Marjorie Kinnan Rawlings leaves her journalist husband and goes to live in the Florida backwoods, where she hopes to write a Gothic romance.
Elongated study of writer's block (though the subject did eventually write The Yearling*). Altogether too typical of its producer and director – and too slow – to hold much surprise or interest.*
w Dalene Young *memoirs* Marjorie Kinnan Rawlings *d* Martin Ritt *ph* John A. Alonzo *m* Leonard Rosenman *pd* Walter Scott Herndon
☆ Mary Steenburgen, Rip Torn, Peter Coyote, Dana Hill, Ike Eisenmann, Alfre Woodard

'The landscapes are attractive, but much too lushly filmed with lyrical inserts in which the wonders of the bayou are contemplated. Good performances fail to mask the fact that the characters are stereotypes from start to finish.' – *Tom Milne, MFB*

'Everything is lighted to look holy, and when the score isn't shimmering and burnishing, nature is twittering.' – *New Yorker*

Academy Award nomination: Rip Torn, Alfre Woodard, Leonard Rosenman

Cross My Heart *

US 1945 83m bw
Paramount (Harry Tugend)

A romantic girl confesses to murder, is acquitted, and finds the real murderer.
Modest remake of True Confession *(qv), with frenetic pace but not much style.*
w Claude Binyon, Harry Tugend, Charles Schnee *d* John Berry *ph* Charles Lang Jnr *m* Robert Emmett Dolan
☆ Betty Hutton, Sonny Tufts, Michael Chekhov, Rhys Williams, Ruth Donnelly, Al Bridge, Howard Freeman, Iris Adrian

Cross My Heart

US 1987 90m DeLuxe
Universal (Lawrence Kasdan)

As they begin to fall in love, a man and a woman are unable to be honest with each other on a date that first goes disastrously wrong and then miraculously right.
Slight romantic comedy that needed the injection of a little more pace and variation to hold an audience's attention; it has a certain charm, though.
w Armyan Bernstein, Gail Parent *d* Armyan Bernstein *ph* Thomas del Ruth *m* Bruce Broughton *pd* Lawrence G. Paull *ed* Mia Goldman
☆ Martin Short, Annette O'Toole, Paul Reiser, Joanna Kerns

Cross My Heart *

Canada 1990 105m colour
Belbo (Ludi Boeken, Jacques Fansten)

original title: *La Fracture du Myocarde*

Frightened of being sent to an orphanage, a 12-year-old boy tries to conceal the death of his mother.
Enjoyable comedy that stretches credulity at times but at least presents believable children living in a recognizable world.
wd Jacques Fansten *ph* Jean-Claude Saillier *m* Jean Marie Senia *pd* Gilbert Gagneux
☆ Sylvain Copans, Nicolas Parodi, Cecilia Rouaud, Lucie Blossier, Delphine Gouttman

'Delightfully offbeat first feature ... Few will remain unmoved.' – *Variety*

Cross of Iron *

GB/West Germany 1977 133m Technicolor
EMI-Rapid Film/Terra Filmkunst (Wolf. C. Hartwig)

Militarily and emotionally at the end of its tether, a German battalion is decimated while fighting the Russians in 1943.
Painful to follow, occasionally beautiful to watch, this quite horrid film offers too much opportunity for its director to wallow in unpleasant physical details, and its main plot of bitter rivalry offers no relief.
w Julius J. Epstein, Herbert Asmodi *novel* *The Willing Flesh* by Willi Heinrich *d* Sam Peckinpah *ph* John Coquillon *m* Ernest Gold
☆ James Coburn, James Mason, Maximilian Schell, David Warner, Klaus Löwitsch, Senta Berger

'Morally dubious but technically brilliant.' – *Michael Billington, Illustrated London News*

The Cross of Lorraine *

US 1944 91m bw
MGM (Edwin Knopf)

In a German camp for French prisoners, an escape leads to a rising by local villagers.
Standard war propaganda piece, made with enthusiasm on unconvincing sets.
w Michael Kanin, Ring Lardner Jnr, Alexander Esway, Robert Andrews *d* Tay Garnett *ph* Sidney Wagner *m* Bronislau Kaper
☆ Gene Kelly, Jean-Pierre Aumont, Cedric Hardwicke, Peter Lorre, Joseph Calleia, Richard Whorf, Hume Cronyn

'Half a football team worked on the story, yet except for a foolish coda it is one of the most edged, well-characterized, and naturally cinematic scripts of the year.' – *James Agee*

Cross Shot

Italy 1976 95m colour
P.A.C. (Teodoro Agrimi)

A quick-tempered police inspector, a sensational journalist and a gangster attempt to track down a young cop-killer.
Portentous, studiedly slow thriller with nothing to recommend it, not even Lee J. Cobb (in a minor role, despite his star billing) as a blind Mafioso.
w Lucio de Caro, Piero Poggio, Maurizio Mengoni, Dardano Sacchetti, Ted Rusoff *story* Lucio de Caro *d* Stelvo Massi *ph* Mario Vulpiani *m* Piero Pintucci *pd* Carlo Leva *ed* Mauro Bonanni
☆ John Saxon, Lee J. Cobb, Renzo Palmer, Rosanna Fratello, Antonella Lualdi, Lino Capolicchio

Crossed Swords

Italy/USA 1954 83m Pathécolor
Viva Films (J. Barrett Mahon, Vittorio Vassarotti)

original title: *Il Maestro di Don Giovanni*

The son of an Italian duke prevents an uprising.
A thin swashbuckler showing the perils of early co-production.
wd Milton Krims *ph* Jack Cardiff
☆ Errol Flynn, Gina Lollobrigida, Cesare Danova, Nadia Gray, Paola Mori

Crossed Swords: see *The Prince and the Pauper (1977)*

'Sensational? No, it's dynamite!'

Crossfire ****

US 1947 86m bw
RKO (Adrian Scott)

A Jew is murdered in a New York hotel, and three soldiers are suspected.
Tense, talky thriller shot entirely at night with pretty full expressionist use of camera technique; notable for style, acting, experimentation, and for being the first Hollywood film to hit out at racial bigotry.
w John Paxton *novel* *The Brick Foxhole* by Richard Brooks *d* *Edward Dmytryk* *ph* J. Roy Hunt *m* Roy Webb
☆ *Robert Young*, Robert Mitchum, *Robert Ryan*, Gloria Grahame, *Paul Kelly*, Sam Levene, Jacqueline White, Steve Brodie

'Another murder story that holds its own with any on the basis of suspense and speed.' – *Richard Winnington*

Academy Award nomination: best picture; John Paxton; Edward Dmytryk; Robert Ryan; Gloria Grahame

The Crossing

Australia 1990 92m colour
Beyond (Sue Seeary)

A young man returns home from the city, hoping to marry the girl he left behind, and disrupts a small community.
Heavy-handed domestic melodrama that looks like an imitation of American films of teenage rebellion and unsatisfactory parent–child relationships.
w Ranald Allan *d* George Ogilvie *ph* Jeff Darling *m* Martin Armiger *pd* Igor Nay *ed* Henry Dangar
☆ Russell Crowe, Robert Mammone, Danielle Spencer, Emily Lumbers, Rodney Bell, Ben Oxenbould, Myles Collins

'A funny movie about getting serious.'

Crossing Delancey *

US 1988 97m DuArt
Warner (Michael Nozik)

A bookshop manager vacillates between an author and a pickle manufacturer as a suitable lover.
Small but enjoyable celebration of the simple life.
w Susan Sandler *play* Susan Sandler *d* Joan Micklin Silver *ph* Theo Van de Sande *m* Paul Chihara, The Roches *pd* Dan Leigh *ed* Rick Shaine
☆ Amy Irving, Peter Riegert, Reizl Bozyk, Jeroen Krabbe, Sylvia Miles, George Martin, John Bedford Lloyd

The Crossing Guard *

US 1995 114m DeLuxe
Buena Vista/Miramax (Sean Penn, David S. Hamburger)

An alcoholic jeweller plans to kill the man, just released from prison, who killed his daughter in a drunk-driving accident six years previously.
Grim, over-emphatic, slow-moving drama of loss and guilt, but one that elicts some good performances from the principals.
wd Sean Penn *ph* Vilmos Zsigmond *m* Jack Nitzsche, Joseph Vitarelli *pd* Michael Haller *ed* Jay Cassidy
☆ Jack Nicholson, David Morse, Anjelica Huston, Robin Wright, Piper Laurie, Richard Bradford, Robbie Robertson, John Savage

'A tough guy's weepie ... It's a trademark of the tough guy's weepie, incidentally, that it takes emotion seriously, but only among people who fight against it, i.e. men. Women get paradoxically short shrift, because they're meant to be good at that stuff.' – *Adam Mars-Jones, Independent*

The Crossing of the Rhine *
France/Italy/West Germany 1960 125m bw
Franco-London-Gibe-Jonia-UFA (Ralph Baum)
original title: *Le Passage du Rhin*
Two French soldiers escape from the Germans in 1940 and after various adventures meet up again in Paris in 1945.
Two crowded plots and not a great deal of point emerge from this watchable war film full of conventional set-pieces.
w André Cayatte, Armand Jammot *d* André Cayatte *ph* Roger Fellous *m* Louiguy
☆ Charles Aznavour, Nicole Courcel, Georges Rivière, Cordula Trantow

Crossing the Line: see *The Big Man*

Crossplot
GB 1969 97m Eastmancolor
UA/Tribune (Robert S. Baker)
An advertising executive gets involved in a spy ring.
Old-fashioned, London-set amalgam of secret codes, disappearing bodies, helicopter attacks, and a finale frustrating the assassination of a statesman in Hyde Park.
w Leigh Vance *d* Alvin Rakoff *ph* Brendan J. Stafford *m* Stanley Black
☆ Roger Moore, Martha Hyer, Alexis Kanner, Francis Matthews, Bernard Lee

Crossroads **
Japan 1928 80m approx bw silent
Shochiku
original title: *Jujiro*
A woman kills her seducer. Her brother thinks he has killed a man and takes refuge with her, only to die of shock when he sees the man alive.
The only widely distributed Japanese silent film, this curious piece is fragmentarily told and will remind many of Rashomon *with its mixture of flashbacks and dreams.*
wd Teinosuke Kinugasa *ph* Kohei Sugiyama
☆ J. Bandoha, A. Tschihaya, Yujiko Ogawa, I. Sohma

Crossroads *
US 1942 84m bw
MGM (Edwin Knopf)
A French diplomat who once lost his memory is blackmailed by crooks who claim he was once a criminal.
Smooth mystery melodrama adapted from the French film Carrefour.
w Guy Trosper *story* Howard Emmett Rogers, John Kafka *d* Jack Conway *ph* Joseph Ruttenberg *m* Bronislau Kaper
☆ William Powell, Hedy Lamarr, Basil Rathbone, Claire Trevor, Margaret Wycherly, Felix Bressart, Sig Rumann
'Well directed and acted with polish, delightful romantic moments breaking up the general atmosphere of excitement and suspense.' – *Picturegoer*

Crossroads
US 1986 96m Technicolor
Delphi IV/Columbia (Mark Carliner)
Urged by a young musician, an old blues singer travels the South in search of his legendary companion's lost music.
Rather specialized and unsatisfactory road pic which loses its way well before the end.
w John Fusco *d* Walter Hill *ph* John Bailey *m* Ry Cooder *ad* Albert Heschong *ed* Freeman Davies
☆ Ralph Macchio, Joe Seneca, Jami Gertz, Joe Morton
'You can tell what's wrong with *Crossroads* when you try to describe it to friends. Half-way through the plot description, their eyes glaze over.' – *People*

'Dreams change. Friends are forever.'
Crossroads
US 2002 93m DeLuxe
Paramount/Zomba/MTV (Ann Carli)
Three girls make a trip to Los Angeles to celebrate their graduation from high school.
Exceptionally bland star vehicle for a pop singer and celebrity virgin.
w Shonda Rhimes *d* Tamra Davis *ph* Eric Edwards *m* Trevor Jones *pd* Waldemar Kalinowski *ed* Melissa Kent *cos* Wendy Schecter
☆ Britney Spears (Lucy), Anson Mount (Ben), Zoe Saldana (Kit), Taryn Manning (Mimi), Kim Cattrall (Caroline), Dan Aykroyd (Pete), Justin Long (Henry), Beverly Johnson (Kit's Mom)
'Innocuous in the extreme and very poorly written even on the teen trauma-lite level on which it operates.' – *Todd McCarthy, Guardian*

Crossworlds
US 1996 91m colour
Trimark (Rupert Harvey, Lloyd Segan)
A youth is hunted by beings from another dimension, who want the crystal left to him by his father, which unlocks the boundaries between worlds.
Low-budget, brainless science-fiction; it displays a paucity of imagination, as well as a paunchy Hauer, looking uncomfortable in the role of an action hero.
w Raman Rao, Krishna Rao *d* Krishna Rao *ph* Christopher Walling *m* Christopher Beck *pd* Aaron Osborne *ed* Anita Brandt-Burgoyne
☆ Rutger Hauer (A.T.), Josh Charles (Joe), Stuart Wilson (Ferris), Andrea Roth (Laura), Perry Anzilotti (Rebo), Richard McGregor (Stu), Jack Black (Steve)

Crouching Tiger, Hidden Dragon **
Hong Kong/Taiwan/US 2000 120m Technicolor
Columbia TriStar/UCV/SPC/Good Machine/Edko/Zoom Hunt (Bill Kong, Hsu Li Kong, Ang Lee)
original title: *Wo Hu Zang Long*
A master swordsman and a female security escort investigate the theft of a antique sword and find themselves engaged in a struggle to the death with a rebellious girl and an evil witch.
Following in the footsteps of King Hu and Tsai Hark, Lee's stylish fantasy of doomed love revives a familiar genre of flying swordsmen: it excels in the exuberant, airborne fight sequences, but its contrasting romances are both unsatisfactory, particularly in an protracted desert sequence, which resembles an Asian version of The Sheik.
w James Schamus, Wang Hui Ling, Tsai Kuo Jung *novel* Wang Du Lu *d* Ang Lee *ph* Peter Pau *m* Tan Dun *pd* Tim Yip *ed* Tim Squyres *sp* MVFX *cos* Tim Yip *action ch* Yuen Wo-Ping
☆ Chow Yun-fat (Li Mu Bai), Michelle Yeoh (Yu Shu Lien), Zhang Ziyi (Jen), Chang Chen (Lo), Lung Sihung (Sir Te), Cheng Pei-pei (Jade Fox), Li Fazeng (Governor Yu), Gao Xian (Bo), Hai Yan (Madam Yu), Wang Deming (Tsai), Li Li (May)
'It's pulp fiction presented in a grand, knowingly humorous style distinguished by star power, a strong female slant and the latest in stunts and effects.' – *Todd McCarthy, Variety*
'Ang Lee's beautiful, intimate epic is–one would have though self-evidently–a luminous work of art.' – *Salman Rushdie*
foreign language film; Peter Pau; Tan Dun; Tim Yip (art direction)
picture; Ang Lee; script (Wang Hui Ling, James Schamus, Tsai Kuo Jung); Tim Squyres; Tim Yip (costumes); song 'A Love Before Time' (*m* Jorge Calandrelli, Tan Dun, *l* James Schamus)
foreign film; Ang Lee; Tan Dun; Tim Yip (costumes)

'He hates cheats.'
'Hang On Tightly... Let Go Lightly.'
Croupier
GB/Ireland/France/Germany 1997 94m colour
BFI/Little Bird/Tatfilm/Compagnie des Phares & Balises/La Sept/Channel4 (Jonathan Cavendish)
A would-be novelist and former croupier returns to working in a casino where he avoids the temptation to be dishonest.
Cool, impersonal thriller that keeps its distance from the events it shows, becoming a somewhat arid account of a man trapped in a world he understands but dislikes.
w Paul Mayersberg *d* Mike Hodges *ph* Mike Garfath *m* Simon Fisher Turner *pd* Jon Bunker *ed* Les Healey
☆ Clive Owen (Jack Manfred), Kate Hardie (Bella), Alex Kingston (Jani de Villiers), Gina McKee (Marion Neil), Nicholas Ball (Jack Manfred Snr), Nick Reding (Giles Cremorne), Alexander Morton (David Reynolds)
'Lurches from stylish tension and dry comedy to toe-curling awkwardness with perplexing regularity.' – *Tom Doyle, Empire*
'One of the niftiest noir character studies to have come along in a long time.' – *Andrew Sarris, New York Observer*

'Believe In Angels.'
'Darker than the bat.'
The Crow *
US 1994 101m DeLuxe
Entertainment/Jeff Most/Edward R. Pressman
Accompanied by a crow, a rock guitarist returns from the dead to kill those responsible for the murders of him and his girlfriend.
Accomplished comic-book action which looks good but rarely takes flight, following an all-too-predictable pattern.
w David J. Schow, John Shirley *comic book* James O'Barr *d* Alex Proyas *ph* Dariusz Wolski *m* Graeme Revell *pd* Alex McDowell *ed* Dov Hoenig, Scott Smith *visual effects* Andrew Mason *make-up* Lance Anderson
☆ Brandon Lee, Ernie Hudson, Michael Wincott, Angel David, David Patrick Kelly, Rochelle Davis, Laurence Mason, Bai Ling, Tony Todd, Jon Polito
'A stunning work of visual style – the best version of a comic book universe I've seen.' – *Roger Ebert, Chicago Sun-Times*
'A seamless, pulsating, dazzlingly visual revenge fantasy that stands as one of the most effective live-actioners derived from a comic strip.' – *Todd McCarthy, Variety*
† Brandon Lee died in a shooting accident during filming. The film was completed using computer techniques of digital compositing, in which Lee's image was placed in scenes in which he did not appear, and his face substituted for that of his body double in some scenes. The sell-through video release included an on-camera interview with Lee made a few days before his death.

'Believe in the power of another...'
The Crow: City of Angels
GB/US 1996 86m DeLuxe
Buena Vista/Bad Bird/Miramax/Dimension (Edward R. Pressman, Jeff Most)
A drowned man returns to life to revenge his, and his baby's, death at the hands of a gang of bikers.
Less a sequel than a rehash of the original, but without its visual power or even narrative interest.
w David Goyer *comic book* James O'Barr *d* Tim Pope *ph* Jean Yves Escoffier *m* Graeme Revell *pd* Alex McDowell *ed* Michael N. Knue, Anthony Redman, Barry Dresner, Neil Eric Wenger
☆ Vincent Perez, Mia Kirshner, Richard Brooks, Vincent Castellanos, Ian Dury, Tracey Ellis, Thomas Jane, Iggy Pop
'Offers the usual fragmentary "visions" of apocalypse, all mashed together into an occult junkyard that makes an average horror-trash music video look like a model of coherence.' – *Owen Gleiberman, Entertainment Weekly*
† The British release had 20 feet of film cut.

The Crowd ***
US 1928 98m bw silent
MGM (King Vidor)
Episodes in the life of a city clerk.
A deliberately humdrum story, chosen to show that drama can exist in the lowliest surroundings, retains much of its original power, though some of the director's innovations have become clichés.
w King Vidor, John V. A. Weaver, Harry Behn *d* King Vidor *ph* Henry Sharp *ad* Cedric Gibbons, Arnold Gillespie *ed* Hugh Wynn
☆ James Murray, Eleanor Boardman, Bert Roach, Estelle Clark
'No picture is perfect, but this comes as near to reproducing reality as anything you have ever witnessed.' – *Photoplay*
King Vidor; Unique and Artistic Picture

The Crowd Roars *
US 1932 85m bw
Warner
A star motor-racing driver tries to prevent his young brother from following in his footsteps.
Typical early Cagney vehicle, still spectacularly pacy but dated in its dialogue scenes.
w Kubec Glasmon, John Bright, Niven Busch *d* Howard Hawks *ph* Sid Hickox, John Stumar *md* Leo Forbstein
☆ James Cagney, Joan Blondell, Ann Dvorak, Eric Linden, Guy Kibbee, Frank McHugh, Regis Toomey
'A thin and uneventful story, but a majority of the footage is devoted to three stirring contests.' – *Variety*
'As so often Hawks seems bitter at the world men have created but respects those who have to attempt to live it to the full.' – *NFT, 1963*
'The story is not precisely exciting ... the closing episode is the best, for it reveals a certain originality in having the injured automobile racers eager to continue the race in ambulances on the way to hospital.' – *Mordaunt Hall, New York Times*
† Remade in 1939 as *Indianapolis Speedway*.

The Crowd Roars *
US 1938 90m bw
MGM (Sam Zimbalist)
A young boxer becomes involved with the underworld.
Standard star vehicle with efficient trimmings.
w Thomas Lennon, George Bruce, George Oppenheimer *d* Richard Thorpe *ph* John Seitz *m* Edward Ward
☆ Robert Taylor, Frank Morgan, Edward Arnold, Maureen O'Sullivan, William Gargan, Frank Craven, Jane Wyman, Lionel Stander, Nat Pendleton
'Exciting melodrama with plenty of ring action, some plausible romance and several corking good characterizations.' – *Variety*
† Remade as *Killer McCoy*.

The Crowded Day
GB 1954 82m bw
Advance
Problems of five assistants in a department store during the Christmas rush.
Naïve little portmanteau which suited its purpose.
w Talbot Rothwell *d* John Guillermin
☆ Joan Rice, John Gregson, Freda Jackson, Patricia Marmont, Josephine Griffin, Sonia Holm, Rachel Roberts, Thora Hird, Dora Bryan, Edward Chapman, Sid James, Richard Wattis

The Crowded Sky
US 1960 104m Technicolor
Warner (Michael Garrison)
As two planes fly unwittingly towards each other, the passengers muse on their personal problems. An emergency landing averts total disaster.
The format goes back as far as Friday the Thirteenth, *and forward to* Airport 75, *but this was in fact a cut-rate rehash of* The High and the Mighty, *with dull characters and insufficiently tense handling, not to mention a second team cast.*
w Charles Schnee *d* Joseph Pevney *ph* Harry Stradling *m* Leonard Rosenman
☆ Dana Andrews, Rhonda Fleming, Efrem Zimbalist Jnr, John Kerr, Anne Francis, Keenan Wynn, Troy Donahue, Joe Mantell, Patsy Kelly

Crows and Sparrows *
China 1949 113m bw
Peak Film Industries (Xia Yunhu, Ren Zongde)
original title: *Wuya Yu Maque*
Preparing to flee from the victorious Red Army, a landlord decides to sell his house and evict the tenants.
Lively slice-of-Chinese-life, made just before the Communist revolution.
w Shen Fu, Xu Tao, Zhao Dan, Lin Gu, Chen Baichen, Zheng Junli *d* Zheng Junli *ph* Miao Zhenhua, Hu Zhenhua *md* Wang Yunjie
☆ Zhao Dan, Wu Yin, Sun Daoling, Shangguan Yunzhu, Wei Heling, Li Tianji, Huang Zongying, Wang Pei

'What Some Hearts Desire They Must Possess.'
'Arthur Miller's Timeless Tale Of Truth On Trial.'
The Crucible **
US 1996 123m Technicolor
TCF (Robert A. Miller, David V. Picker)
In Salem in the 1690s, a young woman claims that the wife of the married man she loves is a witch.
Powerful historical drama of the power of superstition when allied to the processes of an inquisition, though it has lost some of its contemporary relevance along the way.

w Arthur Miller *play* Arthur Miller *d* Nicholas Hytner *ph* Andrew Dunn *m* George Fenton *pd* Lilly Kilvert *ed* Tariq Anwar
☆ Daniel Day-Lewis, Winona Ryder, *Paul Scofield*, *Joan Allen*, Bruce Davison, Rob Campbell, Jeffrey Jones, Peter Vaughan, Karron Graves, Charlaine Woodard, George Gaynes

'Still possesses the power to stir up wrenching emotion through its elemental crises and conflicts. But neither the establishing dramatic linchpin nor the final conversion of conscience is terribly convincing, leaving this pared-down rendition of the original work diminished in power and meaning as well.' – *Todd McCarthy, Variety*

Joan Allen; Arthur Miller
Paul Schofield

Crucible of Terror
GB 1971 91m Eastmancolor
Glendale (Tom Parkinson)

An art dealer and his girlfriend visit a reclusive artist with a penchant for murdering his models and turning them into bronze statues.
Slow-moving and dreary drama, with cliché-ridden dialogue and dull direction.
w Ted Hooker, Tom Parkinson *d* Ted Hooker *ph* Peter Newbrook *m* Paris Rutherford *ad* Arnold Chapkis *ed* Maxine Julius
☆ Mike Raven, Mary Maude, James Bolam, Ronald Lacey, Melissa Stribling, John Arnatt, Beth Morris, Judy Matheson, Betty Alberge

'What You Can't Have, You Can't Resist.'
Cruel Intentions *
US 1999 95m DeLuxe
Columbia/Original/Newmarket (Neal H. Moritz)

Annoyed at losing her boyfriend, a rich girl wagers that her stepbrother cannot seduce two virgins.
A teenage version of a novel about world-weary adults; the attitudes of ennui and malice are an awkward fit on the young cast (even though they look too old to be still at school); but it has a little more bite than most movies aimed at a teen audience.
wd Roger Kumble *novel Les liaisons dangereuses* by Choderlos de Laclos *ph* Theo Van de Sande *m* Edward Shearmur *pd* Jon Gary Steele *ed* Jeff Freeman
☆ Sarah Michelle Gellar, Ryan Phillippe, Reese Witherspoon, Selma Blair, Louise Fletcher, Joshua Jackson, Eric Mabius, Sean Patrick Thomas, Swoosie Kurtz, Christine Baranski

'Nasty, profane and wickedly entertaining for the most part.' – *Emanuel Levy, Variety*

† Other recent films based on the novel include *Dangerous Liaisons* and *Valmont* (qqv).

Cruel Passion
GB 1977 97m Eastmancolor
Target International (Chris Boger)

Two sisters are sent away from a convent school: one becomes an aristocrat's mistress, the other is raped by him.
Good-looking but tedious and downbeat period drama, which owes little to de Sade and more to the British sex film industry of the 70s; its scenes of lesbian nuns, brothels and rape are not likely to find favour with the dirty macintosh brigade, and there is little to interest anyone else.
w Ian Cullen, Chris Boger, Peter Delfgou *novel Justine* by the Marquis de Sade *d* Chris Boger *ph* Roger Deakins *pd* Tony Curtis *ed* Peter Delfgou
☆ Koo Stark (Justine), Martin Potter (Lord Carlisle), Lydia Lisle (Juliette), Katherine Kath, Hope Jackman, Louis Ife, Barry McGinn

The Cruel Sea **
GB 1953 126m bw
Ealing (Leslie Norman)

Life and death on an Atlantic corvette during World War II.
Competent transcription of a bestselling book, cleanly produced and acted; a huge box-office success.
w Eric Ambler *novel* Nicholas Monsarrat *d Charles Frend ph* Gordon Dines *m* Alan Rawsthorne *ad* Jim Morahan *ed* Peter Tanner
☆ *Jack Hawkins* (Capt. Ericson), Donald Sinden (Lt Lockhart), Stanley Baker (Bennett), John Stratton (Ferraby), Denholm Elliott (Sub-Lt Morell), John Warner (Baker), Bruce Seton (Bob Tallow), Virginia McKenna (Julie Hallam), Moira Lister (Elaine Morell), June Thorburn (Doris Ferraby), Alec McCowen (Tonbridge), Glyn Houston (Phillips)

'This is a story of the battle of the Atlantic, a story of an ocean, two ships and a handful of men. The men are the heroes. The heroines are the ships. The only villain is the sea – the cruel sea – that man has made even more cruel.' – *opening narration*

'One is grateful nowadays for a film which does not depict war as anything but a tragic and bloody experience, and it is this quality which gives the production its final power to move.' – *John Gillett*

'Sensitivity, faithfulness, and almost inevitable tedium.' – *Time Out, 1984*

Eric Ambler

Cruise Missile
Germany/Italy/Spain 1978 90m colour
Noble Productions/Echberg Film (Ika Panajotovic)
An American and Russian agent team up with the local police to prevent a terrorist blowing up a peace conference in Iran.
Substandard thriller, in which the Iranian police are portrayed as wonderful.
w Clarke Reynolds, Elio Romano *d* Leslie H. Martinson *ph* Claudio Catozzo *m* Alberto Baldan *ed* Enzio Monachesi
☆ Peter Graves, Curt Jurgens, Michael Dante, John Carradine

Cruisin' Down the River
US 1953 79m colour
Columbia
A night-club singer inherits a riverboat.
Slim excuse for a musical variety bill.
w Blake Edwards, Richard Quine *d* Richard Quine
☆ Dick Haymes, Audrey Totter, Billy Daniels, Cecil Kellaway, the Bell Sisters, Erze Ivan

Cruising
US 1980 106m Technicolor
Lorimar (Jerry Weintraub)

A New York cop becomes degraded in his search among homosexuals for a sadistic killer.
Alleged thriller with phoney pretensions and repellent detail.
wd William Friedkin *ph* James Contner *m* Jack Nitzsche
☆ Al Pacino, Paul Sorvino, Karen Allen, Richard Cox, Don Scardino, Joe Spinell

'Like any approach to the bizarre, it's fascinating for about fifteen minutes. After that, it suffers from the same boring repetition that makes porno so uninteresting generally.' – *Variety*

Crumb ***
US 1994 120m colour
Artificial Eye/Superior (Lynn O'Donnell, Terry Zwigoff)

Robert Crumb, celebrated underground cartoonist and creator of Fritz the Cat and Mr Natural, discusses his life and work and plays ragtime and jazz from his vast collection of 78 rpm records as he leaves California to settle in France; his mother and brother and other cartoonists are also interviewed.
Fascinating documentary on an artist called 'the Breughel of the 20th century' by one interviewee, critic Robert Hughes, seen in context with his somewhat dysfunctional brothers who, also talented, have failed to come to terms with society in the way that he has. (Charles, his older brother, committed suicide a year after being filmed.)
d Terry Zwigoff *ph* Maryse Alberti *ed* Victor Livingston
☆ Robert Crumb, Charles Crumb, Maxon Crumb, Aline Kominsky, Dana Crumb, Beatrice Crumb

'By turns gripping and appalling, *Crumb* is one of the most complete pictures of an artist ever made.' – *Clark Collis, Empire*

'Wonders to dazzle the human imagination – in a flaming love story set in titanic world conflict!'
The Crusades **
US 1935 127m bw
Paramount/Cecil B. de Mille
Spurred by his wife Berengaria, Richard the Lionheart sets off on his holy wars.
Heavily tapestried medieval epic, spectacular sequences being punctuated by wodges of uninspired dialogue. A true de Mille pageant.
w Harold Lamb, Waldemar Young, Dudley Nichols *d Cecil B. de Mille ph Victor Milner m* Rudolph Kopp *sp* Gordon Jennings
☆ Henry Wilcoxon, Loretta Young, C. Aubrey Smith, Ian Keith, Katherine de Mille, Joseph Schildkraut, Alan Hale, C. Henry Gordon, George Barbier, Montagu Love, Lumsden Hare, William Farnum, Hobart Bosworth, Pedro de Cordoba, Mischa Auer

'Mr de Mille's evangelical films are the nearest equivalent today to the glossy German colour prints which decorated mid-Victorian bibles. There is the same lack of a period sense, the same stuffy horsehair atmosphere of beards and whiskers, and, their best quality, a childlike eye for detail.' – *Graham Greene*

'Cinema addicts by now have some idea what to expect in a de Mille version of the Holy Wars. *The Crusades* should fulfil all expectations. As a picture it is historically worthless, didactically treacherous, artistically absurd. None of these defects impairs its entertainment value. It is a hundred-million-dollar sideshow which has at least three features to distinguish it from the long line of previous de Mille extravaganzas. It is the noisiest; it is the biggest; it contains no baths.' – *Time*

'Probably only de Mille could make a picture like this and get away with it. It's long, and slow, and the story is not up to some of his previous films, but the production has sweep and spectacle.' – *Variety*

Victor Milner

Crush
New Zealand 1992 96m colour
Metro/Hibiscus/NZFC/NFU/NZ On Air/Movie Partners (Bridget Ikin)

While she is in hospital recovering from a car crash, a female journalist is angered to discover that her best friend has begun an affair with a novelist she planned to interview.
A bisexual revenge thriller that attempts to expose bourgeois values, but fails to convince.
w Alison Maclean, Anne Kennedy *d* Alison Maclean *ph* Dion Beebe *m* JPS Experience, Antony Partos *pd* Meryl Cronin *ed* John Gilbert
☆ Marcia Gay Harden, William Zappa, Donogh Rees, Caitlin Bossley, Pete Smith, Jon Brazier

'Often as murky as the bubbling New Zealand mud springs Maclean cuts to in order to underscore the otherworldly ambience.' – *Empire*

'He thought it was just a crush. He was dead wrong.'
The Crush
US 1993 89m Technicolor
Warner/Morgan Creek (James G. Robinson)

A teenage girl develops a crush on her new neighbour, a writer, and becomes violent when he ignores her advances.
Predictable and unintelligent thriller, recycling familiar themes in an uninspired fashion.
wd Alan Shapiro *ph* Bruce Surtees *m* Graeme Revell *pd* Michael Bolton *ed* Ian Crafford
☆ Cary Elwes, Alicia Silverstone, Jennifer Rubin, Amber Benson, Kurtwood Smith, Gwynyth Walsh, Matthew Walker

'Another by-the-numbers thriller longer on suspense than brains. Silly and predictable.' – *Variety*

'Could Mr. Wrong... be Mr. Right?'
Crush
GB 2001 111m Fujicolor Panavision
FilmFour/Film Council/Senator/Industry Entertainment/Pipedream (Lee Thomas)

A middle-aged headmistress upsets her two 40-ish female friends when she begins an affair with a younger man.
Tart comedy of older women looking towards a possibly lonely old age, which gives it a melacholy edge.
wd John McKay *ph* Henry Braham *m* Kevin Sargent *pd* Amanda MacArthur *ed* Anne Sopel
☆ Andie MacDowell (Kate), Imelda Staunton (Janine), Anna Chancellor (Molly), Kenny Doughty (Jed), Bill Paterson (Rev. Gerald Marsden)

'For women in the midst of otherwise v. successful adult lives, these ladies are awfully stupid about love, sex, friendship, menstrual cycles, and the attributes of a good boyfriend or a bad script.' – *Lisa Schwarzbaum, Entertainment Weekly*

Crusoe *
US 1988 94m Technicolor
Virgin/Island Pictures (Andrew Braunsberg)

A slave-owner, shipwrecked on a desert island, makes friends with a cannibal.
Deft variation on the original familiar story.
w Walon Green, Christopher Logue *novel Robinson Crusoe* by Daniel Defoe *d* Caleb Deschanel *ph* Tom Pinter *m* Michael Kamen *pd* Velco Despotovic *ed* Humphrey Dixon
☆ Aidan Quinn, Elvis Payne, Richard Sharp, Colin Bruce, William Hootkins, Shane Rimmer, Jimmy Nail, Patrick Monkton, Chris Pitt, Ade Sapara

The Cry: see *Il Grido*

Cry Baby Killer
US 1958 62m bw
Roger Corman/AA
A gunman on the run barricades himself and hostages in a storeroom.
Modest second feature which served its purpose.
w Leo Gordon, Melvin Levy *d* Jus Addiss
☆ Jack Nicholson, Harry Lauter, Carolyn Mitchell, Brett Halsey

Cry Danger *
US 1951 79m bw
RKO/Olympic (Sam Wiesenthal, W. R. Frank)

After serving five years for robbery, a man gets out on parole and clears his name.
Slick little slice of thick ear, very lively all round.
w William Bowers *story* Jerome Cady *d* Robert Parrish *ph* Joseph F. Biroc *m* Emil Newman, Paul Dunlap *ad* Richard Day
☆ Dick Powell, Rhonda Fleming, Richard Erdman, William Conrad, Regis Toomey, Jay Adler

Cry for Happy
US 1961 110m Eastmancolor Cinemascope
Columbia (William Goetz)
Four navy cameramen in Japan help geishas to found an orphanage.
As bad as it sounds, a repellent mixture of sentiment and knockabout.
w Irving Brecher *d* George Marshall *ph* Burnett Guffey *m* George Duning
☆ Glenn Ford, Donald O'Connor, Miiko Taka, James Shigeta, Miyoshi Umeki, Joe Flynn, Howard St John

'Any film which expends most of its energies on a protracted joke about how far you can go with a geisha could hardly fail to be as charmless and witless as this.' – *MFB*

Cry Freedom **
GB 1987 158m colour Panavision
Marble Arch/Universal (Richard Attenborough)

South African journalist Donald Woods is forced to flee the country after attempting to investigate the death in custody of his friend the black activist Steve Biko.
Part thriller, part social conscience tract, the film has magnificent set-pieces typical of the director's work. However, it failed to satisfy either opponents or supporters of apartheid.
w John Briley *d* Richard Attenborough *ph* Ronnie Taylor *m* George Fenton, Jonas Gwangwa *pd* Stuart Craig
☆ Kevin Kline, Penelope Wilton, Denzel Washington, Alec McCowen, Kevin McNally, Zakes Mokae

Denzel Washington; music; song 'Cry Freedom' (m/ly George Fenton, Jonas Gwangwa)

A Cry from the Streets
GB 1958 100m bw
Film Traders (Ian Dalrymple)

Episodes from the work of child welfare officers.
Mildly pleasing but unconvincing semi-documentary, with children competing with the star at scene-stealing.
w Vernon Harris *novel The Friend in Need* by Elizabeth Coxhead *d* Lewis Gilbert *ph* Harry Gilliam *m* Larry Adler

☆ Max Bygraves, Barbara Murray, Colin Petersen, Dana Wilson, Kathleen Harrison, Eleanor Summerfield, Mona Washbourne

Cry Havoc
US 1943 97m bw
MGM (Edwin Knopf)
War nurses are caught up in the Bataan retreat.
An all-woman cast adequately handles a stagey melodrama about a tragic situation.
w Paul Osborn *play* *Proof thro' the Night* by Allen R. Kenward *d* Richard Thorpe *ph* Karl Freund *m* Daniele Amfitheatrof
☆ Margaret Sullavan, Joan Blondell, Ann Sothern, Fay Bainter, Marsha Hunt, Ella Raines, Frances Gifford, Diana Lewis, Heather Angel, Connie Gilchrist
'A sincere fourth-rate film made from a sincere fifth-rate play.' – *James Agee*
'Its popularity will stem less from its probably factual record of nurses starving, sweating and dying in the beleaguered Philippine jungle than from the impressive all-woman cast which MGM has rounded up for the occasion.' – *Newsweek*

A Cry in the Dark *
Australia 1988 121m colour Panavision
Pathé/Evil Angels/Cannon International (Verity Lambert)
A woman is tried for the murder of her baby daughter, who was carried off by a wild dog during a family camping expedition.
Skilful reconstruction of a sensational true-life court case.
w Robert Caswell, Fred Schepisi *book* *Evil Angels* by John Bryson *d* Fred Schepisi *ph* Ian Baker *m* Bruce Smeaton *pd* Wendy Dickson, George Liddle *ed* Jill Bilcock
☆ Meryl Streep, Sam Neill, Dale Reeves, David Hoflin, Jason Reason, Michael Wetter, Kane Barton, Trent Roberts, Brian Jones, Dorothy Alison
'May be the most quietly uncondescending film ever made about religious fundamentalists.' – *Peter Rainer, Los Angeles Herald Examiner*
Meryl Streep

A Cry in the Night
US 1956 75m bw
Warner/Jaguar (George C. Bertholon)
A peeping Tom, caught by a teenage couple, abducts the girl and threatens rape.
Odd little domestic thriller, with parents and police working together. Watchable, but a bit over the top.
w David Dortort *novel* Whit Masterson *d* Frank Tuttle *ph* John Seitz *m* David Buttolph
☆ Edmond O'Brien, Brian Donlevy, Natalie Wood, Raymond Burr, Richard Anderson, Irene Hervey, Anthony Caruso

Cry of the Banshee
GB 1970 87m Movielab
AIP (Gordon Hessler)
A 16th-century magistrate is cursed by a witch, who sends a devil in the form of a young man to destroy him.
Modest horror film which fails to do justice to its interesting plot.
w Tim Kelly, Christopher Wicking *d* Gordon Hessler *ph* John Coquillon *m* Les Baxter
☆ Vincent Price, Elisabeth Bergner, Patrick Mower, Essy Persson, Hugh Griffith, Hilary Dwyer, Sally Geeson

The Cry of the Black Wolves
West Germany 1972 90m colour
Hillenbrand (Gunter Eulan)
In Alaska, a fur-trapper is accused of killing the man who stole his dog-team.
Standard Western in an icy setting, complete with the bad guys in black hats.
w Kurt Nachmann, Rolf Olsen *story* Jack London *d* Harald Reinl *ph* Franz X. Lederle *m* Gerhard Heinz *ad* Rolf Zehetbauer, Herbert Strabel *ed* Eva Zeyn
☆ Ron Ely, Raimund Harmstorf, Gila von Weitershausen, Heinrich Schweiger

Cry of the City **
US 1948 96m bw
TCF (Sol C. Siegel)
A ruthless gangster on the run is pursued by a policeman who was once his boyhood friend.
Very well produced but relentlessly miserable New York thriller on the lines of Manhattan Melodrama *and* Angels with Dirty Faces.
w Richard Murphy *novel* *The Chair for Martin Rome* by Henry Helseth *d* *Robert Siodmak* *ph* *Lloyd Ahern* *m* Alfred Newman
☆ Victor Mature, Richard Conte, Mimi Aguglia, Shelley Winters, Tommy Cook, Fred Clark, Debra Paget
'When the city cries in a movie, it's with the desolate wail of police sirens and with rain-streaked sidewalks; but most of all with poetic justification.' – *Paul Taylor, Time Out, 1980*

The Cry of the Owl: *see Le Cri de Hibou*

Cry Terror **
US 1958 96m bw
MGM/Andrew Stone, Virginia Stone
As security against ransom money being delivered, an airline bomber kidnaps a family.
Unabashed suspenser which screws panic situations as far as they will go and farther.
wd *Andrew Stone* *ph* Walter Strenge *m* Howard Jackson *ed* Virginia Stone
☆ James Mason, Rod Steiger, Inger Stevens, Neville Brand, Angie Dickinson, Kenneth Tobey, Jack Klugman, Jack Kruschen
'The story is launched with dizzying speed and suspenseful pursuit that hardly relaxes until the final frame.' – *Variety*

Cry the Beloved Country *
GB 1951 96m bw
London Films (Alan Paton)
US title: *African Fury*
In South Africa, a white farmer and a black preacher find friendship through linked family tragedies.
Well-intentioned, earnest, rather high-flown racial drama.
w Alan Paton *novel* Alan Paton *d* Zoltan Korda *ph* Robert Krasker *m* Raymond Gallois-Montbrun
☆ Canada Lee, Sidney Poitier, Charles Carson, Charles McRae, Joyce Carey, Geoffrey Keen, Michael Goodliffe, Edric Connor
† Screenwriter John Howard Lawson was excluded from the credits of the film because he was blacklisted at the time.

Cry Vengeance
US 1954 81m bw
Allied Artists (Lindsley Parsons)
An innocent man is released from jail and seeks vengeance against the man who framed him and killed his wife and child.
Adequate toughie with no particular flair.
w Warren Douglas, George Bricker *d* Mark Stevens *ph* William Sickner *m* Paul Dunlap
☆ Mark Stevens, Martha Hyer, Skip Homeier, Joan Vohs, Douglas Kennedy

Cry Wolf
US 1947 83m bw
Warner (Henry Blanke)
A widow claims her husband's estate and finds his mysterious uncle very difficult to deal with…
Rather obvious old dark house mystery with a not very interesting solution, all relying too heavily on star performances.
w Catherine Turney *novel* Marjorie Carleton *d* Peter Godfrey *ph* Carl Guthrie *m* Franz Waxman
☆ Barbara Stanwyck, Errol Flynn, Geraldine Brooks, Richard Basehart, Helene Thimig

Cry Wolf
GB 1980 31m bw
Picture Partnership/Paramount
A scientist accidentally imbibes a canine serum and turns into a werewolf.
Flattish comedy which is mainly indistinguishable from the low-budget British shockers it satirizes, but manages a few good moments.
w Stan Hey *d* Leszek Burzynski *ph* Robert Krasker
☆ Paul Maxwell, Rosalind Ayres, Stephen Greif

Cry-Baby
US 1990 85m DeLuxe
UIP/Imagine Entertainment (Rachel Talalay)
A delinquent rock 'n' roll singer falls in love with an upper-class girl.
Kitsch celebration of the early 60s that soon grows tedious.
wd John Waters *ph* David Insley *m* Patrick Williams *pd* Vincent Peranio *ad* Delores Deluxe *ed* Janice Hampton
☆ Johnny Depp, Amy Locane, Susan Tyrrell, Polly Bergen, Iggy Pop, Ricki Lake, Traci Lords, Kim McGuire, Darren E. Burrows

Crying Freeman
France/Canada 1995 101m CFI color Super 35
Davis/Ozla/Brian Yuzna/Toei (Samuel Hadida, Brian Yuzna)
An enigmatic hitman, who weeps for his victims, travels to Vancouver to eliminate a Japanese gangster and a female artist who witnessed his murders.
Slick transfer to live action of a comic-book hero, with some stylish action sequences.
w Christophe Gans, Thierry Casals *comic book* Kazuo Koike, Ryoichi Ikegami *d* Christophe Gans *ph* Thomas Burstyn *m* Pat O'Hearn *pd* Douglas Higgins, Alex McDowell *ed* David Wu, Chris Roth
☆ Mark Dacascos, Julie Condra Douglas, Tcheky Karyo, Rae Dawn Chong, Byron Mann, Masaya Kato, Yoko Shimada, Mako
'A satisfying mix of smooth Asian chop-socky and smooth Western tech wizardry.' – *Variety*

Crying Freeman, Chapter 1: Portrait of a Killer (dubbed)
Japan 1992 50m colour
Toei (Shoko Takahashi, Akira Sasaki, Tomirou Kuriyama)
A 29-year-old Japanese artist who witnessed a Japanese assassin, working for the Chinese Mafia, kill three people awaits her own death at his hands.
A gore-filled cartoon for an adult audience that enjoys indifferent animation, sex and violence.
w Higashi Shimizu *d* Daisuke Nishio *ph* Hisao Shirai *m* Hiroaki Yoshino *ad* Mitsutaka Nakamura *ed* Shigeru Nishiyama
☆ Featuring Voices of Stephen Tremblay, Edita Brychta, Vincent Marzello, Bob Sherman, Burt Kwouk

Crying Freeman, Chapter 2: The Enemy Within (dubbed)
Japan 1992 50m colour
Toei (Shoko Takahashi, Akira Sasaki, Tomirou Kuriyama)
A Japanese hitman, who cries whenever he kills, suspects that the élite corps of killers he commands for the Chinese Mafia contains a traitor.
Another gore-filled cartoon for an adult audience that enjoys indifferent animation, sex and violence.
w Kazuo Kioke, Toichi Ikegami *d* Nishizawa Nobukata *ph* Yoshijuki Tamagawa *m* Hiroaki Yoshino *ed* Shigeru Nishiyama
☆ Featuring Voices of Stephen Tremblay, Edita Brychta, Vincent Marzello, John Baddeley

Crying Freeman, Chapter 3: Retribution (dubbed)
Japan 1992 50m colour
Toei (Akira Sasaki, Tomirou Kuriyama)
Crying Freeman finds himself confronting a group of African terrorists, while his wife gains a mystical sword.
The mixture as before: rudimentary animation and comic strip heroics, featuring much sudden and bloody death.
w Kazuo Koike, Toichi Ikegami *d* Johei Matsuura *ph* Yoichi Takanashi *m* Hiroaki Yoshino *ad* Tomoshi Urushibana *ed* Shigeru Nishiyama
☆ Featuring Voices of Stephen Tremblay, Edita Brychta, John Baddeley, Rosemary Miller, Deborah Weston

'Desire Is A Danger Zone.'
The Crying Game ***
GB 1992 112m Metrocolor Panavision
Palace/Channel 4/Eurotrustees/NDF/British Screen (Stephen Woolley)
An IRA gunman makes friends with a black British soldier who is taken hostage and, after the soldier's death, goes to London where he falls for the man's lover.
Complex and brilliantly successful examination of matters of identity and gender.
wd *Neil Jordan* *ph* Ian Wilson *m* Anne Dudley *pd* Jim Clay *ed* Kant Pan
☆ *Stephen Rea, Miranda Richardson, Forest Whitaker, Jim Broadbent*, Ralph Brown, Adrian Dunbar, *Jaye Davidson*, Tony Slattery
'An astonishingly good and daring film.' – *Variety*
'Every so often, a "little" film hits the collective heart. *The Crying Game* is one of these, because it shows that a man is never so naked as when he reveals his secret self.' – *Richard Corliss, Time*
Neil Jordan (as writer)
best picture; Neil Jordan (as director); Kant Pan; Stephen Rea; Jaye Davidson

Crypt of the Living Dead
US 1972 83m Metrocolor Scope
Golden Era/Coast Industries (Lou Shaw)
GB title: *Vampire Woman*
A female vampire comes back to life after her tomb is opened.
Uninteresting low-budget horror that fails to raise a shiver.
w Lou Shaw *d* Ray Danton *ph* Juan Gelpi *m* Phillip Lambro *ad* Juan Alberto *ed* David Rawlins
☆ Andrew Prine, Mark Damon, Patty Sheppard, Teresa Gimpera, Ihsan Genik, Mariano Rey, Frank Brana
'A dismal sortie into sanguineous legend.' – *Sight and Sound*

The Crystal Ball *
US 1943 82m bw
UA/Richard Blumenthal
A failed beauty contestant becomes a fortune teller and is involved in a land swindle.
Pleasant comedy with fanciful moments, ending with a pie-throwing contest.
w Virginia Van Upp *d* Elliott Nugent *ph* Leo Tover *m* Victor Young
☆ Paulette Goddard, Ray Milland, Gladys George, Virginia Field, Cecil Kellaway, William Bendix, Ernest Truex

Crystal Heart
US 1987 103m Technicolor
New World/Izaro/Eagle (Carlosa Vasallo)
A young musician, who has to live isolated in a plastic bubble, falls in love with a rock singer.
Dull and sentimental romantic drama intercut with a succession of uninspired music videos of routine songs; its chief interest is in observing Tawny Kitaen's succession of curious hairstyles and outfits.
w Linda Shayne *story* Alberto Vazquez-Figueroa *d* Gil Bettman *ph* Alexander Ulloa *m* Joel Goldsmith *pd* Jose Maria Alarcon *ed* Nicholas Wentworth
☆ Tawny Kitaen, Lee Curreri, Lloyd Bochner, Simon Andreu, May Heatherly, Lagena Lookabill, Marina Saura

Cuba
US 1979 122m Technicolor
UA/Alex Winitsky, Arlene Sellers
Upper-crust characters are caught in Havana when the Castro revolution starts.
Aimless romantic melodrama which gets absolutely nowhere and might have been better played in the Casablanca vein.
w Charles Wood *d* Richard Lester *ph* David Watkin *m* Patrick Williams *pd* Gil Parrando
☆ Sean Connery, Brooke Adams, Jack Weston, Hector Elizondo, Denholm Elliott, Martin Balsam, Chris Sarandon

Cuba Si! *
France 1961 58m bw
Films de la Pléiade
A documentary on the Cuban revolution and Castro's rise to power.

Remarkable and influential at the time for its use of techniques which are now the commonplaces of television, this documentary still has its flashes of interest.
m E. G. Mantici, J. Calzada *ed* Eva Zora
wd/ph Chris Marker
'An eloquent, personal record of history in the making.' – *Georges Sadoul*

Cuban Love Song
US 1931 86m bw
MGM (Albert Lewin)
A marine on leave in Cuba falls in love; years later he returns to retrieve his illegitimate child, whose mother has died.
Pathetic musical melodrama which did not advance its singing star's film career.
w John Lynch *d* W. S. Van Dyke *ph* Harold Rosson *m* Charles Maxwell *m/ly* various
☆ Lawrence Tibbett, Lupe Velez, Jimmy Durante, Ernest Torrence, Karen Morley, Louise Fazenda
'Tibbett may be a sensation on the concert stage, but it's not the same in pictures.' – *Variety*

'Don't Look For A Reason...Look For A Way Out.'
Cube *
Canada 1997 90m colour
Trimark/Cineplex Odeon/Cube Libre (Mehra Meh, Betty Orr)
Six people find themselves lost in a dangerous maze of interlocking metal boxes.
Teasing low-budget science-fiction movie that makes the most of its puzzling qualities.
w Vincenzo Natali, Andre Bijelic, Graeme Manson *d* Vincenzo Natali *ph* Derek Rogers *m* Mark Korven *pd* Jasna Stefanovic *ed* John Sanders *sp* CORE Digital Pictures
☆ Maurice Dean, Nicole deBoer, Nicky Guadagni, David Hewlett, Wayne Robson, Andrew Miller, Julian Richings
'Brilliant set design and smart plotting are let down by pedestrian dialogue.' – *Ken Eisner, Variety*

A Cuckoo in the Nest *
GB 1933 85m bw
Gaumont (Ian Dalrymple, Angus MacPhail)
A newlywed husband is forced to spend a night at an inn with an old flame pretending to be his wife.
Classic Aldwych farce with the stage company in excellent form; directorial style on the stagey side.
w Ben Travers, A. R. Rawlinson *play* *Ben Travers* *d* Tom Walls *ph* Glen MacWilliams *ad* Alfred Junge *ed* Helen Lewis
☆ *Ralph Lynn, Tom Walls, Yvonne Arnaud, Mary Brough*, Veronica Rose, Gordon James, Cecil Parker, Roger Livesey, Robertson Hare
† Remade 1955 as *Fast and Loose*.

The Cuckoos
US 1930 90m bw (Technicolor sequences)
RKO
Two tramps become fortune tellers.
The most ambitiously staged, and probably the most popular of this team's gag marathons.
w Cy Woods *musical comedy* *The Ramblers* by Guy Bolton, *Harry Ruby, Bert Kalmar* *d* Paul Sloane
☆ Bert Wheeler, Robert Woolsey, Jobyna Howland, June Clyde, Hugh Trevor, Dorothy Lee
'It holds little between the laughs and doesn't need anything else.' – *Variety*

'Terror Has A New Name...'
Cujo
US 1983 91m CFI color
ITC/Sunn Classic/Taft (Daniel H. Blatt)
A St Bernard dog is bitten by a rabies-infected bat, and becomes a vicious killer.
Not much of a basis for a horror film, and this is not much of a horror film.
w Don Carlos Dunaway, Lauren Currier *novel* Stephen King *d* Lewis Teague *ph* Jan de Bont *m* Charles Bernstein *pd* Guy Comtois *ed* Neil Travis
☆ Dee Wallace, Daniel Hugh Kelly, Danny Pintauro, Ed Lauter, Christopher Stone

Cul de Sac
GB 1966 111m bw
Compton-Tekli (Gene Gutowski)
Two gangsters on the run take refuge in an old castle on a desolate Northumbrian island, but find their nemesis in the effeminate owner and his voluptuous wife.
Overlong, eccentric black comedy, more perplexing than entertaining.
w Roman Polanski, Gerard Brach *d* Roman Polanski *ph* Gilbert Taylor *m* Komeda
☆ *Lionel Stander*, Donald Pleasence, Jack MacGowran, Françoise Dorléac, William Franklyn, Robert Dorning, Renée Houston
'A voyeur's wallow in schizophrenia and murder to no point beyond sensation – but one could not deny the creative talent at work.' – *Judith Crist*

The Culpeper Cattle Company *
US 1972 92m DeLuxe
TCF (Paul A. Helmick)
A 16-year-old would-be cowboy joins a cattle trail but is shocked at the harsh realities of Western life.
Excellent moody photography helps to convince us that the old west was really like this, but the story is more brutal than interesting.
w Eric Bercovici, Gregory Prentiss *d* Dick Richards *ph* *Lawrence Edward Williams, Ralph Woolsey* *m* Tom Scott, Jerry Goldsmith
☆ Gary Grimes, Billy 'Green' Bush, Luke Askew, Bo Hopkins, Geoffrey Lewis, Wayne Sutherlin

Cult of the Cobra
US 1955 79m bw
Universal-International
Six GIs are cursed by the high priest of an Indian cobra cult. Back in New York, a mysterious woman brings about their deaths, and when the survivor kills a cobra, it turns into her.
Glossy but wholly unconvincing and unexciting non-horror potboiler.
w Jerry Davis, Cecil Maiden, Richard Collins *d* Francis D. Lyon *ph* Russell Metty *ed* Milton Carruth
☆ Faith Domergue, Richard Long, Marshall Thompson, Kathleen Hughes, Jack Kelly

'Buddhism is their philosophy. Soccer is their religion.'
The Cup **
Australia 1999 94m Fujicolor
Alliance/Palm/Coffee Stain (Malcolm Watson, Raymond Steiner)
original title: *Phörpa*
Two football-crazed teenage Tibetan monks persuade their abbot to allow them to raise money to buy a satellite dish so that they can watch the final of the World Cup.
An enjoyable and unexpected movie that allows audiences to see the odd ways of the West through other eyes.
wd Khyentse Norbu *ph* Paul Warren *m* Douglas Mills *pd* Raymond Steiner *ed* John Scott
☆ Jamyang Lodro (Orgyen), Orgyen Tobgyal (Geko), Neten Chokling (Lodo), Lama Chonjor (Abbot), Godu Lama (Old lama)
'Beautifully observed and exquistely played, this is one to treasure.' – *David Parkinson, Empire*
† The film uses a cast of real Buddhist monks and it is directed by a lama.

'No Winners In This Game.'
'A soldier from Israel, captured in the Lebanon, but his goal was to be at the...'
Cup Final
Israel 1992 110m colour
(Michael Sharfshstein)
original title: *G'mar Giviya*
An Israeli soldier finds common ground with his PLO captors in talk of football.
A story of coexistence that may mean more to Israeli audiences than others. It points out the similarities that exist between enemies, but does little else to advance one's understanding.
w Eyal Halfon *d* Eran Riklis *ph* Amnon Salomon *m* Raviv Gazit *ed* Anat Lubarsky
☆ Moshe Ivgi, Muhammed Bakri, Suheil Haddad
'Exciting, touching and politically even-handed.' – *Empire*

A Cup of Kindness
GB 1934 81m bw
Gaumont (Michael Balcon)
Young lovers marry despite parental disapproval on both sides.
Farcical updating of Romeo and Juliet; *it hasn't worn too well, but the stars are at their peak.*
w Ben Travers *play* Ben Travers *d* Tom Walls *ph* Phil Tannura *ad* Alfred Junge *ed* A. W. Roome
☆ Tom Walls, Ralph Lynn, Robertson Hare, Claude Hulbert, Dorothy Hyson, Eva Moore

Cupid in the Rough: see *Aggie Appleby Maker of Men*

Curdled
US 1996 88m DeLuxe
Miramax/A Band Apart/Tinderbox (John Maass, Raul Puig)
A maid, who works for a service that cleans up after murders, discovers the identity of a serial killer.
Interminable comedy thriller with a script that is too thin to sustain the joke for long.
w John Maass, Reb Braddock *d* Reb Braddock *ph* Steven Bernstein *m* Joseph Julian Gonzalez *pd* Sherman Williams *ed* Mallory Gottlieb
☆ William Baldwin, Angela Jones, Bruce Ramsay, Mel Gorham, Lois Chiles, Daisy Fuentes, Barry Corbin
'Would have been better off remaining the short film it was to begin with.' – *Variety*
† The film began life as a short whose subject matter then inspired part of Tarantino's *Pulp Fiction*; in turn, Tarantino backed its reworking as a feature.

The Cure ****
US 1917 20m approx bw silent
Mutual/Charles Chaplin
A dipsomaniac sent to a spa gets his booze mixed up with the spa water.
One of the funniest of the Chaplin shorts, with no pathos intervening (nor come to that much plot); it is simply a succession of balletic slapstick scenes of the highest order.
wd *Charles Chaplin* *ph* William C. Foster, Rollie Totheroh
☆ *Charles Chaplin*, Edna Purviance, Eric Campbell, Henry Bergman

The Cure *
GB 1950 18m bw
Richard and Betty Massingham
A health nut tries every possible remedy for lumbago.
Richard Massingham huffs and puffs in his endearing way through a short which is too long by far to be effective in his particular vein; but it does identify his particular persona.
wd Richard and Betty Massingham

'Two boys found a way to make one summer last a lifetime.'
The Cure
US 1995 98m DeLuxe
Polygram/Universal/Island (Mark Burg, Eric Eisner)
Two young boys go in search of a cure for AIDS, which one of them contracted through a blood transfusion.
An earnest, well-acted narrative of childhood friendship that is sabotaged by the implausibilities of its plot.
w Robert Kuhn *d* Peter Horton *ph* Andrew Dintenfass *m* David Grusin *pd* Armin Ganz *ed* Anthony Sherin, Saar Klein
☆ Joseph Mazzello, Brad Renfro, Bruce Davison, Annabella Sciorra, Diana Scarwid, Aeryk Egan
'Reeks of staple television dramatic fare and, even if it represents the zenith of the form, it's very much rooted in small-screen, earnest, low-key human emotion.' – *Leonard Klady, Variety*

The Cure for Love
GB 1949 98m bw
London Films (Robert Donat)
An ex-soldier goes home and tries to get married.
Thin Lancashire comedy which seemed an astonishing choice for Robert Donat, whose acting and direction are equally ill at ease.
w Robert Donat, Alexander Shaw, Albert Fennell *play* Walter Greenwood *d* Robert Donat *ph* Jack Cox *m* William Alwyn
☆ Robert Donat, Renée Asherson, Dora Bryan, Marjorie Rhodes, Charles Victor, Thora Hird, Gladys Henson
'Antediluvian regional farce.' – *MFB*

The Cure Show
GB 1993 96m bw/colour
Rank/Fiction/Polygram Video (Steve Swartz)
Documentary on the British rock group The Cure performing at two concerts in Detroit in July 1992.
A concert recording strictly for fans of the group, with the cameras staying at a distance from the on-stage action, revealing nothing more than could be seen from the auditorium.
d Aubrey Powell, Leroy Bennett *ph* Jeff Zimmerman *ed* Ian Mallett, Liam Hall
'So depressingly ordinary – it could fill a late night TV slot and attract no reaction – that it is hard to see why it was made at all.' – *Sight and Sound*

The Curious Doctor Humpp: see *La Venganza Del Sexo*

'Big laughs come in small packages.'
Curly Sue
US 1991 101m Technicolor
Warner (John Hughes)
A con man and a nine-year-old orphan win the heart of a successful woman lawyer.
Gruesomely sentimental and manipulative comedy.
wd John Hughes *ph* Jeffrey Kimball *m* Georges Delerue *pd* Doug Kraner *ed* Peck Prior, Harvey Rosenstock
☆ James Belushi, Kelly Lynch, Alisan Porter, John Getz
'With its mix of childish gags and shameless melodrama, *Curly Sue* could make off with a tidy box-office take.' – *Variety*
'John Hughes here graduates from the most successful comedy in film history to scripting and directing a large piece of non-biodegradable tosh.' – *Nigel Andrews, Financial Times*
'Lacks the charm, good jokes or vigour to hide its contrivances.' – *Geoff Brown, The Times*

Curly Top *
US 1935 78m bw
Fox (Darryl F. Zanuck, Winfield Sheehan)
An orphan waif is adopted by a playboy, and not only sets his business right but fixes his romantic interest in her sister.
Archetypal Temple vehicle, a loose remake of Daddy Longlegs.
w Patterson McNutt, Arthur Beckhard *d* Irving Cummings *ph* John Seitz *m/ly* Ray Henderson, Ted Koehler, Edward Heyman, Irving Caesar
☆ *Shirley Temple*, John Boles, Rochelle Hudson, Jane Darwell, Rafaela Ottiano, Esther Dale, Arthur Treacher, Etienne Girardot
'Cinch b.o. for almost any house.' – *Variety*

Curry and Pepper
Hong Kong 1990 96m colour
Movie Impact (Ho-Sun Chan)
Two irresponsible cops fall out as partners when both fall for a glamorous TV reporter.
Crudely comic and violent action movie, which is closer to the Three Stooges or Police Academy *than to John Woo, and all the worse for that.*
w James Yuen *d* Blacky Ko (Ko Shuo Liang) *ph* Andrew Lau *m* Richard Lo *ad* Ben Luk *ed* Chan Ki Hop
☆ Jacky Cheung, Ann Bridgewater, Eric Tsang, Blacky Ko, Chow Mei-Yan, Barry Wong

The Curse: see *Xala*

Curse of Dark Shadows: see *House of Dark Shadows*

'The creature created by man is forgotten by nature!'
The Curse of Frankenstein **
GB 1957 83m Eastmancolor
Warner/Hammer (Anthony Hinds)
A lurid revamping of the 1931 *Frankenstein*, this time with severed eyeballs and a peculiarly unpleasant and uncharacterized creature, all in gory colour.
It set the trend in nasty horrors from which we have all suffered since, and launched Hammer Studios on a long and profitable career of charnelry. But it did have a gruesome sense of style.
w *Jimmy Sangster* *d* *Terence Fisher* *ph* Jack Asher *m* *James Bernard* *ad* Ted Marshall *ed* James Needs

☆ *Peter Cushing, Christopher Lee*, Hazel Court, Robert Urquhart, Valerie Gaunt, Noel Hood

'Among the half-dozen most repulsive films I have encountered in the course of some 10,000 miles of film reviewing. Indeed, at the moment, I can only think of two which sickened me more.' – *C. A. Lejeune*

'A tender tale of terror!'

The Curse of the Cat People *

US 1944 70m bw

RKO (Val Lewton)

A child is haunted by the spirit of the cat people.

A gentle film ordered by the studio as a sequel to Cat People *but turned by Lewton into a fantasy of childhood. Slow to start but finally compelling, it's a pleasing and unusual film in a minor key.*

w De Witt Bodeen *d* Robert Wise, Gunther von Fritsch *ph* Nicholas Musuraca *m* Roy Webb

☆ Kent Smith, Simone Simon, Jane Randolph, Julia Dean, Ann Carter, Elizabeth Russell

'Full of the poetry and danger of childhood.' – *James Agee*

'A clumsy coming together of unrealized ideas, gothic effects, and stiff, dull acting.' – *New Yorker, 1979*

Curse of the Crimson Altar

GB 1968 89m Eastmancolor

Tigon/AIP (Tony Tenser)

aka: *The Crimson Cult*

Witchcraft, diabolism and mystery in an English country house.

A derivative, muddled scribble of a horror film, making no sense and wasting much talent.

w Mervyn Haisman, Henry Lincoln *d* Vernon Sewell *ph* John Coquillon *m* Peter Knight

☆ Boris Karloff, Christopher Lee, Rupert Davies, Mark Eden, Barbara Steele, Michael Gough

Curse of the Demon: see *Night of the Demon*

The Curse of the Ellanbys: see *She Wolf of London*

'Entombed for eons – turned to stone – seeking women, women, women!'

Curse of the Faceless Man

US 1958 67m bw

Vogue/United Artists

An encrusted man, found in the earth near Pompeii, is revived and goes on the rampage, but is eventually dissolved by water.

Absurd chiller with the saving grace of not taking itself seriously.

w Jerome Bixby *d* Edward L. Cahn

☆ Richard Anderson, Elaine Edwards, Adele Mara, Gar Moore, Felix Locher

'Love stings.'

The Curse of the Jade Scorpion

US 2001 101m Technicolor

DreamWorks/VCLGravier (Letty Aronson)

In 1940, an insurance investigator and an efficiency expert become jewel thieves under the influence of a stage hypnotist.

Mild comedy in the style of yesteryear's crime melodramas; pleasant in a semi-soporific way, it is nevertheless a disappointment from its writer-director.

wd Woody Allen *ph* Zhao Fei *pd* Santo Loquasto *ed* Alisa Lepselter *cos* Suzanne McCabe

☆ Woody Allen (CW Briggs), Dan Aykroyd (Chris Magruder), Elizabeth Berkley (Jill), Helen Hunt (Betty Ann Fitzgerald), Brian Markinson (Al), Wallace Shawn (George Bond), David Ogden Stiers (Voltan), Charlize Theron (Laura Kensington)

'A charming trifle that flatters the good taste of everyone involved.' – *A. O. Scott, New York Times*

Curse of the Living Corpse

US 1963 78m bw

TCF (Del Tenney)

A millionaire vows to return and kill all his relatives if he is buried alive, which he is...

Gothic cheapie made in Stamford, Connecticut, where they have little experience of such things.

wd Del Tenney

☆ Roy Scheider, Candace Hilligoss

'Half bone, half bandage ... all bloodcurdling terror!'

Curse of the Mummy's Tomb

GB 1964 80m Technicolor Techniscope

Columbia/Swallow/Hammer (Michael Carreras)

An Egyptian mummy taken to London goes on the rampage, and meets its own wicked brother who has been cursed to eternal life.

Absurd farrago which takes too long to set up its plot and then finds little to do with its monster.

w Henry Younger (Michael Carreras) *d* Michael Carreras *ph* Otto Heller *m* Carlo Martelli *ad* Bernard Robinson *ed* James Needs, Eric Boyd-Perkins

☆ Ronald Howard, Terence Morgan, *Fred Clark*, Jeanne Roland, George Pastell, Jack Gwillim, John Paul

Curse of the Pink Panther

GB 1983 110m Technicolor Panavision

MGM-UA/Titan/Jewel (Blake Edwards, Gerald T. Nutting)

Inspector Clouseau has disappeared, and Dreyfus selects the world's worst detective to replace him.

Unspeakably awful attempt at prolonging a series whose star died two episodes ago. Crude, tasteless and unfunny throughout.

w Blake Edwards, Geoffrey Edwards *d* Blake Edwards *ph* Dick Bush *m* Henry Mancini *pd* Peter Mullins

☆ Ted Wass, Joanna Lumley, Herbert Lom, David Niven, Robert Wagner, Capucine, Harvey Korman, Burt Kwouk

'Another bout of film-making as grave robbing.' – *Sight and Sound*

'The ultimate version of deadpan humour ... the most tedious of the whole series.' – *Richard Combs, MFB*

Curse of the Undead

US 1959 79m bw

Universal-International

A black-clad stranger in a Western town turns out to be a vampire of Spanish origin.

Abysmal attempt to substitute Wyoming for Transylvania; more skill and sensitivity were required.

wd Edward Dein

☆ Michael Pate, Eric Fleming, Kathleen Crowley, John Hoyt

'He had but one body – yet lived with two souls!'

The Curse of the Werewolf

GB 1961 92m Technicolor

U-I/Hotspur/Hammer (Anthony Hinds)

A beggar rapes a servant girl and their offspring grows up to be a werewolf.

Doleful Hammer horror in a Spanish setting, with an absurd but predictable plot and a lack of sympathy for its fancy, hairy hero.

w John Elder (Anthony Hinds) *novel The Werewolf of Paris* by Guy Endore *d* Terence Fisher *ph* Arthur Grant *m* Benjamin Frankel *ad* Bernard Robinson *ed* James Needs, Alfred Cox

☆ Oliver Reed, Clifford Evans, Catherine Feller, Yvonne Romain, Anthony Dawson, Richard Wordsworth, Warren Mitchell, Peter Sallis

The Curse of the Wraydons

GB 1946 94m bw

Bushey

The Victorian story of Spring-heeled Jack, here depicted as a mad inventor out for revenge.

Too long and stagey to be one of its star's better barnstormers, especially as by this time his girth made the notion of his springing about somewhat hilarious.

w Michael Barringer *d* Victor M. Gover

☆ Tod Slaughter, Bruce Seton, Gabriel Toyne

Curtain Call *

US 1940 63m bw

RKO

Two Broadway producers buy an awful play in order to get even with a temperamental star, but she likes it.

Amusing second feature, a kind of flashforward to The Producers. *A reprise the following year,* Footlight Fever, *did not work.*

w Dalton Trumbo *d* Frank Woodruff *ph* Russell Metty *m* Roy Webb

☆ *Alan Mowbray, Donald MacBride*, Helen Vinson, Barbara Read, John Archer

Curtain Call at Cactus Creek *

US 1949 83m Technicolor

U-I (Robert Arthur)

GB title: *Take the Stage*

A travelling repertory company in the old west exposes a gang of bank robbers.

Cheerful minor comedy with good pace and amusing burlesques of old melodramas.

w Oscar Brodney *d* Charles Lamont *ph* Russell Metty *m* Walter Scharf

☆ Donald O'Connor, Gale Storm, Eve Arden, Vincent Price, Walter Brennan, Chick Chandler

Curtain Up *

GB 1952 85m bw

Rank/Constellation (Robert Garrett)

A seaside repertory company runs into trouble when the producer is at loggerheads with the author of next week's play.

Fairly amusing farce which has now acquired historical value for the light it throws on the old weekly reps.

w Michael Pertwee, Jack Davies *play On Monday Next* by Philip King *d* Ralph Smart *ph* Stanley Pavey *m* Malcolm Arnold

☆ *Margaret Rutherford*, Robert Morley, Olive Sloane, Joan Rice, Charlotte Mitchell, Kay Kendall, Liam Gaffney, Michael Medwin

Custer of the West

US 1967 146m Technicolor Super Technirama 70

Cinerama/Security (Louis Dolivet, Philip Yordan, Irving Lerner)

After the Civil War, Custer is offered a cavalry command, becomes disillusioned, and is massacred with his troops at Little Big Horn.

Gloomily inaccurate spectacular with pauses for Cinerama carnival thrills and dour bits of melodrama.

w Bernard Gordon, Julian Halevy (Julian Zimet) *d* Robert Siodmak *ph* Cecilio Paniagua *m* Bernardo Segall

☆ Robert Shaw, Mary Ure, Robert Ryan, Jeffrey Hunter, Ty Hardin, Lawrence Tierney, Kieron Moore

† Screenwriter Zimet used a pseudonym because he was blacklisted at the time.

'They just have to finish the film... before it finishes them.'

Cut

Australia/Germany/US 2000 79m colour

Beyond/MBP/Mushroom/SAFC (Martin Fabinyi, Bill Bennett, Jennifer Bennett)

Film students decide to complete an abandoned low-budget slasher movie that appears to be cursed: those who have tried to finish it have been murdered.

Brutal and bloody horror that sticks to the usual slasher movie conventions, and does so without any subtlety.

w Dave Warner *d* Kimble Rendall *ph* David Foreman *m* Guy Gross *pd* Steven Jones-Evans *ed* Henry Dangar

☆ Molly Ringwald (Vanessa Turnbill/Chloe), Jessica Napier (Raffy), Simon Bossell (Bobby), Sarah Kants (Hester Ryan), Kylie Minogue (Hilary), Geoff Revell (Lossman), Stephen Curry (Rick), Matt Russell (Paulie), Frank Roberts (Brad/Scarman)

A Cut Above: see *Gross Anatomy*

Cutter and Bone

US 1981 109m Technicolor

United Artists/Gurian

GB title: *Cutter's Way*

A California failure witnesses the aftermath of murder, and with a crippled ex-Vietnam veteran turns detective.

Heavy-going melodrama which tries very hard to be something more than a thriller, and manages only to imply that the world stinks; so it might as well have stuck to Philip Marlowe.

w Jeffrey Alan Fiskin *novel* Newton Thornburg *d* Ivan Passer *ph* Jordan Cronenweth *m* Jack Nitzsche *ed* Caroline Ferriol

☆ Jeff Bridges, John Heard, Lisa Eichhorn, Ann Dusenberry, Stephen Elliott, Nina Van Pallandt

Cutter's Way: see *Cutter and Bone*

Cutthroat Island

US 1995 93m Technicolor Panavision, Technovision

Guild/Carolco/Forge/Canal (Renny Harlin, Joel B. Michaels, Laurence Mark, James Gorman)

Determined to beat her dastardly uncle, a female pirate goes in search of buried treasure with the aid of a literate slave.

Dull and confused action film that swiftly sinks with all hands lost.

w Robert King, Marc Norman *story* Michael Frost Beckner, James Gorman, Bruce A. Evans, Raynold Gideon *d* Renny Harlin *ph* Peter Levy *m* John Debney *pd* Norman Garwood *ed* Frank J. Urioste, Ralph E. Winters

☆ Geena Davis, Matthew Modine, Frank Langella, Maury Chaykin, Patrick Malahide, Stan Shaw, Rex Linn, Harris Yulin

'This sort of film gives excitement a bad name.' – *Derek Malcolm, Guardian*

'A hoary pastiche of pirate movies of old, tricked out in cast-off clichés (inscrutable maps, monkey sidekicks, quicksand) and groaning under the strain of being driven so hard (breathless chases, an endless final battle), it is a sorry hulk of a film.' – *Leslie Felperin, Sight and Sound*

Cutting Class

US 1989 91m colour

April (Donald R. Beck, Rudy Cohen)

An axe murderer terrorises a high school.

Inadequate horror spoof for insomniacs.

w Steve Slavkin *d* Rospo Pallenberg *ph* Avraham Karpick *m* Jill Fraser *pd* Richard Sherman *ed* Bill Butler, Natan Zahavi

☆ Donovan Leitch (Brian Woods), Jill Schoelen (Paula Carson), Brad Pitt (Dwight Ingalls), Roddy McDowall (Mr Dante), Martin Mull (William Carson III), Brenda Lynn Klemme (Colleen), Mark Barnet (Gary)

'The King Of The Rink Is About To Meet America's Ice Queen.'

The Cutting Edge

US 1992 110m DeLuxe

UIP/MGM/Interscope (Ted Field, Karen Murphy, Robert W. Cort)

A tough former ice-hockey player becomes the partner of a spoiled and wealthy figure-skater.

Predictable romantic teen movie of winning against the odds.

w Tony Gilroy *d* Paul M. Glaser *ph* Elliot Davis *m* Patrick Williams *pd* David Gropman *ed* Michael E. Polakow

☆ D. B. Sweeney, Moira Kelly, Roy Dotrice, Terry O'Quinn, Dwier Brown, Chris Benson, Kevin Peeks, Barry Flatman

Cybèle ou les Dimanches de Ville d'Avry: see *Sundays and Cybèle*

Cyberjack

Canada/Japan 1995 96m colour

Catalyst/Fuji Eight (John A. Curtis)

US title: *Virtual Assassin*

An ex-cop turned janitor foils a criminal's attempt to steal a super-virus.

Routine low-budget science fiction, substituting action for characterization.

w Eric Poppen, John A. Curtis *d* Robert Lee *ph* Allan Trow *m* George Blondheim *pd* Richard Paris, Linda del Rosario *ed* Derek Whelan *sp* Paller Special Effects, Magic Camera Co.

☆ Michael Dudikoff, Brion James, Suki Kaiser, Jon Cuthbert, James Thom

'The acting's not much, and the script is notably lacking in wit, but the set-in-the-near-future saga looks way better than its $2 million budget.' – *Ken Eisner, Variety*

† The movie was released direct to video.

'He's the first hero of the 21st century.'

Cyborg

US 1989 85m colour

Cannon/Golan-Globus

A martial arts expert accompanies a female cyborg, holding information to save mankind, across post-apocalyptic America.

Charmless, cliché-packed action movie, carrying the explicit message that violence is good for you.

w Kitty Chalmers *d* Albert Pyun *ph* Philip Alan Waters *m* Kevin Bassinson *pd* Douglas Leonard *ed* Rozanne Zingale, Scott Stevenson
☆ Jean-Claude Van Damme, Deborah Richter, Vincent Klyn, Alex Daniels, Rolf Muller, Jackson Pinckney, Dayle Haddon

'He was programmed to kill ... Nobody can stop him.'

Cyborg Cop
US 1993 93m colour
Nu Image/Nu World (Danny Lerner)

An ex-cop goes to the rescue of his brother, who has been captured and turned into a killer cyborg by a mad millionaire drug dealer on a Caribbean island.
Dim standard robot action fodder, remarkable only for its violent, cliché-ridden plot and dialogue.
w Greg Latter *d* Sam Firstenberg *ph* Joseph Wein *m* Paul Fishman *pd* John Rosewarne *ed* Alan Patillo
☆ David Bradley, Todd Jensen, Alonna Shaw, Rufus Swart, John Rhys-Davies
'Some effective special effects make this watchable trash' – *Sight and Sound*

Cyborg Cop II
US 1994 97m colour
New World

A cop battles with a pyschotic killer who is turned into a cyborg and decides to wipe out the world.
A remake with a similar plot to the original film, and even less watchable this time around.
w Jon Stevens *d* Sam Firstenberg *ph* Joseph Wein *m* Bob Mithoff *ed* Marcus Manton
☆ David Bradley, Morgan Hunter, Jill Pierce
'Low budget schlock, directed without grace and displaying the offensive sexist exploitation which gave the horror genre such a bad reputation in the 70s.' – *Sight and Sound*

Cyclo **
France/Vietnam 1995 129m colour
Entertainment/Lazannec/Lumière/La Sept/La SFP (Christophe Rossignon)

original title: *Xich Lo*
After a pedicab driver has his vehicle stolen, his employer recruits him as a member of a criminal gang involved in robbery and drug-dealing.
A lovingly detailed drama of street life and the way in which old cultural values are eroded by modern commercial pressures.
w Nguyen Trung Binh, Tran Anh Hung *d Tran Anh Hung ph Benoit Delhomme m* Ton That Tiet *ad* Daniel Zalay *ed* Nicole Dedieu, Claude Ronzeau
☆ Le Van Loc, Tony Leung, Tran Nu Yen Khe, Nguyen Nhu Quynh, Nguyen Hoang Phuc, Ngo Vu Quang Hai
'A remarkable film, superbly performed, shot and designed with real distinction.' – *Derek Malcolm, Guardian*
† It won the Golden Lion as best film at the 1995 Venice Film Festival.

The Cyclops
US 1956 65m bw
B and H (Bert I. Gordon)
Explorers in Mexico find animals turned by radiation into monsters, plus a one-eyed 25-foot-tall human.
Modest monster movie, quite palatable of its kind.
wd Bert I. Gordon *ph* Ira Morgan *m* Albert Glasser
☆ James Craig, Lon Chaney Jnr, Gloria Talbott, Tom Drake

Cynara **
US 1932 78m bw
Samuel Goldwyn
A London barrister has an affair with a young girl who commits suicide when he goes back to his wife.
Solidly carpentered, effective star vehicle of the old school, now dated but preserving its dignity.
w Frances Marion, Lynn Starling *novel An Imperfect Lover* by Robert Gore Brown *play* Cynara by H. M. Harwood, *Robert Gore Brown d* King Vidor *ph* Ray June *md* Alfred Newman *ad* Richard Day
☆ *Ronald Colman*, Kay Francis, Phyllis Barry, *Henry Stephenson*, Paul Porcasi
'The values it involves are wholly unlike those which US audiences are usually called upon to comprehend.' – *Time*
† The film's title comes from Ernest Dowson's lines: 'I have been faithful to thee, Cynara, in my fashion.'

Cynthia
US 1947 98m bw
MGM (Edwin H. Knopf)
GB title: *The Rich Full Life*
An over-protected girl finds an outlet in music and her parents finally allow her to lead her own life.
An overlong domestic drama in which thin writing and acting are backed by unsound psychology.
w Harold Buchman, Charles Kaufman *play* Vina Delmar *d* Robert Z. Leonard *ph* Charles Schoenbaum *m* Bronislau Kaper
☆ Elizabeth Taylor, George Murphy, Mary Astor, S. Z. Sakall, James Lydon, Gene Lockhart, Spring Byington

Cyrano de Bergerac *
US 1950 112m bw
Stanley Kramer

In the 17th century a long-nosed poet, philosopher and buffoon writes letters enabling a friend to win the lady he loves himself.
The classic romantic verse play does not take kindly to a hole-in-corner black-and-white production, but at the time it was lapped up as a daring cultural breakthrough.
w Brian Hooker *play* Edmond Rostand *d* Michael Gordon *ph* Franz Planer *m* Dimitri Tiomkin
☆ *José Ferrer*, Mala Powers, William Prince, Morris Carnovsky, Ralph Clanton, Virginia Farmer, Edgar Barrier, Elena Verdugo
'Vigorous, respectful, full of lively movement, and pictorially well-composed.' – *C. A. Lejeune*
José Ferrer

Cyrano de Bergerac ***
France 1990 138m colour
Hachette Première/Camera One/Films A2/D.D. Productions/UGC (Rene Cleitman, Michael Seydoux)

A dashing soldier and noted duellist, handicapped by his long nose, helps a handsome friend make love to the woman he adores from afar.
Exuberant version of the romantic French classic, using the rhymed couplets of the original. The English subtitles, in a rhyming translation by Anthony Burgess, are a distraction, though.
w Jean-Paul Rappeneau, Jean-Claude Carrière *play* Edmond Rostand *d Jean-Paul Rappeneau ph Pierre Lhomme m* Jean-Claude Petit *ad* Ezio Frigerio *ed* Noëlle Boisson
☆ *Gérard Depardieu*, Anne Brochet, Vincent Perez, Jacques Weber, Roland Bertin, Philippe Morier-Genoud, Philippe Volter, Pierre Maguelon
'A near-perfect balance of verbal and visual flamboyance.' – *Variety*
'Cyrano? Bravo!' – *Le Monde*
Gérard Depardieu; best foreign film; best art direction; best costume design; best make-up
Pierre Lhomme; Jean-Claude Petit

Czar of the Slot Machines: see *King of Gamblers*

Czarina: see *A Royal Scandal*

Czlowiek Z Marmur: see *Man of Marble*

Czlowiek Z Zelaza: see *Man of Iron*

D2: The Mighty Ducks
US 1994 106m Astrocolor
Walt Disney (Jon Avnet, Jordan Kerner)

A coach gathers together a group of misfits and moulds them into an ice-hockey team to compete in the Junior Goodwill Games.
A lacklustre sequel of little interest to anyone.
w Steven Brill *d* Sam Weisman *ph* Mark Irwin *m* J. A. C. Redford *ed* John F. Link, Eric A. Sears
☆ Emilio Estevez, Kathryn Erbe, Michael Tucker, Jan Rubes, Carsten Norgaard, Maria Ellingsen, Joshua Jackson
'A pretty sorry follow-up.' – *Variety*
† It is a sequel to *The Mighty Ducks* (qv).

D3: Mighty Ducks
US 1996 104m Technicolor
Buena Vista/Disney (Jordan Kerner, Jon Avnet)

A hockey team gain scholarships to a snobbish private school.
Slight and sentimental comedy in which tedium sets in early.
w Steven Brill, Jim Burnstein *d* Ron Lieberman *ph* David Hennings *m* J. A. C. Redford *pd* Steven Storer *ed* Patrick Lussier, Colleen Halsey
☆ Emilio Estevez, Jeffrey Nordling, David Selby, Heidi Kling, Joshua Jackson, Joss Ackland
'This amazingly resilient film franchise continues to be entertaining in a shamelessly manipulative way.' – *Leonard Klady, Variety*

D. C. Cab
US 1983 99m Technicolor
RKO-Universal (Topper Carew)

GB title: *Street Fleet*
Cab drivers for a run-down Washington company capture kidnappers.
Brainless extravaganza with aspirations somewhere between Taxi *and* Carry On.
wd Joel Schumacher *ph* Dean Cundey, Ron Van Nostrand *m* Giorgio Moroder *pd* John Lloyd *ed* David Blewitt
☆ Mr T, Max Gail, Adam Baldwin, Charlie Barnett, Gary Busey, Gloria Gifford
'Artificial energy used to bolster wretched material.' – *Steve Jenkins, MFB*

The DI
US 1957 106m bw
Warner/Mark VII (Jack Webb)
A tough marine drill instructor takes a special interest in a backward member of his platoon.
Noisy recruiting poster heroics in which the producer gives himself a loud but boring part. The drill sequences are well done, but the film is overlong and repetitive.
w James Lee Barrett *d* Jack Webb *ph* Edward Colman *m* David Buttolph
☆ Jack Webb, Don Dubbins, Jackie Loughery, Lin McCarthy, Monica Lewis

DNA
US 1996 93m colour
InterLight (Patrick D. Choi, Nile Niami)

A doctor's discovery in Borneo is stolen by a power-crazed genetic scientist who uses it to bring back to life a long-dead monster.
Undemanding action fare in a jungle setting, with borrowings from many horrors, from King Kong *to* Alien *and* Predator.
w Nick Davis *d* William Mesa *ph* Gerry Lively *m* Christopher L. Stone *pd* Charles Wood *ed* Edward R. Abroms
☆ Mark Dacascos, Jürgen Prochnow, Robin McKee, Roger Aaron Brown, John H. Brennan, Thomas Taus Jnr

D.O.A. **
US 1950 83m bw
UA/Leo C. Popkin

The victim of a slow poison tracks down his own killer.
Semi-classic suspense drama, sufficiently original to be remembered though the plot details become hazy.
w Russel Rouse, Clarence Greene (partly from a 1931 German film Der Mann der seinen Mörder Sucht) d Rudolph Maté *ph* Ernest Laszlo *m Dimitri Tiomkin*
☆ *Edmond O'Brien*, Pamela Britton, Luther Adler, Neville Brand, Beverly Campbell
† The title is a police abbreviation for 'dead on arrival'
†† Remade as *Colour Me Dead* (qv) and see below.

D.O.A.
US 1988 97m CFI color
Warner/Touchstone/Silver Screen Partners III (Ian Sander, Laura Ziskin)

A college professor, discovering that he has been poisoned, and with less than 48 hours to live, solves the mystery of his murder.
Ambitious but inept remake, lacking in suspense.
w Charles Edward Pogue *story* Charles Edward Pogue, Russel Rouse, Clarence Greene *d* Rocky Morton, Annabel Jankel *ph* Yuri Neyman *m* Chaz Jankel *pd* Richard Amend *ed* Michael R. Miller, Raja Gosnell
☆ Dennis Quaid, Meg Ryan, Charlotte Rampling, Daniel Stern, Jane Kaczmarek, Christopher Neame, Robin Johnson, Rob Knepper, Jay Patterson

D-Day the Sixth of June
US 1956 106m Eastmancolor Cinemascope
TCF (Charles Brackett)

On the way to invade France in 1944, a British colonel and an American captain reminisce about their love for the same woman.
Turgid war romance with some good action scenes and the usual hilarious Hollywood view of London. General effect very wooden.
w Ivan Moffat, Harry Brown *novel* Lionel Shapiro *d* Henry Koster *ph* Lee Garmes *m* Lyn Murray
☆ Robert Taylor, Richard Todd, Dana Wynter, Edmond O'Brien, John Williams, Jerry Paris, Richard Stapley
'Reminiscent of *Mrs Miniver* in style and feeling.' – *MFB*

'Survival is a killer'
D-Tox
US 2002 96m DeLuxe Panavision
UIP/Universal/KC Medien/Capella (Ric Kidney)

A heavy-drinking FBI agent, who is receiving treatment at a detox clinic, becomes convinced that one of the other patients is a serial killer.
Gruesome but ineffectual thriller with thin characterisation, stolid acting and a narrative littered with implausibilities.
w Ron L. Brinkerhoff, Patrick Kelly *novel Jitter Joint* by Howard Swindle *d* Jim Gillespie *ph* Dean Semler *m* John Powell, James McKee Smith, Geoff Zanelli *pd* Gary Wissner *ed* Steve Mirkovich
☆ Sylvester Stallone (Jake Malloy), Tom Berenger (Hank), Charles S. Dutton (Chuck Hendricks), Sean Patrick Flanery (Connor), Christopher Fulford (Frank Slater), Dina Meyer (Mary), Robert Patrick (Pete Noah), Robert Prosky (McKenzie), Courtney B. Vance (Willie Jones), Polly Walker (Jenny Munroe), Jeffrey Wright (Jaworski), Kris Kristofferson (Dr John Mitchell)
'Will somebody please put Sly Stallone's career out of its misery. Unplug the life support, sign whatever form it takes… I know a persistent vegetative state when I see one and this is it.' – *Donald Clarke, Irish Times*

Da **
US 1988 102m colour
Premier/Film Dallas/A. J. Corman-Sheen/Greenblatt/Auerbach (Julie Corman)

A playwright, returning to Ireland for his father's funeral, finds himself discussing life with his father's ghost.
An autobiographical work which runs deep with emotion.
w Hugh Leonard *play* Hugh Leonard *d* Matt Clark *ph* Alar Kivilo *m* Elmer Bernstein *pd* Frank Conway *ed* Nancy Nuttal Beyda
☆ *Barnard Hughes*, Martin Sheen, William Hickey, Doreen Hepburn, Karl Hayden, Hugh O'Conor, Ingrid Craigie, Joan O'Hara, Jill Doyle

Da Uomo a Uomo: see *Death Rides a Horse*

Da Yuebing: see *The Big Parade (1986)*

Daayraa: see *The Square Circle*

'Sometimes the greatest man you ever meet… is the first one.'
Dad
US 1989 118m DeLuxe
UIP/Universal/Amblin Entertainment (Joseph Stern, Gary David Goldberg)

A son helps his father face up to death.
Excessively sentimental family drama.
wd Gary David Goldberg *novel* William Wharton *ph* Jan Kiesser *m* James Horner *pd* Jack DeGovia *ed* Eric Sears
☆ Jack Lemmon, Ted Danson, Olympia Dukakis, Kathy Baker, Kevin Spacey, Ethan Hawke, Zakes Mokae, J. T. Walsh, Peter Michael Goetz
'Emotional exploitation at its most objectionable.' – *MFB*

Dad Rudd films: see *On Our Selection*

Dad Savage
GB 1997 104m Technicolor Super 35
Polygram/Sweet Child/Dad Savage (Gwynneth Lloyd, Robert Jones)

In Norfolk, a gangster attempts to discover which of his accomplices killed his son and tried to steal his buried loot.
Derivative, brutal thriller that would seem more at home in the United States than rural England; its narrative overload gets in the way of any suspense.
w Steven Williams *d* Betsan Morris Evans *ph* Gavin Finney *pd* Michael Carlin *ed* Guy Bensley
☆ Patrick Stewart, Kevin McKidd, Helen McCrory, Joe McFadden, Marc Warren, Jake Wood
'Truly awful … another nail in the British Film Industry's revival coffin.' – *Alan Jones, Film Review*

Daddy Day Care
US 2003 92m DeLuxe
Columbia/Revolution (John Davis, Matt Berenson, Wyck Godfrey)
An out-of-work advertising executive, who is forced to stay at home with his young son while his wife works, decides to open a day-care centre with a friend.
Woefully weak comedy with cute kids and unfunny adults.
w Geoff Rodkey *d* Steve Carr *ph* Steven Poster *m* David Newman *pd* Garreth Stover *ed* Christopher Greenbury;
☆ Eddie Murphy (Charlie Hinton), Jeff Garlin (Phil), Steve Zahn (Marvin), Regina King (Kim Hinton), Kevin Nealon (Bruce), Jonathan Katz (Mr Dan Kubitz), Siobhan Fallon Hogan (Peggy), Lisa Edelstein (Crispin's Mom), Anjelica Huston (Miss Gwyneth Harridan), Khamani Griffin (Ben Hinton)
'A comedy that would have to work harder even to justify the appellation uninspired.' – *Elvis Mitchell, New York Times*

Daddy Longlegs *
US 1931 80m bw
Fox
An orphan girl grows up to fall in love with her mysterious benefactor.
Cinderella-like romance, adequately adapted from a novel which became the classic American version of the January–May romance.
w Sonya Levien *novel* Jean Webster *d* Alfred Santell *ph* Lucien Andriot
☆ Janet Gaynor, Warner Baxter, Una Merkel, John Arledge, Claude Gillingwater, Louise Closser Hale
'A smash … one of those rare talkers with universal appeal.' – *Variety*
† Other versions were made in 1919 with Mary Pickford and Mahlon Hamilton, directed by Marshall Neilan; in 1935 disguised as *Curly Top* (qv) and in 1955 (see below).

Daddy Longlegs *
US 1955 126m Technicolor Cinemascope
TCF (Samuel G. Engel)

Overlong and unsuitably wide-screened musical version of a popular story (see above).
Generally clumsy and dispirited, but Astaire is always worth watching and a couple of the dances are well staged.
w Phoebe and Henry Ephron *d* Jean Negulesco *ph* Leon Shamroy *m* Alfred Newman *m/ly* Johnny Mercer
☆ *Fred Astaire*, Leslie Caron, *Fred Clark*, Thelma Ritter, Terry Moore, Charlotte Austin, Larry Keating
Alfred Newman; song 'Something's Gotta Give'

Daddy Nostalgie **
France 1990 106m Eastmancolor Panavision
Clea/Little Bear/Solyfic Eurisma (Adolphe Viezzi)

aka: *These Foolish Things*
A screenwriter returns home to be close to her invalid father.
Gently understated domestic drama.
w Colo Tavernier O'Hagan *d* Bertrand Tavernier *ph* Denis Lenoir *m* Antoine Duhamel *pd* Jean-Louis Poveda *ed* Ariane Boeglin
☆ *Dirk Bogarde*, Jane Birkin, Emmanuelle Bataille, Charlotte Kady, Michele Minns
'A miniature jewel of a film … acted and directed with great subtlety.' – *Variety*

Daddy's Dyin', Who's Got the Will?
US 1990 95m DeLuxe
Palace/Propaganda Films/Artist Circle Entertainment (Sigurjon Sighvatsson, Steve Golin, Monty Montgomery)

Children gather at home after their father has a stroke.
Raucous comedy of family relationships that ends in sentimentality.
w Del Shores *play* Del Shores *d* Jack Fisk *ph* Paul Elliot *m* David McHugh *pd* Michelle Minch *ed* Edward A. Warschilka Jnr
☆ Beau Bridges, Beverly D'Angelo, Tess Harper, Judge Reinhold, Amy Wright, Patrika Darbo, Bert

Remsen, Molly McClure, Keith Carradine, Newell Alexander

Daddy's Gone A-Hunting
US 1969 108m Technicolor
Warner/Red Lion (Mark Robson)

A child and its mother are threatened by her deranged ex-husband.
Unpleasant and protracted suspenser with the emphasis on sex rather than thrills.
w Larry Cohen, Lorenzo Semple Jnr *d* Mark Robson *ph* Ernest Laszlo *m* John Williams
☆ Carol White, Paul Burke, Scott Hylands, Mala Powers, Andrea King

Dad's Army **
GB 1971 95m Technicolor
Columbia/Norcon (John R. Sloan)

Misadventures of a number of elderly gents in Britain's wartime Home Guard.
Expanded big-screen version of the long-running TV series, a pleasant souvenir but rather less effective than was expected because everything is shown – the town, the Nazis, the wives – and thus the air of gentle fantasy disappears, especially in the face of much coarsened humour.
w Jimmy Perry, David Croft *d* Norman Cohen *ph* Terry Maher *m* Wilfred Burns
☆ *Arthur Lowe, John Le Mesurier, John Laurie, James Beck,* Ian Lavender, *Arnold Ridley,* Liz Fraser, *Clive Dunn,* Bill Pertwee, Frank Williams, Edward Sinclair

Daens *
Belgium/France/Netherlands 1992 138m colour
Mayfair/Favourite/Investco/Kredietbank Luxembourg/Films Dérive/Titane/Shooting Star/BRTN/KRO (Dick Impens)

At the turn of the century, a Catholic priest champions the half-starved, underpaid workers in the city of Aalst.
Dogged biopic celebrating a remarkable man, but without much flair in its telling.
w François Chevallier, Stijn Coninx *novel Pieter Daens* by Louis Paul Boon *d* Stijn Coninx *ph* Wather Vanden Ende *m* Dirk Brossé *pd* Allan Starski *ed* Ludo Troch
☆ Jan Decleir, Gérard Desarthe, Antje de Boeck, Michael Pas, Johan Leysen, Idwig Stéphane, Wim Meuwissen

'A bit of a pudding, and long with it. It says all the right things ... But it says them so slowly and deliberately that your patience is at times sorely tested.' – *Derek Malcolm, Guardian*

'A bit of a plod. But it does have dramatic force, a passionate central performance and the great virtue of clarity.' – *Adam Mars-Jones, Independent*

best foreign film

Dagon, Sect of the Sea
Spain 2001 94m colour
Fantastic Factory/Castelao/Via Digital (Julio Fernandez, Brian Yuzna)

In Spain, survivors of a boating accident go for help to a fishing village where the locals worship an octopus-like monster.
Gory low-budget horror with a few effective moments.
w Dennis Paoli *story* H. P. Lovecraft *d* Stuart Gordon *ph* Carlos Suarez *m* Carles Cases *ad* Llorenc Miquel *ed* Jaume Villalta *sp* DDT
☆ Ezra Godden, Francisco Rabal, Raquel Merono, Macarena Gomez, Brendan Price, Birgit Bofarull

'An enjoyably mindless ride.' – *Variety*

Dahong Denglong Gaogao Gua: see *Raise The Red Lantern*

Daisies **
Czechoslovakia 1966 80m colour
Bohumil Smida (Lasislav Fikar)

original title: *Sedmikrásky*
Bored by their lives, two girls go in search of decadence.
Witty, playful, visually exuberant attack on conformity and a materialistic society that the Czech authorities banned for a time.
w Ester Krumbachova, Vera Chytilova *d Vera Chytilova ph* Jaroslav Kucera *pd* Ester Krumbachova

☆ Jitka Cerhova, Ivana Karbanova, Julius Albert

'What makes this film particularly distasteful is its idiot yearning for Western beatnikdom, its slobbering (and, I suspect, lesbian) adulation of its ghastly heroines.' – *John Simon*

Daisy Kenyon
US 1947 99m bw
TCF (Otto Preminger)
A fashion designer has two men in her life.
Adequate woman's picture which hardly justifies its cast.
w David Hertz *novel* Elizabeth Janeway *d* Otto Preminger *ph* Leon Shamroy *m* David Raksin
☆ Joan Crawford, Henry Fonda, Dana Andrews, Ruth Warrick, Martha Stewart, Peggy Ann Garner

Daisy Miller *
US 1974 92m Technicolor
Paramount/Copa de Oro (Peter Bogdanovich)

In the 19th century, an American girl tourist in Europe falls in love but dies of the Roman fever.
Curious attempt to film a very mild and uneventful Henry James story, with careful production but inadequate leads. The first sign that Bogdanovich was getting too big for his boots.
w Frederic Raphael *story* Henry James *d* Peter Bogdanovich *ph* Alberto Spagnoli *m* classical themes *ad* Ferdinando Scarfiotti
☆ Cybill Shepherd, Barry Brown, Cloris Leachman, Mildred Natwick, Eileen Brennan, James MacMurtry

'A historical film bereft of any feeling for history, and a literary adaptation which reveals a fine contempt for literary subtlety.' – *Jan Dawson*

'Appallingly crass ... directed with all the subtlety of a sledgehammer.' – *Michael Billington, Illustrated London News*

'Trying to make that little thing he's with into Daisy Miller was hilarious. God almighty couldn't do that. She's so coy.' – *Henry Hathaway*

Dakota
US 1945 82m bw
Republic (Joseph Kane)

The daughter of a railroad tycoon elopes with a cowboy and becomes involved in a land war.
Adequate star Western.
w Lawrence Hazard *story* Carl Foreman *d* Joseph Kane *ph* Jack Marta *m* Walter Scharf
☆ John Wayne, Vera Hruba Ralston, Walter Brennan, Ward Bond, Ona Munson, Hugo Haas, Mike Mazurki, Paul Fix, Grant Withers, Jack La Rue

Dakota Incident
US 1956 88m bw
Republic

Strangers take cover when they are attacked by Indians.
A formula older than Stagecoach *is played out to humdrum results.*
w Frederic Louis Fox *d* Lewis R. Foster
☆ Linda Darnell, Dale Robertson, Regis Toomey, John Lund, Ward Bond, Skip Homeier, Irving Bacon, John Doucette, Whit Bissell

Dakota Road
GB 1990 89m colour
Mayfair/Dakota Road/Working Title/Film Four/British Screen (Donna Grey)
In East Anglia a 15-year-old girl suffers from her father's suicide, her family's eviction from their home and an unsatisfactory love affair with a local youth.
Rural melodrama so unrelievedly tragic that it hovers on the edge of parody.
wd Nick Ward *ph* Ian Wilson *m* Paul Stacey *pd* Careen Hertzog *ed* William Diver
☆ Charlotte Chatton, Jason Carter, Rachel Scott, Amelda Brown, Matthew Scurfield, Alan Howard, David Warrilow

'A melodrama with the *angst* button set to full volume, all the way through.' – *Sheila Johnston, Independent*

'Though the film is splendidly shot by Ian Wilson, making the most of the exposed landscape and its patches of unexpected lushness, it founders on a relentless rural miserabilism.' – *Hugo Davenport, Daily Telegraph*

Dal Polo all'Equatore: see *From The Pole to The Equator*

Daleks: Invasion Earth 2150 AD: see *Dr Who and the Daleks*

Dallas *
US 1950 94m Technicolor
Warner (Anthony Veiller)

A renegade ex-Confederate colonel is pardoned for bringing law and order to Dallas.
Routinely competent top-of-the-bill Western.
w John Twist *d* Stuart Heisler *ph* Ernest Haller *m* Max Steiner *ed* Clarence Kolster
☆ Gary Cooper, Ruth Roman, Raymond Massey, Steve Cochran, Barbara Payton, Leif Erickson, Antonio Moreno, Jerome Cowan

Dallas Doll
Australia 1994 104m Eastmancolor
Metro Tartan/Dallas Doll/ABC/BBC (Ross Matthews)

A female American golf instructor causes dissension in an Australian family by seducing the husband, wife and son.
Dim would-be satirical comedy, a variation on Pasolini's Theorem, *which falls very flat.*
wd Ann Turner *ph* Paul Murphy *m* David Hirschfelder *pd* Marcus North *ed* Michael Honey
☆ Sandra Bernhard, Frank Gallacher, Victoria Longley, Jake Blundell, Rose Byrne, Jonathon Leahy, Douglas Hedge, Melissa Thomas

'An out-of-control mess.' – *Independent*

The Dam Busters **
GB 1954 125m bw
ABPC (Robert Clark)

In 1943 the Ruhr dams are destroyed by Dr Barnes Wallis's bouncing bombs.
Understated British war epic with additional scientific interest and good acting and model work, not to mention a welcome lack of love interest.
w R. C. Sherriff books Guy Gibson and Paul Brickhill *d* Michael Anderson *ph* Erwin Hillier *m Leighton Lucas, Eric Coates ad* Robert Jones *ed* Richard Best *sp* George Blackwell
☆ *Michael Redgrave* (Dr B. N. Wallis), Richard Todd (Wing Commander Guy Gibson), Basil Sydney (Air Chief Marshal Sir Arthur Harris), Derek Farr (Group Capt J. N. H. Whitworth), Patrick Barr (Capt. Joseph Summers), Ernest Clark (Air Vice-Marshal the Hon Ralph Cochrane), Raymond Huntley (Official), Ursula Jeans (Mrs Wallis), Brewster Mason (Flight Lt R. D. Trevor-Roper), Anthony Doonan (Flight Lt R. E. G. Hutchison), Nigel Stock (Flying Officer F. M. Spafford), Brian Nissen (Flight Lt A. T. Taerum), Robert Shaw (Flight Sgt J. Pulford), Peter Assinder (Flying Officer G. A. Deering)

A dama do cine Shanghai: see *The Lady from the Shanghai Cinema*

Dama sSobachkoi: see *The Lady with the Little Dog*

'Desire. Deceit.'
Damage
GB/France 1992 111m Technicolor
Entertainment/Skreba/NEF/Canal (Louis Malle)

A Conservative minister is destroyed by his obsessive love for his son's girlfriend.
Disappointingly thin tale that carries very little conviction.
w David Hare *novel* Josephine Hart *d* Louis Malle *ph* Peter Biziou *m* Zbigniew Preisner *pd* Brian Morris *ed* John Bloom
☆ Jeremy Irons, Juliette Binoche, *Miranda Richardson,* Rupert Graves, Leslie Caron, Ian Bannen, Gemma Clarke, Julian Fellowes, Tony Doyle, Benjamin Whitrow

'A cold, brittle film about raging, traumatic emotions.' – *Variety*

'A carefully controlled picture about uncontrollable passion, in which precise camera movements and unobtrusive editing subtly complement the immaculate acting.' – *Philip French, Observer*

Miranda Richardson
Miranda Richardson

La Dame aux Camélias: see *The Lady of the Camelias*

Dames **
US 1934 90m bw
Warner (Robert Lord)

A millionaire purity fanatic tries to stop the opening of a Broadway show.
Typical Warner musical of the period: its real raison d'être is to be found in the splendidly imaginative numbers at the finale, but it also gives very full rein to the roster of comic actors under contract at the time.
w Delmer Daves *d* Ray Enright *ph* Sid Hickox, George Barnes *m* various *ch Busby Berkeley*
☆ *Joan Blondell, Hugh Herbert, Guy Kibbee, ZaSu Pitts,* Dick Powell, Ruby Keeler

'That Warners was able to fashion so zestful an entertainment under post-Haysian restrictions is a credit to the collective ingenuities of the studio artificers ... Swell entertainment, no matter how you slice it.' – *Variety*

† Originally intended as *Gold Diggers of 1934*.

Les Dames du Bois de Boulogne *
France 1946 90m bw
Consortium du Film (Raoul Ploquin)

US title: *Ladies of the Park*
A woman revenges herself on her faithless lover by inveigling him into a marriage with a nightclub dancer-cum-prostitute.
An austerely directed romantic melodrama that fails to satisfy.
w Jean Cocteau, Robert Bresson *story* Diderot *d* Robert Bresson *ph* Philippe Agostini *m* Jean-Jacques Grunenwald *pd* Max Douy
☆ Paul Bernard, Maria Casarès, Elina Labourdette, Lucienne Bogaert, Jean Marchat

'The first time was only a warning!'
Damien: Omen Two
US 1978 109m DeLuxe Panavision
TCF (Harvey Bernhard)

The antichrist who got rid of the entire cast of *The Omen* now, as a teenager, starts in on his foster parents.
Once was enough.
w Stanley Mann, Michael Hodges *d* Don Taylor *ph* Bill Butler *m* Jerry Goldsmith
☆ William Holden, Lee Grant, Jonathan Scott-Taylor, Robert Foxworth, Lucas Donat, Lew Ayres, Sylvia Sidney, Elizabeth Shepherd
† It was followed by *The Final Conflict* (qv).

Damn the Defiant: see *HMS Defiant*

Damn Yankees **
US 1958 110m Technicolor
Warner (George Abbott, Stanley Donen)

GB title: *What Lola Wants*
The devil interferes in the fortunes of a failing baseball team.
Smartly-styled but very American musical based on Faust; *brilliant moments but some tedium.*
w George Abbott *novel* Douglass Wallop *d* George Abbott, Stanley Donen *ph* Harold Lipstein *m/ly* Richard Adler, Jerry Ross *md* Ray Heindorf
☆ Gwen Verdon, Tab Hunter, Ray Walston, Russ Brown, Shannon Bolin
Ray Heindorf

Damnation Alley
US 1977 95m DeLuxe Panavision
TCF/Hal Landers, Bobby Roberts, Jerome M. Zeitman
Four survivors from World War Three try to reach a colony of fellow-survivors in New York.
Feeble attempt at a low-budget blockbuster.
w Alan Sharp, Lukas Heller *novel* Roger Zelazny *d* Jack Smight *ph* Harry Stradling Jnr *m* Jerry Goldsmith *pd* Preston Ames
☆ Jan-Michael Vincent, George Peppard, Dominique Sanda, Paul Winfield

The Damned *
GB 1963 87m bw HammerScope
Columbia/Hammer-Swallow (Anthony Hinds)
US title: *These Are the Damned*
A scientist keeps radioactive children in a cliff cave, sealed off from the world's corruption.

Absurdly pompous, downcast and confused sci-fi melodrama set in Weymouth, with a secondary plot about motor-cycling thugs.
w Evan Jones *novel* The Children of Light by H. L. Lawrence *d* Joseph Losey *ph* Arthur Grant *m* James Bernard *pd* Bernard Robinson
☆ Macdonald Carey, Shirley Anne Field, Alexander Knox, Viveca Lindfors, Oliver Reed, Walter Gotell, James Villiers
'*A folie de grandeur*.' – *Tom Milne*
'Out of this wild mishmash some really magnificent images loom.' – *John Coleman*

The Damned **
West Germany/Italy 1969 164m
Eastmancolor
Praesidens/Pegaso
original title: *Götterdämmerung*
A family of German industrialists divides and destroys itself under Nazi influence.
A film which has been called baroque, Wagnerian, and just plain unpleasant; it is also rather a strain to watch, with exaggerated colour and make-up to match the rotting theme.
w Nicola Badalucco, Enrico Medioli, Luchino Visconti *d Luchino Visconti ph* Armando Nannuzzi, Pasquale de Santis *m* Maurice Jarre *ad* Enzo del Prato, Pasquale Romano
☆ Dirk Bogarde, Ingrid Thulin, Helmut Berger, Renaud Verley, Helmut Griem, René Kolldehoff, Albrecht Schönhals, Umberto Orsini
'One is left lamenting that such a quondam master of realism as Visconti is making his films look like operas from which the score has been inexplicably removed.' – *MFB*
'The ludicrous flailings of puny puppets in inscrutable wooden frenzies.' – *John Simon*
script

'The private lady of a public enemy!'
The Damned Don't Cry
US 1950 103m bw
Warner (Jerry Wald)
A middle-class housewife leaves her husband for a gambler, and becomes involved with gangsters, but eventually reforms.
Rather dreary stimulation for female audiences who like safe dreams of danger.
w Harold Medford, Jerome Weidman *novel* Case History by Gertrude Walker *d* Vincent Sherman *ph* Ted McCord *m* Daniele Amfitheatrof
☆ Joan Crawford, Kent Smith, David Brian, Steve Cochran, Hugh Sanders, Selena Royle, Morris Ankrum, Richard Egan

'Mad adventure! Daring deeds! White hot love with music!'
A Damsel in Distress *
US 1937 101m bw
RKO (Pandro S. Berman)
An American dancing star falls for an aristocratic young Englishwoman.
Astaire without Rogers, but the style is the same and there are some very good numbers.
w P. G. Wodehouse, S. K. Lauren, Ernest Pagano *d* George Stevens *ph* Joseph H. August *m/ly* George and Ira Gershwin *ch* Hermes Pan *ad* Carroll Clark
☆ *Fred Astaire, George Burns, Gracie Allen*, Joan Fontaine, Reginald Gardiner, Constance Collier, Ray Noble, Montagu Love
'Plenty for the b.o. – dancing, comedy, marquee values, the usual sumptuous investiture accorded by Pandro Berman, and those Gershwin songs.' – *Variety*
† Rogers had demanded a break from musicals, so she was replaced by the demure Miss Fontaine, who was generally thought disappointing.
Hermes Pan
Carroll Clark

Dance Band
GB 1935 75m bw
BIP (Walter Mycroft)
A band leader who croons falls for the boss of an all-ladies orchestra.
Fairly slick light musical fare of its period.
w Roger Burford, Jack Davies, Denis Waldock *d* Marcel Varnel *ph* Bryan Langley *md* Harry Acres *ad* David Rawnsley *ed* Sidney Cole
☆ Buddy Rogers, June Clyde, Fred Duprez, Richard Hearne, Steve Geray, Magda Kun
'Popular entertainment from start to finish, cut to a point where there is hardly a draggy moment.' – *Variety*

Dance Fools Dance
US 1931 82m bw
MGM
A lady reporter in Chicago proves her worth.
Bizarrely-titled gangster thriller based on the Jake Lingle killing. Very moderate of its kind.
w Richard Schayer, Aurania Rouverol *d* Harry Beaumont *ph* Charles Rosher
☆ Joan Crawford, Lester Vail, Cliff Edwards, William Bakewell, William Holden (the other one), Clark Gable, Earle Foxe, Joan Marsh
'It will rock the b.o … sex, romance, punch, suspense, and everything a deluxer can sell.' – *Variety*

Dance, Girl, Dance *
US 1940 88m bw
RKO (Erich Pommer)
Private problems of the members of a night-club dance troupe.
Competent and sometimes interesting formula drama with a harder edge than usual.
w Tess Slesinger, Frank Davis *story* Vicki Baum *d Dorothy Arzner ph* Russell Metty *m* Edward Ward
☆ Maureen O'Hara, Louis Hayward, Lucille Ball, Maria Ouspenskaya, Ralph Bellamy, Virginia Field, Mary Carlisle, Walter Abel, Edward Brophy, Harold Huber

The Dance Goes On
Canada 1991 103m colour
Quest (Paul Almond)
A brash young man learns to appreciate rustic values after he travels from Malibu to the family farm in Quebec with the ashes of his uncle.
Amiable family drama of a familiar kind, dealing with tensions between father and son.
wd Paul Almond *ph* Peter Benison *m* Claude Léveillée, James Smith *pd* Reuben Freed
☆ James Keach, Matthew James Almond, Geneviève Bujold, Leslie Hope, Bryan Hennessy, Deborah Freeland, Cary Lawrence

Dance Hall *
GB 1950 80m bw
Ealing (Michael Balcon, E. V. H. Emmett)
Four factory girls seek relaxation and various kinds of romance at the local palais.
Untypically flat Ealing slice of life, now watchable only with a smile as musical nostalgia.
w E. V. H. Emmett, Diana Morgan, Alexander Mackendrick *d* Charles Crichton *ph* Douglas Slocombe *m* Joyce Cochran *md* Ernest Irving *ed* Seth Holt
☆ Natasha Parry, Donald Houston, Diana Dors, Bonar Colleano, Jane Hylton, Petula Clark, Gladys Henson, Sydney Tafler, Geraldo and his band, Ted Heath and his band
'Not a film that will please everyone. Its story is tiresome and not varied enough for the length of the picture.' – *A. Jympson Harman*

Dance Little Lady
GB 1954 87m Eastmancolor
George Minter/Renown
An ambitious man tries to turn his balletomane daughter into a film star.
Artless melodrama in poor colour.
w Val Guest, Doreen Montgomery *d* Val Guest
☆ Terence Morgan, Mai Zetterling, Mandy Miller, Guy Rolfe, Eunice Gayson

Dance Me Outside *
Canada 1994 84m colour
Yorktown/Shadow Shows (Brian Dennis, Bruce McDonald)
In Ontario, an 18-year-old Indian, compelled to write a story in order to get into mechanics school, recalls events following the rape and murder of an Indian girl by a white man.
Effective drama of racial tensions and resentment that touches with humour and insight on many other aspects of life.
w Bruce McDonald, Don McKellar, John Frizzell *novel* W. P. Kinsella *d* Bruce McDonald *ph* Miroslaw Baszak *m* Mychael Danna *pd* John Dondertman *ed* Michael Pacek
☆ Ryan Rajendra Black, Adam Beach, Lisa LaCroix, Michael Greyeyes, Kevin Hicks, Jennifer Podemski, Sandrine Holt
'Bolstered by a winning, youthful cast, the film is a droll ensemble piece that makes its serious points skillfully and effortlessly.' – *Leonard Klady, Variety*

The Dance of Death *
GB 1968 149m Technicolor
BHE/National Theatre (John Brabourne)
Edgar and Alice live alone on an island, their marriage having become a constant war.
Too-literal film transcription of an applauded theatrical production, with the camera anchored firmly in the middle of the stalls.
w August Strindberg (translation C. D. Locock)
d David Giles *ph* Geoffrey Unsworth
☆ *Laurence Olivier*, Geraldine McEwan, Robert Lang, Carolyn Jones

Dance of the Vampires: see *The Fearless Vampire Killers*

Dance of the Wind *
Germany/GB/France/Netherlands/India/Switzerland 1997 86m colour
Artificial Eye/Pandora/Elephant Eye/Illumination/JBA/Filmcompany/NFDC (Karl Baumgartner)
In New Delhi, a singer of classical Hindustani music loses her voice when her mother dies, and goes to find the guru who was her mother's teacher.
A fable about individuality within a culture, accessible to a sympathetic Western audience.
w Robin Mukherjee *d* Rajan Khosa *ph* Piyush Shah *pd* Amardeep Behl *ed* Emma Matthews
☆ Kitu Gidwani, Bhaveen Gossain, B. C. Sanyal, Roshan Bano, Kapila Vatsyayan, Vinod Nagpal, Punamava Mehta, Ami Arora, Bhunvar Lal
'A little gem.' – *Empire*

Dance with a Stranger *
GB 1985 101m Technicolor
Goldcrest/NFFC/First Picture Co (Roger Randall-Cutler)
Ex-prostitute Ruth Ellis, infatuated with a worthless sponger, shoots him dead rather than lose him.
Muddled account of the last woman to hang in Great Britain; no sympathies are aroused and no clear viewpoint taken.
w Shelagh Delaney *d* Mike Newell *ph* Peter Hannan *m* Richard Hartley *pd* Andrew Mollo *ed* Mick Audsley
☆ *Miranda Richardson*, Rupert Everett, Ian Holm, Matthew Carroll, Stratford Johns

Dance with Me
US 1998 126m CFI color
Columbia/Mandalay (Lauren C. Weissman, Shinya Egawa, Randa Haines)
A young Cuban travels to the United States to find his father and a partner for a Las Vegas dance competition.
Lively romantic drama, with most of the action taking place on the dance-floor, but it is both forgettable and predictable.
w Daryl Matthews *d* Randa Haines *ph* Fred Murphy *m* Michael Convertino *pd* Waldemar Kalinowski *ed* Lisa Fruchtman
☆ Vanessa L. Williams, Chayanne, Kris Kristoffersen, Joan Plowright, Jane Krakowski, Beth Grant, William Marquez
'*Flashdance* for the 1990s, for good and ill.' – *Variety*

Dancer in the Dark **
Denmark/Sweden/France 2000 140m colour
Film4/Zentropa/Trust/Film i Vast/Liberator (Vibeke Windelov)
A factory worker, trying to raise money for an operation to save her son's sight, is threatened with her own blindness, eviction, unemployment, and the death penalty for killing the man who robbed her.
A film to divide audiences into those who will respond to the intense emotions on display, many of them heightened by anguished sequences of song and dance, and those who will find the jerky handheld photography a needless distraction, and will reject the melodramatic sob-story as shameless manipulation. Björk throws herself into the role of the most self-sacrificing mother since Stella Dallas with complete conviction.
wd Lars Von Trier *ph* Robby Mueller *m/ly* Bjork; Lars Von Trier, Sjon Sigurdsson *pd* Karl Juliusson *ed* Molly Malene Stensgaard, Francois Gedigier *cos* Manon Rasmussen *ch* Vincent Paterson
☆ *Björk* (Selma), Catherine Deneuve (Kathy), David Morse (Bill), Peter Stormare (Jeff), Joel Grey (Oldrich Novy), Vincent Paterson (Director), Cara Seymour (Jean), Jean-Marc Barr (Foreman), Vladica Kostic (Gene), Udo Kier (Doctor), Zeljko Ivanek (D.A.)
'Occasionally riveting folly.' – *Adam Mars-Jones, Times*
'I was simultaneously struck by the film's preposterousness and astounded by its intensity and audacity.' – *Edward Porter, Sunday Times*
'A demo of auteurist self-importance that's artistically bankrupt on almost every level.' – *Derek Elley, Variety*
† The film won the Palme D'Or, and Björk won the Best Actress award, at the Cannes Festival in 2000. It also won the Best Film award, and Björk the Best Actress award, at the European Film Awards of 2000.
song 'I've Seen It All' (*m* Björk, *l* Lars von Trier, Sjon Sigurdsson)

Dancers
US 1987 99m colour
Cannon/Hera/Baryshnikov/Golan/Globus
On tour in Italy, a leading dancer recovers his inspiration when a young ballerina joins the company.
Trite script, dull romance and moments of exciting dance.
w Sarah Kernochan *d* Herbert Ross *ph* Ennio Guarnieri *m* Pino Donnagio *pd* Gianni Quaranta *ed* William Reynolds
☆ Mikhail Baryshnikov, Alessandra Ferri, Leslie Browne, Thomas Rall, Lynn Seymour, Victor Barbee, Julie Kent

Dances with Wolves **
US 1990 180m DeLuxe Panavision
Guild/Tig Productions/Jim Wilson, Kevin Costner
A cavalry officer is adopted by the Sioux Indians.
A liberal Western – the Indians (or Native Americans) are the good guys – sentimental and over-long, but nonetheless affecting. A version of 'the director's cut' was promised for videocassette, with a running time of 240 minutes.
w Michael Blake *novel* Michael Blake *d* Kevin Costner *ph* Dean Semler *m* John Barry *pd* Jeffrey Beecroft *ad* William Ladd Skinner *ed* Neil Travis
☆ Kevin Costner, Mary McDonnell, Graham Greene, Rodney A. Grant, Floyd Red Crow Westerman, Tantoo Cardinal, Robert Pastorelli, Charles Rocket, Maury Chaykin, Jimmy Herman, Nathan Lee Chasing His Horse
'*Dances with Wolves* would be easier to love if screenwriter Blake had resisted the temptation to plug every positive stereotype about Native Americans. The characters, alternately stoic, are ecologically aware and brave. Even Hollywood Indians don't have to be like this.' – *Michael Dorris, Premiere*
'Long, simplistic and lacking in irony, though not in pawky humour. The action set-pieces (two ambushes, two pitched battles, a grand buffalo hunt) are dynamically handled. But the picture lacks the visual and dramatic authority of the best Westerns.' – *Philip French, Observer*
'Costner has feathers in his hair and feathers in his head.' – *Pauline Kael*
† A special edition of the film with an extra 53 minutes added was given a London cinema release in 1991 and later released on video.
best film; Kevin Costner (as director); Michael Blake; John Barry; Dean Semler; Neil Travis; best sound
Kevin Costner (as actor); Mary McDonnell; Graham Greene; best costume design; best art direction

Dancin' thru the Dark **
GB 1990 95m colour
Palace/BBC Films/Formost Films (Andre Molyneux)
On the night before her wedding, a woman goes out with her girl-friends for a celebration at a

night-club, only to meet there her former lover, now a successful rock singer, and her fiancé, drunk from his stag-night party.
High-spirited and witty domestic drama.
w Willy Russell *play Stags and Hens* by Willy Russell *d* Mike Ockrent *ph* Philip Bonham-Carter *m* Willy Russell *pd* Paul Joel
☆ Claire Hackett, Con O'Neill, Angela Clarke, Mark Womack, Julia Deakin, Simon O'Brien, Louise Duprey, Andrew Naylor, Sandy Hendrickse, Peter Watts
'A satisfying and enjoyable work.' – *Variety*

'Five sisters embrace the spirit of a people.'
Dancing at Lughnasa
Ireland/GB/US 1998 92m Rank Colour
Ferndale/Capitol/Sony/Channel 4 Films (Noel Pearson)
Five unmarried sisters contemplate their future in rural Donegal in the mid-30s.
A dull transfer of an atmospheric play about Irish identity to the screen; only the landscape holds the interest.
w Frank McGuinness *play* Brian Friel *d* Pat O'Connor *ph* Kenneth MacMillan *m* Bill Whelan *pd* Mark Geraghty *ed* Humphrey Dixon
☆ Meryl Streep, Michael Gambon, Catherine McCormack, Kathy Burke, Sophie Thompson, Brid Brennan, Rhys Ifans, Darrell Johnston, Lorcan Cranitch, Peter Gowen
'Middlebrow, bland film, lacking in emotional or intellectual bite.' – *Claire Monk, Sight and Sound*

Dancing at the Blue Iguana
US 2000 123m DeLuxe
Miracle/Moonstone/Bergman Listig/Dragon/Gallery
Five women who work as pole dancers in an LA club confront their bleak lives.
Downbeat drama, based on a series of improvisational workshops, that bares bodies but not lives: its cast proffers stereotypes instead of realities.
w Michael Radford, David Linter *d* Michael Radford *ph* Ericson Core *m* Tal Bergman, Renato Neto *pd* Martina Buckley *ed* Roberto Perpignani
☆ Charlotte Ayanna (Jessie), Daryl Hannah (Angel), Sheila Kelley (Stormy), Elias Koteas (Sully), Vladimir Mashkov (Sacha), Sandra Oh (Jasmine), Jennifer Tilly (Jo), Robert Wisdom
'Far too much of the running time is devoted to relatively routine behavioral matters devoid of dramatic urgency or import.' – *Todd McCarthy, Variety*
'Much of the movie is funny, and almost all of it is sad.' – *Gaby Wood, Observer*

Dancing Co-ed
US 1939 90m bw
MGM (Edgar Selwyn)
GB title: *Every Other Inch a Lady*
A college girl makes it in show business as well as the groves of academe.
Mindless vehicle for a 19-year-old star.
w Albert Mannheimer *story* Albert Treynor *d* S. Sylvan Simon *ph* Alfred Gilks *m* David Snell, Edward Ward
☆ Lana Turner, Richard Carlson, Artie Shaw, *Leon Errol*, Ann Rutherford, Lee Bowman, Monty Woolley, Roscoe Karns, June Preisser, Walter Kingsford
'Better than average programme entertainment.' – *Variety*

Dancing Fool: see *Harold Teen*

Dancing in the Dark
Canada 1986 98m colour
Brightstar/Film Arts/Film House/CBC (Anthony Kramreither)
A housewife recalls the events that led to her breakdown and the murder of her husband.
Virtually a monologue, well performed by Henry, of a woman who thoughtlessly follows a conventional life with a conventional husband and begins to wonder why it is so unfulfilling; the theme has been worked so often that its appeal has begun to pall.
wd Leon Marr *novel* Joan Barfoot *ph* Vic Sarin *pd* Lillian Sarafinchan *ed* Tom Berner
☆ *Martha Henry*, Neil Munro, Rosemary Dunsmore, Richard Monette

Dancing Lady *
US 1933 94m bw
MGM (David O. Selznick)
A successful dancer chooses between a playboy and her stage manager.
Routine backstage semi-musical with interesting talent applied rather haphazardly.
w Allen Rivkin, P. J. Wolfson *novel* James Warner Bellah *d* Robert Z. Leonard *ph* Oliver T. Marsh *m* various *md* Louis Silvers
☆ *Joan Crawford*, Clark Gable, *Fred Astaire*, Franchot Tone, May Robson, Ted Healy and his Stooges (the Three Stooges), Winnie Lightner, Robert Benchley, Nelson Eddy
'Very potent b.o. in the screen musical cycle.' – *Variety*

The Dancing Masters
US 1943 63m bw
TCF (Lee Marcus)
Laurel and Hardy run a ballet school, and get involved with gangsters and inventors.
Insubstantial star comedy featuring reworkings of old routines, and a back-projected runaway bus climax.
w Scott Darling *story* George Bricker *d* Malcolm St Clair *ph* Norbert Brodine *m* Arthur Lange *ad* James Basevi, Chester Gore *ed* Norman Colbert
☆ Stan Laurel, Oliver Hardy, Trudy Marshall, Bob Bailey, Margaret Dumont, Matt Briggs, Robert Mitchum

The Dancing Years
GB 1949 97m Technicolor
ABPC (Warwick Ward)
A composer loves a singer who leaves him after a misunderstanding but later bears his son … all in the Alps pre-1914.
Lamentable transcription of an operetta; precisely the ingredients which worked so well on stage seem embarrassing on film, and the performances and direction do not help.
w Warwick Ward, Jack Whittingham *operetta* Ivor Novello *d* Harold French *ph* Stephen Dade *m Ivor Novello*
☆ Dennis Price, Gisèle Préville, Patricia Dainton, Anthony Nicholls, Grey Blake, Muriel George, Olive Gilbert

Dandin **
France 1988 110m colour
Films du Losange/Selena Audiovisuel/Sept/A2 (Margaret Menegoz)
A rich peasant faces constant humiliation when he marries the daughter of an aristocrat; she refuses to consummate the marriage and her parents treat him with snobbish disdain.
A sumptuous-looking but tough and exhilaratingly uncompromising approach to a classic comedy of greed and desire so that, for all its period setting, it has a contemporary bite.
wd Roger Planchon *play Georges Dandin* by Molière *ph* Bernard Lutic
☆ Claude Brasseur, Zabou, Nelly Borgeaud, Evelyne Buyle, Jean-Claude Adelin, Daniel Gélin, Marco Bisson, Vincent Garanger

Dandy Dick
GB 1935 72m bw
BIP (Walter Mycroft)
A country vicar becomes innocently involved with racehorse doping.
Flatly-handled farce which helped to introduce Will Hay to the screen, though not in his accustomed role.
w William Beaudine, Frank Miller, Clifford Grey, Will Hay *play* Sir Arthur Wing Pinero *d* William Beaudine *ph* Jack Parker *ad* Duncan Sutherland *ed* A. C. Hammond
☆ Will Hay, Nancy Burne, Esmond Knight, Davy Burnaby

'His mission is murder! His victim – himself!'
A Dandy in Aspic
GB 1968 107m Technicolor Panavision
Columbia (Anthony Mann)
A double agent in Berlin is given orders to kill himself.
Muddled, pretentious spy thriller; flat, nebulous and boring.
w Derek Marlowe *novel* Derek Marlowe *d* Anthony Mann *ph* Christopher Challis *m* Quincy Jones
☆ Laurence Harvey, Tom Courtenay, Lionel Stander, Mia Farrow, Harry Andrews, Peter Cook, Per Oscarsson
† Anthony Mann died during shooting, and Laurence Harvey completed the direction.

Dandy the All-American Girl
US 1976 90m Metrocolor Panavision
MGM
GB title: *Sweet Revenge*
A much convicted woman car thief determines to become the legitimate owner of a Dino Ferrari.
The American dream gone sour again, this time offering in its wake a curious stream of moral values.
w B. J. Perla, Marilyn Goldin *d* Jerry Schatzberg
☆ Stockard Channing, Sam Waterston, Richard Doughty, Franklyn Ajaye

Danger: Diabolik
Italy/France 1967 105m Technicolor
Dino de Laurentiis/Marianne (Bruno Todini)
International police bait a golden trap for a master criminal.
Superior Batman-type adventures with a comic strip hero-villain.
w Dino Maiuri, Adriano Baracco, Mario Bava *d* Mario Bava *ph* Antonio Rinaldi *m* Ennio Morricone
☆ John Phillip Law, Marisa Mell, Michel Piccoli, Adolfo Celi, Terry-Thomas

Danger Lights *
US 1930 87m bw
RKO (William LeBaron)
Railroad owners face various problems.
Routine would-be thriller intended to show off a wide screen system called Spoor-Bergen Natural Vision; it failed owing to cost and the thin quality of the film.
w James Ashmore Creelman *d* George B. Seitz *ph* Karl Struss
☆ Louis Wolheim, Robert Armstrong, Jean Arthur, Hugh Herbert

Danger List
GB 1957 22m bw
Exclusive/Hammer (Anthony Hinds)
At a hospital dispensary, three out-patients are given a fatal drug by mistake.
Uneventful programme filler with predictable twists in its little tales.
w J. D. Scott *d* Leslie Arliss *ph* Arthur Grant *m* Edwin Astley *ad* Ted Marshall *ed* James Needs
☆ Philip Friend, Honor Blackman, Mervyn Johns, Alexander Field, Constance Fraser, Muriel Zillah

Danger, Love at Work *
US 1937 84m bw
TCF (Harold Wilson)
A young lawyer needs the signature of a rich crazy family to conclude a land sale.
The title doesn't suggest it, but this is a not inconsiderable comedy in the tradition of My Man Godfrey *and* You Can't Take It With You. *A highly competent cast does its best.*
w James Edward Grant, Ben Markson *d* Otto Preminger *ph* Virgil Miller *md* David Buttolph
☆ Ann Sothern, Jack Haley, Edward Everett Horton, Mary Boland, Walter Catlett, John Carradine, Maurice Cass, Alan Dinehart, E. E. Clive
'Not important enough to be a main feature but a very good dualler.' – *Variety*

Danger on My Side: see *Danger by My Side*

Danger Patrol
US 1937 58m bw
RKO
Life among 'soup handlers' – lorry drivers who deliver nitro-glycerine to oil wells.
An interesting notion slackly handled, with suspense losing out to romance.
w Sy Bartlett *story* Helen Vreeland, Hilda Vincent *d* Lew Landers *ph* Nicholas Musuraca *ad* Van Nest Polglase *ed* Ted Cheesman
☆ Sally Eilers, John Beal, Harry Carey, Frank M. Thomas, Crawford Weaver, Lee Patrick, Edward Gargan

Danger Route
GB 1967 92m DeLuxe
UA/Amicus (Max J. Rosenberg, Milton Subotsky)
An 'eliminator' for the British secret service finds after a series of adventures that he must dispose of his own girlfriend.
Dour sub-Bondian thriller with little to commend it.
w Meade Roberts *novel The Eliminator* by Andrew York *d* Seth Holt *ph* Harry Waxman *m* John Mayer
☆ Richard Johnson, Diana Dors, Sylvia Syms, Carol Lynley, Barbara Bouchet, Gordon Jackson, Sam Wanamaker, Maurice Denham, Harry Andrews

'Four hundred plan to escape – one plans to betray!'
Danger Within **
GB 1958 101m bw
British Lion/Colin Lesslie
US title: *Breakout*
Escape plans of officers in a prisoner-of-war camp are threatened by an informer.
Familiar comedy and melodrama with an added whodunnit element, smartly handled and very entertaining.
w Bryan Forbes, Frank Harvey novel Michael Gilbert *d Don Chaffey ph* Arthur Grant *m* Francis Chagrin
☆ Richard Todd, Bernard Lee, Michael Wilding, Richard Attenborough, Dennis Price, Donald Houston, William Franklyn, Vincent Ball, Peter Arne

Danger Zone
US 1995 92m Foto-Kem
Nu Image (Danny Lerner, Elie Samaha)
In East Africa, a disgraced American mining engineer, blamed for poisoning communities with toxic waste, goes to find his friend who was involved and discovers that the real purpose of his search has been kept from him.
Deplorable and ludicrous thriller that condemns ignorance about Africa, while at the same time exploiting its more exotic aspects, and revelling in violence; you might feel sympathy towards Billy Zane for being involved in such garbage if he were not also one of the movie's co-producers.
w Jeff Albert *story* Danny Lerner *d* Allan Eastman *ph* Yossi Wein *m* Daniel Pelfrey *pd* Leith Ridley, David Varod *ed* Alain Jakubowicz
☆ Billy Zane, Ron Silver, Cary-Hiroyuki Tagawa, Robert Downey Jnr, Lisa Collins

Dangerous *
US 1935 78m bw
Warner (Harry Joe Brown)
An alcoholic actress is rehabilitated.
Unconvincing and only adequately handled melodrama which won the star her first Oscar, presumably from sympathy at her losing it the previous year for Of Human Bondage.
w Laird Doyle *d* Alfred E. Green *ph* Ernest Haller
☆ Bette Davis, Franchot Tone, Margaret Lindsay, Alison Skipworth, John Eldredge, Dick Foran
'Well-acted and directed drama with *femme* appeal.' – *Variety*
† Remade 1941 as *Singapore Woman*.
Bette Davis

Dangerous Afternoon
GB 1961 92m bw
Bryanston/Theatrecraft
The owner of a boarding house for elderly criminals is blackmailed by an ex-convict who knows her true identity.
An interesting notion —a retirement home for genteel female crooks—becomes mired in an uninteresting story of blackmail and murder.
w Brandon Fleming *play* Gerald Anstruther *d* Charles Saunders
☆ Ruth Dunning, Nora Nicholson, Joanne Dunham, Howard Pays, May Hallatt, Gwenda Wilson, Ian Colin, Gladys Henson, Barbara Everest, Jerold Wells

Dangerous Beauty
US 1998 111m Technicolor Panavision
Warner/Regency/Bedford Falls (Arnon Milchan, Marshall Herskovitz, Edward Zwick, Sarah Kaplan)
GB title: *The Honest Courtesan*
In 16th-century Venice, a woman becomes a celebrated courtesan when the man she loves marries for money.
Sumptuous historical romance, which is based on fact but plays as if it were invented by a sentimental novelist.
w Jeannine Dominy *biography* The Honest Courtesan by Margaret Rosenthal *d* Marshall Herskovitz *ph* Bojan Bazelli *m* George Fenton *pd* Norman Garwood *ed* Steven Rosenblum, Arthur Coburn
☆ Catherine McCormack, Rufus Sewell, Jacqueline Bisset, Oliver Platt, Moira Kelly, Fred Ward, Naomi Watts, Jeroen Krabbe, Joanna Cassidy, Peter Eyre
'An odd mix of high-toned intentions and cornball romance that works in fits and bursts.' – *Leonard Klady, Variety*

Dangerous Corner *
US 1934 67m bw
RKO
After dinner conversation reveals what might have been if friends had spoken the truth about a long-ago suicide.
A fascinating trick play makes interesting but scarcely sparkling cinema.
w Anne Morrison Chapin, Madeleine Ruthven *play* J. B. Priestley *d* Phil Rosen *ph* J. Roy Hunt *m* Max Steiner
☆ Melvyn Douglas, Conrad Nagel, Virginia Bruce, Erin O'Brien Moore, Ian Keith, Betty Furness, Henry Wadsworth, Doris Lloyd
'Confusing mixture of a mystery and problem play ... doubtful as to general fan appeal.' – *Variety*

Dangerous Crossing *
US 1953 75m bw
TCF (Robert Bassler)
At the start of an Atlantic sea voyage a woman's husband disappears, and she is assured that he never existed. He does, and is trying to murder her.
Adequately handled twist on the vanishing lady story: grade A production covers lapses of grade B imagination.
w Leo Townsend *story* John Dickson Carr *d* Joseph M. Newman *ph* Joseph LaShelle *md* Lionel Newman
☆ Jeanne Crain, Michael Rennie, Carl Betz, Casey Adams, Mary Anderson, Willis Bouchey

Dangerous Curves
US 1929 75m bw
Paramount
A bareback rider loves a high wire artist.
Obvious circus melodrama, a modest star vehicle.
w Donald Davis, Florence Ryerson *d* Lothar Mendes *ph* Harry Fischbeck
☆ Clara Bow, Richard Arlen, Kay Francis, David Newell, Anders Randolf

Dangerous Days: see *Wild Boys of the Road*

Dangerous Exile
GB 1957 90m Eastmancolor Vistavision
Rank (George H. Brown)
After the French Revolution, the young would-be Louis XVII is brought across the Channel and hidden in Pembrokeshire, where enemies attack him.
Historical romance, ineptly plotted but quite well produced.
w Robin Estridge *novel* Vaughan Wilkins *d* Brian Desmond Hurst *ph* Geoffrey Unsworth *m* Georges Auric
☆ Louis Jourdan, Belinda Lee, Keith Michell, Richard O'Sullivan, Martita Hunt, Finlay Currie, Anne Heywood, Jacques Brunius

Dangerous Female: see *The Maltese Falcon (1931)*

Dangerous Game: see *Snake Eyes (1993)*

Dangerous Ground
South Africa/US 1996 96m DeLuxe
Entertainment/Investec/New Line (Gillian Gorfil, Darrell Roodt)
Returning to his home after a dozen years in America, a South African goes in search of his missing brother and discovers that he is involved with drug dealers.
Trite tale of revenge, a dreary gangster movie that gains nothing from its South African setting.
w Greg Latter, Darrell Roodt *d* Darrell Roodt *ph* Paul Gilpin *m* Stanley Clarke *pd* Dimitri Repanis *ed* David Heitner
☆ Ice Cube, Elizabeth Hurley, Sechaba Morojele, Eric 'Waku' Miyeni, Ving Rhames, Thokozani Nkosi, Ron Smerczak
'Don't see this film.' – *Film Review*

Dangerous Liaisons **
US 1988 120m Eastmancolor
Warner/Lorimar/NFH (Norma Heyman, Hank Moonjean)
Two jaded French aristocrats play games of sexual politics.
A cool dissection of sexual feeling.
w Christopher Hampton *play* Christopher Hampton *novel* Choderlos de Laclos *d* Stephen Frears *ph* Philippe Rousselot *m* George Fenton *pd* Stuart Craig *ed* Mick Audsley
☆ Glenn Close, John Malkovich, Michelle Pfeiffer, Swoosie Kurtz, Keanu Reeves, Mildred Natwick, Uma Thurman
'Beautifully acted (by Glenn Close in particular), elegantly phrased, carefully shot on location in an appropriate selection of chateaux, directed with a limpidly formalised serenity, it's a handsome and intelligent piece of work.' – *Tom Milne, MFB*
Christopher Hampton; Stuart Craig
best picture; Glenn Close; Michelle Pfeiffer; George Fenton
adapted screenplay; Michelle Pfeiffer

Dangerous Millions
US 1946 69m bw
TCF
GB title: *The House of Tao Ling*
Eight would-be inheritors of a millionaire's estate find themselves at the mercy of a warlord in the Chinese mountains.
Odd little second feature confusion of The Cat and the Canary *and* Shanghai Express*; quite watchable.*
w Irving Cummings Jnr, Robert G. North *d* James Tinling
☆ Kent Taylor, Dona Drake, Tala Birell, Leonard Strong, Konstantin Shayne

Dangerous Minds
US 1995 99m Technicolor
Buena Vista/Hollywood (Don Simpson, Jerry Bruckheimer)
An ex-marine becomes an English teacher at a tough inner-city school where she confronts raucous students who don't want to learn.
Despite its basis in fact, this comes across as bland and unbelievable wish-fulfilment, just another feel-good fantasy about tough, restive delinquents being tamed by poetry.
w Ronald Bass *book* My Posse Don't Do Homework by LouAnne Johnson *d* John N. Smith *ph* Pierre Letarte *m* Wendy & Lisa *pd* Donald Graham Burt *ed* Tom Rolf
☆ Michelle Pfeiffer, George Dzundza, Courtney B. Vance, Robin Bartlett, Bruklin Harris, Renoly Santiago, John Neville
'This earnest, sweet-natured inspirational drama almost seems like something from another, more innocent era.' – *Variety*
'This is one of those sham inspirational-teacher fables that worships the idea of knowledge without actually bothering to put any on screen. We're supposed to clasp our hands to our hearts when the kids learn a few lines of Dylan Thomas.' – *Owen Gleiberman, Entertainment Weekly*
† Andy Garcia's role as Michelle Pfeiffer's boyfriend was left on the cutting-room floor.

'An Avalanche Of Thrills And Excitement!'
'A Desperate Woman Hunt From Manhattan To The Wilds of Montana!'
Dangerous Mission
US 1954 75m Technicolor 3-D
RKO (Irwin Allen)
In Montana's Glacier National Park, a policeman tries to protect an innocent girl witness from big city gangsters.
Tolerable routine double-bill thriller with a predictable cable car climax.
w Horace McCoy, W. R. Burnett, Charles Bennett, James Edmiston *d* Louis King *ph* William Snyder *m* Roy Webb *ad* Albert S. D'Agostino, Walter E. Keller *ed* Gene Palmer
☆ Victor Mature (Det Matt Hallett), Piper Laurie (Louise Graham), Vincent Price (Paul Adams), William Bendix (Chief Ranger Joe Parker), Betta St John (Mary Tiller), Dennis Weaver (Pruitt), Steve Darrell (Katoonai Tiller), Marlo Dwyer (Mrs Elster)
'The scenery received the best notices.' – *James Robert Parish, 1976*

'This is your melody – you gave it to me. I'll never play it again without thinking of you!'
Dangerous Moonlight *
GB 1941 98m bw
RKO (William Sistrom)
US title: *Suicide Squadron*
A Polish pianist escapes from the Nazis and loses his memory after flying in the Battle of Britain.
Immensely popular wartime romance which introduced Richard Addinsell's Warsaw Concerto*. Production values and script somewhat below par.*
w Shaun Terence Young, Brian Desmond Hurst, Rodney Ackland *d* Brian Desmond Hurst *ph* Georges Périnal, Ronald Neame *m* Richard Addinsell
☆ *Anton Walbrook*, Sally Gray, Derrick de Marney, Cecil Parker, Percy Parsons, Keneth Kent, Guy Middleton, John Laurie, Frederick Valk

Dangerous Moves *
Switzerland 1985 100m colour
Enterprise/Spectrafilm (Arthur Cohn)
The world championship chess showdown is between the Soviet title holder and an exiled dissident challenger.
Interesting, rather specialized actor's piece with political overtones.
wd Richard Dembo *ph* Raoul Coutard *m* Gabriel Yared *ad* Ivan Maussion *ed* Agnès Guillemot
☆ Michel Piccoli, Leslie Caron, Liv Ullmann, Alexandre Arbatt
best foreign film

A Dangerous Profession
US 1949 79m bw
RKO
An ex-detective tries to help a beautiful woman and becomes involved in murder and the bail bond racket.
Undistinguished crime melodrama providing a satisfactory vehicle for its stars.
w Martin Rackin, Warren Duff *d* Ted Tetzlaff
☆ Pat O'Brien, George Raft, Ella Raines, Jim Backus, Bill Williams

A Dangerous Summer
Australia 1982 94m colour Panavision
McElroy and McElroy
In a Blue Mountain resort, a partner decides to burn down the buildings for the insurance.
Modest melodrama with spectacular fire sequences.
w David Ambrose, Quentin Masters *novel* Kit Denton *d* Quentin Masters
☆ James Mason, Tom Skerritt, Ian Gilmour, Wendy Hughes, Kim Deacon

Dangerous When Wet **
US 1953 95m Technicolor
MGM (George Wells)
An entire Arkansas family is sponsored to swim the English Channel.
A bright and lively vehicle for an aquatic star, who in one sequence swims with Tom and Jerry. Amusing sequences give opportunities to a strong cast.
w Dorothy Kingsley d Charles Walters *ph* Harold Rosson *m/ly* Johnny Mercer, Arthur Schwartz *md* George Stoll
☆ *Esther Williams, Charlotte Greenwood, William Demarest*, Fernando Lamas, Jack Carson, Denise Darcel, Barbara Whiting

'The truth hurts. But a lie can kill.'
A Dangerous Woman *
US 1993 101m Eastmancolor
First Independent/Amblin/Island World/Gramercy/Rollercoaster (Naomi Foner)
An ungainly woman who finds it impossible to lie is faced with a situation where telling the truth will mean her imprisonment.
An unusual and sometimes affecting drama, dealing with moral dilemmas and skewed relationships, but heavy-handed in its methods.
w Naomi Foner *novel* Mary McGarry Morris *d* Stephen Gyllenhaal *ph* Robert Elswit *m* Carter Burwell *pd* David Brisbin *ed* Harvey Rosenstock
☆ Debra Winger, Barbara Hershey, Gabriel Byrne, David Strathairn, John Terry, Chloe Webb
'Pic will register deeply with some viewers, especially women, but it's the kind of odd and muted tale for which it is difficult to drum up theatrical interest these days.' – *Todd McCarthy, Variety*
'At times something of a ponderous bore and has enough characters and plots to keep a soap opera going for a few months.' – *Kim Newman, Empire*

Dangerous Youth: see *These Dangerous Years*

Dangerously They Live
US 1941 77m bw
Warner (Ben Stoloff)
American Nazi agents try to get a secret memorized by a British girl agent injured in a car crash.
Watchable, routine spy propaganda fare.
w Marion Parsonnet *d* Robert Florey *ph* William O'Connell
☆ John Garfield, Raymond Massey, Nancy Coleman, Moroni Olsen, Lee Patrick, Christian Rub, Frank Reicher

Daniel
US 1983 129m Technicolor
World Film Services (John Van Eyssen)
The children of executed spies are traumatized by the past.
Patchwork vision of thirties America, with Jewishness thrown in for added weight. Not easy to watch.
w E. L. Doctorow *novel* The Book of Daniel by E. L. Doctorow *d* Sidney Lumet *ph* Andrzej Bartkowiak *m* Bob James *pd* Philip Rosenberg
☆ Timothy Hutton, Mandy Patinkin, Lindsay Crouse, Ed Asner, Ellen Barkin, Tovah Feldshuh
'Only with the last scene does one realize that it has collapsed into an empty liberal squeak.' – *Tom Milne, MFB*

Daniel and the Devil: see *All that Money Can Buy*

Daniel Boone, Trail Blazer
US 1956 76m Trucolor
Republic (Albert C. Gannaway)
Daniel Boone, battling against the Indians, makes the wilderness safe for settlers.
Stolidly acted story of the pioneer days of America, dully directed.
w Tom Hubbard, Jack Patrick *d* Albert C. Gannaway, Ismael Rodriguez *ph* Jack Draper *m* Raul Lavista *ed* Fernando A. Martinez.
☆ Bruce Bennett, Lon Chaney, Faron Young, Kem Dibbs, Damian O'Flynn, Jacqueline Evans, Nancy Rodman, Freddy Fernandez

Danny Boy: see *Angel (1982)*

Danny the Champion of the World *
GB 1989 99m colour
Portobello Productions (Eric Abraham)
A poacher's son devises a plan to discomfit the obnoxious squire.
Pleasant film aimed at a family audience, if it still exists.
w John Goldsmith *novel* Roald Dahl *d* Gavin Millar *ph* Oliver Stapleton *m* Stanley Myers *pd* Don Homfray *ed* Peter Tanner, Angus Newton
☆ Jeremy Irons, Robbie Coltrane, Samuel Irons, Cyril Cusack, Michael Hordern, Lionel Jeffries,

Ronald Pickup, Jean Marsh, Jimmy Nail, William Armstrong, John Woodvine

Dans la Poussière du Soleil: see *Lust in the Sun*

Dans la Ville Blanche: see *In the White City*

'It Will Burn Itself Into Your Memory Forever!'
Dante's Inferno **
US 1935 89m bw
Fox (Sol M. Wurtzel)
A ruthless carnival owner gets too big for his boots, and has a vision of hell induced by one of his own attractions.
Curiously unpersuasive melodrama with a moral, but the inferno sequence is one of the most unexpected, imaginative and striking pieces of cinema in Hollywood's history.
w Philip Klein, Robert Yost *d Harry Lachman ph Rudolph Maté m* Hugo Friedhofer, Samuel Kaylin, R. H. Bassett, Peter Brunelli *sp Fred F. Sersen, Ralph Hammeras sets Willy Pogany, from drawings by Gustav Doré*
☆ Spencer Tracy, Claire Trevor, Henry B. Walthall, Alan Dinehart, Scotty Beckett, Rita Hayworth
'A pushover for vigorous exploitation ... accentuate the inferno sequence and forget the rest, including the story.' – *Variety*
'We depart gratefully, having seen papier mâché photographed in more ways than we had thought possible.' – *Robert Herring*
'One of the most unusual and effectively presented films of the thirties.' – *John Baxter, 1968*
'The spectacle is shattering.' – *Sunday Times*
'Immediately following the 10-minute picturization of Hell, the story reverts to its native dullness.' – *Variety*
† Rita Hayworth's performance, as a dancer, was her first on the screen.

'The most awesome sight you'll ever see may be your last.'
Dante's Peak
US 1997 108m DeLuxe Panavision
Universal/Western Pacific (Gale Anne Hurd, Joseph M. Singer)
A vulcanologist warns an unheeding town of an impending disaster.
Disaster movie that follows a familiar narrative of a lone voice crying out against ignorance and complacency before the inevitable catastrophe; the eruption is spectacular, but hardly worth waiting for.
w Leslie Bohem *d* Roger Donaldson *ph* Andrzej Bartkowiak *m* John Frizzell, John Newton Howard *pd* Dennis Washington *ed* Howard Smith, Conrad Buff, Tina Hirsch *sp* Digital Domain
☆ Pierce Brosnan, Linda Hamilton, Charles Hallahan, Grant Heslov, Elizabeth Hoffman, Jamie Renee Smith, Jeremy Foley, Arabella Field
'Thanks to its predictable plot and boneheaded dialogue ("It's just like riding a bicycle," Brosnan assures a long-abstemious Hamilton about sex), Peak never reaches a peak among disaster films.' – *Leah Rozen, People Weekly*

Danton *
France/Poland 1982 136m colour
Losange/Group X (for Gaumont/TFI)
Robespierre quarrels with his colleague Danton, who hopes for a new spirit of tolerance.
Vivid historical re-creation which finally exhausts the spectator and is a little too concerned to make political points.
w Jean-Claude Carrière *play The Danton Affair* by Stanlislawa Przybyszewska *d Andrzej Wajda ph* Igor Luther *m* Jean Prodromides
☆ Gérard Depardieu, Wojciech Pszoniak, Anne Alvaro, Roland Blanche
'The temptation to see it in terms of Solidarity is unavoidable.' – *Philip Strick, MFB*
'By any reasonable standard, terrible.' – *New Yorker*
best foreign-language film

Danzón *
Spain 1991 96m colour
Metro/Instituto Mexicano Cinematografia/Macondo Cine Video/Fondo de Fomento a la Calidad Cinematografia/Televisión Española/Tabasco/ Gobierno del Estado de Veracruz (Jorge Sanchez)
A telephone operator goes in search of her ballroom dancing partner, who has fled Mexico City after being accused of a crime, and finds new friends and excitement before returning home.
Slight but charming film of a woman finding herself.
w Beatriz Navaro, Maria Novaro *d* Maria Novaro *ph* Rodrigo Garcia *ad* Marisa Pecarlins, Noberto Sanchez-Mejorada *ed* Nelson Rodriguez, Maria Novaro
☆ Maria Rojo, Carmen Salinas, Blanca Guerra, Tito Vasconcelos, Victor Carpinteiro, Margarita Isabel
'Despite its lack of pace, and sometimes because of it, this is a lovely film which will remain in the memory longer than most.' – *Derek Malcolm, Guardian*

Darby O'Gill and the Little People *
US 1959 90m Technicolor
Walt Disney
An Irish caretaker falls down a well and is captured by leprechauns, who allow him three wishes to rearrange his life.
Pleasantly barmy Irish fantasy with brilliant trick work but some tedium in between.
w Lawrence Edward Watkin *stories* H. T. Kavanagh *d* Robert Stevenson *ph* Winton C. Hoch *m* Oliver Wallace *ad* Carroll Clark *ed* Stanley Johnson *sp Peter Ellenshaw, Eustace Lycett, Joshua Meador*
☆ Albert Sharpe, *Jimmy O'Dea*, Sean Connery, Janet Munro, Kieron Moore, Estelle Winwood, Walter Fitzgerald, Denis O'Dea, J. G. Devlin, Jack MacGowran
'One of the best fantasies ever put on film.' – *Leonard Maltin*

Darby's Rangers
US 1957 121m bw
Warner (Martin Rackin)
GB title: *The Young Invaders*
A tough American commando unit is trained in Britain before seeing action in Africa and Sicily.
Standard World War II actioner, adequately executed.
w Guy Trosper *book* Major James Altieri *d* William Wellman *ph* William H. Clothier *m* Max Steiner
☆ James Garner, Etchika Choureau, Jack Warden, Edd Byrnes, Venetia Stevenson, Torin Thatcher, Stuart Whitman, Andrea King, Frieda Inescort, Reginald Owen, Adam Williams

D'Ardenelle: see *Harem*

'He is the man without fear.'
Daredevil
US 2003 103m DeLuxe 'Scope
TCF/Regency/MarvelNew Regency/Horseshoe Bay (Arnon Milchan, Gary Foster, Avi Arad)
A lawyer, who was blinded in a childhood accident that sharpened his other senses, becomes a vigilante superhero by night, taking on New York's lowlife.
Daredevil follows in the mould of recent Batman movies: a hero who had a traumatic childhood that resulted in a troubled adult doing good in a Gothic city. The movie is intended as the beginning of a new franchise – let's hope future episodes offer more excitement than is on view here.
wd Mark Steven Johnson *ph* Ericson Core *m* Graeme Revell *pd* Barry Chusid *ed* Dennis Virkler, Armen Minasian *sp* Rich Thorne; Rhythm & Hues; Digital Domain; Pixel Magic
☆ Ben Affleck (Matt Murdock/Daredevil), Jennifer Garner (Elektra Natchios), Michael Clarke Duncan (Kingpin/Fisk), Colin Farrell (Bullseye), Joe Pantoliano (Urich), Jon Favreau (Franklin Nelson), David Keith (Jack Murdock), Erick Avari (Natchios)
'The movie is, in short, your money's worth, better than we expect, more fun than we deserve.' – *Roger Ebert, Chicago Sun-Times*
'The movie is derivative, flat, halfhearted, its squareness unrelieved by irony or fantasy.' – *David Denby, New Yorker*
† Budgeted at around $75m, the film took more than $102m at the US box-office.

The Dark: see *The Haunted House of Horror (1969)*

The Dark
US 1979 92m DeLuxe Panavision
Film Ventures International (Dick Clark, Edward L. Montoro)
A homicidal alien stalks Los Angeles, ripping off people's heads.
Unconsidered shocker with nothing to it but the shocks.
w Stanford Whitmore *d* John Cardos *ph* John Morrill *m* Roger Kellaway *ad* Rusty Rosene *ed* Martin Dreffke
☆ William Devane, Cathy Lee Crosby, Richard Jaeckel, Keenan Wynn, Vivian Blaine

The Dark Angel *
US 1925 83m (24 fps) bw silent
First National (Samuel Goldwyn)
During World War I, a blinded officer tries to persuade his fiancée to marry another man, without her knowing of his own infirmity.
Vilma Banky's first American film, her first teaming with Colman and a mid-twenties hit of colossal proportions.
w Frances Marion *play* Guy Bolton *d* George Fitzmaurice *ph* George Barnes
☆ Ronald Colman, Vilma Banky, Wyndham Standing, Frank Elliott, Charles Lane, Florence Turner, Helen Jerome Eddy

The Dark Angel *
US 1935 105m bw
Samuel Goldwyn
Rivalry between two friends over a woman comes to a head during the First World War.
Tearstained melodrama from another age, a remake of a 1925 film, neatly packaged for the romantic 1935 public.
w Lillian Hellman, Mordaunt Shairp *d* Sidney Franklin *ph* Gregg Toland *m* Alfred Newman *ad* Richard Day
☆ Merle Oberon, Fredric March, Herbert Marshall, Janet Beecher, John Halliday, Henrietta Crosman, Frieda Inescort, George Breakston, Claud Allister
'A sockaroo woman's picture.' – *Variety*
'A highly literate screen adaptation, telling the story with feeling and good taste.' – *New York Times*
'It makes a systematic and skilful appeal to those untrustworthy emotions which may suddenly cause the most hardened intellects to dissolve before the most obvious sentimentality.' – *The Times*
Richard Day
Merle Oberon

'Good Cop. Bad Alien. Big Trouble.'
Dark Angel *
US 1990 93m DeLuxe
Vision/Damon/Saunders (Jeff Young)
US title: *I Come in Peace*
A maverick cop and the FBI chase after a killer from another planet.
A cut above the usual aliens-on-the-rampage action, thanks to occasional wit and a narrative with unexpected twists.
w Jonathan Tydor, Leonard Maas Jnr *d* Craig R. Baxley *ph* Mark Irwin *m* Jan Hammer *pd* Phillip M. Leonard *ad* Nino Candido *ed* Mark Helfrich
☆ Dolph Lundgren, Brian Benben, Betsy Brantley, Matthias Hues, Jay Bilas, Jim Haynie, David Ackroyd, Sherman Howard, Sam Anderson
'This undemanding cinematic comic book may come in peace but doesn't seem likely to go all that quietly.' – *Variety*

'Every time a woman turns her face away because she's tired or unwilling, there's someone waiting like me...'
The Dark at the Top of the Stairs **
US 1960 124m Technicolor
Warner (Michael Garrison)
Twenties small town drama about a young boy's awakening to the sexual tensions around him.
Archetypal family drama set in that highly familiar American street. The perfect essence of this playwright's work, with high and low spots, several irrelevancies, but a real feeling for the people and the place.
w Harriet Frank Jnr, Irving Ravetch *play* William Inge *d* Delbert Mann *ph* Harry Stradling *m* Max Steiner
☆ *Robert Preston, Dorothy McGuire*, Angela Lansbury, *Eve Arden*, Shirley Knight, Frank Overton, Lee Kinsolving, Robert Eyer
† The curious title turns out to be a synonym for life, which one should never be afraid of.
Shirley Knight

The Dark Avenger *
GB 1955 85m Eastmancolor Cinemascope
Allied Artists (Vaughan N. Dean)
US title: *The Warriors*
The Black Prince quells some French rebels.
Good-humoured historical romp with the ageing star in his last swashbuckling role, helped by a good cast and brisk pace.
w Daniel B. Ullman *d* Henry Levin *ph* Guy Green *m* Cedric Thorpe Davie
☆ Errol Flynn, Peter Finch, Joanne Dru, Yvonne Furneaux, Patrick Holt, Michael Hordern, Moultrie Kelsall, Robert Urquhart, Noel Willman

Dark Blue World
Czech Republic/GB 2001 115m colour
Columbia TriStar/Biograf/Portobello (Eric Abraham, Jan Sverak)
aka: *Trmavomodry Svet*
During the Second World War, two Czech pilots become rivals in love when they join the Royal Air Force.
The sense of irony evident at the end of the film – with a Czech pilot imprisoned in his homeland and guarded by former S.S. men – is sadly lacking elsewhere, in a trite romance against the background of war.
w Zdenek Sverak *d* Jan Sverak *ph* Vladimir Smutny *m* Ondrej Soukup *pd* Jan Vlasak *ed* Alois Fisarek
☆ Ondrej Vetchy (Lt Franta Slama), Krystof Hadek (Karel Vojtisek), Oldrich Kaiser (Machaty), Susan Whitmore (Tara Fitzgerald), Jorg Assmann (Doctor), Charles Dance (Wing Commander Bentley), Anna Massey (English teacher)
'Derivative and not compelling.' – *Roger Ebert*
† The film re-uses aerial dogfights from the 1969 movie *Battle of Britain*.

Dark City
US 1950 97m bw
Paramount/Hal B. Wallis
A bookmaker finds himself on the run from a revenge-seeking psychopath.
Unattractive and heavily-handled underworld melodrama, a disappointment from the talents involved.
w John Meredyth Lucas, Larry Marcus *d* William Dieterle *ph* Victor Milner *m* Franz Waxman
☆ Charlton Heston, Lizabeth Scott, Viveca Lindfors, Dean Jagger, Don Defore, Jack Webb, Ed Begley, Henry Morgan, Mike Mazurki
'A jaded addition to a type of thriller which has become increasingly tedious and unreal.' – *MFB*

'They built a city to see what makes us tick. Last night one of us went off.'
Dark City *
US 1998 101m DeLuxe Panavision
Polygram/New Line/Mystery Clock (Andrew Mason)
An amnesiac man in a strange night-time city discovers that aliens are carrying out an experiment by manipulating his life and that of its other inhabitants.
Paranoid fantasy that owes its visual style to graphic novels such as The Crow, and its tone to film noir; its narrative, though, is more muddled and, ultimately, somewhat forgettable.
w Alex Proyas, Lem Dobbs, David S. Goyer *d* Alex Proyas *ph* Dariusz Wolski *m* Trevor Jones *pd* George Liddle, Patrick Tatopolous *ed* Dov Hoenig
☆ Rufus Sewell, Kiefer Sutherland, Jennifer Connelly, William Hurt, Richard O'Brien, Ian Richardson, Colin Friels, Bruce Spence, John Bluthal

'Engaging mostly in the degree to which it creates and sustains a visually startling alternate universe.' – *Todd McCarthy, Variety*

Dark Command *
US 1940 92m bw
Republic (Sol C. Siegel)
In pre-Civil War Kansas, an ambitious ex-schoolteacher named Cantrill organizes guerrilla bands to pillage the countryside.
Semi-historical hokum, quite well done with a good cast.
w Grover Jones, Lionel Houser, F. Hugh Herbert *novel* W. R. Burnett *d* Raoul Walsh *ph* Jack Marta *m* Victor Young *ad* John Victor Mackay
☆ John Wayne, Claire Trevor, Walter Pidgeon, Roy Rogers, George 'Gabby' Hayes, Porter Hall, Marjorie Main
'It's the highest budgeter for Republic to date, running in neighbourhood of 700,000 dollars in negative cost. In the family and action houses, it's a natural to roll up good grosses.' – *Variety*
Victor Young; art direction

The Dark Corner *
US 1946 98m bw
TCF (Fred Kohlmar)
A private eye with a criminal record thinks he is being menaced by an old adversary, but the latter is found murdered.
Moody, brutish, well-made thriller with a plot put together from bits and pieces of older, better movies, notably Clifton Webb's reprise of his Laura performance and William Bendix ditto The Glass Key.
w Jay Dratler, Bernard Schoenfeld *story* Leo Rosten *d Henry Hathaway ph Joe MacDonald* *m* Cyril Mockridge
☆ Mark Stevens, Clifton Webb, Lucille Ball, William Bendix, Kurt Kreuger, Cathy Downs, Reed Hadley, Constance Collier
CATHCART (CLIFTON WEBB): 'I hate the dawn. The grass always looks as though it's been left out all night.'
BRAD (MARK STEVENS): 'There goes my last lead. I feel all dead inside. I'm backed up in a dark corner, and I don't know who's hitting me.'
'Not so much a whodunnit as a whodunnwhat ... all seem bent on "getting" each other and their internecine plottings add up to an alpha thriller.' – *Daily Mail*

The Dark Crystal **
GB 1982 94m Technicolor Panavision
Universal/AFD/ITC (David Lazer)
Two young people defeat the evil creatures who have taken over the world by replacing a shard which has been taken from the Dark Crystal.
Surprisingly effective piece of mysticism performed entirely by puppets from the Muppet stable.
w David Odell d Jim Henson, Frank Oz *ph* Oswald Morris *pd Harry Lange ed* Ralph Kemplen *conceptual designer Brian FroudMD0*
'A dazzling technological and artistic achievement ... could teach a lesson in morality to youngsters at the same time as it is entertaining their parents.' – *Variety*

Dark Days **
US 2000 81m bw
Optimum/Picture Farm (Marc Singer)
Documentary on a community of homeless people who made their own shantytown in an Amtrak underground railway tunnel in Manhattan.
Disturbing, diverting documentary, made over a period of two years, among derelicts and drug addicts, who still find life worth living, even in subterranean dark.
d Marc Singer *ph* Marc Singer *m* DJ Shadow *ed* Melissa Neidich
'Manages the tricky feat of humanizing its subjects without overly sentimentalizing them.' – *Stephen Holden, New York Times*

Dark Eyes: see *Black Eyes*

Dark Eyes of London *
GB 1939 75m bw
Pathé/Argyle (John Argyle)
US title: *The Human Monster*
The proprietor of a home for the blind uses a mute giant to drown insured victims.
Reasonably effective British horror, a rarity at the time.
w John Argyle, Walter Summers, Patrick Kirwan *novel* Edgar Wallace *d* Walter Summers *ph* Bryan Langley *m* Guy Jones *ad* Duncan Sutherland *ed* E. G. Richards
☆ *Bela Lugosi*, Hugh Williams, Greta Gynt, Wilfrid Walter, Edmon Ryan
'Though it creaks a bit and some of the performances are stilted, this is actually one of Lugosi's better vehicles.' – *The Dark Side*
† It was the first British film to be given an H (for Horror) certificate.

Dark Forces: see *Harlequin*

Dark Habits
Spain 1983 100m colour
Metro/Tesauro (Luis Calvo)
original title: *Entre Tinieblas*
A drug-addicted singer takes refuge from the police in a convent full of decadent nuns.
High spirited, but for the easily amused only.
wd Pedro Almodóvar *ph* Angel L. Fernandez *m* Cam España *pd* Pin Morales, Roman Arango *ed* José Salcedo
☆ Cristina S. Pascual, Marisa Paredes, Mari Carrillo, Lina Canalejas, Manuel Zarzo, Carmen Maura, Chus Lampreave
'A rather labored series of jokes.' – *Pauline Kael, New Yorker*

The Dark Half
US 1991 122m DeLuxe
Orion/Dark Half (Declan Baldwin)
A writer has two personalities – one an unsuccessful novelist, the other a disreputable bestselling author who is also a killer.
A literary twist on Dr Jekyll and Mr Hyde, but only of minor interest; it neither shocks nor thrills.
wd George A. Romero *novel* Stephen King *ph* Tony Pierce-Roberts *m* Christopher Young *pd* Cletus Anderson *ed* Pasquale Buba *sp* make-up: John Vulich, Everett Burrell; visual effects: VCE/Peter Kuran; Video Image
☆ Timothy Hutton, Amy Madigan, Michael Rooker, Julie Harris, Robert Joy, Kent Broadhurst, Beth Grant, Chelsea Field, Royal Dano
'Features enough gruesome killings and special effects to satisfy hardcore horror fans, but also has sufficient narrative and thematic substance to keep more mainstream viewers interested.' – *Variety*
'A classy psychological horror movie, this delivers its share of visual shock moments, but relies for the most part on a controlled build-up of cumulative tension.' – *Nigel Floyd, The Dark Side*

The Dark Horse
US 1932 75m bw
Warner
A nitwit runs for governor and nearly makes it.
Mild political satire; closer to farce, really.
w Joseph Jackson, Wilson Mizner *d* Alfred E. Green
☆ Guy Kibbee, Bette Davis, Warren William, Frank McHugh

Dark Journey *
GB 1937 82m bw
London Films/Victor Saville
In 1915 Stockholm, a French woman spy masquerading as a traitor falls in love with her German spy contact.
Unconvincing but entertaining romantic adventure with good star performances.
w Lajos Biro, Arthur Wimperis *play* Lajos Biro *d* Victor Saville *ph* Georges Périnal, Harry Stradling *m* Richard Addinsell *ad* Andrei Andreiev *ed* William Hornbeck, Hugh Stewart
☆ *Conrad Veidt, Vivien Leigh*, Joan Gardner, Anthony Bushell, Ursula Jeans, Eliot Makeham, Austin Trevor, Edmund Willard
'An exceptional quantity of carefully thought out direction ... the financial success will depend on whether the general public will understand and keep pace with the plot.' – *Variety*

'One twin loves – and one twin loves to kill!'
The Dark Mirror **
US 1946 85m bw
Universal
A police detective works out which of identical twin girls is a murderer.
Unconvincing but highly absorbing thriller with all credits plus; the best brand of Hollywood moonshine.
w Nunnally Johnson *story* Vladimir Pozner *d Robert Siodmak ph* Milton Krasner *m* Dimitri Tiomkin
☆ *Olivia de Havilland, Lew Ayres*, Thomas Mitchell, Garry Owen
'Smooth and agreeable melodrama ... the detective work involves inkblot and word association tests and an amusingly sinister tandem of oscillating pens which register concealed emotions as one of the sisters talks.' – *James Agee*
Vladimir Pozner

Dark Obsession: see *Diamond Skulls*

Dark of the Night: see *Mr Wrong*

Dark of the Sun: see *The Mercenaries*

The Dark Page: see *Scandal Sheet*

Dark Passage **
US 1947 106m bw
Warner (Jerry Wald)
A convicted murderer escapes from jail and proves his innocence.
Loosely assembled, totally unconvincing star thriller which succeeds because of its professionalism, some good cameos, and a number of narrative tricks including subjective camera for the first half hour.
w Delmer Daves *novel* David Goodis *d Delmer Daves ph Sid Hickox m* Franz Waxman
☆ *Humphrey Bogart, Lauren Bacall*, Agnes Moorehead, Bruce Bennett, *Tom D'Andrea, Houseley Stevenson*
'An almost total drag.' – *New Yorker, 1977*

The Dark Past **
US 1948 75m bw
Columbia (Buddy Adler)
A psychiatrist turns the tables on convicts who break into his home.
Tense, economical remake of Blind Alley *(qv); a fresh look at a familiar situation (*The Small Voice, The Desperate Hours*, etc.) helped by excellent performances.*
w Philip Macdonald, Malvin Wald, Oscar Saul *d Rudolph Maté ph* Joseph Walker *m* George Duning
☆ *William Holden, Lee J. Cobb, Nina Foch*, Adele Jergens, Stephen Dunne
'A picture so packed with skill and imagination that every minute is absorbing.' – *Richard Mallett, Punch*

Dark Sands: see *Jericho*

The Dark Side of Love
Italy 1985 88m colour
Globe/Dania/Filmes International (Pietro Innocenzi)
original title: *Fotografando Patrizia*
A sickly, isolated teenager is introduced to sex by his promiscuous sister.
Slick, glossily presented soft-core porn.
w Riccardo Ghione, Edith Bruck, Salvatore Samperi, Lewis E. Cianelli, Massimo di Luzio *d* Salvatore Samperi *ph* Dante Spinotti *m* Fred Bongusto *pd* Maria Chiara Gamba *ed* Sergio Montanari
☆ Monica Guerritore, Lorenzo Lena, Gianfranco Manfredi, Gilla Novak, Saverio Vallone
'Surprisingly well shot, boasting first rate interiors, lighting and cinematography in the style of Tony Scott.' – *Sight and Sound*

The Dark Side of the Moon
Denmark 1986 94m colour
Cannon/Film-Cooperative Denmark (Per Arman)
original title: *Manden I Manen*
A wife murderer, released from prison, tries to effect a reconciliation with his daughter.
Ponderously slow and introverted, with darkly expressionistic camerawork.
wd Eric Clausen *ph* Morten Bruus *m* John Hoybe *pd* Leif Sylvester *ed* Ghita Beckendorff
☆ Peter Thiel, Catherine Poul Dupont, Christina Bengtsson, Kim Jansson, Yavuzer Cetinkaya, Royt Richards, Berthe Qvistgaard, Erik Truxa

'The mission of the Strangelove generation!'
Dark Star ***
US 1974 83m Metrocolor
Jack H. Harris (John Carpenter)
In the 22nd century, the bored crew of a starship on an intergalactic mission become prey to their own phobias and to the alien mascot they are taking back to Earth.
A semi-professional film which turned out to be one of the screen's neatest low-budget entries in the pulp science fiction genre. That doesn't make it wholly entertaining, but its credentials are impeccable.
w John Carpenter, Dan O'Bannon d John Carpenter *ph* Douglas Knapp *m* John Carpenter *pd/ed* Dan O'Bannon
☆ Brian Narelle, Dre Pahich, Cal Kuniholm, Dan O'Bannon

Dark Summer
GB 1994 85m colour CinemaScope
2C/Activate (Charles Teton)
In Liverpool, a black youth turns professional boxer, only to lose his first fight and his wife.
An ambitious first feature in which style triumphs over content.
wd Charles Teton *ph* Charles Teton *m* Clive Chin *pd* Elouise Attwood *ed* Charles Teton
☆ Steve Ako, Joeline Garnier-Joel, Chris Darwin, Bernie Deasy, Wayne Ako, Sylvia Amon, Tom Williamson
'Despite the difficulties put in front of your average impatient viewer, who may wonder why the film is so painfully slow without looking under its surface, Teton is very clearly a film-maker to watch. Whether many will watch *Dark Summer* is more open to question.' – *Derek Malcolm, Guardian*

'Never a love so exquisite! She smiled at the cost, and bravely paid the reckoning when her heart's happy dancing was ended!'
Dark Victory **
US 1939 106m bw
Warner (David Lewis)
A good-time society girl discovers she is dying of a brain tumour.
A highly commercial tearjerker of its day, this glutinous star vehicle now works only fitfully.
w Casey Robinson *play* George Brewer Jnr, Bertram Bloch *d* Edmund Goulding *ph* Ernest Haller *m* Max Steiner
☆ *Bette Davis, George Brent*, Humphrey Bogart, Ronald Reagan, Geraldine Fitzgerald, Henry Travers, Cora Witherspoon, Dorothy Peterson
JUDITH (BETTE DAVIS): 'Nothing can hurt us now. What we have can't be destroyed. That's our victory – our victory over the dark. It is a victory because we're not afraid.'
'If it were an automobile, it would be a Rolls-Royce with the very best trimmings.' – *Time*
'Will turn in a good account of itself at the box office, though not rating socko proportions.' – *Variety*
'A completely cynical appraisal would dismiss it all as emotional flim-flam ... but it is impossible to be that cynical about it.' – *Frank S. Nugent*
'A gooey collection of clichés, but Davis slams through them in her nerviest style.' – *New Yorker, 1976*
† Remade 1963 as *Stolen Hours*, with Susan Hayward; 1975 as *Dark Victory* (TV movie) with Elizabeth Montgomery.
best picture; Bette Davis; Max Steiner

Dark Water *
GB 1980 28m colour
Dragonfly/ITC
A girl locked in a swimming pool is terrorized by a mad killer.

Agreeably watchable thriller full of shadows and shocks.
w Andrew Bogle, Tony Grisoni d Andrew Bogle
☆ Phil Davis, Gwyneth Strong, David Beames

Dark Waters **
US 1944 90m bw
Benedict Bogeaus

Recovering from being torpedoed, an orphan girl visits her aunt and uncle in Louisiana and has some terrifying experiences.
Competent frightened-lady melodrama helped by its bayou surroundings. Possibly discarded by Hitchcock, but with sequences well in his manner.
w Joan Harrison, Marian Cockrell d *André de Toth* ph *John Mescall* m Miklos Rozsa
☆ Merle Oberon, Franchot Tone, *Thomas Mitchell, Fay Bainter, John Qualen*, Elisha Cook Jnr, Rex Ingram

Dark Wind
US 1991 111m Technicolor
Guild/Carolco/North Face Motion Picture Company (Patrick Markey)

Hassled by corrupt FBI agents, a Navajo cop investigates drugs-related murders.
Despite its unusual hero, a disappointingly mundane thriller.
w Neal Jimenez, Eric Bergren, Mark Horowitz novel Tony Hillerman d Errol Morris ph Stefan Czapsky m Michel Colombier pd Ted Bafaloukos ed Susan Crutcher, Freeman Davies
☆ Lou Diamond Phillips, Gary Farmer, Fred Ward, Guy Boyd, John Karlen, Jane Loranger, Gary Basaraba, Blake Clark
'A smooth genre piece, well acted, slickly written and benefiting from the natural beauty of the setting.' – *Kim Newman, Empire*

Darker than Amber
US 1970 96m Technicolor
Cinema Center/Major Films (Walter Seltzer)

A Florida private eye rescues a girl who is subsequently murdered and turns out to be part of a confidence racket.
Routine suspenser from the Travis McGee books; not very stimulating.
w Ed Waters novel John D. MacDonald d Robert Clouse ph Frank Phillips m John Parker
☆ Rod Taylor, Suzy Kendall, Theodore Bikel, James Booth, Jane Russell, Janet McLachlan, William Smith

The Darkest Light *
GB 1999 92m colour
Pathé/Canal+/BBC/Footprint/Arts Council (Mark Blaney)

While her brother is ill with leukaemia and her father's sheep and cattle are slaughtered because of foot and moth disease, an 11-year-old Yorkshire farmer's daughter sees a bright light and believes she has had a vision of the Virgin Mary.
A drama about birth and death, faith and fantasy, but its small-scale approach is likely to work better on TV than the big screen.
w Simon Beaufoy d Bille Eltringham, Simon Beaufoy ph Mary Farbrother m Adrian Johnston pd Chris Townsend ed Ewa J. Lind cos Ffion Elinor
☆ Stephen Dillane (Tom), Kerry Fox (Sue), Keri Arnold (Catherine), Kavita Sungha (Uma), Jason Walton (Matthew), Nisha K. Nayar (Nisha), Nicholas Hope (Father Mark)
'Despite some powerful moments, the movie's overall feel and emotional range are more reminiscent of Brit telepics, equipping this more for a small-screen career than a theatrical one.' – *Derek Elley, Variety*

Darklands
GB 1996 90m Sohoimages
Metrodome/Darklands/Lluniau Lliw Cyf (Paul Brooks)

A journalist investigating the murder of a steelworker in South Wales uncovers a pagan cult involved in human sacrifice.
Dire, cheapskate Gothic horror movie, in thrall to the cult The Wicker Man *(qv).*
wd Julian Richards ph Zoran Djordjevic m John Murphy, David Hughes pd Hayden Pearce ed Mark Talbot-Butler
☆ Craig Fairbrass, Rowena King, Jon Finch, David Duffy, Richard Lynch, Nicola Branson, Beth Morris, William Thomas
'The acting fails to rise above a creaking script, and the visual style would shame a 30-year-old *Look at Life*.' – *Richard Williams, Guardian*

'They destroyed everything he had, everthing he was. Now, crime has a new enemy, and justice has a new face.'
Darkman
US 1990 91m DeLuxe
UIP/Universal (Robert Tapert)

A hideously deformed scientist invents a synthetic skin that makes him a master of disguise.
Relentlessly silly horror movie full of extravagantly pointless camera movements.
w Chuck Pfarrer, Sam Raimi, Ivan Raimi, Daniel Goldin, Joshua Goldin d Sam Raimi ph Bill Pope m Danny Elfman pd Randy Ser ed David Stiven
☆ Liam Neeson, Frances McDormand, Colin Friels, Larry Drake, Nelson Mashita, Jesse Lawrence Ferguson, Rafael H. Robledo, Danny Hicks, Theodore Raimi

Darkman 2: The Return of Durant
US/Canada 1994 93m colour
Universal/Renaissance (David Roessell)

A hideously disfigured scientist works on a formula to give himself new skin while fending off the attacks of a crooked property developer.
A bad direct-to-video sequel, with plodding performances and script.
w Steven McKay, Chuck Pfarrer d Bradford May ph Bradford May m Randy Miller ad Ian Brock ed Daniel Cahn cos Noreen Landry
☆ Arnold Vosloo (Dr Peyton Westlake/Darkman), Larry Drake (Robert G. Durant), Kim Delaney (Jill Randall), Renée O'Connor (Laurie Brinkman), Rod Wilson (Ivan Druganov), Lawrence Dane (Dr Hathaway), Jesse Collins (Dr David Brinkman), Jack Langedijk (Rollo Latham)

Darkman III: Die Darkman Die
US 1995 87m colour
MCA/Renaissance (David Roessell)

While trying to perfect his formula for a liquid skin, a disfigured doctor falls foul of a gangster.
Cheap and nasty sequel, with much ham acting and a narrative that is never less than ridiculous.
w Michael Colleary, Mike Werb d Bradford May ph Bradford May m Randy Miller pd Ian Brock ed Daniel Cahn makeup fx Kurtzman, Nicotero & Berger EFX
☆ Jeff Fahey (Peter Rooker), Arnold Vosloo (Dr Peyton Westlake), Darlanne Fluegel (Bridget Thorne), Roxann Biggs-Dawson (Angela Rooker), Nigel Bennett (Nico), Alicia Panetta (Jenny Rooker), Ronn Sarosiak (Mack), Peter Graham (Joey)

Darkness Falls
GB 1998 96m colour
Downtown/Vine International/Hoseplace (Alan Latham, Clifford Haydn-Tovey)

A businessman has problems: he has 24 hours to repay a £10m loan, and he is confronted by a gunman accusing him of adultery.
An uninteresting thriller about uninteresting people.
w John Howlett play *Dangerous Obsession* by N. J. Crisp d Gerry Lively ph Adam Santelli m Guy Farley pd Edward Thomas ed David Spiers
☆ Sherilyn Fenn, Ray Winstone, Tim Dutton, Anita Dobson, Bryan Pringle, Robin McCaffrey, Michael Praed, Oliver Tobias
'A nasty, common little film.' – *Danny Leigh, Sight and Sound*

Darkness in Tallinn **
Finland/USA/Sweden/Estonia 1993 99m bw/Eastmancolor
Metro/FilmZolfo/Upstream/FilmLance/Teknik/EXITfilm (Lasse Saarinen)

original title: *Tallinn Pimeduses*
In 1991, ruthless gangsters decide to grab $970m in gold being returned to Tallinn, the capital of newly independent Estonia, from Paris, where it had been hidden for 50 years; but their plan depends on persuading a reluctant electrician to fix a city-wide power-cut at the time of the theft.
A deft and intriguing thriller, set against wider themes of freedom and responsibility. Järvilaturi builds the suspense to a tense climax while still allowing space for his actors to create individual characters.
w Paul Kolsby d *Ilkka Järvilaturi* ph Rein Kotov m Mader pd Toomas Hörak ed Christopher Tellefsen
☆ Ivo Uukkivi, Milena Gulbe, Enn Klooren, Jüri Järvet, Väino Laes, Peeter Dja, Monika Mäger
'A modest but quite ingenious genre pic with an unusual setting and plenty of atmosphere.' – *Variety*
'A compelling and densely plotted heist movie.' – *Sight and Sound*

'When she was good she was very very good. When she was bad, she was...'
Darling **
GB 1965 127m bw
Anglo-Amalgamated/Vic/Appia (Joseph Janni, Victor Lyndon)

An ambitious young woman deserts her journalist mentor for a company director, an effeminate photographer and an Italian prince.
Fashionable mid-sixties concoction of smart swinging people and their amoral doings. Influential, put over with high style, and totally tiresome in retrospect.
w Frederic Raphael d *John Schlesinger* ph Ken Higgins m John Dankworth pd Ray Simm
☆ *Julie Christie*, Dirk Bogarde, Laurence Harvey, Roland Curram, Alex Scott, Basil Henson, Pauline Yates
BOGARDE TO CHRISTIE: 'Your idea of being fulfilled is having more than one man in bed at the same time.'
'As empty of meaning and mind as the empty life it's exposing.' – *Pauline Kael*
'A cool, clear and devastating look at the glossy success set.' – *Judith Crist*
Frederic Raphael; Julie Christie
best picture; John Schlesinger
Frederic Raphael; Ray Simm; Dirk Bogarde; Julie Christie

Darling I am Growing Younger: see *Monkey Business*

Darling Lili *
US 1970 136m Technicolor Panavision
Paramount/Geoffrey (Owen Crump)

During World War I, an American air ace falls for a German lady spy, and waits till the war is over to marry her.
Farce and romance mix oddly with aerial acrobatics in this expensive and dull extravaganza which bore the sub-title Where Were You the Night I Shot Down Baron von Richthofen? *(which probably sums up its aims and its failure). A coffee table film, good to look at and with occasional striking moments.*
w Blake Edwards, William Peter Blatty d Blake Edwards ph *Russell Harlan, Harold E. Wellman* m Henry Mancini pd Fernando Carrere
☆ Julie Andrews, Rock Hudson, Jeremy Kemp, Lance Percival, Michael Witney, Jacques Marin, André Maranne
Henry Mancini; song 'Whistling Away the Dark' (m Henry Mancini, ly Johnny Mercer)

'A Conspiracy To Overthrow The King...Leads to Courage, Passion & Adventure!'
D'Artagnan's Daughter *
France 1994 130m colour
Artificial Eye/CiBy 2000/Little Bear/TF1 (Véronique Bourboulon)

original title: *La Fille de D'Artagnan*
D'Artagnan's daughter sets out to revenge the murder of a nun, an act which brings back into action the ageing three musketeers, who foil a plot to kill the King.
An enjoyable romp that does not take history or itself too seriously.
w Michel Leviant, Jean Cosmos, Bertrand Tavernier idea Riccardo Freda, Eric Poindrom d Bertrand Tavernier ph Patrick Blossier m Philippe Sarde ad Geoffroy Larcher ed Ariane Boeglin
☆ Sophie Marceau, Philippe Noiret, Claude Rich, Sami Frey, Jean-Luc Bideau, Raoul Billerey, Charlotte Kady, Nils Tavernier
'In an era where comedy wears hob-nailed boots, Tavernier's gentle, almost inconsequential touch gladdens the heart.' – *Geoff Brown, The Times*
† Italian Riccardo Freda, whose original idea it was, was set to direct, but a week before shooting began Sophie Marceau refused to work with him and he was replaced by the producer, Bertrand Tavernier.

The Darwin Adventure *
GB 1971 91m Eastmancolor
TCF/Palomar (Joseph Strick, Irving Lerner)
In 1831, Charles Darwin becomes ship's naturalist on the *Beagle* and studies wildlife in South America.
Rather naïve biopic of Darwin which tries to cover too much with too slender resources but makes a pleasant introduction to the subject.
w William Fairchild d Jack Couffer ph Denys Coop, Jack Couffer m Marc Wilkinson
☆ Nicholas Clay, Susan Macready, Ian Richardson, Christopher Martin, Robert Flemyng, Aubrey Woods, Hugh Morton
'The biopic plague, which has ravaged the screen lives of Pasteur, Juarez, Cole Porter and countless others, has now struck down the memory of famed naturalist Charles Darwin. The filmgoing public's own version of Darwin's natural selection theory will immediately weed out this inferior species.' – *Variety*

D.A.R.Y.L.
US 1985 99m TVC Color Panavision
Columbia (Burt Harris, Gabrielle Kelly)

A mysterious young man is really a robot, 'data analysing robot youth lifeform'; but he begins to have feelings...
Muddled sentimental fantasy which doesn't seem to know where it's going.
w David Ambrose, Allan Scott, Jeffrey Ellis d Simon Wincer ph Frank Watts m Marvin Hamlisch pd Alan Cassie ed Adrian Carr
☆ Mary Beth Hurt, Michael McKean, Kathryn Walker, Colleen Camp
'The kind of project that must have looked great on paper.' – *Variety*

A Date with a Lonely Girl: see *T.R. Baskin (1971)*

A Date with Destiny: see *The Mad Doctor (1941)*

A Date with Destiny: see *The Return of October (1948)*

A Date with Judy
US 1948 113m Technicolor
MGM (Joe Pasternak)

A teenager wrongly suspects her friend of an illicit affair.
Ambitious but flat comedy musical which neatly wraps up all kinds of forties people and institutions: teenagers, small towns, families, Carmen Miranda and Miss Taylor, not to mention the producer.
w Dorothy Cooper, Dorothy Kingsley d Richard Thorpe ph Robert Surtees m/ly various md George Stoll
☆ Wallace Beery, Elizabeth Taylor, Jane Powell, Carmen Miranda, Xavier Cugat, Robert Stack, Selena Royle, Scotty Beckett, Leon Ames

A Date with the Falcon
US 1941 63m bw
RKO (Howard Benedict)
The Falcon attempts to save his forthcoming marriage and find a missing scientist with a formula for synthetic diamonds.
Slick comic thriller with a few amusing moments.
w Lynn Root, Frank Fenton *character created by* Michael Arlen d Irving Reis ph Robert de Grasse m Paul Sawtell ad Albert D'Agostino, Al Herman ed Harry Marker
☆ George Sanders, Wendy Barrie, James Gleason, Allen Jenkins, Mona Maris

Daughter of Dr Jekyll
US 1957 74m bw
Allied Artists

An evil doctor tells his ward that she is the daughter of the unfortunate Dr Jekyll and therefore responsible for a series of werewolf killings.

Bathetic cheapie with risible views of England and a tendency to mix up several myths in one package.
w Jack Pollexfen *d* Edgar G. Ulmer
☆ Arthur Shields, John Agar, Gloria Talbott, John Dierkes

Daughter of Luxury: see *Five and Ten*

The Daughter of Rosie O'Grady *
US 1950 104m Technicolor
Warner (William Jacobs)
A girl determines to follow in her dead mother's musical comedy footsteps against the wishes of her still-grieving father.
Absolutely standard period musical, quite pleasantly handled but with below-par musical numbers.
w Jack Rose, Mel Shavelson, Peter Milne
d David Butler *ph* Wilfred M. Cline *md* David Buttolph
☆ June Haver, Gordon MacRae, *James Barton*, S. Z. Sakall, Gene Nelson, Debbie Reynolds, Sean McClory, Jane Darwell

Daughter of the Dragon
US 1931 70m bw
Paramount
Fu Manchu continues to seek revenge on Dr Petrie for the loss of his wife in the Boxer rebellion.
Muddled thriller with too much plot and too little action.
w Lloyd Corrigan, Monte Katterjohn *d* Lloyd Corrigan
☆ Warner Oland, Anna May Wong, Sessue Hayakawa, Bramwell Fletcher, Holmes Herbert
'Chinese blunderings, murders, and silly acting. Best for the combos where the kids may get a kick out of it.' – *Variety*

Daughter of the Nile *
Taiwan 1988 91m colour
Artificial Eye/Fu Film Productions (Li Xianchang)
original title: *Nilouhe, Nuer*
A lovesick schoolgirl on the fringes of gangster society escapes from her workaday chores by reading a comic, *Daughter of the Nile*.
Impressively controlled direction and well observed characters flesh out a minimal story.
w Zhu Tianwen *d* Hou Hsiao-Hsien *ph* Chen Huai'en *m* Chen Zhiyuan, Zhang Hongyi *pd* Liu Zhihua, Lin Ju *ed* Liao Qingsong, Chen Liyu
☆ Yang Lin, Gao Jie, Yang Fan, Xin Shufen, Li Tianlu, Cui Fusheng
'By far the most achieved and mature of the cycle of "young criminal" films in recent Taiwanese cinema.' – *Tony Rayns, MFB*

'Twice in a Lifetime: A Motion Picture Like This...'
Daughters Courageous *
US 1939 107m bw
Warner (Hal B. Wallis)
A prodigal father returns to his family and sorts out their problems.
Following the success of Four Daughters *(qv) the cast was reassembled to make this amiable rehash about a different family.*
w Julius and Philip Epstein *play Fly Away Home* by Dorothy Bennett, Irving White *d* Michael Curtiz *ph James Wong Howe* *m* Max Steiner *ad* John Hughes *ed* Ralph Dawson
☆ *Claude Rains*, John Garfield, Jeffrey Lynn, Fay Bainter, Priscilla Lane, Rosemary Lane, Lola Lane, Gale Page, Donald Crisp, May Robson, Frank McHugh, Dick Foran, Berton Churchill
'Suited to the family trade anywhere ... but there's something to be said against a running time of an hour and 47 minutes.' – *Variety*
'For its intelligent use of small town locations, its skilled acting, fine camerawork and evenly paced, sympathetic direction, it surpasses everything of its type.' – *John Baxter, 1968*
'Attractive people, good dialogue and camerawork, and skilful direction can work wonders.' – *Richard Mallett, Punch*

'They Hunger For Your Blood!'
Daughters of Darkness *
Belgium/France/Germany 1970 96m colour
Roxy/Showking/Cinevog/Maya (Paul Collet, Alain Guillaume)
original title: *Le Rouge aux Lèvres*
A seaside hotel in the dead season is visited by an elegant lesbian countess and her companion.
Surrealist and gory horror, stylishly directed and often visually intriguing.
w Harry Kumel, Pierre Drouot *d* Harry Kumel *ph* Eddy van der Enden *m* François de Roubiaix *ad* Françoise Hardy *ed* Gust Verschueren
☆ Delphine Seyrig, John Karlen, Daniele Ouimet, Andrea Rau, Paul Esser, Georges Jamin, Joris Collet, Fons Rademakers

Daughters of Destiny: see *Love, Soldiers and Women*

Daughters of the Dust *
US 1991 112m colour
BFI/American Playhouse/WMG/Geechee Girls (Julie Dash)
At the turn of the century, a family of Gullahs, descendants of African slaves living on islands off South Carolina, prepare to make a journey to the mainland to travel to the North.
A commemoration and celebration of black experience in America and its African roots, told in overlapping voices of the old and the unborn, and shot with an eye for beauty.
wd Julie Dash *ph* A. Jaffa Fielder *m* John Barnes *pd* Kerry Marshall *ed* Amy Carey, Joseph Burton
☆ Adisa Anderson, Barbara-O, Cheryl Lynn Bruce, Cora Lee Day, Geraldine Dunston, Vertamae Grosvenor, Tommy Hicks, Trula Hoosier, Kaycee Moore, Eartha D. Robinson, Alva Rodgers, Cornell Royal, Catherine Tarver, Bahni Turpin
'This is balletic, operatic cinema, and a celebration of cinema itself.' – *Lizzie Francke, Sight and Sound*

'In a country where anybody can become President, anybody just did.'
'Dave Kovic was an ordinary guy who was asked to impersonate the president. When they gave him a chance to make the country better ... he did.'
Dave *
US 1993 110m colour
Warner (Luaren Schuler-Donner, Ivan Reitman)
After the President of the United States has a stroke, a Baltimore businessman is recruited by the White House to impersonate him.
A slight but amusing comedy of political life that nevertheless manages to evade most of the issues it raises.
w Gary Ross *d* Ivan Reitman *ph* Adam Greenberg *m* James Newton Howard *pd* J. Michael Riva *ed* Sheldon Kahn
☆ Kevin Kline, Sigourney Weaver, Frank Langella, Kevin Dunn, Ben Kingsley, Charles Grodin, Ving Rhames, Faith Prince, Laura Linney
'A dear and funny movie.' – *Richard Corliss, Time*
'A delightful, buoyant new take on an old theme that will win at the polls because it never strikes a false note.' – *Variety*
Gary Ross

'For this woman – he broke God's own commandments! The fire and tempest of their love still flames across 3000 years!'
David and Bathsheba *
US 1951 116m Technicolor
TCF (Darryl F. Zanuck)
King David loves the wife of one of his captains, and ensures that the latter is killed in battle.
Deliberately sober bible-in-pictures, probably intended as a riposte to Cecil B. de Mille. Somewhat lacking in excitement, but you can't call it gaudy.
w Philip Dunne *d* Henry King *ph* Leon Shamroy *m* Alfred Newman *ad* Lyle Wheeler, George Davis
☆ Gregory Peck, Susan Hayward, James Robertson Justice, Raymond Massey, Kieron Moore, Jayne Meadows, John Sutton, Dennis Hoey, Francis X. Bushman, George Zucco
'Hardly a single unintentional laugh.' – *Richard Mallett, Punch*
Philip Dunne; Leon Shamroy; Alfred Newman; art direction

David and Lisa *
US 1962 94m bw
Continental (Paul M. Heller)
Two disturbed adolescents at a special school fall in love.
Case history drama, earnest and well meaning rather than exciting.
w Eleanor Perry book Theodore Isaac Rubin *d Frank Perry ph* Leonard Hirschfield *m* Mark Lawrence
☆ Keir Dullea, Janet Margolin, Howard da Silva, Neva Patterson, Clifton James, Richard McMurray
'It recognises and probes the wounds of the mind and the heart and the power of love to penetrate even the most private of worlds.' – *Judith Crist*
† Made for 180,000 dollars, it took more than one million dollars in its first run in the States.
Eleanor Perry; Frank Perry

'One of the greatest stories of love and adventure ever told is brought to the screen as Dickens himself would wish it!'
David Copperfield ****
US 1934 132m bw
MGM (David O. Selznick)
Disliked by his cruel stepfather and helped by his eccentric aunt, orphan David grows up to become an author and eventually to marry his childhood sweetheart.
Only slightly faded after sixty years, this small miracle of compression not only conveys the spirit of Dickens better than the screen has normally managed but is a particularly pleasing example of Hollywood's handling of literature and of the deployment of a great studio's resources. It also overflows with memorable character cameos, and it was a box-office giant.
w Hugh Walpole, Howard Estabrook
novel Charles Dickens *d George Cukor ph* Oliver T. Marsh *m* Herbert Stothart *ad Cedric Gibbons* *ed* Robert J. Kern *montage* Slavko Vorkapich
☆ *Freddie Bartholomew* (young David), *Frank Lawton* (David as a man), *W. C. Fields* (Micawber), *Roland Young* (Uriah Heep), *Edna May Oliver* (Aunt Betsy), *Lennox Pawle* (Mr Dick), *Basil Rathbone* (Mr Murdstone), Violet Kemble Cooper (Miss Murdstone), Maureen O'Sullivan (Dora), Madge Evans (Agnes), Elizabeth Allan (Mrs Copperfield), *Jessie Ralph* (Peggotty), Lionel Barrymore (Dan Peggotty), Hugh Williams (Steerforth), Lewis Stone (Mr Wickfield) and also *Herbert Mundin* (Barkis), Elsa Lanchester (Clickett), Jean Cadell (Mrs Micawber), Una O'Connor (Mrs Gummidge), John Buckler (Ham), Hugh Walpole (the Vicar), Arthur Treacher (donkey man)
'One of the best ensembles ever ... unusually good production which will win general approval.' – *Variety*
'Though half the characters are absent, the whole spectacle of the book, Micawber always excepted, is conveyed.' – *James Agee*
'The most profoundly satisfying screen manipulation of a great novel that the camera has ever given us.' – *André Sennwald*
'Perhaps the finest casting of all time.' – *Basil Wright, 1972*
† Charles Laughton was originally cast as Micawber, but resigned from the role after two days of shooting. It was said at the time that 'he looked as though he were about to molest the child'.
best picture; editing

Davy *
GB 1957 84m Technirama
Ealing (Basil Dearden)
A member of a family music hall act auditions at Covent Garden.
Curiously unsuccessful vehicle for a popular singing comic; the script and continuity are simply poor, and swamped by the wide screen.
w William Rose *d* Michael Relph *ph* Douglas Slocombe *m* various classics
☆ Harry Secombe, Ron Randell, George Relph, Alexander Knox, Susan Shaw, Bill Owen

Davy Crockett *
US 1955 93m Technicolor
Walt Disney
Episodes in the career of the famous Tennessee hunter and Indian scout who died at the Alamo.
Disjointed and naïve but somehow very fresh and appealing adventures; made for American television (as 3 50m episodes) but elsewhere an enormous hit in cinemas.
w Tom Blackburn *d* Norman Foster *ph* Charles Boyle *m* George Bruns
☆ *Fess Parker*, Buddy Ebsen, Basil Ruysdael, William Bakewell, Hans Conried, Kenneth Tobey, Nick Cravat
† 1956 sequel on similar lines: *Davy Crockett and the River Pirates*

Dawandeh: see *The Runner*

Dawg: see *Bad Boy*

Dawn *
GB 1928 90m approx bw silent
British and Dominions (Herbert Wilcox)
In 1914 Brussels, Nurse Edith Cavell helps 210 English soldiers to escape before the Germans catch and execute her.
Inspirational piece, totally dated now; remade by the same producer in 1939 as Nurse Edith Cavell, *with Anna Neagle.*
w Herbert Wilcox, Robert J. Cullen
play Reginald Berkeley *d* Herbert Wilcox
☆ Sybil Thorndike, Marie Ault, Mary Brough, Haddon Mason

Dawn!
Australia 1979 115m colour
Aquataurus/SAFC (Joy Cavill)
Dawn Fraser reflects on her career as a swimmer which took her from a working-class Sydney suburb to international success and the winning of three Olympic gold medals.
A biopic that celebrates a bloody-minded heroine, forever at war with authority, but, with an inexperienced actress in the title role and a style that smooths away the rough edges, the result is too bland to engage the interest for long.
w Joy Cavill *d* Ken Hannam *ph* Russell Boyd *m* Michael Carlos *pd* Ross Major *ed* Max Lemon
☆ Bronwyn Mackay-Payne, Ron Haddrick, Bunney Brooke, Tom Richards, John Diedrich, Gabrielle Hartley

'When there's no more room in Hell, the dead will walk the earth...'
Dawn of the Dead
US 1979 127m Technicolor
Target International/Laurel Group/Dawn Associates (Richard P. Rubinstein)
GB title: *Zombies*
America is filled by legions of carnivorous zombies.
Seemingly endless horror comic with absurd pretensions to be an allegory of something or other; occasionally laughable, otherwise sickening or boring.
wd George A. Romero *ph* Michael Gornick *m* The Goblins, Dario Argento *ad* Josie Caruso, Barbara Lifsher *ed* George A. Romero *sp* Tom Savini
☆ David Emge, Ken Foree, Scott H. Reiniger, Gaylen Ross

'Roaring into the blood-red dawn – fighting for women they had never seen – for love they might never know!'
'Forty youngsters sporting with fate!'
The Dawn Patrol **
US 1930 90m bw
Warner
In France during World War I, flying officers wait their turn to leave on missions which may mean death.
The second 1938 version is more watchable today, but this early talkie was highly effective in its time, and much of its aerial footage was re-used.
w John Monk Saunders *d Howard Hawks*
ph Ernest Haller *m* Leo Forbstein *ed* Ray Curtiss
☆ *Richard Barthelmess* (Dick Courtney), *Douglas Fairbanks Jnr* (Douglas Scott), Neil Hamilton (Major Brand), William Janney (Gordon Scott), *James Finlayson* (Field Sergeant), Clyde Cook (Bott), Edmund Breon (Lt Bathurst), Frank McHugh (Flaherty)
'No women and few laughs, so needs good surrounding comedy shorts.' – *Variety*
'Bare, cleancut, uncluttered technique, a stark story line, terse dialogue ... and a pervasive atmosphere of hopelessness captured with economy and incisiveness.' – *Andrew Sarris, 1963*
† TV title is *Flight Commander*, which was the title of Saunders's original story.
John Monk Saunders

'There's no chance for a flight to get through, but one man – flying low, hedgehopping – might make it!'

The Dawn Patrol **

US 1938 103m bw
Warner (Hal B. Wallis)

In the First World War, new recruits are given minimal training as pilots before being sent on dangerous missions.
A remarkably early but trim and competent remake of the 1930 movie, using much of the same aerial footage.
w Seton I. Miller, Dan Totheroh *story* John Monk Saunders *d* *Edmund Goulding* *ph* Tony Gaudio *m* Max Steiner *ad* John Hughes *ed* Ralph Dawson
☆ *Errol Flynn* (Courtney), *Basil Rathbone* (Major Brand), David Niven (Scott), Melville Cooper (Watkins), Donald Crisp (Phipps), Barry Fitzgerald (Bott), Carl Esmond (Von Mueller)
'A powerful, red-corpuscled drama ... geared for top grosses.' – *Variety*
'A great deal of self-pity and romanticism have gone into the making of this excellent ham sandwich.' – *Graham Greene*

The Dawn Rider

US 1935 56m bw
Lone Star (Paul Malvern)

A cowboy revenges the murder of his father.
Standard quickie Western with little to recommend it.
wd Robert N. Bradbury *ph* Archie Stout
☆ John Wayne, Marion Burns, Yakima Canutt, Reed Howes, Denny Meadows, Bert Dillard

The Dawning *

GB 1988 97m colour
Enterprise/TVS (Sarah Lawson)

In the 1920s in Southern Ireland, at the beginning of the Troubles between the Irish and the English, a teenage girl becomes involved with a mysterious stranger, to the annoyance of her English fiancé.
A small-scale but affecting film of the end of innocence.
w Moira Williams *novel* *The Old Jest* by Jennifer Johnson *d* Robert Knights *ph* Adrian Biddle *m* Simon May *pd* Mike Porter *ed* Max Lemon
☆ Trevor Howard, Hugh Grant, Anthony Hopkins, Rebecca Pidgeon, Jean Simmons, Adrian Dunbar, Tara MacGowran

A Day at the Races ****

US 1937 109m bw/blue-tinted ballet sequence
MGM (Lawrence Weingarten)

The Marxes help a girl who owns a sanatorium and a racehorse.
Fashions in Marxism change, but this top quality production, though lacking their zaniest inspirations, does contain several of their funniest routines and a spectacularly well integrated racecourse climax. The musical and romantic asides are a matter of taste but delightfully typical of their time.
w *Robert Pirosh, George Seaton, George Oppenheimer* *d* *Sam Wood* *ph* *Joseph Ruttenberg* *m* Franz Waxman *ch* Dave Gould
☆ *Groucho, Chico, Harpo, Margaret Dumont*, Maureen O'Sullivan, Allan Jones, *Douglass Dumbrille, Esther Muir, Sig Rumann*
'The money is fairly splashed about; the capitalists have recognized the Marx Brothers; ballet sequences, sentimental songs, amber fountains, young lovers. Easily the best film to be seen in London, but all the same I feel a nostalgia for the old cheap rickety sets.' – *Graham Greene*
Academy Award nomination: Dave Gould

Day for Night ****

France/Italy 1973 116m Eastmancolor
Films du Carrosse/PECF/PIC (Marcel Bébert)

original title: *La Nuit Américaine*
Frictions and personality clashes beset the making of a romantic film in Nice.
Immensely enjoyable, richly detailed, insider's-eye-view of the goings-on in a film studio. A fun film with melodramatic asides.
w François Truffaut, Jean-Louis Richard, Suzanne Schiffman *d* *François Truffaut* *ph* Pierre-William Glenn *m* Georges Delerue
☆ Jacqueline Bisset, Valentina Cortese, Jean-Pierre Aumont, Jean-Pierre Léaud, Dani, Alexandra Stewart, Jean Champion, François Truffaut, David Markham
'I thought I'd had my last dram of enjoyment out of the Pagliacci theme and studio magic, and Truffaut shows there's life in the old whirl yet.' – *Stanley Kauffmann*
'Made with such dazzling craftsmanship and confidence that you can never quite believe Truffaut's point that directing a movie is a danger-fraught experience.' – *Michael Billington, Illustrated London News*
† Graham Greene, as Henry Graham, played an insurance representative.
Academy Award: best foreign film
Academy Award nomination: script; François Truffaut (as director); Valentina Cortese
BAFTA: best picture; François Truffaut; Valentina Cortese

The Day I Became A Woman: *see Roozi Khe Zan Shodam*

A Day in the Country: see *Une Partie de Campagne*

A Day in the Death of Joe Egg ***

GB 1971 106m Eastmancolor
Columbia/Domino (David Deutsch)

A teacher and his wife are frustrated by their own inability to cope with the problem of their spastic daughter.
A well-filmed version of a sincerely human play, with humour and fantasy sequences leavening the gloom.
w *Peter Nichols* *play* Peter Nichols *d* *Peter Medak* *ph* Ken Hodges *m* Elgar
☆ *Alan Bates, Janet Suzman*, Peter Bowles, Sheila Gish, *Joan Hickson*
'It's unsatisfying, and it's not to be missed.' – *Stanley Kauffmann*

A Day of Fury

US 1956 78m Technicolor
Universal (Robert Arthur)
A marshal is reluctant to shoot a wandering gunman who once saved his life.
Fair little Western with more tension than usual.
w James Edmiston, Oscar Brodney *d* Harmon Jones
☆ Dale Robertson, Jock Mahoney, Mara Corday, Carl Benton Reid

The Day of the Animals

US 1976 98m DeLuxe Todd-AO 35
Film Ventures International (Edward L. Montero)

In the Californian High Sierras, animals of all kinds suddenly turn on human beings, but a day later are all found dead.
Irritatingly pointless horror fable borrowing heavily from The Birds*; basically an exploitation shocker, most efficient when most unpleasant.*
w William and Eleanor Norton *d* William Girdler *ph* Tom McHugh *m* Lalo Schifrin
☆ Christopher George, Lynda Day George, Leslie Nielsen, Robert Sorrentino, Richard Jaeckel, Michael Ansara, Ruth Roman, Paul Mantee, Gil Lamb

Day of the Badman

US 1957 82m Eastmancolor Cinemascope
Universal-International
A circuit judge stands up against threatening outlaws.
Uninvolving Western which can't fill the wide screen.
w Irving Glassberg *d* Harry Keller
☆ Fred MacMurray, Joan Weldon, John Ericson, Robert Middleton, Edgar Buchanan

The Day of the Beast

Spain/Italy 1995 104m colour
Metro Tartan/Sogetel/Iberoamericana/M.G. SRL/Canal (Antonio Saura, Claudio Gaeta)

original title: *El Dia de la Bestia*
With the aid of a heavy metal fan and a fake Satanist, a priest acts uncharitably in order to be able to track down the Anti-Christ, who is about to be born in Madrid.
Exuberant horror movie with a political subtext – the Devil finds work for idle fascists – and a blackly comic tone, but it fails to cohere into a satisfactory whole.
w Alex de la Iglesia, Jorge Guerricaechevarria *d* Alex de la Iglesia *ph* Flavio Martinez Labiano *m* Battista Lena *pd* José Luis Arrizabilaga *ed* Teresa Font *sp* make-up: José Antonio Sanchez
☆ Alex Angulo, Armando de Razza, Santiago Segura, Terele Pavez, Nathalie Sesaña, Jaime Blanch
'A rough piece that shows how low the New Spanish Cinema is prepared to grovel in its post-Franco search for international box-office.' – *Alexander Walker, London Evening Standard*
'The funniest Spanish film of the decade is also one of the most serious.' – *Sight and Sound*

Day of the Dead

US 1985 102m colour
Laurel/United (Richard P. Rubinstein)

Zombies outnumber normal humans by 400,000 to one, but a doctor is trying to domesticate them.
Gory but very talkative successor to Dawn of the Dead*; not for regular audience consumption.*
wd George A. Romero *ph* Michael Gornick *m* John Harrison *pd* Cletus Anderson *ed* Pasquale Buba
☆ Lori Cardille, Terry Alexander, Jarlath Conroy, Joseph Pilato

The Day of the Dolphin *

US 1973 104m Technicolor Panavision
Avco-Embassy/Icarus (Robert E. Relyea)

A marine biologist researching dolphins off the Florida coast discovers they are being used in a plot to blow up the President's yacht.
A strangely unexpected and unsuccessful offering from the talent involved: thin and repetitive as scientific instruction (the dolphins' language in any case topples it into fantasy), and oddly childlike as spy adventure.
w Buck Henry *novel* Robert Merle *d* Mike Nichols *ph* *William A. Fraker* *m* Georges Delerue *pd* Richard Sylbert
☆ George C. Scott, Trish Van Devere, Paul Sorvino, Fritz Weaver
'The whole thing seems to have been shoved through the cameras as glibly as possible, so that everyone concerned could grab the money and run.' – *Stanley Kauffmann*
'An eight and a half million dollar Saturday afternoon special for sheltered nine-year-olds.' – *Judith Crist*
'Dolphins may live in a state of ecstasy, but the cast of this film seems lost in a state of confusion, wondering whether they are in an enlightened documentary, juvenile fantasy, or lurid soap opera.' – *Les Keyser, Hollywood in the Seventies*
'The most expensive Rin Tin Tin movie ever made.' – *Judith Crist*
Academy Award nomination: Georges Delerue

The Day of the Evil Gun *

US 1968 93m Metrocolor Panavision
MGM (Jerry Thorpe)
Returning home after three years, a rancher finds that his wife and child have been carried off by Indians.
Competent standard Western which resolves itself into a duel of wits between the hero and his rival.
w Charles Marquis Warren, Eric Bercovici *d* Jerry Thorpe *ph* W. Wallace Kelley *m* Jeff Alexander
☆ Glenn Ford, Arthur Kennedy, Dean Jagger, Paul Fix, John Anderson, Nico Minardos

The Day of the Jackal ***

GB/France 1973 142m Technicolor
Universal/Warwick/Universal France (John Woolf, David Deutsch)

British and French police combine to prevent an OAS assassination attempt on de Gaulle by use of a professional killer.
An incisive, observant and professional piece of work based on a rather clinical bestseller. Lack of a channel for sympathy, plus language confusions, are its main drawbacks.
w Kenneth Ross *novel* Frederick Forsyth *d* *Fred Zinnemann* *ph* *Jean Tournier* *m* Georges Delerue *ed* Ralph Kemplen
☆ *Edward Fox*, Michel Lonsdale, Alan Badel, Eric Porter, Cyril Cusack, Delphine Seyrig, Donald Sinden, Tony Britton, Timothy West, Olga Georges-Picot, Barrie Ingham, Maurice Denham, Anton Rodgers
'Before *Jackal* is five minutes old, you know it's just going to be told professionally, with no flavour and no zest.' – *Stanley Kauffmann*
'All plot, with scarcely a character in sight.' – *Michael Billington, Illustrated London News*
'A better than average thriller for those who haven't read the book.' – *Judith Crist*
'A rare lesson in film-making in the good old grand manner.' – *Basil Wright, 1972*
Academy Award nomination: Ralph Kemplen

'It happened in Hollywood – but it could have happened in Hell!'

The Day of the Locust **

US 1974 143m Technicolor
Paramount/Long Road (Jerome Hellman, Sheldon Shrager)

In Hollywood in the 1930s, a novice is bewildered by the eccentricities of life and an innocent man is martyred by the crowd.
A curious and interesting work from a savagely satirical novel; full of stimulating scenes and characters, it barely succeeds as a whole and was a disaster at the box-office.
w Waldo Salt *novel* Nathanael West *d* *John Schlesinger* *ph* Conrad Hall *m* John Barry *pd* Richard MacDonald *ed* Jim Clark
☆ Donald Sutherland, William Atherton, Karen Black, Burgess Meredith, Geraldine Page, Richard A. Dysart, Bo Hopkins, Lelia Goldoni, Billy Barty
'The sense of horror which the film excites is all the sharper because the monstrosities of action are man-produced. In this brilliantly devised film it is the human heart, not some freak of an indifferent nature, which kills.' – *Dilys Powell*
Academy Award nomination: Conrad Hall; Burgess Meredith

The Day of the Outlaw **

US 1958 96m bw
UA/Security Pictures (Sidney Harmon)
Two rival cattlemen forget their differences to fight six outlaws who ride into town.
Bleak and wintry Western, well done and sufficiently unusual to stick in the mind.
w Philip Yordan *novel* Lee Wells *d* *André de Toth* *ph* *Russell Harlan* *m* Alexander Courage
☆ Robert Ryan, Burl Ives, Tina Louise, Nehemiah Persoff, David Nelson, Venetia Stevenson, Jack Lambert, Lance Fuller
'In the best William S. Hart tradition.' – *MFB*

'Spine Chilling Terror!'

The Day of the Triffids *

GB 1962 95m Eastmancolor Cinemascope
Philip Yordan (George Pitcher)

Almost everyone in the world is blinded by meteorites prior to being taken over by intelligent plants.
Rough and ready adaptation of a famous sci-fi novel, sometimes blunderingly effective and with moments of good trick work.
w Bernard Gordon *novel* John Wyndham *d* Steve Sekely *ph* Ted Moore *m* Ron Goodwin
☆ Howard Keel, Nicole Maurey, Kieron Moore, Janette Scott, Alexander Knox
† The script was originally credited to Philip Yordan because Bernard Gordon was blacklisted at the time.

Day of Wrath ***

Denmark 1943 105m bw
Palladium

original title: *Vredens Dag*
In a 17th-century village an old woman is burned as a witch and curses the pastor who judged her. He dies and his mother accuses her daughter-in-law, in love with another man, of using witchcraft to kill him.
Harrowing, spellbinding melodrama with a message, moving in a series of Rembrandtesque compositions from one horrifying sequence to another. Depressing, but marvellous.
w Carl Dreyer, Poul Knudsen, Mogens Skot-Hansen *play* *Anne Pedersdotter* by Hans Wiers Jenssen *d* *Carl Dreyer* *ph* *Carl Andersson* *m* Poul Schierbeck *ad* Erik Ases, Lis Fribert
☆ Thorkild Roose, Lisbeth Movin, Sigrid Neiiendam, Preben Lerdoff Rye, Anna Svierkier
'An exceptional piece of cinema ... the film will, I think, be remembered for its realistic treatment of the incredible; for its vicious tension; for the

unrivalled horror of its picture of human callousness.' – *Dilys Powell*

The Day the Earth Caught Fire **
GB 1961 99m bw with filters Dyaliscope
British Lion/Pax (Val Guest)

Nuclear tests knock the world off its axis and send it careering towards the sun.
A smart piece of science fiction told through the eyes of Fleet Street journalists and showing a sharp eye for the London scene. Rather exhaustingly talkative, but genuinely frightening at the time.
w Wolf Mankowitz, Val Guest *d* Val Guest
ph Harry Waxman *m* Monty Norman
☆ Edward Judd, Janet Munro, Leo McKern, Arthur Christiansen *(ex-editor of the Daily Express)*, Michael Goodliffe, Bernard Braden, Reginald Beckwith, Austin Trevor, Renée Asherson, Edward Underdown
† A remake went into production in 1995.
screenplay

'From out of space – a warning and an ultimatum!'
The Day the Earth Stood Still **
US 1951 92m bw
TCF (Julian Blaustein)

A flying saucer arrives in Washington and its alien occupant, aided by a robot, demonstrates his intellectual and physical power, warns the world what will happen if wars continue, and departs.
Cold-war wish-fulfilment fantasy, impressive rather than exciting but very capably put over with the minimum of trick work and the maximum of sober conviction. 'Klaatu barada nikto', the command given to the robot, has achieved cult status.
w Edmund H. North *d* Robert Wise *ph* Leo Tover *m* Bernard Herrmann
☆ Michael Rennie, Patricia Neal, Hugh Marlowe, Sam Jaffe, Billy Gray
'Quite wry and alarmingly smooth.' – *New Yorker, 1977*

The Day the Fish Came Out
GB/Greece 1967 109m DeLuxe
TCF/Michael Cacoyannis
Atomic material contaminates a Mediterranean island.
Addle-pated, would-be satirical mod fantasy with establishment figures cast as world villains.
wd Michael Cacoyannis *ph* Walter Lassally
m Mikis Theodorakis
☆ Tom Courtenay, Colin Blakely, Sam Wanamaker, Candice Bergen, Ian Ogilvy, Patricia Burke

The Day the Hot Line Got Hot
US 1968 92m Eastmancolor
Commonwealth United

Russian and American agents are outwitted by their go-between.
Feeble espionage comedy teaming two big stars at the end of their careers.
w Paul Jarrico, Dominique Fabre, M. Trueblood
d Etienne Périer
☆ Charles Boyer, Robert Taylor, George Chakiris, Marie Dubois

The Day the Sun Turned Cold *
Hong Kong 1994 100m colour
Artificial Eye/Pineast (Cherie Wong)

original title: *Tianguo Niezi*
In China, a young man recalls to the police his troubled childhood, which ended with his mother poisoning his father.
Bleak and angry story of familial betrayal, which gains interest from its exoticism.
w Wang Xing Dong, Wang Zhe Bin *d* Yim Ho
ph Hou Yong, Shang Yong *m* Otomo Yoshihide
ad Gong Ming Hui *ed* Wong Yee-shun, Zhou Ying Wu, Yun Jiang Chun
☆ Si Ching Gao Wa, Tao Chung Wa, Ma Jing Wu, Wu'ai Zi, Shu Zi'ong, Li Hu
'A haunting film, magnificently filmed and perfectly scored, a splendid example of the new Eastern cinema.' – *Nigel Robinson, Film Review*

'A new high in naked shrieking terror.'
Day the World Ended
US 1955 82m bw Superscope
AIP/Golden State (Roger Corman)

Survivors of the nuclear war take refuge in a mountain hideout where they are attacked by three-eyed, cannibalistic mutants.
Small-scale, paranoid science-fiction thriller from what the film calls 'the age of anxiety'.
w Lou Rusoff *d* Roger Corman *ph* Jock Feindel
m Ronald Stein *ed* Ronald Sinclair
☆ Richard Denning, Lori Nelson, Adele Jurgens, Touch Connors, Paul Birch, Raymond Hatton

The Day They Gave Babies Away: see *All Mine to Give*

The Day They Robbed the Bank of England *
GB 1960 85m bw
MGM/Summit (Jules Buck)
In 1901 Irish patriots plan a coup against the British government…
Small-scale, well-detailed period caper story, marred by a slow-starting script and unsympathetic acting.
w Howard Clewes, Richard Maibaum *novel* John Brophy *d* John Guillermin *ph* Georges Périnal
m Edwin Astley
☆ Peter O'Toole, Aldo Ray, Elizabeth Sellars, Kieron Moore, Albert Sharpe, Hugh Griffith, John Le Mesurier, Joseph Tomelty, Miles Malleson, Colin Gordon

A Day to Remember
GB 1953 92m bw
Rank/Box-Thomas/GFD
A darts team takes a day trip to France.
Pleasant compendium of mini-stories with an agreeable cast.
w Robin Estridge *novel* The Hand and Flower by Jerrard Tickell *d* Ralph Thomas *ph* Ernest Steward *m* Clifton Parker *ed* Gerald Thomas
☆ Stanley Holloway, Donald Sinden, Joan Rice, Odile Versois, James Hayter, Edward Chapman, Harry Fowler, Peter Jones, Bill Owen

The Day Will Dawn *
GB 1942 98m bw
Niksos (Paul Soskin)

US title: *The Avengers*
Norwegian freedom fighters destroy a U-boat base and are saved by commandos.
Dated propaganda piece with an interesting cast.
w Terence Rattigan, Anatole de Grunwald, Patrick Kirwan *d* Harold French *ph* Bernard Knowles *m* Richard Addinsell
☆ Ralph Richardson, Deborah Kerr, Hugh Williams, Griffith Jones, Francis L. Sullivan, Roland Culver, Niall MacGinnis, Finlay Currie, Bernard Miles, Patricia Medina

Daybreak: see *Le Jour Se Lève (1939)*

'He's the kind of guy women fall for. She's the kind of girl men fall over. Is this any way to fall in love?'
Daydream Believer
Australia 1991 82m colour
Beyond/Ben Gannon

A scatterbrained actress with a fellow feeling for horses falls for a Cockney show-business entrepreneur with a stud farm.
Fluffy romantic comedy that is occasionally amusing but more often irritating, with its concentration on a charmless couple.
w Saturday Rosenberg *d* Kathy Mueller
ph Andrew Lesnie *m* Todd Hunter, Johanna Pigott *pd* Roger Ford *ed* Robert Gibson
☆ Miranda Otto, Martin Kemp, Gia Carides, Anne Looby, Bruce Venables, Peter Hehir

Dayereh ***
Iran/Italy/Switzerland 2000 90m colour
Artificial Eye/Mikado/Lumiere/Jafar Panahi

aka: *The Circle*
In Teheran, women – from a mother distraught at having given birth to a girl, to prisoners on parole and a prostitute – attempt to cope in a society where men make the law.
Urgent, understated drama with a documentary feel: its considerable power derives from its matter-of-fact, non-histrionic approach.
w Kambozia Partovi *d* Jafar Panahi *ph* Bahram Badakhshani *ad* Iraj Raminfar *ed* Jafar Panahi
☆ Maryiam Parvin (Arezou), Nargess Mamizadeh (Nargess), Fereshteh Sadr Orafai (Pari), Monir Arab (Ticket seller), Elham Saboktakin (Nurse), Fatemeh Naghavi (Mother), Mojgan Faramarzi (Prostitute)
'Whatever its political significance, this is a dark, sustained, and wrenching film.' – *J. Hoberman, Village Voice*
'A compelling, humane and deeply serious film.' – *Peter Bradshaw, Guardian*
† It won the Golden Lion at the Venice Film Festival in 2000.

'Hold Your Breath.'
Daylight
US 1996 115m DeLuxe
Universal/Davis Entertainment/Joseph M. Singer

A diverse group of people is trapped in Manhattan's Holland Tunnel.
Stolid and claustrophobic disaster movie, in which Stallone flexes his muscles to little effect.
w Leslie Bohem *d* Rob Cohen *ph* David Eggby
m Randy Edelman *pd* Benjamin Fernandez
ed Peter Amundson
☆ Sylvester Stallone, Amy Brenneman, Viggo Mortensen, Dan Hedaya, Jay O. Sanders, Karen Young, Claire Bloom
'Just too limited in scope, imagination and excitement.' – *Variety*
† The film cost more than $80m to make, and took around $33m at the US box-office and a further $111m worldwide.
sound effects editing

The Days
China 1993 80m bw
ICA/Yinxiang Dianying Gongzuoshi (Liu Jie, Zhang Hongtao)
original title: *Dongchun De Rizi*
Two thirtysomething art teachers, bored with life and each other, decide to part.
A doom-laden study of a dysfunctional couple in which the most interesting things happen off-screen and are described in a voice-over; its interest and novelty lie in the fact that it is the first Chinese film to show aimless characters, alienated from their society but too indifferent to what is happening to them to rebel.
wd Wang Xiaoshuai *ph* Liu Jie, Wu Di *m* Liang Heping *ed* Qingqing
☆ Yu Hong, Liu Xiadong
'The net impression is of inertia; the characters are bored with each other and we're bored with them.' – *Sheila Johnston, Independent*
† The film was made on a budget of $10,000 which the director raised from his friends and his savings.

Days and Nights in the Forest: see *Aranyer Din Ratri*

Days of Being Wild **
Hong Kong 1991 93m Agfacolor
Made in Hong Kong/In-Gear (Rover Tang)

original title: *Ahfei Zhenjuang*
In 1960, the lives of a womanizing playboy searching for his real mother, the abandoned girlfriend who pursues him, and a cop who realizes his ambition of becoming a sailor, cross in Hong Kong and Manila.
A stylish account of the disaffected and rootless young which eschews straightforward narrative for a more complex approach, strong on atmosphere and period re-creation.
wd Wong Kar-Wai *ph* Christopher Doyle
pd William Chang *ed* Kai Kit-Wai
☆ Leslie Cheung, Maggie Cheung, Andy Lau, Carina Lau, Jacky Cheung, Rebecca Pan, Tony Leung
'As an existential account of solitary souls in random orbits, the film blows away the entire body of recent French "designer cinema". As a touchstone for Hong Kong's specific identity and psyche, it's close to sublime.' – *Tony Rayns, Sight and Sound*
† This version was the director's cut following the film's original release in 1990, when despite winning the Hong Kong Film Awards for best film, best director, best actor (Leslie Cheung) and best art direction, it flopped at the local box-office.

Days of Glory
US 1944 86m bw
RKO (Casey Robinson)

Russian peasants fight the invading Nazis.
Lower-berth wartime propaganda piece chiefly notable for introducing Gregory Peck to the screen.
w Casey Robinson *story* Melchior Lengyel
d Jacques Tourneur *ph* Tony Gaudio *m* Daniele Amfitheatrof
☆ Tamara Toumanova, Gregory Peck, Alan Reed, Maria Palmer, Lowell Gilmore, Hugo Haas

'Your eyes – your ears – your senses will be overwhelmed!'
Days of Heaven ****
US 1978 95m Metrocolor
Paramount/OP (Bert and Harold Schneider)

In the early 20th century, three young immigrants leave Chicago for the wheatfields.
Visually a superb slice of period life, it has an emotional force that emerges slowly from the conjunction of the vast landscape and its reticent intruders, who have fled from the dark of the city to find no peace in the country.
wd Terrence Malick *ph* Nestor Almendros *m* Ennio Morricone
☆ Richard Gere, Brooke Adams, Sam Shepard, Linda Manz
'It's serious, yes, very solemn, but not depressing.' – *Roger Ebert*
'Superbly directed and acted; see it for a second time and its hold is still more relentless.' – *Dilys Powell, Punch*
'One of the great cinematic achievements of the 1970s.' – *Variety*
'Terrence Malick's innocently convoluted parable of love lost and found, and reconciliation achieved and then fatally broken, is superbly counterpointed, thanks to Nestor Almendros' photography, by the burgeoning expansiveness of Texas during the First War.' – *Sight and Sound*
Nestor Almendros
Ennio Morricone
Ennio Morricone

Days of Hope: see *Espoir*

Days of Thrills and Laughter ***
US 1961 93m bw
TCF (Robert Youngson)

Appealing if rather miscellaneous silent film compilation with the accent on action and thrills as well as comedy.
Like the other Youngson histories, a boon to film archivists despite a facetious commentary.
m Jack Shaindlin *narrator* Jay Jackson
☆ Stan Laurel, Oliver Hardy, Snub Pollard, Douglas Fairbanks, Charles Chaplin, Pearl White, Houdini, Harry Langdon, Ben Turpin, Charlie Chase, Boris Karloff, Warner Oland, Fatty Arbuckle, Keystone Kops

Days of Thunder
US 1990 107m Technicolor Panavision
Paramount (Don Simpson, Jerry Bruckheimer)

An eager young stock car driver challenges the champion. Guess who wins?
An over-familiar story rendered no more interestingly than usual. Despite its star, it flopped at the box-office.
w Robert Towne *story* Robert Towne, Tom Cruise
d Tony Scott *ph* Ward Russell *m* Hans Zimmer
ad Benjamin Fernandez, Thomas E. Sanders
ed Billy Weber, Chris Lebenzon
☆ Tom Cruise, Robert Duvall, Nicole Kidman, Randy Quaid, Michael Rooker, Cary Elwes, Fred Dalton Thompson, John C. Reilly, J. C. Quinn, Don Simpson
'Simply a flashy, noisy star vehicle for Tom Cruise, one which – like the stock cars he drives – goes around in circles getting nowhere.' – *MFB*

'They Will Let Him Up Soon And He Will Look For His Wife And He May Pray That He Doesn't Find Her…'
Days of Wine and Roses **
US 1962 117m bw
Warner (Martin Manulis)

A PR man becomes an alcoholic; his wife gradually reaches the same state, but he recovers and she does not.

Smart satirical comedy confusingly gives way to melodrama, then sentimentality; quality is evident throughout, but all concerned are happiest with the first hour.
w J. P. Miller *d* Blake Edwards *ph* *Philip Lathrop* *m* *Henry Mancini*
☆ *Jack Lemmon, Lee Remick, Charles Bickford, Jack Klugman*, Alan Hewitt, Debbie Megowan, Jack Albertson

'The film fails. The fault is not an upbeat ending, but the mere fact that there is any ending at all. The ending, here, denatures the alcoholism, turning it from grim reality to dramatic device, and escaping from the battle of the bottle into a more manageable battle of the sexes.' – *Newsweek*

title song (*m* Henry Mancini, *ly* Johnny Mercer)
Jack Lemmon; Lee Remick

A Day's Pleasure *
US 1919 20m bw silent
First National/Charles Chaplin

Mishaps of a family picnic.
Very mild Chaplin, reaching for but not achieving a kind of lyric quality. Amusing bits rather than scenes.
wd Charles Chaplin *ph* Rollie Totheroh
☆ Charles Chaplin, Edna Purviance, Jackie Coogan, Henry Bergman, Babe London

Daytime Wife
US 1939 71m bw
TCF
A young wife finds that her husband is still dating his secretary, and retaliates by dating his colleague.
Hollywood version of a French farce; not terrific, but watchable.
w Art Arthur, Robert Harari *d* Gregory Ratoff
☆ Tyrone Power, Linda Darnell, Warren William, Binnie Barnes, Wendy Barrie, Joan Davis, Leonid Kinskey

'Will give a good account of itself in the key runs.' – *Variety*

Dayton's Devils
US 1968 103m Eastmancolor
Madison/Harold Goldman (Robert W. Stabler)

A former USAF colonel assembles a group of misfits and adventurers to steal an army payroll.
Overlong, routine caper film with a surprisingly crisp climax (when it comes).
w Fred de Gorter *d* Jack Shea *ph* Brick Marquard *m* Marlin Skiles
☆ Leslie Nielsen, Rory Calhoun, Lainie Kazan, Hans Gudegast

'What a day. What a trip.'
The Daytrippers **
US 1996 87m colour
Metrodome/Fiasco/Trick Films (Nancy Tenenbaum, Steven Soderbergh)

The adventures of a wronged wife and her family as she drives from Long Island to confront her husband in Manhattan.
Clever road movie, which wittily dissects troubled relationships.
wd Greg Mottola *ph* John Inwood *m* Richard Martinez *pd* Bonnie J. Brinkley *ed* Anne McCabe
☆ Hope Davis, Pat McNamara, Anne Meara, Parker Posey, Liev Schreiber, Stanley Tucci, Campbell Scott, Marcia Gay Harden, Andy Brown

'Has more wit than countless studio movies.' – *Sunday Times*

Dazed and Confused **
US 1993 102m DeLuxe
Feature/Universal/Gramercy/Alphaville (James Jacks, Sean Daniel, Richard Linklater)

In 1976, a group of high school students celebrate their last day by victimizing younger kids.
Enjoyable and truthful comedy of adolescents trying to avoid facing up to the inevitable future.
wd *Richard Linklater* *ph* Lee Daniel *pd* John Frick *ed* Sandra Adair
☆ Jason London, Wiley Wiggins, Milla Jovovich, Rory Cochrane, Shawn Andrews, Adam Goldberg, Anthony Rapp, Sasha Jenson, Matthew McConaughey, Ben Affleck

'A very clever piece of retro 70s anti-nostalgia which scrupulously avoids sentimentality. It just wants to tell us how genuinely strange the 70s were.' – *Steve Beard, Empire*

De eso no se habla: see *We Don't Want to Talk about It*

'He made evil an art, a vice a virtue and pain a pleasure!'
De Sade *
US/Germany 1969 113m Movielab
AIP/CCC/Transcontinental (Louis M. Heyward, Artur Brauner)
The unbalanced Marquis de Sade is tormented by his wicked uncle with thoughts of his past.
Mildly interesting attempt by AIP at European debauchery, with a good theatrical framework for the fantasies but too much flailing about by all concerned, especially in the slow motion orgy sequences, which are relentlessly boring, as is the film.
w Richard Matheson *d* Cy Endfield *ph* *Heinz Pehlke* *m* Billy Strange *ad* *Jurgen Kiebach*
☆ Keir Dullea, *John Huston*, Lilli Palmer, Senta Berger, Anna Massey, Uta Levka

The Dead ****
GB 1987 83m Foto-Kem
Vestron/Zenith/Liffey Films (Wieland Schulz-Keil, Chris Sievernich)

Two Irish spinster sisters throw a winter dinner for their relatives and friends.
Its director's last film is a warm and somehow invigorating reminiscence of things past.
w Tony Huston *book* *Dubliners* by James Joyce *d* *John Huston* *ph* Fred Murphy *m* Alex North *pd* Stephen Grimes, Dennis Washington *cos* Dorothy Jeakins
☆ Anjelica Huston, Donal McCann, Rachel Dowling, Cathleen Delany, Dan O'Herlihy, Helena Carroll, Donal Donnelly

'A delicate coda in a minor key to an illustrious 46-year career.' – *Daily Variety*
'A small masterpiece, perfectly achieved.' – *Time Out*

best adapted screenplay; Dorothy Jeakins

'How many times can you die for love?'
Dead Again *
US 1991 108m Technicolor/bw
UIP/Paramount/Mirage (Lindsay Doran, Charles H. Maguire)

A private detective is hired to investigate an amnesiac who can only remember a past life as a concert pianist murdered by her husband.
Tricksy thriller, switching between past and present, which is frequently too clever for its own good.
w Scott Frank *d* Kenneth Branagh *ph* Matthew F. Leonetti *m* Patrick Doyle *pd* Tim Hervey *ed* Peter E. Berger
☆ Kenneth Branagh, Emma Thompson, Andy Garcia, Derek Jacobi, Robin Williams, Wayne Knight, Hanna Schygulla

'Briskly entertaining enough to generate mostly positive word of mouth among mature audiences.' – *Variety*
'A monstrous cinematic folly.' – *Geoff Brown, Sight and Sound*

Dead Alive: see *Braindead*

Dead and Buried
US 1981 95m colour
GTO/Avco Embassy (Ronald Shusett, Robert Fentress)

A sheriff investigates killings in a small town where the locals are not what they seem.
Cheap horror movie along familiar and predictable lines.
w Ronald Shusett, Dan O'Bannon *story* Jeff Millar, Alex Stern *d* Gary A. Sherman *ph* Steve Poster *m* Joe Renzetti *ad* Bill Sandell, Joe Aubel *ed* Alan Balsam
☆ James Farentino, Melody Anderson, Jack Albertson, Dennis Redfield, Nancy Locke Hauser, Lisa Blount, Robert Englund, Bill Quinn

'The gratuitously explicit death-dealing mounts up, the reductive echoes of superior ventures into similar territory grow stronger, and it all peters out in a welter of speciously manufactured hysteria.' – *Tim Pulleine, MFB*

The Dead and the Deadly **
Hong Kong 1982 95m colour 'Scope
Raymond Chow
original title: *Ren Xia Ren*
Murdered by his greedy colleagues after faking his own death to inherit a fortune, a wastrel returns as a ghost to seek his revenge.
Engaging black kung-fu comedy in which the humour and the conventions of the spirit world are more accessible than usual to Western audiences.
w Sammo Hung, Barry Wong *d* Wu Ma
☆ Sammo Hung, Wu Ma, Lam Ching-ying, Cherie Chung, Chung Fat

Dead Babies
GB 2001 101m DeLuxe Panavision
Redbus/Gruber/Civilian Content/Outer Edge (Richard Holmes, Neil Peplow)

A group of British and American friends spend a drug-fuelled weekend at a country house, where they are threatened with death by an anarchist gang.
Amis's novel of the mid-70s has been updated here, without gaining either topicality or relevance; the tone suggests the unlovely excesses of the Swinging Sixties cycle of bad British movies.
wd William Marsh *novel* Martin Amis *ph* Daniel Cohen *m* Mark Pember, Marvin Beaver *pd* Mark Tanner *ed* Eddie Hamilton
☆ Paul Bettany (Quentin), Katy Carmichael (Lucy), Hayley Carr (Roxanne), Charlie Condou (Giles Coldstream), Alexandra Gilbreath (Celia), William Marsh (Marvell), Kris Marshall (Skip), Andy Nyman (Keith), Cristian Solimeno (Andy), Olivia Williams (Diana)

'A wannabe black comedy with a handful of grotesque laughs amid an ocean of clumsy misfires.' – *Derek Elley, Variety*

† The film was made in 1999.

Dead Calm *
Australia 1988 96m colour Panavision
Warner/Kennedy Miller Productions (Terry Hayes, Doug Mitchell, George Miller)

A couple bring a dangerous stranger aboard their yacht.
Effectively suspenseful.
w Terry Hayes *novel* Charles Williams *d* Phillip Noyce *ph* Dean Semler *m* Graeme Revell *pd* Graham 'Grace' Walker *ed* Richard Francis-Bruce
☆ Nicole Kidman, Sam Neill, Billy Zane, Rod Mulliner, Joshua Tilden, George Shevtsov, Michael Long

The Dead Can't Lie
US 1988 97m colour
Cannon/Showtime (David Latt)
A private eye is hired to prevent a millionaire being harassed by his dead wife.
Silly supernatural thriller, dead from the neck up.
wd Lloyd Fonvielle *ph* Michael Chapman *m* George Clinton *pd* Carol Spier *ed* Evan Lottman
☆ Tommy Lee Jones, Virginia Madsen, Colin Bruce, Kevin Jarre, Frederic Forrest

Dead Cert
GB 1974 99m DeLuxe
UA/Woodfall (Neil Hartley)
A gentleman jockey investigates the death of his friend, a horse owner and fellow amateur rider, during a steeplechase.
Dull and implausible thriller, not helped by its uncharismatic hero, though the climax, at the Grand National, generates a little excitement.
w Tony Richardson, John Oaksey *novel* Dick Francis *d* Tony Richardson *ph* Freddie Cooper *m* John Addison *ad* David Brockhurst *ed* John Glen
☆ Scott Anthony, Judi Dench, Michael Williams, Nina Thomas, Julian Glover, Mark Dignam, John Bindon, Ian Hogg, Bill Fraser

'Unfortunately, wonderful reads don't necessarily make wonderful scripts.' – *Tony Richardson*

The Dead Don't Dream
US 1947 62m bw
UA/Hopalong Cassidy Productions (Lewis J. Rachmil)
Hoppy goes to be best man at a wedding and instead solves the mystery of multiple murders at an inn.
Slow-paced, amiable but unremarkable Western with the emphasis on detection.
w Francis Rosenwald *d* George Archainbaud *ph* Mack Stengler *m* Darrell Calker *ad* Jerome Pycha Jnr *ed* Fred W. Berger
☆ William Boyd, Andy Clyde, Rand Brooks, John Parrish, Leonard Penn, Mary Tucker

'You may not like these people, nor pity them, but you'll never forget this picture!'
Dead End ***
US 1937 92m bw
Samuel Goldwyn

A slice of life in New York's east side, where slum kids and gangsters live in a river street next to a luxury apartment block.
Highly theatrical film of a highly theatrical play, more or less preserving the single set and overcoming the limitations of the script and setting by sheer cinematic expertise. It is chiefly remembered, however, for introducing the Dead End Kids to a delighted world.
w Lillian Hellman *play* *Sidney Kingsley* *d* *William Wyler* *ph* *Gregg Toland* *m* Alfred Newman *ad* *Richard Day*
☆ Joel McCrea, Sylvia Sidney, *Humphrey Bogart*, Wendy Barrie, Claire Trevor, Allen Jenkins, *Marjorie Main*, James Burke, Ward Bond, *The Dead End Kids (Billy Halop, Leo Gorcey, Bernard Punsley, Huntz Hall, Bobby Jordan, Gabriel Dell)*

'Tense and accurate transcription, but sordid and depressing … in for a disappointing career.' – *Variety*

best picture; Gregg Toland; Claire Trevor; Richard Day

The Dead End Kids
The films in which the original gang of young 'hooligans' (see above) appeared were as follows:
1937 Dead End
1938 Crime School, Angels with Dirty Faces
1939 They Made Me a Criminal, Hell's Kitchen, Angels Wash Their Faces, On Dress Parade
Subsequently they broke up into the LITTLE TOUGH GUYS, the EAST SIDE KIDS, and the BOWERY BOYS (all qv).

Dead Fire
Canada/Czechoslovakia 1996 96m colour
North American/Do or Die (Lloyd A. Simandl)

In 2060 AD, after the world has been laid waste, a maverick security man on an orbiting space station is the only person who can defeat a criminal conspiracy to rule the future.
Cliché-ridden science fiction, with risible hard-boiled dialogue ('You've got big balls, Brody. I'll give you that. But you just tripped over them for the last time.') and performances to match.
w Christopher Hyde, Andrew McEvoy, Nicholas Racz *d* Robert Lee *ph* Dave Pelletier *m* Peter Allen *ed* Richard Benwick
☆ Matt Frewer, C. Thomas Howell, Colin Cunningham, Monika Schnarre, Rachel Hayward, Robert Russel, Jim Thorburn, Lucie Zednickova, Gerard Whelan

Dead Heart *
Australia 1996 103m colour
AFFC/New Town (Bryan Brown, Helen Watts)

A police constable in an isolated aboriginal community finds himself caught between upholding the law and conforming to the demands of tribal custom.
Interesting but muddled drama of a clash between cultures and between attitudes within cultures; it just fails to cohere into a satisfying experience.
wd Nick Parsons *ph* James Bartle *m* Stephen Rae *pd* Brian Edmonds *ed* Henry Dangar
☆ Bryan Brown, Ernie Dingo, Angie Milliken, Gnarnayarrahe Waitaire, Aaron Pedersen, John Jarratt, Lewis Fitz-Gerald, Anne Tenney, Lafe Charlton, David Gulpilil

Dead Heat
US 1988 83m Technicolor
Entertainment/New World Pictures (Michael Meltzer, David Helpern)

Two zombie cops track down their killer.
Asinine comic combination of DOA *and* The Night of the Living Dead.

w Terry Black *d* Mark Goldblatt *ph* Robert D. Yeoman *m* Ernest Troost *pd* Craig Stearns *ed* Harvey Rosenstock
☆ Treat Williams, Joe Piscopo, Lindsay Frost, Darren McGavin, Vincent Price, Clare Kirkconnell, Keye Luke, Ben Mittleman

Dead Heat on a Merry Go Round
US 1967 108m Technicolor
Columbia (Carter de Haven)
An ex-con breaks parole and plans to rob Los Angeles Airport.
Boringly arty caper comedy-melodrama, concentrating less on the robbery than on its hero's sexual prowess. All very superficially flashy, and what the title means is anybody's guess.
wd Bernard Girard *ph* Lionel Lindon *m* Stu Phillips
☆ James Coburn, Camilla Sparv, Aldo Ray, Nina Wayne, Robert Webber, Rose Marie, Todd Armstrong, Marian Moses, Severn Darden
'Just fills the space between a frisky title and a tricky TV-comedy ending, but doesn't fill it with any revels that require a viewer's complete attention.' – *Time*

Dead Image: see *Dead Ringer*

Dead Innocent
Canada 1996 92m colour
Blackwatch/Mariani (Michael Doherty, William R. Mariani)
A workaholic lawyer returns home late to discover her maid and daughter murdered.
A thriller that sets up an intriguing situation, but then fails to develop it satisfactorily.
w Dolores Payne, Mort Pattigo *d* Sarah Botsford *ph* Rodney Gibbons *m* David Findlay *pd* Donna Noonan *ed* Michael Doherty
☆ Genevieve Bujold, Nancy Beatty, Graham Greene, Emily Hampshire, Jonathan Scarfe, Neil Kroetsch, Benz Antoine

Dead Letter Office
Australia 1998 95m colour
BBC/AFFC/Artist Services/Film Victoria (Denise Patience)
Impelled by memories of her father, who left home when she was small, a young woman gets a job at the dead letter office, where she forms an uneasy relationship with her boss, a Chilean émigré.
Muted, elegiac movie about loss, given to over-heavy symbolism.
w Deb Cox *d* John Ruane *ph* Ellery Ryan *m* Roger Mason *pd* Chris Kennedy *ed* Denise Haratzis
☆ Miranda Otto, George DelHoyo, Nicholas Bell, Syd Brisbane, Georgina Naidu, Jane Hall, Barry Otto

'No One Can Survive Becoming A Legend.'
Dead Man **
US/Germany 1996 121m bw
Electric/12-Gauge/Pandora (Demetra J. MacBride)
An unemployed accountant goes into the lawless West and becomes a hunted man and a killer.
Enjoyable existential Western, slow-moving but providing an interesting and eccentric ride on the trail from civilization to savagery.
wd Jim Jarmusch *ph* Robby Müller *m* Neil Young *pd* Robert Ziembicki *ed* Jay Rabinowitz
☆ Johnny Depp, Gary Farmer, Lance Henriksen, Robert Mitchum, Crispin Glover, Gabriel Byrne, John Hurt, Alfred Molina, Michael Wincott, Mili Avital, Iggy Pop, Jared Harris, Billy Bob Thornton
'Only a few script drafts or some ruthless re-editing away from being rather good.' – *Adam Mars-Jones, Independent*

'The Drop-Dead Funniest Movie Of The Decade!'
Dead Man on Campus
US 1998 93m colour
Paramount/MTV/Pacific Western (Gale Anne Hurd)
Two partying medical students, on the verge of being expelled, discover that they will be awarded perfect grades if a room-mate commits suicide, and go in search of a suitable candidate.
Limp comedy that is too eager not to offend, and so fails to come to terms with its subject-matter.
w Michael Traeger, Mike White *story* Anthony Abrams, Adam Larson Broder *d* Alan Cohn *ph* John Thomas *m* Mark Mothersbaugh *pd* Carol Winstead Wood *ed* Debra Chiate
☆ Tom Everett Scott, Mark-Paul Gosselaar, Poppy Montgomery, Lochlyn Munro, Randy Pearlstein, Corey Page, Alyson Hannigan, Mari Morrow, Dave Ruby
'A modestly amusing trifle that merits a passing grade as lightweight entertainment.' – *Joe Leydon, Variety*
† A similar starting point was used in the movie *Dead Man's Curve* (qv).

Dead Man Walking **
US 1995 122m DuArt
Polygram/Working Title/Havoc (John Kilik, Tim Robbins, Rudd Simmons)
A murderer on Death Row repents of his crime after visits from a Catholic nun.
A tense and gripping meditation on death and the taking of lives, handled with sensitivity and an avoidance of sensationalism.
wd Tim Robbins *book* Sister Helen Prejean *ph* Roger A. Deakins *m* David Robbins *pd* Richard Hoover *ed* Lisa Zeno Churgin
☆ Susan Sarandon, *Sean Penn*, Robert Prosky, Raymond J. Barry, R. Lee Ermey, Celia Weston, Lois Smith, Scott Wilson
'As drama, *Dead Man Walking* is dead on its feet.' – *Tom Shone, Sunday Times*
'A film that carefully eschews the usual Hollywood sentimentality.' – *Derek Malcolm, Guardian*
Susan Sarandon
Sean Penn; song 'Dead Man Walking' (*m/ly* Bruce Springsteen)

Dead Man's Curve
US 1998 90m colour
Hope Street Entertainment/Mount Royal (Michael Amato, Theodore Schipper, Jeremy Lew)
Two college students discover that they can get a perfect grade if their room-mate kills himself; so they decide to murder him and make it look like suicide.
Black thriller on the theme that winners take all; but there is an unpleasant, gloating tone to it, and its twists are predictable.
wd Dan Rosen *ph* Joey Forstyte *m* Shark *pd* Robert Harbour *ed* William Mercer
☆ Matthew Lillard, Michael Vartan, Randall Batinkoff, Keri Russell, Tamara Craig Thomas, Anthony Griffin, Bo Dietle, Kevin Huff, Henry Strozier, Dana Delany
'Isn't clever enough to hit the mark as an intended diabolical black comedy.' – *Dennis Harvey, Variety*
† A similar plot device was used in the comedy *Dead Man on Campus* (qv).

Dead Man's Eyes
US 1944 64m bw
Universal
In order to trap a murderer, a blind artist pretends to have recovered his sight.
Cheerless lower-case thriller from the disappointing Inner Sanctum series.
w Dwight V. Babcock *d* Reginald LeBorg *ph* Paul Ivano *md* Paul Sawtell *ad* John B. Goodman, Martin Obzina *ed* Milton Carruth
☆ Lon Chaney Jnr, Jean Parker, Paul Kelly, Thomas Gomez, Jonathan Hale, Edward Fielding, George Meeker, Acquanetta

Dead Man's Shoes
GB 1939 67m bw
Associated British (Walter Mycroft)
A wealthy Paris manufacturer is accused of being a criminal who once disappeared.
Sufficiently absorbing courtroom/amnesia melodrama, with British actors in a French setting.
w Hans Kafka, Nina Jarvis *d* Thomas Bentley *ph* Gunther Krampf *ad* Ian White *ed* Monica Kimmick
☆ Leslie Banks, Joan Marion, Geoffrey Atkins, Wilfrid Lawson, Judy Kelly, Nancy Price, Peter Bull, Walter Hudd, Ludwig Stossel
'Goes straight into tense situations, and there are unexpected twists ... should do well.' – *Variety*

Dead Men Don't Die
US 1991 94m colour
Trans Atlantic/Waymar (Wayne Marmorstein)
After he is killed by drug dealers, a TV newscaster is brought back to life as a zombie.
Terrible, heavy-handed comedy, stuffed with ham acting.
☆ Elliott Gould, Melissa Anderson, Mark Moses, Mabel King, Philip Bruns, Jack Betts, Robert Dryer, Robert Covarrubias, Phil Shipko

Dead Men Don't Wear Plaid *
US 1982 88m bw
Universal/Aspen Film Society (David V. Picker, William E. McEuen)
A private eye is hired by a beautiful girl to find her father's murderer.
Ingenious but overstretched prank in which the hero apparently (by intercutting) gets involved with famous crime stars of the forties: Bogart, Ladd, Bacall, Stanwyck, etc. The basic script is simply not funny enough to support the superstructure, though the selection of lines from the oldies is often ingenious.
w Carl Reiner, George Gipe, Steve Martin *d* Carl Reiner *ph* Michael Chapman *m* Miklos Rozsa *pd* John DeCuir *ed* Bud Molin
☆ Steve Martin, Rachel Ward, Carl Reiner, Reni Santoni
'The content is undergraduate facetiousness at its worst, but at least the excerpts themselves provide a pleasant *noir* anthology.' – *Sight and Sound*

Dead Men Tell No Tales
GB 1938 80m bw
British National (John Corfield)
The matron of a school for boys is murdered after winning a lottery.
Reasonably intriguing mystery.
w Walter Summers, Stafford Dickens, Emlyn Williams *novel* *The Norwich Victims* by Francis Beeding *d* David MacDonald *ph* Bryan Langley *md* W. L. Trytel *ed* James Corbett
☆ Emlyn Williams, Hugh Williams, Marius Goring, Lesley Brook, Sara Seegar

Dead Men Walk
US 1943 64m bw
PRC
A vampire returns from death to destroy his twin brother.
Incompetent chiller partly sustained by its star performance.
w Fred Myton *d* Sam Newfield
☆ George Zucco, Mary Carlisle

Dead of Night: see *Lighthouse*

'Like Nothing In This World You've Ever Thrilled To Before.'
Dead of Night ****
GB 1945 104m bw
Ealing (Sidney Cole, John Croydon)
An architect is caught up in an endless series of recurring dreams, during which he is told other people's supernatural experiences and finally murders the psychiatrist who is trying to help him.
Chillingly successful and influential compendium of the macabre, especially effective in its low-key handling of the linking sequence with its circular ending.
w John Baines, Angus MacPhail, *based on stories by themselves, H. G. Wells, E. F. Benson* *d* *Alberto Cavalcanti, Charles Crichton, Robert Hamer, Basil Dearden* *ph* Douglas Slocombe, Stan Pavey *m* *Georges Auric* *ad* *Michael Relph*
☆ *Mervyn Johns, Roland Culver*, Mary Merrall, Judy Kelly, Anthony Baird, *Sally Ann Howes, Frederick Valk, Googie Withers*, Ralph Michael, Esmé Percy, Basil Radford, Naunton Wayne, Miles Malleson, *Michael Redgrave*, Hartley Power and also Elizabeth Welch
'In a nightmare within a nightmare are contained five separate ghost stories ... they have atmosphere and polish, they are eerie, they are well acted.' – *Richard Winnington*
'One of the most successful blends of laughter, terror and outrage that I can remember.' – *James Agee*
'The five ghost stories accumulate in intensity until the trap closes in the surrealist climax.' – *Pauline Kael, 1968*

Dead of Winter
US 1986 100m Metrocolor
UIP/MGM-UA (John Bloomgarden, Marc Shmuger)
An actress finds herself cast for a role which involves her being trapped in a country house with two villains.
Oddball suspenser with talent which seems to have expected something better.
w Marc Shmuger, Mark Malone *d* Arthur Penn *ph* Jan Weincke *m* Richard Einhorn *pd* Bill Brodie *ed* Rick Shaine
☆ Mary Steenburgen, Roddy McDowall, Jan Rubes, William Russ

Dead on Sight
US 1994 96m Foto-Kem
MCEG Sterling (Roxanne Messina Captor)
A university professor, trying to find the serial killer who murdered his wife, enlists the aid of a student who sees future murders in her dreams.
Extremely dull and silly thriller, remarkable only for its lack of suspense.
w Lewis Green *d* Ruben Preuss *ph* Levie Isaacks *m* Harry Manfredini *pd* Jo-Ann Chorney *ed* David Kern
☆ Jennifer Beals, Daniel Baldwin, Kurtwood Smith, William H. Macy, Kent Williams, Ed Beechner

Dead or Alive
Italy/US 1967 89m Eastmancolor
Documento/Selmur (Albert Band)
US title: *A Minute to Pray, a Second to Die*
A gunman with a paralysed right arm helps a state governor rid a town of bandits.
Semi-spaghetti Western with a strong cast and violent action scenes.
w Ugo Liberatore, Louis Garfinkle *d* Franco Giraldi *ph* Aiace Parolin *m* Carlo Rustichelli
☆ Robert Ryan, Arthur Kennedy, Alex Cord, Nicoletta Machiavelli

Dead or Alive: Hanzaisha
Japan 1999 105m colour
Daiei Co./Toei Video (Katsumi Ono, Makoto Okada, Toshiki Kimura)
A tough cop with problems becomes involved with a tougher gangster who is trying to take over the drug trade.
Delirious frenetic thriller, violent and frequently unpleasant, with a joke ending; it will no doubt become a cult film.
w Ichiro Ryu *d* Takashi Miike *ph* Hideo Yamamoto *m* Kouji Endou *ad* Akira Ishige *ed* Taiji Shimamura
☆ Riki Takeuchi (Ryuuichi), Show Aikawa (Detective Jojima), Renji Ishibashi (Aoki), Hitoshi Ozawa (Satake), Shingo Turumi (Chen), Kaoru Sugita (Mrs Jojima)
'Adrenaline-charged, anarchic thriller with more flash than finesse.' – *David Rooney, Variety*
'A soulless compilation of thrills. It may raise the temperature of cynical teenage boys, for whom it seems to have been made.' – *Elvis Mitchell, New York Times*

Dead Pigeon on Beethoven Street
West Germany 1972 103m DeLuxe
Bavaria Atelier
An American private eye is shot dead in Germany by an international extortion gang, and his partner arrives to seek revenge.
Cheapskate thriller of interest only to addicts of the director.
wd Samuel Fuller
☆ Glenn Corbett, Christa Lang, Anton Diffring

Dead Poets Society **
US 1989 129m Metrocolor
Warner/Touchstone/Silver Screen Partners IV/Witt-Thomas Productions (Steven Haft, Paul Junger Witt, Tony Thomas)
A new English teacher subverts tradition by encouraging his students to enjoy life.
Heartfelt, but a little too manipulative to be totally successful.
w Tom Schulman *d* Peter Weir *ph* John Seale *m* Maurice Jarre *pd* Wendy Stites *ed* William Anderson, Lee Smith, Priscilla Nedd

☆ Robin Williams, Robert Sean Leonard, Ethan Hawke, Josh Charles, Gale Hansen, Dylan Kussman, Allelon Ruggiero, James Waterston, Norman Lloyd
Academy Award: Tom Schulman
Academy Award nomination: best picture; Robin Williams; Peter Weir
BAFTA: best picture; Maurice Jarre

The Dead Pool
US 1988 91m Technicolor
Warner/Malpaso (David Valdes)

Inspector Callahan investigates a murder and the game of Dead Pool, in which people bet on certain celebrities dying within a specified time.
Fifth and worst in the series involving a tough cop that began with Dirty Harry.
w Steve Sharon *story* Steve Sharon, Durk Pearson, Sandy Shaw *d* Buddy Van Horn *ph* Jack N. Green *m* Lalo Schifrin *pd* Edward C. Carfagno *ed* Ron Spang
☆ Clint Eastwood, Patricia Clarkson, Liam Neeson, Evan C. Kim, David Hunt, Michael Currie, Michael Goodwin, Darwin Gillett, Anthony Charnota

Dead Presidents *
US 1995 119m Technicolor Super 35
Buena Vista/Hollywood/Caravan/Underworld (Allen Hughes, Albert Hughes)

After serving in Vietnam, a black man turns to crime to support himself, his girlfriend and child.
Downbeat thriller that struggles to marry social comment with the familiar form of a gangster movie; the union is not a happy one.
w Michael Henry Brown *story Specialist No. 4 Haywood T. 'The Kid' Kirkland* by Wallace Terry *d* Allen Hughes, Albert Hughes *ph* Lisa Rinzler *m* Danny Elfman *pd* David Brisbin *ed* Dan Lebental
☆ Larenz Tate, Keith David, Chris Tucker, Freddy Rodriguez, Rose Jackson, N'Bushe Wright, Bokeem Woodbine, Martin Sheen (uncredited)
'The outlook is bleak, the pessimism and the fatalism show that political consciousness without social outlets only leads to blanket nihilism.' – *Alexander Walker*

Dead Reckoning *
US 1947 100m bw
Columbia (Sidney Biddell)

Two war veterans are on their way to be decorated in Washington when one disappears.
Dour, complexly plotted thriller, a typical Hollywood film noir of the post-war years but a long way behind Gilda *in likeability. The hero confesses the plot to a priest, and all the way it is more glum than fun.*
w Oliver H. P. Garrett, Steve Fisher *d John Cromwell ph* Leo Tover *m* Marlin Skiles *md* Morris Stoloff
☆ Humphrey Bogart, Lizabeth Scott, *Morris Carnovsky*, Charles Cane, William Prince, Marvin Miller, Wallace Ford, James Bell
'The atmosphere is fraught with sinister suggestion.' – *Sunday Express*

Dead Ringer *
US 1964 116m bw
Warner (William H. Wright)

GB title: *Dead Image*
A woman shoots her rich twin sister and assumes her identity.
High camp star vehicle, full of memories of long ago but rather drearily assembled and far too long, though Miss Davis as ever is in fighting form.
w Albert Beich, Oscar Millard *d* Paul Henreid *ph* Ernest Haller *m* André Previn
☆ *Bette Davis*, Karl Malden, Peter Lawford, Philip Carey, Jean Hagen, Estelle Winwood, George Chandler, Cyril Delevanti

Dead Ringers *
Canada 1988 115m colour
Rank/The Mantle Clinic II/Morgan Creek Productions (David Cronenberg, Marc Boyman)

Identical twins, top gynaecologists, indulge in confusing their identities.
Downbeat and grisly, though possessing a certain elegance of style.
w David Cronenberg, Norman Snider *book Twins* by Barry Wood *d* David Cronenberg *ph* Peter Suschitzky *m* Howard Shore *pd* Carol Spier *ed* Ronald Sanders
☆ Jeremy Irons, Geneviève Bujold, Heidi von Palleske, Barbara Gordon, Shirley Douglas, Stephen Lack, Nick Nicholas, Lynne Cormack
'Its disturbing impact derives from a laying bare of male fantasies in such a way that masculinity itself is revealed as fragile, unstable, even impossible.' – *Pam Cook, MFB*

Dead Run
France 1967 100m colour
SNC (René Picneres)
original title: *Deux Billets pour Mexico*
A pickpocket steals top-secret papers and is chased across Europe by the CIA and a ruthless freelance espionage outfit.
Lightweight thriller, with performances to match, and of little interest, even on the level of a travelogue.
w Christian-Jaque, Michael Levine, Pascal Jardin *novel Dead Run* by Robert Sheckley *d* Christian-Jaque *ph* Pierre Petit *m* Gerard Calvi *ad* Jurgen Kiebach *ed* Jacques Desagneaux
☆ Peter Lawford, Ira Furstenberg, Georges Geret, Maria Bucella, Werner Peters, Wolfgang Kieling, Horst Frank

The Dead that Walk: see *The Zombies of Mora Tau*

'In his mind, he has the power to see the future. In his hands, he has the power to change it.'
The Dead Zone *
US 1983 103m Technicolor
Lorimar/Dino de Laurentiis (Debra Hill)

The survivor of a road accident discovers that he has psychic powers.
Glum thriller with a fairly predictable outcome but some well-staged episodes.
w Jeffrey Boam *novel* Stephen King *d David Cronenberg ph* Mark Irwin *m* Michael Kamen *pd* Carol Spier
☆ Christopher Walken, Brooke Adams, Tom Skerritt, Herbert Lom, Anthony Zerbe, Colleen Dewhurst

Dead-Bang
US 1989 102m Metrocolor
Warner/Lorimar (Steve Roth)

A detective, hunting a killer, uncovers a white racist organization.
Loud and undistinguished thriller.
w Robert Foster *d* John Frankenheimer *ph* Gerry Fisher *m* Gary Chang, Michael Kamen *pd* Ken Adam *ed* Robert F. Shugrue
☆ Don Johnson, Penelope Ann Miller, William Forsythe, Bob Balaban, Frank Military, Tate Donovan, Antoni Stutz, Mickey Jones, Ron Campbell
'John Frankenheimer's boldest, most enjoyable, and at least partially successful attempt both to recreate the halcyon days of his early 60s reputation, and to adapt them to changing times.' – *Richard Coombs, MFB*

Deadbolt
US 1992 95m colour
Allegro/Image (Tom Berry, Franco Battista)

A divorced woman finds herself sharing an apartment with a manipulative homicidal maniac.
Risible, violent, dreary thriller on a threadbare theme; in order for the narrative to work, it requires intelligent people to behave stupidly.
w Mara Trafficante, Frank Rehwaldt *d* Douglas Jackson *ph* Rodney Gibbons *m* Milan Kymlicka *pd* Perri Gorrara *ed* Yves Langlois
☆ Justine Bateman, Adam Baldwin, Michelle Scarabelli, Chris Mulkey, Anthony Sherwood, Ellen Cohen, Colin Fox, Cyndi Pass
† The film was released direct to video in the US.

Deadfall
GB 1968 120m DeLuxe
TCF/Salamanda (Paul Monash, Jack Rix)

Robbery turns sour when a cat burglar falls in love with the wife of his homosexual partner.
Drearily fashionable romantic melodrama with far too few high spots and generally dull performances.
wd Bryan Forbes *novel* Desmond Cory *ph* Gerry Turpin *m* John Barry
☆ Michael Caine, Eric Portman, Giovanna Ralli, Nanette Newman, David Buck
'Exhausted no doubt by their past passions and childhood traumas, the principal protagonists move like so many somnambulists through the turgid labyrinth ... whatever the intention, *Deadfall* merely falls flat on its somewhat ludicrous face.' – *MFB*

Deadlier than the Male
GB 1966 101m Techniscope
Rank/Sydney Box (Betty E. Box)
Bulldog Drummond traces the death of oil company executives to a master criminal using glamorous female assassins.
Just about tolerable recreation of Drummond in the modern world, with too little style, too much violence and sex, and an almost total lack of self-mockery. A sequel Some Girls Do *(qv) was an unmitigated disaster.*
w Jimmy Sangster, David Osborn, Liz Charles-Williams *d* Ralph Thomas *ph* Ernest Steward *m* Malcolm Lockyer *ad* Alex Vetchinsky
☆ *Richard Johnson, Nigel Green*, Elke Sommer, Sylva Koscina, Suzanna Leigh, Zia Mohyeddin, Steve Carlson
'The original Drummond would have found the whole thing rather distasteful.' – *MFB*

Deadline: see *Deadline USA*

Deadline at Dawn
US 1946 82m bw
RKO (Adrian Scott)
A sailor on leave passes out, finds the girl he was with has been murdered, and is helped by a philosophical taxi driver and a girl.
This could have been another Crossfire, *but is smothered by pretentious writing and uncertain direction. The credits are interesting, though.*
w Clifford Odets *novel* William Irish (Cornell Woolrich) *d* Harold Clurman *ph* Nicholas Musuraca *m* Hanns Eisler
☆ Paul Lukas, Bill Williams, Susan Hayward, Osa Massen, Lola Lane

Deadline Midnight: see *–30–*

Deadline USA *
US 1952 87m bw
TCF (Sol C. Siegel)
GB title: *Deadline*
Despite threats and the killing of a witness, a crusading newspaper goes ahead with a story about the crimes of a powerful gangster.
Watchable newspaper melodrama with nothing much to say except that America must wake up to the enemy within. Smooth production, but too much semi-pretentious talk.
wd Richard Brooks *ph* Milton Krasner *m* Cyril Mockridge
☆ Humphrey Bogart, Kim Hunter, Ethel Barrymore, Ed Begley, Paul Stewart, Warren Stevens, Martin Gabel, Joe de Santis, Audrey Christie, Jim Backus

Deadlock: see *Wedlock*

Deadly
Australia 1990 99m colour
Beyond/AFFC/Moirstorm (Richard Moir)
A city cop in trouble goes to a small town to cover up the killing of an aborigine artist, found hanged in a police cell.
An angry drama of institutionalized racism and bigotry, but genuine emotion is soon submerged in the slickly melodramatic contrivances of the narrative.
w Esben Storm, Richard Moir, Ranald Allan *d* Esben Storm *ph* Geoffrey Simpson *m* Graeme Revell *pd* Peta Lawson *ed* Ralph Strasser
☆ Jerome Ehlers, Frank Gallacher, Lydia Miller, John Moore, Alan David Lee, Caz Lederman, Tony Barry, Julie Nihill, Martin Vaughan, Bill Hunter

Deadly Advice
GB 1994 90m colour
Mayfair/Zenith (Nigel Stafford-Clark)

An unhappy woman has visions of famous murderers of the past, who advise her on how to kill her domineering mother and others who annoy her.
Flat attempt at a black comedy; it lacks the necessary style and wit and succeeds only in being depressing.
w Glenn Chandler *d* Mandie Fletcher *ph* Richard Greatrex *m* Richard Harvey *pd* Christopher Hobbs *ed* John Jarvis
☆ Jane Horrocks, Brenda Fricker, Jonathan Pryce, Imelda Staunton, Edward Woodward, Billie Whitelaw, Hywel Bennett, John Mills, Eleanor Bron, Jonathan Hyde
'Squanders a gaggle of British character actors on a nothing script that's desperately in need of a laugh track.' – *Derek Elley, Variety*

The Deadly Affair **
GB 1966 106m Technicolor
Columbia/Sidney Lumet
A Foreign Office man apparently commits suicide; his colleague is unconvinced and finally uncovers a spy ring.
Compulsive if heavy-going thriller from the sour-about-spies era, deliberately glum, photographed against the shabbiest possible London backgrounds in muddy colour. Solidly entertaining for sophisticated grown-ups.
w Paul Dehn novel Call for the Dead by John Le Carré *d Sidney Lumet ph* Frederick A. Young *m* Quincy Jones
☆ *James Mason*, Simone Signoret, Harry Andrews, Maximilian Schell, Harriet Andersson, Kenneth Haigh, *Max Adrian*, Robert Flemyng, Roy Kinnear, Lynn Redgrave
'The whole film is a most skilful organisation of action, motive and character.' – *Dilys Powell*

The Deadly Bees
GB 1966 83m Technicolor
Amicus
A pop singer goes on holiday to a remote farm and finds herself menaced by killer bees.
Flat little thriller with one very obvious twist and no monster: just those bees.
w Robert Bloch, Anthony Marriott *d* Freddie Francis
☆ Frank Finlay, Guy Doleman, Suzanna Leigh, Catherine Finn

'To the valley of mystery came the shadow of death!'
Deadly Blessing
US 1981 102m Metrocolor
Polygram/Interplanetary (William Gilmore)

A strict Hittite sect in Pennsylvania is disrupted by the murderous activities of an incubus.
Further developments from the school of Alien, Omen *and* The Exorcist; *basically a succession of well-engineered shocks punctuated by long periods of boredom.*
w Glenn M. Benest, Matthew Barr, Wes Craven *d* Wes Craven *ph* Robert Jessup *m* James Horner *sp* Jack Bennett
☆ Maren Jensen, Susan Buckner, Jeff East, Ernest Borgnine, Lisa Hartman, Lois Nettleton

The Deadly Companions *
US 1961 90m Pathécolor Panavision
Warner/Pathé America (Charles B. Fitzsimmons)

An army sergeant, a deserter, a trigger-happy gunman and a saloon hostess join forces to rob a bank.
Disjointed but rather attractive little Western let down by corny moments in the script.
w A. S. Fleischman *novel* A. S. Fleischman *d Sam Peckinpah ph* William H. Clothier *m* Marlin Skiles, Raoul Kraushaar
☆ Brian Keith, Maureen O'Hara, Chill Wills, Steve Cochran, Strother Martin

Deadly Force
US 1983 95m CFI color
Hemdale/Sandy Howard

An ex-cop returns to Los Angeles to hunt a serial killer, to the annoyance of local police, gangsters and his estranged wife.
Tacky, dim-witted thriller, never less than implausible and hardly watchable.
w Ken Barnett, Barry Schneider, Robert Vincent O'Neil *d* Paul Aaron *ph* Norman Leigh, David Myers *m* Gary Scott *pd* Alan Roderick-Jones *ed* Roy Watts
☆ Wings Hauser, Joyce Ingalls, Paul Shenar, Al Ruscio, Arlen Dean Snyder, Lincoln Kilpatrick

Deadly Friend
US 1986 99m Technicolor
Warner/Pan Arts Layton (Robert M. Sherman)

A bright kid robotizes a victimized girl and helps her get her revenge.
Silly but nasty horror flick of the Elm Street genre.
w Bruce Joel Rubin *novel* Friend by Diana Henstell *d* Wes Craven *ph* Philip Lathrop *m* Charles Bernstein *pd* Daniel Lomino *ed* Michael Eliot
☆ Matthew Laborteaux, Kristy Swanson, Michael Sharrett, Anne Twomey

Deadly Game: see *The Manhattan Project (1986)*

Deadly is the Female: see *Gun Crazy*

'See a 1000-ton insect monster hungering for human prey!'
The Deadly Mantis
US 1957 78m bw
Universal-International

A 'prehistoric' mantis escapes from Arctic ice and travels rapidly towards New York.
Absurd and poorly crafted monster movie.
w Martin Berkeley *d* Nathan Juran
☆ Craig Stevens, Alix Talton, William Hopper

Deadly Peacemaker: see *Man with the Gun*

Deadly Pursuit: see *Shoot to Kill*

Deadly Roulette: see *How I Spent My Summer Vacation*

Deadly Strangers
GB 1974 93m Eastmancolor
Rank/Silhouette (Peter Miller)

A girl accepts a lift from a motorist at a time when a mad strangler is on the loose.
Sub-Hitchcock melo-thriller with enough red herrings to sink a ship. Smartly enough done, but the grisliness needed balancing by humour.
w Philip Levene *d* Sidney Hayers *ph* Graham Edgar *m* Ron Goodwin
☆ Hayley Mills, Simon Ward, Sterling Hayden, Ken Hutchison, Peter Jeffrey

The Deadly Trackers
US 1973 104m Technicolor
Warner/Cine Film (Ed Rosen, Fouad Said)

A sheriff stalks the bandits who killed his wife and son.
Lurid and ludicrous Western started, and abandoned, by Samuel Fuller; the challenge need not have been taken up.
w Lukas Heller *d* Barry Shear *ph* Gabriel Torres *m* various
☆ Rod Taylor, Richard Harris, Al Lettieri, Neville Brand, William Smith
'It is no more than the outline of a shadow.' – *Tony Rayns*
'An incoherent, blood-soaked chase story.' – *New Yorker, 1977*

The Deadly Trap
France/Italy 1971 100m Eastmancolor
Corona/Pomereu/Oceania

The children of an American couple in Paris are kidnapped.
Smoothly made thriller which spends rather too much time being chic.
w Sidney Buchman, Eleanor Perry *novel The Children are Gone* by Arthur Cavanaugh *d* René Clément
☆ Faye Dunaway, Frank Langella, Barbara Parkins

Deadwood '76
US 1965 97m Technicolor Techniscope
Ember/Fairway (Nicholas Meriwether)
In Deadwood, a young man who is mistaken for Billy the Kid finds himself at odds with the townspeople.
Poor acting and production values do nothing to aid an incoherent and convoluted narrative.
w Arch Hall Jnr *d* James Landis *ph* William Zsigmond, Lewis Guinn *m* Manuel Francisco *ad* D. Reed III *ed* Anthony M. Lanza
☆ Arch Hall Jnr, Jack Lester, Melissa Morgan, William Watters, Robert Dix, La Donna Cottier
'It looks like a carbon copy of the worst of the Italian Westerns.' – *David McGillivray, MFB*
† Unshown in its home country, the film received a British release six years after it was made.

Deadwood Dick
US 1940 bw serial: 15 eps
Columbia
A crusading editor in disguise takes on a gang of renegades led by The Skull.
Mildly hilarious Western serial, under the gun of Laurel and Hardy's old director.
d James W. Horne
☆ Don Douglas, Lane Chandler, Harry Harvey

Deal of the Century
US 1983 98m Technicolor
Warner (Bud Yorkin)

An arms dealer is urged not to sell a new weapon to a warmongering dictator.
Complex comedy, descending into farce when the visiting general is bribed by the availability of American women. Not a success.
w Paul Brickman *d* William Friedkin *ph* Richard H. Kline *m* Arthur B. Rubinstein *pd* Bill Malley *ed* Bud Smith
☆ Chevy Chase, Sigourney Weaver, Gregory Hines, Vince Edwards, William Jarvis, William Marquez

Dealers
GB 1989 91m colour
Rank/Euston Films (William P. Cartlidge)

An ambitious young dealer in the City makes good.
An admiring look at the unacceptable face of capitalism.
w Andrew MacLear *d* Colin Bucksey *ph* Peter Sinclair *m* Richard Hartley *pd* Peter J. Hampton *ed* Jon Costelloe
☆ Paul McGann, Rebecca de Mornay, Derrick O'Connor, John Castle, Paul Guilfoyle, Rosalind Bennett, Adrian Dunbar, Nicholas Hewetson

Dear Brigitte
US 1965 100m DeLuxe Cinemascope
TCF (Henry Koster)

The small son of an American professor writes a love letter to Brigitte Bardot, and when they finally go to Paris she is charming to them.
Mild family comedy quaintly set around a decaying Mississippi riverboat home; despite assured performances, it all gets a bit icky at times.
w Hal Kanter *novel Erasmus with Freckles* by John Haase *d* Henry Koster *ph* Lucien Ballard *m* George Duning
☆ James Stewart, Glynis Johns, Fabian, Cindy Carol, Billy Mumy, John Williams, Jack Kruschen, Brigitte Bardot, Ed Wynn, Alice Pearce

Dear Diary ***
Italy 1994 100m colour
Artificial Eye/Sacher/Banfilm/La Sept/Canal (Angelo Barbagallo, Nanni Moretti, Nella Banfi)

original title: *Caro Diario*
A filmed diary in three chapters: the first involves a trip around Rome on a scooter, a chance meeting with actress Jennifer Beals and a visit to the place where Pasolini was killed; the second an island-hopping trip with a friend who stopped watching television in the 60s but becomes obsessed by it again; the third hospital treatment for a form of cancer.
A brilliant essay in autobiography, often bordering on the inconsequential but always interesting, full of charm and humour which remains even when deepening into a confrontation with the likelihood of imminent death.
wd Nanni Moretti *ph* Giuseppe Lanci *m* Nicola Piovani *pd* Marta Maffucci *ed* Mirco Garrone
☆ Nanni Moretti, Jennifer Beals, Alexandre Rockwell, Renato Carpentieri, Antonio Neiwiller
'The film seems slight and a little slapdash until the final episode, when Moretti faces mortality with a deadpan humanism that, under the circumstances, is bracing, even heroic.' – *Time*
'Appearing to be about nothing very much, it manages to encompass an awful lot, and it would be a strange viewer who didn't, somewhere in the film, identify with its major concern, which is how to survive in an increasingly frustrating and impersonal world.' – *Derek Malcolm, Guardian*

Dear God
US 1996 112m DeLuxe
Paramount/Rysher (Steve Tisch)
A repentant con man answers letters addressed to God at the post office's dead letter office.
Soft-centred, extraordinarily sentimental hokum, enough to make you wish for a little curdling of the milk of human kindness.
w Warren Leight, Ed Kaplan *d* Garry Marshall *ph* Charles Minsky *m* Jeremy Lubbock, James Patrick Dunne *pd* Albert Brenner *ed* Debra Neil-Fisher
☆ Greg Kinnear, Laurie Metcalf, Tim Conway, Maria Pitillo, Roscoe Lee Browne, Jon Seda, Anna Maria Horsford, Hector Elizondo
'Plays very much like a good first draft for a much better movie than the one on view.' – *Leonard Klady, Variety*

Dear Heart *
US 1964 114m bw
Warner (Martin Manulis)
At a postmasters' convention in New York, two middle-aged delegates fall in love.
Charming, understated, overlong romantic drama in the Marty tradition; all quite professional and satisfying.
w Tad Mosel *d* Delbert Mann *ph* Russell Harlan *m* Henry Mancini
☆ Glenn Ford, Geraldine Page, Angela Lansbury, Michael Anderson Jnr, Barbara Nichols, Patricia Barry, Charles Drake, Ruth McDevitt, Neva Patterson, Alice Pearce, Richard Deacon
title song (*m* Henry Mancini, *ly* Jay Livingston, Ray Evans)

Dear Inspector *
France 1977 105m Eastmancolor
Ariane/Mondex (Alexander Mnouchkine)

original title: *Tendre Poulet*
A female detective chases a murderer, helped by her professor boyfriend.
Very likeable comedy-thriller with neat performances. Popular in America, it was translated into a series for television, but didn't run.
w Michel Audiard, Philippe de Broca *novel* Jean-Paul Rouland, Claude Olivier *d Philippe de Broca* *ph* Jean-Paul Schwartz *m* Georges Delerue
☆ *Annie Girardot, Philippe Noiret*, Catherine Alric, Hubert Deschamps

Dear John *
Sweden 1964 111m bw
Sandrew (Bo Jonsson)
original title: *Kare John*
An unmarried mother in a seaside village falls for a seaman.
A slight story effectively tricked out with all manner of cinematic devices including a multitude of flashbacks. Very watchable if a little self-conscious.
wd Lars Magnus Lindgren *novel* Olle Lansburg *ph* Rune Ericson *m* Bengt-Arne Wallin
☆ Jarl Kulle, Christina Schollin, Helena Nilsson, Morgan Anderson
'It shines with the cool clear light of the Swedish summer, and despite its glossy surface manages also to convey strong sensual pleasure.' – *Brenda Davies*
best foreign film

Dear Mr Prohack
GB 1949 91m bw
GFD/Wessex (Ian Dalrymple, Dennis Van Thal)

A treasury official copes admirably with public money but is helpless when he comes into a private fortune.
Flat little comedy in which the minor amusements are incidental to the story.
w Ian Dalrymple, Donald Bull *novel* Arnold Bennett *d* Thornton Freeland *ph* H. E. Fowle *m* Temple Abady
☆ Cecil Parker, Hermione Baddeley, Dirk Bogarde, Sheila Sim, Glynis Johns, Heather Thatcher, Henry Edwards, Judith Furse

Dear Murderer
GB 1947 94m bw
GFD/Gainsborough (Betty E. Box)

Plot and counterplot among an adulterous triangle.
Thoroughly artificial pattern play set among the unreal rich, from one of those unaccountable West End successes, here boringly filmed.
w Muriel and Sydney Box, Peter Rogers *play* St John L. Clowes *d* Arthur Crabtree *ph* Stephen Dade *m* Benjamin Frankel *md* Muir Mathieson *ad* George Provis, John Elphick *ed* Gordon Hales
☆ Eric Portman (Lee Warren), Greta Gynt (Vivien Warren), Dennis Price (Richard Fenton), Maxwell Reed (Jimmy Martin), Jack Warner (Inspector Pembury), Hazel Court (Avis Fenton), Andrew Crawford (Sgt Fox), Jane Hylton (Rita)
'A quite alarming little picture.' – *Alan Dent, News Chronicle*

Dear Octopus **
GB 1943 86m bw
GFD/Gainsborough (Edward Black)
US title: *The Randolph Family*
Members of a well-to-do British family reunite for Golden Wedding celebrations.
Traditional upper-class British comedy drama, and very well done too, with opportunities for excellent character acting.
w R. J. Minney, Patrick Kirwan *play* Dodie Smith *d* Harold French *ph* Arthur Crabtree
☆ Margaret Lockwood, Michael Wilding, *Helen Haye, Frederick Leister, Celia Johnson, Roland Culver, Athene Seyler*, Basil Radford, Nora Swinburne, Jean Cadell, Kathleen Harrison, Ann Stephens, Muriel George, Antoinette Cellier, Graham Moffatt

'The screen's gayest love story!'
Dear Ruth *
US 1947 95m bw
Paramount (Paul Jones)
A schoolgirl causes confusion when she writes love letters to a soldier using her elder sister's photograph.
Smoothly amusing family comedy from a Broadway success.
w Arthur Sheekman *play* Norman Krasna *d* William D. Russell *ph* Ernest Laszlo *m* Robert Emmett Dolan
☆ Joan Caulfield, William Holden, Mona Freeman, Billy de Wolfe, Edward Arnold, Mary Philips, Virginia Welles
'It is unlikely that 1947 will bring a more satisfying comedy ... so many surprising and funny twists.' – *John Thompson, New York Mirror*
† Two less amusing sequels were made using virtually the same cast: *Dear Wife* (1949, 88m, *d* Richard Haydn); *Dear Brat* (1951, 82m, *d* William A. Seiter).

Dearest Love: see *Le Souffle au Coeur*

'Tonight, mercy will be buried with the past.'
Death and the Maiden **
GB/US/France 1995 103m colour
Electric/Capitol/Channel 4/Flach/Canal (Thom Mount, Josh Kramer)

In a South American country, a woman realizes that her neighbour is the man who raped and tortured her in prison during a previous regime and decides to try him for his crimes.
Electrifying debate on matters of morality, with acting and directing tightening the sense of unease and suspense to the end.
w Rafael Yglesias, Ariel Dorfman *play* Ariel Dorfman *d Roman Polanski* *ph* Tonino delli Colli *m* Wojciech Kilar *pd* Pierre Guffroy *ed* Herve de Luze
☆ *Sigourney Weaver*, Ben Kingsley, Stuart Wilson, Krystia Mova
'A tense, taut exercise in psychological menace that offers the audience barely a moment's respite.' – *Colin Brown, Screen International*

Death at Broadcasting House *
GB 1934 71m bw
ABFD/Phoenix (Hugh Perceval)
A radio actor is murdered during a broadcast.
Intriguing little murder mystery with an unusual background.
w Basil Mason *novel* Val Gielgud *d* Reginald Denham *ph* Gunther Krampf *md* Geoffrey Goodhardt *ad* R. Holmes Paul
☆ Ian Hunter, Austin Trevor, Mary Newland, Henry Kendall, Val Gielgud, Peter Haddon, Betty Ann Davies, Jack Hawkins, Donald Wolfit

'Your basic black comedy.'
Death Becomes Her
US 1992 104m colour
UIP/Universal (Robert Zemeckis, Steve Starkey)
An ageing Broadway star and a novelist, both rivals for the same man, take an elixir that gives eternal life.
A small comedy overwhelmed by its impressive special effects and suffering from its director's belief that louder and faster is funnier.
w Martin Donovan, David Koepp *d* Robert Zemeckis *ph* Dean Cundey *m* Alan Silvestri *pd* Rick Carter *ed* Arthur Schmidt *sp* Industrial Light and Magic
☆ Meryl Streep, Goldie Hawn, Bruce Willis, Isabella Rossellini, Ian Ogilvy, Adam Storke, Nancy Fish, Alaina Reed Hall, Michelle Johnson, Mary Ellen Trainor
'A black comedy that is so pleased with its own blackness that it frequently forgets to be funny.' – *Kenneth Turan, Los Angeles Times*
Visual effects

Death before Dishonor
US 1986 95m DeLuxe
Kubik/MPI/BIMA/New World
The Marines fight terrorists in an Arab country.
Violent exploitation actioner which will satisfy its audience.
w Frank Capra Jnr, Lawrence Kubik, John Gatliff *d* Terry J. Leonard *m* Brian May
☆ Fred Dryer, Brian Keith, Paul Winfield, Joanna Pacula

Death by Hanging ***
Japan 1968 117m bw VistaVision
Academy/Connoisseur/Sozosha (Masayuki Nakajima, Takuji Yamaguchi, Nagisa Oshima)
original title: *Koshikei*
A Korean student survives being hanged for the rape and killing of two Japanese girls but loses his memory and refuses to accept responsibility for his past actions.
A complex, challenging and blackly comic examination of racism, guilt and justice, filmed as a succession of re-enacted episodes, complete with chapter headings, in the life of the central character.
w Tsutomu Tamura, Mamoru Sasaki, Michinori Faukao, Nagisa Oshima *d* Nagisa Oshima *ph* Yasuhiro Yoshioka *m* Hikaru Hayashi *ad* Jusho Toda *ed* Sueko Shiraishi
☆ *Nagisa Oshima* (narrator), Yun-Do Yun, Kei Sato, Fumio Watanabe, Toshiro Ishido, Masao Adachi, Mutsuhiro Toura
'For three-quarters of its length, the film can be read as a brilliantly, insolently witty Brechtian parable; an alienation effect taking one away from the appalling realities of death by hanging, the better to make one understand the implications of those realities.' – *Tom Milne*

Death Drums along the River
GB 1963 83m Technicolor Techniscope
Big Ben Films/Hallam
US title: *Sanders*
In Africa, a police commissioner foils a murderous diamond smuggler.
Stilted, often facetious cut-price version of the old warhorse, and one that should have been put out to grass.
w Lawrence Huntington, Kevin Kavanagh, Nicolas Roeg, Harry Alan Towers *novel Sanders of the River* by Edgar Wallace *d* Lawrence Huntington *ph* Bob Huke *ed* Allan Morrison
☆ Richard Todd, Marianne Cook, Albert Lieven, Walter Rilla, Jeremy Lloyd, Robert Arden, Vivi Bach, Bill Brewer, Simon Sabela

Death Hunt
US 1981 97m Technicolor
Golden Harvest (Murray Shostak)
In 1931 Yukon, a reclusive trapper turns to violence when goaded by other wanderers and drunken mounties.
An arctic cross between Straw Dogs *and* Death Wish, *and not even so good as either.*
w Michael Grais, Mark Victor *d* Peter Hunt *ph* James Devis *m* Jerrold Immel
☆ Charles Bronson, Lee Marvin, Angie Dickinson, Andrew Stevens, Ed Lauter, Carl Weathers, Henry Beckman

Death in a French Garden *
France 1985 101m Eastmancolor
Artificial Eye/Gaumont (Emmanuel Schlumberger)
original title: *Péril en la Demeure*
aka: *Péril*
A music teacher, seduced by the mother of his pupil, finds himself embroiled in other sexual entanglements and murder.
Elegantly stylish thriller.
w Michel Déville, Rosalinde Damamme *novel Sur la Terre Comme au Ciel* by Rene Belletto *d* Michel Déville *ph* Martial Thury *ad* Philippe Combastel *ed* Raymonde Guyot
☆ Michel Piccoli, Nicole Garcia, Anemone, Christophe Malavoy, Richard Bohringer, Anaïs Jeanneret, Jean-Claude Jay

Death in Brunswick **
Australia 1990 109m Eastmancolor
Meridian/Film Victoria/Australian Film Finance Corp (Timothy White)
The new cook in a sleazy night-club accidentally kills his drunken assistant and asks an old friend to help him get rid of the body.
Witty black comedy of losers adrift in a world they cannot control.
w John Ruane, Boyd Oxlade *novel* Boyd Oxlade *d* John Ruane *ph* Ellery Ryan *m* Philip Judd *pd* Chris Kennedy *ed* Neil Thumpston
☆ Sam Neill, Zoe Carides, John Clarke, Yvonne Lawley, Deborah Kennedy
'An unusual, intelligent black comedy. Some will find the film outrageous, but word-of-mouth should give the pic legs on the international art-house circuit.' – *Variety*

Death in Venice ***
Italy 1971 128m Technicolor Panavision
Warner/Alfa (Mario Gallo)
original title: *Morte a Venezia*
In a lush Venetian hotel one summer in the early years of the century, a middle-aged German composer on holiday falls for the charms of a silent young boy, and stays in the city too long to escape the approaching plague.
Incredibly extended and rather pointless fable enriched by moments of great beauty and directorial style; these do not quite atone for the slow pace or the muddled storyline.
w Luchino Visconti, Nicola Badalucco *novel* Thomas Mann *d Luchino Visconti* *ph* Pasquale de Santis *m* Gustav Mahler *md* Franco Mannino *ad Ferdinando Scarfiotti*
☆ Dirk Bogarde, Bjorn Andresen, Silvana Mangano, Marisa Berenson, Mark Burns
'Maybe a story as elusive as *Death in Venice* simply can't be filmed. Visconti has made a brave attempt, always sensitive to the original; but it's finally not quite the same thing.' – *David Wilson, MFB*
'Camp and miscalculated from start to finish ... a prime contender for the title Most Overrated Film of All Time.' – *Time Out, 1985*
costumes (Piero Tosi)
Pasquale de Santis; Ferdinando Scarfiotti

Death is My Trade **
West Germany 1977 145m colour
Contemporary/WDR/Iduna (Fred Ilgner)
original title: *Aus Einem Deutschen Leben*
A working class man rises through the Nazi hierarchy to become commandant at Auschwitz.
Dispassionate and chilling account of the banality of evil.
wd Theodor Kotulla *novel* Robert Merle *ph* Dieter Naujeck *m* Eberhard Weber *ad* Wolfgang Schunke *ed* Wolfgang Richter
☆ Gotz George, Kai Taschner, Elisabeth Schwartz, Kurt Hubner, Hans Korte, Sigurd Fitzek, Peter Franke, Wilfried Elste, Matthias Fuchs

Death Japanese Style **
Japan 1984 124m colour/bw
Yashushi Tamaoki, Yutaka Okada
original title: *Ososhiki*
aka: *The Funeral*
An actress arranges the three-day wake and funeral of her father.
Witty and well-observed account of domestic dramas.
wd Juzo Itami *ph* Yonezo Yuasa *ad* Hiroshi Tokuda *ed* Akira Suzuki
☆ Nobuko Miyamoto, Tsutomu Yamazaki, Kin Sugai, Shuji Otaki, Ichiro Zaitsu

The Death Kiss
US 1932 74m bw
KBS/World Wide
During the making of a film an actor is murdered.
Promising murder mystery which becomes more and more muddled as it progresses; it wasn't helped by advertising suggesting that Lugosi was again playing a vampire instead of a red herring.
w Barry Barringer, Gordon Kahn *novel* Madelon St Dennis *d* Edwin L. Marin
☆ David Manners, Adrienne Ames, Bela Lugosi, John Wray, Vince Barnett, Edward Van Sloan

Death Line
GB 1972 87m Technicolor
Rank/Jay Kanter-Alan Ladd Jnr (Paul Maslansky)
aka: *Raw Meat*
Police investigating missing persons at a London underground station discover the existence of cannibals living in abandoned tunnels.
Tightly constructed thriller, unpleasant but effective, and revelling in violence and decaying flesh.
w Ceri Jones *story* Gary Sherman *d* Gary Sherman *ph* Alex Thomson *m* Jeremy Rose *ad* Denis Gordon-Orr *ed* Geoffrey Foot *sp* John Horton
☆ Donald Pleasence, Christopher Lee, Norman Rossington, David Ladd, Sharon Gurney, Hugh Armstrong, Clive Swift, James Cossins
'The film, a coherent whole in which the parts inter-relate suggestively rather than schematically, and rich in mythological overtones, represents one of the most remarkable debuts of recent years.' – *Robin Wood, MFB*

'Man's Deadliest Invention Is About To Show Its Metal.'
'In subterranean level 10 of the Chaank Corporation Building there are 23.2 billion dollars of bonds ... And in vault No. 10...'
Death Machine *
US 1994 111m Eastmancolor
Entertainment/JVC Victor/Fugitive (Dominic Anciano)
After he is fired, a hi-tech armament company's mad scientist sets the Warbeast, an unstoppable killer robot, after his former boss and a gang of activists, who are trapped in the headquarters building.
Knowing, blackly humorous, extremely gory science-fiction thriller that borrows from Blade Runner, Robocop *and* Terminator, *among others, but does so with more style than might have been expected.*
wd Stephen Norrington *ph* John de Borman *m* Crispin Merrell *pd* Chris Edwards *ed* Paul Endacott *sp* Peter Hutchinson; make-up: Dave Elsey, Creature FX; animatronics: Nik Williams, Animated Extras
☆ Brad Dourif, Ely Pouget, William Hootkins, John Sharian, Martin McDougall, Andreas Wisniewski, Richard Brake
'Great fun.' – *Film Review*
† The film features characters called John Carpenter, Sam Raimi and Scott Ridley, and the credits include, after a long list of Special Thanks, the line 'No Thanks to They Know Who They Are'.

Death of a Bureaucrat **
Cuba 1966 84m bw
ICAIC
original title: *La muerte de un burocrata*
When the widow of a stonemason discovers that to obtain her state pension she needs his work card, which has been buried with him, her nephew decides to take action.
Witty and irreverent satire at the expense of all bureaucracies and jobsworths, directed with a light hand and in a style that owes much to silent comedy.
w Alfredo L. del Cueto, Ramón F. Suárez, Tomás Guitiérrez Alea *story* Tomás Gutiérrez Alea *d Tomás Gutiérrez Alea* *ph* Ramón F. Suárez *m* Leo Brower *md* Manuel Duchesne Cuzán *ad* Luis Márquez *ed* Mario González
☆ Salvador Wood, Silvia Planas, Manuel Estanillo, Gaspar de Santelices, Carlos Ruiz de la Tejera
† The film is dedicated to 'Luis Buñuel, Oliver Hardy, Stan Laurel, Ingmar Bergman, Harold Lloyd, Akira Kurosawa, Orson Wells [sic], Juan Carlos Tabio, Elia Kazan, Buster Keaton, Jean Vigo, Marilyn Monroe and all those who, in one way or another, have taken part in the film industry since the days of Lumière.'

Death of a Cyclist *
Spain/Italy 1955 85m bw
Guion-Suevia/Trionfalcine
original title: *Muerte de un Ciclista*
An accident – a cyclist is knocked down and killed by an adulterous couple – tragically affects the lives of many people.
Rather like a politically conscious version of An Inspector Calls, *this mannered and unemotional film was most interesting because of its almost Hollywoodian self-assurance.*
wd Juan Antonio Bardem *story* Luis de Igoa *ph* Alfredo Fraile *m* Isrido Maiztegui
☆ Lucia Bose, Alberto Closas, Otello Toso, Carlos Casaravilla
'I can remember no other film which succeeds without either jealousy or absurdity in presenting a serious convincing picture of sophisticated European society.' – *Dilys Powell*

'Is it love or guilt that's making you marry me after all these years?'
Death of a Gunfighter *
US 1969 100m Technicolor
Universal (Richard E. Lyons)
An unpopular marshal refuses to resign, and the situation leads to gunplay.
Downcast character Western set in the early years of the century.
w Joseph Calvelli *d* Robert Totten, Don Siegel *ph* Andrew Jackson *m* Oliver Nelson
☆ Richard Widmark, Lena Horne, John Saxon, Carroll O'Connor, Larry Gates, Kent Smith

'A salesman's got to dream – it comes with the territory!'
'One mistake – seen by his son – unleashes with overwhelming power the great drama of our day!'
Death of a Salesman ***
US 1951 112m bw
Columbia (Stanley Kramer)
An ageing travelling salesman recognizes the emptiness of his life and commits suicide.
A very acceptable screen version of a milestone play which has become an American classic; stage conventions and tricks are cleverly adapted to cinematic use, especially when the hero walks from the present into the past and back again.
w Stanley Roberts *play Arthur Miller* *d Laslo Benedek* *ph* Franz Planer *m* Alex North *md* Morris Stoloff
☆ *Fredric March, Kevin McCarthy,* Cameron Mitchell, Mildred Dunnock, Howard Smith, Royal Beal, Jesse White
MRS LOMAN: 'Attention must finally be paid to such a man. He's not to be allowed to fall into his grave like an old dog.'
WILLY LOMAN: 'A salesman is somebody way up there in the blue, riding on a smile and a shoeshine...'
'Its time shifts with light, which were poetic in the theatre, seemed shabby in a medium that can dissolve time and space so easily.' – *Stanley Kauffmann*
Franz Planer; Alex North; Fredric March; Kevin McCarthy; Mildred Dunnock

Death of a Scoundrel *
US 1956 119m bw
RKO/Charles Martin
A Czech in New York becomes rich by fraud.
Unconvincing but intermittently entertaining melodrama, a vehicle for a male Bette Davis.
wd Charles Martin *ph* James Wong Howe *m* Max Steiner
☆ George Sanders, Yvonne de Carlo, Coleen Gray, Victor Jory, Zsa Zsa Gabor, Nancy Gates, John Hoyt, Tom Conway
'Vague moralizing and some attempts at social comment scarcely enliven this protracted study in megalomania.' – *MFB*

Death of a Soldier
Australia 1986 93m colour Panavision
Suatu/Scotti
The story of Edward J. Leonski, a psychopathic GI hanged in 1942 for the murders of three women.

Case history, most interesting for its re-creation of a period.
w William Nagle *d* Philippe Mora *ph* Louis Irving *ad* Geoff Richardson
☆ James Coburn, Reb Brown, Bill Hunter, Maurie Fields, Michael Pate, Terence Donovan

The Death of Mario Ricci *
Switzerland/France/West Germany 1983 101m Eastmancolor
Pegase/TSR/Swanie/FR3/Tele München
A Swiss TV journalist arrives in a remote village to record an interview with a malnutrition expert, and finds himself in the middle of a mystery about the death of an Italian immigrant worker.
A rather uncontrolled drama which begins by suggesting Bad Day at Black Rock *but becomes less interesting as it proceeds.*
w Claude Goretta, Georges Haldas *d* Claude Goretta *ph* Hans Liechti *m* Arie Dzierlatka
☆ Gian-Maria Volonte, Magali Noel, Mimsy Farmer, Heinz Bennent, Jean-Michael Dupuis

Death on the Diamond
US 1934 69m bw
MGM
Murder during a baseball game.
The story isn't much, so the picture's appeal depends on one's addiction to baseball.
w Harvey Thew, Joseph Sherman, Ralph Spence, Cortland Fitzsimmons *d* Edward Sedgwick
☆ Robert Young, Madge Evans, Nat Pendleton, Ted Healy, C. Henry Gordon, Paul Kelly, Edward Brophy, Mickey Rooney, David Landau
'Due to plot, miscasting and some minor league technical preparation, it was two strikes to the bad before the cameras started to grind.' – *Variety*

Death on the Nile *
GB 1978 140m Technicolor
EMI (John Brabourne, Richard Goodwin)
Hercule Poirot solves the mystery of who killed the spoilt heiress on a steamer cruising down the Nile.
A pleasant thirties atmosphere and the travel poster backgrounds are the chief assets of this rather hesitant whodunnit which plays fair enough with the audience but gives its popular cast too little to do, while its constant repetitions of the crime become rather ghoulish. On the whole, though, a very passable representation of an old-fashioned genre, and a few points up on Murder on the Orient Express.
w Anthony Shaffer *novel* Agatha Christie *d* John Guillermin *ph* Jack Cardiff *m* Nino Rota *pd* Peter Murton *ed* Malcolm Cooke
☆ *Peter Ustinov*, Bette Davis, Mia Farrow, Angela Lansbury, Jane Birkin, David Niven, George Kennedy, Jack Warden, Simon MacCorkindale, Lois Chiles, Jon Finch, Maggie Smith, Olivia Hussey, Harry Andrews, *I. S. Johar*
costumes (Anthony Powell)

Death Race 2000 *
US 1975 79m colour
New World (Roger Corman)
In the year 2000, the world's most popular sport involves motor racers who compete for the highest total of human casualties.
Cheaply made macabre satire, quite well enough made to please addicts of the blackest of black comedy.
w Robert Thom, Charles Griffith, Ib Melchior *d* Paul Bartel *ph* Tak Fujimoto *m* Paul Chihara
☆ David Carradine, Simone Griffeth, Sylvester Stallone, Mary Woronov
'The script is hardly Swiftian and therefore treads a thin delicate line between mockery and exploitation.' – *Michael Billington, Illustrated London News*

Death Rides a Horse
Italy 1967 115m Technicolor Techniscope
PEC (Alfonso Sansone, Henryk Chroscicki)
original title: *Da Uomo a Uomo*
After his family is massacred, a young gunfighter tracks down the killers with the aid of a bandit who has his own reasons for seeking revenge.
Spaghetti Western that sticks close to the usual formula of over-dramatic gunfights.
w Luciano Vincenzoni, Giulio Petroni *d* Giulio Petroni *ph* Carlo Carlini *m* Ennio Morricone *ad* Franco Bottari, Rosa Sansone *ed* Eraldo Da Roma
☆ Lee Van Cleef, John Phillip Law, Anthony Dawson (Antonio Margheriti), Mario Brega, Luigi Pistilli, Jose Torres, Carlo Cassola
† The plot was used again in 1971 as the basis of *Viva Django*.

Death Ship
Canada 1980 91m CFI color
Astral Bellevue Pathé/Bloodstar
Survivors of a shipwreck take refuge on a mysterious empty ship which sets about killing them one by one.
Yes, that's the synopsis, in the wake of Killdozer *and* The Car, *and this film is stupider than either.*
w John Robins *d* Alvin Rakoff
☆ George Kennedy, Richard Crenna, Nick Mancuso, Sally Ann Howes, Kate Reid

'No woman ever loved such a man! The whole world waited while he made love!'
Death Takes a Holiday *
US 1934 78m bw
Paramount (E. Lloyd Sheldon)
In the form of a mysterious prince, Death visits an Italian noble family to see why men fear him so.
A somewhat pretentious classic from a popular play of the twenties; interesting handling and performances, but a slow pace by modern standards.
w Maxwell Anderson, Gladys Lehman, Walter Ferris *plays Maxwell Anderson and Alberto Casella d Mitchell Leisen ph* Charles Lang *m* Bernhard Kaun, Sigmund Krumgold *ad* Ernst Fegte
☆ Fredric March, Evelyn Venable, Sir Guy Standing, Katherine Alexander, Gail Patrick, Helen Westley, Kathleen Howard, Henry Travers, Kent Taylor
'Highly fantastic, but well done ... likely to have greater appeal among the intelligentsia.' – *Variety*
† It was remade in 1998 as *Meet Joe Black* (qv).

Death Trap
US 1976 89m colour
Mars (Mohammed Rustam)
video title: *Eaten Alive*
The proprietor of a motel on the edge of a swamp is a maniac who murders his guests and feeds them to his pet crocodile.
Pretty sick rip-off of Psycho, *with no holds barred; a typical and regrettable example of the so-called Gothic horrors of the independent American cinema in the late seventies.*
w Alvin L. Fast, Mardi Rustam *d* Tobe Hooper *ph* Jack Beckett *m* Tobe Hooper, Wayne Bell
☆ Neville Brand, Mel Ferrer, Carolyn Jones, Marilyn Burns, William Finley, Stuart Whitman

Death Trap: see *Deathtrap (1982)*

'Not even a scream escapes!'
Death Valley
US 1981 88m Technicolor
Universal (Elliott Kastner)
A boy on vacation in Arizona finds himself being chased by a murderer.
Tedious shocker with little in the way of scenic background to relieve the unpleasant monotony.
w Richard Rothstein *d* Dick Richards *ph* Stephen H. Burum *m* Dana Kaproff *ed* Joel Cox
☆ Paul Le Mat, Catherine Hicks, Stephen McHattie, A. Wilford Brimley, Edward Herrmann

Death Vengeance: see *Fighting Back*

Death Warrant
US 1990 89m DeLuxe
UIP/MGM/Pathé (Mark DiSalle)
A Canadian Mounted Policeman goes undercover to discover who is responsible for a series of prison murders.
An implausible thriller, given little sense of reality but affording opportunities, readily taken, for violence.
w David S. Goyer *d* Deran Sarafian *ph* Russell Carpenter *m* Gary Chang *pd* Curtis Schnell *ed* G. Gregg McLaughlin, John A. Barton
☆ Jean-Claude Van Damme, Robert Guillaume, Cynthia Gibb, George Dickerson, Art LaFleur, Patrick Kilpatrick, Joshua Miller
'Unusually sadistic even by genre standards, this well-made exploitation yarn unravels under the weight of its dim-witted carnage.' – *Variety*

'It began with a rape. It ended with a massacre'
Death Weekend
Canada 1976 94m Eastmancolor Panavision
Reitman/Dunning/Link (Ivan Reitman)
Four louts take revenge on a lady driver by following her to a secluded country house.
Hoary shocker chiefly concerned with rape, the threat of rape, and various unpleasant methods of murder.
wd William Fruet *ph* Robert Saad *ad* Roy Forge Smith *ed* Jean Lafleur, Debbie Karjala
☆ Brenda Vaccaro, Don Stroud, Chuck Shamata
'Exploitation of the emptiest and most blatant kind.' – *MFB*

'Vigilante, city style ... judge, jury and executioner!'
Death Wish *
US 1974 94m Technicolor
Paramount/Dino de Laurentiis (Hal Landers, Bobby Roberts, Michael Winner)
When his wife dies and his daughter becomes a vegetable after an assault by muggers, a New York businessman takes the law into his own hands.
After a highly unpleasant and sensational opening, this curious and controversial film settles down into what amounts to black comedy, with the audience well on the vigilante's side. It's not very good, but it keeps one watching.
w Wendell Mayes *novel* Brian Garfield *d* Michael Winner *ph* Arthur J. Ornitz *m* Herbie Hancock
☆ *Charles Bronson*, Hope Lange, Vincent Gardenia, Stuart Margolin, Steven Keats, William Redfield
'This urban version of *Walking Tall* transcends its violence to satisfy every base instinct that "we liberals" are heir to.' – *Judith Crist*

Death Wish 2
US 1981 95m colour
Golan-Globus/Landers-Roberts
His maid gang-raped and killed, his handicapped daughter driven to her death, Paul Kersey resumes his stalking of urban thugs.
A badly made exercise in the exploitation of the most repellent aspects of violence, without the first film's saving grace of slickness and humour.
w David Engelbach *d* Michael Winner *ph* Richard L. Kline, Tom Del Ruth *m* Jimmy Page
☆ Charles Bronson, Jill Ireland, Vincent Gardenia, J. D. Cannon, Anthony Franciosa
'Bad art is one thing, but *Death Wish II* is ludicrous.' – *Variety*
'The sort of sequel which makes you realize that the original wasn't half so bad as you thought.' – *Margaret Hinxman, Daily Mail*
'It doesn't contain an ounce of life. It slinks onto the screen and squirms for a while, and is over.' – *Roger Ebert*

Death Wish 3
US 1985 90m colour
Cannon (Menahem Golan, Yoram Globus)
Paul Kersey, the urban vigilante, eliminates a gang of thugs terrorizing an apartment block.
The killing sprees have become routine, and there's nothing else of interest in this boring sequel to a sequel.
w Michael Edmonds *d* Michael Winner *ph* John Stanier *m* Jimmy Page *pd* Peter Mullins *ed* Arnold Crust
☆ Charles Bronson, Deborah Raffin, Ed Lauter, Martin Balsam, Gavan O'Herlihy

Death Wish 4: The Crackdown
US 1987 99m colour
Cannon (Pancho Kohner)
The ageing vigilante attacks drug dealers in Los Angeles.
Repetitious violence, with little narrative, other than villains being set up so that they can be mown down.
w Gail Morgan Hickman *d* J. Lee-Thompson *ph* Gideon Porath *m* Paul McCallum, Valentine McCallum, John Bisharat *ad* Whitney Brooke Wheeler *ed* Peter Lee Thompson
☆ Charles Bronson, Kay Lenz, John P. Ryan, Perry Lopez, Soon-Teck Oh, George Dickerson, Dana Barron, Jesse Dabson

'The Vigilante Is Back...'
Death Wish 5: The Face of Death
US 1993 90m colour
21st Century (Damian Lee)
A university professor seeks revenge after his girlfriend is first disfigured and then killed by her former lover, a gangster.
A rerun of the original movie, adding little that is new and nothing that is interesting.
wd Allan A. Goldstein *ph* Curtis Petersen *m* Terry Plumeri *pd* Csaba A. Kertesz *ed* Patrick Rand
☆ Charles Bronson, Lesley-Anne Down, Michael Parks, Saul Rubinek, Kenneth Welsh
'Comes off as a flat-footed, by-the-numbers programmer that, judging from what's on-screen, failed to spark much enthusiasm among the people who made it.' – *Variety*
† The film was released direct to video in Britain.

Deathcheaters
Australia 1976 96m colour
Australian Film Commission/Roadshow/D. L. Taffner/Trenchard Productions (Brian Trenchard Smith)
Two Vietnam veterans turned stuntmen are hired to infiltrate a Filipino fortress guarded by 150 men.
Jocular romp that provides an excuse for a succession of low-cost stunts, from car crashes to hang gliding.
w Michael Cove *story* Brian Trenchard Smith *d* Brian Trenchard Smith *ph* John Seale *m* Peter Martin *ad* Darrell Lass *ed* Ron Williams
☆ John Hargreaves, Grant Page, Margaret Gerard, Noel Ferrier, Judith Woodroffe

The Deathmaster
US 1973 88m DeLuxe
RF World Entertainment/AIP
California surfers cheerfully adopt a local mystic, not knowing that he is a vampire.
Modestly budgeted teenage screamer, competently made but of interest only to avid bibliographers of Count Dracula.
w R. L. Grove *d* Ray Danton
☆ Robert Quarry, Brenda Dickson, Bill Ewing, John Fiedler

Deathsport
US 1978 83m Metrocolor
New World (Roger Corman)
A popular game of the future involves gladiators willing to lose their lives against lethal motorcyclists.
Low-budget shocker for teenagers, by Rollerball *out of* Death Race. *Of no possible interest except as exploitation.*
w Henry Suso, Donald Stewart *d* Henry Suso, Allan Arkush *ph* Gary Graver *m* Andrew Stein
☆ David Carradine, Claudia Jennings, Richard Lynch, William Smithers

Deathstalker
Argentina 1984 80m colour
New World (James Sbardellati)
original title: *El Cazador de la Muerte*
A muscular hero battles against an evil wizard.
Low-budget, low-intelligence sword and sorcery, lacking any imagination, but offering a plethora of female nudity. It surprisingly spawned several sequels.
w Howard R. Cohen *d* John Watson (James Sbardellati) *ph* Leonardo Rodriguez Solis *m* Oscar Cardozo Ocampo *ad* Emilio Basaldua *ed* John Adams, Silvia Ripoli
☆ Richard Hill, Barbi Benton, Richard Brooker, Victor Bo, Lana Clarkson, Bernard Erhard

Deathstalker 2
US 1987 77m colour
New Horizons (Frank Isaac)
aka: *Deathstalker 2: Duel of the Titans*
Deathstalker goes to the aid of an exiled princess who has been robbed of her throne.
Sword-and-sorcery action played for laughs, which makes it no more entertaining.
w Neil Ruttenberg, R. J. Robertson *d* Jim Wynorski *ph* Leonard Solis *m* Oscar Cardozo

Campo, Christopher Young *ad* Marta Albert *ed* Steve Barnett
☆ John Terlesky, Monique Gabrielle, John Lazar, Toni Naples, Maria Socas, Queen Kong

Deathstalker and the Warriors from Hell
US 1989 86m colour
Concorde/New Horizons/Triana (Alfonso Corona, Antonio de Noriega)
aka: *Deathstalker III*
The outlaw Deathstalker honours the wish of a dying princess to search for a fabled city made of precious jewels and metals.
Tongue-in-cheek sword and sorcery, workmanlike but unimaginative and generally tedious.
w Howard Cohen *d* Alfonso Corona *ph* Xavier Cruz *m* Israel Torres, Alejandro Rulfo *ad* Francisco Magallon *ed* Ernesto Guillen
☆ John Allen Nelson, Carla Herd, Terri Treas, Thom Christopher, Aaron Hernan, Roger Cudney, Claudia Inchaurregui
† *Deathstalker IV: Match of the Titans*, produced, written and directed by Howard Cohen, followed in 1989.

Deathtrap *
US 1982 116m Technicolor
Warner/LAH (Burtt Harris)
A playwright past his best conceives a plan to murder an upcoming rival and steal his script.
This thriller on the lines of Sleuth *was enjoyable enough on stage, but on the screen, despite pretensions to style, it takes far too long to unravel its very few twists, the last of which is badly fumbled.*
w Jay Presson Allen *play* Ira Levin *d* Sidney Lumet *ph* Andrzej Bartkowiak *m* Johnny Mandel *pd* Tony Walton
☆ Michael Caine, Christopher Reeve, Dyan Cannon, Irene Worth, Henry Jones
'It plays absolutely fair, more or less, and yet fools us every time, more or less.' – *Roger Ebert*

Deathwatch **
France/West Germany 1980 128m Fujicolour Panavision
Contemporary/Quartet (Gabriel Boustiani, Janine Rubeiz)
In the future, a TV documentary producer has a cameraman, who has the apparatus implanted in his brain, follow every moment in the life of a dying woman.
Grim fable of media manipulation and sensationalist pressures on popular entertainment that retains its resonance.
w Bertrand Tavernier, David Rayfiel *novel The Continuous Katherine Mortenhoe* by David Compton *d* Bertrand Tavernier *ph* Pierre-William Glenn *m* Antoine Duhamel *ad* Tony Pratt *ed* Armand Psenay, Michael Ellis
☆ Romy Schneider, Harvey Keitel, Harry Dean Stanton, Max von Sydow, Therese Liotard

Deathwatch
GB/Germany 2002 94m colour
Pathé/OdysseyApollo/Media/F&ME (Sam Taylor, Mike Downey, Frank Huebner)
In the First World War, British soldiers take refuge in an abandoned German trench occupied by supernatural forces.
Atmospheric low-budget horror that gets bogged down in its muddy location and fails to develop satisfactorily.
d Michael J. Bassett *ph* Hubert Taczanowski *m* Curt Cress, Chris Weller *pd* Aleksandar Denic *ed* Anne Sopel
☆ Jamie Bell (Charlie Shakespeare), Ruaidhri Conroy (Chevasse), Laurence Fox (Capt. Jennings), Torben Liebrecht (Friedrich), Dean Lennox Kelly (McNess), Kris Marshall (Starinski), Hans Matheson (Hawkstone), Hugh O'Conor (Bradford), Matthew Rhys ('Doc' Fairweather), Andy Serkis (Quinn), Hugo Speer (Sgt Tate)
'As so often, a dull script lets it down. Simply picking off the cast one by one doesn't mean the plot is progressing satisfactorily.' – *Peter Bradshaw, Guardian*
† Other movies with a similar theme include *Castle Keep*, 1969, *The Keep*, 1983, and *The Bunker*, 2000.

'Some debts can never be paid'
The Debt Collector **
GB 1999 110m Eastmancolor
Film4/GFF/Dragon (Graham Broadbent, Damian Jones)
A bitter policeman is determined that an artist and writer shall not live down his violent past as a loan shark and murderer.
Violent , intensely-acted melodrama of hatred, rivalry and obsession that also casts an ironic sidelight on the current cult of the gangster as celebrity.
wd Anthony Neilson *ph* Dick Pope *m* Adrian Johnston *pd* Mark Geraghty *ed* John Wilson
☆ Billy Connolly (Dryden), Ken Stott (Keltie), Francesca Annis (Val), Iain Robertson (Flipper), Annette Crosbie (Lana), Alastair Galbraith (Colouhdun)
'Hardly a note rings false in this tightly paced, scorching thriller.' – *Marianne Gray, Film Review*

'Degenerate, disgusting, and ... deliciously funny!'
Decadence
GB/Germany 1993 108m colour
Mayfair/Vendetta (Lance W. Reynolds, Christoph Meyer-Weil)
A newly rich, upwardly mobile couple indulge in affairs: the husband with an upper-class woman, the wife with an investigator she has hired to spy on her husband.
An intensely theatrical work transfers unsuccessfully to film, with Berkoff playing a philandering husband and a private eye who mixes sex and business, and Collins as both a wealthy and a nouveau-riche woman; its stylized, over-the-top acting seems merely grotesque on the big screen and its satire on the get-rich-quick decade of the 80s is without bite.
wd Steven Berkoff *ph* Denis Lenoir *m* Stewart Copeland *pd* Yolanda Sonnabend, Simon Holland *ed* John Wilson
☆ Steven Berkoff, Joan Collins, Christopher Biggins, Michael Winner, Marc Sinden
'A ripe, belching, heaving, power-drill satire of 1980s Thatcherite Britain that's as full of excesses as the passé targets it parodies.' – *Variety*
'This offers very little to keep you glued to your seat for what is, in reality, two rather uncomfortable hours.' – *Kim Newman, Empire*

The Decameron *
Italy/France/W. Germany 1971 111m colour
UA/PEA/Artemis (Franco Rossellini)
original title: *Il Decamerone*
Eight of the bawdier stories from Boccaccio's cycle.
The first of Pasolini's excursions into folk-tales, emphasizing their earthiness and sexuality.
wd Pier Paolo Pasolini *book The Decameron* by Giovanni Boccaccio *ph* Tonino delli Colli *m* Ennio Morricone, Pier Paolo Pasolini *pd* Dante Ferretti *ed* Nino Baragli, Tatiana Morigi
☆ Franco Citti, Ninetto Davoli, Angela Luce, Patrizia Capparelli, Pier Paolo Pasolini, Jovan Jovanovic, Gianni Rizzo
'A film which finds comedy and beauty in all aspects of human vitality.' – *MFB*
† It was followed by similar adaptations of *The Canterbury Tales* and *Arabian Nights* (qqv).

Decameron Nights
GB 1952 94m Technicolor
Film Locations (M. J. Frankovich)
Young Boccaccio entertains a glamorous widow and her three guests with stories.
Feeble costume charade with all the cuckolding off-screen: insipid and artificial.
w George Oppenheimer *d* Hugo Fregonese *ph* Guy Green *m* Antony Hopkins
☆ Louis Jourdan, Joan Fontaine, Binnie Barnes, Joan Collins, Godfrey Tearle, Eliot Makeham, Noel Purcell
'The sort of hybrid international production of which experience has made one mistrustful.' – *Gavin Lambert*

Deceived
US 1991 108m Eastmancolor
Warner/Touchstone/Silver Screen Partners IV (Michael Finnell, Wendy Dozoretz, Ellen Collett)
A happily married New York art dealer discovers that her husband is not the person he claims to be.
An interesting premise is ignored in preference to an increasingly predictable narrative.
w Mary Agnes Donoghue, Derek Saunders *d* Damian Harris *ph* Jack N. Green *m* Thomas Newman *pd* Andrew McAlpine *ed* Neil Travis, Lisa M. Citron
☆ Goldie Hawn, John Heard, Ashley Peldon, Robin Bartlett, Tom Irwin, Amy Wright, Jan Rubes, Kate Reid
'A visually interesting but essentially made-to-order thriller.' – *Sight and Sound*

Deceiver: see *Liar*

The Deceivers
GB/India 1988 112m colour
Merchant-Ivory/Michael White/Cinecom/Film Four (Ismail Merchant, Tim Van Rellim)
An English army officer serving in India in the 1820s infiltrates the cult of Thuggee, a secret society of murderers.
Muddled melodrama that fails to carry any conviction.
w Michael Hirst *novel* John Masters *d* Nicholas Meyer *ph* Walter Lassally *m* John Scott *pd* Ken Adam *ed* Richard Trevor
☆ Pierce Brosnan, Saeed Jaffrey, Shashi Kapoor, Helena Michell, Keith Michell, David Robb

'Two men loved her ... she loved them both'
December Bride *
GB 1990 90m colour
BFI/Film Four/CTE/British Screen/Little Bird (Jonathan Cavendish)
A servant girl with an illegitimate daughter defies local and religious feeling when she refuses to marry either of the two brothers who might be the father.
Engaging drama of individual struggle.
w David Rudkin *novel* Sam Hanna Bell *d* Thaddeus O'Sullivan *ph* Bruno de Keyzer *m* Jurgen Knieper *pd* Adrian Smith *ed* Rodney Holland
☆ Donal McCann, Saskia Reeves, Ciaran Hinds, Patrick Malahide, Brenda Bruce, Michael McKnight, Geoffrey Golden, Dervla Kirwan

Deception: see *Reindeer Games*

Deception **
US 1947 112m bw
Warner (Henry Blanke)
A European cellist returning to America after the war finds that his former girlfriend has a rich and jealous lover.
Downcast melodrama made when its star was beginning to slide; today it seems irresistible bosh with a background of classical music, done with intermittent style especially by Claude Rains as the egomaniac lover.
w John Collier *play Monsieur Lamberthier* by Louis Verneuil *d* Irving Rapper *ph* Ernest Haller *m* Erich Wolfgang Korngold
☆ Bette Davis, *Claude Rains*, Paul Henreid, John Abbott, Benson Fong
'It's like grand opera, only the people are thinner ... I wouldn't have missed it for the world.' – *Cecelia Ager*
'Exquisitely foolish: a camp classic.' – *New Yorker, 1977*
† Previously filmed in 1929 as *Jealousy*, with Fredric March and Jeanne Eagels.

Decision Against Time: see *The Man in the Sky*

Decision at Sundown
US 1957 77m Technicolor
Columbia (Harry Joe Brown)
A cowboy tracks down the badman who has seduced his wife.
Routine small-town Western, efficiently done.
w Charles Lang Jnr *d* Budd Boetticher *ph* Burnett Guffey *m* Heinz Roemheld
☆ Randolph Scott, John Carroll, Karen Steele, Valerie French, Noah Beery Jnr, Andrew Duggan

Decision before Dawn *
US 1951 119m bw
TCF (Anatole Litvak, Frank McCarthy)
In 1944, anti-Nazi German POWs are parachuted into Germany to obtain information.
Meticulous, well made but unexciting spy story which seldom comes vividly to life.
w Peter Viertel *novel Call It Treason* by George Howe *d* Anatole Litvak *ph* Franz Planer *m* Franz Waxman *ed* Dorothy Spencer
☆ *Oskar Werner*, Richard Basehart, Gary Merrill, Hildegarde Neff, Dominique Blanchar, Helene Thimig, O. E. Hasse, Hans Christian Blech
best picture; editing

The Decks Ran Red
US 1958 84m bw
MGM/Andrew and Virginia Stone
Unscrupulous sailors plan to murder the entire crew of a freighter and claim the salvage money.
Solidly crafted but basically uninteresting melodrama.
w Andrew and Virginia Stone *d* Andrew Stone *ph* Meredith M. Nicholson
☆ James Mason, Broderick Crawford, Dorothy Dandridge, Stuart Whitman

Decline and Fall
GB 1968 113m DeLuxe
TCF/Ivan Foxwell
aka: *Decline and Fall of a Birdwatcher*
An innocent, accident-prone Oxford undergraduate is expelled and after various adventures in high and low society is convicted as a white slaver.
Flabby, doomed attempt to film a satirical classic which lives only on the printed page. Odd moments amuse.
w Ivan Foxwell *novel* Evelyn Waugh *d* John Krish *ph* Desmond Dickinson *m* Ron Goodwin
☆ Robin Phillips, Donald Wolfit, Genevieve Page, Robert Harris, Leo McKern, Colin Blakely, Felix Aylmer, Donald Sinden, Griffith Jones
'The British *Graduate*.' – *New Yorker*
'Literate, lavishly furnished, tastefully faithful.' – *Observer*

Decline and Fall of a Birdwatcher: see *Decline and Fall*

Decline of the American Empire ***
Canada 1986 101m colour
Malofilm/National Film Board Of Canada (Rene Malo, Roger Frappier)
original title: *Le Déclin de l'Empire Américain*
A group of intellectuals discuss their attitudes to gender, sex and love.
Witty, perceptive conversation piece that won the Film Critics' award at the Cannes Film Festival in 1986.
wd Denys Arcand *ph* Guy Dufaux *md* François Dompierre, based on themes by Handel *ad* Gaudeline Sauriol *ed* Monique Forcier
☆ Dorothée Berryman, Louise Portal, Pierre Curzi, Rémy Girard, Yves Jacques, Genevieve Rioux, Daniel Briere, Gabriel Arcand
'Arcand isn't out to expose these people as spiritually empty; he's trying to present a truthful look at how they live. There's nothing weighty in his approach; it's a lovely, very unassuming picture, yet there is enough drama so that by the end a subtle shift in all the relationships is necessary.' – *New Yorker*
foreign film

The Decline of Western Civilization *
US 1981 100m colour
Nu-Image (Penelope Spheeris)
A documentary of punk rock in Los Angeles in the late 70s, with disenchanted and alienated teenagers both as performers and audience.
Quirky and fascinating study of some of the unlovelier aspects of youthful rebellion; it makes an interesting companion piece to the director's first feature film, Suburbia.
d Penelope Spheeris *ph* Steve Conant, Bill Muerer, Penelope Spheeris *m* Fear, Black Flag, Germs, X, Alice Bag Band, The Circle Jerks, Catholic Discipline *ed* Charles Mullin, Peter Wiehl, David Colburn

The Decline of Western Civilization Part II: The Metal Years *
US 1988 90m colour
New Line (Jonathan Dayton, Valerie Faris)
Documentary on the bands and personalities of heavy metal rock.
Lively documentary of one of the noisier forms of popular entertainment, including interviews with some of its wilder practitioners.

d Penelope Spheeris *ph* Jeff Zimmerman, Julio Macat *ed* Earl Ghaffari
☆ Aerosmith, Alice Cooper, Kiss, Ozzy Osborne, Megadeath

'Harry Block Wrote A Bestseller About His Friends. Now, His Best Friends Are About To Become His Worst Enemies.'

Deconstructing Harry **

US 1997 96m DuArt
Fine Line (Jean Doumanian)

A writer, who makes use of the lives of his friends and family in his novels, goes to a ceremony in his honour at his old school.
Witty, discursive comedy, shuttling between the realities of a novelist's life and the fictions he makes from them; it has some excellent jokes and moments of hilarious farce, but there is no centre to hold it all together.
wd Woody Allen *ph* Carlo DiPalma *pd* Santo Loquasto *ed* Susan E. Morse
☆ Woody Allen, Caroline Aaron, Kirstie Alley, Bob Balaban, Richard Benjamin, Eric Bogosian, Billy Crystal, Judy Davis, Hazelle Goodman, Mariel Hemingway, Amy Irving, Julie Kavner, Julia Louis-Dreyfus, Tobey Maguire, Demi Moore and also Elisabeth Shue, Stanley Tucci, Robin Williams
'Abrasive, complex, lacerating and self-revelatory. It's also very funny, most of the time.' – *David Strattan, Variety*
Woody Allen (script)

Decoy

US 1947 76m bw
Monogram
The girlfriend of an executed gangster tries to get her hands on his buried loot.
Surprisingly tough little co-feature of its day; even more surprisingly, the leading lady is British.
w Nedrick Young *d* Jack Bernhard
☆ Jean Gillie, Edward Norris, Herbert Rudley, Robert Armstrong

Decoy: see *Mystery Submarine (1962)*

Dédée: see *Dédée d'Anvers*

Dédée d'Anvers *

France 1948 95m bw
Sacha Gordine (André Paulvé)
aka: *Woman of Antwerp*
aka: *Dédée*
A dockside prostitute falls for a sailor and arouses the jealousy of her protector.
Seamy low life melodrama, presented con brio, *but rather like a tenth copy of* Quai des Brumes.
w Yves Allégret, Jacques Sigurd *d* Yves Allégret *ph* Jean Bourgoin *m* Jacques Besse
☆ Simone Signoret, Marcel Pagliero, Bernard Blier, Marcel Dalio, Jane Marken

The Deep

US 1977 124m Metrocolor Panavision
Columbia/EMI/Casablanca (Peter Guber)

Underwater treasure seekers off Bermuda clash with black villains seeking a lost consignment of morphine.
An expensive action picture which is singularly lacking in action and even in plot, but oozes with brutality and overdoes the splendours of submarine life, forty per cent of it taking place under water.
w Peter Benchley, Tracy Keenan Wynn *novel* Peter Benchley *d* Peter Yates *ph* Christopher Challis, Al Giddings, Stan Waterman *m* John Barry *pd* Tony Masters
☆ Jacqueline Bisset, Robert Shaw, Nick Nolte, Lou Gossett, Eli Wallach
'The ultimate disco experience ... it dances on the spot for two hours, taking voodoo, buried treasure, morphine, violence and sea monsters in its stride.' – *Time Out*
'Peter Yates has knocked himself out doing masterly underwater action sequences in the service of a woefully crummy book.' – *Russell Davies, Observer*

The Deep Blue Sea *

GB 1955 99m Eastmancolor Cinemascope
TCF/London Films (Anatole Litvak)
A judge's wife attempts suicide when jilted by her ex-RAF lover.
Undistinguished adaptation of a very good play, hampered by wide screen and muddy colour, helped by thoughtful performances.
w Terence Rattigan *play* Terence Rattigan *d* Anatole Litvak *ph* Jack Hildyard *m* Malcolm Arnold
☆ *Vivien Leigh, Kenneth More*, Eric Portman, *Emlyn Williams*, Moira Lister, Arthur Hill, Dandy Nichols, Jimmy Hanley, Miriam Karlin

Deep Blue Sea

US 1999 105m Technicolor Super 35
Warner/Village Roadshow/Groucho III (Alan Riche, Tony Ludwig, Akiva Goldsman)

Sharks with enhanced intelligence threaten the staff of an underwater research facility.
Basically a B movie on steroids, this delivers all the expected, and more than familiar, thrills and spills, but lacks surprise.
w Duncan Kennedy, Donna Powers, Wayne Powers *d* Renny Harlin *ph* Stephen Windon *m* Trevor Rabin *pd* William Sandell, Joseph Bennett *ed* Frank J. Urioste, Derek G. Brechin, Dallas S. Puett *sp* ILM; Hammerhead
☆ Thomas Jane (Carter Blake), Saffron Burrows (Dr Susan McAlester), Samuel L. Jackson (Russell Franklin), Jacqueline McKenzie (Janice Higgins), Michael Rapaport (Tom Scoggins), Stellan Skarsgard (Jim Whitlock), LL Cool J (Preacher), Aida Turturro (Brenda Kerns)
'Leave your brain at the popcorn concession stand and you'll just cope with this ridiculous but intermittently pleasurable waterlogged action thriller.' – *Charles Gant, Heat*

'He'd be the perfect criminal if he wasn't the perfect cop.'

Deep Cover **

US 1992 112m DeLuxe
First Independent/Image Organisation (Pierre David)

A cop finds himself in trouble when he is recruited to infiltrate the operation of a Los Angeles drug dealer with powerful South American connections.
Vigorous, intelligent thriller that offers more complexity than most of its type.
w Michael Tolkin, Henry Bean *d* *Bill Duke* *ph* Bojan Bazelli *m* Michel Colombier *pd* Pam Warner *ed* John Carter
☆ *Larry Fishburne*, Jeff Goldblum, Victoria Dillard, Charles Martin Smith, Gregory Sierra, Clarence Williams III, Sydney Lassick
'Deeply cynical, almost despairing second feature from Bill Duke features enough promotable hard action, rough violence and bad attitude to make a small spring stash.' – *Variety*
'A formulaic police thriller with a hip-hop musical tail that constantly wags the cinematic dog.' – *Philip French, Observer*

Deep Crimson **

Mexico/France/Spain 1996 115m colour
Metro/Tartan/Ivania/MCINE/MK2/Wanda (Miguel Necoechea, Pablo Barbachano)

original title: *Profundo Carmesi*
aka: *Carmin Profond*
In Mexico in the late 40s, a fat nurse and a con man join forces to cheat lonely widows of their money.
Slick, slightly camp, deeply romantic account of a couple of ruthless serial killers.
w Paz Alicia Garciadiego *d* Arturo Ripstein *ph* Guillermo Granillo *m* David Mansfield *ad* Mónica Chirinos, Patricia Nava *ed* Rafael Castanedo
☆ Daniel Gimenez Cacho, Regina Orozco, Marisa Paredes, Veronica Merchant, Julieta Egurrola, Rosa Furman
'It's not a comfortable watch, but it is a compelling one.' – *Kim Newman, Empire*
† The same true story was also the basis of *The Honeymoon Killers* (qv), directed by Leonard Kastle, to whom this film is dedicated.

Deep End *

West Germany/USA 1970 88m Eastmancolor
Maran/Kettledrum/Bavaria Atelier (Judd Bernard)
Sexual problems of two young people on the staff of a London municipal bathhouse.
Interestingly made but rather dreary and vaguely symbolic modern fable.
w Jerzy Skolimowski, Jerzy Gruza, Boleslaw Sulik *d* Jerzy Skolimowski *ph* Charly Steinberger *m* Cat Stevens
☆ Jane Asher, John Moulder-Brown, Diana Dors, Karl Michael Vogler, Christopher Sandford
'A study in the growth of obsession that is both funny and frighteningly exact.' – *Nigel Andrews, MFB*

The Deep End *

US 2001 99m Foto-Kem Panavision
TCF/i5 (Scott McGehee, David Siegel)

A mother covers up a murder that she believes was committed by her gay teenage son.
Cool thriller that is better on the domestic detail of everyday life than on the messy details of blackmail and death.
wd Scott McGehee, David Siegel *novel* *The Blank Wall* by Elizabeth Sanxay Holding *ph* Giles Nuttgens *m* Peter Nashel *pd* Kelly McGehee *ed* Lauren Zuckerman
☆ Tilda Swinton (Margaret Hall), Goran Visnjic (Alek Spera), Jonathan Tucker (Beau Hal), Raymond Barry (Carlie Nagle), Josh Lucas (Darby Reese), Peter Donat (Jack Hall), Tamara Hope (Paige Hall), Jordan Dorrance (Dylan Hall)
'An absorbing, beautifully made melodrama that succeeds on formal levels more than it does with suspense or emotion.' – *Todd McCarthy, Variety*
† Elizabeth Sanxay Holding's novel was also the basis for Max Ophuls's 1949 movie *The Reckless Moment.*

The Deep End of the Ocean **

US 1999 105m Technicolor
Columbia/Mandalay/Via Rosa (Kate Guinzberg, Steve Nicolaides)

A family struggles to survive the sudden disappearance of their three-year-old son.
Engrossing domestic drama exploring the meaning of family values which is elevated out of the ordinary by its central performances.
w Stephen Schiff *novel* Jacquelyn Mitchard *d* Ulu Grosbard *ph* Stephen Goldblatt *m* Elmer Bernstein *pd* Dan Davis *ed* John Bloom
☆ *Michelle Pfeiffer* (Beth Cappadora), *Treat Williams* (Pat Cappadora), Whoopi Goldberg (Candy Bliss), Jonathan Jackson (Vincent Cappadora), Ryan Merriman (Sam), John Kapelos (George Karras), Michael McElroy (Ben Cappadora), Cory Buck (Vincent Cappadora, aged 7), Alexa Vega (Kerry Cappadora), Michael McGrady (Jimmy Daugherty), Brenda Strong (Ellen), Rose Gregorio (Rosie)
'Restrained and unsentimental, this astute drama deals thoughtfully with the chasm between real and idealized family lives.' – *Janet Maslin, New York Times*

'Oceans Rise. Cities Fall. Hope Survives.'

Deep Impact *

US 1998 125m DeLuxe 'Scope
Paramount/DreamWorks (Richard D. Zanuck, David Brown)

When a huge asteroid is spotted on a collision course for Earth, astronauts are sent to try to destroy it while contigency plans are made to save the lives of a few.
Something of a feel-bad disaster movie, in which the world is almost destroyed, while the audience is slowly drowned in the sticky syrup of sentimentality. What is truly striking is the poverty of imagination: the end of all life is a theme worth more than the trivial psycho-dramas on display.
w Bruce Joel Rubin, Michael Tolkin *d* Mimi Leder *ph* Dietrich Lohmann *m* James Horner *pd* Leslie Dilley *ed* David Rosenbloom *sp* Industrial Light and Magic
☆ Robert Duvall, Téa Leoni, Elijah Wood, Vanessa Redgrave, Maximilian Schell, Morgan Freeman, James Cromwell, Ron Eldard, Jon Favreau
'This devastating, deadly-serious glimpse at the emotional impact of Earth's possible destruction is a bold experiment, superbly realized – a gripping, thoughtful big-budget Summer movie about real people.' – *Jason Caro, Film Review*
'Spectacular enough in its cataclysmic scenes of the planet being devastated by an unstoppable fireball, but proves far from thrilling in the down time spent with a largely dull assortment of troubled human beings.' – *Todd McCarthy, Variety*

Deep in My Heart *

US 1954 132m Eastmancolor
MGM (Roger Edens)

Sigmund Romberg, a composer-waiter in New York, is helped by writer Dorothy Donnelly and showman Florenz Ziegfeld to become a famous writer of musicals.
Standard fictionalized biopic with plenty of good turns and a sharper script than usual.
w Leonard Spigelgass *d* Stanley Donen *ph* George Folsey *m* Sigmund Romberg *ch* Eugene Loring *ad* Cedric Gibbons, Edward Carfagno
☆ *José Ferrer* (Sigmund Romberg), Merle Oberon (Dorothy Donnelly), Paul Henreid (Florenz Ziegfeld), Walter Pidgeon (J.J. Shubert), Helen Traubel (Anna Mueller), Doe Avedon (Lillian Ziegfeld), Tamara Toumanova (Gaby Deslys), Paul Stewart, Isobel Elsom, David Burns, Jim Backus and also Gene Kelly, Fred Kelly, Rosemary Clooney, Jane Powell, Ann Miller, Cyd Charisse, James Mitchell, Howard Keel, Tony Martin, Joan Weldon

Deep in the Woods: see *Promenons-Nous Dans Les Bois*

'When was the last time you were really scared!!!?'
'You will never forget it!!!'

Deep Red **

Italy 1975 120m Eastmancolor 'Scope
Rizzoli Film/SEDA Spettacoli/Salvatore Argento

original title: *Profondo Rosso*
aka: *The Hatchet Murders*
A jazz pianist who witnesses a horrific murder obsessively and ineffectually tracks down the killer.
Slick, stylish, decadent, suspenseful thriller, with a disquieting atmosphere that continually puts its audience, like its victims, off-balance. Hemmings's character owes much to his role in Antonioni's Blow Up.
w Dario Argento, Bernardino Zapponi *d* Dario Argento *ph* Luigi Kuveiller *m* Giorgio Gaslini, Goblin *ad* Giuseppe Bassan *ed* Franco Fraticelli *sp* Germano Nobile, Carlo Rambaldi
☆ David Hemmings, Daria Nicolodi, Gabriele Lavia, Macha Meril, Eros Pagni, Giuliana Calandra, Glauco Mauri, Clara Calamai
'An Argento movie to treasure.' – *The Dark Side*
'A director of incomparable incompetence.' – *Vincent Canby, New York Times*
† The current British video release is of the subtitled original version. The film has also been released in an inferior dubbed version cut to 98m, which robs it of much of its narrative structure. The shorter version has been available on video.

Deep Rising

US 1998 106m Technicolor Panavision
Buena Vista/Hollywood Pictures (Laurence Mark, John Baldecchi)

Pirates rescue a few survivors from a luxury liner that has been attacked by a gigantic octopus-like creature.
Glossy monster movie, with most of the budget going on special effects; the script appears to have been cobbled together after a hasty viewing of 50s horror movies.
wd Stephen Sommers *ph* Howard Atherton *m* Jerry Goldsmith *pd* Holger Gross *ed* Bob Ducsay, John Wright *sp* creature design: Rob Bottin
☆ Treat Williams, Famke Janssen, Anthony Heald, Kevin J. O'Connor, Wes Studi, Derrick O'Connor, Jason Flemying, Djimon Hounsou, Cliff Curtis, Clifton Powell
'An old-fashioned B movie with A-budget effects, but the quality sheen can't disguise the cheap-thrills hokum.' – *Leonard Klady, Variety*

The Deep Six

US 1958 110m Warnercolor
Jaguar (Martin Rackin)

A Quaker is unhappy at being drafted into the navy, but after initial unpopularity becomes a hero.
An ageing star contends with many hazards: slipshod production, poor colour, a dull script, and an unplayable part.

w John Twist, Martin Rackin, Harry Brown *novel* Martin Dibner *d* Rudolph Maté *ph* John Seitz *m* David Buttolph
☆ Alan Ladd, William Bendix, Efrem Zimbalist Jnr, Dianne Foster, Keenan Wynn, James Whitmore, Joey Bishop, Jeanette Nolan

Deep Valley
US 1947 104m bw
Warner (Henry Blanke)
The daughter of a poor California farmer falls for a convict on a work gang.
Downright peculiar melodrama, a cross between Tobacco Road *and* Cold Comfort Farm, *with touches of* High Sierra. *For collectors.*
w Salka Viertel, Stephen Morehouse Avery *novel* Dan Totheroh *d* Jean Negulesco *ph* Ted McCord *m* Max Steiner
☆ Ida Lupino, Dane Clark, Wayne Morris, Henry Hull, Fay Bainter, Willard Robertson

Deep Waters
US 1948 85m bw
TCF
A problem orphan boy is content when adopted by a lobster fisherman.
Forgettable family film, smoothly directed and photographed.
w Richard Murphy *d* Henry King *ph* Joseph LaShelle *m* Cyril Mockridge
☆ Jean Peters, Dana Andrews, Dean Stockwell, Cesar Romero, Anne Revere

'Not All Aliens Come From Space. Save Your Last Breath...To Scream.'
Deepstar Six *
US 1989 100m Technicolor
Tri-Star (Sean S. Cunningham, Patrick Markey)
Underwater workers blow a hole in the sea-floor that releases a monster from the depths.
Modest, moderately suspenseful thriller with an excess of gore.
w Lewis Abernathy, Geoff Miller *d* Sean S. Cunningham *ph* Mac Ahlberg *m* Harry Manfredini *pd* John Reinhart *ed* David Handman
☆ Taurean Blacque, Nancy Everhard, Greg Evigan, Miguel Ferrer, Matt McCoy, Nia Peeples, Cindy Pickett, Marius Weyers

The Deer Hunter *
US 1978 182m Technicolor Panavision
Universal/EMI (Barry Spikings, Michael Deeley, Michael Cimino, John Peverall)
Three friends from a small Pennsylvania town go to fight in Vietnam.
The three-hour running time is taken up with crosscutting of a wedding, a deer hunt and a game of Russian roulette. Presumably the audience has to guess the point, if any; meanwhile it may be repelled by this long and savage if frequently engrossing film.
w Deric Washburn *story* Michael Cimino, Louis Garfinkle, Quinn K. Redeker and Deric Washburn *d Michael Cimino ph* Vilmos Zsigmond *m* Stanley Myers
☆ *Robert DeNiro*, John Cazale, John Savage, Christopher Walken, Meryl Streep
'A hollow spectacle, less about war than its effect on a community, full of specious analogies, incoherent sentimentality and belief in its own self-importance.' – *Time Out*
best picture; direction; Christopher Walken
Deric Washburn; Vilmos Zsigmond; Robert DeNiro; Meryl Streep
Vilmos Zsigmond

Def by Temptation
US 1990 95m Technicolor
BFI/Troma/Orpheus/Bonded Filmworks (James Bond III)
A young black man, intent on becoming a preacher, meets a woman possessed by a demon.
Slow-moving, low-budget occult thriller, more concerned with male/female relationships than horror, and showing promise of better movies to come from its first-time writer-director.
wd James Bond III *ph* Ernest Dickerson *m* Paul Laurence *pd* David Carrington *ed* Li-Shin Yu *sp* Rob Benevides
☆ James Bond III, Kadeem Hardison, Bill Nunn, Samuel L. Jackson, Minnie Gentry, Rony Clanton, Melba Moore, Stephen Van Cleef
'An instant addition to the canon of so-bad-it's-good classics and, inadvertently, a fascinating glimpse into the contradictions of contemporary American black culture.' – *John Lyttle, Independent*
'Sharp, funny and borderline creepy socio-sexual horror story.' – *Kim Newman, Sight and Sound*

Def Jam's How to Be a Player: see *How to Be a Player*

Defcon-4
Canada 1984 90m colour
New World/Salter Street (B. A. Gillian, Maura O'Connell, Paul Donovan)
aka: *Ground Zero*
Astronauts from an orbiting defence system return to Earth after a nuclear war to discover that savage tribes are fighting for control of the world.
Post-apocalyptic science-fiction of a familiar kind, but done with a certain unlovely intensity.
wd Paul Donovan *ph* Doug Connell, Les Krizsan *m* Chris Young *ad* J. W. Walsh, Emanuel Jannasch *ed* Todd Ramsay
☆ Lenore Zann, Maury Chaykin, Kate Lynch, Tim Choate, Kevin King, John Walsch, Jeff Pustil, Donna King

The Defector
France/West Germany 1966 101m Eastmancolor
PECF/Rhein Main (Raoul Lévy)
original title: *L'Espion*
An American physicist in East Germany gets involved in the spy game.
Disenchanted espionage 'realism', not very well styled and hampered by a star at the end of his tether.
w Robert Guenette, Raoul Lévy *novel* The Spy by Paul Thomas *d* Raoul Lévy *ph* Raoul Coutard *m* Serge Gainsbourg
☆ Montgomery Clift, Hardy Kruger, Macha Meril, Roddy McDowall, David Opatoshu, Christine Delaroche, Jean-Luc Godard
'All that we're finally left with is the cliché, a relatively new one, along with the triple-viced hero, that spying is not a nice profession but the good guys have to go in and win for our team. Well, East, West, or Western, what this country needs, moviewise, is a good cliché-breaker – and hang the expense.' – *Judith Crist*

Defence of the Realm **
GB 1985 96m colour
(Rank) Enigma/NFFC (David Puttnam) (Linda Miles)
A journalist tries to check the relationship between an MP and a Russian agent.
Efficient political melodrama, basically too old-fashioned to start a cult.
w Martin Stellman d David Drury ph Roger Deakins *m* Richard Hartley *pd* Roger Murray-Leach *ed* Michael Bradsell
☆ Gabriel Byrne, Greta Scacchi, Denholm Elliott, Ian Bannen, Fulton Mackay, Bill Paterson
best supporting actor, Denholm Elliott

Defenceless
US 1991 104m colour
New Visions (Renee Missel, David Bombyk)
A female attorney is hired to defend the wife of her lover, who is accused of his murder.
Moderately engaging thriller, in which the acting is better than the plot.
w James Hicks *story* James Hicks, Jeff Burkhart *d* Martin Campbell *ph* Phil Meheux *m* Curt Sobel *pd* Curtis A. Schnell *ed* Lou Lombardo, Chris Wimble
☆ Barbara Hershey, Sam Shepard, Mary Beth Hurt, J. T. Walsh, Kellie Overbey, Sheree North, Randy Brooks
'Effective (if somewhat predictable) thriller … Tense and engrossing.' – *Sight and Sound*
'A trite whodunnit dressed up with some good performances and an unusually emotional finale.' – *Empire*
† The film was released direct to video in Britain.

'The First True Story Of What Happens After You Die.'
Defending Your Life **
US 1991 111m Technicolor
Warner/Geffen (Michael Grillo)
Killed in a car crash, an advertising executive finds himself in Judgement City where he must defend what he did with his life in a trial to decide his ultimate fate.
Enjoyable comedy of modern manners, less concerned with the afterlife than with the here-and-now.
wd Albert Brooks *ph* Allen Daviau *m* Michael Gore *pd* Ida Random *ed* David Finfer, Spencer Gross
☆ Albert Brooks, Meryl Streep, Rip Torn, Lee Grant, Buck Henry, Michael Durrell, James Eckhouse, Gary Beach, Julie Cobb
'Original in concept, funny in spasms and pretty good about the American propensity to examine themselves in such minute detail that Judgement Day is likely to seem like just another spell on the analyst's couch.' – *Derek Malcolm, Guardian*

Defiance
US 1980 102m Movielab
AIP
A young seaman staying in New York fights back against the power of an urban gang.
Belated and unnecessary addition to the gang cycle; violent nonsense.
w Thomas Michael Donnelly *d* John Flynn *ph* Ric Waite *m* Dominic Frontiere *pd* Bill Malley *ed* David Finfer
☆ Jan Michael Vincent, Theresa Saldana, Danny Lopez, Rudy Ramos, Lenny Montana, Art Carney

The Defiant Ones **
US 1958 96m bw
UA/Stanley Kramer
A black and a white convict escape from a chain gang, still linked together but hating each other.
Schematic melodrama with a moral, impeccably done and with good performances.
w Nathan E. Douglas (Nedrick Young), Harold Jacob Smith *d Stanley Kramer ph Sam Leavitt m* Ernest Gold *ed* Frederic Knudtson
☆ *Tony Curtis, Sidney Poitier*, Theodore Bikel, Charles McGraw, Lon Chaney Jnr, King Donovan, Claude Akins, Lawrence Dobkin, Whit Bissell, Carl 'Alfalfa' Switzer, Cara Williams
'Probably Kramer's best picture. The subject matter is relatively simple, though "powerful"; the action is exciting; the acting is good. But the singleness of purpose behind it all is a little offensive.' – *Pauline Kael*
† Nathan E. Douglas was a pseudonym for the blacklisted writer Nedrick Young.
Nathan E. Douglas, Harold Jacob Smith; Sam Leavitt
picture; Stanley Kramer; Tony Curtis; Sidney Poitier; Theodore Bikel; Cara Williams; editing
Sidney Poitier

Le Défroqué *
France 1953 111m bw
SFC/SNEG
A defrocked priest performs a gallant action which persuades an acquaintance to become a priest himself and try to draw his friend back into the fold.
Curious but holding moral melodrama embellished by good acting.
w Leo Joannon, Denys de la Patellière *d Leo Joannon ph* Nicolas Torporkoff *m* Jean-Jacques Grunenwald
☆ *Pierre Fresnay*, Pierre Trabaud, Nicole Stéphane, Marcelle Geniat, Guy Decomble, Leo Joannon, René Blancard

Déjà Vu
GB 1985 90m colour
Cannon (Michael Kagan)
Lovers discover that they are reincarnations of a couple who perished 50 years ago in a fire.
Muddling, over-talkative supernatural thriller with dollops of sex.
w Ezra D. Rappaport, Anthony Richmond *book* Trevor Meldal-Johnsen *d* Anthony Richmond *ph* David Holmes *m* Pino Donaggio *pd* Tony Wollard *ed* Richard Trevor
☆ Jaclyn Smith (Maggie Rogers/Brooke Ashley), Nigel Terry (Gregory Thomas/Michael Richardson), Claire Bloom (Eleanor Harvey), Shelley Winters (Olga Nabokov)

'Sometimes your head has to listen to your heart.'
Déjà Vu
US 1997 115m DeLuxe
UIP/Rainbow/Revere/Jagtoria (John Goldstone)
A chance encounter leads to an American woman abandoning her fiancé for a new lover.
An involved and rarely believable tale of passion, in the style of a superior home movie; it may be enjoyed by those who believe that passion excuses bad behaviour.
w Henry Jaglom, Victoria Foyt *d* Henry Jaglom *ph* Hanania Baer *m* Gaili Schoen *pd* Helen Scott *ed* Henry Jaglom
☆ Stephen Dillane, Victoria Foyt, Vanessa Redgrave, Glynis Barber, Michael Brandon, Vernon Dobtcheff, Graydon Gould, Noel Harrison, Rachel Kempson, Aviva Marks, Anna Massey
'Ludicrously contrived and monumentally indulgent.' – *Guardian*

Déjeuner sur l'Herbe: see *Lunch on the Grass*

Delbaran **
Iran/Japan 2001 97m colour
ICA/Office Kitano/Bandai VisualFilm-e-Aval/T-Mark (Abolfazl Jalili, Shozo Ichiyama)
A young, orphaned Afghan refugee tries to survive by working in a remote Iranian roadside café.
Moving account of a boy forced to live on his wits in a hostile world, told with great humanity and visual directness.
wd Abolfazl Jalili *story* Reza Saberi *ph* Mohammad Ahmadi *ed* Abolfazl Jalili
☆ Kaim Alizadeh, Rahmatollah Ebrahimi, Hossein Hashemian, Ahmad Mahdavi
'Full of bizarre, often mysterious incidents, cruelty, kindness and wry humour.' – *Philip French, Observer*

'A comedy with the works!'
The Deli
US 1997 96m colour
Golden Monkey (Sylvia Caminer)
Facing financial ruin, a delicatessen owner risks everything by frantic gambling, while customers come and go.
Amiable, ramshackle comedy with little narrative but a succession of quirky characters to entertain in one way or another.
w John Dorrian, John Gallagher *d* John Gallagher *ph* Robert Lechterman *m* Ernie Mannix *pd* Lisa Frantz *ed* Sue Blainey
☆ Mike Starr (Johnny), Matt Keeslar (Andy), Judith Malina (Mrs Amico), Brian Vincent (Pinky), Ice T (Phil the Meat Man), Michael Imperioli (Matty), David Johansen (Cabbie), Heather Matarazzo (Sabrina), Debi Mazur (Teresa), Jerry Stiller (Petey Cheesecake), Frank Vincent (Tommy Tomatoes), Burt Young (J. C.)
'On this deli's menu, there's way too much ham.' – *Janet Maslin, New York Times*

A Delicate Balance *
US 1975 134m colour
American Express/Ely Landau/Cinevision
A quarrelsome Connecticut family is dominated by an ageing matriarch, and tensions mount to a climax of fear and threats.
Honourable but slightly boring film version of an essentially theatrical play: the acting is the thing.
w Edward Albee *play* Edward Albee *d* Tony Richardson *ph* David Watkin *m* none
☆ *Katharine Hepburn, Paul Scofield*, Joseph Cotten, Lee Remick, Kate Reid, Betsy Blair

The Delicate Delinquent
US 1956 101m bw Vistavision
Paramount/Jerry Lewis
A New York policeman tries to make friends with an eccentric youth who mixes with thugs; the boy decides to train as a policeman.
Jerry Lewis's first film without Dean Martin: a sobering experience combining zany comedy, sentiment, pathos and social comment. The mixture fails to rise.
wd Don McGuire *ph* Haskell Boggs *m* Buddy Bregman
☆ Jerry Lewis, Darren McGavin, Martha Hyer, Robert Ivers, Horace McMahon

Delicatessen ***
France 1990 99m colour
Electric/Constellation/UGC/Hachette Première (Claudie Ossard)
In a decaying city of the future, a butcher, who flourishes by killing his workers and selling their flesh, is attacked by underground vegetarian terrorists.
A gruesome theme given exuberant, witty, cartoon-like treatment.
wd Jean-Pierre Jeunet, Marc Caro *ph* Darius Khondji *m* Carlos D'Alessio *ad* Marc Caro *ed* Hervé Schneid
☆ Dominique Pinon, Marie-Laure Dougnac, Jean-Claude Dreyfus, Karin Viard, Ticky Holgado, Anne-Marie Pisani, Jacques Mathou
'Beautifully textured, cleverly scripted and eerily shot ... a zany little film that should get terrific word of mouth.' – *Variety*
'An impressive achievement and extremely funny.' – *Philip French, Observer*

Delicious
US 1931 106m bw
Fox
An Irish girl in New York falls for a rich man.
Early musical, very thin, but an agreeable museum piece for collectors.
w Guy Bolton, Sonya Levien *d* David Butler *ph* Ernest Palmer *m/ly George and Ira Gershwin*
☆ Janet Gaynor, Charles Farrell, El Brendel, Lawrence O'Sullivan, Virginia Cherrill, Mischa Auer
'Cream puffs, applesauce, and plenty of nuts ... should do the team's business on its name strength.' – *Variety*

Delightfully Dangerous
US 1945 93m bw
UA (Charles R. Rogers)
A straitlaced girl discovers that her eldest sister is a burlesque dancer.
Mild family comedy with music.
w Walter de Leon, Arthur Phillips *d* Arthur Lubin
☆ Jane Powell, Constance Moore, Ralph Bellamy, Arthur Treacher

The Delinquents
Australia 1989 101m colour
Warner/Village Roadshow (Alex Cutler, Michael Wilcox)
Two teenagers ignore adult disapproval and fall in love.
Tiresome account of adolescent angst.
w Mac Gudgeon, Clayton Frohman *novel* Criena Rohan *d* Chris Thomson *ph* Andrew Lesnie *m* Miles Goodman *pd* Laurence Eastwood *ed* John Scott
☆ Kylie Minogue, Charlie Schlatter, Angela Punch McGregor, Bruno Lawrence, Todd Boyce, Desiree Smith, Melissa Jaffer

'What did happen on the Cahulawassee River?'
Deliverance ****
US 1972 109m Technicolor Panavision
Warner/Elmer Enterprises (John Boorman)
Four men spend a holiday weekend canoeing down a dangerous river, but find that the real danger to their lives comes from themselves and other humans.
Vigorous, meaningful, almost apocalyptic vision of man's inhumanity, disguised as a thrilling adult adventure.
w James Dickey novel James Dickey *d John Boorman ph* Vilmos Zsigmond *m* Eric Weissberg
☆ Burt Reynolds, Jon Voight, Ned Beatty, Ronny Cox, James Dickey
'There is fundamentally no view of the material, just a lot of painful grasping and groping.' – *Stanley Kauffmann*
best picture; John Boorman

Dellamorte Dellamore: see *Cemetery Man*

'The distance between two men is ... The Delta.'
The Delta *
US 1996 85m colour
Charlie Guidance (Margot Bridger)
In Memphis, a male prostitute, a Vietnamese immigrant of mixed race, involves a white, middle-class teenager in his seedy world of hustling for a living.
A gritty, documentary-style drama of disillusionment and alienated youth that just about overcomes its cheap production values.
wd Ira Sachs *ph* Benjamin P. Speth *m* Michael Rohatyn *pd* Bernhard Blythe *ed* Alfonso Goncalves
☆ Shayne Gray, Thang Chan, Rachel Zan Huss
'Confronts issues of race and sexuality with a frankness rarely seen in the cinema, marrying a minimalist, almost intrusive, style to a naturalistic dialogue.' – *James Mottram, Film Review*

Delta Force
US 1986 129m colour
Cannon (Menahem Golan)
A TWA plane is hijacked in Athens and rescued by an elite force.
What starts more or less as a recapitulation of fact turns at the half-way point into macho fantasy. Oddly enough, the paying customers rejected the mix.
w James Bruner, Menahem Golan *d* Menahem Golan *ph* David Gurfinkel *m* Alan Silvestri *pd* Luciano Spadoni *ed* Alain Jakubowicz *cos* Tamy Mor
☆ Chuck Norris (Major Scott McKay), Lee Marvin (Col Nick Alexander), Martin Balsam (Ben Kaplan), Joey Bishop (Harry Goldman), Shelley Winters (Edie Kaplan), Robert Forster (Abdul), Lainie Kazan (Sylvia Goldman), George Kennedy (Father O'Malley), Hanna Schygulla (Ingrid), Susan Strasberg (Debra Levine), Bo Svenson (Capt Campbell), Robert Vaughn (Gen Woolbridge), Kim Delaney (Sister Mary)
'An exercise in wish fulfilment ... it's easy to get off on all this, as millions surely will, so long as you are willing to put your brain in hibernation for more than two hours.' – *Variety*

Delta Force 2: Operation Stranglehold
US 1990 111m colour
UIP/Cannon (Yoram Globus, Christopher Pearce)
US commandos go into action against a South American drug baron.
Ridiculous action film with a superhuman hero and a high body-count.
w Lee Reynolds *d* Aaron Norris *ph* Joâo Fernandes *m* Frederic Talgorn *pd* Ladislav Wilheim *ed* Michael J. Duthie, Daniel Candib *cos* Kady Dover
☆ Chuck Norris (Col Scott McCoy), Billy Drago (Ramon Cota), John P. Ryan (Gen Taylor), Richard Jaeckel (John Page), Begonia Plaza (Quinquina), Paul Perri (Major Bobby Chavez), Hector Mercado (Miguel), Mark Margolis (Gen Olmedo)

'A new generation of action-adventure excitement!'
Delta Force 3: The Killing Game
US 1991 97m Agfacolor
Global (Christopher Pearce, Boaz Davidson)
US and Russian special units combine to snatch an Arab terrorist who has planted an atom bomb in an American city.
Standard bang-bang action, with the usual gun fights and explosions, though it does occasionally work up a modicum of suspense.
w Boaz Davidson, Greg Latter *d* Sam Firstenberg *ph* Avi Karpik *m* Robert Thomas Mein *pd* Luciano Spadoni *ed* Michael Duthie
☆ Nick Cassavetes (Charlie), Eric Douglas (Sam), Mike Norris (Greg), Matthew Penn (Richard), John Ryan (Sergei), Hanna Azulai-Haspari (Irenia), Sandy Ward (General Wilson), Candice Brecker (Wendy Jackson), Jonathan Cherchi (Kadal), Dan Turgeman (Anwar Hussein)

'When A Hollywood Cop Teams Up With A Detective From The Swamps Of New Orleans ... All Hell Is About To Break Loose.'
Delta Heat
US 1992 91m colour
Harkham/Karen/Sawmill Entertainment (Richard L. Albert, Rudy Cohen)
A Los Angeles detective goes to New Orleans to track down the killer of his partner with the help of a one-armed renegade ex-cop.
Energetic and occasionally amusing thriller providing some engaging, if mindless, entertainment.
w Sam A. Scribner *d* Michael Fischa *ph* Avi Karpik *m* Christopher Tyng, Rockin' Dopsie *pd* Don Day *ed* Robert Edwards, Robert Gordon
☆ Anthony Edwards, Lance Henriksen, Betsy Russell, Linda Doná, Rod Masterson, John 'Spud' McConnell, Clyde R. Jones
'Nothing special, but not an ordeal.' – *Empire*

Delta of Venus
US 1994 100m Foto-Kem
New Line/Alliance/Evzen Kolar
After an unhappy love affair, an American woman, who has come to Paris to write in 1940, begins to invent erotic stories for a private collector.
Trivial soft-core porn from a director whose notion of sophistication is accompanying sexual activity with classical music.
w Elisa Rothstein, Louisianna Knop *novel* Anaïs Nin *d* Zalman King *ph* Eagle Egilsson *m* George S. Clinton *pd* Zdenek Flemming *ed* James Gavin Bedford, Marc Grossman
☆ Audie England, Costas Mandylor, Eric Da Silva, Marek Vasut, Zette, Emma Louise Moore, Raven Snow, Rory Campbell
† The film was made in Prague.

'Love and murder. The first time is always the hardest.'
Delusion *
US 1991 100m CFI color
Cineville/Seth M. Willenson (Daniel Hassid)
aka: *Mirage*
An ambitious businessman, driving to Reno with $240,000 stolen from his employers, picks up a psychotic hitman and his girlfriend along the way.
Deft thriller, a little short on narrative twists, but filled with some enjoyably quirky characters.
w Carl Colpaert, Kurt Voss *d* Carl Colpaert *ph* Geza Sinkovics *m* Barry Adamson *pd* Ildiko Toth *ed* Mark Allan Kaplan
☆ Jim Metzler, Jennifer Rubin, Kyle Secor, Tracey Walter, Robert Costanzo, Jerry Orbach

Demasiado Miedo a la Vida, O Plaff: see *Plaff! Or Too Afraid Of Life*

Dementia 13 *
US/Eire 1963 81m bw
Filmgroup/AIP (Roger Corman)
GB title: *The Haunted and the Hunted*
An axe murderer attacks members of a noble Irish family at their lonely castle.
Nastily effective macabre piece with interesting credits.
wd Francis Ford Coppola ph Charles Hannawalt *m* Ronald Stein
☆ Luana Anders, William Campbell, Bart Patton, Mary Mitchell, Patrick Magee, Eithne Dunn

Demetrius and the Gladiators **
US 1954 101m Technicolor Cinemascope
TCF (Frank Ross)
A Greek slave who keeps Christ's robe after the crucifixion is sentenced to be one of Caligula's gladiators and becomes involved in Messalina's wiles.
Lively, efficient sequel to The Robe, *with emphasis less on religiosity than on the brutality of the arena and our hero's sexual temptations and near-escapes. Good Hollywood hokum.*
w Philip Dunne d Delmer Daves ph Milton Krasner *m* Franz Waxman *ed* Dorothy Spencer, Robert Fritch
☆ Victor Mature (Demetrius), Susan Hayward (Messalina), Michael Rennie (Peter), Debra Paget, Anne Bancroft, Jay Robinson (Caligula), Barry Jones, William Marshall, Richard Egan, Ernest Borgnine
'An energetic attempt to fling the mantle of sanctity over several more millions of the entertainment dollar.' – *The Times*

The Demi-Paradise *
GB 1943 114m bw
Two Cities (Anatole de Grunwald)
US title: *Adventure for Two*
In 1939, a Russian inventor is sent to observe the British way of life.
Pleasant, aimless little satirical comedy in which this blessed plot seems to be peopled entirely by eccentrics.
w Anatole de Grunwald *d* Anthony Asquith *ph* Bernard Knowles *m* Nicholas Brodszky
☆ *Laurence Olivier*, Penelope Dudley Ward, *Margaret Rutherford*, Leslie Henson, Marjorie Fielding, Felix Aylmer, Guy Middleton, Michael Shepley, George Thorpe, Edie Martin, Muriel Aked, Joyce Grenfell
'A backhanded way of showing us poor juvenile-minded cinemagoers that the England of Mr Punch and Mrs Malaprop lives forever.' – *Richard Winnington*

Demobbed
GB 1944 96m bw
Butcher/Mancunian (F. W. Baker, John E. Blakeley)
Four incompetent ex-servicemen prevent a crooked manager from robbing a factory.
A rudimentary comedy from one of Britain's regional film companies that retains a slight interest by showcasing the performances of once popular variety theatre and radio performers.
w Roney Parsons, Anthony Toner *d* John E. Blakeley *ph* Geoffrey Faithfull, G. Gibbs *md* Percival Mackey *ad* Jim Carter *ed* Ted Richards
☆ Norman Evans, Nat Jackley, Dan Young, Betty Jumel, Webster Booth, Anne Ziegler, Tony Dalton, James Plant

The Democratic Terrorist *
Sweden/Norway 1992 98m colour
Sonet (Hans Iveberg)
original title: *Den Demokratiske Terroristen*
Carl Hamilton, a left-wing, CIA-trained Swedish naval officer, goes undercover in Hamburg to infiltrate a terrorist group.
A tough, and ultimately tense, thriller featuring Sweden's answer to James Bond, only bleaker, more brutal (and probably more realistic), and with less sex; Skarsgard makes a somewhat glum hero.
w Hans Iveberg *novel* Jan Guillou *d* Pelle Berglund *ph* Erling Thurmann-Andersen *m* Björn J:son Lindh *ad* Rainer Schaper *ed* Sylvia Ingmarsson, Christin Loman
☆ Stellan Skarsgard, Katja Flint, Burkhard Driest, Heikko Deutschmann, Karl Heinz Maslo, Susanne Lothar, May Buchgraber

Les Demoiselles de Rochefort: see *The Young Girls of Rochefort*

Demolition Man **
US 1993 115m Technicolor Panavision
Warner/Silver Pictures (Joel Silver, Michael Levy, Howard Kazanjian)
In the non-violent, politically correct world of the 21st century, a violent criminal from the 1990s escapes after being thawed out from his cryo-prison – and his arch-enemy, a cop framed on a murder charge, is brought back to life to catch him.
An exciting adventure, clever and violent, that has fun at the expense of a sanitized future, complete with the President Schwarzenegger Memorial Library, and also indulges in self-parody without compromising the action.
w Daniel Waters, Robert Reneau, Peter M. Lenkov *d Marco Brambilla ph* Alex Thomson *m* Elliot Goldenthal *pd* David L. Snyder *ed* Stuart Baird
☆ Sylvester Stallone, Wesley Snipes, Sandra Bullock, Nigel Hawthorne, Benjamin Bratt, Bob Gunton, Denis Leary
'A noisy, soulless, self-conscious pastiche that mixes elements of sci-fi, action-adventure and romance, then pours on a layer of comedy replete with Hollywood in-jokes.' – *Variety*
'Decently constructed, almost witty at times and a genuine attempt to make an action thriller that's halfway intelligent.' – *Derek Malcolm, Guardian*

The Demolitionist
US 1995 93m CFI color
A-Pix/Planet/Le Monde (Donald P. Borchers)
After she is killed by a violent criminal, an undercover cop is brought back to life as an unstoppable crime fighter.
Cheap and nasty exploitation flick; it borrows heavily from Robocop, but never rises above the level of sadistic and unoriginal trash.
w Brian DiMuccio, Dino Vindeni *story* Robert Kurtzman, Anne Kurtzman *d* Robert Kurtzman *ph* Marcus Hahn *m* Shawn Patterson *pd* Charley

Cabrera *ed* Paolo Mazzucato *sp* John Hartigan, KNB EFX, Flash Film Works
☆ Nicole Eggert, Richard Grieco, Bruce Abbott, Susan Tyrrell, Peter Jason, Heather Langenkamp, Jack Nance, Tom Savini, Bruce Campbell (uncredited)

Demon: see *God Told Me To*

Demon Seed
US 1977 95m Metrocolor Panavision
MGM (Herb Jaffe)
A scientist invents too perfect a computer: it locks up his wife, rapes her, and incubates a child...
Science fiction at the end of its tether, all very smart and self-conscious, but at this length very tasteless. Hitchcock would have got it into a television half-hour.
w Robert Jaffe, Roger O. Hirson *novel* Dean R. Koontz *d* Donald Cammell *ph* Bill Butler *m* Jerry Fielding *pd* Edward Carfagno
☆ Julie Christie, Fritz Weaver, Gerrit Graham, Berry Kroeger, Lisa Lu

The Demons (dubbed)
Portugal/France 1972 116m Eastmancolor Techniscope
Interfilme/Comptoir (Victor de Costa)
original title: *Os Demonios*
Two nuns, the daughters of a witch burned at the stake, revenge their mother's death.
Bizarre and low-budget horror, exploiting sex and violence.
w Jesús Franco *novel* David Kuhne (Jesús Franco) *d* Clifford Brown (Jesús Franco) *ph* Raoul Artigot *m* Jean-Bernard Raiteux
☆ Anne Libert, Britt Nichols, Doris Thomas, John Foster, Howard Vernon, Karin Field, Alberto Dalbes
† The film was cut to 97m for its British release.

Demons
Italy 1985 89m colour
Dacfilm (Dario Argento)
original title: *Demoni*
Members of an audience watching a horror movie about demons ravaging the world are themselves transformed into murderous monsters.
Gore-filled horror, derivative of modern American zombie movies.
w Lamberto Bava, Dario Argento, Dardano Sacchetti, Franco Ferrini *d* Lamberto Bava
☆ Urbano Barberini, Natasha Harvey, Karl Zinny, Fiore Argento, Paolo Cozzo, Fabiola Toledo

Demons 2
Italy 1987 91m colour
Avatar (Dario Argento)
original title: *Demoni 2*
The occupants of an apartment block, watching a TV documentary about demons, are turned into rampaging monsters.
A sequel that repeats, with a slight twist, the events of the original, and also its gore-filled content, with less effect.
w Lamberto Bava, Dario Argento, Franco Ferrini, Dardano Sacchetti *d* Lamberto Bava *ph* Gianlorenzo Battaglia *pd* Davide Bassan *ed* Franco Fraticelli, Pietro Bozza
☆ David Knight, Nancy Brilli, Coralina Cataldi Tassoni, Bobby Rhodes, Asia Argento, Virginia Bryant

'The Demon Is Loose Again... And No One Is Safe!'
Demons of the Mind
GB 1972 89m Technicolor
Hammer (Frank Godwin)
aka: *Black Evil*
aka: *Nightmare of Terror; Blood Will Have Blood*
Crazed by the suicide of his wife, a Victorian aristocrat believes that his children are possessed by evil.
Lurid psychological thriller, with a rather better cast than it deserves.
w Christopher Wicking *d* Peter Sykes *ph* Arthur Grant *m* Harry Robinson *ad* Michael Stringer *ed* Chris Barnes
☆ Paul Jones, Patrick Magee, Gillian Hills, Robert Hardy, Michael Hordern, Yvonne Mitchell, Shane Briant, Kenneth J. Warren, Thomas Heathcote

Demons of the Swamp: see *Attack of the Giant Leeches*

Den Goda Viljan: see *The Best Intentions*

Den Sedmy – Osma Noc: see *Seventh Day, Eighth Night*

Denise Calls Up
US 1995 80m colour
Artificial Eye/Off the Hook/Davis/Skyline/Dark Matter (J. Todd Harris)
A pregnant woman phones the man who provided the sperm for her baby.
A clever notion, of a group of people who fail to meet face to face but are linked by the technology of telephone and e-mail, is here stretched well beyond its limits, so that it fails to communicate much at all.
wd Hal Salwen *ph* Michael Mayers *pd* Susan Bolles *ed* Gary Sharfin
☆ Tim Daly, Caroleen Feeney, Dan Gunther, Dana Wheeler Nicholson, Liev Schreiber, Aida Turturro, Alanna Ubach
'Alas, with only one idea, the film soon has nowhere to go, and the cast, each acting in isolation with only a telephone to talk to, cannot give depth to the characters.' – *George Perry*

Dennis the Menace
US 1993 96m Technicolor
Warner (John Hughes, Richard Vane)
GB title: *Dennis*
A mischievous six-year-old boy makes his neighbours' life a misery.
Dull and saccharine comedy, indulging in the broadest slapstick and with Matthau going through his grumpiest grimaces.
w John Hughes, based on characters created by Hank Ketchum *d* Nick Castle *ph* Thomas Ackerman *m* Jerry Goldsmith *pd* James Bissell *ed* Alan Heim
☆ Walter Matthau, Mason Gamble, Joan Plowright, Christopher Lloyd, Lea Thompson, Robert Stanton, Amy Sakasitz, Kellen Hathaway, Paul Winfield
'Very young children may find the numbskull, by-the-numbers gags here amusing, but teens will consider this kids' stuff and adults will be pained.' – *Variety*

La Dentellière: see *The Lacemaker*

The Dentist **
US 1932 19m bw
Paramount/Sennett
Classic star short with W. C. Fields working up briskly to a dentist sketch in which he deals summarily with a variety of patients.
d Leslie Pearce

The Dentist
US 1996 89m colour
Trimark (Pierre David)
A marital break-up propels a dentist into madness and some unconventional surgery.
Macabre and gory horror that plays expertly on a common phobia.
w Dennis Paoli, Stuart Gordon, Charles Finch *d* Brian Yuzna *ph* Levie Isaacks *m* Alan Howarth *pd* William V. Ryder *ed* Christopher Roth
☆ Corbin Bernsen, Linda Hoffman, Molly Hagen, Michael Stadvec, Ken Foree, Tony Noakes, Patty Toy

'Sweet Dreams.'
The Dentist 2
US 1998 94m colour
Trimark (Pierre David)
Escaping from a mental institution, a mad dentist settles down in a small town and gets to work on the locals.
An unsettling, unpleasant sequel that extracts more gruesome horror from teeth.
w Dennis Paoli, Stuart Gordon, Charles Finch *d* Brian Yuzna *ph* Levie Isaacks *m* Alan Howarth *pd* William B. Ryder *ed* Christopher Roth *sp* make-up fx: Anthony C. Ferrante
☆ Corbin Bernsen, Jillian McWhirter, Linda Hoffman, Jeff Douchette, Suzanne Wright, Jim Antonio
'How this mild-mannered and softly spoken filmmaker handles the material puts him head and shoulders above almost everybody working in the field today, from the past-it Argento to the unfulfilled Anthony Hickox.' – *Martyn Carroll, Dark Side*

Dentist in the Chair
GB 1960 88m bw
Briand (Bertram Ostrer)
Students at a dental college discover that the instruments they have sold to their colleagues were stolen and try to recover them with the aid of a burglar.
Routine and dispiriting farce, much in the manner of the Carry On *and* Doctor *series.*
w Val Guest, Bob Monkhouse, George Wadmore *novel* Matthew Finch *d* Don Chaffey *ph* Reginald Wyer *m* Ken Jones *ad* Bill Andrews *ed* Bill Lenny
☆ Bob Monkhouse, Peggy Cummins, Kenneth Connor, Eric Barker, Ronnie Stevens, Vincent Ball, Eleanor Summerfield, Reginald Beckwith, Stuart Saunders
† It was followed by a less amusing sequel, *Dentist on the Job*, directed by C. M. Pennington-Richards in 1961.

Dentist on the Job
GB 1961 88m bw
Bertram Ostrer
US title: *Get On with It!*
Two incompetent, freshly graduated dentists are hired to promote a new toothpaste and decide to create their own superior brand.
Tired slapstick comedy that will not raise many smiles.
w Hazel Adair, Hugh Woodhouse, Bob Monkhouse *d* C. M. Pennington-Richards *ph* Stephen Dade *m* Ken Jones *ad* Tony Masters *ed* Bill Lenny
☆ Bob Monkhouse, Kenneth Connor, Shirley Eaton, Eric Barker, Richard Wattis, Ronnie Stevens, Reginald Beckwith, Charles Hawtrey, Graham Stark, Jeremy Hawk

Denver and Rio Grande
US 1952 89m Technicolor
Nat Holt/Paramount
Railroad companies compete to lay track through a narrow gorge.
Adequate Western thick ear.
w Frank Gruber *d* Byron Haskin
☆ Edmond O'Brien, Sterling Hayden, Dean Jagger, Laura Elliott, ZaSu Pitts, Lyle Bettger, J. Carrol Naish

Deported
US 1950 88m bw
Universal-International
A gangster is sent back to his native Italy and tries to smuggle in his stolen money, but is finally redeemed.
Slightly unusual from this studio at this time, but not very interesting.
w Robert Buckner *d* Robert Siodmak
☆ Jeff Chandler, Marta Toren, Claude Dauphin, Marina Berti, Richard Rober

The Depraved
GB 1957 63m bw
The Danzigers
An American officer helps his beloved kill her unattractive husband.
Shades of Double Indemnity, *but only shades.*
w Brian Clemens *d* Paul Dickson
☆ Anne Heywood, Robert Arden, Carroll Levis, Basil Dignam

Derby Day
GB 1952 84m bw
British Lion/Wilcox-Neagle (Maurice Cowan)
US title: *Four Against Fate*
Intercut comic and melodramatic stories of four people who go to the Derby.
Quietly efficient, class-conscious entertainment on the lines of Friday the 13th *and* The Bridge of San Luis Rey. *No surprises, but plenty of familiar faces.*
w John Baines, Monckton Hoffe, Alan Melville *d* Herbert Wilcox *ph* Max Greene *m* Anthony Collins
☆ Anna Neagle, Michael Wilding, Googie Withers, Gordon Harker, John McCallum, Peter Graves, Suzanne Cloutier, Gladys Henson, Ralph Reader, Alfie Bass, Edwin Styles, Nigel Stock
'Excessive loyalty to a formula has produced far from happy results.' – *Penelope Houston, MFB*

Derelict
US 1930 73m bw
Paramount
Two sea dogs battle over a ship and a girl.
Well-filmed melodrama, with plenty of location work.
w Max Marcin, William Slavens McNutt, Grover Jones *d* Rowland V. Lee
☆ George Bancroft, William Boyd, Jessie Royce Landis, Donald Stuart
'One of the best sea pictures filmed ... a cinch for the deluxers.' – *Variety*

Le Dernier Combat: see *The Last Battle*

Le Dernier Milliardaire *
France 1934 100m bw
Pathé-Natan
The queen of a small principality invites a financial wizard to pay court to her daughter. The girl elopes with a bandleader, the financier is engaged to the queen, and is then revealed as a sham.
Rather too determined to be satirical, this comedy sadly lacks the pace and flair of the director's best work but there are several sequences of interest.
wd René Clair *ph* Rudolph Maté, Louis Née *m* Maurice Jaubert
☆ Max Dearly, Renée Saint-Cyr, Marthe Mellot, Raymond Cordy
'This film is so unpopular here that the crowd is rioting against it nightly – partly because they think it's rotten and partly because they don't like the way it kids the State ... despite flop here, American specialized houses should do well with it.' – *Variety, Paris*

Le Dernier Tournant *
France 1939 90m bw
Lux
A woman persuades the man she seduces to help her murder her husband.
Interesting, but not remarkable, French version of The Postman Always Rings Twice.
w Charles Spaak, Henry Torres *novel* James M. Cain *d* Pierre Chenal
☆ Fernand Gravet, Corinne Luchaire, Michel Simon, Marcel Vallée, Florence Marly
'Class B at best.' – *Variety*

Les Dernières Vacances *
France 1947 95m bw
Pathé
During a country house holiday in the twenties, the last before the house is sold, old friends conduct amorous intrigues, and so do their teenage progeny.
A moderately charming little fable making a rather obscure social point.
w R. Breuil, Roger Leenhardt *d* Roger Leenhardt *ph* Philippe Agostini
☆ Berthe Bovy, Renée Devillers, Pierre Dux, Jean d'Yd, Odile Versois, Michel François

Derrière la Façade *
France 1939 90m bw
Filmsonor
A judge, his son, a soldier and a prostitute are involved in a night of attempted and actual murders.
Complex puzzle drama which made its mark.
d Yves Mirade, Georges Lacombe
☆ Lucien Baroux, Jacques Baumer, Jules Berry, Gaby Morlay, Michel Simon, Betty Stockfeld, Erich von Stroheim, Carette, André Lafaur

Dersu Uzala *
USSR/Japan 1975 140m colour Sovscope 70
Mosfilm/Toho
A Russian surveyor mapping Siberian wastes becomes friendly with a wily Mongolian hunter.
Magnificent vistas punctuate an essentially plodding propaganda piece which does not rank with its director's best work.

w Yuri Nagibin, Akira Kurosawa *d* Akira Kurosawa
☆ Maxim Munzuk, Juri Solomine
best foreign film

Desert Attack: see *Ice Cold in Alex*

Desert Bloom
US 1985 104m Metrocolor
Columbia/Carson/Delphi IV (Michael Hausman)
In 1950 Las Vegas, an ex-GI runs a gas station, illtreats his stepdaughters and falls for his sister-in-law.
Why do paying customers need to know all this? A downbeat enterprise which never got released.
wd Eugene Corr *story* Linda Remy *ph* Reynaldo Villalobos *m* Brad Fiedel
☆ Jon Voight, JoBeth Williams, Ellen Barkin, Allen Garfield, Annabeth Gish
'Viewers looking for sensitive, discreetly handled fare will be amply rewarded.' – *Variety*

The Desert Fox **
US 1951 88m bw
TCF (Nunnally Johnson)
GB title: *Rommel, Desert Fox*
Rommel returns, disillusioned, to Hitler's Germany after his North African defeat, and is involved in the July plot.
Vivid but scrappy account of the last years of a contemporary hero. At the time it seemed to show a new immediacy in film-making, and was probably the first film to use an action sequence to arrest attention before the credit titles.
w Nunnally Johnson *book* Rommel by Desmond Young *d* *Henry Hathaway* *ph* *Norbert Brodine* *m* Daniele Amfitheatrof *ad* Lyle Wheeler, Maurice Ransford *ed* James B. Clark
☆ *James Mason* (Rommel), Jessica Tandy (Frau Rommel), Cedric Hardwicke (Dr Karl Strolin), Luther Adler (Hitler), Everett Sloane (General Bergdorf), *Leo G. Carroll* (Field Marshall Von Rundstedt), *George Macready* (General Fritz Bayerlein), Richard Boone (Aldinger), Eduard Franz (Colonel Von Stauffenberg), Desmond Young (himself)

'Two men wanted her love – the third wanted her life!'
Desert Fury
US 1947 96m Technicolor
Paramount (Hal B. Wallis)
Against advice, a girl is attracted to a neurotic gambler who may have murdered his first wife.
Muddled melodrama slightly helped by Arizona colour settings; unconvincing characters mouth unspeakable lines in an airless tedium.
w Robert Rossen *novel* *Desert Town* by Ramona Stewart *d* Lewis Allen *ph* Charles Lang, Edward Cronjager *m* Miklos Rozsa
☆ Lizabeth Scott, Wendell Corey, Burt Lancaster, John Hodiak, Mary Astor, Kristine Miller
'The only fury I could sense was in my corner of the balcony.' – C. A. *Lejeune*

The Desert Hawk
US 1950 77m Technicolor
Universal-International
Against an Arabian Nights background, a cheerful outlaw abducts a princess.
Tolerable cloak-and-sandal action comedy.
w Aubrey Wisberg, Jack Pollexfen, Gerald Drayson Adams *d* Frederick de Cordova
☆ Richard Greene, Yvonne de Carlo, Jackie Gleason, George Macready, Rock Hudson, Carl Esmond

Desert Hearts
US 1985 91m colour
Desert Heart Productions (Donna Deitch)
A would-be divorcée in Reno becomes a lesbian.
A fairly accessible piece of special pleading, nicely made and good to look at.
w Natalie Cooper *novel* *Desert of the Heart* by Jane Rule *d* Donna Deitch *ph* Robert Elswit *m* various *pd* Jeannine Oppewall *ed* Robert Estrin
☆ Helen Shaver, Patricia Charbonneau, Audra Lindley, Andra Akers

'Left for dead. Burning for revenge.'
Desert Heat
US 1999 96m colour
Long Road/KPI (Evzen Kolar, Lawrence Levy, Jean-Claude Van Damme)
aka: *Inferno*
aka: *Coyote Moon*
Left for dead by a vicious gang, a loner takes his revenge.
Cheap and not very cheerful variation on Yojimbo. *Amid the dozen or so killings, there's a dash of Native American mysticism and comedy relief from a bunch of eccentric old men.*
w Tom O'Rourke *d* Danny Mulroon *ph* Ross A. Maehl *m* Bill Conti *pd* Michael Novotny *ed* J. Douglas Seelig
☆ Jean-Claude Van Damme (Eddie Lomax), Pat Morita (Jubal Early), Danny Trejo (Johnny), Gabrielle Fitzpatrick (Rhonda), Larry Drake (Ramsey Hogan), Vincent Schiavelli (Mr Singh), David 'Shark' Fralick (Matt Hogan), Silas Weir Mitchell (Jesse Hogan), Jaime Pressly (Dottie)
† It was released direct to video.

'An Assassin Accepts An Impossible Mission... To Save A Young Boy'
Desert Law
Italy 1990 155m Eastmancolor
Titanus/Reteitalia/International Dean Film (Rossella Angeletti, David Pash)
A New York businesswoman hires an ex-CIA agent to rescue her son, who has been kidnapped by his Arab grandfather to become the future leader of a tribe of desert warriors.
Glossy and competent thriller, most likely to appeal to 10-year-olds who can identify with the central character of a young boy.
w Adriano Bolzoni, Sergio Donati, Luigi Montefiori *d* Duccio Tessari *ph* Giorgio Di Battista *m* Ennio Morricone *pd* Luciano Sagoni *ed* Maria Morra
☆ Rutger Hauer, Carol Alt, Omar Sharif, Elliott Gould, Kabir Bedi, Brett Halsey, Peter Sands

'The Legion's my life. A girl doesn't fit into it. Especially a girl like you!'
Desert Legion
US 1953 86m Technicolor
Universal (Ted Richmond)
A Foreign Legion captain rids a lost city of menacing bandits.
Schoolboy stuff, impudent in its silly story and its unconvincing Shangri-La, but quite entertaining for those prepared to let their hair down.
w Irving Wallace, Lewis Meltzer *d* Joseph Pevney *ph* John Seitz *m* Frank Skinner
☆ Alan Ladd, Richard Conte, Arlene Dahl, Akim Tamiroff, Leon Askin

Desert Mice
GB 1959 83m bw
Artna/Welbeck/Sydney Box (Michael Relph, Basil Dearden)
Adventures of a concert party sent to entertain the troops in North Africa during World War II.
A most promising idea is wasted on a singularly unfunny script which leaves its actors all at sea.
w David Climie *d* Michael Relph *ph* Ken Hodges *m* Philip Green *pd* Peter Froud *ed* Reginald Beck
☆ Alfred Marks, Sid James, Patricia Bredin, Dick Bentley, Dora Bryan, Irene Handl, Kenneth Fortescue, Reginald Beckwith, Joan Benham, Marius Goring

Desert Passage
US 1952 60m bw
RKO (Herman Schlom)
A paroled bank robber hires a stagecoach owner to take him over the border with his recovered loot, while being chased by five other crooks.
Slow-moving Western, made near the end of Holt's long career; he seems as tired as his audience is likely to feel.
w Norman Houston *d* Lesley Selander *ph* J. Roy Hunt *m* Paul Sawtell *ad* Albert D'Agostino, Feild Gray *ed* Paul Weatherwax
☆ Tim Holt, Richard Martin, Joan Dixon, Walter Reed, Dorothy Patrick, John Dehner, Clayton Moore, Denver Pyle

Desert Patrol: see *Sea of Sand*

The Desert Rats *
US 1953 88m bw
TCF (Robert L. Jacks)
An English captain commands an Australian detachment in the siege of Tobruk, and survives an encounter with Rommel.
Actioner made to cash in on the success of The Desert Fox *(qv). Stars and battle scenes survive a studio look.*
w Richard Murphy *d* Robert Wise *ph* Lucien Ballard *m* Leigh Harline *md* Nathaniel Finston *ad* Lyle Wheeler, Addison Hehr *ed* Barbara McLean
☆ James Mason (Rommel), Richard Burton (Captain MacRoberts), Robert Newton (Bartlett), Robert Douglas (General), Torin Thatcher (Barney), Chips Rafferty (Smith), Charles Tingwell (Lt Carstairs), Charles Davis (Pete)
Richard Murphy

The Desert Song
US 1929 106m bw (Technicolor sequences)
Warner
A romantic figure leads North African natives against evil Arabs.
Primitive sound version of the highly successful 1926 operetta.
w Harvey Gates *play* Otto Harbach, Laurence Schwab, Frank Mandel *d* Roy del Ruth *ph* Barney McGill *m/ly* *Sigmund Romberg, Oscar Hammerstein II*
☆ John Boles, Carlotta King, Louise Fazenda, Johnny Arthur, Edward Martindel, Jack Pratt

The Desert Song
US 1943 96m Technicolor
Warner (Robert Florey)
A mysterious figure recruits followers to take action against the Nazis.
Mundane version of the Romberg operetta, updated to provide light-hearted propaganda.
w Robert Buckner *play* Otto Harbach, Laurence Schwab, Frank Mandel *d* Robert Florey *ph* Bert Glennon *m* Heinz Roemheld *m/ly* Sigmund Romberg, Oscar Hammerstein II, Otto Harbach
☆ Dennis Morgan, Irene Manning, Bruce Cabot, Lynne Overman, Gene Lockhart, Victor Francen, Faye Emerson, Curt Bois, Jack La Rue, Marcel Dalio, Nestor Paiva, Gerald Mohr

'The Best Loved Of All Musical Adventures!'
The Desert Song
US 1953 110m Technicolor
Warner (Rudi Fehr)
The Red Shadow leads the Riffs against evil Arabs.
Well staged straight version of the musical, with full score.
w Roland Kibbee *play* Otto Harbach, Laurence Schwab, Frank Mandel *d* H. Bruce Humberstone *ph* Robert Burks *m/ly* Sigmund Romberg, Oscar Hammerstein II, Otto Harbach *md* Max Steiner
☆ Gordon MacRae, Kathryn Grayson, Steve Cochran, Raymond Massey, Dick Wesson, Allyn McLerie, Ray Collins, Paul Picerni, William Conrad
♫ The Riff Song; Romance; The Desert Song; Gay Parisienne; Azuri's Dance; One Flower Grows Alone in Your Garden; One Alone; Love Live the Night

Desert Tanks: see *The Battle of El Alamein*

The Desert Trail
US 1935 54m bw
Lone Star (Paul Malvern)
A cowboy and a womanizing gambler hunt down the man who framed them for the murder of a rodeo owner in Rattlesnake Gulch.
Sub-standard semi-comic Western.
w Lindsley Parsons *d* Cullen Lewis *ph* Archie Stout *ed* Carl Pierson
☆ John Wayne, Mary Kornman, Paul Fix, Eddy Chandler, Carmen LaRoux, Lafe McKee, Al Ferguson, Henry Hall

Desert Victory ***
GB 1943 60m bw
Ministry of Information/British Army Film Unit
Montgomery's army chases the Nazis through Tripoli.
Classic war documentary.
w anonymous *d* *Roy Boulting, David MacDonald* *m* *William Alwyn* *ed* A. Best, F. Clarke *narrator* James Langdale Hodson
'The greatest battle film of the war ... it puts the audience right in the middle ... Americans who see this film will be anxiously waiting for the next – and a US equivalent.' – *Variety*
'A first rate work of art.' – *Time*
'The finest factual film ever made.' – *Daily Telegraph*
'Profoundly moving, and fierce in its impact upon imagination, eye and ear.' – *Scotsman*
† A few shots were reconstructed in the studio.
documentary feature

The Deserter
Italy/Yugoslavia/USA 1970 99m Technicolor Panavision
Dino de Laurentiis/Jadran/Heritage (Norman Baer, Ralph Serpe)
original title: *La Spina Dorsale del Diavolo*
In the South-west in 1886, a cavalry captain tracks down the Apaches who tortured his wife to death.
Brutal revenge Western, as muddled as its international credits would suggest.
w Clair Huffaker *d* Burt Kennedy *ph* Aldo Tonti *m* Piero Piccione *pd* Mario Chiari
☆ Bekim Fehmiu, John Huston, Richard Crenna, Chuck Connors, Ricardo Montalban, Ian Bannen, Brandon de Wilde, Slim Pickens, Albert Salmi, Woody Strode, Patrick Wayne, Fausto Tozzi

Il Deserto Rosso: see *The Red Desert*

'Three people who loved each other very much!'
Design for Living **
US 1933 88m bw
Paramount (Ernst Lubitsch)
Two friends love and are loved by the same worldly woman, and they set up house together.
Elegant but miscast version of a scintillating play, with all the sex and the sting removed (at the insistence of the Legion of Decency, then coming into power). Ben Hecht claimed to have removed all but one line of Coward's dialogue: 'For the good of our immortal souls!'
w Ben Hecht *play* Noël Coward *d* *Ernst Lubitsch* *ph* Victor Milner *m* Nathaniel Finston *ad* Hans Dreier
☆ Gary Cooper, Fredric March, Miriam Hopkins, Edward Everett Horton, Franklin Pangborn, Isabel Jewell
'Can't miss because it holds plenty ... an improvement on the original.' – *Variety*
'A delightfully smart, crisp piece of entertainment, cleverly conceived and delightfully executed.' – *New York American*
'A partial cleansing for the screen of a stage story notorious for its wealth and variety of moral code infractions.' – *Martin Quigley*

Design for Lust: see *Confessions of a Sex Maniac*

Design for Scandal
US 1941 85m bw
MGM
A reporter is assigned by his boss to get a lady judge disbarred.
Mechanical star comedy.
w Lionel Houser *d* Norman Taurog
☆ Rosalind Russell, Walter Pidgeon, Edward Arnold, Guy Kibbee, Lee Bowman

The Designated Mourner *
GB 1997 94m colour
First Look/Greenpoint/BBC (Donna Grey, David Hare)
Living under a repressive regime, a man, his wife and her father, a poet whose political views are not liked, discuss their relationships.
No attempt has been made to open up this stage play, which mainly consists of static monologues, and it does not transfer easily to the screen, though it will reward patient audiences.
w Wallace Shawn *play* Wallace Shawn *d* David Hare *ph* Oliver Stapleton *m* Richard Hartley *pd* Bob Crowley *ed* George Akers
☆ *Mike Nichols*, Miranda Richardson, David de Keyser
'Insidiously superb.' – *Stanley Kauffmann, New Republic*

Designing Woman *
US 1957 118m Metrocolor Cinemascope
MGM (Dore Schary)

A sports reporter marries a dress designer and finds that their common interests are few.
Lumbering comedy which aims for sophistication but settles for farce: tolerable for star watchers who have dined well.
w George Wells *d* Vincente Minnelli *ph* John Alton *m* André Previn
☆ Gregory Peck, Lauren Bacall, Dolores Gray, Sam Levene, Tom Helmore, Mickey Shaughnessy, Jesse White, Chuck Connors, Jack Cole
George Wells

Desire **
US 1936 89m bw
Paramount (Ernst Lubitsch)

In Spain, an American car designer falls for a glamorous jewel thief.
Romantic comedy which the producer should have worked on longer: it begins brilliantly and keeps its style, but the pace and wit ebb away.
w Edwin Justus Mayer, Waldemar Young, Samuel Hoffenstein, from a German film Die schönen Tage von Aranjuez play Hans Szekely, R. A. Stemmle *d Frank Borzage ph* Charles Lang, Victor Milner *m* Frederick Hollander *ad* Hans Dreier, Robert Usher
☆ *Marlene Dietrich*, Gary Cooper, *John Halliday*, William Frawley, Ernest Cossart, Akim Tamiroff, Alan Mowbray, Zeffie Tilbury
'It sparkles and twinkles ... one of the most engaging pictures of the season.' – *Frank S. Nugent, New York Times*
'A sure, beautifully written piece about the usual Lubitsch trifles, about crooks and fake countesses breathless before the dawn of romance.' – *Alistair Cooke*
'Brilliant treatment, superb staging and inspiring acting. Irresistible entertainment.' – *CEA Film Report*

Desire in the Dust
US 1960 102m bw Cinemascope
TCF/Associated Producers (William F. Claxton)
A wealthy Southern aristocrat is involved in a fatal car crash and persuades a young farmhand to take the blame.
Derivative hothouse drama, a little better than its title, with a cast breathing heavily in imitation of refugees from Tennessee Williams or William Faulkner.
w Charles Lang *novel* Harry Whittington *d* William F. Claxton *ph* Lucien Ballard *m* Paul Dunlap
☆ Raymond Burr, Martha Hyer, Joan Bennett, Ken Scott, Brett Halsey, Anne Helm, Jack Ging, Edward Binns

Desire Me
US 1947 91m bw
MGM (Arthur Hornblow Jnr)
The wife of a Normandy villager hears that he has died in a concentration camp. She marries the bearer of the news, who turns out to be a psychotic who has left her husband for dead ... but he is not.
Dreary drama, troubled during production and offering little for the actors to chew on.
w Marguerite Roberts, Zoë Akins, Casey Robinson *novel* Leonhard Frank *d* not credited, but mostly by George Cukor, Mervyn Le Roy, Jack Conway *ph* Joseph Ruttenberg *m* Herbert Stothart
☆ Greer Garson, Robert Mitchum, Richard Hart, George Zucco, Morris Ankrum
'The supporting cast includes a number of characters who give the appearance of having come out of a dusty cupboard marked "French Types – Assorted".' – *MFB*
† Robert Montgomery shot a few scenes before bowing out to be replaced by Richard Hart.

Desire under the Elms
US 1958 111m bw Vistavision
Paramount (Don Hartman)

A New England farmer brings home a young bride and causes friction with his son.
This bid for culture turns out like a hoary and very slow melodrama, not exactly risible but annoying because it teeters between several styles.
w Irwin Shaw *play* Eugene O'Neill *d* Delbert Mann *ph* Daniel L. Fapp *m* Elmer Bernstein
☆ Sophia Loren, Burl Ives, Anthony Perkins, Frank Overton, Pernell Roberts, Anne Seymour
'The film is consistently and unhappily out of its depth.' – *Penelope Houston*
'A challenging and inspiring picture.' – *News of the World*
Daniel L. Fapp

'Their story is not in the history books. It has never been seen on the screen – until now!'
Desirée
US 1954 110m DeLuxe Cinemascope
TCF (Julian Blaustein)

Fictionalized biopic of one of Napoleon's mistresses.
Heavy-going costume piece, with all contributors distinctly uncomfortable.
w Daniel Taradash *novel* Annemarie Selinko *d* Henry Koster *ph* Milton Krasner *m* Alex North *ad* Lyle Wheeler, Leland Fuller
☆ Jean Simmons, Marlon Brando, Merle Oberon, Michael Rennie, Cameron Mitchell, Elizabeth Sellars, Cathleen Nesbitt, Isobel Elsom
art direction

Desk Set **
US 1957 103m Eastmancolor Cinemascope
TCF (Henry Ephron)

GB title: *His Other Woman*
Ladies in a broadcasting company's reference section are appalled when an electronics expert is sent to improve their performance.
Thin comedy, altered from a Broadway success; patchy as a whole, but with several splendid dialogue scenes for the principals.
w Phoebe and Henry Ephron *play* William Marchant *d* Walter Lang *ph* Leon Shamroy *m* Cyril Mockridge
☆ *Spencer Tracy, Katharine Hepburn*, Joan Blondell, Gig Young, Dina Merrill, Neva Patterson
'They lope through this trifling charade like a couple of oldtimers who enjoy reminiscing with simple routines.' – *Bosley Crowther, New York Times*

Despair *
West Germany/France 1978 119m Eastmancolor
NF Geria/Bavaria/SFP (Peter Märthesheimer)

West German title: *Eine Reise ins Licht*
In 1930 Berlin, a Russian immigrant businessman leads a fantasy life which drives him to murder and insanity.
Filmed in English, this curious cross between Lolita *and* Repulsion *found surprisingly little critical favour, considering its participants.*
w Tom Stoppard *novel* Vladimir Nabokov *d* Rainer Werner Fassbinder *ph* Michael Ballhaus *m* Peer Raben *pd* Rolf Zehetbauer
☆ Dirk Bogarde, Andrea Ferreol, Volker Spengler, Klaus Löwitsch, Bernhard Wicki
'It begins magnificently, remains sporadically brilliant throughout, but grows heavier and heavier until it finally sinks into inertia.' – *Tom Milne, MFB*

'He came back to settle the score with someone. Anyone. Everyone.'
Desperado
US 1995 105m Technicolor
Columbia/Los Hooligans (Bill Borden, Robert Rodriguez)

A man carrying a guitar case full of weapons walks into a small Mexican town and starts shooting.
This is more or less an expensive remake of El Mariachi, *and a disappointing one in its failure to develop the original in any significant way; it is one long gun battle, filmed in a style that owes much to the balletic tradition of John Woo and other Hong Kong film-makers.*
wd Robert Rodriguez *ph* Guillermo Navarro *m* Los Lobos *pd* Cecilia Montiel *ed* Robert Rodriguez
☆ Antonio Banderas, Salma Hayek, Joaquin de Almeida, Cheech Marin, Steve Buscemi, Carlos Gomez, Quentin Tarantino, Tito Larriva, Carlos Gallardo
'A film so insanely unambitious, so childishly unheeding of the normal rigours of film-making, it's almost cheering. It's got the crazed, obsessive squint of one of Roy Lichtenstein's immaculate dot paintings of a single explosion – it's pop art Peckinpah.' – *Tom Shone, Sunday Times*
† Its DVD release also includes its low-budget predecessor *El Mariachi* (qv).

Desperadoes
US 1943 85m Technicolor
Columbia (Harry Joe Brown)
A gunman rides into town to cause trouble, but finds romance and renews an old friendship.
Lively star Western of its day.
w Max Brand, Robert Carson *d* Charles Vidor *ph* George Meehan *m* John Leipold *md* M. W. Stoloff *ad* Lionel Banks, Perry Smith *ed* Gene Havlik *cos* Travilla
☆ Randolph Scott, Glenn Ford, Evelyn Keyes, Edgar Buchanan, Claire Trevor, Guinn Williams
† This was Columbia's first film in colour.

'Hang on to your money, your woman, and your life!'
The Desperados
US 1968 90m Technicolor
Columbia/Meadway (Irving Allen)

After the Civil War, a fanatic 'parson' leads a tribe of violent outlaws including his three sons.
Rough-and-tumble Western in the modern savage manner; made in Spain.
w Walter Brough *d* Henry Levin *ph* Sam Leavitt *m* David Whitaker
☆ Vince Edwards, Jack Palance, George Maharis, Neville Brand, Sylvia Syms, Christian Roberts, Kate O'Mara, Kenneth Cope, John Paul

Desperate *
US 1947 73m bw
RKO (Michel Kraike)

A trucker becomes innocently involved in a robbery and goes on the run.
Lively second feature from the studio's best period, with plenty of burgeoning talent.
w Harry Essex, Martin Rackin *story* Dorothy Atlas, Marston Mann *d Anthony Mann* *ph* George E. Diskant *m* Paul Sawtell
☆ Steve Brodie, Audrey Long, Raymond Burr, Jason Robards Snr, Douglas Fowley, William Challee, Ilka Gruning
'Amazingly watchable within its formulary limits.' – *Tom Milne, MFB, 1982*

Desperate Characters *
US 1971 106m colour
ITC/TDJ (Frank D. Gilroy)

Residents of New York's east side find the rigours of life hard to take.
Curious but interesting suburban drama, a kind of deglamorized and updated City for Conquest.
wd Frank D. Gilroy *novel* Paula Fox *ph* Urs Furrer *m* Lee Konitz, Ron Carter, Jim Hall
☆ Shirley MacLaine, Gerald S. O'Loughlin, Kenneth Mars, Sada Thompson, Jack Somack
'The most blistering indictment of New York City since *Midnight Cowboy*.' – *Rex Reed*
'A film of authenticity, of delicately realized intangibles.' – *Stanley Kauffmann*

The Desperate Hours *
US 1955 112m bw Vistavision
Paramount (William Wyler)

Three escaped convicts take over a suburban house but are finally outwitted by the family.
Ponderous treatment of an over-familiar situation with only the acting and an 'A' picture look to save it.
w Joseph Hayes *play* Joseph Hayes *novel Joseph Hayes d* William Wyler *ph* Lee Garmes *m* Gail Kubik
☆ *Fredric March*, Humphrey Bogart, Martha Scott, Arthur Kennedy, Gig Young, Dewey Martin, Mary Murphy, Robert Middleton, Richard Eyer
'A solid, deliberate and long-drawn-out exercise in the mechanics of suspense.' – *Penelope Houston*
† Bogart's role had been played on stage by Paul Newman. March's role had been offered to Spencer Tracy, but he wouldn't take second billing.

Desperate Hours
US 1990 105m Technicolor
TCF/Dino de Laurentiis (Michael Cimino)

An armed robber on the run with two friends takes a family hostage.
A failure, even by the ponderous standards of the 1955 version of Hayes' novel.
w Lawrence Konner, Mark Rosenthal, Joseph Hayes *novel* Joseph Hayes *d* Michael Cimino *ph* Doug Milsome *m* David Mansfield *pd* Victoria Paul *ed* Peter Hunt
☆ Mickey Rourke, Anthony Hopkins, Mimi Rogers, Lindsay Crouse, Kelly Lynch, Elias Koteas, David Morse, Shawnee Smith
'A coldly mechanical and uninvolving remake.' – *Variety*

Desperate Journey **
US 1942 109m bw
Warner (Hal B. Wallis)

Three POWs in Nazi Germany fight their way back to freedom.
When you pit Errol Flynn against the Nazis, there's no doubt who wins; and the last line is 'Now for Australia and a crack at those Japs!' Exhilarating adventure for the totally uncritical; professional standards high.
w Arthur Horman *d Raoul Walsh ph* Bert Glennon *m* Max Steiner
☆ *Errol Flynn, Alan Hale*, Ronald Reagan, Nancy Coleman, Raymond Massey, Arthur Kennedy, Ronald Sinclair, Albert Basserman, Sig Rumann, Ilka Gruning, Pat O'Moore
'Yarn is an extreme strain on anyone's credulity, and yet it's so exciting that the preposterousness of it all is only something to be thought about on the way home from the theatre.' – *Variety*
'A 1942 treatment of *The Three Musketeers*, packed with action, shorn of romance, and utilizing the Third Reich for terrain. Folks who sacrifice reason for fast action and the joy of seeing Nazis foiled, will find it entirely gratifying.' – *New York Times*

Desperate Living
US 1977 95m colour
New Line/Charm City (John Waters)

A paranoid housewife kills her husband with the aid of her maid and flees to a community of murderers and degenerates.
A typical Waters work, concerned with obesity, transvestism, transsexuality and nudity. It also features bad acting, uninspired direction, unimaginative camera-work and adolescent notions of what is shocking.
wd John Waters *ph* Thomas Loizeaux *m* Chris Lobinger *ad* Vincent Peranio *ed* Charles Roggero
☆ Mink Stole, Susan Lowe, Edith Massey, Mary Vivian Pearce, Jean Hill

'Detective Frank Connor is forced to choose between the badge he wears and the son he loves ... no contest.'
Desperate Measures
US 1998 100m Technicolor
Entertainment/Mandalay (Barbet Schroeder, Susan Hoffman, Gary Foster, Lee Rich)

A policeman is desperate to keep alive a violent escaped criminal because he needs him as a bone-marrow donor for his dying son.
Risible action movie, in which two uninteresting characters interminably stalk one another.
w David Klass *d* Barbet Schroeder *ph* Luciano Tavoli *m* Trevor Jones *pd* Geoffrey Kirkland *ed* Lee Percy
☆ Michael Keaton, Andy Garcia, Brian Cox, Marcia Gay Harden, Erik King, Efrain Figueroa, Joseph Cross
'As hackneyed and instantly forgettable as its title.' – *Variety*

Desperate Moment
GB 1953 88m bw
GFD/Fanfare (George H. Brown)
In Poland, a man imprisoned for murder finds he didn't do it, escapes, and tracks down the real criminal, his best friend.
Cliché-ridden melodrama climaxing in a car chase; poor in all departments.
w Patrick Kirwan, George H. Brown *novel* Martha Albrand *d* Compton Bennett *ph* C. Pennington-Richards *m* Ronald Binge

☆ Dirk Bogarde, Mai Zetterling, Philip Friend, Albert Lieven, Carl Jaffe, Gerard Heinz

Desperate Remedies *

New Zealand 1993 93m colour
Electric/NFU Studios/NZ on Air/New Zealand Film Commission/James Wallace

In the 19th century, a bisexual wealthy woman finds herself involved in deceit and murder when she attempts to buy a husband for her sex- and drug-addicted sister.
A swooning parody of period romances, deliberately larger than life (more, in fact, similar to an Imitation of Life*) and over-elaborate in its approach to costume and plot, enjoyable if you're in the mood for tongue-in-cheek melodrama.*
wd Stewart Main, Peter Wells *ph* Leon Narbey *m* Peter Scholes *pd* Michael Kane *ed* David Coulson
☆ Jennifer Ward-Lealand, Kevin Smith, Lisa Chappell, Cliff Curtis, Michael Hurst, Kiri Mills, Bridget Armstrong, Timothy Raby
'An extravagant, opulent and mostly enjoyable exercise in high camp (or low kitsch).' – *Variety*
'The cumulative effect is to make costume melodrama's classic preoccupations with strict social hierarchy and sexual propriety seem hilariously gratuitous, irrational and redundant.' – *Claire Monk, Sight and Sound*

Desperate Siege: see *Rawhide*

Desperately Seeking Susan *

US 1985 104m DeLuxe
Orion/Sarah Pillsbury, Midge Sanford

A bored housewife causes confusion and mayhem when out of curiosity she tracks down what's behind some intriguing ads in the personal column.
Mildly diverting romantic mystery which could have been both funnier and more thrilling.
w Leona Barish *d* Susan Seidelman *ph* Edward Lachman *m* Thomas Newman *pd* Santo Loquasto *ed* Andrew Mondshein
☆ Rosanna Arquette, Madonna, Aidan Quinn, Mark Blum, Robert Joy
'Simply easy entertainment, with a lively cast caught up in a silly situation.' – *Variety*
Rosanna Arquette

'Roaring across the land of Marco Polo and Genghis Khan come Uncle Sam's sailors on camels!'

Destination Gobi *

US 1953 90m Technicolor
TCF (Stanley Rubin)
American sailors get Mongol help against the Japanese in the Gobi desert.
A curious war adventure, a kind of camel opera, apparently based on fact; mildly enjoyable, though the outlandish is gradually replaced by the predictable.
w Everett Freeman *d* Robert Wise *ph* Charles G. Clarke *m* Sol Kaplan
☆ Richard Widmark, Don Taylor, Casey Adams, Murvyn Vye, Darryl Hickman, Martin Milner, Ross Bagdasarian, Rodolfo Acosta

Destination Moon *

US 1950 91m Technicolor
Universal/George Pal

An American inventor gets private backing to build a rocket so that the US can reach the moon before the Russians.
Semi-documentary prophecy with impressive gadgetry encased in a tedious and totally unsurprising script.
w Rip Van Ronkel, Robert Heinlein, James O'Hanlon *d* Irving Pichel *ph* *Lionel Lindon* *m* Leith Stevens
☆ Warner Anderson, John Archer, Tom Powers, Dick Wesson
'Heavy-handed, unimaginative and very badly acted.' – *MFB*

Destination Tokyo *

US 1943 135m bw
Warner (Jerry Wald)

A US submarine is sent into Tokyo harbour.
Solid, well acted war suspenser, but overlong.
w Delmer Daves, Albert Maltz *story* Steve Fisher *d* Delmer Daves *ph* Bert Glennon *m* Franz Waxman
☆ Cary Grant, John Garfield, Alan Hale, John Ridgely, Dane Clark, Warner Anderson, William Prince, Robert Hutton, Tom Tully, Peter Whitney, Faye Emerson, John Forsythe
'We don't say it is credible; we don't even suggest that it makes sense. But it does make a pippin of a picture from a purely melodramatic point of view.' – *Bosley Crowther*
'Even moviegoers who have developed a serious allergy for service pictures should find it high among the superior films of the war.' – *Newsweek*
Steve Fisher

Destination Unknown

US 1933 69m bw
Universal
Bootleggers, in a crippled ship with a mutinous crew, are saved by a mysterious stranger.
Curious melodrama which turns halfway through into The Passing of the Third Floor Back.
w Tom Buckingham *d* Tay Garnett *ph* Edward Snyder *ed* Milton Carruth
☆ Pat O'Brien, Ralph Bellamy, Alan Hale, Russell Hopton, Tom Brown, Betty Compson, Noel Madison
'Good sea melodrama ruined by change of intent.' – *Variety*

Destinées: see *Love, Soldiers and Women*

Les Destineés Sentimentales *

France/Switzerland 2000 180m colour
Pathé/Arena/TF1/CAB (Bruno Pesery)

A former Protestant minister divorces his wife, falls in love, and runs a porcelain factory.
An old-fashioned period romance covering the first thirty years or so of the 20th century; it does not justify its inordinate length.
w Olivier Assayas, Jacques Fieschi *novel* Jacques Chardonne *d* Olivier Assayas *ph* Eric Gautier *m* Guillaume Lekeu *pd* Katia Wyszkop *ed* Luc Barnier *cos* Anais Romand
☆ Emmanuelle Béart (Pauline), Charles Berling (Jean Barnery), Isabelle Huppert (Nathalie), Olivier Perrier (Philippe Pommerel), Dominique Reymond (Julie Desca), André Marcon (Paul Desca), Alexandra London (Louise Desca), Julie Depardieu (Marcelle)
'The appeal of the sunny landscapes and elegant costumes wears diaphanously thin, exposing us to the full brunt of the script's monotony.' – *Edward Porter, Sunday Times*

Destiny *

Germany 1921 100m approx bw silent
Decla-Bioscop
original title: *Der Müde Tod*
In the 19th century a young woman tries to save her lover from the presence of Death, who shows her that whatever she does it is inevitable.
A solemn fantasy on the lines of Appointment in Samarra*, the framing story being more effective than the 'illustrations'.*
w Thea von Harbou, Fritz Lang *d* Fritz Lang *ph* Fritz Arno Wagner, Erich Nitschmann, Hermann Saalfrank
☆ Lil Dagover, Rudolf Klein-Rogge, Bernhard Götzke, Walter Janssen

Destiny *

US 1944 65m bw
Universal (Roy William Neill)
An escaped convict on the run finds refuge with a blind girl on a lonely farm.
Curious second feature, interesting because it began as a story eliminated from Flesh and Fantasy *(qv); extra footage was added to bring it up to the required length. The original footage is mainly the nightmare suffered by the girl. Curtis died in the original, but survives here.*
w Roy Chanslor (F and F Ernest Pascal) *d* Reginald Le Borg (F and F Julien Duvivier) *ph* George Robinson (F and F Paul Ivano) *m* Frank Skinner
☆ *Gloria Jean*, Alan Curtis, Frank Craven, Grace McDonald

Destiny of a Man **

USSR 1959 98m bw
Sovexportfilm/Mosfilm (G. Kuznetsov)
original title: *Sudba Cheloveka*
During World War II a Russian is captured by Nazis but escapes and returns home only to find his family dead.
Strikingly styled sob story whose very glumness prevented it from being hailed as a masterpiece; in technique however it is in the best Russian tradition.
w Y. Lukin, F. Shakhmagonov *story* Mikhail Sholokhov *d* *Sergei Bondarchuk* *ph* Vladimir Monakhov *m* V. Basnov
☆ Sergei Bondarchuk, Zinaida Kirienko, Pavlik Boriskin
'Of all Soviet post-war films, this will be looked on as the greatest and most original work of the period.' – *MFB*

'The craziest, wackiest journey you'll ever take!'
'A romantic adventure of mystical proportion.'

Destiny Turns on the Radio

US 1995 101m CFI color
Entertainment/Savoy (Gloria Zimmerman)

A bank robber gets out of jail and goes to a Las Vegas motel to find his partner and the loot, but discovers that the money has been stolen by a mysterious stranger.
Oddball movie that obstinately refuses to come to life; it just lies there, leaving its cast and director stranded.
w Robert Ramsey, Matthew Stone *d* Jack Baran *ph* James L. Carter *m* Steve Soles *pd* Jean-Philippe Carp *ed* Raul Davalos
☆ James LeGros, Dylan McDermott, Quentin Tarantino, Nancy Travis, James Belushi, Janet Carroll, David Cross, Bobcat Goldthwait
'The plot is incomprehensible and the dialogue cheapjack. This piece of cod-pulp fiction is neither credible nor incredible. It's just dull.' – *Derek Malcolm, Guardian*
'The intended tone of romantic, magical comedy is spectacularly misjudged.' – *Independent*

'What nation will survive?'

Destroy all Monsters

Japan 1968 89m colour Tohoscope
Toho/AIP

Moon invaders gain control of Godzilla and his friends.
Typically inept Japanese monster rally full of men in rubber suits.
w Kaoru Mabuchi *d* Inoshiro Honda *ph* Taiichi Kankura *m* Akira Ifukube
☆ Akira Kubo, Jun Tazaki, Kyoko Ai

'Her only rival is his ship!'

Destroyer

US 1943 99m bw
Columbia (Louis F. Edelmann)

An old sea dog talks himself into a job on a World War II destroyer but works his men too hard.
Flat propaganda piece, not too well made.
w Frank Wead, Lewis Meltzer, Borden Chase *d* William A. Seiter *ph* Franz Planer *m* Anthony Collins
☆ Edward G. Robinson, Glenn Ford, Marguerite Chapman, Edgar Buchanan, Leo Gorcey, Regis Toomey, Ed Brophy

The Destructors: see *The Marseilles Contract*

Destry *

US 1954 95m Technicolor
U-I (Stanley Rubin)
Almost scene-for-scene remake of *Destry Rides Again* (qv), in which a peaceable sheriff tames a tough town.
Well enough made and tolerably acted, but it doesn't have the sparkle, despite employing the same director.
w Edmund H. North, D. D. Beauchamp *d* George Marshall *ph* George Robinson *m* Joseph Gershenson *ed* Ted J. Kent
☆ Audie Murphy, Mari Blanchard, Lyle Bettger, Thomas Mitchell, Edgar Buchanan, Wallace Ford, Lori Nelson, Alan Hale Jnr, Mary Wickes
'The impression is of a school revival of the original production.' – *MFB*

'They make the fighting sinful west blaze into action before your eyes!'

Destry Rides Again ****

US 1939 94m bw
Universal (Joe Pasternak)

A mild-mannered sheriff finally gets mad at local corruption and straps on his guns.
Classic Western which manages to encompass suspense, comedy, romance, tenderness, vivid characterization, horseplay, songs and standard Western excitements, without moving for more than a moment from a studio main street set. It starts with a sign reading 'Welcome to Bottleneck' and an outburst of gunfire; it ends with tragedy followed by a running joke. Hollywood expertise at its very best.
w *Felix Jackson, Gertrude Purcell, Henry Myers* *novel* Max Brand *d* *George Marshall* *ph* *Hal Mohr* *m* *Frank Skinner* *m/ly* *Frederick Hollander, Frank Loesser* *md* Charles Previn *ad* Jack Otterson *ed* Milton Carruth *cos* Vera West
☆ *James Stewart, Marlene Dietrich, Brian Donlevy, Charles Winninger, Samuel S. Hinds, Mischa Auer,* Irene Hervey, Jack Carson, *Una Merkel*, Allen Jenkins, Warren Hymer, *Billy Gilbert*
'Makes the b.o. grade in a big way ... just plain, good entertainment.' – *Variety*
'I think it was Lord Beaverbrook who said that Marlene Dietrich standing on a bar in black net stockings, belting out *See What the Boys in the Back Room Will Have*, was a greater work of art than the Venus de Milo.' – *Richard Roud*
† An early sound version in 1932 starred Tom Mix; *Frenchie* (1950) was a slight variation. See also *Destry*.

Det Regnar Pa Var Kärlek: see *It Rains on Our Love*

The Detective: see *Father Brown (1954)*

The Detective **

US 1968 114m DeLuxe Panavision
TCF/Arcola/Millfield (Aaron Rosenberg)

A New York police detective fights crime and corruption.
Determinedly sleazy and 'frank' cop stuff, quite arrestingly narrated and with something to say about police methods. Good violent entertainment, with just a shade too many homosexuals and nymphomaniacs for balance.
w *Abby Mann* *novel* Roderick Thorp *d* *Gordon Douglas* *ph* Joseph Biroc *m* Jerry Goldsmith
☆ *Frank Sinatra*, Lee Remick, Jacqueline Bisset, Ralph Meeker, Jack Klugman, Horace MacMahon, Lloyd Bochner, William Windom, Tony Musante, Al Freeman Jnr, Robert Duvall
'It vacillates uncertainly between murder mystery, political allegory, and a psychological study of the hero.' – *Jan Dawson*

Detective *

France 1985 98m colour
Sara/JLG

Four groups of people find their paths intersecting in a Paris hotel while the hotel detective tries to solve a murder.
Eccentric Grand Hotel-style compendium with many baffling asides presumably attributable to the director. One suspects that the audience is expected to be a detective too.
w Alain Sarde, Philippe Setbon, Anne-Marie Mieville, Jean-Luc Godard *d* Jean-Luc Godard
☆ Claude Brasseur, Nathalie Baye, Johnny Hallyday, Laurent Terzieff, Jean-Pierre Léaud, Alain Cuny

'A man whose wife was more woman than angel!'

Detective Story **

US 1951 103m bw
Paramount (William Wyler)
A day in a New York precinct police station, during which a detective of almost pathological righteousness discovers a stain on his family and himself becomes a victim of violence.
Clever, fluent transcription of a Broadway play with some of the pretensions of Greek tragedy; it could have been the negation of cinema, but professional handling makes it the essence of it.
w *Philip Yordan, Robert Wyler* *play* *Sidney Kingsley* *d* *William Wyler* *ph* *Lee Garmes*
☆ *Kirk Douglas*, Eleanor Parker, William Bendix, Cathy O'Donnell, George Macready, Horace MacMahon, Gladys George, *Joseph Wiseman*, Lee Grant, Gerald Mohr, Frank Faylen, Luis Van Rooten
'The admirably directed interaction of movement and talk all over the big room is what gives the thing its satisfying texture.' – *Richard Mallett, Punch*
† No music was used.
Philip Yordan, Robert Wyler; William Wyler; Eleanor Parker; Lee Grant

Determination of Death
US 2001 100m colour
WIN/Papazian Hirsch (Skip Beaudine)
Insurance investigators suspect a woman of killing her abusive husband.
Dull thriller that lacks plausibility in its many narrative twists.
w Sharon Barry McTigue, James G. Hirsch *d* Michael Miller *ph* Geoffrey Schaaf *m* Dana Kaproff *pd* Peter Wooley *ed* Daniel Cahn
☆ Veronica Hamel (Virginia Halloran), Marc Singer (Reese Williams), Michele Greene (Katie Williams), John Ratzenberger (Charlie Halloran), William Katt (John Logan), Alice Hirson (Edith), Bradford English (Col Black), George Dzundza (Mac)

'Suspense As Startling As A Strangled Scream!'
Detour *
US 1945 68m bw
PRC (Leon Fromkess)
On his way to Hollywood to meet a girlfriend, a night-club pianist assumes the identity of a dead man.
A minor cult movie with as much doomladen dialogue and film noir angles as could be shovelled into a Poverty Row 'B' at the time. On the whole, less than meets the eye.
w Martin Goldsmith *d* Edgar G. Ulmer *ph* Benjamin H. Kline *m* Leo Erdody
☆ Tom Neal, Ann Savage, Claudia Drake, Edmund MacDonald, Tim Ryan

'Kiss the rules goodbye.'
Detroit Rock City
US 1999 95m DeLuxe Super 35
Entertainment/New Line/Takoma/Base-12/Kissnation (Gene Simmons, Barry Levine, Kathleen Haase)
In the late 70s, four highschool students overcome numerous problems in order to see their favourite rock group Kiss give a concert in Detroit.
Sex, drugs and rock are all mixed together in a slight drama that is only likely to be enjoyed by Kiss's fans.
w Carl V. Dupré *d* Adam Rifkin *ph* John R. Leonetti *m* J. Peter Robinson *ed* Mark Goldblatt
☆ Edward Furlong (Hawk), Giuseppe Andrews (Lex), James DeBello (Trip), Sam Huntington (Jeremiah 'Jam' Bruce), Gene Simmons (Himself), Paul Stanley (Himself), Ace Frehley (Himself), Peter Criss (Himself), Melanie Lynskey (Beth Bumsteen), Nick Scotti (Kenny), Shannon Tweed (Amanda Finch)
'Cruel, fast-paced, slapstick fun with an ace rock soundtrack.' – *Andrew Collins, Empire*

'He's not very good-looking. But when the lights go out... he's still not very good-looking.'
Deuce Bigalow: Male Gigolo
US 1999 88m Technicolor
Buena Vista/Touchstone/Happy Madison/Out of the Blue (Sid Ganis, Barry Bernardi)
After he trashes a gigolo's expensive aquarium, a dim-witted fish fancier is forced to become a 'man-whore', servicing unattractive women.
With Adam Sandler among the executive producers, no one should be surprised that this is a gross, no-brow comedy lacking wit and sense, consisting merely of a series of crudely-done gags on bodily functions.
w Harris Goldberg, Rob Schneider *d* Mike Mitchell *ph* Peter Lyons Collister *m* Teddy Castellucci *pd* Alan Au *ed* George Bowers, Lawrence Jordan
☆ Rob Schneider (Deuce Bigalow), William Forsythe (Det Chuck Fowler), Eddie Griffin (T.J. Hicks), Arija Bareikis (Kate), Oded Fehr (Antoine Laconte), Gail O'Grady (Claire), Richard Riehle (Bob Bigalow), Jacqueline Obradors (Elaine Fowler)
'The pic is a sign that the Sandler comedy empire is expanding and reaching new depths of pure gross-out stupidity.' – *Robert Koehler, Variety*

Deus e o Diabo na Terra do Sol: see *Black God, White Devil*

Les Deux Anglaises et le Continent: see *Anne and Muriel*

Deux ou trois choses que je sais d'elle: see *Two or Three Things I Know about Her*

'A grand saga of timeless love'
Devdas *
India 2002 182m colour 'scope
Eros/Mega Bollywood (Bharat Shah)
A London-educated lawyer turns to drink when his wealthy family stop him marrying the woman he loves.
Lavishly over-the-top Bollywood epic that overwhelms its classic love story with silks and satins.
w Prakash Kapadia, Sanjay Leela Bhansali *novel* Sarat Chandra Chattopadhye *d* Sanjay Leela Bhansali *ph* Binod Pradhan *m* Monty *m/ly* Ismail Darbar, Birju Maharaj, Nusrat Badr, Sameer *ch* Birju Maharaj, Saroj Khan, Vaibhavi Merchant, Pappu-Mallu *pd* Nitin Chandrakant Desai *ed* Bela Segal *cos* Abu Jani, Sandeep Khosla, Neeta Lulla, Reza Shariffi
☆ Shah Rukh Khan (Devdas Mukherjee), Madhuri Dixit (Chandramukhi), Aishwarya Rai (Parvati), Jackie Shroff (Chunnilal), Kiron Kher (Sumitra), Smita Jayakar (Kaushalya), Vijayendra Ghatge (Bhuvan Choudhry), Ananya Khare (Kumud)
'Tthe glitz, glamour and slightly tacky luxury on display almost strangles the life out of its relatively simple story.' – *Derek Malcolm, Guardian*

Devi *
India 1960 93m bw
Satyajit Ray Productions
aka: *The Goddess*
While his son is away at university, a farmer persuades his daughter-in-law that she is a goddess, and the events which follow, including the death of her son, are too much for her reason.
A curious, 'foreign' story which does not have the usual Ray tempo or feeling for character, but wins one's attention by its very strangeness.
wd Satyajit Ray *story* Prabhat Kumar Mukherjee *ph* Subrata Mitra *m* Ali Akbar Khan *ad* Bansi Chandragupta *ed* Dulal Dutta
☆ Chhabi Biswas, Sharmila Tagore, Soumitra Chatterjee, Karuna Banerjee

The Devil and Daniel Webster: see *All That Money Can Buy*

The Devil and Max Devlin
US 1981 95m Technicolor
Walt Disney (Jerome Courtland)
An unscrupulous apartment manager is knocked down by a bus. Finding himself in hell, he is offered freedom if he can buy three young souls within two months.
Frowsty Freudian comedy, a very unhappy indication of the depths to which Disney productions have sunk since Walt's death. To carry this kind of thing off requires a hundred times more style than is evidenced here.
w Mary Rodgers *d* Steven Hilliard Stern *ph* Howard Schwartz *m* Buddy Baker
☆ Elliott Gould, Bill Cosby, Susan Anspach, Adam Rich, Charles Shamata, Ronnie Schell

The Devil and Miss Jones **
US 1941 97m bw
RKO/Frank Ross, Norman Krasna
A millionaire masquerades as a clerk in his own department store to investigate worker complaints.
Attractive comedy with elements of the crazy thirties and the more socially conscious forties.
w Norman Krasna *d* Sam Wood *ph* Harry Stradling *m* Roy Webb
☆ Jean Arthur, Charles Coburn, Robert Cummings, Spring Byington, S. Z. Sakall, William Demarest
Norman Krasna; Charles Coburn

'Greatest Thrill Ever Screened!'
'Her sin – their death?'
Devil and the Deep *
US 1932 73m bw
Paramount (Emmanuel Cohen)
A submarine commander goes mad with jealousy of his faithless wife.
A turgid melodrama notable for its stars.
w Benn Levy *d* Marion Gering *ph* Charles Lang
☆ Tallulah Bankhead, Charles Laughton, Gary Cooper, Cary Grant, Paul Porcasi
'Of femme interest despite lukewarm performance of Tallulah Bankhead … a fair commercial release.' – *Variety*

The Devil and the Nun *
Poland 1960 108m bw
Kadr
original title: *Matka Joanna od Aniolow*
aka: *Mother Joan of the Angels*
In a 17th-century convent nuns are possessed by devils. A priest who tries to help is burned at the stake; another becomes possessed himself.
Reasonably dispassionate and fairly stylized version of the same facts that were treated so hysterically by Ken Russell in The Devils.
w Tadeusz Konwicki, Jerzy Kawalerowicz *novel* Jaroslav Iwaszkiewicz *d* Jerzy Kawalerowicz *ph* Jerzy Wojcik *m* Adam Walacinski
☆ Lucyna Winnicka, Mieczyslaw Voit, Anna Ciepielewska

The Devil at Four o'Clock
US 1961 126m Eastmancolor
Columbia/Leroy/Kohlmar (Fred Kohlmar)
A drunken missionary and three convicts save a colony of leper children from a South Seas volcano.
Muddled adventure melodrama with a downbeat ending long delayed.
w Liam O'Brien *novel* Max Catto *d* Mervyn Le Roy *ph* Joseph Biroc *m* George Duning
☆ Spencer Tracy, Frank Sinatra, Kerwin Mathews, Jean-Pierre Aumont, Grégoire Aslan, Alexander Scourby, Barbara Luna

The Devil Bat
US 1941 70m bw
PRC
A crazed scientist trains bats to kill at the scent of a certain perfume.
Horror comic hokum from the bottom of the barrel.
w John Neville *d* Jean Yarbrough
☆ Bela Lugosi, Suzanne Kaaren, Dave O'Brien
† The DVD release also included *Scared to Death* (qv).

Devil Bat's Daughter
US 1946 67m bw
PRC
A girl who thinks she is the daughter of a vampire consults a psychiatrist, who encourages her to murder his wife.
Tolerable, potboiling shocker.
w Griffin Jay *story* Frank Wisbar, Ernst Jaeger *d* Frank Wisbar
☆ Rosemary La Planche, John James, Michael Hale, Nolan Leary

The Devil Came from Akasava
West Germany 1970 85m colour
CCC Films/Fenix Films (Karl-Heinz Mannchen)
Rival groups attempt to control a stone with mystic powers.
Nonsensical adventure, barely competent in all departments.
w Paul Andre, Lladislas Fedor *d* Jess Frank (Jesús Franco) *ph* Manuel Merino *m* Manfred Hubler, Siegfried Schwab
☆ Fred Williams, Susann Korda, Horst Tappert, Ewa Stroemberg, Siefried Schurenberg, Walter Rilla, Paul Muller

The Devil Commands *
US 1941 65m bw
Columbia (Wallace MacDonald)
An electrical scientist tries to communicate with his dead wife through a medium.
Modestly effective horror thriller, though rather too deliberately paced.
w Robert D. Andrews, Milton Gunzberg *story* *The Edge of Running Water* by William Sloane *d* Edward Dmytryk *ph* Allan G. Siegler *md* Morris Stoloff
☆ Boris Karloff, Richard Fiske, Amanda Duff, Anne Revere, Ralph Penney

Devil Dogs of the Air *
US 1935 86m bw
Warner (Lou Edelman)
Rivalry and romance in the Marine Flying Corps.
Standard, lively vehicle for Cagney and O'Brien, with excellent stunt flying sequences.
w Malcolm Stuart Boylan, Earl Baldwin *novel* John Monk Saunders *d* Lloyd Bacon *ph* Arthur Edeson *md* Leo F. Forbstein
☆ *James Cagney, Pat O'Brien*, Margaret Lindsay, Frank McHugh, Helen Lowell, John Arledge, Robert Barrat, Russell Hicks, Ward Bond
'Exhibs should have no squawks and may even cheer if they put a little steam behind their selling.' – *Variety*
'A loud and roughneck screen comedy, both amusing and exciting.' – *André Sennwald*

'What Is The Strange Terrifying Evil Secret Of The Dummy … and why is it locked in a cage every night?'
'Can You Keep The Secret Of The Most Diabolical Ending Ever Filmed?'
Devil Doll
GB 1963 70m bw
Galaworld/Gordon (Lindsay Shonteff)
A hypnotist and ventriloquist uses his doll, containing the trapped soul of a human, to carry out his evil purposes.
Competent but uninspired thriller, too silly to be effective and too obviously indebted to the much superior Dead of Night *(qv).*
w George Barclay (Ronald Kinnoch), Lance Z. Hargreaves (Charles Vetter) *story* Frederick Escreet Smith *d* Lindsay Shonteff *ph* Gerald Gibbs *ad* Stan Shields *ed* Ernest Bullingham
☆ William Sylvester, Bryant Halliday, Yvonne Romain, Sandra Dorne, Nora Nicholson, Alan Gifford, Karel Stepanek, Francis de Wolff

'Earth menaced by fantastic powers!'
Devil Girl from Mars
GB 1954 76m bw
Edward J. and Harry Lee Danziger
A female Martian is sent to Earth to bring back a stock of men for breeding purposes.
Absurd attempt to cash in on the then new space fiction craze. The budget matches the imagination.
w John C. Maher, James Eastwood *d* David MacDonald *ph* Jack Cox *m* Edwin Astley
☆ Patricia Laffan, Hugh McDermott, Joseph Tomelty, Adrienne Corri, Peter Reynolds, Hazel Court, John Laurie, Sophie Stewart
'There is really no fault in this film that one would like to see eliminated. Everything, in its way, is quite perfect.' – *Gavin Lambert, Sight and Sound*

'Private detective Easy Rawlins has been caught on the wrong side of the most dangerous secret in town.'
Devil in a Blue Dress **
US 1995 102m Technicolor
TriStar/Clinica Estetico/Mundy Lane (Jesse Beaton, Gary Goetzman)
In Los Angeles in the late 40s, private eye Easy Rawlins is hired to find a missing woman.
Deft and engrossing thriller of corrupt politics and racial and sexual tensions, well acted, and directed with economy and style.
wd Carl Franklin *novel* Walter Mosley *ph* Tak Fujimoto *m* Elmer Bernstein *pd* Gary Frutkoff *ed* Carole Kravetz
☆ Denzel Washington, Tom Sizemore, Jennifer Beals, Don Cheadle, Maury Chaykin, Terry Kinney, Mel Winkler, Albert Hall
'The most enjoyable private-eye film in a long time: a modest, skillful, unfussy genre film that tells an exciting story and lets its more serious concerns remain just below the surface.' – *Terrence Rafferty, New Yorker*

Devil in the Flesh: see *Le Diable au Corps*

Devil in the Flesh
US 1998 99m colour
Le Monde/Prostar/Unapix (Kurt Anderson, Richard Brandes)
A unbalanced teenage girl develops an obsessive crush on one of her teachers.
Mundane thriller with nothing to distinguish from similar run-other-mill movies offering a modicum of sex and violence.
w Steve Cohen, Robert McCall, Kelly Carlin-McCall, Michael Michand *story* Kurt Anderson, Richard Brandes *d* Steve Cohen *ph* Joseph

Montgomery *m* Michael Burns, Steve Gurevitch *pd* Radha Mehta *ed* Michael Thibault
☆ Rose McGowan (Debbie Strand), Alex McArthur (Peter Rinaldi), Peg Shirley (Fiona Long), J.C. Brandy (Janie Magray), Phil Morris (Det Joe Rosales), Robert Silver (Det Phil Archer), Sherrie Rose (Marilyn)
† Its narrative was recycled in a sequel in 2000, under the title *Teacher's Pet* (qv).

Devil in the Flesh 2: see *Teacher's Pet (2000)*

The Devil Is a Sissy
US 1936 92m bw
MGM (Frank Davis)
aka: *The Devil Takes the Count*
The young son of divorcing parents gets into bad company.
Adequate juvenile melodrama.
w John Lee Mahin, Richard Schayer, Rowland Brown *d* W. S. Van Dyke *ph* Harold Rosson, George Schneiderman *m* Herbert Stothart
☆ Freddie Bartholomew, Jackie Cooper, Mickey Rooney, Ian Hunter, Peggy Conklin, Katherine Alexander, Gene Lockhart, Dorothy Peterson

'Men are my slaves – and glad to be!'
The Devil Is a Woman *
US 1935 82m bw
Paramount
In Seville in the 1890s, a *femme fatale* has several admirers.
The last Dietrich vehicle to be directed by von Sternberg, and rather splendid in its highly decorative and uncommercial way; a treat for addicts.
w John Dos Passos, S. K. Winston *novel La Femme et le Pantin* by Pierre Louÿs *d Josef von Sternberg ph Josef von Sternberg, Lucien Ballard m* from Rimsky-Korsakov *ad Hans Dreier*
☆ Marlene Dietrich, Lionel Atwill, Cesar Romero, Edward Everett Horton, Alison Skipworth, Don Alvarado, Morgan Wallace, Tempe Piggott
'A somewhat monotonous picture … sophisticated audiences are its best bet.' – *Variety*
'One of the most sophisticated films ever produced in America.' – *André Sennwald, New York Times*
'Light and shadow are splashed liberally around over the white-painted sets; cafés, tobacco factories, stairs and balconies are decorated with every conceivable device and camera-level.' – *Peter John Dyer, 1964*
'A clever, perversely dehumanized picture said to be one of von Sternberg's favourites.' – *New Yorker, 1977*

The Devil Is Driving
US 1937 69m bw
Columbia
An attorney protects a friend's son from a drunk driving charge, but finally indicts himself for perjury.
Standard moral melodrama with the star in good form.
w Jo Milward, Richard Blake *d* Harry Lachman
☆ Richard Dix, Joan Perry, Nana Bryant, Frank C. Wilson, Ian Wolfe, Elisha Cook Jnr, Henry Kolker, Ann Rutherford, Walter Kingsford
'Carries a good deal of punch, but not enough to lug it above the moderate biz bracket.' – *Variety*

The Devil Makes Three
US 1952 90m bw
MGM (Richard Goldstone)
An American intelligence officer in post-war Germany becomes involved with neo-Nazis.
A curious break from dancing for Gene Kelly, this obscurely titled thriller has little to commend it but authentic locations.
w Jerry Davis *story* Lawrence Bachmann *d* Andrew Marton *ph* Vaclav Vich *m* Rudolph G. Kopp
☆ Gene Kelly, Pier Angeli, Richard Rober, Richard Egan, Claus Clausen

The Devil Never Sleeps: see *Satan Never Sleeps*

Devil on Horseback
GB 1954 89m bw
Group 3 (John Grierson, Isobel Pargiter)
A teenage jockey gets to the top the hard way.
Highly resistible compendium of racetrack clichés and sentiment, not at all what one expected from Group 3.
w Neil Paterson, Montagu Slater *d* Cyril Frankel *ph* Denny Densham *m* Malcolm Arnold
☆ Googie Withers, John McCallum, Jeremy Spenser, Meredith Edwards, Liam Redmond, Sam Kydd

The Devil, Probably *
France 1977 95m Eastmancolor
Sunchold/GMF (Stéphane Tchalgadchieff)
original title: *Le Diable, Probablement*
A young Parisian goes to the devil and arranges to have himself shot.
A despairing vision of an arid world, seen through unpleasant details of city life. A fascinating but enervated film very typical of its director.
wd Robert Bresson ph Pasqualino de Santis *m* Philippe Sarde *pd* Eric Simon
☆ Antoine Monnier, Tina Irissari, Henri de Maublanc

The Devil Rides Out *
GB 1968 95m Technicolor
Warner/Hammer (Anthony Nelson-Keys)
US title: *The Devil's Bride*
The Duc de Richleau rescues a friend from a group of Satanists.
Rather stodgy adaptation of a frightening novel; moments of suspense.
w Richard Matheson *novel* Dennis Wheatley *d* Terence Fisher *ph* Arthur Grant *m* James Bernard *ad* Bernard Robinson *ed* James Needs, Spencer Reeve
☆ Christopher Lee, *Charles Gray*, Leon Greene, Patrick Mower, Gwen Ffrangcon-Davies

Devil Ship Pirates
GB 1964 96m Technicolor Hammerscope
ABP/Hammer (Anthony Nelson-Keys)
At the time of the Armada, Spanish privateers terrorize a Cornish seaside village.
Lacklustre pirate yarn with not much action and some elements of Hammer horror.
w Jimmy Sangster *d* Don Sharp *ph* Michael Reed *m* Gary Hughes *ad* Bernard Robinson, Don Mingaye *ed* James Needs
☆ Christopher Lee, John Cairney, Barry Warren, Ernest Clark, Andrew Keir, Duncan Lamont

The Devil Takes the Count: see *The Devil Is a Sissy*

The Devil Thumbs a Ride
US 1947 63m bw
RKO
A commercial traveller gives a lift to a man who turns out to be wanted for murder.
Predictable suspenser without much entertainment value.
wd Felix Feist
☆ Ted North, Lawrence Tierney, Nan Leslie

The Devil to Pay *
US 1930 72m bw
Samuel Goldwyn
The prodigal son of a snooty English family returns to cheer them all up.
Agreeably lighthearted star comedy in the drawing-room tradition.
w Frederick Lonsdale *d* George Fitzmaurice *ph* Gregg Toland, George Barnes *m* Alfred Newman
☆ *Ronald Colman*, Loretta Young, Myrna Loy, Frederick Kerr
'Snappy British comedy that should please everywhere … a set-up for femmes.' – *Variety*
'Six reels of Mr Colman being charming … a polished, tasteful and entirely likeable screen comedy.' – *New York Herald Tribune*

The Devil with Hitler
US 1942 44m bw
Hal Roach
Hell's board of directors want to sack Satan and bring in Hitler.
Somewhat infantile war farce, one of this producer's very few successful medium-length 'screenliners'.
w Cortland FitzSimmons, Al Martin *d* Gordon Douglas
☆ Alan Mowbray, Bobby Watson, George E. Stone, Joe Devlin
† The Hays Office gave special permission, in a just cause, for the use of the word 'Hell'.

Devil within Her (dubbed)
Italy 1974 109m Technicolor
UA/AR Cinematografica (Ovisio Assonitis, Giorgio C. Rossi)
original title: *Chi Sei?*
US title: *Beyond the Door*
The Devil gives a black magician ten days to obtain the unborn child of his former mistress.
An unoriginal and unexciting variation on The Exorcist*, repeating to lesser effect that film's tricks.*
w Sonia Molteni, Antonio Troisio, Giorgio Marini, Aldo Crudo, Robert D'Ettore Piazzoli *d* Oliver Hellman *ph* Robert D'Ettore Piazzoli *m* Franco Micalizzi *ad* Piero Filippone, Franco Pellecchia Velchi *ed* Angelo Curi
☆ Juliet Mills, Richard Johnson, Gabriele Lavia, Barbara Fiorini, David Colin Jnr, Joan Acti
'A disastrous foray into the fashionable area of demonic possession, unencumbered with any trace of subtlety or conviction.' – *Verina Glaessner*

The Devil within Her: see *I Don't Want to Be Born (1975)*

Devil-Doll **
US 1936 79m bw
MGM (E. J. Mannix)
A refugee from Devil's Island disguises himself as an old lady who sells human dolls which murder those responsible for his imprisonment.
Interesting rather than exciting tall tale with a Paris backdrop; despite impressive moments it does not quite have the right frisson.
w Tod Browning, Garrett Fort, Erich von Stroheim, Guy Endore *novel Burn Witch Burn* by A. A. Merritt *d Tod Browning ph Leonard Smith m* Franz Waxman *ad* Cedric Gibbons
☆ *Lionel Barrymore*, Maureen O'Sullivan, Frank Lawton, Henry B. Walthall, Rafaela Ottiano, Grace Ford, Arthur Hohl
'Grotesque, slightly horrible and consistently interesting.' – *Frank Nugent, New York Times*

'Hell holds no surprises … for them!'
The Devils **
GB 1970 111m Technicolor Panavision
Warner/Russo (Robert H. Solo, Ken Russell)
An account of the apparent demoniacal possession of the 17th-century nuns of Loudun, climaxing in the burning of their priest as a sorcerer.
Despite undeniable technical proficiency this is its writer-director's most outrageously sick film to date, campy, idiosyncratic and in howling bad taste from beginning to end, full of worm-eaten skulls, masturbating nuns, gibbering courtiers, plague sores, rats and a burning to death before our very eyes … plus a sacrilegious dream of Jesus.
wd Ken Russell *play* John Whiting *book The Devils of Loudun* by *Aldous Huxley ph David Watkin m* Peter Maxwell Davies *ad* Robert Cartwright
☆ Vanessa Redgrave, Oliver Reed, Dudley Sutton, Max Adrian, Gemma Jones, Murray Melvin, Michael Gothard, Graham Armitage
'Ken Russell doesn't report hysteria, he markets it.' – *New Yorker, 1976*
'Russell's swirling multi-colored puddle … made me glad that both Huxley and Whiting are dead, so that they are spared this farrago of witless exhibitionism.' – *Stanley Kauffmann*
'A garish glossary of sado-masochism … a taste for visual sensation that makes scene after scene look like the masturbatory fantasies of a Roman Catholic boyhood.' – *Alexander Walker*

The Devil's 8
US 1968 98m Pathécolor
AIP/Burt Topper
A federal agent on the trail of a moonshine gang recruits a gang of hardened convicts and arranges for them to escape.
The Dirty Dozen *all over again, and not good.*
w James Gordon White, Willard Huyck, John Milius *d* Burt Topper *ph* Richard C. Glouner *m* Mike Curb
☆ Christopher George, Ralph Meeker, Fabian, Tom Nardini, Leslie Parrish, Ross Hagen

The Devil's Advocate
West Germany 1977 109m colour
Geria (Lutz Hengst)
A dying priest is summoned to Rome to investigate the cult of a dead partisan nominated for sainthood.
Well-meaning but rather tepid and inconclusive adaptation of a bestseller which presumably made its points more firmly.
w Morris West *novel* Morris West *d* Guy Green *ph* Billy Williams *m* Bert Grund
☆ John Mills, Stéphane Audran, Jason Miller, Timothy West, Patrick Mower, Paola Pitagora, Daniel Massey, Leigh Lawson, Raf Vallone, Jack Hedley

'Evil Has Its Winning Ways.'
Devil's Advocate
US 1997 144m Technicolor Panavision
Warner (Arnon Milchan, Arnold Kopelson, Anne Kopelson)
A successful young lawyer is tempted to join a big New York firm that is run by the Devil.
A perfunctory thriller that seems mainly designed to provide Al Pacino with an opportunity to overact, which he accepts with relish.
w Jonathan Lemkin, Tony Gilroy *novel* Andrew Neiderman *d* Taylor Hackford *ph* Andrzej Bartkowiak *m* James Newton Howard *pd* Bruno Rubeo *ed* Mark Warner
☆ Keanu Reeves, Al Pacino, Charlize Theron, Jeffrey Jones, Judith Ivey, Connie Neilsen, Craig T. Nelson, Delroy Lindo (uncredited)
'A fairly entertaining supernatural potboiler that finally bubbles over with a nearly operatic sense of absurdity and excess.' – *Todd McCarthy, Variety*

The Devil's Backbone: see *El Espinazo del Diablo*

Devil's Bait
GB 1959 58m bw
Rank/Independent Artists
A baker accidentally bakes a loaf containing poison.
B-feature thriller of minimal interest.
w Peter Johnson, Diana K. Watson *d* Peter Graham Scott *ph* Michael Reed *m* William Alwyn *md* Muir Mathieson *ad* Eric Saw *ed* John Trumper
☆ Geoffrey Keen, Jane Hylton, Gordon Jackson, Rupert Davies, Dermot Kelly

The Devil's Bride: see *The Devil Rides Out*

The Devil's Brigade
US 1968 132m DeLuxe Panavision
UA/David L. Wolper
For combat in Norway and Italy during World War II a US officer assembles a platoon of thugs and misfits to work with crack Canadian commandos.
Flagrant but routine imitation of The Dirty Dozen, *quite undistinguished.*
w William Roberts *book* Robert H. Adleman, George Walton *d* Andrew V. McLaglen *ph* William Clothier *m* Alex North
☆ William Holden, Cliff Robertson, Vince Edwards, Andrew Prine, Claude Akins, Carroll O'Connor, Richard Jaeckel
'After nearly three decades of World War II films, it is hardly surprising that Hollywood is beginning to suffer from combat fatigue.' – *Time*

The Devil's Brother: see *Fra Diavolo*

'Fighting like jungle beasts for the love of one woman!'
Devil's Canyon
US 1953 92m Technicolor Natural Vision 3-D
RKO/Edmund Grainger
Life in a notorious Arizona prison in the 1880s; a marshal is unjustly convicted but wins his pardon.
Fairly brutal Western, quite unmemorable.
w Frederick Hazlitt Brennan, Harry Essex *story* Bennett R. Cohen, Norton S. Parker *d* Alfred Werker *ph* Nicholas Musuraca *m* Daniele Amfitheatrof *md* Constantin Bakaleinikoff *ad* Albert S. D'Agostino, Jack Okey *ed* Gene Palmer

☆ Dale Robertson (Billy Reynolds), Virginia Mayo (Abby Nixon), Stephen McNally (Jesse Gorman), Arthur Hunnicutt (Frank Taggert), Robert Keith (Steve Morgan), Jay C. Flippen (Captain Wells), Whit Bissell (Virgil), William Phillips (Red), Morris Ankrum (Sheriff), George J. Lewis (Colonel Gomez)

The Devil's Disciple *
GB 1959 82m bw
UA/Hecht-Hill-Lancaster/Brynaprod (Harold Hecht)
In 1777 an American ne'er-do-well almost allows himself to be hanged by the British in mistake for a rebel pastor.
Star-studded but indifferently staged adaptation of a minor Shavian frolic. Patchy, with good moments.
w John Dighton, Roland Kibbee *play* Bernard Shaw *d* Guy Hamilton *ph* Jack Hildyard *m* Richard Rodney Bennett *ad* Terence Verity, Edward Carere
☆ Burt Lancaster, Kirk Douglas, Laurence Olivier (General Burgoyne), Eva Le Gallienne, Janette Scott, Harry Andrews, Basil Sidney, George Rose, Neil McCallum, David Horne, Mervyn Johns

Devil's Doorway
US 1950 84m bw
MGM (Nicholas Nayfack)
A Shoshone Indian fights valiantly in the Civil War but on his return to Wyoming finds himself hated and threatened by his former colleagues.
Dull pro-Indian Western with a most unsuitable star.
w Guy Trosper *d* Anthony Mann *ph* John Alton *m* Daniele Amfitheatrof
☆ Robert Taylor, Louis Calhern, Paula Raymond, Marshall Thompson, James Mitchell, Edgar Buchanan, Rhys Williams, Spring Byington

The Devil's Envoys: see *Les Visiteurs du Soir*

The Devil's Eye *
Sweden 1960 90m bw
Svensk Filmindustri
An old proverb says that a woman's chastity is a stye in the devil's eye. So when Satan has a sore eye he comes down to earth to put things right.
Surprisingly shoddily-made comedy with just a few of the sharpnesses of technique and mystifications of plot which one had come to expect from this maestro.
wd Ingmar Bergman *ph* Gunnar Fischer *m* Domenico Scarlatti
☆ Jarl Kulle, Bibi Andersson, Nils Poppe, Stig Järrel, Gunnar Björnstrand

The Devil's General
West Germany 1955 121m bw
Ryal (Gyula Trebitsch)
In 1941 a German air ace becomes estranged from the high command and is tortured by the Gestapo. On release he helps a Jewish couple …
Heavy-going melodrama which nevertheless paints a convincing picture of Berlin during the war.
w George Hurdalek, Helmut Kautner *play* Carl Zuckmayer *d* Helmut Kautner *ph* Albert Benitz
☆ Curt Jurgens, Victor de Kowa, Karl John, Eva-Ingeborg Scholz

The Devil's Hairpin
US 1957 83m Technicolor Vistavision
Paramount/Cornel Wilde
A former motor racing champion makes a comeback, and redeems his past boorish behaviour.
Efficient routine melodramatics with good action sequences.
w James Edmiston, Cornel Wilde *d* Cornel Wilde *ph* Daniel Fapp *m* Van Cleave
☆ Cornel Wilde, Jean Wallace, Arthur Franz, *Mary Astor*, Paul Fix

The Devil's Impostor: see *Pope Joan*

Devil's Island *
US 1939 63m bw
Warner (Bryan Foy)
A surgeon is sent to Devil's Island for aiding an escaped convict.
Sharply-made exposé of the notorious French penal colony; commendable pace and vigour all round.
w Kenneth Gamet, Don Ryan *story* The Return of Doctor X by Anthony Coldeway, Raymond L. Schrock *d* William Clemens *ph* George Barnes *ed* Frank Magee
☆ *Boris Karloff, James Stephenson*, Nedda Harrigan, Adia Kuznetzoff, Robert Warwick, Pedro de Cordoba
'It is being touted as an "uncensored" version. But there is nothing in it that could startle a well-protected child of seven or give pause even to a censor.' – *Variety*

Devil's Island **
Iceland/Norway/Germany/Denmark 1996 103m colour
Theatrical Experience/IFC/Zentropa (Fridrik Thor Fridricksson, Egil ödergaard, Peter Rommel)
original title: *Djöflaeyjan*
In Iceland in the 50s, a man returns from America to live with his poverty-stricken family in an abandoned US military barracks.
Engaging, episodic domestic drama, an effective mix of comedy and tragedy, among society's misfits.
w Einar Kárason *d* Fridrik Thor Fridriksson *ph* Ari Kristinsson *m* Hilmar örn Hilmarsson *pd* Arni Páll Jóhansson *ed* Steingrimur Karlsson, Skule Eriksen
☆ Baltasar Kormakur, Sveinn Geirsson, Gisli Halldorsson, Sigurveig Jonsdottir, Halldora Geirhardsdottir

The Devil's Kiss (dubbed)
Spain/Andorra 1974 104m colour
Andros
original title: *La Perversa Caricia De Satan*
With the aid of a telepath, a woman uses occult powers to seek revenge on those who wronged her and caused the death of her husband.
Dull horror movie, taken at a plodding pace; the music, dialogue, and acting are its true terrors.
wd Georges Gigo (Jorge Luis Gigo) *ph* Julio Peréz de Rozas *m* Albert Argudo *ed* Albert Gasset Nicolau
☆ Silvia Solar, Oliver Matthau (Olivier Mathot), Evelyne Scott, Daniel Martin, Jose Nieto, Ronnie Harp, Wendy Asher

The Devil's Nightmare
Belgium/France 1971 95m colour
Delfino/Cetelci
original title: *La Plus Longue Nuit du Diable*
Seven stranded travellers take shelter in a mansion occupied by a cursed family.
Predictable horror in which one murder follows another, whenever one of the seven deadly sins is committed; the overemphatic direction kills any suspense.
w Jean Brismée, Charles Lecocq, Patrice Rhomm, André Hunnebelle *d* Jean Brismée *ph* André Goeffers
☆ Erika Blanc, Jean Servais, Jacques Monseau, Lucien Raimbourg, Daniel Emilfork, Ivana Novak, Shirley Corrigan

Devils of Darkness
GB 1964 90m Eastmancolor
Planet (Tom Blakeley)
A writer discovers that mysterious deaths in Brittany are caused by Count Sinistre and his gypsy bride, vampires who are protected by the locals.
Lacklustre low-budget horror, given a modern setting apart from its prologue; the script pits English rectitude against French perversity.
w Lyn Fairhurst *d* Lance Comfort *ph* Reg Wyer *m* Bernie Fenton *ad* John St John Earl *ed* John Trumper
☆ William Sylvester, Hubert Noel, Carole Gray, Tracy Reed, Diana Decker, Rona Anderson, Eddie Byrne, Gerard Heinz, Peter Illing, Brian Oulton
'Flat direction and cheap sets and camerawork make this one of the least atmospheric British horror movies of all time.' – *The Dark Side*

The Devil's Own: see *The Witches (1966)*

'One man trapped by destiny, and another bound by duty. They're about to discover what they're willing to live, to fight, and to die for.'
The Devil's Own
US 1997 110m Technicolor Panavision
Columbia (Lawrence Gordon, Robert F. Colesberry)
An IRA hitman goes to America to buy missiles and lodges with a New York cop who hates violence.
Dull glamorization of thuggery and male bonding.
w David Aaron Cohen, Vincent Patrick, Kevin Jarre *d* Alan J. Pakula *ph* Gordon Willis *m* James Horner *pd* Jane Musky *ed* Tom Rolf, Dennis Virkler
☆ Harrison Ford, Brad Pitt, Margaret Colin, Ruben Blades, Treat Williams, George Hearn, Mitchell Ryan, Natascha McElhone
'From the opening caterwauling … you can tell this film is going to be rubbish, and it is.' – *Andrew Harrison, Neon*
† The film cost some \$95m and grossed around \$42.9m in the US.

The Devil's Playground
US 1946 66m bw
UA/Hopalong Cassidy (Lewis J. Rachmil)
Hoppy and his friends save a girl and stolen gold from a crooked judge and his gang.
Pleasant 'B' Western that mixes comedy and action to amiable effect.
w Ted Wilson *d* George Archainbaud *ph* Mack Stengler *m* David Chudnow *ad* Harvey T. Gillett *ed* Fred W. Berger
☆ William Boyd, Andy Clyde, Rand Brooks, Elaine Riley, Robert Elliott, Joseph J. Greene, Francis McDonald, Ned Young

The Devil's Playground *
Australia 1976 107m Eastmancolor
The Feature Film House (Fred Schepisi)
Tensions between masters and boys in a Catholic seminary in the fifties.
Well made but rather dislikeable intrusion into Mr Perrin and Mr Traill *country with the addition of modern frankness.*
wd Fred Schepisi *ph* Ian Baker *m* Bruce Smeaton
☆ Arthur Dignam, Nick Tate, Simon Burke, Charles McCallum, John Frawley

'Heaven help us all when'
The Devil's Rain
US 1975 86m colour Todd-AO 35
Rank/Sandy Howard (James V. Cullen, Michael S. Glick)
Witchcraft in the modern west causes victims to melt; the son of one of them takes arms against the leading Satanist.
Interestingly cast example of the low-budget seventies exploitation picture, with more nastiness than logic.
w Gabe Essoe, James Ashton, Gerald Hopman *d* Robert Fuest *ph* Alex Phillips Jnr *m* Al de Lory
☆ Ernest Borgnine, Ida Lupino, Eddie Albert, William Shatner, Keenan Wynn, Tom Skerritt

The Devil's Wanton *
Sweden 1949 80m bw
Terrafilm
original title: *Fängelse*
aka: *Prison*
Film-makers discuss some rather unpleasant projects but put them aside as unsatisfactory.
A bit of a Scandinavian wallow, with heavy expressionism and low-life themes.
wd Ingmar Bergman *ph* Göran Strindberg *m* Erland von Koch
☆ Doris Svedlund, Birger Malmsten, Eva Henning, Hasse Ekman
'It employs all the paraphernalia associated with Scandinavian angst.' – *John Gillett, MFB*

The Devil's Widow: see *Tam-Lin*

Devlin
US 1992 106m colour
Viacom (Paula de Oliviera, Craig Roessler)
A cop fights back when he discovers he is being framed for the murder of his brother-in-law, a leading politician.
An unoriginal movie that is acted and directed with enough pace and energy to make it enjoyable.
w David Taylor *novel* Roderick Thorp *d* Rick Rosenthal *ph* Neil Roach *m* John Altman *pd* Barbara Dunphy *ed* Tony Gibbs
☆ Bryan Brown, Roma Downey, Lloyd Bridges, Whip Hubley, Lawrence Dane, Lisa Eichhorn, Carole Shelley, Jan Rubes, Frances Fisher
'A slick thriller that really does thrill.' – *Alan Frank, Movies*

'It tells ALL about those Brontë sisters! … They didn't dare call it love – they tried to call it devotion!'
Devotion **
US 1946 107m bw
Warner (Robert Buckner)
A highly romanticized account of the lives of the Brontë sisters and their brother Branwell.
An enjoyable bad example of a big-budget Hollywood production which tampers with things it cannot understand, in this case life in a Yorkshire parsonage in Victorian times. An excuse is found to give the curate an Austrian accent to fit the available actor, but this and other faux pas are atoned for by the vividness of Emily's recurrent dream of death as a silhouetted man on horseback. In general, an interesting period piece in more senses than one.
w Keith Winter *d Curtis Bernhardt ph* Ernest Haller *m* Erich Wolfgang Korngold
☆ *Ida Lupino* (Emily), Olivia de Havilland (Charlotte), Nancy Coleman (Anne), Arthur Kennedy (Branwell), Montagu Love (Revd Brontë), Paul Henreid (Revd Nicholls), Ethel Griffies (Aunt Branwell), Sydney Greenstreet (Thackeray), Eily Malyon, Forrester Harvey, Victor Francen
'I found it painless. It never got nearer to the subject than names and consequently didn't hurt. But I would like to know who was devoted to whom and why.' – *Richard Winnington*
† More items from the extraordinary publicity campaign devised by Warner for this placid Victorian romance:
Emily: she ruled in that strange quiet house! None could resist the force of her will!
The man in black (i.e. the Revd Nicholls): he fled from her demands into her sister's arms!
Charlotte: the sweetness of love and the meaning of torment – she learned them both together!
The 'friend' – the furious fat man (i.e. William Makepeace Thackeray): they couldn't fool him – they couldn't trust him!
Dialogue includes the celebrated exchange between two celebrated London literary figures:
Dickens: 'Morning, Thackeray.'
Thackeray: 'Morning, Dickens.'
†† Made in 1943, but not released until later.

Dharmaga Tongjoguro Kan Kkadalgun?: see *Why Did Bodhi-Dharma Leave for the East?*

El Dia de la Bestia: see *The Day of the Beast*

Le Diable au Corps *
France 1946 110m bw
Transcontinental
US title: *Devil in the Flesh*
When her husband is away at war, a young married woman falls for a college student with tragic consequences.
A love story of World War I; a great commercial success, but tending to be slow and dreary.
w Jean Aurenche, Pierre Bost *novel* Raymond Radiguet *d* Claude Autant-Lara *ph* Michel Kelber *m* René Cloërec *pd* Max Douy *ed* Madeleine Gug
☆ Micheline Presle, Gérard Philipe, Jean Debucourt, Denise Grey, Jacques Tati

Le Diable, Probablement: see *The Devil, Probably*

Diabolique: see *Les Diaboliques*

Diabolique
US 1996 107m Technicolor
Warner/Morgan Creek/Marvin Worth/ABC (Marvin Worth, James G. Robinson)
The wife and mistress of an unpleasant schoolmaster conspire to murder him, with unexpected results.
An appalling remake of Henri-Georges Clouzot's masterly Les Diaboliques*; it is boring, badly made and miserably acted.*
w Don Roos *novel* Celle qui n'était plus by Pierre Boileau and Thomas Narcejec *d* Jeremiah Chechik *ph* Peter James *m* Randy Edelman *pd* Leslie Dilley *ed* Carol Littleton
☆ Sharon Stone, Isabelle Adjani, Chazz Palminteri, Kathy Bates, Spalding Gray, Shirley Knight, Allen Garfield
'As mouldy as anything ever laid before an audience.' – *Tom Hutchinson, Film Review*

'While the original grabbed you by the synapses and shook hard, this amounts to watchable nonsense enacted by unbelievable people in a preposterous scenario.' – *Ian Nathan, Empire*
'The filmmakers have turned silk into a sow's ear, giving people new reason to fear Hollywood remakes of quality foreign films.' – *Variety*

Les Diaboliques ***
France 1954 114m bw
Filmsonor (Henri-Georges Clouzot)
aka: *Diabolique*
GB title: *The Fiends*
A sadistic headmaster's wife and mistress conspire to murder him; but his body disappears and evidence of his presence haunts them.
Highly influential, suspenseful and scary thriller with a much-copied twist typical of its authors. Slow to start and shabby-looking as befits its grubby school setting, it gathers momentum with the murder and turns the screw with fine professionalism.
w Henri-Georges Clouzot, G. Geronimi *novel* *The Woman Who Was* by Pierre Boileau and Thomas Narcejac *d* *Henri-Georges Clouzot* *ph* Armand Thirard *m* Georges Van Parys
☆ Simone Signoret, Vera Clouzot, Charles Vanel, Paul Meurisse
'Scary, but so calculatedly sensational that it's rather revolting.' – *New Yorker, 1978*
'It depends very much on the intimate details of the seedy fourth-rate school, with its inadequate education and uneatable food, its general smell of unwashed children, hatred and petty perversions.' – *Basil Wright, 1972*
† Remade in 1976 as a TV movie, *Reflections of Murder*.

Diagnosis: Murder
GB 1974 90m Eastmancolor
Silhouette (Patrick Dromgoole, Peter Miller)
A psychiatrist's wife disappears, and the police suspect her husband.
Well-upholstered but sadly old-fashioned domestic crime thriller; one is vaguely surprised to see it in colour, having seen it so often in black-and-white.
w Philip Levene *d* Sidney Hayers *ph* Bob Edwards *m* Laurie Johnson *ed* David Williams
☆ Jon Finch (Inspector Lomax), Judy Geeson (Helen), Christopher Lee (Dr Stephen Hayward), Tony Beckley (Sgt Green), Dilys Hamlett (Julia Hayward), Jane Merrow (Mary Dawson), Colin Jeavons (Bob Dawson)

'If a woman answers...hang on for dear life!'
Dial M For Murder **
US 1954 105m Warnercolor 3-D
Warner (Alfred Hitchcock)
An ageing tennis champion tries to arrange the death of his wife so that he will inherit, but his complex plan goes wrong.
Hitchcock did not try very hard to adapt this highly commercial play for the cinema, nor did he exploit the possibilities of 3-D. But for a one-room film with a not very exciting cast the film holds its grip pretty well.
w *Frederick Knott* *play* Frederick Knott *d* *Alfred Hitchcock* *ph* Robert Burks *m* Dimitri Tiomkin *md* Ray Heindorf *ad* Edward Carrere *ed* Rudi Fehr
☆ *Ray Milland* (Tony Wendice), *John Williams* (Chief Inspector Hubbard), Grace Kelly (Margot Wendice), Robert Cummings (Mark Halliday), Anthony Dawson (Capt Swan Lesgate), Patrick Allen (Pearson), George Leigh (Williams), Leo Britt (narrator)
'All this is related with Hitchcock's ghoulish chic but everyone in it seems to be walking around with tired blood.' – *Pauline Kael, 1968*
† Although shot in 3-D, it was never released in that form.

Diamond Head
US 1962 107m Eastmancolor Panavision
Columbia (Jerry Bresler)
A domineering Hawaiian landowner almost ruins the lives of his family.
Predictable, heavy-going transcription of a bestseller.
w Marguerite Roberts *novel* Peter Gilman *d* Guy Green *ph* Sam Leavitt *m* Johnny Williams
☆ Charlton Heston, Yvette Mimieux, George Chakiris, France Nuyen, James Darren, Aline MacMahon, Elizabeth Allen, Richard Loo

Diamond Horseshoe
US 1945 104m Technicolor
TCF (William Perlberg)
aka: *Billy Rose's Diamond Horseshoe*
A night-club singer gives up her career for a medical student.
Lavish but humourless star vehicle with standard numbers.
wd George Seaton *play* *The Barker* by Kenyon Nicholson *ph* Ernest Palmer *m/ly* Mack Gordon, Harry Warren
☆ Betty Grable, Dick Haymes, *William Gaxton*, Phil Silvers, Beatrice Kay, Carmen Cavallero, Margaret Dumont

Diamond Jim *
US 1935 93m bw
Universal (Edmund Grainger)
A fantasia on the life of the 1890s millionaire who sailed pretty close to the wind in business, adored Lillian Russell, and developed a gargantuan appetite.
Cheerful period comedy drama with plenty of gusto.
w Preston Sturges *d* A. Edward Sutherland *ph* George Robinson *m* Ferde Grofe, Franz Waxman
☆ Edward Arnold, Jean Arthur, Binnie Barnes, Cesar Romero, Eric Blore
'Good picture and title. Lacks real pull names.' – *Variety*

The Diamond Mercenaries
Switzerland/Ireland/South Africa 1975 101m colour
Michelangelo (Nat Wachsberger)
aka: *Killer Force*
A patrol guard joins a group of mercenaries to steal diamonds from a mine where there is a ruthless head of security.
Muddled and routine action movie which lacks a clear focus.
w Michael Winder, Gerald Sanford, Val Guest *d* Val Guest *ph* David Millin *m* Georges Garvarentz *ad* Peter Church *ed* Bill Butler
☆ Peter Fonda, Telly Savalas, Hugh O'Brian, Christopher Lee, Maud Adams, O. J. Simpson, Ian Yule
'Disappointingly fails to gel.' – *MFB*

Diamond Skulls
GB 1989 87m Technicolor
Virgin Vision/Working Title/British Screen/Channel 4 (Tim Bevan)
US title: *Dark Obsession*
An aristocrat kills a woman in a hit-and-run accident and lets his friend take the blame.
Confused melodrama of sex and the old boy network that seems uncertain of what kind of film it wants to be.
w Tim Rose Price *d* Nick Broomfield *ph* Michael Coulter *m* Hans Zimmer *pd* Jocelyn James *ed* Rodney Holland
☆ Gabriel Byrne, Amanda Donohoe, Michael Hordern, Judy Parfitt, Douglas Hodge, Sadie Frost, Matthew Marsh, Ian Carmichael
'All in all, a promising portrait of aristocratic thuggery in changing times, yet ultimately too diffuse to deliver its punch with the force it needs.' – *Julian Petley, MFB*

Diamonds
US 1975 108m Eastmancolor
Avco Embassy/AmeriEuro (Menahem Golan)
A London diamond merchant sets himself up to be robbed so that he can blackmail the culprits into a raid on the Tel Aviv diamond repository.
Cheerful but unremarkable caper movie with an upbeat ending.
w David Paulsen, Menahem Golan *d* Menahem Golan *ph* Adam Greenberg *m* Roy Budd
☆ Robert Shaw, Richard Roundtree, Barbara Seagull, Shelley Winters

Diamonds Are Forever *
GB 1971 120m Technicolor Panavision
UA/Eon/Danjaq (Harry Saltzman, Albert R. Broccoli)
Seeking a diamond smuggler, James Bond has adventures in Amsterdam, a Los Angeles crematorium, various Las Vegas gambling parlours, and a secret installation in the desert.
Campy, rather vicious addition to a well-worn cycle, with an element of nastiness which big-budget stunts cannot conceal. Panavision does not help, and Connery's return to the role is disappointing.
w Richard Maibaum, Tom Mankiewicz *novel* Ian Fleming *d* Guy Hamilton *ph* Ted Moore *m* John Barry *pd* Ken Adam
☆ Sean Connery, Jill St John, Charles Gray, Lana Wood, Jimmy Dean, Bruce Cabot, Bernard Lee, Lois Maxwell
'It has been claimed that the plot is impossible to describe, but I think I could if I wanted to. I can't think why anyone would want to, though.' – *Roger Ebert*

Diamonds for Breakfast
GB 1968 102m Eastmancolor
Paramount/Bridge Films (Carlo Ponti, Pierre Rouve)
An impoverished Russian aristocrat decides to retrieve from a museum the crown jewels of his ancestors, and seduces seven female accomplices.
Yawning caper yarn embellished with sex and slapstick.
w N. F. Simpson, Pierre Rouve, Ronald Harwood *d* Christopher Morahan *ph* Gerry Turpin *m* Norman Kay
☆ Marcello Mastroianni, Rita Tushingham, Elaine Taylor, Warren Mitchell, Nora Nicholson, Bill Fraser, Leonard Rossiter

Diane
US 1956 110m Eastmancolor
Cinemascope
MGM (Edwin H. Knopf)
Diane de Poitiers becomes a consultant to the king and falls in love with his son.
Solidly boring slice of Hollywood history, with all concerned out of their depth.
w Christopher Isherwood *d* David Miller *ph* Robert Planck *m* Miklos Rozsa
☆ Lana Turner, Roger Moore, Cedric Hardwicke, Pedro Armendariz, Marisa Pavan

Diary for My Children ***
Hungary 1982 107m bw
Artificial Eye/Mafilm/Hungarofilm
original title: *Napló Gyermekeimnek*
An orphan, returning to Budapest in 1947, recalls her happy childhood while dealing with a less enjoyable present.
Three generations of a family encapsulate the modern history of Hungary in a gripping film. Withheld from the West for two years, it won a special jury prize at the Cannes Film Festival in 1984.
w Márta Mészáros, Balàzs Fakan, András Szeredás *d* *Márta Mészáros* *ph* Miklós Jancsó Jnr *m* Zsolt Döme
☆ Zsusza Czinkóczi, Anna Polony, Jan Nowicki, Mari Szémes, Pàl Zolnay

Diary for My Father and Mother **
Hungary 1990 93m colour/bw
Budapest Film Studio/Hungarofilm
original title: *Napló Apámnak Anyámnak*
In 1956, a woman film-maker returns to Budapest from Moscow at a time of recrimination and betrayal, just after the Russians crush the Hungarian revolution.
Moving and emotional finale to an impressive, semi-autobiographical trilogy, tracing Hungary's changing fortunes through the experience of one woman; even if more recent events have made it seem like ancient history, it retains its power and interest through its emphasis on individual lives and feelings, though it will be most enjoyed by those familiar with the earlier films in the sequence.
w Márta Mészáros, Éva Pataki *d* Márta Mészáros *ph* Nyika Jancsó *m* Zsolt Döme *ed* Éva Kármentö
☆ Zsusza Czinkóczi, Jan Nowicki, Anna Polony, Mari Töröcsik, Ildiko Bánsági

Diary for My Loves **
Hungary 1987 130m bw
Artificial Eye/Mafilm/Hungarofilm/Magyar Film/Zespoly Filmowe
original title: *Napló Szerelmeimnek*
An eighteen-year-old Hungarian girl goes to Moscow to become a film-maker and to search for her father.
Absorbing sequel to Diary for my Children*, tracing the end of Stalinism.*
w Márta Mészáros, Éva Pataki *d* Márta Mészáros *ph* Nyika Jancsó *pd* Éva Martin *ed* Éva Kármentö
☆ Zsuzsa Czinkóczi, Anna Polony, Jan Nowicki, Irina Kouberskaya, László Szabó, Pál Zolnay, Adél Kováts, Erzsébet Kútvölgyi

A Diary for Timothy ***
GB 1945 40m bw
Basil Wright/Crown Film Unit
A baby is born as the war ends, and the narrator ponders its future.
Brilliant sentimental documentary, a summing up of the aims and feelings of Britain at the time.
w E. M. Forster *d* Humphrey Jennings *narrator* Michael Redgrave

Diary of a Bride: see *I, Jane Doe*

The Diary of a Chambermaid *
US 1946 86m bw
Benedict Bogeaus (Burgess Meredith, Paulette Goddard)
A 19th-century serving girl causes sexual frustration and other troubles in two households.
Hollywood notables were all at sea in this wholly artificial and unpersuasive adaptation of a minor classic.
w Burgess Meredith *novel* Octave Mirbeau *d* *Jean Renoir* *ph* Lucien Andriot *m* Michel Michelet *pd* Eugene Lourié
☆ Paulette Goddard, Burgess Meredith, Hurd Hatfield, Francis Lederer, Judith Anderson, Florence Bates, Irene Ryan, Reginald Owen, Almira Sessions
'I do not mean to disparage Renoir's direction of the piece; erratic and with a curious element of flippancy and even vulgarity at the start, it advances with the melodramatic development of the plot to a fine climax of excitement, movement, terror. But the theme is incurably novelettish.' – *Dilys Powell*

The Diary of a Chambermaid *
France/Italy 1964 98m bw Franscope
Speva/Ciné Alliance/Filmsonor/Dear (Serge Silberman, Michel Sabra)
original title: *Le Journal d'une Femme de Chambre*
A new maid disrupts the lives of a middle-class family.
Interesting but not especially successful Buñuel version: the subject is certainly up his street, but the novel seems to restrict him and the visual quality is unattractive.
w Luis Buñuel, Jean-Claude Carrière *d* Luis Buñuel *ph* Roger Fellous *m* none
☆ Jeanne Moreau, Georges Géret, Michel Piccoli, Françoise Lugagne
'The film remains notable but inconclusive: a half-Buñuel.' – *Dilys Powell*

Diary of a Cloistered Nun: see *Story of a Cloistered Nun*

The Diary of a Country Priest ***
France 1950 120m bw
Union Générale Cinématographique (Léon Carré)
original title: *Journal d'un Curé de Campagne*
A lonely young priest fails to make much impression in his first parish; and, falling ill, he dies alone.
Striking, depressing, slow and austere, with little dialogue but considerable visual beauty; a very typical work of its director.
wd *Robert Bresson* *novel* Georges Bernanos *ph* L. Burel *m* Jean-Jacques Grunenwald
☆ *Claude Laydu*, Jean Riveyre, Armand Guibert, Nicole Ladmiral

'Nothing personal, purely business.'
Diary of a Hitman
US 1992 91m Technicolor
Vision International/Continental (Amin Q. Chaudhri)
A hired killer begins to have doubts when a husband pays him to murder his wife and baby.
A wordy, claustrophobic thriller that betrays its stage origins and strains credulity.
w Kenneth Pressman *play* *Insider's Price* by Kenneth Pressman *d* Roy London *ph* Yuri Sokol *m* Michel Colombier *pd* Stephen Hendrickson *ed* Brian Smedley-Aston
☆ Forest Whitaker, John Bedford-Lloyd, James Belushi, Seymour Cassel, Lois Chiles, Lewis Smith, Sharon Stone, Sherilyn Fenn

Diary of a Lost Girl **
Germany 1929 110m approx bw silent
G. W. Pabst Film

original title: *Tagebuch einer Verlorenen*
A rich man's daughter is seduced, has an illegitimate child, is placed in a house of correction and finds herself later in a brothel.
Heavily Germanic Road to Ruin, superbly mounted in best cinematic style, with several memorable sequences. Heavily mutilated by censors; according to the screenwriter the film ends just after the middle of his script.
w Rudolf Leonhardt *novel* Margaret Böhme *d* G. W. Pabst *ph* Sepp Allgeier
☆ *Louise Brooks*, Fritz Rasp, Josef Ravensky
† A previous version had been made in 1918, written and directed by Richard Oswald.

Diary of a Mad Housewife **
US 1970 95m Technicolor
Universal/Frank Perry

The bored and repressed wife of a lawyer tries an affair, walks out on her husband, and opts for group therapy.
An agreeably mordant view of the contemporary American scene, with good dialogue and performances, but the little bits of satire do not really add up to a satisfactory film.
w *Eleanor Perry* *novel* Sue Kaufman *d* *Frank Perry* *ph* Gerald Hirschfeld
☆ *Carrie Snodgress*, *Richard Benjamin*, Frank Langella, Lorraine Cullen, Frannie Michel
'A prototypical contemporary American artifact … all its assorted talents and technological smartness are turned to the varnishing of mediocrity.' – *Stanley Kauffmann*
Academy Award nomination: Carrie Snodgress

Diary of a Madman
US 1962 96m Technicolor
UA/Admiral (Robert E. Kent)

A murderer explains to a magistrate that he was possessed by an evil spirit.
Ponderous transcription of Maupassant stories with a few moments of horror.
w Robert E. Kent *d* Reginald Le Borg *ph* Ellis W. Carter *m* Richard La Salle *ad* Daniel Haller
☆ Vincent Price, Nancy Kovack, Chris Warfield, Stephen Roberts

The Diary of a Married Woman
Germany 1953 83m bw
Magna
original title: *Tagebuch einer Verliebten*
A wife divorces her adulterous husband, but their small son brings them together again.
One long Hollywood cliché, assembled with some spirit; notable only as one of the rare post-war German films to get distribution in English-speaking countries.
w Emil Burri, Johann Mario Simmel *d* Josef von Baky *ph* Oskar Snirch *m* Alois Melichar
☆ Maria Schell, O. W. Fischer, Franco Andrei

Diary of a Shinjuku Thief *
Japan 1969 94m bw/Eastmancolor
Sozosha (Masayuki Nakajima)
original title: *Shinjuku Dorobo Nikki*
A minor theft in a bookstore brings a young man in contact with a mysterious girl who leads him into various sexual experiments.
Inexplicable but quite fascinating piece of oriental mystification in which sex equates to some extent with revolution.
w Tsutomu Tamura and others *d* Nagisa Oshima *ph* Yasuhiro Yamaguchi *m* none
☆ Tadanori Yokoo, Rie Yokoyama, Moichi Tanabe

The Diary of Anne Frank **
US 1959 170m bw Cinemascope
TCF/George Stevens

In 1942, a Jewish family hides from the Nazis in an Amsterdam attic; just before the war ends, they are betrayed and sent to concentration camps.
Based on the diaries of a girl who died at Bergen-Belsen, this solemn adaptation is elephantine in its length, its ponderousness and its use of Cinemascope when the atmosphere is supposed to be claustrophobic.
w Frances Goodrich, Albert Hackett from their play based on Anne Frank's diaries *d* George Stevens *ph* *William C. Mellor* *m* Alfred Newman *ad* Lyle R. Wheeler, George W. Davis
☆ Millie Perkins, *Joseph Schildkraut*, *Shelley Winters*, *Ed Wynn*, Richard Beymer, Gusti Huber, Lou Jacobi, Diane Baker
Academy Award: William C. Mellor; Shelley Winters; art direction
Academy Award nomination: best picture; George Stevens; Alfred Newman; Ed Wynn

The Diary of Lady M
Switzerland/Belgium/Spain/France 1993 112m colour
Filmograph/Nomad/Messidor/Lazennec (Alain Tanner, Jacques de Clercq, Dimitri de Clercq, Gerardo Herrero, Marta Esteban, Christophe Rossignon)

original title: *Le Journal de Lady M*
A Parisian singer begins a passionate affair with a Spanish painter and, discovering that he is married, invites his wife and family to join them.
Supposedly based on the star's diaries, this is a throwback to the sad sex films of the 60s, a drearily egocentric, uninteresting drama.
w Myriam Mézières *d* Alain Tanner *ph* Denis Jutzeler *m* Arie Dzierlatka *ad* Jordi Canora, Alain Chennaux *ed* Monica Goux
☆ Myriam Mézières, Juanjo Puligcorbé, Félicité Wouassi, Antoine Basler, Makeda, Marie Peyrucq-Yamou, Gladys Gambie
'A preposterously clichéd, would-be (but not-at-all) titillating film that charts the sad decline of Alain Tanner … I started noting down the worst lines but soon gave up; I was transcribing the script.' – *Sheila Johnston, Independent*
'Pic's extremely frank sex scenes have a shocking realism and seem a natural outgrowth of Mézières' honesty in recounting her feelings. A scene in which Lady M shaves her pubic hair and dances for her lover clothed only in a long, dangling earring must set some kind of art-film precedent.' – *Variety*

The Diary of Major Thompson
France 1955 83m bw
SNE Gaumont/Paul Wagner
original title: *Les Carnets de Major Thompson*
US title: *The French They Are a Funny Race*
An Englishman married to a Frenchwoman keeps notes on the French way of life.
Tatty filming of a mildly amusing book; it falls away into a number of badly-timed and presented gags, and one can't believe that its creator was once the top comedy genius of Hollywood.
wd Preston Sturges *ph* Maurice Barry, Christian Matras *m* Georges Van Parys
☆ Jack Buchanan, Martine Carol, Noel-Noel, Genevieve Brunet
'Even allowing for the appalling editing and the frequently incomprehensible dubbed soundtrack, there is little evidence to suggest that this film could ever have been anything but a shambles.' – *Peter John Dyer, MFB*

Il Diavolo e il Morto: see *Lisa and The Devil*

Dice Rules
US 1991 83m Foto-Kem
Seven Arts/Fleebin Dabble (Fred Silverstein)

A 20-minute short on the emergence of the comedian is followed by footage of a concert performance in Madison Square Gardens.
Like strychnine, an acquired and less than enjoyable taste.
w Lenny Shulman, Andrew Dice Clay *d* Jay Dubin *ph* Michael Negrin *ed* Mitchell Sinoway
☆ Andrew Dice Clay, Eddie Griffin, Sylvia Harman, Lee Lawrence, Noodles Levenstein, Maria Parkinson
'A pretty accurate snapshot of the comedian's standup act – crude, sexist, racist, homophobic and designed to shock.' – *Variety*

'A humorous look at man's greatest asset … and liability.'
Dick *
US 1990 13m bw
Island (Jo Menell)

Documentary in which photographs of multifarious flaccid male organs are flashed on screen to the accompaniment of women's voices answering such questions as 'Would you want one?'
Amusing novelty, although one that was denied a television showing in Britain.
d Jo Menell, B. Moel *ph* Paul Latoures *m* John Cale
'Menell's liberating, wholly unprurient film should put an end to Freud's theory of penis envy.' – *Philip French, Observer*

'He was tricky. They were better.'
Dick *
US 1999 95m Technicolor
Columbia/Phoenix/Pacific Western (Gale Anne Hurd)

Two vapid teenage girls became inadvertently involved in exposing President Richard Nixon's cover-up of the break-in at the Watergate building in Washington.
Genial, fitfully amusing comedy of innocent bunglers helping to change the course of history; there are some good jokes at the expense of politicians and journalists.
w Andrew Fleming, Sheryl Longin *d* Andrew Fleming *ph* Alexander Gruszynski *m* John Debney *pd* Barbara Dunphy *ed* Mia Goldman *cos* Deborah Everton
☆ Kirsten Dunst (Betsy Jobs), Michelle Williams (Arlene Lorenzo), Dan Hedaya (Dick), Jim Breuer (John Dean), Will Ferrell (Bob Woodward), Dave Foley (Bob Haldeman), Teri Garr (Helen Lorenzo), Ana Gasteyer (Rose Mary Woods), Bruce McCulloch (Carl Bernstein), Ted McGinley (Roderick), Ryan Reynolds (Chip), Saul Rubinek (Henry Kissinger), Harry Shearer (G. Gordon Liddy), G.D. Spradlin (Ben Bradlee)
'This audaciously imaginative political comedy will have Watergate buffs in particular and baby boomers in general laughing loud and long.' – *Todd McCarthy, Variety*

Dick Barton
The radio detective was created by Edward J. Mason in the mid-forties, and three rough-and-ready film versions were subsequently made by Hammer/Exclusive. They were *Dick Barton Special Agent* (1948); *Dick Barton Strikes Back* (1949); and *Dick Barton at Bay* (1950); all with Don Stannard. *Critical comment would be irrelevant.*

Dick Tracy
US 1945 61m bw
RKO (Herman Schlom)

GB title: *Splitface*
The jut-jawed detective routs a disfigured criminal named Splitface.
Vigorous second feature from the comic strip.
w Eric Taylor *comic strip* Chester Gould *d* William Berke *ph* Frank Redman *m* Roy Webb
☆ Morgan Conway, Jane Greer, Mike Mazurki, Anne Jeffreys, Lyle Latell, Joseph Crehan, Trevor Bardette
† Sequels: *Dick Tracy vs Cueball* (1946) with Morgan Conway, *d John Rawlins*; *Dick Tracy Meets Gruesome* (1947) with Ralph Byrd, Boris Karloff, *d John Rawlins*; *Dick Tracy's Dilemma* (1947), with Ralph Byrd, *d John Rawlins*.
†† There had been several Republic serials featuring Tracy, and in the fifties a cartoon series appeared.

Dick Tracy *
US 1990 103m Technicolor
Touchstone/Silver Screen Partners IV (Warren Beatty)

Detective Dick Tracy tangles with a master criminal.
A limp narrative is bolstered by a lavish and stylized production design, using comic-book primary colours, and by the careful re-creation of the bizarre appearance of the gangsters from the original newspaper strip-cartoon.
w Jim Cash, Jack Epps Jnr *comic strip* Chester Gould *d* Warren Beatty *ph* Vittorio Storaro *m* Danny Elfman *m/ly* Stephen Sondheim *pd* Richard Sylbert *ad* Harold Michelson *ed* Richard Marks *sp* character make-up by John Caglione Jnr, Doug Drexler
☆ Warren Beatty, Charlie Korsmo, Glenne Headly, Madonna, Al Pacino, Dustin Hoffman, William Forsythe, Charles Durning, Mandy Patinkin, Paul Sorvino, R. G. Armstrong, Dick Van Dyke
'This is no ready-to-wear movie; it's the work of a cinematic couturier. Take it for what it is: a simple gift, consummately wrapped.' – *David Ansen, Newsweek*
'A charming and beautifully designed work of American popular art.' – *David Denby, New York Magazine*
'A grand exercise in cinema imagination and wit for their own sake.' – *Vincent Canby, New York Times*
'A major disappointment.' – *Variety*
Academy Award: best art direction; best song 'Sooner or Later'; best make-up
Academy Award nomination: Al Pacino; Vittorio Storaro; best costume design; best sound
BAFTA: Richard Sylbert

Dick Tracy Meets Gruesome
US 1947 65m bw
RKO (Herman Schlom)

Tracy tracks down a criminal who robs a bank with the aid of a paralysing gas.
Effective little thriller, once you accept the implausibilities of the plot.
w Robertson White, Eric Taylor *story* William H. Graffis, Robert E. Kent *cartoon strip* Chester Gould *d* John Rawlins *ph* Frank Redman *m* Paul Sawtell *md* C. Bakaleinikoff *ad* Albert S. D'Agostino, Walter E. Keller *ed* Elmo Williams
☆ Boris Karloff, Ralph Byrd, Anne Gwynne, Edward Ashley, June Clayworth, Lyle Latell, Skelton Knaggs, Lex Barker
'Employs almost serial-type action … with surprisingly good results.' – *Variety*
† The script's in-joke: one cop says of Gruesome, the character played by Karloff, 'He's weird. I tell you that if I didn't know better I swear we were doing business with Boris Karloff.'

Dick Tracy vs Cueball
US 1946 62m bw
RKO (Herman Schlom)

Dick Tracy solves the murder of a diamond dealer by a bald-headed crook.
Occasionally entertaining 'B' feature with a few colourful characters to compensate for Conway's blandness, though Tracy's detective skills seem limited to tailing suspects and arriving at the scene a few minutes after a crime has been committed.
w Dane Lussier, Robert E. Kent *story* Luci Ward *cartoon strip* Chester Gould *d* Gordon M. Douglas *ph* George E. Diskant *m* Phil Ohman *md* C. Bakaleinikoff *ad* Albert S. D'Agostino, Lucius O. Croxton *ed* Philip Martin Jnr
☆ Morgan Conway, Anne Jeffreys, Lyle Latell, Rita Corday, Ian Keith, Dick Wessel

Dick Tracy's Dilemma
US 1947 60m bw
RKO (Herman Schlom)

Dick Tracy investigates a murder at a fur warehouse and uncovers an insurance scam.
Enjoyable little thriller, with quirkier characters than are usually found in such low-budget excursions.
w Robert Stephen Brode *cartoon strip* Chester Gould *d* John Rawlins *ph* Frank Redman *m* Paul Sawtell *md* C. Bakaleinikoff *ad* Albert S. D'Agostino, Lucius O. Croxton *ed* Marvin Coil
☆ Ralph Byrd, Lyle Latell, Kay Christopher, Jack Lambert, Ian Keith, Bernadene Hayes, Jimmy Conlin, William B. Davidson, Tony Barrett, Richard Powers

Dick Turpin
GB 1933 79m bw
Stoll-Stafford (Clyde Cook)
Highwayman Dick Turpin rides to York is to prevent an enforced marriage.
Mild British costume piece which sent its star to Hollywood.
w Victor Kendall *novel* *Rookwood* by Harrison Ainsworth *d* Victor Hanbury, John Stafford *ph* Desmond Dickinson *ad* Wilfred Arnold
☆ Victor McLaglen, Jane Carr, Frank Vosper, James Finlayson, Gillian Lind

Dick Turpin's Ride: see *The Lady and the Bandit*

Did You Hear the One about the Traveling Saleslady?
US 1967 96m Techniscope
Universal (Si Rose)
In a Kansas town in 1910 an eccentric saleslady offers pianolas which tend to go berserk.
Cornbelt comedy vehicle for an unappealing star.

w John Fenton Murray *d* Don Weis *ph* Bud Thackery *m* Vic Mizzy
☆ Phyllis Diller, Bob Denver, Joe Flynn, Jeanette Nolan

Die Another Day *

GB/US 2002 133m colour Panavision
TCF/OdysseyApollo/Media/F&ME (Sam Taylor, Mike Downey, Frank Huebner)

Disgraced after being imprisoned by the North Koreans, James Bond determines to clear his name and discover who betrayed him.
Bond's adventures have grown more risible with the years and this, which has him driving around an ice-palace in an invisible car, is more ridiculous than any that have gone before; Brosnan carries it off with suave charm, with some sex appeal added by Halle Berry.
w Neal Purvis, Robert Wade *d* Lee Tamahori *ph* David Tattersall *m* David Arnold *pd* Peter Lamont *ed* Christian Wagner *cos* Lindy Hemming
☆ Pierce Brosnan (James Bond), Halle Berry (Jinx), Toby Stephens (Gustav Graves), Rosamund Pike (Miranda Frost), Rick Yune (Zao), Judi Dench (M), John Cleese (Q), Michael Madsen (Falco), Samantha Bond (Moneypenny)

'As strong on action as it is weak on the interpersonal stuff. If Bond can get a new car for each episode, how about some new pickup lines?' – *Jami Bernard, New York Daily News*

'Flat, distressingly witless – To put it bluntly – the thrill is gone. Nobody did it better. But that was then.' – *David Ansen, Newsweek*

† The film took $161m at the US box-office, and $57m in the United Kingdom.

Die! Die! My Darling: see *Fanatic*

'40 Stories Of Sheer Adventure!'

Die Hard **

US 1988 132m DeLuxe Panavision
Fox/Gordon Company/Silver Pictures (Lawrence Gordon, Joel Silver)

A cop battles with terrorists who have taken over the skyscraper where his wife is among the hostages.
Powerful, suspenseful action movie, with splendid special effects, although it goes on rather too long.
w Jeb Stuart, Steven E. de Souza *novel* *Nothing Lasts Forever* by Roderick Thorp *d* John McTiernan *ph* Jan de Bont *m* Michael Kamen *pd* Jackson DeGovia *ed* Frank J. Urioste, John F. Link
☆ Bruce Willis, Bonnie Bedelia, Reginald VelJohnson, Paul Gleason, De'Voreaux White, William Atherton, Hart Bochner, James Shigeta, Alan Rickman, Alexander Godunov

Die Hard 2 *

US 1990 124m DeLuxe Panavision
Fox/Gordon Co./Silver Pictures (Lawrence Gordon, Joel Silver, Charles Gordon)

A cop, going to meet his wife at an airport, discovers that terrorists have taken it over.
Frenetically unsubtle, and very bloody, action movie.
w Steven E. de Souza, Doug Richardson *novel* *58 Minutes* by Walter Wager *d* Renny Harlin *ph* Oliver Wood *m* Michael Kamen *pd* John Vallone *ad* Christiaan Wagener *ed* Stuart Baird, Robert A. Ferretti
☆ Bruce Willis, Bonnie Bedelia, William Atherton, Reginald VelJohnson, Franco Nero, William Sadler, John Amos, Dennis Franz, Art Evans, Fred Dalton Thompson
† The film was advertised with the title *Die Hard 2: Die Harder*.

'It's Boomtime In The Big Apple.'

Die Hard with a Vengeance

US 1995 128m Technicolor Panavision
Buena Vista/Cinergi (Michael Tadross, John McTiernan)

A mad bomber plays explosive games with a New York detective and his black aide.
A sequel that abandons the formula of a lone cop battling against overwhelming odds in an isolated situation, substituting something closer to the Lethal Weapon *films, with an edgy, racially tinged relationship at its centre, a convoluted, confusing, schematic narrative, and lots of big bangs.*
w Jonathan Hensleigh *d* John McTiernan *ph* Peter Menzies *m* Michael Kamen *pd* Jackson DeGovia *ed* John Wright
☆ Bruce Willis, Jeremy Irons, Samuel L. Jackson, Graham Greene, Colleen Camp, Larry Bryggman, Sam Phillips

'After a frenetic, razzley-dazzley first half hour, the film quickly fizzles into formula ... with a vengeance.' – *Andy Webster, Premiere*

† The film took more than $353m at the box-office worldwide.

Die Laughing

US 1980 108m Technicolor
Orion/Warner (Jon Peters)

After the murder of a nuclear scientist, a young musician who knows too much is chased by the murderers and the FBI.
Witless black comedy rehash of The 39 Steps.
w Jerry Segal, Robby Benson, Scott Parker *d* Jeff Werner *ph* David Myers *m* Craig Safan *pd* James H. Spencer *ed* Neil Travis
☆ Robby Benson, Linda Grovenor, Charles Durning, Elsa Lanchester, Bud Cort

Dieu A Besoin des Hommes *

France 1950 100m bw
Transcontinental (Paul Graetz)
aka: *Isle of Sinners*
aka: *God Needs Men*

The priest of a Breton island leaves in horror at the sinfulness of his flock, and the fisherfolk appoint one of their number as priest.
Cold, gloomy, rather pointless fable, often a pleasure to look at.
w Jean Aurenche, Pierre Bost *novel* *Un Recteur de l'Ile de Sein* by H. Queffiec *d* Jean Delannoy *ph* *Robert Le Fèbvre* *m* René Cloërc
☆ Pierre Fresnay, Madeleine Robinson, Daniel Gélin, Andrée Clément, Sylvie, Jean Brochard

Diexue Shuang Xiong: see *The Killer*

'He's not half the man she used to be.'

Different for Girls *

GB 1996 97m colour
NTFC/X Pictures/BBC (John Chapman)

A motorcycle courier falls in love with a schoolboy friend who has changed sex.
A heady and gritty mix of transsexual romance, police corruption and social comment, it at least ventures into new territory.
w Tony Marchant *d* Richard Spence *ph* Sean Van Hales *m* Stephen Warbeck *pd* Grenville Horner *ed* David Gamble
☆ Rupert Graves, Steven MacKintosh, Saskia Reeves, Neil Dudgeon, Charlotte Coleman, Miriam Margolyes, Ian Dury

'One of the best British films of the decade.' – *Andy Medhurst, Sight and Sound*

'Would be infinitely more likeable if it wasn't for some irritatingly unreal plot development.' – *Rob Driscoll, Empire*

A Different Story

US 1978 106m CFI color
Avco/Alan Belkin

A homosexual falls in love with a lesbian.
One supposes it had to come, but one doesn't really have to watch it.
w Henry Olek *d* Paul Aaron *ph* Philip Lathrop *m* David Frank
☆ Perry King, Meg Foster, Valerie Curtin, Peter Donat

'There's something in *A Different Story* to turn off audiences of every sexual persuasion – and movie lovers most of all.' – *Richard Schickel, Time*

La Diga sul Pacifico: see *This Angry Age*

Digby: the Biggest Dog in the World

GB 1973 88m Technicolor
TCF/Walter Shenson

An old English sheepdog accidentally eats a chemical intended to increase the size of vegetables...
Nice to see this kind of gimmick used for comedy instead of horror, but the result is rather tame and old-fashioned, though for several years it made a pleasant television offering for Christmas.
w Michael Pertwee *story* Charles Isaacs *book* *Hazel* by Ted Key *d* Joe McGrath *ph* Harry Waxman *m* Edwin T. Astley *ad* Maurice Fowler *ed* Jim Connock *sp* Tom Howard
☆ Jim Dale (Jeff Eldon), Spike Milligan (Dr Harz), Angela Douglas (Janine), Milo O'Shea (Dr Jameson), Dinsdale Landen (Col Masters), Garfield Morgan (Rogerson), Victor Spinetti (Professor Ribart), Bob Todd (The Great Manzini), John Bluthal (Jerry), Norman Rossington (Tom), Richard Beaumont (Billy White), Harry Towb (Ringmaster), Kenneth J. Warren (General Frank), Victor Maddern (Dogs' Home Manager)

Digging to China

US 1998 98m colour
Moonstone/David/Ministry of Film (Alan Mruvka, Marilyn Vance, John Davis, J. Todd Harris)

In the 60s, a mentally retarded man forms a friendship with an unhappy young girl whose mother runs a rural motel.
Soft-centred character study that skims the surface of things.
w Karen Janszen *d* Timothy Hutton *ph* Jorgen Persson *m* Cynthia Miller *pd* Robert de Vico *ed* Dana Congdon, Alain Jakubowicz
☆ Kevin Bacon, Mary Stuart Masterson, Cathy Moriarty, Evan Rachel Wood, Marian Seldes

'Will ultimately move only those inclined to cry on cue.' – *Variety*

Diggstown *

US 1992 98m DeLuxe
UIP/MGM/Electric (Robert Schaffel)
GB title: *Midnight Sting*

Two con men journey to a town noted for unofficial prize fights and take a $1 million bet that their boxer can beat 10 local fighters in a period of 24 hours.
Enjoyable enough caper, though it risks monotony with its repeated fights; it flopped at the box-office.
w Steven McKay *novel* *The Diggstown Ringers* by Leonard Wise *d* Michael Ritchie *ph* Gerry Fisher *m* James Newton Howard *pd* Steve Hendrickson *ed* Don Zimmerman
☆ James Woods, Louis Gossett Jnr, Bruce Dern, Oliver Platt, Heather Graham, Randall 'Tex' Cobb, Thomas Wilson Brown, Duane Davis, Willie Green

'This crowd-pleaser mixes it up with boxing, revenge and salty one-liners that should satisfy audiences.' – *Variety*

Digimon: The Movie

Japan 2000 88m DeLuxe
TCF/Saban/Toei Animation (Terry-Lei O'Malley, Hiromi Seki)

Children become keepers of digital monsters who exist within computers.
A movie cobbled together from three Japanese shorts, which accounts for a disjointed narrative, though all suffer from lurid, rudimentary animation.
w Reiko Yoshida *English adaptation* Jeff Nimoy, Bob Buchholz *d* Mamoru Hosoda, Shigeyasu Yamauchi *ph* Shigeru Ando *m* Udi Harpaz, Amotz Plessner *ed* Douglas Purgason, Gary A. Friedman
☆ voices of: Lara Jill Miller, Joshua Seth, Colleen O'Shaughnessy, Philece Sampler, Bob Glouberman, Mona Marshall, Michael Lindsay

'These imports sound like adverts rather than children's entertainment.' – *Rupert Laight, Film Review*

Dilemma

GB 1962 90m bw
Bryanston/ACT (Ted Lloyd)

On returning home from school, a teacher finds his wife missing and a dying man in his bathroom.
An interesting concept, of a man being continually interrupted as he tries to get rid of a corpse, that is given lacklustre treatment; it might have worked better as a black comedy.
wd Peter Maxwell *story* Pip and Janet Baker *ph* Gerald Moss *ad* Wilfred Arnold *ed* Tom Simpson
☆ Peter Halliday, Ingrid Hafner, Patricia Burke, Joan Heath, Patrick Jordan, Barbara Lott, William Sherwood

'His Story Is Written In Bullets, Blood And Blondes!'

Dillinger *

US 1945 70m bw
Monogram (Frank and Maurice King)

The life of American public enemy number one who was shot by the police in 1934.
Slick, speedy gangster thriller, possibly the most tolerable movie to come from this low-budget studio.
w Philip Yordan *d* *Max Nosseck* *ph* Jackson Rose *m* Dimitri Tiomkin
☆ *Lawrence Tierney, Edmund Lowe*, Anne Jeffreys
Philip Yordan

Dillinger *

US 1973 107m Movielab
AIP (Buzz Feitshans)

Violence-soaked version, with black comedy touches, of the last year of Dillinger's life.
Not badly done, with a style reminiscent of Bonnie and Clyde.
wd *John Milius* *ph* Jules Brenner *m* Barry Devorzon *ad* Trevor Williams *ed* Fred R. Feitshans Jnr
☆ Warren Oates (John Dillinger), Ben Johnson (Melvin Purvis), Michelle Phillips, Cloris Leachman, Harry Dean Stanton, Richard Dreyfuss

Dim Sum: a Little Bit of Heart *

US 1985 89m colour
CIM (Tom Sternberg, Wayne Wang, Danny Yung)

Convinced that she will soon die, a Chinese widow living in San Francisco tries to persuade her daughter to marry.
Domestic drama full of a gentle, rambling charm.
w Terrel Seltzer *d* Wayne Wang *ph* Michael Chin *m* Todd Boekelheide *ad* Danny Yung *ed* Ralph Wikke
☆ Lauren Chew, Kim Chew, Victor Wong, Ida F. O. Chung, Cora Miao, John Nishio

Un Dimanche à la Campagne: see *Sunday in the Country*

Dimension 5

US 1966 88m colour
United Pictures Corporation

CIA agents use a time converter to jump ahead three weeks and prevent the Chinese from bombing Los Angeles.
Silly spy fantasy with inadequate effects.
w Arthur C. Pierce *d* Franklin Adreon
☆ Jeffrey Hunter, France Nuyen, Harold Sakata, Donald Woods

Dimples **

US 1936 82m bw
TCF (Darryl F. Zanuck, Nunnally Johnson)

In the New York Bowery in pre-Civil War days, a child and her reprobate grandfather win the hearts of high society.
Excellent Temple vehicle with good period flavour.
w Arthur Sheekman, Nat Perrin *d* William A. Seiter *ph* Bert Glennon *m* Louis Silvers *m/ly* Jimmy McHugh, Ted Koehler
☆ *Shirley Temple, Frank Morgan, Helen Westley*, Berton Churchill, Robert Kent, Delma Byron, Astrid Allwyn

'What they wanted most wasn't on the menu'

Diner **

US 1982 110m Technicolor
MGM/SLM (Jerry Weintraub)

In 1959 Baltimore, college students congregate at their old meeting place and find themselves more occupied by adult problems than of yore.
Generally amusing group character study, an awkward attempt to divine the meaning of life through the accumulation of detail. A little masterpiece of observation, for those with ears to hear; but not necessarily a great film.
wd *Barry Levinson* *ph* Peter Sova *m* Bruce Brody, Ivan Kral *pd* Leon Harris *ed* Stu Linder
☆ Steve Guttenberg, Daniel Stern, Mickey Rourke, Kevin Bacon, Timothy Daly, Ellen Barkin, Paul Reiser, Kathryn Dowling, Michael Tucker, Jessica James

'A terrific movie – a gentle, lyrical, magically funny portrait of the games young men play to keep from growing up, and of the oddly childish society that encourages them.' – *Stephen Schiff* original screenplay

Le Diner de Cons **
France 1998 80m colour Technovision
Pathé/Gaumont/Efve/TFI (Alain Poiré)
aka: *The Dinner Game*
A publisher attends a weekly dinner to which he and his friends invite the most boring people they encounter; but he becomes incapacitated and is trapped in his flat with a man who makes models of buildings out of matchsticks.
Enjoyable, expertly constructed, cruel farce of misunderstandings in which a sophisticated man's life is unravelled by a well-meaning fool.
wd Francis Veber *play* Francis Veber *ph* Luciano Tovoli *m* Vladimir Cosma *ad* Hugues Tissandier *ed* Georges Klotz
☆ *Jacques Villeret* (François Pignon), Thierry Lhermitte (Pierre Brochant), Francis Huster (Leblanc), Alexandra Vandernoot (Christine), Daniel Prévost (Cheval), Catherine Frot (Marlène), Edgar Givry (Cordier), Christian Pereira (Sorbier)
'Veber delivers a marvellously wrought plot at exactly the length it can sustain, and manages consistently to pull out situations that provoke laughter and astonishment.' – *Kim Newman, Empire*

Dingaka
South Africa 1965 97m Technicolor Cinemascope
Embassy (Jamie Uys)
Tribal antagonisms cause a simple native to seek revenge in the city.
Unconvincing and now very dated melodrama with rather too much local colour.
wd Jamie Uys *ph* Manie Botha *m* Bertha Egnos, Eddie Domingo, Basil Gray
☆ Ken Gampu, Stanley Baker, Juliet Prowse, Siegfried Mynhardt, Paul Makgoba

Dinner at Eight ***
US 1933 113m bw
MGM (David O. Selznick)
Guests at a society dinner party all find themselves in dramatic circumstances.
Artificial but compelling pattern play from a Broadway success.
w Frances Marion, Herman J. Mankiewicz *play* George S. Kaufman, Edna Ferber *d George Cukor* *ph* William Daniels *m* William Axt
☆ *Marie Dressler*, John Barrymore, Lionel Barrymore, Billie Burke, Wallace Beery, *Jean Harlow*, Lee Tracy, Edmund Lowe, Madge Evans, Jean Hersholt, Karen Morley, Louise Closser Hale, Phillips Holmes, May Robson, Grant Mitchell and also Elizabeth Patterson
KITTY (JEAN HARLOW): 'You know, I read a book the other day. It's all about civilization or something – a nutty kind of a book. Do you know that the guy said machinery is going to take the place of every profession?'
CARLOTTA (MARIE DRESSLER): 'Oh, my dear. That's something you need never worry about!'
'Marquee speaks for itself. It spells money, and couldn't very well be otherwise.' – *Variety*

Dinner at the Ritz
GB 1937 77m bw
New World (Robert T. Kane)
A French girl exposes swindlers who faked her father's suicide.
Once-diverting comedy melodrama with an international cast.
w Roland Pertwee, Romney Brent *d* Harold Schuster *ph* Philip Tannura *m* Lee Sims *ad* Frank Wells *ed* James B. Clark
☆ Annabella, Paul Lukas, David Niven, Romney Brent, Stewart Rome, Francis L. Sullivan, Nora Swinburne, Frederick Leister
'Slow and shoddily made British product.' – *Variety*
'It moves with old world decorum and occasional touches of gout.' – *New York Times*

'Revenge is a dish best served cold.'
Dinner Rush **
US 2000 98m Technicolor
Pathé/Giraldi Suarez Digiaimo/Dinner Rush (Lou DiGiaimo, Patti Greaney)
On the night an influential food critic comes to dine, a restaurant manager is faced by gangsters who want to take over the place, a rebellious chef and a awkward waitress.
Enjoyable movie which uses food as an indicator of changing tastes and moral values, though everyone here gets their just desserts.
w Brian Kalata, Rick Shaughnessy *d* Bob Giraldi *ph* Tim Ives *m* Alexander Lasarenko *pd* Andrew Bernard *ed* Allyson C. Johnson
☆ Danny Aiello (Louis Cropa), Edoardo Ballerini (Udo), Vivian Wu (Nicole), Michael McGlone (Carmen), Kirk Acevedo (Duncan), Sandra Bernhard (Jennifer Freely), John Corbett (Ken), Jamie Harris (Sean), Summer Phoenix (Marti), Polly Draper (Natalie), Mark Margolis (Fitzgerald)
'A mouth-watering display of talent, technique and patience.' – *Elvis Mitchell, New York Times*

Dino
US 1957 93m bw
AA/Bernice Block
A juvenile delinquent released from prison has trouble reforming.
Adequately made social drama with good credentials.
w Reginald Rose *play* Reginald Rose *d* Thomas Carr *ph* Wilfrid M. Cline *m* Gerald Fried *ad* David Milton *ed* William Austin
☆ Sal Mineo (Dino), Brian Keith (Sheridan), Susan Kohner (Shirley), Frank Faylen (Mandel), Joe DeSantis (Mr Minetta), Penny Santon (Mrs Minetta)

Dinosaur *
US 2000 82m Technicolor
Buena Vista/Walt Disney (Pam Marsden)
An orphaned iguanadon is adopted by lemurs and helps save other dinosaurs after a meteorite destroys their habitat.
Superb and often breath-taking hyper-realistic computer animation is thrown away on an unexciting, over-familiar narrative told in crass dialogue.
w John Harrison, Robert Nelson Jacobs *screenplay* Walon Green *d* Ralph Zondag, Eric Leighton *ph* Steven Douglas Smith, Dave Hardberger *m* James Newton Howard *pd* Walter P. Martishius *ed* H. Lee Peterson
☆ voices of: D.B. Sweeney (Aladar), Alfre Woodard (Plio), Ossie Davis (Zini), Hayden Panettiere (Suri), Samuel E. Wright (Kron), Julianna Margulies (Neera), Peter Siragusa (Bruton), Joan Plowright (Baylene), Della Reese (Eema)
'Beneath its talk of high tech triumphs, this is just a mediocre dinosaur cartoon that took four years to make–and five minutes to forget.' – *Cosmo Landesman, Sunday Times*
† The film cost $127m to make, and took $318m at the box office worldwide.

Dinosaurus!
US 1960 85m DeLuxe Cinemascope
Jack H. Harris, Irvin S. Yeaworth Jnr
Workers on a tropical island bring up from the seabed a frozen Neanderthal man and two dinosaurs, who promptly thaw out.
Risible monster movie with effects that are more comic than horrific.
w Dan E. Weisburd, Jean Yeaworth *d* Irvin S. Yeaworth Jnr *ph* Stanley Cortez *m* Ronald Stein *ad* Jack Senter *ed* John A. Bushelman *sp* Tim Baar, Wah Chang, Gene Warren
☆ Ward Ramsey, Paul Lukather, Kristina Hanson, Alan Roberts, Gregg Martell

The Dion Brothers: see *The Gravy Train*

Diplomaniacs
US 1933 59m bw
RKO
Two halfwits are offered a fortune to go to Geneva and make the peace delegates stop fighting.
Fatuous comedy which never gets going.
w Joseph Mankiewicz, Henry Meyers *d* William Seiter *ph* Edward Cronjager *m* Max Steiner *ch* Larry Ceballos *ad* Van Nest Polglase, Al Herman *ed* William Hamilton
☆ Bert Wheeler, Robert Woolsey, Hugh Herbert, Marjorie White, Phyllis Barry, Louis Calhern
'A baddie; rhymed dialogue no help for inane plot.' – *Variety*

The Diplomatic Corpse
GB 1958 65m bw
Rank/ACT Films (Francis Searle)
A crime reporter, investigating the identity of a corpse found in the Thames, uncovers a drug-smuggling ring.
Programme filler of a thriller, involving a great deal of talk and not much action.
w Sidney Nelson, Maurice Harrison *d* Montgomery Tully *ph* Philip Grindrod *ad* Joseph Bato *ed* James Connock
☆ Robin Bailey, Susan Shaw, Liam Redmond, Harry Fowler, André Mikhelson, Bill Shine, Charles Farrell

Diplomatic Courier *
US 1952 98m bw
TCF (Casey Robinson)
American and Russian agents clash on a train between Salzburg and Trieste; an unexpected master spy is revealed after several chases.
Lively cold war intrigue, well produced and played with relish.
w Casey Robinson, Liam O'Brien *novel Sinister Errand* by Peter Cheyney *d* Henry Hathaway *ph* Lucien Ballard *m* Sol Kaplan *md* Lionel Newman
☆ Tyrone Power, Patricia Neal, Stephen McNally, Hildegarde Neff, Karl Malden, James Millican, Herbert Berghof
'A reversion to the oldest tradition of spy fiction.' – *Penelope Houston*

Dirigible *
US 1931 102m bw
Columbia
The story of an airship disaster.
Economical epic with a few Capra touches.
w Jo Swerling, Dorothy Howell *story* Frank 'Spig' Wead *d* Frank Capra *ph* Joe Wilbur, Elmer Dyer, Joseph Walker
☆ Jack Holt, Fay Wray, Ralph Graves, Hobart Bosworth, Roscoe Karns
'Plenty of everything expected in a flying film spectacle.' – *Variety*

The Dirt Bike Kid
US 1985 90m colour
Cinema/Concorde (Julie Corman)
A boy acquires a motor-bike with magical powers and defeats the plans of a wicked banker.
Trivial and predictable film, intended for a childish audience.
w Lewis Colick, David Brandes *d* Hoite C. Caston *ph* Daniel Lacambre *m* Bill Bowersock *ad* Betty Block *ed* Jeff Freeman
☆ Peter Billingsley (Jack Simmons), Stuart Pankin (Mr Hodgkins), Anne Bloom (Janet Simmons), Patrick Collins (Mike), Sage Parker (Miss Clavell), Chad Sheets (Bo), Daniel Breen (Flaherty)

'Have The Time Of Your Life.'
Dirty Dancing *
US 1987 97m colour
Vestron (Linda Gottlieb)
In 1963, kids go dance crazy at a borscht belt resort.
Mildly agreeable variant on Saturday Night Fever, *almost equally successful at the box-office.*
w Eleanor Bergstein *d* Emile Ardolino *ph* Jeff Jur *m* John Morris *pd* David Chapman *ed* Peter C. Frank
☆ Jennifer Grey, Patrick Swayze, Jerry Orbach, Cynthia Rhodes, Jack Weston
song 'I've Had the Time of My Life' (Franke Previte, John DeNicola, Donald Markowitz)

Dirty Dingus Magee
US 1970 91m Metrocolor Panavision
MGM (Burt Kennedy)
A likeable Western outlaw crosses swords with an old enemy.
Fair burlesque Western often stooping to vulgarity.
w Tom Waldman, Frank Waldman, Joseph Heller *novel* David Markson *d* Burt Kennedy *ph* Harry Stradling *m* Jeff Alexander
☆ Frank Sinatra, George Kennedy, Anne Jackson, Lois Nettleton, Jack Elam, John Dehner, Henry Jones, Harry Carey Jnr, Paul Fix
'Skittish burlesque, scripted in the brash and undisciplined style of a TV show ... heavily reliant on the *Carry On* brand of humour.' – *David McGillivray*

'Damn them or praise them – you'll never forget them!'
The Dirty Dozen **
US/Spain 1967 150m Metrocolor 70mm
MGM/Kenneth Hyman
In 1944, twelve convicts serving life sentences are recruited for a commando suicide mission.
Professional, commercial but unlikeable slice of wartime thick ear; pretensions about capital punishment are jettisoned early on in favour of frequent and violent bloodshed. Much imitated, e.g. by The Devil's Brigade, A Reason to Live, a Reason to Die, *etc.*
w Nunnally Johnson, Lukas Heller *novel* E. M. Nathanson *d Robert Aldrich* *ph* Edward Scaife *m* Frank de Vol
☆ Lee Marvin, Ernest Borgnine, Robert Ryan, Charles Bronson, Jim Brown, John Cassavetes, George Kennedy, Richard Jaeckel, Trini Lopez, Telly Savalas, Ralph Meeker, Clint Walker, Robert Webber, Donald Sutherland
John Cassavetes

Dirty Hands: see *Les Mains Sales*

'You don't assign him to murder cases – you just turn him loose!'
Dirty Harry ***
US 1971 103m Technicolor Panavision
Warner/Malpaso (Don Siegel)
A violently inclined San Francisco police inspector is the only cop who can bring to book a mad sniper. When the man is released through lack of evidence, he takes private revenge.
A savage cop show which became a cult and led to a spate of dirty cop movies, including four sequels, Magnum Force, The Enforcer, Sudden Impact *and* The Dead Pool *(qqv). Well done for those who can take it.*
w Harry Julian Fink, Rita M. Fink, Dean Riesner *d Don Siegel* *ph* Bruce Surtees *m* Lalo Schifrin *ad* Dale Hennesy *ed* Carl Pingitore
☆ *Clint Eastwood* (Harry Callahan), Harry Guardino (Lt Bressler), Reni Santoni (Chico), John Vernon (The Mayor), Andy Robinson (Killer), John Larch (Chief), John Mitchum (De Georgio), Mae Mercer (Mrs Russell)
HARRY CALLAHAN (CLINT EASTWOOD): 'I know what you're thinking, punk. You're thinking, "Did he fire six shots or only five?" Now, to tell you the truth I've forgotten myself in all this excitement. But being this is a .44 Magnum, the most powerful handgun in the world, and will blow your head clean off, you've gotta ask yourself a question, "Do I feel lucky?" Well, do ya, punk?'

Dirty Little Billy
US 1972 92m Eastmancolor
Columbia/WRG/Dragoti (Jack L. Warner)
The violent young life of Billy the Kid.
Squalid little Western with few attractive aspects except that it presents its hero as the mentally retarded delinquent which history says he was.
w Charles Moss, Stan Dragoti *d* Stan Dragoti *ph* Ralph Woolsey *m* Sascha Burland
☆ Michael J. Pollard, Lee Purcell, Richard Evans, Charles Aidman
'The gap between its ostensible aims and its manner of realizing them continually leaves the film bogged down in its own scrupulously realistic mud.' – *Tony Rayns*

Dirty Mary, Crazy Larry
US 1974 92m DeLuxe
Academy Pictures Corporation (Norman T. Herman)
Two racing drivers and a kooky groupie rob a supermarket and almost elude their police pursuers.
Elaborately stunted chase film, agreeable enough to watch if the characters were not so disagreeable.

w Leigh Chapman, Antonio Santean novel The Chase by Richard Unekis d John Hough ph Mike Margulies m Jimmie Haskell
☆ Peter Fonda, Susan George, Adam Roarke, Vic Morrow, Kenneth Tobey, Roddy McDowall, Eugene Daniels
'The film's general delight in destruction and despoliation makes one wonder if it is the cinema that reflects the ugliness of modern society or the ugliness of modern society that reflects trends in the cinema.' – *Michael Billington, Illustrated London News*

Dirty Money (dubbed) *
France/Italy 1972 98m Eastmancolor
Columbia-Warner/Corona/Oceania/Euro (Robert Dorfmann)
original title: *Un Flic*
While investigating a drug-running operation, a police inspector solves a robbery and discovers that his mistress is double-crossing him.
Glum investigation of betrayal in which atmosphere is all, but not enough to sustain interest.
wd Jean-Pierre Melville ph Walter Wottitz m Michel Colombier pd Théo Muerisse ed Patricia Renaut
☆ Alain Delon, Catherine Deneuve, Richard Crenna, Riccardo Cucciolla, Michael Conrad, André Pousse
'It is curiously fitting that Melville's last feature should reaffirm the genre's hardiest conventions in a context of disenchantment and failure; and happy that this final, equivocal embrace of the genre should be distinguished by the director's most adventurous experiments with form.' – *Tony Rayns, MFB*

Dirty Pretty Things **
GB 2002 94m Technicolor
Buena Vista/Miramax/BBC/Celador (Tracey Seaward, Robert Jones)
In a seedy London hotel, two illegal immigrants discover that the place is a front for criminal activities.
Engrossing movie that marries a dark thriller to some uncomfortable insights into the underside of London life.
w Steven Knight d Stephen Frears ph Chris Menges m Nathan Larson pd Hugo Luczyc-Wyhowski ed Mick Audsley
☆ Chiwetel Ejiofor (Okwe), Audrey Tautou (Senay), Sergi Lopez (Sneaky), Sophie Okonedo (Juliette), Benedict Wong (Guo Yi), Sotigui Kouyate (Shinti), Abi Gouhad (Shinti's son), Jean-Philippe Ecoffey (Jean Luc)
'An intelligent and extremely well-made romantic drama.' – *David Stratton, Variety*
'A gently entertaining crowd-pleaser.' – *Jonathan Romney, Independent*

Dirty Rotten Scoundrels
US 1988 110m DeLuxe
Rank/Orion (Bernard Williams)
Two con men compete in a contest of skills.
Heavy-handed remake of Ralph Levy's Bedtime Story*, made in 1964.*
w Dale Launer, Stanley Shapiro, Paul Henning d Frank Oz ph Michael Ballhaus m Miles Goodman pd Roy Walker ed Stephen A. Rotter, William Scharf
☆ Steve Martin, Michael Caine, Glenne Headly, Anton Rodgers, Barbara Harris, Ian McDiarmid, Dana Ivey, Meagen Fay, Frances Conroy, Nicole Calfan

Dirty Weekend
GB 1993 103m colour
UIP/Scimitar (Michael Winner, Robert Earl)
A woman, harassed by a succession of lecherous males, decides to kill them.
A sleazy little tale of a female vigilante, directed and acted in a perfunctory, over-emphatic manner.
w Michael Winner, Helen Zahavi novel Helen Zahavi d Michael Winner ph Alan Jones m David Fanshawe pd Crispian Sallis ed Arnold Crust
☆ Lia Williams, Rufus Sewell, Michael Cule, David McCallum, Christopher Ryan, Sean Pertwee, Ian Richardson
'Michael Winner aims low and half misses.' – *Variety*
'The film is uniquely awful ... sheer murder to watch.' – *Nick James, Sight and Sound*

Dirty Work ***
US 1933 20m bw
Hal Roach
Chimney sweeps cause havoc in the house of an eccentric scientist.
Hilarious star comedy with splendid timing and comedy touches.
w H. M. Walker d Lloyd French ph Kenneth Peach ed Bert Jordan
☆ Laurel and Hardy, Lucien Littlefield, Sam Adams

Dirty Work
GB 1934 78m bw
Gaumont (Michael Balcon)
Shop assistants pose as crooks in order to catch thieves.
Rather thin Ben Travers farce with some authentic moments.
w Ben Travers play Ben Travers d Tom Walls ph Phil Tannura md Louis Levy ad Alfred Junge ed Alfred Roome
☆ Ralph Lynn, Gordon Harker, Robertson Hare, Lillian Bond, Basil Sydney, Cecil Parker, Margaretta Scott, Gordon James, Peter Gawthorne

The Disappearance
GB/Canada 1977 102m Eastmancolor
Trofar/Tiberius (David Hemmings)
An international hit man finds that his wife has disappeared.
Confusing and pretentious thriller which spends more time on introspection than action and ends up not satisfying anybody.
w Paul Mayersberg novel Echoes of Celandine by Derek Marlowe d Stuart Cooper ph John Alcott m Robert Farnon
☆ Donald Sutherland, Francine Racette, David Hemmings, John Hurt, David Warner, Peter Bowles, Virginia McKenna, Christopher Plummer

The Disappearance of Finbar
Ireland/GB/Sweden/France 1997 102m colour
Film Four/Pandora/First City/Samson/Victoria (Bertil Ohlsson, Martin Bruce-Clayton)
A detective and his best friend go looking for an unsettled Irish teenager who disappears from his home.
An aimless road movie that gets lost in Scandinavia.
w Dermot Bolger, Sue Clayton novel The Disappearance of Rory Brophy by Carl Lombard d Sue Clayton ph Eduardo Serra m Davy Spillane ad Ned McLoughlin, Connor Devlin, Bengt Froderberg ed J. Patrick Duffner, Alan Strachan
☆ Jonathan Rhys Meyers (credited as Rhys-Myers), Luke Griffin, Fanny Risberg, Lorraine Pilkington, Eleanor Methven, Sean Lawlor, Sean McGinley
'Ambitious and sloppy, yet occasionally likeable, cross-European fable.' – *Caroline Westbrook, Empire*

'The Movie Hollywood Doesn't Want You To See.'
Disappearance of Kevin Johnson *
US 1995 106m Foto-Kem
Bedford/Makani Kai/Wobblyscope (Scott Richard Wolf)
A British documentary team, who are making a feature on expatriates in Hollywood, investigate the disappearance of a missing producer on the brink of the big time.
An amusing look at the seedier side of the dream factory, done in the muck-raking style of the sleazier television documentaries.
wd Francis Megahy ph John C. Newby m John Coda ad Sandy Grass ed Hudson Legrand
☆ Alexander Folk, Bridget Baiss, Carl Sundstrom, Michael Brandon, Keely Sims, Hector Elias, Pierce Brosnan (himself), James Coburn (himself), Dudley Moore (himself)
'This exercise in witty Hollywood-bashing is subtler than most.' – *Kim Newman*

Disbarred
US 1938 58m bw
Paramount
A lady lawyer is paid by a crime czar to defend a gangster.
Slick mini-melo of the kind at which this studio excelled at the time.
w Lillie Hayward, Robert Presnell d Robert Florey
☆ Otto Kruger, Gail Patrick, Robert Preston, Sidney Toler, Charles D. Brown
'Moderately entertaining drama; nicely fills the lower brackets.' – *Variety*

'Sex is power.'
Disclosure *
US 1994 127m Technicolor Panavision
Warner/Baltimore/Cónstant c (Barry Levinson, Michael Crichton)
A female executive in a computer company accuses a male colleague of sexual harassment after he rejects her advances.
Entertaining nonsense, abandoning all pretence to be ostensibly exploring matters of social concern in favour of sensationalism and the trappings of a computer thriller; it is a movie of virtual unreality.
w Paul Attanasio novel Michael Crichton d Barry Levinson ph Anthony Pierce-Roberts m Ennio Morricone pd Neil Spisak ed Stu Linder sp visual effects: Industrial Light and Magic
☆ Michael Douglas, Demi Moore, Donald Sutherland, Caroline Goodall, Dylan Baker, Roma Maffia, Dennis Miller, Allan Rich
'This is the kind of well-made and highly professional entertainment which relies as much on techno-babble, a virtual reality encounter between the two principals and screens which tell you how to run your lives than on the moral dilemma.' – *Derek Malcolm, Guardian*
'If the viewer can get past the stupidity of *Disclosure*'s plot and casting, the movie isn't all that bad.' – *Joe Queenan*

'90 Minutes You Will Never Forget.'
Disco Pigs
GB/Ireland 2000 93m colour
Entertainment/Renaissance/IFB/Temple (Ed Guiney)
Two teenagers, close friends from birth, turn to violence when others try to separate them.
Melodramatic drama of an intense relationship, so claustrophobic that it leaves no room for an audience.
w Enda Walsh play Enda Walsh d Kirsten Sheridan ph Igor Jadue-Lillo m Gavin Friday, Maurice Seezer pd Zoe MacLeod ed Ben Yeates
☆ Elaine Cassidy (Sinead, 'Runt'), Cillian Murphy (Darren, 'Pig'), Geraldine O'Rawe (Runt's Mam), Eleanor Methven (Pig's Mam), Brian O'Byrne (Runt's Dad), Darren Healy (Marky), Tara Lynne O'Neill (Mags), Michael Rawley (Foxy)
'An extremely ugly experience indeed.' – *James Mottram, Film Review*

The Discreet Charm of the Bourgeoisie ****
France/Spain/Italy 1972 105m Eastmancolor
Greenwich (Serge Silberman)
original title: *Le Charme Discret de la Bourgeoisie*
The efforts of a group of friends to dine together are continually frustrated.
A frequently hilarious, sometimes savage surrealist fable which makes all its points beautifully and then goes on twenty minutes too long. The performances are a joy.
w *Luis Buñuel, Jean-Claude Carrière* d *Luis Buñuel* ph Edmond Richard ad Pierre Guffroy ed Hélène Plemiannikov
☆ *Fernando Rey, Delphine Seyrig, Stéphane Audran,* Bulle Ogier, Jean-Pierre Cassel, Paul Frankeur, Julien Bertheau
'A perfect synthesis of surreal wit and blistering social assault.' – *Jan Dawson, MFB*
best foreign film
Luis Buñuel, Jean-Claude Carrière (script)
Stéphane Audran; script

The Disembodied
US 1957 73m bw
Allied Artists
In the tropics, a doctor's wife is really a voodoo queen who is trying to kill him by supernatural means.
Verbose rubbish with more yawns than thrills.
w Jack Townley d Walter Grauman
☆ Allison Hayes, Paul Burke, John Wengraf

'As Neil Armstrong set foot on the moon, our only link was a satellite dish in rural Australia with a few bugs. (And a few hundred sheep.)'
The Dish **
Australia 2000 100m colour
Icon/Working Dog/Dish (Santo Cilauro, Tom Gleisner, Jane Kennedy, Rob Sitch)
A power cut threatens the success of a team of Australian engineers, working under NASA supervision, who have been assigned to track Apollo II and relay to the world TV pictures of the first lunar landing.
Engaging small-scale comedy that casts a gently ironic eye on history and those who make it.
w Santo Cilauro, Tom Gleisner, Jane Kennedy, Rob Sitch d Rob Sitch ph Graeme Wood m Edmund Choi, Jane Kennedy pd Carrie Kennedy ed Jill Bilcock
☆ Sam Neill (Cliff Buxton), Kevin Harrington (Ross 'Mitch' Mitchell), Tom Long (Glenn Latham), Patrick Warburton (Al Burnett), Genevieve Mooy (May McIntyre), Tayler Kane (Rudi Kellerman), Bille Brown (Prime Minister), Roy Billing (Mayor Bob McIntyre)
'A feel-good comic ensembler that's hard to resist.' – *Dennis Harvey, Variety*

Dishonored **
US 1931 91m bw
Paramount
An officer's widow turned streetwalker is hired by the German government as a spy.
Rather gloomy melodrama which helped to establish its star as a top American attraction; but the heavy hand of her Svengali, von Sternberg, was already evident.
w Daniel N. Rubin story Josef von Sternberg d *Josef von Sternberg* ph *Lee Garmes* m Karl Hajos
☆ *Marlene Dietrich,* Victor McLaglen, Lew Cody, Gustav von Seyffertitz, Warner Oland, Barry Norton, Wilfred Lucas
'Miss Dietrich rises above her director ... should make the money grade of an A1 draw talker.' – *Variety*
'The most exciting movie I have seen in several months ... yet I hope I may die young if I ever again have to listen to a manuscript so full of recusant, stilted, outmoded theatrical mouthings.' – *Pare Lorentz*
'The whole film has a kind of magnificent grandeur embellished, of course, by its shining central performance.' – *John Gillett, 1964*

'She insulted her soul!'
Dishonored Lady
US 1947 85m bw
Mars Film (Hedy Lamarr)
A girl with a past is cleared of a murder charge by her psychiatrist.
Melodramatic showpiece designed for herself by a glamorous star; OK for the silly season.
w Edmund H. North play Edward Sheldon, Margaret Ayer Barnes d Robert Stevenson ph Lucien Andriot m Carmen Dragon
☆ Hedy Lamarr, John Loder, Dennis O'Keefe, Paul Cavanagh, William Lundigan, Natalie Schafer, Morris Carnovsky

Dishonour Bright *
GB 1936 82m bw
GFD/Cecil (Herman Fellner, Max Schach)
An ageing playboy is blackmailed about a past affair.
Interesting semi-smart comedy of the period, tailored for its star.
w Ben Travers d Tom Walls ph Phil Tannura
☆ Tom Walls, Eugene Pallette, Betty Stockfeld, Diana Churchill, Arthur Wontner, Cecil Parker, George Sanders, Henry Oscar, Basil Radford

Disney's First Kid: see *First Kid*

'Nobody ever grows up quite like they imagined.'
Disney's The Kid
US 2000 104m Technicolor
Buena Vista/Walt Disney/Junction (Jon Turteltaub, Christina Steinberg, Hunt Lowry)
A middle-aged image consultant meets himself at the age of 8: each decides the other needs a make-over.
Lacklustre comedy of time-travel that hardly tries to get the most out of an intriguing concept; it is content to settle for dewy-eyed nostalgia.

w Audrey Wells *d* Jon Turteltaub *ph* Peter Menzies Jnr *m* Marc Shaiman *pd* Garreth Stover *ed* Peter Honess, David Rennie *sp* James E. Price; Secret Lab
☆ Bruce Willis (Russ Duritz), Spencer Breslin (Rusty Duritz), Emily Mortimer (Amy), Lily Tomlin (Janet), Chi McBride (Kenny), Jean Smart (Deirdre Lafever), Dana Ivey (Dr Alexander), Daniel von Bargen (Sam Duritz), Stanley Anderson (Bob Riley), Susan Dalian (Giselle)
'Insufferably cloying and sickly sweet for anyone with the least intolerance to "find the inner child" saccharinity.' – *Todd McCarthy, Variety*
'Has a pleasant, unforced air, aided by the professionalism of the actors.' – *A. O. Scott, New York Times*

Disorderly Conduct
US 1932 82m bw
Fox
A cop turns crook after being demoted.
Heavy-going melodrama apparently intended as a tribute to the New York police.
w William Anthony McGuire *d* John W. Considine Jnr
☆ Spencer Tracy, Sally Eilers, El Brendel, Dickie Moore, Ralph Bellamy, Ralph Morgan, Alan Dinehart
'Good entertainment ... mother-love sentiment with some kid atmosphere.' – *Variety*

The Disorderly Orderly
US 1964 89m Technicolor
Paramount/York (Paul Jones)
A hospital orderly creates havoc by his inefficiency and his sympathy for other people's predicaments.
Spasmodic farce with far too much pathos between its highlights.
wd Frank Tashlin *ph* W. Wallace Kelley *m* Joseph Lilley
☆ Jerry Lewis, Glenda Farrell, Everett Sloane, Kathleen Freeman, Karen Sharpe, Susan Oliver, Alice Pearce

Disorganized Crime
US 1989 98m Metrocolor
Touchstone/Silver Screen Partners IV (Lynn Bigelow)
A gang of incompetent crooks await the arrival of their leader, who has escaped from prison, so that they can attempt the perfect bank robbery.
Dull and uninteresting crime caper with stereotyped characters that flopped at the box-office.
wd Jim Kouf *ph* Ron Garcia *m* David Newman *pd* Waldemar Kalinowski *ed* Frank Morriss, Dallas Puett
☆ Hoyt Axton, Corbin Bernsen, Ruben Blades, Fred Gwynne, Ed O'Neill, Lou Diamond Phillips, Daniel Roebuck, William Russ

Les Disparus de St Agil *
France 1938 95m bw
Vog Films
Students disappear in a school whose headmaster is a forger and murderer.
Curious black comedy: a half-success.
w J. H. Blanchon *novel* Pierre Véry *d* Christian-Jaque
☆ Michel Simon, Erich von Stroheim, Aimé Clariond, Armand Bernard

A Dispatch from Reuters **
US 1940 90m bw
Warner (Henry Blanke)
GB title: *This Man Reuter*
The story of the man who provided Europe's first news service.
Acceptable if slightly dull addition to Warner's prestige biopics; well made and acted.
w Milton Krims *d William Dieterle ph James Wong Howe m* Max Steiner
☆ Edward G. Robinson, Edna Best, Eddie Albert, Albert Basserman, Gene Lockhart, Otto Kruger, Montagu Love, Nigel Bruce, James Stephenson

Disputed Passage *
US 1939 90m bw
Paramount (Harlan Thompson)
A young scientist who wants to marry meets resistance from his mentor.
Adequate screen version of a bestseller.
w Anthony Veiller, Sheridan Gibney *novel* Lloyd C. Douglas *d* Frank Borzage *ph* William C. Mellor *m* Frederick Hollander, James Leopold
☆ Dorothy Lamour, John Howard, Akim Tamiroff, Judith Barrett, William Collier Snr, Victor Varconi, Keye Luke, Elizabeth Risdon
'Fine drama of medical science: a top-of-the-bill attraction.' – *Variety*
'I should describe the flavour as a rather nauseating blend of iodine and glucose.' – *Graham Greene*

'It dwarfs the stage!'
Disraeli *
US 1929 89m bw
Warner
Fictionalized episodes in the life of the Victorian statesman, including his activities as a matchmaker.
Very early star talkie, of primarily archival interest; Arliss had appeared in a silent version in 1921.
w Julien Josephson *play* Louis N. Parker *d* Alfred E. Green *ph* Lee Garmes *md* Louis Silvers
☆ George Arliss, Joan Bennett, Florence Arliss, Anthony Bushell, David Torrence, Ivan Simpson, Doris Lloyd
'Those seeking a fuller assessment of the man and his work would have been better off in a library.' – *Clive Hirschhorn, 1982*
🏆 George Arliss
🏅 best picture; Julian Josephson

'The rescue ... the throbbing jungle drums ... the man-devouring marsh wilderness aflame with unseen menace!'
Distant Drums
US 1951 101m Technicolor
United States Pictures (Milton Sperling)
In 1840 Florida, an army officer rescues prisoners from an Indian fort and decimates the Seminoles who threaten their return journey.
Overlong action saga, with dull stretches compensated by a dominating star and some lively incident.
w Niven Busch, Martin Rackin *d* Raoul Walsh *ph* Sid Hickox *m* Max Steiner
☆ Gary Cooper, Mari Aldon, Richard Webb, Ray Teal, Arthur Hunnicutt, Robert Barrat
'Don't look for surprises. Mr Cooper is kept steady and laconic throughout, the action is serio-comic, and the pace is conventionally maintained.' – *Bosley Crowther, New York Times*

Distant Thunder ***
India 1973 100m colour
Balaka (Sarbani Bhattacharya)
original title: *Asani Sanket*
In 1943 a Brahmin teacher-priest and his wife experience in their small village the beginnings of a famine in Bengal.
A potent account of the breakdown of traditional values under the pressure of terrible events.
wd Satyajit Ray *novel* Bibhutibhusan Banerjee *ph* Soumendu Ray *m* Satyajit Ray *ad* Asok Bose *ed* Dulal Dutta
☆ Soumitra Chatterjee, Babita, Ramesh Mukherjee, Chitra Banerjee, Gobinda Chakravarti, Sandhya Roy
'I don't know when I've been so moved by a picture that I knew was riddled with flaws. It must be that Ray's vision comes out of so much hurt and guilt and love that the feeling pours over all the cracks in *Distant Thunder* and fills them up.' – *Pauline Kael, New Yorker*
† It won the Golden Bear award for Best Film at the Berlin Film Festival in 1973.

Distant Thunder
US/Canada 1988 114m Technicolor
Paramount (Robert Schaffel)
A Vietnam veteran who, after his wartime experiences, lives on the fringes of society renews contact with the 18-year-old son he abandoned years before.
Soft-centred drama of male bonding through violence which might have been made for television; it is small in scale and scope, despite its melodramatic climax.
w Robert Stitzel, Deedee Wehle *d* Rick Rosenthal *ph* Ralf Bode *m* Maurice Jarre *ed* Dennis Virkler
☆ John Lithgow, Ralph Macchio, Kerrie Keane, Reb Brown, Janet Margolin, Denis Arndt, Jamey Sheridan, Tom Bower

A Distant Trumpet
US 1964 116m Technicolor Panavision
Warner (William H. Wright)
The new commander of a cavalry outpost tightens up discipline, which serves him well when Indian trouble erupts.
Moderate Western, quite well staged but with a second team cast.
w John Twist *novel* Paul Horgan *d* Raoul Walsh *ph* William Clothier *m* Max Steiner
☆ Troy Donahue, Suzanne Pleshette, James Gregory, Diane McBain, William Reynolds, Claude Akins, Kent Smith, Judson Pratt

Distant Voices, Still Lives *
GB 1988 84m colour
BFI/Film Four International (Colin MacCabe)
Working-class family life in Liverpool in the 40s and 50s.
Low-budget labour of love filmed at intervals over two years, succeeding through close, unsentimental observation and excellent performances by a cast of unknowns.
wd Terence Davies *ph* William Diver, Patrick Duval *pd* Miki van Zwanenberg
☆ Freda Dowie, Pete Postlethwaite, Angela Walsh
'While its pacing and structure may exasperate some, should envelop receptive audiences with its special magic.' – *Variety*

The Distinguished Gentleman *
US 1992 112m Technicolor
Buena Vista/Hollywood Pictures (Leonard Goldberg, Michael Peyser)
A con man decides that the best place for his talents is in government.
Enjoyable, broad comedy, which gives Murphy a good opportunity to display his fast-talking talents.
w Marty Kaplan *d* Jonathan Lynn *ph* Gabriel Beristain *m* Randy Edelman *pd* Leslie Dilley *ed* Tony Lombardo, Barry B. Leirer
☆ Eddie Murphy, Lane Smith, Sheryl Lee Ralph, Joe Don Baker, Victoria Rowell, Grant Shaud, Kevin McCarthy
'A lazily slung together collection of clichés, mixing diet politics with laughter-free comedy.' – *Kim Newman, Empire*

Disturbing Behavior
US 1998 84m DeLuxe
MGM/Village Roadshow/Hoyts/Beacon Communications (Armyan Bernstein, Jon Shestack)
A new high-school student discovers something odd about the school's athletic élite, who are able to get away with murder.
A somewhat dumb variation on The Stepford Wives *(qv), played as a comedy and designed for a teenage audience.*
w Scott Rosenberg *d* David Nutter *ph* John S. Bartley *m* Mark Snow *pd* Nelson Coates *ed* Randy Jon Morgan
☆ James Marsden (Steve Clark), Katie Holmes (Rachel Wagner), Nick Stahl (Gavin Strick), Steve Railsback (Officer Cox), Bruce Greenwood (Dr. Caldicott), William Sadler (Dorain Newberry), Chad E. Donella (U.V.), Ethan Embry (Allen Clark), Katherine Isabelle (Lindsay Clark)
'Brisk, slick, sloppily plotted, cliché-ridden script pic won't win many critical allies.' – *Dennis Harvey, Variety*

Ditte, Child of Man *
Denmark 1946 106m bw
Nordisk
original title: *Ditte Menneskebarn*
An unmarried mother abandons her daughter, who grows up to be a servant and to be seduced in her turn.
Impressive, doom-laden Scandinavian saga, highly thought of on its release.
wd Astrid and Bjarne Henning-Jensen *novel* Martin Andersen *ph* Werner Jenssen *m* Herman Koppel
☆ Tove Maes, Rasmus Ottesen, Karen Poulsen

Ditte Menneskebarn: see *Ditte, Child of Man*

Diva *
France 1981 117m Eastmancolor
Galaxie/Greenwich/Antenne 2 (Irene Silberman)
A black prima donna in Paris becomes accidentally involved in drug smuggling and murder.
A curious hybrid of violence and surrealism which doesn't seem to know what effect it's aiming at, or at least doesn't let the viewer in on the secret, being content to entertain in a flashy and sometimes shocking way.
w Jean-Jacques Beineix, Jean Van Hamme *novel* Delacorta *d Jean-Jacques Beineix ph* Philippe Rousselot *m* Vladimir Cosma *pd Hilton McConnico*
☆ Frederic Andrei, Roland Bertin, Richard Bohringer, Wilhelmenia Wiggins Fernandez, Jean-Jacques Moreau, Chantal Deruaz
'It's a mixture of style and chic hanky-panky, but it's genuinely sparkling.' – *New Yorker*

The Dive
GB/Norway 1989 95m colour
Filmeffekt/Millennium/British Screen (Dag Alveberg, Patrick Cassavetti)
Deep-sea divers are trapped underwater while attempting to repair a pipeline.
Standard rescue melodrama, more lethargically directed than most.
w Leidulv Risan, Carlos Wiggen *d* Tristan de Vere Cole *ph* Harald Paalgard *m* Geir Bîhren, Bent Aserud *pd* Jarle Blesvik *ed* Russell Lloyd
☆ Bjîrn Sundquist, Frank Grimes, Eindride Eidsvold, Marika Lagercrantz, Nils Ole Oftebro, Michael Kitchen, Sverre Anker Ousdal

Dive Bomber *
US 1941 133m Technicolor
Warner (Hal B. Wallis)
Aviation scientists work to eliminate pilot blackout.
Somewhat rarefied propaganda piece with too many reels of romantic banter but tense climactic scenes and good star performances.
w Frank 'Spig' Wead, Robert Buckner *d* Michael Curtiz *ph* Bert Glennon, Winton C. Hoch *m* Max Steiner *md* Leo F. Forbstein
☆ *Errol Flynn*, Fred MacMurray, Ralph Bellamy, Alexis Smith, Regis Toomey, Robert Armstrong, Allen Jenkins, Craig Stevens, Moroni Olsen, Gig Young, William Hopper, Charles Drake, Russell Hicks, Addison Richards, Ann Doran and also Herbert Anderson
🏅 Bert Glennon, Winton C. Hoch

The Divided Heart **
GB 1954 89m bw
Ealing (Michael Truman)
A boy believed to be a war orphan is lovingly brought up by foster parents; then his real mother turns up and wants him back.
Effective 'woman's picture' set in Europe and giving a genuine sense of post-war feelings and problems.
w Jack Whittingham d Charles Crichton ph Otto Heller *m* Georges Auric
☆ *Cornell Borchers, Yvonne Mitchell*, Armin Dahlen, Alexander Knox, Geoffrey Keen, Michel Ray, Liam Redmond, Eddie Byrne
BAFTA Yvonne Mitchell; Cornell Borchers

'In a war-torn village, one couple makes the ultimate sacrifice to save another.'
Divided We Fall **
Czech Republic 2000 123m colour
Total HelpArt THA/Czech TV (Ondrej Trojan, Pavel Borovan)
aka: *Musime si Pomàhat*
During the Nazi occupation of Czechoslovakia, a couple risk their lives to shelter a Jewish friend.
Deft black tragi-comedy of ordinary people in extraordinary times, and the compromises life forces upon them.
w Petr Jarchovsky *novel* Petr Jarchovsky *d* Jan Hrebejk *ph* Jan Malir *m* Alec Brezina *ad* Milan Bycek *ed* Vladimir Barak
☆ Boleslav Polivka (Josef Cizek), Csongor Kassai (David Wiener), Jaroslav Dusek (Horst Prohaska), Anna Siskova (Marie Cizkova), Jiri Pecha (Frantisek Simacek), Martin Huba (Dr Kepk), Simona Stasova (Libuse Simackova)
'Pervaded with humor that serves not to sentimentalize or sugarcoat the monstrosity of

Naziism, but to explain it. The filmmakers explore not only the banality of evil, but also the banality of goodness, and the ridiculousness, as well as the tragedy, of their collision.' – *A. O. Scott, New York Times*

The Dividing Line: see *The Lawless*

The Divine Lady *
US 1929 100m bw
Warner
The adventures of Emma, Lady Hamilton.
Historical charade which titillated at the time.
w Agnes Christine Johnston, Forrest Halsey *d* Frank Lloyd *ph* John Seitz
☆ Corinne Griffith, Victor Varconi, H. B. Warner, Montagu Love, Marie Dressler
Frank Lloyd
John Seitz; Corinne Griffith

Divine Madness
US 1980 93m Technicolor Panavision
Ladd Company/Warner
A record of a Bette Midler concert performance. 'Since this is the time capsule version of my show, I may as well do everything I know.'
It certainly isn't a movie.
d Michael Ritchie *ph* William A. Fraker

'Mothers. Daughters. The neverending story of good vs evil.'
Divine Secrets of the Ya-Ya Sisterhood
US 2002 116m Technicolor Panavision
Warner/Gaylord/All Girl (Bonnie Bruckheimer, Hunt Lowry)
Childhood friends of a heavy-drinking, pill-popping mother attempt to reconcile her with her daughter, an outspoken writer.
Talky chick-flick of a generational clash that quickly palls, mainly because it resembles no known reality.
wd Callie Khouri *adaptation* Mark Andrus *novels* *Divine Secrets of the Ya-Ya Sisterhood; Little Altars Everywhere* by Rebecca Wells *ph* John Bailey *m* T Bone Burnett, David Mansfield *pd* David J. Bomba *ed* Andrew Marcus *cos* Gary Jones
☆ Sandra Bullock (Sidda), Ellen Burstyn (Vivi), Fionnula Flanagan (Teensy), James Garner (Shep Walker), Cherry Jones (Buggy), Ashley Judd (Younger Vivi), Shirley Knight (Necie), Angus MacFadyen (Connor), Maggie Smith (Caro)
'There must be a reason that the sort of comic caricatures of Southern womanhood as displayed here have weathered the test of time, so there may be kernels of truth buried behind all the studied glances, poses and play-acting' – *Todd McCarthy, Variety*
'Why do gifted actresses appear in such slop?' – *Roger Ebert*

The Divine Woman *
US 1927 95m approx (24 fps) bw silent
MGM
The loves of Sarah Bernhardt.
Garbo's first star role; a typical Hollywood melodramatization of facts.
w Dorothy Farnum *play* *Starlight* by Gladys Unger *d* Victor Sjostrom
☆ *Greta Garbo*, Lars Hanson, Lowell Sherman, John Mack Brown, Polly Moran

Divorce
US 1945 71m bw
Monogram/Jeffrey Bernerd/Kay Francis
A much-married woman tries to break up another happy family.
This somewhat elementary tract was the star's first independent production, and not a success.
w Sidney Sutherland, Harvey Gates *d* William Nigh
☆ Kay Francis, Bruce Cabot, Helen Mack, Jonathan Hale, Jerome Cowan
'A lacklustre script grooves it for the duals.' – *Variety*

'In America the ring costs two dollars to put on – and a fortune to take off!'
Divorce American Style **
US 1967 109m Technicolor
Columbia/Tandem (Norman Lear)
Well-heeled Los Angeles suburbanites toy with divorce but eventually resume their domestic bickering.
Rather arid and patchy but often sharply sardonic comedy about a society in which people can't afford to divorce.
w *Norman Lear* *d* Bud Yorkin *ph* Conrad Hall *m* *David Grusin* *pd* Edward Stephenson
☆ *Dick Van Dyke, Debbie Reynolds, Jean Simmons,* Jason Robards Jnr, Van Johnson, Joe Flynn, Shelley Berman, Martin Gabel, Lee Grant, Tom Bosley, Dick Gautier
Norman Lear

'A delightfully daring plan to give marriage a surprise ending!'
Divorce Italian Style **
Italy 1961 108m bw
Lux/Vides/Galatea (Franco Cristaldi)
original title: *Divorzio all'Italiana*
A Sicilian nobleman explains how, wishing to be rid of his wife, he arranged for her to be seduced and later shot by a jealous lover.
Sardonic, stylized comedy which, rather in the manner of Kind Hearts and Coronets, *manages while retailing a black comedy plot to satirize Italian manners and institutions.*
w *Ennio de Concini, Pietro Germi, Alfredo Gianetti* *d* *Pietro Germi* *ph* Leonida Barboni *m* Carlo Rustichelli
☆ *Marcello Mastroianni*, Daniela Rocca, Stefania Sandrelli, Leopoldo Trieste
script
Pietro Germi; Marcello Mastroianni
Marcello Mastroianni

The Divorce of Lady X **
GB 1938 92m Technicolor
London Films (Alexander Korda)
A nobleman's daughter wins a barrister by posing as a divorce client.
Pleasing comedy with high production standards of its time, deftly performed by a distinguished cast.
w Lajos Biro, Arthur Wimperis, Ian Dalrymple *play* *Counsel's Opinion* by Gilbert Wakefield *d* *Tim Whelan* *ph* Harry Stradling *m* Miklos Rozsa *ad* Lazare Meerson, Paul Sheriff *ed* William Hornbeck
☆ *Laurence Olivier, Merle Oberon,* Binnie Barnes, Ralph Richardson, Morton Selten, J. H. Roberts

'Her sin was no greater than his, but she was a woman! If the world permits the husband to philander – why not the wife?'
The Divorcee *
US 1930 83m bw
MGM (Robert Z. Leonard)
Would-be liberal young marrieds divorce when she puts up with his affairs but he can't tolerate hers. She falls in love with another married man but sends him back to his wife.
Rather wan illustration of the double standard which was being much discussed in society at the time.
w John Meehan, Nick Grinde, Zelda Sears *novel* *Ex-Wife* by Ursula Parrott *d* Robert Z. Leonard *ph* Norbert Brodine *ad* Cedric Gibbons
☆ Norma Shearer, Chester Morris, Conrad Nagel, Robert Montgomery, Florence Eldridge
'Shearer's specialty was sexy suffering in satin gowns by Adrian; here, she almost seems to want to abandon herself to naughtiness, but one line after another stops her.' – *Pauline Kael, 70s*
Norma Shearer
best picture; Robert Z. Leonard; John Meehan, Nick Grinde, Zelda Sears

Divorcing Jack **
GB/France 1998 100m Rank Colour
BBC/Winchester/Scala (Robert Cooper)
In an independent Northern Ireland, a journalist goes on the run after being framed for a murder, and is hunted by Loyalists and the IRA.
Tense, tough thriller that thumbs its nose at gunmen of all persuasions, served up with some wit and a gun-toting stripper-nun.
w Colin Bateman *novel* Colin Bateman *d* David Caffrey *ph* James Welland *m* Adrian Johnston *pd* Claire Kenny *ed* Nick Moore
☆ David Thewlis, Rachel Griffiths, Robert Lindsay, Jason Isaacs, Laura Fraser, Richard Gant, Bronagh Gallagher
'An out-and-out chase movie, stuffed with visual gags and boasting a fine comedy script which bends the ear with delight.' – *Jake Hamilton, Empire*

Divorzio all'Italiana: see *Divorce Italian Style*

Dixiana
US 1930 100m bw (Technicolor sequences)
RKO
A Dutchman from Pennsylvania tries to run a plantation in Louisiana.
Lavish but utterly witless musical comedy which just lies there and dies there.
wd Luther Reed *play* Ann Caldwell
☆ Bebe Daniels, Bert Wheeler, Robert Woolsey, Everett Marshall, Joseph Cawthorn, Jobyna Howland, Dorothy Lee, Bill Robinson
'Not much but bigness for exploiting.' – *Variety*

Dixie *
US 1943 90m Technicolor
Paramount (Paul Jones)
The life of old-time minstrel man Dan Emmett.
Lighter-than-air fictionalized biography with pleasing mid-19th-century settings.
w Karl Tunberg, Darrell Ware *d* A. Edward Sutherland *ph* William C. Mellor *m* Robert Emmett Dolan *m/ly* Johnny Burke, Jimmy Van Heusen
☆ Bing Crosby, Dorothy Lamour, Marjorie Reynolds, *Lynne Overman, Eddie Foy Jnr, Billy de Wolfe, Raymond Walburn*, Grant Mitchell

Django **
Italy/Spain 1966 95m colour
BRC/Tecisa (Manolo Bolognini)
A gunfighter who carries a machine-gun in a coffin rids a town of its gangs of Mexican bandits and the Ku Klux Klan.
One of the earliest, most notorious and influential of spaghetti Westerns, marked by a high level of violence but nevertheless watchable for its operatic style.
w Sergio Corbucci, Bruno Corbucci, Franco Rossetti, José G. Naesso, Piero Vivarelli *d* Sergio Corbucci *ph* Enzo Barboni *m* Luis Enrique Bacalov
☆ Franco Nero, Eduardo Fajardo, Loredana Nusciak, José Bodalo, Angel Alvarez
'After Leone, Corbucci was the genius of the spaghettis.' – *Empire*

Django against Sartana (dubbed)
Italy 1970 90m Telecolor
P.A.C./B.C.R. (Roberto Bessi)
original title: *Django Sfida Sartana*
Django avenges the death of his brother, hanged for a crime he did not commit.
Mundane spaghetti Western, a sequel lacking the excesses of the original and content to provide the minimum in interest or excitement.
wd William Redford (Pasquale Squitieri) *ph* Eugenio Bentivoglio *m* Piero Umiliani
☆ George Ardisson, Tony Kendall, José Torres, Bernard Faber, Adler Gray, John Alvar

Django, Kill! (dubbed)
Italy/Spain 1967 120m colour Techniscope
GIA/Hispamer (Alex J. Rascal)
original title: *Sei Sei Vivo, Spara!*
aka: *If You Live Shoot!*
A vengeful gunman, who was among Mexicans double-crossed and shot down by American bandits, tracks the gang to a town controlled by Zorro, a homosexual bandit, and his followers.
Sprawling, decadent spaghetti Western in a rococo style, given over to brutal deaths; it is not often screened uncut.
w Franco Arcalli, Giulio Questi, Benedetto Benedetti *idea* Ma del Carmen, M. Roman *d* Giulio Questi *ph* Franco delli Colli *m* Ivan Vandor *ed* Franco Arcalli
☆ Tomas Milian, Marilu Tolo, Piero Lulli, Milo Quesada, Roberto Camardiel, Patrizia Valturri, Raymond Lovelock
† The film exists in several other, shorter versions, cut for reasons of violence or length.

Django Sfida Sartana: see *Django against Sartana*

Django Spara per Primo
Italy 1966 95m Technicolor Techniscope
Gala/Fida (Edmondo Amati)
aka: *He Who Shoots First*
Django is framed for a bank robbery by the man who murdered his father.
Tedious re-run of the usual theme of vengeance, done without style or originality.
w Sandro Continenza, Massimiliano Capriccoli, Florenzo Carpi, Vincenzo Flamini, Alberto de Martino *d* Alberto de Martino *ph* Ricardo Pallottini *m* Bruno Nicolai *ad* Pier Vittorio Marchi *ed* Otello Colangeli
☆ Glenn Saxon, Fernando Sancho, Evelyn Stewart (Ida Galli), Nando Gazzolo, Lee Burton (Guido Lollobrigida)
'A lifeless Italian Western ... plods wearily through the required rituals.' – *MFB*

En Djunselsaga: see *The Flute and the Arrow*

The Do It Yourself Cartoon Kit **
GB 1961 6m Eastmancolor
Biographic
A commercial for the kit in question, poking fun at all comers in a Monty Pythonish way.
Great stuff for those who like zany humour well controlled.
w Colin Pearson *d* Bob Godfrey

'What should a girl do when opportunity knocks ... twice?'
Do Not Disturb
US 1965 102m DeLuxe Cinemascope
TCF/Melcher/Arcola (Aaron Rosenberg, Martin Melcher)
An American wool executive is posted to London; his dizzy wife makes him jealous by flirting with a French antique dealer.
Silly farce which paints a lunatic picture of English and French life but occasionally raises a wild laugh or two. Thin script and production.
w Milt Rosen, Richard Breen *play* William Fairchild *d* Ralph Levy *ph* Leon Shamroy *m* Lionel Newman
☆ Doris Day, Rod Taylor, *Sergio Fantoni*, Reginald Gardiner, Hermione Baddeley, Leon Askin

Do the Right Thing ***
US 1989 120m colour
UIP/Forty Acres And A Mule Filmworks/Spike Lee
A white pizza parlour owner in a black neighbourhood sparks off a riot.
Complex, witty, street-wise and passionate film about racism.
w Spike Lee *d* *Spike Lee* *ph* Ernest Dickerson *m* Bill Lee *pd* Wynn Thomas *ed* Barry Alexander Brown
☆ Danny Aiello, Ossie Davis, Ruby Dee, Richard Edson, Giancarlo Esposito, Spike Lee, Bill Nunn, John Turturro, John Savage, Rosie Perez
'A very unusual movie experience – two hours of bombardment with New York-style stimuli.' – *Terrence Rafferty, New Yorker*
best original screenplay; Danny Aiello

Do You Like Women?
France/Italy 1964 100m bw CinemaScope
Francoriz/Number One/Federiz (Pierre Kalfon)
original title: *Aimez-Vous Les Femmes?*
Secret rival sects of woman-eaters cause an outbreak of murders in Paris.
Bizarre black comedy that doesn't quite work but provides ghoulish fun along the way.
w Roman Polanski, Gérard Brach *novel* Georges Bardawil *d* Jean Léon *ph* Sacha Vierny *m* Ward Swingle
☆ Sophie Daumier, Guy Bédos, Edwige Feuillère, Grégoire Aslan, Roger Blin
'It has the provoking quality of a carefully-prepared firework display which, due to faulty timing or bad connections, is never actually ignited.' – *MFB*

Do You Love Me?
US 1946 91m Technicolor
TCF (George Jessel)
The lady dean of a music school gets herself glamorized.
Thin, mildly agreeable but forgettable musical.
w Robert Ellis, Helen Logan *d* Gregory Ratoff *ph* Edward Cronjager *m/ly* various
☆ Maureen O'Hara, Dick Haymes, Harry James and his Orchestra, Reginald Gardiner, Richard Gaines, Stanley Prager
'Written for errand boys and nursemaids, junior clerks and typists.' – *James Agate, Tatler*

The Doberman Gang
US 1972 87m Eastmancolor
Fox-Rank/Rosamond (David Chudnow)

After his accomplices bungle a robbery, a crook trains six Dobermans to rob a bank.
The dogs run away with the picture, but invention and budget are both on too tight a leash to offer much more than the equivalent of an over-long pet-food commercial.
w Louis Garfinkle, Frank Ray Perilli *d* Byron Ross Chudnow *ph* Robert Caramico *m* Bradford Craig, Alan Silvestri *ad* Budd Costello *ed* Herman Freedman
☆ Byron Mabe, Hal Reed, Julie Parrish, Simmy Bow, Jojo D'Amore
'The film hovers uncertainly between straight thriller and comedy.' – *MFB*
† It was followed by two sequels with similar plots, *The Daring Dobermans*, 1973, and the bigger-budget *The Amazing Dobermans*, 1976 (qv), in which the dogs were on the side of the law.

Dobermann *
France 1997 103m colour 'Scope
Polygram/Noé/La Chauve Souris/Tawak/Canal+/France 3/Comstock (Frederique Dumas, Eric Neve)

A violent bank-robber, his deaf girlfriend and psychotic gang are hunted down by a brutal and sadistic cop.
Frenetic, black thriller, a fast-moving romp in the manner of an exuberant comic strip; its style almost compensates for its unremitting violence.
w Joel Houssin *novels* Joel Houssin *d* Jan Kounen *ph* Michel Amathieu *m* Schyzomaniac *pd* Michel Barthelemy *ed* Benedicte Brunet *sp* Mac Guff Ligne
☆ Vincent Cassel, Monica Belluci, Tcheky Karyo, Antoine Basler, Dominique Bettenfeld, Chick Ortéga, Stephane Metzger
'Ultraviolent, sexist, scatological and drug-drenched… Astoundingly high-voltage entertainment.' – *Stephen O'Shea, Variety*

Doc *
US 1971 96m DeLuxe
UA/Frank Perry
Doc Holliday goes to Tombstone to die of TB, but is drawn into the feud between the Clantons and his friend Wyatt Earp, whose motives are not of the highest.
A somewhat glum debunking of the west's most heroic myth, backing dour character study with grubby pictures. The result lacks excitement but maintains interest.
w Pete Hamill *d* Frank Perry *ph* Gerald Hirschfeld *m* Jimmy Webb
☆ Stacy Keach (Doc), Harris Yulin (Earp), Faye Dunaway (Kate Elder), Mike Witney, Denver John Collins, Dan Greenberg
'The physical realism that *Doc* is at pains to establish becomes simply a convention of its own.' – *Richard Combs*

Doc Hollywood *
US 1991 103m Technicolor
Warner (Susan Solt, Deborah D. Johnson)

On the way to a new job as a plastic surgeon in Hollywood, a young doctor crashes his car in a small town and is sentenced to work at the local hospital.
Amiable, inoffensive comedy in a familiar vein.
w Jeffrey Price, Peter S. Seaman, Daniel Pyne *novel What? … Dead Again* by Neil B. Shulman *d* Michael Caton-Jones *ph* Michael Chapman *m* Carter Burwell *pd* Lawrence Miller *ed* Gregg London
☆ Michael J. Fox, Julie Warner, Barnard Hughes, Woody Harrelson, David Ogden Stiers, Frances Sternhagen, George Hamilton, Bridget Fonda, Mel Winkler, Helen Martin, Roberts Blossom
'This serving of recycled Capracorn has no real taste of its own, but, in its mildness and predictability, offers the reassurance of a fast-food or motel chain.' – *Variety*

'Have no fear, Doc Savage is here!'
Doc Savage, Man of Bronze
US 1975 100m Technicolor
Warner (George Pal)

A thirties superman and his assistants the Amazing Five fly to South America to avenge the death of Doc's father.
Stolid, humourless adaptation from a comic strip, totally lacking in the necessary panache.
w George Pal, Joe Morhaim *stories* Kenneth Robeson *d* Michael Anderson *ph* Fred Koenekamp *m* John Philip Sousa
☆ Ron Ely, Paul Gleason, Bill Lucking, Michael Miller, Eldon Quick
'A slick, ultra-self-conscious camp that denies the material its self-respect.' – *Colin Pahlow*
'Nothing in this unfortunate enterprise is likely to please anyone: former Savage fans will be enraged, newcomers bored, and children will probably feel superior to the whole mess…' – *New Yorker*

The Dock Brief
GB 1962 88m bw
MGM/Dimitri de Grunwald

US title: *Trial and Error*
An incompetent barrister defends his client on a murder charge. The client is found guilty but the sentence is quashed on the grounds of inadequate defence.
Flat filming of a TV play which was a minor milestone; the film is twice the length and half as funny, and both stars quickly become tiresome.
w John Mortimer, Pierre Rouve *play* John Mortimer *d* James Hill *ph* Ted Scaife *m* Ron Grainer
☆ Peter Sellers, Richard Attenborough, Beryl Reid, David Lodge, Frank Pettingell

Docks of New York **
US 1928 80m (24 fps) bw silent
Paramount
A stoker marries a girl he has saved from suicide. Further unfortunate incidents result in his going to prison, but she waits for him.
Glum melodrama chiefly remarkable for its sets and lighting, reminiscent of the later Quai des Brumes.
w Jules Furthman *story The Dock Walloper* by John Monk Saunders *d Josef von Sternberg ph Harold Rosson ad Hans Dreier*
☆ George Bancroft, Betty Compson, Olga Baclanova, Clyde Cook, Gustav von Seyffertitz
'One comes away with the memory of a film impregnated with a life whose essential is in its energy and force.' – *Louis Chavance*

Docks of New York
US 1945 61m bw
Pathé/Monogram/Banner (Sam Katzman, Jack Dietz)
Mugs and Glimpy become involved in espionage and skulduggery when they try to help two refugees, who turn out to be European royalty being hunted by secret foreign agents.
Average programmer, broadly acted and with a patriotic propaganda message. It was one of the last films in the East Side Kids series (qv).
w Harvey Gates *d* Wallace Fox *ph* Ira Morgan *md* Edward Kay *ed* William Austin
☆ Leo Gorcey (Mugs), Huntz Hall (Glimpy), Billy Benedict (Skinny), Gloria Pope, Carlyle Blackwell Jnr, Betty Blythe, Cyrus Kendall, George Meeker

The Doctor **
US 1991 125m Technicolor
Buena Vista/Touchstone/Silver Screen Partners IV (Laura Ziskin)

A repressed surgeon alters his attitudes after he becomes a cancer patient at his own hospital.
Well-made drama of personal redemption.
w Robert Caswell *book A Taste of My Own Medicine* by Ed Rosenbaum *d* Randa Haines *ph* John Seale *m* Michael Convertino *pd* Ken Adam *ed* Bruce Green, Lisa Fruchtman
☆ William Hurt, Christine Lahti, Elizabeth Perkins, Mandy Patinkin, Adam Arkin, Charlie Korsmo, Wendy Crewson, Bill Macy
'Grapples powerfully with themes seldom faced in today's escapist marketplace: mortality, compassion, social responsibility.' – *Variety*

The Doctor and the Debutante: see *Dr Kildare's Victory*

The Doctor and the Devils
GB 1985 93m Rank Colour Panavision
Brooksfilm (Jonathan Sanger)

In the late 18th century an Edinburgh surgeon starts to pay for bodies as specimens, and doesn't ask their provenance.
Yet another version (see The Body Snatcher, The Flesh and the Fiends, Burke and Hare*) of the tale of Dr Knox, and this time a pretty poor one, justified by the use of Dylan Thomas's script.*
w Ronald Harwood, from Dylan Thomas *d* Freddie Francis *ph* Gerry Turpin, Norman Warwick *m* John Morris *pd* Robert Laing
☆ Timothy Dalton, Jonathan Pryce, Twiggy, Julian Sands, Lewis Fiander, Stephen Rea
'Unrelentingly serious treatment of a gruesome subject is unlikely to attract many warm bodies to the box office.' – *Variety*

The Doctor and the Girl
US 1949 98m bw
MGM (Pandro S. Berman)
A young doctor renounces specialization to help the poor.
Antediluvian medical romance full of the nicest people. Technically very competent.
w Theodore Reeves, from 'a literary work' by Maxene Van Der Meersch *d* Curtis Bernhardt *ph* Robert Planck *m* R. G. Kopp
☆ Glenn Ford, Charles Coburn, Gloria de Haven, Janet Leigh, Bruce Bennett, Warner Anderson

Doctor at Large
GB 1957 104m Eastmancolor
Rank (Betty E. Box)

Simon Sparrow tries two country practices, but returns at last to St Swithin's.
Hit-or-miss medical comedy with honours about even.
w Nicholas Phipps *novel* Richard Gordon *d* Ralph Thomas *ph* Ernest Steward *m* Bruce Montgomery
☆ Dirk Bogarde, Muriel Pavlow, James Robertson Justice, Donald Sinden, Shirley Eaton, Derek Farr, Michael Medwin, Edward Chapman, Barbara Murray, Gladys Henson, Lionel Jeffries, A. E. Matthews, Athene Seyler, George Coulouris

Doctor at Sea *
GB 1955 93m Technicolor
VistaVision
Rank/Group Films (Betty E. Box)

Simon Sparrow becomes medical officer on a cargo steamer.
Reasonably lively comedy of errors with nice seascapes and predictable jokes.
w Nicholas Phipps, Jack Davies *d* Ralph Thomas *ph* Ernest Steward *m* Bruce Montgomery
☆ Dirk Bogarde, Brigitte Bardot, Brenda de Banzie, James Robertson Justice, Maurice Denham, Michael Medwin, Hubert Gregg, Raymond Huntley, Geoffrey Keen, George Coulouris, Jill Adams, James Kenney
'Brisk professional humour has given way to the more elementary business of traditional British farce.' – *Penelope Houston, MFB*

Doctor Blood's Coffin
GB 1960 92m Eastmancolor
UA/Caralan (George Fowler)

A disbarred doctor sets up in a Cornish tin mine and begins to emulate Dr Frankenstein.
Lurid horror piece which makes no sort of sense.
w Jerry Juran, James Kelly, Peter Miller *d* Sidney J. Furie *ph* Stephen Dade *m* Buxton Orr
☆ Kieron Moore, Hazel Court, Ian Hunter, Gerald C. Lawson, Kenneth J. Warren, Fred Johnson
'It lacks style, suspense and imagination and will scarcely satisfy even the most naive necrophiliac.' – *MFB*

Dr Christian
Following the success of THE COUNTRY DOCTOR (qv), a rival studio (RKO) made a series of second features about a fictional country doctor, the rights to Dr Dafoe's life story being unavailable. Jean Hersholt again played the leading role and the films were immensely popular in small towns. A TV series followed in the fifties, starring Macdonald Carey.
1939 Meet Dr Christian
1940 The Courageous Dr Christian, Dr Christian Meets the Women, Remedy for Riches
1941 Melody for Three, They Meet Again

Dr Crippen *
GB 1962 98m bw
ABP/John Clein

A quiet doctor murders his wife and elopes with a typist.
Straightforward account of a famous and rather unsurprising Edwardian murder case; well enough made but with no special raison d'être.
w Leigh Vance *d* Robert Lynn *ph* Nicolas Roeg *m* Kenneth Jones
☆ Donald Pleasence, Coral Browne, Samantha Eggar, Donald Wolfit

'Diabolical dictator … devastating discoverer of the most frightening invention in the history of civilized man!'
'The picture made behind locked doors!'
Dr Cyclops *
US 1940 76m Technicolor
Paramount (Merian C. Cooper)

Jungle travellers are captured and miniaturized by a mad scientist.
Splendid special effects and an appropriately sombre atmosphere are hampered by a slow-paced narrative in this minor horror classic.
w Tom Kilpatrick *d* Ernest Schoedsack *ph Henry Sharp, Winton Hoch m* Ernst Toch, Gerard Carbonara, Albert Hay Malotte
☆ *Albert Dekker*, Janice Logan, Victor Kilian, Thomas Coley, Charles Halton

Doctor Death: Seeker of Souls
US 1973 89m Movielab
Fox-Rank/Freedom Arts (Eddie Saeta)

Doctor Death, who has the power to pass his and others' souls into the bodies of those he kills, attempts to re-animate a woman at the request of her grieving husband.
Bizarre low-budget horror which, judging from a brief turn by one of the Three Stooges, is presumably meant to amuse, though, seeing its general ineptitude, it is hard to be sure.
w Sal Ponti *d* Eddie Saeta *ph* Kent Wakeford, Emil Oster *m* Richard LaSalle *ad* Ed Graves *ed* Tony DiMarco
☆ John Considine, Barry Coe, Cheryl Miller, Stewart Moss, Leon Askin, Jo Morrow, Moe Howard
'The spectator who brings a properly black frame of mind to it may well be entertained.' – *Jonathan Rosenbaum, MFB*

Dr Dolittle
US 1967 152m DeLuxe Todd-AO
TCF/APJAC (Arthur P. Jacobs)

In a Victorian English village, Dr Dolittle is a veterinary surgeon who talks to his patients; escaping from a lunatic asylum, he travels with friends to the South Seas in search of the Great Pink Sea Snail.
Lumpish family spectacular with no imagination whatever, further handicapped by charmless performances and unsingable songs.
novels Hugh Lofting *d* Richard Fleischer *ph* Robert Surtees *md* Lionel Newman, Alex Courage *pd* Mario Chiari *w/songs* Leslie Bricusse
☆ Rex Harrison, Anthony Newley, Samantha Eggar, *Richard Attenborough*, William Dix, Peter Bull
song 'Talk to the Animals'; special effects (L. B. Abbott)
best picture; Robert Surtees; Lionel Newman, Alex Courage; Leslie Bricusse (*m*)

'He doesn't just talk to the animals!'
Dr Dolittle
US 1998 85m DeLuxe
TCF (John Davis, Joseph M. Singer, David T. Friendly)

A doctor who can talk to animals is put in an asylum by jealous colleagues.
The second unsuccessful attempt to make a movie of Hugh Lofting's creation; this time, there's talking animatronic animals and crude jokes, but it lacks charm.
w Nat Mauldin, Larry Levin *stories* Hugh Lofting *d* Betty Thomas *ph* Russell Boyd *m* Richard

Gibbs *pd* William Elliott *ed* Peter Teschner *sp* animatronics: Jim Henson's Creature Shop
☆ Eddie Murphy, Ossie Davis, Oliver Platt, Peter Boyle, Richard Schiff, Kristen Wilson, Jeffrey Tambor, Kyla Pratt, Raven-Symoné, Steven Gilborn and also the voices of: Norm Macdonald, Albert Brooks, Chris Rock, Reni Santoni, John Leguizamo, Julie Kavner, Garry Shandling

'This is as self-conscious and iconoclastic as story-telling gets. What kids will make of it, is anyone's guess.' – *Charlotte O'Sullivan, Sight and Sound*

'Slim on story and rife with scatological jokes, the film may strike a chord with pre-teens but misses for an older crowd despite some nifty effects and broad humor.' – *Leonard Klady, Variety*

'The doctor is in again.'

Dr Dolittle 2

US 2001 87m DeLuxe
TCF (John Davis)

Dr Dolittle is asked by forest animals to save their environment from destruction by a timber company.
Amiable, light-weight entertainment for the undemanding, with Murphy in relaxed and mellow mode.
w Larry Levin *stories* Hugh Lofting *d* Steve Carr *ph* Daryn Okada *m* David Newman *pd* William Sandell *ed* Craig P. Herring *sp* Rhythm & Hues
☆ Eddie Murphy (Dr Dolittle), Kristen Wilson (Lisa Dolittle), Jeffrey Jones (Joseph Potter), Kevin Pollak (Jack Riley), Raven-Symone (Charisse Dolittle), Kyla Pratt (Maya Dolittle), Lil' Zane (Eric Wilson), voices of: Steve Zahn (Archie), Norm Macdonald (Lucky), Lisa Kudrow (Ava), Jacob Vargas (Pepito), Michael Epps (Sonny), Michael Rapaport (Joey the Raccoon), Isaac Hayes (Possum), Richard C. Sarafian (God Beaver)

'Abounds in funny business that auds of all ages can enjoy.' – *Variety*

Dr Ehrlich's Magic Bullet ***

US 1940 103m bw
Warner (Wolfgang Reinhardt)
aka: *The Story of Dr Ehrlich's Magic Bullet*

A German scientist develops a cure for venereal disease.
Excellent period biopic: absorbing, convincing and extremely well put together.
w John Huston, Heinz Herald, Norman Burnside *d William Dieterle ph James Wong Howe m* Max Steiner
☆ Edward G. Robinson, Ruth Gordon, Otto Kruger, Donald Crisp, Maria Ouspenskaya, Montagu Love, Sig Rumann, Donald Meek, Henry O'Neill, Albert Basserman, Edward Norris, Harry Davenport, Louis Calhern, Louis Jean Heydt

'A superb motion picture.' – *Pare Lorentz*

John Huston, Heinz Herald, Norman Burnside

Dr Faustus

GB 1967 93m Technicolor
Columbia/Oxford University Screen Productions/Nassau Films/Venfilms (Richard Burton, Richard McWhorter)

A medieval scholar conjures up Mephistopheles and offers his soul in exchange for a life of voluptuousness.
Marlowe's play has been adapted and 'improved', and there is some good handling of the poetry, but the production is flat, dingy and uninspired, as well as ludicrous when Miss Taylor makes her silent appearances.
w Nevill Coghill *play* Christopher Marlowe *d* Richard Burton, Nevill Coghill *ph* Gabor Pogany *m* Mario Nascimbene *pd* John DeCuir
☆ *Richard Burton, Andreas Teuber*, Ian Marter, Elizabeth Donovan, Elizabeth Taylor (Helen of Troy)

'It is of an awfulness that bends the mind. The whole enterprise has the immense vulgarity of a collaboration in which academe would sell its soul for a taste of the glamour of Hollywood, and the stars are only too happy to appear a while in academe.' – *John Simon*

'It turns out to be the story of a man who sold his soul for Elizabeth Taylor.' – *Judith Crist*

Doctor from Seven Dials: see *Corridors of Blood*

'A new prescription for terror.'

Dr Giggles

US 1992 95m DeLuxe Super 35
Universal (Stuart M. Besser)

A mad doctor takes his revenge on those who lynched his equally murderous father.
Predictably grisly horror played for laughs.
w Manny Coto, Graeme Whifler *d* Manny Coto *ph* Robert Draper *m* Brian May *pd* Bill Malley *ed* Debra Neil *sp* Phil Cory Special EFX, Digital Fantasy
☆ Larry Drake, Holly Marie Combs, Cliff de Young, Glenn Quinn, Keith Diamond, Richard Bradford, Michelle Johnson

'Picture is aimed at the low end of the shock audience.' – *Variety*

'A piece of excrement.' – *Nigel Floyd*

'What this project really needs is major script surgery.' – *The Dark Side*

Dr Gillespie's Criminal Case

US 1943 89m bw
MGM
GB title: *Crazy to Kill*

The elderly doctor solves a murder for which an innocent man is in prison.
Skilled programme filler with beloved characters.
w Martin Berkeley, Harry Ruskin, Lawrence Bachmann *d* Willis Goldbeck
☆ Lionel Barrymore, Margaret O'Brien, Donna Reed, Van Johnson, Keye Luke, Marilyn Maxwell
† See also *Dr Kildare*.

Dr Gillespie's New Assistant

US 1942 88m bw
MGM

Shorn of young Dr Kildare, Gillespie chooses a new support from three interns, and meanwhile concentrates on an amnesia case.
Slick series entry which played widely as top of the bill.
w Willis Goldbeck, Harry Ruskin, Lawrence Bachmann *d* Willis Goldbeck
☆ Lionel Barrymore, Van Johnson, Keye Luke, Richard Quine, Susan Peters
† See also *Dr Kildare*.

Dr Goldfoot and the Bikini Machine

US 1965 90m Pathécolor Panavision
AIP (Anthony Carras)

Dr G. makes girl robots programmed to lure wealthy men into their clutches.
Way-out farce for the jaded end of the teenage market; a few lively touches and a climactic chase partly atone for the general tastelessness.
w Elwood Ullman, Robert Kaufman *d* Norman Taurog *ph* Sam Leavitt *m* Les Baxter *ad* Daniel Haller
☆ Vincent Price, Fred Clark, Frankie Avalon, Dwayne Hickman, Susan Hart, Jack Mullaney

'Meet the girls with the thermo-nuclear navels! The most titillating time bombs you've ever been tempted to trigger!'

Dr Goldfoot and the Girl Bombs

US/Italy 1966 86m colour
AIP

The evil mastermind teams up with Red China to cause trouble between Russia and the USA.
Inane teenage nonsense, almost enough to make one swear off movies.
w Louis M. Heyward, Robert Kaufman *d* Mario Bava
☆ Vincent Price, Fabian Forte, Franco Franchi, Laura Antonelli

Dr Heckyl and Mr Hype

US 1980 99m Metrocolor
Golan-Globus

An ugly scientist is transformed into a handsome young sadist.
Would-be comic variation on a well-worn theme; the level of comedy is indicated by the title.
wd Charles B. Griffith
☆ Oliver Reed, Sunny Johnson, Mel Wells, Maia Danziger

Doctor in Clover

GB 1966 101m Eastmancolor
Rank/Betty E. Box-Ralph Thomas

Grimsdyke goes back to his old hospital for a refresher course and finds a rejuvenating drug useful in his philandering.
Depressing mixture of smut and slapstick.
w Jack Davies *novel* Richard Gordon *d* Ralph Thomas *ph* Ernest Steward *m* John Scott
☆ Leslie Phillips, James Robertson Justice, Shirley Anne Field, Joan Sims, John Fraser, Arthur Haynes, Fenella Fielding, Noel Purcell, Jeremy Lloyd, Eric Barker, Terry Scott, Alfie Bass

'Everything is reduced to clichés and stereotypes.' – *Ken Russell*

Doctor in Distress

GB 1963 102m Eastmancolor
Rank/Betty E. Box-Ralph Thomas

Simon Sparrow goes back to work for Sir Lancelot Spratt and finds his old mentor in love.
Tedious flummery whose characters fail to perform with the old pizazz.
w Nicholas Phipps, Ronald Scott Thorn *d* Ralph Thomas *ph* Ernest Steward *m* Norrie Paramor
☆ Dirk Bogarde, James Robertson Justice, Mylene Demongeot, Samantha Eggar, Barbara Murray, Donald Houston, Jessie Evans, Ann Lynn, Leo McKern, Dennis Price

Doctor in Love

GB 1960 97m Eastmancolor
Rank/Betty E. Box-Ralph Thomas

Dr Burke and Dr Hare have various adventures, mostly amorous, in city and country practices.
Virtually plotless collection of weak sketches based on schoolboy smut.
w Nicholas Phipps *novel* Richard Gordon *d* Ralph Thomas *ph* Ernest Steward *m* Bruce Montgomery
☆ Michael Craig, Leslie Phillips, James Robertson Justice, Virginia Maskell, Nicholas Phipps, Reginald Beckwith, Joan Sims, Liz Fraser, Ambrosine Philpotts, Irene Handl

Doctor in the House **

GB 1954 91m Eastmancolor
Rank (Betty E. Box)

Amorous and other misadventures of medical students at St Swithin's Hospital.
A comedy with much to answer for: several sequels and an apparently endless TV series. The original is not bad, as the students, though plainly over age, constitute a formidable mass of British talent at its peak.
w Nicholas Phipps novel Richard Gordon d Ralph Thomas *ph* Ernest Steward *m* Bruce Montgomery
☆ *Dirk Bogarde, Kenneth More*, Donald Sinden, Donald Houston, Kay Kendall, Muriel Pavlow, *James Robertson Justice*, Geoffrey Keen

'Works its way with determined high spirits through the repertoire of medical student jokes.' – *MFB*

'An uproarious, devil-may-care, almost wholly ruthless picture.' – *Dilys Powell*

† Sequels, of increasing inanity and decreasing connection with the original characters, were: *Doctor at Sea, Doctor at Large, Doctor in Love, Doctor in Distress, Doctor in Clover* and *Doctor in Trouble. Carry on Doctor* and *Carry on Again Doctor* were horses of a different colour.

Kenneth More

Doctor in the Village *

Holland 1958 92m bw
Nationale Filmproductie Maatschappij (Bobby Roosenboom)
original title: *Dorp aan de Rivier*

Stories are recalled of an eccentric but respected country doctor at the turn of the century.
Tragi-comic incidents in the vein of Pagnol, a little too rich in farce and melodrama to be convincingly human.
w Hugo Claus *novel* Antoon Coolen *d* Fons Rademakers *ph* Eduard J. R. van der Enden *m* Jurriaan Andriessen
☆ Max Croiset, Mary Dresselhuys, Bernhard Droog, Jan Teulings

'Scenes which should have had disturbing power crowd one upon another with an almost repellent relish which falls over into parody.' – *Peter John Dyer, MFB*

Doctor in Trouble

GB 1970 90m Technicolor
Rank/Betty E. Box

Dr Burke inadvertently becomes a stowaway on an Atlantic cruise.
Witless tailpiece to the Doctor saga, like a half-hearted wrapping-up of discarded jokes from the other episodes.
w Jack Davies *novel Doctor on Toast* by Richard Gordon *d* Ralph Thomas *ph* Ernest Steward *m* Eric Rogers
☆ Leslie Phillips, Harry Secombe, Angela Scoular, Irene Handl, Robert Morley, Simon Dee, Freddie Jones, James Robertson Justice, Joan Sims, John Le Mesurier, Fred Emney

'The cinematic equivalent of an end-of-the-pier summer show.' – *Films and Filming*

Doctor Jack *

US 1922 72m approx (24 fps) bw silent
Pathé/Rolin

A quack country doctor does more good than the licensed medicos.
Pleasing but not hilariously funny star vehicle.
w Sam Taylor, Jean Havez *d* Fred Newmeyer
☆ Harold Lloyd, Mildred Davis, John Prince, Eric Mayne

'The greatest drama of dual identity ever written!'

Dr Jekyll and Mr Hyde **

US 1921 63m (24 fps) bw silent
Paramount Artcraft

A respected London physician experiments with a drug which separates out the evil part of his soul.
A lively star vehicle which renewed John Barrymore's popularity with film audiences. Some scenes still grip, and Barrymore accomplished some transformations in full view of the camera, by facial contortions.
w Clara S. Beranger *novel* Robert Louis Stevenson *d* John S. Robertson
☆ *John Barrymore*, Nita Naldi, Martha Mansfield, Louis Wolheim

'Strange desires! Loves and hates and secret yearnings ... hidden in the shadows of a man's mind!'

Doctor Jekyll and Mr Hyde ****

US 1931 98m bw
Paramount (Rouben Mamoulian)

A Victorian research chemist finds a formula which separates the good and evil in his soul; when the latter predominates, he becomes a rampaging monster.
The most exciting and cinematic version by far of the famous horror story; the make-up is slightly over the top, but the gas-lit London settings, the pace, the performances and clever camera and sound tricks make it a film to enjoy over and over again. Subjective camera is used at the beginning, and for the first transformation the actor wore various layers of make up which were sensitive to different colour filters and thus produced instant change.
w Samuel Hoffenstein, Percy Heath novel Robert Louis Stevenson *d Rouben Mamoulian ph Karl Struss ad Hans Dreier*
☆ *Fredric March*, Miriam Hopkins, Rose Hobart, Holmes Herbert, Halliwell Hobbes, Edgar Norton

'Promises abundant shocks and returns now that the fan public is horror conscious. Probably loses something on popular appeal by highbrow treatment.' – *Variety*

'As a work of cinematic imagination this film is difficult to fault.' – *John Baxter, 1968*

† The screenplay with 1,400 frame blow-ups was published in 1976 in the Film Classics Library (editor Richard J. Anobile).
†† The film was subsequently edited down to 80m, and this is the only version remaining.

Fredric March

Samuel Hoffenstein, Percy Heath; Karl Struss

'A romantic gentleman by day – a love-mad beast at night!'

Dr Jekyll and Mr Hyde **

US 1941 122m bw
MGM (Victor Saville, Victor Fleming)

Curiously misconceived, stately, badly cast version with elaborate production including Freudian dream sequences.
Always worth watching, but not a success.
w John Lee Mahin *d* Victor Fleming *ph* Joseph Ruttenberg *m* Franz Waxman *ed* Harold F. Kress
☆ Spencer Tracy, Ingrid Bergman, Lana Turner, Ian Hunter, C. Aubrey Smith, Donald Crisp, Sara Allgood

'Not so much evil incarnate as ham rampant ... more ludicrous than dreadful.' – *New York Times*

† Other versions: *The Two Faces of Dr Jekyll* (1960), *I Monster* (1970). Variations: *Daughter of Dr Jekyll* (1957), Abbott and Costello Meet Dr Jekyll

and Mr Hyde (1954), *Son of Dr Jekyll* (1951), *The Ugly Duckling* (1960), *House of Dracula* (1945), *The Nutty Professor* (1963), *Dr Jekyll and Sister Hyde* (1971).
Joseph Ruttenberg; Franz Waxman; Harold F. Kress

Dr Jekyll and Ms Hyde
US 1995 89m Technicolor
Rank/Rastar/Savoy/Leider-Shapiro
An under-achieving chemist experiments on a formula he finds in his grandfather's scientific journals, which turns him into an ambitious, seductive woman.
A concept that first surfaced in Hammer's Dr Jekyll and Sister Hyde; *time has not lent it any enchantment, even when it is played for laughs as it is here – unfortunately few are forthcoming.*
w Tim John, Oliver Butcher, William Davies, William Osborne *story* David F. Price *d* David F. Price *ph* Tom Priestley *m* Mark McKenzie *pd* Gregory Melton *ed* Tony Lombardo *sp make-up: Kevin Yagher; visual effects: Dream Quest Images*
☆ Sean Young, Tim Daly, Lysette Anthony, Stephen Tobolowsky, Harvey Fierstein, Polly Bergen, Stephen Shellen
'A typical thesaurus includes some 350 synonyms for the word *bad* – an alarming number of which apply to this thoroughly misbegotten outing.' – *Premiere*
'The film is littered with embarrassingly ham-fisted farce.' – *Kim Newman, Sight and Sound*

Dr Jekyll and Sister Hyde *
GB 1971 97m Technicolor
MGM-EMI/Hammer (Albert Fennell, Brian Clemens)
A twist: Jekyll now turns into a young and beautiful woman, and kills prostitutes so that he can continue his research.
Half-successful attempt to link the legend with Jack the Ripper, killed by gore and overlength.
w Brian Clemens *d* Roy Ward Baker *ph* Norman Warwick *m* David Whitaker *pd* Robert Jones *ed* James Needs
☆ Ralph Bates, Martine Beswick, Gerald Sim, Lewis Fiander, Dorothy Alison

Dr Kildare
This long-running screen hero was a young intern at Blair Hospital, under the cranky tutelage of old Dr Gillespie. Created by Max Brand in a series of novels, he first appeared on the screen in a 1937 Paramount double-biller called INTERNS CAN'T TAKE MONEY, played by Joel McCrea with Barbara Stanwyck, no less, providing the love interest. Kildare came up against gangsters; Gillespie did not appear. MGM then took over the property and went to town with it, making fifteen films in ten years. They were as follows:
1938 Young Dr Kildare
1939 Calling Dr Kildare, The Secret of Dr Kildare
1940 Dr Kildare's Strange Case (qv), Dr Kildare Goes Home (qv), Dr Kildare's Crisis (qv)
1941 The People vs Dr Kildare
1942 Dr Kildare's Wedding Day (qv)
1942 Dr Kildare's Victory (qv), Calling Dr Gillespie, Dr Gillespie's New Assistant (qv)
1943 Dr Gillespie's Criminal Case (qv)
1944 Three Men in White, Between Two Women
1947 Dark Delusion (qv)
Lew Ayres played Kildare, but in 1942 declared himself a conscientious objector and was dropped. The emphasis shifted to Gillespie, played by Lionel Barrymore from a wheelchair, and he proceeded to deal with a whole series of interns. The films were well enough made on medium budgets; nine were directed by Harold S. Bucquet and the last five by Willis Goldbeck, one by W. S. Van Dyke. In 1961 a TV series began with Richard Chamberlain and Raymond Massey, and ran for seven years.

Dr Kildare Goes Home
US 1940 79m bw
MGM
Young Dr Kildare temporarily deserts Blair Hospital to help his father establish a small-town clinic.
Rather below par episode with obvious outcome.
w Willis Goldbeck, Harry Ruskin *d* Harold S. Bucquet
☆ Lew Ayres, Lionel Barrymore, Laraine Day, Samuel S. Hinds, Gene Lockhart

Dr Kildare's Crisis
US 1940 75m bw
MGM
Dr Kildare's fiancée may have epilepsy in the family.
The series at its peak.
w Willis Goldbeck, Harry Ruskin *d* Harold S. Bucquet
☆ Lew Ayres, Lionel Barrymore, Robert Young, Laraine Day, Nat Pendleton, Marie Blake

Dr Kildare's Strange Case
US 1940 77m bw
MGM
The young doctor cures a mental patient by the newest methods.
Crisp series episode.
w Willis Goldbeck, Harry Ruskin *d* Harold S. Bucquet
☆ Lew Ayres, Lionel Barrymore, Laraine Day, Shepperd Strudwick, Samuel S. Hinds

Dr Kildare's Victory
US 1942 92m bw
MGM
GB title: *The Doctor and the Débutante*
Back at Blair, Dr Kildare fights ambulance zoning regulations.
Rather heavy-going episode, its star's last before becoming a conscientious objector and leaving Hollywood for the duration.
w Harry Ruskin, Willis Goldbeck *d* W. S. Van Dyke
☆ Lew Ayres, Lionel Barrymore, Ann Ayars, Robert Sterling

Dr Kildare's Wedding Day
US 1941 83m bw
MGM
GB title: *Mary Names the Day*
Dr Kildare's fiancée is killed in a road accident.
Rather deliberately downbeat episode, well enough assembled.
w Lawrence Bachmann, Ormond Ruthven *d* Harold S. Bucquet
☆ Lew Ayres, Lionel Barrymore, Laraine Day, Red Skelton, Nils Asther

Dr Knock *
France 1936 74m bw
Pathé-Natan
A sly young doctor takes over a country practice and turns the townsfolk into hypochondriacs.
Amusing version of a modern French comedy classic.
w Jules Romains play Jules Romains *d* Louis Jouvet, Roger Goupillières
☆ *Louis Jouvet*, Palau, Le Vigan, Moor, Alexandre Rignault
'Once under way it scoots along like a Bermuda sloop, and holds right till the surprise fadeout.' – *Variety*

'Death is the ultimate vacation.'
Dr M
West Germany/France/Italy 1989 116m colour
Hobo/NEF/Ellepi Film/Clea Productions (Ingrid Windisch)
US title: *Camp Extinction*
A doctor indoctrinates holidaymakers with the desire to commit suicide.
Limp thriller.
w Sollace Mitchell *story* Thomas Bauermeister *d* Claude Chabrol *ph* Jean Rabier *m* Paul Hindemith *pd* Wolfgang Hundhammer, Dante Ferretti *ed* Monique Fardoulis
☆ Alan Bates, Jennifer Beals, Jan Niklas, Hanns Zischler, Benoit Regent, William Berger, Alexander Radszun, Peter Fitz, Daniela Poggi

Doctor Mabuse the Gambler ***
Germany 1922 101m (24 fps) bw silent
UFA (Erich Pommer)
original title: *Doktor Mabuse, der Spieler*
A criminal mastermind uses hypnotism and blackmail in his efforts to obtain world domination, but when finally cornered is discovered to be a raving maniac.
A real wallow in German post-war depression and melodrama, in the form of a Fu Manchu/Moriarty type thriller. Fascinating scene by scene, but by now a slightly tiresome whole.
w Thea von Harbou, Fritz Lang *novel* Norbert Jacques *d Fritz Lang ph* Carl Hoffman *ad* Otto Hunte, Stahl-Urach, Erich Kettelhut, Karl Vollbrecht
☆ Rudolf Klein-Rogge, Alfred Abel, Gertrude Welcker, Lil Dagover, Paul Richter
† Originally issued in Germany in two parts, *Der Grosse Spieler* and *Inferno*, adding up to a much longer running time.
†† See sequels, *The Testament of Dr Mabuse* and *The Thousand Eyes of Dr Mabuse.*

Dr Monica
US 1934 80m bw
Warner (Henry Blanke)
A lady doctor allows her husband to fall for another woman.
Heavy-handed 'woman's picture' which did well at the time.
w Charles Kenyon *play* Marja Morozowicz *d* William Keighley
☆ Kay Francis, Warren William, Jean Muir, Verree Teasdale, Philip Reed, Emma Dunn

Doctor No ***
GB 1962 111m Technicolor
UA/Eon (Harry Saltzman, Albert R. Broccoli)
A British secret service agent foils a master criminal operating in the West Indies.
First of the phenomenally successful James Bond movies, mixing sex, violence and campy humour against expensive sets and exotic locales. Toned down from the original novels, they expressed a number of sixties attitudes, and proved unstoppable box-office attractions for nearly twenty-five years. The first was, if not quite the best, reasonably representative of the series.
w Richard Maibaum, Johanna Harwood, Berkely Mather novel Ian Fleming *d* Terence Young *ph* Ted Moore *m Monty Norman*
☆ *Sean Connery, Ursula Andress*, Jack Lord, Joseph Wiseman, John Kitzmiller, Bernard Lee, Lois Maxwell, Zena Marshall, Eunice Gayson, Anthony Dawson
† The subsequent titles, all qv, were *From Russia with Love* (1963), *Goldfinger* (1964), *Thunderball* (1965), *You Only Live Twice* (1967), *On Her Majesty's Secret Service* (1969), *Diamonds Are Forever* (1971), *Live and Let Die* (1973), *The Man with the Golden Gun* (1974), *The Spy Who Loved Me* (1977), *Moonraker* (1979), *For Your Eyes Only* (1981), *Octopussy* (1983), *A View To A Kill* (1985), *The Living Daylights* (1987), *Licence To Kill* (1989), *Golden Eye* (1995). *Never Say Never Again* (1984) was not part of the series, though it brought back Sean Connery as Bond. *Casino Royale* (1967) was a Bond spoof made by other hands.

Dr Petiot
France 1990 102m colour/bw
Electric/MS/Sara/Cine 5 (Alain Sarde, Philippe Chapelier-Dehesdin)
In wartime Paris, a doctor who claims to help Jews to escape the Nazis kills them instead.
An unflinching examination of a serial killer, filmed in the style of an old-fashioned horror movie.
w Dominique Garnier, Christian de Chalonge *d* Christian de Chalonge *ph* Patrick Blossier *m* Michel Portal *ad* Yves Brover *ed* Anita Fernandez
☆ Michel Serrault, Pierre Romans, Zbigniew Horoks, Berangere Bonvoisin, Aurore Prieto, André Chaumeau, Axel Bogousslavski

'The sting's in the tale!'
Dr Phibes Rises Again *
GB 1972 89m DeLuxe
AIP (Richard Dalton)
The immortal Phibes and his wife rise from the dead to seek an Egyptian elixir of life, and cross swords with a satanic Egyptologist.
Uncertainly paced but generally zippy comic strip for adults, with all concerned entering gleefully into the evil spirit of the thing. See prequel, The Abominable Dr Phibes.
w Robert Fuest, Robert Blees *d* Robert Fuest *ph* Alex Thomson *m* John Gale *ad Brian Eatwell*
☆ *Vincent Price, Robert Quarry*, Valli Kemp, Fiona Lewis, Peter Cushing, Beryl Reid, Terry-Thomas, Hugh Griffith, *Peter Jeffrey*, Gerald Sim, John Thaw, John Cater, Lewis Fiander

'It's refreshing to find a sequel which is better than its prototype.' – *Philip Strick, MFB*

Dr Renault's Secret
US 1942 58m bw
TCF
A scientist turns an ape into a semi-human, which runs amok.
Fairly well done horror support.
w William Bruckner, Robert F. Metzler *d* Harry Lachman
☆ George Zucco, J. Carrol Naish, John Shepperd, Lynne Roberts

Dr Rhythm *
US 1938 80m bw
Paramount
A veterinary surgeon goes into show business.
Easy-going star musical with pleasant songs.
w Jo Swerling, Richard Connell *story* O. Henry *d* Frank Tuttle
☆ Bing Crosby, Beatrice Lillie, Mary Carlisle, Andy Devine, Laura Hope Crews, Rufe Davis

'You'd better watch out!'
Dr Seuss' How the Grinch Stole Christmas *
US 2000 105m CFI
Universal/Imagine (Brian Grazer, Ron Howard)
aka: *The Grinch*
A hairy Christmas-hating creature steals all the presents from Whoville before he learns the error of his ways with the help of a small girl.
A singularly charmless variation on A Christmas Carol, *with a great deal of dull material added to bulk out Seuss' slim book; it, however, found an appreciative mass audience.*
w Jeffrey Price, Peter S. Seaman *book* Dr Seuss *d* Ron Howard *ph* Don Peterman *m* James Horner *pd* Michael Corenblith *ed* Dan Hanley, Mike Hill *sp* makeup fx: Rick Baker, Gail Ryan *cos* Rita Ryack
☆ Jim Carrey (Grinch), Jeffrey Tambor (May Who), Christine Baranski (Martha May Whovier), Bill Irwin (Lou Lou Who), Molly Shannon (Betty Lou Who), Taylor Momsen (Cindy Lou Who), Clint Howard (Whobris), Kelley (Max the Dog), Frank Welker (Voice of Max the Dog), Anthony Hopkins (Narrator)
'The movie is so clogged with kooky gadgetry and special effects and glitter and goo that watching it feels like being gridlocked at Toys 'R' Us during the Christmas rush.' – *Stephen Holden, New York Times*
'A sweet and simple tale gone enormously sour. Shrill, strenuous and entirely without charm, Ron Howard's attempt at a Christmas classic is an elaborately wrapped empty box that will fool many people into buying it.' – *Todd McCarthy, Variety*
† It was the most successful film at the US box office in 2000, taking more than $253m.
make-up (Rick Baker, Gail Ryan)
art direction (Michael Corenblith, Merideth Boswell); Rita Ryack
make-up

'Armed with a doctor's kit, he fought a thousand killers!'
Dr Socrates *
US 1935 70m bw
Warner (Robert Lord)
A small-town doctor is forced to help wounded gangsters, and becomes involved.
Good star melodrama.
w Robert Lord *novel* W. R. Burnett *d* William Dieterle *ph* Tony Gaudio *md* Leo F. Forbstein
☆ *Paul Muni*, Ann Dvorak, Barton MacLane, Robert Barrat, John Eldredge, Hobart Cavanaugh, Mayo Methot, Samuel S. Hinds, Henry O'Neill
'Arriving at the tail end of the G-man and gangster cycle, *Dr Socrates* is a graceful valedictory.' – *Variety*
'Rapid, strong and exciting.' – *Sunday Times*
† Remade as *King of the Underworld* and *Bullet Scars.*

'The hot line suspense comedy!'

Dr Strangelove; or, How I Learned to Stop Worrying and Love the Bomb ★★★★
GB 1963 93m bw
Columbia/Stanley Kubrick (Victor Lyndon)

A mad USAF general launches a nuclear attack on Russia, and when recall attempts fail, and retaliation is inevitable, all concerned sit back to await the destruction of the world.
Black comedy resolving itself into a series of sketches, with the star playing three parts (for no good reason): the US president, an RAF captain, and a mad German-American scientist. Historically an important film in its timing, its nightmares being those of the early sixties, artistically it clogs its imperishable moments by untidy narrative.
w Stanley Kubrick, Terry Southern, Peter George *novel* Red Alert by Peter George *d* Stanley Kubrick *ph* Gilbert Taylor *m* Laurie Johnson *ad* Ken Adam
☆ *Peter Sellers, George C. Scott*, Peter Bull, Sterling Hayden, Keenan Wynn, Slim Pickens, James Earl Jones, Tracy Reed
GENERAL (GEORGE C. SCOTT): 'I don't say we wouldn't get our hair mussed, but I do say no more than ten to twenty million people killed.'
'Scarcely a picture of relentless originality; seldom have we seen so much made over so little.' – *Joan Didion*
'The double-face of the story – serious events broken up into farcical incidents – is expressed in double-face acting of a high order.' – *Dilys Powell*
'Irreverent to the point of savagery; it is funny and it is engrossing. And it's heady stuff for moviegoers, for Kubrick, boy genius that he is, assumes that we're grown-up enough to share his bitter laughter.' – *Judith Crist*
† *Fail Safe* (qv), which took the same theme more seriously, was released almost simultaneously.
best picture; script; Stanley Kubrick (as director); Peter Sellers
best picture; best British film; Ken Adam

Dr Syn ★
GB 1937 80m bw
Gaumont (Michael Balcon)
The vicar of Dymchurch in 1780 is really a pirate believed dead.
This now obscure, lively pirate yarn was its star's last film.
w Michael Hogan, Roger Burford *novel* Russell Thorndike *d* Roy William Neill *ph* Jack Cox *md* Louis Levy *ad* Vetchinsky *ed* R. E. Dearing, Alfred Roome
☆ George Arliss, Margaret Lockwood, John Loder, Roy Emerton, Graham Moffatt, Frederick Burtwell, Meinhart Maur, George Merritt
'With Arliss in the name part it doesn't ring true.' – *Variety*

Dr Syn Alias the Scarecrow
GB 1963 98m Technicolor
Walt Disney (Bill Anderson)

The vicar of Dymchurch is really a smuggler who manages to outwit a rascally general and save a prisoner from Dover Castle.
Oddly released the same year as another version of the story, Captain Clegg, *this rather set-bound adventure yarn turns its hero into a Robin Hood figure. It was originally made to be shown in three parts on American TV.*
w Robert Westerby *novel* Christopher Syn by Russell Thorndike, William Buchanan *d* James Neilson *ph* Paul Beeson *m* Gerard Schurmann
☆ Patrick McGoohan, George Cole, Tony Britton, Geoffrey Keen, Kay Walsh, Patrick Wymark, Alan Dobie, Eric Pohlmann, Michael Hordern

Dr T and the Women
US 2000 122m DeLuxe Panavision
Columbia TriStar/Sandcastle 5 (Robert Altman, James McLindon)

A popular gynaecologist to Dallas's upper crust has problems with his patients, daughters and wife.
Rambling social comedy that lacks any particular point.
w Anne Rapp *d* Robert Altman *ph* Jan Kiesser *m* Lyle Lovett *pd* Stephen Altman *ed* Geraldine Peroni
☆ Richard Gere (Dr Sullivan Travis), Helen Hunt (Bree), Farrah Fawcett (Kate), Laura Dern (Peggy), Shelley Long (Carolyn), Tara Reid (Connie), Kate Hudson (Dee Dee), Liv Tyler (Marilyn), Robert Hays (Harlan), Matt Malloy (Bill), Andy Richter (Eli)
'Altman orchestrates Dr T's odyssey with the precision, heart and lively wit of a virtuoso.' – *Peter Travers, Rolling Stone*

The Doctor Takes a Wife ★
US 1940 89m bw
Columbia (William Perlberg)
A young doctor has to pretend to be the husband of a socialite.
Typical high life comedy of its period, quite brisk and diverting.
w George Seaton, Ken Englund *d* Alexander Hall *ph* Sid Hickox *m* Frederick Hollander *md* Morris Stoloff
☆ Loretta Young, Ray Milland, Edmund Gwenn, Reginald Gardiner, Gail Patrick, Frank Sully, George Metaxa, Charles Halton, Chester Clute

Dr Terror's House of Horrors
GB 1965 98m Technicolor Techniscope
Amicus (Milton Subotsky, Max J. Rosenberg)

An eccentric, who turns out to be Death himself, tells the fortunes of five men in a railway carriage.
One of the first Amicus horror compendiums and a weak one, not helped by wide screen, a couple of naïve scripts and ho-hum acting. The book-ends are quite pleasant, though.
w Milton Subotsky *d* Freddie Francis *ph* Alan Hume *m* Elisabeth Lutyens, Tubby Hayes *ad* Bill Constable *ed* Thelma Connell *sp* Ted Samuels
☆ *Peter Cushing, Ursula Howells, Max Adrian*, Roy Castle, Alan Freeman, Bernard Lee, Jeremy Kemp, Kenny Lynch, Christopher Lee, Michael Gough, Donald Sutherland
† Later collections from the same stable include *Torture Garden, Tales from the Crypt, Vault of Horror* and *Asylum*.

Dr Who and the Daleks
GB 1965 83m Techniscope
British Lion/Regal/Aaru (Milton Subotsky, Max J. Rosenberg)

Three children and their grandfather accidentally start his time machine and are whisked away to a planet where villainous robots rule.
Junior science fiction from the BBC series. Limply put together, and only for indulgent children.
w Milton Subotsky *d* Gordon Flemyng *ph* John Wilcox *m* Malcolm Lockyer
☆ Peter Cushing, Roy Castle, Jennie Linden, Roberta Tovey, Barrie Ingham
† A sequel, no better, emerged in 1966: *Daleks: Invasion Earth 2150 AD*, with similar credits except that Bernard Cribbins instead of Roy Castle provided comic relief.

'A full moon was his signal to kill!'

Doctor X ★★
US 1932 82m Technicolor
Warner (Hal Wallis)

A reporter investigates a series of moon murders and narrows his search to one of several doctors at a medical college.
Fascinating, German-inspired, overblown and generally enjoyable horror mystery whose armless villain commits murders by growing limbs from 'synthetic flesh'.
w Earl Baldwin, Robert Tasker *play* Howard W. Comstock, Allen C. Miller *d* Michael Curtiz *ph* Richard Towers *md* Leo Forbstein
☆ Lee Tracy, Lionel Atwill, Preston Foster, Fay Wray, George Rosener, Mae Busch, Arthur Edmund Carewe, John Wray
'The settings, lighting and final battle with the man-monster are quite stunning.' – *NFT, 1974*
'It almost makes Frankenstein seem tame and friendly.' – *New York Times*

Doctor You've Got to be Kidding
US 1967 93m Metrocolor Panavision
MGM/Trident (Douglas Laurence)
A girl arrives at a maternity hospital chased by three prospective husbands.
Wild and wacky farce which leaves little impression.
w Phillip Shuken *novel* Patte Wheat Mahan *d* Peter Tewkesbury *ph* Fred Koenekamp *m* Kenyon Hopkins
☆ Sandra Dee, George Hamilton, Celeste Holm, Bill Bixby, *Dwayne Hickman*, Dick Kallman, Mort Sahl, Allen Jenkins

'A love caught in the fire of revolution!'

Doctor Zhivago ★★★
US 1965 192m Metrocolor Panavision 70
MGM/David Lean/Carlo Ponti

A Moscow doctor is caught up in World War I, exiled for writing poetry, forced into partisan service and separated from his only love.
Beautifully photographed and meticulously directed, this complex epic has been so reduced from the original novel that many parts of the script simply do not make any kind of sense. What remains is a collection of expensive set-pieces, great for looking if not listening.
w Robert Bolt *novel* Boris Pasternak *d* David Lean *ph* Frederick A. Young *m* Maurice Jarre *pd* John Box *ed* Norman Savage
☆ Omar Sharif, Julie Christie, Rod Steiger, Alec Guinness, Rita Tushingham, Ralph Richardson, Tom Courtenay, Geraldine Chaplin, Siobhan McKenna, Noel Willman, Geoffrey Keen, Adrienne Corri
'A long haul along the road of synthetic lyricism.' – *MFB*
'David Lean's *Doctor Zhivago* does for snow what his *Lawrence of Arabia* did for sand.' – *John Simon*
'It isn't shoddy (except for the music); it isn't soap opera; it's stately, respectable, and dead. Neither the contemplative Zhivago nor the flow of events is intelligible, and what is worse, they seem unrelated to each other.' – *Pauline Kael*
Robert Bolt; Frederick A. Young; Maurice Jarre
best picture; David Lean; Tom Courtenay

A Doctor's Diary
US 1937 77m bw
Paramount
The resident physician of a privately-endowed hospital is impatient with the niceties of procedure.
Unsurprising medical drama which adequately filled half a bill.
w Sam Ornitz, Joseph Anthony *d* Charles Vidor
☆ George Bancroft, John Trent, Helen Burgess, Ruth Coleman, Charles Waldron, Ra Hould, Sidney Blackmer
'Packs enough drama to hold attention.' – *Variety*

The Doctor's Dilemma ★
GB 1958 99m Metrocolor
MGM/Anatole de Grunwald
Eminent Harley Street surgeons debate the case of a devoted wife and her tubercular artist husband.
Well acted but curiously muffled filming of Shaw's Edwardian play about ethics and human values.
w Anatole de Grunwald *play* Bernard Shaw *d* Anthony Asquith *ph* Robert Krasker *m* Joseph Kosma *ad* Paul Sheriff
☆ Leslie Caron, Dirk Bogarde, *John Robinson*, Alastair Sim, Felix Aylmer, Robert Morley, Michael Gwynn, Maureen Delany, Alec McCowen

Doctors' Wives
US 1970 102m Eastmancolor
Columbia/M. J. Frankovich

When Dr Dellman shoots his unfaithful wife, his colleagues reconsider their sex lives.
Adult soap opera from talents who at other times have found better things to do. In the sensational circumstances, two sanguinary operation sequences are tastelessly irrelevant.
w Daniel Taradash *novel* Frank G. Slaughter *d* George Schaefer *ph* Charles B. Lang *m* Elmer Bernstein
☆ Richard Crenna, Janice Rule, Gene Hackman, John Colicos, Dyan Cannon, Diana Sands, Rachel Roberts, Carroll O'Connor, Cara Williams, Ralph Bellamy, Richard Anderson
'Crisis follows hard on crisis to breathlessly ludicrous effect.' – *Tom Milne*

Dodes'ka-den ★★
Japan 1970 140m Eastmancolor
Essential Cinema/Yonki-No-Kai/Toho (Akira Kurosawa, Keisuke Kinoshita, Kon Ichikawa, Masaki Kobayashi)

In a shanty town on the outskirts of Tokyo, a group of down-and-outs go about the daily business of surviving.
Fascinating, detailed portrait of ordinary and eccentric lives in the lower depths.
w Akira Kurosawa, Hideo Orguni, Shinobu Hashimoto *novel* Kisetsu No Nai Machi by Shugoro Yamamoto *d* Akira Kurosawa *ph* Takao Saito, Yasumichi Fukusawa *m* Toru Takemitsu *ad* Yoshiro Muraki, Shinobu Muraki *ed* Reiko Keneko
☆ Yoshitaka Zushi, Kin Sugai, Kaou Kato, Junzaburo Ban, Kiyoko Tange, Michiko Hino, Tatsuhei Shimokawa
Foreign language film

'West of Chicago there was no law! West of Dodge City there was no God!'

Dodge City ★★★
US 1939 104m Technicolor
Warner (Robert Lord)

An ex-soldier and trail boss helps clean up the west's great railroad terminus.
Standard, satisfying big-scale Western with all clichés intact and very enjoyable, as is the soft, rich early colour. The story is plainly inspired by the exploits of Wyatt Earp.
w Robert Buckner *d* Michael Curtiz *ph* Sol Polito, Ray Rennahan *m* Max Steiner
☆ Errol Flynn, Olivia de Havilland, Ann Sheridan, Bruce Cabot, Alan Hale, Frank McHugh, John Litel, Victor Jory, William Lundigan, Henry Travers, Henry O'Neill, Guinn Williams, Gloria Holden
'A lusty Western, packed with action, including some of the dandiest mêlée stuff screened.' – *Variety*
'It looks programmed and underpopulated, though in an elegantly stylized way.' – *New Yorker, 1980*

Dodsworth ★★★
US 1936 101m bw
Samuel Goldwyn

An American businessman takes his wife on a tour of Europe, and their lives are changed.
Satisfying, well-acted drama from a bestselling novel; production values high.
w Sidney Howard *novel* Sinclair Lewis *d* William Wyler *ph* Rudolph Maté *m* Alfred Newman *ad* Richard Day
☆ *Walter Huston, Mary Astor*, Ruth Chatterton, David Niven, Paul Lukas, Gregory Gaye, *Maria Ouspenskaya*, Odette Myrtil, Spring Byington, John Payne
'No one, I think, will fail to enjoy it, in spite of its too limited and personal plot, the sense it leaves behind of a very expensive, very contemporary, Bond Street vacuum flask.' – *Graham Greene*
'William Wyler has had the skill to execute it in cinematic terms, and a gifted cast has been able to bring the whole alive to our complete satisfaction.' – *New York Times*
'A smoothly flowing narrative of substantial interest, well-defined performances and good talk.' – *New York Times*
'An offering of dignity and compelling power to provide you with a treat you can rarely experience in a picture house.' – *Hollywood Spectator*
Richard Day
best picture; Sidney Howard; William Wyler; Walter Huston; Maria Ouspenskaya

The Does: see *Les Biches*

Dog Day Afternoon ★★★
US 1975 130m Technicolor
Warner/AEC (Martin Bregman, Martin Elfand)

Two incompetent robbers are cornered in a Brooklyn bank.
Recreation of a tragi-comic episode from the newspaper headlines; for half its length a fascinating and acutely

observed film which then bogs itself down in a surplus of talk and excessive sentiment about homosexuality.
w Frank Pierson *book* Patrick Mann *d* Sidney Lumet *ph* Victor J. Kemper *m* none
☆ Al Pacino, John Cazale, Charles Durning, Sully Boyar, James Broderick, Chris Sarandon

'There is plenty of Lumet's vital best here in a film that at least glancingly captures the increasingly garish pathology of our urban life.' – *Jack Kroll*

'Scattered moments of wry humour, sudden pathos and correct observation.' – *John Simon*

'The mask of frenetic cliché doesn't spoil moments of pure reporting on people in extremity.' – *New Yorker*

'A long and wearying case history of the beaten, sobbing, despairing and ultimately powerless anti-hero.' – *Karyn Kay, Jump Cut*

'Full of galvanic mirth rooted in human desperation.' – *Michael Billington, Illustrated London News*

'Brisk, humorous and alive with urban energies and angers fretting through the 92 degree heat.' – *Sight and Sound*

Frank Pierson
best picture; Sidney Lumet; Al Pacino; Chris Sarandon
Al Pacino

Dog Days **
Austria/Germany 2001 121m colour
Metro Tartan/Allegro (Helmut Grasser, Philippe Bober)
original title: *Hundstage*
In the summer heat, the middle-class residents of a suburb of Vienna lead bleak lives.
The first feature of a director known for his documentaries, this turns an unblinking eye on discontented people: there are joyless couplings, ritualistic and obsessive behaviour, brutality and sadness. Occasionally humour breaks through, but it is of a melancholy kind. It is a film not easy to forget, nor to watch.
w Ulrich Seidl, Veronika Franz *d* Ulrich Seidl *ph* Wolfgang Thaler *pd* Andreas Donhauser, Renate Martin *ed* Andrea Wagner, Christof Schertenlieb
☆ Maria Hofstatter (Hitchhiker), Christine Jirku (Teacher), Victor Hennemann (Teacher), Georg Friedrich (Lucky), Alfred Mrva (Alarm Man), Erich Finsches (Old Man), Gerti Lehner (Housekeeper), Franziska Weiss (Klaudia)

'Treats the chemistry of human relationships like a cancer, an enormous growth that, unchecked, leads to disease.' – *Elvis Mitchell, New York Times*

'Vibrantly inventive, aesthetically rigorous, sardonic and occasionally quite brilliant.' – *Deborah Young, Variety*

Dog Eat Dog
GB/Germany 2000 94m colour
Film4/Senator/Tiger Aspect/Shoma (Dalziel Douglas)
Four penniless would-be London DJs try various ways to raise money, but only displease a local gangster.
Hapless, episodic, small-minded caper of petty criminals.
w Moody Shoaibi, Mark Tonderai *d* Moody Shoaibi *ph* John Daly *m* Mark Hinton Stewart *pd* Greg Shaw *ed* Luke Dunkley
☆ Mark Tonderai (Rooster), Nathan Constance (Jess), David Oyelowo (C. J.), Crunski (Changarcy), Alan Davies (Phil), Melanie Blatt (Kelly), Gary Kemp (Jesus), Steve Toussaint (Darcy)

'An obnoxious sub-Guy Ritchie caper entirely made up of foul language and loutish doings.' – *Alexander Walker, London Evening Standard*

A Dog of Flanders
US 1959 97m DeLuxe Cinemascope
TCF/Associated Producers (Robert B. Radnitz)
A small boy wants to be an artist; when he runs away in frustration, his shaggy dog, formerly a stray, leads his family to him.
Old-fashioned tear-jerker for well-brought-up children, previously filmed as a silent; quite accomplished in presentation.
w Ted Sherdeman *novel* Ouida *d* James B. Clark *ph* Otto Heller *m* Paul Sawtell, Bert Shefter
☆ David Ladd, Donald Crisp, Theodore Bikel, Max Croiset, Monique Ahrens

Dog Soldiers: see *Who'll Stop the Rain?*

'Six Soldiers. Full Moon. No chance.'
Dog Soldiers
GB/Luxembourg 2002 104m
Pathé/Kismet/Noel Gay Motion Picture Co/Victor Film/Carousel (Christopher Figg, Tom Reeve, David Allen)
In the Scottish Highlands, an army patrol on a training mission is besieged by werewolves.
Bloody, visceral horror movie that plays like a low-budget, less inventive version of John Carpenter's Assault on Precinct 13.
wd Neil Marshall *ph* Sam McCurdy *m* Mark Thomas *pd* Simon Bowles *ed* Neil Marshall *sp* Bob Keen, Image Effects
☆ Sean Pertwee (Sgt Harry Wells), Kevin McKidd (Rfn Lawrence Cooper), Emma Cleasby (Megan), Liam Cunningham (Capt. Richard Ryan), Darren Morfitt (Rfn Phil Witherspoon), Chris Robson (Rfn Joe Kirkley), Leslie Simpson (Terry Milburn), Thomas Lockyer (Corp. Bruce Campbell)

'An unashamedly cheesy, high-octane werewolf movie that remains true to its B-movie inspiration.' – *Derek Elley, Variety*

'Get "touched" by an angel.'
Dogma **
US 1999 135m DeLuxe Panavision
Miramax/View Askew (Scott Mosier)
Two fallen angels plan to take advantage of a theological loophole to re-enter heaven by passing through the entrance to a New Jersey cathedral, an act that will bring the world to an end.
A bizarre comedy that is on the side of the angels (the heavenly host, that is). In part an attack on the dumbing down of religious faith, it is also a hodge-podge of cinematic genres and styles, taking in road and chase movies, surreal and comic encounters, and theological musings.
wd Kevin Smith *ph* Robert Yeoman *m* Howard Shore *pd* Robert 'Ratface' Holtzman *ed* Kevin Smith, Scott Mosier *sp* Bellissimo, Belardinelli Effects; Vincent Guastini; Station X Studios
☆ Ben Affleck (Bartleby), Matt Damon (Loki), Linda Fiorentino (Bethany), Salma Hayek (Serendipity), Jason Lee (Azrael), Jason Mewes (Jay), Alan Rickman (Metatron), Chris Rock (Rufus), George Carlin (Cardinal Glick), Bud Cort (John Doe Jersey), Alanis Morissette (God), Kevin Smith (Silent Bob), Janeane Garofalo (Clinic girl)

'Mr Smith enjoys shock value, but this time he makes it mercilessly funny and places it in the context of an obviously devout, enlightened parable.' – *Janet Maslin, New York Times*

† The film caused controversy among Catholic organisations, as a result of which Miramax sold the film to distributor Lion's Gate.

Dogpound Shuffle
Canada 1974 97m Eastmancolor
Elliott Kastner/Bulldog
aka: *Spot*
An old Irish hobo lives on the earnings of his dancing dog.
Dog-eared 'family film' which didn't seem to entertain many families.
wd Jeffrey Bloom
☆ Ron Moody, David Soul, Ray Stricklyn

Dogs In Space *
Australia 1986 108m colour Panavision
Recorded Releasing/Skouras/Atlantic (Glenys Rowe)
Punks and hippies gather in a squat in Melbourne in the late 1970s.
Episodic, rambling film with a raucous rock soundtrack, but with an engaging affection for its lost tribe of teenagers.
wd Richard Lowenstein *ph* Andrew de Groot *m* Iggy Pop, Dogs In Space and others *ad* Jody Borland *ed* Jill Bilcock
☆ Michael Hutchence, Saskia Post, Nique Needles, Deanna Bond, Tony Helou, Chris Haywood, Peter Walsh, Laura Swanson

A Dog's Life *
US 1918 30m approx bw silent
First National/Charles Chaplin
A tramp and a stray mongrel help each other towards a happy ending.
Threatening sentiment is kept at bay by amusing sight gags in this pleasing star featurette.
wd Charles Chaplin *ph* Rollie Totheroh
☆ Charles Chaplin, Edna Purviance, Chuck Riesner, Henry Bergman, Albert Austin, Scraps

A Dog's Life: see *Mondo Cane (1961)*

The Dogs of War
GB 1980 118m Technicolor
UA/Silverwold (Larry De Waay)
A disenchanted mercenary becomes involved in a plot to take over an impoverished West African state.
Tough but seemingly dated modern irony, somewhat lacking in action and surprise.
w Gary DeVore, George Malko *novel* Frederick Forsyth *d* John Irvin *ph* Jack Cardiff *m* Geoffrey Burgon *pd* Peter Mullins *ed* Antony Gibbs
☆ Christopher Walken, Tom Berenger, Colin Blakely, Hugh Millais, Paul Freeman, Robert Urquhart

Dogtown and Z-Boys *
US 2001 90m bw/colour
Columbia Tri-Star/Vans Off the Wall/Agi Orsi
Documentary on a group of working-class Los Angeles skateboarders who revolutionised the sport in the mid-1970s by introducing surfboarding techniques.
Intermittently interesting hagiography of a group of youthful slackers who gained fame and, in some cases, wealth by their aggressive athleticism.
w Stacy Peralta, Craig Stecyk *d* Stacy Peralta *ph* Peter Pilafian *pd* C. R. Stecyk *ed* Paul Crowder
☆ Sean Penn (Narrator)

'Loopy, spacey, hugely endearing and exciting documentary.' – *Peter Bradshaw, Guardian*

Doing Time: see *Porridge*

Doktor Mabuse, der Spieler: see *Doctor Mabuse*

La Dolce Vita ****
Italy/France 1960 173m bw Totalscope
Riama/Pathé Consortium (Giuseppe Amato)
aka: *The Sweet Life*
A journalist mixes in modern Roman high society and is alternately bewitched and sickened by what he sees.
Episodic satirical melodrama, a marathon self-indulgent wallow with a wagging finger never far away. Full of choice moments such as a statue of Christ being flown by helicopter over the city.
w Federico Fellini, Tullio Pinelli, Ennio Flaiano, Brunello Rondi *d* Federico Fellini *ph* Otello Martelli *m* Nino Rota *ad* Piero Gherardi
☆ Marcello Mastroianni, Anita Ekberg, Anouk Aimée, Alain Cuny, Yvonne Furneaux, Magali Noel, Nadia Gray, Lex Barker

'Its personification of various familiar symbols – love, death, purity, sin, reason and so on – never succeeds in reflecting human values or creating intellectual excitement ... Its actual significance rests in the way its (albeit specious) social attack has stirred the imagination of other Italian film-makers, as well as public interest in their work.' – *Robert Vas, MFB*

'An awesome picture, licentious in content but moral and vastly sophisticated in its attitude and what it says.' – *Bosley Crowther, New York Times*

'One of the few films that one feels can be seen with increasing enjoyment a second or third time.' – *Paul V. Backley, New York Herald Tribune*

script; Federico Fellini

Doll Face
US 1945 80m bw
TCF (Bryan Foy)
GB title: *Come Back to Me*
A burlesque queen goes to Broadway.
Lower case musical of minimal interest.
w Leonard Praskins *d* Lewis Seiler *ph* Joseph LaShelle *m/ly* Harold Adamson, Jimmy McHugh
☆ Vivian Blaine, Dennis O'Keefe, Carmen Miranda, Perry Como, Martha Stewart, Michael Dunne, Reed Hadley, George E. Stone, Donald McBride, Edgar Norton

The Doll Squad
US 1973 101m Eastmancolor
Nationwide/Feature-Faire (Ted V. Mikels)
A female team of CIA agents track down the man who sabotaged an American space project.
Badly made, poorly scripted and acted comedy thriller.
w Jack Richesin, Pam Eddy, Ted V. Mikels *d* Ted V. Mikels *ph* Anthony Salinas *m* Nicholas Carras *pd* Mike McCloskey *ed* Ted V. Mikels
☆ Michael Ansara, Francine York, Anthony Eisley, John Carter, Rafael Campos, William Bagdad, Lillian Garrett

'The endless running, jumping and kicks-to-the-groin stunts of this bevy of Emma Peels are conceived and executed with about as much conviction as knockabout comedy.' – *David Pirie, MFB*

Dollar
Sweden 1938 80m bw
Svensk Filmindustri
An American millionairess upsets the lives of three married couples.
A sour and brittle little comedy of romantic misunderstandings.
w Stina Bergman *play* Hjalmar Bergman *d* Gustaf Molander *ph* Åke Dahlquist
☆ Ingrid Bergman, Georg Rydeberg, Tutta Rolfe, Kotti Chave, Birgit Tengroth, Håkan Westergren, Edvin Adolphson, Elsa Burnett

The Dollar Bottom
GB 1981 33m Eastmancolor
Rocking Horse Films/Paramount
A sharp-witted public schoolboy sells his friends insurance against being beaten.
Ingenious but thinly acted short, with the added hazard of impenetrable accents.
w Shane Connaughton *story* James Kennaway *d* Roger Christian
☆ Rikki Fulton, Robert Urquhart, Jonathan McNeil

Dollars *
US 1971 120m Technicolor
Columbia/M. J. Frankovich
GB title: *The Heist*
An American security expert installs an electronic system in a Hamburg bank which he plans to rob himself.
Overlong caper comedy-drama which is quite good to watch when it starts moving, though the quick cutting, short takes and deliberately obscure narrative leave one breathless.
wd Richard Brooks *ph* Petrus Schloemp *m* Quincy Jones
☆ Warren Beatty, Goldie Hawn, Gert Frobe, Robert Webber, Scott Brady, Arthur Brauss

'An essay in virtuoso film construction ... rather as if one were watching a perfect machine in full throttle but with nowhere to go.' – *John Gillett*

Dolls
US 1986 77m colour
Empire Pictures/Taryn Productions (Brian Yuzna)
On a dark and stormy night, stranded travellers take refuge in an old house inhabited by an elderly couple and their killer dolls.
Risible, low-budget horror with more clichés than corpses.
w Ed Naha *d* Stuart Gordon *ph* Mac Ahlberg *m* Fuzzbee Morse, Victor Spiegel *pd* Giovanni Natalucci *ed* Lee Percy
☆ Stephen Lee, Guy Rolfe, Hilary Mason, Ian Patrick Williams, Carolyn Purdy-Gordon, Cassie Stuart, Bunty Bailey, Carrie Lorraine

A Doll's House *
GB 1973 95m Eastmancolor
Elkins/Freeward (Hillard Elkins)
A wife begins to resist her husband's will. Ibsen's feminist play was always good value; set in Norway in the 1890s, it was taken up eighty years later as a precursor of women's lib, which accounts for two film versions in one year.
This one is simply staged and well performed, but suffers from a bad translation.
w Christopher Hampton *play* Henrik Ibsen *d* Patrick Garland *ph* Arthur Ibbetson *m* John Barry

☆ Claire Bloom, Anthony Hopkins, Ralph Richardson, Denholm Elliott, Anna Massey, Edith Evans

A Doll's House
GB/France 1973 106m Eastmancolor
World Film Services/Les Films de la Boétie (Joseph Losey)

Opened out but less effective version of the above, with too much solemnity and the central part miscast.
w David Mercer *play* Henrik Ibsen *d* Joseph Losey *ph* Gerry Fisher *m* Michel Legrand
☆ Jane Fonda, David Warner, Trevor Howard, Edward Fox, Delphine Seyrig, Anna Wing

The Dolly Sisters **
US 1945 114m Technicolor
TCF (George Jessel)
The lives of a Hungarian sister act in American vaudeville.
Fictionalized biographical musical, only fair in the script department but glittering to look at in superb colour, and enriched by splendid production values. Undoubtedly among the best of its kind.
w John Larkin, Marian Spitzer *d* Irving Cummings *ph Ernest Palmer m/ly* various *md* Alfred Newman, Charles Henderson *ch* Seymour Felix *ad Lyle Wheeler, Leland Fuller*
☆ Betty Grable, June Haver, John Payne, S. Z. Sakall, Reginald Gardiner, Frank Latimore, Gene Sheldon, Sig Rumann, Trudy Marshall
song 'I Can't Begin to Tell You' (*m* James Monaco, *ly* Mack Gordon)

'They Were Separated By A Death … And Reunited By A Murder.'
Dolores Claiborne **
US 1995 131m Technicolor Panavision
Rank/Castle Rock (Taylor Hackford, Charles Mulvehill)

When an elderly woman dies, her housekeeper, who had earlier been acquitted of killing her husband, is arrested for her murder, an event that brings home her estranged daughter, whom she has not seen for 15 years.
Effective melodrama with feminist overtones: all the women are abused or misunderstood, all the men are abusers; what saves it from too much over-simplification is the revelation of the reasons for the edgy relationship between mother and daughter.
w Tony Gilroy *novel* Stephen King *d* Taylor Hackford *ph* Gabriel Beristain *m* Danny Elfman *pd* Bruno Rubeo *ed* Mark Warner
☆ Kathy Bates (Dolores Claiborne), Jennifer Jason Leigh (Selena St George), Judy Parfitt (Vera Donovan), Christopher Plummer (Det. John Mackey), David Strathairn (Joe St George), Eric Bogosian (Peter), John C. Reilly (Frank Stamshaw), Bob Gunton (Mr Pease)
'Highly engrossing psychological study that manages to be both raw and finally tender in its treatment.' – *Lizzie Franke*
'The sensible formality of Taylor Hackford's direction has the effect of cooling the film's narrative frenzies and helping the actors dig some simple, truthful stuff out of the hubbub.' – *Richard Schickel, Time*

Dom Za Vesanje: see *Time Of the Gypsies*

Domani è Troppo Tardi
Italy 1950 101m bw
Rizzoli (Giuseppe Amato)
GB title: *Tomorrow Is Too Late*
Inquisitive pupils and repressive teachers at a co-educational school almost cause a tragedy.
Possibly well intentioned, but in effect an old-fashioned melodrama which works well enough on its level.
w Alfred Machard, Leonide Moguy *d* Leonide Moguy *ph* Mario Craveri, Renato del Frate *m* Alessandro Cicognini
☆ Vittorio de Sica, Lois Maxwell, Gabrielle Dorziat, Anna Maria Pierangeli, Gino Leurini

Domenica d'Agosto **
Italy 1950 75m bw
Colonna (Sergio Amidei)
GB title: *Sunday in August*
Various Romans enjoy Sunday by the sea at Ostia.
Fragmented comedy-drama which succeeds in being charming throughout, every detail being freshly observed through an inquisitive eye.
w Franco Brusati, Luciano Emmer, Giulio Macchi, Cesare Zavattini *d Luciano Emmer ph* Domenico Scala, Leonida Barboni, Ubaldo Marelli *m* Roman Vlad *ed* Jolanda Benvenuti
☆ Anna Baldini, Franco Interlenghi, Elvy Lissiak, Massimo Serato, Marcello Mastroianni, Corrado Verga

'He will do anything to protect his family.'
Domestic Disturbance
US 2001 90m DeLuxe 'Scope
Paramount (Donald De Line, Jonathan D. Krane)

A twelve year-old boy realises that his new stepfather is a sadist, but only his father will believe him.
Uninteresting family drama involving a set of cardboard characters.
w Lewis Colick *d* Harold Becker *ph* Michael Seresin *m* Mark Mancina *pd* Clay A. Griffith *ed* Peter Honess
☆ John Travolta (Frank Morrison), Vince Vaughn (Rick Barnes), Teri Polo (Susan), Matt O'Leary (Danny Morrison), Ruben Santiago-Hudson (Sgt Edgar Stevens), Susan Floyd (Diane), Angelica Torn (Patty), Steve Buscemi (Ray Coleman)
'An engaging if predictable thriller.' – *Observer*
'A low-end example of family imperilment hokum.' – *Todd McCarthy, Variety*

Domicile Conjugal: see *Bed and Board*

The Dominant Sex
GB 1937 71m bw
BIP (Walter Mycroft)
A woman demands the right to her own individuality after marriage.
Tepid comedy drama from a popular stage play.
w Vina de Vesci, John Fernald *play* Michael Egan *d* Herbert Brenon *ph* J. J. Cox, Roy Clark *ad* Cedric Dawe
☆ Phillips Holmes, Diana Churchill, Carol Goodner, Romney Brent, Hugh Miller, Billy Milton

Dominick and Eugene: see *Nicky and Gino*

Dominion Tank Police Acts I & II (dubbed)
Japan 1989 80m colour
Masamune Shirow/Hakusensha/Agent 21/Toshiba Video (Ritsuko Kakita, Kazuhiko Inomata, Tomaki Harada)

A girl who joins the Tank Police in its fight against crime accidentally destroys a large tank and builds a smaller, cute one.
Japanese animated comic-book fare, revealing a debt to American strip cartoons, done with less violence and more humour than usual. The story, such as it is, is continued in Dominion Tank Police Acts III & IV.
w Kouichi Mashimo *story* Masamune Shirow *d* Kouichi Mashimo *ad* Matsuharu Miyamae
☆ Featuring the voices of Toni Barry, Stephen Graf, Sean Barrett, Jesse Vogel, Bill Armstrong, John Bull, Marc Smith
† The film was released direct to video.

Dominion Tank Police Acts III & IV (dubbed)
Japan 1989 70m colour
Masamune Shirow/Hakusensha/Agent 21/Toshiba Video (Kazuhiko Inomata, Tomaki Harada)

An android criminal and his two cat-like female accomplices who steal a priceless painting and kidnap a policewoman are hunted down by the Tank Police and a private security organization.
Bizarre animated movie, mixing comedy, violence, science fiction and mysticism in a manner that is unlikely to engage the interest of occidental audiences, despite its slick, cartoon-like style.
w Dai Kohno *story* Masamune Shirow *d* Takaaki Ishiyama *ph* Kazushi Torigoe *m* Brown Eyes *ad* Osamu Honda
☆ Featuring the voices of Toni Barry, Stephen Graf, Sean Barrett, Jesse Vogel, Bill Armstrong, John Bull, Marc Smith, Alison Dowling, Garrick Hagon
† The film was released direct to video.

'Dominique will make you shriek!'
Dominique
GB 1978 100m colour
Grand Prize/Melvin Simon (Milton Subotsky, Andrew Donally)

A woman who was convinced that her husband was deliberately driving her mad is found dead, and buried, but seemingly returns…
The old Diabolique syndrome revamped in a very parsimonious production with little to hold the interest.
w Edward and Valerie Abraham *novel What Beckoning Ghost* by Harold Lawlor *d* Michael Anderson *ph* Ted Moore *m* David Whitaker
☆ Cliff Robertson, Jean Simmons, Jenny Agutter, Simon Ward, Ron Moody, Judy Geeson, Michael Jayston, Flora Robson, David Tomlinson, Jack Warner

The Domino Killings: see *The Domino Principle*

'Trust no one. No one!'
The Domino Principle
US 1977 100m CFI color
Associated General Films (Lew Grade, Martin Starger)

GB title: *The Domino Killings*
A murderer is offered his freedom if he will assassinate a national figure.
Fashionable, complex and rather boring political thriller.
w Adam Kennedy *novel* Adam Kennedy *d* Stanley Kramer *ph* Fred Koenekamp, Ernest Laszlo *m* Billy Goldenberg
☆ Gene Hackman, Richard Widmark, Candice Bergen, Mickey Rooney, Edward Albert, Eli Wallach, Ken Swofford, Neva Patterson
'Terrible movies tend to start with a preposterous premise and then laboriously work their way to an impossible conclusion. This one however starts with an arrant impossibility and works its way to whatever lies beyond and below that.' – *John Simon*

Don Camillo e l'Onorevolo Peppone: see *Don Camillo's Last Round*

Don Camillo's Last Round *
Italy 1955 98m bw
Rizzoli
original title: *Don Camillo e l'Onorevole Peppone*
The village Catholic priest tries to stop the re-election of the communist mayor.
Pleasant third collection of encounters with familiar characters.
w Giovanni Guareschi and others *books* Giovanni Guareschi *d* Carmine Gallone *ph* Anchise Brizzi *m* Alessandro Cicognini
☆ Fernandel, Gino Cervi, Claude Silvain, Leda Gloria
'The episodic narrative is full of mildly amusing incident.' – *MFB*

Don Giovanni
France/Italy/Germany 1979 184m colour
Gaumont-Opera-Camera One (Michel Seydoux)

Grandiose but artistically somewhat hesitant version of Mozart's opera; little here for film buffs.
d Joseph Losey *ph* Gerry Fisher *ad* Alexander Trauner *cinematic conception* Rolf Lieberman
☆ Ruggero Raimondi, John Macurdy, Edda Moser, Kiri Te Kanawa

The Don Is Dead
US 1973 117m Technicolor
Universal/Hal B. Wallis (Paul Nathan)

Cross and double cross among Mafia families.
A failed attempt to cash in on The Godfather, *this endless melodrama is boringly violent and totally predictable.*
w Marvin H. Albert *novel* Marvin H. Albert *d* Richard Fleischer *ph* Richard H. Kline *m* Jerry Goldsmith
☆ Anthony Quinn, Frederic Forrest, Robert Forster, Al Lettieri, Angel Tompkins, Charles Cioffi

Don Juan **
US 1926 126m bw
Warner

Exploits of the famous lover and adventurer at Lucretia Borgia's court.
Lithe swashbuckler in the best silent tradition, but with a synchronized score (by William Axt) which made it a sensation and led directly to the talkie revolution.
w Bess Meredyth *d* Alan Crosland *ph Byron Haskin*
☆ *John Barrymore*, Mary Astor, Warner Oland, Estelle Taylor, Myrna Loy, Phyllis Haver, Willard Louis, Montagu Love

'The story of a man who thought he was the greatest lover in the world … and the people who tried to cure him of it!'
Don Juan de Marco *
US 1995 90m colour
Entertainment/New Line/American Zoetrope (Francis Ford Coppola, Fred Fuchs, Patrick Palmer)

A young man wearing a mask and cape who claims to be a legendary lover is examined by a psychiatrist.
A dashingly romantic, modern-day variation on the old swashbuckling movies, enabling audiences to enjoy the fantasy while it is being explained away.
wd Jeremy Leven *ph* Ralf Bode *m* Michael Kamen *pd* Sharon Seymour *ed* Tony Gibbs
☆ Marlon Brando, *Johnny Depp*, Faye Dunaway, Geraldine Pailhas, Bob Dishy, Rachel Ticotin, Talisa Soto, Richard Sarafian
'Great Lover spoof is a long-winded bore.'– *Alexander Walker, London Evening Standard*
'Romantic without being super-sweet and avoids the heaviness of most Hollywood attempts to spring a tear.' – *Derek Malcolm, Guardian*
song 'Have You Ever Really Loved A Woman' (*m/ly* Michael Kamen, Bryan Adams, Robert John Lange)

Don Juan Quilligan
US 1945 76m bw
TCF
A would-be romantic bargee becomes engaged to two girls simultaneously, one on each side of the Hudson.
Thin comedy of bigamy, similar to The Captain's Paradise, *which came later.*
w Arthur Kober, Frank Gabrielson *d* Frank Tuttle
☆ William Bendix, Phil Silvers, Joan Blondell, Mary Treen, Anne Revere, George Macready

'The finest adventure tale ever screened!'
Don Q Son of Zorro *
US 1925 170m (16 fps) bw silent
United Artists
Further adventures in the manner of the star's 1920 hit (see *The Mark of Zorro*).
w Jack Cunningham *novel* K. and H. Prichard *d* Donald Crisp *ph* Henry Sharp
☆ *Douglas Fairbanks*, Mary Astor, Donald Crisp, Jack McDonald, Jean Hersholt

Don Quixote *
France 1933 82m bw
Vandor/Nelson/Wester

An adequate potted version starring Fedor Chaliapin and in the English version George Robey (French version: Dorville).
w Paul Morand, Alexandre Arnoux, from Cervantes *d* G. W. Pabst *ph* Nikolas Farkas, Paul Portier *m* Jacques Ibert *ad* Andrei Andreiev
'Strictly for the arty clientele … for general consumption tedious and dull. Americans in general may feel that the story scarcely rates retelling.' – *Variety*

Don Quixote **
USSR 1957 105m Agfacolor Sovscope
Lenfilm
An extremely handsome version with a commanding star performance.
w E. Schwarz *d* Grigori Kozintsev *ph* Andrei Moskvin, Apollinari Dudko *m* Kara-Karayev *ad* Yevgeny Yenei
☆ *Nikolai Cherkassov*, Yuri Tolubyev
† Other versions came from France in 1902 and 1908, Italy in 1910, France in 1911, USA in 1915, Britain in 1923, Denmark in 1926, Spain in 1947,

Britain in 1972, and Britain (ballet version with Nureyev) in 1975.

Dona Flor and Her Two Husbands
Brazil 1976 110m Eastmancolor
Carnaval (Luis Carlos Barreto)

A young widow remarries, and has to share her bed with her late husband's ghost.
Semi-pornographic comedy which achieved some fashionable success.
wd Bruno Barreto *novel* Jorge Amado
ph Maurito Salles *m* Chico Buarque de Holanda
☆ Sonia Braga, Jose Wilker, Mauro Mendonca

Dona Herlinda and Her Son *
Mexico 1986 90m colour
Clasa Films Mondiales (Manuel Barbachano Ponce)
original title: *Doña Herlinda y Su Hijo*
A mother insists that her homosexual son, a doctor, get married, whereupon he sets up home with his wife and boyfriend.
An amusing comedy of manners, on how to remain gay in a masculine society.
wd Jaime Humberto Hermosillo *ph* Miguel Erhenberg *ed* Luis Kelly
☆ Arturo Meza, Marco Antonio Treviño, Leticia Lupercio, Guadalupe Del Toro, Angelica Guerrero, Donato Casteñeda, Guillermina Alba

Donald Cammell's Wild Side *
US 2000 DeLuxe
Nu Image (Elie Cohn, John Langley)

A bank executive who moonlights as a prostitute becomes involved with a millionaire money launderer and his wife.
Oblique, melodramatic tale of homoerotic intrigue and betrayal among crazed individuals, in which normality never intrudes; Walken gives one of his notably eccentric, over-the-edge performances.
w Donald Cammell, China Kong *d* Donald Cammell *ph* Sead Mutarevic *m* Ryuichi Sakamoto *pd* Claire Bowin *ed* Frank Mazzola *cos* Alison Hirsch
☆ Christopher Walken (Bruno Buckingham), Joan Chen (Virginia Chow), Steven Bauer (Tony), Anne Heche (Alex Lee), Allen Garfield (Dan Rackman), Adam Novack (Lyle Litvak), Zion (Hiro Sakamoto), Richard Palmer (Cop Driver), Randy Crowder (Federal Agent), Marcus Aurelius (James Reed), Lewis Arquette (The Chief)
'An extraordinary piece of work.' – *Sight and Sound*
† The film exists in two versions. It was originally released direct to video in 1995 in a version cut by the producers and repudiated by Donald Cammell. After Cammell's suicide, editor Frank Mazzola recreated the film's original cut, which ran for 20 minutes longer and was first shown in British cinemas in 2000. This director's cut was produced by Hamish McAlpine and Nick Jones.
†† The original score by Jon Hassell and Jaimie Muhoberac was replaced by a new score by Sakamoto for the director's cut.

Dondi
US 1960 80m bw
Allied Artists
GIs in Italy adopt an orphan boy, who stows away to be with them in America.
Glutinous, sentimental comedy-drama.
w Albert Zugsmith, Gus Edson, from a comic strip *d* Albert Zugsmith
☆ David Janssen, Patti Page, Walter Winchell, Mickey Shaughnessy, Robert Strauss, Arnold Stang, Gale Gordon

Dongchun De Rizi: see *The Days*

La Donna del Fiume: see *Woman of the River*

Donna Donna
Holland 1987 90m colour
Movies Film (Chris Brouwer, Haig Balian)
Distressed by his inability to attract a girlfriend, a bright but inept student falls in love with a girl on a poster.
A small-scale, lackadaisical comedy, amiable enough in its casual way.
w Luc Van Beek *d* Hans Van Beek, Luc Van Beek *ph* Peter de Bont *m* Bert Hermelink *ad* Harry Ammerlaan *ed* Wim Louwrier
☆ René Van 'Thof, Simone Walraven, Glenn Durfort, Guusje Van Tilborgh, Bridget George, Joke Tjalsma, Lou Landré, Heleen Van Meurs

'1978. The US Government Waged A War Against Organised Crime. One Man Was Left Behind The Lines.'
Donnie Brasco ***
US 1997 126m Technicolor Panavision
Entertainment/Mandalay/Baltimore (Mark Johnson, Barry Levinson, Louis DiGiaimo, Gail Mutrux)

After he successfully infiltrates the Mafia, an undercover agent for the FBI finds himself torn between duty and friendship for the gangster who vouched for him.
A Mob movie, based on a true story, that takes an almost academic interest in the rituals and manners of its denizens, concerned less with their actions than their characters, which gives it an effectively tragic intensity as two different sets of loyalties collide.
w Paul Attanasio *book* Joseph D. Pistone with Richard Woodley *d Mike Newell ph* Peter Sova *m* Patrick Doyle *pd* Donald Graham Burt *ed* Jon Gregory
☆ *Al Pacino, Johnny Depp,* Michael Madsen, Bruno Kirby, James Russo, Anne Heche, Zeljko Ivanek, Gerry Becker, Zach Grenier
'One of the best gangster movies you'll see this year, bursting with tension and filled with rewarding moments.' – *John Patterson, Neon*
Paul Attanasio

'Dark, Darkest, Darko'
Donnie Darko ***
US 2001 113m DeLuxe Panavision
Metrodome/Pandora/Flower (Sean McKittrick, Nancy Juvonen, Adam Fields)

In the late 1980sw, a troubled teenage boy, who is prone to sleepwalking, is visited by a large rabbit, who tells him that the world is soon going to end.
An engaging, darkly comic look at growing up in suburbia; lurid and deliberately confusing in its circular narrative, it is also bracingly original.
wd Richard Kelly *ph* Steven Poster *m* Michael Andrews *pd* Alexander Hammond *ed* Sam Bauer, Eric Strand
☆ Jake Gyllenhaal (Donnie Darko), Jena Malone (Gretchen Ross), Drew Barrymore (Karen Pomeroy), James Duval (Frank), Maggie Gyllenhaal (Elizabeth Darko), Mary McDonnell (Rose Darko), Holmes Osborne (Eddie Darko), Katharine Ross (Dr Lillian Thurman), Patrick Swayze (Jim Cunningham), Noah Wyle (Dr Monnitoff)
'What a refreshingly different, distinctive piece of work it is.' – *Peter Bradshaw, Guardian*
'Kelly is unable to give the movie the kind of pacing that would make us laugh and shock us simultaneously, because he's too infatuated with an aura of hand-me-down gloom.' – *Elvis Mitchell, New York Times*

The Donor
Canada 1994 94m colour
MCEG Sterling (Damian Lee)

A stuntman spends the night with an attractive woman and wakes up to find that he is missing a kidney.
Part action film, part psychological thriller: neither works – the action sequences include a bicycle chase, and script and acting aren't up to emotional depth.
w Neal Dobrofsky, Tippi Dobrofsky *d* Damian Lee *ph* Gerald R. Goozee *m* Ronald J. Weiss *pd* John Gillespie *ed* David Ransley
☆ Jeff Wincott, Michelle Johnson, Gordon Thomson, Richard Zeppieri, Joseph Scorsiani, Amanda Tapping, Geza Kovacs

Donovan's Brain *
US 1953 81m bw
UA/Dowling (Tom Gries)

An unscrupulous tycoon is fatally injured, but his brain is kept alive by a surgeon who finds himself dominated by it.
Modest competence marks this version of a much filmed novel, with quiet suspense and a firm central performance.
wd Felix Feist *novel* Curt Siodmak *ph* Joseph Biroc *m* Eddie Dunstedter
☆ *Lew Ayres,* Gene Evans, Nancy Davis, Steve Brodie, Lisa K. Howard
† It was a remake of *The Lady and the Monster* (qv).

Donovan's Reef
US 1963 108m Technicolor
Paramount (John Ford)

War veterans settle down on a South Sea island; when the daughter of one of them comes to visit, his reputation must be protected.
Good-humoured but finally enervating mixture of rough-house and slapstick, with the appearance of an old friends' benefit and the director in familiar sub-standard form.
w Frank Nugent, James Edward Grant *d* John Ford *ph* William H. Clothier *m* Cyril Mockridge
☆ John Wayne, Lee Marvin, Jack Warden, Elizabeth Allen, Dorothy Lamour, Cesar Romero, Mike Mazurki

Don's Party *
Australia 1976 90m Eastmancolor
Miracle/Double Head/AFC (Philip Adams)

In suburban Sydney, a political celebration party turns into a pretence of wife-swapping.
Fairly acute observation of middle-class antipodean mores, interrupted with predictable bouts of antipodean crudeness.
w David Williamson *play* David Williamson *d* Bruce Beresford
☆ Ray Barrett, Clare Binney, Pat Bishop, Graeme Blundell, John Hargreaves

Don't Be a Menace to South Central While Drinking Your Juice in the Hood
US 1996 88m DeLuxe
Miramax/Island/Ivory Way (Keenen Ivory Wayans, Eric L. Gold)

A son moves in with his irresponsible father and gun-toting cousin.
Broad-humoured satire that sends up socially conscious movies of black experience; the jokes are usually coarse and sometimes funny.
w Shawn Wayans, Marlon Wayans, Phil Beauman *d* Paris Barclay *ph* Russ Brandt *m* John Barnes *pd* Aaron Osborne *ed* William Young
☆ Shawn Wayans, Marlon Wayans, Tracey Cherelle Jones, Chris Spencer, Suli McCullough, Darrell Heath, Keenen Ivory Wayans
'Full of obvious spoofery and funnier in the concept than in execution.' – *Variety*

Don't Bother to Knock *
US 1952 76m bw
TCF (Julian Blaustein)

A deranged girl gets a baby-sitting job in a hotel and terrifies all concerned by threatening to kill her charge.
Curious vehicle for the emergent Monroe, who is not up to it, as who would be? Technical credits par, but entertainment value small.
w Daniel Taradash *novel* Charlotte Armstrong *d* Roy Baker *ph* Lucien Ballard *m* Lionel Newman
☆ Marilyn Monroe, Richard Widmark, Anne Bancroft, Donna Corcoran, Jeanne Cagney, Lurene Tuttle, Jim Backus, Elisha Cook Jnr

Don't Bother to Knock
GB 1961 89m Technicolor Cinemascope
ABP/Haileywood (Frank Godwin)

US title: *Why Bother to Knock*
A Casanova travel agent gives each of his girlfriends a key to his Edinburgh flat.
Poorly developed and self-conscious sex farce.
w Denis Cannan, Frederic Gotfurt, Frederic Raphael *novel* Clifford Hanley *d* Cyril Frankel *ph* Geoffrey Unsworth *m* Elisabeth Lutyens
☆ Richard Todd, *Judith Anderson,* Elke Sommer, June Thorburn, Nicole Maurey, Rik Battaglia, Eleanor Summerfield, John Le Mesurier

Don't Drink the Water
US 1969 100m Berkeley-Pathé
Avco Embassy (Jack Rollins, Charles H. Joffe)

Americans, visiting Europe for the first time, are stranded in Bulgaria, where they are mistaken for spies and forced to take refuge in the American embassy staffed by incompetents.
Frenetic and stagey version of the play, with broad acting that diminishes what is left of the comedy.
w R. S. Allen, Harvey Bullock *play* Woody Allen *d* Howard Morris *ph* Harvey Genkins *m* Pat Williams *ad* Robert Gundlach *ed* Ralph Rosenblum
☆ Jackie Gleason, Estelle Parsons, Ted Bessell, Joan Delaney, Michael Constantine, Howard St John, Danny Meehan

Don't Ever Leave Me
GB 1949 85m bw
Triton/Rank

A kidnapped teenager falls for her abductor.
No Orchids for Miss Blandish played as a family comedy; quite unmemorable.
w Robert Westerby *novel The Wide Guy* by Anthony Armstrong *d* Arthur Crabtree
☆ Jimmy Hanley, Petula Clark, Edward Rigby, Hugh Sinclair, Linden Travers, Anthony Newley

Don't Get Me Started
GB/Germany 1994 76m colour
BFI/TiMe Medienvertreibs/Skyline (Steve Clark-Hall)
A murderer who has got away with his crime finds the strain of giving up smoking too much for him.
A strange, unenthralling thriller that suggests repression is bad for you; it certainly doesn't do much for the film.
wd Arthur Ellis *ph* Gil Taylor *m* Roger Bolton *pd* Caroline Amies *ed* Mike Bradsell
☆ Trevor Eve, Steve Waddington, Marion Bailey, Ralph Brown, Marcia Warren, Alan David, Patrick O'Connell, Lorna Heilbron
'A neat idea on paper that doesn't survive its journey to the screen.' – *Variety*
† It was first shown at Cannes in 1993 under the title *Psychotherapy* in a version that ran for 98m. It was withdrawn, re-cut, and some additional scenes added, under the direction of Paul Cowan and Martin Walsh.

Don't Give Up the Ship
US 1959 89m bw
Hal Wallis (Paramount)

A dim-witted naval lieutenant is accused of stealing a destroyer.
Feeble American service farce.
w Herbert Baker, Edmund Beloin, Henry Garson *d* Norman Taurog *ph* Haskell Boggs
☆ Jerry Lewis, Dina Merrill, Diana Spencer, Mickey Shaughnessy, Robert Middleton, Gale Gordon

Don't Go Breaking My Heart
GB 1998 94m colour
Polygram/Bill Kenright

As the result of a hypnotic suggestion going wrong, a widow with teenage children falls for an American sports therapist.
Dire romantic comedy; it is slick and glossy, and also clumsy and dull.
w Geoff Morrow *d* Willi Patterson *ph* Vernon Lawton *m* Rolfe Kent *pd* Tony Noble *ed* Peter Beston
☆ Anthony Edwards, Jenny Seagrove, Charles Dance, Jane Leeves, Tom Conti, Linford Christie (himself), Ben Reynolds, Ace Ryan, Amanda Holden
'One of those little British films that is so mind-bogglingly bad you will weep with boredom and frustration and beg for mercy – and that's even before the opening credits are over.' – *Cosmo Landesman, Sunday Times*

Don't Go in the House
US 1980 90m DeLuxe
Film Ventures/Turbine (Ellen Hammill)

In revenge for being burned as a child, a mother-dominated man incinerates women to whom he is attracted.
Extraordinarily unpleasant horror movie, influenced for the bad by Psycho.
w Joseph Ellison, Ellen Hammill, Joseph R. Masefield *d* Joseph Ellison *ph* Oliver Wood *m* Richard Einhorn *ad* Sarah Wood *ed* Jane Kurson
☆ Dan Grimaldi, Robert Osth, Ruth Dardick, Charles Bonet, Bill Ricci, Dennis M. Hunter

Don't Go Near the Water *
US 1957 107m Metrocolor Cinemascope
MGM/Avon (Lawrence Weingarten)
The US Navy sets up a public relations unit on a South Pacific island.
*Loosely cemented service farce full of fumbling lieutenants and bumbling commanders, a more light-hearted M*A*S*H. Boring romantic interludes separate some very funny farcical sequences.*
w Dorothy Kingsley, George Wells *novel* William Brinkley *d* Charles Walters *ph* Robert Bronner *m* Bronislau Kaper
☆ *Glenn Ford*, *Fred Clark*, Gia Scala, Romney Brent, Mickey Shaughnessy, Earl Holliman, Anne Francis, Keenan Wynn, Eva Gabor, Russ Tamblyn, Jeff Richards, Mary Wickes

'Drop everything! And see the cheekiest comedy of the year!'
Don't Just Lie There, Say Something!
GB 1973 91m Eastmancolor
Comocroft/Rank
By a strange chapter of accidents, a politician finds himself in bed with his under-secretary and a lady not his wife.
Stupefying from-the-stalls rendering of a successful stage farce; in this form it simply doesn't work.
w Michael Pertwee *play* Michael Pertwee *d* Bob Kellett
☆ Brian Rix, Leslie Phillips, Joan Sims, Joanna Lumley, Derek Royle, Peter Bland

Don't Just Stand There
US 1967 99m Techniscope
Universal (Stan Margulies)
A mild-mannered watch smuggler gets himself involved with kidnapping, murder, and finishing a sex novel.
Frantic but ineffective farce which keeps on the move but does not arrive anywhere.
w Charles Williams *novel* *The Wrong Venus* by Charles Williams *d* Ron Winston *ph* Milton Krasner *m* Nick Perito
☆ Mary Tyler Moore, Robert Wagner, *Barbara Rhoades*, Glynis Johns, Harvey Korman
'Paris locations might have helped, but we're stuck with the San Fernando Valley.' – *Robert Windeler*

'The Kings of Rock are rollin' back to the screen in their biggest!'
Don't Knock the Rock *
US 1956 84m bw
Columbia/Clover (Sam Katzman)
A singer returns to his home town to show adults that rock is harmless fun.
Cheap exploitation movie, most notable for Little Richard's performances of 'Long Tall Sally', 'Rip It Up' and 'Tutti Frutti'.
w Robert E. Kent, James B. Gordon *d* Fred F. Sears *ph* Benjamin H. Kline *ad* Paul Palmentola *ed* Edwin Bryant, Paul Borofsky
☆ Alan Dale, Alan Freed, Bill Haley and the Comets, Jimmy Ballard, Little Richard, the Treniers, Dave Appell and his Applejacks

Don't Look Now ****
GB 1973 110m Technicolor
BL/Casey/Eldorado (Peter Katz)
After the death of their small daughter, the Baxters meet in Venice two old sisters who claim mediumistic connection with the dead girl. The husband scorns the idea, but repeatedly sees a little red-coated figure in shadowy passages by the canals. Then he confronts it…
A macabre short story has become a puzzling piece of high cinema art full of vague suggestions and unexplored avenues. Whatever its overall deficiencies, it is too brilliant in surface detail to be dismissed. Depressingly but fascinatingly set in wintry Venice, it has to be seen to be appreciated.
w Allan Scott, Chris Bryant *story* Daphne du Maurier *d Nicolas Roeg* *ph Anthony Richmond* *m* Pino Donaggio *ad* Giovanni Soccol
☆ Donald Sutherland, Julie Christie, Hilary Mason, Clelia Matania, Massimo Serrato
'The fanciest, most carefully assembled enigma yet seen on the screen.' – *New Yorker*
'A powerful and dazzling visual texture.' – *Penelope Houston*
Anthony Richmond

Don't Look Now ... We're Being Shot At! *
France 1966 130m Eastmancolor Panavision
Les Films Corona (Robert Dorfmann)
original title: *La Grande Vadrouille*
During World War II three members of a British bomber crew bale out over Paris and make a frantic escape to the free zone by means of various wild disguises.
Freewheeling star farce, a shade lacking in control, but with some funny sequences.
wd Gérard Oury *ph* Claude Renoir *m* Georges Auric
☆ Terry-Thomas, Bourvil, Louis de Funès, Claudio Brook, Mike Marshall
'Both the sight gags and the characters evoke pale echoes of Laurel and Hardy, but it is not familiarity that breeds contempt here so much as the debasement of the familiar.' – *MFB*

Don't Lose Your Head: see *Carry On – Don't Lose Your Head*

Don't Make Waves
US 1967 97m Metrocolor Panavision
MGM/Filmways (John Calley, Martin Ransohoff)
A swimming-pool salesman attempts to get his own back on an impulsive young woman who has wrecked his car.
Malibu beach farce for immature adults, made by professionals helpless in the face of a weak script, but boasting a funny climax with a house teetering on the edge of a cliff.
w Ira Wallach, George Kirgo *novel* *Muscle Beach* by Ira Wallach *d* Alexander Mackendrick *ph* Philip Lathrop *m* Vic Mizzy
☆ Tony Curtis, Claudia Cardinale, Robert Webber, Joanna Barnes, Sharon Tate, Jim Backus, Mort Sahl

Don't Move, Die and Rise Again!: see *Zamri, Umri, Voskresni!*

Don't Open the Window: see *The Living Dead at the Manchester Morgue*

Don't Open till Christmas
GB 1983 86m colour
21st Century
A maniac goes about killing Father Christmases.
Tawdry horror film of marginal interest because of subject and cast,
w Derek Ford, Al McGoohan *d* Edmund Purdom
☆ Edmund Purdom, Alan Lake, Gerry Sundquist, Belinda Mayne, Mark Jones

Don't Panic, Chaps!
GB 1959 85m bw
Columbia/Hammer/ACT (Teddy Baird)
British and German units are sent to set up observation posts on the same Adriatic island, and agree to sit out the war in comfort.
An ingenious idea is ill-served by a poorly written script and a rather bored cast.
w Jack Davies *story* Michael Corston, Ronald Holroyd *d* George Pollock *ph* Arthur Graham *m* Philip Green *ad* Scott MacGregor *ed* Harry Aldous
☆ Dennis Price, George Cole, Thorley Walters, Harry Fowler, Nicholas Phipps, Percy Herbert, Nadja Regin

'The fun never sets on the British Empire!'
Don't Raise the Bridge, Lower the River
GB 1967 100m Technicolor
Columbia/Walter Shenson
An American turns his English wife's home into a discotheque.
Dreary comedy apparently intent on proving that its star can be just as unfunny abroad as at home.
w Max Wilk *d* Jerry Paris *ph* Otto Heller *m* David Whitaker
☆ Jerry Lewis, Terry-Thomas, Jacqueline Pearce, Bernard Cribbins, Patricia Routledge, Nicholas Parsons, Michael Bates

'...I'll never tell.'
Don't Say a Word
US/Australia 2001 113m DeLuxe Panavision
TCF/Regency/Village Roadshow/NPV/Further (Arnon Milchan, Arnold Kopelson, Anne Kopelson)
Ruthless criminals give a psychiatrist eight hours to save his young daughter's life by uncovering a secret locked in the mind of a mental patient.
Slick, unpleasant thriller that sacrifices logic for suspense.
w Anthony Peckham, Patrick Smith Kelly *novel* Andrew Klavan *d* Gary Fleder *ph* Amir Mokri *m* Mark Isham *pd* Nelson Coates *ed* William Steinkamp, Armen Minasian *cos* Ellen Mirojnick
☆ Michael Douglas (Dr Nathan Conrad), Sean Bean (Patrick B. Koster), Brittany Murphy (Elisabeth Burrows), Skye McCole Bartusiak (Jessie Conrad), Guy Torry (Martin J. Dolen), Jennifer Esposito (Detective Sandra Cassidy), Shawn Doyle (Russel Maddox), Victor Argo (Sydney Simon), Famke Janssen (Aggie Conrad), Oliver Platt (Dr Louis Sachs)
'Smart, stylish and, most important, satisfying.' – *Kevin Thomas, Los Angeles Times*
'It's hard to care about characters who make cardboard look complex and multifaceted.' – *Jay Carr, Boston Globe*

Don't Take it to Heart *
GB 1944 90m bw
GFD/Two Cities (Sydney Box)
A genial castle ghost is unleashed by a bomb and affects the love affair of a researcher with the daughter of the house.
Amiably lunatic British-upper-class extravaganza with eccentric characters and some felicitous moments.
wd Jeffrey Dell *ph* Eric Cross *m* Mischa Spoliansky
☆ Richard Greene, *Edward Rigby*, Patricia Medina, Alfred Drayton, Richard Bird, Wylie Watson, Moore Marriott, Brefni O'Rorke, Amy Veness, Claude Dampier, Joan Hickson, Joyce Barbour, Ronald Squire, Ernest Thesiger
'A cheerful and rewarding entertainment.' – *Richard Mallett, Punch*
'Not funny accidental but funny deliberate, and nine times out of ten the joke comes off.' – *Observer*

Don't Talk to Strange Men
GB 1962 65m bw
British Lion-Bryanston/Derick Williams
A girl begins a romance via a telephone call-box with a man she has never met.
Undramatic little warning to the young about the dangers of accepting lifts from strange men.
w uncredited *story* Gwen Cherrell *d* Pat Jackson *ph* Stephen Dade *ad* Brian Herbert *ed* Helen Wiggins
☆ Christina Gregg, Cyril Raymond, Gillian Lind, Conrad Phillips, Janina Faye, Dandy Nichols, Gwen Nelson

Don't Tell Her It's Me
US 1990 102m CFI color
Rank/Sovereign (George Braunstein, Ron Hamady)
A romantic novelist persuades her wimpish brother, who is recovering from radiation treatment, to pretend to be a biker in order to get a girlfriend.
Trivial, depressingly unsubtle comedy with matching performances.
w Sarah Bird *novel* *The Boyfriend School* by Sarah Bird *d* Malcolm Mowbray *ph* Reed Smoot *m* Michael Gore *pd* Linda Pearl, Daryl Kerrigan *ed* Marshall Harvey
☆ Shelley Long, Steve Guttenberg, Jami Gertz, Kyle MacLachlan, Madchen Amick, Kevin Scannell
'Takes the germ of an amusing notion about the division between realistic and fantastic romantic hero and hammers it painfully into the ground.' – *Kim Newman, Sight and Sound*
'Grotesquely unfunny comedy.' – *Variety*

Don't Tell Mom the Babysitter's Dead
US 1991 105m DeLuxe
Warner/HBO/Cinema Plus/Outlaw/Mercury/Douglas (Robert Newmyer, Brian Reilly, Jeffrey Silver)
A young girl supports her siblings while their mother is away on holiday.
Lamentably silly comedy.
w Neil Landau, Tara Ison *d* Stephen Herek *ph* Tim Suhrstedt *m* David Newman, Brian Nazarian *pd* Stephen Marsh *ed* Larry Bock
☆ Christina Applegate, Joanna Cassidy, John Getz, Josh Charles, Keith Coogan, Concetta Tomei, David Duchovny, Kimmy Robertson

Don't Trust Your Husband
US 1948 90m bw
James Nasser/United Artists
An executive conceals from his wife the sex of the client with whom he has to spend a lot of time.
Ho-hum comedy with a laborious plotline and a flagging cast.
w Lou Breslow, Joseph Hoffman *d* Lloyd Bacon
☆ Fred MacMurray, Madeleine Carroll, Charles Rogers

The Doolins of Oklahoma
US 1949 90m bw
Columbia (Harry Joe Brown)
GB title: *The Great Manhunt*
When his old gang claims his return to lawlessness, Bill Doolin walks into the sheriff's guns rather than cause his wife unhappiness.
Moderate Western with an unusually less-than-sympathetic role for its star.
w Kenneth Gamet *d* Gordon Douglas *ph* George Lawton *m* Paul Sawtell, George Duning
☆ Randolph Scott, George Macready, Louise Allbritton, John Ireland, Noah Beery Jnr, Dona Drake

The Doom Generation
US/France 1995 83m colour
Metro Tartan/Union Générale/Teen Angst/Desperate/Blurco/Why Not (Andresa Sperling, Gregg Araki)
A young drifter involves two teenagers in sex, robbery and murder.
Randomly violent road movie, which seems to be deliberately devoid of meaning.
wd Gregg Araki *ph* Jim Fealy *pd* Therese Deprez *ed* Gregg Araki
☆ James Duval, Rose McGowan, Johnathon Schaech, Cress Williams, Skinny Puppy, Parker Posey, Heidi Fleiss
'A stunning film with superlative production values … pic is bold not only in its art design, but also in its narrative and tone, a mixture of satire and horror.' – *Emanuel Levy, Variety*

Doomed: see *Ikiru*

The Doomed Battalion *
US/Germany 1932 74m bw
Universal
Austrians fight Italians high in the Alps.
Interesting but not very effective attempt to internationalize a German 'bergfilm'.
w Luis Trenker, Carl Harth *d* Cyril Gardner *ph* Sepp Allgeier *m* Giuseppe Becce *ad* Walter R. Koessler *ed* Clarence Kolster
☆ Luis Trenker, Tala Birell, Victor Varconi, Albert Conti, C. Henry Gordon, Gibson Gowland, Henry Armetta, Gustav von Seyffertitz
'Beaucoup snow and ice stuff for hot weather appeal … capable of sustaining bally.' – *Variety*

Doomed Cargo: see *Seven Sinners*

Doomed to Die: see *Mr Wong*

Doomsday Man
US 1998 89m CFI
G&G/Downhome/Symphony/WIN (Sam L. Grogg)
A scientist, who is concerned about military research into biological weapons, steals a virulent killer virus and goes on the run.
Predictable, uninteresting low-budget thriller that exploits its serious subject matter for trivial purposes.
w Andrew Stein *d* William R. Greenblatt *ph* Alton Chewning *m* Billy Lincoln, John Nau *pd* Dan Hall *ed* Sherwood Jones
☆ Esai Morales (Mike), Yancy Butler (Kate), James Marshall (Dr Tom Banks), Renee Allman

(Jill), Randell Haynes (Lyons), Barry Bell (Prentiss), Todd Sandler (Carter), Rhoda Griffis (Mrs Prentiss), Adoley Odunton (Sharon), Gina Stewart (Dolores), Roy Lind (Dr Reinhardt), Jill Galloway (Melissa)

Doomwatch
GB 1972 92m colour
Tigon (Tony Tenser)
An investigator of coastal pollution discovers a village in which dumped chemicals have given all the inhabitants a distorting disease called acromegaly.
An unsatisfactory horror film is drawn from a moderately serious TV series about ecology.
w Clive Exton *d* Peter Sasdy *ph* Kenneth Talbot *m* John Scott
☆ Ian Bannen, Judy Geeson, John Paul, Simon Oates, George Sanders, Percy Herbert, Geoffrey Keen, Joseph O'Conor

The Door in the Wall *
GB 1956 29m Technicolor Vistavision
AB Pathé/BFI/Lawrie (Howard Thomas)
A man is obsessed by a childhood dream of a green door which leads into a beautiful garden.
The story is chosen to experiment with Dynamic Frame, a system in which the picture changes shape and size according to the subject matter. In this case the results are entertaining enough.
wd Glenn H. Alvey Jnr *ph* Jo Jago *m* James Bernard
☆ Stephen Murray, Ian Hunter

The Door with Seven Locks
GB 1940 89m bw
Rialto (John Argyle)
US title: *Chamber of Horrors*
A mad doctor abducts an heiress in the hope of gaining her wealth.
Old-fashioned barnstormer, ineptly made.
w Norman Lee, John Argyle, Gilbert Gunn *novel* Edgar Wallace *d* Norman Lee *ph* Desmond Dickinson
☆ Leslie Banks, Lilli Palmer, Romilly Lunge, Gina Malo, Richard Bird, David Horne, Cathleen Nesbitt

'The Ceremony Is About To Begin.'
The Doors **
US 1991 134m DeLuxe Panavision
Guild/Carolco/Imagine (Bill Graham, Sasha Harari, A. Kitman Ho)
A film school drop-out and poet becomes a drug-abusing, self-destructive rock star.
Despite the title, the focus of this grandiose biopic is The Doors' singer Jim Morrison. Fans will enjoy it most; others are likely to find it noisy, overlong and over-busy.
w J. Randal Johnson, Oliver Stone *d* Oliver Stone *ph* Robert Richardson *m* The Doors *pd* Barbara Ling *ed* David Brenner, Joe Hutshing
☆ Val Kilmer, Frank Whaley, Kevin Dillon, Meg Ryan, Kyle MacLachlan, Billy Idol, Dennis Burkley, Josh Evans, Michael Madsen, Michael Wincott, Kathleen Quinlan
'It is folly to lavish $40 million (that's $10 million a Door!) and 2hr 15 min. of your time on a proposition – some guys can't handle fame – that was evident two decades ago. Maybe it was fun to bathe in decadence back then. But this is no time to wallow in that mire.' – *Richard Corliss, Time*

Doorway to Hell
US 1930 79m approx bw
Warner
GB title: *A Handful of Clouds*
A young gangster tries to go straight but is driven back into crime.
Vividly written but dramatically evasive crime-does-not-pay story, trying to eat its cake and have it.
w George Rosener *story* A Handful of Clouds by Rowland Brown *d* Archie Mayo *ph* Barney McGill *md* Leo Forbstein
☆ Lew Ayres, Charles Judels, James Cagney, Dorothy Matthews, Leon Janney, Robert Elliott
'Swell gang picture, handled so as to just slip by the censors.' – *Variety*
original story

Dop Bey Kuan Wan: see *One Armed Boxer*

Doppelganger: see *Journey to the Far Side of the Sun*

Doro No Kawa: see *Muddy River*

Dorp aan de Rivier: see *Doctor in the Village*

Dosshouse *
GB 1933 53m bw
MGM/Sound City (John Baxter)
An escaped convict is captured by a reporter and detective posing as tramps.
Low-budget featurette which deserves a footnote in film history for its social consciousness, rare at the time, especially in the dosshouse scenes.
w Herbert Ayres *d* John Baxter *ph* George Stretton *md* Colin Wark *ad* D. W. L. Daniels *ed* R. Gardener, R. Swan
☆ Frank Cellier, Arnold Bell, Herbert Franklyn, J. Hubert Leslie

Dou San: see *God of Gamblers*

The Double: see *Kagemusha*

Double Bunk
GB 1960 92m bw
British Lion/Bryanston (George H. Brown)
Newlyweds live in an old houseboat.
Thin comedy which turns out not to be leakproof.
wd C. M. Pennington-Richards *ph* Stephen Dade *m* Stanley Black
☆ Ian Carmichael, Janette Scott, Liz Frazer, Sid James, Dennis Price, Reginald Beckwith, Irene Handl, Noel Purcell, Naunton Wayne

Double Confession
GB 1950 85m bw
ABP/Harry Reynolds
At a seaside resort, a man finds his wife dead and tries to frame her lover, but becomes confused with two real murderers with a different purpose.
Confused and unlikely melodrama which signally lacks the ancient mariner's eye.
w William Templeton *novel* All on a Summer's Day by John Garden *d* Ken Annakin *ph* Geoffrey Unsworth *m* Benjamin Frankel
☆ Derek Farr, Peter Lorre, William Hartnell, Joan Hopkins, Naunton Wayne, Ronald Howard, Kathleen Harrison, Leslie Dwyer, Edward Rigby

Double Deal
Australia 1981 90m colour Panavision
Rychemond Film Productions (Brian Kavanagh, Lynn Barker)
A wealthy businessman plans an elaborate scheme to rid himself of his disenchanted wife.
Silly thriller in the style of Sleuth.
wd Brian Kavanagh ph Ross Berryman *m* Bruce Smeaton *ad* Jill Eden *ed* Tim Lewis
☆ Louis Jourdan, Angela Punch McGregor, Diane Craig, Warwick Comber, Peter Cummins, Bruce Spence, June Jago, Kerry Walker

'Frankenstein, Dracula and other screen monsters pale by comparison with this fiendish, decadent woman!'
Double Door
US 1934 75m bw
Paramount
A selfish, wealthy Fifth Avenue spinster takes a dislike to her brother's girlfriend and locks her up in a vault.
Silly, rather boring melodrama which may have worked on the stage but did not take to the screen.
w Gladys Lehman, Jack Cunningham *play* Elizabeth McFadden *d* Charles Vidor
☆ Mary Morris (the American one), Evelyn Venable, Kent Taylor, Sir Guy Standing, Anne Revere, Colin Tapley, Halliwell Hobbes
'Not likely to get anywhere at the b.o ... dull, drab and incredible.' – *Variety*

Double Dragon
US 1994 95m CFI color
Gramercy/Imperial Entertainment/Scanbox/Greenleaf (Sunil R. Shah, Ash R. Shah, Alan Schechter, Jan Hamsher, Don Murphy)
In the future, when Los Angeles has been reduced to rubble by an earthquake, two brothers fight an evil ruler who wants to control the world.
Martial arts mayhem based on a successful video game, consisting only of endless noisy fights.
w Michael Davis, Peter Gould *d* James Yukich *ph* Gary Kibbe *m* Jay Ferguson *pd* Mayne Berke *ed* Florent Retz
☆ Robert Patrick, Mark Dacascos, Scott Wolf, Kristina Malandro Wagner, Julia Nickson, Alyssa Milano
'Even kids won't get much of a kick out of this high-energy, low-IQ futuristic slugfest.' – *Brian Lowry, Variety*

Double Dynamite
US 1951 80m bw
RKO (Irving Cummings Jnr)
aka: *It's Only Money*
A bank teller wins a fortune at the race track but is afraid his winnings will be thought the proceeds of a bank robbery.
Insultingly mild comedy, nearly saved by a few quips from Groucho.
w Melville Shavelson, Harry Crane, Leo Rosten *d* Irving Cummings *ph* Robert de Grasse *m* Leigh Harline
☆ Frank Sinatra, Jane Russell, Groucho Marx, Don McGuire, Howard Freeman
† Made in 1948.

'What Starts With A Kiss Will End With A Killing...'
Double Exposure
US 1993 93m CFI color
New Age/Falcon Arts & Entertainment/Joey Walker (Joanne Watkins)
A jealous husband, who suspects his wife of having an affair, hires a private detective with troubles of his own to investigate.
Exceedingly dull and trivial thriller, acted and directed without conviction.
w Claudia Hoover, Bridget Hoffman *story* Christine Colfer *d* Claudia Hoover *ph* John Connor *m* Paolo Rustichelli *pd* Tim Keating *ed* Tom Meshelski
☆ Ron Perlman, Ian Buchanan, Jennifer Gatti, Dedee Pfeiffer, William R. Moses, James McEachin, Bridget Hoffman

Double Harness
US 1933 70m bw
RKO
A girl sets out to trick a rich man into marriage.
Mildly amusing comedy which in its time was considered risqué.
w Jane Murfin *play* Edward Montgomery *d* John Cromwell
☆ Ann Harding, William Powell, Henry Stephenson, Lillian Bond, Reginald Owen, George Meeker, Kay Hammond
'Managed with such reticence that at no time is there a note of offence ... this class actress again triumphs over her surroundings, and the picture will please her large following.' – *Variety*

'Twin brothers torn apart by violence. On a mission of revenge. One packs a punch. One packs a piece. Together they deliver...'
Double Impact
US 1991 109m DeLuxe
Columbia TriStar/Stone Group (Ashok Amritaj, Jean-Claude Van Damme)
Twin brothers, separated when young, get together when grown up to avenge their parents' murder by gangsters.
Two Van Dammes for the price of one merely doubles the incoherence of this otherwise ordinary martial arts movie.
w Sheldon Lettich, Jean-Claude Van Damme *story* Sheldon Lettich, Jean-Claude Van Damme, Steve Meerson, Peter Krikes *d* Sheldon Lettich *ph* Richard Kline *m* Arthur Kempel *pd* John Jay Moore *ed* Mark Conte, Brent White
☆ Jean-Claude Van Damme, Geoffrey Lewis, Alan Scarfe, Alonna Shaw, Cory Everson, Philip Can Yan Kin, Bolo Yeung, Sarah-Jane Varley
'Turns on a typically lame revenge plot while dragging out unimaginatively shot action sequences until no one will give a good Van Damme. Tedious story-telling should mute the pic's b.o. impact.' – *Variety*

'You can't kiss away a murder!'
Double Indemnity ****
US 1944 107m bw
Paramount (Joseph Sistrom)
An insurance agent connives with the glamorous wife of a client to kill her husband and collect.
Archetypal film noir of the forties, brilliantly filmed and incisively written, perfectly capturing the decayed Los Angeles atmosphere of a Chandler novel but using a simpler story and more substantial characters. The hero/villain was almost a new concept.
w Billy Wilder, Raymond Chandler novel James M. Cain *d Billy Wilder ph John Seitz m Miklos Rozsa*
☆ *Fred MacMurray, Barbara Stanwyck, Edward G. Robinson*, Tom Powers, Porter Hall, Jean Heather, Byron Barr, Richard Gaines
'The sort of film which revives a critic from the depressive effects of bright epics about the big soul of America or the suffering soul of Europe and gives him a new lease of faith.' – *Richard Winnington*
'The most pared-down and purposeful film ever made by Billy Wilder.' – *John Coleman, 1966*
'Profoundly, intensely entertaining.' – *Richard Mallett, Punch*
'One of the highest summits of *film noir* ... without a single trace of pity or love.' – *Charles Higham, 1971*
best picture; script, direction; John Seitz; Miklos Rozsa; Barbara Stanwyck

Double Indemnity: see *The River's Edge (1956)*

'Murder Isn't Always A Crime.'
Double Jeopardy
US 1999 105m DeLuxe Panavision
Paramount (Leonard Goldberg)
Sentenced to prison for killing her husband, a wife discovers he framed her and that, when she gets out, she can kill him with impunity because she cannot be tried twice for the same offence.
Idiotically implausible thriller; if you can accept its premise, there are mild pleasures to be had.
w David Weisberg, Douglas S. Cook *d* Bruce Beresford *ph* Peter James *m* Normand Corbeil *pd* Howard Cummings *ed* Mark Warner
☆ Tommy Lee Jones (Travis Lehman), Ashley Judd (Libby Parsons), Bruce Greenwood (Nick Parsons), Annabeth Gish (Angie), Roma Maffia (Margaret Skolowski), Davenia McFadden (Evelyn Lake), Jay Brazeau (Bobby), Gillian Barber (Rebecca Tingely), Benjamin Weir (Matty Parsons, age 4), Spencer Treat Clark (Matty Parsons, age 11)
'It will hold your attention, but it does nothing to win your admiration.' – *Cosmo Landesman, Sunday Times*
† The film was a hit, taking more than $100m at the US box-office.

'This woman inspired him – this woman feared him!'
A Double Life **
US 1947 103m bw
Universal/Kanin Productions (Michael Kanin)
An actor playing Othello is obsessed by the role and murders a woman he imagines to be Desdemona.
An old theatrical chestnut (cf Men Are Not Gods*) is decked out with smartish backstage dialogue but despite a pleasant star performance remains unrewarding if taxing, and the entertainment value of the piece is on the thin side considering the mighty talents involved.*
w Ruth Gordon, Garson Kanin *d* George Cukor *ph* Milton Krasner *m* Miklos Rozsa
☆ Ronald Colman, Shelley Winters, Signe Hasso, Edmond O'Brien, Millard Mitchell
'As a piece of film story-telling it is generally skilled. Yet the central situation is artificial.' – *Dilys Powell*
Miklos Rozsa; Ronald Colman
Ruth Gordon, Garson Kanin; George Cukor

The Double Life of Véronique **
France/Poland 1991 98m colour
Gala/Sidéral/Canal Plus/TOR/Norsk Film (Leonardo de la Fuente)
original title: *La Double Vie de Véronique*
Two young women, one Polish, the other French, seem to share a single existence.
A complex, finely acted and directed puzzle of a film, but one that grips the attention throughout.

w Krzysztof Kieślowski, Krzysztof Piesiewicz *d* Krzysztof Kieślowski *ph* Slawomir Idziak *m* Zbigniew Preisner *pd* Patrice Mercier, Halina Dobrowolska *ed* Jacques Witta
☆ Irène Jacob, Halina Gryglaszewska, Kalina Jedrusik, Aleksander Bardini, Wladyslaw Kowalski, Jerzy Gudejko
'Despite pic's many-splendoured outbursts of filmic creativity and intense emotion, final result remains a head-scratching cipher with blurred edges.' – *Variety*

The Double Man *
GB 1967 105m Technicolor
Warner/Hal E. Chester
A CIA agent investigates the death of his son on a Swiss skiing holiday and finds the murder was a lure to get him there so that an enemy lookalike can substitute for him.
Rather ruthless but good-looking and generally watchable spy melodrama.
w Frank Tarloff, Alfred Hayes *novel* Henry S. Maxfield *d* Franklin Schaffner *ph* Denys Coop *m* Ernie Freeman
☆ Yul Brynner, Clive Revill, Anton Diffring, Britt Ekland, Moira Lister

The Double McGuffin
US 1979 100m colour
Mulberry Square/Joe Camp
Kids turn into amateur detectives when they find that a visiting foreign leader is to be assassinated.
Barely tolerable lightweight mystery for an audience which probably doesn't exist.
wd Joe Camp *ph* Don Reddy *m* Euel Box *pd* Harland Wright
☆ Ernest Borgnine, George Kennedy, Elke Sommer, Rod Browning

Double Negative
Canada 1980 96m colour
Quadrant
A photo journalist tries to find the murderer of his wife, and discovers he's an amnesiac and did it himself.
Ho-hum mystery thriller centring on an ancient wheeze; treatment resolutely plodding.
w Thomas Hedley Jnr, Janis Allen, Charles Dennis *novel* *The Three Roads* by Ross Macdonald *d* George Bloomfield
☆ Michael Sarrazin, Susan Clark, Anthony Perkins, Howard Duff, Kate Reid

Double or Nothing
US 1937 90m bw
Paramount
Inheritors under a trick will must double their bequests or lose them.
Flat comedy with music; none of the elements are really up to scratch.
w Charles Lederer and others *d* Theodore Reed
☆ Bing Crosby, Martha Raye, Andy Devine, William Frawley, Mary Carlisle, Benny Baker
'Due for big openings and tapering-off business. Will squeeze through.' – *Variety*

Double Team
US 1997 91m Technicolor Panavision
Columbia/Mandalay/Moshe Diamant/One Story
A top agent who wants to quit the game discovers that his wife and unborn child are threatened by the terrorist he failed to kill.
Frenetic action movie that throws in everything but the towel and the kitchen sink.
w Don Jacoby, Paul Mones *d* Tsui Hark *ph* Peter Pau *m* Gary Chang *pd* Marek Dobrowolski *ed* Bill Pankow
☆ Jean-Claude Van Damme, Dennis Rodman, Mickey Rourke, Paul Freeman, Natacha Lindinger, Valeria Cavalli, Jay Benedict, Rob Diem
'Action-packed, often campy and colorful amusement park of a movie.' – *Variety*

Double Wedding
US 1937 87m bw
MGM (Joseph L. Mankiewicz)
A bohemian artist makes a play for the lady of his choice by romancing her sister.
Zany star comedy which doesn't quite come off.
w Jo Swerling *play* *Great Love* by Ferenc Molnar *d* Richard Thorpe *ph* William Daniels *m* Edward Ward
☆ William Powell, Myrna Loy, John Beal, Florence Rice, Jessie Ralph, Edgar Kennedy, Sidney Toler, Barnett Parker, Katherine Alexander, Donald Meek
'OK for topflight business ... would be funnier if it were shorter.' – *Variety*

Double Whoopee **
US 1928 20m bw silent
Hal Roach
Incompetent doormen at a swank hotel cause havoc.
Simple-minded but pleasing star farce.
w Leo McCarey, H. M. Walker *d* Lewis R. Foster *ph* George Stevens, Jack Roach *ed* Richard Currier
☆ Laurel and Hardy, Jean Harlow, Charlie Hall

Double X
GB 1991 97m Technicolor
Feature/String of Pearls (Shani S. Grewal)
A reformed safebreaker asks a former Chicago cop-turned-hitman to help him rescue his kidnapped daughter from a vicious gangleader.
Dismal thriller, with a dreary plot and uninspired direction and acting, which suggests that the British film industry is bent on committing ritual suicide.
wd Shani S. Grewal *story* *Vengeance* by David Fleming *ph* Dominique Grosz *m* Raf Ravenscroft *pd* Colin Pocock *ed* Michael Johns
☆ Simon Ward, William Katt, Norman Wisdom, Bernard Hill, Gemma Craven, Leon Herbert, Derren Nesbitt, Vladek Sheybal, Chloe Annett
'An inept low-budget suspenser. Reliable cast is double-crossed by a laughable script and clumsy helming. Result, which hardly cuts it even as a TV pic, should expire fast.' – *Variety*

Doubting Thomas
US 1935 78m bw
Fox
Small-town 'society' puts on an amateur show.
Slight but attractive star vehicle.
w William Conselman, Bartlett Cormack *novel* *The Torch Bearers* by George Kelly *d* David Butler
☆ Will Rogers, Billie Burke, Alison Skipworth, Sterling Holloway, Andrew Tombes, Gail Patrick
'There is one thing that Rogers knows, and that is how to get laughs with any sort of a situation, and he didn't learn that just from reading the papers.' – *Variety*

Douce *
France 1943 106m bw
Société Parisienne de l'Industrie Cinématographique
In 1887 Paris a sheltered young rich girl falls for a steward and encounters family opposition.
A charming old-fashioned story which provides a well-taken opportunity for a portrait of the old bourgeoisie.
w Jean Aurenche, Pierre Bost *d* Claude Autant-Lara *ph* Gaston Thonnart *m* René Cloërc
☆ Odette Joyeux, Jean Debucourt, Marguerite Moreno, Roger Pigaut, Madeleine Robinson
'Direction and camerawork constantly reveal touches of felicity.' – *MFB*

Doucement Les Basses: see *Take It Easy*

Doughboys *
US 1930 80m approx bw
MGM/Buster Keaton (Lawrence Weingarten)
GB title: *Forward March*
A young eccentric joins the army.
Simple-minded farce with a few good routines for the star.
w Richard Schayer *d* Edward Sedgwick *ph* Leonard Smith
☆ Buster Keaton, Sally Eilers, Cliff Edwards, Edward Brophy
'Keaton's first talker is comedy with a kick.' – *Variety*

The Doughgirls *
US 1944 102m bw
Warner (Mark Hellinger)
In a crowded wartime Washington hotel, a honeymoon is frustrated by constant interruption, not to mention the discovery that the wedding was not legal.
Frantic farce, generally well adapted, and certainly played with gusto.
w James V. Kern, Sam Hellman *play* Joseph Fields *d* James V. Kern *ph* Ernest Haller *m* Adolph Deutsch
☆ Alexis Smith, Jane Wyman, Jack Carson, Ann Sheridan, Irene Manning, *Eve Arden*, Charlie Ruggles, John Alexander, John Ridgely, Craig Stevens, Alan Mowbray, Donald MacBride
'There's nothing so good in it that you must attend, just as there is nothing bad enough to keep you away.' – *Archer Winsten*

Doug's 1st Movie
US 1999 77m Technicolor
Buena Vista/Walt Disney/Jumbo (Jim Jenkins, David Campbell, Melanie Grisanti, Jack Spillum)
Schoolfriends discover a monster, created from pollutants, in their local lake.
A spinoff from a long-running US TV series, this is a leisurely, adequately animated movie of minimal appeal.
w Ken Scarborough *characters created by* Jim Jenkins *d* Maurice Joyce *m* Mark Watters *ed* Alysha Nadine Cohen, Christopher K. Gee
☆ Featuring voices: Thomas McHugh, Fred Newman, Chris Phillips, Constance Shulman, Frank Welker, Doug Preis, Guy Hadley
'I can't believe kids will tolerate this boring *ET/Free Willy* knock-off.' – *Peter Bradshaw, Guardian*

The Dove *
US 1968 15m bw
Coe/Davis Ltd
Back in the countryside of his childhood, a Nobel prize winner recalls the events of a summer...
Elaborate Ingmar Bergman spoof complete with subtitles and pidgin Swedish. Hilarious at the time for those who had just seen Wild Strawberries.
w Sidney Davis *d* George Coe, Anthony Lover *ph* Anthony Lover
☆ David Zirlin, George Coe, Pamela Burrell, Madeline Kahn

The Dove *
US 1974 104m Technicolor
Panavision
St George Productions (Gregory Peck)
Yachtsman Robin Lee Graham makes a five-year voyage around the world.
Bland, rather stolid adventure story for boat-niks, based on real incidents; good to look at.
w Peter Beagle, Adam Kennedy *book* Robin Lee Graham, Derek Gill *d* Charles Jarrott *ph* *Sven Nykvist* *m* John Barry
☆ Joseph Bottoms, Deborah Raffin, John McLiam, Dabney Coleman
'Postcard views flick by to the strains of a saccharine score.' – *David McGillivray*

The Dover Road: see *Where Sinners Meet*

Down among the Sheltering Palms
US 1952 86m Technicolor
TCF (Fred Kohlmar)
An American army unit takes over a South Sea island, but fraternization is forbidden.
Tolerable comedy-musical with familiar jokes and situations.
w Claude Binyon, Albert Lewin, Burt Styler *d* Edmund Goulding *ph* Leon Shamroy *m* Leigh Harline *m/ly* Harold Arlen, Ralph Blane
☆ William Lundigan, Jane Greer, Mitzi Gaynor, David Wayne, Gloria de Haven, Gene Lockhart, Jack Paar, Billy Gilbert

Down among the Z Men
GB 1952 71m bw
New Realm (E. J. Fancey)
US title: *Stand Easy*
A detective turned soldier keeps an atomic formula out of enemy hands.
A missed opportunity to transfer the appeal of The Goons from their successful radio show to the screen; it was not helped by the conventional script, the dancing girls and Secombe's straight role.
w Jimmy Grafton, Francis Charles *d* Maclean Rogers *ph* Geoffrey Faithfull *m* Jack Jordan *ed* Peter Mayhew
☆ Peter Sellers, Michael Bentine, Harry Secombe, Spike Milligan, Carole Carr, Andrew Timothy, Graham Stark, Miriam Karlin, Eunice Gayson, The Television Toppers

Down and Out in Beverly Hills *
US 1985 97m Technicolor
Touchstone (Paul Mazursky)
A wandering con artist is taken in by an insecure Beverly Hills family.
Somewhat bumbling but sporadically effective rehash of Renoir's Boudu Sauvé des Eaux *(qv), with a few modern jabs and effectively eccentric performances.*
w Paul Mazursky, Leon Capetanos *play* René Fauchois *d* Paul Mazursky *ph* Donald McAlpine *m* Andy Summers *pd* Pato Guzman
☆ Nick Nolte, Richard Dreyfuss, Bette Midler, Little Richard, Tracy Nelson, Elizabeth Pena
'What makes this picture so enjoyable is not the exaggerations of its narrative but the richness of its texture. Every inch of every frame is utilized. While, in the foreground, the actors are doing or saying one thing, behind them a television screen is telling us something else. The audience is completely embroiled in every incident.' – *Quentin Crisp*

Down Argentine Way *
US 1940 94m Technicolor
TCF (Harry Joe Brown)
A wealthy American girl falls in love with an Argentinian horse-breeder.
A very moderate musical which happened to bring both Grable and Miranda to star stature and set Fox off on their successful run of forties extravaganzas, reasonably pleasant to look at but empty-headed.
w Karl Tunberg, Darrell Ware *d* Irving Cummings *ph* Ray Rennahan, Leon Shamroy *m/ly* Harry Warren, Mack Gordon *ad* Richard Day, Joseph C. Wright
☆ Betty Grable, Carmen Miranda, Don Ameche, Charlotte Greenwood, J. Carrol Naish, Henry Stephenson, Leonid Kinskey, The Nicholas Brothers
'I dislike Technicolor in which all pinks resemble raspberry sauce, reds turn to sealing wax, blues shriek of the washtub, and yellows become suet pudding.' – *James Agate*
'So outrageous – that it's hard to believe it isn't at least partly intentional – but why would anybody make this picture on purpose.' – *New Yorker, 1976*
Ray Rennahan, Leon Shamroy; title song (*m* Harry Warren, *ly* Mack Gordon); art direction

'It's not where you start – It's where you start again.'
Down by Law *
US 1986 107m bw
Island Pictures/Black Snake/Grokenburger Films (Alan Kleinberg)
A disc jockey and a pimp, framed for crimes they did not commit, escape from jail with an Italian who has a minimal grasp of English.
Engaging lowlife comedy.
wd Jim Jarmusch *ph* Robby Müller *m* John Lurie, Tom Waits *ed* Melody London
☆ Tom Waits, John Lurie, Roberto Benigni, Ellen Barkin, Billie Neal, Rockets Redglare, Vernel Bagneris, Nicoletta Braschi

Down from the Mountain **
US 2000 94m FotoKem
Momentum/Pennebaker Hegedus/Mike Zoss (Bob Neuwirth, Frazer Pennebaker)
Documentary of the rehearsals and performance in Nashville, Tennessee, of a concert by some of the singers and musicians involved in the soundtrack of the Coen brothers' film *O Brother, Where Art Thou?*
Enjoyable account of the country musicians whose soundtrack album became an enormous hit: highlights include the veteran Ralph Stanley, one of the last performances by singer-songwriter and fiddle-player John Hartford, who died soon after, and the gospel singing of the Fairfield Four.
d Nick Doob, Chris Hegedus, D. A. Pennebaker *ph* Joan Churchill, Jim Desmond, Doob, Chris Hegedus, Bob Neuwirth, Jehane Noujaim, D.A. Pennebaker, John Paul Pennebaker *md* T-Bone Burnett *ed* Nick Doob, D. A. Pennebaker
☆ John Hartford, Dr Ralph Stanley, Fairfield Four, Emmylou Harris, The Cox Family, Chris Thomas

King, Alison Kraus and Union Station, Colin Linden, The Nashville Bluegrass Band, The Peasall Sisters, Gillian Welch, Ethan Coen, Joel Coen, T-Bone Burnett, Tim Blake Nelson

'Brings us close to some likeable, gifted people and the roots of their music in poverty, religion and social isolation.' – *Philip French, Observer*

Down Memory Lane *
US 1949 70m bw
Aubrey Schenck
A kaleidoscope of Mack Sennett comedy shorts, linked by Steve Allen as a disc jockey. Much Bing Crosby; Fields in *The Dentist*; an appearance by Sennett himself.
d Phil Karlson

Down Periscope
US 1996 93m DeLuxe
TCF (Robert Lawrence)
A submarine commander is given a broken-down ship, crewed by misfits, with which to prove his abilities.
Low comedy that sends up submarine movies, but sinks under the weight of some leaden jokes.
w Hugh Wilson, Andrew Kurtzman, Eliot Wald *d* David S. Ward *ph* Victor Hammer *m* Randy Edelman, Mark McKenzie *pd* Michael Corenblith *ed* William Anderson, Armen Minasian
☆ Kelsey Grammer, Lauren Holly, Rob Schneider, Harry Dean Stanton, Bruce Dern, William H. Macy, Ken Hudson Campbell, Rip Torn

'A curiously sterile effort which, although by no means unwatchable, still manages to reinvent good old-fashioned bland.' – *Bob McCabe, Empire*

Down Three Dark Streets *
US 1954 85m bw
UA/Edward Small (Arthur Gardner, Jules V. Levy)
An FBI agent is shot on duty, and his friend avenges him in the course of clearing up three cases in which he was involved.
Competent, enjoyable police film with three cases for the price of one.
w The Gordons, Bernard C. Schoenfeld *book Case File FBI* by the Gordons *d Arnold Laven ph* Joseph Biroc *m* Paul Sawtell
☆ Broderick Crawford, Ruth Roman, Martha Hyer, Marisa Pavan, Casey Adams, Kenneth Tobey
† One of the first collaborations of the prolific production company Laven-Gardner-Levy.

Down to Earth
US 1932 79m bw
Nouveau riche Americans return from Europe and find themselves misfits at home.
Thin sequel to They Had to See Paris.
w Edwin Burke *story* Homer Croy *d* David Butler
☆ Will Rogers, Dorothy Jordan, Irene Rich, Matty Kemp, Mary Carlisle

'Will need support ... the least powerful in draw of all Rogers' pictures.' – *Variety*

Down to Earth *
US 1947 101m Technicolor
Columbia (Don Hartman)
The muse Terpsichore comes down to help a Broadway producer fix a new show in which she is featured.
Pleasant but undistinguished musical fantasy, a sequel to Here Comes Mr Jordan. *The heavenly sequences promise more amusement than they produce.*
w Edwin Blum, Don Hartman *d* Alexander Hall *ph* Rudolph Maté *m* Heinz Roemheld
☆ *Rita Hayworth, Larry Parks, Roland Culver* (Mr Jordan), *Edward Everett Horton*, Marc Platt, James Gleason

'Just the film to make the spectator forget the troubles of life.' – *MFB*

'Celestial whimsy musical, with arch acting and a dull score.' – *New Yorker, 1977*

† Rita Hayworth's singing was dubbed by Anita Ellis.

'A story of premature reincarnation.'
Down to Earth
US 2001
Paramount/Village Roadshow/NPV/Alphaville 3 Arts (Sean Daniel, Michael Rotenberg, James Jacks)
A black unsuccessful standup comedian arrives in heaven too soon, and is sent back to occupy the body of a murder victim, a rich and elderly white man.
Feeble comedy that wastes Rock's talents and does not compare to the two earlier versions of the same story; it lacks finesse and style.
w Chris Rock, Lance Crouther, Ali LeRoi, Louis CK *screenplay Heaven Can Wait* by Elaine May, Warren Beatty *play Halfway to Heaven* by Harry Segall *d* Chris Weitz, Paul Weitz
☆ Chris Rock (Lance Barton), Regina King (Sontee), Chazz Palminteri (King), Eugene Levy (Keyes), Frankie Faison (Whitney Daniels), Mark Addy (Cisco), Greg Germann (Sklar), Jennifer Coolidge (Mrs Wellington), Wanda Sykes (Wanda), John Cho (Phil Quon)

'Disappointingly poor.' – *Empire*

† Harry Segall's play was first filmed in 1941 as *Here Comes Mr Jordan*, starring Robert Montgomery; Warren Beatty starred in a remake *Heaven Can Wait* in 1978.

Down to the Sea in Ships *
US 1948 120m bw
TCF (Elmer Clifton)
An old whaling skipper wants his grandson to follow in his footsteps.
Seagoing spectacle with strong characters; all concerned show Hollywood in its most professional form, but the film somehow fails to catch the imagination or live in the memory.
w John Lee Mahin, Sy Bartlett *d* Henry Hathaway *ph Joe MacDonald m* Alfred Newman
☆ *Lionel Barrymore*, Dean Stockwell, Richard Widmark, *Cecil Kellaway*, Gene Lockhart

Down to You
US 2000 92m colour
Miramax/Open City (Jason Kliot, Joana Vicente)
Two high-school students fall in love.
Teen soap opera that follows the usual formula, gaining a little interest from the charm of its protagonists.
wd Kris Isacsson *ph* Robert Yeoman *m* Edmund Choi *pd* Kevin Thompson *ed* Stephen A. Rotter *cos* Michael Clancy
☆ Freddie Prinze Jnr (Al Connelly), Julia Stiles (Imogen), Selma Blair (Cyrus), Shawn Hatosy (Eddie Hicks), Zak Orth (Monk Jablonski), Jim Morrison (Ashton Kutcher), Rosario Dawson (Lana), Henry Winkler (Chef Ray), Lucie Arnaz (Judy Connelly)

'The latest addition to the teen-pic boom has all the elements in place to please its target demo and leave most everyone else underwhelmed.' – *Brendan Kelly, Variety*

Down Went McGinty: see *The Great McGinty*

'The ultimate catch has met his match.'
Down with Love *
US 2003 94m DeLuxe Panavision
TCF/Fox 2000/Regency (Bruce Cohen, Dan Jinks)
In the early 60s, a womanising journalist bets that he can bed the author of a bestselling book that announces the arrival of a new kind of woman who is not dependent upon men.
A throwback to the kind of innocent romantic movies that teamed Rock Hudson and Doris Day; this comes out as a pale carbon copy.
w Eve Ahlert, Dennis Drake *d* Peyton Reed *ph* Jeff Cronenweth *m* Marc Shaiman *pd* Andrew Laws *ed* Larry Bock *cos* Daniel Orlandi
☆ Renee Zellweger (Barbara Novak), Ewan McGregor (Catcher Block), Sarah Paulson (Vicki Hiller), David Hyde Pierce (Peter McMannus), Rachel Dratch (Gladys), Jack Plotnick (Maurice), Tony Randall (Theodore Banner)

'In spite of all the manic high jinks, the laughter here arises not from confusion and hysteria, but from complacency, which is not as funny.' – *A. O. Scott, New York Times*

'Made by people with a genuine love for the entertainment they're bringing back to life. You'd have to be a real prude not to go for it.' – *Shawn Levy, Oregonian*

Downhill
GB 1927 80m approx (24 fps) bw silent
Gainsborough (Michael Balcon)
US title: *When Boys Leave Home*
A sixth-form schoolboy, accused of theft, is expelled and goes to the bad in Marseilles before being found innocent.
Absurd novelette with only marginal glimpses of the director's emerging talent.
w Eliot Stannard *play* David Lestrange (Ivor Novello, Constance Collier) *d* Alfred Hitchcock *ph* Claude McDonnell *ed* Ivor Montagu
☆ Ivor Novello, Ben Webster, Robin Irvine, Sybil Rhoda, Lilian Braithwaite, Isabel Jeans, Ian Hunter

FAMOUS LINE: 'Does this mean, sir, that I shall not be able to play for the Old Boys?'

Downhill Racer *
US 1969 101m Technicolor
Paramount/Wildwood (Richard Gregson)
An ambitious American skier gains a place on the team competing in Europe.
Virtually plotless, casually assembled study of a man and a sport, good to look at, often exciting, but just as frequently irritating in its throwaway style.
w James Salter *novel* Oakley Hall *d* Michael Ritchie *ph Brian Probyn m* Kenyon Hopkins
☆ Robert Redford, Gene Hackman, Camilla Sparv, Joe Jay Jalbert, Timothy Kirk, Dabney Coleman
BAFTA Robert Redford

Downstairs
US 1932 77m bw
MGM
A villainous chauffeur blackmails the other servants.
Failed attempt by a falling star to do something different.
w Melville Baker, Lenore Coffee *story* John Gilbert *d* Monta Bell
☆ John Gilbert, Virginia Bruce, Paul Lukas, Hedda Hopper, Reginald Owen, Olga Baclanova

'Next Time Take The Stairs.'
Downtime **
GB/France 1997 91m colour
Film Four/Scala/Channel 4/Arts Council/Moving Image/Pandora (Richard Johns)
A former police psychologist is trapped in a lift in a gang-ridden tower block on a run-down housing estate with the suicidal woman he fancies, her young son and an epileptic old man.
A low-budget thriller grounded in a slum-ridden social reality which delivers on downbeat suspense, apart from its unconvincing ending.
w Caspar Berry *d* Bharat Nalluri *ph* Tony Imi *m* Simon Boswell *pd* Chris Townsend *ed* Les Healey
☆ Paul McGann, Susan Lynch, Tom Georgeson, David Roper, Denise Bryson, Adam Johnston, David Horsefield, Stephen Graham, Birdy Sweeney

'It's a game try with some splendid moments.' – *Variety*

Downtown
US 1990 96m DeLuxe
TCF (Charles H. Maguire)
An idealistic young white cop is transferred from a genteel suburb to a tough black inner-city neighbourhood.
Unarresting buddy movie that is an uneasy mix of broad comedy, violence and far too many narrative clichés.
w Nat Mauldin *d* Richard Benjamin *ph* Richard H. Kline *m* Alan Silvestri *pd* Charles Rosen *ed* Jacqueline Cambas, Brian Chambers
☆ Anthony Edwards, Forest Whitaker, Penelope Ann Miller, Joe Pantoliano, David Clennon, Art Evans

Drachenfutter: see *Dragon's Food*

'The strangest love a woman has ever known ... a livid face bent over her in the ghostly mist!'
Dracula ***
US 1931 84m bw
Universal (Carl Laemmle Jnr)
A Transylvanian vampire count gets his come-uppance in Yorkshire.
A film which has much to answer for. It started its star and its studio off on horror careers, and it launched innumerable sequels (see below). In itself, after two eerie reels, it becomes a pedantic and slow transcription of a stage adaptation, and its climax takes place offscreen; but for all kinds of reasons it remains full of interest.
w Garrett Fort *play* Hamilton Deane, John Balderston *novel Bram Stoker d Tod Browning ph Karl Freund m* Tchaikovsky *ad* Charles D. Hall *ed* Milton Carruth, Maurice Pivar
☆ *Bela Lugosi*, Helen Chandler, David Manners, *Dwight Frye, Edward Van Sloan*

'Must have caused much uncertainty as to the femme fan reaction ... as it turns out the signs are that the woman's angle is all right and that sets the picture for better than average money ... it comes out as a sublimated ghost story related with all surface seriousness and above all with a remarkably effective background of creepy atmosphere.' – *Variety*

'A too literal adaptation of the play (not the book) results in a plodding, talkative development, with much of the vital action taking place off-screen.' – *William K. Everson*

'The mistiest parts are the best; when the lights go up the interest goes down.' – *Ivan Butler*

'It'll chill you and fill you with fears. You'll find it creepy and cruel and crazed.' – *New York Daily News*

† Later advertising variations concentrated on the horror element: 'In all the annals of living horror one name stands out as the epitome of evil! So evil, so fantastic, so degrading you'll wonder if it isn't all a nightmare! Innocent girls lured to a fate truly worse than death!

†† Lugosi was not the first choice for the role of the Count. Ian Keith and William Powell were strongly favoured.

††† Sequels include *Dracula's Daughter* (qv), *Son of Dracula* (qv); the later Hammer sequence consists of *Dracula* (see below), *Brides of Dracula* (qv), *Dracula Prince of Darkness* (qv), *Dracula Has Risen From the Grave* (qv), *Taste the Blood of Dracula* (qv), *Scars of Dracula* (qv), *Dracula AD 1972* (qv), *The Satanic Rites of Dracula* (qv). Other associated films in which the Count or a disciple appears include (all qv) *Return of the Vampire* (1944), *House of Frankenstein* (1945), *House of Dracula* (1945), *Abbott and Costello Meet Frankenstein* (1948), *The Return of Dracula* (1958), *Kiss of the Vampire* (1963), *The Fearless Vampire Killers* (1967), *Count Yorga Vampire* (1969), *Countess Dracula* (1970), *Vampire Circus* (1970), *The House of Dark Shadows* (1970), *Vampire Lovers* (1971), *Blacula* (1972), *Dracula* (1974), *Martin* (1978), *Dracula* (1979), *Salem's Lot* (1979), *Nosferatu The Vampyre* (1979), *The Hunger* (1983), *The Lost Boys* (1987), *Bram Stoker's Dracula* (1992). Minor potboilers are legion.

'Who will be his bride tonight?'
Dracula ***
GB 1958 82m Technicolor
Rank/Hammer (Anthony Hinds)
US title: *Horror of Dracula*
A remake of the 1931 film.
Commendably brief in comparison with the later Hammer films, this was perhaps the best horror piece they turned out as well as the most faithful to its original. Decor and colour were well used, and the leading performances are striking.
w Jimmy Sangster novel Bram Stoker *d Terence Fisher ph Jack Asher m James Bernard ad Bernard Robinson ed* James Needs, Bill Lenny
☆ *Peter Cushing* (Van Helsing), *Christopher Lee* (Dracula), Melissa Stribling, Carol Marsh, Michael Gough, John Van Eyssen, Valerie Gaunt, Miles Malleson

Dracula
Italy 1974 93m colour
Andrew Braunsberg
aka: *Andy Warhol's Dracula*
aka: *Blood for Dracula*
In this sick and gory version, Dracula becomes ill if he feasts on anything but pure virgin's blood. The hero saves the heroine in the predictable way.
Not for the squeamish.
wd Paul Morrissey
☆ Udo Kier, Arno Juerging, Vittorio de Sica, Maxime McEmory, Joe Dallesandro

Dracula *
GB 1979 112m Technicolor Panavision
Universal/Mirisch (Marvin Mirisch/Tom Pevsner)

A lush, expensive and romantic version which presents the count as a matinée idol and spends too much time on the romantic scenes to distract attention from an old old story.
w W. D. Richter *d* John Badham *ph* Gilbert Taylor *m* John Williams *pd* Peter Murton
☆ Frank Langella, Laurence Olivier, Donald Pleasence, Kate Nelligan, Trevor Eve
'A triumphantly lurid creation that seems bound to be either under-valued for its circus effects or over-valued for the stylishness with which it steers between the reefs of camp and theatrical indulgence.' – *Richard Combs, MFB*

Dracula: see *Bram Stoker's Dracula (1992)*

'The most seductive evil of all time has now been unleashed in ours.'
Dracula 2000
US 2000 98m DeLuxe
Buena Vista/Dimension/Neo Art & Logic (W.K. Border, Joel Soisson)

GB title: *Dracula 2001*
After Dracula is released when his coffin is stolen and opened, a centenarian Van Helsing follows his old adversary to New Orleans to save his estranged daughter from the vampire's clutches.
Despite being given the blessing of Wes Craven, this is just another vampire movie, even though it manages to identify Dracula with Judas Iscariot.
w Joel Soisson *d* Patrick Lussier *ph* Peter Pay *m* Marco Beltrami *pd* Carol Spier *ed* Patrick Lussier, Peter Devaney Flanagan *cos* Denise Cronenberg
☆ Christopher Plummer (Van Helsing), Gerard Butler (Dracula), Jonny Lee Miller (Simon), Justine Waddell (Mary), Jennifer Esposito (Solina), Omar Epps (Marcus), Colleen Ann Fitzpatrick (Lucy), Sean Patrick Harris (Trick), Danny Masterson (Nightshade), Lochlyn Munro (Eddie), Tig Fong (Dax), Jeri Ryan (Valerie Sharp)
'Thudding, suspense-free montage of unshocking shock effects and more severed heads than toppled during the French Revolution.' – *Stephen Holden, New York Times*

Dracula 2001: see *Dracula 2000*

Dracula 71: see *Bram Stoker's Count Dracula*

'The Count is back, with an eye for London's hot pants, and a taste for everything!'
Dracula AD 1972
GB 1972 95m Eastmancolor
Warner/Hammer (Josephine Douglas)

Dracula reappears among Chelsea teenagers practising black magic.
Depressed attempt to update a myth; the link with modern sin makes it seem not only tarnished but tasteless, and the film itself is lamentably short on excitement.
w Don Houghton *d* Alan Gibson *ph* Richard Bush *m* Michael Vickers *pd* Don Mingaye *ed* James Needs
☆ Peter Cushing, Christopher Lee, Stephanie Beacham, Michael Coles, Christopher Neame, William Ellis

Dracula contra Frankenstein: see *Dracula – Prisoner of Frankenstein*

'You'll die laughing. Then you'll rise from the dead and laugh once more.'
Dracula: Dead and Loving It
US 1995 90m Technicolor
Polygram/Castle Rock/Gaumont/Brooksfilms (Mel Brooks)

Dracula comes to London to seek fresh blood.
A feeble comedy, poking fun at British repression while sticking surprisingly closely to the plot of the original novel.
w Mel Brooks, Rudy de Luca, Steve Haberman *d* Mel Brooks *ph* Michael D. O'Shea *m* Hummie Mann *pd* Roy Forge Smith *ed* Adam Weiss
☆ Leslie Nielsen, Peter MacNicol, Steven Weber, Amy Yasbeck, Lysette Anthony, Harvey Korman, Mel Brooks, Anne Bancroft, Clive Revill
'As thin as bat wing.' – *Sunday Times*

'You just can't keep a good man down!'
Dracula Has Risen from the Grave
GB 1968 92m Technicolor
Hammer (Aida Young)

Dracula again terrorizes the village in the shadow of his castle, and is routed by a bishop.
Tedious, confined and repetitive shocker with little conventional action and an unusual emphasis on sex.
w John Elder (Anthony Hinds) *d* Freddie Francis *ph* Arthur Grant *m* James Bernard *ad* Bernard Robinson *ed* James Needs, Spencer Reeve
☆ Christopher Lee, Rupert Davies, Veronica Carlson, Barbara Ewing, Barry Andrews, Ewan Hooper
'A bloody bore.' – *Judith Crist*

Dracula is Alive and Well and Living in London: see *The Satanic Rites of Dracula*

Dracula Prince of Darkness
GB 1966 90m Techniscope
Warner/Hammer/Seven Arts (Anthony Nelson-Keys)

Stranded travellers are made welcome at the late count's castle by his sinister butler, who proceeds to use the blood of one of them to revivify his master.
Ingenious rehash of incidents from the original story, largely dissipated by poor colour and unsuitable wide screen.
w John Sansom *story* John Elder *d* Terence Fisher *ph* Michael Reed *m* James Bernard *pd* Bernard Robinson *ed* James Needs, Chris Barnes
☆ Christopher Lee, *Philip Latham*, Barbara Shelley, Thorley Walters, Andrew Keir, Francis Matthews, Suzan Farmer, Charles Tingwell
'Run-of-the-coffin stuff ... only for ardent fang-and-cross fans.' – *Judith Crist*

Dracula – Prisoner of Frankenstein (dubbed)
Spain/France 1972 90m Telecolor 'Scope
Interfilme/Fenix/Prodif ETS
original title: *Dracula contra Frankenstein*
aka: *The Screaming Dead*
Frankenstein revives Dracula in order to create an army of vampires to take over the world.
Horrendous not for its subject matter but for its total incompetence, including an incoherent narrative and a directorial style that consists of meaningless zooms and out-of-focus close-ups. An ailing Price plays Frankenstein as a somnambulistic zombie and the acting honours go to a rubber bat.
w Jess Franco, Paul D'Ales *d* Jess Franco (Jesús Franco) *ph* José Climent *m* Bruno Nicolai *ed* R. Aventer
☆ Howard Vernon (Mario Lippert), Dennis Price, Genevieve Deloir, Josiane Gilbert, Albert D'Albes, Mary Francis

Dracula versus Frankenstein (dubbed)
Spain/West Germany/Italy 1971 87m Eastmancolor Totalvision
Monarch/Eichberg/International Jaguar/Jaime Prades
aka: *El Hombre que Vino de Ummo*
Aliens attempt to conquer Earth by reviving Dracula, Frankenstein's monster, the Mummy and a werewolf.
Dire mix of horror and science fiction, cheaply and unimaginatively made.
w Jacinto Molina Alvarez *d* Tulio Demicheli *ph* Godofredo Pachecho *m* Franco Salina *ad* Adolfo Cofiño *ed* Emilio Rodriguez *sp* Antonio Molna
☆ Michael Rennie, Karin Dor, Craig Hill, Patty Sheppard, Paul Naschi
'The film's sole claim on anyone's attention is the unabashed sadism of several sequences ... As for the English title, Dracula and Frankenstein are never in the same shot together, let alone in conflict.' – *Tony Rayns*

'More sensational than her unforgettable father!'
Dracula's Daughter **
US 1936 70m bw
Universal (E. M. Asher)

The daughter of the old count follows his remains to London.
Lively sequel which develops in the manner of a Sherlock Holmes story.
w Garrett Fort *d Lambert Hillyer ph* George Robinson *m* Heinz Roemheld *ad* Albert S. D'Agostino *ed* Milton Carruth
☆ *Otto Kruger*, Marguerite Churchill, Edward Van Sloan, Gloria Holden, Irving Pichel, Nan Grey, Hedda Hopper, Gilbert Emery, Claud Allister, E. E. Clive, Halliwell Hobbes, Billy Bevan

'There's more to the legend than meets the throat!'
Dracula's Dog
US 1977 88m DeLuxe
Vic (Albert Band, Frank Ray Perelli)

GB title: *Zoltan, Hound of Dracula*
The resurrected servant of Dracula tries to use his vampire dog to create a new master.
Ingenious but unattractive addition to the saga, with dogs as chief villains; the style varies between spoof and rather nasty horror.
w Frank Ray Perelli *d* Albert Band *ph* Bruce Logan *m* Andrew Belling
☆ José Ferrer, Reggie Nalder, Michael Pataki, Jan Shutan

Draegerman Courage
US 1937 59m bw
Warner
Problems of a Nova Scotian gold mine cave-in.
Adequate action fare inspired by a real event. (Draegermen are burrowers.)
w Anthony Coldeway *d* Louis King
☆ Jean Muir, Barton MacLane, Henry O'Neill, Robert Barrat. Addison Richards, Gordon Oliver
'Vivid and often thrilling.' – *Variety*

Dragao da Maldade contra o Santo Guerreiro: see *Antonio das Mortes*

The Dragnet *
US 1928 77m approx (24 fps) bw silent
Paramount

When his buddy is killed, a detective resigns from the force and takes to the bottle.
Obviously interesting sequel to Underworld. *It can't be evaluated because no print is known to exist.*
w Jules and Charles Furthman *story Night Stick* by Oliver H. P. Garrett *d* Josef von Sternberg *ph* Harold Rosson *ad* Hans Dreier
☆ George Bancroft, Evelyn Brent, William Powell, Fred Kohler, Francis McDonald, Leslie Fenton

Dragnet *
US 1954 93m Warnercolor
Mark VII (Stanley Meyer)

Sgt Joe Friday solves the murder of an ex-convict.
Moderately interesting but overlong attempt to transfer television techniques to the big screen; laconic dialogue, question and answer, cheap sets, close-ups and convenient Los Angeles locations.
w Richard Breen *d Jack Webb ph* Edward Colman *m* Walter Schumann
☆ Jack Webb, Ben Alexander, Richard Boone, Stacy Harris, Ann Robinson, Virginia Gregg

Dragnet
US 1987 106m DeLuxe
Universal/Applied Action/Bernie Brillstein

The nephew of Sgt Joe Friday gets involved in a murder case.
Overlong parody with some obvious amusements before the whole thing becomes tiresome.
w Dan Aykroyd, Alan Zweibel, Tom Mankiewicz *d* Tom Mankiewicz *ph* Matthew F. Leonetti *m* Ira Newborn *pd* Robert F. Boyle
☆ Dan Aykroyd, Tom Hanks, Christopher Plummer, Harry Morgan, Alexandra Paul, Elizabeth Ashley, Dabney Coleman

Dragon Seed *
US 1944 144m bw
MGM (Pandro S. Berman)

Chinese peasants fight the Japanese.
Ill-advised attempt to follow the success of The Good Earth; *badly cast actors mouth propaganda lines in a mechanical script which provokes more boredom and unintentional laughter than sympathy.*
w Marguerite Roberts, Jane Murfin *novel* Pearl S. Buck *d* Jack Conway, Harold S. Bucquet *ph* Sidney Wagner *m* Herbert Stothart
☆ Katharine Hepburn, Walter Huston, Turhan Bey, Aline MacMahon, Akim Tamiroff, Hurd Hatfield, Frances Rafferty, Agnes Moorehead, Henry Travers, J. Carrol Naish
'A kind of slant-eyed *North Star*. Often awkward and pretentious, it nevertheless has moments of moral and dramatic grandeur.' – *Time*
'A fine film in anybody's sweepstakes. It'll wow 'em at the box office.' – *Variety (It didn't.)*
Sidney Wagner; Aline MacMahon

'The Mystery. The Life. The Love. The Legend.'
Dragon: The Bruce Lee Story *
US 1993 120m DeLuxe Panavision
Universal (Raffaella de Laurentiis)

A boy who trains in martial arts grows up to become a star of kung-fu movies, haunted by a vision of a dragon representing his inner fears, and dies young.
Enjoyable, if unenlightening, biopic of Bruce Lee that does little to explain why he became the genre's most famous performer, but notable for starring an interesting actor, the unrelated Jason Scott Lee.
w Edward Khmara, John Raffo, Rob Cohen *book Bruce Lee: The Man Only I Knew* by Linda Lee Cadwell *d* Rob Cohen *ph* David Eggby *m* Randy Edelman *pd* Robert Ziembicki *ed* Peter Amundson
☆ Jason Scott Lee, Lauren Holly, Robert Wagner, Michael Learned, Nancy Kwan, Kay Tong Lim, Ric Young, John Cheung
'Seemingly contrary elements and styles nonetheless mesh into an entertaining whole and the result provides extremely touching and haunting material.' – *Variety*
'It's less about daring deeds than about Lee's triumph over adversity.' – *Vincent Canby, New York Times*
'Cheerful, downmarket hagiography.' – *Derek Malcolm, Guardian*

Dragonfly: see *One Summer Love*

'When someone you love dies... are they gone forever?'
Dragonfly
US 2002 103m DeLuxe Panavision
Universal/Spyglass/Gran Via/Shady Acres (Mark Johnson, Tom Shadyac, Roger Birnbaum, Gary Barber)

In Chicago, a doctor becomes convinced that his dead wife is trying to send him a message through patients who have had a near-death experience.
Limp, lugubrious movie of mourning and loss that provides Costner with the opportunity, quickly seized, to look soulful.
w David Seltzer, Brandon Camp, Mike Thompson *d* Tom Shadyac *ph* Dean Semler *m* John Debney *pd* Linda DeScenna *ed* Don Zimmerman *cos* Judy Ruskin Howell
☆ Kevin Costner (Joe Darrow), Joe Morton (Hugh Campbell), Ron Rifkin (Charlie Dickinson), Linda Hunt (Sister Madeline), Susanna Thompson (Emily Darrow), Jacob Vargas (Pilot), Kathy Bates (Miriam Belmont), Robert Bailey Jnr (Jeffrey Reardon)
'It is impossible to find the film anything but appalling, shamelessly manipulative and contrived, and totally lacking in conviction. It is high grade Hollywood hokum.' – *Kevin Thomas, Los Angeles Times*

Dragonheart *
US 1996 103m DeLuxe Panavision
UIP/Universal (Raffaella de Laurentiis)

In the late 900s, a knight forms an alliance with the last dragon to rid Britain of a tyrant.
A thin medieval fantasy saved from mediocrity by its splendid dragon, voiced by Connery.
w Charles Edward Pogue *d* Rob Cohen *ph* David Eggby *m* Randy Edelman *pd* Benjamin Fernandez *ed* Peter Amundson *sp* Industrial Light and Magic; Tippett Studio
☆ Dennis Quaid, Sean Connery (voice), David Thewlis, Pete Postlethwaite, Dina Meyer, Jason Isaacs, Julie Christie, John Gielgud (voice)
'A blunted sword-and-sorcery fantasy which never gets it together.' – *Tom Hutchinson, Film Review*
visual effects

Dragon's Food **
West Germany 1987 75m bw
Novoskop Film Jan Schutte/Probst Film (Eric Nellessen)
original title: *Drachenfutter*
aka: *Spicy Rice*
A Pakistani and a Chinese immigrant struggle to open their own restaurant in Hamburg.
The dialogue mixes half-a-dozen languages, but succeeds in communicating its message of lives wasted by prejudice and intolerance.
w Jan Schutte, Thomas Strittmatter *d Jan Schütte ph* Lutz Konermann *m* Claus Bantzer *ed* Andreas Schreitmiller
☆ Bhaskar, Ric Young, Buddy Uzzaman, Wolf-Dieter Springer, Ulrich Wildgruber

Dragons Forever (dubbed)
Japan 1988 90m colour
Golden Harvest (Leonard K. C. Ho)
A lawyer discovers, when he falls in love, that he is on the wrong side in a case involving pollution and drug-dealing.
Comic martial arts adventure with romantic overtones and spectacular combat, for the undemanding.
w Szeto Cheuk-Hon *story* Gordon Chan, Leung Yiu Ming *d* Samo Hung *ph* Jimmy Leung, Cheung Yiu Tso *m* James Wong *pd* Oliver Wong *ed* Peter Cheung, Josephy Chiang
☆ Jackie Chan, Samo Hung, Yuen Biao, Deannie Yip, Pauline Yeung, Crystal Kwok

'Only sorcery can destroy it!'
Dragonslayer
† US 1981 110m Metrocolor Panavision
Walt Disney/Paramount (Howard W. Koch, Hal Barwood)
A sorcerer's apprentice uses his master's magic amulet to ward off various dangers.
Heavy-going sword-and-sorcery fable, not helped at all by slow plotting and dark photography. The dragons, however, are genuinely fierce.
w Hal Barwood, Matthew Robbins *d* Matthew Robbins *ph* Derek Vanlint *m* Alex North *pd* Elliot Scott *sp* Thomas Smith
☆ Peter MacNicol, Caitlin Clarke, Ralph Richardson, John Hallam, Peter Eyre, Albert Salmi
'Verges on the nasty for the nippers; sails too close to *déjà vu* for fantasy fans.' – *Time Out*
Alex North; visual effects (Dennis Muren and others)

Dragonwyck *
US 1946 103m bw
TCF (Darryl F. Zanuck)
In the 1840s a farmer's daughter marries her rich cousin, not knowing that he has poisoned his first wife.
Good-looking but rather tedious romance of the Jane Eyre/Rebecca school: tyrannical recluse, mystery upstairs, spooky house, etc. Heavy going.
wd Joseph L. Mankiewicz *novel* Anya Seton *ph Arthur Miller m* Alfred Newman
☆ Gene Tierney, Vincent Price, Glenn Langan, Walter Huston, Anne Revere, Spring Byington, Henry Morgan, Jessica Tandy

Dragoon Wells Massacre *
US 1957 88m DeLuxe CinemaScope
Allied Artists (Lindsley Parsons)
A group of travellers are stranded in hostile Indian territory.
Moderately suspenseful Western on a familiar theme.
w Warren Douglas *story* Oliver Drake *d* Harold Schuster *ph* William Clothier *m* Paul Dunlap *ed* Maurice Wright
☆ Barry Sullivan, Dennis O'Keefe, Mona Freeman, Katy Jurado, Sebastian Cabot, Jack Elam

'Car crazy, speed crazy, boy crazy!'
Dragstrip Girl
US 1957 69m bw
AIP/Golden State (Alex Gordon)
Two young hot-rodders are rivals for a new girl in town.
Stalled low-budget drive-in movie, requiring minimal attention from its audience.
w Lou Rusoff *d* Edward L. Cahn *ph* Frederick E. West *m* Ronald Stein *ad* Don Ament *ed* Ronald Sinclair
☆ Fay Spain, Steve Terrell, John Ashley, Frank Gorshin, Russ Bender, Tommy Ivo

Drake of England
GB 1935 104m bw
BIP (Walter C. Mycroft)
US title: *Drake the Pirate*
US title: *Elizabeth of England*
Sir Francis Drake is knighted by Queen Elizabeth for his seafaring exploits, and defeats the Spanish Armada.
Stiffly moving historical pageant; you can smell the mothballs.
w Clifford Grey, Akos Tolney, Marjorie Deans, Norman Watson *play Drake* by Louis N. Parker *d* Arthur Woods *ph* Claude Friese-Greene, Ronald Neame, Jack Parker *m* G. H. Clutsam *ad* Duncan Sutherland, Clarence Elder *ed* E. B. Jarvis
☆ Matheson Lang, Athene Seyler, Jane Baxter, Donald Wolfit, Henry Mollison, George Merritt, Amy Veness, Sam Livesey, Ben Webster

Drake the Pirate: see *Drake of England*

A Drama of Jealousy: see *Jealousy Italian Style*

'Yearning Youth – Behind the Scenes of a Parisian Dramatic School.'
Dramatic School *
US 1938 80m bw
MGM (Mervyn Le Roy)
Young actresses compete for success.
Another, less lively, Stage Door; *tolerable but not exciting.*
w Ernst Vajda, Mary McCall Jnr *play School of Drama* by Hans Szekely, Zoltan Egyed *d* Robert B. Sinclair Jnr *ph* William Daniels *m* Franz Waxman
☆ Luise Rainer, Paulette Goddard, Alan Marshal, Lana Turner, Anthony Allan (later John Hubbard), Henry Stephenson, Genevieve Tobin, Gale Sondergaard, Melville Cooper, Erik Rhodes, Ann Rutherford, Margaret Dumont, Virginia Grey, Hans Conried
'A disappointing effort which arouses little interest in its unfolding.' – *Variety*

Dramma della Gelosia – Tutti i Particolari in Cronaca: see *Jealousy Italian Style*

Drango
US 1957 92m bw
UA/Hall Bartlett
After the Civil War, a Union Army officer is assigned to bring law and order to a Georgia community.
Eccentric, downbeat semi-Western with aspirations to be some kind of film noir; does not come off.
w Hall Bartlett *d* Hall Bartlett, Jules Bricken *ph James Wong Howe m* Elmer Bernstein
☆ Jeff Chandler, Ronald Howard, Joanne Dru, Julie London, Donald Crisp, John Lupton, Morris Ankrum

The Draughtsman's Contract **
GB 1982 108m colour
BFI/Channel 4 (David Payne)
In 1694 a young draughtsman receives a curious commission from a country gentlewoman, his rewards to include bed and bawd.
Pleasantly unusual, stylized puzzle film which involves both sex and murder while maintaining a detached attitude to both. The period costumes help to give it an air of fantasy which was presumably intended.
wd Peter Greenaway ph Curtis Clark *m* Michael Nyman *ed* John Wilson
☆ Anthony Higgins, Janet Suzman, Anne Louise Lambert, Neil Cunningham, Hugh Fraser, Dave Hill
'Mannered and idiosyncratic, the speeches are so arch and twitty that they seem to be pitched higher than a dog whistle.' – *Pauline Kael, New Yorker*
'Perhaps the four-hour version which may one day become available is clearer if not more concise.' – *Guardian*
'Best enjoyed as a sly piece of double bluff, a puzzle without a solution, an avant garde hoax in the spirit of Dada and the surrealists.' – *Observer*

Dream Demon
GB 1988 89m colour
Palace (Paul Webster)
A woman begins to have horrific nightmares before her marriage to a hero of the Falklands War.
A moderately effective psychological thriller, though over-reliant on shock effects.
w Harley Cokliss, Christopher Wicking *d* Harley Cokliss *ph* Ian Wilson *m* Bill Nelson *pd* Hugo Luczyc-Wyhowski *ed* Ian Crafford, David Martin
☆ Jemma Redgrave, Jimmy Nail, Timothy Spall, Kathleen Wilhoite, Annabelle Lanyon, Susan Fleetwood, Nickolas Grace
'One of this, or any year's, worst ... proof of the low levels the genre can sink to.' – *Stefan Jaworzyn, Shock Xpress*

Dream Girl
US 1947 86m bw
Paramount (P. J. Wolfson)
A girl revels in her own romantic dreams, one of which nearly comes true.
Potentially pleasant comedy about a female Walter Mitty does not work because the director has run out of ideas, the star is miscast and Hollywood has insisted on making the girl rich to begin with, which robs the dreams of any point.
w Arthur Sheekman *play* Elmer Rice *d* Mitchell Leisen *ph* Daniel L. Fapp *m* Victor Young
☆ Betty Hutton, Macdonald Carey, Walter Abel, Patric Knowles, Virginia Field, Peggy Wood, Lowell Gilmore

Dream Lover
US 1986 104m Technicolor
MGM-UA/Alan J. Pakula, Jon Boorstin
A dream researcher is assigned to the case of a girl who has fatally stabbed an intruder.
Flabby and overlong case history with no very interesting conclusion.
w Jon Boorstin *d* Alan J. Pakula *ph* Sven Nykvist *m* Michael Small
☆ Kristy McNichol, Ben Masters, Paul Shenar, John McMartin, Gayle Hunnicutt, Justin Deas

Dream Lover
US 1994 103m DeLuxe
Rank/Polygram/Propaganda/Nicita/Lloyd/Edward R. Pressman (Sigurjon Sighvatsson, Wallis Nicita, Lauren Lloyd)
An architect begins to suspect that his model wife is not who she claims to be.
An uninvolving drama of identity, exploring interesting territory but making no new discoveries.
wd Nicholas Kazan *ph* Jean-Yves Escoffier *m* Christopher Young *pd* Richard Hoover *ed* Jill Savitt, Susan Crutcher
☆ James Spader, Mädchen Amick, Bess Armstrong, Larry Miller, Frederic Lehne, William Shockley
'Looks more like the thing you might get out of the video store but would balk at paying for in the cinema. It's a bit basic really, playing one tune over and over again.' – *Derek Malcolm, Guardian*

Dream Machine
US 1991 86m Hawk
DM (Lyman Dayton)
A college student is given a Porsche by a wealthy, vengeful wife; unknown to either, her philandering husband's body is hidden in its boot, and his murderer wants it back.
Inane wish-fulfilment for teenage drivers: a love story about a boy and his car, though a comedy thriller was intended.
w Eric Hendershot *d* Lyman Dayton *ph* T. C. Christenson *m* Lex de Azevedo *pd* Michael C. Ayers *ed* Steve Johnson
☆ Corey Haim, Evan Richards, Jeremy Slate, Randall England, Tracy Fraim, Brittney Lewis, Susan Seaforth Hayes

The Dream of a Rarebit Fiend *
US 1906 4m (24 fps) bw silent
Early trick film depicting a nightmare resulting from overeating.
w Winsor McCay *d* Edwin S. Porter

A Dream of Kings
US 1969 110m Technicolor
National General (Jules Schermer)
Episodes in the life of an improvident, lusty, poetical Chicago Greek with a dying son.
The part screamed for Anthony Quinn and got him, with the result that it has all been seen before, too frequently. Well made, with strong appeal to Chicago Greeks.
w Harry Mark Petrakis, Ian Hunter *novel* Harry Mark Petrakis *d* Daniel Mann *ph* Richard H. Kline *m* Alex North
☆ Anthony Quinn, Irene Papas, Inger Stevens, Sam Levene, Val Avery, Tamara Daykarhanova

A Dream of Life: see *Life Begins*

The Dream of Light: see *The Quince Tree Sun*

The Dream of Olwen: see *While I Live*

A Dream of Passion
Greece 1978 110m Eastmancolor
Branfilm/Melinafilm (Jules Dassin)
A woman who, Medea-like, has killed her children is drawn into an eccentric relationship with an actress playing Medea on the stage.
Weird and ineffective character drama which badly needs discipline.
wd Jules Dassin *ph* George Arvanitis *m* Ionnis Markopoulos
☆ Melina Mercouri, Ellen Burstyn, Andreas Voutsinas, Despo Diamantidou

Dream Street *
US 1921 89m (24 fps) bw silent
D. W. Griffith Inc
Three Limehouse folk, torn between good and evil, act out their dreams.
Trilogy of moral tales, fancifully and often charmingly assembled by the master director who often reminds one of a Victorian lace maker.
wd D. W. Griffith stories Thomas Burke *ph Henrik Sartov*
☆ Carol Dempster, Ralph Graves, Charles Emmett Mack, Edward Peil, Tyrone Power Snr, W. J. Ferguson

The Dream Team *
US 1989 113m DeLuxe Panavision
UIP/Imagine Entertainment (Christopher W. Knight)
On a day trip to New York, four inmates of a psychiatric hospital foil a murder plot.
Enjoyable sentimental comedy that avoids most of the pitfalls of its subject matter.
w Jon Connolly, David Loucka *d* Howard Zieff *ph* Adam Holender *m* David McHugh *pd* Todd Hallowell *ad* Christopher Nowak *ed* C. Timothy O'Meara
☆ Michael Keaton, Christopher Lloyd, Peter Boyle, Stephen Furst, Dennis Boutsikaris, Lorraine Bracco, Milo O'Shea, Philip Bosco, James Remar
'Sharp and punchily acted.' – *John Pym, MFB*

Dream Wife
US 1953 99m bw
MGM (Dore Schary)
An executive leaves his ambitious wife for a sheik's daughter schooled in the art of pleasing men, but naturally finds drawbacks.
Very moderate comedy with strained situations and few laughs. The stars work hard.
w Sidney Sheldon, Herbert Baker, Alfred L. Levitt *d* Sidney Sheldon *ph* Milton Krasner *m* Conrad Salinger
☆ Cary Grant, Deborah Kerr, Walter Pidgeon, Betta St John, Eduard Franz, Buddy Baer, Les Tremayne

Dream with the Fishes *
US 1997 97m Foto-Kem
Columbia TriStar/3 Ring Circus (Johnny Wow, Mitchell Stein)
A terminally ill man offers to help a would-be suicide kill himself in return for financing some of his fantasies, which include nude bowling and public drug-taking.
Sometimes engaging, somewhat schematic celebration of life that harks back to the style of 70s movies.

wd Finn Taylor *ph* Barry Stone *m* Tito Larriva *pd* Justin McCartney *ed* Nick LeCompte
☆ David Arquette, Brad Hunt, Kathryn Erbe, Cathy Moriarty, J. E. Freeman, Allyce Beasley
'Refreshing, unexpectedly profound comedy.' – *Variety*

Dreamboat *
US 1952 83m bw
TCF (Sol C. Siegel)

A romantic star of the silent film era is embarrassed when his old movies turn up on television.
Hollywood rather blunderingly makes fun of its arch enemy in this sometimes sprightly but often disappointing comedy which should have been a bull's-eye.
wd Claude Binyon *ph* Milton Krasner *m* Cyril Mockridge
☆ Clifton Webb, Ginger Rogers, Anne Francis, Jeffrey Hunter, Elsa Lanchester, Fred Clark, Ray Collins, Paul Harvey
'A merry comedy filled with uproarious laughter from beginning to end.' – *Hollywood Reporter*

Dreamchild **
GB 1985 94m Technicolor
Thorn EMI/PFH (Rick McCallum, Kenith Trodd)

Travelling to New York for the centenary of Lewis Carroll's birth, Alice Hargreaves, the original of his Alice, remembers her relationship with him.
Complex and intriguing drama of a woman coming to terms with her past and present.
w Dennis Potter *d* Gavin Millar *ph* Billy Williams *m* Stanley Myers *pd* Roger Hall *ed* Angus Newton *sp* Jim Henson's Creature Shop
☆ *Coral Browne*, Peter Gallagher, Ian Holm, Jane Asher, Nicola Cowper, Caris Corfman, Amelia Shankley
'Not a movie for a wide audience: it simply isn't conceived in the broad narrative patterns that please most moviegoers. Yet it's very enjoyable; it has a twinkling subtext, and in some scenes it achieves levels of feeling that the new mainstream films don't get near.' – *Pauline Kael, New Yorker*
'Ambitious but unsatisfying and gimmicky.' – *Variety*

Dreamer
US 1979 86m Eastmancolor
TCF (Michael Lobell)

A young man dreams of becoming a professional bowling champion.
Faced with the impossible task of making tenpin bowling visually or dramatically interesting, the makers focus instead on a stormy romance and a sentimental relationship with an elderly mentor; they are no more effective in gaining an audience's attention.
w James Proctor, Harry Bischof *d* Noel Nosseck *ph* Bruce Surtees *m* Bill Conti *ad* Archie Sharp *ed* Fred Chulack
☆ Tim Matheson, Susan Blakely, Jack Warden

Dreaming
GB 1944 78m bw
Ealing

A soldier on leave gets a bump on the head, and dreams ...
Rather elementary series of sketches with a few good laughs and interesting guest appearances.
w Bud Flanagan, Reginald Purdell *d* John Baxter
☆ Flanagan and Allen, Hazel Court, Dick Francis, Philip Wade, Teddy Brown, Reginald Foort, Gordon Richards, Alfredo Campoli

Dreaming Lips *
GB 1936 94m bw
Trafalgar (Max Schach, Paul Czinner)

The wife of an invalid musician has an affair with another man and commits suicide.
Standard star fare, possibly Miss Bergner's most notable film, also available in a German version.
w Margaret Kennedy, Lady Cynthia Asquith, Carl Mayer *play* Melo by Henry Bernstein *d* Paul Czinner, Lee Garmes *ph* Roy Clark *m* William Walton *ad* Andrei Andreiev, Tom Morahan *ed* David Lean
☆ Elisabeth Bergner, Romney Brent, Raymond Massey, Joyce Bland, Sydney Fairbrother, Felix Aylmer, Donald Calthrop
'In many respects one of the finest productions ever made in England ... made in Hollywood, the story would be whitewashed and much of its strength weakened.' – *Variety*

'Even with her eyes wide open, she never stopped...'

Dreaming of Joseph Lees
US/GB 1999 92m Technicolor
TCF/Midsummer/IoMFC (Chris Milburn)

In Somerset in the 1950s, a young woman is obsessed by her one-legged cousin.
Unhappy, underwritten rural melodrama that fails to sustain its attempt at a romantic tragedy.
w Catherine Linstrum *d* Eric Styles *ph* Jimmy Dibling *m* Zbigniew Preisner *pd* Humphrey Jaeger *ed* Caroline Limmer *cos* Maggie Chappelhow
☆ Samantha Morton (Eva), Lee Ross (Harry), Rupert Graves (Joseph Lees), Holly Aird (Maria), Miriam Margolyes (Signora Caldoni), Frank Finlay (Eva's father), Nick Woodeson (Mr Dian), Lauren Richardson (Janie), Felix Billson (Robert)
'A humourless symphony of false notes.' – *Philip French, Observer*

The Dreamlife of Angels ***
France 1998 113m colour
Bagheera/Diaphana/France3 (François Marquis)

original title: *La Vie Rêvée des Anges*
Two young women, trying to survive in Lille, form an uneasy friendship with each other and with two bouncers at rock concerts.
Engrossing and frequently surprising narrative of French working-class life, with two protagonists with contrasting personalities: one happy to take life as it comes, the other striving for material success.
w Erick Zonca, Roger Bohbot *d* Erick Zonca *ph* Agnes Godard *m* Yann Thiersen *pd* Jimmy Vansteenkiste *ed* Yannick Kergoat
☆ *Elodie Bouchez, Natacha Regnier*, Gregoire Colin, Jo Prestia, Patrick Mercado
'A passionate and unpretentious gem.' – *Film Review*
† In France, it won the Prix Méliès as the best French film of the year. Elodie Bouchez and Natacha Regnier were joint winners of the best actress award at the 1998 Cannes Film Festival.

Dreams That Money Can Buy *
US 1946 81m Technicolor
Art of the Century (Hans Richter, Peggy Guggenheim, Kenneth MacPherson)

A young itinerant sells dreams to people who need them.
Semi-underground surrealist film, momentarily of interest, but disjointed and with no real apparent purpose.
wd Hans Richter *ph* Arnold Eagle *md* Louis Applebaum
'Arch, snobbish and sycophantic, about as genuinely experimental as a Chemcraft set.' – *James Agee*
† The individual dreams are Max Ernst, Man Ray, Fernand Leger, Marcel Duchamp and Alexander Calder as well as Richter.

Dreamscape
US 1984 99m CFI color
Thorn-EMI/Zuplein-Curtis/Bella (Bruce Cohn Curtis)

Experiments prove that it is possible for a dreamer to enter the dreams of others, and a subject finds himself being used for a plot against the president of the US.
Complex fantasy melodrama with a cold war basis; neither exciting nor praiseworthy.
w David Loughery, Joseph Ruben, Chuck Russell *d* Joseph Ruben *ph* Brian Tufano, Kevin Kutchaver *m* Maurice Jarre *ad* Jeff Stags *ed* Richard Halsey
☆ Dennis Quaid, Max von Sydow, Christopher Plummer, Eddie Albert, Kate Capshaw

Drei von der Tankstelle *
Germany 1930 80m bw
UFA

Three penniless young men find happiness as petrol station attendants.
Light-hearted operetta of the Depression era, well received at the time.
w Franz Schultz, Paul Frank *d William Thiele* *ph* Franz Planer *m* Werner Heymann
☆ Willy Fritsch, Lilian Harvey, Oskar Karlweis, Heinz Ruhmann, Olga Tchekhova
'When leaving this charming talker operetta, one feels in good humour, humming the catchy hits of its talented composer ... constant laughter and enthusiasm.' – *Variety*
† Remade 1955 by Hans Wolff, with a cast still led by Willy Fritsch.

Die Dreigroschenoper **
Germany 1931 114m bw
Warner/Tobis/Nero

US title: *The Threepenny Opera*
In turn-of-the-century London, Mack the Knife marries the daughter of the beggar king and runs into trouble.
Heavy-footed but interesting updating of The Beggar's Opera*, with splendid sets.*
w Bela Balazs, Leo Lania, Ladislas Vajda *play* Bertolt Brecht *d G. W. Pabst* *ph* Fritz Arno Wagner *m Kurt Weill* *ad Andrei Andreiev*
☆ *Lotte Lenya, Rudolf Forster*, Fritz Rasp, Caroline Neher, Reinhold Schunzel, Valeska Gert, Vladimir Sokoloff
† Brecht disliked the film and sued the makers, but lost.
†† A French version was also released under the title *L'Opéra de Quat'sous*, with Albert Préjean.

Dressage (dubbed)
France 1985 90m Eastmancolor
Samourai

A woman sets out to corrupt her father's 17-year-old daughter while her friend attempts to ruin a would-be politician by seducing him and his son.
Glossy soft-core porn, slickly done but uninteresting.
w Jean-Philippe Berger, J. C. Roy *d* Pierre B. Reinhard *ph* Denis Lenoir *m* Philippe Brejean *ad* Jean-Claude Roy
☆ Véronique Catanzaro, Patrick Guillemin, Marc Henry, Henri-Jacques Huet, André Nader, Sylvie Novak, Katya Strambi, Cornélia Wilms

Dressed to Kill
US 1946 72m bw
Universal (Roy William Neil)

aka: *Sherlock Holmes: Dressed to Kill*
Sherlock Holmes pits his wits against a murderous gang searching for the location of printing plates stolen from the Bank of England.
Unremarkable end to an enjoyable series, with some barely adequate performances, apart from the central duo of Rathbone and Bruce.
w Frank Gruber, Leonard Lee *d* Roy William Neill *ph* Maury Gertsman *m* Milton Rosen *ad* Jack Otterson, Martin Obzina *ed* Saul A. Goodkind
☆ Basil Rathbone, Nigel Bruce, Patricia Morison, Edmund Breon, Frederick Worlock, Carl Harbord, Mary Gordon, Anita Glyn

'Every nightmare has a beginning. This one never ends!'

Dressed to Kill **
US 1980 105m Technicolor Panavision
Filmways/Samuel Z. Arkoff/Cinema 77 (George Litto)

A sexually disturbed matron under analysis is murdered by a transvestite slasher, who then goes after a witness.
Occasionally brilliant, generally nasty suspenser clearly derived from many viewings of Psycho*. Certainly not for the squeamish.*
wd Brian de Palma *ph* Ralf Bode *m* Pino Donaggio *pd* Gary Weist *ed* Gerald Greenberg
☆ Michael Caine, Angie Dickinson, Nancy Allen, Keith Gordon, Dennis Franz
'De Palma goes right for the audience jugular ... it fully milks the boundaries of its "R" rating.' – *Variety*
'By casting a halo of excitement around killing, a glow of degradation around living, and linking the two in a queasy, guilty partnership, de Palma is asking us to celebrate the joys of barbarism in a world already drunk on rape, torture, murder and war.' – *Sunday Times*
'De Palma earns the title of master, all right ... but Hitch remains the grand master.' – *Roger Ebert*

The Dresser ***
GB 1983 118m colour
Columbia/Goldcrest/World Film Services (Peter Yates)

An exhausted Shakespearean actor-manager has a wild last day on tour, comforted and restrained by his homosexual dresser.
A strained film, but a valuable record of a play based on the touring career of Donald Wolfit, whose dresser the author was.
w Ronald Harwood *play* Ronald Harwood *d Peter Yates* *ph* Kelvin Pike *m* James Horner *pd* Stephen Grimes
☆ *Albert Finney, Tom Courtenay*, Edward Fox, Zena Walker, Eileen Atkins, Michael Gough, Betty Marsden, Lockwood West
'The best sort of drama, fascinating us on the surface with colour and humour and esoteric detail, and then revealing the truth underneath.' – *Roger Ebert*
'It is not an American picture; it is not like *42nd Street*. It is British and therefore tells a tale not of effortless overnight success but of day by day humiliation and defeat ... It is utterly joyless. I can only claim that it tells its grim tale with sparks of humor and in merciless detail.' – *Quentin Crisp*
best picture; Tom Courtenay; Albert Finney; Peter Yates as director; Ronald Harwood (adaptation)

The Dressmaker *
GB 1988 91m colour
Rank/Film Four International/British Screen (Ronald Shedlo)

Tensions arise in wartime within a puritanical working-class family with the arrival of American GIs.
Well acted, but depressing.
w John McGrath *novel* Beryl Bainbridge *d* Jim O'Brien *ph* Michael Coulter *m* George Fenton *pd* Caroline Amies *ed* William Diver
☆ *Joan Plowright, Billie Whitelaw*, Jane Horrocks, Tim Ransom, Pete Postlethwaite, Pippa Hinchley, Rosemary Martin, Tony Haygarth
'A masterpiece of minimalist compression.' – *Hal Hinson, Washington Post*

Dreyfus *
GB 1931 80m bw
BIP (F. W. Kraemer)

US title: *The Dreyfus Case*
In 1894 France, a Jewish officer is accused of spying.
Primitive version of a much-filmed story (cf The Life of Emile Zola, I Accuse*).*
w Reginald Berkeley, Walter C. Mycroft *play The Dreyfus Case* by Hans Rehfisch, Wilhelm Herzog *d* F. W. Kraemer, Milton Rosmer *ph* Willy Minterstein *ed* Langford Reed, Betty Spiers
☆ Cedric Hardwicke (Captain Alfred Dreyfus), George Merritt (Emile Zola), Charles Carson (Colonel Picquart), Sam Livesey (Labori), Garry Marsh (Major Esterhazy), Randle Ayrton (President of Court Martial), George Zucco
'A picture of the documentary class, well out of the ordinary.' – *Variety*

Drifters *
GB 1929 40m approx bw
Empire Marketing Board (John Grierson)

A documentary of the North Sea fishing fleet.
A highly influential documentary, made at a time when British films were totally unrealistic and studio-bound. Unfortunately it now seems extremely dull.
wd John Grierson *ph* Basil Emmott *ed* John Grierson

Drifting Clouds **
Finland 1996 93m Eastmancolor
Metro/Tartan/Sputnik Oy/YLE TV-1/Pandora/Pyramide (Aki Kaurismäki)

original title: *Kauas Pilvet Karkaavat*
A tram-driver and his wife, a head waiter, face difficulties when they lose their jobs and decide to try to open their own restaurant.
A bleakly humorous account of domestic difficulties with, for a change, a feel-good ending; it all has an inconsequential charm.
wd Aki Kaurismäki *ph* Timo Salminen *ad* Markku Pätilä, Jukka Salmi *ed* Aki Kaurismäki

☆ Kati Outinen, Kari Väänänen, Elina Salo, Sakari Kuosmanen, Matti Onnismaa, Markku Peltola

'There are small quirky pleasures to cherish from this warm, comical and optimistic tribute to the human spirit.' – *Caroline Rees, Empire*

† The film is dedicated to Matti Pellonpää, an actor who died in 1995 and appeared in many of Kaurismäki's movies; he appears here as the child in a photograph.

Driftwood

US 1947 90m bw
Republic

An orphan is adopted by a kindly doctor.
Lavender-scented family yarn with pleasant backgrounds and expert performances.
w Mary Loos, Richard Sale *d* Allan Dwan *ph* John Alton *m* Nathan Scott
☆ Natalie Wood, Ruth Warrick, Walter Brennan, Dean Jagger, Charlotte Greenwood

'An erotic dream of obsession.'

Driftwood

Ireland/GB 1996 100m Technicolor
Blue Dolphin/Goldcrest/Deadwood/Setanta (Mary Breen-Farrelly)

A French sculptor discovers an injured man on a remote beach in Ireland and takes him home to keep.
A cliché-ridden situation and a script that is beyond redemption.
w Richard M. N. Waring *d* Ronan O'Leary *ph* Billy Williams *m* John Cameron *pd* Tim Hutchinson *ed* Malcolm Cooke
☆ James Spader, Anne Brochet, Barry McGovern, Anna Massey, Aiden Grenell, Kevin McHugh

'Banal and dreary.' – *Sight and Sound*

'The blood runs in rivers, and the drill keeps tearing through flesh and bone.'

The Driller Killer

US 1979 85m colour
Navaron (Rochelle Weisberg)

A disturbed artist murders vagrants with an electric drill.
Gruesome movie of frustration and sordid city life; it was among the first so-called 'video nasties' to be banned in Britain, until its re-release in 1999.
w Nicholas St John, Louis Mascolo *d* Abel Ferrara *ph* Ken Kelsch *m* Joseph Delia *ad* Louis Mascolo *ed* Orlando Gallini, Bonnie Constant, Michael Constant, Jimmy Laine (Abel Ferrara) *sp* David Smith
☆ Jimmy Laine (Abel Ferrara), Carolyn Marz, Baybi Day, Harry Schultz, Alan Wynroth, Maria Helhoski, Bob DeFrank

'Ferrara's films may be rough, but there's no denying the cheapskate proficiency with which he puts them together, or the painful accuracy of his probing for the unhealthy nerve.' – *Kim Newman, MFB*

Drive

US/Japan 1997 99m CFI Super 35
Overseas/Neo

A Chinese man, who has been fitted with a bio-mechanical device that increases his physical abilities, is hunted by gangsters after he flees to the US.
Frenetic, stunt-crammed, tongue-in-cheek, over-the-top martial arts thriller with an invincible hero and gun-toting bad guys who couldn't hit a barn door at three paces; it is the sort of film where a gang of killers burst through the windows of a nightclub on motorbikes, while firing automatic weapons, in order to take out one man.
w Scott Phillips *d* Steve Wang *ph* Michael G. Wojciechowski *m* Walter Werzowa *pd* Terrence Foster *ed* Ivan Ladizinsky
☆ Mark Dacascos, Kadeem Hardison, John Pyper-Ferguson, Brittany Murphy, Tracey Walter, James Shigeta, Masaya Kato

'She needed the money – and I needed her!'

Drive a Crooked Road

US 1954 82m bw
Columbia (Jonie Taps)

A garage mechanic falls in with bank robbers.
Terse crime melodrama, quite watchable.
w Blake Edwards *d* Richard Quine *ph* Charles Lawton Jnr *md* Ross di Maggio
☆ Mickey Rooney, Kevin McCarthy, Dianne Foster

Drive He Said

US 1970 90m colour
Columbia/Drive Productions/BBS (Steve Blauner)

An easygoing college basketball star is helped by an eccentric rebel to ensure his own unfitness for military service. Both run into trouble.
Flabby celebration of against-the-government attitudes, expressed partly through sex and bad language. Defiantly hard to like.
w Jeremy Larner, Jack Nicholson *d* Jack Nicholson *ph* Bill Butler *m* David Shire
☆ Michael Margotta, William Tepper, Bruce Dern, Karen Black, Robert Towne, Henry Jaglom

'They got dumped. They needed dates. They got more than they bargained for.'

Drive Me Crazy

US 1999 91m DeLuxe
TCF (Amy Robinson)

A popular girl grooms a scruffy, carefree boy, who lives next door, so that he can get together again with his estranged girlfriend.
Limp teenaged romantic comedy that lacks any sense of reality or fun.
w Rob Thomas *novel How I Created My Perfect Prom Date* by Todd Strasser *d* John Schultz *ph* Kees Van Oostrum *m* Greg Kendall *pd* Aaron Osborne *ed* John Pace *cos* Genevieve Tyrrell
☆ Melissa Joan Hart (Nicole Maris), Adrian Grenier (Chase Hammond), Susan May Pratt (Alicia), Kris Park (Ray Neeley), Mark Webber (Dave), Ali Larter (Dulcie), Stephen Collins (Mr Maris), Gabriel Carpenter (Brad), Mark Metcalf (Mr Rope), William Converse-Roberts (Mr Hammond), Faye Grant (Mrs Maris)

'Sloppy and dull in equal measures.' – *Variety*

Drive-in

US 1976 96m Technicolor
Columbia (George Litto)

In Texas, various illicit activities find their climax at a drive-in movie.
Mild sex-and-destruction comedy which raises few laughs and makes little sense.
w Bob Peete *d* Rod Amateau *ph* Robert Jessup *m* various
☆ Lisa Lemole, Glenn Morshower, Gary Cavagnaro, Billy Milliken, Lee Newsome, Regan Kee

'Welcome to The Human Race'

Driven

US 2001 117m DeLuxe Panavision
Warner/Franchise (Elie Samaha, Sylvester Stallone, Renny Harlin)

A veteran sports car driver helps turn a young hotshot into a winner.
Noisy, messy movie about sleek, fast cars and very dull people.
w Sylvester Stallone *story* Jan Skrentny, Neal Tabachnick *d* Renny Harlin *ph* Mauro Fiore *m* BT *pd* Charles Wood *ed* Stuart Levy, Steve Gilson
☆ Sylvester Stallone (Joe Tanto), Burt Reynolds (Carl Henry), Kip Pardue (Jimmy Bly), Stacy Edwards (Lucretia Clans), Til Schweiger (Beau Brandenburg), Gina Gershon (Cathy Moreno), Estella Warren (Sophia Simone), Cristian de la Fuente (Memo Heguy), Brent Briscoe (Crusher), Robert Sean Leonard (DeMille Bly)

'A movie about Americans oblivious to the rest of the world, looking only inwards, at themselves, their macho culture and their can-do competence, and finding the prospect good, arrogantly self-satisfying and uncritical.' – *Alexander Walker, London Evening Standard*

'A movie by, for and about the Attention Deficit Disordered.' – *Roger Ebert*

The Driver ****

US 1978 91m DeLuxe
TCF/EMI/Lawrence Gordon

A detective determines to catch an old enemy, a getaway driver.
Deft and clever thriller that has been stripped of all redundancies and reduced to its core, of two obsessional men on different sides of the law locked in deadly conflict. It is a simple, spare story of bleak lives, brilliantly told.
wd Walter Hill *ph* Philip Lathrop *m* Michael Small
☆ Ryan O'Neal, Bruce Dern, Isabelle Adjani, Ronee Blakley

'Comic book cops and robbers existentialism.' – *Pauline Kael*

'Because of the quiet and mysterious mood of this picture, it has a pretentious quality to it.' – *Variety*

Driving Force

Australia/US/Philippines 1989 90m colour
J & M/Eastern (Howard Grigsby, Rod Confesor)

In a future post-industrial world, an honest trucker battles with a violent gang of scavengers.
Incoherent action film that fails in its recreation of a believable future (although virtually all goods are recycled or secondhand, petrol is plentiful), and is not helped by having an uncharismatic star.
w Patrick Edgeworth *d* A. J. Prowse *ph* Kevan Lind, Richard Michalak *m* Paul Schutze *pd* Toto Castillo *ed* Tony Paterson
☆ Sam Jones, Catherine Bach, Don Swayze, Gerald Gordon, Angel Cook, Renata Scott, Robert Marius, Billy Blanks

Driving Me Crazy: see *Dutch*

Driving Miss Daisy *

US 1989 99m Technicolor Panavision
Warner/Zanuck Company/Richard Zanuck, Lili Fini Zanuck

A elderly rich Jewish widow at first resists, and then succumbs to, the obsequious attentions of her black chauffeur.
Old-fashioned and charming, but slight to the point of inconsequentiality.
w Alfred Uhry *play* Alfred Uhry *d* Bruce Beresford *ph* Peter James *m* Hans Zimmer *pd* Bruno Rubeo *ed* Mark Warner
☆ Morgan Freeman, Jessica Tandy, Dan Aykroyd, Patti LuPone
Academy Award: best picture; best makeup; Alfred Uhry; Jessica Tandy
Academy Award nomination: Morgan Freeman; Dan Aykroyd; best art direction; best costume design
BAFTA: Jessica Tandy

Le Droit d'Aimer: see *Brainwashed*

Drôle de Drame *

France 1936 100m approx bw
aka: *Bizarre, Bizarre (84m American version)*

A complicated chain of bizarre events is set in motion when a botanist pretends not to be a detective story writer, a bishop tries to be a detective, and a murderer seeks revenge for libel.
A curious satirical comedy which is never quite as funny as it seems about to be, but should be seen for its downright peculiar London sets and its array of actors in top form.
w Jacques Prévert *novel The Lunatic at Large* by J. Storer Clouston *d* Marcel Carné *ph* Eugene Schufftan *m* Maurice Jaubert *pd* Alexandre Trauner
☆ *Françoise Rosay, Michel Simon, Louis Jouvet, Jean-Louis Barrault*, Jean-Pierre Aumont

'Art theatres and foreign-language houses will do fair business.' – *Variety*

'No one with any taste for nonsense should miss it.' – *Richard Mallett, Punch*

Drôle d'endroit pour une Rencontre *

France 1988 98m colour
Artificial Eye/Hachette/A2/DD/Deneuve/Orly/Editions Sidonie (Patrick Bordier)

GB title: *A Strange Place to Meet*

A doctor falls in love with an abandoned wife, who is waiting for her husband to return.
An unconvincing romance, full of longueurs.
w François Dupreyron, Dominique Faysse *d* François Dupreyron *ph* Charlie Van Damme *ad* Carlos Conti *ed* Françoise Collin
☆ Catherine Deneuve, Gérard Depardieu, André Wilms, Nathalie Cardone, Jean-Pierre Sentier, Alain Rimoux, Vincent Martin

Drop Dead Darling

GB 1966 100m Technicolor Panavision
Seven Arts (Ken Hughes)
US title: *Arrivederci Baby*

A con man who marries and murders rich women meets a con lady with similar intentions.
Loud, restless black comedy which squanders its moments of genuine inventiveness among scenes of shouting, confusion and action for action's sake.
wd Ken Hughes *story The Careful Man* by Richard Deming *ph* Denys Coop *m* Dennis Farnon
☆ Tony Curtis, Rosanna Schiaffino, Lionel Jeffries, Zsa Zsa Gabor, Nancy Kwan, Fenella Fielding, Anna Quayle, Warren Mitchell, Mischa Auer

'He creates the havoc. She takes the blame.'

Drop Dead Fred

US 1991 99m colour
Rank/Working Title/Polygram (Paul Webster)

A young woman in difficulties is revisited by her imaginary, destructive childhood friend.
Singularly tasteless comedy, lacking any vestige of wit or even humour.
w Carlos Davis, Anthony Fingleton *story* Elizabeth Livingston *d* Ate de Jong *ph* Peter Deming *m* Randy Edelman *pd* Joseph T. Garrity *ed* Marshall Harvey
☆ Phoebe Cates, Rik Mayall, Marsha Mason, Tim Matheson, Bridget Fonda, Carrie Fisher, Keith Charles, Ashley Peldon, Daniel Gerroll

'Harvey reimagined for the Beetlejuice generation, with strident gags standing in for magic and relentless obviousness overriding the disturbing ambiguity that might have made the film work.' – *Kim Newman, Sight and Sound*

'This celebration of mental retardation is where the nadirs of two current Hollywood cycles – the regression to childhood/life swap movie and the ghost/revenant picture – intersect.' – *Philip French, Observer*

'If Looks Could Kill...'
'The Battle Between The Good And The Bad Is About To Get Ugly.'

Drop Dead Gorgeous

US/Germany 1999 98m DeLuxe
New Line/Capella/KC Medien (Gavin Pallone, Judy Hofflund)

A documentary film crew follow the events leading up to a beauty contest, which the town's wealthiest woman is determined that her daughter will win.
Heavy-handed satire on small town life and the beauty business; the narrative becomes too contrived to provide much satisfaction.
w Lona Williams *d* Michael Patrick Jann *ph* Michael Spiller *m* Mark Mothersbaugh *pd* Ruth Ammon *ed* David Codron, Janice Hampton
☆ Kirsten Dunst (Amber Atkins), Ellen Barkin (Annette Atkins), Allison Janney (Loretta), Denise Richards (Becky Leeman), Kirstie Alley (Gladys Leeman), Sam McMurray (Lester Leeman), Amy Adams (Leslie Miller), Tara Redepenning (Molly Howard), Shannon Nelson (Tess Weinhaus), Sarah Stewart (Jenelle Betz), Michael McShane (Harold Vilmes)

'Crude mockery that thinks it's satire.' – *Lisa Schwarzman, Entertainment Weekly*

Drop Squad

US 1994 86m colour
Universal/Gramercy/40 Acres & A Mule (Shelby Stone, Butch Robinson)

A group of black vigilantes – Deprogramming and Restoration of Pride – kidnap people to bring them back to a sense of community.
A satire aimed at those who forget their roots and adopt attitudes that destroy ethnic communities, but one that is too slapdash and crude to convince.
w David C. Johnson, Butch Robinson *story* David Taylor *d* D. Clark Johnson *ph* Ken Kelsch *m* Michael Bearden *pd* Ina Mayhew *ed* Kevin Lee
☆ Eriq LaSalle, Vondie Curtis-Hall, Ving Rhames, Kasi Lemmons, Leonard Thomas, Vanessa Williams, Nicole Powell, Eric A. Payne, Spike Lee

'Something Dangerous Is In The Air.'

Drop Zone

US 1994 101m DeLuxe Panavision
UIP/Nicita/Lloyd

A discredited US marshal goes undercover to expose a gang of skydiving crooks who killed his brother, kidnapped his prisoner and escaped from a 747 jet in mid-flight.

A stunt-driven thriller, in which breathtaking aerial acrobatics do not make up for the absence of a suspenseful narrative.

w Peter Barsocchini, John Bishop, Tony Griffin, Guy Manos *d* John Badham *ph* Roy H. Wagner *m* Hans Zimmer *pd* Joe Alves *ed* Frank Morriss

☆ Wesley Snipes, Gary Busey, Yancy Butler, Michael Jeter, Corin Nemec, Kyle Secor, Luca Bercovici, Grace Zabriskie

'Little more than a by-the-numbers programmer, reasonably diverting and briskly paced but thinly written and utterly predictable.' – *Variety*

'Skydiving may be spectacular, but one hopes its participants are less rip-roaringly boorish than they appear in *Drop Zone*. I kept hoping their parachutes wouldn't open.' – *Derek Malcolm, Guardian*

Drowning by Numbers **

GB 1988 119m Kodak Color
Film Four International/Elsevier Vendex

Three women (all with the same name) murder their respective husbands with the collusion of the local coroner.

Cynical black comedy, beautifully played and more accessible than this director's earlier work, although with some obscure formalism.

wd Peter Greenaway *ph* Sacha Vierny *m* Michael Nyman *pd* Ben Van Os, Jan Roelfs

☆ Bernard Hill, Joan Plowright, Juliet Stevenson, Joely Richardson, Jason Edwards

The Drowning Pool

US 1975 108m Technicolor Panavision
Warner/Coleytown (Lawrence Turman, David Foster)

Private eye Lew Harper goes to New Orleans to investigate an anonymous letter which ends in murder.

Dreary sequel to Harper *(qv), full of boring characters uninventively deployed.*

w Tracy Keenan Wynn, Lorenzo Semple Jnr, Walter Hill *novel* John Ross MacDonald *d* Stuart Rosenberg *ph* Gordon Willis *m* Michael Small

☆ Paul Newman (Lew Harper), Joanne Woodward (Iris Devereaux), Coral Browne, Anthony Franciosa (Chief Broussard), Murray Hamilton (J. J. Kilbourne), Gail Strickland (Mavis Kilbourne), Linda Hayes (Gretchen), Richard Jaeckel, Melanie Griffith (Schulyer Devereaux)

'The impenetrable mystery is not particularly gripping; and the general air of pointlessness is only intensified by the sudden rush of clarifications at the end.' – *Tom Milne*

'It recycles every private eye cliché known to civilized man as it crawls through Louisiana talking all the way.' – *Paul D. Zimmermann*

'All the clichés of cheapjack TV private eye capers have been added to MacDonald's book; whatever separates him from the paperback hacks has been deleted.' – *Judith Crist*

Drugstore Cowboy **

US 1989 100m colour
Avenue Pictures (Nick Wechsler, Karen Murphy)

A drug-addict, his wife and two friends travel across America, robbing drug-stores to support their habit.

Low-key, effective melodrama with an unconvincing ending.

w Gus Van Sant, Daniel Yost *novel* James Fogle *d* Gus Van Sant *ph* Robert Yeoman *m* Elliot Goldenthal *pd* David Brisbin *ed* Curtiss Clayton

☆ Matt Dillon, Kelly Lynch, James Remar, James Le Gros, Heather Graham, William S. Burroughs

'A rather thoughtless and unenlightening film about drug addiction.' – *MFB*

The Drum *

GB 1938 96m Technicolor
UA/London Films (Alexander Korda)

US title: *Drums*

The British army helps an Indian prince to resist his usurping uncle.

Reasonably entertaining story of the Raj, with adequate excitement after a meandering start.

w Lajos Biro, Arthur Wimperis, Patrick Kirwan, Hugh Gray *novel* A. E. W. Mason *d* Zoltan Korda *ph* Georges Périnal, Osmond Borradaile *m* John Greenwood, Miklos Rozsa *ad* Vincent Korda *ed* William Hornbeck, Henry Cornelius

☆ Sabu, Roger Livesey, Raymond Massey, Valerie Hobson, Desmond Tester, David Tree, Francis L. Sullivan, Roy Emerton, Edward Lexy

'Looks like a 100% commercial bet.' – *Variety*

Drum

US 1976 100m Metrocolor Panavision
Dino de Laurentiis (Ralph Serpe)

In 1860 New Orleans, a bordello house slave faces all manner of sexual predators.

Tediously single-minded sequel to the appalling Mandingo.

w Norman Wexler *novel* Kyle Onstott *d* Steve Carver *ph* Lucien Ballard *m* Charles Smalls

☆ Warren Oates, Ken Norton, Isela Vega, Yaphet Kotto, John Colicos, Royal Dano

'Shamelessly it exploits the factors which explain the success of the prototype: a feeble pretence at outraged historical exposé of the abuses of the slave trade provides the excuse for an orgy of wish dreams, of sadism, flagellation, domination, sexuality of all tastes, popular fantasies of negro potency.' – *David Robinson, The Times*

Drum Beat

US 1954 111m Warnercolor CinemaScope
Jaguar (no producer credited)

An Indian fighter sets out to make peace with a renegade.

Long, dull Western, stolid all round.

wd Delmer Daves *ph* J. Peverell Marley *m* Victor Young *ed* Clarence Kolster

☆ Alan Ladd, Audrey Dalton, Marisa Pavan, Robert Keith, Rodolfo Acosta, Charles Bronson, Warner Anderson, Elisha Cook Jnr, Anthony Caruso

Drum Crazy: see *The Gene Krupa Story*

Drums: see *The Drum*

Drums Across the River

US 1954 78m Technicolor
Universal-International (Melville Tucker)

A young Westerner who hates Indians finally helps them to overthrow a white crook.

Slick little Western with almost every familiar ingredient.

w John K. Butler, Lawrence Roman *d* Nathan Juran *ph* Harold Lipstein *m* Joseph Gershenson

☆ Audie Murphy, Walter Brennan, Lyle Bettger, Lisa Gaye, Hugh O'Brian, Jay Silverheels, Emile Meyer

Drums Along the Amazon: see *Angel on the Amazon*

Drums Along the Mohawk **

US 1939 103m Technicolor
TCF (Raymond Griffith)

Colonists survive Indian attacks in upstate New York during the Revolutionary War.

Patchy, likeable period adventure story with domestic and farming interludes; in its way a key film in the director's canon.

w Lamar Trotti, Sonya Levien *novel* Walter Edmonds *d John Ford ph Bert Glennon, Ray Rennahan m* Alfred Newman

☆ Claudette Colbert, Henry Fonda, *Edna May Oliver*, Eddie Collins, John Carradine, Dorris Bowdon, Jessie Ralph, Arthur Shields, Robert Lowery, Roger Imhof, Ward Bond

'Outdoor spec, a top-bracketer, though not in the smash division.' – *Variety*

'No one appears to know why the picture is being made, or what its point is, exactly.' – *Pauline Kael, 70s*

Edna May Oliver

Drums in the Deep South

US 1951 87m Supercinecolor
RKO/King Brothers

A Confederate officer finds himself fighting a lonely battle with his best friend from West Point.

Barely stimulating semi-Western in appalling colour.

w Philip Yordan, Sidney Harmon *d* William Cameron Menzies *pd* William Cameron Menzies

☆ James Craig, Barbara Payton, Guy Madison, Barton MacLane, Craig Stevens, Tom Fadden, Taylor Holmes

Drums of Fu Manchu *

US 1940 bw serial: 15 eps
Republic

The Yellow Peril seeks the long-lost sceptre of Genghis Khan, which will allow him to rule the eastern hordes.

Spirited rendering of an ideal serial theme.

d William Witney, John English

☆ Henry Brandon, William Royle, Robert Kellard, Gloria Franklin, Olaf Hytten, Luana Walters, Dwight Frye

'A volcano erupts! A hurricane strikes! A man ... a woman ... discover passion in each other's arms!'

Drums of Tahiti

US 1953 73m Technicolor 3D
Columbia (Sam Katzman)

In 1877 an American helps the queen of Tahiti, who doesn't want to become a French possession.

Cheapskate potboiler with an extended volcanic climax (courtesy of older, better movies).

w Douglas Heyes, Robert E. Kent *d* William Castle

☆ Dennis O'Keefe, Patricia Medina, Francis L. Sullivan, Sylvia Lewis

Drunken Angel **

Japan 1948 102m bw
Toho

original title: *Yoidore Tenshi*

A gruff, hot-tempered, alcoholic doctor befriends a young gangster who is dying of tuberculosis.

Moving drama of sacrifice and redemption, filmed in an understated, realistic style.

w Keinosuke Uekusa, Akira Kurosawa *d* Akira Kurosawa *ph* Takeo Ito *m* Fumio Hayasaka

☆ Takashi Shimura, *Toshiro Mifune*, Reizaburo Yamamoto, Chieko Nakakita, Michiyo Kogure

Dry Rot

GB 1956 87m bw
Romulus (Jack Clayton)

Three bookmakers plot to make a fortune by substituting a doped horse for the favourite.

Flat filming of a long-running theatrical farce.

w John Chapman *play* John Chapman *d* Maurice Elvey *ph* Arthur Grant *m* Peter Akister

☆ Ronald Shiner, Brian Rix, Sid James, Michael Shepley, Joan Haythorne, Joan Sims, Heather Sears, Lee Patterson, Peggy Mount

A Dry White Season *

US 1989 107m DeLuxe
UIP/MGM/Star Partners II (Paula Weinstein)

A white South African is transformed into a radical after investigating the death of his gardener at the hands of the police.

Filmed with a passion that does not always communicate to the audience.

w Colin Welland, Euzhan Palcy *novel* André Brink *d* Euzhan Palcy *ph* Kelvin Pike, Pierre William Glenn *pd* John Fenner *ed* Sam O'Steen, Glenn Cunningham

☆ Donald Sutherland, Janet Suzman, Zakes Mokae, Jurgen Prochnow, Susan Sarandon, Marlon Brando, Winston Ntshona, Thoko Ntshinga, Leonard Maguire

Marlon Brando

Du Barry, Woman of Passion

US 1930 88m bw
United Artists (Talmadge)

Incidents in the life of the mistress of Louis XV.

Tedious early talkie which marked the virtual end of its star's career.

play David Belasco *d* Sam Taylor *ph* Oliver T. Marsh

☆ Norma Talmadge, William Farnum, Hobart Bosworth, Conrad Nagel, Alison Skipworth

'Wholly unimpressive ... nix for kids and the sticks.' – *Variety*

Du Rififi chez les Hommes: see *Rififi*

Du Skal Aere Din Hustru: see *Master of the House*

Dual Alibi

GB 1947 81m bw
British National (Louis H. Jackson)

Twin trapezists fall out over a lottery ticket and a worthless woman, but later extract a unique revenge.

Sprightly circus melodrama, shot on a shoestring.

w Alfred Travers, Stephen Clarkson *d* Alfred Travers *ph* James Wilson *m* Hans May *ad* R. Holmes-Paul *ed* Monica Kimick

☆ Herbert Lom (Jules and Georges de Lisles), Phyllis Dixey (Penny), Ronald Frankau (Vincent Barney), Terence de Marney (Mike Bergen), Abraham Sofaer (French Judge), Eugene Deckers (French Ring Master), Harold Berens (Ali), Sebastian Cabot (Loterry Official)

Dubarry Was a Lady

US 1943 101m Technicolor
MGM (Arthur Freed)

A New Yorker imagines himself back at the court of Louis XIV.

Dull, stiff adaptation of a Broadway musical comedy, with changed songs.

w Irving Brecher *book* B. G. de Sylva, Herbert Fields *d* Roy del Ruth *ph* Karl Freund *m/ly* Cole Porter *md* George Stoll

☆ Gene Kelly, Lucille Ball, Red Skelton, Virginia O'Brien, Zero Mostel, Rags Ragland, Tommy Dorsey and his Orchestra

'If the rustlers didn't get you ... the hustlers did!'

The Duchess and the Dirtwater Fox

US 1976 104m DeLuxe Panavision
TCF (Melvin Frank)

A Barbary Coast con man and a saloon singer have various hectic adventures.

Wild and woolly spoof Western which fires off aimlessly in a variety of styles and becomes merely tiresome despite good scenes.

w Melvin Frank, Barry Sandler *d* Melvin Frank *ph* Joseph Biroc *m* Charles Fox

☆ George Segal, Goldie Hawn, Conrad Janis, Thayer David, Roy Jenson, Bob Hoy, Bennie Dobbins

'The classic Western has now been shot to death by Sam Peckinpah, laughed to death by Mel Brooks and pondered to death by Arthur Penn, and Frank is like a scavenger picking up stray relics from its body.' – *Newsweek*

'The relentless vulgarity of the enterprise suggests that Mr Frank, having been so long constrained by the Hollywood Production Code when churning out vehicles for Bob Hope and Danny Kaye, is still making up for lost time.' – *Philip French*

The Duchess of Idaho

US 1950 98m Technicolor
MGM (Joe Pasternak)

Romantic misunderstandings among candidates for Miss Idaho Potato.

Lightweight musical, quite pleasant if routine, with guest spots.

w Dorothy Cooper, Jerry Davis *d* Robert Z. Leonard *ph* Charles Schoenbaum *md* Georgie Stoll

☆ Esther Williams, Van Johnson, John Lund, Paula Raymond, Clinton Sundberg, Eleanor Powell, Lena Horne, Red Skelton

Duck Soup ****

US 1933 68m bw
Paramount

An incompetent becomes President of Fredonia and wages war on its scheming neighbour.

The satirical aspects of this film are fascinating but appear to have been unintentional. Never mind, it's

also the most satisfying and undiluted Marx Brothers romp, albeit the one without instrumental interludes. It does include the lemonade stall, the mirror sequence, and an endless array of one-liners and comedy choruses.
w Bert Kalmar, Harry Ruby, Arthur Sheekman, Nat Perrin *d* Leo McCarey *ph* Henry Sharp *m/ly* Bert Kalmar, Harry Ruby *ad* Hans Dreier, Wiard Ihnen *ed* LeRoy Stone
☆ Groucho Marx (Rufus T. Firefly), Chico Marx (Chicolini), Harpo Marx (Pinky), Zeppo Marx (Bob Roland), Margaret Dumont (Mrs Teasdale), Louis Calhern (Ambassador Trentino), Edgar Kennedy (Lemonade man), Raquel Torres (Vera Marcal)
'Practically everybody wants a good laugh right now, and this should make practically everybody laugh.' – *Variety*
'So much preliminary dialogue is necessary that it seems years before Groucho comes on at all; and waiting for Groucho is agony.' – *E. V. Lucas, Punch*
'The most perfect of all Marxist masterpieces.' – *Time Out, 1984*
♫ Hail. Hail Freedonia; His Excellency is Due; Just Wait 'til I Get Through With It; Freedonia's Going to War.

Duck, You Sucker: see *A Fistful of Dynamite*

'After a night they can't remember, comes a day they'll never forget.'
Dude, Where's My Car?
US 2000 83m DeLuxe
TCF (Wayne Rice, Broderick Johnson, Andrew Kusove, Gil Netter)
Two young men wake up unable to remember where they parked their car, which is also a topic of interest for their girlfriends, some odd aliens and members of a strange cult.
Adolescent comedy that ambles along at a low level of bewilderment at the adult world.
w Philip Stark *d* Danny Leiner *ph* Robert Stevens *m* Dave Kitay *pd* Charles Breen *ed* Kimberly Ray
☆ Ashton Kutcher (Jesse), Seann William Scott (Chester), Kristy Swanson (Christie Boner), Jennifer Garner (Wanda), Marla Sokoloff (Wilma), David Herman (Nelson), Christian Middelthon (Nordic Dude No 1), David W. Bannick (Nordic Dude No 2), Charlie O'Connell (Tommy), Teressa Tunney (Tania)
'Aimed squarely at adolescents who might find *Bill & Ted's Excellent Adventure* too intellectually taxing.' – *Joe Leydon, Variety*
'A surprisingly sweet, mild-mannered movie for a teenage comedy spoof, and that's not a good thing.' – *Stephen Holden, New York Times*

Dudes
US 1987 90m colour
Recorded Releasing/New Century/Vista (Herbert Jaffe, Miguel Tejada Flores)
Three punk rockers, on their way to California, fall foul of a gang of murderous rednecks.
Haphazard, absurdist account of a violent culture clash.
w John Randall Johnson *d* Penelope Spheeris *ph* Robert Richardson *m* Charles Bernstein *pd* Robert Ziembicki *ed* Andy Horvitch
☆ Jon Cryer, Daniel Roebuck, Flea, Catherine Mary Stewart, Lee Ving

Dudley Do-Right
US 1999 77m DeLuxe
Universal (John Davis, Joseph M. Singer, J. Todd Harris)
An inept Royal Canadian Mountie and his clever horse attempt to deal with a bad man who starts a gold rush in order to grow rich.
This live-action version of a 60s TV cartoon gives Fraser a chance to reprise his George of the Jungle act as a good-natured idiot; it provides some mild amusement.
wd Hugh Wilson *based on characters developed by* Jay Ward *ph* Donald E. Thorin *m* Steve Dorff *ch* Adam Shankman *pd* Bob Ziembicki *ed* Don Brochu
☆ Brendan Fraser (Dudley Do-Right), Sarah Jessica Parker (Nell Fenwick), Alfred Molina (Snidely Whiplash), Eric Idle (The Prospector), Robert Prosky (Inspector Fenwick), Alex Rocco (The Chief), Corey Burton (The Voice of the Announcer), Jack Kehler (Howard), Louis Mustillo (Standing Room Only), Regis Philbin (Regis), Kathie Lee Gifford (Kathie Lee)
'A silly bit of tiptop tomfoolery with cross-generational appeal.' – *Joe Leydon, Variety*

Due Soldi di Speranza *
Italy 1952 98m bw
Universalcine (Sandro Ghenzi)
GB title: *Two Pennyworth of Hope*
Demobilized after World War II, Antonio finds life in his native village hard to take.
Neo-realist comedy-melodrama full of gesticulating rustics; good for those who like this sort of thing.
w Renato Castellani, Titina de Filippo *d* Renato Castellani *ph* Arturo Gallea *m* Alessandro Cicognini
☆ Vincenzo Musolino, Maria Fiore, Filumena Russo, Luigi Astarita

Le Due Vite di Mattia Pascal: see *The Two Lives of Mattia Pascal*

Duel **
US 1971 90m colour
Universal (George Eckstein)
A travelling salesman discovers that the driver of the petrol tanker following him is determined to kill him.
Tense, suspenseful drama that made Spielberg's name as a bright young director.
w Richard Matheson *story* Richard Matheson *d* Steven Spielberg
☆ Dennis Weaver, Jacqueline Scott, Eddie Firestone, Lou Frizzell
† Made for television, the film received a UK release in 1972, but was not seen in American cinemas until 1983.

Duel at Diablo *
US 1966 103m DeLuxe
UA/Nelson/Engel/Cherokee/Rainbow/Brien
White and black man fight together as Apaches attack.
Well-paced, old-fashioned, shoot-'em-up star Western.
w Marvin H. Albert, Michel M. Grilikhes *d* Ralph Nelson *ph* Charles F. Wheeler *m* Neal Hefti
☆ Sidney Poitier, James Garner, Bibi Andersson, Bill Travers, William Redfield, John Hoyt, John Hubbard

Duel at Silver Creek
US 1952 77m Technicolor
U-I (Leonard Goldstein)
An honest man is murdered by claim jumpers, and the Silver Kid is suspected.
Modest, efficient Western.
w Gerald Drayson Adams, Joseph Hoffman *d* Don Siegel *ph* Irving Glassberg *m* Hans Salter
☆ Audie Murphy, Stephen McNally, Faith Domergue, Susan Cabot, Gerald Mohr, Eugene Iglesias, Lee Marvin, Walter Sande

Duel at the Rio Grande: see *The Mark of Zorro (1963)*

Duel in the Jungle
GB 1954 101m Technicolor
ABP/Marcel Hellman
An African explorer intends to defraud an insurance company and sets traps for the investigator who pursues him.
Lackadaisical romp in the studio jungle, none of it with much style or film sense.
w Sam Marx, T. J. Morrison *d* George Marshall *ph* Erwin Hillier *m* Mischa Spoliansky
☆ Dana Andrews, Jeanne Crain, David Farrar, Patrick Barr

Duel in the Sun **
US 1946 138m Technicolor
David O. Selznick
A half-breed girl causes trouble between two brothers.
Massive Western, dominated and fragmented by its producer, who bought the best talent and proceeded to interfere with it, so that while individual scenes are marvellous, the narrative has little flow. The final gory shoot-up between two lovers was much discussed at the time.
w David O. Selznick, Oliver H. P. Garrett *novel* Niven Busch *d* King Vidor (and others) *ph* Lee Garmes, Harold Rosson, Ray Rennahan *m* Dimitri Tiomkin *pd* J. McMillan Johnson *ad* James Basevi *second unit* B. Reeves Eason, Otto Brower
☆ Jennifer Jones, Joseph Cotten, Gregory Peck, Lionel Barrymore, Lillian Gish, Walter Huston, Herbert Marshall, Charles Bickford, Tilly Losch, Joan Tetzel, Harry Carey, Otto Kruger, Sidney Blackmer
'A knowing blend of oats and aphrodisiac.' – *Time*
'Cornographic is a word that might have been coined for it.' – *Daily Mail*
'As sexual melodrama with a spectacular background it is in its way remarkable.' – *New Statesman*
'A razzmatazz of thunderous naïvety simmering into a kind of majestic dottiness.' – *Basil Wright, 1972*
'A lavish, sensual spectacle, so heightened it becomes a cartoon of passion.' – *Pauline Kael, 70s*
† The uncredited directors included Josef von Sternberg, William Dieterle, B. Reeves Eason, and Selznick himself.
Jennifer Jones; Lillian Gish

The Duellists *
GB 1977 101m colour
Scott Free/NFFC/David Puttnam
In the early 1800s, two Hussar Officers challenge each other to a series of duels; after sixteen years an ironic truce is called.
A singularly pointless anecdote; its main virtue is that it is coldly attractive to look at.
w Gerald Vaughan-Hughes *story* The Point of Honour by Joseph Conrad *d* Ridley Scott *ph* Frank Tidy *m* Howard Blake *pd* Peter J. Hampton
☆ Keith Carradine, Harvey Keitel, Albert Finney, Edward Fox, Cristina Raines, Tom Conti, Robert Stephens, John McEnery

Duet for One
GB 1987 107m Rank Colour
Cannon (Menahem Golan, Yoram Globus)
A leading lady violinist contracts multiple sclerosis.
Lamentable opening out of a two-character play, all gloom and doom and overstatement.
w Tom Kempinski, Jeremy Lipp, Andrei Konchalovsky *play* Tom Kempinski *d* Andrei Konchalovsky *ph* Alex Thomson *pd* John Graysmark *ed* Henry Richardson
☆ Julie Andrews, Alan Bates, Max von Sydow, Rupert Everett, Margaret Courtenay

'Six lost souls in search of a little harmony.'
Duets
US 2000 112m Technicolor
Buena Vista/Hollywood/Seven Arts/Beacon (Kevin Jones, Bruce Paltrow, John Byrum)
Three couples travel to a karaoke contest in Omaha, Nebraska.
Rambling, bland road movie with a few effective moments.
w John Byrum *d* Bruce Paltrow *ph* Paul Sarossy *m* David Newman *pd* Sharon Seymour *ed* Jerry Greenberg *cos* Mary Claire Hannan
☆ Maria Bello (Suzi Loomis), Andre Braugher (Reggie Kane), Paul Giamatti (Todd Woods), Huey Lewis (Ricky Dean), Gwyneth Paltrow (Liv), Scott Speedman (Billy), Marian Seldes (Harriet Gahagan), Kiersten Warren (Candy Woods), Angie Phillips (Arlene), Angie Dickinson (Blair)
'Empty is how this well-meaning little film feels in the end.' – *Peter Bradshaw, Guardian*

'Some helpful hints for those who are very rich, very beautiful, very hip, elaborately oversexed, tuned in, turned on and bored to death!'
Duffy
GB 1968 101m Technicolor
Columbia/Martin Manulis
Two half-brothers plan to rob their millionaire father.
Would-be with-it caper film, all flashy fragments and pop art, like sitting through a feature-length commercial. Exasperating.
w Donald Cammell, Harry Joe Brown Jnr *d* Robert Parrish *ph* Otto Heller *m* Ernie Freeman
☆ James Coburn, James Mason, James Fox, Susannah York, John Alderton, Guy Deghy, Tutte Lemkow, Carl Duering, Marne Maitland

Duffy's Tavern
US 1945 97m bw
Paramount (Danny Dare)
The owner of a bar is helped by Hollywood stars.
Flat comedy based on a radio show and not helped by dismal guest star appearances.
w Melvin Frank, Norman Panama *d* Hal Walker *ph* Lionel Lindon *m* Robert Emmett Dolan
☆ Ed Gardner, Victor Moore, Marjorie Reynolds, Barry Sullivani, Bob Hope, Bing Crosby, Betty Hutton, Alan Ladd, Dorothy Lamour, Veronica Lake, William Bendix, Joan Caulfield

'Two thousand men and a girl!'
The Duke of West Point *
US 1938 112m bw
Edward Small
An extrovert army cadet finds the going tough.
Dated romantic flagwaver which pleased at the time.
w George Bruce *d* Alfred E. Green *ph* Robert Planck
☆ Louis Hayward, Joan Fontaine, Tom Brown, Richard Carlson, Alan Curtis, Don Barry, Gaylord Pendleton, Jed Prouty, Marjorie Gateson
'Fairly good entertainment. Much human interest, but the comedy relief is rather light.' – *Variety*

The Duke Wore Jeans
GB 1958 89m bw
Insignia (Peter Rogers)
An aristocrat persuades his Cockney double to woo a princess on his behalf.
Moderately lively comedy with songs, tailored for Britain's new musical star.
w Norman Hudis *story* Lionel Bart, Michael Pratt *d* Gerald Thomas *ph* Otto Heller *m* Bruce Montgomery
☆ Tommy Steele, June Laverick, Michael Medwin, Alan Wheatley, Eric Pohlmann

Dulcima
GB 1971 98m Technicolor
EMI (Basil Rayburn)
A farmer's daughter reluctantly moves in with a persistent, lecherous old miser.
Weird sex melodrama from Cold Comfort Farm *country, more risible than interesting.*
wd Frank Nesbitt *story* H. E. Bates *ph* Tony Imi *m* Johnny Douglas *ad* Ray Sim
☆ John Mills, Carol White, Stuart Wilson, Bernard Lee, Dudley Foster

Dulcimer Street: see *London Belongs to Me*

'For Harry And Lloyd Every Day Is A No-Brainer.'
Dumb & Dumber
US 1994 106m Film House colour
First Independent/New Line/MPCA (Charles B. Wessler, Brad Krevoy, Steve Stabler)
A dim-witted chauffeur travels across America with his dimmer-witted friend in order to return a briefcase to someone who does not want it back.
In comparison with Jerry Lewis, the comedian he most resembles, there is something sweetly innocent about the personality of the relentlessly mugging Jim Carrey, which can wear down resistance to what is no more than a succession of bad jokes on such matters as farting. It makes the most basic Carry On movie look sophisticated and was among the most successful releases of the year.
w Peter Farrelly, Bennett Yellin, Bobby Farrelly *d* Peter Farrelly *ph* Mark Irwin *m* Todd Rundgren *pd* Sidney Bartholomew Jnr *ed* Christopher Greenbury
☆ Jim Carrey, Jeff Daniels, Lauren Holly, Karen Duffy, Teri Garr, Mike Starr, Charles Rocket, Victoria Rowell
'*D and D* – in comparison with which Jim Carrey's other pictures look as if they were scripted by Oscar Wilde – makes you laugh out loud for almost its entire running time.' – *Richard Schickel, Time*

'A flat-out celebration of stupidity, bodily functions and pratfalls … ideal fare for those who want to laugh themselves sick' – *Variety*

Dumbo ****
US 1941 64m Technicolor
Walt Disney
A baby circus elephant finds that his big ears have a use after all.
Delightful cartoon feature notable for set-pieces such as the drunken nightmare and the crows' song.
w various *d* Ben Sharpsteen *m* Frank Churchill, Oliver Wallace
☆ Featuring the voices of Sterling Holloway, Edward Brophy, Verna Felton, Herman Bing, Cliff Edwards
music
song, 'Baby Mine' (*m* Frank Churchill, *ly* Ned Washington)

The Dummy Talks
GB 1943 85m bw
British National
A ventriloquist turns to blackmail and is murdered backstage.
Curious, oddly cast murder mystery, not unentertaining at the time.
w Michael Barringer *d* Oswald Mitchell
☆ Jack Warner, Claude Hulbert, Beryl Orde, G. H. Mulcaster, Ivy Benson, Manning Whiley

Dune
US 1984 140m Technicolor Todd-AO
Dino de Laurentiis (Raffaella de Laurentiis)
Armies from several planets descend on another which has valuable spice guarded by monster worms.
A basically simple space fiction plot is immensely complicated by a welter of characters who are not properly introduced and who indeed are mostly irrelevant. The result, which cost nearly 50 million dollars, is inaudible, invisible (because of dim lighting) and unentertaining: a disaster of the very first order.
wd David Lynch *novel* Frank Herbert *ph* Freddie Francis *m* Toto *pd* Anthony Masters *ed* Antony Gibbs
☆ Francesca Annis, Jose Ferrer, Sian Phillips, Brad Dourif, Dean Stockwell, Freddie Jones, Linda Hunt, Kenneth McMillan, Richard Jordan, Kyle MacLachlan, Silvana Mangano, Jurgen Prochnow, Max Von Sydow, Sting
'Huge, hollow, imaginative and cold.' – *Variety*
'This movie is a real mess, an incomprehensible, ugly, unstructured, pointless excursion into the murkier realms of one of the most confusing screenplays of all time.' – *Roger Ebert*

'This is no game.'
Dungeons and Dragons
US 2000 108m DeLuxe
Entertainment/New Line/Sweetpea (Courtney Solomon, Kia Jam, Tom Hammel)
In a medieval world, a thief becomes a hero in a battle between his empress and a wicked wizard to control the world.
Based on the popular role-playing game, this is risible sword and sorcery, with cheap and lurid effects, hammy role-playing from its cast, and, on the few occasions it can be heard, corny dialogue.
w Topper Lilien, Carroll Cartwright *d* Courtney Solomon *ph* Doug Milsome *m* Justin Caine Burnett *pd* Bryce Perrin *ed* Caroline Ross *cos* Barbara Lane
☆ Justin Whalin (Ridley Freeborn), Marlon Wayans (Snails), Zoe McLellan (Marina Pretensa), Thora Birch (Empress Savina), Bruce Payne (Damodar), Jeremy Irons (Profion), Kristen Wilson (Norda), Richard O'Brien (Xilus), Tom Baker (Halvarth)
'Stunningly bad sci-fi/fantasy hokum.' – *Variety*

Dunkirk **
GB 1958 135m bw
MGM/Ealing (Michael Balcon)
In 1940 on the Normandy beaches, a small group gets detached from the main force.
Sober, small-scale approach to an epic subject; interesting but not inspiring, with performances to match.
w W. P. Lipscomb, David Divine *d* Leslie Norman *ph* Paul Beeson *m* Malcolm Arnold
☆ John Mills, Richard Attenborough, Bernard Lee, Robert Urquhart, Ray Jackson

Dunston Checks In *
Canada 1996 88m DeLuxe
TCF (Joe Wizan, Todd Black)
An aristocratic hotel burglar has an unusual accomplice: an orang-utan, who prefers the company of the manager's two young sons.
Enjoyable, smartly written farce that also charms; the laughs keep coming.
w John Hopkins, Bruce Graham *d* Ken Kwapis *ph* Peter Collister *m* Miles Goodman *pd* Rusty Smith *ed* Jon Poll
☆ Jason Alexander, Faye Dunaway, Eric Lloyd, Rupert Everett, Graham Sack, Paul Reubens, Glenn Shadix, Sam
'It all works very smoothly, mostly because the sight gags are just predictable enough for comfort, and partly because of a cast who gamely suffer simian-inflicted indignities.' – *Guardian*

'Men invoke its horror! Women invite its shame!'
The Dunwich Horror *
US 1970 90m Movielab
AIP (Roger Corman, Jack Bohrer)
A young warlock plans to use his girlfriend in a fertility rite.
Bookish horror story, quite well done against a village background.
w Curtis Lee Hanson, Henry Rosenbaum, Ronald Silkosky *story* H. P. Lovecraft *d Daniel Haller* *ph* Richard C. Glouner *m* Les Baxter
☆ Dean Stockwell, Sandra Dee, Ed Begley, Sam Jaffe, Lloyd Bochner
'A bit psychedelic in places, but with a real feeling for sinister rites and strange manifestations.' – *Sight and Sound*

Duoluo Tianshi: see *Fallen Angels*

Duped Till Doomsday *
East Germany 1957 97m bw
DEFA (Adolf Fischer)
original title: *Betrogen bis zum Jungsten Tag*
Three Nazi NCOs go to the bad.
Propagandist anti-Nazi war melodrama, very well made in parts.
w Kurt Bortfeldt *novel Kameraden* by Franz Fuhmann *d* Kurt Jung-Alsen *ph* Walter Fehdmer
☆ Wolfgang Kieling, Rudolph Ulrich, Hans-Joachim Martens

Dust
Belgium/France 1985 87m Fujicolour
Mans/Daska/Flach/FR3
On an isolated South African farm, a girl murders her adulterous father.
Doomladen saga redeemed by strong pictorial style.
wd Marion Hansel *novel In the Heart of the Country* by J. M. Coetzee
☆ Jane Birkin, Trevor Howard, John Matshikiza

Dust *
GB/Germany/Italy/Macedonia 2001 124m colour
Pathé/History/Dreams/ena/Fandango/Shadow/Film Council/BSkyB/British Screen (Chris Auty, Vesna Jovanoska, Domenico Procacci)
In an Manhattan apartment an old woman holds a burglar at gunpoint while she tells him how her father and his brother left the American west to fight in Macedonia.
Good-looking, bloody, dramatically incoherent movie that is unduly influenced by Sergio Leone and Sam Peckinpah, reproducing all their faults and none of their virtues.
wd Milcho Manchevski *ph* Barry Ackroyd *m* Kiril Dzajkovski *pd* David Munns *ed* Nic Gaster
☆ Joseph Fiennes (Elijah), David Wenham (Luke), Adrian Lester (Edge), Anne Brochet (Lilith), Nikolina Kujaca (Neda), Rosemary Murphy (Angela)
'Very tiresome, overblown piece of machismo.' – *Peter Bradshaw, Guardian*

Dust Be My Destiny *
US 1939 88m bw
Warner (Lou Edelman)
A young misfit tries to find himself in the country.
Dated but well made social melodrama.
w Robert Rossen *story* Jerome Odlum *d* Lewis Seiler *ph* James Wong Howe *m* Max Steiner
☆ John Garfield, Priscilla Lane, Alan Hale, Frank McHugh, John Litel, Charles Grapewin, Billy Halop, Bobby Jordan, Stanley Ridges
'Strong programmer, though overlong and episodic.' – *Variety*
'You can tell from the title that John Garfield has his usual part – the angry, bitter, tough poor young man with slight persecution mania.' – *Richard Mallett, Punch*
† Remade 1942 as *I Was Framed*, with Michael Ames.

Dust Devil: The Final Cut
GB 1992 103m Technicolor
Polygram/Palace/Film Four/Richard Stanley
An alien, which has to kill in order to return to its own world, journeys to a ghost town, where he is attracted by two people with a death-wish: a battered wife fleeing her husband and a black cop who has lost his wife and son.
Confused science-fiction thriller that never quite comes to life; whatever message the director is striving to impart, it remains obscure.
wd Richard Stanley *ph* Steven Chivers *m* Simon Boswell *pd* Joseph Bennett *ed* Derek Trigg, Paul Carlin *sp* The Dream Machine, Rick Cresswell
☆ Robert Burke, Chelsea Field, Zakes Mokae, John Matshikiza, Marianne Sagebrecht, William Hootkins, Rufus Swart
'Overflowing with ideas, visual invention and genre references but saddled by a weak, unfocused script.' – *Variety*
'In any of its several versions, this is a considerable and remarkable film.' – *Kim Newman*
† The film exists in several versions. The above is the director's preferred version, which he restored with his own money. A shorter version, cut by its American distributor, was released in Europe under the title *Demonica*. The US version of the film was re-dubbed and had a new voice-over added.

Dust in the Wind *
Taiwan 1987 100m colour
ICA/Central Motion Picture (Ling Deng Fei, Xu Guo Liang)
original title: *Lien-lien feng-ch'en*
Instead of going to high school, a youth leaves his mining village to seek work in the big city, where his girlfriend joins him.
A leisurely, intermittently insightful examination of the tensions and pleasures of family life and the problems of surviving without much education in an unsympathetic urban environment.
w Wu Nien-jen, Chu Tien-wen *d* Hou Hsiao-hsien *ph* Li Ping-pin *pd* Zhao Qi Bin
☆ Wang Ching-Wen, Hsing Shu-fen, Ch'en Shu-fang, Li Tien-lu

'The Competition Will Kill You.'
Dusting Cliff 7
US 1996 88m colour
Silvertime (Leman Cetiner, Axel Munch)
video title: *Last Assassins*
After her daughter is taken hostage, a former CIA hitwoman is forced to help an old colleague steal a hidden arsenal of nuclear weapons.
A by-the-numbers action movie with lots of big explosions and gunfights; nothing out of the ordinary.
w Jim Menza, William H. Molina, Charles Philip Moore, Justin J. Stanley *d* William H. Molina *ph* William H. Molina *m* David Wurst, Eric Wurst *ed* William H. Molina
☆ Lance Henriksen (Roger McBride), Nancy Allen (Anne Bishop), Scott Lincoln (Brock Daniels), Dean Scofield (Mitch Stevens), Ashley Buccile (Carrie Bishop), Floyd 'Red Crow' Westerman (Indian Bob), Zahn McClarnon (Indian Louis), Shashawnee Hall (Wayne)

Dusty
Australia 1982 85m colour
Panavision
Kestrel Films/Dusty Productions (Gil Brealey)
An old shepherd takes to the bush to save his half-wild dog from being shot by sheep farmers.
Sentimental tale with pleasant landscape photography.
w Sonia Berg *novel* Frank Dalby Davison *d* John Richardson *ph* Alex McPhee *m* Frank Strangio *pd* Robbie Perkins *ad* Ivana Perkins *ed* David Greig
☆ Bill Kerr, Noel Trevarthen, Carol Burns, John Stanton, Nicholas Holland

Dusty Ermine
GB 1938 74m bw
Julius Hagen/Twickenham
US title: *Hideout in the Alps*
Scotland Yard chases counterfeiters to Switzerland, and the hunt ends in a ski chase.
Modestly effective melodrama with dated romantic leads.
w Paul Hervey Fox *play* Neil Grant *d* Bernard Vorhaus
☆ Jane Baxter, Anthony Bushell, Ronald Squire, Margaret Rutherford, Athole Stewart, Katie Johnson, Austin Trevor, Felix Aylmer
'The humour is of the British kind – not too hilarious but still tickling.' – *Variety*

Dutch
US 1991 107m DeLuxe
TCF (John Hughes, Richard Vane)
GB title: *Driving Me Crazy*
An arrogant and snobbish twelve-year-old boy is reformed by his divorced mother's working-class boyfriend.
Inert comedy of class warfare, part of the cycle of buddy-buddy movies in which antagonists at the beginning become friends by the end.
w John Hughes *d* Peter Faiman *ph* Charles Minsky *m* Alan Silvestri *pd* Stan Jolley *ed* Paul Hirsch, Adam Bernardi
☆ Ed O'Neill, Ethan Randall, Christopher McDonald, Ari Meyers, E. G. Daily, L. Scott Caldwell, Kathleen Freeman

Dutchman *
GB 1966 56m bw
Gene Persson
On a New York subway train a woman humiliates a black man and finally knifes him.
An allegory for addicts who can ferret out the meaning; on the surface, vaguely Pinterish and mainly boring.
w LeRoi Jones *play* LeRoi Jones *d* Anthony Harvey *ph* Gerry Turpin *m* John Barry
☆ Shirley Knight, Al Freeman Jnr

D'Ye Ken John Peel?
GB 1935 81m bw
AP&D/Twickenham (Julius Hagen)
US title: *Captain Moonlight*
In the early 1800s, an army officer prevents a villain from marrying the girl he loves.
A muddled melodrama of highwaymen and skulduggery with musical interludes; it provided Stanley Holloway with an opportunity to perform one of his best-known monologues, 'Sam, Pick Up Thy Musket', and also contains the English equivalent of cavalry riding to the rescue with a charge of fox-hunters.
w H. Fowler Mear *story* Charles Cullum *d* Henry Edwards *ph* Sydney Blythe, William Luff *m* W. L. Trytel *ad* James A. Carter *ed* Jack Harris, Lister Laurence
☆ John Garrick, Winifred Shotter, Stanley Holloway, John Stuart, Leslie Perrins, Mary Lawson, Charles Carson

'Just when she'd given up on love, she fell for a guy who'd given up on life.'
Dying Young
US 1991 111m
TCF/Fogwood (Sally Field, Kevin McCormick)
A man suffering from leukaemia falls in love with the nurse he hires to look after him.
Inane romance, meandering and glossily sentimental, and coming to the conclusion that death is nothing to worry about if you've Julia Roberts by your side.
w Richard Friedenberg *novel* Marti Leimbach *d* Joel Schumacher *ph* Juan Ruiz Anchia *m* James Newton Howard *ad* Guy J. Comtois, Richard Johnson *ed* Robert Brown, Jim Prior
☆ Julia Roberts, Campbell Scott, Vincent D'Onofrio, Colleen Dewhurst, David Selby, Ellen Burstyn, Dion Anderson, George Martin
'Starpower should carry this rather thin and maudlin weeper through some heated weeks, but the only real legs likely to be shown are those amply exposed by the femme lead.' – *Variety*

Dynamite ★★
US 1929 129m bw
MGM (Cecil B. de Mille)
In order to gain an inheritance, a socialite marries a man about to be executed ... but he is reprieved.
Dated but still dynamic social melodrama of the early talkie period.

w Jeanie Macpherson *d* Cecil B. de Mille
ph Peverell Marley *m* Herbert Stothart
ad Mitchell Leisen
☆ Kay Johnson, Charles Bickford, Conrad Nagel, Julia Faye, Joel McCrea

'A pot-pourri of all previous de Mille efforts crammed into one picture.' – *Variety*
'Exuberant, wonderfully vigorous, the film skilfully evokes the look and character of the Jazz Age.' – *Charles Higham*
'An astonishing mixture, with artificiality vying with realism and comedy hanging on the heels of grim melodrama.' – *Mordaunt Hall, New York Times*

Academy Award nomination: Mitchell Leisen

Dynamite Man from Glory Jail: see *Fools Parade*

Dyrygent: see *The Conductor*

E la Nave Va: see *And the Ship Sails On*

...E Poi Lo Chiamarono Il Magnifico: see *Man of the East*

E.T. The Extra-Terrestrial ****
US 1982 115m DeLuxe
Universal (Steven Spielberg, Kathleen Kennedy)

When an alien spacecraft is disturbed in a Los Angeles suburb, one of its crew members is left behind and befriended by a small boy.
Stupefyingly successful box-office fairy tale by the current wonder kid Spielberg, taken to the world's heart because he dares to make films without sex, violence or bad language. This one could hardly be simpler, but it works; and the ailing cinema would love to know how to repeat the trick several times a year.
w Melissa Mathison *d* Steven Spielberg *ph* Allen Daviau *m* John Williams *pd* James D. Bissell *ed* Carol Littleton *sp* Creator of E.T.: Carlo Rambaldi
☆ Dee Wallace (Mary), Henry Thomas (Elliott), Peter Coyote (Keys), Robert MacNaughton (Michael), Drew Barrymore (Gertie), K. C. Martel (Greg), Sean Frye (Steve), Tom Howell (Tyler)
'The most moving science-fiction movie ever made on earth.' – *Pauline Kael, New Yorker*
'E.T. is the closest film to my own sensibilities, my own fantasies, my own heart.' – *Steven Spielberg*
† The movie was reissued in 2002 with its special effects enhanced, and walkie-talkies substituted for the FBI agents' guns. One line of dialogue was also changed in the Halloween scene. Spielberg explained, 'There's no reason why the word terrorist belongs in a film like *ET*, and we were being glib in the early 80s with Mary saying, "You will not go out dressed as a terrorist."' Now she says, "You will not go out dressed as a hippy."'
John Williams; visual effects (Carlo Rambaldi, Dennis Murren, Kenneth F. Smith); sound (Buzz Knudson, Robert Glass, Don Digirolamo, Gene Cantamessa); sound effects editing (Charles L. Campbell, Ben Burtt)
picture; Steven Spielberg; Melissa Matheson; Allen Daviau; Carol Littleton
John Williams

E Tornato Sabata ... Hai Chiuso un'Altra Volta: see *Return of Sabata*

Each Dawn I Die *
US 1939 84m bw
Warner (David Lewis)

original title: *Killer Meets Killer*
A crusading reporter is framed for manslaughter and becomes a hardened prisoner.
Efficient, vigorous yet slightly disappointing star vehicle; the talents are in the right background, but the script is wobbly.
w Norman Reilly Raine, Warren Duff, Charles Perry *novel* Jerome Odlum *d* William Keighley *ph* Arthur Edeson *m* Max Steiner *ad* William Cameron Menzies
☆ James Cagney, George Raft, Jane Bryan, George Bancroft, Maxie Rosenbloom, Stanley Ridges, Alan Baxter, Victor Jory
'Rich in horror and brutality.' – *New York Sunday Mirror*
'In addition to its crackling screenplay, it is made memorable by the easy mastery of its two principals.' – *Time*
'Towards the end of the thirties Warners' underworld pictures began to get hazy and high-minded, and in this one the pre-Second World War spiritual irradiation blurs the conventions of the prison genre.' – *Pauline Kael, 70s*

The Eagle **
US 1925 80m approx (24 fps) bw silent
United Artists/Joseph M. Schenck

A Cossack lieutenant turns masked outlaw when his father's lands are annexed.
Enjoyable romp in the wake of Robin Hood, the Scarlet Pimpernel and Zorro; the eye-flashing star is somewhere near his best.
w Hans Kraly *story* Dubrowsky by Alexander Pushkin *d* Clarence Brown *ph* George Barnes
☆ *Rudolph Valentino*, Vilma Banky, Louise Dresser

The Eagle and the Hawk **
US 1933 72m bw
Paramount

In 1918 France, two American army flyers dislike each other but come together before the death of one of them.
Dawn Patrol *melodrama, well done with unusually vivid dialogue and acting.*
w Bogart Rogers, Seton I. Miller *story* John Monk Saunders *d* Stuart Walker *ph* Harry Fischbeck
☆ Fredric March, Cary Grant, Carole Lombard, Sir Guy Standing, Jack Oakie, Forrester Harvey
'Will make good with those it attracts, but is handicapped by the mass of earlier flight pictures.' – *Variety*

The Eagle and the Hawk
US 1949 86m bw
(Paramount)
During the Mexican wars, a US government agent tracks down a traitor who is supplying arms to the rebel Juarez.
Stolid adventure yarn, energetically played.
w Geoffrey Homes, Lewis R. Foster *d* Lewis R. Foster *ph* James Wong Howe *m* David Chudnow
☆ John Payne, Dennis O'Keefe, Rhonda Fleming, Thomas Gomez, Fred Clark, Frank Faylen, Eduardo Noriega

The Eagle Has Landed *
GB 1976 135m Eastmancolor Panavision
ITC/Associated General (Jack Wiener, David Niven Jnr)

During World War II, enemy aliens infiltrate an English village in the hope of killing Churchill.
Elaborately plotted but uninvolving spy melodrama, lethargically directed, muddily coloured and too concerned to create some good Germans.
w Tom Mankiewicz *novel* Jack Higgins *d* John Sturges *ph* Anthony Richmond *m* Lalo Schifrin
☆ Michael Caine, Donald Sutherland, Robert Duvall, Jenny Agutter, Donald Pleasence, Anthony Quayle, Jean Marsh, Sven-Bertil Taube, John Standing, Judy Geeson, Larry Hagman, Maurice Roeves

Eagle Squadron
US 1942 102m bw
Universal (Walter Wanger)
During World War II, American flyers join the RAF.
Studio-bound air epic, leavened with conventional romance but little humour or sympathy.
w Norman Reilly Raine *story* C. S. Forester *d* Arthur Lubin *ph* Stanley Cortez *m* Frank Skinner
☆ Robert Stack, Diana Barrymore, John Loder, Eddie Albert, Nigel Bruce, Leif Erickson, Edgar Barrier, Jon Hall, Evelyn Ankers, Isobel Elsom, Alan Hale Jnr, Don Porter, Frederick Worlock, Gladys Cooper

Eagle's Wing
GB 1979 111m Eastmancolor Panavision
Rank/Peter Shaw (Ben Arbeid)

A Comanche chief pursues a white man who has stolen a prize Indian horse.
Would-be poetic Western which emerges as very pretty but stultifyingly dull; an odd thing indeed to come from a moribund British studio.
w John Briley *d* Anthony Harvey *ph* Billy Williams *m* Marc Wilkinson *pd* Herbert Westbrook
☆ Martin Sheen, Sam Waterston, Harvey Keitel, Stephane Audran, John Castle

The Ear *
Czechoslovakia 1970 93m bw
Barrandov (Erich Svabik, Jan Prochazka)
original title: *Ucho*
An unhappily married couple return to their bugged home from an official reception, at which the husband, a government minister, has discovered that he is to be purged.
A skilled but claustrophobic domestic and political drama, which is partly filmed in semi-darkness to emphasize its atmosphere of betrayal, guilt and general malaise; though when characters emerge into the light it is for a sinister purpose.
w Jan Prochazka, Karel Kachyna *d* Karel Kachyna *ph* Joseph Illik *m* Svatopluk Havelka *ed* Stansikav Petrek
☆ Jirina Bohdalova, Radoslav Brzobohaty, Gustav Opecensky, Miroslav Holub, Lubor Tokos, Borivoj Navratil, Jiri Cisler
† Russian authorities suppressed the film for 20 years.

The Earl of Chicago *
US 1939 87m bw
MGM (Victor Saville)
An American gangster accedes to an English earldom but is tried for murder.
Unusual but unsatisfactory comedy-drama which rambles to a dismal conclusion but has entertaining passages.
w Lesser Samuels *novel* Brock Williams *d* Richard Thorpe *ph* Ray June *m* Werner Heymann
☆ Robert Montgomery, Edward Arnold, Reginald Owen, Edmund Gwenn
† This had been planned as a British production, but the war intervened.

The Early Bird
GB 1965 98m Eastmancolor
Rank/Hugh Stewart

A milkman gets involved in an inter-company war.
Star farcical comedy; not the worst of Wisdom, but overlong and mainly uninventive.
w Jack Davies, Norman Wisdom, Eddie Leslie, Henry Blyth *d* Robert Asher *ph* Jack Asher *m* Ron Goodwin
☆ Norman Wisdom, Edward Chapman, Jerry Desmonde, Paddie O'Neil, Bryan Pringle, Richard Vernon, John Le Mesurier, Peter Jeffrey

Early Frost
Australia 1982 90m colour
Filmco (David Hannay)
A private investigator discovers that a series of apparently accidental deaths are the work of a serial killer who hates mothers.
A psychological horror story that tries hard to scare, but becomes more ludicrous the longer it lasts.
w Terry O'Connor *d* uncredited *ph* David Eggby *m* Mike Harvey *ad* Bob Hilditch *ed* Tim Street
☆ Diana McLean, Jon Blake, Jan Kingsbury, Kit Taylor, David Franklin, Joanne Samuel, Danny Adcock, Daniel Cumerford, Guy Doleman

Early Spring *
Japan 1956 108m bw
Shochiku
original title: *Soshun*
The marriage of an office worker breaks down when he begins an affair with a typist.
A slight, unengaging tale of the dreariness of domestic and office life.
w Kogo Noda, Yasujiro Ozu *d* Yasujiro Ozu *ph* Yuharu Atsuta *m* Kojun Saito *ad* Tatsuo Hamada *ed* Yoshiyasu Hamamura
☆ Chikage Awajima, Ryo Ikebe, Keiko Kishi, Teiji Takahashi, Chishu Ryu, So Yamamura, Haruko Sugimura, Takako Fujino

Early Summer ***
Japan 1951 125m bw
Shochiku

original title: *Bakushu*
A family breaks up when the daughter rejects the man chosen as her husband and marries someone else.
A complex, compassionate, beautifully observed study of family tensions, traced over three generations living together.
w Kogo Noda, Yasujiro Ozu *d* *Yasujiro Ozu* *ph* Yuharu Atsuta *m* Senji Ito *ad* Toshio Hamada *ed* Yoshiyasu Hamamura
☆ *Setsuko Hara, Chishu Ryu*, Chikage Awajima, Kuniko Miyake, Ichiro Sugai, Chieko Higashiyama, Haruko Sugimura

Early to Bed
US 1928 20m bw silent
Hal Roach

Stan becomes Ollie's butler but rebels when his friend's fortune goes to his head.
One of the most untypical and seldom seen of the stars' comedies, with both prankishly out of character. On its own account however it is mainly very funny.
w H. M. Walker *d* Emmett Flynn *ph* George Stevens *ed* Richard Currier
☆ Stan Laurel, Oliver Hardy

The Earrings of Madame De...: see *Madame De...*

Earth ***
USSR 1930 63m approx (24 fps) bw silent
VUFKU

original title: *Zemlya*
Trouble results in a Ukrainian village when a landowner refuses to hand over his land for a collective farm.
The melodramatic little plot takes second place to lyrical sequences of rustic beauty, illustrating life, love and death in the countryside.
wd *Alexander Dovzhenko* *ph* *Danylo Demutsky* *ed* Alexander Dovzhenko
☆ Semyon Svashenko, Stephan Shkurat, Mikola Nademsky, Yelena Maximova
'Stories in themselves do not interest me. I choose them in order to get the greatest expression of essential social forms.' – *Dovzhenko*
'A picture for filmgoers who are prepared to take their cinema as seriously as Tolstoy took the novel.' – *James Agate*

Earth **
Canada 1999 colour 106
Pathé/Cracking the Earth (Deepa Mehta, Anne Masson)

In Lahore in 1947 at the time of independence, a young Parsee girl watches the end of friendships between Muslims and Hindus who are companions of her ayah when it is known that the city will become part of Pakistan.

A narrative with a tragic dimension, with events recalled by a woman whose life was changed by her uncomprehending actions as a child; it gains immeasurably from its limited, personal perspective on a national cataclysm.
wd Deepa Mehta *book Cracking India* by Bapsi Sidhwa *ph* Giles Nuttgens *m* A.R. Rahman *pd* Aradhana Seth *ed* Barry Farrell
☆ Maia Sethna (Lenny Sethna), Nandita Das (Shanta, the Ayah), Kitu Gidwani (Bunty Sethna), Arif Zakaria (Rustom Sethna), Eric Peterson (Mr Rogers), Kulbhushan Kharbanda (Imam Din), Pavan Malhotra (Butcher), Sunil Mehra (Toto Ramji)

Earth Girls Are Easy
US 1988 100m colour Panavision
Fox/De Laurentiis/Kestrel Films (Tony Garnett)
Three aliens crashland on Earth and learn to enjoy disco dancing.
Ineffectual teenage musical.
w Julie Brown, Charlie Coffey, Terrence E. McNally *d* Julien Temple *ph* Oliver Stapleton *md* Nile Rodgers *pd* Dennis Gassner *ed* Richard Halsey
☆ Geena Davis, Jeff Goldblum, Jim Carrey, Damon Wayans, Julie Brown, Michael McKean, Charles Rocket, Larry Linville, Rick Overton

Earth Versus the Flying Saucers
US 1956 83m bw
Columbia (Charles H. Schneer)
Saucermen from another planet try to disintegrate the Earth.
Elementary science fiction with special effects in a similar if enthusiastic vein.
w George Worthing Yates, Raymond T. Marcus (Bernard Gordon) *story* Curt Siodmak *book Flying Saucers from Outer Space* by Major Donald E. Keyhoe *d* Fred F. Sears *ph* Fred Jackman Jnr *sp Ray Harryhausen*
☆ Hugh Marlowe, Joan Taylor, Donald Curtis, Morris Ankrum
† Screenwriter Gordon used a pseudonym because he was blacklisted at the time.

Earth vs The Spider
US 1958 72m bw
AIP (Bert I. Gordon)
A seemingly dead giant spider is brought back to life by the playing of a high-school rock 'n' roll group.
Ineffably silly horror movie with poor special effects.
w Laszlo Gorog, George Worthing Yates *story* Bert I. Gordon *d* Bert I. Gordon *ph* Jack Marta *m* Albert Glasser *ad* Walter Keller *ed* Ronald Sinclair *sp* Bert I. Gordon
☆ Ed Kemmer, June Kenney, Gene Persson

'When The Big One Finally Hits L.A.'
Earthquake *
US 1974 123m Technicolor Panavision
Universal/Jennings Lang/Mark Robson
Various personal stories intertwine in a Los Angeles earthquake.
Dreary drama with very variable special effects, gimmicked up by Sensurround. A box-office bonanza.
w George Fox, Mario Puzo *d* Mark Robson *ph* Philip Lathrop *m* John Williams *pd* Alexander Golitzen, E. Preston Ames *ed* Dorothy Spencer *sp* Albert Whitlock, Frank Brendel, Glen Robinson
☆ Charlton Heston (Graff), Ava Gardner (Remy), Lorne Greene (Royce), Marjoe Gortner (Jody), Barry Sullivan (Stockle), George Kennedy (Slade), Richard Roundtree (Miles), Geneviève Bujold (Denise), Walter Matuschanskayasky (Walter Matthau) (Drunk), Lloyd Nolan (Dr Vance), Victoria Principal
'The picture is swell, but it isn't a cheat. It's an entertaining marathon of Grade A destruction effects, with B-picture stock characters spinning through it.' – *Pauline Kael*
sound; visual effects
Philip Lathrop; Alexander Golitzen, E. Preston Ames; Dorothy Spencer

Earthworm Tractors
US 1936 69m bw
Warner
GB title: *A Natural Born Salesman*
A salesman whose fiancée wants him to think big turns to tractors.
One of the star's livelier comedies.
w Richard Macaulay, Joe Traub, Hugh Cummings *d* Ray Enright
☆ *Joe E. Brown*, June Travis, Guy Kibbee, Dick Foran

'The frank fearless drama of a woman who sinned!'
The Easiest Way
US 1931 86m bw
MGM
A hard-working slum girl falls into the lap of luxury but her easy virtue finally causes her to be rejected.
Familiar moral melodrama which got past the Hays Office only after some heavy deletions.
w Edith Ellis *play* Eugene Walter *d* Jack Conway *ph* John Mescall
☆ *Constance Bennett*, Robert Montgomery, Adolphe Menjou, Anita Page, Marjorie Rambeau, J. Farrell MacDonald, Clark Gable, Clara Blandick
'Gilded wickedness played by flawless cast: will entice.' – *Variety*

East End Chant: see *Limehouse Blues*

'A Comedy Of Families, A Chip Shop... And A Very Randy Dog.'
East is East ***
GB 1999 96m DeLuxe
FilmFour/Assassin/BBC (Leslee Udwin)
The children of a strict Pakistani father, who is married to an Englishwoman, rebel when he arranges marriages for them.
Often broad but always enjoyable comedy that, for all its use of stereotypical characters and situations, manages to be truthful about family relationships.
w Ayub Khan-Din play Ayub Khan-Din *d Damien O'Donnell ph* Brian Tufano *m* Deborah Mollison *pd* Tom Conroy *ed* Michael Parker
☆ *Om Puri*, Linda Bassett, Jordan Routledge, Archie Panjabi, Emil Marwa, Chris Bisson, Jimi Mistry, Raji James, Ian Aspinall, Lesley Nicol, Gary Damer, John Bardon, Emma Rydal, Ruth Jones
† It is the most successful fully-funded British film so far.
British film

East L.A.: see *My Family*

East Lynne
US 1931 102m bw
Fox
A Victorian lady is unjustly divorced by her husband, and later loses both her lover and her sight.
Much caricatured melodrama, here presented in stolidly acceptable form.
w Bradley King, Tom Barry *novel* Mrs Henry Wood *d* Frank Lloyd *ph* John Seitz *m* Richard Fall
☆ Ann Harding, Clive Brook, O. P. Heggie, Conrad Nagel, Cecilia Loftus, Beryl Mercer, Flora Sheffield
'A lavish production, some corking direction, and the elemental appeal of all dramatic hokum.' – *Variety*
† Previous versions had been made by Fox, in 1916 with Theda Bara and in 1925 with Alma Rubens.
best picture

'Of what a boy did ... what a girl did ... of ecstasy and revenge!'
'The most shocking revenge a girl ever let one brother take on another!'
East of Eden **
US 1955 115m Warnercolor Cinemascope
Warner (Elia Kazan)
In a California farming valley in 1917 a wild adolescent rebels against his stern father and discovers that his mother, believed dead, runs a nearby brothel.
Turgid elaboration of Genesis with strong character but nowhere to go. Heavily over-directed and rousingly acted.
w Paul Osborn *novel* John Steinbeck *d Elia Kazan ph* Ted McCord *m* Leonard Rosenman *ad* James Basevi, Malcolm Bert
☆ *Raymond Massey, James Dean*, Julie Harris, Dick Davalos, *Jo Van Fleet*, Burl Ives, Albert Dekker
'The first distinguished production in Cinemascope.' – *Eugene Archer*
Jo Van Fleet
Paul Osborn; Elia Kazan; James Dean

East of Elephant Rock
GB 1976 92m colour
Boyd's Company/Kendon (Don Boyd)
In 1948 Malaya a womanizing civil servant is shot by his jealous mistress.
Style-less and quite uncredited re-hash of The Letter, *striving vainly to recreate the spirit of Somerset Maugham.*
wd Don Boyd *ph* Keith Goddard *m* Peter Skellern
☆ Judi Bowker, Jeremy Kemp, John Hurt, Christopher Cazenove, Anton Rodgers, Vajira, Tariq Yunus
'Punishingly inept in every department.' – *David Badder, MFB*

East of Java: see *South Sea Sinner (1949)*

East of Shanghai: see *Rich and Strange*

East of Sumatra *
US 1953 82m Technicolor
U-I (Albert J. Cohen)
A mining engineer has trouble with the ruthless chief of a Pacific island.
A good example of routine Hollywood hokum, efficiently staged and acted.
w Frank Gill Jnr *novel* Louis L'Amour *d Budd Boetticher ph* Clifford Stine *md* Joseph Gershenson
☆ Jeff Chandler, Anthony Quinn, Marilyn Maxwell, John Sutton

East of the Rising Sun: see *Malaya*

The East Side Kids
US 1940 62m bw
Monogram (Sam Katzman)
Street kids reform after helping to catch counterfeiters.
See entry for The Dead End Kids; *this is the first attempt at a splinter group, and one that did not suggest longevity.*
Later, the East Side Kids were boosted by the addition of members of the original Dead End Kids, Leo Gorcey and Bobby Jordan, soon followed by Huntz Hall and Gabriel Dell. They made the following movies before the group was re-formed as The Bowery Boys (qv):
1940 Boys of the City, That Gang of Mine
1941 Pride of the Bowery, Spooks Run Wild
1942 Mr Wise Guy, Let's Get Tough!, Smart Alecks, 'Neath Brooklyn Bridge
1943 Kid Dynamite, Clancy Street Boys (qv), Ghosts on the Loose, Mr Muggs Steps Out, Million Dollar Kid
1944 Follow the Leader, Block Busters (qv), Bowery Champs
1945 Docks of New York, Mr Muggs Rides Again, Come Out Fighting (qv)
w Robert Lively *d* Bob Hill
☆ Leon Ames, Dave O'Brien, Joyce Bryant, Harris Burger, Frankie Burke, Donald Haines, David Durand, Hally Chester (later Hal E. Chester, producer)
'An absurdly poor picture that will command little interest even from the vast army of Dead End Kids devotees.' – *Variety*

East Side West Side *
US 1949 108m bw
MGM (Voldemar Veltuguin)
A New York businessman is torn between his wife and another woman.
High-class soap opera with all the production stops pulled out; generally well acted and reasonably entertaining.
w Isobel Lennart *novel* Marcia Davenport *d* Mervyn Le Roy *ph* Charles Rosher *m* Miklos Rozsa
☆ *James Mason, Barbara Stanwyck*, Van Heflin, Ava Gardner, *Gale Sondergaard*, Cyd Charisse, Nancy Davis, William Conrad
'No company is quite so adept as MGM at presenting basically uninteresting material with such style, and such a strong cast, that it cannot fail to entertain.' – *Penelope Houston*

East-West *
France/Russia/Bulgaria/Spain 1999 125m colour
Gala/UGC/France3/NVC/Mate (Yves Marmion)
original title: *Est-Ouest*
In 1946, A Russian doctor and his French wife and son are enticed back to the Soviet Union, where their marriage begins to suffer.
A romantic melodrama, set against the repressions of Stalinism, that comes to life only fitfully.
w Sergei Bodrov, Rustam Ibragimbekov, Louis Gardel, Regis Wargnier *d* Regis Wargnier *ph* Laurent Dailland *m* Patrick Doyle *ad* Vladimir Svetozarov, Alexei Levchenko *ed* Herve Schneid *cos* Pierre-Guillaume Sciama, Dominique Dalmasso
☆ Sandrine Bonnaire (Marie), Oleg Menhikov (Alexei Golovin), Catherine Deneuve (Gabrielle Develay), Sergei Bodrov Jnr (Sasha), Ruben Tapiero (Seryozha, age 7), Erwan Baynaud (Seryozha, age 14), Grigori Manukov (Pirogov), Tatyana Dogilova (Olga), Bogdan Stupka (Colonel Boyko), Meglena Karalambova (Nina Fyodorovna)
'Pitched unashamedly as a broad-brushstroke historical melodrama. But the historical part of the equation is underdeveloped.' – *Michael Witt, Sight and Sound*
foreign-language film

Easter Parade **
US 1948 109m Technicolor
MGM (Arthur Freed)
A song and dance man quarrels with one partner but finds another.
A musical which exists only in its numbers, which are many but variable. All in all, an agreeable lightweight entertainment without the style to put it in the top class.
w Sidney Sheldon, Frances Goodrich, Albert Hackett *d* Charles Walters *ph* Harry Stradling *m/ly Irving Berlin md* Roger Edens, Johnny Green
☆ *Fred Astaire, Judy Garland*, Ann Miller, Peter Lawford, Clinton Sundberg, Jules Munshin
'The important thing is that Fred Astaire is back, with Irving Berlin calling the tunes.' – *Newsweek*
† Fred Astaire was actually second choice, replacing Gene Kelly who damaged an ankle.
♫ 'Happy Easter'; 'Drum Crazy'; 'It Only Happens When I Dance With You'; 'A Fella with an Umbrella'; 'I Love a Piano'; 'When the Midnight Choo-Choo Leaves for Alabam''; 'Steppin' Out With My Baby'; 'A Couple of Swells'; 'Easter Parade'
Roger Edens, Johnny Green

Easy Come, Easy Go
US 1966 97m Technicolor
Paramount/Wallis-Hazen
A frogman tries to salvage a treasure from a wreck off the California coast.
Empty-headed star vehicle, almost indistinguishable from many of the others.
w Allan Weiss, Anthony Lawrence *d* John Rich *ph* William Margulies *m* Joseph J. Lilley
☆ Elvis Presley, Dodie Marshall, Pat Priest, Pat Harrington, Skip Ward, Frank McHugh, Elsa Lanchester

'Where there's smoke, there must be somebody smoking!'
Easy Living **
US 1937 91m bw
Paramount (Arthur Hornblow Jnr)
A fur coat is thrown out of a window and lands on a typist…
Amusing romantic comedy with farcical trimmings; it now stands among the semi-classic crazy comedies of the thirties.
w Preston Sturges d Mitchell Leisen *ph* Ted Tetzlaff *md* Boris Morros

☆ *Jean Arthur*, Ray Milland, *Edward Arnold*, Luis Alberni, Mary Nash, Franklin Pangborn, William Demarest, Andrew Tombes

'Slapstick farce which does not fulfil the box office possibilities of its stars.' – *Variety*

'Secretaries, millionaires, jokes, sight gags, furies, attacks of cool sense – there are always three things going on at once.' – *New Yorker, 1977*

Easy Living

US 1949 77m bw

RKO (Robert Sparks)

An ageing football star wants to retire but has to satisfy the living standards of his ambitious wife.

Dim drama.

w Charles Schnee *story* *Education of the Heart* by Irwin Shaw *d* Jacques Tourneur *ph* Harry J. Wild *m* Roy Webb

☆ Victor Mature, Lucille Ball, Lizabeth Scott, Sonny Tufts, Lloyd Nolan, Paul Stewart, Jack Paar, Jeff Donnell

Easy Money

US 1983 100m bw

Orion

A baby photographer is left a fortune provided that he totally reforms.

Overlong and increasingly feeble comedy with a star who quickly outstays his welcome.

w Rodney Dangerfield, Michael Endler, P. J. O'Rourke, Dennis Blair *d* James Signorelli

☆ Rodney Dangerfield, Joe Pesci, Geraldine Fitzgerald, Candy Azzara, Val Avery

'A man went looking for America and couldn't find it anywhere!'

Easy Rider ★★★★

US 1969 94m Technicolor

Columbia/Pando/Raybert (Peter Fonda)

Two drop-outs ride across America on motorcycles.

Happening to please hippies and motor-cycle enthusiasts as well as amateur politicians, this oddball melodrama drew freakishly large audiences throughout the world and was much imitated though never equalled in its casual effectiveness.

w Peter Fonda, Dennis Hopper, Terry Southern *d* Dennis Hopper *ph* Laszlo Kovacs *m* various recordings

☆ Peter Fonda, Dennis Hopper, *Jack Nicholson*

'*Cinéma-vérité* in allegory terms.' – *Peter Fonda*

'Ninety-four minutes of what it is like to swing, to watch, to be fond, to hold opinions and to get killed in America at this moment.' – *Penelope Gilliatt*

🏆 script; Jack Nicholson

Easy Street ★★★★

US 1917 22m approx bw silent

Mutual/Charles Chaplin

In a slum street, a tramp is reformed by a dewy-eyed missionary, becomes a policeman, and tames the local bully.

Quintessential Chaplin, combining sentimentality and social comment with hilarious slapstick.

wd Charles Chaplin *ph* William C. Foster, Rollie Totheroh

☆ *Charles Chaplin*, Edna Purviance, Albert Austin, Eric Campbell

Easy to Love

US 1953 96m Technicolor

MGM (Joe Pasternak)

The romances of an aqua-queen in Florida's Cypress Gardens.

Thin, humourless and forgettable musical vehicle sustained by spectacular water ballets.

w Laslo Vadnay, William Roberts *d* Charles Walters *ph* Ray June *md* Lennie Hayton, George Stoll *ch* Busby Berkeley

☆ Esther Williams, Tony Martin, Van Johnson, John Bromfield, Carroll Baker

Easy to Wed ★

US 1946 110m Technicolor

MGM (Jack Cummings)

A socialite threatens a newspaper with libel; he postpones his own wedding and sets a friend to compromise her.

Bright but tasteless remake of Libelled Lady, *with a second team cast trying hard.*

w Dorothy Kingsley, Maurine Watkins, Howard Emmett Rogers, George Oppenheimer *d* Edward Buzzell *ph* Harry Stradling *m* Johnny Green

☆ Van Johnson, Esther Williams, *Lucille Ball*, Keenan Wynn, Cecil Kellaway, Carlos Ramirez, Ben Blue, Ethel Smith

Easy Virtue

GB 1927 73m (24 fps) bw silent

Gainsborough (Michael Balcon)

A drunkard's wife falls for a young man who kills himself. Her past then prevents her attempts to lead a respectable life.

Vapid social melodrama with minimal points of interest despite its credits.

w Eliot Stannard *play* Noël Coward *d* Alfred Hitchcock *ph* Claude McDonnell *ed* Ivor Montagu

☆ Isabel Jeans, Franklin Dyall, Eric Bransby Williams, Ian Hunter, Violet Farebrother, Robin Irvine

The Easy Way: see *Room for One More*

'A Taste Of Life In America.'

Eat a Bowl of Tea ★★

US 1989 104m DeLuxe Panavision

Artificial Eye/American Playhouse Theatre (Tom Sternberg)

A young Chinese-American brings back to New York a Chinese-born bride, but finds that family pressures to produce children make him impotent.

Sharply observed, witty domestic drama, set in the 1940s when Chinese immigrants were first allowed to bring their wives to America.

w Judith Rascoe *novel* Louis Chu *d* Wayne Wang *ph* Amir Mokri *m* Mark Adler *pd* Bob Ziembicki *ed* Richard Candib

☆ Cora Miao, Russell Wong, Victor Wong, Lau Siu Ming, Eric Tsang Chi Wai

'An engaging and welcome picture. Good-humoured, sincere, it is nothing more than it modestly aspires to be.' – *MFB*

'A comedy with taste.'

Eat and Run

US 1985 86m colour

New World (Jack Briggs)

A cop investigates when an obese alien lands on earth and begins to eat Italians.

A send-up of science-fiction and police movies, but done with little style and overusing its one joke – a voice-over narration spoken out loud by the characters.

w Stan Hart, Christopher Hart *d* Christopher Hart *ph* Dyanna Taylor *m* Scott Harper *pd* Robert Kracik, Anne C. Patterson *ed* Pamela Scott Arnold

☆ Ron Silver, Sharon Schlarth, R. L. Ryan, John J. Fleming, Derek Murcott, Robert Silver

† The British video release runs for 80m.

'A comedy to arouse your appetite.'

Eat Drink Man Woman ★★

Taiwan 1994 124m DuArt

Buena Vista/Central Motion Picture/Good Machine/Ang Lee (Li-Kong Hsu)

original title: *Yinshi Nan Nu*

A widowed chef who has lost his sense of taste recovers it once he gets his three daughters off his hands.

Gentle comedy of food and family life, reasserting primary needs over more ephemeral desires.

w Hui-Ling Wang, Ang Lee, James Schamus *d Ang Lee* *ph* Jong Lin *m* Mader *pd* Fu-Hsiung Lee *ed* Tim Squyres

☆ Sihung Lung, Kuei-Mei Yang, Chien-Lien Wu, Yu-Wen Wang, Winston Chao, Ah-Leh Gua, Sylvia Chang, Lester Chen

'The movie is more likeable than memorable; you come out running for the nearest restaurant.' – *Terrence Rafferty, New Yorker*

'A feel-good movie, to be sure – but is that a stigma when so many young film-makers seem hell-bent on making us feel bad?' – *Sheila Johnston, Independent*

🏆 Best Foreign Film

Eat the Peach ★

Eire 1986 95m Technicolor

Strongbow/Film Four International (David Collins)

Out-of-work Irish devise a mad scheme to construct a motorcycle Wall of Death.

Fairly amusing comedy, like an Irish version of an Ealing movie.

w Peter Ormrod, John Kelleher *d* Peter Ormrod *ph Arthur Wooster* *m* Donal Lummy

☆ Stephen Brennan, Eamon Morrissey, Catherine Byrne, Niall Toibin, Joe Lynch, Tony Doyle

Eaten Alive: see *Death Trap*

Eating Raoul ★

US 1982 83m Pacific Color

Bartel Film (Anne Kimmel)

A restaurateur kills a drunken swinger, and finds that he has a profitable sideline on his hands...

Black comedy with insufficient humour to offset tastelessness.

w Richard Blackburn, Paul Bartel *d* Paul Bartel *ph* Gary Thieltges *m* Arlon Ober

☆ Paul Bartel, Mary Woronov, Robert Beltran, Susan Saiger, Richard Blackburn

'I wanted to make a film about two greedy, uptight people who are at the same time not so unlike you and me and Nancy and Ronnie, to keep it funny and yet communicate something about the psychology and perversity of these values ... My movie touches on many things: the perversion of middle class values, the resurgence of Nixonism, machismo versus WASP fastidiousness, *film noir*...' – *Paul Bartel*

L'Eau Froide

France 1994 92m colour

Ima/La Sept/Arte/SPF (Georges Benayoun, Paul Rozenberg)

aka: *Cold Water*

On the outskirts of Paris in the early 70s, two unhappy teenagers seek solace with each other after abrasive confrontations with parents and teachers.

A muted study in alienation and misery, much of it shot with a handheld camera to provide a sense of immediacy and intimacy; adult sympathies may be moderated by its youthful delight in unmotivated delinquency.

wd Olivier Assayas *ph* Denis Lenoir *ad* Gilbert Gagneux *ed* Luc Barnier

☆ Virginie Ledoyen, Cyprien Fouquet, Laszlo Szabo, Jean-Pierre Darroussin, Dominique Faysse, Smail Mekki, Jackie Berroyer

'Delivers a sustained emotional pummeling, underscored by a steady whisper of despair.' – *David Rooney, Variety*

'The story of a man who thought he was God!'

Ebb Tide ★★

US 1937 92m Technicolor

Paramount (Lucien Hubbard)

Sailors are stranded with a dangerous fanatic on a South Sea island.

Interesting adaptation of Stevenson, notable both for its early colour and its genuinely sour, anti-romantic mood, almost unique for Hollywood in this period.

w Bertram Millhauser *novel* R. L. Stevenson, Lloyd Osbourne *d* James Hogan *ph* Leo Tover *m* Victor Young

☆ Ray Milland, Frances Farmer, Oscar Homolka, Barry Fitzgerald, Lloyd Nolan

'More pretentious as to production than dramatically. Does not suggest big b.o.' – *Variety*

† Remade 1946 as *Adventure Island.*

Ebbtide

Australia 1994 90m colour

Ambroco/Genesis (Craig Lahiff, Paul Davies, Helen Leake)

A lawyer, who takes over the clients of his dead partner, finds himself mixed up in murder when he investigates a case involving toxic waste.

Glossy, melodramatic and implausible thriller, with rather too much time spent on shots of Hamlin staring moodily into the far distance.

w Robert Ellis, Peter Goldsworthy, Warwick Hind *idea* Craig Lahiff, Helen Leake *d* Craig Lahiff *ph* Steve Arnold *m* Peter Best *pd* Ross Major *ed* Peter Carrodus

☆ Harry Hamlin, Judy McIntosh, John Waters, Susan Lyons, John Gregg, Frankie J. Holden

Ebirah, Horror of the Deep

Japan 1966 85m Eastmancolor Tohoscope

Toho (Tomoyuki Tanaka)

Scientists creating nuclear weapons on an island guarded by a giant lobster are foiled with the aid of Godzilla.

The usual hokum, enlivened by fight sequences that have Godzilla heading rocks with the aplomb of a football striker, and a giant moth that looks as if it has been made from an old carpet.

w Shinichi Sekizawa *d* Jun Fukuda *ph* Kazuo Yamada *ad* Takeo Kita *sp* Eiji Tsuburaya

☆ Akira Takarada, Kumi Mizuno, Akihiko Hirata, Jun Tazaki, Hideo Sunazuka, Chotaro Togin, Toru Watanabe

Echo Park ★

Austria 1985 92m colour

Sasha Wein/Walter Shenson

In a rundown area of Los Angeles, three unsuccessful youngsters await the big break.

Vaguely entertaining slice-of-life drama with good observational touches.

w Michael Ventura *d* Robert Dornhelm *ph* Karl Kofler *m* David Rickets

☆ Susan Dey, Thomas Hulce, Michael Bowen, Christopher Walker

Echoes of a Summer

US/Canada 1975 98m Eastmancolor

Beata/Castle/Astral/Bryanston (Robert L. Joseph)

An 11-year-old girl dying of heart disease spends her last summer with her parents on holiday in a Nova Scotian village.

Excruciating.

w Robert L. Joseph *d* Don Taylor *ph* John Coquillon *m* Terry James

☆ Jodie Foster, Richard Harris, Lois Nettleton, Geraldine Fitzgerald, William Windom, Brad Savage

'The only honest thing about this movie is its desire to make a buck.' – *Frank Rich, New York Post*

The Eclipse ★★

Italy/France 1962 125m bw

Interopa-Cineriz/Paris Film (Robert and Raymond Hakim)

original title: *L'Eclisse*

A young Roman woman breaks off one affair and begins another.

A portrait in depth, rather tiresomely long and with at least one totally irrelevant stock-market sequence; but superbly done for connoisseurs.

wd Michelangelo Antonioni, Tonino Guerra, Elio Bartolini, Ottiero Ottieri *ph* Gianni di Venanzo *m* Giovanni Fusco

☆ *Monica Vitti*, Alain Delon, Francisco Rabal

'The first time I saw the film I thought it magnificent but chill, played glitteringly ... At a second visit the passion breaks through.' – *Dilys Powell*

Eclipse ★

Canada/Germany 1994 95m colour/bw

Pagemedia/Fire Dog/Time Medienvertieb (Camelia Frieberg, Jeremy Podeswa)

As a solar eclipse approaches in Toronto, ten people are linked through their various sexual encounters.

A stylish exercise in voyeurism and abortive relationships, in which pleasure is swiftly followed by disillusionment.

wd Jeremy Podeswa *ph* Miroslaw Baszak *m* Ernie Tollar *ad* Tamara Deverell *ed* Susan Maggi

☆ Von Flores, John Gilbert, Pascale Montpetit, Manuel Aranguiz, Maria Del Mar, Greg Ellwand, Matthew Ferguson, Earl Pastko, Daniel MacIvor, Kirsten Johnson

'Don't go near this film. It's about as interesting as watching a sunbather peel.' – *Tom Shone, Sunday Times*

'Powerful blend of casual sex, eye-catching, arty camera work and witty, sophisticated dialogue.' – *Variety*

L'Eclisse: see *The Eclipse*

L'école Buissonière *
France 1948 89m bw
UGC/CGCF
US title: *I Have a New Master*
At a provincial village school, a new teacher introduces new methods and takes a while to win over the locals.
Rustic comedy-drama of a kind the French do well.
w Jean-Paul Le Chanois, Elise Freinet *d* Jean-Paul Le Chanois *ph* Marc Fossard, Maurice Pecqueux, André Dumaître *m* Joseph Kosma
☆ Bernard Blier, Juliette Fabre, Edouard Delmont

L'école des Facteurs **
France 1947 14m bw
Cady (Fred Orain)
A village postman puts into practice what he has learned at training school.
Amusing short, full of a humane humour, which was to blossom a year later into the wonderful Jour de Fête.
wd Jacques Tati *m* Jean Yatove *ed* Marcel Moreau
☆ Jacques Tati, Paul Demange
† It was released on video together with *Cours du Soir* and *Soigne Ton Gauche* as *Tati Shorts*.

Ecologia del Delitto: see *A Bay of Blood*

Ecstasy: see *Extase*

Ed
US 1996 94m DeLuxe
Universal/Longview (Rosalie Swedlin)
An unsuccessful baseball player discovers a chimpanzee with a talent for the game.
A sporting comedy so thin that the most human and engaging character is an animatronic ape.
w David Mickey Evans *d* Bill Couturie *ph* Alan Caso *m* Stephen D. Endelman *pd* Curtis A. Schnell *ed* Robert K. Lambert
☆ Matt LeBlanc, Jayne Brook, Bill Cobbs, Jack Warden, Doren Fein, Patrick Kerr, Charlie Schlatter

'Almost painfully modest in its ambition and accomplishment, this slow-pitch offering might tolerably amuse the under-10 crowd, but will prove borderline intolerable for everyone else.' – *Todd McCarthy, Variety*

'Before Dahmer, Before Gacy There Was Ed.'
Ed Gein
US 2001 89m FotoKem
Metro Tartan/Tartan (Hamish McAlpine, Michael Muscal)
Biopic of the Wisconsin grave-robber and murderer, whose life was the inspiration for *Psycho*.
Fact may be stranger than fiction; here it is less enthralling than what Hitchcock and others created. The understated approach to real-life horrors may be laudable, but it fails to grip.
w Stephen Johnston *d* Chuck Parello *ph* Vanja Cernjul *m* Robert McNaughton *pd* Mark Harper *ed* Elena Maganini *sp* Perpetual Motion Pictures
☆ Steve Railsback (Ed Gein), Carrie Snodgress (Augusta Gein), Sally Champlin (Mary), Carol Mansell (Colette), Nancy Linehan Charles (Eleanor), Pat Skipper (Sheriff Jim Stillwell), Travis McKenna (Ronnie), Craig Zimmerman (Pete)

'A disappointingly mild re-creation of true events.' – *Variety*

Ed Wood **
US 1994 124m bw
Buena Vista/Touchstone (Denise di Novi, Tim Burton)
Biopic of the film director who has become posthumously notorious for writing and directing some of the worst movies ever made (most of which, ironically, are now available on video and laser disc).
A delightful, charming, straight-faced account of a hopelessly obsessive film-maker and transvestite, which turns his ineffectual life and career into some sort of triumphant celebration of the American dream, making a success of failure; its appeal, though, may be limited to those who have experienced Wood's films.
w Scott Alexander, Larry Karaszewski *book* *Nightmare of Ecstasy: The Life and Art of Edward D. Wood* by Rudolph Grey *d* Tim Burton *ph* Stefan Czapsky *m* Howard Shore *pd* Tom Duffield *ed* Chris Lebenzon
☆ Johnny Depp (Ed Wood), *Martin Landau* (Bela Lugosi), Sarah Jessica Parker, Patricia Arquette, Jeffrey Jones, Vincent D'Onofrio (Orson Welles), Bill Murray, Lisa Marie, George 'The Animal' Steele, G. D. Spradlin

'There's a strong whiff of pointlessness to the whole enterprise.' – *Terrence Rafferty, New Yorker*

'Wood was an obsessive without taste, an artist without art, and Burton, forgoing irony, celebrates the innocence, the energy, the perfection of ineptitude.' – *New York*

† Edward D. Wood Jnr (1922–1978) is best known for making *Plan 9 from Outer Space* (qv). His other films include *Bride of the Monster, Glen or Glenda?* and *Night of the Ghouls* (qqv).
Martin Landau; make-up (Rick Baker, Ve Neill, Yolanda Toussieng)

Las Edades de Lulu: see *The Ages of Lulu*

'The Newest Coach In The NBA Has Got The Knicks Right Where She Wants Them.'
Eddie
US 1996 100m Technicolor
Buena Vista/Hollywood (David Permut, Mark Burg)
A female baseball fan is made coach of the New York Knicks by the team's new owner.
Dumb comedy of minor interest, and one that fails to exploit its central fantasy.
w Jon Connolly, David Loucka, Eric Champnella, Keith Mitchell, Steve Zacharias, Jeff Buhai *d* Steve Rash *ph* Victor Kemper *m* Stanley Clarke *pd* Dan Davis *ed* Richard Halsey
☆ Whoopi Goldberg, Frank Langella, Dennis Farina, Richard Jenkins, Lisa Ann Walter, John Benjamin Hickey

'Especially uninspired.' – *Variety*

Eddie and the Cruisers
US 1983 95m Technicolor
Embassy/Aurora (Joseph Brooks, Robert K. Lifton)
A high-school teacher recalls his days as a member of a 60s rock group, prompted by a journalist investigating the suicide of its charismatic lead singer.
A dully nostalgic drama, interspersed with some energetic rock and hampered by a convoluted narrative that leads nowhere; it toys with themes of change and decay but fails to develop them.
w Martin Davidson, Arlene Davidson *novel* P. F. Kluge *d* Martin Davidson *ph* Fred Murphy *m* John Cafferty *ad* Gary Weist *ed* Priscilla Nedd
☆ Tom Berenger, Michael Paré, Joe Pantoliano, Matthew Laurance, Helen Schneider, David Wilson, Michael Antunes, Ellen Barkin
† It was followed by an even less successful sequel in 1989, *Eddie and the Cruisers II: Eddie Lives*, directed by Jean-Claude Lord, with Michael Paré reprising his role as Eddie.

'It's big and bright as those banjo eyes!'
The Eddie Cantor Story
US 1953 116m Technicolor
Warner (Sidney Skolsky)
After a tough childhood on New York's east side, Israel Iskowitz becomes a famous entertainer.
Deliberately patterned after the success of The Jolson Story, *this is an unhappy example of how close are success and failure; the elements are the same, but this film suffers from unsure timing, lack of humour, rather apologetic numbers, a really dismal script and a caricature performance in the lead.*
w Jerome Weidman, Ted Sherdeman, Sidney Skolsky *d* Alfred E. Green *ph* Edwin DuPar *m/ly* various *md* Ray Heindorf *ch* Le Roy Prinz
☆ Keefe Brasselle, Marilyn Erskine, Aline MacMahon, Arthur Franz, Alex Gerry, Gerald Mohr, William Forrest (Florenz Ziegfeld), Will Rogers Jnr (Will Rogers), Eddie Cantor

'When I saw the rushes, I realized there was something wrong. When I read the reviews, I knew what it was: everything.' – *Keefe Brasselle*

'If that's my life, I didn't live.' – *Eddie Cantor*

† Eddie Cantor sings the songs off screen.

Eddie Holm's Second Life **
Denmark 1985 95m colour
Scenograf (Poul Arnt Thomsen)
original title: *Eddie Holms Andet Liv*
A suicidal musician is taken back through his life to discover what drove him to end it.
Witty, black comedy of love, death and family life.
w Bjarne Henriksen, Gert Henriksen *d* Esben Hùilund Carlsen *ph* Ole Schultz *m* Bo Lykke Jùrgensen *ed* Jette Allarp
☆ Kristian Halken, Pernille Hansen, Lisbet Lundquist, Claus Nissen, Holger Boland, Karen Marie Lowert, Frederik Esbensen

Eddie Macon's Run
US 1983 95m Technicolor
Universal/Martin Bregman (Louis A. Stroller)
A man innocently convicted escapes and hotfoots it back home.
Old-style chase film marred by passages of sex and crude backwoods violence.
wd Jeff Kanew *novel* James McLendon *ph* James A. Contner *m* Norton Buffalo *ed* Jeff Kanew
☆ John Schneider, Kirk Douglas, Lee Purcell, Leah Ayres

The Eddy Duchin Story
US 1956 123m Technicolor Cinemascope
Columbia (Jonie Taps, Jerry Wald)
The success story of a pianist who died of leukemia.
Predictable, glossy, sentimental musical biopic.
w Samuel Taylor *story* Leo Katcher *d* George Sidney *ph* Harry Stradling *m* George Duning *piano* Carmen Cavallero
☆ Tyrone Power, Kim Novak, Victoria Shaw, James Whitmore, Shepperd Strudwick, Frieda Inescort, Gloria Holden, Larry Keating
Leo Katcher; Harry Stradling; George Duning

Eden Valley
GB 1994 95m colour
Amber/Channel 4/NDR/Northern Arts
A youth, arrested for theft, is given six months to redeem himself, and goes to stay with his father on some isolated fields where he breeds trotting horses.
An austere slice-of-life drama, closer to the British documentary traditions than to normal features; the narrative ends at the point where it begins to get interesting.
☆ Brian Hogg, Darren Bell, Mike Elliott, Jimmy Killeen, Wayne Buck, Kevin Buck, Rose Laidler, Brian Laidler

'The major investment here has been made in terms of time and energy rather than money and the dividend – a self-contained, distinctive film which eschews clichés and sentimentality – pays off.' – *Jo Comino, Sight and Sound*

† Amber Films is a collective and does not provide individual production credits. Its team was: Richard Grassick, Ellen Hare, Sirkka Lisa Konttinen, Murray Martin, Pat McCarthy, Lorna Powell, Pete Roberts.

Edes Emma, Draga Böbe – Vazlatok, Aktok: see *Dear Emma, Sweet Böbe*

Edgar Wallace
Between 1960 and 1966 no fewer than 46 second features emerged from Jack Greenwood's production unit at the London suburban studios of Merton Park, under the Edgar Wallace banner and prefaced by a sinister revolving bust of the author (though few had very much to do with his original stories).

All maintained a better standard than any other crime second features of the period, and a few were seized on with delight by the critics. They were subsequently popular on television, though the Independent Broadcasting Authority banned repeats on the grounds that they were without merit. In this complete list, details are given for the more interesting items:

The Clue of the Twisted Candle
A Marriage of Convenience
The Man Who Was Nobody
The Clue of the New Pin*, *w* Philip Mackie, *d* Allan Davis, with Paul Daneman, Bernard Archard
Partners in Crime
The Fourth Square
The Man at the Carlton Tower
The Clue of the Silver Key
Attempt to Kill
The Sinister Man*, *w* Philip Mackie , *d* Clive Donner, with Patrick Allen, John Bentley
Never Back Losers
Man Detained
Ricochet
The Double
The Rivals
To Have and to Hold
The Partner
Five to One
Accidental Death
We Shall See
Downfall
The Verdict
Who Was Maddox?*, *w* Roger Marshall , *d* Geoffrey Nethercott, with Bernard Lee, Finlay Currie
Act of Murder*, *w* Lewis Davidson , *d* Alan Bridges, with John Carson, Anthony Bate
Face of a Stranger
Never Mention Murder*, *w* Robert Banks Stewart , *d* John Nelson Burton, with Maxine Audley, Dudley Foster
The Main Chance
Game for Three Losers
Dead Man's Chest
Change Partners
Strangler's Web*, *w* George Baxt , *d* John Moxey, with Griffith Jones, Gerald Harper
Backfire
Candidate for Murder*, *w* Lukas Heller , *d* David Villers, with Michael Gough, John Justin
Flat Two
The Share-Out
Number Six
Time to Remember
Playback*, *w* Robert Banks Stewart , *d* Quentin Lawrence, with Barry Foster, Dinsdale Landen, Margit Saad
Solo for Sparrow
Locker 69
Death Trap
The Set-Up
On the Run
The £20,000 Kiss
Incident at Midnight
Return to Sender

'They were fighting over a woman until the plane went down. Now, their only chance for survival is each other.'
The Edge *
US 1997 117m DeLuxe Panavision
TCF (Art Linson)
When their plane crashes, a billionaire and a fashion photographer, whom he suspects of lusting after his wife, a fashion model, are stranded in an Alaskan wilderness inhabited by a ferocious bear.
Enjoyable hokum amidst splendid scenery, concentrating on the battle for supremacy between two very different men.
w David Mamet *d* Lee Tamahori *ph* Donald M. McAlpine *m* Jerry Goldsmith *pd* Wolf Kroeger *ed* Neil Travis
☆ Anthony Hopkins, Alec Baldwin, Elle Macpherson, Harold Perrineau, L. Q. Jones, Kathleen Wilhoite

'A tense, pleasurably visceral battle-of-wits thriller played out against a spectacular wilderness background.' – *Todd McCarthy, Variety*

Edge of Darkness *
US 1943 124m bw
Warner (Henry Blanke)
Norwegian village patriots resist the Nazis.
High-intentioned, ambitiously cast but ultimately bathetic resistance melodrama, high principled down to its tragic finale but compromised by backlot shooting and the presence of Errol Flynn.
w Robert Rossen *d* Lewis Milestone *ph* Sid Hickox *m* Franz Waxman
☆ Errol Flynn, Ann Sheridan, Walter Huston, Judith Anderson, Ruth Gordon, Nancy Coleman, Helmut Dantine, Morris Carnovsky, Charles Dingle, John Beal, Richard Fraser, Helene Thimig

'It is not a tea party. It is an icy shower turned loose on audiences in the hope of driving home what this war is about.' – *Motion Picture Herald*

Edge of Divorce: see *Background*

Edge of Doom
US 1950 97m bw
Samuel Goldwyn
GB title: *Stronger than Fear*
A desperate youth kills a priest and struggles with his conscience.

A sanctimonious weirdie, extremely odd coming from this producer, and unhappily re-edited before release. Someone was interested enough to want to make it, but it seems to have been killed by the cast and the front office.
w Philip Yordan *novel* Leo Brady *d* Mark Robson *ph* Harry Stradling *m* Hugo Friedhofer
☆ Dana Andrews, Farley Granger, Joan Evans, Robert Keith, Paul Stewart, Mala Powers, Adele Jergens, Harold Vermilyea, Mabel Paige

Edge of Eternity *
US 1959 80m Technicolor Cinemascope
Columbia/Thunderbird (Kendrick Sweet)
A Grand Canyon sheriff traces three murders to an ownership struggle over a disused mine.
Routine but suspenseful thriller with splendid locations.
w Knut Swenson, Richard Collins *d Don Siegel ph Burnett Guffey m* Daniele Amfitheatrof
☆ Cornel Wilde, Victoria Shaw, Edgar Buchanan, Mickey Shaughnessy, Jack Elam

Edge of Honor *
US 1991 92m Western Cine colour
Merit Badge/Guerilla Film Unit (Jay B. Davis, Peter Garrity, David O'Malley)
Scouts are attacked by a gang of ruthless arms smugglers after they discover a cache of weapons hidden in a forest.
A violent but effective action adventure intended for a teenage audience.
w Mark Rosenbaum, Michael Spence, David O'Malley *d* Michael Spence *ph* Billy Dickson *m* William Stromberg *pd* Charles Armstrong *ed* Ellen Keneshea
☆ Corey Feldman, Meredith Salenger, Scott Reeves, Ken Jenkins, Don Swayze, Christopher Neame
'A great action movie with a gung-ho performance by Don Swayze.' – *Sight and Sound*

Edge of Sanity
GB 1988 90m Eastmancolor
Palace/Allied Vision (Edward Simons, Harry Alan Towers)
Dr Jekyll, under the influence of drugs, becomes Jack the Ripper.
Dire variation on Robert Louis Stevenson's classic.
w J. P. Felix, Ron Raley *d* Gerard Kikoine *ph* Tony Spratling *m* Frederic Talgorn *pd* Jean Charles Dedieu *ed* Malcolm Cooke
☆ Anthony Perkins, Glynis Barber, Sarah Maur-Thorp, David Lodge, Ben Cole, Ray Jewers, Jill Melford

Edge of the City **
US 1957 85m bw
MGM/Jonathan (David Susskind, Jim di Ganci)
GB title: *A Man is Ten Feet Tall*
Racial tensions lead to tragedy in the railroad yards of New York's waterfront.
Tense, brutal melodrama, which has historical interest as an effective opening-up in cinematic terms of a TV play, in its imitation of On the Waterfront, *and in its rebel hero and relaxed black friend.*
w Robert Alan Aurthur play Robert Alan Aurthur *d Martin Ritt ph* Joseph Brun *m* Leonard Rosenman
☆ *Sidney Poitier, John Cassavetes*, Jack Warden, Kathleen Maguire, Ruby Dee, Robert Simon, Ruth White

The Edge of the Horizon *
France/Portugal/Spain 1993 90m colour
Films do Principe Real/CTN/Origen (António da Cunha Telles)
original title: *Le Fil de l'Horizon*
A Lisbon mortuary worker is puzzled to discover that the body of a murdered 25-year-old man resembles him as he was 30 years ago.
Intriguing, slow-paced psychological and philosophical mystery, heavily reliant on the melancholy charm of Brasseur's performance as a man who feels he should not be alive.
w Christopher Frank, Jean Nachbaur *novel Il Fillo dell'Orizonte* by Antonio Tabucchi *d* Fernando Lopes *ph* Javier Aguirresarobe *m* Zbigniew Preisner *ad* Jasmim de Matos *ed* Jacques Witta
☆ Claude Brasseur, Andrea Ferreol, Antonio Valero, Ana Padrão, Miguel Guilherme

Edge of the World **
GB 1937 80m bw
GFD/Rock (Joe Rock)
Life, love and death on Foula, a remote Shetland island.
Rare for its time, a vigorous location drama in the Flaherty tradition; sometimes naïve, usually exhilarating.
wd Michael Powell ph Ernest Palmer, Monty Berman, Skeets Kelly *m* Lambert Williamson *ed* Derek Twist
☆ Niall MacGinnis, Belle Chrystal, John Laurie, Finlay Currie, Eric Berry
'Scant of plot and unlikely to be hailed by the public at large.' – *Variety*

'The love of a woman ... the courage of a fighting America ... lifted him from obscurity to thrilling fame!'
Edison the Man **
US 1940 107m bw
MGM (John W. Considine Jnr)
Edison struggles for years in poverty before becoming famous as the inventor of the electric light bulb.
Standard, well-made biopic following on from Young Tom Edison; *reasonably absorbing, but slightly suspect in its facts.*
w Dore Schary, Talbot Jennings, Bradbury Foote, Hugo Butler *d Clarence Brown ph* Harold Rosson *m* Herbert Stothart
☆ *Spencer Tracy*, Rita Johnson, Lynne Overman, Charles Coburn, Gene Lockhart, Henry Travers, Felix Bressart
🏆 Dore Schary, Hugo Butler (original story)

Edith and Marcel *
France 1984 140m Eastmancolor
Gala/Cannon/Film 13/Parafrance/Miramax (Tania Zazulinsky)
Two French idols indulge in a tragic love affair.
Effective biopic based on the affair between singer Edith Piaf and boxer Marcel Cerdan.
wd Claude Lelouch *ph* Jean Boffety *m* Francis Lai *ed* Hugues Darmois
☆ Evelyne Bouix, Jacques Villeret, Francis Huster, Jean-Claude Brialy, Jean Bouise, Charles Gérard, Marcel Cerdan Jnr

Edouard et Caroline **
France 1951 99m bw
UGC/CICC
A young pianist and his wife quarrel while preparing for an important recital.
Gay, slight, charming comedy, a two-hander taking place within the course of a few hours.
w Annette Wademant, Jacques Becker d Jacques Becker ph Robert Le Fèbvre *m* Jean-Jacques Grunenwald
☆ *Daniel Gélin, Anne Vernon*, Jacques François, William Tubbs, Jean Galland, Elina Labourdette, Betty Stockfeld
'It lifts its weighty trivialities into a world of enchantment.' – *Sunday Times*

Ed's Next Move
US 1996 88m DeLuxe
Orion/Ed's Films (Sally Roy)
A young, socially inept scientist moves from Wisconsin to New York and falls in love with a singer.
Slight romantic comedy that tries too hard to charm; it most resembles a situation comedy stretched slowly beyond its limits.
wd John Walsh *ph* Peter Nelson *m* Benny Golson *pd* Kristin Vallow *ed* Pamela Martin
☆ Matt Ross, Callie Thorne, Kevin Carroll, Ramsey Faragallah, Nina Sheveleva
'A delightful, sweet first film.' – *Variety*

'The Story Of A Nobody Everybody Is Watching!'
EdTV *
US 1999 122m DeLuxe
Universal/Imagine (Brian Grazer, Ron Howard)
A video-store clerk becomes a star when his life is shown on cable television 24 hours a day.
Mildly amusing comedy about modern-day celebrity and the public fascination with people who are famous for being famous.
w Lowell Ganz, Babaloo Mandel *screenplay Louis XIX: Roi des ondes* by *Emile Gaudreault, Sylvie Bouchard d* Ron Howard *ph* John Schwartzman *m* Randy Edelman *pd* Michael Corenblith *ed* Mike Hill, Dan Hanley
☆ Matthew McConaughey, Jenna Elfman, Woody Harrelson, Ellen DeGeneres, Sally Kirkland, Martin Landau, Rob Reiner, Dennis Hopper, Elizabeth Hurley, Clint Howard
'Good humored, deceptively easygoing satire.' – *Janet Maslin, New York Times*

Educating Rita *
GB 1983 110m Technicolor
Rank/Acorn (Lewis Gilbert)
A cheerful young hairdresser improves her knowledge of English Literature by enrolling on an Open University course.
Rather dismal, thinly characterized and ill-lit variation on Pygmalion, *with endless talk leading nowhere (it was originally a two-character play). Due to its Liverpudlian modishness it achieved surprising box-office success.*
w Willy Russell *play* Willy Russell *d* Lewis Gilbert *ph* Frank Watts *m* David Hentschel
☆ Michael Caine, Julie Walters, Michael Williams, Maureen Lipman
'If only I'd been able to believe they were actually reading the books, everything else would have fallen into place.' – *Roger Ebert*
🏆 Michael Caine; Julie Walters; Willy Russell
🎭 best picture; Michael Caine; Julie Walters

Edvard Munch *
Norway/Sweden 1976 215m colour
New Yorker/SR
The life of the 19th-century Norwegian expressionist painter.
A yawn for the majority but a delight for connoisseurs of a certain kind; with a wholly non-professional cast.
wd Peter Watkins
☆ Geir Westby, Gro Fraas, Johan Halsborg, Lotte Teig

'A Classic Tale of Sex, Revenge, and Love.'
Edward II **
GB 1991 90m colour
Palace/Edward II/Working Title/British Screen/BBC (Steve Clark-Hall, Antony Root)
Edward II's love for Piers Gaveston leads to his downfall.
An explicitly homosexual reworking of Marlowe's play, done in modern dress and given a contemporary twist.
w Derek Jarman, Stephen McBride, Ken Butler *play* Christopher Marlowe *d Derek Jarman ph* Ian Wilson *m* Simon Fisher Turner *pd* Christopher Hobbs *ed* George Akers
☆ Steven Waddington, Kevin Collins, Andrew Tiernan, John Lynch, Dudley Sutton, Tilda Swinton, Jerome Flynn, Jody Graber, Nigel Terry, Annie Lennox
'Provocative and challenging ... likely will be the director's most commercial production to date.' – *Variety*
'Through the miracle of cinema, two sensibilities and centuries become wondrously fused. Bold, passionate and savagely beautiful.' – *Geoff Brown, The Times*

Edward My Son
GB 1949 112m bw
MGM (Edwin H. Knopf)
A rich, unscrupulous man remembers the people he has made unhappy, and the son to whom he never behaved as a father should.
Unsatisfactory, rather ugly-looking adaptation of a gripping piece of theatre, with casting and direction remarkably uncertain from such professionals.
w Donald Ogden Stewart *play* Robert Morley *d* George Cukor *ph* F. A. Young *m* John Wooldridge, Malcolm Sargent
☆ Spencer Tracy, Deborah Kerr, Ian Hunter, James Donald, Leueen McGrath, Mervyn Johns
🏆 Deborah Kerr

Edward Scissorhands **
US 1990 98m colour
Fox (Denise de Novi, Tim Burton)
A boy with artificial hands upsets the community in which he lives.
Bizarre fairy-tale with a good deal of charm.
w Caroline Thompson *story* Tim Burton *d* Tim Burton *ph* Stefan Czapsky *m* Danny Elfman *pd* Bo Welch *ad* Tom Duffield *ed* Richard Halsey
☆ Johnny Depp, Winona Ryder, Dianne Wiest, Anthony Michael Hall, Alan Arkin, Kathy Baker, Robert Oliver, Conchata Ferrell, Vincent Price
'A delightful and delicate comic fable.' – *Variety*
🏆 best makeup
🎭 Bo Welch

The Eel **
Japan 1996 117m colour
Artificial Eye/KSS/Eisei Gekijo/Groove/Shochiku (Hisa Iino)
When he is released from prison, an introverted wife-murderer opens a barber's shop and takes an unstable woman as his assistant.
Enigmatic, though simple-seeming, drama of a man coming to terms with himself and his actions; the narrative takes on a dream-like quality.
w Motofumi Tomikawa, Daisuke Tengan, Shohei Imamura *story Glittering in the Dark* by Akira Yoshimura *d* Shohei Imamura *ph* Shigeru Komatsubara *m* Shinichiro Ikebe *pd* Hisao Inagaki *ed* Hajime Okayasu
☆ Koji Yakusho, Misa Shimizu, Fujio Tsuneta, Mitsuko Baisho, Makoto Sato, Akira Emoto, Sho Aihara, Ken Kobayashi, Sabu Kawahara, Etsuko Ichihara
'What starts out as intriguing turns into simply baffling.' – *Empire*
'It's too early to be sure whether *The Eel* is a great Imamura film or merely a good one.' – *Tony Rayns, Sight and Sound*
† The film won the Palme d'Or at the 1997 Cannes Film Festival.

The Effect of Gamma Rays on Man-in-the-Moon Marigolds
US 1972 101m DeLuxe
Newman-Foreman (Paul Newman)
A slatternly middle-aged woman dreams of better times for herself and her children.
Well-written but essentially banal and pretentious domestic drama, the kind of film that only gets made when powerful stars see in it a juicy role.
w Alvin Sargent *play* Paul Zindel *d* Paul Newman *ph* Adam Holender *m* Maurice Jarre
☆ *Joanne Woodward*, Nell Potts, Roberta Wallach, Judith Lowry

Effi Briest *
West Germany 1974 140m bw
Tango Film (Rainer Werner Fassbinder)
original title: *Fontane Effi Briest*
A teenage girl is married to a rich baron, but fails to understand what is expected of her.
Overlong but often fascinating picture of a vanished society in which not the slightest weakening of structure is permitted.
wd Rainer Werner Fassbinder *novel* Theodor Fontane *ph* Jürgen Jürges, Dietrich Lohmann *m* from Saint-Saëns
☆ Hanna Schygulla, Wolfgang Schenck, Ulli Lommel, Karl-Heinz Böhm, Ursula Strätz
'Beautiful. It renders the book as fully and texturally as could be possible in 140 minutes, and it's a work, in and of itself, intrinsically cinematic.' – *Stanley Kauffmann*

The Efficiency Expert: see *Spotswood*

L'Effrontée: see *The Impudent Girl*

The Egg and I *
US 1947 104m bw
U-I (Chester Erskine)
A city couple try to become gentleman farmers.
Mild, pleasant comedy notable chiefly for introducing a hillbilly couple, Ma and Pa Kettle, who went on, in the personae of Main and Kilbride, to make several later features. (See under Kettles.)
w Chester Erskine, Fred Finklehoffe *novel* Betty Macdonald *d* Chester Erskine *ph* Milton Krasner *m* Frank Skinner
☆ Claudette Colbert, Fred MacMurray, *Marjorie Main, Percy Kilbride*, Louise Allbritton, Richard Long, Billy House, Ida Moore, Donald MacBride
'Marjorie Main, in an occasional fit of fine, wild comedy, picks the show up and brandishes it as if she were wringing its neck. I wish to God she had.' – *James Agee*

Marjorie Main

Egon Schiele: Excess and Punishment
(dubbed)
Austria/Germany/France 1980 90m colour
Gamma/Stand'Art/Cineproduction/Profinanz/Jadran/V-Film/Dieter Geissler
original title: *Egon Schiele: Exzess und Bestrafung*
In prison awaiting trial for corrupting a minor, an artist recalls his past, while his model attempts to obtain his release.
Uninvolving biopic of the Austrian Expressionist artist Egon Schiele (1890–1918), which gives the impression that he never painted anything other than naked women.
w Herbert Vesely, Leo Tichat *d* Herbert Vesely *ph* Rudolf Blahaček *m* Brian Eno, Anton von Webern, Felix Mendelssohn-Bartholdy
☆ Mathieu Carrière, Jane Birkin, Nina Fallenstein, Kristina Van Eyck, Marcel Ophuls
† The British video release runs for 81m.

Egymásra Nézve: see *Another Way*

'10,965 pyramids! 5,337 dancing girls! One million swaying bulrushes! 802 sacred bulls!'
The Egyptian *
US 1954 140m DeLuxe Cinemascope
TCF (Darryl F. Zanuck)
In ancient Egypt an abandoned baby grows up to be physician to the pharaoh.
More risible than reasonable, sounding more like a parody than the real thing, this pretentious epic from a bestseller flounders helplessly between its highlights but has moments of good humour and makes an excellent example of the pictures they don't make 'em like any more.
w Philip Dunne, Casey Robinson *novel* Mika Waltari *d* Michael Curtiz *ph* Leon Shamroy *m* Bernard Herrmann, Alfred Newman *ad* Lyle Wheeler, George W. Davis
☆ Edmund Purdom, Victor Mature, *Peter Ustinov*, Bella Darvi, Gene Tierney, Michael Wilding, Jean Simmons, Judith Evelyn, Henry Daniell, John Carradine, Carl Benton Reid
'The novel ... supplied the reader with enough occurrences and customs of Akhnaton's time ... to hide some of the more obvious contrivances of the story. The film does not do this.' – *Carolyn Harrow, Films in Review*
Leon Shamroy

Die Ehe der Maria Braun: see *The Marriage of Maria Braun*

Ehi, Amico ... C'è Sabata, Hai Chiuso: see *Sabata*

The Eiger Sanction *
US 1975 125m Technicolor Panavision
Universal/Malpaso (Jennings Lang)
An art teacher returns to the CIA as an exterminator, and finds himself in a party climbing the Eiger.
Silly spy melodrama with some breathtaking mountain sequences.
w Warren B. Murphy, Hal Dresner, Rod Whitaker *novel* Trevanian *d* Clint Eastwood *ph* Frank Stanley, John Cleare, Jeff Schoolfield, Peter Pilafian, Pete White *m* John Williams
☆ Clint Eastwood, George Kennedy, Vonetta McGee, Jack Cassidy, Heidi Bruhl, Thayer David
'All the villains have been constructed from prefabricated Bond models.' – *Richard Combs*

'You can't prepare for where the truth will take you.'
8mm
US 1999 119m Technicolor Super 35
Columbia (Gavin Polone, Judy Hofflund, Joel Schumacher)
A wealthy widow discovers among her dead husband's possessions a videocassette showing the apparent murder of a teenage girl, and hires an investigator to find out the girl's identity.
A gloating, exploitative thriller about pornography in Los Angeles; it develops a hectoring tone that cannot be justified by script, direction or acting.
w Andrew Kevin Walker *d* Joel Schumacher *ph* Robert Elswit *m* Mychael Danna *pd* Gary Wissner *ed* Mark Stevens
☆ Nicolas Cage, Joaquin Phoenix, James Gandolfini, Peter Stormare, Anthony Heald, Chris Bauer, Catherine Keener, Myra Carter, Amy Morton
'Loathsome crap ... Coming generations of late-night video hounds may recognize it, along with Oliver Stone's *The Doors*, as one of the most unintentionally hilarious attempts at serious filmmaking in cinema history.' – *Andrew O'Hehir, Salon*
'Delves into the perverse underworld of the pornography business, shocking audiences with the realization that sex and violence can be so dull.' – *Janet Maslin, New York Times*

Eight and a Half ****
Italy 1963 138m bw
Cineriz (Angelo Rizzoli)
original title: *Otto e Mezzo*
A successful film director on the verge of a nervous breakdown has conflicting fantasies about his life.
A Fellini self-portrait in which anything goes.
w Federico Fellini, Ennio Flaiano, Tullio Pinelli, Brunello Rondi *d Federico Fellini* *ph* Gianni di Venanzo *m* Nino Rota *ad* Piero Gherardi
☆ *Marcello Mastroianni*, Claudia Cardinale, Anouk Aimée, Sandra Milo, Rossella Falk, Barbara Steele, Madeleine Lebeau
'The whole may add up to a magnificent folly, but it is too singular, too candid, too vividly and insistently alive to be judged as being in any way diminishing.' – *Peter John Dyer, MFB*
'Fellini's intellectualizing is not even like dogs dancing; it is not done well, nor does it surprise us that it is done at all. It merely palls on us, and finally appals us.' – *John Simon*
'A de luxe glorification of creative crisis, visually arresting but in some essential way conventional-minded.' – *Pauline Kael, 70s*
best foreign film
script; direction

'When sexual desire becomes an obsession, it's every man for himself'
Eight and a Half Women *
Netherlands/GB/Luxembourg/Germany 1999 121m colour
Pathé/Woodline/Movie Masters/Continent (Kees Kasander)
A wealthy English businessman, mourning the death of his wife, goes with his son on a voyage of sexual discovery in Kyoto and Geneva.
A stylised and visually and verbally witty movie, in which women become toys for two rich men to play with; sexual relationships are reduced to commodities to be bargained over and paid for.
wd Peter Greenaway *ph* Sacha Vierny, Reinier Van Brummelen *pd* Wilbert Van Dorp, Emi Wada *ed* Elmer Leupen
☆ John Standing, Matthew Delamerie, Vivian Wu, Shizuka Inoh, Barbara Sarafian, Kirina Mano, Toni Collette, Amanda Plummer, Natacha Amal, Manna Fujiwara, Polly Walker
'I was left to conclude that what Greenaway is really expressing is the shame of a filmmaker who longs, in his guilty heart, to make a dirty movie, and who must then kill that impulse by cold-showering his audience into an unholy stupor.' – *Owen Gleiberman, Entertainment Weekly*

Eight Crazy Nights: see *Adam Sandler's Eight Crazy Nights*

8 Femmes: see *8 Women*

'A Mindless Comedy.'
8 Heads in a Duffell Bag
US 1997 95m DeLuxe
Rank/Orion (Brad Krevoy, Steve Stabler, John Bertolli)
A gangster attempts to find his bag, containing the heads of his boss's enemies, after it is mixed up with one belonging to a medical student.
Gruesome and tasteless comedy that hasn't even the saving grace of being amusing.
wd Tom Schulman *ph* Adam Holender *m* Andrew Gross *pd* Paul Peters *ed* David Holden
☆ Joe Pesci, Kristy Swanson, David Spade, George Hamilton, Dyan Cannon, Andy Comeau, Todd Luiso
'A charmless mess.' – *Richard Williams, Guardian*
'About as funny as being a guest at the St Valentine's Day Massacre.' – *Philip French, Observer*

'Do you hate spiders? Do you really hate spiders? Well they don't like you either.'
Eight Legged Freaks *
US 2002 99m Technicolor
Warner/Village Roadshow/NPV/Electric Entertainment (Dean Devlin, Bruce Berman)
Contaminated by biochemical waste, giant spiders threaten an isolated Arizona mining town.
Slickly made, old-fashioned exploitation movie with a leavening of humour.
w Jesse Alexander, Ellory Elkayem, Randy Kornfield *d* Ellory Elkayem *ph* John Bartley *m* John Ottman *pd* Charles Breen *ed* David J. Siegel *sp* Karen E. Goulekas, Thomas Dadras; CFX
☆ David Arquette (Chris), Kari Wuhrer (Sam), Scott Terra (Mike), Scarlett Johansson (Ashley), Doug E. Doug (Harlan), Rick Overton (Deputy Pete), Leon Rippy (Wade)
'Instantly disposable, artistically worthless, expertly crafted trash.' – *Christopher Tookey, Daily Mail*
'Just what the average 12-year-old boy wants from for his multiplex dollars.' – *Dennis Harvey, Variety*

Eight Men Out ***
US 1988 119m colour
Rank/Orion (Sarah Pillsbury, Midge Sandford)
In 1919 members of the great Chicago White Sox baseball team take bribes to lose the World Series.
Absorbing drama, excellently filmed, with good ensemble acting.
w John Sayles *book* Eliot Asinof *d* John Sayles *ph* Robert Richardson *m* Mason Daring *pd* Nora Chavooshian *ed* John Tintori
☆ John Cusack, Clifton James, Michael Lerner, Christopher Lloyd, John Mahoney, Charlie Sheen, David Strathairn, D. B. Sweeney

'Every moment is another chance.'
8 Mile **
US/Germany 2002 110m DeLuxe
Universal/Imagine (Brian Grazer, Curtis Hanson, Jimmy Iovine)
A poor white boy overcomes obstacles and gains respect by winning a rap contest.
Successful attempt to make a rapper into a movie star with a gritty, semi-autobiographical drama; in the process, though, Eminem has been tamed.
w Scott Silver *d* Curtis Hanson *ph* Rodrigo Prieto *m* Eminem *pd* Philip Messina *ed* Jay Rabinowitz, Craig Kitson
☆ Eminem (Jimmy Smith Jnr), Kim Basinger (Stephanie), Brittany Murphy (Alex), Mekhi Phifer (Future), Evan Jones (Cheddar Bob), Omar Benson Miller (Sol George)
'The rough power, as well as the humor and sensitivity, of pop phenom Eminem is delivered intact.' – *Todd McCarthy, Variety*
'Because it rejects easy victories, this may be one of the few inspirational movies that could actually inspire someone, somewhere, sometime.' – *Richard Shickel, Time*
song 'Lose Yourself' (*m* Eminem, Jeff Bass, Luis Resto *l* Eminem)

8 Million Ways to Die
US 1986 115m bw
Tri-Star/PSO (Steve Roth)
An alcoholic ex-cop tries to discover the killer of a prostitute who had asked him to protect her.
Dreary thriller of redemption from the low life; its pace is numbingly slow, despite the insistent score trying to impose a faster rhythm.
w Oliver Stone, David Lee Henry *novel* Lawrence Block *d* Hal Ashby *ph* Stephen H. Burum *m* James Newton Howard *pd* Michael Haller *ed* Stuart Pappé, Robert Lawrence
☆ Jeff Bridges, Rosanna Arquette, Alexandra Paul, Andy Garcia, Randy Brooks

Eight O'Clock Walk
GB 1953 87m bw
British Lion/George King
A young barrister proves a taxi driver innocent of murder.
Minor-league courtroom stuff, an adequate time-passer.
w Katherine Strueby, Guy Morgan *story* Jack Roffey, Gordon Harbord *d* Lance Comfort *ph* Brendan Stafford *m* George Melachrino
☆ Richard Attenborough, Derek Farr, Cathy O'Donnell, Ian Hunter, Maurice Denham, Bruce Seton, Harry Welchman

Eight on the Lam
US 1966 107m DeLuxe
United Artists/Hope Enterprises (Bill Lawrence)
GB title: *Eight on the Run*
A bank teller is suspected of embezzlement and goes on the run with his seven children.
Feeble comedy punctuated by even feebler chases; the star had lost his comic character.
w Albert E. Lewin, Burt Styler, Bob Fisher, Arthur Marx *d* George Marshall *ph* Alan Stensvold *m* George Romanis
☆ Bob Hope, Phyllis Diller, Jonathan Winters, Shirley Eaton, Jill St John

Eight on the Run: see *Eight on the Lam*

'The sport made him a Legend. His heart made him a Hero.'
8 Seconds
US 1994 105m Film House colour
First Independent/New Line/Jersey Films (Michael Shamberg)
The former world bull-riding champion wins back his title and his wife after losing both to booze.
Based on the life of Lane Frost, this is a mundane biopic of limited interest.
w Monte Merrick *d* John G. Avildsen *ph* Victor Hammer *m* Bill Conti *pd* William J. Cassidy *ed* J. Douglas Seelig
☆ Luke Perry, Stephen Baldwin, James Rebhorn, Red Mitchell, Ronnie Claire Edwards, Linden Ashby, Cynthia Geary, Carrie Snodgress
'Never more than occasionally diverting, and in spite of some spirited playing is strictly for Luke Perry fans and rodeo nuts.' – *Anwar Brett, Film Review*

8 Women **
France 2001 colour
UGC/Fidelite/France 2/Mars (Olivier Delbosc, Marc Missonnier)
original title: *8 Femmes*
In a house cut off by a snow storm, a man's family try to discover which of them was responsible for his death.
Highly artificial, witty, enjoyable pastiche of a country house murder mystery, with bravura performances from its stellar cast., representing four generations of French acting, who burst into song at unexpected moments.
w François Ozon, Marina de Van *play* Robert Thomas *d* François Ozon *ph* Jeanne Lapoirie *m* Krishna Levy *pd* Arnaud de Moleron *ed* Laurence Bawedin
☆ Catherine Deneuve (Gaby), Isabelle Huppert (Augustine), Emmanuelle Béart (Louise), Fanny Ardant (Pierrette), Virginie Ledoyen (Suzon), Danielle Darrieux (Mamy), Ludivine Sagnier (Catherine), Firmine Richard (Mme Chanel)
'Indefensible, cynical, even grotesque; it is also pure – that is to say innocent and uncorrupted – fun.' – *A. O. Scott, New York Times*

1871
GB 1989 100m Metrocolor
ICA/Looseyard/Film Four/La Sept/Palawood/Animatografo (Stewart Richards)
An Irish rebel, in love with an actress-cum-prostitute whom he is forced to share with an English aristocrat and spy, takes part in the doomed Paris Commune of 1871.
Blinkered and fussy look at a failed revolution.
w Terry James, James Leahy, Ken McMullen *d* Ken McMullen *ph* Elso Roque *m* Barrie Guard *pd* Paul Cheetham *ed* William Diver
☆ Roshan Seth, John Lynch, Timothy Spall, Alexandre de Sousa, Ian McNeice, Alan Braine,

Maria João Toscano, Maria de Medeiros, Ana Padrao, Jacqueline Dankworth

'Another melancholy example of rigid radicalism lacking mainstream and popular sophistication.' – *Raymond Durgnat, Sight and Sound*

'Has all the elements of terrific television: romance, revolution, murder, a good cast and top-notch production values.' – *Variety*

18 Again!
US 1988 100m DeLuxe
Entertainment/New World (Walter Coblenz)

After a car crash, the mind of an 81-year-old grandfather is switched into the body of his 18-year-old grandson.
Feeblest of the body-swap cycle of films, with little to entertain.
w Josh Goldstein, Jonathan Prince *d* Paul Flaherty *ph* Stephen M. Katz *m* Billy Goldenberg *pd* Dena Roth *ed* Danford B. Greene
☆ George Burns, Charlie Schlatter, Tony Roberts, Anita Morris, Miriam Flynn, Jennifer Runyon, Red Buttons

'The Crow Flies. The Clock Strikes. And the Devil is Due.'
The Eighteenth Angel
US 1997 85m DeLuxe
Rysher (William Hart, Douglas Curtis)

An Italian sect of devil worshippers, who need eighteen beautiful women to help bring about the return of Satan, make as their final choice the daughter of an American academic.
Supernatural thriller that, with its subpolot of genetic experiments, attempts to be topical but fails to rise above mediocrity.
w David Seltzer *d* William Bindley *ph* Thomas E. Ackerman *m* Starr Parodi, Jeff Eden Fair *pd* Stefano Maria Ortolani *ed* William Hoy *sp* visual fx: Jon Townley *cos* Ornella Campanale
☆ Christopher McDonald (Hugh Stanton), Rachael Leigh Cook (Lucy Stanton), Stanley Tucci (Todd Stanton), Wendy Crewson (Nora Stanton), Maximilian Schell (Father Simeon), Cosimo Fusco (Florian)

The Eighth Day *
France 1996 114m colour
Polygram/Pan-Européene/Home Made/TF1/RTL/TVI/Working Title/DA (Philippe Godeau)

original title: *Le Huitième Jour*
A salesman brefriends a young runaway with Downs syndrome.
Accomplished and sentimental comedy, with an unpleasant shock ending, of one man's redemption, in which emotional manipulation predominates.
wd Jaco Van Dormael *ph* Walther Van Ende *m* Pierre Van Dormael *ad* Hubert Pouille *ed* Susana Rossberg
☆ Daniel Auteuil, Pascal Duquenne, Miou-Miou, Isabelle Sadoyan, Henri Garcin, Michele Maes

'The result is a European film aiming at sophistication that becomes more and more like a Hollywood epic about idiots savants.' – *Derek Malcolm, Guardian*

† Daniel Auteuil and Pascal Duquenne shared the best actor award at the 1996 Cannes Film Festival.

84 Charing Cross Road **
GB 1986 97m Rank Colour
Columbia/Brooksfilm (Geoffrey Helman)

A New York woman conducts a long correspondence with an antiquarian bookseller in London.
Pleasant picturization of a now famous book which had already been seen on TV and stage.
w Hugh Whitemore *book* Helene Hanff *d David Jones ph* Brian West *m* George Fenton *pd* Eileen Diss, Edward Pisoni
☆ *Anne Bancroft*, Anthony Hopkins, Judi Dench, Maurice Denham, Jean de Baer, Eleanor David
Anne Bancroft

84 Charlie Mopic *
US 1989 95m colour
Charlie Mopic Company (Michael Nolin)

An army cameraman and an inexperienced officer accompany a reconnaissance patrol in Vietnam.
A documentary-style account of war as it affects the individual, as seen from the subjective viewpoint of the cameraman.
wd Patrick Duncan *ph* Alan Casco *m* Donovan *ad* Douglas Dick *ed* Stephen Purvis
☆ Jonathan Emerson, Nicholas Cascone, Jason Tomlins, Christopher Burgard, Glenn Morshower, Richard Brooks, Byron Thames

80,000 Suspects *
GB 1963 113m bw Cinemascope
Rank/Val Guest
A smallpox epidemic terrorizes the city of Bath.
Predictable melodrama which adequately passes the time.
wd Val Guest *novel The Pillars of Midnight* by Elleston Trevor *ph* Arthur Grant *m* Stanley Black *ad* Geoffrey Tozer *ed* Bill Lenny
☆ Claire Bloom, Richard Johnson, Yolande Donlan, Cyril Cusack, Michael Goodliffe, Mervyn Johns, Kay Walsh, Basil Dignam, Ray Barrett

Einmal Ku'damm und Zurück: see *Girl In a Boot*

Él **
Mexico 1952 91m bw
Nacional Film (Oscar Dancigers)
aka: *This Strange Passion*
aka: *Torments*
A middle-aged aristocrat marries a beautiful young girl and falls victim to insane jealousy.
A tragi-comic case history with chilling and memorable details; not one of its director's great works, but an engaging minor one.
w Luis Buñuel, Luis Alcoriza *novel Pensamientos* by Mercedes Pinto *d Luis Buñuel ph* Gabriel Figueroa *m* Luis Hernandez Breton
☆ *Arturo de Cordova*, Delia Garces, Luis Beristain, Aurora Walker

El Chucho, Quién Sabe?: see *A Bullet for the General*

El Cid *
US/Spain 1961 184m Super Technirama
Samuel Bronston

A legendary 11th-century hero drives the Moors from Spain.
Endless glum epic with splendid action sequences as befits the high budget.
w Fredric M. Frank, Philip Yordan, Ben Barzman *d* Anthony Mann *ph* Robert Krasker *m* Miklos Rozsa
☆ Charlton Heston, Sophia Loren, Raf Vallone, Genevieve Page, John Fraser, Gary Raymond, Herbert Lom, Hurd Hatfield, Massimo Serato, Andrew Cruickshank, Michael Hordern, Douglas Wilmer, Frank Thring

'A Lone Ranger liberation tale.' – *Judith Crist*

† Ben Barzman, a screenwriter who was blacklisted in the 50s, had his name restored to the credits in 1999.

Miklos Rozsa; song 'The Falcon and the Dove' (*m* Miklos Rozsa, *ly* Paul Francis Webster)

El Condor
US 1970 102m Technicolor
National General/Carthay Continental (André de Toth)

An escaped convict and a con man seek a fortune in gold believed to be hidden in a fortress in the Mexican desert.
Blood and guts Western with few moments of interest.
w Larry Cohen, Steven Carabatsos *d* John Guillermin *ph* Henri Persin *m* Maurice Jarre
☆ Jim Brown, Lee Van Cleef, Patrick O'Neal, Marianna Hill, Iron Eyes Cody, Elisha Cook Jnr

'The kind of fun you can find at your friendly neighbourhood abattoir.' – *Judith Crist, 1977*

'The big one with the big two!'
El Dorado *
US 1967 126m Technicolor
Paramount/Laurel (Howard Hawks)

A gunfighter and a drunken sheriff tackle a villainous cattle baron.
Easy-going, semi-somnolent, generally likeable but disappointing Western … an old man's movie all round.
w Leigh Brackett *novel The Stars in Their Courses* by Harry Joe Brown *d* Howard Hawks *ph* Harold Rosson *m* Nelson Riddle *ad* Hal Pereira, Carl Anderson *ed* John Woodcock
☆ John Wayne (Cole Thornton), Robert Mitchum (Sheriff J. B. Harrah), James Caan (Mississippi), Charlene Holt (Maudie), Michele Carey (Josephine MacDonald), Ed Asner (Bart Jason), Arthur Hunnicutt (Bull), R. G. Armstrong (Kevin MacDonald), Paul Fix (Dr Miller), Christopher George (Nelse McLeod)

'A rumbustious lament for the good days of the bad old west.' – *Tom Milne*

'A claustrophobic, careless and cliché-ridden thing, wavering constantly between campy self-deprecation and pretentious pomposity.' – *Richard Schickel*

'Wayne and Mitchum, parodying themselves while looking exhausted.' – *Pauline Kael, 70s*

'The Son of Rio Bravo Rides Again.' – *Leigh Brackett*

† Harry Joe Brown wanted his novel removed from the credits because the film bore little resemblance to his book.

El Dorado *
France/Spain 1988 123m colour 'Scope
Palace/Iberoamericana/Chrysalide/UGC-Top1/FR3/Canal Plus (Victor Albarran)

Conquistadores set out from Peru to find El Dorado, the fabled land of gold.
Ambitious but flawed epic, handicapped by its ponderous approach.
d Carlos Saura *ph* Teo Escamilla *md* Alejandro Masso *ad* Terry Pritchard *ed* Pedro del Rey
☆ Omero Antonutti, Eusebio Poncela, Lambert Wilson, Gabriela Roel, Jose Sancho, Feodor Atkine, Patxi Bisquert, Francisco Algora, Francisco Merino

El Greco
Italy/France 1964 94m Eastmancolor Cinemascope
(TCF) Artistiche Internazionale/Arco-Films du Siècle (Alfredo Bini, Mel Ferrer)

In the 16th century, a Greek-Italian painter finds favour in Spain and falls in love with an aristocratic girl.
Heavily embellished history with a few good scenes.
w Guy Elmes, Massimo Franciosa, Luigi Magni, Luciano Salce *d* Luciano Salce *ph* Leonida Barboni *m* Ennio Morricone
☆ Mel Ferrer, Rosanna Schiaffino, Adolfo Celi, Angel Aranda

El Mariachi **
US 1992 81m Technicolor
Columbia/Los Hooligans (Robert Rodriguez, Carlos Gallardo)

In a small Mexican town a wandering musician with his guitar-case is mistaken for a hitman.
Witty, visually inventive low-budget thriller, cleverly taking apart the conventions of Westerns and reassembling them in a quirky and individual way.
wd Robert Rodriguez ph Robert Rodriguez *m* Marc Trujillo, Alvaro Rodriguez, Chris Knudson, Cecilio Rodriguez, Eric Guthrie *ed* Robert Rodriguez
☆ Carlos Gallardo, Consuelo Gómez, Reinol Martinez, Peter Marquardt, Jaime de Hoyos, Ramiro Gómez, Jesus Lopez, Luis Baro

'Uses a broad genre to make subtle points: about change and tradition, about Mexicans and Chicanos with separate values and voices. Despite its superficial sense of low-budget genre-as-usual, this project offers something truly new for American film.' – *Sight and Sound*

'Has an exhilarating rawness that works for, rather than against it, its kinetic pacing, visceral editing and bravura camerawork revealing the presence of a director with unbridled visual panache. A minor masterpiece.' – *Empire*

† The film, by a 24-year-old director born in Texas, is said to have cost $7,000 (coming in $2,000 under budget) to shoot in 14 days and became the cheapest movie to be given international distribution by Columbia. He was signed to remake the film with a budget of $6m.
†† It was released on DVD together with its bigger budget remake *Desperado* (qv).

El Paso
US 1949 92m Cinecolor
Paramount/Pine-Thomas
After the civil war, a young lawyer brings a corrupt township to its senses by learning to outshoot the badmen.
Lively, fairly tough Western with all the familiar ingredients.
wd Lewis R. Foster *ph* Ellis Carter *m* Darrell Calker
☆ John Payne, Gail Russell, Dick Foran, Sterling Hayden, George 'Gabby' Hayes

El Topo *
Mexico 1971 124m Eastmancolor
Producciones Panic

An evil gunfighter rides through the old west and has various encounters, after which he sets himself on fire.
Curious, perverse, powerful surrealist allegory which takes in the life of Christ and the fate of man among some exceedingly unpleasant violence. A treat for connoisseurs of the unpleasantly absurd.
ph Raphael Corkidi *md* Nacho Mendez *ed* Lilia Lupercio *wd/m/ad Alejandro Jodorowsky*
☆ Alejandro Jodorowsky (El Topo), Brontis Jodorowsky (Brontis as a child), Mara Lorenzio (Mara), David Silva (The Colonel), Paula Roma (Woman in Black), Hector Martinez (First Master), Juan José Gurrola (Second Master), Victor Fosado (Third Master), Agustin Izunza (Fourth Master), Robert John (Brontis as a man)

'Reading. Writing. Revenge.'
Election ***
US 1999 103m DeLuxe Super 35
Paramount/MTV/Bonafide (Albert Berger, Ron Yerxa, David Gale, Keith Samples)

The star pupil at a Midwest high school is determined to become president of the student government; a disgruntled teacher is determined that she should fail.
Witty, inventive satire that, although given a high-school setting, makes telling points about the politics and underhand methods involved in all kinds of power struggles.
w Alexander Payne, Jim Taylor novel Tom Perrotta *d Alexander Payne ph* James Glennon *m* Rolfe Kent *pd* Jane Ann Stewart *ed* Kevin Tent
☆ Matthew Broderick (Jim McAllister), *Reese Witherspoon* (Tracy Flick), Chris Klein (Paul Metzler), Jessica Campbell (Tammy Metzler), Mark Harelik (Dave Novotny), Phil Reeves (Walt Hendricks), Molly Hagan (Diane McAllister), Delaney Driscoll (Linda Novotny), Colleen Camp (Judith R. Flick)

'If Billy Wilder had been assigned to make a teen comedy, he might well have come up with a film as sour and witty as this.' – *Geoffrey Macnab, Sight and Sound*

'Pertinent, fiendishly funny… A modern classic.' – *Peter Bradshaw, Guardian*

script (Alexander Payne, Jim Taylor)

'He's a good cop on a big bike on a bad road!'
Electra Glide in Blue *
US 1973 113m DeLuxe Panavision
UA/James William Guercio/Rupert Hitzig

A small-town motor-cycle cop becomes disillusioned.
Agreeable desert melodrama in the wake of Easy Rider, *freshly observed with mordant humour, marred by a fashionable downbeat ending.*
w Robert Boris ph Conrad Hall m James William Guercio *d/m* James William Guercio
☆ *Robert Blake*, Billy Green Bush, Mitch Ryan, Jeannine Riley, Elisha Cook Jnr, Royal Dano

'The most unusual triangle in the history of love. A boy, a girl, and a computer.'
Electric Dreams
GB 1984 112m Metrocolor
Virgin/MGM-UA (Rusty Lemorande, Larry de Waay)

A computer becomes jealous of its owner's love affair.
Gruesomely extended revue sketch which totally fails to develop its characters and offers instead a very sparing amount of cleverness.
w Rusty Lemorande *d* Steve Barron *ph* Alex Thomson *m* Giorgio Moroder *pd* Richard MacDonald

☆ Lenny von Dohlen, Virginia Madsen, Maxwell Caulfield, Bud Cort, Don Fellows

The Electric Horseman *
US 1979 120m Technicolor Panavision
Columbia/Universal (Ray Stark/Wildwood)

A horseman advertising breakfast cereal in Las Vegas suddenly tires of it all and heads for the wilderness.
Pretty but slightly sheepish moral saga with too much technique for its own good.
w Robert Garland *d* Sydney Pollack *ph* Owen Roizman *m* Dave Grusin *pd* Stephen Grimes
☆ Robert Redford, Jane Fonda, Valerie Perrine, Willie Nelson, John Saxon, Nicolas Coster
'Overlong, talky and diffused.' – *Variety*

The Electric Man: see *Man Made Monster*

Electric Moon
GB 1991 103m Technicolor
Winstone/Grapevine Media/Channel 4/Times Television (Sundeep Singh Bedi)
Rivalry between an Indian hotelier, a former Maharajah, and the director of the national park in which the hotel is situated causes problems for a group of Western tourists.
Uncertain comedy that mocks the expectations and preconceptions of tourists in India.
w Arundhati Roy *d* Pradip Krishen *ph* Giles Nuttgens *m* Basaya Khan, Zakab Khan, Deepak Castelino, Sanjee Saith *pd* Arundhati Roy *ed* Pradip Krishen
☆ Roshan Seth, Naseeruddin Shah, Leela Naidu, Gerson Da Cunha, Raghubir Yadav, Alice Spivak, Frances Helm, James Fleet, Francesca Brill
'Loses its shine early on. This amiable, good-humored satire on cultural stereotypes on both sides of the Indian tourist fence is too low-voltage to create much of a theatrical buzz.' – *Variety*

Element of Crime
Denmark 1984 104m Eastmancolor
Per Holst (Lars von Trier)

original title: *Forbrydelsens Element*
In Cairo, a retired policeman recalls how he tried to think himself into the mind of a killer while investigating the murders of young girls.
Bizarre English language film noir from a Danish director, which may account for its incomprehensible narrative, with Elphick moodily wandering in the wet around an apparantly war-ravaged Europe.
w Niels Vørsel, Lars von Trier (English translation by William Quarshie, Steven Wakelam *d* Lars von Trier *ph* Tom Elling *m* Henrik Blichmann, Mogens Dam, Bo Holten *pd* Peter Høimark *ed* Tomas Gislason
☆ Michael Elphick (Fisher), Esmond Knight (Osborne), Kim (MeMe Lai), Jerold Wells (Kramer), Ahmed El Shenawi (Therapist), Astrid Henning-Jensen (House Keeper), Jànos Herskó (Coroner), Lars von Trier (Schmuck of Ages)

Elementary School **
Czechoslovakia 1991 97m colour
Barrandov (Jaromir Lukas)
original title: *Obecna Skola*
Episodes in the life of a 10-year-old boy at home and with his unruly school-friends, just after the end of the Second World War.
A gently comic, nostalgic, semi-autobiographical movie; it has a quiet charm, enhanced by its romantic visual style.
w Zdenek Sverak *d* Jan Sverak *ph* F. A. Brabec *m* Jiri Traxler *ad* Vladimir Labsky, Gabriella Kubenove *ed* Alois Fisarek
☆ Jan Triska, Rudolf Hrusinsky, Zdenek Sverak, Libuse Safrankova, Vaclav Jakoubek, Daniela Kolarova, Boleslav Polivka, Petr Cepek
foreign-language film

Eleni
US 1985 117m colour
CBS/Vanoff/Pick/Gage

A journalist back in Greece investigates his mother's death in the civil war of the late 1940s.
Deadeningly boring true life drama with flashbacks which fail to communicate the author's sense of revenge.
w Steve Tesich *book* Nicholas Gage *d* Peter Yates *ph* Billy Williams *m* Bruce Smeaton *pd* Roy Walker *ed* Ray Lovejoy
☆ Kate Nelligan, John Malkovich, Linda Hunt, Oliver Cotton, Ronald Pickup, Rosalie Crutchley
'As lofty in ambition as it is deficient in accomplishment.' – *Variety*

Elenya *
GB 1992 82m colour
Frankfurter Film/S4C/BFI/Ffilmian/ZDF (Heidi Ulmke)

An elderly woman remembers how, as a young girl living in Wales in 1940, she tried to hide and care for a German pilot she discovered wounded in a wood.
Pleasant low-budget feature, but lacking in any particular individuality or originality.
wd Steve Gough *ph* Patrick Duval *m* Simon Fisher Turner *pd* Hayden Pearce *ed* Alan Smithee
☆ Margaret John, Pascale Delafouge Jones, Seirol Tomos, Sue Jones Davies, Iago Wynn Jones, Lilo Milward, Catrin Llwyd, Edward Elwyn Jones, Ioan Meredith, Klaus Behrendt
'Very quiet, acutely sensitive in some areas and a debut from which much could spring.' – *Derek Malcolm, Guardian*

The Elephant and the Bicycle **
Cuba 1995 85m colour/bw
ICAIC/Channel 4 (Rafael Rey)
original title: *El Elefante y la Bicicleta*
In 1925, a former prisoner returns to his island village with a movie projector and a film of Robin Hood which, as the villagers watch it every night, becomes a film about their own oppression by the local landowner.
A charming, sophisticated fable of the transforming power of art, or the ability of people to read into it what they want; in one witty scene, the villagers, in critical mode, debate whether cinema should be escapist or reflect reality – this manages to do both.
w Eliseo Alberto Diego, Juan Carlos Tabío *d* Juan Carlos Tabío, Rapi Diego *ph* Julio Valdes *m* Jose Vitier *ad* Onelio Larralde *ed* Lina Baniela
☆ Luis Alberto Garcia, Lilian Vega, Martha Farre, Raul Pomares, Daisy Granados, Adolfo Llaurado, Patricio Wood, Fidelio Torres

Elephant Boy **
GB 1937 91m bw
London Films (Alexander Korda)

In India, a boy elephant keeper helps government conservationists.
Documentary drama which seemed fresh and extraordinary at the time, has dated badly since, but did make an international star of Sabu.
w John Collier, Akos Tolnay, Marcia de Sylva *novel Toomai of the Elephants* by Rudyard Kipling *d Robert Flaherty, Zoltan Korda ph* Osmond Borradaile *m* John Greenwood *ed* William Hornbeck, Charles Crichton
☆ Sabu, Walter Hudd, Allan Jeayes, W. E. Holloway, Wilfrid Hyde-White
'Should draw anywhere in the world.' – *Variety*
'This is a fractured film, its skeleton is awry, its bones stick out through the skin.' – *Richard Griffith, 1941*
'It has gone the way of *Man of Aran*: enormous advance publicity, director out of touch with the press for months, rumours of great epics sealed in tins, and then the disappointing diminutive achievement.' – *Graham Greene*

Un Eléphant ça Trompe Enormément: see *Pardon Mon Affaire*

Elephant Gun: see *Nor the Moon by Night*

'It's not what you say, it's how you say it!'
Elephant Juice
GB/US 1999 86m Technicolor Panavision
Miramax/Film4/HAL (Sheila Fraser Milne)
After agreeing to help find a partner for their single friend, three couples find their own relationships are less permanent than they thought.
This take on the love-lives of Londoners old enough to know better is both dull and empty of emotion.
w Amy Jenkins *d* Sam Miller *ph* Adrian Wild *m* Tim Atack *pd* Grant Hicks *ed* Elen Pierce Lewis *cos* Jill Taylor
☆ Emmanuelle Béart (Jules), Sean Gallagher (Billy), Daniel Lapaine (Will), Daniela Nardini (Daphne), Mark Strong (Frank), Kimberly Williams (Dodie), Lennie James (Graham), Lee Williams (George)
'But for the odd cuss word and fleeting flash of breast, they might have had a neat coffee commercial on their hands.' – *Peter Bradshaw, Guardian*
'As phony as a three-dollar bill — and about as worthless.' – *Derek Elley, Variety*

The Elephant Man ***
US 1980 124m bw Panavision
EMI/Brooksfilms (Stuart Cornfeld)

In 1884 London, a penniless man deformed by a rare illness is rescued by a doctor from a fairground freak show, and becomes a member of fashionable society.
A curious story which happens to be true; the film sets its scene superbly, has splendid performances and a fascinating make-up. Yet it fails to move quite as it should, perhaps because the central figure is treated as a horrific come-on, like the hunchback of Notre Dame.
w Christopher de Vore, Eric Bergren, David Lynch, from various memoirs *d David Lynch ph* Freddie Francis *m* John Morris *pd* Stuart Craig
☆ *Anthony Hopkins, John Hurt,* John Gielgud, Anne Bancroft, Freddie Jones, Wendy Hiller, Michael Elphick, Hannah Gordon
'If there's a wrong note in this unique movie – in performance, production design, cinematography or anywhere else – I must have missed it.' – *Paul Taylor, Time Out*
'In an age of horror movies this is a film which takes the material of horror and translates it into loving kindness.' – *Dilys Powell, Punch*
best film; screenplay; David Lynch; editing (Anne V. Coates); art direction (Stuart Craig, Bob Cartwright, Hugh Scaife); John Morris; costume design (Patricia Norris); John Hurt
best film; production design; John Hurt

Elephant Walk *
US 1954 103m Technicolor
Paramount (Irving Asher)

The owner of a Ceylon tea plantation takes back an English wife who finds the atmosphere strange and turns to a friendly overseer for comfort.
Echoes of Jane Eyre *and* Rebecca*, with stampeding elephants instead of a mad or dead wife.*
w John Lee Mahin *novel* Robert Standish *d* William Dieterle *ph* Loyal Griggs *m* Franz Waxman
☆ Elizabeth Taylor, Peter Finch, Dana Andrews, Abraham Sofaer
'The climactic elephant stampede's a rouser – if you're still awake.' – *Judith Crist*

Elephants Never Forget: see *Zenobia*

11' 09" 01 September 11 **
France/Iran/Egypt/Bosnia-Herzegovina/Burkina Faso/GB/Mexico/Israel//India/US/Japan 2002 134m colour
Artificial Eye/StudioCanal

Short films by 11 international directors inspired by the terrorist destruction of the World Trade Centre on 11 September 2001. Each film is 9 minutes, 11 seconds and one frame long.
A mixed bag of reactions, ranging from the self-indulgent to the moving. The most effective are Samira Makhmalbaf's, showing an Afghan teacher trying to explain the tragedy to a class of uncomprehending children while their elders build shelters from clay bricks to protect themselves from American bombers, Amos Gitai's account of a TV journalist outraged that her account of a bombing in Tel Aviv has been upstaged, and Ken Loach's remembrance, by a Chilean writer, of September 11, 1973, when a CIA-backed coup overthrew the democractically elected government of Chile, replacing it with a military dictatorship.
Episode 1 *wd* Samira Makhmalbaf with Maryam Karimi
Episode 2 *w* Pierre Uytterhoeven, Claude Lelouch *d* Claude Lelouch with Emmanuelle Laborit, Jerome Horry
Episode 3 *wd* Youssef Chahine with Nour el-Cherif, Ahmed Seif Eldine
Episode 4 *wd* Danis Tanovic with Dzana Pinjo, Aleksandar Seksan
Episode 5 *wd* Idrissa Ouedraogo with Lionel Zizreel Guire, Rene Aime Bassinga
Episode 6 *w* Paul Laverty, Ken Loach, Vladimir Vega *d* Ken Loach with Vladimir Vega
Episode 7 *wd* Alejandro Gonzalez Inarritu
Episode 8 *w* Amos Gitai, Marie-Jose Sanselme *d* Amos Gitai with Keren Mor, Liron Levo
Episode 9 *w* Sabrina Dhawan d Mira Nair with Tanvi Azmi, Kapil Bawa
Episode 10 *wd* Sean Penn with Ernest Borgnine
Episode 11 *w* Daisuke Tengan *d* Shohei Imamura with Tomorowo Taguchi, Kumiko Aso, Akira Emoto
'A bold attempt to define the terrorist attack as a global event, and a global tragedy.' – *Peter Bradshaw, Guardian*

Eleven Harrowhouse *
GB 1974 108m DeLuxe Panavision
TCF/Harrowhouse (Elliott Kastner)

An American diamond merchant is robbed of a valuable jewel, and finds himself in the middle of an ingenious plot.
Amusing caper story marred by sudden changes of mood.
w Jeffrey Bloom *novel* Gerald A. Browne *d* Aram Avakian *ph* Arthur Ibbetson *m* Michael J. Lewis
☆ Charles Grodin, *James Mason,* Trevor Howard, John Gielgud, Candice Bergen, Peter Vaughan, Helen Cherry, Jack Watson, Jack Watling
'This lackadaisical caper comedy is inoffensive, but the comic ideas don't build or erupt, and since the director fails to get any suspense going, it becomes a bumbling and stupid romp.' – *Pauline Kael*

Elinor Norton
US 1935 71m bw
Fox
A wife has a jealous husband and a South American lover.
Underwritten triangle drama which never comes to boiling point.
w Rose Franken, Philip Klein *novel The State versus Elinor Norton* by Mary Roberts Rinehart *d* Hamilton McFadden
☆ Claire Trevor, Gilbert Roland, Hugh Williams, Henrietta Crosman, Norman Foster
'No cast for b.o. and results look mild.' – *Variety*

Elisa *
France 1994 114m colour
Gala/Christian Fechner/Solo/TF1 (Henri Brichetti)

A street-smart teenager, whose mother committed suicide when she was a baby, blames the father who abandoned them for the tragedy and sets out to find him.
A vehicle designed to establish Paradis as film star as well as a singer, in which it succeeds: she is convincing as an amoral flirt, and more interesting than the film itself.
w Jean Becker, Fabrice Carazo *d* Jean Becker *ph* Etienne Becker *m* Zbigniew Preisner *ad* Thérèse Ripaux *ed* Jacques Witta
☆ *Vanessa Paradis,* Gérard Depardieu, Clothilde Courau, Sekkou Sall, Florence Thomassin
'A subtly structured, often whimsical personal odyssey.' – *Empire*
† The title is taken from a song by Serge Gainsbourg, to whom the film is dedicated.

Eliza Fraser
Australia 1976 127m colour
Hexagon (Tim Burstall)
A shipwrecked couple have to live with Aborigines; later she becomes a fairground attraction.
Would-be bawdy historical romp on the lines of Tom Jones*; it seldom works.*
w David Williamson *d* Tim Burstall
☆ Susannah York, Trevor Howard, Noel Ferrier, John Waters, Charles Tingwell

'Declared Illegitimate Aged 3. Tried For Treason Aged 21. Crowned Queen Aged 25.'
'Absolute Power Demands Absolute Loyalty.'

Elizabeth ***
GB 1998 121m colour
Polygram/Channel 4/Working Title (Alison Owen, Eric Fellner, Tim Bevan)

Amid plots and counter-plots, the hatred of her Catholic sister, Queen Mary, and the loss of her lover, Elizabeth survives to become absolute ruler of England.
Fast-moving drama which, while it rearranges historical events, seems accurate in spirit to the political upheavals of the time; against the background of religious persecution and overweening ambitions, it charts Elizabeth's emotional life, as she moves from frightened and passionate girl to a frightening and passionless queen.
w Michael Hirst *d* Shekhar Kapur *ph* Remi Adefarasin *m* David Hirschfelder *pd* John Myhre *ed* Jill Bilcock
☆ *Cate Blanchett, Geoffrey Rush,* Christopher Eccleston, Joseph Fiennes, Richard Attenborough, Fanny Ardant, Kathy Burke, Eric Cantona, James Frain, Vincent Cassel, Daniel Craig, John Gielgud, Angus Deayton, Edward Hardwicke, Terence Rigby
'The very model of a successful historical drama – imposingly beautiful, persuasively resonant, unfailingly entertaining.' – *Richard Williams, Guardian*
'A horror film masquerading as a historical pageant.' – *David Denby, New Yorker*
Jenny Shircore (make-up)
best picture; Cate Blanchett; Remi Adefarasin; David Hirschfelder; John Myhre; Alexandre Byrne (costumes)
best British film; Cate Blanchett; Remi Adefarasin; David Hirschfelder; Jenny Shircore (make-up)

Elizabeth and Essex: see *The Private Lives of Elizabeth and Essex*

Elizabeth of England: see *Drake of England*

Elizabeth the Queen: see *The Private Lives of Elizabeth and Essex*

Ella Cinders **
US 1926 83m approx bw silent
First National

A servant girl wins a trip to Hollywood.
Famous and still pleasing comedy from the comic strip Cinderella in the Movies.
w Frank Griffin, Mervyn Le Roy *d* Alfred E. Green *ph* Arthur Martinelli
☆ Colleen Moore, Lloyd Hughes, Vera Lewis, Doris Baker

Ellen: see *The Second Woman*

Ellery Queen
The debonair detective created by Manfred B. Lee and Frederic Dannay was seen in several unremarkable second features, usually with his secretary Nikki and his police inspector father. The first two were made for Republic, the rest for Columbia.
1935 The Spanish Cape Mystery with Donald Cook
1936 The Mandarin Mystery (Eddie Quillan)
1940 Ellery Queen Master Detective (Ralph Bellamy)
1941 Ellery Queen's Penthouse Mystery, Ellery Queen and the Perfect Crime, Ellery Queen and the Murder Ring (all Bellamy)
1942 A Close Call for Ellery Queen, A Desperate Chance for Ellery Queen, Enemy Agents Meet Ellery Queen (all William Gargan)
In 1971 Peter Lawford starred in a TV pilot, *Don't Look Behind You*, and in 1975 a one-season series starred Jim Hutton. The books, pseudonymously authored by Ellery Queen, were far more popular than any of the movies.

Ellery Queen, Master Detective
US 1940 66m bw
Columbia
Searching for the missing daughter of a dying health food tycoon, Ellery Queen finds the wrong girl and solves the mystery of a murder in a locked room.
A slow-moving mystery, bland and uninteresting, with a great deal of talk and very little action, being mainly confined to a couple of interior sets.
w Eric Taylor *story* Ellery Queen *d* Kurt Neumann *ph* James S. Brown Jnr *m* Lee Zahler *ed* Dwight Caldwell
☆ Ralph Bellamy (Ellery Queen), Margaret Lindsay (Nikki Porter), Charley Grapewin, James Burke, Michael Whalen

Elles n'oublient pas: see *Love in the Strangest Way*

'From a book that shook a nation with its sledgehammer theme ... From a Nobel Prize-winning author ... comes the raging story of the man who used the Holy Bible and broke every rule in it!'

Elmer Gantry **
US 1960 146m Eastmancolor
UA/Bernard Smith

The exploits of an American evangelist in the twenties.
Mainly gripping but overlong exposé of commercialized small-town religion.
wd Richard Brooks novel Sinclair Lewis *ph John Alton m* André Previn *ad Edward Carrere*
☆ *Burt Lancaster,* Jean Simmons, Arthur Kennedy, *Shirley Jones,* Dean Jagger, Edward Andrews, Patti Page, John McIntire
Richard Brooks (as writer); Burt Lancaster; Shirley Jones
best picture; André Previn

Elmer the Great
US 1933 74m bw
Warner (Ray Griffith)
A country hick turns out to be a great baseball hitter.
Best and most farcical version of a play also filmed in 1929 as Fast Company *and in 1939 as* The Cowboy Quarterback.
w Tom Geraghty *play* Ring Lardner, George M. Cohan *d* Mervyn Le Roy
☆ Joe E. Brown, Patricia Ellis, Frank McHugh, Claire Dodd, Sterling Holloway, Emma Dunn, Douglass Dumbrille, Jessie Ralph, J. Carrol Naish

Elmore Leonard's Gold Coast
US 1997 105m DuArt
Paramount/Chanticleer/Mancat/Richard Maynard

In Florida, a petty crook falls for the widow of a Mafia boss, who is being threatened by a hired killer.
Tart, spare thriller, slickly made but underpowered.
w Harley Peyton *novel* Elmore Leonard *d* Peter Weller *ph* Jacek Laskus *m* Peter Harris *pd* Maria Caso *ed* Dean Goodhill
☆ David Caruso, Marg Helgenberger, Jeff Kober, Barry Primus, Wanda de Jesus, Richard Bradford, Rafael Baez, Melissa Raven
† The film was made for cable television.

Éloge De L'Amour
France/Switzerland 2001 98m bw/colour
Optimum/Peripheria

US title: *In Praise of Love*
After his leading actress dies, the author of a work on the subject of love realises he had met her two years before, in discussions about a Hollywood movie of the French resistance.
There are welcome flashes of the Godard of the 60s here, but you have to sit through a great deal of sloganeering and windy philosophising first.
wd Jean-Luc Godard *ph* Christophe Pollock, Julien Hirsch *ed* Raphaele Urtin
☆ Bruno Putzulu (Edgar), Cecile Camp (Elle), Jean Davy (Grandfather), Françoise Verney (Grandmother), Audrey Klebaner (Eglantine), Jeremy Lippman (Perceval), Claude Baigneres (Mr Rosenthal)
'His work over the past 30 years has been incoherent, self-indulgent and barely watchable and *Éloge De L'Amour* is no exception.' – *Philip French, Observer*

Elstree Calling *
GB 1930 95m bw/Pathécolour
Wardour/BIP (John Maxwell)
A film studio mounts a television show.
Slender excuse for an all-star revue which luckily preserves much light entertainment talent of the time.
w Adrian Brunel, Walter C. Mycroft, Val Valentine *d* Adrian Brunel, Alfred Hitchcock, Jack Hulbert, André Charlot, Paul Murray *ph* Claude Friese-Greene *m* Reg Casson, Vivian Ellis, Chick Endor, Ivor Novello, Jack Strachey *ed* Emile de Ruelle, A. C. Hammond
☆ Tommy Handley, Jack Hulbert, Cicely Courtneidge, Will Fyffe, Lily Morris, Teddy Brown, Anna May Wong, Gordon Harker, Donald Calthrop, John Longden, Jameson Thomas, Bobbie Comber

The Elstree Story *
GB 1952 61m bw
ABPC (Gilbert Gunn)
A compilation drawn from 25 years of filmmaking at Elstree Studios.
Highlights include Hitchcock's Number Seventeen; The White Sheik; Piccadilly; Bulldog Drummond; Arms and the Man; The Informer; Blossom Time; *and* Poison Pen. *Commentary and presentation are adequate.*
d Gilbert Gunn *m* Philip Green

The Elusive Pimpernel *
GB 1950 109m Technicolor
BL/London Films (Michael Powell, Emeric Pressburger)

US title: *The Fighting Pimpernel*
A foppish 18th-century London dandy is actually the hero who rescues French aristocrats from the guillotine.
Expensive remake of The Scarlet Pimpernel *which fails to please, apparently because the talents were not congenial to the subject. Interesting detail, though.*
wd Michael Powell, Emeric Pressburger *novel* Baroness Orczy *ph* Christopher Challis *m* Brian Easdale *pd* Hein Heckroth *ed* Reginald Mills
☆ David Niven (Sir Percy Blakeney), Margaret Leighton (Lady Blakeney), Cyril Cusack (Chauvelin), Jack Hawkins (Prince of Wales), David Hutcheson (Lord Anthony Dewhurst), Robert Coote (Sir Andrew ffoulkes), Arlette Marchall (Countess de Tournai), Gérard Nery (Philippe de Tournai), Danielle Godet (Suzanne), Edmond Audran (Armand St. Juste), Charles Victor (Colonel Winterbotham), Eugene Deckers (Captain Merières), David Oxley (Captain Duroc), Patrick Macnee (Hon John Bristow), Terence Alexander (Duke of Dorset)
'The quality of excitement which should carry the film is quite lost. *The Elusive Pimpernel* is highly – often too highly – coloured, and has an artificiality quite different in character from that of the original.' – *Penelope Houston*
'I never thought I should feel inclined to leave a Powell and Pressburger film before the end; but I did here.' – *Richard Mallett, Punch*
'Niven plays the Scarlet Pimpernel with the sheepish lack of enthusiasm of a tone deaf man called upon to sing solo in church. His companions lumber through their parts like schoolboys about to go down with mumps.' – *Daily Express*

Elvira Madigan *
Sweden 1967 95m Eastmancolor
Europa Film (Waldemar Bergendahl)

A married army officer runs off with a tightrope dancer; when they run out of money they live in the woods and finally commit suicide rather than part.
A simple Victorian romantic idyll, based on a true incident; a director's and photographer's piece which entrances the eyes and ears while starving the mind.
ph Jörgen Persson m Mozart *wd/ed* Bo Widerberg
☆ Thommy Berggren, Pia Degermark

Elvira, Mistress of the Dark
US 1988 96m CFI color
Entertainment/New World/NBC/Queen B (Eric Gardner, Mark Pierson)

The hostess of a TV horror show discovers that she has magic powers.
Camp nonsense, limply performed.
w Sam Egan, John Paragon, Cassandra Peterson *d* James Signorelli *ph* Hanania Baer *m* James Campbell *pd* John DeCuir Jnr *ed* Battle Davis
☆ Cassandra Peterson, W. Morgan Sheppard, Daniel Greene, Susan Kellermann, Jeff Conaway, Edie McClurg, Kurt Fuller, Pat Crawford Brown

Elvis! Elvis!
Sweden 1977 100m colour
Moviemakers/SF1/SR-TV2 (Bert Sundberg)
A sensitive seven-year-old boy tries to cope with a mother obsessed by Elvis Presley.
Unimaginative family drama.
w Maria Gripe, Kay Pollak *novel* Maria Gripe *d* Kay Pollak *ph* Mikael Salomon *m* Ralph Lundsten *ed* Lasse Lundberg
☆ Lele Dorazio, Lena-Pia Bernhardsson, Fred Gunnarsson, Elisaveta, Allan Adwall

Embassy *
US 1972 90m colour
Hemdale/Triad/Weaver (Mel Ferrer)
At the US Embassy in Beirut, a Soviet official seeking asylum is in danger from a KGB killer.
Goodish suspenser with reasonably literate dialogue and several Hitchcockian sequences.
w William Fairchild d Gordon Hessler ph Raoul Coutard *m* Jonathan Hodge
☆ Richard Roundtree, Chuck Connors, Max von Sydow, Broderick Crawford, Ray Milland

Embryo
US 1976 104m colour
Cine Artists (Arnold H. Orgolini, Anita Doohan)

A researcher experiments on foetuses with growth hormones, and lives to regret it.
Rather unpleasant mixture of science fiction and old-fashioned horror; slickness can't conceal a total lack of taste.
w Anita Doohan, Jack W. Thomas *d* Ralph Nelson *ph* Fred Koenekamp *m* Gil Melle
☆ Rock Hudson, Diane Ladd, Barbara Carrera, Roddy McDowall

The Emerald Forest **
GB 1985 113m Technicolor Panavision
Embassy/John Boorman

An American engineer sets off to find his lost son in the jungles of Brazil.
Heavy-going, dazzling to look at, finally uncomforting dalliance with themes originally explored in Tarzan the Ape Man, *e.g. would man do better to return to nature?*
w Rospo Pallenberg *d John Boorman ph* Philippe Rousselot *m* Junior Homrich, Brian Gascoyne *pd* Simon Holland
☆ Powers Boothe, Meg Foster, Charley Boorman
'Begins as a breathtaking fable and ends as a routine action movie. Somewhere along the way, there was a failure of the imagination.' – *Roger Ebert*

The Emigrants *
Sweden 1970 191m Technicolor
Svensk Filmindustri (Bengt Forslund)

original title: *Utvandrarna*
A family of farmers leaves famine-stricken 19th-century Sweden for America, and builds a homestead in Minnesota.
Solemn, forceful, overlong epic which while full of trial and tribulation is sufficiently well made to cast a hypnotic spell and was a major hit among Swedish-Americans.
w Jan Troell, Bengt Forslund *novels* Vilhelm Moberg *m* Erik Nordgren *ed* Jan Troell *d/ph/ed Jan Troell*
☆ Max von Sydow, Liv Ullmann, Eddie Axberg, Svenolof Bern
'A Fordian canvas without the Fordian warmth.' – *Sight and Sound*
† A sequel, *The New Land*, shortly appeared, and this was also the title of a short-lived TV series on the subject.
best picture; best foreign film; Jan Troell (direction and script); Liv Ullmann

Emil and the Detectives *
Germany 1931 80m bw
UFA
City children discover and chase a crook, who is finally arrested.
A pleasing fable for children which has survived several subsequent versions; the original is probably the best.
w Billy Wilder *novel* Erich Kästner *d* Gerhard Lamprecht *ph* Werner Brandes *m* Allan Grey
☆ Fritz Rasp, Kathe Haack
† Other versions: Britain 1935, directed by Milton Rosmer, with George Hayes; West Germany 1954, directed by R. A. Stemmle, with Kurt Meisel; US

1964 (Walt Disney), directed by Peter Tewkesbury, with Walter Slezak.

Emma *
US 1932 73m bw
MGM
A servant marries into the family.
Predictably cosy family drama tailored for its star.
w Frances Marion, Leonard Praskins, Zelda Sears *d* Clarence Brown *ph* Oliver T. Marsh
☆ *Marie Dressler*, Richard Cromwell, Jean Hersholt, Myrna Loy, John Miljan, Purnell E. Pratt
'A hoke story saved by the star.' – *Variety*
Marie Dressler

'A new comedy from Jane Austen's timeless classic.'
Emma *
GB/US 1996 120m Eastmancolor
Buena Vista/Matchmaker/Miramax/Haft (Patrick Cassavetti, Steven Haft)
A rich young woman's matchmaking goes amiss, but she finds happiness where she least expects it.
Pleasant but stolid adaptation that skates lightly over the moral concerns of the original.
wd Douglas McGrath *novel* Jane Austen *ph* Ian Wilson *m* Rachel Portman *pd* Michael Howells *ed* Lesley Walker
☆ *Gwyneth Paltrow*, Toni Collette, Jeremy Northam, Alan Cumming, Ewan McGregor, Greta Scacchi, Juliet Stevenson, Polly Walker, Sophie Thompson, Phyllida Law
'Jane Austen cooked up a full-banquet romantic comedy in her happiest, best-known masterpiece; writer-director Douglas McGrath offers a light, sunny, American-style tea party.' – *Lisa Schwarzbaum, Entertainment Weekly*
'Pretty and pleasing, but there are less patronising ways of spending your time.' – *Tom Shone, Sunday Times*
Rachel Portman
Ruth Myers (costumes)

Emmanuelle *
France 1974 94m Eastmancolor
Trinacra/Orphée (Yves Rousset-Rouard)
The bored bride of a French Embassy official in Siam is initiated by well-meaning friends into various forms of sexual activity.
Not much sexier than a Sunday colour supplement, this fashionable piece of suberoticism took off like a bomb and spawned half-a-dozen so-called sequels. Future students may well wonder why.
w Jean-Louis Richard *novel* Emmanuelle Arsan *d* Just Jaeckin *ph* Richard Suzuki, Marie Saunier *m* Pierre Bachelet
☆ Sylvia Kristel, Marika Green, Daniel Sarky, Alain Cuny
'Much hazy, soft-focus coupling in downtown Bangkok.' – *Michael Billington, Illustrated London News*

Emma's War
Australia 1985 96m colour
Curzon/Belinon (Clytie Jessop, Andrena Finlay)
In the 40s, a 14-year-old girl befriends a runaway conscientious objector, after her mother takes her away from the dangers of wartime Sydney to live in a cottage in the mountains.
Mundane domestic drama of life's little disappointments.
w Peter Smalley, Clytie Jessop *d* Clytie Jessop *ph* Tom Cowan *m* John Williams *ad* Jane Norris *ed* Sonia Hofmann
☆ Lee Remick, Miranda Otto, Mark Lee, Terence Donovan, Donal Gibson

L'Emmerdeur **
France/Italy 1973 84m Eastmancolor
Miracle/Les Films Ariane/Mondex/OPIC (George Dancigers)
aka: *A Pain in the A–*
A hit-man, waiting in a Paris hotel to kill a witness, befriends a suicidal husband and is unable to get rid of him.
Amusing character comedy of a strong, silent man and a chattering weakling.
w Edouard Molinaro, Francis Veber *play Le Contrat* by Francis Veber *d* Edouard Molinaro *ph* Raoul Coutard *m* Jacques Brel, François Gabuber *ad* Jacques Brizzio *ed* Robert Isnardon, Monique Isnardon
☆ Lino Ventura, Jacques Brel, Caroline Cellier, Nino Castelnuovo, Jean-Pierre Darras, André Vallardy
'A black comedy par excellence. All that really need be said about it is that it begins well, sustains its chosen mood efficiently, builds to a satisfying climax and is in other words a delight from start to finish.' – *David McGillivray, Films and Filming*
† The film was remade by Billy Wilder as *Buddy Buddy*.

The Emperor and the Assassin *
China/Japan/France 1999 162m colour
Canal+/Pricel/Shin/NDF/New Wave/CFC (Chen Kaige, Shirley Kao, Satoru Iseki)
original title: *Jing Ke Ci Qin Wang*
In 229 BC, a Chinese king's attempt to unite all of the country's kingdoms under his rule is opposed by his concubine after he seizes her homeland.
An epic of the violent emergence of the first Emperor of China, with some spectacular battle scenes; but the narrative gets bogged down in detail.
w Chen Kaige, Wang Peigong *d* Chen Kaige *ph* Zhao Fei *m* Zhao Jiping *pd* Tu Juhua, Lin Qi *ed* Zhou Xinxia *cos* Mo Xiaomin, Huang Qiuping *martial arts d* Liu Jiacheng
☆ Gong Li (Lady Zhao), Zhang Fengyi (Jing Ke), Li Xuejian (Ying Zheng, King of Qin), Sun Zhou (Dan, Prince of Yan), Wang Zhiwen (Marquis Changxin), Chen Kaige (Lu Buwei), Lu Xiaohe (General Fan Yuqi), Gu Yongfei (Queen Mother), Ding Haifeng (Qin Wuyang), Zhao Benshan (Gao Jianli), Pan Changjiang (Prison official), Zhou Xun (Blind Girl)
'A string of striking set pieces hung on a dramatically shaky clothesline.' – *Derek Elley, Variety*

The Emperor Jones *
US 1933 72m bw
UA
A train porter becomes king of the Haitian jungle.
Stagey transcript of a stagey play, with acting of some interest at the time.
w DuBose Heyward *play* Eugene O'Neill *d* Dudley Murphy *ph* Ernest Haller *m* Frank Tours
☆ *Paul Robeson, Dudley Digges*, Frank Wilson
'For the classes rather than the masses, and questionable commercially.' – *Variety*

Emperor of the North: see *Emperor of the North Pole*

Emperor of the North Pole *
US 1973 119m DeLuxe
TCF/Inter Hemisphere (Robert Aldrich)
GB title: *Emperor of the North*
In 1933 Oregon, freeloading hobos are brutally attacked by a sadistic train guard.
Unlikely melodrama with vicious but exhilarating high spots separating acres of verbiage.
w Christopher Knopf *d* Robert Aldrich *ph* Joseph Biroc *m* Frank de Vol
☆ Lee Marvin, Ernest Borgnine, Keith Carradine, Charles Tyner, Malcolm Atterbury, Elisha Cook Jnr
'It's hard, contrived, pointless in its thesis, repulsive in its people, and it's singularly joyless and contemptible in its glorification of the bum and freeloader.' – *Judith Crist*

'The biggest thing that ever happened to Bing – or to you!'
The Emperor Waltz
US 1948 106m Technicolor
Paramount (Charles Brackett)
In 1901 Austria, a countess falls for an American phonograph salesman.
Thin to the point of emaciation, this witless comedy with music, dully set-bound, proved its director's strangest and most unsatisfactory choice.
w Charles Brackett, Billy Wilder *d* Billy Wilder *ph* George Barnes *m* Victor Young *m/ly* Johnny Burke, Jimmy Van Heusen *ad* Hans Dreier, Franz Bachelin
☆ Bing Crosby, Joan Fontaine, Roland Culver, Lucile Watson, Richard Haydn, Harold Vermilyea, Sig Rumann, Julia Dean
Victor Young

The Emperor's Candlesticks *
US 1937 89m bw
MGM (John Considine Jnr)
In old Russia, spies on opposite sides fall in love.
Lavish romantic comedy drama, generally well handled; superior Hollywood moonshine.
w Monckton Hoffe, Herman J. Mankiewicz, Harold Goldman *novel* Baroness Orczy *d* George Fitzmaurice *ph* Harold Rosson *m* Franz Waxman
☆ William Powell, Luise Rainer, Maureen O'Sullivan, Robert Young, Frank Morgan, Douglass Dumbrille
'It's about international spies in evening dress during that long ago period when Russia had a Czar, Vienna was the scene of brilliant *valasques*, and the favour of royalty was something to get excited over … it's acted with unusual seriousness midst settings of unusual extravagance.' – *Variety*

The Emperor's New Groove **
US 2000 79m Technicolor
Buena Vista/Walt Disney (Randy Fullmer)
A selfish Inca emperor, who is turned into a llama by his evil advisor, tries to regain his humanity and his throne with the aid of a friendly peasant.
Genial slapstick comedy, closer in spirit and style to Chuck Jones's cartoons than Disney's other recent features, but none the worse for that.
w David Reynolds *story* Chris Williams, Mark Dindal *original story* Roger Allers, Matthew Jacobs *d* Mark Dindal *m* John Debney, Sting, David Hartley *pd* Paul Felix *ed* Pamela Ziegenhagen-Shefland
☆ voices of: David Spade (Kuzco/Kuzco Llama), John Goodman (Pacha), Eartha Kitt (Yzma), Patrick Warburton (Kronk), Wendie Malick (Chica), Kellyann Kelso (Chaca), Eli Russell Linnetz (Tipo)
'A funny, breezy romp.' – *Time*
† In its four years of development, the movie went from a serious spectacular musical to a comedy. Along the way, six songs were dropped.
song 'My Funny Friend and Me' (m/l Sting, David Hartley)

L'Empire des Sens: see *Ai No Corrida*

Empire of Passion: see *Ai No Borei*

'For they shall inherit the earth… sooner than you think!'
Empire of the Ants
US 1977 89m Movielab
AIP/Cinema 77 (Bert I. Gordon)
Giant ants menace a stretch of the Florida coast.
A long way behind Them, but as exploitation it could be worse.
w Jack Turley *story* H. G. Wells *d* Bert I. Gordon *ph* Reginald Morris *m* Dana Kaproff
☆ Joan Collins, Robert Lansing, John David Carson, Albert Salmi, Jacqueline Scott

Empire of the Passions: see *Ai No Corrida*

Empire of the Sun ***
US 1987 152m Technicolor
Robert Shapiro/Amblin (Steven Spielberg, Kathleen Kennedy, Frank Marshall)
Semi-autobiographical story of an 11-year-old English boy learning to grow up in a Japanese internment camp during World War II.
Intelligent and thought-provoking movie about the loss of childhood innocence through the horrors of war. Bale, as the boy, gives an extraordinarily believable performance
w Tom Stoppard *novel* J. G. Ballard *d* Steven Spielberg *ph* Allen Daviau *m* John Williams *pd* Norman Reynolds *ed* Michael Kahn
☆ Christian Bale, John Malkovich, Miranda Richardson, Nigel Havers, Joe Pantoliano
'A masterpiece of popular cinema.' – *MFB*
Allen Daviau; editing; Norman Reynolds; John Williams; costumes (Bob Ringwood); sound
Allen Daviau; John Williams

'Selling records but not selling out.'
Empire Records
US 1995 91m colour Super 35
Warner/New Regency (Tony Ludwig, Alan Riche, Michael Nathanson, Arnon Milchan)
A day in the life of the staff of a record shop as they fight off an attempt to buy the business.
Drearily inane comedy, with uncertain performers enunciating unspeakable dialogue to an overpowering soundtrack.
w Carol Heikkinen *d* Allan Moyle *ph* Walt Lloyd *m* Mitchell Leib *pd* Peter Jamison *ed* Michael Chandler
☆ Anthony LaPaglia, Liv Tyler, Johnny Whitworth, Robin Cochrane, Renee Zellweger, Robin Tunney, Ethan Randall, Maxwell Caulfield, Debi Mazar
'A soundtrack in search of a movie.' – *Variety*

Empire State
GB 1987 104m colour
Miracle/Virgin (Norma Heyman)
An American gangster tries to infiltrate London's East End.
Over-the-top melodrama with an irritating pictorial style.
w Ron Peck, Mark Ayres *d* Ron Peck *ph* Tony Imi *m* Steve Parsons *pd* Adrian Smith *ed* Chris Kelly
☆ Cathryn Harrison, Jason Hoganson, Elizabeth Hickling, Jamie Foreman, Martin Landau, Ray McAnally

The Empire Strikes Back ***
US 1980 124m Eastmancolor
Panavision
TCF/Lucasfilm (Gary Kurtz)
The Rebel Alliance takes refuge from Darth Vader on a frozen planet.
More exhilarating interplanetary adventures, as mindless as Star Wars *but just as enjoyable for aficionados.*
w Leigh Brackett, Lawrence Kasdan *story* George Lucas *d* Irvin Kershner *ph* Peter Suschitzky *m* John Williams *pd Norman Reynolds*
☆ Mark Hamill, Harrison Ford, Carrie Fisher, Billy Dee Williams
'Slightly encumbered by some mythic and neo-Sophoclean overtones, but its inventiveness, humour and special effects are scarcely less inspired than those of its phenomenally successful predecessor.' – *New Yorker*
John Williams; art direction
music

L'Emploi du Temps **
France 2001 134m colour
Artificial Eye/Haut et Court/Arte France/Havas/Rhones-Alpes Cinema (Caroline Benjo)
aka: *Time Out*
When he loses his job, a professional man is unable to tell his family the truth and pretends he is still employed.
Engrossing study of a man whose job is his identity; when it ceases to exist he re-invents himself.
w Robin Campillo, Laurent Cantet *d* Laurent Cantet *ph* Pierre Milon *m* Jocelyn Pook *ad* Romain Denis *ed* Robin Campillo
☆ Aurelien Recoing (Vincent), Karin Viard (Muriel), Serge Livrozet (Jean-Michel), Jean-Pierre Mangeot (Vincent's father), Monique Mangeot (Vincent's mother), Nicolas Kalsch (Julien)
'Suspense can spring from action: here it's generated by inaction. And Hitchcock couldn't do it better.' – *Alexander Walker*
'Like an Ingmar Bergman film with the loss of religious faith replaced with a sort of socioeconomic nebulousness.' – *David Edelstein, Slate*

Employees' Entrance *
US 1933 75m bw
Warner
A ruthless department store manager gets his come-uppance.
Smart comedy-melodrama with solidly familiar cast.
w Robert Presnell *play* David Boehm *d* Roy del Ruth
☆ *Warren William*, Loretta Young, Alice White, Wallace Ford, Allen Jenkins, Marjorie Gateson

'Here's one that calls for preferred dating ... plenty to sell for the mobs.' – *Variety*

The Empty Beach
Australia 1985 100m Eastmancolor
Jethro (John Edwards, Timothy Read)
A private eye searches around Bondi Beach for a businessman who went missing in mysterious circumstances two years earlier.
A conventional and, for the most part, unsurprising thriller with the occasional witty line of dialogue; its hero is beaten up so often that it is clear he is in the wrong business.
w Keith Dewhurst *novel* Peter Corris *d* Chris Thomson *ph* John Seale *m* Martin Armiger, Red Symons *pd* Lawrence Eastwood *ed* Lindsay Frazer
☆ Bryan Brown, Anna Maria Monticelli, Ray Barrett, John Wood, Belinda Giblin, Peter Collingwood, Nick Tate, Kerry Mack

The Empty Canvas
Italy/France 1964 118m bw
CC Champion/Concordia (Joseph E. Levine, Carlo Ponti)
original title: *La Noia*
A young painter, obsessed by his own spiritual emptiness, becomes paranoically jealous of his promiscuous young mistress.
An extraordinarily boring film version of a novel which needed Buñuel, if anybody, to handle it.
w Tonino Guerra, Ugo Liberatore, Damiano Damiani *novel* Alberto Moravia *d* Damiano Damiani *ph* Roberto Gerardi *m* Luis Enriquez Bacalov
☆ Horst Buchholz, Catherine Spaak, Bette Davis, Isa Miranda, Lea Padovani

The Empty Table
Japan 1985 142m colour
Electric Pictures/Marugen Building Group/Haiyu-za Film/Herald Ace (Ginichi Kishimoto, Kyoto Oshima)
original title: *Shokutaku No Nai Ie*
A family disintegrates when the eldest son is arrested for terrorism.
Slow and ponderous, without much to interest a Western audience.
wd Masaki Kobayashi *story* Fumiko Enji *ph* Kozo Okazaki *md* Toru Takemitsu *pd* Shigemasha Toda *ed* Nobuo Ogawa
☆ Tatsuya Nakadai, Mayumi Ogawa, Kie Nakaj, Kiichi Nakai, Takeyuki Takemoto, Shima Iwashita

En Cas de Malheur *
France/Italy 1958 120m bw
Iena/UCIL/Incom
aka: *Love Is My Profession*
A wealthy, middle-aged lawyer leaves his wife for a worthless young wanton whom he is defending on a robbery charge.
Good solid melodrama with excellent credits: it caught all concerned on top form and had international success, but the theme is not in itself very interesting.
w Jean Aurenche, Pierre Bost *novel* Georges Simenon *d Claude Autant-Lara* *ph* Jacques Natteau *m* René Cloërc
☆ *Jean Gabin, Edwige Feuillère, Brigitte Bardot*, Franco Interlenghi

En Compagnie de Max Linder: see *Laugh with Max Linder*

En Effeuillant la Marguerite: see *Plucking the Daisy*

En Face
France 1999 90m colour
Cinemane/M6 (Guillaume Godard, Patrick Gouyou Beauchamps, Thierry Peronne, Claude Carrere)
aka: *Facing*
aka: *Across the Road*
Life takes a sinister turn when a happily married young couple unexpectedly inherit a large house, on condition that they continue to employ the housekeeper.
Creepy psychological thriller finally overcome by its own absurdities.
w Valérie Guignabodet *d* Mathias Ledoux *ph* Stéphane Leparc *m* Gekko *pd* Jean-Jacques Gernolle *ed* Jean-Pierre Baiesi
☆ Jean-Hugues Anglade (Jean Dorset), Clotilde Courau (Michelle Dorset), Christine Boisson (Clemence Richbourg), José Garcia (Hugo), Jean Benguigui (Henri de Villard), Emmanuel Salinger (Inspector Ruault), Laurence Février (Ghislaine de Villard)
'A tasty treat for the thriller lover.' – *Variety*

En Plein Coeur *
France 1998 101m colour Panavision
Pathé/Légende/France2 (Alain Goldman)
aka: *In All Innocence*
A lawyer, who has made it to the top of his profession, leaves his wife for a young girl who is accused of armed robbery.
Enjoyably old-fashioned melodrama of a man's humiliation at the hands of a street-smart petty thief.
w Roselyne Bosch *novel En Cas de Malheur* by Georges Simenon *d* Pierre Jolivet *ph* Pascal Ridao *m* Serge Perathoner, Jannick Top *pd* Thierry Flamand *ed* Yves Deschamps *cos* Valerie Pozzo di Borgo
☆ Gerard Lanvin (Michel), Virginie Ledoyen (Cecile), Carole Bouquet (Viviane), Guillaume Canet (Vincent), Aurélie Vérillon (Samira), Denis Podalydes (Martorel), Jean-Pierre Lorit (Antoine)
† Simenon's novel was first filmed in 1958 by Claude Autant-Lara as *Love Is My Profession/En Cas de Malheur* (qv) with Jean Gabin, Edwige Feuillère and Brigitte Bardot.

En Rade *
France 1927 60m approx bw silent
Neofilm
A Marseilles docker dreams of escaping his pent-in existence and fleeing with his mistress to the South Seas.
More realistic than Pagnol's Marius trilogy, which used the same setting, this remains an interesting slice of romantic realism, with good attention to detail.
w Alberto Cavalcanti, Claude Heymann *d* Alberto Cavalcanti *ph* Jimmy Rogers, A. Fairli, P. Enberg
☆ Catherine Hessling, Philippe Heriat, Georges Charlia

Enchanted April
US 1935 66m bw
RKO
A woman becomes lonely when her husband turns into a successful novelist.
Thin marital comedy-drama for fans of the star.
w Samuel Hoffenstein, Ray Harris *novel* Elizabeth von Arnim *d* Harry Beaumont
☆ Ann Harding, Frank Morgan, Katharine Alexander, Reginald Owen, Jane Baxter, Jessie Ralph
'Very British in background and proceeding at all times with a lifted eyebrow.' – *Variety*

'Escaping From Winter In London, They Planned A Holiday In Paradise ... Everything Was Going Perfectly, Until The Men Arrived.'
Enchanted April
GB 1991 99m colour
Curzon/Miramax/BBC/Greenpoint (Ann Scott)
In the 1920s four Englishwomen, bored with their lives, take a holiday in Italy.
Stilted period movie that is pretty to look at but has little to engage the mind.
w Peter Barnes *novel* Elizabeth von Arnim *d* Mike Newell *ph* Rex Maidment *m* Richard Rodney Bennett *pd* Malcolm Thornton *ed* Dick Allen
☆ Miranda Richardson, Josie Lawrence, Polly Walker, Joan Plowright, Alfred Molina, Michael Kitchen, Jim Broadbent
'A slim comedy of manners about Brits discovering their emotions in Italy ... Strong cast's reliable playing is undercut by a script that dawdles over well-trod territory.' – *Variety*
'Crude, fussy, bland stuff gauged to please American anglophiles who watch Masterpiece Theatre.' – *Philip French, Observer*
Joan Plowright; Peter Barnes; costumes (Sheena Napier)

The Enchanted Cottage *
US 1945 92m bw
RKO (Harriet Parsons)
A plain girl and a disfigured man are beautiful to each other.
Wartime updating of a sentimental old play; insufficiently well considered to be more than tolerable.
w De Witt Bodeen, Herman J. Mankiewicz *play* Sir Arthur Wing Pinero *d* John Cromwell *ph* Ted Tetzlaff *m* Roy Webb *ad* Albert D'Agostino, Carroll Clark *ed* Joseph Noriega
☆ Dorothy McGuire, Robert Young, Herbert Marshall, Mildred Natwick, Spring Byington, Hillary Brooke
'A silly film with considerable charm. It will be liked by millions, who are fully aware of its silliness while being captivated by its charm. It will be liked for the best of reasons; because it is based on a solid and humane truth.' – *C. A. Lejeune*
† A silent version in 1924 starred Richard Barthelmess and May McAvoy.
Roy Webb

The Enchanted Forest *
US 1945 77m Cinecolor
PRC
Old John the Hermit talks to trees and animals, and rescues a lost child.
Surprising piece of Victorian whimsy, remarkably effective in its unambitious way, especially as a product of this studio. The best known example of Cinecolor.
w Robert Lee Johnson, John Le Bar, Lou Brock *d* Lew Landers *ph* Marcel Le Picard *m* Alfred Hay Malotte
☆ Harry Davenport, Edmund Lowe, Brenda Joyce, Billy Severn

Enchantment *
US 1948 101m bw
Samuel Goldwyn
A London house tells the story of three generations.
Yes, a house tells the story, and the leading characters are called Rollo and Lark, but this is a very appealing piece of period romantic nonsense, with the highest possible gloss upon it.
w John Patrick *novel A Fugue in Time* by Rumer Godden *d Irving Reis* *ph Gregg Toland* *m* Hugo Friedhofer *ed* Daniel Mandell
☆ David Niven, Teresa Wright, Evelyn Keyes, Farley Granger, Jayne Meadows, Leo G. Carroll
'Deliberate in pace, and artfully contrived as an emotional holiday, yet genuinely moving on its own terms.' – *Newsweek*
'Genuinely moving on its own terms, produced with a careful good taste that should disarm the critics of lachryma and old lace.' – *Newsweek*

Encino Man
US 1992 88m Technicolor
Warner/Hollywood Pictures/Touchwood Pacific Partners 1 (George Zaloom)
GB title: *California Man*
Two high-school students revive a frozen prehistoric youth who quickly adapts to the prevailing life-style.
A depressing youth comedy, though those with a Neanderthal sense of humour may be amused.
w Shawn Schepps *story* George Zaloom, Shawn Schepps *d* Les Mayfield *ph* Robert Brickmann *m* J. Peter Robinson *pd* James Allen *ed* Eric Sears, Jonathan Siegel
☆ Sean Astin, Brendan Fraser, Pauly Shore, Megan Ward, Robin Tunney, Michael DeLuise, Patrick Van Horn, Dalton James, Rick Ducommun
'Mindless would-be comedy ... insulting even within its own no-effort parameters.' – *Variety*
'Less funny than your own funeral.' – *Washington Post*

Encore *
GB 1951 88m bw
GFD/Two Cities (Antony Darnborough)
Three more Somerset Maugham short stories introduced by the author.
The final follow-up to the success of Quartet *and* Trio*; television playlets quickly made this kind of short story seem old-fashioned, but the standard here was high.*
w T. E. B. Clarke, Arthur Macrae, Eric Ambler *stories The Ant and the Grasshopper* by Somerset Maugham *d* Pat Jackson, Anthony Pelissier, Harold French *ph* Desmond Dickinson *m* Richard Addinsell
☆ *Nigel Patrick*, Roland Culver, *Kay Walsh*, Noel Purcell, Ronald Squire, John Laurie, Glynis Johns, Terence Morgan, David Hutcheson

Encounter: see *Stranger On the Prowl*

Encounter at Raven's Gate
Australia 1989 93m colour J-D-C Scope
Castle Premier/Hemdale/FGH/International Film Management (Rolf de Heer, Marc Rosenberg)
A strange scientist appears to orchestrate a series of bizarre happenings at an isolated farming community.
Low budget science fiction non-thriller that rarely explains what is happening but staggers from one spooky event to the next.
w Rolf de Heer, Marc Rosenberg *screenplay* James Michael Vernon *d* Rolf de Heer *ph* Richard Michalak *m* Graham Tardif, Roman Kronen *pd* Judith Russell *ed* Suresh Ayyar
☆ Steven Vidler, Celine Griffin, Ritchie Singer, Vince Gil, Saturday Rosenberg, Max Cullen, Terry Camilleri

'A comedy for you and your next of kin!'
The End
US 1978 100m DeLuxe
UA/Lawrence Gordon (Hank Moonjean)
A selfish man finds he is dying and unsuccessfully tries to change what remains of his life.
Presumably intended as an ironic black comedy, this comes over as tasteless ham; nobody involved, least of all the director-star, has any idea how to handle it.
w Jerry Belson *d* Burt Reynolds *ph* Bobby Byrne *m* Paul Williams *pd* Jan Scott
☆ Burt Reynolds, Dom DeLuise, Sally Field, Strother Martin, David Steinberg, Joanne Woodward, Norman Fell, Myrna Loy, Pat O'Brien, Robby Benson, Carl Reiner

End as a Man: see *The Strange One*

The End of August *
US 1981 107m Metrocolor
Sewanee (Martin Jurow)
In 1900, a bored young wife takes a lover beneath her station.
Unexpectedly nostalgic wallow in days gone by, the background detail seeming more important than the personal story, and certainly very good to look at.
w Eula Seaton, Leon Heller *novel The Awakening* by Kate Chopin *d* Bob Graham *ph Robert Elswit* *m* Shirley Walker *pd* Warren Jacobson, Erin Jo Jurow
☆ Sally Sharp, Lilia Skala, David Marshall Grant, Kathleen Widdoes, Paul Roebling, Paul Shenar
'Reminiscent of nothing so much as the turning of pages in a family album.' – *Jo Imeson, MFB*

End of Days
US 1999 120m DeLuxe Panavision
Universal/Beacon (Armyan Bernstein, Bill Borden)
In the final moments before the new millennium, an alcoholic ex-cop must prevent Satan from impregnating a young woman and bringing about the end of days, as foretold in the Book of Revelation.
As pumped-up as its hero, this is a riotous, over-the-top mish-mash of religiosity and shock effects, like The Omen *on steroids.*
w Andrew W. Marlowe *d* Peter Hyams *ph* Peter Hyams *m* John Debney *pd* Richard Holland *ed* Steve Kemper *sp* creature fx: Stan Winston; makeup fx: Kurtzman, Nicotero & Berger EFX Group
☆ Arnold Schwarzenegger (Jericho Cane), Gabriel Byrne (The Man), Kevin Pollak (Chicago), Robin Tunney (Christine York), CCH Pounder (Detective Margie Francis), Rod Steiger (Father Kovak), Derrick O'Connor (Thomas Aquinas), Miriam Margolyes (Mabel), Udo Kier (Head Priest), Victor Varnado (Albino)
'Pointlessly nasty would-be thriller. The material is so derivative that it amounts to a tag sale of used parts from better apocalyptic movies.' – *Janet Maslin, New York Times*
'Dreadful enough to make most viewers consider gouging out their eyes in order to avoid seeing a second time the spectacle of the world's most wooden actor pretending to undergo a spiritual crisis.' – *Mark Kermode, Sight and Sound*
'A fun, all-out action movie with a sexy millennial edge.' – *Bob McCabe, Empire*

The End of St Petersburg **

USSR 1927 110m approx bw silent
Mezhrabpom-Russ

original title: *Konyets Sankt-Peterburga*

A peasant comes to live in St Petersburg in 1914, understands the workers' problems, and joins in the revolution.

Exhilarating propaganda, reprehensible but superbly conceived, with an especially rousing climax.

w Nathan Zarkhi *d* V. I. Pudovkin *ph* Anatoli Golovnya, K. Vents *ad* S. Kozlovsky

☆ Ivan Chuvelov, Vera Baranovskaya, A. P. Christiakov

† The film was officially commissioned as part of the 10th anniversary celebrations.

The End of the Affair

GB 1954 106m bw
Columbia/Coronado (David Lewis)

In wartime London, a repressed wife has an affair with a writer but develops religious guilt which leads indirectly to her death.

Glum sinning in Greeneland; over-ambitious, miscast, and poor-looking.

w Lenore Coffee *novel* Graham Greene
d Edward Dmytryk *ph* Wilkie Cooper
m Benjamin Frankel

☆ Deborah Kerr, Van Johnson, Peter Cushing, John Mills, Stephen Murray, Nora Swinburne, Charles Goldner

'The end was just the beginning'

The End of the Affair *

GB 1999 109m Technicolor
Columbia (Stephen Woolley, Neil Jordan)

In 1946, a writer tries to understand why his wartime affair with a married woman came to a sudden end.

On one level, this is an effective movie of love among the emotionally repressed; but the changes made to Greene's novel negate its original purpose, in demonstrating the power and purpose of religious faith.

wd Neil Jordan *novel* Graham Greene *ph* Roger Pratt *m* Michael Nyman *pd* Anthony Pratt
ed Tony Lawson

☆ Ralph Fiennes (Maurice Bendrix), Julianne Moore (Sarah Miles), Stephen Rea (Henry Miles), Ian Hart (Mr Parkis), Samuel Bould (Lance Parkis), Jason Isaacs (Father Smythe), James Bolam (Mr Savage), Deborah Findlay (Miss Smythe)

'An awkward, edgy, tormented novel has been upholstered for comfort.' – *Philip Kemp, Sight and Sound*

'A movie to make you think and to feel and to live another life for nearly two hours alongside as compelling, flawed and real a group of characters as any movie can offer.' – *Anwar Brett, Film Review*

Julianne Moore; Roger Pratt
Neil Jordan (screenplay)

End of the Game *

US/West Germany 1976 104m colour
TCF/Maximilian Schell

A retiring police inspector intensifies his vendetta against the crooked industrialist who thirty years earlier killed the woman they both loved.

Chess-like revenge melodrama very typical of its author, with no light relief and a few existentialist touches added for general confusion. Well made and sometimes fascinating, but finally annoying.

w Maximilian Schell, Friedrich Dürrenmatt *novel* The Judge and his Hangman by Friedrich Dürrenmatt *d* Maximilian Schell *ph* Ennio Guarnieri, Klaus Koenig, Roberto Gerardi

☆ Jon Voight, Robert Shaw, Martin Ritt, Jacqueline Bisset

'A more addled, overreaching, misjudged, ill-made, wasteful, posturizing, uninteresting and tedious little epic has not toddled into town in years.' – *Charles Champlin, Los Angeles Times*

'It was a time when anything seemed possible–even miracles.'

The End of the Golden Weather

New Zealand 1992 103m colour
Blue Dolphin/South Pacific/New Zealand Film Commission/TV New Zealand (Christina Milligan, Ian Mune)

During a summer holiday a lonely boy becomes friendly with a retarded youth with Olympic ambitions.

A slight and uninvolving movie of the dawning of maturity.

w Ian Mune, Bruce Mason *play* Bruce Mason *d* Ian Mune *ph* Alun Bollinger *m* Stephen McCurdy *pd* Ron Highfield *ed* Michael Horton

☆ Stephen Fulford, Stephen Papps, Paul Gittins, Gabrielle Hammond, David Taylor, Alexandra Marshall

'An intimate and gentle coming-of-age comedy drama.' – *Variety*

End of the Rainbow: see *Northwest Outpost*

The End of the River *

GB 1947 83m bw
GFD/The Archers (Michael Powell, Emeric Pressburger)

A South American Indian boy flees to the outside world and finds life in the city as dangerous as in the jungle.

Strange but oddly impressive departure for British film-makers at this time. A commercial and critical disaster.

w Wolfgang Wilhelm *novel* Desmond Holdridge *d* Derek Twist *ph* Christopher Challis *m* Lambert Williamson *ad* Fred Pusey *ed* Brereton Porter

☆ Sabu (Manoel), Esmond Knight (Dantos), Bibi Ferreira (Teresa), Robert Douglas (Jones), Antoinette Cellier (Conceicao), Raymond Lovell (Porpino), Torin Thatcher (Lisboa), James Hayter (Chico), Orlando Martins (Harrigan), Maurice Denham (Defending Counsel), Alan Wheatley (Irygoyen), Charles Hawtrey (Raphael)

The End of the Road *

GB 1954 77m bw
Group Three (Alfred Shaughnessy)

A retired engineer becomes frustrated by idleness, and his family contemplate sending him to an old people's home.

Reasonably absorbing study of old age, suffering from a contrived end.

w James Forsyth, Geoffrey Orme *d* Wolf Rilla *ph* Arthur Grant *m* John Addison

☆ *Finlay Currie*, Duncan Lamont, Naomi Chance, David Hannaford

End of the Road *

US 1970 110m Eastmancolor
Contemporary/Allied Artists (Stephen F. Kesten, Terry Southern)

Released from a sanitarium, a teacher takes a job at a local university and impregnates a professor's wife.

Determinedly offbeat, intermittently successful movie that was very much of its time, with the mad being regarded as truly sane.

w Aram Avakian, Dennis McGuire, Terry Southern *novel* John Barth *d* Aram Avakian *ph* Gordon Willis *m* Teo Macero *pd* John K. Wright *ed* Robert Q. Lovett

☆ Stacy Keach, Harris Yulin, Dorothy Tristan, James Earl Jones, Grayson Hall, Ray Brock, James Coco

'The cinematography by Gordon Willis is often beautiful, the optical effects are sometimes elegant, and the sets and details are often remarkably fine, but the absurdist point of view has too self-congratulatory a tone.' – *Pauline Kael*

End of the World *

France 1930 105m bw
Ecran d'Art (Abel Gance)
original title: *La Fin du Monde*

Social and economic panic is caused when a comet is about to hit the Earth.

Massive attempt by Gance to rival his Napoleon in scope. Made in German, French and English, it cost a phenomenal sum which it never regained; Gance found work hard to get in future, especially since he set himself up as a prophet.

wd Abel Gance

☆ Abel Gance, Colette Darfeuil, Sylvia Grenade, Victor Francen

'A megalomaniac's effort turned out without consideration for financial results, and containing a strange mixture of crazy stuff, with successfully directed spectacular sequences.' – *Variety*

† The full title is *The End of the World as Seen, Heard and Rendered by Abel Gance.*

The End of the World (in our usual bed in a night full of rain)

Italy 1978 104m colour
Gil Shiva/Liberty/Warner

aka: *Night Full of Rain*

An American lady photographer has a bumpy romance with an Italian communist journalist with expensive tastes.

Pretentious talk-piece which slowly gets nowhere.

wd Lina Wertmüller

☆ Candice Bergen, Giancarlo Giannini

The End of Violence *

US/Germany/France 1997 122m DeLuxe
Otto Nemenz Cameras
Artificial Eye/CiBy 2000/Road Movies/Kintop (Deepak Nayar, Wim Wenders, Nicholas Klein)

A Hollywood producer of violent action movies goes into hiding after being kidnapped and nearly killed by incompetent hitmen.

A stylish, enigmatic, paranoid thriller that touches on themes of movie violence and real-life surveillance without being particularly illuminating about either.

w Nicholas Klein *d* Wim Wenders *ph* Pascal Rabaud *m* Ry Cooder *pd* Patricia Norris
ed Peter Przygodda

☆ Bill Pullman, Andie MacDowell, Gabriel Byrne, Loren Dean, Traci Lind, Daniel Benzali, K. Todd Freeman, Pruitt Taylor Vince, Peter Horton, Udo Kier, Samuel Fuller

'A cool, contemplative consideration of a hot contemporary topic.' – *Variety*

Endangered Species

US 1982 97m Metrocolor
MGM/Alive Enterprises (Carolyn Pfeiffer)

Citizens of a small Wyoming town discover that their cattle are being systematically murdered.

Curious melodrama which never really explains itself but seems to be carrying a message about chemical warfare. With a proper ending it could have been a good suspenser.

w Alan Rudolph, John Binder *story* Judson Klinger, Richard Woods *d* Alan Rudolph *ph* Paul Lohmann *m* Gary Wright *pd* Trevor Williams

☆ Robert Urich, JoBeth Williams, Paul Dooley, Hoyt Axton, Peter Coyote

'It's not over ... it's not over!'

Endless Love

US 1981 110m Technicolor
Polygram (Keith Barish)

A high school student's love for a 15-year-old girl is thwarted by circumstance and accident.

Overheated melodrama with unbelievable and unlikeable characters. Why this director should choose to make it is mysterious.

w Judith Rascoe *novel* Scott Spencer *d* Franco Zeffirelli *ph* David Watkin *m* Jonathan Tunick *pd* Ed Wittstein

☆ Brooke Shields, Martin Hewitt, Shirley Knight, Don Murray, Richard Kiley, Beatrice Straight

title song (m/ly Lionel Richie)

Endless Night *

GB 1971 99m Eastmancolor
BL/EMI (Leslie Gilliat)

An American girl buys an English stately home and marries a chauffeur, but is later frightened to death.

Bumpy British thriller, structurally weak and peopled by the dullest conceivable characters, but with watchably scary sequences.

wd Sidney Gilliat *novel* Agatha Christie *ph* Harry Waxman *m* Bernard Herrmann

☆ Hayley Mills, Hywel Bennett, George Sanders, Britt Ekland, Per Oscarsson, Lois Maxwell

The Endless Summer

US 1966 95m Technicolor
Bruce Brown Films/Columbia

A study of surfing round the world.

A documentary which became a cult for those influenced by this Californian obsession; smashing photography hardly atones for an approach so naïve as to become fatuous.

wd/ph/ed Bruce Brown

'When Was The Last Time You Stood Up And Cheered At A Movie?'

Endurance *

US 1998 83m DeLuxe Super 35
Buena Vista/Hollywood/La Junta/Film Four/Helkon (Edward R. Pressman, Terrence Malick, Max Palevsky)

A biopic of the Ethiopian long distance runner Haile Gebrselassie.

Framed by his winning performance over 10,000 metres at the 1996 Olympics, Haile Gebrselassie's life is told in flashback in a mix of documentary and dramatic re-creation, revealing him as a natural athlete who has rarely stopped running and has managed to outpace the poverty in which he began.

wd Leslie Woodhead *ph* Ivan Strasburg *m* John Powell *ed* Saar Klein, Oral Norrie Ottey

☆ Haile Gebrselassie (Himself), Shawananness Gebrselassie (Haile's Mother), Yonas Zergaw (Young Haile), Tedesse Haile (Young Haile's Father), Gebrselassie Bekele (Himself), Alem Tellahun (Herself)

'Its mixture of biographical hype and social studies quickly curdles.' – *Stephen Holden, New York Times*

† The producers signed up eight runners in the 10,000 metres at the Atlanta Olympics so that they could make a documentary about the winner.

Enemies, a Love Story *

US 1989 120m colour
Fox/Morgan Creek Productions (Paul Mazursky)

The life of a Jew who survived the concentration camps becomes tragically entangled with that of three women: his first wife, whom he thought was dead, his second wife and his mistress.

Rushed in its telling, despite its length, and lacking in conviction.

w Roger L. Simon, Paul Mazursky *novel* Isaac Bashevis Singer *d* Paul Mazursky *ph* Fred Murphy *m* Maurice Jarre *pd* Pato Guzman *ed* Stuart Pappe

☆ Anjelica Huston, Ron Silver, Lena Olin, Margaret Sophie Stein, Judith Malina, Alan King, Rita Karin, Phil Leeds

Anjelica Huston, Lena Olin; screenplay

Enemies of the Public: see *Public Enemy*

Enemy Agent: see *British Intelligence (1940)*

'A battle between two nations became a conflict between two men.'

Enemy at the Gates *

Germany/GB/Ireland/US 2001 131m DeLuxe
Panavision
Pathé/Mandalay/KC Medien/MP Film/DOS/Swanford/Little Bird

At the siege of Stalingrad, a duel develops between two snipers, one a Russian worker, the other a German aristocrat.

Muddled war movie with some effective moments, but suffering fatally from hackneyed dialogue and miscasting.

w Alain Godard, Jean-Jacques Annaud *d* Jean-Jacques Annaud *ph* Robert Fraisse *m* James Horner *pd* Wolf Kroeger *ed* Noelle Boisson, Humphrey Dixon

☆ Jude Law (Vassili Zaitsev), Joseph Fiennes (Danilov), Rachel Weisz (Tania), Bob Hoskins (Krushchev), Ed Harris (Major Koenig), Ron Perlman (Kulikov), Gabriel Marshall-Thomson (Sasha), Eva Mattes (Mrs Filipov)

'Any flaws in execution pale against those moments when the film brings history to vital life.' – *Peter Travers, Rolling Stone*

The Enemy Below *

US 1957 98m Technicolor Cinemascope
TCF (Dick Powell)

During World War II an American destroyer in the South Atlantic is involved in a cat-and-mouse operation with a U-boat.

Well-staged, unsurprising naval thriller with good pace and a pat let's-not-be-nasty-to-each-other ending.

w Wendell Mayes *novel* Commander D. A. Rayner *d* *Dick Powell* *ph* Harold Rosson *m* Leigh Harline
☆ Robert Mitchum, Curt Jurgens, Theodore Bikel, David Hedison

Enemy from Space: see *Quatermass II*

Enemy Mine
US 1985 108m DeLuxe Amiflex Widescreen
Kings Road/TCF (Stephen Friedman)
A space pilot goes down on Dracon and makes friends with his lizard-like captor.
All talk and little action, this is a way-out piece of do-goodery which tests the patience.
w Edward Khmara *story* Barry Longyear *d* Wolfgang Petersen *ph* Tony Imi *m* Maurice Jarre *pd* Rolf Zehetbauer *ed* Hannes Nikel
☆ Dennis Quaid, Lou Gossett Jnr, Brion James, Richard Marcus, Carolyn McCormick

An Enemy of the People *
US 1977 103m Metrocolor
First Artists (George Schaefer)
A small-town doctor discovers that for commercial reasons his colleagues propose to conceal the fact that the local spa is contaminated by tannery waste.
Ibsen's plot is well intentioned but well worn – it more or less served as the starting point for Jaws – so in any modern version the acting is all. Here it isn't enough, though the star so badly wanted to do it that arguments and sulks kept him off the screen for three years.
w Alexander Jacobs *play* Arthur Miller's version of the play by Henrik Ibsen *d* George Schaefer *ph* Paul Lohmann *m* Leonard Rosenman
☆ Steve McQueen, Charles Durning, Bibi Andersson, Eric Christmas, Richard Bradford, Richard A. Dysart
'The main thing I was shooting for was not to make bucks but to have something I could believe in.' – *Steve McQueen*

An Enemy of the People *
India 1989 100m Eastmancolor
Contemporary/Electric/National Film Development Corp of India (Anil Gupta)
original title: *Ganashatru*
A doctor encounters local hostility when he complains of polluted water supplies.
Less than successful transfer of Ibsen's play to modern-day India, in a studio-bound production.
wd Satyajit Ray *play* Henrik Ibsen *ph* Barun Raha *m* Satyajit Ray *ad* Ashok Bose *ed* Dulal Dutta
☆ Soumitra Chatterjee, Dhritiman Chatterjee, Ruma Guhathakurta, Mamata Shankar, Dipankar Dey, Subhendu Chatterjee

Enemy of the State
US 1998 127m Technicolor Panavision
Buena Vista/Touchstone/Scott Free (Don Simpson/ Jerry Bruckheimer)
Government agents target a lawyer who inadvertently has incriminating evidence against them.
Energetic, paranoid thriller preoccupied with surveillance methods; its narrative becomes increasingly implausible and substitutes speed for sense.
w David Marconi *d* Tony Scott *ph* Dan Mindel *m* Trevor Rabin, Harry Gregson-Williams *pd* Benjamin Fernandez *ed* Chris Lebenzon
☆ Will Smith, Gene Hackman, Jon Voight, Lisa Bonet, Regina King, Stuart Wilson, Tom Sizemore, Loren Dean, Barry Pepper, Ian Hurt, Jake Busey, Scott Caan, Jason Lee, Gabriel Byrne, James Le Gros
'The movie goes like the wind, but it's more a technological exercise than anything else.' – *David Denby, New Yorker*

L'Enfance Nue **
France 1968 80m colour
Stephan Films (Mag Bodard, François Truffaut, Claude Berri, Jo and Samy Siritzky)
aka: *Naked Childhood*
US title: *Me*
Rejected by his foster parents because of his difficult behaviour, a 10-year-old boy finds temporary refuge with an elderly couple.
A restrained, unsentimental account of a troubled and troublesome childhood, shot in a naturalistic style with a non-professional cast.
w Maurice Pialat, Arlette Langmann *d* Maurice Pialat *ph* Claude Beausoleil *m* Wagner
☆ Michel Tarrazon, Rene Thierry, Marie-Louis Thierry, Henri Puff, Maurice Coussoneau, Marie Marc, Michel Soulé

L'Enfant Sauvage *
France 1970 84m bw
UA/Films du Carrosse (Marcel Berbert)
US title: *The Wild Child*
In 1797, a scientist tames and studies a young boy who has mysteriously been living wild in the forest.
Slightly flat but generally interesting reconstruction of a true event, the same one which subsequently inspired TV projects such as Stalk the Wild Child *and* Lucan.
w François Truffaut, Jean Gruault *d* François Truffaut *ph* Nestor Almendros *m* Vivaldi
☆ Jean-Pierre Cargol, François Truffaut, Jean Dasté, Françoise Seigner

Les Enfants du Marais ***
France 1998 110m colour Panavision
UGC/Fechner/France2/Rhone-Alpes/KJB (Jean-Claude Bourlat)
GB title: *Children of the Marshland*
An old woman remembers life when she was young in the 1920s, living in a hut on the marshes.
Charming, nostalgic recreation of a vanished rural life, and the enjoyment of friendship and simple pleasures, tinged with a sense of melancholy and loss.
w Sebastian Japrisot *novel* Georges Montforez *d* Jean Becker *ph* Jean-Marie Dreujou *m* Pierre Bachelet *ad* Therese Ripaud *ed* Jacques Witta *cos* Sylvie de Segonzac
☆ Jacques Villeret (Riton), Jacques Gamblin (Garris), Andre Dussollier (Amedée), Michel Serrault (Pépé), Isabelle Carré (Marie), Eric Cantona (Jo Sardi)
'The values celebrated seem stale and contrived rather than warm and vibrant.' – *Ginette Vincendeau, Sight and Sound*

Les Enfants du Paradis ****
France 1945 195m bw
Pathé (Fred Orain, Raymond Borderic)
US title: *Children of Paradise*
In the 'theatre street' of Paris in the 1840s, a mime falls in love with the elusive Garance, but her problems with other men keep them apart.
A magnificent evocation of a place and a period, this thoroughly enjoyable epic melodrama is flawed only by its lack of human warmth and of a real theme. It remains nevertheless one of the cinema's most memorable films.
w Jacques Prévert d Marcel Carné ph Roger Hubert *m* Maurice Thiriet, Joseph Kosma, G. Mouque *ad Alexandre Trauner, Léon Barsacq, Raymond Gabutti*
☆ *Arletty, Jean-Louis Barrault, Pierre Brasseur, Marcel Herrand, Maria Casarès,* Louis Salou, Pierre Renoir, Gaston Modot, Jane Marken
'A magnificent scenario ... Prévert is as adept with wit as with poignancy ... I don't believe a finer group of actors was ever assembled on film' – *John Simon*
🏆 Jacques Prévert

Les Enfants Terribles *
France 1950 100m bw
Jean-Pierre Melville
aka: *The Strange Ones*
The hothouse relationship of an adolescent brother and sister leads to tragedy.
Rough-edged, stage-bound but occasionally quite powerful exploration into familiar Cocteau territory.
wd Jean-Pierre Melville *novel* Jean Cocteau *ph* Henri Decaë *m* Bach, Vivaldi
☆ Nicole Stéphane, Edouard Dermithe, Renée Cosima, Jacques Bernard

L'Enfer **
France 1993 100m Eastmancolor
Mayfair/MK2/CED/France 3/Cinemanuel/Canal (Marin Karmitz)
aka: *Torment*
A hotelier becomes insanely jealous of his wife and imagines that she is having affairs with locals and the guests.
Chilling study of a disintegrating marriage, and a husband's descent into a mad hell of his own making, though the ambiguous ending is not entirely satisfactory.
w Henri-Georges Clouzot, Jose-Andre Lacour, Claude Chabrol *d* Claude Chabrol *ph* Bernard Zitzermann *m* Matthieu Chabrol *ad* Emile Ghigo *ed* Monique Fardoulis
☆ Emmanuelle Béart, François Cluzet, Nathalie Cardone, André Wilms, Marc Lavoine, Christiane Minazzoli, Dora Doll, Mario David, Jean-Pierre Cassel
'Under the film's sunny surface and vacational locations this is a winter's tale about the long autumn of love that has a casebook darkness to it.' – *Tom Hutchinson, Film Review*
† Director Henri-Georges Clouzot began making the film from his script in 1964, with Romy Schneider and Serge Reggiani, but had to stop when Reggiani became ill. He was rehearsing with a new star, Jean-Louis Trintignant, when he suffered a heart attack and had to abandon the production; he never tried again, despite living for another 13 years.

'The first story of the double-fisted DA who tore apart the evil dynasty that peddled murder for a price!'
The Enforcer ***
US 1950 87m bw
United States Pictures (Milton Sperling)
GB title: *Murder, Inc*
A crusading District Attorney tracks down the leader of a gang which murders for profit.
Extremely suspenseful and well-characterized police yarn based on fact. One of the very best of its kind.
w Martin Rackin d Bretaigne Windust ph Robert Burks *m* David Buttolph *ed* Fred Allen
☆ *Humphrey Bogart, Everett Sloane, Zero Mostel,* Ted de Corsia, Roy Roberts, King Donovan
'A tough, very slickly-made thriller with a host of fine character parts.' – *NFT, 1969*
'Absorbing and exciting, with little of the violence that so often disfigures films of this kind.' – *Richard Mallett, Punch*
'The first fifteen minutes is as powerful and rapid a sketch of tension as I can recall for seasons. The last fifteen might make Hitch weep with envy.' – *Observer*
† Raoul Walsh directed much of the film, uncredited.

The Enforcer
US 1976 96m DeLuxe Panavision
Warner/Malpaso (Robert Daley)
Brutal Inspector Callahan of the San Francisco police redeems himself by rounding up a group of psychopathic hoodlums.
Dirty Harry, *phase three: for hardened veterans only.*
w Stirling Silliphant, Dean Riesner *d* James Fargo *ph* Richard Glouner *m* Jerry Fielding
☆ Clint Eastwood, Tyne Daly, Harry Guardino, Bradford Dillman, John Mitchum, DeVeren Bookwalter, John Crawford
'A new low in mindless violence is reached in this film, which is so bad it would be funny if it were not for the gut-thumping killings from beginning to end.' – *William F. Fore, Film Information*

'An Undercover Agent With Fists Of Fury!'
The Enforcer (dubbed)
Hong Kong 1995 100m colour
Dimension/Win's Entertainment (Wong Jing, Tiffeny Chen)
original title: *Gei Ba Ba De Xin*
aka: *Jet Li's The Enforcer*
An undercover Beijing cop leaves his sick wife and young son to go to Hong Kong to infiltrate the gang of the local crime boss.
A film that is unlikely to appeal greatly to Li's action fans: the emphasis of a familiar, though confusing, narrative is on a sentimental family drama.
w Sandy Shaw *story* Wong Jing *d* Corey Yuen (Yeun Kwai) *ph* Tom Lau *m* Nicholas Rivera, Chow Kam-Cheung *ad* Ben Lau *ed* Angie Lin
☆ Jet Li (Kung Wei), Anita Mui (Inspector Fong), Xie Miao (Kung Ku), Yu Rong-Guang, Ko Shou-Lian, Damien Lau, Low Houi-Kang, Lo Hen-Chow

The Engagement *
GB 1970 44m Technicolor
Memorial (David Barber)
A young executive spends a devastating afternoon trying to borrow money to pay for an engagement ring which cost more than he expected.
Brisk little comedy which doesn't wear out its welcome.
w Tom Stoppard *d* Paul Joyce *ph* Tony Spratling *m* John Dankworth
☆ David Warner, Michael Bates, George Innes, Juliet Harmer, Paul Curran, Barbara Couper, Peter Copley

England Made Me ***
GB 1972 100m Eastmancolor Panavision
Hemdale/Atlantic (Jack Levin)
In 1935 a sponging Englishman becomes involved through his sister with a German financier.
Somewhat altered from the novel, this unusual film remains a lively, intelligent character melodrama.
w Desmond Cory, Peter Duffell *novel* Graham Greene *d Peter Duffell* *ph* Ray Parslow *m* John Scott
☆ *Peter Finch,* Michael York, Hildegarde Neil, *Michael Hordern,* Joss Ackland

'In memory, love lies forever.'
The English Patient **
US 1996 162m DeLuxe
Buena Vista/Tiger Moth/Miramax (Saul Zaentz)
Tended by a devoted nurse in a deserted Italian villa at the end of the Second World War, a dying Austrian count recalls his doomed affair with the English wife of a colleague.
Those who believe that love excuses any behaviour will succumb to this glossy romance, made on an epic scale and in that Hollywood tradition where heroes emerge from a three-day walk across the desert looking slightly tousled, and derelict pianos remain miraculously in tune; others, despite the skills on display, may find its celebration of betrayal less entrancing.
wd Anthony Minghella *novel* Michael Ondaatje *ph John Seale m Gabriel Yared pd Stuart Craig ed Walter Murch*
☆ *Ralph Fiennes, Juliette Binoche,* Willem Dafoe, *Kristin Scott-Thomas, Naveen Andrews,* Colin Firth, Julian Wadham, Jürgen Prochnow
'A respectable, intelligent, but less-than-stirring adaptation of an imposingly dense and layered novel.' – *Todd McCarthy, Variety*
'*A tour de force* so haunting that other films can't exorcise the memory of its radiant cast, exquisite craftsmanship or complex system of metaphors.' – *Rita Kempley, Washington Post*
† Juliette Binoche won the best actress award for her performance at the Berlin Film Festival in 1997.
🏆 Best picture; Anthony Minghella (as director); Juliette Binoche; John Seale; Walter Murch; Gabriel Yared; Ann Roth (costumes); Stuart Craig; sound
🏆 Kristin Scott-Thomas; Ralph Fiennes; Anthony Minghella (as adaptor)
🏆 Best film; Anthony Minghella (best adapted screenplay); Juliette Binoche; John Seale; Gabriel Yared; Walter Murch

English without Tears *
GB 1944 89m bw
GFD/Two Cities (Anatole de Grunwald, Sydney Box)
US title: *Her Man Gilbey*
During World War II a rich ATS girl falls for her butler who has become a lieutenant.
Wispy satirical comedy with amusing moments, chiefly interesting for the pre-war League of Nations sequences.
w Terence Rattigan, Anatole de Grunwald *d* Harold French *ph* Bernard Knowles
☆ Lilli Palmer, Michael Wilding, *Margaret Rutherford,* Penelope Dudley Ward, Albert Lieven, Roland Culver, Peggy Cummins

The Englishman Who Went Up a Hill But Came Down a Mountain *
GB 1995 99m colour Panavision
Buena Vista/Parallax (Sarah Curtis)
In 1917, two English surveyors working in a Welsh village discover that the highest local point cannot be classified as a mountain because it is 16 feet short of the necessary 1,000 feet; the outraged villagers decide to make good the discrepancy.
Amiable comedy in a quaintly English tradition, with shrewd rural characters outwitting smarter urban outsiders; inevitably, it suggests Ealing comedies, but the best of those avoided period settings.
wd Christopher Monger *story* Ifor David Monger, Ivor Monger *ph* Vernon Layton *m* Stephen Endelman *pd* Charles Garrad *ed* David Martin
☆ Hugh Grant, Tara Fitzgerald, Colm Meaney, Ian McNeice, Ian Hart, Kenneth Griffith, Tudor Vaughn, Hugh Vaughn
'Certainly a charming piece of work, a film that fits in tidily with our pseuding national cinema.' – *Adam Mars-Jones, Independent*

Enid Is Sleeping
US 1989 102m DeLuxe
First Independent/Vestron/Davis (John A. Davis, Howard Malin)
GB title: *Over Her Dead Body*
Having accidentally killed her sister, who discovered her in bed with her husband, a woman tries to dispose of the body without arousing suspicion.
Unoriginal attempt at a black comedy, lacking wit and timing; Hitchcock did it far better with The Trouble With Harry.
w Maurice Phillips, A. J. Tipping, James Whaley *d* Maurice Phillips *ph* Affonso Beato *m* Craig Safan *pd* Paul Peters *ed* Malcolm Campbell
☆ Elizabeth Perkins, Judge Reinhold, Jeffrey Jones, Rhea Perlman, Michael J. Pollard, Brion James, Charles Tyner
'Neither farcical enough nor sufficiently outrageous to justify the sterling efforts of the cast to inject some much-needed energy into the flatly directed scenes.' – *Nigel Floyd, Sight and Sound*

Enigma
GB/France 1982 101m colour
Embassy/Filmcrest/Peter Shaw
An East German refugee is recruited by the CIA to return to East Berlin.
Threadbare spy stuff with an indecipherable plot.
w John Briley *novel* Michael Barak *d* Jeannot Szwarc *ph* Jean-Louis Picavet *m* Marc Wilkinson
☆ Martin Sheen, Brigitte Fossey, Sam Neill, Derek Jacobi, Michel Lonsdale, Frank Finlay, Michael Williams, Warren Clarke
'Well made but insufficiently exciting.' – *Variety*
'The mystery is why they bothered.' – *Guardian*

'Crack the Code.'
Enigma
GB/US/Netherlands/Germany 2001 118m Technicolor Panavision
Buena Vista/Intermedia/Senator/Meespierson/Jagged Films/Broadway (Lorne Michaels, Mick Jagger)
In 1943, at the headquarters of British intelligence, a mathematician tries to break a new German code while searching for his missing lover.
Stolidly old-fashioned movie, in the style of Second World War propaganda films, that segues into an even more old-fashioned spy yarn of derring-do.
w Tom Stoppard *d* Michael Apted *ph* Seamus McGarvey *m* John Barry *pd* John Beard *ed* Rick Shaine *cos* Shirley Russell
☆ Dougray Scott (Tom Jericho), Kate Winslet (Hester Wallace), Saffron Burrows (Claire Romilly), Jeremy Northam (Wigram), Nikolaj Coster Waldau (Puck), Tom Hollander (Logie), Corin Redgrave (Admiral Trowbridge), Matthew MacFadyen (Cave), Robert Pugh (Skynner)
'It's an impatient film-goer who won't be hooked by the tale of deception, treachery and double (or treble) dealing.' – *Alexander Walker, London Evening Standard*
'A flat, plodding picture…the movie is a muddle.' – A. O. Scott, *New York Times*

The Enigma of Kaspar Hauser ****
West Germany 1974 110m colour
Contemporary/Zud Deutscher Rudfunk/Werner Herzog
original title: *Jeder für sich und Gott gegen alle*
aka: *The Mystery of Kaspar Hauser; Every Man for Himself and God against All*
In the 1820s, a 16-year-old boy, who has spent his life isolated from others, is found abandoned in the town square of Nuremberg.
Based on a true story, a disturbing and affecting account of an untouched mind confronting humanity at its best and worst and exposing the limitations of society's response, with a fiercely convincing performance in the title role.
wd Werner Herzog ph Jörg Schmidt-Reitwein *m* Pachelbel, Albinoni and others *ad* Henning V. Gierke *ed* Beate Mainke-Jellinghaus
☆ *Bruno S.*, Walter Ladengast, Brigitte Mira, Willy Semmelrogge, Gloria Dör, Volker Prechtel, Hans Musaus
'A double fable, intermingling the stultifying effects of bourgeois society and the cruelty of a demonic universe.' – *Pauline Kael*
'Herzog's direction is not free of the hallmarks of contemporary German film-making, an estheticism, a slow pace, an arrogance toward dramatic concept that almost supply an imaginary soundtrack accompanying the picture saying: "You can see that this film was made by an intellectual, can't you?"' – *Stanley Kauffmann*
† The film was awarded the Special Jury Prize at the Cannes Film Festival in 1975.

L'Ennui **
France 1998 122m colour
Artificial Eye/Gemini/Ima (Paulo Branco)
A depressed philosopher, who has eschewed love in order to finish writing a book, begins an affair with a young girl who bores, but obsesses, him.
Intriguing drama of two people who can only communicate in bed, of an intellectual almost destroyed by his jealousy and desire for a sensual, unthinking woman.
w Laurence Ferreira Barbosa, Cédric Kahn *novel* Alberto Moravia *d* Cédric Kahn *ph* Pascal Marti *pd* François Abelanet *ed* Yann Dedet *cos* Françoise Clavet
☆ Charles Berling (Martin), Sophie Guillemin (Cécilia), Arielle Dombasle (Sophie), Robert Kramer (Meyers), Alice Grey (Cécilia's Mother), Maurice Antoni (Cécilia's Father), Tom Ouedraogo (Momo)
'This devastating film goes as far as a movie ever has in exploring the kind of eroticized panic that can explode into violence.' – *Stephen Holden, New York Times*

'Everyone has a limit.'
Enough
US 2002 115m DeLuxe Panavision
Columbia/Irwin Winkler, Rob Cowan
A woman goes on the run from her abusive husband and learns to stand up for herself.
Contrived and tacky domestic drama of a familiar kind that is always predictable and never interesting.
w Nicholas Kazan *d* Michael Apted *ph* Rogier Stoffers *m* David Arnold *pd* Doug Kraner *ed* Rick Shaine
☆ Jennifer Lopez (Slim), Billy Campbell (Mitch), Juliette Lewis (Ginny), Dan Futterman (Joe), Fred Ward (Jupiter), Bill Cobbs (Jim Toller), Tessa Allen (Gracie), Noah Wyle (Robbie)
'The latest model in the recent spate of underwhelming female star vehicles.' – *Robert Koehler, Variety*
'Clumsy, obvious, preposterous, the movie will likely set the cause of woman warriors back decades.' – *Peter Rainer, New York*

Ensayo de un Crimen: see *The Criminal Life of Archibaldo de la Cruz*

Ensign Pulver
US 1964 104m Technicolor Panavision
Warner (Joshua Logan)
Further naval misadventures of the character from *Mr Roberts*.
Threadbare naval comedy with every expected cliché.
w Joshua Logan, Peter S. Feibleman *play* Joshua Logan, Thomas Heggen *d* Joshua Logan *ph* Charles Lawton *m* George Duning
☆ Robert Walker, Burl Ives, Walter Matthau, Tommy Sands, Millie Perkins, Kay Medford, Larry Hagman, James Farentino, James Coco, Al Freeman Jnr

Entebbe: Operation Thunderbolt: see *Operation Thunderbolt*

Enter Laughing *
US 1966 111m Technicolor
Columbia/Acre/Sajo (Carl Reiner, Joseph Stein)
In New York in the thirties, a young man about to train as a pharmacist decides to become an actor instead.
Strident Jewish comedy based on the writer-director's own youthful experiences, which might have been more effectively strained by another hand. The talent is there, though.
w Joseph Stein, Carl Reiner *play* Carl Reiner *d* Carl Reiner *ph* Joseph Biroc *m* Quincy Jones
☆ Reni Santoni, José Ferrer, Shelley Winters, Elaine May, Jack Gilford, Janet Margolin, David Opatoshu, Michael J. Pollard, Rob Reiner

Enter the Dragon *
US/Hong Kong 1973 99m Technicolor Panavision
Warner/Concord (Fred Weintraub, Paul Heller)
A master of martial arts is enlisted by British intelligence to stop opium smuggling.
The first Hollywood-based Kung Fu actioner; not bad, on the lines of a more violent James Bond.
w Michael Allin *d* Robert Clouse *ph* Gilbert Hubbs *m* Lalo Schifrin
☆ Bruce Lee, John Saxon, Shih Kien, Jim Kelly, Bob Wall
'A good-natured example of the pleasures of schlock art.' – *Pauline Kael*

The Entertainer *
GB 1960 96m bw
BL/Bryanston/Woodfall/Holly (John Croydon)
A faded seaside comedian reflects on his failure as an entertainer and as a man.
Even with Olivier repeating his stage triumph, or perhaps because of it, this tragi-comedy remains defiantly theatrical and does not take wing on film.
w John Osborne, Nigel Kneale *play* John Osborne *d* Tony Richardson *ph* Oswald Morris *m* John Addison
☆ *Laurence Olivier*, Joan Plowright, Brenda de Banzie, *Roger Livesey*, Alan Bates, Shirley Anne Field, Albert Finney, Thora Hird, Daniel Massey
'No amount of deafening sound effects and speciously busy cutting can remove one's feeling that behind this distracting façade of heightened realism lurks a basic lack of confidence.' – *Peter John Dyer*
† A 1975 version for television starred Jack Lemmon.
Laurence Olivier

Entertaining Angels: The Dorothy Day Story
US 1996 111m DeLuxe
Warner/Paulist (Ellwood E. Kieser)
A left-wing journalist and intellectual becomes a Catholic, founds the crusading *The Catholic Worker* newspaper and establishes soup kitchens and shelters for the homeless.
A bland biopic about an interesting woman, short on conflict, but big on uplift.
w John Wells *d* Michael Ray Rhodes *ph* Michael Fash *m* Bill Conti, Ashley Irwin *ed* George Folsey Jnr, Geoffrey Rowland
☆ Moira Kelly, Heather Graham, Melinda Dillon, Martin Sheen, Lenny von Dohlen, Paul Lieber, Boyd Kestner, James Lancaster, Brian Keith
'A stultifying bore.' – *Film Review*
† The film's production company is a branch of the Paulist Fathers, 'dedicated to the communication of spiritual values through modern media'.

Entertaining Mr Sloane *
GB 1969 94m Technicolor
Pathé/Canterbury (Douglas Kentish)
A lodger attracts the amorous attention of both the middle-aged daughter and older son of the house.
A Gothic tour de force of bad taste which worked better on the stage but has its moments.
w Clive Exton *play* Joe Orton *d* Douglas Hickox *ph* Wolfgang Suschitzky *m* Georgie Fame
☆ Beryl Reid, Harry Andrews, Peter McEnery, Alan Webb
'What works as an offbeat comedy in the theatre fails to grip in the cinema where the darkness is made light. The direction becomes as brash as the dayglo colours of Beryl Reid's see-through mini-dress.' – *Ken Russell, Fire over England*

The Entity
US 1981 125m Technicolor Panavision
TCF/Pelleport Investors/American Cinema (Harold Schneider)
A young mother is attacked and raped by an invisible entity which may come from her own id.
Unpleasant nonsense, way overlong but with the occasional well-staged scene for those who can stay the course.
w Frank DeFelitta *novel* Frank DeFelitta *d* Sidney J. Furie *ph* Stephen H. Burum *m* Charles Bernstein *pd* Charles Rosen *ed* Frank J. Urioste
☆ Barbara Hershey, Ron Silver, David Labiosa, George Coe, Jacqueline Brookes

Entr'acte **
France 1924 20m approx bw silent
Ballets Suédois
Various eccentric characters become involved in a crazy chase.
Hilarious nonsense short, devised originally to be shown between the acts of a Dadaist ballet. Very clearly the start of a famous directorial career.
w Francis Picabia *ph* J. Berliet *d/ed René Clair*
☆ Jean Borlin, Inge Fries, Francis Picabia, Man Ray, Georges Auric, Marcel Achard, Marcel Duchamp

'The trap is set.'
Entrapment *
US/Germany 1999 110m DeLuxe Panavision
TCF/New Regency/Fountainbridge (Michael Hertzberg, Sean Connery, Rhonda Tollefson)
A female insurance investigator sets a trap for the world's greatest thief by asking him to steal a Chinese mask worth millions.
A thriller-cum-romantic-comedy with the emphasis on glamour; it has little else to offer.
w Ron Bass, William Broyles *d* Jon Amiel *ph* Phil Meheux *m* Christopher Young *pd* Norman Garwood *ed* Terry Rawlings
☆ Sean Connery (Robert 'Mac' MacDougal), Catherine Zeta-Jones (Virginia 'Gin' Baker), Ving Rhames (Thibadeaux), Will Patton (Hector Cruz), Maury Chaykin (Conrad Greene), Kevin McNally (Haas), Terry O'Neill (Quin), David Yip (Chief of Police)
'No need to believe the outlandish details of the story; there's enough verve and charisma to the stars to make the escapade easy on the eyes.' – *Janet Maslin, New York Times*
'Preposterous whimsy that sort of gets by thanks to lustrous settings, slick production values and, especially, its ultra-attractive stars.' – *Todd McCarthy, Variety*

Entre Nous: see *Coup de Foudre*

Entre Onze Heures et Minuit *
France 1948 103m bw
Francinex (Jacques Roitfeld)
A police detective solves his case by impersonating one of the victims.
Twisty, elaborate murder mystery, very competently performed but a little overlong.
w Henri Decoin, Marcel Rivet *novel Le Sosie de la Morgue* by Claude Luxel *d* Henri Decoin *ph* Nicolas Hayer *m* Henri Saguet
☆ Louis Jouvet, Madeleine Robinson, Robert Arnoux, Gisèle Casadesus

Entre Tinieblas: see *Dark Habits*

Entrée des Artistes *
France 1938 100m bw
Regina
Jealousies among the students at the Paris Conservatory lead to murder.
Predictable but well-made audience pleaser.
w Henri Jeanson, André Cayatte *d* Marc Allégret
☆ Louis Jouvet, Odette Joyeux, Claude Dauphin, Janine Darcy, Carette, Dalio, Sylvie

Equilibrium
US 2002 107m colour
Momentum/Blue Tulip (Jan De Bont, Lucas Foster)
In a future totalitarian state, where the population takes emotion-suppressing drugs, an enforcer turns against the system.
Risible science-fiction that borrows from classic works without understanding them and substitutes sentimentality for sense; the frequent fights look like rehearsals from The Matrix.
wd Kurt Wimmer *ph* Dion Beebe *m* Klaus Badelt *pd* Wolf Kroeger *ed* Tom Rolfe, William Yeh
☆ Christian Bale (John Preston), Emily Watson (Mary O'Brian), Taye Diggs (Brandt), Angus MacFayden (Dupont), Sean Bean (Partridge), Matthew Harbour (Robbie Preston), William Fichtner (Jurgen)
'The fight scenes are technically impressive, but as for the rest: you may find yourself heading for the perfect equilibrium of sleep.' – *Peter Bradshaw, Guardian*
'Like a remake of "1984" by someone who's seen "The Matrix" 25 times while eating Twinkies and doing methamphetamines.' – *Stephen Hunter, Washington Post*

'Everyone Has A Dark Side. Henry's About To Meet His.'
Equinox *
US 1992 110m colour Panavision
Metro Tartan/SC Entertainment (David Blocker)
A shy and timid garage mechanic discovers that he has a twin brother who is a killer.
Quirky, stylized but insubstantial tale of people damaged by, or fearful of, life; but it cannot bear as much weight as its director intended.
wd Alan Rudolph *ph* Elliot Davis *m* Rachmaninov and others *pd* Steven Legler *ed* Michael Ruscio
☆ Matthew Modine, Lara Flynn Boyle, Marisa Tomei, Fred Ward, Tyra Ferrell, Kevin J. O'Connor, Tate Donovan, Lori Singer, M. Emmet Walsh, Gailard Sartain
'A film which needs several viewings to be appreciated. Although the battle between dark and light is obvious, the finer touches are buried in a visual tapestry to be discovered by the devoted (perhaps obsessive) viewer.' – *Sight and Sound*

L'Equipage *
France 1935 107m bw
Pathé-Natan
A World War I flyer finds that the love of his life is the wife of his colleague.
Tense romantic drama with aerial sequences, subsequently remade in Hollywood as The Woman I Love.
story Joseph Kessel *d Anatole Litvak*
☆ *Charles Vanel, Jean-Pierre Aumont,* Annabella
'A gripping human story, beautifully told.' – *Variety*

Equus *
GB 1977 137m colour
UA/Winkast (Denis Holt)
A middle-aged psychiatrist tries to find out why a 17-year-old boy blinded six horses.
Overlong film version of a play which was a succès d'estime; *it makes the fatal mistake of showing the tragic events realistically instead of stylistically as was done on the stage, and as a study in abnormal psychology it is scarcely gripping or revealing.*
w Peter Shaffer *play* Peter Shaffer *d* Sidney Lumet *ph* Oswald Morris *m* Richard Rodney Bennett *pd* Tony Walton
☆ *Richard Burton,* Peter Firth, Colin Blakely, Joan Plowright, Harry Andrews, Eileen Atkins, Jenny Agutter, Kate Reid
'It sets Peter Shaffer's worst ideas on a pedestal.' – *Pauline Kael*
Peter Shaffer; Richard Burton; Peter Firth
Jenny Agutter

'He will erase your past to protect your future.'
Eraser
US 1996 115m Technicolor Panavision
Warner (Arnold Kopelson, Anne Kopelson)
An agent for the Federal Witness Protection Program discovers that he can trust no one.
Predictable recycling of the themes of modern paranoid thrillers, punctuated by the furious sound of monstrous gun battles.
w Tony Puryear, Walon Green *d* Chuck Russell *ph* Adam Greenberg *m* Alan Silvestri *pd* Bill Kenney *ed* Michael Tronick
☆ Arnold Schwarzenegger, James Caan, Vanessa Williams, James Coburn, Robert Pastorelli, James Cromwell, Andy Romano, Danny Nucci
'If *Mission: Impossible* failed to make any sense to you, you could look on *Eraser* as the world's fastest remake, since its plot, its characters and its big set pieces are exactly the same.' – *Mark Steyn, Spectator*
'Filmgoers may feel that they've been there, seen that: fans will still flock.' – *Alexander Walker*
† It was a box-office success in 1996, grossing around $234m worldwide.
sound effects editing

Eraserhead
US 1976 89m bw
David Lynch
A nondescript man has a number of increasingly nightmarish experiences including becoming pregnant and being consumed by a planet.
Tediously elongated piece of schlock surrealism. At least Buñuel and Dali didn't take so long about their nonsense.
wd David Lynch *ph* David Elmes, Herbert Cardwell
☆ John Nance, Charlotte Stewart, Allen Joseph
'A compulsive hybrid mix of punk surrealism and B picture.' – *Time Out*

Erbin des Dracula: see *Vampyros Lesbos*

Ercole e la Regina di Lidia: see *Hercules Unchained*

L'Erdita Ferramonti: see *The Inheritance*

Erendira *
France/Mexico/Germany 1982 105m colour
Les Films du Triangle/A2/Cine Qua Non/Atlas Saskia Film (Alain Queffelean)
An intolerant woman tries to restore the family fortune by prostituting her young granddaughter after she accidentally burns down their home.
Bizarre, surrealist fable of thwarted love and domination.
w Gabriel García Marquez *d* Ruy Guerra *ph* Denys Clerval *m* Maurice Lecoeur *pd* Pierre Cadiou *ed* Kenout Peltier
☆ Irene Papas, Claudia Ohana, Michel Lonsdale, Oliver Wehe, Rufus, Blanca Guerra, Ernesto Gomez Cruz

Erik the Viking
GB 1989 108m Technicolor
UIP/Erik The Viking Productions/Prominent Features/ AB Svensk Filmindustri (Terry Glinwood)
A Viking sails on an expedition to wake the Gods.
Uneasy mix of fantasy and humour.
wd Terry Jones *novel* Terry Jones *ph* Ian Wilson *m* Neil Innes *pd* John Beard *ed* George Akers
☆ Tim Robbins, Mickey Rooney, Eartha Kitt, Terry Jones, Imogen Stubbs, John Cleese, Tsutomu Sekine, Anthony Sher, Gary Cady, Charles McKeown, Tim McInnerny, John Gordon Sinclair
'A thunderous, unfunny jumble.' – *MFB*

'She brought a small town to its feet and a huge corporation to its knees.'
Erin Brockovich ***
US 2000 131m CFI
Columbia TriStar/Universal/Jersey (Danny DeVito, Michael Shamberg, Stacey Sher)
A working-class mother, who talks her way into a job in a law firm, organises a winning investigation into industrial pollution that has devastated a community.
Unexpectedly lively and amusing movie of a heartening true story, one that gives Julia Roberts her best and most convincing role so far, as a feisty but vulnerable mother who refuses to be intimidated by anyone.
w Susannah Grant d Steven Soderbergh ph Ed Lachman *m* Thomas Newman *pd* Phil Messina *ed* Anne V. Coates *cos* Jeffrey Kurland
☆ *Julia Roberts* (Erin Brockovich), Albert Finney (Ed Masry), Aaron Eckhart (George), Marg Helgenberger (Donna Jensen), Cherry Jones (Pamela Duncan), Veanne Cox (Theresa Dallavale), Conchata Ferrell (Brenda), Tracey Walter (Charles Embry), Peter Coyote (Kurt Potter), Scotty Leavenworth (Matthew), Gemmenne De la Pena (Katie), Jamie Harrold (Scott)
'A movie that is both intensely funny and emotionally satisfying.' – *Ian Nathan, Empire*
'An exhilarating tale about a woman discovering her full potential and running with it.' – *Todd McCarthy, Variety*
† Erin Brockovich herself appears briefly as a waitress in a coffee shop.
Julia Roberts
picture; Steven Soderbergh; Susannah Grant; Albert Finney
Julia Roberts

Ermo ***
China/Hong Kong 1994 98m colour
ICA/Ocean/Shanghai Studio (Jimmy Tan, Chen Kunming)
A wife with an elderly and impotent husband works hard in order to buy a big-screen television set to impress the neighbours.
Biting comedy of village and peasant life, which also asks some tough questions on what gives meaning and purpose to a person's existence.
w Lang Yun *story* Xu Baoqi *d* Zhou Xiaowen *ph* Lu Gengxin *m* Zhoi Xiaowen *ad* Zhang Daqian *ed* Zhong Furong
☆ Ailiya, Liu Peiqi, Ge Zhijun, Zhang Haiyan, Zan Zhenguo
'A lively, constantly diverting film: it has amusing, colourful characters, a generous dash of humour and not a jot of sentimentality.' – *Independent*

Ernest Rides Again
US 1994 92m CFI color
Emsell (Stacy Williams)
Ernest discovers that a cannon contains the British Crown Jewels.
There are few experiences more depressing than attempting to sit through an Ernest movie: it's not just that the jokes are poor, the comic timing is off and its hero has all the charm of an over-ripe skunk; it is just the pervasive feeling that no one is having fun, on either side of the camera.
w John Cherry, William M. Akers *d* John Cherry *ph* David Geddes *m* Bruce Arntson *ed* Craig Bassett
☆ Jim Varney, Ron James, Linda Kash, Tom Butler, Xuke Ernsberger, Jeff Pillars

Ernest Saves Christmas
US 1988 91m Metrocolor
Warner/Touchstone/Silver Screen Partners III (Stacy Williams, Doug Claybourne)
Santa Claus goes to America to find someone to take over his job.
Inept and witless from start to finish.
w B. Kline, Ed Turner *d* John Cherry *ph* Peter Stein *m* Mark Snow *ad* Ian Thomas *ed* Sharyn L. Ross
☆ Jim Varney, Douglas Seale, Oliver Clark, Noelle Parker, Gailard Sartain, Billie Bird, Bill Byrge, Robert Lesser, Key Howard

L'Eroe di Babylon: see *The Hero of Babylon*

Eroica *
Poland 1957 83m bw
Kadr
aka: *Heroism*
Two ironic episodes of war; in the 1944 Warsaw uprising and in a POW camp.
Nicely-judged little stories with a sting.
w Jerzy Stefan Stawinski *novels Jerzy Stefan Stawinski d* Andrzej Munk *ph* Jerzy Wojcik *m* Jan Krenz
☆ Barbara Polomska, L. Niemszyk, Edward Dziewonski, K. Rudzki, Roman Klosowski, Josef Nowak

The Erotic Dreams of Cleopatra (dubbed)
Italy/France 1983 85m colour
2T/Naja (Victor Beniard)
Cleopatra, a captive in Rome, becomes caught up in the power struggle to control the Empire.
An oddity: a risible, would-be erotic exploitation movie that opens with a quote from Cicero, followed by the assassination of Julius Caesar in a thick fog (a dream by Cleopatra) and then departs from known history with its cast simultaneously engaging in energetic couplings and banal political discussions.
w Rino di Silvestro *d* Cesar Todd *ph* Giovanni Bergamini *m* Romuald *ad* Mario Ambrosino *ed* Adriano Tagliavia
☆ Marcella Petrelli, Rita Silva, Jacques Stany, Andrea Coppola, Maurizio Faraoni

Erotikon *
Sweden 1920 85m approx bw silent
Svensk Filmindustri
When a professor discovers that his wife is unfaithful, he consoles himself with his young niece.
Sophisticated comedy drama filled with material which might later have appealed to Lubitsch; a little faded now, but it still has charm.
w Gustav Molander, Mauritz Stiller *play* Franz Herzeg *d Mauritz Stiller ph* Henrik Jaenzon
☆ Lars Hanson, Karin Molander, Tora Teje, Anders de Wahl

Erotikon *
Czechoslovakia 1929 85m approx bw silent
Gem Film
A stationmaster's daughter takes a rich lover.
Atmospheric little sex drama which sufficiently justified its title to be a big international success.
wd Gustav Machaty ph Vaclav Vich
☆ Ita Rina, Karel Schleichert, Olaf Fjord, Theo Pistek

The Errand Boy
US 1961 92m bw
Paramount/Jerry Lewis (Ernest D. Glucksman)
A dimwit paperhanger causes havoc in a Hollywood studio but is eventually signed up as a comic to rival Jerry Lewis.
Feeble comedy with the star at his self-satisfied worst.
wd Jerry Lewis *ph* W. Wallace Kelley *m* Walter Scharf
☆ Jerry Lewis, Brian Donlevy, Sig Rumann, Fritz Feld, Isobel Elsom, Iris Adrian

Es Geschah am 20 Juli: see *Jackboot Mutiny*

Escapade
US 1935 87m bw
MGM (Bernard Hyman)
Affairs of a Viennese artist.
Turgid romantic drama copied from the more successful German film Maskerade.
w Herman J. Mankiewicz *original* Walter Reisch *d* Robert Z. Leonard *ph* Ernest Haller *m* Bronislau Kaper, Walter Jurmann
☆ William Powell, Luise Rainer, Virginia Bruce, Mady Christians, Reginald Owen, Frank Morgan, Laura Hope Crews, Henry Travers
'A triumph of studio slickness.' – *Variety*

Escapade: see *Robinson Crusoeland (1950)*

Escapade *
GB 1955 87m bw
Pinnacle (Daniel Angel)
Parents row with a headmaster when their three sons steal an aeroplane, but all is well when it turns out that they are on a peace mission.
Whimsical comedy-drama with a rather foolish point; the cast however can hardly fail to provide entertaining moments.
w Gilbert Holland (Donald Ogden Stewart) *play* Roger MacDougall *d* Philip Leacock *ph* Eric Cross *m* Bruce Montgomery

☆ John Mills, Alastair Sim, Yvonne Mitchell, Colin Gordon, Marie Lohr
† Stewart used his father's name as screenwriter because he was blacklisted at the time.

Escapade in Florence
US 1962 80m Technicolor
Walt Disney (Bill Anderson)
Two American students in Florence uncover art thefts.
Cheerful adventure for children, well enough produced on location, but quite unmemorable.
w Maurice Tombragel *novel* The Golden Doors by Edward Fenton *d* Steve Previn *ph* Kurt Grigoleit *m* Buddy Baker
☆ Ivan Desny, Tommy Kirk, Annette Funicello, Nino Castelnuovo

Escapade in Japan
US 1957 93m Technirama
RKO (Arthur Lubin)
An American boy survives a plane crash in Tokyo and the crisis reunites his parents.
Nicely photographed travelogue with a thread of plot; pleasant but hardly sustaining.
w Winston Miller *d* Arthur Lubin *ph* William Snyder *m* Max Steiner
☆ Cameron Mitchell, Teresa Wright, Jon Prevost, Philip Ober

'There is a love from which no man can escape!'
Escape **
US 1940 104m bw
MGM (Lawrence Weingarten)
reissue title: *When the Door Opened*
An American gets his mother out of a Nazi concentration camp before World War II.
Ingenious but somewhat slow-moving melodrama with an exciting climax and good production values.
w Arch Oboler, Marguerite Roberts *novel* Ethel Vance *d* *Mervyn Le Roy* *ph* Robert Planck *m* Franz Waxman
☆ Norma Shearer, Robert Taylor, *Conrad Veidt*, *Nazimova*, Felix Bressart, Albert Basserman, Philip Dorn, Bonita Granville
'It takes an hour to get started and makes just another feeble fable from headlines.' – *Otis Ferguson*
'Far and away the most dramatic and hair-raising picture yet made on the sinister subject of persecution in a totalitarian land.' – *Bosley Crowther, New York Times*
'One of the most poignant dramatic films of the year.' – *Modern Screen*
'The director takes forever to set up the manoeuvres, and the villain is so much more attractive than the hero that the whole thing turns into a feeble, overproduced joke.' – *Pauline Kael, 70s*

The Escape Artist *
US 1982 93m Technicolor
Zoetrope Studios (Doug Claybourne, Buck Houghton)
A young boy justifies his descent from 'the world's greatest escape artist'.
Curiously unfulfilled fable, too vague to satisfy the family audience it seems to aim at, but with pleasant moments.
w Melissa Mathison, Stephen Zito. *novel* David Wagoner *d* Caleb Deschanel *ph* Stephen H. Burum *m* Georges Delerue *pd* Dean Tavoularis
☆ Griffin O'Neal, Raul Julia, Teri Garr, Joan Hackett, Gabriel Dell, Desi Arnaz

Escape from Alcatraz *
US 1979 112m DeLuxe
Paramount/Malpaso (Don Siegel)
The allegedly true story of a 1960 escape from the prison on a rock in San Francisco Bay.
A dour, terse, depressing prison movie which makes an uncomfortable star vehicle and not very much of an entertainment, but does preserve a certain integrity right to its ambiguous ending.
w Richard Tuggle *book* J. Campbell Bruce *d* Don Siegel *ph* Bruce Surtees *m* Jerry Fielding *pd* Allen Smith
☆ Clint Eastwood, Patrick McGoohan, Roberts Blossom, Jack Thibeau, Larry Hankin
'An almost entirely interior film masquerading as an exterior one.' – *Tom Milne, MFB*

Escape from East Berlin
Germany/US 1962 94m bw
MGM/Walter Wood/Hans Albin
aka: *Tunnel 28*
An East German chauffeur is persuaded to help an escape attempt by digging and tunnelling under the Berlin Wall.
Cheerless escape melodrama, thinly based on fact but without much suspense.
w Gabrielle Upton, Peter Berneis, Millard Lampell *d* Robert Siodmak *ph* Georg Krause *m* Hans-Martin Majewski
☆ Don Murray, Christine Kaufmann, Werner Klemperer, Ingrid van Bergen

Escape from Fort Bravo *
US 1953 98m Anscocolor
MGM (Nicholas Nayfack)
A girl helps her Confederate lover to escape from a Yankee fort in Arizona; the commander then tries to save them from Indians.
Grade A Western, effectively shot in Death Valley.
w Frank Fenton *d* John Sturges *ph* Robert Surtees *m* Jeff Alexander
☆ William Holden, Eleanor Parker, John Forsythe, William Demarest

'Snake is Back.'
Escape from L.A.
US 1996 100m DeLuxe Panavision
Paramount/Rysher (Kurt Russell, Debra Hill)
aka: *John Carpenter's Escape from L.A.*
In 2013, an outlaw is sent to the island of Los Angeles to eliminate the President's daughter, who has stolen a device to shut down the world's power sources and joined a revolution against her father's right-wing government.
No more than a weary rehash of Carpenter's Escape from New York; *the plot has aged in the 15-year gap between the two movies, and one might have hoped that its star and director would have moved on to something less stale.*
w John Carpenter, Debra Hill, Kurt Russell *d* John Carpenter *ph* Gary B. Kibbe *m* Shirley Walker, John Carpenter *pd* Lawrence G. Paull *ed* Edward Warschilka
☆ Kurt Russell, Stacy Keach, Steve Buscemi, Peter Fonda, George Corraface, Valeria Golino, Pam Grier, Michelle Forbes, Cliff Robertson
'Easily the crappiest-looking, cheesiest FX-toting, shoddiest excuse for a $50 million action epic ever foisted on unsuspecting audiences.' – *Guardian*
† The film took $25m at the US box-office.

Escape from New York *
US 1981 99m Metrocolor Panavision
Avco Embassy/International Film Investors/Goldcrest (Larry Franco, Debra Hill)
In 1997 the whole of Manhattan Island has become a vast security prison; a president has to bale out over it and is taken hostage.
Inventive but too complex melodrama with unattractive detail; its director's biggest production but not his most rewarding.
w John Carpenter, Nick Castle *d* *John Carpenter* *ph* Jim Lucas *m* John Carpenter *pd* Joe Alves
☆ Kurt Russell, Lee Van Cleef, Ernest Borgnine, Donald Pleasence, Isaac Hayes, Season Hubley, Adrienne Barbeau, Harry Dean Stanton

Escape from the Dark
GB 1976 104m Technicolor
Walt Disney (Ron Miller)
US title: *The Littlest Horse Thieves*
In 1909 Yorkshire, two boys save pit ponies from the slaughterhouse.
Efficient family fare with plenty of suspense and good character cameos.
w Rosemary Anne Sisson *d* Charles Jarrott *ph* Paul Beeson *m* Ron Goodwin
☆ Alastair Sim, Peter Barkworth, Maurice Colbourne, Susan Tebbs, Geraldine McEwan, Prunella Scales, Leslie Sands, Joe Gladwin

'A New Generation Of Incredible Apes In The Most Exciting Suspense Film Of Them All.'
Escape from the Planet of the Apes
US 1971 97m DeLuxe Panavision
TCF/APJAC (Arthur P. Jacobs, Frank Capra Jnr)
Three educated apes travel back from the disaster-strewn future to warn mankind of what lies ahead. Mankind naturally misunderstands.
Predictable third in the series, with infantile humour alternating with a downbeat trend.
w Paul Dehn *d* Don Taylor *ph* Joseph Biroc *m* Jerry Goldsmith
☆ Roddy McDowall, Kim Hunter, Bradford Dillman, Ricardo Montalban, Natalie Trundy, Eric Braeden, William Windom, Sal Mineo
† See also *Planet of the Apes*.

Escape from Zahrain
US 1961 93m Technicolor Panavision
Paramount (Ronald Neame)
Prisoners escape across the desert from an oil sheikdom.
Slow, boring adventure film; good to look at, with James Mason unbilled in a tiny part.
w Robin Estridge *d* Ronald Neame *ph* Ellsworth Fredricks *m* Lyn Murray
☆ Yul Brynner, Sal Mineo, Madlyn Rhue, Jack Warden, Jay Novello

Escape If You Can: see *St Benny the Dip*

Escape in the Desert
US 1945 81m bw
Warner (Alex Gottlieb)
An American flyer outwits renegade Nazis.
Oddball remake of The Petrified Forest, *with Nazis sitting in for gangsters. Of no interest in itself.*
w Thomas Job *play* Robert E. Sherwood *d* Edward A. Blatt *ph* Robert Burks *m* Adolph Deutsch
☆ Philip Dorn, Helmut Dantine, Alan Hale, Jean Sullivan, Irene Manning, Samuel S. Hinds

Escape Me Never *
GB 1935 95m bw
B and D (Herbert Wilcox)
The mother of an illegitimate baby marries a composer who loves someone else.
Archetypal romantic weepie which has probably the star's most memorable and likeable performance.
w Carl Zuckerman, Robert Cullen *play* Margaret Kennedy *d* Paul Czinner *ph* Georges Périnal *m* Erich Wolfgang Korngold *ad* Carl Jules Weyl *ed* Clarence Kolster
☆ *Elisabeth Bergner*, Hugh Sinclair, Griffith Jones, Penelope Dudley Ward, Irene Vanbrugh, Leon Quartermaine, Lyn Harding
'Story stirs audience resentment, yet its able presentation commands attention.' – *Variety*
'That it is a thoroughly British film is proved by the fact that among the staff one can see names like Andrejiev, Allgeier and Strassner, that the principal actress is German, and the producer is German too.' – *James Agate*
🎗 Elisabeth Bergner

Escape Me Never
US 1947 104m bw
Warner (Henry Blanke)
A composer marries a widow and her child, but falls for another woman.
Muddled remake of the 1935 movie of Margaret Kennedy's play, with shifted emphasis; it is so ill-conceived it's like watching through frosted glass.
w Thomas Williamson *d* Peter Godfrey *ph* Sol Polito *m* Erich Wolfgang Korngold
☆ Errol Flynn, Ida Lupino, Eleanor Parker, Gig Young, Reginald Denny, Isobel Elsom, Albert Basserman, Ludwig Stossel, Helene Thimig

The Escape of Mechagodzilla: see *Monsters from an Unknown Planet*

Escape of the Amethyst: see *Yangtse Incident*

Escape to Athena
GB 1979 117m Eastmancolor Panavision
ITC/Pimlico (David Niven Jnr, Jack Wiener)
Prisoners-of-war on a Greek island during World War II recruit the aid of their sympathetic camp commandant in harassing the SS.
Expensive but not very involving thick ear, hampered by tediously typecast actors and an uninventive script.
w Edward Anhalt, Richard S. Lochte *d* George Pan Cosmatos *ph* Gil Taylor *m* Lalo Schifrin
☆ Roger Moore, David Niven, Elliott Gould, Sonny Bono, Telly Savalas, Claudia Cardinale, Stefanie Powers, Richard Roundtree, Anthony Valentine
'Performing as though they had met up by chance on holiday ... the clutch of box office stars do what they can in a situation where they are the stand-ins and the stuntmen (especially the motorcyclists) dominate the screen.' – *Martyn Auty, MFB*

Escape to Burma
US 1955 88m Technicolor Superscope
Benedict Bogeaus
An adventurer suspected of murder hides out on the tea plantation of an indomitable American woman.
Far Eastern hokum in which the heroine has a way with elephants.
w Talbot Jennings, Herbert Donovan *d* Allan Dwan *ph* John Alton *m* Louis Forbes
☆ Barbara Stanwyck, Robert Ryan, David Farrar, Murvyn Vye, Reginald Denny

Escape to Danger
GB 1943 92m bw
RKO (William Sistrom)
A British schoolmistress becomes a spy.
Adequate propaganda hokum.
w Wolfgang Wilhelm, Jack Whittingham *d* Lance Comfort *ph* Max Greene *m* William Alwyn
☆ Eric Portman, Ann Dvorak, Karel Stepanek, Ronald Ward, Ronald Adam, Lily Kann, David Peel, Felix Aylmer, A. E. Matthews

Escape to Glory
US 1940 74m bw
Columbia (Sam Bischoff)
aka: *Submarine Zone*
A merchant ship with a variety of passengers is stalked by a Nazi submarine.
Minor Grand Hotel *afloat: quite brisk and watchable.*
w P. J. Wolfson *d* John Brahm *ph* Franz Planer
☆ Pat O'Brien, Constance Bennett, John Halliday, Alan Baxter, Melville Cooper, Edgar Buchanan, Marjorie Gateson

Escape to Happiness: see *Intermezzo*

Escape to Victory: see *Victory*

Escape to Witch Mountain *
US 1974 97m Technicolor
Walt Disney (Jerome Courtland)
Two mysterious orphan children have extraordinary powers, are chased by a scheming millionaire, and prove to come from another planet.
Mildly ingenious story frittered away by poor scripting and special effects. A stimulating change in children's films, however.
w Robert Malcolm Young *novel* Alexander Key *d* John Hough *ph* Frank Phillips *m* Johnny Mandel *sp* Art Cruickshank, Danny Lee
☆ Ray Milland, Donald Pleasence, Eddie Albert, Kim Richards, Ike Eisenmann, Walter Barnes, Reta Shaw, Denver Pyle

Escapement
GB 1957 72m bw
Anglo Amalgamated/Merton Park Studios (Alec C. Snowden)
An insurance investigator traces some mysterious deaths in France to a health clinic where doctors are experimenting with mind-altering techniques.
Efficient and slightly unconventional low-budget thriller.
w Charles Eric Maine, J. Maclaren-Ross *d* Montgomery Tully *ph* Bert Mason, Teddy Catford *m* Soundrama *md* Richard Taylor *ad* Wilfred Arnold *ed* Geoffrey Muller
☆ Rod Cameron, Mary Murphy, Meredith Edwards, Peter Illing, Carl Jaffé, Kay Callard, Carl Duering, Roberta Huby

The Escort: see *La Scorta*

'I'll be your friend. I'll be your lover, but it's strictly by the hour.'

The Escort
France/GB 1999 106m colour
Pathé/Renn/France3 (Claude Berri)
original title: *Mauvaise Passe*
After leaving his job and family and coming to London to write a novel, a Parisian professor becomes a successful gigolo.
Glum and faintly ridiculous drama of a writer in search of a subject; an audience needs to share the director's belief that French lovers are irresistible.
wd Michel Blanc *idea* Hanif Kureishi *additional script work* Nick Love *ph* Barry Ackroyd *m* Barry Adamson *pd* Gary Williamson *ed* Maryline Monthieux *cos* Ralph Holes
☆ Daniel Auteuil (Pierre), Stuart Townsend (Tom), Liza Walker (Kim), Noah Taylor (Gem), Frances Barber (Jessica), Claire Skinner (Patricia), Béatrice Agenin (Catherine), Keith Allen (Jessica's husband), Ben Wishaw (Jay), Amanda Ryan (Ann), Peter Mullan (Patricia's husband)
'Like watching a high-brow version of Jackie Collins's *The Stud*, only it's not as good... Pay not to see it.' – *Cosmo Landesman, Sunday Times*

Escort Girls
GB 1974 95m Eastmancolor
Variety/Donwin (Donovan Winter)
Six stories of encounters between clients and escorts hired for the night from an agency, which frequently end in rape or seduction.
Glossily made but empty sexploitation movie, hampered by a script that never deviates from the obvious.
wd Donovan Winter *ph* Gus Coma, Austin Parkinson *ed* Donovan Winter
☆ David Dixon, Maria O'Brien, Marika Mann, Gil Barber, Helen Christie, Richard Wren

Escort West
US 1958 75m bw Cinemascope
Batjac/Romina/UA
An ex-Confederate soldier helps the survivors of a Union wagon train attack.
Watchable lower-berth Western.
w Leo Gordon, Fred Hartsook *d* Francis D. Lyon *ph* William H. Clothier *m* Henry Vars
☆ Victor Mature, Elaine Stewart, Faith Domergue, Noah Beery Jnr, Rex Ingram, John Hubbard

Eskimo *
US 1933 120m bw
MGM
The life of an Eskimo hunter and his family.
Curious fated attempt by a major studio to do a northern version of the successful White Shadows in the South Seas. *Despite a melodramatic plot and gripping documentary sequences, the locale chilled audiences to the marrow.*
w John Lee Mahin, Peter Freuchen *d* W. S. Van Dyke *ed* Conrad Nervig
☆ Mala, Peter Freuchen
'Igloo whoopee variations not sufficiently hotcha to spell b.o.' – *Variety*
editing

'The living will always be more dangerous than the dead.'

El Espinazo del Diablo **
Spain/Mexico 2001 108m colour
Optimum/El Deseo/Tequila GangAnhelo/Sogepaq/Canal+ (Agustin Almodovar, Bertha Navarro)
aka: *The Devil's Backbone*
After his father has been killed in the Republican cause during the Spanish Civil War, a boy is sent to an isolated orphanage haunted by the ghost of a murdered child.
Elegant, chilling tale of greed and repression that also serves as a political allegory of the times.
w Guillermo del Toro, Antonio Trashorras, David Munoz *d* Guillermo del Toro *ph* Guillermo Navarro *m* Javier Navarrete *ad* Cesar Macarron *ed* Luis de la Madrid
☆ Marisa Paredes (Carmen), Eduardo Noriega (Jacinto), Federico Luppi (Casares), Fernando Tielve (Carlos), Irene Visedo (Conchita), Inigo Garces (Jaime)
'For the most part, creepy, meaty, crafty and fun.' – *Shawn Levy, Oregonian*
'Provokes your screams and shudders, but he also earns your tears.' – *A. O. Scott, New York Times*

L'Espion: see *The Defector*

Les Espions
France 1957 136m bw
Cinedis (L. de Mazure)
aka: *The Spies*
Spies from all sides converge on a psychiatric clinic where an atomic scientist is being hidden.
Unsatisfactory thriller with some aims to be both a whimsy and a parable. Not one of its director's successes.
w Henri-Georges Clouzot, Gerome Geronomi *d* Henri-Georges Clouzot *ph* Christian Matras *m* Georges Auric
☆ Martita Hunt, Peter Ustinov, Sam Jaffe, Vera Clouzot, Gabrielle Dorziat, Curt Jurgens, Gerard Sety, O. E. Hasse

El Espiritu de la Colmene: see *The Spirit of the Beehive*

Espoir *
France/Spain 1938 73m bw
Cornignion/Moligniec
aka: *Days of Hope*
aka: *Man's Hope*
Events of the Spanish Civil War, recreated by surviving combatants.
Anti-fascist propaganda which seems a good deal less inspiring than on its first release, but has some vivid cinematic ideas.
wd André Malraux *ph* Louis Page *m* Darius Milhaud
☆ Mejuto, Nicolas Rodriguez, Jose Lado

Esprit d'Amour
Hong Kong 1983 100m colour
Cinema City (Dean Shek, Raymond Wong)
A hen-pecked insurance investigator is haunted by the spirit of a young girl who died in an accidental fall.
Insubstantial and heavy-handed comedy, though attractive to look at.
w Ko Chi Sum, Lo Kin, Raymond Fung *story* Raymond Wong *d* Ringo L. T. Lam *m* Tang Siu Lam *pd* Nansun Shi, Raymond Fung *ed* Tony Chow
☆ Alan Tam, Cecilia Chan, Ni Shu Chun

'If You Know What Happened... You'd Better Keep Your Mouth Shut.'

Essex Boys
GB 2000 102m Technicolor
Pathé/Granada (Jeff Pope)
A taxi driver becomes involved with rival gangs of drug dealers and pushers.
Violent gangster movie, in part based on a actual murder of three men, found shot dead in a car in an Essex wood in 1995, but otherwise a familiar fantasy of betrayal and revenge among thugs.
w Jeff Pope, Terry Winsor *d* Terry Winsor *ph* John Daly *m* Colin Towns *pd* Chris Edwards *ed* Edward Mansell *cos* Sarah Lubel
☆ Sean Bean (Jason Locke), Alex Kingston (Lisa Locke), Charlie Creed-Miles (Billy Reynolds), Tom Wilkinson (John Dyke), Larry Lamb (Peter Chase), Michael McKell (Wayne Lovell), Billy Murray (Perry Elley), Amelia Lowdell (Nicole), Holly Davidson (Suzy Welch), Terence Rigby (Henry Hobbs)
'Just another disappointing British film.' – *Jo Berry, Empire*
'A movie of quiet menace with a definite character of its own.' – *Derek Elley, Variety*

'And it was written – gather together all the fair young virgins unto the palace – and let the maiden which pleaseth the king be queen.'

Esther and the King
US 1960 109m Technicolor Cinemascope
TCF/Galatea (Raoul Walsh)
A Persian king selects a new bride who helps defend him from his enemies.
Tedious biblical hokum with a muddled script and the usual co-production deficiencies.
w Raoul Walsh, Michael Elkins *d* Raoul Walsh *ph* Mario Bava *m* Francesco Lavagnino, Roberto Nicolosi
☆ Richard Egan, Joan Collins, Denis O'Dea, Sergio Fantoni, Rik Battaglia

Esther Kahn
GB/France 2000 163m colour
Winchester/Why Not/France2/France 3/Zephyr/Arts Council of England/BSkyB/British Screen (Alain Sarde)
In Victorian London, a young working-class Jewish girl overcomes personal tragedy to become a great actress.
Unsatisfactory, badly-scripted movie about theatre: it fails on the most basic level, with the cast's uniformly poor performances.
w Arnaud Desplechin, Emmanuel Bourdieu *story* Arthur Symons *d* Arnaud Desplechin *ph* Eric Gautier *m* Howard Shore *pd* Jon Henson *ed* Herve de Luze
☆ Summer Phoenix (Esther Kahn), Ian Holm (Nathan Quellen), Philippe Haygard (Fabrice Desplechin), Frances Barber (Rivka Kahn), Laszlo Szabo (Ytzhok Kahn), Emmanuelle Devos (Sylvia l'Italienne), Akbar Kurtha (Samuel Kahn), Claudia Solti (Mina Kahn), Kika Markham (Trish), Anton Lesser (Sean)
'A very long, very unsuccessful two hours and 40 minutes in the cinema.' – *Peter Bradshaw, Guardian*

Esther Waters
GB 1947 108m bw
GFD/Wessex (Ian Dalrymple)
In the 1870s, a maid is seduced by a squire but insists on bringing up her child without help.
Faded costumer with tentative performances and little else to recommend it.
w Michael Gordon, William Rose, Gerard Tyrrell *novel* George Moore *d* Ian Dalrymple, Peter Proud *ph* C. Pennington-Richards, H. E. Fowle *m* Gordon Jacob
☆ Kathleen Ryan, Dirk Bogarde, Cyril Cusack, Ivor Barnard, Fay Compton, Mary Clare, Morland Graham

Et Dieu Créa la Femme: see *And God Created Woman*

Et Mourir de Plaisir: see *Blood and Roses*

L'Eté Meurtrier: see *One Deadly Summer*

The Eternal Sea
US 1955 96m bw
Republic (John H. Auer)
The career of an aircraft carrier captain in World War II and Korea.
Solemn biopic of John Hoskins: competent but quite uninspired.
w Allen Rivkin *d* John H. Auer *ph* John L. Russell Jnr *m* Elmer Bernstein
☆ Sterling Hayden, Alexis Smith, Dean Jagger, Virginia Grey

Eternally Yours *
US 1939 95m bw
Walter Wanger
A magician's wife thinks he is too interested in his tricks.
Slightly scatty romantic comedy, amiable if not quite good enough to stand the test of time, but with a great cast.
w Gene Towne, Graham Baker *d* Tay Garnett *ph* Merritt Gerstad *m* Werner Janssen
☆ Loretta Young, David Niven, Broderick Crawford, Hugh Herbert, Billie Burke, C. Aubrey Smith, Raymond Walburn, ZaSu Pitts, Virginia Field, Eve Arden, Herman the Rabbit
'Will have to depend on the name power to get it by.' – *Variety*
'An amusing and irresponsible picture, though on the whole more irresponsible than amusing.' – *New York Times*
Werner Janssen

L'Eternel Retour: see *Love Eternal*

Eternity and a Day **
Greece/France/Italy 1998 134m colour
Theo Angelopoulos/Greek Film Centre/ERT/Paradis/La Sept/Intermedias (Theo Angelopoulos, Eric Heumann, Giorgio Silvagni, Amedeo Pagani)
original title: *Mia Eoniotita Ke Mia Mera*
A dying Greek writer ponders on the past while attempting to return an Albanian boy to his homeland.
Lyrical, elegiac meditation on the purpose of life; a slow-moving, deeply felt journey into the soul of man.
w Theo Angelopoulos, Tonino Guerra, Petros Markaris, Giorgio Silvagni *d* Theo Angelopoulos *ph* Giorgos Arvanitis, Andreas Sinani *m* Eleni Karaindrou *pd* Giorgos Patsos, Giorgos Ziakas *ed* Yannis Tsitsopoulos
☆ Bruno Ganz, Isabelle Renauld, Achileas Skevis, Despina Bebedeli, Iris Chatziantoniou, Helene Gerasimidiou, Fabrizio Bentivoglio, Vassilis Siemenis
'Give it time and Theo Angelopolous's sedate but eloquent tone-poem will reward your patience.' – *Nigel Cliff, The Times*
† The film won the Palme d'Or at the Cannes Film Festival in 1998.

Ethan Frome
US 1993 99m DuArt
American Playhouse/Richard Price/BBC (Stan Wlodkowski)
The new minister in a small and repressive Massachusetts community hires a crippled farmer to be his driver and discovers the story of love and hate that lies behind the man's injury.
A somewhat inert version of a rural tragedy, a grim tale of requited love, though it is strikingly photographed.
w Richard Nelson *novel* Edith Wharton *d* John Madden *ph* Bobby Bukowski *m* Rachel Portman *pd* Andrew Jackness *ed* Katherine Wenning
☆ Liam Neeson, Patricia Arquette, Joan Allen, Tate Donovan, Katharine Houghton, Stephen Mendillo
'Careful, literary, restrained, nicely acted and more than a bit dry.' – *Variety*

L'étoile du Nord *
France 1982 124m Fujicolour
Gala/Sara Films/Antenne 2 (Alain Sarde)
A lodger entrances his landlady with stories of his Egyptian adventures, neglecting to mention his involvement in a murder there.
Two well-dovetailed performances lift this odd little thriller above the ordinary.
w Jean Aurenche, Michel Grisolia, Pierre Granier-Deferre *novel* *Le Locataire* by Georges Simenon *d* Pierre Granier-Deferre *ph* Pierre-William Glenn *m* Philippe Sarde *ad* Dominique André *ed* Jean Revel
☆ *Simone Signoret*, *Philippe Noiret*, Fanny Cottençon, Julie Jezequel, Liliana Gerace, Gamil Ratib

'One Woman. Four Sons. Three Fathers. No one said love was simple.'

Eu Tu Eles *
Brazil/US/Portugal 2000 106m colour
Columbia TriStar/Conspiracao (Leonardo M. De Barros, Pedro B. De Hollanda, Andrucha Waddington, Favio R. Tambelinni)
aka: *Me You Them*
A pregnant and abandoned bride marries an elderly, miserly bachelor, and also takes in two other lovers, producing a child by each of them.
A repetitious, intermittently enjoyable comedy of rural life, apparently based on a true story.
w Elena Soarez *d* Andrucha Waddington *ph* Breno Silveira *m* Gilberto Gil *ad* Toni Vanzolini *ed* Vicente Kubrusly
☆ Regina Case (Darlene), Lima Duarte (Osias), Stenio Garcia (Zezinho), Luis Carlos Vasconcelos (Ciro), Nilda Spencer (Raquel)
'An unexpected delight, a film that weds the humor and magic of a folk tale with a very modern feel for the psychological dynamics between men and women.' – *A. O. Scott, New York times*

Eureka
GB/USA 1982 129m Technicolor
MGM/UA/RPC/JF (Jeremy Thomas)
An immensely rich gold striker becomes a recluse and is murdered by Mafia hoods.
Unpleasant in detail and obscure in meaning, this is the sort of film of which the fact that it was financed at all is the most interesting thing about it.
w Paul Mayersberg *book* *Who Killed Sir Harry Oakes?* by Marshall Houts *d* Nicolas Roeg *ph* Alex Thomson *m* Stanley Myers *pd* Michael Seymour
☆ Gene Hackman, Theresa Russell, Rutger Hauer, Jane Lapotaire, Mickey Rourke, Ed Lauter

'A Roeg elephant film.' – *Variety*
'Between them Roeg and Mayersberg have worked an astonishing alchemy through which an abstraction of the basic patterns of human intercourse is rendered wholly concrete. Embodying Vico's cyclical theory of history, it expounds the despair of humanity's vicious circle from ecstasy to agony, as the impulse to love and possession leads inevitably to loss and destruction.' – *Tom Milne, Monthly Film Bulletin*
'I've a feeling it will become a cult movie, but no one will convince me that it isn't just the poshest kind of tosh.' – *Margaret Hinxman, Daily Mail*

Eureka ★
Japan/France 2000 218m bw/colour Panavision
Artificial Eye/Dentsu/Imagica/Suncent/Tokyo Theaters (Takenori Sento)
The three survivors of a bus hijacking try to come to terms with their traumatic experience.
A remarkable minimalist movie, filmed in sepia-toned black annd white, that has as its protagonists two virtually mute teenagers and a monosyllabic bus driver. Its emphasis on the ordinary holds the attention for much of its great length, until it loses its way in a subplot about a serial killer.
wd Shinji Aoyama *ph* Masaki Tamra *m* Isao Yamada, Shinji Aoyama *pd* Takeshi Shimizu *ed* Shinji Aoyama
☆ Koji Yakusho (Makoto Sawai), Aoi Miyazaki (Kozue Tamara), Masaru Miyazaki (Naoki Tamura), Yohichiroh Saitoh (Akihiko), Ken Mitsuishi (Shigeo), Go Riju (Hijacker), Yutaka Matsushige (Matsuoka), Sansei Shiomi (Yoshiyuki Sawai)
'A mysterious and sometimes maddening movie. Some spectators may find it too slow and ambiguous. But others will hail Aoyama's intelligent examination of the interplay between kinship and friendship.' – *David Sterritt, Christian Science Monitor*
'This allegory of modern anomie turns ludicrously pretentious. In pursuing its aesthetic agenda so single-mindedly, the movie leaves the characters behind in the muck.' – *Stephen Holden, New York Times*

Eureka Stockade
GB 1948 103m bw
Ealing (Leslie Norman)
US title: *Massacre Hill*
In 1854, Australian gold miners revolt against a harsh governor.
Unconvincingly made historical actioner from Ealing's antipodean period.
w Harry Watt, Walter Greenwood, Ralph Smart *d* Harry Watt *ph* Gerald Heath *m* John Greenwood
☆ Chips Rafferty, Jane Barrett, Gordon Jackson, Jack Lambert, Peter Illing, Ralph Truman, Peter Finch

Europa ★★
Denmark 1991 114m bw/colour 'Scope
Electric/Nordisk/Eurimages (Peter Aalbaek Jensen, Bo Christensen)
US title: *Zentropa*
In Germany in 1945, an idealistic young American finds work as a sleeping-car attendant and falls in love with a Nazi sympathizer.
Witty and exuberant tragi-comedy of the clash between New World innocence and European sophistication.
w Lars von Trier, Niels Vïrsel, Tomas Gislason *d* Lars von Trier *ph* Henning Bendtsen, Jean-Paul Meurisse, Edward Klosinsky *m* Joakim Holbek *pd* Henning Bahs *ed* Herve Schneid
☆ Jean-Marc Barr, Barbara Sukowa, Udo Kier, Ernst-Hugo Järegård, Erik Mïrk, Jïrgen Reenberg, Henning Jensen, Eddie Constantine, Max von Sydow (narrator)

Europa 51 ★
Italy 1952 110m bw
Ponti/de Laurentiis
An American society woman living in Rome seeks vainly for truth in the chaotic post-war world and is committed to an asylum by her husband.
A despairing, ironic comment on a period which unfortunately does not convince on the personal level.
w Roberto Rossellini and others *d* Roberto Rossellini *ph* Aldo Tonti *m* Renzo Rossellini
☆ Ingrid Bergman, Alexander Knox, Ettore Giannini, Giulietta Masina

Europa Europa ★★
France/Germany 1991 110m Eastmancolor
Les Films du Losange/CCC Filmkunst/Perspektywa (Margaret Menegoz, Artur Brauner)
A young Polish Jew, captured by the Germans, pretends to be a loyal Nazi in order to stay alive.
A fascinating true story with the qualities of a thriller, filmed with sensitivity.
wd Agnieszka Holland *book* Salomon Perel *ph* Jacek Petrycki *m* Zbigniew Priesner *pd* Allan Starski *ed* Ewa Smal
☆ Marco Hofschneider, Julie Delpy, André Wilms, Aschley Wanninger, Hanns Zischler, Klaus Kowatsch, Hanna Labornaska
'Filled with suspense and touches of humour, pic brings a fresh approach to familiar themes and should find an appreciative arthouse audience in many parts of the world.' – *Variety*
† Controversy erupted over the German committee's failure to nominate the film for an Oscar for best foreign film. Most leading German directors signed a letter protesting about its decision.
Agnieszka Holland (screenplay adaptation)

European Nights ★
France/Italy 1959 79m Technicolor
Avers Film (Fabio Jegher)
A collection of cabaret acts from various European cities are seen in live performances.
A film of some historical interest, showing the sort of entertainment that once flourished in big cities. The highlight is the immaculate magic of Channing Pollock, effortlessly producing doves out of thin air. Also on show are The Platters, Italian singer-songwriter Domenico Modugno, French ventriloquist Robert Lamouret, and some lesser acts, such as Belgium's junior xylophone champion and Colin Hicks (Tommy Steele's less successful brother).
w Ennio de Concini, Gualtiero Jacopetti, Richard Wadleigh *d* Alessandro Blasetti *ph* Gabor Pogany *m* Carlo Savina *ad* Flavio Mogherini *ed* Mario Serandrei
☆ Carmen Sevilla, Henry Salvador, Domenico Modugno, The Platters, Channing Pollock, Robert Lamouret, Colin Hicks, The Rastellis, Le Charley Ballet, Ukrainian Orlyck Dance Group, Eddie Gray, The Three Monarchs

The Europeans ★
GB 1979 83m colour
Merchant Ivory (Ismail Merchant)
In 1850, a European baroness arrives in Boston in search of a husband.
Charming if rather tentative period mood piece, probably the most professional and judicious of all the overpraised Merchant Ivory offerings.
w Ruth Prawer Jhabvala *novel* Henry James *d* James Ivory *ph* Larry Pizer *m* Richard Robbins *ad* Jeremiah Rusconi
☆ Lee Remick, Robin Ellis, Tim Woodward, Wesley Addy, Lisa Eichhorn
'A film of astonishing delicacy and richness in which the tiniest gesture or intonation reverberates with a world of meanings.' – *Tom Milne, MFB*

Eva
France/Italy 1962 135m bw
Paris/Interopa (Robert and Raymond Hakim)
A raw Welsh novelist in Venice is humiliated by a money-loving Frenchwoman who erotically ensnares him.
Foolish story of a femme fatale; elegantly Freudian at moments, it long outstays its welcome.
w Hugo Butler, Evan Jones *novel* James Hadley Chase *d* Joseph Losey *ph* Gianni di Venanzo *m* Michel Legrand
☆ Stanley Baker, Jeanne Moreau, Virna Lisi, James Villiers
'They don't hardly make 'em like Joseph Losey's *Eva* anymore, not even in Hollywood, not since Elinor Glyn passed from the script scene and Theda Bara quit as head vamp.' – *Judith Crist*

Eve Knew Her Apples
US 1945 64m bw
Wallace McDonald/Columbia
A radio singer sets off incognito for a vacation.
Mild musical support whose plot owes something to It Happened One Night.
w E. Edwin Moran *d* Will Jason
☆ Ann Miller, William Wright, Robert Williams, Ray Walker

The Eve of St Mark
US 1944 95m bw
TCF (William Perlberg)
A small-town boy goes to war and his sweetheart waits for him.
Poetic propaganda based on a sticky play which however had a tragic ending that the film eschews. Smartly made is all one can say.
w George Seaton *play* Maxwell Anderson *d* John M. Stahl *ph* Joseph LaShelle *m* Cyril Mockridge
☆ William Eythe, Anne Baxter, Michael O'Shea, Vincent Price, Ruth Nelson, Ray Collins, Stanley Prager, Henry Morgan

Eve Wants to Sleep ★
Poland 1957 98m bw
Film Polski (Wislaw Mincer)
An innocent country girl arrives in a city overrun by subversives.
Curious yet sympathetic black farce, like a cross between Hellzapoppin *and* M. *One on its own.*
wd *Tadeusz Chmielewski* *ph* Stefan Matyjaskiewicz *m* Henryk Czyz
☆ Barbara Kwiatkowska, Stanislaw Mikulski, Ludwik Benoit

Evel Knievel
US 1971 90m Metrocolor
(MGM) Fanfare (George Hamilton)
Episodes from the life of a motor-cycle stuntman.
Mildly entertaining ragbag of action sequences and fragments of philosophy which might have been more tolerable had EK played himself.
w Alan Caillou, John Milius *d* Marvin Chomsky *ph* David Walsh *m* Pat Williams
☆ George Hamilton, Sue Lyon, Bert Freed, Rod Cameron

'The story of a father's love that changed a nation.'
Evelyn ★
Ireland/GB 2002 95m colour Panavision
Pathé/First Look/Cinerenta/Irish DreamTime (Pierce Brosnan, Beau St. Clair, Michael Ohoven)
In Dublin in the 1950s, a house-painter fights to regain custody of his three young children after they are taken away from him when his wife leaves him.
Based on a true story that brought an alteration to Irish law, this small-scale domestic drama is sweet enough to rot the teeth and is played for more than it's worth by its cast.
w Paul Pender *d* Bruce Beresford *ph* Andre Fleuren *m* Stephen Endelman *pd* John Stoddart *ed* Humphrey Dixon
☆ Pierce Brosnan (Desmond Doyle), Aidan Quinn (Nick Barron), Julianna Margulies (Bernadette Beattie), Stephen Rea (Michael Beattie), Sophie Vavasseur (Evelyn Doyle), Alan Bates (Tom Connolly)
'Slight and dogged; its surprises are likable but minor.' – *Elvis Mitchell, New York Times*
'We are deep in the land of OT – Oirish Twaddle – where the pipes trill plaintively, the fiddles weep in sympathy, and no opportunity is missed to milk pathos from the soulful looks of cute moppet Evelyn and her daft but loveable Da.' – *Anthony Quinn, Independent*

Evelyn Prentice
US 1934 80m bw
MGM (John W. Considine Jnr)
The wife of a criminal lawyer has an affair with a man who blackmails her.
Moderate domestic-cum-courtroom melodrama, heavily reliant on its popular stars.
w Lenore Coffee *novel* W. E. Woodward *d* William K. Howard *ph* Charles G. Clarke *md* Oscar Radin
☆ Myrna Loy, William Powell, Una Merkel, Harvey Stephens, Isabel Jewell, Rosalind Russell, Henry Wadsworth, Edward Brophy
'Uneven film but extra heavy cast and strong femme sob yarn will put it in the money class.' – *Variety*

'There have been many great drivers, but only one great passenger.'
Even Cowgirls Get the Blues
US 1993 96m Alpha Cine
Rank/New Line/Fourth Vision (Laurie Parker)
The adventures of the world's greatest hitchhiker, a woman with large thumbs and a penchant for dressing as a cowgirl.
A cult novel of the 70s fails to become a cult film of the 90s; the world has moved on and stranded its characters in some whimsical no-man's land.
wd Gus Van Sant *novel* Tom Robbins *ph* John Campbell, Eric Alan Edwards *m* k. d. lang, Ben Mink *pd* Missy Stewart *ed* Curtiss Clayton
☆ Uma Thurman, Lorraine Bracco, Angie Dickinson, Noriyuki 'Pat' Morita, Keanu Reeves, John Hurt, Rain Phoenix, Roseanne Arnold, Ed Begley Jnr, Crispin Glover, Buck Henry, Carol Kane, Sean Young
'Result is at best amusing; at worst, uninvolving, often confusing and sometimes a little boring.' – *Variety*
'A mess, but a fitfully interesting one.' – *Sheila Johnston, Independent*

Even Dwarfs Started Small
West Germany 1970 96m bw
Werner Herzog
original title: *Auch Zwerge Haben Klein Angefangen*
Dwarfs in a prison settlement on a volcanic island stage an unsuccessful revolt.
Bizarre and off-putting movie that attempts to say something about the human condition but muddles its message.
wd Werner Herzog *ph* Thomas Mauch *m* Florian Fricke *ed* Beate Mainka-Jellinghaus
☆ Helmut Doring, Paul Glauer, Gisela Hertwig, Hertel Minkner, Gertraud Piccini, Marianne Saar, Brigitte Saar
'There is little arresting in the visual images and the determined obliqueness of treatment is finally unsatisfying.' – *Films and Filming*

Evening Dress: see *Tenue de Soirée*

'A story about friends, family and other natural disasters.'
The Evening Star
US 1996 128m DeLuxe
Paramount/Rysher (David Kirkpatrick, Polly Platt, Keith Samples)
In the 80s, a grandmother tries to cope with the lives and loves of her three adult grandchildren.
Routine soap opera, which lacks the spice of the first instalment, though the actors are again encouraged to go over the top in their performances.
wd Robert Harling *novel* Larry McMurtry *ph* Don Burgess *m* William Ross *pd* Bruno Rubeo *ed* Priscilla Nedd-Friendly, David Moritz
☆ Shirley MacLaine, Bill Paxton, Juliette Lewis, Miranda Richardson, Ben Johnson, Scott Wolf, George Newbern, Marion Ross, Mackenzie Astin, Donald Moffat, Jack Nicholson
'A vastly disappointing sequel to a superlative original.' – *Variety*
† It is a sequel to *Terms of Endearment* (qv).

Evenings
Netherlands 1989 126m colour
Concorde/Praxino (René Solleveld, Peter Weijdeveld)
original title: *De Avonden*
In 1946 in Amsterdam a young man, unhappy at home and work, contemplates his unsatisfactory life before deciding to write about it.
Tiresome account of an obsessive adolescent's refusal to grow up.
w Jean Ummels, Rudolf van den Berg *novel* Gerard Reve *d* Rudolf van den Berg *ph* Willy Stassen *m* Bob Zimmerman *ad* Freek Bissiot *ed* Maria Steenburgen
☆ Thom Hoffman, Rijk de Gooijer, Viviane de Muynck, Sylvia de Leur, Leen Jongewaard, Kees Coolen Pierre Bokma, Eljer Pelgrom, Jobet Schnibbe, Gija Scholten-van Aschat

Evensong *
GB 1934 84m bw
Gaumont (Michael Balcon)
At the turn of the century, an Austrian prima donna gives up her career for love.
Well-made romantic drama of its type, notable as the best of its star's few films.
w Edward Knoblock, Dorothy Farnum *play* Beverley Nichols, Edward Knoblock *novel* *Beverley Nichols* *d* Victor Saville *ph* Max Greene *m/ly* Mischa Spoliansky, Edward Knoblock *ad* Alfred Junge *ed* Otto Ludwig
☆ *Evelyn Laye*, Fritz Kortner, Carl Esmond, Alice Delysia, Emlyn Williams, Muriel Aked
'A highly absorbing and intelligently produced musical … looks like money.' – *Variety*

'Infinite Space. Infinite Terror.'
Event Horizon
US 1997 95m Rank Colour Panavision
Paramount/Golar/Impact (Lawrence Gordon, Lloyd Levin, Jeremy Bolt)
In 2047, the crew of a spaceship, who go to the rescue of an apparently lifeless experimental ship, experience terrible hallucinations.
Creepy horror movie in outer space that delivers the requisite shocks; a little less predictability would have been welcome, though.
w Philip Eisner *d* Paul Anderson *ph* Adrian Biddle *m* Michael Kamen *pd* Joseph Bennett *ed* Martin Hunter
☆ Laurence Fishburne, Sam Neill, Kathleen Quinlan, Joely Richardson, Richard T. Jones, Jack Noseworthy, Jason Isaacs, Sean Pertwee
'A muddled and curiously uninvolving sci-fi horror show.' – *Joe Leydon, Variety*
'Essentially *The Old Dark House* in outer space.' – *George Perry*

'Desire. Defy. Escape.'
Ever After: A Cinderella Story *
US 1998 122m Technicolor Panavision
TCF (Mireille Soria, Tracey Trench)
A prince falls in love with a beautiful girl who disguises her true identity.
A swooningly romantic version of Cinderella, done as a period drama.
w Susannah Grant, Andy Tennant, Rick Parks *d* Andy Tennant *ph* Andrew Dunn *m* George Fenton *pd* Michael Howells *ed* Roger Bondelli
☆ Drew Barrymore, Anjelica Huston, Dougray Scott, Patrick Godfrey, Megan Dodds, Melanie Lynskey, Jeanne Moreau, Timothy West, Judy Parfitt, Jeroen Krabbe
'A rather pompous, overlong, only thinly charming love story.' – *Ian Nathan, Empire*

'She'd say yes, but she no's him too well!'
Ever Since Eve
US 1937 80m bw
Warner (Earl Baldwin)
A publisher falls for a pretty girl, not realizing that she is his own plain secretary in disguise.
Silly romantic comedy which sadly lacks wit, style and believability.
w Lawrence Riley, Earl Baldwin, Lillie Hayward *d* Lloyd Bacon *ph* George Barnes *m* Heinz Roemheld
☆ Marion Davies, Robert Montgomery, Frank McHugh, Patsy Kelly, Louise Fazenda, Barton MacLane, Mary Treen
'A highly incredible script, and badly handled … it just doesn't jell.' – *Variety*
† It was Marion Davies's last film.

Ever Since Venus
US 1944 74m bw
Columbia
The inventors of a new lipstick formula can't get production facilities.
Modestly effective wartime comedy with good talent not ill-used.
w Arthur Dreifuss, McElbert Moore *d* Arthur Dreifuss
☆ Hugh Herbert, Billy Gilbert, Ina Ray Hutton, Glenda Farrell, Ann Savage, Ross Hunter, Alan Mowbray, Fritz Feld, Thurston Hall, Marjorie Gateson

Evergreen **
GB 1934 90m bw
Gaumont (Michael Balcon)
A star's daughter takes her mother's place, with romantic complications.
Pleasant musical with more wit and style than might be expected.
w Emlyn Williams, Marjorie Gaffney *play* *Ever Green* by Benn W. Levy *d* *Victor Saville* *ph* Glen Mac Williams *m/ly* Rodgers and Hart ('Dancing on the Ceiling', 'Dear Dear'); all other songs Harry Woods *md* Louis Levy *ad* Alfred Junge, Peter Proud *ed* Ian Dalrymple
☆ Jessie Matthews, Sonnie Hale, Betty Balfour, Barry Mackay, Ivor McLaren, Hartley Power

An Everlasting Piece *
US 2000 103m Technicolor
Columbia TriStar/DreamWorks/Bayahibe/Baltimore/Spring Creek (Mark Johnson, Louis DiGiaimo, Jerome O'Connor, Barry Levinson, Paula Weinstein)
In Belfast in the 1980s, a Protestant and a Catholic team up to sell toupees to the locals.
Tart little comedy that throws an ironic sidelight on the sectarian problems in Northern Ireland.
w Barry McEvoy *d* Barry Levinson *ph* Seamus Deasy *m* Hans Zimmer *pd* Nathan Crowley *ed* Stu Linder
☆ Barry McEvoy (Colm), Brian F. O'Byrne (George), Anna Friel (Bronagh), Colum Convey (IRA Man), Billy Connolly (Scalper), Pauline McLynn (Gerty), Ruth McCabe (Mrs O'Neill), Laurence Kinlan (Mickey), Des McAleer (Mr Black)
'Great fun, since it is heartless, cheekier by far than non-Irish film-makers would risk even in these low-intensity times, and shows everyone in a cold North light.' – *Alexander Walker, London Evening Standard*
† The film took $75,000 at the US box office.
†† Producer Jerome O'Connor accused DreamWorks of failing to give the film proper distribution because the studio did not wish to upset the British.

Eversmile New Jersey
US/Argentina 1989 103m Technicolor
J&M Entertainment/Los Films del Camino (Oscar Kramer)
A cavity-obsessed Irish dentist travelling around Patagonia acquires a female assistant en route.
An extraordinarily dreary attempt at a comic road movie, impossible to enjoy without anaesthetic.
w Jorge Goldenberg, Roberto Scheuer, Carlos Sorin *d* Carlos Sorin *ph* Esteban Courtalon *m* Steve Levine *ad* Coca Oderigo, Maria Julia Bertotto *ed* Bryan Oates
☆ Daniel Day-Lewis, Mirjana Jokovic, Gabriela Acher, Julio de Grazia, Ignacio Quiros

Every Day's a Holiday *
US 1937 79m bw
Paramount (Emmanuel Cohen)
A confidence girl in the old Bowery sells Brooklyn Bridge to suckers.
The most satisfactory example of post-Legion of Decency Mae West, the smut being replaced by a lively cast of comedians.
w *Mae West* *d* A. Edward Sutherland *ph* Karl Struss *m/ly* various *ad* Wiard Ihnen
☆ Mae West, Edmund Lowe, Charles Butterworth, Charles Winninger, Walter Catlett, Lloyd Nolan, Herman Bing, Roger Imhof, Chester Conklin
'A lively, innocuously bawdy, and rowdy entertainment.' – *Variety*
Wiard Ihnen

'When the dreamers meet the screamers it's the swingin'est hit that ever swung!'
Every Day's a Holiday
GB 1964 94m Technicolor Techniscope
Grand National (Maurice J. Wilson, Ronald J. Kahn)
US title: *Seaside Swingers*
Young people who want a showbusiness career take jobs at a holiday camp so that they can enter a talent competition.
Lively lightweight 'teen musical of the time, featuring some briefly successful groups and singers; it must be one of the last movies to feature a performer in blackface, when John Leyton imitates Nat 'King' Cole.
w Anthony Marriott, Jeri Matos, James Hill *d* James Hill *ph* Nicolas Roeg *m* Tony Osborne *ch* Gillian Lynne *ad* Edward Carrick *ed* Tristam Cones
☆ John Leyton (Gerry), Michael Sarne (Tim), Ron Moody (Professor), Liz Fraser (Miss Slightly), Grazina Frame (Christina), Susan Baker (Susan), Jennifer Baker (Jennifer), Nicholas Parsons (Julian Goddard), Michael Ripper (Mr Pulman), Hazel Hughes (Mrs Barrington de Witt), Richard O'Sullivan (Jimmy), Charles Lloyd Pack (Mr Close), Freddie and the Dreamers, The Mojos, The Leroys

Every Girl Should Be Married
US 1948 84m bw
RKO (Don Hartman, Dore Schary)
A determined girl sets her cap at a bachelor pediatrician.
Woefully thin star comedy with few laughs.
w Stephen Morehouse Avery, Don Hartman *d* Don Hartman *ph* George E. Diskant *m* Leigh Harline
☆ Cary Grant, Betsy Drake, Franchot Tone, Diana Lynn, Alan Mowbray, Elizabeth Risdon, Richard Gaines
'In the past, Cary Grant has shown a talent for quietly underplaying comedy. In this picture, he has trouble finding comedy to play.' – *Time*

Every Home Should Have One
GB 1970 94m Eastmancolor
British Lion/Example (Ned Sherrin)
An advertising man goes berserk when he tries to think up an erotic way of selling porridge.
Tiresomely frenetic star comedy with the emphasis on smut.
w Marty Feldman, Barry Took, Denis Norden *d* James Clark *ph* Ken Hodges *m* John Cameron
☆ Marty Feldman, Shelley Berman, Judy Cornwell, Julie Ege, Patrick Cargill, Jack Watson, Patience Collier, Penelope Keith, Dinsdale Landen

Every Little Crook and Nanny
US 1972 92m Metrocolor
MGM (Leonard J. Ackerman)
A Mafia chief finds his child's new nanny has a grudge against him.
Sporadically amusing farce.
w Cy Howard, Jonathan Axelrod, Robert Klane *d* Cy Howard *ph* Philip Lathrop *m* Fred Karlin
☆ Victor Mature, Lynn Redgrave, Paul Sand, Maggie Blye, Austin Pendleton, John Astin, Dom DeLuise

Every Man for Himself: see *Sauve Qui Peut (La Vie)*

Every Man for Himself and God against All: see *The Enigma of Kasper Hauser*

Every Minute Counts: see *Count the Hours*

Every Night at Eight
US 1935 80m bw
Paramount (Walter Wanger)
Three sisters become a successful radio singing team.
Forgettable comedy musical with a mildly interesting cast.
w Gene Towne, Graham Baker *d* Raoul Walsh *ph* James Van Trees *m/ly* Dorothy Fields, Jimmy McHugh
☆ George Raft, Alice Faye, Frances Langford, Patsy Kelly, The Radio Rogues, Walter Catlett, Herman Bing
'Looks like another case of missed opportunity … a routine show world romance.' – *Variety*

Every Other Inch a Lady: see *Dancing Co-Ed*

Every Saturday Night: see *The Jones Family*

Every Second Counts: see *Les Assassins du Dimanche*

Every Time We Say Goodbye
US 1986 95m colour
Tri-Star (Jacob Kotzky, Sharon Harel)
In 1942 Jerusalem, an American pilot falls for a Sephardic Jewish girl.
Patchy and spasmodically developed story of love across the cultures: TV movie stuff.
w Moshe Mizrahi, Rachel Fabien, Leah Appet *d* Moshe Mizrahi *ph* Giuseppe Lanci *m* Philippe Sarde *ad* Micky Zahar *ed* Mark Burns
☆ Tom Hanks, Cristina Marsillach, Benedict Taylor, Anat Atzmon

Every Which Way but Loose
US 1978 114m DeLuxe
Warner/Malpaso (Robert Daley)
A Los Angeles trucker wins an orang-utan in a prize fight and becomes involved in sundry brawls and chases.
Easy-going, shambling star vehicle which was liked by nobody but the public.
w Jeremy Joe Kronsberg *d* James Fargo *ph* Rexford Metz *md* Steve Dorff
☆ Clint Eastwood, Sondra Locke, Ruth Gordon, Geoffrey Lewis, Walter Barnes
† The 1980 sequel, almost indistinguishable, was *Any Which Way You Can* (qv).

Every Woman's Man: see *The Prizefighter and the Lady*

Everybody Does It
US 1949 98m bw
TCF (Nunnally Johnson)
A stage-struck wife is chagrined to see her dull husband accidentally become an opera singer.
Very mild remake of Wife, Husband and Friend; *everyone tries to be zany, but the result is often just silly.*
w Nunnally Johnson *story* James M. Cain *d* Edmund Goulding *ph* Joseph LaShelle *md* Alfred Newman
☆ Paul Douglas, Celeste Holm, Linda Darnell, Charles Coburn, Millard Mitchell, Lucile Watson, John Hoyt, George Tobias, Leon Belasco
'For sheer momentary enjoyment it would be hard to beat.' – *Richard Mallett, Punch*

Everybody Sing *
US 1937 80m bw
MGM (Harry Rapf)
An eccentric theatrical family is upstaged by its servants, who put on a Broadway show.
Agreeably zany comedy with music.
w Florence Ryerson, Edgar Allan Woolf *d* Edwin L. Marin *ph* Joseph L. Ruttenberg *m* William Axt
☆ Allan Jones, *Fanny Brice*, *Judy Garland*, Reginald Owen, Billie Burke, Lynne Carver, Monty Woolley, Reginald Gardiner, Henry Armetta
'Excellent film musical with fresh ideas and a corking cast … for the top spots.' – *Variety*
♫ 'Swing Mister Mendelssohn'; 'The One I Love'; 'Cosi Cosa'; 'I'm Gonna Pack My Bag'; 'The Show Must Go On'; 'Why? Beacause'; 'Ever Since the World Began'; 'Shall I Sing a Melody?'

Everybody Wins
GB 1990 97m DuArt
Virgin/Recorded Picture Company (Jeremy Thomas)
A private eye is seduced by the unstable woman who has hired him to clear a youth of a murder charge.
Old-fashioned, unsubtle and wordy exploration of small-town corruption.
w Arthur Miller *d* Karel Reisz *ph* Ian Baker *m* Leon Redbone *pd* Peter Larkin *ed* John Bloom
☆ Debra Winger, Nick Nolte, Will Patton, Judith Ivey, Jack Warden, Kathleen Wilhoite, Frank Converse
'For a brief period in the late sixties and early seventies, moviegoers seemed willing to be guided through a movie by their intuition and imagination; if this slyly funny movie about the spread of corruption had been released then, it might have been considered a minor classic.' – *Pauline Kael, New Yorker*

Everybody's All-American: see *When I Fall In Love*

Everybody's Cheering: see *Take Me Out to the Ball Game*

Everybody's Fine: see *Stanno Tutti Bene*

Everyone Says I Love You **
US 1996 101m DuArt
Sweetland/Jean Doumanian (Robert Greenhut)
A teenager observes the year-long romantic entanglements of her mother, her divorced father, and her half-brothers and -sisters.
A slightly sour romantic comedy, and a musical for people who don't like musicals, with its cast warbling and dancing in an amateurish manner; it has a certain charm, though, even if the old songs deserve better.
wd Woody Allen *ph* Carlo Di Palma *m* Dick Hyman *ch* Graciela Daniele *pd* Santo Loquasto *ed* Susan E. Morse
☆ Woody Allen, Alan Alda, Drew Barrymore, Goldie Hawn, Julia Roberts, Tim Roth, Lukas Haas, Gaby Hoffman, Edward Norton, Natalie Portman, David Ogden Stiers, Natasha Lyonne
'A cinematic oxymoron – complex, bold and audacious and simultaneously simple, guileless and sublime.' – *Leonard Klady, Variety*
'Perhaps it isn't only the musical that is a highly artificial form, but Allen's particular blend of romanticism, therapy, middlebrow comedy and undemanding art film.' – *Adam Mars-Jones, Independent*

Everything But the Truth
US 1956 83m Technicolor
U-I (Howard Christie)
A small boy embarrasses his family by telling the truth at all times.
Dum-dum formula comedy made with jaded professionalism.
w Herb Meadow *d* Jerry Hopper *ph* Maury Gertsman *m* Milton Rosen
☆ Maureen O'Hara, John Forsythe, Tim Hovey, Frank Faylen, Barry Atwater

Everything Happens at Night
US 1939 77m bw
TCF (Harry Joe Brown)
Two reporters fall for the daughter of a Nobel Peace Prize winner on the run from the Gestapo.
The star's sixth American film plays down the music and skating in favour of rather jaded spy comedy. Modest entertainment.
w Art Arthur, Robert Harari *d* Irving Cummings *ph* Edward Cronjager *m* various
☆ Sonja Henie, Ray Milland, Robert Cummings, Maurice Moscovich, Leonid Kinskey, Alan Dinehart, Fritz Feld, Victor Varconi
'At no time does very much happen that is of interest.' – *Variety*

Everything I Have Is Yours
US 1952 92m Technicolor
MGM (George Wells)
A song and dance team is disrupted when the wife decides to become a mother.
Uninventive but lively musical vehicle for the Champions.
w George Wells *d* Robert Z. Leonard *ph* William V. Skall *md* David Rose *ch* Nick Castle, Gower Champion
☆ Marge and Gower Champion, Dennis O'Keefe, Eduard Franz

Everything Is Rhythm
GB 1936 73m bw
Joe Rock
A dance band leader wins a European princess.
Modest programme filler remarkable only for its record of a top band of its time.
w Syd Courtenay, Jack Byrd, Stanley Haynes *story* Tom Geraghty *d* Alfred Goulding *ph* Ernest Palmer *ad* A. L. Mazzei, George Provis
☆ Harry Roy and his Band, Princess Pearl, Ivor Moreton, Dave Kaye

Everything Put Together **
US 2000 85m FotoKem
ICA/Furst
A young wife tries to come to terms with the unexpected death of her newborn baby.
A difficult film to watch, given its subject matter and the director's intensely focused approach that is sometimes closer to a horror movie in its sense of dread and alienation than the usual domesticated drama; but it is rewarding if you can bear it.
w Adam Forgash, Catherine Lloyd Burns, Marc Forster *d* Marc Forster *ph* Roberto Schaefer *m* Thomas Koppel *pd* Paul Jackson *ed* Matt Chessé
☆ Radha Mitchell (Angie), Megan Mullally (Barbie), Justin Louis (Russ), Catherine Lloyd Burns (Judith), Alan Ruck (Kessel), Michele Hicks (April), Matt Malloy (Dr Reiner)
'Finely acted expressionistic critique of the suburban baby culture and its joys, fears and fetishes.' – *Stephen Holden, New York Times*

Everything You Always Wanted to Know about Sex *
US 1972 87m DeLuxe
UA (Charles H. Joffe)
Seven sketches on sexual themes.
Dishevelled revue with a reasonable number of laughs for broadminded audiences.
wd Woody Allen *book* Dr David Reuben *ph* David M. Walsh *m* Mundell Lowe *pd* Dale Hennesy
☆ Woody Allen, Lynn Redgrave, Anthony Quayle, John Carradine, Lou Jacobi, Louise Lasser, Tony Randall, Burt Reynolds, Gene Wilder

Everything's Ducky
US 1961 81m bw
Barboo/Columbia
Two naval ratings adopt a talking duck.
Anything-goes service farce, with material below the standard of the talent available.
w John Fenton Murray, Benedict Freedman *d* Don Taylor *ph* Carl Guthrie *m* Bernard Green
☆ Mickey Rooney, Buddy Hackett, Jackie Cooper, Joanie Summers, Roland Winters

'The secrets that hold us together can also tear us apart.'
Eve's Bayou **
US 1997 108m colour
Alliance/Trimark (Caldecot Chubb, Samuel L. Jackson)
In the early 60s, a 10-year-old girl with psychic powers vows to kill her philandering father for sexually assaulting her sister.
A family saga seen through the distancing eyes of a child; it is an intriguing story of shifting memories and blame, as the truth of situations changes.
wd Kasi Lemmons *ph* Amy Vincent *m* Terence Blanchard *pd* Jeff Howard *ed* Terilyn A. Shropshire
☆ Jurnee Smollett, Megan Good, Samuel L. Jackson, Lynn Whitfield, Debi Morgan, Jake Smollett, Diahann Carroll, Ethel Ayler, Vondie Curtis Hall
'If it's not nominated for Academy Awards then the Academy is not paying attention.' – *Roger Ebert, Chicago Sun-Times*

The Evictors
US 1979 92m Movielab Panavision
AIP (Charles B. Pierce)
Axe murders abound when a young couple move into an old house with a history.
Old-hat horror, out of Psycho *and* The Amityville Horror*: strictly for drive-ins.*
w Charles B. Pierce, Gary Rusoff, Paul Fisk *d* Charles B. Pierce *ph* Chuck Bryant *m* Jaime Mendoza-Nava *ed* Shirak Khojayan
☆ Michael Parks, Jessica Harper, Vic Morrow, Sue Ane Langdon

The Evil
US 1978 89m Movielab
New World/Rangoon (Ed Carlin)
A psychologist takes a team to investigate a haunted house, and is soon sorry he meddled.
Another variation on the theme of The Haunting *and* The Legend of Hell House*; more this time on the horror comic level, but reasonably effective.*
w Donald G. Thompson *d* Gus Trikonis *ph* Mario Di Leo *m* Johnny Harris
☆ Richard Crenna, Joanna Pettet, Andrew Prine, Cassie Yates, Victor Buono, Lynne Moody

'The Ultimate Experience In Gruelling Terror.'
The Evil Dead
US 1983 85m DuArt
Palace/Renaissance (Robert G. Tapert)
Five youngsters in a remote cabin find an old book which helps them summon up dormant demons from a nearby forest.
Semi-professional horror rubbish, blown up from 16mm and looking it. When released in England, it was prosecuted as unsuitable for public showing and gained a cult following. It was released on video in a cut version.
wd Sam M. Raimi *ph* Tim Philo *m* Joe LoDuca *ed* Edna Ruth Paul
☆ Bruce Campbell, Ellen Sandweiss, Betsy Baker, Hal Delrich
'The *ne plus ultra* of low-budget gore and shock effects.' – *Variety*
† Originally made in 1980, but not released publicly for 3 years.

Evil Dead 2: Dead by Dawn
US 1987 85m Technicolor
Renaissance/De Laurentiis (Robert G. Tapert)
Trapped in a lonely cabin, a couple fight off ferocious hordes of the spirits of the dead.
Fast-moving horror movie with flashy camerawork and an exuberant taste in sick jokes.
w Sam Raimi, Scott Spiegel *d* Sam Raimi *ph* Peter Deming *m* Joseph LoDuca *ad* Philip Duffin, Randy Bennett *ed* Kaye Davis *sp* make-up: Mark Shostrom
☆ Bruce Campbell, Sarah Berry, Dan Hicks, Kassie Wesley, Theodore Raimi, Denise Bixler
'More an absurdist comedy than a horror film.' – *Variety*
† It was followed by a sequel, *Army of Darkness* (qv).

Evil Ed (dubbed) *
Sweden 1995 90m colour/bw
Evil Ed Productions (Göran Lundström)
A mild-mannered film editor becomes increasingly deranged after he goes to work in his studio's splatter-and-gore department to remove excessive violence from the company's movies.
Exuberant, over-the-top satire of bloody horror flicks, done with some wit; but the lashings of gore overwhelm whatever serious intentions may have been lurking beneath its surface.
w Anders Jacobsson, Göran Lundström, Christer Ohlsson *d* Anders Jacobsson *ph* Anders Jacobsson *m* Henriksson & Lindh *ed* Anders Jacobsson
☆ Johan Rudebeck, Per Löfberg, Olof Rhodin, Camela Leierth, Gert Fylking, Cecilia Ljung

Evil Fingers: see *The Fifth Cord*

'The monster's back and no one can stop him!'
The Evil of Frankenstein
GB 1964 94m Eastmancolor
Rank/Hammer (Anthony Hinds)
Frankenstein returns to his derelict castle and finds the Monster preserved in a glacier.
For their third Frankenstein film Hammer made a distribution deal with Universal and thus for the first time were able to use fragments of the old plots as well as something approximating to the Karloff make-up. Production and writing, however, are sadly dispirited except when relying on sadism.
w John Elder (Anthony Hinds) *d* Freddie Francis *ph* John Wilcox *m* Don Banks *ad* Don Mongaye *ed* James Needs
☆ Peter Cushing (Baron Frankenstein), Peter Woodthorpe (Zoltan), Sandor Eles (Hans), Kiwi Kingston (The Monster), Duncan Lamont (Chief of Police), Katy Wild, David Hutcheson

Evil Senses (dubbed)
Italy 1986 90m colour
DMV/Globe/Dania/Filmes International/National Cinematografica (Pietro Innocenzi)
A hitman on the run from other killers takes refuge in a high-class brothel and begins an obsessive relationship with a mysterious part-time prostitute.
Glossy but unremarkable thriller, with a flimsy plot and some ludicrous sexual interludes.
w Gianfranco Clerici, Gabriele Lavia, Vincenzo Mannino, Dardano Sacchetti *d* Gabriele Lavia *ph* Mario Vulpiani *m* Fabio Frizzi *ad* Giovanni Agostinucci *ed* Daniele Alabiso
☆ Monica Guerritore, Gabriele Lavia, Mimsy Farmer, Lewis Eduard Ciannelli, Dario Mazzoli, Gioia Maria Scola, Jean René Masrevery, Ragnhild Aslaksen
'Sleekly shot, and has enough narrative twists to maintain a modicum of interest despite the risibly melodramatic sex scenes.' – *Sight and Sound*

The Evil that Men Do
US 1984 90m CFI color
ITC/Capricorn/Zuleika Farms (Pancho Kohner)
A professional killer is asked to eliminate a sadistic political torturer in Guatemala.
More than usually turgid and unpleasant vehicle for a star who is now too old for this kind of thing.
w David Lee Henry, John Crowther *novel* R. Lance Hill *d* J. Lee-Thompson *ph* Javier Ruvalcaba Cruz *m* Ken Thorne
☆ Charles Bronson, Theresa Saldana, Joseph Maher, José Ferrer, René Enriquez, John Glover, Raymond St Jacques

Evil under the Sun
GB 1982 117m Technicolor Panavision
EMI/Mersham/Titan (John Brabourne, Richard Goodwin)
Hercule Poirot solves the murder of a film star on an Adriatic holiday island.
Very competent but somehow too bland package in the Agatha Christie series, not quite so lively as Death on the Nile.
w Anthony Shaffer *novel* Agatha Christie *d* Guy Hamilton *ph* Christopher Challis *m* Cole Porter *pd* Elliot Scott
☆ Peter Ustinov, James Mason, Diana Rigg, Maggie Smith, Colin Blakely, Jane Birkin, Nicholas Clay, Roddy McDowall, Sylvia Miles, Denis Quilley
'They have swapped elegant English menace for a splurge of theatrical camp.' – *Time Out*
'Temperance beverage Noël Coward.' – *Sunday Times*

Evil Woman: see *Saving Silverman*

Evils of Chinatown: see *Confessions of an Opium Eater*

Evita *
US 1996 134m Eastmancolor
Entertainment/Cinergi/Robert Stigwood/Dirty Hands (Alan Parker, Andrew G. Vajna, Robert Stigwood)
The progress to fame and political power of Eva Duarte, who rises from poverty to become a model, film actress and wife of the president of Argentina.
Epic version of the stage musical with a star performance in the title role, and providing some sweep and power, while still retaining the clumsy narrative and uninteresting music of the original.
w Alan Parker, Oliver Stone *musical* Andrew Lloyd Webber, Tim Rice *d* Alan Parker *ph* Darius Khondji *m/ly* Andrew Lloyd Webber, Tim Rice *md* John Mauceri *ch* Vincent Paterson *pd* Brian Morris *ed* Gerry Hambling
☆ Madonna, Antonio Banderas, Jonathan Pryce, Jimmy Nail, Victoria Sus, Julian Littman, Olga Merediz
'No effort or expense has been spared in transforming the stage musical into a Hollywood spectacular. As such, the film is, as the hype would have it, a triumph. The problems start, however, as soon as one has lost interest in the sumptuous clothes, virtuoso tango-dancing and necrophiliac display. There is very little dramatic tension.' – *Linda Holt, TLS*
† The film was one of the few to be subtitled in non-English speaking countries. Even such musicals as *The Sound of Music* have been dubbed in the past for most Spanish- and Italian-speaking countries.
song 'You Must Love Me' (*m* Andrew Lloyd-Webber, *ly* Tim Rice)
Darius Khondji; Brian Morris; Gerry Hambling; sound

'Have a nice end of the world.'
Evolution
US 2001 102m Technicolor
Columbia/Montecito (Ivan Reitman, Daniel Goldberg, Joe Medjuck)
Two incompetent scientists investigate a meteor that contains rapidly-evolving, hostile alien life.
Enjoyable enough romp with juvenile jokes, though it finally mutates into a advertisement for anti-dandruff shampoo; only Hollywood could regard that as progress.

w David Diamond, David Weissman, Don Jakoby *d* Ivan Reitman *ph* Michael Chapman *m* John Powell *pd* J. Michael Riva *ed* Sheldon Kahn, Wendy Greene Bricmont *sp* Phil Tippett *cos* Aggie Guerard Rodgers
☆ David Duchovny (Dr Ira Krane), Orlando Jones (Harry Block), Seann William Scott (Wayne), Julianne Moore (Allison), Ted Levine (Gen Woodman), Ethan Suplee (Deke), Katharine Towne (Nadine), Dan Aykroyd (Governor Lewis)
'A consistently amusing action romp that easily passes muster as a summertime diversion.' – *Todd McCarthy, Variety*

Ex-Flame
US 1930 68m bw
Liberty
A modernized version of *East Lynne*.
With so many American accents attached to the British peerage, this is mainly for laughs – unintentional ones.
wd Victor Halperin
☆ Neil Hamilton, Marian Nixon, Norman Kerry, Roland Drew, Snub Pollard
'Old-fashioned mush stuff for the woman.' – *Variety*

'We don't dare tell you how daring it is!'
Ex-Lady *
US 1933 70m bw
Warner
A lady artist has ultra-modern views on sex and marriage, but turns conventional when she falls in love.
Mildly shocking in its day, this romantic drama was one of the contributing factors to the onslaught of the Legion of Decency which transformed Hollywood output in the following year.
w David Boehm *story* Edith Fitzgerald, Robert Riskin *d* Robert Florey
☆ Bette Davis, Gene Raymond, Frank McHugh, Monroe Owsley, Claire Dodd
† Previously filmed in 1931 as *Illicit*.

The Ex-Mrs Bradford *
US 1936 87m bw
RKO (Edward Kaufman)
A doctor's scatty ex-wife involves him in solving a murder plot.
Amusing crime comedy, just a little way behind The Thin Man.
w Anthony Veiller, James Edward Grant *d* Stephen Roberts *ph* J. Roy Hunt *m* Roy Webb
☆ *William Powell, Jean Arthur*, James Gleason, Eric Blore, Robert Armstrong, Lila Lee, Grant Mitchell, Ralph Morgan

'Forged by a god! Foretold by a wizard! Found by a king!'
'No mortal could possess it! No kingdom could command it!'
Excalibur *
US 1981 140m Technicolor
Warner/Orion (John Boorman)
The story of King Arthur, Merlin, Uther Pendragon, the Holy Grail and the Lady of the Lake.
Curiously pointless retelling of a legend with unexplained flashes of realism and bouts of gore alternating with romance and modern wisecracks. Of mainly visual interest.
w Rospo Pallenberg, John Boorman *d* John Boorman *ph* Alex Thomson *m* Trevor Jones *pd Anthony Pratt ed* John Merritt
☆ Nigel Terry, Helen Mirren, Nicol Williamson, Nicholas Clay, Cherie Lunghi, Paul Geoffrey, Liam Neeson, Patrick Stewart
'Left entirely to his own devices, Boorman seems to run in self-defeating circles.' – *Richard Combs, MFB*
'It tries overhard to be simultaneously critical and credulous, magical and earthy, inspiring and entertaining.' – *Sunday Times*
'A record of the comings and goings of arbitrary, inconsistent, shadowy figures who are not heroes but simply giants run amok.' – *Roger Ebert*
Alex Thomson

Excess Baggage
US 1997 98m Technicolor
Columbia/First Kiss (Bill Borden, Carolyn Kessler)
A bored rich girl who fakes her own kidnapping becomes involved with a car thief, who is being hunted by crooked debt-collectors.
Trivial comedy that is about nothing in particular, and has no particular place to go.
w Max D. Adams, Dick Clement, Ian La Frenais *d* Marco Brambilla *ph* Jean Yves Escoffier *m* John Lurie *pd* Missy Stewart *ed* Stephen Rivkin
☆ Alicia Silverstone, Benicio del Toro, Christopher Walken, Jack Thompson, Harry Connick Jnr, Nicholas Turturro, Michael Bowen, Sally Kirkland
'A film so airy that viewers will forget about it even while they're watching it.' – *Timothy M. Gray, Variety*

Excessive Force
US 1993 90m DeLuxe
New Line/3 Arts/Ian Page (Oscar L. Costo, Thomas Ian Griffith, Erwin Stoff)
A maverick Chicago cop finds himself framed for the murder of a gangster.
Excessively violent, cliché-ridden movie with no redeeming qualities.
w Thomas Ian Griffith *d* Jon Hess *ph* Donald M. Morgan *m* Charles Bernstein *pd* Michael Z. Hanan *ed* Alan Baumgarten
☆ Thomas Ian Griffith (Terry McCain), Lance Henriksen (Devlin), Tom Hodges (Dylan), James Earl Jones (Jake), Charlotte Lewis (Anna Gilmour), Tony Todd (Frankie Hawkins), Burt Young (Sal DiMarco), Earl Brown (Vinnie DiMarco)
'The only surprising thing about this by-the-numbers effort is the talent squandered in supporting roles.' – *Joe Leydon, Variety*
† It was followed in 1995 by *Excessive Force 2: Force on Force*, an equally violent but otherwise unconnected film set in Los Angeles.

'Racket rule sweeps midwest city!'
Exclusive
US 1937 76m bw
Paramount
Journalist sacrifices himself for daughter whose views he despises.
Solid newspaper drama jinxed by the excellent tragic performance of a star too long regarded as a comedian.
w John C. Moffitt, Sidney Salkow, Rian James *d* Alexander Hall
☆ *Charles Ruggles*, Fred MacMurray, Frances Farmer, Lloyd Nolan
'Hokey newspaper-gangster yarn of old-fashioned meller calibre.' – *Variety*
'In the tough race it falls behind – it can't make the 1937 speed in murder, and the result, like lavender, is not unagreeable.' – *Graham Greene*

Excuse My Dust *
US 1951 82m Technicolor
MGM (Jack Cummings)
The inventor of a horseless carriage loves the daughter of a livery stable owner.
Innocuous small-town 1890s comedy with a race climax. Quite pleasant.
w George Wells *d* Roy Rowland *ph* Alfred Gilks *m* Arthur Schwartz
☆ Red Skelton, Sally Forrest, Macdonald Carey, William Demarest

'Every day he loves, somebody else dies!'
The Executioner *
GB 1970 107m Technicolor Panavision
Columbia/Ameran (Charles H. Schneer)
A British spy suspects a colleague of being a double agent.
Dour espionage thriller with a reasonably holding narrative and predictable performances.
w Jack Pulman *d* Sam Wanamaker *ph* Denys Coop *m* Ron Goodwin
☆ George Peppard, Nigel Patrick, Joan Collins, Judy Geeson, Oscar Homolka, Charles Gray, Keith Michell, George Baker, Alexander Scourby, Peter Bull, Ernest Clark, Peter Dyneley
'Does not escape from the well-worn shallow groove in which the contemporary spy film is in danger of becoming stuck.' – *Russell Campbell*

Executioner of Venice
Italy 1963 90m colour
Liber (Ottavio Poggi)
original title: *Il Boia di Venezia*
On the day of his marriage the son of the Doge of Venice discovers that his true father was a pirate and is arrested for treason on the orders of the power-hungry Grand Inquisitor.
Standard swashbuckler with glossy production values.
d Luigi Capuano *ph* Alvardo Mancori *ed* Antonietta Zita
☆ Lex Barker, Guy Madison, Alessandro Panaro, Alberto Farnese, Mario Petri, Giulio Marchetti

'Assassination Conspiracy? The Possibility Is Frightening.'
Executive Action *
US 1973 91m colour
EA Enterprises/Wakefield Orloff (Edward Lewis)
An imaginative version of the facts behind the 1963 assassination of President Kennedy.
Interesting but rather messy mixture of fact and fiction; makes one sit up while it's unreeling.
w Dalton Trumbo *story* Mark Lane, Donald Freed *d* David Miller *ph* Robert Steadman *m* Randy Edelman
☆ Burt Lancaster, Robert Ryan, Will Geer, Gilbert Green, John Anderson
'A dodo bird of a movie, the winner of the *Tora Tora Tora* prize.' – *Variety*

Executive Decision
US 1996 132m Technicolor Panavision
Warner/Silver Pictures (Joel Silver)
An élite team of commandos goes into action when Islamic militants, carrying a nerve gas that could kill everyone in Washington, hijack an aeroplane and demand a $50m ransom.
This is everything you would expect from a movie produced by Joel Silver: glossy, loud, fast and empty, but at least Steven Seagal disappears halfway through the action.
w Jim Thomas, John Thomas *d* Stuart Baird *ph* Alex Thomson *m* Jerry Goldsmith *pd* Terence Marsh *ed* Dallas Pruitt, Frank J. Urioste, Stuart Baird
☆ Kurt Russell (David Grant), Halle Berry (Jean), John Leguizamo (Rat), Steven Seagal (Lt Col Austin Travis), Oliver Platt (Cahill), Joe Morton, David Suchet (Nagi Hassan), B. D. Wong, Len Cariou, Whip Hubley, J. T. Walsh
'The acting is all first base, the script a laughable stream of gung ho-isms, the action merely solid and the effects indifferent. Yet, you still stroll out with a grin a mile wide.' – *Ian Nathan*

'High up in the skyscraper beauty and power clash in conflict!'
Executive Suite **
US 1954 104m bw
MGM (John Houseman)
When the president of a big company dies, the boardroom sees a battle for control.
First of the boardroom films of the fifties, a calculatedly commercial mixture of business ethics and domestic asides, with an all-star cast working up effective tensions.
w Ernest Lehman novel Cameron Hawley *d* Robert Wise *ph* George Folsey *m* none *ad* Cedric Gibbons, Edward Carfagno
☆ *Fredric March*, William Holden, June Allyson, *Barbara Stanwyck*, Walter Pidgeon, Shelley Winters, Paul Douglas, *Louis Calhern*, Dean Jagger, *Nina Foch*, Tim Considine
'Not a classic, not a milestone in movie making, but it does suggest a standard of product that could bring back to the box office those vast audiences long alienated by trivia.' – *Arthur Knight*
'The only trouble with all these people is that they are strictly two-dimensional. They give no substantial illusion of significance, emotion or warmth.' – *Bosley Crowther, New York Times*
† A TV series followed in 1976.
George Folsey; Nina Foch; art direction

The Exile *
US 1948 90m bw
U-I (Douglas Fairbanks Jnr)
The man who is to return to the English throne as Charles II hides in Holland, receives his friends and despatches his enemies.
Curious, talkative swashbuckler with only a few moments of action; the available talents are simply not used, though the director imposes a nice pictorial style.
w Douglas Fairbanks Jnr *novel His Majesty the King* by Cosmo Hamilton *d Max Ophüls ph* Franz Planer *m* Frank Skinner *ad* Hilyard Brown, Bernard Herzbrun *ed* Ted J. Kent
☆ Douglas Fairbanks Jnr, Maria Montez, Paula Corday, Henry Daniell, Nigel Bruce, Robert Coote
† Originally released in sepia.

'Play It. Live It. Kill For It.'
'Plug Into The Most Dangerous Fantasy Ever Created.'
eXistenZ *
US 1999 97m DeLuxe
Miramax/Alliance Atlantis/Serendipity Point/Natural Nylon (Robert Lantos, Andras Hamori, David Cronenberg)
A leading video-game designer, demonstrating her latest creation, is threatened with death by a group who object to artificial realities.
The problem here is that the video game is one that you can imagine only Cronenberg wanting to play, and underneath the hi-tech trimmings, which look like leftovers from his Naked Lunch, are themes on the relativity of truth that were handled rather better by Pirandello 70 years ago; but perhaps that is to take the movie more seriously than was intended.
wd David Cronenberg *ph* Peter Suschitzky *m* Howard Shore *pd* Carol Spier *ed* Ronald Sanders *sp* Jim Isaac
☆ Jennifer Jason Leigh, Jude Law, Willem Dafoe, Ian Holm, Don McKellar, Callum Keith Rennie, Sarah Polley, Christopher Eccleston
'Unquestionably Cronenberg Lite, but there is plenty of fun to be had from the absurdities and convoluted plotting, and a solid cast lends stature to the far-fetched fantasies.' – *David Stratton, Variety*

Exit Smiling **
US 1926 71m (24 fps) bw silent
MGM (Sam Taylor)
The worst actress in a stock company saves the show.
Amusing comedy for a star who never quite made it in films: this is the best of her vehicles.
w Sam Taylor, Tim Whelan *play* Marc Connelly *d* Sam Taylor *ph* André Barlatier
☆ *Beatrice Lillie*, Jack Pickford, Harry Myers, Doris Lloyd, DeWitt Jennings, Louise Lorraine, Franklin Pangborn

Exit to Eden
US 1994 113m Technicolor
Guild/Savoy (Alex Rose, Garry Marshall)
Undercover detectives track a diamond smuggler to a holiday island devoted to gratifying sado-masochistic sexual fantasies.
Drear, unbelievably bad comedy; the actors seem embarrassed, as well they might, and the director is obviously uncomfortable with any fantasy more explicit than his Pretty Woman.
w Deborah Amelon, Bob Brunner *novel* Anne Rice *d* Garry Marshall *ph* Theo Van de Sande *m* Patrick Doyle *pd* Peter Jamison *ed* David Finfer
☆ Dana Delany, Paul Mercurio, Rosie O'Donnell, Dan Aykroyd, Hector Elizondo, Stuart Wilson, Iman
'The film is awful.' – *Derek Malcolm, Guardian*
'It has the sophistication of an adolescent bathroom joke indifferently told.' – *Variety*

'What Can Two Men Do Against A Gang Of Crooked Cops? Whatever It Takes.'
'This Is Gonna Hurt.'
Exit Wounds
US 2001 103m Technicolor Panavision
Warner/Village Roadshow/NPV/Silver Pictures (Joel Silver, Dan Cracchiolo)
In Detroit, a maverick cop cleans up corruption in the force.
Routine, utterly forgettable action movie with a ponderous star.
w Ed Horowitz, Richard D'Ovidio *novel* John Westermann *d* Andrzej Bartkowiak *ph* Glen Macpherson *m* Jeff Rona, Damon 'Grease' Blackman *pd* Paul Denham Austerberry *ed* Derek G. Brechin

☆ Steven Seagal (Orin Boyd), DMX (Latrell Walker), Isaiah Washington (George Clark), Anthony Anderson (T.K.), Michael Jai White (Strutt), Bill Duke (Hinges), Jill Hennessy (Mulcahy), Tom Arnold (Henry Wayne), Bruce McGill (Daniels), David Vadim (Montini), Eva Mendes (Trish)

'Seeing Steven Seagal in "Exit Wounds," his first bigscreen actioner in a few years, makes one wonder how he ever managed to be regarded as anything resembling a movie star.' – *Todd McCarthy, Variety*

Exodus *
US 1960 220m Technicolor Super Panavision 70
UA/Carlyle/Alpha (Otto Preminger)

The early years of the state of Israel, seen through various eyes.
Heavy-going modern epic, toned down from a passionate novel.
w Dalton Trumbo *novel* Leon Uris *d* Otto Preminger *ph* Sam Leavitt *m* Ernest Gold
☆ Paul Newman, Eva Marie Saint, Ralph Richardson, Peter Lawford, Lee J. Cobb, Sal Mineo, John Derek, Hugh Griffith, Gregory Ratoff, Felix Aylmer, David Opatoshu, Jill Haworth, Alexandra Stewart, Martin Benson, Martin Miller

'Professionalism is not enough – after three and a half hours the approach seems more exhausting than exhaustive.' – *Penelope Houston*

† Jewish comedian Mort Sahl, invited by the director to a preview, is said to have stood up after three hours and said: 'Otto – let my people go!'
Academy Award: Ernest Gold
Academy Award nomination: Sam Leavitt; Sal Mineo

The Exorcist *
US 1973 122m Metrocolor
Warner/Hoya (William Peter Blatty)

A small girl is unaccountably possessed by the devil and turned into a repellent monster who causes several violent deaths before she is cured.
Spectacularly ludicrous mishmash with uncomfortable attention to physical detail and no talent for narrative or verisimilitude. Its sensational aspects, together with a sudden worldwide need for the supernatural, assured its enormous commercial success.
w William Peter Blatty *novel* William Peter Blatty *d* William Friedkin *ph* Owen Roizman *m* Jack Nitzsche *pd* Bill Malley *ed* Jordan Leandopoulos, Evan Lottman, Norman Gay, Bud Smith
☆ Ellen Burstyn, Max von Sydow, Jason Miller, Linda Blair, Lee J. Cobb, Kitty Winn, Jack MacGowran

'No more nor less than a blood and thunder horror movie, foundering heavily on the rocks of pretension.' – *Tom Milne*

'*The Exorcist* makes no sense, [but] if you want to be shaken, it will scare the hell out of you.' – *Stanley Kauffmann*

'It exploits the subject of diabolic possession without telling you anything about it ... just a stylistic exercise.' – *Michael Billington, Illustrated London News*

'There is a little exposition, some philosophy and theology, a quiet interlude, and then pandemonium reigns: rooms shake, heads turn full circle on bodies, wounds fester, vomit spews forth in bilious clouds besmirching a saintly priest, a possessed adolescent girl masturbates bloodily on a crucifix as she barks blasphemies and obscenities, and hoary demons freeze the soul.' – *Les Keyser, Hollywood in the Seventies*

'I know how to do it. I just throw everything at the audience and give them a real thrill. That's what they want. They don't want to go into a theater and treat it like a book. They don't even read books!' – *William Peter Blatty*

'This one was scheduled for 105 days. It wound up 200 days. We were plagued by strange and sinister things from the beginning.' – *William Peter Blatty*

'...raw and painful experience. Are people so numb that they need movies of this intensity in order to feel anything at all?' – *Roger Ebert*

† Published 1974: *The Story Behind the Exorcist* by Peter Travers and Stephanie Reiff; 1999, *The Exorcist: Out of the Shadows, The Full Story Of The Film* by Bob McCabe.
Academy Award: William Peter Blatty; sound (Robert Knudson, Chris Newman)
Academy Award nomination: best picture; William Friedkin; Owen Roizman; Ellen Burstyn; Jason Miller; Linda Blair; Bill Malley; editing

'It's four years later. What does she remember?'
Exorcist II: The Heretic
US 1977 117m Technicolor
Warner (Richard Lederer, John Boorman)

Father Lamont, investigating the case related in *The Exorcist*, finds that the evil in Regan, apparently exorcized, is only dormant.
Highly unsatisfactory psychic melodrama which, far from the commercial route of the shocker followed by its predecessor, falls flat on its face along some wayward path of metaphysical and religious fancy. A commercial disaster, it was released in two versions and is unintelligible in either.
w William Goodhart *d* John Boorman *ph* William A. Fraker *m* Ennio Morricone *pd* Richard MacDonald
☆ Richard Burton, Linda Blair, Louise Fletcher, Kitty Winn, Max von Sydow, Paul Henreid, James Earl Jones, Ned Beatty

'Do You Dare Walk These Steps Again?'
The Exorcist III
US 1990 110m DeLuxe
Fox/Morgan Creek/Carter DeHaven (James G. Robinson, Joe Roth)

A cop investigates a series of strange killings with the aid of an exorcist.
Unexciting and confused sequel that follows on from the first film in the series.
wd William Peter Blatty *novel* *Legion* by William Peter Blatty *ph* Gerry Fisher *m* Barry DeVorzon *pd* Leslie Dilley *ed* Tom Ramsay, Peter-Lee Thompson
☆ George C. Scott, Ed Flanders, Brad Dourif, Jason Miller, Nicol Williamson, Scott Wilson, Nancy Fish, George DiCenzo, Don Gordon

Exotica **
Canada 1994 104m colour
Artificial Eye/Alliance/Ego (Atom Egoyan, Camelia Frieberg)

A murder and an attempt to smuggle eggs bring together five disparate people in a club specializing in striptease and lap-dancing.
Elegantly devious drama about sex and voyeurism and the unexpected connections between people, told in a deliberately enigmatic way, gradually revealing the secrets that link one person to the next.
wd Atom Egoyan *ph* Paul Sarossy *m* Mychael Danna *pd* Linda del Rosario, Richard Paris *ed* Susan Shipton
☆ Bruce Greenwood, Elias Koteas, Don McKellar, Mia Kirshner, Arsinée Khanjian, Sarah Polley

'Egoyan promises us a sleazy tabloid sex thriller, then gives us an altogether sobering psychological thriller.' – *Jonathan Romney, Guardian*

† The film won a Genie award as the best Canadian film of 1994.

The Experiment: see *Das Experiment*

Das Experiment
Germany 2000 119m colour
Metrodome/Typhoon/Fanes/Senator/SevenPictures (Norbert Preuss, Marc Conrad, Friedrich Wildfeuer)

aka: *The Experiment*
In a scientific experiment, volunteers take on the roles of guards and prisoners; but those who are the guards begin to brutalise the others.
Taking its inspiration from an experiment conducted at Stanford University in the early 70s, which showed that power corrupted, this merely exploits the opportunity for action-movie violence.
w Mario Giordano, Christoph Darnstaedt, Don Bohlinger *novel* *Black Box* by Mario Giordano *d* Oliver Hirschbiegel *ph* Rainer Klausmann *m* Alexander Bubenheim *ad* Andrea Kessler, Uli Hanisch *ed* Hans Funck
☆ Moritz Bleibtreu (Tarek Fahd, No 77), Maren Eggert (Dora), Christian Berkel (Robert Steinhoff, No 38), Justus von Dohnanyi (Berus), Oliver Stokowski (Günther Schütte, No 82), Andrea Sawatzki (Dr Jutta Grimm), Edgar Selge (Professor Dr Klaus Thon), Timo Dierkes (Eckert)

'Shallow, unedifying and self-important ... silly and obtuse nonsense.' – *Peter Bradshaw, Guardian*

Experiment in Terror **
US 1962 123m bw
Columbia/Geoffrey-Kate Productions (Blake Edwards)

GB title: *The Grip of Fear*
An asthmatic stranger threatens the life of a bank teller and her sister if she does not help him commit a robbery.
Detailed, meticulous police thriller with San Francisco locations. Good stuff, a bit long.
w The Gordons *novel* *Operation Terror* by The Gordons *d* *Blake Edwards* *ph* Philip Lathrop *m* Henry Mancini
☆ Glenn Ford, Lee Remick, Ross Martin

Experiment Perilous *
US 1944 91m bw
RKO (Warren Duff)

A wealthy husband becomes insanely jealous of his wife.
Enjoyable mystery melodrama which takes itself with a pinch of salt.
w Warren Duff *novel* Margaret Carpenter *d* *Jacques Tourneur* *ph* Tony Gaudio *m* Roy Webb *ad* Albert S. D'Agostino, Jack Okey
☆ Hedy Lamarr, Paul Lukas, George Brent, Albert Dekker, Margaret Wycherly
Academy Award nomination: art direction

'It's time to enter the new dragon.'
Expert Weapon
US 1993 90m colour
Silver Screen/Cine Excel (David Hue, K. Y. Lim)

A convicted killer is offered freedom if he turns assassin for a secret government organization.
Incoherent action flick, made on a minuscule budget, and with talents to match.
w Steven Austin, Henry Clay *d* Steven Austin *ph* Dwight F. Lay *m* H. Schuyler Collins *ed* James Fletcher
☆ Joe Estevez, Ian Jacklin, Sam J. Jones, Judy Landers, Julie Merrill, Mel Novak

The Experts
US 1989 83m Alpha Cine
Paramount (James Keach)

Two trendy New Yorkers think they have been hired to open a night-club in Nebraska; in reality, they are transported to the USSR to teach American manners to Russian spies living in a replica of a US town.
Feeble and simple-minded comedy that is almost enough to restart the Cold War.
w Nick Thiel, Steven Greene, Eric Alter *d* Dave Thomas *ph* Ronnie Taylor *m* Marvin Hamlisch *pd* David Fischer *ed* Bud Molin
☆ John Travolta, Arye Gross, Kelly Preston, Deborah Foreman, James Keach, Jan Rubes, Brian Doyle Murray, Mimi Maynard, Eve Brent, Charles Martin Smith

Explorers
US 1985 109m Technicolor
Paramount/Edward S. Feldman/Industrial Light and Magic

Two boys make off in a space craft and encounter an alien race whose culture consists of intercepted American television programmes.
Slightly interesting but overlong fantasy spoof, probably not for popular consumption.
w Eric Luke *d* Joe Dante *ph* John Hora *m* Jerry Goldsmith *pd* Robert F. Boyle
☆ Ethan Hawke, River Phoenix, Jason Presson, Amanda Peterson

'One of the weirdest and most endearingly offbeat alien pix to have surfaced in recent years.' – *Variety*

Exposed
US 1983 99m Metrocolor
MGM-UA (James Toback)

A fashion model falls for a concert violinist who turns out to be a notorious terrorist.
A glossy absurdity confected from reading too many indigestible headlines.
wd James Toback *ph* Henri Decae *m* Georges Delerue *pd* Brian Eatwell *ed* Robert Lawrence, Annie Charvein
☆ Nastassja Kinski, Rudolf Nureyev, Harvey Keitel, Ian McShane, Bibi Andersson, Ron Randell, Pierre Clementi

'It often seems to be working out of a tension between sophisticated ambition and the capabilities of a tyro director, a kind of neo-primitivism (with a hint, perhaps, of Fuller, especially in its cultural name-dropping – Bach, Bosch, Dostoievsky, Heifetz, Perlman, Stern, to name a few).' – *Richard Combs, MFB*

'Johnny never had it so good – or lost it so fast!'
Expresso Bongo *
GB 1959 111m bw Dyaliscope
BL/Britannia/Conquest (Val Guest)

A Soho agent turns a nondescript teenage singer into an international star.
Heavily vulgarized version of a stage skit on the Tommy Steele rock phenomenon, divested of most of its satirical barbs and only intermittently amusing.
w Wolf Mankowitz *play* Wolf Mankowitz *d* Val Guest *ph* John Wilcox *m/ly* David Heneker, Monty Norman *md* Robert Farnon
☆ Laurence Harvey, Sylvia Syms, Yolande Donlan, Cliff Richard, *Meier Tzelniker*, Gilbert Harding, Ambrosine Philpotts, Eric Pohlmann, Wilfrid Lawson, Hermione Baddeley, Reginald Beckwith, Martin Miller

'What the cinema offers is a sardonic rattle with music ... The approach may be satirical or flippant; and yet one finds oneself half-beginning to believe in the subject; even minding about it.' – *Dilys Powell*

The Exquisite Sinner
US 1926 80m approx (24 fps) bw silent
MGM
A young French industrialist becomes bored with his society and takes off with a band of gypsies.
Curious and unsatisfactory farrago with extensive retakes by Phil Rosen (who also took credit the following year for an almost exactly similar film with a different title, Heaven on Earth, *but featuring the same stars).*
w Josef von Sternberg, Alice Duer Miller *d* Josef von Sternberg, Phil Rosen *ph* Max Fabian *ad* Cedric Gibbons
☆ Conrad Nagel, Renee Adoree, Myrna Loy

'First Jason...Then Freddy...Finally, A Professional.'
Exquisite Tenderness
Germany/US 1994 100m CFI color
Guild/Connexion (Alan Beattie, Chris Chesser, Willi Baer)

aka: *The Surgeon*
A mad doctor runs amok in a hospital, killing patients in order to obtain the ingredients for his miracle cure.
Bizarre horror movie that gives the impression that the participants improvised the increasingly risible plot; it runs out of originality within minutes.
w Patrick Cirillo, based on a screenplay by Bernard Sloane *d* Carl Schenkel *ph* Thomas Burstyn *m* Christopher Franke *pd* Douglas Higgins *ed* Jimmy B. Frazier *sp* Gary Paller; make-up: Steve Johnson
☆ Isabel Glasser, James Remar, Sean Haberle, Peter Boyle, Malcolm McDowell, Charles Dance

'A slick, sadistic horror film which is about as exquisite and tender as a medical textbook.' – *Tom Shone, Sunday Times*

'Over-excited camerawork barely dispels one's impression that the script and indeed the movie were thrown together in five minutes.' – *Independent*

Extase *
Czechoslovakia 1932 90m bw
Universal Elektra Film

aka: *Ecstasy*
A country girl takes a lover.
Simple love story with Freudian sequences, quite successfully and cinematically done. It caused a sensation at the time and was issued in various censored versions; the star's husband later tried to destroy all the copies.

wd Gustav Machaty *story* Viteslav Nezval *ph* Jan Stallich *m* Giuseppe Becce
☆ *Hedy Kiesler (later Hedy Lamarr)*, Aribert Mog
'The first important film to come out of Czechoslovakia since *Erotikon*, and what a hornet's nest it has stirred up! Critics and public are divided into two camps. Some proclaim it the world's worst, others rank it among the best productions of the year. It would never get by the censor in America.' – *Variety*

Extension du Domaine de la Lutte: see *Whatever*

The Exterminating Angel ***
Mexico 1962 95m bw
Uninci Films 59 (Gustavo Alatriste)
original title: *El Angel Exterminador*
High society dinner guests find themselves unable to leave the room, stay there for days, and go totally to the bad before the strange spell is broken; when they go to church to give thanks, they find themselves unable to leave.
Fascinating surrealist fantasia on themes elaborated with even more panache in The Discreet Charm of the Bourgeoisie. *Nevertheless, one of its director's key films.*
wd Luis Buñuel *(story assistance from Luis Alcoriza) ph* Gabriel Figueroa *ad* Jesus Bracho
☆ Silvia Pinal, Enrique Rambal, Jacqueline Andere, Jose Baviera
'An unsound and unsightly mixture of spurious allegory and genuine craziness.' – *John Simon*

The Exterminator
US 1980 102m Movielab
Interstar (Mark Buntzman)
An ex-Vietnam vet goes berserk when his friend is killed by a street gang, and vows revenge.
Vigilante movie with aspects of the modern horror-comic tradition; not much doubt that its real purpose is exploitation. It aroused some anger in America when a murder seemed to be based on its methods, but it was quickly succeeded by even more violent films.
wd James Glickenhaus *ph* Robert M. Baldwin *m* Joe Renzetti
☆ Robert Ginty, Christopher George, Samantha Eggar, Steve James
'Glickenhaus has plundered the iconographic treasury of recent American cinema, wrenching the images of war, sexuality and street crime out of their contexts and deploying them portentously so as to lend spurious significance to his film.' – *Martyn Auty, MFB*

Exterminator 2
US 1984 90m TVC Color
Cannon
An unemployed Vietnam veteran in New York eliminates punks with a flame thrower.
Violence fantasy, an extreme form of Death Wish; *quite reprehensible, and not for the squeamish.*
w Mark Buntzman, William Sachs *d* Mark Buntzman
☆ Robert Ginty, Deborah Geffner, Mario Van Peebles, Frankie Faison

The Extra Day
GB 1956 83m Eastmancolor
British Lion/William Fairchild (E. M. Smedley Aston)
The personal problems of five film extras who are recalled when a scene has to be reshot.
Thin excuse for portmanteau drama, only amusing in its depiction of a British movie being made with mostly foreign talent.
wd William Fairchild *ph* Arthur Grant *m* Philip Green
☆ Richard Basehart, Simone Simon, Sid James, Josephine Griffin, George Baker, Colin Gordon, Laurence Naismith, Charles Victor, Olga Lindo, Beryl Reid, Dennis Lotis

The Extra Girl *
US 1923 69m bw silent
Mack Sennett
A small town girl wins a beauty contest and goes to Hollywood.
A comparatively restrained comedy with slapstick interludes, this charming film shows its star at her best and admirably illustrates Hollywood in the early twenties.
w Bernard McConville *d* Mack Sennett
ph Homer Scott, Eric Crockett
☆ *Mabel Normand*, Max Davidson, Ralph Graves, George Nicholls

The Extraordinary Seaman
US 1968 80m Metrocolor Panavision
MGM/John Frankenheimer/Edward Lewis (John H. Cushingham, Hal Dresner)
Four stranded sailors come upon the ghostly Royal Navy captain of a ghostly World War II ship.
Curious sixties attempt at forties fantasy; obviously, from its short running time and fragmented style, something went sadly adrift during its making, and the wide screen does not help, but there are scattered funny moments.
w Philip Rock, Hal Dresner *d* John Frankenheimer *ph* Lionel Lindon *m* Maurice Jarre
☆ David Niven, Faye Dunaway, Alan Alda, Mickey Rooney, Jack Carter, Juano Hernandez, Barry Kelley
'A cleverly made curiosity, not so much produced as manufactured.' – *Marjorie Bilbow*

Extreme Justice
US 1993 96m Foto-Kem
Reflective/Arica (Frank Sacks)
aka: *S.I.S. Extreme Justice*
A young cop joins the Special Investigations Section of the Los Angeles police, a secret unit that tracks known dangerous criminals, but becomes concerned about their methods of shooting first and not bothering to ask questions later.
Despite its claim to be based on fact (which annoyed the LAPD), the movie sticks to the familiar exploitation routines of young idealistic recruit versus older cynical cop, car chases, violence and gratuitous gore.
w Frank Sacks, Robert Boris *d* Mark L. Lester *ph* Mark Irwin *m* David Michael Frank *pd* Richard L. Johnson *ed* Donn Aron
☆ Lou Diamond Phillips, Scott Glenn, Chelsea Field, Yaphet Kotto, Andrew Divoff, Richard Grove, William Lucking, Ed Lauter
'Lester's direction is leaden and the script, while raising some intriguing moral questions, lacks subtlety or grace.' – *Sight and Sound*
† Originally intended for cinema release, it was first shown on cable TV, and was released direct to video in Britain.

'Not all surgery is intended to cure.'
Extreme Measures
GB/US 1996 117m Technicolor Panavision
Columbia/Castle Rock/Simian (Elizabeth Hurley)
A doctor working in a New York hospital discovers that unethical experiments are being carried out on patients.
An unsuccessful medical thriller about a mad scientist, notable mainly as an attempt to broaden Grant's appeal to encompass action.
w Tony Gilroy *novel* Michael Palmer *d* Michael Apted *ph* John Bailey *m* Danny Elfman *pd* Doug Kramer *ed* Rick Shaine
☆ Hugh Grant, Gene Hackman, Sarah Jessica Parker, David Morse, Bill Nunn, John Toles-Bey, Paul Guilfoyle, Debra Monk
'Can never quite make up its mind whether it's a horror movie, an action thriller, or a reasonably serious medical drama. In fact, it is not quite any of these things and its screenplay betrays a fundamental lack of confidence.' – *Derek Malcolm, Guardian*
† The first production from Hugh Grant and Elizabeth Hurley's company, the film was a box-office flop, grossing just over $17m in the US.

Extreme Prejudice
US 1987 104m Technicolor
Carolco/Tri-Star (Buzz Feitshans)
A Texas Ranger pins down a drug trafficker.
Ordinary urban thriller with overplayed violence.
w Deric Washburn, Harry Kleiner *story* John Milius, Fred Rexer *d* Walter Hill *ph* Matthew F. Leonetti *m* Jerry Goldsmith *pd* Albert Heschong *ed* Freeman Davies
☆ Nick Nolte, Powers Boothe, Michael Ironside, Rip Torn, Clancy Brown, Maria Conchita Alonso

Extremities
US 1986 90m colour
Atlantic Releasing (Burt Sugarman)
A girl takes revenge on the man who raped her.
Unpleasant when it's not verbose; anything but entertaining.
w William Mastrosimone *play* William Mastrosimone *d* Robert M. Young *ph* Curtis Clark *m* J. A. C. Redford *pd* Chester Kaczenski *ed* Arthur Coburn
☆ Farrah Fawcett, James Russo, Diana Scarwid, Alfre Woodard

'What if the reflection you see is not yours'
The Eye
Hong Kong 2002 99m colour
Metro Tartan/Fortissimo/Applause/Raintree (Peter Ho-Sun Chan, Lawrence Tan-Shui Cheng)
original title: *Gin Gwai*
In Hong Kong, a blind woman has cornea transplants and begins to see ghosts of the recently dead.
Strange psychological horror story that requires more than the usual suspension of disbelief.
w Jojo Yuet-Chun Hui *story* Danny Pang, Oxide Pang *d* Danny Pang, Oxide Pang *ph* Decha Seementa *m* Orange Music *ad* Simon So, Kritapas Suttinet *ed* Danny Pang, Oxide Pang
☆ Lee Sin-Je (Mann), Lawrence Chou (Wah), Chutcha Rujinanon (Ying Ying), Candy Lo (Mann's Sister), Pierre Png (Ed), Ko Yin Ping (Mann's Grandmother), Dr Lo (Edmund Chen)
'This lugubrious, self-conscious film is an odd mixture of the corny and the cornea.' – *Philip French, Observer*

An Eye for an Eye
France/Italy 1956 93m Technicolor VistaVision
UGC/Jolly (André Cayatte)
A doctor finds himself trekking across the desert with a demented man whose wife has died in his care.
Initially striking melodrama which becomes increasingly unconvincing and has a tendency to harp on unpleasant detail.
wd André Cayatte *novel* Vahe Katcha *ph* Christian Matras *m* Louiguy
☆ Curt Jurgens, Folco Lulli, Lea Padovani

An Eye for an Eye
US 1981 104m CFI color
Avco Embassy/Adams Apple/South Street/Westcom (Frank Capra Jnr)
An undercover cop resigns from the force but uncovers a drug ring.
Tedious and violent actioner with a martial arts champion for hero.
w William Gray, James Bruner *d* Steve Carver *ph* Roger Shearman *m* William Goldstein *ad* Vance Lorenzini *ed* Anthony Redman
☆ Chuck Norris (Sean Kane), Christopher Lee (Morgan Canfield), Richard Roundtree (Capt. Stevens), Matt Clark (Tom McCoy), Mako (James Chan), Maggie Cooper (Heather Sullivan), Rosalind Chao (Linda Chan), Toru Tanaka (Giant)

'What do you do when justice fails?'
Eye for an Eye
US 1996 101m DeLuxe
Paramount (Michael I. Levy)
When the rapist and killer of her teenage daughter is freed on a legal technicality, a mother decides to kill him herself.
Contrived and unpleasant little pro-vigilante movie that loads the scales of justice while providing Sally Field with an opportunity to display prolonged hysteria.
w Amanda Silver, Rick Jaffa *novel* Erika Holzer *d* John Schlesinger *ph* Amir M. Mokri *m* James Newton Howard *pd* Stephen Hendrickson *ed* Peter Honess
☆ Sally Field, Kiefer Sutherland, Ed Harris, Beverly D'Angelo, Charlaine Woodard, Joe Mantegna, Olivia Burnette, Alexandra Kyle
'A virtually worthless piece of film-making. It's a crude and paranoid scare story dressed up as moral sensitivity.' – *Tom Shone, Sunday Times*

'A Journey Into Obsession.'
Eye of the Beholder *
GB/Canada 1999 107m colour
TCF/Behaviour Worldwide/Village Roadshow/Ambridge/Hit & Run/Filmline/Eye of the Beholder (Nicolas Clermont, Tony Smith)
A burnt-out investigator, haunted by the memory of his missing young daughter, compulsively tracks a woman who enjoys killing men for their money.
Sporadically intriguing thriller with intellectual pretensions and more than a few irritations; as it becomes increasingly risible, the main pleasure lies in Judd's characterisation of a ruthless, unhappy woman.
wd Stephan Elliott *novel* Marc Behm *ph* Guy Dufaux *m* Marius De Vries *pd* Jean-Baptiste Tard *ed* Sue Blainey *cos* Lizzy Gardiner
☆ Ewan McGregor (The Eye), *Ashley Judd* (Joanna), Patrick Bergin (Alex Leonard), k.d. lang (Hilary), Jason Priestley (Gary), Genevieve Bujold (Dr Brault)
'An empty bit of confusing rubbish.' – *Alexander Walker*

'Terror that tears the scream right out of your throat!'
Eye of the Cat *
US 1969 102m Technicolor
Universal/Joseph M. Schenck (Bernard Schwarz, Philip Hazelton)
A young man who hates cats goes to stay with his crippled aunt who keeps a house full of them.
Odd, Psycho*-like thriller (from the same screen writer) with plenty of scary sequences but an inadequate resolution.*
w Joseph Stefano *d* David Lowell Rich *ph* *Russell Metty, Ellsworth Fredricks* *m* Lalo Schifrin *cat trainer* Ray Berwick
☆ Eleanor Parker, Michael Sarrazin, Gayle Hunnicutt, Tim Henry, Laurence Naismith
'Not so much a good film as an extravagantly enjoyable one.' – *MFB*

Eye of the Devil *
GB 1967 92m bw
MGM/Filmways (John Calley, Ben Kadish)
A French nobleman is obsessed by a family tradition of pagan self-sacrifice.
Diabolical goings-on in a spooky castle, not really helped by a glittering supporting cast any more than by miscast stars, sluggish direction or a general atmosphere of gloom rather than suspense.
w Robin Estridge, Dennis Murphy *novel* *Day of the Arrow* by Philip Loraine *d* J. Lee-Thompson *ph* Erwin Hillier *m* Gary McFarland
☆ David Niven, Deborah Kerr, Emlyn Williams, Flora Robson, Donald Pleasence, Edward Mulhare, David Hemmings, Sharon Tate, John Le Mesurier, Donald Bisset
'It is hard to say why the total effect is so constantly hilarious.' – *MFB*
† The film had a chequered career. The first attempt to make it was abandoned because of Kim Novak's inadequacy; it then went through three titles and a lot of trouble with the censor.

'To love a stranger is easy ... to kill a lover is not!'
Eye of the Needle
GB 1981 113m Technicolor
UA/Kings Road (Stephen Friedman)
In London in 1940 a German agent murders his landlady but is eventually cornered by a girl on a Scottish island.
Listless espionage narrative with very little drive or interest: the shape of the story defies suspense.
w Stanley Mann *novel* Ken Follett *d* Richard Marquand *ph* Alan Hume *m* Miklos Rozsa
☆ Donald Sutherland, Kate Nelligan, Christopher Cazenove, Ian Bannen, Alex McCrindle

Eye of the Tiger
US 1986 90m United Color
Scotti Brothers (Tony Scotti)
A vigilante avenges his wife's murder.
Predictable thriller with video in mind.
w Michael Montgomery *d* Richard Sarafian *ph* Peter Collister *ad* Wayne Springfield *ed* Greg Prange
☆ Gary Busey, Yaphet Kotto, Seymour Cassel, Bert Remsen, William Smith

Eye Witness: see *Your Witness (1950)*

Eye Witness

GB 1956 82m bw

Rank/Sydney Box

A maniacal burglar pursues a witness of his crime into the emergency ward of a local hospital.

Naïve but adequate suspenser with too many character cameos getting in the way of the plot.

w Janet Green *d* Muriel Box *ph* Reg Wyer *m* Bruce Montgomery

☆ Donald Sinden, Muriel Pavlow, Belinda Lee, Michael Craig, Nigel Stock, Susan Beaumont, David Knight, Ada Reeve

Eyes in the Night *

US 1942 80m bw

MGM (Jack Chertok)

A blind detective sets out to discover whether a mysterious man engaged to an heiress is really a Nazi spy.

Tolerable wartime puzzler.

w Guy Trosper, Howard Emmett Rogers *novel* *Odor of Violets* by Baynard Kendrick *d* Fred Zinnemann *ph* Robert Planck, Charles Lawton *m* Lennie Hayton

☆ Edward Arnold, Ann Harding, Donna Reed, Allen Jenkins, John Emery, Stephen McNally, Reginald Denny, Rosemary de Camp, Stanley Ridges

'They have converted a basically humdrum yarn into a tense and tingling little thriller.' – *New York Times*

† Edward Arnold appeared once more as Duncan Maclain, in *The Hidden Eye* (1944) (qv).

Eyes of Laura Mars

US 1978 104m Metrocolor

Columbia/Jon Peters (Jack H. Harris)

A fashion photographer has violent premonitions about a series of murders.

Silly and often unpleasant suspenser which despite its chic appearance never bothers to explain itself.

w John Carpenter, David Zelag Goodman *d* Irvin Kershner *ph* Victor J. Kemper *m* Artie Kane

☆ Faye Dunaway, Tommy Lee Jones, Brad Dourif, René Auberjonois, Raul Julia, Frank Adonis

'Long on trendy settings, high-priced actors and vicious murders, but devoid of narrative thrills.' – *Richard Schickel, Time*

'Moves so fast, with such delicate changes of rhythm, that its excitement has a subterraneum sexiness.' – *Pauline Kael, New Yorker*

Eyes Wide Shut **

US/GB 1999 159m DeLuxe

Warner/Pole Star/Hobby (Stanley Kubrick)

Distressed by his wife's account of a sexual fantasy, a New York doctor goes on an erotic odyssey through the city.

An atmospheric account of sexual jealousy, temptation and fidelity, meticulously made and with an oddly dreamlike quality about it; but, while being faithful to its slim source, it is also overlong and much too portentous.

w Stanley Kubrick, Frederic Raphael *novella* *Dream Story/Traumnovelle* by Arthur Schnitzler *d* Stanley Kubrick *ph* Larry Smith *m* Jocelyn Pook *pd* Les Tomkins, Roy Walker *ed* Nigel Galt

☆ Tom Cruise (Dr William Harford), Nicole Kidman (Alice Harford), Sydney Pollack (Victor Ziegler), Marie Richardson (Marion), Rade Sherbedgia (Milich), Todd Field (Nick Nightingale), Vinessa Shaw (Domino), Alan Cumming (Desk Clerk), Sky Dumont (Sandor Szavost), Fay Masterson (Sally), Leelee Sobieski (Milich's Daughter), Thomas Gibson (Carl), Madison Eginton (Helena Harford)

'An uncanny masterpiece.' – *Glenn Kenny, Premiere*

'This musty tale feels exactly what it is: a small-scale arthouse movie way past its sell-by date, exhumed from a bygone era of Freudian fascination.' – *Matt Mueller, Total Film*

'The batsqueak of hysteria and absurdity is essential to this fable of erotic paranoia and erotic discontent within a bourgeois marriage.' – *Peter Bradshaw, Guardian*

† The film took $31m in its first week at the US box-office, after which audiences fell away; its final take was $55.7m.

Eyes without a Face *

France/Italy 1959 90m bw

Champs Elysées/Lux (Jules Borkon)

original title: *Les Yeux sans Visage*

US title: *The Horror Chamber of Dr Faustus*

When his daughter is mutilated in a car accident, a mad professor murders young girls in the process of grafting their faces onto hers.

Unpleasant horror film which its director seems to have made as a joke; the years have made it a cult.

w Jean Redon *novel* Jean Redon *d* Georges Franju *ph* Eugen Schüfftan *m* Maurice Jarre

☆ Pierre Brasseur, Alida Valli, Edith Scob, François Guérin

'Perhaps the most austerely elegant horror film ever made.' – *Pauline Kael*

Eyewitness *

GB 1970 91m Technicolor

ITC/ABP (Paul Maslansky)

aka: *Sudden Terror*

A boy is the sole witness to an assassination, but no one believes him except the assassins.

The Window *all over again, the standard clichés being tricked out with fancy photography, sub-Hitchcock set-ups and Mediterranean locations, which make it all very tolerable.*

w Ronald Harwood *novel* Mark Hebden *d* John Hough *ph* David Holmes *m* Fairfield Parlour, David Whitaker

☆ Mark Lester, Lionel Jeffries, Susan George, Tony Bonner, Jeremy Kemp, Peter Vaughan, Peter Bowles, Betty Marsden

Eyewitness

US 1981 108m Technicolor

TCF (Peter Yates)

GB title: *The Janitor*

A bashful janitor with a crush on a TV star finds himself hunted down by a murderer afraid of identification.

Odd little character thriller which despite pleasant touches never really seems to have its mind on its plot.

w Steve Tesich *d* Peter Yates *ph* Matthew F. Leonetti *m* Stanley Silverman *pd* Philip Rosenberg

☆ William Hurt, Christopher Plummer, Sigourney Weaver, Irene Worth, James Woods, Kenneth McMillan, Steven Hill

The FBI Story *
US 1959 149m Technicolor
Warner (Mervyn Le Roy)

An FBI agent thinks back on his career with the bureau.
Predictable mix of domestic sentimentality (very trying) and competent crime capsules: mad bomber, Ku Klux Klan, thirties hoodlums, Nazi spy rings and the cold war.
w Richard L. Breen, John Twist *d* Mervyn Le Roy *ph* Joseph Biroc *m* Max Steiner *ad* John Beckman
☆ James Stewart, Vera Miles, Larry Pennell, Nick Adams, Murray Hamilton
'Insufferably cosy.' – *MFB*

F for Fake *
France/Iran/West Germany 1973 85m colour
Astrophore/Saco/Janus (Dominique Antoine, François Reichenbach)

French title: *Vérités et Mensonges*
Orson Welles, at a railway station, lectures the audience in truth and falsehood, in art, in films and in life.
A ragbag of an entertainment, cannibalizing as it does more than one unsold documentary, shredded at the editing table to match the narrator's illusionist style. Despite the raptures of some critics, this is an irritating effusion, and Welles now looks more like a clever charlatan than a master film-maker.
w Orson Welles, Oja Palinkas *d* Orson Welles *ph* Gary Graver, Christian Odasso *m* Michel Legrand
'Welles stretches his material and his legend just about as thin as possible in this tedious treatise on truth and illusion.' – *Kevin Thomas, Los Angeles Times*
† Joseph Cotten, Paul Stewart and Laurence Harvey make fleeting appearances.

'No Static At All!'
FM
US 1978 104m Technicolor Panavision
CIC/Universal (Rand Holston)

aka: *Citizens' Band*
Problems of a commercial radio station whose disc jockeys seek integrity above commerce.
Footling cause-pleading is all this 'with-it' movie has to offer apart from its picture of commercial radio in the late seventies, which should be of interest to social historians.
w Ezra Sacks *d* John A. Alonzo *ph* David Myers *m* Steely Dan, Linda Ronstadt, Jimmy Buffett and others *pd* Lawrence G. Paull *ed* Jeff Gourson
☆ Michael Brandon, Eileen Brennan, Alex Karras, Cleavon Little, Martin Mull

F. T. W.
US 1994 100m colour
Nu Image/HKM/Red Ruby (Tom Mickel)

A cowboy gets out of prison and meets a girl on the run from a bank robbery.
Glum little road movie that goes nowhere interesting.
w Mari Kornhauser *d* Michael Karbelnikoff *ph* James L. Carter *m* Gary Chang *pd* J. K. Reinhart *ed* Joe D'Augustine
☆ Mickey Rourke (Frank T. Wells), Aaron Neville (Snake), Peter Berg (Clem Stuart), Lori Singer (Scarlett Stuart), Ron Peterson (Checklist Guard), John Enos (Joe Palmieri), Brion James (Sheriff Rudy Morgan)

F/X
US 1985 106m Technicolor
Orion (Dodi Fayed, Jack Wiener)

GB title: *Murder by Illusion*
A special effects man is paid to stage a phony assassination, then finds himself the target of hit men.
Initially mysterious premise settles down into a long chase, which of its kind isn't badly done but goes on forever.
w Robert T. Megginson, Gregory Fleeman *d* Robert Mandel *ph* Miroslav Ondricek *m* Bill Conti *pd* Mel Bourne *ed* Terry Rawlings
☆ Bryan Brown, Brian Dennehy, Diane Venora, Cliff DeYoung, Mason Adams, Jerry Orbach
'Delivers high-gear excitement from start to finish.' – *Bruce Williamson, Playboy*

'Outgunned by the mob, outmanned by the cops ... their effects had better be special!'
F/X2: The Deadly Art of Illusion
US 1991 108m DeLuxe
Columbia TriStar/Orion (Jack Wiener, Dodi Fayed)

A former special effects man and a private eye team up to recover some stolen Michelangelo medallions.
Virtually a repeat of the first movie, but done with much less panache and little attempt at plausibility.
w Bill Condon *d* Richard Franklin *ph* Victor J. Kemper, David M. Walsh, Tonino Delli Colli *m* Lalo Schifrin *pd* John Jay Moore *ed* Andrew London, Michael Tronick *sp* Eric Allard
☆ Bryan Brown, Brian Dennehy, Rachel Ticotin, Joanna Gleason, Philip Bosco, Kevin J. O'Connor, Tom Mason
'With all the ingenuity that went into toys and gadgetry in this five-years-removed sequel, it's a shame no-one bothered to hook up a brain to the plot.' – *Variety*

Fa Talai Jone: see *Tears of the Black Tiger*

'She'll change your life.'
Le Fabuleux Destin d'Amélie Poulain **
France/Germany 2001 123m bw/colour Super 35
Momentum/Victoires/Tapioca/France3/MMC (Claudie Ossard)

GB and US title: *Amélie*
In Monmartre, a young woman has an improving effect on the lives of those around her.
Paris and love are seen through rose-coloured spectacles in this aggressively charming movie that has a puppy-dog eagerness to please, when not licking its audience into submission with candied tongue.
w Guillaume Laurant, Jean-Pierre Jeunet *d* Jean-Pierre Jeunet *ph* Bruno Delbonnel *m* Yann Tiersen *pd* *Aline Bonetto* *ed* Herve Schneid *cos* Emma Lebail
☆ *Audrey Tautou* (Amélie), Mathieu Kassovitz (Nino Quincampoix), Rufus (Raphael Poulain), Yolande Moreau (Madeleine Wallace), Artus Penguern (Hipolito), Urbain Cancellier (Collignon), Dominique Pinon (Joseph), Maurice Benichou (Bretodeau), Andre Dussollier (Narrator)
'It is overwritten and overdirected for the quaint, simple feelings it attempts to project.' – *Andrew Sarris*
'Redefines what is possible in the cinema. A paean to feel-good entertainment, buttressed by a wonderful story, remarkable imagery, haunting music and a heart-stopping performance.' – *James Cameron-Wilson, Film Review*
foreign language film; Guillaume Laurent, Jean-Pierre Jeunet (screenplay); Aline Bonetto; Bruno Delbonnel; sound (Vincent Arnardi, Guillaume Leriche, Jean Umansky)
Guillaume Laurent, Jean-Pierre Jeunet (screenplay); Aline Bonetto

The Fabulous Adventures of Marco Polo
France/Italy/Yugoslavia/Egypt/Afghanistan 1964 115m Eastmancolor Franscope
Ittac/Prodi/Avala/Mounir Rafla/Italaf Kaboul (Raoul Lévy)
aka: *Marco the Magnificent*
In 1271 Marco Polo carries a message of peace to Kubla Khan.
Curious mixture of melodrama and pantomime, with a star cast half playing for laughs.
w Raoul Lévy, Denys de la Patellière *d* Denys de la Patellière, Noel Howard *ph* Armand Thirard *m* George Garvarentz
☆ Horst Buchholz, Anthony Quinn, Orson Welles, Akim Tamiroff, Robert Hossein, Omar Sharif, Elsa Martinelli, Grégoire Aslan, Massimo Girotti, Folco Lulli

The Fabulous Baker Boys *
US 1989 113m colour
Rank/Gladden (Paula Weinstein, Sydney Pollack, Mark Rosenberg)

Two piano-playing brothers hire a female singer to enliven their dying night-club act.
Enjoyable excursion into the lower depths of showbusiness.
wd Steve Kloves *ph* Michael Ballhaus *m* Dave Grusin *pd* Jeffrey Townsend *ed* Bill Steinkamp
☆ Jeff Bridges, *Michelle Pfeiffer*, Beau Bridges, Ellie Raab, Jennifer Tilly
Michelle Pfeiffer; Michael Ballhaus; Dave Grusin; Bill Steinkamp

The Fabulous Dorseys
US 1947 91m bw
UA (Charles R. Rogers)

Two quarrelling bandleader brothers are reunited on the death of their father.
Slight, comedic biopic with the Dorseys playing well and trying hard.
w Richard English, Art Arthur, Curtis Kenyon *d* Alfred E. Green *ph* James Van Trees *m* Leo Shuken
☆ Tommy Dorsey, Jimmy Dorsey and their bands, Janet Blair, Paul Whiteman, William Lundigan

The Fabulous Texan
US 1947 97m bw
Republic
Confederate officers after the Civil War return home to find Texas overrun by carpetbaggers and despotic state police.
Fairly handsome Western which gets by without ever being memorable.
w Lawrence Hazard, Horace McCoy *d* Edward Ludwig
☆ William Elliott, John Carroll, Catherine McLeod, Andy Devine, Albert Dekker, Ruth Donnelly, Harry Davenport, Douglass Dumbrille

Faccia a Faccia: see *Face to Face (1967)*

The Face ***
Sweden 1958 100m bw
Svensk Filmindustri (Allan Ekelund)

original title: *Ansiktet*
US title: *The Magician*
In 19th-century Sweden, a mesmerist and his troupe are halted at a country post to be examined by three officials. Partly exposed as a fraud, he takes a frightening revenge.
A virtually indecipherable parable which may be about the survival of Christianity (and may not), this wholly personal Bergman fancy has to be enjoyed chiefly for its surface frissons, for its acting and its look, which are almost sufficient compensation.
wd *Ingmar Bergman* *ph* *Gunnar Fischer* *m* Erik Nordgren *ad* P. A. Lundgren *ed* Oscar Rosander
☆ *Max von Sydow*, Ingrid Thulin, *Gunnar Björnstrand*, Naima Wifstrand, Uke Fridell, Lars Ekborg, Bengt Ekerot

'The blag to kill for. Only one of them meant it for real.'
Face *
GB 1997 103m colour
UIP/BBC/Distant Horizon (David M. Thompson, Elinor Day)

A thief who sets up a robbery with four others tries to discover which of them is a traitor.
A streetwise thriller with political overtones, too old-fashioned and heavy-handed to carry much conviction.
w Ronan Bennett *d* Antonia Bird *ph* Fred Tamms *pd* Chris Townsend *ed* St John O'Rorke
☆ Robert Carlyle, Ray Winstone, Steven Waddington, Philip Davis, Damon Albarn, Lena Headey, Peter Vaughan, Sue Johnston, Gerry Conlon
'The soundtrack is full of blurred and sombre beats, while the yellow overalls worn by the gang for the raid make the job look designed as much as planned. But this is only top dressing when the script is full of howling clichés.' – *Adam Mars-Jones, Independent*

The Face at the Window *
GB 1939 65m bw
Pennant/Ambassador (George King)

In 1880 Paris, a murderer uses his moronic half-brother to distract his victims but is foiled when a dead man apparently incriminates him.
Roistering melodrama which provided Tod Slaughter with one of his juiciest roles and is here effectively presented, which is more than can be said for the screen treatments of most of his other vehicles.
w A. R. Rawlinson, Ronald Fayre *play* F. Brooke Warren *d* George King *ph* Hone Glendining *md* Jack Beaver *ad* Philip Bawcombe *ed* Jack Harris
☆ *Tod Slaughter*, Marjorie Taylor, John Warwick, Leonard Henry, Aubrey Mallalieu
'One of the best English pictures I have seen ... leaves the American horror films far behind.' – *Graham Greene*

The Face behind the Mask *
US 1941 69m bw
Columbia (Wallace MacDonald)
When his face is disfigured in a fire, an immigrant turns to a life of crime.
Effective second feature melodrama with a good star performance.
w Allen Vincent, Paul Jarrico *play* Thomas O'Connell *d* Robert Florey *ph* Franz Planer *md* Sidney Cutner
☆ *Peter Lorre*, Evelyn Keyes, *Don Beddoe*, George E. Stone

A Face in the Crowd ***
US 1957 126m bw
(Warner) Newton (Elia Kazan)

A small-town hick becomes a megalomaniac when television turns him into a cracker-barrel philosopher.
Brilliantly cinematic melodrama of its time which only flags in the last lap and paints a luridly entertaining picture of modern show business.
w *Budd Schulberg* *story* *Your Arkansas Traveller* by Budd Schulberg *d* *Elia Kazan* *ph* *Harry Stradling*, *Gayne Rescher* *m* Tom Glazer
☆ *Andy Griffith*, *Lee Remick*, *Walter Matthau*, *Patricia Neal*, Anthony Franciosa, Percy Waram, Marshall Neilan

'Savagery, bitterness, cutting humour.' – *Penelope Houston*
'If Kazan and Schulberg had been content to make their case by implication, it might have been a completely sophisticated piece of movie-making. Instead, everything is elaborately spelled out, and the film degenerates into preposterous liberal propaganda.' – *Andrew Sarris*
'Some exciting scenes in the first half, but the later developments are frenetic, and by the end the film is a loud and discordant mess.' – *Pauline Kael, 70s*

Face of a Fugitive *
US 1959 81m Eastmancolor
Columbia/Morningside
A man falsely accused of murder makes a new life in a frontier town.
Lively Western melodrama with good atmosphere.
w David T. Chantler *d Paul Wendkos ph* Wilfrid M. Cline *m* Jerry Goldsmith
☆ Fred MacMurray, Lin McCarthy, Alan Baxter, James Coburn

Face of a Stranger: see *The Promise*

The Face of Fu Manchu **
GB 1965 96m Techniscope
Anglo-EMI/Hallam (Harry Alan Towers)
In the twenties, Nayland Smith of Scotland Yard links an oriental crime wave with evil mastermind Fu Manchu.
A splendidly light touch and attention to detail make this entertaining spoof like a tuppenny blood come to life.
w Peter Welbeck (Harry Alan Towers) *d Don Sharp ph* Ernest Steward *m* Chris Whelan *ad Frank White*
☆ *Nigel Green*, Christopher Lee, Tsai Chin, Howard Marion Crawford

The Face of Marble
US 1946 70m bw
Monogram (Jeffrey Bernard)
A scientist revives the dead through voodoo.
Grade Z shocker with entertaining moments.
w Michel Jacoby *d* William Beaudine
☆ John Carradine, Robert Shayne, Claudia Drake, Maris Wrixon

Face/Off **
US 1997 138m DeLuxe Panavision
Buena Vista/Douglas/Reuther/WCG (David Permut, Barrie M. Osborne, Terence Chang, Christopher Godsick)
In order to discover the location of a bomb planted in Los Angeles, an FBI man assumes a false identity by having his own face replaced by that of a criminal.
Delirious thriller, in which the two male stars play each other as well as themselves in a pas de deux of elaborately choreographed violence.
w Mike Werb, Michael Colleary *d* John Woo *ph* Oliver Wood *m* John Powell *pd* Neil Spisak *ed* Christian Wagner, Steven Kemper
☆ John Travolta, Nicolas Cage, Joan Allen, Alessandro Nivola, Gina Gershon, Dominique Swain, Nick Cassavetes, Harve Presnell, Colm Feore
'Woo clearly thinks he's onto something big and mythic about male identity but, in truth, the film never really rises above the shin-kicking level of a pubescent bun fight – like the surgery itself, the film only goes skin deep.' – *Tom Shone, Sunday Times*
'It takes a lot of patience and stamina to watch more than two hours of this brazen rubbish.' – *Geoff Brown, The Times*
† The film was originally written as a vehicle for Arnold Schwarzenegger and Sylvester Stallone.
†† It was the tenth most commercially successful movie of the year, grossing some $112m in the US, and another $115m elsewhere.
♙ sound effects editing

Face the Music
GB 1954 84m bw
Exclusive/Hammer (Michael Carreras)
US title: *The Black Glove*
An American musician in London solves the murder of a night-club singer.
Minor thriller in a sub-Chandler manner, improved by its music featuring the trumpet-playing of Kenny Baker.
w Ernest Borneman *novel* Ernest Borneman *d* Terence Fisher *ph* Jimmy Harvey *m* Kenny Baker's Dozen *ad* J. Elder Wills *ed* Maurice Rootes
☆ Alex Nicol, Eleanor Summerfield, John Salew, Paul Carpenter, Geoffrey Keen, Ann Hanslip

Face to Face *
Italy/Spain 1967 110m Technicolor Techniscope
PEA/Arturo Gonzalez (Alberto Grimaldi)
original title: *Faccia a Faccia*
A consumptive university professor goes to Texas for a cure and becomes the ruthless leader of a gang of outlaws.
Political spaghetti Western that can be taken as an allegory for the rise of fascism and the doctrine that ten violent men are bandits, but hundreds are an army and thousands are history.
w Sergio Donati, Sergio Sollima *d* Sergio Sollima *ph* Raphael Pacheco *m* Ennio Morricone *ad* Carlo Simi *ed* Eugenio Alabiso
☆ Gian Maria Volonte, Tomas Milian, William Berger, Jolanda Modio, Gianni Rizzo, Carol André, Lidya Alfonsi

Face to Face ****
Sweden 1976 136m Eastmancolor
Ingmar Bergman/De Laurentiis/Sveriges Radio (Ingmar Bergman, Lars-Owe Carlberg)
A psychiatrist staying with her grandparents finds herself in need of guidance.
Fascinating material edited down from a TV series; too long as a film.
wd Ingmar Bergman ph Sven Nykvist *m* Mozart *ad* Anne Terselius-Hagegòrd, Anna Asp, Maggie Strindberg *ed* Siv Lundgren
☆ *Liv Ullmann*, Erland Josephson, Gunnar Björnstrand, Aino Taube-Henrikson
'After one has detailed its shortcomings, a wonderful fact remains: it's a work possible only to a first-class artist who has invested his life with other artists.' – *Stanley Kauffmann*
♙ Ingmar Bergman (as director); Liv Ullmann

The Faceless Monster: see *Night of the Doomed*

Faces *
US 1968 130m bw
Maurice McEndree
A discontented Los Angeles executive tries but fails to go through with a divorce.
A personal, probing study of middle-aged loneliness, made with the director's usual long-winded relentlessness but quite frequently compelling.
wd John Cassavetes *m* Jack Ackerman *ph/ed* Al Ruban
☆ *John Marley, Gena Rowlands*, Lynn Carlin, Fred Draper, Seymour Cassel
'The cast are all painfully and overpoweringly real.' – *Jan Dawson*
♙ John Cassavetes (as writer); Lynn Carlin; Seymour Cassel

Facing: see *En Face*

The Facts of Life *
US 1960 103m bw
UA/HLP (Norman Panama)
Two middle-aged married suburbanites have an abortive affair.
Star comedy with muted slapstick and earnest acting, a good try, but less effective than their normal pratfalls.
w Norman Panama, Melvin Frank *d* Melvin Frank *ph* Charles Lang Jnr *m* Leigh Harline *ad* Joseph McMillan Johnson, Kenneth A. Reid
☆ *Bob Hope, Lucille Ball*, Ruth Hussey, Don Defore, Louis Nye, Philip Ober
'Random shots of mockery aimed effectively at the American middle-class way of life.' – *Peter John Dyer*
♙ Norman Panama, Melvin Frank (script); Charles Lang Jnr; title song (*m/ly* Johnny Mercer); art direction

The Faculty *
US 1998 102m colour
Dimension/Los Hooligans (Elizabeth Avellan)
High-school students notice that teachers and classmates are behaving oddly.
An adolescent variation on Invasion of the Body Snatchers, *done with immense energy and a little wit.*
w Kevin Williamson *story* David Wechter, Bruce Kimmel *d* Robert Rodriguez *ph* Enrique Chediak *m* Marco Beltrami *pd* Cary White *ed* Robert Rodriguez *sp* make-up and creature fx: Robert Kurtzman, Gregory Nicotero, Howard Berger, KNB EFX
☆ Jordana Brewster, Clea DuVall, Laura Harris, Josh Harnett, Shawn Hatosy, Salma Hayek, Famke Janssen, Piper Laurie, Chris McDonald, Bebe Neuwirth, Robert Patrick, Usher Raymond, Jon Stewart, Daniel von Bargen, Elijah Wood
'A rip-snorting hunk of giddy, self-aware genre trash.' – *Dennis Harvey, Variety*
'It isn't the least bit scary or particularly involving, but that seems to be the point.' – *Peter Matthews, Sight and Sound*

Fade to Black
US 1980 100m colour
Compass International/Leisure Investment/Movie Ventures (George Braunstein, Ron Hamady)
A film buff becomes known as the 'Celluloid Killer' for murdering his victims while disguised as his favourite movie characters.
Violent, off-beat thriller that makes black jokes at the expense of movies.
wd Vernon Zimmerman *story* Irving Yablans *ph* Alex Phillips Jnr *ed* Howard Kunin *sp* James Wayne
☆ Dennis Christopher, Linda Kerridge, Tim Thomerson, Morgan Paull, Hennen Chambers, Marya Small, Mickey Rourke
† The film won the Critics' Prize at the Avoriaz Festival of Fantastic Films in 1981.

Fahrenheit 451 *
GB 1966 112m Technicolor
Rank/Anglo Enterprise/Vineyard (Lewis M. Allen)
In a fascist future state, a fireman's job is to burn books.
1984 stuff, a little lacking in plot and rather tentatively directed, but with charming moments.
w François Truffaut, Jean-Louis Richard *novel* Ray Bradbury *d* François Truffaut *ph* Nicolas Roeg *m* Bernard Herrmann *design consultant* Tony Walton
☆ *Oskar Werner*, Julie Christie, Cyril Cusack, Anton Diffring, Jeremy Spenser
'He barely dramatizes the material at all, and though there are charming, childlike moments, the performers seem listless, and the whole enterprise is a little drab.' – *Pauline Kael*
† All the credits in this film are spoken.

'It will have you sitting on the brink of eternity!'
Fail Safe ***
US 1964 111m bw
Columbia/Max E. Youngstein/Sidney Lumet
An American atomic bomber is accidentally set to destroy Moscow, and the president has to destroy New York in retaliation.
Despite a confusing opening, this deadly earnest melodrama gets across the horror of its situation better than the contemporaneous Dr Strangelove *which treated the same plot as black comedy. Here the details are both terrifying and convincing.*
w Walter Bernstein *novel* Eugene Burdick, Harvey Wheeler *d Sidney Lumet ph* Gerald Hirschfeld *m* none
☆ *Henry Fonda*, Walter Matthau, Dan O'Herlihy, Frank Overton, Fritz Weaver, Edward Binns, Larry Hagman, Russell Collins

Fair Game: see *Mamba (1988)*

Fair Game
US 1995 90m Technicolor
Warner/Silver Pictures (Joel Silver)
A Miami lawyer is targeted by a former KGB killer.
A star vehicle built around Cindy Crawford: as long as she's in motion, it works as a low-level, senseless action film; when she stops, not even the many loud explosions can hide her lack of acting ability.
w Charles Fletcher *novel* Paula Gosling *d* Andrew Sipes *ph* Richard Bowen *m* Mark Mancina *pd* James Spencer *ed* David Finfer, Christian Wagner, Steven Kemper
☆ William Baldwin, Cindy Crawford, Steven Berkoff, Christopher McDonald, Miguel Sandoval, Johann Carlo, Salma Hayek
'Notable only for its jaw-dropping stupidity, the sort of action yarn that hopes nonstop mayhem will help cloud just how nonsensical it is.' – *Brian Lowry, Variety*
'A thriller primarily about the movement of Cindy Crawford's breasts beneath a succession of ever-smaller T-shirts.' – *Entertainment Weekly*
† The novel was first filmed in 1986 as *Cobra* (qv), starring Sylvester Stallone.

Fair Wind to Java
US 1952 92m Trucolor
Republic (Joseph Kane)
A sailor with a mutinous crew seeks a South Sea treasure.
Routine adventure culminating in a volcanic explosion.
w Richard Tregaskis *novel* Garland Roark *d* Joseph Kane *ph* Jack Marta *m* Victor Young
☆ Fred MacMurray, Vera Hruba Ralston, Robert Douglas, Victor McLaglen

'Believe.'
Fairytale – A True Story
US 1997 99m DeLuxe
Warner/Icon (Wendy Finerman, Bruce Davey)
Two young girls cause a sensation by taking photographs of fairies.
Sentimental drama that swoons into fantasy and stays there, limp and apparently lifeless.
w Ernie Contreras *story* Albert Ash, Tom McLoughlin *d* Charles Sturridge *ph* Michael Coulter *m* Zbigniew Preisner *pd* Michael Howells *ed* Peter Coulson *sp* Tim Webber
☆ Florence Hoath, Elizabeth Earl, Paul McGann, Phoebe Nicholls, Peter O'Toole (Sir Arthur Conan Doyle), Harvey Keitel (Houdini), Anton Lesser, Bill Nighy, Bob Peck, Tim McInnerny, Mel Gibson (uncredited)
† The film is based on the true story of the Cottingley Fairies, when two young girls faked photographs of fairies in 1917, which was also the basis of another film, *Photographing Fairies*.

'20 years ago Jack and Margaret said, "Till death us do part." Tonight they close the deal.'
Faithful *
US 1996 88m Technicolor
Miramax/Savoy/Tribeca (Jane Rosenthal, Robert DeNiro)
While waiting for a signal to kill the wife of a philandering husband, a hitman chats to his victim.
A profane conversation piece that shows its stage origins too obviously, but the dialogue has an amusing bite about it.
w Chazz Palminteri *play* Chazz Palminteri *d* Paul Mazursky *ph* Fred Murphy *m* Philip Johnston *pd* Jeffrey Townsend *ed* Nicholas C. Smith
☆ Cher, Chazz Palminteri, Ryan O'Neal, Paul Mazursky, Amber Smith, Elisa Leonetti
'This determinedly offbeat comedy drama too often seems talky and static.' – *Variety*

Faithful in My Fashion
US 1946 81m bw
MGM
A soldier on leave causes havoc in a department store where his girlfriend is manager.
Sentimental comedy, forgettable for itself but containing endearing performances by a number of favourite character actors.
w Lionel Houser *d* Sidney Salkow
☆ Tom Drake, Donna Reed, Edward Everett Horton, Spring Byington, Harry Davenport, Sig Rumann, Margaret Hamilton, Hobart Cavanaugh

Faithless
US 1932 76m bw
MGM
A spoiled rich girl and her beau both descend to working-class level and almost further.
Would-be sensational drama ruined by censorship and miscasting.

w Carey Wilson *novel* *Tinfoil* by Mildred Cram *d* Harry Beaumont *ph* Oliver T. Marsh
☆ Tallulah Bankhead, Robert Montgomery, Hugh Herbert, Maurice Murphy, Louise Closser Hale, Lawrence Grant, Henry Kolker

'They pile the suffering on so thick that any but the most naive theatregoers are going to revolt and scoff.' – *Variety*

Faithless **
Sweden 2000 154m colour
Metro Tartan/SVT/AB Svensk/NRK,/Classic SRL/RAI/ZDF (Kaj Larsen)
original title: *Trolösa*
An ageing film director, trying to write a script about infidelity, recalls a director's obsessive affair with a married woman that wrecked the lives of her, her daughter and her husband.
Intense, slow-moving drama of marital disruption and vengeful behaviour that gains resonance from its apparently autobiographical origins.
w Ingmar Bergman *d* Liv Ullmann *ph* Jorgen Persson *pd* Göran Wassberg *ed* Sylvia Ingemarsson
☆ Lena Endre (Marianne Vogler), Erland Josephson (Bergman), Krister Henriksson (David), Thomas Hanzon (Markus), Michelle Gylemo (Isabelle), Juni Dahr (Margareta), Philip Zanden (Martin Goldman), Therese Brunnander (Petra Holst), Marie Richardson (Anna Berg)

'An unanswerably powerful film–a film for intelligent grown-ups.' – *Peter Bradshaw, Guardian*

The Falcon
A debonair solver of crime puzzles allegedly created by Michael Arlen but owing much to The Saint and resulting from a need by RKO for more of the same. Helped by a tough/comic manservant, he flourished during the forties in sixteen second features (the last three for Film Classics). After three episodes George Sanders tired of the role and was written out by being 'shot' and having his real-life brother Tom Conway take over as his fictional one. The performances of these two actors are pleasant, though the films are now fairly unwatchable, but John Calvert who took over for the last three was not a success.
1941 The Gay Falcon, A Date with the Falcon
1942 The Falcon Takes Over (the plot was borrowed from Raymond Chandler's Farewell My Lovely) (qv), The Falcon's Brother (qv)
1943 The Falcon Strikes Back (qv), The Falcon and the Co-Eds (qv), The Falcon in Danger
1944 The Falcon in Hollywood (qv), The Falcon in Mexico (qv), The Falcon Out West
1945 The Falcon in San Francisco (qv)
1946 The Falcon's Alibi (qv), The Falcon's Adventure
1948 The Devil's Cargo, Appointment with Murder, Search for Danger

The Falcon and the Co-Eds
US 1943 68m bw
RKO (Maurice Geraghty)
The Falcon is called to a girl's school to investigate the murder of a teacher, forecast by a psychic student.
Flimsy programmer, with less wit and more implausibility than usual.
w Ardel Wray, Gerald Geraghty *d* William Clemens *ph* Roy Hunt *md* C. Bakaleinikoff *ad* Albert S. D'Agostino *ed* Theron Warth
☆ Tom Conway, Jean Brooks, Rita Corday, Amelita Ward, Isabel Jewell, George Givot, Cliff Clark, Ed Gargan

The Falcon and the Snowman
US 1984 123m DeLuxe
Orion/Gabriel Katzka, John Schlesinger (John Daly)
A college dropout and a drug pusher sell secrets to the Russians.
A true case is made to seem not merely impossible but uninteresting by flaccid cinematic treatment.
w Steven Zaillian *book* Robert Lindsey *d* John Schlesinger *ph* Allen Daviau *m* Pat Metheny, Lyle Mays *pd* James D. Bissell *ed* Richard Marden
☆ Timothy Hutton, Sean Penn, David Suchet, Lori Singer, Pat Hingle, Dorian Harewood

The Falcon in Hollywood
US 1944 67m bw
RKO (Maurice Geraghty)
Holidaying in Hollywood, the Falcon reluctantly investigates an actor's murder.
Light thriller, well enough done in its low-budget way, with a narrative device that prefigures The Producers.
w Gerald Geraghty *d* Gordon Douglas *ph* Nicholas Musuraca *m* C. Bakaleinikoff *ad* Albert S. D'Agostino, L. O. Croxton *ed* Gene Milford
☆ Tom Conway, Barbara Hale, Veda Ann Borg, John Abbott, Sheldon Leonard, Rita Corday

The Falcon in Mexico
US 1944 70m bw
RKO (Maurice Geraghty)
The Falcon, suspected of murdering an art dealer and stealing a valuable painting, goes to Mexico to solve the mystery.
Moderate thriller, though the Falcon's capacity for being knocked unconscious at inopportune moments seems inexhaustible.
w George Worthing Yates, Gerald Geraghty *d* William Berke *ph* Frank Redmon *md* C. Bakaleinikoff *ad* Albert S. D'Agostino *ed* Joseph Noriega
☆ Tom Conway, Mona Maris, Martha MacVicar, Nestor Paiva, Mary Currier, Joseph Vitale

The Falcon in San Francisco
US 1945 66m bw
RKO (Maurice Geraghty)
The Falcon goes to the rescue of a small girl and uncovers a smuggling ring.
One of the best of the series, an entertaining mix of thriller and comedy.
w Robert Kent, Ben Markson *d* Joseph H. Lewis *ph* Virgil Miller, William Sickner *m* Paul Sawtell *ad* Albert S. D'Agostino, Charles Pyke *ed* Ernie Leadlay
☆ Tom Conway, Rita Corday, Edward S. Brophy, Sharyn Moffett, Fay Helm, Robert Armstrong, Carl Kent

The Falcon Strikes Back
US 1943 66m bw
RKO (Maurice Geraghty)
The Falcon, framed for stealing war bonds and shooting a bank messenger, tracks down the real culprit.
Thriller that tries rather too hard to be amusing, although it occasionally succeeds.
w Edward Dein, Gerald Geraghty *story* Stuart Palmer *d* Edward Dmytryk *ph* Jack Mackenzie *md* Roy Webb *ad* Albert S. D'Agostino, Walter E. Keller *ed* George Crone
☆ Tom Conway, Harriet Hilliard, Jane Randolph, Edgar Kennedy, Cliff Edwards, Cliff Clark, Ed Gargan

The Falcon Takes Over *
US 1942 62m bw
RKO (Howard Benedict)
The Falcon goes after a killer and finds himself vamped by a *femme fatale* with his death on her mind.
The best of the Falcon series, taking Chandler's complex plot and compressing it into a fast-moving little thriller with comic overtones.
w Lynn Root, Frank Fenton *novel* *Farewell My Lovely* by Raymond Chandler *d* Irving Reiss *ph* George Robinson *md* C. Bakaleinikoff *ad* Albert S. D'Agostino, Feild M. Gray *ed* Harry Marker
☆ George Sanders, Lynn Bari, James Gleason, Allen Jenkins, Helen Gilbert, Ward Bond, Edward Gargan
† Chandler's novel was refilmed in 1944 as the classic *Farewell My Lovely* (aka *Murder, My Sweet*) and again in 1975.

The Falcon's Alibi
US 1946 62m bw
RKO (William Berke)
The Falcon foils a gang of jewel thieves.
Dull episode that lacks the usual comedy and provides very little mystery.
w Paul Yawitz *story* Dane Lussier, Manny Seff *d* Ray McCarey *ph* Frank Redman *md* C. Bakaleinikoff *ad* Albert S. D'Agostino, Lucius Croxton *ed* Phillip Martin Jnr
☆ Tom Conway, Rita Corday, Vince Barnett, Jane Greer, Elisha Cook Jnr, Emory Parnell, Al Bridge, Jason Robards

The Falcon's Brother
US 1942 63m bw
RKO (Maurice Geraghty)
The Falcon's brother helps him bring to justice a Nazi spy-ring in America.
One of the dullest films in the series, with Sanders in a coma for most of the time and Conway not yet into his stride as his replacement.
w Stuart Palmer, Craig Rice *d* Stanley Logan *ph* Russell Metty *m* Roy Webb *ad* Albert S. D'Agostino, Walter E. Keller *ed* Mark Robson
☆ George Sanders, Tom Conway, Jane Randolph, Don Barclay, Cliff Clark, Edward Gargan, Eddie Dunn, Charlotte Wynters, Keye Luke
† Sanders was persuaded to make the fourth in the Falcon series only because a part was written for his brother Tom Conway, who took over as the Falcon. To RKO's surprise, Conway was a success in the role.

The Fall *
Argentina 1958 86m bw
Argentine Sono (Leopoldo Torre Nilsson)
original title: *La Caida*
A strictly brought-up college girl lodges with an eccentric family whose strange world comes to mean more to her than the love of a young lawyer.
Odd, claustrophobic melodrama from a very personal film-maker.
w Beatriz Guido, Leopoldo Torre Nilsson *novel* Beatriz Guido *d* Leopoldo Torre Nilsson *ph* Alberto Etchebehere *m* Juan Carlos Paz
☆ Elsa Daniel, Duilio Marzia, Lydia Lamaison, Carlos Lopez Monet

The Fall of the House of Usher
France 1928 48m (24 fps) bw silent
Roderick Usher's sister, prone to catalepsy, is buried alive; her unexpected return to life is instrumental in setting the house ablaze.
The original story is not so much stated as inferred in this very impressionistic version, of limited interest only to art movie buffs.
wd Jean Epstein, Luis Buñuel *story* Edgar Allen Poe *ad* Pierre Kefer
☆ Marguerite Gance, Jean Debucourt, Charles Lamy

The Fall of the House of Usher: see *House of Usher (1960)*

The Fall of the Roman Empire **
US/Spain 1964 187m Technicolor Ultra Panavision 70
Samuel Bronston
After poisoning the Emperor Marcus Aurelius his mad son Commodus succumbs to dissipation and allows Rome to be ravaged by pestilence and the Barbarians.
Would-be distinguished epic with an intellectual first hour; unfortunately the hero is a priggish bore, the villain a crashing bore, the heroine a saintly bore, and the only interesting character is killed off early. A chariot race, a javelin duel, some military clashes and a mass burning at the stake keep one watching, and the production values are high indeed.
w Ben Barzman, Basilio Franchina, Philip Yordan *d* *Anthony Mann* *ph* Robert Krasker *m* Dimitri Tiomkin *pd* Veniero Colasanti, John Moore *ed* Robert Lawrence
☆ *Alec Guinness*, Christopher Plummer, Stephen Boyd, James Mason, Sophia Loren, John Ireland, Eric Porter, Anthony Quayle, Mel Ferrer, Omar Sharif

CHRISTOPHER PLUMMER TO SOPHIA LOREN: 'Sister! And I thought you'd retired as a vestal virgin!'

'The film works from a restricted palette, and the result is weirdly restraining and severe, a dignified curb on absurdities.' – *John Coleman*

'You have to hand it to Bronston for thinking and making it big – both in spectacle and silliness.' – *Judith Crist*

† The forum set in this film is said to be the largest ever built.
♫ Dimitri Tiomkin

'Today ... innocence is about to die.'
Fall Time **
US 1994 88m colour
Polygram/Capitol (Edward Bates)
Three teenagers who stage a fake murder in a small town as a prank find themselves caught up with vicious bank robbers.
Clever, darkly ironic thriller that moves from a pastiche of such movies and its clichés into something more real and frightening.
w Steve Alden, Paul Skemp *d* Paul Warner *ph* Mark J. Gordon *m* Hummie Mann *pd* Andrew Precht *ed* Steve Nevius
☆ Mickey Rourke, Stephen Baldwin, Sheryl Lee, Jason London, David Arquette, Jonah Blechman, J. Michael Hunter

'Wry, witty and unsettling ... takes on major themes without ever slowing its pace or loosening its dramatic grip.' – *Philip Kemp, Sight and Sound*

'Nasty, mean-spirited and leaden. The only point of interest is that it marks another stage in the weird decline of Mickey Rourke.' – *Jonathan Romney, Guardian*

'Don't Trust A Soul.'
Fallen
US 1998 124m Technicolor Panavision
Warner/Turner/Atlas (Charles Roven, Dawn Steel)
A police detective discovers that the serial killer he is tracking is a demon with the ability to transfer its soul from one person to another.
A supernatural thriller that offers little in the way of frisson; the Devil may have the best tunes, but he still has the worst films.
w Nicholas Kazan *d* Gregory Hoblit *ph* Newton Thomas Sigel *m* Tan Dun *pd* Terence Marsh *ed* Lawrence Jordan
☆ Denzel Washington, John Goodman, Donald Sutherland, Embeth Davidtz, James Gandolfini, Elias Koteas, Gabriel Casseus, Michael J. Pagan

'A convoluted picture that's only intermittently suspenseful and not very engaging emotionally or intellectually.' – *Emanuel Levy, Variety*

'Even now she stood between us – the taunt of her smile like a black curse on our love!'
Fallen Angel *
US 1945 97m bw
TCF (Otto Preminger)
A man plans to get rid of his wife and marry another woman, but it is the latter who is murdered.
Oddly sleazy melodrama, not more successful then because it was unexpected than now because it is miscast. Some good sequences, though.
w Harry Kleiner *novel* Marty Holland *d* *Otto Preminger* *ph* *Joseph LaShelle* *m* David Raksin
☆ Dana Andrews, Alice Faye, Linda Darnell, Charles Bickford, Anne Revere, Bruce Cabot, John Carradine, Percy Kilbride

'It holds you by its undertones of small-town life and frustration.' – *Richard Winnington*

'It isn't in the class of *Laura*, but it's tolerable, in a tawdry sort of way.' – *Pauline Kael, 70s*

Fallen Angels **
Hong Kong 1995 96m colour
Electric/Jet Tone (Jeff Lau)
original title: *Duoluo Tianshi*
A hitman and a former convict look for love.
A stylish, elliptical narrative about lonely people, veering from doom-laden despair to loud comedy; probably an acquired taste, but an interesting and unusual one.
wd Wong Kar-Wai *ph* Christopher Doyle *m* Frankie Chan, Roel A. Garcia *pd* William Chang *ed* William Chan, Wong Ming-Lam
☆ Leon Lai, Michele Reis, Takeshi Kaneshiro, Charlie Young, Karen Mong

'Takes every risk known to film-making, and succeeds triumphantly a whole lot more often than it fails.' – *Tony Rayns, Sight and Sound*

The Fallen Idol ***
GB 1948 94m bw
British Lion/London Films (Carol Reed)
US title: *The Lost Illusion*
An ambassador's small son nearly incriminates his friend the butler in the accidental death of his shrewish wife.

A near-perfect piece of small-scale cinema, built up from clever nuances of acting and cinematic technique.
w Graham Greene *story* The Basement Room by Graham Greene *d* Carol Reed *ph* Georges Périnal *m* William Alwyn *ad* Vincent Korda *ed* Oswald Haffenrichter
☆ *Ralph Richardson*, Michèle Morgan, *Bobby Henrey*, Sonia Dresdel, Jack Hawkins

'A short story has become a film which is compact without loss of variety in pace and shape.' – *Dilys Powell*

'It's too deliberate and hushed to be much fun ... you wait an extra beat between the low-key lines of dialogue.' – *Pauline Kael, 70s*

Graham Greene; Carol Reed

British film

The Fallen Sparrow *

US 1943 93m bw
RKO (Robert Fellows)

An American veteran of the Spanish Civil War finds himself hounded in New York by Nazis seeking the Spanish flag of freedom.
Obscure melodrama, very good to look at but hardly worth unravelling; a precursor of Hollywood's post-war films noirs.
w Warren Duff *novel* Dorothy B. Hughes *d* Richard Wallace *ph* Nicholas Musuraca *md* Roy Webb, Constantin Bakaleinikoff
☆ John Garfield, Maureen O'Hara, Walter Slezak, Martha O'Driscoll, Patricia Morison, Bruce Edwards, John Banner, John Miljan

'One of the uncommon and provocatively handled melodramas of recent months.' – *New York Times*

Roy Webb, Constantin Bakaleinikoff

'The adventures of an ordinary man at war with the everyday world.'

Falling Down **

US 1992 112m Technicolor Panavision
Warner (Arnold Kopelson, Herschel Weingrod, Timothy Harris)

A redundant defence worker abandons his car on the Los Angeles freeway and attempts to make his way to the home of his former wife and their daughter. Confronted with the problems of urban life, from recalcitrant shopkeepers to unnecessary roadworks and would-be muggers, his behaviour becomes increasingly violent.
A fascinating movie on urban life, with a protagonist who is both hero and villain. It can be seen as a vigilante film, an attempt to claim a position for White Anglo-Saxon Protestants as among the victims of modern society, or a satire on over-reaction to city living. It remains a slightly queasy but enjoyable experience.
w Ebbe Roe Smith *d* Joel Schumacher *ph* Andrzej Bartkowiak *m* James Newton Howard *pd* Barbara Ling *ed* Paul Hirsch
☆ Michael Douglas, *Robert Duvall*, Barbara Hershey, Rachel Ticotin, Tuesday Weld, Frederic Forrest, Lois Smith

'At first comes across like a mean-spirited black comedy and then snowballs into a reasonably powerful portrait of social alienation.' – *Variety*

'Glitzy, casually cruel, hip and grim. It's sometimes very funny, and often nasty in the way it manipulates one's darkest feelings.' – *Vincent Canby, New York Times*

'It's hard to decide whether it's a fascist movie made by a liberal or a liberal film made by a fascist. Sometimes it's hard to tell the difference between a hawk on good behaviour or a dove on steroids.' – *Adam Mars-Jones*

Falling From Grace

US 1992 100m Technicolor
Columbia (Harry Sandler)

A country singer returns home with his wife and child and begins an affair with his first girlfriend, who is now married to his brother and having an affair with his father.
Dull domestic drama of an Oedipal conflict that leads nowhere interesting, accompanied by a soundtrack of country songs.
w Larry McMurtry *d* John Mellencamp *ph* Victor Hammer *pd* George Corsillo *ed* Dennis Virkler
☆ John Mellencamp (Bud Parks), Mariel Hemingway (Alice Parks), Claude Akins (Speck Parks), Dub Taylor (Grandpa Parks), Kay Lenz (P.J. Parks), Larry Crane (Ramey Parks), Kate Noonan (Linda), Deirdre O'Connell (Sally Cutler), John Prine (Mitch Cutler), Brent Huff (Parker Parks)

Falling in Love *

US 1984 107m Technicolor
Paramount/Marvin Worth

Meeting as commuters, Frank and Molly, each married to someone else, think about having an affair.
Rather tedious rehash of Brief Encounter, *with no real interest in the characters or their backgrounds.*
w Michael Cristofer *d* Ulu Grosbard *ph* Peter Suschitzky *m* Dave Grusin *pd* Santo Loquasto *ed* Michael Kahn
☆ Robert DeNiro, Meryl Streep, Harvey Keitel, Jane Kaczmarek, George Martin

'The effect of this talented pair acting in such a lightweight vehicle is akin to having Horowitz and Rubinstein improvise a duet on the theme of Chopsticks.' – *Variety*

Falling in Love Again *

US 1980 103m colour
International Picture Show of Atlanta (Steven Paul)

A middle-aged New Yorker remembers his young romances and his dreams of success.
Warm little independent production harking back to the days of H. M. Pulham Esquire *and none the worse for that.*
w Steven Paul, Ted Allan, Susannah York *d* Steven Paul *ph* Michael Mileham, Dick Bush, Wolfgang Suschitzky *m* Michel Legrand
☆ Elliott Gould, Susannah York, Stuart Paul, Kaye Ballard

Die Fälschung: see *Circle of Deceit*

False Faces: see *Let 'Em Have It*

False Witness: see *Zigzag*

Falstaff: see *Chimes at Midnight*

Fame *

US 1980 133m Metrocolor
MGM (David de Silva, Alan Marshall)

Assorted teenagers attend Manhattan's High School for the Performing Arts.
Cleverly shot and edited slice of life which unfortunately features people whose language and personalities are fairly repellent. The result is like A Chorus Line *without the music.*
w Christopher Gore *d* Alan Parker *ph* Michael Seresin *m* Michael Gore *pd* Geoffrey Kirkland *ed* Gerry Hambling
☆ Irene Cara, Lee Curreri, Laura Dean, Paul McCrane, Barry Miller, Gene Anthony Ray

'Our film, I hope, will be a microcosm of New York ... a dozen races pitching in and having their own crack at the American dream.' – *Alan Parker*

'Its soft-centred view of human relationships is periodically undercut by what can only be described as the grotesque.' – *John Pym*

Michael Gore; song 'Fame' (*m* Michael Gore, *ly* Dean Pitchford)

screenplay; song 'Out Here On My Own' (*m* Michael Gore, *ly* Lesley Gore); editing

Fame Is the Spur *

GB 1947 116m bw
GFD/Two Cities/Charter Films (John Boulting)

The rise to political eminence of a working-class socialist.
Disappointingly flat historical drama from a novel allegedly based on the career of Ramsay MacDonald. Interesting moments.
w Nigel Balchin *novel* Howard Spring *d* Roy Boulting *ph* Gunther Krampf, Harry Waxman *m* Alan Rawsthorne *ad* John Howell *ed* Richard Best *cos* Honoria Plesch
☆ Michael Redgrave (Hamer Radshaw), Rosamund John (Ann), Bernard Miles (Tom Hannaway), Carla Lehmann (Lady Lettice), Hugh Burden (Arnold Ryerson), Marjorie Fielding (Aunt Lizzie), Seymour Hicks (Old Buck), David Tomlinson (Lord Liskeard), Brian Weske (The Boy Ryerson), Anthony Wager (The Boy Hamer), Wylie Watson (Pendleton)

'The film is not merely a misfortune, it is a symbol of something mislaid. But for an absence of aplomb and background choruses it might have been made by an average Hollywood director.' – *Richard Winnington*

La Famiglia: see *The Family (1987)*

The Family: see *Violent City (1970)*

The Family **

Italy/France 1987 127m colour
Maasfilm/Cinecitta/Cinemax/Ariane (Franco Committeri)

original title: *La Famiglia*
A man of 80 recalls the events of his long life, centred on the Rome apartment where he and his family still live.
An intriguing family saga of love, laughter and disappointment that is both a character and a social study.
w Ruggero Maccari, Furio Scarpelli, Ettore Scola *d* Ettore Scola *ph* Ricardo Aronovich *m* Armando Trovajoli *ad* Luciano Ricceri *ed* Ettore Scola
☆ Vittorio Gassman, Fanny Ardant, Stefania Sandrelli, Andrea Occhipinti, Jo Champa

A Family Affair *

US 1937 69m bw
MGM (Lucien Hubbard)

A small-town judge faces a few family problems.
The second feature that started the highly successful Hardy family series (qv under Hardy). In this case the judge and his wife were played by actors who did not persevere into the series, but the stage was otherwise set for a long run, and the town of Carvel came to mean home to many Americans abroad.
w Kay Van Riper *play* Skidding by Aurania Rouverol *d* George B. Seitz *ph* Lester White *m* David Snell
☆ Lionel Barrymore, Spring Byington, *Mickey Rooney*, Eric Linden, Cecilia Parker, Sara Haden, Charles Grapewin, Julie Haydon

'Family trade and tops in dual locations.' – *Variety*

Family Business

US 1989 110m colour
Palace/Tri-Star (Lawrence Gordon)

Three generations of crooks take part in a robbery.
Dull comedy that never convinces and certainly doesn't amuse.
w Vincent Patrick *novel* Vincent Patrick *d* Sidney Lumet *ph* Andrzej Bartkowiak *m* Cy Coleman *pd* Philip Rosenberg *ed* Andrew Mondshein
☆ Sean Connery, Dustin Hoffman, Matthew Broderick, Rosana DeSoto, Janet Carroll, Victoria Jackson, Bill McCutcheon, Deborah Rush, Marilyn Cooper

Family Doctor: see *RX Murder*

Family Honeymoon

US 1948 90m bw
U-I (John Beck, Z. Wayne Griffin)
A college professor marries a widow whose three children join them on their Grand Canyon honeymoon.
Very ordinary and predictable star comedy.
w Dane Lussier, Homer Croy *d* Claude Binyon *ph* William Daniels *m* Frank Skinner *ad* Bernard Herzbrun, Richard H. Riedel *ed* Milton Carruth
☆ Claudette Colbert, Fred MacMurray, Rita Johnson, Gigi Perreau, Peter Miles, Jimmy Hunt, Hattie McDaniel, Chill Wills

The Family Jewels

US 1965 100m Technicolor
Paramount/York/Jerry Lewis

A child heiress chooses a new father from among her five uncles.
Unfunny star farce with multiple impersonations.
w Jerry Lewis, Bill Richmond *d* Jerry Lewis *ph* W. Wallace Kelley *m* Pete King
☆ Jerry Lewis, Donna Butterworth, Sebastian Cabot, Robert Strauss

Family Life ***

GB 1971 108m Technicolor
EMI/Kestrel (Tony Garnett)

A 19-year-old girl is driven into a mental collapse by emotional and family problems.
A slice of suburban life and an indictment of it, put together with unknown actors and probing TV techniques. Somewhat too harrowing for fiction, but extraordinarily vivid.
w David Mercer *play* In Two Minds by David Mercer *d* Ken Loach *ph* Charles Stewart *m* Marc Wilkinson
☆ Sandy Ratcliff, Bill Dean, Grace Cave

'What If Fate Gave You The Glimpse Of The Road Not Taken?'

The Family Man *

US 2000 125m DeLuxe Panavision
Universal/Beacon (Marc Abraham, Zvi Howard Rosenman, Tony Ludwig, Alan Riche)

A wealthy, Ferrari-driving bachelor banker finds himself transformed into a suburban husband and father, married to the woman he left thirteen years earlier.
Slick, sentimental retread of It's A Wonderful Life, *in which a selfish man is redeemed; it has the disadvantage that his bachelor existence seems the more preferable of the two, and that, while the earlier film was concerned with the effect of one man on a community, this deals with a person changing only himself–but that's progress for you.*
w David Diamond, David Weissman *d* Brett Ratner *ph* Dante Spinotti *m* Danny Elfman *pd* Kristi Zea *ed* Mark Helfrich *cos* Betsy Herman
☆ Nicolas Cage (Jack Campbell), Tea Leoni (Kate), Don Cheadle (Cash), Jeremy Piven (Arnie), Saul Rubinek (Alan Mintz), Josef Sommer (Lassiter), Makenzie Vega (Annie), Jake Milkovich/Ryan Milkovich (Josh), Lisa Thornhill (Evelyn), Harve Presnell (Big Ed), Mary Beth Hurt (Adelle), Amber Valletta (Paula), Francine York (Lorraine)

'Derivative, humourless and unbelievably icky sentimental comedy.' – *Peter Bradshaw, Guardian*

'A piece of moldy wax fruit if ever there was one.' – *Elvis Mitchell, New York Times*

'There's no body in the family plot!'

Family Plot **

US 1976 126m Technicolor
Universal (Alfred Hitchcock)

A fake medium tries for easy money by producing a lost heir.
Talkative, complex, patchy, low-key but always interesting Hitchcock suspenser in an unusually friendly vein.
w Ernest Lehman *novel* The Rainbird Pattern by Victor Canning *d* Alfred Hitchcock *ph* Leonard J. South *m* John Williams *pd* Henry Bumstead
☆ Karen Black, Bruce Dern, Barbara Harris, William Devane, Ed Lauter, Cathleen Nesbitt

'Full of benign mischief, beautiful craftsmanship and that elusive sense of cinematic rhythm that has always been Hitchcock's trump card.' – *Michael Billington, Illustrated London News*

'The picture bogs down in one talky, undramatic sequence after another, and the plot, with all its exposition and loose ends, is involved beyond belief.' – *De Witt Bodeen, Films in Review*

Family Portrait **

GB 1950 24m bw
Festival of Britain/Wessex (Ian Dalrymple)

A study of the English tradition and spirit through history.
The last work of a director-poet; not his most vivid movie, yet an accurate distillation of the themes which concerned him and of a dreamlike patriotism which now seems lost.
wd Humphrey Jennings ph Martin Curtis *ed* Stewart MacAllister *commentary* Michael Goodliffe

'Perhaps the most polished in style of all Jennings' films ... continuously fascinating, sharp and evocative.' – *MFB*

Family Resemblances: see *Un Air de Famille*

A Family Thing
US 1996 109m DeLuxe
United Artists/Butcher's Run (Todd Black, Randa Haines, Robert Duvall)

A white Arkansas man discovers that he has a black half-brother, a Chicago cop.
Despite the best efforts of its cast, an uninvolving, melodramatic family drama that skirts around the issue of race.
w Billy Bob Thornton, Tom Epperson *d* Richard Pearce *ph* Fred Murphy *m* Charles Gross *ed* Mark Warner *pf* Linda DeScenna
☆ Robert Duvall, James Earl Jones, Michael Beach, *Irma P. Hall*, Grace Zabriskie, Regina Taylor

Family Viewing
Canada 1988 86m colour
The Other Cinema/Ego Film (Atom Egoyan)
A television- and video-obsessed family live lives of quiet desperation.
Interesting low-budget film, originally shot on video, and as obsessed as its characters with electronic media.
wd Atom Egoyan *ph* Robert Macdonald *m* Michael Danna *ad* Linda del Rosario *ed* Atom Egoyan, Bruce Macdonald
☆ David Hemblen, Aidan Tierney, Gabrielle Rose, Arsinee Khanjian, Selma Keklikian, Rose Sarkisyan, Jeanne Sabourin

'There are streaks of filmmaking talent visible through the pretentious murk of this disjointed story.' – *Variety*

The Family Way *
GB 1966 115m Eastmancolor
BL/Jambox (John Boulting)

There is consternation in a Lancashire family when the son cannot consummate his marriage.
Overstretched domestic farce-drama. Good scenes and performances, but it was all much sharper as a one-hour TV play.
w Bill Naughton play Honeymoon Deferred by Bill Naughton *d* Roy Boulting *ph* Harry Waxman *m* Paul McCartney
☆ John Mills, *Marjorie Rhodes*, Hywel Bennett, Hayley Mills, *Avril Angers*, Murray Head, Wilfred Pickles, Barry Foster, Liz Fraser

The Fan *
US 1949 79m bw
TCF (Otto Preminger)
GB title: *Lady Windermere's Fan*
Scandal almost results when Lady Windermere loses her fan.
Reasonably polished, rather dull version of an old play, not really helped by modern bookends.
w Walter Reisch, Dorothy Parker, Ross Evans *play Lady Windermere's Fan* by Oscar Wilde *d* Otto Preminger *ph* Joseph LaShelle *m* Daniele Amfitheatrof
☆ George Sanders, Madeleine Carroll, Jeanne Crain, Richard Greene, Martita Hunt, John Sutton, Hugh Dempster, Richard Ney

The Fan
US 1981 95m Technicolor
Paramount/Robert Stigwood/Filmways

A Broadway actress is threatened by a disturbed admirer.
Ruthless, witless thriller with no suspense cliché unturned.
w Priscilla Chapman, John Hartwell *d* Edward Bianchi *ph* Dick Bush *m* Pino Donaggio *pd* Santo Loquasto
☆ Lauren Bacall, James Garner, Maureen Stapleton, Hector Elizondo, Michael Biehn, Anna Maria Horsford

'Horror comic mechanics ... the theatrical milieu fails to register, either individually or collectively.' – *Gilbert Adair, MFB*

The Fan
US 1996 115m Technicolor Panavision
Entertainment/TriStar/Mandalay/Scot Free (Wendy Finerman)

An unemployed, frustrated baseball fan kidnaps the son of a star player and threatens to kill him.
A hyperactive thriller that makes little effort to investigate the fraught relationship between fan and hero; the emphasis here is on shock and sensation.
w Phoef Sutton *novel* Peter Abrahams *d* Tony Scott *ph* Dariusz Wolski *m* Hans Zimmer *pd* Ida Random *ed* Christian Wagner, Claire Simpson
☆ Robert DeNiro, Wesley Snipes, Ellen Barkin, John Leguizamo, Benicio del Toro, Patti D'Arbanville, Chris Mulkey

'Fails even as pulp. It's all urgency and no pace, and the climax is an insult.' – *Tom Shone, Sunday Times*

Fanatic *
GB 1965 96m Technicolor
Hammer/Seven Arts (Anthony Hinds)

US title: *Die! Die! My Darling*
An American girl in England visits the mother of her dead fiancé and finds herself the prisoner of a religious maniac.
Boringly overlong Grand Guignol which even defeats its gallantly unmade-up and deathly-looking star; mildly notable however as a record of one of her last performances.
w Richard Matheson *novel Nightmare* by Anne Blaisdell *d* Silvio Narizzano *ph* Arthur Ibbetson *m* Wilfrid Josephs *pd* Peter Proud *ed* James Needs, John Dunsford
☆ *Tallulah Bankhead*, Stefanie Powers, Peter Vaughan, Yootha Joyce, Donald Sutherland

The Fanatics *
France 1957 92m bw
Cinégraphe-Regent (Pierre Lévy)
Patriots quarrel over the assassination by bomb of a South American dictator when he travels by public plane.
Suspense melodrama with many artificial twists, but slick and well acted.
w Alex Joffé, Jean Levitte *d* Alex Joffé *ph* L. H. Burel *m* Paul Misraki
☆ Pierre Fresnay, Michel Auclair, Grégoire Aslan, Betty Schneider

Fancy Pants **
US 1950 92m Technicolor
Paramount (Robert Welch)

A British actor stranded in the far west poses as a butler.
Lively Western comedy remake of Ruggles of Red Gap *(qv), one of the star's better vehicles.*
w Edmund Hartmann, Robert O'Brien *d George Marshall ph* Charles Lang Jnr *m* Van Cleave
☆ *Bob Hope, Lucille Ball*, Bruce Cabot, Jack Kirkwood, Lea Penman, Eric Blore, John Alexander, Norma Varden

Fandango
US 1984 91m Technicolor
Warner/Amblin (Tim Zinnemann)

In the early 1970s, a group of college friends drive across Texas for a final weekend of fun before graduation and army service in Vietnam looms.
Slight but enjoyable movie that began life as a small student film before being expanded under the auspices of Steven Spielberg's production company.
wd Kevin Reynolds *ph* Thomas Del Ruth *m* Alan Silvestri *ad* Peter Lansdown Smith *ed* Arthur Schmidt, Stephen Semel
☆ Kevin Costner, Judd Nelson, Sam Robards, Chuck Bush, Brian Cesak, Marvin J. McIntyre, Suzy Amis, Glenne Headly

Fanfan la Tulipe *
France 1951 98m bw
Filmsonor/Ariane/Amato (Alexandre Mnouchkine)
Recruited into the army of Louis XV by a prophecy that he will marry the king's daughter, a young braggart does everything he can to live up to it.
Rather like a spoof Errol Flynn effort, this likeable swashbuckler can't quite summon up enough buckle or swash to be the minor classic it clearly intends.
w Christian-Jaque, Henri Jeanson, René Wheeler *story* René Wheeler, René Fallet *d* Christian-Jaque *ph* Christian Matras *m* Georges Van Parys, Maurice Thiriet *ad* Robert Gys *ed* Jacques Desagneaux
☆ Gérard Philipe, Gina Lollobrigida, Marcel Herrand, Olivier Hussenot, Henri Rollan, Nerio Bernardi, Jean Marc Tennberg, Jean Parédès, Noël Roquevert, Geneviève Page, Sylvia Pelayo

'A daring and delightful piece of work.' – *The Times*

† The film won Christian-Jaque the award for best director at the Cannes Film Festival in 1952.

Fängelse: see *The Devil's Wanton*

Fanny ***
France 1932 128m bw
Les Films Marcel Pagnol/Braunberger-Richebé

After her lover returns to sea, Fanny discovers that she is pregnant and agrees to marry a wealthy widower.
The second instalment of Pagnol's trilogy of Marseilles life, suffused with acute observation, warmth and humanity.
w Marcel Pagnol play Marcel Pagnol *d Marc Allégret ph* Nicolas Toporkoff, André Dantan, Roger Hubert, Georges Benoit, Coutelain *m* Vincent Scotto *ed* Raymond Lamy
☆ *Raimu*, Orane Demazis, Pierre Fresnay, *Fernand Charpin*, Alida Rouffe, Robert Vattier, Auguste Mouriès, Milly Mathis, Maupi, Edouard Delmont
† This was the first film Pagnol made as his own producer. After its success he was able to build his own studio. An Italian version, directed by Mario Almirante, was made in 1933 and a German version starring Emil Jannings in 1934. It followed on from *Marius* and was followed by a sequel, *César* (qqv).

'There are three men in her life. The one she married ... the young adventurer ... and the baby they all shared!'
Fanny *
US 1961 133m Technicolor
Warner/Mansfield (Joshua Logan)

Life on the Marseilles waterfront, and in particular the story of two old men and two lovers.
Lumbering adaptation of three Pagnol films of the thirties (Marius, Fanny, César – *see* Marius) *previously seen as a 1938 Hollywood film* (Port of Seven Seas) *and later as a Broadway musical. This is the dullest version despite fine photography and a couple of good performances.*
w Julius J. Epstein *play* S. N. Behrman, Joshua Logan *films Marcel Pagnol d* Joshua Logan *ph Jack Cardiff m* Harold Rome *md* Morris Stoloff, Harry Sukman
☆ *Charles Boyer, Maurice Chevalier*, Leslie Caron, Horst Buchholz, Georgette Anys, Salvatore Baccaloni, Lionel Jeffries, Raymond Bussières, Victor Francen
† The film was proudly advertised as 'Joshua Logan's Fanny' until the press pointed out the double meaning.
best picture; Jack Cardiff; Morris Stoloff, Harry Sukman; Charles Boyer

Fanny and Alexander ****
Sweden/France/West Germany 1982 188m Eastmancolor
AB Cinematograph/Swedish Film Institute/Swedish TV One/Gaumont/Persona Film/Tobis (Jörn Donner)

A well-to-do Uppsala family comes together to celebrate Christmas 1907.
An interesting mixture of Dear Octopus *and* Wild Strawberries *turns into something more akin to* The Face *or* The Night Comers. *A kind of Bergman compendium, and impossible to describe exactly for those who have not seen it.*
wd Ingmar Bergman ph Sven Nykvist m Daniel Bell *pd Anna Asp*
☆ Gunn Walgren, Ewa Fröling, Jarl Kulle, Erland Josephson, Allan Edwall, Börje Ahlstedt, Mona Malm, Gunnar Björnstrand, Jan Malmsjö

'It's as if Bergman's neuroses had been tormenting him for so long that he cut them off and went sprinting back to Victorian health and domesticity.' – *New Yorker*

cinematography; best foreign-language film; art direction; costume
direction; screenplay
cinematography

Fanny and Elvis
GB 1999 111m colour
UIP/Scala/Film Consortium/Ima (Laurie Borg)

Two seemingly unsuited people, both deserted by their partners, begin a tentative relationship.
Contrived and implausible romantic comedy; its only interest lies in the unorthodox casting of its leads.
wd Kay Mellor *ph* John Daly *m* Stephen Warbeck *pd* Maria Djurkovic *ed* Chris Blunden
☆ Kerry Fox (Kate), Ray Winstone (Dave), Ben Daniels (Andrew), David Morrissey (Rob), Jennifer Saunders (Roanna), Colin Salmon (Alan), Gaynor Faye (Samantha), William Ash (Rick)

'Trawls every known cliché in its tale of a mismatched pair thrown together under circumstances beyond their control.' – *Alexander Walker, London Evening Standard*

Fanny by Gaslight **
GB 1944 108m bw
GFD/Gainsborough (Edward Black)

US title: *Man of Evil*
The illegitimate daughter of a cabinet minister is saved from a lustful lord.
Highly-coloured Victorian romantic melodrama, enjoyably put over with no holds barred and a pretty high budget for the time.
w Doreen Montgomery, Aimée Stuart *novel* Michael Sadleir *d Anthony Asquith ph* Arthur Crabtree *m* Cedric Mallabey
☆ James Mason, Phyllis Calvert, Stewart Granger, Wilfrid Lawson, John Laurie, Margaretta Scott, Stuart Lindsell, Jean Kent

'Seldom have I seen a film more agreeable to watch, from start to finish.' – *William Whitebait*

'Mr Asquith does not seem to have made much effort to freshen it by interesting treatment, so that the rare unusual device seems quite out of key among so much that is simple, obvious, hackneyed.' – *Richard Mallett, Punch*

† One of several costume melodramas patterned after the success of *The Man in Grey* (qv).

Fanny Hill
West Germany 1965 104m bw
Albert Zugsmith/Pan World
Adventures of an 18th-century woman of pleasure.
Tacky exploitation piece half-spoofing a suddenly fashionable piece of pornography.
w Robert Heel *d* Russ Meyer
☆ Miriam Hopkins, Leticia Roman, Walter Giller, Alex D'Arcy, Helmut Weiss

Fanny (Pagnol): see *Marius*

Fantasia ****
US 1940 135m Technicolor
Walt Disney

A concert of classical music is given cartoon interpretations.
Brilliantly inventive for the most part, the cartoons having become classics in themselves. The least part (the Pastoral Symphony) can be forgiven.
The pieces are:
Bach: Toccata and Fugue in D Minor
Tchaikovsky: The Nutcracker Suite
Dukas: The Sorcerer's Apprentice
Stravinsky: The Rite of Spring
Beethoven: The Pastoral Symphony
Ponchielli: Dance of the Hours
Moussorgsky: Night on a Bald Mountain
Schubert: Ave Maria
md Edward H. Plumb *supervisor* Ben Sharpsteen
☆ Leopold Stokowski, the Philadelphia Orchestra, Deems Taylor

'Dull as it is towards the end, ridiculous as it is in the bend of the knee before Art, it is one of the strange and beautiful things that have happened in the world.' – *Otis Ferguson*

'It is ambitious, and finely so, and one feels that its vulgarities are at least unintentional.' – *James Agate*

'Disney sometimes at his worst, often at his very best; and the best is on a level which no other cinematographic designer has reached. It takes over two hours, but somehow or other I'm afraid you will have to find the time.' – *Dilys Powell*

† Multiplane cameras, showing degrees of depth in animation, were used for the first time. The film was re-released in a print restored to its original freshness in 1990.
Special Award to Walt Disney, Leopold Stokowski

Fantasia 2000 **
US 2000 75m CFI
Buena Vista/Walt Disney (Donald W. Ernst)

A long-awaited sequel, following the same format as the original, of animated sequences to classical music.
A disappointment, given a period of 60 years in which Disney's style of animation –heavy on cute and kitsch–

seems hardly to have developed: the one sequence held over from the original Fantasia, Mickey Mouse as the sorcerer's apprentice, easily holds its own. The most successful new sequence, to Rhapsody in Blue, utilises the style of caricaturist Al Hirschfeld; perhaps the animators' imaginations might have been freed by a more adventurous choice of music.
Symphony No 5:
d,ad Pixote Hunt *m* Ludwig Van Beethoven
Pines of Rome:
d Hendel Butoy *m* Ottorino Respighi *ad* Dean Gordon, William Perkins
Rhapsody in Blue:
d, story Eric Goldberg *m* George Gershwin *md* Bruce Broughton (*piano* Ralph Grierson) *ad* Susan McKinsey Goldberg
Piano Concerto No 2, Allegro Opus 102:
d Hendel Butoy *story* The Steadfast Tin Soldier by Hans Christian Andersen *m* Dmitri Shostakovich (*piano* Yefim Bronfman) *ad* Michael Humphries *ch* Kendra McCool
Carnival of the Animals, Finale:
d, story Eric Goldberg *concept* Joe Grant *m* Camille Saint-Saens *ad* Susan McKinsey Goldberg
The Sorcerer's Apprentice:
d James Algar *m* Paul Dukas *md* Leopold Stokowski *ad* Tom Codrick, Charles Philippi, Zack Schwartz
Pomp and Circumstance – Marches 1, 2, 3, 4:
d Francis Glebas *m* Edward Elgar *ad* Daniel Cooper
Firebird Suite – 1919 version:
d, story Gaetan Brizzi, Paul Brizzi. *m* Igor Stravinsky *ad* Carl Jones
ph Tim Suhrstedt *md* James Levine *pd* Pixote Hunt *ed* Jessica Ambinder Rojas, Lois Freeman-Fox
☆ Hosts: Steve Martin, Itzhak Perlman, Quincy Jones, Bette Midler, James Earl Jones, Penn & Teller, James Levine, Angela Lansbury

'A light buffet of tasty morsels rather than a full and satisfying meal; all the episodes are more or less agreeable, but as a whole it lacks a knockout punch, one dynamite sequence that will galvanize viewers.' – *Todd McCarthy, Variety*

† The film was originally released in a version for Imax cinemas.

The Fantasist
Ireland 1987 98m colour
Blue Dolphin (Mark Forstater)

A psychopathic killer stalks a young country girl who goes to work in Dublin.
Occasionally suspenseful thriller, but it offers little out of the ordinary and is muddled in its intentions, attempting to be a more serious film than it actually is.
wd Robin Hardy *novel* Goosefoot by Patrick McGinley *ph* Frank Gell *m* Stanislas Syrewicz *ed* Thomas Schwalm
☆ Moira Harris, Christopher Cazenove, Timothy Bottoms, John Kavanagh, Mick Lally

The Fantastic Disappearing Man: see *The Return of Dracula*

Fantastic Invasion of Planet Earth: see *The Bubble*

Fantastic Planet **
France/Czechoslovakia 1970 72m colour
Armorial/Ceskoslovensky Filmexport (S. Damiani, A. Valio-Cavaglione)

original title: *La Planète Sauvage*
On a distant planet, a race of meditating giants use humans as slaves and playthings.
A witty fable of the worth of liberty, elegantly animated in a semi-surrealist style.
w Roland Topor, Rene Laloux *novel* Oms en Serie by Stefan Wul *d* Rene Laloux *ph* Lubomir Rejthar, Boris Baromyk *m* Alain Goraguer *pd* Roland Topor *ed* Rich Harrison, Dick Elliott
☆ Featuring the voices of: Cynthia Adler, Barry Bostwick, Mark Gruner, Nora Heflin, Marvin Miller

† The film was shot in the animation studios of Jiri Trnka in Prague.

'Journey Into The Living Body Of A Man!'
Fantastic Voyage *
US 1966 100m DeLuxe Cinemascope
TCF (Saul David)

When a top scientist is shot and suffers brain damage, a team of doctors and a boat are miniaturized and injected into his blood stream ... but one is a traitor.
Engagingly absurd science fiction which keeps its momentum but is somewhat let down by its décor.
w Harry Kleiner *d* Richard Fleischer *ph* Ernest Laszlo *m* Leonard Rosenman *ad* Dale Hennesy, Jack Martin Smith *sp* L. B. Abbott, Art Cruickshank, Emil Kosa Jnr
☆ Stephen Boyd, Raquel Welch, Edmond O'Brien, Donald Pleasence, Arthur Kennedy, Arthur O'Connell, William Redfield

'The process shots are so clumsily matted ... that the actors look as if a child has cut them out with blunt scissors.' – *Pauline Kael*

art direction; special visual effects (Art Cruickshank)
Ernest Laszlo

Fantomas *
France/Italy 1964 104m bw
SNEG
A master crook is also a master of disguise.
One of several films made in the sixties in affectionate imitation of a French silent serial.
w Jean Halain, Pierre Foucaud *d* André Hunebelle *ph* Marcel Grignon *m* Michel Magne
☆ Jean Marais, Louis de Funes, Mylene Demongeot, Jacques Dynam

Le Fantôme de la Liberté: see *The Phantom of Liberty*

'What They Needed Was A Country Big Enough For Their Dreams.'
Far and Away
US 1992 140m DeLuxe Panavision Super 70
UIP/Universal/Imagine (Brian Grazer, Ron Howard)

A young Irish woman, daughter of a landowner, runs away to America, taking one of her father's tenants with her as an unwilling servant.
A romance conceived on an epic scale, but still-born; an uninteresting molehill of a movie.
w Bob Dolman *story* Bob Dolman, Ron Howard *d* Ron Howard *ph* Mikael Salomon *m* John Williams *pd* Jack T. Collis, Allan Cameron *ed* Michael Hill, Daniel Hanley
☆ Tom Cruise, Nicole Kidman, Thomas Gibson, Robert Prosky, Barbara Babcock, Cyril Cusack, Eileen Pollock, Colm Meaney, Niall Toibin

'A doddering bloated bit of corn, and its characters and situations so obviously hackneyed, that we can't give in to the story and allow ourselves to be swept away.' – *Washington Post*

'The plot and characters seem sometimes to have been borrowed from a picture storybook for teenage girls.' – *Iain Johnstone, Sunday Times*

'Unrepentant and vapid nonsense, celebrated with inappropriate splendour.' – *Philip Strick, Sight and Sound*

The Far Country *
US 1954 97m Technicolor
U-I (Aaron Rosenberg)

Two cowboys on their way to the Alaska goldfields are beset by swindlers.
Sturdy star Western with good production values.
w Borden Chase *d* Anthony Mann *ph* William Daniels *m* Hans Salter
☆ *James Stewart*, Walter Brennan, Ruth Roman, Corinne Calvet, John McIntire

Far East
Australia 1982 100m colour
Filmco Australia/Alfred Road (Richard Mason)
An Australian bar owner in an Asian city rampant with violence is confronted by a girl from his past.
A disappointing attempt to redo Casablanca *without the wit or style.*
wd John Duigan *ph* Brian Probyn *m* Sharon Calcraft *pd* Ross Major *ed* Henry Dangar
☆ Bryan Brown, Helen Morse, John Bell, Raina McKeon, Henry Duval, Sinan Leong, Bill Hunter

Far from Heaven
US/France 2002 107m CFI
Entertainment/Focus/Vulcan/Killer/John Wells/Section Eight (Christine Vachon, Jody Patton)

In 1957, in a wealthy suburb, a wife who discovers that her marriage is a sham begins to feel love for her black gardener.
Elegantly designed and shot and acted, and made in the style of a Douglas Sirk melodrama, this subverts the form by bringing to the fore what would have been the subtext of the movie in the 1950s; it is undeniably clever, but too often feels like an exercise in style.
d Todd Haynes *ph* Edward Lachman *m* Elmer Bernstein *pd* Mark Friedberg *ed* James Lyons *cos* Sandy Powell
☆ Julianne Moore (Cathy Whitaker), Dennis Quaid (Frank Whitaker), Dennis Haysbert (Raymond Deagan), Patricia Clarkson (Eleonor Fine), Viola Davis (Sybil), James Rebhorn (Dr Bowman), Celia Weston (Mona Lauder)

'Would have been one of the great American films of the '50s; it is certainly the finest American melodrama of our time.' – *Shawn Levy, Oregonian*

'With its stilted dialogue not quite kitschy enough to be funny and not quite authentic enough to be realistic, the whole movie feels as if it's taking place in formaldehyde.' – *Stephen Hunter, Washington Post*

Todd Haynes (as writer); Julianne Moore; Edward Lachman; Elmer Bernstein

'One Boy Wants Her Love. One Boy Wants Her Dead.'
Far from Home
US 1989 86m CFI color
Vestron/Lightning (Donald P. Borchers)

While on holiday with her father, an adolescent girl is stalked by a serial killer.
Drear little film that follows the standard pattern for the over-familiar genre.
w Tommy Lee Wallace *story* Ted Gershuny *d* Meiert Avis *ph* Paul Elliott *m* Jonathan Elias *ed* Marc Grossman
☆ Matt Frewer, Drew Barrymore, Richard Masur, Karen Austin, Susan Tyrrell, Anthony Rapp, Jennifer Tilly, Dick Miller

'Partners in survival. Friends for life.'
Far from Home: The Adventures of Yellow Dog *
US 1994 81m colour
TCF (Peter O'Brian)

After being shipwrecked, a 14-year-old boy survives a fortnight in the wilderness of British Columbia with the help of his labrador.
Enjoyable, if simple-minded, adventure story in imposing landscapes which should set a few tails wagging.
wd Phillip Borsos *ph* James Gardner *m* John Scott *pd* Mark S. Freeborn *ed* Sidney Wolinsky
☆ Mimi Rogers, Bruce Davison, Jesse Bradford, Tom Bower, Joel Palmer, Josh Wanamaker, Dakotah

'Predictability doesn't overshadow the movie's appeal since it is deftly handled by Borsos, striking such a basic emotional chord that you'd have to have a heart of stone not to get pulled in. This really is miles better than you would expect.' – *Julie Stevens, Empire*

Far from the Madding Crowd *
GB 1967 175m Technicolor Panavision 70
EMI/Vic/Appia (Joseph Janni)

In Victorian Wessex a headstrong girl causes unhappiness and tragedy.
Good-looking but slackly handled version of a melodramatic and depressing novel.
w Frederic Raphael *novel* Thomas Hardy *d* John Schlesinger *ph* *Nicolas Roeg* *m* Richard Rodney Bennett *pd* Richard Macdonald
☆ Julie Christie, Peter Finch, Alan Bates, Terence Stamp, Prunella Ransome

'In this rather plodding film the insufficiency of the foreground is partly offset by the winsomeness of the backgrounds. The very sheep are so engaging as to entice our gaze into some extremely amiable woolgathering.' – *John Simon*

Richard Rodney Bennett

The Far Horizons
US 1955 108m Technicolor Vistavision
(Paramount)
The story of Lewis and Clark's 1803 expedition west through the Louisiana Purchase territory.
Flabbily-handled historical hokum; potential interest quickly dissipated.
w Winston Miller, Edmund H. North *d* Rudolph Maté *ph* Daniel L. Fapp *m* Hans Salter
☆ Fred MacMurray, Charlton Heston, Donna Reed, Barbara Hale, William Demarest

Far North
US 1988 89m colour
Rank/Alive Films/Nelson/Circle JS (Malcolm R. Harding, Carolyn Pfieffer)

A family squabbles around the bed of their sick father.
Inconsequential film that marked the directorial debut of writer/actor Shepard.
wd Sam Shepard *ph* Robbie Greenberg *m* The Red Clay Ramblers, J. A. Deane *pd* Peter Jamison *ed* Bill Yahraus
☆ Jessica Lange, Tess Harper, Charles Durning, Donald Moffat, Ann Wedgeworth, Patricia Arquette, Nina Draxten

A Far Off Place *
US 1993 116m Technicolor Panavision
Buena Vista/Walt Disney/Amblin (Eva Monely, Elaine Sperber)

A teenage boy and girl, pursued by murderous ivory poachers, are guided across the Kalahari desert by a young bushman.
Old-fashioned children's movie about discovering maturity through an understanding of the natural world; the photography has charm.
w Robert Caswell, Jonathan Hensleigh, Sally Robinson *book* A Story Like the Wind *and* A Far Off Place by Laurens van der Post *d* Mikael Salomon *ph* *Juan Ruiz-Anchia* *m* James Horner *pd* Gemma Jackson *ed* Ray Lovejoy
☆ Reese Witherspoon, Ethan Randall, Jack Thompson, Sarel Bok, Robert Burke, Patricia Kalember, Maximilian Schell

'A coming-of-age yarn that should hold the attention of kids and patient adults.' – *Variety*

'Potential date movie material for environmentally aware 13-year-olds.' – *Matt Mueller, Empire*

Far Out Man
US 1990 85m Foto-Kem
New Line/CineTel (Lisa M. Hansen)

An ageing, permanently stoned hippie searches for his former girlfriend and their child.
A Chong family home movie inflicted upon a wider public, it is only worth watching if you are related to the writer/director and even then you must be prepared to be indulgent.
wd Thomas Chong *ph* Greg Gardiner, Eric Woster *m* Jay Chattaway *ed* Stephen Myers, Gilberto Costa Nunes
☆ Thomas Chong, C. Thomas Howell, Rae Dawn Chong, Shelby Chong, Paris Chong, Martin Mull, Bobby Taylor, Al Mancini, Judd Nelson, Cheech Marin, Paul Bartel

'Technically, pic is a mess. Two lensers are credited, so it may be that one held the camera while the other held the film and the director never came out of character long enough to tell them what to do with either.' – *Variety*

Faraway, So Close *
Germany 1993 144m colour/bw
Columbia TriStar/Road Movies/Tobis (Wim Wenders)

original title: *In Weiter Ferne, So Nah!*
An angel watching over the citizens of Berlin decides to become human but finds that life is too difficult for him to survive.
A bungled and often sentimental sequel to Wings of Desire *which suddenly switches into a confused thriller about arms dealing; it does have some superlative moments, but not enough.*
w Wim Wenders, Ulrich Zieger, Richard Reitinger *d* Wim Wenders *ph* Jürgen Jürges *m* Laurent Petitgirard *pd* Albrecht Konrad *ed* Peter Pryzgodda
☆ Otto Sander, Peter Falk, Bruno Ganz, Horst Buchholz, Nastassja Kinski, Heinz Rühmann, Solveig Dommartin, Rudiger Vogler, Lou Reed, Willem Dafoe, Henri Alekan, Mikhail Gorbachev

'Occasionally veers into pretension, wavers between perfect black-and-white and striking washed-out colour, and discusses politics and eternity, but is filled with moments that will stay with you forever.' – *Kim Newman, Empire*

Farewell *
USSR 1981 126m colour
Artificial Eye/Mosfilm (A. Rasskazov, G. Sokolova)
original title: *Proshchanie*
A peasant community is resettled, against its will, into modern apartments to make way for a new dam.
Emotional and detailed look at the destruction of a community and its relationships.
w Lorisa Shepitko, Rudolf Tyurin, German Klimov *novel* Valentin Rasputin *d* Elem Klimov *ph* Alexei Rodionov, Yuri Skhirtladze, Sergei Taraskin *m* V. Artyomov *ad* V. Petrov *ed* V. Byelova
☆ Stefaniya Stayuta, Lev Durov, Alexei Petrenko, Leonid Kryuk, Vadim Yakovenko, Yuri Katin-Yartsev, Denis Luppov

Farewell Again **
GB 1937 85m bw
Pendennis/London Films (Erich Pommer)
US title: *Troopship*
Soldiers returning from India have six hours' shore leave to sort out their problems.
Dated but sharply made compendium drama, a solid success of its time.
w Clemence Dane, Patrick Kirwan *story* Wolfgang Wilhelm *d* *Tim Whelan* *ph* James Wong Howe, Hans Schneeberger *m* Richard Addinsell *ad* Frederick Pusey *ed* Jack Dennis
☆ Flora Robson, Leslie Banks, Robert Newton, René Ray, Patricia Hilliard, Sebastian Shaw, Leonora Corbett, Anthony Bushell, Edward Lexy, Wally Patch, Edmund Willard, Martita Hunt, John Laurie

The Farewell: Brecht's Last Summer: see *Abschied aus Buckow*

Farewell My Concubine ***
Hong Kong/China 1993 156m colour
Artificial Eye/Thomson/China Film/Beijing Film (Hsu Feng)
Two boys who train together at the Peking Opera form a lifelong relationship, both on-stage – one playing masculine roles, the other in feminine parts – and off, through the political upheavals from the 1930s onwards until their final performance in the 60s.
A beautiful and epic film that records the social changes of Chinese life with an unblinking eye and from the viewpoint of the endlessly persecuted.
w Lilian Lee, Lu Wei *novel* Lilian Lee *d* *Chen Kaige* *ph* *Gu Changwei* *m* Zhaao Jiping *ad* Chen Huaikai *ed* Pei Xiaonan
☆ *Leslie Cheung, Zhang Fengyi*, Gong Li, Lu Qi, Ying Da, Ge You, Lin Chun, Lei Han, Tong Di
'Chinese cinema ceases to be an acquired taste and becomes a required one … Its vast running time contains some episodes of pleasure, pain, adventure, vice or instructive insight for every taste or brow – high and low.' – *Alexander Walker, London Evening Standard*
'Chen's attempt to reach a wider audience with a bigger, less ambiguous film is still a formidable success. It's a kind of opera in itself, conducted by a director whose visual power is matched by an emotional force that few others in world cinema can match.' – *Derek Malcolm*
'A big, eventful historical soap opera of the *Doctor Zhivago* school.' – *Terrence Rafferty, New Yorker*
† The film was joint winner of the Palme d'Or at the Cannes Film Festival in 1993.
best foreign-language film; Gu Changwei

Farewell My Lovely ***
US 1944 95m bw
RKO (Adrian Scott)
aka: *Murder My Sweet*
A private eye searches for an ex-convict's missing girlfriend.
A revolutionary crime film in that it was the first to depict the genuinely seedy milieu suggested by its author. One of the first films noirs of the mid-forties, a minor masterpiece of expressionist film making, and a total change of direction for a crooner who suddenly became a tough guy.
w John Paxton *novel* Raymond Chandler *d Edward Dmytryk* *ph Harry J. Wild* *m Roy Webb*
☆ *Dick Powell*, Claire Trevor, Anne Shirley, *Mike Mazurki, Otto Kruger*, Miles Mander, Douglas Walton, Ralf Harolde, Don Douglas, Esther Howard
MARLOWE (DICK POWELL): '"Okay Marlowe," I said to myself. "You're a tough guy. You've been sapped twice, choked, beaten silly with a gun, shot in the arm until you're crazy as a couple of waltzing mice. Now let's see you do something really tough – like putting your pants on."'
MARLOWE: 'I caught the blackjack right behind my ear. A black pool opened up at my feet. I dived in. It had no bottom.'
MARLOWE: 'My fingers looked like a bunch of bananas.'
'A nasty, draggled bit of dirty work, accurately observed.' – *C. A. Lejeune*

Farewell, My Lovely ***
US 1975 95m Technicolor
Avco Embassy/Elliott Kastner/ITC (George Pappas, Jerry Bruckheimer)
A private eye realises that two separate cases he is working on concern the same woman.
A pretty sharp remake of the 1944 movie, with the plot slightly rewritten but tightened, and an excellent performance from a rather over-age star.
w David Zelag Goodman *d Dick Richards* *ph* John A. Alonzo *m* David Shire *pd* Dean Tavoularis
☆ *Robert Mitchum*, Charlotte Rampling, John Ireland, Sylvia Miles, Anthony Zerbe, Jack O'Halloran, Kate Murtagh
'A moody, bluesy, boozy recreation of Marlowe's tacky, neon-flashed Los Angeles of the early forties.' – *Judith Crist*
'A delicious remake with a nice, smoky 1940s atmosphere.' – *Michael Billington, Illustrated London News*
Sylvia Miles

A Farewell to Arms **
US 1932 78m bw
(Paramount)
In World War I, a wounded American ambulance driver falls in love with his nurse.
Now very dated but important in its time, this romantic drama was one of the more successful Hemingway adaptations to be filmed.
w Benjamin Glazer, Oliver H. P. Garrett *novel Ernest Hemingway* *d Frank Borzage* *ph* Charles Lang *m* W. Franke Harling *ad* Hans Dreier, Roland Anderson
☆ Gary Cooper, *Helen Hayes*, Adolphe Menjou, Mary Philips, Jack La Rue, Blanche Frederici, Henry Armetta
'Too much sentiment and not enough strength.' – *Mordaunt Hall, New York Times*
'Borzage has invested the war scenes with a strange, brooding expressionist quality … indeed, the overall visual style is most impressive.' – *NFT, 1974*
'Corking femme film fare at any angle or price.' – *Variety*
† Remade as *Force of Arms* (qv) and see below.
Charles Lang
best picture; art direction

A Farewell to Arms
US 1957 150m DeLuxe Cinemascope
TCF/David O. Selznick
In the First World War, a wounded ambulance driver falls for a nurse.
Elaborate ill-fated remake which tried to make an adventure epic out of a low-key war drama. Its failure caused David O. Selznick to produce no more films.
w Ben Hecht *d* Charles Vidor *ph* Piero Portalupi, Oswald Morris *m* Mario Nascimbene *pd* Alfred Junge
☆ Rock Hudson, Jennifer Jones, Vittorio de Sica, Alberto Sordi, Kurt Kasznar, Mercedes McCambridge, Oscar Homolka, Elaine Stritch, Victor Francen
'If there were a supreme Bad Taste Award for movies, *A Farewell to Arms* would win it hands down. This smutty version of Ernest Hemingway's novel will set thousands of stomachs to turning.' – *William K. Zinsser, New York Herald-Tribune*
† The film's original director, John Huston, was fired after clashing with Selznick. Cinematographer Oswald Morris quit after Selznick claimed that Hudson was being favoured over Jennifer Jones, his wife.
Vittorio de Sica

Farewell to the King
US 1988 117m Technicolor
Vestron/Orion/Film Plan Financing Number 1 (Albert S. Ruddy, Andre Morgan)
In the Second World War, an American ruler of a tribe of headhunters in Borneo helps the British attack the Japanese.
Ineffectual Kiplingesque adventure with a confusing narrative.
wd John Milius *novel* *L'Adieu au Roi* by Pierre Schoendoerffer *ph* Dean Semler *m* Basil Poledouris *ed* Anne V. Coates, Timothy O'Meara
☆ Nick Nolte, Nigel Havers, Frank McRae, James Fox, Marilyn Tokuda, Marius Weyers, William Wise, John Bennett Perry, Elan Oberon, Gerry Lopez, Choy Chang Wing
'Thematically speaking, the admixture of the *Heart of Darkness* and *The Man Who Would Be King* promises a heady brew, but what emerges, alas, is a cup of weak tea.' – *Tom Milne, MFB*

Fargo
US 1964 99m Technicolor
Universal/Pennebaker (Al Ruddy)
aka: *Wild Seed*
A teenage girl hitch-hikes from New York to Los Angeles and is befriended by a young tramp.
Peripatetic romance in the modern manner, with no conclusions drawn and not much entertainment value beyond the scenery.
w Les Pine *d* Brian G. Hutton *ph* Conrad Hall *m* Richard Markowitz
☆ Michael Parks, Celia Kaye, Ross Elliott, Woodrow Chambliss, Eva Novak

'Small Town … Big Crime … Dead Cold.'
Fargo ****
US 1996 98m DuArt
Polygram/Working Title (Ethan Coen)
In a small Minnesotan town, a car salesman with money troubles hires two criminals to kidnap his wife so that her wealthy father will pay a ransom.
Deft, witty and original thriller which pits a pregnant, rural police chief against two city slickers; the violence, when it comes, is properly shocking, but it's the humanity that you will remember.
w Joel and Ethan Coen *d Joel Coen* *ph Roger Deakins* *m* Carter Burwell *pd* Rick Heinrichs *ed Roderick Jaynes (Joel and Ethan Coen)*
☆ *Frances McDormand, William H. Macy*, Steve Buscemi, *Peter Stormare*, Harve Presnell, Kristin Rudrüd, Tony Denman
'Written and directed with the verve, painstaking nuance and outrageously black humour that have become the mainstay of a Coen movie.' – *Ian Nathan, Empire*
'I came away feeling what a great film it was as it had managed to make the basically bland triumph of decency over evil a most rivetting affair.' – *Marianne Gray, Film Review*
† A subtitle claims that the film is based on a true story, but it is more likely an invention of its authors.
Frances McDormand; Ethan and Joel Coen (screenplay)
best picture; William H. Macy; Joel Coen (as director); Roger Deakins; Roderick Jaynes
Joel Coen (as director)

Farinelli Il Castrato *
Italy/Belgium 1994 111m colour
Guild/Stephan/Alinea/Canal/France 2/Images/K2/RTL/TV1 (Vera Belmont)
Europe's most famous singer, a castrato who has a love-hate relationship with his more virile brother, becomes involved in a feud with Handel.
Enjoyably over-the-top biopic, made in a style that veers from high camp to low opera; it's good to look at and, sometimes, to listen to.
w André Corbiau, Gérard Corbiau, Marcel Beaulieu *d* Gérard Corbiau *ph* Walther Vanden Ende *md* Christophe Rousset *pd* Gianni Quaranta *ed* Joelle Hache
☆ Stéfano Dionisi, Enrico Lo Verso, Elsa Zylberstein, Caroline Cellier, Marianne Basler, Jeroen Krabbé, Graham Valentine, Omero Antonutti
'Not since *Amadeus* has a film made classical music so accessible or yesteryear's people so understandable.' – *Tom Hutchinson, Film Review*
† The unusual vocal sound of the castrated Farinelli was created by digitally combining the singing of counter-tenor Derek Lee Ragin and soprano Ewa Mallas-Godlewska.

The Farmer Takes a Wife *
US 1935 91m bw
TCF (Winfield Sheehan)
By the Erie Canal in the 1820s, a wandering girl finds security with a farmer.
Pleasantly 'different' romantic drama, quite ably executed and introducing Henry Fonda to the screen.
w Edwin Burke *play* Frank B. Elser, Marc Connelly *novel* *Rome Haul* by *Walter D. Edmonds* *d* Victor Fleming *ph* John Seitz *m* Arthur Lange
☆ Janet Gaynor, Henry Fonda, Charles Bickford, Slim Summerville, Andy Devine, Roger Imhof, Jane Withers, Margaret Hamilton, Sig Rumann, John Qualen
'It will pull in the Gaynor fans, and do much to return her to favour.' – *Variety*

The Farmer Takes a Wife *
US 1953 81m Technicolor
TCF (Frank P. Rosenberg)
A cook on a canal barge has a low opinion of farmers.
Musical remake of a1935 movie with an agreeably stylized look, hampered by a slowish script and dull cast.
w Walter Bullock, Sally Benson, Joseph Fields *d* Henry Levin *ph* Arthur E. Arling *m* Cyril Mockridge *m/ly* Harold Arlen, Dorothy Fields *ad Lyle Wheeler, Addison Hehr*
☆ Betty Grable, Dale Robertson, Thelma Ritter, Eddie Foy Jnr, John Carroll

'Now she's raising eyebrows instead of corn!'
The Farmer's Daughter **
US 1947 97m bw
RKO (Dore Schary)
The Swedish maid of a congressman becomes a political force.
Well-made Cinderella story with a touch of asperity and top notch production values and cast.
w Allen Rivkin, Laura Kerr *d* H. C. Potter *ph Milton Krasner* *m* Leigh Harline
☆ *Loretta Young, Joseph Cotten, Ethel Barrymore*, Charles Bickford, Rose Hobart, Rhys Williams, Harry Davenport, Tom Powers
'Patricians, politicians, even peasants are portrayed with unusual perception and wit.' – *James Agee*
Loretta Young
Charles Bickford

The Farmer's Wife
GB 1928 67m approx bw silent
BIP (John Maxwell)
A farmer seeks a wife and after three disappointments settles for his housekeeper.
A simple and not very interesting silent screen version of a stage success which depended largely on dialogue.
wd Alfred Hitchcock *play* Eden Philpotts *ph* Jack Cox *ed* Alfred Booth
☆ Jameson Thomas, Gordon Harker, Lilian Hall-Davis, Maud Gill
'Some pleasant photography and a subtle impression of rural life rescued the picture from complete failure.' – *George Perry, 1966*

Farrebique **
France 1947 85m bw
L'Ecran Français/Les Films Etienne Lallier
Problems of a peasant family in central France.
Superbly-filmed semi-documentary, acted by a real family.
wd Georges Rouquier *ph André Dantan* *m* Henri Sauguet
'Definitely a film for posterity.' – *MFB*

Fashions of 1934 *
US 1934 78m bw
Warner (Henry Blanke)
A confidence trickster conquers the French fashion world.
Slight musical comedy with a couple of splendid Berkeley numbers.
w F. Hugh Herbert, Carl Erickson *d* William Dieterle *ph* William Rees *m/ly* Sammy Fain, Irving Kahal *ch Busby Berkeley* *ad* Jack Okey

☆ William Powell, Bette Davis, Verree Teasdale, Frank McHugh, Reginald Owen, Hugh Herbert, Henry O'Neill

Fast and Furious: see *Fast Company (1938)*

Fast and Loose *
US 1939 80m bw
MGM (Frederick Stephani)
Married detectives and rare book experts solve the mystery of a missing Shakespeare manuscript.
Pleasing comedy mystery in the wake of The Thin Man.
w Harry Kurnitz *d* Edwin L. Marin *ph* George Folsey
☆ Robert Montgomery, Rosalind Russell, Ralph Morgan, Reginald Owen, Etienne Girardot, Alan Dinehart, Joan Marsh, Sidney Blackmer

The Fast and the Furious
US 2001 107m DeLuxe Super 35
Universal/Mediastream (Neal H. Moritz)
An undercover cop joins a Los Angeles gang of street racers to investigate a hijacking racket.
Enjoyably old-fashioned exploitation flick, one that lives up to its title and makes the most of obsessions with fast cars and macho attitudes.
w Gary Scott Thompson, Erik Bergquist, David Ayer *d* Rob Cohen *ph* Ericson Core *m* BT *pd* Waldemar Kalinowski *ed* Peter Honess
☆ Paul Walker (Brian O'Conner), Vin Diesel (Dominic Toretto), Michelle Rodriguez (Letty), Jordana Brewster (Mia Toretto), Rick Yune (Johnny Tran), Chad Lindberg (Jesse), Johnny Strong (Leon), Matt Schulze (Vince), Ted Levine (Sgt Tanner)
'It's all zoomed up with nowhere to go and nothing much to say.' – *Cosmo Landesman, Sunday Times*
'A gritty and gratifying cheap thrill.' – *Todd Mccarthy, Variety*
† The film was a surprise hit: budgeted at $38m, it took more than $145m at the US box-office.

Fast Company *
US 1938 75m bw
MGM
A couple in the rare book business are implicated in the murder of a rival.
First of three whodunnits featuring Joel and Garda Page, whose style was not at all dissimilar from that of Nick and Nora Charles in the Thin Man *series. A polished time-passer.*
w Marco Page (Harry Kurnitz) *d* Edward Buzzell
☆ Melvyn Douglas, Florence Rice, Claire Dodd, Louis Calhern, George Zucco
† The follow-ups had different stars as the pair of sleuths. *Fast and Loose* (qv) featured Robert Montgomery and Rosalind Russell; Sidney Blackmer, Ralph Morgan and Reginald Owen supported. *Fast and Furious*, also released in 1939, starred Franchot Tone and Ann Sothern, with Ruth Hussey, Lee Bowman and Allyn Joslyn.

Fast Food
GB 1998 97m colour
Optimum/Twin/Fast Food (Phil Hunt)
A telephone engineer gets together with his old gang to rob a criminal who keeps his money in a local sweetshop and be re-united with his former girlfriend.
Hapless thriller composed of the less interesting elements from every other gangster movie; the ending is simply silly.
wd Stewart Sugg *ph* Simon Reeves *m* Ben Lee-Delisle *pd* Katie Franklyn-Thompson *ed* Jeremy Gibbs
☆ Douglas Henshall (Benny), Emily Woof (Letitia/Claudia), Miles Anderson (Dwayne), Gerard Butler (Jacko), Danny Midwinter (Bisto), Stephen Lord (Flea)
'It takes a certain ingenuity to make a film as bad as this.' – *James Christopher, Times*

Fast Getaway
US 1991 90m Foto-Kem
New Line/CineTel (Lisa M. Hansen, Paul Hertzberg)
A father and son team of bank robbers is betrayed by the girlfriend the son abandoned.
Energetic though mindless action film, with Rothrock demonstrating her high-kicking abilities.
w James Dixon *d* Spiro Razatos *ph* Jacques Haitkin *m* Bruce Rowland *ed* David Kern
☆ Corey Haim, Cynthia Rothrock, Leo Rossi, Ken Lerner, Marcia Strassman, Shelli Lether, Richard Jewkes, Jeff Olsen
'Will appeal to video fans tired of overblown, hyped-up cinema.' – *Variety*

Fast Getaway II
US 1994 90m Foto-Kem
CineTel/Live Entertainment (Russell D. Markowitz)
A former thief hunts the female bank robber who frames him for her crimes.
Dull action film, with the emphasis on Haim's reformed crook and his relationships with his father and girlfriend, neither of which will interest anyone outside the immediate family.
w Mark Sevi *d* Oley Sassone *ph* Mark Parry *m* David Robbins *pd* Jeannie M. Lomma *ed* Glenn Garland
☆ Corey Haim, Cynthia Rothrock, Sarah Buxton, Leo Rossi, Peter Liapis
'Action buffs won't be busting down the doors for this one.' – *Variety*

The Fast Lady **
GB 1962 95m Eastmancolor
Rank/Group Films (Julian Wintle, Leslie Parkyn)
A bashful suitor buys an old Bentley, becomes a roadhog, passes his test, captures some crooks and gets the girl.
Spirited if aimless farcical comedy which crams in all the jokes about cars anyone can think of.
w Jack Davies, Henry Blyth *d* Ken Annakin *ph* Reg Wyer *m* Norrie Paramor
☆ Stanley Baxter, James Robertson Justice, Leslie Phillips, Julie Christie, Dick Emery

The Fast Runner: see *Atanarjuat The Fast Runner*

Fast Talking
Australia 1984 95m Eastmancolor
Ross Matthews/Oldata
The youngest son of a shiftless and semi-criminal Sydney family gets into trouble and finally drives off on his motor cycle to an uncertain future.
Depressingly downbeat comedy-drama about characters of whom any audience must quickly tire.
wd Ken Cameron *ph* David Gribble *m* Sharon Calcraft
☆ Rod Zuanic, Toni Allaylis, Chris Truswell, Gail Sweeny, Steve Bisley

'It's Awesome! Totally Awesome!'
Fast Times at Ridgemont High
US 1982 92m Technicolor
Universal/Refugee (C. O. Erickson)
Students at a California high school aim to lose their virginity.
The tiresome content of this teen comedy is slightly offset by bright handling. But only slightly.
w Cameron Crowe *book* Cameron Crowe *d* Amy Heckerling *ph* Matthew F. Leonetti *m/songs* Rob Fahey
☆ Sean Penn, Jennifer Jason Leigh, Judge Reinhold, Phoebe Cates, Brian Backus, Robert Romanus, Ray Walston

Fast-Walking
US 1981 116m Metrocolor
Lorimar
Racial disharmony and violence prevail at a midwest state prison.
Curious black comedy dealing entirely with unpleasant types.
wd James B. Harris *novel* *The Rap* by Ernest Brawley
☆ James Woods, Tim McIntire, Kay Lenz, Robert Hooks, M. Emmet Walsh
'What do people think of when they write a script these days? Don't they have any sense of human values or human decency?' – *Arthur Knight*

Faster, Pussycat! Kill! Kill!
US 1966 84m bw
Eve (Russ and Eve Meyer)
Three homicidal exotic dancers drive around the Californian desert.
Meyer's best movie, with his usual ingredients of big-breasted women and lustful, ineffectual men.
w Jack Moran *story* Russ Meyer *d* Russ Meyer *ph* Walter Schenk *m* Paul Sawtell, Bert Shefter *ed* Russ Meyer
☆ Tura Satana, Haji, Stuart Lancaster, Lori Williams, Paul Trinka, Susan Bernard, Dennis Busch

The Fastest Guitar Alive
US 1968 87m Metrocolor
Sam Katzman/MGM
Inept Confederate soldiers are sent on a spy mission.
Ham-handed farce with music, unappealing on either count.
w Robert E. Kent *d* Michael Moore
☆ Roy Orbison, Sammy Jackson, Maggie Pierce, Joan Freeman, Lyle Bettger

The Fastest Gun Alive *
US 1956 89m bw
MGM (Clarence Greene)
A mild-mannered Western storekeeper proves to be the son of a famous gunfighter, and is put to the test.
Flimsily contrived mini-Western helped by good performances.
w Frank D. Gilroy, Russel Rouse *d* Russel Rouse *ph* George Folsey *m* André Previn
☆ Glenn Ford, Broderick Crawford, Jeanne Crain, Russ Tamblyn, Allyn Joslyn, Leif Erickson, John Dehner

Fat City **
US 1972 96m Eastmancolor
Columbia/Rastar (Ray Stark)
In a small Californian town, a has-been boxer tries to get back to the top, but loses his self respect and becomes a hobo.
Vivid but over-casual exploration of failure, with more interest in the characters than the sport.
w Leonard Gardner *novel* Leonard Gardner *d* John Huston *ph* Conrad Hall *md* Marvin Hamlisch *pd* Richard Sylbert
☆ Stacy Keach, Jeff Bridges, Susan Tyrrell, Candy Clark
'Huston has confronted a piece of material and a milieu perfectly suited to his insights and talents. The result is his best film in years and one of the best he has ever done: a lean, compassionate, detailed, raucous, sad, strong look at some losers and survivors on the side streets of small-city Middle America.' – *Charles Champlin*
Susan Tyrrell

Fat Girl: see *À Ma Soeur!*

The Fat Man
US 1950 77m bw
U-I (Aubrey Schenck)
The murder of a dentist leads to the circus.
Dense murder mystery featuring a gourmet 17-stone detective; understandably, no series resulted.
w Harry Essex, Leonard Lee *d* William Castle *ph* Irving Glassberg *m* Bernard Green
☆ J. Scott Smart, Rock Hudson, Julie London, Clinton Sundberg, Jerome Cowan, Jayne Meadows

Fat Man and Little Boy: see *Shadow Makers*

Fatal Attraction
Canada 1980 88m colour
Greentree/Michael Grant
aka: *Head On*
In Toronto, after an academic psychologist has a head-on crash with a car driven by a married female psychiatrist, the two begin a torrid affair in which they act out their erotic desires.
Uninvolving drama, notable, given the protagonists' professions, for the banality of its sexual fantasies, concerning as they do nursery rhymes, shaving cream, sex in the office and playing at gangsters.
w James Sanderson, Paul Illidge *d* Michael Grant *ph* Anthony Richmond *m* Peter Mann *pd* Antonin Dimitrov *ed* Gary Oppenheimer
☆ Sally Kellerman, Stephen Lack, Lawrence Dane, John Peter Linton, John Huston

Fatal Attraction **
US 1987 119m Technicolor
Paramount/Jaffe-Lansing (Stanley Jaffe, Sherry Lansing)
A married man finds it difficult to shed his nearly homicidal light of love.
A kind of rehash of Play Misty for Me, *and a sensational success at the box-office: the timing must have been right, even if the details aren't always persuasive.*
w James Dearden *d* Adrian Lyne *ph* Howard Atherton *m* Maurice Jarre *pd* Mel Bourne *ed* Michael Kahn, Peter E. Berger
☆ Michael Douglas, Glenn Close, Anne Archer, Fred Gwynne
'A predictable dog's dinner of thriller clichés – will appeal strongly to those who think women should be kept on a short leash.' – *Time Out*
'This shrewd film also touches on something deeper than men's fear of feminism: their fear of women, their fear of women's emotions, of women's hanging on to them. *Fatal Attraction* doesn't treat the dreaded passionate woman as a theme; she's merely a monster in a monster flick.' – *Pauline Kael*
† A video release of the movie included an alternative ending to the film.
Glenn Close; Anne Archer; Adrian Lyne; best picture; James Dearden; film editing

Fatal Beauty
US 1987 104m colour
Enterprise/MGM/CST Communications (Leonard Kroll)
A female cop tracks down a drug dealer.
A violent formula film with nothing new to offer.
w Hilary Henkin, Dean Riesner *story* Bill Svanoe *d* Tom Holland *ph* David M. Walsh *m* Harold Faltermeyer *pd* James William Newport *ed* Don Zimmerman
☆ Whoopi Goldberg, Sam Elliott, Ruben Blades, Harris Yulin, John P. Ryan, Jennifer Warren, Brad Dourif, Mike Jolly, Charles Hallahan, David Harris

Fatal Bond
Australia 1991 89m colour
Avalon Films/Phillip Avalon
A hairdresser begins to suspect that her mysterious new boyfriend is killing and raping young girls.
Overblown, under-budgeted thriller, of interest only to followers of the declining career of Linda Blair.
w Phillip Avalon *d* Vincent Monton *ph* Ray Henman *m* Art Phillips *ad* Keith Holloway *ed* Ted ötton
☆ Linda Blair, Jerome Ehlers, Joe Bugner, Donal Gibson, Stephen Leeder, Caz Lederman, Teo Gerbert, Penny Pederson

The Fatal Glass of Beer *
US 1933 18m bw
Paramount/Sennett
The prodigal son returns to a snowbound cabin in the Yukon.
Absurd star comedy with appeal to addicts only: most of the humour consists of repeats of one line, ''Taint a fit night out for man nor beast.'
w W. C. Fields *d* Clyde Bruckman
☆ W. C. Fields, Rosemary Theby, Rychard Cramer, George Chandler

'Torn between his wife, a seductress and a pet skunk ... he's a private eye in danger of spreading himself too thin!'
Fatal Instinct
US 1993 88m DeLuxe
MGM (Katy Jacobs, Pierce Gardner)
A double-crossing wife plans to murder her husband, a cop-cum-lawyer who is seduced by her twin sister and being chased by a tattooed ex-convict.
Clumsy farce that attempts to parody film noir and such modern thrillers as Fatal Attraction, Basic Instinct *and* Body Heat; *about one joke in twenty raises a hint of a smile.*
w David O'Malley *d* Carl Reiner *ph* Gabriel Beristain *m* Richard Gibbs *pd* Sandy Veneziano *ed* Bud Molin, Stephen Myers
☆ Armand Assante, Sherilyn Fenn, Kate Nelligan, Sean Young, Christopher McDonald, James Remar, Tony Randall

'The insane collision of plot climaxes *is* funny, but as collections of cinematic jests go, it's even thinner than most.' – *Angie Errigo, Empire*

† It was released direct to video in Britain.

'You have a date with fate!'

Fate Is the Hunter

US 1964 106m bw Cinemascope

TCF/Arcola (Aaron Rosenberg)

An airline executive investigates the cause of a fatal crash in which his friend the pilot was a victim.

Watchable how-did-it-happen melodrama marred by pretentious dialogue.

w Harold Medford *novel* Ernest K. Gann *d* Ralph Nelson *ph* Milton Krasner *m* Jerry Goldsmith

☆ Glenn Ford, Rod Taylor, Nehemiah Persoff, Nancy Kwan, Suzanne Pleshette, Jane Russell

Milton Krasner

Father

Australia 1989 100m colour

Leftbank/Barron (Damien Parer, Tony Cavanaugh, Graham Hartley, Paul D. Barron)

In modern-day Australia, a grandfather is accused of being an SS officer who massacred an entire village in the Second World War.

Moderately engaging but overly manipulative drama, concentrating on family relationships rather than the larger issues it raises.

w Tony Cavanaugh, Graham Hartley *d* John Power *ph* Dan Burstall *m* Peter Best *pd* Phil Peters *ed* Kerry Regan

☆ Max von Sydow, Carol Drinkwater, Julia Blake, Steve Jacobs, Simone Robertson, Kahli Sneddon

'Boasts a good screenplay, firm direction and a couple of very strong performances.' – *Variety*

Father and Master: see *Padre Padrone*

Father and Son

Hong Kong 1981 96m Eastmancolor

BFI/Feng Huang Motion Picture Company (Wong Kai-Chuen)

original title: *Fuzi Qing*

Returning home for his father's funeral, a film-maker reflects on his childhood.

A gently observant semi-autobiographical domestic drama, but lacking individuality.

w Chan Chiu, Cheung Kin-Ting, Lee Bik-Wah *d* Fong Yuk-Ping (Allen Fong) *ph* Patrick Wong *m* Violet Lam *ad* Wong Huk-Sun, Wong Kwai-Ping

☆ Shek Lui, Lee Yu-Tin, Cheng Yu-Or, Chan Sun, Cheung Kwok-Ming, Kung Yee, Yan Sin-Mei, Yung Wai-Man, Chung Hung, Lo Tai-Wai

Father Brown ***

GB 1954 91m bw

Columbia/Facet (Vivian A. Cox)

US title: *The Detective*

A Catholic clergyman retrieves a priceless church cross from master thief Flambeau.

Delightfully eccentric comedy based closely on the famous character, with a sympathetic if rather wandering script, pointed direction and some delicious characterizations. A thoroughly civilized entertainment.

w Thelma Schnee, Maurice Rapf, Robert Hamer story The Blue Cross by G. K. Chesterton *d Robert Hamer ph* Harry Waxman *m* Georges Auric

☆ *Alec Guinness, Joan Greenwood, Peter Finch,* Sidney James, *Cecil Parker, Bernard Lee, Ernest Thesiger,* Marne Maitland

'It has wit, elegance, and kindly humour – all somewhat rare commodities in the 1954 cinema.' – *Star*

† Maurice Rapf was not credited as one of the screenwriters at the time of the film's release as he was blacklisted.

Father Came Too

GB 1963 93m Eastmancolor

Rank/Independent Artists

Honeymooners agree to live with her overbearing actor-manager father.

Less funny sequel to The Fast Lady, *with comic household disasters striking every couple of minutes. Easy-going, and predictably amusing in spots.*

w Jack Davies, Henry Blyth *d* Peter Graham Scott *ph* Reg Wyer *m* Norrie Paramor

☆ Stanley Baxter, James Robertson Justice, Leslie Phillips, Sally Smith, Ronnie Barker, Timothy Bateson, Philip Locke

Father, Dear Father

GB 1972 99m Eastmancolor MultiVista

Sedgemoor-MM (Peter J. Thompson)

A divorced, middle-aged writer, who has problems with his two teenage daughters, decides he should get married.

Trivial comedy, based on a TV sitcom, and looking and sounding like it.

w Johnnie Mortimer, Brian Cooke *d* William G. Stewart *ph* Alan Hume *m* Nachum Heiman *pd* Michael Bastow *ed* Timothy Gee

☆ Patrick Cargill, Natasha Pyne, Ann Holloway, Noël Dyson, Ursula Howells, Joyce Carey, Richard O'Sullivan, Joseph O'Conor, Jack Watling, Jill Melford, Beryl Reid, Donald Sinden

Father Goose *

US 1964 116m Technicolor

U-I/Granox (Robert Arthur)

During World War II a South Seas wanderer is compelled by the Australian navy to act as sky observer on a small island, where he finds himself in charge of six refugee schoolchildren and their schoolmistress.

Eager-to-please but unsatisfactory film which wanders between farce, adventure and sex comedy, taking too long about all of them.

w Peter Stone, Frank Tarloff *story A Place of Dragons* by S. H. Barnett *d* Ralph Nelson *ph* Charles Lang Jnr *m* Cy Coleman *ad* Alexander Golitzen, Henry Bumstead *ed* Ted J. Kent

☆ Cary Grant, Leslie Caron, Trevor Howard, Jack Good, Verina Greenlaw, Pip Sparke, Stephanie Berrington, Jennifer Berrington

CARY GRANT: 'Let me tell you I am not a father figure. I am not a brother figure or an uncle figure or a cousin figure. In fact, the only figure I intend being is a total stranger figure.'

'Reasoning would indicate a made-to-order Christmas package for the family trade. However, the more sophisticated may be bored and exasperated after some of the initial brightness wears off.' – *Cue*

'Cary Grant wrings what there is to be wrung from the role, but never quite enough to conceal the fact that *Father Goose* is a waste of his talent and the audience's time.' – *Arthur Knight*

Peter Stone, Frank Tarloff

Ted J. Kent; sound (Waldon O. Watson)

Father Hood

US 1993 94m Technicolor

Buena Vista/Hollywood (Nicholas Pileggi, Anant Singh, Gillian Gorfil)

A petty crook kidnaps his children from their foster home and takes them on a cross-country journey.

Inane and clumsy road movie, uninteresting to watch and with the explicit message that robbery is fun.

w Scott Spencer *d* Darrell James Roodt *ph* Mark Vicente *m* Patrick O'Hearn *pd* David Barkham *ed* David Heitner

☆ Patrick Swayze, Halle Berry, Diane Ladd, Brian Bonsall, Sabrina Lloyd, Michael Ironside, Bob Gunton

'A train wreck from start to finish.' – *Variety*

Father Is a Bachelor

US 1950 85m bw

Columbia (S. Sylvan Simon)

A young tramp cares for a family of orphaned children.

Boringly sentimental semi-Western.

w Aleen Leslie, James Edward Grant *d* Norman Foster, Abby Berlin *ph* Burnett Guffey *m* Arthur Morton

☆ William Holden, Coleen Gray, Charles Winninger, Stuart Erwin, Sig Rumann

'Saccharine, paper thin. At least one spectator at the Palace yesterday couldn't take it – a tot of about four, wearing a cowboy suit, who aimed a toy pistol at the screen and popped off the cast one by one.' – *New York Times*

Father Is a Prince: see *Big Hearted Herbert*

'The bride gets the thrills! Father gets the bills!'

Father of the Bride **

US 1950 93m bw

MGM (Pandro S. Berman)

A dismayed but happy father surveys the cost and chaos of his daughter's marriage.

Fragmentary but mainly delightful suburban comedy which finds Hollywood in its best light vein and benefits from a strong central performance.

w Frances Goodrich, Albert Hackett novel Edward Streeter d Vincente Minnelli *ph* John Alton *m* Adolph Deutsch

☆ *Spencer Tracy,* Joan Bennett, Elizabeth Taylor, Don Taylor, Billie Burke, Moroni Olsen, Leo G. Carroll, Taylor Holmes, Melville Cooper

'The idealization of a safe sheltered existence, the good life according to MGM: 24 carat complacency.' – *New Yorker, 1980*

† Jack Benny badly wanted the role but was thought unsuitable.

best picture; Frances Goodrich, Albert Hackett; Spencer Tracy

'Love is wonderful. Until it happens to your only daughter.'

Father of the Bride

US 1991 105m Technicolor

Touchstone/Touchwood Pacific Partners I (Nancy Myers, Carol Baum, Howard Rosenman)

A father is upset by his daughter's announcement that she is engaged – and even more horrified by the arrangements for an expensive wedding.

Lacklustre remake with flat or exaggerated performances, few jokes and a great deal of sentimentality.

w Frances Goodrich, Albert Hackett, Nancy Myers, Charles Shyer *novel* Edward Streeter *d* Charles Shyer *ph* John Lindley *m* Alan Silvestri *pd* Sandy Veneziano *ed* Richard Marks

☆ Steve Martin, Diane Keaton, Kimberly Williams, Martin Short, Kieran Culkin, George Newbern, B. D. Wong, Peter Michael Goetz

'Little more than a mildly entertaining diversion.' – *Empire*

Father of the Bride 2

US 1995 106m Technicolor

Buena Vista/Touchstone/Sandollar/Meyers/Shyer

As they are on the point of becoming grandparents, a couple find that they are also about to be parents again.

Broad and undistinguished comedy, though audiences that enjoyed the previous film will find this no worse, though no better either.

w Nancy Meyers, Charles Shyer *screenplay* Albert Hackett, Frances Goodrich *d* Charles Shyer *ph* William A. Fraker *m* Alan Silvestri *pd* Linda DeScenna *ed* Stephen A. Rotter

☆ Steve Martin, Diane Keaton, Martin Short, Kimberly Williams, George Newbern, Kieran Culkin, B. D. Wong, Peter Michael Goetz

'Pleasant enough, assuming a reasonably high tolerance for saccharine in one's diet.' – *Variety*

† The film is a remake of *Father's Little Dividend.*

Father Takes a Wife *

US 1941 80m bw

RKO (Lee S. Marcus)

A famous actress marries a shipping magnate and runs into resentment from his children.

Disappointing comedy with a script too flat for the stars to make interesting.

w Dorothy and Herbert Fields *d* Jack Hively *ph* Robert de Grasse *m* Roy Webb

☆ Gloria Swanson, Adolphe Menjou, Desi Arnaz, John Howard, Helen Broderick, Florence Rice, Neil Hamilton

'One kid. Two dads. A who done it?'

Fathers' Day

US 1997 98m Technicolor Panavision

Warner/Silver/Northern Lights (Joel Silver, Ivan Reitman)

Two men – one a suicidal writer, the other a successful lawyer – search for a missing 16-year-old youth, each believing that he is the boy's father.

Tiresome comedy, slick and soulless, with little evidence of life or interest from its cast.

w Lowell Ganz, Babaloo Mandel *film Les Compres* by Francis Veber *d* Ivan Reitman *ph* Stephen H. Burum *m* James Newton Howard *pd* Thomas Sanders *ed* Sheldon Kahn, Wendy Green Bricmont

☆ Robin Williams (Dale Putney), Billy Crystal (Jack Lawrence), Julia Louis-Dreyfus (Carrie Lawrence), Nastassja Kinski (Collette Andrews), Charlie Hofheimer (Scott Andrews), Bruce Greenwood (Bob Andrews), Jared Harris (Lee), Louis Lombardi, Patti D'Arbanville (Shirley Trainor)

'A brainless feature-length sitcom with too much sit and no com.' – *Roger Ebert, Chicago Sun-Times*

Father's Doing Fine

GB 1952 83m Technicolor

Marble Arch/ABP (Victor Skutezky)

An impoverished lady has trouble with her daughters, one of whom is pregnant.

Agreeable madcap farce from a long-running stage success (so why did they change the title?).

w Anne Burnaby *play Little Lambs Eat Ivy* by Noel Langley *d* Henry Cass *ph* Erwin Hillier *ad* Don Ashton

☆ Heather Thatcher, Richard Attenborough, Susan Stephen, Noel Purcell, George Thorpe

Father's Little Dividend

US 1951 81m bw

MGM (Pandro S. Berman)

Sequel to *Father of the Bride*, in which the newlyweds have a baby.

A very flat follow-up, palatable enough at the time but quite unmemorable.

w Frances Goodrich, Albert Hackett *d* Vincente Minnelli *ph* John Alton *m* Albert Sendrey

☆ Spencer Tracy, Joan Bennett, Elizabeth Taylor, Don Taylor, Billie Burke, Moroni Olsen, Frank Faylen, Marietta Canty, Russ Tamblyn

'The world's most uncovered undercover agent!'

Fathom

GB 1967 99m DeLuxe Franscope

TCF (John Kohn)

Adventures of a glamorous sky-diving spy.

Watchable romp with nothing memorable about it.

w Lorenzo Semple Jnr *novel* Larry Forrester *d* Leslie Martinson *ph* Douglas Slocombe, Jacques Dubourg *m* Johnny Dankworth

☆ *Raquel Welch,* Tony Franciosa, Clive Revill, Ronald Fraser, Greta Chi, Richard Briers, Tom Adams

'Belongs not in the category of High Camp but in that of Good Wholesome Fun.' – *MFB*

Le Fatiche di Ercole: see *Hercules*

Fatso

US 1980 93m DeLuxe

TCF/Brooksfilms

A fat man fails to make much headway at slimming, and gives up.

Unappealing mixture of sentiment, satire, shouting and crude humour.

wd Anne Bancroft

☆ Dom DeLuise, Anne Bancroft, Ron Carey, Candice Azzara

'As bumbling and sluggish as its title might suggest, a lamentable affair which ricochets uncontrollably between attempts at hilarity and pathos.' – *Variety*

Fatto di Sarigne fra due vomini per causa di una vedora – si sospettano moventi politici: see *Blood Feud*

Faust **

Germany 1926 100m approx bw silent

UFA

A man sells his soul to the devil in exchange for his heart's desire.

A superbly stylish version of the legend, the best of many silent versions. See also All That Money Can Buy.

w Hans Kyser *d F. W. Murnau ph* Carl Hoffman

☆ Emil Jannings, Gosta Ekman, Camilla Horn, Yvette Guilbert, William Dieterle

'A magical tale of love, friendship and dreams that come true.'

Fausto

France 1992 81m colour
Mayfair/Amorces/Lili/BBD/France 2 (Christine de Jekel)

In mid-60s Paris, a 17-year-old orphan falls in love and becomes a successful fashion designer.
Slight and frivolous first feature by an advertising director which is full of pretty images but has nothing of interest to sell; it gets by for a while on charm.
w Richard Morgiève, Rémy Duchemin
novel Richard Morgiève *d* Rémy Duchemin
ph Yves Lafaye *m* Denis Barbier *ad* Fouillet & Wieber *ed* Maryline Monthieux
☆ Florence Darel, Jean Yanne, Ken Higelin, François Hautesserre, Maite Nahyr, Maurice Bénichou, Bruce Myers
'Sadly, fragile whimsy cannot sustain a whole movie.' – *Kim Newman, Empire*

Faustrecht der Freiheit: see *Fox*

'Two Women. Three Men. One Secret.'
'An outrageous romantic comedy.'

The Favor

US 1994 97m DeLuxe
Nelson (Lauren Shuler-Donner)

A bored but happily married woman asks a friend to make real her fantasy, by bedding her high school sweetheart.
Tiresome romantic drama that needed a lighter touch and a better script; it is heavy-handed and heavy-going.
w Sara Parriott, Josann McGibbon *d* Donald Petrie *ph* Tim Suhrstedt *m* Thomas Newman
pd David Chapman *ed* Harry Keramidas
☆ Elizabeth McGovern, Harley Jane Kozak, Bill Pullman, Brad Pitt, Ken Wahl, Larry Miller, Holland Taylor
'Delicate material, and unfortunately it's executed by comparative barbarians.' – *Variety*
† The film was made in 1991 and its release delayed by Orion's financial difficulties.

Les Favoris de la Lune: see *Favourites of the Moon*

'A romantic comedy beyond normal experience.'

The Favour, the Watch & the Very Big Fish

France/GB 1991 87m colour
Rank/Sovereign/Ariane/Fildebroc/Umbrella (Michelle de Broca)

A religious photographer, who gets an ex-criminal to pose as Christ for him, falls in love with an actress who dubs pornographic films.
Flaccid farce in which most of the cast give the impression that they would rather be somewhere else.
wd Ben Lewin *story Rue Saint-Sulpice* by Marcel Ayme *ph* Bernard Zitzermann *m* Vladimir Cosma
pd Carlos Conti *ed* John Grover
☆ Bob Hoskins, Jeff Goldblum, Natasha Richardson, Michel Blanc, Jacques Villeret, Jean-Pierre Cassel, Angela Pleasence
'Mildy intriguing title, stultifyingly dull film.' – *Empire*

Favourites of the Moon *

France 1984 102m Eastmancolor
Philippe Dussart/FR3
original title: *Les Favoris de la Lune*
Characters in Paris find that their paths cross as they pursue their obsessions.
Buñuel-like surrealism without Buñuel's intensity of vision results in a film which sometimes pleases but eventually becomes tiresome.
w Otar Iosseliani, Gerard Brach *d* Otar Iosseliani
ph Philippe Theaudiere
☆ Katia Rupe, Hans Peter Cloos, Alix de Montaigu, François Michel

The Fear: see *City of The Living Dead*

Fear

US 1946 68m bw
Monogram
A student kills his professor, and a detective taunts him to the point of confession.
Cheeky second feature version of Crime and Punishment, *with a twist ending. Not too bad in its way.*
w Alfred Zeisler, Dennis Cooper *d* Alfred Zeisler
ph Jackson Rose
☆ Warren William, Peter Cookson, Anne Gwynne, Nestor Paiva

'Your First Impulse. Your Last Sensation.'

Fear

US 1989 95m CFI color Super 35
First Independent/Richard Kobritz-Rockne S. O'Bannon

A psychic detective discovers that the killer she is hunting is also a powerful psychic.
Mindless thriller that offers nothing new.
wd Rockne S. O'Bannon *ph* Robert Stevens
m Henry Mancini *pd* Joseph Nemec III *ed* Kent Beyda
☆ Ally Sheedy, Pruitt Taylor Vince, Lauren Hutton, Michael O'Keefe, Stan Shaw, Dina Merrill, John Agar
'Treads an increasingly uninspiring road to nowhere.' – *MFB*

Fear

US 1996 96m DeLuxe Panavision
Universal/Imagine (Brian Grazer, Ric Kidney)

An architect's teenage daughter falls for a psychopath.
Uninteresting teen thriller, predictable from its opening to its closing moments.
w Christopher Crowe *d* James Foley *ph* Thomas Kloss *m* Carter Burwell *pd* Alex McDowell
ed David Brenner
☆ Mark Wahlberg, Reese Witherspoon, William Petersen, Amy Brenneman, Alyssa Milano, Christopher Gray
'Stylishly crafted suspenser doesn't hold many surprises for those familiar with the genre.' – *Variety*

Fear and Loathing in Las Vegas

US 1998 119m Rank Colour 'Scope
Universal/Rhino (Laila Nabulsi, Patrick Cassavetti)

In 1971, a journalist and his attorney binge on drugs in Las Vegas.
A surreal trip into bad drugs makes for a queasy film that is unlikely to attain the cult status of the original book.
w Terry Gilliam, Tony Grisoni, Tod Davies, Alex Cox *book* Hunter S. Thompson *d* Terry Gilliam
ph Nicola Pecorini *m* Ray Cooper *pd* Alex McDowell *ed* Lesley Walker *sp* Kent Houston; make-up fx: Rob Bottin
☆ Johnny Depp, Benicio Del Toro, Craig Bierko, Ellen Barkin, Gary Busey, Cameron Diaz, Flea, Mark Harmon, Katherine Helmond, Michael Jeter, Penn Jillette, Lyle Lovett, Tobey Maguire, Christina Ricci, Harry Dean Stanton and also Tim Thomerson
'It's hard to imagine any segment of the public embracing this off-putting, unrewarding slog through the depths of the drug culture.' – *Todd McCarthy, Variety*

Fear City

US 1985 93m colour
Zupnik-Curtis Enterprises (Bruce Cohn Curtis)

A psychopathic killer terrorizes strippers working in the Times Square area of New York.
Sleazy, violent, low-life thriller, of minimal interest despite an interesting cast.
w Nicholas St John *d* Abel Ferrara *ph* James Lemmo *m* Dick Halligan *ed* Jack Holmes, Anthony Redman
☆ Tom Berenger, Billy Dee Williams, Jack Scalia, Melanie Griffith, Rossano Brazzi, Rae Dawn Chong, Joe Santos

Fear Eats the Soul *

West Germany 1974 92m colour
Tango Film (Christian Hohoff)

original title: *Angst essen Seele auf*
A Moroccan immigrant in Munich comes up against social and racial prejudice when he marries a sixty-year-old charwoman.
Unexceptionable moral tale which can hardly have been necessary in view of the infrequency of such cases.
wd Rainer Werner Fassbinder *ph* Jürgen Jürges
ed Thea Eymèsz
☆ Brigitte Mira, El Hedi Ben Salem, Barbara Valentin, Irm Hermann, Rainer Werner Fassbinder

Fear in the Night **

US 1947 72m bw
Paramount (William H. Pine, William C. Thomas)

A man suffering from a strange nightmare discovers he has been hypnotized into committing a murder.
Intriguing small-scale puzzler later remade to less effect as Nightmare *(qv). Adequate performances and handling, but the plot's the thing.*
wd Maxwell Shane *ph* Jack Greenhalgh *m* Rudy Schrager
☆ Paul Kelly, DeForest Kelley, Ann Doran, Kay Scott

Fear in the Night *

GB 1972 85m Technicolor
MGM-EMI/Hammer (Jimmy Sangster)

A girl recovering from a nervous breakdown is deluded into committing a murder.
Yet another variant on Les Diaboliques, *ingeniously worked out with good touches of detail to produce an air of general competence.*
w Jimmy Sangster, Michael Syson *d* Jimmy Sangster *ph* Arthur Grant *m* John McCabe
ad Don Picton *ed* Peter Weatherley
☆ Peter Cushing, Judy Geeson, Joan Collins, Ralph Bates

Fear Is the Key *

GB 1972 108m Technicolor Panavision
EMI/KLK (Alan Ladd Jnr, Elliott Kastner)

A man conceives an elaborate plot to track down those responsible for killing his wife and family in a plane crash.
Reasonably absorbing, surprise-plotted thriller.
w Robert Carrington *novel* Alistair MacLean
d Michael Tuchner *ph* Alex Thomson *m* Roy Budd
☆ Suzy Kendall, Barry Newman, John Vernon, Dolph Sweet, Ben Kingsley, Ray McAnally

Fear o' God: see *The Mountain Eagle*

Fear of a Black Hat *

US 1993 86m colour
Oakwood (Darin Scott)

A mock documentary on the progress of a tough rap group, NWH (Niggas With Hats), and its members, Ice Cold, Taste Taste and Tone Def.
Witty demolition of rap's pretensions, in the style of This Is Spinal Tap, *that hits the target more often than the similar, rival movie* CB4.
wd Rusty Cundieff *ph* John Demps *m* Larry Robinson *pd* Stuart Blatt *ed* Karen Horn
☆ Larry B. Scott, Christopher Lawrence, Rusty Cundieff, Kasi Lemmons, Howie Gold, Barry Heins, Eric Laneuville
'A midnight movie. But wild irreverent humor and exuberant music may also help this spoof find a larger, hip public.' – *Variety*

Fear Strikes Out

US 1957 100m bw Vistavision
Paramount/Alan Pakula

A father wants his son to become a professional baseball player, and the son in consequence suffers a nervous breakdown.
Rather flat biopic of Jim Piersall; well-intentioned and careful in its psychological insights, but too often just plain dull.
w Ted Berkman, Raphael Blau *d* Robert Mulligan
ph Haskell Boggs *m* Elmer Bernstein
☆ Anthony Perkins, Karl Malden, Norma Moore, Perry Wilson

Fearless **

US 1993 122m Technicolor
Warner/Spring Creek (Paula Weinstein, Mark Rosenberg)

The survivor of a plane crash loses all sense of fear in his everyday life, but also all feelings of responsibility to his wife and son.
A refreshingly different mainstream Hollywood film, tackling matters of life and death and individual freedom and obligation, but failing to resolve them satisfactorily.
w Rafael Yglesias *d* Peter Weir *ph* Allen Daviau
m Maurice Jarre *pd* John Stoddart *ed* William Anderson
☆ Jeff Bridges, Isabella Rossellini, Rosie Perez, Tom Hulce, John Turturro, Deirdre O'Connell, Benicio del Toro
'It always feels like it could become a breathtaking, thought provoking film that does everything that the run-of-the-mill Hollywood drama so singularly fails to do. Unfortunately, and not a little ironically, about halfway through it gets cold feet and bottles out of saying anything remotely meaningful or even logical with regards to all that has gone before.' – *Anwar Brett, Film Review*

The Fearless Vampire Killers, or Pardon Me, Your Teeth Are in My Neck *

US 1967 124m Metrocolor Panavision
MGM/Cadre Films/Filmways (Gene Gutowski)

aka: *Dance of the Vampires*
A professor and his assistant stake a Transylvanian vampire.
Heavy, slow spoof of Dracula, *most of which shows that sense of humour is very personal; a few effective moments hardly compensate for the prevailing stodge.*
w Gerard Brach, Roman Polanski *d* Roman Polanski *ph Douglas Slocombe* *m* Krzystof Komeda
pd Wilfrid Shingleton
☆ Jack MacGowran, Roman Polanski, Alfie Bass, Sharon Tate, *Ferdy Mayne*, Iain Quarrier, Terry Downes
'An engaging oddity ... long stretches might have been lifted intact from any Hammer horror.' – *Tom Milne*
† A credit ran: Fangs by Dr Ludwig von Krankheit.

Fearless Young Boxer: see *The Avenging Boxer*

The Fearmakers

US 1958 85m bw
Pacemaker (Martin H. Lancer)
A brainwashed Korean War veteran returns to Washington and finds that his PR firm has been taken over by communist racketeers.
Unusual but cheaply made anti-Red propaganda, too talkative to be very entertaining.
w Elliot West, Chris Appley *novel* Darwin Teilhet
d Jacques Tourneur *ph* Sam Leavitt *m* Irving Gertz
☆ Dana Andrews, Dick Foran, Mel Tormé

A Feast at Midnight

GB 1995 106m colour
Entertainment/Kwai River (Yoshi Nishio)

A new boarder at a public school, where there is a regime of healthy eating, becomes popular by producing gourmet food and cakes.
Shades of Billy Bunter arise in this old-fashioned school story that is presumably someone's nostalgic fantasy of childhood, one that an audience is unlikely to share.
w Justin Hardy, Yoshi Nishio *d* Justin Hardy
ph Tim Maurice-Jones *m* David Hughes, John Murphy *pd* Christiane Ewing *ed* Michael Johns
☆ Freddie Findlay, Christopher Lee, Aled Roberts, Andrew Lusher, Robert Hardy, Samuel West, Edward Fox, Carol Macready, Lisa Faulkner
'Nothing about it suggests that it should have been made for the big screen, so modest is its scope.' – *Empire*

'There is no escape from the past.'

Feast of July

GB/US 1995 113m Technicolor Super 35
Buena Vista/Touchstone/Merchant Ivory (Henry Herbert, Christopher Neame)

In the 1890s, a woman, abandoned by her lover, finds brief happiness with a simple-minded youth.
Glum tale of working-class suffering and loss that never comes fully to life, muting any emotional response.
w Christopher Neame *novel* H. E. Bates
d Christopher Menaul *ph* Peter Sova
m Zbigniew Preisner *pd* Christopher Robilliard
ed Chris Wimble
☆ Embeth Davidtz, Tom Bell, Gemma Jones, James Purefoy, Ben Chaplin, Kenneth Anderson, Greg Wise, David Neal

'Sadly, script and direction give the actors little chance to develop their characters and they remain ciphers.' – *George Perry*

Feather Your Nest *

GB 1937 86m bw

ATP (Basil Dean)

A gramophone record technician substitutes his own voice for a star and becomes world famous.

The star in less farcical vein than usual; this is the one in which he sings 'Leaning on a Lamp-post'.

w Austin Melford, Robert Edmunds, Anthony Kimmins *story* Ivar and Sheila Campbell

d William Beaudine *ph* Ronald Neame *m* Leslie Sarony, Leslie Holmes and others *ad* R. Holmes Paul *ed* Ernest Aldridge

☆ *George Formby*, Polly Ward, Enid Stamp Taylor, Val Rosing, Davy Burnaby

Fedora *

West Germany/France 1978 110m Eastmancolor

Geria/SFP (Billy Wilder)

An ageing star who seems miraculously to have kept her beauty comes out of retirement.

Sunset Boulevard *revisited, with a less bitter approach and less effectiveness; but any civilized film is welcome in the late seventies.*

w I. A. L. Diamond, Billy Wilder *story* Crowned Heads by Tom Tryon *d* Billy Wilder *ph* Gerry Fisher *m* Miklos Rozsa

☆ William Holden, Marthe Keller, Hildegarde Knef, José Ferrer, Mario Adorf, Henry Fonda, Michael York

'Rife with Wilderean gallows humour and a sumptuous sense of decay in never-never land.' – *Sight and Sound*

'Sleep Tight America. These Women Carry Guns.'

Feds

US 1988 82m colour

Warner (Ilona Herzberg, Len Blum)

Two women – one academic, the other athletic – meet masculine prejudice when they train to become FBI agents.

A mild, unarresting comedy, too predictable and unmemorable to cause more than a very occasional smile.

w Len Blum, Dan Goldberg *d* Dan Goldberg *ph* Timothy Suhrstedt *m* Randy Edelman *pd* Randy Ser *ed* Donn Cambern

☆ Rebecca DeMornay, Mary Gross, Ken Marshall, Fred Dalton Thompson, Larry Cedar, Raymond Singer, James Luisi, Rex Ryon, Tony Longo

Feel the Motion (dubbed)

West Germany 1985 98m colour

Atlas International/Solaris/Bavaria Atelier/Neue Constantin (Peter Zenk)

A female car mechanic tries to persuade a television pop show to listen to her demo tape.

Trivial story of a pop romance interspersed with forgettable songs and heavy-handed rock parodies.

w Wolfgang Büld, Rochus Hahn, Peter Zemann *d* Wolfgang Büld *ph* Roland Willaert *pd* Twyla Weixl *ed* Inge Kuhnert

☆ Sissy Kelling, Frank Meyer-Brockmann, Ingolf Lück, Dietmar Bär, Kurt Raab, Meatloaf, Falco, The Flirts, Pia Zadora, Limahl, Die Toten Hosen

'She met the man of her dreams. Then her husband showed up and ruined everything.'

Feeling Minnesota *

US 1996 95m DeLuxe Super 35

Entertainment/New Line/Jersey (Danny DeVito, Michael Shamberg, Stacy Sher)

An ex-convict goes on the run with his brother's bride.

Over-the-top, small-town, family melodrama of double-dealing gangsters, less interesting than it sounds.

wd Steven Baigelman *ph* Walt Lloyd *pd* Naomi Shohan *ed* Martin Walsh

☆ Keanu Reeves, Vincent D'Onofrio, Cameron Diaz, Delroy Lindo, Courtney Love, Tuesday Weld, Dan Aykroyd, Levon Helm

'Suggests Sam Shepard trying to be Quentin Tarantino. It makes even gun battles seem pretentious.' – *Owen Gleiberman, Entertainment Weekly*

'A thrill a minute! A laugh a second! A comedy cyclone!'

Feet First **

US 1930 88m bw

Harold Lloyd

A shoe salesman gets entangled with crooks and has a narrow escape when hanging from the side of a building.

Very funny early talkie comedy, probably the comedian's last wholly satisfactory film.

w Lex Neal, Felix Adler, Paul Gerard Smith

d *Clyde Bruckman* *ph* Walter Lundin, Henry Kohler

☆ Harold Lloyd, Robert McWade, Barbara Kent

'That Lloyd was a bit pressed for laughs may be guessed from the fact that he is again dangling from the front of a skyscraper.' – *Variety*

Feiying Gaiwak: see *Operation Condor*

Felicia's Journey ***

GB/Canada 1999 116m DeLuxe Panavision

Icon/Marquis/Screen Ventures XLIII

A pregnant Irish girl comes to England to search for the father of her child, and is taken in by a middle-aged catering manager who lives alone in the family house once occupied by his mother, a TV cook.

Creepy drama of the unloved searching for redemption, an unsettling insight into the mind of a serial killer.

wd *Atom Egoyan* *novel* William Trevor *ph* Paul Sarossy *m* Mychael Danna *pd* Jim Clay *ed* Susan Shipton *cos* Sandy Powell

☆ *Bob Hoskins* (Hilditch), Elaine Cassidy (Felicia), Arsinee Khanjian (Gala), Peter McDonald (Johnny), Gerard McSorley (Felicia's Father), Brid Brennan (Mrs Lysaght), Danny Turner (Young Hilditch), Claire Benedict (Miss Calligary)

'An altogether amazing work; it creates a world and then leaves it with you, what's more, in a manner that you might find difficult to forget.' – *Andrew O'Hagan, Daily Telegraph*

'Very well-made, but cold and hollow at its core.' – *Stephen Farber, Movieline*

Felix the Cat: The Movie

US 1989 82m colour

Transatlantic/Felix The Cat Creations/Productions Inc (Don Oriolo, Christian Schneider, Janos Schenk)

Felix rescues a princess from another dimension.

Laboured attempt to update the classic cartoon figure.

w Don Oriolo, Pete Brown *d* Tibor Hernadi *ph* Laszlo Radocsay *pd* Tibor A. Belay, Tibor Hernadi

☆ Featuring the voices of Chris Phillips, Maureen O'Connell, Peter Neuman, Alice Playten, Susan Montanaro, Don Oriolo, Christian Schneider, David Kolin

'More likely to bury the ingratiating Felix beyond revival than to stimulate fresh legions of fans.' – *Philip Strick, MFB*

Fellini's Casanova: see *Casanova*

'The decline and fall of the Roman Empire, 1931–1972!'

Fellini's Roma **

Italy/France 1972 119m Technicolor

Ultra/Artistes Associés (Turi Vasile)

aka: *Roma*

A small boy learns about Rome at school and then grows up to visit a city that does not resemble the place of his imagination; later, as a film director, he films the city of the 1970s in all its chaos and confusion.

Delightful mix of documentary and autobiography, combining fantasy and reality, artifice and actuality; it is a record of the director's love affair with Rome, recalled with nostalgic affection for the past and distress for its future.

w Federico Fellini, Bernardino Zapponi

d Federico Fellini *ph* Giuseppe Rotunno *m* Nino Rota *ad* Danilo Donati *ed* Ruggero Mastroianni

☆ Peter Gonzales, Fiona Florence, Britta Barnes, Pia de Doses, Marne Maitland, Renato Giovannoli

'Fellini shows a Rome which reflects his own feelings and experiences, in short himself. The film is a huge dream, an offshoot of his *Satyricon*, grotesque, horrible, beautiful.' – *Dily Powell, Sunday Times*

Fellini's Satyricon: see *Satyricon*

Fellow Traveller **

GB/US 1989 97m colour

BFI/BBC Films/HBO (Michael Wearing)

A blacklisted American scriptwriter ponders the suicide of his closest friend, a Hollywood star, and the role played in it by their Marxist psychotherapist.

Intelligent political thriller, despite some melodramatic moments.

w Michael Eaton *d* Philip Saville *ph* John Kenway *m* Colin Towns *pd* Gavin Davies *ed* Greg Miller

☆ Ron Silver, Imogen Stubbs, Hart Bochner, Daniel J. Travanti, Katherine Borowitz, Julian Fellowes, Richard Wilson, Doreen Mantle, David O'Hara

'Thought-provoking, entertaining and visually pleasurable … one of the most original and impressive British films of the 80s' – *Julian Petley, MFB*

'One of the most politically sophisticated, visually imaginative British pictures of the past decade.' – *Philip French, Observer*

Female *

US 1933 60m bw

Warner

A high-powered lady president of a motor car company has a secret night life.

Slick star vehicle reminiscent of Peg's Paper *but absorbing while on screen.*

w Gene Markey, Kathryn Scola *story* Donald Henderson Clarke *d* Michael Curtiz, William Dieterle

☆ Ruth Chatterton, George Brent, Johnny Mack Brown, Ruth Donnelly, Douglass Dumbrille, Lois Wilson

'The story is worthy neither of this actress nor of the high-grade production.' – *Variety*

The Female Animal

US 1957 82m bw Cinemascope

U-I (Albert Zugsmith)

A beach bum becomes the lover of a film star, then falls in love with her daughter.

Dreary and humourless melodrama notable only for the comeback appearance of one of the screen's legendary glamour queens.

w Robert Hill *d* Harry Keller *ph* Russell Metty *m* Hans Salter *ad* Robert Clatworthy, Alexander Golitzen *ed* Milton Carruth

☆ Hedy Lamarr, Jan Sterling, Jane Powell, George Nader, James Gleason

Female Jungle

US 1956 69m bw

Burt Kaiser

aka: *The Hangover*

An off-duty cop, too drunk to remember his actions, begins to suspect that he might have been guilty of the murder of an actress.

Minor pulp thriller that attempts a hard-boiled tone, but succeeds only in being corny, with overblown dialogue.

w Burt Kaiser, Bruno Ve Sota *d* Bruno Ve Sota *ph* Elwood Bredell *m* Nicholas Carras *pd* Ben Roseman *ed* Carl Pingitore

☆ Kathleen Crowley, Lawrence Tierney, John Carradine, Jayne Mansfield, Burt Kaiser, James Kodl, Rex Thorsen, Jack Hill, Bruno Ve Sota

'Once she was too hungry for love to be afraid – but now – it was too late!'

The Female on the Beach

US 1955 97m bw

U-I (Albert Zugsmith)

A wealthy widow visits her late husband's beach house and falls for the gigolo next door, who later seems intent on murdering her.

Absurd and jaded melodrama, a rehash of Love from a Stranger, *enlivened by some hilarious love-hate dialogue.*

w Robert Hill, Richard Alan Simmons *d* Joseph Pevney *ph* Charles Lang *m* Joseph Gershenson

☆ Joan Crawford, Jeff Chandler, Jan Sterling, Cecil Kellaway, Natalie Schafer

JOAN CRAWFORD TO JEFF CHANDLER: 'I wouldn't have you if you were hung with diamonds, upside down!'

Female Perversions

US/Germany 1996 113m Foto-Kem

Feature/MAP/Trans Atlantic/Kinowelt/Degeto (Mindy Affrime)

An ambitious Los Angeles lawyer finds herself facing a crisis about her sexuality and her relationship with her academic sister, a compulsive thief.

Stylish but uninvolving feminist critique of male attitudes towards women and women's attitudes towards themselves, though its concentration on nudity, underwear and erotic fantasies suggests that it is aimed at the usual audience for the work of Zalman King, one of its executive producers, who directed Red Shoe Diaries *(for cable TV) and* Wild Orchid *(qv).*

w Julie Herbert, Susan Streitfeld *book* Female Perversions: The Temptations of Emma Bovary by Louise J. Kaplan *d* Susan Streitfeld *ph* Teresa Medina *m* Debbie Wiseman *pd* Missy Stewart *ed* Curtiss Clayton, Leo Trombetta

☆ Tilda Swinton (Eve), Amy Madigan (Madelyn), Karen Sillas (Renee), Frances Fisher (Annunciata), Laila Robins (Emma), Clancy Brown (John), Paulina Porizkova (Langley), Lisa Jane Persky (Margot)

'One of the most disturbing, intriguing feminist films in years … unsettlingly recognisable and often cynically funny.' – *Claire Monk, Sight and Sound*

Female Vampire

France/Belgium 1973 101m Technicolor 'Scope

General Films/Eurocine (Marius Lesoeur)

aka: *Les Avaleuses*

aka: *The Bare Breasted Countess; La Comtesse Noire; La Comtesse aux Seins Nus; Jacula; The Last Thrill; Yacula*

Irina, a mute and frequently naked female vampire, fellates her partners to death.

An attempt to combine horror and soft-core porn, marked by its prolific director's usual out-of-focus zooms; the content is negligible when not risible.

wd J. P. Johnson (Jesús Franco) *ph* Joan Vincent (Jesús Franco) *m* Daniel White *ed* P. Querut (Jesús Franco)

☆ Lina Romay, Jack Taylor, Alice Arno, Monica Swin, Jess Franck (Jesús Franco)

'Even in its original version, one might have grave doubts about a film which relies on such gambits as the question put to Irina by a journalist, "Do you feel ill at ease being descended from a family of vampires?"' – *David McGillivray, MFB*

† The movie exists in several versions, some concentrating on its sexual content, others on horror. The dubbed British video release runs for 94m, while the version shown in UK cinemas in 1978 ran for 59m.

The Feminine Touch

US 1941 97m bw

MGM (Joseph L. Mankiewicz)

A professor gets into woman trouble when he writes a book about jealousy.

Matrimonial comedy rather less interesting than its credits suggest.

w George Oppenheimer, Edmund L. Hartmann, Ogden Nash *d* W. S. Van Dyke *m* Franz Waxman

☆ Rosalind Russell, Don Ameche, Kay Francis, Van Heflin, Donald Meek, Henry Daniell, Sidney Blackmer

La Femme de l'Aviateur: see *The Aviator's Wife*

La Femme de Mon Pote: see *My Best Friend's Girl*

La Femme de Nulle Part *

France 1922 70m approx bw silent

aka: *The Woman from Nowhere*

A woman who feels that her life has been ruined through love returns home and persuades a young girl not to do the same.

A minor atmospheric piece of some power, comparable with Partie de Campagne *and cinematically very interesting.*

wd Louis Delluc *ph* Lucas Gibory *ad* F. Jourdain

☆ Eve Francis, Roger Karl, Gine Avril

Une Femme Disparait *
France 1944 104m bw
Mayer-Burstyn
aka: *A Woman Disappeared*
aka: *Portrait of a Woman*
When a body is found, four people believe it to be that of a loved one who has disappeared; their stories are told in flashback.
Virtually a short story portmanteau to accommodate five performances by its star.
wd Jacques Feyder *novel* Jacques Viot
☆ *Françoise Rosay*, Henri Guisol, Jean Nohain, Claire Gérard

Une Femme Douce **
France 1969 88m Eastmancolor
Academy/Parc/Marianne (Mag Bodard)
aka: *A Gentle Creature*
A husband attempts to explain to the maid the events of his married life which led to his wife's suicide.
A cool and subtle exploration of the gap between a person's understanding of life and reality.
wd Robert Bresson *story* A Gentle Soul by Fyodor Dostoevsky *ph* Ghislain Cloquet *m* Jean Wiener *ad* Pierre Charbonnier *ed* Raymond Lamy
☆ Dominique Sanda, Guy Frangin, Jane Lobre
'One of Bresson's big films, and, like all his others, it is really about confinement and flight – an account of a character pledged to escape.' – *New Yorker*

La Femme du Boulanger **
France 1938 110m bw
Marcel Pagnol
aka: *The Baker's Wife*
Villagers put a stop to the infidelity of the baker's wife because her husband no longer has the heart to make good bread.
Best-known of Pagnol's rustic fables, this rather obvious and long-drawn-out joke is important because international critics hailed it as a work of art (which it isn't) and because it fixed an image of the naughty bucolic French.
wd Marcel Pagnol novel Jean Le Bleu by Jean Giono *ph* Georges Benoit, R. Lendruz, N. Daries *m* Vincent Scotto *ed* Suzanne de Troeye
☆ *Raimu*, Ginette Leclerc, Charles Moulin, Charpin, Maximilienne
'It is a long film with a small subject, but the treatment is so authentic that it seems over far too soon, and the acting is superb.' – *Graham Greene*

Une Femme Est une Femme: see *A Woman Is a Woman*

'A secret life. A deadly passion.'
Femme Fatale
US 1991 96m Foto-Kem
Republic/Gibraltar Entertainment (Andrew Lane, Nancy Rae Stone)
After his wife leaves him at the start of their honeymoon, a husband discovers that she has more than one identity.
Anonymous thriller that stumbles to a lame conclusion.
w Michael Ferris, John D. Brancato *d* André Guttfreund *ph* Joey Forsyte *m* Parmer Fuller *pd* Pam Warner *ed* Richard Candib
☆ Colin Firth, Lisa Zane, Billy Zane, Scott Wilson, Lisa Blount, Suzanne Snyder

Une Femme Française *
France/GB/Germany 1995 98m Eastmancolor
UGC/TF1/Recorded Pictures/DA/Studio Babelsberg (Yves Marmion)
aka: *A French Woman*
During and after the Second World War, the wife of a French soldier has numerous affairs while her husband serves in Germany, Syria, Indochina and Algeria.
A glossy, highly charged, sometimes diverting, episodic account of an unhappy relationship over a period of 15 years; its restless, promiscuous heroine may be intended as a symbol of France during a period of social upheaval and, on this wider level, it fails to convince.
w Regis Wargnier, Alain Le Henry *d* Regis Wargnier *ph* François Catonné *m* Patrick Doyle *pd* Jacques Bufnoir *ed* Genevieve Winding, Agnes Schwab
☆ Emmanuelle Beart, Daniel Auteuil, Gabriel Barylli, Jean-Claude Brialy, Genevieve Casile, Michel Etcheverry, Heinz Bennent
'A painless slice of handsome moviemaking that offers goodly guilty pleasures.' – *Variety*

La Femme Infidèle **
France/Italy 1968 98m Eastmancolor
La Boëtie/Cinegay (André Génovès)
aka: *The Unfaithful Wife*
A middle-aged insurance broker, set in his ways, murders his wife's lover; when she suspects the truth, they are drawn closer together.
Almost a Buñuel-like black comedy, spare and quiet, with immaculate performances.
wd Claude Chabrol ph Jean Rabier *m* Pierre Jansen *ed* Jacques Gaillard
☆ Stéphane Audran, Michel Bouquet, Maurice Ronet
'On any level, this bizarre murder framed by whiskies emerges as Chabrol's most flawless work to date.' – *Jan Dawson, MFB*

Une Femme Mariée: see *A Married Woman*

La Femme Nikita: see *Nikita*

Une Femme ou Deux
France 1985 97m colour
AAA/Hachette/Philippe Dussart/FR3/DD (Michel Choquet)
aka: *One Woman or Two*
An advertising woman uses an archaeologist as basis for a new campaign, then falls in love with him.
Lighthearted, not to say light-headed, romantic comedy with silly asides: Doris Day and Rock Hudson, where are you?
w Daniel Vigne, Elizabeth Rappeneau *d* Daniel Vigne *ph* Carlo Varini *m* Kevin Mulligan, Evert Verhees, Toots Thielemans *ad* Jean-Pierre Kohut-Svelko *ed* Marie-Josèphe Yoyotte
☆ Gérard Depardieu, Sigourney Weaver, Michel Aumont, Dr Ruth Westheimer, Zabou, Jean-Pierre Bisson
'Unsatisfactory on all levels.' – *Quentin Crisp*

La Femme-flic *
France 1979 100m Eastmancolor
Sara/Antenne 2 (Alain Sarde)
aka: *The Lady Cop*
A female police inspector who becomes a political embarrassment is transferred to the provinces, where she is subjected to high-level interference when she uncovers a child pornography racket.
Tough and cynical political thriller which comes to the conclusion that honesty is far from the best policy.
w Claude Veillot *story* Claude Veillot, Yves Boisset *d* Yves Boisset *ph* Jacques Loiseleux *m* Philippe Sarde *pd* Maurice Sergent, Jimmy Vansteenkiste *ed* Albert Jurgenson, Nadine Muse, Martine Fleury
☆ Miou-Miou, Jean-Marc Thibault, Leny Escudero, Jean-Pierre Kalfon, François Simon, Alex Lacast, Niels Arestrup, Henri Garçin, Philippe Caubere

Femmes de Paris *
France 1954 85m approx Agfacolor
Optimax-Lux (Edgar Bacquet)
aka: *Ah! Les Belles Bacchantes*
A touring revue is almost run out of town for indecency.
A rather crude but quite valuable record of Dhéry's stage revue, which convulsed London in the fifties.
w Robert Dhéry *d* Jean Loubignac *ph* René Colas *m* Gérard Calvi
☆ Robert Dhéry, Colette Brosset, Louis de Funès, Raymond Bussières, the Bluebell Girls

The Fencing Master ***
Spain 1992 88m colour
Mayfair/Majestic/Origen/Altube Filmeak/ICAA (Antonio Cardenal, Pedro Olea)
original title: *El Maestro de Esgrima*
In Madrid in the 1860s, at a time of extreme political upheaval, a fencing master becomes involved with a beautiful woman and finds himself caught up in a situation he does not understand.
Elegant, erotically charged story of love and loyalty and of different codes of behaviour, told with subtlety, dash and elegance.
w Antonio Larreta, Francisco Prada, Arturo Pérez Reverte, Pedro Olea *novel* Arturo Pérez Reverte *d Pedro Olea ph* Alfredo Mayo *m* José Nieto *ad* Luis Valles *ed* José Salcedo
☆ *Omero Antonutti, Assumpta Serna*, Joaquim de Almeida, José Luis Lopez Vázquez, Alberto Closas, Miguel Rellán
'Stellar performances ... a distinguished and literate script, fine plot development and accomplished direction and lensing.' – *Variety*
'A deeply romantic Spanish thriller with two performances at its centre that do more than catch the eye. At times they catch the breath.' – *Derek Malcolm, Guardian*

Fengyue: see *Temptress Moon*

La Ferme du Pendu *
France 1946 90m bw
Corona
aka: *Hanged Man's Farm*
The lecherous son of a farming family brings tragedy to the lives of himself and his brothers and sister.
Cold Comfort Farm with a vengeance, appropriately played: arrant melodrama, but watchable.
w André-Paul Antoine *d* Jean Dréville *ph* André Thomas *m* Marcel Delannoy
☆ Alfred Adam, Charles Vanel, Arlette Merry

FernGully: The Last Rainforest
Australia 1992 76m DeLuxe
TCF/FAI/Youngheart (Wayne Young, Peter Faiman)
A fairy, a fruit-bat and a miniaturized lumberjack save the rainforest from the evil spirit who would destroy it.
Moderately enjoyable animated feature with an ecological moral: be kind to trees.
w Jim Cox *story* Diana Young *d* Bill Kroyer *m* Alan Silvestri *ad* Susan Kroyer *ed* Gillian Hutshing
☆ Featuring the voices of: Tim Curry, Samantha Mathis, Christian Slater, Jonathan Ward, Robin Williams, Grace Zabriskie, Geoffrey Blake, Robert Pastorelli, Cheech Marin, Thomas Chong, Tone-Loc
'As lectures on the environment go, this one is less likely to induce adult narcolepsy than most.' – *Ian Johnstone, Sunday Times*
'Pic will amply entertain tykes while feeding them an environmental lesson, and features enough amusing jokes and clever songs to make it palatable for adults.' – *Variety*

Ferris Bueller's Day Off *
US 1986 103m Metrocolor
Panavision
Paramount/John Hughes, Tom Jacobson
A teenage student enjoys an aimless day playing truant.
Aimless it is, and juvenile, but people have found pleasing things in it.
wd John Hughes *ph* Tak Fujimoto *m* Ira Newborn *pd* John W. Corso *ed* Paul Hirsch
☆ Matthew Broderick, Alan Ruck, Mia Sara, Jeffrey Jones, Cindy Pickett, Jennifer Grey

Ferry to Hong Kong
GB 1958 113m Eastmancolor
Cinemascope
Rank (George Maynard)
An Austrian layabout can land at neither of the Hong Kong ferry's ports of call, but shows his true worth when a typhoon strikes.
Silly storyline and rampant bad acting ruin the Rank Organization's first attempt at an international epic.
w Vernon Harris, Lewis Gilbert *d* Lewis Gilbert *ph* Otto Heller *m* Kenneth V. Jones
☆ Curt Jurgens, Sylvia Syms, Orson Welles, Jeremy Spenser, Noel Purcell

Festen ***
Denmark 1998 105m colour
October/Nimbus/DR TV/SVT Drama (Brigitte Hald)
aka: *The Celebration*
At a formal dinner to celebrate a patriarch's 60th birthday, his eldest son makes a speech claiming that his father sexually abused him as a child, and drove his twin sister to kill herself.
Unsettling, nervy drama, in which the edgy acting and twitchy camera combine to give a raw, emotional power to the narrative.
w Thomas Vinterberg, Mogens Rukov *d* Thomas Vinterberg *ph* Anthony Dod Mantle *ed* Valdis Oskarsdottir
☆ Ulrich Thomsen, Henning Moritzen, Thomas Bo Larsen, Paprika Steen, Birthe Neumann, Trine Dyrholm, Helle Dolleris, Therese Glahn, Klaus Bondam, Bjarne Henriksen, Gbatokai Dakinah
'As smart, sharp and stinging as a slap around the face.' – *Tom Shone, Sunday Times*
† The film was made under the dictates of Dogma 95, of which Vinterberg was a signatory; its conditions laid down for film-making include location shooting, direct sound, and hand-held camerawork.

La Fête à Henriette *
France 1952 113m bw
Regina-Filmsonor
aka: *Holiday for Henrietta*
Two screenwriters disagree whether or not to give their hero and heroine a happy ending.
A rather heavy-handed romantic joke which does have its moments and was later – fatally – Americanized as Paris When It Sizzles.
w Julien Duvivier, Henri Jeanson *d* Julien Duvivier *ph* Roger Hubert *m* Georges Auric
☆ Dany Robin, Michel Auclair, Hildegarde Neff, Michel Roux, Saturnin Fabre, Julien Carette

Le Feu Follet ***
France 1963 107m bw
Lux/Nouvelles éditions (Jean Pieuchot)
US title: *The Fire Within*
aka: *Will-O'-The-Wisp; A Time to Live and a Time to Die*
A recovering alcoholic, urged to be positive, visits his old friends and, horrified by the compromises they have made, kills himself.
A compassionate and fascinating film, shot in an understated way; though, with its downbeat ending, it is not easy viewing.
wd Louis Malle novel Pierre Drieu La Rochelle *ph* Ghislain Cloquet *m* Erik Satie *ad* Bernard Evein *ed* Suzanne Baron, Monique Nana
☆ *Maurice Ronet*, Léna Skerla, Jeanne Moreau, Yvonne Clech, Hubert Deschamps, Alexandra Stewart
'An epitaph for all the beautiful young men, the semi-intellectual "gilded mediocrities" who skim through their days to their doom unchanged save for a surface tarnish. A latter-day parable of a Dorian Gray, superbly acted and beautifully filmed.' – *Judith Crist*

A Fever in the Blood
US 1960 117m bw
Warner (Roy Huggins)
Candidates for governor sharpen their campaigns on a murder trial.
Interestingly-cast, flabbily-written melodrama.
w Roy Huggins, Harry Kleiner *novel* William Pearson *d* Vincent Sherman *ph* J. Peverell Marley *m* Ernest Gold
☆ Efrem Zimbalist Jnr, Angie Dickinson, Don Ameche, Herbert Marshall, Jack Kelly, Ray Danton, Jesse White, Rhodes Reason, Robert Colbert

Fever Pitch
US 1985 96m Metrocolor
MGM-UA/Freddie Fields
A compulsive Vegas gambler gets in deep with loan sharks.
You might think there was more to the plot than that, but no; and the whole thing is just glum.
wd Richard Brooks *ph* William Fraker *m* Thomas Dolby *pd* Raymond G. Storey
☆ Ryan O'Neal, Catherine Hicks, Giancarlo Giannini, Bridgette Andersen, Chad Everett, John Saxon
'The cards are stacked against it.' – *Variety*

'Life Gets Complicated When You Love One Woman and Worship Eleven Men.'

Fever Pitch *

GB 1996 102m Rank Colour
Film Four/Wildgaze (Amanda Posey)

A soccer-mad London comprehensive school English teacher neglects his girlfriend in his obsession for Arsenal Football Club.
A small-scale attempt at a romantic comedy, which finds its climax in a real-life event – Arsenal's triumph in the last moment of their last game to win the league championship – but otherwise indulges in a fantasy of a man behaving badly and getting away with it.
w Nick Hornby *book* Nick Hornby *d* David Evans *ph* Chris Seager *pd* Michael Carlin *ed* Scott Thomas
☆ Colin Firth, Ruth Gemmell, Neil Pearson, Lorraine Ashbourne, Mark Strong, Holly Aird, Ken Stott, Stephen Rea
'Should do as well as Arsenal – though, like them, it is a little dull to watch.' – *Derek Malcolm, Guardian*

A Few Good Men **

US 1992 138m Technicolor Panavision
Columbia TriStar/Castle Rock (David Brown, Rob Reiner, Andrew Scheinman)

A lawyer known for plea bargaining decides to defend two marines accused of killing a fellow marine, a case that depends on discrediting their martinet of a commanding officer.
Slick, engrossing courtroom drama, in which audiences can cheer the hero and hiss the villain, even though it seems little more than a more portentous re-run of The Caine Mutiny.
w Aaron Sorkin *play* Aaron Sorkin *d* Rob Reiner *ph* Robert Richardson *m* Marc Shaiman *pd* J. Michael Riva *ed* Robert Leighton
☆ Tom Cruise, Jack Nicholson, Demi Moore, Kevin Bacon, Kiefer Sutherland, Kevin Pollak, James Marshall, J. T. Walsh, Christopher Guest, J. A. Preston
'A big-time, mainstream Hollywood movie par excellence.' – *Variety*
'A slick, entertaining, flashily-acted courtroom drama replete with all the standard ingredients.' – *Philip French, Observer*
Best picture; Jack Nicholson; Robert Leighton

ffoulkes: see *North Sea Hijack*

Fiddler on the Roof **

US 1971 180m Technicolor Panavision 70
UA/Mirisch (Norman Jewison)

In a pre-revolutionary Russian village, Tevye the Jewish milkman survives family and political problems and when the pogroms begin cheerfully emigrates to America.
Self-conscious, grittily realistic adaptation of the stage musical, with slow and heavy patches in its grossly overlong celebration of a vanished way of life. The big moments still come off well though the songs tend to be thrown away and the photography is unnecessarily murky.
w Joseph Stein *play* Joseph Stein *story* *Tevye and his Daughters* by *Sholom Aleichem* *d* Norman Jewison *ph* Oswald Morris *m/ly* *Jerry Bock, Sheldon Harnick* *md* John Williams *pd* Robert Boyle
☆ *Topol*, Norma Crane, Leonard Frey, Molly Picon
'Jewison hasn't so much directed a film as prepared a product for world consumption.' – *Stanley Kauffmann*
Oswald Morris; John Williams
best picture; Norman Jewison (as director); Topol; Leonard Frey

Fiddlers Three *

GB 1944 87m bw
Ealing (Robert Hamer)

Sailors struck by lightning on Salisbury Plain are transported back to ancient Rome.
Sequel to Sailors Three; *despite a harsh and unattractive look, every conceivable joke about old Romans is deftly mined and the good humour flows free.*
w *Diana Morgan, Angus Macphail* *d* Harry Watt *ph* Wilkie Cooper *m* Spike Hughes
☆ *Tommy Trinder, Sonnie Hale, Frances Day, Francis L. Sullivan*, Ernest Milton, Diana Decker, Elisabeth Welch, Mary Clare, Kay Kendall

'It Owns Him. It Possesses Him. It Could Even Destroy Him.'

The Field *

GB 1990 110m colour
Granada (Noel Pearson)

A farmer is prepared to kill in order to keep a rented field which his family has farmed for generations and which an American wishes to buy.
Melodramatic domestic drama trying for a tragic dimension it cannot quite encompass.
wd Jim Sheridan *play* John B. Keane *ph* Jack Conroy *m* Elmer Bernstein *pd* Frank Conway *ad* Frank Hallinan Flood *ed* J. Patrick Duffner
☆ Richard Harris, John Hurt, Tom Berenger, Sean Bean, Frances Tomelty, Brenda Fricker
'Superb acting and austere visual beauty are offset by a somewhat overheated screenplay.' – *Variety*
Richard Harris

Field of Dreams ***

US 1989 106m DeLuxe
Guild/Universal/Carolco (Lawrence Gordon, Charles Gordon)

A farmer builds a baseball pitch to summon the ghosts of past players.
A gentle fantasy with the power to charm.
wd Phil Alden Robinson *book* *Shoeless Joe* by W. P. Kinsella *ph* John Lindley *m* James Horner *pd* Dennis Gassner *ed* Ian Crafford
☆ Kevin Costner, Amy Madigan, James Earl Jones, Timothy Busfield, Ray Liotta, Burt Lancaster, Gaby Hoffman, Frank Whaley, Dwier Brown
best film; best adapted screenplay; best original score

'It's a sickness of the soul!'

The Fiend

GB 1971 87m colour
Miracle/World Arts Media (Robert Hartford-Davis)

US title: *Beware My Brethren*
A journalist investigates a religious cult that may harbour a serial killer of young girls.
Trivial slasher movie with an inadequate script and a heavy-handed directorial approach, forever cutting back and forth between two separate but similar events.
w Brian Comport *d* Robert Hartford-Davis *ph* Desmond Dickinson *m* Tony Osborne, Richard Kerr *ad* George Provis *ed* Alan Patillo
☆ Ann Todd (Birdy Wemys), Patrick Magee (Minister), Tony Beckley (Kenny Wemys), Madeleine Hinde (Brigitte Lynch), Percy Herbert (Commissionaire), Suzanna Leigh (Paddy Lynch), David Lodge (CID Inspector), Ronald Allen (Paul)
'Flat and colourless.' – *MFB*

'Don't be ashamed to scream! Everyone in the theatre will be screaming with you!'

The Fiend Who Walked the West

US 1958 101m bw Cinemascope
TCF (Herbert B. Swope Jnr)

A sadistic killer released from prison tracks down the associates of a cellmate and terrorizes the district.
Western remake of Kiss of Death, *with babyface Robert Evans in the Widmark role. Violent and dull.*
w Harry Brown, Philip Yordan *d* Gordon Douglas *ph* Joe MacDonald *m* Leon Klatzkin
☆ Hugh O'Brian, Dolores Michaels, Robert Evans, Linda Cristal, Stephen McNally, Edward Andrews

'New Horrors! Mad Science Spawns Evil Fiends!'

Fiend without a Face

GB 1957 75m bw
Eros/Producers Associates (John Croydon)

A scientist working on materialized thought produces monsters from his own id.
Tepid shocker with well-organized mobile brains.
w Herbert J. Leder *story* Amelia Reynolds Long *d* Arthur Crabtree *ph* Lionel Banes *m* Buxton Orr *md* Frederic Lewis *ad* John Elphick *ed* R.O. McNaughton *sp* Ruppel & Nordhoff, Peter Neilson
☆ Marshall Thompson (Major Cummings), Kynaston Reeves (Prof. Walgate), Terence Kilburn (Capt. Chester), Kim Parker (Barbara Griselle), Stanley Maxted (Col Butler), James Dyrenforth (Mayor), Robert MacKenzie (Constable Gibbons), Michael Balfour (Sgt Kasper)

The Fiendish Plot of Dr Fu Manchu

US 1980 108m Technicolor
Warner/Orion/Playboy (Hugh Hefner)

The 'yellow peril' returns to the western world to mastermind diamond thefts.
Feeble spoof with a history of production troubles; clearly the only thing in anybody's mind was to get it over with.
w Jim Moloney, Rudy Dochtermann *d* Piers Haggard *ph* Jean Tournier *m* Marc Wilkinson *pd* Alexander Trauner
☆ Peter Sellers, Helen Mirren, David Tomlinson, Sid Caesar, Simon Williams, Steve Franken, Stratford Johns, John Le Mesurier, Clive Dunn

The Fiends: see *Les Diaboliques*

'Don't Pet Them.'

Fierce Creatures

GB/US 1997 95m Rank Colour Panavision
Universal/Fish Productions/Jersey Films (Michael Shamberg, John Cleese)

A megalomaniacal tycoon puts an incompetent ex-policeman in charge of running an English zoo.
A floundering comedy that never gets its act together; its running jokes are lame, and the satire is heavy-handed.
w John Cleese, Ian Johnstone *d* Robert Young, Fred Schepisi *ph* Adrian Biddle, Ian Baker *m* Jerry Goldsmith *pd* Roger Murray-Leach *ed* Robert Gibson
☆ John Cleese (Rollo Lee), Jamie Lee Curtis (Willa Weston), Kevin Kline (Vince McCain/Rod McCaine), Michael Palin (Adrian Malone), Ronnie Corbett (Reggie Sealions), Carey Lowell (Cub Felines), Robert Lindsay (Sydney Small Mammals)
'A distracting little comedy with an Ealing-esque theme and a clutch of star names giving their all to a script which they know is beneath them.' – *Independent*
† After previews in December 1995, the film's release was delayed by more than a year so that new scenes could be shot, in which Kline, as the tycoon's son, does not die. It took six months to reassemble the cast, by which time director Robert Young was busy elsewhere. So Fred Schepisi replaced him for the three weeks, filming additional material.

Fiesta

US 1947 102m Technicolor
MGM (Jack Cummings)

A young Mexican wants to be a musician though his father insists he should be a bullfighter.
An extremely boring idea for a musical which at best is a tedious time-passer.
w George Bruce, Lester Cole *d* Richard Thorpe *ph* Sidney Wagner, Charles Rosner, William Cline *m* Aaron Copland *md* John Green
☆ Esther Williams, Ricardo Montalban, Cyd Charisse, Mary Astor, John Carroll, Akim Tamiroff, Hugo Haas
John Green

Fièvre *

France 1921 50m approx bw silent
Alhambre

A brawl in a Marseilles bar ends in murder.
A dramatic sketch, filmed with remarkable detail and artistry.
wd *Louis Delluc* *ph* A. Gibory *ad* Bécan
☆ Eve Francis, Edmond Van Daele, Gaston Modot

Fifi la Plume

France 1964 80m bw
Les Films Montsouris (Albert Lamorisse)

A burglar becomes a circus bird-man, learns to fly, and is everywhere mistaken for an angel.
A likeable fantasy idea which doesn't quite come off, alternating uneasily between slapstick and sentiment.
wd Albert Lamorisse *ph* Pierre Petit *m* Jean-Michel Defaye
☆ Philippe Avron, Mireille Nègre, Henri Lambert, Raoul Delfosse

'America's had enough.'

15 Minutes *

US 2000 120m DeLuxe Panavision
New Line/Industry Entertainment/New Redemption/Tribeca (Nick Wechsler, Keith Addis, David Blocker, John Herzfeld)

A publicity-loving detective and a fire investigator team up to solve murders committed by an Eastern European pair who videotape a killing and sell the footage to a TV news show.
An action thriller is combined with an angry satire on those who seek their 15 minutes of fame and the celebrity-worshipping media that encourages them; it doesn't cohere and the violence panders to the audience it condemns, but at least it is thought-provoking.
wd John Herzfeld *ph* Jean Yves Escoffier *m* Anthony Marinelli, J. Peter Robinson *pd* Mayne Berke *ed* Steven Cohen
☆ Robert De Niro (Eddie Flemming), Edward Burns (Jordy Warsaw), Kelsey Grammer (Robert Hawkins), Avery Brooks (Leon Jackson), Melina Kanakaredes (Nicolette Karas), Karel Roden (Emil Slovak), Oleg Taktarov (Oleg Razgul), Daphne Handlova (Vera Farmiga), John DiResta (Bobby Korfin), James Handy (Captain Duffy), Charlize Theron (Rose Hearn), Kim Cattrall (Cassandra), David Alan Grier (Mugger)
'A thriller more contrived than it is exciting.' – *Todd McCarthy, Variety*
'It expands Warhol's witticism to say, more or less, "In the future, everyone will be a world-famous psycho killer for 15 minutes, and everyone will also be a world-famous psycho killer's victim for roughly the same amount of time."' – *Jonathan Rosenbaum, Chicago Reader*

Fifth Avenue Girl *

US 1939 83m bw
RKO (Gregory La Cava)

An unemployed girl is persuaded by a millionaire to pose as a gold digger and annoy his avaricious family.
Brightish comedy of the Cinderella kind.
w Allan Scott *d* Gregory La Cava *ph* Robert de Grasse
☆ Ginger Rogers, Walter Connolly, Verree Teasdale, Tim Holt, James Ellison, Franklin Pangborn, Kathryn Adams, Louis Calhern
'Substantial comedy drama for top grosses.' – *Variety*

The Fifth Chair: see *It's in the Bag*

The Fifth Cord (dubbed)

Italy 1971 100m Eastmancolor
Jumbo/BRC/Dario (Manolo Bolognini)

original title: *Giornata Nera per L'Ariete*
aka: *Evil Fingers*
A journalist investigating a crime becomes a murder suspect when people he questions are murdered.
Uninteresting thriller with cardboard characters and a teasing narrative.
w Mario di Nardo, Mario Fenelli, Luigi Bazzoni *novel* D. M. Devine *d* Luigi Bazzoni *ph* Vittorio Storaro *m* Ennio Morricone *ad* Gastone Carsetti *ed* Eugenio Alabiso
☆ Franco Nero, Silvia Monti, Wolfgang Preiss, Ira Furstenberg, Edmund Purdom, Maurizio Bonuglia, Pamela Tiffin, Renato Romano
'Shoals of red herrings do little to make up for … meagre characterisation, the scrambled course of its plot, or its shamefully deceptive ending.' – *David McGillivray, MFB*
† The British release in 1973 was cut by the censor to 80m. The UK video release runs for 89m.

The Fifth Element *

France 1997 127m Technicolor Super 35
Columbia/Gaumont (Patrice Ledoux)

original title: *Le Cinquième Elément*
In 2214, a taxi driver, a monk and a supreme being (a willowy blonde with garishly dyed red hair) save the world from total destruction.
Juvenile space hokum that derives from pulp writing of the 30s; its visual style and simple action narrative attracted a mass audience, presumably hungering for mindless entertainment, since that is what it successfully delivers.

w Luc Besson, Robert Mark Kamen *d* Luc Besson *ph* Thierry Arbogast *m* Eric Serra *pd* Dan Weil *ed* Sylvie Landra *sp* Digital Domain
☆ Bruce Willis (Korben Dallas), Gary Oldman (Zorg), Ian Holm (Cornelius), Milla Jovovich (Leeloo), Chris Tucker (Ruby Rhod), Luke Perry (Billy), Brion James (General Munro), John Neville, John Bluthal, Mathieu Kassovitz, Lee Evans

'This mishmash of half-baked futuristic, mythological, quasi-religious, big-scale action and would-be romantic motifs. Despite the hefty production coin, there is something left to be desired about nearly every aspect of the picture, from the narrative line and vision of the future to the score and execution of the special effects, that will combine to turn off all but the most avid teen sci-fi fans long before the pic comes in for its final landing.' – *Todd McCarthy, Variety*

'A massively bad, massively stupid film.' – *Jim Schembri, Melbourne Age*

† The film, at a cost of around $89m, was the most expensive so far made in France, and had its origins in a script Besson wrote at the age of 16. It took around $63m at the US box-office and more than $200m elsewhere in the world.

sound effects editing

The Fifth Monkey

US 1990 93m Rank Colour
21st Century (Menahem Golan)

In Brazil, a snake hunter finds four chimpanzees and travels across country in search of a buyer for them so that he can earn enough to get married.

Pleasant but inconsequential drama; the exotic setting appears to have interested its makers more than the episodic and clichéd narrative, though Kingsley brings his customary intensity to his role in an attempt to prevent the apes from stealing the film.

wd Eric Rochat *novel* Le Cinquième Singe by Jacques Zibi *ph* Gideon Porath *m* Robert O. Ragland *ad* Pedro Nanni *ed* Alain Jakubowicz, Fabien D. Tordjmann
☆ Ben Kingsley, Mika Lins, Silvia de Carvalho, Vera Fischer, Carlos Kroeber, Julio Levy

The Fifth Musketeer

Austria 1978 106m Eastmancolor
Sascha-Wien Film/Ted Richmond

aka: *Behind the Iron Mask*

Louis XIII and his twin brother Philippe vie for the crown of France.

Virtually a remake of The Man in the Iron Mask, *with patchy style and a few excisable sex scenes added. The 1939 version was better.*

w David Ambrose *d* Ken Annakin *ph* Jack Cardiff *m* Riz Ortolani
☆ Beau Bridges, Sylvia Kristel, Ursula Andress, Cornel Wilde (D'Artagnan), Lloyd Bridges, Alan Hale Jnr, José Ferrer, Rex Harrison (Colbert), Olivia de Havilland (Queen Anne), Ian McShane, Helmut Dantine

'Nice Wheels. Dirty Deals. And One Mean Mother In A Kilt.'

The 51st State

GB/Canada 2001 92m DeLuxe 'Scope
Momentum/Focus/51st/Alliance Atlantis (David Pupkewitz, Malcolm Kohll, Andras Hamori, Seaton McLean, Jonathan Debin)

US title: *Formula 51*

The American creator of a new drug goes to Liverpool to sell the formula for $20m to the local drug baron.

Loud and pointless gangster movie with over-the-top acting and a dim-witted, foul-mouthed script.

w Stel Pavlou *d* Ronny Yu *ph* Poon Hang-sang *m* Headrillaz *pd* Alan MacDonald *ed* David Wu
☆ Samuel L. Jackson (Elmo McElroy), Robert Carlyle (Felix DeSouza), Emily Mortimer (Dakota Phillips), Rhys Ifans (Iki), Meatloaf (The Lizard), Sean Pertwee (Det. Virgil Kane), Ricky Tomlinson (Leopold Durant), Steven Walters (Blowfish)

'Ferociously entertaining comic thriller.' – *James Cameron-Wilson, Film Review*

'It is truly, utterly and irreparably dreadful.' – *Derek Malcolm, Guardian*

55 Days at Peking *

US/Spain 1963 154m Super Technirama 70
Samuel Bronston

In 1900 Peking, Boxer fanatics are encouraged by the Empress to take over the city and besiege the international diplomatic quarter; an American major leads the defence.

Spasmodically lively action spectacular weighed down by romantic stretches.

w Philip Yordan, Bernard Gordon *d* Nicholas Ray, Andrew Marton *ph* Jack Hildyard, Manuel Berenguer *m* Dimitri Tiomkin *ad* Venerio Colasanti, John Moore
☆ Charlton Heston, David Niven, Ava Gardner, Flora Robson, Robert Helpmann, Leo Genn, Paul Lukas, John Ireland, Harry Andrews, Elizabeth Sellars, Massimo Serrato, Jacques Sernas, Geoffrey Bayldon

'An open-air western in Chinese.' – *David Niven*

'Pictorially this is a beautiful film, but the characters are conventional siege figures.' – *Sunday Times*

Dimitri Tiomkin; song 'So Little Time' (*m* Dimitri Tiomkin, *ly* Paul Francis Webster)

'The Story That Seduced The World Is Now The Most Provocative Film Of The Year.'

54

US 1998 92m DeLuxe
Miramax/Redeemable Features/Dollface/Film Colony (Richard N. Gladstein, Dolly Hall, Ira Deutchman)

In the late 70s, a working-class youth gets a job in New York's most fashionable disco, where he observes the decadent, drug-fuelled lifestyle of the wealthy.

Tame, inhibited biopic of club-owner Steve Rubell, entrepreneur of the disco culture of the 70s; the real thing must have been more interesting, otherwise no one would ever have gone to Studio 54.

wd Mark Christopher *ph* Alexander Gruszynski *m* Marco Beltrami *pd* Kevin Thompson *ed* Lee Percy
☆ Ryan Phillippe, Salma Hayek, Neve Campbell, Mike Myers, Sela Ward, Breckin Meyer, Sherry Stringfield, Ellen Albertini Dow, Heather Matarazzo, Skipp Sudduth, Aemillia Robinson, Lauren Hutton, Michael York

'Those expecting any real insight into the 70s club scene will come away hugely disappointed.' – *Caroline Westbrook, Empire*

'His Wife... His Mistress... His Career... A Deadly Trap.'

52 Pick-up

US 1986 114m TVC Color
Cannon (Henry T. Weinstein)

A businessman rounds on blackmailers who take films of his sex life.

Uninteresting melodrama based on the same novel as The Ambassador, *released two years earlier by the same company.*

w Elmore Leonard, John Steppling *novel* Elmore Leonard *d* John Frankenheimer *ph* Jost Vacano *m* Gary Chang
☆ Roy Scheider, Ann-Margret, Vanity, John Glover, Robert Trebor, Lonny Chapman

'There is no rush of energy to propel the film past its improbability.' – *Variety*

'Mischief. Mayhem. Soap.'

Fight Club *

US 1999 139m Technicolor Panavision
TCF/Fox 2000/Regency (Art Linson, Cean Chaffin, Ross Grayson Bell)

Tired of his life as a cog in a corporate and consumer society, an insomniac businessman sets up secret clubs where men indulge in bare-knuckle fighting and anarchist activities.

It is impossible to take seriously the film's sado-masochistic posturing, its insistence that inflicting and suffering pain is redemptive; but as a blackly comic updating of Dr Jekyll and Mr Hyde, a sick fantasy of a man in two minds, it has its moments.

w Jim Uhls *novel* Chuck Palahniuk *d* David Fincher *ph* Jeff Cronenweth *m* Dust Brothers *pd* Alex McDowell *ed* James Haygood
☆ Brad Pitt (Tyler Durden), Edward Norton (Narrator), Helena Bonham Carter (Marla Singer), Meat Loaf (Robert Paulsen), Jared Leto (Angel Face)

'There are sequences in this film I never thought I would see on a screen; ideas I never believed a responsible Hollywood corporation would permit to be voiced as popular entertainment.' – *Alexander Walker, London Evening Standard*

'A fascist rhapsody posing as a metaphor of liberation… a laborious and foolish waste of time.' – *David Denby, New Yorker*

'Witless mishmash of whiny, infantile philosophising and bone-crunching violence' – *Kenneth Turan*

† The BBFC cut eight seconds from the film for its UK release.

sound effects editing (Ren Klyce, Richard Hymns)

The Fighter

US 1952 78m bw
GH (Alex Gottlieb)

A Mexican fisherman whose family is murdered by government troops becomes a prizefighter to earn money for the rebels.

A rather glum attempt to turn a few ringside clichés.

w Aben Kandel, Herbert Kline *story* The Mexican by Jack London *d* Herbert Kline *ph* James Wong Howe *m* Vincente Gomez
☆ Richard Conte, Vanessa Brown, Lee J. Cobb, Frank Silvera

Fighter Squadron

US 1948 96m Technicolor
Warner (Seton I. Miller)

In World War II, a dedicated flyer risks his friends' lives.

Routine aerial actioner.

w Seton I. Miller *d* Raoul Walsh *ph* Sid Hickox, Wilfrid M. Cline *m* Max Steiner
☆ Edmond O'Brien, Robert Stack, John Rodney, Tom D'Andrea, Henry Hull, Walter Reed, Shepperd Strudwick, Rock Hudson

The Fighting 69th *

US 1940 89m bw
Warner (Hal B. Wallis)

During World War I in the trenches, a cocky recruit becomes a hero and loses his life in the process.

Recruiting poster stuff, all well enough done but bewildering in its changes of mood.

w Norman Reilly Raine, Fred Niblo Jnr, Dean Franklin *d* William Keighley *ph* Tony Gaudio *m* Adolph Deutsch
☆ James Cagney, Pat O'Brien, George Brent, Jeffrey Lynn, Alan Hale, Frank McHugh, Dennis Morgan, Dick Foran, William Lundigan, Guinn Williams, John Litel, Henry O'Neill

'The picture is better if you can manage to forget the plot and think of it instead as the human, amusing and frequently gripping record of a regiment marching off to war.' – *Frank Nugent, New York Times*

'Enough is enough!'

Fighting Back

US 1982 98m Technicolor
Dino de Laurentiis (D. Constantine Conte)

GB title: *Death Vengeance*

After his wife and mother are both injured in crimes of violence, a delicatessen owner forms a vigilante group and is backed to some extent by police and businessmen.

Smartly made but ethically muddled urban shocker.

w Tom Hedley, David Zelag Goodman *d* Lewis Teague *ph* Franco DiGiacomo *m* Piero Piccioni
☆ Tom Skerritt, Michael Sarrazin, Patti LuPone, Yaphet Kotto, David Rasche

Fighting Father Dunne

US 1948 93m bw
RKO (Phil L. Ryan)

A clergyman looks after unfortunate boys.

A slum melodrama which all concerned could have made with their eyes closed, and probably did.

w Martin Rackin, Frank Davis *d* Ted Tetzlaff *ph* George E. Diskant *m* Roy Webb
☆ Pat O'Brien, Darryl Hickman, Charles Kemper, Una O'Connor

The Fighting Guardsman

US 1945 84m bw
Columbia

Under the tyrannical reign of Louis XVI a young nobleman leads a peasants' revolt.

Stiff swashbuckler in which the actors appear to have been only recently introduced to their clothes.

w Franz Spencer, Edward Dein *d* Henry Levin
☆ Willard Parker, Anita Louise, George Macready, John Loder

Fighting Justice: see *True Believer*

The Fighting Kentuckian

US 1949 100m bw
Republic (John Wayne)

In 1810 a farmer combats land-grabbing criminals.

Standard star Western for the family.

wd George Waggner *ph* Lee Garmes *m* George Antheil
☆ John Wayne, Vera Ralston, Oliver Hardy, Philip Dorn, Marie Windsor, Mae Marsh

Fighting Mad

US 1976 90m DeLuxe
TCF/Santa Fe (Roger Corman)

A rancher and his son are murdered by a local industrialist who wants their land, and the rancher's city-bred son takes revenge.

Another vigilante Western in modern dress, very laborious and violent without being very exciting.

wd Jonathan Demme *ph* Bill Birch *m* Bruce Langhorne
☆ Peter Fonda, Lynn Lowry, John Doucette, Philip Carey, Scott Glenn

'Demme has allowed violence to outweigh ideas to such a degree that the picture becomes a turnoff, little more than a blatantly obvious play to the yahoo mentality.' – *Kevin Thomas, Los Angeles Times*

The Fighting O'Flynn

US 1949 94m bw
U-I (Douglas Fairbanks Jnr)

In 18th-century Ireland, a penniless young adventurer aborts Napoleon's plan for invasion.

Lively minor-league adventure.

w Douglas Fairbanks Jnr, Robert Thoeren *novel* Justin Huntly McCarthy *d* Arthur Pierson *ph* Arthur Edeson *m* Frank Skinner
☆ Douglas Fairbanks Jnr, Helena Carter, Richard Greene, Patricia Medina, Arthur Shields, J. M. Kerrigan

'Fairbanks plays the irrepressible O'Flynn with unflagging energy and tongue in cheek good humour; the rest of the cast stolidly refuses to see the joke.' – *MFB*

The Fighting Pimpernel: see *Pimpernel Smith (1941)*

The Fighting Pimpernel: see *The Elusive Pimpernel (1950)*

The Fighting Prince of Donegal

GB 1966 104m Technicolor
Walt Disney (Bill Anderson)

Adventures of an Irish rebel in the reign of Elizabeth I.

Adequate Boys' Own Paper romp.

w Robert Westerby *novel* Red Hugh, Prince of Donegal by Robert T. Reilly *d* Michael O'Herlihy *ph* Arthur Ibbetson *m* George Bruns
☆ Peter McEnery, Susan Hampshire, Tom Adams, Gordon Jackson, Andrew Keir, Norman Wooland, Richard Leech

The Fighting Seabees

US 1944 100m bw
Republic (Albert J. Cohen)

During World War II in the Pacific, construction workers attack the Japanese.

Routine, studio-staged war melodrama, heavily fleshed out with love interest.

w Borden Chase, Aeneas Mackenzie *d* Edward Ludwig *ph* William Bradford *m* Walter Scharf, Roy Webb
☆ John Wayne, Susan Hayward, Dennis O'Keefe, William Frawley, Duncan Renaldo, Addison Richards, Leonid Kinskey, Paul Fix

Walter Scharf, Roy Webb

The Fighting Seventh: see *Little Big Horn*

The Fighting Sullivans: see *The Sullivans*

The Figurehead *
GB 1952 8m Technicolor
A carved saint is turned into a figurehead and can't respond when a mermaid falls in love with him.
Pleasant whimsy, one of the better jobs from this team of animators.
poem Crosbie Garstin *pd* John Halas, Joy Batchelor *animation* John Halas, Joy Batchelor
☆ *Robert Beatty* (narrator)

Figures in a Landscape
GB 1970 110m Technicolor Panavision
Cinecrest (John Kohn)
Two men on the run are pursued by soldiers and helicopters; only one crosses the frontier.
Portentous Pinterish parable, very long-winded and relentlessly boring though good to look at. Everything is symbolic, nothing is specific, not even the country.
w Robert Shaw *novel* Barry England *d* Joseph Losey *ph* Henri Alekan *m* Richard Rodney Bennett
☆ Robert Shaw, Malcolm McDowell

Le Fil de l'Horizon: see *The Edge of the Horizon*

The File of the Golden Goose
GB 1969 109m DeLuxe
UA/Theme/Caralan/Dador (David E. Rose)
An American agent works with Scotland Yard to track down counterfeiters.
Incredibly predictable spy thriller which almost makes an eccentricity out of collecting so many clichés and so many tourist views of London. Like ten TV episodes cut together.
w John C. Higgins, James B. Gordon *d* Sam Wanamaker *ph* Ken Hodges *m* Harry Robinson
☆ Yul Brynner, Edward Woodward, Charles Gray, John Barrie, Bernard Archard, Ivor Dean, Adrienne Corri, Graham Crowden, Karel Stepanek
'The film plods wearily homewards through an exceptionally uninteresting batch of fights, intrigues and sinister encounters.' – *MFB*

The File on Thelma Jordon *
US 1949 100m bw
Paramount (Hal B. Wallis)
aka: *Thelma Jordon*
A district attorney falls for a murder suspect and has her acquitted by losing the case.
Stylishly made, murkily plotted melodrama and a superior star vehicle of its time.
w Ketti Frings *d* Robert Siodmak *ph* George Barnes *m* Victor Young
☆ Barbara Stanwyck, Wendell Corey, Paul Kelly, Joan Tetzel, Stanley Ridges, Richard Rober, Minor Watson, Barry Kelley

La Fille de D'Artagnan: see *D'Artagnan's Daughter*

'An Ordinary Woman. An Extraordinary Love. A Daring Adventure.'
La Fille de l'Air **
France 1992 106m colour
Ciby 2000/TF1 (Farid Chaouche)
A woman learns to fly a helicopter so that she can help her husband to break out of a Paris prison.
A unusual romantic drama, celebrating a wife's fierce and determined love and ignoring her dubious morality and that of her friends; it is nevertheless an extraordinary story, based on fact and told with conviction.
w Florence Quentin, Maroun Bagdadi, Dan Franck *book* Nadine Vaujour *d* Maroun Bagdadi *ph* Thierry Arbogast *m* Gabriel Yared *ad* Michael Vandestien *ed* Luc Barnier
☆ *Beatrice Dalle*, Thierry Fortineau, Hippolyte Girardot, Roland Bertin, Jean-Claude Dreyfus, Catherine Jacob, Liliane Rovere, Jean-Paul Roussillon, Louis-Laure Mariani
'Delivers on action and suspense.' – *Variety*

La Fille du Puisatier *
France 1946 131m bw
Marcel Pagnol
aka: *The Well-Digger's Daughter*
A stern old well-digger feels bound to send his daughter away when she becomes pregnant.
More country matters from Pagnol, this time with an East Lynne type plot getting in the way of some fine acting. Not much comedy.
wd Marcel Pagnol *m* Vincent Scotto
☆ Raimu, Fernandel, Charpin, Josette Day
'There is a feeling in France that such films are made for the foreigner and exploit the eccentricities of French rural life rather than the realities.' – *MFB*

La Fille sur la Pont: see *The Girl on the Bridge*

Film
GB 1979 26m Eastmancolor
BFI
No synopsis is possible for this speechless parable about a poor old man fighting (presumably) against personal obscurity, but its credits make it interesting; it was originally written for Buster Keaton.
w Samuel Beckett *d* David Rayner Clark *ph* Mike Tomlinson *pd* Ariane Gastambide
☆ Max Wall, Patricia Hayes

Film ohne Titel *
West Germany 1947 100m bw
Camera Film (Erwin Gitt)
aka: *Film without Title*
Scriptwriters discuss how it is possible to make a comedy film in post-war Germany, and evolve a story with alternative endings.
Elegantly conceived but rather humourlessly executed, this interesting film was one of the first post-war German exports, but failed to start a trend. It has similarities to La Fête à Henriette *and* Rashomon.
w Helmut Kautner, Ellen Fechner, Rudolf Jugert d Rudolf Jugert *ph* Igor Oberberg *m* Bernard Eichhorn
☆ Hans Söhnker, Hildegarde Knef, *Irene von Meyendorff*, Willy Fritsch

Film without Title: see *Film ohne Titel*

Filofax: see *Taking Care of Business*

The Filth and the Fury **
GB/US 2000 108m DeLuxe
FilmFour/Sex Pistols/Jersey Shore/Nitrate Film (Anita Camarata, Amanda Temple)
Documentary on the rise and fall of the Sex Pistols, who present themselves as a working-class rebellion against the failures of the Labour government and the forces of conservatism, influenced by Olivier's Richard III and the Hunchback of Notre Dame in their public stance
Diverting account of the beginnings of punk rock, as told by its participants, who acknowledge the tensions within the group that kept high their levels of aggression, though the habit of filming the interviewees against the light, so that their faces are obscured, becomes wearisome after a while.
d Julien Temple *ed* Niven Howie
☆ Paul Cook, Steve Jones, Glen Matlock, Johnny Rotten, Sid Vicious
'Proves an obituary for the Seventies every bit as extreme as the group itself. It penetrates the perfidy and politics of the pop business as well as providing plenty of up-front excerpts from the gigs, including previously unseen footage from their US tour.' – *Alexander Walker, London Evening Standard*

Fin Août, Début Septembre: see *Late August, Early September*

Fin de Semana para los Muertos: see *The Living Dead at the Manchester Morgue*

La Fin du Jour **
France 1939 106m bw
Filmsonor/Regina
Tensions mount in a home for retired actors.
Fascinating opportunity for three fine actors to play off each other.
w Charles Spaak, Julien Duvivier *d* Julien Duvivier *ph* Christian Matras *m* Maurice Jaubert
☆ *Michel Simon, Louis Jouvet, Victor Francen*, Gabrielle Dorziat, Madeleine Ozeray, Sylvie

La Fin du Monde: see *End of the World*

'A psychiatrist and two beautiful sisters playing the ultimate mind game. Someone was seduced. Someone was set up. And before it was over ... someone was dead.'
'Hot-blooded passion. Cold-blooded murder.'
Final Analysis
US 1992 124m Technicolor
Warner/Roven-Cavallo (Charles Roven, Paul Junger Witt, Anthony Thomas)
A psychiatrist begins a passionate affair with a patient's married sister, with the result that she decides she no longer wants her husband around.
Drearily derivative thriller that fails to engage the attention.
w Wesley Strick *story* Robert Berger, Wesley Strick *d* Phil Joanou *ph* Jordan Cronenweth *m* George Fenton *pd* Dean Tavoularis *ed* Thom Noble
☆ Richard Gere (Dr Isaac Barr), Kim Basinger (Heather Evans), Uma Thurman (Diana Baylor), Eric Roberts (Jimmy Evans), Paul Guilfoyle (Mike O'Brien), Keith David (Detective Higgins), Robert Harper (Alan Lowenthal), Harris Yulin (Attorney)
'A crackling good melodrama in which star power and slick surfaces are used to potent advantage.' – *Variety*
'Nothing rings very true in this slick, vacuous Hitchcockian thriller.' – *Newsday*

Final Combination
US 1993 92m Foto-Kem
Rank/Polygram/Propaganda (Steve Golin, Gregg Fienberg)
A cop tracks down an ex-boxer turned serial killer.
Mundane thriller that makes all the expected moves in a clumsy fashion.
w Larry Golin *story* Jonathan Tydor *d* Nigel Dick *ph* David Bridges *m* Rolfe Kent *pd* Gary Steele *ed* Henry Richardson, Jonathan Shaw
☆ Michael Madsen, Lisa Bonet, Gary Stretch, Damian Chapa, Tim Russ, Clarence Landry, Carmen Argenziano, Susan Byun, Alan Toy
'Dim.' – *Observer*

'Any time, any place, at any game – Samson Shillitoe can outfox them all!'
'The power of evil is no longer in the hands of a child!'
The Final Conflict
US 1981 108m DeLuxe Panavision
TCF/Mace Neufeld (Harvey Bernhard)
aka: *Omen III: The Final Conflict*
The Antichrist, now head of Thorn Industries, arranges to become US Ambassador in London.
The devil as an adult proves somehow less chilling than the devil as a child, and all the elaborate mayhem seems decidedly old hat in this sequel to The Omen *and* Damien: Omen II.
w Andrew Birkin *d* Graham Baker *ph* Robert Paynter, Phil Meheux *m* Jerry Goldsmith *pd* Herbert Westbrook *ed* Alan Strachan
☆ Sam Neill (Damien Thorn), Rossano Brazzi (Father DeCarlo), Don Gordon (Harvey Dean), Lisa Harrow (Kate Reynolds), Mason Adams (President), Robert Arden (American Ambassador), Barnaby Holm (Peter Reynolds), Tommy Duggan (Brother Matteus)
'If Armageddon is as boring as this movie, we'll need a program to tell the players.' – *Roger Ebert*

The Final Countdown *
US 1980 105m TVC Color Panavision
UA/Bryna (Peter Vincent Douglas)
An aircraft carrier on manoeuvres near Hawaii passes through a strange storm and finds itself back at Pearl Harbor.
Quite an enjoyable bit of schoolboy science fiction, but containing no more body than an episode of Twilight Zone. *The ending, as so often, is impenetrable.*
w David Ambrose, Gerry Davis, Thomas Hunter, Peter Powell *d* Don Taylor *ph* Victor J. Kemper *m* John Scott *pd* Fernando Carrere
☆ Kirk Douglas, Martin Sheen, Katharine Ross, James Farentino, Ron O'Neal, Charles Durning

'Have you ever wondered about your wife? Jude did. so he decided to find out, and now... Jude Is Dead.'
Final Cut
GB 1998 93m colour
Downtown/Fugitive (Dominic Anciano, Ray Burdis)
Gathering at a wake for a dead actor, guests watch a video he made secretly of them indulging in drugs, sex and petty mischief.
Narcissistic, semi-improvised, trivial thriller that resembles one of those home movies, of a game of charades, that is better left unseen.
wd Dominic Anciano, Ray Burdis *ph* John Ward *m* Feelybooth, Thierry Lang *pd* Sabina Sattar *ed* Sam Sneade
☆ Ray Winstone (Ray), Sadie Frost (Sadie), Jude Law (Jude), Holly Davidson (Holly), John Beckett (John), Mark Burdis (Mark), Perry Benson (Tony), Lisa Marsh (Lisa), William Scully (Bill), Ray Burdis (Burdis), Dominic Anciano (Dominic)
'A contrived and ultimately preposterous film, redeemed by its voracious cynicism.' – *Steve Grant, Sunday Times*
'Regrettable, self-indulgent mush that skirts the odd telling insight into the two-facedness of close friendships in favour of the worst kind of vérité arse.' – *Ian Nathan, Empire*

'No Accidents. No Coincidences. No Escapes.'
'I'll See You Soon.'
Final Destination
US 2000 97m DeLuxe
New Line (Warren Zide, Craig Perry, Glen Morgan)
After saving his friends from a plane crash in which there were no survivors, a psychic student discovers that it is difficult to cheat death.
Intriguing and gory horror that begins well but finally runs out of control.
w Glen Morgan, James Wong, Jeffrey Reddick *d* James Wong *ph* Robert McLachlan *m* Shirley Walker *pd* John Willet *ed* James Coblentz *sp* Ariel Velasco Shaw; Terry Sonderhoff
☆ Devon Sawa (Alex Browning), Ali Larter (Clear Rivers), Kerr Smith (Carter Horton), Kristen Cloke (Valerie Lewton), Daniel Roebuck (Agent Weine), Roger Guenveur Smith (Agent Schreck), Chad E. Donella (Tod Waggner), Seann William Scott (Billy Hitchcock), Tony Todd (Bludworth), Amanda Detmer (Terry Chaney)
'As subtle as a brick, but sometimes obvious silly, shrieky fun is all you want from a film. This one will have you laughing all the way to the end.' – *Cam Winstanley, Total Film*
† Many of the characters' names derive from participants in classic horror movies, including Tod Browning, Lon Chaney, Alfred Hitchcock, Val Lewton, Max Schreck, George Waggner, and Robert Wiene.

'For every beginning there is an end.'
Final Destination 2 *
US 2003 90m DeLuxe
Entertainment/New Line (Warren Zide, Craig Perry)
After a psychic saves motorists from being killed in a crash, the survivors die one by one.
Gruesome, darkly comic retread of the first movie, in which horrific deaths are gleefully presented.
w J. Mackye Gruber, Eric Bress *d* David R. Ellis *ph* Gary Capo *m* Shirley Walker *pd* Michael Bolton *ed* Eric Sears *sp* Pixel Magic, Digital Dimension
☆ Ali Larter (Clear Rivers), A. J. Cook (Kimberly Corman), Michael Landes (Officer Thomas Burke), T. C. Carson (Eugene Dix), Jonathan Cherry (Rory), Keegan Connor Tracy (Kat), Sarah Carter (Shania), Lynda Boyd (Nora Carpenter), Tony Todd (Mr Bludworth)
'Suffers from the same rancid dialogue and acting problems as the original but with a much funnier pulse.' – *Robert Koehler, Variety*

Final Fantasy: The Spirits Within *
Japan/US 2001 106m DeLuxe
Columbia TriStar/Square/Amuse/Bandai/Dentsu/Digicube/GaGa/Humax (Hironobu Sakaguchi, Jun Aida, Chris Lee)
In 2065, a female scientist searches for the spirits that she believes will rid the world of powerful aliens known as phantoms.
Some excellent animation, coming close to creating actors as real as many flesh-and-blood stars, is not

enough to save a narrative that is both clichéd and unconvincingly mystical.
w Al Reinert, Jeff Vintar *d* Hironobu Sakaguchi, Motonori Sakakibara *m* Elliot Goldenthal *ed* Christopher S. Capp
☆ voices of: Ming-Na (Dr Aki Ross), Alec Baldwin (Captain Gray Edwards), Ving Rhames (Ryan), Steve Buscemi (Neil), Peri Gilpin (Jane), Donald Sutherland (Dr Sid), James Woods (General Hein), Keith David (Council Member), Jean Simmons (Council Member), Major Elliot (Matt McKenzie)

Final Impact
US 1992 102m Foto-Kem
PM (Richard Pepin, Joseph Merhi)
A former kick-boxing champion trains his protégé to fight the new champion.
Undistinguished action flick, with the same moves and narrative that have been seen dozens of times before.
w Stephen Smoke *d* Joseph Merhi, Stephen Smoke *m* John Gonzalez *pd* Richard Dearborn *ed* Geraint Bell, John Weidner
☆ Lorenzo Lamas, Kathleen Kinmont, Jeff Langton, Kathrin Lautner, Mike Toney, Michael Worth

The Final Option: see *Who Dares Wins*

'The future is cancelled!'
The Final Programme
GB 1973 89m Technicolor
Goodtimes/Gladiole (John Goldstone, Sanford Lieberson)
US title: *The Last Days of Man on Earth*
In the future, when the world is torn by famine and war, a scientist awaits a new messiah.
Intellectualized sci-fi, hard to take as entertainment but very glossy.
wd Robert Fuest *novel* Michael Moorcock *ph* Norman Warwick *m* Paul Beaver, Bernard Krause
☆ Jon Finch, Jenny Runacre, Sterling Hayden, Hugh Griffith
'Clumsy and almost incomprehensible.' – *Sight and Sound*

The Final Test
GB 1953 90m bw
Rank/ACT (R. J. Minney)
A cricketer looks forward to his last game but is out for a duck; he is however cheered by the crowd and comforted by his son.
Flat character study some way below the author's best style, cluttered up with real cricketers and stymied by lack of action.
w Terence Rattigan *d* Anthony Asquith *ph* Bill McLeod *m* Benjamin Frankel
☆ Jack Warner, Robert Morley, George Relph

Finally, Sunday *
France 1983 111m bw
Films du Carrosse/Films A2/Soprofilms (Armand Barbault)
French title: *Vivement Dimanche*
When his friend is murdered, a small-town estate agent becomes a prime suspect.
Agreeable Hitchcock parody which goes on too long and runs out of steam.
w François Truffaut, Suzanne Schiffman, Jean Aurel *novel The Long Saturday Night* by Charles Williams *d* François Truffaut *ph* Nestor Almendros *m* Georges Delerue *pd* Hilton McConnico
☆ Fanny Ardant, Jean-Louis Trintignant, Philippe Laudenbach, Caroline Sihol
'Devoid of interest or distinction, a comedy-thriller that is not funny and most emphatically not thrilling. Ardant and Trintignant fancy themselves as Carole Lombard and Fredric March, an illusion not likely to be shared by anyone else…' – *Gilbert Adair, MFB*

Find the Lady
Canada/GB 1976 79m colour Panavision
Quadrant/Impact (Gerald Flint-Shipman, David Main, John Trent)
aka: *Call the Cops!*
aka: *Kopek and Broom*
Two incompetent cops go on the track of two bumbling crooks.
Coarse slapstick comedy that yields very few laughs.
w David Main, John Trent *d* John Trent *ph* Harry Waxman *m* Robert Sharples *pd* Karen Bromley *ed* Al Gell
☆ Lawrence Dane, John Candy, Dick Emery, Mickey Rooney, Peter Cook, Alexandra Bastedo, Richard Monette, Bob Vinci, Ed McNamara, Tim Henry

Finders Keepers
GB 1966 94m Eastmancolor
UA/Interstate (George H. Brown)
The Americans lose an atomic bomb off the Spanish coast, and it's found by a pop group.
Harmless youth musical without much style. Tunes poor, comedy rather too easy-going.
w Michael Pertwee *d* Sidney Hayers *ph* Alan Hume *m* The Shadows, Norrie Paramor
☆ Cliff Richard, The Shadows, Robert Morley, Peggy Mount, Viviane Ventura, Graham Stark, John Le Mesurier, Robert Hutton

Finders Keepers
US 1984 96m Technicolor
CBS (Sandra Marsh, Terence Marsh)
On a train from California to New York, various factions try to grab stolen money hidden in a coffin.
Yawnworthy comedy-thriller with a zany streak; all the elements have been better done in other movies.
w Ronny Graham, Charles Dennis, Terence Marsh *novel The Next to Last Train Ride* by Charles Dennis *d* Richard Lester *ph* Brian West *m* Ken Thorne *pd* Terence Marsh
☆ Michael O'Keefe, Beverly D'Angelo, Lou Gossett Jnr, Pamela Stephenson, Ed Lauter, David Wayne, Brian Dennehy, John Schuck

Finders Keepers, Lovers Weepers!
US 1968 71m Eastmancolor
Eve (Russ Meyer)
A brothel-keeper organizes the robbery of a club belonging to one of her lovers.
Typical Meyer fare, in which larger-breasted women get the better of less virile men, and a bad time is had by all.
w Richard Zachary *story* Russ Meyer *d* Russ Meyer *ph* Russ Meyer *md* Igor Kantor *ed* Russ Meyer, Richard Brummer
☆ Anne Chapman, Paul Lockwood, Gordon Westcourt, Duncan McLeod, Robert Rudelson, Lavelle Roby

'In an ordinary place, he found the one person to make his life extraordinary.'
Finding Forrester
US 2000 133m DeLuxe Panavision
Columbia/Fountainbridge (Laurence Mark, Sean Connery, Rhonda Tollefson)
A reclusive Scottish novelist becomes the mentor of a talented, athletic black teenager.
A recycling of familiar themes with no hint of originality in its sentimental narrative and easy resolution.
w Mike Rich *d* Gus Van Sant *ph* Harris Savides *pd* Jane Musky *ed* Valdis Oskarsdottir *cos* Ann Roth
☆ Sean Connery (William Forrester), Rob Brown (Jamal), F. Murray Abraham (Crawford), Anna Paquin (Claire), Busta Rhymes (Terrell), April Grace (Ms Joyce)
'Van Sant, emptily employing the realist manner of his early films, is goodwill hunting in all the wrong places.' – *Richard Schickel, Time*

'Not your ordinary fairy tale.'
Finding North
US 1997 95m colour
Millivres/SoNo (Steven A. Jones, Stephen Dyer)
A gay man, grieving over the death from AIDS of his lover, forms a friendship with a lonely woman looking for love.
Slight sentimental tale of a self-obsessed man finding an unlikely redemption.
w Kim Powers *d* Tanya Wexler *ph* Michael Barrett *m* Café Noir *pd* James B. Smythe *ed* Thom Zimny
☆ Wendy Makkena (Rhonda Portelli), John Benjamin Hickey (Travis Furlong), Anne Bobby (Debi), Rebecca Creskoff (Gina), Angela Pietropinto (Mama Portelli), Freddie Roman (Papa Portelli), Molly McClure (Aunt Bonnie Tucker)
'It glibly uses gay men's experience of bereavement as an easy passport to the touchy-feely values of empathy.' – *Peter Bradshaw, Guardian*

Fine and Dandy: see *West Point Story*

A Fine Madness *
US 1966 104m Technicolor
Warner Seven Arts (Jerome Hellman)
A frustrated New York poet has outbursts of violence.
Patchy, interesting, with-it comedy which suffers from too many changes of mood.
w Elliott Baker *novel* Elliott Baker *d* Irvin Kershner *ph* Ted McCord *m* John Addison
☆ Sean Connery, Jean Seberg, Joanne Woodward, Patrick O'Neal, Colleen Dewhurst, Clive Revill
'Straddling a no man's land somewhere between the nouvelle vague and the crazy comedies of Old Hollywood.' – *Tom Milne*

A Fine Mess
US 1985 88m DeLuxe Panavision
Columbia/BEE/Delphi V (Tony Adams)
Two private eyes who accidentally know too much are chased by gangsters.
Not enough plot for a feature, and not enough comedy talent for a comedy, despite the dedication to Laurel and Hardy.
wd Blake Edwards *ph* Harry Stradling *m* Henry Mancini *pd* Rodger Maus *ed* John F. Burnett
☆ Ted Danson, Howie Mandel, Richard Mulligan, Stuart Margolin, Paul Sorvino
'Word of mouth is unlikely to be favourable … mechanically contrived funny business, most of which falls pretty flat.' – *Variety*
'The plot needn't be the thing, but then the gags and setpieces aren't much either.' – *Sight and Sound*

A Fine Pair
Italy 1968 115m Technicolor Panavision
Vides (Franco Cristaldi)
original title: *Ruba al Prossimo Tua*
A New York detective falls for an Italian girl jewel thief.
Tedious, meandering comedy-thriller with nothing to offer apart from a good robbery sequence.
w Francesco Maselli, Luisa Montagnana, Larry Gelbart, Virgil C. Leone *d* Francesco Maselli *ph* Alfio Contino *m* Ennio Morricone
☆ Rock Hudson, Claudia Cardinale, Tomas Milian, Leon Askin, Ellen Corby

The Finest Hour
US 1991 105m colour
21st Century (Menahem Golan)
Two tough Navy SEALS, who are rivals for the same woman, are sent on a dangerous assignment in the Gulf War.
Gung-ho tedium, full of noisy, macho posturing.
w Shimon Dotan, Stuart Schoffman *d* Shimon Dotan *ph* Avi Karpik *m* Walter Christian Rothe *pd* Avi Avivi *ed* Netaya Anbar, Bob Ducsay
☆ Rob Lowe, Gale Hansen, Tracy Griffith, Eb Lottimer
'Just ignore the boisterous propaganda, suspend disbelief and enjoy the roller-coaster ride.' – *Empire*

The Finest Hours *
GB 1964 116m Technicolor
(Jack Le Vien)
The life of Winston Churchill is built up from newsreels plus a few feature film clips and some original location shooting.
Generally excellent documentary, a handy introduction to Churchill's own writing and rather more entertaining than the later Young Winston.
w Victor Wolfson *d* Peter Baylis
best documentary

Finger of Guilt: see *The Intimate Stranger*

The Finger Points
US 1931 88m bw
Warner
A crime reporter succumbs to pressures from the underworld.
Humourless and low-geared exposé-style melodrama.
w John Monk Saunders, W. R. Burnett, Robert Lord *d* John Francis Dillon
☆ Richard Barthelmess, Clark Gable, Fay Wray, Regis Toomey

Fingers *
US 1977 90m Technicolor
Gala/Brut (George Barrie)
A would-be concert pianist gets involved with his father's gangster friends, and violence results.
Lively and interesting skirmish with an overworked and essentially downbeat subject.
wd James Toback *ph* Mike Chapman *pd* Gene Rudolf *ed* Robert Lawrence
☆ Harvey Keitel, Tisa Farrow, Jim Brown, Marian Seldes, Danny Aiello

Fingers at the Window
US 1942 90m bw
MGM (Irving Asher)
A stage magician hypnotizes lunatics into murdering all those who stand between him and an inheritance.
Slow-starting thriller which never achieves top gear.
w Rose Caylor, Lawrence P. Bachmann *d* Charles Lederer *ph* Harry Stradling, Charles Lawton *m* Bronislau Kaper
☆ Basil Rathbone, Lew Ayres, Laraine Day, Walter Kingsford, Miles Mander, Russell Gleason
'The kind of picture actors do when they need work.' – *Lew Ayres*

Finian's Rainbow *
US 1968 140m Technicolor Panavision 70
Warner Seven Arts (Joseph Landon)
A leprechaun tries to retrieve a crock of gold from an old wanderer who has taken it to America.
Musical whimsy-whamsy, a long way after a 1947 Broadway success; in this overlong and overblown screen version the elements and the style do not jell and there is too much sentimental chat, but moments of magic shine through.
w E. Y. Harburg, Fred Saidy *play* E. Y. Harburg, Fred Saidy *d* Francis Ford Coppola *ph* Philip Lathrop *m/ly* Burton Lane, E. Y. Harburg *md* Ray Heindorf *pd* Hilyard M. Brown
☆ Fred Astaire, Petula Clark, Tommy Steele, Don Francks, Keenan Wynn, Barbara Hancock, Al Freeman Jnr
Ray Heindorf

Finis Terrae *
France 1929 90m approx bw silent
Société Générale des Films
A re-enacted account of the lives of fishermen on remote Brittany islands.
A feature documentary which was impressive at the time; very similar to Flaherty's Man of Aran.
wd Jean Epstein *ph* Joseph Barth, Joseph Kottula

Finishing School
US 1934 73m bw
RKO (Kenneth MacGowan)
A girl at an exclusive school falls for an intern.
Modest pap for the teenage audience.
w Wanda Tuchock, Laird Doyle *d* George Nicholls Jnr *ph* J. Roy Hunt *m* Max Steiner
☆ Frances Dee, Ginger Rogers, Billie Burke, Bruce Cabot, John Halliday, Beulah Bondi, Sara Haden

The Finishing Touch *
US 1928 20m bw silent
Hal Roach
Stan and Ollie accidentally destroy the house they are building.
Excellent early star slapstick with predictable but enjoyable gags.
w H. M. Walker *d* Clyde Bruckman *ph* George Stevens *ed* Richard Currier
☆ Stan Laurel, Oliver Hardy, Edgar Kennedy, Dorothy Coburn

Finyé: see *The Wind*

Il Fiore delle Mille e una Notte *

Italy 1974 155m Technicolor
UA/PEA/Artistes Associés (Alberto Grimaldi)

aka: *Arabian Nights*

Stories of love and betrayal are framed by the tale of a slave girl who chooses as her owner and lover a handsome youth but is only reunited with him after fantastic adventures.

A shifting narrative in exotic settings, in which stories collide and elide, gives a dreamlike quality to Pasolini's individual approach, where the erotic dominates.

wd Pier Paolo Pasolini *ph* Giuseppe Ruzzolini *m* Ennio Morricone *ad* Dante Ferretti *ed* Enzo Ocone *cos* Danilo Donati

☆ Ninetto Davoli (Aziz), Franco Merli, Ines Pellegrini (Zumurrud), Luigina Rocchi, Franco Citti (Demon), Margaret Clementi, Tessa Bouché

'Even without its extraordinary visual beauties, and the innovative aesthetic position it represents, *Arabian Nights* would go down in film history as the first movie whose scenes of carnality were smothered in the sounds of laughter.' – *Tony Rayns, MFB*

† After its initial screenings, Pasolini cut the film to 130m by dropping two of the stories. The British release ran for 128m.

††† The film forms part of Pasolini's trilogy of films based on great collections of stories, together with *The Decamaron* and *The Canterbury Tales.*

Fiorile **

Italy/France/Germany 1993 122m colour
Arrow/Filmtre-Gierre/Pemnta/Flordia/La Sept/Canal/Roxy/KS (Grazia Volpi, Jean-Claude Cecile, Luggi Waldleitner, Karl Spiehs)

On a car journey, a father tells his children the story of a curse on the family that began more than two hundred years before, when their peasant forebears became rich with the theft of a chest of gold belonging to Napoleon's army.

A compelling tale of unfulfilled love and political expediency, and of past events influencing the future, delivered by master storytellers.

w Sandro Petraglia, Paolo and Vittorio Taviani *d* Paolo and Vittorio Taviani *ph* Giuseppe Lanci *m* Nicola Piovani *ad* Gianni Sbarra *ed* Roberto Perpignani

☆ Claudio Bigagli, Galatea Ranzi, Michael Vartan, Renato Carpentieri, Lino Capolicchio, Costanze Engelbrecht, Chiara Caselli, Athina Cenci

'Remains worth seeing, as an example of how it is still possible to make a film that means to do no more than just entertain. I wish I could say, however, that it was more like the best of the Tavianis' work than it actually is.' – *Derek Malcolm, Guardian*

'Beneath the surface lies a burning secret.'

Fire *

India 1996 104m DeLuxe
Trial By Fire (Bobby Bedi, Deepa Mehta)

Starved of affection in her arranged marriage to an indifferent and philandering husband, a new bride begins a sexual relationship with her sister-in-law, whose infertility has caused her husband to become celibate.

A movie that caused controversy in India, where it was banned; in the wider world, it seems a lushly romantic but somewhat inconsequential drama of thwarted affections and macho posturing.

wd Deepa Mehta *ph* Giles Nuttgens *m* A.A. Rahman *pd* Aradhana Seth *ed* Barry Farrell

☆ Shabana Azmi (Radha), Nandita Das (Sita), Kulbushan Kharbanda (Ashok), Jaaved Jaaferi (Jatin), Ranjit Chowdhry (Mundu), Kushal Rekhi (Biji), Alice Poon (Julie), Ram Gopal Bajaj (Swamiji)

Fire and Ice

US 1982 82m colour
Fox/PSO (Ralph Bakshi, Frank Frazetta)

Evil Lord Nekron uses black magic to subdue the good King Jarol.

Fair cartoon feature, using rotoscoping, in the mould of Conan the Barbarian.

w Roy Thomas, Gerry Conway *d* Ralph Bakshi *m* William Kraft *ed* E. Davis Marshall

☆ Featuring the voices of Susan Tyrrell, Maggie Rosewell, William Ostrander, Stephen Mendel, Clare Nono, Alan Koss

'Three of the biggest in one of the best!'

Fire Down Below

GB 1957 116m Technicolor Cinemascope
Columbia/Warwick (Irving Allen, Albert Broccoli)

Partners in a Caribbean fishing and smuggling business fall out over a woman.

Overheated melodrama with thin characters, predictable incident and ill-advised casting.

w Irwin Shaw *novel* Max Catto *d* Robert Parrish *ph* Desmond Dickinson *m* Arthur Benjamin

☆ Rita Hayworth, Robert Mitchum, Jack Lemmon, Herbert Lom, Bonar Colleano, Bernard Lee, Edric Connor, Peter Illing

'A fast-paced adventure yarn laced around a taut interlude of high drama.' – *Time*

Fire Down Below

US 1997 105m Technicolor
Warner (Steven Seagal, Julius Nasso)

An environmental protection agent investigates the dumping of toxic waste in the Kentucky hills.

Self-regarding action movie with moments of moralizing; neither makes much impact.

w Jeb Stuart *d* Felix Enriquez Alcala *ph* Tom Houghton *m* Nick Glennie-Smith *pd* Joe Alves *ed* Robert A. Ferretti

☆ Steven Seagal (Jack Taggart), Marg Helgenberger (Sarah Kellogg), Harry Dean Stanton (Cotton), Stephen Lang (Earl), Kris Kristofferson (Orin Snr.), Levon Helm (Rev. Goodall), Ed Bruce (Sherrif Lloyd), Richard Masur (Pratt)

'Slick, shallow good-guy/bad-guy stuff interrupted from time to time with some ill-conceived sermonizing. It tries hard to generate heat but is actually no more substantive than a puff of smoke.' – *Leonard Klady, Variety*

Fire Festival

Japan 1985 120m Eastmancolor
Recorded Releasing/Gunro/Seibu/Cine Saison (Kazuo Shimizu)

original title: *Himatsuri*

A nature-loving lumberjack turns killer after observing the effects of pollution on the locality.

Fairly impenetrable to Western audiences, despite its ecological message.

w Kanji Nakagami *d* Mitsuo Yanagimachi *ph* Masaki Tamura *m* Toru Takemitsu *ad* Takeo Kimura *ed* Sachiko Yamaji

☆ Kinya Kitaoji, Kiwako Taichi, Ryota Nakamoto, Norihei Miki, Rikiya Yasuoka, Seiji Kurasaki, Maiko Kawakami

Fire in the Sky

US 1993 109m DeLuxe Panavision
Paramount (Joe Wizan, Todd Black)

A lumberjack is suspected of murder when a friend goes to investigate a flying saucer and disappears.

A close encounter of the boring kind, in which small-town values are made to seem even more alien than tadpoles from outer space.

w Tracy Tormé *book* *The Walton Experience* by Travis Walton *d* Robert Lieberman *ph* Bill Pope *m* Mark Isham *pd* Laurence Bennett *ed* Steve Mirkovich *sp* Industrial Light and Magic

☆ D. B. Sweeney, Robert Patrick, Craig Sheffer, Peter Berg, Henry Thomas, Bradley Gregg, Noble Willingham, James Garner

'This unappealing pic is likely to attract only a few curiosity seekers.' – *Variety*

The Fire in the Stone

Australia 1983 100m colour
South Australian Film Corp (Pamela H. Vanneck)

A teenager foils a murderer, finds some opals and re-unites her parents.

Unexceptional and undemanding entertainment.

w Graeme Koetsveld *novel* Colin Thiele *d* Gary Conway *ph* Ross Berryman *m* Garry and Anita Hardman *ad* Derek Mills *ed* Philip Reid

☆ Alan Cassell, Paul Smith, Ray Meagher, Linda Hartley, Leo Taylor, Andrew Gaston, Theo Pertsinidis

'A world of women seeking male partners to carry on their race!'

Fire Maidens from Outer Space

GB 1956 80m bw
Criterion Films/Eros (George Fowler)

Space explorers find that the thirteenth moon of Jupiter is inhabited solely by sixteen beautiful girls and an aged patriarch.

A strong contender for the title of worst movie ever made, with diaphanously clad English gals striking embarrassed poses against cardboard sets. Must be seen to be believed.

wd Cy Roth *ph* Ian Struthers

☆ Susan Shaw, Anthony Dexter, Harry Fowler, Sydney Tafler, Owen Berry, Paul Carpenter

'Even the most dedicated connoisseurs of the artless are likely to find this something of a strain on their patience.' – *MFB*

Fire over Africa: see *Malaga*

Fire over England ***

GB 1937 92m bw
London Films/Pendennis (Erich Pommer)

Elizabeth I and her navy overcome the Spanish Armada.

Though the film has a faded air and the action climax was always a bath-tub affair, the splendid cast keeps this pageant afloat and interesting.

w Clemence Dane, Sergei Nolbandov *novel* A. E. W. Mason *d* William K. Howard *ph* James Wong Howe *m* Richard Addinsell *ad* Lazare Meerson, Frank Wells *ed* Jack Dennis

☆ Flora Robson, Laurence Olivier, Leslie Banks, Vivien Leigh, Raymond Massey, Tamara Desni, Morton Selten, Lyn Harding, James Mason

'Should bring much artistic acclaim but, outside of the urban class spots, business will be stubborn … if it had marquee strength it would stand an excellent chance.' – *Variety*

'Pommer and Howard have done one remarkable thing: they have caught the very spirit of an English public schoolmistress's vision of history.' – *Graham Greene*

'Swashbuckling nonsense, but with a fine spirit.' – *Pauline Kael, 70s*

Fire over Rome

Italy 1968 94m colour
GMC (Giorgio Marzelli)

original title: *L'incendio di Roma*
aka: *Revenge of the Gladiators*

A Roman consul defies Nero's order to massacre Christians.

One of Italy's interminable gladiatorial epics of the period, consisting mainly of a series of sword fights, although Jesus gets a walk-on role right at the end.

d Guido Malatesta *ph* Aldo Greci *ad* Oscar D'Amico *ed* Enzo Alfonsi

☆ Lang Jeffries, Cristina Gaioni, Moira Orfei, Mario Feliciani, Luciano Marin, Evi Maltagliati

Fire Sale *

US 1977 88m DeLuxe
TCF (Marvin Worth)

Misadventures of a frantic, eccentric New York-Jewish family who own a department store.

Frenzied black farce for ethnic audiences.

w Robert Klane *novel* Robert Klane *d* Alan Arkin *ph* Ralph Woolsey *m* Dave Grusin

☆ Alan Arkin, Rob Reiner, Vincent Gardenia, Anjanette Comer, Kay Medford, Sid Caesar, Alex Rocco

'It moves fast enough to carry the occasional lapses from its own high standards of tastelessness.' – *Jan Dawson, MFB*

Fire with Fire

US 1986 103m Metrocolor
Paramount (Gary Nardino)

aka: *Captive Hearts*

A girl at an expensive Catholic boarding school falls in love with a boy at a nearby parole camp.

Sluggish teen romance that not even its melodramatic finale can save.

w Bill Phillips, Warren Skaaren, Paul and Sharon Boorstin *d* Duncan Gibbins *ph* Hiro Narita *m* Howard Shore *pd* Norman Newberry *ed* Peter E. Berger

☆ Virginia Madsen, Craig Sheffer, Kate Reid, Jeffrey Jay Cohen, Jon Polito, Jean Smart, David Harris

The Fire Within: see *Le Feu Follet*

The Fireball

US 1950 84m bw
Thor/TCF

A juvenile delinquent becomes a ruthless roller-skating champion.

Predictable and unattractive star character drama with sporting asides.

w Tay Garnett, Horace McCoy *d* Tay Garnett *ph* Lester White *m* Victor Young

☆ Mickey Rooney, Pat O'Brien, Beverly Tyler, Glenn Corbett

Firecreek

US 1967 104m Technicolor Panavision
Warner Seven Arts (Philip Leacock)

The people of Firecreek protect themselves from wandering gunmen.

Dour, predictable little Western which does not show its stars at their best.

w Calvin Clements *d* Vincent McEveety *ph* William Clothier *m* Alfred Newman

☆ James Stewart, Henry Fonda, Inger Stevens, Gary Lockwood, Dean Jagger, Ed Begley, Jay C. Flippen, Jack Elam, James Best, Barbara Luna

'This cramped and clumsy western grinds to a standstill in its attempts to give Firecreek symbolic status … while the gunmen roister like mad and the townsfolk rhubarb glumly in the background.' – *MFB*

'It will make 1937 remembered always as the year of the first romantic dramatic musical film!'

The Firefly *

US 1937 131m bw
MGM (Hunt Stromberg)

Adventures of a Spanish lady spy during the Napoleonic war.

Solid production of a romantic operetta; splendid stuff for connoisseurs.

w Frances Goodrich, Albert Hackett, Ogden Nash *original book/ly* Otto Harbach *d* Robert Z. Leonard *ph* Oliver Marsh *m/ly* Rudolf Friml, Otto Harbach, Gus Kahn *md* Herbert Stothart *ch* Albertina Rasch

☆ Jeanette MacDonald, *Allan Jones*, Warren William, Billy Gilbert, Henry Daniell, George Zucco, Douglass Dumbrille

'The sepia tint is monotonous … the length will seriously militate against popularity.' – *Variety*

'A lavish musical monstrosity.' – *New Yorker, 1978*

'The musical film par excellence … resplendent and gorgeous.' – *Evening News*

♫ Love is Like a Firefly; The Donkey Serenade; Giannina Mia; He Who Loves and Runs Away; Sympathy; When a Maid Comes Knocking at Your Heart

Firefox

US 1982 136m DeLuxe Panavision
Warner/Malpaso (Clint Eastwood)

An American pilot is disguised as a businessman and sent to Moscow to steal a new supersonic Soviet fighter.

Dreary melodrama with doleful acting and very little action or suspense.

w Alex Lasker, Wendell Willman *novel* Craig Thomas *d* Clint Eastwood *ph* Bruce Surtees *m* Maurice Jarre *sp* John Dykstra

☆ Clint Eastwood, Freddie Jones, David Huffman, Warren Clarke, Ronald Lacey, Kenneth Colley, Nigel Hawthorne

'What is most curious about this farrago is that Eastwood, the actor and the director, should have walked through it all with scarcely a thought for each other.' – *Richard Combs, MFB*

'Despite the tense mission being depicted, there's no suspense, excitement or thrills to be had, and lackadaisical pacing gives the viewer plenty of time to ponder the gaping implausibilities that skilful execution could have rendered irrelevant.' – *Variety*

'Immensely long, unfailingly dull, and not even silly enough to be funny.' – *Sunday Times*

'Passion has no limits.'
Firelight
US/GB 1997 103m colour 'Scope
Miramax/Capitol/Wind Dancer/Carnival (Brian Eastman)
In the 1840s, a Swiss governess goes in search of the child she had by an English aristocrat.
Unconvincing romantic melodrama, a poor man's Jane Eyre.
wd William Nicholson *ph* Nic Morris
m Christopher Gunning *pd* Rob Harris *ed* Chris Wimble
☆ Sophie Marceau, Stephen Dillane, Kevin Anderson, Joss Ackland, Lia Williams, Dominique Belcourt
'First time director and veteran screenwriter never puts a foot wrong in this powerful and moving story of forbidden love and all-consuming passion.' – *Nick Briggs, Film Review*

Fireman Save My Child
US 1932 67m bw
Warner/First National
A fireman is more interested in baseball but becomes a hero all the same.
Thin star comedy.
w Ray Enright, Robert Lord, Arthur Caesar
d Lloyd Bacon
☆ Joe E. Brown, Evalyn Knapp, Lillian Bond, Guy Kibbee

The Firemen's Ball *
Czechoslovakia/Italy 1967 73m Eastmancolor
Barrandov/Carlo Ponti
original title: *Hori, Ma Panenko*
In a small provincial town, arrangements for the firemen's annual ball go wrong at every turn.
Vaguely amusing Tati-esque comedy with not quite enough funny moments and a prevailing atmosphere of pessimism.
w Milos Forman, Ivan Passer, Jaroslav Papousek
d Milos Forman *ph* Miroslav Ondricek *m* Karel Mares
☆ Jan Vostrcil, Josef Kolb, Josef Svet, Frantisek Debelka
'A compendium of superb items.' – *Philip Strick*
Ꝗ best foreign film

Firepower
GB 1979 104m Technicolor
ITC/Michael Winner
A chemist about to expose contaminated drugs is murdered; his widow persuades the US Justice Department to hire her ex-lover, a gangster, to track down his killers.
Globe-trotting kaleidoscope of the familiar patterns of violence; tolerable for those who haven't been here a hundred times before.
w Gerald Wilson *d* Michael Winner *ph* Robert Paynter, Dick Kratina *m* Gato Barbieri *md* Jay Chattaway *pd* John Blezard, Robert Gundlach
ed Arnold Crust
☆ Sophia Loren, James Coburn, Anthony Franciosa, O. J. Simpson, Eli Wallach, George Grizzard, Vincent Gardenia, Victor Mature
'The nearest thing yet to film-making by numbers, with identikit characters jet-setting across a travel brochure landscape to an orchestration of gunfire, car smashes and colourful explosions.' – *Clyde Jeavons, MFB*

Fires on the Plain **
Japan 1959 108m bw Daieiscope
Daiei (Masaichi Nagata)
original title: *Nobi*
In the Philippines during World War II, a half-demented Japanese private takes to the hills, becomes a cannibal, and is shot by the Americans when he tries to surrender.
Stomach-turning anti-war epic with fine scenes and performances but dubious intent.
w Natto Wada *novel* Shohei O-oka *d* Kon Ichikawa *ph* Setsuo Kobayashi *m* Yasushi Akatagawa
☆ *Eiji Funakoshi*, Osamu Takizawa, Micky Curtis

Fires Were Started **
GB 1943 63m bw
Crown Film Unit (Ian Dalrymple)
aka: *I Was a Fireman*
One day and night in the life of a National Fire Service unit during the London blitz.
Thoughtful, slow-moving, poetic documentary originally intended as a training film but generally released to boost morale. Not its director's finest work, but perhaps his most ambitious.
wd Humphrey Jennings ph C. Pennington-Richards *m* William Alwyn
'An astonishingly intimate portrait of an isolated and besieged Britain ... an ... unforgettable piece of human observation, affectionate, touching, and yet ironic.' – *Georges Sadoul*
'It transforms its observation into a personal, epic celebration of the courage and dignity of ordinary people in times of stress.' – *Time Out, 1984*
† The firemen were real firemen, but the scenes were re-enacted.

Fires Within
US 1991 87m colour Panavision
MGM/Pathé (Wallis Nicita, Lauren Lloyd)
In Miami, a Cuban woman is forced to choose between her husband, returning to her after eight years as a political prisoner, and the man she has come to love.
Lacklustre drama, mixing romance and politics, but with little conviction; the emphasis is on local colour and music.
w Cynthia Cidre *d* Gillian Armstrong *ph* David Gribble *m* Maurice Jarre *pd* Robert Ziembicki
ed John Scott
☆ Jimmy Smits, Greta Scacchi, Vincent D'Onofrio, Luis Avalos, Bertila Damas, Raul Davila
'A cold narrative that never lingers on any situation long enough to generate either suspense or romance.' – *Variety*

Firestarter
US 1984 114m Technicolor J-D-C Scope
Universal (Frank Capra Jnr)
A young girl is capable of starting fires by pyrokinesis, and the government wants to use her as a weapon.
Complicated and dislikeable piece of political science fiction.
w Stanley Mann *novel* Stephen King *d* Mark L. Lester *ph* Giuseppe Ruzzolini *m* Tangerine Dream
☆ Drew Barrymore, George C. Scott, David Keith, Martin Sheen, Freddie Jones, Heather Locklear, Art Carney, Louise Fletcher, Moses Gunn
'The most astonishing thing in the movie is how boring it is.' – *Roger Ebert*

Firestorm
US 1998 89m DeLuxe Panavision
TCF (Joseph Loeb III, Matthew Weisman, Thomas H. Hammel)
A fire-fighter is parachuted into a forest to fight a blaze set by a group of hardened criminals in order to break out of prison.
A lacklustre thriller, which tries in vain to breathe a little life into disaster movies.
w Chris Soth *d* Dean Semler *ph* Stephen F. Windon *m* J. Peter Robinson *pd* Richard Paris, Linda del Rosario *ed* Jack Hofstra
☆ Howie Long, Scott Glenn, William Forsythe, Suzy Amis, Christianne Hirt, Garwin Sanford, Sebastian Spence
'A half-baked B movie.' – *Variety*

Firewalker
US 1986 104m TVC Color
Cannon (Menahem Golan, Yoram Globus)
Adventurers seek gold in an Aztec temple.
Old hat heroics and violence in the wake of Raiders of the Lost Ark. *Not a happy outcome.*
w Robert Gosnell *d* J. Lee-Thompson *ph* Alex Phillips *m* Gary Chang *pd* Jos Rodriguez
ed Richard Marx
☆ Chuck Norris, Lou Gossett Jnr, Melody Anderson, John Rhys-Davies, Will Sampson

'Power can be murder to resist.'
The Firm *
US 1993 154m DeLuxe
Paramount (Sydney Pollack, Scott Rudin, John Davis)
A bright young lawyer finds himself trapped between becoming an informant for the FBI and being killed by the ruthless Mafia gangsters who control his firm.
An attention-holding thriller for the most part, though its conclusion, diverging from the tougher stance of the novel, is unsatisfactory.
w David Rabe, Robert Towne, David Rayfiel
novel John Grisham *d* Sydney Pollack *ph* John Seale *m* David Grusin *pd* Richard Macdonald
ed William Steinkamp, Frederic Steinkamp
☆ Tom Cruise, Jeanne Tripplehorn, Gene Hackman, Hal Holbrook, Terry Kinney, Wilford Brimley, Ed Harris, Holly Hunter, David Strathairn, Gary Busey, Steven Hill, Tobin Bell
'A vacuous upper-middle-class success story about a fresh-faced lad outwitting both sides of the law while securing wealth and safety for his family.' – *Michael Sragow, New Yorker*
'There is sufficient conviction from everyone before and behind the camera to provide an absorbing, pulpy, old-fashioned movie experience.' – *Variety*
Ꝗ Holly Hunter; Dave Grusin

First a Girl
GB 1935 94m bw
Gaumont (Michael Balcon)
A messenger girl attracts attention by posing as a boy, and becomes a star.
Moderate light star vehicle.
w Marjorie Gaffney *play Viktor und Viktoria* by Reinhold Schunzel *d* Victor Saville *ph* Glen MacWilliams *md* Louis Levy *ad* Oscar Werndorff
ed Al Barnes
☆ Jessie Matthews, Sonnie Hale, Griffith Jones, Anna Lee, Alfred Drayton, Martita Hunt, Eddie Gray
† Julie Andrews starred in a remake entitled *Victor/Victoria* in 1982.

The First and the Last: see *Twenty-One Days*

First Blood
US 1982 94m Technicolor Panavision
Carolco (Buzz Feitshans)
A former Green Beret gets into trouble in a small Californian community and sets himself against the forces of law.
Pure blood and thunder with some decent action sequences.
w Michael Kozoll, William Sackheim, Sylvester Stallone *novel* David Morell *d* Ted Kotcheff
ph Andrew Laszlo *m* Jerry Goldsmith
☆ Sylvester Stallone, Richard Crenna, Brian Dennehy, David Caruso, Jack Starrett
'Socially irresponsible ... there are enough nuts out there without giving them a hero to cheer for.' – *Variety*
† It was followed by two sequels: *Rambo: First Blood II* and *Rambo III*.

The First Deadly Sin
US 1980 112m TVC Color
Filmways/Artanis/Cinema Seven (Elliott Kastner)
A police lieutenant tracks down a homicidal lunatic but is unable to save his own wife who is dying in hospital from an obscure ailment.
The two halves of this depressing cop show don't seem to relate, and it offers little in the way of entertainment value beyond the traditional tracking down of the murderer.
w Mann Rubin *novel* Lawrence Sanders *d* Brian G. Hutton *ph* Jack Priestley *m* Gordon Jenkins
☆ Frank Sinatra, Faye Dunaway, David Dukes, George Coe, Brenda Vaccaro, Martin Gabel, Anthony Zerbe, James Whitmore
'An odd collection of pretensions seem to be rattling round in an overlength TV film.' – *Mark Lefanu, MFB*
'Mystery without meaning, despite a froth of intercutting and religious iconography.' – *Sight and Sound*

The First Gentleman *
GB 1948 111m bw
Columbia (Joseph Friedman)
US title: *Affairs of a Rogue*
The affairs and foibles of the Prince Regent.
Dullish adaptation of a successful West End play about 18th-century court life; script and performances still entertain.
w Nicholas Phipps, Reginald Long *play Norman Ginsbury d* Alberto Cavalcanti *ph* Jack Hildyard
m Lennox Berkeley *md* Sir Thomas Beecham
ad C. P. Norman *ed* Margary Saunders
☆ *Cecil Parker*, Jean-Pierre Aumont, Joan Hopkins, Margaretta Scott, Jack Livesey, Ronald Squire, Athene Seyler, Hugh Griffith

The First Great Train Robbery *
GB 1978 108m Technicolor Panavision
UA/Starling (John Foreman)
US title: *The Great Train Robbery*
In 1855, an elegant but ruthless crook picks out a gang to help him rob the Folkestone express of gold bullion.
Patchy but generally very likeable period crime story, with just a few lapses of pace and taste.
wd Michael Crichton novel Michael Crichton
ph Geoffrey Unsworth m Jerry Goldsmith
pd Maurice Carter
☆ Sean Connery, Donald Sutherland, Lesley-Anne Down, Alan Webb, Robert Lang, Malcolm Terris
'My dream was that the historical world was going to be lovingly recreated, and then I was going to shoot *The French Connection* inside it.' – *Michael Crichton*

First Kid
US 1996 101m Continental Color
Buena Vista/Walt Disney/Caravan (Roger Birnbaum, Riley Kathryn Ellis)
aka: *Disney's First Kid*
An agent is given the task of guarding the US President's bored teenage son.
Occasionally amusing, sentimental comedy of the bonding of two misfits.
w Tim Kelleher *d* David Mickey Evans
ph Anthony Richmond *m* Richard Gibbs
pd Chester Kaczenski *ed* Harry Keramidas
☆ Sinbad, Robert Guillaume, Timothy Busfield, Brock Pierce, Blake Boyd, Art La Fleur, Lisa Eichhorn, James Naughton
'The film has a lot of heart and humor.' – *Variety*

'Their greatest battle would be for her love.'
First Knight
US 1995 134m Technicolor
Columbia/Zucker Brothers (Jerry Zucker, Hunt Lowry)
Guinevere marries King Arthur to protect her lands and finds herself torn between her love for Lancelot and her respect for her husband.
This is less the medieval epic it attempts to be, and closer in spirit to A Yankee in King Arthur's Court, *thanks to Gere's American gigolo masquerading as Lancelot; it lacks passion and there is no feeling that anything is worth fighting or dying for.*
w William Nicholson *d* Jerry Zucker *ph* Adam Greenberg *m* Jerry Goldsmith *pd* John Box
ed Walter Murch
☆ Sean Connery, Richard Gere, Julia Ormond, Ben Cross, Liam Cunningham, Christopher Villiers, Valentine Pelka, John Gielgud
'It is not often that the genuine Hollywood vulgarian adds a new chapter to our national heritage. The event should be commemorated somehow. But I do not believe this will be achieved at the historic site called a box-office.' – *Alexander Walker, London Evening Standard*
'May look impressive on the surface; inside it is a mediocrity *de luxe*.' – *Geoff Brown, The Times*
† The film cost $60m and took $37m at the US box-office.

First Lady *
US 1937 82m bw
Warner (Hal B. Wallis)
The President's wife is a power behind the scenes.
Solidly entertaining Washington comedy.
w Rowland Leigh *play* George S. Kaufman, Katherine Dayton *d* Stanley Logan *ph* Sid Hickox *m* Max Steiner

☆ Kay Francis, Preston Foster, Anita Louise, Walter Connolly, Verree Teasdale, Victor Jory, Marjorie Rambeau, Louise Fazenda
'Smart stuff but generally palatable.' – *Variety*

The First Legion *
US 1951 86m bw
Sedif (Douglas Sirk)
Priests are bewildered when one of their number is the centre of an apparent miracle.
Talkative religious drama of a peculiarly American kind which likes to have its cake and eat it; watchable for the performances.
w Emmet Lavery *play* Emmet Lavery *d* Douglas Sirk *ph* Robert de Grasse *m* Hans Sommer
☆ Charles Boyer, William Demarest, Lyle Bettger, Barbara Rush, Leo G. Carroll, Walter Hampden, George Zucco, Taylor Holmes

First Love *
US 1939 84m bw
Universal (Joe Pasternak)
An orphaned teenager goes to live with her uncle and his snobbish family, and falls for a local bigwig's son.
A vehicle carefully conceived to introduce its star to grown-up romance. The compromises show, but it's palatable enough.
w Bruce Manning, Lionel Houser *d* Henry Koster *ph* Joseph Valentine *m* Frank Skinner *md* Charles Previn *ad* Jack Otterson, Martin Obzina
☆ Deanna Durbin, Robert Stack, Eugene Pallette, Helen Parrish, Lewis Howard, Leatrice Joy
'A top-bracketer for general audiences in keys and subsequents.' – *Variety*
'The most obvious Cinderella story I ever met with, apart from *Cinderella*.' – *Richard Mallett, Punch*
'There is nothing at all to resent in the picture: it is admirably directed, amusingly written, and acted with immense virtuosity by a fine cast.' – *Graham Greene*
Charles Previn; art direction

First Love
US 1977 92m Metrocolor
Paramount (Lawrence Turman, David Foster)
A romantic, inhibited student falls in love with a girl who is involved with an older, married man.
Dull, unoriginal and uninvolving drama that spends a great deal of time spelling out the obvious.
w Jane Stanton Hitchcock, David Freeman *story* *Sentimental Education* by Harold Brodkey *d* Joan Darling *ph* Bobby Byrne *pd* Robert Luthardt *ed* Frank Morriss
☆ William Katt, Susan Dey, John Heard, Beverly D'Angelo, Robert Loggia, Tom Lacy, Swoosie Kurtz

First Man into Space
GB 1958 78m bw
Producers' Associates (John Croydon)
An astronaut runs into a cloud of meteor dust and returns to Earth a vampirish killer.
Quatermass-like shocker with modest budget but firm control.
w John C. Cooper, Lance Z. Hargreaves *d* Robert Day *ph* Geoffrey Faithfull *m* Buxton Orr
☆ Marshall Thompson, Marla Landi, Bill Edwards

First Men in the Moon *
GB 1964 103m Technicolor Panavision
Columbia/Ameran (Charles H. Schneer)
A Victorian eccentric makes a voyage to the moon and is forced to stay there.
Rather slack in plot development, but an enjoyable schoolboy romp with a good eye for detail and tongue firmly in cheek.
w Nigel Kneale, Jan Read *novel* H. G. Wells *d* Nathan Juran *ph* Wilkie Cooper *m* Laurie Johnson *sp* Ray Harryhausen
☆ Lionel Jeffries, Edward Judd, Martha Hyer
† Uncredited, Peter Finch played the bit part of a process server.

'In the Supreme Court, there are only eight of them against all of her!'
First Monday in October
US 1981 99m Metrocolor Panavision
Paramount (Paul Heller, Martha Scott)
Ruth Loomis becomes the first woman to be appointed to the US Supreme Court, and wins over her severest critic.
Fairly yawnworthy comedy which has nowhere to go from its initial situation, and has detail too complex for any but politically minded Americans.
w Jerome Lawrence, Robert E. Lee *play* Jerome Lawrence, Robert E. Lee *d* Ronald Neame *ph* Fred J. Koenekamp *m* Sousa, Handel, arr. Ian Fraser *pd* Philip M. Jefferies
☆ Jill Clayburgh, Walter Matthau, Barnard Hughes, Jan Sterling, James Stephens, Joshua Bryant
'Any attempts to inject a little healthy subversion or a few dangerous thoughts are soon smothered by the plot demands of middle-aged romantic whimsy.' – *Sunday Times*

First Name Carmen *
France 1983 85m colour
Sara/A2/JLG Films (Alain Sarde)
original title: *Prénom Carmen*
The niece of a mad film director pretends to be making a film in order to organize an armed robbery.
A quirky film, in which Godard enjoys himself playing a film director at the end of his tether, but which is otherwise disorganized and disjointed.
w Jean-Luc Godard, Anne-Marie Miéville *d* Jean-Luc Godard *ph* Raoul Coutard *m* Beethoven
☆ Maruschka Detmers, Jacques Bonnaffé, Myriem Roussel, Christophe Odent, Pierre-Alain Chapuis, Bertrand Liebert, Jean-Luc Godard
'From the way this new film is made, it appears that Godard feels hurt on some deep level and he thinks the movies did it to him – and he's not going to let himself be hurt again. He won't throw himself into this project. He gives the story a dry, flat treatment and entertains himself with Beethoven and the rolling surf and with a limited palette – soft, somber tones and subdued golden ones – that suggest the classics (but not of movies).' – *Pauline Kael*

The First of the Few **
GB 1942 117m bw
Melbourne/British Aviation (Leslie Howard, George King, Adrian Brunel, John Stafford)
US title: *Spitfire*
The story of R. J. Mitchell who saw World War II coming and devised the Spitfire.
Low-key but impressive biopic with firm acting and good dialogue scenes. Production values slightly shaky.
w Anatole de Grunwald, Miles Malleson, Henry C. James, Katherine Strueby *d* Leslie Howard *ph* Georges Perinal *m* William Walton
☆ *Leslie Howard*, David Niven, Rosamund John, Roland Culver, David Horne
'Full of action, Schneider Trophy races, test flying and flashes from the Battle of Britain.' – *Sunday Times*

The First Power
US 1990 98m DeLuxe
Castle Premier/Nelson Entertainment/Interscope Communications (David Madden)
A serial killer comes back from the dead to continue his murders.
Silly, predictable tale of the supernatural.
wd Robert Resnikoff *ph* Theo Van de Sande *pd* Joseph T. Garrity *ed* Michael Bloecher
☆ Lou Diamond Phillips, Tracy Griffith, Jeff Kober, Mykel T. Williamson, Elizabeth Arlen, Dennis Lipscomb, Carmen Argenziano, Julianna McCarthy

The First Rebel: see *Allegheny Uprising*

First Strike: see *Jackie Chan's First Strike*

The First Texan
US 1956 82m Technicolor Cinemascope
Allied Artists (Walter Mirisch)
The Governor of Tennessee helps Texas win its independence.
Generally well done biopic of Sam Houston, with the usual Western excitements.
w Daniel B. Ullman *d* Byron Haskin *ph* Wilfrid Cline *m* Roy Webb
☆ Joel McCrea, Felicia Farr, Jeff Morrow, Wallace Ford, Abraham Sofaer

The First Time
US 1968 90m DeLuxe
UA/Mirisch/Rogallan (Roger Smith, Allan Carr)
GB title: *You Don't Need Pajamas at Rosie's*
Three teenage boys who fantasize about sex help a stranded girl under the impression that she is a prostitute.
Embarrassingly sentimental teenage sex comedy, all the more irritating by its restraint. Not a patch on Summer of '42.
w Jo Heims, Roger Smith *d* James Nielson *ph* Ernest Laszlo *m* Kenyon Hopkins
☆ Jacqueline Bisset, Wes Stern, Rick Kelman, Wink Roberts, Sharon Acker

First to Fight
US 1967 97m Technicolor Panavision
Warner (William Conrad)
A World War II hero is taken home and fêted, but on returning to the front he loses his nerve.
War film in the guise of a psychological study; competently done but very American in its sentiments and a bit shaky on period detail.
w Gene L. Coon *d* Christian Nyby *ph* Harold Wellman *m* Fred Steiner
☆ Chad Everett, Gene Hackman, Dean Jagger, Marilyn Devin, Claude Akins

The First Traveling Saleslady
US 1956 92m Technicolor
RKO (Arthur Lubin)
Two women set out to sell barbed wire in the old west.
Strained comedy with very few effective moments.
w Devery Freeman, Stephen Longstreet *d* Arthur Lubin *ph* William Snyder *m* Irving Gertz
☆ Ginger Rogers, Carol Channing, Barry Nelson, James Arness, David Brian, Clint Eastwood

'Don't get mad. Get Everything.'
The First Wives Club *
US 1996 96m DeLuxe
UIP/Paramount (Scott Rudin)
Three women, dumped by their husbands for younger women, decide to get their own back.
Old-fashioned, brightly played, sugar-coated, sitcom-styled farce of marital revenge.
w Robert Harling *novel* Olivia Goldsmith *d* Hugh Wilson *ph* Donald Thorin *m* Marc Shaiman *pd* Peter Larkin *ed* John Bloom
☆ Goldie Hawn, Bette Midler, Diane Keaton, Maggie Smith, Dan Hedaya, Victor Garber, Bronson Pinchot, Marcia Gay Harden, Eileen Heckart, Philip Bosco, Elizabeth Berkley
'Whisks us along. But then the dumb revenge plot takes over, and the comedy leaks out of the movie like helium from a balloon.' – *Owen Gleiberman, Entertainment Weekly*
Marc Shaiman

First Yank into Tokyo
US 1945 82m bw
RKO (J. Robert Bren)
An army pilot undergoes plastic surgery so that he can infiltrate the Japanese lines.
Highly unconvincing spy fiction ripped off from the headlines as the war ended.
w J. Robert Bren *d* Gordon Douglas *ph* Harry J. Wild *m* Leigh Harline
☆ Tom Neal, Richard Loo, Marc Cramer, Barbara Hale, Keye Luke

Firstborn
US 1984 100m Technicolor
Paramount (Paul Junger Witt, Tony Thomas)
A divorced woman's children defend her against her malevolent second husband.
Heavy-handed melodrama with no clue to what inspired its making.
w Ron Koslow *d* Michael Apted *ph* Ralf D. Bode *m* Michael Small *pd* Paul Sylbert *ed* Arthur Schmidt
☆ Teri Garr, Peter Weller, Christopher Collet, Corey Haim, Sarah Jessica Parker

Fish and Elephant
China 2001 106m colour
Cheng Yong
original title: *Jin Nian Xiatian*
A lesbian elephant keeper at Beijing Zoo is visited by her match-making mother and a former girlfriend who is on the run after killing her father.
Low-budget movie using a non-professional cast
wd Li Yu *ph* Fei Xiaoping *ad* Wang Nan *ed* Jiang Jianwei, An Na
☆ Pan Yi (Xiaoqun), Shitou (Xiaoling), Zhang Jilian (Mother), Zhang Qianqian (Wujujun)

A Fish Called Wanda **
US 1988 108m Technicolor
MGM (Michael Shamberg)
Diamond-heist comedy depending on Anglo-American rivalries for its laughs.
Deft, blackish comedy with a little romance thrown in; its humour relied too much on Cleese's familiar, if expert, performance as an overbearing, uptight buffoon.
w John Cleese, Charles Crichton *d* Charles Crichton *ph* Alan Hume *m* John Du Prez *pd* Roger Murray-Leach
☆ John Cleese, Jamie Lee Curtis, Kevin Kline, Michael Palin, Maria Aitken
Kevin Kline
Charles Crichton; best original screenplay
John Cleese (as actor); Michael Palin (supporting actor)

The Fish that Saved Pittsburgh
US 1979 104m colour
United Artists (David Dashev, Gary Stromberg)
An inept baseball team improves its performance by recruiting players born under the sign of Pisces.
Uninteresting comedy to a disco beat.
w Jaison Starkes, Edmond Stevens *d* Gilbert Moses *ph* Frank Stanley *m* Thom Bell *ad* Herbert Spencer Deverill *ed* Peter Zinner
☆ Julius Erving, Jonathan Winters, Meadowlark Lemon, Jack Kehoe, Margaret Avery, James Bond III, Michael V. Gazzo, M. Emmet Walsh, Stockard Channing, Flip Wilson

'A Modern Day Tale About The Search For Love, Sanity, Ethel Merman And The Holy Grail.'
The Fisher King **
US 1991 137m Technicolor
Columbia TriStar (Debra Hill, Linda Obst)
A former disc jockey seeking salvation becomes involved in the mystic quest of a tramp who was once a medieval historian.
Enjoyable more for its director's extravagances than for its attempt at modern myth-making, and finally too diffuse to be taken seriously.
w Richard LaGravenese *d* Terry Gilliam *ph* Roger Pratt *m* George Fenton *pd* Mel Bourne *ed* Lesley Walker
☆ Robin Williams, Jeff Bridges, Amanda Plummer, Mercedes Ruehl, Michael Jeter
'Has all the ingredients of a major critical and commercial event: two actors at the top of their form, and a compelling, well-directed and well-produced story.' – *Variety*
'At heart, the film is no different from a whole string of Hollywood movies centering on mysterious madmen who may be legendary heroes ... A peculiarly irritating failure – a leaden piece of uplift.' – *New Yorker*
Mercedes Ruehl
Robin Williams; Richard LaGravenese; George Fenton; Mel Bourne

F.I.S.T. *
US 1978 145m Technicolor
UA/Norman Jewison (Gene Corman)
The rise and fall of a union boss.
Reminiscent of All the King's Men *and* On the Waterfront, *this much overlong melodrama has compelling passages, but the star is not quite equal to it and parts are both repetitive and obscure.*
w Joe Eszterhas, Sylvester Stallone *d* Norman Jewison *ph* Laszlo Kovacs *m* Bill Conti *pd* Richard MacDonald
☆ Sylvester Stallone, Rod Steiger, Peter Boyle, Melinda Dillon, David Huffman, Tony Lo Bianco, Cassie Yates, Peter Donat, Henry Wilcoxon
'Stallone exerts the same compulsive presence we saw in *Rocky* – and this time there is the

added bonus that you can understand what he's saying.' – *Variety*

Fist of Fury (dubbed)
Hong Kong 1972 106m Eastmancolor Dyaliscope
Cathay/Golden Harvest (Raymond Chow)
aka: *The Chinese Connection*
aka: *The Iron Hand*
A kung-fu fighter revenges himself on a gang of Japanese karate experts who have murdered his old teacher.
Violent martial arts movie, enlivened by Lee's style in the frequent fight scenes.
wd Lo Wei *ph* Chen Ching Cheh *m* Joseph Koo *pd* Lo Wei *ed* Chang Yao Chung
☆ Bruce Lee, Nora Miao, James Tien, Robert Baker

Fist of the North Star (dubbed)
Japan 1986 112m colour
Tohi (Shoji Kishimoto)
In a world after a nuclear holocaust, grotesquely muscled thugs with mystic powers battle for supremacy.
Repellently violent animated feature, full of exploding heads, popping eyeballs and gushers of blood; as if that were not bad enough, it also lacks any narrative coherence.
w Buronson, Tetsuo Hara *graphic novel* Buronson, Tetsuo Hara *d* Toyoo Ashida *ph* Tamiyo Hosoda *m* Katsuhisa Haltori *ad* Shiko Tanaka
☆ Featuring the voices of John Vickery, Michael McConnohie, Melodee Spivack, Dan Woren, Tony Oliver, Wally Burr, Gregory Snegoff
† The film was released direct to video.

Fist of the North Star
US/Japan 1995 88m Foto-Kem
Overseas/First Look/Ozla/Zeta/Neo (Mark Yellen, Aki Komine)
The last champion of a martial arts studio battles against a ruthless dictator who plans to rule a post-apocalyptic world.
A live-action remake of the animated film which simplifies the narrative but retains the unpleasantly over-the-top comic-book violence with gouts of blood and exploding heads; the acting is resolutely one-dimensional.
w Peter Atkins, Tony Randel *graphic novels Buronson, Tetsuo Hara* *d* Tony Randel *ph* Jacques Haitkin *m* Christopher L. Stone *pd* Clark Hunter *ed* Sonny Baskin
☆ Gary Daniels, Costas Mandylor, Chris Penn, Malcolm McDowell, Isako Washio, Melvin Van Peebles, Downtown Julie Brown
'This ludicrously cramped nonsense, which presents the regulation post-Apocalypse wasteland on what is obviously a very small sound stage.' – *Sight and Sound*

A Fistful of Dollars ***
Italy/Germany/Spain 1964 100m Techniscope
UA/Jolly/Constantin/Ocean (Arrigo Colombo, Georgio Papi)
original title: *Per un Pugno di Dollari*
An avenging stranger, violent and mysterious, cleans up a Mexican border town.
A film with much to answer for: it began the craze for 'spaghetti Westerns', took its director to Hollywood, and made a TV cowboy into a world star. It turned the Western into a brutal baroque opera, a violent clash between individuals.
w Sergio Leone, Duccio Tessari *d Sergio Leone* *ph* Massimo Dallamano *m* Ennio Morricone
☆ *Clint Eastwood*, Gian Maria Volonte, Marianne Koch
'A film with no purpose beyond its ninety-five-minute Technicolor close-up portrayals of men being shot, gouged, burned, beaten and stomped to death.' – *Judith Crist*
† Direct sequels by Leone, apart from numerous imitations, are *For a Few Dollars More* and *The Good, the Bad and the Ugly.*

A Fistful of Dynamite
Italy 1971 150m Techniscope
UA/Rafran/San Marco/Miura (Fulvio Morsella)
original title: *Giu' la Testa*
aka: *Duck, You Sucker*
In 1913 a Mexican bandit and an ex-IRA explosives expert join forces to rob a bank.
Overblown action spectacular, far too long to be sustained by its flashes of humour and excitement. A good instance of what happens to a small talent when success goes to its head.
wd Sergio Leone *ph* Giuseppe Ruzzolini *m* Ennio Morricone
☆ Rod Steiger, James Coburn, Romolo Valli, Maria Monti

Fists in the Pocket *
Italy 1965 113m bw
Doria (Ezio Passadore)
original title: *I Pugni in Tasca*
One of a family of epileptics murders most of the others in order to help his normal eldest brother.
Complex black melodrama which makes its points, if it has any, with great style.
wd Marco Bellocchio *ph* Alberto Marrama *m* Ennio Morricone
☆ Lou Castel, Paola Pitagora, Liliana Gerace
'There have been few débuts as exciting as this in recent years.' – *Tom Milne, MFB*

Fists of Fury: see *The Big Boss*

Fitzcarraldo ****
West Germany 1982 158m colour
Werner Herzog/ProjectFilmproduktion/Zweite Deutsches Fernsehen/Wildlife Films, Peru (Werner Herzog, Lucki Stipetic)
In Peru at the turn of the century, an eccentric Irishman succeeds against all odds in establishing an opera house in the jungle.
A strange and brilliant film centring on the hero's successful attempt to drag his massive boat from one river to another.
wd Werner Herzog *ph Thomas Mauch* *m Popol Vuh*
☆ *Klaus Kinski*, Claudia Cardinale, Jose Lewgoy, Paul Hittscher
† 'Fitzcarraldo' is the nearest the natives can get to 'Fitzgerald'.

Fitzwilly *
US 1967 102m DeLuxe Panavision
UA/Dramatic Features Inc/Walter Mirisch
GB title: *Fitzwilly Strikes Back*
A New York butler, in order to keep his lady in style, has to organize the staff into a crime syndicate.
Moderately inventive, good-looking comedy with rather too much plot and not enough funny lines.
w Isobel Lennart *novel A Garden of Cucumbers* by Poyntz Tyler *d* Delbert Mann *ph* Joseph Biroc *m* Johnny Williams
☆ *Dick Van Dyke, Edith Evans*, Barbara Feldon, John McGiver, Harry Townes, John Fiedler, Norman Fell, Cecil Kellaway, Anne Seymour, Sam Waterston, Billy Halop

Fitzwilly Strikes Back: see *Fitzwilly*

Five
US 1951 89m bw
Columbia (Arch Oboler)
There are only five survivors of an atomic holocaust, and their political and racial tensions soon reduce the number to two.
Gutless talkfest which becomes interesting only when the camera moves out of doors; otherwise, too pretentious and dull by half.
wd Arch Oboler *ph* Lou Stoumen, Ed Spiegel, Sid Lubow *m* Henry Russell
☆ William Phipps, Susan Douglas, James Anderson, Charles Lampkin, Earl Lee
'The talk leaves one with a strong impression that in this case the fittest did not survive.' – *Penelope Houston*

Five Against the House
US 1955 84m bw
Columbia (Stirling Silliphant, John Barnwell)
College students try to rob a casino.
Meandering caper melodrama with too much flabby dialogue.
w Stirling Silliphant, John Barnwell *novel* Jack Finney *d* Phil Karlson *ph* Leslie White *m* George Duning
☆ Guy Madison, Kim Novak, Brian Keith, Kerwin Mathews, William Conrad

Five and Ten
US 1931 88m bw
MGM
GB title: *Daughter of Luxury*
A chain store heiress elopes with a married man, but is tamed by family misfortune.
Solid star drama which maintains points of interest.
w A. P. Younger, Edith Fitzgerald *novel* Fannie Hurst *d* Robert Z. Leonard
☆ Marion Davies, Leslie Howard, Richard Bennett, Irene Rich, Kent Douglass, Halliwell Hobbes

Five Angles on Murder: see *The Woman in Question*

Five Boys from Barska Street *
Poland 1953 115m Agfacolor
Film Polski
original title: *Piatka z Ulicy Barskiej*
Five city boys are placed on probation and gradually change their attitudes towards life and society.
Rather dated propaganda piece with a plot which surprisingly follows Western models.
wd Aleksander Ford *novel* Kazimierz Kozniewski *ph* Jaroslav Tuzar *m* Kazimierz Serocki
☆ Tadeusz Janczar, Aleksandra Slaska, Andrzej Kozak

Five Branded Women
Italy/US 1960 100m bw
Paramount/Dino de Laurentiis
Five Yugoslav girls have their heads shaved for associating with German soldiers, and after various adventures join the partisans.
Rough, tough war adventure which makes a few boring points about love and war.
w Michael Wilson, Paul Jarrico, Ivo Perelli *novel* Ugo Pirro *d* Martin Ritt *ph* Giuseppe Rotunno *m* Francesco Lavagnino
☆ Silvana Mangano, Van Heflin, Vera Miles, Barbara Bel Geddes, Jeanne Moreau, Richard Basehart, Harry Guardino, Steve Forrest, Alex Nicol
'For the most part the film is devoted to unexciting guerrilla action and uninviting partisan life ... obstinately unreal despite lashings of blood, mutilation, childbirth and death.' – *MFB*
† Michael Wilson and Paul Jarrico were omitted from the film's original credits because they were blacklisted at the time.

Five Came Back **
US 1939 75m bw
RKO (Robert Sisk)
A passenger plane crashlands in the jungle. It can carry back only five survivors, and headhunters are coming closer...
A minor film which gradually achieved cult status and was remade as Back to Eternity *as well as being the starting point for many variations. Still gripping in its dated way.*
w Jerry Cady, Dalton Trumbo, Nathanael West *d John Farrow* *ph* Nicholas Musuraca *m* Roy Webb
☆ Chester Morris, Lucille Ball, C. Aubrey Smith, Elizabeth Risdon, Wendy Barrie, John Carradine, Joseph Calleia, Allen Jenkins, Kent Taylor, Patric Knowles
'Exceptionally well-made adventure yarn, out of the B category and almost rates A ... looks like a solid click.' – *Variety*

Five Card Stud
US 1968 103m Technicolor
Paramount/Hal. B. Wallis
Members of a lynching party are murdered one by one.
Would-be nonchalant murder mystery Western: the stars just about hold it together, but it's an uphill fight.
w Marguerite Roberts *novel* Ray Gaulden *d* Henry Hathaway *ph* Daniel L. Fapp *m* Maurice Jarre
☆ Dean Martin, Robert Mitchum, Inger Stevens, Roddy McDowall, Katherine Justice, John Anderson, Yaphet Kotto
'Marginally watchable ... but destined to sink without trace minutes after one leaves the cinema.' – *Gavin Millar*
'So mediocre you can't get mad at it.' – *Judith Crist*

Five Corners *
US 1988 93m colour
Handmade Films (Tony Bill, Forest Murray)
Four old friends meet again when one of them is released from prison.
Set in the 1960s, a perceptive period piece that unhappily segues into an unconvincing melodrama.
w John Patrick Shanley *d* Tony Bill *ph* Fred Murphy *m* James Newton Howard *ed* Andy Blumenthal
☆ Jodie Foster, Tim Robbins, Todd Graff, John Turturro, Elizabeth Berridge, Rose Gregorio, Gregory Rozakis, John Seitz

Five Days One Summer *
US 1982 108m Technicolor
Warner/Ladd (Fred Zinnemann)
In 1932 a middle-aged Scots doctor takes his young mistress on an Alpine climbing holiday, and she falls for the guide.
Superbly photographed and crafted mountain movie, akin to the German epics of the early thirties. Alas, the content is very thin.
w Michael Austin *story Maiden Maiden* by Kay Boyle *d Fred Zinnemann* *ph Giuseppe Rotunno* *m* Elmer Bernstein *pd* Willy Holt *ed* Stuart Baird
☆ Sean Connery, Betsy Brantley, Lambert Wilson, Jennifer Hilary, Isabel Dean, Anna Massey
'Dawdling and eventually silly, though the veteran director's tenacity and craftsmanship provide muted applause.' – *Variety*

Five Dolls for an August Moon (dubbed)
Italy 1970 88m colour
PAC
original title: *Cinque Bambole per la Luna d'Agosto*
A group of wealthy industrialists and their entourages are murdered one by one when they go to an island mansion to bid for the rights to a valuable formula.
Although the plot is based on Agatha Christie's Ten Little Indians, *Bava shows little interest in its thriller aspects, preferring to concentrate on fashionable gloss, flashy photography and the occasional grisly image.*
w Mario Di Nardo *d* Mario Bava *ph* Antonio Rinaldi *m* Piero Umiliani *ad* Giuseppe Aldobranc
☆ William Berger, Ira Furstenberg, Edwige Fenech, Howard Ross (Renato Rossini), Helena Ronée, Teodoro Corrá, Maurice Poli
'A pleasure to watch even when the plot flags and the zooms proliferate.' – *Tom Milne*
† The British video release runs for 80m.

Five Easy Pieces **
US 1970 98m Technicolor
Columbia/Bert Schneider (Bob Rafelson, Richard Wechsler)
A middle-class drifter jilts his pregnant mistress for his brother's fiancée, but finally leaves both and hitches a ride to nowhere in particular.
Echoes of Easy Rider, The Graduate *and* Charlie Bubbles *abound in this generally likeable but insubstantial modern anti-drama which at least takes place in pleasant surroundings and is firmly directed.*
w Adrien Joyce *d* Bob Rafelson *ph* Laszlo Kovacs *m* various
☆ *Jack Nicholson*, Karen Black, Susan Anspach, Lois Smith, Billy 'Green' Bush, Fannie Flagg
best picture; Adrien Joyce; Jack Nicholson; Karen Black

'There are many kinds of love, but are there any without guilt?'
Five Finger Exercise
US 1962 109m bw
Columbia/Sonnis (Frederick Brisson)
A snobbish wife falls in love with a young house guest, with dire effect on her husband and son.
This West End study of a neurotic family is probably not good film material, certainly not adaptable to

California, and above all not suitable to this star's whizzbang dramatics. Numbing hysteria arrives early and stays till the end.
w Frances Goodrich, Albert Hackett *play* Peter Shaffer *d* Daniel Mann *ph* Harry Stradling *m* Jerome Moross
☆ Rosalind Russell, Jack Hawkins, Maximilian Schell, Richard Beymer

Five Fingers **
US 1952 108m bw
TCF (Otto Lang)

The valet of the British ambassador in Ankara sells military secrets to the Germans, who pay him but never use the information.
Absorbing, lightweight film adaptation of a true story of World War II; civilized suspense entertainment with all talents contributing nicely.
w Michael Wilson book Operation Cicero by L. C. Moyzisch *d Joseph L. Mankiewicz ph* Norbert Brodine *m* Bernard Herrmann *ad* Lyle Wheeler, George W. Davis
☆ *James Mason*, Danielle Darrieux, Michael Rennie, Walter Hampden, Oscar Karlweis, Herbert Berghof, John Wengraf, Michael Pate
'One of the highest, fastest and most absorbing spy melodramas since Hitchcock crossed the Atlantic.' – *Arthur Knight*
Michael Wilson; Joseph L. Mankiewicz

Five Gates to Hell
US 1959 98m bw Cinemascope
TCF
A Vietcong warlord carries off a nun and seven nurses; the latter escape by brutal means.
Unpleasant shocker showing no signs of talent in any department.
wd James Clavell *ph* Sam Leavitt *m* Paul Dunlap
☆ Dolores Michaels, Patricia Owens, Neville Brand, Kevin Scott, Nobu McCarthy, Nancy Kulp, Shirley Knight, Irish McCalla
'This grimly amateurish war film exploits sex and violence with an emotional arrest bordering on paranoia.' – *MFB*

Five Golden Dragons
GB 1965 92m Techniscope
Harry Alan Towers

An American playboy in Hong Kong becomes involved in the affairs of five master criminals preparing to sell out to the Mafia.
Anything-goes comedy-thriller, patchy at best, unintelligible at worst, and filled with ageing stars.
w Harry Alan Towers *d* Jeremy Summers
☆ Robert Cummings, Rupert Davies, Margaret Lee, Maria Perschy, Klaus Kinski, Dan Duryea, Brian Donlevy, Christopher Lee, George Raft

Five Golden Hours
GB/Italy 1960 90m bw
Columbia/Anglofilm/Fabio Jegher (Mario Zampi)

A con man tries to murder three widows who have invested money in one of his schemes.
Ill-judged black comedy, sadly lacking style.
w Hans Wilhelm *d* Mario Zampi *ph* Christopher Challis *m* Stanley Black
☆ Ernie Kovacs, Cyd Charisse, Kay Hammond, George Sanders, Dennis Price, Reginald Beckwith, Martin Benson, Ron Moody, Finlay Currie, Avice Landone, Sydney Tafler, John Le Mesurier, Clelia Matania

Five Graves to Cairo ***
US 1943 96m bw
Paramount (Charles Brackett)

During the North Africa campaign, British spies try to destroy Rommel's secret supply dumps.
Intriguing spy melodrama set in a desert hotel, a notable example of Hollywood's ability to snatch polished drama from the headlines.
w Charles Brackett, Billy Wilder play Lajos Biro *d Billy Wilder ph* John Seitz *m* Miklos Rozsa *ad* Hans Dreier, Ernst Fegte *ed* Doane Harrison
☆ Franchot Tone, Anne Baxter, *Erich von Stroheim* (Rommel), Akim Tamiroff, Peter Van Eyck, Miles Mander
'Von Stroheim has all the other movie Huns backed completely off the screen.' – *Variety*
'Billy Wilder must have had something a little grander in mind: the cleverness lacks lustre.' – *New Yorker, 1978*
'A fabulous film fable, but it has been executed with enough finesse to make it a rather exciting pipe dream.' – *Howard Barnes, New York Herald Tribune*
† Locations representing the African desert include California's Salton Sea and Yuma, Arizona.
John Seitz; art direction; editing

Five Guns West
US 1955 78m Pathécolor
Palo Alto (Roger Corman)

Five criminals are recruited into the Southern army to catch a traitor and some Union gold.
Western trial run for The Dirty Dozen; *cheapjack actioner, quite tolerable of its kind.*
w R. Wright Campbell *d* Roger Corman *ph* Floyd Crosby *m* Buddy Bregman *ed* Ronald Sinclair
☆ John Lund, Dorothy Malone, Chuck Connors, Paul Birch

The Five Heartbeats *
US 1991 121m DeLuxe
TCF (Loretha C. Jones)

The ups and downs of a vocal group in the 1960s and 70s.
A dramatic and witty account of the tribulations of a black group fighting for recognition in a world controlled by whites.
w Robert Townsend, Keenen Ivory Wayans *d* Robert Townsend *ph* Bill Dill *m* Stanley Clarke *pd* Wynn Thomas *ed* John Carter
☆ Robert Townsend, Michael Wright, Leon, Harry J. Lennix, Tico Wells, Diahann Carroll, Harold Nicholas, Tressa Thomas, John Canada Terrell
'Convincing only in its sweet and dazzling musical sequences, this overly sincere effort otherwise misses its mark.' – *Variety*

Five Miles to Midnight *
France/Italy 1962 110m bw
UA/Filmsonor/Dear Film (Anatole Litvak)
A neurotic believed dead forces his terrified wife to collect his life insurance.
Hysterical melodrama, smoothly made with all the familiar expressionist devices, but far too long for its content.
w Peter Viertel, Hugh Wheeler *d Anatole Litvak ph Henri Alekan m* Mikis Theodorakis
☆ Sophia Loren, Anthony Perkins, Gig Young, Jean-Pierre Aumont, Yolande Turner, Tommy Norden
'From the polished immediacy of the cars, streets, shop windows and café tables to the off-focus vertigo shots of panic, from the overhead view of neighbours on stairs ... to the close-ups of hands in filing trays touching off the details of fear and guilt, there is a thread of colour to keep you watching.' – *MFB*
'One of those movies without a country that are becoming as fixed a part of the international scene as the Duke and Duchess of Windsor.' – *Arthur Schlesinger Jnr, Show*

Five Million Years to Earth: see *Quatermass and the Pit*

The Five Pennies *
US 1959 117m Technicolor Vistavision
Paramount/Dena (Jack Rose)

The rags-to-riches success story of cornet player Red Nichols.
The only touch of originality in this biopic is that the subject is given touches of irascibility. Production values reach a good standard.
w Jack Rose, Melville Shavelson *d* Melville Shavelson *ph* Daniel L. Fapp *m* cornet solos: Red Nichols *m/ly* Sylvia Fine *md* Leith Stevens *ad* Hal Pereira, Tambi Larsen
☆ Danny Kaye (Red Nichols), Barbara Bel Geddes, *Louis Armstrong*, Bob Crosby, Harry Guardino, Tuesday Weld, Ray Anthony
Daniel L. Fapp; Leith Stevens; title song

Five Savage Men: see *The Animals*

Five Star Final **
US 1931 89m bw
Warner
A sensation-seeking newspaper causes tragedy.
Dated but still powerful melodrama which set the pattern for all the newspaper films of the thirties.
w Robert Lord, Byron Morgan play Louis Weitzenkorn *d Mervyn Le Roy ph* Sol Polito *md* Leo F. Forbstein
☆ *Edward G. Robinson*, H. B. Warner, Marian Marsh, Anthony Bushell, George E. Stone, Ona Munson, Aline MacMahon, Boris Karloff
'All the elements to make a hit attraction.' – *Variety*
† Remade in 1936 with Humphrey Bogart, as *Two Against the World.*
best picture

The 5000 Fingers of Doctor T *
US 1953 88m Technicolor
Columbia (*Stanley Kramer*)

A boy who hates piano lessons dreams of his teacher as an evil genius who keeps five hundred boys imprisoned in a castle of musical instruments.
Badly scripted fantasy with gleaming sophisticated dream sequences which deserve a better frame. A real oddity to come from Hollywood at this time, even though Dr Seuss's books were and are bestsellers.
w Dr Seuss (Theodore Geisel), Allan Scott *d* Roy Rowland *ph Franz Planer m* Frederick Hollander *ch* Eugene Loring *pd Rudolph Sternad ly* Dr Seuss
☆ Hans Conried, Tommy Rettig, Peter Lind Hayes, Mary Healy
Frederick Hollander

Five Weeks in a Balloon
US 1962 101m DeLuxe
Cinemascope
TCF (Irwin Allen)

In 1862 a professor is financed on a balloon trip into central Africa.
Would-be humorous semi-fantasy which strives to equal Journey to the Center of the Earth *but unfortunately falls flat on its face despite the interesting talent available. Limp comedy situations, poor production values.*
w Charles Bennett, Irwin Allen, Albert Gail *novel* Jules Verne *d* Irwin Allen *ph* Winton Hoch *m* Paul Sawtell *ad* Jack Martin Smith, Alfred Ybarra
☆ Cedric Hardwicke, Peter Lorre, Red Buttons, Fabian, Richard Haydn, Billy Gilbert, Herbert Marshall, Reginald Owen, Henry Daniell

Fixed Bayonets! *
US 1951 93m bw
TCF (Jules Buck)
An American platoon in Korea fights a rearguard action.
Downbeat war melodrama of a familiar kind, with more characterization than action.
wd Samuel Fuller *ph* Lucien Ballard *m* Roy Webb
☆ Richard Basehart, Gene Evans, Michael O'Shea, Richard Hylton, Craig Hill

The Fixer
US 1968 130m Metrocolor
MGM/Edward Lewis, John Frankenheimer
A Jew in Tsarist Russia denies his race but becomes a scapegoat for various crimes and is imprisoned without trial until he becomes a *cause célèbre.*
Worthy but extremely dreary realist melodrama.
w Dalton Trumbo *novel* Bernard Malamud *d* John Frankenheimer *ph* Marcel Grignon *m* Maurice Jarre
☆ Alan Bates, Dirk Bogarde, Georgia Brown, Jack Gilford, Hugh Griffith, Elizabeth Hartman, Ian Holm, David Warner, Carol White, Murray Melvin, Peter Jeffrey, Michael Goodliffe
'The kind of film in which one has to admire much of the acting simply because it is all there is to admire.' – *David Pirie*
'A totally false film, devoid of a breath of human life or truth.' – *Arthur Schlesinger Jnr*
'Alan Bates's bare posterior, known to us from *Georgy Girl* and *King of Hearts*, makes another timely appearance here, thus becoming one of the most exposed arses in cinematic annals.' – *John Simon*
Alan Bates

The Fixer Uppers
US 1935 20m bw
Hal Roach

Christmas card salesmen try to help a bored wife, but her jealous husband challenges Ollie to a duel.
Rather flat comedy marking a tailing-off from the stars' best period.
w uncredited *d* Charles Rogers *ph* Art Lloyd *ed* Bert Jordan
☆ Stan Laurel, Oliver Hardy, Mae Busch, Charles Middleton, Arthur Housman, Noah Young
† A remake of an early silent, *Slipping Wives.*

Fixing the Shadow
US 1992 101m Technicolor
Columbia TriStar/Polar/Capitol (John Fiedler, Mark Tarlov)

A sacked cop is recruited by the FBI to infiltrate a violent gang of drug-pushing bikers.
Dreary action picture that runs through all the clichés of the genre without any conviction.
wd Larry Ferguson *ph* Robert Stevens *m* Cory Lerios, John D'Andrea *pd* James L. Schoppe *ed* Robert C. Jones, Don Brochu
☆ Charlie Sheen, Linda Fiorentino, Michael Madsen, Courtney B. Vance, Rip Torn
'Trashy dialogue, indifferent performances and shoddy construction make it strictly minor league stuff.' – *Film Review*

The Flame and the Arrow *
US 1950 88m Technicolor
Warner/Norma (Harold Hecht, Frank Ross)

In medieval Italy, a rebel leader seeks victory over a tyrant.
Good-humoured Robin Hood stuff with the star at his most acrobatic.
w Waldo Salt *d* Jacques Tourneur *ph* Ernest Haller *m* Max Steiner *ad* Edward Carrere
☆ *Burt Lancaster*, Virginia Mayo, Robert Douglas, Aline MacMahon, Frank Allenby, Nick Cravat
'I never found a Technicolor costume picture so entertaining.' – *Richard Mallett, Punch*
Ernest Haller; Max Steiner

A Flame In My Heart
France/Switzerland 1987 110m bw
Mainline/Garance/Le Sept/Filmograph (Paulo Branco)
original title: *Une Flamme dans Ma Coeur*
An actress ditches her working-class Arab lover for a journalist.
Pretentious and tasteless, always straining for the arty effect.
w Myriam Mezières, Alain Tanner *d* Alain Tanner *ph* Acacio de Almeida *m* Bach *ed* Laurent Uhler
☆ Myriam Mezières, Benoit Regent, Aziz Kabouche, André Marcon, Jean-Gabriel Nordman, Jean-Yves Berteloot, Anne Rucki, Douglas Ireland

Flame in the Streets
GB 1961 93m colour Cinemascope
Rank/Somerset (Roy Baker)

A liberal-minded union man erupts when his daughter proposes to marry a black man.
Predictable East End problem picture, unconvincingly set and acted and boring into the bargain.
w Ted Willis *play Hot Summer Night* by Ted Willis *d* Roy Baker *ph* Christopher Challis *m* Phil Green
☆ John Mills, Brenda de Banzie, Sylvia Syms, Earl Cameron, Johnny Sekka, Ann Lynn, Wilfrid Brambell
'Its methods belong more to the writer's study than to life.' – *John Gillett*

The Flame of New Orleans *
US 1941 79m bw
Universal (Joe Pasternak)
A European adventuress settles in America.
Fluffy comedy romance with the exiled director scarcely in top form.
w Norman Krasna *d* René Clair *ph* Rudolph Maté *m* Frank Skinner *ad* Martin Obzina, Jack Otterson
☆ Marlene Dietrich, Roland Young, Bruce Cabot, Mischa Auer, Andy Devine, Frank Jenks, Eddie Quillan, Laura Hope Crews, Franklin Pangborn
† Remade as *Scarlet Angel.*
art direction

Flame of the Barbary Coast
US 1945 97m bw
Republic (Joseph Kane)

In old San Francisco, a cowboy becomes involved with a night-club queen, and their fortunes are resolved by the earthquake.
Tolerable period melodrama, and the one in which Wayne played a character named Duke: the nickname stuck.
w Borden Chase *d* Joseph Kane *ph* Robert de Grasse *m* Dale Butts *sp* Howard and Theodore Lydecker
☆ John Wayne, Ann Dvorak, Joseph Schildkraut, William Frawley, Virginia Grey, Russell Hicks, Jack Norton, Paul Fix, Marc Lawrence
Dale Butts

Flame Over India: see *Northwest Frontier*

The Flame Within
US 1935 73m bw
MGM
A lady psychiatrist falls for the husband of one of her patients.
Decent star melodrama.
wd Edmund Goulding
☆ Ann Harding, Maureen O'Sullivan, Louis Hayward, Henry Stephenson, Herbert Marshall

Flaming Brothers
Hong Kong 1988 117m colour
In-Gear/Rover K. C. Tang (Alan Tang)

Two orphans, lifelong friends who grow up to be successful crooks in Macao, run into problems: one wishes to go straight so that he can marry, the other provokes a war with the local gang boss.
Romantic comedy, religiosity and the extreme violence on view here make for a gruesome mix; the abrupt changes from sentimentality to brutality will be hard to take for all but devout aficionados of the genre.
w Kelvin Wang *d* Tony Velesco *ph* Ma Chor Shing *m* Lam Mun Ye *ad* William Cheung *ed* Poon Hung
☆ Chow Yun-Fat, Alan Tang, Jenny Yen, Pat Ha, Tse Yin, Philip Chan, Kent Tsui

Flaming Feather
US 1951 78m Technicolor
Paramount (Nat Holt)
Arizona is harassed by an outlaw called The Sidewinder who leads a troupe of pillaging Indians.
Spot-the-villain Western; not much to detain one.
w Gerald Drayson Adams *d* Ray Enright *ph* Ray Rennahan
☆ Sterling Hayden, Forrest Tucker, Barbara Rush, Richard Arlen, Victor Jory, Edgar Buchanan

Flaming Star *
US 1960 92m DeLuxe Cinemascope
TCF (David Weisbart)

A half-breed family is torn between two loyalties.
Solemn, unusual Civil War Western with a downbeat ending.
w Clair Huffaker, Nunnally Johnson *novel* Clair Huffaker *d* Don Siegel *ph* Charles G. Clarke *m* Cyril Mockridge
☆ *Elvis Presley, Dolores del Rio*, Steve Forrest, Barbara Eden, John McIntire, Rodolfo Acosta
'Despite familiar absurdities, it has more than its share of good moments.' – *MFB*

The Flaming Torch: see *The Bob Mathias Story*

The Flamingo Kid
US 1984 100m DeLuxe
Palace/Mercury/ABC (Michael Phillips)

In 1963, a teenager comes of age while working at a beach club.
Innocent but unexciting comedy-drama about matters which scarcely concern grown-ups.
w Neal Marshall, Garry Marshall (no relation) *d* Garry Marshall *ph* James A. Contner *pd* Lawrence Miller *ed* Priscilla Nedd
☆ Matt Dillon, Richard Crenna, Hector Elizondo, Jessica Walter, Fisher Stevens

'A wrong girl from the right side of the tracks!'
Flamingo Road *
US 1949 94m bw
Warner (Jerry Wald)

A tough carnival dancer is stranded in a small town and soon affects the lives of the local politicians.
Standard melodrama from a bestseller, absurd but well performed.
w Robert Wilder *play* Robert Wilder, Sally Wilder *d* Michael Curtiz *ph* Ted McCord *m* Max Steiner
☆ Joan Crawford, David Brian, Sydney Greenstreet, Zachary Scott, Gladys George, Virginia Huston, Fred Clark

Une Flamme Dans Mon Coeur: see *A Flame In My Heart*

The Flanagan Boy
GB 1953 81m bw
Exclusive/Hammer (Anthony Hinds)
US title: *Bad Blonde*
A young merchant seaman becomes a boxer and is corrupted by a hard-boiled blonde.
Competent British imitation of an American B movie.
w Guy Elmes, Richard Landau *novel* Max Catto *d* Reginald LeBorg *ph* Walter Harvey *m* Ivor Slaney *ad* Wilfred Arnold *ed* James Needs
☆ Tony Wright, Barbara Payton, Sidney James, John Slater, Frederick Valk, Marie Burke

Flap
US 1970 106m Technicolor Panavision
Warner (Jerry Adler)
GB title: *The Last Warrior*
A drunken Indian on a dilapidated modern reservation starts a public relations war and leads a march on the city.
Unendearing comedy with a tragic end tacked on, not very entertaining as whimsy, farce or social conscience.
w Clair Huffaker *novel Nobody Loves a Drunken Indian* by Clair Huffaker *d* Carol Reed *ph* Fred Koenekamp *m* Marvin Hamlisch
☆ Anthony Quinn, Claude Akins, Tony Bill, Victor Jory, Shelley Winters

Flare Up
US 1969 98m Metrocolor
MGM/GMF (Leon Fromkes)
A man kills his wife and threatens her friends who he feels are responsible for the break-up of his marriage.
Sensationally violent melodrama with a plot that goes back to Sudden Fear *and further. Adequately made.*
w Mark Rodgers *d* James Neilson *ph* Andrew J. McIntyre *m* Les Baxter
☆ Raquel Welch, James Stacy, Luke Askew, Don Chastain, Ron Rifkin

Flash Gordon *
The hero of the 25th century was created in comic strip form by Alex Raymond and his chief claims to film fame are three wild and woolly serials made by Universal: *Flash Gordon* (1936), *Flash Gordon's Trip to Mars* (1938), and *Flash Gordon Conquers the Universe* (1940), all starring Buster Crabbe with Charles Middleton as the wily Emperor Ming.
Their cheap and cheerful futuristic sets and their non-stop action have kept them popular with film buffs through the years. In 1974 a semi-porno spoof, Flesh Gordon, *appeared.*

'Pathetic Earthlings... Who Can Save You Now?'
Flash Gordon
GB 1980 115m Technicolor Todd-AO
EMI/Famous/Starling (Dino de Laurentiis)

A football hero, his girlfriend, and Dr Zarkov have adventures on the planet Mongo.
Lively comic strip addition to the increasing numbers of such things being restaged at enormous expense fifty years after their prime.
w Lorenzo Semple Jnr, from characters created by Alex Raymond *d* Michael Hodges *ph* Gil Taylor *m* Queen *pd* Danilo Donati
☆ Sam J. Jones, Melody Anderson, Topol, Max von Sydow, Timothy Dalton, Brian Blessed, Peter Wyngarde
'An expensively irrelevant gloss on its sources.' – *Richard Combs, MFB*

'The yippie and yuppie. Only a vowel stands between them.'
Flashback *
US 1990 108m colour
Paramount (Marvin Worth)

An uptight young FBI agent is chosen to escort to prison a hero of the counter-culture who has been caught after 20 years on the run.
A lightweight comedy of a culture clash, but too contrived to afford lasting amusement, particularly as everyone ends up on the same side.
w David Loughery *d* Franco Amurri *ph* Stefan Czapsky *m* Barry Goldberg *pd* Vincent Cresciman *ed* C. Timothy O'Meara
☆ Dennis Hopper, Kiefer Sutherland, Carol Kane, Paul Dooley, Cliff de Young, Richard Masur, Michael McKean, Kathleen York, Tom O'Brien

'Don't you understand? When you give up the dream, you die!'
Flashdance *
US 1983 98m Movielab
Paramount/Polygram (Don Simpson, Jerry Bruckheimer)

A female welder in a Pittsburgh factory has ambitions to be a ballet dancer.
Slickly-made, disco-style but dramatically empty entertainment.
w Tom Hedley, Joe Eszterhas *d* Adrian Lyne *ph* Don Peterman *m* Giorgio Moroder *ed* Bud Smith, Walt Mulconery
☆ Jennifer Beals, Michael Nouri, Lilia Skala, Sunny Johnson, Kyle T. Heffner, Belinda Bauer
'It resembles an extended video for a record album.' – *Observer*
'A preposterous success.' – *Guardian*
'Basically, a series of rock videos.' – *New Yorker*
song, 'Flashdance … What a Feeling' (*m* Giorgio Moroder, *ly* Keith Forsey, Irene Cara)
cinematography; editing; song, 'Maniac' (*m/ly* Michael Sembello, Dennis Matkosky)

'You never know anything about anybody until they're dead.'
Flashfire
US 1994 90m colour
Silver Lion/Avondale (Lance Hool)

Police detectives investigate the activities of an arsonist.
Unoriginal paranoid thriller, about corruption in high places; it offers nothing new or interesting.
w John Warren, Dan York *d* Elliot Silverstein *ph* Bert Dunk *m* Sylvester Lay *pd* Gregory Melton *ed* Mark Conte
☆ Billy Zane, Louis Gossett Jnr, Kristin Minter, Tom Mason
'Pleasant and inoffensive, but decidedly unexciting.' – *Variety*

Flashpoint
US 1984 94m Metrocolor
Home Box Office/Silver Screen (Skip Short)

Border patrolmen discover treasure and decide to make off with it.
Competent action melodrama which doesn't quite hang together in the later stretches but has plenty of lively moments.
w Dennis Shryack, Michael Butler *novel* George La Fountaine *d* William Tannen *ph* Peter Moss *m* various, performed by Tangerine Dream
☆ Kris Kristofferson, Treat Williams, Rip Torn, Kevin Conway, Miguel Ferrer

Flatliners
US 1990 114m DeLuxe Panavision
Columbia-Tri-Star/Stonebridge (Michael Douglas, Rick Bieber)

Medical students experiment to discover whether there is life after death.
Hectic fantasy, filmed in a restless manner.
w Peter Filardi *d* Joel Schumacher *ph* Jan de Bont *m* James Newton Howard *ed* Robert Brown
☆ Kiefer Sutherland, Julia Roberts, Kevin Bacon, William Baldwin, Oliver Platt, Kimberly Scott, Joshua Rudoy, Benjamin Mouton
'Filmed like an epic, packed with crisis, shock and suspense, it's a small tale that has been spectacularly escalated into a tall one.' – *Philip Strick, MFB*

Flavia Priestess of Violence: see *Flavia the Heretic*

Flavia the Heretic (dubbed)
Italy/France 1974 97m Technicolor
Eagle/PAC/ROC

original title: *Flavia la Monaca Musulmana*
aka: *Flavia la Nonne Musulmana; Flavia Priestess of Violence; The Rebel Nun*
Forced to become a nun by her father and appalled by the violence of masculine society, a young woman takes her revenge by joining a force of invading Muslims.
An unpleasant mixture of religiosity and sadism, masquerading as a feminist tract. Some images are extraordinary – a naked woman crawling into the hanging carcase of a cow – but hardly compensate for its general lack of narrative drive.
w Fabrizio Onofri, Gianfranco Mingozzi, Bruno Di Geronimo, Sergio Tau *story* Raniero Di Giovanbattista, Sergio Tau, Francesco Vietri *d* Gianfranco Mingozzi *ph* Alfio Contini *m* Nicola Piovani *ad* Guido Josia *ed* Ruggero Mastroianni
☆ Florinda Bolkan, Maria Casares, Claudio Cassinelli, Anthony Corlan, Spiros Focas

'They couldn't like each other less, or need each other more.'
Flawless *
US 1999 111m DeLuxe
MGM/Tribeca (Joel Schumacher, Jane Rosenthal)

After he suffers a stroke, a macho security guard takes therapeutic singing lessions from his neighbour, a drag artiste saving for a sex-change operation.
Genial comedy of opposites grudgingly coming to respect one another, with two good performances helping to cover up its formulaic qualities.
wd Joel Schumacher *ph* Declan Quinn *m* Bruce Roberts *pd* Jan Roelfs *ed* Mark Stevens *cos* Daniel Orlandi
☆ Robert De Niro (Walt Koontz), Philip Seymour Hoffman (Rusty), Barry Miller (Leonard Wilcox), Chris Bauer (Jacko), Skipp Sudduth (Tommy), Wilson Jermaine Heredia (Cha-Cha), Nashom Benjamin (Amazing Grace), Scott Allen Cooper (Ivana), Rory Cochrane (Pogo), Daphne Rubin-Vega (Tia), Wanda De Jesus (Karen)
'A film that should be seen for the acting talent on board rather than its originality (or lack thereof).' – *Empire*

Flaxy Martin
US 1948 86m bw
Warner (Saul Elkins)
A lawyer falls for a racketeer's girlfriend and finds himself framed for murder.
Flatly-handled melodrama with unsympathetic characters.
w David Lang *d* Richard Bare *ph* Carl Guthrie
☆ Zachary Scott, Virginia Mayo, Dorothy Malone, Tom d'Andrea, Elisha Cook Jnr

A Flea in Her Ear *
US/France 1968 94m DeLuxe Panavision
TCF (Fred Kohlmar)
Various suspicious wives and husbands converge on the notorious Hotel Coq d'Or.
Disappointing filming of a Feydeau farce, which needs to be much more cleverly handled to come over with its full theatrical force.
w John Mortimer *play La Puce à l'Oreille* by Georges Feydeau *d* Jacques Charon *ph* Charles Lang *m* Bronislau Kaper *pd Alexander Trauner*
☆ Rex Harrison, Rachel Roberts, Rosemary Harris, Louis Jourdan, John Williams, Grégoire Aslan, Edward Hardwicke, Frank Thornton, Victor Sen Yung
'The plunge into madness never comes, and one is left with the sight of a group of talented players struggling with alien material.' – *Michael Billington, Illustrated London News*

'See how they run.'
Fled
US 1996 105m DeLuxe
MGM (Frank Mancuso Jnr)

Two convicts escape, chased by a hitman hired by a gangster, who wants to get back incriminating evidence that one of them possesses.

Chase thriller that borrows heavily from predecessors, consisting of a sequence of shoot-outs, none of them of any particular interest.
w Preston A. Whitmore II *d* Kevin Hooks *ph* Matthew F. Leonetti *m* Graeme Revell *pd* Charles Bennett *ed* Richard Nord, Joseph Gutowski
☆ Laurence Fishburne, Stephen Baldwin, Will Patton, Robert John Burke, Robert Hooks, Victor Rivers, David Dukes, Salma Hayek
'Devotes itself to one mindless macho bang-bang sequence after another.' – *Ty Burr, Entertainment Weekly*

'Gobs of glee! A boatload of beauties! A shipful of songs!'

The Fleet's In *
US 1942 93m bw
Paramount (Paul Jones)
A sailor on leave in San Francisco takes a bet that he can kiss the glamorous singer at a swank nightclub.
Mindless wartime musical which happened to set the seal of success on a number of young talents.
w Walter de Leon, Sid Silvers, Ralph Spence *play Sailor Beware* by Kenyon Nicholson *story Monte Price, J. Walter Ruben d* Victor Schertzinger *ph* William Mellor *m/ly* Victor Schertzinger, Johnny Mercer *ed* Paul Weatherwax
☆ Dorothy Lamour, William Holden, *Eddie Bracken, Betty Hutton*, Cass Daley, Gil Lamb, Leif Erickson, Betty Jane Rhodes
'A slim and obvious comedy with some good tunes. Much of the film is a roughhouse; several reels towards the end are turned over to straight vaudeville.' – *Eileen Creelman, New York Sun*
† Previously a Clara Bow vehicle, it was later remade as *Sailor Beware* starring Dean Martin and Jerry Lewis
♫ 'I Remember You'; 'When You Hear the Time Signal'; 'The Fleet's In'; 'Tomorrow You Belong to Uncle Sam'; 'Arthur Murray Taught Me Dancing in a Hurry'; 'If You Build a Better Mousetrap'; 'Tangerine'; 'Conga from Honga'

'He sacrificed his career for the sake of a woman's lying lips!'

Flesh *
US 1932 95m bw
MGM
A German wrestler in the US falls for a street waif.
Unusual, rather unattractive, but vivid melodrama.
w Leonard Praskins, Edgar Allan Woolf, Moss Hart *story* Edmund Goulding *d* John Ford *ph* Arthur Edeson *ed* William S. Gray
☆ Wallace Beery, Ricardo Cortez, Karen Morley, John Miljan, Jean Hersholt, Herman Bing, Edward Brophy
'Not bad, could have been better ... that it takes 95 minutes to get home is the big fault.' – *Variety*

Flesh *
US 1968 105m colour
Vaughn/Score Movies (Andy Warhol)
aka: *Andy Warhol's Flesh*
A day in the life of a male prostitute.
A revelation at the time, for putting New York street life and unabashed sexuality on the screen. It wears better than most underground movies of its time.
wd Paul Morrissey
☆ Joe Dallesandro, Geraldine Smith, Patti D'Arbanville, Candy Darling, Jackie Curtis, Geri Miller
'With this strangely kindly and sympathetic film obscenity is only in the beholder's eye.' – *David Robinson, Financial Times*
'Totally obscene from the conventional point of view.' – *John Weightman, Encounter*

Flesh & Blood
US 1985 126m DeLuxe Technovision
Riverside/Impala (Gys Versluys)
In a dark medieval world, a young bride-to-be is kidnapped and raped, but grows to like it.
Unpleasant wallow in a decadent world of the imagination.
w Gerard Soeteman, Paul Verhoeven *d* Paul Verhoeven *ph* Jan de Bont *m* Basil Poledouris *ad* Felix Murcia *ed* Ine Schenkkan
☆ Rutger Hauer, Jennifer Jason Leigh, Tom Burlinson, Jack Thompson, Susan Tyrrell, Ronald Lacey

'An Appalling Amalgam of Carnage and Carnality...'

The Flesh and Blood Show
GB 1972 96m Eastmancolor
Tigon/Peter Walker
Actors rehearsing a play in a derelict seaside theatre are killed off one by one.
A low-budget horror-cum-whodunnit, with a few interesting moments before it succumbs to banality.
w Alfred Shaughnessy *d* Peter Walker *ph* Peter Jessop *m* Cyril Ornadel *ed* Ron Pope
☆ Jenny Hanley, Ray Brooks, Luan Peters, Judy Matheson, Candace Glendenning, Robin Askwith, Patrick Barr, Jess Conrad
'Has an unexpectedly pleasing, old-fashioned quality about it.' – *David Pirie, MFB*
† The film was partly made in 3D.
†† The 1997 video release runs for 86m.

Flesh and Bone *
US 1993 124m DeLuxe
Paramount/Mirage/Spring Creek (Mark Rosenberg, Paula Weinstein)
A vending machine operator realizes that the woman he meets on the road is the only survivor of a family killed by his crooked father 30 years earlier.
Tense, intriguing psychological drama of love and betrayal, although its conclusion is not altogether satisfactory.
wd Steve Kloves *ph* Philippe Rousselot *m* Thomas Newman *pd* Jon Hutman *ed* Mia Goldman
☆ Dennis Quaid, Meg Ryan, James Caan, Gwyneth Paltrow, Scott Wilson, Christopher Rydell
'Offbeat but emotionally stunted piece ... Trying to shoehorn a cute romance of temperamental opposites into an essentially somber, violent format.' – *Variety*

Flesh and Fantasy *
US 1943 94m bw
Universal (Charles Boyer, Julien Duvivier)
A club bore tells three strange stories.
A portmanteau with ingredients of varying interest, attempting to emulate the success of Tales of Manhattan. *The fourth episode planned was deleted and turned up as* Destiny *(qv). All quite stylish, the best section being* Lord Arthur Savile's Crime.
w Ernest Pascal, Samuel Hoffenstein, Ellis St Joseph *story* Ellis St Joseph, Oscar Wilde, Laslo Vadnay *d Julien Duvivier ph Paul Ivano, Stanley Cortez m* Alexandre Tansman
☆ Robert Benchley, *Edward G. Robinson*, Barbara Stanwyck, Charles Boyer, Betty Field, Robert Cummings, *Thomas Mitchell*, C. Aubrey Smith, Dame May Whitty, Edgar Barrier, David Hoffman

Flesh and the Devil *
US 1926 109m bw silent
MGM
A temptress toys with three men.
Hokey but good-looking star melodrama, climaxing with death on an ice floe. A huge commercial success because of the off-screen Garbo-Gilbert romance.
w Benjamin Glazer *novel The Undying Past* by Hermann Sudermann *d Clarence Brown ph* William Daniels
☆ *Greta Garbo, John Gilbert*, Lars Hanson, Marc McDermott, Barbara Kent
'A film of more than passing cleverness ... the theme is sheer undiluted sex, and Brown uses a series of close-ups to get this across with considerable effect.' – *Paul Rotha, The Film Till Now*

The Flesh and the Fiends
GB 1959 97m bw Dyaliscope
Regal/Triad (Robert Baker, Monty Berman)
US title: *Mania*
In 1820 Edinburgh, 'resurrection men' commit murders to keep anatomists supplied.
Dr Robert Knox rides again, in a version more bloody but less entertaining than The Body Snatcher.
w John Gilling, Leon Griffiths *d* John Gilling *ph* Monty Berman *m* Stanley Black
☆ Peter Cushing, June Laverick, George Rose, Donald Pleasence, Renée Houston, Billie Whitelaw, Dermot Walsh

The Flesh of the Orchid
France/Italy/Germany 1974 100m Eastmancolor
VMP/Paris Cannes Productions/F. Meric/L'Astrophone/ORTF/Oceana/TIT (Vincent Malle)
original title: *La Chair de l'Orchidée*
A young heiress, incarcerated in a mental institution by her aunt who wants her fortune, goes on the run with a man being hunted by contract killers.
A baroque and overwrought stew of sex and death, likely to be too rich for most tastes.
w Jean-Claude Carrière, Patrice Chéreau *novel* James Hadley Chase *d* Patrice Chéreau *ph* Pierre Lhomme *m* Fiorenzo Carpi *ad* Richard Peduzzi *ed* Pierre Gillette
☆ Charlotte Rampling, Bruno Cremer, Edwige Feuillère, Alida Valli, Hans Christian Blech, François Simon, Hugues Quester, Simone Signoret

Fletch *
US 1985 96m Technicolor
Universal/Douglas/Greisman
A newspaper columnist with a penchant for disguise tracks down a nefarious con man.
A lightness of touch unusual for the eighties makes this comedy mystery more welcome than most.
w Andrew Bergman *novel* Gregory McDonald *d Michael Ritchie ph* Fred Schuler *m* Harold Faltermeyer
☆ Chevy Chase, Dana Wheeler-Nicholson, Tim Matheson, Joe Don Baker, Richard Libertini, Kenneth Mars, M. Emmet Walsh

Fletch Lives
US 1989 95m colour
UIP/Universal/Greisman/Douglas
An investigative reporter inherits trouble along with a Southern mansion.
Dire comedy with nothing to recommend it.
w Leon Capetanos *d* Michael Ritchie *ph* John McPherson *m* Harold Faltermeyer, Buckwheat Zydeco *ed* Richard A. Harris
☆ Chevy Chase, Hal Holbrook, Julianne Phillips, R. Lee Ermey, Richard Libertini, Randall 'Tex' Cobb, Cleavon Little

Les Fleurs Sauvages
Canada 1982 153m bw/colour
Cinegate/Cinak (Marguerite Duparc)
A seventy-year-old widow visits her married daughter for a holiday.
Excessively drawn-out and introspective view of family relationships that loses interest long before the end.
wd Jean Pierre Lefèbvre *ph* Guy Dufaux *m* Raoul Duguay, Jean Corriveau *ed* Marguerite Duparc
☆ Marte Nadeau, Michell Magny, Pierre Curzi, Claudia Aubin, Eric Beausejour, Georges Belisle, Sarah Mills

Un Flic: see *Dirty Money*

'What would you do if the man you loved wanted you to love his pal?'
'The first all-talking drama of the air!'

Flight
US 1929 110m bw
Columbia (Harry Cohn)
Two rival flyers join a mission to rescue US Marines ambushed in Nicaragua.
Pale stuff now, but in its time an ambitious action movie showing a new suppleness in its young director.
w Frank Capra, Ralph Graves *d* Frank Capra *ph* Joseph Walker *ad* Harrison Wiley
☆ Jack Holt, Lila Lee, Ralph Graves, Alan Roscoe, Harold Goodwin, Jimmy de la Cruze

Flight Angels
US 1940 74m bw
Edmund Grainger/Warner
Airline stewardesses compete for the favours of a romantic pilot.
An efficient potboiler, now most interesting for its depiction of 1939 air travel.
w Maurice Leo *d* Lewis Seiler
☆ Virginia Bruce, Dennis Morgan, Wayne Morris, Ralph Bellamy, Jane Wyman, John Litel

Flight Command
US 1940 116m bw
MGM (J. Walter Ruben)
A cocky recruit makes good in the naval air arm.
Routine flagwaver.
w Wells Root, Cmdr Harvey Haislip *d* Frank Borzage *ph* Harold Rosson *m* Franz Waxman
☆ Robert Taylor, Ruth Hussey, Walter Pidgeon, Paul Kelly, Nat Pendleton, Red Skelton, Shepperd Strudwick, Dick Purcell

Flight Commander: see *The Dawn Patrol (1930)*

Flight for Freedom
US 1943 101m bw
RKO (David Hempstead)
Biography of an intrepid aviatrix and her husband.
Patchy job based on the life of Amelia Earhart, suggesting that her final disappearance was on a government mission. Dull production.
w Oliver H. P. Garrett, S. K. Lauren *story* Horace McCoy *d* Lothar Mendes *ph* Lee Garmes *m* Roy Webb *ad* Albert S. D'Agostino, Carroll Clark
☆ Rosalind Russell, Fred MacMurray, Herbert Marshall, Eduardo Ciannelli, Walter Kingsford
art direction

Flight from Ashiya *
US/Japan 1963 102m Eastmancolor Panavision
UA/Harold Hecht/Daiei
When a cargo vessel sinks off the coast of Japan during a typhoon, the helicopter rescue service springs into action.
Conventional Grade A action thriller with flashbacks to earlier disasters in the lives of its heroes.
w Elliott Arnold, Waldo Salt *d* Michael Anderson *ph* Joe MacDonald, Burnett Guffey *m* Frank Cordell *pd* Eugène Lourié
☆ Yul Brynner, Richard Widmark, George Chakiris, Shirley Knight, Daniele Gaubert, Suzy Parker

Flight from Destiny
US 1941 74m bw
Warner
An elderly professor with six months to live determines on one good deed ... which includes murder.
Likeable minor melodrama, well put together.
w Barry Trivers *play* Anthony Berkeley *d* Vincent Sherman
☆ Thomas Mitchell, Geraldine Fitzgerald, Jeffrey Lynn, Mona Maris

Flight from Glory *
US 1937 66m bw
Robert Sisk/RKO
Tensions mount among flyers who cross the Andes daily between secluded mines and their supply base.
Tense 'B' picture which looks like a trial run for Only Angels Have Wings.
w David Silverstein, John Twist *d* Lew Landers
☆ Chester Morris, Whitney Bourne, Onslow Stevens, Van Heflin, Richard Lane, Paul Guilfoyle
'Better than the average programmer and worth strong exhibitor plugging. In tone the picture may be fairly described as semi-sophisticated, which for rank and file purposes is probably just the right amount of sophistication.' – *Variety*

Flight of the Doves *
US 1971 101m colour
Columbia/Rainbow (Ralph Nelson)
Two children run away from their bullying stepfather to join their Irish grandmother, but are chased by a wicked uncle who knows they are heirs to a fortune.
Pantomimish whimsy which works in fits and starts, but has little real humour or charm.
w Frank Gabrielson, Ralph Nelson *novel* Walter Macken *d* Ralph Nelson *ph* Harry Waxman *m* Roy Budd
☆ *Ron Moody*, Dorothy McGuire, Helen Raye, Dana, Jack Wild, Stanley Holloway, William Rushton

The Flight of the Dragon
US 1982 98m colour
Rankin/Bass Productions (Arthur Rankin Jnr, Jules Bass)
An author is plucked from modern times back into a mythic past to help save magic in the world.
Children's cartoon with an ecological message. By modern standards, the animation is above average.

w Romeo Muller *book* *The Flight of Dragons* by Peter Dickinson *d* Arthur Rankin Jnr, Jules Bass *m* Maury Laws *pd* Wayne Anderson
☆ Featuring the voices of Victor Buono, James Gregory, James Earl Jones, Harry Morgan, John Ritter

Flight of the Innocent
Italy 1993 105m Technicolor
Buena Vista/Cristaldi/Fandango/Raitre/Fildebroc (Franco Cristaldi, Domenico Procacci)
original title: *Corsa dell'Innocente*
A 10-year-old boy, witness to a gang killing, goes on the run followed by killers.
An unoriginal and violent chase movie with a sickly ending, done with skill but hardly worth the doing; it represents the neo-realist tradition at its most decadent.
w Carlo Carlei, Gualtiero Rosella *d* Carlo Carlei *ph* Raffaele Mertes *m* Carlo Siliotto *pd* Franco Ceraolo *ed* Carlo Fontana, Claudio di Mauro
☆ Manuel Colao, Federico Pacifici, Nicola di Pinto, Francesca Neri, Jacques Perrin
'Carlei has a strong eye for comic book images but he doesn't know when to stop, and the whole thing soon turns into a shapeless, hysterical melodrama.' – *Derek Malcolm, Guardian*
'This despicable docuthriller … the film's only agenda is finding pretexts to photograph people lifted out of their shoes and blown across the room, farmyard, or plaza by a shotgun blast to the chest, preferably in gold-suffused backlight.' – *Richard T. Jameson, Film Comment*

'The only thing they can count on is each other.'
Flight of the Intruder
US 1991 113m Technicolor Panavision
Paramount/Mace Neufeld, Robert Rehme
Pilots aboard an aircraft carrier during the Vietnam war decide to bomb Hanoi.
Dated and dull, with nothing to recommend it.
w Robert Dillon, David Shaber *novel* Stephen Coonts *d* John Milius *ph* Fred J. Koenekamp *m* Basil Poledouris *pd* Jack T. Collis *ad* E. Albert Heschong *ed* C. Timothy O'Mears, Steve Mirkovich, Peck Prior
☆ Danny Glover, Willem Dafoe, Brad Johnson, Rosanna Arquette, Tom Sizemore, J. Kenneth Campbell

Flight of the Navigator *
US 1986 90m colour
Buena Vista/Walt Disney (Robby Wald, Dimitri Villard)
Kidnapped by aliens, a 12-year-old boy returns home after an eight-year absence without having grown any older.
Science fiction aimed at a family audience and providing blandly innocuous, occasionally amusing entertainment.
w Michael Burton, Matt Macmanus *story* Mark H. Baker *d* Randal Kleiser *ph* James Glennon *m* Alan Silvestri *pd* William J. Creber *ed* Jeff Gourson
☆ Joey Cramer (David Freeman), Veronica Cartwright (Helen Freeman), Cliff DeYoung (Bill Freeman), Sarah Jessica Parker (Carolyn McAdams), Matt Adler (Jeff), Howard Hesseman (Dr Faraday), Paul Mall (Paul Reubens) (Max), Robert Small (Troy)

The Flight of the Phoenix *
US 1965 149m DeLuxe
TCF/Associates and Aldrich
A cargo passenger plane crashes in the desert, and the survivors try to avert disaster.
Achingly slow character adventure; an all-star cast works desperately hard but the final flight of the rebuilt plane seems almost an anticlimax after the surfeit of personal melodramatics.
w Lukas Heller *novel* Elleston Trevor *d* Robert Aldrich *ph* Joseph Biroc *m* Frank de Vol
☆ James Stewart, Richard Attenborough, Hardy Kruger, Peter Finch, Dan Duryea, Ernest Borgnine, Ian Bannen, Ronald Fraser, Christian Marquand, George Kennedy
Academy Award nomination: Ian Bannen

The Flight of the White Stallions: see *The Miracle of the White Stallions*

The Flight that Disappeared
US 1961 73m bw
UA/Harvard (Robert E. Kent)
Atomic scientists on an airliner find themselves in 'heaven' being tried by people of the future.
Eccentric anti-bomb curiosity, a second feature Outward Bound.
w Ralph Hart, Judith Hart, Owen Harris *d* Reginald Le Borg *ph* Gilbert Warrenton *m* Richard La Salle
☆ Gregory Morton, Addison Richards, Craig Hill, Paula Raymond, Dayton Lummis

Flight to Mars
US 1951 75m Cinecolor
Monogram
After a rocket flight, four scientists discover that the inhabitants of Mars speak perfect American, learned by radio.
Pioneering science-fiction entry with nothing going for it but being first: writing, production and acting are alike abysmal.
w Arthur Strawn *d* Lesley Selander *ph* Harry Newman *m* Marlin Skiles
☆ Cameron Mitchell, Marguerite Chapman, Arthur Franz, Virginia Huston, John Litel

'The Year's Most Exciting Action Drama!'
Flight to Tangier
US 1953 90m Technicolor 3-D
Paramount (Nat Holt)
A female FBI agent chases a three million dollar letter of credit.
Forced and boring action romance without much of either element.
wd Charles Marquis Warren *ph* Ray Rennahan *m* Paul Sawtell *ad* Hal Pereira, John B. Goodman *ed* Frank Bracht
☆ Joan Fontaine (Susan Lane), Jack Palance (Gil Walker), Corinne Calvet (Nicole), Robert Douglas (Danzar), Marcel Dalio (Gogo), Jeff Morrow (Colonel Wier), Murray Matheson (Franz Kovac), John Doucette (Sgt Tirera)

The Flim Flam Man *
US 1967 104m DeLuxe Panavision
TCF/Lawrence Turman
GB title: *One Born Every Minute*
An army deserter joins forces with an elderly con man.
Folksy comedy in a small-town setting; none of it really comes to the boil after a couple of early chase sequences.
w William Rose *novel* Guy Owen *d* Irvin Kershner *ph* Charles Lang *m* Jerry Goldsmith *Stunt director* Yakima Canutt
☆ George C. Scott, Michael Sarrazin, Sue Lyon, Harry Morgan, Jack Albertson, Alice Ghostley, Albert Salmi

'Yabba Dabba Do!'
The Flintstones
US 1994 93m DeLuxe
Universal/Amblin/Hanna-Barbera (Bruce Cohen)
In the Stone Age town of Bedrock, quarry worker Fred Flintstone is promoted to vice-president so that he can be the fall guy for his boss's crooked schemes.
The only appeal of this live-action version of Hanna-Barbera's dated, animated TV sitcom lies in the actual re-creation of a cartoon environment and creatures. In the absence of anything approaching wit or humour, that soon palls; but the film found favour with the public, who flocked to see it.
w Tom S. Parker, Jim Jennewein, Steven E. de Souza *d* Brian Levant *ph* Dean Cundey *m* David Newman *pd* William Sandell *ed* Kent Beyda *sp* Industrial Light and Magic
☆ John Goodman, Elizabeth Perkins, Rick Moranis, Rosie O'Donnell, Elizabeth Taylor, Kyle MacLachlan, Halle Berry, Jonathan Winters, Sam Raimi
'Yabba Dabba Doo-doo.' – *Philadelphia Inquirer*
'Yabba Dabba Don't.' – *USA Today*
'Yabba Dabba Dud.' – *New York Daily Post*
'Yabba Dabba Poo!' – *Empire*
† The film's script was worked on by more than 30 writers, many of them in 'round table' sessions, in the style of TV sitcom scriptwriting.

'Get ready to rock!'
The Flintstones in Viva Rock Vegas
US 2000 90m DeLuxe
Universal/Hanna-Barbera/Amblin (Bruce Cohen)
An alien observes the mating habits of Earthlings and sees how Fred and Wilma, and friends Barney and Betty, became couples.
A prequel to the first Flintstones' movie, and even more a crude slapstick comedy in which its live action cast turn themselves into one dimensional versions of the original cartoon creations.
w Deborah Kaplan, Harry Elfont, Jim Cash, Jack Epps Jnr *d* Brian Levant *ph* Jamie Anderson *m* David Newman *pd* Christopher Burian-Mohr *ed* Kent Beyda *sp* Rhythm & Hues; creature fx: Jim Henson's Creature Shop *cos* Robert Turturice
☆ Mark Addy (Fred Flintstone), Stephen Baldwin (Barney Rubble), Kristen Johnston (Wilma Slaghoople), Jane Krakowski (Betty O'Shale), Thomas Gibson (Chip Rockefeller), Joan Collins (Pearl Slaghoople), Alan Cumming (Gazoo/Mick Jagged), Harvey Korman (Col Slaghoople), Alex Meneses (Roxie)
'Utterly disarming.' – *James Christopher, Times*
'Guaranteed to bore the entire family.' – *Cosmo Landesman, Sunday Times*

Flipper
US 1963 87m Metrocolor
(MGM)
A fisherman's son on the Florida Keys befriends a dolphin.
Harmless boy-and-animal adventure which spawned two sequels and a TV series.
w Arthur Weiss *d* James B. Clark *ph* Lamar Boren, Joseph Brun *m* Henry Vars
☆ Chuck Connors, Luke Halpin, Kathleen Maguire, Connie Scott
† *Flipper's New Adventure* followed in 1964.

'Sandy thought he was in for another boring summer. Instead, he got the adventure of a lifetime.'
Flipper
US 1996 96m DeLuxe Super 35
Universal/Bubble Factory/American Film (James J. McNamara, Perry Katz)
A 14-year-old boy, staying with his uncle on a Florida island, makes friends with a young dolphin.
Lacklustre movie in which nothing much happens very slowly; even dolphin lovers will be disappointed.
wd Alan Shapiro *ph* Bill Butler *m* Joel McNeely *pd* Thomas A. Walsh *ed* Peck Prior
☆ Paul Hogan, Elijah Wood, Chelsea Field, Isaac Hayes, Jonathan Banks, Jason Fuchs, Jessica Wesson
'You just can't get away with this sort of lack of invention any more.' – *Empire*

Flirtation Walk *
US 1934 97m bw
Warner (Frank Borzage)
Love affairs of West Point cadets.
Light musical very typical of its period, with a few agreeable numbers.
w Delmer Daves *d* Frank Borzage *ph* Sol Polito, George Barnes *m/ly* Allie Wrubel, Mort Dixon *ch* Bobby Connolly
☆ Dick Powell, Ruby Keeler, Pat O'Brien, Ross Alexander, John Arledge, Henry O'Neill, Guinn Williams
'A rousing recruiting poster … and a splendid laboratory specimen of the adolescent cinema.' – *André Sennwald, New York Times*
Academy Award nomination: best picture

Flirting *
Australia 1989 99m colour
Warner/Kennedy Miller (George Miller, Doug Mitchell, Terry Hayes)
A 17-year-old Australian schoolboy falls in love with a Ugandan girl at a neighbouring school.
A less effective, though occasionally affecting, sequel to The Year My Voice Broke.
wd John Duigan *ph* Geoff Burton *pd* Roger Ford *ed* Robert Gibson, Marcus D'Arcy
☆ Noah Taylor, Thandie Newton, Nicole Kidman, Bartholomew Rose, Felix Nobis, Josh Picker, Kiri Paramore
'Such rites of passage movies are common currency nowadays, but Duigan's ability to summon up the past with conviction, get good performances from his cast and to apply a sense of humour as well as a feeling of horror at what Australians did to their young *circa* 1965, makes the film universal in its appeal.' – *Derek Malcolm, Guardian*

The Flirting Widow
US 1930 70m bw
First National
A girl invents a lover, then kills him off … but his friend shows up.
Whimsical comedy which outstays its welcome.
w John F. Goodrich *story* *Green Stockings* by A. E. W. Mason *d* William A. Seiter
☆ Dorothy Mackaill, Basil Rathbone, Leila Hyams, Claude Gillingwater, William Austin
'Slim for the key houses and really built for neighbourhoods.' – *Variety*

Flirting with Disaster **
US 1996 92m DeLuxe
Buena Vista/Miramax (Dean Silvers)
After his wife gives birth to their son, the new father decides it is time to find his biological parents.
Witty road movie about a search for identity and new possibilities.
wd David O. Russell *ph* Eric Edwards *m* Stephen Endelman *pd* Kevin Thompson *ed* Christopher Tellefsen
☆ Ben Stiller, Patricia Arquette, Téa Leoni, Mary Tyler Moore, George Segal, Alan Alda, Lily Tomlin, Richard Jenkins, Josh Brolin
'Packed to the roof with genuinely chucklesome humour … manages to keep you laughing for at least two-thirds of its running time.' – *Total Film*

Flood Tide
US 1958 82m bw 'Scope
Universal
A boy is jealous of his widowed mother's interest in a neighbour.
Modest melodrama, typical of its studio at the time.
w Dorothy Cooper *d* Abner Biberman *ph* Arthur E. Arling *m* William Lava, Henry Mancini *ad* Alexander Golitzen, Bill Newberry *ed* Ted J. Kent
☆ George Nader, Cornell Borchers, Michel Ray, Judson Pratt, Joanna Moore, Charles Arnt, Russ Conway

Floodtide
GB 1949 90m bw
Aquila/Rank
A Clydebank apprentice becomes a ship designer.
Boring inspirational drama hindered by the Independent Frame method.
w Donald B. Wilson, George Blake *d* Frederick Wilson
☆ Gordon Jackson, Rona Anderson, John Laurie, Jack Lambert, Elizabeth Sellars

La flor de mi secreto: see *The Flower of My Secret*

The Florentine Dagger
US 1935 69m bw
Warner
A mysterious Borgia influence is brought to bear on the murder of an art dealer.
Vaguely unsatisfactory whodunnit with some intriguing and some pretentious elements.
w Brown Holmes, Tom Reed *novel* Ben Hecht *d* Robert Florey
☆ Margaret Lindsay, Donald Woods, C. Aubrey Smith, Robert Barrat, Henry O'Neill

Florian
US 1940 91m bw
MGM (Winfield Sheehan)
In 1910 Austria, a poor boy and a rich girl are united by their love of a Lippizaner stallion.
Not kinky, but strangely dull.
w Noel Langley, Geza Herczeg, James K. McGuinness *d* Edwin L. Marin *ph* Karl Freund, Richard Rosson *m* Franz Waxman
☆ Robert Young, Helen Gilbert, Charles Coburn, Lee Bowman, Reginald Owen, S. Z. Sakall, Lucile Watson, Irina Baronova

The Florodora Girl
US 1930 75m bw (Technicolor sequence)
MGM
GB title: *The Gay Nineties*
The romance of the last remaining Florodora girl.
Not a musical but a period farce which laughs at rather than with the fashions of 1900. It doubtless succeeded with the audiences of its time.
w Gene Markey, Ralph Spence, Al Boasberg, Robert Hopkins *d* Harry Beaumont
☆ Marion Davies, Lawrence Gray, Walter Catlett, Ilka Chase, Vivian Oakland, Jed Prouty
'Good hoke entertainment ... an all-type audience picture with no limitations.' – *Variety*

Flower Drum Song *
US 1961 133m Technicolor Panavision
U-I/Rodgers and Hammerstein/Joseph Fields (Ross Hunter)
Romantic problems among the immigrants in San Francisco's Chinatown.
A Broadway musical which on the screen seems old-fashioned, remorselessly cute, and even insulting to the Chinese characters. Within its limits, however, it is well enough staged and performed.
w Joseph Fields *d* Henry Koster *ph* Russell Metty *m/ly* Richard Rodgers, Oscar Hammerstein II *md* Alfred Newman, Ken Darby *ch* Hermes Pan *ad* Alexander Golitzen, Joseph Wright *ed* Milton Carruth *cos* Irene Sharaff
☆ Nancy Kwan, James Shigeta, Juanita Hall, Miyoshi Umeki, Jack Soo, Sen Yung, Kam Tong, Reiko Sato
† Nancy Kwan's singing was dubbed by B. J. Baker, Kam Tong's by John Dodson, and Reiko Sato's by Marilyn Horne.
Alfred Newman, Ken Darby; Russell Metty

The Flower of My Secret *
Spain/France 1995 107m Eastmancolor
Electric/CiBy 2000/El Deseo (Esther Garcia)
original title: *La flor de mi secreto*
A best-selling romantic novelist has a mid-life crisis: she takes to drink, tries a different kind of fiction, and rids herself of her quarrelsome husband.
Rather like his heroine, Almodóvar abandons his camp frivolities for something more mundane; it is sometimes effective, but as artificial as ever and not entirely convincing.
wd Pedro Almodóvar *ph* Affonso Beato *m* Alberto Iglesias *ad* Wolfgang Burmann *ed* José Salcedo
☆ Marisa Paredes, Juan Echanove, Imanol Arias, Carmen Elias, Rossy de Palma, Chus Lampreave, Joaquin Cortes
'From a director whose wackiness had begun to seem irritatingly predictable, it's a thoughtful and provocative new departure.' – *Sheila Johnston, Independent*

Flowers in the Attic
US 1987 92m colour
Entertainment/New World (Sy Levin, Thomas Fries)
Four children are kept locked in an attic by their deranged grandmother.
Tame melodrama that tones down the horrors of the novel and settles for a soporific approach to its sensational material.
wd Jeffrey Bloom *novel* Virginia C. Andrews *ph* Frank Byers, Gil Hubbs *m* Christopher Young *pd* John Muto *ed* Gregory F. Plotts
☆ Louise Fletcher, Victoria Tennant, Jeb Stuart Adams, Ben Granger, Lindsay Parker, Marshall Colt, Nathan Davis

The Flowers of St Francis: see *Francis, God's Jester*

Flubber
US 1997 93m Technicolor Panavision
Buena Vista/Walt Disney/Great Oaks (John Hughes, Ricardo Mestres)
An absent-minded scientist accidentally invents a substance that is lighter than air.
The change of title in this sequel reflects the altered emphasis, which is now firmly on special effects that suggest Hughes should be making animated films. Playing stooge to a green jelly, Williams lacks gravity and also humour.
w John Hughes, Bill Walsh *story* Samuel W. Taylor *d* Les Mayfield *ph* Dean Cundey *m* Danny Elfman *pd* Andrew McAlpine *ed* Harvey Rosenstock, Michael A. Stevenson *sp* Industrial Light and Magic
☆ Robin Williams (Professor Philip Brainard), Marcia Gay Harden (Sara Jane Reynolds), Christopher McDonald (Wilson Croft), Raymond J. Barry (Chester Hoenicker), Clancy Brown (Smith), Ted Levine (Wesson), Wil Wheaton (Bennett Hoenicker), Edie McClurg (Martha George)
'Old-fashioned family entertainment.' – *The Times*
† It is a remake of the 1961 movie *The Absent-Minded Professor* (qv), starring Fred MacMurray, which was followed by a sequel, *Son of Flubber*.

'Love Is Hard.'
The Fluffer
US 2001 94m DeLuxe
Metrodome/Fluff and Fold (John Sylla, Victoria Robinson)
In Los Angeles, a naive young man becomes obsessed by a porn star and gets a job in the industry so that he can be close to him.
Slight drama of unrequited love that aims high and scores low.
w Wash West *d* Richard Glatzer, Wash West *ph* Mark Putnam *m* The Bowling Green, Micko Westmoreland, John Vaughn *pd* Devorah Herbert *ed* John Binninger
☆ Scott Gurney (Michael Rossini/'Johnny Rebel'), Michael Cunio (Sean McGinnis), Roxanne Day (Babylon), Taylor Negron (Tony Brooks), Richard Riehle (Sam Martins), Deborah Harry (Marcella), Robert Walden (Chad Cox)
'A well-produced and packaged item that could achieve minor cult status despite the relative thinness of the material.' – *David Stratton, Variety*

Fluffy
US 1964 92m Eastmancolor
U-I/Scarus (Gordon Kay)
A biologist manages to tame a lion.
Mindless, cheerful animal comedy.
w Samuel Rocca *d* Earl Bellamy *ph* Clifford Stine *m* Irving Gertz
☆ Tony Randall, Shirley Jones, Edward Andrews, Ernest Truex, Howard Morris, Jim Backus, Frank Faylen

'Have you ever met someone you felt you already knew?'
Fluke
US 1995 96m colour
MGM/Rocket (Paul Maslansky, Lata Ryan)
After dying in a car crash, a man is reincarnated as a dog and tries to find his way home.
Doggedly sentimental fantasy; it sits up and begs to be liked, but lacks bite.
w Carlo Carlei, James Carrington *novel* James Herbert *d* Carlo Carlei *ph* Raffaele Mertes *m* Carlo Siliotto *pd* Hilda Stark *ed* Mark Conte
☆ Matthew Modine, Nancy Travis, Eric Stoltz, Jon Polito, Tom Coleman

'Once it was human ... even as you and I ... this monster created by atoms gone wild!'
The Fly
US 1958 94m Eastmancolor Cinemascope
TCF (Kurt Neumann)
A scientist invents a method of transmitting and reassembling atoms. He transmits himself and does not notice a fly in the compartment...
Unpleasant horror film which becomes ludicrous but not funny.
w James Clavell *story* George Langelaan *d* Kurt Neumann *ph* Karl Struss *m* Paul Sawtell
☆ David Hedison, Patricia Owens, Herbert Marshall, Vincent Price
'It might be possible, I suppose, to take this preposterous piece of merchandise as a monstrous joke. Even so, it would be a joke in deplorably bad taste.' – *C. A. Lejeune*
† Sequels were *Return of the Fly* (1959) and *Curse of the Fly* (1965), neither worth noting in detail. And see below.

'Be afraid. Be very afraid.'
The Fly *
US 1986 100m DeLuxe
TCF/Brooksfilm (Stuart Cornfeld)
A scientist experimenting with transmitting matter transforms himself into a half human-half fly.
A deliberately gruesome update of the 1958 horror movie, with much unpleasant detail carried along by a certain style.
w Charles Edward Pogue, David Cronenberg *d* David Cronenberg *ph* Mark Irwin *m* Howard Shore *pd* Carol Spier *ed* Ronald Sanders
☆ Jeff Goldblum, Geena Davis, John Getz
'One does not have to be totally warped to appreciate this film, but it does take a particular sensibility to embrace it.' – *Variety*
'Stylish acrobatics, cowgum gore.' – *Sight and Sound*
make-up (Chris Walas, Stephen Dupuis)

Fly Away Home **
US 1996 106m Technicolor
Columbia/Sandollar (John Veitch, Carol Baum)
After her mother dies, a 13-year-old goes to Canada to live with her estranged father and adopts a family of motherless goslings.
Charming, understated film about loss and love, which reaches a splendid climax as the young girl teaches geese to migrate to their winter haunts.
w Robert Rodat, Vince McKewin *autobiography* Bill Lishman *d* Carroll Ballard *ph* Caleb Deschanel *m* Mark Isham *pd* Seamus Flannery *ed* Nicholas C. Smith *sp* CORE Digital
☆ Jeff Daniels, Anna Paquin, Dana Delany, Terry Kinney, Holter Graham, Jeremy Ratchford
'It's a genuine delight, and a definite thumbs aloft for kids of about six upwards.' – *Philip Thomas, Empire*
Caleb Deschanel

'Like father. Like son.'
The Fly II
US 1989 105m colour
Fox/Brooksfilms (Steven-Charles Jaffe)
The precocious son of The Fly takes his revenge on the scientist who exploits him.
An uneasy mix of sentimentality and gore, but otherwise a standard monster movie.
w Mick Garris, Jim and Ken Wheat, Frank Darabont *d* Chris Walas *ph* Robin Vidgeon *m* Christopher Young *pd* Michael S. Bolton *ed* Sean Barton *sp* Chris Walas
☆ Eric Stoltz, Daphne Zuniga, Lee Richardson, Harley Cross, Gary Chalk, Ann Marie Lee, Frank C. Turner, John Getz
'Constructed with a refreshing intricacy and visual panache.' – *Philip Strick, MFB*

The Flying Deuces *
US 1939 67m bw
Boris Morros
Laurel and Hardy join the Foreign Legion.
Patchy comedy from the end of the comedians' period of glory, and showing signs of decline.
w Ralph Spence, Harry Langdon, Charles Rogers, Alfred Schiller *d* A. Edward Sutherland *ph* Art Lloyd, Elmer Dyer *m* Leo Shuken *md* Edward Paul *ed* Jack Dennis
☆ Stan Laurel, Oliver Hardy, Jean Parker, James Finlayson, Reginald Gardiner, Charles Middleton
'Mechanical stuff ... seemed like *Beau Hunks* and *Bonnie Scotland* all over again.' – *William K. Everson*

Flying Down to Rio **
US 1933 89m bw
RKO (Merian C. Cooper, Lou Brock)
A dance band is a big success in Rio de Janeiro.
A thin musical electrified by the finale in which girls dance on the wings of moving airplanes, and by the teaming of Astaire and Rogers for the first time. Now an irresistible period piece.
w Cyril Hume, H. W. Hanemann, Erwin Gelsey *play* Anne Caldwell *story* Louis Brock *d* Thornton Freeland *ph* J. Roy Hunt *m/ly* Vincent Youmans, Edward Eliscu, Gus Kahn *md* Max Steiner *ch* Dave Gould *ad* Van Nest Polglase, Carroll Clark *ed* Jack Kitchin
☆ Dolores del Rio, Gene Raymond, Raul Roulien, *Ginger Rogers, Fred Astaire*, Blanche Frederici, Walter Walker, Franklin Pangborn, Eric Blore
'Its main point is the screen promise of Fred Astaire ... the others are all hoofers after him.' – *Variety*
♫ 'Music Makes Me'; 'Orchids in the Moonlight'; 'Flying Down to Rio'
song 'The Carioca'

Flying Elephants
US 1927 20m bw silent
Hal Roach
A caveman has the toothache.
Fragmentary and generally unsatisfactory comedy starring Laurel and Hardy before they properly teamed, but released after their joint success.
w Hal Roach, H. M. Walker *d* Frank Butler *sp* Roy Seawright
☆ Stan Laurel, Oliver Hardy, James Finlayson, Viola Richard, Dorothy Coburn
† According to Hal Roach, he directed the film, with Butler only doing a day's work on retakes.

'Marine air-devils in hot pursuit ... Blood-red trails streak the sky!'
'Bares the hearts of women who wait!'
Flying Leathernecks
US 1951 102m Technicolor
RKO (Edmund Grainger)
Two marine officers fight the Japs and each other on Guadalcanal.
Empty, violent war actioner full of phoney heroics.
w James Edward Grant *d* Nicholas Ray *ph* William E. Snyder *m* Roy Webb
☆ John Wayne, Robert Ryan, Janis Carter, Don Taylor, Jay C. Flippen, William Harrigan, James Bell
'Ray's treatment is depressingly second rate and does nothing to alleviate the unpleasant impression of this disturbingly violent production.' – *Penelope Houston*

Flying Saucer
US 1949 60m bw
Film Classics (Mikel Conrad)
Russians try to steal the secret of a flying saucer from its inventor.
A film whose title brought the term into general use; otherwise it is a standard paranoid Cold War thriller.
w Mikel Conrad, Howard Irving Young *d* Mikel Conrad *ph* Phil Tannura *m* Darrell Calker *ed* Robert Crandall
☆ Mikel Conrad, Pat Garrison, Lester Sharpe, Russell Hicks, Frank Draper, Virginia Hewitt, Hantz von Teuffen

The Flying Scotsman
GB 1929 63m bw
Warner/BIP
An ex-employee tries to wreck a crack train.
Fairly presentable example of an early talkie film originally shot silent; one or two climactic thrills.
w Victor Kendall, Garnett Weston *story* Joe Grossman *d* Castleton Knight *ph* Theodor Sparkuhl *m* Idris Lewis, John Reynders *ad* T. H. Gibbins *ed* A. C. Hammond
☆ Moore Marriott, Pauline Jameson, Ray Milland, Alec Hurley, Dino Galvani

'Relic of an ancient terror born a billion years ago!'
The Flying Serpent
US 1945 59m bw
PRC (Sigmund Neufeld)
A crazed archaeologist uses a rare bird as a murder instrument.
Ineffective low-key horror despite an always interesting star.
w John T. Neville *d* Sherman Scott (Sam Newfield)
☆ George Zucco, Ralph Lewis, Hope Kramer, Eddie Acuff

'A bomber squadron wouldn't get through ... but one ship might make it!'

Flying Tigers
US 1942 100m bw
Republic (Edmund Grainger)
American airmen fight the Japs over World War II China.
More mock heroics with noisy but unconvincing action sequences.
w Kenneth Gamet, Barry Trivers d David Miller ph Jack Marta m Victor Young
☆ John Wayne, John Carroll, Anna Lee, Paul Kelly, Mae Clarke
Victor Young

The Fog *
US 1979 91m Metrocolor Panavision
Rank/Avco Embassy (Debra Hill)
A small Californian town is invaded by the leprous ghosts of mariners wrecked on the coast a hundred years before.
Silly but beguiling horror film with shock effects typical of its director.
w John Carpenter, Debra Hill d John Carpenter ph Dean Cundey m John Carpenter pd Tommy Lee Wallace ed Tommy Lee Wallace, Charles Bornstein
☆ Adrienne Barbeau, Hal Holbrook, John Houseman, Janet Leigh, Jamie Lee Curtis, Tom Atkins
'An uneasy venture down a blind alley.' – *Tom Milne, MFB*

Fog Island
US 1945 70m bw
PRC (Leon Fromkess)
A wealthy ex-convict gathers on a foggy island all the people he considers responsible for his downfall.
Very tolerable minor mystery lifted without permission from Agatha Christie's And There Were None.
w Pierre Gendron d Terry Morse
☆ George Zucco, Lionel Atwill, Jerome Cowan, Sharon Douglas, Veda Ann Borg, Ian Keith

Fog over Frisco ***
US 1934 68m bw
Warner (Henry Blanke)
A San Francisco heiress gets herself murdered.
Silly whodunnit highly notable for its cinematic style, all dissolves, wipes and quick takes. Probably the fastest moving film ever made, and very entertaining despite its plot inadequacy.
w Robert N. Lee novel George Dyer d *William Dieterle* ph *Tony Gaudio* md Leo F. Forbstein ed *Harold McLernon*
☆ Bette Davis, Donald Woods, Margaret Lindsay, Lyle Talbot, Hugh Herbert, Arthur Byron, Robert Barrat, Douglass Dumbrille, Henry O'Neill, Irving Pichel, Alan Hale
'Another racketeering story, mild in entertainment. No marked names of strength.' – *Variety*
'It reveals those qualities of pace and velocity and sharpness which make the Hollywood product acceptable even when the shallow content of ideas makes you want to scream.' – *Robert Forsythe*
'Its speed is artificially created by pacing, wipes, opticals, overlapping sound, camera movement and placing of characters, and by its habit of never having time really to begin or end scenes.' – *William K. Everson*
† Remade 1942 as *Spy Ship*, a second feature.

Folies Bergère ***
US 1935 84m bw
Twentieth Century (William Goetz, Raymond Griffith)
GB title: *The Man from the Folies Bergère*
A Parisian banker persuades a music hall artist to impersonate him, but the wife and girlfriend become involved in the confusion.
Amusing star vehicle with inventive Berkeleyish numbers and some remarkably sexy dialogue.
w Bess Meredyth, Hal Long play *The Red Cat* by Rudolph Lothar, Hans Adler d Roy del Ruth ph Barney McGill, Peverell Marley md Alfred Newman ch Dave Gould
☆ *Maurice Chevalier*, Merle Oberon, Ann Sothern, Eric Blore
† Remade as *That Night in Rio*, with Don Ameche, and *On the Riviera*, with Danny Kaye (both qv).
Dave Gould

The Folies of Elodie (dubbed)
France 1981 90m Fujicolour
AGC/MMP
aka: *Naughty Blue Knickers*
A pair of satin panties tells the story of the adventures of its owner with her lover, maid, godson, her godson's mother and a truck driver.
Trite comic erotica, despite its high-powered scriptwriters, done with no style, merely soft-focus photography of banal images.
w Paul Gegauff, Gerard Croce, Andre Genoves novel *Les Mémoires d'une Culotte* by Aymé Dubois-Jolly d Andre Genoves ph Jean G. Charruyer m C. Pimper ad Michel Debats ed Aline Asseo
☆ Marcha Grant, Andre Genoves, Caroline Aguilar, Bruno Du Louvat, Charlotte Walior, Yves Massard, Marthe Mercadier

'Jon Aldrich is about to come face to face with the most terrifying force known to man... His parents.'

Folks!
US 1992 106m Technicolor
First Independent/Penta (Victor Drai, Malcolm R. Harding)
At his ailing mother's suggestion, a businessman tries to kill her and his senile father for the insurance money.
Embarrassingly bad comedy, not merely tasteless but, what is worse, devoid of humour.
w Robert Klane d Ted Kotcheff ph Larry Pizer m Michel Colombier pd William J. Creber ed Joan E. Chapman
☆ Tom Selleck, Don Ameche, Anne Jackson, Christine Ebersole, Wendy Crewson, Robert Pastorelli, Michael Murphy
'Marking severe career setbacks for Ameche and Selleck, *Folks!* obviously miscalculates the low intelligence of the mass audience.' – *Variety*

Follies Girl
US 1943 71m bw
PRC
An army private visits the forces canteen but falls for the burlesque dancer next door.
Feebly developed romance with music, mostly notable for its specialities.
w Marcy Klauber, Charles Robinson d William Rowland
☆ Wendy Barrie, Doris Nolan, Gordon Oliver, Anne Barrett, Cora Witherspoon

Follow a Star
GB 1959 104m bw
Rank (Hugh Stewart)
A shy amateur singer allows a fading star to mime to his voice.
Star comedy with an antique plot and a superfluity of pathos.
w Jack Davies, Henry Blyth, Norman Wisdom d Robert Asher ph Jack Asher m Philip Green
☆ Norman Wisdom, Jerry Desmonde, June Laverick, Hattie Jacques, Richard Wattis, John Le Mesurier, Fenella Fielding, Ron Moody
'Such comedy as there is is mostly muffed by the lack of any sense of comic timing.' – *MFB*

Follow Me
GB 1971 93m Technicolor Panavision
Universal/Hal B. Wallis (Paul Nathan)
US title: *The Public Eye*
An eccentric private eye is hired to follow an accountant's wife, and she finds him fascinating.
Dullish, whimsical rendering of a dullish, whimsical one-act play; it never springs to life or interest.
w Peter Shaffer play Peter Shaffer d Carol Reed ph Christopher Challis m John Barry
☆ Topol, Michael Jayston, Mia Farrow
'An uneasy mixture of broad comedy and high romance.' – *Sight and Sound*

Follow Me Boys
US 1966 132m Technicolor
Walt Disney (Winston Hibler)
The domestic trials and tribulations of a smalltown schoolmaster.
Sentimental family saga full of patriotic fervour.
w Louis Pelletier novel *God and My Country* by Mackinlay Kantor d Norman Tokar ph Clifford Stine m George Bruns
☆ Fred MacMurray, Vera Miles, Lillian Gish, Charlie Ruggles, Elliott Reid, Kurt Russell, Luana Patten, Ken Murray
'Demands an extremely strong stomach.' – *MFB*
'One of the worst films to emanate from the Disney studios, a near parody of all the lowbrow small-townery that has given Disney's features a bad name among intellectuals who never go to Disney movies. It is unworthy of the Disney trademark.' – *Judith Crist*

Follow Me Quietly *
US 1949 60m bw
RKO (Herman Schlom)
Police track down a killer who strangles whenever it rains.
Effective little urban thriller with nice sense of detail.
w Lillie Hayward d Richard Fleischer ph Robert de Grasse
☆ William Lundigan, Dorothy Patrick, Jeff Corey, Nestor Paiva, Charles D. Brown, Paul Guilfoyle

Follow That Camel: see *Carry On – Follow That Camel*

Follow That Dream
US 1962 110m DeLuxe Panavision
UA/Mirisch (David Weisbart)
A wandering family sets up house on a Florida beach.
Tiresomely cute comedy vehicle for a resistible star.
w Charles Lederer novel *Pioneer Go Home* by Richard Powell d Gordon Douglas ph Leo Tover m Hans Salter
☆ Elvis Presley, Arthur O'Connell, Joanna Moore, Anne Helm, Jack Kruschen

Follow That Guy with the One Black Shoe: see *Le Grand Blond avec une Chaussure Noire*

Follow the Band
US 1943 60m bw
Universal (Paul Malvern)
A farm worker on his first visit to New York becomes a trombonist in a night-club.
Minor musical filler which packs in a surprising range of talent.
w Warren Wilson, Dorothy Bennett d Jean Yarbrough ph Elwood Bredell md Charles Previn ch Louis DaPron ad John B. Goodman ed Milton Carruth
☆ Eddie Quillan, Leon Errol, Mary Beth Hughes, Samuel S. Hinds, Robert Mitchum, Frances Langford, Leo Carrillo, Hilo Hattie, the King Sisters, Skinnay Ennis and his band

Follow the Boys *
US 1944 109m bw
Universal (Charles K. Feldman)
A song and dance man organizes entertainment for the US troops during World War II.
Scrappy, unattractive propaganda tribute by the stars to the stars, enlivened only by a few guest spots.
w Lou Breslow, Gertrude Purcell d A. Edward Sutherland ph David Abel m Leigh Harline and others
☆ George Raft, Vera Zorina, Charley Grapewin, Grace MacDonald, Charles Butterworth, George Macready, Elizabeth Patterson; and Orson Welles, Marlene Dietrich, Jeanette MacDonald, Dinah Shore, Donald O'Connor, Peggy Ryan, W. C. Fields, the Andrews Sisters, Artur Rubinstein and also Sophie Tucker, Ted Lewis and his band, etc
song 'I'll Walk Alone' (m Jule Styne, ly Sammy Cahn)

Follow the Boys
US 1963 95m Metrocolor Panavision
MGM/Franmet (Lawrence P. Bachmann)
An American warship is diverted from Cannes to Santa Margarita, and the waiting wives have to follow by road.
Harmless star comedy musical.
w David T. Chantler, David Osborn d Richard Thorpe ph Ted Scaife
☆ Connie Francis, Paula Prentiss, Dany Robin, Russ Tamblyn, Richard Long

Follow the Fleet **
US 1936 110m bw
RKO (Pandro S. Berman)
Sailors on shore leave romance a couple of girl singers.
Amiable star musical which makes heavy weather of a listless and overlong script, but has good numbers for those who can wait.
w Dwight Taylor play *Shore Leave* by Hubert Osborne, Allan Scott d Mark Sandrich ph David Abel m/ly *Irving Berlin* md Max Steiner
☆ *Fred Astaire, Ginger Rogers*, Randolph Scott, Harriet Hilliard, Astrid Allwyn, Harry Beresford, Lucille Ball, Betty Grable, Tony Martin
'The running time is way overboard ... dialogue is good and can be depended on for laughs, with the Astaire-Rogers dancing sure to do the rest. But cutting it would have helped a lot more.' – *Variety*
♫ 'I'm Putting All My Eggs in One Basket'; 'We Saw the Sea'; 'Let's Face the Music and Dance'; 'Let Yourself Go'; 'But Where Are You?'; 'I'd Rather Lead a Band'; 'Get Thee Behind Me Satan'; 'With a Smile on My Face'.

Follow the Leader
US 1944 64m bw
Monogram/Banner (Sam Katzman, Jack Dietz)
Muggs, unhappy at being unable to stay in the Army, escapes a murder rap and exposes a thief robbing Army stores.
Despite a violent death, this is a sentimental addition to the East Side Kids series, substituting flag-waving and mother-love for the more usual comedy.
w William X. Crowley, Beryl Sachs story Ande Lamb d William Beaudine ph Marcel LePicard md Edward Kay ad Ernest Hickson ed Carl Pierson
☆ Leo Gorcey, Huntz Hall, Gabriel Dell, Billy Benedict, Joan Marsh, Jack LaRue, Dave Durand, Gene Austin, Sherrill Sisters

Follow the Sun
US 1951 93m bw
TCF (Samuel G. Engel)
Ben Hogan, a professional golfer, recovers slowly and painfully from a car crash and for the first time gains the affection of the crowd.
Modest sporting biopic, generally watchable but rising to no great heights.
w Frederick Hazlitt Brennan d Sidney Lanfield ph Leo Tover m Cyril Mockridge
☆ Glenn Ford, Anne Baxter, Dennis O'Keefe, June Havoc, Larry Keating, Nana Bryant, Roland Winters

Follow Thru
US 1930 93m Technicolor
Paramount
Two women are after the same pro golfer.
Flat film version of a Broadway show.
w De Sylva, Brown, Henderson, from their show d Laurence Schwab, Lloyd Corrigan
☆ Charles Rogers, Nancy Carroll, Zelma O'Neal, Jack Haley, Eugene Pallette, Thelma Todd
'Paramount has tossed away a heavy money picture.' – *Variety*
♫ 'Button Up Your Overcoat'; 'You Wouldn't Fool Me Would You'; 'I'm Hard to Please'; 'A Peach of a Pair'; 'It Must be You'.

Folly to be Wise *
GB 1952 91m bw
London Films/Launder and Gilliat
A brains trust at an army unit starts off a battle of the sexes.
Typical James Bridie comedy which starts brightly and whimsically, then peters out and is saved by the acting.
w Frank Launder, John Dighton play *It Depends What You Mean* by James Bridie d Frank Launder ph Jack Hildyard m Temple Abady
☆ *Alastair Sim* (Rev William Paris), Roland Culver (George Prout), Elizabeth Allan (Angela Prout), Martita Hunt (Lady Dodd), Colin Gordon (Professor Mutch), Janet Brown (Jessie), Peter Martyn (Walter), Miles Malleson (Dr Hector McAdam), Edward Chapman (Joseph Byrne MP), Cyril Chamberlain (Drill Sergeant), Michael Ripper (Drill Corporal), Robin Bailey (Intellectual Corporal), Michael Kelly (Staff Sergeant)
'It seems to get funnier the longer it's spun out.' – *Pauline Kael, 70s*

Fong Sai Yuk *
Hong Kong/China 1993 112m colour
Eastern (Chui Po Chu)

aka: *The Legend of Fong Sai Yuk*
US title: *The Legend*
With the help of his fighting mother, a martial arts expert wins a bride and joins a revolution to overthrow the Manchu dynasty.
Exuberant mix of broad comedy and acrobatic martial arts, encompassing mistaken identity, gender confusion and romance.
w Kay On, Chan Kim Chung *d* Corey Yuen *ph* Jingle Ma *m* James Wong *pd* Ann Hui *ed* Cheung Yim Chung
☆ Jet Li, Josephine Siao, Michele Reis, Adam Cheng, Sibelle Hu, Paul Chu Kong

Fong Sai Yuk II
Hong Kong 1993 colour
Eastern

aka: *The Legend of Fong Sai Yuk II*
US title: *The Legend II*
Fong Sai Yuk defeats a traitor's attempt to rule a triad opposed to the Manchu dynasty, while two women battle for his love.
A lively though scrappy sequel with the emphasis on comedy and romantic passion and disappointment; it climaxes with some spectacular, acrobatic fight sequences, including Jet Li's blindfolded sword-wielding and a battle with benches to prevent his mother's death by hanging.
☆ Jet Li, Michelle Reis, Amy Kwok, Josephine Siao, Adam Cheng

Fontan **
USSR 1988 101m colour
BFI/Lenfilm (Boris Pavlov-Silvanski)
aka: *The Fountain*
The eccentric inhabitants of a Leningrad apartment block take matters into their own hands when their water and electricity are cut off.
Satirical comedy poking fun at most aspects of Gorbachev's Russia.
w Vladimir Vardunas *d* Yuri Mamin *ph* Anatoli Lapshov *m* Aleksei Zalivalow *ad* Yuri Pugach *ed* O. Adrianova
☆ Asankul Kuttubaev, Sergei Dontsov, Zhanna Kerimtaeva, Viktor Mikhailov, Anatoli Kalmikov, Liudmila Samokhvalova

Fontane Effi Briest: see *Effi Briest*

Food of Love
GB/France 1997 109m colour
Channel 4/Arts Council/Intrinsica/MP/Canal+ (Karim Bamborough)
An assistant bank manager recruits his old student friends to return to their past and stage again, with the aid of a few young punks, a performance of *Twelfth Night* in a village that has changed and grown antagonistic since their earlier visit.
A drama of middle-aged angst, nostalgia and culture clashes that never seems more than a diagrammatic sketch for a movie; it obstinately refuses to come to life.
wd Stephen Poliakoff *ph* Wit Dabal *m* Adrian Johnston *pd* Michael Pickwoad *ed* Anne Sopel
☆ Richard E. Grant (Alex Salmon), Nathalie Baye (Michèle), Joe McGann (Sam), Juliet Aubrey (Madeline), Lorcan Cranitch (Luke), Penny Downie (Mary), Holly Davidson (Jessica), Temeka Empson (Alice), John Ramm (Donald), Mark Tandy (Robin), Sylvia Syms (Mrs Harvey-Brown)

The Food of the Gods
US 1976 88m Movielab
AIP (Bert I. Gordon)
A curious substance which oozes out of the ground turns common beasts into monsters.
Rather crude horror movie which has little affinity with its literary original.
wd Bert I. Gordon *story* H. G. Wells *ph* Reginald Morris *m* Elliot Kaplan
☆ Marjoe Gortner, Pamela Franklin, Ida Lupino, Ralph Meeker, John McLiam
'Not only sick, but sickening.' – *Arthur Knight*
'I wish I hadn't seen the movie, so I could avoid it like the plague.' – *John Simon*
'More plot holes than any movie in recent memory, and enough dopey lines to make a Saturday night audience howl in all the wrong places.' – *David Sterritt, Christian Science Monitor*

Food of the Gods II
Canada 1989 91m colour
Rose & Ruby (David Mitchell, Damian Lee)

Giant man-eating rats are let loose on a college campus.
Risibly bad horror with a catch-penny title; it was not a sequel to the first film nor does it in any way resemble Wells's original story.
w Richard Bennett, E. Kim Brewster *d* Damian Lee *ph* Curtis Petersen *ed* David Mitchell *sp* Ted Rae
☆ Paul Coufos, Lisa Schrage, Colin Fox, Frank Moore, Real Andrews, Jackie Burroughs

The Fool **
GB 1990 140m colour
Hobo/Sands Films/Richard Goodwin, Christine Edzard
A Victorian clerk enjoys a double life as a businessman moving in the best social circles.
Its meticulous evocation of Victorian life, drawing on the books of Henry Mayhew, sometimes overwhelms the slender plot, but it is never less than watchable.
w Christine Edzard, Olivier Stockman *d* Christine Edzard *ph* Robin Vidgeon *m* Michael Sanvoisin *ed* Olivier Stockman
☆ Derek Jacobi, Cyril Cusack, Ruth Mitchell, Maria Aitken, Irina Brook, Paul Brooke, Richard Caldicot, James Cairncross, Jim Carter, Jonathan Cecil, Maria Charles

Fool for Love
US 1985 106m colour
Cannon/Golan-Globus

In a decaying motel, a half-brother and sister pick over the scab of their unsatisfactory, incestuous relationship.
Basically a filmed play, claustrophobic and taken at an excessively slow tempo.
w Sam Shepard *play* Sam Shepard *d* Robert Altman *ph* Pierre Mignot *m* George Burt *pd* Stephen Altman *ed* Luce Grunenwaldt, Steve Dunn
☆ Sam Shepard, Kim Basinger, Randy Quaid, Harry Dean Stanton

The Fool Killer
US 1964 100m bw
Landau/AA

An orphan suspects his friend is an axe murderer.
Post-Civil War fable with good performances but not much point.
w David Friedkin, Morton Fine *novel* Helen Eustis *d* Servando Gonzalez
☆ Anthony Perkins, Edward Albert, Dana Elcar, Henry Hull, Salome Jens

Foolin' Around
US 1979 101m DeLuxe
Columbia/Arnold Kopelson
A country bumpkin wins a runaway heiress.
Uneasy harkback to the innocence of It Happened One Night, *with willing performers in search of a script and setting.*
w Mike Kane, David Swift *d* Richard T. Heffron *ph* Philip Lathrop *m* Charles Bernstein
☆ Gary Busey, Annette O'Toole, John Calvin, Eddie Albert, Cloris Leachman, Tony Randall

Foolish Wives **
US 1921 85m approx (24 fps) bw silent
Universal

In Monte Carlo, a fake count seduces and blackmails rich women.
Weird melodrama with memorable moments and a vast set; Stroheim's most vivid star performance and one of his most lavish productions.
wd Erich von Stroheim ph Ben Reynolds, William Daniels *ad Erich von Stroheim, Richard Day*
☆ *Erich von Stroheim, Mae Busch*, Maude George, Cesare Gravina
'A very superior piece of photoplay craftsmanship, original in ideas and treatment and deserving of higher rating than *Orphans of the Storm, Loves of Pharaoh, The Storm* and other second-class material which however brought forth applause and bravos from screen public and scribes.' – *Tamar Lane, What's Wrong with the Movies*
† The film was released in Latin America at a length of 6hrs 48m.

Fools
US 1970 93m Eastmancolor
Translor

An unsuccessful actor has an idyllic love affair with a girl he meets in a park; but her jealous millionaire husband shoots her dead.
Foolish is the word for those who concocted this tedious parable about the innocence of love and the sickness of society.
w Robert Rudelson *d* Tom Gries
☆ Jason Robards Jnr, Katharine Ross, Scott Hylands

Fools of Fortune *
GB 1990 109m Technicolor
Palace/Polygram/Working Title/Film Four International (Sarah Radclyffe)

An Anglo-Irish family becomes caught up in the troubles of the 1920s.
Understated story of family tragedy, with a quiet appeal.
w Michael Hirst *novel* William Trevor *d* Pat O'Connor *ph* Jerzy Zielinski *m* Hans Zimmer *pd* Jamie Leonard *ed* Michael Bradsell
☆ Iain Glen, Mary Elizabeth Mastrantonio, Julie Christie, Michael Kitchen, Niamh Cusack, Tom Hickey, John Kavanagh, Mick Lally, Niall Toibin
'A piece of classically-British film-making in the television style: restrained, elliptical, curiously reticent.' – *David Wilson, MFB*

Fools Parade **
US 1971 98m Eastmancolor
Columbia/Stanmore/Penbar (Andrew V. McLaglen)
GB title: *Dynamite Man from Glory Jail*
An ex-con has trouble cashing a cheque for his prison savings, especially as outlaws are after it.
Curious admixture of comedy, adventure and violence with a thirties setting, from the author of Night of the Hunter; *generally gripping entertainment.*
w James Lee Barrett novel Davis Grubb d Andrew V. McLaglen *ph* Harry Stradling Jnr *m* Henry Vars *ad* Alfred Sweeney *ed* David Bretherton, Robert Simpson
☆ James Stewart, George Kennedy, Strother Martin, Anne Baxter, Kurt Russell, William Windom, Mike Kellin
'A quintessentially American tribute to the quiet heroism of the self-made man.' – *Nigel Andrews*

'An impulsive love story'
Fools Rush In
US 1997 108m Technicolor
Columbia (Doug Draizin)

Boy meets girl, boy loses girl, boy gets girl and a baby.
Unexciting, formulaic romantic comedy of minimal interest.
w Katherine Reback *d* Andy Tennant *ph* Robbie Greenberg *m* Alan Silvestri *pd* Edward Pisoni *ed* Roger Bondelli
☆ Matthew Perry (Alex Whitman), Salma Hayek (Isabel Fuentes), Jon Tenney (Jeff), Carlos Gomez (Chuy), Tomas Milian (Tomas), Siobhan Fallon (Lanie), John Bennett Perry (Richard), Jill Clayburgh (Nan)
'The intended humorous moments aren't very funny, while the scenes stressing pathos and drama seem tentative and unconvincing.' – *Todd McCarthy, Variety*

Football Crazy
Italy 1974 106m colour
Documento Films (Gianni Hecht Lucara)
A small-town football referee, who dreams of making the big time, has an affair with a glamorous journalist.
An ineffectual comedy that requires an audience to believe that referees are heroes in their community and that Joan Collins offers erotic promise.
w G. Scarniaci, R. Vianello, S. Continenza, Luigi Filipo D'Amico *d* Luigi Filipo D'Amico *ph* Sergio D'Offizi *m* Guido and Maurizio de Angelis *pd* Walter Patriarca *ed* Marisa Mengoli
☆ Lando Buzzanca, Joan Collins, Gabriella Pallotta, Ignazio Leone, Daniele Vargas

'Can you even think of missing it?'
'1,000 surprises! 300 beauties! 20 big stars!'
Footlight Parade ***
US 1933 104m bw
Warner (Robert Lord)

A determined producer of cine-variety numbers gets the show going despite great difficulty.
Classic putting-on-a-show musical distinguished by rapid-fire dialogue, New York setting, star performances and some of the best Busby Berkeley numbers.
w Manuel Seff, James Seymour *d Lloyd Bacon ph* George Barnes *m/ly* Harry Warren, Al Dubin, Sammy Fain, Irving Kahal *ch Busby Berkeley ad* Anton Grot, Jack Okey *ed* George Amy
☆ *James Cagney*, Joan Blondell, Ruby Keeler, Dick Powell, Frank McHugh, Guy Kibbee, Ruth Donnelly, Hugh Herbert, Claire Dodd, Herman Bing
'Bevies of beauty and mere males disport themselves in a Honeymoon Hotel, by (and in) a Waterfall, and over several acres of Shanghai.' – *C. A. Lejeune*
† The Chester Kent studio was a take-off of Fanchon and Marco, who had just such a studio on Sunset Boulevard
♫ 'By a Waterfall'; 'Ah, the Moon Is Here'; 'Sittin' on a Backyard Fence'; 'Shanghai Lil'; 'Honeymoon Hotel'

Footlight Serenade
US 1942 80m bw
TCF (William LeBaron)

A boxer romances a showgirl.
Indifferent star musical.
w Robert Ellis, Helen Logan, Lynn Starling *d* Gregory Ratoff *ph* Lee Garmes *m/ly* Ralph Rainger, Leo Robin *md* Charles Henderson
☆ Betty Grable, John Payne, Victor Mature, James Gleason, Phil Silvers, Jane Wyman, Cobina Wright Jnr, June Lang, Mantan Moreland

'He's A Big-City Kid In A Small Town. They Said He'd Never Win. He Knew He Had To.'
Footloose
US 1984 107m Movielab
Paramount/Indieprod (Lewis J. Rachmil, Craig Zadan)

The domination of an old-fashioned local preacher is slackened by a young newcomer who insists on arranging a dance.
Odd fable which seeks to combine Flashdance *with* Rebel without a Cause, *and misses out on both.*
w Dean Pitchford *d* Herbert Ross *ph* Ric Waite *m* various *pd* Ron Hobbs
☆ Kevin Bacon, Lori Singer, John Lithgow, Dianne Wiest, Christopher Penn
'The celebration of teenage frustration as dance reduces the issues to the level of platitude.' – *Donald Greig, MFB*
title song (*m/ly* Kenny Loggins, Dean Pitchford); song 'Let's Hear It for the Boy' (*m/ly* Dean Pitchford, Tom Snow)

Footsteps in the Dark
US 1941 96m bw
Warner (Robert Lord)
A would-be detective novelist on the lookout for story material finds himself solving a murder.
Lethargic modern vehicle for Flynn between his swashbucklers, a poor imitation of the Thin Man *style.*
w Lester Cole, John Wexley *play Blondie White* by Ladislas Fodor *d* Lloyd Bacon *ph* Ernest Haller *m* Frederick Hollander
☆ Errol Flynn, Brenda Marshall, Ralph Bellamy, Alan Hale, Lucile Watson, Allen Jenkins, Lee Patrick, William Frawley, Roscoe Karns, Grant Mitchell
'The footsteps were those of restless patrons on their way out to buy popcorn.' – *Clive Hirschhorn*

'When he comes to her room at midnight, is it to kiss or kill?'
Footsteps in the Fog *
GB 1955 90m Technicolor
Film Locations/Mike Frankovich (Maxwell Setton)
A Victorian murderer plans to eliminate a blackmailing maid.
This variation on Gaslight *turns into a black comedy without laughs, but it has effective moments and is efficiently if charmlessly made.*

w Dorothy Reid, Lenore Coffee *story* The Interruption by W. W. Jacobs *d* Arthur Lubin *ph* Christopher Challis *m* Benjamin Frankel *ad* Wilfrid Shingleton
☆ Stewart Granger, Jean Simmons, Bill Travers, Ronald Squire, Finlay Currie, Peter Bull

For a Few Dollars More **
Italy/Spain/West Germany 1965 130m Techniscope
PEA/Gonzales/Constantin (Alberto Grimaldi)
original title: *Per Qualche Dollari in Più*
Bounty hunters in El Paso agree to work together.
Vague, inflated, sometimes good-looking sequel to A Fistful of Dollars, *with customary violence and predictably mean performances.*
wd Sergio Leone *ph* Massimo Dallamano *m* Ennio Morricone
☆ Clint Eastwood, Lee Van Cleef, Gian Maria Volonte, Klaus Kinski

For Better For Worse
GB 1954 84m Eastmancolor
Kenwood (Kenneth Harper)
US title: *Cocktails in the Kitchen*
Tribulations of a young married couple.
Undernourished comedy with an agreeable cast but no surprises.
wd J. Lee-Thompson *play* Arthur Watkyn *ph* Guy Green *m* Wally Stott
☆ Dirk Bogarde, Susan Stephen, Cecil Parker, Dennis Price, Athene Seyler, Eileen Herlie, Thora Hird, James Hayter, Pia Terri, Sid James, Charles Victor

For Better, For Worse: see *Zandy's Bride (1974)*

For Heaven's Sake
US 1950 92m bw
TCF (William Perlberg)
Two angels are sent to earth to mend a Broadway producer's marriage.
Silly, flat whimsy of the Here Comes Mr Jordan *school, and originating from the same author. Stale beer, but historically interesting.*
wd George Seaton *play* Harry Segall *ph* Lloyd Ahern *m* Alfred Newman
☆ Clifton Webb, Edmund Gwenn, Robert Cummings, Joan Bennett, Joan Blondell, Gigi Perreau, Jack La Rue

For Keeps: see *Maybe Baby*

For Love of Ivy
US 1968 100m Perfectcolor
Cinerama/Palomar (Edgar J. Scherick, Jay Weston)
An invaluable coloured maid gives notice, and the family blackmails a likeable black ne'er-do-well to make love to her so that she will stay.
Unhappy whimsy with an extremely laboured script and no jokes, notable only as Hollywood's first bow towards a black love affair.
w Robert Alan Aurthur *story* Sidney Poitier *d* Daniel Mann *ph* Joseph Coffey *m* Quincy Jones
☆ Sidney Poitier, Abbey Lincoln, Beau Bridges, Carroll O'Connor, Nan Martin, Lauri Peters
title song (*m* Quincy Jones, *ly* Bob Russell)

'Billy Chapel must choose between the woman he loves and the game he lives for.'
For Love of the Game
US 1999 137m DeLuxe Panavision
Universal/Beacon/Tig/Mirage (Armyan Bernstein, Amy Robinson)
A baseball player, who is facing the end of his career, recalls the events of the past five years and a romance that is also over.
A movie with limited international appeal, except for those who can take baseball as a metaphor for life; part of the problem is that the life on view here is composed of clichés.
w Dana Stevens *novel* Michael Shaara *d* Sam Raimi *ph* John Bailey *m* Basil Poledouris *pd* Neil Spisak *ed* Eric L. Beason, Arthur Coburn *cos* Judianna Makovsky
☆ Kevin Costner (Billy Chapel), Kelly Preston (Jane Aubrey), John C. Reilly (Gus Sinski), Jena Malone (Heather), Brian Cox (Gary Wheeler), J.K. Simmons (Frank Perry), Vin Scully (Himself), Steve Lyons (Himself), Carmine D. Giovinazzo (Ken Strout), Bill Rogers (Davis Birch), Hugh Ross (Mike Udall)
'Calculating and generic, with a screenplay drafted by a committee of script doctors.' – *Joe Queenan*
'As all-American and all-Hollywood as a movie can get in the late '90s.' – *Variety*

For Love or Money
US 1963 108m Technicolor
U-I (Robert Arthur)
A rich widow hires a lawyer to look after the affairs of her three wayward daughters; he picks the eldest for himself.
Slow, thin, overlong comedy with a surfeit of witless chat.
w Larry Marks, Michael Morris *d* Michael Gordon *ph* Clifford Stine *m* Frank de Vol
☆ Kirk Douglas, Mitzi Gaynor, Thelma Ritter, William Bendix, Gig Young

'He thought there was nothing as seductive as money. He was wrong.'
For Love or Money
US 1993 96m DeLuxe
Universal (Brian Grazer)
GB title: *The Concierge*
A concierge's dreams of owning his own hotel come true.
A dim romantic comedy that wastes a likeable star.
w Mark Rosenthal, Lawrence Konner *d* Barry Sonnenfeld *ph* Oliver Wood *m* Bruce Broughton *pd* Peter Larkin *ed* Jim Miller
☆ Michael J. Fox, Gabrielle Anwar, Anthony Higgins, Michael Tucker, Bob Balaban, Isaac Mizrahi, Udo Kier, Dan Hedaya
'No amount of good humor can deter the thin tale from evaporating before the final clinch.' – *Variety*
'A faceless bit of professionalism, occasionally sparked by incidental bits of business, which coasts too heavily on Fox's boyish charm.' – *Kim Newman*

For Me and My Gal ***
US 1942 104m bw
MGM (Arthur Freed)
Just before World War I, a girl vaudevillian chooses between two partners.
A routine musical romance at the time of its production, this film now stands out because of its professional execution, its star value, and the fact that they don't make 'em like that any more.
w Richard Sherman, Sid Silvers, Fred Finklehoffe *d Busby Berkeley ph William Daniels md* Georgie Stoll, Roger Edens
☆ *Judy Garland, Gene Kelly, George Murphy,* Marta Eggerth, Ben Blue, Richard Quine, Stephen McNally
'A touch of imagination and a deal more than a touch of energy.' – *The Times*
♫ 'Oh, You Beautiful Doll'; 'For Me and My Gal'; 'When You Wore a Tulip'; 'After You've Gone'; 'Till We Meet Again'; 'Ballin' the Jack'.
Georgie Stoll, Roger Edens

For My Sister: see *À Ma Soeur!*

For Pete's Sake *
US 1974 90m Eastmancolor
Columbia/Rastar/Persky-Bright-Barclay (Martin Erlichmann, Stanley Shapiro)
A New York taxi driver's wife borrows money and finds herself heavily committed to work off the debt.
Involved farcical comedy with amusing passages.
w Stanley Shapiro, Martin Richlin *d* Peter Yates *ph* Laszlo Kovacs *m* Artie Butler
☆ Barbra Streisand, Michael Sarrazin, Estelle Parsons, William Redfield, Molly Picon
'Revives memories of how much more inventively they used to do it thirty years ago.' – *Sight and Sound*

For Queen and Country
GB/US 1988 106m Eastmancolor
UIP/Zenith/Atlantic/Working Title (Tim Bevan)
A black soldier returns to a squalid civilian life in Britain.
Turgid political drama that alienates the sympathies it attempts to arouse.
w Martin Stellman, Trix Worrell *d* Martin Stellman *ph* Richard Greatrex *m* Michael Kamen, Geoff MacCormack, Simon Goldenberg *pd* Andrew McAlpine *ed* Stephen Singleton
☆ Denzel Washington, Dorian Healy, Amanda Redman, Sean Chapman, Bruce Payne, Geff Francis, George Baker

For Roseanna: see *Roseanna's Grave*

'For The Laughter. For The Tears. For The Boys.'
For the Boys
US 1991 145m DeLuxe
TCF/All Girl (Bette Midler, Bonnie Bruckheimer, Margaret South)
A singer reminisces about her forty years in showbusiness and her partnership with a song-and-dance man.
Designed mainly as a showcase for Bette Midler, it becomes instead a sentimental wallow in cheap emotions.
w Marshall Brickman, Neal Jimenez, Lindy Laub *d* Mark Rydell *ph* Stephen Goldblatt *m* Dave Grusin *pd* Assheton Gorton *ed* Jerry Greenberg, Jere Huggins
☆ Bette Midler, James Caan, George Segal, Patrick O'Neal, Christopher Rydell, Arye Gross, Norman Fell, Rosemary Murphy, Bud Yorke
'Strong on period décor, weak and dishonest on social history. What it makes you loathe is the ethos of show business.' – *Philip French, Observer*
Bette Midler

For the Defense *
US 1930 62m bw
Paramount
Exploits of a New York criminal lawyer.
Slick programme picture of its day; it gave a lift to its star's career.
w Oliver H. P. Garrett (based on the career of William J. Fallon) *d* John Cromwell
☆ William Powell, Kay Francis, Scott Kolk, Thomas E. Jackson, William B. Davidson
'Certain to hold its head up on grosses.' – *Variety*

For the First Time
US 1959 97m Technirama
MGM/Corona/Orion (Alexander Gruter)
A famous tenor slips off incognito to Capri and falls in love with a deaf girl.
Slipshod co-production (with West Germany) with a hoary sentimental plot, a fat star, and some agreeable picture postcard views.
w Andrew Solt *d* Rudolph Maté *ph* Aldo Tonti *md* Georgie Stoll
☆ Mario Lanza, Johanna von Koczian, Kurt Kasznar, Zsa Zsa Gabor, Hans Sohnker

For the Love of Ada
GB 1972 88m Eastmancolor
LMG/Tigon (Peter J. Thompson)
An elderly grave-digger and his wife celebrate their first wedding anniversary.
A mild comedy, consisting of a series of tiny jokes, stretched well beyond its ability to amuse or entertain.
w Harry Driver, Vince Powell *TV serial* Harry Driver, Vince Powell *d* Ronnie Baxter *ph* Alan Hume *m* Frank Barber *pd* Bill Palmer *ed* Anthony Palk
☆ Irene Handl, Wilfred Pickles, Barbara Mitchell, Jack Smethurst, Arthur English, Patsy Kensit
'A boneless jelly of a film, setting up pointless little heartbreaks so that it can dissolve them in a flood of coy sentimentality.' – *Tom Milne, MFB*
† It was a spin-off from a TV sitcom that ran from 1970 to 1971.

For the Love of Benji
US 1977 84m colour
Mulberry Square
A small dog gets lost in the Greek islands.
Adequate follow-up to Benji; *what more can one say?*
w Ben Vaughn, Joe Camp *d* Joe Camp
☆ Patsy Garrett, Cynthia Smith, Peter Bowles, Ed Nelson

For the Love of Mary
US 1948 90m bw
Universal (Robert Arthur)
A White House switchboard operator gets tangled up in politics when the president helps cure her hiccups.
Tedious comedy with music, a hasty vehicle for a star past her peak.
w Oscar Brodney *d* Frederick de Cordova *ph* William Daniels *m* Frank Skinner *ed* Ted J. Kent
☆ Deanna Durbin, Edmond O'Brien, Harry Davenport, Don Taylor, Jeffrey Lynn, Ray Collins, Hugo Haas
'A warning to all interfering presidents.' – *MFB*

For the Love of Mike *
US 1960 84m DeLuxe Cinemascope
TCF/Shergari (George Sherman)
GB title: *None But the Brave*
An Indian boy in New Mexico is helped by a priest to care for sick animals.
Sentimental outdoor film for young people with a pleasantly light touch.
w D. D. Beauchamp *d* George Sherman *ph* Alex Phillips *m* Raul Lavista
☆ Richard Basehart, Stuart Erwin, Arthur Shields, Armando Silvestre

For Them That Trespass
GB 1948 93m bw
ABP (Victor Skutezky)
A man proves himself innocent of the crime for which he has served fifteen years in prison.
Tedious melodrama which served to introduce Richard Todd to the screen.
w J. Lee-Thompson *d* Alberto Cavalcanti *ph* Derick Williams *m* Philip Green
☆ Richard Todd, Stephen Murray, Joan Dowling, Patricia Plunkett, Michael Laurence, Rosalyn Boulter

For Those Who Think Young
US 1964 96m Techniscope
UA/Aubrey Schenck-Howard W. Koch (Hugh Benson)
College students save their favourite club from closure.
Tedious beach party frolic, very typical of its day, with some odd cameo appearances.
w James and George O'Hanlon, Dan Beaumont *d* Leslie H. Martinson *ph* Harold E. Stine *m* Jerry Fielding
☆ James Darren, Pamela Tiffin, Woody Woodbury, Nancy Sinatra, Tina Louise, Paul Lynde, Bob Denver, Jack La Rue, George Raft, Allen Jenkins, Robert Armstrong, Roger Smith

For Valour *
GB 1937 95m bw
GFD/Capitol (Max Schach)
Adventures in two wars of a major, his shady friend, and their sons.
Agreeable adult farce with the stars each playing father and son.
w Ben Travers d Tom Walls *ph* Phil Tannura *md* Van Phillips *ad* Oscar Werndorff *ed* E. B. Jarvis
☆ *Tom Walls, Ralph Lynn,* Veronica Rose, Joan Marion, Hubert Harben
'A very pleasant antidote to the Coronation, though a little marred by its inability to remain wholly flippant.' – *Graham Greene*

'168 minutes of breathless thrills and romance!'
For Whom the Bell Tolls **
US 1943 168m Technicolor
Paramount (Sam Wood)
An American joins partisan fighters in the Spanish Civil War and falls in love with a refugee girl before going on a suicide mission.
Portentous, solemn adventure story based on a modern classic but without much cinematic impetus despite careful handling and useful performances. It looks expensive, though.
w Dudley Nichols *novel* Ernest Hemingway *d* Sam Wood *ph* Ray Rennahan *m* Victor Young *pd* William Cameron Menzies *ed* Sherman Todd, John Link
☆ Gary Cooper, Ingrid Bergman, Akim Tamiroff, Arturo de Cordova, *Katina Paxinou,* Vladimir Sokoloff, Mikhail Rasumny, Victor Varconi, Joseph Calleia, Alexander Granach
MARIA (INGRID BERGMAN): 'I do not know how

to kiss, or I would kiss you. Where do the noses go?'

'Everybody must have thought they were making a classic … but what with the typical Hollywood compromises, plus the political pressures from Spain and from Catholics – or the fears of such pressures – the whole thing became amorphous and confused.' – *Pauline Kael, 70s*

'The rhythm of this film is the most defective I have ever seen in a super-production … colour is very nice for costume pieces and musical comedies, and has a great aesthetic future in films, but it still gets fatally in the way of any serious imitation of reality.' – *James Agee*

Katina Paxinou

best picture; Ray Rennahan; Victor Young; Gary Cooper; Ingrid Bergman; Akim Tamiroff; Sherman Todd, John Link

For You Alone: see *When You're in Love (1937)*

For You Alone
GB 1944 98m bw
Butcher's
Romance of a naval officer and a vicar's daughter.
Sentimental drama with music; you can smell the lavender a mile off, but it was probably the most ambitious production of this indefatigable Poverty Row production company.
w Montgomery Tully *d* Geoffrey Faithfull
☆ Lesley Brook, Jimmy Hanley, Dinah Sheridan, G. H. Mulcaster, Manning Whiley

For Your Eyes Only *
GB 1981 127m Technicolor Panavision
UA/Eon (Albert R. Broccoli)
James Bond traces a top secret device sunk in a surveillance vehicle off the Greek coast.
Lively set-pieces can't quite redeem this wholly uninventive addition to the Bond canon. Fun while it's on, but next morning there's nothing left to remember.
w Richard Maibaum, Michael G. Wilson *d* John Glen *ph* Alan Hume *m* Bill Conti *pd* Peter Lamont
☆ Roger Moore, Carole Bouquet, Topol, Lynn-Holly Johnson, Julian Glover, Jill Bennett, Jack Hedley, Lois Maxwell, Desmond Llewelyn, Geoffrey Keen

'Roger Moore fronts for a succession of stunt men with all the relaxed, lifelike charm of a foyer poster of himself.' – *Sunday Times*

'Pretty boring between the stunts, as if the director isn't interested in actors, and Broccoli forgot to commission a screenplay.' – *Guardian*

† The first Bond in which original author Ian Fleming doesn't even rate a credit.

title song (*m* Bill Conti, *ly* Mick Leeson)

Forbidden
US 1953 85m bw
Universal-International
A detective falls in love with the woman a mobster has hired him to find.
Would-be intense film noir; talent does not enable it to register.
w William Sackheim, Gil Doud *d* Rudolph Maté
☆ Tony Curtis, Joanne Dru, Lyle Bettger, Marvin Miller, Sen Yung

Forbidden Alliance: see *The Barretts of Wimpole Street (1934)*

The Forbidden Dance: see *Lambada: Forbidden Dance*

Forbidden Fruit *
France 1952 103m bw
Gray Film
original title: *Le Fruit Défendu*
A widowed doctor marries again, then falls for a prostitute.
One of the rather solemn romantic melodramas in which the star insisted from time to time in becoming involved.
w Jacques Companeez, Henri Verneuil, Jean Manse *novel Lettre à Mon Juge* by Georges Simenon *d* Henri Verneuil *ph* Henri Alekan *m* Paul Durand
☆ Fernandel, Claude Nollier, Françoise Arnoul, Sylvie

Forbidden Games: see *Jeux Interdits*

Forbidden Music: see *Land without Music*

Forbidden Paradise
US 1924 60m (24 fps) bw silent
Paramount
GB title: *Czarina*
The amorous intrigues of Catherine the Great of Russia.
Seldom seen these days, this was judged at the time a scintillating satire, with its sly innuendo and modern references such as motor cars and bobbed hair. Remade, more or less, as A Royal Scandal
w Hans Kraly, Agnes Christine Johnston *play The Czarina* by Melchior Lengyel, Lajos Biro *d Ernst Lubitsch ph* Charles Van Enger *ad* Hans Dreier
☆ Pola Negri, Adolphe Menjou, Rod La Rocque, Pauline Starke, Fred Malatesta

'Lubitsch's most brilliant film' – *Paul Rotha, 1949*

'More than a year in production!'

Forbidden Planet **
US 1956 98m Eastmancolor Cinemascope
MGM (Nicholas Nayfack)
In AD 2200 a space cruiser visits the planet Altair Four to discover the fate of a previous mission.
Intriguing sci-fi with a plot derived from The Tempest *and a Prospero who unwittingly creates monsters from his own id. High spirits and suspense sequences partially cancelled out by wooden playing from the younger actors and some leaden dialogue.*
w Cyril Hume d Fred M. Wilcox ph George Folsey *m* Louis and Bebe Barron *ad* Cedric Gibbons, Arthur Lonergan
☆ Walter Pidgeon, Anne Francis, Leslie Nielsen, Warren Stevens, Jack Kelly, Richard Anderson, Earl Holliman

'It's a pity they didn't lift some of Shakespeare's language.' – *New Yorker, 1977*

Forbidden Relations
Hungary 1983 92m Eastmancolor
Cinegate/Objektiv Filmstudio/Mafilm (Jozsef Marx)
original title: *Visszaesök*
In a peasant community, a step-brother and sister fall in love.
Relentless account of an uninteresting incest.
wd Zsolt Kézdi-Kovacs *ph* János Kende *ad* Tamas Banovich *ed* Andrasne Karmento
☆ Lili Monori, Miklós B. Székely, Mari Töröcsik, József Horváth, József Tóth, Tibor Molnar

The Forbidden Street: see *Britannia Mews*

Forbidden Valley
US 1938 67m bw
Universal
After the death of a rancher, who lived in hiding after being accused of murder, his son vows to find the real killer.
Melodramatic Western with stilted dialogue and clumsy direction. (Gittens was a writer-director of silents, and has an overemphatic style.)
wd Wyndham Gittens *novel The Mountains Are My Kingdom* by Stuart Hardy *ph* Elwood Bredell *md* Charles Previn *ad* Jack Otterson *ed* Frank Gross
☆ Noah Beery Jnr, Frances Robinson, Robert Barrat, Fred Kohler, Alonzo Price, Samuel S. Hinds, Stanley Andrews
† It was remade as *Sierra* in 1950.

The Forbin Project **
US 1969 100m Technicolor Panavision
Universal (Stanley Chase)
GB title: *Colossus, The Forbin Project*
An enormous computer takes over the defence of the western world; but it goes into collaboration with the Russian one.
Good-looking sci-fi for intellectual addicts.
w James Bridges *novel Colossus* by D. F. Jones *d* Joseph Sargent *ph* Gene Polito *m* Michel Colombier
☆ Eric Braeden, Gordon Pinsent, Susan Clark, William Schallert

Forbrydelsens Element: see *Element of Crime*

Force 10 from Navarone
GB 1978 118m Technicolor Panavision
Columbia/AIP/Guy Hamilton (Oliver A. Unger)
During World War II, commandos are detailed to blow up a vital bridge separating the Germans and partisans in Yugoslavia.
Routine war hokum with plenty of explosions and sudden death, but not much sense. Nothing, really, to do with The Guns of Navarone.
w Robin Chapman *novel* Alistair MacLean *d* Guy Hamilton *ph* Chris Challis *m* Ron Goodwin *pd* Geoffrey Drake
☆ Robert Shaw, Edward Fox, Franco Nero, Harrison Ford, Barbara Bach, Richard Kiel

Force Majeure *
France 1989 85m colour
CAPAC/Fildebroc/Investimage (Paul Claudon, Michelle de Broca)
Two Frenchmen are faced with a dilemma: to continue with their lives or face imprisonment in South-East Asia, where a casual acquaintance has been sentenced to death for being in possession of drugs that they gave to him.
Intriguing, though slightly plodding, drama of conscience and commitment.
w Pierre Jolivet, Olivier Schatzky *d* Pierre Jolivet *ph* Bertrand Chatry *m* Serge Perathoner, Jannick Top *ad* Eric Simon
☆ Patrick Bruel, François Cluzet, Kristin Scott-Thomas, Alan Bates, Thom Hoffman, Sabine Haudepin

Force of Arms *
US 1951 100m bw
Warner (Anthony Veiller)
A soldier in the Italian campaign falls in love with his nurse.
Routine variation on A Farewell to Arms, *adequately but unexcitingly mounted.*
w Orin Jannings *story* Richard Tregaskis *d* Michael Curtiz *ph* Ted McCord *m* Max Steiner
☆ William Holden, Nancy Olson, Frank Lovejoy, Gene Evans, Dick Wesson, Paul Picerni

'The romance rings true and the battle scenes are dangerously alive.' – *Variety*

The Force of Destiny: see *La Forza del Destino*

Force of Evil **
US 1948 80m bw
MGM/Enterprise (Bob Roberts)
A lawyer is corrupted by the easy money provided by his clients, gangsters who are opposed by his brother in their plans to take over the city's numbers racket.
Bleak and powerful melodrama, an attack on capitalism that is here personified by racketeers.
w Abraham Polonsky, Ira Wolfert *novel Tucker's People* by Ira Wolfert *d* Abraham Polonsky *ph* George Barnes *m* David Raksin *ad* Richard Day *ed* Art Seid
☆ John Garfield, Thomas Gomez, Beatrice Pearson, Roy Roberts, Marie Windsor, Howland Chamberlain, Barry Kelley, Paul Fix

A Force of One
US 1979 90m colour
American Cinema (Alan Belkin)
A karate expert tackles drug pushers in California.
Standard undistinguished action fare.
w Ernest Tidyman *story* Pat Johnson, Ernest Tidyman *d* Paul Aaron *ph* Roger Shearman *m* Dick Halligan *ad* Norman Baron *ed* Bert Lovitt
☆ Chuck Norris, Jennifer O'Neill, Clu Gulager, Ron O'Neal, James Whitmore Jnr, Clint Ritchie, Pepe Serna
† A sequel to *Good Guys Wear Black* (qv).

Forced Vengeance
US 1982 90m colour
MGM (John B. Bennett)
In Hong Kong, a casino security chief seeks revenge when his boss is shot and his girlfriend raped and killed by gangsters who want to take over the business.
The modern equivalent of the second-feature Western of the 40s, as the Stetson-wearing Norris stomps woodenly through an uninteresting narrative, dispensing rough justice and preferring fists to guns; the main difference is the gloating here over the scenes of violence.
w Franklin Thompson *d* James Fargo *ph* Rexford Metz *m* William Goldstein *pd* George B. Chan *ed* Irving C. Rosenblum
☆ Chuck Norris, Mary Louise Weller, Michael Cavanaugh, David Opatoshu, Camila Griggs, Seiji Sakaguchi, Frank Michael Liu

Forces of Nature
US 1999 104m Technicolor Panavision
DreamWorks (Susan Arnold, Donna Arkoff Roth, Ian Bryce)
Attempting to get to his wedding through catastrophic accidents and bad weather, an uptight man becomes involved with a free-spirited woman.
Trivial attempt at a screwball comedy, one that lacks any kind of sparkle or wit despite its engaging stars.
w Marc Lawrence *d* Bronwen Hughes *ph* Elliot Davis *m* John Powell *pd* Lester Cohen *ed* Craig Wood
☆ Sandra Bullock, Ben Affleck, Maura Tierney, Steve Zahn, Blythe Danner, Ronny Cox, Michael Fairman, Janet Carroll, Richard Schiff, David Strickland, Meredith Scott Lynn

'Who on earth left the handbrake on?' – *Empire*

A Foreign Affair **
US 1948 116m bw
Paramount (Charles Brackett)
A deputation of American politicians goes to visit post-war Berlin and a congresswoman finds herself in an emotional triangle with a captain and his German mistress.
Bleakly sophisticated comedy from this team's headline-grabbing period; full of interest and amusement, it never quite sparkles enough to remove the doubtful taste.
w Charles Brackett, Billy Wilder, Richard Breen story David Shaw *d Billy Wilder ph* Charles Lang Jnr *m* Frederick Hollander
☆ *Jean Arthur, Marlene Dietrich, John Lund, Millard Mitchell*, Peter von Zerneck, Stanley Prager

'This deliberately cynical political farce … often seems on the verge of being funny, but the humour is too clumsily forced.' – *New Yorker, 1980*

'What really shocks me about this Hollywood film is the attitude towards life that it reflects; the casual acceptance of irresponsibility and bad manners, of lawlessness and boorishness and mischief-making.' – *C. A. Lejeune*

script; Charles Lang Jnr

Foreign Affaires
GB 1935 71m bw
Gainsborough (Michael Balcon, Tom Walls)
A gambler and a car salesman get mixed up with a phoney casino.
Mild star farce.
w Ben Travers *d* Tom Walls *ph* Roy Kellino *md* Louis Levy *ad* Vetchinsky *ed* Alfred Roome
☆ Tom Walls, Ralph Lynn, Robertson Hare, Norma Varden, Marie Lohr, Diana Churchill, Cecil Parker

'A well-written film in which Mr Tom Walls gives a really lovely performance.' – *Graham Greene*

Foreign Correspondent ****
US 1940 120m bw
Walter Wanger
An American journalist is sent to Europe in 1938 and becomes involved with spies.
Thoroughly typical and enjoyable Hitchcock adventure with a rambling script which builds up into brilliantly managed suspense sequences: an assassination, a windmill, an attempted murder in Westminster Cathedral, a plane crash at sea. The final speech was an attempt to encourage America into the war.
w Charles Bennett, Joan Harrison, James Hilton, Robert Benchley novel Personal History by Vincent Sheean *d Alfred Hitchcock ph Rudolph Maté m* Alfred Newman *pd* William Cameron Menzies *ad* Alexander Golitzen *sp* Lee Zavitz
☆ *Joel McCrea, Laraine Day, Herbert Marshall, Albert Basserman, Edmund Gwenn, George Sanders, Eduardo Ciannelli, Robert Benchley, Harry Davenport*, Martin Kosleck

HAVERSTOCK (JOEL MCCREA): 'I've been watching a part of the world blown to pieces! I can't read the rest of the speech I had because the lights have gone out. It is as if the lights were out everywhere, except in America. Keep those lights burning there! Cover them with steel! Ring them with guns! Build a canopy of battleships and bombing planes around them! Hello, America! Hang on to your lights, they're the only lights left in the world!'

'If you have any interest in the true motion and sweep of pictures, watching that man work is like listening to music ... If you would like a seminar in how to make a movie travel the lightest and fastest way, in a kind of beauty that is peculiar to movies alone, you can see this once, and then again to see what you missed, and then study it twice.' – *Otis Ferguson*

'The most excitingly shot and edited picture of the year.' – *Basil Wright*

'A masterpiece of propaganda, a first class production which no doubt will make a certain impression upon the broad masses of the people in enemy countries.' – *Joseph Goebbels*

'This juxtaposition of outright melodramatics with deadly serious propaganda is eminently satisfactory ... Hitchcock uses camera tricks, cinematic rhythm and crescendo to make his points.' – *Howard Barnes, New York Herald Tribune*

'Easily one of the year's finest pictures.' – *Time*

🎗 best picture; script; Rudolph Maté; Albert Basserman; Alexander Golitzen

Foreign Intrigue *
US 1956 100m Eastmancolor
UA/Sheldon Reynolds

A press agent investigates the death of a man who had been blackmailing potential traitors.
Location espionage melodrama of the cold war fifties, quite well done in a rather dismal vein, but a long way from Foreign Correspondent.
wd Sheldon Reynolds *ph* Bertil Palmgren *m* Paul Durand
☆ Robert Mitchum, Genevieve Page, Ingrid Thulin, Eugene Deckers

Foreign Student
US 1994 96m colour
Universal/Carthago/Libra/Featherstone (Mark Lombardo)

In the mid-50s, a French student goes to study at an American university in Virginia, where he falls in love with a local black teacher and maidservant.
Rose-coloured, nostalgic view of material – involving culture clash and colour prejudice – that might have benefited from a tougher treatment; even abrasive blues singer Howling Wolf, in a brief appearance, appears to have succumbed to the all-enveloping mellowness.
w Menno Meyjes *novel* Philippe Labro *d* Eva Sereny *ph* Franco Di Giacomo *m* Jean-Claude Petit *pd* Howard Cummings *ed* Peter Hollywood
☆ Marco Hofschneider, Robin Givens, Rick Johnson, Charlotte Ross, Anthony Herrera, Jack Coleman, Hinton Battle, Charles Dutton, Edward Herrmann

The Foreman Went to France **
GB 1941 87m bw
Ealing (Alberto Cavalcanti)

US title: *Somewhere in France*
Before Dunkirk, a Welsh foreman is sent on a mission to salvage secret French machinery.
Fresh, appealing comedy drama based on a true incident of World War II.
w John Dighton, Angus Macphail, Leslie Arliss, Roger Macdougall, Diana Morgan *story* J. B. Priestley *d* Charles Frend *ph* Wilkie Cooper *m* William Walton
☆ Tommy Trinder, Constance Cummings, Clifford Evans, Robert Morley, Gordon Jackson, Ernest Milton

'The thrilling story of women who play with fire, and men who fight it!'

The Forest Rangers *
US 1942 85m Technicolor
Paramount (Robert Sisk)

A socialite marries a district ranger and rescues her disgruntled rival during a forest blaze.
Routine, competent, box-office actioner of its time, with popular stars, adequate plot, but precious little inventiveness.
w Harold Shumate *d* George Marshall *ph* Charles Lang *m* Victor Young
☆ Fred MacMurray, Paulette Goddard, Susan Hayward, Lynne Overman, Albert Dekker, Eugene Pallette, Regis Toomey, Rod Cameron

'Another tale of the tall timbers, complete with conflagrations, he-men, and women like cats.' – *New York Times*

Forever Amber *
US 1947 137m Technicolor
TCF (William Perlberg)

Adventures of a desirable young lady during the reign of Charles II.
Much-bowdlerized version of a sensational novel of the forties; pretty but rather thin, with a colourless cast, saved by lively action sequences.
w Philip Dunne, Ring Lardner Jnr *novel* Kathleen Winsor *d* Otto Preminger *ph* *Leon Shamroy* *m* David Raksin *ad* *Lyle Wheeler*
☆ Linda Darnell, Cornel Wilde, *George Sanders* (Charles II), Richard Greene, Glenn Langan, Richard Haydn, Jessica Tandy, Anne Revere, Robert Coote, John Russell, Leo G. Carroll
🎗 David Raksin

Forever and a Day **
US 1943 104m bw
RKO (Herbert Wilcox, Victor Saville)

The history of a London house from 1804 to the blitz of World War II.
Made for war charities by a combination of the European talents in Hollywood, this series of sketches was unavoidably patchy but gave good opportunities to several familiar performers and stands as a likeable quick reference to their work at this period.
w Charles Bennett, C. S. Forester, Lawrence Hazard, Michael Hogan, W. P. Lipscomb, Alice Duer Miller, John Van Druten, Alan Campbell, Peter Godfrey, S. M. Herzig, Christopher Isherwood, Gene Lockhart, R. C. Sherriff, Claudine West, Norman Corwin, Jack Hartfield, James Hilton, Emmet Lavery, Frederick Lonsdale, Donald Ogden Stewart, Keith Winter *d* René Clair, Edmund Goulding, Cedric Hardwicke, Frank Lloyd, Victor Saville, Robert Stevenson, Herbert Wilcox *ph* Robert de Grasse, Lee Garmes, Russell Metty, Nicholas Musuraca *m* Anthony Collins *ad* Albert D'Agostino, Lawrence Williams, Al Herman
☆ Anna Neagle, Ray Milland, *Claude Rains*, *C. Aubrey Smith*, Dame May Whitty, Gene Lockhart, Edmund Gwenn, Ian Hunter, *Jessie Matthews*, *Charles Laughton*, Montagu Love, *Cedric Hardwicke*, Reginald Owen, *Buster Keaton*, Wendy Barrie and also Ida Lupino, *Brian Aherne*, Edward Everett Horton, June Duprez, Eric Blore, Merle Oberon, Una O'Connor, Nigel Bruce, *Roland Young*, *Gladys Cooper*, Robert Cummings, Richard Haydn, Elsa Lanchester, Sara Allgood, Robert Coote, Donald Crisp, Ruth Warrick, Kent Smith, Herbert Marshall, Victor McLaglen, and many others in bit parts

'One of the most brilliant casts of modern times has been assembled to bolster up one of the poorest pictures.' – *James Agate*

'It is holding and entertaining ... a production of outstanding quality.' – *CEA Film Report*

† The film is notable for having the longest-ever list of credited co-writers.

Forever Darling
US 1956 91m Eastmancolor
MGM/Zanra (Desi Arnaz)

A couple's matrimonial difficulties are solved by her guardian angel.
Cutesy-pie comedy with all concerned embarrassed by their material.
w Helen Deutsch *d* Alexander Hall *ph* Harold Lipstein *m* Bronislau Kaper
☆ Lucille Ball, Desi Arnaz, James Mason (the angel), John Emery, Louis Calhern, John Hoyt, Natalie Schafer

Forever England: see *Brown on Resolution*

Forever Female
US 1953 93m bw
Paramount (Pat Duggan)

A young writer sells his play to a Broadway producer who wants to transform it into a vehicle for his ex-wife; she falls for the writer but eventually discourages him.
Talky romantic comedy without much style or sense of Broadway; a long way from All About Eve.
w Julius J. Epstein, Philip G. Epstein *play* *Rosalind* by J. M. Barrie *d* Irving Rapper *ph* Harry Stradling *m* Victor Young
☆ Ginger Rogers, William Holden, Paul Douglas, James Gleason, Pat Crowley

Forever in Love: see *Pride of the Marines*

Forever Lulu
US/Germany 1986 90m Precision colour
Lulu/TV60/TV-80/Bayerischer Rundfunk/Dieter Geissler (Amos Kollek)

US video title: *Crazy Streets*
In New York, a struggling German-born writer finds fame and fortune when she becomes inadvertently involved in murder.
An experience as depressing as the life of its protagonist: the script is implausible when it is not ridiculous, the direction dull and the performances mostly inadequate.
wd Amos Kollek *ph* Lisa Rinzler *pd* Stephen McCabe *ed* Jay Freund
☆ Hanna Schygulla, Deborah Harry, Alec Baldwin, Paul Gleason, Annie Golden, Dr Ruth Westheimer, Amos Kollek

Forever Mary: see *Mery per sempre*

Forever Young
GB 1984 84m colour
Goldcrest (Chris Griffin)

Father Michael finds himself influenced by sexual tensions among his flock.
Rather slight drama chiefly concerning a twelve-year-old boy who idolizes his fallible priest.
w Ray Connolly *d* David Drury *ph* Norman Langley *md* Anthony King
☆ James Aubrey, Nicholas Gecks, Alec McCowen, Karen Archer

'Fifty years ago he volunteered for a dangerous experiment. All in the name of love.'
'Time waits for no man, but true love waits forever.'

Forever Young *
US 1992 102m Technicolor
Warner/Icon (Bruce Davey)

A pilot, who is frozen in an experiment in 1939, wakes up to find that it is 1992.
Pleasant, light-hearted romantic movie, a throwback to the past.
w Jeffrey Abrams *d* Steve Miner *ph* Russell Boyd *m* Jerry Goldsmith *pd* Gregg Fonseca *ed* Jon Poll
☆ Mel Gibson, Jamie Lee Curtis, Elijah Wood, Isabel Glasser, George Wendt, Joe Morton, Nicholas Surovy, David Marshall Grant, Robert Hy Gorman, Millie Slavin

'A big, rousing, old-fashioned romance ... A perfect "women's picture" alternative to action fare and kid-oriented sequels.' – *Variety*

Forever Yours: see *Forget Me Not*

Forfaiture: see *The Cheat*

Forget Me Not
GB 1936 72m bw
UA/Itala/London Films (Alberto Giacolone, Alexander Korda)

US title: *Forever Yours*
On the rebound from a shipboard romance, a young girl marries a widowed tenor.
Bland romance, notable only for the star's singing.
w Hugh Gray, Arthur Wimperis *d* Zoltan Korda, Stanley Irving *ph* Hans Schneeberger *m* Mischa Spoliansky *ed* O. H. Cornelius
☆ Beniamino Gigli, Joan Gardner, Ivan Brandt, Hugh Wakefield

'As a larynx exercise it possesses an appeal for those audiences which go for singing.' – *Variety*

'A Comedy About Love ... After Marriage.'

Forget Paris
US 1995 101m
Rank/Castle Rock/Face (Billy Crystal)

An on-and-off romance of a basketball referee and the married woman he meets in Paris, when he goes there to bury his father.
Dreary romantic comedy, with the focus on Crystal's unlovable character, who is meant to be charmingly offbeat, but is just irritating; forget to watch it.
w Billy Crystal, Lowell Ganz, Babaloo Mandel *d* Billy Crystal *ph* Don Burgess *m* Marc Shaiman *pd* Terence Marsh *ed* Kent Beyda
☆ Billy Crystal, Debra Winger, Joe Mantegna, Julie Kavner, Richard Masur, Cathy Moriarty, William Hickey, Cynthia Stevenson

'Lots of big laughs and a sweet if sometimes sticky take on love amongst the regular folks will satisfy the date-night crowd.' – *Variety*

Forgotten Commandments *
US 1932 75m bw
Paramount

In a Russia which has renounced Christianity, a scientist who considers himself above emotion is led by jealousy into the murder of his mistress.
Vague, feeble and absurd modern parable which takes in its stride a 20-minute excerpt from de Mille's 1923 The Ten Commandments.
w J. B. Fagan, Agnes Brand Leahy *d* Louis Gasnier, William Schoor *ph* Karl Struss
☆ Gene Raymond, Sari Maritza, Irving Pichel, Marguerite Churchill, Edward Van Sloan, Harry Beresford

'Hardly a single dramatic sequence and not over three laughs at the New York opening – and one of them at, not with, the picture.' – *Variety*

The Formula
US 1980 117m Metrocolor
MGM/CIP (Steve Shagan)

A cop follows a murder trail to West Germany and finds that it all hinges on a secret formula for turning coal into petrol.
Convoluted thriller which is all McGuffin and no interest.
w Steven Shagan *novel* Steven Shagan *d* John G. Avildsen *ph* James Crabe *m* Bill Conti
☆ George C. Scott, Marlon Brando, Marthe Keller, John Gielgud, Beatrice Straight, Richard Lynch
🎗 James Crabe

Formula 51: see *The 51st State (2001)*

'The world will never be the same once you've seen it through the eyes of Forrest Gump.'

Forrest Gump **
🏆 US 1994 142m colour Panavision

A retarded boy grows up to become an All-American footballer, a Vietnam hero, champion ping-pong player and a millionaire, while the woman he loves finds that her progress is mostly downhill.
A slick comedy as simple-minded as its hero, worth watching for the clever manner in which it slots Gump into the same historical frame as Kennedy, Johnson and Nixon. He remains a blank on which an audience can project any feelings it chooses, while the film's opprobrium is vented on the less conservative values represented by the woman he loves, whose fate is a lingering death. The movie's point is obscure, unless it is to suggest that you have to be an idiot to believe in the American dream, and its success took even its makers by surprise.
w Eric Roth *novel* Winston Groom *d* *Robert Zemeckis* *ph* Don Burgess *m* Alan Silvestri *pd* Rick Carter *ed* Arthur Schmidt
☆ Tom Hanks, Robin Wright, Gary Sinise, Sally Field, Mykelti Williamson, Michael Conner Humphreys, Hanna R. Hall

'Warm, wise and wearisome as hell.' – *New Yorker*

'An unembarrassed celebration of stupidity.' – *Gilbert Adair, Sunday Times*

'Marred by sentiment and cant and much flattery of the audience.' – *David Denby, New York*

'A film which would make saccharine taste sour. It goes beyond the further shores of the glutinous, with just enough historical wit to dampen the nausea.' – *Martin Walker, Sight and Sound*

† A book of the sayings of Forrest Gump was published following the film's success, of which the best-known (as well as the most banal) is 'Life is like a box of chocolates. You never know what you're gonna get.'

†† It is the third most successful film so far, having taken more than \$325m at the US box-office and a total of more than \$635m worldwide. The video sold more than 15 million copies in the United States.

best picture; Robert Zemeckis; Tom Hanks; Eric Roth; Arthur Schmidt; visual effects (Ken Ralston, George Murphy, Stephen Rosenblum, Allen Hall)
Gary Sinise; Alan Silvestri; art direction; cinematography; sound; sound effects editing; make-up

'The night... has an appetite.'
The Forsaken
US 2001 91m colour
Columbia TriStar/Screen Gems/Sandstone (Carol Kottenbrook, Scott Einbinder)

A van driver picks up two victims of a gang of vampires, who plan to cure themselves by killing the master vampire.
A cheap horror movie that sucks the blood out of the familiar story, leaving only a pale corpse behind.
wd J. S. Cardone *ph* Steven Bernstein *m* Johnny Lee Schell, Tim Jones *pd* Martina Buckley *ed* Norman Buckley
☆ Kerr Smith (Sean), Brendan Fehr (Nick), Izabella Miko (Megan), Phina Oruche (Cym), Simon Rex (Pen), Carrie Snodgress (Ina), Johnathon Schaech (Kit), Alexis Thorpe (Teddy)
'Shamelessly derivative and exuberantly junky.' – *Joe Leydon, Variety*

Forsaking All Others *
US 1934 84m bw
MGM (Bernard H. Hyman)

A woman almost marries the wrong man twice.
Star power carries this thin comedy drama.
w Joseph L. Mankiewicz *play* Edward Barry Roberts, Frank Morgan Cavett *d* W. S. Van Dyke *ph* Gregg Toland, George Folsey *m* William Axt
☆ Clark Gable, Joan Crawford, Robert Montgomery, *Charles Butterworth*, Billie Burke, Frances Drake, Rosalind Russell, Arthur Treacher
'Stock romantic comedy despite some messy hokum.' – *Variety*
'Contrary to expectation, sophistication is at a minimum.' – *Time*

The Forsyte Saga: see *That Forsyte Woman*

Fort Apache **
US 1948 127m bw
RKO/Argosy (John Ford, Merian C. Cooper)

In the old west, a military martinet has trouble with his family as well as the Indians.
Rather stiff and unsatisfactory epic Western which yet contains sequences in its director's best manner.
w Frank S. Nugent *story Massacre* by James Warner Bellah *d John Ford ph* Archie Stout *m* Richard Hageman *ad* James Basevi *ed* Jack Murray
☆ *Henry Fonda*, John Wayne, Shirley Temple, Pedro Armendariz, Ward Bond, Irene Rich, George O'Brien, John Agar, Victor McLaglen, Anna Lee, Dick Foran, Guy Kibbee
'A visually absorbing celebration of violent deeds.' – *Howard Barnes*
'The whole picture is bathed in a special form of patriotic sentimentality: scenes are held so that we cannot fail to appreciate the beauty of the American past.' – *New Yorker, 1976*
'Shirley Temple and her husband handle the love interest as though they were sharing a soda fountain special, and there is enough Irish comedy to make me wish Cromwell had done a more thorough job.' – *James Agee*

Fort Apache, the Bronx
US 1980 123m DeLuxe
Time Life/Producer Circle (Martin Richards, Tom Fiorello)

A veteran policeman deals with various violent crimes in New York.
This instantly forgettable movie unspools like an ultra-violent Dixon of Dock Green, but Newman is no Jack Warner.
w Heywood Gould *d* Daniel Petrie *ph* John Alcott *m* Jonathan Tunick *pd* Ben Edwards
☆ Paul Newman, Ed Asner, Ken Wahl, Danny Aiello, Rachel Ticotin, Pam Grier, Kathleen Beller

Fort Defiance
US 1951 81m Cinecolor
Ventura/UA
Ben Shelby comes back from the Civil War to avenge his brother's death.
Complicated lower-berth Western, crudely executed.
w Louis Lantz *d* John Rawlins
☆ Dane Clark, Ben Johnson, Peter Graves, Tracey Roberts, George Cleveland

Fort Massacre
US 1958 80m DeLuxe Cinemascope
Mirisch/UA
A cavalry sergeant becomes reckless when he has to lead to safety the survivors of an Indian attack.
Psychological Western without the skill necessary to realize its pretensions.
w Martin M. Goldsmith *d* Joseph Newman
☆ Joel McCrea, Forrest Tucker, Susan Cabot, John Russell

Fort Ti
US 1953 73m Technicolor 3-D
Columbia (Sam Katzman)
In 1759 a platoon of Rogers' Rangers marches north to defend their territory against Indians.
Cheap and feeble Western memorable only for the amount of miscellaneous objects thrown at the audience via 3-D photography.
w Robert E. Kent *d* William Castle *ph* Lester E. White, Lathrop B. Worth *md* Ross di Maggio
☆ George Montgomery, Joan Vohs, Irving Bacon, James Seay
'The lack of restraint is remarkable. To the injury of tomahawks, rifle shots, cannon balls, flaming arrows, broken bottles and blazing torches is added the insult of grubby redskins hurled judo style into one's lap.' – *David Robinson*

Fort Worth
US 1951 80m Technicolor
Warner

A newspaper editor combats a would-be dictator.
Satisfying star Western.
w John Twist *d* Edwin L. Marin *ph* Sid Hickox *ed* Clarence Kolster
☆ Randolph Scott, Phyllis Thaxter, David Brian, Dick Jones, Paul Picerni

Fortress
Australia/US 1993 89m CFI color
Village Roadshow/Davis Entertainment (John Davis, John Flock)

In the future, a couple who break the law by having more than one child are incarcerated in a huge underground prison, run by a harsh private corporation.
An efficient action film in a science-fiction setting, but one that is unable to escape from its own over-familiar scenario.
w Steve Feinberg, Troy Neighbors, Terry Curtis Fox *d* Stuart Gordon *ph* David Eggby *m* Frederic Talghorn *pd* David Copping *ed* Timothy Wellburn *sp* Tad Pride, Paul Gentry
☆ Christopher Lambert, Kurtwood Smith, Loryn Locklin, Lincoln Kilpatrick, Clifton Gonzalez Gonzalez, Jeffrey Combs, Tom Towles, Vernon Wells
'A grim, sometimes bloody, futuristic prison picture that has been well produced and directed within the limitations of a predictable, uninspired screenplay.' – *Variety*

'Locked in a prison orbiting 26,000 miles above earth. Escape was never thought possible...until now.'
Fortress 2: Re-entry
US/Luxembourg 2000 93m DeLuxe
Columbia TriStar/Gower/Carousel (John Flock)

A recaptured prisoner is incarcerated with others in a space station, where the governor plans to use their labour for illegal purposes.
Depite its futuristic setting, this is the usual prison fare, with lots of tough talk and much macho swaggering.
w John Flock, Peter Doyle *story* Steven Feinberg, Troy Neighbors *d* Geoff Murphy *ph* Hiro Narita *m* Christopher Franke *pd* Rob Stratfold *ed* James R. Symons *cos* Cynthia Dumont
☆ Christopher Lambert (John Brennick), Pam Grier (Susan Mendenall), Patrick Malahide (Peter Teller), Liz May Brice (Elena Rovera), Willie Garson (Stanley Nussbaum), Yuji Okumoto (Sato), Nick Brimble (Max Polk), Beth Toussaint (Karen Brennick), David Robertson (Nestor Tubman), Aidan Rea (Danny Brennick), Anthony C. Hall (Marcus Jackson)
'Shot entirely on four or five claustrophobic sets with special effects which seem to have been created on a ZX-81, it absolutely fails to entertain.' – *Grant Kempster, Film Review*

The Fortune
US 1975 88m Technicolor Panavision
Columbia (Hank Moonjean)
A twenties heiress elopes with her lover and his dim-witted friend but discovers that they mean to murder her for her money.
Bungled black comedy with top talent over-confident of carrying it.
w Adrien Joyce (Carol Eastman) *d* Mike Nichols *ph* John A. Alonzo *m* various songs *pd* Richard Sylbert
☆ Jack Nicholson, Warren Beatty, Stockard Channing, Florence Stanley, Richard B. Shull, John Fiedler
'Like the ill-assorted styles of the film generally, the stars themselves frequently seem to belong in different movies.' – *Richard Combs*
'A silly, shallow, occasionally enjoyable comedy trifle ... classy 20's production values often merit more attention than the plot.' – *Variety*

Fortune and Men's Eyes
Canada/US 1971 102m Metrocolor
MGM/Cinemex/CFD (Lester Persky, Lewis M. Allen)

Life among homosexuals in a Canadian jail.
A welter of sensational incident outweighs any point the author may have had; this prison seems to be beyond reform.
w John Herbert *play* John Herbert *d* Harvey Hart *ph* Georges Dufaux *m* Galt McDermot
☆ Wendell Burton, Michael Greer

The Fortune Cookie *
US 1966 125m bw Panavision
UA/Mirisch/Phalanx/Jalem (Billy Wilder)

GB title: *Meet Whiplash Willie*
A crooked lawyer forces his slightly injured client to sue for a million dollars.
Flat, stretched-out, only occasionally effective comedy which relies too much on mordant attitudes and a single star performance.
w Billy Wilder, I. A. L. Diamond *d* Billy Wilder *ph* Joseph LaShelle *m* André Previn
☆ *Walter Matthau*, Jack Lemmon, Ron Rich, Cliff Osmond, Lurene Tuttle
'A jackhammer of a film savagely applied to those concrete areas of human spirit where cupidity and stupidity have been so long entrenched.' – *Richard Schickel*
Walter Matthau
Billy Wilder, I. A. L. Diamond (script); Joseph LaShelle

Fortune Is a Woman *
GB 1957 95m bw
Columbia/Frank Launder, Sidney Gilliat
US title: *She Played with Fire*
An insurance assessor investigates a fire, finds a murder, marries the victim's widow, and is blackmailed...
Slackly-handled mystery thriller, a disappointment from the talents involved.
w Frank Launder, Sidney Gilliat *novel* Winston Graham *d* Sidney Gilliat *ph* Gerald Gibbs *m* William Alwyn
☆ Jack Hawkins, Arlene Dahl, Dennis Price, Geoffrey Keen, Violet Farebrother, John Robinson, Bernard Miles, Greta Gynt

Fortunes of Captain Blood
US 1950 91m bw
Columbia (Harry Joe Brown)
The famous Caribbean pirate eludes his pursuers by taking over their own ship.
Lethargic adventures on a low budget; the cast was there for something better.
w Michael Hogan, Robert Libbott, Frank Burt *d* Gordon Douglas
☆ Louis Hayward, Patricia Medina, George Macready, Dona Drake, Alfonso Bedoya

Forty Carats *
US 1973 109m Metrocolor
Columbia/M. J. Frankovich

A 40-year-old divorcee on holiday in Greece has a brief affair with a 22-year-old man.
Curiously miscast and mishandled comedy for the smart set; scores a laugh or two but never really takes off.
w Leonard Gershe *play* Pierre Barillet, Jean-Pierre Gredy *d* Milton Katselas *ph* Charles Lang Jnr *m* Michel Legrand
☆ Liv Ullmann, Edward Albert, Gene Kelly, Billy 'Green' Bush, Binnie Barnes, Nancy Walker, Deborah Raffin, Don Porter, Natalie Schafer, Rosemary Murphy

'One man is about to do the unthinkable. No sex. Whatsoever. For...'
40 Days and 40 Nights
US 2002 94m DeLuxe
Universal/StudioCanal/Working Title/Milo (Tim Bevan, Eric Fellner, Michael London)

An unmarried young computer expert finds it hard to keep to his vow to abstain from sex for the 40 days of Lent.
Amiable comedy in the style of a TV sitcom.
w Robert Perez *d* Michael Lehmann *ph* Elliot Davis *m* Rolfe Kent *pd* Sharon Seymour *ed* Nicholas C. Smith
☆ Josh Hartnett (Matt), Shannyn Sossamon (Erica Sutton), Vinessa Shaw (Nicole), Paulo Costanzo (Ryan), Maggie Gyllenhaal (Sam), Michael Maronna (Bagel Guy), Glenn Fitzgerald (Chris), Mary Gross (Mom), Stanley Anderson (Father Maher), Adam Trese (John), Barry Newman (Dad), Griffin Dunne (Jerry)
'The movie contains some smart writing, funny dialogue, a cheeky production design, attractive leading actors and only occasional lapses into tastelessness.' – *Kirk Honeycutt, Hollywood Reporter*

Forty Eight Hours: see *Went the Day Well? (1942)*

48 Hours
US 1982 96m Movielab
Paramount/Lawrence Gordon

A cop and a criminal on parole combine to track down the latter's former associates.
Reasonable action melodrama with comedy asides and San Francisco locations; but too violent for its own good.
w Roger Spottiswoode, Walter Hill, Larry Gross, Steven E. de Souza *d* Walter Hill *ph* Ric Waite *m* James Horner *pd* John Vallone
☆ Nick Nolte, Eddie Murphy, Annette O'Toole, Frank McRae
'It's like *The French Connection*, *Dirty Harry* and *Butch Cassidy* all put in a compactor and pressed into cartoon form.' – *New Yorker*
† It was followed, after a long gap, by a sequel *Another 48 Hours* (qv).

The Forty First *
USSR 1927 80m approx bw silent
Mezhrabpom
original title: *Sorok Pervyi*
During the Civil War in Turkestan, a girl sniper for the Reds becomes the companion in adventure of a White lieutenant. But in the end he becomes her 41st victim.
Strong action melodrama which found an international audience.
w Boris Lavryenov *novel* Boris Lavryenov *d* Yakov Protazanov *ph* Pyotr Yermolov
☆ Ada Voitsik, Ivan Kovan-Samborsky
† Remade in 1956 by Grigori Chukrai, in colour.

Forty Guns *
US 1957 80m bw Cinemascope
TCF/Globe (Samuel Fuller)
A powerful ranchwoman protects her hoodlum brother.
Heavily melodramatic and slow-moving Western with a few effective moments.
wd Samuel Fuller *ph* Joseph Biroc *m* Harry Sukman
☆ Barbara Stanwyck, Barry Sullivan, Dean Jagger, Gene Barry, John Ericson

Forty Guns to Apache Pass
US 1966 95m Technicolor
Admiral/Columbia
A cavalry captain protects homesteaders when Cochise attacks.
Flat and overlong star Western compounded of excessively familiar elements.
w Willard and Mary Willingham *d* William Witney *ph* Jacques R. Marquette *m* Richard La Salle
☆ Audie Murphy, Michael Burns, Kenneth Tobey, Laraine Stephens

Forty Little Mothers
US 1940 90m bw
MGM (Harry Rapf)
A teacher in a girls' school finds himself in charge of a baby.
Ill-advised star vehicle composed largely of whimsy ... and no musical numbers.
w Dorothy Yost, Ernest Pagano *d* Busby Berkeley *ph* Charles A. Lawton Jnr
☆ Eddie Cantor, Judith Anderson, Bonita Granville, Rita Johnson, Diana Lewis, Nydia Westman, Martha O'Driscoll

Forty Naughty Girls
US 1937 68m bw
RKO (William Sistrom)
Hildegarde Withers solves a murder backstage.
Weak addition to a faltering series.
w John Grey, Stuart Palmer *d* Edward F. Cline
☆ ZaSu Pitts, James Gleason, Marjorie Lord, George Shelley, Joan Woodbury

'Decidedly tame, and won't cause much ripple on nether side of duals, where it'll undoubtedly land.' – *Variety*

49th Parallel ★★★
GB 1941 123m bw
GFD/Ortus (John Sutro, Michael Powell)
US title: *The Invaders*
In Canada, five stranded U-boat men try to escape into the US.
Episodic, effective propaganda piece which develops some nice Hitchcockian touches and allows a range of star actors to make impact.
w Emeric Pressburger, Rodney Ackland *d* Michael Powell *ph* F. A. Young *m* Ralph Vaughan Williams *ad* David Rawnsley *ed* David Lean
☆ *Eric Portman*, Laurence Olivier, *Anton Walbrook*, *Leslie Howard*, *Raymond Massey*, Glynis Johns, Niall MacGinnis, Finlay Currie, Raymond Lovell, John Chandos

'Some of the plotting and characterization look rather rusty at this remove, but the sense of landscape and figures passing through it remains authoritatively dynamic.' – *Tony Rayns, Time Out, 1979*

'An admirable piece of work from every point of view.' – *MFB*

original story (Emeric Pressburger)
best picture; script

The Forty Niners
US 1954 70m bw
Allied Artists
A marshal tracks down three men who were accomplices to a murder.
Very tolerable minor Western.
w Dan Ullman *d* Thomas Carr
☆ Wild Bill Elliott, Virginia Grey, Henry Morgan, John Doucette, Lane Bradford

Forty Pounds of Trouble ★
US 1963 105m Eastmancolor Panavision
U-I/Curtis Enterprises (Stan Margulies)
A casino manager is chased by his ex-wife's detective for alimony payments, and also has to look after an abandoned six-year-old girl.
Standard sentimental comedy with some verve and a lively climactic chase through Disneyland.
w Marion Hargrove *d* Norman Jewison *ph* Joe MacDonald *m* Mort Lindsey
☆ Tony Curtis, Phil Silvers, Suzanne Pleshette, Edward Andrews

'Mightier than Broadway ever beheld.'
'Most important entertainment event since Warner Bros gave you Vitaphone!'

42nd Street ★★★
US 1933 89m bw
Warner (Hal B. Wallis)
A Broadway musical producer has troubles during rehearsal but reaches a successful opening night.
Archetypal Hollywood putting-on-a-show musical in which the leading lady is indisposed and a chorus girl is told to get out there and come back a star. The clichés are written and performed with great zest, the atmosphere is convincing, and the numbers when they come are dazzlers.
w James Seymour, Rian James novel Bradford Ropes *d Lloyd Bacon ph Sol Polito m/ly Al Dubin, Harry Warren ch Busby Berkeley*
☆ *Warner Baxter* (Julian Marsh), *Ruby Keeler* (Peggy Sawyer), *Bebe Daniels* (Dorothy Brock), George Brent (Pat Denning), Una Merkel (Lorraine Fleming), Guy Kibbee (Abner Dillon), Dick Powell (Billy Lawler), *Ginger Rogers* (Anytime Annie), *Ned Sparks*, George E. Stone, Allen Jenkins

(WARNER BAXTER): 'Sawyer, you listen to me, and you listen hard. Two hundred people, two hundred jobs, two hundred thousand dollars, five weeks of grind and blood and sweat depend upon you. It's the lives of all these people who've worked with you. You've got to go on, and you've got to give and give and give. They've got to like you. Got to. Do you understand? You can't fall down. You can't because your future's in it, my future and everything all of us have is staked on you. All right, now I'm through, but you keep your feet on the ground and your head on those shoulders of yours and go out, and Sawyer, you're going out a youngster but you've got to come back a star!'

'The story has been copied a hundred times since, but never has the backstage atmosphere been so honestly and felicitously caught.' – *John Huntley, 1966*

'It gave new life to the clichés that have kept parodists happy.' – *New Yorker, 1977*

♫ 'Forty-Second Street'; 'It Must Be June'; 'Shuffle Off to Buffalo'; 'Young and Healthy'; 'You're Getting to Be a Habit with Me'
best picture

Forty Thousand Horsemen
Australia 1940 100m bw
Famous Feature Films (Charles Chauvel)
The story of the Australian Light Horse in Palestine during World War I.
One of the first Australian bids for the world market; in itself, just a competent little war movie, and too long.
w Charles Chauvel, Elsa Chauvel *d* Charles Chauvel
☆ Chips Rafferty, Betty Bryant, Grant Taylor, Pat Twohill

'Almost unbelievably primitive in these days of stream-lined talkies. It is also most uncannily exciting. I don't remember enjoying a film quite in this way since the first cowboys rode the range.' – *C. A. Lejeune*

Forty-Five Fathers
US 1937 71m bw
TCF (John Stone)
A show business orphan becomes the personal ward of the Gun and Spear Club.
Palatable vehicle for a growing child star.
w Frances Hyland, Albert Ray, Mary Bickel *d* James Tinling
☆ Jane Withers, Paul and Grace Hartman, Thomas Beck, Louise Henry, Richard Carle, Nella Walker, Andrew Tombes

Forward March: see *Doughboys*

La Forza del Destino ★
Italy 1950 100m bw
Union Film Gallone (Ottavio Poggi)
The Duke of Rivas, a political prisoner, is inspired by an 18th-century manuscript to write a play about the doomed love affair between Don Alvaro and Leonora.
A voice-over narration is used to compress and contain Verdi's sprawling melodrama, in which most of the principals are pretending to be someone else. It has been effectively opened up and framed within the story of how Saavedra's original came to be written, but remains of interest mainly for Tito Gobbi, the bass of Giulio Neri and as an example of Italian opera of its time.
w Mario Corsi, Ottavio Poggi, Lionello de Felice *play* Angelo Saavedra *d* Carmine Gallone *ph* Aldo Giordani *m* Giuseppe Verdi *md* Gabriele Santini *ad* Gastone Medin *ed* Nicolo Lazzari
☆ Nelly Carradi, Tito Gobbi, Gino Sinimberghi, John Kitzmiller, Giulio Neri, Vito de Taranto
† The singers are: Tito Gobbi, Caterina Mancini, Fausto Tomei, Galliano Masini, Giulio Neri

Foul Play ★
US 1978 116m Movielab
Paramount/Thomas L. Miller, Edward K. Milkis
Two innocents in San Francisco get involved in a plot to assassinate the visiting pope.
Sometimes sprightly, sometimes tired rehash of Hitchcock elements, rather on the level of the similar Silver Streak.
wd Colin Higgins *ph* David M. Walsh *m* Charles Fox
☆ Goldie Hawn, Chevy Chase, Burgess Meredith, Rachel Roberts, Eugene Roche, Dudley Moore, Billy Barty
song, 'Ready to Take a Chance Again' (*m* Charles Fox, *ly* Norman Gimbel)

The Fountain: see *Fontan*

The Fountainhead ★★
US 1949 114m bw
Warner (Henry Blanke)
An idealistic architect clashes with big business.
Overripe adaptation of a rather silly novel, full of Freudian symbols and expressionist techniques with which the star really can't cope; but an enjoyable field day for the director and the rest of the cast.
w Ayn Rand *novel* Ayn Rand *d* King Vidor *ph Robert Burks m* Max Steiner
☆ Gary Cooper, *Patricia Neal*, *Raymond Massey*, Kent Smith, Robert Douglas, Henry Hull, Ray Collins, Moroni Olsen, Jerome Cowan

'If you like deep thinking, hidden meanings, plus pure modern architecture, then this is something for which you have been waiting a long time.' – *Screenland*

'The most bizarre movie in both Vidor's and Cooper's filmographies, this adaptation mutes Ms Rand's neo-Nietzschian philosophy of "objectivism" but lays on the expressionist symbolism with a "free enterprise" trowel.' – *Time Out, 1980*

Four Adventures of Reinette and Mirabelle ★★
France 1986 99m colour
Artificial Eye/CER/Les Films du Losange (Eric Rohmer)
original title: *Quatre Aventures de Reinette et Mirabelle*
Four stories involving two contrasted students, one from the country, the other from the city.
Charming small-scale work, full of incidental pleasures.
wd Eric Rohmer *ph* Sophie Maintigneux *m* Ronan Girre, Jean-Louis Valero *ed* Marie-Luisa Garcia
☆ Joëlle Miquel, Jessica Forde, Philippe Laudenbach, Yasmine Haury, Marie Rivière, Beatrice Romand, Gérard Courant, David Rocksavage

Four Against Fate: see *Derby Day*

Four Clowns ★★
US 1970 96m bw
Robert Youngson Productions (Herb Gelbspan)
Studies of four silent comedians. Laurel and Hardy in excerpts from *Putting Pants on Philip, The Second Hundred Years, Their Purple Moment, Big Business, Two Tars* and *Double Whoopee*; Charley Chase in *Us, What Price Goofy, Fluttering Hearts, The Family Group* and *Limousine Love*; Buster Keaton in *Seven Chances*.
An essential compendium, especially for the Charley Chase revaluation which was long overdue.
w Robert Youngson *m* Manny Alban
☆ Jay Jackson (narrator)

Four Dark Hours: see *The Green Cockatoo*

Four Daughters ★★★
US 1938 90m bw
Warner (Henry Blanke)
Domestic and romantic adventures of a small-town family.
Standard small-town hearth-fire hokum, impeccably done and really quite irresistible. Garfield is a sensation in his first role.
w Julius Epstein, Lenore Coffee *novel Sister Act* by Fannie Hurst *d Michael Curtiz ph* Ernest Haller *m* Max Steiner *ad* John Hughes *ed* Ralph Dawson
☆ *Claude Rains* (Adam Lemp), *John Garfield* (Mickey Borden), Priscilla Lane (Ann Lemp), Rosemary Lane (Kay Lemp), Lola Lane (Thea Lemp), Gale Page (Emma Lemp), Jeffrey Lynn (Felix Deitz), Frank McHugh (Ben Crowley), *May Robson* (Aunt Etta), Dick Foran (Ernest)

'It may be sentimental, but it's grand cinema.' – *New York Times*

'It simply, yet powerfully, brings into focus a panorama of natural but startling events.' – *Motion Picture Herald*

† An immediate sequel was required, but the Garfield character had been killed off, so to accommodate him a variation was written under the title *Daughters Courageous*; then came two proper sequels without him, *Four Wives* and *Four Mothers*. In 1955 the original was remade as *Young at Heart* (qv).
best picture; script; Michael Curtiz; John Garfield

The Four Days of Naples ★
Italy 1962 119m bw
Titanus-Metro (Goffredo Lombardo)
A reconstruction of the 1943 city battle in which the Nazis were driven out by civilian fury.
A kind of update of Open City*: much admired, but a little ill-timed.*
w Nanni Loy and others *d Nanni Loy ph* Marcello Gatti *m* Carlo Rustichelli
☆ Lea Massari, Frank Wolff, Domenico Formato, Raffaele Barbato
best foreign film; script

Four Desperate Men: see *The Siege of Pinchgut*

'A girl in your lap.'

The Four Dimensions of Greta
GB 1972 89m Eastmancolor/bw
Hemdale/Peter Walker
A reporter from Berlin comes to London to investigate the disappearance of a German au pair girl.
Flat soft-core sex flick; its only novelty is the inclusion of some uninteresting 3-D sequences in black and white, in which characters hold objects at arm's length close to the lens. In an attempt to disarm criticism, one character remarks, 'This is just like a very cheap British sex film!', and so it is.
w Murray Smith *d* Peter Walker *ph* Peter Jessop *m* Harry South *ed* Matt McCarthy
☆ Tristan Rogers, Karen Boyes, Alan Curtis, Robin Askwith, Leena Skoog, Kenneth Hendel, John Clive, Godfrey Kenton, Pearl Hackney, Bill Maynard, Myna Bird

'Tepid and tedious sexploitation picture.' – *Nigel Andrews, MFB*

Four Faces West
US 1948 90m bw
Enterprise (David Loewe, Charles Einfeld)
aka: *They Passed This Way*
A young man turns bandit to save his father's ranch.
Thoughtful minor Western, nicely made.
w Graham Baker, Teddi Sherman *novel Paso por aqui* by Eugene Rhodes *d* Alfred E. Green *ph* Russell Harlan *m* Paul Sawtell
☆ Joel McCrea, Frances Dee, Charles Bickford, Joseph Calleia

The Four Feathers ★★
US 1929 83m bw
Paramount (David O. Selznick)
During the Sudan campaign of the 1890s, a stay-at-home receives four white feathers as a symbol of cowardice; but he goes undercover, becomes a hero, and rescues his best friend.

Ambitious early talkie based on a famous adventure novel, partly filmed in Africa; interesting but now very stilted.
w Howard Estabrook *novel* A. E. W. Mason
d Lothar Mendes, Merian C. Cooper, Ernest Schoedsack *ph* Robert Kurrle, Merian C. Cooper, Ernest Schoedsack *m* William F. Peters
☆ Richard Arlen, Fay Wray, Clive Brook, William Powell, George Fawcett, Theodore Von Eltz, Noah Beery

The Four Feathers ********
GB 1939 130m Technicolor
London (Alexander Korda, Irving Asher)
A man accused of cowardice by his friends proves himself to be a hero.
The standard version of the story, perfectly cast and presented, with battle scenes which have since turned up in a score of other films from Zarak *to* Master of the World; *also a triumph of early colour.*
w R. C. Sherriff, Lajos Biro, Arthur Wimperis
d Zoltan Korda ph Georges Périnal, Osmond Borradaile, Jack Cardiff *m* Miklos Rozsa
ad Vincent Korda *ed* William Hornbeck, Henry Cornelius
☆ *John Clements, Ralph Richardson,* C. Aubrey Smith, June Duprez, Allan Jeayes, Jack Allen, Donald Gray, Henry Oscar, John Laurie
'It cannot fail to be one of the best films of the year ... even the richest of the ham goes smoothly down, savoured with humour and satire.' – *Graham Greene*
'Keeps the screen packed with movement, spectacle, and excitement. Beyond these box-office virtues, however, it has another quality. It tells a thumping good personal story.' – *C. A. Lejeune*
† Remade 1956 as *Storm over the Nile* (qv). An effective TV movie, *The Four Feathers*, was made in 1977, directed by Don Sharp and starring Beau Bridges, Robert Powell, Simon Ward, Richard Johnson, Jane Seymour and Harry Andrews.

Four for Texas
US 1963 124m Technicolor
Warner/Sam Company (Robert Aldrich)
Two survivors of a stagecoach raid doublecross each other for the loot and become rival saloon owners.
Flabby Western comedy, tediously directed and casually performed.
w Teddi Sherman, Robert Aldrich *d* Robert Aldrich *ph* Ernest Laszlo *m* Nelson Riddle
☆ Dean Martin, Frank Sinatra, Anita Ekberg, Ursula Andress, Charles Bronson, Victor Buono, the Three Stooges
'The major laughs come from the Three Stooges doing an ancient routine and an old lady falling out of her wheelchair. Zowie.' – *Judith Crist*
'One suspects that the most amusing antics were those that went on off-screen.' – *Films and Filming*

Four Friends
US 1981 115m Technicolor
Filmways/Cinema 77/Geria (Arthur Penn, Gene Lasko)
GB title: *Georgia's Friends*
A Yugoslavian boy grows up in Indiana and is influenced by the adult behaviour of his three friends.
Mildly interesting semi-autobiographical nostalgia movie, a vein which has been mined twice too often.
w Steve Tesich *d* Arthur Penn *ph* Ghislain Cloquet *m* Elizabeth Swados *pd* David Chapman
☆ Craig Wasson, Jodi Thelen, Michael Huddleston, Jim Metzler

'They threw away conventions with their tattered clothes!'
Four Frightened People *
US 1934 78m bw
Paramount/Cecil B. de Mille
A bubonic plague outbreak on board ship causes four survivors to escape via a lifeboat and trek through dangerous jungle.
Studio-bound but interesting action melodrama, of a type unusual from this director.
w Bartlett Cormack, Lenore Coffee *novel* E. Arnot Robertson *d Cecil B. de Mille ph* Karl Struss *m* Karl Hajos and others
☆ Claudette Colbert, Herbert Marshall, William Gargan, Mary Boland, Leo Carrillo, Nella Walker, Tetsu Komai, Ethel Griffies

'The adventures are episodic and disjointed, running the gamut from stark tragedy to unbelievable farce.' – *Variety*
'A cumbersome sort of melodrama ... despite some mildly entertaining jungle scenes.' – *Literary Digest*

Four Girls in Town
US 1956 85m Technicolor Cinemascope
U-I (Aaron Rosenberg)
Girls from various countries are chosen for Hollywood screen tests.
Formula romantic comedy adequately exposing young talent.
wd Jack Sher *ph* Irving Glassberg *m* Alex North
☆ George Nader, Julie Adams, Marianne Cook, Elsa Martinelli, Gia Scala, Sydney Chaplin, Grant Williams, John Gavin

Four Girls in White
US 1938 88m bw
MGM (Nat Levine)
Drama among the student nurses.
Standard hospital fare designed as a try-out for budding talent.
w Dorothy Yost *story* Nathalie Bucknall, Endre Bohem *d* S. Sylvan Simon
☆ Florence Rice, Alan Marshal, Ann Rutherford, Una Merkel, Buddy Ebsen, Mary Howard, Kent Taylor, Jessie Ralph, Sara Haden, Philip Terry, Tom Neal

Four Guns to the Border
US 1954 83m Technicolor
Universal-International
Things go wrong for four bank robbers after a raid.
Rather downbeat Western with insufficient excitement.
w George Van Marter, Franklin Coen *d* Richard Carlson *ph* Russell Metty
☆ Rory Calhoun, Walter Brennan, Colleen Miller, George Nader, Nina Foch, John McIntire, Charles Drake

The Four Horsemen of the Apocalypse **
US 1921 150m approx bw silent
Metro
A young Argentinian fights for his father's country, France, in World War I.
Highly derivative dramatic spectacle, almost a pageant, from a fairly unreadable novel. Despite its variable if exotic style, it made a star of Rudolph Valentino.
w June Mathis *novel* Vicente Blasco-Ibanez
d Rex Ingram ph John F. Seitz
☆ *Rudolph Valentino,* Alice Terry, Nigel de Brulier, Alan Hale, Jean Hersholt, Wallace Beery
'A blend of exotic settings, striking composition, dramatic lighting, and colourful if sordid atmosphere.' – *Lewis Jacobs*
'Not only was it marvellously effective in its appeal to the eye, but the logical and dramatic unfolding of the basic story was a striking revelation of the valuable service that an expert scenario-writer may render to the professional writer of novels.' – *Edward S. Van Zile, That Marvel the Movie*

The Four Horsemen of the Apocalypse *
US 1961 153m Metrocolor Cinemascope
MGM (Julian Blaustein)
In this ill-fated modernization of a dated novel, the idle grandson of an Argentinian beef tycoon finds his manhood at last as a member of the French resistance during World War II.
The visionary skyriding figures of death and pestilence simply do not fit in with bombs and concentration camps. Glum acting by a too elderly company, ugly colour and the usual hindrances of Cinemascope.
w Robert Ardrey, John Gay *d* Vincente Minnelli *ph* Milton Krasner *m* André Previn
☆ Glenn Ford, Ingrid Thulin, Charles Boyer, Paul Henreid, Lee J. Cobb, Paul Lukas, Karl Boehm, Yvette Mimieux
'An elephantine helping of hysteria and hokum.' – *Judith Crist, 1973*

Four Hours to Kill **
US 1935 74m bw
Paramount (Arthur Hornblow Jnr)
A psychopathic gangster gets loose during an evening at the theatre.
Tense, well-handled melodrama making full use of its setting.

w Norman Krasna play Small Miracle by Norman Krasna *d Mitchell Leisen ph* Theodor Sparkuhl
☆ Richard Barthelmess, Ray Milland, Gertrude Michael, Joe Morrison, Helen Mack, Dorothy Tree, Roscoe Karns, Henry Travers
'It fails to grip and isn't long on laughs.' – *Variety*

The Four Hundred Blows **
France 1959 94m bw Dyaliscope
Films du Carrosse/SEDIF (Georges Charlot)
original title: *Les Quatre Cents Coups*
A 12-year-old boy, unhappy at home, finds himself in a detention centre but finally escapes and keeps running.
Little more in plot terms than a piece of character observation, this engaging film is so controlled and lyrical as to be totally refreshing; and it gives a very vivid picture of the Paris streets.
wd François Truffaut ph Henri Decaë m Jean Constantin *ad* Bernard Evein *ed* Marie-Josèph Yoyotte
☆ *Jean-Pierre Léaud,* Claire Maurier, Albert Rémy
'The narrative is boldly fluent. Sympathetic, amused, reminded, occasionally puzzled, you are carried along with it. I don't think you will get away before the end.' – *Dilys Powell*
† The film is said to be based on Truffaut's own childhood.
script

Four in a Jeep *
Switzerland 1951 96m bw
Praesensfilm (Lazar Wechsler)
In the post-war international zone of Vienna, the four nationals of a police patrol come to blows over the cases they encounter.
Historically interesting but rather bland illustration of an untenable and even tragic political situation which was treated more melodramatically in The Third Man.
w Richard Schweizer *d* Leopold Lindtberg *ph* Emil Barna *m* Robert Blum
☆ Viveca Lindfors, Ralph Meeker, Yoseph Yadin, Michael Medwin

Four in the Morning *
GB 1965 94m bw
West One (John Morris)
Four personal stories are intercut during one London night.
Attractive minor effort which takes the eye without engaging the mind.
wd Anthony Simmons ph Larry Pizer *m* John Barry
☆ Ann Lynn, Judi Dench, Norman Rodway, Brian Phelan, Joe Melia
Judi Dench

Four Jacks and a Jill
US 1941 68m bw
RKO (John Twist)
Four struggling musicians adopt a down-and-out girl.
Flimsy remake of That Girl from Paris; *the talent is given little opportunity to rise.*
w John Twist *d* Jack Hively *ph* Russell Metty *m/ly* Mort Greene, Harry Revel
☆ Anne Shirley, Ray Bolger, Desi Arnaz, Jack Durant, June Havoc, Eddie Foy Jnr, Fritz Feld

Four Jills in a Jeep
US 1944 89m bw
TCF (Irving Starr)
Four Hollywood glamour girls entertain the troops.
Condescending, dispirited 'semi-documentary' war musical.
w Robert Ellis, Helen Logan, Snag Werris
d William A. Seiter *ph* Peverell Marley *md* Emil Newman
☆ Kay Francis, Martha Raye, Carole Landis, Mitzi Mayfair, Jimmy Dorsey and his band, John Harvey, Phil Silvers, Dick Haymes, Betty Grable, Carmen Miranda, George Jessel, Alice Faye
'It gives the painful impression of having been tossed together in a couple of hours.' – *Bosley Crowther*

The Four Just Men *
GB 1939 85m bw
Ealing-Capad (Michael Balcon, S. C. Balcon)
US title: *The Secret Four*
To save the Empire, four stalwart Britishers agree to murder a villainous MP.
Bright, unusual but dated thriller from a popular novel.
w Roland Pertwee, Angus Macphail, Sergei Nolbandov *novel* Edgar Wallace *d* Walter Forde *ph* Ronald Neame *m* Ernest Irving *ad* Wilfred Shingleton *ed* Charles Saunders
☆ Hugh Sinclair, Francis L. Sullivan, Frank Lawton, Griffith Jones, Anna Lee, Basil Sydney, Alan Napier, Athole Stewart, Edward Chapman, Garry Marsh, Ellaline Terriss, Lydia Sherwood, George Merritt
† The TV series of the late fifties restrained its heroes from criminal acts; the men were Jack Hawkins, Richard Conte, Dan Dailey, Vittorio de Sica.

Four Men and a Prayer *
US 1938 85m bw
TCF (Kenneth MacGowan)
Four young Englishmen set out to clear the name of their dishonoured father.
Pleasantly performed mystery which improves after a slowish start.
w Richard Sherman, Sonya Levien, Walter Ferris *novel* David Garth *d John Ford ph* Ernest Palmer *md* Louis Silvers
☆ Loretta Young, Richard Greene, George Sanders, David Niven, William Henry, C. Aubrey Smith, J. Edward Bromberg, John Carradine, Alan Hale, Reginald Denny, Barry Fitzgerald, Berton Churchill, John Sutton
'Better cast than story ... the pace is so uneven that the general effect at times is bewildering.' – *Variety*
'Energetically told, compactly presented.' – *New York Times*

Four Mothers
US 1940 86m bw
Warner (Henry Blanke)
The four Lemp sisters, all happily married, have financial problems.
Third and last in the Four Daughters *trilogy; quite attractively made but very routine.*
w Stephen Morehouse Avery *d* William Keighley *m* Heinz Roemheld
☆ Priscilla Lane, Rosemary Lane, Lola Lane, Gale Page, Claude Rains, Dick Foran, Frank McHugh, Jeffrey Lynn, Eddie Albert, Vera Lewis

'What has eight legs, feathers, and is usually seen coming to the rescue?'
The Four Musketeers (The Revenge of Milady) *
Panama 1974 103m Technicolor
TCF/Film Trust/Este (Alexander Salkind, Michael Salkind)
Athos, Porthos, Aramis and D'Artagnan have a final battle with Rochefort.
Perfunctory sequel to the same team's The Three Musketeers; *allegedly the two films were intended as one, but if so the first ten reels were by far the best, though this section has its regulation quota of high spirits and lusty action.*
w George MacDonald Fraser *d* Richard Lester *ph* David Watkin *m* Lalo Schifrin *pd* Brian Eatwell
☆ Michael York, Oliver Reed, Frank Finlay, Richard Chamberlain, Raquel Welch, Faye Dunaway, Charlton Heston, Christopher Lee, Simon Ward, Geraldine Chaplin, Jean-Pierre Cassel, Roy Kinnear
'The whole sleek formula has rolled over to reveal a very soft, very flabby underside.' – *Tony Rayns*

Four Rooms
US 1995 97m DeLuxe
Buena Vista/Miramax (Lawrence Bender)
On New Year's Eve, the bell-hop at a run-down hotel deals with customers in four rooms: in the first, he is asked to supply some semen for witches attempting to bring the goddess Diana back to life (*The Missing Ingredient*); in the second, he deals with a gun-toting, drug-taking husband who has tied up his wife (*The Wrong Man*); in the third, he baby-sits some young delinquents (*The*

Misbehavers); in the fourth, some movie executives are recreating a moment from a Hitchcock television story, in which Peter Lorre bet Steve McQueen his car against McQueen's little finger that McQueen could not light his cigarette lighter ten times in a row (*The Man from Hollywood*).
One of those occasions where the film-makers may have enjoyed themselves, but audiences won't. Four feeble anecdotes suffer from sloppy writing and unfocused acting; it should have remained a home movie.
☆ Tim Roth, Jennifer Beals, David Proval, Antonio Banderas, Kathy Griffin, Marc Lawrence, Marisa Tomei, Sammi Davis, Amanda de Cadenet, Valeria Golino, Madonna, Quentin Tarantino, Lawrence Bender

'This showcase folly by four of Hollywood's "hottest" stars plumbs new depths.' – *Mark Kermode, Sight and Sound*

'Here's to our friends – and the strength to put up with them!'

The Four Seasons **
US 1981 108m Technicolor
Universal (Martin Bregman)

Three married couples take seasonal holidays together, and remain united despite various tensions.
Rueful sexual comedy which maintains considerable momentum and actually makes us laugh at its sympathetic characters.
wd Alan Alda *ph* Victor J. Kemper *m* Antonio Vivaldi
☆ Alan Alda, Carol Burnett, Len Cariou, Sandy Dennis, Rita Moreno, Jack Weston, Bess Armstrong

'An odd mingling of perspicuity and histrionics ... a real middle-of-the-road film.' – *Geoff Brown, MFB*

'Unfailingly amusing, touchingly honest, and in the end refreshingly decent.' – *Margaret Hinxman, Daily Mail*

'See! a strange and beautiful woman created before your eyes!'

Four Sided Triangle
GB 1953 81m bw
Exclusive/Hammer (Michael Carreras, Alexander Paal)

When a scientist's girlfriend marries another, he creates a clone but finds that it has the same preferences.
A very early entry in this field; not too well done, but faithful to its silly theme.
w Paul Tabori, Terence Fisher *novel* William F. Temple *d* Terence Fisher *ph* Reg Wyer *m* Malcolm Arnold *ad* J. Elder Wills *ed* Maurice Rootes
☆ Stephen Murray, Barbara Payton, James Hayter, John Van Eyssen, Percy Marmont, Kynaston Reeves

The Four Skulls of Jonathan Drake
US 1959 70m bw
UA/Vogue (Robert E. Kent)
A family is cursed by a head-hunting Equadorian medicine man.
Cheaply made but full-blooded occult horror, rather effectively done by a cast that knows how.
w Orville H. Hampton *d* Edward L. Cahn *ph* Maury Gertsman *m* Paul Dunlap
☆ Henry Daniell, Eduard Franz, Valerie French, Grant Richards, Paul Cavanagh

'Amazonian Indians may find the plot a shade far-fetched.' – *MFB*

Four Sons *
US 1940 89m bw
TCF (Darryl F. Zanuck)
A Czech family is divided when the Nazis take over.
Predictable po-faced anti-Hitler melodrama released to an indifferent public well before America entered the war. A remake of a silent film set during World War I.
w John Howard Lawson *d* Archie Mayo *ph* Leon Shamroy *m* David Buttolph
☆ Don Ameche, Eugenie Leontovich, Mary Beth Hughes, Alan Curtis, George Ernest, Robert Lowery, Sig Rumann, Lionel Royce, Ludwig Stossel

'It partakes more of sentimental melodrama than of tragedy ... Neither in its performance nor its writing does the film ever rise to any passion.' – *New York Times*

Four Steps in the Clouds *
Italy 1942 90m bw
Cines Amato
original title: *Quattro Passi fra le Nuvole*
A travelling salesman on a bus gets involved with the problems of a pregnant girl, but misunderstandings are finally cleared up to general satisfaction.
A comedy on the American model which was a great success in wartorn Italy. Not particularly remarkable in itself, it was remade in 1957, as The Virtuous Bigamist, *with Fernandel. It does show the lighter side of Italian neo-realism.*
w Cesare Zavattini, Giuseppe Amato, Piero Tellini, Aldo de Benedetti *d* Alessandro Blasetti *ph* Vaclav Vich *m* Alessandro Cicognini
☆ Gino Cervi, Adriana Benetti, Giuditta Rissone

'A gay tender ironic story of a brief encounter; a small film with an effervescent belief in life.' – *Richard Winnington*

Four Times That Night: see *Quante Volte... Quella Notte*

'Five Good Reasons To Stay Single.'

Four Weddings and a Funeral ***
GB 1994 117m Eastmancolor
Rank/Polygram/Channel 4/Working Title (Duncan Kenworthy)

A confirmed bachelor chases the woman of his dreams from one wedding to another.
Enjoyable, episodic comedy with expert comic performances, occasionally hindered by its lapses into broad farce and ancient jokes.
w Richard Curtis d Mike Newell ph Michael Coulter *m* Richard Rodney Bennett *pd* Maggie Gray *ed* Jon Gregory
☆ *Hugh Grant*, Andie MacDowell, *Kristin Scott Thomas*, Simon Callow, James Flett, David Bower, Charlotte Coleman, John Hannah, Anna Chancellor, Robert Lang, Jeremy Kemp, Rosalie Crutchley, Rowan Atkinson

'Old-fashioned in its essence, and highly conservative: there will certainly be some British viewers who find the languid mating rites of the moneyed upper-middle-classes less than compulsive.' – *Sheila Johnston, Independent*

'Highly expert and entertaining comedy.' – *Derek Malcolm, Guardian*

† The film is the most successful British movie so far, having taken more than £130m at the box-office worldwide. Its British video release was available for sale for five weeks only.
†† Following the recitation of one of his poems in the film, a slim paperback of love poems by W. H. Auden became a best-seller.
Academy Award nomination: picture; Richard Curtis
BAFTA: film; Mike Newell; Hugh Grant; Kristin Scott Thomas

Four Wives *
US 1939 110m bw
Warner (Henry Blanke)
Three of the Lemp girls find a new husband for their widowed sister.
Lively and thickly textured sequel to Four Daughters; *predecessor of the less interesting* Four Mothers.
w Julius J. and Philip G. Epstein, Maurice Hanline *novel Sister Act* by Fannie Hurst *d* Michael Curtiz *ph* Sol Polito *m* Max Steiner
☆ *Claude Rains*, Priscilla Lane, Rosemary Lane, Lola Lane, Gale Page, Jeffrey Lynn, Eddie Albert, May Robson, Frank McHugh, Dick Foran, John Garfield

'Will ride along on momentum to excellent box office.' – *Variety*

The Four-Poster
US 1952 103m bw
Columbia/Stanley Kramer
The history of a marriage told in a series of bedroom scenes.
Hastily shot and rather tatty looking version of a stage play; unfortunately film can't contrast the comedy of the opening and the tragedy of the close within one small set, and the UPA cartoon bridges, though smart in themselves, are merely an irritation.
w Allan Scott *play* Jan de Hartog *d* Irving Reis *ph* Hal Mohr *m* Dimitri Tiomkin
☆ Rex Harrison, Lilli Palmer
Academy Award nomination: Hal Mohr

Four's a Crowd
US 1938 91m bw
Warner (Hal B. Wallis/David Lewis)
A public relations man has the job of promoting a mean-spirited millionaire, and falls in love with his daughter.
Floppy comedy, neither very witty nor as crazy as might have been expected. However, it ambles along quite engagingly.
w Casey Robinson, Sig Herzig *novel All Rights Reserved* by Wallace Sullivan *d* Michael Curtiz *ph* Ernest Haller *m* Heinz Roemheld, Ray Heindorf *ad* Max Parker *ed* Clarence Kolster *cos* Orry-Kelly
☆ Errol Flynn, Rosalind Russell, Olivia de Havilland, Patric Knowles, Walter Connolly, Hugh Herbert, Melville Cooper, Franklin Pangborn, Herman Bing, Margaret Hamilton

'Goofy click comedy that moves along to a whirlwind laugh finish.' – *Variety*

'Centuries Before The Exploration Of Space, There Was Another Voyage Into The Unknown.'

1492: Conquest of Paradise **
US 1992 155m colour Panavision
Guild/Touchstone (Ridley Scott, Alain Goldman)

Columbus persuades the Spanish court to back his expedition to reach the East by sailing west, but his attempts to live in peace with the natives in the New World are sabotaged by his followers.
A box-office flop, it is nevertheless a handsome-looking film and one that sustains one's interest throughout, despite some narrative ambiguity.
w Roselyne Bosch *d* Ridley Scott *ph* Adrian Biddle *m* Vangelis *pd* Norris Spencer *ed* William Anderson, Françoise Bonnot
☆ Gérard Depardieu, Armand Assante, Sigourney Weaver, Loren Dean, Angela Molina, Fernando Rey, Michael Wincott, Tcheky Karyo, Kevin Dunn, Frank Langella

Fourteen Hours ***
US 1951 92m bw
TCF (Sol C. Siegel)
A man stands on the ledge of a tall building and threatens to jump.
Well-made documentary drama based on a true occurrence but given a happy ending. First class detail gives an impression of realism.
w John Paxton article Joel Sayre *d Henry Hathaway ph* Joe MacDonald *m* Alfred Newman *ad* Lyle Wheeler, Leland Fuller
☆ Richard Basehart, Paul Douglas, Barbara Bel Geddes, Grace Kelly, Debra Paget, Agnes Moorehead, Robert Keith, Howard da Silva, Jeffrey Hunter, Martin Gabel, Jeff Corey

'A model of craftsmanship in all departments.' – *Penelope Houston*

'A highly enjoyable small scale picture, with a strength immensely greater than its size would suggest.' – *Richard Mallett, Punch*

Academy Award nomination: art direction

The Fourth Man **
Netherlands 1983 102m colour
Mainline/De Verenigde Nederlandsche Filmcompagnie/Spectrafilm (Rob Houwer)

original title: *De Vierde Man*
A novelist makes love to a widow as the first step to seducing her boyfriend.
Inventive, exuberant black comedy.
w Gerard Soeteman *novel* Gerard Reve *d* Paul Verhoeven *ph* Jan de Bont *m* Loek Dikker *ad* Roland de Groot *ed* Ine Schenkkan
☆ Jeroen Krabbé, Renee Soutendijk, Thom Hoffman, Dolf de Vries, Geert de Jong, Hans Veerman, Hero Muller, Caroline de Beus

'A highbrow debauch of depravity, destruction, sex and blasphemy.' – *Quentin Crisp*

The Fourth Protocol *
GB 1987 119m Rank Colour 'Scope
Rank (Timothy Burrill)

Vying masterspies narrowly avert nuclear disaster.
Very competent but somehow old hat espionage thriller, from a best seller.
w Frederick Forsyth *novel* Frederick Forsyth *d* John Mackenzie *ph* Phil Meheux *m* Lalo Schifrin *pd* Alan Cameron
☆ Michael Caine, Pierce Brosnan, Joanna Cassidy, Ned Beatty, Betsy Brantley, Ray McAnally, Ian Richardson, Anton Rodgers

'There is an uneasy feeling that the whole affair could have been better made into an excellent miniseries.' – *Daily Variety*

'It's no longer East vs West ... Just two proud heroes with no one to fight ... but each other.'

The Fourth War
US 1990 91m DeLuxe
Kodiak (Wolf Schmidt)

A violent feud develops between an American and a Soviet colonel, each in charge of a border post between Czechoslovakia and East Germany.
Moderate thriller, somewhat overtaken by events.
w Stephen Peters, Kenneth Ross *novel* Stephen Peters *d* John Frankenheimer *ph* Gerry Fisher *m* Bill Conti *pd* Alan Manzer *ed* Robert F. Shugrue
☆ Roy Scheider, Jürgen Prochnow, Tim Reid, Lara Harris, Harry Dean Stanton, Dale Dye, Bill MacDonald

'A simple moral story, directly told without adornment and relying on old-fashioned effects.' – *MFB*

The Fourth Wish
Australia 1976 105m colour
Galaxy/South Australian Film Corp (John Morris)
A single father sets out to grant three wishes to his 12-year-old son, who is dying from leukaemia.
Effective domestic drama, cut down from a three-part television series, held together by Meillon's strong central performance.
w Michael Craig *d* Don Chaffey *ph* Geoff Burton *m* Tristram Cary *ad* David Copping *ed* G. Turney Smith
☆ *John Meillon*, Robert Bettles, Michael Craig, Anne Haddy, Ron Haddrick, Robyn Nevin

Les Fous de Bassan: see *In the Shadow of the Wind*

'Between Ellen and Jill came Paul...'

The Fox *
US/Canada 1968 110m DeLuxe
Warner/Raymond Stross/Motion Pictures International (Howard Koch)
On an isolated farm, two lesbians are disturbed by the arrival of a wandering seaman.
Rather obvious sexual high jinks full of symbolism and heavy breathing.
w Lewis John Carlino, Howard Koch *novel* D. H. Lawrence *d* Mark Rydell *ph* Bill Fraker *m* Lalo Schifrin
☆ *Anne Heywood*, Sandy Dennis, Keir Dullea
Academy Award nomination: Lalo Schifrin

Fox *
West Germany 1975 123m Eastmancolor
Tango Film (Rainer Werner Fassbinder)

original title: *Faustrecht der Freiheit*
aka: *Fox and His Friends*
The decline of a homosexual sideshow performer.
Ironic, semi-autobiographical melodrama in the Blue Angel *tradition, with sidelong glances at Hollywood glamour. In its way very memorable, but overlong.*
w Rainer Werner Fassbinder, Christian Hohoff *d Rainer Werner Fassbinder ph* Michael Ballhaus *m* Peer Raben
☆ Rainer Werner Fassbinder, Karl-Heinz Boehm, Peter Chatel, Harry Bär, Adrian Hoven, Ulla Jacobsson

Fox and His Friends: see *Fox*

The Fox and the Hound *
US 1981 83m Technicolor
Walt Disney (Wolfgang Reitherman, Art Stevens)

A fox cub makes friends with a hound puppy, but their friendship is tested when they grow up.
Not unpleasant but somewhat heavy-going for a feature cartoon, made with some of the old Disney style but none of the old inventiveness.
w various *novel* Daniel P. Mannix *d* Art Stevens, Ted Berman, Richard Rich
☆ Featuring the voices of Mickey Rooney, Kurt Russell, Pearl Bailey, Jack Albertson, Sandy Duncan, Jeanette Nolan

'Laughs are few and far between ... the whole enterprise lacks vitality.' – *Brenda Davies, MFB*

Fox Movietone Follies of 1929
US 1929 82m bw (colour sequences)
Fox
GB title: *Movietone Follies of 1929*
An all-star review.
Every studio had its early talkie musical using up its contract stars; this was perhaps the least interesting.
wd David Butler, William K. Wells *ph* Charles Van Enger *m* Con Conrad, Sidney Mitchell, Archie Gottlieb *md* Arthur Kay
☆ Sue Carol, Lola Lane, Dixie Lee, Sharon Lynn, Stepin Fetchit

Foxes
US 1980 106m Technicolor
UA/Polygram (David Puttnam, Gerald Ayres)
Four teenage girls battle with sex, drugs and life in general.
Well-meaning but entirely resistible melodrama from behind the headlines.
w Gerald Ayres *d* Adrian Lyne *ph* Leon Bijou *m* Giorgio Moroder *ad* Michael Levesque *ed* Jim Coblentz
☆ Jodie Foster, Scott Baio, Sally Kellerman, Randy Quaid, Adam Faith
'Almost nil adult appeal.' – *Variety*

The Foxes of Harrow
US 1947 117m bw
TCF (William A. Bacher)
In 1820 New Orleans, a philanderer seeks advancement by breaking up his marriage.
Tolerable but rather flat adaptation of a bestseller, stultified by central miscasting.
w Wanda Tuchock *novel* Frank Yerby *d* John M. Stahl *ph* Joseph LaShelle *m* Alfred Newman
☆ Rex Harrison, Maureen O'Hara, Richard Haydn, Victor McLaglen, Vanessa Brown, Patricia Medina, Gene Lockhart, Hugo Haas
† Rex Harrison's role had been turned down by Tyrone Power.

'I don't care what they call you! I only care that you are all man – and all mine!'
Foxfire
US 1955 92m Technicolor
U-I (Aaron Rosenberg)
A rich New York girl on holiday in Arizona is attracted to a half-Apache miner.
Romantic melodrama with action asides; watchable for those who like that sort of thing.
w Ketti Frings *novel* Anya Seton *d* Joseph Pevney *ph* William Daniels *m* Frank Skinner *ad* Robert Clatworthy, Alexander Golitzen *ed* Ted J. Kent
☆ Jane Russell, Jeff Chandler, Frieda Inescort, Dan Duryea, Mara Corday, Robert F. Simon, Barton MacLane, Charlotte Wynters

Foxhole in Cairo
GB 1960 80m bw
Omnia (Steven Pallos, Donald Taylor)
A German agent in Libya is allowed to get back to Rommel with false information.
Interesting true spy story deflated by muddled handling.
w Leonard Mosley *novel* *The Cat and the Mice* by Leonard Mosley *d* John Moxey *ph* Desmond Dickinson *m* Wolfram Rohrig, Douglas Gamley, Ken Jones
☆ James Robertson Justice, Adrian Hoven, Albert Lieven (Rommel), Niall MacGinnis, Peter Van Eyck, Robert Urquhart, Fenella Fielding

Foxtrot
Mexico/Switzerland 1977 91m Technicolor
New World (Gerald Green)
Rich people retreat to a desert island to avoid World War II, but their servants revolt.
A more or less direct attempt to remake La Règle du Jeu; *it sinks into boredom.*
w Arturo Ripstein, José Emilio Pacheco, H. A. L. Craig *d* Arturo Ripstein
☆ Peter O'Toole, Charlotte Rampling, Max von Sydow, Jorge Luke, Helena Rojo, Claudio Brook

Foxy Brown
US 1974 91m Movielab
AIP (Buzz Feitshans)
After her boyfriend, a cop, is killed by drug dealers, a woman survives prostitution, rape, torture and drugs to get her revenge.
Unlikeable, sour-toned thriller, which puts the emphasis on brutality.
wd Jack Hill *ph* Brick Marquard *m* Willie Hutch *ad* Kirk Axtell *ed* Chuck McClelland *cos* Ruthie West
☆ Pam Grier (Foxy Brown), Antonio Fargas (Link Brown), Peter Brown (Steve Elias), Terry Carter (Michael Anderson), Kathryn Loder (Katherine Wall), Harry Holcombe (Judge Fenton), Sid Haig (Hays), Juanita Brown (Claudia), Sally Ann Stroud (Deb)
'Even by the gutter-high standards of the genre, Foxy Brown is something of a mess.' – *Variety*

Fra Diavolo **
US 1933 90m bw
MGM/Hal Roach
aka: *The Devil's Brother*
Two incompetent bandits are hired as manservants by a real bandit.
Auber's 1830 operetta becomes a vehicle for Laurel and Hardy, setting a pattern they followed with Babes in Toyland *and* The Bohemian Girl. *They have excellent sequences, but overall the film lacks pace.*
w Jeanie Macpherson *d* Hal Roach, Charles Rogers *ph* Art Lloyd, Hap Depew *md* LeRoy Shield *ed* Bert Jordan, William Terhune
☆ *Stan Laurel, Oliver Hardy*, Dennis King, *James Finlayson*, Thelma Todd
'An early 19th-century comic opera doesn't make for particularly good film fare despite its hoking.' – *Variety*

La Fracture du Myocarde: see *Cross My Heart*

Fragment of an Empire *
USSR 1929 100m approx bw silent
Sovkino
A young man who lost his memory in World War I regains it in 1928 and surveys the changed social order.
Mildly satirical propaganda piece with a vivid impression of Leningrad at the time.
w Friedrich Ermler, Katerina Vinogradskaya *d* Friedrich Ermler *ph* Yevgeni Schneider
☆ Fyoder Nikitin, Yakov Gudkin, Ludmila Semyonova

Fragment of Fear *
GB 1970 95m Technicolor
Columbia (John R. Sloan)
A young writer investigates the murder of his aunt, but finds that he may himself be mad.
What appears to be a whodunnit turns into a flashy, fashionable, sub-Antonioni puzzle with no ending, but despite the considerable irritation this causes, the details and character cameos are excellent.
w Paul Dehn *novel* John Bingham *d* Richard C. Sarafian *ph* Oswald Morris *m* Johnny Harris
☆ David Hemmings, Gayle Hunnicutt, Roland Culver, Daniel Massey, Flora Robson, Wilfrid Hyde-White, Adolfo Celi, Mona Washbourne

'No Soul Is Safe.'
Frailty *
US 2002 99m FotoKem
Lions Gate/American Entertainment/Cinerenta/Cinedelta (David Kirschner, David Blocker, Corey Sienega)
In Texas, a man tells his two sons that an angel has ordered him to kill demons who are disguised as ordinary people; years later one of the sons tells of the serial killings to an FBI agent.
Chilling little horror story of fundamentalist religion gone mad, stylishly made.
w Brent Hanley *d* Bill Paxton *ph* Bill Butler *m* Brian Tyler *ad* Nelson Coates, Kevin Cozen *ed* Arnold Glassman
☆ Bill Paxton (Dad), Matthew McConaughey (Adam Meiks), Powers Boothe (Agent Wesley Doyle), Matt O'Leary (Young Fenton Meiks), Luke Askew (Sheriff Smalls), Jeremy Sumpter (Young Adam Meiks), Derk Cheetwood (Agent Griffin Hul), Melissa Crider (Becky)
'Something altogether weird and worrying: a mad axe-murderer movie that the Christian right can enjoy.' – *Peter Bradshaw, Guardian*
'A well-crafted, disturbing Texas gothic thriller, a completely spooky piece of business that gets under your skin.' – *Kenneth Turan, Los Angeles Times*

Framed
US 1947 82m bw
Columbia
GB title: *Paula*
A drunken out-of-work engineer is used as fall guy by two thieves planning an elaborate coup.
Lugubrious mixture of puzzle, character drama and gloomy philosophizing, complete with femme fatale who is handed over to the cops at the end.
w Ben Maddow *d* Richard Wallace
☆ Glenn Ford, Janis Carter, Barry Sullivan

Framed
US 1974 106m Metrocolor
Paramount
A Tennessee gambler inadvertently kills a sheriff, is sent to prison, gets out on parole and wreaks revenge on those who framed him.
Violent thick-ear update of The Count of Monte Cristo, *of interest only to connoisseurs of gratuitous nastiness.*
w Mort Briskin *d* Phil Karlson
☆ Joe Don Baker, Conny Van Dyke, Gabriel Dell, Brock Peters, John Marley, John Larch

Frances
US 1982 140m Technicolor
EMI/Brooksfilm (Jonathan Sanger)
The downhill career of 30s actress Frances Farmer.
Long, glum, and not particularly convincing in its inferences, this exhaustive study of a person who didn't deserve all this fuss is illuminated only by a strong star performance.
w Eric Bergren, Christopher Devore, Nicholas Kazan *d* Graeme Clifford *ph* Laszlo Kovacs *m* John Barry *pd* Richard Sylbert
☆ *Jessica Lange*, Kim Stanley, Sam Shepard, Bart Burns, Jeffrey de Munn
Jessica Lange; Kim Stanley

Francesco, Giullare di Dio: see *Francis, God's Jester*

The Franchise Affair *
GB 1950 88m bw
ABP (Robert Hall)
A young girl accuses two gentlewomen of kidnapping and ill-treating her.
Unusual and absorbing mystery based on a true 18th-century case; the treatment however is rather too mild.
w Robert Hall, Lawrence Huntington *novel* Josephine Tey *d* Lawrence Huntington *ph* Gunther Krampf *m* Philip Green
☆ Michael Denison, Dulcie Gray, Anthony Nicholls, Marjorie Fielding, Athene Seyler, Ann Stephens, Hy Hazell, John Bailey, Kenneth More

Francis *
US 1949 90m bw
U-I (Robert Arthur)
An army private makes friends with a talking mule who causes him some embarrassment.
Simple-minded, quite agreeable if rather slow-moving fantasy farce which was popular enough to spawn several sequels and later a TV series called Mister Ed.
Sequels (the first six with Donald O'Connor):
1951 Francis Goes to the Races
1952 Francis Goes to West Point
1953 Francis Covers Big Town
1954 Francis Joins the WACS
1955 Francis in the Navy
1956 Francis in the Haunted House (with Mickey Rooney)
w David Stern *novel* David Stern *d* Arthur Lubin *ph* Irving Glassberg *m* Frank Skinner *ad* Bernard Herzbrun, Richard H. Reidel *ed* Milton Carruth
☆ Donald O'Connor, Patricia Medina, ZaSu Pitts, Ray Collins, John McIntire, Eduard Franz, Robert Warwick, Chill Wills (voice of Francis)

Francis, God's Jester **
Italy 1950 75m bw
Cineriz (Giuseppe Amato)
original title: *Francesco, Giullare di Dio*
aka: *The Flowers of St Francis*
An anecdotal and episodic account of the beginnings of the Franciscan order and its first members as they go to preach their faith.
Using mainly non-professional actors, and with Franciscan monks playing the founders of their order, Rossellini, with compassion and humour, affirms that the great virtues are innocence and simplicity.
w Roberto Rossellini, Federico Fellini *book* *The Little Flowers of St Francis* and *The Life of Brother Ginepro* *d* Roberto Rossellini *ph* *Otello Martelli* *m* Renzo Rossellini, Father Enrico Buondonno *ed* Jolanda Benvenuti
☆ Aldo Fabrizi, Arabella Lemaitre, Brother Nazario Gerardi (St Francis)

Francis of Assisi
US 1961 107m DeLuxe Cinemascope
TCF/Perseus (Plato A. Skouras)
The son of a medieval cloth merchant takes a vow of poverty, cares for animals and dies a hermit.
Tedious biopic.
w Eugene Vale, Jack Thomas, James Forsyth *d* Michael Curtiz *ph* Piero Portalupi *m* Mario Nascimbene
☆ Bradford Dillman, Dolores Hart, Stuart Whitman, Eduard Franz, Pedro Armendariz, Cecil Kellaway, Finlay Currie, Mervyn Johns, Athene Seyler

Françoise Steps Out: see *Rue de l'Estrapade*

'A Terrifying Tale Of Sluts And Bolts.'
'Where Sex Can Cost You An Arm And A Leg.'
Frankenhooker
US 1990 90m colour
Shapiro/Glickenhaus (Edgar Levens)
A mad scientist uses the bodies of prostitutes to rebuild his girlfriend, cut to pieces in a lawnmower accident.
Odd mix of uninventive comedy and gore, relying on its tastelessness to amuse.
w Robert Martin, Frank Henenlotter *d* Frank Henenlotter *ph* Robert M. Baldwin *m* Joe Renzetti *ed* Kevin Tent *sp* Gabe Bartalos
☆ James Lorintz, Patty Mullen, Charlotte Helmkamp, Shirley Stoler, Louise Lasser
† The film was cut to 81m on its British video release.

'To have seen it is to wear a badge of courage!'
'A monster science created but could not destroy!'
Frankenstein ****
US 1931 71m bw
Universal (Carl Laemmle Jnr)
A research scientist creates a living monster from corpses, but it runs amok.
Whole books have been written about this film and its sequels. Apart from being a fascinating if primitive cinematic work in its own right, it set its director and star on interesting paths and established a Hollywood attitude towards horror (mostly borrowed from German silents such as The Golem). *A seminal film indeed, which at each repeated viewing belies its age.*
w *Garrett Fort, Francis Edwards Faragoh, John L. Balderston* *play* Peggy Webling *novel* *Mary Wollstonecraft Shelley* *d* *James Whale* *ph* *Arthur Edeson* *m* David Broekman *ad* Charles D. Hall *ed* *Clarence Kolster, Maurice Pivar*
☆ *Boris Karloff, Colin Clive, Mae Clarke,* John Boles, *Edward Van Sloan, Frederick Kerr, Dwight Frye*
'Still the most famous of all horror films, and deservedly so.' – *John Baxter, 1968*
'The horror is cold, chilling the marrow but never arousing malaise.' – *Carlos Clarens*
† Direct sequels by the same studio (all qv) include *The Bride of Frankenstein, Son of Frankenstein, Ghost of Frankenstein, Frankenstein Meets the Wolf Man, House of Frankenstein, House of Dracula, Abbott and Costello Meet Frankenstein.* The later Hammer series, which told the story all over again in gorier vein, includes (all qv) *The Curse of Frankenstein, The Revenge of Frankenstein, The Evil of Frankenstein, Frankenstein Created Woman, Frankenstein Must be Destroyed, Horror of Frankenstein, Frankenstein and the Monster from Hell.* Other Frankenstein films date from as early as 1908, and scores have been made in various languages. *Young Frankenstein* (qv) is a partly effective spoof on the Hollywood series; *The Munsters* was a sixties comedy series for TV which used the monster as its leading character in a domestic setting.
Robert Florey is said to have contributed to the script, having been the first choice for director.

Frankenstein '70
US 1958 83m bw Cinemascope
Allied Artists (Aubrey Schenck)

Television film-makers descend on Castle Frankenstein; the current Count needs the money to finance some monster making of his own.
Boringly talkative and very silly 'futuristic' blot on an honourable name, apart from a rather frightening pre-credits sequence.
w Richard Landau, G. Worthing Yates *d* Howard W. Koch *ph* Carl Guthrie *m* Paul Dunlap
☆ Boris Karloff, Tom Duggan, Jana Lund, Mike Lane (The monster)

Frankenstein and the Monster from Hell
GB 1973 99m Technicolor
Hammer/Avco (Roy Skeggs)

The Baron turns an injured lunatic into a hairy ape man.
Cheaply made and very ghoulish horror comic in the unattractive setting of an asylum; very little entertainment is provided.
w John Elder (Anthony Hinds) *d* Terence Fisher *ph* Brian Probyn *ad* Scott MacGregor *ed* James Needs
☆ Peter Cushing (Baron Frankenstein), Shane Briant (Dr Helder), Madeleine Smith (The Angel, Sarah), John Stratton (The Director), Bernard Lee (Tarmut), Dave Prowse (The monster), Patrick Troughton (Body snatcher)

'A beautiful woman with the soul of a devil!'
Frankenstein Created Woman
GB 1966 86m Technicolor
Warner/Hammer-Seven Arts (Anthony Nelson-Keys)

The Baron invests the body of a dead girl with the soul of her dead lover, and a murder spree results.
Crude and gory farrago, with the central laboratory sequence apparently excised at the last moment.
w John Elder (Anthony Hinds) *d* Terence Fisher *ph* Arthur Grant *m* James Bernard *pd* Bernard Robinson *ad* Don Mingaye *ed* James Needs, Spencer Reeve
☆ Peter Cushing (Baron Frankenstein), Thorley Walters (Dr Hertz), Susan Denberg (Christina), Robert Morris (Hans), Duncan Lamont (The prisoner)

'Titans of terror, clashing in mortal combat!'
Frankenstein Meets the Wolf Man **
US 1943 73m bw
Universal (George Waggner)

Lawrence Talbot, the wolf man, travels to Vasaria in the hope of a cure, and finds the Frankenstein monster being reactivated.
Once one recovered from the bargain basement combination of two monsters in one picture, this was a horror comic with stylish sequences, weakened by cuts in the script and a miscast Bela Lugosi.
w Curt Siodmak *d Roy William Neill* *ph* George Robinson *m* Hans Salter
☆ Lon Chaney Jnr, Ilona Massey, Bela Lugosi (The monster), Patric Knowles, *Maria Ouspenskaya*

Frankenstein Must Be Destroyed
GB 1969 96m Technicolor
Warner-Pathé/Hammer (Anthony Nelson-Keys)

The Baron transplants the brain of one colleague into the body of another.
Spirited but decidedly unpleasant addition to the cycle, made more so by a genuine note of pathos.
w Bert Batt *d* Terence Fisher *ph* Arthur Grant *m* James Bernard *ad* Bernard Robinson *ed* Gordon Hales
☆ Peter Cushing (Baron Frankenstein), Freddie Jones (Professor Richter), Veronica Carlson (Anna Spengler), Simon Ward (Karl Holst), Thorley Walters (Inspector Fritsch), Maxine Audley (Ella Brandt)

Frankenstein Unbound
US 1990 85m DeLuxe
Fox/Mount Company (Roger Corman, Thom Mount, Kabi Jaeger)

A scientist is transported back in time to Switzerland in the 1800s where he meets Mary Godwin, Byron, Shelley and Dr Frankenstein and his monster.
Odd mix of science fiction and horror that fails to cohere.
w Roger Corman, F. X. Feeney *novel* Brian Aldiss *d* Roger Corman *ph* Armando Nannuzzi, Michael Scott *m* Carl Davis *pd* Enrico Tovaglieri *ed* Jay Cassidy, Mary Bauer
☆ John Hurt, Raul Julia, Bridget Fonda, Nick Brimble, Catherine Rabett, Jason Patric, Michael Hutchence
'Competent but uninspired.' – *Variety*

Frankie and Johnny *
US 1966 87m Technicolor
UA/F and J (Edward Small)

On a Mississippi riverboat, a gambling singer is the despair of his lady partner.
Mildly amusing pastiche both of the old song and of the various riverboat dramas.
w Alex Gottlieb *d* Frederick de Cordova *ph* Jacques Marquette *m* Fred Karger
☆ Elvis Presley, Donna Douglas, Sue Ane Langdon, Harry Morgan, Nancy Kovack, Audrey Christie, Jerome Cowan

'He's no knight in shining armor. She's no princess. But who says life is a fairytale anyway?'
Frankie and Johnny *
US 1991 118m Technicolor
UIP/Paramount (Garry Marshall)

A short-order cook ardently woos a reluctant waitress.
Soft-centred romance with its stars trying hard to persuade an audience that they are damaged and unlovable until the final clinch.
w Terrence McNally *play Frankie and Johnny in the Clair de Lune* by Terrence McNally *d* Garry Marshall *ph* Dante Spinotti *m* Marvin Hamlisch *pd* Albert Brenner *ed* Battle Davis, Jacqueline Cambas
☆ Al Pacino, Michelle Pfeiffer, Hector Elizondo, Nathan Lane, Jane Morris, Greg Lewis, Al Fann, Glenn Plummer, Sean O'Bryan, Kate Nelligan
'The layers of artifice are just too thick for the film's warm glow to last long.' – *Geoff Brown, The Times*
'This is a vehicle of Pacino and Pfeiffer, and they're more glamorous than the characters they're playing, but, in a weird way, their star power is perfectly appropriate here: it's the meat-and-potatoes stuff of big-budget movie entertainment.' – *New Yorker*
Kate Nelligan

Frankie Starlight *
US 1995 100m colour
Film Four/Ferndale (Noel Pearson)

A dwarf becomes a successful author with an autobiographical novel about his French mother, who arrived in Ireland in the late 40s, pregnant by a GI.
Offbeat romantic drama about the power of dreams.
w Chet Raymo, Ronan O'Leary *novel The Dork of Cork* by Chet Raymo *d* Michael Lindsay-Hogg *ph* Paul Laufer *m* Elmer Bernstein *pd* Frank Conway *ed* Ruth Foster
☆ Anne Parillaud, Matt Dillon, Gabriel Byrne, Corban Walker, Rudi Davies, Georgina Cates, Alan Pentony, Niall Toibin, Dearbhla Molloy
'A noble effort whose ambitious, unorthodox approach limits it to a rarefied crowd.' – *Variety*

Frantic: see *Lift to the Scaffold (1957)*

Frantic *
US 1988 120m colour
Warner/Mount (Thom Mount, Tim Hampton)

An American cardiologist in Paris hunting for his kidnapped wife becomes embroiled with Arab terrorists.
Amiable thriller with Hitchcockian touches, quite untypical of this director.
w Roman Polanski, Gérard Brach *d* Roman Polanski *ph* Witold Sobocinski *m* Ennio Morricone *pd* Pierre Guffroy *ed* Sam O'Steen
☆ Harrison Ford (Dr Richard Walker), Betty Buckley (Sondra Walker), Emmanuelle Seigner (Michelle), John Mahoney (Williams), Jimmy Ray Weeks (Shaap), Yorgo Voyagis (Kidnapper), David Huddleston (Peter)
'Disappointingly conventional mystery.' – *Variety*

Fratelli e Sorelle
Italy 1992 101m colour Technovision
Duea/Filmauro/RAI-1 (Antonio Avati, Luigi and Aurelio De Laurentiis)
Leaving her adulterous husband, an Italian woman takes her teenage sons and goes to St. Louis to visit her sister, who lives with an Italian and his two American daughters.
Dysfunctional families meet in an enclosed Italian community; the result resembles an overlong soap opera episode.
wd Pupi Avati *ph* Roberto D'Ettorre Piazzoli *m* Riz Ortolani *ad* Carlo Simi *ed* Amedeo Salfa
☆ Franco Nero, Paola Quattrini, Anna Bonaiuto, Lino Capolicchio, Luciano Federico, Stefano Accorsi, Kelly Evinston, Barbara Wilder
'Phony, contrived and awkward.' – *Variety*

Fraternally Yours: see *Sons of the Desert*

Fraternity Row *
US 1977 101m colour
Paramount (Charles Gary Allison)
In the early 1950s, students indulge in dangerous fraternity initiations at an exclusive Eastern university.
Efficient, well-acted drama of college life.
w Charles Gary Allison *d* Thomas J. Tobin *ph* Peter Gibbons *m* Michael Corner, Don McLean *ad* James Sbardellati *ed* Eugene A. Fournier
☆ Peter Fox, Gregory Harrison, Scott Newman, Nancy Morgan, Wendy Phillips, Robert Emhardt, Robert Matthews, Bernard R. Kantor, Cliff Robertson

Frau im Mond: see *The Woman in the Moon*

'He's No Ordinary Insurance Man. You Can Bet Your Life On It!'
Frauds
Australia 1992 94m colour
First Independent/Latent Image/AFFC (Andrena Finlay, Stuart Quin)

A manic practical-joke-playing insurance agent, who tosses dice to decide his next action, torments a couple who decide to play him at his own game.
A frantic comedy that remains unsympathetic viewing; it is simply not funny, despite the strenuous efforts of everyone involved.
wd Stephan Elliott *ph* Geoff Burton *m* Guy Gross *pd* Brian Thomson *ed* Frans Vandenburg
☆ Phil Collins, Hugo Weaving, Josephine Byrnes, Peter Mochrie, Helen O'Connor, Rebel Russell, Colleen Clifford
'Chronically over-designed and over-directed, each angle containing something cute and clever.' – *Sheila Johnston, Independent*
'A comedy designed to set teeth on edge.' – *Sight and Sound*

Fräulein
US 1958 100m Eastmancolor
Cinemascope
TCF (Walter Reisch)
During World War II an American prisoner of war escapes and is helped by the daughter of a German professor.
Studio-bound war heroics with little conviction achieved or aimed at.
w Leo Townsend *novel* James McGowan *d* Henry Koster *ph* Leo Tover *m* Daniele Amfitheatrof
☆ Dana Wynter, Mel Ferrer, Margaret Hayes, Dolores Michaels, Theodore Bikel, Helmut Dantine

Fräulein Doktor
Italy/Yugoslavia 1968 104m Technicolor
(Paramount)
In World War I, a German lady spy outwits British intelligence.
Rather glum international action melodrama.
w Duilio Coletti, H. A. L. Craig, Stanley Mann, Vittoriano Petrilli, Alberto Lattuada *d* Alberto Lattuada *ph* Luigi Kuveiller *m* Ennio Morricone
☆ Suzy Kendall, Kenneth More, James Booth, Capucine, Alexander Knox, Nigel Green, Roberto Bisacco
† A similar story was filmed in 1936 as *Mademoiselle Docteur.*

Freaked
US 1993 79m DeLuxe
TCF/Tommy (Harry Ufland, Mary Jane Ufland)

A glib spokesman for a polluting chemical company is turned into a monster by a freak-show proprietor.
A comic horror movie, in which most of the energy and imagination went into the creation of a succession of bizarre characters.
w Tim Burns, Tom Stern, Alex Winter *d* Tom Stern, Alex Winter *ph* Jamie Thompson *m* Kevin Kiner *pd* Catherine Hardwicke *ed* Malcolm Campbell *sp* Thomas Rainone
☆ Alex Winter, Megan Ward, Randy Quaid, Brooke Shields, Mr T, Michael Stoyanov, William Sadler, Alex Zuckerman, Derek McGrath
'An anarchic mix of hip comedy, vague, socially correct, eco politics and overstated make-up effects ... disproves the old saw that brevity is the soul of wit.' – *Leonard Klady, Variety*
† Keanu Reeves makes a brief, uncredited appearance as a Dog Boy.

Freaks **
US 1932 64m bw
MGM (Tod Browning)

A lady trapeze artist marries a midget, then attempts to poison him; his abnormal friends take revenge by turning her into a freak.
Made but disowned by MGM after accusations of tastelessness, this strident and silly melodrama has dated badly but has sequences of great power, especially the final massing of the freaks, slithering to their revenge in a rainstorm. It would have been better as a silent; the dialogue kills it.
w Willis Goldbeck, Leon Gordon *novel Spurs* by Tod Robbins *d Tod Browning* *ph* Merritt B. Gerstad
☆ Wallace Ford, Olga Baclanova, Leila Hyams, Roscoe Ates, Johnny Eck, Daisy Hilton, Violet Hilton
'Either too horrible or not sufficiently so.' – *Variety*
'It is a skilfully presented production but of a character which in consideration of the susceptibilities of mass audiences should be avoided.' – *Martin Quigley*
'For pure sensationalism it tops any picture yet produced.' – *Louella Parsons*
'I want something that out-horrors Frankenstein.' – *Irving Thalberg*
'Touching and funny and made with a miraculous delicacy.' – *Evening Standard, 1964*

Freaky Friday
US 1976 100m Technicolor
Walt Disney (Ron Miller)

A 13-year-old and her mother, each discontented with their lot, express a wish to change places – and do.
A trendy update of Vice Versa, padded out with Disney irrelevancies and long outstaying its welcome.
w Mary Rodgers *novel* Mary Rodgers *d* Gary Nelson *ph* Charles F. Wheeler *m* Johnny Mandel
☆ Jodie Foster, Barbara Harris, John Astin, Patsy Kelly, Dick Van Patten, Sorrell Booke, Marie Windsor

Freckles
US 1935 69m bw
RKO (Pandro S. Berman)
A mild teenager gets a job as a timber guard.
Unsensational version of a rustic classic.
w Dorothy Yost *novel* Gene Stratton-Porter *d* Edward Killy, William Hamilton
☆ Tom Brown, Carol Stone, Virginia Weidler, Lumsden Hare, James Bush, Addison Richards, George Lloyd
'The novel, published in 1875, is shown to have sold 2,000,000 copies. It will have a tough time making the same grade as a picture ... its appeal is of a past generation.' – *Variety*
† A 1960 remake for Fox starred Martin West.

Freddie as F.R.0.7
GB 1992 91m colour
Rank/Hollywood Road Films

A human-sized frog, a French secret agent, investigates the disappearance of such British institutions as Buckingham Palace and the Tower of London.

Dated, animated parody of James Bond. It was intended as the first of a series starring Freddie, but its box-office failure led to a sequel being abandoned.
w Jon Acevski, David Ashton *d* Jon Acevski *ph* Rex Neville *m/ly* David Dundas, Rick Wentworth, Don Black, Jon Acevski, David Ashton *ad* Paul Shardlow *ed* Alex Rayment, Mick Manning
☆ Featuring the voices of Ben Kingsley, Jenny Agutter, Brian Blessed, Nigel Hawthorne, Michael Hordern, Edmund Kingsley, Phyllis Logan, Victor Maddern, Jonathan Pryce, Prunella Scales, John Sessions, Billie Whitelaw
'This likeable enough saga of a super-agent frog looks unlikely to hop into the big time.' – *Variety*

'This Time You Can't Change The Channel.'
Freddy Got Fingered
US 2001 87m DeLuxe
TCF/Epsilon/New Regency/MBST (Larry Brezner, Lauren Lloyd, Howard Lapides)
A 28-year-old would-be cartoonist, still living at home, becomes rich enough to ship his house and comatose father to Pakistan.
Flaunting a script so infantile it could have been written by a foetus, Green displays an unloveable persona behaving badly, and expects to be applauded for it.
w Tom Green, Derek Harvie *d* Tom Green *ph* Mark Irwin *m* Mike Simpson *pd* Bob Ziembicki *ed* Jacqueline Cambas
☆ Tom Green (Gord Brody), Rip Torn (Jim Brody), Marisa Coughlan (Betty), Eddie Kaye Thomas (Freddy Brody), Harland Williams (Darren), Anthony Michael Hall (Mr Davidson), Julie Hagerty (Julie Brody)
'Just as Eminem disarms anyone who bothers to listen to his songs (rather than quoting them secondhand for the purposes of punditry) with his verbal wit and rhythmic dexterity, so does Mr Green stage his gross-outs with a demented but unmistakable integrity. Like it or not, he's an artist.' – A. O. Scott, *New York Times*
'Jaw-dropping, head-pounding, tumor-inducing, apocalypse-summoning bad.' – *Michael Rechtshaffen, Hollywood Reporter*
'A vomitorium… of Tom Green doing things that a geek in a carnival sideshow would turn down.' – *Roger Ebert, Chicago Sun-Times*
'One of the most brutally awful comedies ever to emerge from a major studio.' – *Robert Koehler, Variety*

'They saved the best … for last.'
Freddy's Dead: The Final Nightmare
US 1991 90m DeLuxe Part 3-D
Guild/New Line (Robert Shaye, Aron Warner)
With the aid of some disturbed teenagers, Freddy Krueger's daughter ends her father's life.
Sixth and, with luck, the last of the Nightmare On Elm Street *series, which has little to offer other than the gimmick of an ineffectual 3-D climax.*
w Michael DeLuca *story* Rachel Talalay *d* Rachel Talalay *ph* Declan Quinn *m* Brian May *pd* C. J. Strawn *ed* Janice Hampton
☆ Robert Englund, Lisa Zane, Shon Greenblatt, Lezlie Deane, Ricky Dean Logan, Breckin Meyer, Yaphet Kotto, Roseanne Arnold, Tom Arnold, Alice Cooper
'Delivers enough violence, black humor and even a final reel in 3-D to hit paydirt with horror-starved audiences.' – *Variety*
'The dream logic of Wes Craven's ground-breaking original has been reduced to sloppy plotting and a string of unrelated special-effects set-pieces. It is sadly apt therefore that the manner of Freddy's passing should be as unimaginative as the enervated sequels themselves.' – *Sight and Sound*
† It was followed by *Wes Craven's New Nightmare* (qv)

Free and Easy
US 1930 75m bw
MGM (Edward Sedgwick)
A beauty contest winner is taken to Hollywood by her accident-prone manager.
Primitive talkie showing a great silent comedian all at sea with the new techniques, and the MGM studio offering entertainment on the level of a very bad school concert.
w Al Boasberg, Richard Schayer *d* Edward Sedgwick *ph* Leonard Smith
☆ Buster Keaton, Anita Page, Robert Montgomery, Trixie Friganza

Free and Easy
US 1941 56m bw
MGM
In British high society, father and son both seek rich wives.
A remarkable cast is all at sea in a potted version of Ivor Novello's The Truth Game.
w Marvin Borowsky *d* George Sidney
☆ Nigel Bruce, Robert Cummings, Ruth Hussey, Judith Anderson, C. Aubrey Smith, Reginald Owen, Tom Conway, Forrester Harvey
'This one must have slipped through the Metro wringer while the brains department was out to lunch.' – *Variety*

'Only One Man In The Universe Can Get Them On The Right Trek…'
'Live Long And Party.'
Free Enterprise *
US 1999 100m colour
Regent/Mindfire/Triad (Dan Bates, Mark A. Altman, Allan Kaufman)
Two aspiring film makers who want to make a movie about a serial killer meet a self-important star determined to film a musical of *Julius Caesar* starring himself in most of the roles
Enjoyable comedy that makes a joke of ageing adolescents and the excesses of fandom and pop culture, with Shatner poking fun at Captain Kirk and Star Trek.
w Mark A. Altman, Robert Meyer Burnett *d* Robert Meyer Burnett *ph* Charles L. Barbee *m* Scott Spock *pd* Cynthia Halligan *ed* Robert Meyer Burnett
☆ Rafer Weigel (Robert), Eric McCormack (Mark), Audie England (Claire), Patrick Van Horn (Sean), William Shatner (Bill), Jonathan Slavin (Dan Vebber), Phil LaMarr (Eric Wallace), Deborah Van Valkenberg (Marlena), Marilyn Kentz (Gail), Holly Gagnier (Laura), Jennifer Sommerfield (Tricia)
'The fun…occasionally runs a bit thin but is mostly sustained by the filmmakers' verve and wit.' – *New York Times*
† The end credits contain various references to trivia, such as 'Wise Guy Vinne Terranova' (a reference to Ken Wuhl's role in the TV series *Wiseguy*), 'Seen Things You People Wouldn't Believe Roy Batty' (the name of the character played by Rutger Hauer in *Blade Runner*) and Forgotten Coon Gene L. Coon (a producer and writer of *Star Trek*).

A Free Soul *
US 1931 91m bw
MGM
An unconventional lawyer regrets allowing his daughter to consort with a gangster.
Heavy melodrama with outdated attitudes, but an impressive example of the studio's style in the early thirties.
w John Meehan *novel* Adela Rogers St Johns *d* Clarence Brown *ph* William Daniels *m* William Axt
☆ Lionel Barrymore, Norma Shearer, Leslie Howard, Clark Gable, Lucy Beaumont, James Gleason
'An ungainly, rambling and preposterous theme, awkwardly brought to the screen.' – *Variety*
† Remade 1953 as *The Girl Who Had Everything.*
🏆 Lionel Barrymore (who had a 14-minute speech)
Ⓝ Clarence Brown; Norma Shearer

Free to Live: see *Holiday (1938)*

'A 12 Year Old Street Kid. A 3 Ton Killer Whale. A Friendship You Could Never Imagine. An Adventure You'll Never Forget.'
Free Willy *
US 1993 112m Technicolor Panavision
Warner/Canal/Regency/Alcor (Jennie Lew Tugend, Lauren Shuler-Donner)
A young, disturbed boy forms a friendship with a killer whale threatened with death.
Sentimental animal story with a little charm and some appeal to the under-10s, but no more than a damp update of Lassie.
w Keith A. Walker, Corey Blechman *d* Simon Wincer *ph* Robbie Greenberg *m* Basil Poledouris *pd* Charles Rosen *ed* O. Nicholas Brown
☆ Jason James Richter, Lori Petty, Jayne Atkinson, August Schellenberg, Michael Madsen, Michael Ironside, Keiko
'An exhilarating drama of boy and nature that unabashedly pulls at the heart-strings. Thankfully, its creators know just what to do emotionally and technically to pull off this old-fashioned sentimental yarn.' – *Variety*
'The movie hits every emotional button with a firm fist.' – *Richard Corliss, Time*

Free Willy 2: The Adventure Home
US 1995 96m Technicolor Panavision
Warner (Lauren Shuler-Donner, Jennie Lew Tugend)
A teenage boy and his young brother save a family of whales from an oil spillage and those who plan to exploit them.
Mundane sequel, using animatronic whales, which settles for simple thrills together with familiar teenage problems of growing up.
w Karen Janszen, Corey Blechman, John Mattson *d* Dwight Little *ph* Laszlo Kovacs *m* Basil Poledouris *pd* Paul Sylbert *ed* Robert Brown, Dallas Puett
☆ Jason James Richter, August Schellenberg, Michael Madsen, Jayne Atkinson, Mary Kate Schellhardt, Francis Capra, Jon Tenney, Elizabeth Pena, M. Emmet Walsh
'Somebody set us straight on this: When did killer whales become the stuff of cute and cuddly animal-buddy movies? Last we checked, Orca was noshing on Bo Derek's leg.' – *Premiere*

'A new friend. A new threat. A new adventure that will capture your heart.'
Free Willy 3: The Rescue
US 1997 86m Technicolor
Warner/Regency (Jennie Lew Tugend)
A friendship between a 17-year-old youth and a 10-year-old boy, whose father is illegally hunting whales, saves Willy and his pregnant mate from death.
The mixture much as before, with a killer whale acting as the unwitting saviour of unhappy kids; those who enjoyed the earlier episodes should gain an equal amount of pleasure this time around.
w John Mattson *d* Sam Pillsbury *ph* Tobias Schliesser *m* Cliff Eidelman *pd* Brent Thomas *ed* Margie Goodspeed
☆ Jason James Richter, August Schellenberg, Annie Corley, Vincent Berry, Patrick Kilpatrick, Tasha Simms
'Whether Willy can fuel any more screen vehicles remains in serious doubt. But if he's to be put out to pasture, he couldn't have asked for a better *bon voyage*.' – *Leonard Klady, Variety*
'This may well be the worst sequel of all time.' – *Mark Steyn, Spectator*
† The two leading whales, Willy and Nikki, were animatronic creations and not real animals.

'Today they demolished 23 cars, four motor cycles and one apartment building. But don't call the cops. They *are* the cops!'
Freebie and the Bean *
US 1974 113m Technicolor Panavision
Warner (Richard Rush)
Two vaguely incompetent cops try to link a mobster with the numbers racket.
Violent comedy melodrama with a high mortality rate, amoral outlook, and the usual seventies reliance on incoherent plot, bumbled dialogue and excessive background noise. Occasionally funny all the same.
w Richard Kaufman *d* Richard Rush *ph* Laszlo Kovacs *m* Dominic Frontière
☆ Alan Arkin, James Caan, Loretta Swit, Jack Kruschen, Mike Kellin
'It summarizes Hollywood's favourite thematic elements of the early seventies: platonic male love affair, police corruption, comic violence, cynicism in high places, San Francisco, gay villains, the car chase. A return to the Keystone Kops, with character trimmings and lashings of sado-masochistic mayhem.' – *Clyde Jeavons*
'A tasteless film from a spitball script.' – *Variety*
'There is a beating or a killing, or at least a yelling scene, every couple of minutes.' – *New Yorker, 1980*

Freedom Is Paradise: see *SER*

Freejack
US 1992 108m Technicolor Panavision
Warner/Morgan Creek (Ronald Shusett, Stuart Oken)
A racing-car driver on the point of death is taken eighteen years into the future so that his body can house the mind of a terminally ill millionaire.
Predictable science fiction about a sleazy future that lacks the wit and originality of the novel on which it is based.
w Steven Pressfield, Ronald Shusett, Dan Gilroy *novel* *Immortality Inc* by Robert Sheckley *d* Geoff Murphy *ph* Amir Mokri *m* Trevor Jones *pd* Joe Alves *ed* Dennis Virkler *sp* Richard Hoover
☆ Emilio Estevez, Mick Jagger, René Russo, Anthony Hopkins, Jonathan Banks, David Johansen, Amanda Plummer
'Chalk it up as one of life's little ironies that a pic about mind transfers would be so mindless.' – *Variety*

Freeway
US 1996 108m DeLuxe
Kushner-Locke/Samuel Hadida/August/Davis/Illusion (Chris Hanley, Brad Wyman)
On the run after her mother, a drug-addicted prostitute, is arrested, an illiterate 15-year-old girl is picked up by a serial killer.
The opening credits, showing a sex-obsessed wolf chasing Red Riding Hood, suggest some sort of satire is intended; but what follows is a sleazily violent, unsubtle melodrama.
wd Matthew Bright *ph* John Thomas *m* Danny Elfman, Tito Larriva *pd* Pam Warner *ed* Maysie Hoy
☆ Kiefer Sutherland, Reese Witherspoon, Wolfgang Bodison, Dan Hedaya, Amanda Plummer, Brooke Shields, Michael T. Weiss, Bokeem Woodbine
'A thoroughly nasty piece of work, the product of a filmmaker with a ludicrously misplaced confidence in his own cleverness. Pic is so cartoonish and mean-spirited, it is impossible to work up any sympathy for anyone on screen.' – *Joe Leydon, Variety*

Freeway II Confessions of a Trickbaby
US/France/Canada 1999 98m FotoKem
Metro Tartan/Kushner-Locke/Davis/Muse/Incognito (Brad Wyman, Chris Hanley)
aka: *Confessions of a Trickbaby*
A bulimic drug-dealer and prostitute, who beats and robs her clients, goes on the run from juvenile prison with a psychotic serial killer.
Trashy exploitation movie, an unholy stew of vomit, sexual molestation, masturbation, transvestism, necrophilia, cannibalism, murder and general sleaziness, with a climax straight out of Hansel and Gretel.
wd Matthew Bright *ph* Joel Ransom *m* Kennard Ramsey *pd* Brian Davie *ed* Suzanne Hines
☆ Natasha Lyonne (White Girl (Crystal)), María Celedonio (Cyclona (Angela)), Vincent Gallo (Sister Gomez), David Alan Grier (Mr Butz), Michael T. Weiss (Drifter), John Landis (Judge), Max Perlich (Flacco), Bob Dawson (Detective Creldo), Jenn Griffin (Detective Dollar), April Telek (Mrs Wilson)
'It really is bad. It's beyond bad.' – *Rupert Laight, Film Review*

Freeze Frame
US 1989 78m colour
Film Indiana/Creative Edge (Martin Wiley)
aka: *The Homeroom News*
A high-school reporter exposes a crooked would-be politician.
Uninteresting and silly drama, written, directed and acted without noticeable flair and with little to interest any audience.
wd William Bindley *ph* Craig Somers *m* John Cascella *ad* Todd Hatfield *ed* Jeffrey Neuman
☆ Shannen Doherty, Charles Haid, Ryan Lambert, Adam Carl, Robyn Douglass, Seth Michaels

'Revenge Has Never Been So Cold'

Freeze Me

Japan 2000

Nikkatsu/KSS (Takashi Ishii, Nobuaki Nagae, Taketo Niitsu)

video title: *Freezer*

A woman takes her revenge when, after being released from prison, the gang that raped her turn up at her flat to repeat the crime.

Grim little shocker about a woman's descent into madness that has a touch of black humour, but rather too much repetitive violence to maintain interest.

wd Takashi Ishii *ph* Yasushi Sasakibara *m* Goro Yasukawa *pd* Teru Yamazaki *ed* Kawashima Akimasa

☆ Harumi Inoue (Chihiro), Shingo Tsurumi (Kojima), Kazuki Kitamura (Hirokawa), Shunsuke Matsuoka (Nogami), Naoto Takenaka (Baba)

'The violent scenes veer vertiginously between slapstick, soft-core pornography and raw documentary, leaving you repelled and confused, as well as fascinated.' – *A. O. Scott, New York Times*

French Can-Can **

France/Italy 1955 105m Technicolor

Franco-London/Jolly (Louis Wipf)

How the can-can was launched in Paris night-clubs.

A dramatically thin vehicle splendidly evoking a vision of vanished Paris: a feast for the eyes.

w André-Paul Antoine *d* Jean Renoir *ph* Michel Kelber *m* Georges Van Parys

☆ *Jean Gabin*, Françoise Arnoul, Maria Félix, Jean-Roger Caussimon, Edith Piaf, Patachou

'Doyle is bad news ... but a good cop!'

The French Connection ****

US 1971 104m DeLuxe

TCF/Philip D'Antoni

New York police track down a consignment of drugs entering the country in a car.

Lively semi-documentary based on the true exploits of a tough cop named Eddie Egan who liked to break a few rules. Most memorable for a car chase scene involving an elevated railway, for showing the seamy side of New York more or less as it is.

w Ernest Tidyman *book* Robin Moore *d* *William Friedkin* *ph* Owen Roizman *m* Don Ellis *ad* Ben Kazaskow *ed* Jerry Greenberg

☆ *Gene Hackman* (Jimmy 'Popeye' Doyle), Roy Scheider (Buddy Russo), *Fernando Rey* (Alain Charnier), Tony Lo Bianco (Sal Boca), Marcel Bozzufi (Pierre Nicoli)

'The only thing this movie believes in is giving the audience jolts, and you can feel the raw, primitive responses in the theater.' – *Pauline Kael, New Yorker*

Academy Award: best picture; Ernest Tidyman; William Friedkin; Gene Hackman

Academy Award nomination: Owen Roizman; Roy Scheider

BAFTA: Gene Hackman

French Connection II

US 1975 119m DeLuxe

TCF (Robert L. Rosen)

The New York cop who in *The French Connection* smashed most of a drug ring arrives in Marseilles to track down its elusive leader.

Sleazy, virtually plotless and unattractive sequel which rises to a few good action moments but is bogged down by bad language, unconvincing characterization and an interminable and irrelevant 'cold turkey' sequence.

w Robert Dillon, Laurie Dillon, Alexander Jacobs *d* John Frankenheimer *ph* Claude Renoir *m* Don Ellis *pd* Jacques Saulnier *ed* Tom Rolf

☆ Gene Hackman (Popeye Doyle), Fernando Rey (Alain Charnier), Bernard Fresson (Barthelemy), Jean-Pierre Castaldi (Raoul Diron), Charles Millot (Miletto), Cathleen Nesbitt (Old Lady)

'Visually as well as morally the film makes you uncertain where its feet are.' – *New Yorker*

French Dressing

GB 1963 86m bw 'Scope

ABP/Kenwood (Kenneth Harper)

A deckchair attendant and a local reporter believe that what Bardot can do for St Tropez they can do for Gormleigh-on-Sea.

Cinema's enfant terrible directs this his first theatrical film at breakneck speed with echoes of Tati, Keaton and the Keystone Kops. Alas, lack of star comedians and firm control make its exuberance merely irritating.

w Peter Myers, Ronald Cass, Peter Britt *d* *Ken Russell* *ph* Ken Higgins *m* Georges Delerue

☆ James Booth, Roy Kinnear, Marisa Mell, Bryan Pringle

'Saddled with lousy dialogue and a director who seems more concerned with composition than content ... I actually heard the director compare his film with Jacques Tati's *Monsieur Hulot's Holiday*. What arrogance! Dream on, Mr Director, dream on.' – *Ken Russell*

'Kate's stuck in a place where anything can happen with a guy who'll make sure that it does.'

French Kiss

US 1995 111m DeLuxe Panavision

Polygram/TCF/Working Title/Prufrock (Tim Bevan, Eric Fellner, Meg Ryan, Kathryn F. Galan)

An American woman goes to Paris, in search of her fiancé who has fallen for a Frenchwoman, and becomes romantically involved with a French thief.

A tourist trip around the more photogenic parts of Paris, providing a background to a lacklustre love story between two incompatible people, which offers nothing that hasn't been done rather better before.

w Adam Brooks *d* Lawrence Kasdan *ph* Owen Roizman *m* James Newton Howard *pd* Jon Hutman *ed* Joe Hutshing

☆ Meg Ryan, Kevin Kline, Timothy Hutton, Jean Reno, François Cluzet, Susan Anbeh, Renee Humphrey

'A romantic comedy that's neither very romantic nor very comic.' – *Derek Malcolm, Guardian*

'She was lost from the moment she saw him...'

The French Lieutenant's Woman *

GB 1981 123m Technicolor

UA/Juniper (Leon Clore)

In 1867 Lyme Regis, a gentleman forsakes his fiancée for the abandoned mistress of a French seaman.

Vaguely unsatisfactory and muddily coloured adaptation of a novel which set its thin story against the entire social background of the Victorian age as related to our own. The attempt to replace this by an equally thin modern story about actors playing the Victorian roles fails rather dismally; but the enterprise supplies points of interest along the way.

w Harold Pinter *novel* John Fowles *d* Karel Reisz *ph* Freddie Francis *m* Carl Davis *pd* *Assheton Gorton*

☆ *Jeremy Irons, Meryl Streep*, Leo McKern, Patience Collier, Peter Vaughan, Hilton McRae

'Pinter's reduction not only shears away the sliding historical perspective, but robs the narrative of its Victorian charisma.' – *Tom Milne, MFB*

'There are some lovely moments, and a few have magical undertones, but most of the picture might be taking place in a glass case.' – *Pauline Kael*

'If you see the movie, the book will still surprise you, and that's as it should be.' – *Roger Ebert*

Academy Award nomination: Harold Pinter; editing (John Bloom); Meryl Streep

BAFTA: best sound; Carl Davis; Meryl Streep

'It'll knock both your eyes out!'

The French Line

US 1953 102m Technicolor 3-D

RKO (Edmund Grainger)

A cheery Texas oil heiress finds a husband while travelling to France.

Very thinly plotted but quite attractive light musical with a good-humoured star wearing costumes once thought censorable.

w Mary Loos, Richard Sale *d* Lloyd Bacon *ph* Harry J. Wild *m* Walter Scharf *md* Lionel Newman *ch* Jack Cole, Billy Daniel *ad* Albert S. D'Agostino, Carroll Clark *ed* Robert Ford *cos* Michael Woulfe, Howard Greer

☆ Jane Russell (Mary Carson), Gilbert Roland (Pierre du Quesne), Arthur Hunnicutt (Waco Mosby), Mary McCarty (Madame Farelli), Joyce MacKenzie (Myrtle Brown), Paul Corday (Celeste), Scott Elliott (Bill Harris), Craig Stevens (Bill Harris)

'A slouching Amazon, her clothes appear to stay put just as long as she agrees not to burst out of them; essentially a good sort, she has an ever-annihilating sneer for the false, the pretentious and the fresh.' – *MFB*

A French Mistress

GB 1960 98m bw

British Lion/Charter (John Boulting)

An attractive new mistress causes havoc at a boys' school.

Sloppy, predictable comedy with practised performers getting a few easy laughs. The producers tried to excuse its imperfections by promoting it as 'a romp'.

w Roy Boulting, Jeffrey Dell *play* Robert Monro (Sonnie Hale) *d* Roy Boulting *ph* Max Greene *m* John Addison *ad* Albert Witherick *ed* John Jympson

☆ James Robertson Justice (Robert Martin), Cecil Parker (Headmaster), Raymond Huntley (Rev Edwin Peake), Ian Bannen (Colin Crane), Agnes Laurent (Madeleine Lafarge), Thorley Walters (Colonel Edmond), Edith Sharpe (Matron), Athene Seyler (Beatrice Peake), Kenneth Griffith (Mr Meade), Irene Handl (Staff Sgt Hodges), Cardew Robinson (Ambulance Attendant), Christopher Sandford (Poole), Michael Crawford (Kent), Christopher Beeney (Stephenson)

The French They Are a Funny Race: see *The Diary of Major Thompson*

French Twist **

France 1995 107m colour

Guild/Renn/TF1/Les Films Flam (Claude Berri)

original title: *Gazon Maudit*

A lesbian musician forms a *menage à trois* with a married couple.

An enjoyable comedy at the expense of male philandering, performed with excellent comic timing; it was, perhaps surprisingly, a box-office success in France.

wd *Josiane Balasko* *ph* Gérard de Battista *m* Manuel Malou *ad* Carlos Conti *ed* Claudine Merlin

☆ *Victoria Abril, Josiane Balasko*, Alain Chabat, Ticky Holgado, Miguel Bosé, Catherine Hiegel, Catherine Samie

'Funny, breezy, erotic, and so matter-of-fact about the infinite variety of human sexuality, it could only be baked in France.' – *Lisa Schwarzbaum, Entertainment Weekly*

A French Vampire in America: see *Innocent Blood*

French without Tears **

GB 1939 85m bw

Paramount/Two Cities (David E. Rose)

Young Britons at a French crammer fall for the young sister of one of their number.

Pleasant light comedy from a successful West End play.

w Terence Rattigan, Anatole de Grunwald, Ian Dalrymple *play* *Terence Rattigan* *d* Anthony Asquith *ph* Bernard Knowles, Jack Hildyard *m* Nicholas Brodszky *ad* Paul Sheriff, Carmen Dillon *ed* David Lean

☆ Ray Milland, Ellen Drew, *Guy Middleton, Roland Culver*, David Tree, Jim Gerald, Janine Darcy, Kenneth Morgan

'There is always something a little shocking about English levity. The greedy exhilaration of these blithe young men when they learn that another fellow's girl is to join them at the establishment where they are learning French, the scramble over her luggage, the light-hearted badinage, the watery and libidinous eye – that national mixture of prudery and excitement – would be unbearable if it were not for Mr Asquith's civilized direction.' – *Graham Greene*

† Incredibly, Paramount had purchased the property as a vehicle for Marlene Dietrich.

Frenchie

US 1950 80m Technicolor

U-I (Michel Kraike)

A saloon queen sets up shop in Bottleneck, her real aim being to track down her father's murderers.

Modest Western of the Destry Rides Again school.

w Oscar Brodney *d* Louis King *ph* Maury Gertsman *m* Hans Salter *ed* Ted J. Kent

☆ Shelley Winters, Joel McCrea, Paul Kelly, Elsa Lanchester, Marie Windsor, John Emery, George Cleveland, John Russell

'For 24 reckless hours the arms of adventure embraced her – and she knew the thrill of true love!'

Frenchman's Creek *

US 1944 112m Technicolor

Paramount (B. G. de Sylva)

In Restoration England, a lady flees from a lascivious nobleman to her family home in Cornwall, where she falls in love with a French pirate.

Enjoyable Girls' Own Paper *romance, dressed to kill and entertaining despite its many palpable absurdities.*

w Talbot Jennings *novel* Daphne du Maurier *d* Mitchell Leisen *ph* George Barnes *m* Victor Young *ad* Hans Dreier, Ernst Fegte

☆ Joan Fontaine, Arturo de Cordova, Basil Rathbone, Nigel Bruce, *Cecil Kellaway*, Ralph Forbes, Moyna McGill

'Masturbation fantasy triple distilled.' – *James Agee*

Academy Award: art direction

Frenzy *

Sweden 1944 101m bw

Svensk Filmindustri

original title: *Hets*

aka: *Torment*

A sadistic Latin teacher and his sensitive pupil find themselves competing for the same girl.

Hothouse melodrama of the Blue Angel *school: it seemed pretty powerful at the time.*

w Ingmar Bergman *d* *Alf Sjöberg* *ph* Martin Bodin *m* Hilding Rosenberg

☆ *Stig Jarrel, Alf Kjellin, Mai Zetterling*

'In spite of being always moving and sincere and pictorially satisfying, the film seems to miss the revelation it strives for. The lack – of passion, of inspiration – is inherent in the picture, and that is judging it by those very high standards it fails by so narrow a margin to reach.' – *Richard Winnington*

Frenzy: see *Latin Quarter (1945)*

'From the master of shock, a shocking masterpiece!'

Frenzy *

GB 1972 116m Technicolor

Universal/Alfred Hitchcock

A disillusioned and aggressive ex-RAF officer is suspected through circumstantial evidence of being London's 'necktie murderer'.

Has-been, unconvincing, cliché-ridden thriller, an old man's sex suspenser, which would have been derided if anyone but Hitchcock had made it. As it is, a few comic and suspenseful touches partly atone for the implausibilities and lapses of taste.

w Anthony Shaffer *novel* *Goodbye Piccadilly, Farewell Leicester Square* by Arthur La Bern *d* Alfred Hitchcock *ph* Gilbert Taylor *m* Ron Goodwin *pd* Syd Cain *ed* John Jympson

☆ Jon Finch (Richard Blaney), *Alec McCowen* (Chief Inspector Oxford), *Barry Foster* (Robert Rusk), Vivien Merchant (Mrs Oxford), Anna Massey (Babs Milligan), Barbara Leigh-Hunt (Brenda Blaney), Billie Whitelaw (Hetty Porter), Clive Swift (Johnny Porter), Bernard Cribbins (Felix Forsythe)

'Hitchcock's most stodgy piece since *Dial M for Murder* and possibly his least interesting film from any period.' – *William S. Pechter*

'There is suspense, and local colour, and always, Hitchcock smacking his lips and rubbing his hands and delighting in his naughtiness.' – *Roger Ebert*

'The future is listening.'

Frequency *

US 2000 118m DeLuxe Super 35

Entertainment/New Line (Hawk Koch, Gregory Hoblit, Bill Carraro, Toby Emmerich)

During freak electric storms, a modern day cop is able to communicate by ham radio with his father in 1969, so that together they can change the past and the present.

Supernatural tale of father-son relationships and male-bonding that becomes an increasingly silly thriller involving a serial killer. Its appeal appears to lie in the evasion at its centre: its refusal to accept the fact of death.

w Toby Emmerich *d* Gregory Hoblit *ph* Alar Kivilo *m* Michael Kamen *pd* Paul Eads *ed* David Rosenbloom

☆ Dennis Quaid (Frank Sullivan), Jim Caviezel (John Sullivan), Andre Braugher (Satch DeLeon), Elizabeth Mitchell (Julia Sulliva), Noah Emmerich (Gordo Hersch), Shawn Doyle (Jack Shepard), Jordan Bridges (Graham Gibson), Melissa Errico (Samantha Thomas), Daniel Henson (Johnny Sullivan)

'An oddly schizophrenic fantasy thriller that ultimately succumbs to a fatal case of sentimentality.' – *Todd McCarthy, Variety*

Fresa y Chocolate: see *Strawberry and Chocolate*

'In a world where criminals make the rules, one kid is out to beat them at their own game.'

Fresh **

US/France 1994 112m DeLuxe

Entertainment/Lumière (Randy Ostrow, Lawrence Bender)

In Brooklyn, a 12-year-old black youth, who divides his time between drug-running for local dealers and attending to his schoolwork, devises a desperate plan to obtain a better life for himself and his addicted sister.

A tough tale of street life lived on the edge, violent, foul-mouthed and full of casual slaughter, told with a raw authenticity; it is a brutal urban tragedy that touches on real emotions of loss and despair.

wd Boaz Yakin *ph* Adam Holender *m* Stewart Copeland *pd* Dan Leigh *ed* Dorian Harris

☆ *Sean Nelson*, Giancarlo Esposito, Samuel L. Jackson, N'Bushe Wright, Ron Brice, Jean LaMarre

'This taut little thriller is brutal and unformulaic, a real surprise.' – *Alexander Walker, London Evening Standard*

'This portrait of a childhood both incredibly resourceful and tragically deprived is memorable.' – *Variety*

Fresh Horses

US 1988 103m colour

Columbia TriStar/Weintraub Entertainment (Dick Berg)

A wealthy student falls in love with a married 16-year-old girl.

Insignificant romance, no more than adequate.

w Larry Ketron *play* Larry Ketron *d* David Anspaugh *ph* Fred Murphy *m* David Foster, Patrick Williams *pd* Paul Sylbert *ed* David Rosenbloom

☆ Molly Ringwald, Andrew McCarthy, Patti D'Arbanville, Ben Stiller, Leon Russom, Molly Hagen, Viggo Mortensen, Doug Hutchinson, Chiara Peacock

The Freshman **

US 1925 75m (24 fps) bw silent

Harold Lloyd

An awkward college student accidentally becomes a star football player.

A rather slow but striking star vehicle with assured set-pieces. The football game climax was later used as the first reel of Mad Wednesday.

w Sam Taylor, Ted Wilde, Tim Whelan, John Grey *d* Fred Newmeyer, Sam Taylor *ph* Walter Lundin, Henry Kohler

☆ *Harold Lloyd*, Jobyna Ralston, Brooks Benedict

'Next time they make you an offer you can't refuse ... refuse!'

The Freshman **

US 1990 102m Technicolor

Tri-Star/Mike Lobell, Andrew Bergman

A student of gangster movies goes to work for a real-life criminal.

A genial spoof of The Godfather *films, with Brando parodying his own performance as an ageing patriarch of crime.*

wd Andrew Bergman *ph* William A. Fraker *m* David Newman *ed* Barry Malkin

☆ Marlon Brando, Matthew Broderick, Bruno Kirby, Penelope Ann Miller, Frank Whaley, Jon Polito, Paul Benedict, Richard Gant, Kenneth Welsh, Pamela Payton-Wright

Freud **

GB 1962 140m bw

U-I (Wolfgang Reinhardt)

Vienna 1885; Dr Sigmund Freud, a neurologist, uses hypnotism to treat hysteria, and finds new interest in the case of a boy whose hatred of his father springs from incestuous love of his mother, a failing which Freud finds in himself.

Earnest and competent biopic harking back to Warner's similar films of the 30s, with the addition of franker language. Generally absorbing, but undeniably hard tack.

w Charles Kaufman, Wolfgang Reinhardt *d* John Huston *ph* Douglas Slocombe *m* Jerry Goldsmith

☆ *Montgomery Clift, Larry Parks*, Susannah York, Eileen Herlie, Susan Kohner, David McCallum

'The dream sequences, photographed mostly in negative or overexposure, belong not on the couch of Dr Freud but in the Cabinet of Dr Caligari.' – *John Simon*

'It is impossible, I would think, for any educated person to sit through *Freud* without bursting into laughter at least once.' – *Ernest Callenbach, Film Quarterly*

script; Jerry Goldsmith

Die Freudlose Gasse: see *Joyless Street*

Fric Frac *

France 1939 95m bw

Maurice Lehmann

A provincial jeweller's assistant falls in with underworld characters.

Well-prized French comedy with dialogue entirely in thieves' slang.

w Michel Duran *play* Edouard Bourdet *d* Maurice Lehmann

☆ Michel Simon, Fernandel, Arletty, Helene Robert

'Prepare to be seduced.'

Frida **

US 2002 123m colour

Buena Vista/Miramax/Ventanarosa/Lions Gate (Sarah Green, Salma Hayek, Jay Polstein, Lizz Speed)

Biopic of the artist Frida Kahlo and her tempestuous marriage to fellow artist Diego Rivera.

Colourful and inventively directed, this tries to cram in the whole of a life, so that it becomes too hectic and crowded to be as affecting as it should.

w Clancy Sigel, Diane Lake, Gregory Nava, Anna Thomas *book* Hayden Herrera *d* Julie Taymor *ph* Rodrigo Prieto *m* Elliot Goldenthal *pd* Felipe Fernández del Paso *ed* Francoise Bonnot *cos* Julie Weiss

☆ *Salma Hayek* (Frida Kahlo), Alfred Molina (Diego Rivera), Geoffrey Rush (Leon Trotsky), Ashley Judd (Tina Modotti), Antonio Banderas (David Alfaro Siqueiros), Edward Norton (Nelson Rockefeller), Valeria Golino (Lupe Marin), Mia Maestro (Cristina Kahlo), Roger Rees (Guillermo Kahlo)

'Endlessly interesting. It's about people who thought ideas and art mattered, which makes it a rarity today.' – *Stephen Hunter, Washington Post*

'A revolutionary life has rarely felt less edgy, or the biography of an iconoclast more bourgeois.' – *Lisa Schwarzbaum, Washington Post*

Elliot Goldenthal; make-up (John E. Jackson, Beatrice De Alba)

Salma Hayek; Felipe Fernández del Paso (with Hannia Robledo); Julie Weiss; song 'Burn It Blue' (*m* Elliot Goldenthal *l* Julie Taymor)

make-up/hair (Judy Chin, Beatrice De Alba, John E. Jackson, Regina Reyes)

Friday

US 1995 89m Foto-Kem

Entertainment/New Line/Priority (Patricia Charbonnet)

Two friends, one unemployed, the other having problems with his drug dealer, watch the neighbourhood go by in South Central Los Angeles.

A sort of extended sitcom with an improvised air, this consists of idle gossip interspersed with moments of brisker action; despite being written and performed by rappers, it has little sense of urgency or aggression apart from that supplied by its soundtrack.

w Ice Cube, DJ Pooh *d* F. Gary Gray *ph* Gerry Lively *m* Hidden Faces *pd* Bruce Bellamy *ed* John Carter

☆ Ice Cube, Chris Tucker, Nia Long, Tiny 'Zeus' Lister Jnr, John Witherspoon, Anna Maria Horsford

'A crudely made, sometimes funny bit of porchfront humor from the 'hood.' – *Variety*

'Broad, unsophisticated, appallingly sexist stuff.' – *Independent*

† It was followed by a sequel *Next Friday* (qv).

'Fridays will never be the same again.'

Friday the 13th

US 1980 95m colour

Georgetown (Sean S. Cunningham)

When a summer camp is reopened after many years, the grisly murders which closed it down begin again.

Horror suspense story with no raison d'être but a series of inventively gory shock moments, which were enough for it to ring the box-office bell.

w Victor Miller *d* Sean S. Cunningham *ph* Barry Abrams *m* Harry Manfredini *ad* Virginia Field *ed* Bill Freda

☆ Betsy Palmer, Adrienne King, Jeannine Taylor, Robbi Morgan

'An oversexed couple makes love in the bottom bunk, there's a dead body in the top bunk and the rest of the bunk is in the television commercials.' – *Variety*

Friday the 13th Part II

US 1981 87m DeLuxe

CIC/Georgetown (Steve Miner, Dennis Murphy)

The sole survivor of the massacre at Camp Crystal Lake is murdered, and five years later the mayhem begins again, the villain being the son of the woman who committed the former killings.

Virtually a remake of the first film, starting with a long flashback to it; short sharp shocks punctuate slabs of tedium.

w Ron Kurz *d* Steve Miner *ph* Peter Stein *m* Harry Manfredini *pd* Virginia Field *ed* Susan E. Cunningham

☆ Amy Steel, John Furey, Adrienne King, Kirsten Baker, Stu Charno

Friday the 13th Part III

US 1982 95m Movielab 3D

UIP/Jason Productions (Frank Mancuso Jnr)

Crazy Jason is still murdering kids up at Crystal Lake.

No better than its predecessors for being in three dimensions; in fact, half as bad again.

w Martin Kitrosser, Carol Watson *d* Steve Miner *ph* Gerald Feil *m* Harry Manfredini *ad* Robb Wilson *ed* George Hively

☆ Dana Kimmell, Richard Brooker, Catherine Parks, Paul Kratka

'The first was dreadful and took seventeen million. The second was just as bad and took more than ten million. No doubt the distributor will be happy to learn that the third is terrible too.' – *Variety*

Friday the 13th Part V – A New Beginning

US 1985 92m colour

UIP/Paramount (Timothy Silver)

A mass murderer stalks a private hospital, killing the inmates.

Gory return of a series that could only offer a repetition of its previous killings, poverty-stricken in imagination and everything else.

w Martin Kitrosser, David Cohen, Danny Steinmann *d* Danny Steinmann *ph* Stephen L. Posey *m* Harry Manfredini *pd* Robert Howland *ed* Bruce Green

☆ John Shepard, Shavar Ross, Melanie Kinnaman, Richard Young, Corey Feldman, Corey Parker

'Kill or be killed!'

Friday the 13th Part VI – Jason Lives

US 1986 87m Metrocolor

Paramount (Don Behrns)

The corpse of the exhumed Jason is brought to life after being hit by lightning and, to the surprise only of the cast, begins killing teenagers yet again.

Tedious re-run of previous movies in the series without even a hint of originality to be discovered.

wd Tom McLoughlin *ph* Jon Kranhouse *m* Harry Manfredini *pd* Joseph T. Garrity *ed* Bruce Green *sp* Martin Becker

☆ Thom Mathews, Jennifer Cooke, David Kagen, Renee Jones, C. J. Graham, Tony Goldwyn

'Jason Is Back. But This Time Someone's Waiting.'

Friday the 13th Part VII – The New Blood

US 1988 90m Technicolor

Paramount/Friday Four (Iain Paterson)

A woman with telekinetic powers attempts to stop the axe-wielding Jason continuing his killing spree.

Lacklustre continuation, still offering no variation on its basic theme of killing teenagers, especially those who display any sexual feelings. There is, though, less gore than usual; perhaps make-up was in as short supply as imagination.

w Daryl Haney, Manuel Fidello *d* John Carl Buechler *ph* Paul Elliott *m* Harry Manfredini, Fred Mollin *pd* Richard Lawrence *ed* Barry Zetlin, Maureen O'Connell, Martin Jay Sadoff

☆ Lar Park Lincoln, Kevin Blair, Susan Blu, Terry Kiser, Kane Hodder

Friday the 13th Part VIII – Jason Takes Manhattan

US 1989 96m Technicolor

Paramount/Horror, Inc. (Randolph Cheveldave)

An underwater electrical accident re-animates the corpse of Jason, who clambers aboard the cruise ship Lazarus to murder its young passengers.

The interminable story retold in the standard manner, though with less gore than usual; fans of the series, if any remain, are likely to be disappointed at the way the film cuts away from the action at the many moments of teenage death.

wd Rob Hedden *ph* Bryan England *m* Fred Mollin *pd* David Fischer *ed* Steve Mirkovich *sp* make-up effects: Jamie Brown; mechanical effects: Martin Becker

☆ Jensen Daggett, Scott Reeves, Barbara Bingham, Peter Mark Richman, Kane Hodder, Sharlene Martin

Friday the 13th: The Final Chapter

US 1984 91m Movielab

Paramount (Frank Mancuso Jnr)

aka: *Friday the 13th Part IV*

Supposedly dead Jason escapes from cold storage at the morgue and goes on another rampage.

The awful mixture as before: would that the title meant what it says.

w Barney Cohen *d* Joseph Zito *ph* Joao Fernandes *m* Harry Manfredini *pd* Shelton H. Bishop III *ed* Joel Goodman

☆ E. Erich Anderson, Judie Aronson, Peter Barton, Kimberly Beck

'Yet another catalogue of mindless slaughter which doesn't even offer the courtesy of a story.' – *Daily Mail*

'The censor says you have to be 18 to see it. I would suggest you merely have to be daft.' – *Sunday Times*

Friday the Thirteenth ***

GB 1933 84m bw

Gainsborough (Michael Balcon)

Several people are involved in a bus crash, and we turn back the clock to see how they came to be there.

Highly competent compendium of comedies and dramas looking back to The Bridge of San Luis Rey *and forward to the innumerable all-star films of the forties.*

w G. H. Moresby-White, *Sidney Gilliat, Emlyn Williams* *d* *Victor Saville* *ph* Charles Van Enger *ad* Alfred Junge, Vetchinsky *ed* R. E. Dearing

☆ Sonnie Hale, Cyril Smith, *Eliot Makeham*, Ursula Jeans, *Emlyn Williams*, Frank Lawton, Belle Chrystal, *Max Miller*, Alfred Drayton, Edmund Gwenn, Mary Jerrold, Gordon Harker, *Robertson Hare*, Martita Hunt, Leonora Corbett and also Jessie Matthews, Ralph Richardson

'The secret of life? The secret's in the sauce.'

Fried Green Tomatoes at the Whistle Stop Café *

US 1991 130m DeLuxe
Rank/Act III/Electric Shadow (Jordan Kerner, Jon Avnet)

A middle-aged housewife is encouraged to be more self-assertive after listening to an old woman recalling her past.
A pleasant wallow in nostalgia for a less complicated age.
w Fannie Flagg, Carol Sobieski *novel* Fannie Flagg *d* Jon Avnet *ph* Geoffrey Simpson *m* Thomas Newman *pd* Barbara Ling *ed* Debra C. Neil
☆ Kathy Bates, Jessica Tandy, Mary-Louise Parker, Mary Stuart Masterson, Cicely Tyson, Gailard Sartain, Stan Shaw

'Absorbing and life-affirming quality fare.' – *Variety*

Jessica Tandy; Fannie Flagg, Carol Sobieski

'Would you take Frieda into *your* home?'

Frieda *

GB 1947 97m bw
Ealing (Michael Relph)

An RAF officer marries and takes home a girl who helped him escape from a POW camp.
Stuffy and dated drama about how one English family learned to love one particular German. Timely when it appeared, however, and well made within its conventions.
w Angus MacPhail, Ronald Millar *play* Ronald Millar *d* Basil Dearden *ph* Gordon Dines *m* John Greenwood *ad* Jim Morahan *ed* Leslie Norman
☆ Mai Zetterling (Frieda), David Farrar (Robert), Glynis Johns (Judy), Flora Robson (Nell), Albert Lieven (Richard), Barbara Everest (Mrs Dawson), Gladys Henson (Edith), Ray Jackson (Tony), Patrick Holt (Alan), Milton Rosmer (Merrick), Barry Jones (Holliday), Garry Marsh (Beckwith)

'Something of a cinema rarity – a film which stimulates intelligent thought and argument.' – *Dick Richards, Sunday Pictorial*

Friendly Persuasion **

US 1956 139m DeLuxe
AA (William Wyler)

At the outbreak of the Civil War, a family of Quakers has to consider its position.
Sentimental, homespun Western fare, well done without being especially engrossing.
w Michael Wilson *novel* Jessamyn West *d* William Wyler *ph* Ellsworth Fredericks *m* Dimitri Tiomkin
☆ Gary Cooper, Dorothy McGuire, Anthony Perkins, Marjorie Main, Richard Eyer, Robert Middleton, Walter Catlett

'The material is a little tenuous … but Wyler's sure-handed direction constantly illuminates it with a humour, a gentle charm and a feeling for fundamental values that are rare indeed.' – *Moira Walsh, America*

† It was successfully remade as a TV movie in 1975, directed by Joseph Sargent and starring Richard Kiley and Shirley Knight.

best picture; Michael Wilson; William Wyler; Anthony Perkins; song 'Thee I Love' (*m* Dimitri Tiomkin, *ly* Paul Francis Webster)

'Who needs the world when you own the moon and stars?'

Friends

GB 1971 102m Technicolor
Paramount (Lewis Gilbert)

Teenage lovers run away to a country cottage and have a child.
Peculiar idyll given corny 'poetic' treatment: a real non-starter.
w Jack Russell, Vernon Harris *d* Lewis Gilbert *ph* Andreas Winding *m* Elton John
☆ Sean Bury, Anicee Alvina, Toby Robbins, Ronald Lewis

'In a world ripped apart friends are all you can trust.'

Friends *

GB/France 1993 109m Technicolor
Metro Tartan/Friends/Chrysalide/Rio/Channel 4 (Judith Hunt)

Three friends from university – two white, one black – follow divergent paths in the political life of South Africa in the 1980s.
A complex film of an impossible situation and personal responses to it, although a schematic approach – the three female protagonists are an Afrikaner, a wealthy white who turns to terrorism, and a poor black – lessens its impact.
wd Elaine Proctor *ph* Dominique Chapuis *m* Rachel Portman *pd* Carmel Collins *ed* Tony Lawson
☆ Kerry Fox, Dambisa Kente, Michele Burgers, Marius Weyers, Tertius Meintjes, Dolly Rathebe, Wilma Stockenstrom

'This powerful, moving and uplifting film uses its unfailingly human story to convey its anti-apartheid message without a hint of the righteousness which so often accompanies such statements. Intelligent, affecting and thoroughly thought-provoking cinema.' – *Yvette Huddleston, Empire*

Friends and Husbands **

West Germany 1982 106m colour
Miracle/Bioskop/Les Films du Losange/Westdeutscher Rundfunk (Eberhard Junkersdorf)
original title: *Heller Wahn*

Two women engage in a friendship that destroys them both.
Slow-moving, but intense and absorbing.
wd Margarethe von Trotta *ph* Michael Ballhaus *m* Nicolas Economou *ad* Jurgen Henze, Werner Mink *ed* Dagmar Hirtz
☆ Hanna Schygulla, Angela Winklet, Peter Striebeck, Christine Fersen, Franz Buchrieser, Jochen Striebeck, Therese Affolter, Werner Eichhorn

Friends and Lovers

US 1931 67m bw
RKO (William Le Baron)

A society wife causes several hearts to flutter illicitly.
Unsatisfactory comedy-drama which lurches along from one mood to another and may have been intended as satire.
w Wallace Smith *novel* The Sphinx Has Spoken by Maurice Dekobra *d* Victor Schertzinger *ph* J. Roy Hunt *m* Victor Schertzinger, Max Steiner
☆ Adolphe Menjou, Laurence Olivier, Lili Damita, Erich von Stroheim, Hugh Herbert, Frederick Kerr, Blanche Friderici

'Dumb sentimental romance … the people never once display motives that are understandable or reasonable.' – *Variety*

The Friends of Eddie Coyle *

US 1973 102m Technicolor
Paramount (Paul Monash)

An ageing hoodlum agrees to become a police informer and is hunted down by his former associates.
Dour gangster melodrama held together by its central performance.
w Paul Monash *novel* George V. Higgins *d* Peter Yates *ph* Victor J. Kemper *m* Dave Grusin
☆ *Robert Mitchum*, Peter Boyle, Richard Jordan, Steven Keats, Mitch Ryan, Alex Rocco

'It's a grubby, violent, dangerous world. But it's the only world they know. And they're the only friends Eddie has.'

Friends of Mr Sweeney *

US 1934 68m bw
Warner

A brow-beaten reporter gets drunk, faces life, and changes his personality.
Amusing minor comedy of a kind no longer made.
w Warren Duff, Sidney Sutherland *novel* Elmer Davis *d* Edward Ludwig
☆ *Charles Ruggles*, Eugene Pallette, Berton Churchill, Robert Barrat, Ann Dvorak

'Old situations given a new comedy coating … positive all-round fun for every family.' – *Variety*

Fright

GB 1971 87m Eastmancolor
Fantale/British Lion (Harry Fine, Michael Style)

A babysitter is menaced by a psychotic.
Unattractive screamer which starts on a hysterical note and never lets up.
w Tudor Gates *d* Peter Collinson
☆ Susan George, Ian Bannen, Dennis Waterman, Honor Blackman, John Gregson, Maurice Kaufmann

Fright Night

US 1985 105m Metrocolor Panavision
Columbia/Vista (Herb Jaffe)

A vampire moves in next door to a teenage horror film buff.
Fairly agreeable mixture of modest comedy and genuine scares; but no classic.
wd Tom Holland *ph* Jan Kiesser *m* Brad Fiedel *pd* John DeCuir Jnr *ed* Kent Beyda
☆ Chris Sarandon, William Ragsdale, Amanda Bearse, Roddy McDowall

Fright Night Part 2

US 1988 104m DeLuxe Panavision
Columbia TriStar/Vista (Herb Jaffe, Mort Engelberg)

A college student is attacked by vampires.
Virtually a remake of the first film, and much less effective the second time around.
w Tim Metcalfe, Miguel Tejada-Flores, Tommy Lee Wallace *d* Tommy Lee Wallace *ph* Mark Irwin *ed* Jay Lash Cassidy, Jonathan P. Shaw, Duwayne Dunham
☆ Roddy McDowall, William Ragsdale, Traci Lin, Julie Carmen, Jonathan Gries, Russell Clark, Brian Thompson

'Strictly an identikit remake of Tom Holland's already derivative original.' – *Kim Newman, MFB*

The Frightened Bride: see *The Tall Headlines*

Frightened City: see *The Killer That Stalked New York (1950)*

Frightened City

GB 1961 98m bw
Anglo Amalgamated/Zodiac (John Lemont)

Gangsters fall out over a protection racket.
Reasonably terse racketeer melodrama rather surprisingly set in London.
w Leigh Vance *d* John Lemont *ph* Desmond Dickinson *m* Norrie Paramor
☆ Herbert Lom, Sean Connery, John Gregson, Alfred Marks, Yvonne Romain, Kenneth Griffith

The Frightened Lady

GB 1932 87m bw
Gainsborough/British Lion (Michael Balcon)
US title: *Criminal at Large*

A mad young lord is protected by his mother.
Modest chiller remade later as The Case of the Frightened Lady *(qv).*
w Angus MacPhail, Bryan Edgar Wallace *play The Case of the Frightened Lady* by Edgar Wallace *d* T. Hayes Hunter *ph* Bernard Knowles, Alex Bryce *ad* Norman Arnold *ed* Ralph Kemplen
☆ Norman McKinnel, Cathleen Nesbitt, Emlyn Williams, Gordon Harker, Belle Chrystal, Finlay Currie

The Frightened Man

GB 1952 69m bw
Eros/Tempean (Robert S. Baker, Monty Berman)

An antique dealer's ambitious plans for his son go wrong after he is sent down from university.
Crisp, competent drama, nominally a thriller but less interested in action than in the relationships between its characters.
wd John Gilling *ph* Monty Berman *m* John Lanchbery *md* Eric Robinson *ad* Andrew Mazzei *ed* Jack Slade
☆ Dermot Walsh, Barbara Murray, *Charles Victor*, John Blythe, Michael Ward, Thora Hird, Ballard Berkeley

The Frighteners *

New Zealand/US 1996 109m colour Super 35
UIP/Universal/Wingnut (Jamie Selkirk, Peter Jackson)

Accompanied by three ghosts, a dubious psychic investigator turns himself into a spirit so he can discover what evil is killing the inhabitants of a small town.
An odd horror movie that mixes jokes and shocks in a special-effects extravaganza; at its best it is unsettling, but it too often borders on the incoherent.
w Fran Walsh, Peter Jackson *d* Peter Jackson *ph* Alun Bolinger, John Blick *m* Danny Elfman *pd* Grant Major *ed* Jamie Selkirk *sp* WETA *creature & make-up design* Richard Taylor
☆ Michael J. Fox, Trini Alvarado, Peter Dobson, John Astin, Jeffrey Combs, Dee Wallace Stone

'A smart, subtle movie disguised as a dumb, noisy one … a rare horror film that gets better as it proceeds.' – *Ken Tucker, Entertainment Weekly*

'Worse than your most shocking nightmare!'

Frightmare

GB 1974 86m Eastmancolor
Miracle/Peter Walker
aka: *Frightmare II*

The daughter of a couple who were once committed to an asylum after a series of cannibalistic killings, notices that her sister and mother are beginning to behave oddly.
Dark and gruesome little shocker, aided by some chilling performances.
w David McGillivray *story* Peter Walker *d* Peter Walker *ph* Peter Jessop *m* Stanley Myers *ad* Chris Burke *ed* Robert Dearberg
☆ Rupert Davies (Edmund), Sheila Keith (Dorothy), Deborah Fairfax (Jackie), Paul Greenwood (Graham), Kim Butcher (Debbie), Fiona Curzon (Merle), Jon Yule (Robin), Trisha Mortimer (Lilian)

'The film has a distinct power out of all proportion to its subject.' – *David Pirie, MFB*

Fringe Dwellers

Australia 1986 98m colour
Virgin/Damien Nolan/Ozfilm (Sue Milliken)

Two sisters of an aboriginal family persuade their parents to move from their shantytown to a house on a new estate, where they encounter prejudice and miss the community they have left.
A sharp look at racism that avoids simple-mindedness – the young black woman at the centre of the action resents allowances being made for her, and her father is a lazy, feckless drunk – but fails to energize its subject, becoming bogged down in petty detail.
w Bruce Beresford, Rhoisin Beresford *novel* Nene Gare *d* Bruce Beresford *ph* Don McAlpine *m* George Dreyfus *pd* Herbert Pinter *ed* Tim Wellburn
☆ Justine Saunders, Kristina Nehm, Bob Maza, Kylie Belling, Ernie Dingo, Malcom Silva, Kath Walker, Denis Walker, Bill Sandy

Frisco Jenny

US 1933 73m bw
Warner

A Barbary Coast lady is prosecuted for murder by her own son.
Antediluvian melodramatic plot, borrowed from Madame X, *provides an adequate star vehicle.*
w Wilson Mizner, Robert Lord *d* William A. Wellman
☆ Ruth Chatterton, Donald Cook, Louis Calhern, J. Carrol Naish, James Murray

The Frisco Kid *

US 1935 77m bw
Warner (Samuel Bischoff)

A Shanghaied sailor rises to power among the riff raff of the Barbary Coast in the 1860s.
Fair melodrama with the star in action and (less interestingly) in love.
w Warren Duff, Seton I. Miller *d* Lloyd Bacon *ph* Sol Polito *md* Leo F. Forbstein
☆ *James Cagney*, Margaret Lindsay, Ricardo Cortez, Lili Damita, Donald Woods, Barton MacLane, George E. Stone, Addison Richards

'So similar to *Barbary Coast* as almost to be its twin … nevertheless, good entertainment.' – *Variety*

The Frisco Kid
US 1979 108m Technicolor
Warner (Howard W. Koch Jnr)

In the old west, a rabbi heading for San Francisco makes friends with an outlaw.
Unsuccessful episodic comedy, unreasonably alternating farce with sentimentality.
w Michael Elias, Frank Shaw *d* Robert Aldrich *ph* Robert B. Hauser *m* Frank de Vol
☆ Gene Wilder, Harrison Ford, Ramon Bieri, Leo Fuchs, Penny Peyser
'A very forced comedy, made all the worse by the fact that Aldrich seems to time and edit comedy as though it were a melodrama only played a little slower.' – *Richard Combs, MFB*

Frisco Lil
US 1942 62m bw
Universal
A girl law student traps a killer and clears her dad.
Formula second feature, quite adequate in its way.
w George Bricker, Michel Jacoby *d* Erle C. Kenton
☆ Irene Hervey, Kent Taylor, Minor Watson, Jerome Cowan

Frisco Sal
US 1945 63m bw
Universal
A New England girl goes to California to avenge her brother's murder.
Minor musical vehicle for a star being groomed as a rival to Deanna Durbin.
w Curt Siodmak, Gerald Geraghty *d* George Waggner
☆ Susanna Foster, Turhan Bey, Alan Curtis, Andy Devine, Thomas Gomez, Samuel S. Hinds

Frisk
US 1995 83m colour
Dangerous to Know/Strand/Industrial Eye (Marcus Hu, Jon Gerrans)
An adult homosexual acts out his youthful fantasies of killing his sexual partners.
A story of sado-masochistic lust somewhat unimaginatively filmed; had it been better, it would have probably been even less watchable.
w Jim Dwyer, George LaVoo *novel* Dennis Cooper *d* Todd Verow *ph* Greg Watkins *m* Coil et al *pd* Jennifer Graber *ed* Todd Verow
☆ Michael Gunther, Craig Chester, Parker Posey, James Lyons, Alexis Arquette, Raoul O'Connell, Jaie Laplante, Michael Stock
'Though intelligent and daring in its own right, does little to disprove the adage that great novels rarely make great films.' – *José Arroyo, Sight and Sound*

Le Frisson des Vampires (dubbed)
France 1970 90m colour
Films ABC/Filmes Modernes (Jean Rollin)

aka: *Sex and the Vampire*
aka: *The Terror of the Vampires; Vampire Thrills*
A newly married couple break their journey to stay at an ancient chateau, where a vampire errant has changed its two owners from vampire hunters into bourgeois vampires.
A ridiculous, high-camp horror, which consists mainly of actresses removing their clothes, usually to indulge in a little lesbian lovemaking. An attempt at a crepuscular atmosphere, all guttering candles and flaming torches against old stone, is not helped by a rock music soundtrack or by the trance-like acting and banal dialogue.
wd Jean Rollin *ph* Jean-Jacques Renon *m* Acanthus *ad* Michel Delesalles *ed* Olivier Gregoire
☆ Sandra Julien, Jean-Marie Durand, Jacques Robiolles, Michel Delahaye, Marie-Pierre, Kuelan Herce, Nicole Nancel, Dominique
'It combines the triteness of a typical Hammer plot with stretches of decidedly unerotic skinflick writhing, but is redeemed by Rollin's quirky descent into surrealist imagery.' – *Empire*

Fritz the Cat **
US 1971 78m DeLuxe
Fritz Productions/Aurica (Steve Krantz)

An alleycat student in New York seeks new and varied experience.
Cartoon feature which applies the old anthropomorphism to the contemporary scene, and whips up more obscenity and violence than Disney ever dreamed of. A fast-moving orgy of outrage which could never have got by in live form.
comic strip R. H. Crumb *m* Ed Bogas, Ray Shanklin *wd/animator* Ralph Bakshi
'A bitter and snarling satire that refuses to curl up in anyone's lap.' – *Bruce Williamson*

The Frog *
GB 1937 75m bw
Herbert Wilcox
The mysterious leader of a criminal organization is unmasked.
Lively old-fashioned mystery melodrama.
w Ian Hay, Gerald Elliott *novel The Fellowship of the Frog* by Edgar Wallace *d* Jack Raymond *ph* Frederick A. Young
☆ *Gordon Harker*, Carol Goodner, Noah Beery, Jack Hawkins, Richard Ainley, Esmé Percy, Felix Aylmer
'Badly directed, badly acted, it is like one of those plays produced in country towns by stranded actors. It has an old-world charm: Scotland Yard is laid up in lavender.' – *Graham Greene*
† Sequel 1938: *The Return of the Frog.*

The Frog Prince *
GB 1984 90m Eastmancolor
Warner/Goldcrest/Enigma (Iain Smith)

In Paris in the early 1960s an English girl studying at the Sorbonne decides to lose her virginity to a handsome young Frenchman.
Quietly charming, though unmemorable, romantic drama.
w Brian Gilbert, Posy Simmonds *d* Brian Gilbert *ph* Clive Tickner *m* Enya Ni Bhraonain *pd* Anton Furst *ed* Jim Clark
☆ Jane Snowden, Alexandre Sterling, Diana Blackburn, Oystein Wiik

The Frogmen
US 1951 96m bw
TCF (Samuel G. Engel)
Underwater demolition experts pave the way for the invasion of a Japanese-held island.
Standard, efficient war fare.
w John Tucker Battle *d* Lloyd Bacon *ph* Norbert Brodine *m* Cyril Mockridge
☆ Richard Widmark, Dana Andrews, Gary Merrill, Jeffrey Hunter, Warren Stevens, Robert Wagner, Harvey Lembeck
'Competent, unpretentious and free from jingoism.' – *MFB*
original story (Oscar Millard); Norbert Brodine

'Frogs lay millions and millions of eggs each year! What if they all hatched? Today the pond – tomorrow the world!'
Frogs *
US 1972 91m Movielab
AIP (George Edwards, Peter Thomas)

A remote, inhabited island in the southern States is overtaken by amphibians.
As Hitchcock might have said, the frogs is coming; instead of monsters, ordinary creepy-crawlies in their thousands devour most of the cast. Well enough done for those with strong stomachs.
w Robert Hutchison, Robert Blees *d* George McCowan *ph* Mario Tosi *m* Les Baxter
☆ Ray Milland, Joan Van Ark, Sam Elliott, Adam Roarke, Judy Pace
'One of the most remarkable and impressive onslaughts since *King Kong*.' – *David Pirie*

'A mind is a terrible thing to waste.'
From Beyond *
US 1986 85m colour
Empire (Brian Yuzna)

aka: *H. P. Lovecraft's From Beyond*
A physicist's experiment to stimulate the pineal gland and create a sixth sense summons man-eating monsters from another dimension.
Slickly directed, and extremely gory, horror that comes closer than most to recreating the nauseating, tentacled nightmares of Lovecraft's decadent imagination and an addiction to the search for forbidden knowledge.
w Dennis Paoli *story* H. P. Lovecraft, adapted by Brian Yuzna, Dennis Paoli, Stuart Gordon *d* Stuart Gordon *ph* Mac Ahlberg *m* Richard Band *pd* Giovanni Natalucci *ed* Lee Percy *sp* John Buechler, Mark Shostrom, John Naulin, Anthony Doublin
☆ Jeffrey Combs, Barbara Crampton, Ken Foree, Ted Sorel, Carolyn Purdy-Gordon, Bunny Summers, Bruce McGuire

From Beyond the Grave *
GB 1973 98m Technicolor
Warner/Amicus (Milton Subotsky)

The proprietor of an East End antique shop involves his customers in horrific situations.
Reasonably lively portmanteau of tall tales from a familiar stable.
w Robin Clarke, Raymond Christodoulou *stories* R. Chetwynd-Hayes *d* Kevin Connor *ph* Alan Hume *m* David Gamley *pd* Maurice Carter
☆ David Warner, Donald Pleasence, Ian Bannen, Diana Dors, Margaret Leighton, Ian Carmichael, Nyree Dawn Porter, Ian Ogilvy

From Dusk till Dawn *
US 1995 198m Technicolor
Dimension/Los Hooligans/A Band Apart (Gianni Nunnari, Meir Teper)

Two ruthless robbers take a preacher and his children hostage and drive with them to Mexico, where they stumble into a den of vampires.
Extraordinarily gory horror that begins, and might have been better advised to have continued, as a tense, hyper-kinetic thriller; even so, it has a power and energy that put it a cut above most movies of its kind.
w Quentin Tarantino *story* Robert Kurtzman *d* Robert Rodriguez *ph* Guillermo Navarro *m* Graeme Revell *pd* Cecilia Montiel *ed* Robert Rodriguez *make-up fx* Kurtzman, Nicotero & Berger EFX
☆ Harvey Keitel, George Clooney, Quentin Tarantino, Juliette Lewis, Salma Hayek, Brenda Hillhouse, Marc Lawrence, Cheech Marin, Michael Parks, Kelly Preston, Fred Williamson, John Saxon, Tom Savini, Ernest Liu
'Pure juvenilia that should have remained true to its origins as a straight-to-video low-budget project.' – *Lizzie Franke, Sight and Sound*

'You Think You Know Terror But You Don't Know Jack.'
'Only the legend will survive.'
From Hell *
US 2001 121m DeLuxe Panavision
TCF/Underworld (Don Murphy, Jane Hamsher)

In London in the 1880s, a psychic, drug-addicted police inspector discovers that the serial killer known as Jack the Ripper has royal connections.
Lurid melodrama, in which London becomes a city of myth and occult forces; it never quite convinces and much of the narrative will seem familiar to those who saw the 1978 Sherlock Holmes mystery Murder By Decree.
w Terry Hayes, Rafael Yglesias *graphic novel* Alan Moore, Eddie Campbell *d* Allen Hughes, Albert Hughes *ph* Peter Deming *m* Trevor Jones *pd* Martin Childs *ed* Dan Lebental, George Bowers *cos* Kym Barrett
☆ Johnny Depp (Insp. Fred Abberline), Heather Graham (Mary Kelly), Ian Holm (Sir William Gull), Robbie Coltrane (Sgt Peter Godley), Ian Richardson (Sir Charles Warren), Jason Flemyng (Netley), Katrin Cartlidge ('Dark Annie' Chapman), Terence Harvey (Ben Kidney), Susan Lynch (Liz Stride), Lesley Sharp (Kate Eddowes), Annabelle Apsion (Polly)
'Extraordinarily violent, in addition to being one of the most breathtaking leaps of directing skills I've seen in years.' – *Elvis Mitchell, New York Times*
'For the most part this is an engrossing, hard-hitting, consistently well-acted picture.' – *Philip French, Observer*

From Hell It Came
US 1957 71m bw
Milner Brothers/Allied Artists
An executed native of Kalai returns to life in the form of a vengeful tree stump.
Absolute rubbish, just about worth sitting through for the unintentional laughs.
w Richard Bernstein *d* Dan Milner *ph* Brydon Baker
☆ Tod Andrews, Tina Carver, Linda Watkins

From Hell to Heaven
US 1933 67m bw
Paramount
Stories of a racetrack hotel.
Very minor Grand Hotel, *neatly made for its time.*
w Percy Heath, Sidney Buchman *story* Lawrence Hazard *d* Erle C. Kenton
☆ Carole Lombard, Jack Oakie, Sidney Blackmer, Adrienne Ames, David Manners

From Hell to Texas
US 1958 100m Eastmancolor
Cinemascope
TCF (Robert Buckner)
GB title: *Manhunt*
After accidentally killing a man, a cowboy is vengefully pursued by the victim's father.
Competent chase Western with a stand against violence.
w Robert Buckner, Wendell Mayes *d* Henry Hathaway *ph* Wilfrid Cline *m* Daniele Amfitheatrof
☆ Don Murray, Diane Varsi, Chill Wills, Dennis Hopper, R. G. Armstrong, Margo, Jay C. Flippen

'The Boldest Book Of Our Time ... Honestly, Fearlessly On The Screen!'
From Here to Eternity ***
US 1953 118m bw
Columbia (Buddy Adler)

Life in a Honolulu barracks at the time of Pearl Harbor.
Cleaned up and streamlined version of a bestseller in which the mainly sexual frustrations of a number of unattractive characters are laid bare. As a production, it is Hollywood in good form, and certainly took the public fancy as well as establishing Sinatra as an acting force.
w Daniel Taradash *novel* James Jones *d* Fred Zinnemann *ph* Burnett Guffey *m* George Duning *ed* William Lyon
☆ Burt Lancaster, Deborah Kerr, *Frank Sinatra*, Donna Reed, Ernest Borgnine, Montgomery Clift, Philip Ober, Mickey Shaughnessy
'This is not a theme which one would expect Zinnemann to approach in the hopeful, sympathetic mood of his earlier films; but neither could one expect the negative shrug of indifference with which he seems to have surrendered to its hysteria.' – *Karel Reisz, Sight and Sound*
† The story was remade for TV in 1979 as a six-hour mini-series.
†† Frank Sinatra got his key role after Eli Wallach dropped out.
best picture; Daniel Taradash; Fred Zinnemann; Burnett Guffey; Frank Sinatra; Donna Reed; William Lyon
George Duning; Burt Lancaster; Deborah Kerr; Montgomery Clift

From Hollywood to Deadwood *
US 1988 102m DuArt
Island/Night Film (Jo Peterson)

Two impecunious tough-talking private detectives are hired by a Hollywood production company to find an actress who has gone missing.
Entertaining dark-toned thriller in a pulp fiction style, with hard-boiled private eyes cracking wise when they are not being set up.
wd Rex Pickett *ph* Peter Deming *m* Alex Gibson, Gregory Kuehn *ad* Tori Nourafchan *ed* Steve Adrianson, Robert Erickson
☆ Scott Paulin, Jim Haynie, Barbara Schock, Chris Mulkey, Jurgen Doeres, Michael Genovese, Norbert Weisser, Tom Dahlgren, Campbell Scott

From Noon Till Three
US 1976 99m DeLuxe
UA/Frankovich-Self

A bank robber becomes a local legend when he interrupts a raid to dally with an attractive widow. Later, when someone else is shot in mistake for him, he is reduced to penury, unable to prove his identity or live up to his own legend.
Curious, shapeless, lumpy Western satire, difficult to synopsize or analyse. Despite effort all round, it's just plain unsatisfactory.
wd Frank D. Gilroy *novel* Frank D. Gilroy *ph* Lucien Ballard *m* Elmer Bernstein
☆ Charles Bronson, Jill Ireland, Douglas Fowley, Stan Haze, Damon Douglas

'It squanders its early sparkle for a pot of message.' – *Michael Billington, Illustrated London News*
'The main thing – hell, the only thing – worth noting about *From Noon Till Three* is that it is profoundly weird, which is not quite the same thing as being good.' – *Frank Rich, New York Post*

From Russia with Love ***
GB 1963 118m Technicolor
UA/Eon (Harry Saltzman, Albert Broccoli)
A Russian spy joins an international crime organization and develops a plan to kill James Bond and steal a coding machine.
The second Bond adventure and possibly the best, with Istanbul and Venice for backdrops and climaxes involving a speeding train and a helicopter. Arrant nonsense with tongue in cheek, on a big budget.
w Richard Maibaum, Johanna Harwood *novel* Ian Fleming *d* Terence Young *ph* Ted Moore *m* John Barry *titles* Robert Brownjohn
☆ *Sean Connery, Robert Shaw, Pedro Armendariz,* Daniela Bianchi, *Lotte Lenya,* Bernard Lee, Eunice Gayson, Lois Maxwell
Ted Moore

From Soup to Nuts *
US 1928 20m bw silent
Hal Roach
Two temporary waiters wreck a dinner party.
Very funny slapstick which the stars subsequently reworked into A Chump at Oxford.
w H. M. Walker *story* Leo McCarey *d* Edgar Kennedy *ph* Len Powers *ed* Richard Currier
☆ Laurel and Hardy, Anita Garvin, Tiny Sandford

From the Earth to the Moon
US 1958 100m Technicolor
Waverley (Benedict Bogeaus)
In the 1880s an armaments millionaire finances a trip to the moon in a projectile fired by his own invention.
Cardboard science fiction, with an imposing cast at sea in an unspeakable script and an unseaworthy production.
w Robert Blees, James Leicester *novel* Jules Verne *d* Byron Haskin *ph* Edwin DuPar *m* Louis Forbes *ad* Hal Wilson Cox
☆ Joseph Cotten, George Sanders, Henry Daniell, Carl Esmond, Melville Cooper, Don Dubbins, Debra Paget, Patric Knowles

From the Edge of the City: see *Apo Tin Akri Tis Polis*

From the Hip
US 1987 112m Technicolor J-D-C Scope
De Laurentiis Entertainment Group/Indian Neck (René Dupont, Bob Clark)
An ambitious and unscrupulous young lawyer defends an academic accused of murder.
An unfortunate mix of courtroom drama and romantic comedy that fails on all levels.
w David E. Kelley, Bob Clark *d* Bob Clark *ph* Dante Spinotti *m* Paul Zaza *pd* Michael Stringer *ed* Stan Cole
☆ Judd Nelson, Elizabeth Perkins, John Hurt, Darren McGavin, Dan Monahan, David Alan Grier, Ray Walston

From the Life of Marionettes: see *Aus Dem Leben Der Marionetten*

From the Mixed-Up Files of Mrs Basil E. Frankweiler
US 1973 105m colour
Cinema 5
Two children hide out in New York's Metropolitan Museum of Art and befriend a rich woman.
An unusual idea makes ho-hum entertainment for well-brought-up children.
w Blanche Hanalis *novel* E. L. Konigsberg *d* Fielder Cook *ph* Victor J. Kemper *m* Donald Devor
☆ Ingrid Bergman, Sally Prager, Johnny Doran, George Rose, Richard Mulligan

From The Pole to The Equator *
W. Germany/Italy 1986 96m bw/colour
ZDF (Gianikian & Ricci Lucchi)
original title: *Dal Polo all'Equatore*
Deteriorating documentary footage, taken in the early 1900s by a forgotten pioneer, the much-travelled Luca Comerio (died 1940), was rescued, reprinted, tinted, speeded up and slowed down to recreate a psychedelic vision of the past.
A curiosity, a silent film, with electronic musical accompaniment, of images from another age; they flicker, fade and disintegrate as you watch, though the memories they contain are often less than nostalgic. Yesterday has seldom seemed so remote.
wd Gianikian & Ricci Lucchi *ph* Luca Comerio *m* Keith Ullrich, Charles Anderson

From the Terrace
US 1960 144m DeLuxe Cinemascope
TCF/Linebrook (Mark Robson)
Life among Pennsylvania's idle rich.
Heavy-going family melodrama from a bestseller peopled with boorish characters.
w Ernest Lehman *novel* John O'Hara *d* Mark Robson *ph* Leo Tover *m* Elmer Bernstein
☆ Paul Newman, Joanne Woodward, Myrna Loy, Ina Balin, Leon Ames, Felix Aylmer, George Grizzard, Patrick O'Neal, Elizabeth Allen

From This Day Forward ***
US 1946 95m bw
RKO (William L. Pereira)
After World War II, a New York couple think back to their early years in the poverty-stricken thirties.
Effective sentimental realism coupled with Hollywood professionalism made this film more memorable than it may sound.
w Hugo Butler, Garson Kanin *novel* All Brides Are Beautiful by Thomas Bell *d* John Berry *ph* George Barnes *m* Leigh Harline
☆ Joan Fontaine, Mark Stevens, Rosemary de Camp, Henry Morgan, Wally Brown, Arline Judge, Bobby Driscoll, Mary Treen
'Distinguished from the usual film about Young Love and Young Marriage by irony, poetry and realism.' – *Richard Winnington*

The Front *
US 1976 95m Metrocolor
Columbia/Persky-Bright, Devon (Martin Ritt, Charles H. Joffe)
For a small commission, a bookmaker puts his name to scripts by blacklisted writers.
Rather bland satire on the communist witch hunts of the fifties; interesting, but neither funny nor incisive enough.
w Walter Bernstein *d* Martin Ritt *ph* Michael Chapman *m* Dave Grusin
☆ Woody Allen, Zero Mostel, Herschel Bernardi, Michael Murphy, Andrea Marcovicci, Lloyd Gough
'The pacing is off, the sequences don't flow, and the film seems sterile, unpopulated and flat.' – *New Yorker*
'A light comedy forged out of dark and authentic pain.' – *Frank Rich, New York Post*
'It catches the anguish of America's creative community with wit and feeling.' – *Sunday Express*
Walter Bernstein

The Front Page ***
US 1931 101m bw
Howard Hughes
A Chicago reporter wants to retire and marry, but is tricked by his scheming editor into covering one last case.
Brilliant early talkie perfectly transferring into screen terms a stage classic of the twenties. Superficially a shade primitive now, its essential power remains.
w Bartlett Cormack, Charles Lederer *play* Charles MacArthur, Ben Hecht *d* Lewis Milestone *ph* Glen MacWilliams
☆ *Adolphe Menjou* (Walter Burns), *Pat O'Brien* (Hildy Johnson), Mary Brian (Peggy), Edward Everett Horton (Bensinger), Walter Catlett (Murphy), George E. Stone (Earl Williams), Mae Clarke (Molly), Slim Summerville (Pincus), Matt Moore (Kruger), Frank McHugh (McCue)
'Sure money-getter … it will universally entertain and please.' – *Variety*
'The most riproaring movie that ever came out of Hollywood.' – *Pare Lorentz*
'It excelled most of the films of its day by sheer treatment. The speedy delivery of lines and business and the re-emphasis upon cutting as a prime structural element made the film a model of mobility for confused directors who did not know yet how to handle sound.' – *Lewis Jacobs, The Rise of the American Film*
† Remade in 1940 as *His Girl Friday* (qv) and in 1988 as *Switching Channels* (qv). And see below.
best picture; Lewis Milestone; Adolphe Menjou

'It's the hottest story since the Chicago fire … and they're sitting on it.'
The Front Page **
US 1974 105m Technicolor Panavision
U-I (Paul Monash)
Disappointing Billy Wilder remake, relying overmuch on bad language and farcical intrusions, while tending to jettison the plot in the latter half. Some laughs nevertheless.
w Billy Wilder, I. A. L. Diamond *d* Billy Wilder *ph* Jordan S. Cronenweth *m* Billy May *ad* Henry Bumstead *ed* Ralph E. Winters
☆ *Walter Matthau* (Walter Burns), Jack Lemmon (Hildy Johnson), Susan Sarandon (Peggy Grant), *David Wayne* (Bensinger), Carol Burnett (Mollie Malloy), Vincent Gardenia (Sheriff), Allen Garfield (Kruger), Herb Edelman (Schwartz), Charles Durning (Murphy), *Austin Pendleton* (Earl Williams)
'The signs of coarsening in Wilder's comedy technique are unmistakable.' – *MFB*
'I can't think of a better tonic for the winter glooms.' – *Michael Billington, Illustrated London News*

Front Page Story *
GB 1953 99m bw
British Lion/Jay Lewis
A day in the life of a Fleet Street newspaper, when the editor is torn between several big stories and nearly loses his wife.
Dogged 'slice of life' drama with few excitements but some incidental entertainment and a production of routine competence.
w Jay Lewis, Jack Howells *novel* Final Night by Robert Gaines *d* Gordon Parry *ph* Gilbert Taylor *m* Jackie Brown
☆ Jack Hawkins, Elizabeth Allan, Derek Farr, Michael Goodliffe, Martin Miller

Front Page Woman **
US 1935 82m bw
Warner (Samuel Bischoff)
Rival reporters try to outshine each other.
Lively comedy-melodrama very typical of its style and time.
w Laird Doyle, Lillie Hayward, Roy Chanslor *d* Michael Curtiz *ph* Tony Gaudio *m* Heinz Roemheld *md* Leo Forbstein
☆ *Bette Davis, George Brent,* Roscoe Karns, Wini Shaw, J. Carrol Naish, Walter Walker
'Completely screwy but will get fair b.o.' – *Variety*
'A swift-moving, unsensational, unsentimental, honest piece of cynicism which is really good value for money.' – *MFB*

La Frontera *
Chile/Spain 1991 115m colour
Metro Tartan/Cine XXI (Eduardo Larrain S., Ricardo Larrain P.)
Because of his outspokenness, a Santiago schoolteacher is exiled to a remote seaside town in the mid-80s.
An interesting look back at Chile's recent political past from a left-wing standpoint; it was a big hit in Chile, but is unlikley to mean as much outside the country, other than as an indication of a revitalized cinema.
w Jorge Goldenberg, Ricardo Larrain *d* Ricardo Larrain *ph* Hector Rios *m* Jaime de Aguirre *ad* Juan Carlos Castillo *ed* Claudio Martinez
☆ Patricio Contreras, Gloria Laso, Hector Noguera, Alonso Venegas, Aldo Bernales, Patricio Bunster
'Despite the extraordinary wild scenery and unhistrionic performances, the movie tends to get bogged down in its melancholy mood and ends up rather cheerless and dull.' – *Caroline Rees, Empire*

Frontier: see *Aerograd*

Frontier Badmen
US 1943 74m bw
Ford Beebe Universal
Texas ranchers try to break a cattle-buying monopoly.
The good guys and the bad guys at it again, with fair results.
w Gerald Geraghty, Morgan B. Cox *d* William McGann
☆ Robert Paige, Anne Gwynne, Lon Chaney Jnr, Noah Beery Jnr, Diana Barrymore, Leo Carrillo, Andy Devine, Thomas Gomez, William Farnum

Frontier Gal
US 1945 84m Technicolor
Universal (Michael Fessier, Ernest Pagano)
GB title: *The Bride Wasn't Willing*
An outlaw weds a saloon girl at pistol point; emerging five years later from prison, he finds he has a daughter.
Rambling Western with some pretensions to humour and sentiment; not a success, but it established de Carlo as a star.
w Michael Fessier, Ernest Pagano *d* Charles Lamont *ph* George Robinson, Charles Boyle *m* Frank Skinner
☆ Yvonne de Carlo, Rod Cameron, Sheldon Leonard, Andy Devine, Fuzzy Knight, Andrew Tombes, Clara Blandick

Frontier Marshal *
US 1933 66m bw
Fox
A marshal cleans up Tombstone.
Interesting trial run for the 1939 film, which was subsequently done over as My Darling Clementine.
w William Conselman, Stuart Anthony *book* Stuart N. Lake *d* Lewis Seiler
☆ George O'Brien, Irene Bentley, George E. Stone, Ruth Gillette.
† For legal reasons in this version the marshal is called Michael Wyatt instead of Wyatt Earp.

Frontier Marshal *
US 1939 70m bw
TCF (Sol M. Wurtzel)
Wyatt Earp cleans up Tombstone.
Simple-minded, pleasing Western, later worked over by Ford as My Darling Clementine.
w Sam Hellman *book* Stuart N. Lake *d* Allan Dwan *ph* Charles Clarke *m* Samuel Kaylin
☆ Randolph Scott, Nancy Kelly, Cesar Romero (Doc Holliday), Binnie Barnes, John Carradine, Joe Sawyer, Lon Chaney Jnr, Ward Bond, Edward Norris, Eddie Foy Jnr
'Strong programme western, in-betweener for key duals, but a top biller in subsequents.' – *Variety*
† Eddie Foy Jnr appeared as his father, who historically did perform in Tombstone at the time. The equivalent in *My Darling Clementine* was the Shakespearean actor played by Alan Mowbray.

Frou Frou: see *The Toy Wife*

'At First Family Sperm Bank, she banks on babies, he banks on bucks.'
Frozen Assets
US 1992 93m Eastmancolor
RKO (Don Klein)
A financial expert takes a job in a small town and discovers that he's expected to run a sperm bank.
A coy and extremely predictable comedy that treats its subject-matter with sniggers.
w Don Klein, Tom Kartozian *d* George Miller *ph* Ron Lautore, Geza Sinkovics *m* Michael Tavera *pd* Dorian Vernacchio *ed* Larry Bock
☆ Shelley Long, Corbin Bernsen, Larry Miller, Dody Goodman, Matt Clark, Jeanne Cooper, Paul Sand, Gloria Camden, Teri Copley
'Yet another waste of the talents of Shelley Long, but she's the film's one real asset.' – *Variety*
† It was released direct to video in Britain.

The Frozen Dead
GB 1966 95m Eastmancolor
Goldstar/Seven Arts
In an English laboratory, a scientist is trying to revive the frozen corpses of Nazi leaders.

Flatfooted horror piece providing very little of interest to pass the time.
wd Herbert J. Leder
☆ Dana Andrews, Anna Palk, Philip Gilbert, Karel Stepanek, Kathleen Breck

The Frozen Ghost *
US 1945 61m bw
Universal
When a drunk dies while under his influence, a hypnotist fears he has the will and power to kill.
Absurdly titled and insufficiently vigorous entry in the Inner Sanctum *series.*
w Bernard Schubert, Luci Ward d Harold Young
☆ Lon Chaney Jnr, Evelyn Ankers, Martin Kosleck, Milburn Stone, Tala Birell, Douglass Dumbrille

The Frozen Limits *
GB 1939 84m bw
Gainsborough (Edward Black)
Six impecunious comedians hear of the Yukon gold rush, and join it ... forty years too late.
The Crazy Gang not quite at its best, but working hard, with a few hilarious moments and a special assist from Moore Marriott.
w Marriott Edgar, Val Guest, J. O. C. Orton d Marcel Varnel ph Arthur Crabtree md Louis Levy ad Vetchinsky ed R. E. Dearing, Alfred Roome
☆ Bud Flanagan, Chesney Allen, Jimmy Nervo, Teddy Knox, Charlie Naughton, Jimmy Gold, Moore Marriott, Eileen Bell, Anthony Hulme, Bernard Lee, Eric Clavering
'The funniest English picture yet produced ... it can bear comparison with *Safety Last* and *The General*.' – *Graham Greene*

Frühlingssinfonie: see *Spring Symphony*

Le Fruit Défendu: see *Forbidden Fruit*

The Fruit Machine
GB 1988 103m colour
Vestron/Granada/Ideal (Steve Morrison)
Two mixed-up teenagers run away after witnessing a murder.
Unsuccessful mixture of fantasy and thriller.
w Frank Clarke d Philip Saville ph Dick Pope m Hans Zimmer pd David Brockhurst ed Richard Bedford
☆ Emile Charles, Tony Forsyth, Robert Stephens, Clare Higgins, Bruce Payne, Robbie Coltrane, Kim Christie, Julie Graham

Fu Manchu
The Yellow Peril, or evil Oriental master criminal, was created by Sax Rohmer in a 1911 novel, which led to 13 more plus some short stories.
A long series of British two-reelers was made in the twenties, and talking films are as follows:
1929 The Mysterious Dr Fu Manchu, with Warner Oland (Paramount)
1930 The Return of Dr Fu Manchu (ditto)
1931 Daughter of the Dragon (ditto)
1932 The Mask of Fu Manchu (qv) with Boris Karloff (MGM)
1939 Drums of Fu Manchu, with Henry Brandon (Republic serial)
The following are British productions by Harry Alan Towers, with Christopher Lee:
1965 The Face of Fu Manchu (qv)
1966 Brides of Fu Manchu (qv)
1968 The Vengeance of Fu Manchu (qv)
1969 Sax Rohmer's The Blood of Fu Manchu (qv)
1970 The Castle of Fu Manchu (qv)
A feeble spoof, starring Peter Sellers, effectively killed off the character:
1979 Fiendish Plot of Fu Manchu (qv)

Fu Manchu and the Kiss of Death: see *Sax Rohmer's The Blood of Fu Manchu*

Fucking Amal **
Sweden/Denmark 1998 89m colour
Alliance/Memfis (Lars Jönsson)
aka: *Show Me Love*
In a dull Swedish suburb of Amal, an unhappy 16-year-old has a secret crush on her school's most popular girl.
Gentle, believable story of adolescent ennui and trauma which retains its interest despite its lack of action.
wd Lukas Moodysson ph Ulf Brantas ad Lina Strand, Heidi Saikkonen ed Michal Leszczylowski, Bernhard Winkler
☆ Alexandra Dahlström (Elin), Rebecca Liljeberg (Agnes Ahlberg), Mathias Rust (Johan Hult), Erica Carlson (Jessica), Stefan Hörberg (Markus), Josefin Nyberg (Viktoria), Ralph Carlsson (Olof), Maria Hedborg (Karin), Axel Widegren (Oskar), Jill Ung (Birgitta)
'I've never been so moved by the loneliness of growing pains.' – *James Christopher, Times*
'I urge everyone who likes good film-making to go and see this film.' – *Mike Figgis*

Fuddy Duddy Buddy **
US 1952 7m Technicolor
UPA
Mr Magoo mistakes a walrus for his friend the colonel.
Top drawer Magoo adventure climaxing with the celebrated line: 'I don't care if he is a walrus. I like him. I like him!'
wd John Hubley m William Lava

The Fugitive: see *On the Night of the Fire (1939)*

The Fugitive *
US 1947 104m bw
Argosy (Merian C. Cooper, John Ford)
In an anti-clerical country, a priest is on the run.
Ford's attempt to do a Mexican Informer *is slow and rather boring, but the pictures are nice to look at even though the original novel has been totally emasculated.*
w Dudley Nichols novel *The Power and the Glory* by Graham Greene d John Ford ph Gabriel Figueroa m Richard Hageman ad Alfred Ybarra ed Jack Murray
☆ Henry Fonda, Dolores del Rio, Pedro Armendariz, J. Carrol Naish, Leo Carrillo, Ward Bond, Robert Armstrong, John Qualen
'A symphony of light and shade, of deafening din and silence, of sweeping movement and repose.' – *Bosley Crowther*
'The most pretentious travesty of a literary work since *For Whom the Bell Tolls*.' – *Richard Winnington*

'A murdered wife. A one-armed man. An obsessed detective. The chase begins.'
The Fugitive ***
US 1993 127m Technicolor
Warner (Keith Barish, Arnold Kopelson)
A surgeon, unjustly accused of his wife's murder, goes on the run to find the real killer, while being hunted by a ruthless cop.
Tense and exciting thriller that sticks closely to the plot of the original television series and, despite its many improbabilities, remains compulsively watchable.
w Jeb Stuart, David Twohy story David Twohy *based on characters created by* Roy Huggins *(for the TV series)* d *Andrew Davis* ph Michael Chapman m James Newton Howard pd Dennis Washington ed Dennis Virkler, David Finfer, Dean Goodhill, Don Brochu, Richard Nord, Dov Hoenig
☆ Harrison Ford, *Tommy Lee Jones*, Sela Ward, Joe Pantoliano, Jeroen Krabbé, Andreas Katsulas, Julianne Moore
'A consummate nail-biter that never flags, it leaves you breathless from the chase yet anxious for the next bit of mayhem or clever plot twist.' – *Variety*
'A remarkably successful Hollywood product, with a brilliantly contrived star double act pursuing different paths through the central plot.' – *Kim Newman, Sight and Sound*
† The TV series ran from 1963 to 1967 and starred David Janssen.
Tommy Lee Jones
best picture; Michael Chapman; James Newton Howard; editing; sound; sound effects editing

The Fugitive Kind
US 1960 121m bw
UA/Martin Jurow/Richard A. Shepherd/Pennebaker
A Mississippi drifter in a small strange town runs into trouble with women.
Doom-laden melodrama, almost a parody of the author's works, full of cancer patients, nympho-dipsos, and cemetery seductions; we are however spared the final castration.
w Tennessee Williams, Meade Roberts play *Orpheus Descending* by Tennessee Williams d Sidney Lumet ph Boris Kaufman m Kenyon Hopkins pd Richard Sylbert
☆ Marlon Brando, Anna Magnani, Joanne Woodward, Victor Jory, Maureen Stapleton, R. G. Armstrong
'A series of mythological engravings, determined by a literary text and a lurid concept of hell on earth.' – *Peter John Dyer*
'Sidney Lumet is usually clever at least part of the time – an acquisitive magpie who has picked up, along with the selly trash, a few small gems. This time he brings us nothing but bits of coloured glass.' – *Stanley Kauffmann*

Fugitive Lovers
US 1934 74m bw
MGM
A convict escapes on a transcontinental bus.
Unsatisfactory comedy drama with a miscast star; chiefly interesting for showing the form of travel, but It Happened One Night *did it better in the following year.*
w Ferdinand Reyher, Frank Wead d Richard Boleslawski
☆ Robert Montgomery, Madge Evans, Ted Healy and the Three Stooges, Nat Pendleton, C. Henry Gordon
'Acceptable for lesser houses but not de luxe quality.' – *Variety*

Full Circle
GB/Canada 1976 97m Eastmancolor
Paramount/Fetter-Classic (Peter Fetterman, Alfred Parisier)
After the death of her small daughter, a woman leaves home to live in an old house which is haunted by the malevolent spirit of another dead child.
Unpleasant and incompetent supernatural nonsense, seeking a niche somewhere between Don't Look Now *and* The Exorcist.
w Dave Humphries novel *Julia* by Peter Straub d Richard Loncraine ph Peter Hannan m Colin Towns
☆ Mia Farrow, Keir Dullea, Tom Conti, Jill Bennett, Robin Gammell, Cathleen Nesbitt, Mary Morris, Edward Hardwicke

Full Confession
US 1939 73m bw
RKO
A priest bound by the sanctity of confession urges a murderer to give himself up.
Neat little melodrama with a plot much copied subsequently.
wd John Farrow
☆ Victor McLaglen, Barry Fitzgerald, Sally Eilers, Joseph Calleia
'Rather interesting, but not strong enough for the upper bracket.' – *Variety*

Full Contact
Hong Kong 1992 97m colour
Made in Hong Kong/Golden Princess (Ringo Lam)
original title: *Xia Dao Gao Fei*
Two friends fall out over guns and the wife of one of them.
Violent, action-packed drama of revenge of a familiar kind.
w Nam Yin d Ringo Lam ph Lau Hung Chun, Joe Chan m Teddy Robin Kwan ad Ray Lam ed Tony Chow
☆ Chow Yun-Fat, Simon Yam, Ann Bridgewater, Anthony Wong, Bonnie Fu, Lee Kin-Sang, Frankie Chin
'The movie is such a catalogue of inventively inflicted bodily harm and casual sordid behaviour, it's almost like watching a sustained piece of Theatre of Cruelty.' – *David Tse, Sight and Sound*

A Full Day's Work *
France 1973 90m Eastmancolor
President/Cinetel/Euro International (Jacques-Eric Strauss)
original title: *Une Journée Bien Remplie*
A baker sets out to kill in one day the jurors who found his son guilty of murder.
Mildly amusing black comedy, though it is too self-conscious for its own good.
wd Jean-Louis Trintignant ph William Lubtchansky m Bruno Nicolai ed Nicole Lubtchansky
☆ Jacques Dufilho, Luce Marquand, Denise Peron, Antoine Marin, Jacques Doniol-Valcroze, Vittorio Caprioli

Full Eclipse
US 1993 93m colour
HBO/Citadel (Peter Abrams, Robert L. Levy)
A detective discovers that an élite group of cops, concerned about 'animals ruling the streets', become werewolves in order to deal with them outside the law.
Daft thriller that begins as if the director had overdosed on John Woo's shoot-outs and then becomes like any other cheap horror movie.
w Richard Christian Matheson, Michael Reaves d Anthony Hickox ph Sandi Sissel m Gary Chang pd Gregory Melton ed Peter Amundson sp make-up effects: Alterian Studios
☆ Mario Van Peebles, Patsy Kensit, Anthony John Denison, Jason Beghe, Paula Marshall, John Verea, Dean Norris, Willie C. Carpenter, Bruce Payne
'Daft but pleasurable.' – *Sight and Sound*

Full House: see *O. Henry's Full House*

'In Vietnam The Wind Doesn't Blow. It Sucks.'
Full Metal Jacket **
GB 1987 116m Rank Colour
Warner/Stanley Kubrick
After rigorous training, US marines land in Vietnam.
Smartly ordered but rather ordinary and predictable war film to come from one of the cinema's acknowledged masters after seven years of silence.
w Stanley Kubrick, Michael Herr, Gustav Hasford novel *The Short Timers* by Gustav Hasford d *Stanley Kubrick* ph Douglas Milsome m Abigail Mead pd Anton Furst
☆ Matthew Modine, Adam Baldwin, Vincent D'Onofrio, R. Lee Ermey, Dorian Harewood, Arliss Howard
best adapted screenplay

'The year's most revealing comedy.'
The Full Monty ***
GB/US 1997 91m Metrocolor
TCF/Redwave (Uberto Pasolini)
A group of unemployed Sheffield steelworkers decide to become male strippers in order to raise some money.
Clever, enjoyable comedy about salvaging self-respect and baring all, emotionally as well as physically; it struck a chord not only in Britain, but around the world.
w *Simon Beaufoy* d *Peter Cattaneo* ph John de Borman m *Anne Dudley* pd Max Gottlieb ed David Freeman, Nick More
☆ Robert Carlyle (Gaz), Tom Wilkinson (Gerald), Mark Addy (Dave), Lesley Sharp (Jean), Emily Woof (Mandy), Steve Huison (Lomper), Paul Barber (Horse), Hugo Speer (Guy), Deirdre Costello
'The particular magic of the film is the way in which it draws credible characters in a recognizable setting but elevates them and their story into crowd-pleasing fare without losing sight of the big social picture.' – *Derek Elley, Variety*
'The fault of the film is not that it deals in wishful thinking but that its style of wishful thinking – assertive, benignly narcissistic, dedicated to overcoming fear – is imported, a graft job. The people in the film would be much more likely to see success as a form of class betrayal and defeat than as a badge of solidarity.' – *Adam Mars-Jones, Independent*
† The film cost $3.5m and grossed $35m in the US, and another $132m elsewhere. It was, briefly, the biggest-grossing film at the British box-office, and is now second only to *Titantic*.
†† Two origins are given for the title phrase. 'Monty' was the nickname given to Field Marshal Montgomery. The Full Monty is either slang to describe the three-piece suits provided to soldiers on demobilization at the end of the Second World War, or to the Field Marshal's insistence on being served with a full English breakfast on the battlefield.
††† The story was turned into a Broadway musical, with the action relocated to Buffalo, N.Y., in 2000.

Anne Dudley
picture; Peter Cattaneo; Simon Beaufoy
film; Robert Carlyle; Tom Wilkinson

Full Moon High
US 1981 94m colour
Filmways/Larco (Larry Cohen)
After a visit to Romania, a high-school student turns into a werewolf and ceases to age.
Tame and trivial teen comedy.
wd Larry Cohen *ph* Daniel Pearl *m* Gary William Friedman *ad* Robert Burns *ed* Armond Lebowitz
☆ Adam Arkin, Roz Kelly, Ed McMahon, Joanne Nail, Elizabeth Hartman, Louis Nye, Kenneth Mars, Alan Arkin, Tom Aldredge, Pat Morita

Full Moon in Blue Water
US 1988 95m Technicolor
Entertainment/Trans World Entertainment (Lawrence Turman, David Foster, John Turman)
A Texan restaurateur foils plans by property developers to buy his diner.
Weak and sentimental comedy, resembling a TV sitcom.
w Bill Bozzone *d* Peter Masterson *ph* Fred Murphy *m* Phil Marshall *ed* Jill Savitt
☆ Gene Hackman, Teri Garr, Burgess Meredith, Elias Koteas, Kevin Cooney, David Doty, Gil Glasgow, Becky Gelke, Marietta Marich, Lexie Masterson
'A comedy as soft-centred as they come ... just about insufferable' – *MFB*

Full Moon in Paris *
France 1984 102m colour
original title: *Les Nuits de la Pleine Lune*
Striving for independence, a girl divides her time between her boyfriend in the suburbs and a flat in Paris.
One of Rohmer's talkier Comedies and Proverbs, taking as its epigraph 'He who has two women loses his soul. He who has two houses loses his mind.'
w Eric Rohmer *ph* Renato Berta *m* Elli and Janco *ed* Cecile Decugis
☆ Pascale Ogier, Tcheky Karyo, Fabrice Luchini, Virginie Thevenet, Christian Vadim, Laszlo Szabo

Full of Life *
US 1956 91m bw
Columbia (Fred Kohlmar)
A poor New York/Italian couple expect a baby.
Domestic comedy drama with good scenes but fatally uncertain mood.
w John Fante *novel* John Fante *d* Richard Quine *ph* Charles Lawton Jnr *m* George Duning
☆ Judy Holliday, Richard Conte, Esther Minciotti, Salvatore Baccaloni

'A new experience in screen suspense!'
The Full Treatment
GB 1960 109m bw Megascope
Columbia/Hilary/Falcon (Val Guest)
US title: *Stop Me Before I Kill*
A racing driver crashes and subsequently tries to murder his wife; psychiatric help leads to further gruesome goings-on.
Variation on Les Diaboliques, *with very little mystery and too much talk from boring characters.*
w Val Guest, Ronald Scott Thorn *novel* Ronald Scott Thorn *d* Val Guest *ph* Gilbert Taylor *m* Stanley Black
☆ Ronald Lewis, Diane Cilento, Claude Dauphin, Françoise Rosay, Bernard Braden

The Fuller Brush Girl *
US 1950 85m bw
Columbia (S. Sylvan Simon)
GB title: *Affairs of Sally*
A cosmetics saleslady gets involved in murder.
Fairly amusing slapstick mystery with the star in good form.
w Frank Tashlin *d* Lloyd Bacon *ph* Charles Lawton *m* Heinz Roemheld
☆ *Lucille Ball*, Eddie Albert, Carl Benton Reid, Gale Robbins, Jeff Donnell, John Litel, Jerome Cowan, Lee Patrick

The Fuller Brush Man *
US 1948 93m bw
Columbia (S. Sylvan Simon)
GB title: *That Mad Mr Jones*
A door-to-door salesman gets involved in homicide.
Bright star comedy with slow patches.
w Frank Tashlin, Devery Freeman *d* S. Sylvan Simon *ph* Leslie White *m* Heinz Roemheld
☆ *Red Skelton*, Janet Blair, Don McGuire, Adele Jergens

Fun
US 1994 105m DeLuxe/bw
Metro Tartan/Prerogative/Lighthouse/Neo Modern (Rafal Zielinski)
Two teenage girls become friends and enjoy themselves by killing an old lady.
A voyeuristic look at the lives of amoral youngsters, providing little in the way of insight and too keen to shock.
w James Bosley *play* James Bosley *d* Rafal Zielinski *ph* Jens Sturup *m* Marc Tschanz *pd* Vally Mestroni *ed* Monika Lightstone
☆ Alicia Witt, Renee Humphrey, William R. Moses, Leslie Hope, Ania Suli
'A queasy contribution to the current "bad seed" exploitation flicks.' – *Alexander Walker, London Evening Standard*

Fun and Fancy Free *
US 1947 73m Technicolor
Walt Disney (Ben Sharpsteen)
Cartoon stories told by and to Jiminy Cricket and Edgar Bergen.
Variable Disney ragbag including Bongo the Bear, *and a lengthy version of* Jack and the Beanstalk.
w various *d* various

Fun Down There
US 1988 88m colour
Metro/Angelina/Stigliano
A young homosexual leaves home to enjoy life in New York.
Full of grainy, low-budget sincerity, but slight to the point of boredom.
w Roger Stigliano, Michael Waite *d* Roger Stigliano *ph* Peggy Ahwesh *ed* Roger Stigliano, Keith Sanbourn
☆ Michael Waite, Nickolas Nagurney, Martin Goldin, Jeanne Sobkowski, Gretschen Somerville, Elizabeth Waite, Harold Waite
'Low-budget Woody Allen without the angst and wit.' – *MFB*

Fun in Acapulco
US 1963 97m Technicolor
Paramount/Hal B. Wallis
A trapeze artist becomes a lifeguard and is pursued by a lady bullfighter.
Dim comedy musical.
w Allan Weiss *d* Richard Thorpe *ph* Daniel Fapp *m* Joseph J. Lilley
☆ Elvis Presley, Ursula Andress, Paul Lukas

Fun on a Weekend
US 1947 93m bw
United Artists
A girl with self-confidence persuades a penniless man to pose as a millionaire.
Weakish comedy with good moments.
wd Andrew Stone
☆ Eddie Bracken, Priscilla Lane, Tom Conway, Allen Jenkins, Arthur Treacher, Clarence Kolb

Fun with Dick and Jane
US 1976 100m Metrocolor
Columbia/Peter Bart, Max Pelevsky
When an aerospace executive is fired, in order to keep up with the Joneses he and his wife embark on a life of crime.
This being a 1970s satire, they actually get away with it, providing some, but not enough, fun on the way.
w David Giler, Jerry Belson, Mordecai Richler *story* Gerald Gaiser *d* Ted Kotcheff *ph* Fred J. Koenekamp *m* Ernest Gold
☆ George Segal, Jane Fonda, Ed McMahon, Dick Gautier, Alan Miller
'A nitwit mixture of counterculture politics, madcap comedy and toilet humour.' – *New Yorker*
† The sequence in which the heroine discusses the family predicament while sitting on a toilet was later deleted, reducing the running time by two minutes.

The Funeral: see *Death Japanese Style*

The Funeral
US 1996 100m DuArt
Guild/October/MDP/C&P (Mary Kane)
In New York in the 30s, the psychopathic brothers of a murdered gangster hunt his killer.
A brutal movie with pretentions, mixing windy philosophizing with sudden violence.
w Nicholas St John *d* Abel Ferrara *ph* Ken Kelsch *m* Joe Delia *pd* Charles M. Lagola *ed* Mayin Lo, Bill Pankow
☆ Christopher Walken, Chris Penn, Annabella Sciorra, Isabella Rossellini, Vincent Gallo, Benicio del Toro
'A dull, unimpressive experience.' – *George Perry*

Funeral in Berlin *
GB 1967 102m Technicolor Panavision
Paramount/Harry Saltzman (Charles Kasher)
Harry Palmer is sent to Berlin to check a story that a Russian colonel wants to defect.
Initially intriguing, finally confusing, always depressing spy yarn in the sixties manner, i.e. with every character devious and no one a hero. Good production.
w Evan Jones *novel* Funeral in Berlin by Len Deighton *d* Guy Hamilton *ph* Otto Heller *m* Konrad Elfers *pd* Ken Adam
☆ Michael Caine, *Oscar Homolka*, Eva Renzi, Paul Hubschmid, *Hugh Burden*, Guy Doleman, Rachel Gurney
'So many twists that even Sherlock Holmes might have been baffled ... before long it becomes difficult to remember who is watching whom and why, or indeed whether anybody was watching anybody at any given moment.' – *Tom Milne*
† Second in the Harry Palmer series, of which the first was *The Ipcress File* and the third *Billion Dollar Brain* (both qv).

The Funhouse
US 1981 96m Technicolor Panavision
Universal/Mace Neufeld (Derek Power, Steven Bernhardt)
aka: *Carnival of Terror*
Four teenagers decide to spend the night in the Haunted House of a travelling fair.
A violent, freak-show horror that tries for black humour but misses most of the time; it sticks to the usual equation: teenage sex equals gruesome death.
w Larry Block *d* Tobe Hooper *ph* Andrew Laszlo *m* John Beal *pd* Morton Rabinowitz *ed* Jack Hofstra *sp* Rick Baker, Craig Reardon
☆ Elizabeth Berridge, Shawn Carson, Jeanne Austin, Jack McDermott, Cooper Huckabee, Largo Woodruff, David Carson, Sylvia Miles

The Funniest Man in the World *
US 1967 102m bw
Funnyman Inc
Moderately intelligent compilation of sequences from the films of Charlie Chaplin, including *Making a Living, Kid Auto Races at Venice, Tillie's Punctured Romance, The Tramp, A Night Out, The Rink, The Immigrant* and *Easy Street*. The later shorts and features, on which Chaplin himself claimed full copyright, are not included.
wd Vernon P. Becker

Funny about Love
US 1990 101m colour
Paramount (John Avnet, Jordan Kerner)
A cartoonist and his wife experience marital problems when they fail to have a child.
Misconceived and mawkish romantic comedy which fails to extract much humour from its treatment of infertility.
w Norman Steinberg, David Frankel *story* Bob Greene *d* Leonard Nimoy *ph* Fred Murphy *m* Miles Goodman *pd* Stephen Storer *ed* Peter E. Berger
☆ Gene Wilder, Christine Lahti, Mary Stuart Masterson, Robert Prosky, Stephen Tobolowsky, Anne Jackson, Susan Ruttan

'Beware. Comic geniuses at work.'
Funny Bones *
GB 1995 126m Technicolor
Buena Vista/Hollywood Pictures (Simon Fields, Peter Chelsom)
A failing American comedian, son of a successful comic, goes to Blackpool, where he spent his childhood, to rediscover himself and improve his act; there he discovers the truth about his father and the difference between his comedy and that of his English half-brother, a natural clown.
The adventurousness of the film and the refusal by its director to play safe are to be applauded, as is his investigation of the nature of comedy; unfortunately there is a problem: it simply isn't ever funny, not even when it is intended to be.
w Peter Chelsom, Peter Flannery *d* Peter Chelsom *ph* Eduardo Serra *m* John Altman *pd* Caroline Hanania *ed* Martin Walsh
☆ Oliver Platt, Lee Evans, Richard Griffiths, Oliver Reed, George Carl, Leslie Caron, Jerry Lewis
'A complex saga of vaudeville and schtick, pathos and absurdity. One can only quarrel with the density of the effort, which stuffs far too much story and sideshow into its modest frame.' – *Leonard Klady, Variety*
'A nostalgic homage to the art of slapstick, its nostalgia somehow feels closer to a disinterment, its homage more of an autopsy. It's comedy on the slab.' – *Tom Shone, Sunday Times*

A Funny Dirty Little War **
Argentina 1983 79m Eastmancolor
ICA/Aries Cinematografica Argentina (Fernando Ayala, Luis Osvaldo)
Small town rebels defy the army as Perón is returned to power in 1974.
A brutal black farce of civilians succumbing to military terror, it won the special jury prize at the Berlin Film Festival in 1984.
w Roberto Cossa, Hector Olivera *novel* Osvaldo Soriano *d* Hector Olivera *ph* Leonardo Rodriguez *m* Oscar Cadoza Ocampo *ed* Eduaro Lopez
☆ Federico Luppi, Hector Bidonde, Victor Laplace, Rodolfo Ranni, Miguel Angel Sola, Julio de Grazia, Lautaro Murua

Funny Face: see *Bright Lights (1935)*

Funny Face **
US 1956 103m Technicolor Vistavision
Paramount (Roger Edens)
A fashion editor and photographer choose a shy bookstore attendant as their 'quality woman'.
Stylish, wistful musical with good numbers but drawn-out dialogue; finally a shade too sophisticated and a whole lot too fey.
w Leonard Gershe *d* *Stanley Donen* *ph* *Ray June* *m/ly* *George and Ira Gershwin* *ad* Hal Pereira, George W. Davis *art consultant* Richard Avedon
☆ Fred Astaire, Audrey Hepburn, Kay Thompson, Michel Auclair, Robert Flemyng
Leonard Gershe; Ray June; art direction

Funny Farm
US 1988 101m colour
Warner/Cornelius-Pan Arts (Robert L. Crawford)
A New York sports writer moves to live in the country, and regrets it.
Leisurely comedy, in which old jokes are recycled slowly.
w Jeffrey Boam *book* Jay Cronley *d* George Roy Hill *ph* Miroslav Ondricek *m* Elmer Bernstein *pd* Henry Bumstead *ed* Alan Heim
☆ Chevy Chase, Madolyn Smith, Joseph Maher, Jack Gilpin, Brad Sullivan, Macintyre Dixon, Audrie Neenan, Kevin O'Morrison, Caris Corfman

Funny Games **
Germany 1997 108m colour
Metro Tartan/Wega (Veit Heiduschka)
A wealthy family in their holiday home are terrorized by two strangers.
A disturbing film, intended as a polemic against film-makers and audiences who enjoy gratuitous violence; the violence here is presented in a way to make it seem painful rather than thrilling.
wd Michael Haneke *ph* Jurgen Jurges *pd* Christoph Kanter *ed* Andreas Prochaska

☆ Susanne Lothar, Ulrich Muhe, Frank Giering, Arno Frisch, Stefan Clapczynski
'Why would anyone stay when the film so explicitly challenges them to leave?' – *Mark Kermode, Sight and Sound*

Funny Girl **
US 1968 169m Technicolor Panavision 70
Columbia/Rastar (Ray Stark)

Fanny Brice, an ugly Jewish girl from New York's east side, becomes a big Broadway star but loses her husband in the process.
Interminable cliché-ridden musical drama relieved by a few good numbers, high production gloss and the unveiling of a new powerhouse star.
w Isobel Lennart *play* Isobel Lennart *d* William Wyler *ph* Harry Stradling *m/ly* *Jule Styne*, Bob Merrill *md* Walter Scharf *pd* Gene Callahan
☆ *Barbra Streisand*, Omar Sharif, Walter Pidgeon, Kay Medford, Anne Francis, Lee Allen, Gerald Mohr, Frank Faylen
Barbra Streisand
best picture; Harry Stradling; Walter Scharf; Kay Medford; title song

'How Lucky Can You Get.'
Funny Lady *
US 1975 138m Eastmancolor Panavision
Columbia/Rastar/Persky-Bright/Vista (Ray Stark)

Fanny Brice marries Billy Rose.
Unnecessary sequel to Funny Girl entirely predictable and far from the truth, but with the occasional pleasures that a high budget brings.
w Jay Presson Allen, Arnold Schulman *d* Herbert Ross *ph James Wong Howe* *m/ly* various *md* Peter Matz *pd* George Jenkins
☆ Barbra Streisand, James Caan, *Ben Vereen*, Omar Sharif, Roddy McDowall, Larry Gates
'The plot line is as slackly handled as the milieu.' – *Geoff Brown*
'As Fanny Brice, Streisand is no longer human; she's like a bitchy female impersonator imitating Barbra Streisand.' – *New Yorker*
James Wong Howe; Peter Matz; song 'How Lucky Can You Get' (m/ly Fred Ebb, John Kander)

A Funny Thing Happened on the Way to the Forum **
GB 1966 99m DeLuxe
UA/Quadrangle (Melvin Frank)

In ancient Rome, a conniving slave schemes to win his freedom.
Bawdy farce from a Broadway musical inspired by Plautus but with a New York Jewish atmosphere. The film pays scant attention to the comic numbers that made the show a hit, but adds some style of its own, including a free-for-all slapstick climax.
w Melvin Frank, Michael Pertwee *musical comedy* Burt Shevelove, Larry Gelbart *d Richard Lester* *ph Nicolas Roeg* *m/ly Stephen Sondheim* *md* Ken Thorne *pd* Tony Walton *titles* Richard Williams
☆ Zero Mostel, Phil Silvers, Michael Crawford, Jack Gilford, *Michael Hordern*, Buster Keaton, Patricia Jessel, Leon Greene, Beatrix Lehmann
'Actors have to be very fast and very sly to make themselves felt amid the flash and glitter of a characteristic piece of Lester film-mosaic.' – *John Russell Taylor*
'He proceeds by fits and starts and leaves jokes suspended in mid-air ... like coitus interruptus going on forever.' – *Pauline Kael*
Ken Thorne

Funnyman
US 1967 100m bw/colour
Korty Films (Hugh McGraw, Stephen Schmidt)
A satirical comedian seeks some better occupation in life, but finally agrees he's best as a comic.
One suspects Korty has seen Sullivan's Travels *several times; but even though his film tries hard, it finally provides more yawns than appreciative chuckles.*
w John Korty, Peter Bonerz *d John Korty* *ph* John Korty *m* Peter Schickele
☆ Peter Bonerz, Sandra Archer, Carol Androsky, Gerald Hiken
'It has its dull patches, but it made me laugh louder and more often than any other film this year.' – *Michael Billington, Illustrated London News*

Funnyman
GB 1994 93m Technicolor
Feature/Nomad (Nigel Odell)

A record producer and his friends are killed one by one when they visit the stately home he won in a poker game.
Gruesome, low-budget, jokey horror that features a Punch-like killer, but its incoherent narrative lacks impact.
wd Simon Sprackling *ph* Tom Ingle Jnr *m* Parsons/Haines *pd* David Endley *ed* Ryan L. Driscoll *sp* Neill Gorton, Jim Francis
☆ Tim James, Christopher Lee, Benny Young, Pauline Chan, Ingrid Lacey, Matthew Devitt, Chris Walker
'Isn't half as funny as it thinks it is, but has enough chuckles to draw the six-pack and frozen-dinner contingent.' – *Derek Elley, Variety*

The Furies *
US 1950 109m bw
Paramount/Hal B. Wallis
A cattle baron feuds with his tempestuous daughter.
Interesting but heavy-going Western, more solemn than stimulating despite its Freudian excesses.
w Charles Schnee *novel* Niven Busch *d* Anthony Mann *ph* Victor Milner *m* Franz Waxman
☆ Barbara Stanwyck, *Walter Huston*, Wendell Corey, Judith Anderson, Gilbert Roland, Thomas Gomez, Beulah Bondi, Wallace Ford, Albert Dekker, Blanche Yurka
'An immoral saga, capably mounted, with some pretentious psychological trimmings.' – *MFB*
Victor Milner

The Further Adventures of Tennessee Buck
US 1988 90m colour
Sarlui/Diamant/Sri Lanka Film Location Services (Gideon Amir)

A big white hunter in Borneo leads a rich couple into cannibal country.
Charmless action adventure with a leering emphasis on the female body.
w Barry Jacobs, Stuart Jacobs, Paul Mason *d* David Keith *ph* Avraham Karpick *m* John Debney *pd* Errol Kelly *ed* Anthony Redman
☆ David Keith, Kathy Shower, Brant Van Hoffmann, Sydney Lassick

A Further Gesture
GB/Germany/Ireland/Japan 1997 101m Metrocolor
Film Four/Channel 4/NDF/Pony Canyon/Zephyr/Samson/Road Movies (Chris Curling)

An IRA prisoner escapes to America, falls in love, and agrees to assassinate the dictator who killed his girlfriend's father.
Melancholy tale of a violent man who cannot escape his past; it offers little that is new or interesting.
w Ronan Bennett *idea* Stephen Rea *d* Robert Dornhelm *ph* Andrzej Sekula *m* John Keane *pd* Kalina Ivanov, Tom McCullagh *ed* Masahiro Hirakubo
☆ Stephen Rea (Dowd), Rosana Pastor (Monica), Alfred Molina (Tulio), Brendan Gleeson (Richard), Jorge Sanz (Paco), Pruitt Taylor Vince (Scott), Maria Doyle Kennedy (Roisin)
'Mostly fires from only one barrel.' – *Variety*

The Further Perils of Laurel and Hardy ***
US 1967 99m bw
TCF/Robert Youngson

A compilation of longish extracts from the stars' silent comedies, including *Early to Bed*, *The Second Hundred Years*, *Should Married Men Go Home*, *You're Darn Tootin'*, *Habeas Corpus*, *That's My Wife*, and *Leave 'Em Laughing*. The producer is to be congratulated on refurbishing so many deteriorating negatives, though the commentary leaves much to be desired.
m John Parker *w/ed* Robert Youngson
☆ Stan Laurel, Oliver Hardy

Fury ***
US 1936 94m bw
MGM (Joseph L. Mankiewicz)

A traveller in a small town is mistaken for a murderer and apparently lynched; he escapes in a fire but determines to have his persecutors hanged for his murder.
Powerful drama which becomes artificial in its latter stages but remains its director's best American film.
w Bartlett Cormack, Fritz Lang *story* Norman Krasna *d Fritz Lang* *ph Joseph Ruttenberg* *m* Franz Waxman
☆ *Spencer Tracy*, Sylvia Sidney, Bruce Cabot, Walter Abel, Edward Ellis, Walter Brennan, Frank Albertson
'The surface of American life has been rubbed away: *Fury* gets down to the bones of the thing and shows them for what they are.' – *C. A. Lejeune*
'Since the screen began to talk, no other serious film except *The Front Page* has so clearly shown that here is a new art and what this new art can do.' – *John Marks*
'Everyday events and people suddenly took on tremendous and horrifying proportion; even the most insignificant details had a pointed meaning.' – *Lewis Jacobs*
'For half its length a powerful and documented piece of fiction about a lynching, and for the remaining half a desperate attempt to make love, lynching and the Hays Office come out even.' – *Otis Ferguson*
'Astonishing, the only film I know to which I have wanted to attach the epithet of *great*.' – *Graham Greene*
Norman Krasna

The Fury *
US 1978 117m DeLuxe
TCF/Frank Yablans (Ron Preissman)

The head of a government institute for psychic research finds that his own son is wanted by terrorists who wish to use his lethal psychic powers.
Flashy, kaleidoscopic nonsense which never even begins to make sense but is used as the basis for the director's showing-off, which is occasionally worth a glance for those with hardened stomachs.
w John Farris *novel* John Farris *d* Brian de Palma *ph* Richard H. Kline *m* John Williams *pd* Bill Malley *ed* Paul Hirsch
☆ Kirk Douglas, John Cassavetes, Carrie Snodgress, Charles Durning, Andrew Stevens, Amy Irving, Fiona Lewis
'A conception of cinema that is closer to Ken Russell than Alfred Hitchcock.' – *Richard Combs, MFB*

Fury at Furnace Creek *
US 1948 88m bw
TCF
A Westerner clears the name of his father, a general accused of diverting a wagon train into hostile Indian territory.
Adequate old-fashioned Western with a good story line and standard excitements.
w Charles G. Booth *d* H. Bruce Humberstone *ph* Harry Jackson *m* David Raksin *md* Alfred Newman
☆ Victor Mature, Coleen Gray, Glenn Langan, Reginald Gardiner

Fury at Smugglers' Bay
GB 1960 96m Eastmancolor Panascope
Regal/Mijo (Michael Green, Joe Vegoda)
The squire of a Cornish village is being blackmailed by the vicious leader of a gang of wreckers.
Watchable, then forgettable variation on Jamaica Inn.
wd John Gilling *ph* Harry Waxman *m* Harold Geller
☆ Peter Cushing, John Fraser, Bernard Lee, William Franklyn, June Thorburn, Miles Malleson, Michele Mercier, George Coulouris

Fuss over Feathers: see *Conflict of Wings*

Futtock's End *
GB 1969 49m Eastmancolor
Paradine/Gannet/British Lion
Adventures of a weekend in an English country mansion.
A collection of visual gags, rather thinly spread, with dialogue replaced by squeaks and mumblings. Like all Barker's subsequent comedies on similar lines (The Picnic, By the Sea, *etc) one chuckles in constant anticipation of guffaws which never come.*
w Ronnie Barker *d* Bob Kellett
☆ Ronnie Barker, Michael Hordern, Roger Livesey, Julian Orchard, Kika Markham, Mary Merrall, Richard O'Sullivan

Future Cop: see *Trancers*

The Future of Emily
France/West Germany 1984 116m colour
Mainline/Les Films du Losannge/Helma Sanders/Literarisches Colloquium/ ZDF/BMI/FFA/Berliner Film (Nicole Flipo, Ursula Ludwig)
original title: *L'Avenir D'Emilie*
Mother and daughter (a film star) discuss their attitudes to life.
Conversation piece of limited interest.
wd Helma Sanders-Brahms *ph* Sacha Vierney *m* Jürgen Knieper *ad* Jean-Michel Hugon, Rainer Schaper *ed* Ursula West
☆ Brigitte Fossey, Hildegarde Knef, Ivan Desny, Herman Treusch, Camille Raymond, Mathieu Carrière

Futureworld *
US 1976 107m Metrocolor
AIP (James T. Aubrey Jnr, Paul Lazarus III)

The robot factory seen in *Westworld* (qv) now aims at world domination by duplicating influential figures.
Amusing and fairly suspenseful fantasy with a bigger budget than its predecessor.
w Mayo Simon, George Schenck *d* Richard T. Heffron *ph* Howard Schwartz, Gene Polito *m* Fred Karlin
☆ Peter Fonda, Blythe Danner, Arthur Hill, Yul Brynner, John Ryan, Stuart Margolin, Jim Antonio

Fuzi Qing: see *Father and Son*

Fuzz *
US 1972 93m DeLuxe
UA/Filmways/Javelin (Jack Farren)

Detectives of Boston's 87th precinct try to catch a rapist.
A black farce devoted to police incompetence, though taken from a straight 'Ed McBain' story. Brisk and sometimes funny.
w Evan Hunter ('Ed McBain') *d* Richard A. Colla *ph* Jacques Marquette *m* Dave Grusin
☆ Burt Reynolds, Raquel Welch, Jack Weston, Yul Brynner, Tom Skerritt, James McEachin

GI Blues
US 1960 104m Technicolor
Paramount/Hal B. Wallis (Paul Nathan)

A guitar-playing gunner with the American army in West Germany falls for a cabaret dancer.
Routine star vehicle marking Presley's return from military service.
w Edmund Beloin, Henry Garson *d* Norman Taurog *ph* Loyal Griggs *m* Joseph J. Lilley
☆ Elvis Presley, Juliet Prowse, Robert Ivers, Letitia Roman, Arch Johnson

'Failure Is Not an Option.'
G.I. Jane
US 1997 124m Technicolor Panavision
Buena Vista/Hollywood/Scott Free/Largo (Roger Birnbaum, Demi Moore, Suzanne Todd)

In the face of much male hostility, a female intelligence officer attempts to become the first woman to join the élite Navy SEALS, which involves a gruelling training programme.
Noisy, incoherent and thuggish movie that finds something redemptive in pain and violence.
w David Twohy, Danielle Alexandra *d* Ridley Scott *ph* Hugh Johnson *m* Trevor Jones *pd* Arthur Max *ed* Pietro Scalia
☆ Demi Moore, Viggo Mortensen, Anne Bancroft, Jason Beghe, Scott Wilson, Lucinda Jenney, Morris Chestnut, Daniel von Bargen
'A very entertaining get-tough fantasy with political and feminist underpinnings.' – *Todd McCarthy, Variety*
'It indulges the drive for physical perfection that Moore has so consistently mistaken for screen acting.' – *Tom Shone, Sunday Times*

G Man's Wife: see *Public Enemy's Wife*

'G' Men ***
US 1935 85m bw
Warner (Lou Edelman)

A young lawyer becomes a G-man to avenge the murder of his best friend, and finds himself tracking down another old friend who is a gangster.
In the face of mounting criticism of their melodramas making heroes of gangsters, Warner pulled a clever switch by showing the same crimes from a different angle, that of the law enforcer. As an action show it became pretty good after a slow start.
w Seton I. Miller *d* William Keighley *ph* Sol Polito *md* Leo F. Forbstein
☆ *James Cagney*, Ann Dvorak, Margaret Lindsay, Robert Armstrong, Barton MacLane, Lloyd Nolan, William Harrigan
'Cagney joins the government and cleans up the gangsters. Just loads of action, knocked off in bing-bang manner. Strong b.o.' – *Variety*
'The gangster is back, racing madly through one of the fastest melodramas ever made.' – *New York Sun*
'The headiest dose of gunplay that Hollywood has unleashed in recent months.' – *André Sennwald, New York Times*
'It is not violence alone which is in the air; there is also a skilfully contrived and well-maintained suspense, and throughout a feeling of respect for the men who are paid to die in the execution of necessary work.' – *The Times*
'A swell show: the construction is swift and staccato.' – *New York World Telegraph*
'Not for the kiddies, but see it if your nerves are good.' – *Photoplay*

'Time starts here...'
G:MT Greenwich Mean Time
GB 1998 118m DeLuxe
Icon/Anvil/GMT (Taylor Hackford)
Three members of a London rock group fall out over the type of music they should play.
Slick and confused account of would-be musicians becoming involved with drugs and gangsters as they try to hold on to their integrity, a quality nowhere evident in the movie itself.
w Simon Mirren *d* John Strickland *ph* Alan Almond *m* Guy Sigsworth *pd* Luana Hanson *ed* Patrick Moore
☆ Alec Newman (Charlie), Melanie Gutteridge (Lucy), Georgia MacKenzie (Rachel), Chiwetel Ejiofor (Rix), Steve John Shepherd (Sam), Alicya Eyo (Bobby), Benjamin Waters (Bean), Anjela Lauren Smith (Sherry)
'This must be the worst coming-of-age/life-in-a-band yoof film ever made, with a rare and ruthless power to irritate and embarrass.' – *Cosmo Landesman, Sunday Times*

Gabbeh **
Iran 1995 74m colour
MK2/Sanayeh Dasti (Khalil Daroudchi, Khalil Mahmoudi)

A young woman tells the story of her frustrated love for a mysterious horseman, and her father's reluctance to let her marry, to an elderly woman, whom she resembles, and her querulous husband.
Set among a nomadic tribe of carpet weavers, this fable mixes magic realism with a documentary approach; its power derives from its ambiguous narrative, which may be a ghost story, and from the exotic beauty of its images, especially of figures dwarfed by the landscapes through which they move.
ph Mahmoud Kalari *m* Houssein Alizadeh
☆ Abbas Sayah, Shaghayegh Djodat, Hossein Moharami, Rogheih Moharami, Parvaneh Ghalandari, Hassen Kermi, Zineb Kermi

'They had more than love ... they had fame!'
Gable and Lombard
US 1976 131m Technicolor
Universal (Harry Korshak)
After Carole Lombard's death in a 1942 air crash, Clark Gable recalls their years together.
Vulgar and inaccurate representation of two Hollywood stars of the thirties; it fails even as titillation.
w Barry Sandler *d* Sidney J. Furie *ph* Jordan S. Cronenweth *m* Michel Legrand *pd* Edward Carfagno *ed* Argyle Nelson
☆ James Brolin (Clark Gable), Jill Clayburgh (Carole Lombard), Allen Garfield (Louis B. Mayer), Red Buttons, Joanne Linville
'A limply raunchy, meaningless movie with nothing to say about the movies, about love, or about stardom.' – *New Yorker*
'An uneven combination of smut and sentimentality.' – *Les Keyser, Hollywood in the Seventies*

Gabriel and Me
GB 2001 84m colour 'Scope
Pathé/Film Consortium/Film Council/FilmFour/IoMFC (Marc Samuelson, Peter Samuelson)

In Newcastle, a sensitive 11-year-old boy applies to the Angel Gabriel for a job as an angel in order to impress his dying father.
Although eschewing sentimentality for the most part, this movie never takes wing and flops in the dust of the similarly-themed Billy Elliot by the same writer.
w Lee Hall *radio play I Luv You Jimmy Spud* by Lee Hall *d* Udayan Prasad *ph* Alan Almond *pd* Andy Harris *ed* Barry Vince
☆ Iain Glen (Dad), David Bradley (Granddad), Sean Landless (Jimmy), Rosie Rowell (Mam), Billy Connolly (Gabriel), Ian Cullen (Ridley), Jordan Routledge (Scout)
'It's just another "it's grim oop North" retread with a little originality to commend it.' – *Alan Jones, Film Review*

'It comes like a marching army to thrill the nation!'
'The picture that will make 1933 famous!'
Gabriel over the White House *
US 1933 87m bw
MGM/Walter Wanger

A crook becomes president and mysteriously reforms.
Pleasing, dated New Deal fantasy.
w Carey Wilson, Bertram Bloch *novel Rinehard* by T. F. Tweed *d* Gregory La Cava *ph* Bert Glennon *m* William Axt
☆ Walter Huston, Karen Morley, Franchot Tone, C. Henry Gordon, Samuel S. Hinds, Jean Parker, Dickie Moore
'Flag-waving flapdoodle, shrewdly dished up for the man in the street and his best girl. Beautifully produced, cannily hoked, and looks like money all round.' – *Variety*

Gabriela
Brazil 1983 99m colour
Sultana

In a coastal town in 1925, the sensual Gabriela marries a bar owner but becomes involved again with her old gangster cronies.
Ethnic melodrama of familiar type, a spin-off from an immensely popular Brazilian TV series.
w Leopoldo Sarran, Bruno Barreto *novel* Jorge Amada *d* Bruno Barreto
☆ Sonia Braga, Marcello Mastroianni, Antonio Cantafora

Gaby
US 1956 97m Eastmancolor Cinemascope
MGM (Edwin H. Knopf)
During the Second World War, a couple meet and fall in love; but before they can marry he is reported killed in action and she becomes a prostitute.
Flabby remake of Waterloo Bridge *(qv); saccharine, fussy and outmoded, despite updated settings and a happy ending.*
w Albert Hackett, Frances Goodrich, Charles Lederer *d* Curtis Bernhardt *ph* Robert Planck *m* Conrad Salinger
☆ Leslie Caron, John Kerr, Cedric Hardwicke, Taina Elg, Margalo Gillmore

Gaby – A True Story *
US 1987 114m colour
Columbia TriStar (Pinchas Perry)

A Mexican girl suffering from cerebral palsy struggles to overcome her disabilities.
Well-acted and touching.
w Martin Salinas, Michael James Love *d* Luis Mandoki *ph* Lajos Koltai *m* Maurice Jarre *ad* Alejandro Luna *ed* Garth Craven
☆ Liv Ullmann, Norma Aleandro, Robert Loggia, Rachel Levin, Lawrence Monoson, Robert Beltran, Beatriz Sheridan, Tony Goldwyn
Norma Aleandro

Gadael Lenin: see *Leaving Lenin*

Gaiety George
GB 1946 98m bw
Embassy (George King)
US title: *Showtime*
The career in the London theatre of Irish impresario George Howard in the early part of the century.
Tepid musical biopic.
w Katherine Strueby *d* George King *ph* Otto Heller *md* Jack Beaver
☆ Richard Greene, Ann Todd, Peter Graves, Hazel Court, Leni Lynn, Ursula Jeans, Morland Graham, Frank Pettingell

Gaiety Girls: see *Paradise for Two*

Gaily, Gaily **
US 1969 117m DeLuxe
UA/Mirisch/Cartier (Norman Jewison)
GB title: *Chicago, Chicago*
The early life on a Chicago newspaper of screenwriter and dramatist Ben Hecht.
Busy, farcical, melodramatic, always interesting biopic of the formative years of a celebrated literary figure.
w Abram S. Ginnes *book* Ben Hecht *d* Norman Jewison *ph* Richard Kline *m* Henry Mancini *pd* Robert Boyle
☆ Beau Bridges, Melina Mercouri, *Brian Keith*, George Kennedy, Hume Cronyn, Margot Kidder, Wilfrid Hyde-White, Melodie Johnson, John Randolph

The Gal Who Took the West
US 1949 84m Technicolor
Universal-International
In 1890, an opera singer travels west and is the object of romantic rivalry.
Lame attempt to equal the splendid idiocy of Salome Where She Danced.
w William Bowers, Oscar Brodney *d* Frederick de Cordova *ph* William H. Daniels *m* Frank Skinner
☆ Yvonne de Carlo, Charles Coburn, Scott Brady, John Russell, James Millican

'The Show Was Cancelled..But The Adventure Has Only Begun.'
Galaxy Quest *
US 1999 104m Technicolor Panavision
DreamWorks (Mark Johnson, Charles Newirth)

The fading stars of a cult TV science-fiction series are approached by gullible aliens who need help in defeating an extraterrestrial terrorist.
Enjoyable comedy at the expense of space operas such as Star Trek *and the trivia-obsessed fans of the genre.*
w David Howard, Robert Gordon *d* Dean Parisot *ph* Jerzy Zielinski *m* David Newman *pd* Linda DeScenna *ed* Don Zimmerman *sp* make and creature fx: Stan Winston *cos* Albert Wolsky
☆ Tim Allen (Jason Nesmith), Sigourney Weaver (Gwen DeMarco), Alan Rickman (Alexander Dane), Tony Shalhoub (Fred Kwan), Sam Rockwell (Guy Fleegman), Daryl Mitchell (Tommy Webber), Enrico Colantoni (Mathesar), Robin Sachs (Sarris), Patrick Breen (Quellek), Missi Pyle (Laliari)
'A mischievously clever and slickly commercial sci-fi comedy with strong cross-generational appeal.' – *Joe Leydon, Variety*

Galileo *
GB 1975 145m Eastmancolor
Ely Landau/Cinevision
In the 17th century, a poor Italian mathematics teacher has trouble establishing his 'heretical' astronomical theories.
Overlong play-on-celluloid for the American Film Theatre: very decently made and acted, it lacks inspiration.
w Barbara Bray, Joseph Losey *play* Bertolt Brecht *d* Joseph Losey *ph* Michael Reed *m* Hanns Eisler
☆ *Topol*, Edward Fox, Michel Lonsdale, Richard O'Callaghan, Tom Conti, Judy Parfitt, Patrick Magee, Michael Gough, John Gielgud, Colin Blakely, Margaret Leighton, Clive Revill
'The whole feeling is something like a modestly produced star touring-show. Without the star.' – *Stanley Kauffmann*

Gallant Bess
US 1946 99m Cinecolor
MGM
A soldier's horse saves his life and becomes his peacetime friend.
Boy-and-horse story with a wartime setting; good for small towns.

w Jeanne Bartlett *d* Andrew Marton
☆ Marshall Thompson, George Tobias, Clem Bevans, Donald Curtis

The Gallant Blade

US 1948 81m Cinecolor
Columbia
In France in 1648, a dashing young lieutenant rescues his general from the plot of a would-be revolutionary.
Pinchpenny swashbuckler which maintains a commendable verve.
w Walter Ferris, Morton Grant *d* Henry Levin
☆ Larry Parks, Marguerite Chapman, Victor Jory, George Macready

The Gallant Hours *

US 1959 115m bw
UA/James Cagney/Robert Montgomery
Episodes in the career of Admiral William F. Halsey.
Adulatory but physically restrained biopic which covers World War II with barely a scene outside control room sets: interesting but finally too talky.
w Beirne Lay Jnr, Frank D. Gilroy *d* Robert Montgomery *ph* Joe MacDonald *m* Roger Wagner
☆ James Cagney, Dennis Weaver, Richard Jaeckel, Ward Costello, Carl Benton Reid
'Imaginatively conceived but erroneously realized.' – *Robert Vas*

Gallant Journey

US 1946 86m bw
Columbia (William A. Wellman)
The life of an early American aviation pioneer.
Curious biopic, very tentatively done, about an inventor so obscure as to be virtually fictitious. Sentimental, artificial, but harmless.
w Byron Morgan, William A. Wellman
d William A. Wellman *ph* Burnett Guffey
m Marlin Skiles
☆ Glenn Ford, Janet Blair, Charles Ruggles, Henry Travers, Arthur Shields

Gallant Lady

US 1933 84m bw
UA/Twentieth Century (Darryl F. Zanuck)
A woman allows her illegitimate son to be adopted, but years later marries his stepfather.
A tearjerker very typical of its time, moderately well assembled; later remade as Always Goodbye *(qv).*
w Sam Mintz *story* Gilbert Emery, Doug Doty
d Gregory La Cava *ph* Peverell Marley *m* Alfred Newman
☆ Ann Harding, Clive Brook, Otto Kruger, Tullio Carminati, Dickie Moore, Janet Beecher

Gallant Sons

US 1940 71m bw
MGM
Schoolboys club together to get the father of one of them off a murder charge.
Unlikely and undemanding but pleasant filler.
w William R. Lipman, Marion Parsonnet
d George B. Seitz
☆ Jackie Cooper, Bonita Granville, Gene Reynolds, Gail Patrick, Ian Hunter, June Preisser, Leo Gorcey, William Tracy, El Brendel

'From a place you may never have heard of, a story you'll never forget!'

Gallipoli *

Australia 1981 111m Eastmancolor Panavision
Associated RandR (Martin Cooper, Ben Gannon)
In 1915, two friends trek from Perth across the desert to join up, and one dies in the Dardanelles.
Consistently interesting aspects of the 1914–18 war, but rather broken-backed as a story.
w David Williamson *d Peter Weir ph* Russell Boyd *md* Brian May
☆ Mark Lee, Mel Gibson, Bill Hunter, Robert Grubb, Tim McKenzie, Bill Kerr
'Like so many of Weir's films it promises more than it delivers.' – *Time Out, 1984*

Gallivant **

GB 1996 104m colour
Electric/Tall Stories/BFI/Channel 4 (Ben Woolford)
A director travels around the coast of Britain in a camper van with his 85-year-old grandmother and seven-year-old daughter, who suffers from Joubert's Syndrome, a condition that restricts her ability to speak.
Quirky documentary on a 10-week tour of Britain, including interviews with a variety of everyday eccentrics met on the way; but the concentration is on the relationship between the generations of a family, particularly between the busily signalling young girl and her great-grandmother.
wd Andrew Kötting *ph* N. G. Smith *m* David Burnand *ed* Cliff West
☆ Gladys Morris, Eden Kötting
'That rare thing, a celebratory film that never turns sugary or mawkish.' – *Philip Kemp, Sight and Sound*

The Galloping Major *

GB 1951 82m bw
British Lion/Romulus (Monja Danischewsky)
A group of suburbanites form a syndicate to buy a racehorse.
Rather contrived and imitative sub-Ealing comedy which fails to generate much steam.
w Monja Danischewsky, Henry Cornelius
d Henry Cornelius *ph* Stan Pavey *m* Georges Auric
☆ *Basil Radford*, Janette Scott, Hugh Griffith, Jimmy Hanley, René Ray, Joyce Grenfell, Sydney Tafler, Charles Victor, A. E. Matthews

Gambit **

US 1966 109m Techniscope
Universal (Leo L. Fuchs)
A Cockney thief conspires with a Eurasian girl to rob a multi-millionaire of a prize statue.
An enjoyably light pattern of cross and double cross is well sustained to the end.
w Jack Davies, Alvin Sargent story Sidney Carroll
d Ronald Neame *ph* Clifford Stine *m* Maurice Jarre
☆ *Michael Caine*, Shirley MacLaine, Herbert Lom, John Abbott, Roger C. Carmel, Arnold Moss

'He's been bruised, blackmailed, sliced and slammed. But nothing can stop him from going after the big money!'

The Gambler *

US 1975 111m Eastmancolor
Paramount (Irwin Winkler, Robert Chartoff)
A compulsive gambler has a will to lose.
Flashily made but basically uninteresting sub-Freudian study, vaguely based on Dostoievsky.
w James Toback *d* Karel Reisz *ph* Victor J. Kemper *m* Mahler *md* Jerry Fielding
☆ James Caan, Paul Sorvino, Lauren Hutton, Morris Carnovsky, Jacqueline Brookes, Burt Young
'The script is pretentious and empty. Reisz's quality, apparent in his early films and writings, seems to have atrophied with disuse and tension.' – *Stanley Kauffmann*

'In The Grip Of Obsession, Reason Is Suspended.'

The Gambler

GB/Netherlands/Hungary 1997 97m colour
Film Four/Channel 4/Image/Hungry Eye/KRO (Charles Cohen, Marc Vlessing)
As an ageing Dostoyevsky struggles to complete a novel before his deadline, his young stenographer becomes fascinated by him and the story he tells, of a man who gambles to save those he loves.
A complex tale that intertwines life and art but illuminates neither.
w Katharine Ogden, Charles Cohen, Nick Dear
d Karoly Makk *ph* Jules van den Steenhoven
m Brian Lock, Gerard Schurmann *pd* Ben van Os
ed Kevin Whelan
☆ Michael Gambon, Jodhi May, Polly Walker, Dominic West, Luise Rainer, John Wood, Johan Leysen, Angeline Ball, Tom Jansen
'To put it bluntly, the gloomy Russian scribe isn't the sexiest subject for a frock movie.' – *Derek Elley, Variety*

The Gambler and the Lady

GB 1952 74m bw
Exclusive/Hammer (Anthony Hinds)
A tough American gambler and club-owner in London is ruined by his attempt to move in aristocratic circles.
Enjoyable if routine thriller with its contrast between a streetwise American losing his way among the upper-class English.
w uncredited *d* Patrick Jenkins *ph* Walter Harvey *m* Ivor Slaney *ad* J. Elder Wills
ed Maurice Rootes
☆ Dane Clark, Kathleen Byron, Naomi Chance, Meredith Edwards, Anthony Forwood, Eric Pohlmann, Julian Somers, Thomas Gallagher, Max Bacon, Mona Washbourne

Gambler from Natchez

US 1954 88m Technicolor
TCF (Leonard Goldstein)
A professional gambler returns to New Orleans to avenge his father's murder, and disposes of his enemies one by one.
Mildly watchable semi-Western with a plot borrowed from The Count of Monte Cristo.
w Gerald Drayson Adams, Irving Wallace
d Henry Levin *ph* Lloyd Ahern *md* Lionel Newman
☆ Dale Robertson, Debra Paget, Thomas Gomez, Kevin McCarthy

Gambling *

US 1934 82m bw
Fox/Harold B. Franklin
A professional gambler ferrets out the killer of his ward.
Transcript of a George M. Cohan play, with the star in good form; but the presentation is uncinematic and tedious.
w Garrett Graham *play* George M. Cohan
d Rowland V. Lee
☆ *George M. Cohan*, Wynne Gibson, Dorothy Burgess, Theodore Newton
'It moves too slowly towards an intelligent but almost wholly mental climax.' – *Variety*

Gambling Lady *

US 1934 66m bw
Warner (Henry Blanke)
The daughter of a gambling suicide follows in father's footsteps and becomes involved in murder.
Fast-paced melodrama with a happy ending: smart entertainment of its time.
w Ralph Block, Doris Malloy *d* Archie Mayo
ph George Barnes
☆ Barbara Stanwyck, Joel McCrea, Pat O'Brien, Claire Dodd, C. Aubrey Smith, Robert Barrat, Philip Reed

'Are You Ready To Play?'

The Game ***

US 1997 128m Technicolor Panavision
Polygram/Propaganda (Steve Golin, Cean Chaffin)
A middle-aged workaholic millionaire is, for his birthday, given a gift that casts him as a participant in a mysterious game that turns his life upside down.
A high-energy paranoid thriller that plunges its protagonist, and the audience, into a world where nothing is to be trusted; the result is some dazzling sleight-of-hand.
w John Brancato, Michael Ferris *d* David Fincher
ph Harris Savides *m* Howard Shore *pd* Jeffrey Beecroft *ed* James Haygood
☆ Michael Douglas (Nicholas Van Orton), Sean Penn (Conrad), Deborah Kara Unger (Christine), James Rebhorn (Jim Feingold), Peter Donat (Samuel Sutherland), Carroll Baker (Ilsa), Anna Katarina (Elizabeth), Armin Mueller-Stahl (Anson Baer)
'A high-toned mind-game of a movie.' – *Variety*

A Game for Vultures

GB 1979 106m colour
Columbia
In Rhodesia, a sanctions-buster comes to understand a black freedom fighter.
After a lot of violence and attitudinizing, that is, in this unattractively pretentious piece of bloodthirsty hokum.
w Phillip Baird *novel* Michael Hartmann
d James Fargo
☆ Richard Harris, Richard Roundtree, Ray Milland, Joan Collins, Sven Bertil Taube, Denholm Elliott

A Game of Death

US 1945 72m bw
RKO
Cheap remake of *The Most Dangerous Game* (qv); excitement dissipated by poor handling.
w Norman Houston *d* Robert Wise *ph* J. Roy Hunt *m* Paul Sawtell
☆ John Loder, Audrey Long, Edgar Barrier, Russell Wade, Russell Hicks

Games *

US 1967 100m Techniscope
Universal (George Edwards)
A sophisticated New York couple play complex games, one of which turns out to have a deadly effect.
Tedious variation on Les Diaboliques, *with interesting moments.*
w Gene Kearney *d Curtis Harrington ph* William A. Fraker *m* Samuel Matlovsky
☆ Simone Signoret, James Caan, Katharine Ross, Don Stroud, Kent Smith, Estelle Winwood, Marjorie Bennett
'A cheap-jack mélange of *Angel Street* and *Diabolique* in a New York brownstone.' – *Judith Crist*

The Games *

GB 1970 97m DeLuxe Panavision
TCF (Lester Linsk)
Four men in various parts of the world prepare to take part in the marathon at the Rome Olympics.
Tepid multi-drama with good locations and a well-shot and exciting climactic race.
w Erich Segal *novel* Hugh Atkinson *d* Michael Winner *ph Robert Paynter m* Francis Lai
☆ Stanley Baker, Michael Crawford, Ryan O'Neal, Charles Aznavour, Jeremy Kemp, Elaine Taylor, Kent Smith, Mona Washbourne
'Dramatically captures the tension, the physical agony and the almost religious fervour of the Olympics.' – *Daily Mail*

The Gamma People

GB 1955 79m bw
Warwick/Columbia
Journalists in a Balkan state uncover a plot by a mad scientist to control the minds of children by gamma rays.
Artless serial-like thriller with little suspense.
w John Gilling, John Gossage *d* John Gilling
☆ Paul Douglas, Leslie Phillips, Eva Bartok, Walter Rilla, Philip Leaver

Gamyuk Muntong: see *The Chinese Feast*

Ganashatru: see *An Enemy of the People*

'His goal was freedom ... his strategy was peace ... his weapon was his humanity!'

Gandhi ***

GB 1982 188m Technicolor Panavision
Columbia/Goldcrest/Indo-British/International Film Investors/National Film Development Corporation of India (*Richard Attenborough*)
The life of the young Indian advocate who became a revolutionary, a saint and a martyr.
A straightforward treatment with the odd twists and turns expected of this director; but the remarkable things about the film are first, that it was made at all in an age which regards inspirational epics as very old hat; and secondly, that it has brought into life so splendid a leading performance. Beside these factors the sluggish pace and the air of schoolbook history seem comparatively unimportant.
w John Briley *d* Richard Attenborough *ph* Billy Williams, Ronnie Taylor *m* George Fenton
pd Stuart Craig *ed* John Bloom
☆ *Ben Kingsley*, Candice Bergen, Edward Fox, John Mills, John Gielgud, Trevor Howard, Martin Sheen, Ian Charleson, Athol Fugard, Saeed Jaffrey
'It reminds us that we are, after all, human, and thus capable of the most extraordinary and wonderful achievements, simply through the use of our imagination, our will, and our sense of right.' – *Roger Ebert*
† Opening dedication: 'No man's life can be encompassed in one telling ... what can be done is to be faithful in spirit to the record and try to find one's way to the heart of the man.'
best picture; Ben Kingsley; Richard Attenborough as director; John Briley; cinematography; costume design (John Mollo, Bhanu Athalya); art direction (Stuart Craig, Bob Laing); editing (John Bloom)
music
best film; best direction; best actor; best supporting actress (Rohini Hattangady); outstanding newcomer (Ben Kingsley)

'The best place to hide is behind a badge.'

Gang Related ★
US 1997 122m DeLuxe Super 35
MGM/Orion (John Bertolli, Brad Krevoy, Steven Stabler)

Two crooked cops frame a vagrant for their murder of an undercover agent.
Familiar fare of police corruption, drugs and inner-city deprivation, enlivened by its direction and dry wit.
wd Jim Kouf *ph* Brian H. Reynolds *m* Mickey Hart *pd* Charles Breen *ed* Todd C. Ramsay
☆ James Belushi (Davinci), Tupac Shakur (Rodriguez), Lela Rochon (Cynthia), Dennis Quaid (William), James Earl Jones (Arthur Baylor), David Paymer (Elliot Goff), Wendy Crewson (Helen Eden), Gary Cole (Richard Simms)
'Little more than a TV movie with a bad mouth.' – *James Cameron-Wilson, Film Review*

The Gang That Couldn't Shoot Straight
US 1971 96m Metrocolor
MGM (Robert Chartoff, Irwin Winkler)
Members of the New York Mafia organize a cycle race and start antagonisms that end in mass murder.
Unfunny black comedy with all concerned gesticulating wildly.
w Waldo Salt *novel* Jimmy Breslin *d* James Goldstone *ph* Owen Roizman *m* Dave Grusin
☆ Jerry Orbach, Leigh Taylor-Young, Jo Van Fleet, Lionel Stander, Robert DeNiro, Herve Villechaize, Joe Santos

Gang War: see *Odd Man Out (1946)*

Gang War ★
US 1958 75m bw RegalScope
Fox (Harold E. Knox)
When his wife is killed by gangsters a reluctant witness seeks revenge.
Minor prototype for Death Wish *and the star's other vehicles in similar vein.*
w Louis Vittes *novel* *The Hoods Take Over* by Ovid Demaris *d* Gene Fowler Jnr
☆ Charles Bronson, Kent Taylor, Jennifer Holden, John Doucette, Gloria Henry

The Gang's All Here ★
GB 1939 77m bw
ABPC/Jack Buchanan (Walter C. Mycroft)
US title: *The Amazing Mr Forrest*
An insurance investigator goes undercover among gangsters.
Lively comedy-melodrama.
w Ralph Spence *d* Thornton Freeland *ph* Claude Friese-Greene *ad* John Mead, Cedric Dawe *ed* E. B. Jarvis
☆ Jack Buchanan, Googie Withers, Edward Everett Horton, Syd Walker, Otto Kruger, Jack La Rue, Walter Rilla
† Buchanan played the same character in *Smash and Grab.*

The Gang's All Here ★★
US 1943 103m Technicolor
TCF (William Le Baron)
GB title: *The Girls He Left Behind*
A serviceman is caught between a fiery entertainer and a Park Avenue socialite.
Frenetic wartime musical with some of Busby Berkeley's most outré choreography (e.g. 'The Lady in the Tutti Frutti Hat') and gleamingly effective Technicolor.
w Walter Bullock *ph* Edward Cronjager *m/ly* Leo Robin, Harry Warren *md* Alfred Newman *ad* James Basevi, Joseph C. Wright *d/ch* Busby Berkeley
☆ Alice Faye, Carmen Miranda, James Ellison, Phil Baker, Benny Goodman, Charlotte Greenwood, Eugene Pallette, Edward Everett Horton
'Those who consider Berkeley a master consider this film his masterpiece.' – *New Yorker, 1976*
'Mainly made up of Busby Berkeley's paroxysmic production numbers, which amuse me a good deal.' – *James Agee*
Ꞵ art direction

'America Was Born In The Streets.'

Gangs of New York ★★
US 2002 168m Technicolor 'Scope
Entertainment/Miramax/Alberto Grimaldi

In the mid 1800s, two gangs – one made up of New Yorkers, the other of Irish immigrants – meet in violent battles to control the poor Manhattan district in which they live.
Sprawling epic account of the making of modern New York, enlivened by a roistering performance from Day-Lewis, who overshadows a miscast DiCaprio; Scorsese's ambition is evident, but its adherence to conventional devices of revenge and romance pull it down.
w Jay Cocks, Steven Zaillian, Kenneth Lonergan *d* Martin Scorsese *ph* Michael Ballhaus *m* Howard Shore *pd* Dante Ferretti *ed* Thelma Schoonmaker *sp* ILM *cos* Sandy Powell
☆ Leonardo DiCaprio (Amsterdam Vallon), *Daniel Day-Lewis* (William 'Bill the Butcher' Cutting), Cameron Diaz (Jenny Everdeane), Liam Neeson (Priest Vallon), Jim Broadbent (William 'Boss' Tweed), John C. Reilly (Happy Jack), Henry Thomas (Johnny Sirocco), Brendan Gleeson (Walter 'Monk' McGinn), Gary Lewis (McGloin), Stephen Graham (Shang), Alec McCowe (Reverend Raleigh)
'A great love letter to a lost New York, but a mediocre movie.' – *Cosmo Landesman, Sunday Times*
'An ironic, emotional, gory revision of the American Experiment, marred by narrative problems but sufficiently awesome in its ambitious scale and intentions to rate as a must-see.' – *Angie Errigo, Empire*
'Falls somewhat short of great film status, but is still a richly impressive and densely realized work that bracingly opens the eye and mind to untaught aspects of American history.' – *Todd McCarthy, Variety*
Ꞵ picture; Jay Cocks, Steven Zaillian, Kenneth Lonergan; Martin Scorsese; Daniel Day-Lewis; Michael Ballhaus; Dante Ferretti (with Francesca LoSchiavo); Thelma Schoonmaker; Sandy Powell; song 'The Hands That Built America' (*m/l* Bono,The Edge, Adam Clayton, Larry Mullen Jnr); sound (Tom Fleischman, Eugene Gearty, Ivan Sharrock)
BAFTA: Daniel Day-Lewis

Gangsta's Paradise: see *Stiletto Dance*

The Gangster
US 1947 84m bw
Monogram/King Bros (Maurice King)

A gangster begins to go to pieces as a rival moves in on his territory.
Shoddy-looking Poverty Row melodrama with little rhyme, reason or interest.
w Daniel Fuchs *novel* *Low Company* by Daniel Fuchs *d* Gordon Wiles *ph* Paul Ivano *m* Louis Gruenberg *md* Irving Talbot *ad* F. Paul Sylos *ed* Walter Thompson
☆ Barry Sullivan (Shubunka), Akim Tamiroff (Nick Jammey), Belita (Nancy Starr), John Ireland (Karty), Harry Morgan (Shorty), Joan Lorring (Dorothy), Fifi D'Orsay (Mrs Ostroleng), Virgina Christine (Mrs Karty), Sheldon Leonard (Comell), Leif Erickson (Beaumont), Elisha Cook (Oval), Shelley Winters (Hazel)

'It's Not Who You Know, It's Who You Kill.'

Gangster No 1 ★
GB/Germany 2000 103m Technicolor
FilmFour/Pagoda/Road Movies (Norma Heyman, Jonathan Cavendish)

A London gangster remembers how, in the late 1960s, as a ruthlessly ambitious young man he betrayed his boss, a crook known as the Butcher of Mayfair.
Effective thriller that catches the sleazy glamour of the period, with its conjunction of showbusiness and crime, but then declines into less convincing melodrama.
w Johnny Ferguson *play* Louis Mellis, David Scinto *d* Paul McGuigan *ph* Peter Sova *m* John Dankworth *pd* Richard Bridgland *ed* Andrew Hulme *cos* Jany Temine
☆ Malcolm McDowell (Gangster 55), David Thewlis (Freddie Mays), Paul Bettany (Young Gangster), Saffron Burrows (Karen), Kenneth Cranham (Tommy), Jamie Foreman (Lennie Taylor), Razaaq Adoti (Roland), Doug Allen (Mad John), Eddie Marsan (Eddie Miller), David Kennedy (Fat Charlie), Andrew Lincoln (Maxie King), Cavan Clerkin (Billy), Johnny Harris (Derek), Anton Valensi (Trevor)
'Plausible and sure-footed, a film with a canny yet appalled sense of the repulsive realities of crime and the unlovely, unfunny people involved in it.' – *Peter Bradshaw, Guardian*
'Have punters the stomach for slaughter presented as crowd-pleasing pornography?' – *Alexander Walker*

The Gangster's Moll: see *Minbo No Onna*

Gangway ★
GB 1937 89m bw
GFD/Gaumont (Michael Balcon)
A girl reporter poses as a star's maid and is accused of theft.
Mildly pleasing star vehicle.
w Lesser Samuels, Sonnie Hale *d* Sonnie Hale *ph* Glen MacWilliams
☆ Jessie Matthews, Barry Mackay, Nat Pendleton, Noel Madison, Alastair Sim

Gangway for Tomorrow
US 1943 69m bw
RKO
Five defence workers with problematical pasts unite in the cause of war.
Naïve but oddly stirring little propaganda piece.
w Arch Oboler *d* John H. Auer
☆ Robert Ryan, Margo, John Carradine

Garbo Talks ★
US 1984 103m Technicolor
MGM-UA/Elliott Kastner (Burtt Harris)

A dying woman's last obsession is to meet her idol Greta Garbo.
New Yorkish wry comedy which doesn't seem entirely clear of its point but is smartly acted and produced.
w Larry Grusin *d* Sidney Lumet *ph* Andrzej Bartkowiak *m* Cy Coleman *pd* Philip Rosenberg *ed* Andrew Mondshein
☆ Anne Bancroft, Ron Silver, Carrie Fisher, Catherine Hicks, Steven Hill, Howard Da Silva, Harvey Fierstein, Dorothy Loudon, Hermione Gingold
'A sweet and sour film clearly not for all tastes.' – *Variety*

La Garce: see *The Bitch (1984)*

Garde à Vue: see *The Inquisitor*

The Garden ★
GB 1990 90m colour
Artificial Eye/Basilisk/Channel 4/British Screen/ZDF/Uplink (James McKay)

A sequence of images – of Jesus, the Last Supper, the director tending his garden, and a homosexual couple being persecuted – create the effect of a series of semi-religious tableaux.
AIDS and homosexual suffering are the main themes of an intensely personal film most likely to find favour with those who share the director's preoccupations or who can admire his visual flair.
wd Derek Jarman *ph* Christopher Hughes *m* Simon Fisher Turner *pd* Derek Brown, Christopher Hobbs *ed* Peter Cartwright
☆ Kevin Collins, Roger Cook, Jody Graber, Pete Lee-Wilson, Philip Macdonald, Johnny Mills, Tilda Swinton

'Dangerous love in a desert paradise!'

The Garden of Allah ★★
US 1936 80m Technicolor
Selznick International (David O. Selznick)

A disenchanted socialite falls in love with a renegade monk in the Algerian desert.
Arty old-fashioned romantic star vehicle; great to look at, and marking a genuine advance in colour photography, but dramatically a bit of a drag.
w W. P. Lipscomb, Lynn Riggs *novel* Robert Hichens *d* Richard Boleslawski *ph* W. Howard Greene, Harold Rosson *m* Max Steiner *ad* Sturges Carne, Lyle Wheeler, Edward Boyle
☆ Marlene Dietrich, Charles Boyer, Basil Rathbone, Tilly Losch
'The last word in colour production, but a pretty dull affair.' – *Variety*
'Hopelessly dated folderol.' – *J. R. Parish*
'The juiciest tale of woe ever, produced in poshly lurid colour, with a Max Steiner score poured on top.' – *Judith Crist*
'Alas! my poor church, so picturesque, so noble, so superhumanly pious, so intensely dramatic. I really prefer the *New Statesman* view, shabby priests counting pesetas on their dingy fingers before blessing tanks.' – *Graham Greene*
† Previous, silent, versions had been made in 1917, with Tom Santschi and Helen Ware, and in 1927 with Ivan Petrovich and Alice Terry.
Academy Award: special award for colour cinematography
Ꞵ Max Steiner

Garden of Evil ★
US 1954 100m Technicolor Cinemascope
TCF (Charles Brackett)

En route to the Californian goldfields an ex-sheriff and a gambler help a woman to rescue her husband from a mine, but are trapped by Indians.
High-flying Western melodrama with the principals glowering at each other. Stock situations quite skilfully compiled.
w Frank Fenton *d* Henry Hathaway *ph* Milton Krasner *m* Bernard Herrmann
☆ Susan Hayward, Gary Cooper, Richard Widmark, Hugh Marlowe, Cameron Mitchell

The Garden of the Finzi-Continis ★★
Italy/West Germany 1970 95m Eastmancolor
Documento Film/CCC Filmkunst (Gianni Hecht Lucari, Arthur Cohn)

In 1938, a family of wealthy Italian Jews sees its world collapse, with a concentration camp as the next destination.
A dreamlike, poignant, and very beautiful film.
w Tullio Pinelli, Valerio Zurlini, Franco Brusati, Ugo Pirro, Vittorio Bonicelli, Alain Katz *novel* Giorgio Bassani *d* *Vittorio de Sica* *ph* *Ennio Guarnieri* *m* Manuel de Sica
☆ *Dominique Sanda*, Lino Capolicchio, Helmut Berger, Romolo Valli, Fabio Testi
'I lived through the period. The same feelings I experienced in life I transposed to the picture: that is the definition of the artist.' – *Vittorio de Sica*
'This extraordinary film, with its melancholy glamour, is perhaps the only one that records the halfhearted anti-Jewish measures of the Mussolini period.' – *New Yorker*
Academy Award: best foreign film
Ꞵ script

Garden of the Moon
US 1938 94m bw
Warner (Lou Edelman)
A night-club owner vies with his bandleader for the affections of his leading singer.
Pleasant talent can't turn this script into anything but a tedious small-scale musical, especially since both director and songwriters are operating below par.
w Jerry Wald, Richard Macaulay *d* Busby Berkeley *m/ly* Al Dubin, Harry Warren
☆ Pat O'Brien, Margaret Lindsay, John Payne, Melville Cooper, Isabel Jeans

Gardens of Stone
US 1987 111m DeLuxe
Tri-Star/ML Delphi (Michael I. Levy, Francis Coppola)

A soldier trains youngsters for the Vietnam War despite his conviction that the war is wrong.
Muddled talk-piece which fails to make any point.
w Ronald Bass *novel* Nicholas Proffitt *d* Francis Coppola *ph* Jordan Cronenweth *m* Carmine Coppola *pd* Dean Tavoularis *ed* Barry Malkin
☆ James Caan, Anjelica Huston, James Earl Jones, D. B. Sweeney, Dean Stockwell, Mary Stewart Masterson, Dick Anthony Williams

Garm Hava ★
India 1973 136m Eastmancolor
Unit 3 MM/Film Finance Corp. (Abu Siwani, Ishan Arya, M. S. Sathyu)
aka: *Hot Winds*
aka: *Scorching Winds*
After India's independence and partition, some members of a prosperous Muslim family leave to live in Pakistan while others choose to remain in India, where they face hostility and prejudice.
Sprawling family drama, engrossing, despite its occasional clumsinesses, in exploring the impact of public events on private lives.

w Kaifi Azmi, Shama Zaidi *story* Ismat Chugtai *d* M. S. Sathyu *ph* Ishan Arya *md* Ustad Bahadur Khan *ed* S. Chakraborty, Herman Topno
☆ Balraj Sahni, Jalal Agha, Jamal Hashmi, Gita, A. K. Hangal, Yunus Parwaiz, Shaukat Kalfi, Vikas Anand, Rajendra Raghuvanshi

The Garment Jungle *
US 1957 88m bw
Columbia (Harry Kleiner)
Union and gangster problems abound for a family in the New York clothing business.
Reasonably powerful melodrama fashioned from familiar material in the wake of On the Waterfront.
w Harry Kleiner *d* Robert Aldrich, Vincent Sherman *ph* Joseph Biroc *m* Leith Stevens
☆ Lee J. Cobb, Kerwin Mathews, Gia Scala, Richard Boone, Valerie French, Robert Loggia, Joseph Wiseman

Gas Food Lodging **
US 1991 101m DeLuxe
Mainline/Cineville Partners (Daniel Hassid, Seth M. Willenson, William Ewart)
A mother and her two disaffected daughters look for love in a small town.
Engrossing domestic drama of three women struggling to survive and searching for something to make life worthwhile.
wd Allison Anders *novel* *Don't Look and It Won't Hurt* by Richard Peck *ph* Dean Lent *m* J. Mascis *pd* Jane Ann Stewart *ed* Tracy S. Granger
☆ Brooke Adams, Ione Skye, Fairuza Balk, James Brolin, Robert Knepper, David Lansbury, Jacob Vargas, Donovan Leitch, Chris Mulkey
'Anders's film is sometimes stilted, at times over-contrived, but it invariably rings true both socially and psychologically.' – *Philip French, Observer*

Gas House Kids
US 1946 71m bw
PRC
Young New Yorkers help a crippled veteran buy a chicken ranch.
First of three forgotten attempts to stretch out the Dead End Kids genre; not good. (The other titles, both in 1947, were Gas House Kids Go West *and* Gas House Kids in Hollywood.*)*
w Raymond Schrock, George and Elsie Bricker *d* Sam Newfield *ph* Jack Greenhalgh
☆ Billy Halop, Alfalfa Switzer, Robert Lowery, Teala Loring, Rex Downing, David Reed

Gas! or It Became Necessary to Destroy the World in Order to Save It
US 1970 79m Movielab
AIP/San Jacinto (Roger Corman)
A gas which speeds up the ageing process is accidentally released and kills everyone over twenty-five.
Psychedelic sci-fi for the Easy Rider set. Very mildly diverting.
w Graham Armitage *d* Roger Corman *ph* Ron Dexter *m* Country Joe and the Fish
☆ Robert Corff, Elaine Giftos, Pat Patterson, Graham Armitage, Alex Wilson, Ben Vereen, Bud Cort

Gasbags *
GB 1940 77m bw
Gainsborough (Edward Black)
Airmen stranded in Germany by a barrage balloon return in a captured secret weapon.
Fast-moving knockabout from the Crazy Gang; often inventive despite reach-me-down script and production.
w Val Valentine, Val Guest, Marriott Edgar *d* Marcel Varnel *ph* Arthur Crabtree *md* Louis Levy *ad* Vetchinsky *ed* R. E. Dearing
☆ Bud Flanagan, Chesney Allen, Jimmy Nervo, Teddy Knox, Charlie Naughton, Jimmy Gold, Moore Marriott, Wally Patch, Peter Gawthorne, Frederick Valk

Gaslight ****
GB 1940 88m bw
British National (John Corfield)
US title: *Angel Street*
A Victorian schizophrenic drives his wife insane when she seems likely to stumble on his guilty secret of an old murder and hidden rubies.
Modest but absolutely effective film version of a superb piece of suspense theatre.
w A. R. Rawlinson, Bridget Boland *play* *Patrick Hamilton* *d* *Thorold Dickinson* *ph* Bernard Knowles *m* *Richard Addinsell*
☆ *Anton Walbrook, Diana Wynyard, Frank Pettingell*, Cathleen Cordell, Robert Newton, Jimmy Hanley
'For one who has seen the stage play, much of the tension is destroyed by the insistence on explaining everything rather than hinting at it.' – *Dilys Powell*
'The electric sense of tension and mid-Victorian atmosphere are entirely cinematic.' – *Sequence, 1950*
† MGM is said to have tried to destroy the negative of the film when it made its version four years later. See below.

'A melodrama of a strange love!'
'This is love ... clouded by evil ... darkened by a secret no one dared to guess! The strange drama of a captive sweetheart!'
Gaslight **
US 1944 114m bw
MGM (Arthur Hornblow Jnr)
GB title: *The Murder in Thornton Square*
Grossly overblown and less effective version of the above, but with moments of power, effective performances and superior production.
w John Van Druten, Walter Reisch, John L. Balderston *play* *Patrick Hamilton* *d* *George Cukor* *ph* *Joseph Ruttenberg* *m* Bronislau Kaper *ad* *Cedric Gibbons, William Ferrari*
☆ *Charles Boyer, Ingrid Bergman*, Joseph Cotten, Dame May Whitty, Barbara Everest, *Angela Lansbury*, Edmund Breon, Halliwell Hobbes
† Irene Dunne and Hedy Lamarr were previously offered the Ingrid Bergman part, and turned it down.
Ingrid Bergman; art direction
best picture; script; Joseph Ruttenberg; Charles Boyer; Angela Lansbury

The Gate
Canada 1987 92m colour
Vista (John Kemeny)
Two young boys dig a hole in their back yard which opens a gate to hell.
Enjoyable low-budget horror, with some amusing moments.
w Michael Nankin *d* Tibor Takacs *ph* Thomas Vamos *m* Michael Hoenig, J. Peter Robinson *pd* William Beeton *ed* Rit Wallis *sp* Randall William Cook
☆ Stephen Dorff, Christa Denton, Louis Tripp, Kelly Rowan, Jennifer Irwin, Scott Denton
'Sort of an Evil Dead for pre-teen nerds.' – *Stefan Jaworzyn, Shock Xpress*

Gate II
Canada 1992 95m Film House colour
Alliance/Andras Hamori
A teenager and his two friends summon demons who possess them.
Predictable horror aimed at teen audiences, but too tame to attract them.
w Michael Nankin *d* Tibor Takacs *ph* Brian England *m* George Blondheim *pd* William Beeton *ed* Ronald Sanders *sp* Randall William Cook
☆ Louis Tripp, Simon Reynolds, Pamela Segall, James Villemaire, Neil Munro
'An idiotic horror film boasting good monster effects.' – *Variety*

Gate of Hell *
Japan 1953 90m Eastmancolor
Daiei (Masaichi Nagata)
original title: *Jigokumon*
After a 12th-century war, a soldier demands as his prize a woman who has helped him; but she is married.
Curious traditional Japanese saga, its emphases strange to western eyes and ears. Its colour, however, is devastatingly beautiful.
wd Teinosuke Kinugasa *novel* Kan Kikuchi *ph* *Kohei Sugiyama* *m* Yasushi Akutagawa
☆ Machiko Kyo, Kazuo Hasegawa, Isao Yamagata
best foreign film

Gate of Lilacs: see *Porte des Lilas*

Gates of Hell: see *City of The Living Dead*

Gates of Night: see *Les Portes de la Nuit*

Gates of Paris: see *Porte des Lilas*

Gateway *
US 1938 75m bw
TCF (Darryl F. Zanuck)
An Irish girl emigrating to the US is helped on board ship by a war correspondent.
Brisk romantic drama which provides an interesting recreation of the Ellis Island procedures still effective in the thirties.
w Lamar Trotti *d* Alfred Werker *ph* Edward Cronjager *m* Arthur Lange, Charles Maxwell
☆ Don Ameche, Arleen Whelan, Gregory Ratoff, Raymond Walburn, Binnie Barnes, Gilbert Roland, John Carradine, Harry Carey
'*Grand Hotel* treatment applied to Ellis Island ... should look to fair b.o.' – *Variety*

A Gathering of Eagles
US 1963 115m Eastmancolor
U-I (Sy Bartlett)
A colonel becomes unpopular when he strives to improve the efficiency of a Strategic Air Command base.
Tame revamp of Twelve O'clock High *without the justification of war; all strictly routine and perfectly dull.*
w Robert Pirosh *d* Delbert Mann *ph* Russell Harlan *m* Jerry Goldsmith
☆ Rock Hudson, Mary Peach, Rod Taylor, Barry Sullivan, Kevin McCarthy

'Come and get him!'
Gator
US 1976 116m DeLuxe Todd-AO 35
UA/Levy-Gardner-Laven
A convicted moonshiner is blackmailed into becoming a government undercover man in the organization of a hoodlum.
Shambling mixture of action, violence, and raw humour.
w William Norton *d* Burt Reynolds *ph* William A. Fraker *m* Charles Bernstein
☆ Burt Reynolds, Jack Weston, Lauren Hutton, Jerry Reed, Alice Ghostley, Dub Taylor, Mike Douglas
'The relentless violence, the sentimentality, the raucous stag party humour, the inability to cut off a scene once it has made its point, attest to the influence of Robert Aldrich.' – *Philip French*

'There Is No Gene For The Human Spirit.'
Gattaca
US 1997 106m Technicolor Super 35
Columbia TriStar/Jersey (Danny DeVito, Michael Shamberg, Stacey Sher)
In the future, when genetically engineered people control the world, an ordinary person takes another's identity to succeed.
Glossy science fiction with a very soft centre under its hard surface.
wd Andrew Niccol *ph* Slawomir Idziak *m* Michael Nyman *pd* Jan Roelfs *ed* Lisa Zeno Churgin
☆ Ethan Hawke (Vincent/Jerome), Uma Thurman (Irene), Alan Arkin (Detective Hugo), Jude Law (Jerome/Eugene), Loren Dean (Anton), Gore Vidal (Director Joseph), Ernest Borgnine (Caesar), Blair Underwood, Xander Berkeley (Lamar), Tony Shalhoub (German)
'For all its style and promise, *Gattaca* is far easier to look at than actually watch.' – *Neil Jeffries, Empire*
Jan Roelfs

Il Gatto Dogli Occhi Di Gioda: see *The Cat's Victims*

Il Gatto Nero: see *The Black Cat (1981)*

Il Gattopardo: see *The Leopard*

The Gaucho *
US 1928 115m approx bw silent
Douglas Fairbanks
An outlaw reforms when he falls for the Girl of the Shrine.
Subdued star swashbuckler leading up to a fine climax.
w Lotta Woods *story* Douglas Fairbanks *d* F. Richard Jones
☆ Douglas Fairbanks, Lupe Velez, Geraine Greer, Gustav von Seyffertitz

The Gaunt Stranger *
GB 1938 73m bw
Northwood/Capad (Ealing) (Michael Balcon, S. C. Balcon)
US title: *The Phantom Strikes*
A criminal master of disguise threatens to kill a much more despicable criminal at an appointed hour ... and does so despite police protection.
A highly reliable suspenser of which this is perhaps the best film version.
w Sidney Gilliat *play and novel* *The Ringer* by *Edgar Wallace* *d* Walter Forde *ph* Ronald Neame *ad* Oscar Werndorff *ed* Charles Saunders
☆ Sonnie Hale, Wilfrid Lawson, Alexander Knox, Louise Henry, Patricia Roc, Patrick Barr, John Longden, George Merritt
'Dialogue, humour and suspense are effectively alternated ... the film is in fact capital crime fiction.' – *Kine Weekly*
† Other versions, as *The Ringer*, appeared in 1931 and 1953.

The Gauntlet *
US 1977 109m DeLuxe Panavision
Warner/Malpaso (Robert Daly)
A disreputable cop is assigned to escort a foul-mouthed prostitute to a courtroom across country, through the gauntlet of baddies who want them both dead.
The epitome of seventies violence, with no excuse except to stage one detailed shoot-up or explosion after another. Well done for those who like this sort of thing.
w Michael Butler, Dennis Shryack *d* Clint Eastwood *ph* Rexford Metz *m* Jerry Fielding
☆ Clint Eastwood, Sondra Locke, Pat Hingle, William Prince
'At times the whole world seems to be firing at them. Buildings and cars are turned to lace. You look at the screen even though there's nothing to occupy your mind...' – *Pauline Kael*
† This was the first film to give a credit for first aid.

Gawain and the Green Knight *
GB 1973 93m Technicolor Panavision
UA/Sancrest (Philip Breen)
The medieval legend of a supernatural knight who challenges the king's men to kill him.
Enterprising if unsuccessful low-budget attempt to create a medieval world; too long by half.
w Philip Breen, Stephen Weeks *d* Stephen Weeks *ph* Ian Wilson *m* Ron Goodwin *ad* *Anthony Woollard*
☆ Murray Head, Ciaran Madden, Nigel Green, Anthony Sharp, Robert Hardy, Murray Melvin

The Gay Adventure: see *Golden Arrow*

The Gay Bride
US 1934 80m bw
MGM (John Considine Jnr)
A gold-digging chorus girl marries a racketeer but soon becomes a widow.
Misfiring satirical melodrama which quickly becomes tedious.
w Bella and Samuel Spewack *story* *Repeal* by Charles Francis Coe *d* Jack Conway *ph* Ray June
☆ Carole Lombard, Chester Morris, ZaSu Pitts, Nat Pendleton, Leo Carrillo
'Gangster pictures are gone, and this won't do anything to bring them back.' – *Variety*

The Gay Deception *
US 1935 79m bw
Fox (Jesse L. Lasky)
A Ruritanian prince becomes a doorman at a swank New York hotel, and marries a secretary.
Lightly-handled Cinderella story showing most of its director's accomplishment.
w Stephen Morehouse Avery, Don Hartman *d* *William Wyler* *ph* Joseph Valentine *m* Louis de Francesco

☆ Francis Lederer, Frances Dee, Benita Hume, Alan Mowbray, Akim Tamiroff, Lennox Pawle, Richard Carle, Lionel Stander

'Doesn't lean too much to sophistication to miss appreciation in the hamlet houses.' – *Variety*

story

The Gay Desperado **

US 1936 85m bw

Mary Pickford

An heiress is held for ransom by a romantic bandit.

Very light, quite amusing, sometimes irritatingly skittish musical spoof sparked by the director's ideas.

w Wallace Smith *story* Leo Birinski *d Rouben Mamoulian* *ph* Lucien Andriot *m* Alfred Newman

☆ Ida Lupino, Nino Martini, Leo Carrillo, Harold Huber, Mischa Auer

'Fairly diverting Mexican western ... it'll do spotty trade, depending on locale.' – *Variety*

'One of the best light comedies of the year ... Mr Mamoulian's camera is very persuasive.' – *Graham Greene*

'While some of the show is fetching, the ideas mostly misfire and the spell is fitful and unsure.' – *Otis Ferguson*

'It has the lightness of touch which goes into the making of the perfect meringue.' – *Basil Wright*

The Gay Divorce: see *The Gay Divorcee*

'The gayest of mad musicals!'

'The dance-mad musical triumph of two continents!'

The Gay Divorcee ****

US 1934 107m bw

RKO (Pandro S. Berman)

GB title: *The Gay Divorce*

A would-be divorcee in an English seaside hotel mistakes a dancer who loves her for a professional co-respondent.

Wildly and hilariously dated comedy musical with splendidly archaic comedy routines supporting Hollywood's great new dance team in their first big success. Not much dancing, but 'The Continental' is a show-stopper.

w George Marion Jnr, Dorothy Yost, Edward Kaufman *play* Dwight Taylor, J. Hartley Manners *musical comedy Samuel Hoffenstein, Kenneth Webb, Cole Porter* *d Mark Sandrich* *ph* David Abel *m/ly* various *md* Max Steiner *ad* Van Nest Polglase, Carroll Clark *ed* William Hamilton *sp Vernon Walker*

☆ *Fred Astaire, Ginger Rogers, Edward Everett Horton, Alice Brady, Erik Rhodes, Eric Blore,* Lillian Miles, Betty Grable

'Cinch box office anywhere and certain of big foreign grosses.' – *Variety*

'The plot is trivial French farce, but the dances are among the wittiest and most lyrical expressions of American romanticism on the screen.' – *New Yorker, 1977*

† 'Night and Day' was the only Cole Porter song to survive from the stage musical.

song 'The Continental' (*m* Con Conrad, *ly* Herb Magidson)

best picture; musical score (Ken Webb, Samuel Hoffenstein); art direction

The Gay Dog

GB 1954 87m bw

Coronet/Eros

A miner trains a pet greyhound to win races.

Modest, set-bound regional comedy.

w Peter Rogers *play* Joseph Colton *d* Maurice Elvey *ph* James Wilson *m* Edwin Astley

☆ Wilfred Pickles, Petula Clark, Megs Jenkins, John Blythe

The Gay Duellist: see *Meet Me at Dawn*

The Gay Imposters: see *Gold Diggers in Paris*

The Gay Intruders

US 1948 68m bw

TCF

Quarrelling stage marrieds consult psychiatrists, who end up more confused than the patients.

Unusual second feature comedy with a few good laughs; allegedly based on Tallulah Bankhead.

w Francis Swann *d* Ray McCarey

☆ Tamara Geva, John Emery, Leif Erickson, Virginia Gregg

The Gay Lady: see *Trottie True*

The Gay Mrs Trexel: see *Susan and God*

The Gay Nineties: see *The Floradora Girl*

Gay Purree *

US 1962 85m Technicolor

UPA (Henry Saperstein)

A country cat goes to Paris and is Shanghaied.

Feature cartoon similar to Disney's later The Aristocats *and about as good, i.e. not quite up to the best standards.*

w Dorothy and Chuck Jones *d* Abe Levitow *m/ly* Harold Arlen, E. Y. Harburg *md* Mort Lindsey

☆ Featuring the voices of Judy Garland, Robert Goulet, Hermione Gingold

The Gay Sisters *

US 1942 110m bw

Warner (Henry Blanke)

Three sisters refuse to sell their aristocratic New York mansion to make way for development.

Slowish but quite interesting family drama with Chekhovian touches.

w Lenore Coffee *novel* Stephen Longstreet *d* Irving Rapper *ph* Sol Polito *m* Max Steiner

☆ Barbara Stanwyck, George Brent, Geraldine Fitzgerald, Donald Crisp, *Gig Young*, Nancy Coleman, Gene Lockhart, Larry Simms, Donald Woods, Grant Mitchell

† Gig Young took his name from his part in this film; he was formerly Byron Barr.

The Gazebo *

US 1959 102m bw CinemaScope

MGM/Avon (Lawrence Weingarten)

A TV writer kills a blackmailer (he thinks) and hides his body in the garden.

Frenetic black comedy which must have worked better on the stage but produces a few laughs.

w George Wells *play* Alec Coppel *d* George Marshall *ph* Paul C. Vogel *m* Jeff Alexander

☆ Glenn Ford, Debbie Reynolds, Carl Reiner, John McGiver, Mabel Albertson, Doro Merande, ZaSu Pitts, Martin Landau

Gazon Maudit: see *French Twist*

Gei Ba Ba De Xin: see *The Enforcer (1995)*

The Geisha Boy

US 1958 98m Technicolor Vistavision

Paramount (Jerry Lewis)

A third-rate magician joins a USO entertainment tour in Japan.

Disconnected farce which amuses only fitfully, and actively displeases when it becomes sentimental with the star drooling over a baby.

wd Frank Tashlin *ph* Haskell Boggs *m* Walter Scharf

☆ Jerry Lewis, Marie MacDonald, Barton MacLane, Sessue Hayakawa, Suzanne Pleshette

The Gene Krupa Story

US 1959 101m bw

Columbia (Philip A. Waxman)

GB title: *Drum Crazy*

A successful jazz drummer is convicted on a drugs charge and falls from grace.

Dreary biopic with the expected music track.

w Orin Jannings *d* Don Weis *ph* Charles Lawton Jnr *m* Leith Stevens

☆ Sal Mineo, Susan Kohner, James Darren, Susan Oliver, Yvonne Craig, Lawrence Dobkin, Celia Lovsky, Shelly Manne, Buddy Lester, Red Nichols

'Everybody laughs but Buster!'

The General ****

US 1926 80m approx (24 fps) bw silent

UA/Buster Keaton (Joseph M. Schenck)

A confederate train driver gets his train and his girl back when they are stolen by Union soldiers.

Slow-starting, then hilarious action comedy, often voted one of the best ever made. Its sequence of sight gags, each topping the one before, is an incredible joy to behold.

w Al Boasberg, Charles Smith d Buster Keaton, Clyde Bruckman ph J. Devereux Jennings, Bert Haines

☆ *Buster Keaton*, Marion Mack, Glen Cavander

'It has all the sweet earnestness in the world. It is about trains, frontier America, flower-faced girls.' – *New Yorker, 1977*

'The production itself is singularly well mounted, but the fun is not exactly plentiful ... here he is more the acrobat than the clown, and his vehicle might be described as a mixture of cast iron and jelly.' – *Mordaunt Hall, New York Times*

† The story is based on an actual incident of the Civil War, treated more seriously in *The Great Locomotive Chase* (qv).

†† The screenplay with 1,400 freeze frames was issued in 1976 in the Film Classics Library (editor, Richard Anobile).

The General ***

Ireland/GB 1998 123m bw Panavision

Warner/Merlin Films/J&M (John Boorman)

In Dublin of the early 90s, Martin Cahill, a charming and brutal gangster, pulls off a succession of daring robberies until he betrays himself and is killed by an IRA gunman.

A knowing, witty throwback to the street-smart, socially aware gangster films of the 30s. Although 'torn from today's headlines', it follows a classic tragic trajectory, of a man taking on the world until he is undone by his own overweening pride.

wd John Boorman ph Seamus Deasy *m* Richie Buckley *pd* Derek Wallace *ed Ron Davis*

☆ *Brendan Gleeson*, Adrian Dunbar, Sean McGinley, Maria Doyle Kennedy, Angeline Ball, Jon Voight

'Both challenges and entertains the audience at a variety of levels, as well as reviving the vitality and freshness of the helmer's earliest, mid-'60s pics.' – *Derek Elley, Variety*

† John Boorman won the prize for best director at the 1998 Cannes Film Festival.

General Della Rovere **

Italy 1959 130m bw

Gaumont/Zebra (Morris Ergas)

original title: *Il Generale Della Rovere*

A petty thief, forced by the Nazis to pose as a Resistance leader to flush out the real leaders, begins to take the role seriously.

De Sica's bravura performance saves a slickly made but emotionally hollow film, one that its director seems not to have liked.

w Sergio Amidei, Diego Fabbri, Indro Montanelli, Roberto Rossellini *d* Roberto Rossellini *ph* Carlo Carlini *m* Renzo Rossellini *ad* Piero Zuffi *ed* Cesare Cavagna

☆ Vittorio de Sica, Hannes Messemer, Sandra Milo, Giovanna Ralli

† The film was co-winner of the Golden Lion at the Venice Film Festival in 1959.

story and screenplay

'Gary goes to town for the best-looking gal in China!'

The General Died at Dawn **

US 1936 93m bw

Paramount (William le Baron)

A mercenary in China overcomes an evil warlord and falls in love with a spy.

Heavy-going but very decorative studio-bound intrigue which seems to take place on the old Shanghai Express sets with an extra infusion of dry ice. An intellectual's picture of its day.

w Clifford Odets *novel* Charles Booth *d Lewis Milestone* *ph Victor Milner* *m* Werner Janssen, Gerard Carbonara

☆ Gary Cooper, Madeleine Carroll, *Akim Tamiroff, Dudley Digges*, Porter Hall, *William Frawley*

'If it were not for a rather ludicrous ending, this would be one of the best thrillers for some years.' – *Graham Greene*

'In terms of cinematic invention, a fascinating technical exercise.' – *John Baxter, 1968*

'A curious study in exoticism.' – *NFT, 1974*

'In direction and photography it has undeniable class ... but like most movies, it is empty of any ideas or characters that stay with you longer than it takes to reach the nearest subway entrance.' – *Brooklyn Daily Eagle*

Victor Milner; Werner Janssen; Akim Tamiroff

The General Line **

USSR 1929 90m (24 fps) bw silent

Sovkino

original title: *Staroye i Novoye*

aka: *Old and New*

A country woman helps to start a village co-operative.

A slight piece of propaganda, put together with all of Eisenstein's magnificent cinematic resources: the cream separator demonstration is one of the most famous montage sequences in cinema history.

w Sergei Eisenstein *d* Sergei Eisenstein, Grigori Alexandrov *ph* Edouard Tissé

☆ Marta Lapkina and a cast of non-professionals

General Spanky

US 1936 73m approx bw

MGM/Hal Roach

A small boy is instrumental in a famous Civil War victory.

Uneasy sentimental melodrama vehicle for one of the moppet stars of 'Our Gang'.

w Richard Flournoy, Hal Yates, John Guedel *d* Gordon Douglas, Fred Newmeyer

☆ Spanky McFarland, Phillips Holmes, Hobart Bosworth, Ralph Morgan, Irving Pichel

'Desultory, overlong ... built for the lesser family trade.' – *Variety*

'To Find The Truth, Follow the Lies.'

'Her Murder Was Just The Beginning.'

The General's Daughter

US/Germany 1999 116m DeLuxe Panavision

Paramount (Mace Neufeld)

A detective has 36 hours in which to solve the rape and murder of a general's daughter.

Ponderous, loquacious whodunnit, with an involved narrative that becomes more unbelievable, and less involving, by the minute.

w Christopher Bertolini, William Goldman *novel* Nelson DeMille *d* Simon West *ph* Peter Menzies Jnr *m* Carter Burwell *pd* Dennis Washington *ed* Glen Scantlebury

☆ John Travolta (Paul Brenner), Madeleine Stowe (Sarah Sunhill), James Cromwell (General Campbell), Timothy Hutton (Colonel Kent), Leslie Stefanson (Elisabeth Campbell), Daniel von Bargen (Chief Yardley), Clarence Williams III (Colonel Fowler), James Woods (Colonel Moore), Peter Weireter (Belling), Mark Boone Jnr (Elkins)

'Misogynist nonsense' – *Guardian*

'The cinematic equivalent of a disposable airplane read, a hokey, kinky military thriller that's twisty and compelling enough to hook viewers in the mood for a trashy good time.' – *Variety*

† It grossed more than $102m at the US box-office.

Generation *

Poland 1954 90m bw

Film Polski

original title: *Pokolenie*

In occupied Warsaw in 1942 a teenager becomes hardened by life and joins the resistance.

Heavy-going but quite striking propaganda piece, amply demonstrating its director's talents.

w Bohdan Czeszko *novel* Bohdan Czeszko *d Andrzej Wajda* *ph* Jerzy Lipman *m* Andrzej Markowski

☆ Tadeusz Lomnicki, Urszula Modrzynska, Roman Polanski, Zbigniew Cybulski

Generation

US 1969 104m Technicolor

Avco Embassy/Frederick Brisson

GB title: *A Time for Giving*

A Denver advertising executive is horrified by his daughter's ideas of modern marriage.

Lame generation-gap comedy centring on a couple who intend to deliver their own baby.

w William Goodhart *play* William Goodhart *d* George Schaefer *ph* Lionel Lindon *m* Dave Grusin

☆ David Janssen, Kim Darby, Carl Reiner, Pete Duel, Andrew Prine, James Coco, Sam Waterston, Don Beddoe

'Slightly too sticky for comfort.' – *MFB*

Genevieve ****
GB 1953 86m Technicolor
GFD/Sirius (Henry Cornelius)
Two friendly rivals engage in a race on the way back from the Brighton veteran car rally.
One of those happy films in which for no very good or expected reason a number of modest elements merge smoothly to create an aura of high style and memorable moments. A charmingly witty script, carefully pointed direction, attractive actors and locations, an atmosphere of light-hearted British sex and a lively harmonica theme turned it, after a slowish start, into one of Britain's biggest commercial hits and most fondly remembered comedies.
w *William Rose* d *Henry Cornelius* ph Christopher Challis m *Larry Adler (who also played it)*
md Muir Mathieson ad Michael Stringer
☆ *Dinah Sheridan, John Gregson, Kay Kendall, Kenneth More, Geoffrey Keen, Joyce Grenfell, Reginald Beckwith, Arthur Wontner*
'One of the best things to have happened to British films over the last five years.' – *Gavin Lambert*
† On American prints, Muir Mathieson was credited as the composer and with the Oscar nomination rather than Larry Adler, who was blacklisted at the time.
William Rose; Larry Adler
British film

'In the eight centuries since he ruled the world, no man has matched the magnificence of his adventure!'
Genghis Khan *
US 1964 126m Technicolor Panavision
Columbia/Irving Allen/CCC/Avala
Temujin raises a Mongol army and revenges himself on his old enemy Jamuga.
Meandering epic in which brutality alternates with pantomimish comedy and bouts of sex. Necessarily patchy but reasonably watchable.
w Clarke Reynolds, Beverley Cross d Henry Levin ph Geoffrey Unsworth m Ducan Radic
☆ Omar Sharif, Stephen Boyd, Françoise Dorléac, *James Mason*, Robert Morley, Telly Savalas, Woody Strode, Eli Wallach, Yvonne Mitchell

Genius at Work
US 1946 61m bw
RKO (Herman Schlom)
Radio detectives expose a killer.
Rackety vehicle for a comedy team which never even approached Abbott and Costello.
w Robert E. Kent, Monte Brice d Leslie Goodwins ph Robert De Grasse
☆ Wally Brown, Alan Carney, Anne Jeffreys, Bela Lugosi, Lionel Atwill

A Genius in the Family: see *So Goes My Love*

Genou de Claire: see *Claire's Knee*

Les Gens de la Rizière: see *Rice People*

Gente di rispetto: see *The Masters*

A Gentle Creature: see *Une Femme Douce*

The Gentle Giant
US 1967 93m Eastmancolor
Ivan Tors/Paramount
A small boy in Florida befriends a bear, which later saves his disapproving father's life.
Lumbering family movie which provided the impetus for a TV series.
w Edward J. Lakso, Andy White novel *Gentle Ben* by Walt Morey d James Neilson ph Howard Winner
☆ Dennis Weaver, Clint Howard, Vera Miles, Ralph Meeker, Huntz Hall

The Gentle Gunman
GB 1952 88m bw
GFD/Ealing (Michael Relph)
Tensions mount in an IRA family where one brother believes in peace.
Stilted and unconvincing pattern play which wouldn't have done at all once the Troubles restarted.
w Roger MacDougall play Roger MacDougall d Basil Dearden ph Gordon Dines m John Greenwood ed Peter Tanner
☆ John Mills, Dirk Bogarde, Elizabeth Sellars, Barbara Mullen, Robert Beatty, Eddie Byrne, Joseph Tomelty, Gilbert Harding, Liam Redmond, Jack MacGowran

The Gentle Sergeant: see *Three Stripes in the Sun*

The Gentle Sex **
GB 1943 93m bw
Rank/Two Cities/Concanen (Leslie Howard, Derrick de Marney)
Seven girls from different backgrounds are conscripted into the ATS.
Unassuming war propaganda, quite pleasantly done and historically very interesting.
w Moie Charles, Aimée Stuart, Phyllis Rose, Roland Pertwee d Leslie Howard, Maurice Elvey ph Robert Krasker m John Greenwood
☆ Rosamund John, Joan Greenwood, Joan Gates, Jean Gillie, Lilli Palmer, Joyce Howard, Barbara Waring, John Justin, Frederick Leister, Mary Jerrold, Everley Gregg
† Leslie Howard is heard as narrator and recognizably glimpsed in two scenes photographed from behind.

A Gentleman after Dark
US 1942 74m bw
Edward Small
A jewel thief comes out of prison to pay back his vindictive wife for shopping him.
Efficient melodrama of a dated kind.
w Patterson McNutt, George Bruce story *A Whiff of Heliotrope* by Richard Washburn Child d Edwin L. Marin ph Milton Krasner m Dimitri Tiomkin
☆ Brian Donlevy, Miriam Hopkins, Preston Foster, Harold Huber, Philip Reed, Gloria Holden, Douglass Dumbrille, Ralph Morgan
† Previously filmed in 1920 as *Heliotrope* with Fred Burton; in 1928 as *Forgotten Faces* with Clive Brook; and in 1936 as *Forgotten Faces* with Herbert Marshall.

Gentleman for a Day: see *Union Depot*

Gentleman Jim **
US 1942 104m bw
Warner (Robert Buckner)
The rise to fame of boxer Jim Corbett.
Cheerful biopic of an 1890s show-off, mostly played for comedy.
w Vincent Lawrence, Horace McCoy book *The Roar of the Crowd* by James J. Corbett d *Raoul Walsh* ph Sid Hickox m Heinz Roemheld
☆ *Errol Flynn, Alan Hale*, Alexis Smith, John Loder, Jack Carson, *Ward Bond*, William Frawley, Rhys Williams, Arthur Shields
'Good-natured enough, but it lacks flavour.' – *New Yorker, 1976*

'Now! It comes to the screen with nothing left unsaid and no emotion unstressed!'
Gentleman's Agreement **
US 1947 118m bw
TCF (Darryl F. Zanuck)
A journalist poses as a Jew in order to write about anti-semitism.
Worthy melodrama which caused a sensation at the time but as a film is alas rather dull and self-satisfied.
w Moss Hart novel Laura Z. Hobson d Elia Kazan ph Arthur Miller m Alfred Newman ed Harmon Jones
☆ Gregory Peck, Dorothy McGuire, *John Garfield*, Celeste Holm, *Anne Revere*, June Havoc, Albert Dekker, Jane Wyatt, Dean Stockwell
best picture; Elia Kazan; Celeste Holm
Moss Hart; Gregory Peck; Dorothy McGuire; Anne Revere; editing

Gentleman's Fate
US 1931 90m bw
MGM
A man goes to the bad after his wife walks out on him.
Dismal early talkie, one of several which killed off its star's career.
w Leonard Praskins story Ursula Parrott d Mervyn Le Roy
☆ John Gilbert, Louis Wolheim, Leila Hyams, Anita Page, John Miljan, Marie Prevost
'It got a laugh at the Strand Saturday afternoon, where all of the audience probably thought the same thing, that Gilbert died too late as the picture had been dying since its start.' – *Variety*

Gentlemen Don't Eat Poets: see *The Grotesque*

Gentlemen Marry Brunettes
US 1955 95m Technicolor Cinemascope
UA/Russ-Field (Richard Sale, Robert Waterfield)
Two American shopgirls seek rich husbands in Paris, and find that their aunts were notorious there.
Jaded sequel to Gentlemen Prefer Blondes; *it barely raises a smile and the numbers are dismal.*
w Mary Loos, Richard Sale d Richard Sale ph Desmond Dickinson m Robert Farnon ch Jack Cole ad Paul Sheriff
☆ Jane Russell, Jeanne Crain, Alan Young, Scott Brady, Rudy Vallee
† Jeanne Crain's vocals were dubbed by Anita Ellis.

Gentlemen of the Navy: see *Annapolis Farewell*

Gentlemen Prefer Blondes *
US 1953 91m Technicolor
TCF (Sol C. Siegel)
A dumb blonde and a showgirl go to Paris in search of rich husbands.
Musicalized and updated version of the twenties satire; no real vigour, but not too bad.
w Charles Lederer novel Anita Loos d Howard Hawks ph Harry J. Wild m/ly Jule Styne, Leo Robin md Lionel Newman ch Jack Cole
☆ *Jane Russell, Marilyn Monroe, Charles Coburn*, Tommy Noonan, Norma Varden, Elliott Reid, George Winslow

Geordie *
GB 1955 99m Technicolor
British Lion/Argonaut (Sidney Gilliat, Frank Launder)
US title: *Wee Geordie*
A weakly Scottish boy takes a physical culture course and becomes an Olympic hammer-thrower.
Slight comic fable, good to look at but without the necessary style to follow it through.
w Sidney Gilliat, Frank Launder novel David Walker d Frank Launder ph Wilkie Cooper m William Alwyn
☆ Bill Travers, Alastair Sim, Norah Gorsen, Raymond Huntley, Brian Reece, Miles Malleson, Stanley Baxter

George and Mildred
GB 1980 93m colour
Chips/ITC (Roy Skeggs)
A suburban husband on a weekend package holiday is mistaken for a hired killer.
Abysmal TV spinoff, seeming even more lugubrious since it was released after the death of the female star.
w Dick Sharples d Peter Frazer Jones ph Frank Watts m Philip Martell ad Carolyn Scott ed Peter Weatherley
☆ Yootha Joyce, Brian Murphy, Stratford Johns, Norman Eshley, Sheila Fearn, Kenneth Cope
'Flaccid entertainment even by routine sit-com standards.' – *Martyn Auty, MFB*

George in Civvy Street
GB 1946 79m bw
Columbia (Marcel Varnel, Ben Henry)
A soldier returns to his country pub and finds himself in the middle of a beer war.
The star's last film was oddly lacklustre and compared very badly with his earlier successes.
w Peter Fraser, Ted Kavanagh, Max Kester, Gale Pedrick d Marcel Varnel ph Phil Grindrod
☆ George Formby, Rosalyn Boulter, Ronald Shiner, Ian Fleming, Wally Patch

George of the Jungle *
US 1997 91m colour
Buena Vista/Walt Disney/Mandeville (David Hoberman, Jordan Kerner, Jon Avnet)
A dim-witted ape-man meets his first humans and falls in love.
An affectionate send-up of Tarzan, with a talking ape and a puppy-like elephant; Fraser, too, has a puppy-dog manner that gives this juvenile stuff a slight charm.
w Dana Olsen, Audrey Wells *characters developed by* Jay Ward d Sam Weisman ph Thomas Ackerman m Marc Shaiman pd Stephen Marsh ed Stuart Pappé, Roger Bondelli
☆ Brendan Fraser, Leslie Mann, Thomas Haden Church, Richard Roundtree, Greg Cruttwell, John Cleese (voice)
'Sporadically playful, it ends up wearing as thin as any film geared to a pre-teen sense of humor is bound to.' – *Kenneth Turan, Los Angeles Times*
† The film was based on an animated series for television that ran from 1967 to 1970.
†† It grossed \$105m at the US box-office, and \$35m elsewhere.

The George Raft Story
US 1961 105m bw
Allied Artists (Ben Schwab)
GB title: *Spin of a Coin*
In twenties New York, a dancer falls in with gangsters, but eludes them when he goes to Hollywood, where his acting career is harmed by temperament.
Tepid, unconvincing biopic, rather shoddily made but with flashes of interest.
w Crane Wilbur d Joseph M. Newman ph Carl Guthrie m Jeff Alexander
☆ *Ray Danton* (George Raft), Julie London, Jayne Mansfield, Frank Gorshin, Neville Brand (Al Capone)

George Washington **
US 2000 90m colour 'Scope
BFI/Youandwhatarmy Filmed Challenges/Blue Moon/Down Home (David Gordon Green, Sacha Mueller, Lisa Muskat)
In a run-down North Carolina town, a group of teenagers attempt to cover up a tragedy.
Delicate, dreamy movie with its own slow rhythms, of inertia punctuated by small bursts of energy.
wd David Gordon Green ph Tim Orr m Michael Linnen, David Wingo pd Richard Wright ed Steven Gonzales, Zene Baker
☆ Candace Evanofski (Nasia), Donald Holden (George), Curtis Cotton III (Buddy), Eddie Rouse (Damascus), Paul Schneider (Rico), Damian Jewan Lee (Vernon), Rachel Handy (Sonya), Jonathan Davidson (Euless), Janet Taylor (Aunt Ruth)
'An almost awe-inspiringly accomplished movie with an absolute faith in its own aesthetic sense, and an unapologetic preoccupation with finding beauty in the look of ordinary places, people and things.' – *Peter Bradshaw, Guardian*

George Washington Slept Here
US 1942 93m bw
Warner (Jerry Wald)
A New York couple move to a dilapidated country house.
Disappointingly stiff and ill-timed version of a play that should have been a natural.
w Everett Freeman play George Kaufman, Moss Hart d William Keighley ph Ernest Haller m Adolph Deutsch ad Max Parker, Mark-Lee Kirk
☆ Jack Benny, Ann Sheridan, Percy Kilbride, Charles Coburn, Hattie McDaniel, William Tracy, Lee Patrick, John Emery, Charles Dingle
art direction

George White's 1935 Scandals *
US 1935 83m bw
Fox (Winfield Sheehan)
A small-town star is discovered by a Broadway producer.
Again, basic plot serves to introduce some pretty good acts.
w Jack Yellen, Patterson McNutt d George White ph George Schneiderman m/ly various
☆ George White, Alice Faye, James Dunn, Eleanor Powell, Ned Sparks, Lyda Roberti, Cliff Edwards, Arline Judge

George White's Scandals *
US 1934 79m bw
Fox (Winfield Sheehan)
Romance blossoms backstage during the production of a big musical.
Revue with minimum plot and some impressive numbers.

w Jack Yellen, from the Broadway show directed by George White *d* Thornton Freeland, Harry Lachman, George White *ph* Lee Garmes, George Schneiderman *m/ly* various
☆ George White, Rudy Vallee, Alice Faye, Jimmy Durante, Dixie Dunbar, Adrienne Ames, Cliff Edwards, Gertrude Michael, Gregory Ratoff

George White's Scandals *
US 1945 95m bw
RKO (Jack J. Gross, Nat Holt, George White)
Ex-Scandals girls get together, and one disappears.
Lively comedy-musical with vaudeville orientations.
w Hugh Wedlock, Parke Levy, Howard Green *d* Felix E. Feist *ph* Robert de Grasse *m* Leigh Harline *m/ly* various
☆ Joan Davis, Jack Haley, Philip Terry, Martha Holliday, Ethel Smith, Margaret Hamilton, Glenn Tryon, Jane Greer, Fritz Feld, Rufe Davis

Georgia
Australia 1988 93m colour
Jethro (Bob Weis)
A tough tax investigator tries to find out the truth about how her mother died when she was a baby.
Implausible and uninteresting thriller that comes to no satisfactory conclusion.
w Ben Lewin, Joanna Murray-Smith, Bob Weis *story* Mac Gudgeon *d* Ben Lewin *ph* Yuri Sokol *m* Paul Grabowsky *pd* Jon Dowding *ed* Edward McQueen-Mason
☆ Judy Davis, John Bach, Julia Blake, Alex Menglet, Marshall Napier, Lewis Fiander
'A rather silly piece of hokum.' – *Scott Murray, Australian Cinema*

Georgia *
US/France 1995 117m Technicolor
CiBy 2000 (Ulu Grosbard, Barbara Turner, Jennifer Jason Leigh)
A self-destructive woman with ambitions, but not the talent, to be a rock performer envies her elder sister who is a successful singer.
Intense study of family tensions within the life of an unhappy alcoholic who cannot come to terms with her own failings; it is affecting and irritating in equal measure.
w Barbara Turner *d* Ulu Grosbard *ph* Jan Kiesser *pd* Lester Cohen *ed* Elizabeth Kling
☆ Jennifer Jason Leigh, Mare Winningham, Ted Levine, John Doe, John C. Reilly, Jimmy Witherspoon
'A nearly perfect movie about a nearly total screw-up.' – *Entertainment Weekly*
'Performed to maximum effect by a host of top-flight actors.' – *Variety*
Mare Winningham

Georgia's Friends: see *Four Friends*

Georgy Girl *
GB 1966 100m bw
Columbia/Everglades (Otto Plaschkes, Robert A. Goldston)
An unattractive girl is fancied by her middle-aged employer but escapes to look after the illegitimate baby of her ungrateful friend.
Frantic black farce which seems determined to shock, but has a few good scenes once you get attuned to the mood. A censorship milestone.
w Margaret Forster, Peter Nichols *novel* Margaret Forster *d* *Silvio Narizzano* *ph* Ken Higgins *m* Alexander Faris
☆ *James Mason, Lynn Redgrave, Charlotte Rampling,* Alan Bates, Bill Owen, Clare Kelly, Rachel Kempson
'Another swinging London story filled with people running through London late at night, dancing madly in the rain, and visiting deserted children's playgrounds to ride on the roundabouts.' – *MFB*
'So glib, so clever, so determinedly kinky that everything seems to be devalued.' – *Pauline Kael*
'A bit of 1960s camp about a fat girl who finds love. At a preview, the director asked me, "Who the hell is going to pay to see this?" "All the fat girls?" I suggested.' – *Peter Nichols, Diaries 1969-1977*
Ken Higgins; James Mason; Lynn Redgrave; title song (*m* Tom Springfield, *ly* Jim Dale)

Gerald McBoing Boing ***
US 1951 7m Technicolor
UPA
A small boy becomes famous because he can't speak words: 'he goes boing-boing instead'.
Highly influential cartoon in what was then a new style; told with a light touch which is still extremely funny. Followed less successfully by Gerald McBoing Boing's Symphony and Gerald McBoing Boing On Planet Moo.
w *Dr Seuss (Theodore Geisel)* *d* *Robert Cannon* *m* *Gail Kubik* *pd* *John Hubley*
best cartoon

The German Sisters *
West Germany 1981 107m Fujicolour
Bioskop Film/ (Eberhard Junkersdorf)
original title: *Die Bleierne Zeit*
Based on a real-life case, this is a suppositional account of how two well-brought-up girls can develop so differently.
wd *Margarethe von Trotta* *ph* *Franz Rath* *m* Nicolas Economou *ed* Dagmar Hirtz
☆ Jutta Lampe, Barbara Sukowa, Rudiger Vogler, Doris Schade, Verenice Rudolph
'Beautifully acted and strikingly shot, it all has a calculated, crowd-pleasing fervour.' – *Tom Milne, MFB*

Germany Year Zero *
France/Italy 1947 78m bw
Union Générale Cinématographique/DEFA
original title: *Germana Anno Zero*
Life in post-war Germany is so appalling that a boy kills his father and then himself.
Both realistic and pessimistic, this depressing film has a savage power of its own but totally fails to be constructive.
w Roberto Rossellini, Carlo Lizzani, Max Kolpet *d* Roberto Rossellini *ph* Robert Juillard *m* Renzo Rossellini *ad* Piero Filippone *ed* Eraldo Da Roma
☆ Edmund Moeschke, Ernst Pittschau, Franz Krüger, Ingetraud Hintze
'Sloppy, over-hasty and careless without even appearing to be informed by sincerity.' – *Paul Dehn*
'A film of inescapable irony and pity.' – *William Whitebait*

Germinal ***
France/Italy 1993 158m colour Panavision
AMLF/Renn/France 2/DD/Alternative Films/Nuova Artisti (Claude Berri)
In the 1870s, an unemployed railroad engineer finds work as a miner and joins a strike against poverty and appalling working conditions; the result is tragedy as the workers are starved, soldiers are called in, and the mine is sabotaged.
Detailed and sweeping epic evocation of Zola's novel, an impassioned portrait of exploitation and a plea for a more just society that retains much of the force of the original.
w Claude Berri, Arlette Langmann *novel* Emile Zola *d* *Claude Berri* *ph* *Yves Angelo* *m* Jean-Louis Roques *ad* Thanh At Hoang, Christian Marti *ed* Hervé de Luze
☆ Gérard Depardieu, *Miou-Miou*, Renaud, Jean Carmet, Judith Henry, Jean-Roger Milo, Laurent Terzieff
'One of those truly great examples of European filmmaking, a monumental statement of a movie about the fundamental struggles for life, love, freedom and the pursuit of even the most fragile happiness.' – *Phillipa Bloom, Empire*
'Strangely flat and matter-of-fact, this earnest depiction of class struggle will be a struggle for many viewers as well.' – *Variety*
† It was the most expensive film so far made in France, at a cost of 172m francs ($30m).

'Ten thousand red raiders roar into battle!'
Geronimo!
US 1939 89m bw
Paramount
The seventh cavalry gives the Indians a run for their money.
Muddled Western of no discernible merit.
wd Paul H. Sloane *ph* Henry Sharp *m* Gerard Carbonara
☆ Ellen Drew, Preston Foster, Andy Devine, Gene Lockhart, Ralph Morgan, William Henry
'Lusty and actionful melodrama geared to hit popular appeal.' – *Variety*

Geronimo
US 1962 101m Technicolor Panavision
UA/Laven-Gardner-Levy
In 1883 Geronimo and his remaining Apaches seek peace but are betrayed.
Moderate Western held back by script and performances.
w Pat Fielder *d* Arnold Laven *ph* Alex Phillips *m* Hugo Friedhofer
☆ Chuck Connors, Ross Martin, Kamala Devi

'A Warrior. A Leader. A Legend.'
Geronimo: An American Legend *
US 1994 115m Technicolor Panavision
Columbia (Walter Hill, Neil Canton)
GB title: *Geronimo*
A young cavalry officer is assigned to a patrol to track down Geronimo, after the Chiricahua Apache leader breaks out of a reservation and defies attempts to recapture him and his small band of warriors.
Handsome, moderately gripping Western, although the story, told often in voice-over from the viewpoint of a white Texan participant, distances the audience from its central character, treating him from the start as mythic, and also provides for a degree of self-congratulation in the making of a comparatively Indian-free America.
w John Milius, Larry Gross *d* Walter Hill *ph* Lloyd Ahern *m* Ry Cooder *pd* Joe Alves *ed* Freeman Davies, Carmel Davies, Donn Aron
☆ Wes Studi (Geronimo), Gene Hackman, Jason Patric, Robert Duvall, Matt Damon, Rodney A. Grant, Kevin Tighe, Steve Reevis
'A physically impressive, well-acted picture whose slightly stodgy literary quality holds it back from even greater impact.' – *Todd McCarthy, Variety*

Gert and Daisy's Weekend
GB 1941 79m bw
Butcher's
Gert and Daisy accompany a crowd of Cockney children who are being evacuated to a stately home in the country.
Low-budget wartime comedy starring a popular double-act from the radio; their humour has lost its appeal, and the script and direction lack polish and style.
w Kathleen Butler, Maclean Rogers, H. F. Maltby *d* Maclean Rogers *ph* Stephen Dade *md* Percival Mackey *ad* W. J. Hemsley
☆ Elsie Waters, Doris Waters, Iris Vandeleur, Elizabeth Hunt, John Slater, Wally Patch, Annie Esmond, Aubrey Mallalieu, Gerald Rex

Gertrud *
Denmark 1966 115m bw
Pathé Contemporary/Palladium
A lawyer's wife leaves him for an unhappy affair with a young musician.
Austere psychological drama, better to look at than to listen to.
wd Carl Theodor Dreyer *play* Hjalmar Soderberg
☆ Nina Pens Rode, Bendt Rothe, Ebbe Rode, Axel Strobye

Gervaise *
France 1956 116m bw
Agnès Delahaye-Silver Films-CLCC
In 19th-century Paris, a laundrymaid is deserted by her lover, settles with another man and is able to open her own laundry, but they both take to drink.
The French equivalent of David Lean's Dickens films, superbly detailed and wonderful to look at, but with a plot which finally seems worthless and depressing.
w Jean Aurenche, Pierre Bost *novel* *L'Assommoir* by Emile Zola *d* *René Clément* *ph* *René Juillard* *m* Georges Auric *ad* *Paul Bertrand*
☆ Maria Schell, François Périer, Suzy Delair, Mathilde Casadesus
'A tremendous *tour de force* of literal realism … a piece for the admiration of technicians, or for those whose consciences are purged and hands kept clean by the vicarious contemplation of how the other half lived – once upon a time.' – *David Robinson, MFB*
† Other French versions were made in 1902, 1909, 1911 and 1933.
foreign film
film; François Périer

Gestapo: see *Night Train to Munich*

Get Back
GB 1991 89m colour/bw
Entertainment/Allied Filmmakers/Front Page/MPL (Henry Thomas, Philip Knatchbull)
Documentary of a world tour by Paul McCartney and his band.
An extended music video that is a far cry from Lester's exuberant earlier treatment of the Beatles; he and McCartney are obviously older and staider.
d Richard Lester *ph* Jordan Cronenweth, Robert Paynter *ed* John Victor Smith
'Heavy on nostalgia and light on visual zap. Low-tech item will score limited biz in specialized play-off … By MTV standards, this is somewhere in a stone age.' – *Variety*

Get Carter **
GB 1971 112m Metrocolor
MGM/Mike Klinger
A racketeer goes to Newcastle to avenge his brother's death at the hands of gangsters.
Brutal British crime melodrama with faint echoes of Raymond Chandler. Sex and thuggery unlimited.
wd Mike Hodges *novel* *Jack's Return Home* by Ted Lewis *ph* Wolfgang Suschitzky *m* Roy Budd
☆ Michael Caine, John Osborne, Ian Hendry, Britt Ekland
'TV on the big screen – more sex, more violence, but no more attention to motivation or plot logic.' – *Arthur Knight*
'So calculatedly cool and soulless and nastily erotic that it seems to belong to a new era of virtuoso viciousness.' – *Pauline Kael*
'A cracking good movie.' – *Ken Russell*

'The Truth Hurts.'
Get Carter
US 2000 104m DeLuxe Panavision
Warner/Morgan Creek/Franchise (Mark Canton, Elie Samaha, Neil Canton)
A Las Vegas gangster goes to his hometown to kill the murderers of his brother.
Tedious remake of the 70s British thriller, all flash and no substance, with Stallone at his most ponderous.
w David McKenna *novel* *Jack's Return Home* by Ted Lewis *d* Stephen Kay *ph* Mauro Fiore *m* Tyler Bates *pd* Charles J.H. Wood *ed* Jerry Greenberg
☆ Sylvester Stallone (Jack Carter), Miranda Richardson (Gloria), Rachael Leigh Cook (Doreen), Alan Cumming (Jeremy Kinnear), Mickey Rourke (Cyrus Paice), John C. McGinley (Con McCarty), Rhona Mitra (Geraldine), Michael Caine (Cliff Brumby)
'Lacks excitement, credibility, suspense, character insight or anything else that might conceivably engage viewers.' – *Todd McCarthy, Variety*

Get Charlie Tully: see *Ooh, You Are Awful*

Get Cracking *
GB 1942 96m bw
Columbia (Ben Henry)
George joins the home guard.
Adequate star comedy.
w L. DuGarde Peach *d* Marcel Varnel *ph* Stephen Dade *md* Harry Bidgood
☆ George Formby, Edward Rigby, Frank Pettingell, Dinah Sheridan, Ronald Shiner, Wally Patch, Irene Handl

Get Off My Back: see *Synanon*

Get Off My Foot
GB 1935 83m bw
Warner (Irving Asher)
A Smithfield porter becomes a butler, and later finds himself heir to a fortune.
The nearest Max Miller came to being a genuine film star was in this first of eight Warner comedies, but the screen simply couldn't contain him.
w Frank Launder, Robert Edmunds *play* *Money By Wire* by Edward Paulton *d* William Beaudine *ph* Basil Emmott *ad* Peter Proud
☆ Max Miller, Chili Bouchier, Morland Graham, Jane Carr, Norma Varden, Reginald Purdell, Wally Patch

Get On the Bus **
US 1996 120m Technicolor
Columbia/40 Acres & A Mule (Reuben Cannon, Bill Borden, Barry Rosenbush)

A varied group of black men travel to Washington together for the Million Man March, called by the Black Muslim leader Louis Farrakhan, in October 1995.
An effective, talky movie that overcomes the schematic problems of its representative passengers – ranging from the elderly to the delinquent young, from a cop to a killer, gay to heterosexual – to engage in a worthwhile debate on the difficulties of masculinity which transcends race.
w Reggie Rock Blythewood *d* Spike Lee *ph* Elliot Davis *m* Terence Blanchard *pd* Ina Mayhew *ed* Leander T. Sales
☆ Richard Belzer, DeAundre Bonds, Andre Braugher, Thomas Jefferson Byrd, Gabriel Casseus, Albert Hall, Ossie Davis, Charles S. Dutton
'Will prove enormously entertaining to black audiences and should get many former Lee fans of all stripes back on board.' – *Todd McCarthy, Variety*
† The film was shot on a budget of $2.5m raised from 15 black men: Larkin Arnold, Jheryl Busby, Reggie Rock Blythewood, Reuben Cannon, Johnnie L. Cochran Jnr, Lemuel Daniels, Danny Glover, Calvin Grigsby, Robert Guillaume, Robert Johnson, Olden Lee, Spike Lee, Charles D. Smith, Will Smith, and Wesley Snipes.

Get Out Your Handkerchiefs **
France 1978 108m Eastmancolor
Les Films Ariane/CAPAC/Belga/SODEP (Georges Dancigers, Alexandre Mnouchkine, Paul Claudon)

original title: *Préparez Vos Mouchoirs*
A frigid wife is provided with a handsome lover by her doting husband but finds satisfaction only when she meets a bright 13-year-old boy.
Mildly amusing comedy, helped by some deft performances from the leading actors.
wd Bertrand Blier *ph* Jean Penzer *m* Georges Delerue *ad* Eric Moulard *ed* Claudine Merlin
☆ *Gérard Depardieu, Patrick Dewaere*, Carole Laure, Michel Serrault, Eleonore Hirt, Jean Rougerie, Sylvie Jolly, Riton
'Flagrantly funny in a slangy, buoyant, unpredictable way.' – *New Yorker*
best foreign film

'Get Dumped. Get Pumped. Get Even!'
Get Over It
US 2001 87m colour
Miramax/Ignite/Morpheus (Michael Burns, Marc Butan, Paul Feldsher)

Dumped by his girlfriend, a highschool student hopes to win her back by auditioning for a rock version of Shakespeare's *A Midsummer Night's Dream*.
Amiable 'teen romantic comedy that is at least lively and, occasionally, amusing.
w R. Lee Fleming Jnr *d* Tommy O'Haver *ph* Maryse Alberti *m* Steve Bartek *m/ly* Marc Shaiman, Scott Wittman *pd* Robin Standefer *ed* Jeff Betancourt *cos* Mary Jane Fort
☆ Kirsten Dunst (Kelly), Ben Foster (Berke Landers), Melissa Sagemiller (Allison McAllister), Sisqo (Dennis), Shane West (Bentley), Colin Hanks (Felix), Swoosie Kurtz (Beverly Landers), Ed Begley Jnr (Frank Landers), Martin Short (Dr Oates), Carmen Electra (Mistress Moira)
'Mild, harmless and occasionally affecting, possessing the fizz of diet soda and the sweet snap of slightly stale bubble gum.' – *A. O. Scott, New York Times*

'What if you can't avoid sexuality virginity bigotry stupidity insecurity hormones heavies prats liars rumours confusion and big big trouble? Don't get angry...'
Get Real *
GB/South Africa 1999 110m Rank Colour Panavision
Paramount/Distant Horizon/Graphite (Stephen Taylor)

A gay sixth-former begins a covert relationship with the school's star athlete.
Earnest coming-of-age and coming-out drama, effectively written and acted for the most part, but a little glib.
w Patrick Wilde *play What's Wrong with Angry* by Patrick Wilde *d* Simon Shore *ph* Alan Almond *m* John Lunn *pd* Bernd Lepel *ed* Barrie Vince
☆ Ben Silverstone, Brad Gorton, Charlotte Brittain
'Ends up being merely likable and rather quaint.' – *José Arroyo, Sight and Sound*

Get Shorty **
US 1995 105m DeLuxe
MGM/Jersey

A Miami debt collector for the Mob goes to Las Vegas after a defecting client and discovers that his talents fit him to become a successful film producer.
Enjoyable thriller that makes fun of Hollywood's hustlers and pretentions, but its impact is lessened by dull direction.
w Scott Frank *novel* Elmore Leonard *d* Barry Sonnenfeld *ph* Don Peterman *m* John Lurie *pd* Peter Larkin *ed* Jim Miller
☆ John Travolta, Gene Hackman, René Russo, Danny DeVito, Dennis Farina, Delroy Lindo, James Gandolfini, Jon Gries, David Paymer
'The pleasures of *Get Shorty* are genuine, but they remain stubbornly on the surface.' – *Entertainment Weekly*
† Bette Midler and Harvey Keitel appear uncredited.

Get to Know Your Rabbit
US 1972 91m Technicolor
Warner/Bernhardt-Gaer
A bored businessman enrols in a school of magic.
Whimsical satire which never takes off.
w Jordon Crittenden *d* Brian de Palma
☆ Tom Smothers, John Astin, Suzanne Zenor, Orson Welles, Samantha Jones, Allen Garfield, Katharine Ross

The Getaway
US 1941 89m bw
MGM
A lawman goes to jail, gets to know an imprisoned mob leader, and breaks out with him.
Routine rehash of 1935's Public Hero Number One.
w Wells Root, W. R. Burnett *d* Edward Buzzell
☆ Robert Sterling, Dan Dailey, Donna Reed, Charles Winninger, Henry O'Neill

'It takes two to make it. The big two!'
The Getaway **
US 1972 122m Technicolor Todd-AO 35
Solar/First Artists (David Foster, Mitchell Brower)

A convict leaves jail and promptly joins his wife in a bank robbery.
Violent, amoral, terse and fast-moving action melodrama which generally holds the interest despite its excesses.
w Walter Hill *novel* Jim Thompson *d* Sam Peckinpah *ph* Lucien Ballard *m* Quincy Jones
☆ Steve McQueen, Ali MacGraw, Ben Johnson, Sally Struthers, Al Lettieri, Slim Pickens
'This pair have no mission or "meaning". As in all romances, *The Getaway* simply extracts one element of reality and dwells on it. Nor is the violence "American". Pictures like this don't fail overseas.' – *Stanley Kauffmann*

The Getaway *
US 1994 115m DeLuxe Panavision
Warner/Largo/JVC (David Foster, Lawrence Turman, John Alan Simon)

A crook, released from jail with the help of a gangster, promises his wife that their next robbery will be their last.
Slick, fast-moving thriller, an involved tale of duplicity and deception, but no improvement on the original and hardly worth re-making.
w Walter Hill, Amy Jones *novel* Jim Thompson *d* Roger Donaldson *ph* Peter Menzies Jnr *m* Mark Isham *pd* Joseph Nemec III *ed* Conrad Buff
☆ Alec Baldwin, Kim Basinger, Michael Madsen, James Woods, David Morse, Jennifer Tilly, James Stephens, Richard Farnsworth
'A pretty good remake of a pretty good action thriller.' – *Variety*
'Like a digitally remastered CD of a Top Forty hit that you never much cared for.' – *Terrence Rafferty, New Yorker*

Getting Away with Murder
US 1996 92m Technicolor
Rank/Peter V. Miller/Savoy (Penny Marshall, Frank Price)

An ethics professor discovers that his kindly next-door neighbour is a Nazi war criminal who ran a concentration camp, and decides to poison him.
Feeble sitcom treatment of the Holocaust; it is a mystery why it was even made, or ever released. If it has a moral, it appears to be that murder is good for your sex life.
wd Harvey Miller *ph* Frank Tidy *m* John Debney *pd* John Jay Moore *ed* Richard Nord
☆ Dan Aykroyd, Lily Tomlin, Jack Lemmon, Bonnie Hunt, Brian Kerwin, Jerry Adler, Andy Romano
'A distasteful affair that should embarrass all concerned.' – *Daniel M. Kimmel, Variety*
† The film was released direct to video in Britain. In the US it took under $198,000 at the box-office.

Getting Even with Dad
US 1994 108m DeLuxe
MGM (Katie Jacobs, Pierce Gardner)

An 11-year-old hides the proceeds of his father's latest robbery and refuses to return it unless he promises to give him a good time and then return the money.
Crushingly dull comedy of father–son bonding and role reversal, in which the infant phenomenon that is Macaulay Culkin turns in a smug and charmless performance.
w Tom S. Parker, Jim Jennewein *d* Howard Deutch *ph* Tim Suhrstedt *m* Miles Goodman *pd* Virginia L. Randolph *ed* Richard Halsey
☆ Macaulay Culkin, Ted Danson, Glenne Headly, Gailard Sartain, Saul Rubinek, Hector Elizondo, Sam McMurray, Kathleen Wilhoite
'A dim affair, lacking even the gooey conviction of Hollywood's usual efforts to make one the better convinced of family values.' – *Derek Malcolm, Guardian*

Getting Gertie's Garter
US 1945 73m bw
UA (Edward Small)
A businessman tries all manner of wiles to retrieve an incriminating garter.
Silly variation on Up in Mabel's Room, *with similar team and cast. A few laughs are inevitable.*
w Allan Dwan, Karen de Wolf *play* Wilson Collison, Avery Hopwood *d* Allan Dwan *ph* Charles Lawton Jnr
☆ Dennis O'Keefe, Marie McDonald, Binnie Barnes, Barry Sullivan, J. Carrol Naish

Getting It Right
US 1989 102m Fujicolour

A hairdresser becomes involved with three contrasting women.
Mildly amusing, old-fashioned, romp.
w Elizabeth Jane Howard *novel* Elizabeth Jane Howard *d* Randal Kleiser *ph* Clive Tickner *pd* Caroline Amies *ad* Frank Walsh *ed* Chris Kelly
☆ Jesse Birdsall, Helena Bonham Carter, Peter Cook, John Gielgud, Jane Horrocks, Lynn Redgrave, Shirley Anne Field, Pat Heywood, Bryan Pringle, Nan Munro
'A contemporary London romance that vacillates between the relishable and the acutely embarrassing.' – *Kim Newman, MFB*

Getting It Up: see *Les Valseuses*

The Getting of Wisdom **
Australia 1977 101m Eastmancolor
Southern Cross/AFC/Victorian Film Corporation/9 Television Network (Phillip Adams)

In 1897 a backwoods girl is sent to an exclusive Melbourne ladies' college and eventually wins a music scholarship.
Praiseworthy period piece which thankfully seems to have no axe to grind and is all the better for it.
w Eleanor Witcombe *novel* Henry Handel Richardson (Ethel Richardson) *d* *Bruce Beresford* *ph* Donald McAlpine *m* various *pd* John Stoddart
☆ Susannah Fowle, Sheila Helpmann, Patricia Kennedy, John Waters, Barry Humphries, Kerry Armstrong

Getting Straight *
US 1970 125m Eastmancolor
Columbia/The Organization (Richard Rush)

A political activist returns to college in order to teach and discovers the foolishness of most contemporary attitudes.
Modish comedy, too long, far too pleased with itself, and now irrevocably dated.
w Robert Kaufman *novel* Ken Kolb *d* Richard Rush *ph* Laszlo Kovacs *m* Ronald Stein
☆ *Elliott Gould*, Candice Bergen, Robert F. Lyons, Jeff Corey, Max Julien, Cecil Kellaway

'Witness History.'
'In The Tradition Of "Gone With The Wind".'
Gettysburg **
US 1993 254m Foto-Kem
Mayfair/Turner (Robert Katz, Moctesuma Esparza)

In July 1863, during three days of fighting that left more than 50,000 dead, Confederate General Robert E. Lee's troops are defeated at Gettysburg in the decisive battle in the American Civil War.
A stirring and epic historical re-creation of the event as seen from the point of view of the commanders and their officers, concentrating on strategy as well as the actual bloody fighting; it ignores the wider causes of the war and does little to explain how such slaughter could come about among men of apparent goodwill.
wd *Ronald F. Maxwell* *novel The Killer Angels* by Michael Shaara *ph* Kees van Oostum *m* Randy Edelman *pd* Cary White *ed* Corky Ehlers
☆ Tom Berenger, Martin Sheen, Stephen Lang, Richard Jordan, Jeff Daniels, Sam Elliott, C. Thomas Howell, Kevin Conway, Andrew Prine, Maxwell Caulfield, James Lancaster, Royce Applegate, Brian Mallon, Buck Taylor, Patrick Stuart
'Succeeds as a motion picture event, and as a re-creation of a pivotal chapter of American history.' – *Variety*
† The film was shown on TV in a longer version as a three-part mini-series and also released on video in a version that runs for just under six hours.

Ghare-Baire: see *The Home and the World*

Ghost **
US 1990 127m Technicolor
UIP/Paramount/Howard W. Koch (Lisa Weinstein)

A murdered stockbroker returns as a ghost to hunt down his killers.
Deftly made, romantic, sentimental, sometimes silly thriller that was the surprise hit of 1990, either because of its fundamentalist view of heaven and hell or its underlying theme that revenge is good for the soul.
w Bruce Joel Rubin *d* Jerry Zucker *ph* Adam Greenberg *pd* Jane Musky *ed* Walter Murch *sp* Industrial Light and Magic
☆ Patrick Swayze, Demi Moore, Tony Goldwyn, Whoopi Goldberg, Stanley Lawrence, Christopher J. Keene, Susan Breslau, Martina Degnan
'Amiable entertainment, even for those not looking for reassurances that the afterlife still permits use of the subway.' – *David Robinson, The Times*
Whoopi Goldberg; Bruce Joel Rubin
best picture; best score; best film editing
Whoopi Goldberg

The Ghost and Mr Chicken
US 1965 90m Techniscope
Universal (Edward J. Montagne)
An incompetent small-town reporter finds ghosts in a local murder mansion.
Old-fashioned scare comedy starring a highly resistible comic. A big hit in American small towns.
w James Fritzell, Everett Greenbaum *d* Alan Rafkin *ph* William Margulies *m* Vic Mizzy
☆ Don Knotts, Skip Homeier, Joan Staley, Liam Redmond, Dick Sargent, Reta Shaw

'Doin' what comes supernaturally ... it's the man-woman affair that's like nothing on earth!'

The Ghost and Mrs Muir *

US 1947 104m bw

TCF (Fred Kohlmar)

A widow refuses to be frightened away from her seaside home by the ghost of a sea captain, with whom she falls in love.

Charming sentimental fable in Hollywood's best style.

w Philip Dunne *novel* R. A. Dick *d* Joseph L. Mankiewicz *ph* Charles Lang *m* Bernard Herrmann *ad* Richard Day, George Davis

☆ Gene Tierney, Rex Harrison, George Sanders, Edna Best, Vanessa Brown, Anna Lee, Robert Coote, Natalie Wood, Isobel Elsom

'A not at all disagreeable piece of whimsy.' – *News Chronicle*

'A jolly caper, gently humorous and often sparkling.' – *New York Times*

† A half-hour TV series followed in 1968.

Charles Lang

The Ghost and the Darkness

US 1996 109m DeLuxe Panavision

Paramount/Constellation (Gale Anne Hurd, Paul Radin, A. Kitman Ho)

In the 1890s, an engineer and a big-game hunter stalk two man-eating lions who are terrorizing the locals and preventing the building of a railway across Africa.

A stilted, curiously old-fashioned colonial adventure, broadly acted and dully written.

w William Goldman *d* Stephen Hopkins *ph* Vilmos Zsigmond *m* Jerry Goldsmith *pd* Stuart Wurtzel *ed* Robert Brown, Steve Mirkovich *sp* Stan Winston Studio

☆ Michael Douglas, Val Kilmer, Bernard Hill, John Kani, Tom Wilkinson, Brian McCardie, Henry Cele, Om Puri

'A blatantly trashy film that marks time until its climax.' – *Kim Newman, Sight and Sound*

sound effects editing (Bruce Stambler)

The Ghost Breakers ***

US 1940 85m bw

Paramount (Arthur Hornblow Jnr)

A girl inherits a West Indian castle and finds herself up to her neck in ghosts, zombies and buried treasure.

Archetypal comedy horror, very well done; a follow-up to the success of The Cat and the Canary, *and just about as entertaining.*

w Walter de Leon *play* Paul Dickey, Charles W. Goddard *d* George Marshall *ph* Charles Lang *m* Ernst Toch *ad* Hans Dreier, Robert Asher

☆ Bob Hope, Paulette Goddard, Paul Lukas, Willie Best, Richard Carlson, Lloyd Corrigan, Anthony Quinn, Noble Johnson, Pedro de Cordoba

'Bob Hope can joke, apparently, even with a risen corpse.' – *MFB*

'Paramount has found the fabled formula for making audiences shriek with laughter and fright at one and the same time.' – *New York Times*

† Previously filmed in 1914 with H. B. Warner; in 1922 with Wallace Reid; and remade in 1953 as *Scared Stiff*.

The Ghost Camera

GB 1933 68m bw

H & S Films/Real Art (Julius Hagen)

A chemist investigates how a camera containing film of a murder came into his possession.

Mundane, stagey thriller with much talk and little action.

w H. Fowler Mear *story* Jefferson Farjeon *d* Bernard Vorhaus *ph* Ernest Palmer *ad* James A. Carter *ed* David Lean

☆ Ida Lupino, Henry Kendall, John Mills, S. Victor Stanley, George Merritt, Felix Aylmer

Ghost Catchers

US 1944 68m bw

Universal

A Southern colonel and his beautiful daughters have spooks in their mansion – or bats in the belfry.

Lower-case farce made when the stars' contract was being allowed to run out.

w Edmund L. Hartmann *story* Milt Gross, Edward Cline *d* Edward F. Cline

☆ Ole Olsen, Chic Johnson, Gloria Jean, Leo Carrillo, Martha O'Driscoll, Andy Devine, Lon Chaney Jnr, Walter Catlett, Henry Armetta

Ghost Chase

West Germany 1987 89m colour

Medusa/Contropolis/pro-ject Film/Hessischer Rundfunk (Dean Heyde)

Horror movie-makers summon a ghost to help them find treasure.

Its convoluted plot seems designed to confuse the young audience at which it is presumably aimed, though it misses the target anyway.

w Roland Emmerich, Thomas Kubisch *story* Roland Emmerich, Oliver Eberle *d* Roland Emmerich *ph* Karl Walter Lindenlaub *pd* Ekkehard Schroeer, Sonja B. Zimmer *ed* Brigitte Pia Fritsche *sp* Joachim Grueninger, Hubert Bartholomae

☆ Jason Lively, Jill Whitlow, Tim McDaniel, Paul Gleason, Chuck Mitchell, Leonard Lansink, Ian McNaughton, Toby Kaye, Cynthia Frost, Julian Curry

Ghost Dad

US 1990 84m DeLuxe

Universal/SAH (Terry Nelson)

A frantic businessman, killed in a traffic accident, is given three days to sort out his affairs and see that his orphaned children are provided for.

A sentimental comedy dependent on its special effects for laughs; otherwise the jokes are so thin as to be almost invisible.

w Chris Reese, Brent Maddock, S. S. Wilson *d* Sidney Poitier *ph* Andrew Laszlo *m* Henry Mancini *pd* Henry Bumstead *ed* Pembroke Herring

☆ Bill Cosby, Kimberly Russell, Denise Nicholas, Ian Bannen, Christine Ebersole, Barry Corbin, Salim Grant, Brooke Fontaine

'All assassins live beyond the law. Only one follows the code.'

Ghost Dog: The Way of the Samurai ***

US/Japan/France/Germany 1999 116m DeLuxe

Film4/JVC/Bac Films/Canal+/Pandora/ARD/Degeto/Plywood (Richard Guay, Jim Jarmusch)

A reclusive, pigeon-fancying hitman, who leads his life as if he were a samurai warrior, becomes a target for assassination after killing a member of a Mafia gang.

A film that is likely to divide audiences: some will find its literary structure pretentious, others will enjoy a slyly comic movie about a clash between two different codes of honour.

wd Jim Jarmusch *ph* Robby Muller *m* RZA *pd* Ted Berner *ed* Jay Rabinowitz

☆ Forest Whitaker (Ghost Dog), John Tormey (Louie), Cliff Gorman (Sonny Valerio), Henry Silva (Vargo), Isaach de Bankolé (Raymond), Tricia Vessey (Louise Vargo), Victor Argo (Vinny), Gene Ruffini (Old Consigliere), Richard Portnow (Handsome Frank), Camille Winbush (Pearline)

'A playful but exceedingly wispy piece of doodling.' – *Todd McCarthy, Variety*

The Ghost Goes West ***

GB 1935 85m bw

London Films (Alexander Korda)

When a millionaire buys a Scottish castle and transports it stone by stone to America, the castle ghost goes too.

Amusing whimsy which is always pleasant but never quite realizes its full potential; fondly remembered for its star performance.

w Robert E. Sherwood, Geoffrey Kerr *story* Eric Keown *d* René Clair *ph* Harold Rosson *m* Mischa Spoliansky

☆ Robert Donat, Jean Parker, Eugene Pallette, Elsa Lanchester, Ralph Bunker, Patricia Hilliard, Morton Selten

'Fine business likely in the keys, but not for the tanks.' – *Variety*

'Although the film is not cast in the fluid, rapidly paced style of Clair's typical work, it has a sly wit and an adroitness of manner that make it delightful.' – *André Sennwald, New York Times*

'It is typical of the British film industry that M. René Clair should be brought to this country to direct a Scottish film full of what must to him be rather incomprehensible jokes about whisky and bagpipes, humorous fantasy without any social significance, realistic observation, or genuine satire.' – *Graham Greene*

The Ghost in the Invisible Bikini

US 1966 82m Pathécolor Panavision

American International

A motor cycle gang gets mixed up with a rejuvenated corpse in a haunted mansion.

Mindless beach party stuff suffering under one of Hollywood's most inane titles.

w Louis M. Heyward, Elwood Ullman *d* Don Weis

☆ Boris Karloff, Basil Rathbone, Patsy Kelly, Tommy Kirk, Deborah Walley, Aron Kincaid, Quinn O'Hara, Jesse White

'They said the killer was better off dead. They were wrong.'

Ghost in the Machine

US 1993 95m DeLuxe

TCF (Paul Schiff)

The spirit of a serial killer escapes into cyber-space at the moment of his death, so that he can continue his killing spree.

Paranoid fantasy about computers aimed at a teenage audience; it is a familiar and silly horror story that is dependent upon some gruesome moments to maintain interest.

w William Davies, William Osborne *d* Rachel Talalay *ph* Phil Meheux *m* Graeme Revell *pd* James Spencer *ed* Janice Hampton, Erica Huggins *sp* make-up: Alterian Studios; visual effects: VIFX

☆ Karen Allen, Chris Mulkey, Ted Marcoux, Wil Horneff, Jessica Walter, Brandon Quintin Adams, Rick Ducommun, Nancy Fish, Jack Laufer

'The film's social statement may be hopelessly muddy, but its adroit sense of fun and thrills cannot be discounted.' – *Variety*

† The film was released direct to video in Britain.

Ghost in the Shell

Japan/GB 1995 83m Eastmancolor

Straight/Kodansha/Bandai/Manga

aka: *Kokaku Kidotai*

In Tokyo in 2029, a cyborg cop investigates a master criminal and discovers that he is a government-controlled entity that is trying to escape and become human.

Spectacular-looking Japanese animated film, but one that, like so many of its kind, involves a confusing narrative and peculiar metaphysics that reduce interest in its depiction of a corrupt future.

w Kazunori Ito *graphic novel* Shirow Masamune *d* Mamoru Oshii *ph* Hisao Shirai *m* Kenji Kawai *ad* Hiromasa Ogura *ed* Shuichi Kakesu

☆ Featuring the voices of: Richard George, Mimi Woods, William Frederick, Abe Lasser, Christopher Joyce, Mike Sorich, Ben Isaacson

'This is exactly the kind of film that James Cameron would make if Disney ever let him through the front gates.' – *Empire*

'You can't keep a good monster down!'

The Ghost of Frankenstein

US 1942 67m bw

Universal (George Waggner)

Frankenstein's second son implants evil shepherd Igor's brain into the monster.

The rot set in with this flatly-handled potboiler, which had none of the literary mood or cinematic interest of Bride *or* Son *which preceded it, and suffered from a particularly idiotic script.*

w W. Scott Darling *story* Eric Taylor *d* Erle C. Kenton *ph* Milton Krasner, Woody Bredell *m* Charles Previn *md* Hans J. Salter *ad* Jack Otterson *ed* Ted J. Kent

☆ Cedric Hardwicke, Lon Chaney Jnr (The monster), Bela Lugosi, Lionel Atwill, Evelyn Ankers, Ralph Bellamy

† See *Frankenstein* for other episodes in the series.

The Ghost of St Michael's **

GB 1941 82m bw

Ealing (Basil Dearden)

A school is evacuated to the Isle of Skye, and the local ghost turns out to be an enemy agent.

The star's schoolmaster character is here at its seedy best, and he is well supported in a comedy-thriller plot.

w Angus Macphail, John Dighton *d* Marcel Varnel *ph* Derick Williams

☆ Will Hay, Claude Hulbert, Felix Aylmer, Raymond Huntley, Elliot Mason, Charles Hawtrey, John Laurie, Hay Petrie, Roddy Hughes, Manning Whiley

The Ghost Ship

US 1943 69m bw

RKO (Val Lewton)

The captain of a merchant ship is driven mad by isolation.

Long unavailable because of legal problems, this very minor Val Lewton thriller inevitably disappoints because it has no supernatural elements and must compare unfavourably with both The Caine Mutiny *and* The Sea Wolf, *which plotwise it closely resembles.*

w Donald Henderson Clarke *d* Mark Robson *ph* Nicholas Musuraca *m* Roy Webb

☆ Richard Dix, Russell Wade, Edith Barrett, Ben Bard, Edmund Glover, Skelton Knaggs

'Sea Evil'

Ghost Ship

US/Australia 2002 91m Technicolor

Warner/Village Roadshow/NPV/Dark Castle (Joel Silver, Robert Zemeckis, Gilbert Adler)

A salvage crew discover an old abandoned ship that is haunted by the ghosts of its former passengers.

Predictable horror movie that fails to make interesting either its characters or their predicament.

w Mark Hanlon, John Pogue *d* Steve Beck *ph* Gale Tattersall *m* John Frizzell *pd* Graham 'Grace' Walker *ed* Roger Barton

☆ Julianna Margulies (Epps), Ron Eldard (Dodge), Desmond Harrington (Ferriman), Isaiah Washington (Greer), Gabriel Byrne (Murphy), Alex Dimitriades (Santos), Karl Urban (Munder)

'Collapses under the weight of its own dull conception and weak direction, dialogue and character portraits.' – *Robert Koehler, Variety*

'She'll never rest till her tale is told!'

Ghost Story *

GB 1974 89m Fujicolour

Stephen Weeks

Former college acquaintances spend a weekend at a country house, and one of them is drawn into tragic events of forty years before.

Overlong chiller, ingeniously shot in India but very variably acted; aims for the M. R. James style and sometimes achieves it, but badly needs cutting.

w Rosemary Sutcliff, Stephen Weeks *d* Stephen Weeks *ph* Peter Hurst *m* Ron Geesin

☆ Murray Melvin, Larry Dann, Vivian Mackerall, Marianne Faithfull, Anthony Bate, Leigh Lawson, Barbara Shelley

Ghost Story

US 1981 110m Technicolor

Universal (Ronald G. Smith)

Four old men tell each other ghost stories, but are haunted by a guilty secret of their own.

Bizarre vehicle for four welcome old actors, ruined by the director's insistence on frequent shock cuts to the rotting spectre. A subtler treatment akin to that of The Uninvited *might have produced a little masterpiece.*

w Lawrence D. Cohen *novel* Peter Straub *d* John Irvin *ph* Jack Cardiff *m* Philippe Sarde

☆ Fred Astaire, Melvyn Douglas, John Houseman, Douglas Fairbanks Jnr, Craig Wasson, Patricia Neal, Alice Krige, Jacqueline Brookes

The Ghost that Never Returns *

USSR 1929 80m approx (24 fps) bw silent

Sovkino

original title: *Prividenie, Kotoroe ne Vozvrashchaetsya*

After ten years' imprisonment for leading a strike, a South American worker is given a day's leave which may result in his death.

Unsatisfactory communist propaganda of its time, probably rescued from obscurity by its title. A few strikingly visual moments stand out, but the narrative is needlessly obscure.

w Valentin Turkin *story* Henri Barbusse *d* Abram Room *ph* Dmitri Feldman

☆ B. Ferdinandov, Olga Zhizneva, Maxime Straukh

The Ghost Train **
GB 1931 72m bw
Gainsborough (Michael Balcon)
Passengers stranded at a haunted station in Cornwall include a detective posing as a silly ass in order to trap smugglers.
Excellent early sound version of a comedy-thriller play which has not only been among the most commercially successful ever written but also provided the basic plot for many another comedy: Oh Mr Porter, The Ghost of St Michael's, Back Room Boy, Hold That Ghost, *etc. Previously filmed as a silent in 1927, with Guy Newall.*
w Angus MacPhail, Lajos Biro play Arnold Ridley d Walter Forde ph Leslie Rowson *ad* Walter Murton *ed* Ian Dalrymple
☆ *Jack Hulbert*, Cicely Courtneidge, Donald Calthrop, Ann Todd, Cyril Raymond, Angela Baddeley, Allan Jeayes

The Ghost Train *
GB 1941 85m bw
Gainsborough (Edward Black)
Adequate remake with the lead split into two characters, which doesn't work quite so well.
w Marriott Edgar, Val Guest, J. O. C. Orton *d* Walter Forde *ph* Jack Cox
☆ *Arthur Askey*, Richard Murdoch, Kathleen Harrison, Morland Graham, Linden Travers, Peter Murray Hill, *Herbert Lomas*

'Accentuate the negative.'
Ghost World ***
US 2001 111m colour
United Artists/Granada/Jersey Shore (Lianne Halfon, John Malkovich, Russel Smith)
In an American suburb, two teenagers leave high school and feel like misfits in the adult world.
Witty, perceptive comedy of the confusions of adolescence, experiments in love, and the discovery of a wider world beyond the restrictions of suburbia.
w Daniel Clowes, Terry Zwigoff *comic book* Daniel Clowes *d* Terry Zwigoff *ph* Affonso Beato *m* David Kitay *pd* Edward T. McAvoy *ed* Carole Kravetz *cos* Mary Zophres
☆ Thora Birch (Enid), Scarlett Johansson (Rebecca), Steve Buscemi (Seymour), Brad Renfro (Josh), Illeana Douglas (Roberta), Bob Balaban (Dad), Teri Garr (Maxine)
'A film like no other, an artful spellbinder that cuts deep.' – *Peter Travers, Rolling Stone*
'One of the biggest disappointments of the summer, though I would give it points for projecting its own heart of darkness with apparent conviction.' – *Andrew Sarris, New York Observer*
Daniel Clowes, Terry Zwigoff (screenplay)

Ghostbusters *
US 1984 105m Metrocolor Panavision
Columbia/Delphi (Ivan Reitman)
Unemployed academic parapsychologists set themselves up as ghostbusters and destroy several monstrous apparitions on the streets of New York.
Crude farce with expensive special effects. It took more money – millions more – than Indiana Jones and the Temple of Doom, *which must say something about the age we live in.*
w Dan Aykroyd, Harold Ramis *d* Ivan Reitman *ph* Laszlo Kovacs, Herb Wagreitch *m* Elmer Bernstein *pd* John DeCuir *ed* Sheldon Kahn, David Blewitt
☆ Bill Murray, Dan Aykroyd, Harold Ramis, Sigourney Weaver, Rick Moranis, Annie Potts, William Atherton
title song (m/ly Ray Parker)

Ghostbusters II
US 1989 108m DeLuxe Panavision
Columbia TriStar (Ivan Reitman)
The disbanded Ghostbusters reform to deal with supernatural threats to New York.
Rambling, disjointed sequel of little amusement.
w Harold Ramis, Dan Aykroyd *d* Ivan Reitman *ph* Michael Chapman *m* Randy Edelman *pd* Bo Welch *ed* Sheldon Kahn, Donn Cambern
☆ Bill Murray, Dan Aykroyd, Sigourney Weaver, Harold Ramis, Rick Moranis, Ernie Hudson, Annie Potts, Peter MacNicol, Harris Yulin, David Margulies

Ghostly Love
Hong Kong 1990 92m colour
Kam Chung Kuey
A man's love for the spirit of a dead girl brings her back to life.
A ghost story that mixes crude sex and cruder acting in an incomprehensible plot which is rendered in confusing subtitles: 'I counted something is happening recently. You better watch out lately,' says one character in an attempt to explain events.
d Wu Kwo Rem
☆ Emily Chu, Hui Tien Chee, Lam Wei, Mark Long

Ghosts from the Past: see *Ghosts of Mississippi*

The Ghosts of Berkeley Square *
GB 1947 89m bw
British National (Louis H. Jackson)
Two 18th-century ghosts are doomed to haunt a London house until royalty visits.
Thin, skittish whimsy with pleasant moments.
w James Seymour *novel No Nightingales* by S. J. Simon, Caryl Brahms *d* Vernon Sewell *ph* Ernest Palmer *m* Hans May *ad* C. Wilfred Arnold *ed* Dan Birt *cos* Beresford Egan
☆ Robert Morley (General Burlap), Claude Hulbert (Merryweather), Felix Aylmer (Colonel Kelsoe), Yvonne Arnaud (Millie), Abraham Sofaer (Disraeli), Ernest Thesiger (Investigator), Marie Lohr (Lottie), Martita Hunt (Lady Mary), A. E. Matthews (General Bristow), John Longden (Mortimer Digby), Ronald Frankau (Tex), Wilfrid Hyde-White (Staff Captain), Esmé Percy (Vizier), Mary Jerrold (Lettie), Wally Patch (Foreman) and also Martin Miller (Professor)

'You Don't Stand A Ghost Of A Chance'
Ghosts of Mars
2001 98m
Columbia TriStar/Screen Gems (Sandy King)
aka: *John Carpenter's Ghosts of Mars*
In the matriarchal world of Mars in 2176, a cop explains how the inhabitants of a mining town were possessed by killer ghosts.
Quaint old-fashioned sf adventure, with a feeble premise for some unexciting action.
w Larry Sulkis, John Carpenter *d* John Carpenter *ph* Gary B. Kibbe *m* John Carpenter *pd* William Elliott *ed* Paul Warschilka
☆ Ice Cube (James 'Desolation' Williams), Natasha Henstridge (Melanie Ballard), Jason Statham (Jericho Butler), Clea Duvall (Bashira Kincaid), Pam Grier (Helena Braddock), Joanna Cassidy (Whitlock), Richard Cetrone (Big Daddy Mars), Rosemary Forsyth (Inquisitor)
'This movie's soul lies somewhere deep in a teenage wasteland before CD players.' – *Robert Koehler, Variety*

Ghosts of Mississippi
US 1996 130m Technicolor Panavision
Rank/Castle Rock (Frederick Zollo, Nicholas Paleologos, Andrew Scheinman, Rob Reiner)
GB title: *Ghosts from the Past*
In the 80s, an assistant district attorney decides to reopen the case of a racist who killed black civil rights activist Medgar Evans in 1963 and was exonerated by two all-white juries.
A Hollywood re-creation of a real trial, in which all the participants, save the murderer Beckwith, are reduced to stereotypes; Woods's intense performance as the killer overwhelms the surrounding, self-congratulatory blandness.
w Lewis Colick *d* Rob Reiner *ph* John Seale *m* Marc Shaiman *pd* Lilly Kilvert *ed* Robert Leighton
☆ Alec Baldwin, Whoopi Goldberg, *James Woods*, Craig T. Nelson, Susanna Thompson, Lucas Black, William H. Macy, Virginia Madsen
'Tepid and two dimensional in the manner of many telepics.' – *Godfrey Cheshire, Variety*

Ghosts ... of the Civil Dead
Australia 1988 93m colour
Electric/Correctional Services/Outlaw Values (Evan English)
Prisoners react violently against a repressive regime.
A confused narrative weakens a brutal drama, filmed in a documentary style.
w Gene Conkie, John Hillcoat, Evan English, Nick Cave, Hugo Race *d* John Hillcoat *ph* Paul Goldman, Graham Wood *m* Nick Cave, Mick Harvey, Blixa Bargeld *pd* Chris Kennedy *ed* Stewart Young
☆ Dave Field, Mike Bishop, Chris de Rose, Nick Cave, Freddo Dierck, Vincent Gil, Bogdan Koca, Kevin Mackey, Dave Mason

The Ghoul **
GB 1933 79m bw
Gaumont (Michael Balcon)
An Egyptologist returns from the tomb to uncover stolen jewels and a murderer.
Fascinating minor horror piece reminiscent of The Old Dark House, *with many effective moments and a ripe cast.*
w Frank King, Leonard Hines, L. DuGarde Peach, Roland Pertwee, John Hastings Turner, Rupert Downing *novel* Frank King *d T. Hayes Hunter ph* Gunther Krampf *make-up* Heinrich Heitfeld
☆ Boris Karloff, Cedric Hardwicke, Ralph Richardson, Kathleen Harrison, Ernest Thesiger, Dorothy Hyson, Anthony Bushell, D. A. Clarke-Smith
'Lacks general US appeal because of bad plot mechanics, mostly bad acting, and colourless camerawork.' – *Variety*
† Remade after a fashion as *What A Carve Up* (1961).

The Ghoul
GB 1975 87m Eastmancolor
Tyburn (Kevin Francis)
In the twenties, a group of stranded travellers is reduced in number when they take shelter in the house of a former clergyman.
The build-up is too slow, the revelation too nasty, and the whole thing is a shameless rip-off of the structure of Psycho.
w John Elder (Anthony Hinds) *d* Freddie Francis *ph* John Wilcox *m* Harry Robinson
☆ Peter Cushing, Alexandra Bastedo, John Hurt, Gwen Watford, Veronica Carlson, Don Henderson
'Peter Cushing brings out his violin for a soothing spot of the classics, the local copper mutters veiled warnings before trundling off on his bike, and thick fog swirls round the exterior sets at the drop of a canister.' – *Geoff Brown*

Ghoulies
US 1985 88m colour
Empire (Jefery Levy)
After a youth invokes a Satanic ritual, vicious imp-like creatures are loosed on the world.
Cheap and nasty rip-off of Gremlins, *lacking wit and style and even failing at slapstick comedy.*
w Luca Bercovici, Jefery Levy *d* Luca Bercovici *ph* Mac Ahlberg *m* Richard Band, Shirley Walker
☆ Peter Liapis, Lisa Pelikan, Michael Des Barres, Jack Nance, Peter Risch, Tamara de Treaux
† It was followed by *Ghoulies 2*, directed by Albert Band, in 1988, and *Ghoulies 3: Ghoulies Go to College*, directed by John Carl Buechler, in 1991, both conforming to the usual law of diminishing returns. Both were also released direct to video. Ghoulies 4 (1993), directed by Jim Wynorski, continued the downward trend.

Giant **
US 1956 197m Warnercolor
Warner (George Stevens, Henry Ginsburg)
The life of a Texas cattle rancher through two generations.
Sprawling, overlong family saga with unconvincing acting but good visual style.
w Fred Guiol, Ivan Moffat *novel* Edna Ferber *d George Stevens ph* William C. Mellor, Edwin DuPar *m* Dimitri Tiomkin *ad* Boris Leven *ed* William Hornbeck, Philip W. Anderson, Fred Bohanan
☆ Rock Hudson, Elizabeth Taylor, James Dean, Mercedes McCambridge, Carroll Baker, Chill Wills, Jane Withers, Dennis Hopper, Sal Mineo, Rod Taylor, Judith Evelyn, Earl Holliman, Alexander Scourby, Paul Fix
George Stevens
best picture; script; Dimitri Tiomkin; Rock Hudson; James Dean; Mercedes McCambridge; art direction; editing

The Giant Behemoth
GB 1959 70m bw
Artistes Alliance/Stratford
aka: *Behemoth the Sea Monster*
A radioactive palaeosaurus menaces London.
Underfed monster, undercast melodramatics.
w Eugène Lourié *d* Eugène Lourié, Douglas Hickox
☆ Gene Evans, André Morell, Leigh Madison, John Turner, Jack MacGowran

The Giant Claw
US 1957 71m bw
Clover (Sam Katzman)
A monstrous bird threatens New York.
Incompetent horror item: the bird is mostly talons and sound track.
w Samuel Newman, Paul Gangelin *d* Fred F. Sears
☆ Jeff Morrow, Mara Corday, Morris Ankrum

'A giant among men in a gigantic color spectacle.'
The Giant of Marathon (dubbed) *****
Italy/France 1960 92m Eastmancolor Dyaliscope
MGM/Titanus/Galatea/Lux (Bruno Vailati)
original title: *La Battaglia di Maratona*
Philippides, an Olympic athlete, encourages the Spartans to fight the invading Persian army at Marathon and goes to Athens to organize a sea battle against the invaders.
Inaccurate history, but enjoyable as a lively example of an Italian epic.
w Ennio de Concini, Augusto Frassonetti, Bruno Vailati *idea* Alberto Barsanti, Raffaelo Pacini *d* Jacques Tourneur *ph* Mario Bava, Massimo Terzano *m* Roberto Nicolosi *ad* Marcello Del Prato *ed* Mario Serandrei
☆ Steve Reeves, Mylène Demongeot, Sergio Fantoni, Alberto Lupo, Ivo Garrani, Philippe Hersent, Daniella Rocca
† Tourneur directed only the main dialogue scenes, with the rest of the film being shot by Bava and Vailati.

The Giant Spider Invasion
US 1975 76m Eastmancolor
Hemdale/Transcentury/Cinema Group 75 (Bill Rebane, Richard L. Huff)
Nuclear fall-out causes giant spiders to breed and go on the rampage.
Thinly scripted reprise of one of those small-town horror thrillers of the fifties.
w Richard L. Huff, Robert Easton *d* Bill Rebane
☆ Barbara Hale, Steve Brodie, Leslie Parrish, Alan Hale

Gideon of Scotland Yard: see *Gideon's Day*

Gideon's Day *
GB 1958 91m Technicolor
Columbia/John Ford (Michael Killanin)
US title: *Gideon of Scotland Yard*
A Scotland Yard Inspector has an eventful but frustrating day.
Pleasant, ordinary little TV style police yarn showing no evidence of its director's particular talents.
w T. E. B. Clarke *novel* John Creasey *d* John Ford *ph* Frederick C. Young *m* Douglas Gamley *ad* Ken Adam
☆ Jack Hawkins, Dianne Foster, Anna Lee, Andrew Ray, Anna Massey, Frank Lawton, John Loder, Cyril Cusack

Gidget
US 1959 95m Eastmancolor Cinemascope
Columbia (Lewis J. Rachmil)
A 16-year-old girl falls for a surfer; her parents disapprove until he turns out to be the son of their best friend.
Commercial mixture of domestic comedy and beach athletics, for nice teenagers and their moms and pops.
w Gabrielle Upton *novel* Frederick Kohner *d* Paul Wendkos *ph* Burnett Guffey *m* George

Duning *md* Morris Stoloff *ad* Ross Bellah *ed* William A. Lyon
☆ Sandra Dee, Cliff Robertson, James Darren, Arthur O'Connell
† Sequels include *Gidget Goes Hawaiian* (V*, 1961) with Deborah Walley; *Gidget Goes to Rome* (V*, 1962) with Cindy Carol; and two TV movies.

'The Only Witness To The Crime Was Not Even There.'
The Gift
US 2000 110m DeLuxe
Redbus/Paramount Classics, Alphaville, Lakeshore (Sean Daniel, Ted Tannebaum, Gregory Goodman, Rob Tapert)
Trying to help people in trouble, a young widow with psychic abilities becomes involved in a murder investigation.
Engaging hokum in the Deep Southern Gothic style, given a modicum of credibility by the strength of Cate Blanchett's performance; despite her gift for foresight, though, most of the audience will anticipate the narrative twists long before she does.
w Billy Bob Thornton, Tom Epperson *d* Sam Raimi *ph* Jamie Anderson *m* Christopher Young *pd* Neil Spisak *ed* Arthur Coburn, Bob Murawsk
☆ Cate Blanchett (Annie Wilson), Giovanni Ribisi (Buddy Cole), Keanu Reeves (Donnie Barksdale), Katie Holmes (Jessica King), Greg Kinnear (Wayne Collins), Hilary Swank (Valerie Barksdale), Michael Jeter (Gerald Weems), Kim Dickens (Linda), Gary Cole (David Duncan), Rosemary Harris (Annie's Granny), J. K. Simmons (Sheriff Pearl Johnson), Chelchie Ross (Kenneth King), John Beasley (Albert Hawkins)
'A solid tale well told.' – *Variety*

A Gift for Heidi
US 1958 71m Eastmancolor
RKO/Chabert (Robert Goodstein)
A young girl learns about faith, hope and charity.
An excruciatingly sentimental family film, based on the character created by Johanna Spyri, which is given to plodding moralistic homilies and features one of the least endearing of child actresses.
w Eugene Vale, David Dortort *d* George Templeton *ph* Bruno Stephan *m* Bert Grund *ad* Hans Berthel, Willi Schatz *ed* Jack Ogilvie
☆ Sandy Descher, Douglas Fowley, Peter Capell, Van Dyke Parks, Eric Jelde, Rolf Wanka

The Gift Horse *
GB 1952 100m bw
British Lion/Molton (George Pitcher)
US title: *Glory at Sea*
In 1940 an old US destroyer is given to Britain, and an officer reluctantly takes charge of it.
Conventional, popular seafaring war adventure.
w William Fairchild, Hugh Hastings, William Rose *story* Ivan Goff, Ben Roberts *d* Compton Bennett *ph* Harry Waxman *m* Clifton Parker
☆ Trevor Howard, Richard Attenborough, Sonny Tufts, James Donald, Joan Rice, Bernard Lee, Dora Bryan, Hugh Williams, Robin Bailey

The Gift of Gab
US 1934 71m bw
Universal
A conceited radio announcer gets his comeuppance.
Odd little comedy drama notable only for its long list of stars making cameo appearances.
w Rian James, Lou Breslow *d* Karl Freund *m* Albert von Tilzer, Con Conrad, Charles Tobias
☆ Edmund Lowe, Gloria Stuart, Ruth Etting, Phil Baker, Alexander Woollcott, Ethel Waters, Victor Moore, Boris Karloff, Bela Lugosi, Paul Lukas, Chester Morris, Binnie Barnes, Douglass Montgomery, Wini Shaw
'A hodge-podge, an elongated short.' – *Variety*

The Gift of Love
US 1958 105m Eastmancolor Cinemascope
TCF (Charles Brackett)
A dying wife adopts an orphan girl so that her husband will not be lonely.
Incredibly cloying and miscast remake of Sentimental Journey *(qv).*
w Luther Davis *d* Jean Negulesco *ph* Milton Krasner *m* Cyril Mockridge
☆ Lauren Bacall, Robert Stack, Evelyn Rudie, Lorne Greene

The Gig
US 1985 92m colour
McLaughlin, Piven, Vogel (Norman I. Cohen)
A group of amateur Dixieland musicians take a professional job at a holiday resort, which is not quite as they had imagined.
Gently humorous drama of the male menopause; it has some charm and avoids easy resolutions, but is a little thin.
wd Frank D. Gilroy *ph* Jeri Sopanen *md* Warren Vaché *ed* Rick Shaine
☆ Wayne Rogers, Cleavon Little, Andrew Duncan, Jerry Matz, Daniel Nalbach, Joe Silver, Warren Vaché

Gigi *
France 1948 109m bw
Codo Cinema (Claude Dolbert)
In Paris in the 1890s, a young girl is trained by her aunt to be a cocotte, but when married off to a rake she reforms him.
Charming, overlong, non-musical version of a famous story, chiefly memorable for its local colour.
w Pierre Laroche *novel* Colette *d Jacqueline Audry ph* Gérard Perrin *m* Marcel Landowski
☆ Daniele Delorme, *Gaby Morlay, Yvonne de Bray*, Frank Villard, Jean Tissier, Madeleine Rousset

Gigi ***
US 1958 119m Metrocolor Cinemascope
MGM (Arthur Freed)
Laundered and musicalized version; delightfully set, costumed and performed, but oddly lacking dance numbers.
w Alan Jay Lerner d Vincente Minnelli ph Joseph Ruttenberg m/ly Frederick Loewe, Alan Jay Lerner md André Previn *ed* Adrienne Fazan *pd/cos* Cecil Beaton
☆ *Leslie Caron, Louis Jourdan, Maurice Chevalier, Hermione Gingold,* Isabel Jeans, Jacques Bergerac, Eva Gabor, John Abbott
'It has the sureness expected when a group of the most sophisticated talents are able to work together on material entirely suited to them.' – *Penelope Houston*
† Leslie Caron's vocals were dubbed by Betty Wand.
best picture; Alan Jay Lerner; Vincente Minnelli; Joseph Ruttenberg; André Previn; Cecil Beaton; editing; Preston Ames and William A. Horning (art directors); title song; Maurice Chevalier (special award)

Gigot
US 1962 104m DeLuxe
TCF/Seven Arts (Kenneth Hyman)
The mute caretaker of a Montmartre boarding house looks after an ailing prostitute and her child.
From Paris, Hollywood, comes a grotesque piece of self-indulgence, the arch example of the clown who wanted to play Hamlet. Plotless, mawkish and wholly unfunny.
w John Patrick, Jackie Gleason *d* Gene Kelly *ph* Jean Bourgoin *m* Jackie Gleason *md* Michael Magne *ad* Auguste Capelier
☆ Jackie Gleason, Katherine Kath, Gabrielle Dorziat, Jean Lefebvre, Jacques Marin
'Chaplinesque pretensions have proved fatal before to artists who will not accept their own limitations.' – *Gavin Lambert*
Michael Magne

'There never was a woman like Gilda!'
Gilda ***
US 1946 110m bw
Columbia (Virginia Van Upp)
A gambler in a South American city resumes a love-hate relationship with an old flame … but she is now married to his dangerous new boss.
Archetypal Hollywood film noir, wholly studio-bound and the better for it, with dialogue that would seem risible if it did not happen to be dealt with in this style and with these actors, who keep the mood balanced between suspense and absurdity.
w Marion Parsonnet story E. A. Ellington *d Charles Vidor ph Rudolph Maté m* Hugo Friedhofer *md* Morris Stoloff, Marlin Skiles
☆ *Rita Hayworth, Glenn Ford, George Macready, Steve Geray, Joseph Calleia,* Joe Sawyer, Gerald Mohr, Ludwig Donath
'From a quietly promising opening the film settles into an intractable obscurity of narrative through which as in a fog three characters bite off at each other words of hate.' – *Richard Winnington*
† Rita Hayworth's singing was dubbed by Anita Ellis.

'He fed her popcorn and kisses on a park bench!'
The Gilded Lily *
US 1935 85m bw
Paramount (Albert Lewis)
A poor stenographer who meets her reporter boyfriend on a park bench is wooed by a British peer.
Good depression era romantic comedy with the heroine inevitably choosing poverty.
w Claude Binyon *d* Wesley Ruggles *ph* Victor Milner
☆ *Claudette Colbert*, Fred MacMurray, Ray Milland, C. Aubrey Smith, Luis Alberni, Donald Meek
'Breezy romance … should carry box-office draught.' – *Variety*

'Altamont changed a lot of people's heads.'
Gimme Shelter ***
US 1970 90m colour
Cinema 5 (Ronald Schneider)
Documentary of the Rolling Stones' free concert at Altamont Speedway in December 1969, when a member of the audience was killed by Hell's Angels who had been hired as security for the event.
An excellently photographed concert film that unexpectedly turned out to be the obverse of Woodstock, *revealing the darker side of rock and the revolutionary fervour that once accompanied it.*
d Albert Maysles, David Maysles, Charlotte Zwerin
☆ The Rolling Stones, Ike and Tina Turner, Jefferson Airplane, The Flying Burrito Brothers

Gin Gwai: see *The Eye*

Ginger and Fred ***
Italy/France/West Germany 1986 126m colour
PEA/Revcom/Stella/RAI (Alberto Grimaldi)
An ageing pair of dancers is brought out of retirement to appear on a TV show.
Melancholy comedy with resonances, chiefly taking the side of age against youth, with 'Fred' as an image of Fellini himself.
w Federico Fellini, Tonino Guerra, Tullio Pinelli *d Federico Fellini ph Tonino Delli Colli, Ennio Guarnieri m* Nicola Piovani *pd* Dante Ferretti
☆ *Giulietta Masina, Marcello Mastroianni,* Franco Fabrizi, Frederick von Ledebur

'They Don't Call It The Curse For Nothing.'
Ginger Snaps *
Canada 2000 108m DeLuxe
Optimum/Copper Heart/Water Pictures/TVA/Lions Gate (Steve Hoban, Karen Lee Hall)
In a Canadian suburb, a teenage girl discovers that her older sister is becoming a werewolf.
Engaging, feminist addition to an overworked genre, though it does not escape from the obligatory overkill of contemporary horror.
w Karen Walton *d* John Fawcett *ph* Thom Best *m* Michael Shields *pd* Todd Cherniawsky *ed* Brett Sullivan *sp* creature fx: Paul Jones
☆ Emily Perkins, Katharine Isabelle, Kris Lemche, Mimi Rogers, Jesse Moss, Danielle Hampton, Peter Keleghan, John Bourgeois
'The movie is much at its best when dealing merely with suspicions, rather than when later laying out the lycanthropy and laying on the gore.' – *Philip French, Observer*

The Gingerbread Man
US 1997 113m CFI color
Polygram/Island/Enchanter (Jeremy Tannenbaum)
A lawyer is accused of murdering his girlfriend's father, a cult leader who kidnapped his children.
Routine thriller, in which the director's usual quirkiness has been reined in by the script.
w Al Hayes *story* John Grisham *d* Robert Altman *ph* Changwei Gu *m* Mark Isham *pd* Stephen Altman *ed* Geraldine Peroni
☆ Kenneth Branagh, Embeth Davidtz, Robert Downey Jnr, Daryl Hannah, Robert Duvall, Tom Berenger, Famke Janssen, Clyde Hayes, May Whitman
'A thoroughly run-of-the-mill thriller.' – *Stephen Amidon, Sunday Times*
'Superbly visualised, broodingly atmospheric, blessed with emotional and moral resonances far beyond the squeaks expected from Grisham's usual band of lawyers in trouble.' – *Geoff Brown, The Times*

Giornata Nera per L'Ariete: see *The Fifth Cord*

The Gipsy: see *Le Gitan*

Girl
US 1998 94m Foto-Kem
Feature Film/Kushner-Locke/HSX Films/Muse (Jeff Most, Brad Wyman, Chris Hanley)
In her last year in high school, a girl from a wealthy family is determined to lose her virginity to the local rock star.
Routine rites-of-passage movie, most likely to interest a teen audience, and given an occasional fillip by the contrast between our heroine's voice-over commentary, which swings between naivety and perceptiveness, and her wilder actions.
w David E. Tolchinsky *novel* Blake Nelson *d* Jonathan Kahn *ph* Tami Reiker *m* Michael Tavera *pd* Magda Lavandez-Berliner *ed* Gillian Hutshing
☆ Dominique Swain (Andrea Marr), Sean Patrick Flanery (Todd Sparrow), Summer Phoenix (Rebecca), Tara Reid (Cybil), Selma Blair (Darcy), Channon Roe (Kevin), Portia Di Rossi (Carla), Christopher Masterson (Richard), David Moslow (Greg), Rosemary Forsyth (Mother), James Karen (Father)
'A well-cast, modestly effective pic aimed squarely at the younger set.' – *David Stratton, Variety*
'Trite, clichéd and thoroughly condescending.' – *Sight and Sound*

'Six Is For Sex…'
Girl 6 *
US 1996 108m DeLuxe
TCF/Fox Searchlight/40 Acres and a Mule (Spike Lee)
An unsuccessful actress finds employment providing sex chats on the phone, and begins to enjoy her work too much until she is threatened by a man whose fantasies are about killing prostitutes.
A curious soft-centred movie that begins with confident satire, but tends to exploit what it also condemns, though its inclusion of fantasy sequences involving stereotyped roles in popular entertainment, from Carmen Jones *to blaxploitation movies and sitcoms, suggests Lee wants to make some wider point. He moves away from his documentary style to something that attempts, without great success, to incorporate the self-referential and the surreal; what holds the disparate parts together is the performance of Theresa Randle.*
w Suzan-Lori Parks *d* Spike Lee *ph* Malik Hassan Sayeed *m* Prince *pd* Ina Mayhew *ed* Sam Pollard
☆ *Theresa Randle*, Isaiah Washington, Spike Lee, Jenifer Lewis, Debi Mazar, Peter Berg, Michael Imperioli, Naomi Campbell, Quentin Tarantino, Madonna, John Turturro, Ron Silver
'Lee's film both has its cheesecake and eats it.' – *Sunday Times*

A Girl, a Guy and a Gob
US 1941 91m bw
RKO/Harold Lloyd
GB title: *The Navy Steps Out*
A secretary and her sailor boyfriend teach her stuffy boss how to enjoy life.
Did producer Lloyd intend himself for the role played by O'Brien? If so, he would have needed a stronger script to prevent this Capraesque comedy from falling flat.
w Frank Ryan, Bert Granet *d* Richard Wallace *ph* Russell Metty *m* Roy Webb
☆ Lucille Ball, Edmond O'Brien, George Murphy, George Cleveland, Henry Travers, Franklin Pangborn, Marguerite Churchill, Lloyd Corrigan

The Girl and the General
Italy/France 1967 113m Technicolor
MGM/Champion/Corcordia (Carlo Ponti)
During World War I, a captured Austrian general escapes with a girl partisan.
Turgid war epic veering from melodrama to comedy.

w Luigi Malerba, Pasquale Festa Campanile *d* Pasquale Festa Campanile *ph* Ennio Guarnieri *m* Ennio Morricone
☆ Rod Steiger, Virna Lisi, Umberto Orsini

A Girl Called Katy Tippel: see *Keetje Tippel*

The Girl Can't Help It *
US 1956 97m Eastmancolor
Cinemascope
TCF (Frank Tashlin)
A theatrical agent grooms a gangster's dumb girlfriend for stardom.
Scatty, garish pop scene spoof with a plot borrowed from Born Yesterday *and a lot of jokes about its new star's superstructure. Some scenes are funny, and it puts the first rock and roll stars in pickle for all time.*
w Frank Tashlin, Herbert Baker *story* *Do Re Mi* by Garson Kanin *d* *Frank Tashlin* *ph* Leon Shamroy *md* Lionel Newman
☆ *Jayne Mansfield, Tom Ewell, Edmond O'Brien,* Henry Jones, John Emery; and Julie London, Ray Anthony, Fats Domino, Little Richard, The Platters
'Add to this shimmering example of fifties femininity a massive dose of rock 'n' roll, a crazy plot, mix it up with swirling style and colour, fast humour and neat timing, and you get a bundle of joy whichever way you look at it.' – *Judith Williamson, City Limits*

Girl Crazy
US 1932 75m bw
RKO
Romance at a desert college.
Early talkie version of the musical comedy (see below), here redesigned as a weak vehicle for two comedy stars.
w Tim Whelan, Herman J. Mankiewicz
d William A. Seiter
☆ Bert Wheeler, Robert Woolsey, Eddie Quillan, Dorothy Lee, Mitzi Green, Arline Judge
'A weak sister ... after a while it all becomes too silly.' – *Variety*

Girl Crazy *
US 1943 99m bw
MGM (Arthur Freed)
aka: *When the Girls Meet the Boys*
Romance at a desert college.
Predictable star musical with good tunes.
w Fred Finklehoffe *play* Guy Bolton, Jack McGowan *d* Norman Taurog *ph* William Daniels, Robert Planck *m/ly* *George and Ira Gershwin* *md* Georgie Stoll
☆ *Judy Garland, Mickey Rooney,* Guy Kibbee, Gil Stratton, Robert E. Strickland, Rags Ragland, June Allyson, Nancy Walker, Tommy Dorsey and his band
† Busby Berkeley was replaced as director during filming. Remade 1965 as *When the Boys Meet the Girls.*
♫ 'Treat Me Rough'; Bidin' My Time'; 'Could You Use Me?'; Embraceable You'; 'But Not For Me'; I Got Rhythm'; 'Fascinating Rhythm'

The Girl Downstairs
US 1938 77m bw
MGM
A rich bachelor in Europe chooses the maid instead of the mistress.
Feeble rewrite of Cinderella.
w Harold Goldman, Felix Jackson, Karl Noti
d Norman Taurog
☆ Franchot Tone, Franciska Gaal, Walter Connolly, Rita Johnson, Reginald Owen, Reginald Gardiner, Franklin Pangborn, Robert Coote
'Keen direction and fine performances highlight moderate programmer.' – *Variety*

The Girl Friend
US 1935 67m bw
Columbia
An actor and two songwriters become rural con men.
Thin comedy with music.
w Gertrude Purcell, Benny Rubin *d* Edward Buzzell *ph* Joseph Walker
☆ Ann Sothern, Jack Haley, Roger Pryor, Thurston Hall, Victor Kilian
'Enough hoke to make it a welcome laugh picture for lesser towns.' – *Variety*

The Girl Friends: see *Le Amiche*

A Girl from Lorraine
France 1980 112m colour
Gala/Phoenix/Gaumont/FR3/SSR (Yves Peyrot, Raymond Pousaz)
aka: *La Provinciale*
A woman from the country finds heartbreak in Paris.
Over-solemn in its determination to discover the disillusion of city life.
w Claude Goretta, Jacques Kirsner, Rosine Rochette *d* Claude Goretta *ph* Philippe Rousselot *m* Arié Dzierlatka *ad* Jacques Bufnoir *ed* Joele Van Effenterre
☆ Nathalie Baye, Angela Winkler, Bruno Ganz, Pierre Vernier, Patrick Chesnais, Dominique Paturel, Roland Monod

The Girl from Manhattan
US 1948 81m bw
UA/Benedict Bogeaus
A model returns home to help her uncle with his mortgaged boarding house.
Mouldy comedy-drama full of kind thoughts, charming failures and worldly priests. Interesting for cast.
w Howard Estabrook *d* Alfred E. Green
ph Ernest Laszlo *m* Heinz Roemheld *md* David Chudnow
☆ Dorothy Lamour, Charles Laughton, George Montgomery, Ernest Truex, Hugh Herbert, Constance Collier, Sara Allgood, Frank Orth, Howard Freeman, Adeline de Walt Reynolds, George Chandler, Maurice Cass

The Girl from Mexico: see *Mexican Spitfire*

The Girl from Missouri *
US 1934 75m bw
MGM (Bernard H. Hyman)
aka: *100% Pure*
original titles: *Born to be Kissed; Eadie was a Lady*
A chorus girl determines to remain virtuous until the right millionaire comes along.
Smart, amusing comedy very typical of its period.
w *Anita Loos, John Emerson* *d* Jack Conway
ph Ray June *m* William Axt
☆ *Jean Harlow,* Franchot Tone, Lionel Barrymore, Lewis Stone, Patsy Kelly, Alan Mowbray, Clara Blandick, Henry Kolker
'It's going to be in the money ... one that plenty of purity crusaders will see and like.' – *Variety*
'Noisily defiant, rip-roaring and raucous in spots ... fast and furious adult fare.' – *Photoplay*

The Girl from Paris *
France/Belgium 2001 103m colour
Artificial Eye/Nord-Ouest/StudioCanal/Artemis/Rhône-Alpes/Mars/MS (Christophe Rossignon)
original title: *Une Hirondelle A Fait Le Printemps*
A Parisian woman leaves her job in computing to become a farmer.
Slow-moving drama of agricultural life, dependent for interest on its odd-couple pairing of stubborn young city woman and a crusty old farmer who doesn't hold with new-fangled ways.
w Christian Carion, Eric Assous *d* Christian Carion *ph* Antoine Heberle *m* Philippe Rombi *ad* Jean-Michel Simonet *ed* Andrea Sedlackova
☆ Michel Serrault (Adrien Rochas), Mathilde Seigner (Sandrine Dumez), Jean-Paul Roussillon (Jean Farjon), Frederic Pierrot (Gérard Chauvin), Marc Berman (Stéphane), Françoise Bette (Sandrine's mother)
'Gets nowhere much beyond looking picturesque.' – *Philip French, Observer*

The Girl from Petrovka
US 1974 103m Technicolor
Universal/Richard Zanuck, David Brown
An American correspondent in Moscow falls for a Russian girl.
Lugubrious and lethargic romantic comedy-drama.
w Allan Scott, Chris Bryant *d* Robert Ellis Miller *m* Henry Mancini
☆ Goldie Hawn, Hal Holbrook. Anthony Hopkins, Grégoire Aslan, Anton Dolin

The Girl from Scotland Yard
US 1937 61m bw
Paramount
A female agent tracks down the cause of mysterious explosions.
Lacklustre second feature.
w Doris Anderson, Dore Schary *d* Robert Vignola *ph* Robert Pittack *md* George Stoll
☆ Karen Morley, Robert Baldwin, Katherine Alexander, Eduardo Ciannelli
'Weak thriller ... only for the back seat in duals.' – *Variety*

The Girl from Tenth Avenue
US 1935 69m bw
Warner (Robert Lord)
GB title: *Men on Her Mind*
A jilted attorney drowns his sorrows and marries on the rebound.
Watchable 'woman's picture'.
w Charles Kenyon *play* Hubert Henry Davies
d Alfred E. Green *ph* James Van Trees
☆ Bette Davis, Ian Hunter, Colin Clive, Alison Skipworth, Katherine Alexander, John Eldredge, Philip Reed
'Bette Davis' first starring venture ... she should pull the picture through to good returns.' – *Variety*

Girl Happy
US 1965 96m Metrocolor
Panavision
MGM/Euterpe (Joe Pasternak)
A pop singer in Florida is forced to chaperone a group of college girls including a gangster's daughter.
Standard star vehicle, quite professionally made and totally forgettable.
w Harvey Bullock, R. S. Allen *d* Boris Sagal
ph Philip Lathrop *m* George Stoll
☆ Elvis Presley, Harold J. Stone, Shelley Fabares, Gary Crosby, Nita Talbot

The Girl He Left Behind
US 1956 103m bw
Warner (Frank P. Rosenberg)
The army makes a man of a spoiled youth.
Platitudinous recruiting comedy for dim American teenagers.
w Guy Trosper *book* Marion Hargrove *d* David Butler *ph* Ted McCord *m* Roy Webb
☆ Tab Hunter, Natalie Wood, Jessie Royce Landis, Jim Backus, Henry Jones, Murray Hamilton, Alan King, James Garner, David Janssen

The Girl Hunters
GB 1963 100m bw Panavision
Present Day (Robert Fellows)
Private eye Mike Hammer solves a few murders plus the disappearance of his own ex-secretary.
Comic strip thuggery with the author playing his own slouchy hero; the general incompetence gives this cheap production an air of Kafkaesque menace.
w Mickey Spillane, Roy Rowland, Robert Fellows
d Roy Rowland *ph* Ken Talbot *m* Phil Green
☆ Mickey Spillane, Shirley Eaton, Lloyd Nolan

Girl in a Boot
West Germany 1983 96m colour
Cannon/Cinecom/Neue Filmproduktion/Sender Freies (Axel Bar, Franz Thies)
aka: *Einmal Ku'damm Und Zurück*
An East Berlin woman falls in love with a Swiss cook but opts to stay her side of the Wall.
Soberly shot romance which has dated more than somewhat.
w Jurgen Engert *d* Herbert Ballman *ph* Ingo Hamer *m* Jurgen Knieper *ed* Hans Otto Kruger, Ruth Kusche
☆ Ursula Monn, Christian Kohlund, Evelyn Meyka, Peter Schiff

The Girl in Black
Greece 1955 93m bw
Hermes
original title: *To Koritsi me ta Mavra*
A writer holidaying on a remote fishing island causes tension and tragedy when he falls for a local maiden.
Watchable mood piece benefiting from its star female performance.
wd Michael Cacoyannis *ph* Walter Lassally
m Argyris Kounadis, Manos Hadji Bredkis
☆ Ellie Lambetti, Georges Foundas, Dimitri Horna

The Girl in Black Stockings
US 1957 71m bw
Bel Air/UA
Suspects abound when a young woman is killed in a Utah hotel.
Tolerable murder mystery.
w Richard Landau *story* *Wanton Murder* by Peter Godfrey *d* Howard W. Koch
☆ Anne Bancroft, Lex Barker, Mamie Van Doren, John Dehner, Ron Randell, Marie Windsor

Girl in Distress: see *Jeannie*

A Girl in Every Port *
US 1928 62m (24 fps) bw silent
Fox
Two sailors brawl over women.
Adventure comedy with themes typical of its director.
w Seton Miller, James K. McGuinness
story Howard Hawks *d* Howard Hawks *ph* R. J. Berquist, L. William O'Connell *ed* Ralph Dixon
☆ Victor McLaglen, Robert Armstrong, Natalie Joyce, Dorothy Matthews, Maria Casajuana, Louise Brooks, Francis McDonald
'Brief and essentially anecdotal, it now looks more than anything else like a preliminary sketch for concerns which Hawks would later elaborate.' – *Tim Pulleine, MFB*

A Girl in Every Port
US 1951 87m bw
RKO (Irwin Allen, Irving Cummings Jnr)
Two accident-prone sailors have trouble with a racehorse.
Dismally mechanical farce.
wd Chester Erskine *ph* Nicholas Musuraca
m Roy Webb
☆ Groucho Marx, William Bendix, Marie Wilson, Don Defore, Gene Lockhart

The Girl in Overalls: see *Maisie (Swing Shift Maisie)*

The Girl in Pawn: see *Little Miss Marker (1934)*

The Girl in Room 17: see *Vice Squad*

The Girl in the Headlines *
GB 1963 93m bw
Bryanston/Viewfinder (John Davis)
US title: *The Model Murder Case*
Scotland Yard investigates the murder of a model.
Standard police mystery, well enough done.
w Vivienne Knight, Patrick Campbell *novel* *The Nose on My Face* by Laurence Payne *d* Michael Truman *ph* Stan Pavey *m* John Addison
ad Alan Withy *ed* Frederick Wilson
☆ Ian Hendry, Ronald Fraser, Margaret Johnston, Natasha Parry, Jeremy Brett, Kieron Moore, Jane Asher, Rosalie Crutchley

The Girl in the Kremlin
US 1957 81m bw
Universal
An OSS agent infiltrates the Iron Curtain to assist a plot to overthrow Stalin.
Boring cold war nonsense with the leading lady for some reason playing three parts.
w Gene L. Coon, Robert Hill *d* Russell Birdwell
ph Carl Guthrie *ad* Alexander Golitzen
☆ Lex Barker, Zsa Zsa Gabor, Jeffrey Stone, Maurice Manson, William Schallert

The Girl in the News *
GB 1940 78m bw
TCF (Edward Black)
A nurse is framed for the death of her employer.
Easy-going British mystery of the Agatha Christie school.
w Sidney Gilliat *novel* Roy Vickers *d* Carol Reed
ph Otto Kanturek *md* Louis Levy
☆ Margaret Lockwood, Barry K. Barnes, Emlyn Williams, Margaretta Scott, Roger Livesey, Basil Radford, Wyndham Goldie, Irene Handl, Mervyn Johns, Kathleen Harrison, Richard Bird, Michael Hordern, Roland Culver, Edward Rigby

The Girl in the Painting: see *Portrait from Life*

The Girl in the Red Velvet Swing *
US 1955 109m DeLuxe Cinemascope
TCF (Charles Brackett)

In New York at the turn of the century, a rich unstable man shoots his mistress's former lover.
Plushy but not very interesting recounting of a celebrated murder case in which the victim was a famous architect, Stanford White.
w Walter Reisch, Charles Brackett *d* Richard Fleischer *ph* Milton Krasner *m* Leigh Harline *ad* Lyle R. Wheeler, Maurice Ransford
☆ Ray Milland, Farley Granger, Joan Collins, Glenda Farrell, Luther Adler, Cornelia Otis Skinner, Philip Reed, John Hoyt
'A needlessly long-winded piece of lush sensationalism.' – *Penelope Houston*

The Girl in the Taxi
GB 1937 72m bw
ABFD/British Unity (Eugene Tuscherer, Kurt Bernhardt)
The head of the purity league is drawn into an adulterous flirtation.
Moderately piquant comedy shot in English and French versions.
w Austin Melford, Val Valentine and Fritz Gottfurcht *play* Georg Okonowsky *d* André Berthomieu *ph* Roy Clark *md* Jean Gilbert *ad* D'Eaubonne *ed* Ray Pitt
☆ Frances Day, Henri Garat, Lawrence Grossmith, Jean Gillie, Mackenzie Ward, Helen Haye, Albert Whelan

The Girl in White *
US 1952 93m bw
MGM (Armand Deutsch)
GB title: *So Bright the Flame*
The story of Dr Emily Dunning, the first woman to become an intern in one of New York's hospitals.
Bland biopic, modestly produced, with predictable plot crises.
w Irmgard von Cube, Allen Vincent *book Bowery to Bellevue* by Emily Dunning Barringer *d* John Sturges *ph* Paul C. Vogel *m* David Raksin
☆ June Allyson, Arthur Kennedy, Gary Merrill, Mildred Dunnock, Jesse White, Marilyn Erskine

'Sometimes the only way to stay sane is to go a little crazy'
Girl, Interrupted *
US 1999 127m DeLuxe
Columbia/Red Wagon/Global (Douglas Wick, Cathy Konrad)

In the mid-60s, a teenage girl is wrongly institutionalized in a hospital for the mentally ill.
An only occasionally interesting rites-of-passage drama, contrasting two young women, one vulnerable, the other out-of-control; but it says little of interest about the times or the use of such institutions to dump those who did not accept the way things were.
w James Mangold, Lisa Loomer, Anna Hamilton Phelan *book* Susanna Kaysen *d* James Mangold *ph* Jack Green *m* Mychael Danna *pd* Richard Hoover *ed* Kevin Tent *cos* Arianne Phillips
☆ Winona Ryder (Susanna), Angelina Jolie (Lisa), Clea Duvall (Georgina), Brittany Murphy (Daisy), Elisabeth Moss (Polly), Jared Leto (Tobias Jacobs), Jeffrey Tambor (Dr Potts), Vanessa Redgrave (Dr Wick), Whoopi Goldberg (Valerie), Mary Kay Place (Mrs Gilcres)
'A lopsided, often dull movie.' – *Variety*
Angelina Jolie

Girl Loves Boy
US 1937 77m bw
ABFD/Grand National (B. F. Zeidman)
In the early 1900s, a rich, spoilt young man, after being tricked into marriage by a crooked woman, finds true love.
A sickly mix of sentimentality and heavy-handed humour, hardly watchable.
w Duncan Mansfield, Carroll Graham *story* Karl Brown, Hinton Smith *d* Duncan Mansfield *ph* Edward Snyder *md* Abe Meyer *ad* Edward Jewell *ed* Edward Schroeder
☆ Eric Linden, Cecilia Parker, Roger Imhof, Dorothy Peterson, Pedro de Cordoba, Bernadene Hayes

The Girl Most Likely
US 1958 98m Technicolor RKOscope
RKO (Stanley Rubin)

A girl finds herself engaged to three men at the same time, and envisions marriage with each.
Dully cast, quite brightly handled remake of Tom, Dick and Harry, *with modest songs and dances.*
w Paul Jarrico, Devery Freeman *d* Mitchell Leisen *ph* Robert Planck *m* Nelson Riddle *m/ly* Ralph Blane, Hugh Martin
☆ Jane Powell, Cliff Robertson, Keith Andes, Tommy Noonan, Kaye Ballard, Una Merkel
† For Mitchell Leisen and RKO studios, their last film.
†† Paul Jarrico was omitted from the original screenwriting credits because he was blacklisted at the time.

A Girl Must Live **
GB 1939 92m bw
Gainsborough-20th Century (Edward Black)
A runaway schoolgirl falls among chorus girls planning to marry into the nobility.
Light, peppery comedy with a strong cast.
w Frank Launder, Michael Pertwee *novel* Emery Bonnet *d* Carol Reed *ph* Jack Cox *m/ly* Eddie Pola, Manning Sherwin *md* Louis Levy *ad* Vetchinsky *ed* R. E. Dearing
☆ Margaret Lockwood, Renée Houston, Lilli Palmer, George Robey, Hugh Sinclair, Naunton Wayne, Moore Marriott, Mary Clare, David Burns, Kathleen Harrison, Martita Hunt, Helen Haye
'An unabashed display of undressed femininity, double-meaning dialogue alternating between piquancy and vulgarity, and hearty knockabout involving scantily attired young viragos who fight furiously in a whirligig of legs and lingerie.' – *Kine Weekly*

'He was half-oriental ... but he used the women of two continents without shame or guilt!'
A Girl Named Tamiko
US 1962 119m Technicolor Panavision
Paramount/Hal B. Wallis (Paul Newman)
A Eurasian photographer uses his women in an attempt to get American nationality.
Humdrum romantic melodrama with dim performances.
w Edward Anhalt *novel* Ronald Kirkbride *d* John Sturges *ph* Charles Lang Jnr *m* Elmer Bernstein
☆ Laurence Harvey, France Nuyen, Martha Hyer, Michael Wilding, Miyoshi Umeki

The Girl Next Door
US 1953 92m Technicolor
TCF (Robert Bassler)

A Broadway musical star falls for her suburban neighbour.
Mild musical linked by UPA cartoon sequences.
w Isobel Lennart *d* Richard Sale *ph* Leon Shamroy *m/ly* Josef Myrow, Mack Gordon *md* Lionel Newman *ch* Richard Barstow
☆ Dan Dailey, June Haver, Natalie Schafer, Dennis Day, Cara Williams

The Girl of the Golden West
US 1930 81m bw
Warner (Robert North)
A gun-toting, saloon-owning girl marries an outlaw and saves him from the sheriff.
Straight version of a dusty old Broadway success, later musicalized under the same title (see below).
w Waldemar Young *play* David Belasco *d* John Francis Dillon *ph* Sol Polito
☆ Ann Harding, James Rennie, Harry Bannister, Ben Hendricks Jnr, J. Farrell MacDonald
† A silent version was made in 1923 by First National, with Sylvia Breamer and J. Warren Kerrigan, directed by Edwin Carewe.

The Girl of the Golden West
US 1938 121m bw/sepia release
MGM (William Anthony McGuire)

In backwoods Canada, a girl loves a bandit who is being chased by the Mounties.
Solemn musical melodrama in which the stars seem miscast and a bit of pep is badly needed. Taken from a hoary David Belasco spectacular, and looks it.
w Isabel Dawn, Boyce DeGaw *d* Robert Z. Leonard *ph* Oliver Marsh *m/ly* Sigmund Romberg, Gus Kahn
☆ Jeanette MacDonald, Nelson Eddy, Walter Pidgeon, Leo Carrillo, Buddy Ebsen, Olin Howland
'This musical mustanger finds the stars not only out of their element, but hemmed in by a two-hour mélange of the great outdoors, Mexican bandits, early Spanish-Californian atmosphere and musical boredom ... a spotty entry.' – *Variety*

Girl of the Year: see *The Petty Girl*

The Girl on a Motorcycle
GB/France 1968 91m Technicolor
Mid Atlantic/Ares (William Sassoon)

US title: *Naked under Leather*
French title: *La Motocyclette*
A married woman leaves her husband, zooms off on her motorcycle to see her lover, and crashes to her death while indulging in sexual reverie.
An incredibly plotless and ill-conceived piece of sub-porn claptrap, existing only as a long series of colour supplement photographs.
w Ronald Duncan *novel La Motocyclette* by André Pieyre de Mandiargues *d* Jack Cardiff *ph* Jack Cardiff, René Guissart *m* Les Reed *md* Douglas Gamley *ad* Russell Hagg, Jean D'Eaubonne *ed* Peter Musgrave
☆ Marianne Faithfull (Rebecca), Alain Delon (Daniel), Roger Mutton (Raymond), Marius Goring (Rebecca's Father)

The Girl on the Boat
GB 1962 91m bw
UA/Knightsbridge (John Bryan)
In the 20s, a shipboard romance develops between an upper-class Englishman and an American girl.
A misfiring attempt at a satirical comedy with a miscast star, who looks unhappy in its period setting.
w Reuben Ship *novel* P. G. Wodehouse *d* Henry Kaplan *ph* Denys Coop *m* Kenneth Jones *ad* Tony Masters *ed* Noreen Ackland
☆ Norman Wisdom, Millicent Martin, *Richard Briers*, Sheila Hancock, Bernard Cribbins, Athene Seyler, Philip Locke, Reginald Beckwith, Peter Bull, Ronald Fraser

The Girl on the Bridge **
France 1998 92m bw Panavision
Pathé/UGCF/France2/Christian Fechner

original title: *La Fille sur la Pont*
A knife-thrower rescues a suicidal girl and offers her a job as a human target.
Witty, enjoyable, escapist romantic drama, done with elegance and style.
w Serge Frydman *d* Patrice Leconte *ph* Jean-Marie Dreujou *m* various *ad* Ivan Maussion *ed* Joelle Hache
☆ Daniel Auteuil (Gabor), Vanessa Paradis (Adele), Demetre Georgalas (Takis), Isabelle Petit-Jacques (The Bride), Frederic Pfluger (The Contortionist)
'Like a pocket anthology of your favorite foreign movies (or mine, anyway), a meticulous cut-and-paste collage of a half-dozen half-remembered, dreamed-up movies by Godard, Truffaut and, above all, Fellini.' – A. O. Scott, *New York Times*

The Girl on the Canal: see *Painted Boats*

The Girl Rosemarie
West Germany 1958 100m bw
Roxy
original title: *Das Mädchen Rosemarie*
Corrupt industrialists and investigators alike are relieved when a girl who had been the mistress of all of them is murdered.
Slick melodrama based on an actual case; almost a documentary exposé.
w Erich Kuby, Rolf Thiele, Joe Herbst, Rolf Urich *d* Rolf Thiele *ph* Klaus von Rautenfeld *m* Norbert Schultze
☆ Nadja Tiller, Peter Van Eyck, Carl Raddatz, Gert Frobe, Mario Adorf, Horst Frank

The Girl Rush
US 1955 85m Technicolor Vistavision
Paramount (Frederick Brisson, Robert Alton)
A gambler's daughter inherits a half share in a Las Vegas hotel.
Dull charmless semi-musical vehicle for a star who can't quite carry it.
w Phoebe and Henry Ephron *d* Robert Pirosh *ph* William Daniels *m* Herbert Spencer, Earle Hagen *ch* Robert Alton
☆ Rosalind Russell, Eddie Albert, Fernando Lamas, James Gleason, Gloria de Haven, Marion Lorne

Girl Shy **
US 1924 65m bw silent
Pathé/Harold Lloyd

A bashful, stuttering apprentice tailor in a small town writes a book on love-making, despite being terrified of girls.
A comedy of character that only comes to life in its final slapstick chase sequence, one that has few rivals for invention and complexity as Lloyd transfers from car to horse, fire-engine, tram, speeding car, motorcycle and collapsing horse and cart in order to get to the church on time.
story Sam Taylor, Ted Wilde, Tim Whelan *d* Fred Newmeyer, Sam Taylor *ph* Walter Ludin *ad* Liell K. Vedder *ed* Allen McNeil
☆ Harold Lloyd, Jobyna Ralston, Richard Daniels, Carlton Griffin
† The film was the first of Lloyd's own productions.

Girl Stroke Boy
GB 1971 88m Eastmancolor
Hemdale/Virgin (Ned Sherrin, Terry Glinwood)
A well-to-do couple try to find out whether their son's house guest is male or female.
Initially funny but appallingly extended one-joke comedy which many will find merely embarrassing.
w Caryl Brahms, Ned Sherrin *play Girlfriend* by David Percival *d* Bob Kellett *ph* Ian Wilson *m* John Scott
☆ Joan Greenwood, Michael Hordern, Clive Francis, Patricia Routledge, Peter Bull, Rudolph Walker, Elizabeth Welch

A Girl Was Young: see *Young and Innocent*

The Girl Who Had Everything
US 1953 69m bw
MGM (Armand Deutsch)

The daughter of a wealthy criminal lawyer falls in love with one of her father's crooked clients.
Glossy melodrama of purely superficial interest.
w Art Cohn *novel* Adela Rogers St Johns *d* Richard Thorpe *ph* Paul Vogel *m* André Previn
☆ Elizabeth Taylor, William Powell, Fernando Lamas, Gig Young
† Remake of *A Free Soul*.

The Girl with Brains in Her Feet
GB 1997 98m Metrocolor
Alliance/Lexington (Don Boyd)

In the early 70s, an athletic teenage girl discovers sex with a Leicestershire farmworker.
Low-budget movie about the pains and pleasures of growing up that will probably seem more watchable on the small screen.
w Jo Hodges *d* Robert Bangura *ph* Peter Butler *m* Rob Lane *pd* Lynn Bird *ed* Adam Ross
☆ Amanda Mealing, Joanna Ward, Jamie McIntosh, Jodie Smith, Richard Claxton, John Thompson, Garth Tudor-Price, Samantha Wheatley

Girl with Green Eyes **
GB 1963 91m bw
UA/Woodfall (Oscar Lewenstein)

An artless young Dublin girl falls for a middle-aged writer.
Lyrical romance which just about preserves its charm by good location sense.
w Edna O'Brien *novel The Lonely Girl* by Edna O'Brien *d Desmond Davis ph Manny Wynn m John Addison*
☆ *Peter Finch, Rita Tushingham, Lynn Redgrave*
'A beautiful and eloquent first directorial effort ... embodies all that is naive and silly and noble and wonderful and heartbreaking and funny about being young.' – *Judith Crist*

The Girl with Red Hair
Netherlands 1981 116m Fujicolour
Blue Dolphin/Movies Filmproductions/VNU/Trio/Vara TV/Querido/Meteor (Chris Brouwer, Haig Balian)
original title: *Het Meisje Met Het Rode Haar*
The life and death of a member of the Dutch resistance at the hands of the Nazis is recalled by a friend.
Muddled attempt to explain actions from a feminist point of view.
w Ben Verbong, Peter de Vos *novel* Theun de Vries *d* Ben Verbong *ph* Theo Van de Sande *m* Nicola Piovani *ad* Dorus Van Der Linden *ed* Ton de Graff
☆ Renee Soutendijk, Peter Tuinman, Loes Luca, Johan Leysen, Robert Delhez, Ada Bouwman, Lineke Rijxman, Maria de Booy

The Girl-Getters: see *The System (GB)*

'Prove Them Wrong'
Girlfight **
US 2000 113m Technicolor
Columbia TriStar/Independent Film Channel (Sarah Green, Martha Griffin, Maggie Renzi)
An aggressive high school girl finds an outlet for her temper and pride by becoming a boxer.
A feminist take on a familiar Rocky*-like story, but one that seems new and fresh this time around, helped by a knockout performance from Michelle Rodriguez.*
wd Karyn Kusama ph Patrick Cady *m* Theodore Shapiro *pd* Stephen Beatrice *ed* Plummy Tucker
☆ *Michelle Rodriguez* (Diana), Jaime Tirelli (Hector), Paul Calderon (Sandro), Santiago Douglas (Adrian), Ray Santiago (Tiny), Elisa Bocanegra (Marisol), Shannon Walker Williams (Veronica), Iris Little-Thomas (Ms Martinez), John Sayles (Science Teacher)
'A near-irresistible button-pusher that's agile enough to hold a mirror to its own aspirations.' – *J. Hoberman, Village Voice*

The Girlfriend: see *La Amiga*

Girlfriends *
US 1978 86m DuArt
Cyclops (Claudia Weill, Jan Saunders)
A Jewish girl photographer in New York is ditched by her girlfriend and considers men.
Mild, amusing, well-observed little comedy-drama which goes nowhere in particular and slightly outstays its welcome.
w Vicki Polon *d* Claudia Weill *ph* Fred Murphy *m* Michael Small
☆ Melanie Mayron, Eli Wallach, Anita Skinner, Bob Balaban
'A quiet triumph ... There is no tedium, there is realization; involvement; pleasure. The more I think about this film, the warmer I feel.' – *Stanley Kauffmann*

The Girls: see *Les Bonnes Femmes*

Les Girls *
US 1957 114m Metrocolor Cinemascope
MGM (Sol. C. Siegel)
One member of a dancing troupe sues another over her memoirs.
Disappointing, talent-laden comedy-musical with a Rashomon-like flashback plot and a curious absence of the expected wit and style.
w John Patrick *novel* Vera Caspary *d* George Cukor *ph* Robert Surtees *m/ly* Cole Porter *md* Adolph Deutsch *ch* Jack Cole
☆ Gene Kelly, *Kay Kendall*, Mitzi Gaynor, Taina Elg, Jacques Bergerac, Leslie Phillips, Henry Daniell, Patrick MacNee

Girls about Town
US 1931 80m bw
Paramount
Gold diggers find true love.
A laugh, a tear and a wisecrack in the big city: very dated, but may have seemed fresh at the time.
w Raymond Griffith, Brian Marlow *story* Zoë Akins *d* George Cukor
☆ Kay Francis, Joel McCrea, Lilyan Tashman, Eugene Pallette, Alan Dinehart, George Barbier
'Generally only fair b.o. as ultra sophistication may be small-town setback.' – *Variety*

Girls' Dormitory *
US 1936 66m bw
TCF
A college girl falls for her headmaster.
Old-fashioned romance for nice young people, smoothly produced in the Fox mid-30s manner.
w Gene Markey *story* Ladislaus Fodor *d* Irving Cummings *ph* Merritt B. Gerstad *m* Arthur Lange
☆ Herbert Marshall, *Simone Simon*, Ruth Chatterton, Constance Collier, J. Edward Bromberg, Dixie Dunbar, Tyrone Power
'The picture, dewy as it is, has merit even apart from Mlle Simon (it is well directed and the performance of Mr Edward Bromberg as a cruel, warped pedagogic type is admirable), but I am afraid its concentrated atmosphere of young innocence (even the bathing-costumes are white like the nightdresses) defeats its own purpose.' – *Graham Greene*

'The Swingin'-est Elvis! The Fastest-Movin' Fun'n'Music! And The World's Curviest Girls! Girls! Girls!'
Girls! Girls! Girls!
US 1962 106m Technicolor
Wallis-Hazen (Hal B. Wallis)
A night-club singer runs a fishing boat as a hobby.
Empty-headed, lighter than air vehicle for star fans.
w Edward Anhalt, Allan Weiss *d* Norman Taurog *ph* Loyal Griggs *m* Joseph J. Lilley
☆ Elvis Presley, Stella Stevens, Laurel Goodwin, Jeremy Slate

The Girls He Left Behind: see *The Gang's All Here (1943)*

Girls in the Night
US 1953 82m bw
Universal
GB title: *Life After Dark*
The son of a New York tenement family falls under suspicion of murder.
Very mildly sensational low-life melodrama, like a citified Tobacco Road.
w Ray Buffum *d* Jack Arnold *ph* Carl Guthrie *ad* Alexander Golitzen
☆ Glenda Farrell, Harvey Lembeck, Joyce Holden, Glen Roberts, Don Gordon

Girls in the Street: see *London Melody*

Girls in Uniform: see *Maedchen in Uniform*

Girls Just Want to Have Fun
US 1985 87m CFI color
New World/James G. Robinson (Chuck Russell)
A new girl at high school defies her strict father to take part in a TV dance contest.
High-spirited but vapid comedy; of minimal interest outside its target audience of girls in their early teens.
w Amy Spies *d* Alan Metter *ph* Thomas Ackerman *m* Thomas Newman *pd* Jeffrey Staggs *ed* David Rawlins, Lorenzo Destefano
☆ Sarah Jessica Parker, Lee Montgomery, Helen Hunt, Morgan Woodward, Ed Lauter, Jonathan Silverman, Holly Gagnier, Shannen Doherty

Girls Night
GB/US 1997 102m Technicolor
Granada/Showtime (Bill Boyes)
Two sisters-in-law, one dying of cancer, take off for Las Vegas to spend their bingo winnings.
Derivative movie of terminal illness that has all the attractions, and most of the emotions, of a television soap opera.
w Kay Mellor *d* Nick Hurran *ph* David Odd *m* Ed Shearmur *pd* Taff Batley *ed* John Richards
☆ Brenda Blethyn, Julie Walters, Kris Kristofferson, George Costigan, James Gaddas, Philip Jackson, Sue Cleaver, Myra Syal
'A film so forcibly aimed at a particular audience it becomes offensive.' – *Gaby Wood, Guardian*

The Girls of Pleasure Island
US 1953 96m Technicolor
Paramount (Paul Jones)
In 1945 the Marines land on a tiny Pacific island, disturbing the life of an English gentleman and his three inexperienced but beautiful daughters.
Tedious and wholly artificial comedy with a leaden touch, devised as a try-out for young talent.
w F. Hugh Herbert *d* F. Hugh Herbert, Alvin Ganzer *ph* Daniel Fapp *m* Lyn Murray
☆ Leo Genn, Gene Barry, Don Taylor, Elsa Lanchester, Dorothy Bromiley, Audrey Dalton, Joan Elan

The Girls of Summer: see *Satisfaction*

Girls on Probation
US 1938 63m bw
Warner
A lawyer falls in love with a young girl in trouble.
Formula B picture that was re-released a few years later when its two stars were more familiar to the public.
w Crane Wilbur *d* William McGann *ph* Arthur Todd *ad* Hugh Reticker *ed* Frederick Richards
☆ Jane Bryan, Ronald Reagan, Sheila Bromley, Anthony Averill, Henry O'Neill, Elisabeth Risdon
'A creditable job.' – *Variety*

Girls Town
US 1996 89m DuArt
Metrodome/AC Hundred/Boomer (Lauren Zalaznick)
Three high-school friends take action when another friend kills herself because she was raped.
A confrontational drama, worked out in improvisationary workshops before it was shot, that has some effective moments, but lacks a solid narrative base.
w Jim McKay, Denise Casano, Anna Grace, Bruklin Harris, Lili Taylor *d* Jim McKay *ph* Russell Lee Fine *m* Guru *pd* David Doernberg *ed* Jim McKay, Alex Hall
☆ Lili Taylor, Brucklin Harris, Anna Grace, Aunjanue Ellis, Ramya Pratt, Asia Minor, Carl Kwaku Ford, Guillermo Diaz
'This indie's attraction lies in its raw, unpredictable plot.' – *Jessica Mellor, Empire*

Girly: see *Mumsy, Nanny, Sonny and Girly*

Giro City *
GB 1982 102m colour
Silvarealm/Rediffusion/Channel 4 (Sophie Balhetchet, David Payne)
A television documentary team tries to present honest programmes about Ireland and about local government corruption.
Smartly made if somewhat predictably and stridently left-wing slice of so-called realism.
wd Karl Francis *ph* Curtis Clark *m* Alun Francis *ed* Kent Pan
☆ Glenda Jackson, Jon Finch, Kenneth Colley, James Donnelly, Emrys James, Simon Jones

Le Gitan
France/Italy 1975 94m Eastmancolor
Lara/Adel (Raymond Danon, Alain Delon)
aka: *The Gipsy*
On the run from the police, an alienated gypsy commits a series of daring robberies with the aid of two accomplices.
A tired, plodding thriller-cum-protest about society's persecution of gypsies that settles for making its murderous hero into a figure of alluring glamour.
wd José Giovanni *novel* *Histoire de Fou* by José Giovanni *ph* Jean-Jacques Tarbes *m* Django Reinhardt, Claude Bolling, Lick *ad* Willy Holt *ed* Jacqueline Thiedot
☆ Alain Delon, Annie Girardot, Paul Meurisse, Marcel Bozzuffi, Maurice Barrier, Maurice Giraud, Bernard Giraudeau, Renato Salvatori

Giulietta degli Spiriti: see *Juliet of the Spirits*

Give a Girl a Break *
US 1953 84m Technicolor
MGM (Jack Cummings)
A Broadway star walks out on a show and three girls audition as replacements.
Minor musical vehicle for the Champions; an agreeable time-passer.
w Frances Goodrich, Albert Hackett *d* Stanley Donen *ph* William Mellor *m/ly* Burton Lane, Ira Gershwin *md* André Previn *ch* Stanley Donen, Gower Champion
☆ Marge and Gower Champion, Debbie Reynolds, Bob Fosse, Kurt Kasznar

Give Me a Break: see *Life with Mikey*

Give Me a Sailor
US 1938 80m bw
Paramount (Jeff Lazarus)
An ugly girl envies her sister her beaux, but ends up winning a competition for beautiful legs.
One of the double bill comedies which got Bob Hope's career off to a shaky start.
w Doris Anderson, Frank Butler *play* Anne Nichols *d* Elliott Nugent *ph* Victor Milner *m/ly* Leo Robin, Ralph Rainger *md* Boris Morros
☆ Martha Raye, Bob Hope, Betty Grable, Jack Whiting, Clarence Kolb
'Not so funny farce.' – *Variety*

Give My Regards to Broad Street *
GB 1984 108m colour
TCF/MPL (Andros Epimanondas)
An international rock star fears that the priceless tapes of his new album have been stolen, and searches London for them.
An absurdly thin premise even for a musical which is essentially an ego trip for Paul McCartney, who at least squandered his own money on it and not the bank's. Some of the numbers have merit but the mood never connects.
w Paul McCartney *d* Peter Webb *ph* Ian McMillan *m* Paul McCartney *pd* Anthony Pratt
☆ Paul McCartney, Bryan Brown, Ringo Starr, Barbara Bach, Tracey Ullman, Ralph Richardson, George Martin, John Bennett

Give My Regards to Broadway *
US 1948 89m Technicolor
TCF (Walter Morosco)
An old-time vaudevillian yearns to get back into show business.
Pleasantly performed, sentimental family comedy with familiar tunes.
w Samuel Hoffenstein, Elizabeth Reinhardt *d* Lloyd Bacon *ph* Harry Jackson
☆ Dan Dailey, *Charles Winninger*, Fay Bainter, Charles Ruggles, Nancy Guild
'Vaudeville is dead. I wish to God someone would bury it.' – *James Agee*

Give Us the Moon
GB 1944 95m bw
GFD/Gainsborough (Edward Black)
In post-war London a club is opened for idle members only.
Whimsical comedy which fell with a dull thud.
wd Val Guest *novel* *The Elephant is White* by Caryl Brahms, S. J. Simon
☆ Margaret Lockwood, Vic Oliver, Peter Graves, Max Bacon, Roland Culver, Frank Cellier, Jean Simmons

Give Us This Day
GB 1949 120m bw
Plantagenet (Rod E. Geiger, N. A. Bronsten)
US title: *Salt to the Devil*
Depression struggles of an Italian immigrant family in New York.
An unconvincing, self-pitying wallow, a very curious enterprise for a British studio.
w Ben Barzman *story* *Christ in Concrete* by Pietro di Donato *d* Edward Dmytryk *ph* C. Pennington Richards *m* Benjamin Frankel
☆ Sam Wanamaker, Lea Padovani, Kathleen Ryan, Charles Goldner, Bonar Colleano, William Sylvester, Karel Stepanek, Sidney James
'Dmytryk insisted on cutting the film himself and he has left in at least three spare reels.' – *Richard Winnington*
'Worth making and worth seeing, but cramped by its symbolism and its language.' – *Richard Mallett, Punch*

The Gladiator
US 1938 70m bw
Columbia
A poor boy wins a prize and becomes a college football hero.
Elementary star farce.
w Charles Melson, Arthur Sheekman *novel* Philip Wylie *d* Edward Sedgwick
☆ Joe E. Brown, Man Mountain Dean, June Travis, Dickie Moore, Lucien Littlefield
'Goofy but a lot of fun.' – *Variety*

Gladiator *
US 1992 102m Technicolor
Columbia TriStar/Columbia/Price Entertainment (Frank Price, Steve Roth)

A white teenage amateur boxer is forced to turn professional by a crooked promoter and forms a friendship with a young black fighter.
Enjoyable boxing movie that nevertheless sticks to all the usual moves; it could never have been a contender but on its modest level it holds the interest.
w Lyle Kessler, Robert Mark Kamen *story* Djordje Milicevic, Robert Mark Kamen *d* Rowdy Herrington *ph* Tak Fujimoto *m* Brad Fiedel *pd* Gregg Fonseca *ed* Peter Zinner, Harry B. Miller III
☆ James Marshall, Cuba Gooding Jnr, Brian Dennehy, Robert Loggia, Ossie Davis, Jon Seda, Cara Buono, Lance Slaughter
'An exercise in audience manipulation that probably will get a thumbs-down from the targetted younger audience.' – *Variety*

'What We Do In Life Echoes In Eternity.'
Gladiator ***
US 2000 154m Technicolor Panavision
Universal/DreamWorks/Scott Free (Douglas Wick, David Franzoni, Branko Lustig)

Condemned to die by a power-mad Emperor, a Roman general escapes to become a slave and a gladiator before he gains an opportunity for vengeance.
Lavish, spectacular, action-packed epic that re-invigorated a moribund genre, though in contrast to its predecessors it is somewhat glum in its approach; in its attempt at a tragic dimension, it eschews the camp decadence and fun of previous excursions into ancient Rome.
w David Franzoni, John Logan, William Nicholson *d Ridley Scott ph John Mathieson m* Hans Zimmer, Lisa Gerrard *pd Arthur Max ed* Pietro Scalia *sp* John Nelson, Neil Corbould, Tim Burke, Rob Harvey; Mill Film *cos* Janty Yates
☆ *Russell Crowe* (Maximus), Joaquin Phoenix (Commodus), Connie Nielsen (Lucilla), *Oliver Reed* (Proximo), Derek Jacobi (Gracchus), Djimon Hounsou (Juba), Richard Harris (Marcus Aurelius), David Schofield (Falco), John Shrapnel (Gaius), Tomas Arana (Quintus), Ralf Moeller (Hagen), Spencer Treat Clark (Lucius), David Hemmings (Cassius)
'So entertaining and carried off with such chutzpah, you forgive the odd absurdity and wonder where this genre has been all your life.' – *Peter Bradshaw, Guardian*
'A muscular and bloody combat picture, a compelling revenge drama and a truly transporting trip back nearly 2,000 years.' – *Todd McCarthy, Variety*
† The film cost $100m to make and took $449m at the box office world wide.
picture; Russell Crowe; Janty Yates; sound (Scott Millan, Bob Beemer, Ken Weston) ; visual effects (John Nelson, Neil Corbould, Tim Burke, Rob Harvey)
Ridley Scott; Joaquin Phoenix; John Mathieson; Pietro Scalia; script (David Franzoni, John Logan, William Nicholson); art direction (Arthur Max, Crispian Sallis); Hans Zimmer
film; John Mathieson; Arthur Max; Pietro Scalia

Glamorous Night
GB 1937 81m bw
BIP/ABP (Walter C. Mycroft)
An opera singer and her gypsy friends save a Ruritanian king from his scheming prime minister.
Modest transcription of a popular stage musical.
w Dudley Leslie, Hugh Brooke, William Freshman *play* Ivor Novello *d* Brian Desmond Hurst *ph* Fritz Arno Wagner *m/ly* Ivor Novello, Christopher Hassall *md* Harry Acres *ad* Cedric Dawe *ed* Flora Newton
☆ Mary Ellis, Otto Kruger, Victor Jory, Barry Mackay, Trefor Jones, Finlay Currie, Felix Aylmer
† Although several of the original songs are either sung or heard, much of the background music is not Novello's.

Glamour Boy *
US 1941 79m bw
Colbert Clark/Paramount
GB title: *Hearts in Springtime*
An ex-child star finds himself tutoring his successor.
Quite an appealing peep inside Hollywood, and especially wry at the time because the star was still a household word.
w Bradford Ropes, Val Burton *d* Ralph Murphy
☆ Jackie Cooper, Susanna Foster, Walter Abel, Darryl Hickman, Ann Gillis, William Demarest
'One of the happiest "idea" pictures turned out by Hollywood in a long time.' – *Variety*

'Underwater ... undercover ... under any circumstances ... you must see the wildest, funniest new comedy!'
The Glass Bottom Boat
US 1966 110m Metrocolor Panavision
MGM/Arwin-Reame (Martin Melcher)

A young widow gets involved with spies.
Frantic spy spoof, pleasantly set on the Californian coast, but overflowing with pratfalls, messy slapstick and pointless guest appearances.
w Everett Freeman *d* Frank Tashlin *ph* Leon Shamroy *m* Frank de Vol
☆ Doris Day, Rod Taylor, Arthur Godfrey, Paul Lynde, John McGiver, Edward Andrews, Eric Fleming, Dom DeLuise

The Glass Cage
GB 1954 59m bw
Exclusive/Hammer (Anthony Hinds)
US title: *The Glass Tomb*
A freak-show promoter solves the murder of a circus girl.
Moderate programmer with an interesting cast.
w Richard Landau *novel The Outsiders* by A. E. Martin *d* Montgomery Tully *ph* Walter Harvey *m* Leonard Salzedo *md* John Hollingsworth *ad* J. Elder Wills *ed* James Needs
☆ John Ireland, Honor Blackman, Geoffrey Keen, Eric Pohlmann, Sidney James, Liam Redmond, Sydney Tafler, Sam Kydd, Ferdy Mayne, Tonia Bern

'Be Careful Who You Trust.'
'When Her Parents Died Their Best Friends Welcomed Her Into Their Home... And Their Deadly Game.'
The Glass House
US 2001 106m DeLuxe Panavision
Columbia TriStar/Original (Neal H. Moritz)

Two young orphans begin to suspect the motives of the couple who have given them a home.
Risibly melodramatic thriller that never rises out of the rut of predictability.
w Wesley Strick *d* Daniel Sackheim *ph* Alar Kivilo *m* Christopher Young *pd* Jon Gary Steele *ed* Howard E. Smith
☆ LeeLee Sobieski (Ruby), Diane Lane (Erin), Stellan Skarsgard (Terry), Bruce Dern (Begleiter), Kathy Baker (Nancy Ryan), Trevor Morgan (Rhett), Chris Noth (Uncle Jack), Michael O'Keefe (Dave Baker), Rita Wilson (Grace Baker)
'A thriller that does not mean to be comical but that inspires more howls of laughter than shivers of dread.' – A. O. Scott, *New York Times*
'So laughably awful that it begs to have stones thrown at it; it's a wonder it got made at all.' – *Kevin Thomas, Los Angeles Times*

'He carries his love in his iron fists!'
The Glass Key **
US 1935 87m bw
Paramount (E. Lloyd Sheldon)
A slightly corrupt but good-natured politician is saved by his henchman from being implicated in a murder.
Lively transcription of a zesty crime novel.
w Kathryn Scola, Kubec Glasmon, Harry Ruskin *novel Dashiell Hammett d* Frank Tuttle *ph* Henry Sharp
☆ Edward Arnold, George Raft, Claire Dodd, Rosalind Keith, Guinn Williams, Ray Milland
'Will have to struggle to strike above average grosses.' – *Variety*

The Glass Key **
US 1942 85m bw
Paramount (Fred Kohlmar)

Nifty remake of the above which finds some limited talents in their best form, helped by a plot which keeps one watching.
w Jonathan Latimer *d* Stuart Heisler *ph* Theodor Sparkuhl *m* Victor Young
☆ *Brian Donlevy, Alan Ladd, Veronica Lake*, Bonita Granville, *William Bendix*, Richard Denning, Joseph Calleia, Moroni Olsen
MADVIG (BRIAN DONLEVY): 'I'm going to society. He's practically given me the key to his house.'
BEAUMONT (ALAN LADD): 'Yeah, a glass key. Be sure it doesn't break up in your hand.'

The Glass Menagerie **
US 1950 107m bw
Warner/Charles K. Feldman (Jerry Wald)
A shy crippled girl seeks escape from the shabby reality of life in St Louis and from her mother's fantasies.
Pleasantly moody version of one of its author's lighter and more optimistic plays; fluent and good-looking production, memorable performances.
w Tennessee Williams, Peter Berneis play Tennessee Williams *d Irving Rapper ph Robert Burks m* Max Steiner
☆ *Gertrude Lawrence*, Jane Wyman, Kirk Douglas, Arthur Kennedy
† An excellent TV movie of the play, directed by Anthony Harvey and starring Katharine Hepburn, was made in 1973.

The Glass Menagerie *
US 1987 135m DuArt
Cineplex (Burtt Harris)

A son longs to escape from his stifling home, where his genteel mother worries about the future prospects of his lame, shy sister.
Well-acted and faithful to the original stage play, this version still obstinately refuses to come to life on the screen.
w Tennessee Williams *play* Tennessee Williams *d* Paul Newman *ph* Michael Ballhaus *m* Henry Mancini *pd* Tony Walton *ed* David Ray
☆ Joanne Woodward, John Malkovich, Karen Allen, James Naughton

The Glass Mountain
GB 1949 98m bw
Victoria (John Sutro, Joseph Janni, Fred Zelnik)
In the Dolomites, a married composer loves an Italian girl who saved his life during the war.
Tedious sudser, ineptly produced; an enormous British box-office success because of its theme music.
w Joseph Janni, John Hunter, Emery Bonnet, Henry Cass, John Cousins *d* Henry Cass *ph* Otello Martelli, William McLeod *m* Nino Rota
☆ Michael Denison, Dulcie Gray, Valentina Cortese, Tito Gobbi, Sebastian Shaw

The Glass Shield *
US 1995 108m Foto-Kem
CiBy 2000 (Tom Byrnes, Carolyn Schroeder)

The first black cop at a Los Angeles station is tempted to collude in the framing of a black man for murder.
Intense study of the corruption of a police force within a violent society, but too heavy-handed to be entirely successful.
wd Charles Burnett *screenplay One of Us* by *Ned Welsh ph* Elliot Davis *m* Stephen Taylor *pd* Penny Barrett *ed* Curtiss Clayton
☆ Michael Boatman, Lori Petty, Richard Anderson, Ice Cube, Michael Ironside, Bernie Casey, Elliott Gould, M. Emmet Walsh
'A powerful moral drama that tries to deal with the racism at the root of many problems in contemporary American society.' – *Todd McCarthy, Variety*

The Glass Slipper
US 1954 94m Eastmancolor
MGM (Edwin H. Knopf)

The story of Cinderella.
To those used to the pantomime version this is dull, dreary, high-flown stuff: limbo sets, ballets, psychological rationalization and virtually no comedy.
d Charles Walters *ph* Arthur E. Arling *m* Bronislau Kaper *ch* Roland Petit *w/ly* Helen Deutsch
☆ Leslie Caron, Michael Wilding, Elsa Lanchester, Barry Jones, *Estelle Winwood* (Fairy Godmother)

The Glass Tomb: see *The Glass Cage*

The Glass Web
US 1953 81m bw 3-D
U-I (A. J. Cohen)
A TV executive kills a blackmailing actress and allows a young scriptwriter to be accused.
Boring thriller set in a TV studio.
w Robert Blees, Leonard Lee *d* Jack Arnold *ph* Maury Gertsman *m* Joseph Gershenson *ad* Bernard Herzbrun, Eric Orbom *ed* Ted J. Kent
☆ Edward G. Robinson, John Forsythe, Marcia Henderson, Richard Denning, Kathleen Hughes, Hugh Sanders, Jean Willes

Glastonbury The Movie
GB 1996 92m colour Panavision
Starlight/GTM/Space Baby/Arts Council
Documentary of three rock music festivals staged at Glastonbury in the late 80s and early 90s.
A film that goes with the flow, not imposing much editorial control over a collage of images of a festival noted for its slightly mystical, New Age slant; the emphasis is rarely on performances by the various groups involved.
d Robin Mahoney, Matthew Salkeld, William Beaton et al ph Aubrey Fagon, Robin Mahoney, William Beaton et al ed Robin Mahoney, Matthew Salkeld, William Beaton

Gleaming the Cube
US 1988 105m Deluxe
Rank/Gladden Entertainment (Lawrence Turman)

A teenage skateboarder tracks down the killers of his adopted Vietnamese brother.
Likely to appeal only to those who know what the film's title means.
w Michael Tolkin *d* Graeme Clifford *ph* Reed Smoot *m* Jay Ferguson *pd* John Muto *ed* John Wright
☆ Christian Slater, Steven Bauer, Richard Herd, Le Tuan, Min Luong, Art Chudabala, Ed Lauter, Micole Mercurio, Peter Kwong

Glen or Glenda?
US 1953 61m bw
Edward D. Wood Jnr

aka: *I Changed My Sex*
aka: *He or She; The Transvestite; I Led Two Lives*
A doctor relates stories about transvestites and sex-change operations.
Notorious grade Z exploitation piece, often counted among the worst films ever made. See for yourself.
wd Edward D. Wood Jnr *ph* William C. Thompson *ad* Jack Miles *ed* Bud Schelling
☆ Lyle Talbot, Timothy Farrell, Bela Lugosi, Dolores Fuller

'A Story For Everyone Who Works For A Living.'
Glengarry Glen Ross **
US 1992 100m Eastmancolor Super 35
Rank/Zupnik Enterprises (Jerry Tokofsky, Stanley R. Zupnik)

Four real-estate salesmen are in competition to see who can sell the most, with the sack facing the two losers.
A brilliant stage play seems a little claustrophobic on its transfer to the screen, but provides opportunities for some excellent acting.
w David Mamet play David Mamet *d* James Foley *ph* Juan Ruiz Anchia *m* James Newton Howard *pd* Jane Musky *ed* Howard Smith
☆ *Al Pacino*, Jack Lemmon, Alec Baldwin, Ed Harris, Alan Arkin, Kevin Spacey, Jonathan Pryce
'The prize-winning comedy of outrage is brought to the screen, intact and enhanced.' – *Time*
'An entertaining but slightly uncomfortable marriage both of different stage traditions and of movie ways of dealing with them.' – *Richard Combs, Sight and Sound*
† Jack Lemmon won the best actor award at the 1992 Venice Film Festival for his performance.
Al Pacino

The Glenn Miller Story **
US 1953 116m Technicolor
U-I (Aaron Rosenberg)

The life of the unassuming trombonist and bandleader whose plane disappeared during World War II.
Competent musical heartwarmer with a well-cast star and successful reproduction of the Miller sound. A big box-office hit.
w Valentine Davies, Oscar Brodney *d Anthony Mann ph William Daniels md* Henry Mancini, Joseph Gershenson *ad* Bernard Herzbrun, Alexander Golitzen *ed* Russell Schoengarth
☆ *James Stewart* (Glenn Miller), June Allyson (Helen Burger Miller), Harry Morgan (Chummy MacGregor), Charles Drake (Don Haynes), Frances Langford (herself), Louis Armstrong (himself), Gene Krupa (himself)
† Jimmy Stewart's trombone playing was dubbed by Murray MacEachern and Joe Yukl.
sound recording
script; music direction

Gli Occhi, La Bocca: see *Those Eyes, That Mouth*

The Glimmer Man
US 1996 91m Technicolor Panavision
Warner (Steven Seagal, Julius R. Nasso)

A cop and a martial arts expert, who team up to catch a serial killer who crucifies his victims, discover that the murders are part of a larger conspiracy.
Unoriginal and ever-predictable action movie; isn't it time someone thought up a slightly better plot than this paranoid nonsense?
w Kevin Brodbin *d* John Gray *ph* Rick Bota *m* Trevor Rabin *pd* William Sandell *ed* Donn Cambern
☆ Steven Seagal, Keenen Ivory Wayans, Bob Gunton, Brian Cox, John M. Jackson, Michelle Johnson, Stephen Tobolowsky
'The clichés pile up as fast as the bodies.' – *George Perry*

'In music she found her dream, her love, herself.'
Glitter
US/Canada 2001 104m DeLuxe
Columbia TriStar/Maroon (Laurence Mark)

In the 1980s, a girl becomes a successful pop singer with the help of a DJ.
Vapid star vehicle for a pop singer with no visible acting ability.
w Kate Lanier *story* Cheryl L. West *d* Vondie Curtis-Hall *ph* Geoffrey Simpson *m* Terence Blanchard *ch* Neisha Folkes *pd* Dan Bishop *ed* Jeff Freeman
☆ Mariah Carey (Billie Frank), Max Beesley (Julian Dice), Da Brat (Louise), Tia Texada (Roxanne), Valarie Pettiford (Lillian Frank), Ann Magnuson (Kelly), Terrence Howard (Timothy Walker), Dorian Harewood (Guy Richardson)
'As phony a vehicle as one could possibly concoct for a wannabe movie star.' – *Robert Koehler, Variety*
† The movie cost around $22m and took around $4.3m at the US box-office. The failure of the soundtrack album led EMI to pay around $32m to Mariah Carey to end her recording contract with the company.

A Global Affair
US 1963 84m bw
Seven Arts/Hall Bartlett

A United Nations official has to look after an abandoned baby.
Flat sentimental farce which embarrassingly tries to say something about the UN.
w Arthur Marx, Bob Fisher, Charles Lederer *d* Jack Arnold *ph* Joseph Ruttenberg *m* Dominic Frontière
☆ Bob Hope, Lilo Pulver, Michèle Mercier, Yvonne de Carlo
'Squaresville incarnate, with a side trip into Leersville.' – *Judith Crist, 1973*

La Gloire de Mon Père *
France 1990 110m Eastmancolor
Palace/Gaumont International/La Guéville/TF1 (Marc Goldstaub, Guy Azzi)

aka: *My Father's Glory*
A young city boy goes on holiday to Provence with his family and falls in love with the countryside.
Charm and nostalgia are laid on thickly in a movie based on the childhood of Marcel Pagnol, who grew up to become an influential film-maker.
w Jérôme Tonnerre, Louis Nucera, Yves Robert *autobiography* Marcel Pagnol *d* Yves Robert *ph* Robert Alazraki *m* Vladimir Cosma *ad* Jacques Dugied *ed* Pierre Gillette
☆ Philippe Caubère, Nathalie Roussel, Didier Pain, Thérèse Liotard, Julien Ciamaca, Victorien Delamare, Joris Molinas, Paul Crauchet, Jean-Pierre Darras (narrator)
'The weave of inner drama, family album, and discursive sceneries is gentle and lightly enchanting.' – *Raymond Durgnat, Sight and Sound*
† The story is continued in a sequel, *Le Château de Ma Mère* (qv).

Gloria *
US 1980 121m Technicolor
Columbia (Sam Shaw)

In the Bronx, an innocent woman finds she has to meet violence with violence in order to protect a small boy from the mob.
Overlong but lively and oddly entertaining; however, one is never quite sure what if anything it is getting at.
wd John Cassavetes *ph* Fred Schuler *m* Bill Conti *ad* Rene D'Auriac *ed* George C. Villasenor
☆ *Gena Rowlands*, John Adames, Buck Henry, Julie Carmen, Tony Knesich, Gregory Cleghorn
Gena Rowlands

'Gloria. Big mouth. Big attitude. But who knew she had a big heart.'
Gloria
US 1998 108m Technicolor
Entertainment/Mandalay/Eagle Point (Gary Foster, Lee Rich)

A woman flees from her gangster boyfriend, taking with her a young child, the sole survivor of a mob hit, and an incriminating computer disc.
A lacklustre chase movie that plods towards total inertia and ennui; the only suspense it provides is wondering whether one will still be awake at the end.
w Steven Antin *d* Sidney Lumet *ph* David Watkin *m* Howard Shore *pd* Mel Bourne *ed* Tom Swartwout *cos* Dona Granata
☆ Sharon Stone (Gloria), Jean-Luke Figueroa (Nicky), Jeremy Northam (Kevin), Cathy Moriarty (Diane), George C. Scott (Ruby), Mike Starr (Sean), Barry McEvoy (Terry), Don Billett (Raymond), Jerry Dean (Mickey), Tony DiBenedetto (Zach), Bonnie Bedelia (Brenda), Teddy Atlas (Ian)
'A travesty trying to be a Sharon Stone vehicle, this wooden crime yarn easily qualifies as the most tired, unexciting mob movie in recent memory.' – *Godfrey Cheshire, Variety*
† Although there is no mention of it in the credits, the movie is a remake of John Cassavetes' *Gloria* (qv).

Glorifying the American Girl *
US 1929 87m bw (colour sequence)
Paramount (Florenz Ziegfeld)

A chorus girl rejects her boyfriend for the sake of stardom.
Archetypal show-must-go-on musical.
w J. P. McEvoy, Millard Webb *d* Millard Webb, John Harkrider *ph* George Folsey *md* Frank Tours
☆ Mary Eaton, Edward Crandall, Helen Morgan, Rudy Vallee, Florenz Ziegfeld, Adolph Zukor, Otto Kahn, Texas Guinan, Mayor Jimmy Walker, Ring Lardner, Noah Beery, Johnny Weissmuller, Eddie Cantor

The Glorious Adventure *
GB 1921 100m approx Prizmacolor silent
Stoll/J.Stuart Blackton
Various lives are affected by the Great Fire of London in 1666.
Stagey costume drama, notable only as the first British film in colour.
w Felix Orman *d* J. Stuart Blackton *ph* William T. Crespinal
☆ Lady Diana Manners, Victor McLaglen, Gerald Lawrence, Cecil Humphreys, Alex Crawford, Lennox Pawle (Pepys)

Glory **
US 1989 122m Technicolor Panavision
Columbia TriStar (Freddie Fields)

A young and inexperienced Union officer is given command of the first black regiment recruited to fight in the Civil War.
Moving, if sometimes sanitised, account of the stirrings of black freedom.
w Kevin Jarre *book Lay This Laurel* by Lincoln Kirstein, *One Gallant Rush* by Peter Burchard, the letters of Robert Gould Shaw *d* Edward Zwick *ph Freddie Francis m* James Horner *pd* Norman Garwood *ed* Steven Rosenblum
☆ Matthew Broderick, Denzel Washington, Cary Elwes, Morgan Freeman, Jihmi Kennedy, Andre Braugher, John Finn, Donovan Leitch, John David Cullum
Freddie Francis; Denzel Washington
art direction; editing

Glory at Sea: see *The Gift Horse*

The Glory Brigade
US 1953 82m bw
TCF (William Bloom)
Greek soldiers fight in Korea alongside the Americans.
Modest war adventure with predictable racial tensions.
w Franklin Coen *d* Robert D. Webb *ph* Lucien Andriot *md* Lionel Newman
☆ Victor Mature, Alexander Scourby, Lee Marvin, Richard Egan

The Glory Guys *
US 1965 112m DeLuxe Panavision
UA/Levy-Gardner-Laven

Officers of the US cavalry disagree about dealing with the Indians.
Standard big-budget Western.
w Sam Peckinpah *novel The Dice of God* by Hoffman Birney *d* Arnold Laven *ph* James Wong Howe *m* Riz Ortolani
☆ Tom Tryon, Harve Presnell, Senta Berger, Andrew Duggan, James Caan, Slim Pickens, Michael Anderson Jnr

G'mar Giviya: see *Cup Final*

The Gnome-Mobile *
US 1967 90m Technicolor
Walt Disney (James Algar)

A millionaire and his family go for a forest picnic and help a colony of gnomes.
Cheerful adventures for small children, with good trick work.
w Ellis Kadison *novel* Upton Sinclair *d* Robert Stevenson *ph* Edward Colman *m* Buddy Baker
☆ Walter Brennan, Matthew Garber, Karen Dotrice, Richard Deacon, Sean McClory, Ed Wynn, Jerome Cowan, Charles Lane

'A weekend wasted is never a wasted weekend.'
Go **
US 1999 103m DeLuxe Panavision
Columbia/Banner/Saratoga (Paul Rosenberg, Mickey Liddell, Matt Freeman)

The lives of a supermarket checkout girl, four friends on a weekend in Vegas, two actors and a drug dealer collide with one another.
Enjoyably hectic caper with three interlocking stories of rave-ups and drug deals going wrong, deftly done with just enough wit and style.
w John August *d* Doug Liman *ph* Doug Liman *m* BT *pd* Tom Wilkins *ed* Stephen Mirrione
☆ Desmond Askew (Simon Baines), Taye Diggs (Marcus), William Fichtner (Burke), J.E. Freeman (Victor Sr), Katie Holmes (Claire Montgomery), Breckin Meyer (Tiny), Jay Mohr (Zack), Timothy Olyphant (Todd Gaines), Sarah Polley (Ronna Martin), Scott Wolf (Adam)
'An overly calculated concoction that nonetheless delivers a pretty good rush.' – *Variety*

Go Fish *
US 1994 83m bw
Mainline/Islet/Can I Watch Pictures/KVPI (Rose Troche, Guinevere Turner)

A young lesbian would-be writer looks for love and finds it.
Wry, witty and sometimes charming account of a community of lesbians, though their interests rarely stray from talk of sex, and gossip about who is making it with whom.
w Guinevere Turner, Rose Troche *d* Rose Troche *ph* Ann T. Rossetti *m* Brendan Dolan, Jennifer Sharpe *ed* Rose Troche
☆ V. S. Brodie, Guinevere Turner, T. Wendy McMillan, Migdalia Melendez, Anastasia Sharp
'A low-budget *When Sally Met Sally*.' – *Sight and Sound*
'By turns charming and tedious, this proves that no matter what your sexual preferences may be, we are all faced with the same problems in life.' – *Empire*

Go for a Take
GB 1972 90m colour
Rank/Century Films (Roy Simpson)
Two waiters in debt to a gangster take refuge in a film studio.
Painful British farce.
w Alan Hackney *d* Harry Booth *ph* Mark McDonald *m* Glen Mason
☆ Reg Varney, Norman Rossington, Sue Lloyd, Dennis Price, Julie Ege, Patrick Newell, David Lodge

Go for Broke
US 1951 93m bw
MGM (Dore Schary)
World War II exploits of Japanese-American soldiers.
Absolutely unsurprising war film with all the anti-Japs converted by the end. Production quite good.
wd Robert Pirosh *ph* Paul C. Vogel *m* Alberto Colombo
☆ Van Johnson, Lane Nakano, George Miki, Akira Fukunaga, Warner Anderson, Don Haggerty
Robert Pirosh (as writer)

Go Into Your Dance **
US 1935 89m bw
Warner (Sam Bischoff)

GB title: *Casino de Paree*
A big-headed star gets his come-uppance and finds happiness.
Moderate backstage musical notable for the only teaming of Jolson and Keeler, who were then married.
w Earl Baldwin *story* Bradford Ropes *d* Archie Mayo *ph* Tony Gaudio, Sol Polito *m/ly* Harry Warren, Al Dubin *ch* Bobby Connolly
☆ *Al Jolson*, Ruby Keeler, Glenda Farrell, Benny Rubin, Phil Regan, Barton MacLane, Sharon Lynne, Akim Tamiroff, Helen Morgan, Patsy Kelly
'It has everything for the box office.' – *Variety*
Bobby Connolly

Go, Johnny Go!
US 1958 75m bw
Hal Roach (Alan Freed)

A former choirboy becomes a rock singer.
Typical teen fare of its time; if it retains any interest, it is due to Berry singing the title song, 'Little Queenie' and 'Memphis Tennessee', and to Ritchie Valens's only film performance.
w Gary Alexander *d* Paul Landres
☆ Alan Freed, Chuck Berry, Jimmy Clanton, Sandy Stewart, Herb Vigran, Eddie Cochrane, Ritchie Valens

Go Man Go
US 1954 82m bw
Alfred Palca (Anton M. Leader)
How Abe Saperstein moulded and trained the Harlem Globetrotters basketball team.
Not so much a film as an athletic demonstration with some actors round the edges.
w Arnold Becker (Alfred Palca) *d James Wong Howe ph* Bill Steiner *m* Alex North
☆ Dane Clark, Sidney Poitier, Pat Breslin, Edmon Ryan
† Arnold Becker fronted for Alfred Palca because Palca was blacklisted.

Go Naked in the World
US 1960 103m Metrocolor Cinemascope
MGM/Arcola (Aaron Rosenberg)
A prostitute causes a rift between son and millionaire father.
Antediluvian melodrama with overblown performances.
wd Ranald MacDougall *novel* Tom Chamales
ph Milton Krasner *m* Adolph Deutsch
☆ Gina Lollobrigida, Tony Franciosa, Ernest Borgnine, Luana Patten, Will Kuluva, Philip Ober
'A good example of how the increased liberation of Hollywood can be misused.' – *MFB*

Go Tell the Spartans
US 1978 114m CFI color
Spartan Company (Allan F. Bodoh, Mitchell Cannold)
In Vietnam, a seasoned commander tries to get a platoon of raw soldiers out of a Vietcong ambush.
We have been here before, in other wars, and since there is little heroism to be had from Vietnam it is difficult to see why we are invited again.
w Wendell Mayes *story* Daniel Ford *d* Ted Post
ph Harry Stradling Jnr *m* Dick Halligan
☆ Burt Lancaster, Craig Wasson, Jonathan Goldsmith, Marc Singer
'No earth-shaking masterpieces, but in its small-scale way it's strong, hard, forthright.' – *Stanley Kauffmann*
'Has the virtues of its defects. It is understated, lacking in powerful dramatic incidents and high human emotion, and rather flatly written and directed. As a result, it has about it a realistically antiheroic air that is rare enough in any movie about any war.' – *Richard Schickel, Time*

Go to Blazes
GB 1961 84m Technicolor Cinemascope
ABP (Kenneth Harper)
Ex-convicts become firemen, intending to use the engine for smash and grab raids.
Mild comedy ruined by wide screen.
w Patrick Campbell, Vivienne Knight *d* Michael Truman *ph* Erwin Hillier *m* John Addison
☆ Dave King, Daniel Massey, Norman Rossington, Wilfrid Lawson, Maggie Smith, Robert Morley, Coral Browne

'Laughter is what it has nothing else but!'
Go West *
US 1925 70m (24 fps) bw silent
Metro-Goldwyn/Buster Keaton (Joseph M. Schenck)
A tenderfoot makes friends with a cow and takes it everywhere.
Disappointingly slow star comedy with splendid moments.
w Raymond Cannon *d* Buster Keaton *ph* Bert Haines, E. Lessley
☆ Buster Keaton, Howard Truesdall, Kathleen Myers

Go West **
US 1940 82m bw
MGM (Jack Cummings)
Three zanies tackle a Western villain.
Minor Marx comedy with a good start (the ticket office sketch) and a rousing finale as they take a moving train to bits, but some pretty soggy stuff in between.
w Irving Brecher *d* Edward Buzzell *ph* Leonard Smith *m* Bronislau Kaper *md* Georgie Stoll
☆ Groucho Marx, Harpo Marx, Chico Marx, John Carroll, Diana Lewis, Robert Barrat

'How you gonna keep 'em down on the farm, after they've seen Mae West?'
Go West Young Man
US 1936 80m bw
Paramount (Emanuel R. Cohen)
A movie star has a car breakdown in Pennsylvania and falls for a local lad.
Cleaned-up Mae West vehicle, all rather boring.
w Mae West *play* Personal Appearance by Lawrence Riley *d* Henry Hathaway *ph* Karl Struss *m* George Stoll
☆ Mae West, Randolph Scott, Warren William, Lyle Talbot, Alice Brady, Isabel Jewell, Elizabeth Patterson
'On the way to snug profits.' – *Variety*
'Quite incredibly tedious, as slow and wobbling in its pace as Miss West's famous walk. The wisecracks lack the old impudence, and seldom have so many feet of film been expended on a mere dirty look.' – *Graham Greene*

The Go-Between ***
GB 1970 116m Technicolor
EMI/World Film Services (John Heyman, Norman Priggen)
Staying at a stately home around the turn of the century, 12-year-old Leo carries love letters from a farmer to his friend's sister.
A rather tiresome plot sustains a rich picture of the Edwardian gentry, a milieu with which however the director is not at home and treats far too slowly and tricksily.
w Harold Pinter *novel* L. P. Hartley *d* Joseph Losey *ph* Geoffrey Fisher *m* Michel Legrand
ad Carmen Dillon
☆ Alan Bates, Julie Christie, Michael Redgrave, Dominic Guard, Michael Gough, Margaret Leighton, Edward Fox
'It's an almost palpable recreation of a past environment, and that environment is the film's real achievement, not the drama enacted within it.' – *Stanley Kauffmann*
Margaret Leighton
Harold Pinter; Edward Fox; Margaret Leighton; Dominic Guard

The Go-Getter
US 1937 90m bw
Warner (Sam Bischoff)
A one-legged navy veteran is determined that his injury will not prevent him from becoming a success.
Moderate comedy-drama, agreeably played.
w Delmer Daves, Peter B. Kyne *d* Busby Berkeley
ph Arthur Edeson *md* Leo F. Forbstein
☆ George Brent, Charles Winninger, Anita Louise, John Eldredge, Henry O'Neill, Willard Robertson, Eddie Acuff
'A fair amount of comedy within a story bordering on the ridiculous.' – *Variety*

The Goalie's Anxiety at the Penalty Kick: see *The Goalkeeper's Fear of the Penalty Kick*

The Goalkeeper's Fear of the Penalty Kick **
West Germany 1971 101m colour
Filmverlag der Autoren/Osterreichischer Telefilm (Thomas Schamoni, Peter Genee)
original title: *Die Angst des Tormanns beim Elfmeter*
Sent off during a game, an ageing goalkeeper commits a motiveless murder.
Disturbing film of the failure of communication; difficult but rewarding for the patient.
wd Wim Wenders *story* Peter Handke *ph* Robby Muller *m* Jurgen Knieper *ed* Peter Przygodda
☆ Arthur Brauss, Kai Fischer, Erika Pluhar, Libgart Schwartz, Rudiger Vogler, Marie Bardischewski

God Gave Him a Dog: see *The Biscuit Eater (1940)*

God Needs Men: see *Dieu a Besoin des Hommes*

God of Gamblers
Hong Kong 1990 120m colour
Wins (Charles Heung)
original title: *Dou San*
A successful globe-trotting gambler loses his intelligence in an accident and becomes involved with petty crooks.
Over-long thriller with its emphasis on broad comedy, although it livens up for the last half-hour. The subtitling is sub-standard, getting every idiom wrong, as in 'Let's be frankly', 'I'll put him dead' and 'I was self-defencing'.
d Wong Ching
☆ Chow Yun-Fat, Andy Leung
'The action is great and the gambling scenes are crazy. Recommended.' – *Sight and Sound*
† The film was a big local success and gave a boost in Hong Kong to movies about gambling.

God Told Me To
US 1976 89m colour
Larco
GB title: *Demon*
A detective investigates the death of a mad sniper and finds it to be a case of demonic possession.
Unsavoury mix of several genres, insufficiently well written to compel.
wd Larry Cohen *ph* Paul Glickman *m* Frank Cordell
☆ Tony Lo Bianco, Deborah Raffin, Sandy Dennis, Sylvia Sidney, Sam Levene, Robert Drivas, Richard Lynch, Harry Bellaver

The Goddess *
US 1958 105m bw
Columbia/Carnegie (Milton Perlman)
A small-town girl becomes a Hollywood sex symbol and lives to regret it.
Savage attack on the Marilyn Monroe cult, a bit lachrymose and compromised by miscasting, but with interesting detail.
w Paddy Chayefsky *d* John Cromwell *ph* Arthur J. Ornitz *m* Virgil Thomson
☆ Kim Stanley, Lloyd Bridges, Steven Hill, Betty Lou Holland
Paddy Chayefsky

The Goddess: see *Devi (1960)*

The Godfather ****
US 1972 175m Technicolor
Paramount/Alfran (Albert S. Ruddy)
When, after ruling for two generations, the Mafia's New York head dies of old age, his son takes over reluctantly but later learns how to kill.
A brilliantly-made film with all the fascination of a snake pit: a warm-hearted family saga except that the members are thieves and murderers. Cutting would help, but the duller conversational sections do heighten the cunningly judged moments of suspense and violence.
w Francis Ford Coppola, Mario Puzo *novel* Mario Puzo *d* *Francis Ford Coppola* *ph* Gordon Willis
m Nino Rota *pd* Dean Tavoularis
☆ Marlon Brando, *Al Pacino*, Robert Duvall, James Caan, Richard Castellano, Diane Keaton, Talia Shire, Richard Conte, John Marley
'The immorality lies in his presentation of murderers as delightful family men – the criminal is the salt of the earth – and to our shame we rub it into the wounds of our Watergate-world mortality and even ask for more.' – *Judith Crist, 1974*
'They have put padding in Brando's cheeks and dirtied his teeth, he speaks hoarsely and moves stiffly, and these combined mechanics are hailed as great acting ... Like star, like film, the keynote is inflation. *The Godfather* was made from a big bestseller, a lot of money was spent on it, and it runs over three hours. Therefore it's important.' – *Stanley Kauffmann*
'The greatest gangster picture ever made.' – *Pauline Kael*
best picture; script; Marlon Brando
Francis Ford Coppola (as director); Al Pacino; Robert Duvall; James Caan
Nino Rota

The Godfather of Harlem: see *Black Caesar*

The Godfather Part II ****
US 1974 200m Technicolor
Paramount/the Coppola Company (Francis Ford Coppola)
In 1958, Michael Corleone reflects on the problems of himself and his father before him.
Complex gangster movie, explaining the present in terms of the past and providing a comprehensive view of American society, full of good scenes and performances.
w Francis Ford Coppola, Mario Puzo *d* *Francis Ford Coppola* *ph* Gordon Willis *m* Nino Rota, Carmine Coppola *pd* Dean Tavoularis
☆ Al Pacino, *Robert DeNiro*, Diane Keaton, Robert Duvall, John Cazale, Lee Strasberg, Michael V. Gazzo, Talia Shire, Troy Donahue
'The daring of Part II is that it enlarges the scope and deepens the meaning of the first film ... It's an epic vision of the corruption of America.' – *Pauline Kael, New Yorker*
† The two films were eventually combined and extended for television into a ten-hour serial, *The Godfather Saga*.
best picture; script; Francis Ford Coppola (as director); Nino Rota, Carmine Coppola; Robert DeNiro
Al Pacino; Lee Strasberg; Michael V. Gazzo; Talia Shire
Al Pacino

'Real Power Can't Be Given. It Must Be Taken.'
The Godfather Part III **
US 1990 161m Technicolor
Paramount/Zoetrope (Francis Ford Coppola)
Michael Corleone attempts to become a legitimate businessman while grooming his brother's violent and illegitimate son as his successor.
Overlong, often confusing to those who cannot remember the earlier films, and hampered by at least one wretched performance, it fails to reach the standard of the first two movies in the series. But for all that it retains one's interest most of the time.
w Mario Puzo, Francis Ford Coppola *d* Francis Ford Coppola *ph* Gordon Willis *m* Carmine Coppola, Nino Rota *pd* Dean Tavoularis *ad* Alex Tavoularis *ed* Barry Malkin, Lisa Fruchtman, Walter Murch
☆ Al Pacino, Diane Keaton, Talia Shire, Andy Garcia, Eli Wallach, Joe Mantegna, George Hamilton, Bridget Fonda, Sofia Coppola, Raf Vallone, Franc D'Ambrosio, Donal Donnelly, Richard Bright, Helmut Berger, Don Novello
'While certain flaws may prevent it from being regarded as the full equal of its predecessors ... it nonetheless matches them in narrative intensity, epic scope, sociopolitical analysis, physical beauty and deep feeling for its characters and milieu.' – *Variety*
'This engrossing movie is conceived and executed on a grand scale. In these inflationary times, the numbers of killings and the sums of money under discussion are much greater than before. But, oddly enough, Michael seems to shrink in stature as the picture proceeds and the *Lear*-like tragedy at which Coppola aims is not realised.' – *Philip French, Observer*
'As in the second film, a fearful price is paid for power, and Michael is left alone to consider the cost. It is here, in the ruined face of such a man, that *The Godfather Part III* locates an emotional gravity rare in American movies. The film is a slow fuse with a big bang – one that echoes through every family whose own tragedy is an aching for things past and loved ones lost.' – *Richard Corliss, Time*
best picture; Francis Ford Coppola; Andy Garcia; best song 'Promise Me You'll Remember'; best art direction; best cinematography, best film editing

'Sometimes It's Hard To Tell Them Apart.'
Gods and Monsters **
US 1998 105m colour/bw Super 35
Regent (Paul Colichman, Gregg Fienberg, Mark Harris)
Ailing film director James Whale looks back on his life while attempting a seduction of his young gardener.
Enjoyable, if fictional, account of the last days of a director who reinvented himself in America as a middle-class Englishman and a master of horror; if the material is sometimes a little thin, the acting carries it through.
wd Bill Condon *novel* *Father of Frankenstein* by Christopher Bram *ph* Stephen M. Katz *m* Carter Burwell *pd* Richard Sherman *ed* Virginia Katz
☆ *Ian McKellen* (James Whale), Brendan Fraser, Lynn Redgrave, Lolita Davidovich, Kevin J. O'Connor, David Dukes, Brandon Kleyla, Jack Plotnick
'Beautifully acted, witty and heart-tugging film.' – *Janet Maslin, New York Times*
'I dare say some people will find it all touchingly affectionate. To me, its posthumous libelling of James Whale, without a shred of evidence for most of its fictions, proves that death is not the last thing one has to fear.' – *Alexander Walker, London Evening Standard*
Bill Condon (script)
Ian McKellen; Lynn Redgrave

God's Army: see *The Prophecy*

God's Country and the Woman
US 1936 80m Technicolor
Warner (Lou Edelman)
The junior partner of a lumber company goes to work undercover in an opponent's camp, causes trouble, and falls in love.
Adequate outdoor melodrama in early colour.
w Norman Reilly Raine *novel* James Oliver Curwood *d* William Keighley *ph* Tony Gaudio *m* Max Steiner
☆ George Brent, Beverly Roberts, Barton MacLane, Robert Barrat, Alan Hale, Addison Richards, El Brendel, Roscoe Ates, Billy Bevan
'Great outdoors in Technicolor, but not likely for much b.o.' – *Variety*

God's Gun
Italy/Israel 1976 94m colour
Cannon/Rovi/Golan/Globus
aka: *Pistola di Dio*
When bandits kill a priest, a young boy goes to find the man's brother, a gunfighter, so that he can seek revenge.
Dull and violent Western, in which Lee Van Cleef plays two roles, indistinguishable one from the other, and neither cast nor director displays any enthusiasm for the tired material.
wd Frank Kramer (Gianfranco Parolini) *story* John Fonseca *ph* Sandro Mancori *m* Sante Maria Romitelli *pd* Claudio Desantis *ed* Manlio Camastro
☆ Jack Palance, Lee Van Cleef, Richard Boone, Sybil Danning, Leif Garrett, Robert Lipton, Cody Palance, Ian Sander

'The story that no one dared film till now becomes the most adult motion picture ever made!'
God's Little Acre *
US 1958 110m bw
Security (Sidney Harmon)
A poor white farmer in Georgia neglects his land in a fruitless search for gold.
Tobacco Road *under another name, and not so lively: bowdlerized and eventually tedious despite a welter of sensational incident and depraved characters.*
w Philip Yordan *novel* Erskine Caldwell *d* Anthony Mann *ph* Ernest Haller *m* Elmer Bernstein
☆ Robert Ryan, Aldo Ray, Tina Louise, Buddy Hackett, Jack Lord, Vic Morrow, Rex Ingram

The Gods Must Be Crazy
South Africa 1980 109m colour Panavision
New Realm/Mimosa/CAT (Jamie Uys)
A Coca-Cola bottle falls from a plane and becomes a religious object to Kalahari bushmen.
Unexpected throwback farce with the blacks behaving almost as stupidly as Mantan Moreland in an old Charlie Chan movie. One for the Race Relations Board.
wd Jamie Uys *ph* Jamie Uys, Buster Reynolds *m* John Boshoff *ad* Caroline Burls
☆ N'xau, Marius Weyers, Sandra Prinsloo, Nic de Jager, Michael Thys

The Gods Must Be Crazy II
South Africa 1988 98m colour
Fox/Elrina Investment Corp (Boet Troskie)
A bushman searching for his lost children finds a New York lawyer in the desert.
Implausible tale, as condescending as the first film to its black cast.
wd Jamie Uys *ph* Buster Reynolds *m* Charles Fox *ed* Renee Engelbrecht, Ivan Hall
☆ N'xau, Lena Farugia, Hans Strydom, Eiros, Nadies, Erick Bowen, Treasure Tshabalala, Pierre Van Pletzen, Lournes Swanepoel, Richard Loring

The Godson: see *The Samurai*

'The gospel according to today!'
Godspell *
US 1973 102m TVC Color
Columbia/Lansbury/Duncan/Beruh (Edgar Lansbury)
The Gospel according to St Matthew played out musically by hippies in the streets of New York.
Wild and woolly film version of the successful theatrical fantasy, surviving chiefly by virtue of its gleaming photography.
w David Greene, John Michael Tebelak *play* John Michael Tebelak *d* David Greene *ph* Richard G. Heimann *m/ly* Stephen Schwartz
☆ Victor Garber, David Haskell, Jerry Sroka, Lynne Thigpen, Robin Lamont
'A patch of terra incognita somewhere between *Sesame Street* and the gospel according to *Laugh-In*.' – *Bruce Williamson*

Godzilla
Japan 1955 80m bw
Toho (Tomoyuki Tanaka)
original title: *Gojira*
A prehistoric monster is awakened by H-bomb tests and menaces Tokyo.
Tepid forerunner of scores of Japanese monster movies peopled by men in rubber suits.
w Takeo Murato, Inoshiro Honda *d* Inoshiro Honda *ph* Masao Tamai *m* Akira Ifukube
☆ Raymond Burr, Takashi Shimura, Momoko Kochi
† Sequels included *Godzilla vs the Thing, King Kong vs Godzilla, Godzilla vs the Sea Monster, Godzilla vs the Smog Monster, Destroy All Monsters*. Other monstrous creations included *Rodan, Manda* and *Mothra*.

'Size Does Matter.'
Godzilla
US 1998 138m Technicolor
Columbia TriStar/Centropolis/Fried/Independent (Dean Devlin)
The result of French nuclear tests in the Pacific, a giant lizard invades Manhattan to lay its eggs.
An expensive, but dull, remake of the first Godzilla movie, in which the monster is a baddie; unlike the Japanese original, the lizard king is here created by computer graphics; it is the remainder of the cast who seem to be played by men in rubber suits.
w Dean Devlin, Roland Emmerich, Ted Elliott, Terry Rossio *d* Roland Emmerich *ph* Ueli Steiger *m* David Arnold *pd* Oliver Scholl *ed* Peter Amundson, David J. Siegel
☆ Matthew Broderick, Jean Reno, Maria Pitillo, Hank Azaria, Kevin Dunn, Michael Lerner, Harry Shearer, Arabella Field, Vicki Lewis
'Despite all the flash and filigree, this monster movie is curiously – and conspicuously – lacking in heart.' – *Joe Leydon, Variety*
'An overblown action montrosity with no surprises, no exhilaration and no thrills.' – *Mick LaSalle, San Francisco Chronicle*
'To many, Godzilla has become the ultimate example of a marketing campaign in search of a movie. The movie was seemingly made, not to entertain audiences, but to help sell tacos and T-shirts.' – *Peter Bart, Variety*

Godzilla on Monster Island: see *Godzilla versus Gigan*

Godzilla versus Gigan
Japan 1972 89m colour Tohoscope
Toho Productions (Tomoyuki Tanaka)
aka: *Godzilla on Monster Island*
With the aid of Godzilla and his friends, a comic-book artist foils a plot by giant alien cockroaches to take over the world.
The usual nonsense, with the novelty of talking monsters, although their dialogue is no more interesting than that of the humans.
w Shinichi Sekizawa *d* Jun Fukuda *m* Akira Ifukube *pd* Yoshifumi Honda *ed* Yoshio Tamura *sp* Akiyoshi Nakano
☆ Hiroshi Ishikawa, Tomoko Umeda, Yuriko Hishimi, Minora Takashima, Zan Fujita, Toshiaki Nishizawa, Kunio Murai

Godzilla versus Hedora (dubbed)
Japan 1971 96m colour
Toho
original title: *Gojira Tai Hedora*
US title: *Godzilla vs The Smog Monster*
In a polluted sea, the human sludge and waste encourage the growth of an alien, metallic creature, exhaling sulphuric acid, that only Godzilla can challenge.
Dull and heavy-handed fable of ecological disaster with a hectoring tone and a risible monster.
w Karou Mabuchi, Yoshimitsu Banno *d* Yoshimitsu Banno *ph* Yoichi Manoda *m* Riichiro Manabe
☆ Akira Yamauchi, Hiroyuki Kawase, Toshie Kimura, Keiko Mari, Toshio Shibamoto, Yoshie Yoshida, Kengo Nakayama

Godzilla versus Mechagodzilla
Japan 1974 84m colour Tohoscope
Toho (Tomoyuki Tanaka)
original title: *Gojira Tai Mekagojira*
Aliens from the Third Planet of the Black Hole build a mechanical Godzilla from space titanium to destroy the world; in order to save it, Godzilla needs the help of a royal monster.
Vapid fantasy, with an often incoherent narrative and not much action.
w Hiroyasu Yamaura, Jun Fukuda *story* Shinichi Sekizawa, Masatoyo Fukushima *d* Jun Fukuda *ph* Jo Aizawa *m* Masaru Sato *ad* Kazuo Satsuya *sp* Teruyoshi Nakano
☆ Masaaki Daimon, Kazuya Aoyama, Reiko Tajima, Bellbella Leen, Hiromi Matsushita, Akihiko Hirata, Mamoru Kusumi, Isami Zushi, Issei Mori

Godzilla versus Megalon
Japan 1976 80m colour Tohoscope
Toho Studios (Tomoyuki Tanaka)
Angered by nuclear tests, the ruler of an underwater world sends a monster, a sort of winged lobster, to destroy Tokyo.
Most ridiculous, and, for that reason, the most enjoyable of the Godzilla series, notable for the Seatopians, a submarine race given to wearing togas with knee-length boots, and the tag-team wrestling style of the monster combats.
w Shinichi Sekizawa *d* Jun Fukuda *ph* Yuzuru Aizawa *m* Riichiro Manabe *ad* Yoshibumi Honda *ed* Michiko Ikeda *sp* Akiyoshi Nakano
☆ Katsuhiko Sasaki, Yutaka Hayashi, Hiroyuki Kawase

Godzilla versus Monster Zero: see *Invasion of the Astro-Monsters*

Godzilla vs King Ghidorah
Japan 1998 100m colour
Toho (Shogo Tomiyama)
Time-travelling aliens try to prevent Godzilla from interfering with the monster King Ghidorah which they create to take over the world.
This attempt to re-create Godzilla in a more modern style has a bigger budget than usual, but the narrative and acting remain perfunctory.
wd Kazuki Omori *ph* Yoshinori Sekiguchi *m* Akira Ifukube *ed* Michiko Ikeda *sp* Koichi Kawakita
☆ Anna Nakagawa, Isao Toyohara, Megumi Odaka, Chuck Wilson, Yoshio Tsuchiya, Katsuhiko Sasaki, Richard Berger

'Stay Behind Locked Doors... Gog is on the loose!'
'The Creature of Tomorrow!'
Gog *
US 1954 85m Color Corporation 3D
Ivan Tors
In an underground laboratory in New Mexico, a giant computer controls two robots, and a spy programs it to kill.
Brisk, imaginative low-budget sci-fi in gleaming colour, well staged and developed.
w Tom Taggart *story* Ivan Tors *adaptation* Richard G. Taylor *d* Herbert L. Strock *ph* Lothrop B. Worth *m* Harry Sukman *ad* William Ferrari
☆ Richard Egan (David Sheppard), Constance Dowling (Joanna Merritt), Herbert Marshall (Dr Van Hess), John Wengraf (Dr Zietman), Philip Van Zandt (Dr Elzevir), Valerie Vernon (Madame Elzevir), Steve Roberts (Major Howard), Byron Kane (Dr Carter)

Goha
France/Tunisia 1957 90m Agfacolor
Films Franco-Africains
A young Arab helps a blind musician and falls in love with a wise man's young bride.
Curiously winning, good-looking little romance which, apart from an unexpected sad ending, plays like an update of the Arabian Nights.
w Georges Schéhadé *novel* Le Livre de Goha le Simple by A. Ades, A. Jospiovici *d* Jacques Baratier *ph* Jean Bourgoin *m* Maurice Ohana
☆ Omar Chérif (later Sharif), Zina Bouzaiane, Lauro Gazzolo

Gohatto **
Japan/France/GB 1999 100m colour
Momentum/Shochiku/BAC/Canal+/Recorded Picture (Eiko Oshima, Shigehiro Nakagawa, Kazuo Shimizu)
aka: *Taboo*
In Japan of the 1860s, a beautiful young man causes problems when he joins a samurai troop in Kyoto.
Absorbing drama of homosexuality, murder and betrayal in a fiercely masculine society on the edge of disintegration.
wd Nagisa Oshima *novellas* Maegami No Sozaburo, Sanjogawara Ranjin by Ryotaro Shiba *ph* Toyomichi Kurita *m* Ryuichi Sakamoto *pd* Yoshinobu Nishioka *ed* Tomoyo Oshima
☆ Beat Takeshi (Capt. Toshizo Hijikata), Ryuhei Matsuda (Samurai Sozaburo Kano), Shinji Takeda (Lt Soji Okita), Tadanobu Asano (Samurai Hyozo Tashiro), Koji Matoba (Samurai Heibei Sugano), Tommies Masa (Inspector Jo Yamazaki), Masatoh Eve (Officer Koshitaro Ito), Uno Kanda (Geisha Nishikigi-Dayu)
'Has the musty air of a "scandalous" film from another era...it's hard to say that there is much substance to the tale.' – *Todd McCarthy, Variety*

'Saved from the hangman for a fate worse than death!'
Goin' South
US 1978 101m Metrocolor
Paramount (Henry Gittes, Harold Schneider)
An unwashed outlaw is saved from the rope when a young girl promises to marry and reform him, for no very good reason
Curious semi-comic Western which might have made a good two-reeler.
w John Herman Shaner, Al Ramrus, Charles Shyer, Alan Mandel *d* Jack Nicholson *ph* Nestor Almendros *m* Van Dyke Parks, Perry Botkin Jnr
☆ Jack Nicholson, Mary Steenburgen, Christopher Lloyd, John Belushi, Veronica Cartwright, Richard Bradford

'Mae's a lady now and she'll lick anyone in the house who says she ain't!'
Goin' to Town *
US 1935 74m bw
Paramount (William Le Baron)
A Western oil heiress moves into society.
Reasonably satisfactory Mae West vehicle, but not in the old bawdy style.
w Mae West *d* Alexander Hall *ph* Karl Struss *m/ly* Sammy Fain, Irving Kahal *md* Andrea Setaro
☆ Mae West, Paul Cavanagh, Ivan Lebedeff, Tito Coral, Marjorie Gateson, Fred Kohler Snr, Monroe Owsley
'No amount of epigrammatic hypoing can offset the silly story.' – *Variety*

Going All the Way *
US 1997 103m Foto-Kem
Polygram/Lakeshore/Gramercy (Tom Gorai, Sigurjon Sighvatsson)
In the mid-50s, two young GIs – one sexually shy, the other confident – become friends.
Amiable rites-of-passage drama that looks back on the period with regretful nostalgia.
w Dan Wakefield *novel* Dan Wakefield *d* Mark Pellington *ph* Bobby Bukowski *m* Tomandandy *pd* Thérèse DuPrez *ed* Leo Trombetta
☆ Jeremy Davies, Ben Affleck, Amy Locane, Rose McGowan, Rachel Weisz, John Lordan, Bob Swan, Jill Clayburgh, Lesley Ann Warren
'Has charm, but it certainly doesn't linger in the mind.' – *Edward Porter, Sunday Times*

Going Bye Bye **
US 1934 20m bw
Hal Roach
A violent convict escapes to take vengeance on the two innocents whose evidence sent him up.
Splendid star comedy displaying most of the team's most endearing aspects.
w Stan Laurel, Charles Rogers, Frank Terry *d* Charles Rogers *ph* Francis Corby *ed* Bert Jordan
☆ Stan Laurel, Oliver Hardy, Walter Long, Mae Busch

Going Hollywood *
US 1933 80m bw
MGM
A crooner is pursued by a girl who poses as a French maid.
Lively comedy with a studio setting; anything goes.
w Donald Ogden Stewart *d* Raoul Walsh
☆ Bing Crosby, Marion Davies, Patsy Kelly, Stuart Erwin
'Lavishly produced musical with everything but a story.' – *Variety*

Going Home
US 1971 98m colour
MGM (Herbert B. Leonard)
An ex-convict who killed his wife while drunk assumes an ambivalent relationship with his son.
Thoroughly uninteresting melodrama which was barely released.
w Lawrence Marcus *d* Herbert B. Leonard *ph* Fred Jackman *m* Bill Walker
☆ Robert Mitchum, Jan-Michael Vincent, Brenda Vaccaro

Going in Style
US 1979 97m Technicolor
Warner/Tony Bill
Three bored elderly men decide to plan a bank robbery.
Curiously aimless sentimental comedy-drama which is simply neither funny enough, thrilling enough or moving enough to hold the interest.
wd Martin Brest *ph* Billy Williams *m* Michael Small
☆ George Burns, Art Carney, Lee Strasberg

Going My Way **
US 1944 126m bw
Paramount (Leo McCarey)
A young priest comes to a New York slum parish and after initial friction charms the old pastor he is to succeed.
Sentimental comedy which got away with it wonderfully at the time, largely through careful casting, though it seems thin and obvious now.
w Frank Butler, Frank Cavett, Leo McCarey *d* Leo McCarey *ph* Lionel Lindon *m* Robert Emmett Dolan *m/ly Johnny Burke, James Van Heusen, J. R. Shannon* *ed* Leroy Stone
☆ *Bing Crosby, Barry Fitzgerald*, Rise Stevens, Frank McHugh, James Brown, Gene Lockhart, Jean Heather, Porter Hall
'I should not feel safe in recommending it to anyone but a simple-hearted sentimentalist with a taste for light music.' – *Richard Mallett, Punch*
'The lessons, if I read them right, are that leisureliness can be excellent, that if you take a genuine delight in character the universe is opened to you, and perhaps above all that a movie, like any other genuine work of art, must be made for love. But I am willing to bet that the chief discernible result of *Going My Way* will be an anxiety-ridden set of vaudeville sketches about Pat and Mike in cassocks.' – *James Agee*
† Father O'Malley reappeared in *The Bells of St Mary's* and *Say One for Me* (both qv).
Academy Award: best picture; script; original story (Leo McCarey); Leo McCarey (direction); Bing Crosby; Barry Fitzgerald (best supporting actor); song, 'Swinging on a Star' (mJames Van Heusen, lyJohnny Burke)
Academy Award nomination: Lionel Lindon; Barry Fitzgerald (best actor); Leroy Stone

Going Off Big Time
GB 2000 87m colour Panavision
Entertainment/KT/Catalysm/SpinOff (Ian Brady)
In Liverpool, a ruthless gangster explains how his career began with an accidental spell in prison.
Watchable drama of a slacker who goes wrong, but one that offers little insight into criminal psychology, or even a fresh approach to stories of urban crime.
w Neil Fitzmaurice *d* Jim Doyle *ph* Damian Bromley *m* Andy Roberts *pd* David Butterworth *ed* Julian Day
☆ Neil Fitzmaurice (Mark Clayton), Dominic Carter (Ozzi Shepherd), Sarah Alexander (Stacey Bannerman), Nick Lamont (Paul), Vinnie Adams (John), Gabbi Barr (Natasha), Nick Moss (Charlie), Peter Kay (Flipper), Huggy Leaver (Mario), Del Henney (George Hannassey), Bernard Hill (Murray), Stan Boardman (Arthur McCann)
'Not quite as bad as its appalling title might suggest.' – *Film Review*

'The love boat was never quite like this.'
Going Overboard
US 1989 93m colour
Theater Technologies/LA Dreams (Randolf L. Turrow)
aka: *The Unsinkable Shecky Moskowitz*
A struggling comedian joins a cruiise ship as a waiter.
Terrible, self-described 'no budget' movie, with what is intended as disarming, direct-to-camera comments from Sandler, which merely point up the desperation of it all.
wd Valerie Breiman *ph* Ron Jacobs *m* Steven Scott Smalley *pd* Alex Tavoularis *ed* Randy. Wiles
☆ Adam Sandler (Schecky Moskowitz), Scott LaRose (Dickie Diamond), Liza Collins Zane (Ellen), Tom Hodges (Bob), Adam Rifkin (Croaker), Billy Zane (King Neptune), Billy Bob Thornton (Dave), Burt Young (General Noriega)

Going Places
US 1938 84m bw
Warner (Hal Wallis)
A sporting goods salesman poses as a jockey and has to ride a horse to victory.
Thin musical spurred by the hit song 'Jeepers Creepers', here sung by Louis Armstrong to the race horse.
w Jerry Wald, Sig Herzig, Maurice Leo *play The Hottentot* by Victor Mapes, William Collier *d* Ray Enright *ph* Arthur L. Todd *md* Leo F. Forbstein *ad* Hugh Reticker *ed* Clarence Kolster
☆ Dick Powell, Anita Louise, Ronald Reagan, Louis Armstrong, Allen Jenkins, Walter Catlett
'Satisfactory but not smash.' – *Variety*
Academy Award nomination: song 'Jeepers Creepers' (mHarry Warren, lyJohnny Mercer)

Going Places: see *Les Valseuses (1974)*

Going Undercover: see *Yellow Pages*

Gojira No Gyakushu
Japan 1955 82m bw
Toho (Tomoyuki Tanaka)
aka: *Godzilla Raids Again*
A new Godzilla appears on a deserted island and lays waste to Osaka.
Standard monster movie, made quickly to cash in on the success of the first Godzilla film; this time, the makers didn't make the mistake of killing the monster, just immobilising him while another sequel was planned.
w Shigeaki Hidaka, Takeo Murata *story* Shigeru Kayama *d* Motoyoshi Oda *ph* Seiichi Endo *m* Masaru Sato *ad* Morio Kita *ed* Kazuji Taira *sp* Eiji Tsuburaya
☆ Hiroshi Koizumi, Setsuko Wakayama, Minoru Chiaki, Takashi Shimura, Masao Shimizu, Seizaburo Onda, Munenosuke Sawamura, Tomonosuke Yamada
† A badly dubbed version was released in the US by Warner.

Gold *
GB 1974 124m Technicolor Panavision
Hemdale/Avton (Michael Klinger)
A South African mining engineer falls for the boss's granddaughter and exposes a conspiracy.
Old-fashioned thick ear with spectacular underground sequences and a rousing finale.
w Wilbur Smith, Stanley Price *novel Goldmine* by Wilbur Smith *d Peter Hunt* *ph Ousama Rawi* *m* Elmer Bernstein
☆ Roger Moore, Susannah York, Ray Milland, Bradford Dillman, John Gielgud, Tony Beckley
Academy Award nomination: song 'Wherever Love Takes Me' (mElmer Bernstein, lyDon Black)

The Gold and the Glory
Australia 1984 112m colour Panavision
Alpine/Noble (John Weiley)
aka: *The Coolangatta Gold*
A son defies his father by challenging his elder brother in the Iron Man marathon race.
A film of Oedipal conflict that never quite escapes from its parochial concerns.
w Peter Shreck, Ted Robinson *idea* Max Oldfield *d* Igor Auzins *ph* Keith Wagstaff *m* Bill Conti *pd* Bob Hill *ed* Tim Wellburn
☆ Josh McWilliam, Nick Tate, Robyn Nevin, Josephine Smulders, Grant Kenny, Colin Friels

'Here They Come On A Million Dollar Spree To Wake and Make and Take Paree!'
Gold Diggers in Paris *
US 1938 95m bw
Warner (Sam Bischoff)
GB title: *The Gay Imposters*
Three girls chase rich husbands abroad.
A thin end to the series, saved by an agreeable cast.
w Earl Baldwin, Warren Duff *d* Ray Enright *ph* Sol Polito, George Barnes *m/ly* Harry Warren, Al Dubin, Johnny Mercer *ch Busby Berkeley*
☆ Rudy Vallee, Rosemary Lane, Hugh Herbert, Allen Jenkins, Gloria Dickson, Melville Cooper, Fritz Feld, Ed Brophy, Curt Bois

'Your dream of perfect beauty come true!'
Gold Diggers of 1933 ***
US 1933 96m bw
Warner (Robert Lord)
Cheerful, competent, well-cast remake of the above; numbers include 'My Forgotten Man', 'We're in the Money' and 'Pettin' in the Park'.
w Erwin Gelsey, James Seymour, David Boehm, Ben Markson *play The Gold Diggers* by Avery Hopwood *d Mervyn Le Roy* *ph Sol Polito* *m/ly Harry Warren, Al Dubin* *ch Busby Berkeley*
☆ Warren William, Joan Blondell, *Aline MacMahon*, Ruby Keeler, Dick Powell, Guy Kibbee, Ned Sparks, Ginger Rogers, Clarence Nordstrom
'It sums up what is meant by the phrase "pure thirties": electrically wired chorus girls singing "In the Shadows Let Me Come and Sing to You" merge to form a big illuminated violin.' – *New Yorker, 1979*
'It is memorable chiefly because Busby Berkeley created a mad geometry of patterned chorines ... The innocent vulgarity of the big numbers is charming and uproarious, and aesthetically preferable to the pretentious ballet finales of fifties musicals like *An American in Paris*. Even those of us who were children at the time did not mistake *Gold Diggers* for art – and certainly no one took it for life.' – *Pauline Kael, 1968*

Gold Diggers of 1935 **
US 1934 95m bw
Warner (Robert Lord)
A socialite puts on a Broadway show at her country home, and is taken in by a swindler.
Heavy-handed but laugh-provoking comedy with familiar faces of the day, climaxed by big numbers including 'Lullaby of Broadway'.
w Manuel Seff, Peter Milne, Robert Lord *ph George Barnes* *m/ly Harry Warren, Al Dubin* *md* Ray Heindorf *d/ch* Busby Berkeley
☆ Dick Powell, Adolphe Menjou, Gloria Stuart, Alice Brady, Hugh Herbert, Glenda Farrell, Frank McHugh, Grant Mitchell, Wini Shaw
'Busby Berkeley, the master of scenic prestidigitation, continues to dazzle the eye and stun the imagination.' – *André Sennwald, New York Times*
'A decidedly heady mixture.' – *Pare Lorentz*
Academy Award: song 'Lullaby of Broadway'
Academy Award nomination: choreography

Gold Diggers of 1937 *
US 1936 100m bw
Warner (Hal B. Wallis)
A group of insurance salesmen back a show.
Mild tailing-off of the Gold Diggers series, though with the accustomed production polish.
w Warren Duff *play* Richard Maibaum, Michael Wallach, George Haight *d* Lloyd Bacon *ph* Arthur Edeson *m/ly* Harry Warren, Al Dubin, E. Y. Harburg, Harold Arlen *ch Busby Berkeley*
☆ Dick Powell, Joan Blondell, Glenda Farrell, Victor Moore, Lee Dixon, Osgood Perkins, Charles D. Brown
Academy Award nomination: Busby Berkeley

'Exceeds in pretentiousness and beauty anything which has yet appeared on the screen!'
Gold Diggers of Broadway *
US 1929 98m Technicolor
Warner
Three Broadway chorus girls seek rich husbands.
Fascinating primitive musical that includes the songs 'Tiptoe Through the Tulips' and 'Painting the Clouds With Sunshine'.
w Robert Lord *play The Gold Diggers* by Avery Hopwood *d* Roy del Ruth *ph* Barney McGill, Ray Rennahan *m/ly* Al Dubin, Joe Burke *ch* Larry Ceballos
☆ Nancy Welford, Conway Tearle, Winnie Lightner, Ann Pennington, Lilyan Tashman, William Bakewell, Nick Lucas
† Other versions of the play include *The Gold Diggers* (1923), *Gold Diggers of 1933* (qv), *Painting the Clouds with Sunshine* (qv).

Gold Diggers: The Secret of Bear Mountain
US 1995 94m DeLuxe
Universal (Martin Bregman, Michael S. Bregman, Rolf Deyhle)
Two young girls go in search of a buried treasure.
Predictable drama of feisty children and dim-witted adults, stuck in a narrative that gives away its climax in the opening moments and thereafter dwindles into incoherence.
w Barry Glasser *d* Kevin James Dobson *ph* Ross Berryman *m* Joel McNeely *pd* Michael Bolton *ed* Stephen W. Butler
☆ Christina Ricci (Beth Easton), Anna Chlumsky (Jody Salerno), Polly Draper (Kate Easton), Brian Kerwin (Sheriff Matt Hollinger), Diana Scarwid (Lynette Salerno), David Keith (Ray Karnisak), Gillian Barber (Grace Briggs), Ashleigh Aston Moore (Tracey Briggs)
'A series of ill-fitting clichés and hackneyed plotting.' – *Variety*

Gold Is Where You Find It *
US 1938 90m Technicolor
Warner (Sam Bischoff)
Gold rush miners settle as California farmers.
Agreeable Western in excellent early colour.
w Warren Duff, Clements Ripley, Robert Buckner *d* Michael Curtiz *ph* Sol Polito *m* Max Steiner *ed* Clarence Kolster
☆ George Brent, Olivia de Havilland, Claude Rains, Margaret Lindsay, John Litel, Marcia Ralston, Barton MacLane, Tim Holt, Sidney Toler
'It's jam but good jam – with a few better moments you don't often find in films like this.' – *Graham Greene*

Gold of Naples
Italy 1955 135m bw
Ponti-de Laurentiis
original title: *L'Oro di Napoli*
Six sketches, comic and tragic, give an impression of Naples today.
A variable collection, mainly shown around the world in abridged versions.
w Cesare Zavattini, Vittorio de Sica, Giuseppe Marotta *d* Vittorio de Sica *ph* Otello Martelli *m* Alessandro Cicognini
☆ Vittorio de Sica, Eduardo de Filippo, Toto, Sophia Loren, Paolo Stoppa, Silvana Mangano

Gold of the Seven Saints
US 1961 89m bw Warnerscope
Warner (Leonard Freeman)
Cowboys compete in a search for lost gold.
Adequate minor Western using TV stars.
w Leigh Brackett, Leonard Freeman *d* Gordon Douglas *ph* Joseph Biroc *m* Howard Jackson
☆ Clint Walker, Roger Moore, Letitia Roman, Robert Middleton, Chill Wills, Gene Evans

The Gold Rush ***
US 1925 72m bw
Charles Chaplin
A lone prospector in the Yukon becomes rich after various adventures.
Essentially a succession of slowly but carefully built visual gags, this is Chaplin's finest example of comedy drawn from utter privation; as such it appealed vastly to the poor of the world. As a clown, Chaplin himself is near his best, though as usual there is rather too much straining for pathos.

ph Rollie Totheroh *md* Max Terr (1942 version) *ad* Charles D. Hall *ed* Harold McGhean (1942 version) *wd/p/m Charles Chaplin*
☆ *Charles Chaplin*, Georgia Hale, Mack Swain, Tom Murray
Max Terr

The Golden Age of Buster Keaton **
US 1975 97m bw
Jay Ward (Raymond Rohauer)
A useful introductory package to the shorts and features of Buster Keaton, with most of the great silent scenes present.
commentary Bill Scott

The Golden Age of Comedy ****
US 1957 78m bw
Robert Youngson Productions
First of the scholarly compilations of silent comedy which saved many negatives from destruction, this is a fast-paced general survey which despite a facetious sound track does provide a laugh a minute.
It particularly brought Laurel and Hardy back into public notice, and includes sections from Two Tars *and* The Battle of the Century.
wd Robert Youngson m George Steiner
narrators Dweight Weist, Ward Wilson
☆ Stan Laurel, Oliver Hardy, Harry Langdon, Ben Turpin, Will Rogers, Billy Bevan, Charley Chase, Andy Clyde

Golden Arrow
US 1936 68m bw
Warner
An heiress tricks a newspaper reporter into a marriage of convenience.
Dull, schematic romantic comedy.
w Charles Kenyon, Michael Arlen *d* Alfred E. Green
☆ Bette Davis, George Brent, Eugene Pallette, Dick Foran

Golden Balls *
Spain 1993 95m colour Panavision
UIP/Lolafilms/Ovideo/Filmauro/Hugo/Lumiere (Marivi de Villanueva)
original title: *Huevos de Oro*
An entrepreneur who regards the erection of the tallest skyscraper in Benidorm as an extension of his own virility is ruined by the complications of his sexual involvement with four women.
Engaging comedy, much concerned with sex, death, food, and the limitations of machismo, and a satire at the expense of Spanish icons, from Salvador Dali to Julio Iglesias.
w Cuca Canals, Bigas Luna *d* Bigas Luna *ph* José Luis Alcaine *m* Nicola Piovani *ad* Antxón Gómez *ed* Carmen Frias
☆ Javier Bardem, Maria de Medeiros, Maribel Verdú, Elisa Touati, Raquel Bianca, Maria Martin, Francisco Casares
'It will doubtless find a following among the designer raincoat brigade who don't mind subtitles over bedroom scenes, but slobberers would probably enjoy it more without the jamón-fisted analysis of the crisis of Spanish masculinity and the huevos-up Luna makes of telling his story.' – *Kim Newman, Empire*
'Script is weak, with numerous false leads that are never followed up. The sex scenes may help pic chalk up some sales for this meretricious and ultimately non-erotic film.' – *Variety*

'His blade of gold, a legend in battle – her kiss of surrender, the prize of victory!'
The Golden Blade
US 1953 80m Technicolor
U-I (Richard Wilson)
With the help of a magic sword, Harun saves a princess and captures a rebel.
Standard cut-rate Arabian Nights adventure, very typical of its studio during the fifties.
w John Rich *d* Nathan Juran *ph* Maury Gertsman *m* Joseph Gershenson *ad* Bernard Herzbrun, Eric Orbom *ed* Ted J. Kent
☆ Rock Hudson, Piper Laurie, George Macready, Gene Evans, Kathleen Hughes, Steven Geray, Edgar Barrier, Anita Ekberg

The Golden Bowl *
GB/France/US 2000 134m Technicolor Panavision
Merchant Ivory/TF1/Miramax (Ismail Merchant)
An adulterous Italian aristocrat learns to regret resuming his affair with his former American lover, now married to his millionaire father-in-law.
Stolid, stately, uninvolving period drama that rarely suggests any depth of emotion under its formal surface; it is not helped by the obtrusively nudging musical score.
w Ruth Prawer Jhabvala *novel* Henry James *d* James Ivory *ph* Tony Pierce-Roberts *m* Richard Robbins *pd* Andrew Sanders *ed* John David Allen *cos* John Bright
☆ Uma Thurman (Charlotte Stant), Jeremy Northam (Prince Amerigo), Kate Beckinsale (Maggie Verver), Nick Nolte (Adam Verver), Anjelica Huston (Fanny), James Fox (Bob Assingham), Madeleine Potter (Lady Castledan), Peter Eyre (Jarvis)
'Its use of film language is entirely conventional, making no attempt to reproduce one of the most mannered styles in all of prose. After 40-odd years of film-making, Ivory doesn't seem to trust himself to achieve the most basic effect.' – *Adam Mars-Jones, Times*

Golden Boy *
US 1939 101m bw
Columbia (William Perlberg)
A poor boy is torn between two absorbing interests: prizefighting and the violin.
Personalized version of a socially conscious play; moderately effective with smooth production and good cast.
w Lewis Meltzer, Daniel Taradash, Sarah Y. Mason, Victor Heerman *play* Clifford Odets *d Rouben Mamoulian ph* Nicholas Musuraca, Karl Freund *m* Victor Young *md* Morris Stoloff *ad* Lionel Banks *ed* Otto Meyer
☆ Barbara Stanwyck, *William Holden*, Adolphe Menjou, Joseph Calleia, Lee J. Cobb, Sam Levene, Edward Brophy, Don Beddoe
'Strong entertainment with general audience appeal.' – *Variety*
'A slick, swift, exciting but insensitive movie.' – *Gordon Sager*
'Interesting, entertaining, dramatic, but scarcely first-rate.' – *Frank Nugent, New York Times*
Victor Young

Golden Braid *
Australia 1990 91m colour
Artificial Eye/Illumination/Australian Film Commission/Film Victoria (Paul Cox, Paul Ammitzboll, Santhana Naidu)
A clock restorer, obsessed by death and time, falls in love with a braid of hair he discovers in the secret drawer of an antique cabinet.
Slow-paced account of a man trying to decide between fantasy and reality that at times comes near to showing that one man's obsession is another's tedium.
w Paul Cox, Barry Dickens *story La Chevelure* by Guy de Maupassant *d* Paul Cox *ph* Nino G. Marinetti *pd* Neil Angwin *ed* Russell Hurley
☆ Chris Haywood, Gosia Dobrowolska, Paul Chubb, Norman Kaye, Marion Heathfield, Monica Maughan, Robert Menzies, Jo Kennedy

The Golden Child
US 1986 93m Metrocolor
Paramount/Feldman-Meeker/Eddie Murphy
A social worker is assigned to look for a mystic child who will bring peace to the Earth.
Astonishingly inept fantasy.
w Dennis Feldman *d* Michael Ritchie *ph* Donald E. Thorin *m* Michel Colombier
☆ Eddie Murphy, Charles Dance, Charlotte Lewis, Victor Wong

The Golden Coach
Italy/France 1953 100m Technicolor
Hoche/Panaria (Valentine Brosio, Giuseppe Bordognoi)
original title: *Le Carrosse d'Or*
In Spanish South America in the 18th century, the leading lady of a band of strolling players turns all heads including that of the viceroy, who scandalizes all by making her a present of his official golden coach.
The director seems to have been chiefly interested in the colour and the backgrounds: the story is a bore and the leading lady ill-chosen.
w Jean Renoir, Jack Kirkland, Renzo Avanzo, Giulio Macchi *play* Prosper Merimée *d* Jean Renoir *ph Claude Renoir m* Vivaldi
☆ Anna Magnani, Duncan Lamont, Paul Campbell, Ricardo Rioli, William Tubbs

The Golden Disc
GB 1958 78m bw
Butchers (W. G. Chalmers)
An unsuccessful singer helps her aunt transform a rundown coffee bar and start a record company, making a star of a stagehand.
Tired British second feature, aimed at a young audience at a time when Gaggia espresso machines and juke boxes playing rock and skiffle were the height of fashion; the music is bland and the guitars are acoustic.
w Don Nicholl, Don Sharp *story* Gee Nicholl *d* Don Sharp *ph* Geoffrey Faithfull *md* Philip Green *ad* John Jones *ed* Eily Boland
☆ Lee Patterson, Mary Steele, Terry Dene, Linda Gray, Ronald Adam, Peter Dyneley, David Jacobs
† Apart from Dene, artists featured are Nancy Whiskey, Dennis Lotis, the Sonny Stewart Skiffle Kings, Terry Kennedy Group, Murray Campbell, Sheila Buxton, Les Hobeaux and the Phil Seamen (misspelt Seamon on the credits) Jazz Group

'Now you know the way a gypsy loves!'
Golden Earrings *
US 1947 95m bw
Paramount (Harry Tugend)
A British Intelligence officer is helped by a gypsy to sneak a poison gas formula out of Nazi Germany.
One of the silliest stories of all time, despite the presence of Quentin Reynolds asserting that he believed it; also lacking in the humour which might have saved it, but produced with polish and interesting for the two stars at this stage in their careers.
w Abraham Polonsky, Frank Butler, Helen Deutsch *novel* Yolanda Foldes *d Mitchell Leisen ph* Daniel L. Fapp *m* Victor Young
☆ *Ray Milland, Marlene Dietrich*, Murvyn Vye, Bruce Lester, Dennis Hoey, Reinhold Schunzel, Ivan Triesault
'A good deal of torso work goes on which I can't help feeling they're a bit old for.' – *Richard Winnington*

The Golden Falcon (dubbed)
Italy 1955 90m colour
Ottavio Poggi
original title: *Il Falco d'Oro*
Rivalry between two powerful Italian families becomes more intense when plans go wrong over an arranged marriage to end the fighting.
Comic swashbuckler, performed without much panache and not helped by unsympathetic dubbing.
d Carlo Ludovico Bragaglia *ph* Alvaro Mancori
☆ Anna Maria Ferrero, Nadia Gray, Massimo Serato

Golden Gate
US 1993 90m colour
American Playhouse (Michael Brandman)
An FBI agent, feeling guilty over the suicide of an innocent Chinese laundry worker, whom he put in prison for 10 years, seduces the man's daughter.
Confused, heavy-handed, tendentious drama that gets itself into a moral muddle with its crass characterizations.
w David Henry Hwang *d* John Madden *ph* Bobby Bukowski *m* Elliot Goldenthal *pd* Andrew Jackness *ed* Sean Barton
☆ Matt Dillon, Joan Chen, Bruno Kirby, Teri Polo, Tzi Ma, Stan Egi, Jack Shearer, Peter Murnick, George Guidall

Golden Girl *
US 1951 108m Technicolor
TCF (George Jessel)
The story of Lotta Crabtree, who after the Civil War determined to become a great musical star.
Harmless semi-Western biopic with good tunes.
w Walter Bullock, Charles O'Neal, Gladys Lehman *d* Lloyd Bacon *ph* Charles G. Clarke *md* Lionel Newman *ch* Seymour Felix
☆ Mitzi Gaynor, Dale Robertson, Dennis Day, James Barton, Una Merkel, Raymond Walburn, Gene Sheldon
song 'Never' (*m*Lionel Newman, *ly*Eliot Daniel)

The Golden Hawk
US 1952 83m Technicolor
Columbia (Sam Katzman)
A pirate determines to avenge his mother's death at the hands of the governor of Cartagena.
Clean-cut period romp for boys who don't demand realism.
w Robert E. Kent *novel* Frank Yerby *d* Sidney Salkow *ph* William B. Skall *md* Mischa Bakaleinikoff
☆ Sterling Hayden, Rhonda Fleming, John Sutton, Helena Carter, Paul Cavanagh

The Golden Head
US/Hungary 1964 115m Technirama 70
Cinerama/Hungarofilm (Alexander Paal)
Passengers on a Danube pleasure boat become involved in the theft of the golden head of St Laszlo.
Travelogue with a thin plot, somewhat slow moving but suitable for children.
w Stanley Boulder, Ivan Boldizsar *d* Richard Thorpe *ph* Istvan Hildebrand *m* Peter Fenyes
☆ George Sanders, Buddy Hackett, Douglas Wilmer, Jess Conrad, Robert Coote

The Golden Heist: see *Inside Out*

The Golden Horde
US 1951 76m Technicolor
U-I (Howard Christie)
aka: *The Golden Horde of Genghis Khan*
Crusaders meet Mongols in Samarkand, and Sir Guy wins a princess.
Rather priceless idiocies are perpetrated in this variation on the studio's favourite Arabian Nights theme, but somehow they fail to make one laugh, which should be the only possible response to such a farrago.
w Gerald Drayson Adams *d* George Sherman *ph* Russell Metty *m* Hans Salter
☆ David Farrar, Ann Blyth, George Macready, Henry Brandon, Richard Egan, Marvin Miller

The Golden Horde of Genghis Khan: see *The Golden Horde*

The Golden Hour: see *Pot o' Gold*

The Golden Madonna
GB 1949 88m bw
IFP/Pendennis (John Stafford)
Two young people search Italy for a religious painting stolen by thieves.
Stilted but eager to please, this romantic comedy-drama seemed a bit lacking in drive.
w Akos Tolnay *d* Ladislas Vajda *ph* Anchise Brizzi
☆ Phyllis Calvert, Michael Rennie, Tullio Carminati, David Greene, Aldo Silvani

Golden Marie: see *Casque d'Or*

The Golden Mask: see *South of Algiers*

The Golden Mistress *
US 1954 80m Technicolor
UA/RK (Richard Kay, Harry Rybnick)
An American and his girlfriend search the sea bed for the forbidden treasure of a Haitian tribe.
Curious independent production, an adventure in the style of silent serials; amateur in many ways, yet with a freshness of photography and location plus some powerful voodoo scenes.
wd Joel Judge (Abner Biberman) *ph William C. Thompson m* Raoul Kraushaar
☆ John Agar, Rosemarie Bowe, Abner Biberman

'Whoever owns them can rule the world!'
Golden Needles
US 1974 92m Movielab Panavision
AIP/Sequoia (Fred Weintraub, Paul Heller)
Various factions seek a Hong Kong statue showing seven miraculous acupuncture points.
Youth/sex/Kung Fu/James Bond action amalgam.
w S. Lee Pogostin, Sylvia Schneble *d* Robert Clouse *ph* Gilbert Hubbs *m* Lalo Schifrin
☆ Joe Don Baker, Elizabeth Ashley, Jim Kelly, Burgess Meredith, Ann Sothern

Golden Rendezvous
US 1977 109m colour
Film Trust/Milton Okun (Andre Pieterse)

Murderous mercenaries take over a freighter, but reckon without the courageous first officer.
Blood-and-thunder hokum with many casualties but not much sense.
w Stanley Price *novel* Alistair MacLean
d Ashley Lazarus *ph* Ken Higgins *m* Jeff Wayne
☆ Richard Harris, Ann Turkel, David Janssen, Burgess Meredith, John Vernon, Gordon Jackson, Keith Baxter, Dorothy Malone, John Carradine, Robert Flemyng, Leigh Lawson, Robert Beatty

The Golden Seal *
US 1983 94m Metrocolor
Samuel Goldwyn Jnr (Russell Thatcher)

On a bleak Aleutian island a boy stops hunters from killing a seal once thought mythical.
Rather chilling and thinly plotted moral fable for children, who may, however, be bored. The seals, the scenery and the music just about save it.
w John Groves *novel* *A River Ran out of Eden* by James Vance Marshall *d* Frank Zuniga *ph* Eric Saarinen *m* Dana Kaproff, John Barry
☆ Steve Railsback, Michael Beck, Penelope Milford, Torquil Campbell

The Golden Virgin: see *The Story of Esther Costello*

The Golden Voyage of Sinbad *
GB 1973 105m Eastmancolor
Columbia/Morningside (Charles H. Schneer)

Sinbad finds a strange map and crosses swords with a great magician.
Routine, rather uninspired fantasy enlivened by grotesque trick effects.
w Brian Clemens, Ray Harryhausen *d* Gordon Hessler *ph* Ted Moore *m* Miklos Rozsa *pd* John Stoll *sp* *Ray Harryhausen*
☆ John Phillip Law, Caroline Munro, Tom Baker, Douglas Wilmer, Grégoire Aslan

'No limits. No fears. No substitutes.'
GoldenEye **
US 1995 130m DeLuxe Panavision
UIP/United Artists/Danjaq/Eon (Michael G. Wilson, Barbara Broccoli)

Bond goes to Russia to defeat a criminal mastermind who controls a secret satellite that can disable the world's electronic devices.
The mixture much as before, except that the makers give a few nods and winks to the audience so that everyone is in on the joke of this suave agent saving the world yet again; the stunts are spectacular, Brosnan well conveys a slightly weary sophistication, and the jokes are familiar, which should be enough to keep its new audience happy.
w Jeffrey Caine, Bruce Feirstein *story* Michael France *d* Martin Campbell *ph* Phil Meheux *m* Eric Serra *pd* Peter Lamont *ed* Terry Rawlings
☆ Pierce Brosnan, Sean Bean, Izabella Scorupco, Famke Janssen, Joe Don Baker, Judi Dench, Robbie Coltrane, Tcheky Karyo, Gottfried John, Alan Cumming, Desmond Llewelyn, Samantha Bond, Michael Kitchen
'The very definition of escapist fare.' – *Variety*
'At last, you think, somebody has had the courage to make a Bond film as it should be made nowadays: as period drama.' – *Tom Shone, Sunday Times*
'Proves that the dinosaur can change its spots.' – *Adam Mars-Jones, Independent*
'Fast cars! Exotic games of baccarat! Double entendres that might have been cribbed from a 20-year-old copy of *Playboy*! Are we having fun now or what?' – *Owen Gleiberman, Entertainment Weekly*
† The film took more than $219m at the box-office worldwide.

Goldengirl
US 1979 104m colour
Avco Embassy (Danny O'Donovan)

A scientist uses experimental drugs on his daughter to turn her into an Olympic champion runner.
Ridiculous and overblown fantasy with a cast busily distancing themselves from the script.
w John Kohn *novel* Peter Lear *d* Joseph Sargent *ph* Steven Larner *m* Bill Conti *ad* Syd Litwack *ed* George Nicholson
☆ Susan Anton, James Coburn, Curt Jurgens, Leslie Caron, Robert Culp, James A. Watson Jnr, Harry Guardino, Ward Costello, Michael Lerner

'James Bond 007 Back In Action!'
Goldfinger ***
GB 1964 112m Technicolor
UA/Eon (Harry Saltzman, Albert R. Broccoli)

James Bond prevents an international gold smuggler from robbing Fort Knox.
Probably the liveliest and most amusing of the Bond spy spoofs, with a fairly taut plot between the numerous highlights. The big budget is well used.
w Richard Maibaum, Paul Dehn novel Ian Fleming *d Guy Hamilton ph Ted Moore m John Barry pd Ken Adam titles Robert Brownjohn*
☆ *Sean Connery, Honor Blackman,* Gert Frobe, Harold Sakata, Shirley Eaton, Bernard Lee, Lois Maxwell, Desmond Llewelyn
'A dazzling object lesson in the principle that nothing succeeds like excess.' – *Penelope Gilliatt*
'A diverting comic strip for grown-ups.' – *Judith Crist*

The Goldwyn Follies **
US 1938 115m Technicolor
Samuel Goldwyn

A Hollywood producer seeks the average girl to test his scripts.
Goldwyn's failure to become Ziegfeld, chiefly due to a lack of humour in the script, still has a soupçon of effective Hollywood satire and some excellent numbers.
w Ben Hecht *d* George Marshall *ph* Gregg Toland *m* Alfred Newman *ch* George Balanchine *ad* Richard Day
☆ Kenny Baker, Vera Zorina, *the Ritz Brothers, Adolphe Menjou,* Edgar Bergen and Charlie McCarthy, Helen Jepson, Phil Baker, Ella Logan, Bobby Clark, Jerome Cowan, Nydia Westman, Andrea Leeds
'An advance glimpse at next Sunday's amusement section from any metropolitan newspaper.' – *Variety*
'The bizarre in musical pretentiousness.' – *Commonweal*
'Many features to suit all tastes and not enough of them to suit anybody's.' – *Time*
Alfred Newman; Richard Day

The Golem ***
Germany 1920 75m approx bw silent
UFA

In 16th-century Prague a Jewish rabbi constructs a man of clay to defend his people against a pogrom.
There were several versions of this story (Germany 1913, sequel 1917; Czechoslovakia 1935 and 1951), but this is almost certainly the best, its splendid sets, performances and certain scenes all being clearly influential on later Hollywood films, especially Frankenstein.
w Paul Wegener, Henrik Galeen *d Paul Wegener, Carl Boese ph Karl Freund, Guido Seeber ad Hans Poelzig*
☆ Paul Wegener, Albert Steinruck, Ernst Deutsch

The Golem *
Czechoslovakia 1936 95m bw
AB
GB title: *The Legend of Prague*
Rather disappointing remake with entirely French crew.
w André Paul Antoine, Julien Duvivier *novel* Gustav Meyrinck *d* Julien Duvivier *ph* Vaclav Vich, Jan Stallich *m* Joseph Kumok
☆ Harry Baur, Roger Karl, Ferdinand Hart, Charles Dorat
'Sequences are scattered; there's no build-up, and no human interest is created.' – *Variety*
'It is all rich and spacious, and rather exquisite, and the big scene at the end should do nicely. If one can forget that Wegener once did it so much better, with nothing but a robot, a child and a flower.' – C. A. *Lejeune*

Golem – The Wandering Soul
France/Germany/Netherlands/Italy/GB 1992 colour
Agav (Laurent Truchot)
original title: *Golem – L'Esprit de l'Exil*
An Israeli woman living in Paris suffers after her husband dies in an accident and her two sons are killed by racists.
Dully experimental movie on the theme of narrow chauvinism, mainly composed of uninteresting images combined with dialogue taken from the Old Testament, but all is vanity.
wd Amos Gitai *ph* Henri Alekan *m* Simon Stockhausen, Markus Stockhausen *ad* Thierry François *ed* Anna Ruiz
☆ Hanna Schygulla, Opra Shemesh, Mireille Perrier, Sotigui Kouyate, Samuel Fuller, Bernardo Bertolucci, Fabienne Babe, Bernard Eisenschitz, Antonio Carallo, Bernard Levy

The Golf Specialist **
US 1930 18m bw
RKO
A film version of a classic vaudeville golfing sketch (also reprised in *You're Telling Me*).
d Monte Brice
☆ *W. C. Fields*

Golgotha *
France 1935 100m bw
D'Agular

The trial and passion of Jesus Christ.
Impressive version made at a time when the portrayal of Christ was still virtually taboo.
wd Julien Duvivier *m* Jacques Ibert
☆ Harry Baur (Herod), Jean Gabin (Pilate), Robert le Vigan (Jesus), Charles Granval (Caiaphas), Edwige Feuillère (Claudia)
'An accomplishment that should bring world-wide prestige to the French film industry.' – *Variety*

'A Thousand And One Women Dream Of His Embrace.'
Goliath and the Barbarians (dubbed)
Italy/US 1959 88m Eastmancolor Totalscope
Standard/AIP (Emimmo Salvi)
original title: *Il Terrore dei Barbari*
In AD 568, a man vows vengeance and disguises himself as a monster when barbarian hordes, invading northern Italy, massacre his father and other villagers.
A garish Italian epic adapted for an American audience with a voice-over narration, and concentrating on spectacle and action.
w Gino Mangini, Carlo Campogalliani, Nino Stresa, Giuseppe Taffarel, Emimmo Salvi *d* Carlo Campogalliani *ph* Alberto Albertini *m* Les Baxter, Carlo Innocenzi *ad* Camillo del Signore, Emilio D'Andria *ed* Franco Fraticelli
☆ Steve Reeves, Chelo Alonso, Bruce Cabot, Giulia Rubini, Luciano Marin, Livio Lorenzon

Goliath, King of Slaves: see *The Hero of Babylon*

Golpes a Mi Puerta: see *Knocks at My Door*

Gomar the Human Gorilla: see *Night of the Bloody Apes*

Gone Fishin'
US 1997 94m Technicolor
Buena Vista/Hollywood/Caravan (Roger Birnbaum, Julie Bergman Sender)

Two slow-witted friends win a trip to the Everglades, where everything goes wrong.
A dim and ever dimmer comedy, in which stupidity substitutes for wit.
w Jill Mazurzky Cody, Jeffrey Abrams
d Christopher Cain *ph* Dean Semler *m* Randy Edelman *pd* Lawrence Miller *ed* Jack Hofstra
☆ Joe Pesci, Danny Glover, Rosanna Arquette, Lynn Whitfield, Willie Nelson, Nick Brimble, Gary Grubbs, Carol Kane
'Comes across as an unwitting tribute to the films of Huntz Hall.' – *Variety*
† Louise Fletcher and Maury Chaykin appear uncredited.

'Ice Cold. Hot Wired'
Gone In 60 Seconds
US 2000 117m Technicolor Panavision
Buena Vista/Touchstone/Jerry Bruckheimer

A car thief comes out of retirement to steal 50 cars in four days.
This is little more than a prolonged car chase, and is about as exciting as a motorway gridlock.
w Scott Rosenberg *screenplay* H.B. Halicki
d Dominic Sena *ph* Paul Cameron *m* Trevor Rabin *pd* Jeff Mann *ed* Tom Muldoon, Chris Lebenzon
☆ Nicolas Cage (Memphis Raines), Angelina Jolie (Sara 'Sway' Wayland), Giovanni Ribisi (Kip Raines), Delroy Lindo (Det Roland Castlebeck), Will Patton (Atley Jackson), Christopher Eccleston (Raymond Calitri), Chi McBride (Donny Astricky), Robert Duvall (Otto Halliwell), Scott Caan (Tumbler), Timothy Olyphant (Det Drycoff), William Lee Scott (Toby), Vinnie Jones (The Sphinx), James Duval (Freb), TJ Cross (Mirror Man), Frances Fisher (Junie)
'By far the silliest motion picture of the summer season, but it is by no means the least entertaining.' – *Joe Queenan*
† It was based on a little-known 1974 B-movie of the same name, written and directed by, and starring, H.B. Halicki.

Gone to Earth
GB 1950 110m Technicolor
London Films/David O. Selznick (Michael Powell, Emeric Pressburger)
US title: *The Wild Heart*
In the 1890s, a wild Shropshire girl is desired by the local squire.
Unintentionally funny film version of an intractable novel.
wd Michael Powell, Emeric Pressburger
novel Mary Webb *ph* Christopher Challis
m Brian Easdale *pd* Hein Heckroth
☆ Jennifer Jones, David Farrar, Cyril Cusack, Esmond Knight, Sybil Thorndike, Edward Chapman, George Cole, Hugh Griffith, Beatrice Varley
'It tries hard to be a powerful work of art, but it is intrinsically artificial and pretentious.' – *Richard Mallett, Punch*
† For the version shown in US, additional scenes were directed by Rouben Mamoulian.

'The most magnificent picture ever!'
Gone with the Wind ****
US 1939 220m Technicolor
MGM/Selznick International (David O. Selznick)

An egotistic Southern girl survives the Civil War but finally loses the only man she cares for.
The only film in history which could be profitably revived for forty years: 'still pure gold', said the Daily Mirror *in 1975. Whole books have been written about it; its essential appeal is that of a romantic story with strong characters and an impeccable production. The widescreen version produced in the late sixties ruined its composition and colour, but it is to be hoped that the original negative still survives.*
w Sidney Howard (and others) *novel Margaret Mitchell d Victor Fleming (and George Cukor, Sam Wood) ph Ernest Haller, Ray Rennahan m Max Steiner pd William Cameron Menzies ad Lyle Wheeler ed* Hal C. Kern, James E. Newcom
sp Jack Cosgrove, Fred Albin, Arthur Johns
☆ *Clark Gable* (Rhett Butler), *Vivien Leigh* (Scarlet O'Hara), Olivia de Havilland (Melanie Hamilton), Leslie Howard (Ashley Wilkes), Thomas Mitchell (Gerald O'Hara), Barbara O'Neil (Ellen O'Hara), *Hattie McDaniel* (Mammy), *Butterfly McQueen*, Victor Jory, Evelyn Keyes, Ann Rutherford, Laura Hope Crews, Harry Davenport, Jane Darwell, Ona Munson and also Ward Bond
'A major event in the history of the industry but only a minor event in motion picture art. There are moments when the two categories meet on good terms, but the long stretches between are filled with mere spectacular efficiency.' – *Franz Hoellering, The Nation*
'Shakespeare's *The Taming of the Shrew* seems to have got mixed up with one of the novels of Ethel M. Dell.' – *James Agate*
'Perhaps the key plantation movie.' – *Time Out, 1980*
'Forget it, Louis, no Civil War picture ever made a nickel.' – *Irving Thalberg to Louis B. Mayer, 1936*

† The best account of the film's making is in Gavin Lambert's 1975 book, *GWTW*
♫ In the early seventies a stage musical version toured the world, with music by Harold Rome.
♛ best picture; Sidney Howard; Victor Fleming; best cinematography; Lyle Wheeler; Vivien Leigh; Hattie McDaniel; best film editing; William Cameron Menzies (special award)
♛ Max Steiner; Clark Gable; Olivia de Havilland; special effects

The Gong Show Movie
US 1980 89m colour
Chuck Barris Productions (Bud Granoff)
The trials and tribulations of the host of a TV talent show for untalented amateurs.
A once-successful television show transfers unsuccessfully to the screen.
w Chuck Barris, Robert Downey *d* Chuck Barris *ph* Richard C. Glouner *m* Milton Delugg *ad* Robert J. Kinoshita *ed* James Mitchell
☆ Chuck Barris, Robin Altman, Brian O'Mullin, Mabel King, James B. Douglas, Jaye P. Morgan

Good Burger
US 1997 95m DeLuxe
Paramount/Nickelodeon (Mike Tollin, Brian Robbins)
A tiny fast-food restaurant is faced with overwhelming competition from a corporate giant.
Developed from a series of comedy sketches on cable television, this inept slapstick will not satisfy comic appetites outside the United States.
w Dan Schneider, Kevin Kopelow, Heather Seifert *d* Brian Robbins *ph* Mac Ahlberg *m* Stewart Copeland *pd* Steven Jordan *ed* Anita Brandt-Burgoyne
☆ Kel Mitchell, Kenan Thompson, Sinbad, Abe Vigoda, Shar Jackson, Dan Schneider, Jan Schweiterman
'This winning comedy serves up a hearty helping of fun and wholesome values.' – *Leonard Klady, Variety*
'When this movie was screened to a selection of 15 hardened filmic hacks, a record total of nine walked out ... this stodge is beyond help.' – *Bob McCabe, Empire*

The Good Companions **
GB 1933 113m bw
Gaumont/Welsh-Pearson (Michael Balcon, George Pearson)
Three ill-assorted people take to the road and in various capacities join the Dinky Doos pierrot troupe.
Gallant, mini-budgeted version of Priestley's popular picaresque novel. A little faded now, it retains some of its vigour, and the performances please.
w W. P. Lipscomb, Angus MacPhail, Ian Dalrymple *play* J. B. Priestley, Edward Knoblock *novel* J. B. Priestley *d* Victor Saville *ph* Bernard Knowles *m/ly* George Posford, Douglas Furber *md* Louis Levy *ad* Alfred Junge *ed* Frederick Y. Smith
☆ *Edmund Gwenn*, Mary Glynne, John Gielgud, *Jessie Matthews*, Percy Parsons, A. W. Baskcomb, Dennis Hoey, Richard Dolman, Frank Pettingell, Finlay Currie, *Max Miller*, Jack Hawkins, George Zucco
'Has come to the screen just as it was written, honest and sentimental and episodic, with the smell of the tarmac and the railway buffet, the tinny rapture of the pavilion piano, the jostling pageantry of insignificant faces.' – *C. A. Lejeune*

The Good Companions *
GB 1956 104m Technicolor Cinemascope
ABP (Hamilton Inglis, J. Lee-Thompson)
Faint-hearted remake of the above, unwisely Cinemascoped and leaving no impression.
w T. J. Morrison *d* J. Lee-Thompson *ph* Gilbert Taylor *m* Laurie Johnson
☆ Eric Portman, Celia Johnson, John Fraser, Janette Scott, Hugh Griffith, Bobby Howes, Rachel Roberts, John Salew, Thora Hird
† A stage musical version (*m André Previn, ly* Johnny Mercer) had moderate success in London in 1974.
††† .

Good Cop Bad Cop: see *Raw Justice*

Good Day for a Hanging
US 1959 85m Columbia Color
Columbia
A young outlaw is arrested and seems destined to be lynched; the marshal tries to see fair play.
Moody Western in which the protected hero turns out to be very guilty after all.
w Daniel B. Ullman, Maurice Zimm *d* Nathan Juran
☆ Fred MacMurray, Robert Vaughn, Maggie Hayes, Joan Blackman, James Drury

The Good Die Young *
GB 1954 98m bw
Remus (Jack Clayton)
Four crooks, all with private problems, set out to rob a mail van.
Glum all-star melodrama which set a pattern for such things; worth waiting for is the climactic chase through underground stations.
w Vernon Harris, Lewis Gilbert *d* Lewis Gilbert *ph* Jack Asher *m* Georges Auric
☆ Laurence Harvey, Margaret Leighton, Gloria Grahame, Richard Basehart, Joan Collins, John Ireland, René Ray, Stanley Baker, Robert Morley

'To the memory of Irving Grant Thalberg we dedicate this picture – his last great achievement!'
The Good Earth ***
US 1937 138m bw
MGM (*Irving Thalberg*)
A Chinese peasant grows rich but loses his beloved wife.
A massive, well-meaning and fondly remembered production which is nevertheless artificial, unconvincing and pretty undramatic in the second half. The star performances impress to begin with, then wear thin, but the final locust attack is as well done as it originally seemed. Historically valuable as a Hollywood prestige production of the thirties.
w Talbot Jennings, Tess Schlesinger, Claudine West *play* Owen and Donald Davis *novel Pearl S. Buck d Sidney Franklin ph Karl Freund m* Herbert Stothart *ad* Cedric Gibbons *ed* Basil Wrangell *montage* Slavko Vorkapich
☆ *Paul Muni, Luise Rainer*, Walter Connolly, Tilly Losch, Jessie Ralph, Charley Grapewin, Keye Luke, Harold Huber
'A true technical achievement with names enough to send it across. But it's not going to be easy to get the three-million-dollar investment back. And if it does come back it's going to take a long time.' – *Variety*
'Performances, direction and photography are of a uniform excellence, and have been fused perfectly into a dignified, beautiful, but soberly dramatic production.' – *New York Times*
'One of the superb visual adventures of the period.' – *John Baxter, 1968*
'Prestigious boredom, and it goes on for a very long time.' – *New Yorker, 1977*
♛ Karl Freund; Luise Rainer
♛ best picture; Sidney Franklin; Basil Wrangell

The Good Fairy *
US 1935 90m bw
Universal (Henry Henigson)
A beautiful but naïve cinema usherette ensnares three rich men.
Unusual, rather lumpy romantic comedy using top talent.
w Preston Sturges play Ferenc Molnar *d William Wyler ph* Norbert Brodine
☆ *Margaret Sullavan*, Herbert Marshall, Frank Morgan, Reginald Owen, Alan Hale, Beulah Bondi, Cesar Romero, Eric Blore, Al Bridge
'It's rather slapsticking a master but it's for the box office. Will not please those who cherish memories of the play but it will please a more important audience.' – *Variety*
† Remade as *I'll Be Yours* (qv).

The Good Father **
GB 1986 90m Technicolor
Channel 4/Greenpoint (Ann Scott)
Two divorced men become bitter about the way their marriages ended, estranging them from their children.
An astringent study of masculine rage and emotional impotence, and of the difficulty of maintaining honest relationships.
w Christopher Hampton *novel* Peter Prince *d* Mike Newell *ph* Michael Coulter *m* Richard Hartley *pd* Adrian Smith *ed* Peter Hollywood
☆ Anthony Hopkins, Jim Broadbent, Harriet Walter, Frances Viner, Simon Callow, Miriam Margolyes, Joanne Whalley-Kilmer, Michael Byrne, Jennie Stoller, Stephen Fry
'Though the emotional perceptions might speak to a wider audience, its practical concerns are those of that newly-important consumer class, the well-meaning, hard-done-by professionals.' – *Judith Williamson, New Statesman*

'It's her last best chance... is she going to take it?'
'Is finding what you could have, worth losing what you've got?'
The Good Girl
US/Germany/Netherlands 2002 93m DeLuxe
TCF/Myriad/In-Motion/WMF V (Matthew Greenfield)
At a Texas chain store, a bored, married sales assitsant begins an affair with a younger man.
Enjoyable, offbeat comedy about bleak lives and unrealisable dreams.
w Mike White *d* Miguel Arteta *ph* Enrique Chediak *pd* Daniel Bradford *ed* Jeff Betancourt *cos* Nancy Steiner
☆ Jennifer Aniston (Justine Last), Zooey Deschanel (Cheryl), Jake Gyllenhaal (Holden Worther), John C. Reilly (Phil Last), Tim Blake Nelson (Bubba), Mike White (Corny), Deborah Rush (Gwen Jackson), John Carroll Lynch (Jack Field)
'Droll, well-acted, character-driven comedy with unexpected deposits of feeling.' – *J. Hoberman, Village Voice*

Good Girls Go to Paris *
US 1939 75m bw
Columbia (William Perlberg)
After several zany adventures, a Greek professor marries a gold digger.
Amusingly crazy comedy, one of the last of its type.
w Gladys Lehman, Ken Englund *d* Alexander Hall *ph* Henry Freulich *md* Morris Stoloff
☆ Melvyn Douglas, Joan Blondell, Walter Connolly, Alan Curtis, Joan Perry, Isabel Jeans, Alexander D'Arcy, Clarence Kolb
'It can't stand analysis much, but it pleases while you're there.' – *Variety*

The Good Guys and the Bad Guys *
US 1969 90m Technicolor Panavision
Warner (Ronald M. Cohen, Dennis Shryack)
An ageing sheriff and a train robber have one last showdown.
Good-humoured, black-flavoured Western set in the early days of automobiles.
w Ronald M. Cohen, Dennis Shryack *d* Burt Kennedy *ph* Harry Stradling Jnr *m* William Lava
☆ Robert Mitchum, George Kennedy, David Carradine, Tina Louise, Douglas Fowley, Martin Balsam, Lois Nettleton, John Davis Chandler, John Carradine, Marie Windsor

Good Guys Wear Black
US 1977 95m CFI color
Enterprise/Mar Vista/Action One Film Partners (Allan F. Bodoh)
The former leader of a commando raid into North Vietnam sets out to discover who in Washington betrayed him and his men.
Lacklustre martial arts action in an unsuccessful American attempt to create a local star to replace Bruce Lee.
w Bruce Cohn, Mark Medoff *story* Joseph Fraley *d* Ted Post *ph* Bob Steadman *m* Craig Safan *ad* B. B. Neal *ed* William and Millie Moore
☆ Chuck Norris, Anne Archer, James Franciscus, Lloyd Haynes, Dana Andrews, Jim Backus
† The film was followed by a sequel, *A Force of One* (qv).

Good Little Girls: see *Les Petites Filles Modèles*

'Deep In The Heart Of Africa The British Practise Bizarre Rituals. They Call It Diplomacy.'
A Good Man in Africa
US 1994 95m Technicolor
UIP/Polar/Capitol/Southern Sun (John Fiedler, Mark Tarlov)
A British diplomat in Africa decides, after dubious political and sexual manoeuvres, that he will try to be a better man.
A flaccid comedy satirizing colonial corruption and the lessons learnt by local politicians, acted and directed without distinction.
w William Boyd *novel* William Boyd *d* Bruce Beresford *ph* Andrzej Bartkowiak *m* John du Prez *pd* Herbert Pinter *ed* Jim Clark
☆ Colin Friels, Joanne Whalley-Kilmer, Sean Connery, Louis Gossett Jnr, John Lithgow, Diana Rigg, Maynard Eziashi, Sarah Jane Fenton
'Has a good cast, and that's all that can be claimed for it.' – *Alexander Walker, London Evening Standard*
'Stumbles its way through a series of comic mishaps and manages to upturn every cliché in its path.' – *Screen International*

A Good Marriage: see *Le Beau Mariage*

Good Morning Babylon *
Italy/France 1987 115m colour
Filmtre/MK2/Pressman/RAI/Films A2 (Giuliani G. de Negri)
Italian film-makers set out for Hollywood to restore the family fortunes.
Likeable but sometimes inept fantasia on Hollywood's early silent days.
wd Paolo and Vittorio Taviani ph Giuseppe Lanci *m* Nicola Piovani *ad* Gianni Shara *ed* Roberto Perpignanni
☆ Vincent Spano, Joaquim de Almeida, Greta Scacchi, Desiree Becker, Charles Dance (D. W. Griffith)
'They have made a molehill of a picture out of a mountain of an idea.' – *Daily Variety*

Good Morning Boys **
GB 1937 79m bw
GFD/Gainsborough (Edward Black)
A schoolmaster takes his troublesome pupils to Paris and becomes involved with an art theft.
Sprightly vehicle for the star's seedy schoolmaster persona: it established him as a major draw in British films.
w Marriott Edgar, Val Guest, Anthony Kimmins d Marcel Varnel ph Arthur Crabtree *md* Louis Levy *ad* Vetchinsky *ed* R. E. Dearing, Alfred Roome
☆ *Will Hay*, Graham Moffatt, Lilli Palmer, Mark Daly, Peter Gawthorne, Martita Hunt, Charles Hawtrey, Will Hay Jnr
† Remade with Ronald Shiner as *Top of the Form*.

Good Morning, Doctor: see *You Belong to Me*

Good Morning, Miss Dove
US 1955 107m Eastmancolor Cinemascope
TCF (Samuel G. Engel)
While recovering from an operation, a small-town schoolmistress looks back on her career.
A fairly spirited weepie with a happy ending and a strong sense of cynicism behind the scenes.
w Eleanore Griffin *novel* Frances Gray Patton *d* Henry Koster *ph* Leon Shamroy *m* Leigh Harline
☆ Jennifer Jones, Robert Stack, Robert Douglas, Kipp Hamilton, Peggy Knudsen, Marshall Thompson, Chuck Connors, Mary Wickes
'Mr Chips has changed sex and habitat while preserving intact his ability to provoke epidemics of sentimentality.' – *MFB*

Good Morning, Vietnam *
US 1987 120m DeLuxe
Touchstone (Mark Johnson, Larry Brezner)
Exploits of an Armed Forces Radio disc-jockey in Saigon at the height of the Vietnam War.
Largely a vehicle for the frenetic irreverence of Robin Williams, enjoyed by many for the 60s hits used copiously on the soundtrack.
w Mitch Markowitz *d* Barry Levinson *ph* Peter Sova *m* Alex North *pd* Roy Walker
☆ Robin Williams, Forest Whitaker, Tung Thanh Tran, Chintara Sukapatana, Bruno Kirby
♛ Robin Williams

The Good Mother
US 1988 103m colour
Warner/Touchstone/Silver Screen Partners IV (Arnold Glimcher)
GB video title: *The Price of Passion*
A separated husband claims his daughter has been sexually abused by his wife's lover.
Dull domestic drama.
w Michael Bortman *novel* Sue Miller *d* Leonard Nimoy *m* Elmer Bernstein *pd* Stan Jolley *ed* Peter Berger
☆ Diane Keaton, Liam Neeson, Jason Robards, Ralph Bellamy, Teresa Wright, James Naughton, Asia Vieira, Joe Morton, Katey Sagal, Margaret Bard, Nancy Beatty
'An over-simplified addendum to a series of recent works in which mothers are taken to task and sometimes pilloried.' – *MFB*

'It's All About That Laff-Whoppin' Eye Poppin' Suburban Switcheroo!'
Good Neighbour Sam
US 1964 130m Eastmancolor
Columbia/David Swift
A prissy suburban advertising man becomes innocently involved in a pretence to be the husband of the divorcee next door.
A promising comic idea is here ruined by lengthiness, lack of funny lines, and no apparent idea of how to film a farce. The actors are driven to repeating every trick a dozen times.
w James Fritzell, Everett Greenbaum, David Swift *novel* Jack Finney *d* David Swift *ph* Burnett Guffey *m* Frank de Vol
☆ Jack Lemmon, Romy Schneider, Dorothy Provine, Senta Berger, Edward G. Robinson, Mike Connors, Edward Andrews, Louis Nye
'Lemmon and company breathlessly toss gags from bedrooms to advertising offices with verve and vigor.' – *New York Times*

Good News
US 1930 85m approx bw
MGM
Fraternity tensions are sorted out in time for the big football game.
Spirited early talkie musical.
w Frances Marion, Joe Farnham *d* Nick Grinde, Edgar McGregor *ph* Percy Hilburn *m/ly* De Sylva, Brown, Henderson and others *md* Abe Lyman
☆ Bessie Love, Stanley Smith, Gus Shy, Mary Lawlor, Lola Lane, Dorothy McNulty (aka Penny Singleton), Cliff Edwards
'Not the smash hit the show was. Too fast, too peppy, too entertaining to flop, though.' – *Variety*
♫ 'He's a Ladies' Man'; 'The Best Things in Life Are Free'; 'Varsity Drag'; 'Good News'; 'Tait Song'; 'Students Are We'; 'If You're Not Kissing Me'; 'Football'; 'I Feel Pessimistic'; 'I'd Like to Make You Happy'

Good News *
US 1947 83m Technicolor
MGM (Arthur Freed)
Bright, good-humoured remake of the above.
w Betty Comden, Adolph Green *d* Charles Walters *ph* Charles Schoenbaum *m/ly* De Sylva, Brown, Henderson and others *md* Lennie Hayton *ad* Cedric Gibbons, Edward Carfagno *ed* Albert Akst
☆ June Allyson, Peter Lawford, Patricia Marshall, *Joan McCracken*, Mel Tormé
song 'Pass that Peace Pipe' (*m/ly* Ralph Blane, Hugh Martin, Roger Edens)

The Good Old Days
GB 1939 79m bw
Warner (Jerome Jackson)
A noble child is kidnapped by a chimney sweep and saved by strolling players.
Curious Victorian vehicle for a snappy 20th-century star.
w Austin Melford, John Dighton *story* Ralph Smart *d* Roy William Neill *ph* Basil Emmott
☆ Max Miller, Hal Walters, Kathleen Gibson, H. F. Maltby, Martita Hunt, Allan Jeayes, Roy Emerton

Good Old Schooldays: see *Those Were the Days*

Good Sam
US 1948 114m bw
Rainbow (Leo McCarey)
A small-town business man is so charitable that he finds himself bankrupt.
Poor, disjointed, overlong and obvious comedy in the Capra style.
w Ken Englund *d* Leo McCarey *ph* George Barnes *m* Robert Emmett Dolan
☆ Gary Cooper, Ann Sheridan, Ray Collins, Edmund Lowe, Joan Lorring, Ruth Roman, Clinton Sundberg
'A bit too long, but in its incidentals often very enjoyable.' – *Richard Mallett, Punch*

The Good Son
US 1993 87m DeLuxe Panavision
TCF (Mary Anne Page, Joseph Ruben)
A sweet-seeming 10-year-old boy is actually an amoral, murderous child.
A slick but uninvolving updating of the themes of The Bad Seed
w Ian McEwan *d* Joseph Ruben *ph* John Lindley *m* Elmer Bernstein *pd* Bill Groom *ed* George Bowers
☆ Macaulay Culkin, Elijah Wood, Wendy Crewson, David Morse, Daniel Hugh Kelly, Jacqueline Brooks, Quinn Culkin
'This rather peculiar thriller doesn't deliver enough jolts to leave the audience screaming.' – *Variety*
'If this film were a teenager, it would be the one who always did his homework, never pranged the family car, and then one day quietly shot everyone with a rifle made in his metalwork class.' – *Leslie Felperin Sharman, Sight and Sound*

The Good, the Bad and the Ugly ***
Italy 1966 180m Techniscope
PEA (Alberto Grimaldi)
original title: *Il Buono, il Brutto, il Cattivo*
During the American Civil War, three men seek hidden loot.
Intermittently lively, very violent, and interminably drawn-out Western with a number of rather hilarious stylistic touches.
w Age Scarpelli, Luciano Vincenzoni, Sergio Leone *d* *Sergio Leone* *ph* Tonino delli Colli *m* *Ennio Morricone*
☆ Clint Eastwood, Eli Wallach, Lee Van Cleef

'He doesn't want money. He wants what money can't buy.'
Good Thief *
GB/France/Ireland 2002 109m Technicolor
Momentum/Alliance Atlantis/TNVO/ Sarl/Double Down/Metropolitan (Stephen Woolley, John Wells, Seaton McLean)
An American gambler and thief becomes involved with a gang who plan to rob the casino at Monte Carlo.
A crepuscular account of a lucky streak in the life of a world-weary man who has seen too much; there is a dogged quality about it that makes for less than engaging viewing.
wd Neil Jordan *ph* Chris Menges *m* Elliot Goldenthal *pd* Anthony Pratt *ed* Tony Lawson *cos* Penny Rose
☆ Nick Nolte (Bob), Tcheky Karyo (Roger), Said Taghmaoui (Paulo), Gerard Darmon (Raoul), Emir Kusturica (Vladimir), Marc Lavoine (Remi), Ouassini Embarek (Said)
'It's all been done before, but seldom with this degree of vigor and panache.' – *Eddie Cockrell, Variety*

Good Time Girl
GB 1948 93m bw
Triton/Rank (Sydney Box)
A girl escapes from a remand home and starts on the road to ruin.
Risible vehicle for a rising star; at the time it set the box-offices clicking.
w Muriel and Sydney Box, Ted Willis *novel* *Night Darkens the Street* by Arthur La Bern *d* David MacDonald *ph* Stephen Dade *m* Lambert Williamson *ad* George Provis
☆ Jean Kent, Dennis Price, Flora Robson, Griffith Jones, Diana Dors, Herbert Lom, Bonar Colleano, Michael Hordern

Good Times
US 1967 92m DeLuxe
Motion Picture International
A singing duo in Hollywood imagines starring in films of various types.
Mildly agreeable light fantasy.
w Tony Barrett *d* William Friedkin
☆ Sonny and Cher, George Sanders, Norman Alden, Larry Duran

Good to Go
US 1986 91m Technicolor
Island Visual Arts (Doug Dilge, Sean Ferrer)
aka: *Short Fuse*
An alcoholic journalist begins to acquire a social conscience as he watches a cop hunt down an innocent black man accused of rape and murder.
Little more than a failed attempt to market Go-Go groups, a music that failed to find an audience outside Washington: a coarse-toned and uninteresting drama, in which any narrative momentum is lost in order to showcase the music.
wd Blaine Novak *ph* Peter Sinclair *m* Trouble Funk, Redds & The Boys, Chuck Brown and the Soul Searchers *ad* Ron Downing *ed* Gib Jaffe, Kimberly Logan, D. C. Stringer
☆ Art Garfunkel, Robert Doqui, Harris Yulin, Reginald Daughtry, Richard Brooks, Richard Bauer, Paula Davis, Michael White, Hattie Winston, Anjelica Huston

The Good Wife
Australia 1987 92m Eastmancolor
Entertainment/Laughing Kookaburra (Jan Sharp, Helen Watts)
Australian title: *The Umbrella Woman*
In 1939, a wife is bored with her backwater life, and takes a lover.
Heavy-going domestic drama with an interesting setting.
w Peter Kenna *d* Ken Cameron *ph* James Bartle *m* Cameron Allan *pd* Sally Campbell *ed* John Scott
☆ Rachel Ward, Bryan Brown, Sam Neill, Steven Vidler

Good Will Hunting **
US 1997 126m colour
Miramax (Lawrence Bender)
A delinquent working-class youth with a gift for mathematics has a difficult choice to make: to continue working as a janitor, and drinking and brawling with his friends, or become a highly paid resident genius with a powerful corporation.
The analogue to the narrative on the screen is one about an unknown actor who dreams of being admired, and writes a script with a star part for himself about a boy who is loved by all, however he behaves; in Matt Damon's case, the wish fulfilment worked.
w Matt Damon, Ben Affleck *d* Gus Van Sant *ph* Jean Yves Escoffier *m* Danny Elfman *pd* Melissa Stewart *ed* Pietro Scalia
☆ Matt Damon, Robin Williams, Ben Affleck, Minnie Driver, Stellan Skarsgard, Casey Affleck, Cole Hauser
'To see it is to fall under its spell. Never do you doubt that everybody connected with this film cares. It works – satisfyingly, urgently and richly – because it comes to us as felt knowledge.' – *Jay Carr, Boston Globe*
'Schematic, predictable and somewhat tedious.' – *Alexander Walker, London Evening Standard*
'Robin Williams, disproving optimistic predictions that he might be back on track, plays not just restrained, but restrained and noble. At the same time.' – *Emma Forrest, Guardian*
Matt Damon, Ben Affleck (as writers); Robin Williams
best picture; Matt Damon (as actor); Minnie Driver; Gus Van Sant; Pietro Scalia; Danny Elfman; song 'Miss Misery' (*m/ly* Elliott Smith)

Goodbye Again
US 1933 66m bw
Warner
An author's secretary is jealous of his rekindled interest in an old flame.
Unassuming star comedy which entertained at the time.
w Ben Markson *play* George Haight, Allan Scott *d* Michael Curtiz
☆ Warren William, Joan Blondell, Genevieve Tobin, Hugh Herbert, Helen Chandler, Ruth Donnelly
† *Honeymoon for Three* in 1941 (qv) was a leaden remake.

Goodbye Again *
US 1961 120m bw
UA/Mercury/Argus/Anatole Litvak
A woman of forty swaps her rich lover for a young law student.
Melancholy romantic drama, well produced and staged on Paris locations.
w Samuel Taylor *novel* *Aimez-vous Brahms* by Françoise Sagan *d* Anatole Litvak *ph* *Armand Thirard* *m* Georges Auric
☆ *Ingrid Bergman*, Anthony Perkins, Yves Montand, Jessie Royce Landis, Jackie Lane
'A grey-toned Sagan novella, spread wide and lush over two hours of screen time.' – *MFB*
'The kind of "woman's picture" that gives women a bad name.' – *Judith Crist, 1973*

Goodbye Charlie *
US 1964 116m DeLuxe Cinemascope
TCF/Venice (David Weisbart)
A philandering gangster, shot dead by an irate husband, is reincarnated in his friend's house as a dishy blonde.
Overlong but amusing Broadway comedy for wisecrackers, uninventively adapted.
w Harry Kurnitz *play* George Axelrod *d* Vincente Minnelli *ph* Milton Krasner *m* André Previn
☆ *Debbie Reynolds*, Pat Boone, Walter Matthau, Tony Curtis

Goodbye Charlie Bright *
GB 2001 86m DeLuxe
Metrodome/Flashpoint/Bonaparte/Cowboy/Imagine (Charles Steel, Lisa Bryer)
One summer, on a South London housing estate, two adolescent friends realise that one of them is going to break free into a wider world, while the other will never escape from poverty and petty crime.
Lively coming-of-age drama of teenagers seeking any form of excitement to stave off boredom, while shades of the prison-house close around them.
w Nick Love, Dominic Eames *d* Nick Love *ph* Tony Imi *m* Ivor Guest *pd* Eve Stewart *ed* Patrick Moore
☆ Paul Nicholls (Charlie), Roland Manookian (Justin), Phil Daniels (Eddie), Jamie Foreman (Tony Immaculate), Danny Dyer (Francis), Dani Behr (Blondie), Richard Driscoll (Hector), David Thewlis (Charlie's dad), Alexis Rodney (Damien), Sid Mitchell (Tommy), Frank Harper (Tommy's dad)
'An excellent cast, fluid direction and perceptive writing make it rattle persuasively. The estate that no one leaves voluntarily – only in a police car or a hearse – is the territorial villain, rather than any single member of it.' – *Alexander Walker, London Evening Standard*

'Every father's daughter is a virgin!'
Goodbye Columbus **
US 1969 105m Technicolor
Paramount/Willow Tree (Stanley Jaffe)
A young Jewish librarian has an affair with the wilful daughter of a *nouveau riche* family.
An amusing and well-observed delineation of two kinds of Jewish life in New York; the story, despite its frank talk of penises and diaphragms, leaves much to be desired, and the style is post-Graduate.
w Arnold Schulman *novel* Philip Roth *d* *Larry Peerce* *ph* Gerald Hirschfeld *m* Charles Fox
☆ *Richard Benjamin, Ali MacGraw*, Jack Klugman, Nan Martin, Michael Meyers, Lori Shelle
Arnold Schulman

Goodbye Gemini
GB 1970 89m colour
Cinerama/Josef Shaftel (Peter Snell)
A 20-year-old brother and sister share a world of petulant fantasy which leads to murder.
Abysmally over-the-top melodrama with a swinging London backdrop. Its immaculate appearance only makes matters worse.

w Edmund Ward *novel Ask Agamemnon* by Jenni Hall *d* Alan Gibson *ph* Geoffrey Unsworth *m* Christopher Gunning *pd* Wilfrid Shingleton
☆ Judy Geeson, Martin Potter, Michael Redgrave, Alexis Kanner, Mike Pratt, Freddie Jones, Peter Jeffrey

'Every man she ever loved thought a permanent relationship was a three-day weekend!'

The Goodbye Girl *
US 1977 110m Metrocolor
Warner/Rastar (Ray Stark)

A misunderstanding about the lease of an apartment results in a girl dancer agreeing to share it with a would-be actor.
A very moderate script assisted by excellent acting and the usual array of Neil Simon one-liners. Nothing at all new, but enjoyable.
w Neil Simon *d* Herbert Ross *ph* David M. Walsh *m* Dave Grusin
☆ *Richard Dreyfuss, Marsha Mason, Quinn Cummings*, Paul Benedict, Barbara Rhoades
Richard Dreyfuss
best picture; Neil Simon; Marsha Mason; Quinn Cummings
Richard Dreyfuss

Goodbye, Lover
US/Germany 1998 101m Technicolor Panavision
Warner/Arnon Milchan/Gotham/Lightmotive (Alexandra Milchan, Patrick McDarrah, Joel Rodman, Chris Daniel)

A Los Angeles advertising executive plots with his wife to collect millions on his brother's life.
Convoluted, comic thriller of double-cross and deception that is heavy-handed and obtuse.
w Ron Peer, Joel Cohen, Alec Sokolow *d* Roland Joffé *ph* Dante Spinotti *m* John Ottman *pd* Stewart Starkin *ed* William Steinkamp
☆ Patricia Arquette (Sandra Dunmore), Dermot Mulroney (Jake Dunmore), Ellen DeGeneres (Rita Pompano), Mary-Louise Parker (Peggy Blane), Don Johnson (Ben Dunmore), Ray McKinnon (Nathaniel Rollins), Alex Rocco (Detective Crowley), André Gregory (Rev. Finlayson), John Neville (Bradley)
'Once the thud of its wooden dialogue has settled into a deadly mechanical clomp – about 10 minutes into the film – you wonder why this risible movie didn't go straight to video.' – *Stephen Holden, New York Times*
'Unmitigated ordure.' – *Peter Bradshaw, Guardian*

Goodbye Mr Chips ***
GB 1939 114m bw
MGM (Victor Saville)

The life of a shy schoolmaster from his first job to his death.
Sentimental romance in MGM's best style, a long-standing favourite for its performances and humour; but the production seems slightly unsatisfactory these days.
w R. C. Sherriff, Claudine West, Eric Maschwitz *novel* James Hilton *d Sam Wood ph* Frederick A. Young *m* Richard Addinsell *ed* Charles Frend
☆ *Robert Donat, Greer Garson, Paul Henreid*, Lyn Harding, Austin Trevor, Terry Kilburn, John Mills, Milton Rosmer, Judith Furse
'Charming, quaintly sophisticated ... more for the big situations than the smaller towns.' – *Variety*
'The whole picture has an assurance, bears a glow of popularity like the face of a successful candidate on election day. And it is wrong to despise popularity in the cinema.' – *Graham Greene*
'The picture has no difficulty in using two hours to retell a story that was scarcely above short story length. *Mr Chips* is worth its time.' – *New York Times*
'The novel became an American best seller when that old sentimentalist Alexander Woollcott touted it on the radio ... the movie clogs the nose more than necessary.' – *Pauline Kael, 70s*
Robert Donat
best picture; script; Sam Wood; Greer Garson; editing

'He is a shy schoolmaster. She is a music hall star. They marry and immediately have 283 children – all boys!'

Goodbye Mr Chips *
GB 1969 147m Metrocolor Panavision 70
MGM/APJAC (Arthur P. Jacobs)

Elaborate musical remake of the 1939 movie about the life of a stern schoolmaster softened by marriage.
Slow and slushy treatment, with no improvement visible whatever; but a few of the trimmings please.
w Terence Rattigan *d* Herbert Ross *ph* Oswald Morris *m* Leslie Bricusse *md* John Williams *pd* Ken Adam
☆ Peter O'Toole, Petula Clark, Michael Bryant, Michael Redgrave, George Baker, Jack Hedley, Sian Phillips, Alison Leggatt
'The sum total is considerably less than the parts.' – *Variety*
'An overblown version with songs where they are not needed (and Leslie Bricusse's songs are never needed).' – *Pauline Kael, New Yorker*
† Originally sought for the title role, in order of preference, were Richard Burton and Rex Harrison; for the female lead, Samantha Eggar and Lee Remick.
Leslie Bricusse, John Williams; Peter O'Toole

Goodbye My Fancy
US 1951 107m bw
Warner (Henry Blanke)
A congresswoman returns to her old college for an honorary degree, and falls in love.
Tolerable romantic flim-flam.
w Ivan Goff, Ben Roberts *play* Fay Kanin *d* Vincent Sherman *ph* Ted McCord *m* Daniele Amfitheatrof
☆ Joan Crawford, Robert Young, Frank Lovejoy, Eve Arden, Janice Rule

Goodbye My Lady *
US 1956 95m bw
Warner/Batjac (William Wellman)

A Mississippi swamp boy finds a valuable dog but eventually returns it to its owner.
Reliable, slightly unusual family film.
w Sid Fleischman *novel* James Street *d* William Wellman *ph* William H. Clothier, Archie Stout *m* Laurindo Almeida, George Field
☆ Brandon de Wilde, Walter Brennan, Phil Harris, Sidney Poitier, William Hopper, Louise Beavers

Goodbye New York
US/Israel 1985 90m colour
Kole-Hill (Amos Kollek)

An accident-prone New York businesswoman, who decides her life lacks adventure, sets out for Paris and ends up in Israel.
Pleasant but unremarkable comedy of cultural misunderstandings; it sinks under its own weightlessness.
wd Amos Kollek *ph* Amnon Salomon *m* Michael Abene *ed* Alan Heim
☆ Julie Hagerty, Amos Kollek, David Topaz, Aviva Ger, Shmuel Shiloh, Jennifer Babtist, Christopher Goutman

The Goodbye People
US 1984 104m DeLuxe
Embassy/Coney Island (David V. Picker)

Middle-aged eccentrics meet on a beach.
Saroyanesque talk piece which never quite comes off, and will probably be seen only at festivals.
wd Herb Gardner *play* Herb Gardner *ph* John Lindley *pd* Tony Walton *ed* Rick Shaine
☆ Martin Balsam, Judd Hirsch, Pamela Reed, Ron Silver, Michael Tucker, Gene Saks

Goodbye Pork Pie *
New Zealand 1980 105m Eastmancolor
NZ Film Commission/NZ United Corporation/Nigel Hutchinson, Geoff Murphy

Three young people go on an illegal road spree and are arrested one by one.
Familiar high jinks with a moral conclusion. Fun up to a point, and good to look at.
w Geoff Murphy, Ian Mune *d* Geoff Murphy *ph* Alun Bollinger *m* John Charles
☆ Tony Barry, Kelly Johnson, Claire Oberman
'Displays encouraging physical flair in its cross-country sweep of action.' – *Tim Pulleine, MFB*

'Three Decades of Life in the Mafia.'

GoodFellas ****
US 1990 146m Technicolor
Warner (Irwin Winkler)

An Irish-Italian boy grows up to become a gangster.
Brilliant, unsparing delineation of the sub-culture of crime and the corruption of the spirit it entails.
w Martin Scorsese, Nicholas Pileggi *novel Wiseguy* by Nicholas Pileggi *d Martin Scorsese ph* Michael Ballhaus *pd* Kristi Zea *ad* Maher Ahmad *ed* Thelma Schoonmaker
☆ Robert DeNiro, *Ray Liotta, Joe Pesci*, Lorraine Bracco, Paul Sorvino, Frank Sivero, Tony Darrow, Mike Starr, Frank Vincent, Chuck Low
'Simultaneously fascinating and repellent.' – *Variety*
'In its own narrow, near-claustrophobic perspective, however, driven along by a classic soundtrack and with no shortage of master directorial brush strokes, it is hard to imagine a bigger picture than this.' – *Empire*
Joe Pesci
film; Martin Scorsese; script (Martin Scorsese, Nicholas Pileggi); Lorraine Bracco; Thelma Schoonmaker
film; Martin Scorsese; script (Martin Scorsese, Nicholas Pileggi)

Goodnight Vienna
GB 1932 76m bw
British and Dominions (Herbert Wilcox)
US title: *Magic Night*
In 1913 Vienna, a general's son falls for a shopgirl.
Already dated when it was made, this thin musical romance nevertheless made a star of Anna Neagle and re-established Jack Buchanan on the screen.
w Holt Marvel, George Posford *play* Holt Marvel, George Posford *d* Herbert Wilcox *ph* F. A. Young *m* George Posford, Eric Maschwitz *ad* L. P. Williams *ed* E. Aldridge
☆ Jack Buchanan, Anna Neagle, Gina Malo, Clive Currie, William Kendall

A Goofy Movie
US 1995 78m Technicolor
Buena Vista/Walt Disney (Dan Rounds)

Goofy takes his slacker son on holiday and ends up in Los Angeles.
Minor animated feature; it may be of some social interest that Goofy is a single parent, but this tale of male bonding otherwise has little to offer.
w Jymn Magon, Chris Matheson, Brian Pimental *d* Kevin Lima *m* Carter Burwell *pd* Fred Warter *ed* Gregory Perler, Catherine Rascon
☆ Featuring the voices of: Bill Farmer, Jason Marsden, Jim Cummings, Kellie Martin, Rob Paulsen, Wallace Shawn
'The strength lies in the storytelling, and while this is slight, it's still a lot of fun.' – *Empire*

The Goonies
US 1985 111m Technicolor Panavision
Warner/Steven Spielberg

Kids discover a pirate map and set out on a fantasy treasure hunt.
The bottomless pit of the Spielberg genre, a silly tale which takes forever to get going and is acted by children who have not studied elocution. The trick effects when they come are OK, but it's a long annoying haul to that point.
w Chris Columbus *story* Steven Spielberg *d* Richard Donner *ph* Nick McLean *m* Dave Grusin *pd* J. Michael Riva *ed* Michael Kahn
☆ Sean Astin, Josh Brolin, Jeff Cohen, Corey Feldman, Kerri Green, Martha Plimpton, Ke Huy Kwan

The Goose and the Gander
US 1935 65m bw
Warner
A divorcee can't leave her ex-husband's life alone.
Tolerable farcical goings-on which just fail to come to the boil.
w George Kenyon *d* Alfred E. Green
☆ Kay Francis, George Brent, Genevieve Tobin, John Eldredge, Claire Dodd
'Well-played little farce with too much story for its own good.' – *Variety*

The Goose Steps Out *
GB 1942 79m bw
Ealing (S. C. Balcon)
To steal a secret weapon, an incompetent teacher is sent into Germany in place of his Nazi double.
Quite amusing star vehicle, not up to his best standards.
w Angus Macphail, John Dighton *d* Will Hay, Basil Dearden *ph* Ernest Palmer *m* Bretton Byrd
☆ *Will Hay, Charles Hawtrey*, Frank Pettingell, Julien Mitchell, Peter Croft, Jeremy Hawk, Peter Ustinov, Raymond Lovell, Barry Morse

The Goose Woman
US 1925 90m approx bw silent
Universal
A young actress falls for the son of an embittered old one.
Interesting character melodrama of which prints have survived.
w Melville Brown *story* Rex Beach *d* Clarence Brown *ph* Milton Moore
☆ Louise Dresser, Jack Pickford, Constance Bennett, James Barrows

The Gorbals Story
GB 1949 75m bw
Eros/New World (Ernest Gartside)
A successful artist remembers his unhappy youth in a tenement in the slums of Glasgow.
Well-meaning, low-budget proletarian melodrama, featuring actors from the Glasgow Unity theatre. Set mainly in a couple of tenement rooms, it would have benefited from opening up with more exterior scenes; as it is, it remains a photographed stage play.
w David MacKane *play* Robert McLeish *d* David MacKane *ph* Stanley Clinton *m* John Bath *ad* George Haslam *ed* Helen Wiggins
☆ Russell Hunter, Betty Henderson, Howard Connell, Marjorie Thomson, Roddy McMillan, Isobel Campbell, Carl Williamson, Lothar Lewinsohn, Andrew Keir

Gordon's War
US 1973 90m TVC Color
TCF/Palomar (Robert L. Schaffel)
A black Vietnam veteran returns to Harlem and avenges the death of his wife.
Violent vigilante melodrama with vivid locations.
w Howard Friedlander, Ed Spielman *d* Ossie Davis *ph* Victor J. Kemper *m* Andy Bodale, Al Ellis
☆ Paul Winfield, Carl Lee, David Downing

Gorgeous
Hong Kong 1999 121m colour
Golden Harvest/Golden Pictures (Raymond Chow)

original title: *Bolei Cheun*
A Taiwanese girl goes to Hong Kong in search of romance and falls for a multi-millionaire.
Glossy romantic comedy of little interest, in which the decorative Shu Qi giggles and simpers a great deal, and Jackie Chan glowers; there's little to interest fans of his stunt-filled action movies, merely a couple of exhibition-style martial arts contests, which he loses.
w Vincent Kuk, Jackie Chan, Lo Yiu-fai *story* Ivy Ho *d* Vincent Kuk *ph* Cheung Man-po *m* Wong Dan-yi *ad* Yee Chung-man *ed* Kwong Chi-leung, Cheung Ka-fai *cos* Shirley Chan, Dora Ng
☆ Jackie Chan (C.N. Chan), Shu Qi (Bu), Tony Leung Chiu-wai (Albert), Emil Chow (L.W. Lo), Jen Hsien-chi (Bu's Suitor), Elaine Jin (Bu's Mother), Chen Sung-yung (Bu's Father), Bradley James Allan (Martial Artist)
'A good old-fashioned heart-warmer.' – *Derek Elley, Variety*

A Gorgeous Bird Like Me: see *Une Belle Fille comme Moi*

'An unbeatable cast in an unequalled drama! Metro's successor to The Great Ziegfeld!'

The Gorgeous Hussy *
US 1936 105m bw
MGM (Joseph L. Mankiewicz)
The love life of Peggy O'Neal, protégée of President Andrew Jackson.
Bowdlerized all-star historical drama; the production values are better than the script.

w Ainsworth Morgan, Stephen Morehouse Avery *novel* Samuel Hopkins Adams *d Clarence Brown ph* George Folsey *m* Herbert Stothart
☆ Joan Crawford, Lionel Barrymore, Franchot Tone, Melvyn Douglas, Robert Taylor, James Stewart, Alison Skipworth, Louis Calhern, Beulah Bondi, Melville Cooper, Sidney Toler, Gene Lockhart
† A foreword read: 'This story of Peggy Eaton and her times is not presented as a precise account of either, rather as fiction founded upon historical fact.'
George Folsey; Beulah Bondi

'This is the big one! Two years in the making!'
Gorgo
GB 1960 78m Technicolor
King Brothers (Wilfrid Eades)
A prehistoric monster is caught in Irish waters and brought to London, but rescued by its mother.
Amiable monster hokum with a happy ending but not much technical resource.
w John Loring, Daniel Hyatt (Robert L. Richards, Daniel James) *d* Eugène Lourié *ph* Frederick A. Young *m* Angelo Lavagnino *sp* Tom Howard
☆ Bill Travers, William Sylvester, Vincent Winter, Christopher Rhodes, Joseph O'Conor, Bruce Seton, Martin Benson
† The script was written under pseudonyms because of the blacklist.

The Gorgon *
GB 1964 83m Technicolor
Columbia/Hammer (Anthony Nelson-Keys)
A castle ruin near a German village is infested by Megaera, the gorgon of ancient myth, whose gaze turns people to stone and who can take over the form of an unknowing villager.
Writhing snakes in the hair-do being too great a challenge to the make-up man, the monster is barely glimpsed and the film becomes a who-is-it, all quite suspenseful despite the central idea being too silly for words.
w John Gilling *story* J. Llewellyn Devine *d* Terence Fisher *ph* Michael Reed *m* James Bernard *ad* Bernard Robinson *ed* James Needs, Eric Boyd-Perkins
☆ Peter Cushing, Christopher Lee, Barbara Shelley, Richard Pasco, Patrick Troughton, Michael Goodliffe, Jack Watson

The Gorilla *
US 1939 66m bw
TCF (Harry Joe Brown)
A murderer blames an escaped gorilla for his crimes.
Spooky house mystery comedy revamped as a Ritz Brothers vehicle; not much suspense, but it all looks good and the cast is highly satisfactory.
w Rian James, Sid Silvers *play* Ralph Spence *d Allan Dwan ph Edward Cronjager md* David Buttolph
☆ *The Ritz Brothers*, Bela Lugosi, Lionel Atwill, Patsy Kelly, Joseph Calleia, Anita Louise, Edward Norris, Wally Vernon
'A good programmer that will get by for normal biz where the Ritzes can attract.' – *Variety*
† There were two previous versions, in 1927 with Charlie Murray and 1931 with Joe Frisco.

'Get out of the way – before it's too late!'
Gorilla at Large
US 1954 93m Technicolor 3-D
TCF/Panoramic (Robert L. Jacks)
A circus gorilla is used as a cover for murder.
Silly thriller with the gorilla as unconvincing as the story.
w Leonard Praskins, Barney Slater *d* Harmon Jones *ph* Lloyd Ahern *m* Lionel Newman
☆ Anne Bancroft, Lee J. Cobb, Cameron Mitchell, Lee Marvin, Raymond Burr, Charlotte Austin, Peter Whitney, Warren Stevens

The Gorilla Man
US 1942 63m bw
Warner
A wounded commando discovers that his hospital is run by Nazis, who then try to prove him insane so that he won't be believed.
There must have been less laborious ways, one assumes, but at least this farrago is good for a few unintentional laughs.
w Anthony Coldeway *d* D. Ross Lederman
☆ John Loder, Ruth Ford, Richard Fraser, Paul Cavanagh, John Abbott

Gorillas in the Mist *
US 1988 129m Technicolor
UIP/Warner (Arnold Glimcher, Terence Clegg)
Researching into the lives of gorillas, a reclusive female scientist antagonizes local poachers.
Respectful, unenlightening biopic.
w Anna Hamilton Phelan *story* Anna Hamilton Phelan, Tab Murphy *book Dian Fossey (article by Harold T. P. Hayes) d* Michael Apted *ph* John Seale *m* Maurice Jarre *pd* John Graysmark *ed* Stuart Baird *sp* Rick Baker
☆ Sigourney Weaver, Bryan Brown, Julie Harris, John Omirah Miluwi, Iain Cuthbertson, Constantin Alexandrov, Waigwa Wachira, Iain Glen, David Lansbury
Sigourney Weaver; Maurice Jarre; Anna Hamilton Phelan; Stuart Baird; best sound

Gorky Park *
US 1983 128m Technicolor
Orion/Eagle (Gene Kirkwood, Howard W. Koch Jnr)
The Moscow police link murders with a sable-smuggling operation.
Bleak thriller which doggedly makes its way through a conventional plot but fails to convey the book's detail of life in Moscow today. (The film was shot in Helsinki.)
w Dennis Potter *novel* Martin Cruz Smith *d* Michael Apted *ph* Ralf D. Bode *m* James Horner *pd* Paul Sylbert
☆ Lee Marvin, William Hurt, Brian Dennehy, Ian Bannen, Joanna Pacula, Michael Elphick, Richard Griffiths, Alexander Knox

'Tea At Four. Dinner At Eight. Murder By Midnight.'
Gosford Park ****
US/GB 2001 137m Technicolor Panavision
Entertainment/Capitol/Film Council/Sandcastle 5/ Chicagofilms/Medusa (Robert Altman, Bob Balaban, David Levy)
During a country house weekend in the early 1930s, aristocratic guests and their servants come under suspicion when their host is killed twice.
Witty, acute, splendidly acted dissection of a way of life at the point of its disintegration; it captures not only the antagonism between the working- and upper-classes, but also their complicity in the continuation of a decadent social system.
w Julian Fellowes idea Robert Altman, Bob Balaban *d Robert Altman ph* Andrew Dunn *m* Patrick Doyle *pd* Stephen Altman *ed* Tim Squyres *cos* Jenny Beavan
☆ Eileen Atkins (Mrs Croft), Michael Gambon (Sir William McCordle), Jeremy Northam (Ivor Novello), Clive Owen (Robert Parks), Bob Balaban (Morris Weissman), Maggie Smith (Constance, Countess of Trentham), Ryan Phillippe (Henry Denton), Alan Bates (Jennings), Helen Mirren (Mrs Wilson), Kelly Macdonald (Mary Maceachran), Richard E. Grant (George), Tom Hollander (Lt Commander Anthony Meredith), Kristin Scott Thomas (Lady Sylvia McCordle), Emily Watson (Elsie), James Wilby (The Hon. Freddie Nesbitt) and also Derek Jacobi (Probert), Geraldine Somerville (Louisa, Lady Stockbridge), Sophie Thompson (Dorothy), Camilla Rutherford (Isobel McCordle), Claudie Blakley (Mabel Nesbitt), Stephen Fry (Inspector Thompson), Ron Webster (Constable Dexter)
'A virtuoso ensemble piece to rival the director's "Nashville" and "Short Cuts" in its masterly interweaving of multiple characters and subplots.' – *Stephen Holden, New York Times*
'Witty, moving, intriguing, it is accurate in its social and physical detail and performed by the most outstanding British cast ever assembled.' – *Philip French, Observer*
Julian Fellowes
picture; Robert Altman; Helen Mirren; Maggie Smith; Stephen Altman; Jenny Beavan
British film; Jenny Beavan

The Gospel According to St Matthew *
Italy/France 1964 142m bw
Arco/Lux (Alfredo Bini)
original title: *Il Vangelo Secondo Matteo*
The life of Christ seen almost as a ciné-vérité documentary.
The tone is realist but not notably iconoclastic.
wd Pier Paolo Pasolini *ph* Tonino delli Colli *m* Bach, Mozart, Prokofiev, Webern *md* Luis Enrique Bacalov *ad* Luigi Scaccianoce *ed* Nino Baragli
☆ Enrique Irazoqui, Susanna Pasolini, Mario Socrate
Luis Enrique Bacalov

The Gospel According to Vic: see *Heavenly Pursuits*

'It can turn you on, or turn on you.'
Gossip
US/Australia 2000 90m Technicolor Super 35
Warner/Village Roadshow/NPV/Outlaw (Jeffrey Silver, Bobby Newmyer)
As an experiment, three students spread the false news that a chaste girl had sex with her boyfriend.
An interesting concept swiftly goes wrong; no one seems to know how to develop the narrative and, despite the occasional slick dialogue, the film founders.
w Gregory Poirier, Theresa Rebeck *d* Davis Guggenheim *ph* Andrzej Bartkowiak *m* Graeme Revell *pd* David Nichols *ed* Jay Cassidy *cos* Louise Mingenbach
☆ James Marsden (Derrick Webb), Lena Headey (Cathy Jones), Norman Reedus (Travis), Kate Hudson (Naomi Preston), Marisa Coughlan (Sheila), Sharon Lawrence (Detective Kelly), Eric Bogosian (Professor Goodwin), Edward James Olmos (Detective Curtis), Joshua Jackson (Beau Edson)
'Preposterous twists and motives turn a potentially gripping and thought-provoking movie into an utterly daft one.' – *Jo Berry, Empire*

Gösta Berlings Saga: see *The Atonement of Gösta Berling*

Una Gota De Sangre Para Morir Amando (dubbed) *
Spain/France 1973 110m colour Techniscope
Jose Frade (Angel Parrondo)
aka: *Murder in a Blue World*
While the state attempts to cure criminals by electric shock treatment, and delinquents roam the streets, a serial killer targets young men.
A quirky, low-budget attack on social and sexual repression, one that acknowledges its debt to Kubrick's A Clockwork Orange.
w Eloy de la Iglesia, Jose Luis Garci, Antonio Fos, Antonio Artero, George Lebourg *d* Eloy de la Iglesia *ph* Francisco Fraile *m* George Garvarent *ad* Eduardo Torre De La Fuente *ed* Jose Luis Matesanz
☆ Sue Lyon, Christopher Mitchum, Jean Sorel, Charlie Bravo, Ramon Pons, Alfredo Alba, Antionio Real, David Carpenter
† In an in-joke, during the film Sue Lyon reads Nabokov's *Lolita*, the role that began her screen career.

Gothic
GB 1986 90m Eastmancolor
Virgin Visions (Penny Corke)
Byron, the Shelleys and Dr Polidori spend a weekend thinking up ghost stories.
Somewhat unhinged version of a famous occurrence in 1816, full of nauseous detail typical of its director.
w Stephen Volk *d* Ken Russell *ph* Mike Southon *m* Thomas Dolby *pd* Christopher Hobbs
☆ Gabriel Byrne, Julian Sands, Natasha Richardson, Miriam Cyr, Timothy Spall
'The thinking man's *Nightmare on Elm Street*.' – *Daily Variety*

Götterdämmerung: see *The Damned (1969)*

Goupi Mains Rouges *
France 1943 95m bw
Minerva
US title: *It Happened at the Inn*
A French village is largely populated by members of the same family, and one of them murders another.
An odd little black comedy which strengthened its director's reputation.
w Pierre Véry, Jacques Becker *novel* Pierre Véry *d* Jacques Becker *ph* Pierre Montazel, Jean Bourgoin *m* Jean Alfaro
☆ Fernand Ledoux, Georges Rollin, Blanchette Brunoy, Robert Le Vigan

'The Sexy Comedy About Good Taste... And Bad Manners!'
Le Goût des Autres *
France 2000 113m colour 'Scope
Pathé/Telema/A4/France 2 (Christian Berard, Charles Gassot)
aka: *The Taste of Others*
A married, philistine factory owner begins to take an interest in artistic pursuits after he falls in love with an actress.
Amiable comedy of manners about the attraction of opposites, the culture of commerce, and the commerce of culture.
w Agnes Jaoui, Jean-Pierre Bacri *d* Agnes Jaoui *ph* Jean-Paul Dumas-Grillet *m* Jean-Charles Jarrell *ad* Francois Emmanuelli *ed* Herve de Luze *cos* Anne Dunsford-Varenne
☆ Jean-Pierre Bacri (Jean-Jacques Castella), Anne Alvaro (Clara Devaux), Agnes Jaoui (Manie), Gerard Lanvin (Moreno), Alain Chabat (Deschamps), Brigitte Catillon (Beatrice), Christiane Millet (Angelique), Wladimir Yordanoff (Antoine)
'It seems to come down off the screen to sit with us and become friendly.' – *Stanley Kaufmann, New Republic*
foreign language film

Gouttes d'eau sur pierres brulantes: see *Water Drops On Burning Rocks*

The Governess
GB/France 1997 114m colour Super 35
Alliance/Pandora/Parallax (Sarah Curtis)
In the 1840s, a Jewish woman, who disguises her origins, becomes governess to a Scottish family.
A feminist variation on Jane Eyre *that says little that is new or interesting.*
wd Sandra Goldbacher *ph* Ashley Rowe *m* Edward Shearmur *pd* Sarah Greenwood *ed* Isabel Lorente
☆ Minnie Driver, Tom Wilkinson, Harriet Walter, Florence Hoath, Bruce Myers, Jonathan Rhys Meyers, Arlene Cockburn, Emma Bird
'Pictorially, the movie is never less than sophisticated; only on a dramatic level is it silly.' – *Peter Matthews, Sight and Sound*

Government Girl
US 1943 94m bw
RKO
War Department secretaries find their love lives confused in wartime Washington, where rooms have to be shared.
Thin variation on a theme curiously dear to Hollywood at the time.
wd Dudley Nichols *story* Adela Rogers St Johns, Budd Schulberg
☆ Olivia de Havilland, Sonny Tufts, Anne Shirley, James Dunn, Paul Stewart, Agnes Moorehead, Harry Davenport, Una O'Connor, Sig Rumann, Jane Darwell

Goya in Bordeaux **
Spain/Italy 1999 104m colour
Dowtown/Mainline/Lolafilms/Italian Intl (Andres Vicente Gomez)
original title: *Goya en Bordeos*
Dying in France, the exiled Spanish artist Francisco de Goya recalls the events of his life to his daughter, while around him his paintings come to life.
This is more a homage from one artist to another than a conventional movie, climaxing as it does in the recreation by a Spanish theatre troupe of Goya's series of engravings, Disasters of War; *visually, it entrances.*
wd Carlos Saura *ph Vittorio Storaro m* Roque Banos *ad Pierre-Louis Thevenet ed* Julia Juaniz *cos* Pedro Moreno
☆ Francisco Rabal (Goya), Jose Coronado (Goya as a Young Man), Dafne Fernandez (Rosario), Maribel Verdu (Duchess of Alba), Eulalia Ramon (Leocadia), Joaquin Climent (Moratin), Cristina Espinosa (Pepita Tudo), Jose Maria Pou (Godoy), Saturnino Garcia (Priest/San Antonio), Carlos Hipolito (Juan Valdes)

'The absence of narrative drive and characterisation makes the experience of the film akin to leafing through a de luxe volume of illustrations.' – *Paul Julian Smith, Sight and Sound*

Le Graal: see *Lancelot du Lac*

The Grace Moore Story: see *So This Is Love*

Grace of My Heart *
US 1996 115m CFI color
Universal/Gramercy/Cappa (Ruth Charny, Daniel Hassid)

A would-be singer becomes a successful songwriter in New York's Brill Building in the 50s and 60s.
Amiable trot through the pop music styles of the period in a movie that is loosely based on the career of Carole King; it is enjoyable, but as evanescent as the music it celebrates.
wd Allison Anders *ph* Jean-Yves Escoffier
m Larry Klein, Elvis Costello, Burt Bacharach
pd François Seguin *ed* Thelma Schoonmaker, James Kwei, Harvey Rosenstock
☆ Illeana Douglas, John Turturro, Eric Stoltz, Patsy Kensit, Bridget Fonda, Matt Dillon, Bruce Davison, Lucinda Jenney, Jennifer Leigh Warren, Christina Pickles
'Art with heart and rhythm, this is irresistibly wonderful. We're unlikely to see many films that are more entertaining all year.' – *Angie Errigo, Empire*
† Illeana Douglas's singing is dubbed by Kristen Vigard.

Grace Quigley
US 1984 95m colour
Cannon/Northbrook (Menahem Globus, Yoram Globus)

aka: *The Ultimate Solution of Grace Quigley*
An aged widow blackmails a hit man into performing his services for all her elderly and miserable friends.
Yukky black comedy which ill befits its star and is an embarrassment from start to finish.
w A. Martin Zweiback *d* Anthony Harvey
ph Larry Pizer *m* John Addison
☆ Katharine Hepburn, Nick Nolte, Elizabeth Wilson, Walter Abel, Kit Le Fever, Chip Zuen
† The *Grace Quigley* version has a contrived happy ending. In the original, Grace walks into the sea and the hit man is drowned trying to save her.

The Gracie Allen Murder Case *
US 1939 74m bw
George K. Arthur/Paramount
Gracie Allen helps Philo Vance solve the murder of an escaping convict.
At the time of Gracie Allen's radio eminence, this was a cute comedy idea.
w Nat Perrin *novel* S. S. Van Dine *d* Alfred E. Green *ph* Charles Lang *ad* Hans Dreier, Earl Hedrick *ed* Paul Weatherwax
☆ Gracie Allen, Warren William, Ellen Drew, Kent Taylor, Jed Prouty, Jerome Cowan, Donald McBride, H. B. Warner, William Demarest
'Smacko for general audiences ... one of the top comedies of the season.' – *Variety*

Gracious Living: see *La Vie de Château*

'This is Benjamin ... he's a little worried about his future!'
The Graduate ****
US 1967 105m Technicolor Panavision
UA/Embassy (Lawrence Turman)

A rich Californian ex-student is led into an affair with the wife of his father's friend, then falls in love with her daughter.
Richly reflecting the anything-goes mood of the late sixties, this lushly-filmed sex comedy opened a few new doors, looked ravishing, was well acted and had a popular music score. A comedy of its time, it has also stood the test of time.
w Calder Willingham, Buck Henry *novel Charles Webb d Mike Nichols ph Robert Surtees m* Dave Grusin *m/ly Paul Simon (sung by Simon and Art Garfunkel) pd Richard Sylbert*
☆ *Dustin Hoffman, Anne Bancroft,* Katharine Ross, Murray Hamilton, William Daniels, Elizabeth Wilson
BENJAMIN: 'Mrs Robinson, if you don't mind my saying so, this conversation is getting a little strange.'
'Seeing *The Graduate* is a bit like having one's most brilliant friend to dinner, watching him become more witty and animated with every moment, and then becoming aware that what one may really be witnessing is the onset of a nervous breakdown.' – *Renata Adler*
'Yes, there are weaknesses ... But in cinematic skill, in intent, in sheer connection with us, *The Graduate* is a milestone in American film history.' – *Stanley Kauffmann*
Mike Nichols
best picture; script; Robert Surtees; Dustin Hoffman; Anne Bancroft; Katharine Ross
best picture; Mike Nichols; Calder Willingham, Buck Henry; Dustin Hoffman

Graffiti Bridge
US 1990 95m colour
Warner/Paisley Park (Arnold Stiefel, Randy Phillips)

Two clubowners quarrel over the type of music they should be featuring.
Little more than an excuse for Prince to perform his songs, and strictly for fans.
wd Prince *ph* Bill Butler *m* Prince *pd* Vance Lorenzini *ed* Rebecca Rose
☆ Prince, Ingrid Chavez, Morris Day, Jerome Benton, Mavis Staples

The Grail: see *Lancelot du Lac*

Le Grand Blond avec une Chaussure Noire (dubbed) *
France 1972 89m Eastmancolor
Fox-Rank/Gaumont International/Productions de la Guéville/Madeleine (Alain Poire, Yves Robert)

aka: *Follow That Guy with the One Black Shoe*
aka: *The Tall Blond Man with One Black Shoe*
A disaster-prone violinist is the victim of a set-up by the head of the secret service who is attempting to discredit his second-in-command.
Mildly amusing comedy that makes fun of spies and their suspicious attitudes, though it suffers from being dubbed.
w Yves Robert, Francis Véber *d* Yves Robert
ph René Mathelin *m* Vladimir Cosma
ed Ghislaine Desjonquères
☆ Pierre Richard, Bernard Blier, Jean Rochefort, Mireille Darc, Jean Carmet, Colette Castel

Grand Canyon *
US 1991 134m DeLuxe Panavision
TCF (Lawrence Kasdan, Charles Okun, Michael Grillo)

After a black truck driver comes to the aid of a white lawyer, the two men form a friendship despite the disparity between them.
A sentimental account of urban unease, and one that offers glib answers to the questions it raises, but at least it does raise questions.
w Meg and Lawrence Kasdan *d* Lawrence Kasdan
ph Owen Roizman *m* James Newton Howard
pd Bo Welch *ed* Carol Littleton
☆ Danny Glover, Kevin Kline, Steve Martin, Mary McDonnell, Mary-Louise Parker, Alfre Woodard
'As a study of survival strategies in a disintegrating metropolis, pic brings a welcome seriousness and maturity to subject matter too often treated with flippancy and mindless romanticism.' – *Variety*
'It is hard to think of another American movie that has so directly, even naively, confronted the basic source of our existential unease.' – *Richard Schickel, Time*
Meg and Lawrence Kasdan (screenplay)

Le Grand Chemin **
France 1987 107m colour
Warner/Flach/Selena Audio Visuel/TFI (Pascal Hommais, Jean-François Lepetit)

A nine-year-old boy spends the summer with a childless couple.
Charming account of a child trying to cope with the adult world which was a big hit in France.
wd Jean-Loup Hubert *ph* Claude Lecomte
m Georges Granier *pd* Farid Chaouche
ed Raymonde Guyot
☆ Anemone, Richard Bohringer, Antoine Hubert, Vanessa Guedi, Christine Pascal, Raoul Billerey, Pascale Roberts, Marie Matheron, Daniel Railet

'The greatest cast in stage or screen history!'
Grand Hotel **
US 1932 115m bw
MGM (Irving Thalberg)

The lives of various hotel guests become intertwined and reach their climaxes.
It's a little faded now, but much of the magic still works in this first of the portmanteau movies; the production is opulent yet somehow stiff, and the performances have survived with varying success.
w William A. Drake *novel* Vicki Baum
d Edmund Goulding ph William Daniels
ad Cedric Gibbons
☆ Greta Garbo, *John Barrymore*, Lionel Barrymore, Joan Crawford, Wallace Beery, Jean Hersholt, Lewis Stone
DOCTOR (LEWIS STONE): 'Grand Hotel. Always the same. People come, people go. Nothing ever happens.'
GRUSINSKAYA (GRETA GARBO): 'I want to be alone ... I think I have never been so tired in my life.'
† Remade as *Weekend at the Waldorf* (qv).
best picture

Le Grand Jeu *
France 1934 115m bw
Films de France
A young man joins the Foreign Legion to forget a woman, meets another who reminds him of her, and is condemned to death for murdering the second woman's lover.
Hokey melodrama whose great interest lay in its picture of life in the Legion.
w Charles Spaak, Jacques Feyder *d* Jacques Feyder
ph Harry Stradling, Maurice Forster *m* Hanns Eisler
☆ Pierre-Richard Wilm, Marie Bell, Françoise Rosay, Charles Vanel
'At last a good French film.' – *Variety*
† A remake appeared in 1953, directed by Robert Siodmak and starring Jean-Claude Pascal, Gina Lollobrigida and Arletty. Sometimes known as *Card of Fate*, it is of little interest.

Le Grand Meaulnes **
France 1967 110m Eastmancolor Techniscope
Fair Enterprises/Madeleine/Awa (Gilbert de Goldschmidt)
aka: *The Wanderer*
An adolescent's frantic search for a beautiful young girl he met by chance ends in tragedy.
A bitter-sweet romance that is faithful to the original but, for all its attractions, lacks imagination in its transfer to the screen.
w Isabelle Rivière, Jean-Gabriel Albicocco
novel Alain-Fournier *d* Jean-Gabriel Albicocco
ph Quinto Albicocco *m* Jean-Pierre Bourtayre
ad Daniel Louradour *ed* Georges Klotz
☆ Brigitte Fossey, Jean Blaise, Alain Libolt, Alain Noury, Juliette Villard, Christian de Tillière
'Photographed for the most part in unforgettable scenery, and acted with convincing delicacy and charm, it carries a real poetic power and retains an amazing amount of the original's intensely romantic quality of loss and fragile innocence.' – *David Pirie, MFB*

Le Grand Méliès *
France 1952 30m bw
Armor Films (Fred Orain)
The life of Georges Méliès, conjuror and pioneer film maker, is told in a series of vignettes separated by clips from his films.
An interesting documentary reconstruction.
wd Georges Franju
☆ André Méliès

Grand National Night
GB 1953 80m bw
Talisman (George Minter)
US title: *The Wicked Wife*
A stable owner accidentally kills his drunken wife, but fate and a complex series of events clear him.
Slightly dubious morally, but otherwise an adequate detective story with the outcome hinging on train timetables and the like.
w Dorothy and Campbell Christie *play* Dorothy and Campbell Christie *d* Bob McNaught *ph* Jack Asher *m* John Greenwood
☆ Nigel Patrick, Moira Lister, Beatrice Campbell, Betty Ann Davies, Michael Hordern, Noel Purcell, Leslie Mitchell, Barry Mackay, Colin Gordon

Grand Prix *
US 1966 179m Metrocolor Super Panavision
MGM/Douglas and Lewis (Edward Lewis)

Motor racers converge on Monte Carlo and other European centres.
Seemingly endless montage, mostly in multisplit screens, of motor races, with some very jaded personal footage between. It looks a dream but quickly becomes a bore.
w Robert Alan Aurthur *d John Frankenheimer ph Lionel Lindon m* Maurice Jarre *pd Richard Sylbert*
☆ James Garner, Eva Marie Saint, Brian Bedford, Yves Montand, Toshiro Mifune, Jessica Walter, Françoise Hardy, Adolfo Celi, Claude Dauphin, Genevieve Page
'The same old story with the same types we've seen flying planes and riding horses in dozens of fast, cheap, hour-and-a-quarter movies.' – *Pauline Kael*
'Nothing more nor less than a paean to the racing car ... off the track, though, the film is firmly stuck in bottom gear.' – *MFB*

Grand Rue: see *Calle Mayor*

Il Grand Silencio: see *The Big Silence*

Grand Slam
US 1933 65m bw
Warner
A Russian waiter is called in to make a fourth at bridge and proves to be an expert.
Able spoof of the bridge craze then sweeping America; precise knowledge unnecessary.
w David Boehm, Ernest Gelsey *novel* B. Russell Herts *d* William Dieterle
☆ Paul Lukas, Loretta Young, Frank McHugh, Glenda Farrell, Helen Vinson, Walter Byron, Ferdinand Gottschalk
'It just about makes three spades doubled, which isn't bad when you're vulnerable, and that should be enough to show a profit.' – *Variety*

Grand Slam
Italy/Spain/West Germany 1967 120m Techniscope
Paramount/Jolly-Coral-Constantin (Harry Columbo, George Papi)
original title: *Ad Ogni Costo*
A retired professor has a plan for a diamond robbery, but recruits his aides unwisely.
Long-drawn-out caper melodrama with good sequences but nothing at all new; a very poor man's Rififi.
w Mino Roli, Caminito, Marcello Fondato, Antonio de la Loma *d* Giuliano Montaldo
ph Antonio Macasoli *m* Ennio Morricone
☆ Janet Leigh, Edward G. Robinson, Klaus Kinski, Robert Hoffman, Georges Rigaud, Adolfo Celi

La Grande Bouffe: see *Blow-Out*

La Grande Illusion ***
France 1937 117m bw
Réalisations d'Art Cinématographique (Frank Rollmer, Albert Pinkovitch)

During World War I, three captured French pilots have an uneasy relationship with their German commandant.
Celebrated mood piece with much to say about war and mankind; more precisely, it is impeccably acted and directed and has real tragic force.
w Jean Renoir, Charles Spaak d Jean Renoir
ph Christian Matras *m* Joseph Kosma
m/ly Vincent Telly, Albert Valsien *ad Eugène Lourie ed* Marguerite Renoir, Marthe Huguet
☆ *Pierre Fresnay, Erich von Stroheim, Jean Gabin,* Julien Carette, Marcel Dalio, Gaston Modot, Jean Dasté, Dita Parlo
'The story is true. It was told to me by my friends in the war ... notably by Pinsard who flew fighter planes. I was in the reconnaissance squadron. He saved my life many times when the German fighters became too persistent. He himself was shot down seven times. His escapes are the basis for the story.' – *Jean Renoir*
'Artistically masterful.' – *Variety*
'One of the true masterpieces of the screen.' – *Pauline Kael, 70s*
best picture

La Grande Vadrouille: see *Don't Look Now ... We're Being Shot At!*

Les Grandes Manoeuvres *
France/Italy 1955 106m Eastmancolor
Filmsonor/Rizzoli
aka: *Summer Manoeuvres*
In 1913, an army lieutenant takes a bet that he can win any woman in the town in which his regiment is quartered during manoeuvres.
An elegant, but surprisingly unwitty film from this director, saddled with a well-worn and very predictable plot.
wd René Clair *ph* Robert Le Fèbvre, Robert Juillard *m* Georges Van Parys
☆ Gérard Philipe, Michèle Morgan, Brigitte Bardot, Yves Robert, Jean Desailly, Pierre Dux

Grandma's Boy *
US 1922 50m approx (24 fps) bw silent
Associated Exhibitors (Hal Roach)
Inspired by the heroism of his own grandpa, a meek and mild young fellow subdues a terrifying tramp.
Modest second-feature-length comedy of a burgeoning star, no great shakes by his later standards.
w Harold Lloyd, Sam Taylor, Jean Havez *d* Fred Newmeyer
☆ Harold Lloyd, Dick Sutherland, Anna Townsend

Granny Get Your Gun
US 1939 56m bw
Warner
An indomitable old lady turns sheriff to get her granddaughter off the hook for murder.
Energetic second feature comedy mystery from a Perry Mason story; pleasant performances.
w Kenneth Gamet *d* George Amy
☆ May Robson, Harry Davenport, Margot Stevenson, Hardie Albright

'The thousands who have read the book will know why WE WILL NOT SELL ANY CHILDREN TICKETS to see this picture!'
The Grapes of Wrath ****
US 1940 128m bw
TCF (Darryl Zanuck, Nunnally Johnson)
After the dust-bowl disaster of the thirties, Oklahoma farmers trek to California in the hope of a better life.
A superb film which could scarcely be improved upon. Though the ending is softened from the book, there was too much here for filmgoers to chew on. Acting, photography, direction combine to make this an unforgettable experience, a poem of a film.
w Nunnally Johnson novel John Steinbeck *d John Ford ph Gregg Toland m* Alfred Newman *ad* Richard Day, Mark Lee Kirk *ed* Robert Simpson
☆ *Henry Fonda* (Tom Joad), *Jane Darwell* (Ma Joad), *John Carradine* (Casy), Charley Grapewin (Grandpa), Dorris Bowdon (Rosasharn), Russell Simpson (Pa Joad), Zeffie Tilbury (Grandma), O. Z. Whitehead (Al), John Qualen (Muley), Eddie Quillan (Connie), Grant Mitchell

TOM (HENRY FONDA) READING GRAVE MARKER: 'This here's William James Joad, died of a stroke, old, old man. His fokes bured him because they got no money to pay for funerls. Nobody kilt him. Just a stroke and he died.'

MA (JANE DARWELL): 'Rich fellas come up, an' they die, an' their kids ain't no good, an' they die out. But we keep a-comin'. We're the people that live. Can't lick us. We'll go on forever, Pa, because we're the people.'

MA: 'Well, Pa, woman can change better'n a man. Man lives – well, in jerks. Baby born or somebody dies, that's a jerk. Gets a farm or loses one, an' that's a jerk. With a woman, it's all one flow, like a stream – little eddies, little waterfalls – but the river, it goes right on. Woman looks at it that way.'

'A genuinely great motion picture which makes one proud to have even a small share in the affairs of the cinema.' – *Howard Barnes*
'The most mature motion picture that has ever been made, in feeling, in purpose, and in the use of the medium.' – *Otis Ferguson*
'A sincere and searing indictment of man's cruel indifference to his fellows.' – *Basil Wright*
🏆 John Ford; Jane Darwell
🎗 best picture; Nunnally Johnson; Henry Fonda; Robert Simpson

Grass *
US 1925 50m approx bw silent
Famous Players-Lasky
Nomadic Iranian tribes make an annual migration in search of fresh pasture.
Striking early documentary marred by facetious subtitles.
wd/ph Merian C. Cooper, Ernest Schoedsack *titles* Terry Ramsaye

The Grass Harp *
US 1995 106m colour
Pathé/Grass Harp/Fine Line (Charles Matthau, Jerry Tokofsky, John Davis, James J. Davis)
In America in the 30s, a teenage boy goes to live with his two aunts whose quarrel splits the neighbourhood.
Slight, ineffectual, anecdotal account of small-town life; its pleasures, too, are small.
w Sterling Silliphant, Kirk Ellis *novel* Truman Capote *d* Charles Matthau *ph* John A. Alonzo *m* Patrick Williams *pd* Paul Sylbert *ed* Sidney Levin, C. Timothy O'Leary
☆ Piper Laurie, Sissy Spacek, Walter Matthau, Edward Furlong, Nell Carter, Jack Lemmon, Mary Steenburgen, Sean Patrick Flanery, Joe Don Baker, Charles Durning, Roddy McDowall, Mia Kirshner
'A tale steeped in tragic loss tempered with a wit that engages and meanders to almost equal effect.' – *Bob McCabe, Empire*

The Grass Is Greener *
GB 1960 104m Technirama
Grandon (Stanley Donen)
The wife of an English earl falls for an American millionaire tourist.
Heavy-going and unsuitably widescreened version of an agreeable piece of West End fluff. Performances just about save it.
w Hugh and Margaret Williams *play* Hugh and Margaret Williams *d* Stanley Donen *ph* Christopher Challis *m/ly* Noël Coward *md* Muir Mathieson
☆ Cary Grant, Deborah Kerr, Robert Mitchum, *Jean Simmons, Moray Watson*
'It's too bad Coward couldn't have written the wisecracks too.' – *Philip T. Hartung*
'The stars do not glitter or even glow. Instead of being liberated and propelled by the screenplay, they are chained and sunk. It is one of the year's most disappointing films.' – *James Powers, Hollywood Reporter*

The Grasshopper
US 1969 98m Technicolor
NGP (Jerry Belson, Garry Marshall)
A small-town girl goes from man to man in Los Angeles and Las Vegas, finally becoming a call girl.
The road to ruin in modern dress; nicely made and quite entertaining in its gaudy way.
w Jerry Belson *novel The Passing of Evil* by Mark MacShane *d* Jerry Paris *ph* Sam Leavitt *m* Billy Goldenberg
☆ Jacqueline Bisset, Jim Brown, Joseph Cotten, Corbett Monica

Grave Indiscretions: see *The Grotesque*

'4 kids. 3 bodies. 2 fights. 1 night. No $!*'
Gravesend *
US 1997 85m Technicolor
Manga/Island/Brooklynwood/Gravesend (Salvatore Stabile)
Four Brooklyn layabouts attempt to dispose of the body when one accidentally shoots his friend's brother.
Oliver Stone endorsed this slice of street life, which has an authenticity, as well as a touch of slickness, about its account of losers losing what little they have.
wd Salvatore Stabile *ph* Joseph Dell'Olio *m* Bill Laswell *ed* Miranda Davin
☆ Tony Tucci, Michael Parducci, Tom Malloy, Thomas Brandise, Sean Quinn, Macky Aquilino
'This is about as cutting edge as movies get.' – *Ian Freer, Empire*
† Stabile shot his film on the streets of New York with the aid of a $5,000 inheritance, though it cost another $60,000 to bring it to its final polish.

The Graveyard: see *Persecution*

Graveyard Shift
US 1990 86m DeLuxe
Columbia TriStar/Graveyard Inc (William J. Dunn, Ralph S. Singleton)
Workers in a rat-infested, run-down mill investigate a mysterious killer beast in the cellars.
Dreary, badly made horror movie that fails on every level.
w John Esposito *story* Stephen King *d* Ralph S. Singleton *ph* Peter Stein *m* Anthony Marinelli, Brian Banks *pd* Gary Wissner *ed* Jim Gross, Randy Jon Morgan
☆ David Andrews, Kelly Wolf, Stephen Macht, Andrew Divoff, Vic Polizos, Brad Dourif, Robert Alan Beuth, Ilona Margolis
'Miserably inept.' – *Sight and Sound*

The Gravy Train *
US 1974 96m Eastmancolor
Columbia-Warner/Tomorrow Entertainment (Jonathan T. Taplin)
aka: *The Dion Brothers*
Two working-class brothers throw up their jobs and take to crime with bloody results.
Moderately entertaining caper, which manages to mix comedy and mayhem with some success.
w Bill Kerby, David Whitney (Terrence Malick) *d* Jack Starrett *ph* Jerry Hirshfeld *pd* Stan Jolley *ed* John Horger
☆ Stacy Keach, Frederic Forrest, Margot Kidder, Barry Primus, Richard Romanus, Denny Miller

Gray Lady Down
US 1978 111m Technicolor Panavision
Universal/Mirisch (Walter Mirisch)
After a collision, an American submarine lodges in the neck of an underwater canyon.
A rather boring update of Morning Departure *with added technology.*
w James Whittaker, Howard Sackler *novel Event 1000* by David Levallee *d* David Greene *ph* Stevan Larner *m* Jerry Fielding
☆ Charlton Heston, David Carradine, Stacy Keach, Ned Beatty, Stephen McHattie, Ronny Cox, Dorian Harewood, Rosemary Forsyth
'The crew eventually reach the surface, but the film deserves to sink without trace.' – *Nicholas Wapshott, The Times*

Grayeagle
US 1977 104m Movielab Panavision
Orion/AIP (Charles B. Pierce)
In Montana in the 1840s, a settler tracks the Indian who kidnapped his daughter.
Overlong Western, which owes something to The Searchers, *though it is less complex and not hung up on matters of race; the acting, for the most part, and for most parts, is so ripe that it is almost rotten.*
wd Charles B. Pierce *story* Brad White, Mike Sajbel *ph* Jim Roberson *m* Jaime Mendoza-Nava *ed* Jim Roberson
☆ Ben Johnson, Iron Eyes Cody, Lana Wood, Jack Elam, Paul Fix, Alex Cord, Jacob Daniels, Jimmy Clem, Charles B. Pierce

Gray's Anatomy *
US/GB 1996 80m colour
Independent Film Channel/BBC (John Hardy)
Spalding Gray describes his medical experiences, conventional and alternative, when he discovered that he had a problem with the vision in his left eye.
Moderately engaging monologue, with some distracting direction and ineffectual vox pop interviews. It has about it an air of contrivance, as if the various therapies were tried in order to provide good material for an amusing monologue.
w Spalding Gray *d* Steven Soderbergh *ph* Elliot Davies *m* Cliff Martinez *pd* Adele Plauché *ed* Susan Littenberg
☆ Spalding Gray

Grease **
US 1978 110m Metrocolor Panavision
Paramount/Robert Stigwood, Allan Carr
The path of true love in a fifties high school does not run smoothly.
Amiable 'period' musical for teenagers: a highly fashionable exploitation of the new star John Travolta, its commercialism was undeniable, and it carefully built in appeal to older age groups.
w Bronte Woodard *stage musical* Jim Jacobs, Warren Casey *d* Randal Kleiser *ph* Bill Butler *m/ly* Jim Jacobs, Warren Casey *md* Louis St Louis *ch* Patricia Birch *pd* Phil Jefferies *ed* John F. Burnett *titles* John Wilson
☆ *John Travolta, Olivia Newton-John,* Stockard Channing, Eve Arden, Frankie Avalon, Joan Blondell, Edd Byrnes, Sid Caesar, Alice Ghostley, Sha Na Na, Jeff Conaway, Barry Pearl, Michael Tucci
'A bogus, clumsily jointed pastiche of late fifties high school musicals, studded with leftovers from *West Side Story* and *Rebel Without A Cause.*' – *New Yorker*
🎗 song, 'Hopelessly Devoted to You' (*m/ly* John Farrar)

Grease 2
US 1982 114m Metrocolor Panavision
Paramount (Robert Stigwood, Allan Carr)
In 1961 an English boy causes emotional problems when he joins the senior class of Rydell High School.
Despite the mixture as before, this sequel was a resounding flop in all departments, perhaps proving that the success of the original was only a fluke of timing.
w Ken Finkleman *d* Patricia Birch *ph* Frank Stanley *md* Louis St Louis *songs* various
☆ Maxwell Caulfield, Michelle Pfeiffer, Adrian Zmed, Lorna Luft, Eve Arden, Sid Caesar, Tab Hunter, Connie Stevens
'It's like being cooped up for two hours inside a combination of juke box and pinball machine, with you as the ball.' – *Daily Mail*

Greased Lightning
US 1977 96m Movielab
Third World (Hannah Weinstein)
A black Virginian moonshiner becomes a famous stock car racer.
Fashionable action hokum based on a real character.
w Kenneth Vose, Lawrence DuKore, Melvin Van Peebles, Leon Capetanos *d* Michael Schultz *ph* George Bouillet *m* Fred Karlin
☆ Richard Pryor, Beau Bridges, Pam Grier, Cleavon Little, Vincent Gardenia

The Great Adventure: see *The Adventurers (1950)*

The Great Adventure **
Sweden 1953 73m bw
Arne Sucksdorff
Two boys on a farm rescue an otter and keep it as a pet.
Superbly photographed wildlife film featuring a variety of small animals.
m Lars Erik Larsson *wd/ed/ph* Arne Sucksdorff
☆ Anders Norberg, Kjell Sucksdorff, Arne Sucksdorff

The Great Alaskan Mystery *
US 1944 bw serial: 13 eps
Universal
Dr Miller invents a defence weapon called the Peratron, and goes to Alaska, followed by evil fascists, in search of the one element which will make it work.
Good serial stuff with a remarkably recognizable cast, and Ralph Morgan for once not the villain.
d Ray Taylor, Lewis D. Collins
☆ Milburn Stone, Marjorie Weaver, Edgar Kennedy, Ralph Morgan, Samuel S. Hinds, Martin Kosleck, Joseph Crehan, Fuzzy Knight, Harry Cording

The Great American Broadcast *
US 1941 90m bw
TCF (Kenneth MacGowan)
A romantic triangle set against the burgeoning years of the radio industry.
Pleasant musical, amusing if historically inaccurate.
w Don Ettlinger, Edwin Blum, Robert Ellis, Helen Logan *d* Archie Mayo *ph* Leon Shamroy, Peverell Marley *m/ly* Mack Gordon, Harry Warren

☆ Alice Faye, John Payne, Jack Oakie, Cesar Romero, The Ink Spots, The Nicholas Brothers, The Wiere Brothers

The Great American Pastime
US 1956 89m bw
MGM (Henry Berman)
A mild lawyer takes over a junior baseball team but incurs parental jealousy.
Thin lower-bracket comedy.
w Nathaniel Benchley *d* Herman Hoffman
ph Arthur E. Arling *m* Jeff Alexander
☆ Tom Ewell, Anne Francis, Ann Miller, Dean Jones, Raymond Bailey

The Great Awakening: see *New Wine*

The Great Balloon Adventure: see *Olly Olly Oxen Free*

Great Balls of Fire!
US 1989 107m colour
Rank/Orion (Adam Fields)
Biopic of the country rock singer Jerry Lee Lewis.
Unimaginative, unfactual treatment that conveys little of the performer's qualities.
w Jack Baran, Jim McBride *book* Myra Lewis, Murray Silver *d* Jim McBride *ph* Affonso Beato *pd* David Nichols *ed* Lisa Day, Pembroke Herring, Bert Lovitt
☆ Dennis Quaid, Winona Ryder, John Doe, Joe Bob Briggs, Stephen Tobolowsky, Trey Wilson, Alec Baldwin, Steve Allen, Lisa Blount, Joshua Sheffield

The Great Bank Robbery *
US 1969 98m colour Panavision
Warner (Malcolm Stuart)
Would-be bank robbers turn up in a Western town disguised as priests.
Western spoof without the courage of its convictions, but easy enough to watch.
w William Peter Blatty *novel* Frank O'Rourke *d* Hy Averback *ph* Fred J. Koenekamp *m* Nelson Riddle
☆ Kim Novak, Zero Mostel, Clint Walker, Claude Akins, Akim Tamiroff, Larry Storch, John Anderson, Sam Jaffe, Ruth Warrick, Elisha Cook Jnr

The Great Caruso **
US 1951 109m Technicolor
MGM (Joe Pasternak)
Semi-fictional biography of the Italian tenor.
Dramatically flat but opulently staged biopic, turned into a star vehicle and a huge commercial success.
w Sonya Levien, William Ludwig *d* Richard Thorpe *ph* Joseph Ruttenberg *md* Johnny Green, Peter Herman Adler
☆ Mario Lanza, Ann Blyth, Dorothy Kirsten, Jarmila Novotna, Carl Benton Reid, Eduard Franz, Richard Hageman, Ludwig Donath, Alan Napier
'Sounds like a recorded programme of excerpts from "Operas You Have Loved" which indeed it is.' – *C. A. Lejeune*
Johnny Green, Peter Herman Adler

Great Catherine
GB 1968 98m Technicolor
Warner/Keep Films (Jules Buck)
An English captain visits the court of Catherine the Great.
Chaos results from the attempt to inflate an ill-considered Shavian whimsy into a feature film: the material is simply insufficient and the performances flounder in irrelevant production values.
w Hugh Leonard *play* Bernard Shaw *d* Gordon Flemyng *ph* Oswald Morris *m* Dimitri Tiomkin *pd* John Bryan
☆ Jeanne Moreau, Peter O'Toole, Zero Mostel, Jack Hawkins, Marie Lohr, Akim Tamiroff, Marie Kean, Kenneth Griffith
'All Shaw's jokes work very well, but the film has been padded out with Cossack dances, frantic chases, and unfunny slapstick.' – *Michael Billington, Illustrated London News*

The Great Dan Patch
US 1949 92m bw
United Artists (W. R. Frank)
The career of a famous racehorse at the turn of the century.
Modest small-town crowd-pleaser.
w John Taintor Foote *d* Joseph Newman
☆ Dennis O'Keefe, Gail Russell, Ruth Warrick, Charlotte Greenwood, Henry Hull, John Hoyt, Arthur Hunnicutt

Great Day
GB 1945 79m bw
RKO British (Victor Hanbury)
A village Women's Institute prepares for a visit by Mrs Roosevelt.
Modestly pleasing little drama from a successful play.
w Wolfgang Wilhelm, John Davenport *play* Lesley Storm *d* Lance Comfort *ph* Erwin Hillier
☆ Eric Portman, Flora Robson, Sheila Sim, Isabel Jeans, Walter Fitzgerald, Philip Friend, Marjorie Rhodes, Maire O'Neill, Beatrice Varley

A Great Day in Harlem **
US 1995 bw/colour
Flo-Bert/NYFA (Jean Bach)
The story of the day in 1958 when Art Kane gathered more than 50 leading jazz musicians together to take a now-famous photograph for *Esquire*, as remembered by some of those involved.
A heart-warming documentary, using still photography, by Dizzy Gillespie, Mary Lou Williams, Mike Lipskin and others, and 8mm colour film shot by bassist Milt Hinton and his wife Mona, and performances from the television documentary The Sound of Jazz. *What comes through most strongly is the participants' respect and affection for one another; it is essential viewing for anyone interested in jazz or in the pleasure artists can take in the abilities of their peers.*
w Jean Bach, Susan Peehl, Matthew Seig *d* Jean Bach *ph* Steve Petropoulos *ed* Susan Peehl
☆ Quincy Jones (narrator)
'A likeable, intelligently original and moving documentary.' – *Sight and Sound*

Great Day in the Morning
US 1955 92m Technicolor Superscope
RKO/Edmund Grainger
At the outbreak of the Civil War, Denver has divided loyalties.
Solemn semi-Western without much excitement.
w Lesser Samuels *novel* Robert Hardy Andrews *d* Jacques Tourneur *ph* William Snyder *m* Leith Stevens
☆ Robert Stack, Virginia Mayo, Ruth Roman, Alex Nicol, Raymond Burr, Regis Toomey

The Great Dictator **
US 1940 129m bw
United Artists/Charles Chaplin
A Jewish barber is mistaken for dictator Adenoid Hynkel.
Chaplin's satire on Hitler has a few funny moments, but the rest is heavy going, the production is cheeseparing, and the final speech to the world is a grave mistake.
wd Charles Chaplin *ph* Karl Struss, Rollie Totheroh *m* Meredith Willson *ad* J. Russell Spencer *ed* Willard Nico
☆ *Charles Chaplin* (Hynkel/a Jewish barber), Paulette Goddard (Hannah), *Jack Oakie* (Napaloni), Reginald Gardiner (Schultz), Henry Daniell (Garbitsch), Billy Gilbert (Herring), Maurice Moscovich (Mr Jaeckel)
'For this film he takes on more than a mimed representation of common humanity; he states, and accepts, the responsibility of being one of humanity's best and most widely-known representatives.' – *Basil Wright*
'The last impassioned speech about peace and serenity still wrecks everything that has gone before: Chaplin mawkish can always overrule Chaplin the innocent mime.' – *New Yorker, 1978*
'You must go back to *Intolerance* for another motion picture that is so completely one man's personal expression of his attitude on something about which he feels deeply and passionately.' – *James Shelley Hamilton, National Board of Review*
'No time for comedy? Yes, I say, time for comedy. Time for Chaplin comedy. No time ever for Chaplin to preach as he does in those last six minutes, no matter how deeply he may feel what he wrote and says. He is not a good preacher. Indeed, he is frighteningly bad.' – *John O'Hara*
'Some moments actually work, but they are very few and far between.' – *Time Out, 1984*
best picture; Charles Chaplin (as writer and actor); Meredith Willson; Jack Oakie

The Great Escape **
US 1963 173m DeLuxe Panavision
UA/Mirisch/Alpha (John Sturges)
Allied prisoners plan to escape from a German prison camp.
Pretty good but overlong POW adventure with a tragic ending that gave Steve McQueen his defining role.
w James Clavell, W. R. Burnett *book* Paul Brickhill *d* John Sturges *ph Daniel Fapp* *m* Elmer Bernstein
☆ James Garner, *Steve McQueen*, Richard Attenborough, James Donald, Charles Bronson, Donald Pleasence, James Coburn, David McCallum, Gordon Jackson, John Leyton, Nigel Stock

Great Expectations
US 1934 100m bw
Universal
A poor boy becomes unexpectedly rich and mistakes the source of his good fortune.
Solidly carpentered but never inspired version of a sprawling novel later tackled with much more style by David Lean. See below.
w Gladys Unger *novel* Charles Dickens *d* Stuart Walker *m* Edward Ward
☆ Phillips Holmes (Pip), Jane Wyatt (Estella), Henry Hull (Magwitch), Florence Reed (Miss Havisham), Alan Hale (Joe Gargery), Rafaela Ottiano (Mrs Joe), Francis L. Sullivan (Jaggers)
'First half represents a fine achievement … and then it all falls apart.' – *Variety*

Great Expectations ****
GB 1946 118m bw
Rank/Cineguild (Anthony Havelock-Allan)
A boy meets an escaped convict on the Romney Marshes, with strange consequences for both of them.
Despite the inevitable simplifications, this is a superbly pictorial rendering of a much-loved novel, with all the famous characters in safe hands and masterly judgement in every department.
w Ronald Neame, David Lean, Kay Walsh, Cecil McGivern, Anthony Havelock-Allan *d David Lean* *ph Guy Green* *m* Walter Goehr *ad* John Bryan *ed* Jack Harris
☆ *John Mills* (Pip), Bernard Miles (Joe Gargery), *Finlay Currie* (Abel Magwitch), *Martita Hunt* (Miss Havisham), Valerie Hobson (Estella), *Jean Simmons* (Young Estalla), Alec Guinness (Herbert Pocket), Francis L. Sullivan (Jaggers), Anthony Wager (Young Pip), Ivor Barnard (Wemmick), Freda Jackson (Mrs Joe Gargery), Hay Petrie (Uncle Pumblechook), O. B. Clarence (Aged Parent), George Hayes (Compeyson), Torin Thatcher (Betley Drummle) and also Eileen Erskine (Biddy)
'The first big British film to have been made, a film that sweeps our cloistered virtues out into the open.' – *Richard Winnington*
'The best Dickens adaptation, and arguably David Lean's finest film.' – *NFT, 1969*
'It does for Dickens what *Henry V* did for Shakespeare. That is, it indicates a sound method for translating him from print to film … almost never less than graceful, tasteful and intelligent, and some of it better than that.' – *James Agee*
† It was remade as a less than memorable TV movie in 1974, directed by Joseph Hardy and starring Michael York, Sarah Miles and James Mason.
†† Robert Krasker was the original cinematographer, but was replaced after Lean found his photography flat and uninteresting.
Guy Green; John Bryan
best picture; script; David Lean (as director)

'She'll only break your heart – yet you'll still pursue her.'
Great Expectations
US 1998 111m DeLuxe Panavision
TCF (Art Linson)
In Florida, an orphan helps an escaped convict and his life is transformed.
A modern version of Charles Dickens's novel, with its hero turned into a brooding artist; despite the care lavished upon it, the picture is devoid of life.
w Mitch Glazer *novel* Charles Dickens *d* Alfonso Cuaron *ph* Emmmanuel Lubezki *m* Patrick Doyle *pd* Tony Burrough *ed* Steven Weisberg
☆ Ethan Hawke, Gwyneth Paltrow, Hank Azaria, Chris Cooper, Ann Bancroft, Robert de Niro, Josh Mostel, Kim Dickens, Nell Campbell
'Despite the dream-team production, despite the star-packed cast and its strong back-up characters, despite some ravishing camera-work, the film *Great Expectations* is a turkey. The actors can't get inside their characters.' – *John Sutherland, Guardian*

The Great Flamarion
US 1945 78m bw
Republic
A jealous vaudeville sharpshooter hunts down and kills the woman he loves because she prefers another.
Heavy-handed melodrama reminiscent of German silents but without their flair.
w Heinz Harald, Ann Wigton, Richard Weil *d* Anthony Mann
☆ Erich von Stroheim, Dan Duryea, Mary Beth Hughes

The Great Flirtation
US 1934 71m bw
Paramount
An actor is jealous of his wife's stardom.
Would-be sophisticated comedy with far too many loose ends.
w Humphrey Pearson *story* Gregory Ratoff *d* Ralph Murphy
☆ Adolphe Menjou, Elissa Landi, David Manners, Lynne Overman, Raymond Walburn, Paul Porcasi, Akim Tamiroff
'Hardly a picture of strong audience appeal.' – *Variety*

The Great Gabbo
US 1929 88m bw
Sono Art
A ventriloquist's personality is taken over by that of his dummy.
Yes, that old chestnut, here in tedious and primitive early talkie form.
w F. Hugh Herbert *story* Ben Hecht *d* James Cruze
☆ Erich von Stroheim, Betty Compson, Margie Kane

The Great Garrick **
US 1937 91m bw
Warner (Mervyn Le Roy)
When Garrick goes to act in Paris, members of the Comédie Française take over a wayside inn and try to teach him a lesson, but the plan goes awry.
A pleasant unhistorical conceit makes a rather literary film to have come from Hollywood, but it is all very winning and cast and director keep the fun simmering happily.
w Ernest Vajda *d James Whale* *ph* Ernest Haller *m* Adolph Deutsch
☆ *Brian Aherne*, Edward Everett Horton, Olivia de Havilland, Lionel Atwill, *Melville Cooper*, *Luis Alberni*, *étienne Girardot*, Marie Wilson, Lana Turner, Albert Dekker, Fritz Leiber, Dorothy Tree, Chester Clute
'Finely made period romantic comedy, but its reception at the paygate is extremely problematical.' – *Variety*
'As elegantly witty as anything Whale ever did.' – *Tom Milne*
'A jestful and romantic piece.' – *Frank S. Nugent, New York Times*

The Great Gatsby *
US 1949 90m bw
Paramount (Richard Maibaum)
Events leading to the death of a retired gangster and mysterious Long Island plutocrat.

Rather bland and uninteresting attempt to accommodate a unique author to a formula star.
w Richard Maibaum novel F. Scott Fitzgerald d Elliott Nugent ph John Seitz m Robert Emmett Dolan
☆ Alan Ladd, Macdonald Carey, Betty Field, Barry Sullivan, Howard da Silva
† A silent version in 1926 had starred Warner Baxter.

The Great Gatsby **
US 1974 146m Eastmancolor
Paramount/Newdon (David Merrick)
Plush version with lavish production values and pleasing period sense but not much grip on the story or characters. Overlong footage is not made to seem shorter by snail's pace and dull performances.
w Francis Ford Coppola d Jack Clayton ph Douglas Slocombe m Nelson Riddle pd John Box
☆ Robert Redford, Mia Farrow, Karen Black, Scott Wilson, *Sam Waterston*, Lois Chiles
'Pays its creator the regrettable tribute of erecting a mausoleum over his work.' – *Richard Combs*
'Leaves us more involved with six-and-a-half-million dollars' worth of trappings than with human tragedy.' – *Judith Crist*
'A total failure of every requisite sensibility.' – *Stanley Kauffmann*
'Profoundly unfilmable: a poetic and ultimately pessimistic comment on the American dream is transformed by cinematic realism into pure prose.' – *Michael Billington, Illustrated London News*
Academy Award: Nelson Riddle; costumes (Theoni V. Aldredge)
BAFTA: Douglas Slocombe; John Box

The Great Gilbert and Sullivan: see *The Story of Gilbert and Sullivan*

The Great Gildersleeve
US 1942 61m bw
RKO (Herman Schlom)
A small town loudmouth is always in hot water.
Unremarkable film début for a radio character from Fibber McGee and Molly. Three more second features followed.
w Jack Townley, Joseph Josephson d Gordon Douglas
☆ Harold Peary, Jane Darwell, Nancy Gates, Charles Arnt, Thurston Hall

Great Guns *
US 1941 74m bw
TCF (Sol M. Wurtzel)
A young millionaire's retainers join the army with him.
Disappointing Laurel and Hardy comedy, their first for Fox and the beginning of their decline. A few good jokes, but no overall control or inventiveness.
w Lou Breslow d Monty Banks ph Glen MacWilliams m Emil Newman ed Al de Gaetano
☆ Stan Laurel, Oliver Hardy, Sheila Ryan, Dick Nelson, Edmund Macdonald, Charles Trowbridge, Ludwig Stossel, Mae Marsh

Great Guy *
US 1936 73m bw
Grand National (Douglas Maclean)
GB title: *Pluck of the Irish*
An ex-prizefighter joins the bureau of weights and measures and fights corruption.
Rather tame racket film, Cagney's first independent venture away from Warner. He atones for rather thin production values.
w Henry McCarthy, Henry Johnson, James Edward Grant, Harry Ruskin d John G. Blystone ph Jack McKenzie m Marlin Skiles
☆ James Cagney, Mae Clarke, James Burke, Edward Brophy, Henry Kolker
'It's all typical Cagney stuff, and that's the trouble with it. Cagney apparently is doing the things he likes best, but they're repetitious and apt to disappoint a public anticipating something finer from this star after his quite lengthy absence.' – *Variety*

The Great Impersonation *
US 1935 81m bw
Universal (Edmund Grainger)
During World War I, a German murders an English nobleman and, being his double, takes over.
Reliable espionage melodrama with atmospheric country house asides, from a sturdily compelling novel.
w Frank Wead, Eve Greene novel E. Phillips Oppenheim d Alan Crosland ph Milton Krasner m Franz Waxman
☆ Edmund Lowe, Valerie Hobson, Wera Engels, Henry Mollison, Lumsden Hare, Spring Byington, Charles Waldron, Dwight Frye
'They giggled a bit when Lowe went to bed with candles, and an hour later a sliding panel attempt on his life has him pushing an electric light switch ... probably doesn't matter that the 1914 characters are dressed throughout in 1935 modishness and drive around in streamlined automobiles.' – *Variety*
† It was previously filmed in 1921 with James Kirkwood.

The Great Impersonation *
US 1942 71m bw
Universal (Paul Malvern)
Okay quickie updating of the above, serviceable rather than inventive.
w W. Scott Darling d John Rawlins ph George Robinson m Hans Salter
☆ *Ralph Bellamy*, Evelyn Ankers, Aubrey Mather, Edward Norris, Karen Verne, Henry Daniell, Ludwig Stossel

The Great Imposter *
US 1961 112m bw
U-I (Robert Arthur)
The career of Ferdinand Waldo Demara, a marine and Trappist monk who also impersonated a Harvard research fellow, a prison warden, a naval doctor and a schoolteacher.
Uncertain mood hampers this biopic of a likeable fantasist.
w Liam O'Brien book Robert Crichton d Robert Mulligan ph Robert Burks m Henry Mancini
☆ *Tony Curtis*, Raymond Massey, Karl Malden, Edmond O'Brien, Arthur O'Connell, Gary Merrill, Frank Gorshin, Joan Blackman, Robert Middleton

Great – Isambard Kingdom Brunel *
GB 1975 28m Eastmancolor
British Lion
A musical, animated biography of the great Victorian engineer.
Quite unexpected, and therefore the more delightful.
w Bob Godfrey d *Bob Godfrey*

The Great John L.
US 1945 96m bw
UA/Bing Crosby Productions (Frank Mastroly, James Edward Grant)
GB title: *A Man Called Sullivan*
Women in the life of prizefighter John L. Sullivan.
Very mild period biopic without the zest of Gentleman Jim.
w James Edward Grant d Frank Tuttle ph James Van Trees m Victor Young
☆ Greg McClure, Linda Darnell, Barbara Britton, Lee Sullivan, Otto Kruger, Wallace Ford, Robert Barrat

'Sometimes there's a terrible penalty for telling the truth...'
The Great Lie ***
US 1941 107m bw
Warner (Hal B. Wallis, Henry Blanke)
A determined girl loses the man she loves, believes him dead in a plane crash, and takes over the baby which his selfish wife does not want.
Absurd melodrama becomes top-flight entertainment with all concerned in cracking form and special attention on the two bitchy female leads, splendidly played. Classical music trimmings, too.
w Lenore Coffee novel *January Heights* by Polan Banks d *Edmund Goulding* ph *Tony Gaudio* m *Max Steiner*
☆ *Bette Davis, Mary Astor, George Brent*, Lucile Watson, Hattie McDaniel, Grant Mitchell, Jerome Cowan
Academy Award: Mary Astor

The Great Locomotive Chase *
US 1956 76m Technicolor Cinemascope
Walt Disney (Lawrence Edward Watkin)
During the Civil War, Union spies steal a train and destroy track and bridges behind them.
A serious version of Buster Keaton's The General, *based on a true incident; good sequences but no overall pace.*
w Lawrence Edward Watkin d Francis D. Lyon ph Charles Boyle m Paul Smith
☆ Fess Parker, Jeffrey Hunter, Jeff York, John Lupton, Kenneth Tobey

The Great Lover *
US 1949 80m bw
(Paramount) Hope Enterprises (Edmund Beloin)
On a transatlantic liner, a timid scoutmaster catches a strangler.
Amusing suspense comedy, a good star vehicle.
w Edmund Beloin, Melville Shavelson, Jack Rose d Alexander Hall ph Charles Lang m Joseph J. Lilley
☆ *Bob Hope*, Rhonda Fleming, *Roland Young*, Jim Backus, Roland Culver, George Reeves

The Great Man **
US 1956 92m bw
U-I (Aaron Rosenberg)
A memorial programme to a much-loved TV personality turns into an exposé.
Patchy melodrama with a Citizen Kane *framework; the best bits are very effective.*
w *José Ferrer, Al Morgan* novel Al Morgan d José Ferrer ph Harold Lipstein m Herman Stein
☆ José Ferrer, Dean Jagger, Keenan Wynn, *Julie London*, Joanne Gilbert, *Ed Wynn*, Jim Backus
'Its distinction is in its unwavering tone – one of blunt and frequently savage irony and cynicism.' – *MFB*
'The movie is almost over before one realizes what a slick, fast sell it is (resembling nothing so much as what it is attacking).' – *Pauline Kael, 1968*

The Great Man Votes *
US 1938 72m bw
RKO (Cliff Reid)
A drunken professor turns out to have the casting vote in a local election.
Slow-starting but progressively funny political comedy with some favourite talents in good form.
w John Twist story Gordon Malherbe Hillman d *Garson Kanin* ph Russell Metty m Roy Webb
☆ *John Barrymore*, Virginia Weidler, Peter Holden, *William Demarest, Donald MacBride*
'It will be hailed by class audiences as a fine example of the film art, yet carrying sock appeal for mass patronage.' – *Variety*

The Great Manhunt: see *The Doolins of Oklahoma (1949)*

The Great Manhunt: see *State Secret (1950)*

The Great Man's Lady *
US 1941 90m bw
Paramount (William A. Wellman)
A Western pioneer is inspired and encouraged by his wife.
Adequate but unsurprising flashback family drama starting with its star as a lady of 109.
w W. L. Rivers story Vina Delmar d William A. Wellman ph William C. Mellor m Victor Young
☆ *Barbara Stanwyck*, Joel McCrea, Brian Donlevy, Katharine Stevens, Thurston Hall, Lloyd Corrigan

'He'll give you the biggest heart sock, laugh shock you ever thrilled to!'
The Great McGinty **
US 1940 83m bw
Paramount (Paul Jones)
GB title: *Down Went McGinty*
A hobo and a crook have a hectic political career.
Lively comedy-drama which signalled the arrival as director of a new and stimulating Hollywood talent.
wd *Preston Sturges* ph William C. Mellor m Frederick Hollander
☆ *Brian Donlevy, Akim Tamiroff*, Muriel Angelus, Louis Jean Heydt, Arthur Hoyt
PROLOGUE: 'This is the story of two men who met in a banana republic. One of them never did anything dishonest in his life except for one crazy minute. The other never did anything honest in his life except for one crazy minute. They both had to leave the country.'
'This is his first directing job and where has he been all our lives? He has that sense of the incongruous which makes some of the best gaiety.' – *Otis Ferguson*
'The tough dialogue is matched by short, snappy scenes; the picture seems to have wasted no time, no money.' – *Gilbert Seldes*
'A director as adroit and inventive as any in the business ... it starts like a five-alarm fire and never slackens pace for one moment until its unexpected conclusion.' – *Pare Lorentz*
'Sturges takes the success ethic and throws it in the face of the audience.' – *James Orsini*
'Capra with the gloves off.' – *Raymond Durgnat*
Academy Award: script

The Great McGonagall
GB 1974 89m Eastmancolor
Darlton
An unemployed Scot aims to become Queen Victoria's Poet Laureate.
Appalling tribute to a minor figure of sub-literature.
w Joe McGrath, Spike Milligan d Joe McGrath
☆ Spike Milligan, Peter Sellers, Julia Foster, Julian Chagrin, John Bluthal, Valentine Dyall, Victor Spinetti

The Great Missouri Raid
US 1950 81m Technicolor
Nat Holt/Paramount
Jesse and Frank James are seen as Civil War guerrillas, subsequently forced into crime by a vengeful officer.
Unsuccessful whitewash job, tediously told.
w Frank Gruber d Gordon Douglas
☆ Macdonald Carey, Wendell Corey, Ward Bond, Ellen Drew, Bruce Bennett, Bill Williams, Anne Revere, Edgar Buchanan

'They booed him to greatness!'
The Great Moment **
US 1944 83m bw
Paramount
How anaesthetics may have been invented.
Curious biopic of Dr W. T. G. Morgan, poised somewhere between utter seriousness and pratfall farce. The beginning of its director's decline, but always interesting in itself.
wd *Preston Sturges* book *Triumph over Pain* by René Fulop-Miller ph Victor Milner m Victor Young
☆ Joel McCrea, Betty Field, William Demarest, Harry Carey, Franklin Pangborn, Porter Hall, Grady Sutton
'Mr Sturges has triumphed over stiffness in screen biography.' – *New York Times*
'The careless, careful authority is there ... the contrivance is smart enough.' – *Sunday Times*

Great Moments in Aviation
GB 1994 92m colour
BBC Films (Phillippa Giles)
En route to London, a young West Indian woman begins a shipboard romance with a mysterious Scotsman who is accused of theft and murder by a fellow passenger.
Incoherent and arcane romantic drama with leaden dialogue that not even its talented cast can make meaningful.
w Jeanette Winterson d Beeban Kidron ph Remi Adefarasin m Rachel Portman pd Tony Burrough ed John Stothart
☆ Vanessa Redgrave, John Hurt, Jonathan Pryce, Dorothy Tutin, Rakie Ayola
'Damaged beyond repair by a mannered scripting style and evident recutting, this wingless relic looks commercially to stay confined to its hangar.' – *David Rooney, Variety*

The Great Mouse Detective *
US 1986 80m Technicolor
Walt Disney/Silver Screen Partners II (Burny Mattinson)
GB title: *Basil, The Great Mouse Detective*
A mouse who has studied Sherlock Holmes solves the mystery of a missing mouse toymaker and outwits the evil Professor Rattigan.

One of the better recent Disney cartoon features, but the texture will probably never again be so rich as in the days of Pinocchio *and* Bambi.
w Pete Young, Steven Hulett, John Musker, Matthew O'Callaghan, Dave Michener, Vance Gerry, Ron Clements, Bruce M. Morris, Melvin Shaw, Burney Mattinson *novel* *Basil of Baker Street* by Eve Titus *d* John Musker, Ron Clements, Dave Michener, Burney Mattinson *ph* Ed Austin *m* Henry Mancini *pd* Guy Vasilovich *ed* Roy M. Brewer Jnr, James Melton
☆ Featuring the voices of Barrie Ingham, Vincent Price, Val Bettin, Alan Young

The Great Mr Handel *
GB 1942 103m Technicolor
Rank/GHW (James B. Sloan)
How the 18th-century composer came to write the Messiah.
Earnest, unlikely biopic, naïve but rather commendable.
w Gerald Elliott, Victor MacClure *play* L. DuGarde Peach *d* Norman Walker *ph* Claude Friese-Greene, Jack Cardiff *md* Ernest Irving
☆ Wilfrid Lawson, Elizabeth Allan, Malcolm Keen, Michael Shepley, Hay Petrie, A. E. Matthews
'A graceful addition to the ranks of prestige pictures.' – *Kine Weekly*

The Great Muppet Caper **
GB 1981 97m Technicolor
ITC (David Lazer, Frank Oz)
Kermit and Fozzie are reporters sent to solve a jewel robbery.
Considerably livelier than The Muppet Movie *but a badly timed flop at the box-office, this genial caper has a pleasant collection of guest stars as well as showing the familiar puppets at their most typical.*
w Tom Patchett, Jay Tarses, Jerry Juhl, Jack Rose *d* Jim Henson *ph* Oswald Morris *m* Joe Raposo *pd* Harry Lange
☆ Diana Rigg, Charles Grodin, John Cleese, Robert Morley, Trevor Howard, Peter Ustinov, Jack Warden
'Large chunks are pleasingly daft.' – *Sight and Sound*
song 'The First Time It Happened' (*m/ly* Joe Raposo)

The Great Northfield Minnesota Raid *
US 1971 91m Technicolor
Universal/Robertson and Associates/Jennings Lang
In 1876 a gang of bandits, technically pardoned, plan a bank robbery.
'Realistic' Western in which the settings and photography have an impressively rough look but the script leaves much to be desired.
wd Philip Kaufman *ph* Bruce Surtees *m* Dave Grusin
☆ Cliff Robertson, Robert Duvall, Luke Askew, Elisha Cook Jnr

The Great O'Malley
US 1937 77m bw
Warner (Harry Joe Brown)
An overzealous cop cares for the wife and child of a petty criminal whom he has sent to prison.
Considering the talent involved, an astonishingly routine programmer.
w Milton Krims, Tom Reed *story* *The Making of O'Malley* by Gerald Beaumont *d* William Dieterle *ph* Ernest Haller *m* Heinz Roemheld
☆ Pat O'Brien, Humphrey Bogart, Ann Sheridan, Sybil Jason, Frieda Inescort, Donald Crisp, Henry O'Neill, Hobart Cavanaugh, Mary Gordon
'Familiar sentimental police theme: little action or appeal.' – *Variety*
† Previously filmed in 1923 with Milton Sills, as *The Making of O'Malley*.

The Great Outdoors
US 1988 90m CFI color Panavision
Universal/Hughes Entertainment (Arne L. Schmidt)
A family's holiday in the woods is disrupted by a surprise visit from their wealthy in-laws.
Broad and tiresome comedy in which its participants flail around noisily to no particular purpose.
w John Hughes *d* Howard Deutch *ph* Ric Waite *m* Thomas Newman *pd* John W. Corso *ed* Tom Rolf, William Gordean, Seth Flaum
☆ Dan Aykroyd, John Candy, Stephanie Faracy, Annette Bening, Chris Young, Ian Giatti, Hilary Gordon, Rebecca Gordon, Robert Prosky

The Great Profile *
US 1940 82m bw
TCF (Raymond Griffith)
A dissipated actor disgraces his family and becomes an acrobat.
Shapeless farce in which a great talent on his last legs parodies himself.
w Milton Sperling, Hilary Lynn *d* Walter Lang *ph* Ernest Palmer *m* Cyril Mockridge
☆ *John Barrymore*, Mary Beth Hughes, Gregory Ratoff, Anne Baxter, John Payne, Lionel Atwill, Edward Brophy, Willie Fung

'The greatest comedy ever made!'
The Great Race ***
US 1965 163m Technicolor Super Panavision
Warner/Patricia/Jalem/Reynard (Martin Jurow)
In 1908, the Great Leslie and Professor Fate are leading contenders in the first New York to Paris car race.
Elaborate comedy spectacular with many good moments, notably the early disasters, a Western saloon brawl, and a custard pie fight. Elsewhere, there is more evidence of an oversize budget than of wit or finesse, and the entire Prisoner of Zenda spoof could have been omitted. Excellent production detail and general good humour.
w Arthur Ross *d* Blake Edwards *ph* *Russell Harlan* *m* *Henry Mancini* *pd* *Fernando Carrere*
☆ *Jack Lemmon, Tony Curtis, Peter Falk, Natalie Wood*, George Macready, Ross Martin, Vivian Vance, Dorothy Provine
'The most expensive comedy ever filmed; but there the superlatives end: it is not exactly the worst.' – *Time*
Russell Harlan; song 'The Sweetheart Tree' (*m* Henry Mancini, *ly* Johnny Mercer)

The Great Rupert
US 1950 87m bw
Eagle Lion (George Pal)
A family of impoverished acrobats are assisted by a pet squirrel which proves lucky in more ways than one.
Modest whimsical comedy which outstays its welcome.
w Laslo Vadnay *d* Irving Pichel
☆ Jimmy Durante, Terry Moore, Tom Drake, Sara Haden, Frank Orth
† The squirrel was part puppet.

The Great St Trinian's Train Robbery
GB 1966 94m Eastmancolor
British Lion/Braywild (Leslie Gilliat)
The staff of St Trinian's is infiltrated by would-be train robbers.
Flat-footed farce with a sense of strain evident from first to last shot.
w Frank Launder, Ivor Herbert *d* Frank Launder, Sidney Gilliat *ph* Ken Hodges *m* Malcolm Arnold
☆ Frankie Howerd, Dora Bryan, Reg Varney, Desmond Walter-Ellis, Raymond Huntley, Richard Wattis, George Benson, Eric Barker, Godfrey Winn, George Cole, Colin Gordon, Barbara Couper, Elspeth Duxbury

The Great Santini *
US 1979 115m Technicolor
Warner/Orion/Bing Crosby Productions (Charles A. Pratt)
A crack fighter pilot has difficulty adjusting to peacetime domestic life.
Overlong but generally absorbing star character drama.
wd Lewis John Carlino *novel* Pat Conroy *ph* Ralph Woolsey *m* Elmer Bernstein *pd* Jack Poplin
☆ *Robert Duvall*, Blythe Danner, Michael O'Keefe, Lisa Jane Persky, Julie Anne Haddock
Robert Duvall; Michael O'Keefe (supporting actor)

'They were not forgotten by history – they were left out on purpose!'
The Great Scout and Cathouse Thursday
US 1976 102m Technicolor
AIP (Jules Buck and David Korda)
reissue title: *Wildcat*
While trying to revenge himself on an absconding partner, an old cowboy falls for a young prostitute.
Downright peculiar comedy Western which never seems to make up its mind what it's trying to be, and too often is merely embarrassing.
w Richard Shapiro *d* Don Taylor *ph* Alex Phillips Jnr *m* John Cameron *pd* Jack Martin Smith
☆ Lee Marvin, Oliver Reed, Kay Lenz, Robert Culp, Elizabeth Ashley, Strother Martin, Sylvia Miles
'It takes more than a dollop or two of sentiment and acres of dirty talk to make a movie.' – *Michael Billington, Illustrated London News*
'It sounds like the latest in the cute twosome series launched by *Butch Cassidy and the Sundance Kid*. In fact it features not two but seven wacky westerners who all seem addicted to stealing, hee-hawing, falling into puddles and punching each other in the privates.' – *Janet Maslin, Newsweek*

The Great Sinner *
US 1949 110m bw
MGM (Gottfried Reinhardt)
A serious young writer becomes a compulsive gambler.
Rather pointless and heavy-handed but extremely good-looking and splendidly cast period drama vaguely based on Dostoievsky.
w Ladislas Fodor, Christopher Isherwood *d* Robert Siodmak *ph* *George Folsey* *m* Bronislau Kaper *ad* *Cedric Gibbons, Hans Peters*
☆ Gregory Peck, *Walter Huston*, Ava Gardner, Agnes Moorehead, Ethel Barrymore, Melvyn Douglas, Frank Morgan

The Great Sioux Massacre
US 1965 93m Eastmancolor Cinemascope
Columbia/FF (Leon Fromkess)
Two officers are court-martialled after Custer's last stand.
Fragmentary flashback Western let down by production and performances.
w Fred C. Dobbs *d* Sidney Salkow *ph* Irving Lippman *m* Emil Newman, Edward B. Powell
☆ Joseph Cotten, Darren McGavin, Phil Carey, Nancy Kovack, Julie Sommars, Michael Pate

The Great Smokey Roadblock
US 1976 106m colour
Marvista (Ingo Preminger, Allan F. Bodoh)
original title: *The Last Of The Cowboys*
A truckdriver avoiding the finance company picks up an assortment of eccentrics and starts on a wild chase.
What possessed Henry Fonda to appear in this hick action melodrama will be forever unclear.
wd John Leone *ph* Ed Brown Snr *m* Craig Safan *ed* Corky Ehlers
☆ Henry Fonda, Eileen Brennan, John Byner, Dub Taylor, Susan Sarandon, Dana House, Robert Englund, Melanie Mayron, Valerie Curtin

The Great Spy Mission: see *Operation Crossbow*

The Great Stone Face *
US 1968 93m bw
Funnyman Productions
A very acceptable biography of Buster Keaton, with unusual emphasis on the very early films.
wd Vernon P. Becker

The Great Train Robbery ***
US 1903 10m approx bw silent
Edison
Bandits tie up a telegraph operator and rob a train, but are arrested.
In its day this was a real pioneer. It was among the longest films then made, it had the most complicated story line, it was the first Western and it used new technical tricks such as the pan and the close-up. Needless to say, it must now be viewed with sympathy.
wd Edwin S. Porter
☆ Marie Murray, Broncho Billy Anderson, George Barnes

The Great Train Robbery: see *The First Great Train Robbery (1978)*

'The grandest of love stories told to the tunes of the grandest musical score ever written!'
The Great Victor Herbert *
US 1939 91m bw
Paramount (Andrew L. Stone)
At the turn of the century a famous composer plays cupid to two young singers.
Pleasant minor musical with excellent songs and an infectious cheerfulness.
w Russel Crouse, Robert Lively *d* *Andrew L. Stone* *ph* Victor Milner *md* Phil Boutelje, Arthur Lange
☆ Walter Connolly, Allan Jones, Mary Martin, Susanna Foster, Lee Bowman
'Elaborately produced, visually effective ... but audiences will learn from it very little about Victor Herbert.' – *Variety*
'Not highbrow, not lowbrow, but strictly on the beam for both mass and class audiences.' – *Motion Picture Herald*
Phil Boutelje, Arthur Lange

'What do you do when the war is over and you're the second best pilot in the world?'
The Great Waldo Pepper *
US 1975 108m Technicolor Todd-AO 35
Universal (George Roy Hill)
In the twenties, a World War I flyer becomes an aerial stuntman.
Whimsical spectacular which concentrates less on the mystique of flying than on a series of splendid stunts.
w William Goldman *d* *George Roy Hill* *ph* *Robert Surtees* *m* Henry Mancini
☆ Robert Redford, Bo Svenson, Bo Brundin, Susan Sarandon, Geoffrey Lewis
'Charged with enthralling balletic precision.' – *Tom Milne*
'One hundred per cent pure plastic adolescent male fantasy.' – *New Yorker*

A Great Wall
US 1987 102m colour
Mainline/W and S/Nanhai (Shirley Sun)
A Chinese-American executive takes his family to visit China and the sister he has not seen for twenty years.
The first American film to be made in China since the revolution turns out to be a small and pleasant comedy of cultural misunderstandings.
w Peter Wang, Shirley Sun *d* Peter Wang *ph* Peter Stein, Robert Primes *m* David Laing, Ge Ganru *ad* Wing Lee, Feng Yuan, Moing Ming Cheung *ed* Graham Weinbren
☆ Peter Wang, Sharon Iwai, Kelvin Han Yee, Li Qinqin, Hu Xiaoguang, Shen Guanglan

'Miliza Korjus – rhymes with gorgeous!'
The Great Waltz ***
US 1938 103m bw
MGM (Bernard Hyman)
Young Johann Strauss becomes Vienna's waltz king.
Exhilarating old-fashioned studio-set musical located in Hollywood's endearing vision of Old Vienna, assisted by streamlined production and excellent cast. Musical schmaltz.
w Walter Reisch, Samuel Hoffenstein *story* Gottfried Reinhardt *d* *Julien Duvivier* *ph* Joseph Ruttenberg *m* Dimitri Tiomkin *ed* Tom Held
☆ Fernand Gravet, Luise Rainer, Miliza Korjus, Lionel Atwill, Hugh Herbert, Herman Bing, Curt Bois
'Should click nicely, but in these swingaroo days the waltz part may slow down anticipated b.o. enthusiasm.' – *Variety*
'A film to set the feet itching, and to make you want to grab a partner and join in.' – *Film Weekly*
Joseph Ruttenberg
Miliza Korjus; Tom Held

The Great Waltz *
US 1972 134m Metrocolor Panavision 70
MGM (Andrew L. Stone)
Heavy-going remake set on real locations and hampered by them, styled in the manner of the same director's *Song of Norway*, i.e. with no real style at all.

The music survives.
wd Andrew L. Stone *ph* David Boulton *m* the Strauss family, adapted by Robert Wright, Chet Forrest *ch* Onna White *ad* William Albert Havenmeyer *ed* Ernest Walter
☆ Horst Buchholz, Nigel Patrick, Mary Costa, Rossano Brazzi, Yvonne Mitchell
'Take a box of chocolates – soft-centred, of course.' – *Michael Billington, Illustrated London News*

'He could beat any white man in the world. He just couldn't beat all of them!'
The Great White Hope **
US 1970 103m DeLuxe Panavision
TCF (Lawrence Turman)
In 1910, a black boxer becomes world heavyweight champ but has trouble through his affair with a white girl.
Vivid, slightly whitewashed biopic of Jack Johnson (called Jefferson). Dramatic deficiencies outweighed by excellent period detail and a spellbinding central performance.
w Howard Sackler *play* Howard Sackler *d Martin Ritt ph Burnett Guffey md* Lionel Newman *pd* John DeCuir
☆ *James Earl Jones*, Jane Alexander, Lou Gilbert, Joel Fluellen, Chester Morris, Robert Webber, Hal Holbrook
James Earl Jones; Jane Alexander

'If you can't find the perfect contender ... make one.'
The Great White Hype
US 1996 91m DeLuxe
TFC/Atman (Fred Berner, Joshua Donen)
Worried about falling revenues for fights featuring his black heavyweight champion, a fraudulent promoter builds up an inept white boxer as a leading contender.
While boxing is certainly ripe for a hard-hitting exposé of its behind-the-scenes machinations, this movie isn't it, settling instead for some inoffensive comedy.
w Tony Hendra, Ron Shelton *d* Reginald Hudlin *ph* Ron Garcia *m* Marcus Miller *pd* Charles Rosen *ed* Earl Watson
☆ Samuel L. Jackson, Jeff Goldblum, Peter Berg, Jon Lovitz, Damon Wayans, Corbin Bernsen, Cheech Marin, John Rhys-Davies, Salli Richardson, Jamie Foxx
'Thin, uneven scripting and unfocused direction create the impression of a TV sketch stretched to feature length.' – *Godfrey Cheshire, Variety*

The Great Ziegfeld **
US 1936 179m bw
MGM (Hunt Stromberg)
The growth and Broadway fame of impresario Florenz Ziegfeld.
Mammoth biopic which despite a few show-stopping numbers never takes off dramatically and becomes something of an endurance test; interesting, however, as a spectacular of its time.
w William Anthony McGuire *d* Robert Z. Leonard *ph* Oliver T. Marsh, Ray June, George Folsey, Karl Freund *m/ly* Irving Berlin, Walter Donaldson, Harold Adamson *md* Arthur Lange *ch* Seymour Felix *ad* Cedric Gibbons, Eddie Imazu, Edwin B. Willis *ed* William S. Gray *cos* Adrian
☆ William Powell (Florenz Ziegfeld), Luise Rainer (Anna Held), Myrna Loy (Billie Burke), Frank Morgan (Billings), Reginald Owen (Sampston), Nat Pendleton (Sandow), Virginia Bruce (Audrey Lane), *Ray Bolger* (himself), Harriet Hoctor (herself), Ernest Cossart (Sidney), *Fanny Brice*, Robert Greig, Gilda Gray, Leon Errol, Stanley Morner (Dennis Morgan)
'This huge inflated gas-blown object bobs into the critical view as irrelevantly as an airship advertising somebody's toothpaste at a south coast resort. It lasts three hours. That is its only claim to special attention.' – *Graham Greene*
'Everything should have been tightened – not in the team job of cutting those miles of negative, but in boiling down the script, saving a line here, combining two scenes into one.' – *Otis Ferguson*
best picture; Luise Rainer; Seymour Felix
William Anthony McGuire; Robert Z. Leonard; art direction

The Greatest
US/GB 1977 101m Metrocolor
Columbia/EMI (John Marshall)
The life and times of Muhammad Ali.
Bland confection of rags to riches in the boxing ring, its only plus being that Ali plays himself and offers a predictable array of enjoyable one-liners.
w Ring Lardner Jnr *book The Greatest* by Muhammed Ali *d* Tom Gries *ph* Harry Stradling *m* Michael Masser
☆ *Muhammad Ali*, Ernest Borgnine, Roger E. Mosley, Lloyd Haynes, Malachi Throne, John Marley, Robert Duvall, David Huddleston, Ben Johnson, James Earl Jones, Dina Merrill, Paul Winfield

The Greatest Attack
France 1978 96m colour
Adel Productions/Films 21/Eota Films/Antenne 2
original title: *Le Toubib*
An introspective surgeon falls for a sickly nurse during a European war in the 1980s.
Moodily self-indulgent melodrama.
w Pascal Jardin, Pierre Granier-Deferre *novel Harmonie ou les horreurs de la guerre* by Jean Freustie *d* Pierre Granier-Deferre *ph* Claude Renoir *m* Phillipe Sarde *ad* Maurice Sargent *ed* Jean Revel
☆ Alain Delon, Veronique Jannot, Bernard Giraudeau, Bernard Le Coq, Catherine Lachens, Francine Berge, Michel Auclair

The Greatest Show on Earth *
US 1952 153m Technicolor
Paramount/Cecil B. de Mille (Henry Wilcoxon)
Various dramas come to a head under the big top.
Moribund circus drama with bad acting, stilted production, an irrelevant train crash climax and a few genuinely spectacular and enjoyable moments.
w Fredric M. Frank, Theodore St John, Frank Cavett, Barre Lyndon *d* Cecil B. de Mille *ph* George Barnes, Peverell Marley, Wallace Kelley *m Victor Young ad* Hal Pereira, Walter Tyler *ed* Anne Bauchens
☆ Betty Hutton, Cornel Wilde, James Stewart, Charlton Heston, Dorothy Lamour, Gloria Grahame, Lyle Bettger, Henry Wilcoxon, Emmett Kelly, Lawrence Tierney, John Kellogg, John Ringling North
best picture; original story (Fredric M. Frank, Theodore St John, Frank Cavett)
Cecil B. de Mille (as director); editing

The Greatest Story Ever Told **
US 1965 225m Technicolor Ultra Panavision 70
UA/George Stevens
Solemn spectacular with an elephantine pace, shot in Utah because allegedly it looked more like Palestine than Palestine did.
All frightfully elegant and reverent, but totally unmoving, partly because of the fatal casting of stars in bit parts. (John Wayne looks in merely to say 'Truly this man was the son of God.')
w James Lee Barrett, George Stevens *d* George Stevens *ph William C. Mellor, Loyal Griggs m* Alfred Newman *ad Richard Day, William Creber*
☆ *Max von Sydow*, Dorothy McGuire, Claude Rains, José Ferrer, David McCallum, Charlton Heston, Sidney Poitier, Donald Pleasence, Roddy McDowall, Gary Raymond, Carroll Baker, Pat Boone, Van Heflin, Sal Mineo, Shelley Winters and also Ed Wynn, John Wayne, Telly Savalas, Angela Lansbury, Joseph Schildkraut, Victor Buono, Nehemiah Persoff
'George Stevens was once described as a water buffalo of film art. What this film more precisely suggests is a dinosaur.' – *MFB*
'God is unlucky in *The Greatest Story Ever Told*. His only begotten son turns out to be a bore ... the photography is inspired mainly by Hallmark Cards ... as the Hallelujah Chorus explodes around us stereophonically and stereotypically it becomes clear that Lazarus was not so much raised from the tomb as blasted out of it. As for pacing, the picture does not let you forget a single second of its four hours.' – *John Simon*
'No more than three minutes have elapsed before we suspect that Stevens' name and fame have been purchased by the Hallmark Greeting Card Company, and that what we are looking at is really a lengthy catalogue of greeting cards for 1965 – for Those Who Care Enough to Send the Very Best.' – *Stanley Kauffmann*
'Who but an audience of diplomats could sit through this thing? As the picture ponderously unrolled, it was mainly irritation that kept me awake.' – *Shana Alexander, Life*
'If the subject-matter weren't sacred, we would be responding to the picture in the most charitable way by laughing at it from start to finish.' – *Brendan Gill, New Yorker*
'A big windy bore.' – *Bruce Williamson, Playboy*
† The film was originally released at 4 hours 20 minutes. Subsequent versions were at 3 hours 58 minutes, 3 hours 17 minutes, 2 hours 27 minutes and 2 hours 7 minutes.
William C. Mellor, Loyal Griggs; Alfred Newman

Greed ***
US 1924 110m (24 fps) bw silent
MGM/Goldwyn Company (Erich von Stroheim, Irving Thalberg)
An ex-miner dentist kills his avaricious wife. Later in Death Valley he also kills her lover, but is bound to him by handcuffs.
This much-discussed film is often cited as its director's greatest folly: the original version ran eight hours. Re-edited by June Mathis, it retains considerable power sequence by sequence, but is necessarily disjointed in development. However, it must be seen to be appreciated.
wd Erich von Stroheim novel McTeague by Frank Norris *ph* Ben Reynolds, William Daniels *ad* Richard Day, Cedric Gibbons, Erich von Stroheim *ed* Erich Von Stroheim, Rex Ingram, June Mathis, Jos W. Farnham
☆ *Gibson Gowland, ZaSu Pitts, Jean Hersholt*, Chester Conklin, Dale Fuller
'The end leaves one with an appalling sense of human waste, of futility, of the drabness and cruelty of lives stifled by genteel poverty. Every character in the film is overwhelmed by it.' – *Gavin Lambert*
'Von Stroheim is a genius – *Greed* established that beyond all doubt – but he is badly in need of a stopwatch.' – *Robert E. Sherwood*
'Nothing more morbid and senseless, from a commercial picture standpoint, has been seen on the screen for a long time ... Never has there been a more out-and-out box-office flop.' – *Variety*
† In 1972 Herman G. Weinberg published a complete screenplay with 400 stills.
†† The original length at the première is said to have been 420m.

Greedy *
US 1994 113m DeLuxe
Imagine
A family waiting for their aged millionaire uncle to die begins to worry when he hires an attractive young nurse.
A heartless black comedy that might have been funnier had it been taken at a brisker pace; the compensations include Kirk Douglas as the hard-hearted invalid.
w Lowell Ganz, Babaloo Mandel *d* Jonathan Lynn *ph* Gabriel Beristain *m* Randy Edelman *pd* Victoria Paul *ed* Tony Lombardo
☆ Michael J. Fox, Kirk Douglas, Nancy Travis, Olivia D'Abo, Bob Balaban, Ed Begley Jnr, Phil Hartman, Jere Burns, Colleen Camp, Kevin McCarthy, Austin Pendleton, Jonathan Lynn
'Nicely nasty farce succeeds by humiliating all its characters.' – *Sight and Sound*
† The family is named McTeague, after the one in Erich von Stroheim's *Greed*, while the plot owes a debt to Charles Dickens's *Martin Chuzzlewit*.

The Greek Tycoon
US 1978 106m Technicolor Panavision
Universal/ABKCO (Allan Klein, Ely Landau)
A billionaire shipping tycoon marries the widow of an American president.
Rather messy 'faction' based on Onassis and Jacqueline Kennedy; entirely uninteresting save for glossy backgrounds and the relentlessness with which the characters swear at each other.
w Mort Fine *d* J. Lee-Thompson *ph* Tony Richmond *m* Stanley Myers *pd* Michael Stringer
☆ Anthony Quinn, Jacqueline Bisset, Raf Vallone, Edward Albert, James Franciscus, Camilla Sparv
† Among its other idiocies, this is the first film to credit 'Assistant to the assistant to the Unit Publicist'.

The Greeks Had a Word for Them *
US 1932 77m bw
UA/Samuel Goldwyn
Adventures of three New York gold diggers.
Smart early talkie which helped launch the Gold Diggers *series and TCF's parallel* Three Little Mice/Moon over Miami/How to Marry a Millionaire *series.*
w Sidney Howard *play* Zoe Akins *d* Lowell Sherman *ph* George Barnes *m* Alfred Newman
☆ Joan Blondell, Madge Evans, Ina Claire, David Manners, Lowell Sherman, Phillips Smalley, Betty Grable
'Grand rowdy comedy ... a revel in femme clothes and a picture calculated to fascinate women. Backwater clienteles questionable.' – *Variety*

'Their badge of honour was a green beret, and it said they had lived it all ... the night jumps, the ambushes, the hand-to-hand combat, and the long nights of terror they filled with courage!'
The Green Berets
US 1968 141m Technicolor Panavision
Warner/Batjac (Michael Wayne)
After extensive training, two tough army detachments see service in Vietnam.
Overlong actioner criticized for unquestioningly accepting the Vietnam cause; in itself, violent, exhausting and dull.
w James Lee Barrett *novel* Robin Moore *d* John Wayne, Ray Kellogg *ph* Winton C. Hoch *m* Miklos Rozsa
☆ John Wayne, David Janssen, Jim Hutton, Aldo Ray, Raymond St Jacques, Jack Soo, Bruce Cabot, Patrick Wayne, Irene Tsu, Jason Evers, Luke Askew
'Propaganda as crude as this can only do damage to its cause.' – *David Wilson*
'A film best handled from a distance and with a pair of tongs.' – *Penelope Gilliatt*

Green Card *
Australia/France 1990 108m Technicolor
Touchstone (Peter Weir)
A Frenchman marries a New Yorker in order to stay in the United States.
Amiable romantic tale of an odd couple.
wd Peter Weir *ph* Geoffrey Simpson *m* Hans Zimmer *pd* Wendy Stites *ad* Christopher Nowak *ed* William Anderson
☆ Gérard Depardieu, Andie MacDowell, Bebe Neuwirth, Gregg Edelman, Robert Prosky, Jessie Keosian, Ethan Phillips, Mary Louise Wilson, Lois Smith, Conrad McLaren
Peter Weir (as writer)

The Green Cockatoo
GB 1940 65m bw
TCF/New World (Robert T. Kane)
aka: *Four Dark Hours*
aka: *Race Gang*
A man seeks revenge on the gangsters who killed his brother.
Sleazy little Soho-set thriller, mainly remarkable for cast and credits.
w Edward O. Berkman, Arthur Wimperis *story* Graham Greene *d* William Cameron Menzies *ph* Osmond Borradaile *m* Miklos Rozsa
☆ John Mills, Robert Newton, Rene Ray, Bruce Seton, Charles Oliver
† The film was made in 1937 but not shown for three years.

'A fiery girl dares the dangers of the sea and a strange land – fighting for the love of a bold adventurer!'
Green Dolphin Street
US 1947 141m bw
MGM (Carey Wilson)
A Channel Islander emigrates to New Zealand and sends home for the wrong bride.
Silly 19th-century romance climaxed by rather a good earthquake. Expensively but falsely produced.
w Samson Raphaelson *novel* Elizabeth Goudge *d* Victor Saville *ph* George Folsey *m* Bronislau Kaper *ed* George White

☆ Lana Turner, Richard Hart, Edmund Gwenn, Van Heflin, Donna Reed

'The actors in this stupefyingly flimsy epic seem to be in competition for booby prizes.' – *Pauline Kael, 70s*

George Folsey; George White

Green Eyed Woman: see *Take a Letter Darling*

Green Fire

US 1954 100m Eastmancolor Cinemascope
MGM (Armand Deutsch)

Two engineers disagree over their mining of Colombia emeralds.

Routine adventure story with good action highlights including landslide, flood and storm, all deadened by dull dialogue and romantic complications.

w Ivan Goff, Ben Roberts *d* Andrew Marton *ph* Paul Vogel *m* Miklos Rozsa *ad* Cedric Gibbons, Malcolm Brown *ed* Harold F. Kress *cos* Helen Rose

☆ Stewart Granger (Rian X. Mitchell), Paul Douglas (Catherine Knowland), Grace Kelly (Vic Leonard), John Ericson (Donald Knowland), Murvyn Vye (El Moro), Jose Torvay (Manuel), Robert Tafur (Father Ripero)

Green for Danger ***

GB 1946 93m bw
Rank/Individual (Frank Launder, Sidney Gilliat)

A mysterious murderer strikes on the operating table at a wartime emergency hospital.

Classic comedy-thriller, with serious detection balanced by excellent jokes and performances, also by moments of fright.

w Sidney Gilliat, Claud Guerney novel Christianna Brand *d Sidney Gilliat ph Wilkie Cooper* *m* William Alwyn *pd* Peter Proud *ed* Thelma Myers

☆ *Alastair Sim* (Inspector Cockrill), *Sally Gray* (Nurse Linley), *Rosamund John* (Nurse Sanson), *Trevor Howard* (Dr Barnes), *Leo Genn* (Mr Eden), *Megs Jenkins* (Nurse Woods), *Judy Campbell* (Sister Bates), Ronald Adam (Dr White), *Moore Marriott* (Joseph Higgins), George Woodbridge (Det Sgt Hendricks)

'Slick, witty and consistently entertaining.' – *Daily Telegraph*

'Launder and Gilliat have told an exciting story excitingly.' – *Times*

The Green Glove

US/France 1952 89m bw
UA/Benagoss (George Maurer)

A paratrooper against all odds returns a jewelled relic to its proper place in a French church.

An unsatisfactory concoction by people who have clearly seen The Maltese Falcon *as well as lots of Hitchcock films, this interestingly cast and credited independent production never really takes off.*

w Charles Bennett *d* Rudolph Maté *ph* Claude Renoir *m* Joseph Kosma

☆ Glenn Ford, Cedric Hardwicke, Geraldine Brooks, George Macready, Gaby André, Roger Treville

The Green Goddess *

US 1930 80m bw
Warner

An Indian potentate holds Britishers prisoner.

Early talkie star vehicle which was also successful on the stage and as a silent but has little appeal now.

w Julien Josephson *play* William Archer *d* Alfred E. Green *ph* James Van Trees

☆ *George Arliss*, Alice Joyce, H. B. Warner, Ralph Forbes, David Tearle

'Nice programme fare, but it suggests too many synthetic thrillers that have gone before.' – *Variety*

† Remade 1942 as *Adventure in Iraq*.

George Arliss

Green Grass of Wyoming

US 1948 88m Technicolor
TCF

A rancher captures his runaway white stallion and wins the local trotting races.

Predictable, good-looking family film shot on location; a second sequel to My Friend Flicka.

w Martin Berkeley *novel* Mary O'Hara *d* Louis King *ph* Charles G. Clarke *m* Cyril Mockridge

☆ Peggy Cummins, Charles Coburn, Robert Arthur, Lloyd Nolan

Charles G. Clarke

Green Grow the Rushes

GB 1951 77m bw
ACT Films (John Gossage)

Civil servants discover that a Kentish village is devoted to smuggling.

Amiable but disappointingly feeble imitation of Ealing comedy by a company formed from the technicians' union; it simply hasn't got the right snap in any department.

w Derek Twist, Howard Clewes *novel* Howard Clewes *d* Derek Twist *ph* Harry Waxman *m* Lambert Williamson

☆ Roger Livesey, Richard Burton, Honor Blackman, Frederick Leister, John Salew, Colin Gordon, Geoffrey Keen, Harcourt Williams, Vida Hope

Green Hell *

US 1940 87m bw
Universal (Harry Edington)

Explorers seek Inca treasure in the South American jungle.

Studio-bound potboiler unworthy of its director but mainly enjoyable as a romp.

w Frances Marion *d* James Whale *ph* Karl Freund *ed* Ted J. Kent

☆ Douglas Fairbanks Jnr, Joan Bennett, George Sanders, Vincent Price, Alan Hale, Gene Garrick, George Bancroft, John Howard

'It's the old nickelodeon mellerdrammer, at higher prices.' – *Picture Play*

'It was one of the funniest films ever shot anywhere in the world. About five of the worst pictures ever made are all in that picture.' – *Vincent Price*

† The temple set was re-used the same year in *The Mummy's Hand*.

The Green Helmet

GB 1961 88m bw
MGM (Charles Francis Vetter)

A race driver with shattered nerves makes his last job the introduction of an American car of new design.

Totally conventional motor racing thriller. Most of the work could just as effectively have been phoned in.

w Jon Cleary *novel* Jon Cleary *d* Michael Forlong *ph* Geoffrey Faithfull *m* Ken Jones

☆ Bill Travers, Ed Begley, Sidney James, Nancy Walters, Ursula Jeans, Megs Jenkins

Green Ice

GB 1981 116m colour
ITC/Lew Grade (Jack Wiener)

An aimless American in Mexico becomes involved with emerald thieves.

Dismally routine punch-ups and car chases are enlivened by a mildly original theft by balloon, but the overall effect is soporific.

w Edward Anhalt, Ray Hassett, Anthony Simmons, Robert de Laurentiis *novel* Gerald Browne *d* Ernest Day *ph* Gilbert Taylor *m* Bill Wyman

☆ Ryan O'Neal, Anne Archer, Omar Sharif, Philip Stone

'It should not tempt anyone away from doubtlessly superior versions of the same material on television.' – *Geoff Brown, MFB*

Green Light *

US 1936 85m bw
Warner (Henry Blanke)

A dedicated doctor gives up his practice when a patient dies.

Adequate star melodrama.

w Milton Krims *novel* Lloyd C. Douglas *d* Frank Borzage *ph* Byron Haskin *m* Max Steiner

☆ Errol Flynn, Anita Louise, Margaret Lindsay, Cedric Hardwicke, Henry O'Neill, Spring Byington

'Customer lure in the title and the player names ... it will carry a weak sister nicely.' – *Variety*

The Green Man *

GB 1956 80m bw
BL/Grenadier (Frank Launder, Sidney Gilliat)

A professional assassin stalks a pompous politician.

Cheerful but not very subtle black comedy, suffering from the attempt to make a star part out of a very minor character.

w Sidney Gilliat, Frank Launder *play* Meet a Body by Sidney Gilliat, Frank Launder *d* Robert Day *ph* Gerald Gibbs *m* Cedric Thorpe Davie

☆ Alastair Sim, George Cole, Jill Adams, Terry-Thomas, Avril Angers, John Chandos, Dora Bryan, Colin Gordon, Raymond Huntley

Green Mansions

US 1959 104m Metrocolor Cinemascope
MGM/Avon (Edmund Grainger)

In a remote Amazon forest an adventurer encounters Rima, a child of nature who takes him on a quest for truth.

Absurd studio-bound Shangri-La story based on an Edwardian fantasy that may well have suited the printed page, but not the wide screen. Dismally photographed in shades of green, with all concerned looking acutely uncomfortable.

w Dorothy Kingsley *novel* W. H. Hudson *d* Mel Ferrer *ph* Joseph Ruttenberg *m* Bronislau Kaper, Heitor Villa-Lobos

☆ Anthony Perkins, Audrey Hepburn, Lee J. Cobb, Henry Silva

'Paul Edgecomb did not believe in miracles...until he met one.'

The Green Mile **

US 1999 187m Technicolor
Warner/Castle Rock (David Valdes, Frank Darabont)

A retired prison warden recalls how his life dealing with prisoners condemned to die in the electric chair was changed by a giant convict with mystical healing powers.

Immaculately done, well-acted fantasy of redemption, suffused with a sickly religiosity; it fails to justify its inordinate length.

wd Frank Darabont *novel* Stephen King *ph* David Tattersall *m* Thomas Newman *pd* Terence Marsh *ed* Richard Francis-Bruce

☆ Tom Hanks (Paul Edgecomb), David Morse (Brutus 'Brutal' Howell), Bonnie Hunt (Jan Edgecomb), *Michael Clarke Duncan* (John Coffey), James Cromwell (Warden Hal Moores), Michael Jeter (Eduard Delacroix), Graham Greene (Arlen Bitterbuck), Doug Hutchison (Percy Wetmore), Sam Rockwell ('Wild Bill' Wharton), Barry Pepper (Dean Stanton), Jeffrey DeMunn (Harry Terwilliger), Harry Dean Stanton (Toot-Toot), Gary Sinise (Burt Hammersmith)

'A well-populated drama with a relatively simple story, one that could have been told with more economy and fewer talky bits of business around the cellblock.' – *Janet Maslin, New York Times*

'If you can stand this three-hour-plus stretch of saccharine gibberish and patronising racial politics, you've got a stronger stomach than me.' – *Peter Bradshaw, Guardian*

† The film was a commercial success, taking more than 132m at the US box-office.

picture; Michael Clarke Duncan; Frank Darabont (as writer); sound (Robert J. Litt, Elliot Tyson, Michael Herbick, Willie D. Burton)

The Green Pastures ***

US 1936 93m bw
Warner (Henry Blanke)

Old Testament stories as seen through simple-minded negro eyes.

Though recently attacked as setting back the cause of black emancipation, this is a brilliantly sympathetic and humorous film, very cunningly adapted for the screen in a series of dramatic scenes which make the material work even better than it did on the stage.

w Marc Connelly play Marc Connelly *stories Roark Bradford d William Keighley, Marc Connelly ph Hal Mohr m Erich Wolfgang Korngold*

☆ *Rex Ingram, Oscar Polk, Eddie Anderson*, Frank Wilson, George Reed

'I imagine God has a sense of humour, and I imagine that He is delighted with *The Green Pastures*.' – *Don Herold*

'That disturbance around the Music Hall yesterday was the noise of shuffling queues in Sixth Avenue and the sound of motion picture critics dancing in the street.' – *Bosley Crowther, New York Times*

'This is as good a religious play as one is likely to get in this age from a practised New York writer.' – *Graham Greene*

Green Promise

US 1949 88m bw
RKO/Glenn McCarthy (Robert Paige, Monty F. Collins)

GB title: *Raging Waters*

A farmer refuses to move from the dust bowl area, and a landslide causes a flood.

Curiously stilted independent production which doesn't really bear comparison with The Grapes of Wrath.

w Monty F. Collins *d* William D. Russell *ph* John Russell *m* David Chudnow

☆ Marguerite Chapman, Walter Brennan, Robert Paige, Natalie Wood, Ted Donaldson, Connie Marshall

The Green Ray **

France 1986 98m colour
Les Films du Losange (Margaret Menegoz)

original title: *Le Rayon Vert*
aka: *Summer*

A lonely secretary goes on holiday alone and, after days of tedium, falls in love.

With its improvised dialogue and less than sympathetic heroine, the movie lacks the precision and interest of Rohmer's best work, even if the theme remains the same.

w Eric Rohmer, Marie Rivière *d* Eric Rohmer *ph* Sophie Maintigneux *m* Jean-Louis Valero *ed* Marie-Luisa Garcia

☆ Marie Rivière, Lisa Heredia, Béatrice Romand, Vincent Gautier, Eric Hamm, Rosette, Vanessa Leleu, Irene Skobline, Carita

The Green Scarf

GB 1954 96m bw
B and A (Bertram Ostrer, Albert Fennell)

An elderly French lawyer takes on the defence of a blind, deaf and dumb murder suspect.

Plodding courtroom drama with familiar faces in unconvincing French guise.

w Gordon Wellesley *novel* The Brute by Guy des Cars *d* George More O'Ferrall *ph* Jack Hildyard *m* Brian Easdale

☆ Michael Redgrave, Ann Todd, Leo Genn, Kieron Moore

The Green Years *

US 1946 127m bw
MGM (Leon Gordon)

A young boy brought up strictly in Ireland makes friends with his mischievous grandfather.

Period family film in familiar style, sparked only by its scene-stealing star performance.

w Robert Ardrey, Sonya Levien *novel* A. J. Cronin *d* Victor Saville *ph* George Folsey *m* Herbert Stothart *ad* Cedric Gibbons, Hans Peters

☆ *Charles Coburn*, Dean Stockwell, Tom Drake, Beverly Tyler, Hume Cronyn, Gladys Cooper, Selena Royle, Jessica Tandy, Richard Haydn, Andy Clyde

'It has been described in the ads as "wonderful" by everyone within Louis B. Mayer's purchasing power except his horses, so I hesitate to ask you to take my word for it: the picture is awful.' – *James Agee*

George Folsey; Charles Coburn

Greenfingers

GB/US 2000 90m colour
Winchester/Boneyard/Overseas Filmgroup/Xingu (Travis Swords, Daniel J. Victor)

A paroled murderer goes back inside an open prison to help inmates create a flower garden.

Corny comedy of an isolated group of macho men gaining self-respect in an unexpected way; it is loosely based on a true story but has little connection with reality.

wd Joel Hershman *ph* John Daly *m* Guy Dagul *pd* Tim Hutchinson *ed* Justin Krish

☆ Clive Owen (Colin Briggs), Helen Mirren (Georgina Woodhouse), David Kelly (Fergus Wilks), Warren Clarke (Governor Hodge), Danny Dyer (Tony), Adam Fogerty (Raw), Paterson Joseph (Jimmy), Natasha Little (Primrose Woodhouse)

'Slightly racy, but pretty unexciting.' – *Guardian*

'Suck all the integrity out of *The Full Monty* and you've got *Greenfingers*... This shameless knockoff.' – *Dennis Harvey, Variety*

The Greengage Summer *
GB 1961 99m Technicolor
Columbia/PKL (Victor Saville, Edward Small)
US title: *Loss of Innocence*
A young girl staying at a hotel falls in love with a jewel thief but is accidentally responsible for his capture.
Old-fashioned and not very interesting story with an appeal, one supposes, to well-brought-up young women. Decently made.
w Howard Koch *novel* Rumer Godden *d* Lewis Gilbert *ph* Frederick A. Young *m* Richard Addinsell
☆ Kenneth More, Danielle Darrieux, Susannah York, Claude Nollier, Jane Asher, Elizabeth Dear, Maurice Denham

Greenwich Village *
US 1944 82m Technicolor
TCF (William Le Baron)
In the twenties, a hick composer in New York allows his concerto to be used in a jazz musical.
Lightweight musical romp.
w Michael Fessier, Ernest Pagano *d* Walter Lang *ph* Leon Shamroy, Harry Jackson *m/ly* Leo Robin, Nacio Herb Brown
☆ Carmen Miranda, Don Ameche, William Bendix, Vivian Blaine, Felix Bressart, Tony and Sally de Marco, Adolph Green, Betty Comden, Alvin Hammer, Judy Holliday

Greetings *
US 1968 88m Eastmancolor
West End Films
A draftee tries every which way to be exempted, then subjects himself to a whirl of physical experience.
Kaleidoscopic stringing together of fleeting satirical bits; talent undeniable but equally uncontrolled.
w Charles Hirsch, Brian de Palma *d* Brian de Palma *ed* Brian de Palma
☆ Jonathan Warden, Robert DeNiro, Gerrit Graham, Megan McCormick

Grégoire Moulin Contre L'Humanité **
France 2001 91m colour 'Scope
Millennium/LitswaLGM/M6/SFP/Rhone Alpes/TPS/Litsva (Cyrille Colbeau-Justin)
On the night of an important soccer match, a shy office worker has to overcome a series of obstacles and accidents in order to return a stolen wallet to the girl he has admired from afar.
Exuberantly misanthropic comedy of thwarted hopes and football fanaticism, in which bad behaviour is the norm.
w Artus De Penguern, Jerome L'Hotsky *d* Artus De Penguern *ph* Vincent Mathias *m* Benoit Pimont *ad* Sylvie Olive *ed* Corrine Cahour, Claude-France Husson, Christophe Marthoud
☆ Artus De Penguern (Grégoire Moulin), Pascale Arbillot (Odile), Didier Benureau (Jean-François), Clovis Cornillac (Jacky), Antoine Dulery (Emmanuel Lacarriere), Serge Riaboukine (Cab Driver), Elisabeth Vitali (Hélène)
'Extremely funny and well-cast bout of sustained lunacy. A comic *cri de coeur* for sensitive guys in a macho world.' – *Lisa Nesselson, Variety*

Gregorio
Peru 1985 95m colour
Grupo Chaski (Maria Barea)
The young son of a peasant farmer turns to crime in the big city.
The documentary-style work of a film collective, well-meaning but only intermittently interesting.
w Maria Barea, Fernando Espinoza, Stefan Kaspar, Alejandro Legaspi, Margreth Noth, Susi Pastor *d* Alejandro Legaspi *m* Arturo Ruiz del Pozo *ad* Rafael Hernandez *ed* Alejandro Legaspi, Stefan Kasper, Gaby Faura
☆ Marino Leon de La Torre, Vetzy Perez-Palma, Augusto Varillas, Manuel Acosta Ojeda, Rafael Hernandez

Gregory's Girl ***
GB 1980 91m colour
Lake/NFFC/STV (Davina Belling, Clive Parsons)
In a Scottish new town, a school footballer becomes aware of sex.
Curiously diverting comedy peopled by dreamers but handicapped by impenetrable accents. An unexpected world-wide success.
wd Bill Forsyth *ph* Michael Coulter *m* Colin Tully *ad* Adrienne Coulter *ed* John Gow
☆ Gordon John Sinclair (later John Gordon Sinclair), Dee Hepburn, Jake D'Arcy, Claire Grogan
best script

Gregory's Two Girls
GB 1999 116m DeLuxe
FilmFour/SAC/NLF/Kinowelt/Young Lake (Christopher Young)
A left-wing English teacher at a Scottish school muddles through life, lusting after a schoolgirl and ignoring the maturer love offered by a colleague.
Disappointing sequel from a director who seems to have lost much of his interest in people; the narrative veers from an observant study of the life of a hapless teacher into an unlikely, ill-handled story of industrial espionage and illegal immigration.
wd Bill Forsyth *ph* John de Borman *m* Michael Gibbs *pd* Andy Harris *ed* John Gow
☆ John Gordon Sinclair (Gregory Underwood), Carly McKinnon (Frances), Dougray Scott (Fraser Rowan), Maria Doyle Kennedy (Bel), Kevin Anderson (Jon), Martin Schwab (Dimitri), Fiona Bell (Maddy Underwood), Hugh McCue (Douglas), John Murtagh (Headmaster), Matt Costello (Det Gorrie), Jane Stabler (Det Ritchie)
'A perfect example of why well-loved nostalgia should never be updated.' – *Sarah Cohen, Heat*

Gremlins *
US 1984 106m Technicolor
Warner/Amblin (Michael Finnell)
Small furry creatures called mogwais prove to be immensely prolific and dangerous when wet.
Juvenile horror comic, a kind of deliberate inversion of E.T. Slow to start, and a little too knowingly nasty, with variable special effects; but a pretty hot commercial success.
w Chris Columbus *d* Joe Dante *ph* John Hora *m* Jerry Goldsmith *ed* Tina Hirsch *sp* Gremlin designer: Chris Walas
☆ Zach Galligan, Phoebe Cates, Hoyt Axton, Polly Holliday, Keye Luke, Scott Brady, Edward Andrews
'Don't go if you still believe in Santa Claus.' – *Roger Ebert*

Gremlins 2: The New Batch **
US 1990 105m Technicolor
Warner/Amblin (Michael Finnell)
A mogwai, captured by mad research scientists, produces hundreds of violent gremlins who run amuck in a megalomaniac property developer's skyscraper.
A sequel more entertaining than the original, stuffed with in-jokes for movie buffs.
w Charlie Haas *d* Joe Dante *ph* John Hora *m* Jerry Goldsmith *pd* James Spencer *ad* Joe Lucky *ed* Kent Beyda *sp* Gremlin and mogwai effects: Rick Baker
☆ Zach Galligan, Phoebe Cates
'An hilarious sequel featuring equal parts creature slapstick and satirical barbs for adults.' – *Variety*

The Grey Fox *
Canada 1982 91m Eastmancolor
Mercury (Peter O'Brian)
The more or less true story of a turn-of-the-century stagecoach bandit who in 1901 was released from a long prison term, genially committed more crimes, and disappeared.
Likeable semi-Western with an excellent sense of place and time.
w John Hunter *d* Phillip Borsos *ph* Frank Tidy *m* Michael Conway
☆ Richard Farnsworth, Jackie Burroughs, Ken Pogue, Wayne Robson

'He Fought To Change The World'
Grey Owl *
GB/Canada 1998 118m colour Panavision
TCF/Largo/Transfilm/Beaver (Richard Attenborough, Jake Eberts, Claude Leger)
An Englishman re-invents himself as a Native American and preaches the conservation of nature.
A timely biopic of a once-influential writer, but suffering from the miscasting of the lead role.
w William Nicholson *d* Richard Attenborough *ph* Roger Pratt *m* George Fenton *pd* Anthony Pratt *ed* LesleyWalker
☆ Pierce Brosnan (Archibald Belaney/Grey Owl), Annie Galipeau (Anahareo/Pony), Nathaniel Arcand (Ned White Bear), Vlasta Vrana (Harry Champlin), David Fox (Jim Wood), Charles Powell (Walter Perry), Stephanie Cole (Ada Belaney), Renée Asherson (Cary Belaney), Graham Greene (Jim Bernard)
'So drab you start miserably taking sides with urban development.' – *Empire*

Greyfriars Bobby *
GB 1961 91m Technicolor
Walt Disney (Hugh Attwooll)
A Skye terrier keeps persistent vigil over his master's grave and is made a freeman of the city of Edinburgh.
Adequately produced film of a charming old Victorian story.
w Robert Westerby *book* Eleanor Atkinson *d* Don Chaffey *ph* Paul Beeson *m* Francis Chagrin
☆ Donald Crisp, Laurence Naismith, Alexander Mackenzie, Kay Walsh, Andrew Cruickshank, Vincent Winter, Moultrie Kelsall, Duncan Macrae
'The better Disney qualities of exact period detail and childlike directness are apparent.' – *MFB*
† The story was previously filmed as *Challenge to Lassie*.

Greystoke: The Legend of Tarzan, Lord of the Apes
GB 1984 130m Eastmancolor Panavision
Warner/WEA Records (Hugh Hudson, Stanley S. Canter)
In the 1880s, an English lord and lady are killed in Africa, and their son is brought up by apes.
An absurd attempt to treat the story seriously after 70 years of hokum, this meandering chronicle, cut down from something much longer and even less endurable, has men in ape suits, an eye for unpleasant detail, and Ralph Richardson sliding down the stairs on a tray. The attempt to moralize at the end is emetic.
w P. H. Vazak (Robert Towne), Michael Austin *novel* *Tarzan of the Apes* by Edgar Rice Burroughs *d* Hugh Hudson *ph* John Alcott *m* John Scott *pd* Stuart Craig
☆ Ralph Richardson, Ian Holm, James Fox, Christopher Lambert, Andie MacDowell, Cheryl Campbell, Paul Geoffrey, John Wells, Nigel Davenport, Ian Charleson, Richard Griffiths
'A unique mixture of pomposity and ineptitude ... in the second half the movie simply loses its mind, and dribbles to a pathetically indecisive conclusion.' – *Pauline Kael, New Yorker*
† Andie MacDowell's voice was dubbed by Glenn Close.
Ralph Richardson (supporting actor); adapted screenplay

Gridlock'd *
US 1997 91m DeLuxe
Polygram/Interscope/DEF/Webster and Dragon (Damian Jones, Paul Webster, Erica Huggins)
After their singer suffers from an overdose, her two drug-addicted accompanists try to kick the habit.
Engaging streetwise narrative which depends for its moderate success on the interaction between its two leads.
wd Vondie Curtis-Hall *ph* Bill Pope *m* Stewart Copeland, The Angel *pd* Dan Bishop *ed* Charles Koefoed
☆ Tim Roth, Tupac Shakur, Thandie Newton, Charles Fleischer, Howard Hesseman, James Pickens Jnr, John Sayles
'There is the nagging feeling that the film has neither been quite as funny or as truly involving as it might have been.' – *Todd McCarthy, Variety*

Il Grido *
Italy 1957 102m bw
SPA Cinematografica/Robert Alexander
aka: *The Cry*
A man whose wife has left him travels across the Po Valley with his daughter in search of new happiness, but fails to find it and commits suicide.
Watchable but rather aimlessly depressing character drama.
w Michelangelo Antonioni, Elio Bartolini, Ennio de Concini *d* Michelangelo Antonioni *ph* Gianni di Venanzo *m* Giovanni Fusco
☆ Steve Cochran, Alida Valli, Dorian Gray, Betsy Blair, Lynn Shaw

Grief *
US 1993 87m colour
ICA/Grief (Ruth Charny, Yoram Mandel)
Romantic entanglements and power struggles during a week at a TV production company creating sensational drama set in a divorce court.
Enjoyable, often comic drama which begins as a gay soap opera and develops into an exploration of friendship.
wd Richard Glatzer *ph* David Dechant *m* Tom Judson *pd* Don Diers *ed* Robin Katz, William W. Williams
☆ Craig Chester, Jackie Beat, Illeana Douglas, Alexis Arquette, Carlton Wilborn, Shawn Hoffman, Lucy Gutteridge
'Isn't a dazzling debut technique-wise, but its drollery and genuine warmth are of another, perhaps deeper stripe. As "feel-good" sleepers go, this one is funny, smart and sweet.' – *Dennis Harvey, Variety*

La Grieta
Spain 1989 83m colour
Warner/Dister (Jose Escriva, Francesca de Laurentiis)
aka: *The Rift*
Submariners discover mutated monsters under the sea.
Feeble fantasy with poor special effects.
w J. P. Simon, Mark Klein *d* J. P. Simon *ph* Manuel Rojas *m* Joel Goldsmith *pd* Gonzalo Gonzalo *ed* Isaac Sehayek, Earl Watson
☆ Jack Scalia, R. Lee Ermey, Ray Wise, Deborah Adair, John Toles Bey, Ely Pouget, Emilio Linder, Tony Isbert, Alvaro Labra, Luis Lorenzo
'The characterisation is predictably shallow and the romantic interest distinctly soggy, while the model work and creature effects plumb new depths of ineptitude.' – *Nigel Floyd, MFB*

Grievous Bodily Harm *
Australia 1988 96m colour
International Film Management/Smiley/FGH (Richard Brennan)
A teacher goes on a killing spree in an attempt to discover the whereabouts of his missing wife, tracked by an unscrupulous journalist and a crooked cop.
Clever, slick thriller that maintains its momentum despite its shallow characterization.
w Warwick Hind *d* Mark Joffe *ph* Ellery Ryan *m* Chris Neal *pd* Roger Ford *ed* Marc Van Buren
☆ Colin Friels, John Waters, Bruno Lawrence, Shane Briant, Caz Lederman, Sandy Gore, Kerry Armstrong, Joy Bell

'Just another day of lying, cheating and stealing.'
The Grifters ***
US 1990 110m CFI color
Palace/Cineplex Odeon (Martin Scorsese, Robert Harris)
A mother, who is robbing her gangster boss, is reunited with her son and his girlfriend, both confidence tricksters.
Bleakly invigorating vision of the underside of the American dream.
w Donald Westlake *novel* Jim Thompson *d* Stephen Frears *ph* Oliver Stapleton *m* Elmer Bernstein *pd* Dennis Gassner *ed* Mick Audsley
☆ Anjelica Huston, John Cusack, Annette Bening, Pat Hingle, Henry Jones, Michael Laskin, Eddie Jones, J. T. Walsh, Charles Napier
'A brilliant, immensely seductive mix of *Kammerspiel*, film noir and naturalistic slice-of-life.' – *Tom Milne, MFB*
Anjelica Huston; Stephen Frears; Annette Bening; Donald Westlake

Grim Prairie Tales *
US 1990 94m colour
East West Film Partners (Richard Hahn)
Two drifters, who meet by chance on the prairie, pass the night by telling each other stories.
A clever compendium movie, a mix of Western and atmospheric horror, which is stylish and imaginative enough to rise above its low-budget limitations, helped by strong performances from its two leads.

wd Wayne Coe *ph* Janusz Kaminski *m* Steve Dancz *pd* Anthony Zierhut *ed* Earl Ghaffari
☆ James Earl Jones, Brad Dourif, William Atherton, Lisa Eichhorn, Marc McClure, Scott Paulin, Will Hare, Michelle Joyner, Wendy Cooke

The Grim Reaper *
Italy 1962 100m bw
Cineriz/Compagnia/Cervi (Antonio Cervi)
original title: *La Commare Secca*
After a prostitute is found murdered in a park, a series of suspects account for their movements to the police.
Intermittently interesting drama of restricted lives, with an emotional impact that is dulled by its repetitious structure.
w Bernardo Bertolucci, Sergio Citti *story* Pier Paolo Pasolini *d* Bernardo Bertolucci *ph* Gianni Narzisi *m* Piero Piccioni *ed* Nino Baragli
☆ Francesco Ruiu, Giancarlo de Rosa, Vincenzo Ciccora, Alfredo Leggi, Gabriella Giorgelli, Marisa Solinas, Romano Labate, Alvaro D'Ercole
'At once a gritty documentary-style drama about life on the streets and a dewy-eyed evocation of adolescence, this ranks alongside its director's best work.' – *Sight and Sound*

The Grinch: see *Dr Seuss' How the Grinch Stole Christmas*

The Grip of Fear: see *Experiment in Terror*

Grip of the Strangler *
GB 1958 78m bw
Producers' Associates (John Croydon)
US title: *The Haunted Strangler*
A novelist investigating an old murder case finds that he was himself the murderer.
Moderate thriller with a predictable but efficient plot.
w Jan Read *d* Robert Day *ph* Lionel Banes *m* Buxton Orr
☆ Boris Karloff, Elizabeth Allan, Jean Kent, Vera Day, Anthony Dawson

The Grissom Gang
US 1971 128m Metrocolor
Associates and Aldrich/ABC
In 1931, a New York heiress is kidnapped by gangsters and comes to like it.
Unpleasant remake of No Orchids for Miss Blandish *(previously filmed under that title, incredibly badly, in GB in 1948), with too much footage of lush blonde being slobbered over by psychotic thug, and an inevitable emphasis on violence.*
w Leon Griffiths *novel* James Hadley Chase *d* Robert Aldrich *ph* Joseph Biroc *m* Gerald Fried *ad* James Dowell Vance
☆ Scott Wilson, Kim Darby, Tony Musante, Robert Lansing, Irene Dailey, Connie Stevens, Wesley Addy
'Offensive, immoral and perhaps even lascivious.' – *Vincent Canby*

Gritos en la Noche: see *The Awful Dr Orloff*

'18 feet of towering fury! The most dangerous jaws on land!'
Grizzly
US 1976 91m Movielab Todd-AO 35
Film Ventures International (David Sheldon, Harvey Flaxman)
aka: *Killer Grizzly*
A mammoth bear preys upon campers in a national park.
Inept and boring shocker in the wake of Jaws.
w Harvey Flaxman, David Sheldon *d* William Girdler *ph* William Asman *m* Robert O. Ragland
☆ Christopher George, Andrew Prine, Richard Jaeckel, Joan McCall

'Are you feeling it?'
Groove
US 2000 83m FotoKem
Columbia TriStar/415.com (Danielle Renfrew, Greg Harrison)
Various young people congregate for a rave in an abandoned warehouse in San Francisco.
A movie aimed squarely at a young audience similar to those it depicts dancing the night away in a drugged condition, though they may prefer the actual experience to this ersatz one.
wd Greg Harrison *ph* Matthew Irving *pd* Chris Ferriera *ed* Greg Harrison *cos* Kai Hashinoguchi, Elizabeth Rodriguez
☆ Lola Glaudini (Leyla Heydel), Hamish Linklater (David Turner), Denny Kirkwood (Colin Turner), MacKenzie Firgens (Harmony Stitts), Rachel True (Beth Anderson), Steve Van Wormer (Ernie Townsend), Nick Offerman (Sgt Channaham), Ari Gold (Cliff Rafferty), DJ John Digweed (Himself)
'Doesn't have much on its mind but a good time. It delivers one, though crustier critics are unlikely to do much raving themselves.' – *Dennis Harvey, Variety*

Gross Anatomy
US 1989 107m Technicolor
Touchstone/Silver Screen Partners IV (Howard Rosenman, Debra Hill)
aka: *A Cut Above*
A fisherman's son, who becomes a medical student because he wants to be rich, discovers compassion and love in his first year.
A light romantic comedy that cannot encompass the darker moments it attempts, relying too heavily on the charm of its star to compensate for the conceited brat he plays.
w Ron Nyswaner, Mark Spragg *story* Mark Spragg, Howard Rosenman, Alan Jay Glueckman, Stanley Isaacs *d* Thom Eberhardt *ph* Steve Yaconelli *m* David Newman *pd* William F. Matthews *ed* Bud Smith, Scott Smith
☆ Matthew Modine, Daphne Zuniga, Christine Lahti, Todd Field, John Scott Clough, Alice Carter, Robert Desiderio, Zakes Mokae

'Even A Hit Man Deserves A Second Shot.'
Grosse Pointe Blank *
US 1997 108m Technicolor
Buena Vista/Hollywood/Caravan/New Crime (Susan Arnold, Donna Arkoff Roth, Roger Birnbaum)
A professional killer with work problems goes to his old school reunion.
Slick romantic comedy with added violence; it has a few amusing moments amid the bloodshed.
w Tom Jankiewicz, D. V. DeVincentis, Steve Pink, John Cusack *d* George Armitage *ph* Jamie Anderson *m* Joe Strummer *pd* Stephen Altman *ed* Brian Berdan
☆ John Cusack, Minnie Driver, Alan Arkin, Dan Aykroyd, Joan Cusack, Jeremy Piven, Hank Azaria, Barbara Harris, Mitchell Ryan
'Very enjoyable. It is also very insubstantial … Strategically, the film has been conceived as a vehicle to advance Cusack's career.' – *John Sutherland, TLS*

'Beneath the surface of respectability lies the shadow of our darker side.'
The Grotesque
GB 1996 98m Technicolor
Starlight/Xingu (Trudie Styler)
US title: *Gentlemen Don't Eat Poets*
US video title: *Grave Indiscretions*
In the late 40s, a new, devious butler and his alcoholic wife bring death and destruction to the household of an eccentric, aristocratic palaeontologist.
Limp social satire that never touches on any sort of reality, which may be why its cast resorts to mannered performances.
w Patrick McGrath, John-Paul Davidson *novel* *The Grotesque* by Patrick McGrath *d* John-Paul Davidson *ph* Andrew Dunn *m* Anne Dudley *pd* Jan Roelfs, Michael Seirton *ed* Tariq Anwar
☆ Alan Bates (Sir Hugo Coal), Theresa Russell (Lady Harriet Coal), Sting (Fledge), Lena Headey (Cleo Coal), Jim Carter (George Lecky), Anna Massey (Mrs Giblet), Trudie Styler (Doris Fledge), Maria Aitken (Lavinia Freebody), James Fleet (Inspector Limp), Steven Mackintosh (Sydney Giblet), John Mills
'The genre props – thunderstorms, marshes, family retainers both *compos* and *non-compos mentis* – ensure that it's closer to a game of Cluedo than a genuinely engaging drama.' – *Adam Mars-Jones, Independent*
'This bizarre shambles of a film.' – *George Perry, Sunday Times*

'No Radar. No Contact. No Control.'
Ground Control *
US 1998 93m FotoKem
Green/Hard Work (Talaat Captan, Vince Ravine)
video title: *Jet*
A former air traffic controller, traumatised after a crash, is recalled to work during an emergency, in which a storm hits, an airliner runs into difficulties, some of the controllers lose their cool, the computers go down and Henry Winkler is the repairman.
Overheated drama, but one that keeps the tension and suspense high so that it remains eminently watchable.
w Mark Shepherd, Robert Moreland, Talaat Captan *d* Richard Howard *ph* Henner Hofmann *m* Randy Miller *pd* Michael Perry *ed* Edward R. Abroms
☆ Kiefer Sutherland (Jack Harris), Robert Sean Leonard (Cruise), Kristy Swanson (Julie Albrecht), Kelly McGillis (Susan Stratton), Henry Winkler (John Quinn), Bruce McGill (T.C. Bryant), Michael Gross (Murray), Margaret Cho (Amanda), Ruben Paul (Sam), Charles Fleischer (Randy)

Ground Zero *
Australia 1987 109m Eastmancolor Panavision
BDB/Pattinson-Burrowes
A cinematographer stumbles on dangerous secrets when investigating his father's death 30 years previously.
Smart contemporary thriller with a political theme.
w Jan Sardi, Mac Gudgeon *d* Michael Pattinson, Bruce Myles
☆ Colin Friels, Jack Thompson, Donald Pleasence, Natalie Bate

'He's having the day of his life … over and over again.'
Groundhog Day ***
US 1993 101m Technicolor Panavision
Columbia TriStar/Columbia (Trevor Albert, Harold Ramis)
A cynical weatherman, sent to cover an annual small-town Groundhog ceremony, finds himself reliving his day over and over again until he becomes a better person.
A 90s version of It's A Wonderful Life*: tougher, smarter, more knowing and successfully avoiding corn to provide an unexpectedly witty and warming comedy.*
w Danny Rubin, Harold Ramis d Harold Ramis *ph* John Bailey *m* George Fenton *pd* David Nichols *ed* Pembroke J. Herring
☆ *Bill Murray*, Andie MacDowell, Chris Elliott, Stephen Tobolowsky, Brian Doyle-Murray, Marita Geraghty, Angela Paton, Rick Ducommun
'A major studio Hollywood comedy that both delights and surprises.' – *Sight and Sound*
'Something of a comedy classic, and a film which, for sheer entertainment value, you'd be hard pushed to beat.' – *Empire*
best original screenplay

'We challenge you to guess the ending!'
The Groundstar Conspiracy *
US 1972 96m Technicolor Panavision
Universal/Hal Roach International (Trevor Wallace)
An explosion rips apart a top secret space project, and the surviving scientist loses his memory.
Gimmicky but generally compulsive sci-fi mystery yarn, with an effective though predictable climax.
w Matthew Howard *novel* *The Alien* by L. P. Davies *d* Lamont Johnson *ph* Michael Reed *m* Paul Hoffert
☆ George Peppard, Michael Sarrazin, James Olson, Christine Belford, Tim O'Connor, James McEachin

The Group ***
US 1966 152m DeLuxe
UA/Famous Artists (Sidney Buchman)
The subsequent love lives of a group of girls who graduate from Vassar in 1933.
Patchy but generally fascinating series of interwoven sketches and character studies, with mainly tragic overtones; good attention to period detail, and dazzling array of new talent.
w Sidney Buchman novel Mary McCarthy d Sidney Lumet ph Boris Kaufman *m* Charles Gross *pd Gene Callahan*
☆ *Joanna Pettet*, Candice Bergen, *Jessica Walter, Joan Hackett*, Elizabeth Hartman, Mary Robin-Redd, *Kathleen Widdoes*, Shirley Knight, Larry Hagman, *Hal Holbrook, Robert Emhardt*, Richard Mulligan, James Congdon, James Broderick
'Although it is a strange, inclusive, no-holds-barred movie that runs the gamut from scenes that are almost soap-operaish, to amusing scenes that are almost satire, to outrageously frank scenes that are almost voyeuristic, it is still greatly exhilarating while it provokes thought and pushes the viewer into examining his own conscience.' – *Philip T. Hartung, Commonweal*

Grumpier Old Men
US 1995 100m Technicolor
Warner/John Davis/Lancaster Gate
Two elderly rivals intensify their feud when an Italian widow and her daughter move into the neighbourhood.
A sequel that is a virtual rerun of the original movie, with Lemmon and Matthau showing surprising enthusiasm for the familiar material.
w Mark Steven Johnson *d* Howard Deutch *ph* Tak Fujimoto *m* Alan Silvestri *pd* Gary Frutkoff *ed* Billy Weber, Seth Flaum, Maryann Brandon
☆ Jack Lemmon, Walter Matthau, Ann-Margret, Sophia Loren, Kevin Pollak, Daryl Hannah, Burgess Meredith
'Lazily scripted and crude in every sense of the word, without the two wily leads it would be nothing. With them it's a double tonic.' – *Sight and Sound*
† The film was released direct to video in Britain.

Grumpy Old Men
US 1993 104m Technicolor
Warner/Lancaster Gate (John Davis, Richard C. Berman)
A long feud between two ageing neighbours is intensified when an attractive widow moves into the neighbourhood.
Mildy amusing comedy, providing an opportunity for Lemmon, Matthau and Meredith to do their party pieces, which they do as well as their somewhat thin material will allow.
w Mark Steven Johnson *d* Donald Petrie *ph* Johnny E. Jensen *m* Alan Silvestri *pd* David Chapman *ed* Bonnie Koehler
☆ Jack Lemmon, Walter Matthau, Ann-Margret, Burgess Meredith, Daryl Hannah, Kevin Pollak, Ossie Davis, Buck Henry, Christopher McDonald
'Light, reasonably pleasant and undoubtedly sappy holiday entertainment.' – *Variety*

Gruppo di Famiglia in un Interno: see *Conversation Piece*

Guadalcanal Diary *
US 1943 93m bw
TCF (Bryan Foy)
Marines fight for a vital Pacific base.
Standard war propaganda, with good action scenes.
w Lamar Trotti *book* Richard Tregaskis *d* Lewis Seiler *ph* Charles G. Clarke *m* David Buttolph
☆ Preston Foster, Lloyd Nolan, William Bendix, Richard Conte, Anthony Quinn, Richard Jaeckel, Roy Roberts, Minor Watson, Ralph Byrd, Lionel Stander, Miles Mander, Reed Hadley

'A Comedy About Life, Death, Cars And … Cuba!'
Guantanamera
Cuba/Spain/Germany 1995 102m colour
Film Four/Tornasol/Alta/CAICICAA (Gerardo Herrero)
A bureaucrat gets the opportunity to test his scheme for transporting dead bodies around the island when his aunt dies.
Disappointing comedy of red tape and bungled chances, too tame to be effective.
w Eliseo Alberto Diego, Tomás Gutiérrez Alea, Juan Carlos Tabío *d* Tomás Gutiérrez Alea, Juan Carlos Tabío *ph* Hans Burmann *m* José Nieto *pd* Onelio Larralde *ed* Carmen Frias
☆ Carlos Cruz, Mirtha Ibarra, Jorge Perugorria, Raul Eguren, Pedro Fernández, Luis Alberto Garcia
'While the obscure humour takes time to weave its magic, this is a film to be cherished for its ingenious plot and its sheer mischievousness.' – *Empire*

'Tonight, while the world is asleep ... an ancient evil is about to awaken.'

The Guardian
US 1990 93m Technicolor
UIP/Universal (Joe Wizan)

A nanny sacrifices her charges to a tree.
Ridiculous horror of no discernible interest.
w Stephen Volk, Dan Greenburg *novel The Nanny* by Dan Greenburg *d* William Friedkin *m* Jack Hues *pd* Gregg Fonseca *ed* Seth Flaum *sp* Phil Cory, Ray Svedin, Hans Metz
☆ Jenny Seagrove, Dwier Brown, Carey Lowell, Brad Hull, Miguel Ferrer, Natalia Nogulich, Pamela Brull, Gary Swanson
'An ill-conceived, simple-minded horror flick' – *Variety*

'The Mission: Protect The Former President's Wife. The Danger: The Former President's Wife.'
'A Comedy Beyond The Call Of Duty.'

Guarding Tess *
US 1994 96m Technicolor
TriStar/Channel (Ned Tanen, Nancy Graham Tanen)

A secret service agent engages in a battle of wills with a temperamental former First Lady.
Likeable comedy of conflicting personalities, played with a lightness and charm by its two leads; its later plunge into melodrama is a mistake.
w Hugh Wilson, Peter Torokvei *d* Hugh Wilson *ph* Brian Reynolds *m* Michael Convertino *pd* Peter Larkin *ed* Sidney Levin
☆ *Shirley MacLaine, Nicolas Cage,* Austin Pendleton, Edward Albert, James Rebhorn, Richard Griffiths, John Roselius, David Graf
'Comedy, pathos and thrills alternately collide, creating problems in both pacing and developing a consistent tone. Ultimately, its thinness works against it.' – *Leonard Klady, Variety*

The Guardsman *
US 1931 83m bw
MGM (Albert Lewin)
A jealous actor tests his wife's fidelity.
Theatrically effective comedy filmed for the sake of its stars; later remade as a musical, The Chocolate Soldier *(qv).*
w Ernest Vajda, Claudine West *play* Ferenc Molnar *d* Sidney Franklin *ph* Norbert Brodine
☆ *Alfred Lunt, Lynn Fontanne,* Roland Young, ZaSu Pitts, Maude Eburne, Herman Bing, Ann Dvorak
'Looks like a smash engagement on Broadway and less than moderate returns on general release.' – *Variety*
🏆 Alfred Lunt; Lynn Fontanne

Guelwaar **
Senegal/France 1992 115m colour
Domireew/Galatee/FR3 (Ousmane Sembène, Jacques Perrin)
A Catholic family discover when they come to bury their father that his corpse has disappeared and he has been given a Muslim funeral by mistake.
A comic and ironic tone pervades an engaging tale of bureaucratic bungling, chauvinism, parochial intransigence and civic and national corruption.
wd Ousmane Sembène *ph* Dominique Gentil *m* Baaba Mall *pd* François Laurent Sulva *ed* Marie-Aimée Debril
☆ Omar Seck, Ndiawar Diop, Mame Ndoumbe Diop, Isseu Niang, Thierno Niaye, Joseph Baloma Sane, Abou Camara, Samba Wane, Moustapha Diop
'One of the more accessible African films to emerge in the last couple of years.' – *Variety*
† Sample dialogue: Man to young widow, 'For you, I'll divorce my four wives.'

Les Guerisseurs
Ivory Coast/France 1988 90m colour
Afriki Projection/Cote d'Ivoire Films/DEA/Alain Depardieu (Ayala Bakaba)
aka: *Aduefue, Lords of the Street*
In order to get money to finance his extravagant lifestyle, a black businessman plans a robbery with the aid of a French pimp.
A rambling, ill-constructed narrative on corruption, semi-satirical in tone and influenced for the worse by American action movies.
wd Sijiri Bakaba *ph* Mohammed Soudani *m* Serge Franklin *ad* Alama Kanate *ed* Olivier Morel
☆ Pierre Loup Rajot, Georges T. Benson, Nayanka Bell, Mory Traore, Sijiri Bakaba, Alpha Blondy, Salifou Keita

La Guerra di Troia: see *The Trojan War*

La Guerre Est Finie
France/Sweden 1966 122m bw
Sofracima/Europa Film

aka: *The War Is Over*
A Spanish revolutionary maintains his ideals even though he is warned that he will be sold out.
Dreary drama with romantic interludes and a fussy technique involving what appears to be the first use of flashforwards.
w Jorge Semprun *d* Alain Resnais *ph* Sacha Vierny *m* Giovanni Fusco
☆ Yves Montand, Ingrid Thulin, Geneviève Bujold, Michel Piccoli
'The most sophisticated work Alain Resnais has yet provided us, perfecting his technique in dealing cinematically with the interrelation of time and place, and never before has he brought such lyricism to the harshness of everyday living or given such scope to the probing of the inner man – all this within the framework of a suspense thriller.' – *Judith Crist*
🏆 Jorge Semprun

Guess Who's Coming to Dinner **
US 1967 112m Technicolor
Columbia/Stanley Kramer

A well-to-do San Francisco girl announces that she is going to marry a black man, and her parents find they are less broad-minded than they thought.
The problem picture that isn't really, since everyone is so nice and the prospective bridegroom is so eligible. It looks like a photographed play, but isn't based on one; the set is unconvincing; but the acting is a dream.
w William Rose *d* Stanley Kramer *ph* Sam Leavitt *md* Frank de Vol *pd* Robert Clatworthy
☆ *Spencer Tracy, Katharine Hepburn,* Katharine Houghton, *Sidney Poitier,* Cecil Kellaway, Roy E. Glenn Snr, Beah Richards, Isabel Sanford, Virginia Christine
'Suddenly everybody's caught up in a kind of integrated drawing-room comedy, and unable to decide whether there's anything funny in it or not.' – *Ann Birstein, Vogue*
'A load of embarrassing rubbish. In the circumstances there is little that director Stanley Kramer can do but see that his camera plod from room to room and make the most of people sitting down and getting up again.' – *Penelope Mortimer*
'What Rose and Kramer have done is to create a number of elaborate Aunt Sallies, arrange them in attractive patterns, and dispose of them with the flick of a feather.' – *Basil Wright, 1972*
'Mendacious and sanctimonious drivel.' – *John Simon*
† Katharine Houghton is the niece of Katharine Hepburn.
🏆 William Rose; Katharine Hepburn
🏆 best picture; Stanley Kramer; Frank de Vol; Spencer Tracy; Cecil Kellaway; Beah Richards
BAFTA: Spencer Tracy; Katharine Hepburn

The Guest: see *The Caretaker*

Guest House Paradiso
GB 1999 89m colour Arriscope
UIP/Universal (Phil McIntyre)

Two manic, light-fingered sadists run a seedy boarding house near a nuclear power station.
Gross and excessively aggressive comedy, mainly concerned with vomit and violent assaults on the more delicate parts of the human anatomy; banging your head hard against a brick wall would be considerably more entertaining, and would also capture the spirit of the movie.
w Adrian Edmondson, Rik Mayall *d* Adrian Edmondson *ph* Alan Almond *m* Colin Towns *pd* Tom Brown *ed* Sean Barton
☆ Rik Mayall (Richard Twat), Adrian Edmondson (Eddie Elizabeth Ndingombaba), Vincent Cassel (Gino Bolognese), Hélène Mahieu (Gina Carbonara), Bill Nighy (Mr Johnson), Simon Pegg (Mr Nice), Fenella Fielding (Mrs Foxfur), Lisa Palfrey (Mrs Nice), Kate Ashfield (Mrs Hardy), Steve O'Donnell (Chef)
'Years of barrel-scraping could not produce a film more hackneyed and lacklustre than this celluloid toilet paper.' – *James Christopher, Times*
'Horrifyingly unfunny, it is naff, smug, cynical, ugly and charmless.' – *Peter Bradshaw, Guardian*

Guest in the House *
US 1944 121m bw
Hunt Stromberg
A seemingly pleasant young woman is invited to stay with a family and brings tragedy and hatred to them.
Theatrical and rather unconvincing melodrama.
w Ketti Frings *play Dear Evelyn* by Dale Eunson, Hagar Wilde *d* John Brahm *ph* Lee Garmes *m* Werner Janssen *pd* Nicolai Remisoff
☆ Anne Baxter, Ralph Bellamy, Aline MacMahon, Ruth Warrick, Scott McKay, Jerome Cowan, Marie McDonald, Percy Kilbride, Margaret Hamilton
🏆 Werner Janssen

Guest Wife
US 1945 90m bw
UA/Greentree (Jack H. Skirball)

For business purposes a man allows his wife to pretend to be the wife of another.
Stereotyped star farce which seemed tolerable at the time.
w Bruce Manning, John Klorer *d* Sam Wood *ph* John Valentine *md* Daniele Amfitheatrof
☆ Claudette Colbert, Don Ameche, Dick Foran, Charles Dingle, Grant Mitchell
'Mr Wood is a big gun to be trained on so trivial a target, but the result justifies the choice.' – *Richard Mallett, Punch*
🏆 Daniele Amfitheatrof

'For the married man who's thinking single – or the single man who's just thinking!'

A Guide for the Married Man **
US 1967 91m DeLuxe Panavision
TCF (Frank McCarthy)

A practised wolf explains to a perfect husband how to be unfaithful.
Generally funny revue with as many hilarious moments as flat spots.
w Frank Tarloff *d* Gene Kelly *ph* Joe Macdonald *m* Johnny Williams
☆ *Walter Matthau,* Inger Stevens, *Robert Morse,* Sue Ane Langdon, Lucille Ball, Art Carney, Jack Benny, Polly Bergen, Joey Bishop, Sid Caesar, Wally Cox, Jayne Mansfield, Carl Reiner, Phil Silvers, Jeffrey Hunter and also Terry-Thomas, Ben Blue
'One of the funniest films of the last several seasons ... it has sense enough to sit down when it's through.' – *Robert Windeler*

Guilty?
GB 1956 93m bw
Grand National/Gibraltar (Charles A. Leeds)
An ex-resistance heroine is on trial for murder at the Old Bailey; her young solicitor goes to Avignon to prove her innocence.
Solidly cast old-fashioned mystery with a courtroom climax.
w Maurice J. Wilson *novel Death Has Deep Roots* by Michael Gilbert *d* Edmond T. Gréville *ph* Stan Pavey *m* Bruce Montgomery
☆ John Justin, Barbara Laage, Donald Wolfit, Stephen Murray, Norman Wooland, Frank Villard, Sydney Tafler, Betty Stockfeld

Guilty as Charged
US 1991 95m Foto-Kem
Copeland/Colichman (Randolph Gale)

A mad tycoon turned vigilante sets up his own electric chair to execute murderers who escape the law.
Over-the-top performances help distract attention from the predictable events.
w Charles Gale *d* Sam Irvin *ph* Richard Michalak *m* Steve Bartek *pd* Byrnadette DiSanto *ed* Kevin Tent
☆ Rod Steiger, Lauren Hutton, Heather Graham, Lyman Ward, Isaac Hayes, Zelda Rubinstein, Irwin Keyes, Michael Beach

Guilty as Sin
US 1993 107m Technicolor
Buena Vista/Hollywood (Martin Ransohoff)

An ambitious lawyer agrees to defend a man accused of murdering his wife and discovers that he is a serial killer.
Elegant but empty thriller, taken at too easy a tempo to create any suspense or tension.
w Larry Cohen *d* Sidney Lumet *ph* Andrzej Bartkowiak *m* Howard Shore *pd* Philip Rosenberg *ed* Evan Lottman
☆ Rebecca DeMornay, Don Johnson, Stephen Lang, Jack Warden, Dana Ivey, Ron White
'This has the empty, varnished vacuity of any old American TV movie, masquerading as one of those lesser Hitchcock courtroom sagas. The director is Sidney Lumet. I have absolutely no idea why he dunnit.' – *Derek Malcolm, Guardian*

'All it took was a whisper.'

Guilty by Suspicion *
US 1990 105m DeLuxe
Warner (Arnon Milchan)

In the 1950s, a successful film director finds himself without work after refusing to co-operate with the House Un-American Activities Committee investigating 'communist subversion' in Hollywood.
A weak, if well-meaning, attempt to deal with the period of blacklisting in Hollywood, but one that comes close to ignoring the complicity of the majority of studios in HUAC's activities. Martin Scorsese makes a brief appearance playing Joe Lesser, a director based on Joseph Losey, who fled to Europe to avoid testifying to the committee.
wd Irwin Winkler *ph* Michael Ballhaus *m* James Newton Howard *pd* Leslie Dilley *ed* Priscilla Nedd
☆ Robert DeNiro, Annette Bening, George Wendt, Patricia Wettig, Sam Wanamaker
'Once again, a producer has confused earnestness with seriousness, and felt that displaying good intentions could serve as a substitute for the low cunning of entertainment.' – *Sight and Sound*

Guilty Hands
US 1931 60m bw
MGM
A district attorney commits murder and tries to frame a girl, but is killed when rigor mortis makes the gun go off in his victim's hand.
Risible melodrama which might with better writing have been effective.
w Bayard Veiller *d* W. S. Van Dyke
☆ Lionel Barrymore, Kay Francis, Madge Evans, William Bakewell, C. Aubrey Smith, Polly Moran, Alan Mowbray
'Someone missed here, and plenty.' – *Variety*

The Guinea Pig **
GB 1948 97m bw
Pilgrim (John Boulting)

US title: *The Outsider*
The first poor boy to win a scholarship to a famous public school has a hard time.
Enjoyable though unrealistic school drama with chief interest centring on the staff. A rude word ('kick up the arse') ensured its popularity.
w Bernard Miles, Warren Chetham Strode *play* Warren Chetham Strode *d* Roy Boulting *ph* Gilbert Taylor *m* John Wooldridge
☆ Richard Attenborough, *Robert Flemyng, Cecil Trouncer,* Sheila Sim, Bernard Miles, Joan Hickson

Guling Jie Shaonian Sha Ren Shijan: see *A Brighter Summer Day*

Gulliver's Travels **
US 1939 74m Technicolor
Paramount/Max Fleischer

Animated cartoon version which invents a Romeo-Juliet romance between Lilliput and Blefuscu and has the usual trouble with romantic humans.
At the time it represented a genuine challenge to Disney, but has not worn well in terms of pace or inventiveness. Fleischer made one more feature cartoon, Mr Bug Goes to Town.
d Dave Fleischer *m* Victor Young *m/ly* Ralph Rainger, Leo Robin

☆ Featuring the voices of Lanny Ross, Jessica Dragonette
'Effective entertainment, but may not reach the grosses of *Snow White*.' – *Variety*
song 'Faithful Forever'; Victor Young

Gulliver's Travels
GB 1976 81m Eastmancolor
EMI/Valeness-Belvision (Josef Shaftel)
An ineffective treatment, again aimed at children, in which Gulliver is the only human element and all the Lilliputians are cartooned.
w Don Black *d* Peter Hunt *ph* Alan Hume *m* Michel Legrand *pd* Michael Stringer
☆ Richard Harris, Catherine Schell, Norman Shelley
'Bonelessly inoffensive.' – *Sight and Sound*

The Gumball Rally
US 1976 107m Technicolor
Warner/First Artists (Chuck Bail)
A variety of vehicles take part in a crazy race from New York to Long Beach.
The stuntmen are the real stars of this good-looking but dramatically deficient chase and destruction extravaganza.
w Leon Capetanos *d* Chuck Bail *ph* *Richard Glouner* *m* Dominic Frontière *stunt coordinator* Eddie Donno
☆ Michael Sarrazin, Norman Burton, Gary Busey, John Durren, Susan Flannery

Gummo
US 1997 88m DeLuxe
Entertainment/Fine Line (Cary Woods)
Unhappy adolescents search for ways of passing the time in a dull Ohio town devastated by a tornado.
Deliberately haphazard account of fractured lives which seems intended as a freak show for idle minds.
wd Harmony Korine *ph* Jean Yves Escoffier *pd* Dave Doernberg *ed* Christopher Tellefsen
☆ Jacob Reynolds, Nick Sutton, Jacob Sewell, Darby Dougherty, Chloe Sevigny, Carisa Bara, Linda Manz, Max Perlich
'A puzzlingly idiosyncratic, and not entirely effective, feature.' – *Variety*
'On one level *Gummo* represents a high watermark of 90s White Trash Chic, on another its resurrection and flagrant deforming of the neo-realist impulse harbours a longing to invent a Cinema of Abjection.' – *Gavin Smith, Sight and Sound*

Gumshoe **
GB 1971 85m Eastmancolor
Columbia/Memorial (David Barber)
A Liverpool bingo caller dreams of becoming a Bogart-like private eye and finds himself in the middle of a murder case.
A likeable spoof which is never quite as funny as it means to be. Billy Liar did it better, but there's plenty of amusing detail.
w Neville Smith *d* Stephen Frears *ph* Chris Menges *m* Andrew Lloyd Webber
☆ *Albert Finney*, Billie Whitelaw, Fulton Mackay, Frank Finlay, Janice Rule

Gun Crazy *
US 1949 87m bw
King Brothers/Universal-International
reissue title: *Deadly Is the Female*
A boy and girl set off on a trail of armed robbery and murder.
Modernized Bonnie and Clyde story which has become a minor cult film.
w Dalton Trumbo, Mackinlay Kantor *story* Mackinlay Kantor *d* *Joseph H. Lewis* *ph* Russell Harlan *m* Victor Young
☆ John Dall, Peggy Cummins, Morris Carnovsky, Berry Kroeger, Annabel Shaw, Harry Lewis, Russ Tamblyn

Gun for a Coward
US 1956 88m Technicolor Cinemascope
U-I (William Campbell)
Three brothers join forces on a cattle drive, but one is killed.
Slightly pretentious Western co-feature.
w R. Wright Campbell *d* Abner Biberman *ph* George Robinson
☆ Fred MacMurray, Jeffrey Hunter, Dean Stockwell, Chill Wills, Janice Rule

'One Against The Killers!!!'
Gun Fury
US 1953 80m Technicolor 3-D
Columbia (Lewis J. Rachmil)
Outlaws rob a stagecoach and abduct a girl; her fiancé follows and takes revenge.
Adequate Western programmer.
w Irving Wallace, Roy Huggins *novel* *Ten Against Caesar* by Kathleen, George and Robert Granger *d* Raoul Walsh *ph* Lester H. White *md* Mischa Bakaleinikoff *ad* Ross Bellah *ed* Jerome Thoms, James Sweeney
☆ Rock Hudson (Ben Warren), Donna Reed (Jennifer Ballard), Phil Carey (Frank Slayton), Lee Marvin (Blinky), Neville Brand (Brazos), Roberta Haynes (Estella Moralez), Ray Thomas (Doc), Robert Herron (Curly Jordan)

Gun Glory
US 1957 89m Metrocolor Cinemascope
MGM (Nicholas Nayfack)
A gunfighter returns home to settle down, but finds his wife dead and his son resentful.
Dull, unexciting star Western.
w William Ludwig *novel* *Man of the West* by Philip Yordan *d* Roy Rowland *ph* Harold J. Marzorati *m* Jeff Alexander
☆ Stewart Granger, Rhonda Fleming, Chill Wills, Steve Rowland, James Gregory

'She Was Nobody Until Somebody Found...'
The Gun in Betty Lou's Handbag
US 1992 89m Technicolor
Buena Vista/Touchstone/Interscope/Nomura Babcock & Brown (Scott Kroopf)
An unassertive librarian, tired of being ignored by everyone, confesses to a murder she did not commit.
Drear and dim-witted comedy, short on laughs, long on longeurs and with a few moments of unpleasant violence to ensure its failure as entertainment.
w Grace Cary Bickley *d* Allan Moyle *ph* Charles Minsky *m* Richard Gibbs *pd* Michael Corenblith *ed* Janice Hampton, Erica Huggins
☆ Penelope Ann Miller, Eric Thal, William Forsythe, Cathy Moriarty, Julianne Moore, Alfre Woodard
'Figures to fire a blank into the box-office till' – *Variety*

The Gun Runner: see *Santiago*

The Gun Runners *
US 1958 82m bw
UA/Seven Arts (Clarence Greene)
The owner of a Florida motor cruiser innocently rents it to a gun merchant.
Modestly effective action melodrama, the third version of To Have and Have Not (qv).
w Daniel Mainwaring, Paul Monash *d* *Don Siegel* *ph* *Hal Mohr* *m* Leith Stevens
☆ Audie Murphy, Eddie Albert, Patricia Owens, Everett Sloane

'They've been hit before, but never in the heart.'
Gun Shy
US 2000 102m Technicolor
Buena Vista/Hollywood/Fortis (Sandra Bullock)
An undercover agent goes into group therapy to help him deal with investigating a money-laundering deal.
A farce in which the humour depends upon inverting stereotypical characterisations of Colombian cocaine dealers, gangsters and tough agents; its tone is too genial to encompass its occasional lurches into violence.
wd Eric Blakeney *ph* Tom Richmond *m* Rolfe Kent *pd* Maher Ahmad *ed* Pamela Martin *cos* Mary Claire Hannan
☆ Liam Neeson (Charlie), Oliver Platt (Fulvio Nesstra), Sandra Bullock (Judy Tipp), Jose Zuniga (Fidel Vaillar), Richard Schiff (Elliott), Andy Lauer (Jason Cane), Mitch Pileggi (Dexter Helvenshaw), Paul Ben-Victor (Howard), Mary McCormack (Gloria Nesstra), Frank Vincent (Carmine Minetti), Gregg Daniel (Jonathan)
'Alternately hits its target and fires blanks as the latest comedy crime pic to explore the vulnerabilities of tough guys.' – *Robert Koehler, Variety*

Gun Smoke
US 1931 64m bw
Paramount
Cowboys defeat a gang of big city crooks who plan to ransack a small town.
Odd little western, in which the crooks are defined as 'capitalists', modernity is mocked, and the good guys are even more ruthless than the gangsters, arguing that 'the only thing to do with killers is to kill 'em.'
w Grover Jones, William McNutt *d* Edward Sloman *ph* Archie Stout
☆ Richard Arlen, Mary Brian, Eugene Pallette, Louise Fazenda, Charles Winninger, Guy Oliver, James Durkin, Brooks Benedict, William 'Stage' Boyd, J. Carrol Naish

Gunbus
aka: *Sky Bandits*

Guncrazy
US 1992 93m Foto-Kem
Zeta/First Look (Zane W. Levitt, Diane Firestone)
A parentless 16-year-old marries a paroled murderer and the two take to the road, robbing and killing as they go.
An uninvolving thriller set in a depressed and depressing red-neck community; it may interest for the light it sheds on the darker edges of American society, but it is hardly entertaining.
w Matthew Bright *d* Tamra Davis *ph* Lisa Rinzler *m* Ed Tomney *ed* Kevin Tent
☆ Drew Barrymore, James LeGros, Billy Drago, Rodney Harvey, Joe Dallesandro, Michael Ironside, Ione Skye
'A shoot-'em-up exploitationer with a few interesting ideas ... settles into a surprisingly somber mood that suppresses the possibilities latent in the story and actors.' – *Variety*

Guney's The Wall: see *The Wall*

'In the bullring at Bajo Rio, Mexico, on Saturday at 4 pm, they'll pay to see two men kill each other!'
A Gunfight *
US 1970 94m Technicolor
Harvest/Thoroughbred/Bryna (Ronnie Lubin, Harold Jack Bloom)
Two famous gunfighters on their uppers stage a duel for money.
Austere and anti-climactic Western supposedly against popular blood lust.
w Harold Jack Bloom *d* Lamont Johnson *ph* David M. Walsh *m* Laurence Rosenthal
☆ Kirk Douglas, Johnny Cash, Karen Black, Raf Vallone, Jane Alexander

Gunfight at Comanche Creek
US 1963 90m DeLuxe Panavision
Allied Artists (Ben Schwalb)
In 1875 a detective goes undercover to unmask the brains behind a robber gang with complex methods.
Ingenious but over-emphatic Western programmer.
w Edward Bernds *d* Frank McDonald *ph* Joseph Biroc *m* Marlin Skiles *ad* Edward Jewell *ed* William Austin
☆ Audie Murphy, Ben Cooper, Colleen Miller, John Hubbard, DeForest Kelley
† It was a remake of *Last of the Badmen* (qv).

Gunfight at Dodge City
US 1958 81m DeLuxe Cinemascope
UA/Mirisch
After various problems, Bat Masterson is elected sheriff of Dodge City.
Fair standard Western with emphasis on plot and character.
w Daniel B. Ullman, Martin M. Goldsmith *d* Joseph M. Newman *ph* Carl Guthrie *m* Hans Salter
☆ Joel McCrea, Julie Adams, John McIntire, Richard Anderson, Nancy Gates

Gunfight at the OK Corral **
US 1957 122m Technicolor Vistavision
Paramount/Hal Wallis
Wyatt Earp and Doc Holliday defeat the Clanton Gang.
Watchable, ambitious, but vaguely disappointing super-Western.
w Leon Uris *d* John Sturges *ph* Charles B. Lang *m* Dimitri Tiomkin
☆ *Burt Lancaster, Kirk Douglas*, Jo Van Fleet, Rhonda Fleming, John Ireland, Frank Faylen, Kenneth Tobey, Earl Holliman
'Carefully and lavishly mounted, but overlong and overwrought.' – *John Cutts*
† The legendary gunfight was tackled again in the 1994 Western *Tombstone* (qv).

Gunfight in Abilene
US 1967 86m Technicolor Techniscope
Universal
After the Civil War, an officer goes home to find strife between farmers and cattlemen.
Fairly sensible and pleasing lower-berth Western.
w Berne Giler, John D. F. Black *d* William Hale
☆ Bobby Darin, Emily Banks, Leslie Nielsen, Donnelly Rhodes, Don Galloway, Michael Sarrazin

'His only friend was his gun – his only refuge, a woman's heart!'
The Gunfighter **
US 1950 84m bw
TCF (Nunnally Johnson)
A gunfighter fails to shake off his past.
Downbeat, small-scale but very careful adult Western set in a believable community.
w William Bowers, William Sellers *d* *Henry King* *ph* *Arthur Miller* *m* Alfred Newman
☆ Gregory Peck, Helen Westcott, Millard Mitchell, Jean Parker, Karl Malden, Skip Homeier, Mae Marsh
'Preserves throughout a respectable level of intelligence and invention.' – *Lindsay Anderson*
'Not merely a good western, a good film.' – *Richard Mallett, Punch*
'The movie is done in cold, quiet tones of gray, and every object in it – faces, clothing, a table, the hero's heavy moustache – is given an air of uncompromising authenticity, suggesting those dim photographs of the nineteenth-century west...' – *Robert Warshow, The Immediate Experience*
original story (William Bowers, André de Toth)

Gunfighters
US 1947 87m Cinecolor
Columbia
GB title: *The Assassin*
A retired gunfighter is suspected of the murder of his best friend.
Presentable star Western.
w Alan Le May *novel* *Twin Sombreros* by Zane Grey *d* George Waggner
☆ Randolph Scott, Barbara Britton, Dorothy Hart, Bruce Cabot, Forrest Tucker

Gunfire: see *China 9, Liberty 37*

Gung Ho!
US 1943 88m bw
Universal/Walter Wanger
Adventures of the Marines in the Pacific War.
Trite flagwaver, popular at the time.
w Lucien Hubbard, based on the experiences of Captain W. S. LeFrançois USMC *d* Ray Enright *ph* Milton H. Krasner *m* Frank Skinner, Hans Salter *ad* Alexander Golitzen, John B. Goodman *ed* Milton Carruth
☆ Randolph Scott, Grace MacDonald, Alan Curtis, Noah Beery Jnr, J. Carrol Naish, David Bruce, Peter Coe, Robert Mitchum

Gung Ho
US 1986 111m Technicolor Panavision
Paramount (Tony Ganz, Deborah Blum)
Japanese management takes over an American small town.
Basically old-fashioned hands-across-the-sea stuff, without any very clear attitude except gentle fun. It rapidly led to a TV series, which folded, and that's about its level.
w Lowell Ganz, Babaloo Mandel *d* Ron Howard *ph* Don Peterman *m* Thomas Newman *pd* James Schoppe *ed* Daniel Hanley, Michael Hill
☆ Michael Keaton, Gedde Watanabe, George Wendt, Mimi Rogers, John Turturro
'A film that's not much of anything except two hours long.' – *People*

'Thrills for a thousand movies plundered for one mighty show!'
'Romance aflame through dangerous days and nights of terror! In a land where anything can happen – most of all to a beautiful girl alone!'

Gunga Din ***
US 1939 117m bw
RKO (George Stevens)
Three cheerful army veterans meet adventure on the North-West Frontier.
Rousing period actioner with comedy asides, one of the most entertaining of its kind ever made.
w Joel Sayre, Fred Guiol, Ben Hecht, Charles MacArthur *poem* Rudyard Kipling *d* George Stevens *ph* Joseph H. August *m* Alfred Newman *ad* Van Nest Polglase
☆ *Cary Grant, Victor McLaglen, Douglas Fairbanks Jnr, Sam Jaffe,* Eduardo Ciannelli, Joan Fontaine, Montagu Love, Robert Coote, Cecil Kellaway, Abner Biberman, Lumsden Hare
'One of the big money pictures this year ... will recoup plenty at the box office window.' – *Variety*
'One of the most enjoyable nonsense-adventure movies of all time.' – *Pauline Kael, 1968*
'Bravura is the exact word for the performances, and Stevens' composition and cutting of the fight sequences is particularly stunning.' – *NFT, 1973*

Gunhed (dubbed)
Japan 1989 99m colour
Manga/Toho/Sunrise (Yoshishige Shimatani, Tetsuhisha Yamada)
In 2039, engineers patch up warrior-robots to disarm a super-computer that is trying to take over the world.
Comic-book science fiction, frequently risible and always over the top.
w Masato Harada, James Bannon *d* Masato Harada *ph* Jinichi Fujisawa *m* Toshiyuki Honda *ed* Yoshitami Kuroiwa *sp* Koichi Kawakita, Imagica Group
☆ Masahiro Takashima, Brenda Bakke, Yujin Harada, Kaori Mizushima, Aya Enyoji, Mickey Curtis, James B. Thompson, Doll Nguyen, Landy Leyes
'A hokey slab of Nipponese sci-fi that's OK for buffs but not high-key enough to break into wider markets.' – *Variety*
'This is the computer game as cinema.' – *Derek Malcolm, Guardian*

Gunman's Walk *
US 1958 97m Technicolor Cinemascope
Columbia (Fred Kohlmar)
A tough Westerner has two sons, one of whom follows too literally in his footsteps.
Competent action melodrama with good characterization.
w Frank Nugent *d* Phil Karlson *ph* Charles Lawton *m* George Duning
☆ Van Heflin, Tab Hunter, James Darren, Kathryn Grant

Gunmen
US 1992 90m DeLuxe Panavision
Dimension/Davis (Laurence Mark, John Davis, John Flock)
Ruthless killers search for a fortune of $400m stolen from a powerful South American drug dealer and hidden on a boat.
Ludicrously overheated and violent thriller with some moments of sanctimonious moralizing that only emphasize its inherent sleaziness.
w Stephen Sommers *d* Deran Sarafian *ph* Hiro Narita *m* John Debney *pd* Michael Seymour *ed* Bonnie Koehler
☆ Christopher Lambert, Mario Van Peebles, Denis Leary, Kadeem Hardison, Sally Kirkland, Richard Sarafian, Robert Harper, Brenda Bakke, Patrick Stewart, Deran Sarafian
'A routine, vacuous actioner that tries to mix thrills with humor.' – *Variety*
'Charmless.' – *Empire*

Gunn *
US 1967 95m Technicolor
Paramount/Geoffrey (Owen Crump)
A private eye is hired to find a gangster's killer.
Tongue-in-cheek violence from the television series, with Craig Stevens doing a Cary Grant imitation.
w Blake Edwards, William Peter Blatty *d* Blake Edwards *ph* Philip Lathrop *m* Henry Mancini
☆ Craig Stevens, Laura Devon, Ed Asner, Sherry Jackson, Helen Traubel, J. Pat O'Malley, Regis Toomey
'Falters between parody and straight action.' – *MFB*

Gunpoint: see *At Gunpoint*

Gunpoint
US 1965 86m Technicolor
Universal
A Colorado sheriff goes after train robbers.
Simple-minded but quite professional and good-looking Western programmer.
w Mary and Willard Willingham *d* Earl Bellamy *ph* William Margulies *m* Hans Salter
☆ Audie Murphy, Joan Staley, Warren Stevens, Edgar Buchanan, Denver Pyle, Royal Dano

Guns at Batasi *
GB 1964 103m bw Cinemascope
TCF/George H. Brown
The headquarters of an Anglo-African regiment is threatened by rebels.
Basically the old chestnut about a group of disparate types trapped in a dangerous situation, this is given shape and stature by the star's lively performance as the martinet of an RSM.
w Robert Holles *novel* The Siege of Battersea by Robert Holles *d* John Guillermin *ph* Douglas Slocombe *m* John Addison
☆ *Richard Attenborough,* Flora Robson, Mia Farrow, Jack Hawkins, Cecil Parker, Percy Herbert, Errol John, John Leyton, Earl Cameron
BAFTA: Richard Attenborough

Guns for San Sebastian
France/Mexico/Italy 1967 111m Metrocolor Franscope
MGM/Cipra/Filmes/Ernesto Eniques (Jacques Bar)
In Mexico in 1746, a rebel on the run stays to defend a besieged village.
Multi-national actioner, violent but quite undistinguished.
w James R. Webb *book* A Wall for San Sebastian by William B. Flaherty *d* Henri Verneuil *ph* Armand Thirard *m* Ennio Morricone
☆ Anthony Quinn, Charles Bronson, Sam Jaffe, Anjanette Comer, Silvia Pinal, Fernand Gravet

Guns in the Afternoon: see *Ride the High Country*

Guns in the Heather
US 1968 90m Technicolor
Walt Disney
An American schoolboy in Ireland finds that his elder brother is a CIA agent.
Tolerable kiddie-fodder from the Disney treadmill; later desiccated for TV.
w Herman Groves *novel* Lockhart Amerman *d* Robert Butler *ph* Michael Reed *m* Buddy Baker
☆ Glenn Corbett, Alfred Burke, Kurt Russell, Patrick Barr

Guns of Darkness
GB 1962 102m bw
ABP/Cavalcade (Thomas Clyde)
A British plantation boss in Latin America escapes with his wife when rebels strike.
Chase/escape film with a few tiny comments about violence.
w John Mortimer *novel* Act of Mercy by Francis Clifford *d* Anthony Asquith *ph* Robert Krasker *m* Benjamin Frankel
☆ David Niven, Leslie Caron, James Robertson Justice, David Opatoshu

The Guns of Fort Petticoat
US 1957 79m Technicolor
Columbia/Brown-Murphy (Harry Joe Brown)
During the Civil War, a wandering Texan trains townswomen into a fighting force.
Unlikely Western which passes the time.
w Walter Doniger *d* George Marshall *ph* Ray Rennahan *m* Mischa Bakaleinikoff
☆ Audie Murphy, Kathryn Grant, Hope Emerson, Jeff Donnell, Isobel Elsom

The Guns of Loos *
GB 1927 89m (24 fps) bw silent
Stoll/New Era
A blinded hero of the war returns home to run an industrial empire and is confronted by a strike.
One of the better British silents, with a strong plot and an interesting cast.
w L. H. Gordon, Reginald Fogwell, Sinclair Hill *d* Sinclair Hill *ph* Desmond Dickinson
☆ Henry Victor, Madeleine Carroll, Bobby Howes, Hermione Baddeley

The Guns of Navarone **
GB 1961 157m Technicolor Cinemascope
Columbia/Open Road/Carl Foreman (Cecil F. Ford)
In 1943 a sabotage team is sent to destroy two giant guns on a Turkish Island.
Ambitiously produced Boy's Own Paper *heroics, with lots of noise and self-sacrifice; intermittently exciting but bogged down by philosophical chat.*
w Carl Foreman *novel* Alistair MacLean *d* J. Lee-Thompson *ph* Oswald Morris *m* Dimitri Tiomkin *ad* Geoffrey Drake
☆ Gregory Peck, David Niven, Stanley Baker, Anthony Quinn, Anthony Quayle, James Darren, Gia Scala, James Robertson Justice, Richard Harris, Irene Papas, Bryan Forbes
'A desperate imbalance: the moral arguments cut into the action without extending it.' – *Penelope Houston*
Academy Award nomination: best picture; Carl Foreman; J. Lee-Thompson; Dimitri Tiomkin; special effects (Bill Warrington, Vivian C. Greenham)

'The Magnificent Seven are back – and they don't aim to please.'

Guns of the Magnificent Seven
US 1969 106m DeLuxe Panavision
UA/Mirisch (Vincent M. Fennelly)
Seven mercenaries rescue a Mexican Robin Hood.
Stale, flat and unprofitable third serving of this particular hash.
w Herman Hoffman *d* Paul Wendkos *ph* Antonio Macasoli *m* Elmer Bernstein
☆ George Kennedy, Monte Markham, Joe Don Baker, James Whitmore, Bernie Casey, Scott Thomas, Reni Santoni, Michael Ansara, Wende Wagner, Fernando Rey, Frank Silvera

Guns of the Timberland
US 1960 91m Technicolor
Jaguar (Aaron Spelling)
Loggers are opposed by cattle interests.
Routine star Western with tolerable production values.
w Joseph Petracca, Aaron Spelling *novel* Louis L'Amour *d* Robert D. Webb *ph* John Seitz *m* David Buttolph
☆ Alan Ladd, Jeanne Crain, Gilbert Roland, Frankie Avalon, Lyle Bettger, Noah Beery Jnr

Guns of Wyoming: see *Cattle King*

Gunsmoke
US 1953 79m Technicolor
Universal (Aaron Rosenberg)
A cowboy befriends the rancher he has been hired to kill.
Moderate Western with too many pauses for sentiment.
w D. D. Beauchamp *novel* Roughshod by Norman A. Fox *d* Nathan Juran *ph* Charles P. Boyle *ad* Robert Boyle, Alexander Golitzen *ed* Ted J. Kent
☆ Audie Murphy, Paul Kelly, Susan Cabot, Mary Castle, Charles Drake

The Guru
US/India 1969 112m DeLuxe
TCF/Arcadia (Ismail Merchant)
In India, an English pop singer succumbs to the local atmosphere.
Pleasant, affectionate but forgettable anecdote of modern India.
w Ruth Prawer Jhabvala, James Ivory *d* James Ivory *ph* Subrata Mitra *m* Ustad Vilayat Khan
☆ Michael York, Rita Tushingham, Utpal Dutt, Aparna Sen, Barry Foster

'When He Talks Women Listen.'

The Guru
GB/US/France 2002 95m DeLuxe
Universal/StudioCanal/Working Title (Tim Bevan, Eric Fellner, Michael London)
An unsuccessful Indian actor in New York finds fame after he impersonates a guru and begins giving advice on sex,
The clash of two cultures should have produced more amusement than is to be found in this soft-centred romantic comedy that cannot even be funny about pornography or Bollywood.
w Tracey Jackson *story* Shekhar Kapur *d* Daisy von Scherler Mayer *ph* John de Borman *m* David Carbonara *pd* Robin Standefer, Sean Afshar *ed* Cara Silverman, Bruce Green
☆ Heather Graham (Sharonna), Marisa Tomei (Lexi), Jimi Mistry (Ramu Chandra Gupta), Michael McKean (Dwain), Christine Baranski (Chantal), Rob Morrow (Josh), Malachy McCourt (Father Flannagan), Sanjeev Bhaskar (Cook)
'A generally entertaining but rather old-fashioned romantic comedy,' – *Derek Elley, Variety*

Guru in Seven
GB 1997 107m colour
Ratpack/Balhar (Shani Grewal)
After his girlfriend leaves him, an artist bets his friends that he can bed seven women in a week.
Familiar sex comedy routine, given a little twist by being set within a Punjabi community in Britain; it tries, but fails, to be an Alfie for the 90s.
wd Shani Grewal *ph* James Bishop *m* Matthew Best, Neil Hourigan, Sean Maher, Sunny Sehgal *ed* Shani Grewal
☆ Saeed Jaffrey, Jacqueline Pearce, Nitin Chandra Ganatra, Lea Rochelle, Lynne Michelle, Elle Lewis, Amanda Pointer
'Definitely worth seeking out.' – *Empire*

Gus
US 1976 96m Technicolor
Walt Disney (Ron Miller)
A football team co-opts a mule which can kick a hundred yard ball.
Predictable Disney fantasy comedy with a direct line back to The Absent Minded Professor.
w Arthur Alsberg, Don Nelson *d* Vincent McEveety *ph* Frank Phillips *m* Robert F. Brunner
☆ Ed Asner, Don Knotts, Gary Grimes, Tim Conway, Liberty Williams, Bob Crane, Harold Gould, Tom Bosley, Dick Van Patten
'In the current comedy climate, when humour so often hinges on a four-letter word or its lengthier variant, a light-hearted football game spoof is a breath of fresh air.' – *Tatiana Balkoff Lipscomb, Films in Review*

The Guv'nor
GB 1935 88m bw
Gaumont (Michael Balcon)
US title: *Mr Hobo*
By chance a tramp becomes a bank director.
Predictable star vehicle with Arliss a most unlikely tramp.
w Maude Howell, Guy Bolton *d* Milton Rosmer *ph* Max Greene *md* Louis Levy
☆ George Arliss, Gene Gerrard, Viola Keats, Patric Knowles, Frank Cellier, Mary Clare, George Hayes
'His admirers need not fear that he has lost any of his usual refinement or sentiment, his cultured English accent, his Universal certificate.' – *Graham Greene*

Guy
GB/Germany 1996 94m colour
Polygram/Pandora (Renée Missel)
A documentary photographer stalks a car salesman with her camera.
An anecdote of surveillance that goes on for far too long.
w Kirby Dick *d* Michael Lindsay-Hogg *ph* Arturo Smith *m* Jeff Beal *pd* Kara Lindstrom *ed* Dody Dorn
☆ Vincent D'Onofrio, Hope Davis, Kimber Riddle, Diane Salinger, Richard Portnow, Valente Rodriguez, Michael Massee, John O'Donohue
'Lacks enough imagination to make it more than a smart, postgraduate film-making exercise.' – *Liese Spencer, Sight and Sound*

A Guy Named Joe
US 1944 120m bw
MGM (Everett Riskin)
▬
A flyer is killed but comes back as a ghost to supervise his ex-girl's new romance.
Icky romantic comedy-drama with strong propaganda intent; the stars make it tolerable.
w Dalton Trumbo *d* Victor Fleming *ph* George Folsey, Karl Freund *m* Herbert Stothart
☆ Spencer Tracy, Irene Dunne, Ward Bond, Van Johnson, James Gleason, Lionel Barrymore, Barry Nelson, Don Defore, Henry O'Neill

'As far as I could judge, the audience loved it: melodrama, farce, fake philosophy, swimming eyes and all.' – *Richard Mallett, Punch*

'It neatly obtunds death's sting as ordinary people suffer it by not only assuming but photographing a good, busy, hearty hereafter.' – *James Agee*

† The title was explained by one of the characters who observed that 'in the Army Air Corps, any fellow who is a right fellow is called Joe'.
†† It was remade in 1989 as *Always* (qv).
🏆 original story (David Boehm, Chandler Sprague)

The Guy Who Came Back
US 1951 92m bw
TCF
A pro football player hates the thought of retiring.
Sentimental sporting drama without much life in it.
w Allan Scott *d* Joseph Newman
☆ Paul Douglas, Joan Bennett, Linda Darnell, Don Defore, Zero Mostel

Guys and Dolls *
US 1955 149m Eastmancolor
Cinemascope
Samuel Goldwyn
▣ ▬ ◉ ◎
A New York gangster takes a bet that he can romance a Salvation Army lady.
The artifices of Runyonland are made more so by a defiantly studio-bound production and thoroughly flat handling; but the songs and sometimes the performances survive.
wd Joseph L. Mankiewicz *musical* Jo Swerling, Abe Burrows *ph* Harry Stradling *m/ly Frank Loesser* *md* Cyril Mockridge, Jay Blackton *ch* Michael Kidd *pd* Oliver Smith *ad* Joseph Wright
☆ Frank Sinatra, Marlon Brando, Jean Simmons, *Vivian Blaine, Stubby Kaye,* B. S. Pully, Robert Keith, Sheldon Leonard, George E. Stone

'Quantity has been achieved only at the cost of quality.' – *Penelope Houston*

🏆 Harry Stradling; Cyril Mockridge, Jay Blackton; art direction

Gycklarnas Afton: see *Sawdust and Tinsel*

Gymkata
US 1985 90m Metrocolor
MGM/UA (Fred Weintraub)
▣ ▬
An American gymnast trains to win a contest of skill and strength in a small Asian country, mainly populated by ninjas, in order that the US can install a spy satellite there.
Disagreeable and ridiculous gung-ho martial arts nonsense.
w Charles Robert Carner *novel The Terrible Game* by Dan Tyler Moore *d* Robert Clouse *ph* Godfrey Godar *m* Alfi Kabiljo *pd* Veljko Despotovic *ed* Robert A. Ferretti
☆ Kurt Thomas, Tetchie Agbayani, Richard Norton, Edward Bell, John Barrett, Conan Lee

'The girl who became the greatest show in show business!'

Gypsy *
US 1962 149m Technirama
Warner (Mervyn Le Roy)
▣ ▬ ◉ ◎
The early days of stripteaser Gypsy Rose Lee, and the exploits of her ambitious mother.
A vaudeville musical that is nowhere near raucous enough, or brisk enough, for its subject, and is miscast into the bargain. The songs are great, but not here: Miss Russell is as boring as an electric drill in a role that should have been reserved for Ethel Merman.
w Leonard Spigelgass *play* Arthur Laurents *d* Mervyn Le Roy *ph* Harry Stradling *m/ly Jule Styne, Stephen Sondheim* *md* Frank Perkins *ad* John Beckman
☆ Rosalind Russell, Natalie Wood, *Karl Malden,* James Millhollin
† Natalie Wood's singing was dubbed by Marni Nixon.
†† A TV version was made in 1993 directed by Emile Ardolino and starring Bette Midler.
🏆 Harry Stradling; Frank Perkins

The Gypsy and the Gentleman
GB 1957 107m Eastmancolor
Rank (Maurice Cowan)
A penniless Regency rake marries a tempestuous gypsy, with melodramatic and tragic results.
Expensive and typically mistimed Rank attempt to re-do The Man in Grey; *a barnstormer notable only for waste of talent.*
w Janet Greene *novel Darkness I Leave You* by Nina Warner Hooke *d* Joseph Losey *ph* Jack Hildyard *m* Hans May *ad* Ralph Brinton
☆ Melina Mercouri, Keith Michell, Patrick McGoohan, June Laverick, Flora Robson, Helen Haye, Mervyn Johns

Gypsy Colt
🚸 US 1954 72m Anscocolor
MGM (William Grady Jnr, Sidney Franklin Jnr)
A cherished colt has to be sold, but makes its way back home.
Disguised second feature remake of Lassie Come Home; *good for children.*
w Martin Berkeley *story* Eric Knight *d* Andrew Marton *ph* Harold Lipstein *m* Rudolph G. Kopp *ad* Cedric Gibbons
☆ Donna Corcoran, Ward Bond, Frances Dee, Larry Keating, Lee Van Cleef

Gypsy Girl: see *Sky West and Crooked*

The Gypsy Moths *
US 1969 110m Metrocolor
MGM/Frankenheimer-Lewis (Hal Landers, Bobby Roberts)
Sky-diving stuntmen find love and death on a small-town tour.
Brilliantly breathtaking actioner which too frequently gets grounded, and does not find a reason for being so glum.
w William Hanley *novel* James Drought *d* John Frankenheimer *ph* Philip Lathrop *m* Elmer Bernstein *aerial ph Carl Boenisch*
☆ Burt Lancaster, Deborah Kerr, Gene Hackman, Scott Wilson, William Windom, Bonnie Bedelia, Sheree North

'A Bergmanesque world of inner emotions and ambiguous means ... As in many of Frankenheimer's films it rains, and the wind in the trees in the park and the sound of traffic all contribute to the realism that makes his work so satisfying.' – *Gerald Pratley*

Gypsy Wildcat
US 1944 77m Technicolor
Universal (George Waggner)
A Transylvanian gypsy girl is really a long lost countess.
Universal's Frankenstein sets are put to lighter use in a quite incredible piece of downright hokum.
w James Hogan, Gene Lewis, James M. Cain *d* Roy William Neill *ph* George Robinson, W. Howard Greene *m* Edward Ward
☆ Maria Montez, Jon Hall, Leo Carrillo, Gale Sondergaard, Douglass Dumbrille, Nigel Bruce, Peter Coe, Curt Bois

'The picture's so bad, it's bound to make money.' – *Cue*

'Never rises to the wild camp of *Cobra Woman*; it's just *opéra bouffe* without music.' – *Pauline Kael, 70s*

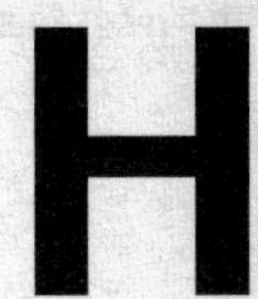

H.M. Pulham Esquire **
US 1940 120m bw
MGM (King Vidor)
A moderately successful Bostonian businessman looks back over his rather stuffy life and has a fling.
Solidly upholstered drama which does not quite do justice to the book on which it is based.
w King Vidor, Elizabeth Hill *novel* John P. Marquand *d* King Vidor *ph* Ray June
m Bronislau Kaper
☆ *Robert Young, Ruth Hussey, Hedy Lamarr,* Charles Coburn, Van Heflin, Fay Holden, Bonita Granville

HMS Defiant *
GB 1962 101m Technicolor Cinemascope
Columbia/GW (John Brabourne)
US title: *Damn the Defiant*
Mutiny erupts on an 18th-century British sailing ship.
Rather unpleasant and unenterprising sea fare reminiscent of the goings-on aboard the Bounty. *Well enough staged and acted but not very remarkable or memorable.*
w Nigel Kneale, Edmund H. North *novel* Mutiny by Frank Tilsley *d* Lewis Gilbert *ph* Christopher Challis *m* Clifton Parker *md* Muir Mathieson *ad* Arthur Kawson *ed* Peter Hunt
☆ Alec Guinness (Captain Crawford), Dirk Bogarde (Lt Scott-Fagett), Anthony Quayle (Vizard), Tom Bell (Evans), Nigel Stock (Senior Midshipman Fitzpatrick), Murray Melvin (Wagstaffe), Victor Maddern (Dawlish), Maurice Denham (Mr Goss), Walter Fitzgerald (Admiral Jackson), Joy Shelton (Mrs Crawford)
'It authentically if superficially recreates the days of press gangs, maggots and the cat.' – *Peter John Dyer*

H. P. Lovecraft's From Beyond: see *From Beyond*

H. P. Lovecraft's The Unnamable Returns: see *The Unnamable Returns*

Habeas Corpus *
US 1928 20m bw silent
Hal Roach
A mad professor sends two vagabonds out to look for a body.
Unusual star comedy, more grotesque and pantomimish than any of the others.
w H. M. Walker *story* Leo McCarey *d* James Parrott *ph* Len Powers *ed* Richard Currier
☆ Stan Laurel, Oliver Hardy, Richard Carle, Charley Rogers
† It was the pair's first sound film, but the discs on which the soundtrack of music and effects were recorded have been lost.

Hable con Ella: see *Talk to Her*

Hachigatsu-no-Kyoshikyoku: see *Rhapsody in August*

Hackers
US 1995 104m colour Panavision
United Artists (Michael Peyser, Ralph Winter)
A teenage hacker and his friends thwart a man attempting a sophisticated and large-scale computer fraud.
A film for 'teens who may enjoy seeing themselves as heroes while adults are portrayed as invariably mean-spirited and nasty; it's childish stuff, with little understanding of how computers actually work.
w Rafael Moreu *d* Ian Softley *ph* Andrzej Sekula *m* Simon Boswell *pd* John Beard *ed* Christopher Blunden, Martin Walsh
☆ Jonny Lee Miller, Angelina Jolie, Jesse Bradford, Matthew Lillard, Laurence Mason, Fisher Stevens, Alberta Watson, Renoly Santiago
'A dismal mess.' – *Entertainment Weekly*

Hadaka no Shima: see *The Island*

Hail the Conquering Hero ***
US 1944 101m bw
Paramount (Preston Sturges)
An army reject is accidentally thought a hero when he returns to his small-town home.
Skilfully orchestrated Preston Sturges romp, slightly marred by an overdose of sentiment but featuring his repertory of comic actors at full pitch.
wd Preston Sturges *ph* John Seitz *m* Werner Heymann
☆ *Eddie Bracken, William Demarest,* Ella Raines, *Franklin Pangborn,* Elizabeth Patterson, *Raymond Walburn, Alan Bridge,* Georgia Caine, Freddie Steele, Jimmy Conlin, Torben Meyer
'Mob scenes, rough-houses and sharply serious passages are played for all the pantomime they are worth ... one of the happiest, heartiest comedies in a twelvemonth.' – *Otis L. Guernsey Jnr*
'First rate entertainment, a pattern of film making, not to be missed.' – *Richard Mallett, Punch*
'The energy, the verbal density, the rush of Americana and the congestion seen periodically in *The Miracle of Morgan's Creek* stagger the senses in this newest film.' – *James Ursini*
'It tells a story so touching, so chock-full of human frailties and so rich in homely detail that it achieves a reality transcending the limitations of its familiar slapstick.' – *James Agee*
'He uses verbal as well as visual slapstick, and his comic timing is so quirkily effective that the dialogue keeps popping off like a string of firecrackers.' – *New Yorker, 1977*
Preston Sturges (as writer)

'The Morning After Was Just The Beginning...'
La Haine **
France 1995 97m bw
Metro Tartan/Lazennec/Canal/La Sept/Kaso (Christophe Rossignon)
aka: *Hate*
A day in the life of three unemployed youths, one black, one Jewish, one Arab, as they join a riot on their rundown suburban housing estate against the brutalities of the police.
Passionate and angry movie, on the side of the dispossessed, filmed in a documentary style that adds authenticity to its account of urban affliction.
wd Mathieu Kassovitz *ph* Pierre Aïm
ad Giuseppe Ponturo *ed* *Mathieu Kassovitz, Scott Stevenson*
☆ Vincent Cassel, Hubert Kounde, Saïd Taghmaoui, Karim Belkhadra, Edouard Montoute, Françoise Levantal, Solo, Marc Duret
'It is hugely energetic, totally convinced of the rightness of its case and pretty angry about everything. It can't possibly be ignored, since it is not about France alone, but about urban and suburban problems almost everywhere in the West.' – *Derek Malcolm, Guardian*
'An exhilarating, thought-provoking triumph.' – *Sunday Times*
† The film caused a sensation in France, with the Prime Minister insisting that his Cabinet watch it. Kassovitz won the best director prize at the Cannes Film Festival in 1995, and the film also won Europe's Felix as the Best Young Film.

Hair *
US 1979 121m Technicolor Panavision
UA/CIP (Lester Persky, Michael Butler)
An Oklahoman on his way to enlist for Vietnam service stops off in New York and becomes embroiled with the flower people.
Slick, vigorous but eventually unsatisfying version of a quickly dated musical frolic with some obvious points to make.
w Michael Weller *musical play* *Galt MacDermot (music) and Gerome Ragni/James Rado (book)*
d Milos Forman *ph* Miroslav Ondricek, Richard Kratina, Jean Talvin *m/ly* Galt MacDermot, Gerome Ragni, James Rado
☆ John Savage, Treat Williams, Beverly D'Angelo, Annie Golden, Dorsey Wright
'The makers of *Hair* have given us some high-spirited reminders of splendid things that film can do and, these days, isn't often asked to.' – *Stanley Kauffmann*
♫ Aquarius; Sodomy; Donna; Hashish; Colonel Spade; Manchester England; I'm Black; Ain't got No; I Got Life; Hair; Electric Bliss; LBJ; Old Fashioned Melody; Hare Krishna; Where Do I Go?; Black Boys/White Boys; Walking in Space; Easy to Be Hard; Good Morning Starshine; Someone to Hold; Let the Sunshine In

The Hairdresser's Husband **
France 1990 80m colour Panavision
Palace/Lambart/TFI/Investimage 2 and 3/Sofica (Thierry de Ganay)
original title: *Le Mari de la Coiffeuse*
A middle-aged man fulfils his childhood erotic fantasy of marrying a hairdresser.
Quirky, witty drama of an obsessive relationship.
w Claude Klotz, Patrice Leconte *d* Patrice Leconte *ph* Eduardo Serra *m* Michael Nyman *ad* Ivan Maussion *ed* Joëlle Hache
☆ Jean Rochefort, Anna Galiena, Roland Bertin, Maurice Chevit, Philippe Clevenot, Jacques Mathou, Claude Aufaure, Henry Hocking

Hairspray
US 1988 90m colour
Palace (Rachel Talalay)
A fat teenager becomes the star of a local TV dance show.
Drear and campy comedy, set in the early days of rock and beehive hair-styles.
wd John Waters *ph* David Insley *m* Kenny Vance *pd* Vincent Peranio *ed* Janice Hampton
☆ Sonny Bono, Ruth Brown, Divine, Colleen Fitzpatrick, Jo Ann Havrilla, Michael St Gerard, Debbie Harry, Ricki Lake, Leslie Ann Powers

The Hairy Ape
US 1944 91m bw
Jules Levy
A ship's stoker aims to kill a socialite who has insulted him.
Patchy treatment of an intractable and dated play.
w Jules Levy *play* Eugene O'Neill *d* Alfred Santell *ph* Lucien Andriot *m* Michel Michelet, Edward Paul
☆ William Bendix, Susan Hayward, John Loder, Dorothy Comingore, Roman Bohnen, Alan Napier
Michel Michelet, Edward Paul

Hakayitz Shel Aviya: see *The Summer of Aviya*

'It's everything a motion picture can be!'
Half a Sixpence *
GB 1967 148m Technicolor Panavision
Paramount/Ameran (Charles H. Schneer, George Sidney)
A draper's assistant inherits a fortune and moves into society.
Mildly likeable but limp and overlong musical which would have benefited from more intimate, sharper treatment than the wide screen can give. The period decor and lively numbers seem insufficient compensation for the longueurs.
w Beverley Cross *play* Beverley Cross *novel* Kipps by H. G. Wells *d* George Sidney *ph* Geoffrey Unsworth *m/ly* David Heneker *ch* *Gillian Lynne* *pd* Ted Haworth
☆ *Tommy Steele,* Julia Foster, Cyril Ritchard, Penelope Horner, Elaine Taylor, Hilton Edwards, Pamela Brown, James Villiers

'The confessions of a female sleepwalker!'
Half Angel
US 1951 80m Technicolor
TCF
A prim and proper nurse has a more forthright personality when she sleepwalks.
Silly romantic comedy with amusing moments.
w Robert Riskin *d* Richard Sale
☆ Loretta Young, Joseph Cotten, Cecil Kellaway, Basil Ruysdael, Jim Backus, Irene Ryan

Half Baked
US 1998 80m DeLuxe
Universal (Robert Simonds)
Stoned friends become drug dealers to raise money to get a friend out of prison.
A modern update of the sort of comedies Cheech and Chong used to make, likely to appeal to ageing hippies.
w Dave Chappelle, Neal Brennan *d* Tamra Davis *ph* Steven Bernstein *m* Alf Clausen *pd* Perry Andelin Blake *ed* Don Zimmerman
☆ Dave Chappelle, Guillermo Diaz, Jim Breuer, Harland Williams, Rachel True, Clarence Williams III
'A couple of hash brownies short of a satisfying cinematic picnic.' – *Variety*

Half Moon Street
US 1986 90m Technicolor
RKO/Edward R. Pressman (Geoffrey Reeve)
A lady PhD turns to prostitution to augment her income, and becomes involved in Middle Eastern schemes.
Totally muddled compromise between thriller and exploitation piece; its message seems to have got left on the cutting room floor.
w Bob Swaim, Edward Behr *novel* Dr Slaughter by Paul Theroux *d* Bob Swaim *ph* Peter Hannan *m* Richard Harvey *pd* Anthony Curtis *ed* Richard Marden
☆ Sigourney Weaver, Michael Caine, Patrick Kavanagh, Keith Buckley
'A half-baked excuse for a film.' – *Variety*

The Half Naked Truth *
US 1932 67m bw
RKO (David O. Selznick)
A publicity agent has trouble with a temperamental actress whose schemes are always over the top.
Amusing wisecracking comedy.
w Bartlett Cormack, Corey Ford *d* Gregory La Cava *ph* Bert Glennon *m* Max Steiner
☆ Lee Tracy, Lupe Velez, Eugene Pallette, Frank Morgan, Bob McKenzie

Half Shot at Sunrise
US 1930 78m bw
Radio (William LeBaron)

In 1918, two American soldiers go absent without leave and chase the girls while they are chased by military police.
Breezily inconsequential comedy, little more than a succession of vaudeville routines, but undemandingly amusing at times.
w Anne Caldwell, Ralph Spence *story* James Ashmore Creelman *d* Paul Sloane *ph* Nick Musuraca *m* Harry Tierney *ad* Max Rée *ed* Arthur Roberts
☆ Bert Wheeler, Robert Woolsey, Dorothy Lee, George McFarlane, Edna May Oliver, Leni Stengel

The Half-Breed
US 1952 81m Technicolor
RKO

A gambler helps a half-breed and wins the respect of the Apaches.
Half-hearted Western which could never be more than the bottom half of a double bill.
w Harold Shumate, Richard Wormser *d* Stuart Gilmore *ph* William V. Skall *m* Paul Sawtell
☆ Robert Young, Jack Buetel, Janis Carter, Barton MacLane, Reed Hadley, Porter Hall, Connie Gilchrist

Halfaouine
Tunisia/France 1990 98m colour
Cine Tele/France Media/Scarabee/RTT/La Sept/WDR (Ahmed Attia, Hassen Daldoul, Elaine Stutterheim)

aka: *The Rooftop Hopper*
In Tunis, a young boy begins to discover sex, a subject that also obsesses his elders.
Slight, episodic narrative of minor interest.
w Férid Boughedir, Maryse Léon Garcia, Nouri Bouzid, Taoufik Jebali *d* Férid Boughedir *ph* George Barsky *m* Anouar Braham *ed* Moufida Tlatli
☆ Mohamed Driss, Mustafa Adueni, Rabia Ben Abdallah, Fatma Ben Saidane, Helène Catazaras, Fathi Al Hadawi, Sélim Boughedir
'Boughedir is a director of broad ideas more than a stylist, yet the pic manages to capture and hold viewers from start to finish.' – *Variety*

The Halfway House *
GB 1944 99m bw
Ealing (Cavalcanti)
Overnight guests at an inn find it was bombed a year before and they have all been given a supernatural chance to reconsider their lives.
Interesting pattern play which would have benefited from lighter handling.
w Angus MacPhail, Diana Morgan *play* *Peaceful Inn* by Denis Ogden *d* Basil Dearden *ph* Wilkie Cooper *m* Lord Berners *ad* Michael Relph
☆ Françoise Rosay, Tom Walls, Alfred Drayton, Sally Ann Howes, Mervyn Johns, Glynis Johns, Esmond Knight, Richard Bird, Guy Middleton

Hallelujah! **
US 1929 106m bw
MGM (King Vidor)

A black cotton worker accidentally kills a man and decides to become a preacher.
Hollywood's unique black melodrama now seems stilted because of its early talkie technique, but at the time its picture of negro life had a freshness and truth which was not reached again for thirty years.
w Wanda Tuchock, King Vidor *d* King Vidor *ph* Gordon Avil *md* Eva Jessye
☆ Daniel Haynes, Nina Mae McKinney, William Fountaine, Fannie Belle de Knight, Harry Gray
'The central theme became swamped by the forty or so singing sequences of folk songs, spirituals, baptism wails, love songs and blues.' – *Peter Noble, The Negro in Films*
King Vidor

Hallelujah, I'm a Bum **
US 1933 80m bw
Lewis Milestone

GB titles: *Hallelujah I'm a Tramp*
aka: *Lazy Bones*
The leader of a group of Central Park tramps smartens himself up for love of a lady who lost her memory. When she recovers it, he becomes a tramp again.
Curious whimsy expressed mainly in recitative, with embarrassing stretches relieved by moments of visual and verbal inspiration. Very typical of the Depression, with the tramps knowing best how life should be lived.
w S. N. Behrman, Ben Hecht *d* Lewis Milestone *ph* Lucien Andriot *ad* Richard Day *rhymes/m/ly* Richard Rodgers, Lorenz Hart
☆ Al Jolson, Harry Langdon, Madge Evans, Frank Morgan, Chester Conklin
'It must rise or fall by Al Jolson's rep ... it won't bore, once in, but it's not a mass play picture.' – *Variety*
'Given a scene or two of high sentiment, he still has you wrapped round his little finger.' – *The Times, 1973*
♫ 'Hallelujah I'm a Bum'; 'You Are Too Beautiful'; 'I'll do It Again'; 'What Do You Want with Money?'; 'I've Got to Get Back to New York'

Hallelujah, I'm a Tramp: see *Hallelujah, I'm a Bum*

The Hallelujah Trail
US 1965 167m Technicolor Ultra Panavision 70
UA/Mirisch/Kappa (John Sturges)

In 1867 a wagonload of whisky bound for Denver is waylaid by Indians, temperance crusaders and the civilian militia.
Absurdly inflated, prolonged, uninventive comedy Western with poor narrative grip; all dressed up and nowhere to go.
w John Gay *novel* Bill Gulick *d* John Sturges *ph* Robert Surtees *m* Elmer Bernstein
☆ Burt Lancaster, Lee Remick, Brian Keith, Jim Hutton, Donald Pleasence, Martin Landau

The Halliday Brand *
US 1956 78m bw
UA/Collier Young
A tough farmer/sheriff conflicts with his son over his attitude to Indians.
Dour, reliable Western melodrama with a good cast.
w George W. George, George F. Slavin *d* Joseph H. Lewis *ph* Ray Rennahan *m* Stanley Wilson
☆ Joseph Cotten, Viveca Lindfors, Ward Bond, Betsy Blair, Bill Williams, Jay C. Flippen

'The Night He Came Home!'
Halloween *
US 1978 91m Metrocolor Panavision
Falcon International (Irwin Yablans)

In a small Illinois town, a mad killer escapes from the asylum.
Single-minded shocker with virtually no plot, just a succession of bloody attacks in semi-darkness. Very well done if you like that kind of thing, though the final suggestion of the supernatural is rather baffling.
w John Carpenter, Debra Hill *d* John Carpenter *ph* Dean Cundey *m* John Carpenter *pd* Tommy Wallace
☆ Donald Pleasence, Jamie Lee Curtis, Nancy Loomis, P. J. Soles
'One of the cinema's most perfectly engineered devices for saying Boo!' – *Richard Combs, MFB*

'Michael Lives, And This Time They're Ready!'
Halloween Five: The Revenge of Michael Myers
US 1989 96m CFI color
Magnum (Ramsey Thomas)

A small girl senses when the Halloween killer is going to strike again.
Lacklustre sequel that goes to some lengths to set up a further instalment of mindless killings at its end.
w Michael Jacobs, Dominique Othenin-Girard, Shem Bitterman *d* Dominique Othenin-Girard *ph* Robert Draper *m* Alan Howarth, John Carpenter *pd* Steven Lee *ed* Jerry Brady
☆ Donald Pleasence, Danielle Harris, Wendy Kaplan, Ellie Cornell, Donald L. Shanks, Jeffrey Landman, Beau Starr
'Pretty stupid and boring fare.' – *Variety*

'Ten Years Ago He Changed The Face Of Halloween. Tonight He's Back!'
Halloween Four: The Return of Michael Myers
US 1988 88m colour Panavision
Fox/Trancas International/Halloween 4 Partnership (Paul Freeman)

The motiveless murderer emerges from a coma to kill again, and again, and again.
A further unnecessary sequel, poorly made.
w Alan B. McElroy *story* Dhani Lipsius, Larry Rattner, Benjamin Ruffner *d* Dwight H. Little *ph* Peter Lyons Collister *m* Alan Howarth *ad* Roger S. Crandall *ed* Curtiss Clayton
☆ Donald Pleasence, Ellie Cornell, Danielle Harris, Michael Pataki, Beau Starr, Kathleen Kinmont, Sasha Jenson, George P. Wilbur, Gene Ross, Carmen Filpi

'This summer, terror won't be taking a vacation.'
Halloween H20
US 1998 85m colour Panavision
Dimension/Nightfall (Paul Freeman)

A homicidal maniac discovers the whereabouts of the sister he terrorized on the night of Halloween 20 years before, and goes after her.
There's not much that's new here in the recycling of a familiar series; the movie is more knowing than its predecessors, in the style of modern horror, and delivers the requisite shocks.
w Robert Zappia, Matt Greenberg *d* Steve Miner *ph* Daryn Okada *m* John Ottman *pd* John Willet *ed* Patrick Lusser
☆ Jamie Lee Curtis, Adam Arkin, Josh Hartnett, Michelle Williams, Adam Hann-Byrd, Jodi Lyn O'Keefe, Janet Leigh, LL Cool J, Joseph Gordon Levitt, Nancy Stephens, Branden Williams, Chris Durand
'Given how dreary the Michael Myers sequels are, it is hardly much of an achievement that *H20* is the best of them.' – *Kim Newman, Empire*

'Evil Finds Its Way Home.'
Halloween Resurrection
US 2002 89m colour
Buena Vista/Nightfall (Paul Freeman)

As part of a reality TV programme, six college students spend the night in an old dark house where serial murders took place.
Dire horror built on the premise that the ending to Halloween H20 was a fantasy. It's just another slasher movie.
w Larry Brand, Sean Hood *d* Rick Rosenthal *ph* David Geddes *m* Danny Lux *pd* Troy Hansen *ed* Robert A. Ferretti *sp* Jamison Goei
☆ Jamie Lee Curtis (Laurie Strode), Brad Loree (Michael Myers), Busta Rhymes (Freddie Harris), Bianca Kajlich (Sara Moyer), Sean Patrick Thomas (Rudy), Daisy McCrackin (Donna), Katee Sackhoff (Jen), Luke Kirby (Jim)
'Even more uselessly redundant and shamelessly money-grubbing than most third-rate horror sequels.' – *Joe Leydon, Variety*

'Terror Never Rests In Peace!'
Halloween: The Curse of Michael Myers
US 1995 88m CFI color
Nightfall (Paul Freeman)

Michael Myers murders the surviving relatives of families he butchered in the past.
Tired and, at times, incomprehensible sequel that adds black magic rituals to the familiar mix but without making it any more interesting.
w Daniel Farrands *d* Joe Chappelle *ph* Billy Dickson *m* Alan Howarth *pd* Bryan Ryman *ed* Randy Bricker *sp* John Carl Buechler
☆ Donald Pleasence, Mitch Ryan, Marianne Hagan, Paul Rudd, Leo Geter, George P. Wilbur, Devin Gardner, Mariah O'Brien
'The producers should take the advice of one of the characters in the film, "Enough of this Michael Myers bullshit!"' – *Shivers*
† The six Halloween films cost in total less than $20m to make. So far they have taken more than $200m at the box-office.

'The Night Nobody Came Home.'
Halloween Three: Season of the Witch
US 1983 98m Technicolor
Dino de Laurentiis (Debra Hill, John Carpenter)

A malicious toy maker intends to restore Halloween to its witch cult origins through magic masks made at his Santa Mira factory. The Halloween zombie-killer makes no appearance: this is a fresh story inspired by *Invasion of the Body Snatchers*.
Alas, its good intentions flounder in a bath of gore.
wd Tommy Lee Wallace *ph* Dean Cundey *m* John Carpenter, Alan Howarth *pd* Peter Jamison
☆ Tom Atkins (Dr Dan Challis), Stacey Nelkin (Ellie), Dan O'Herlihy (Conal), Ralph Strait (Buddy), Michael Currie (Rafferty), Jadeen Barbor (Betty)
† Nigel Kneale wrote the original script but asked to have his name removed from the credits.

'The Nightmare Isn't Over.'
Halloween Two
US 1981 92m Metrocolor Panavision
Dino de Laurentiis (Debra Hill, John Carpenter)

The motiveless murderer from *Halloween* escapes from the asylum fifteen years later.
A totally unnecessary sequel which seems merely an excuse for assorted mayhem at close quarters.
w John Carpenter, Debra Hill *d* Rick Rosenthal *ph* Dean Cundey *m* John Carpenter, Alan Howarth
☆ Donald Pleasence, Jamie Lee Curtis, Charles Cyphers, Jeffrey Kramer

Halls of Anger
US 1969 99m DeLuxe
UA/Mirisch (Herbert Hirschman)
A black basketball star goes to teach in his home town and faces segregation problems.
Schematic melodrama, as well meaning as it is boring.
w John Shaner, Al Ramrus *d* Paul Bogart *ph* Burnett Guffey *m* Dave Grusin
☆ Calvin Lockhart, Janet McLachlan, Jeff Bridges

Halls of Montezuma *
US 1950 113m Technicolor
TCF (Robert Bassler)

Marines fight World War II in the Pacific.
Well-mounted, simple-minded actioner.
w Michael Blankfort *d* Lewis Milestone *ph* Winton C. Hoch, Harry Jackson *m* Sol Kaplan *md* Lionel Newman
☆ Richard Widmark, Jack Palance, Reginald Gardiner, Robert Wagner, Karl Malden, Richard Hylton, Richard Boone, Skip Homeier, Jack Webb, Bert Freed, Neville Brand, Don Hicks, Martin Milner
'By far the noisiest war film I ever encountered.' – *Richard Mallett, Punch*

Hamam *
Italy/Spain/Turkey 1997 101m Cinecitta
Sorpasso/Promete Film/Asbrell (Marco Risi, Maurizio Tedesco)
aka: *The Turkish Bath*
An unhappily married Italian designer moves to Istanbul after he inherits from his aunt a rundown Turkish bath.
Engaging drama of cultural differences, of traditional ways opposed to modern commerce, of dysfunctional families and functioning communities.
w Stefano Tummolini, Ferzan Ozpetek *d* Ferzan Ozpetek *ph* Pasquale Mari *m* Pivio, Aldo de Scalzi *ad* Virginia Vianello, Mustafa Ziya Ulgenciler *ed* Mauro Bonanni
☆ Alessandro Gassman, Francesca d'Aloja, Carlo Cecchi, Halil Ergun, Serif Sezer, Mehmet Gunsur, Basak Koklukaya, Alberto Molinari
'An intelligent and attractive take on cross-cultural confusion and attraction.' – *Paul Julian Smith, Sight and Sound*

Hambone and Hillie
US 1983 90m colour Panavision
Sandy Howard/Adams Apple (Gary Gillingham)

A small dog is lost at New York airport and tracks his aged mistress on foot to California.
Basically a revamp of Lassie Come Home, with a cute dog and some attractive exteriors, but made unsuitable for its presumably intended family audience

by the death of a second dog and a horrific pitchfork sequence in which a heavily pregnant woman is attacked by marauders.
w Sandra K. Bailey, Michael Murphey, Joel Soisson *d* Roy Watts *ph* Jon Kranhouse *m* George Garvarentz
☆ Lillian Gish, Timothy Bottoms, Candy Clark, Robert Walker, O. J. Simpson, Jack Carter, Alan Hale

Hamburger Hill *
US 1987 110m Technicolor
Paramount/RKO (Marcia Nasatir, Jim Carabatsos)
An untried squad goes into action in Vietnam.
One of several Vietnam pics released almost simultaneously; neither the worst nor the best.
w Jim Carabatsos *d* John Irvin *ph* Peter MacDonald *m* Philip Glass *pd* Austen Spriggs *ed* Peter Tanner
☆ Anthony Barrie, Michael Patrick Boatman, Don Cheadle, Michael Dolan, Don James
'Had the filmmakers resisted the temptation to politicise their material they might have made a great war movie. They might also have thought to give us some indication of the strategic significance of the hill. As it is, they've managed to create a deeply affecting, highly accomplished film.' – *Hal Hinson, Washington Post*

Hamlet **
GB 1948 142m bw
Rank/Two Cities (Laurence Olivier)
Prince Hamlet takes too long making up his mind to revenge his father's death.
The play is sharply cut, then time is wasted having the camera prowl pointlessly along gloomy corridors ... but much of the acting is fine, some scenes compel, and the production has a splendid brooding power.
w Alan Dent *play* William Shakespeare *d* Laurence Olivier *ph* *Desmond Dickinson* *m* William Walton *pd* *Roger Furse* *ad* *Carmen Dillon* *ed* Helga Cranston
☆ *Laurence Olivier* (Hamlet), *Eileen Herlie* (Gertrude), *Basil Sydney* (Claudius), *Jean Simmons* (Ophelia), *Felix Aylmer* (Polonius), Norman Wooland (Horatio), Terence Morgan (Laertes), *Stanley Holloway* (Gravedigger), Peter Cushing, Esmond Knight, Anthony Quayle, Harcourt Williams, John Laurie, Niall MacGinnis, Patrick Troughton
'Be you 9 or 90, a PhD or just plain Joe, *Hamlet* is the movie of the year.' – *Washington Times*
'By the end one no longer thinks of the piece as filmed Shakespeare, but accepts it simply as a splendid production of a masterpiece.' – *Dilys Powell*
picture; Laurence Olivier (as actor)
Laurence Olivier (as director); William Walton; Jean Simmons; art direction
picture

Hamlet *
USSR 1964 150m bw Sovscope
Lenfilm
A Russian version of the play, with lowering sets, brooding photography and strong acting.
play William Shakespeare (translation Boris Pasternak) *d* Grigori Kozintsev *ph* I. Gritzys *m* Dmitri Shostakovich
☆ *Innokenti Smoktunovsky* (Hamlet), Mikhail Nazvanov (King), Elsa Radzin (Queen), Anastasia Vertinskaya (Ophelia), Yuri Tolubeyev (Polonius)
'An opportunity almost deliberately missed.' – *Basil Wright, 1972*

Hamlet *
GB 1969 119m Technicolor
Woodfall/Filmways/Columbia (Neil Hartley)
A version which has its moments but fails to impress as a whole.
d Tony Richardson *ph* Gerry Fisher *m* Patrick Gowers *ad* Jocelyn Herbert
☆ Nicol Williamson (Hamlet), Anthony Hopkins (Claudius), Gordon Jackson (Horatio), Judy Parfitt (Gertrude), Marianne Faithfull (Ophelia), Mark Dignam (Polonius), Roger Livesey

Hamlet *
US 1991 135m colour
Warner/Nelson Entertainment/Icon (Dyson Lovell)
A son, inspired by his father's ghost, vows to kill his murdering uncle, who has married his mother and usurped the throne of Denmark.
Decent, unadventurous adaptation that does not challenge Olivier's version.
w Christopher de Vore, Franco Zeffirelli *play* William Shakespeare *d* Franco Zeffirelli *ph* David Watkin *m* Ennio Morricone *pd* Dante Ferretti *ad* Michael Lamont *ed* Richard Marden
☆ Mel Gibson (Hamlet), Glenn Close (Gertrude), Alan Bates (Claudius), Paul Scofield (Ghost), Ian Holm (Polonius), Helena Bonham Carter (Ophelia), Stephen Dillane (Horatio), Nathaniel Parker (Laertes), Sean Murray, Michael Maloney, Trevor Peacock, John McEnery
'A generally flat-footed production, an illustrated gloss on the full Shakespearean text.' – *Variety*
'Funny thing is, Hamlet almost is perfect for Gibson, with his neurotic physicality and urgent baritone ... Zeffirelli goes for the grand. His aim here – nicely realised in a sumptuous production – is to make *Hamlet* so vigorous that the kids will forget it's poetry.' – *Richard Corliss, Time*
best art direction; best costume design

Hamlet **
US 1996 242m Technicolor Panavision Super 70
Rank/Castle Rock (David Barron)
In the 1800s, a Danish prince is slow to take revenge when he discovers that his uncle and stepfather has usurped his father's throne.
Sumptuous version of Shakespeare's play which is notable for presenting an uncut text, though Branagh's vigorous, well-spoken performance makes Hamlet's delay even more inexplicable than usual. Billy Crystal is an excellent gravedigger; some of the other star turns in minor roles would have been better buried.
wd Kenneth Branagh *play* William Shakespeare *ph* Alex Thomson *m* Patrick Doyle *pd* Tim Harvey *ed* Neil Farrell
☆ Kenneth Branagh (Hamlet), Derek Jacobi (Claudius), Julie Christie (Gertrude), Kate Winslet (Ophelia), Richard Briers (Polonius), Nicholas Farrell (Horatio), Michael Maloney (Laertes), Brian Blessed (Ghost), Jack Lemmon (Marcellus), Billy Crystal (1st Gravedigger), Robin Williams (Osric), Gérard Depardieu (Reynaldo), Charlton Heston (Player King), Rosemary Harris (Player Queen), Judi Dench (Hecuba) and also John Gielgud (Priam), Rufus Sewell (Fortinbras), Ken Dodd (Yorick)
'A greatly flawed project – not so much the curate's egg as the curate's 1,000 egg omelette, with good and bad ideas scrambled together on a huge scale.' – *Adam Mars-Jones, Independent*
Kenneth Branagh (as writer); Patrick Doyle; Tim Harvey; Alex Byrne (costumes)

Hamlet **
US 2000 111m bw/colour
Film4/Miramax/Double A (Andrew Fierberg, Amy Hobby)
A son suspects that his father, CEO of Denmark Corp., has been murdered by his second-in-command.
Intriguing modern updating of Shakespeare, in which video cameras, fax machines and instant photographs all play their part; the corporate setting diminishes the tragedy, but it still holds the attention.
wd Michael Almereyda *play* William Shakespeare *ph* John De Borman *m* Carter Burwell *pd* Gideon Ponte *ed* Kristina Boden *cos* Luca Mosca, Marco Cattoretti
☆ Ethan Hawke (Hamlet), Kyle MacLachlan (Claudius), Sam Shepard (Ghost), Diane Venora (Gertrude), Bill Murray (Polonius), Liev Schreiber (Laertes), Julia Stiles (Ophelia), Karl Geary (Horatio), Paula Malcomson (Marcella), Steve Zahn (Rosencrantz), Dechen Thurman (Guildenstern), Rome Neal (Barnardo), Jeffrey Wright (Gravedigger), Paul Bartel (Osric), Casey Affleck (Fortinbras)
'Intelligent, energetic and very refreshing.' – *Peter Bradshaw, Guardian*

Hamlet Goes Business **
Finland 1987 86m bw
Electric/Villealfa Productions/Aki Kaurismäki
original title: *Hamlet Liikemaailmassa*
A son whose father is murdered takes revenge on the killer.
Bizarre and enjoyable modern-day version of Shakespeare's play, which is treated as black comedy and set in the world of business, with company directors attempting to control the rubber duck industry.
wd Aki Kaurismäki *ph* Tino Salminen *m* Shostakovich, Tchaikovsky, Elmore James and others *ed* Raija Talvio
☆ Pirkka-Pekka Petelius, Esko Salminen, Kati Outinen, Elina Salo, Esko Nikkari, Kari Vaananen, Hannu Valtonen, Mari Rantasila

Hamlet Liikemaailmassa: see *Hamlet Goes Business*

Hammerhead
GB 1968 99m Technicolor
Columbia (Irving Allen)
An American secret agent captures a master criminal.
Jaded James Bond imitation, full of would-be fashionable detail.
w William Best, Herbert Baker *novel* James Mayo *d* David Miller *ph* Kenneth Talbot *m* David Whitaker
☆ Vince Edwards, Peter Vaughan, Judy Geeson, Diana Dors, Michael Bates, Beverly Adams, Patrick Cargill, Patrick Holt

Hammersmith Is Out *
US 1972 114m DuArt
Cinerama/J. Cornelius Cream (Alex Lucas)
With the help of a male nurse, a homicidal mental inmate escapes and becomes the most influential man in the country.
Pretentious updating of Faust into a kind of black farce that seldom amuses but is interesting in fits and starts.
w Stanford Whitmore *d* Peter Ustinov *ph* Richard Kline *m* Dominic Frontière
☆ Richard Burton, Elizabeth Taylor, Peter Ustinov, Beau Bridges, Leon Ames, John Schuck, George Raft

Hammett *
US 1982 97m Technicolor
Orion/Zoetrope (Francis Coppola)
San Francisco 1928: Dashiell Hammett is asked to locate a missing Chinese girl and gets involved in sinister goings-on which provide the basis for another mystery book.
Careful and interesting crime thriller in which, however, the rather pretentious framework is largely irrelevant, leaving a detective story slightly off-beat in treatment but otherwise indistinguishable from many others.
w Ross Thomas, Dennis O'Flaherty *novel* Joe Gores *d* *Wim Wenders* *ph* Philip Lathrop, Joseph Biroc *m* John Barry *pd* *Dean Tavoularis, Eugene Lee* *ed* Barry Malkin, Marc Laub, Robert Q. Lovett, Randy Roberts
☆ *Frederic Forrest*, Peter Boyle, Marilu Henner, Roy Kinnear, Elisha Cook Jnr, R. G. Armstrong, Richard Bradford, Sylvia Sidney, Royal Dano, Samuel Fuller
'A symbolic liquidation by Wenders of the massive, but ambivalent patrimony of the American cinematic and cultural tradition that has increasingly dominated his work.' – *Sheila Johnston, MFB*
† The film was actually in pre-production from 1975, though shooting did not begin until 1980. This version was abandoned in rough cut and two-thirds of it was shot again in 1981 with a different crew. Sylvia Miles and Brian Keith were in the first version and not the second.

The Hammond Mystery: see *The Undying Monster*

Hamnstad: see *Port of Call*

Hana-Bi **
Japan 1997 103m colour
Office Kitano/Bandai/Television Tokyo/Tokyo FM (Masayuki Mori, Yasushi Tsuge, Takio Yoshida)
A tough cop, who leaves the force to look after his dying wife and the family of a dead colleague, turns to crime to get the money he needs.
An unusual drama, with dialogue pared to the mimimum and a protagonist whose emotions are kept under strict control, except when they flare into violence; it requires the audience to fill in the gaps it leaves.
wd Takeshi Kitano *ph* Hideo Yamamoto *m* Joe Hisaishi *ad* Norihiro Isoda *ed* Takeshi Kitano, Yoshinori Ota
☆ Beat Takeshi (aka Takeshi Kitano), Kayoko Kishimoto, Ren Osugi, Susumu Terajima, Tetsu Watanabe
'An intriguing and curiously engaging movie.' – *Bob McCabe, Empire*

The Hand
US 1981 104m Technicolor
Warner/Orion (Edward R. Pressman)
A cartoonist loses his hand, which takes on a life of its own to wreak vengeance on his enemies.
Pale imitation of The Beast with Five Fingers, *which wasn't all that good to begin with.*
wd Oliver Stone *novel* *The Lizard's Tail* by Oliver Stone *ph* King Baggot *m* James Horner *pd* John Michael Riva *ed* Richard Marks *sp* Carlo Rambaldi
☆ Michael Caine, Andrea Marcovicci, Viveca Lindfors, Rosemary Murphy, Bruce McGill

Hand in Hand *
GB 1960 80m bw
ABP (Helen Winston)
The friendship of two 7-year-olds is affected by racial prejudice because one is Catholic and the other Jewish; but after misunderstandings their friendship is confirmed by priest and rabbi.
Pleasant, well-meaning drama apparently intended for older children.
w Diana Morgan *d* Philip Leacock *ph* Frederick A. Young *m* Stanley Black
☆ Loretta Parry, Phillip Needs, Sybil Thorndike, John Gregson, Finlay Currie

The Hand of Night
GB 1966 73m Technicolor
Associated British Pathé (Harry Field)
US title: *Beast of Morocco*
In order to recover from the death of his wife and children, an architect holidays in Morocco, where a vampire princess sets out to seduce him.
A psychological horror film, long on talk and short on action.
w Bruce Stewart *d* Frederic Goode *ph* William Jordan *m* Joan Shakespeare *ad* Peter Moll *ed* Frederick Ives
☆ William Sylvester, Diane Clare, William Dexter, Alizia Gur, Edward Underdown, Terence de Marney
'Relies heavily on old Hammer production tricks without contributing any original variations of its own.' – *MFB*

The Hand that Rocks the Cradle *
US 1991 110m Alpha Cine
Buena Vista/Hollywood Pictures/Interscope/Nomura, Babcock & Brown (David Madden)
After her husband's suicide and her miscarriage, a woman becomes nanny to the family she blames for her misfortunes.
A predictable thriller that just manages to hold an audience's interest.
w Amanda Silver *d* Curtis Hanson *ph* Robert Elswit *m* Graeme Revell *pd* Edward Pisoni *ed* John F. Link
☆ Annabella Sciorra, Rebecca de Mornay, Matt McCoy, Ernie Hudson, Julianne Moore, Madeline Zima, John de Lancie, Kevin Skousen
'Diagrammatic script channels the action in a predictable direction toward an inevitable climax, but fine performances and a refusal to pander to the audience's grosser instincts raise this a notch or two above the norm.' – *Variety*
'A rabble-rousing hit, so adept is the movie at exploiting the sinister potential in ordinary

domestic surroundings.' – *Gary Arnold, Washington Times*

A Handful of Clouds: see *Doorway to Hell*

A Handful of Dust **
GB 1988 118m colour
Premier (Derek Granger)
An aristocratic wife, frustrated by the old-fashioned habits of her stately home-owning husband, begins an affair with a young man-about-town.
Glossy production, impeccably acted, although it loses some of the satire of the original.
w Charles Sturridge, Tim Sullivan, Derek Granger *novel* Evelyn Waugh *d* Charles Sturridge *ph* Peter Hannan *m* George Fenton *pd* Eileen Diss *ed* Peter Coulson
☆ James Wilby, Kristin Scott Thomas, Rupert Graves, Anjelica Huston, Judi Dench, Alec Guinness, Stephen Fry, Graham Crowden
best costume design (Jane Robinson)
Judi Dench

Handgun *
US 1982 101m DuArt
EMI/Kestrel (Tony Garnett)
A schoolmistress, raped at gunpoint, takes her revenge.
Novel, feminist revenge drama with a neat twist at the end.
wd Tony Garnett *ph* Charles Stewart *m* Mike Post *pd* Lilly Kilvert
☆ Karen Young, Clayton Day, Suzie Humphreys, Helena Humann

Handgun
US 1994 90m colour
Workin' Man/Odessa/Shooting Gallery (Bob Gosse, Larry Meistritch)
After their father dies, having hidden away half a million stolen dollars, his two crooked sons join forces to find the money before anyone else.
Enjoyably quirky comedy of the low life, slickly written and well acted.
d Whitney Ransick *ph* Michael Spiller *m* Douglas J. Cuomo *pd* Andras Kanegson *ed* Tom McCardle
☆ *Treat Williams*, Seymour Cassel, Paul Schulze, Toby Huss, Angel Caban, Frank Vincent
'Exhibits an unmistakably alert intelligence and cinematic sensibility that announce the arrival of an original American filmmaker.' – *Emanuel Levy, Variety*

Handle with Care *
US 1958 82m bw
MGM (Morton Fine)
Small-town college students stage a mock trial and come up with some embarrassing answers.
Interesting melodrama with a disappointing ending; a well done second feature.
w Morton Fine, David Friedkin d David Friedkin ph Harold J. Marzorati *m* Alexander Courage
☆ Dean Jones, Joan O'Brien, Thomas Mitchell, Walter Abel, John Smith

Handle with Care *
US 1977 98m colour
Paramount (Paul Brickman)
aka: *Citizens Band*
An enthusiast of Citizen's Band radio tries to prevent it being abused in his home town.
Lively and often sharp comedy, but one that failed to find an audience at the time.
w Paul Brickman *d* Jonathan Demme *ph* Jordan Cronenweth *m* Bill Conti *pd* Bill Malley *ed* John F. Link II
☆ Paul LeMat, Candy Clark, Ann Wedgeworth, Bruce McGill, Marcia Rodd, Charles Napier, Alix Elias, Roberts Blossom, Ed Begley Jnr
'A palmy, elegantly deadpan comedy; the jokes aren't pushed, so it takes viewers a few minutes to settle into the comic style, which has the mellow, light touch of thirties Renoir.' – *Pauline Kael, New Yorker*
'For once, the intelligentsia are right about an American genre film; this one is worth serious consideration.' – *Richard Schickel, Time*

The Handmaid's Tale
US/Germany 1990 109m colour
Virgin/Cinecom/Bioskop Film (Daniel Wilson)
In the near future, a woman revolts against her role as child-bearer for the controlling elite.
Barren feminist fantasy.
w Harold Pinter *novel* Margaret Atwood *d* Volker Schlöndorff *ph* Igor Luther *m* Ryuichi Sakamoto *pd* Tom Walsh *ed* David Ray
☆ Natasha Richardson, Robert Duvall, Faye Dunaway, Aidan Quinn, Elizabeth McGovern, Victoria Tennant, Blanche Baker, Traci Lind, David Dukes

Hands across the Table *
US 1935 81m bw
Paramount (E. Lloyd Sheldon)
A manicurist determines to marry a rich man.
Lively romantic comedy, smoothly made and typical of its time.
w Norman Krasna, Vincent Lawrence, Herbert Fields *d Mitchell Leisen ph* Ted Tetzlaff *m* Sam Coslow, Frederick Hollander
☆ Carole Lombard, Fred MacMurray, Ralph Bellamy, Astrid Allwyn, Ruth Donnelly, Marie Prévost, William Demarest, Ed Gargan
'Snappy comedy that should satisfy all over.' – *Variety*
'A happy mixture of brainwork and horseplay and a reminder that when intelligence goes for a walk among even the oldest props, the props may come to life.' – *Otis Ferguson*
† Ray Milland was originally cast, but bowed out saying that he couldn't play comedy.

The Hands of Orlac: see *Mad Love (1935)*

The Hands of Orlac
GB/France 1960 105m bw
Riviera/Pendennis (Steven Pallos, Don Taylor)
A concert pianist's hands are crushed in an accident, and a mad surgeon grafts on those of an executed murderer.
Flatulent remake of the 1926 German silent and the 1935 American Mad Love. *Stilted, hammy, threadbare and overlong.*
w John Baines, Edmond T. Gréville *novel* Maurice Renard *d* Edmond T. Gréville *ph* Desmond Dickinson *m* Claude Bolling
☆ Mel Ferrer, Donald Wolfit, Christopher Lee, Dany Carrel, Felix Aylmer, Basil Sydney, Donald Pleasence

'Jack's Back!'
Hands of the Ripper
GB 1971 85m Technicolor
Rank/Hammer (Aida Young)
Jack the Ripper stabs his wife to death in view of his small daughter, who grows up a sexually repressed murderess.
Gory Hammer horror with well done scenes.
w L. W. Davidson *story* Edward Spencer Shew *d* Peter Sasdy *ph* Kenneth Talbot *m* Christopher Gunning *ad* Roy Stannard *ed* Christopher Barnes
☆ Angharad Rees, Eric Porter, Dora Bryan, Jane Merrow, Derek Godfrey

Hands off the Loot: see *Touchez pas au Grisbi*

Hands over the City
Italy 1963 105m bw Galatea
original title: *Le Mani sulla Città*
A property tycoon wangles local politicians so that he gets development on the property he controls.
An angry political film which is too strident to have much entertainment value.
w Enzo Provenzale, Enzo Forcella, Raffaele La Capria, Francesco Rosi *d* Francesco Rosi *ph* Gianni di Venanzo *m* Piero Piccioni
☆ Rod Steiger, Salvo Randone, and non-professionals

Hands Up *
US 1926 65m (24 fps) bw silent
Paramount
General Lee assigns a spy to prevent a Union man from getting his hands on a gold cache.
Pleasant Civil War comedy with a curious Mormon happy ending.
w Monte Brice, Lloyd Corrigan *d* Clarence Badger
☆ *Raymond Griffith*, Marian Nixon, Virginia Lee Corbin, Mack Swain, Montagu Love

Handsome Antonio: see *Il Bell'Antonio*

Handy Andy
US 1934 82m bw
Fox
A midwestern druggist is married to a snob.
Competent star vehicle overflowing with crackerbarrel philosophy.
w William Conselman, Henry Johnson *play* Merry Andrew by Lewis Beach *d* David Butler *ph* Arthur Miller
☆ *Will Rogers*, Peggy Wood, Conchita Montenegro, Mary Carlisle, Roger Imhof, Robert Taylor, Paul Harvey

'They made two mistakes – they hanged the wrong man, and they didn't finish the job!'
Hang 'em High
US 1967 114m DeLuxe
UA/Malpaso/Leonard Freeman
A cowboy is rescued from lynching and takes revenge on his persecutors.
Hollywood's first attempt to imitate the gore and brutality of spaghetti Westerns and to take back its own errant star. Emetic and interminable.
w Leonard Freeman, Mel Goldberg *d* Ted Post *ph* Leonard South, Richard Kline *m* Dominic Frontière
☆ Clint Eastwood, Inger Stevens, Ed Begley, Pat Hingle, James MacArthur, Arlene Golonka, Charles McGraw, Ben Johnson, L. Q. Jones

Hangar 18
US 1980 97m Technicolor
Sunn Classic
A UFO crashlands and is cared for in secret by the American government.
A cinematic equivalent to the yellow press, supposing villainous behaviour by all concerned but eager only to provide low grade thriller entertainment.
w Steven Thornley *d* James L. Conway *ph* Paul Hipp *m* John Cavacas
☆ Darren McGavin, Robert Vaughn, Gary Collins, Philip Abbott

Hanged Man's Farm: see *La Ferme du Pendu*

'It's gonna be one hell of a night.'
Hangin' with the Homeboys **
US 1991 89m Metrocolor
Palace/New Line (Richard Brick)
In the Bronx, four youths get together for an eventful night out on the town and end up in the unfamiliar surroundings of Manhattan.
Acute and humorous portrait of the immature discovering the beginnings of maturity and self-knowledge.
wd Joseph B. Vasquez *ph* Anghel Decca *ad* Isabel Bau Madden *ed* Michael Schweitzer
☆ Doug E. Doug, Mario Joyner, John Leguizamo, Nestor Serrano, Kimberly Russell, Mary B. Ward, Reggie Montgomery, Christine Claravall, Rosemary Jackson

The Hanging Garden *
Canada 1997 91m colour
Triptych/Galafilm/Emotion (Louise Garfield, Arnie Gelbart, Thom Fitzgerald)
After a decade away, a gay 25-year-old man returns home to Nova Scotia for his sister's wedding.
Slightly surreal domestic drama with a blackly comic edge.
wd Thom Fitzgerald *ph* Daniel Jobin *m* John Roby, Ashley MacIsaac, Heather Rankin, Mary Jane Lamond *ad* Taavo Soodor *ed* Susan Shanks
☆ Chris Leavins, Kerry Fox, Seana McKenna, Peter MacNeill, Christine Dunsworth, Troy Veinotte, Sarah Polley, Joel S. Keller
'A strange, utterly original look at a seriously dysfunctional family.' – *Variety*

The Hanging Tree *
US 1959 106m Technicolor
Warner/Baroda (Martin Jurow, Richard Shepherd)
Life is tough in a Montana gold-mining camp, especially for a doctor who has killed his unfaithful wife.
Lowering Western with a feeling for place and period, plus a welter of melodramatic incident.
w Wendell Mayes, Halsted Welles *novel* Dorothy M. Johnson *d* Delmer Daves *ph* Ted McCord *m* Max Steiner
☆ Gary Cooper, Maria Schell, Karl Malden, Ben Piazza, George C. Scott
title song (*m*Jerry Livingston, *ly*Mack David)

'Every family has a few hang-ups.'
Hanging Up
US 2000 93m DeLuxe
Columbia (Nora Ephron, Laurence Mark)
After their grumpy old father goes into hospital, three middle-aged sisters indulge in sibling rivalries.
Slick, soft-centred soap-opera with the emphasis on glamour and easy sentimentality.
w Delia Ephron, Nora Ephron *book* Delia Ephron *d* Diane Keaton *ph* Howard Atherton *m* David Hirschfelder *pd* Waldemar Kalinowski *ed* Julie Monroe *cos* Bobbie Read
☆ Meg Ryan (Eve), Diane Keaton (Georgia), Lisa Kudrow (Maddy), Walter Matthau (Lou), Adam Arkin (Joe), Duke Moosekian (Omar Kunundar), Ann Bortolotti (Ogmed Kunundar), Cloris Leachman (Pat), Maree Cheatham (Angie), Myndy Crist (Dr Kelly), Jesse James (Jesse)
'An unspeakably bad film.' – *Guardian*

The Hangman
US 1959 86m bw
Paramount (Frank Freeman Jnr)
A marshal with a reputation for getting his man deliberately allows one to escape.
Dour, low-key Western, competent but rather flat and uninteresting.
w Dudley Nichols *d* Michael Curtiz *ph* Loyal Griggs *m* Harry Sukman
☆ Robert Taylor, Jack Lord, Fess Parker, Tina Louise, Mickey Shaughnessy

Hangman's House
US 1928 72m (24 fps) bw silent
Fox
To please her dying father, an Irish girl marries a wastrel instead of the man she loves, but her husband is killed in a duel.
Blarney-filled melodrama, like a sober Quiet Man. *John Wayne can be glimpsed as an extra.*
w Marion Orth *story* Brian Oswald Donn-Byrne *d* John Ford *ph* George Schneiderman
☆ June Collyer, Larry Kent, Earle Foxe, Victor McLaglen, Hobart Bosworth

Hangman's Knot
US 1952 81m Technicolor
Columbia (Harry Joe Brown)
Confederate soldiers returning home with Union booty are waylaid at a way station by renegades.
Adequate suspense Western.
wd Roy Huggins *ph* Charles Lawton Jnr *ad* George Brooks *ed* Gene Havlick
☆ Randolph Scott, Donna Reed, Claude Jarman Jnr, Frank Faylen, Glenn Langan, Richard Denning, Lee Marvin, Jeanette Nolan

Hangmen Also Die! *
US 1943 131m bw
Arnold Pressburger/Fritz Lang (T. W. Baumfield)
reissue title: *Lest We Forget*
The Nazis take revenge for the killing of Heydrich.
Disappointingly heavy-handed, though deeply felt war propaganda set in Hollywood's idea of Czechoslovakia. Only moments of interest remain.
w John Wexley *story* Fritz Lang, Bertolt Brecht *d Fritz Lang ph James Wong Howe m* Hanns Eisler
☆ Brian Donlevy, Anna Lee, Walter Brennan, Gene Lockhart, Dennis O'Keefe, Alexander Granach, Margaret Wycherly, Nana Bryant, Hans von Twardowski (Heydrich), Jonathan Hale, Lionel Stander
'Lang, working with American actors on an American theme, has produced *Fury*. Lang trying to recreate his own Central Europe on a Hollywood set is completely at sea.' – *Paul Rotha, 1949*
'Directed with a skill which excites and delights … brilliant use of the tiny, shocking detail.' – *Dilys Powell*

'They have chosen to use brutality, American gangster idiom, and middle high German cinematic style to get it across, and it is rich with clever melodrama, over-*maestoso* directional touches, and the sort of Querschnitt sophistication for detail which Lang always has.' – *James Agee*

† Working titles included *The Silent City* and *Never Surrender*.

Hanns Eisler

The Hangover: see *Female Jungle*

Hangover Square *

US 1945 77m bw

TCF (Robert Bassler)

In 1903 London, a psychopathic composer murders pretty women.

This rather empty melodrama has almost nothing to do with the book from which it is allegedly taken, but the Hollywoodian evocation of gaslit London is richly entertaining and good to look at.

w Barre Lyndon *novel* Patrick Hamilton *d John Brahm ph Joseph LaShelle m Bernard Herrmann ad Lyle Wheeler, Maurice Ransford*

☆ Laird Cregar, Linda Darnell, George Sanders, Glenn Langan, Faye Marlowe, Alan Napier, Frederick Worlock

'Cregar lumbers around with a Karloffian glare in the spacious mists which happily blur the architectural decor.' – *Richard Winnington*

'Distinguished photography gets the last glint of fancy fright out of the pomps and vanities of the turn of the century.' – *Time*

'A half-chewed collection of reminiscences of *Dr Jekyll and Mr Hyde* and *The Lodger*.' – *Richard Mallett, Punch*

'The worst betrayal of a first class novel that I can remember.' – *James Agate*

'A better than average horror picture up to, but not including, its wildly overloaded climax.' – *James Agee*

† Tragically, Laird Cregar died after slimming for this role, to which he was in any case unsuited.

Hanky Panky

US 1982 107m Metrocolor

Columbia (Martin Ransohoff)

A girl on a spy mission is pursued by assassins and enlists the reluctant aid of an architect she meets in a taxi.

Frantic spoof of North by Northwest, *which was itself as spoofy as all get out. This strained effort lacks wit, substituting shouting, violence and an exasperating hero.*

w Henry Rosenbaum, David Taylor *d* Sidney Poitier *ph* Arthur Ornitz *m* Tom Scott *pd* Ben Edwards *ed* Harry Keller

☆ Gene Wilder (Michael Jordon), Gilda Radner (Kate Hellman), Kathleen Quinlan (Janet Dunn), Richard Widmark (Ransom), Robert Prosky (Hiram Calder), Josef Summer (Adrian Pruitt)

'The plot, rather like Mr Wilder, rushes hither and yon at the slightest excuse without ever adding up to very much. Even McGuffins are supposed to make more sense than this.' – *Richard Combs, MFB*

'A comedy thriller designed solely as a vehicle for Wilder's uninhibited hysteria is bad enough; one that so thoroughly submerges everyone else is so much worse.' – *Sight and Sound*

'One long screech.' – *Ibid.*

Hannah and Her Sisters ***

US 1986 106m Technicolor

Orion/Charles R. Joffe, Jack Rollins (Robert Greenhut)

Relationships intermingle for a New York family over a two-year period between Thanksgiving dinners.

Even though it has nowhere in particular to go, and certain scenes are over the top, this is a brilliantly assembled and thoroughly enjoyable mélange of fine acting and New Yorkish one-liners, with particularly sharp editing and a nostalgic music score.

wd Woody Allen *ph Carlo di Palma m* popular and classical extracts *pd* Stuart Wurtzel *ed Susan E. Morse*

☆ *Woody Allen* (Mickey Sachs), *Mia Farrow* (Hannah), *Dianne Wiest* (Holly), *Michael Caine* (Elliot), Carrie Fisher (April), Barbara Hershey (Lee), Maureen O'Sullivan (Norma), Lloyd Nolan (Evan), Max von Sydow (Frederick), Daniel Stern, Sam Waterston (David), Tony Roberts (Mickey's ex-partner), Julie Kavner (Gail)

'A loosely knit canvas of Manhattan interiors and exteriors.' – *Sight and Sound*

'One of Woody Allen's great films.' – *Variety*

best original screenplay; Dianne Wiest; Michael Caine

best picture; Woody Allen (as director); Susan E. Morse; art direction

best original screenplay; direction

Hanna's War

US 1988 148m colour

Cannon (Menahem Golan, Yoram Globus)

A Jewish poetess, working for the British secret service, is parachuted into Yugoslavia, captured and, after being taken to Budapest, is tortured and executed.

A true and tragic story diminished by its clumsy telling.

wd Menahem Golan *books* The Diaries of Hanna Senesh by Hanna Senesh; A Great Wind Cometh by Yoel Palgi *ph* Elemer Ragalyi *m* Dov Seltzer *pd* Kuli Sander *ed* Alain Jakubowicz

☆ Ellen Burstyn, Maruschka Detmers, Anthony Andrews, Donald Pleasence, David Warner, Vincenzo Ricotta, Christopher Fairbank

Hannibal

Italy 1959 103m Technicolor Supercinescope

Liber Film (Ottavio Poggi)

Hannibal crosses the Alps and falls for the daughter of a Roman senator.

Unhistorical farrago which totally fails to entertain on any level.

w Mortimer Braus *d* Carlo Ludovico Bragaglia, Edgar G. Ulmer *ph* Raffaele Masciocchi *m* Carlo Rustichelli

☆ Victor Mature, Rita Gam, Gabriele Ferzetti, Milly Vitale, Rik Battaglia

'Not even the elephants emerge with dignity.' – *MFB*

'His Genius Undeniable. His Evil Unspeakable. His Name…'

Hannibal *

US 2001 131m Technicolor

Universal/Scott Free (Dino De Laurentiis, Martha De Laurentiis, Ridley Scott)

Hannibal Lecter outwits an old adversary and the FBI.

A movie that edges towards the gruesome style of a big budget Hammer horror, presenting a bogeyman as superhero. No explanation is provided as to how Lecter manages to stay undetected as he moves effortlessly between countries; we have to take his genius on trust, but the rewards of so doing are small.

w David Mamet, Steven Zaillian *novel* Thomas Harris *d* Ridley Scott *ph* John Mathieson *m* Hans Zimmer *pd* Norris Spencer *ed* Pietro Scalia *sp* Keith Vanderlaan's Captive Audience; Greg Cannom

☆ Anthony Hopkins (Hannibal Lecter), Julianne Moore (Clarice Starling), Ray Liotta (Paul Krendler), Frankie R. Faison (Barney), Giancarlo Giannini (Pazzi), Francesca Neri (Allegra Pazzi), Zeljko Ivanek (Dr Cordell Doemling), Hazelle Goodman (Evelda Drumgo), David Andrews (FBI Agent Pearsall), Francis Guinan (FBI Director Noonan), Gary Oldman (Mason Verger)

'Degenerate but devilishly well directed.' – *Alexander Walker*

'Ranging from laughable to just plain boring, *Hannibal* is toothless to the end.' – *Empire*

† It was a sequel to *Silence of the Lambs* and was followed by a prequel *Red Dragon (qqv)*.

Hannibal Brooks

GB 1968 102m DeLuxe

UA/Scimitar (Michael Winner)

A British POW in Germany escapes over the Alps with an elephant.

Curious action adventure which seems undecided whether to take itself seriously. Some passable sequences.

w Dick Clement, Ian La Frenais *d* Michael Winner *ph* Robert Paynter *m* Francis Lai

☆ Oliver Reed, Michael J. Pollard, Wolfgang Preiss, Karin Baal

Hannie Caulder

GB 1971 85m colour Panavision

Tigon/Curtwel (Tony Tenser)

Raped by three outlaws who murdered her husband, a Western woman takes revenge.

Unintentionally comical action melodrama with the star defeating all comers.

w Z. X. Jones (Burt Kennedy, David Haft) *d* Burt Kennedy *ph* Ted Scaife *m* Ken Thorne

☆ Raquel Welch, Robert Culp, Ernest Borgnine, Strother Martin, Jack Elam, Christopher Lee, Diana Dors

Hanover Street

GB 1979 108m Technicolor Panavision

Columbia (Paul N. Lazarus III)

In 1943, an American bomber pilot meets a Red Cross nurse in a bus queue.

Wartime romance of a rather sticky sort, which turns with little warning into escape adventure, with our hero rescuing his loved one's husband from certain death.

wd Peter Hyams *ph* David Watkin *m* John Barry *pd* Philip Harrison

☆ Harrison Ford, Lesley-Anne Down, Christopher Plummer, Alec McCowen, Richard Masur, Michael Sacks, Max Wall

Hans Christian Andersen *

US 1952 112m Technicolor

Samuel Goldwyn

A storytelling cobbler leaves his village to make shoes for the prima ballerina in Copenhagen.

Artificial, sugary confection with little humour and far too little magic of any kind; the star carries it nicely, but he is on his own apart from the songs.

w Moss Hart *d* Charles Vidor *ph* Harry Stradling *m/ly Frank Loesser md* Walter Scharf *ch* Roland Petit *ad Richard Day*

☆ Danny Kaye, Zizi Jeanmaire, Farley Granger, John Qualen, Joey Walsh

'I found it such a charming entertainment, full of happiness and pathos, expert in interpretation yet swinging along with a gay holiday spirit that, when it was all over, I wanted to sit still for a minute and think about it, and then go away and sing its praises.' – C. A. *Lejeune*

† 16 screenplays were written before this one was chosen. Moira Shearer was signed for the role of ballerina but became pregnant. Gary Cooper was thought of for the lead, with William Wyler as director

♫ 'The King's New Clothes'; 'I'm Hans Christian Andersen'; 'Wonderful Copenhagen'; 'The Ugly Duckling'; 'Anywhere I Wander'; 'The Inch Worm'; 'No Two People'.

Harry Stradling; Walter Scharf; song 'Thumbelina'

Hanussen *

Hungary/West Germany 1988 117m Eastmancolor

Columbia TriStar/Objektiv/Mafilm/CCC Filmkunst/ZDF (Arthur Brauner)

An Austrian clairvoyant's predictions are used as Nazi propaganda.

Unusual, if somewhat insubstantial, political drama.

w István Szabó, Péter Dobai *d* István Szabó *ph* Lajos Koltai *m* György Vukan *ed* Zsuzsa Csákány, Eva Szentandrási, Brigitta Kajdácsi, Bettina Rekuc

☆ Klaus Maria Brandauer, Erland Josephson, Ildikó Bánsági, Walter Schmidinger, Károly Eperjes

best foreign film

The Happening

US 1967 101m Technicolor

Columbia/Horizon/Dover (Jud Kinberg)

Four young hippies kidnap a wealthy businessman and don't know what to do with him; he turns the tables.

Freewheeling irresponsible comedy which even at the time of swinging cities seemed very irritating.

w Frank R. Pierson, James D. Buchanan, Ronald Austin *d* Elliot Silverstein *ph* Philip Lathrop *m* Frank de Vol *pd* Richard Day

☆ Anthony Quinn, George Maharis, Michael Parks, Faye Dunaway, Robert Walker, Oscar Homolka, Martha Hyer, Milton Berle, Jack Kruschen

'A wacky comedy à la mode, oddly mixed and only spasmodically effective.' – *Variety*

The Happiest Days of Your Life ***

GB 1950 81m bw

British Lion/Individual (Frank Launder)

A ministry mistake billets a girls' school on a boys' school.

Briskly handled version of a semi-classic postwar farce, with many familiar talents in excellent form.

w Frank Launder, John Dighton *play John Dighton d Frank Launder ph* Stan Pavey *m* Mischa Spoliansky

☆ *Alastair Sim, Margaret Rutherford, Joyce Grenfell, Richard Wattis, Edward Rigby, Guy Middleton, Muriel Aked*, John Bentley, Bernadette O'Farrell

'Absolutely first rate fun.' – *Richard Mallett, Punch*

'Launder couldn't have knocked another laugh out of the situation if he'd used a hockey stick.' – *Sunday Express*

'The best mixed comedy pairing since Groucho Marx and Margaret Dumont.' – *Sunday Chronicle*

The Happiest Millionaire

US 1967 159m Technicolor

Walt Disney (Bill Anderson)

In 1916, a sporting millionaire has several surprising interests but finds time to sort out family problems.

Drearily inept family entertainment with a couple of good songs and an amusing alligator sequence but acres of yawning boredom in between.

w A. J. Carothers *play* Kyle Crichton *book* My Philadelphia Father *by Cornelia Drexel Biddle d* Norman Tokar *ph* Edward Colman *m/ly* Richard M. and Robert B. Sherman *md* Jack Elliott

☆ Fred MacMurray, *Tommy Steele*, Greer Garson, John Davidson, Gladys Cooper, Lesley Ann Warren, Geraldine Page, Hermione Baddeley

Happiness ***

US 1998 139m DuArt

October/Good Machine/Killer Films (Ted Hope, Christine Vachon)

A group of suburbanites seek, but do not find, fulfilment.

A bleak drama, verging on the misanthropic but lightened by a cutting wit, on the unsuccessful pursuit of happiness, and the subsequent discovery of the joylessness of sex and the damage that people can do to one another in unsatisfactory relationships.

wd Todd Solondz *ph* Maryse Alberti *m* Robbie Kondor *pd* Therese Deprez *ed* Alan Oxman

☆ Jane Adams, Dylan Baker, Lara Flynn Boyle, Ben Gazzara, Jared Harris, Philip Seymour Hoffman, Jon Lovitz, Marla Maples, Cynthia Stevenson, Elizabeth Ashley, Louise Lasser

'A disturbing black comedy that, at bottom, is about all the trouble sex causes people … Controversy and critical support will create want-see among discerning and adventurous specialty audiences, but breakout to a wider public will be difficult.' – *Todd McCarthy, Variety*

The Happiness Cage

US 1972 94m Movielab colour

International Film/Latema (George Goodman)

video title: *The Mind Snatchers*

In a German hospital, scientists carry out experiments to control the minds of violent American soldiers.

Small-scale drama debating the morality of brain-washing that does not escape its theatrical origins.

w Ron Whyte *play* Dennis Reardon *d* Bernard Girard *ph* Manny Wynn *m* Chris Dedrick, Phil Ramone *ad* William Molyneaux *ed* Sidney Katz

☆ Christopher Walken (Private James Reese), Joss Ackland (Dr Frederick), Ralph Meeker (The Major), Ronny Cox (Miles), Marco St John (Orderly), Tom Aldredge (Medic), Bette Henritze (Anna Kraus)

The Happiness of Three Women

GB 1954 78m bw

Advance

A village postman and busybody adopts various subterfuges to improve the future happiness of his clients.

Minor Welsh waffle which pleased naïve audiences at the time.

w Eynon Evans *play Wishing Well* by Eynon Evans *d* Maurice Elvey *ph* Stan Pavey *m* Edwin Astley
☆ Brenda de Banzie, Eynon Evans, Petula Clark, Donald Houston, Patricia Burke, Patricia Cutts

Happy

GB 1934 84m bw
ABPC/BIP (Fred Zelnik)
Two musicians find fortune and love in Paris.
Amiable musical, using revue and music-hall talents of the time, although the atmosphere remains resolutely Cockney despite its French setting.
w Austin Melford, Stanley Lupino, Frank Launder *d* Fred Zelnik *ph* Claude Friese-Greene *m* Fred Schwarz *m/ly* Stanley Lupino, Noel Gay and others *md* Harry Acres *ad* Clarence Elder *ed* A. S. Bates
☆ Stanley Lupino, Laddie Cliff, Will Fyffe, Dorothy Hyson, Renee Gadd, Harry Tate, Bertha Belmore, Gus McNaughton
† The script was adapted from French and German films written by Jacques Bachrach, Alfred Halm and Karl Noti.
†† Stanley Lupino and Laddie Cliff formed a notable partnership in several successful stage musicals.

Happy Anniversary

US 1959 83m bw
UA/Ralph Fields
A television set causes family trouble.
Marital farce designed to take a few sideswipes at TV.
w Joseph Fields, Jerome Chodorov *play Anniversary Waltz* by Joseph Fields, Jerome Chodorov *d* David Miller *ph* Lee Garmes *m* Sol Kaplan, Robert Allan
☆ David Niven, Mitzi Gaynor, Carl Reiner, Loring Smith, Patty Duke, Phyllis Povah

Happy Anniversary *

France 1961 13m bw
Capac
A husband is late for his anniversary dinner because of a traffic jam.
Amusing gag comedy, virtually silent and all the better for it.
wd Pierre Etaix
☆ *Pierre Etaix*, Loriot, Nono Zammit

Happy Birthday to Me

Canada 1980 111m Metrocolor
Birthday/CFDC/Famous Players (John Dunning, Andre Link)
Members of the senior class at Crawford Academy are killed off one at a time by one of their number.
Abysmal teenage shocker which grinds on relentlessly for nearly two hours.
w Timothy Bond, Peter Jobin, John Saxton *d* J. Lee-Thompson *ph* Miklos Lente *m* Bo Harwood, Lance Rubin
☆ Melissa Sue Anderson, Glenn Ford, Lawrence Dane, Sharon Acker, Frances Hyland

Happy Birthday Wanda June *

US 1971 105m Technicolor
Columbia (Lester Goldsmith)
An adventurer believed dead returns just as his wife is about to choose one of two suitors.
A farcical situation becomes in this writer's hands an investigation of the hero cult, with many zany jokes, episodes in heaven, and bad language. Interesting in spots, but it would have worked better with a more fluent cinematic technique.
w Kurt Vonnegut Jnr *play* Kurt Vonnegut Jnr *d* Mark Robson *ph* Fred J. Koenekamp
☆ Rod Steiger, Susannah York, George Grizzard, Don Murray
'We can only assume that Mr Robson deserted the filmic instincts that brought him commercial success because here he was, finally, in the presence of Art.' – *Hollis Alpert*
'Nothing more than a miscast film record of the dialogue and plot outline of the stage work.' – *Judith Crist*

Happy Days

US 1930 86m bw Grandeur
Fox
A showboat singer is a hit in New York and helps her old friends.
Virtually a revue, with spectacular effects on the giant screen.
w Sidney Lanfield, Edwin Burke *d* Ben Stoloff *ph* Lucien Andriot and others *m* Hugo Friedhofer *m/ly* various
☆ Marjorie White, Janet Gaynor, Charles Farrell, Victor McLaglen, Edmund Lowe, El Brendel, Walter Catlett, James J. Corbett, Tom Patricola, Dixie Lee, Sharon Lynn, Whispering Jack Smith

'We don't love. We just make love. And damn little of that!'

The Happy Ending *

US 1969 112m Technicolor Panavision
UA/Pax Films (Richard Brooks)
A middle-aged woman reflects over sixteen years of unhappy marriage.
Sometimes glib, sometimes trenchant sophisticated drama with enough interesting scenes to make it more than merely a 'woman's picture'.
wd Richard Brooks ph Conrad Hall *m* Michel Legrand
☆ *Jean Simmons*, John Forsythe, Shirley Jones, Lloyd Bridges, Teresa Wright, Dick Shawn, Nanette Fabray, Bobby Darin, Tina Louise
'Packed with punchy little epigrams floating in a vacuum of glossy superficiality.' – *David Wilson*
'The truth about the process of ageing is what binds this film together like cement.' – *Alexander Walker*
Jean Simmons; song 'What Are You Doing the Rest of Your Life' (*m*Michel Legrand, *ly*Alan and Marilyn Bergman)

Happy Ever After

GB/Germany 1932 86m bw
UFA (Erich Pommer)
Window-cleaners put a young actress on the way to stardom.
Cheerful comedy, set and made in Germany by mainly British talent.
w Jack Hulbert, Douglas Furber *story* Walter Reisch, Billy Wilder *d* Paul Martin, Robert Stevenson
☆ Lilian Harvey, Jack Hulbert, Cicely Courtneidge, Sonnie Hale, Edward Chapman

Happy Ever After *

GB 1954 87m Technicolor
ABP/Mario Zampi
US title: *Tonight's the Night*
Irish villagers draw lots for the privilege of murdering their rascally squire.
Fairly hilarious black comedy with a good cast entering into the spirit of the thing.
w Jack Davies, Michael Pertwee, L. A. G. Strong *d* Mario Zampi *ph* Stan Pavey *m* Stanley Black
☆ David Niven, Yvonne de Carlo, A. E. Matthews, Michael Shepley, George Cole, Barry Fitzgerald

Happy Family: see *The Merry Frinks (1934)*

Happy Gilmore

US 1996 92m DeLuxe
Universal (Robert Simonds)
A bad-tempered ice hockey player, in need of quick money, discovers that he has a talent for golf.
Crude and clumsy slapstick comedy, bone-crunchingly boring.
w Adam Sandler, Tim Herlihy *d* Dennis Dugan *ph* Arthur Albert *m* Mark Mothersbaugh *pd* Perry Andelin Blake *ed* Jeff Gourson
☆ Adam Sandler, Christopher McDonald, Julie Bowen, Frances Bay, Carl Weathers, Alan Covert, Robert Smigel, Richard Kiel, Dennis Dugan
'The laughs come from inflicting injury on anything animate and the hero's answer to every setback he suffers is a bone-crunching punch, a head butt, a kick in the ribs or groin, all gratifyingly amplified on the soundtrack. Maybe the damage this might do to impressionable kids is unproven. But the damage it does to wit, character and story-telling is demonstrable.' – *Alexander Walker*

Happy Go Lovely

GB 1950 97m Technicolor
Excelsior (Marcel Hellman)
A chorus girl meets a millionaire during the Edinburgh Festival.
For a semi-official contribution to the Festival of Britain this is a lamentably unspontaneous musical with no use of cinema techniques or natural locales. Even allowing for the flat handling, it is tedious.
w Val Guest *d* H. Bruce Humberstone *ph* Erwin Hillier *m* Mischa Spoliansky
☆ David Niven, Vera-Ellen, Cesar Romero, Bobby Howes, Diane Hart, Gordon Jackson, Barbara Couper, Gladys Henson, Joyce Carey
† A remake of *Paradise for Two.*

Happy Go Lucky

US 1942 81m Technicolor
Paramount (Harold Wilson)
A cigarette girl chases a millionaire to a Caribbean island.
Flimsy musical for those who like the stars.
w Walter de Leon, Melvin Frank, Norman Panama *d* Curtis Bernhardt *ph* Karl Struss, Wilfrid Cline *m/ly* Frank Loesser, Jimmy McHugh
☆ Mary Martin, Dick Powell, Betty Hutton, Rudy Vallee, Eddie Bracken, Mabel Paige, Eric Blore, Clem Bevans

Happy Gypsies *

Yugoslavia 1967 90m Eastmancolor
Avala
US title: *I Even Met Happy Gypsies*
A handsome, cruel-natured gypsy and his wife have violent adventures and find themselves on the run from the police.
The first film in the gypsy language does not make one too sympathetic to their cause, but some scenes are well managed and the colour is fine.
wd Alexander Petrovic *ph* Tomislav Pinter *m* gypsy melodies
☆ Bekim Fehmiu, Olivera Vuco, Bata Zivojinovic
best foreign film

The Happy Hooker

US 1975 98m Movielab
Double H/Cannon-Happy (Fred Caruso)
A Dutch girl in New York starts a career as a prostitute and finds she enjoys it.
Glum sex comedy based on the supposed exploits of a real madam; crude and not very funny. If this is emancipation, Shirley Temple seems more attractive by the minute.
w William Richert *book* Xaviera Hollander *d* Nicholas Sgarro *ph* Dick Kratina *m* Don Elliott
☆ Lynn Redgrave (hilariously miscast), Jean-Pierre Aumont, Lovelady Powell, Nicholas Pryor, Elizabeth Wilson, Tom Poston, Conrad Janis, Richard Lynch
† Follow-ups: *The Happy Hooker Goes to Washington* (1977), *The Happy Hooker Goes to Hollywood* (1980).

Happy Is the Bride *

GB 1957 84m bw
Panther/Paul Soskin
A couple planning a quiet summer wedding reckon without the intervention of her parents.
Tame remake of Quiet Wedding; *the right spirit but not much sparkle.*
w Jeffrey Dell, Roy Boulting *play* Esther McCracken *d* Roy Boulting *ph* Ted Scaife *m* Benjamin Frankel
☆ Ian Carmichael, Janette Scott, Cecil Parker, Joyce Grenfell, Terry-Thomas, John Le Mesurier, Eric Barker, Edith Sharpe, Athene Seyler

Happy Land *

US 1943 75m bw
TCF (Kenneth MacGowan)
Grandfather's ghost comes back to comfort a family which has lost its son at war.
Sentimental flagwaver very typical of its time; well made, it ensured not a dry eye in the house.
w Kathryn Scola, Julien Josephson *novel* Mackinlay Kantor *d* Irving Pichel *ph* Joseph LaShelle *m* Cyril Mockridge
☆ Don Ameche, Frances Dee, Harry Carey, Ann Rutherford, Cara Williams, Henry Morgan, Richard Crane, Dickie Moore

Happy Landing *

US 1938 102m bw
TCF (David Hempstead)
A Norwegian girl falls for an American flyer who crashes near her home.
Lightweight skating musical, well put together.
w Milton Sperling, Boris Ingster *d* Roy del Ruth *ph* John Mescall *md* Louis Silvers
☆ Sonja Henie, Don Ameche, Cesar Romero, Ethel Merman, Jean Hersholt, Billy Gilbert, Wally Vernon, El Brendel
'Just about everything to ensure entertainment value, shrewdly blended.' – *Variety*

Happy New Year *

France/Italy 1973 115m Eastmancolor
Films 13/Rizzoli (Claude Lelouch)
original title: *La Bonne Année*
A thief is paroled on New Year's Eve in the hope that he will lead police to his confederates. In fact he learns a lot about the world and himself.
Bitter comedy apparently intended to distance the director from the romantic fervour of A Man and a Woman, *a clip from which is screened for the convicts at the beginning.*
m Francis Lai *wd/ph Claude Lelouch*
☆ Lino Ventura, Françoise Fabian, Charles Gérard, André Falcon

'A multi-faceted comedy caper.'

Happy New Year *

US 1987 85m DeLuxe
Columbia/Delphi IV (Jerry Weintraub)
Two middle-aged jewel thieves head for a big score in Florida.
Loose remake of Lelouch's La Bonne Année, *quite watchable in its familiar way.*
w Warren Lane *d* John G. Avildsen *ph* James Crabe *m* Bill Conti *pd* William J. Cassidy *ed* Jane Kuson
☆ Peter Falk, Charles Durning, Wendy Hughes, Tom Courtenay, Joan Copeland

The Happy Road *

US/France 1956 100m bw
MGM/Thor (Gene Kelly)
Two children run away from a Swiss school and are pursued by the American father of one of them.
Whimsical peripatetic comedy which fails to come off despite charming passages.
w Arthur Julian, Joseph Morhaim, Harry Kurnitz *d* Gene Kelly *ph* Robert Juillard *m* George Van Parys
☆ Gene Kelly, Barbara Laage, Michael Redgrave, Bobby Clark, Brigitte Fossey

'Happy, Texas. Where even people on the run find a moment to be fabulous.'

Happy, Texas **

US 1999 104m Foto-Kem
Marked Entertainment (Mark Illsley, Rick Montgomery, Ed Stone)
Two escaped convicts are mistaken for a gay couple who have been hired to stage a beauty pageant in a small town.
Enjoyably eccentric comedy of mistaken identity and sexual confusion.
w Mark Illsley, Ed Stone, Phil Reeves *d* Mark Illsley *ph* Bruce Douglas Johnson *m* Peter Harris *pd* Maurin Scarlata *ed* Norman Buckley
☆ Jeremy Northam (Harry Sawyer), *Steve Zahn* (Wayne Wayne Wayne Jnr), William H. Macy (Sheriff Chappy Dent), Ally Walker (Josephine McLintock), Illeana Douglas (Ms Schaefer), M.C. Gainey (Bob), Ron Perlman (Nalhober), Tim Bagley (David), Michael Hitchcock (Steven), Paul Dooley (Judge)
'A film that, although bright and likeable, is otherwise a touch good-natured for its own good.' – *Philip Kemp, Sight and Sound*

The Happy Thieves

US 1962 88m bw
UA/Hillworth (James Hill, Rita Hayworth)
A gentleman thief and his accomplice become unwittingly involved in murder.
Dreary comedy which turns into equally dreary drama and makes its European backgrounds look ugly.
w John Gay *novel The Oldest Confession* by Richard Condon *d* George Marshall *ph* Paul Beeson *m* Mario Nascimbene
☆ Rex Harrison, Rita Hayworth, Grégoire Aslan, Joseph Wiseman, Alida Valli
'Absolute rubbish.' – *Rex Harrison*

The Happy Time ***
US 1952 94m bw
Columbia/Stanley Kramer (Earl Felton)
Domestic misadventures of a family of French Canadians during the twenties.
Basically concerned with adolescent sexual stirrings, this very agreeable film has a light touch and is most deftly directed and acted.
w Earl Felton *play* Samuel A. Taylor *d* Richard Fleischer *ph* Charles Lawton Jnr *m* Dimitri Tiomkin *pd* Rudolph Sternad
☆ Charles Boyer, Louis Jourdan, Bobby Driscoll, Marsha Hunt, Marcel Dalio, Kurt Kasznar, Linda Christian, Jeanette Nolan, Jack Raine, Richard Erdman

Happy Times: see *The Inspector General*

Happy Times
China 2000 95m colour
TCF/Guangxi/Zhuhai Zhenrong/Beijing NPD (Zhao Yu, Yang Qinglong)
original title: *Xingfu Shiguang*
A retired factory worker sets up a fake hotel room in a deserted warehouse so that he pretend to employ as a masseuse the blind daughter of the woman he wants to marry.
A movie that strives for Chaplinesque charm in the manner of City Lights; *its broad humour seems curiously old-fashioned and out of touch with modern sensibilities.*
w Gui Zi *story* Mo Yan *d* Zhang Yimou *ph* Hou Yong *m* San Bao *ad* Cao Jiuping *ed* Zhai Ru
☆ Zhao Benshan (Zhao), Dong Jie (Wu Ying), Li Xuejian (Li), Dong Lifan (Fat woman), Leng Qibin (Her Son), Niu Ben (Oxhead), Fu Biao (Fu)
'A bland, patronising piece with little in the way of social observation.' – *Philip French, Observer*
'Endows humanist cinema with a heroic moral dimension.' – *Andrew Sarris, New York Observer*

Happy Together
US 1990 96m Metrocolor
Seymour Borde (Jere Henshaw)
Due to a mix-up, a prudish college student finds himself sharing a room with an attractive girl.
Predictable teenage wish-fulfilment comedy unlikely to interest anyone over school-going age.
w Craig J. Nevius *d* Mel Damski *ph* Joe Pennella *m* Robert Folk *pd* Marcia Hinds *ed* O. Nicholas Brown
☆ Patrick Dempsey, Helen Slater, Dan Schneider, Kevin Hardesty, Marius Weyers, Barbara Babcock

Happy Together *
Hong Kong 1997 97m bw/colour
Artificial Eye/Block 2/Prenom H/Seawoo/Jet Tone (Wong Kar-Wai)
original title: *Chunguang Zhaxie*
In Argentina, two Chinese male lovers quarrel and part.
An intense and claustrophobic study of jealousies and passion, done with an excess of style.
wd Wong Kar-Wai *novel* The Buenos Aires Affair by Manuel Puig *ph* Christopher Doyle *m* Danny Chung *pd* William Chang Suk-ping *ed* William Chang Suk-ping, Wong Ming-Lam
☆ Leslie Cheung, Tony Leung, Chang Chen
'In the absence of any genuine emotional wallop, it is the directorial pizzazz that pulls you through. Just about.' – *Ian Freer, Empire*
† The film won Wong Kar-Wai the prize as best director at the 1997 Cannes Film Festival

Happy We *
Sweden 1983 111m colour
AB Svenski Filmindustri
original title: *Tv Killar Och en Tjej*
A dentist recalls how he met his second wife, renewing a friendship begun in student days with her and her former husband.
Pleasantly nostalgic comedy of love and marriage, mainly roses all the way with the occasional thorn of sharp observation.
w Brasse Brännström, Lasse Hallström, Magnus Härenstam *d* Lasse Hallström *ph* Roland Lundin, Torbjörn Andersson *m* Anders Berglund *ad* Lasse Westfelt *ed* Lasse Hallström, Jan Persson
☆ Brasse Brännström, Magnus Härenstam, Lars Amble, Ivan Oljelund, Pia Green

The Happy Years
US 1950 86m bw
MGM (Carey Wilson)
The taming of an unruly pupil at a turn-of-the-century American school.
A curiously unrealized piece of Americana, with only moments to suggest what was being aimed at.
w Harry Ruskin *novel* The Lawrenceville School Stories by Owen Johnson *d* William Wellman *ph* Paul C. Vogel *m* Leigh Harline
☆ Dean Stockwell, Leo G. Carroll, Darryl Hickman, Scotty Beckett, Leon Ames, Margalo Gillmore

Hara Kiri: see *The Battle (1934)*

Hara Kiri *
Japan 1962 135m bw Grandscope
Shochiku (Tatsuo Hosoya)
original title: *Seppuku*
17th-century samurai often pretend to commit hara kiri so that a grand lord will have sympathy and take them on. One of them is forced to go through with it.
Strange, traditional, slow and explicitly brutal costume piece, for specialized western eyes only.
w Shinobu Hashimoto *d* Masaki Kobayashi *ph* Yoshio Miyajima *m* Toru Takemitsu *ad* Junichi Ozumi
☆ Tatsuya Nakadai, Shima Iwashita, Akira Isahama

'As a cop, he has brains, brawn and an instinct to kill.'
Hard Boiled *
Hong Kong 1992 126m colour
Golden Princess/Milestone (Linda Kuk, Terence Chang)
original title: *Lashou Shentan*
A gun-happy cop smashes a smuggling ring.
Spectacularly violent gangster movie, with a body-count in the hundreds and stylishly choreographed, slow-motion deaths and stunts; possibly the best example of John Woo's particular talents for large-scale mayhem.
w Barry Wong *story* John Woo *d* John Woo *ph* Wang Wing-Heng *m* Michael Gibbs, James Wong *ad* James Leung, Joel Chong *ed* John Woo, David Wu, Kai Kit-Wai
☆ Chow Yun-Fat, Tony Leung, Teresa Mo, Philip Chan, Philip Kwok, Anthony Wong, Kwan Hoi-Shan, Tung Wai, Y. Yonemura
'Superbly choreographed violence … Pic delivers ample ammunition with a good dose of humor.' – *Variety*
'A vivid cartoon version of the kinetics and twisted-loyalty themes of Sam Peckinpah.' – *Michael Sragow, New Yorker*
† The film was released on video in a subtitled wide-screen and a dubbed version.

Hard Contract
US 1969 106m DeLuxe Panavision
TCF (Marvin Schwarz)
A professional killer has sexual hang-ups.
Heavy-going modern thriller with lively scenes separated by too much self-analytical chat, not to mention a tour of Europe.
wd S. Lee Pogostin *ph* Jack Hildyard *m* Alex North
☆ James Coburn, Lilli Palmer, Lee Remick, Burgess Meredith, Patrick Magee, Sterling Hayden, Helen Cherry, Karen Black, Claude Dauphin
'Behind it one glimpses a much better film than its surface suggests.' – *MFB*
'Like a flat-footed James Bond story that soaked its feet in a hot bath of existentialism.' – *John Simon*

Hard Country
US 1981 104m CFI color
AFD (David Greene, Mack Bing)
An urban cowboy has no ambitions until he falls in love.
Simple modern Western with music, not at all bad but with a scant potential audience.
w Michael Kane *d* David Greene *ph* Dennis Dalzell *m* Michael Martin Murphey, Jimmie Haskell *pd* Edward Richardson *ed* John A. Martinelli
☆ Jan-Michael Vincent, Kim Basinger, Michael Parks, Tanya Tucker, Gailard Sartain

A Hard Day's Night ****
GB 1964 85m bw
UA/Proscenium (Walter Shenson)
Harassed by their manager and Paul's grandpa, the Beatles embark from Liverpool by train for a London TV show.
Comic fantasia with music; an enormous commercial success with the director trying every cinematic gag in the book, it led directly to all the kaleidoscopic swinging London spy thrillers and comedies of the later sixties, and so has a lot to answer for; but at the time it was a sweet breath of fresh air, and the Beatles even seemed willing and likeable.
w Alun Owen *d* Richard Lester *ph* Gilbert Taylor *m/ly* The Beatles *md* George Martin
☆ The Beatles, Wilfrid Brambell, Norman Rossington, Victor Spinetti
'A fine conglomeration of madcap clowning … with such a dazzling use of camera that it tickles the intellect and electrifies the nerves.' – *Bosley Crowther*
'All technology was enlisted in the service of the gag, and a kind of nuclear gagmanship exploded.' – *John Simon*
'The *Citizen Kane* of Jukebox movies' – *Andrew Sarris*
† It has also been released on CD-ROM for Apple Macintosh computers, together with the script and an essay on the movie.
Alun Owen; George Martin

Hard Driver: see *The Last American Hero*

Hard Eight *
US 1996 101m DeLuxe Super 35
Entertainment/Rysher/Green Parrot (Robert Jones, John Lyons)
A con man has a private reason for taking as a protégé an unsuccessful young gambler.
Tough-talking, low-budget thriller with an atmosphere both claustrophobic and menacing.
wd Paul Thomas Anderson *ph* Robert Elswit *m* Michael Penn, Jon Brion *pd* Nancy Deren *ed* Barbara Tulliver
☆ Philip Baker Hall, John C. Reilly, Gwyneth Paltrow, Samuel L. Jackson, F. William Parker, Philip Seymour Hoffman
'Modern *film noir* of sure touch pivoting round a remarkable performance given by Philip Baker Hall.' – *Richard Williams, Guardian*

Hard, Fast and Beautiful
US 1951 76m bw
RKO/The Filmmakers (Collier Young)
A girl tennis player is influenced by her ambitious mother.
Unusual but not very effective melodrama.
w Martha Wilkerson *novel* John R. Tunis *d* Ida Lupino *ph* Archie Stout *m* Roy Webb
☆ Claire Trevor, Sally Forrest, Carleton Young, Robert Clarke, Kenneth Patterson, Joseph Kearns

Hard Men
GB/France 1996 87m colour
Entertainment/Venture/Dacia (J. K. Amalou, Georges Benayoun)
A London gangster orders two of his enforcers to kill a colleague.
Low-budget movie of a second-hand kind, fashionably violent.
wd J. K. Amalou *ph* Nick Sawyer *pd* Simon Elliott *ed* Victoria Boydell
☆ Vincent Regan, Ross Boatman, Lee Ross, 'Mad' Frankie Fraser, Ken Campbell, Mirella D'Angelo
'A game attempt at a British Tarantino that has its moments but is deep-sixed by lackluster dialogue and uninvolving characters.' – *Derek Elley, Variety*

Hard Promises
US 1991 95m DeLuxe
Columbia/Stone/High Horse (Cindy Chvatal, William Petersen)
An absentee husband, discovering that his wife has divorced him, returns home to prevent her remarriage.
Drear domestic comedy in which it is hard to sympathize with any of the main characters.
w Jule Selbo *d* Martin Davidson *ph* Andrzej Bartkowiak *m* Kenny Vance *pd* Dan Leigh *ed* Bonnie Koehler
☆ Sissy Spacek (Chris Coalter), William Petersen (Joey Coalter), Brian Kerwin (Walt Humphrey), Mare Winningham (Dawn), Jeff Perry (Pinky Kulowski), Olivia Burnette (Beth Coalter), Peter MacNicol (Stuart Haggart), Ann Wedgeworth (Chris's Mom), Amy Wright (Shelley), Lois Smith (Mrs Bell)

Hard Rain
US 1998 96m DeLuxe Panavision
Paramount/Mutual (Mark Gordon, Gary Levinsohn, Ian Bryce)
In a flooded town, a bank robber and an unscrupulous sheriff battle to get their hands on a fortune in stolen notes.
A mix of disaster movie and thriller; the result is a disastrous thriller.
w Graham Yost *d* Mikael Salomon *ph* Peter Menzies Jnr *m* Christopher Young *pd* J. Michael Riva *ed* Paul Hirsch
☆ Morgan Freeman, Christian Slater, Randy Quaid, Minnie Driver, Ed Asner, Richard Dysart, Betty White, Mark Rolston
'A waterlogged would-be thriller deep-sixed by its misguided notion of high concept.' – *Todd McCarthy, Variety*
† The film was made in 1996 and then, according to reports, altered to make less a disaster movie and more a thriller.

Hard Steel
GB 1942 86m bw
GFD/GHW (James B. Sloan)
reissue title: *What Shall It Profit*
A steel worker is promoted and loses his humanity, but comes to his senses when his wife leaves him.
Modest moral drama from the uplift side of the Rank empire.
w Lydia Hayward *novel* Steel Saraband by Roger Dataller *d* Norman Walker *ph* Claude Friese-Greene
☆ Wilfrid Lawson, Betty Stockfeld, John Stuart, George Carney, Joan Kemp-Welch, Hay Petrie

'Don't hunt what you can't kill.'
Hard Target
US 1993 97m DeLuxe
UIP/Alphaville/Renaissance (James Jacks, Sean Daniel)
In New Orleans, a wealthy man organizes the hunting and killing of men for sport.
John Woo, Hong Kong's influential director of action films, makes his American debut with yet another re-make of The Most Dangerous Game; *the experience seems not to have been a happy one for him, or for his audience.*
w Chuck Pfarrer *d* John Woo *ph* Russell Carpenter *m* Graeme Revell *pd* Phil Dagort *ed* Bob Murawski
☆ Jean-Claude Van Damme, Lance Henriksen, Yancy Butler, Arnold Vosloo, Kasi Lemmons, Wilford Brimley, Chuck Pfarrer
'A thuggish, badly scripted thriller.' – *Philip French, Observer*
'Giggles seem as appropriate as shocked gasps. For this film has nothing to do with real life or real violence.' – *Nigel Andrews, Financial Times*

Hard Times *
US 1975 93m Metrocolor Panavision
Columbia (Lawrence Gordon)
GB title: *The Streetfighter*
In New Orleans in the Depression-hit thirties, a prizefighter and a promoter help each other.
Interesting, atmospheric melodrama on the lone stranger theme.
w Walter Hill, Bryan Gindorff, Bruce Henstell *d* Walter Hill *ph* Philip Lathrop *m* Barry DeVorzon
☆ Charles Bronson, James Coburn, Jill Ireland, Strother Martin, Maggie Blye

Hard Times *
Portugal/GB 1988 96m bw
Artificial Eye/Joã Botelho
original title: *Tempos dificeis, este tempo*
A circus child is brought up in the loveless household of a pedant who teaches his children to revere facts.

Dickens is scaled down, but effectively translated to modern-day Portugal.
wd Joã Botelho *novel* Charles Dickens *ph* Elso Roque *m* António Pinho Vargas *ad* Jasmin Matos *ed* Joã Botelho
☆ Luis Estreka, Julia Britton, Isabel de Castro, Ruy Furtado, Inês Medeiros, Henrique Viana, Lia Gama, Joaquim Mendes, Isabel Ruth

Hard to Get
US 1938 80m bw
Warner
An architect is reduced to working at a gas station; here he meets and falls in love with a millionairess.
Arch romantic comedy which failed to enhance its stars.
w Jerry Wald, Maurice Leo, Richard Macaulay *d* Ray Enright *ph* Charles Rosher
☆ Dick Powell, Olivia de Havilland, Charles Winninger, Thurston Hall, Isabel Jeans, Penny Singleton, Allen Jenkins
'Will carry in top brackets mainly due to selling names.' – *Variety*

Hard to Handle **
US 1933 75m bw
Warner (Robert Lord)
The success story of a cheerful public relations man.
Punchy star comedy with interesting sidelights on the social fads of the early thirties including marathon dancing, get-rich-quick schemes and grapefruit diets.
w Wilson Mizner, Robert Lord d Mervyn Le Roy *ph* Barney McGill
☆ *James Cagney, Ruth Donnelly,* Mary Brian, Allen Jenkins, Claire Dodd
'Hokum this time instead of the realism that boosted him to stardom.' – *Variety*
'A violent, slangy, down-to-the-pavement affair which has many a mirthful moment.' – *Mordaunt Hall*

Hard to Kill
US 1989 96m Technicolor
Warner/Lee Rich Productions/Adelson-Todman-Simon
Reviving from a seven-year coma, a former cop and martial arts expert seeks revenge for the massacre of his family.
Formula action film.
w Steve McKay *d* Bruce Malmuth *ph* Matthew F. Leonetti *m* David Michael Frank *pd* Robb Wilson King *ed* John F. Link
☆ Steven Seagal, Kelly Le Brock, Bill Sadler, Frederick Coffin, Bonnie Burroughs, Andrew Bloch, Branscombe Richmond, Charles Boswell

'There are two sides to every story – and every woman!'
The Hard Way *
US 1942 109m bw
Warner (Jerry Wald)
A strong-willed girl pushes her reluctant sister to the heights of show business.
Unconvincing but well-mounted drama.
w Daniel Fuchs, Peter Viertel *d* Vincent Sherman *ph* James Wong Howe *m* Heinz Roemheld *md* Leo F. Forbstein
☆ Ida Lupino, Joan Leslie, Dennis Morgan, Jack Carson, Gladys George, Faye Emerson, Paul Cavanagh, Roman Bohnen

The Hard Way *
US 1991 111m DeLuxe Panavision
UIP/Universal/Badham/Cohen (William Sackheim)
A Hollywood actor who plans to play a cop in his new film teams up with a real-life New York policeman who is obsessed with catching a serial killer.
Amusing comedy that pokes fun at buddy-buddy and cop movies while being both itself.
w Daniel Pyne, Lem Dobbs *story* Lem Dobbs, Michael Kozoll *d* John Badham *ph* Robert Primes, Don McAlpine *m* Arthur B. Rubinstein *pd* Philip Harrison *ed* Frank Morriss
☆ Michael J. Fox, James Woods, Stephen Lang, Annabella Sciorra, Delroy Lindo, Luis Guzman, Mary Mara, Penny Marshall
'Proves that sometimes the system, fuelled here by self-mocking jibes, can turn out films appreciable and enjoyable without adding anything to the cinema.' – *Kim Newman, Sight and Sound*

'Hi-Octane Hi-Calibre Hi-Body Count!'
Hard-Boiled 2: The Last Blood
Hong Kong 1994 89m colour
Movie Impact (Wallace Cheung, Eric Tsang)
In Singapore, a Hong Kong security expert fights to prevent an army of Japanese terrorists killing the one man who can save the life of a visiting Buddhist religious leader (variously called Takka Lama and Daka Lama, and who forgets his principles for long enough to slit the throat of a would-be assassin).
Deliriously silly, over-the-top action thriller, not helped by the poor subtitling (as in: 'Drop that pistol, and let us fight it bear-handed' and 'Many people have bet less but they want it to loss well'); the movie lacks both a coherent narrative and John Woo's panache in its scenes of indiscriminate slaughter, as hostages and bystanders are mown down without compunction.
d Wong Ching (action director: Blackie Ko) *ph* Jingle Ma *ad* Fong Ying *ed* Chang Kwok Kuen
☆ Andy Lau, Alan Tam, Leung Ka Yan, May Lo, Eric Tsang, Chan Pak Cheung
'Tightly-directed set pieces, slow-motion photography and superbly choreographed fights elevate this shaggy dog thriller.' – *Sight and Sound*
† Apart from the title, the film has no connection with John Woo's original.

'The most important thing in life is showing up.'
Hardball
US 2001 106m DeLuxe
Paramount/Fireworks (Tina Nides, Mike Tollin, Brian Robbins)
A compulsive gambler redeems himself by coaching an inner-city kids' baseball team.
Sentimental, manipulative drama that embraces all the usual clichés of the genre and stifles any hint of reality.
w John Gatins *book* Daniel Coyle *d* Brian Robbins *ph* Tom Richmond *m* Mark Isham *pd* Jaymes Hinkle *ed* Ned Bastille
☆ Keanu Reeves (Conor O'Neill), Diane Lane (Elizabeth Wilkes), John Hawkes (Ticky Tobin), Bryan C. Hearne (Andre Ray Peetes), Julian Griffith (Jefferson Albert Tibbs), Michael Jordan (Jamal), A. Delon Ellis Jnr (Miles Pennfield II)
'The movie is so littered with clichés of genre, as well as clichés of artifice in Reeves' pained performance, that any semblance of social reality goes foul.' – *Lisa Schwarzbaum, Entertainment Weekly*

Hardcore
GB 1977 82m Technicolor
Norfolk/Assay (Brian Smedley-Aston)
A vicar's daughter recounts her sexual experiences to a stranger.
Billed as 'the frankly sensational adventures of a liberated lady', it is neither frank nor sensational, but coy, witless and dull, with its cast of familiar character actors giving their worst performances on film, as they try to match the standard set by its star.
w James Kenelm Clarke, Michael Robson *d* James Kenelm Clarke *ph* Mike Molloy *m* James Kenelm Clarke *md* Syd Dale *ad* Roger King *ed* Jim Connock
☆ Fiona Richmond (Fiona), Anthony Steel (Robert), Victor Spinetti (Duncan), Graham Stark (Inspector Flaubert), Graham Crowden (Lord Yardarm), Ronald Fraser (Marty), Percy Herbert (Hubert), Roland Curram (Edward), Harry H. Corbett (Art), Jeremy Child (Tenniel), John Clive, Michael Feast
'A disaster, this is yet another unamusing British sex comedy which misuses all the talents involved.' – *Scott Meek, MFB*

Hardcore ***
US 1979 108m Metrocolor
Columbia/A-Team (John Milius)
GB title: *The Hardcore Life*
A religious man from Michigan journeys to Los Angeles in search of his daughter, who has taken to acting in porno films.
Intense and solemn treatment of a situation that could have gone over the top, and very nearly does; the acting saves it.
wd Paul Schrader *ph* Michael Chapman *m* Jack Nitzsche
☆ *George C. Scott,* Peter Boyle, Season Hubley, Dick Sargent, Leonard Gaines
'Flawed and uneven, it contains moments of pure revelation.' – *Roger Ebert*

The Hardcore Life: see *Hardcore*

The Harder They Come **
Jamaica 1972 110m Metrocolor
International Films (Perry Henzell)
A country boy comes to the city to make it as a reggae singer but finds success only when he turns to crime.
Lively, tough drama of drugs and corruption in which the action is matched by the vigour of the music, which did much to give reggae an international appeal.
w Perry Henzell, Trevor D. Rhone *d* Perry Henzell *ph* David MacDonald, Peter Jessop, Franklyn St Juste *m* Jimmy Cliff, Toots and the Maytalls, Desmond Dekker, The Slickers *ad* Sally Henzell *ed* John Victor Smith, Richard White, Reicland Anderson
☆ *Jimmy Cliff,* Janet Bartley, Carl Bradshaw, Ras Daniel Hartman, Basil Keane, Robert Charlton, Winston Stona
'The film itself is a mess, but the music is redeeming, and Jimmy Cliff's joy in music, along with the whole culture's, stays with you.' – *Pauline Kael*

'No Punches Pulled!'
'If you thought "On the Waterfront" hit hard ... wait till you see this one!'
'This Is A Fighting-Mad Motion Picture!'
The Harder They Fall *
US 1956 109m bw
Columbia (Philip Yordan)
A press agent exposes the crooked fight game.
Wearily efficient sporting melodrama.
w Philip Yordan *novel* Budd Schulberg *d* Mark Robson *ph* Burnett Guffey *m* Hugo Friedhofer
☆ Humphrey Bogart, Rod Steiger, Jan Sterling, Mike Lane, Max Baer, Edward Andrews, Harold J. Stone
† It was Bogart's last performance.
Burnett Guffey

Hardware *
GB/US 1990 92m colour
Palace/Miramax/British Screen/BSB/Wicked Films (Joanne Sellar, Paul Trybits)
Scavengers in a radioactive wasteland unknowingly recover a killer robot.
A low-budget science-fiction horror story, filmed in the style of a rock music video.
wd Richard Stanley *story SHOK!* by Steve McManus, Kevin O'Neill *ph* Steven Chivers *m* Simon Boswell *pd* Joseph Bennett *ed* Derek Trigg *sp* Image Animation
☆ Dylan McDermott, Stacey Travis, John Lynch, William Hootkins, Iggy Pop
'A cacophonic, nightmarish variation on the postapocalyptic cautionary genre.' – *Variety*

The Hardy Family
America's favourite fictional characters just before and during World War II were the family of a small-town judge, who seemed to personify all that everyone was fighting for, especially as the young son was always getting into amusing scrapes. Designed by a delighted MGM as low-budgeters, they paid for many an expensive failure, and introduced, as young Andy's girlfriends, a series of starlets who went on to much bigger things. The basic family was Lewis Stone, Fay Holden, Mickey Rooney, Cecilia Parker and Sara Haden (as the spinster aunt); but in the very first episode Lionel Barrymore and Spring Byington played the judge and his wife. MGM was given a special Academy Award in 1942 'for representing the American Way of Life' in the films.
1937 A Family Affair (qv); 69m, *d* George B. Seitz *w* Kay Van Riper *play* Aurania Rouverol
1938 You're Only Young Once; 78m *d* George B. Seitz *w* Kay Van Riper; introducing Ann Rutherford (who became a regular)
1938 Judge Hardy's Children; 78m *d* George B. Seitz *w* Kay Van Riper; with Ruth Hussey
1938 Love Finds Andy Hardy; 90m *d* George B. Seitz *w* William Ludwig; with Judy Garland, Lana Turner
1938 Out West with the Hardys; 90m *d* George B Seitz *w* Kay Van Riper, Agnes Christine Johnston, William Ludwig
1939 The Hardys Ride High; 81m *d* George B. Seitz *w* as above
1939 Andy Hardy Gets Spring Fever; 85m *d* W. S. Van Dyke II *w* Kay Van Riper
1939 Judge Hardy and Son; 90m *d* George B. Seitz *w* Carey Wilson; with June Preisser, Maria Ouspenskaya
1940 Andy Hardy Meets a Debutante; 89m *d* George B. Seitz *w* Annalee Whitmore, Thomas Seller; with Judy Garland
1941 Andy Hardy's Private Secretary; 101m *d* George B. Seitz *w* Jane Murfin, Harry Ruskin; with Kathryn Grayson, Ian Hunter
1941 Life Begins for Andy Hardy; 100m *d* George B. Seitz *w* Agnes Christine Johnston; with Judy Garland
1942 The Courtship of Andy Hardy; 93m *d* George B. Seitz *w* Agnes Christine Johnston; with Donna Reed
1942 Andy Hardy's Double Life; 92m *d* George B. Seitz *w* Agnes Christine Johnston; with Esther Williams, Susan Peters
1944 Andy Hardy's Blonde Trouble; 107m *d* George B. Seitz *w* Harry Ruskin, William Ludwig, Agnes Christine Johnston; with Bonita Granville, Jean Porter, Herbert Marshall, the Wilde twins
1946 Love Laughs at Andy Hardy; 94m *d* Willis Goldbeck *w* Harry Ruskin, William Ludwig; with Bonita Granville
1958 Andy Hardy Comes Home; 80m *d* Howard Koch *w* Edward Everett Hutshing, Robert Morris Donley; without Lewis Stone

Harem
France 1985 113m colour Panavision
Sara (Alain Sarde)
aka: *D'Ardenelle*
A New York stockbroker is kidnapped by an Arab prince as an addition to his harem, and she likes it.
Glossy but vacuous drama, in which high-priced talents fight against a script devoid of interest, though some swiftly give up the struggle; even by the standards of Valentino's The Sheik, *which it resembles in a retrograde way, it is junk.*
w Arthur Joffé, Tom Rayfiel *d* Arthur Joffé *ph* Pasqualino De Santis *m* Philippe Sarde *pd* Alexandre Trauner *ed* Françoise Bonnot, Ruggero Mastroianni
☆ Nastassja Kinski, Ben Kingsley, Dennis Goldson, Michel Robin, Zohra Segal, Julette Simpson
† The British video release ran for 94m.

Harem Girl
US 1952 70m bw
Columbia
The secretary to a princess vanquishes her employer's Arab ill-wishers.
Dispirited pratfall farce, its star's last movie.
w Edward Bernds, Elwood Ullman *d* Edward Bernds
☆ Joan Davis, Peggie Castle, Arthur Blake, Paul Marion

Harem Holiday: see *Harum Scarum*

Harlem Nights
US 1989 116m Technicolor
UIP/Paramount/Eddie Murphy Productions (Robert D. Wachs, Mark Lipsky)
Two night-club owners fight off a takeover bid by gangsters.
Witless display of self-indulgence by its overparted director-author-star.
wd Eddie Murphy *ph* Woody Omens *m* Herbie Hancock *pd* Lawrence G. Paull *ed* George Bowers, Alan Balsam
☆ Eddie Murphy, Richard Pryor, Redd Foxx, Danny Aiello, Michael Lerner, Della Reese, Berlinda Tolbert, Stan Shaw, Jasmine Guy, Vic Polizos
best costume design (Joe I. Tompkins)

Harlequin
Australia 1980 93m Eastmancolor Panavision
FG Films/Far Flight (Anthony Ginnane)
US title: *Dark Forces*
A faith healer cures a politician's son, seduces his wife, and proves to be of supernatural origin.

Muddled and unsatisfactory fantasy in the manner of The Passing of the Third Floor Back; *in this case far too much is left unexplained, and the film is scarcely entertaining despite effort all round.*
w Everett de Roche *d* Simon Wincer *ph* Gary Hanson *m* Brian May
☆ Robert Powell, David Hemmings, Carmen Duncan, Broderick Crawford

Harley Davidson and the Marlboro Man
US 1991 98m DeLuxe
UIP/MGM (Jere Henshaw)
In the near future, two drifters rob a bank to save their favourite bar from being re-developed.
Tiresome action film on the side of lawlessness and disorder.
w Don Michael Paul *d* Simon Wincer *ph* David Eggby *m* Basil Poledouris *pd* Paul Peters *ed* Corky Ehlers
☆ Mickey Rourke, Don Johnson, Chelsea Field, Daniel Baldwin, Giancarlo Esposito, Vanessa Williams, Robert Ginty, Tia Carrere, Julius Harris, Eloy Casados
'Bone-headed biker Western.' – *Variety*

'She was famous for light dresses, loose living, and trips to the bottom between pictures!'
Harlow
US 1965 125m Technicolor Panavision
Paramount/Embassy/Prometheus (Joseph E. Levine)
In 1929, starlet Jean Harlow is shot to fame by her agent Arthur Landau.
Absurdly whitewashed and excruciatingly boring rags-to-riches yarn with most of the characters fictitious and little to do with the real Jean Harlow. Only the studio scenes are mildly interesting.
w John Michael Hayes *d* Gordon Douglas *ph* Joseph Ruttenberg *m* Neal Hefti *ad* Hal Pereira, Roland Anderson *cos* *Edith Head*
☆ Carroll Baker, Peter Lawford, Mike Connors, Red Buttons, Raf Vallone, Angela Lansbury, *Martin Balsam*
'Hollywood once again succeeds in reducing one of its few fascinating realities to the sleazy turgid level of its more sordid fictions.' – *Judith Crist*
† A rather better television tape drama of the same title, starring Carol Lynley and Ginger Rogers, was made almost simultaneously. It was converted to film ('Electronovision') but had few bookings.

Harmony Parade: see *Pigskin Parade*

'They met at the funeral of a perfect stranger. From then on, things got perfectly stranger and stranger.'
Harold and Maude *
US 1971 92m Technicolor
Paramount/Mildred Lewis/Colin Higgins
A repressed young man, fixated on death and funerals, has an affair with an 80-year-old woman.
Often hilarious black comedy for those who can stand it; the epitome of bad taste, splashed around with wit and vigour, it became a minor cult.
w Colin Higgins d Hal Ashby ph John A. Alonzo *m* Cat Stevens *ad* Michael Haller *ed* William A. Sawyer, Edward Warschilka
☆ *Bud Cort* (Harold), *Ruth Gordon* (Maude), Vivian Pickles (Mrs Chasen), Cyril Cusack (Glaucus), Charles Tyner (Uncle Victor), Ellen Geer (Sunshine Dore), Eric Christmas (Priest)
'Has all the fun and gaiety of a burning orphanage.' – *Variety*

Harold Lloyd's Funny Side of Life ***
US 1963 99m bw
Harold Lloyd (Duncan Mansfield)
Excerpts from twenties comedies plus a shortened version of *The Freshman* (1925).
Excellent compilation, though the mini-feature makes it a little unbalanced.
w Arthur Ross *m* Walter Scharf
☆ *Harold Lloyd*

Harold Lloyd's World of Comedy ****
US 1962 97m bw
Harold Lloyd
Generous clips from the comic climaxes of Lloyd's best silent and sound comedies including *Safety Last, The Freshman, Hot Water, Why Worry, Girl Shy, Professor Beware, Movie Crazy* and *Feet First.*
As Lloyd's work lends itself well to extract, this can hardly fail to be a superb anthology capsuling the appeal of one of America's greatest silent comedians. The timing is just perfect.
w Walter Scharf
☆ Art Ross (narrator)

Harold Teen
US 1934 66m bw
Warner
GB title: *Dancing Fool*
A young reporter saves a small-town bank from collapse.
Teenage romantic comedy.
w Paul Gerard Smith, Al Cohn *comic strip* Carl Ed *d* Murray Roth
☆ Hal Le Roy, Rochelle Hudson, Patricia Ellis, Guy Kibbee, Hobart Cavanaugh
† Previously filmed in 1928 (with Arthur Lake and Mary Brian, directed by Mervyn Le Roy) and here reduced to second feature status.

The Harp of Burma: see *The Burmese Harp*

Harper *
US 1966 121m Technicolor Panavision
Warner/Gershwin-Kastner
GB title: *The Moving Target*
A Los Angeles private eye is hired by a rich woman to find her missing husband.
Formula Californian detection distinguished by its cast rather than by any special talent in the writing or presentation. It seemed likely to produce a new Chandleresque school, but imitations proved very sporadic; the star repeated the role less successfully in The Drowning Pool *(qv).*
w William Goldman *novel The Moving Target* by John Ross Macdonald *d* Jack Smight *ph* Conrad Hall *m* Johnny Mandel
☆ *Paul Newman*, Lauren Bacall, Shelley Winters, Arthur Hill, Julie Harris, Janet Leigh, Pamela Tiffin, Robert Wagner, Robert Webber, Strother Martin
'It isn't a bad try, but it never really slips into overdrive.' – *Penelope Houston*
'Nothing needs justification less than entertainment; but when something planned only to entertain fails, it has no justification. A private-eye movie without sophistication and style is ignominious.' – *Pauline Kael, 1968*

Harper Valley P.T.A.
US 1978 93m colour
April Fools (George Edwards)
An independent woman takes her revenge on those who disapprove of her free-wheeling ways.
A feeble-minded comedy that cannot sustain interest for any longer than the hit song of the 1960s on which it is based.
w George Edwards, Barry Schneider *d* Richard Bennett *ph* Willy Kurant *m* Nelson Riddle *ed* Michael Economu
☆ Barbara Eden, Ronny Cox, Nanette Fabray, Susan Swift, Louis Nye, Pat Paulsen

The Harrad Experiment
US 1973 97m Eastmancolor
Cinerama/Cinema Arts (Dennis F. Stevens)
A college professor conducts a series of tests on sexual relationships.
Low-keyed Kinsey Report for the seventies, pleasantly made but not very stimulating.
w Michael Werner, Ted Cassidy *novel* Robert H. Rimmer *d* Ted Post *ph* Richard Kline *m* Artie Butler
☆ James Whitmore, Tippi Hedren, Don Johnson, Laurie Walters, Robert Middleton
'Ludicrously sober-sided amalgam of nude yoga and extra-curricular groping, which should set sex educational theory back ten years.' – *Sight and Sound*

Harrad Summer
US 1974 105m colour
Cinerama (Dennis F. Stevens)
Students at a sex-education college return home to put their knowledge into practice.
Dull, if inoffensive, drama that never rises above the level of an average soap opera.
w Morth Thaw, Steven Zacharias *d* Steven Hilliard Stern *ph* Richard Kline *m* Pat Williams *ed* Bill Brame
☆ Robert Reiser, Laurie Walters, Richard Doran, Victoria Thompson, Emaline Henry, Bill Dana
† A sequel to *The Harrad Experiment* (qv).

Harriet Craig
US 1950 94m bw
Columbia (William Dozier)
A wife's only real love is her meticulously kept and richly appointed house.
Ho-hum remake of a sturdy thirties film Craig's Wife *(qv).*
w Anne Froelick, James Gunn *play Craig's Wife* by George Kelly *d* Vincent Sherman *ph* Joseph Walker *m* George Duning *md* Morris Stoloff
☆ Joan Crawford, Wendell Corey, Allyn Joslyn, Lucile Watson, William Bishop, K. T. Stevens, Raymond Greenleaf

Harriet the Spy *
US 1996 101m DeLuxe
Paramount/Nickelodeon/Rastar (Marykay Powell)
An 11-year-old girl, who writes down misleading observations on friends and neighbours, learns the error of her ways.
Entertaining family movie with a moral, told with a light touch.
w Douglas Petrie, Theresa Rebeck *novel* Louise Fitzhugh *d* Bronwen Hughes *ph* Francis Kenny *m* Jamshied Sharifi *pd* Lester Cohen *ed* Debra Chiate
☆ Michelle Trachtenberg, Rosie O'Donnell, Vanessa Lee Chester, Gregory Smith, J. Smith-Cameron, Robert Joy, Eartha Kitt, Don Francks
'Thankfully, what could easily have been mawkish claptrap turns out to be smart, good natured and fun.' – *Empire*

'They're two men with nothing in common – they're father and son!'
Harry and Son
US 1984 117m Technicolor
Orion/Paul Newman
An ageing construction worker is at odds with his twenty-one-year-old son, who lives with him.
One can't imagine why Paul Newman wanted to make this boring shouting match between people no one can care for.
w Ronald L. Buck, Paul Newman *novel A Lost King* by Raymond DeCapite *d* Paul Newman *ph* Donald McAlpine *m* Henry Mancini
☆ Paul Newman, Robby Benson, Ellen Barkin, Wilford Brimley

Harry and the Hendersons
US 1987 110m DeLuxe
Universal/Amblin (Richard Vane, William Dear)
GB title: *Big Foot and the Hendersons*
A camping family meets a docile Big Foot.
Elementary kiddie/family pic in the wake of E.T.
w William Dear, William E. Martin, Ezra D. Rappaport *d* William Dear *m* Bruce Broughton *pd* James Bissell *ed* Donn Cambern *sp* Harry designed by Rick Baker
☆ John Lithgow, Melinda Dillon, David Suchet, Don Ameche, Margaret Langrick, Joshua Rudoy
best make-up

Harry and Tonto *
US 1974 115m DeLuxe
TCF (Paul Mazursky)
An elderly New York widower and his cat are evicted and trek to Chicago.
Amiable character study, very watchable but rather pointless.
w Paul Mazursky, Josh Greenfeld *d* Paul Mazursky *ph* Michael Butler *m* Bill Conti
☆ *Art Carney*, Ellen Burstyn, Chief Dan George, Geraldine Fitzgerald, Larry Hagman, Arthur Hunnicutt, Herbert Berghof
'A vivacious and affectionate folk tale.' – *New Yorker*
'It has a life-affirming quality as welcome contrast to the destructive delirium of most modern movies.' – *Michael Billington, Illustrated London News*
Art Carney
Paul Mazursky (as writer)

Harry and Walter Go to New York
US 1976 120m Metrocolor Panavision
Columbia (Don Devlin, Harry Gittes)
In oldtime New York, two carnival entertainers get involved with suffragettes and a safecracker.
Extended period romp in which the high humour soon palls and a general lack of talent makes itself felt.
w John Byrum, Robert Kaufman *d* Mark Rydell *ph* Laszlo Kovacs *m* David Shire *pd Harry Horner*
☆ James Caan, Elliott Gould, Michael Caine, Diane Keaton, Charles Durning, Lesley Ann Warren, Jack Gilford
'A charmless mishmash.' – *Sight and Sound*
'This film fails to work as a light comedy, as a period piece, as a jigsaw puzzle ... mainly, it just sits there and dies.' – *Frank Rich, New York Post*
'Strictly for those who'll laugh at anything.' – *Kevin Thomas, Los Angeles Times*

'The woman or the tiger? He can't have them both!'
Harry Black
GB 1958 117m Technicolor Cinemascope
Mersham (John Brabourne)
US title: *Harry Black and the Tiger*
A famous tiger hunter allows his best friend to prove himself a hero, and falls in love with the friend's wife.
Lethargic melodrama with good Indian backgrounds.
w Sydney Boehm *novel* David Walker *d* Hugo Fregonese *ph* John Wilcox *m* Clifton Parker
☆ Stewart Granger, Anthony Steel, Barbara Rush, I. S. Johar

Harry Black and the Tiger: see *Harry Black*

Harry, He's Here To Help **
France 2000 117m colour Panavision
Artificial Eye/Diaphana (Michel Saint-Jean)
original title: *Harry, Un Ami Qui Vous Veut Du Bien*
US title: *With a Friend Like Harry...*
A psychopath charms his way into the life of a married couple by claiming to have gone to school with the husband.
Ingenious black comedy that invests a familiar scenario with fresh chills.
w Dominik Moll, Gilles Marchand *d* Dominik Moll *ph* Matthieu Poirot-Delpech *m* David Sinclair Whitaker *pd* Michel Barthelemy *ed* Yannick Kergoat
☆ Laurent Lucas (Michel), Sergi Lopez (Harry), Mathilde Seigner (Claire), Sophie Guillemin (Plum)
'An unsettling study of the modern male psyche.' – *Empire*

Harry in Your Pocket
US 1973 103m DeLuxe Panavision
UA/Cinema Video (Bruce Geller)
Adventures of a young, a middle-aged and an old pickpocket.
Partly pleasant but rather aimless comedy drama, agreeably set in Seattle and Salt Lake City.
w Ron Austin, James Buchanan *d* Bruce Geller *ph* Fred Koenekamp *m* Lalo Schifrin
☆ James Coburn, *Walter Pidgeon*, Michael Sarrazin, Trish Van Devere

Harry Munter **
Sweden 1969 101m Eastmancolor
Gala/Sandrew (Göran Lindgren)
A schoolboy inventor rejects the opportunity to move to America with his discontented parents and make his fortune because he feels a responsibility to help the people around him.
Affecting and witty account of the difficulties of adolescent idealism.
wd Kjell Grede *ph* Lars Björne *m* Dvorak *ed* Lars Hagström
☆ Jan Nielsen, Carl-Gustaf Lindstedt, Gun Jönsson, Georg Adelly, Al Simon, Elina Salo
'Some kind of personal vision does emerge to save the film from undiluted monotony.' – *Films and Filming*

'The Chamber of Secrets has been opened. Enemies of the heir... beware!'

Harry Potter and the Chamber of Secrets **

US/GB/Germany 2002 161m Technicolor Panavision
Warner/Heyday/1492 (David Heyman)

A boy wizard investiages a secret chamber containing a petrifying monster that had been sealed for a thousand years.

More interesting than the first film in the series, it still remains a puzzle to the unconverted as to why this bland and resolutely old-fashioned saga should prove so popular.

w Steve Kloves *novel* J. K. Rowling *d* Chris Columbus *ph* Roger Pratt *m* John Williams *pd* Stuart Craig *ed* Peter Honess *sp* Jim Mitchell, Nick Davis; ILM, Mill, Moving Picture Co., Framestore-CFC *cos* Lindy Hemming

☆ Daniel Radcliffe (Harry Potter), Rupert Grint (Ron Weasley), Emma Watson (Hermione Granger), Kenneth Branagh (Gilderoy Lockhart), John Cleese (Nearly Headless Nick), Robbie Coltrane (Hagrid the Giant), Warwick Davis (Professor Flitwick), Richard Griffiths (Uncle Vernon), Richard Harris (Albus Dumbledore), Jason Isaacs (Lucius Malfoy), Fiona Shaw (Aunt Petunia), Maggie Smith (Professor McGonagall)

'May be a bit overlong and unmodulated in pacing, but it possesses a confidence and intermittent flair that begin to give it a life of its own.' – *Todd McCarthy, Variety*

'All that money can buy has been bought, and though that is an accomplishment of a sort, it is not great filmmaking.' – *Kenneth Turan, Los Angeles Times*

† The film is among the Top 20 box office successes, having takwn around $262m in the US.

'Journey beyond your imagination.'
'Let the magic begin.'

Harry Potter and the Philosopher's Stone

US 2001 152m Technicolor Panavision
Warner/Heyday1492/Duncan Henderson (David Heyman)

US title: *Harry Potter and the Sorcerer's Stone*

On his eleventh birthday, an orphan discovers that he is a wizard and goes to school to learn magic.

A curious mish-mash of fairytale, myth, fantasy and British public school ritual – all that seems to be missing, regrettably, is Billy Bunter and the girls from St. Trinian's. Some splendid production design adds visual interest to the bland proceedings, which found favour with the novel's many fans.

w Steve Kloves *novel* J. K. Rowling *d* Chris Columbus *ph* John Seale *m* John Williams *pd* Stuart Craig *ed* Richard Francis-Bruce *cos* Judianna Makovsky

☆ Daniel Radcliffe (Harry Potter), Rupert Grint (Ron Weasley), Emma Watson (Hermione Granger), Robbie Coltrane (Hagrid), Richard Griffiths (Uncle Vernon Dursley), Richard Harris (Albus Dumbledore), Ian Hart (Professor Quirrell/Voldemort), John Hurt (Mr Ollivander), Alan Rickman (Professor Snape), Fiona Shaw (Aunt Petunia Dursley), Maggie Smith (Professor McGonagall), Julie Walters (Mrs Weasley), John Cleese (Nearly Headless Nick), Warwick Davis (Goblin Bank Teller/Professor Flitwick)

'A treat, both visually and emotionally.' – *John Hiscock, Daily Telegraph*

'I went into the movie prejudiced by the hype. I left having enjoyed it immensely and admiring the skill which had gone into the making.' – *Philip French, Observer*

† The film cost $130m. It is the seventh highest-grossing film so far, having taken more than $316m at the US box-office.

Stuart Craig; Judianna Makovsky; John Williams

British film

Harry, Un Ami Qui Vous Veut Du Bien: see *Harry, He's Here to Help (2000)*

'Heroes Are Measured By What They Do.'

Hart's War

US 2002 125m colour Super 35
TCF

In a German POW camp during the Second World War, an inexperienced lieutenant defends a black soldier who is court-martialled for murder.

Heavy-handed, sermonising account of racism and bad behaviour among prisoners of war that should have been kept under lock and key.

w Billy Ray, Terry George *novel* John Katzenbach *d* Gregory Hoblit *ph* Alar Kivilo *m* Rachel Portman *pd* Lily Kilvert *ed* David Rosenbloom

☆ Bruce Willis (Col William McNamara), Colin Farrell (Lt Thomas Hart), Terrence Howard (Lt Lincoln Scott), Cole Hauser (Staff Sgt Vic Bedford), Marcel Iures (Col Werner Visser), Linus Roache (Capt Peter Ross), Rory Cochrane (Sgt Carl Webb), Vicellous Shannon (Lt Lamar Archer), Adrian Grenier (Pvt. Daniel Abrams)

'A film that tries to excel on several levels and falls flat on all of them.' – *Elvis Mitchell, New York Times*

Harum Scarum

US 1965 95m Metrocolor
MGM (Sam Katzman)

GB title: *Harem Holiday*

An American star on the way to the Middle Eastern première of his latest film is kidnapped by assassins.

Flavourless comedy with music; before dull backgrounds the star performs adequately.

w Gerald Drayson Adams *d* Gene Nelson *ph* Fred H. Jackman

☆ Elvis Presley, Mary Ann Mobley, Fran Jeffries, Michael Ansara, Theo Marcuse, Jay Novello, Billy Barty

Harvest

France 1937 122m bw
Marcel Pagnol

original title: *Regain*

A poacher and an itinerant girl set up house in a deserted village and bring it back to life.

Somewhat charming but interminably slow rustic parable.

wd Marcel Pagnol *novel* Jean Giono *ph* Willy Ledru, Roger Ledru *m* Arthur Honegger

☆ Gabriel Gabrio, Fernandel, Orane Demazis, E. Delmont

The Harvest *

US 1993 97m CFI color
Feature Film/Curb Mustfilm/Ron Stone (Morgan Mason, Jason Clark)

A Hollywood screenwriter goes to Mexico to research a script and is kidnapped by a local gang which specializes in selling body parts.

A clever little thriller dealing with many kinds of betrayal: from male-female relationships to Hollywood's way with reality, the arrogance of privilege and the compromises made by hack writers.

wd David Marconi *ph* Emmanuel Lubezki *m* Dave Allen, Rick Boston *pd* Rae Fox *ed* Carlos Puente

☆ Miguel Ferrer, Leilani Sarelle Ferrer, Henry Silva, Anthony John Denison, Tim Thomerson, Harvey Fierstein, Mike Vendrell, George Clooney

'Stylish and satisfying low-budget noir thriller, with a cleverly constructed can-this-really-be-happening-to-me plot that goes on producing surprising twists to the last frame.' – *George Perry*

Harvest of Hate

Australia 1979 80m colour
South Australian Film Corp./Nine Network/Australian Film Commission (Jane Scott)

In the Australian desert Arab guerrillas training to attack Israel take prisoner a couple visiting an isolated house.

Tepid thriller with a ridiculous plot, not helped by its percussive, over-insistent score which attempts to suggest excitement where there is none.

w uncredited *d* Michael Thornhill *ph* David Sanderson *m* uncredited *ad* David Copping *ed* G. Turney Smith

☆ Dennis Grosvenor, Kris McQuade, Richard Meikle, Michael Atkins, Leon Cosak, Moshe Kedein, John Oresik

Harvey ***

US 1950 104m bw
U-I (John Beck)

A middle-aged drunk has an imaginary white rabbit as his friend, and his sister tries to have him certified.

An amiably batty play with splendid lines is here transferred virtually intact to the screen and survives superbly thanks to understanding by all concerned, though the star is as yet too young for a role which he later made his own.

w Mary Chase (*with Oscar Brodney*) *play* Mary Chase *d* Henry Koster *ph* William Daniels *m* Frank Skinner

☆ *James Stewart, Josephine Hull, Victoria Horne,* Peggy Dow, *Cecil Kellaway,* Charles Drake, *Jesse White,* Nana Bryant, Wallace Ford

VETA LOUISE (JOSEPHINE HULL): 'Myrtle Mae, you have a lot to learn, and I hope you never learn it.'

ELWOOD (JAMES STEWART): 'I've wrestled with reality for 35 years, and I'm happy, doctor, I finally won out over it.'

ELWOOD: 'Harvey and I have things to do ... we sit in the bars ... have a drink or two ... and play the juke box. Very soon the faces of the other people turn towards me and they smile. They say: "We don't know your name, mister, but you're all right, all right." Harvey and I warm ourselves in these golden moments. We came as strangers – soon we have friends. They come over. They sit with us. They drink with us. They talk to us. They tell us about the great big terrible things they've done and the great big wonderful things they're going to do. Their hopes, their regrets. Their loves, their hates. All very large, because nobody ever brings anything small into a bar. Then I introduce them to Harvey, and he's bigger and grander than anything they can offer me. When they leave, they leave impressed. The same people seldom come back.'

ELWOOD (DESCRIBING HIS FIRST MEETING WITH HARVEY): 'I'd just helped Ed Hickey into a taxi. Ed had been mixing his drinks, and I felt he needed conveying. I started to walk down the street when I heard a voice saying: "Good evening, Mr Dowd". I turned, and there was this big white rabbit leaning against a lamp-post. Well, I thought nothing of that! Because when you've lived in a town as long as I've lived in this one, you get used to the fact that everybody knows your name...'

Josephine Hull

James Stewart

The Harvey Girls **

US 1946 101m Technicolor
MGM (Arthur Freed)

A chain of 19th-century restaurants hires young ladies to go out west as waitresses.

Sprightly if overlong musical based on fact; a good example of an MGM middle-budget extravaganza.

w Edmund Beloin, Nathaniel Curtis *d* George Sidney *ph* George Folsey *m/ly* Johnny Mercer, Harry Warren *md* Lennie Hayton

☆ *Judy Garland, Ray Bolger,* John Hodiak, Preston Foster, Virginia O'Brien, Angela Lansbury, Marjorie Main, Chill Wills, Kenny Baker, Selena Royle

'Anybody who did anything at all in America up to 1900 is liable to be made into a film by MGM.' – *Richard Winnington*

'An abundance of chromatic spectacle and an uncommonly good score.' – *New York Times*

'A perfect example of what Hollywood can do with its vast resources when it wants to be really showy.' – *New York Herald Tribune*

† Angela Lansbury's singing was dubbed by Virgina Rees, and Cyd Charisse's by Betty Russell

♫ 'The Train Must Be Fed'; 'In the Valley'; 'Wait and See'; 'On the Atchison Topeka and the Santa Fe'; ' It's a Great Big World'; 'The Wild Wild West'

song 'On the Atcheson, Topeka and the Santa Fe'

Lennie Hayton

Has Anybody Seen My Gal? **

US 1952 89m Technicolor
U-I (Ted Richmond)

A multi-millionaire pretends to be poor and moves in with distant relatives to test their worthiness.

Very agreeable comedy set in the twenties and centring on a satisfying star performance.

w Joseph Hoffman *d Douglas Sirk ph* Clifford Stine *m* Joseph Gershenson *ad Bernard Herzbrun, Hilyard Brown*

☆ *Charles Coburn,* Piper Laurie, Rock Hudson, Gigi Perreau, Lynn Bari, Larry Gates, William Reynolds, Skip Homeier, James Dean

Hasards Ou Coincidences: see *Chance or Coincidence*

Hasta Morir

Mexico 1994 90m colour
Imcine/FFCC/Ocixem/Vida (Fernando Sariñana)

aka: *'Til Death*

Two petty crooks fall out after one shoots a cop and is forced to flee; the other assumes his identity for a property swindle.

Lurid melodrama set in an urban wasteland, in which flashy camerawork attempts to compensate for the halting narrative; it has a fashionable gloss, but not much substance.

w Marcela Fuentes-Berain *d* Fernando Sariñana *ph* Guillermo Granillo *m* Enrique Quezadas *ad* Gloria Carrasco *ed* Carlos Bolado

☆ Demian Bichir, Juan Manuel Bernal, Veronica Merchant, Vanessa Bauche, Dolores Beristain, Montserrat Ontiveros, Alfreda Sevilla, Dino Garcia

'Admirably manages to conjure up this marginal world of violence and street gangs.' – *Variety*

The Hasty Heart *

GB 1949 104m bw
ABP (Vincent Sherman)

At an army hospital in Burma, attitudes to an arrogant young Scot change when it is learned that he has only a few weeks to live.

Flat, adequate filming of a successful sentimental stage play.

w Ranald MacDougall *play* John Patrick *d* Vincent Sherman *ph* Wilkie Cooper *m* Jack Beaver

☆ *Richard Todd,* Patricia Neal, Ronald Reagan, Orlando Martins, Howard Marion-Crawford

Richard Todd

Hatari! *

US 1962 158m Technicolor
Paramount/Malabar (Howard Hawks)

International hunters in Tanganyika catch game to send to zoos.

Plotless adventure film with good animal sequences but no shape or suspense; a typical folly of its director, whose chief interest is seeing smart men and women in tough action. The elephants steal this overlong show.

w Leigh Brackett *d* Howard Hawks *ph Russell Harlan m Henry Mancini*

☆ John Wayne, Elsa Martinelli, Red Buttons, Hardy Kruger

'Hawks was taking his friends and cast and crew on a trip he wanted to make personally, and the film is both the incidental excuse for and the record of that experience.' – *Joseph Gelmis, 1970*

Russell Harlan

'A beautiful butterfly broken on the wheel of life!'

The Hatchet Man

US 1932 74m bw
Warner

GB title: *The Honourable Mr Wong*

The executioner of a San Francisco tong dutifully kills his best friend but promises to care for his daughter.

Unconvincing Chinese-American melodrama.

w J. Grubb Alexander *play The Honourable Mr Wong* by Achmed Abdullah, David Belasco *d* William A. Wellman *ph* Sid Hickox

☆ Edward G. Robinson, Loretta Young, Dudley Digges, Leslie Fenton, Edmund Breese, Tully Marshall, J. Carrol Naish, Noel Madison, Blanche Frederici

'Mild gang stuff in oriental trappings ... dynamic action or high voltage drama is missing.' – *Variety*

Hatchet Man

US 1994 100m Foto-Kem
Overseas/Itasca (Daniel Grodnik, Robert Snukal, John Tarnoff)

aka: *The Nature of the Beast*

Two psychopaths meet on the road.

An effective thriller, if you ignore its pretensions to say something significant about the human condition.

wd Victor Salva *ph* Levie Isaacks *m* Bennett Salvay *pd* Stephen Greenberg *ed* W. Peter Miller
☆ Eric Roberts, Lance Henriksen, Brion James, Sasha Jenson, Ana Gabriel, Eloy Casados
† Lance Henriksen is also credited as 'creative consultant'.

The Hatchet Murders: see *Deep Red*

A Hatful of Rain *
US 1957 108m bw Cinemascope
TCF/ (Buddy Adler)

A war veteran becomes a drug addict and upsets his wife and family.
One of the first drug dramas: straightforward, well acted, and quite powerful.
w Michael V. Gazzo, Alfred Hayes, Carl Foreman *play* Alfred Hayes *d* *Fred Zinnemann* *ph* Joe Macdonald *m* Bernard Herrmann
☆ *Eva Marie Saint, Don Murray*, Anthony Franciosa, Lloyd Nolan, Henry Silva
† Carl Foreman was omitted from the film's credits at the time because he was blacklisted.
Anthony Franciosa

'Are you shockproof? Then you will dare to see this famous drama of violence – of hate – of men who teach women the terror of cruelty and mad obsession!'
Hatter's Castle **
GB 1941 102m bw
Paramount British (Isadore Goldsmith)
In the 1890s, a megalomaniac Scottish hatter ruins the lives of his wife and daughter.
Enjoyable period melodrama with a rampant star performance and pretty good detail.
w Rodney Ackland *novel* A. J. Cronin *d* Lance Comfort *ph* Max Greene *m* Horace Shepherd
☆ Robert Newton, Deborah Kerr, James Mason, Beatrice Varley, Emlyn Williams, Henry Oscar, Enid Stamp-Taylor, Brefni O'Rorke

Hatuna Meuheret *
Israel/France 2001 colour
ICA/Transfax,Arte/Morgane/IFF (Marek Rozenbaum, Edgard Tenenbaum)
GB title: *Late Marriage*
In Israel, Jewish parents, determined that their son should marry, are horrified to discover that he is in love with an older, divorced woman who has a young daughter.
Gripping, icy drama of the conflict between traditional and modern ways of life, of parental pressure distorting the lives of future generations.
wd Dover Koshashvili *ph* Dani Schneor *m* Joseph Bardanashvili *pd* Avi Fahima *ed* Yael Perlov
☆ Lior Louie Ashkenazi (Zaza), Ronit Elkabetz (Judith), Moni Moshonov (Yasha), Lili Koshashvili (Lili), Sapir Kugman (Madona)
'It's a little gem: funny, humane, sexy and moving.' – *Peter Bradshaw, Guardian*

Haunted
GB/US 1995 107m colour
Entertainment/Double 'A'/American Zoetrope/ Lumière (Anthony Andrews, Lewis Gilbert)

An academic who debunks psychic phenomena is invited by an old lady to visit a house which she claims is haunted.
Tedious and stultifyingly old-fashioned horror movie whose effect on an audience is more likely to be sedative than scary.
w Tim Prager, Lewis Gilbert, Bob Kellett *novel* James Herbert *d* Lewis Gilbert *ph* Tony Pierce Roberts *m* Debbie Wiseman *pd* John Fenner, Brian Ackland-Snow *ed* Johnny Jympson *sp* Peter Hutchinson
☆ Aidan Quinn, Kate Beckinsale, Anthony Andrews, John Gielgud, Anna Massey, Simon Lowe, Geraldine Somerville, Liz Smith
'Its makers seem to have decided, not to reinvent the horror film, but to deinvent it, to strip it back down to the crude constituent elements from which it was first pieced together: haunted houses, creaking doors, blown-out candles, self-playing pianos, even bumps in the night, if you can believe that, which is more than the characters manage.' – *Tom Shone, Sunday Times*

The Haunted and the Hunted: see *Dementia 13*

Haunted Gold
US 1932 57m bw
Warner (Leon Schlesinger)

A cowboy prevents bandits from taking over a gold mine with the aid of a mysterious rider.
Warner played safe with Wayne's first Western for the studio, remaking The Phantom City, *directed in 1929 by Albert Rogell and starring Ken Maynard and his horse Tarzan; the result is unexciting.*
w Adele Buffington *d* Mack V. Wright *ph* Nicholas Musuraca *m* Leo F. Forbstein *ed* William Clemens
☆ John Wayne, Sheila Terry, Erville Alderson, Harry Wood, Otto Hoffman, Martha Mattox, Blue Washington, Duke

Haunted Honeymoon
US 1986 82m Rank Colour
Orion/Susan Ruskin

A radio actor takes his fiancée to the family's gloomy country estate, where werewolves and transvestites are some of the creatures which abound.
Mainly unfunny spoof: all concerned should have taken a closer look at The Cat and the Canary.
w Gene Wilder, Terence Marsh *d* Gene Wilder *ph* Fred Schuler *m* John Morris *pd* Terence Marsh *ed* Christopher Greenbury
☆ Gene Wilder, Gilda Radner, Dom DeLuise, Jonathan Pryce, Peter Vaughan, Bryan Pringle
'Faintly amusing but singularly uncompelling.' – *Variety*

The Haunted House of Horror
GB/US 1969 90m Eastmancolor
Tigon/AIP (Tony Tenser)
US title: *The Horror House*
aka: *The Dark*
A group of young people try to cover up the murder of one of their number, killed during a night spent at a haunted house.
Wretched attempt to combine a youth movie of swinging London and low-budget horror; neither element works.
w Michael Armstrong, Peter Marcus *d* Michael Armstrong *ph* Jack Atchelor *m* Reg Tilsley *ad* Haydon Pearce *ed* Peter Pitt
☆ Frankie Avalon, Jill Haworth, Dennis Price, George Sewell, Gina Warwick, Richard O'Sullivan, Carol Dilworth, Julian Barnes, Mark Wynter

The Haunted Palace
US 1963 85m Pathécolor Panavision
AIP/Alta Vista (Roger Corman)

In 1875 a New Englander claims an old mansion as his inheritance and is haunted by his vicious ancestor.
Plodding horror comic, too slow to give opportunities to its stalwart cast.
w Charles Beaumont, from material by H. P. Lovecraft and Edgar Allan Poe *d* Roger Corman *ph* Floyd Crosby *m* Ronald Stein
☆ Vincent Price, Lon Chaney Jnr, Debra Paget, Frank Maxwell, Leo Gordon, Elisha Cook Jnr, John Dierkes
'For those of ghoulish bent, or lovers of the perfectly awful.' – *Judith Crist*

The Haunted Strangler: see *Grip of the Strangler*

Haunted Summer
US 1988 106m colour
Pathé/Cannon (Martin Poll)

Byron, Shelley, Mary Godwin and others indulge in drugs and sex in Switzerland.
Unconvincing as history or cinema.
w Lewis John Carlino *novel* Anne Edwards *d* Ivan Passer *ph* Giuseppe Rotunno *m* Christopher Young *pd* Stephen Grimes *ed* Cesare D'Amico, Richard Fields, Steve Peck
☆ Philip Anglim, Laura Dern, Alice Krige, Eric Stoltz, Alexander Winter, Peter Berling, Don Hodson

'You may not believe in ghosts, but you cannot deny terror!'
The Haunting *
GB 1963 112m bw Panavision
MGM/Argyle (Robert Wise)

An anthropologist, a sceptic and two mediums spend the weekend in a haunted Boston mansion.
Quite frightening but exhausting and humourless melodrama with a lot of suspense, no visible spooks, and not enough plot for its length. The wide screen is a disadvantage.
w Nelson Gidding *novel* The Haunting of Hill House by Shirley Jackson *d* Robert Wise *ph* *David Boulton* *m* Humphrey Searle *pd* Elliot Scott *ed* Ernest Walter
☆ Richard Johnson, Claire Bloom, Russ Tamblyn, Julie Harris, Lois Maxwell, Valentine Dyall

The Haunting
US 1999 113m Technicolor Panavision
DreamWorks (Susan Arnold, Donna Arkoff Roth, Colin Wilson)

A doctor studies the effects of fear by gathering together a group of unhappy adults in a haunted house.
Tepid, effects-stuffed horror in which the cast is out-acted by the decor; Neeson wanders through it looking as though he has been hit over the head with a very blunt instrument, such as the script.
w David Self *novel* The Haunting of Hill House by Shirley Jackson *d* Jan De Bont *ph* Karl Walter Lindenlaub *m* Jerry Goldsmith *pd* Dean Tavoularis *ed* Michael Kahn *sp* Phil Tippett, Craig Hayes
☆ Liam Neeson (Dr David Marrow), Catherine Zeta-Jones (Theo), Owen Wilson (Luke Sanderson), Lili Taylor (Nell), Bruce Dern (Mr Dudley), Marian Seldes (Mrs Dudley), Alix Koromzay (Mary Lambetta), Todd Field (Todd Hackett), Virginia Madsen (Jane)
'Worse than awful: desperate. It's a horror flick afraid of its own audience.' – *Lisa Schwarzbaum, Entertainment Weekly*

Havana
US 1990 145m DeLuxe
UIP/Universal/Mirage (Sydney Pollack, Richard Roth)

An American gambler becomes involved in left-wing Cuban politics in the last days of the Batista regime.
Inconsequential, rambling tale with no perceptible point.
w Judith Rascoe, David Rayfiel *d* Sydney Pollack *ph* Owen Roizman *m* Dave Grusin *pd* Terence Marsh *ad* George Richardson *ed* Frederic Steinkamp, William Steinkamp
☆ Robert Redford, Lena Olin, Alan Arkin, Tomas Milian, Raul Julia, Daniel Davis, Tony Plana, Betsy Brantley
'A hollow, handsomely designed reworking of *Casablanca*.' – *Philip French, Observer*
Dave Grusin

Havana Widows *
US 1933 63m bw
First National
Gold diggers seek millionaires in Havana.
Lively second feature with the Warner repertory company.
w Stanley Logan, Earl Baldwin *d* Ray Enright *ph* George Barnes *ad* Esdras Hartley *ed* Clarence Kolster
☆ Joan Blondell, Glenda Farrell, Guy Kibbee, Lyle Talbot, Allen Jenkins, Frank McHugh, Ruth Donnelly, Hobart Cavanaugh
'Hasn't been a picture in weeks with the same content of rapid-fire laughs, all legitimately gained and inescapable.' – *Variety*

Having a Wild Weekend: see *Catch Us If You Can*

Having Wonderful Crime
US 1945 70m bw
RKO

Three amateur detectives solve the mystery of a disappearing magician.
Easy-going comedy thriller.
w Howard J. Green, Stewart Sterling, Parke Levy *d* A. Edward Sutherland
☆ Pat O'Brien, Carole Landis, George Murphy

Having Wonderful Time
US 1938 70m bw
RKO (Pandro S. Berman)

A New York girl falls in love at a summer camp.
Mild comedy which, robbed of its original Jewish milieu, falls resoundingly flat.
w Arthur Kober *play* Arthur Kober *d* Alfred Santell *ph* Robert de Grasse *m* Roy Webb
☆ Ginger Rogers, Douglas Fairbanks Jnr, Peggy Conklin, Lucille Ball, Lee Bowman, Eve Arden, Red Skelton, Donald Meek, Jack Carson

Hawaii *
US 1966 186m DeLuxe Panavision
UA/Mirisch (Lewis J. Rachmil)

In 1820 a pious Yale divinity student becomes a missionary to the Hawaiian islands.
Ambitious attempt to contrast naïve dogma with native innocence, ruined by badly handled sub-plots, storms, a childbirth sequence and other distractions, all fragments of an immense novel. Heavy going.
w Daniel Taradash, Dalton Trumbo *novel* James A. Michener *d* George Roy Hill *ph* Russell Harlan *m* Elmer Bernstein *pd* Cary Odell *second unit* *Richard Talmadge*
☆ Max von Sydow, Julie Andrews, Richard Harris, *Jocelyn La Garde*, Carroll O'Connor, Torin Thatcher, Gene Hackman
'Consistently intelligent humanism gives it a certain stature among the wide screen spectacles.' – *Brenda Davies*
cinematography; Elmer Bernstein; Jocelyn La Garde; song 'My Wishing Doll' (*m* Elmer Bernstein, *ly* Mack David)

The Hawaiians
US 1970 132m DeLuxe Panavision
UA/Mirisch (Walter Mirisch)
GB title: *Master of the Islands*
A young scion of a shipping business leaves after an argument and strikes oil in terrain supposedly barren.
More fragments from Michener, covering 1870 to 1900 and comprising an absolutely uninteresting family chronicle with moments of spectacle.
w James R. Webb *d* Tom Gries *ph* Philip Lathrop *m* Henry Mancini *pd* Cary Odell
☆ Charlton Heston, Tina Chen, Geraldine Chaplin, John Phillip Law, Alec McCowen, Mako, Ann Knight, Lyle Bettger, Keye Luke
'A quickfire succession of corruption, revolution, plague, fire and questions of moral responsibility.' – *MFB*
'Total relaxation – preferably of the brain – is recommended.' – *Judith Crist*

The Hawk: see *Ride Him Cowboy (1932)*

'The First Person You Want To Trust. The Last Person You Want To Suspect.'
The Hawk
GB 1992 86m Rank Colour
Feature Film/BBC/Initial (Ann Wingate, Eileen Quinn)

A wife begins to suspect that her husband is a serial killer.
A thriller that fails to grip the attention and provides little insight.
w Peter Ransley *novel* Peter Ransley *d* David Hayman *ph* Andrew Dunn *m* Nick Bicat *pd* David Myerscough-Jones *ed* Justin Krish
☆ Helen Mirren, George Costigan, Rosemary Leach, Owen Teale, Christopher Madin, Marie Hamer, Melanie Hill, Helen Ryan
'A small film without too much ambition.' – *Derek Malcolm, Guardian*

Hawk the Slayer
GB 1980 93m colour
ITC/Chips (Harry Robertson)

Good and evil brothers compete for possession of a magical flying sword.
Curiously unexciting and rather gloomy sword-and-sorcery epic.
w Terry Marcel, Harry Robertson *d* Terry Marcel *ph* Paul Beeson *m* Harry Robertson
☆ Jack Palance, John Terry, Bernard Bresslaw, Ray Charleson, Annette Crosbie, Cheryl Campbell, Peter O'Farrell

Hawks
GB 1988 109m colour
Rank (Stephen Lanning, Keith Cavele)
Two terminal cancer patients escape from hospital to have a final fling.
Black comedy that lacks the courage of its convictions.
w Roy Clarke *d* Robert Ellis Miller *ph* Doug Milsome *m* Barry Gibb, John Cameron *pd* Peter Howitt *ed* Malcolm Cooke
☆ Timothy Dalton, Anthony Edwards, Janet McTeer, Camille Coduri, Jill Bennett, Robert Lang, Pat Starr, Bruce Boa, Sheila Hancock, Geoffrey Palmer

Hawks and Sparrows **
Italy 1966 88m bw
Arco (Alfredo Bini)
original title: *Uccellacci e Uccellini*
A father and son set out on a quest, accompanied by a talkative crow, a left-wing bird who tells them stories.
A comic fable of a search for faith, sometimes reminiscent of Chaplin in its slapstick identification with the poor and dispossessed, of innocents abroad in a cynical world.
wd Pier Paolo Pasolini *ph* Mario Bernardo, Tonino delli Colli *m* Ennio Morricone *ad* Luigi Scaccianoce *ed* Nino Baragli
☆ *Totò*, Ninetto Davoli, Femi Benussi, Umberto Bevilacqua, Renato Capogna, Alfredo Leggi, Renato Montalbano
'A fantasy, mixing in equal measure frivolity and satire, and for the first half it works well enough or better.' – *John Simon*
† The credits at the beginning of the film are sung as well as shown.

Hawmps
US 1976 127m colour
Mulberry Square
The Texas cavalry experiments with the use of camels in the South-western desert.
Incredibly overstretched and tedious period comedy with some bright patches.
w William Bickley, Michael Warren *d* Joe Camp
☆ James Hampton, Christopher Connelly, Slim Pickens, Denver Pyle, Jennifer Hawkins, Jack Elam

Häxan: see *Witchcraft Through the Ages*

Hazard
US 1948 95m bw
Paramount (Mel Epstein)
A compulsive lady gambler agrees to marry the winner of a dice game, but runs away and is chased by a private detective.
Silly, unamusing romantic comedy-drama.
w Arthur Sheekman, Roy Chanslor *d* George Marshall *ph* Daniel L. Fapp *m* Frank Skinner
☆ Paulette Goddard, Macdonald Carey, Fred Clark, Stanley Clemens, Maxie Rosenbloom, Charles McGraw
'A good bit this side of inspired.' – *New York Times*

He Got Game *
US 1998 134m Technicolor
Buena Vista/Touchstone/40 Acres and a Mule (Jon Kilik, Spike Lee)
A wife-killer is given a week's clandestine parole so that he can persuade his basketball-playing son to sign up for the prison warden's old college.
Drama of a father–son relationship that seems too schematic to carry much conviction.
wd Spike Lee *ph* Malik Hassan Sayeed *m* Aaron Copland, Public Enemy (songs) *pd* Wynn Thomas *ed* Barry Alexander Brown
☆ Denzel Washington, Ray Allen, Milla Jovovich, Rosario Dawson, Hill Harper, Zelda Harris, Jim Brown, Joseph Lyle Taylor, Ned Beatty, Bill Nunn, Michele Shay, Thomas Jefferson Byrd, Lonette McKee, John Turturro
'Demonstrates that Lee sits in the first rank of American film-makers.' – *Anwar Brett, Film Review*

He Knows You're Alone
US 1980 92m Metrocolor
MGM (Lansbury-Beruh)
A sex-starved maniac attacks teenage girls.
Cheapjack horror comic full of fashionable slashing and screaming; of no cinematic interest whatever.
w Scott Parker *d* Armand Mastroianni *ph* Gerald Feil *m* Alexander Peskanov
☆ Don Scardino, Elizabeth Kemp, Caitlin O'Heaney, Tom Hanks
'At this point in the killer-with-a-knife sweepstakes, every company in Hollywood is getting into the act ... more ingenuity is going into the titles and campaigns than into the films.' – *Variety*

'Every love story has two sides.'
He Loves Me... He Loves Me Not *
France 2002 95m
Telema/TF1 (Charles Gassot)
original title: *À La Folie... Pas Du Tout*
An art student's develops an obsessive love for a married cardiologist.
Creepy drama, told from the differing viewpoints of both protagonists, that begins as a lush romance and then becomes something darker.
w Laetitia Colombani, Caroline Thivel *d* Laetitia Colombani *ph* Pierre Aim *m* Jerome Coullet *ad* Jean-Marc Kerdelhue *ed* Veronique Parnet
☆ Audrey Tautou (Angelique), Samuel Le Bihan (Loïc), Isabelle Carre (Rachel), Sophie Guillemin (Heloise), Clement Sibony (David)
'The film holds charms for everyone but in a very unusual way: If some audience members feel cheated at the halfway mark, others will feel that the film is finally getting started. Nifty!' – *Shawn Levy, Oregonian*
'A sugar cube laced with arsenic, a nasty little film whose mean-spiritedness is surpassed only by its mediocrity.' – *Megan Lehmann, New York Post*

He Married His Wife
US 1940 83m bw
TCF (Raymond Griffith)
A divorced wife falls back in love with her husband.
Pleasant minor comedy with screwball touches.
w Sam Hellman, Darrell Ware, Lynn Starling, John O'Hara *story* Erna Lazarus, Scott Darling *d* Roy Del Ruth *ph* Ernest Palmer *m* David Buttolph
☆ Joel McCrea, Nancy Kelly, Roland Young, Mary Boland, Cesar Romero, Lyle Talbot, Elisha Cook Jnr

He or She: see *Glen or Glenda?*

'Dynamite fills the screen with their kind of love!'
He Ran All the Way *
US 1951 78m bw
UA/Bob Roberts
A hoodlum on the run from the police virtually picks up a girl and hides in her family's apartment.
Uninteresting situation melodrama helped by intelligent acting and handling.
w Guy Endore, Hugo Butler *novel* Sam Ross *d* John Berry *ph* James Wong Howe *m* Franz Waxman
☆ John Garfield, Shelley Winters, Wallace Ford, Selena Royle, Gladys George, Norman Lloyd, Bobby Hyatt
'Good production values keep a routine yarn fresh and appealing. Film is scripted, played and directed all the way with little waste motion, so that the suspense is steady and interest constantly sustained.' – *Variety*

He Said, She Said
US 1991 115m Technicolor Panavision
Paramount (Frank Mancuso Jnr)
A couple of TV journalists break up during a programme.
An unusual idea – the story is told first from the man's point of view and then from the woman's – fails to work, owing to a script that provides neither insight nor humour.
w Brian Hohlfeld *d* Ken Kwapis, Marisa Silver *ph* Stephen H. Burum *m* Miles Goodman *pd* Michael Corenblith *ed* Sidney Levin
☆ Kevin Bacon, Elizabeth Perkins, Nathan Lane, Anthony LaPaglia, Sharon Stone, Stanley Anderson, Charlaine Woodard, Danton Stone
'Two awful films rolled into one.' – *Variety*

He Snoops to Conquer
GB 1944 103m bw
Columbia (Ben Henry, Marcel Varnel)
A local handyman exposes a corrupt council.
Spotty star comedy with insufficient zest for its great length.
w Stephen Black, Howard Irving Young, Norman Lee, Michael Vaughan, Langford Reed *d* Marcel Varnel *ph* Roy Fogwell
☆ George Formby, Robertson Hare, Elizabeth Allan, Aubrey Mallalieu

He Stayed for Breakfast
US 1940 89m bw
Columbia (B. P. Schulberg)
A Parisian communist waiter hides out in the apartment of American capitalists, and learns from them.
Post-Ninotchka comedy, not bad but somehow rather uninteresting and mechanical.
w P. J. Wolfson, Michael Fessier, Ernest Vajda *play* *Liberté Provisoire* by Michel Duran *d* Alexander Hall *ph* Joseph Walker *m* Werner Heymann
☆ Melvyn Douglas, Loretta Young, Alan Marshal, Eugene Pallette, Una O'Connor, Curt Bois, Leonid Kinskey

He Walked by Night *
US 1948 80m bw
Eagle-Lion/Bryan Foy
A burglar becomes a cop-killer and is hunted down by the police.
Interesting if rather flatly handled documentary melodrama in clear imitation of Naked City.
w John C. Higgins, Crane Wilbur *d* Alfred Werker *ph* John Alton *m* Leonid Raab
☆ Richard Basehart, Scott Brady, Roy Roberts, Whit Bissell

He Was Her Man
US 1934 70m bw
Warner
A safecracker goes straight in order to get even with old rivals.
Sassy comedy-drama, not quite smart enough to match its star.
w Niven Busch, Tom Buckingham *d* Lloyd Bacon
☆ James Cagney, Joan Blondell, Victor Jory, Frank Craven, Harold Huber
'No help will be President Roosevelt's pronunciamento of last Saturday (May 19) in which he decried the public penchant for romanticizing crime.' – *Variety*

He Who Gets Slapped *
US 1924 80m approx (24 fps) bw silent
MGM
A scientist starts a new life as a circus clown.
Odd poetic tragedy, Metro-Goldwyn-Mayer's very first production; the public took to it surprisingly well.
w Victor Sjostrom, Carey Wilson *play* Leonid Andreyev *d* Victor Sjostrom
☆ Lon Chaney, Norma Shearer, John Gilbert, Tully Marshall, Ford Sterling
'For dramatic value and a faultless adaptation of a play, this is the finest production we have yet seen.' – *New York Times*

He Who Must Die *
France/Italy 1957 126m bw Cinemascope
Indusfilms
original title: *Celui Qui Doit Mourir*
In a Greek village in 1921, preparations for a passion play are interrupted by the arrival of refugees from the mountains.
Occasionally striking, but mainly arty and pretentious parable; however well meant, a bore to watch.
w Ben Barzman, Jules Dassin *novel* Nikos Kazantzakis *d* Jules Dassin *ph* Jacques Natteau *m* Georges Auric
☆ Jean Servais, Carl Mohner, Pierre Vaneck, Melina Mercouri, Fernand Ledoux

He Who Rides a Tiger
GB 1965 103m bw
British Lion/David Newman
A feckless burglar comes out of prison and returns to the old life.
Cliché crime yarn which tries rather desperately after fresh detail but bogs down in romantic asides.
w Trevor Peacock *d* Charles Crichton *ph* John von Kotze *m* Alexander Faris
☆ Tom Bell, Judi Dench, Paul Rogers, Kay Walsh, Ray McAnally, Jeremy Spenser

He Who Shoots First: see *Django Spara per Primo*

Head *
US 1968 85m Technicolor
Columbia (Bert Schneider)
Fantasia on the life of a sixties pop group.
A psychedelic trip of a movie which does for the Monkees what A Hard Day's Night *and* Yellow Submarine *did for the Beatles, and what* Monty Python *did for us all. Sometimes funny, slick and clever; often just plain silly.*
w Jack Nicholson, Bob Rafelson *d* Bob Rafelson *ph* Michel Hugo *m* Ken Thorne *sp* Chuck Gaspar
☆ The Monkees, Victor Mature, Annette Funicello, Timothy Carey
'Random particles tossed around in some demented jester's wind machine.' – *Richard Combs, MFB, 1978*
'A mind-blowing collage of mixed media, a free-for-all freakout of rock music and psychedelic splashes of colour.' – *Daily Variety*

'Murder just became a water sport.'
Head above Water
US/GB 1996 92m colour
Warner/Head above Water/Firmjewel/InterMedia/Fine Line (Jim Wilson, John M. Jacobsen)
A judge's wife tells a passing cop the series of misunderstandings that led to the deaths of her husband and two friends.
Frenetic farce of mounting catastrophes, fatally flawed by its slow pace and broad style.
w Theresa Marie *screenplay* Geir Eriksen, Eirik Ildahl *d* Jim Wilson *ph* Richard Bowen *m* Christopher Young *pd* Jeffrey Beecroft *ed* Michael R. Miller
☆ Harvey Keitel (George), Cameron Diaz (Nathalie), Craig Sheffer (Lance), Billy Zane (Kent), Shay Duffin (Policeman)
'The director may have been told he was doing a comedy. But the cast act as if they think they're doing a drama. A total breakdown in communication is the only explanation for a film of such calamitous ineptitude.' – *Alexander Walker, London Evening Standard*

Head On: see *Fatal Attraction (1980)*

Head On *
Australia 1997 104m colour
Millivres/AFFC/Head On/Film Victoria (Jane Scott)
An unhappy Greek-Australian youth decides it is time to leave home and come to terms with his homosexuality.
A powerful film of drug-filled alienation and self-destruction, given energy not only by its performances but by the disjointed rhythms of its camerawork.
w Andrew Bovell, Ana Kokkinos, Mira Robinson *book* Loaded by Christos Tsiolkas *d* Ana Kokkinos *ph* Jaems Grant *m* Ollie Olsen *pd* Nikki Di Falco *ed* Jill Bilcock
☆ Alex Dimitriades (Ari), Paul Capsis (Johnny), Julian Garner (Sean), Elena Mandalis (Betty), Tony Nikolakopolous (Dimitri), Damien Fotiou (Joe), Eugenia Fragos (Sofia), Dora Kaskanis (Dina)
'Makes all sexual encounters seem futile and banal, and its final message of nihilistic defiance is shrill and unconvincing.' – *Peter Bradshaw, Guardian*

Head over Heels *
GB 1937 81m bw
Gaumont (S. C. Balcon)
US title: *Head Over Heels in Love*
A singing star can't make up her mind between two men.
Interestingly dated light star vehicle.
w Dwight Taylor, Fred Thompson, Marjorie Gaffney *play* *Pierre ou Jack* by François de Croisset *d* Sonnie Hale *ph* Glen McWilliams *m/ly* Harry Revel, Mack Gordon *md* Louis Levy *ad* Alfred Junge
☆ Jessie Matthews, Robert Flemyng, Louis Borell, Romney Brent, Helen Whitney Bourne, Eliot Makeham

'The dialogue has a moral earnestness for which it would be hard to find a parallel even in the Victorian Age.' – *Graham Greene*

Head over Heels
US 1980 97m Technicolor
UA/Triple Play (Mark Metcalf, Amy Robinson, Griffin Dunne)
aka: *Chilly Scenes of Winter*
A government office worker thinks back on his on-again off-again relationship with the woman he loves.
Quirky comedy drama without the zest of Annie Hall, *which it much resembles; too much like a television play for box-office success.*
wd Joan Micklin Silver *novel* *Chilly Scenes of Winter* by Ann Beattie *ph* Bobby Byrne *m* Ken Lauber *pd* Peter Jamison *ed* Cynthia Scheider
☆ John Heard, Mary Beth Hurt, Peter Riegert, Kenneth McMillan, Gloria Grahame

'Four supermodel roommates. One regular girl. The guy next door doesn't stand a chance.'
Head Over Heels
US 2001 86m colour
Universal (Robert Simonds)
An art restorer believes that she has seen her new boy friend commit a murder.
Glossy, fashionable, if less sophisticated, makeover of Hitchcock's Rear Window *for a young audience that likes flatulent jokes.*
w Ron Burch, David Kidd *d* Tommy O'Haver *ph* Mark Plumme *m* Randy Edelman, Steve Porcaro *pd* Perry Andelin Blake *ed* Cara Silverman
☆ Monica Potter (Amanda Pierce), Freddie Prinze Jnr (Jim Winston), Shalom Harlow (Jade), Ivana Milicevic (Roxana), Sarah O'Hare (Candi), Tomiko Fraser (Holly), China Chow (Lisa), Jay Brazeau (Halloran/Strukov), Stanley DeSantis (Alfredo)
'Exists in a realm beyond sense, and it induces in the viewer a trancelike state, leaving the mind free to ponder the mysteries of the universe.' – A. O. Scott, *New York Times*

Head over Heels in Love: see *Head over Heels (1937)*

Health *
US 1979 102m DeLuxe
TCF/Robert Altman
Complications result when a health foods convention is staged in a Florida hotel.
Zany satirical all-star romp on the lines of A Wedding *but by no means as likeable or laughable, considering its cast, as it should be.*
w Robert Altman, Paul Dooley, Frank Barhydt *d* Robert Altman *ph* Edmond L. Koons *m* Joseph Byrd
☆ Lauren Bacall, Glenda Jackson, James Garner, Dick Cavett, Carol Burnett, Paul Dooley, Henry Gibson, Donald Moffat

Hear My Song **
GB 1991 105m Fujicolour
Palace/Film Four/Vision/Limelight/British Screen/Windmill Lane (Alison Owen-Allen)
To revive his flagging business, a 1980s Liverpudlian night-club manager hires a singer who may, or may not, be Joseph Locke, a romantic tenor who was once a variety theatre headliner and fled to Ireland to avoid charges of tax evasion.
A small-scale delight, a film of charm and wit.
w Peter Chelsom, Adrian Dunbar *d* Peter Chelsom *ph* Sue Gibson *m* John Altman *pd* Caroline Hanania *ed* Martin Walsh
☆ *Ned Beatty*, Adrian Dunbar, Shirley Anne Field, Tara Fitzgerald, William Hootkins, Harold Berens, David McCallum, John Dair, Stephen Marcus
'One of the year's most delightful films.' – *Kevin Thomas, Los Angeles Times*
'Far from making an innovative contribution to British cinema, *Hear My Song* relies for the most part on nostalgia, whimsy and sleight of hand.' – *Tom Charity, Sight and Sound*

Hear No Evil
US 1993 97m Technicolor
TCF/Great Movie Ventures (David Matalon)
A deaf fitness trainer becomes a target for crooks trying to recover a stolen priceless coin.
Dull and pointless thriller that looks as if it's been made to be sandwiched between television commercials.
w R. M. Badat, Kathleen Rowell *d* Robert Greenwood *ph* Steven Shaw *m* Graeme Revell *pd* Bernt Capra *ed* Eva Gardos
☆ Marlee Matlin, D. B. Sweeney, Martin Sheen, John C. McGinley, Christina Carlisi, Greg Elam, Charley Lang
'This is filming by numbers, the algebra of the inane.' – *Sight and Sound*

The Hearse
US 1980 95m Metrocolor
Crown International/Marimark (Mark Tenser)
A woman moves into a house that is reputed to be haunted.
Tedious and interminable, lacking suspense and interest.
w Bill Bleich *d* George Bowers *ph* Mori Kawa *m* Webster Lewis *ad* Keith Michl *ed* George Berndt
☆ Trish Van Devere, Joseph Cotten, David Gautreaux, Donald Hotton, Med Flory, Donald Petrie, Christopher McDonald, Perry Lang

Heart
US 1987 90m TVC Color
New World (Randy Jurgensen)
An ageing boxer has one last chance to make the big time, not knowing that his sleazy manager has agreed to throw the fight.
Uninvolving drama that is always predictable; the story has often been told before, and much better than it is here.
w James Lemmo, Randy Jurgensen *d* James Lemmo *ph* Jacek Laskus *m* Geoff Levin, Chris Many *pd* Vicki Paul *ed* Lorenzo Marinelli
☆ Brad Davis, Jesse Doran, Steve Buscemi, Robinson Frank Adu, Sam Gray, Billy Costello, Frances Fisher

'Warning: Jealousy Seriously Damages Your Health.'
Heart *
GB 1998 83m Technicolor
Feature Film/Granada/MFPF (Nicola Shindler)
A mother becomes engrossed with the man, an obsessively jealous husband, who is given her son's heart in a transplant operation.
Intense drama of sex and death that grips the attention, though, on reflection, its melodramatic conclusion teeters on the edge of absurdity.
w Jimmy McGovern *d* Charles McDougall *ph* Julian Court *m* Stephen Warbeck *pd* Stuart Walker, Chris Roope *ed* Edward Mansell
☆ Christopher Eccleston, Saskia Reeves, Kate Hardie, Rhys Ifans, Anna Chancellor, Bill Paterson, Matthew Rhys
'A bizarre and riveting sexual melodrama.' – *Peter Bradshaw, Guardian*

Heart and Souls
US 1993 104m DeLuxe Panavision
Universal/Alphaville/Stampede (Nancy Roberts, Sean Daniel)
Passengers killed in a car and coach crash become guardian angels to the child born of a couple who survive the accident, but he grows up to become a sleazy banker.
Curious and uninvolving movie of obscure intentions.
w Brent Maddock, S. S. Wilson, Gregory and Erik Hansen *d* Ron Underwood *ph* Michael Watkins *m* Marc Shaiman *pd* John Muto *ed* O. Nicholas Brown
☆ Robert Downey Jnr, Charles Grodin, Alfre Woodard, Kyra Sedgwick, Tom Sizemore, David Paymer, Elisabeth Shue
'That the effort is at all watchable is a tribute largely to its performers.' – *Variety*

Heart Beat
US 1979 109m Technicolor
Orion/Warner (Alan Greisman, Michael Shamberg)
The literary career of Jack Kerouac is paralleled with his curious sex life. Hesitant and generally unsatisfactory analysis of the so-called beat generation.
w John Byrum *ph* Laszlo Kovacs *m* Jack Nitzsche *pd* Jack Fisk *ed* Eric Jenkins
☆ John Heard, Nick Nolte, Sissy Spacek, Ray Sharkey, Tony Bill

Heart Condition
US 1990 95m DeLuxe
Enterprise/New Line Cinema (Steve Tisch)
A bigoted white cop who has a heart transplant is haunted by the organ's donor, a suave black lawyer.
Dire comedy, despite likeable performances by its stars.
wd James D. Parriott *ph* Arthur Albert *m* Patrick Leonard *pd* John Muto *ed* David Finfer
☆ Bob Hoskins, Denzel Washington, Chloe Webb, Robert Apisa, Jeffrey Meek, Frank R. Roach, Kieran Mulroney, Lisa Stahl, Ray Baker, Eva Larue, Roger E. Mosley

A Heart in Winter: see *Un Coeur en Hiver*

The Heart Is a Lonely Hunter *
US 1968 123m Technicolor
Warner Seven Arts (Joel Freeman)
Incidents in the life of a gentle deaf mute in a small Southern town.
Wispy film of a wistful novel; quite well done but overlong and hard to cheer at.
w Thomas C. Ryan *novel* Carson McCullers *d* Robert Ellis Miller *ph* James Wong Howe *m* Dave Grusin
☆ Alan Arkin, Sondra Locke, Stacy Keach, Laurinda Barrett, Chuck McCann, Biff McGuire, Percy Rodriguez, Cicely Tyson
Alan Arkin; Sondra Locke

Heart Like a Wheel *
US 1983 113m CFI color
Aurora (Charles Rovin)
The wife of a service station owner stops at nothing to become a racing driver.
Well-made study of an obsession, with the usual racing thrills.
w Ken Friedman *d* Jonathan Kaplan *ph* Tak Fujimoto *m* Laurence Rosenthal *pd* James William Newport
☆ *Bonnie Bedelia*, Beau Bridges, Leo Rossi, Hoyt Axton, Bill McKinney
'An Americanized *Chariots of Fire* for the drive-in market.' – *Observer*

The Heart of a Man
GB 1959 92m bw
Rank (Anna Neagle)
After failing as a bouncer, boxer, and commissionaire, a former merchant seaman becomes a singing star and falls for the mistress of a army officer turned conman.
Odd minor movie that tries, with little success, to combine a gritty story of illegal gaming and a glossy fantasy with musical and sentimental moments.
w Jack Trevor Story, Pamela Bower *story* Rex North *d* Herbert Wilcox *ph* Reginald Wyer *m* Wally Stott *ad* Jack Maxsted *ed* Basil Warren
☆ Frankie Vaughan (Frankie), Anne Heywood (Julie), Tony Britton (Tony), Michael Medwin (Sid), Anthony Newley (Johnnie), Peter Sinclair (Bud), Harry Fowler (Razor), George Rose (Charlie), Harold Kaskett (Oscar), Vanda (Cha Cha), Hogan 'Kid' Bassey (Himself), Leslie Mitchell (Himself)
♫ The Heart of a Man; Walking Tall; Sometime, Somewhere

Heart of a Nation **
France 1940 111m bw
Paul Graetz
original title: *Untel Père et Fils*
The story of a Paris family from the Franco-Prussian war to 1939.
Uneven and episodic but consistently interesting piece completed just as the Nazis moved into Paris and suppressed by them, but later released from America with linking narrative by Charles Boyer.
w Charles Spaak *d* Julien Duvivier *ph* Jules Kruger *m* Jean Wiener
☆ Louis Jouvet, Raimu, Suzy Prim, Lucien Nat, Michèle Morgan

Heart of Dixie
US 1989 105m DeLuxe
Orion (Steve Tisch)
The civil rights movement impinges on the lives of three friends at a college in Alabama in the 1950s.
Trivial stuff, presumably aimed at a teen audience that no longer exists for such mild and inoffensive drama.
w Tom McCown *novel* *Heartbreak Hotel* by Anne Rivers Siddons *d* Martin Davidson *ph* Robert Elswit *m* Kenny Vance, Phillip Namanworth *pd* Glenda Ganis *ed* Bonnie Koehler
☆ Ally Sheedy, Virginia Madsen, Phoebe Cates, Treat Williams, Don Michael Paul, Kyle Secor, Francesca Roberts
'A messy goo of nostalgia, rites of passage and clumsy social conscience with an almost exclusive emphasis on Sheedy's eager smile and breathless enthusiasm.' – *Empire*

Heart of Glass *
West Germany 1976 94m Eastmancolor
Werner Herzog
original title: *Herz aus Glas*
A wandering herdsman with special powers supplies a factory owner with the secret of making a very precious glass.
Apocalyptic visionary parable which may mean everything, or nothing, but amuses fitfully while it's on the screen.
w Werner Herzog, Herbert Achternbusch *d* Werner Herzog *ph* Jörg Schmidt-Reitwin, Michael Gast *m* Popol Vuh *ed* Beate Mainka-Jellinghaus
☆ Josef Bierbichler, Stefan Güttler, Clemens Scheitz, Sonja Skiba

Heart of Midnight
US 1988 105m TVC Color
Vestron/AG Productions (Jon Kurtis)
An emotionally disturbed woman uncovers the dark secrets of a night-club left to her by her uncle.
Unattractive psychological horror.
wd Matthew Chapman *ph* Ray Rivas *m* Yanni *pd* Gene Rudolph *ed* Penelope Shaw
☆ Jennifer Jason Leigh, Denise Dummont, Gale Mayron, James Rebhorn, Sam Schacht, Frank Stallone, Brenda Vaccaro, Peter Coyote, Jack Hallett, Nick Love

Heart of New York *
US 1932 74m bw
Warner
A plumber invents a washing machine and becomes a millionaire.
Ethnic farce set in New York's Jewish quarter; of considerable curiosity value.
w Arthur Caesar, Houston Branch *play* *Mendel Inc* by David Freedman *d* Mervyn Le Roy
☆ Joe Smith, Charles Dale, George Sidney, Anna Apfel, Aline MacMahon, Donald Cook
'Gabby to an extreme … too much dialect and too little animation.' – *Variety*
† Smith and Dale were a famous vaudeville act.

The Heart of the Matter *
GB 1953 105m bw
British Lion/London Films (Ian Dalrymple)
In 1942 in an African colony a police officer has an affair while his wife is away, is blackmailed, and plans suicide despite his staunch Catholic belief.
Rather stodgy attempt to film Graham Greene; perhaps everyone tries a little too hard, and in any case the ending is compromised.
w Ian Dalrymple, Lesley Storm *novel* Graham Greene *d* George More O'Ferrall *ph* Jack Hildyard *m* Brian Easdale
☆ *Trevor Howard*, Maria Schell, Elizabeth Allan, Denholm Elliott, Peter Finch, Gérard Oury, George Coulouris, Earl Cameron, Michael Hordern, Colin Gordon, Cyril Raymond, Orlando Martins
'A curious choice for commercial filming.' – *Lindsay Anderson*

Heart of the North
US 1938 74m Technicolor
Warner (Bryan Foy)
The Canadian Mounties chase after gold and fur thieves.
Routine adventure utilizing early developments in colour processing.

w Lee Katz, Vincent Sherman *novel* William Byron Mowery *d* Lewis Seiler
☆ Dick Foran, Gloria Dickson, Gale Page, Allen Jenkins, Patric Knowles, James Stephenson

Heartbeat
US 1946 102m bw
RKO/Robert and Raymond Hakim
A French gamin just released from reform school becomes a professional pickpocket.
Unamusing remake of Battement de Coeur, *with script and most performances very strained.*
w Hans Wilhelm, Max Kolpe, Michel Duran, Morrie Ryskind *d* Sam Wood *ph* Joe Valentine *m* Paul Misraki
☆ Ginger Rogers, Jean-Pierre Aumont, Adolphe Menjou, *Basil Rathbone*, Mikhail Rasumny, Melville Cooper, Mona Maris, Henry Stephenson
'The heartbeat is irregular and sadly ailing.' – *Photoplay*

Heartbreak Hotel
US 1988 93m colour
Buena Vista/Touchstone (Lyda Obst, Debra Hill)
In 1972, a teenager kidnaps Elvis Presley to please his divorced mother, a long-time fan who runs a run-down hotel bereft of guests.
For the most part this is a risible, deeply sentimental fantasy, though there are a few relishable comic moments, including a parody of early rock movies, a German accordion band serenading Elvis, and his redecoration of the hotel in the style of Graceland.
wd Chris Columbus *ph* Stephen Dobson *m* Georges Delerue *pd* John Muto *ed* Raja Gosnell
☆ David Keith (Elvis Presley), Tuesday Weld, Charlie Schlatter, Angela Goethals, Chris Mulkey, Karen Landry

The Heartbreak Kid *
US 1972 106m DeLuxe
(TCF) Palomar (Edgar J. Scherick)
Disappointed with his honeymoon, a sporting goods salesman promptly sets his cap at a richer, prettier prospective spouse.
Heartless modern comedy reminiscent of The Graduate; *quite well done but unsympathetic and somehow too American to export satisfactorily.*
w Neil Simon *story* A Change of Plan by Bruce Jay Friedman *d* Elaine May *ph* Owen Roizman *m* Garry Sherman
☆ Charles Grodin, Cybill Shepherd, Jeannie Berlin, Eddie Albert, Audra Lindley, William Prince, Art Metrano
'The latest in a relatively new kind of American film – glittery trash.' – *Stanley Kauffmann*
Jeannie Berlin; Eddie Albert

Heartbreak Ridge
US 1986 130m Technicolor
Warner/Malpaso/Jay Weston (Clint Eastwood)
An ageing gunnery sergeant transforms raw recruits into fighting men who become heroes in Grenada.
Dismayingly predictable potboiler with nothing but foul language to pass the time.
w James Carabatsos *d* Clint Eastwood *ph* Jack N. Green *m* Lennie Niehaus
☆ Clint Eastwood, Marsha Mason, Everett McGill, Moses Gunn, Eileen Heckart, Bo Svenson
'Now looking increasingly like an Easter Island statue, he has a voice pickled in Bourbon, a tongue like razor wire and a body so full of shrapnel he can't walk through airport metal detectors.' – *Time Out*

Heartbreakers
US 1984 98m DeLuxe
Orion/Jethro Films (Bob Weis, Bobby Roth)
Two old friends, one an artist, the other a businessman, worry about their relationship, their careers and their love-life.
Mundane drama of male bonding.
wd Bobby Roth *ph* Michael Ballhaus *m* Tangerine Dream *pd* David Nichols *ed* John Carnochan
☆ Peter Coyote, Nick Mancuso, Carole Laure, Max Gail, James Laurenson, Carol Wayne, Jamie Rose, Kathryn Harrold

'Meet the mother and daughter who'll love you for richer... and leave you for poorer'
Heartbreakers
US 2001 124m DeLuxe Panavision
Icon/MGM/Winchester (John Davis, Irving Ong)
Mother-and-daughter confidence tricksters seduce rich men into marriage and a quick divorce settlement.
An uneasy mix of sour and romantic comedy that never finds the right tone, though there is amusement to be had from Hackman's wheezy volcano of a tobacco tycoon.
w Robert Dunn, Paul Guay, Stephen Mazur *d* David Mirkin *ph* Dean Semler *m* John Debney: theme: Danny Elfman *pd* Lilly Kilvert *ed* William Steinkamp
☆ Sigourney Weaver (Angela Nardino/ Max Conners/Ulga Yevanova), Jennifer Love Hewitt (Wendy/Page Conners/Jane Helstrom), Ray Liotta (Dean Cumanno/Vinny Staggliano), Jason Lee (Jack Withrowe), Anne Bancroft (Gloria Vogal/Barbara), Nora Dunn (Miss Madress), Gene Hackman (William B. Tensy)
'Has a slinky, teasing quality that recalls the dressed-up comedies of the studio era.' – A. O. Scott, *New York Times*

Heartburn *
US 1986 108m Technicolor
Paramount/Mike Nichols, Robert Greenhut
Romantic problems of a busy professional couple.
Rather ordinary and overstretched scripting is enlivened by star playing, but the overall feeling is one of disappointment.
w Nora Ephron *novel* Nora Ephron *d* Mike Nichols *ph* Nestor Almendros *m* Carly Simon *pd* Tony Walton *ed* Sam O'Steen
☆ *Meryl Streep, Jack Nicholson,* Jeff Daniels, Maureen Stapleton, Stockard Channing, Richard Masur, Steven Hill, Milos Forman, Catherine O'Hara
'A movie of colossal inconsequence. Heartburn? No, just a bad attack of wind.' – *Time Out*

Heartland *
US 1979 96m DuArt
Wilderness Women Productions/Filmhaus (Annick Smith)
In 1910 Wyoming, a woman with a small daughter takes up her arduous duties as housekeeper to a dour rancher.
Impressive if not very likeable semidocumentary which certainly rubs one's nose in the unfairness of life.
w Beth Ferris, from the papers of Elmore Randall Stewart *d Richard Pearce ph Fred Murphy* *m* Charles Gross
☆ *Conchata Ferrell,* Rip Torn, Barry Primus, Lilia Skala

Heart's Desire
GB 1935 82m bw
BIP (Walter Mycroft)
In old Vienna, a tenor finds that a glamorous socialite wants him for his voice rather than himself.
Dated operetta, but the star still reigns supreme.
w L. DuGarde Peach, Jack Davies, Roger Burford, Bruno Frank *story* Lioni Pickard *d* Paul Stein *ph* Jack Cox *m* Schumann and others *md* Idris Lewis, Stanford Robinson *ad* Clarence Elder *ed* Leslie Norman
☆ *Richard Tauber,* Leonora Corbett, Diana Napier, Frank Vosper

Hearts Divided
US 1936 76m bw
Warner
Napoleon's brother weds a Baltimore beauty.
Uneasy remake of Glorious Betsy *(qv) with a couple of musical numbers added; a splendid cast retires defeated.*
w Laird Doyle, Casey Robinson *d* Frank Borzage
☆ Marion Davies, Dick Powell, Edward Everett Horton, Claude Rains, Charles Ruggles, Arthur Treacher, Henry Stephenson

'What if one of life's great mysteries moved in upstairs?'
Hearts in Atlantis
US 2001 101m Technicolor Panavision
Warner/Castle Rock/Village Roadshow/NPV (Kerry Heysen)
A middle-aged man recalls the time when he was eleven years old, and a strange man with psychic gifts moved into the next apartment.
Soft-centred movie about the beginning of adulthood, bathed in syrupy regret.
w William Goldman *novel* Stephen King *d* Scott Hicks *ph* Piotr Sobocinski *m* Mychael Danna *pd* Barbara C. Ling *ed* Pip Karmel
☆ Anthony Hopkins (Ted Brautigan), Anton Yelchin (Bobby Garfield), Hope Davis (Liz Garfield), Mika Boorem (Carol Gerber), David Morse (Adult Bobby Garfield), Alan Tudyk (Monte Man), Tom Bower (Len Files), Celia Weston (Alana Files)
'Tired and cynical: nostalgia-porn for undemanding baby-boomers.' – *Xan Brooks, Sight and Sound*
'A nostalgic fiasco so shameless it makes movies like *Simon Birch* and *Frequency* seem as austere as the work of Robert Bresson.' – *Stephen Holden, New York Times*

Hearts in Springtime: see *Glamour Boy*

Hearts of Darkness: A Filmmaker's Apocalypse **
US 1991 96m colour
Blue Dolphin/Zaloom Mayfield/Zoetrope (George Zaloom, Les Mayfield)
A documentary on the making of Francis Ford Coppola's *Apocalypse Now* in 1976.
Fascinating glimpse not only of filmmaking on a troubled location with oversized egos in collision, but also of Hollywood attitudes of the time. It bears out Coppola's own summation, 'We had access to too much money, too much equipment, and little by little we went insane.'
wd Fax Bahr, George Hickenlooper *ph* Larry Carney, Eleanor Coppola, Bill Neal, Doug Ryan, Les Blank and others *m* Todd Boekelheide *ed* Michael Hreer, Jay Miracle

Hearts of Fire
US 1987 95m colour J-D-C Scope
UKFD/Lorimar/Phoenix Entertainment/Fox (Richard Marquand, Jennifer Miller, Jennifer Alward)
A female rock singer succeeds with the aid of a reclusive star and a weary British rocker.
Tedious exposé of the world of rock music, lacking in excitement and a sad end to the career of Marquand, who died soon after finishing it.
w Scott Richardson, Joe Eszterhas *d* Richard Marquand *ph* Alan Hume *m* John Barry *pd* Roger Murray-Leach *ed* Sean Barton
☆ Fiona Flanagan, Bob Dylan, Rupert Everett, Lesley Donaldson, Barbara Barnes-Hopkins, Maury Chaykin, Ian Dury, Richie Havens, Julian Glover

Hearts of the West *
US 1975 103m Metrocolor
MGM/Bill-Zieff (Tony Bill)
GB title: *Hollywood Cowboy*
In the early thirties a naïve midwesterner almost accidentally becomes a Hollywood star.
Overstretched comedy poking gentle fun at old Hollywood: likeable but finally disappointing, as it obviously needed a Buster Keaton.
w Rob Thompson *d* Howard Zieff *ph* Mario Tosi *m* Ken Lauber
☆ *Jeff Bridges,* Alan Arkin, Andy Griffith, Blythe Danner, Donald Pleasence, Richard B. Shull, Herb Edelman

Hearts of the World *
US 1918 80m (24 fps) bw silent
Artcraft (David Wark Griffith)
Of various people involved in World War I, the patriotic and dutiful ones come out best.
Rather dim patriotic propaganda made by Griffith at the request of the British government and using a good deal of newsreel as well as reconstruction. The personal stories are on the predictable side.
wd D. W. Griffith *ph* Billy Bitzer *ed* James Smith
☆ Lillian Gish, Dorothy Gish, Robert Harron, Josephine Crowell, Erich von Stroheim, Noël Coward
'Here we have an art of pure emotion which can go beneath thought, beneath belief, beneath ideals, down to the brute fact of emotional psychology, and make a man or a woman who has hated war, all war, even this war, feel the surge of group emotion, group loyalty and group hate.' – *Kenneth MacGowan, The New Republic (1918)*
† For the screenplay credit Griffith used the pseudonym of Gaston de Tolignac.

Heat *
US 1972 100m colour
Score/Sarx (Andy Warhol)
aka: *Andy Warhol's Heat*
An out-of-work television actor and singer moves into a run-down Los Angeles motel and begins an affair with an older, fading actress.
Perverse variation on Sunset Boulevard, *casually presented but offering amusement along the way.*
wd Paul Morrissey *idea* John Hallowell *ph* Paul Morrissey *m* John Cale *ed* Lan Jokel, Jed Johnson
☆ Joe Dallesandro, Sylvia Miles, Andrea Feldman, Pat Ast, Ray Vestal, P. J. Lester, Eric Emerson
'An unsavoury piece of work, laced with sex, lesbianism, self-abuse and perversion.' – *Daily Record, Glasgow*
'Succeeds in being both funny and effortlessly truthful.' – *Derek Malcolm, Guardian*

Heat
US 1987 101m Technicolor
Vista/New Century (Keith Rotman, George Pappas)
A Las Vegas gambler gets into trouble with gangsters.
Unremarkable toughie with the star at his most predictable.
w William Goldman *novel* William Goldman *d* R. M. Richards *ph* James Contner *m* Michael Gibbs *ed* Jeffrey Wolf
☆ Burt Reynolds, Karen Young, Peter MacNicol, Howard Hesseman, Diana Scarwid

Heat **
US 1995 172m Technicolor Panavision
Warner/Monarchy/Forward Pass/Regency (Michael Mann, Art Linson)
A streetwise Los Angeles cop with marital problems comes to respect the ruthless leader of a gang of armed robbers.
A highly polished, lovingly crafted thriller, but overlong, portentous and padded with irrelevant subplots, and one that finally gives birth to a mouse of an idea: that cops and robbers are much alike. Its true subject-matter is no more than male bonding between two boastful and unlovely characters, and its real purpose seems to have been to bring together on-screen Pacino and de Niro. De Niro, perhaps remembering Bogart's not dissimilar duel with Rod Steiger in The Harder They Fall, *goes for a minimalist approach; Pacino shouts a lot.*
wd Michael Mann *ph* Dante Spinotti *m* Elliot Goldenthal *pd* Neil Spisak *ed* Dov Hoenig, Pasquale Buba, William Goldenberg, Tom Rolf
☆ Al Pacino, Robert DeNiro, Val Kilmer, Jon Voight, Tom Sizemore, Diane Venora, Amy Brenneman, Ashley Judd, Wes Studi, Natalie Portman
'Stands apart from other films of its type by virtue of its extraordinarily rich characterizations and its thoughtful, deeply melancholy take on modern life.' – *Todd McCarthy, Variety*
'Proves one thing absolute. If you put great actors and a great script together with a great visionary director, you get a great movie.' – *Empire*
'What is surprising is that the movie is 2 hours and 52 minutes long, and that neither character is entertaining enough to fill the time. Mann's action scenes have an existential, you-are-there jitteriness, but when the characters are just sitting around hatching schemes, *Heat* is a dry, talky movie.' – *Owen Gleiberman, Entertainment Weekly*
† It was based on a TV movie (*L.A. Takedown*), made by Michael Mann in 1989, which has been released on video

Heat and Dust **
GB 1982 130m colour
Merchant Ivory (Ismail Merchant)

A woman discovers India's past through her great-aunt's letters.
Much praised by those who admire the work of this team, but found (as usual) mildly bewildering by others, this has at least a large enough budget to produce interest in its historically re-created backgrounds if not its complex plot structure.
w Ruth Prawer Jhabvala *novel* Ruth Prawer Jhabvala *d* James Ivory *ph* Walter Lassally *m* Richard Robbins
☆ Julie Christie, Christopher Cazenove, Shashi Kapoor, Greta Scacchi, Nickolas Grace, Jennifer Kendal, Julian Glover, Susan Fleetwood
'A likeable patchwork of concepts and cameos.' – *Philip Strick, MFB*
screenplay

Heat and Sunlight
US 1987 98m bw
Stutz/Snowball/New Front Alliance (Steve Burns, Hildy Burns)

A photographer becomes confused when he discovers that his love affair with a dancer is coming to an end.
An improvised low-budget study in neurosis, of interest mainly to its participants.
wd Rob Nilsson *ph* Tomas Tucker *m* David Byrne, Brian Eno *pd* Hildy Burns, Steve Burns *ed* Henk Van Eeghen
☆ Rob Nilsson, Don Bejema, Consuelo Faust, Ernie Fosselius

Heat Lightning
US 1934 63m bw
Warner
A lady gas station attendant in the hot South-west becomes involved with two murderers on the run.
Cautionary tale which does not quite gel despite effort all round.
w Brown Holmes, Warren Duff *play* George Abbott, Leon Abrams *d* Mervyn Le Roy
☆ Aline MacMahon, Ann Dvorak, Preston Foster, Lyle Talbot, Glenda Farrell, Frank McHugh, Ruth Donnelly
'Drab background, little sex appeal and not enough tension. It's a sluffo for deluxers, but can get by elsewhere.' – *Variety*
† Remade in 1941 as *Highway West*.

Heathers
US 1988 103m DeLuxe
Premier Releasing/New World/Cinemarque Entertainment (Denise Di Novi)

A high-school student begins to systematically murder his fellow students.
Black joke that rapidly runs out of interest.
w Daniel Waters *d* Michael Lehmann *ph* Francis Kenny *m* David Newman *pd* Jon Hutman *ed* Norman Hollyn
☆ Winona Ryder, Christian Slater, Shannen Doherty, Lisanne Falk, Kim Walker, Penelope Milford, Glenn Shadix
'The film is not seriously a comedy about high school as a metaphor for society – its false values, its power-hungry cliques, its emotional exploitation.' – *Richard Coombs, MFB*

The Heat's On
US 1943 79m bw
Columbia (Milton Carter)
GB title: *Tropicana*
A star seeks financial backing from an elderly angel whose sister runs the Legion of Purity.
Dim musical vehicle for a fading star; her last film for twenty-seven years.
w Fitzroy Davis, George S. George, Fred Schiller *d* Gregory Ratoff *ph* Franz Planer *m* John Leipold *md* Yasha Bunchuk
☆ Mae West, Victor Moore, William Gaxton, Almira Sessions, Lester Allen, Mary Roche, Hazel Scott, Alan Dinehart, Lloyd Bridges, Xavier Cugat and his Orchestra
'A stale-ale musical in which a lot of good people apathetically support the almost equally apathetic Mae West.' – *James Agee*

Heatwave *
Australia 1982 95m Eastmancolor
M and L Enterprises/Preston Crothers (Hilary Linstead)

Community activists move to prevent the schemes of a Sydney developer.
Rather like an Ealing drama descending into melodrama; a polished piece of committed film journalism masquerading as fiction.
w Marc Rosenberg, Phillip Noyce *d* Phillip Noyce *ph* Vincent Monton *m* Cameron Allan *pd* Ross Major
☆ Judy Davis, Richard Moir, Chris Haywood, Bill Hunter, John Meillon, John Gregg
† A similarly themed Australian film, *The Killing of Angel Street*, came out almost simultaneously.

Heaven *
US 1987 80m colour
Island Pictures/RVP Productions (Joe Kelly)

Interviews with a variety of people about death, after-life and heaven are interspersed with clips from old Hollywood movies and TV programmes that illustrate or contradict the statements made.
Documentary demonstrating the optimism and vagueness of our views on the subject, entertaining in its offbeat fashion despite the manner in which the interviewees are photographed in distracting patterns of light and shade.
d Diane Keaton *ph* Frederick Elmes, Joe Kelly *m* Howard Shore *ad* Barbara Ling *ed* Paul Barnes

'What Would You Risk For Love?'
Heaven
Germany/US 2002 96m colour
Buena Vista/X Filme/Miramax (Maria Koepf, Stefan Arndt)

After she tries to murder a drug dealer and accidentally kills four innocent people, an English teacher goes on the run with the aid of an Italian policeman who has fallen in love with her.
A failure on every level, from the implausibilities of the meandering narrative to the lack of chemistry between its leading players – it is unsurprising that it finally leaves its characters and its audience up in the air.
w Krzysztof Kieslowski, Krzysztof Piesiewicz *d* Tom Tykver *ph* Frank Griebe *m* Arvo Part *pd* Uli Hanisch *ed* Mathilde Bonnefoy
☆ Cate Blanchett (Philippa), Giovanni Ribisi (Filippo), Remo Girone (Father), Stefania Rocca (Regina), Matthia Sbragia (Major Pini), Alberto Di Stasio (Public Prosecutor), Stefano Santospago (Marco Vendice)
'An excruciating middlebrow arthouse drama burdened with flatulent screen imagery and terrible acting.' – *Peter Bradshaw, Guardian*
'One of the most morally reprehensible pieces of work to focus on contemporary society.' – *Alexander Walker, London Evening Standard*
'Engrossing and moving, a poem about a love that breaks barriers and passes understanding.' – *Michael Wilmington, Chicago Tribune*

'From Vietnam to America, one woman's journey from hope, to love, to discovery.'
Heaven & Earth *
US 1993 140m Technicolor Panavision
Warner/Regency/Canal/Alcor (Oliver Stone, Arnon Milchan, Robert Kline, A. Kitman Ho)

A Vietnamese peasant woman endures hardships and torment from both sides in the war, and life is slow to improve after she goes to America as the wife of a US marine.
An ambitious and epic film, but too strident to be successful and one that, although ostensibly dealing with the life of a Vietnamese woman, still manages to make the subject-matter that of the American experience in Vietnam and its aftermath; the balance shifts from the moment Tommy Lee Jones's damaged marine enters the picture.
wd Oliver Stone *books* When Heaven and Earth Changed Place by Le Ly Hayslip, Jay Wurts; Child of War, Woman of Peace by Le Ly Hayslip, James Hayslip *ph* Robert Richardson *m* Kitaro *pd* Victor Kempster *ed* David Brenner, Sally Menke
☆ *Tommy Lee Jones*, Joan Chen, Haing S. Ngor, Hiep Thi Le, Debbie Reynolds, Supak Pititam, Thuan K. Nguyen
'The sledgehammer approach to storytelling merely results in audience numbness and distance from the potentially moving material.' – *Variety*
'Thematically grotesque but visually gorgeous ... if Stone simplifies and distorts, he often does so brilliantly, like a cartoonist with a Fauvist's eye for the drama in color and character.' – *Richard Corliss, Time*
'Cry? I could have wept with boredom.' – *Alexander Walker*

Heaven Can Wait ***
US 1943 112m Technicolor
TCF (Ernst Lubitsch)

On arrival in Hades, an elderly playboy reports his peccadilloes to Satan, who sends him Upstairs.
Charming period piece with fantasy bookends; the essence of the piece is its evocation of American society in the 1890s, and in its director's waspish way with a funny scene.
w Samson Raphaelson play Birthday by Lazlo Bus-Fekete *d Ernst Lubitsch ph Edward Cronjager m* Alfred Newman *ad James Basevi, Leland Fuller*
☆ *Don Ameche*, Gene Tierney, *Laird Cregar, Charles Coburn, Marjorie Main*, Eugene Pallette, *Allyn Joslyn*, Spring Byington, Signe Hasso, Louis Calhern
'It was so good I half believed Lubitsch could still do as well as he ever did, given half a chance.' – *James Agee*
best picture; Ernst Lubitsch; Edward Cronjager

Heaven Can Wait *
US 1978 100m Movielab
Paramount/Warren Beatty (Howard W. Koch Jnr, Charles H. McGuire)

A football star finds himself accidentally in heaven after a car accident; when he is allowed to return, his body has been cremated, so he has to find another.
Unexpectedly commercially successful (the late seventies clearly needed religion) remake of 1941's Here Comes Mr Jordan. *It lacks the sharpness and style of its predecessor, and despite amusing moments is often merely tacky.*
w Warren Beatty, Elaine May *play* Harry Segall *d* Warren Beatty, Buck Henry *ph* William A. Fraker *m* Dave Grusin *pd* Paul Sylbert, Edwin O'Donovan *ed* Robert C. Jones
☆ Warren Beatty (Joe Pendleton), Julie Christie (Betty Logan), James Mason (Mr Jordan), Jack Warden (Mac Corkle), Charles Grodin (Tony Abbott), *Dyan Cannon* (Julia Farnsworth), Buck Henry (Escort), Vincent Gardenia (Lt Krim), Joseph Maher (Sisk)
'Script and direction are very strong, providing a rich mix of visual and verbal humor that is controlled and avoids the extremes of cheap vulgarity and overly esoteric whimsy.' – *Variety*
'It lifts the spirits and makes you feel good about life on earth and even beyond.' – *Rex Reed*
art direction
best picture; script; direction; photography; music; Warren Beatty (as actor); Jack Warden; Dyan Cannon

Heaven Fell That Night
France/Italy 1958 90m Eastmancolor Cinemascope
IENA/CEIAP (Raoul Levy)
original title: *Les Bijoutiers du Clair de Lune*
A young girl becomes involved in a revenge plot and finds herself on the run with a killer.
Heavy going sex-and-violence hokum.
w Roger Vadim, Peter Viertel *novel* Albert Vidalie *d* Roger Vadim *ph* Armand Thirard *m* Georges Auric
☆ Brigitte Bardot, Alida Valli, Stephen Boyd, Pepe Nieto

Heaven Help Us **
US 1985 104m colour
HBO/Silver Screen Partners (Mark Carliner, Dan Wigutow)

GB title: *Catholic Boys*
A new boy discovers friendship, love and tough treatment at a Catholic high school in Brooklyn in the mid-60s.
Engrossing story of adolescent strivings, done with some wit and style.
w Charles Purpura *d* Michael Dinner *ph* Miroslav Ondricek *m* James Horner *pd* Michael Molly *ed* Stephen A. Rotter
☆ Andrew McCarthy, Mary Stuart Masterson, Kevin Dillon, Malcolm Danare, Jennie Dundas, Kate Reid, Wallace Shawn, Jay Patterson, John Heard, Donald Sutherland

Heaven Knows Mr Allison *
US 1957 105m Technicolor Cinemascope
TCF (Buddy Adler, Eugene Franks)

Marooned on a small Pacific island during World War II, a marine and a nun, antagonistic to each other, combine to outwit the Japs.
Silly adventure story with predictably well-handled action sequences separated by even more predictable dialogue, lots of it.
w John Lee Mahin, John Huston *novel* Charles Shaw *d* John Huston *ph* Oswald Morris *m* Georges Auric *ad* Stephen Grimes *ed* Russell Lloyd
☆ Robert Mitchum, Deborah Kerr
script; Deborah Kerr

Heaven on Earth: see *The Exquisite Sinner (1927)*

Heaven Only Knows
US 1947 98m bw
UA (Seymour Nebenzal)
An angel is sent to the old west to reform a bad man.
Whimsical comedy-drama which doesn't work at all, even as a distant cousin of Here Comes Mr Jordan.
w Art Arthur, Rowland Leigh *d* Albert S. Rogell *ph* Karl Struss *m* Heinz Roemheld
☆ Robert Cummings, Brian Donlevy, Marjorie Reynolds, Bill Goodwin, John Litel, Stuart Erwin

Heaven with a Barbed Wire Fence
US 1939 61m bw
TCF (Sol M. Wurtzel)
A New York clerk hitch-hikes his way to Arizona, where he has bought a piece of land.
Subdued flagwaver with everybody behaving just swell in God's own country.
w Dalton Trumbo, Leonard Hoffman, Ben Grauman Kohn *d* Ricardo Cortez *ph* Edward Cronjager *md* Samuel Kaylin
☆ Glenn Ford, Jean Rogers, Richard Conte, Marjorie Rambeau, Raymond Walburn, Eddie Collins, Ward Bond
'A slightly clouded title, with little possibility of propelling many customers through the front door.' – *Variety*
† It was Glenn Ford's first film.

Heaven with a Gun
US 1969 101m Metrocolor Panavision
MGM (King Brothers)
The determined new preacher of a small Western town is an ex-gunfighter.
Solidly carpentered half-a-bill Western.
w Richard Carr *d* Lee Katzin *ph* Fred J. Koenekamp *m* Johnny Mandel
☆ Glenn Ford, Carolyn Jones, David Carradine, J. D. Cannon, Barbara Hershey, Noah Beery Jnr

Heavenly Bodies
Canada 1985 89m Medallion
Alliance/PSO/RSL/Playboy (Robert Lantos, Stephen J.Roth)

Rivalries between two aerobic instructors lead to a marathon workout contest.
Absurd and trivial musical, with all the depth of characterization and narrative interest of a pop video; even those who enjoy watching young women jumping up and down in leotards will tire of it long before it ends.
w Lawrence Dane, Ron Base *d* Lawrence Dane *ph* Thomas Burstyn *md* Paul Hoffert *ch* Brian Foley *pd* Lindsey Goddard
☆ Cynthia Dale, Richard Rebiere, Walter George Alton, Laura Henry, Stuart Stone, Patrica Idlette, Pam Henry

The Heavenly Body
US 1943 93m bw
MGM (Arthur Hornblow Jnr)
An astronomer is too busy to notice his wife, so she takes up astrology and meets a dark handsome stranger as predicted.

Thin romantic comedy which despite crazy touches never actually makes one laugh.
w Michael Arlen, Walter Reisch *d* Alexander Hall *ph* Robert Planck *m* Bronislau Kaper
☆ William Powell, Hedy Lamarr, James Craig, Fay Bainter, Henry O'Neill, Spring Byington, Morris Ankrum, Connie Gilchrist

'Not all angels are innocent.'
'The True Story Of A Crime That Shocked A Nation.'

Heavenly Creatures ***

New Zealand 1994 98m Eastmancolor Super 35
Buena Vista/Wingnut/Fontana/NZFC (Jim Booth)

In New Zealand, two schoolgirls, who form a close relationship, based on a shared fantasy world, decide to kill the mother of one of them to prevent their separation.
Chilling, sensitively directed account of the dangerous mixture of fantasy and reality that precipitated a tragic and violent death. It is a considerable achievement and an unexpected advance from a director hitherto known for slapdash, gore-filled horror movies such as Braindead.
w Frances Walsh, Peter Jackson d Peter Jackson ph Alun Bollinger *m* Peter Dasent *pd* Grant Major *ed* Jamie Selkirk
☆ Melanie Lynskey, Kate Winslet, Sarah Peirse, Diana Kent, Clive Merrison, Simon O'Connor, Jed Brophy

'The sad creatures who Pauline and Juliet must have been in real life are alchemized into figures of horror and beauty. They become the stuff of thrilling popular art.' – *Richard Corliss, Time*

'A striking addition to the cinema of *folie à deux*, the madness for two that is either a perversion of true love or its purest manifestation.' – *Adam Mars-Jones, Independent*

† The real-life Juliet now lives in Scotland and writes, under the name of Anne Perry, mystery novels set in Victorian times.
Frances Walsh, Peter Jackson (screenplay)

Heavenly Days

US 1944 72m bw
RKO (Robert Fellows)

Fibber McGee and Molly go to Washington.
Extension of a radio comedy series about a man who simply can't tell the truth; amusing at the time, but with topical references which mean little today.
wd Howard Estabrook *ph* J. Roy Hunt *m* Leigh Harline
☆ Jim Jordan, Marion Jordan, Eugene Pallette, Gordon Oliver, Raymond Walburn, Barbara Hale, Don Douglas, Frieda Inescort

Heavenly Pursuits

GB 1986 91m colour
Island Films/Skreba/Film Four (Michael Relph)

US title: *The Gospel According to Vic*
A sceptical Scottish teacher is involved with seemingly miraculous happenings at a Catholic school.
Well acted, ineffectual satire on education and religion.
wd Charles Gormley *ph* Michael Coulter *m* B. A. Robinson *pd* Rita McGurn *ed* John Gow
☆ Tom Conti, Helen Mirren, Brian Pettifer, David Hayman, Dave Anderson, Jennifer Black

Heavens Above! *

GB 1963 118m bw
British Lion/Charter (Roy Boulting)

A northern parson with proletarian sympathies is accidentally appointed to a snobby village where he converts the dowager aristocrat to works of absurd charity. Eventually he has the whole country in an uproar and takes the place of an astronaut.
Patchy satirical comedy which takes unsteady aim at too many targets but scores some predictable laughs.
w Frank Harvey, John Boulting *d* John Boulting *ph Max Greene m* Richard Rodney Bennett
☆ Peter Sellers, Isabel Jeans, Cecil Parker, Brock Peters, Ian Carmichael, Irene Handl, Eric Sykes, Bernard Miles

'There are some very amusing verbal and visual jokes, and both are largely aided by some deft acting.' – *Variety*

'What one loves about life are the things that fade...'
'The most talked-about film of the decade!'
'The only thing greater than their passion for America ... was their passion for each other!'

Heaven's Gate

US 1980 219m Technicolor Panavision
UA (Joann Carelli)

1890 Wyoming: established cattlemen fight immigrants.
Totally incoherent, showy Western which was lambasted by the critics and quickly withdrawn. A vital turning point in Hollywood policy, hopefully marking the last time a whiz kid with one success behind him is given a blank cheque to indulge in self-abuse.
wd Michael Cimino *ph* Vilmos Zsigmond *m* David Mansfield *ad* Tambi Larsen *ed* Tom Rolf, William Reynolds, Lisa Fruchtman, Gerald Greenberg
☆ Kris Kristofferson, Christopher Walken, John Hurt, Sam Waterston, Brad Dourif, Isabelle Huppert, Joseph Cotten, Jeff Bridges

'The trade must marvel that directors now have such power that no one, in the endless months since work on the picture began, was able to impose some structure and sense.' – *Variety*

'All too much and not enough.' – *Sunday Times*

'A film which John Ford would have brought in on time and on budget with quite as much social, critical and political comment – and much more entertainment value.' – *Margaret Hinxman, Daily Mail*

'It fails so completely that you might suspect Mr Cimino sold his soul to the devil to obtain the success of *The Deer Hunter*, and the devil has just come around to collect.' – *Vincent Canby, New York Times*

† The film was budgeted at $7.5 million and cost $36 million. The story of what happened is told in Stephen Bach's *Final Cut: Dreams and Disaster in the Making of Heaven's Gate*, published in 1985.
Tambi Larsen

'Trusting the wrong woman can be a deadly choice.'

Heaven's Prisoners

US 1996 132m Technicolor
Rank/New Line/Savoy (Albert S. Ruddy, Andre E. Morgan, Leslie Greif)

A former New Orleans cop is drawn into the world of drugs and mob violence after he rescues a young girl from a crashed aeroplane.
Revenge thriller of no particular distinction; competent is as good as it gets.
w Harley Peyton, Scott Frank *novel* James Lee Burke *d* Phil Joanou *ph* Harris Savides *m* George Fenton *pd* John Stoddart *ed* William Steinkamp
☆ Alec Baldwin, Mary Stuart Masterson, Kelly Lynch, Teri Hatcher, Eric Roberts, Vondie Curtis-Hall, Badja Djola

'An overlong plod, justifying the oxymoronic description a boring thriller.' – *George Perry*

† The film flopped at the US box-office, taking $5m.

Heavy *

US 1995 103m DuArt
Artificial Eye/Mayfair/Available Light (Richard Miller)

A reclusive, overweight, mother-dominated pizza chef falls for a teenage waitress.
A small-scale, slow-moving drama of an unexamined life being sparked into awareness of the world.
wd James Mangold *ph* Michael Barrow *m* Thurston Moore *pd* Michael Shaw *ed* Meg Reticker
☆ *Pruitt Taylor Vince*, Shelley Winters, Liv Tyler, Deborah Harry, Joe Grifasi, Evan Dando

'Well-acted pic dawdles long enough to lose viewers with short attention spans, but delivers modest rewards to those who get in tune with its peculiar rhythms and concerns.' – *Variety*

'A step beyond science fiction!'

Heavy Metal *

US 1981 90m Metrocolor
Columbia/Ivan Reitman, Leonard Vogel

A complicated comic strip/science fiction story, with soft core jokes in the modern manner, is told by international teams of animators each working on an episode.
The experiment is interesting rather than successful.
w Dan Goldberg, Len Blum *story* Richard Corben, Angus McKie, Dan O'Bannon, Thomas Warkentin, Berni Wrightson *d* Gerald Potterton *m* Elmer Bernstein and others *pd* Michael Gross *ed* Janice Brown
☆ Featuring voices of: Roger Bumpass, Jackie Burroughs, John Candy, Joe Flaherty, Don Francks, Eugene Levy, Harold Ramis

'Something of a hodge-podge ... the script is a skeletal, whimsically mystical affair...' – *John Pym, MFB*

Heavy Petting *

US 1988 80m bw/colour
ICA/Fossil (Obie Benz, Carol Noblitt)

An examination of the sexual customs and habits of the 1950s as seen in films of the time and as recalled by interviews with celebrities. It includes excerpts from *Highschool Hellcats*, *Blackboard Jungle*, *Because They're Young* and *Rebel Without a Cause* and from educational films.
An entertaining documentary, although many of the interviews are less revealing than the films of the time.
d Obie Benz, Josh Waletzky *ph* Sandi Sissel *ed* Josh Waletzky, Judith Sobol, Edith Becker
☆ Laurie Anderson, Sandra Bernhard, William Burroughs, Allen Ginsberg, David Byrne, Spalding Gray, Abbie Hoffman, Josh Mostel

Heavyweights

US 1995 97m Technicolor
Buena Vista/Walt Disney/Caravan (Joe Roth, Roger Birnbaum)

A keep-fit fanatic takes over a holiday camp for overweight children.
Tasteless and inane comedy, a clumsy anthology of bad jokes.
w Judd Apatow, Steven Brill *d* Steven Brill *ph* Victor Hammer *m* J. A. C. Redford *pd* Stephen Storer *ed* C. Timothy O'Meara
☆ Tom McGowan, Aaron Schwartz, Ben Stiller, Shaun Weiss, Tom Hodges, Leah Lail, Paul Feig

'The fat gags merely serve to perpetuate offensive and unhelpful stereotypes. It's depressing to think Disney could sink so low.' – *Film Review*

Hedd Wyn *

Wales 1992 125m colour
S4C (Shân Davis)

A Welsh farmer wins a prize for his poetry after he is killed in the First World War.
Glossy period piece, well done but too long for comfort.
w Alan Llwyd *d* Paul Turner *m* John E. R. Hardy *pd* Jane Roberts, Martin Morley *ed* Chris Lawrence
☆ Huw Garmon, Sue Roderick, Judith Humphreys, Nia Dryhurst, Gwen Ellis, Grey Evans, Emlyn Gomer

'With its emphasis on veracity and immaculate production design and costuming, pic lacks enough dramatic smarts to go the two-hour-plus distance.' – *Variety*

best foreign-language film

Hedda *

GB 1975 102m Technicolor
Brut (Robert Enders)

A selfish pregnant woman is bored by her husband and revolted at the idea of carrying his child. She takes an opportunity to revenge herself on an old lover, but the scheme rebounds on herself.
Rather flat rendering of a play which has received more than its due share of attention.
wd Trevor Nunn *play* Henrik Ibsen *ph* Douglas Slocombe *m* Laurie Johnson
☆ Glenda Jackson, Peter Eyre, Timothy West, Jennie Linden, Patrick Stewart
Glenda Jackson

'An anatomically incorrect rock odyssey'

Hedwig and the Angry Inch

US 2001 92m colour
Entertainment/New Line/Killer (Christine Vachon, Katie Roumel, Pamela Koffler)

A transsexual tells, and sings, the story of her life, from boyhood in East Germany to love and betrayal in America.
Based on a off-Broadway success, it transfers to the screen as an energetic, loud rock musical imbued with camp self-pity.
wd John Cameron Mitchell *play* John Cameron Mitchell *ph* Frank DeMarco *m/ly* Stephen Trask *pd* Therese DePrez *ed* Andrew Marcus
☆ John Cameron Mitchell (Hedwig/Hansel), Andrea Martin (Phyllis Stein), Michael Pitt (Tommy Gnosis), Alberta Watson (Hansel's Mom), Stephen Trask (Skszp), Rob Campbell (Krzysztof), Theodore Liscinski (Jacek), Michael Aranov (Schlatko), Miriam Shor (Yitzhak)

'Movingly affirmative...raucous, racy and full of hilarious, lowdown survivor's wit.' – *Kevin Thomas, Los Angeles Times*

Heftig og Begeistret *

Norway/Sweden 2001 105m colour
Artificial Eye/Norsk/Barentsfilm/Giraffilm (Tom Remlov)

aka: *Cool and Crazy*
The male voice choir of Berlevåg, Norway, practise their performance before travelling to a festival at Murmansk, Russia.
Quirky and affectionate documentary of an elderly group of singers, undaunted in enthusiasm by a climate that ranges from cold to freezing blizzards.
d Knut Erik Jensen *ph* Svein Krovel, Aslaug Holm *ed* Aslaug Holm
☆ Members of the Berlevåg Male Choir

'Consistently offbeat and entertaining.' – *New York Times*

Heidi *

US 1937 88m bw
TCF (Raymond Griffith)

An orphan is sent to stay with her crusty grandfather in a mountain village.
Star-tailored version of a favourite children's story; just what the box-office ordered at the time.
w Walter Ferris, Julien Josephson *novel* Johanna Spyri *d* Allan Dwan *ph* Arthur Miller *md* Louis Silvers
☆ Shirley Temple, Jean Hersholt, Arthur Treacher, Helen Westley, Pauline Moore, Mary Nash, Thomas Beck, Sidney Blackmer, Mady Christians, Sig Rumann, Marcia Mae Jones, Christian Rub

'Good for the average Temple draw or better.' – *Variety*

Heimat ***

West Germany 1984 924m bw/colour
Edgar Reitz/WDR/SFB

aka: *Homeland*
An epically conceived story of life in a German village between 1919 and 1982.
Essentially a superior soap opera with pretensions of grandeur, this beautifully photographed serial has moments of magic amid much that is merely pretentious and unexplained. Despite the symbolism and the irony (a village idiot is ever present), an eager if arty audience found that it had much to say, though no one could explain its lapses from colour to black-and-white and back again.
w Edgar Reitz, Peter Steinbach *d Edgar Reitz ph Gernot Roll m* Nikos Mamangakis
☆ Marita Breuer, Michael Lesch, Dieter Schaad, Karin Kienzler, Eva Maria Bayerswaltes, Rüdiger Weigang, Karin Rasenach

The Heir to Genghis Khan: see *Storm Over Asia*

'She was taught to love and hate – by masters!'

The Heiress **

US 1949 115m bw
Paramount (William Wyler)

A plain but rich young woman takes revenge on her fortune-seeking lover.
Richly-decorated and generally pleasing version of a stage success based on a Henry James story set in the 1890s.
w Ruth and Augustus Goetz *play Washington Square* by Ruth and Augustus Goetz *novel Washington Square by Henry James d William Wyler ph* Leo Tover *m* Aaron Copland *ad* John Meehan
☆ *Olivia de Havilland*, Ralph Richardson, Montgomery Clift, Miriam Hopkins, Vanessa Brown, Mona Freeman, Ray Collins

'Wyler is that rarest of craftsmen who can take such a drama, already completely fulfilled in theatre terms, and convert it to film without

ever permitting the play-form to dominate the screen.' – *Hermione Isaacs, Films in Review*
🏆 Aaron Copland; Olivia de Havilland; John Meehan
🎖 best picture; William Wyler; Leo Tover; Ralph Richardson

The Heist: see *Dollars*

'It isn't love that makes the world go round.'
'Love makes the world go round. Love of Gold.'

Heist ☆
US/Canada 2001 109m DeLuxe
Warner/Morgan Creek/Franchise/Indelible (Art Linson, Elie Samaha, Andrew Stevens)

A veteran robber is persuaded by a crooked fence to do one last job before retiring.
Enjoyable but thin caper, with a familiar narrative that springs no surprises after the first double-cross.
wd David Mamet *ph* Robert Elswit *m* Theodore Shapiro *pd* David Wasco *ed* Barbara Tulliver
☆ Gene Hackman (Joe Moore), Danny DeVito (Mickey Bergman), Delroy Lindo (Bobby Blane), Sam Rockwell (Jimmy Silk), Rebecca Pidgeon (Fran), Ricky Jay (Pinky Pincus), Patti LuPone (Betty Croft), Jim Frangione (D. A. Freccia)
'I couldn't believe any of it on any level, though it could be described as "fun."' – *Andrew Sarris, New York Observer*
'The kind of caper movie that was made before special effects replaced wit, construction and intelligence. This movie is made out of fresh ingredients, not cake mix.' – *Roger Ebert, Chicago Sun-Times*

'No star ever climbed higher – no woman ever fell lower!'

The Helen Morgan Story
US 1957 118m bw Cinemascope
Warner (Martin Rackin)
GB title: *Both Ends of the Candle*
A young singer rises from vaudeville to Broadway but becomes an alcoholic.
Moderately truthful biopic with effective 20s trimmings.
w Oscar Saul, Dean Riesner, Stephen Longstreet, Nelson Gidding *d* Michael Curtiz *ph* Ted McCord *m* various *ad* John Beckman
☆ Ann Blyth, Paul Newman, Richard Carlson, Gene Evans, Alan King, Cara Williams, Walter Woolf King (Florenz Ziegfeld)
† Ann Blyth's vocals were sung by Gogi Grant.

'All the tumultuous wonder and tremendous drama in the story of history's most famous runaway lovers! Soon the whole world will know of its greatness!'

Helen of Troy
US/Italy 1955 118m Warnercolor Cinemascope
Warner (Robert Wise)

Helen is kidnapped by Paris and regained by use of the Trojan Horse.
Dingy historical spectacular, stultifyingly boring until the final spectacle, with the actors obviously wishing themselves doing anything but mouthing the doggerel dialogue.
w John Twist, Hugh Gray *d* Robert Wise *ph* Harry Stradling *m* Max Steiner *ad* Edward Carrere *ed* Thomas Reilly *cos* Roger Furse
☆ Rossana Podesta (Helen), Jacques Sernas (Paris), Cedric Hardwicke (Priam), Niall MacGinnis (Menelaus), Stanley Baker (Achilles), Nora Swinburne (Hecuba), Robert Douglas (Agamemnon), Torin Thatcher (Odysseus), Harry Andrews (Hector), Janette Scott (Cassandra), Ronald Lewis (Aeneas), Brigitte Bardot (Andraste)

The Helicopter Spies
US 1967 90m Metrocolor
MGM/Arena (Anthony Spinner)
Spies recruit an expert criminal to open a safe containing a thermal prism, or heat ray, that can destroy the world.
The usual comic-strip mad-scientist scenario with two mad scientists, but entertaining in its undemanding way.
w Dean Hargrove *d* Boris Sagal *ph* Fred Koenekamp *m* Richard Shores *ad* George W. Davis, James W. Sullivan *ed* Joseph Dervin, John B. Rogers
☆ Robert Vaughn, David McCallum, Carol Lynley, Bradford Dillman, Lola Albright, John Dehner, John Carradine, Leo G. Carroll, Julie London, H. M. Wynant

Hell and High Water ☆
US 1954 103m Technicolor Cinemascope
TCF (Raymond A. Klune)
A privately-financed anti-Red scientific expedition sets off for Alaska to prevent a Chinese anti-American plot.
Early scoper which mixes deviously plotted schoolboy fiction with submarine spectacle and cold war heroics.
wd Samuel Fuller *ph* Joe MacDonald *m* Alfred Newman
☆ Richard Widmark, Bella Darvi, Victor Francen, David Wayne, Cameron Mitchell, Gene Evans

'Out of the warm arms of women – into the cold grip of the sea!'

Hell Below
US 1933 105m bw
MGM
Tensions mount at a Mediterranean submarine base during World War I.
Adequate war actioner with appropriate trimmings of heroism, tragedy, comedy and romance.
w John Lee Mahin, John Meehan, Laird Doyle, Raymond Schrock *novel* Pigboats by Commander Edward Ellsberg *d* Jack Conway *ph* Harold Rosson
☆ Robert Montgomery, Walter Huston, Madge Evans, Jimmy Durante, Eugene Pallette, Robert Young, Edwin Styles, John Lee Mahin, Sterling Holloway
'Not a two dollar picture, but will be more than oke in the grinds.' – *Variety*

Hell below Zero
GB 1954 91m Technicolor
Columbia/Warwick (Irving Allen, Albert Broccoli)
An American adventurer accompanies the daughter of a whaling captain to the Antarctic to discover who killed her father.
Adequate outdoor thick ear with an unusual setting and lively cast.
w Alec Coppel, Max Trell *novel* The White South by Hammond Innes *d* Mark Robson *ph* John Wilcox *m* Clifton Parker
☆ Alan Ladd, Joan Tetzel, Basil Sydney, Stanley Baker, Jill Bennett, Niall MacGinnis

Hell Bent for Glory: see *Lafayette Escadrille*

Hell Bent for Leather
US 1960 82m Eastmancolor Cinemascope
Universal (Gordon Kay)
An innocent cowboy is accused of murder.
Energetic but unimaginative Western of a man on the run, relying heavily on star appeal.
w Christopher Knopf *novel* Ray Hogan *d* George Sherman *ph* Clifford Stine *m* William Lava, Irving Gertz *ed* Milton Carruth
☆ Audie Murphy (Clay), Felicia Farr (Janet), Stephen McNally (Deckett), Robert Middleton (Ambrose), Rad Fulton (Moon), Jan Merlin (Travers), Herbert Rudley (Perrick), Malcolm Atterbury (Gamble), John Qualen (Old Ben), Bob Steele (Jared)

Hell Boats
GB 1970 95m Technicolor
UA/Oakmont
An American commander with the British navy is assigned to blockade Malta.
Decently made small-scale war epic.
w Anthony Spinner, Donald and Derek Ford *d* Paul Wendkos *ph* Paul Beeson *m* Frank Cordell
☆ James Franciscus, Elizabeth Shepherd, Ronald Allen, Inigo Jackson

Hell Comes to Frogtown
US 1987 82m Technicolor
New World Entertainment (Donald G. Jackson, Randall Frakes)

In the future, one of the few potent men is sent on a mission to rescue women captured by mutants and impregnate them to provide cannon-fodder for another world war.
Adolescent, misogynistic comedy not helped by having a slob as its hero.
w Donald G. Jackson, Randall Frakes *d* R. J. Kizer, Donald G. Jackson *ph* Donald G. Jackson, Enrico Picard *m* David Shapiro *ed* James Metheny, R. J. Kizer
☆ Roddy Piper, Sandahl Bergman, William Smith, Rory Calhoun, Nicholas Worth, Kristi Somers, Cec Verrell

Hell Divers ☆
US 1931 113m bw
MGM
Friendly rivalry exists between two officers in the Naval Air Force.
Routine romantic melodrama with action highlights; a crowdpuller of its day.
w Harvey Gates, Malcolm Stuart Boylan *story* Frank 'Spig' Wead *d* George Hill *ph* Harold Wenstrom
☆ Wallace Beery, Clark Gable, Conrad Nagel, Dorothy Jordan, Marjorie Rambeau, Marie Prévost, Cliff Edwards
'Fine technical naval aviation display, and no story … unusually long on footage and short on entertainment.' – *Variety*
'It's a matter of squadron after squadron of planes, the mechanics attached thereto, the cutting in and around newsreel material, which Metro does so well, and Beery's excellent personal performance.' – *Hollywood Reporter*

Hell Drivers ☆
GB 1957 108m bw Vistavision
Rank/Aqua (Ben Fisz)
Fast driving on death-trap roads is required of rival lorry drivers for a cheapjack haulage firm.
Absurd, violent, hilarious and constantly surprising melodrama with the silliest of premises backed by a good cast and well handled thrill sequences.
w John Kruse, Cy Endfield *d* Cy Endfield *ph* Geoffrey Unsworth *m* Hubert Clifford
☆ Stanley Baker, Patrick McGoohan, Herbert Lom, Peggy Cummins, William Hartnell, Wilfrid Lawson, Sidney James, Jill Ireland, Alfie Bass, Gordon Jackson
'This extraordinary film may interest future historians for its description of road haulage and masculine social behaviour in the mid-20th century … though produced with efficiency and assurance it is disagreeable and occasionally vicious.' – *MFB*

Hell Harbor
US 1930 90m bw
United Artists
Derelicts congregate in a Caribbean harbour.
Low-life dramatics and scenery, but not much story interest.
w Clarke Silvernail *story* Rida Johnson Young *d* Henry King
☆ Lupe Velez, Jean Hersholt, Gibson Gowland, John Holland, Al St John
'Production of great beauty retarded by a story which fails to retain interest.' – *Variety*

Hell, Heaven and Hoboken: see *I Was Monty's Double*

Hell in Korea: see *A Hill in Korea*

Hell in the Heavens
US 1934 79m bw
Fox
In the 1918 air war, an American helps a French unit to get an ace German flyer.
Routine Dawn Patrol stuff which somehow fails to make an impact.
w Byron Morgan, Ted Parsons *play* The Ace by Herman Rossmann *d* John G. Blystone
☆ Warner Baxter, Conchita Montenegro, Herbert Mundin, Russell Hardie, Andy Devine, Ralph Morgan
'Interesting but probably too familiar at this date.' – *Variety*

Hell in the Pacific ☆
US 1969 104m Technicolor Panavision
Cinerama/Selmur (Reuben Bercovitch)

During World War II, an American pilot and a Japanese naval officer who are stranded on the same tiny Pacific island almost become friends.
Highly artificial and pretentious allegorical two-parter which is occasionally well acted and good to look at.
w Alexander Jacobs, Eric Bercovici *d* John Boorman *ph* Conrad Hall *m* Lalo Schifrin
☆ Lee Marvin, Toshiro Mifune
'No real reverberation and no real excitement, intellectual or physical.' – *Tom Milne*

Hell Is a City ☆
GB 1959 93m bw Hammerscope
ABP/Hammer (Michael Carreras)

A jewel thief breaks jail and is hunted by the Manchester police.
Lively semi-documentary, cameo-filled cop thriller filmed on location.
wd Val Guest *novel* Maurice Proctor *ph* Arthur Grant *m* Stanley Black
☆ Stanley Baker, John Crawford, Donald Pleasence, Maxine Audley, Billie Whitelaw, Joseph Tomelty, George A. Cooper, Vanda Godsell
'A hectic pace, with frequent scene changes, mobility of camera and performers, and much rapid, loud, intense dialogue.' – *MFB*

Hell Is for Heroes ☆
US 1962 90m bw
Paramount (Henry Blanke)

In 1944, embittered GIs fight and die while taking a German pillbox near the Siegfried line.
Fairly routine anti-war film with a strong cast and effectively-directed moments battling a generally artificial look.
w Robert Pirosh, Richard Carr *d* Don Siegel *ph* Harold Lipstein *m* Leonard Rosenman
☆ Steve McQueen, Bobby Darin, Fess Parker, James Coburn, Bob Newhart, Harry Guardino

Hell Is Sold Out
GB 1951 84m bw
Zelstro (Raymond Stross)
A novelist returns from the supposed dead to find that a glamorous woman is posing as his widow and issuing best-sellers under his name.
Downright peculiar comedy-drama which never jells for long enough to be enjoyable. ('Hell Is Sold Out' is the title of a book in the story.)
w Guy Morgan, Moie Charles *d* Michael Anderson *ph* Jack Anderson *m* Sonny Miller
☆ Herbert Lom, Mai Zetterling, Richard Attenborough

Hell Night
US 1981 101m Metrocolor
BLT (Irwin Yablans, Bruce Cohn Curtis)

As an initiation ceremony, four students spend a night in an old mansion where 12 years earlier a man murdered his demented wife and deformed children and then committed suicide, witnessed by his mute son, who then disappeared.
Direly unimaginative teen horror, presumably made for the mentally challenged.
w Randolph Feldman *d* Tom de Simone *ph* Mac Ahlberg *m* Dan Wyman *ad* Steven C. Legler *ed* Tony Di Marco *sp* Court Wizard productions; make-up: Kenneth Horn, Tom Schwartz
☆ Linda Blair, Vincent Van Patten, Kevin Brophy, Jenny Neumann, Suki Goodwin, Jimmy Sturtevant, Peter Barton

Hell on Frisco Bay
US 1955 98m Warnercolor Cinemascope
Jaguar (George Berthelon)

An ex-cop sets out to find the man who framed him for manslaughter.
Tedious actioner enlivened by the character parts and a violent climax.
w Sydney Boehm, Martin Rackin *novel* William P. McGivern *d* Frank Tuttle *ph* John Seitz *m* Max Steiner
☆ Alan Ladd, Edward G. Robinson, Joanne Dru, Paul Stewart, William Demarest, Fay Wray

Hell to Eternity
US 1960 132m bw
Allied Artists/Atlantic (Irving H. Levin)
Marine Guy Gabaldon, brought up by Japanese foster parents, has divided loyalties after Pearl Harbor.
Battle-strewn biopic which after two hours seems to lose its point, if it ever had one, but is efficiently made.
w Ted Sherdeman, Walter Roeber Schmidt *d* Phil Karlson *ph* Burnett Guffey *m* Leith Stevens
☆ Jeffrey Hunter, David Janssen, Vic Damone, Patricia Owens, Richard Eyer, Sessue Hayakawa

Hell up in Harlem
US 1973 96m colour
AIP (Larry Cohen)
A gangster attempts to clean up Harlem by killing everyone.
Tediously violent exploitation movie, showing little of its director's usual quirky style.
wd Larry Cohen *ph* Fenton Hamilton *m* Fonce Mizell, Freddie Perren *pd* Larry Lurin *ed* Franco Guerri, Peter Holmes
☆ Fred Williamson, Julius W. Harris, Gloria Hendry, Margaret Avery, D'Urville Martin.
† A sequel to *Black Caesar* (qv).

'They all had something to sell – courage – sex – corruption!'
The Hell with Heroes
US 1968 102m Techniscope
Universal (Stanley Chase)
Air cargo experts find themselves unwittingly smuggling cigarettes into France, and American counter-intelligence steps in.
Unremarkable, totally predictable action melodrama.
w Halsted Welles, Harold Livingston *d* Joseph Sargent *ph* Bud Thackery *m* Quincy Jones
☆ Rod Taylor, Claudia Cardinale, Harry Guardino, Kevin McCarthy, Pete Deuel, William Marshall

Hellbound
US/Canada/Israel 1993 95m colour
Cannon (Anthony Ridio, Dean Ferrandini)
In Chicago, two cops battle against the resurrected emissary of Satan, who has escaped from being entombed for eight hundred years to bring about the final confrontation between good and evil.
Unsuccessful attempt to broaden Chuck Norris's usual limited range, by mixing a conventional buddy movie with even more conventional moments of horror.
w Brent Friedman, Donald C. Thompson *d* Aaron Norris *ph* Joao Fernandes *m* George S. Clinton *pd* Kuly Sander *ed* Michael J. Duthie
☆ Chuck Norris (Shatter), Calvin Levels (Jackson), Sheree J. Wilson (Leslie), Christopher Neame (Lockley), David Robb (King Richard), Cherie Franklin (Captain Hull), Jack Adalist (Krieger), Erez Atar (Bezi)

Hellbound: Hellraiser II
GB 1988 93m Technicolor
Premier Releasing/Film Futures/New World Pictures (Christopher Figg)
A crazed psychiatrist resurrects a dead woman and ventures into hell with her.
Confused and bloody sequel to Hellraiser *(qv).*
w Peter Atkins *story* Clive Barker *d* Tony Randel *ph* Robin Vidgeon *m* Christopher Young *pd* Mike Buchanan *ed* Richard Marden
☆ Clare Higgins, Ashley Laurence, Kenneth Cranham, Imogen Boorman, Sean Chapman, William Hope, Doug Bradley, Barbie Wilde, Simon Bamford, Nicholas Vince

Hellcamp: see *Opposing Force*

Heller in Pink Tights *
US 1960 100m Technicolor Vistavision
Paramount (Carlo Ponti, Marcello Girosi)
Adventures of a dramatic company touring the west in the 1880s.
Genteel spoof Western which does not quite come off.
w Dudley Nichols, Walter Bernstein *novel Heller with a Gun* by Louis L'Amour *d* George Cukor *ph* Harold Lipstein *m* Daniele Amfitheatrof *ad* Hal Pereira, Eugene Allen
☆ Sophia Loren, Anthony Quinn, Steve Forrest, Eileen Heckart, Edmund Lowe, Margaret O'Brien, Ramon Novarro
'It has a welcome individuality which is never quite smothered by its lapses into convention.' – *Penelope Houston*

Heller Wahn: see *Friends and Husbands*

Hellfighters
US 1968 120m Technicolor Panavision
Universal (Robert Arthur)
Oil well fire-fighting specialists have problems among themselves and with their womenfolk.
Ham-fisted story line and performances are slightly, but only slightly, compensated by excellent special effects.
w Clair Huffaker *d* Andrew V. McLaglen *ph* William H. Clothier *m* Leonard Rosenman
☆ John Wayne, Jim Hutton, Katharine Ross, Vera Miles, Jay C. Flippen, Bruce Cabot, Barbara Stuart
'The overall effect is unpardonably tedious.' – *MFB*

The Hellfire Club *
GB 1960 93m Eastmancolor Dyaliscope
Regal/New World (Robert S. Baker, Monty Berman)
In the 18th century, a nobleman's child escapes from his degenerate father, joins a travelling circus, and later returns to claim his inheritance.
Sprightly historical romantic melodrama lightly based on the nefarious activities of the real Hellfire Club; energetic and entertaining if slightly too jokey.
w Leon Griffiths, Jimmy Sangster *m* Clifton Parker *d/ph* Robert S. Baker, Monty Berman
☆ *Keith Michell, Peter Arne,* Adrienne Corri, Kai Fischer, Bill Owen, Peter Cushing, David Lodge, Francis Matthews

The Hellhounds of Alaska (dubbed)
West Germany 1973 90m colour
A fur-trapper solves a mystery of a missing gold shipment and a lost child.
A snow- and cliché-bound Western, attempting the baroque style of the Italians and missing it entirely.
w Johannes Weiss *d* Harald Reinl *ph* Heinz Hölscher *m* Bruno Nicolai *ad* Zeljko Senecic *ed* Eva Zeyn
☆ Doug McClure, Harald Leipnitz, Angelica Ott, Roberto Blanco, Kristina Nel, Klaus Löwitsch, Kurt Bülau, Heinz Reincke

The Hellions
GB 1961 80m Technirama
Columbia/Irving Allen, Jamie Uys (Harold Huth)
In the 1860s, a family of South African outlaws starts a reign of terror in a small village.
A British attempt to restage the OK Corral; it goes sadly awry.
w Harold Swanton, Patrick Kirwan, Harold Huth *d* Ken Annakin *ph* Ted Moore *m* Larry Adler
☆ Richard Todd, Lionel Jeffries, James Booth, Jamie Uys, Ronald Fraser, Anne Aubrey, Zena Walker, Marty Wilde, Colin Blakely
'Unconvincingly staged and plotted, tediously violent, uncertainly directed and very badly acted.' – *MFB*

Hello Again
US 1987 96m colour
Warner/Touchstone (Frank Perry)
A year after dying, a housewife is brought back by her sister, a medium, to discover that life has changed in her absence.
Moribund comedy that fails to get much mileage from its material.
w Susan Isaacs *d* Frank Perry *ph* Jan Weincke *m* William Goldstein *pd* Edward Pisoni *ed* Peter C. Frank, Trudy Ship
☆ Shelley Long, Judith Ivey, Thor Fields, Corbin Bernsen, Gabriel Byrne, Sela Ward, Austin Pendleton, Carrie Nye

Hello Beautiful: see *The Powers Girl*

Hello Dolly **
US 1969 129m DeLuxe Todd-AO
TCF/Chenault (Ernest Lehman)
In 1890 New York, a widowed matchmaker has designs on a wealthy grain merchant.
Generally agreeable but overblown musical based on a slight but much worked-over farce, fatally compromised by the miscasting of a too-young star. Some exhilarating moments.
w Ernest Lehman *play The Matchmaker* by *Thornton Wilder musical Jerry Herman d Gene Kelly ph Harry Stradling md* Lennie Hayton, Lionel Newman *ch Michael Kidd pd John DeCuir m/l Michael Stewart (book)*
☆ Barbra Streisand, Walter Matthau, *Michael Crawford, Marianne McAndrew,* E. J. Peaker, Tommy Tune, David Hurst
'The film leaves an oddly negative impression; a good deal of synthetic effervescence … but very little real vitality.' – *David Wilson*
† Carol Channing, Ginger Rogers and Betty Grable all fought to get the title role.
music direction; art direction; sound (Jack Solomon, Murray Spivack)
best picture; photography

Hello Down There
US 1969 98m Eastmancolor
MGM (Ivan Tors)
The designer of an underwater house volunteers to live in it for a month.
Curious comedy with predictable obstacles to the happy ending.
w Frank Telford, John McGreevey *d* Jack Arnold *ph* Cliff Poland *m* Jeff Barry
☆ Tony Randall, Janet Leigh, Jim Backus, Roddy McDowall, Merv Griffin, Ken Berry, Richard Dreyfuss

Hello Frisco Hello *
US 1943 98m Technicolor
TCF (Milton Sperling)
On the Barbary Coast, a girl singer becomes a star.
Moderately pleasing period musical with plenty going on but nothing very striking.
w Robert Ellis, Helen Logan, Richard Macaulay *d* H. Bruce Humberstone *ph* Charles Clarke, Allen Davey *m/ly* various *ad James Basevi, Boris Leven*
☆ Alice Faye, John Payne, Jack Oakie, Lynn Bari, Laird Cregar, June Havoc, Ward Bond, Aubrey Mather, George Barbier, Frank Orth
song 'You'll Never Know' (*m* Harry Warren, *ly* Mack Gordon)
Charles Clarke, Allen Davey

Hello Goodbye
US 1970 101m DeLuxe
TCF (André Hakim)
A cheerful young Englishman falls for a mysterious Frenchwoman who turns out to be the wife of a Baron.
Modest, aimless, forgettable romantic comedy, full of old-fashioned clichés imperfectly remembered.
w Roger Marshall *d* Jean Negulesco *ph Henri Decaë m* Francis Lai *pd* John Howell *ad* Auguste Capelier
☆ Michael Crawford, Geneviève Gilles, Curt Jurgens, Ira Furstenberg

Hello Hemingway **
Cuba 1990 88m colour
Metro/ICAIC (Ricardo Guila)
In the 1950s a teenage girl from a poor Havana family enters an examination to win a scholarship to an American university.
Modest and enjoyable movie that marries Hemingway's The Old Man and the Sea *to a narrative of adolescent striving.*
w Maydo Royero *d* Fernando Perez *ph* Julio Valdes *m* Edesio Alejandro *ad* Onelio Larraldi *ed* Jorge Abello
☆ Laura de la Uz, Raul Paz, Herminia Sanchez, Caridad Hernandez, Enrique Molina, Maria Isabel Diaz, Marta Del Rio, Micheline Calvert
'A thoughtful, lovely little film.' – *Variety*

Hello Sister *
US 1933 62m bw
Fox (Winfield Sheehan)
aka: *Walking Down Broadway*
Boy meets girl in New York.
A mild little romance, only notable because it was edited down from an original by Erich von Stroheim, and touches of his work remain.
w Erich von Stroheim, Leonard Spigelgass *novel* Dawn Powell *d* Erich von Stroheim, Alfred Werker *ph* James Wong Howe
☆ James Dunn, Boots Mallory, ZaSu Pitts, Minna Gombell

Hellraiser
GB 1987 93m Technicolor
Cannon/Film Futures/New World Entertainment (Christopher Figg)
A woman tries to bring back her lover from the tortures of hell.
Gloatingly sadistic and unnecessarily gory horror movie.
wd Clive Barker *novel The Hellbound Heart* by Clive Barker *ph* Robin Vidgeon *m* Christopher Young *ad* Jocelyn James *ed* Richard Marden
☆ Andrew Robinson, Clare Higgins, Ashley Laurence, Sean Chapman, Oliver Smith, Robert Hines, Antony Allen, Leon Davis, Michael Cassidy
† It was followed by a sequel, *Hellbound: Hellraiser II* (qv).

Hellraiser: Bloodline
US 1995 85m CFI color
Dimension/Trans Atlantic/Clive Barker (Nancy Rae Stone)
In the past, present and future, members of the same family exhibit the power to summon demons from hell.
A feeble horror movie that attempts to compensate for its many failings with an excess of gore; it is yet another example of a series that has lost its way, bereft of ideas and imagination.
w Peter Atkins *d* Alan Smithee (Kevin Yeager) *ph* Gary Lively *m* Daniel Licht *pd* Ivo Cristante *ed* Ron Dean, Randolph K. Bricker *sp* Kevin Yeager; make-up: Gary Tunnicliffe
☆ Bruce Ramsay, Valentina Vargas, Doug Bradley, Kim Myers, Christine Harnos, Charlotte Chatton, Paul Perri, Mickey Cotrell
'Except for the most undiscriminating gorehound, pic is a pointless mess.' – *Variety*

'What Began In Hell Will End On Earth.'
Hellraiser III: Hell on Earth
US 1992 93m colour
Arrow/Nostradamus (Lawrence Mortorff)
A television journalist battles with Pinhead, a creature from hell.
Gore-filled horror, in which the main intention seems to be to create in Pinhead a demonic figure capable of sustaining a long-running series of such movies.
w Peter Atkins *story* Peter Atkins, Tony Randel *d* Anthony Hickox *ph* Gerry Lively *m* Randy Miller, Christopher Young *pd* Steve Hardie *ed* Christopher Cibelli, James D. R. Hickox *sp* Bob Keen; Cinema Research Corporation
☆ Terry Farrell, Doug Bradley, Paula Marshall, Kevin Bernhardt, Ken Carpenter, Peter Boynton, Aimee Leigh, Lawrence Mortorff
'Film's extremely grotesque gore effects and negative tone will turn off mainstream viewers but hold a hypnotic appeal for hardcore horror aficionados.' – *Variety*
'It is competent and accomplishes the small feat of being better than its predecessor.' – *Sheila Johnston, Independent*

Hell's Angels ***
US 1930 135m bw (colour sequences)
Howard Hughes
Two Americans become flyers in World War I.
Celebrated early talkie spectacular, with zeppelin and flying sequences that still thrill. The dialogue is another matter, but all told this expensive production, first planned as a silent, is a milestone of cinema history.
w Howard Estabrook, Harry Behn *d Howard Hughes ph Tony Gaudio, Harry Perry, E. Burton Steene m* Hugo Reisenfeld
☆ Ben Lyon, James Hall, Jean Harlow, John Darrow, Lucien Prival
'That it will ever pay off for its producer is doubtful … he's in so deep it can't really matter to him now. Minus blue nose interference, it can't miss, but it's up to the brim with sex.' – *Variety*
'It is not great, but it is as lavish as an eight-ring circus, and when you leave the theatre you will know you have seen a movie and not a tinny reproduction of a stage show.' – *Pare Lorentz*
† The film was reissued in 1940 in a 96m version which has not survived.
Tony Gaudio, Harry Perry, E. Burton Steene

Hells Angels on Wheels
US 1967 95m Eastmancolor
Fanfare (Joe Solomon)
A sacked petrol station attendant joins the Hells Angels for a violent ride across country.
Cheap biker movie, lacking plot and maintaining momentum with fights and parties; it employs actual Hells Angels but still achieves an ersatz feeling, perhaps because they cannot act, and Nicholson looks too old for his role as an inexperienced new recruit to the gang.
w R. Wright Campbell *d* Richard Rush *ph* Leslie Kovacs (Laszlo Kovacs) *m* Stu Phillips *ed* William Martin
☆ Adam Roarke, Jack Nicholson, Sabrina Scharf, Jana Taylor, Richard Anders, John Garwood, I. J. Jefferson, Jack Starrett, Sonny Barger
† The British video release was cut to 80m.

Hell's Half Acre
US 1953 91m bw
Republic
A soldier missing after Pearl Harbor turns up years later in Hawaii under a different identity.
Complex melodrama ending in self-sacrifice; amusing bits don't make it hang together.
w Steve Fisher *d* John H. Auer
☆ Wendell Corey, Evelyn Keyes, Elsa Lanchester, Nancy Gates, Philip Ahn, Keye Luke

Hell's Heroes
US 1930 65m bw
Universal
Three cowboys find an abandoned baby.
Yet another version of Three Godfathers; *maybe not the best but the shortest.*
w Tom Reed *novel* Peter Kyne *d* William Wyler *ph* George Robinson
☆ Charles Bickford, Raymond Hatton, Fred Kohler, Fritzi Ridgeway
† Photographed in the Mojave and Panamint Deserts.

Hell's Highway *
US 1932 62m bw
RKO
A convict plans escape from a forced labour gang, under the threat of the lash and the sweatbox.
Well-made but heavy-going melodrama without light relief.
w Samuel Ornitz, Robert Tasker, Rowland Brown *d* Rowland Brown
☆ Richard Dix, Rochelle Hudson, Tom Brown, C. Henry Gordon, Louise Carter
'The story is too sodden to carry a general appeal.' – *Variety*

Hell's House
US 1932 72m bw
Capital Films
A boy is wrongly sentenced to a corrupt reform school.
Primitive cheapie notable only for the early appearance of Bette Davis.
w Paul Gangelin, B. Harrison Orkow *d* Howard Higgin *ph* Alan Siegler
☆ Bette Davis, Pat O'Brien, Junior Durkin, Junior Coghlan, Emma Dunn, Charley Grapewin

Hell's Island *
US 1955 84m Technicolor Vistavision
Paramount/Pine-Thomas
Crooks congregate on a Caribbean island in search of a famous ruby.
Cheeky rehash of The Maltese Falcon, *not bad in its own routine way.*
w Maxwell Shane *d* Phil Karlson *ph* Lionel Lindon *md* Irvin Talbot
☆ John Payne, Mary Murphy, *Francis L. Sullivan*, Arnold Moss

Hell's Kitchen
US 1939 82m bw
Warner (Mark Hellinger, Bryan Foy)
Boys revolt under the cruel headmaster of a reformatory.
Dreary vehicle for the Dead End Kids.
w Crane Wilbur, Fred Niblo Jnr *d* Lewis Seiler, E. A. Dupont *ph* Charles Rosher *ad* Hugh Reticker *ed* Clarence Kolster
☆ Billy Halop, Leo Gorcey, Bobby Jordan, Huntz Hall, Gabriel Dell, Bernard Punsley, Ronald Reagan, Margaret Lindsay, Stanley Fields, Grant Mitchell
'A quagmire of misplaced sentimentality hokum and general incredulousness.' – *Variety*

The Hellstrom Chronicle
US 1971 90m CFI color
David Wolper
A scientist explains the range and variety of insect life.
Odd documentary in fictional bookends; smart and quite sensational for those with strong stomachs.
w David Seltzer *d* Walon Green
☆ Lawrence Pressman (Nils Hellstrom)
best documentary

Hellzapoppin ***
US 1942 84m bw
Universal/Mayfair (Glenn Tryon, Alex Gottlieb)
Two incompetent comics make a picture.
Zany modification of a smash burlesque revue; the crazy jokes are toned down and a romantic interest is added (and tentatively sent up). The result is patchy but often hilarious, and the whole is a handy consensus of forties humour and pop music.
w Nat Perrin, Warren Wilson *d H. C. Potter* *ph* Woody Bredell *m* Frank Skinner *md* Charles Previn *ed* Milton Carruth
☆ *Ole Olsen, Chic Johnson, Hugh Herbert, Martha Raye, Mischa Auer*, Robert Paige, Jane Frazee, Shemp Howard, Elisha Cook Jnr, Richard Lane
'Alive with good gags, mechanical surprise effects, and novelty touches.' – *CEA Report*
† The Frankenstein monster and Man Who Falls into Pool were played by Dale Van Sickel.

Help! *
GB 1965 92m Eastmancolor
UA/Walter Shenson/Suba Films
An oriental high priest chases the Beatles around the world because one of them has a sacred ring.
Exhausting attempt to outdo A Hard Day's Night *in lunatic frenzy, which goes to prove that some talents work better on low budgets. The humour is a frantic cross between* Hellzapoppin, *the Goons, Bugs Bunny and the shade of Monty Python to come. It looks good but becomes too tiresome to entertain.*
w Charles Wood, Marc Behm *d* Richard Lester *ph David Watkin* *m Ken Thorne, The Beatles* *ad Ray Simm* *ed* John Victor Smith
☆ John Lennon (John), Paul McCartney (Paul), George Harrison (George), Ringo Starr (Ringo), Leo McKern (Clang), Eleanor Bron (Ahme), Victor Spinetti (Foot), Roy Kinnear (Algernon), John Bluthal (Bhuta), Patrick Cargill (Superintendent)

Help! I'm a Fish: see *Hjaelp! Jeg er en Fisk*

Helpmates ***
US 1932 20m bw
Hal Roach
Stan helps Ollie clean up after a wild party while the wife was away.
A brilliant succession of catastrophe gags in the stars' best tradition.
w H. M. Walker *d* James Parrott *ph* Art Lloyd *ed* Richard Currier
☆ Stan Laurel, Oliver Hardy, Blanche Payson, Robert Callahan

Helter Skelter
GB 1949 75m bw
GFD/Gainsborough (Anthony Darnborough)
An heiress with hiccups is helped by the staff of the BBC.
Scatty comedy which tries everything, from custard pies and guest stars to a clip from a silent Walter Forde comedy. It isn't the British Hellzapoppin it sets out to be, but hardened buffs will find it worth a look.
w Patrick Campbell *d* Ralph Thomas *ph* Jack Asher *m* Francis Chagrin
☆ Carol Marsh, David Tomlinson, Mervyn Johns, Peter Hammond, Jimmy Edwards, Richard Hearne, Jon Pertwee, Terry-Thomas

Helter Skelter
US 1976 92m Movielab
Hemdale/Lorimar (Tom Gries)
Charles Manson and his followers are charged with the murders of actress Sharon Tate and others.
Dull re-telling of a horrific series of killings from the viewpoint of the prosecutor.
w J. P. Miller *book The Manson Murders* by Vincent Bugliosi with Curt Gentry *d* Tom Gries *ph* Jules Brenner *m* Billy Goldenberg *ad* Phil Barber *ed* Bud S. Isaacs, Byron 'Buzz' Brandt
☆ George DiCenzo, Steve Railsback, Nancy Wolf, Marilyn Burns, Christina Hart, Cathey Paine
† The film was an edited version of an 194m TV mini-series.

Hemingway's Adventures of a Young Man *
US 1962 145m DeLuxe Cinemascope
TCF (Jerry Wald)
aka: *Adventures of a Young Man*
The son of a weak doctor and a religious mother breaks away from his family circle on a voyage of discovery.
Curious mélange of ill-assimilated Hemingway stories based on his Nick Adams character. The film has good intentions but no shape or style, and the guest stars don't help.
w A. E. Hotchner *stories* Ernest Hemingway *d* Martin Ritt *ph* Lee Garmes *m* Franz Waxman
☆ Richard Beymer, Diane Baker, Corinne Calvet, Fred Clark, Dan Dailey, James Dunn, Juano Hernandez, Arthur Kennedy, Ricardo Montalban, Susan Strasberg, Paul Newman, Jessica Tandy, Eli Wallach

'They had killed a woman and destroyed his life. Now he will kill a woman and destroy their nation!'
Hennessy
GB 1975 104m colour
AIP/Marseilles (Peter Snell)
Angered at the death of his family in the Belfast troubles, an Irish revolutionary hurries to London to blow up the Houses of Parliament.
Unattractive, uninventive thriller with a silly script and not an ounce of real suspense.
w John Gay *story* Richard Johnson *d* Don Sharp *ph* Ernest Steward *m* John Scott *pd* Ray Simm
☆ Rod Steiger, Richard Johnson, Lee Remick, Trevor Howard, Eric Porter, Peter Egan, David Collings

Henry Aldrich
Henry was originally a radio character created by Ezra Stone, an awkward small-town youth who like Andy Hardy was always getting into scrapes. Clifford Goldsmith wrote the original play which hit Broadway as well as the radio waves before starting a Hollywood series of amiable Paramount second features, most of them starring Jimmy Lydon with Charles Smith as his friend Dizzy.
1939 What a Life (with Jackie Cooper)
1941 Life with Henry (with Jackie Cooper), Henry Aldrich for President
1942 Henry and Dizzy, Henry Aldrich Editor
1943 Henry Aldrich Gets Glamour, Henry Aldrich Swings It, Henry Aldrich Haunts a House
1944 Henry Aldrich Boy Scout, Henry Aldrich Plays Cupid, Henry Aldrich's Little Secret

Henry and June *
US 1990 136m colour
UIP/Universal/Walrus & Associates (Peter Kaufman)
Anais Nin, married to a banker, has affairs with the writer Henry Miller and his wife.
Complex film of shifting relationships and their transmutation into literature, graphically portrayed.
w Philip Kaufman, Rose Kaufman *book* Anais Nin *d* Philip Kaufman *ph* Philippe Rousselot *m* Mark Adler *pd* Guy-Claude François *ed* Vivien Hillgrove, William S. Scharf, Dede Allen
☆ Fred Ward, Uma Thurman, Maria de Medeiros, Richard E. Grant, Kevin Spacey, Jean-Philippe Ecoffey, Bruce Myers, Jean-Louis Buñuel, Feodor Atkine
'It's like a well-wrapped and luxurious parcel that contains just what you don't want for Christmas.' – *Derek Malcolm, Guardian*
Philippe Rousselot

Henry Fool *
US 1997 141m DuArt
True Fiction/Shooting Gallery (Hal Hartley)
A stranger arrives in a small town and changes the life of a garbage collector and his sister.
Eccentric comedy of liberation that ends up nowhere in particular but provides pleasures along the way.
wd Hal Hartley *ph* Mike Spiller *m* Hal Hartley *pd* Steve Rosenzweig *ed* Steve Hamilton
☆ Thomas Jay Ryan, James Urbaniak, Parker Posey, Maria Porter, James Saito, Kevin Corrigan, Liam Aiken, Miho Nikaido, Gene Riffini, Nicholas Hope, Diana Ruppe
'Poetic, bawdy, contemplative, often side-wrenchingly funny and finally quite touching.' – *Derek Elley, Variety*

Henry Nine Till Five *
GB 1970 6m colour
British Lion
A commuter spends his working days fantasizing about sex.
Typical and very lively cartoon.
w Stan Heyward *d* Bob Godfrey

Henry: Portrait of a Serial Killer **
US 1990 83m colour
Electric/Maljack (John McNaughton, Lisa Dedmond, Steven A. Jones)
Documentary-style account of the life and methods of a motiveless mass murderer.
Oddly compelling, it is often hard to watch because of its violence and, perversely, hard not to watch.
w Richard Fire, John McNaughton *d* John McNaughton *ph* Charlie Lieberman *m* John McNaughton, Ken Hale, Steven A. Jones *pd* Rick Paul *ed* Elena Maganini
☆ Michael Rooker, Tom Towles, Tracy Arnold
'A film of clutching terror that's meant to heighten our awareness instead of dulling it ... This film gives off a dark chill that follows you all the way home.' – *Peter Travers, Rolling Stone*

Henry V ****
GB 1944 137m Technicolor
Rank/Two Cities (Laurence Olivier)
Shakespeare's historical play is seen in performance at the Globe Theatre in 1603; as it develops, the scenery becomes more realistic.
Immensely stirring, experimental and almost wholly successful production of Shakespeare on film, sturdy both in its stylization and its command of more conventional cinematic resources for the battle.
w Laurence Olivier, Alan Dent *play* William Shakespeare *d Laurence Olivier* *ph Robert Krasker* *m William Walton* *ad Paul Sheriff, Carmen Dillon* *ed* Reginald Beck
☆ Laurence Olivier (Henry V), *Robert Newton* (Pistol), *Leslie Banks* (Chorus), *Esmond Knight* (Fluellen), Renée Asherson (Katherine), George Robey (Falstaff), *Leo Genn* (Constable of France), Ernest Thesiger (Duke of Beri), Ivy St Helier (Alice), Ralph Truman (Mountjoy), Harcourt Williams, Max Adrian, Valentine Dyall (Duke of Burgundy), Felix Aylmer (Archbishop of Canterbury), John Laurie and also Roy Emerton, Michael Shepley, George Cole
'His production – it was his first time out as a director – is a triumph of colour, music, spectacle, and soaring heroic poetry, and, as actor, he brings lungs, exultation, and a bashful wit to the role.' – *Pauline Kael, 70s*
'What Shakespeare wrote in *Henry V*, and what the film has splendidly caught in its own fashion, is a fanfare; a flourish; a salute to high adventure; a kind of golden and perennially youthful exaltation of man's grim work.' – *C. A. Lejeune*
Special Award to Laurence Olivier
best picture; William Walton; Laurence Olivier (as actor); art direction

Henry V ***
GB 1989 137m Technicolor
Curzon/Renaissance Films (Bruce Sharman)
After his claim to the throne of France is refused, King Henry invades the country and wins a famous victory.
A darker film than Olivier's, with which it can stand comparison, stressing the brutality of war.
w Kenneth Branagh *play* William Shakespeare *d Kenneth Branagh* *ph* Kenneth MacMillan *m* Patrick Doyle *pd* Tim Harvey *ed* Mike Bradsell
☆ Kenneth Branagh (Henry V), Derek Jacobi (Chorus), Simon Shepherd (Gloucester), James Larkin (Bedford), Brian Blessed (Exeter), James Simmons (York), Paul Gregory (Westmoreland), Charles Kay (Archbishop of Canterbury), Alec McCowen (Bishop of Ely), Edward Jewesbury, Ian Holm, Michael Williams, Geoffrey Hutchings, Robert Stephens, Judi Dench and also Paul Scofield, Harold Innocent, Emma Thompson, Geraldine McEwan
'The film's visual tedium, vulgarity and musical mediocrity would be more bearable if Branagh himself were a more persuasive lead actor.' – *MFB*

'The more I thought about it, the more convinced I became that here was a play to be reclaimed from jingoism and its World War Two associations.' – *Kenneth Branagh*
best costume design (Phyllis Dalton)
Kenneth Branagh (as best actor and best director)
Kenneth Branagh (as director)

Henry VIII and His Six Wives *
GB 1972 125m Technicolor
EMI (Roy Baird)
Dullish historical account of the king's reign, staged as recollections from his deathbed but lacking any of the sparkle of *The Private Life of Henry VIII* made forty years previously.
Accurate sets and costumes fail to compensate for lack of film flair.
w Ian Thorne *d* Waris Hussein *ph* Peter Suschitzky *m* David Munro
☆ *Keith Michell* (Henry VIII), Frances Cuka (Aragon), Charlotte Rampling (Boleyn), Jane Asher (Seymour), Jenny Bos (Cleves), Lynne Frederick (Howard), Barbara Leigh-Hunt (Parr), Donald Pleasence (Thomas Cromwell)
† The production was stimulated by a highly successful BBC TV series, *The Six Wives of Henry VIII.*

Her Alibi
US 1989 94m colour
Warner (Keith Barish)
A thriller writer provides a false alibi for a woman accused of murder.
A romantic comedy without laughs or much love.
w Charlie Peters *d* Bruce Beresford *ph* Freddie Francis *m* Georges Delerue *pd* Henry Bumstead *ed* Anne Goursaud
☆ Tom Selleck, Paulina Porizkova, William Daniels, James Farentino, Hurd Hatfield, Ronald Guttman, Victor Argo, Patrick Wayne, Tess Harper
'Lacking a script able to go beyond the obvious, and direction able to make up for the lack of wit and sophistication.' – *MFB*

Her Cardboard Lover *
US 1942 93m bw
MGM (J. Walter Ruben)
A flirtatious lady hires a lover to make her fiancé jealous.
Paper-thin comedy previously filmed in 1932 with Buster Keaton. It did nobody any good, but preserves some style despite a witless script.
w Jacques Deval, John Collier, Anthony Veiller, William H. Wright *play* Jacques Deval *d* George Cukor *ph* Harry Stradling, Robert Planck *m* Franz Waxman
☆ Norma Shearer, Robert Taylor, George Sanders, Frank McHugh, Elizabeth Patterson, Chill Wills

Her Highness and the Bellboy
US 1945 112m bw
MGM (Joe Pasternak)
A hotel bellboy forsakes his crippled sweetheart to woo a visiting princess.
Glutinous sentimental mishmash; one waits for musical numbers which never happen.
w Richard Connell, Gladys Lehman *d* Richard Thorpe *ph* Harry Stradling *m* Georgie Stoll
☆ Hedy Lamarr, Robert Walker, June Allyson, Rags Ragland, Agnes Moorehead, Carl Esmond, Warner Anderson, Ludwig Stossel

Her Husband's Affairs *
US 1947 83m bw
Columbia (Raphael Hakim)
A husband and wife team of advertising agents promote a depilatory which turns out to grow hair instead.
Mildly amiable crazy comedy.
w Ben Hecht *d* S. Sylvan Simon *ph* Charles Lawton Jnr *m* George Duning
☆ Lucille Ball, Franchot Tone, Edward Everett Horton, Mikhail Rasumny, Gene Lockhart, Nana Bryant, Jonathan Hale, Mabel Paige

'See the mystical hypnotic rites of the white goddess of the jungle! See the plane crash in the tragic typhoon! See the ravening charge of the hundred sacred crocodiles!'
Her Jungle Love *
US 1938 81m Technicolor
Paramount (George M. Arthur)
An aviator crashlands in the jungle, where he is comforted by a lovely lady, a chimp and a lion but distressed by an earthquake, a volcano and assorted villains.
Second of Dorothy Lamour's jungle hokum shows, and the first in colour; despite its fair technical proficiency, the fact that it once packed 'em in is tribute to the changing tastes of mankind.
w Joseph M. March, Lillie Hayward, Eddie Welch *d* George Archainbaud *ph* Ray Rennahan *m* Gregory Stone
☆ Dorothy Lamour, Ray Milland, Lynne Overman, J. Carrol Naish, Dorothy Howe
'Splendid colour job, but there's little more ... only slightly varied from the type of a bygone era.' – *Variety*
† The Lynne Overman character wisecracks: 'Those *Esquire* cartoons must be right: there's always just one girl on a desert island.'
†† The lion cub in this case is called Meewa, the chimp Gaga.

Her Majesty Love
US 1931 76m bw
Warner
A well-born Berliner finds it easier to court the barmaid he loves after she has married a baron.
Heavy-handed musical comedy worth excavating for the odd talents involved.
w Robert Lord, Arthur Caesar *d* William Dieterle
☆ Marilyn Miller, Ben Lyon, W. C. Fields, Leon Errol, Chester Conklin, Ford Sterling
'An exceptionally dismal musical.' – *Clive Hirschhorn, 1983*

Her Man Gilbey: see *English without Tears*

Her Panelled Door: see *The Woman with No Name*

Her Twelve Men
US 1954 91m Anscocolor
MGM (John Houseman)
A woman teacher in a boys' school reforms a difficult class.
Predictable, sugary and artificial school story with the star exuding sweetness and light.
w William Roberts, Laura Z. Hobson *d* Robert Z. Leonard *ph* Joseph Ruttenberg *m* Bronislau Kaper
☆ Greer Garson, Robert Ryan, Richard Haydn, Barry Sullivan

Her Wedding Night
US 1930 78m bw
Paramount
On the Italian riviera a man marries his friend's wife under the impression that they are only booking rooms for the night.
Spicy bedroom farce which crested the wave of its star's notoriety.
w Henry Myers *play* Avery Hopwood *d* Frank Tuttle
☆ Clara Bow, *Charles Ruggles*, Ralph Forbes, Skeets Gallagher
'Deftly handled for smartness and taste ... ought to make women talk.' – *Variety*

Herbie Goes Bananas
US 1980 100m Technicolor
Walt Disney
Two Americans take their magical Volkswagen on a South American holiday.
Listless addition to a series which has already gone on too long.
w Don Tait *d* Vincent McEveety
☆ Charles Martin Smith, Stephan W. Burns, Cloris Leachman, John Vernon

Herbie Goes to Monte Carlo
US 1977 105m Technicolor
Walt Disney (Ron Miller)
The Volkswagen with a mind of its own enters the Monte Carlo rally and routs a gang of thieves.
Utterly predictable, patchily made family comedy.
w Arthur Alsberg, Don Nelson *d* Vincent McEveety *ph* Leonard J. South *m* Frank de Vol
☆ Dean Jones, Don Knotts, Julie Sommars, Jacques Marin, Roy Kinnear, Bernard Fox
† Second sequel to *The Love Bug.*

Herbie Rides Again
US 1974 88m Technicolor
Walt Disney (Bill Walsh)
A Volkswagen with a mind of its own helps an old lady to rout a property developer.
Acceptable sequel to The Love Bug.
w Bill Walsh *d* Robert Stevenson *ph* Frank Phillips *m* George Bruns
☆ Helen Hayes, Ken Berry, Stefanie Powers, John McIntire, Keenan Wynn, Huntz Hall

Hercules
Italy 1959 105m Eastmancolor
Dyaliscope
Oscar/Galatea (Federico Teti)
original title: *Le Fatiche di Ercole*
Hercules helps Jason find the golden fleece.
The strong man epic which started a genre; of little interest in itself.
w Pietro Francisci, Ennio de Concini, Gaio Frattini *d* Pietro Francisci *ph* Mario Bava *m* Enzo Masetti
☆ Steve Reeves, Sylva Koscina, Gianna Maria Canale, Fabrizio Mione

'The man. The myth. The movie.'
Hercules *
US 1997 92m Technicolor
Buena Vista/Walt Disney (Alice Dewey, John Musker, Ron Clements)
Hercules, son of Zeus, is kidnapped by the minions of Hades, ruler of the underworld, and brought up as a mortal; he can only become a god again if he proves himself a hero.
Those with a classical education, or a knowledge of Greek myths, will wince at the crassness of this cartoon feature, though it looks good and provides intermittent pleasures.
w Ron Clements, John Musker, Bob Shaw, Donald McEnery, Irene Mecchi *d* John Musker, Ron Clements *m* Alan Menken *m/ly* Alan Menken, David Zippel *pd* Gerald Scarfe *ed* Tom Finan, Jeff Jones, John K. Carr
☆ Featuring the voices of: Tate Donovan, Danny DeVito, James Woods, John Keaton, Roger Bart, Susan Egan, Bobcat Goldthwait, Matt Frewer, Rip Torn, Samantha Eggar, Barbara Barrie, Hal Holbrook, Charlton Heston (narrator)
'A winning tale, cleverly told and wonderfully voiced.' – *Variety*
'This is Disney's weakest score in a decade and, although the visual style of the picture has a rare distinction, that's not enough to damp down the feeling that the company's run of animated hits is coming to a close.' – *Mark Steyn, Spectator*
† The film grossed some $99m in the US and another $229m elsewhere.
song 'Go the Distance' (*m/ly* Alan Menken, David Zippel)

Hercules against Rome (dubbed)
France/Italy 1965 87m Eastmancolor
Totalscope
Romana/Regina (Fortunato Misiano)
original title: *Ercole contro Roma*
aka: *Hercules in Rome*
Hercules, a blacksmith, goes to the aid of the daughter of the Emperor, in the power of the commander of the Praetorian Guard.
Standard muscle-bound epic, with our hero fighting, not too convincingly, against state corruption.
w Piero Pierotti, Arpad de Riso *story* Arpad de Riso, Nino Scolaro *d* Piero Pierotti *ph* Augusto Tiezzi *m* A. F. Lavagnino *ad* Salvatore Giancotti *ed* Iolanda Benvenuti *d (US version)* Robert Spafford
☆ Alan Steel, Wandisa Guida, Daniele Vargas, Livio Lorenzon, Andrea Aureli, Dina de Santis, Mimmo Palmara

Hercules Goes Bananas: see *Hercules in New York*

Hercules in New York
US 1969 91m Eastmancolor
RAF Industries (Aubrey Wisberg)
aka: *Hercules Goes Bananas*
aka: *Hercules – the Movie*
Hercules drops in on modern-day New York and becomes involved with wrestlers and gamblers.
Schwarzenegger's first film, a dim comedy – and one that no doubt returns to haunt him, particularly his dubbed all-American high tenor voice and the way his muscles do the acting.
w Aubrey Wisberg *d* Arthur A. Seidelman *ph* Leo Lebowitz *m* John Balamos *ad* Perry Watkins *ed* Donald Finamore
☆ Arnold Stang, Arnold Strong (later Schwarzenegger), Deborah Loomis, James Karen, Ernest Graves, Tanny McDonald, Taina Elg, Michael Lipton
'Schwarzenegger as Herc wrestled with a man in a bear suit and when I tell you that the suit was a better actor you will have some conception.' – *Nancy Banks-Smith, Guardian*

Hercules in Rome: see *Hercules against Rome*

Hercules Returns
Australia 1993 80m colour
Metro Tartan/Philm (Philip Jaroslow)
Film enthusiasts reopen a cinema with the last film it showed 30 years before, an Italian muscle-man epic, but, discovering the soundtrack is in Italian, they are forced to dub it in English as it is screened.
An opened-out movie version of an apparently popular live performance by Double Take (Des Mangan and Sally Patience), who improvise new dialogue to bad old films, a joke that requires more wit than is on display here.
w Des Mangan *d* David Parker *ph* David Connell *m* Philip Judd *pd* Jon Dowding *ed* Peter Carrodus
☆ David Argue, Mary Coustas, Michael Carman, Bruce Spence, Brendon Suhr and also the voices of Des Mangan, Sally Patience, Matthew King

Hercules – the Movie: see *Hercules in New York*

Hercules Unchained
Italy/France 1960 105m Eastmancolor
Dyaliscope
Lux/Galatea (Bruno Vailati)
original title: *Ercole e la Regina di Lidia*
Hercules has problems with the king of Thebes and the queen of Lidia.
More comic-strip versions of old legends. This item had more spent on it in publicity than in production cost, and consequently was seen by vast audiences around the world. It isn't very good.
w Pietro Francisci, Ennio de Concini *d* Pietro Francisci *ph* Mario Bava *m* Enzo Masetti
☆ Steve Reeves, Sylva Koscina, Sylvia Lopez, Primo Carnera
† Many sequels followed, the hero sometimes being known as Ursus or Goliath.

Here Come the Coeds
US 1945 88m bw
Universal (John Grant)
Janitors help to forestall a mortgage foreclosure on a college for women.
Routine star vehicle with few highlights.
w Arthur T. Horman, John Grant *d* Jean Yarbrough *ph* George Robinson *m/ly* Jack Brooks, Edgar Fairchild
☆ Bud Abbott, Lou Costello, Lon Chaney Jnr, Peggy Ryan, Martha O'Driscoll, Donald Cook, June Vincent, Charles Dingle

Here Come the Girls *
US 1953 78m Technicolor
Paramount/Hope Enterprises (Paul Jones)
original title: *Champagne for Everybody*
In the 1890s an ageing chorus boy traps a mysterious murderer.
Spotty, ineptly titled star comedy with music; in fact among the last of his passable vehicles, with excellent production backing.
w Edmund Hartmann, Hal Kanter *d* Claude Binyon *ph* Lionel Lindon *md* Lyn Murray *ad Hal Pereira, Roland Anderson*
☆ Bob Hope, Rosemary Clooney, Tony Martin, Arlene Dahl, Millard Mitchell, Fred Clark, William Demarest, Robert Strauss

Here Come the Huggetts *
GB 1948 93m bw
Rank/Gainsborough (Betty Box)
A suburban family has its ups and downs.
Cosy domestic comedy drama, a presage of TV soap operas to come, or Britain's answer to the Hardys, depending how you look at it. Tolerable at the time.
w Mabel and Denis Constanduros, Muriel and Sydney Box, Peter Rogers *d* Ken Annakin
ph Reg Wyer *m* Anthony Hopkins
☆ Jack Warner, Kathleen Harrison, Jane Hylton, Susan Shaw, Petula Clark, Jimmy Hanley, David Tomlinson, Diana Dors, Peter Hammond, John Blythe
† The Huggetts had actually originated in *Holiday Camp* the previous year, and appeared again in *Vote for Huggett* and *The Huggetts Abroad*; Warner and Harrison became an inseparable duo for many years.

Here Come the Nelsons
US 1951 76m bw
Universal
The sons of an advertising agent get involved with gangsters.
Empty-headed family comedy based on the long-running TV show The Adventures of Ozzie and Harriet.
w Ozzie Nelson, Donald Nelson, William Davenport *d* Frederick de Cordova *ph* Irving Glassberg
☆ Ozzie Nelson, Harriet Hilliard, David Nelson, Ricky Nelson, Rock Hudson, Barbara Lawrence, Ann Doran, Jim Backus

Here Come the Waves
US 1944 98m bw
Paramount (Mark Sandrich)
A sailor falls in love with identical twin Waves.
Empty-headed, professionally executed musical recruiting poster.
w Allan Scott, Ken Englund, Zion Myers *d* Mark Sandrich *ph* Charles Lang *m/ly* Harold Arlen, Johnny Mercer *md* Robert Emmett Dolan
☆ Bing Crosby, Betty Hutton, Sonny Tufts, Ann Doran, Gwen Crawford
'An almost totally negligible musical.' – *James Agee*
Academy Award nomination: song 'Accentuate the Positive'

Here Comes Cookie
US 1935 65m bw
Paramount (William le Baron)
Gracie comes into money and opens a theatre-cum-hotel for vaudevillians.
Slight star comedy with its share of laughs.
w Sam Mintz, Don Hartman *d* Norman Z. McLeod
☆ George Burns, Gracie Allen, George Barbier, Betty Furness, Andrew Tombes
'Situation and gag pounding without an ounce of seriousness or sense.' – *Variety*

Here Comes Mr Jordan ***
US 1941 93m bw
Columbia (Everett Riskin)
A prizefighter who is also an amateur saxophonist crashes in his private plane and goes to heaven by mistake: he was supposed to survive and live another forty years. Unfortunately when he goes back for his body it has been cremated, so he has to find another one, recently deceased...
Weird heavenly fantasy which succeeded because of its novelty and because heaven in wartime was a comforting vision. As a movie taken on its own merits, it suffers from illogicalities, a miscast star and a wandering plot, but scene for scene there is enough firmness and control to make it memorable. It certainly had many imitations, including Angel on My Shoulder, Down to Earth, A Guy Named Joe, Heaven Only Knows, The Horn Blows at Midnight *and* That's the Spirit.
w Seton I. Miller, Sidney Buchman *play* Halfway to Heaven *by Harry Segall* *d* Alexander Hall
ph Joseph Walker *m* Frederick Hollander
md Morris Stoloff
☆ Robert Montgomery, Evelyn Keyes, Rita Johnson, *Claude Rains, James Gleason, Edward Everett Horton*, John Emery, *Donald MacBride*, Halliwell Hobbes, Don Costello
'There is something about this original so sweet-spirited and earnest that it transcends its plot devices and shines through its comedic asides to become a true morality play without once becoming either preachy or mawkish.' – *Kit Parker catalogue, 1980*
'Audiences loved this chunk of whimsy ... the slickly hammy Rains gives Mr Jordan a sinister gloss, as if he were involved in some heavenly racket, like smuggling Chinese.' – *Pauline Kael, 70s*
† Remade 1978 as *Heaven Can Wait*.
Academy Award: original story (Harry Segall); script
Academy Award nomination: best picture; Alexander Hall; Joseph Walker; Robert Montgomery; James Gleason

Here Comes the Groom *
US 1951 114m bw
Paramount (Frank Capra)
A journalist adopts war orphans and reforms his selfish fiancée.
Tired attempt by Capra to recapture his prewar mood; despite intermittent pleasures it has neither the right style nor the topical substance.
w Virginia Van Upp, Myles Connolly, Liam O'Brien *story* Robert Riskin *d* *Frank Capra*
ph George Barnes *m/ly* Jay Livingston, Ray Evans *md* Joseph Lilley
☆ Bing Crosby, Jane Wyman, Franchot Tone, Alexis Smith, James Barton, Connie Gilchrist, Robert Keith, Anna Maria Alberghetti
'The general impression is of a loud, strident, rather vulgar comedy in which technique is used to disappointingly mechanical ends, and which a few bright lines of dialogue cannot rescue from tedium.' – *Penelope Houston*
Academy Award: song 'In the Cool Cool Cool of the Evening' (*m* Hoagy Carmichael, *ly* Johnny Mercer)
Academy Award nomination: Robert Riskin

Here Comes the Navy *
US 1934 86m bw
Warner (Lou Edelman)
An aggressive young naval rating fights with his former friend, now Petty Officer.
Breezy comedy melodrama teaming Cagney and O'Brien for the first time and offering star heroics as a sop to the Legion of Decency.
w Ben Markson, Earl Baldwin *d* Lloyd Bacon
ph Arthur Edeson *m* Leo F. Forbstein
☆ James Cagney, Pat O'Brien, Dorothy Tree, Gloria Stuart, Frank McHugh, Robert Barrat
'It's a bit too masculine for matinée appeal and it'll have to be a case of the kids and men dragging the womenfolk along.' – *Variety*
'Rapid and reasonably authentic, a satisfactory addition to a series of cinema cartoons which, because their colour and mood are indigenous and timely, may be more interesting twenty years from now.' – *Time*
Academy Award nomination: best picture

Here Is a Man: see *All That Money Can Buy*

Here We Go Again
US 1942 75m bw
RKO (Allan Dwan)
Various radio celebrities congregate at Silvertip Lodge.
Random excuse for a variety show, with top talent of its day; a sequel to Look Who's Laughing.
w Paul Gerard Smith, Joe Bigelow *d* Allan Dwan
ph Frank Redman *m* Roy Webb *m/ly* Mort Greene, Harry Revel
☆ Jim Jordan, Marion Jordan (Fibber McGee and Molly), Edgar Bergen, Charlie McCarthy, Harold Peary (The Great Gildersleeve), Ginny Simms, Gale Gordon, Ray Noble and his orchestra

Here We Go Round the Mulberry Bush *
GB 1967 96m Technicolor
UA/Giant (Larry Kramer, Clive Donner)
A school-leaver is obsessed by sex and determines to lose his virginity.
Repetitive comedy which certainly opened new avenues in British humour and seemed pretty permissive at the time (pre-Graduate). In itself, however, more modish than sympathetic.
w Hunter Davies, Larry Kramer *novel* Hunter Davies *d* *Clive Donner* *ph* Alex Thomson
m various groups
☆ Barry Evans, Judy Geeson, Angela Scoular, Adrienne Posta, Sheila White, Vanessa Howard, Denholm Elliott, Maxine Audley, Moyra Fraser, Michael Bates
'The only incongruity is that it should have been made by adults, so completely does it enter into the teenager's view of himself.' – *MFB*

The Hero: see *Bloomfield*

Hero *
US 1992 116m Technicolor
Columbia TriStar (Laura Ziskin)
GB title: *Accidental Hero*
A drifter claims to be the saviour of a plane crash while the real hero, a petty crook, goes unrecognized.
An interesting central situation is inadequately developed and finally frittered away.
w David Webb Peoples *story* Laura Ziskin, Alvin Sargent *d* Stephen Frears *ph* Oliver Stapleton
m George Fenton *pd* Dennis Gassner *ed* Mick Audsley
☆ Dustin Hoffman, Geena Davis, Andy Garcia, Joan Cusack, Kevin J. O'Connor, Maury Chaykin, Stephen Tobolowsky
'Peppered with occasional gems but one has to sift through a lot of wreckage to find them.' – *Variety*

A Hero Ain't Nothing but a Sandwich
US 1977 107m CFI color
New World/Radnitz-Mattel (Robert B. Radnitz)
Problems for an urban family in the black ghetto.
Well-intentioned but ultimately wearisome and cliché-strewn melodrama.
w Alice Childress *novel* Alice Childress *d* Ralph Nelson *ph* Frank Stanley *m* Tom McIntosh
☆ Cicely Tyson, Paul Winfield, Larry B. Scott, Helen Martin, Glynn Turman
'The sort of dreaded wholesome film that cultural and societal groups heavily endorse but nobody pays money to go see.' – *Variety*

Hero at Large
US 1980 98m Metrocolor
UA/MGM (Stephen Friedman)
An unemployed actor's bravery while impersonating a comic-book hero is exploited for political gain.
Amiable small-town satire, watchable but forgettable too.
w A. J. Carothers *d* Martin Davidson *ph* David M. Walsh *m* Patrick Williams *pd* Albert Brenner *ed* Sidney Levin, David Garfield
☆ John Ritter, Anne Archer, Bert Convy, Kevin McCarthy, Harry Bellaver, Anita Dangler, Jane Hallaren, Kevin Bacon

The Hero of Babylon
Italy/France 1964 90m Eastmancolor Euroscope
FIA/Gladiator Film (Albino Morandini)
original title: *L'Eroe di Babylone*
aka: *Goliath, King of Slaves*
Prince Nipur returns home to find that his cousin has usurped the throne of Babylon and is ruling as a tyrant.
Typical product of the Italian cycle of movies with an Old Testament setting, given over to sword fights.
w Gianpaolo Callegari, Siro Marcellini, Albert Valentin *d* Siro Marcellini *ph* Pierludovico Pavoni *m* Carlo Franzi *pd* Vittorio Marchi
ed Nella Nannuzzi
☆ Gordon Scott, Moira Orfei, Geneviève Grad, Piero Lulli, Andrea Scotti, Mario Petri

The Heroes
Italy/France/Spain 1972 110m Telecolor Scope
Paladin/Gerico Sound/Finarco/Corona/Transinter/Atlantida (Alfredo Bini)
original title: *Gli Eroi*
In North Africa during the Second World War a former prostitute makes off with £2 million, pursued by German soldiers, a British officer and assorted allies.
Dull caper movie of predictable unoriginality.
w Luciano Vincenzoni, Sergio Donati
novel Albert Kantof, René Harvard *d* Duccio Tessari *ph* Carlo Carlini *m* Riz Ortolani
ad Walter Patriarca, Andrea Crisanti *ed* Mario Morra
☆ Rod Steiger, Rosanna Schiaffino, Rod Taylor, Claude Brasseur, Terry-Thomas
'Treads a well-worn path with a handful of stock characters.' – *Tom Milne, MFB*
† The film was cut to 99m for its British release.

Heroes
US 1977 113m Technicolor
Universal (David Foster, Lawrence Turman)
A Vietnam veteran, made slightly kooky by his experiences, settles down after several adventures when he falls in love.
Just plain awful: a would-be star vehicle that doesn't work.
w James Carabatsos (David Freeman, uncredited) *d* Jeremy Paul Kagan *ph* Frank Stanley *m* Jack Nitzsche, Richard Hazard
☆ Henry Winkler, Sally Field, Harrison Ford, Val Avery

The Heroes Are Tired
France 1955 101m bw
Cila-Terra
original title: *Les Héros Sont Fatigués*
Two ex-wartime pilots, one Free French and the other German, set up an air charter service in Liberia but come to grief over stolen diamonds.
Gloomy post-war film noir set in a peculiarly depressing atmosphere, and not really sharp enough to overcome its squalid plot.
w Yves Ciampi, Jacques-Laurent Bost
novel Christine Garnier *d* Yves Ciampi *ph* Henri Alekan *m* Louiguy
☆ Yves Montand, Maria Félix, Jean Servais, Curt Jurgens, Gérard Oury

Heroes Die Hard: see *Mister Kingstreet's War*

Heroes for Sale
US 1933 73m bw
Warner
A war veteran becomes in turn a drug addict, a millionaire and the central figure in a labour dispute.
Minor social-conscience melodrama with watchable elements.
w Robert Lord, Wilson Mizner *d* William A. Wellman
☆ Richard Barthelmess, Aline MacMahon, Loretta Young, Berton Churchill, Robert Barrat
'This attempted satire on unemployment conditions just prior to the Roosevelt election is not well told ... b.o. doubtful.' – *Variety*

The Heroes of Telemark *
GB 1965 131m Technicolor Panavision
Rank/Benton (Ben Fisz)
Norwegian resistance workers in World War II help the Allies to smash a heavy water plant.
Ambling narrative with big action sequences which often seem irrelevant, so that the story as a whole fails to excite.
w Ivan Moffat, Ben Barzman *d* Anthony Mann
ph *Robert Krasker* *m* Malcolm Arnold
☆ Kirk Douglas, Richard Harris, Ulla Jacobsson, Roy Dotrice, Anton Diffring, Michael Redgrave

Heroic Trio
Hong Kong 1992 88m colour
China Entertainment/Paka Hill (Ching-Siu Tung)
original title: *Dongfang San Xia*
Three superheroines – Wonder Woman, Thief Catcher and Invisible Woman – search for 18 babies that have been kidnapped as future Emperors of China.
Comic-book heroics with plenty of flashy action and some grisly scenes, including cannibalism and child murder.
w Sandy Shaw (Shao Liqiong) *d* Johnny To (Du Qifeng) *ph* Poon Hang-Sang, Tom Lau
m William Hu (Hu Weili) *ad* Bruce Yu, Raymond Chan
☆ Maggie Cheung, Anita Mui, Michelle Yeoh, Damian Lau, Anthony Wong, Paul Chin
'A bravura mix of outrageous acrobatics, over-the-top stunts and superb special effects.' – *Film Review*

The Heroin Gang: see *Sol Madrid*

Heroism: see *Eroica*

Hero's Island *
US 1962 94m Technicolor Panavision
UA/Daystar/Portland (James Mason, Leslie Stevens)
In 1718 bondslaves settle on a Carolina island, are attacked by fishermen and protected by one of the aides of Blackbeard the Pirate.
An oddly personal, patchy, rather mysterious film with a rhetorical script and rather good action sequences.
wd Leslie Stevens *ph* Ted McCord *m* Dominic Frontière
☆ James Mason, Kate Manx, Neville Brand, Rip Torn

Les Héros Sont Fatigués: see *The Heroes Are Tired*

Un Héros Trés Discret: see *A Self-Made Hero*

Herr Puntila and His Servant Matti *
Austria 1955 95m Agfacolor
Bauerfilm
A rich landowner, usually drunk, is rescued from scrapes by his patient valet.
A cogent comedy which its author is said to have approved in this version.
w Alberto Cavalcanti, Vladimir Pozner, Ruth Wieden *play* Bertolt Brecht *d* Alberto Cavalcanti *ph* André Bac, Arthur Hämmerer *m* Hanns Eisler
☆ Curt Bois, Hans Engelmann, Maria Emo, Edith Prager

Hers to Hold
US 1943 94m bw
Universal (Felix Jackson)
A girl decides whether or not to marry a serviceman.
Limp star vehicle, a sequel to Three Smart Girls *(qv).*
w Lewis R. Foster *d* Frank Ryan *ph* Elwood Bredell *m* Frank Skinner *md* Charles Previn *ad* John B. Goodman *ed* Ted J. Kent
☆ Deanna Durbin, Joseph Cotten, Charles Winninger, Nella Walker, Gus Schilling, Ludwig Stossel
song 'Say a Prayer for the Boys Over There' (*m* Jimmy McHugh, *ly* Herb Magidson)

Herz aus Glas: see *Heart of Glass*

Hester Street *
US 1974 89m bw
Midwest Films (Raphael D. Silver)
How Jewish immigrants settled in East Side New York in the 1890s.
Modest, humorous, but not always smooth or dramatically emphatic chronicle of a familiar background; the detail however is excellent.
wd Joan Micklin Silver *story* *Yeki* by Abraham Cahan *ph* Kenneth Van Sickle *m* William Bolcom
☆ Steven Keats, Carol Kane, Mel Howard, Dorrie Kavanaugh, Doris Roberts
'A small, beautifully detailed, slightly shaggy independent film of charm and substance.' – *Judith Crist*
'For old diehards who still go to the cinema seeking humanity, tenderness and insight.' – *Michael Billington, Illustrated London News*
Carol Kane

Hets: see *Frenzy*

Hex
US 1973 93m DeLuxe
TCF (Clark Paylow)
aka: *The Shrieking*
In 1919, when their remote farm in Nebraska is invaded by a gang of bikers, one sister reacts by falling in love while the other uses her occult powers to destroy them.
Odd little adolescent fantasy given a slight twist by its period setting, although the characters' attitudes are strictly from the 60s.
w Leo Garen, Steve Katz *story* Doran William Cannon, Vernon Zimmerman *ph* Charles Rosher Jnr *m* Charles Bernstein *ad* Gary Weist, Frank Sylos *ed* Robert Belcher
☆ Tina Herazo (Cristina Raines), Keith Carradine, Hilarie Thompson, Scott Glenn, Gary Busey, Mike Combs, Dan Haggerty, John Carradine

Hexed
US 1993 90m colour
Columbia/Price Entertainment/Brillstein-Grey (Marc S. Fischer, Louis G. Friedman)
A fantasist of a hotel clerk becomes involved with a murderous model.
Curious black comedy that has the requisite streak of cruelty but not enough momentum to its narrative to entertain.
wd Alan Spencer *ph* James Chressanthis *m* Lance Rubin *pd* Brenton Swift *ed* Debra McDermott
☆ Arye Gross, Claudia Christian, Adrienne Shelly, Ray Baker, R. Lee Ermey, Michael Knight, Robin Curtis, Brandis Kemp, Norman Fell

Hexen geschändet und zu Tode gequält: see *Mark of the Devil*

Hey Arnold! The Movie *
US 2002 75m DeLuxe
Paramount/Nickelodeon/Snee-Oosh (Craig Bartlett, Albie Hecht)
A young boy and his friends try to stop their neighbourhood being demolished and redeveloped.
A movie version of a children's TV favourite: it is overstretched and the stylized, hand-drawn animation palls after a while, but it entertains for the most part.
w Craig Bartlett, Steve Viksten *d* Tuck Tucker *m* Jim Lang *pd* Guy Vasilovich *ed* Christopher Hink
☆ voices of: Spencer Klein (Arnold), Francesca Marie Smith (Helga/Deep Voice), Jamil Walker Smith (Gerald/Rasta Guy), Dan Castellaneta (Grandpa/Nick Vermicelli), Tress MacNeille (Grandma/Mayor Dixie/Red), Paul Sorvino (Scheck), Jennifer Jason Leigh (Bridget), Christopher Lloyd (Coroner)
'it's undeniably smart and appealing in its depiction of everyday superheroes rallying behind a noble cause.' – *Scott Foundas, Variety*

Hey, Good-Lookin'
US 1982 76m Technicolor
Warner (Ralph Bakshi)
Life in 1953 Brooklyn centres round two young womanizers.
Enterprising attempt to use animation to tell a youth melodrama; interesting but not successful.
wd Ralph Bakshi
☆ Featuring the voices of Richard Romanus, David Proval, Jesse Welles, Tina Bowman

Hey! Hey! USA!
GB 1938 92m bw
Gainsborough (Edward Black)
An education expert sails to America, falls in with gangsters, and saves a boy from being kidnapped by them.
Misconceived star vehicle which provides some laughs, but not of the expected kind.
w J. O. C. Orton, Val Guest, G. Marriott Edgar *story* Howard Irving Young, Ralph Spence *d* Marcel Varnel *ph* Arthur Crabtree *m* Cecil Milner *md* Louis Levy *ad* Vetchinsky *ed* R. E. Dearing
☆ Will Hay, Edgar Kennedy, David Burns, Fred Duprez

Hi Diddle Diddle *
US 1943 72m bw
UA/Andrew Stone
aka: *Try and Find It*
Young lovers are hampered by con artist parents.
Scatty comedy with amusing patches and some zest in the telling.
w Edmund L. Hartmann *d* Andrew L. Stone *ph* Charles Van Enger *m* Phil Boutelje
☆ Adolphe Menjou, Pola Negri, Dennis O'Keefe, Billie Burke, Martha Scott, June Havoc
Phil Boutelje

Hi, Mom! *
US 1969 86m Movielab
West End Films
Adventures of a young porno film maker and of the eccentrics who live in the same building.
Busy comedy of the drop-out life, full of random satirical jabs and homages to other film makers.
wd Brian de Palma *ph* Robert Elfstrom *m* Eric Kaz
☆ Robert DeNiro, Allen Garfield, Gerrit Graham, Jennifer Salt, Charles Durning

Hi Nellie *
US 1934 79m bw
Warner (Robert Presnell)
An ex-editor is demoted to advice to the lovelorn and gets involved in city rackets.
Minor, effective star comedy-melodrama.
w Abem Finkel, Sidney Sutherland *d* Mervyn Le Roy *ph* Sol Polito
☆ Paul Muni, Glenda Farrell, Ned Sparks, Robert Barrat, Hobart Cavanaugh, Berton Churchill, Donald Meek, Douglass Dumbrille, Edward Ellis
'Barely gets by as fair entertainment ... it's a better Muni performance than a picture.' – *Variety*
† Remade in 1935 as *Front Page Woman*; 1937 as *Love Is on the Air*; 1942 as *You Can't Escape Forever*; 1949 as *The House across the Street*.

'A Land Without Boundaries. A Passion Without Limits.'
The Hi-Lo Country *
US 1999 114m colour
Universal/Polygram/Working Title/Cappa/De Fina (Barbara De Fina/Martin Scorsese/Eric Fellner/Tim Bevan)
In the late 40s, two cowboys, friends who are in love with the same woman, find it difficult to adapt to the changing ways of the modern world.
Elegiac, overlong movie of the decline of Western traditions that occasionally hints at more complex matters, of men trapped by their own situation, before settling for nostalgia.
w Walon Green *novel* Max Evans *d* Stephen Frears *ph* Oliver Stapleton *m* Carter Burwell *pd* Patricia Norris *ed* Masahiro Hirakubo
☆ Woody Harrelson (Big Boy Matson), Billy Crudup (Pete Calder), Patricia Arquette (Mona), Cole Hauser (Little Brother), Penelope Cruz (Josepha O'Neil), Darren Burrows (Billy Harte), Jacob Vargas (Delfino Mondragon), James Gammon (Hoover Young), Lane Smith (Steve Shaw), Katy Jurado (Meesa), Sam Elliott (Jim Ed Love)
'A good stab at an American genre piece, a modern western.' – *Adam Mars-Jones, Times*

Hickey and Boggs
US 1972 111m DeLuxe
UA/Film Guarantors Ltd (Fouad Said)
Two down and out private eyes, hired to find a girl, keep falling over dead bodies.
Extraordinarily confused thriller with moments of humour and well staged action sequences.
w Walter Hill *d* Robert Culp *ph* Wilmer Butler *m* Ted Ashford *ed* David Berlatsky
☆ Robert Culp (Frank Boggs), Bill Cosby (Al Hickey), Rosalind Cash (Nyona), Sheila Sullivan (Edith Boggs), Isabel Sanford (Nyona's Mother), Ta-Ronce Allen (Nyona's Daughter), Lou Frizzell (Lawyer), Michael Moriarty (Ballard), Vincent Gardenia (Papadakis), James Woods (Lt Wyatt), Ed Lauter (Ted), Bernard Nedell (Used Car Salesman)

The Hidden
US 1988 97m DeLuxe
Palace/New Line-Heron/Third Elm Street Venture (Robert Shaye, Gerald T. Olson, Michael Meltzer)
Detectives hunt down a murderous slug-like alien who possesses the bodies of humans.
Standard action fare, somewhat sillier than the norm.
w Bob Hunt *d* Jack Sholder *ph* Jacques Haitkin *m* Michael Convertino *pd* C. J. Strawn, Mick Strawn *ed* Michael N. Knue
☆ Kyle MacLachlan, Michael Nouri, Claudia Christian, Clarence Felder, Clu Gulager, Ed O'Ross, William Boyett, Richard Brooks, Larry Cedar

Hidden Agenda **
GB 1990 108m Eastmancolor
Enterprise/Hemdale (Eric Fellner)
A police officer discovers that members of the Royal Ulster Constabulary are responsible for murders of IRA sympathizers in Belfast.
Powerful political film, based in part on actual events, that sometimes descends into hectoring agit-prop. It won the Jury Prize at the Cannes Film Festival in 1990.
w Jim Allen *d* Ken Loach *ph* Clive Tickner *m* Stewart Copeland *pd* Martin Johnson *ed* Jonathan Morris
☆ Brian Cox, Frances McDormand, Brad Dourif, Mai Zetterling, Bernard Bloch, John Benfield, Jim Norton, Patrick Kavanagh, Bernard Archard
'*Hidden Agenda*, though it attempts to make an acceptable theatrical entertainment out of a complex political saga, lacks big-screen impact.' – *Variety*

Hidden City
GB 1988 107m colour
Other Cinema/Hidden City/Film Four/ZDF (Irving Teitelbaum)
A writer, persuaded by an out-of-work researcher to investigate mysterious happenings caught on old government information films, finds himself the target of a security operation.
Paranoiac thriller of a cover-up which never achieves credibility.
wd Stephen Poliakoff *ph* Witold Stok *m* Michael Storey *pd* Martin Johnson *ed* Peter Coulson
☆ Charles Dance, Cassie Stuart, Bill Paterson, Richard E. Grant, Alex Norton, Tusse Silberg

The Hidden Fortress **
Japan 1958 123m bw Tohoscope
Toho (Masumi Fujimoto)
original title: *Kakushi Toride No San-Akunin*
In medieval Japan, the heiress of a feudal lord is saved from a bandit by a samurai.
Roistering eastern Western.
w Ryuzo Kikushima, Hideo Oguni, Shinobu Hashimoto, Akira Kurosawa *d* Akira Kurosawa *ph* Ichio Yamazaki *m* Masaru Sato
☆ Toshiro Mifune, Misa Uehara, Minoru Chiaki
† George Lucas has said that the film was his inspiration for *Star Wars*.

The Hidden Room: see *Obsession (1948)*

Hide and Seek
GB 1963 90m bw
British Lion/Albion/Spectrum (Hal E. Chester)
A research scientist is the centre of a kidnap plan designed to make it appear that he has defected.
Too many mysterious happenings with too little explanation sink this comedy-thriller from the start.
w David Stone *d* Cy Endfield *ph* Gilbert Taylor *m* Muir Mathieson, Gary Campbell
☆ Ian Carmichael, Janet Munro, Curt Jurgens, Hugh Griffith, George Pravda, Kieron Moore, Edward Chapman

'It's Not A Game'
Hide and Seek
Canada 2000 100m colour
Trimark/Blue Rider/GFT/Paquin (Gary Howsam, Pieter Kroonenburg)
A couple desperate for a child kidnap a pregnant woman and fake her death.
Luridly implausible thriller of a woman in peril, which leaves much of the action unexplained; it is notable only for a manic performance from Jennifer Tilly.
w Yas Takata, Joel Hladecek *d* Sidney J. Furie *ph* Curtis J. Petersen *m* Robert Carli *pd* Réjean Labrie *ed* Saul Pincus *cos* Darena Sosnowsky
☆ Daryl Hannah (Anne), Jennifer Tilly (Helen), Bruce Greenwood (Jack), Vincent Gallo (Frank), Johanna Black (Emily)
'The script runs out of what steam it had long before the closing credits.' – *Sight and Sound*
† The film was released direct to video.

Hide in Plain Sight
US 1980 92m Metrocolor Panavision
MGM (Robert Christiansen, Rick Rosenberg)
A factory worker searches for his children when his former wife is hidden by the government to protect her husband, an informer.
Unpersuasive melodrama with little more than its unusual plot to commend it.
w Spencer Eastman *book* Leslie Waller *d* James Caan *ph* Paul Lohmann *m* Leonard Rosenman
☆ James Caan, Jill Eikenberry, Robert Viharo

Hideaway
US 1995 103m Technicolor Panavision
TriStar/S/Q (Jerry Baerwitz, Agatha Hanczakowski, Gimel Everett)
An antiques dealer, resuscitated after a car crash, begins to share the experiences of a serial killer, who also has returned from death.
Ordinary horror flick, tricked out with some fancy effects in an attempt to make it watchable; the cast do what they can, but it's dull stuff.
w Andrew Kevin Walker, Neal Jimenez *novel* Dean R. Koontz *d* Brett Leonard *ph* Gale Tattersall *m* Trevor Jones *pd* Michael Bolton *ed* B. J. Sears
☆ Jeff Goldblum, Christine Lahti, Alicia Silverstone, Jeremy Sisto, Alfred Molina, Rae Dawn Chong
'Collapses into a mess of clunking dialogue and computer effects.' – *Sight and Sound*

'Morocco 1972. It's not about escape, it's about discovery...'
Hideous Kinky
GB/France 1998 97m colour 'Scope
Film Consortium/BBC/Arts Council/Greenpoint/L Films/AMLF (Ann Scott)
In the early 70s, an Englishwoman, who is living in Marrakesh with two young daughters, begins an affair with a local acrobat.
Episodic, colourful drama about the illusion of freedom, but a little lacking in substance.
w Billy MacKinnon *novel* Esther Freud *d* Gillies MacKinnon *ph* John de Borman *m* John Keane *pd* Louise Marzaroli, Pierre Gompertz *ed* Pia Di Ciaula
☆ Kate Winslet, Said Taghmaoui, Bella Riza, Carrie Mullan, Pierre Clementi, Sira Stampe
'A pleasant evening in the cinema, but not a great deal more than that.' – *Derek Malcolm, Guardian*

The Hideous Sun Demon
US 1959 74m bw
Clarke-King Enterprises/Robert Clarke
GB title: *Blood on His Lips*
Subjected to a high level of radiation, a scientist turns into a giant two-legged lizard when exposed to sunlight.
Simple-minded science fiction featuring the producer-director-star in an ill-fitting monster costume.
w E. S. Seeley Jnr, Doane Hoag *d* Robert Clarke, Tom Boutrous *ph* John Morrill, Vilis Lapenieks, Stan Follis *m* John Seely *ad* Gianbattista Cassarino *ed* Tom Boutrous
☆ Robert Clarke, Patricia Manning, Nan Peterson, Patrick White

The Hideout: see *The Small Voice (1948)*

Hideout in the Alps: see *Dusty Ermine*

Hider in the House
US 1989 108m CFI color
Vestron/Precision Films (Edward Teets, Michael Taylor)
A murderer, hiding in the attic of a house, spies on the family that lives there.
A thriller lacking in suspense and with nothing else to recommend it.
w Lem Dobbs *d* Matthew Patrick *ph* Jeff Jur *m* Christopher Young *pd* Victoria Paul *ed* Debra T. Smith
☆ Gary Busey, Mimi Rogers, Michael McKean, Kurt Christopher Kinder, Candy Hutson, Elizabeth Ruscio, Chuck Lafont, Bruce Glover

Hiding Out
US 1987 98m Technicolor
DEG/Evenmore/Locomotion (Jeff Rothberg)
A stockbroker on the run from a hitman disguises himself as a high-school student.
Inane attempt at a comic thriller; it lacks suspense and fails to exploit its central situation of an adult trapped in an adolescent environment, concentrating instead on an unlikely love affair.
w Joe Menosky, Jeff Rothberg *d* Bob Giraldi *ph* Daniel Pearl *m* Anne Dudley *pd* Dan Leigh *ed* Edward Warschilka
☆ Jon Cryer, Keith Coogan, Annabeth Gish, Oliver Cotton, Claude Brooks, Tim Quill, Gretchen Cryer, Nancy Fish

Hifazaat: see *In Custody*

High and Dry: see *The Maggie*

High and Low **
Japan 1963 142m bw Tohoscope
Toho (Tomoyuki Tanaka)
A wealthy shoe manufacturer's chauffeur's son is kidnapped in mistake for his own, and he faces a moral dilemma.
Interesting, rather gloomy Japanese version of a light American thriller with all the style expected of the director.
w Hideo Oguni, Ryuzo Kikushima, Eijiro Hisaito, Akira Kurosawa *novel* *The King's Ransom* by Ed McBain *d* Akira Kurosawa *ph* Asakazu Makai, Takao Saito *m* Masaru Sato
☆ Toshiro Mifune, Kyoko Kagawa, Tatsuya Nakadai
'A tapestry of crime, detection and punishment, with vivid vignettes of various strata of society, haunting moments on the waterfront, in an all-night saloon, in an opium den, right down to the confrontation between victim and criminal in the death cell.' – *Judith Crist*

The High and the Mighty *
US 1954 147m Warnercolor Cinemascope
Wayne – Fellows
A big passenger plane is in trouble over the Pacific, and its occupants react in various ways to the prospect of a crash landing.
Compendium fiction with even the pilot having a personal problem which could cloud his judgement. Tolerable, well made hokum.
w Ernest K. Gann *novel* Ernest K. Gann *d* William Wellman *ph* William Clothier *m* Dimitri Tiomkin
☆ John Wayne, Robert Newton, Robert Stack, Doe Avedon, Claire Trevor, Laraine Day, Jan Sterling, Phil Harris, Sidney Blackmer, John Howard
Dimitri Tiomkin
William Wellman; Claire Trevor; Jan Sterling; title song (*m*Dimitri Tiomkin, *ly*Ned Washington)

High Anxiety *
US 1977 94m DeLuxe
TCF/Crossbow (Mel Brooks)
A psychologist taking up a new appointment suspects that his predecessor may have been murdered.
*Elementary but somewhat entertaining spoof of various Hitchcock movies (*Spellbound, North by Northwest, The Birds*), with the level of humour as unsubtle and lavatorial as one has come to expect.*
w Mel Brooks, Ron Clark, Rudy DeLuca, Barry Levinson *d* Mel Brooks *ph* Paul Lohmann *m* John Morris
☆ Mel Brooks, Madeline Kahn, Cloris Leachman, Harvey Korman, Ron Carey, Howard Morris, Dick Van Patten
'It basically just shambles along, in search of the next big set-piece to send up.' – *Richard Combs, MFB*
'Brooks has no idea of how to build a sequence, how to tell a story, when to leave well enough (or ill enough) alone.' – *Philip French, Observer*
'A child's idea of satire – imitations, with a comic hat and a leer.' – *New Yorker*

'A story of ambition, sacrifice, seduction and other career moves.'
High Art *
US 1998 102m colour
October Films (Dolly Hall, Jeff Levy-Hinte, Susan A. Stover)
A young magazine editor leaves her boyfriend for a once-famous, druggy female photographer, who lives with a heroin-addicted actress.
Innocence and experience meet in a not particularly compelling romantic melodrama.
wd Lisa Cholodenko *ph* Tami Reiker *m* Shudder to Think *pd* Bernhard Blythe *ed* Amy E. Duddleston
☆ Ally Sheedy, Radha Mitchell, Patricia Clarkson, Tammy Grimes, Gabriel Mann, Bill Sage, Ann Duong, David Thornton
'Should be wholeheartedly embraced by the lesbian community and, with the right marketing, can cross over to a larger sophisticated audience.' – *Emanuel Levy, Variety*

High Barbaree
US 1947 91m bw
MGM (Everett Riskin)
A pilot crashlands in the Pacific and finds himself drifting towards a Utopian island fancifully described by his favourite uncle.
Thin Hollywood mysticism on Shangri-La *lines but without the solid virtues of plot, dialogue and imagination.*
w Anne Morrison Chapin, Whitfield Cook, Cyril Hume *d* Jack Conway *ph* Sidney Wagner *m* Herbert Stothart
☆ Van Johnson, June Allyson, Thomas Mitchell, Marilyn Maxwell

The High Bright Sun
GB 1965 114m Technicolor
Rank (Betty Box)
US title: *McGuire Go Home*
In 1957 Cyprus the British army is beleaguered by partisans, and an officer tries to contact a leading rebel.
Confused and boring attempt to make romantic drama out of an intractably sad situation.
w Ian Stuart Black *novel* Ian Stuart Black *d* Ralph Thomas *ph* Ernest Steward *m* Angelo Lavagnino
☆ Dirk Bogarde, Susan Strasberg, George Chakiris, Denholm Elliott

The High Command *
GB 1936 88m bw
ABFD/Fanfare/Wellesley/ (Gordon Wellesley)
The general of a West African garrison has a guilty secret known to his young medical officer.
Dated melodrama, rather interestingly performed and directed.
w Katherine Strueby, Walter Meade, Val Valentine *novel* *The General Goes Too Far* by Lewis Robinson *d* *Thorold Dickinson* *ph* Otto Heller, James Rogers *md* Ernest Irving *ad* R. Holmes Paul *ed* Sidney Cole
☆ James Mason, Lionel Atwill, Lucie Mannheim, Steve Geray, Leslie Perrins
'Its avoidance of reality and its slowness make it a first-class soporific.' – *Sunday Times*
'A film critic should be capable of distinguishing, from the faults due to a poor story, an uncertain script and mere poverty, the very high promise of the direction.' – *Graham Greene*
† The cost of the film, including scenes shot in West Africa, was 30,000.

The High Commissioner: see *Nobody Runs Forever*

The High Cost of Loving *
US 1958 87m bw Cinemascope
MGM (Milo O. Frank Jnr)
A happily married middle class couple have doubts about their future.
Pleasant, mildly satirical romantic comedy which doesn't really get anywhere.
w Rip Van Ronkel *d* José Ferrer *ph* George J. Folsey *m* Jeff Alexander
☆ *José Ferrer, Gena Rowlands,* Joanne Gilbert, Jim Backus, Bobby Troup, Philip Ober, Edward Platt, Werner Klemperer

The High Country
Canada 1981 101m colour Panavision
Crown International/Gene Slott (Bruce Mallen)
An escaped convict heads for the mountains accompanied by a simple-minded girl on the run from home.
Tedious drama that will test the patience of the most tolerant; it has nothing to recommend it.
w Bud Townsend *d* Harvey Hart *ph* Robert Ryan *m* Eric Robertson *ad* Reuben Freed *ed* Ron Wisman
☆ Timothy Bottoms, Linda Purl, George Sims

'Everything you trust. Everything you know. May be a lie...'
High Crimes
US 2002 115m DeLuxe Panavision
TCF/New Regency/Manifest/Monarch (Arnon Milchan, Janet Yang, Jesse B'Franklin)
After a female lawyer discovers that her husband is a former marine accused of mass murder in El Salvador, she defends him with the aid of an alcoholic military attorney.
Routine thriller with cover-ups and double-crosses and a predictable twist at the end.
w Yuri Zeltser, Cary Bickley *novel* Joseph Finder *d* Carl Franklin *ph* Theo van de Sande *m* Graeme Revell *pd* Paul Peters *ed* Carole Kravetz-Aykanian
☆ Ashley Judd (Claire Kubik), Morgan Freeman (Grimes), Jim Caviezel (Tom Kubik), Amanda Peet (Jackie), Tom Bower (Mullins), Adam Scott (Embry), Bruce Davison (Brig General Marks), Juan Carlos Hernandez (Major Hernandez)
'Isn't worth the crayons it took to write the script.' – *Stephen Hunter, Washington Posdt*
'Stylish and effective, if slightly overlong, thriller.' – *Jonathan Rosenbaum, Chicago Reader*

High Encounters of the Ultimate Kind: see *Cheech and Chong's Next Movie*

'A comedy about fear of commitment, hating your job, falling in love and other pop favorites.'
High Fidelity **
US/GB 2000 113m Technicolor
Buena Vista/Touchstone/Working Title/Dogstar/New Crime (Tim Bevan, Rudd Simmons)
A record store owner, who is obsessed with the trivia of pop music, revisits old girlfriends to discover how to get back on track with his current relationship.
An exuberant and witty hymn to the potency of cheap music and prolonged adolescence; Hornby's novel has been transferred from London to Chicago without missing a beat.
w D.V. DeVincentis, Steve Pink, John Cusack, Scott Rosenberg *novel* Nick Hornby *d* Stephen Frears *ph* Seamus McGarvey *m* Howard Shore *pd* David Chapman, Therese DePrez *ed* Mick Audsley *cos* Laura Cunningham Bauer
☆ John Cusack (Rob Gordon), Iben Hjejle (Laura), Todd Louiso (Dick), Jack Black (Barry), Lisa Bonet (Marie De Salle), Catherine Zeta-Jones (Charlie), Joan Cusack (Liz), Tim Robbins (Ian), Chris Rehmann (Vince), Ben Carr (Justin), Lili Taylor (Sarah), Joelle Carter (Penny), Natasha Gregson Wagner (Caroline), Sara Gilbert (Anaugh), Bruce Springsteen (Himself)
'Movies this wry and likable rarely get made.' – *Roger Ebert, Chicago Sun-Times*
'The pick of the summer date movies' – *Empire*

High Flyers
US 1937 70m bw
RKO (Lee Marcus)
Two incompetents are duped into smuggling contraband gems.
Feeble finale to the career of two comedians.
w Benny Rubin, Bert Granet *play* Victor Mapes *d* Edward F. Cline *ph* Jack Mackenzie *m* Roy Webb *m/ly* Herman Ruby, Dave Dreyer
☆ Bert Wheeler, Robert Woolsey, Lupe Velez, Marjorie Lord, Margaret Dumont, Jack Carson, Paul Harvey

High Fury: see *White Cradle Inn*

'A mother, a daughter, a lover. Relationships can be murder.'
High Heels
Spain 1991 112m Eastmancolor
El Deseo/Ciby 2000 (Agustin Almadóvar)
original title: *Tacones Lejanos*
A singer restarts an affair with a former lover, who is now married to her daughter.
Camp extravaganza of a showbiz mother-daughter relationship that tries too hard to shock and titillate.
wd Pedro Almodóvar *ph* Alfredo Mayo *m* Ryuichi Sakamoto *ad* Pierre-Louis Thevenet *ed* José Salcedo
☆ Victoria Abril, Marisa Paredes, Miguel Bosé, Feodor Atkine, Pedro Díez del Corral, Ana Lizarán

'One of the finest, most high fashion portrayals of loss and mourning' – *Stuart Klawans, The Nation*

'It's got mad love, a bad-seed child, acrobatic sex, an anchor-woman's on-air announcement of her own arrest for murder, a chorus line in a woman's prison and, of course, cross-dressing. It careers like a runaway circus train over the rickety trestle of melodrama. Yet it already has even true believers – Almodóvar's own camp followers – asking, "Is that all there is?"' – *Richard Corliss, Time*

'Crime has never been so attractive.'

High Heels and Low Lifes

GB/US 2001 85m Technicolor

Buena Vista/Touchstone/Fragile (Uri Fruchtmann, Barnaby Thompson)

A nurse and an actress try to blackmail bank robbers into parting with their loot.

Dispiriting comedy with few bright moments.

w Kim Fuller *story* Georgia Pritchett *d* Mel Smith *ph* Steven Chive *m* Charlie Mole *pd* Michael Pickwoad *ed* Christopher Blunden

☆ Minnie Driver (Shannon), Mary McCormack (Frances), Kevin McNally (Mason), Mark Williams (Tremaine), Danny Dyer (Danny), Kevin Eldon (McGill), Michael Gambon (Kerrigan)

'For this to be an enjoyable, fast-paced, chick comedy, it would first have to be a lot brisker than it is, and secondly, a lot funnier.' – *Jo Berry, Empire*

High Hopes

GB 1988 112m Eastmancolor

Palace/Portman/Film Four International/British Screen (Simon Channing-Williams, Victor Glynn)

A family of contrasting types gather to celebrate their mother's birthday.

A comedy of caricatures.

wd Mike Leigh *m* Andrew Dixon *pd* Diana Charnley *ed* Jon Gregory

☆ Philip Davis, Ruth Sheen, Edna Dore, Philip Jackson, Heather Tobias, Lesley Manville, David Bamber, Jason Watkins, Judith Scott

'When the hands point up ... the excitement starts!'

High Noon **

US 1952 85m bw

Stanley Kramer

A marshal gets no help when he determines to defend his town against revengeful badmen.

A minor Western with a soft-pedalled message for the world, this turned out to be a classic simply because it was well done, with every scene and performance clearly worked out. Cinematically it was pared to the bone, and the theme tune helped.

w Carl Foreman *story* The Tin Star by John W. Cunningham *d* Fred Zinnemann *ph* Floyd Crosby *m* Dimitri Tiomkin *ed* Elmo Williams, Harry Gerstad *singer* Tex Ritter

☆ *Gary Cooper*, Grace Kelly, Thomas Mitchell, Lloyd Bridges, Katy Jurado, Otto Kruger, Lon Chaney, Henry Morgan

'The western form is used for a sneak civics lesson.' – *Pauline Kael, 70s*

'Like nearly all the Kramer productions, this is a neat, well-finished and literate piece of work, though its limitations are more conventional than most.' – *Gavin Lambert*

'A western to challenge *Stagecoach* for the all-time championship.' – *Bosley Crowther*

'A series of crisp and purposeful scenes that interpret each other like the pins on a strategist's war map.' – *Robert L. Hatch*

'It is astonishing how much of the simple western story is told visually by rapid cross-cutting.' – *Films in Review*

'Few recent westerns have gotten so much tension and excitement into the classic struggle between good and evil.' – *Life*

'The most un-American thing I've ever seen in my whole life.' – *John Wayne*

† The leading role was turned down by John Wayne, Charlton Heston, Marlon Brando and Gregory Peck.

Dimitri Tiomkin; Gary Cooper; title song (*m* Dimitri Tiomkin, *ly* Ned Washington); editing

best picture; Carl Foreman; Fred Zinnemann

'They'll never forget the day he drifted into town!'

High Plains Drifter *

US 1972 105m Technicolor Panavision

Universal/Malpaso (Robert Daley)

A mysterious stranger rides into town and terrifies the inhabitants.

Semi-supernatural, mystical revenge Western with an overplus of violence. Very watchable, but irritating.

w Ernest Tidyman *d* Clint Eastwood *ph* Bruce Surtees *m* Dee Barton *ad* Henry Bumstead

☆ Clint Eastwood, Verna Bloom, Marianna Hill, Mitch Ryan, Jack Ging

'Ritualized violence and plodding symbolism make for heavy going.' – *Sight and Sound*

'A nervously humorous, self-conscious near-satire on the prototype Eastwood formula.' – *Variety*

High Pressure *

US 1932 74m bw

Warner

A would-be tycoon believes there's a fortune to be made in artificial rubber.

Amusing con man comedy with good work all round.

w Joseph Jackson *play* Hot Money by Aben Kandel *d* Mervyn Le Roy

☆ *William Powell*, Evelyn Brent, George Sidney, Guy Kibbee, Frank McHugh

'Well acted, but lacks strength to attract much business.' – *Variety*

'Getting In Was Easy ... Getting Out Was War!!!'

High Risk

US 1981 94m colour

American Cinema (Joe Raffill, Gerard Green)

A documentary film-maker enlists three buddies to steal a million dollars from a South American drugs dealer.

Moderately entertaining caper movie which stops too often for action and occasionally for comedy.

wd Stewart Raffill *ph* Alex Phillips Jnr *m* Mark Snow *ed* Tom Walls Jnr

☆ James Brolin, Cleavon Little, Lindsay Wagner, Ernest Borgnine, Bruce Davison, Chick Vennera, Anthony Quinn, James Coburn

High Road to China

US 1983 105m Technicolor

Golden Harvest/Pan Pacific (Fred Weintraub)

In the twenties, an American heiress in Afghanistan has adventures with a drunken flyer.

Abysmal attempt to mate James Bond with a cut-price Raiders of the Lost Ark. *It comes up with nothing at all, and is on the lowest level for continuity, dialogue and direction.*

w Sandra Weintraub Roland, S. Lee Pogostin *novel* Jon Cleary *d* Brian G. Hutton *ph* Ronnie Taylor *m* John Barry *pd* Robert Laing

☆ Tom Selleck, Bess Armstrong, Jack Weston, Robert Morley, Wilford Brimley, Brian Blessed

'An attempt to revive the sort of comedy-adventure romance in which Clark Gable and Jean Harlow would squabble furiously but you knew they were really in love. But as scripted and abominably directed, the thing is as flat as a pancake.' – *Guardian*

High School Confidential!

US 1958 85m bw CinemaScope

MGM (Albert Zugsmith)

A new and obnoxious student turns out to be an undercover narcotics policeman tracking down pot-smokers.

An engagingly silly period piece, with its hysteria about drugs, determination to be up to date with its teenage slang ('Tomorrow is dragsville, cats') and portentous final statement following a fight between students and gun-toting gangsters: 'You have just seen an authentic disclosure of conditions that unfortunately exist in some of our high schools today…'

w Lewis Meltzer, Robert Blees *d* Jack Arnold *ph* Harold J. Marzorati *ad* William J. Horning, Hans Peters *ed* Ben Lewis

☆ Russ Tamblyn, Jan Sterling, John Drew Barrymore, Mamie Van Doren, Jerry Lee Lewis, Ray Anthony, Jackie Coogan, Charles Chaplin Jnr, Diane Jergens, Michael Landon, Burt Douglas

High School High

US 1996 86m Technicolor

Sony/TriStar (David Zucker, Robert LoCash, Gil Netter)

An earnest and idealistic teacher joins the staff of a tough ghetto school.

A spoof of movies such as Dangerous Minds, *but without class; it limps along from one bad joke to another.*

w David Zucker, Robert LoCash, Pat Proft *d* Hart Bochner *ph* Vernon Layton *m* Ira Newborn *pd* Dennis Washington *ed* James R. Symons

☆ Jon Lovitz (Clark), Tia Carrere (Victoria), Mekhi Phifer (Griff), Louise Fletcher (Mrs Doyle), Guillermo Diaz (Paco), John Neville (Thaddeus), Malinda Williams (Natalie), Gil Espinoza (Alonzo), Brian Hooks (Anferny), Natasha Gregson Wagner (Julie)

'The problem isn't that it always goes for the cheap laugh, but that it fails at getting it so often.' – *Variety*

High Season

GB 1987 92m colour

Curzon/British Screen/Film Four/Michael White/Hemdale (Clare Downs)

A female photographer meets strange friends in Rhodes.

Spies, thieves and tourists make an odd lightweight mixture in a movie best suited to TV.

w Mark and Clare Peploe *d* Clare Peploe *ph* Chris Menges *m* Jason Osborn *pd* Andrew McAlpine *ed* Gabriella Cristiani

☆ Jacqueline Bisset, James Fox, Irene Papas, Sebastian Shaw, Kenneth Branagh, Robert Stephens

'The blazing mountain manhunt for Killer Mad-Dog Earle!'

High Sierra *

US 1941 96m bw

Warner (Hal. B. Wallis, Mark Hellinger)

An ex-con gangster plans one last heist in the Californian mountains, but is mortally wounded through his involvement with two women.

Rather dreary action melodrama which gave Bogart his first real star part (after George Raft turned it down). Remade 1955 as I Died a Thousand Times *(qv); also in 1949 as a Western,* Colorado Territory.

w John Huston, W. R. Burnett *novel* W. R. Burnett *d* *Raoul Walsh* *ph* Tony Gaudio *m* Adolph Deutsch

☆ *Humphrey Bogart*, Ida Lupino, Joan Leslie, Alan Curtis, Arthur Kennedy, Henry Hull, Henry Travers, Jerome Cowan

'The last swallow, perhaps, of the gangsters' summer.' – *William Whitebait*

'Like it or not, I'll be damned if you leave before the end, or go to sleep.' – *Otis Ferguson*

'As gangster pictures go, this one has everything – speed, excitement, suspense, and that ennobling suggestion of futility which makes for irony and poetry.' – *New York Times*

High Society

US 1956 107m Technicolor Vistavision

MGM (Sol C. Siegel)

A haughty rich girl chooses between several suitors.

Cold, flat, dull musical reworking of The Philadelphia Story *(qv), with ill-cast performers and just a few bright moments.*

w John Patrick *d* Charles Walters *ph* Paul C. Vogel *m/ly* Cole Porter *md* Johnny Green, Saul Chaplin *ad* Cedric Gibbons, Hans Peters

☆ Bing Crosby, Grace Kelly, Frank Sinatra, Celeste Holm, Louis Armstrong, Sidney Blackmer, Margalo Gillmore, Louis Calhern, Lydia Reed, John Lund

'The principals perform, most of the time, with a kind of glum cheeriness.' – *Hollis Alpert*

'Simply not Top Drawer.' – *Time*

♫ 'Well, Did You Evah'; 'High Society'; 'Who Wants to be a Millionaire?'; 'I Love You, Samantha'; 'Now You Has Jazz'

Johnny Green, Saul Chaplin; song 'True Love'

High Spirits

GB 1988 96m colour

Palace/Vision PDG (Stephen Woolley, David Saunders)

In order to attract tourists, the owner of an Irish castle fakes ghosts and then discovers that he has summoned up some real ones.

Insubstantial comedy that lurches unsuccessfully into supernatural romance.

wd Neil Jordan *ph* Alex Thomson *m* George Fenton *pd* Alex Furst *ed* Michael Bradsell

☆ Peter O'Toole, Donal McCann, Mary Coughlan, Liz Smith, Steve Guttenberg, Beverly D'Angelo, Jennifer Tilly, Peter Gallagher, Daryl Hannah, Liam Neeson, Ray McAnally

High Tide *

Australia 1987 104m colour

Ritzy/FGH/STL/Hemdale (Sandra Levy)

An unsuccessful singer meets the teenage daughter she abandoned years before.

Unsentimental and well acted study of maternal stirrings.

w Laura Jones *d* Gillian Armstrong *ph* Russell Boyd *m* Peter Best *pd* Sally Campbell *ed* Nicholas Beauman

☆ Judy Davis, Jan Adele, Claudia Karvan, Colin Friels, John Clayton, Frankie J. Holden

'There have never been characters like Ally and her mom in movies, and there has never been a film like this emotional riptide.' – *Carrie Rickey, Philadelphia Inquirer*

High Time

US 1960 103m DeLuxe Cinemascope

TCF/Bing Crosby (Charles Brackett)

A middle-aged widower goes back to college.

Flaccid comedy-musical with some undergraduatish jokes.

w Tom and Frank Waldman *d* Blake Edwards *ph* Ellsworth Fredericks *m* Henry Mancini *songs* Jimmy Van Heusen, Sammy Cahn

☆ Bing Crosby, Tuesday Weld, Fabian, Richard Beymer, Nicole Maurey

song 'The Second Time Around'

High Treason *

GB 1951 93m bw

GFD/Conqueror (Paul Soskin)

Saboteurs are routed by the London police.

Unconvincing documentary melodrama which moves fast enough to be entertaining.

w Frank Harvey, Roy Boulting *d* Roy Boulting *ph* Gilbert Taylor *m* John Addison

☆ Liam Redmond, André Morell, Anthony Bushell, Kenneth Griffith, Patric Doonan, Joan Hickson, Anthony Nicholls, Mary Morris, Geoffrey Keen, Dora Bryan

High Vermilion: see *Silver City*

High Wall

US 1947 99m bw

MGM (Robert Lord)

A war veteran is put in an asylum after confessing to killing his wife, but later events prove that he was drugged into saying so.

Adequately entertaining, supremely unconvincing mystery melodrama.

w Sydney Boehm *d* Curtis Bernhardt *ph* Paul C. Vogel *m* Bronislau Kaper

☆ Robert Taylor, Herbert Marshall, Audrey Totter, Dorothy Patrick, H. B. Warner, Warner Anderson

High, Wide and Handsome *

US 1937 110m bw

Paramount (Arthur Hornblow Jnr)

Pennsylvania 1859: a travelling showgirl falls in love with a farmer.

Disappointingly stilted period musical with most of the talent ill at ease until the final reel.

w Oscar Hammerstein II *d* Rouben Mamoulian *ph* Victor Milner, Theodor Sparkuhl *m/ly* Jerome Kern, Oscar Hammerstein II *md* Boris Morros *ch* Le Roy Prinz *ad* Hans Dreier, John Goodman

☆ Irene Dunne, Randolph Scott, Dorothy Lamour, Raymond Walburn, Alan Hale, Elizabeth Patterson, Charles Bickford, William Frawley, Akim Tamiroff, Ben Blue, Irving Pichel, Lucien Littlefield

'Not a road show, but a big picture, and should get nice returns.' – *Variety*

'There are two hours of this long, dumb and dreary picture ... one is left with a few dim distressing memories.' – *Graham Greene*
'Irene Dunne at her cornball primmest, singing alongside a farmhorse when Randolph Scott isn't around.' – *Pauline Kael, 70s*

A High Wind in Jamaica *
GB 1965 104m DeLuxe
Cinemascope
TCF (John Croydon)
In Victorian days, English children en route home from Jamaica are captured by pirates and influence their lives.
Semi-serious adventure story with a highly unlikely ending in which the chief pirate allows himself to be executed for a murder committed by a child. There are however pleasures along the way.
w Stanley Mann, Ronald Harwood, Denis Cannan *novel* Richard Hughes *d* Alexander Mackendrick *ph* Douglas Slocombe *m* Larry Adler
☆ Deborah Baxter, Anthony Quinn, James Coburn, Isabel Dean, Nigel Davenport, Gert Frobe, Lila Kedrova

The High Window: see *The Brasher Doubloon*

High-Ballin'
US 1978 100m Movielab
AIP/Stanley Chase/Pando (Jan Slan)
An independent trucker battles hijackers as well as pressures from a giant trucking firm.
Routine action hokum, a long way behind 1948's Thieves' Highway *and even less entertaining than TV's* Movin' On.
w Paul Edwards *d* Peter Carter *ph* René Verzier *m* Paul Hoffert
☆ Peter Fonda, Jerry Reed, Helen Shaver, Chris Wiggins

Higher and Higher *
US 1943 90m bw
RKO (Tim Whelan)
Servants have an elaborate plan to restore the family fortune.
Unamusing musical which undernourishes several talents.
w Jay Dratler, Ralph Spence *play* Gladys Hurlbut, Joshua Logan *d* Tim Whelan *ph* Robert de Grasse *m/ly* Jimmy McHugh, Harold Adamson *md* Constantin Bakaleinikoff
☆ Michele Morgan, Jack Haley, *Frank Sinatra*, Leon Errol, Marcy McGuire, *Victor Borge*, Mary Wickes, Barbara Hale, Elizabeth Risdon
'There may be some folks who can't figure out the reasons for Sinatra's meteoric rise, or might be wondering whether he's here to stay or not, but in his first screen starring role he at least gets in no one's way.' – *Variety*
Constantin Bakaleinikoff; song 'I Couldn't Sleep a Wink Last Night'

Higher Learning *
US 1994 127m Technicolor
Columbia/New Deal (John Singleton, Paul Hall)
New students at a university campus find themselves in conflict with fellow students according to their colour.
Earnest drama on the complexities and inequalities of the education system, a little too schematic in its oppositions to be entirely persuasive, particularly in its melodramatic finale.
wd John Singleton *ph* Peter Lyons Collister *m* Stanley Clarke *pd* Keith Brian Burns *ed* Bruce Cannon
☆ Omar Epps, Kristy Swanson, Michael Rapaport, Jennifer Connelly, Ice Cube, Laurence Fishburne, Jason Wiles, Tyra Banks, Cole Hauser
'A thoughtful, angry film, but marred by stereotyping and a pervasive self-righteousness.' – *Sheila Johnston, Independent*

The Highest Honour
Australia 1982 143m colour
Southern International Films (Lee Robinson)
aka: *Southern Cross*
In 1942, an Australian spy befriends his captor and finally executioner.
Sombre true story, far too long in the telling.
w Lee Robinson *d* Peter Maxwell *ph* John McLean *m* Eric Jupp
☆ George Mallaby, Michael Aitkens, John Howard, Atsuo Nakamura, Stuart Wilson, Steve Bisley
'Largely fails to ignite.' – *Julian Petley, MFB*

Highlander
GB/US 1986 111m Technicolor
EMI/Highlander (Peter S. Davis, William N. Panzer)
A 14th-century Scotsman apparently dies in battle but finds he is an immortal, and is still crossing swords with his enemy the Kurgan in 20th-century Manhattan.
Muddled, violent and noisy fantasy: the explanation doesn't come until most people will have given up.
w Gregory Widden, Peter Bellwood, Larry Ferguson *d* Russell Mulcahy *ph* Gerry Fisher *m* Michael Kamen *pd* Allan Cameron *ed* Peter Honess
☆ Christopher Lambert, Roxanne Hart, Clancy Brown, Sean Connery
'While there are entertaining moments, total work is a mess.' – *Variety*
'A moody combination of *Blade Runner*, *The Terminator* and your last really good nightmare.' – *People*

'It will take two immortals to face the ultimate evil. But in the end, there can be only one.'
Highlander: Endgame
US 2000 88m DeLuxe
Miramax/Dimension (Peter Davis, William Panzer)
An immortal warrior is determined to kill off all his remaining immortal rivals.
Appallingly nonsensical fantasy without narrative sense or excitement.
w Joel Soisson *story* Eric Bernt, Gillian Horvath, William Panzer *d* Douglas Aarniokoski *ph* Doug Milsome *m* Stephen Graziano *pd* Jonathan Carlson *ed* Christopher Blunden, Michael N. Nue, Robert Feretti, Tracy Granger, Rod Dean, Donald J. Paonessa *martial arts ch* Donnie Yen
☆ Adrian Paul (Duncan MacLeod), Christopher Lambert (Connor MacLeod), Bruce Payne (Jacob Kell), Lisa Barbuscia (Faith/Kate), Donnie Yen (Jin Ke), Jim Byrnes (Dawson), Peter Wingfield (Methos), Damon Dash (Carlos), Beatie Edney (Heather), Sheila Gish (Rachel Ellenstein)
'A farrago on almost every creative level that looks like it was stitched together from three different movies whose cans got mixed up in the editing suite.' – *Derek Elley, Variety*

'It's Time For A New Kind Of Magic.'
Highlander II – The Quickening
US 1990 100m Eastmancolor J-D-C Scope
Entertainment/Lamb Bear/Peter S. Davis, William Panzer
Two immortal aliens join forces to defeat a dictator who controls the Earth.
Incoherent and inconsequential sequel.
w Peter Bellwood *story* Brian Clemens, William Panzer *d* Russell Mulcahy *ph* Phil Meheux *m* Stewart Copeland *pd* Roger Hall *ed* Hubert C. de la Bouillerie, Anthony Redman *sp* John Richardson
☆ Christopher Lambert, Sean Connery, Virginia Madsen, Michael Ironside, Allan Rich, John C. McGinley
'A terrible mess. The film's organization at all levels, from plot down to the cutting of individual action sequences, is so full of holes that there is nothing solid for it to adhere to.' – *Sight and Sound*

'Throughout time they have hunted each other, fulfilling the prophecy that there can be only one.'
'The final conflict.'
Highlander III: The Sorcerer
Canada/France/GB 1994 99m colour
Scope
Entertainment/Transfilm/Initial/Fallingcloud (Claude Léger)
The Highlander is menaced by a fellow immortal, released after being trapped inside a mountain for 400 years.
This third episode of an increasingly woebegone series is set in the time between the first and the second movie and merely adds some oriental trimmings to its unimaginative rerun of a similar narrative.
w Paul Ohl *story* William Panzer, Brad Mirman *d* Andrew Morahan *ph* Steven Chivers *m* J. Peter Robinson *pd* Gilles Aird, Ben Morahan *ed* Yves Langlois *sp* make-up effects: Stephen Dupuis, Charles Carter
☆ Christopher Lambert, Mario Van Peebles, Deborah Unger, Mako, Michael Jayston, Martin Neufeld
'A breakneck, roller-coaster genre ride that's brainless fodder for undiscriminating auds.' – *Variety*

Highly Dangerous
GB 1950 88m bw
Rank/Two Cities (Anthony Darnborough)
A lady entomologist in a Balkan country is suspected of spying but manages to outwit her enemies.
Odd blend of straight adventure and spoof; it doesn't quite come off.
w Eric Ambler *d* Roy Baker *ph* Reg Wyer *m* Richard Addinsell
☆ Margaret Lockwood, Dane Clark, Marius Goring, Naunton Wayne, Eugene Deckers, Wilfrid Hyde-White, Michael Hordern, Gladys Henson

Highpoint
Canada 1984 88m Eastmancolor
Highpoint/New World
An industrialist is on the run from both the Mafia and the CIA.
Routine thriller with a finale atop Toronto's CN Tower.
w Richard Guttman, Ian Sutherland *d* Peter Carter
☆ Richard Harris, Christopher Plummer, Beverly D'Angelo, Kate Reid, Peter Donat
† Filmed in 1979.

Highway 301 *
US 1950 83m bw
Warner (Bryan Foy)
The Tri-State Gang is apprehended by police.
Actionful gangster melodrama of the Bonnie and Clyde *type with plenty of suspenseful situations and slick camerawork.*
wd Andrew Stone *ph* Carl Guthrie *m* William Lava
☆ Steve Cochran, Virginia Grey, Gaby Andre, Edmon Ryan, Richard Egan, Robert Webber
'Several good suspense sequences, some good comic observation, and many pleasing visual moments of the wet-streets-at-night category.' – *Richard Mallett, Punch*

Highway 61 *
Canada/GB 1991 102m colour
Shadow Shows/Telefilm Canada/Film Four International (Colin Brunton, Bruce McDonald)
A guileless small-town Canadian barber and jazz trumpeter travels to New Orleans with a delinquent fugitive rock roadie who has stolen her group's stash of drugs and hidden it in a corpse.
Quirky little movie about the exploited and the exploitative, and those who sell their souls too cheaply.
w Don McKellar *d* Bruce McDonald *ph* Miroslaw Baszak *m* Nash The Slash *ad* Ian Brock *ed* Michael Pacek
☆ Don McKellar, Valerie Buhagiar, Earl Pastko, Peter Breck, Art Bergmann

Highway Dragnet
US 1954 71m bw
Allied Artists (William F. Broidy)
A lady photographer gives a lift to an ex-marine who may or may not be a murderer.
Twisty lower-berth thriller in which all is not as it seems.
w Herb Meadow, Jerome Odlum *story* Roger Corman *d* Nathan Juran *ph* John Martin *md* Edward Kay
☆ Joan Bennett, Richard Conte, Wanda Hendrix, Reed Hadley, Mary Beth Hughes, Iris Adrian

Highway Patrolman *
Mexico 1991 104m colour
Metro Tartan/Cable Hogue/Together Brothers/Ultra (Lorenzo O'Brien)
original title: *El Patrullero*
A newly qualified, poorly paid highway cop finds that maintaining law and order is not as straightforward as he thought during his training, especially when he is offered bribes.
Entertaining, episodic account of low life in Mexico, filmed in a semi-documentary style and concentrating on the small happenings of an existence on the margins.
w Lorenzo O'Brien *d* Alex Cox *ph* Miguel Garzon *m* Zander Schloss *pd* Cecilia Montiel *ed* Carlos Puente
☆ Roberto Sosa, Bruno Bichir, Vanessa Bauche, Zaide Silvia Gutierrez, Pedro Armendariz Jnr, Ernesto Gomez Cruz, Jorge Russek, Karl Braun
'An enjoyable trip and Cox's most accomplished film for a decade.' – *Adam Mars-Jones, Independent*
'It is intelligent, caustic, ironic and humorous all at once, and shows that Cox is a director to match the best of them.' – *Steve Beard, Empire*

Highway to Freedom: see *Joe Smith American*

'Where the toll is your soul.'
Highway to Hell
US 1992 93m CFI color
Sovereign/Hemdale (Mary Anne Page, John Byers)
An eloping couple on the way to Las Vegas run into a demonic cop who abducts the girl.
Hell is an uninventive horror flick.
w Brian Helgeland *d* Ate de Jong *ph* Robin Vidgeon *m* Hidden Faces *pd* Phillip Dean Foreman *ed* Todd Ramsay, Randy Thornton
☆ Patrick Bergin, Adam Storke, Chad Lowe, Kristy Swanson, Pamela Gidley, Jarrett Lennon, C. J. Graham, Richard Farnsworth
'A failed horror comedy in search of a bigger budget and far better script.' – *Variety*
† Made in 1989.

The Highwayman
US 1951 82m Cinecolor
Allied Artists/Jack Dietz (Hal. E. Chester)
A 17th-century nobleman disguises himself as a Quaker and becomes a highwayman to right wrongs.
Curious Poverty Row period actioner with ideas generally above its station, not to mention an unexpected tragic ending.
w Jack DeWitt, Renault Duncan *poem* Alfred Noyes *d* Lesley Selander *ph* Harry Neumann *m* Herschel Burke Gilbert
☆ Philip Friend, Charles Coburn, Victor Jory, Wanda Hendrix, Cecil Kellaway, Scott Forbes, Virginia Huston, Dan O'Herlihy
† The film originally credited Jan Jeffries as the screenwriter because its actual writers were blacklisted.

The Highwayman
Canada 1999 97m colour
Lions Gate/Norstar (Peter R Simpson)
After losing everything, a middle-aged man becomes a criminal by default and goes on the run with an unbalanced teenage girl, who claims that he is her father, her love-struck boyfriend and two psychopaths.
Stylised black comedy that never strikes the right tone, with acting styles that range from naturalistic to over-the-top, and a narrative that runs out of invention long before the end..
w Richard Beattie *d* Keoni Waxman *ph* Kim Derko *m* Ian Thomas *pd* Oleg M Savytskyly *ed* Nick Rotundo
☆ Stephen McHattie (Frank Drake), Laura Harris (Ziggy Watson), Bernie Coulson (Panda), Gordon Michael Woolvett (Walter), Jason Priestley (Breakfast), Louis Gossett Jnr (Phil Bishop)
'There are some things a person should not be forced to watch.' – *Marc Horton, Edmonton Journal*

'The true story of two sisters who shared a passion, a madness and a man.'
Hilary and Jackie **
GB 1998 124m DeLuxe Panavision
Intermedia/Film Four/British Screen/Arts Council/Oxford (Andy Paterson, Nicolas Kent)
The life and loves of cellist Jacqueline Du Pré, whose career ended when she was 27, owing to multiple sclerosis.
Some excellent acting gives an emotional power and rawness to this often conventional biopic, which concentrates on the relationship and rivalry between two sisters.
w Frank Cottrell-Boyce *book* A Genius in the Family by Hilary and Piers Du Pré *d* Anand

Tucker *ph* David Johnson *m* Barrington Pheloung *pd* Alice Normington *ed* Martin Walsh
☆ *Emily Watson* (Jacqueline Du Pré), *Rachel Griffiths* (Hilary Du Pré), James Frain (Daniel Barenboim), David Morrissey, Charles Dance, Celia Imrie, Rupert Penry-Jones, Bill Paterson, Auriol Evans, Keeley Flanders, Nyree Dawn Porter (Dame Margot Fonteyn), Vernon Dobtcheff
'Audiences will find the film an extremely moving and haunting – if ultimately gruelling – experience.' – *James Cameron-Wilson, Film Review*
Emily Watson; Rachel Griffiths

'I want to live like a man – and still be a woman!'

Hilda Crane
US 1956 87m Technicolor Cinemascope
TCF (Herbert B. Swope Jnr)
An unhappy woman marries for the third time and convinces herself it won't work.
Emotional melodrama of the old school: very moderate in all departments.
wd Philip Dunne *play* Samson Raphaelson *ph* Joe MacDonald *m* David Raksin
☆ Jean Simmons, Guy Madison, Jean-Pierre Aumont, *Evelyn Varden*, Judith Evelyn, Peggy Knudsen

'They went up like men! They came down like animals!'

The Hill **
GB 1965 122m bw
MGM/Seven Arts (Kenneth Hyman)
Prisoners rebel against the harsh discipline of a British military detention centre in North Africa during World War II.
Lurid melodrama which descends fairly quickly into black farce with a number of sweaty actors outshouting each other. Enjoyable on this level when you can hear the dialogue through the poor sound recording.
w Ray Rigby play Ray Rigby, R. S. Allen *d* Sidney Lumet *ph* Oswald Morris *m* none *ad* Herbert Smith *ed* Thelma Connell
☆ *Sean Connery*, Harry Andrews, Michael Redgrave, Ian Bannen, Alfred Lynch, *Ossie Davis*, Roy Kinnear, Jack Watson, Ian Hendry
Oswald Morris

Hill 24 Doesn't Answer
Israel 1954 101m bw
Sikor (Thorold Dickinson, Peter Frye)
Four friends defend Hill 24 against the Arabs on the eve of the cease-fire, and are all killed.
Israel's first feature film, a curious amalgam of the slick and the amateur, with long flashbacks which make it resemble The Bridge of San Luis Rey.
w Zvi Kolitz, Peter Frye, Joanna and Thorold Dickinson *d* Thorold Dickinson *ph* Gerald Gibbs *m* Paul Ben-Haim
☆ Michael Wager, Edward Mulhare, Haya Harareet, Arieh Lavi, Michael Shilo

A Hill in Korea
GB 1956 81m bw
British Lion/Wessex (Anthony Squire)
US title: *Hell in Korea*
During the Korean war, a small patrol guards a hill.
Minor war talk-piece, shot in Surrey and looking it.
w Ian Dalrymple, Anthony Squire, Ronald Spencer *novel* Max Catto *d* Julian Amyes *ph* Freddie Francis *m* Malcolm Arnold
☆ George Baker, Harry Andrews, Stanley Baker, Michael Medwin, Ronald Lewis, Stephen Boyd, Victor Maddern, Harry Landis
'Character is adequately sketched into a suitably laconic script.' – *MFB*

Hill's Angels: see *The North Avenue Irregulars*

The Hills Have Eyes
US 1977 90m Movielab
New Realm/Blood Relations (Peter Locke)
Holidaymakers are waylaid and killed by a family of desert cannibals.
Low-grade shocker which mysteriously achieved some cult status.
wd Wes Craven *ph* Eric Saarinen *m* Don Peake *ad* Robert Burns *ed* Wes Craven
☆ John Steadman, Janus Blythe, Arthur King, Russ Grieve, Virginia Vincent
'Simultaneously risible and nauseating.' – *Tim Pulleine, MFB*

The Hills of Home
US 1948 95m Technicolor
MGM
GB title: *Master of Lassie*
A doctor returns to his Scottish village to practise medicine, and brings his faithful collie.
Adequate addition to the Lassie saga, with competent work all round.
w William Ludwig *d* Fred Wilcox
☆ Edmund Gwenn, Tom Drake, Donald Crisp, Rhys Williams, Reginald Owen

Himalaya **
France/Switzerland/GB/Nepal 1999 109m colour
Momentum/BAC/Galatée/France2/Guéville/JMH/Antelope (Jacques Perrin, Christophe Barratier)
original title: *Himalaya: L'Enfance D'Un Chef*
aka: *Caravan*
After his son dies, a dispute over who should lead an all-important yak caravan develops between the elderly village chief, who wants his grandson to become the new leader, and a younger rival.
Visually exciting drama, in a remote and beautiful setting, of an elemental clash between the impetuous young and conservative elders; it's a story as old as time, told in a fresh and vital way.
w Eric Valli, Olivier Dazat, Jean-Claude Guillebaud, Louis Gardel, Nathalie Azoulai, Jacques Perrin *d Eric Valli ph Eric Guichard, Jean Paul Meurisse m* Bruno Coulais *ad* Jérome Krowicki *ed* Marie-Josèphe Yoyotte
☆ Thilen Lhondup (Tinle), Gurgon Kyap (Karma), Lhakpa Tsamchoe (Pema), Karma Wangel (Pasang), Karma Tensing Nyima (Norbou), Labrang Tundup (Labrang), Jampa Kalsang Tamang (Jampa), Tsering Dorjee (Rabkie)
'Epically engaging in its strangeness and yet as accessible as a cattle-drive Western from Howard Hawks' – *Neil Norman, London Evening Standard*
foreign language film

Himatsuri: see *Fire Festival*

Der Himmel über Berlin: see *Wings of Desire*

The Hindenburg *
US 1975 125m Technicolor Panavision
Universal/Filmmakers (Robert Wise)
In 1937, sabotage causes the airship Hindenburg to crash on arrival at New York.
An extremely uninteresting guess at the cause of this famous disaster. The plot and dialogue are leaden, and such actors as have more than a couple of lines look extremely glum. The special effects, however, are fine despite curious blue-rinse photographic processing.
w Nelson Gidding *novel* Michael M. Mooney *d* Robert Wise *ph* Robert Surtees *m* David Shire *pd* Edward Carfagno *sp Albert Whitlock*
☆ George C. Scott, Anne Bancroft, Burgess Meredith, William Atherton, Roy Thinnes, Gig Young, Charles Durning, Robert Clary, René Auberjonois
'The tackiest disaster movie yet – a cheap and chaotic collage of painted drops, wooden actors and not-so-special effects that manages to make one of this century's most sensational real-life catastrophes seem roughly as terrifying as a badly stubbed toe.' – *Frank Rich*
Robert Surtees

Hindle Wakes
GB 1952 82m bw
Monarch
US title: *Holiday Week*
A Lancashire millgirl spends a week at Blackpool with the master's son but causes a scandal when she refuses to marry him.
Modestly competent version of a semi-classic play about class distinctions.
w John Baines *play* Stanley Houghton *d* Arthur Crabtree *ph* Geoffrey Faithfull *m* Stanley Black
☆ Lisa Daniely, Leslie Dwyer, Brian Worth, Sandra Dorne, Ronald Adam, Joan Hickson
† A probably better, but unavailable version was made in 1931 by Victor Saville for Gaumont, with Belle Chrystall, Edmund Gwenn, John Stuart, Ruth Peterson, Norman McKinnel and Sybil Thorndike.

Hips Hips Hooray
US 1934 68m bw
RKO
Two salesmen pitch flavoured lipstick to a beauty parlour chain.
Tired star comedy.
w Harry Ruby, Bert Kalmar *d* Mark Sandrich
☆ Bert Wheeler, Robert Woolsey, Ruth Etting, Thelma Todd, Dorothy Lee, George Meeker
'Femme display chief asset.' – *Variety*

The Hired Hand
US 1971 93m Technicolor
Universal/Pando (William Hayward)
Two Western drifters avenge the killing of their friend and settle down to work on a farm; but violence follows them.
A potentially enjoyable small-scale Western is spoiled by pretentious direction and effects which bore the spectator to death.
w Alan Sharp *d* Peter Fonda *ph* Vilmos Zsigmond *m* Bruce Langhorne
☆ Peter Fonda, Warren Oates, Verna Bloom, Severn Darden
'The first slow-motion western, with endless artsy photography not quite succeeding in obscuring the rambling plot.' – *Judith Crist, 1973*
'When a film begins with a "lyrical" shot, your heart has a right to sink.' – *Stanley Kauffmann*

Hired Wife
US 1940 96m bw
Universal
A secretary who loves her boss saves his company by marrying him so that it can be transferred to her name.
After which the plot has absolutely nowhere to go.
w Richard Connell, Gladys Lehman *d* William A. Seiter *ph* Milton Krasner *ad* Jack Otterson *ed* Milton Carruth
☆ Rosalind Russell, Brian Aherne, Virginia Bruce, Robert Benchley, John Carroll, Hobart Cavanaugh

The Hireling *
GB 1973 108m colour
Columbia/World Film Services (Ben Arbeid)
In the twenties, a lady's chauffeur falls in love with her.
Talkative drama, elegant but not much fun.
w Wolf Mankowitz *novel* L. P. Hartley *d Alan Bridges ph* Michael Reed *m* Marc Wilkinson *pd Natasha Kroll*
☆ Sarah Miles, Robert Shaw, Peter Egan, Elizabeth Sellars, Caroline Mortimer
Natasha Kroll; Peter Egan

Hiroshima Mon Amour *
France/Japan 1959 91m bw
Argos/Comei/Pathé/Daiei
A French actress working in Hiroshima falls for a Japanese architect and remembers her tragic love for a German soldier during the occupation.
Jumbled mixture of flashbacks and flashforwards which can now be recognized as typical of this director and on its first appearance was hailed as a work of art in an innovative new style.
w Marguerite Duras *d Alain Resnais ph* Sacha Vierny, Takahashi Michio *m* Giovanni Fusco, Georges Delerue
☆ Emmanuele Riva, Eiji Okada
'Suddenly a new film. Really new, first-hand: a work which tells a story of its own in a style of its own. One is almost afraid to touch it.' – *Dilys Powell*
Marguerite Duras

His Affair: see *This Is My Affair*

His Brother's Wife
US 1936 91m bw
MGM (Lawrence Weingarten)
A young scientist is helped out of trouble by his brother, on condition he disappears; the brother then weds the scientist's girlfriend.
Heavy romantic melodrama containing everything including jungle fever, flung together to take advantage of the stars' real-life romance.
w Leon Gordon, John Meehan *story* George Auerbach *d* W. S. Van Dyke II *ph* Oliver T. Marsh *m* Franz Waxman
☆ Robert Taylor, Barbara Stanwyck, Joseph Calleia, John Eldredge, Jean Hersholt, Samuel S. Hinds, Leonard Mudie, Jed Prouty

His Butler's Sister *
US 1943 94m bw
Universal (Felix Jackson)
A temporary maid falls for her sophisticated boss.
Pleasant comedy musical: no great shakes, but the principals give the air of enjoying themselves.
w Samuel Hoffenstein, Betty Reinhardt *d* Frank Borzage *ph* Elwood Bredell *m* Hans Salter *ad* John B. Goodman, Martin Obzina *ed* Ted J. Kent
☆ Deanna Durbin, Franchot Tone, Pat O'Brien, Evelyn Ankers, Walter Catlett, Alan Mowbray, Akim Tamiroff, Elsa Janssen, Iris Adrian

His Double Life *
US 1933 63m bw
Paramount (Eddie Dowling)
A famous painter, when his valet dies, takes his identity.
Adequate transcription of a novel later redone as Holy Matrimony.
w Arthur Hopkins, Clara Beranger *novel and play Arnold Bennett d* Arthur Hopkins *ph* Arthur Edeson
☆ Roland Young, Lillian Gish, Lumsden Hare, Lucy Beaumont
'Pleasant little film; big grosses unlikely.' – *Variety*

His Excellency
GB 1951 84m bw
Ealing (Michael Truman)
The Labour government sends a trade union official to govern a Mediterranean colony.
Disappointingly tacky-looking and stagebound version of an unpersuasive West End comedy.
w Robert Hamer, W. P. Lipscomb *play* Dorothy and Campbell Christie *d* Robert Hamer *ph* Douglas Slocombe *m* Handel *md* Ernest Irving
☆ Eric Portman, Cecil Parker, Helen Cherry, Susan Stephen, Edward Chapman, Clive Morton, Robin Bailey, Geoffrey Keen

His Family Tree
US 1935 59m bw
RKO
An Irishman migrates to America and gets involved in politics.
Lively second feature for the Irish halls.
w Joel Sayre, John Twist *play Old Man Murphy* by Patrick Kearney, Harry Wagstaff Gribble *d* Charles Vidor
☆ James Barton, Margaret Callahan, Maureen Delany, Addison Randall, William Harrigan
'With more care, this might have been much better.' – *Variety*

His Girl Friday ****
US 1940 92m bw
Columbia (Howard Hawks)
A remake of *The Front Page* (qv), with Hildy Johnson turned into a woman.
Frantic, hilarious black farce with all participants at their best; possibly the fastest comedy ever filmed, and one of the funniest.
w Charles Lederer play The Front Page by Charles MacArthur, Ben Hecht *d Howard Hawks ph* Joseph Walker *m* Sydney Cutner *md* Morris Stoloff *ad* Lionel Banks *ed* Gene Havlik
☆ *Rosalind Russell* (Hildy Johnson), *Cary Grant* (Walter Burns), *Ralph Bellamy* (Bruce Baldwin), Gene Lockhart (Sheriff Hartwell), Porter Hall (Murphy), *Ernest Truex* (Bensinger), Cliff Edwards (Endicott), *Clarence Kolb* (Mayor), *Roscoe Karns* (McCue), *Frank Jenks* (Wilson), Abner Biberman (Louis), Frank Orth (Duffy), John Qualen (Earl Williams), Helen Mack (Molly Malloy), *Billy Gilbert* (Joe Pettibone) and also Alma Kruger (Mrs Baldwin)
'The kind of terrific verbal slam-bang that has vanished from current film-making.' – *New Yorker, 1975*
'One of the fastest of all movies, from line to line and from gag to gag.' – *Manny Farber, 1971*
'Overlapping dialogue carries the movie along at breakneck speed; word gags take the place of the sight gags of silent comedy, as this vanished race

of brittle, cynical, childish people rush around on corrupt errands.' – *Pauline Kael, 1968*

'The main trouble is that when they made *The Front Page* the first time, it stayed made.' – *Otis Ferguson*

† The Rosalind Russell role had first been turned down by Jean Arthur, Ginger Rogers, Claudette Colbert and Irene Dunne.

His Glorious Night
US 1929 85m bw
MGM
GB title: *Breath of Scandal*
A princess falls in love with a commoner.
Soporific early talkie, remade in 1960 as A Breath of Scandal. *The movie which first exposed its star's high-pitched voice and is credited with killing his career.*
w Willard Mack *play Olimpia* by Ferenc Molnar *d* Lionel Barrymore *ph* Percy Hilburn
☆ John Gilbert, Catherine Dale Owen, Hedda Hopper, Gustav von Seyffertitz, Nance O'Neil

His Kind of Woman *
US 1951 120m bw
RKO (Howard Hughes, Robert Sparks)
At a remote Mexican ranch resort, a gangster on the run holds up residents including a fortune-hunting girl and a fading matinee idol.
Agreeable tongue-in-cheek melodrama which slightly outstays its welcome but is generally good fun.
w Frank Fenton *d* John Farrow *ph* Harry J. Wild *m* Leigh Harline *md* Constantin Bakaleinikoff
☆ Robert Mitchum, Jane Russell, *Vincent Price*, Raymond Burr, Tim Holt, Charles McGraw, Marjorie Reynolds, Jim Backus

His Lordship *
GB 1936 71m bw
Gaumont (S. C. Balcon)
US title: *Man of Affairs*
A politician's twin takes his place to expose an old murder.
Comfortable star comedy-drama.
w Maude Howell, Edwin Greenwood, L. DuGarde Peach *play The Nelson Touch* by Neil Grant *d* Herbert Mason *ph* Gunther Krampf *md* Louis Levy *ad* Alfred Junge
☆ George Arliss, Rene Ray, Romilly Lunge, Jessie Winter, Allan Jeayes

His Majesty O'Keefe
GB 1954 90m Technicolor
Warner/Norma (Harold Hecht)
Native islanders are taught by an easygoing mariner how to exploit their natural resources and defend themselves against pirates.
Thin adventure romance with too little for its star to do.
w Borden Chase, James Hill *novel* Lawrence Kingman, Gerald Green *d* Byron Haskin *ph* Otto Heller *m* Robert Farnon
☆ Burt Lancaster, Joan Rice, André Morell, Abraham Sofaer, Benson Fong, Archie Savage

His Other Woman: see *Desk Set*

His Private Secretary
US 1933 68m bw
Showmen's/Screencraft (Al Alt)
A wealthy playboy falls for minister's granddaughter, much to his father's annoyance.
A curiosity from Wayne's early career, in which he plays a sophisticated man-about-town.
w Lewis D. Collins, Jack Natteford *d* Philip H. Whitman *ph* Abe Scholtz *ed* Bobby Ray
☆ John Wayne (Dick Wallace), Evalyn Knapp (Marion Hall), Alec B. Francis (Dr Hall), Reginald Barlow (Mr Wallace), Natalie Kingston (Polly), Arthur Hoyt (Little), Al 'Fuzzy' St John (Garage owner), Hugh Kidder (Butler)

'From the ends of the earth ... a darling baby brings them together!'
His Woman
US 1931 80m bw
Paramount (Albert Kaufman)
The captain of a tramp freighter finds himself in charge of an abandoned baby and a runaway girl.
Slow, indifferent comedy drama, previously filmed in 1929 as Sal of Singapore.
w Adelaide Heilbron, Melville Baker *novel The Sentimentalist* by Dale Collins *d* Edward Sloman *ph* William Steiner, Arthur Ellis
☆ Gary Cooper, Claudette Colbert, Averill Harris, Richard Spiro, Douglass Dumbrille, Joseph Calleia, Harry Davenport
'Actionless picture ... too many barnacles cling to the script.' – *Variety*

Une Histoire D'Amour *
France 1951 95m bw
Jacques Roitfeld/Cité Films
GB title: *Love Story*
A police inspector discovers that a young couple killed themselves because of parental opposition.
A rather soggy little drama made watchable by its careful detail and immaculate leading performance.
w Michel Audiard *d* Robert Clavel *ph* Louis Page *m* Paul Misraki
☆ Louis Jouvet, Daniel Gélin, Dany Robin

Une Histoire Inventée: see *An Imaginary Tale*

Histoires Extraordinaires *
France/Italy 1968 120m Eastmancolor
Les Films Marceau/Cocinor/PEA (Raymond Eger)
GB title: *Tales of Mystery and Imagination*
aka: *Spirits of the Dead*
Episodic film based on three stories by Edgar Allan Poe.
Only Fellini provides entertainment, and that by abandoning all pretence to be faithful to the original, with a story about a drunken English actor working in Rome.
w Metzengerstein: Roger Vadim, Pascal Cousin, Clement Biddlewood; William Wilson: Louis Malle, Clement Biddlewood; Toby Dammit: Federico Fellini, Bernardino Zapponi *stories* Edgar Allan Poe *d* Metzengerstein: Roger Vadim; William Wilson: Louis Malle; Toby Dammit: Federico Fellini *ph* Metzengerstein: Claude Renoir; William Wilson: Tonino Delli Colli; Toby Dammit: Guiseppe Rotundo *m* Metzengerstein: Jean Prodromides; William Wilson: Diego Masson; Toby Dammit: Nino Rota *ad* William Wilson: Carlo Leva; Toby Dammit: Fabrizio Clerici *ed* Metzengerstein: Helene Plemiannikov; William Wilson: Franco Arcalli, Susanne Baron; Toby Dammit: Ruggiero Mastroianni
☆ Metzengerstein: Jane Fonda, Peter Fonda, Carla Marlier, James Robertson Justice; William Wilson: Alain Delon, Brigitte Bardot, Katia Christina; Toby Dammit: Terence Stamp, Salvo Randone

History Is Made at Night *
US 1937 97m bw
Walter Wanger
A divorcee and her new love have trouble from her ex-husband.
Atmospheric, artificial, generally entertaining romantic comedy-drama of a kind which went out of fashion long ago.
w Gene Towne, Graham Baker *d* Frank Borzage *ph* Gregg Toland *m* Alfred Newman
☆ Charles Boyer, Jean Arthur, *Leo Carrillo*, Colin Clive
'A weird and unbelievable melodrama ... mildly entertaining with good scenes.' – *Variety*
'So souped up with demonic passions and tender glances and elegant photography that it's rather fun.' – *New Yorker, 1978*
'Frank Borzage, who could turn *Frankenstein Meets the Wolf Man* into a romantic reverie, is quite undeterred by the venality rampant in the script and interjects his vision of what Andrew Sarris called love over probability. Oh, there's an iceberg disaster too.' – *Kit Parker catalogue*

The History of Mr Polly *
GB 1948 94m bw
GFD/Two Cities (John Mills)
A draper's assistant buys a small shop but tires of his nagging wife and decides the time has come for a change.
Patchy but generally amusing version of a popular comic novel, very English and rather appealingly done.
w Anthony Pelissier *novel* H. G. Wells *d Anthony Pelissier ph Desmond Dickinson* *m* William Alwyn
☆ John Mills, Sally Ann Howes, Megs Jenkins, Finlay Currie, Betty Ann Davies, Edward Chapman

History of the World Part One
US 1981 92m DeLuxe Panavision
Brooksfilms (Mel Brooks)
Episodes from world history are presented with the author's usual lack of taste or wit: a woeful collection of schoolboy scatology.
wd Mel Brooks *ph* Woody Omens, Paul Wilson *m* John Morris
☆ Mel Brooks, Dom DeLuise, Madeline Kahn, Cloris Leachman, Harvey Korman, Ron Carey, Sid Caesar, Pamela Stephenson, Henny Youngman
'Most of the time it's just expensive sets sitting around waiting for Brooks to do something funny in front of them.' – *Roger Ebert*

Hit!
US 1973 134m Technicolor Panavision
Paramount (Harry Korshak)
A federal agent takes personal action against a drug ring which caused his daughter's death.
Black vigilante melodrama, very violent and interminably padded out with irrelevancies.
w Alan Trustman, David M. Wolf *d* Sidney J. Furie *ph* John A. Alonzo *m* Lalo Schifrin
☆ Billy Dee Williams, Richard Pryor, Paul Hampton, Gwen Welles
'No more under-the-armpit shots, but obscurity is still the keynote of this Sidney Furie effort in the urban vigilante genre.' – *Sight and Sound*

The Hit
GB 1984 98m Technicolor
Zenith/Central/The Recorded Picture Company (Jeremy Thomas)
A supergrass hiding in Spain is sought by two gang executioners.
Old hat thuggery shown in new-style detail. Violently suspenseful but not otherwise interesting.
w Peter Prince *d* Stephen Frears *ph* Mike Molloy *m* Paco de Lucia *pd* Andrew Sanders
☆ John Hurt, Terence Stamp, Tim Roth, Laura del Sol, Fernando Rey, Bill Hunter
'Sensitive editing and seductive camerawork can't disguise that the exercise is heading nowhere, a road movie without fuel.' – *Philip Strick, MFB*

Hit Man
US 1972 90m colour
MGM (Gene Corman)
A professional killer returns home to avenge his brother's death.
An ineffectual reworking of the superior Get Carter, *with an American setting and a black cast.*
wd George Armitage *novel Jack's Return Home* by Ted Lewis *ph* Andrew Davis *m* H. B. Barnum *ad* Lynn Griffin *ed* Morton Tubor
☆ Bernie Casey, Pam Grier, Lisa Moore, Bhetty Waldron, Sam Laws, Don Diamond

Hit Me
US 1996 123m Foto-Kem
Slough Pond (Steven Shainberg)
An ambitious hotel worker succumbs to the attentions of a mysterious woman and a petty crook.
Plodding thriller of double dealing and double-cross, not helped by miscast leads.
w Denis Johnson *novel A Swell-Looking Babe* by Jim Thompson *d* Steven Shainberg *ph* Mark J. Gordon *m* Phillip Manning Robinson *pd* Amy Danger *ed* Donn Aron
☆ Elias Koteas, Laure Marsac, Jay Leggett, Bruce Ramsay, Kevin J. O'Connor, Philip Baker Hall, J. C. Quinn, Haing S. Ngor, William H. Macy
'A bleak, rewarding film noir.' – *Lawrence van Gelder, New York Sunday Times*

Hit Parade of 1941
US 1940 83m bw
Republic (Sol C. Siegel)
The young owner of a radio station subs his singer girlfriend for the sponsor's daughter.
Moderate musical in need of a better script.
w Bradford Ropes, F. Hugh Herbert (no relation), Maurice Leo *d* John H. Auer *m* Cy Feuer
☆ Kenny Baker, Frances Langford, Hugh Herbert, Mary Boland, Ann Miller, Patsy Kelly, Phil Silvers, Sterling Holloway, Donald MacBride, Barnett Parker, Franklin Pangborn, Six Hits and a Miss, Borrah Minevitch and his Harmonica Rascals
Cy Feuer; song 'Who Am I?' (*m*Jule Styne, *ly*Walter Bullock)

Hit Parade of 1943
US 1943 90m bw
Republic (Albert J. Cohen)
aka: *Change of Heart*
A plagiaristic songwriter becomes a model swain.
Lively comedy musical, third and best of the series.
w Frank Gill Jnr *d* Albert S. Rogell *m* Walter Scharf
☆ John Carroll, Susan Hayward, Gail Patrick, Eve Arden, Melville Cooper, Walter Catlett, Mary Treen, Tom Kennedy, Dorothy Dandridge, the Golden Gate Quartet, Count Basie and his orchestra
Walter Scharf; song 'Change of Heart' (*m*Jule Styne, *ly*Harold Adamson)

Hit Parade of 1947
US 1947 90m bw
Republic (Frank McDonald)
A struggling songwriter tries in vain to become sophisticated.
Tolerable musical jamboree with too thin a storyline.
w Mary Loos, Parke Levy *d* Frank McDonald
☆ Eddie Albert, Constance Moore, Joan Edwards, Gil Lamb, Bill Goodwin, William Frawley, Richard Lane, Roy Rogers and Trigger, Woody Herman and his orchestra

Hit the Deck
US 1930 93m bw (colour sequences)
RKO
Navy recruits have girl trouble.
Lumpy production of a stage musical already well worn.
wd Luther Reed *play* Herbert Fields
☆ Jack Oakie, Polly Walker, Roger Gray, Harry Sweet
'No reason why this one should run into trouble on week stands or less.' – *Variety*

Hit the Deck
US 1955 112m Eastmancolor
Cinemascope
MGM (Joe Pasternak)
Romantic adventures of three sailors on shore leave in San Francisco.
Boring situations and performances reduce the temperature of this youth musical which is not another On the Town.
w Sonya Levien, William Ludwig *novel Shore Leave* by Hubert Osborn *musical play Herbert Fields* *d* Roy Rowland *ph* George Folsey *m/ly* Vincent Youmans, Leo Robin *md* George Stoll *ch* Hermes Pan
☆ Tony Martin, Jane Powell, Ann Miller, Debbie Reynolds, Walter Pidgeon, Vic Damone, Gene Raymond

The Hitcher *
US 1986 97m Metrocolor Panavision
Columbia-EMI-Warner/HBO (David Bombyk, Kip Ohman)
A hitchhiker murders all those he meets, implicating a teenage driver in his crimes.
Grim little fable, maintaining a sweaty suspense to the end.
w Eric Red *d* Robert Harmon *ph* John Seale *m* Mark Isham *pd* Dennis Gassner *ed* Frank J. Urioste
☆ Rutger Hauer, C. Thomas Howell, Jennifer Jason Leigh, Jeffrey DeMunn, Billy Greenbush, Jack Thibeau, John Jackson
'Superior exploitation picture.' – *Nigel Floyd, MFB*

Hitler
US 1961 107m bw
Three Crown/E. Charles Straus
A sex-oriented, semi-fictional biopic of the German dictator, from the murder of his niece to his final madness and suicide.
Enterprising sensationalism which deserves a nod for sheer audacity.
w Sam Neuman *d* Stuart Heisler *ph* Joseph Biroc *m* Hans Salter
☆ Richard Basehart, Maria Emo, Martin Kosleck, John Banner

Hitler – Beast of Berlin
US 1939 87m bw
PRC
aka: *Beasts of Berlin*
A spy among Hitler's storm troopers escapes to Switzerland.
Feeble exploitation item which succeeded only as propaganda. Hitler is not seen.
w Shepard Traube *story* Goose Step by Shepard Traube *d* Sherman Scott
☆ Roland Drew, Steffi Duna, Alan Ladd, Greta Granstedt, Lucien Prival
'There are doubtless powerful pictures to be made on the anti-Nazi theme, but this isn't one.' – *Variety*

Hitler – Dead or Alive
US 1942 72m bw
Ben Judell/Charles House
Three Alcatraz graduates try to collect a prize for the capture of Hitler.
Silly mix of farce and propaganda.
w Sam Neumann, Karl Brown *d* Nick Grinde
☆ Ward Bond, Dorothy Tree, Warren Hymer, Paul Fix, Russell Hicks, Bobby Watson

'More morphine for Herr Goering! The greatest gangster picture of all!'
'Did Hitler kill the one woman he loved? What was Hess to Hitler?'
The Hitler Gang **
US 1944 101m bw
Paramount (B. G. de Sylva)
The rise to power of Hitler and his henchmen.
Though at the time it seemed rather like a serious cabaret turn, this fictionalization of historical fact has some good impersonations and dramatically effective scenes.
w Frances Goodrich, Albert Hackett *d* John Farrow *ph* Ernest Laszlo *m* David Buttolph
☆ *Robert Watson*, Martin Kosleck (Goebbels), Victor Varconi (Hess), Luis Van Rooten (Himmler), Alexander Pope (Goering), Roman Bohnen, Ivan Triesault, Helene Thimig, Reinhold Schunzel, Sig Rumann, Alexander Granach

Hitler – The Last Ten Days
GB/Italy 1973 104m Technicolor
MGM/Wolfgang Reinhardt/Westfilm
▬
With Adolf and Eva in the bunker.
Claustrophobic historical reconstruction with an uncomfortable star.
w Ennio de Concini, Maria Pia Fusco, Wolfgang Reinhardt, Ivan Moffat *d* Ennio de Concini *ph* Ennio Guarnieri *m* Mischa Spoliansky
☆ Alec Guinness, Simon Ward, Doris Kunstmann, Adolfo Celi, Diane Cilento, Eric Porter, Joss Ackland

'The truth about the Nazis from the cradle to the battlefront!'
Hitler's Children *
US 1943 83m bw
RKO (Edward A. Golden)
▬
A family reacts to Hitler and the Hitler Youth.
Artificial melodrama set in an unlikely Germany but successful at the time because of its topicality and its refusal to play the Nazis as idiots, which was the usual Hollywood line.
w Emmet Lavery *book* Education for Death by Gregor Ziemer *d* Edward Dmytryk *ph* Russell Metty *m* Roy Webb
☆ Tim Holt, Bonita Granville, Otto Kruger, Kent Smith, H. B. Warner, Lloyd Corrigan, Erford Gage, Gavin Muir, Hans Conried
'A curiously compromised production … strong anti-Nazi propaganda, it has not been woven into a defined and moving show.' – *Howard Barnes, New York Herald Tribune*

Hitler's Gold: see *Inside Out*

Hitler's Hangman: see *Hitler's Madman*

Hitler's Madman *
US 1943 84m bw
MGM/PRC (Seymour Nebenzal)
aka: *Hitler's Hangman*
Heydrich is assassinated in Czechoslovakia and the Nazis take revenge on the village of Lidice.
Cheapjack sensationalism based on a horrifying incident of World War II; despite its imperfections it generates a certain raw power.
w Peretz Hirshbein, Melvin Levy, Doris Malloy *d* Douglas Sirk *m* Karl Hajos
☆ Patricia Morison, *John Carradine*, Alan Curtis, Ralph Morgan, Ludwig Stossel, Edgar Kennedy, Al Shean, Jimmy Conlin, Blanche Yurka, Victor Kilian
'Newspaper accounts of the bombing of German cities will be pleasant antidotes for the unhappy feeling brought on by the final grim scenes of *Hitler's Madman*.' – *New York Herald Tribune*
'Even in its poorly depicted scenes of brutality, it inflames a common anger.' – *Theodore Strauss, New York Times*

'A Potion Put Them In The Ocean.'
Hjaelp! Jeg er en Fisk (dubbed)
Denmark/Germany/Ireland 2000 80m colour
Metrodome/A-Film/Egmont/Munich Animation/EIV/Terraglyph (Christoph Sieciechowicz, Harro Von Have, Gerry Shirren)
GB title: *Help! I'm a Fish*
After drinking a potion that turns them into fish, three children have 48 hours to find the antidote to make them human again.
Lively, simple animated film intended for a young audience, who may enjoy its high spirits and underwater setting.
w Stefan Fjeldmark, Karsten Kulerich, John Stefan Olsen *d* Stefan Fjeldmark, Michael Hegner *m* Søren Hyldgaard *m/ly* Jacob Eriksen, Anders and Lars Twin, Peter Fernando, Jesper Winge Leisner *ad* Matthias Lechner *ed* Per Risager
☆ voices of: Alan Rickman (Joe), Terry Jones (Professor H. O. MacKrill), Aaron Poul (Chuck), Jeff Pace (Fly), Michelle Westerson (Stella), Louise Fribo (Sasha), David Bateson (Crab/Shark), Teryl Rothery (Mother)
'If pre-teen viewers might be expected to have a reasonably good time, there's not much here for adults to get their teeth into.' – *Matthew Leyland, Sight and Sound*

Ho! (dubbed)
France/Italy 1968 107m Eastmancolor
Golden Era/Filmsonor/Marceau/Cocinor/Mega Film
aka: *Criminal Face*
A racing driver turned crook decides to go straight. The title refers to the hero's nickname of Ho.
Ho-hum drama.
w Pierre Pelegri, Lucienna Hamon, Robert Enrico *novel* José Giovanni *d* Robert Enrico *ph* Jean Boffety *m* François de Roubaix *ad* Jacques Saulnier *ed* Jacqueline Meppiel
☆ Jean-Paul Belmondo, Joanna Shimkus, Paul Crauchet, Stéphane Fey, Tony Taffin, Sydney Chaplin

Hobson's Choice ***
GB 1953 107m bw
British Lion/London (Norman Spencer)
In the 1890s a tyrannical Lancashire bootmaker is brought to heel by his plain-speaking daughter and her simple-minded husband.
Brilliantly played version of a famous working-class comedy, memorably set and photographed; one regrets only the slight decline of the predictable third act.
w Norman Spencer, Wynard Browne *play* Harold Brighouse *d* *David Lean* *ph* *Jack Hildyard* *m* *Malcolm Arnold* *ad* *Wilfrid Shingleton*
☆ *Charles Laughton, Brenda de Banzie, John Mills*, Richard Wattis, Helen Haye, Daphne Anderson, Prunella Scales
† Previously filmed in 1931 by Thomas Bentley for BIP from a screenplay by Frank Launder, with James Harcourt, Viola Lyel and Frank Pettingell.
British film

Hocus Pocus
US 1993 96m Technicolor
Buena Vista/Walt Disney (David Kirschner, Steven Haft)
In Salem, three children inadvertently conjure up three wicked witches.
A mildly comic vehicle for Bette Midler, though a kiddies' film is not the best setting for her talents.
w Mick Garris, Neil Cuthbert *story* David Kirschner, Mick Garris *d* Kenny Ortega *ph* Hiro Narita *m* John Debney *pd* William Sandell *ed* Peter E. Berger
☆ Bette Midler, Sarah Jessica Parker, Kathy Najimy, Omri Katz, Thora Birch, Vinessa Shaw, Amanda Shepherd
'The blend of witchcraft and comedy should divert kids without driving the patience of their parents to the boiling point.' – *Variety*

Hoffa
US 1992 140m colour Panavision
TCF/Jersey (Edward R. Pressman, Danny DeVito, Caldecot Chubb)
An aggressive agitator for the Teamster's Union accepts the aid of gangsters and becomes its leader before mysteriously vanishing.
A creakingly old-fashioned biopic that reaches few conclusions and makes no judgements.
w David Mamet *d* Danny DeVito *ph* Stephen H. Burum *m* David Newman *pd* Ida Random *ed* Lynzee Klingman, Ronald Roose
☆ Jack Nicholson, Danny DeVito, Armand Assante, J. T. Walsh, John C. Reilly, Frank Whaley, Kevin Anderson, John P. Ryan, Robert Prosky, Cliff Gorman
'As is so often the case with biopics that attempt to convey decades, something gets sacrificed. Here, it's a human drama one can relate to.' – *Variety*
Stephen H. Burum

'Hope never dies for a man with a good dirty mind.'
Hoffman
GB 1970 113m Technicolor
ABP/Longstone (Ben Arbeid)
A middle-aged misfit blackmails a typist into spending a week with him.
Interminable sex comedy padded out from a short TV play; it quickly becomes claustrophobic, tasteless, and boring.
w Ernest Gebler *play* Ernest Gebler *novel* Ernest Gebler *d* Alvin Rakoff *ph* Gerry Turpin *m* Ron Grainer
☆ Peter Sellers, Sinead Cusack, Jeremy Bulloch, Ruth Dunning

Hog Wild ***
US 1930 20m bw
Hal Roach
Stan helps Ollie to put a radio aerial on the roof of his house.
Brilliantly sustained slapstick makes this one of the best star comedies of Laurel and Hardy.
w H. M. Walker, Leo McCarey *d* James Parrott *ph* George Stevens *ed* Richard Currier
☆ Stan Laurel, Oliver Hardy, Fay Holderness, Dorothy Granger

Hohenfeuer: see *Alpine Fire*

Hol Volt, Hol Nem Volt...: see *A Hungarian Fairy Tale*

The Holcroft Covenant
GB 1985 112m colour
EMI/Ely and Edie Landau
One of the architects of Hitler's Third Reich leaves a bequest which may fall into the wrong hands.
Muddled political thriller which tends to provoke unintended laughs.
w George Axelrod, Edward Anhalt, John Hopkins *novel* Robert Ludlum *d* John Frankenheimer *ph* Gerry Fisher *m* Stanislas *pd* Peter Mullins
☆ Michael Caine, Anthony Andrews, Victoria Tennant, Lilli Palmer, Mario Adorf, Michael Lonsdale, Bernard Hepton
'A narrative deficient in thrills or plausibility.' – *Variety*

'Master of love! He is to all women what each desires him to be!'
Hold Back the Dawn *
US 1941 115m bw
Paramount (Arthur Hornblow Jnr)
A would-be immigrant into the US via Mexico marries a schoolteacher he does not love.
Surprisingly effective romantic melodrama with a nice style and some mordant lines in the script.
w *Charles Brackett, Billy Wilder* *d* *Mitchell Leisen* *ph* Leo Tover *m* Victor Young *ad* Hans Dreier, Robert Usher
☆ Charles Boyer, Olivia de Havilland, Paulette Goddard, Victor Francen, Walter Abel, Curt Bois, Rosemary de Camp, Nestor Paiva, Mitchell Leisen
'All those years with all the others I closed my eyes and thought of you.' – *sample dialogue spoken by Paulette Goddard*
'It has all the vitamins for mass popular appeal.' – *Variety*
† The story is told by Boyer to Mitchell Leisen on a film set where he has just shot a scene from *I Wanted Wings*.
best picture; Charles Brackett, Billy Wilder; Leo Tover; Victor Young; Olivia de Havilland; art direction

Hold Back the Night
US 1956 80m bw
Allied Artists
From World War II to Korea, a marine commander carries with him a lucky whisky bottle.
Pointlessly titled war heroics, competently mounted.
w John C. Higgins, Walter Doniger *novel* Pat Frank *d* Allan Dwan *ph* Ellsworth J. Fredricks *m* Hans Salter
☆ John Payne, Mona Freeman, Peter Graves, Chuck Connors, Audrey Dalton

'It's hard to keep yourself a secret.'
Hold Back the Night
GB/Italy 1999 104m DeLuxe
UIP/Film Consortium/Film4/Arts Council/BIM/Wave/Parallax (Sally Hibbin)
A teenage girl runs away from home and teams up with an environmental activist and a elderly lesbian who is dying from cancer.
A small-scale, gritty road movie with revelations of sexual abuse and parental estrangement along the way; it has nothing fresh to say.
w Steve Chambers *d* Phil Davis *ph* Cinders Forshaw *m* Peter John Vettese *pd* Chris Roope *ed* Adam Ross
☆ Christine Tremarco (Charleen), Stuart Sinclair Blyth (Declan), Sheila Hancock (Vera), Richard Platt (Michael), Julie Ann Watson (Jackie), Kenneth Colley (Bob), Tommy Tiernan (John), Andrew Livingstone (Barman)
'Maladroit, and baffingly without the conviction, sophistication or production values you would expect from the most ordinary television drama.' – *Peter Bradshaw, Guardian*

Hold Everything
US 1930 78m Technicolor
Warner
A comedian becomes a prizefighter.
Pleasant comedy musical which established Joe E. Brown in Hollywood, as it had established Bert Lahr on stage.
w Robert Lord *play* B. G. De Sylva, John McGowan *d* Roy del Ruth
☆ Joe E. Brown, Winnie Lightner, Georges Carpentier, Sally O'Neil, Bert Roach
'Pip laugh picture, the best comedy Warners has turned out since talkers came in.' – *Variety*

Hold Me Thrill Me Kiss Me *
US 1992 92m Foto-Kem
Art House/Mad Dog (Travis Swords)
A burglar, on the run from a shotgun marriage in which he accidentally shot the bride, ends up in a trailer park with a jealous stripper and her virginal sister.
This attempt by its director to add sex and violence to the screwball comedy genre is intermittently amusing, but needed defter comic timing from its cast to succeed.
wd Joel Hershman *ph* Kent Wakeford *m* Gerald Gouriet *pd* Dominic Wymark *ed* Kathryn Himoff
☆ Sean Young, Max Parrish, Diane Ladd, Adrienne Shelly, Andrea Naschak, Timothy Leary, Bela Lehoczky, Ania Suli
'Crazed, larger-than-life and great fun.' – *Empire*

Hold My Hand
GB 1938 76m bw
Associated British (Walter C. Mycroft)
A businessman is engaged to an aristocrat's daughter but marries his secretary instead.
Routine light comedy with a few songs that must have worked better on the stage. It ends with one of the most absurd dance sequences on film.
w Clifford Grey, Bert Lee, William Freshman *play* Stanley Lupino *d* Thornton Freeland

ph Otto Kanturek *md* Harry Acres *ad* Ian White *ed* E. B. Jarvis
☆ Stanley Lupino, Fred Emney, Syd Walker, Barbara Blair, Sally Gray, Polly Ward, Bertha Belmore, Jack Melford, John Wood

Hold That Blonde
US 1945 75m bw
Paramount (Paul Jones)
A psychiatrist suggests that romance may cure a kleptomaniac, but the patient unfortunately chooses a jewel thief.
Thin comedy which erupts into frantic farce, with some energetic slapstick and a Harold Lloyd style finale.
w Walter de Leon, Earl Baldwin, E. Edwin Moran *d* George Marshall *ph* Daniel L. Fapp *m* Werner Heymann
☆ Eddie Bracken, Veronica Lake, Albert Dekker, Frank Fenton, George Zucco, Donald MacBride, Norma Varden, Willie Best

Hold That Co-Ed *
US 1938 80m bw
TCF (David Hempstead)
GB title: *Hold That Girl*
A girl dressed as a boy wins a university football match and thereby helps a governor get re-elected.
Intriguingly-cast crazy comedy which works up into a fine frenzy.
w Karl Tunberg, Don Ettlinger, Jack Yellen *d* George Marshall *ph* Robert Planck *md* Arthur Lange
☆ *John Barrymore*, Joan Davis, George Murphy, Marjorie Weaver, Jack Haley, George Barbier, Donald Meek, Johnny Downs, Guinn Williams
'On the wacky side and fairly amusing, but not quite making the big league.' – *Variety*

Hold That Ghost *
US 1941 86m bw
Universal (Burt Kelly, Glenn Tryon)
A group of strangers are stranded in an apparently haunted house.
Long thought of as Abbott and Costello's best comedy, this now seems pretty strained and slow to start, but it has its classic moments.
w Robert Lees, Fred Rinaldo, John Grant *d* Arthur Lubin *ph* Elwood Bredell, Joe Valentine *m* Hans Salter
☆ *Bud Abbott, Lou Costello, Joan Davis*, the Andrews Sisters, Richard Carlson, *Ted Lewis and his band*, Evelyn Ankers, Marc Lawrence, Mischa Auer

Hold That Girl: see *Hold That Co-Ed*

Hold Your Man *
US 1933 89m bw
MGM (Sam Wood)
A hard-boiled young woman falls for a confidence man, has his baby, and waits for him to emerge from prison.
Briskly-fashioned star comedy-drama with entertaining moments.
w Anita Loos, Howard Emmett Rogers *d* Sam Wood *ph* Harold Rosson *m/ly* Nacio Herb Brown, Arthur Freed
☆ Jean Harlow, Clark Gable, Stuart Erwin, Dorothy Burgess, Muriel Kirkland, Paul Hurst
'A real money picture ... most promising box office prospect in months.' – *Variety*
'The sudden transition from wise-cracking romance to sentimental penitence provides a jolt.' – *Frank S. Nugent*

The Hole *
France/Italy 1959 123m bw
Play-Art/Filmsonor/Titanus (Serge Silberman)
original title: *Le Trou*
Four convicts in a Paris prison dig a tunnel to freedom and almost make it.
Meticulous escape drama nicely shot in very limited sets: hypnotic for those with the patience to adjust to its pace.
w Jacques Becker, José Giovanni, Jean Aurel *novel* José Giovanni *d* Jacques Becker *ph* Ghislain Cloquet
☆ Philippe Leroy, Marc Michel, Jean Kéraudy, Michel Constantin

The Hole: see *Onibaba (1964)*

'Desperate to get in. Dying to get out.'
The Hole
GB/France 2001 102m colour
Pathe/Film Council/Canal+/Cowboy/Granada/Impact (Lisa Bryer, Jeremy Bolt, Pippa Cross)
A schoolgirl explains why she is the only one left alive after being locked into a deserted underground bunker for a weekend party with three friends.
A British movie, lacking any specificity of place, that pretends to be an American horror flick of a familiar, and not very interesting, kind.
w Ben Court, Caroline Ip *novel After the Hole* by Guy Burt *d* Nick Hamm *ph* Denis Crossan *m* Clint Mansell *pd* Eve Stewart *ed* Niven Howie *cos* Verity Hawkes
☆ Thora Birch (Liz Dunn), Desmond Harrington (Mike Steel), Embeth Davidtz (Dr Philippa Horwood), Daniel Brocklebank (Martin Taylor), Laurence Fox (Geoff), Keira Knightley (Frankie Smith), Steven Waddington (DCS Howard)
'The whole enterprise is undercut by a messy script, thoroughly unsympathetic characters and a general lack of tension.' – *Derek Elley, Variety*

A Hole in the Head *
US 1959 120m DeLuxe Cinemascope
UA/Sincap (Frank Sinatra)
A Miami hotelier is threatened with foreclosure and tries to raise the money from his provident elder brother.
Easy-going comedy without much point, but various amusing facets artfully deployed.
w Arnold Shulman *play* Arnold Shulman *d* Frank Capra *ph* William H. Daniels *m* Nelson Riddle
☆ Frank Sinatra, Edward G. Robinson, Eleanor Parker, Eddie Hodges, Carolyn Jones, Thelma Ritter, Keenan Wynn, Joi Lansing
song 'High Hopes' (*m* Jimmy Van Heusen, *ly* Sammy Cahn)

Holiday *
US 1930 99m bw
Pathé (E. B. Derr)
A bright-minded rich girl steals her sister's fiancé, a struggling young lawyer.
Competent early talkie version of a hit play.
w Horace Jackson *play* Philip Barry *d* Edward H. Griffith *ph* Norbert Brodine *m* Josiah Zuro
☆ Ann Harding, Robert Ames, Mary Astor, Edward Everett Horton, Hedda Hopper, Monroe Owsley, William Holden
'A comedy of wide appeal in a finished style.' – *Variety*
Horace Jackson; Ann Harding

'So daring – so tender – so human – so true – that everyone in love will want to see it!'
Holiday ***
US 1938 93m bw
Columbia (Everett Riskin)
GB titles: *Free to Live*
aka: *Unconventional Linda*
A man becomes engaged to a millionaire's daughter but discovers that he loves her unconventional suster.
Elegant, highly successful remake; still a stage play on film, but subtly devised to make the very most of the lines and performances. Horton played the same role in both versions.
w Donald Ogden Stewart d George Cukor ph Franz Planer *m* Sidney Cutner *ad* Stephen Goosson, Lionel Banks
☆ *Katharine Hepburn, Cary Grant,* Doris Nolan, *Edward Everett Horton, Ruth Donnelly, Lew Ayres,* Henry Kolker, Binnie Barnes
'Corking comedy ... exhibitors will pencil in some extra days.' – *Variety*
'The comedy is full of the best of humour, edged with pathos never allowed to drop into sentimentality. It is played with the greatest cheerfulness and a winning skill.' – *Arthur Pollock, Brooklyn Daily Eagle*
'I suppose actually it is a neat and sometimes elegant job, but under its surface of too much brightness and too many words it seems so deadly bored and weary. Hell, save your money and yawn at home.' – *Otis Ferguson*
'Played with the greatest cheerfulness and a winning skill.' – *Brooklyn Daily Eagle*
art direction

Holiday Affair
US 1949 87m bw
RKO (Don Hartman)
A young widow falls for an easy-going boat builder.
Flimsy star-shaped romantic comedy with nice touches.
w Isobel Lennart *story Christmas Gift* by John D. Weaver *d* Don Hartman *ph* Milton Krasner *m* Roy Webb *ad* Albert D'Agostino, Carroll Clark *ed* Harry Marker
☆ Robert Mitchum (Steve), Janet Leigh (Connie), Wendell Corey (Carl), Griff Barnett (Mr Ennis), Esther Dale (Mrs Ennis), Gordon Gebert (Timmy), Henry O'Neill (Mr Crowley), Harry Morgan (Police Lieutenant), Larry J. Blake (Plainsclothesman), Helen Brown (Emily)

Holiday Camp *
GB 1947 97m bw
GFD/Gainsborough (Sydney Box)
At a summer holiday camp, a murderer on the prowl affects people's enjoyment in various ways.
Seminal compendium comedy drama, a bore in itself but establishing several post-war norms of the British cinema, including the Huggetts.
w Muriel and Sydney Box, Ted Willis, Peter Rogers, Mabel and Denis Constanduros *story* Godfrey Winn *d* Ken Annakin *ph* Jack Cox *m* Bob Busby *ad* George Provis *ed* Alfred Roome
☆ Jack Warner (Joe Huggett), Kathleen Harrison (Mrs Huggett), Flora Robson (Esther Harman), Dennis Price (Sqd-Ldr Hardwicke), Hazel Court (Joan Martin), Emrys Jones (Michael Halliday), Yvonne Owen (Angela Kirby), Esmond Knight (Camp Announcer), Jimmy Hanley (Jimmy Gardner), Peter Hammond (Harry Huggett), Esma Cannon (Elsie Dawson), John Blythe (Steve), Susan Shaw (Patsy Crawford), Maurice Denham (Camp Doctor), Patricia Roc (As herself) and also Cheerful Charlie Chester
'It is real – and true – and it will be a smash at the box office.' – *Sunday Chronicle*

Holiday for Henrietta: see *La Fête à Henriette*

Holiday for Lovers
US 1959 103m DeLuxe Cinemascope
TCF (David Weisbart)
To distract his teenage daughter from boys, a Boston psychiatrist organizes a family holiday in South America.
Frail old-fashioned family comedy with entirely predictable situations culminating in a drunk scene for stuffy father.
w Luther Davis *d* Henry Levin *ph* Charles G. Clarke *m* Leigh Harline
☆ Clifton Webb, Jane Wyman, Paul Henreid, Carol Lynley, Jill St John, Gary Crosby, José Greco

Holiday for Sinners
US 1952 72m bw
MGM (John Houseman)
In New Orleans during the Mardi Gras three old friends meet crises in their lives.
Slightly curious but not very interesting portmanteau drama.
w A. I. Bezzerides *novel* Hamilton Basso *d* Gerald Mayer *ph* Paul Vogel *md* Alberto Colombo
☆ Gig Young, Keenan Wynn, Janice Rule, Richard Anderson, William Campbell, Michael Chekhov, Sandro Giglio, Edith Barrett, Porter Hall
'It gives an impression of blurred, rather heavy-going sincerity.' – *MFB*

Holiday in Mexico
US 1946 127m Technicolor
MGM (Joe Pasternak)
The daughter of the American Ambassador to Mexico falls for Jose Iturbi.
Travel brochure musical in which the occasional plums do not redeem the sogginess of the pudding.
w Isobel Lennart *d* George Sidney *ph* Harry Stradling *m* André Previn
☆ Walter Pidgeon, Ilona Massey, Jane Powell, Jose Iturbi, Roddy McDowall

Holiday in Spain: see *Scent of Mystery*

Holiday Inn **
US 1942 101m bw
Paramount (Mark Sandrich)
The joint proprietors of a roadhouse hotel love the same girl.
Plain, simple-minded musical which provided a peg for pleasant performances and good numbers. It hit the box-office spot, especially as it introduced 'White Christmas'.
w Claude Binyon, Elmer Rice *d* Mark Sandrich *ph* David Abel *m/ly Irving Berlin md* Robert Emmett Dolan
☆ Bing Crosby, Fred Astaire, Walter Abel, Marjorie Reynolds, Virginia Dale, Louise Beavers, Irving Bacon, James Bell
'The best musical drama of the year.' – *New York Post*
† Marjorie Reynolds was dubbed by Martha Mears
song 'White Christmas'
original story (Irving Berlin); Robert Emmett Dolan

Holiday on the Buses
GB 1973 85m Technicolor
MGM-EMI/Hammer (Ronald Wolfe, Ronald Chesney)
After losing their jobs on the buses, two drivers and an inspector find work at a holiday camp.
Tired sitcom spin-off in which the cast go half-heartedly through their familiar, poorly timed slapstick routines.
w Ronald Wolfe, Ronald Chesney from their TV series *d* Bryan Izzard *ph* Brian Probyn *m* Denis King *ad* Don Picton *ed* James Needs
☆ Reg Varney (Stan Butler), Stephen Lewis (Inspector Blake), Doris Hare (Mrs Butler), Michael Robbins (Arthur), Anna Karen (Olive), Bob Grant (Jack), Wilfrid Brambell (Bert), Arthur Mullard (Wally Briggs), Henry McGee (Mr Coombs), Kate Williams (Joan), Queenie Watts (Lil Briggs)
'The only concession Wolfe and Chesney have made to avoid being accused of compiling the entire scripts from old *Carry On* situations involves a subsidiary romance between Doris Hare and Wilfred Brambell. One could probably conceive of a more revolting spectacle than Brambell panting after Miss Hare and making jokes about cutting notches on his walking stick, but nothing comes immediately to mind.' – *David McGillivray, Films and Filming*
† It was a sequel to *On the Buses* (qv) and *Mutiny on the Buses* (qv).

Holidays on the River Yarra
Australia 1990 88m colour
Jungle Pictures/AFC/Film Victoria (Fiona Cochrane)
In Melbourne, two young petty thieves, one violent and the other ineffectual, try to raise money to join a group of white supremacists who plan to overthrow the government of an African island.
The one live song – 'Defecate on My Face', performed by TISM – sets the tone of this downbeat account of alienated youth; it may have local resonance, but lacks international appeal.
wd Leo Berkeley *ph* Brendan Lavelle *m* Sam Mallet *ad* Margaret Eastgate, Adele Flere *ed* Leo Berkeley
☆ Craig Adams, Luke Elliot, Alexander Menglet, Tahir Cambis, Claudia Karvan, Ian Scott, Sheryl Munks, Angela McKenna

'What Would You Do If No One Could See You?'
'Think You're Alone? Think Again.'
Hollow Man
US 2000 114m DeLuxe
Columbia (Douglas Wick, Alan Marshall)
A scientist turns himself invisible, but is unable to reverse the process, so he decides to kill his fellow workers.
Violent action movie of little worth, relying on special effects for its impact; it pales beside the original Invisible Man *and is content to be just another predictable monster movie.*
w Andrew W. Marlowe, Gary Scott Thompson *d* Paul Verhoeven *ph* Jost Vacano *m* Jerry Goldsmith *pd* Allan Cameron *ed* Mark Goldblatt *sp* Sony Pictures Imageworks, Tippett Studio *cos* Ellen Mirojnick
☆ Kevin Bacon (Sebastian Caine), Elisabeth Shue (Linda Foster), Josh Brolin (Matt Kensington), Greg Grunberg (Carter Abby), Mary Jo Randle (Janice), Steve Altes (Dad), Kim Dickens (Sarah)
'A tired old tale about the scientist who thinks he is God and goes mad.' – *Cosmo Landesman, Sunday Times*
visual effects (Scott E. Anderson, Craig Hayes, Scott Stokdyk, Stan Parks)

'Not All Marriages Are Made In Heaven.'

Hollow Reed

GB/Germany 1996 106m Rank Colour
Film Four/Scala/Senator/Channel 4 (Elizabeth Karlsen)

A gay father, who discovers that his ex-wife's new lover is physically abusing their son, attempts to gain custody of the boy.

Harsh-toned, old-fashioned problem film that muddles its message.

w Paula Milne *story* Neville Bolt *d* Angela Pope *ph* Remi Adefarasin *m* Anne Dudley *pd* Stuart Walker *ed* Sue Wyatt

☆ Martin Donovan, Joely Richardson, Ian Hart, Jason Flemyng, Sam Bould, Edward Hardwicke, Douglas Hodge, Annette Badland

'A truly disquieting experience because it packs its punch in simple, formal fashion. One cannot be unmoved by the pain at the story's center, especially when it's caused by good intentions.' – *Leonard Klady, Variety*

Hollow Triumph: see *The Scar*

The Holly and the Ivy *

GB 1952 83m bw
British Lion/London (Anatole de Grunwald)

Christmas brings family revelations in a remote Norfolk rectory.

A badly-filmed stage success which succeeds because of its performances.

w Anatole de Grunwald *play* Wynard Browne *d* George More O'Ferrall *ph* Ted Scaife *m* Malcolm Arnold

☆ *Ralph Richardson, Celia Johnson,* Margaret Leighton, Denholm Elliott, John Gregson, Hugh Williams, Margaret Halstan, Maureen Delany, William Hartnell, Robert Flemyng, Roland Culver

'This type of direct translation to the screen, using none of the cinema's resources, can only do harm to the play itself.' – *Penelope Houston*

Hollywood Boulevard *

US 1936 75m bw
Paramount (A. M. Botsford)

A washed-up Hollywood actor writes a sensational memoir for publication, but lives to regret it.

Entertaining melodrama with famous names in bit parts.

w Marguerite Roberts *d* Robert Florey *ph* Karl Struss *m* Gregory Stone

☆ *John Halliday,* Marsha Hunt, Robert Cummings, C. Henry Gordon, Frieda Inescort, Esther Dale; and Gary Cooper, Francis X. Bushman, Maurice Costello, Mae Marsh, Charles Ray, Jane Novak, Bryant Washburn, Jack Mulhall, Creighton Hale, Bert Roach

'A pretty hoary melodrama and a slight enough excuse for a whole series of homilies upon the uncertainty of fame and fortune in the glamour city.' – *New York Times*

Hollywood Boulevard

US 1977 83m colour
New World (Jon Davison)

An inexperienced actress goes to work for makers of low-budget exploitation movies with violent results.

Bizarre action film spoof, with dialogue and a slim narrative added to action sequences taken from previous Roger Corman movies; it will mainly interest fans of Corman or of the other talents involved.

w Patrick Hobby *d* Allan Arkush, Joe Dante *ph* Jamie Anderson *m* Andrew Stein *ad* Jack DeWolfe *ed* Allan Arkush, Joe Dante, Amy Jones

☆ Candice Rialson, Mary Woronov, Rita George, Jeffrey Kramer, Dick Miller, Paul Bartel, Jonathan Kaplan, Charles B. Griffith

† The film began as a bet which Davison made with Roger Corman that he could produce a picture for $90,000, which was less than any other New World movie, providing he could use stock footage from other Corman productions. It was shot in ten days at a cost of $80,000.

Hollywood Canteen *

US 1944 123m bw
Warner (Alex Gottlieb)

The stars give their evenings to entertaining soldiers.

Shoddily made but sociologically fascinating record of Hollywood doing its bit in World War II.

wd Delmer Daves *ph* Bert Glennon *m* Ray Heindorf *md* Leo F. Forbstein

☆ Joan Leslie, Robert Hutton, Dane Clark, Janis Paige; and The Andrews Sisters, Jack Benny, Joe E. Brown, Eddie Cantor, Joan Crawford, Bette Davis, John Garfield, Sydney Greenstreet, Paul Henreid, Peter Lorre, Ida Lupino, Dennis Morgan and also Roy Rogers, S. Z. Sakall, Alexis Smith, Barbara Stanwyck, Jane Wyman, etc etc

'The corporal steps slowly backwards, in his eyes that look of glazed ecstasy which Jennifer Jones wore all through *The Song of Bernadette*. He has just been kissed by Joan Leslie.' – *Richard Winnington*

'To be perfectly blunt about it, this film seems a most distasteful show of Hollywood's sense of its own importance.' – *New York Times*

Ray Heindorf; song 'Sweet Dreams, Sweetheart' (*m* M. K. Jerome, *ly* Ted Koehler)

'It does for the motion picture what Alexander's Ragtime Band did for popular music!'

Hollywood Cavalcade *

US 1939 96m Technicolor
TCF (Harry Joe Brown)

The career of an old-time Hollywood producer.

A lively first half with amusing re-staging of early slapstick comedies gives way depressingly to personal melodrama, but there is enough historical interest to preserve the balance.

w Ernest Pascal *d* Irving Cummings *ph* Allen M. Davey, Ernest Palmer *m* David Raksin, David Buttolph, Cyril Mockridge *md* Louis Silvers *ad* Richard Day, Wiard B. Ihnen

☆ Don Ameche, Alice Faye, *J. Edward Bromberg,* Alan Curtis, Stuart Erwin, Jed Prouty, Buster Keaton, Donald Meek, and the original Keystone Kops

'Surefire ... should score heavily in theatres of every type.' – *Variety*

† Alice Faye did not sing. The Keystone Kops sequence was directed by Mal St Clair. The Ameche/Faye characters were supposedly based on Mack Sennett and Mabel Normand; Mack Sennett's appearance under his own name seemed to be an effort to throw people off the scent.

Hollywood Cowboy: see *Hearts of the West*

Hollywood Hotel

US 1938 109m bw
Warner (Sam Bischoff)

A Hollywood radio show has its problems.

Half-hearted, overlong Warner musical with little of the expected zip.

w Jerry Wald, Maurice Leo, Richard Macaulay *d* Busby Berkeley *ph* Charles Rosher, George Barnes *m/ly* Johnny Mercer, Richard Whiting

☆ Dick Powell, Rosemary Lane, Lola Lane, Hugh Herbert, Ted Healy, Glenda Farrell, Louella Parsons, Alan Mowbray, Frances Langford, Allyn Joslyn, Benny Goodman, Edgar Kennedy

Hollywood or Bust

US 1956 95m Technicolor Vistavision
Paramount/Hal Wallis

Two halfwits win a car and drive across country to Hollywood.

Dopey comedy with more misses than hits; the last film of Martin and Lewis as a team.

w Erna Lazarus *d* Frank Tashlin *ph* Daniel Fapp *m* Walter Scharf

☆ Dean Martin, Jerry Lewis, Pat Crowley, Maxie Rosenbloom, Anita Ekberg

Hollywood Party

US 1934 68m bw (Technicolor sequence)
MGM (Harry Rapf, Howard Dietz)

A mad Russian throws a party which ends in disaster.

Dismal 'all-star' comedy relieved by guest appearances.

w Howard Dietz, Arthur Kober *d* (uncredited) Richard Boleslawski, Allan Dwan, Roy Rowland, George Stevens *ph* James Wong Howe *m/ly* Rodgers, Hart and others *ed* George Boemier

☆ *Laurel and Hardy,* Jimmy Durante, Lupe Velez, Charles Butterworth, Eddie Quillan, Ted Healy and the Stooges, Polly Moran

'A big short ... averagely passable screen divertissement.' – *Variety*

'The picture hardly rates the time and money that MGM has expended.' – *Hollywood Reporter*

† The film was dogged by disaster and was in production for a year. At least eight directors were involved, but no one wanted a credit on the finished film.

The Hollywood Revue of 1929 **

US 1929 116m bw (part Technicolor)
MGM (Harry Rapf)

A variety show featuring most of MGM's talent in slightly surprising acts, this is something of a bore to sit through but an archival must; and just occasionally it boasts surprising vitality.

w Al Boasberg, Robert E. Hopkins *d* Charles F. Reisner *ph* John Arnold, Irving Ries, Maximilian Fabian *m/ly* various *ch* Sammy Lee

☆ Jack Benny, Buster Keaton, Joan Crawford, John Gilbert, Norma Shearer, Laurel and Hardy, Marion Davies, Marie Dressler, William Haines, Lionel Barrymore, Conrad Nagel, Bessie Love, Cliff Edwards, Nils Asther

best picture

Hollywood Shuffle *

US 1987 82m colour
Samuel Goldwyn Company/Conquering Unicorn (Robert Townsend)

A young black actor looks for work in films.

A loosely connected series of satirical sketches that provide fun at the expense of current movie genres and the stereotyping of black actors as gangsters or pimps.

w Robert Townsend, Keenen Ivory Wayans *d* Robert Townsend *ph* Peter Deming *m* Patrice Rushen, Udi Harpaz *ad* Melba Katzman Farquhar *ed* W. O. Garrett

☆ Robert Townsend, Anne-Marie Johnson, Starletta Dupois, Helen Martin, Craigus R. Johnson, John Witherspoon, Keenen Ivory Wayans, Jimmy Woodard

'Scattershot humor misses as much as it hits.' – *Variety*

Hollywood Story *

US 1951 76m bw
U-I (Leonard Goldstein)

A young producer solves a 20-year-old studio murder mystery.

Adequate potboiler with a reasonably absorbing plot and glimpses of silent stars.

w Frederick Kohner, Fred Brady *d* William Castle *ph* Carl Guthrie *m* Joseph Gershenson

☆ Richard Conte, Julie Adams, Richard Egan, Henry Hull, Fred Clark, Jim Backus, Paul Cavanagh; and Francis X. Bushman, William Farnum, Betty Blythe, Helen Gibson, Joel McCrea

Holocaust 2000

GB/Italy 1977 102m Technicolor Technovision
Rank/Aston/Embassy (Edmondo Amati)

aka: *The Chosen*

The executive in charge of a thermonuclear plant in the Middle East is drawn into a legend about the rebirth of the anti-Christ, and discovers that the evil one is his own son.

Extraordinary mishmash of horror, religiosity and social conscience which scarcely works on any level.

w Sergio Donati, Alberto de Martino, Michael Robson *d* Alberto de Martino *ph* Erico Menczer *m* Ennio Morricone

☆ Kirk Douglas, Simon Ward, Agostina Belli, Anthony Quayle, Virginia McKenna, Spiros Focas, Alexander Knox, Adolfo Celi

'The wildest farrago yet to have come out of the demonology genre.' – *Richard Combs, MFB*

Holy Man

US 1998 114m Technicolor Panavision
Buena Vista/Touchstone/Caravan (Roger Birnbaum, Stephen Herek)

A programmer for a TV shopping station discovers a guru who sends ratings and sales figures soaring.

Glib but toothless satire of rampant commercialism.

w Tom Schulman *d* Stephen Herek *ph* Adrian Biddle *m* Alan Silvestri *pd* Andrew McAlpine *ed* Trudy Ship

☆ Eddie Murphy, Jeff Goldblum, Kelly Preston, Robert Loggia, Jon Cryer, Eric McCormack, Sam Kitchin, Robert Small, Marc Macaulay, Morgan Fairchild (as herself), Nino Cerruti (as himself)

'Pulls its punches and winds up caught up in the sort of half-truths it chastises.' – *Leonard Klady, Variety*

Holy Matrimony *

US 1943 87m bw
TCF (Nunnally Johnson)

A famous painter comes back from exile for a knighthood; but when his valet dies of pneumonia, has him buried as himself in Westminster Abbey.

Slightly stilted but generally warmly amusing version of a favourite novel, with excellent star performances.

w Nunnally Johnson *novel* *Buried Alive* by Arnold Bennett *d* John Stahl *ph* Lucien Ballard *m* Cyril Mockridge

☆ Monty Woolley, Gracie Fields, Laird Cregar, Eric Blore, Una O'Connor

'A pleasant hour and a half, very well produced and acted.' – *James Agate*

Nunnally Johnson

Holy Matrimony

US 1994 93m CFI color
Buena Vista/Interscope/Polygram/Aurora (William Stuart, David Madden, Diane Nabatoff)

A woman on the run from a robbery takes refuge in a Hutterite community where her husband has hidden the money and, after his death, marries his 12-year-old brother while she searches for the loot.

Mind-bogglingly silly comedy that is unlikely to appeal to any age group.

w David Weisberg, Douglas S. Cook *d* Leonard Nimoy *ph* Bobby Bukowski *m* Bruce Broughton *pd* Edward Pisoni *ed* Peter E. Berger

☆ Patricia Arquette, Joseph Gordon-Levitt, Armin Mueller-Stahl, Tate Donovan, Lois Smith, John Schuck, Courtney B. Vance

'An unfunny, unholy mess.' – *Guardian*

'Journey into temptation, but be sure you know your way back.'
'He had only one thing on his mind but so did she!'

Holy Smoke *

US 1999 114m colour
Film4/Miramax (Jan Chapman)

An American expert is hired to deprogram a young Australian woman who has become a member of a cult headed by an Indian guru.

A topical subject is explored in depth, with every approach to life equally questioned, but along the way, with its concentration on the relationship between Keitel and Winslet, the impetus is lost and most of the questions raised remain unanswered.

w Anna Campion, Jane Campion *d* Jane Campion *ph* Dion Beebe *m* Angelo Badalamenti *pd* Janet Patterson *ed* Veronika Jenet

☆ Kate Winslet (Ruth), Harvey Keitel (PJ Waters), Pam Grier (Carol), Julie Hamilton (Mum), Sophie Lee (Yvonne), Daniel Wyllie (Robbie), Paul Goddard (Tim), Tim Robertson (Dad), George Mangos (Yani)

'There's something persuasive about being in the hands of such an uncompromising filmmaker who refuses to take a predictable course or make things easy by over-explaining.' – *David Rooney, Variety*

'It is an immense, emotional, engrossing film that nevertheless wears its brilliance casually.' – *Stella Bruzzi, Sight and Sound*

Holy Terror: see *Communion (1978)*

The Holy Virgin versus The Evil Dead

Hong Kong 1990 90m colour
T & M

A university professor is accused of murdering his students after they are attacked at a night-time picnic by a supernatural being, a worshipper of a moustachioed Cambodian goddess.

Gruesome horror-cum-martial arts movie in various cinematic styles, with a little time out for sex; it is unlikely to be found erotic by many, since the nudity is usually accompanied by violent death. The subtitles manage to mix idioms, as in 'You'll get into hot water if you fall into me, got it?'

d Choy Fat (Wang Zhen-Yi)

☆ Donnie Yen, Ken Lo, Pauline Wong, Hui Hoi Chung, Lam Wei Lan

'You'll probably need to lie down in a darkened room for half an hour after this one!' – *The Dark Side*

† It was one of the first films to be issued with Hong Kong's Category III rating (equivalent to the British 18 certificate) because of its sex and nudity.

Homage
US 1995 96m Foto-Kem
Arrow/Skyline (Mark Medoff, Elan Sassoon)

A postgraduate mathematician, working as a caretaker on a widow's small farm, begins an affair with her visiting daughter, a drug-addicted TV star.
Uninvolving domestic drama of three unlovely people: its documentary direct-to-camera approach of TV news broadcasts is at odds with the directorial style, full of flamboyant and distracting flourishes.
w Mark Medoff *play* The Homage that Follows by Mark Medoff *d* Ross Kagan Marks *ph* Tom Richmond *m* W. G. Snuffy Walden *pd* Amy B. Ancona *ed* Kevin Tent
☆ Blythe Danner (Katherine), Frank Whaley (Archie), Sheryl Lee (Lucy), Danny Nucci (Gilbert), Bruce Davison (Joseph)
'Story provides no rooting interest, and the creepiness of the material tries one's patience.' – *Variety*

Hombre **
US 1967 111m DeLuxe Panavision
TCF/Hombre Productions (Martin Ritt, Irving Ravetch)

Stagecoach passengers at the mercy of a robber are helped by a despised half-caste.
Slow but suspenseful Western melodrama which works up to a couple of good climaxes but falls away in an unnecessary tragic ending.
w Irving Ravetch, Harriet Frank *novel* Elmore Leonard *d* Martin Ritt *ph* James Wong Howe *m* David Rose
☆ Paul Newman, Diane Cilento, Fredric March, Richard Boone, Martin Balsam, Barbara Rush, Cameron Mitchell
'A fine array of quirkish characters … and some unusually literate dialogue.' – *Tom Milne*

Hombre Mirando al Sudeste *
Argentina 1986 100m Eastmancolor
Cinequanon (Hugo E. Lauria)
A saxophone-playing psychiatrist is confronted by a patient who claims to come from another planet.
An interesting, if portentously told, fable of a Christ-like character meeting with incomprehension in the modern world.
wd Eliseo Subiela *ph* Ricardo de Angelis *m* Pedro Aznar *pd* Marta Albertinazzi *ed* Luis Cesar D'Angiolillo
☆ Lorenzo Quinteros, Hugo Soto, Ines Vernengo

El Hombre que Vino de Ummo: see *Dracula versus Frankenstein*

Home Alone *
US 1990 102m DeLuxe
TCF/John Hughes

A young boy, inadvertently left behind at Christmas when his parents go on holiday, foils some inept house-breakers.
Swinging uneasily between heavy-handed slapstick and sentimental domestic comedy, this unpretentious movie was, inexplicably, the biggest box-office success of 1990.
w John Hughes *d* Chris Columbus *ph* Julio Macat *m* John Williams *pd* John Muto *ed* Raja Gosnell
☆ Macaulay Culkin, Joe Pesci, Daniel Stern, Catherine O'Hara, John Heard, Roberts Blossom, John Candy
'What is astonishing is that a cute family comedy which takes over an hour really to get going should have provoked such an enthusiastic audience response and gained such a phenomenal word-of-mouth reputation.' – *MFB*
John Williams; best song 'Somewhere In My Memory'

'He's Up Past His Bedtime In The City That Never Sleeps!'
Home Alone 2: Lost in New York
US 1992 120m colour
TCF (John Hughes)

Separated from his family after boarding the wrong plane, a young boy alone in New York thwarts the same two robbers he met at home.
Virtually a re-make of the first film, though the humour has a far more unpleasantly sadistic edge to it. This undistinguished comedy was among the biggest box-office successes of 1992.
w John Hughes *d* Chris Columbus *ph* Julio Macat *m* John Williams *pd* Sandy Veneziano *ed* Raja Gosnell
☆ Macaulay Culkin, Joe Pesci, Daniel Stern, Catherine O'Hara, John Heard, Devin Ratray, Hillary Wolf, Maureen Elisabeth Shay, Brenda Fricker
'An interesting example of formula film-making, making use of a higher budget than before but even lower expectations.' – *Derek Malcolm, Guardian*

Home Alone 3
US 1997 102m DeLuxe
TCF (John Hughes, Hilton Green)

Crooks attempt to recover from a small boy a toy in which a valuable computer chip is hidden.
A dispiriting continuation of the series, featuring much the same old routine of violent slapstick that, this time, borders on the sadistic.
w John Hughes *d* Raja Gosnell *ph* Julio Macat *m* Nick Glennie-Smith *pd* Henry Bumstead *ed* Bruce Green, Malcolm Campbell, David Rennie
☆ Alex D. Linz, Olek Krupa, Rya Kihlstedt, Lenny von Dohlen, David Thornton, Haviland Morris, Kevin Kilner
'A largely pointless experience.' – *Empire*

Home and the World **
India 1984 140m Eastmancolor
Artificial Eye/National Film Development Corp of India

original title: *Ghare-Baire*
A wealthy landowner brings his wife out from purdah into the world, with fatal results.
Elegant and impressively acted, with an undercurrent of despair.
wd Satyajit Ray *novel* Rabindranath Tagore *ph* Soumendu Roy *m* Satyajit Ray *ad* Ashoke Bose *ed* Dulal Dutt
☆ Soumitra Chatterjee, Victor Banerjee, Swatilekha Chatterjee, Gopa Aich, Jennifer Kapoor, Manoj Mitra, Indrapramit Roy, Bimal Chatterjee

Home at Seven
GB 1952 85m bw
British Lion/London (Maurice Cowan)

US title: *Murder on Monday*
A clerk suffers a 24-hour loss of memory and may have been involved in a murder.
Intriguing suburban mystery, well acted but all too flatly transferred from the stage, and with a weak solution.
w Anatole de Grunwald *play* R. C. Sherriff *d* Ralph Richardson *ph* Jack Hildyard, Edward Scaife *m* Malcolm Arnold
☆ Ralph Richardson, Margaret Leighton, Jack Hawkins, Campbell Singer, Michael Shepley, Margaret Withers, Meriel Forbes, Frederick Piper
'A film with a notable absence of imagination in conception, direction and acting is not vindicated because it was made very cheaply in fifteen days … it seems ominous that the technique closely resembles that of television.' – *MFB*

Home before Dark
US 1958 137m bw
Warner (Mervyn Le Roy)
A college professor brings his wife home after a year in a mental hospital, but trouble starts again as the circumstances are unchanged.
Overlong, heavygoing, well-made soap opera, quite unconvincing despite firm performances and a suitably gloomy mise-en-scène.
w Eileen and Robert Bassing *d* Mervyn Le Roy *ph* Joseph Biroc *m* Franz Waxman *md* Ray Heindorf
☆ Jean Simmons, Efrem Zimbalist Jnr, Dan O'Herlihy, Rhonda Fleming, Mabel Albertson

Home Fires Burning: see *The Turning*

'Meet the family that put the fun in dysfunctional!'
Home for the Holidays
US 1995 103m colour
Polygram/Egg (Peggy Rajski, Jodie Foster)

A brother and sister reluctantly return home for a family celebration of Thanksgiving.
Frantic comedy, on the level of a TV sitcom and peopled by eccentrics, whose peculiarities barely raise a smile.
w W. D. Richter *story* Chris Radant *d* Jodie Foster *ph* Lajos Koltai *m* Mark Isham *pd* Andrew McAlpine *ed* Lynzee Klingman
☆ Holly Hunter, Robert Downey Jnr, Anne Bancroft, Charles Durning, Dylan McDermott, Geraldine Chaplin, Cynthia Stevenson, Steve Guttenberg, Claire Danes, Austin Pendleton, David Strathairn
'Likeable in that cosy, wet Sunday afternoon, family sort of way.' – *Empire*

Home from the Hill
US 1960 150m Metrocolor Cinemascope
MGM/Sol C. Siegel (Edmund Grainger)

A Southern landowner with a voracious sexual appetite has trouble with his two sons, legitimate and illegitimate.
Shades of Cold Comfort Farm and Tobacco Road … and this solemn family saga does go on a bit.
w Irving Ravetch, Harriet Frank *novel* William Humphrey *d* Vincente Minnelli *ph* Milton Krasner *m* Bronislau Kaper
☆ Robert Mitchum, George Hamilton, George Peppard, Eleanor Parker, Luana Patten, Everett Sloane, Constance Ford, Ray Teal

Home in Indiana
US 1944 103m Technicolor
TCF (André Daven)
Farmers compete in trotting races and their progeny fall in love.
Archetypal homespun Americana, well enough made according to its lights, but now like something from another world … an innocent one.
w Winston Miller *novel* The Phantom Filly by George Agnew Chamberlain *d* Henry Hathaway *ph* Edward Cronjager *m* Hugo Friedhofer *md* Emil Newman
☆ Jeanne Crain, June Haver, Lon McCallister, Walter Brennan, Charlotte Greenwood, Ward Bond, Charles Dingle, Willie Best
† Remade as *April Love*.
Edward Cronjager

A Home of Our Own
US 1993 104m DeLuxe
Rank/Polygram/A&M (Dale Pollock, Bill Borden)

A widowed mother leaves Los Angeles to settle in the country with her six children in the hope of giving them a better life.
Sentimental, nostalgic drama of family togetherness that seems nearer to wish fulfilment than reality; it passes the time in an unmemorable fashion.
w Patrick Duncan *d* Tony Bill *ph* Jean Lepine *m* Michael Convertino *pd* James Schoppe *ed* Axel Hubert
☆ Kathy Bates, Edward Furlong, Tony Campisi, Soon-Teck Oh, Clarissa Lassig, Sarah Schaub, T. J. Lowther, Miles Feulner, Amy Sakasitz
'Audiences will likely find no particular reason to see such a family drama on the big screen, since in scope, scale and production values it perfectly befits TV, where similar inspirational country tales are often shown.' – *Variety*

Home of the Brave *
US 1949 86m bw
Stanley Kramer

During World War II, a black man finds himself the butt of racist behaviour from the rest of his platoon.
One of the first films to touch the subject of anti-black bias, this now seems pretty tame and dated, and in fact never was much more than a filmed play (in which the butt was originally a Jew).
w Carl Foreman *play* Arthur Laurents *d* Mark Robson *ph* Robert de Grasse *m* Dimitri Tiomkin
☆ Frank Lovejoy, Lloyd Bridges, Douglas Dick, James Edwards, Steve Brodie, Jeff Corey, Cliff Clark
† When Arthur Laurents asked Stanley Kramer why the central character was no longer a Jew, Kramer replied, 'Because Jews have been done.'

A Home of Your Own *
GB 1965 44m bw
Dormar/British Lion
Calamities pile up on a building site.
Genuinely funny silent comedy, with bits from a variety of familiar faces.
w Jay Lewis, John Whyte *d* Bob Kellett *ph* Dennis Coop *m* Ron Goodwin
☆ Ronnie Barker, George Benson, Richard Briers, Janet Brown, Peter Butterworth, Bernard Cribbins, Fred Emney, Bill Fraser, Ronnie Stevens

Home Sweet Home
GB 1945 92m bw
Butcher Empire (F. W. Baker, John E. Blakeley)
A worker in a piano factory tries to cope with his fractious employer and his wife, who gives birth to four sons.
An odd confection: there are a few cherishable moments of Randle's anarchic comedy, with its mix of slapstick and surrealism, but there's also a sickly romance, and the action stops halfway through for an interlude of classical music provided by the then-popular Austrian pianists Rawicz and Landauer.
w Roney Parsons, Anthony Toner, Arthur Mertz *d* John E. Blakeley *ph* Geoffrey Faithfull *md* Percival Mackey *ad* Jim Carter *ed* Vladimir Sagovsky
☆ Frank Randle, Nicolette Roeg, Tony Pendrell, H. F. Maltby, Cecil Frederick, Stan Little, Hilda Bayley, Donovan & Byl, Arnley & Gloria

Homebodies
US 1973 96m colour
Essential/Cinema Entertainment (Marshall Backlar)
Among the old people living in a tenement scheduled for redevelopment are homicidal maniacs.
Bizarre and tasteless horror of little visible merit.
w Larry Yust, Howard Kaminsky, Bennett Sims *d* Larry Yust *ph* Isidore Mankofsky *m* Bernardo Segall *ad* John Retsek *ed* Peter Parasheles
☆ Peter Brocco, Frances Fuller, William Hansen, Ruth McDevitt, Paula Trueman
'The film never finds its right level (and, incidentally, seems at a loss to know how to conclude itself).' – *David McGillivray*

Homeboy
US 1988 116m Technicolor
TCF/Homeboy Productions/Redruby (Alan Marshall, Elliott Kastner)

A down-and-out boxer gets one last chance at the big time.
Dim melodrama of the low life.
w Eddie Cook *story* Mickey Rourke *d* Michael Seresin *ph* Gale Tattersall *m* Eric Clapton, Michael Kamen *pd* Brian Morris *ed* Ray Lovejoy
☆ Mickey Rourke, Christopher Walken, Debra Feuer, Thomas Quinn, Kevin Conway, Anthony Alda, Jon Polito, Bill Slayton, David Taylor, Joseph Ragno

Homecoming
US 1948 113m bw
MGM (Sidney Franklin)

A ruthless society doctor is called up in World War II and has his life changed by a brief affair with a nurse who is killed in action.
Ho-hum romantic melodrama which stumbles most badly when it aims to be serious.
w Paul Osborn *d* Mervyn Le Roy *ph* Harold Rosson *m* Bronislau Kaper *md* Charles Previn
☆ Clark Gable, Lana Turner, Anne Baxter, John Hodiak, Ray Collins, Gladys Cooper, Cameron Mitchell, Marshall Thompson
'Its basic substance, like the base of a perfume, has a terrible smell; but to many moviegoers the end-product will seem quite pleasant.' – *Time*

The Homecoming *
GB 1973 114m colour
American Express/Ely Landau
Tensions mount and sexual revelations abound in the house of a retired London butcher.
Plain treatment of an anything-but-plain Pinter play. The result is a record of a performance rather than a film.
w Harold Pinter *play* Harold Pinter *d* Peter Hall *ph* David Watkin *m* Thelonious Monk *pd* John Bury
☆ Paul Rogers, Cyril Cusack, Michael Jayston, Ian Holm, Vivien Merchant, Terence Rigby
'Shocking in its own lucidity, and fascinating as an arrangement of mutually reflecting prisms … the remarkable control of Pinter's language guarantees that the dramatic situations are

revealed to be even *more* abstract and diagrammatic as they steadily accumulate psychological density.' – *Jonathan Rosenbaum*

Homegrown
US 1998 101m DeLuxe
TriStar/Lakeshore/Rollercoaster (Jason Clark)
In northern California, three marijuana growers decide to go into dope-dealing for themselves when their boss is unexpectedly murdered.
Laid-back, desultory thriller with a comic tone; interesting mainly in its depiction of the drug business away from its usual urban setting.
w Nicholas Kazan, Stephen Gyllenhaal
d Stephen Gyllenhaal *ph* Greg Gardiner
m Trevor Rabin *pd* Richard Sherman *ed* Michael Jablow
☆ Billy Bob Thornton, Hank Azaria, Kelly Lynch, Jon Bon Jovi, Ryan Phillippe, Ted Danson, Judge Reinhold, John Lithgow, Jamie Lee Curtis
'Serious, funny, sinister, sexy, silly and a lot more. But it isn't particularly good in any one of those departments.' – *Leonard Klady, Variety*

Homer
US 1970 91m colour
Palomar/Cinema VI (Terence Dene, Steven North)
As the Vietnam War begins, an 18-year-old would-be rock singer finds small-town life constricting.
An unoriginal plod through the usual teenage angst.
w Claude Harz *d* John Trent *ph* Laszlo G. George *ad* Jack McAdam *ed* M. C. Manne
☆ Don Scardino, Alex Nicol, Tisa Farrow, Lenka Peterson, Tim Henry, Tom Harvey

The Homeroom News: see *Freeze Frame*

Homeward Bound II: Lost in San Francisco
US 1996 88m Technicolor
Buena Vista/Walt Disney (Barry Jossen)
Two dogs and a cat, stranded in San Francisco, evade dog-nappers to find their way home.
A sequel, featuring animals with human voices and emotions, that treads much the same ground as its predecessor; enjoyable enough in its way, unless you like dumb animals.
w Chris Hauty, Julie Hickson *d* David R. Ellis *ph* Jack Conroy *m* Bruce Broughton *pd* Michael Bolton *ed* Peter E. Berger, Michael A. Stevenson
☆ Robert Hays, Kim Greist, Veronica Lauren, Kevin Chevalia, Benj Thall, Max Perlich, Michael Rispoli and also the voices of: Michael J. Fox, Sally Field, Ralph Waite, Jon Polito, Adam Goldberg, Sinbad
'Pic is funny enough to amuse adults who are willing to play along with it.' – *Variety*

Homeward Bound: The Incredible Journey
US 1993 85m Technicolor
Buena Vista/Walt Disney/Touchwood Pacific Partners I (Franklin R. Levy, Jeffrey Chernov)
Two dogs and a cat, separated from their human family, run off to find them.
A remake of Disney's The Incredible Journey *with human voices added for the animals, in the manner of the* Look Who's Talking *films; speech adds a feeling of unreality to the proceedings, but probably young audiences will not mind.*
w Caroline Thompson, Linda Wolverton
book *The Incredible Journey* by Sheila Burnford
d Duwayne Dunham *ph* Reed Smoot *m* Bruce Broughton *pd* Roger Cain *ed* Jonathan P. Shaw, Jay Cassidy, Michael Kelly, Brian Berdan
☆ Featuring the voices of Michael J. Fox, Sally Field, Don Ameche
'A sprightly little entertainment that should enthrall tots without straining the patience of parents.' – *Variety*

Homework: see *La Tarea*

'Can your heart stand the challenge when the clock starts the countdown?'
'All those too timid to take the climax will be welcomed to the cowards' corner!'
Homicidal
US 1961 87m bw
Columbia/William Castle
A murderous blonde and a very strange young man both live in the house of a paralysed old lady.
Transvestite horror comic allegedly based on a true case; made on a low budget and played for cheap shocks.
w Robb White *d* William Castle *ph* Burnett Guffey *m* Hugo Friedhofer
☆ Jean Arless, Glenn Corbett, Patricia Breslin, Eugenie Leontovich, Alan Bunce, Richard Rust
† The film was played with a 'fright break' during which faint-hearted members of the audience might leave before the final onslaught.

'Bob Gold is a cop. A good cop. But tonight, he will betray his friends, disgrace the force, and commit an act of violence because he believes it is the only right thing to do.'
Homicide **
US 1991 102m colour
First Independent/J&M Entertainment/Cinehaus (Michael Hausman, Edward R. Pressman)
A Jewish cop investigating the murder of a storekeeper suspects an anti-Semitic conspiracy.
Engrossing study of one man's disintegration.
wd David Mamet *ph* Roger Deakins *m* Alaric Jans *pd* Michael Merritt *ed* Barbara Tulliver
☆ Joe Mantegna, William H. Macy, Natalija Nogulich, Ving Rhames, Rebecca Pidgeon, J. J. Johnston, Jack Wallace
'Portrayed with a spell-binding skill and precision, the pace of an action-thriller off-set by unexpected patterns of colour and speech, part documentary, part theatrical melodrama.' – *Philip Strick, Sight and Sound*

Un Homme Amoureux: see *A Man in Love*

L'Homme au Chapeau Rond *
France 1946 91m bw
Alcina
When his wife dies, a man becomes obsessed with causing the downfall of her two lovers.
Heavy-going melodrama without much in the way of light relief; chiefly memorable for its central performance.
w Charles Spaak, Jean Loubignac *novel* *The Eternal Husband* by Dostoevsky *d* Pierre Billon *ph* Nicolas Torporkoff *m* Maurice Thiriet
☆ *Raimu*, Aimé Clariond, Lucy Valnor

L'Homme de Ma Vie *
France/Canada 1992 104m colour
Optima/Cineroux/Ciné Cinq/Prodeve (Gabriel Boustani)
aka: *The Man of My Life*
Determined to find a rich husband, a young Parisian woman marries a bad-tempered restaurant critic and suffers in style before deciding that love is better than comfort.
A light and frothy account of male–female relationships.
wd Jean Charles Tacchella *ph* Dominique Le Rigoleur *m* Raymond Alessandrini *ad* Serge Douy *ed* Marie-Aimée Debril
☆ Maria de Medeiros, Thiérry Fortineau, Anne Letourneau, Ginette Garcin, Ginette Mathieu, Alain Doutey, Jean-Pierre Bacri

L'Homme de Rio: see *That Man from Rio*

Un Homme est Mort: see *The Outside Man*

Un Homme et une Femme: see *A Man and a Woman*

Hommes Femmes: Mode d'emploi: see *Men Women: A User's Manual*

'First she was afraid he'd stay–then she was afraid he wouldn't...'
Hondo *
US 1953 93m Warnercolor 3-D
Wayne-Fellows
In 1874 New Mexico a cavalry despatch rider stops to defend a lonely widow and her son against Indians.
Overwritten but pleasant-looking Western, clearly patterned after Shane.
w James Edward Grant *novel* Louis L'Amour
d John Farrow *ph* Robert Burks, Archie Stout
m Emil Newman, Hugo Friedhofer *ad* Alfred C. Ybarra *ed* Ralph K. Dawson
☆ John Wayne (Hondo Lane), Geraldine Page (Angie Lowe), Ward Bond (Buffalo Baker), Michael Pate (Chief Vittorio), Lee Aaker (Johnny Lowe), James Arness (Lennie), Rudolfo Acosta (Silva), Leo V. Gordon (Ed Lowe)
Geraldine Page

'To live outside the law you must be...Honest.'
Honest
GB/France 2000 110m DeLuxe
Pathe/Seven Dials (Eileen Gregory, Michael Peyser)
In London in the 60s, three female thieves get away with their crimes because they disguise themselves as men.
An ill-advised spoof of swinging London, intended as a vehicle for the pop group All Saints, which was enough to seriously damage their careers.
w David A.Stewart, Dick Clement, Ian La Fresnais, Karen Street *d* David A. Stewart
ph David Johnson *m* David A. Stewart
pd Michael Pickwoad *ed* David Martin
☆ Nicole Appleton (Gerry), Natalie Appleton (Mandy), Melanie Blatt (Jo), James Cosmo (Tommy Chase), Jonathan Cake (Andrew Pryce-Stevens), Corin Redgrave (Duggie Ord), Peter Facinelli (Daniel Wheaton)
'A pleasant distraction that builds to an entertaining climax with art, acid and a smidgen of social commentary along the way.' – *Lisa Nesselson, Variety*
'I kept hoping the film would reveal itself to be a parody. No such luck.' – *Nigel Cliff, Times*

The Honest Courtesan: see *Dangerous Beauty*

Honey
US 1930 75m bw
Paramount
A brother and sister rent out their Southern mansion and decide to become the butler and cook.
Comedy with music, a little heavier than it should have been.
w Herman J. Mankiewicz *play* *Come Out of the Kitchen* by Alice Duer Miller, A. E. Thomas
d Wesley Ruggles
☆ Nancy Carroll, Skeets Gallagher, Stanley Smith, Lillian Roth, Harry Green, Mitzi Green, ZaSu Pitts
'Not worthy of a big rave but should satisfy the mob.' – *Variety*

Honey, I Blew Up the Kid
US 1992 89m Technicolor
Buena Vista/Walt Disney (Dawn Steel, Edward S. Feldman)
An inventor inadvertently exposes his two-year-old son to a ray that causes him to grow to 50 feet tall.
Predictable and dull comedy that fails to develop its central notion in interesting ways.
w Thom Eberhardt, Peter Elbling, Garry Goodrow *d* Randal Kleiser *ph* John Hora *m* Bruce Broughton *pd* Leslie Dilley *ed* Michael A. Stevenson, Harry Hitner, Tina Hirsch
☆ Rick Moranis, Marcia Strassman, Robert Oliveri, Daniel Shalikar, Joshua Shalikar, Lloyd Bridges, John Shea, Keri Russell, Ron Canada, Amy O'Neill
'A romp, escapism at its breeziest.' – *Variety*
'Proclaims in its every move that particular blend of crassness and technical expertise that is so often used for Hollywood's more down-market popular successes.' – *Derek Malcolm, Guardian*

Honey, I Shrunk the Kids *
US 1989 93m Metrocolor
Warner/Walt Disney/Doric (Penny Finkelman Cox)
An inventor inadvertently miniaturizes his children and dumps them in the garden.
Amusing comedy with Disney's winsomeness kept at bay for the most part, apart from a brave little ant.
w Ed Naha, Tom Schulman *story* Stuart Gordon, Brian Yuzna, Ed Naha *d* Joe Johnston *ph* Hiro Narita *pd* Gregg Fonseca *ed* Michael A. Stevenson
☆ Rick Moranis, Matt Frewer, Marcia Strassman, Kristine Sutherland, Thomas Brown, Jared Rushton, Amy O'Neill, Robert Oliveri, Carl Steven

'You are cordially invited to a perfectly elegant case of murder!'
The Honey Pot *
US 1966 150m Technicolor
UA/Famous Artists (Charles K. Feldman) (Joseph L. Mankiewicz)
A millionaire pretends to be dying in order to trick three former mistresses; but one of them is murdered.
Uneasy variation, via two other variations, on Ben Jonson's Volpone; *despite bright moments, the mood is fatally inconsistent, and a cloud of pseudo-sophisticated dialogue hangs over the whole thing like a pall.*
wd Joseph L. Mankiewicz *play* *Mr Fox of Venice* by Frederick Knott *novel* *The Evil of the Day* by *Thomas Sterling* *ph* Gianni di Venanzo *m* John Addison *pd* John DeCuir
☆ Rex Harrison, Susan Hayward, *Maggie Smith*, Cliff Robertson, Capucine, Edie Adams, Adolfo Celi, Herschel Bernardi
'One of the talkiest pictures ever made.' – *Stephen Farber*

'Miss Glamorous and Mr Amorous in a gay elopement adventure that makes Mexico City blush!'
Honeymoon
US 1947 74m bw
RKO (Warren Duff)
GB title: *Two Men and a Girl*
An 18-year-old elopes to Mexico City with an army corporal but meets a sophisticated older man.
Emaciated comedy, one of the reasons for Shirley Temple's early retirement.
w Michael Kanin *story* Vicki Baum *d* William Keighley *ph* Edward Cronjager *m* Leigh Harline
☆ Shirley Temple, Franchot Tone, Guy Madison, Lina Romay, Gene Lockhart, Grant Mitchell

Honeymoon
Spain/GB 1959 109m Technicolor
Technirama/Dimension 180
Suevia/Everdene (Cesario Gonzalez, Michael Powell)
Spanish title: *Luna de Miel*
An ex-ballerina in Spain with her new husband is tempted to return to the boards.
Incredibly shapeless travel poster with some dancing and two interpolated ballets to provide moments of musical interest. An unbelievable disaster from the co-creator of The Red Shoes.
w Michael Powell, Luis Escobar *d* Michael Powell *ph* Georges Périnal, Gerry Turpin *m* Mikis Theodorakis
☆ Anthony Steel, Ludmilla Tcherina, Antonio, Leonide Massine

Honeymoon for Three
US 1941 77m bw
Warner
An author is protected from adoring females by his secretary.
Fairly flaccid romantic comedy, a remake of Goodbye Again *(1933).*
w Julius J. Epstein, Philip G. Epstein, Earl Baldwin *d* Lloyd Bacon
☆ George Brent, Ann Sheridan, Osa Massen, Charles Ruggles, Jane Wyman, Lee Patrick

Honeymoon Hotel
US 1964 98m Metrocolor Cinemascope
MGM/Avon (Lawrence Weingarten)
A jilted swain goes off with a philandering friend on what was to have been his honeymoon trip ... only to be followed by his repentant fiancée.
Rather unattractive farce with insufficient funny moments.

w R. S. Allen, Harvey Bullock *d* Henry Levin *ph* Harold Lipstein *m* Walter Scharf
☆ Nancy Kwan, Robert Goulet, Robert Morse, Jill St John, Elsa Lanchester, Keenan Wynn

Honeymoon in Bali
US 1939 95m bw
Paramount (Jeff Lazarus)
GB title: *Husbands or Lovers?*
A department store head intends to pursue her career without marriage, but two swains try to prove her wrong.
Thin romantic comedy which got by on its stars.
w Virginia Van Upp *d* Edward H. Griffith
☆ Madeleine Carroll, Fred MacMurray, Allan Jones, Akim Tamiroff, Helen Broderick, Osa Massen
'Infectiously sparkling ... will click substantially in the regular runs.' – *Variety*
† The original title, *Are Husbands Necessary?*, was discarded when Miss Carroll became involved in a divorce suit.

'A comedy about one bride, two grooms, and 34 flying Elvises.'
Honeymoon in Vegas *
US 1992 96m Technicolor
First Independent/Castle Rock/New Line/Lobell/Bergman (Mike Lobell)
In a poker game a Las Vegas gambler wins a weekend with the fiancée of a New York detective.
Moderately enjoyable comedy, with an amusing running gag about Elvis impersonators.
wd Andrew Bergman *ph* William A. Fraker *m* David Newman *pd* William A. Elliott *ed* Barry Malkin
☆ James Caan, Nicolas Cage, Sarah Jessica Parker, Pat Morita, Johnny Williams, Anne Bancroft, Peter Boyle
'A virtually nonstop scream of benign delirium, pop entertainment as revivifying as anything you're likely to see this year.' – *Vincent Canby, New York Times*
'A very good comedy indeed, a dynamite throwback to those 40s screwball numbers.' – *Jeff Dawson, Empire*

The Honeymoon Killers *
US 1969 108m bw
Warren Steibel
A gigolo and a nurse team up to prey upon women looking for a husband.
Unsparing low-budget film, based on a true story of multiple murderers, that has gained a cult following.
wd Leonard Kastle *ph* Oliver Wood *ed* Stan Warnow
☆ Shirley Stoler, Tony Lo Bianco, Mary Jane Higby, Doris Roberts, Kip McArdle

The Honeymoon Machine
US 1961 91m Metrocolor Cinemascope
MGM/Avon (Lawrence Weingarten)
A naval lieutenant uses the ship's computer to break the bank at the Venice casino.
Stolid, expensive-looking comedy which barely raises a laugh.
w George Wells *play* *The Golden Fleecing* by Lorenzo Semple Jnr *d* Richard Thorpe *ph* Joseph LaShelle *m* Leigh Harline
☆ Steve McQueen, Brigid Bazlen, Jim Hutton, Paula Prentiss, Dean Jagger, Jack Weston, Jack Mullaney

Honeysuckle Rose
US 1980 119m Technicolor
Warner (Sydney Pollack)
A happily married country and western star takes to the bottle whenever he goes on the road.
Glum modern drama with music, a semi-autobiographical star vehicle; for fans only.
w Carol Sobieski, William D. Wittliff, John Binder *d* Jerry Schatzberg *ph* Robby Muller *m/ly* Willie Nelson *pd* Joel Schiller *ed* Aram Avakian, Norman Gay, Marc Laub, Evan Lottman
☆ Willie Nelson, Dyan Cannon, Amy Irving, Slim Pickens
song 'On the Road Again'

Hong Gaoliang: see *Red Sorghum*

Hong Kong
US 1951 91m Technicolor
Paramount/Pine-Thomas
An ex-GI has various adventures with a Chinese orphan and a golden idol.
And a plot that seems to make itself up as they go along. Corn-fed hokum.
w Winston Miller *d* Lewis R. Foster *ph* Lionel Lindon *m* Lucien Cailliet *ad* Lewis H. Creber *ed* Howard Smith
☆ Ronald Reagan, Rhonda Fleming, Nigel Bruce, Marvin Miller, Lowell Gilmore

The Honkers
US 1972 102m DeLuxe
Levy-Gardner-Lavin
An ageing rodeo performer runs into trouble when he returns to his home town.
Mundane and predictable drama of middle-aged regrets and disappointments.
w Steve Ihnat, Stephen Lodge *d* Steve Ihnat *ph* James Crabe *m* Jimmie Haskell *ed* Tom Rolf
☆ James Coburn, Lois Nettleton, Slim Pickens, Anne Archer, Richard Anderson, Joan Huntington, Jim Davis, Ramon Bieri

Honky Tonk
US 1929 80m bw
Warner
A night-club entertainer sacrifices everything for her daughter's education.
Primitive cross between Applause *and* Imitation of Life, *with spirited moments from Sophie Tucker the only plus.*
w C. Graham Baker, Jack Yellen *d* Lloyd Bacon *m/ly* Jack Yellen, Milton Ager *ch* Larry Ceballos
☆ Sophie Tucker, Lila Lee, Audrey Ferris, George Duryea, Mahlon Hamilton

'Every kiss a thrill!'
Honky Tonk *
US 1941 104m bw
MGM (Pandro S. Berman)
A Western con man meets his match in the daughter of a fake judge.
Generally amusing comedy melodrama that ambles along between two styles but leaves a pleasant after-effect.
w Marguerite Roberts, John Sanford *d* Jack Conway *ph* Harold Rosson *m* Franz Waxman
☆ *Clark Gable*, Lana Turner, Frank Morgan, Claire Trevor, Marjorie Main, Albert Dekker, Henry O'Neill, Chill Wills, Betty Blythe
'A lively, lusty western that makes you wish you had been there.' – *Variety*

Honky Tonk Freeway
US 1981 107m Technicolor
EMI/Kendon/HTF Company (Don Boyd, Howard W. Koch Jnr)
The mayor of a small Florida resort town has it painted pink to attract tourists ... but too many of the wrong kind come in.
Zany farce, rather like It's a Mad Mad Mad Mad World *without a proper hook to the story. Not an audience-pleaser, and very expensive.*
w Edward Clinton *d* John Schlesinger *ph* John Bailey *m* George Martin, Elmer Bernstein
☆ William Devane, Beau Bridges, Teri Garr, Beverly D'Angelo, Hume Cronyn, Jessica Tandy, Howard Hesseman, Geraldine Page, George Dzundza
'A shambles, and a more convincing one than the half-hearted affair which brings it to a close.' – *Richard Combs, MFB*
'A film for "now" which seems almost endearingly bereft of any real ideas about the messed-up contemporary world it inhabits.' – *Guardian*

Honkytonk Man
US 1982 122m Technicolor
Warner/Malpaso (Clint Eastwood)
In the thirties, an ageing and alcoholic country singer turns to his rural family for help.
Yet another occasion when the star should have asked for help instead of doing all the chores himself. Not much real entertainment here, just a very few moments that amuse.
w Clancy Carlile *novel* Clancy Carlile *d* Clint Eastwood *ph* Bruce Surtees *m* Steve Dorff *pd* Edward Carfagno
☆ Clint Eastwood, Kyle Eastwood, John McIntire, Verna Bloom, Alexa Kenin, Matt Clark

Honolulu
US 1938 83m bw
MGM (Jack Cummings)
A movie star is mistaken for his double.
Sloppy comedy with a few musical numbers.
w Herbert Fields, Frank Partos *d* Edward Buzzell *ph* Ray June *m* Franz Waxman
☆ Robert Young, Eleanor Powell, George Burns, Gracie Allen, Rita Johnson, Ruth Hussey, Clarence Kolb, Sig Rumann, Eddie Anderson
'Fairly amusing comedy for top brackets in duals.' – *Variety*
'The whole thing seems to have been thrown together so that Eleanor Powell can do a frenetic hula.' – *New Yorker, 1977*

Honor Bound
US 1989 102m Technicolor
Pacific/FilmAccord (Tim Van Relim, Eric A. Weymueller)
Two American soldiers investigate a mysterious happening at a Soviet missile base in East Germany.
Cold War thriller of limited interest.
w Aiken Woodruff *novel* *Recovery* by Steven L. Thompson *d* Jeannot Szwarc *ph* Robert Stevens *m* Mark Shreeve *pd* John Graysmark *ed* John Jympson
☆ John Philbin, Tom Skerritt, Gabrielle Lazure, George Dzundza, Lawrence Pressman, Gene Davis

Honor of the Family
US 1931 66m bw
First National
The young mistress of an aged Budapest resident is after his money.
Tiresome comedy drama.
play Emil Fabre *story* Balzac *d* Lloyd Bacon
☆ Bebe Daniels, Warren William, Frederick Kerr, Alan Mowbray, Blanche Friderici

The Honorary Consul
GB 1983 104m Movielab
World Film Services (Norma Heyman)
US title: *Beyond the Limit*
In northern Argentina, a doctor is drawn into the kidnapping by activists of a drunken British consul.
Self-parodic visit to Greeneland, with everybody drunk or depressed. Bouts of explicit sex don't help much, if at all.
w Christopher Hampton *novel* Graham Greene *d* John MacKenzie *ph* Phil Meheux *m* Stanley Myers *pd* Allan Cameron
☆ *Michael Caine*, Richard Gere, Bob Hoskins, Elpidia Carrillo, Joaquim de Almeida
'Some very old friends: exhausted passion, moral betrayal and relics of religious faith.' – *Sight and Sound*
'All it takes is the character to decide he is a burnt-out case, sleeping with all women but capable of loving none, for all the familiar icons to be ranged in battle array.' – *Tom Milne, MFB*

Honour Among Thieves: see *Touchez pas au Grisbi*

The Honourable Mr Wong: see *The Hatchet Man*

An Honourable Murder *
GB 1959 70m bw
Warner/Danzigers (Edward J. Danziger, Harry Lee Danziger)
Boardroom executives scheme to be rid of their chairman.
Oddball, interesting attempt to play Julius Caesar in modern dress. Not entirely successful, but full marks for trying.
w Brian Clemens, Eldon Howard *play* *Julius Caesar* by William Shakespeare *d* Godfrey Grayson *ph* James Wilson
☆ Norman Wooland (Brutus Smith), Margaretta Scott (Claudia Caesar), Lisa Daniely (Paula), Douglas Wilmer (R. Cassius), Philip Saville (Mark Anthony), John Longden (Julian Caesar)

The Hoodlum
US 1951 63m bw
Jack Schwarz Productions
A convict is paroled but continues his criminal career.
Toughish crime support with interesting moments.
w Sam Neumann, Nat Tanchuck *d* Max Nosseck *ph* Clark Ramsey *m* Darrell Calker
☆ Lawrence Tierney, Lisa Golm, Edward Tierney, Allene Roberts

'They had it all. It cost them everything.'
Hoodlum
US 1997 130m DeLuxe
MGM/UA (Frank Mancuso Jnr)
In the 30s, black gangster Bumpy Johnson fights Dutch Schultz for control of the numbers racket in Harlem.
Tough gangster movie that is enjoyable without being memorable.
w Chris Brancato *d* Bill Duke *ph* Frank Tidy *m* Elmer Bernstein *pd* Charles Bennett *ed* Harry Keramidas
☆ Laurence Fishburne, Tim Roth, Andy Garcia, Vanessa L. Williams, Cicely Tyson, Chi McBride, William Atherton
'The film falls short of its aim for mythic proportion. Still, there's a vibrancy that's engrossing, if uneven.' – *Leonard Klady, Variety*
† The film was released direct to video in Britain.

Hoodlum Empire
US 1952 98m bw
Republic (Joseph Kane)
A Congressional committee investigates a racketeer.
Moderate semi-documentary potboiler inspired by the Kefauver investigations.
w Bruce Manning, Bob Considine *d* Joseph Kane *ph* Reggie Lanning *m* Nathan Scott
☆ Brian Donlevy, Forrest Tucker, Claire Trevor, Vera Ralston, Luther Adler, John Russell, Gene Lockhart, Grant Withers, Taylor Holmes
'Familiar gangster melodramatics and repentances, played out in a rigmarole of flashbacks.' – *MFB*

The Hoodlum Priest *
US 1961 100m bw
UA/Don Murray-Walter Wood
A Jesuit teacher tries to help young criminals, especially a condemned murderer.
Moderately well done, very depressing and downbeat chunk of social conscience based on the life of Charles Dismas Clark.
w Don Mankiewicz, Joseph Landon, 'Don Deer' (i.e. Don Murray) *d* Irvin Kershner *ph* Haskell Wexler *m* Richard Markowitz
☆ Don Murray, Keir Dullea, Larry Gates, Cindi Wood, Logan Ramsey

The Hoodlum Saint
US 1946 93m bw
MGM (Cliff Reid)
A cynical newspaperman turns to religion and succours thieves.
Hard-boiled sentimentality, a downright peculiar and doleful comedy drama in deflated post-war mood.
w Frank Wead, James Hill *d* Norman Taurog *ph* Ray June *m* Nathaniel Shilkret
☆ William Powell, Esther Williams, Angela Lansbury, James Gleason, Lewis Stone, Rags Ragland, Frank McHugh, Slim Summerville, Roman Bohnen, Louis Jean Heydt, Charles Arnt, Charles Trowbridge, Henry O'Neill

The Hook
US 1962 98m bw Panavision
MGM/Perlberg-Seaton
Three GIs escaping from Korea are ordered to execute a prisoner but cannot bring themselves to do it.
Predictable, claustrophobic drama which becomes a slick exercise in morality.
w Henry Denker *novel* *L'Hameçon* by Vahe Katcha *d* George Seaton *ph* Joe Ruttenberg *m* Larry Adler
☆ Kirk Douglas, Robert Walker, Nick Adams, Nehemiah Persoff

Hook *
US 1991 144m DeLuxe Panavision
Columbia TriStar/Amblin (Kathleen Kennedy, Frank Marshall, Gerald R. Molen)

Peter Pan, who has returned to the ordinary world to become a father and a corporate lawyer, returns to Neverland to fight Captain Hook.
Sprawling, overlong, often camp extravaganza with splendid special effects and settings that may appeal to the small child in most of us, even if it is time that Spielberg himself grew up.
w Jim V. Hart, Malia Scotch Marmo *play* Peter Pan by J. M. Barrie *story* Jim V. Hart, Nick Castle *d* Steven Spielberg *ph* Dean Cundey *m* John Williams *pd* Norman Garwood (John Napier was visual consultant) *ed* Michael Kahn *sp* Industrial Light and Magic
☆ Dustin Hoffman, Robin Williams, Julia Roberts, Bob Hoskins, Maggie Smith, Caroline Goodall, Charlie Korsmo, Amber Scott, Laurel Cronin, Phil Collins, David Crosby
'Spirited, rambunctious, often messy and undisciplined, this determined attempt to recast the Peter Pan story in contemporary terms splashes every bit of its megabudget (between $60 and $80 million) onto the screen; commercial elements overflow in such abundance that major hit status seems guaranteed.' – *Variety*
'Peel away the expensive, special effects surface and there's nothing but formula.' – *Washington Post*
† Glenn Close appears in an uncredited role as a bearded pirate.
song 'When You're Alone' (*m* John Williams, *ly* Leslie Bricusse); Norman Garwood; visual effects

Hook Line and Sinker
US 1930 72m bw
RKO

Two insurance agents run a derelict hotel.
Feeble comedy vehicle.
w Tim Whelan, Ralph Spence *d* Edward F. Cline
☆ Bert Wheeler, Robert Woolsey, Hugh Herbert, Dorothy Lee, Jobyna Howland, Ralf Harolde
'Will tickle most in those spots where the price is least.' – *Variety*

Hook, Line and Sinker
US 1968 92m Technicolor
Columbia/Jerry Lewis
A salesman who thinks he is dying goes on a spending spree; when he learns the truth, he has to disappear because of his huge debts.
Miserable comedy with frantic slapstick interludes. The plot might have served Preston Sturges.
w Rod Amateau *d* George Marshall *ph* W. Wallace Kelley *m* Dick Stabile
☆ Jerry Lewis, Peter Lawford, Anne Francis, Pedro Gonzales Gonzales

'The Film That Stunned A Nation!'
Hoop Dreams ***
US 1994 174m colour
Feature/FineLine/Kartemquin/KCTA-TV (Fred Marx, Steve James, Peter Gilbert)

Two black teenagers pursue their hopes of becoming professional basketball players.
A documentary that makes redundant all the recent fictional accounts of basketball heroics; here is the real thing, a brilliant documentary of the conjunction and conflict of the American Dream and the realities of life, following its two protagonists and their families through four years of success and failure.
d Steve James *ph* Peter Gilbert *ed* Fred Marx, Steve James, Bill Haugse
☆ William Gates, Arthur Agee, Emma Gates, Curtis Gates, Sheila Agee
'Has the crackle and density of that elusive beast, the Great American Novel.' – *Geoff Brown, The Times*
'A prodigious achievement that conveys the fabric of modern American life, aspirations and, incidentally, sport in close-up.' – *Todd McCarthy, Variety*
editing

Hooper *
US 1978 99m Metrocolor
Warner/Burt Reynolds, Lawrence Gordon (Hank Moonjean)

An ageing stunt man decides on one last sensational stunt before retiring.
There are some agreeably striking moments, but you can't make a movie out of stunts and loud camaraderie. This one palls half way through.
w Thomas Rickman, Bill Kerby *d* Hal Needham *ph* Bobby Byrne *m* Bill Justis
☆ *Burt Reynolds*, Sally Field, Brian Keith, Jan-Michael Vincent, John Marley, Robert Klein, James Best, Adam West
'Burt Reynolds's annual Kleenex of a movie: something to use and throw away without any thought beyond a certain gratitude for the convenience of the thing.' – *Richard Schickel, Time*

'Clara Bow ... red-headed warm-blooded dynamite ... again releases the torrent of her genius in the most colorful performance of her life.'
Hoopla
US 1933 85m bw
Fox
A hardboiled carnival dancer agrees to seduce the son of the show's manager, but ends by marrying him.
Strained melodrama with the star, in her last film, at the end of her tether.
w Bradley King, J. M. March *play* The Barker by Kenyon Nicholson *d* Frank Lloyd
☆ Clara Bow, Richard Cromwell, Preston Foster, Herbert Mundin, James Gleason, Minna Gombell, Roger Imhof
'Miss Bow seems ripe to come back strongly.' – *Variety*

Hooray for Love
US 1935 75m bw
RKO (Felix Young)
A rich college boy plays angel to a musical comedy.
Thin pot-pourri of familiar elements.
w Lawrence Hazard, Ray Harris *story* Marc Lachmann *d* Walter Lang *ph* Lucien Andriot *m/ly* Dorothy Fields, Jimmy McHugh *md* Albert Colombo *ad* Van Nest Polglase *ed* George Crone
☆ Ann Sothern, Gene Raymond, *Bill Robinson*, Thurston Hall, Pert Kelton, Lionel Stander, *Fats Waller*
'Trouble is entirely traceable to its terribly lethargic tempo and lack of any real production numbers.' – *Variety*

The Hoosegow **
US 1929 20m bw
Hal Roach

Stan and Ollie, in prison, contrive to fell a tree on the cook's tent and to smother the governor in boiled rice.
Splendid slapstick leading up to one of their best tit-for-tat routines.
w Leo McCarey, H. M. Walker *d* James Parrott *ph* George Stevens, Len Powers, Glenn Robert Kershner *ed* Richard Currier
☆ Stan Laurel, Oliver Hardy, James Finlayson, Tiny Sandford, Ellinor Vanderveer

Hoosiers
US 1986 114m CFI color
Orion/Hemdale/Carter de Haven

GB title: *Best Shot*
The training and triumph of an Indiana high school basketball team.
Expertise expended on a subject of very limited interest.
w Angelo Pizzo *d* David Anspaugh *ph* Fred Murphy *m* Jerry Goldsmith
☆ Gene Hackman, Barbara Hershey, Dennis Hopper, Sheb Wooley, Fern Persons
'Both rousing and too conventional.' – *Variety*
Jerry Goldsmith; Dennis Hopper

Hoots Mon *
GB 1939 77m bw
Warner
A Cockney comedian starts a popularity contest with a female impressionist.
Tolerable comedy whose value is that it preserves, albeit in cleaned-up form, portions of Max Miller's variety act. Florence Desmond isn't bad either.
w Roy William Neill, Jack Henley, John Dighton *d* Roy William Neill *ph* Basil Emmott *md* Bretton Byrd *ad* Norman Arnold *ed* Leslie Norman
☆ *Florence Desmond, Max Miller*, Hal Walters, Davina Craig, Garry Marsh

Hopalong Cassidy

Cassidy, a creation of Clarence E. Mulford, was a fictitious gentleman cowboy who oddly enough wore black; 26 books about him were published between 1912 and 1956 when Mulford died. 66 films were made starring William Boyd as Hoppy, with either George Gabby Hayes or Andy Clyde as comic sidekick: Harry Sherman produced them, first for Paramount and then for UA, and they were later edited down for TV, in which medium Boyd became a folk hero and eventually made a further series. The films were easy-going, slow-moving second features which always pointed an admirable moral for children; their main directors were Howard Bretherton, Nate Watt, Lesley Selander and George Archainbaud.
1935 Hopalong Cassidy, The Eagle's Brood, Bar 20 Rides Again
1936 Call of the Prairie, Three on the Trail, Heart of the West, Hopalong Cassidy Returns, Trail Dust
1937 Borderland, Hills of Old Wyoming, North of the Rio Grande, Rustlers' Valley, Hopalong Rides Again, Texas Trail
1938 Heart of Arizona, Bar 20 Justice, Pride of the West, In Old Mexico, Sunset Trail, The Frontiersman, Partners of the Plains, Cassidy of Bar 20
1939 Range War, Law of the Pampas, Silver on the Sage, Renegade Trail
1940 Santa Fe Marshal, The Showdown, Hidden Gold, Stagecoach War, Three Men from Texas
1941 Doomed Caravan, In Old Colorado, Border Vigilantes, Pirates on Horseback, Wide Open Town, Outlaws of the Desert, Riders of the Timberline, Secrets of the Wasteland, Stick to Your Guns, Twilight on the Trail
1942 Undercover Man
1943 Colt Comrades, Bar 20, Lost Canyon, Hoppy Serves a Writ, Border Patrol, The Leather Burners, False Colours, Riders of the Deadline
1944 Mystery Man, Forty Thieves, Texas Masquerade, Lumberjack
1946 The Devil's Playground
1947 Fool's Gold, Hoppy's Holiday, Marauders, Unexpected Guest, Dangerous Venture
1948 Sinister Journey, Silent Conflict, Strange Gamble, Borrowed Trouble, The Dead Don't Dream, False Paradise

Hope and Glory **
GB 1987 113m Technicolor
Columbia/Goldcrest/Nelson (John Boorman)

Adventures of a small boy and his family during World War II in suburban London.
Generally appealing but not too accurate reminiscences of an exciting and emotional time.
wd John Boorman *ph* Philippe Rousselot *m* Peter Martin *pd* Anthony Pratt *ad* Don Dossett
☆ Sarah Miles, Susan Wooldridge, Ian Bannen, David Hayman, Derrick O'Connor, Sebastian Rice-Edwards
Philippe Rousselot; John Boorman as director; best picture; best original screenplay; best art direction – set decoration
Susan Wooldridge

'When life fell apart love fell into place.'
Hope Floats
US 1998 114m DeLuxe
TCF/Fortis (Lynda Obst)

After the revelation on a TV talkshow that her husband is having an affair with her best friend, a woman returns home to Texas and meets a childhood sweetheart.
Leaden, dull, slow-paced, overlong drama of small-town virtues and redemption.
w Steven Rogers *d* Forest Whitaker *ph* Caleb Deschanel *m* Dave Grusin *pd* Larry Fulton *ed* Richard Chew
☆ Sandra Bullock, Harry Connick Jnr, Gena Rowlands, Mae Whitman, Michael Paré, Cameron Finley, Kathy Najimy, Rosanna Arquette (uncredited)
'A by-the-numbers bit of emotional calculation without a single fresh, original or offbeat move in its system.' – *Todd McCarthy, Variety*

Hope Springs
GB/US 2002 92m Technicolor
Buena Vista/Touchstone/Fragile (Barnaby Thompson)
In a New England town, two women fight for the love of an English artist.
Dim romantic comedy that fails to get any amusement out of its clash between English and American attitudes.
wd Mark Herman *novel* New Cardiff by Charles Webb *ph* Ashley Rowe *m* John Altman *pd* Don Taylor *ed* Michael Ellis
☆ Colin Firth (Colin Ware), Heather Graham (Mandy), Minnie Driver (Vera Edwards), Mary Steenburgen (Joanie Fisher), Oliver Platt (Mayor Doug Reed), Frank Collison (Fisher)
'Leaves you feeling a mix of pity and embarrassment for the cast, and contempt for the mediocrities who made it.' – *Cosmo Landesman, Sunday Times*

Hoppity Goes to Town: see *Mr Bug Goes to Town*

Hopscotch *
US 1980 104m Movielab Panavision
Avco/Edie and Ely Landau (Otto Plaschkes)

An ex-CIA man writes a revealing book and foils the consequent attempts on his life.
Genial but patchy spy comedy caper; a filler for all concerned.
w Brian Garfield, Bryan Forbes *novel* Brian Garfield *d* Ronald Neame *ph* Arthur Ibbetson *m* Ian Fraser
☆ Walter Matthau, Glenda Jackson, Ned Beatty, Sam Waterston, Herbert Lom, George Baker

Hori, Ma Panenko: see *The Firemen's Ball*

Horizons West
US 1952 81m Technicolor
U-I (Albert J. Cohen)
After the Civil War, a rancher builds an empire on greed and ruthlessness, and his brother has to bring him to trial.
Rather lugubrious Western with the usual quota of effective action scenes.
w Louis Stevens *d* Budd Boetticher *ph* Charles P. Boyle *md* Joseph Gershenson *ad* Robert Clatworthy, Bernard Herzbrun *ed* Ted J. Kent
☆ Rock Hudson, Robert Ryan, Julia Adams, John McIntire, Raymond Burr, Dennis Weaver, Judith Braun

The Horizontal Lieutenant
US 1962 90m Metrocolor Cinemascope
MGM/Euterpe (Joe Pasternak)
World War II Hawaii; an amorous intelligence officer accidentally captures a Japanese guerrilla.
Very moderate army farce of no great skill or memorability.
w George Wells *d* Richard Thorpe *ph* Robert Bronner *m* George Stoll
☆ Jim Hutton, Paula Prentiss, Jim Backus, Miyoshi Umeki, Jack Carter

L'Horloger de St Paul: see *The Watchmaker of St Paul*

The Horn Blows at Midnight *
US 1945 80m bw
Warner (Mark Hellinger)

An angel is sent to earth to destroy the planet with Gabriel's horn.
Wacky comedy inspired by Here Comes Mr Jordan, *but on a broader slapstick level; much better than its star always pretended.*
w Sam Hellman, James V. Kern *d* Raoul Walsh *ph* Sid Hickox *m* Franz Waxman
☆ *Jack Benny*, Alexis Smith, Dolores Moran, Allyn Joslyn, Guy Kibbee, Reginald Gardiner, *Franklin Pangborn*, John Alexander, Margaret Dumont

Hornet's Nest
US 1969 109m DeLuxe
UA/Triangle (Stanley S. Kanter)
In World War II Italy, a wounded US army demolitions expert is nursed back to health by

child partisans, who help him destroy a German-held dam.
Overlong war exploits with the children used as a tiresome gimmick.
w S. S. Schweitzer *d* Phil Karlson *ph* Gabor Pogany *m* Ennio Morricone
☆ Rock Hudson, Sergio Fantoni, Sylva Koscina, Jacques Sernas

Horriplante Bestia Humana: see *Night of the Bloody Apes*

Horror Express *
GB/Spain 1972 88m Technicolor
Gala/Granada/Benmar (Bernard Gordon)
aka: *Panic on the Trans-Siberian Express*
Spanish title: *Pánico en el Transiberiano*
An alien intelligence, trapped in a humanoid fossil for centuries, escapes and goes on a killing spree in which it absorbs the memories of its victims.
Moderately effective and ingenious low-budget horror.
w Arnaud d'Usseau, Julian Halevy (Julian Zimet) *story* Eugenio Martin *d* Gene Martin *ph* Alejandro Ulloa *m* John Cavacas *ad* Ramiro Gomez Guadiana *ed* Robert Dearberg *sp* Pablo Perez
☆ Christopher Lee, Peter Cushing, Telly Savalas, Silvia Tortosa, Jorge Rigaud, Alberta de Mondoza
'The script unwinds itself with sufficient cunning to keep interest alive, always one step ahead of the audience with a new revelation to come.' – *Tom Milne, MFB*
† Zimet used the pseudonym Julian Halevy because he was blacklisted at the time.

'Black Gloves Of Evil Lay Bare The Ultimate Horror!'
Horror Hospital
GB 1973 91m Eastmancolor
Noteworthy (Richard Gordon)
A songwriter goes to spend a week at a health hotel run by a mysterious crippled doctor, who gives a lobotomy to all his patients.
High-camp, macabre movie that opens with a double decapitation and relishes its recycling of familiar horrors.
w Antony Balch, Alan Watson *d* Antony Balch *ph* David McDonald *m* De Wolfe, Mystic *ad* David Bill *ed* Robert Dearberg
☆ Michael Gough, Robin Askwith, Vanessa Shaw, Dennis Price, Ellen Pollock, Skip Martin, Kurt Christian, Barbara Wendy, Kenneth Benda
'If *Horror Hospital* makes no serious attempt to replace the basic clichés, it at least celebrates their survival with a satirical relish seldom displayed on this side of the Atlantic.' – *Jan Dawson, MFB*

Horror Hotel: see *City of the Dead*

The Horror House: see *The Haunted House of Horror*

Horror Island
US 1941 60m bw
Universal
Various people travel to an island where buried treasure might be hidden.
Feeble little mystery with very little interest in who done what to whom.
w Maurice Tombragel, Victor McLeod *d* George Waggner
☆ Dick Foran, Leo Carrillo, Peggy Moran, Fuzzy Knight, John Eldredge, Walter Catlett, Hobart Cavanaugh

Horror of Dracula: see *Dracula (1958)*

The Horror of Frankenstein
GB 1970 95m Technicolor
EMI/Hammer (Jimmy Sangster)
Victor Frankenstein is not above murdering his acquaintances for the sake of his experiments in bringing the dead back to life.
Ill-advised attempt to remake the original story as a black comedy, with Frankenstein frankly villainous from the start. The last in the Hammer series.
w Jeremy Burnham, Jimmy Sangster *d* Jimmy Sangster *ph* Moray Grant *m* Malcolm Williamson *ad* Scott MacGregor *ed* Chris Barnes
☆ Ralph Bates, Kate O'Mara, Graham James, Veronica Carlson, Bernard Archard, Dennis Price, Joan Rice, Dave Prowse

Horror of Snape Island: see *Tower of Evil*

Horror Planet: see *Inseminoid*

The Horror Show
US 1989 95m DeLuxe
UA (Sean S. Cunningham)
aka: *House III*
A cop and his family become the target for a dead homicidal maniac, resurrected through electricity.
Muddled and confused horror that never sparks into life.
w Alan Smithee (Allyn Warner), Leslie Bohem *d* James Isaac *ph* Mac Ahlberg *m* Harry Manfredini *pd* Stewart Campbell *ed* Edward Anton
☆ Lance Henriksen, Brion James, Rita Taggart, Dedee Pfeiffer, Thom Bray, Matt Clark, Lawrence Tierney

Horrors of the Black Museum
GB 1959 81m Eastmancolor Cinemascope
Herman Cohen
A crime writer is fascinated by murder, and works out his own plots by practice beforehand.
Crude shocker.
w Aben Kandel, Herman Cohen *d* Arthur Crabtree *ph* Desmond Dickinson *m* Gerard Schurmann
☆ Michael Gough, Graham Curnow, Shirley Anne Field, Geoffrey Keen

Hors La Vie
France/Italy/Germany 1991 97m colour
Galatee/A2/Filmalpha/Lamy/Canal Plus/Raidue (Jacques Perrin)
A French photographer working in Beirut is taken hostage.
Based on fact, this is an unsensational but not illuminating account of what it is to be held prisoner.
w Maroun Bagdadi, Didier Decoin, Elias Khoury *book* Roger Auque, Patrick Forestier *d* Maroun Bagdadi *ph* Patrick Blossier *m* Nicola Piovani *ad* Dan Weil *ed* Luc Barnier
☆ Hippolyte Girardot, Rafic Ali Ahmad, Hussein Sbetty, Habib Hammoud, Magdi Machmouchi, Hassan Farhat, Hamzah Nasrullah, Nidal El Achkar
'Sober, uncompromising but never excessive treatment conveys the mental and physical horrors of detention while delineating delicate balance between captors and victim.' – *Variety*
'An assembly-kit political thriller. In a moment of madness the Cannes Jury gave it a Special Jury Prize. Perhaps they liked the telegraphic simplicity of the story.' – *Nigel Andrews, Financial Times*

'A scandalous record of low Marx at college – or life among the thirsty co-eds!'
Horse Feathers ***
US 1932 69m bw
Paramount (Herman J. Mankiewicz)
A college needs to win at football, and its corrupt new president knows just how to do it.
Possibly the Marxes' wildest yet most streamlined kaleidoscope of high jinks and irreverence, with at least one bright gag or line to the minute and lively musical interludes to boot. A classic of zany comedy.
w Bert Kalmar, Harry Ruby, S. J. Perelman, Will B. Johnstone d Norman Z. McLeod ph Ray June *m/ly Bert Kalmar, Harry Ruby*
☆ *Groucho Marx, Chico Marx, Harpo Marx,* Zeppo Marx, *Thelma Todd,* Robert Greig
GROUCHO: 'You have the brain of a four-year-old child, and I'll bet he was glad to get rid of it.'
CHICO: 'There's a man outside with a big black moustache.'
GROUCHO: 'Tell him I've got one.'
GROUCHO (TO ZEPPO): 'You're a disgrace to our family name of Wagstaff, if such a thing is possible.'
GROUCHO: 'For years before my son was born
I used to yell from night till morn
Whatever it is – I'm against it!
And I've been yelling since I first commenced it
– I'm against it!'
'The current Marx comedy is the funniest talkie since the last Marx comedy, and the record it establishes is not likely to be disturbed until the next Marx comedy comes along. As for comparisons, I was too busy having a good time to make any.' – *Philip K. Scheuer*

The Horse in the Grey Flannel Suit
US 1969 112m Technicolor
Walt Disney
A teenager's horse becomes the central figure in an advertising campaign for a stomach pill.
Interminable kiddie movie which in its virtual absence of plot or excitement is likely to bore kiddies to death.
w Louis Pelletier *novel The Year of the Horse* by Eric Hatch *d* Norman Tokar *ph* William Snyder *m* George Bruns
☆ Dean Jones, Fred Clark, Diane Baker, Lloyd Bochner, Morey Amsterdam

The Horse Soldiers *
US 1959 119m DeLuxe
UA/Mirisch (John Lee Mahin, Martin Rackin)
In 1863 a Union cavalry officer is sent three hundred miles into Confederate territory to demolish a railroad junction.
Typically sprawling John Ford cavalry Western with not too many high spots and more sombre ingredients than usual.
w John Lee Mahin, Martin Rackin *d* John Ford *ph* William Clothier *m* David Buttolph
☆ John Wayne, William Holden, Constance Towers, Hoot Gibson
HOLDEN: 'Look here, colonel, I didn't ask to be assigned to this mission...'
'Blemished as many of his films are blemished: patches of horseplay, too much manly chest-beating. But the blemishes proceed from the quality which gives his work its frequent splendours. The horseplay and the over-emphasised masculinity belong to his romantic vision.' – *Dilys Powell*

Horse Thief **
China 1986 88m colour
Xi'an Film Studio (Li Changqing)
Trying to feed his family, a peasant becomes a thief and outcast.
Its stunning visuals, of exotic rituals and broad landscapes, and exuberant style compensate for the slightness of narrative.
w Zhang Rui *d* Tian Zhuangzhuang *ph* Hou Yong, Zhao Fei *m* Qu Xiaosong *ad* Huo Jianqi *ed* Li Jingzhong
☆ Tseshang Rinzim, Dan Jiji, Jayang Jamco

The Horse Whisperer
US 1998 168m Technicolor Panavision
Buena Vista/Touchstone/Wildwood (Robert Redford, Patrick Markey)
When her daughter and horse are both traumatized by a riding accident, a New York magazine editor travels to Montana to seek the help of an equine expert.
Ponderous romantic drama, lushly photographed but never convincing on an emotional level.
w Eric Roth, Richard LaGravenese *novel* Nicholas Evans *d* Robert Redford *ph* Robert Richardson *m* Thomas Newman *pd* Jon Hutman *ed* Tom Rolf, Freeman Davies, Hank Corwin
☆ Robert Redford, Kristin Scott Thomas, Sam Neill, Dianne Wiest, Scarlett Johansson, Chris Cooper, Cherry Jones, Ty Hillman, Catherine Bosworth
'An exquisitely crafted, morally and thematically mature picture.' – *Todd McCarthy, Variety*
'Punishingly dull.' – *Newsweek*
'This stately, aggravating film is set in that hollow universe known only to popular middle-brow novels and Hollywood stars too cocooned by their own eminence to recognise the march of time.' – *Geoff Brown, The Times*
song 'A Soft Place to Fall' (*m/ly* Allison Moorer, Gwil Owen)

The Horse without a Head **
GB 1963 89m Technicolor
Walt Disney (Hugh Attwooll)
Stolen money is hidden in an old toy horse, and crooks trying to get it back clash with police and children.
Excellent children's adventure with scenes on trains and in a toy factory.
w T. E. B. Clarke *d* Don Chaffey *ph* Paul Beeson *m* Eric Rogers
☆ Leo McKern, Jean-Pierre Aumont, Herbert Lom, Pamela Franklin, Vincent Winter

The Horseman on the Roof
France 1995 135m colour Technovision
Hachette/France2/CEC/Canal (René Cleitman)
original title: *Le Hussard sur le Toit*
An Italian hussar hides from his enemies in Provence, where he meets a young woman searching for her husband.
Sweepingly romantic, epic romance that delights the eye more than the mind; handsome is as handsome does, and it doesn't do enough to engage the attention for long.
w Jean-Paul Rappeneau, Nina Companeez, Jean-Claude Carrière *novel* Jean Giono *d* Jean-Paul Rappeneau *ph Thierry Arbogast m* Jean-Claude Petit *ad* François Hamel *ed* Noëlle Boisson
☆ Olivier Martinez, Juliette Binoche, Isabelle Carré, François Cluzet, Jean Yanne, Claudio Amendola, Pierre Arditi, Gérard Depardieu
† It was reportedly the most expensive French film yet made, at a cost of around 176m francs.

The Horsemen
US 1970 109m colour Super Panavision
Columbia/John Frankenheimer-Edward Lewis
An Afghan tribesman is determined to rival his father at horsemanship.
Rather tedious variant on Taras Bulba; *plenty of action but not much characterization, or taste, or interest.*
w Dalton Trumbo *novel* Joseph Kessel *d* John Frankenheimer *ph* Claude Renoir *m* Georges Delerue
☆ Omar Sharif, Jack Palance, Leigh Taylor-Young, Peter Jeffrey, Eric Pohlmann, Despo, David de Keyser

The Horse's Mouth *
GB 1958 93m Technicolor
UA/Knightsbridge (John Bryan)
An obsessive painter is a liability to his friends.
Thin but fitfully amusing light study of a social outcast, with a background of London river and streets. Too slight for real success.
w Alec Guinness *novel* Joyce Cary *d* Ronald Neame *ph Arthur Ibbetson m* K. V. Jones from Prokofiev *paintings* John Bratby
☆ Alec Guinness, Kay Walsh, Renée Houston, Robert Coote, Arthur Macrae, Michael Gough, Ernest Thesiger
'Immensely and joyously successful at what it sets out to do.' – *Evening Standard*
'A work of genius.' – *News of the World*
Alec Guinness (as writer)

'Madness, Murder and Malpractice.'
The Hospital ***
US 1971 101m DeLuxe Panavision
UA/Simcha (Howard Gottfried)
A city hospital is beset by weird mishaps, and it transpires that a killer is on the loose.
*Black comedy with the emphasis on sex and medical ethics; in the same genre as M*A*S*H, and very funny if you can take it.*
w Paddy Chayefsky *d* Arthur Hiller *ph* Victor Kemper *m* Morris Surdin *ad* Gene Rudolf *ed* Eric Albertson
☆ George C. Scott (Dr Herbert Bock), Diana Rigg (Barbara Drummond), Barnard Hughes (Drummond), Nancy Marchand (Mrs Christie), Richard Dysart (Dr Welbeck), Stephen Elliott (Sundstrom), Donald Harron (Milton Mead), Roberts Blossom (Guernsey), Frances Sternhagen (Mrs Cushing)
'A civilian mis-MASH.' – *Variety*
Paddy Chayefsky
George C. Scott

'They're blasting the Nazis – from inside!'
Hostages
US 1943 88m bw
Paramount (Sol C. Siegel)
In occupied Prague, the Nazis seize a variety of hostages and threaten them with death as a reprisal for underground activities.
Modest morale-builder, unfortunately padded out with melodramatics and overacting.
w Lester Cole, Frank Butler *novel* Stefan Heym *d* Frank Tuttle *ph* Victor Milner *m* Victor Young

☆ Luise Rainer, Paul Lukas, William Bendix, Oscar Homolka, Arturo de Cordova, Katina Paxinou, Roland Varno

Hostile Guns
US 1967 91m Techniscope
Paramount (A. C. Lyles)
A marshal has to deliver four dangerous convicts to the penitentiary.
Rather crude addition to the A. C. Lyles series distinguished only by nostalgic casting.
w Steve Fisher, Sloan Nibley *d* R. G. Springsteen
☆ George Montgomery, Tab Hunter, Yvonne de Carlo, Brian Donlevy, Fuzzy Knight, John Russell, Leo Gordon, Robert Emhardt, Richard Arlen

Hostile Hostages: see *The Ref*

Hostile Witness
GB 1968 101m DeLuxe
UA/Caralan/Dador (David E. Rose)
A barrister suffers a nervous breakdown after the death of his daughter and finds himself accused of murder.
Complex courtroom thriller, filmed in a flatly boring way with stagey sets and performances. The plot is the only interest.
w Jack Roffey *play* Jack Roffey *d* Ray Milland *ph* Gerry Gibbs
☆ Ray Milland, Sylvia Syms, Felix Aylmer, Raymond Huntley, Geoffrey Lumsden, Norman Barrs, Percy Marmont, Ewan Roberts

'Be there when Jane Russell shakes her tambourines!' 'If you'd hit me and given me orders on our wedding night, I would have kissed your hand!'
Hot Blood
US 1955 85m Technicolor Cinemascope
Columbia (Howard Welsch)
A dying gypsy king wants his young brother to get married and succeed him.
What promises to be a boring musical proves to be a boring melodrama. Artificial Romany hokum.
w Jesse Lasky Jnr *d* Nicholas Ray *ph* Ray June *m* Les Baxter
☆ Cornel Wilde, Jane Russell, Joseph Calleia, Helen Westcott, Mikhail Rasumny

The Hot Box
US 1972 89m Metrocolor
New Realm/New World (Jonathan Demme)
Three American nurses are kidnapped by a revolutionary leader in Latin America.
Ridiculous exploitation film providing sex and violence.
w Joe Viola, Jonathan Demme *d* Joe Viola *ph* Felipe Sacdalan *m* Resti Umali *ad* Ben Otico *ed* Ben Barcelon
☆ Andrea Cagan, Margaret Markov, Rickey Richardson, Laurie Rose, Carmen Argenziano, Charles Dierkop
'The film emerges as an honourable solution to the problem of taking a left-wing position in an essentially capitalist industry.' – *Tony Rayns, MFB*
† The film was cut to 86m on its British release.

Hot Enough for June
GB 1963 98m Eastmancolor
Rank (Betty E. Box)
US title: *Agent 8 3/4*
A penniless writer is sent to Czechoslovakia on a goodwill mission and finds himself being used as a spy.
Very moderate spoof, neither very funny nor very thrilling.
w Lukas Heller *novel* *The Night before Wenceslas* by Lionel Davidson *d* Ralph Thomas *ph* Ernest Steward *m* Angelo Lavagnino
☆ Dirk Bogarde, Sylva Koscina, Robert Morley, Leo McKern, John Le Mesurier

Hot, Hard and Mean: see *Black Mama, White Mama*

Hot Lead
US 1951 60m bw
RKO (Herman Schlom)
Two cowboys set out to capture the train robbers who killed their friend.
Average supporting Western, with all the usual ingredients of gunfights, fistfights, chases, a cattle stampede, mistaken identity and a little romance and comedy.
w William Lively *d* Stuart Gilmore *ph* Nicholas Musuraca *m* Paul Sawtell *ad* Albert S. D'Agostino, Feild Gray *ed* Robert Golden
☆ Tim Holt, Joan Dixon, Richard Martin, Ross Elliott, John Dehner, Robert Wilke, Paul Marion

Hot Lead and Cold Feet
US 1978 90m colour
Buena Vista (Ron Miller)
Twin brothers, one a tough gunfighter, the other a pacifist, compete in a race to inherit a Western town.
Comic Western showcasing Dale in three differing roles – as the father and his two sons – but with a script that runs out of ideas long before the end.
w Arthur Alsberg, Joe McEveety, Don Nelson *story* Rod Piffath *d* Robert Butler *ph* Frank Phillips *m* Buddy Baker *ad* John Mansbridge, Frank T. Smith *ed* Ray de Leuw
☆ Jim Dale, Karen Valentine, Don Knotts, Jack Elam, Darren McGavin, John Williams, Warren Vanders

Hot Millions *
US 1968 106m colour
MGM/Mildred Freed Alberg
A confidence trickster makes a fortune out of fictitious companies.
Elaborate, talky, overlong comedy with irresistible star performances.
w Ira Wallach, Peter Ustinov *d* Eric Till *m* Laurie Johnson
☆ Peter Ustinov, Maggie Smith, Bob Newhart, Karl Malden, Robert Morley, Cesar Romero
Ira Wallach, Peter Ustinov (script)

Hot Money
Canada 1989 78m colour
Westfront (Zale Magder)
A million-dollar robbery causes problems to the inhabitants of a small town as state police and tax investigators move in.
Totally incoherent drama, with little in the way of narrative or continuity, but a great deal of windy philosophizing. It was Welles's last, and least, performance.
w Carl Desantis, Phyllis Camesano, Joel Cohen, Neil Cohen *d* Selig Usher *ph* Stan Mestel *m* John Jones *pd* C. M. Zaharuk *ed* Murray Jay
☆ Orson Welles, Michael Murphy, Michelle Finney, Henry Ramer, Kenneth Pogue, Bobby Pickett, Ann Lance, Thomas Kopache
† Made in 1986.

The Hot One: see *Corvette Summer*

Hot Pursuit
US 1987 93m Metrocolor
Paramount/RKO (Theodore R. Parvin, Pierre David)
Delayed at the start of a Caribbean holiday, a student tries to catch up with his girlfriend and her family who have gone on ahead.
Predictable and uninteresting teen comedy that veers into unexpected and unnecessary violence at its climax.
w Stephen Lisberger, Steven Carabatsos *d* Stephen Lisberger *ph* Frank Tidy *m* Rareview *pd* William J. Creber *ed* Mitchell Sinoway
☆ John Cusack, Robert Loggia, Wendy Gazelle, Jerry Stiller, Monte Markham, Shelley Fabares

The Hot Rock ***
US 1972 105m DeLuxe Panavision
TCF (Hal Landers, Bobby Roberts)
GB title: *How to Steal a Diamond in Four Uneasy Lessons*
Four crooks plan to rob the Brooklyn Museum of a priceless diamond.
Enjoyable variation on the caper theme, with relaxed comic performances and highly skilled technical back-up. It's refreshing to come across a film which hits its targets so precisely.
w William Goldman *novel* Donald E. Westlake *d* Peter Yates *ph* Ed Brown *m* Quincy Jones
☆ Robert Redford, George Segal, Zero Mostel, Paul Sand, Ron Leibman, Moses Gunn, William Redfield
'A funny, fast-paced, inventive and infinitely clever crime comedy, almost as if *The French Connection* had been remade as a piece of urban humour.' – *Michael Korda*

'Her lips offered what her heart denied!'
Hot Saturday
US 1932 73m bw
Paramount
Malicious gossip in a small town causes a girl to lose her job.
Small town, small potatoes; interesting chiefly for its two budding male stars.
w Seton I. Miller *novel* Harvey Ferguson *d* William A. Seiter
☆ Nancy Carroll, Cary Grant, Randolph Scott, Edward Woods, Lillian Bond, Jane Darwell, William Collier Snr
'Fairly agreeable as entertainment, but will not get preferred playing time.' – *Variety*

Hot Shot
US 1987 90m Precision colour
Arista (Steve Pappas)
A rich, cocky New Yorker, who upsets his family by insisting on playing professional soccer, goes to Brazil to ask Pelé to help him improve his game.
A standard revolting-teenager movie aimed at those who understand little about the sport; knowledgeable audiences are likely to find it unintentionally amusing and may be disappointed that Pelé's contribution is mainly restricted to some limited acting (he even cries at the end).
w Joe Sauter, Rick King, Ray Errol Fox, Bill Guttentag *d* Rick King *ph* Greg Andracke, Edgar Moura *m* William Orbit *pd* Ruth Ammon, Beata Segall *ed* Stan Salfas
☆ Jim Youngs, Pelé, Billy Warlock, Jeremy Green, Weyman Thompson, Mario Van Peebles, Penelope Miller, David Groh

'There's Something Funny In The Air.'
Hot Shots!
US 1991 85m DeLuxe
TCF (Bill Badalato)
A young disturbed pilot joins an élite group to take part in a raid on a nuclear plant or, as secondary target, an accordion factory.
A hit-and-miss send-up of Top Gun *and other Hollywood hits, in which most of the targets are missed.*
w Jim Abrahams, Pat Proft *d* Jim Abrahams *ph* Bill Butler *m* Sylvester Levay *pd* William A. Elliott *ed* Jane Kurson, Eric Sears
☆ Charlie Sheen, Cary Elwes, Valeria Golino, Lloyd Bridges, Jon Cryer, Kevin Dunn, Bill Irwin, William O'Leary, Kristy Swanson, Efrem Zimbalist Jnr

'Re-Armed, Re-United ... Re-Diculous!'
Hot Shots!: Part Deux
US 1993 88m DeLuxe
TCF (Bill Badalato)
A special forces mission is sent to the Middle East to rescue a special forces mission whose mission it was to rescue hostages.
A send-up of Rambo, if that is possible, which also takes in references to dozens of other movies, but without providing much in the way of laughs.
w Jim Abrahams, Pat Proft *d* Jim Abrahams *ph* John R. Leonetti *m* Basil Poledouris *pd* William A. Elliott *ed* Malcolm Campbell
☆ Charlie Sheen, Lloyd Bridges, Valeria Golino, Richard Crenna, Brenda Bakke, Miguel Ferrer, Rowan Atkinson
'To truly enjoy it, the viewer must abandon his or her dignity for at least 90 minutes, and accept the inherent silliness.' – *John Anderson, Newsday*

Hot Spell *
US 1958 86m bw Vistavision
Paramount/Hal Wallis
In a small Southern town, a husband seeks to leave his wife and family for a 20-year-old girl.
Overwrought domestic drama slipping perilously close to farce at times, but a good theatrical vehicle for its stars.
w James Poe *play* *Next of Kin* by Lonnie Coleman *d* Daniel Mann *ph* Loyal Griggs *m* Alex North
☆ Anthony Quinn, Shirley Booth, Shirley MacLaine, Earl Holliman, Eileen Heckart

Hot Spot: see *I Wake Up Screaming (1941)*

The Hot Spot *
US 1990 130m colour
Rank/Orion (Paul Lewis)
A car dealer's wife seduces a drifter and petty crook who goes to work for her husband.
Effective melodrama, much in the manner of a 1940s film noir.
w Nona Tyson, Charles Williams *novel* *Hell Hath No Fury* by Charles Williams *d* Dennis Hopper *ph* Ueli Steiger *m* Jack Nitzsche *pd* Cary White *ed* Wende Phifer Mate
☆ Don Johnson, Virginia Madsen, Jennifer Connelly, Charles Martin Smith, William Sadler, Jerry Hardin, Barry Corbin, Leon Rippy, Jack Nance

Hot Stuff
US 1979 91m Metrocolor
Columbia/Rastar/Mort Engelberg
Members of a Burglary Task Force need convictions, so they set up fences in order to lure criminals, and are embarrassed by the results.
Slightly unusual but rather frantically assembled comedy which wears out its welcome long before the end.
w Michael Kane, Donald E. Westlake *d* Dom DeLuise *ph* James Pergola *m* Patrick Williams
☆ Dom DeLuise, Suzanne Pleshette, Ossie Davis, Jerry Reed, Luis Avalos, Marc Lawrence
'Heavy farce in which a bright comedy is struggling to escape.' – *Tom Milne, MFB*

Hot Summer Night *
US 1957 85m bw
MGM (Morton S. Fine)
A foolhardy reporter determines on an interview with a notorious outlaw, and has to be rescued.
Interesting but disappointing low-budget experiment.
w Morton S. Fine, David Friedkin *d* David Friedkin *ph* Harold S. Marcorati *m* André Previn
☆ Leslie Nielsen, Colleen Miller, Edward Andrews, Jay C. Flippen, James Best, Paul Richards, Robert Wilke, Claude Akins

Hot Sweat: see *Keetje Tippel*

Hot Target
New Zealand 1985 90m colour
Crown International/Endeavour (John Barnett, Bryan Cook)
The bored wife of a ruthless and wealthy businessman begins an affair with a man she meets in a park – and discovers that he is a criminal.
Dull and unexciting thriller, in which even the twist in the tale is predictable.
wd Denis Lewiston *story* Gerry O'Hara *ph* Alec Mills *m* Gil Melle *pd* Jo Ford *ed* Michael Horton
☆ Simone Griffeth, Steve Marachuk, Bryan Marshall, Peter McCauley, Elizabeth Hawthorne, Ray Henwood, John Watson

Hot Water *
US 1924 50m approx (24 fps) bw silent
Harold Lloyd
A young husband has trouble with a turkey, a new car and his in-laws.
Casually structured star comedy with brilliant sequences.
w Harold Lloyd, Sam Taylor *d* Fred Newmeyer, Sam Taylor
☆ Harold Lloyd, Jobyna Ralston, Josephine Crowell

Hot Winds: see *Garm Hava*

Hotel *
US 1967 124m Technicolor
Warner (Wendell Mayes)
Guests at a luxurious New Orleans hotel have various problems.
Old-fashioned omnibus drama from a bestseller, quite brightly done.
w Wendell Mayes *novel* Arthur Hailey *d* Richard Quine *ph* Charles Lang *m* Johnny Keating
☆ Rod Taylor, Catherine Spaak, Karl Malden, Melvyn Douglas, Merle Oberon, Richard Conte, Michael Rennie, Kevin McCarthy, Alfred Ryder

Hotel
GB/Italy 2001 109m colour
ICA/Moonstone'Hotel/Cattleya/Red Mullet (Mike Figgis, Annie Stewart, Etchie Stroh)

Staying at a Venetian hotel where the staff are cannibalistic vampires, a squabbling film crew attempts to make a movie of John Webster's *The Duchess of Malfi*.
An experimental mess, frittering away its talented cast on self-indulgent turns and improvised irrelevancies.
wd Mike Figgis *ph* Patrick Alexander Stewart *m* Mike Figgis, Anthony Marinelli *pd* Franco Fumagalli
☆ Rhys Ifans (Trent Stoken), Saffron Burrows (Duchess of Malfi), David Schwimmer (Jonathan Danderfine), Salma Hayek (Charlee Boux), Burt Reynolds (Flamenco Manager), Julian Sands (Quintus), Danny Huston (Hotel Manager), Lucy Liu (Kawika), Chiara Mastroianni (Nurse), Laura Morante (Gretta), Ornella Muti (Flamenco Manager's Wife), Heathcote Williams (Bosola), Jason Isaacs (Australian Actor), Mia Maestro (Latin Actress), John Malkovich (uncredited)
'Looks like an experiment conducted for the benefit of director and cast, rather than the audience, but it's never boring.' – *Peter Bradshaw, Guardian*
'An addled affair.' – *Observer*

Hotel Berlin *
US 1945 98m bw
Warner (Louis F. Edelman)
Various lives intertwine in a Berlin hotel towards the end of the war.
After five years of total war this view of life on the other side can hardly fail to be unconvincing, but the actors gleefully seize on moments of melodrama.
w Joe Pagano, Alvah Bessie *novel* Vicki Baum *d* Peter Godfrey *ph* Carl Guthrie *m* Franz Waxman
☆ Raymond Massey, Peter Lorre, Faye Emerson, Helmut Dantine, Andrea King, Alan Hale, George Coulouris, Henry Daniell, Helene Thimig, Kurt Kreuger, Steve Geray, Frank Reicher
'The most heavily routine of Warners' political melodramas, stuffed with sympathetic veterans.' – *James Agee*

'A comedy for the romantically confused.'
Hotel de Love *
Australia 1996 93m colour
Village Roadshow/Pratt (Michael Lake, David Parker)

Two brothers compete for the love of the same woman.
Kitsch romantic comedy with a modicum of wit.
wd Craig Rosenberg *ph* Steve Windon *m* Christine Woodruff *pd* Simon Dobbin *ed* Bill Murphy
☆ Simon Bossell, Aden Young, Saffron Burrows, Pippa Grandison, Ray Barrett, Julia Blake
'Stocked with enough solid laugh-lines and feel-good resolutions for a half-dozen romantic comedies.' – *Ken Eisner, Variety*

Hotel du Nord **
France 1938 110m bw
Sedif/Imperial
People with problems congregate at a small hotel.
Melancholy, studio-confined character drama which has its adherents but technically seemed a throwback to earlier standards. The acting rescues it.
w Henri Jeanson, Eugene Dabit *d Marcel Carné* *ph* Armand Thirard *m* Maurice Jaubert
☆ Annabella, *Louis Jouvet*, Jean-Pierre Aumont, *Arletty*, Jeanne Marken, Bernard Blier
'An outstander in this country and possesses good chance abroad.' – *Variety (Paris)*

Hotel du Paradis
GB/France 1986 113m Eastmancolor
Umbrella-Portman Films/Pierson/Film Four/London Trust/Antenne 2 (Simon Perry)
An ageing actor, planning a comeback in a one-man show, revisits a small Parisian hotel that he loves.
Slow, atmospheric but inconsequential drama.
wd Jana Bokova *ph* Gerard de Battista *m* Rodolfo Mederos *pd* Patrick Weibel *ed* Bill Shapter
☆ Fernando Rey, Fabrice Luchini, Berangere Bonvoisin, Hugues Quester, Marika Rivera, Carola Regnier, Raul Gimenez, Michael Medwin, Georges Geret

Hotel for Women
US 1939 83m bw
TCF (Raymond Griffith)
Young city gold diggers are encouraged by a matron.
Slight comedy drama notable for the acting debut of hostess Elsa Maxwell.
w Kathryn Scola, Darrell Ware *d* Gregory Ratoff *ph* Peverell Marley *m* David Buttolph
☆ Elsa Maxwell, Linda Darnell, Ann Sothern, James Ellison, John Halliday, Lynn Bari, Alan Dinehart
'Synthetic Cinderella story ... fluffed up with a generous display of latest fashions.' – *Variety*

Hotel Haywire
US 1937 66m bw
Paramount (Harold Hurley)
An astrologer makes eyes at a dentist's wife, and causes much confusion in a hotel.
Frantic farce which might have been funnier if it had stuck to the original script and cast (it was intended for Burns and Allen).
w Preston Sturges (before studio revision) *d* George Archainbaud *ph* Henry Sharp
☆ Leo Carrillo, Lynne Overman, Mary Carlisle, Benny Baker, Spring Byington, George Barbier, Porter Hall, Lucien Littlefield, John Patterson
'Broad comedy applied with sufficient skill and effect to make the journey on the dual route fairly safe.' – *Variety*

'Flaming love drama of the war-torn Balkans!'
'Her beauty sent men marching to their death with a smile!'
Hotel Imperial
US 1939 78m bw
Paramount
Balkans, 1916: a Polish dancer suspects a Hungarian officer of being responsible for her sister's death.
Dim romantic melodrama with espionage trimmings.
w Gilbert Gabriel, Robert Thoeren *play* Lajos Biro *d* Robert Florey *ph* William Mellor *md* Boris Morros
☆ Ray Milland, Isa Miranda, Reginald Owen, Gene Lockhart, J. Carrol Naish, Curt Bois, Henry Victor, Albert Dekker
'Nothing much to be done about this one ... a weak sister, dated and inconclusive ... never seems to generate any interest.' – *Variety*
'A very competent rehash ... for the unexacting the picture has its moments.' – *Graham Greene*
† Previously made in 1926 by Mauritz Stiller, with Pola Negri. This version was originally announced in 1936 as *I Loved a Soldier*, to star Marlene Dietrich (or Margaret Sullavan) and Charles Boyer.

The Hotel New Hampshire
US 1984 108m Technicolor
Orion/Woodfall (Neil Hartley, Pieter Kroonenburg, David Patterson)

A schoolmaster and his family are obsessed by the fantasy of living in a hotel, and this fantasy is performed with variations.
A parable of life in the manner of Thornton Wilder's The Skin of Our Teeth, *and sometimes even more obscure, but generally quite entertaining along the way.*
wd Tony Richardson *novel* John Irving *ph* David Watkin *m* Jacques Offenbach *pd* Jocelyn Herbert *ed* Robert K. Lambert
☆ Rob Lowe, Jodie Foster, Paul McCrane, Beau Bridges, Nastassja Kinski, Wallace Shawn, Wilford Brimley

Hotel Paradiso *
US 1966 99m Metrocolor Panavision
MGM (Peter Glenville)
Various romantic affairs come to a head one evening at a seedy hotel.
A famous boulevard farce seems jellied in aspic in this good-looking but very flatly handled film version, in which famous artists are left to caper about on an unsuitable wide screen with no help from the director.
w Peter Glenville, Jean-Claude Carrière *play* Georges Feydeau *d* Peter Glenville *ph Henri Decaë* *m* Laurence Rosenthal *pd François de Lamothe*
☆ Alec Guinness, Gina Lollobrigida, Robert Morley, Peggy Mount, Douglas Byng, Akim Tamiroff, Robertson Hare

Hotel Reserve
GB 1944 89m bw
RKO (Victor Hanbury)
An Austrian refugee in the south of France is asked by the police to track down a spy among his fellow hotel guests.
Slow, obvious and poorly made suspenser from a good novel.
w John Davenport *novel Epitaph for a Spy* by Eric Ambler *d* Victor Hanbury, Lance Comfort, Max Greene *ph* Max Greene
☆ James Mason, Lucie Mannheim, Raymond Lovell, Julien Mitchell, Martin Miller, Herbert Lom, Frederick Valk, Valentine Dyall

Hotel Sahara *
GB 1951 96m bw
GFD/Tower (George H. Brown)
In North Africa during World War II, a small hotel changes its loyalties to suit its occupiers.
Overstretched, studio-bound, fitfully amusing comedy.
w George H. Brown, Patrick Kirwan *d* Ken Annakin *ph* Jack Hildyard *m* Benjamin Frankel
☆ Peter Ustinov, Yvonne de Carlo, David Tomlinson, Roland Culver, Albert Lieven, Bill Owen, Sydney Tafler, Ferdy Mayne
'Cheerful, uncomplicated empty stuff ... no more subtle than a music hall sketch.' – *Richard Mallett, Punch*

Hotel Sorrento
Australia 1994 112m Cinevex
Polygram/Bayside/Horizon/AFFC (Richard Franklin)
Three sisters quarrel at a family reunion over an autobiographical novel one of them has written.
Stolid adaptation of a theatrical success, which is little more than a staged debate on the cultural condition of Australia; on this evidence, it's in a bad way.
w Richard Franklin, Peter Fitzpatrick *play* Hannie Rayson *d* Richard Franklin *ph* Geoff Burton *m* Nerida Tyson-Chew *pd* Tracy Watt *ed* David Pulbrook
☆ Caroline Goodall, Caroline Gillmer, Tara Morice, Joan Plowright, Ray Barrett, Nicholas Bell, Ben Thomas, John Hargreaves
'A film which seems determined to shoot itself in the foot at every turn.' – *Sight and Sound*

'The Last Resort'
Hotel Splendide
GB/France 1999 98m DeLuxe
Film4/Renegade/TOC (Ildiko Kemeny)
After the matriarch of the family dies, the remaining members attempt to continue running her island hotel with disastrous results for them and their guests.
An odd, windy black comedy, about a dysfunctional family, that is presumably intended to satirise something, though quite what is hardly worth discovering.
wd Terence Gross *ph* Gyula Pados *m* Marc Tschanz *pd* Alison Dominitz *ed* Michael Ellis *cos* Michelle Pernetta
☆ Toni Collette (Kath), Daniel Craig (Ronald Blanche), Katrin Cartlidge (Cora Blanche), Stephen Tompkinson (Dezmond Blanche), Hugh O'Conor (Stanley Smith), Helen McCrory (Lorna Bull), Peter Vaughan (Morton Blanche), Joerg Stadler (Sergei Gorgomov), Claire Cathcart (Lorraine Bull), John Boswell (Bellboy), Toby Jones (Kitchen boy)
'A strong cast struggles desperately with intractable material.' – *Philip French, Observer*

Houdini *
US 1953 106m Technicolor
Paramount (George Pal)

In the 1890s a fairground magician shows a passionate talent for escapology and finally kills himself by undertaking increasingly impossible tricks.
Superficial biopic with more attention to romance than to interesting detail. Some zest in the playing is killed by claustrophobic studio sets.
w Philip Yordan *d* George Marshall *ph* Ernest Laszlo *m* Roy Webb
☆ Tony Curtis, Janet Leigh, Torin Thatcher, Sig Rumann, Angela Clarke

The Hound Dog Man
US 1959 87m DeLuxe Cinemascope
TCF/Company of Artists (Jerry Wald)
An irresponsible country boy gets his come-uppance.
Mild, competent backwoods comedy drama introducing a teenage rave.
w Fred Gipson, Winston Miller *novel* Fred Gipson *d* Don Siegel *ph* Charles G. Clarke *m* Cyril Mockridge *ad* Lyle Wheeler, Walter M. Simonds *ed* Louis Loeffler
☆ Fabian, Stuart Whitman, Carol Lynley, Arthur O'Connell, Betty Field, Royal Dano, Jane Darwell, Edgar Buchanan, Claude Akins

The Hound of the Baskervilles **
US 1939 80m bw
TCF

Sherlock Holmes solves the mystery of a supernatural hound threatening the life of a Dartmoor baronet.
Basil Rathbone's first appearance as Sherlock Holmes is in a painstaking studio production which achieves good atmosphere and preserves the flavour if not the letter of the book but is let down by a curious lack of pace.
w Ernest Pascal *novel* Arthur Conan Doyle *d* Sidney Lanfield *ph* Peverell Marley *m* Cyril Mockridge *ad* Thomas Little
☆ *Basil Rathbone, Nigel Bruce*, Richard Greene, Wendy Barrie, Lionel Atwill, Morton Lowry, John Carradine, Barlowe Borland, Beryl Mercer, Ralph Forbes, E. E. Clive, Eily Malyon, Mary Gordon
'A startling mystery-chiller ... will find many bookings on top spots of key duallers.' – *Variety*
'Lush dialogue, stagey sets and vintage supporting cast make it a delectable Hollywood period piece.' – *Judith Crist, 1980*
† For Rathbone's other appearances as Holmes see under *Sherlock Holmes*.

The Hound of the Baskervilles *
GB 1959 86m Technicolor
UA/Hammer (Anthony Hinds)

Spirited remake let down by dogged Hammer insistence on promises of horror and sex; good atmosphere also let down by poor colour.
w Peter Bryan *novel* Arthur Conan Doyle *d* Terence Fisher *ph* Jack Asher *m* James Bernard *ad* Bernard Robinson *ed* James Needs
☆ *Peter Cushing, André Morell*, Christopher Lee, Marla Landi, Ewen Solon, Francis de Wolff, Miles Malleson, John Le Mesurier

The Hound of the Baskervilles
GB 1977 85m Technicolor Technovision
Hemdale/Michael White Ltd (John Goldstone)

A pointless, pitiful and vulgar spoof of an enjoyable original.
w Dudley Moore, Peter Cook, Paul Morrissey *d* Paul Morrissey *ph* Dick Bush, John Wilcox *m* Dudley Moore
☆ Peter Cook (Sherlock Holmes), Dudley Moore (Watson), Denholm Elliott (Stapleton), Terry-Thomas (Mortimer), Joan Greenwood, Max Wall, Irene Handl, Kenneth Williams, Hugh Griffith, Roy Kinnear, Penelope Keith, Dana Gillespie, Prunella Scales, Jessie Matthews, Spike Milligan

Hounded: see *Johnny Allegro*

The Hounds of Zaroff: see *The Most Dangerous Game*

'As I held her in my arms, how could I know that she was as vicious as she was beautiful?'
The Hour before the Dawn
US 1944 75m bw
Paramount (William Dozier)
When a pacifist English nobleman discovers during World War II that he has married a Nazi spy, he strangles her and joins the forces.
Stultifyingly absurd, badly made and acted melodrama which its author clearly wished he had never written, as it was later withdrawn from his canon.
w Michael Hogan, Lesser Samuels *novel* W. Somerset Maugham *d* Frank Tuttle *ph* John F. Seitz *m* Miklos Rozsa
☆ Franchot Tone, Veronica Lake, John Sutton, Binnie Barnes, Henry Stephenson, Philip Merivale, Nils Asther, Edmund Breon
'Tedious and generally uneventful ... a weak entry for the duals.' – *Variety*

Hour of Glory: see *The Small Back Room*

'Wyatt Earp – hero with a badge, or cold-blooded killer?'

Hour of the Gun **

US 1967 101m DeLuxe Panavision
UA/Mirisch/Kappa (John Sturges)

After the gunfight at the OK Corral, Wyatt Earp tracks down the rest of the Clanton gang.
Vividly set, slowly developed Western which makes an ambiguous but forceful figure of Earp. Generally confident and interesting.
w Edward Anhalt *d* John Sturges *ph* Lucien Ballard *m* Jerry Goldsmith *ad* Alfred Ybarra *ed* Ferris Webster
☆ *James Garner* (Wyatt Earp), Jason Robards Jnr (Doc Holliday), Robert Ryan (Ike Clanton), Steve Ihnat (Warshaw), Michael Tolan (Pete Spencer), Frank Converse (Vergil Earp), Sam Melville (Morgan Earp), Monte Markham (Sherman McMasters), Albert Salmi (Octavius Roy), Jon Voight (Curly Bill Brocius), William Windom, Charles Aidman

'The case is a dog. The defendant is a pig. And the law is an ass.'

The Hour of the Pig *

GB/France 1993 117m colour
Mayfair/BBC/CiBy 2000 (David M. Thompson)

In medieval France, a young city lawyer is sent to a backward, rural area, to defend a pig on the charge of murdering a Jewish boy.
An original film that manages to cram in comedy, traces of thriller, and high-level corruption in its depiction of the superstitious past; it doesn't work as well as it might, but at least it tries something a little different from the endless reworking of over-familiar material.
wd Leslie Megahey *ph* John Hooper *m* Alexandre Desplat *pd* Bruce Macadie *ed* Isabelle Dedieu
☆ Colin Firth, Ian Holm, Donald Pleasence, Amina Annabi, Nicol Williamson, Michael Gough, Harriet Walter, Jim Carter, Lysette Anthony

'The picture is an off-beat one. A pity that the mix is too rich and the cooking of it frequently too muddled and a lot of the acting is mummery dressed in drama-school accents.' – *Alexander Walker*

The Hour of the Wolf *

Sweden 1968 89m bw
Svensk Filmindustri (Lars-Owe Carlberg)

original title: *Vargtimmen*
A painter, at his summer island home with his wife, is terrorized by monstrous nightmares and by memories of his own adulterous past.
Rather like the gloomy side of Smiles of a Summer Night, *this very typical Bergman melodrama doesn't quite flow as intended, and whatever its meaning may be, its surface is less entertaining than usual.*
wd Ingmar Bergman *ph* Sven Nykvist *m* Lars Johan Werle *ad* Marik Vos-Lundh *ed* Ulla Ryghe
☆ Max von Sydow, Liv Ullmann, Ingrid Thulin, Georg Rydeberg, Erland Josephson

'His time is running out.'

Hourglass

US 1995 90m Metrocolor
Live/Crystal Sky (Steven Paul)

A convict recalls life as a fashion mogul, the murder of his ex-wife and his involvement with a psychotic woman.
Poorly constructed drama of interest to no one outside the cast's immediate family.
w Darren Dalton, C. Thomas Howell *story* Steven Paul *d* C. Thomas Howell *ph* John Lambert *m* Chris Saranec *pd* Jacques Hebert *ed* Frank Sacco
☆ C. Thomas Howell (Michael Jardine), Sofia Shinas (Dara Jensen), Ed Begley Jnr (Det Cecil Dish), Terry Kaiser (Henry Jardine), Timothy Bottoms (Jurgen Brauner), Colette O'Connell (Kami), Anthony Clark (Jimmy Jardine)

'The time to hide is over.'

The Hours ***

US 2002 114m DeLuxe
Buena Vista/Paramount/Miramax (Scott Rudin, Robert Fox)

In three different eras, three women contemplate their lives and the possibilities of death.
Deft, engrossing film built around the suicide of Virgina Woolf and the themes of her novel Mrs Dalloway, which connects with two women – one an unhappy housewife in the 50s, the other a woman caring for a former lover, a homosexual poet dying of AIDS. It is a deeply affecting account of the choices people make in their lives and the consequences.
w David Hare *novel* Michael Cunningham *d* Stephen Daldry *ph Seamus McGarvey m* Philip Glass *pd* Maria Djurkovic *ed Peter Boyle cos* Ann Roth
☆ Meryl Streep (Clarissa Vaughan), Julianne Moore (Laura Brown), Nicole Kidman (Virginia Woolf), Ed Harris (Richard Brown), Toni Collette (Kitty), Claire Danes (Julia Vaughan), Jeff Daniels (Louis Waters), Leonard Woolf (Stephen Dillane)

'The twin themes of *The Hours* are the variety of human bonds, especially the bond of love, and the gift that the dying make to the living. The miracle is that such sombre notions fit together as surely and lightly as the dancers in a Balanchine ballet.' – *David Denby, New Yorker*

'A moving, somewhat depressing film that demands and rewards attention.' – *Philip French, Observer*

'A grim and uninvolving film, for which Philip Glass unwittingly provides the perfect score – tuneless, oppressive, droning, painfully self-important.' – *Richard Shickel, Time*

Nicole Kidman
picture; David Hare; Stephen Daldry; Ed Harris; Julianne Moore; Philip Glass; Peter Boyle; Ann Roth
Nicole Kidman; Philip Glass

The Hours and Times *

US 1991 60m bw
ICA/Antarctic Pictures

On holiday in Spain with Beatle John Lennon, his manager Brian Epstein tries to get him into bed and is as unsuccessful in seducing a hotel bellboy.
Interesting, very low-budget feature exploring the ambivalent relationship of men divided by sex and class.
wd Christopher Münch *ph* Christopher Münch *ed* Christopher Münch
☆ David Angus, Ian Hart, Stephanie Pack, Robin McDonald, Sergio Moreno, Unity Grimwood

'A quality piece of film-making.' – *Derek Malcolm, Guardian*

'A touching, perceptive film and well worth seeing.' – *Philip French, Observer*

House

US 1986 93m colour
New World/Sean Cunningham

An old lady is found dead in her spooky house; her nephew moves in and endures various apparitions.
Silly film in which the creatures look ridiculous and the psychology makes no sense, especially when the whole thing attempts to be a protest about Vietnam.
w Ethan Wiley *d* Steve Miner *ph* Mac Ahlberg *m* Harry Manfredini *pd* Gregg Fonseca
☆ William Katt, George Wendt, Richard Moll, Kay Lenz

'Life's not about winning or losing, it's about crossing the line.'

House!

GB 1999 90m colour 'Scope
Pathé/House/Arts Council NL (Michael Kelk)

In Wales, the owner of a small bingo hall is threatened by competition from a bigger hall run by a large corporation.
A movie in the old Ealing comedy tradition of the little guy winning through; unfortunately, it lacks the Ealing touch, and also resorts to a feeble plot device to make its point.
w Jason Sutton *d* Julian Kemp *ph* Kjell Vassdal *m* David Alldridge, Craig Blake-Jones, Mark Thomas *pd* Kit Line *ed* Jonathon Rudd *cos* Leila Ransley
☆ Kelly MacDonald (Linda), Gwenllian Davies (Peggy), Sue Hopkins (Pam), Eileen Edwards (Mrs Collins), Marlene Griffiths (Enid), Freddie Jones (Mr Anzani), Mossie Smith (Kay), Jason Hughes (Gavin), Miriam Margolyes (Beth), Bruce Forsyth (Himself), Keith Chegwin (Himself)

'Charismatic, audience-friendly film… thoroughly enjoyable from start to finish.' – *Emma Cochrane, Empire*

The House across the Bay

US 1940 88m bw
UA/Walter Wanger

To protect her racketeer husband from his enemies, his wife has him convicted of income tax evasion.
Unpersuasive melodrama, a star potboiler.
w Kathryn Scola *d* Archie Mayo *ph* Merritt Gerstad *m* Werner Janssen
☆ Joan Bennett, George Raft, Lloyd Nolan, Walter Pidgeon, Gladys George, June Knight

House Arrest

US 1996 108m DeLuxe
MGM/UA/Rysher (Judith A. Polone, Harry Winer)

Unhappy with their divorcing parents, children lock them in the basement until they agree to stay together.
Trivial comedy that makes poor jokes about a subject that deserves more serious treatment.
w Michael Hitchcock *d* Harry Winer *ph* Ueli Steiger *m* Bruce Broughton *pd* Peter Jamison *ed* Ronald Roose
☆ Jamie Lee Curtis, Kevin Pollak, Jennifer Tilly, Christopher McDonald, Wallace Shawn, Sheila McCarthy, Caroline Aaron, Jennifer Love Hewitt, Ray Walston

'A tepid and repetitious comedy that won't capture the attention of many ticketbuyers.' – *Variety*

House by the River *

US 1950 88m bw
Republic/Fidelity (Howard Welsch)

A weak and lecherous writer murders his maid and persuades his brother to help cover up the deed.
Intriguing little thriller, atmospheric and suspenseful for the most part, until it topples into melodrama.
w Mel Dinelli *novel* A. P. Herbert *d* Fritz Lang *ph* Edward Cronjager *m* George Antheil *ad* Boris Leven *ed* Arthur D. Hilton
☆ Louis Hayward, Lee Bowman, Jane Wyatt, Dorothy Patrick, Ann Shoemaker, Jody Gilbert, Peter Brocco, Howland Chamberlin

House Calls *

US 1978 98m Technicolor
Universal/Jennings Lang (Alex Winitsky, Arlene Sellers)

A middle-aged doctor finds himself widowed and seeks a new mate.
Spotty comedy which tries to combine conventional romantic spats with medical satire, and comes off only in fits and starts.
w Max Shulman, Julius J. Epstein, Alan Mandel, Charles Shyer *d* Howard Zieff *ph* David M. Walsh *m* Henry Mancini
☆ *Walter Matthau, Glenda Jackson,* Art Carney, Richard Benjamin, Candice Azzara, Thayer David, Dick O'Neill

A House Divided *

US 1931 70m bw
Universal (Paul Kohner)

A tough widowed fisherman seeks a new wife, but she falls in love with his son.
Glum variation on Desire under the Elms, *interesting for early Wyler touches.*
w John P. Clymer, Dale Van Every, John Huston *story* Heart and Hand by Olive Edens *d William Wyler ph* Charles Stumar
☆ *Walter Huston,* Kent Douglass, Helen Chandler, Vivian Oakland, Frank Hagney, Mary Foy

House II: The Second Story

US 1988 88m colour
Entertainment/New World (Sean S. Cunningham)

A former Vietnam veteran moves into an old house where his parents were killed 25 years before and searches for a valuable Aztec skull buried with one of his ancestors.
A movie that has little relationship to the original, other than in its general silliness and incoherence.
wd Ethan Wiley *ph* Mac Ahlberg *m* Harry Manfredini *pd* Gregg Fonseca *ed* Marty Nicholson

☆ Arye Gross, Jonathan Stark, Royal Dano, Bill Maher, Lar Park Lincoln, John Ratzenberger

'Sluggish, nonsensical and a generally pointless venture, replete with animated monsters, unresolved plot convolutions and totally forgettable characters. Ridiculous.' – *Stefan Jaworzyn, Shock Xpress*

House III: see *The Horror Show*

The House in Nightmare Park *

GB 1973 95m Technicolor
EMI/Associated London/Extonation (Clive Exton, Terry Nation)

US title: *Night of the Laughing Dead*
aka: *Crazy House*
In 1907, a ham actor is asked to perform at an old dark house in the country where an axe murderer prowls during the night.
Standard creepy house comedy thriller, well enough done though it would have been better with Bob Hope.
w Clive Exton, Terry Nation *d* Peter Sykes *ph* Ian Wilson *m* Harry Robinson
☆ Frankie Howerd, Ray Milland, Hugh Burden, Kenneth Griffith, John Bennett, Rosalie Crutchley, Ruth Dunning

The House in the Square *

GB 1951 91m Technicolor (bw endpieces)
TCF (Sol C. Siegel)

US title: *I'll Never Forget You*
An American atomic chemist living in London becomes his own ancestor of two hundred years ago, and falls in love.
Slow-starting but thereafter quite acceptable remake of Berkeley Square *(qv), with some interesting dialogue and a genuinely affecting fade-out.*
w Ranald MacDougall play John L. Balderston *d* Roy Baker *ph* Georges Périnal *m* William Alwyn *ad* C. P. Norman
☆ Tyrone Power, Ann Blyth, Michael Rennie, Beatrice Campbell, Dennis Price, Raymond Huntley, Irene Browne, Robert Atkins (Dr Johnson)

A House Is Not a Home

US 1964 98m bw
Paramount/Embassy (Clarence Greene)

The life story of New York's most famous madam, Polly Adler.
Dismal, unappealing, laundered biopic, cheaply made in an unconvincing period setting.
w Russel Rouse, Clarence Greene *d* Russel Rouse *ph* Harold Stine *m* Joseph Weiss
☆ Shelley Winters, Robert Taylor, Cesar Romero, Ralph Taeger, Broderick Crawford

'Home Deadly Home.'

House IV

US 1992 93m DeLuxe
Sean S. Cunningham Films

A widow's brother-in-law attempts to frighten her into abandoning the family mansion.
An improvement over its predecessors, it maintains interest despite its unoriginality.
w Geof Miller, Deirdre Higgins *story* Jim Wynorski, R. J. Robinson *d* Lewis Abernathy *ph* James Mathers *m* Harry Manfredini *ed* Seth Gaven
☆ Terri Treas, William Katt, Scott Burkholder, Melissa Clayton, Denny Dillon, Dabbs Greer, Mark Gash

'The emphasis … is on scares rather than comedy, and the result is satisfying.' – *Variety*

'Representing yet another in the seemingly endless parade of artistically-bankrupt genre sequels … It's really sad that given the high-gloss resources afforded this production, the filmmakers couldn't have done any better.' – *Fangoria*

The House of a Thousand Candles

US 1936 54m bw
Republic

A young man must live in an unfinished mansion to inherit under the terms of his grandfather's will.
Odd but basically unremarkable little mystery; the title is more interesting than the movie.
w H. W. Hanemann, Endre Bohem *novel* Meredith Nicholson *d* Arthur Lubin
☆ Phillips Holmes, Mae Clarke, Irving Pichel, Rosita Moreno

'On the road ... but going nowhere.'

House of America

GB/Netherlands 1997 96m colour

First Independent/September/Bergen (Sheryl Crown)

Living in an isolated house with their unbalanced mother, an incestuous brother and sister dream of being reunited in America with the father who abandoned them long ago.

Bleak and melodramatic drama of the hopeless, unable to escape their miserable fate, done in a Gothic, over-emphatic manner.

w Edward Thomas *play* Edward Thomas *d* Marc Evans *ph* Pierre Aim *m* John Cale *pd* Mark Tildesley *ed* Michael Reichwein

☆ Sian Phillips, Steven Mackintosh, Lisa Palfrey, Matthew Rhys, Pascal Laurent, Richard Harrington, Islwyn Morris

'Evans' debut direction is superb, consisting of a dazzling array of images, and the acting is sound. Yet despite its ironic humour there seems little on show for young filmgoers to connect with.' – *Jake Hamilton, Empire*

House of Angels **

Sweden 1992 119m colour

Mayfair/Memfis/Sveriges Television/TV2/Svenska Filminstitute/Danmarks Radio/Nordisk Film and TV (Lars Jönsson, Lars Dahlquist)

original title: *Anglagård*

Villagers are scandalized when a landowner dies and his farm is inherited by his hitherto unknown granddaughter, a night-club singer who has a bisexual boyfriend.

Highly enjoyable comedy of a culture clash, full of a generosity of spirit.

wd Colin Nutley *ph* Jens Fischer *m* Björn Isfält *pd* Ulla Herdin *ed* Perry Schaffer

☆ Helena Bergström, Rikard Wolff, Sven Wollter, Reine Brynolfsson, Ernst Gunter, Viveka Seldahl, Per Oscarsson, Tord Peterson, Ing-Marie Carlsson

'Nutley's achievement is in finding a delicate balance between satire and sentiment ... a surprising delight.' – *Angie Errigo, Empire*

'The story Tokyo couldn't hide, and Washington couldn't hold back!'

House of Bamboo **

US 1955 102m DeLuxe Cinemascope

TCF (Buddy Adler)

Japanese and American authorities move into undercover action against Tokyo gangsters.

Routine big-budget crime drama given a novel twist by its location and vaguely adapted from The Street with No Name *(qv).*

w Harry Kleiner, Samuel Fuller *d* Samuel Fuller *ph* Joe MacDonald *m* Leigh Harline *pd* Lyle R. Wheeler, Addison Hehr *ed* James B. Clark

☆ Robert Stack, Robert Ryan, Shirley Yamaguchi, Cameron Mitchell, Sessue Hayakawa

House of Cards

US 1968 100m Techniscope

Universal/Westward (Dick Berg)

An American becomes tutor in the Paris household of a French general's widow, and finds himself a pawn in a high-powered game of international intrigue.

Good-looking location thriller which after an intricate opening settles into a 39 Steps-style chase, but makes little of it.

w James P. Bonner *novel* Stanley Ellin *d* John Guillermin *ph* Piero Portalupi *m* Francis Lai

☆ George Peppard, Inger Stevens, Orson Welles, Keith Michell, William Job, Maxine Audley, Peter Bayliss

House of Cards

US 1993 107m Technicolor

Penta/A&M Films (Dale Pollock, Lianne Halfon, Wolfgang Glattes)

After the sudden death of her husband, a woman struggles with the fact that her daughter has stopped talking and begun to act in strange ways.

Mundane domestic drama that veers unerringly towards the sentimental.

wd Michael Lessac *ph* Victor Hammer *m* James Horner *pd* Peter Larkin *ed* Walter Murch

☆ Kathleen Turner, Tommy Lee Jones, Asha Menina, Shiloh Strong, Esther Rolle, Park Overall, Michael Horse, Anne Pitoniak

'Plays like a top-of-the-line disease-of-the-week TV movie.' – *Variety*

† The film was released direct to video in Britain.

House of Connelly: *see Carolina*

House of Dark Shadows *

US 1970 97m Metrocolor

MGM (Dan Curtis)

A 200-year-old vampire is released from the crypt of an old mansion and tries to find a cure for his affliction.

Effectively creepy little horror, done with some style.

w Sam Hall, Gordon Russell *d* Dan Curtis *ph* Arthur Ornitz *m* Robert Cobert *pd* Trevor Williams *ed* Arline Garson

☆ Jonathan Frid, Joan Bennett, Roger Davis, Grayson Hall, Kathryn Leigh Scott, Nancy Barrett, Thayer David

'Despite a few awkward moments in the photography and editing (betraying under-budgeting and hasty shooting), the result is the most satisfyingly convulsive traditional horror film in years.' – *Tony Rayns, MFB*

House of Doom: *see The Black Cat*

House of Dracula *

US 1945 67m bw

Universal (Paul Malvern)

As a result of being visited in one evening by Count Dracula, the Wolf Man and the Frankenstein monster, a sympathetic doctor goes on the rampage. Mind-boggling finale to the first Universal monster cycle, with a happy ending for the Wolf Man.

Cheaply made and not really inventive, but has to be seen to be believed.

w Edward T. Lowe *d* Erle C. Kenton *ph* George Robinson *m* Edgar Fairchild

☆ Onslow Stevens, John Carradine, Lon Chaney Jnr, Glenn Strange, Lionel Atwill, Martha O'Driscoll, Jane Adams

The House of Fear: *see The Last Warning (1929)*

The House of Fear

US 1939 65m bw

Universal

Murder in a haunted theatre: an actor dies and the corpse disappears.

Lively Crime Club whodunnit, a remake of The Last Warning *(1929).*

w Peter Milne *d* Joe May

☆ William Gargan, Irene Hervey, Dorothy Arnold, Alan Dinehart, Harvey Stephens, Walter Woolf King, Robert Coote, El Brendel, Tom Dugan

'Sufficient edge-of-seat suspense to catch lower-bracket bookings in the nabe duallers.' – *Variety*

The House of Fear *

US 1944 68m bw

Universal (Roy William Neill)

Members of a club are murdered one by one.

A knotty problem for Sherlock Holmes, but rather tediously unravelled. Despite the orange pips it owes virtually nothing to Conan Doyle.

w Roy Chanslor *story The Adventure of the Five Orange Pips* by Sir Arthur Conan Doyle *d* Roy William Neill *ph* Virgil Miller *md* Paul Sawtell *ad* John B. Goodman, Eugene Lourie *ed* Saul Goodkind

☆ Basil Rathbone (Sherlock Holmes), Nigel Bruce (Dr Watson), Dennis Hoey (Lestrade), Aubrey Mather (Alastair), Paul Cavanagh (Simon Merrivale), Holmes Herbert (Alan Cosgrave), Gavin Muir (Chalmers), Harry Cording (John Simpson), Sally Shepherd (Mrs Monteith), Florette Hillier (Alison MacGregor), David Clyde (Alex McGregor)

'Mighty monsters, locked in mortal combat!'

House of Frankenstein *

US 1944 71m bw

Universal (Paul Malvern)

A mad doctor thaws out the monster and the Wolf Man (frozen at the end of *Frankenstein Meets the Wolf Man*) but comes to a sticky end.

Originally called Chamber of Horrors, *this was the studio's first attempt to package its monsters (the first two reels are about Dracula). It could have been pacier in view of the possibilities, but it has its interest.*

w Edward T. Lowe, Curt Siodmak *d* Erle C. Kenton *ph* George Robinson *m* Hans Salter

☆ Boris Karloff, John Carradine, Lon Chaney Jnr, George Zucco, J. Carrol Naish, Anne Gwynne, Elena Verdugo, Lionel Atwill, Sig Rumann, Glenn Strange

'A chiller-diller meller.' – *Variety*

House of Fright: *see The Two Faces of Dr Jekyll*

House of Games ***

US 1987 102m Du Art Color

Filmhaus/Orion (Michael Hausman)

A psychiatrist becomes involved with a confidence trickster.

Stylish directorial debut, playing dazzling tricks with its audiences' expectations, by a respected Broadway playwright.

wd David Mamet *ph* Juan Ruiz Anchia *m* Alaric Jans *pd* Michael Merritt *ed* Trudy Ship

☆ Lindsay Crouse, Joe Mantegna, Mike Nussbaum, Lilia Skala

House of Horrors

US 1946 65m bw

Universal

GB title: *Joan Medford Is Missing*

An incompetent sculptor tricks a psychopathic killer into murdering his critics.

Grade Z thriller with a monster element; crude beyond belief.

w George Bricker *d* Jean Yarbrough

☆ Martin Kosleck, Rondo Hatton, Robert Lowery, Virginia Grey, Bill Goodwin

House of Long Shadows: *see House of the Long Shadows*

House of Menace: *see Kind Lady*

House of Mirth **

GB 2000 143m DeLuxe

FilmFour/Granada/Three Rivers/Arts Council/Scottish Arts Council/Showtime (Olivia Stewart)

In the early years of the twentieth century, an American woman without much money tries unsuccessfully to find a wealthy man she can marry.

Bleak period drama of social striving and failure in a society where money rules.

wd Terence Davies *novel* Edith Wharton *ph* Remi Adefarasin *md* Adrian Johnston *pd* Don Taylor *ed* Michael Parker *cos* Monica Howe

☆ Gillian Anderson (Lily Bar), Eric Stoltz (Lawrence Selden), Dan Aykroyd (Gus Trenor), Eleanor Bron (Mrs Peniston), Terry Kinney (George Dorset), Anthony LaPaglia (Sim Rosedale), Laura Linney (Bertha Dorset), Jodhi May (Grace Stepney), Elizabeth McGovern (Judy Trenor)

'A substantial, well-upholstered picture with more sinew and power than almost any other period drama of recent times...a brilliant new film from a great British director.' – *Peter Bradshaw, Guardian*

House of Mortal Sin

GB 1975 104m Technicolor

Columbia-Warner/Pete Walker

A sexually obsessed and murderous Catholic priest attempts to blackmail a young woman over her confession.

A horror film of some originality, but feebly directed and acted.

w David McGillivray *story* Peter Walker *d* Peter Walker *ph* Tony Imi *m* Stanley Myers *ad* Chris Burke *ed* Matt McCarthy

☆ Anthony Sharp, Susan Penhaligon, Stephanie Beacham, Norman Eshley, Sheila Keith, Mervyn Johns, Bill Kerr, Andrew Sachs

House of Mystery: *see Night Monster (1942)*

House of Mystery

GB 1961 56m bw

Anglo Amalgamated/Independent Artists (Julian Wintle, Leslie Parkyn)

A house-hunting couple hear from a mysterious woman why an apparently desirable cottage is being sold at a low price.

Effectively spooky little thriller, a story of jealousy and murder.

wd Vernon Sewell *ph* Ernest Steward *m* Stanley Black *ad* Jack Shampan *ed* John Trumper

☆ Jane Hylton, Peter Dyneley, Nanette Newman, Maurice Kaufmann, Colin Gordon, John Merivale, Ronald Hines, Colette Wilde

House of Numbers

US 1957 92m bw Cinemascope

MGM (Charles Schnee)

A man helps his thuggish twin brother escape from prison.

An original melodramatic idea is frittered away through slow pacing.

w Russel Rouse, Don M. Mankiewicz *novel* Jack Finney *d* Russel Rouse *ph* George J. Folsey *m* André Previn

☆ Jack Palance, Barbara Lang, Harold J. Stone, Edward Platt

The House of Rothschild **

US 1934 87m bw (Technicolor sequence)

Twentieth Century (William Goetz, Raymond Griffith)

The chronicles of the famous banking family at the time of the Napoleonic Wars.

Lavish historical pageant with interesting scenes and performances.

w Nunnally Johnson *play* George Humbert Westley *d* Alfred Werker *ph* Peverell Marley *m* Alfred Newman

☆ George Arliss, Loretta Young, Boris Karloff, Robert Young, C. Aubrey Smith, Arthur Byron, Helen Westley, Reginald Owen, Florence Arliss, Alan Mowbray, Holmes Herbert

'A fine picture on all counts ... one of those occasional 100% smashes which Hollywood achieves.' – *Variety*

'A good dramatic photoplay, finely presented, packed with ripe incident and quite beautiful photography.' – *C. A. Lejeune*

best picture

House of Secrets

GB 1956 97m Technicolor Vistavision

Rank/Julian Wintle (Vivian A. Cox)

US title: *Triple Deception*

A naval officer is asked to impersonate a lookalike counterfeiter and work undercover to expose the gang.

Old-hat Boys' Own Paper adventure story, mindlessly watchable.

w Robert Buckner, Bryan Forbes *novel Storm over Paris* by Sterling Noel *d* Guy Green *ph* Harry Waxman *m* Hubert Clifford

☆ Michael Craig, Julia Arnall, Brenda de Banzie, David Kossoff, Barbara Bates, Gerard Oury, Geoffrey Keen, Anton Diffring

House of Settlement: *see Mr Soft Touch*

The House of Seven Corpses

US 1973 90m colour

TCA (Paul Lewis, Paul Harrison)

A film crew, making a horror movie in a house where seven people met violent ends, decide to incorporate in the script an ancient ritual to raise the dead, with predictable results.

Atmospheric low-budget movie, which builds the tension slowly before its horrific climax.

w Paul Harrison, Thomas J. Kelly *d* Paul Harrison *ph* Don Jones

☆ John Ireland, Faith Domergue, John Carradine, Carole Wells, Jerry Strickler, Charles Macaulay

The House of Seven Gables

US 1940 89m bw

Universal (Burt Kelly)

In 17th-century New England, a jealous brother sends his sister's fiancé to prison.

Flat adaptation of a grim, brooding novel; it never grips.

w Lester Cole *novel* Nathaniel Hawthorne *d* Joe May *ph* Milton Krasner *m* Frank Skinner

☆ George Sanders, Margaret Lindsay, Vincent Price, Alan Napier, Nan Grey, Cecil Kellaway, Dick Foran, Miles Mander

Frank Skinner

House of Strangers **
US 1949 101m bw
TCF (Sol C. Siegel)

An Italian-American banker who rigidly controls his three sons is arrested for illegal practices, and the family ties slacken.
Interesting ethnic melodrama with good script and performances; much remade, e.g. as Broken Lance.
w *Philip Yordan* *novel* Jerome Weidman *d* Joseph L. Mankiewicz *ph* Milton Krasner *m* Daniele Amfitheatrof
☆ *Edward G. Robinson, Richard Conte*, Susan Hayward, *Luther Adler*, Paul Valentine, Efrem Zimbalist Jnr, Debra Paget, Hope Emerson, Esther Minciotti, Diana Douglas

The House of Tao Lin: see *Dangerous Millions*

The House of the Angel **
Argentina 1957 73m bw
Argentina Sono Film (Leopoldo Torre Nilsson)
original title: *La Casa del Angel*
A repressed girl is obsessed for life by the shame of her first love affair.
Fascinating minor classic in a heavily Wellesian style.
w *Beatriz Guido, Leopoldo Torre Nilsson, Martin Rodriguez Mentasti* *novel* Beatriz Guido
d Leopoldo Torre Nilsson *ph* Anibal Gonzalez Paz *m* Juan Carlos Paz
☆ Elsa Daniel, Lautaro Murua, Guillermo Battaglia
'The first major work of a director of individual vision and strongly national style.' – *Robert Vas, MFB*

House of the Damned *
US 1963 63m bw CinemaScope
TCF/Associated Producers (Maury Dexter)
An architect is asked to make a survey of an old empty castle, but he and his wife find that someone or something is in hiding there.
Corny but mildly effective second feature with a few neat touches.
w Harry Spalding *d* Maury Dexter *ph* John Nickolaus Jnr *m* Henry Vars
☆ Ronald Foster, Merry Anders

House of the Long Shadows
GB 1983 101m colour
Cannon (Jenny Craven)
An author takes a bet to isolate himself in a dilapidated house and write a Gothic novel within 24 hours…
Semi-spoof variation on an old chestnut, with aged horror practitioners interrupting the silence. Too restricted in script and production to be really effective.
w Michael Armstrong *play* *Seven Keys to Baldpate* by George M. Cohan *novel* *Earl Derr Biggers*
d Peter Walker *ph* Norman Langley *m* Richard Harvey
☆ Christopher Lee, Peter Cushing, Vincent Price, Desi Arnaz Jnr, John Carradine, Sheila Keith, Julie Peasgood, Richard Todd
'Golan and Globus seem to have inherited Lord Grade's habit of assembling advertising packages with movies appended as an afterthought.' – *Kim Newman, MFB*
'A horror flick which basks in the Hammer tradition without in any way understanding it.' – *Guardian*

House of the Seven Hawks
GB 1959 92m bw
MGM/David E. Rose
An American adventurer becomes involved in a search by criminals for buried Nazi loot.
Cliché-ridden thick ear, adequately produced but of no interest.
w Jo Eisinger *novel* *The House of Seven Flies* by Victor Canning *d* Richard Thorpe *ph* Ted Scaife *m* Clifton Parker
☆ Robert Taylor, Nicole Maurey, Linda Christian, Donald Wolfit, David Kossoff, Eric Pohlmann, Gerard Heinz

'Every Passion … Every Obsession … Caught In The Fire Of Revolution.'
The House of the Spirits
Germany/Denmark/Portugal 1993 138m colour Panavision
Entertainment/Neue Constantin/Spring Creek/House of Spirits/Costa do Castelo (Bernd Eichinger)

In Chile, a saga of a family's rise to power and its fall is played out against a background of political upheaval.
Miscast and misconceived, this tale of magic realism is turned into a stolid drama of mundane fantasy; a disappointment.
wd Bille August *novel* Isabel Allende *ph* Jörgen Persson *m* Hans Zimmer *pd* Anna Asp *ed* Janus Billeskov Jansen
☆ Jeremy Irons, Meryl Streep, Glenn Close, Winona Ryder, Antonio Banderas, Vanessa Redgrave, Maria Conchita Alonso, Armin Mueller-Stahl
'Turgid, overlong, silly, hysterical (and that spells TOSH).' – *Adam Mars-Jones, Independent*
'What we get is a romantic drama set against the tide of history, that looks more and more like Latin-American melodrama traversed by a cast of talented strangers to the culture.' – *Derek Malcolm, Guardian*

House of Unclaimed Women: see *The Smashing Bird I Used to Know*

House of Usher *
US 1960 85m Eastmancolor Cinemascope
AIP/Alta Vista (Roger Corman)

GB title: *The Fall of the House of Usher*
The last of the Usher line, prone to catalepsy, is buried alive by her brother and returns to wreak vengeance.
Stylish but grottily-coloured low-budget horror which started the Poe cycle of the sixties. A bit slow, it would have worked better in the standard screen ratio, but there is a tense and spectacular finale.
w Richard Matheson *story* Edgar Allan Poe
d Roger Corman *ph* Floyd Crosby *m* Les Baxter *ad* Daniel Haller
☆ *Vincent Price*, Myrna Fahey, Mark Damon, Harry Ellerbe

House of Usher
US 1990 90m Rank Colour
21st Century/Breton (Harry Alan Towers)

Roderick Usher attempts to force his nephew's girlfriend to bear his child.
Tedious version of the oft-filmed tale, lacking style and substance.
w Michael J. Murray *story* *The Fall of the House of Usher* by Edgar Allan Poe *d* Alan Birkinshaw *ph* Jossi Wein *m* George S. Clinton, Gary Chang *pd* Leonardo Coen Cagli *ed* Michael J. Duthie
☆ Oliver Reed, Donald Pleasence, Romy Windsor, Rufus Swart, Norman Coombes, Anne Stradi
'This remake offers no suspense and a very weak cast.' – *Variety*

'The most astounding motion picture since motion pictures began! Man turned monster stalking show-world beauties! The ultimate dimension in terror!'
'You've never been scared until you've been scared in 3-D!'
House of Wax **
US 1953 88m Warnercolor 3-D
Warner (Bryan Foy)

Mutilated in a fire at his wax museum, a demented sculptor arranges a supply of dead bodies to be covered in wax for exhibition at his new showplace.
Spirited remake of The Mystery of the Wax Museum *(qv); as a piece of screen narrative it leaves much to be desired, but the sudden shocks are well managed, perhaps because this is the first Grade-A 3-D film, packed with gimmicks irrelevant to the story and originally shown with stereophonic sound.*
w Crane Wilbur *screenplay* *The Mystery of the Wax Museum* by Don Mullaly, Carl Erickson *play* *Charles S. Belden* by *The Wax Museum*
d André de Toth *ph* Bert Glennon *m* David Buttolph *ad* Stanley Fleischer *ed* Rudi Fehr
☆ *Vincent Price* (Professor Jarrod), Carolyn Jones (Cathy Gray), Paul Picerni (Scott Andrews), Phyllis Kirk (Sue Allen), Frank Lovejoy (Lt Tom Brennan), Dabs Greer (Sgt Jim Shane), Paul Cavanagh (Sidney Wallace)
† The director could not see the 3-D effect, being blind in one eye.
†† The film marked the beginning of Price's horror career.

House of Whipcord *
GB 1974 101m Eastmancolor
Miracle/Peter Walker

An elderly couple and their son, who run their own private penal system, sentence to death a French model on charges of immorality.
Low-budget psychological horror that stylishly achieves its object: to disturb.
w David McGillivray *story* Peter Walker *d* Peter Walker *ph* Peter Jessop *m* Stanley Myers *ad* Mike Pickwoad *ed* Matt McCarthy
☆ Barbara Markham, Patrick Barr, Ray Brooks, Ann Michelle, Penny Irving, Sheila Keith, Celia Imrie
'Shows that something worthwhile in the entertainment-horror market can be done for the tiny sum of £60,000.' – *Derek Elley, Films and Filming*

The House on 92nd Street ***
US 1945 88m bw
TCF (*Louis de Rochemont*)
During World War II in New York, the FBI routs Nazi spies after the atomic bomb formula.
Highly influential documentary-style 'now it can be told' spy drama, which borrowed the feel of its producer's March of Time *series and applied them to a fairly true story set on genuine locations though with a modicum of fictional mystery and suspense.*
Highly effective in its own right, it looked forward to The Naked City *three years later; the later film unaccountably got most of the credit for taking Hollywood out into the open air.*
w *Barre Lyndon, Charles G. Booth, John Monks Jnr*
d Henry Hathaway *ph* Norbert Brodine *m* David Buttolph
☆ William Eythe, Lloyd Nolan, Signe Hasso, *Leo G. Carroll*, Gene Lockhart, Lydia St Clair, Harry Bellaver
'Recommended entertainment for those who believe that naïve Americans are no match for wily Europeans in the spy trade, and for those who just like their movies to move.' – *Time*
'Imagine an issue of *The March of Time*. The hard agglomeration of fact; the road drill style; the voice. Prolong it to four times its usual length, throw in a fictional climax, and there you have *The House on 92nd Street*.' – *William Whitebait, New Statesman*
original story (Charles G. Booth)

House on Bare Mountain
US 1962 62m colour
Olympic International/B and M (David Andrew, Wes Don)

The elderly headmistress of a girl's school keeps a werewolf in her cellar, where she brews her own booze.
Very cheap exploitation movie – the lip movements and dialogue don't match — that consists mainly of the usual lingering on the bodies of young women, but also shows a modicum of cynical wit.
w Denver Scott *d* R. L. Frost *ph* Greg Sandor *m* Pierre Martel *ed* Gary Lindsay
☆ Bob Cresse, Leticia Cooper, Laine Carlin, Connie Hudson, Dan Hyland, John Nada, Betty Peters
† Credits include 'Casting Director (Deceased)', which, in the circumstances, must have seemed an excellent career move.

The House on Carroll Street *
US 1988 100m colour
Rank/Orion (Peter Yates, Robert F. Colesberry)

A journalist, forced out of her job in McCarthyite America, uncovers a right-wing political conspiracy.
Moderately effective thriller, in a style close to Hitchcock.
w Walter Bernstein *d* Peter Yates *ph* Michael Ballhaus *m* Georges Delerue *pd* Stuart Wurtzel *ed* Ray Lovejoy
☆ Kelly McGillis, Jeff Daniels, Mandy Patinkin, Christopher Rhode, Jessica Tandy, Jonathan Hogan

House on Haunted Hill
US 1958 75m bw
Allied Artists/William Castle

An old house which has seen several murders is the setting for a millionaire's party.
*Gimmick ghost story with some (unexplained) gruesome moments; the most outlandish of its producer's cheapjack trick films (*Thirteen Ghosts, The Tingler, Macabre, *etc), it was originally billed as being in Emergo, which meant that at an appropriately horrific moment an illuminated skeleton on wires was suddenly trundled over the heads of the audience.*
w Robb White *d* William Castle *ph* Carl Guthrie *m* Von Dexter
☆ Vincent Price, Richard Long, Carol Ohmart, Alan Marshal, Elisha Cook Jnr

'Five strangers have the chance to make $1,000,000 each. All they have to do is make it through the night… Alive'
'Evil Loves to Party!'
House on Haunted Hill
US 1999 96m Technicolor Panavision
Warner/Dark Castle (Robert Zemeckis, Joel Silver, Gilbert Adler)

A multimillionaire offers a prize of $1m to any party guest who can last the night in a haunted house, a former asylum for the criminally insane.
Supernatural horror that is heavy on shocks and special effects, but otherwise offers little that is special, though Rush's Vincent Price impersonation provides a little fun.
w Dick Beebe *story* Robb White *d* William Malone *ph* Rick Bota *m* Don Davis *pd* David F. Klassen *ed* Anthony Adler
sp Bellissimo/Belardinelli; make-up fx: Robert Kurtzman, Gregory Nicotero, Howard Berger
☆ Geoffrey Rush (Stephen Price), Famke Janssen (Evelyn), Taye Diggs (Eddie), Peter Gallagher (Blackburn), Chris Kattan (Pritchett), Ali Larter (Sara), Bridgette Wilson (Melissa Marr), Max Perlich (Schecter), Jeffrey Combs (Dr Vannacutt), Lisa Loeb (Channel 3 Reporter)
'"Hill" was pronounced junk in these pages in 1959. And it is still junk.' – *Lawrence Van Gelder, New York Times*

The House on Telegraph Hill
US 1951 93m bw
TCF (Robert Bassler)
A woman in a concentration camp assumes her dead friend's identity so that on release she can be sent to America; but murder threatens there.
Modernized amalgam of Gaslight *and* Suspicion, *not as good as either, but the complexities of the story hold adequate interest.*
w Elick Moll, Frank Partos *novel* Dana Lyon
d Robert Wise *ph* Lucien Ballard *m* Sol Kaplan *ad* Lyle Wheeler, John DeCuir
☆ Richard Basehart, Valentina Cortesa, William Lundigan, Fay Baker, Gordon Gebert, Steve Geray
art direction

House Party
US 1990 104m Metrocolor
Enterprise/Hudlin Brothers/New Line (Gerald Olsen)

A teenager, whose parents are away, throws a party for his friends.
Low-budget youth movie, likeable enough but unlikely to rouse much enthusiasm on the adult side of the generation gap.
wd Reginald Hudlin *ph* Peter Deming *m* Marcus Miller *pd* Bryan Jones *ed* Earl Watson
☆ Christopher Reid, Robin Harris, Christopher Martin, Martin Lawrence, Tisha Campbell, A. J. Johnson, Paul Anthony

House Party 2
US 1991 94m DeLuxe
New Line (Doug McHenry, George Jackson)

Two rappers leave high school and consider their future.
Dull sequel, as if no one was quite sure of what to do next.
w Rusty Cundieff, Daryl G. Nickens *d* Doug McHenry, George Jackson *ph* Francis Kenny *m* Vassal Benford *pd* Michelle Minch *ed* Joel Goodman
☆ Christopher Reid, Christopher Martin, Tisha Campbell, Iman, Martin Lawrence, D. Christopher Judge, Queen Latifah

'The crowd's the same, but the atmosphere's different in this disappointing followup.' – *Variety*

'Terror Waits For You In Every Room.'

The House that Dripped Blood *
GB 1970 102m Eastmancolor
Amicus (Milton Subotsky)

A Scotland Yard man investigating a disappearance is led to a house with a murderous history.
Quartet of stories in Dead of Night *style, neatly made and generally pleasing despite a low level of originality in the writing.*
w Robert Bloch *d Peter John Duffell ph* Robert Parslow *m* Michael Dress
☆ John Bennett, Christopher Lee, Peter Cushing, Denholm Elliott, Joanna Dunham, Nyree Dawn Porter, Jon Pertwee, Ingrid Pitt

Houseboat
US 1958 110m Technicolor
Vistavision
Paramount/Scribe (Jack Rose)

A widower with three children engages a maid who is really a socialite, and they all set up house on a boat.
Artificial sentimental comedy with A-1 credits but little style or bite.
w Melville Shavelson, Jack Rose *d* Melville Shavelson *ph* Ray June *m* George Duning
☆ Cary Grant, Sophia Loren, Martha Hyer, Eduardo Ciannelli, Harry Guardino
'The kind of picture to which you can take your stuffy maiden aunt, your wicked sophisticated uncle and your ten-year-old child, and they will all have a wonderful time.' – *Ruth Waterbury, Los Angeles Examiner*
script; song 'Almost In Your Arms' (*m/ly* Jay Livingston, Ray Evans)

The Housekeeper's Daughter *
US 1939 71m bw
Hal Roach
A gangster's moll returns to mama for a visit and falls in love with the stuffy son of the household.
Zany crime farce which too often lets its zip fade, but atones in a crazy firework finale.
w Rian James, Gordon Douglas *novel* Donald Henderson Clarke *d* Hal Roach *ph* Norbert Brodine *m* Amedeo de Filippi
☆ Joan Bennett, John Hubbard, Adolphe Menjou, William Gargan, George E. Stone, Peggy Wood, Donald Meek, Marc Lawrence, Lillian Bond, Victor Mature, Luis Alberni
'A smacko laugh generator due for profitable biz up and down the line.' – *Variety*

Housekeeping *
US 1987 115m colour
Columbia (Robert F. Colesberry)
Two orphaned sisters are brought up by their wayward aunt.
In his first American feature, Forsyth's pawky humour is overlaid with a bleaker view and his characters seem more conventional and less well-observed.
wd Bill Forsyth *novel* Marilynne Robinson *ph* Michael Coulter *m* Michael Gibbs *pd* Adrienne Atkinson *ed* Michael Ellis
☆ Christine Lahti, Sara Walker, Andrea Burchill, Anne Pitoniak, Barbara Reese, Bill Smillie, Margo Pinvidic, Wayne Robson
'I wouldn't call it a great film, but it comes very close to being a perfect one in everything that it sets out to do.' – *Jonathan Rosenbaum, Chicago Reader*

Housemaster *
GB 1938 95m bw
ABPC (Walter Mycroft)
A schoolmaster sides with his boys against the new headmaster's dictatorial methods.
Pleasing photographed play with all concerned in good form.
w Dudley Leslie, Elizabeth Meehan *play Bachelor Born* by Ian Hay *d* Herbert Brenon *ph Otto Kanturek ad* Cedric Dawe *ed* Flora Newton
☆ Otto Kruger, Diana Churchill, Phillips Holmes, Joyce Barbour, Kynaston Reeves, Rene Ray, Walter Hudd, John Wood, Cecil Parker, Michael Shepley, Jimmy Hanley

Housesitter
US 1992 102m DeLuxe
UIP/Imagine/Universal (Brian Grazer)

After a one-night stand with an architect, a waitress decides to move into his new house, claiming to be his wife.
A farcical comedy that is too leisurely to provoke laughter.
w Mark Stein, Brian Grazer *d* Frank Oz *ph* John A. Alonzo *m* Miles Goodman *pd* Ida Random *ed* John Jympson
☆ Steve Martin, Goldie Hawn, Dana Delany, Julie Harris, Donald Moffat, Peter MacNicol, Richard B. Shull, Laurel Cronin
'A tediously unfunny screwball comedy ... a career misstep both for Steve Martin and Goldie Hawn.' – *Variety*

Housewife
US 1934 69m bw
Warner (Robert Lord)
For an advertising copywriter, success almost brings divorce.
Modestly efficient romantic programmer of its day.
w Manuel Seff, Lillie Hayward *d* Alfred E. Green *ph* William Rees *m* Leo. F. Forbstein
☆ Bette Davis, George Brent, Ann Dvorak, John Halliday, Ruth Donnelly, Hobart Cavanaugh, Robert Barrat, Phil Regan
'The dramatic punches are not merely telegraphed, but radioed.' – *Frank S. Nugent*

The Houston Story
US 1956 80m bw
Columbia (Sam Katzman)
An oil worker has a plan for stealing oil, and is employed by the syndicate.
Racketeering melodrama of the least interesting kind.
w James B. Gordon *d* William Castle
☆ Gene Barry, Barbara Hale, Edward Arnold, Paul Richards, Frank Jenks

How Do I Love Thee
US 1970 109m Metrocolor
ABC (Robert Enders, Everett Freeman)
A philosophy professor recalls the odd career of his atheist father.
Curious comedy about an eccentric and his family relationships, a kind of Cheaper by the Dozen *with religion added. Not on in 1970.*
w Everett Freeman *novel Let Me Count the Ways* by Peter de Vries *d* Michael Gordon *ph* Russell Metty *m* Randy Sparks
☆ Jackie Gleason, Maureen O'Hara, Shelley Winters, Rick Lenz, Rosemary Forsyth
'Nauseated embarrassment for participants and onlookers alike.' – *Judith Crist*

'Rich is their humor! Deep are their passions! Reckless are their lives! Mighty is their story!'
"'What are you? A man or a saint? I don't want him, I want you!" Her desire scorched both their lives with the vicious breath of scandal!'

How Green Was My Valley ***
US 1941 118m bw
TCF (Darryl F. Zanuck)

Memories of childhood in a Welsh mining village.
Prettified and unconvincing but dramatically very effective tearjerker in the style which lasted from Cukor's David Copperfield *to* The Green Years. *High production values here add a touch of extra class, turning the result into a Hollywood milestone despite its intrinsic inadequacies.*
w Philip Dunne *novel* Richard Llewellyn *d John Ford ph Arthur Miller m* Alfred Newman *ad* Richard Day, Nathan Juran *ed* James B. Clark
☆ Walter Pidgeon, Maureen O'Hara, Roddy McDowall, Donald Crisp, Sara Allgood, Anna Lee, John Loder, Barry Fitzgerald, Patric Knowles, Morton Lowry, Arthur Shields, Frederic Worlock
'Perfection of cinematic narrative ... pure visual action, pictures powerfully composed, dramatically photographed, smoothly and eloquently put together.' – *James Shelley Hamilton*
† The unseen narrator was Irving Pichel.
best picture; John Ford; Arthur Miller; Donald Crisp; art direction
Philip Dunne; Alfred Newman; Sara Allgood; James B. Clark

How He Lied to Her Husband
GB 1930 33m bw
BIP
An early film version of Shaw's playlet about a minor flirtation.
Of historical interest only.
w Frank Launder *play* George Bernard Shaw *d* Cecil Lewis *ph* J. J. Cox *ad* Gladys Calthrop *ed* Sam Simmonds
☆ Edmund Gwenn, Robert Harris, Vera Lennox

How I Got Into College
US 1989 89m colour
TCF (Michael Shamberg)

Dim student applies to go to the same difficult-to-enter college as the girl he loves.
Mildy amusing teenage comedy.
w Terrel Seltzer *d* Savage Steve Holland *m* Joseph Vitarelli *pd* Ida Random *ed* Sonya Sones Tramer, Kaja Fehr
☆ Anthony Edwards, Corey Parker, Lara Flynn Boyle, Finn Carter, Charles Rocket, Christopher Rydell, Brian-Doyle Murray

How I Spent My Summer Vacation
US 1966 120m Technicolor
Universal (Jack Laird)
GB title: *Deadly Roulette*
A socially inept man outsmarts his girlfriend's multi-millionaire father, who keeps humiliating him in public.
A frenetic, but unfunny, comedy that suffers from the miscasting of its star.
w Gene Kearney *d* William Hale *ph* Bud Thackery *m* Lalo Schifrin *ad* Henry Larrecq *ed* Douglas Stewart *cos* Helen Colvig
☆ Robert Wagner (Jack Washington), Peter Lawford (Ned Pine), Lola Albright (Mrs Pine), Walter Pidgeon (Lewis Gannet), Jill St John (Nikki Pine), Michael Ansara (Pucci)
† Made for TV in the United States, the film was given a cinema release in Britain.

How I Won the War
GB 1967 110m Eastmancolor
UA/Petersham (Richard Lester)

During World War II an earnest young man becomes an officer and survives many tribulations including the death of his comrades.
Appalling kaleidoscope of black comedy and the director's own brand of uncontrolled cinematic zaniness, with echoes of Candide *and* Oh What a Lovely War! *Just the way to alienate a paying audience.*
w Charles Wood *novel* Patrick Ryan *d* Richard Lester *ph* David Watkin *m* Ken Thorne
☆ Michael Crawford, John Lennon, Roy Kinnear, Lee Montague, Jack MacGowran, Michael Hordern, Jack Hedley, Karl Michael Vogler, Ronald Lacey, James Cossins, Alexander Knox
'Pretentious tomfoolery.' – *John Simon*
'One feels that Lester has bitten off more than he can chew ... the ideas misfire, lost somewhere between the paper on which they were conceived and the celluloid on which they finally appear.' – *MFB*

How Stella Got Her Groove Back
US 1998 124m DeLuxe
TCF (Deborah Schindler)

A middle-aged stockbroker begins an affair with an unemployed Jamaican half her age.
Bland, boring, glossy romantic drama that never attempts to treat its theme with even a pretence of reality.
w Terry McMillan, Ron Bass *novel* Terry McMillan *d* Kevin Rodney Sullivan *ph* Jeffrey Jur *m* Michel Colombier *ed* George Bowers
☆ Angela Bassett (Stella), Taye Diggs (Winston Shakespeare), Whoopi Goldberg (Delilah), Regina King (Vanessa), Suzzanne Douglas (Angela), Michael J. Pagan (Quincy), Sicily (Chantel), Richard Lawson (Jack), Barry (Shabaka) Henley (Buddy), Lee Weaver (Nate), Glynn Turman, Phyllis Yvonne Stickney
'A pretty horrendous experience. Indeed it's the sort of movie that might very well figure in some cynics' 10 worst lists of the year.' – *Derek Malcolm, Guardian*
'Slick production is an ideal girls-night-out attraction, as well as sure-fire date fare.' – *Todd McCarthy, Variety*

How Sweet It Is *
US 1968 98m Technicolor Panavision
Warner/Cherokee/National General (Garry Marshall, Jerry Belson)

Suspicious of their son's intentions towards his girlfriend on a European holiday, a middle-aged American couple decide to follow.
Good-looking, rather silly comedy, plain spoken in the modern manner but without much entertainment value except when farce gets the upper hand.
w Garry Marshall, Jerry Belson *novel The Girl in the Turquoise Bikini* by Muriel Resnik *d* Jerry Paris *ph* Lucien Ballard *m* Pat Williams
☆ James Garner, Debbie Reynolds, Maurice Ronet, Paul Lynde, Marcel Dalio, Terry-Thomas, Donald Losby, Hilarie Thompson
'One of those slender marital farces in which the behaviour of the adults is consistently more juvenile than that of the teenagers.' – *MFB*

How the West Was Won *
US 1962 162m Technicolor
Cinerama
MGM/Cinerama (Bernard Smith)

Panoramic Western following the daughter of a pioneering family from youth (1830) to old age, with several half-relevant stories along the way.
Muddled spectacular with splendid set-pieces but abysmal dullness in between, especially if not seen in three-strip Cinerama (the Cinemascope prints are muddy and still show the dividing lines). An all-star fairground show of its time.
w James R. Webb *d* Henry Hathaway (first half), John Ford (Civil War), George Marshall (train) *ph* William Daniels, Milton Krasner, Charles Lang Jnr, Joseph LaShelle *m* Alfred Newman *ad* George W. Davis, William Ferrari, Addison Hehr
☆ Debbie Reynolds, Carroll Baker, Lee J. Cobb, Henry Fonda, Carolyn Jones, Karl Malden, Gregory Peck, George Peppard, Robert Preston, James Stewart, Eli Wallach, John Wayne, Richard Widmark, Brigid Bazlen, Walter Brennan and also David Brian, Andy Devine, Raymond Massey, Agnes Moorehead, Henry Morgan, Thelma Ritter, Russ Tamblyn, Spencer Tracy (narrator)
'That goddamned Cinerama ... do you know a waist shot is as close as you could get with that thing?' – *Henry Hathaway*
James R. Webb
best picture; photography; music

How to Be a Player
US 1997 94m colour
Polygram/Island/Outlaw (Mark Burg, Todd Baker, Russell Simmons, Preston Holmes)
A womanizer gets his come-uppance from his six girlfriends.
Glossy, empty comedy of sexual stereotypes; it has a very limited appeal.
w Mark Brown, Demetria Johnson *d* Lionel C. Martin *ph* Ross Berryman *m* Darren Floyd *pd* Bruce Curtis *ed* William Young
☆ Bill Bellamy, Natalie Desselle, Lark Voorhies, Mari Morrow, Pierre, Jermaine 'Big Hugg' Hopkins
'An inept sexist comedy ... It is only too typical of mainstream black American cinema today and makes one feel nostalgic for the gutsy blaxploitation pictures of the early Seventies.' – *Philip French, Observer*

How to Be a Woman and Not Die in the Attempt *
Spain 1991 89m colour Panavision
Mayfair/Iberoamericana/Atrium/Idea (Rafael Fernández)

original title: *Como ser mujer y no morir en el intento*
A three-times-married journalist grows tired of having to be a mother to her husband, his and her children, and her boss.
Pleasant comedy about the shifting relationships between the sexes, tame by feminist standards, but perceptive enough to bring smiles of recognition from most audiences.
w Carmen Rico-Godoy *novel* Carmen Rico-Godoy *d* Ana Belén *ph* Juan Amoros *m* Antonio Garcia de Diego, Pancho Verona, Mariano Diaz *ad* Gerardo Vera *ed* Carmen Frias
☆ Carmen Maura, Antonio Resines, Carmen Conesa, Juanjo Puigcorbe, Miguel Rellan, Tina

Sainz, Asunción Balaguer, Enriqueta Carballeira, Paco Aguilar, José Ma Cañete

'A rather creaking middle-aged affair.' – *Empire*

'The script goes nowhere and the characters are drawn paper-thin.' – *Variety*

How to Be Very Very Popular
US 1955 89m DeLuxe Cinemascope
TCF (Nunnally Johnson)

Two belly dancers on the run from gangsters hide out in a co-ed college.

Wacky remake of She Loves Me Not *(qv); tries hard for a vein of freewheeling lunacy but only occasionally achieves it. A few numbers might have helped.*

wd Nunnally Johnson *ph* Milton Krasner *m* Cyril Mockridge

☆ Betty Grable, Sheree North, *Charles Coburn*, Robert Cummings, Orson Bean, Fred Clark, Tommy Noonan

How to Beat the High Cost of Living
US 1980 110m Movielab
Filmways

Three middle-class women take to robbery when they can't make the housekeeping balance.

Undercast, reprehensible and almost totally unfunny alleged comedy.

w Robert Kaufman *d* Robert Scheerer

☆ Susan Saint James, Jane Curtin, Jessica Lange, Richard Benjamin, Fred Willard, Eddie Albert

How to Commit Marriage
US 1969 98m Technicolor
Cinerama/Naho (Bill Lawrence)

A couple decide to divorce, with repercussions on their family and in-laws.

Tiresome generation-gap comedy.

w Ben Starr, Michael Kanin *d* Norman Panama *ph* Charles Lang *m* Joseph J. Lilley

☆ Bob Hope, Jackie Gleason, Jane Wyman, Leslie Nielsen, Maureen Arthur, Paul Stewart, Tina Louise

How to Get Ahead in Advertising
GB 1989 94m colour
Virgin/HandMade Films (David Wimbury)

An advertising man, in revolt against salesmanship, grows a boil that turns into an alternative head.

Unsuccessful diatribe on the consumer society.

wd Bruce Robinson *ph* Peter Hannan *m* David Dundas, Rick Wentworth *pd* Michael Pickwoad *ed* Alan Strachan

☆ Richard E. Grant, Rachel Ward, Richard Wilson, Jacqueline Tong, John Shrapnel, Susan Wooldridge, Mick Ford, Jacqueline Pearce, Roddy Maude-Roxby

How to Make a Monster
US 1958 74m bw/colour
AIP (Herman Cohen)

A movie make-up man takes his revenge by turning his fake monsters into real ones after the new studio bosses sack him.

A tongue-in-cheek attempt to get more mileage out of I Was a Teenage Frankenstein *and* I Was a Teenage Werewolf, *produced and directed by the same team, and to cash in on the popularity of rock; the result is uninspired.*

w Kenneth Langtry, Herman Cohen *d* Herbert L. Strock *ph* Maury Gertsman *m* Paul Dunlap *ad* Leslie Thomas *sp* make-up: Philip Scheer

☆ Robert H. Harris, Paul Brinegar, Gary Conway, Gary Clarke, Malcolm Atterbury, Morris Ankrum, Walter Reed, Heather Ames, John Ashley

'There's beauty in the patterns of life.'
How to Make an American Quilt **
US 1995 117m DeLuxe
Universal/Amblin (Sarah Pillsbury, Midge Sanford)

A graduate student learns about the loves of her grandmother and her women friends as they sew her wedding quilt.

A formulaic film that manages to be a humane and enjoyable celebration of feminism without being merely an exercise in nostalgia, illuminating the struggles and triumphs of its participants in their unexceptional lives.

w Jane Anderson *novel* Whitney Otto *d* Jocelyn Moorhouse *ph* Janusz Kaminski *m* Thomas Newman *pd* Leslie Dilley *ed* Jill Bilock

☆ Winona Ryder, Anne Bancroft, Ellen Burstyn, Kate Nelligan, Alfre Woodard, Kate Capshaw, Adam Baldwin, Dermot Mulroney, Maya Angelou, Lois Smith, Jean Simmons, Rip Torn, Derrick O'Connor, Johnathon Schaech, Samantha Mathis

'A quality movie that leisurely maps a muted, liberal feminism.' – *Sight and Sound*

How to Make It: see *Target Harry*

How to Marry a Millionaire **
US 1953 96m Technicolor Cinemascope
TCF (Nunnally Johnson)

Three girls rent an expensive New York apartment and set out to trap millionaires.

Cinemascope's first attempt at modern comedy was not quite as disastrous as might have been expected, largely because of the expensiveness of everything and the several stars still brightly twinkling, but the handling of this variation on the old Golddiggers theme, while entirely amiable, is dramatically very slack.

w Nunnally Johnson *d* Jean Negulesco *ph* Joe MacDonald *m* Cyril Mockridge *md* Alfred Newman

☆ *Lauren Bacall, Marilyn Monroe*, Betty Grable, *William Powell*, Cameron Mitchell, David Wayne, Rory Calhoun, Alex D'Arcy, Fred Clark

'Not only educational, but great fun.' – *Star*

† The film has an eight-minute pre-credits concert sequence, which is pretty unnerving when it unspools on TV.

'The last word in do-it-yourself!'
How to Murder a Rich Uncle
GB 1957 80m bw Cinemascope
Columbia/Warwick (Ronald Kinnoch)

An impoverished nobleman decides to murder his rich old uncle.

Feebly-handled black comedy which does not come off at all despite a highly talented cast.

w John Paxton *play* *Il Faut Tuer Julie* by Didier Daix *d* Nigel Patrick *ph* Ted Moore *m* Ken Jones *ed* Bert Rule

☆ Nigel Patrick, Charles Coburn, *Katie Johnson*, Wendy Hiller, Anthony Newley, Athene Seyler, Michael Caine, Noel Hood, Kenneth Fortescue

'When Was The Last Time You Took The Wife To A Movie? (This could be it!)'
How to Murder Your Wife *
US 1964 118m Technicolor
UA/Murder Inc (George Axelrod)

A strip cartoonist tests out his violent scenes in real life; when his wife disappears he finds himself accused of murder.

Amusing preliminaries give way to dreary plot complications and an overlong courtroom scene. Leave after the first hour.

w George Axelrod *d* Richard Quine *ph* Harry Stradling *m* Neal Hefti *pd* *Richard Sylbert* *ed* David Wages

☆ Jack Lemmon, Virna Lisi, *Terry-Thomas, Eddie Mayehoff*, Sidney Blackmer, Claire Trevor

'Decked out with gross gags and humorless witticisms, the film is infinitely more vulgar than a mere summary can convey.' – *John Simon*

How to Rob a Bank: see *A Nice Little Bank That Should Be Robbed*

How to Save a Marriage and Ruin Your Life
US 1968 102m Technicolor Panavision
Columbia/Nob Hill (Stanley Shapiro)

An attorney takes it upon himself to convince his friend of the infidelity of the friend's mistress…

Tedious sex antics without any sex; a few smiles are not enough to endear it.

w Stanley Shapiro, Nate Monaster *d* Fielder Cook *ph* Lee Garmes *m* Michel Legrand

☆ Dean Martin, Eli Wallach, Stella Stevens, Anne Jackson, Betty Field, Jack Albertson, Katharine Bard

'Another variation on Hollywood's patent version of the Restoration comedy, which as usual abandons the lustiness of its 17th-century prototype in favour of guilt-ridden lechery and a fundamental respect for the married state.' – *MFB*

How to Steal a Diamond in Four Uneasy Lessons: see *The Hot Rock*

How to Steal a Million *
US 1966 127m DeLuxe Panavision
TCF/World Wide (Fred Kohlmar)

The daughter of an art forger mistakenly involves a private detective in a robbery.

High-class but rather boring romantic comedy; the credits promise much but interest wanes quickly owing to uncertain handling.

w Harry Kurnitz *story* George Bradshaw *d* William Wyler *ph* Charles Lang *m* Johnny Williams *pd* Alexandre Trauner

☆ Audrey Hepburn, Peter O'Toole, Charles Boyer, Hugh Griffith, Eli Wallach, Fernand Gravet, Marcel Dalio

'Terribly wordy and slow … Wyler hasn't got the touch nowadays.' – *Sight and Sound*

'The picture isn't offensive, and it's handsome enough, but it's just blah.' – *Pauline Kael, New Yorker*

How to Steal the World
US 1968 90m Metrocolor
MGM/Arena (Anthony Spinner)

A renegade American agent sets out to end war by kidnapping six leading scientists to create a special gas that will allow him to control the minds of everyone else.

Glossily vacuous spy caper, rarely rising above an atmosphere of genial stupidity amid mass slaughter.

w Norman Hudis *d* Sutton Roley *ph* Robert B. Hauser *m* Richard Shores *ad* George W. Davis, James W. Sullivan *ed* Joseph Dervin, Harry Knapp

☆ Robert Vaughn, David McCallum, Barry Sullivan, Eleanor Parker, Leslie Nielsen, Tony Bill, Mark Richman, Dan O'Herlihy, Leo G. Carroll

† The film was edited from an episode from the television series *The Man from U.N.C.L.E.* Its scriptwriter is better known for having written the first six *Carry On* movies.

'You gotta practice on a tame one first!'
How to Stuff a Wild Bikini
US 1965 93m Pathécolor Panavision
AIP (Samuel Z. Arkoff, James H. Nicholson)

Serving in the army in Tahiti, a youth asks a witch doctor to ensure that his girlfriend remains faithful to him.

A formula exhibiting tiredness, as a familiar plot and situations – a couple's bland jealousies, some blander vocalizing – are recycled for the umpteenth time.

w William Asher, Leo Townsend *d* William Asher *ph* Floyd Crosby *m* Les Baxter *ad* Howard Campbell *ed* Fred R. Feitshans, Eve Newman

☆ Annette Funicello, Dwayne Hickman, Brian Donlevy, Harvey Lembeck, Beverly Adams, Jody McCrea, John Ashley, Buster Keaton, Mickey Rooney, Brian Wilson, The Kingsmen

How to Succeed in Business without Really Trying **
US 1967 121m DeLuxe Panavision
UA/Mirisch (David Swift)

A window cleaner cajoles his way to the top of a New York company.

Cinematically uninventive but otherwise brisk and glowing adaptation of a sharp, slick Broadway musical.

wd David Swift *book* Shepherd Mead *musical book* *Abe Burrows, Jack Weinstock, Willie Gilbert* *ph* Burnett Guffey *m/ly* *Frank Loesser* *md* Nelson Riddle *ad* Robert Boyle, Mary Blair *ed* Ralph E. Winters, Allan Jacobs

☆ *Robert Morse, Rudy Vallee, Michele Lee*, Anthony Teague, Maureen Arthur, Murray Matheson

'Shows how taste and talent can succeed in bringing a stage musical to the screen with its virtues intact.' – *John Cutts*

† Credits include 'visual gags by Virgil Partch'.

Howard, a New Breed of Hero: see *Howard the Duck*

Howard the Duck
US 1986 111m DeLuxe
Universal/Gloria Katz/George Lucas

GB title: *Howard, a New Breed of Hero*

A duck from outer space comes to Earth and has various uncomfortable adventures.

Toned down from an adult comic strip, this peculiar film has nowhere to go because it's too sexy for kids and too stupid for adults.

w Willard Huyck, Gloria Katz from Steve Gerber's character *d* Willard Huyck *ph* Richard H. Kline *m* John Barry *pd* Peter Jamison

☆ Lea Thompson, Jeffrey Jones, Paul Guilfoyle

Howards End ***
GB 1992 140m Technicolor Super35 Widescreen
Merchant Ivory/Film Four (Ismail Merchant)

The fortunes of two middle-class families overlap and interlock.

The best of the adaptations of Forster's novels, in which the nostalgia is undercut by an examination of the moral bankruptcy of the ruling class.

w *Ruth Prawer Jhabvala* *novel* E. M. Forster *d* *James Ivory* *ph* Tony Pierce-Roberts *m* Richard Robbins *pd* Luciana Arrighi *ed* Andrew Marcus

☆ Anthony Hopkins, Vanessa Redgrave, Helena Bonham Carter, *Emma Thompson*, James Wilby, Sam West, Jemma Redgrave, Nicola Duffett, Prunella Scales, Simon Callow

'A most compelling drama, perhaps the best film made during the 30-year partnership of Ismail Merchant and James Ivory.' – *Variety*

'A handsome and intelligent piece of work: a faithful, well-paced, and carefully crafted dramatization of a very good story.' – *Terrence Rafferty, New Yorker*

Emma Thompson; Ruth Prawer Jhabvala; Luciana Arrighi

Best picture; James Ivory; Vanessa Redgrave; Tony Pierce-Roberts; Richard Robbins; Jenny Beavan, John Bright (costume design)

best picture; Emma Thompson

The Howards of Virginia
US 1940 117m bw
Columbia (Frank Lloyd)

GB title: *The Tree of Liberty*

A Virginian surveyor finds himself involved in the Revolutionary War.

Historical cavalcade in which central miscasting seems to cast a shadow of artifice over the whole. Interesting but seldom stimulating.

w Sidney Buchman *novel* *The Tree of Liberty* by Elizabeth Page *d* Frank Lloyd *ph* Bert Glennon *m* Richard Hageman

☆ Cary Grant, Martha Scott, Cedric Hardwicke, Alan Marshal, Richard Carlson, Paul Kelly, Irving Bacon, Elizabeth Risdon

Richard Hageman

'Imagine your worst fear a reality!'
The Howling *
US 1980 90m CFI color
Avco Embassy/International Film Investors/Wescom (Ron Bottin)

A lady newscaster discovers that the medical retreat at which she stays to recover from a nervous breakdown is likely to give her another.

A plethora of werewolves and a glut of in-jokes pale beside a gallery of convincing and horrifying special effects.

w John Sayles, Terence H. Winkless *novel* Gary Brandner *d* Joe Dante *ph* John Hora *m* Pino Donaggio *make-up* Rick Baker

☆ Dee Wallace, Patrick Macnee, Dennis Dugan, Christopher Stone, Kevin McCarthy, John Carradine, Slim Pickens

† Some of the character names: George Waggner, R. William Neill, Sam Newfield, Fred Francis, Terry Fisher, Erle Kenton, Charlie Barton, Lew Landers…

Howling II … Your Sister Is a Werewolf
US 1985 90m colour
Thorn-EMI /Granite/Hemdale (Steven Lane)

An expert goes to Transylvania to track down the werewolf queen.

Thin attempt at comedy-horror, which barely got released.

w Robert Sarno, Gary Brandner *d* Philippe Mora

☆ Christopher Lee, Annie McEnroe, Reb Brown, Ferdy Mayne, Sybil Danning

† The film, which was shot in Czechoslovakia, has no relation whatsoever to *The Howling*.

'Just When You Thought It Was Safe To Go Down Under...'

The Howling III

Australia 1987 94m colour
Baccanial (Charles Waterstreet, Philippe Mora)

A mad scientist goes in search of marsupial werewolves, which resemble fierce koala bears.
Bizarre horror spoof that somehow manages to incorporate the drag act of Barry Humphries as Australian super-housewife Dame Edna Everage – the result is below average.
wd Philippe Mora *novel* Gary Brandner *ph* Louis Irving *m* Allan Zavod *pd* Ross Major *ed* Lee Smith *sp* Bob McCarron
☆ Barry Otto, Imogen Annesley, Dasha Blahova, Max Fairchild, Ralph Cotterill, Barry Humphries, Michael Pate, Frank Thring

Howling IV: The Original Nightmare

GB 1988 92m colour
IVE (Harry Alan Towers)

A best-selling author has visions of a werewolf and goes to an isolated cottage for a rest cure.
Like the rest of this series, this movie bears little resemblance to its predecessors, other than in its low-budget mediocrity.
w Clive Turner, Freddie Rowe *d* John Hough *ph* Godfrey Godar *m* David George, Barrie Guard *ed* Claudia Finkle, Malcolm Burns-Errington *sp* Steve Johnson
☆ Romy Windsor, Michael T. Weiss, Anthony Hamilton, Suzanne Severeid, Lamya Derval, Norman Anstey, Kate Edwards, Clive Turner
'Poor horror fare.' – *Films and Filming*

Howling V: The Rebirth

US 1989 99m colour
Allied Vision (Clive Turner)

A group of tourists are invited to spend a weekend in an ancient castle in Budapest – and discover that one of them is a werewolf.
Dismal horror that attempts to take the myth more seriously than other films in the series, but succeeds only in being a boring variation on Agatha Christie's Ten Little Indians.
w Clive Turner, Freddie Rowe *novel The Howling 1–3* by Gary Brandner *d* Neal Sundstrom *ph* Arledge Armenaki *m* The Factory
☆ Ben Cole, William Shockley, Mark Siversen, Philip Davis, Elizabeth She, Victoria Catlin, Stephanie Faulkner, Mary Stavin, Clive Turner

The Howling VI: The Freaks

US 1991 102m Foto-Kem
Allied Lane Pringle

A wandering werewolf with kindly intentions arrives in a small Southern town and falls prey to the evil owner of a freak show.
Leisurely, affected and lacklustre horror, with pretentions above its budget and the ability of its cast and director.
w Kevin Rock *novel The Howling 1–3* by Gary Brandner *d* Hope Perello *ph* Edward Pei *m* Patrick Gleeson *pd* Richard Reams *ed* Adam Wolfe *sp* Steve Johnson; make-up effects: Todd Masters
☆ Brendan Hughes, Michele Matheson, Sean Gregory Sullivan, Antonio Fargas, Carol Lynley, Jered Barclay, Bruce Martyn Payne
'Tasteless but effective shocker.' – *Variety*
† During a sequence in which a sheriff is chased by a monster, also visible on-screen are the shadows thrown by the camera and crew.

Hsimeng Rensheng: see *The Puppetmaster*

Huang Tudi: see *Yellow Earth*

Huayang Nianhua: see *In the Mood for Love*

Huck and the King of Hearts

US 1993 94m Foto-Kem
Crystal Sky/Trimark (Steven Paul)
A young boy runs away from home to find his grandfather, and is befriended by a card-sharp fleeing from a hitman.
Charmless updating of Twain into a world of dysfunctional families, drug-dealing and guns.
w Christopher Sturgeon *story* Mark Twain *d* Michael Keusch *ph* Victor Goss *m* Chris Saranec *pd* Mary Patvaldnieks *ed* Jack Tucker
☆ Chauncey Leopardi, Joe Piscopo, Graham Greene, Dee Wallace Stone, Gretchen Becker, John Astin

Huckleberry Finn

US 1931 71m bw
Paramount
The river adventures of Mark Twain's scapegrace hero.
Adequate early talkie family film.
w Grover Jones, William Slavens McNutt *d* Norman Taurog *ph* David Abel
☆ Jackie Coogan, Junior Durkin, Mitzi Green, Jackie Searl, Eugene Pallette

Huckleberry Finn **

US 1939 90m bw
MGM (Joseph L. Mankiewicz)

Solidly competent remake with excellent production values and several entertaining sequences.
w Hugo Butler *d* Richard Thorpe *ph* John Seitz *m* Franz Waxman
☆ Mickey Rooney, Walter Connolly, William Frawley, Rex Ingram

Huckleberry Finn *

US 1960 107m Metrocolor
Cinemascope
MGM (Samuel Goldwyn Jnr)
aka: *The Adventures of Huckleberry Finn*
Another patchy remake.
w James Lee *d* Michael Curtiz *ph* Ted McCord *m* Jerome Moross
☆ Eddie Hodges, Tony Randall, Archie Moore, Neville Brand, Judy Canova, Buster Keaton, Andy Devine

Huckleberry Finn

US 1974 118m DeLuxe Panavision
UA/Apjac/Readers Digest (Robert Greenhut)

Ambitious but lustreless version of the famous story, with songs.
d J. Lee-Thompson *ph* Laszlo Kovacs *pd* Philip Jefferies *w/m/ly* Richard M. Sherman, Robert B. Sherman
☆ Jeff East, Paul Winfield, David Wayne, Harvey Korman, Arthur O'Connell, Gary Merrill, Natalie Trundy
'It expires in a morass of treacle.' – *Tom Milne*
'It transforms a great work of fiction into something bland, boring and tasteless.' – *Michael Billington, Illustrated London News*

The Hucksters **

US 1947 115m bw
MGM (Arthur Hornblow Jnr)

Back from the war, an advertising executive finds it difficult to put up with his clients' tantrums.
Good topical entertainment which still entertains and gives a good impression of its period.
w Luther Davis *novel* Frederic Wakeman *d* Jack Conway *ph* Harold Rosson *m* Lennie Hayton
☆ *Clark Gable*, Deborah Kerr, Ava Gardner, *Sydney Greenstreet*, Adolphe Menjou, Keenan Wynn, Edward Arnold, Aubrey Mather
'A good picture, quick and to the point.' – *Photoplay*

Hud ****

US 1963 112m bw Panavision
Paramount/Salem/Dover (Martin Ritt, Irving Ravetch)

Life is hard on a Texas ranch, and the veteran owner is not helped by his sexually arrogant ne'er-do-well son, who is a bad influence on the household.
Superbly set in an arid landscape, this incisive character drama is extremely well directed and acted.
w Irving Ravetch, Harriet Frank novel Horseman Pass By by Larry McMurtry *d Martin Ritt* *ph James Wong Howe* *m* Elmer Bernstein *ad* Hal Pereira, Tambi Larsen
☆ *Paul Newman, Patricia Neal, Melvyn Douglas*, Brandon de Wilde
'So uncompromising in its portrait of an amoral man and his impact upon three people that I am tempted to reach for that dangerous adjective "unique".' – *Judith Crist*
🏆 James Wong Howe; Patricia Neal; Melvyn Douglas
script; Martin Ritt; Paul Newman; Hal Pereira, Tambi Larsen
Patricia Neal

Huddle

US 1932 104m bw
MGM
GB title: *The Impossible Lover*
A steel worker's son makes good at Harvard, and wants to marry out of his class.
Would-be serious class drama which fell over its own feet.
w Robert Johnson, C. Gardner Sullivan, Arthur Hyman, Walton Smith *d* Sam Wood
☆ Ramon Novarro, Madge Evans, Una Merkel, Conrad Nagel, Arthur Byron, Cliff Edwards
'Football film doing much to defeat its own purpose by extreme length ... the Metro foreign production end is substituting soccer for the football portions for European screenings.' – *Variety*

'For the world's greatest cat burglar nine lives may just not be enough...'

Hudson Hawk

US 1991 100m Technicolor
Columbia TriStar/Silver Pictures/Ace Bone (Joel Silver)

A cat burglar is hired to steal from the Vatican an alchemical formula for turning lead into gold.
Direly unsuccessful attempt at a comedy thriller that was a box-office flop.
w Steven E. de Souza, Daniel Waters *story* Bruce Willis, Robert Kraft *d* Michael Lehmann *ph* Dante Spinotti *m* Michael Kamen, Robert Kraft *pd* Jack DeGovia *ed* Chris Lebenzon, Michael Tronick
☆ Bruce Willis, Danny Aiello, Andie MacDowell, James Coburn, Richard E. Grant, Sandra Bernhard, Donald Burton, Don Harvey, David Caruso
'Ever wondered what a Three Stooges short would look like with a $40 million budget? Then meet *Hudson Hawk*, a relentlessly annoying clay duck that crash-lands in a sea of wretched excess and silliness.' – *Variety*
'Its utter failure can only be explained by some form of madness having overcome the people involved in its making.' – *Philip French, Observer*

Hudson's Bay **

US 1940 95m bw
TCF (Kenneth MacGowan)
Pierre Radisson, a French Canadian trapper, opens up millions of acres of northern wilderness for England.
Well-made historical saga with good production and performances.
w Lamar Trotti d Irving Pichel ph Peverell Marley, George Barnes *m* Alfred Newman *ad* Richard Day, Wiard B. Ihnen
☆ *Paul Muni*, Laird Cregar, Gene Tierney, John Sutton, Virginia Field, Vincent Price (King Charles II), Nigel Bruce, Morton Lowry, Robert Greig, Frederic Worlock, Montagu Love

The Hudsucker Proxy **

US 1994 111m colour
Warner/Polygram/Silver/Working Title (Ethan Coen)

In the 50s, a bright but gullible business school graduate rises from the mailroom to be president of a vast corporation overnight as the result of boardroom devilry and makes good against the odds.
Clever and enjoyable pastiche of Hollywood comedies of the 40s, close in spirit to Preston Sturges with an ending straight out of Frank Capra. It is stylized, stylish and civilized entertainment.
w Ethan Coen, Joel Coen, Sam Raimi d Joel Coen ph Roger Deakins m Carter Burwell, Aram Khachaturian *pd Dennis Gassner ed* Thom Noble
☆ Tim Robbins, Jennifer Jason Leigh, Paul Newman, Charles Durning, Jim True, John Mahoney, Bill Cobbs, Bruce Campbell
'Has little else but spasmodic entertainment value to commend it.' – *Derek Malcolm, Guardian*
'Seems like a wizardly but artificial synthesis of aspects of vintage fare, leaving a hole in the middle where some emotion and humanity ought to be.' – *Todd McCarthy, Variety*

Hue and Cry ***

GB 1946 82m bw
Ealing (Michael Balcon)

East End boys discover that their favourite boys' paper is being used by crooks to pass information.
The first 'Ealing comedy' uses vivid London locations as background for a sturdy comic plot with a climax in which the criminals are rounded up by thousands of boys swarming over dockland.
w T. E. B. Clarke d Charles Crichton ph Douglas Slocombe, John Seaholme *m* Georges Auric *ed* Charles Hasse
☆ Alastair Sim (Felix H. Wilkinson), Jack Warner (Nightingale), Harry Fowler (Joe Kirby), Valerie White (Rhona), Frederick Piper (Mr Kirby), Jack Lambert (Ford), Joan Dowling (Clarry), Douglas Barr (Alec), Stanley Escane (Boy), Vida Hope (Mrs Kirby), Ian Dawson (Norman), Gerald Fox (Dicky), Bruce Belfrage (BBC Announcer)
'Refreshing, bloodtingling and disarming.' – *Richard Winnington*

Huey Long **

US 1985 88m DuArt/bw
Ken Burns, Richard Kilberg
The life and death of the populist American politician Huey Long, who dominated the politics of Louisiana in the 30s and was murdered at a point when he might have gone on to become US President or even dictator.
Fascinating documentary not only on the rise of a politician but on the wider question of the corruption of power, told using archive footage and reminiscences of many of the people involved.
w Geoffrey C. Ward *d* Ken Burns *ph* Ken Burns, Buddy Squires *md* John Colby *ed* Amy Stechler Burns
☆ David McCullough (narrator)

Hugo the Hippo

US 1975 78m colour
Brut (Robert Halmi)

An independently-minded hippo combats a Zanzibar magician.
Uninventive cartoon feature, endearing neither in characterization nor in draughtsmanship.
w Thomas Baum *d* William Feigenbaum *md* Bert Keyes
☆ Featuring the voices of Burl Ives, Marie Osmond, Jimmy Osmond, Robert Morley, Paul Lynde

Hugs and Kisses *

Sweden 1966 96m bw
Sandrews (Göran Lindgren)
original title: *Puss och Kram*
A destitute bohemian takes over the house and the wife of the old executive friend who shelters him out of pity.
Rather like a comedy version of the Dirk Stroeve section of The Moon and Sixpence, *this sophisticated film came under censorship fire for depicting the first full frontal female.*
wd Jonas Cornell *ph* Lars Swanberg *m* Bengt Ernryd
☆ Sven-Bertil Taube, Agneta Ekmanner, Hakan Serner
'The brilliance of the film lies in the way humour and sadness are kept in perfect equilibrium.' – *MFB*

Huis Clos *

France 1954 99m bw
Films Marceau
Two women and a man die, go to hell, and are locked up for ever in an elegant room.
Rather flat intellectual fantasy from a play which made great waves when first performed.
w Pierre Laroche *play* Jean-Paul Sartre *d* Jacqueline Audry *ph* Robert Juillard *m* Joseph Kosma
☆ Arletty, Frank Villard, Gaby Sylvia
'Without the ecstasy, terror and poetic imagination of a Cocteau, the subject becomes a fatally stationary one.' – *Peter John Dyer, MFB*

Huk!

US 1956 83m Eastmancolor
UA (Collier Young)
In 1951, an American fights Philippine guerrillas who murdered his father.

Crude action melodrama which served a purpose.
w Stirling Silliphant *novel* Stirling Silliphant *d* John Barnwell *ph* William Snyder *m* Albert Glasser
☆ George Montgomery, Mona Freeman, John Baer, James Bell

The Human Beast: see *La Bête Humaine*

The Human Comedy *
US 1943 117m bw
MGM (Clarence Brown)
In a small town during the war, a telegram boy brings tragedy to others and is touched by it himself.
Gooey, sentimental morale booster in the best MGM tradition, a variant on the Hardy family series but with all the pretensions of its author.
w Howard Estabrook *novel* William Saroyan *d* *Clarence Brown* *ph* Harry Stradling *m* Herbert Stothart
☆ Mickey Rooney, Frank Morgan, James Craig, Marsha Hunt, Jackie Jenkins, Fay Bainter, Ray Collins, Van Johnson, Donna Reed
OPENING NARRATION BY RAY COLLINS: 'I am Matthew Macauley. I have been dead for two years. So much of me is still living that I know now the end is only the beginning. As I look down on my homeland of Ithaca, California, with its cactus, vineyards and orchards, I see that so much of me is still living there – in the places I've been, in the fields and streets and church and most of all in my home, where my hopes, my dreams, my ambitions still live in the daily life of my loved ones.'
'The dignity and simplicity of the ideas shade off into cheap pretentiousness.' – *Bosley Crowther*
'The best one can say of it ... is that it tries on the whole to be "faithful" to Saroyan; not invariably a good idea.' – *James Agee*
'The Saroyan touch leaves nothing ordinary: the film is electric with the joy of life.' – *Time*
original story
best picture; Clarence Brown; Harry Stradling; Mickey Rooney

Human Desire
US 1954 90m bw
Columbia (Lewis J. Rachmil)
A jealous railway official forces his wife to help him murder her suspected lover.
Drab and unattractive remake of La Bête Humaine.
w Alfred Hayes *d* Fritz Lang *ph* Burnett Guffey *m* Daniele Amfitheatrof
☆ Gloria Grahame, Glenn Ford, Broderick Crawford, Edgar Buchanan

The Human Factor
GB 1975 95m Technicolor
Eton (Terry Lens)
The family of a NATO war planner in Italy is slaughtered by terrorists.
Violent revenge drama, of little interest.
w Tom Hunter, Peter Powell *d* Edward Dmytryk
☆ George Kennedy, John Mills, Raf Vallone, Arthur Franz, Rita Tushingham, Frank Avianca, Barry Sullivan

The Human Factor
GB 1979 114m Technicolor Panavision
Rank/Wheel/Sigma/Otto Preminger
An innocent man is suspected of being the 'mole' in the Foreign Office.
Quietly sardonic scenes of diplomatic chess are played far too broadly and literally in this ill-advised and poorly executed foray into the serious spy scene, which despite its stars becomes merely risible before the end.
w Tom Stoppard *novel* Graham Greene *d* Otto Preminger *ph* Mike Malloy *m* Richard and Gary Logan
☆ Nicol Williamson, Richard Attenborough, Derek Jacobi, Robert Morley, John Gielgud, Ann Todd, Richard Vernon, Joop Doderer, Iman
'Unfortunately, Preminger stages it all as if he was just trying to get all the actors through their line readings in under two hours, allowing no breathing room or time for character nuance in a tale which resolutely calls for quiet moments.' – *Variety*

The Human Jungle
US 1954 82m bw
Allied Artists
A new police captain cleans up a gangster-ridden slum district.
Adequate low-life actioner of the kind later taken over by TV.
w William Sackheim, Daniel Fuchs *d* Joseph M. Newman *ph* Ellis Carter *m* Hans Salter
☆ Gary Merrill, Jan Sterling, Paula Raymond, Emile Meyer, Regis Toomey, Lamont Johnson, Chuck Connors

The Human Monster: see *Dark Eyes of London*

Human Resources *
France/GB 1999 103m colour
NFT/La Sept ARTE/Haut et Court (Caroline Benjo, Carole Scotta)
original title: *Ressources Humaines*
A business school graduate in his first job finds himself caught in a dispute between management and factory workers, who include his father.
French-styled social realism, using mainly a non-professional cast and improvised dialogue: despite slender resources, it packs a considerable punch.
w Laurent Cantet, Gilles Marchand *d* Laurent Cantet *ph* Matthieu Poirot Delpech, Claire Caroff *pd* Romain Denis *ed* Robin Campillo, Stéphanie Leger
☆ Jalil Lespert (Frank), Jean-Claude Vallod (Father), Chantal Barré (Mother), Véronique de Pandelaère (Sylvie), Michel Begnez (Olivier), Lucien Longueville (Boss), Danielle Mélador (Danielle Arnoux), Pascal Sémard (Personnel Manager), Didier Emile-Woldemard (Alain), Françoise Boutigny (Betty)
'Generous, sensitive and innovative. It is a film in which, in the widest possible sense, the personal is political.' – *Ginette Vincendeau, Sight and Sound*

'The Weekend has Landed!'
Human Traffic **
GB/Ireland 1999 95m Fujicolor
Metrodome/Irish Screen/Fruit Salad (Allan Niblo, Emer McCourt)
Five Welsh friends, high on Ecstasy, spend a weekend together in clubs and bedrooms, sorting out their sexual problems.
Energetic youth movie, using lurid fantasy sequences and stylistic excesses of one sort and another to duplicate the druggy experiences of its characters.
wd Justin Kerrigan *ph* David Bennett *m* Rob Mello, Mathew Herbert *pd* David Buckingham *ed* Patrick Moore
☆ John Simm (Jip), Lorraine Pilkington (Lulu), Shaun Parkes (Koop), Danny Dyer (Moff), Nicola Reynolds (Nina), Dean Davies (Lee), Peter Albert (Uncle Eric), Jan Anderson (Karen Benson)
'The accuracy of Kerrigan's observations on rave culture are less in question than the absence of a definable narrative drive, the messily episodic structure, characters which hover above caricature or the film's fundamental validity as compelling cinema.' – *Trevor Lewis, Empire*
† It was released on video and DVD under the title *Human Traffic Remixed* into a version recut by its producer.

Humanoids from the Deep
US 1980 81m Metrocolor
New World (Martin B. Cohen)
GB title: *Monster*
Gruesome amphibious creatures rise from the ocean to stalk and destroy the most nubile women in sight.
Lurid, nonsensical but very violent horror flick, with much rape and nudity; like a Corman quickie of the fifties but with added gore.
w Frederick James *d* Barbara Peeters *ph* Daniele Lacambre *m* James Horner *cos* Rob Bottin
☆ Vic Morrow, Doug McClure, Ann Turkel

Humoresque **
US 1946 125m bw
Warner (Jerry Wald)
An ambitious violinist gets emotionally involved with his wealthy patroness.
Lush soaper about suffering in high society, complete with tragic end and lashings of classical music (Isaac Stern on the sound track).
w Clifford Odets, Zachary Gold *novel* Fannie Hurst *d* *Jean Negulesco* *ph* *Ernest Haller* *md* Franz Waxman
☆ *Joan Crawford, John Garfield, Oscar Levant*, J. Carrol Naish, Joan Chandler, Tom D'Andrea, Craig Stevens, Ruth Nelson
'This brilliantly executed but less well-conceived picture functions like a beautifully made piece of machinery, fascinating to watch in action, powerful, but cold and insensitive.' – *Jympson Harman, London Evening News*
† Clifford Odets recycled some of his rejected script for the Gershwin biopic *Rhapsody in Blue*, about which pianist and wit Oscar Levant had commented 'He's written his own life, but with song hits.'
†† Garfield was unable to fake playing the violin, so in scenes showing him doing so, the fingering is performed by one professional violinist crouching out of sight, and the bowing by another.
Franz Waxman

The Hunchback of Notre Dame **
US 1923 120m approx (24 fps) bw silent
Universal
The deformed Notre Dame bellringer rescues a gypsy girl from the evil intentions of her guardian.
Victorian gothic version with a riveting star performance.
w Percy Poore Sheehan, Edward T. Lowe Jnr *novel* *Notre Dame de Paris* by Victor Hugo *d* Wallace Worsley *ph* Robert S. Newhard, Tony Kornman
☆ *Lon Chaney*, Patsy Ruth Miller, Norman Kerry, Ernest Torrence, Gladys Brockwell, Kate Lester, Brandon Hurst, Tully Marshall

The Hunchback of Notre Dame ****
US 1939 117m bw
RKO (Pandro S. Berman)
This superb remake is one of the best examples of Hollywood expertise at work: art direction, set construction, costumes, camera, lighting and above all direction brilliantly support an irresistible story and bravura acting.
w *Sonya Levien, Bruno Frank* *d* *William Dieterle* *ph* *Joseph H. August* *m* *Alfred Newman* *ad* *Van Nest Polglase*
☆ *Charles Laughton, Cedric Hardwicke, Maureen O'Hara, Edmond O'Brien, Thomas Mitchell, Harry Davenport*, Walter Hampden, Alan Marshal, George Zucco, Katherine Alexander, Fritz Leiber, Rod la Rocque
'A super thriller-chiller. Will roll up healthy grosses at the ticket windows.' – *Variety*
'Has seldom been bettered as an evocation of medieval life.' – *John Baxter, 1968*
'It exceeds in sheer magnificence any similar film in history. Sets are vast and rich in detail, crowds are immense, and camera uses of both are versatile, varied and veracious.' – *Motion Picture Herald*
† Other versions: *Esmeralda* (1906, French); *Notre Dame de Paris* (1911, French); *The Darling of Paris* (1917, US, with Theda Bara); and see above and below.
Alfred Newman

The Hunchback of Notre Dame
France/Italy 1956 107m Eastmancolor Cinemascope
Paris Films/Panitalia (Robert and Raymond Hakim)
original title: *Notre Dame de Paris*
Crude international rehash with nothing to commend it, though the script before dubbing may have been interesting.
w Jacques Prévert, Jean Aurenche *d* Jean Delannoy *ph* Michel Kelber *m* Georges Auric
☆ Anthony Quinn, Gina Lollobrigida, Jean Danet, Alain Cuny, Robert Hirsch

The Hunchback of Notre Dame **
US 1996 91m Technicolor
Buena Vista/Walt Disney (Don Hahn)
The deformed bellringer of Notre Dame saves a gypsy girl from the machinations of his master.
An unlikely subject for animation, and one that, despite moments of brilliance, proves intractable to Disney's soft-centred musical way with classics. Young children are likely to be bored or confused, for the tone is uncertain, and the emotional and sexual subtext too adult for the treatment it receives.
w Tab Murphy, Irene Mecchi, Bob Tzudiker, Noni White, Jonathan Roberts *novel* *Notre Dame de Paris* by Victor Hugo *d* Gary Trousdale, Kirk Wise *m* Alan Menken *m/ly* Alan Menken, Stephen Schwartz *ad* David Goetz *ed* Ellen Keneshea
☆ Featuring the voices of: Tom Hulce, Tony Jay, Paul Kandel, Kevin Kline, Demi Moore, Heidi Mollenhauer, Jason Alexander, David Ogden Stiers, Mary Wickes, Jane Withers
'A mild disappointment; not a disaster but a definite falling off from the studio's series of recent triumphs.' – *Adam Mars-Jones, Independent*
'Beautiful and transporting – the best of Disney's "serious" animated features in the multiplex era.' – *Owen Gleiberman, Entertainment Weekly*
† It was among the box-office successes of 1996, grossing some $284m around the world.
Alan Menken, Stephen Schwartz

The Hundred Pound Window
GB 1943 84m bw
Warner (Max Milder)
A racecourse clerk becomes involved with gamblers who bribe him to rig the totalizator, but he finally exposes them.
Routine programmer notable only for giving a leading role to an old character actor.
w Abem Finkel, Brock Williams, Rodney Ackland *d* Brian Desmond Hurst *ph* Otto Heller *m* Hans May
☆ *Frederick Leister*, Mary Clare, Anne Crawford, Richard Attenborough, David Farrar, Niall MacGinnis, David Hutcheson

Hundred Rifles: see *100 Rifles*

Hundstage: see *Dog Days*

A Hungarian Fairy Tale
Hungary 1986 97m bw
Mafilm/Objektiv
original title: *Hol Volt, Hol Nem Volt ...*
After his mother is killed, a 10-year-old boy runs away to search for his father, not realizing that the person named on his birth certificate is a bureaucratic fiction.
An intermittently successful surreal road movie, using Mozart's Magic Flute *as a counterpart to the on-screen events; its portrait of officialdom run mad does not travel well.*
w Gyula Gazdag, Miklós Györffy *d* Gyula Gazdag *ph* Elemér Ragályi *m* Mozart *md* Mártha István
☆ Eszter Csákányi, Mária Varga, Hušák František, Dávid Vermes, Péter Trokán, Szilvia Tóth

'*The Hunger* is a mood, a look, an ambience created by Tony Scott. It is the lighting of Stephen Goldblatt, it is the production design of Brian Morris, it is the clothes created by Milena Canonero.'
The Hunger
US 1983 99m Metrocolor Panavision
MGM-UA/Richard Shepherd
A couple of ageless vampires are desperate for blood.
Absurd attempt to update Dracula with lashings of sex, rock music and flashy photography. An ordeal.
w Ivan Davis, Michael Thomas *novel* Whitley Strieber *d* Tony Scott *ph* Stephen Goldblatt, Tom Mangravite *m* Michael Rubini, Denny Jaeger *pd* Brian Morris
☆ Catherine Deneuve, Susan Sarandon, David Bowie, Cliff de Young
'One of the most incoherent and foolish pictures of recent months.' – *Observer*

Hungry for Love: see *Adua e le Compagne*

Hungry Hill
GB 1946 92m bw
GFD/Two Cities (William Sistrom)
An Irish family feud spans three generations.
Stolid period melodrama, stuffed with stage Irish clichés, that never sparks into life.
w Daphne du Maurier, Terence Young, Francis Crowdy *novel* Daphne du Maurier *d* Brian Desmond Hurst *ph* Desmond Dickinson *m* John Greenwood *ad* Alec Vetchinsky *ed* Alan Jaggs
☆ Margaret Lockwood (Fanny Rosa), Dennis Price (Greyhound John), Cecil Parker (Copper John), Michael Denison (Henry Brodrick), F. J. McCormick (Old Tim), Dermot Walsh (Wild Johnnie), Jean Simmons (Jane Brodrick), Eileen

Herlie (Katherine), Eileen Crowe (Bridget), Barbara Waring (Barbara Brodrick), Dan O'Herlihy (Harry Brodrick), Siobhan McKenna (Kate Donovan)

'It has got everything – costume, Irish brogues, Irish scenery, family feuds, family curses, love, hate, murder, fights, drink and drugs – everything, in fact, but life, movement and conviction, everything but the power to hold your interest.' – *Richard Winnington, News Chronicle*

Hungry Wives: see *Season of the Witch*

'Deadly. Silent. Stolen.'
The Hunt for Red October **
US 1990 137m Technicolor Panavision
Paramount/Mace Neufeld/Jerry Sherlock

The Soviet commander of a top-secret submarine attempts to defect to the West in his vessel.
An intermittently suspenseful thriller, stronger on hardware than human interest.
w Larry Ferguson, Donald Stewart *novel* Tom Clancy *d* John McTiernan *ph* Jan de Bont *m* Basil Poledouris *pd* Terence Marsh *ad* Dianne Wager *ed* Dennis Virkler, John Wright *sp* Industrial Light & Magic
☆ Sean Connery, Alec Baldwin, Scott Glenn, Sam Neill, James Earl Jones, Joss Ackland, Richard Jordan, Peter Firth, Tim Curry

'A terrific adventure yarn, excitingly filmed.' – *Variety*

best sound effects editing
best film editing; best sound

Hunted *
GB 1952 84m bw
GFD/Independent Artists (Julian Wintle)
US title: *The Stranger In Between*
A runaway boy joins forces with a runaway murderer, and the latter sacrifices himself for the boy's safety.
Predictable pattern melodrama, nicely made and acted.
w Jack Whittingham *d* Charles Crichton *ph* Eric Cross *m* Hubert Clifford
☆ *Dirk Bogarde, Jon Whiteley*, Kay Walsh, Elizabeth Sellars, Frederick Piper, Geoffrey Keen, Julian Somers

'He's trapped in a world where killing is an art and revenge is an obsession.'
The Hunted
US 1995 110m DeLuxe
Universal/Bregman/Bauer/Davis (John Davis, Gary W. Goldstein)

In Tokyo, a New York businessman witnesses a murder by a ninja assassin and goes on the run from the killer.
Risible action thriller, full of casual slaughter, and lacking the high-energy choreography of the genre that might have made it watchable.
wd J. F. Lawton *ph* Jack Conroy *m* Motofumi Yamaguchi *pd* Phil Dagort *ed* Robert A. Ferretti, Eric Strand
☆ Christopher Lambert, John Lone, Joan Chen, Yoshio Harada, Yoko Shimada, Mari Natsuki, Tak Kubota

'This grisly yet often laughable actioner most closely resembles the low-budget martial arts movies that used to air, badly dubbed, on independent TV stations.' – *Brian Lowry, Variety*

Hunted Men *
US 1938 67m bw
Paramount
A killer on the run moves into a private home and is outwitted by the head of the house.
Competent second feature which sticks in the memory.
w Horace McCoy, William R. Lipman *d* Louis King *ph* Victor Milner
☆ Lloyd Nolan, Lynne Overman, Mary Carlisle, J. Carrol Naish, Anthony Quinn, Dorothy Peterson

The Hunter
US 1980 117m Metrocolor
Paramount/Rastar/Mort Engelberg

Episodes in the violent career of an urban bounty hunter.
The action scenes salvage a mysteriously banal screenplay full of continuity lapses and unexplained characters.
w Ted Leighton, Peter Hyams *book* Christopher Keane, and the life of Ralph Thorson *d* Buzz Kulik *ph* Fred J. Koenekamp *m* Michel Legrand
☆ Steve McQueen, Eli Wallach, Kathryn Harrold, LeVar Burton, Ben Johnson

'The final impression is of an extended TV pilot for yet another police-boosting serial with more action than sense.' – *Sunday Times*

The Hunters
US 1958 108m DeLuxe Cinemascope
TCF (Dick Powell)

A fearless American pilot is sent to Korea on a special mission.
Standard war thriller, good to look at when airborne but pretty boring on the ground; propaganda element very strong.
w Wendell Mayes *novel* James Salter *d* Dick Powell *ph* Charles G. Clarke, Tom Tutwiler *m* Paul Sawtell
☆ Robert Mitchum, Robert Wagner, Richard Egan, May Britt

Hunting
Australia 1992 97m colour
Boulevard
A married secretary becomes involved with a ruthless media tycoon.
A mix of business thriller and domestic drama that manages to be both dull and pretentious.
wd Frank Howson *ph* David Connell, Dan Burstall *m* John French, David Herzog *pd* Jon Dowding *ed* Philip Reid
☆ John Savage, Kerry Armstrong, Jeffrey Thomas, Rebecca Rigg, Rhys McConnochie, Guy Pearce

The Hunting Party
US 1971 108m DeLuxe
UA/Brighton/Levy-Gardner-Levy
A sadistic Texas baron sets out to shoot one by one the outlaws who have kidnapped his wife.
Crude, brutish and repellent melodrama: the epitome of permissiveness, replete with gore, rape and sadism.
w William Norton, Gilbert Alexander, Lou Morheim *d* Don Medford *ph* Cecilio Paniagua *m* Riz Ortolani
☆ Gene Hackman, Candice Bergen, Oliver Reed

Huozhe: see *To Live*

Las Hurdes: see *Land Without Bread*

Hurlyburly *
US 1998 122m colour
Fine Line/Storm (Anthony Drazan, Richard Gladstein, David Hamburger)

Two Hollywood casting agents and an unemployed actor dissect their relationships with women and each other.
Acerbic, conversational drama of unlovely people who are living on the edge; the performances manage to engage one's attention through its longeurs.
w David Rabe *play* David Rabe *d* Anthony Drazan *ph* Gu Changwei *m* David Baerwald, Steve Lindsey *pd* Michael Haller *ed* Dylan Tichenor
☆ Sean Penn, Kevin Spacey, Robin Wright Penn, Chazz Palminteri, Garry Shandling, Anna Paquin, Meg Ryan

'Two long hours with three self-absorbed misogynists and the articulate women who allow these guys to treat them like dirt is not most people's idea of a good time.' – *David Rooney, Variety*

'Through miles of raging ocean he defied man's law!'
The Hurricane **
US 1937 110m bw
Samuel Goldwyn (Merritt Hulburd)

The simple life on a South Pacific island is disrupted, not only by a vindictive governor but by a typhoon.
Tolerable island melodrama with a spectacular climax and a generally good cast.
w Dudley Nichols, Oliver H. P. Garrett *novel* Charles Nordhoff, James Norman Hall *d John Ford ph Bert Glennon m* Alfred Newman
☆ Dorothy Lamour, Jon Hall, *C. Aubrey Smith, Mary Astor, Raymond Massey, Thomas Mitchell,* John Carradine, Jerome Cowan

'A big money picture ... a production masterpiece.' – *Variety*

'There's a hurricane all right. It's magnificent ... Few people will bother to remember what the rest of the film is about. It goes with the wind.' – *C. A. Lejeune*

† Remade in 1979.
Alfred Newman; Thomas Mitchell

Hurricane
US 1979 120m Technicolor Todd-AO 70
Dino de Laurentiis/Famous Films (Lorenzo Semple Jnr)

A remake of the 1937 film, lacking the style, the innocence, and even the technical splendour.
w Lorenzo Semple Jnr *d* Jan Troell *ph* Sven Nykvist *m* Nino Rota *pd* Danilo Donati
☆ Jason Robards, Mia Farrow, Trevor Howard, Max von Sydow, Dayton Ka'ne, Timothy Bottoms, James Keach

Hurricane
US 1997 88m Technicolor
First Independent/UA (Galt Niederhoffer, Gill Holland, Morgan J. Freeman)
GB title: *Hurricane Streets*
The relationship between a 15-year-old petty criminal and his girlfriend is hampered by cops and her father.
Gritty drama of a familiar kind, in which teenage love is seen as redeeming criminality and manslaughter.
wd Morgan J. Freeman *ph* Enrique Chediak *m* Theodore Shapiro *pd* Petra Barchi *ed* Sabine Hoffman
☆ Brendan Sexton III, Shawn Elliott, José Zuñiga, David Roland Frank, Carlo Alban, Antoine McLean, Mtume Gant, Lynn Cohen, Edie Falco

'It zooms along with the terrific soundtrack and some very affecting sequences.' – *Marianne Gray, Film Review*

'His Greatest Fight Was For Justice.'
The Hurricane **
US 1999 125m DeLuxe
Buena Vista/Beacon/Azoff/Rudy Langlais (Armyan Bernstein, John Ketcham, Norman Jewison)

After reading his autobiography, a youth campaigns for the release of a former middleweight boxer who spent 19 years in prison for murders he did not commit.
Washington's performance helps lift this often plodding biopic out of the ordinary, but its clumsy construction diminishes its impact.
w Armyan Bernstein, Dan Gordon *book The Sixteenth Round* by Rubin 'Hurricane' Carter *book Lazarus and the Hurricane* by Sam Chaiton and Terry Swinton *d* Norman Jewison *ph* Roger Deakins *m* Christopher Young *pd* Philip Rosenberg *ed* Stephen Rivkin
☆ *Denzel Washington* (Rubin 'Hurricane' Carter), Vicellous Reon Shannon (Lesra), Deborah Kara Unger (Lisa), Liev Schreiber (Sam), John Hannah (Terry), Dan Hedaya (Della Pesca), Debbi Morgan (Mae Thelma), Clancy Brown (Lt Jimmy Williams), David Paymer (Myron Bedlock), Harris Yulin (Leon Friedman), Rod Steiger (Judge Sarokin), Garland Witt (John Artis)

'So intriguingly plotted and captivatingly acted that it's easy to overlook its dramatic flaws and overall soft gaze.' – *Emanuel Levy, Variety*

Denzel Washington

Hurricane Smith
US 1952 90m Technicolor
Paramount/Nat Holt
An adventurer charters a boat to find a South Sea treasure but the boat owner turns the tables on him.
Standard thick ear with plenty of action.
w Frank Gruber *d* Jerry Hopper *ph* Ray Rennahan *m* Paul Sawtell
☆ John Ireland, Yvonne de Carlo, James Craig, Forrest Tucker

Hurricane Streets: see *Hurricane*

'Will the south overcome the bigotry of the hate-laden white aristocrats?'
Hurry Sundown
US 1967 146m Technicolor Panavision
Paramount/Sigma (Otto Preminger)
Post-war racial problems in Georgia farmland, with degenerate whites and noble blacks.
Incredibly cliché-ridden epic melodrama with action and sex asides, from a rock bottom bestseller. It long outstays its welcome even for unintentional hilarity.
w Thomas C. Ryan, Horton Foote *novel* K. B. Gilden *d* Otto Preminger *ph* Loyal Griggs, Milton Krasner *m* Hugo Montenegro
☆ Jane Fonda, Michael Caine, Rex Ingram, Diahann Carroll, Burgess Meredith, John Phillip Law, Robert Hooks, Faye Dunaway, Beah Richards, George Kennedy, Madeleine Sherwood

'Critic Wilfrid Sheed wrote recently that no film is ever so bad that you can't find some virtue in it. He must not have seen *Hurry Sundown*.' – *Rex Reed*

'To criticize it would be like tripping a dwarf.' – *Wilfrid Sheed*

'A pantomime version of Greek tragedy.' – *MFB*

'Preminger's taste is atrocious. His idea of erotic symbolism is Jane Fonda caressing Michael Caine's saxophone.' – *Cue*

Hurry Up, or I'll Be 30 *
US 1973 88m colour
Avco Embassy (Joseph Jacoby)

A failure attempts to find success and love before he reaches the beginning of middle age.
Gentle and sometimes perceptive comedy of manners.
w Joseph Jacoby, David Wiltse *d* Joseph Jacoby *ph* Burleigh Wartes *m* Stephen Lawrence *ed* Stan Warnow
☆ John Lefkowitz, Linda de Coff, Ronald Anton, Maureen Byrnes, Danny DeVito, David Kirk, Frank Quinn

'A comedy about love, death, and freedom!'
Husbands *
US 1970 154m DeLuxe
Columbia/Faces Music Inc (Al Ruban)
Three married men, shocked by the death of their friend, impulsively get drunk, fly to London and set out on a weekend of dissipation.
Irritatingly rough hewn and insanely overlong, this half-improvised tragi-comedy forces three good actors to overplay embarrassingly; but its best moments are memorable.
wd John Cassavetes *ph* Victor Kemper *m* none
☆ Peter Falk, John Cassavetes, Ben Gazzara

Husbands and Wives ***
US 1992 108m DuArt
Columbia TriStar/TriStar (Jack Rollins, Charles H. Joffe)

After their best friends announce that they are splitting up, a writer and his wife decide to separate and he becomes infatuated with a young student.
One of Allen's best films, a clever and insightful examination of the insecurities and often self-destructive behaviour of couples, though the nervy camera-work irritates.
wd Woody Allen ph Carlo Di Palma *pd* Santo Loquasto *ed* Susan E. Morse
☆ Woody Allen, *Judy Davis*, Mia Farrow, Juliette Lewis, Liam Neeson, Blythe Danner, Sydney Pollack, Lysette Anthony

'The thing that moviegoers will realize decades hence is that *Husbands and Wives* is a damn fine film.' – *Richard Corliss, Time*

'Rich in characterisation, waspishly witty and profound in its observations about the frailty and fallibilities of modern marriage.' – *Ian Johnstone, Sunday Times*

Judy Davis; Woody Allen (as writer)
original screenplay

Husband's Holiday
US 1931 70m bw
Paramount
A wife takes a passive attitude to her husband's affair.
Tepid sophisticated comedy which doesn't register.
w Ernest Pascal *play The Marriage Bed* by Ernest Pascal *d* Robert Milton
☆ Clive Brook, Vivienne Osborne, Charles Ruggles, Juliette Compton, Charles Winninger, Elizabeth Patterson

'Mild drawing-room problem play made even milder by repressed acting.' – *Variety*

Hush
US 1998 95m Technicolor
TriStar (Douglas Wick)

A jealous mother tries to wreck her son's marriage.

Dire, risible domestic melodrama, with a hysterical performance from Lange and a bland one from Paltrow.
w Jonathan Darby, Jane Rusconi *d* Jonathan Darby *ph* Andrew Dunn *m* Christopher Young *pd* Thomas A. Walsh, Michael Johnston *ed* Dan Rae, Lynzee Klingman, Robert Leighton
☆ Jessica Lange, Gwyneth Paltrow, Johnathon Schaech, Nina Foch, Debi Mazar, Richard Lineback, Kiaulani Lee, David Thornton, Hal Holbrook

'A tawdry, artistically vacant exercise in class snobbery and crude, objectionable sexism.' – *Sight and Sound*

† The movie was released direct to video in Britain.

'It starts with the most shocking scene of all time – and that's only the beginning!'

Hush Hush Sweet Charlotte *
US 1964 133m bw
TCF/Associates and Aldrich

A Southern belle lives 37 years in a lonely mansion tormented by nightmarish memories of her fiancé's murder. Suddenly, after a series of apparent hauntings and other strange events, she finds she didn't do it.
Padded but generally enjoyable replay of elements from Whatever Happened to Baby Jane, *with a large helping of* Les Diaboliques. *The stars help more than the director.*
w Henry Farrell, Lukas Heller *d* Robert Aldrich *ph* Joseph Biroc *m* Frank de Vol *ad* William Glasgow
☆ *Bette Davis, Olivia de Havilland,* Joseph Cotten, Cecil Kellaway, Victor Buono, William Campbell, Mary Astor, Agnes Moorehead

'The blood is on the cleaver, the madwoman is on the loose, the headless corpse is on the prowl and the Guignol is about as grand as it can get.' – *Judith Crist*

'Aldrich only just manages to keep this side of being disgusting and that side of being ridiculous.' – *Films and Filming*

Joseph Biroc; Frank de Vol; Agnes Moorehead; title song (*m* Frank de Vol, *ly* Mack David)

Le Hussard sur le Toit: see *The Horseman on the Roof*

Hussy
GB 1979 94m Eastmancolor
Boyd/Watchgrove (Jeremy Watt)

A high-class prostitute becomes involved with gangsters but eventually finds a new life for herself and her offspring.
Tedious exploitation melodrama, shot like a ninety-minute commercial.
wd Matthew Chapman *ph* Keith Goddard *pd* Hazel Peizer *ed* Bill Blunden
☆ Helen Mirren, John Shea, Daniel Chasin, Jenny Runacre, Murray Salem, Patti Boulaye, Sandy Ratcliff

Hustle
US 1975 118m Eastmancolor
Paramount/RoBurt (Robert Aldrich)

A police lieutenant lives with a call girl and is drawn into her corrupt life.
Doleful crime melodrama with both eyes in the gutter.
w Steve Shagan *d* Robert Aldrich *ph* Joseph Biroc *m* Frank de Vol
☆ Burt Reynolds, Catherine Deneuve, Ben Johnson, Paul Winfield, Eileen Brennan, Eddie Albert, Ernest Borgnine, Catherine Bach, Jack Carter

'A fine companion piece to *Kiss Me Deadly* in its vision of a journey to the end of the night in quest of a myth.' – *Tim Milne*

'Even with such a meandering script as this, one expects more than the paltry fare Aldrich offers.' – *Paul Coleman*

The Hustler ****
US 1961 135m bw Cinemascope
TCF/Robert Rossen

A pool room con man comes to grief when he falls in love.
Downbeat melodrama with brilliantly handled and atmospheric pool table scenes; the love interest is redundant.
w Robert Rossen, Sidney Carroll *novel* Walter Tevis *d Robert Rossen ph Eugene Schufftan* *m* Kenyon Hopkins
☆ *Paul Newman, Jackie Gleason, George C. Scott, Piper Laurie, Myron McCormick,* Murray Hamilton, Michael Constantine

'There is an overall impression of intense violence, and the air of spiritual decadence has rarely been conveyed so vividly.' – *David Robinson*

'The supreme classic of that great American genre, the low-life movie.' – *Observer*

Eugene Schufftan
best picture; script; Robert Rossen (as director); Paul Newman; Jackie Gleason; George C. Scott; Piper Laurie
best picture; Paul Newman

'See it with someone you've paid for.'

Hustler White
US 1996 79m Monaco Film Lab
ICA/Hustler White (Jürgen Brüning, Bruce LaBruce)

A writer goes in search of a hustler who can introduce him to homosexual life in Los Angeles.
A film intended to shock in its camply defiant depiction of unusual and painful sexual practices; in this, it succeeds.
wd Bruce LaBruce, Rick Castro *ph* James Carman *m* UFO or Die *pd* Bruce LaBruce, Rick Castro *ed* Rider Siphron
☆ Tony Ward, Bruce LaBruce, Alex Austin, Kevin Kramer, Ron Athey, Glen Meadmore

'A grossly prurient show. It doesn't possess the remotest artistic merit; nor the slightest concern for suffering humanity in its heart, mind or loins.' – *Alexander Walker*

Hyenes
Senegal/France/Germany 1992 95m colour
ADR/Thelma/Maag Daan/MK2 (Pierre-Alain Meier, Alain Rozanes)
aka: *Hyenas*

Returning to her poverty-stricken home town, a rich old woman offers a fortune to the people if they will kill the man who wronged her 30 years before.
A naïve and melodramatic version of a familiar story.
wd Djibril Diop Mambéty *play The Visit* by Friedrich Dürrenmatt *ph* Matthias Kälin *m* Wasis Diop *ed* Loredana Cristelli
☆ Mansour Diouf, Ami Diakhate, Mamadou Mahouredia Gueye, Mbaba Diop de Rufisque, Abdoulaye Yama Diop, Calgou Fall, Djibril Diop Mambéty

Hyôryuu-gai
Japan 2000 105m colour
Daiei/Tokuma Shoten/Tohuku Shinsha/Tokyo FM (Kazunari Hashiguchi, Toshiki Kimura)

GB and US title: *City of Lost Souls*

In Tokyo, a Sino-Brazilian gangster and his Chinese girlfriend, an illegal immigrant, try to raise the money to leave the country before the yakuza kill them.
Bizarre, nihilistic thriller with a xenophobic theme, influenced by spaghetti westerns. It is composed of random violence, cartoon-styled cockfighting and unusual camera angles (including the view from the bottom of a lavatory bowl, while it is being used).
w Ichiro Ryu *novel* Seishu Hase *d* Takashi Miike *ph* Naosuke Imaizumi *m* Koji Endo *pd* Akira Ishige *ed* Yasushi Shimamura
☆ Teah (Mario), Michelle Reis (Kei), Patricia Manterola (Lucia), Mitsuhiro Oikawa (Mr Ko), Koji Kikkawa (Fushimi), Anatoli Krasnov (Khodoloskii)

'Miike is less a social philosopher than an unabashed entertainer, ready to do what it takes to hold the attention of his increasingly jaded audience. His formal gifts are evident; the uses he puts them to are trivial.' – *David Kehr, New York Times*

The Hypnotic Eye
US 1960 79m bw
Allied Artists

A mad killer hypnotizes pretty girls into defacing themselves.
Unattractive thriller including much mumbo-jumbo about hypnotism.
w Gitta and William Read Woodfield *d* George Blair *ph* Arch Dalzell *m* Marlin Skiles
☆ Jacques Bergerac, Allison Hayes, Merry Anders, Marcia Henderson

The Hypnotist: see *London After Midnight*

Hysteria
GB 1965 85m bw
MGM/Hammer (Jimmy Sangster)

An American suffering from amnesia is discharged from a London clinic and walks into a murder plot.
Complicated and rather unsympathetic Hammer twister.
w Jimmy Sangster *d* Freddie Francis *ph* John Wilcox *m* Don Banks *pd* Edward Carrick *ed* James Needs
☆ Robert Webber, Lelia Goldoni, Anthony Newlands, Jennifer Jayne, *Maurice Denham*, Peter Woodthorpe

I Accuse *
GB 1957 99m bw Cinemascope
MGM (Sam Zimbalist)
In 1894 Paris, Alfred Dreyfus is tried for treason and later defended by Emile Zola.
A well tried historical incident is stolidly retold and unsuitably wide-screened; the star cast tends to flounder for lack of assistance.
w Gore Vidal *d* José Ferrer *ph* Frederick A. Young *m* William Alwyn *ad* Elliot Scott
☆ José Ferrer (Dreyfus), *Anton Walbrook* (Esterhazy), Emlyn Williams (Zola), Viveca Lindfors, David Farrar, Leo Genn, Herbert Lom, Harry Andrews, Felix Aylmer, George Coulouris, Donald Wolfit

I Aim at the Stars
US 1960 107m bw
Columbia/Morningside/Fama (Charles H. Schneer)
The story of German rocket expert Wernher von Braun and his later work on American space vehicles.
Shaky biopic of a controversial scientist who changed sides.
w Jay Dratler *d* J. Lee-Thompson *ph* Wilkie Cooper *m* Laurie Johnson
☆ Curt Jurgens, Herbert Lom, James Daly, Gia Scala, Victoria Shaw, Adrian Hoven, Karel Stepanek
'Mannered panning shots and crafty cutting abound, leading to a stylistic St Vitus' Dance.' – *John Gillett*

'The biggest double exposure since Adam and Eve!'
I Am a Camera
GB 1955 99m bw
Romulus (Jack Clayton)
A young English writer observes life in Berlin in the early thirties, and has a platonic relationship with an amoral and reckless young English girl.
A rather flat and flabby treatment of the stories by Christopher Isherwood and the play by John Van Druten, all better known these days in the form of Cabaret. *Disappointingly unstylish.*
w John Collier *d* Henry Cornelius *ph* Guy Green *m* Malcolm Arnold
☆ Julie Harris, Laurence Harvey, Shelley Winters, Ron Randell, Anton Diffring
'A truly shocking and disgraceful mess.' – *Christopher Isherwood*

'Six sticks of dynamite that blasted his way to freedom ... and awoke America's conscience!'
I Am a Fugitive from a Chain Gang ****
US 1932 90m bw
Warner (Hal B. Wallis)
An innocent man is convicted and after brutal treatment with the chain gang becomes a vicious criminal on the run.
Horrifying story in the semi-documentary manner; a milestone in Hollywood history and still a fairly compelling piece of shock entertainment.
w Howard J. Green, Brown Holmes book Robert E. Burns d Mervyn Le Roy ph Sol Polito m Bernhard Kaun
☆ *Paul Muni*, Glenda Farrell, Helen Vinson, Preston Foster, Allen Jenkins, Edward J. Macnamara, Berton Churchill, Edward Ellis
'A picture with guts ... everything about it is technically 100% ... shy on romantic angles, but should get nice money all over.' – *Variety*
'To be enthusiastically commended for its courage, artistic sincerity, dramatic vigour, high entertainment concept and social message.' – *Wilton A. Barrett*
'I quarrel with the production not because it is savage and horrible, but because each step in an inevitable tragedy is taken clumsily, and because each character responsible for the hero's doom is shown more as a caricature than as a person.' – *Pare Lorentz*
best picture; Paul Muni

I Am Curious – Yellow *
Sweden 1967 116m bw
Sandrew Film
original title: *Jag är nyfiken – gul*
A drama student playing the role of a sociologist questions Swedish citizens on their attitudes to such matters as class, education, military service and non-violence while also discovering her own sexuality.
An important semi-documentary film of the 60s, influenced in its casual style by the French New Wave, and launching an all-out attack on bourgeois attitudes and morality. Its brief but uninhibited scenes of sex caused controversy at the time of its release and led to it becoming the centrepoint of debates on censorship.
wd Vilgot Sjöman *ph* Peter Wester
☆ Lena Nyman, Börje Ahlstedt, Peter Lindgren, Chris Wahlström, Marie Göranzon, Vilgot Sjöman
'Interesting in its shimmering, multifarious approach to life in Sweden today, in its frankness about sex. and in the considerable step ahead it marks in Vilgot Sjöman's artistic development.' – *John Simon*
'Tame by today's standards and tediously long.' – *Sight and Sound (1994)*
† The film was seized by US Customs and banned following a trial, but the verdict was overturned by the Court of Appeals. Much of the footage shot was used in a less interesting companion film, *I Am Curious – Blue*.

I Am Not Afraid
US 1939 59m bw
Warner (Bryan Foy)
GB title: *The Man Who Dared*
An old man testifies against political terrorists.
Tepid remake of Star Witness.
w Lee Katz *story* Lucien Hubbard *d* Crane Wilbur
☆ Charley Grapewin, Jane Bryan, Henry O'Neill, Elizabeth Risdon
'Filler for the duals.' – *Variety*

'Love is all you need.'
I Am Sam
US 2001 132m DeLuxe
Entertainment/New Line/Bedford Falls/Red Fish, Blue Fish/'Sam' (Jessie Nelson, Richard Solomon, Marshall Herskovitz, Edward Zwick)
A mentally retarded father fights attempts to take his clever, 7-year-old daughter away from him.
Sickly, manipulative drama, with a distressingly bad performance from Penn as the saintly Sam.
w Kristine Johnson, Jessie Nelson *d* Jessie Nelson *ph* Elliot Davis *m* John Powell *pd* Aaron Osborne *ed* Richard Chew
☆ Sean Penn (Sam Dawson), Michelle Pfeiffer (Rita Harrison), Dakota Fanning (Lucy), Dianne Wiest (Annie), Loretta Devine (Margaret Calgrove), Richard Schiff (Turner), Laura Dern (Randy Carpenter), Brad Allan Silverman (Brad)
'Its sentimentality is so relentless and its narrative so predictable that the life is very nearly squeezed out of it.' – *A. O. Scott, New York Times*
'The dumbing down of low-IQ sentimentality.' – *Owen Gleiberman, Entertainment Weekly*
Sean Penn

I Am Sexy: see *The Temptations of Marianne*

I Am the Cheese *
US 1983 95m TVC Color
Almi (David Lange)
With the aid of a therapist, a teenage boy recovers the truth about the death of his parents.
Slight and sometimes confusing psychological drama.
w David Lange, Robert Jiras *novel* Robert Cormier *d* Robert Jiras *ph* David Quaid *m* Jonathan Tunick *ed* Nicholas Smith
☆ Robert Macnaughton, Hope Lange, Don Murray, Robert Wagner, Cynthia Nixon, Sudie Bond, Robert Cormier
† The film was remade in 1992 as *Lapse of Memory* (qv).

I Am the Law *
US 1938 83m bw
Columbia (Everett Riskin)
A law professor is asked by a civic leader to become a special prosecutor cleaning up rackets.
Adequate star potboiler, quite enjoyable.
w Jo Swerling *d* Alexander Hall *ph* Henry Freulich *md* Morris Stoloff
☆ Edward G. Robinson, Otto Kruger, John Beal, Barbara O'Neil, Wendy Barrie, Arthur Loft, Marc Lawrence
'A slam-bang, rip-roaring meller that has all the elements of previous films inspired by District Attorney Thomas E. Dewey's career.' – *Variety*
'The liveliest melodrama in town.' – *New York Times*

I Became a Criminal: see *They Made Me a Fugitive*

I Believe in You *
GB 1952 95m bw
Ealing (Michael Relph)
Interwoven stories of probation officers.
Watchable and reasonable but not very compelling.
w Michael Relph, Basil Dearden, Jack Whittingham, Nicholas Phipps *d* Basil Dearden *ph* Gordon Dines *m* Ernest Irving
☆ Celia Johnson, Cecil Parker, Godfrey Tearle, Harry Fowler, George Relph, Joan Collins, Laurence Harvey, Ernest Jay, Ursula Howells, Sidney James, Katie Johnson, Ada Reeve, Brenda de Banzie

'Most Motorcycles Run on Petrol. This One Runs on Blood!'
I Bought a Vampire Motorcycle
GB 1989 105m colour
Hobo/Dirk Productions (Mycal Miller, John Wolskel)
A biker acquires a motorbike possessed by an evil spirit.
Low-budget tongue-in-cheek horror, full of ancient music-hall jokes.
w Mycal Miller *d* Dirk Campbell *ph* Tom Ingle *m* Dean Friedman *pd* Jose Furtado *ed* Mycal Miller *sp* Image Animation
☆ Neil Morrissey, Amanda Noar, Michael Elphick, Anthony Daniels, Andrew Powell, George Rossi, Midge Taylor, Daniel Peacock, Burt Kwouk
'An exuberant tribute to British comedy culture.' – *Screen International*

'The most spinechilling cry that can freeze the blood!'
I Bury the Living
US 1957 77m bw
UA/Maxim
The honorary chairman of a cemetery seems to have the power to mark people for death.
Unusual enough to be encouraging, sloppy enough to disappoint even mystery lovers.
w Louis Garfinkle *d* Albert Band *ph* Frederick Gately
☆ Richard Boone, Theodore Bikel, Herbert Anderson, Peggy Maurer

I Call First: see *Who's That Knocking at My Door*

I Can Get It for You Wholesale *
US 1951 89m bw
TCF (Sol C. Siegel)
GB title: *This Is My Affair*
US TV title: *Only the Best*
An ambitious young mannequin starts her own dressmaking firm and sets her sights high.
Watchable comedy-drama which quickly sheds the edge of satire which might have made it the dressmaker's All About Eve.
w Abraham Polonsky *novel* Jerome Weidman *d* Michael Gordon *ph* Milton Krasner *m* Sol Kaplan *md* Lionel Newman
☆ *Susan Hayward*, Dan Dailey, George Sanders, Sam Jaffe, Randy Stuart, Marvin Kaplan, Harry von Zell
'There is nothing remarkable about the film, except perhaps the carefree abandon with which pearl necklaces are broken, and the curious sidelight that is cast on the ethics of cutters and salesmen. It hadn't occurred to me before that the male partners of a modest costume house would go into voluntary bankruptcy sooner than let their dress designer live in sin, but I haven't moved much in wholesale circles of the garment trade.' – C. A. *Lejeune*

'I love, I have loved, I will love.'
I Capture the Castle
GB 2003 111m colour 'Scope
IDP/Trademark/BBC Films (Anant Singh, David M. Thompson, David Parfitt)
In the mid 1930s, two daughters of the impoverished family of an unsuccessful writer compete for the same man.
Unexpectedly charming romantic drama of crossed loves, given a precise period feel and a gentle comic touch.
w Heidi Thomas *novel* Dodie Smith *d* Tim Fywell *ph* Richard Greatrex *m* Dario Marianelli *pd* John-Paul Kelly *ed* Roy Sharman
☆ Romola Garai (Cassandra Mortmain), Rose Byrne (Rose Mortmain), Henry Thomas (Simon Cotton), Marc Blucas (Neil Cotton), Bill Nighy (James Mortmain), Tara Fitzgerald (Topaz Mortmain), Sinead Cusack (Mrs Cotton), Henry Cavill (Stephen Colley)
'Pert, good-looking entertainment that feels like a labour of love.' – *Anthony Quinn, Independent*

I Changed My Sex: see *Glen or Glenda*

I Come in Peace: see *Dark Angel*

'Crushed lips don't talk!'
I Confess **
US 1953 94m bw
Warner/Alfred Hitchcock
A priest hears the confession of a murderer and cannot divulge it to the police even though he is himself suspected.
Hitchcock is always worth watching, and although this old chestnut gives him very restricted scope he imbues the story with a strong feeling for its setting (Quebec) and an overpowering sense of doom.
w George Tabori, William Archibald *play* Paul Anthelme *d Alfred Hitchcock ph* Robert Burks *m* Dimitri Tiomkin
☆ Montgomery Clift, Anne Baxter, Brian Aherne, Karl Malden, Dolly Haas, O. E. Hasse
'Whatever its shortcomings, it has the professional concentration of effect, the narrative control, of a story teller who can still

make most of his rivals look like amateurs.' – MFB

I Could Go on Singing *
GB 1963 99m Eastmancolor Panavision
UA/Barbican (Lawrence Turman)

An American singing star in Britain looks up an old lover and tries to take over their illegitimate son, but the call of the footlights proves stronger.
The star enjoys her last specially-tailored role; a banal, old-fashioned agreeable one-woman show.
w Mayo Simon *d* Ronald Neame *ph* Arthur Ibbetson *m* Mort Lindsey
☆ *Judy Garland*, Dirk Bogarde, Aline MacMahon, Jack Klugman
'Merely standard fare in an age without standards.' – *John Simon*
♫ 'I Could Go on Singing'; 'Hello Bluebird'; 'It Never Was You'

I Cover the Waterfront *
US 1933 75m bw
Reliance (Edward Small)

A reporter uses a girl's friendship to expose her father's smuggling activities.
In its time a tough, even daring melodrama, this plot has now become the stuff of every other TV series episode.
w Wells Root, Jack Jevne, Max Miller *d James Cruze ph* Ray June *m* Alfred Newman
☆ Claudette Colbert, Ben Lyon, Ernest Torrence, Hobart Cavanaugh
'Combination of title, picturesque background and three good performances should offset inferior story for favourable business.' – *Variety*
'A bit raw and a bit sentimental and a bit routine, the film does let life in through the cracks.' – *Graham Greene*
† Credited with being the origin of the phrase, 'Not tonight, Josephine!'

'When You Go Undercover Remember One Thing. Who You Are.'
i.d.
GB/Germany 1995 107m colour
Polygram/BBC/Sales Company/Parallax/Metropolis (Sally Hibbin)

An ambitious young policeman, who goes undercover to expose the leaders of a gang of football hooligans, discovers that he enjoys violence.
A frenetic and gritty foray into topicality that avoids exploitation but not melodrama and overstatement.
w Vincent O'Connell *story* James Bannon *d* Philip Davis *ph* Thomas Mauch *m* Will Gregory *pd* Max Gottlieb *ed* Inge Behrens
☆ Reece Dinsdale, Richard Graham, Claire Skinner, Sean Pertwee, Saskia Reeves, Warren Clarke
'A raw-steak drama that packs a wallop when it's on form but suffers an intermittent i.d. crisis of its own in the script department when it comes to delivering the psychological goods.' – *Derek Elley, Variety*

I Didn't Do It
GB 1945 97m bw
Columbia (Ben Henry, Marcel Varnel)
Murder in a theatrical boarding house, with suspicion pointing at Our George.
One of the star's last vehicles: not too bad at all, but without the sweet smell of success.
w Howard Irving Young, Stephen Black, Norman Lee, Peter Fraser, Michael Vaughan *d* Marcel Varnel *ph* Roy Fogwell
☆ George Formby, Billy Caryll, Hilda Mundy, Gaston Palmer, Jack Daly, Carl Jaffe, Marjorie Browne, Wally Patch

I Died a Thousand Times
US 1955 109m Warnercolor Cinemascope
Warner (Willis Goldbeck)

An ex-convict plans a big hotel robbery, but things go wrong within his gang.
Overlong, heavygoing, tedious gangster melodrama with too much talk.
w W. R. Burnett *d* Stuart Heisler *ph* Ted McCord *m* David Buttolph *ad* Edward Carrere *ed* Clarence Kolster
☆ Jack Palance, Shelley Winters, Lori Nelson, Lon Chaney Jnr, Lee Marvin, Gonzales Gonzales, Earl Holliman, Perry Lopez
'This remake of *High Sierra* is scarcely more inspired than its title.' – *MFB*
'It is an insult to the intelligence to pull this old mythological hero out of the archives and set him on a mountaintop again.' – *New York Times*

The I Don't Care Girl *
US 1953 78m Technicolor
TCF (George Jessel)
The life of musical entertainer Eva Tanguay, at her height during World War I, as told by three men in her life.
Breezy, conventional backstage musical biopic.
w Walter Bullock *d* Lloyd Bacon *ph* Arthur Arling *md* Lionel Newman *ch* Jack Cole, Seymour Felix
☆ Mitzi Gaynor, David Wayne, Oscar Levant, *George Jessel*, Warren Stevens

I Don't Kiss: see *J'Embrasse Pas*

'It's Evil...It's Horrific...It's Conceived By The Devil'
I Don't Want to Be Born
GB 1975 94m Eastmancolor
Rank/Unicapital (Norma Corney)

US title: *The Devil within Her*
An ex-stripper gives birth to a monstrous baby which goes on a murderous rampage.
Sick horror stuff with a high death rate and no notable credits.
w Stanley Price *d* Peter Sasdy *ph* Ken Talbot *m* Ron Grainer
☆ Joan Collins, Ralph Bates, Donald Pleasence, Eileen Atkins, George Claydon

I Don't Want to Talk about It: see *We Don't Want to Talk about It*

I Dood It!
US 1943 102m bw
MGM (Jack Cummings)

GB title: *By Hook or by Crook*
A tailor falls for a Hollywood star.
Boring star comedy with interpolated musical numbers.
w Sig Herzig, Fred Saidy *d* Vincente Minnelli *ph* Ray June *md* George Stoll
☆ Red Skelton, Eleanor Powell, John Hodiak, Lena Horne, Jimmy Dorsey and his Orchestra, Hazel Scott, Richard Ainley

I Dream of Jeannie
US 1952 90m Trucolor
Republic
The loves and financial problems of songwriter Stephen Foster.
Low-key musical biopic covering exactly the same ground as Swanee River.
w Alan Le May *d* Allan Dwan *ph* Reggie Lanning
☆ Ray Middleton (E. P. Christy), Bill Shirley, Muriel Lawrence, Rex Allen

I Dream Too Much
US 1935 95m bw
RKO (Pandro S. Berman)

A French girl singer marries an American composer.
Forgettable vehicle for an operatic star.
w Edmund North, James Gow *d* John Cromwell *ph* David Abel *m/ly* Jerome Kern, Dorothy Fields *md* Max Steiner
☆ Lily Pons, Henry Fonda, Eric Blore, Osgood Perkins, Lucien Littlefield, Lucille Ball, Esther Dale, Mischa Auer, Paul Porcasi
'It will be a winner at the box office without breaking any records.' – *Variety*

'Sometimes the adventure of a lifetime becomes life itself.'
I Dreamed of Africa
US/Germany 2000 114m colour
Columbia/Jaffilms (Stanley R. Jaffe, Allyn Stewart)

After surviving a car crash, an Italian woman makes a difficult marriage and goes to Africa with her husband and young son in search of fulfilment.
Glossy, stilted epic that tries for a grand, romantic style but seems merely overblown.
w Paula Milne, Susan Shilliday *book* Kuki Gallmann *d* Hugh Hudson *ph* Bernard Lutic *m* Maurice Jarre *pd* Andrew Sanders *ed* Scott Thomas *cos* Shirley Russell
☆ Kim Basinger (Kuki Gallmann), Vincent Perez (Paolo Gallmann), Liam Aiken (Emanuele, at 7), Garrett Strommen (Emanuele, at 17), Eva Marie Saint (Franca), Daniel Craig (Declan Fielding), Lance Reddick (Simon), Connie Chiume (Wanjiku), James Ngobese (Luka), Ian Robert (Mike Donovan)
'The scenic but ultimately hollow results resemble a dazzling wildlife documentary with a dull melodrama obtrusively attached.' – *Danny Leigh, Sight and Sound*

I Escaped from Devil's Island
US 1973 81m DeLuxe
UA (Roger Corman, Gene Corman)
In 1918, a black convict makes his plans for escape.
Rough, brutish melodrama which plainly aimed to beat Papillon *to the box-office.*
w Richard L. Adams *d* William Witney *ph* Rosalio Solano *m* Les Baxter
☆ Jim Brown, Christopher George, Rick Ely, James Luisi, Richard Rust
'Exploitation's own *Papillon*, mercifully free from big brother's pretentiousness.' – *Sight and Sound*

I Even Knew Happy Gypsies: see *Happy Gypsies*

I Found Stella Parish
US 1935 85m bw
Warner (Harry Joe Brown)
An actress tries to keep her naughty past from her child, but a blackmailer strikes.
One for the ladies, who flocked to it in its day.
w Casey Robinson *d* Mervyn Le Roy
☆ Kay Francis, Paul Lukas, Ian Hunter, Sybil Jason, Jessie Ralph, Barton MacLane
'Will receive widespread support at the box office all the way from the best runs down to the subsequents, in the big keys and in the smallest towns.' – *Variety*

I Have a New Master: see *L'Ecole Buissonière*

I Hired a Contract Killer
Finland/Sweden 1990 79m Metrocolor
Electric/Contemporary/Villealfa/Swedish Film Institute (Aki Kaurismäki)

An unhappy man hires someone to kill him, and then decides he wants to live.
Lacklustre comedy.
wd Aki Kaurismäki *ph* Timo Salminen *pd* John Ebden *ed* Aki Kaurismäki
☆ Jean-Pierre Léaud, Margi Clarke, Kenneth Colley, Trevor Bowen, Imogen Clare, Angela Walsh, Cyril Epstein, Nicky Tesco

I Killed Rasputin
France/Italy 1967 100m Eastmancolor Franscope
Copernic/CGC (Raymond Danon)
The evil monk of the Russian court is killed by Prince Yusopov.
Dull version of a much told story. One of the big international films that never seem to get shown anywhere.
w Alain Decaux, Claude Desailly, Robert Hossein *d* Robert Hossein *ph* Henri Persin *m* André Hossein
☆ Gert Frobe, Peter McEnery, Robert Hossein, Geraldine Chaplin, Ira Furstenberg, Patrick Balkany
'A tedious illustrated history lesson which actually manages to obscure the motivation behind the murder.' – *MFB*
† The script was authorized by Prince Yusopov.

I Killed the Count
GB 1939 89m bw
Grafton (Isadore Goldschmidt)
US title: *Who is Guilty?*
Four people confess to the murder of a philanderer.
Inept version of a West End success.
w Alec Coppel, Lawrence Huntington *play* Alec Coppel *d* Fred Zelnik *ph* Bryan Langley *ed* Sam Simmonds
☆ Syd Walker, Ben Lyon, Terence de Marney, Barbara Blair, Antoinette Cellier, Kathleen Harrison, Athole Stewart, Leslie Perrins, Ronald Shiner

I Know What You Did Last Summer
US 1997 101m Technicolor Panavision
Entertainment/Mandalay (Neal H. Moritz, Erik Feig, Stokely Chaffin)

A fisherman begins to murder a group of young friends, who concealed their involvement in the death of a stranger in a hit-and-run accident.
A knowing but predictable variation on the usual slasher movie; it merely reshuffles the clichés of the genre.
w Kevin Williamson *novel* Lois Duncan *d* Jim Gillespie *ph* Denis Crossan *m* John Debney *pd* Gary Wissner *ed* Steve Mirkovich
☆ Jennifer Love Hewitt, Sarah Michelle Gellar, Ryan Phillippe, Freddie Prinze Jnr, Muse Watson, Anne Heche, Bridgette Wilson, Johnny Galecki
'A polished genre piece with superior fright elements.' – *Variety*
† The film cost $17m and took more than $70m at the US box-office.

I Know Where I'm Going **
GB 1945 91m bw
GFD/The Archers (Michael Powell, Emeric Pressburger)

A determined girl travels to the Hebrides to marry a wealthy old man, but is stranded on Mull and marries a young naval officer instead.
A strange assembling of attractive but disparate elements: romance, comedy, bleak scenery, a trained hawk and a dangerous whirlpool. At the time it seemed to represent the Elizabethan age of the British cinema, and remains entertaining for its parts though a bit of a puzzle as a whole.
wd Michael Powell, *Emeric Pressburger ph* Erwin Hillier
☆ *Wendy Hiller, Roger Livesey*, Pamela Brown, Nancy Price, Finlay Currie, John Laurie, George Carney, Walter Hudd
'Continuously fresh and interesting, intelligently written and played, and full of beautiful photography.' – *Richard Mallett, Punch*
'The sensitive photography and the intelligent if not very imaginative use of sound do more than enough to make eloquent the influence of place on people; and the whole thing is undertaken with taste and modesty.' – *James Agee*

I Led Two Lives: see *Glen or Glenda*

I Like It Like That *
US 1994 105m Technicolor
Columbia TriStar/Think Again (Ann Carli, Lane Janger)

In the Bronx, a feckless husband and his wife begin affairs and separate, though their intention is to make each other jealous.
Stolid romance of raucous life on and off the New York streets, well observed though not straying far from movie conventions in its depiction of working-class existence.
wd Darnell Martin *ph* Alexander Gruszynski *m* Sergio George *pd* Scott Chambliss *ed* Peter C. Frank
☆ Lauren Velz, Jon Seda, Desiree Casado, Tomas Melly, Griffin Dunne, Rita Moreno, Lisa Vidal
'From its wittily choreographed opening shot onwards, the film crackles with unforced comedy and invention. Its freshness is all the more surprising when you consider that the movie is largely built from clichés.' – *Kevin Jackson, Independent*
† Darnell Martin is the first black woman to write and direct a movie for a major Hollywood studio.

I Like Money: see *Mr Topaze*

I Live for Love
US 1935 83m bw
Warner (Bryan Foy)
GB title: *I Live For You*
A socialite has show business leanings.
Minor musical.
w Jerry Wald, Julius Epstein, Robert Andrews *ph* George Barnes *md* Leo F. Forbstein *d/ch* Busby Berkeley
☆ Dolores del Rio, Everett Marshall, Allen Jenkins, Eddie Conrad, Guy Kibbee, Berton Churchill

I Live for You: see *I Live for Love*

I Live in Fear: see *Ikimono No Kiroku*

I Live in Grosvenor Square
GB 1945 113m bw
ABP (Herbert Wilcox)
US title: *A Yank in London*
A duke's daughter falls in love with an American air force sergeant.
Sloppily-made topical romance which was hot box-office at the time and started the producer's 'London' romances: Piccadilly Incident, Spring in Park Lane, Maytime in Mayfair, *etc.*
w Nicholas Phipps, William D. Bayles, Maurice Cowan *d* Herbert Wilcox *ph* Max Greene *m* Anthony Collins
☆ Anna Neagle, *Dean Jagger*, Rex Harrison, Robert Morley, Jane Darwell, Nancy Price, Irene Vanbrugh, Edward Rigby, Walter Hudd
'I take it that the whole thing is an elaborate effort to promote goodwill and understanding between the Americans and ourselves. Good! But must the management, in order to do this, give us quite such an improbable version of English town and country life during the war?' – *James Agate*

I Live My Life
US 1935 85m bw
MGM (Bernard H. Hyman)
A bored society girl falls for a working-class archaeologist.
Standard star romance.
w Joseph L. Mankiewicz *story* *Claustrophobia* by A. Carter Goodloe *d* W. S. Van Dyke II *ph* George Folsey *m* Dimitri Tiomkin
☆ Joan Crawford, Brian Aherne, Frank Morgan, Aline MacMahon, Eric Blore, Jessie Ralph, Arthur Treacher, Hedda Hopper, Etienne Girardot, Ed Brophy
'An amusing romance is backgrounded by clothes, cocktails and butlers.' – *Variety*

I Love a Man in Uniform *
Canada 1993 97m colour
Metro Tartan/Alliance/Miracle (Paul Brown)
An actor who plays the part of a policeman in a television series carries the role over into real life.
A creepy drama, in which reality and illusion become increasingly blurred and sanity declines into madness.
wd David Wellington *ph* David Franco *m* Ron Sures and the Tragically Hip *pd* John Dondertman *ed* Susan Shipton
☆ Tom McCamus, Brigitte Bako, Kevin Tighe, David Hemblen, Alex Karzis, Graham McPherson
'A hugely impressive and highly compelling first feature.' – *Empire*

I Love a Mystery *
US 1945 68m bw
Columbia
An eastern secret society offers a businessman a large sum for his head when he dies, as he resembles their founder whose embalmed head is deteriorating.
Start of a short series of mysteries from a radio series; the production was never up to the ingenious plots.
w Charles O'Neal *d* Henry Levin *ph* Burnett Guffey *m* Mario Castelnuovo-Tedesco
☆ *George Macready*, Jim Bannon, Nina Foch

'She kissed the boys goodbye – until Sonny said hello!'
I Love a Soldier
US 1944 106m bw
Paramount (Mark Sandrich)
A San Francisco girl thinks hard before embarking on a wartime marriage.
Glossy, insubstantial sudser chiefly memorable for casting its leading lady as a welder.
w Allan Scott *d* Mark Sandrich *ph* *Charles Lang* *m* Robert Emmett Dolan
☆ Paulette Goddard, Sonny Tufts, Beulah Bondi, Walter Sande, Mary Treen, Ann Doran, Barry Fitzgerald

I Love Melvin *
US 1953 77m Technicolor
MGM (George Wells)
A photographer's assistant falls for a high-born chorus girl.
Zippy little musical with all concerned working hard with thin material.
w George Wells *d* Don Weis *ph* Harold Rosson *m/ly* Josef Myrow, Mack Gordon *md* George Stoll *ch* Robert Alton
☆ Donald O'Connor, Debbie Reynolds, Una Merkel, Allyn Joslyn

I Love My Wife
US 1970 95m Technicolor
Universal (Robert Kaufman)
The affairs of a successful doctor with a guilt complex about sex.
Frantic, fashionable comedy drama with wildly erratic treatment and performances.
w Robert Kaufman *d* Mel Stuart *ph* Vilis Lapenieks *m* Lalo Schifrin
☆ Elliott Gould, Brenda Vaccaro, Angel Tompkins
'A leer-laden, anti-feminist tract disguised as a comedy.' – *Judith Crist*

I Love Trouble
US 1947 93m bw
Columbia/S. Sylvan Simon
A private eye tries to trace the background of a politician's wife.
Standard urban mystery with loose ends, a few notches below Raymond Chandler.
w Roy Huggins *novel* *The Double Take* by Roy Huggins *d* S. Sylvan Simon
☆ Franchot Tone, Janet Blair, Janis Carter, Adele Jergens, Glenda Farrell, Steve Geray, Tom Powers

I Love Trouble
US 1994 123m Technicolor
Buena Vista/Touchstone/Caravan (Nancy Meyers)
A hard-drinking veteran journalist is scooped on an investigative story by a glamorous new reporter but marries her anyway.
A romantic comedy that misses out on the romance and the wit.
w Nancy Meyers, Charles Shyer *d* Charles Shyer *ph* John Lindley *m* David Newman *pd* Dean Tavoularis *ed* Paul Hirsch, Walter Murch, Adam Bernardi
☆ Julia Roberts, Nick Nolte, Saul Rubinek, Robert Loggia, James Rebhorn, Olympia Dukakis, Marsha Mason, Charles Martin Smith, Kelly Rutherford
'Stands as yet further proof of how hard it is to make a soufflé, as well as to successfully create the pure pleasure of the old movies today's filmmakers so revere.' – *Todd McCarthy, Variety*
'The most run-of-the-mill newspaper picture of 50 years ago was brisker, funnier, more exciting (and an hour shorter) than Charles Shyer's feeble offering.' – *Philip French, Observer*

I Love You Again *
US 1940 99m bw
MGM (Lawrence Weingarten)
A much married man gets amnesia and turns into a gay Lothario.
Sprightly romantic comedy with all concerned letting rip until the pace slows.
w Charles Lederer, George Oppenheimer, Harry Kurnitz *d* W. S. Van Dyke II *ph* Oliver T. Marsh *m* Franz Waxman
☆ *William Powell, Myrna Loy*, Frank McHugh, Edmund Lowe, Donald Douglas, Nella Walker, Pierre Watkin

I Love You, Alice B. Toklas *
US 1968 93m Technicolor
Warner Seven Arts/Paul Mazursky, Larry Tucker
An asthmatic Los Angeles lawyer escapes his bullying fiancée by joining the flower people.
Quite amusing satirical farce about the dangers of marijuana, Gertrude Stein and Jewish mothers, thrown together with no great sense of style but achieving hilarious moments among the longueurs.
w *Paul Mazursky, Larry Tucker* *d* Hy Averback *ph* Philip Lathrop *m* Elmer Bernstein *pd* Pato Guzman
☆ *Peter Sellers*, Jo Van Fleet, Joyce Van Patten, Leigh Taylor-Young, David Arkin, Herb Edelman

I Love You No More: see *Je T'Aime Moi Non Plus*

I Love You to Death
US 1990 97m Technicolor
Columbia TriStar/Chestnut Hill (Jeffrey Lurie, Ron Moler)
Discovering her husband's philandering, a wife decides to have him killed.
Black comedy that runs out of jokes.
w John Kostmayer *d* Lawrence Kasdan *ph* Owen Roizman *m* James Horner *pd* Lilly Kilvert *ed* Anne V. Coates
☆ Kevin Kline, Tracey Ullman, Joan Plowright, River Phoenix, William Hurt, Keanu Reeves, James Gammon, Jack Kehler, Victoria Jackson
'Over-the-top farce.' – *David Robinson, The Times*
'A stillborn attempt at black comedy that wastes considerable acting talent.' – *Variety*

'Lips of thunder on lips of fire!'
I Loved a Woman *
US 1933 90m bw
Warner (Henry Blanke)
The career of a Chicago meat packer is hampered by his social-climbing wife.
Potboiling star melodrama which still holds some interest.
w Charles Kenyon, Sidney Sutherland *d* Alfred E. Green *ph* James Van Trees
☆ Edward G. Robinson, Kay Francis, Genevieve Tobin, J. Farrell MacDonald, Henry Kolker, Robert Barrat
'E.G.R. out of his class; may cut biz.' – *Variety*

I, Madman *
US 1989 89m colour
Sarlui/Diamant (Rafael Eisenman)
A bookshop assistant finds that the trashy novel she is reading about a mad, murderous doctor is coming true.
Above average horror, sillier than most in its premise, but performed and directed with some style.
w David Chaskin *d* Tibor Takacs *ph* Bryan England *m* Michael Hoenig *ed* Marcus Manton *sp* Randall William Cook
☆ Jenny Wright, Clayton Rohner, Randall William Cook, Steven Memel, Stephanie Hodge, Michelle Jordan

I Married a Communist: see *The Woman on Pier 13*

I Married a Dead Man
France 1983 110m colour
Sara/TF1 (Alain Sarde)
original title: *J'ai Épousé une Ombre*
aka: *I Married a Shadow*
Following a train crash, an abandoned pregnant woman assumes the identity of a wealthy mother-to-be.
Moderately effective remake of No Man of Her Own, *which was made in 1950.*
w Patrick Laurent, Robin Davis *novel* William Irish *d* Robin Davis *ph* Bernard Zitzermann *m* Philippe Sarde *ad* Ivan Maussion *ed* Marie Castro Vazquez
☆ Nathalie Baye, Francis Huster, Richard Bohringer, Madeleine Robinson, Guy Trejan, Victoria Abril

I Married a Monster from Outer Space *
US 1958 78m bw
Paramount/Gene Fowler Jnr
A young man is taken over by alien invaders but his wife helps to destroy them and bring him back to normal.
Decent, plodding, reasonably effective low-budget science fiction on a well-trampled theme; its minor virtues have been effaced by its silly title.
w Louis Vittes *d* Gene Fowler Jnr *ph* Haskell Boggs *sp* John P. Fulton
☆ Tom Tryon, Gloria Talbott, Robert Ivers
'Carries imaginative plottage which makes it strong fare.' – *Variety*
'Its underlying messages about society and, more specifically, women, are important ones that are particularly relevant today.' – *Cinefantastique, 1974*

I Married a Nazi: see *The Man I Married*

I Married a Shadow: see *I Married a Dead Man*

'She knows all about love potions ... and lovely motions!'
I Married a Witch ***
US 1942 82m bw
UA/Cinema Guild/René Clair
A Salem witch and her sorcerer father come back to haunt the descendant of the Puritan who had them burned.
Delightful romantic comedy fantasy which shows all concerned at the top of their form. Hollywood moonshine, impeccably distilled.
w *Robert Pirosh, Marc Connelly* *novel* *The Passionate Witch* by Thorne Smith *d* *René Clair* *ph* Ted Tetzlaff *m* Roy Webb
☆ *Fredric March, Veronica Lake, Cecil Kellaway, Robert Benchley*, Susan Hayward, Elizabeth Patterson, Robert Warwick
'A delightful sense of oddity and enchantment.' – *New York World Telegram*
Roy Webb

I Married a Woman
US 1956 85m bw (colour sequence)
RKOscope
RKO
A nervous young advertising executive neglects his wife, who determines to make him jealous.
Simple-minded comedy tailored to unsympathetic stars.
w Goodman Ace *d* Hal Kanter *ph* Lucien Ballard *m* Cyril Mockridge
☆ George Gobel, Diana Dors, Adolphe Menjou, Jessie Royce Landis, Nita Talbot

'It brings laughter and song to the screen as this pair from paradise is joyously reunited!'
I Married an Angel
US 1942 84m bw
MGM (Hunt Stromberg)
An attractive angel lures a playboy from his earthly girlfriends.
Silly musical fantasy which spelled the end of a great musical star partnership.
w Anita Loos *play* Vaszary Janos *d* W. S. Van Dyke *ph* Ray June *m/ly* Richard Rodgers, Lorenz Hart
☆ Jeanette MacDonald, Nelson Eddy, Edward Everett Horton, Binnie Barnes, Reginald Owen, Douglass Dumbrille
'As bland as operetta but without its energy.' – *New Yorker, 1978*

I Met a Murderer *
GB 1939 78m bw
Grand National/Gamma (Roy Kellino, Pamela Kellino, James Mason)
A murderer on the run meets a girl novelist who is touring in her motor caravan.
Semi-professional location melodrama which won commendation at the time but now seems very faded.
w Pamela Kellino, James Mason *d* Roy Kellino *ph* Roy Kellino *m* Eric Ansell *ed* Fergus McDonnell
☆ James Mason, Pamela Kellino, Sylvia Coleridge, William Devlin, Peter Coke
'Graceful, gallant, resourceful ... better and more enjoyable than most studio pictures.' – *James Agee*
'That it has a number of defects does not mean that it is not worthy of serious consideration.' – *Basil Wright*

I Met Him in Paris *
US 1937 86m bw
Paramount (Wesley Ruggles)
A fashion designer spends five years' savings on a fling in Paris and finds herself pursued to Switzerland by two philanderers.
Not very witty but likeable romantic comedy with polished performers near their best.
w Claude Binyon *d* Wesley Ruggles *ph* Leo Tover *m* John Leopold *md* Boris Morros
☆ *Claudette Colbert, Melvyn Douglas, Robert Young*, Lee Bowman, Mona Barrie
'A money picture ... laughs are piled on laughs.' – *Variety*
'At least half the footage is a perfect scream, and if you miss it you are an old sobersides, and who cares.' – *Otis Ferguson*

I Met My Love Again
US 1937 77m bw
Walter Wanger
A small-town girl marries a drunken writer, but on his death returns to her first love, a biology professor.
Mildly pleasing, rather dated romantic drama with good local colour.
w David Hertz *novel* *Summer Lightning* by Aileen Corliss *d* Joshua Logan, Arthur Ripley *ph* Hal Mohr *m* Heinz Roemheld
☆ Henry Fonda, Joan Bennett, Alan Marshal, Dorothy Stickney, Dame May Whitty, Alan Baxter, Louise Platt, Tim Holt, Florence Lake
'Sentimentally as sticky as a gum drop, this sugar-coated romance will have to find its favour with the femmes.' – *Variety*

I, Mobster
US 1958 80m bw Cinemascope
Edward L. Alperson (Roger Corman, Gene Corman)
A slum teenager becomes a top gangster.
Routine gangland thriller.
w Steve Fisher *novel* Joseph Hilton Smith *d* Roger Corman *ph* Floyd Crosby *m* Gerald Fried *ad* Daniel Haller *ed* William B. Murphy
☆ Steve Cochran, Lita Milan, Robert Strauss, Celia Lovsky, Grant Withers

I, Monster *
GB 1971 75m Eastmancolor
Amicus (Milton Subotsky)
A straight remake of *Dr Jekyll and Mr Hyde*, holding closely to the original novel but mysteriously using different names.
Interesting minor work.
w Milton Subotsky *d* Stephen Weeks *ph* Moray Grant *m* Carl Davis *ad* Tony Curtis
☆ Christopher Lee, Peter Cushing, Richard Hurndall, George Merritt, Mike Raven

I Never Promised You a Rose Garden
US 1977 96m colour
New World/Imorh/Fadsin (Roger Corman)
A suicidal teenage girl is treated in a psychiatric hospital.
Careful, thoughtful case history which can't help, after so many TV movies of the kind, seeming rather too simple for a theatrical feature, as well as too heavy-going despite the upbeat ending.
w Gavin Lambert, Lewis John Carlino *novel* Hannah Green *d* Anthony Page *ph* Bruce Logan *m* Paul Chihara *pd* Toby Rafelson
☆ Kathleen Quinlan, Bibi Andersson, Sylvia Sidney, Ben Piazza, Lorraine Gary, Reni Santoni, Signe Hasso
🏆 best adapted screenplay

I Never Sang for My Father *
US 1969 92m Technicolor
Columbia/Jamel (Gilbert Cates)
When his mother dies, a middle-aged widower is saddled with his cantankerous father, who tries to prevent him from remarrying.
Literal transcription of a Eugene O'Neillish play, a fascinating if depressing character study.
w Robert Anderson play Robert Anderson *d Gilbert Cates ph* Morris Hartzband, George Stoetzel *m* Al Gorgoni, Barry Mann
☆ *Melvyn Douglas, Gene Hackman, Dorothy Stickney*, Estelle Parsons
🏆 Robert Anderson; Melvyn Douglas; Gene Hackman

I Only Want You to Love Me *
West Germany 1976 104m colour
Bavaria Atelier (Peter Märthesheimer)
original title: *Ich Will Doch Nur, Das Ihr Mich Liebt*
A man denied parental affection, and discovering the lack of love between his mother and father, finds that he is unable to cope with the pressures of his own marriage.
Affecting small-scale domestic drama, probing the cause of violence, originally made for German television.
wd Rainer Werner Fassbinder *book* *Life Sentence (Lebenslänglich)* by Klaus Antes, Christiane Ehrhardt *ph* Michael Ballhaus *m* Peer Raben *ed* Liesgret Schmitt-Klink
☆ Vitus Zeplichal, Elke Aberle, Alexander Allerson, Ernie Mangold, Johanna Hofer, Wolfgang Hess

I Ought to Be in Pictures *
US 1982 107m DeLuxe
TCF (Herbert Ross, Neil Simon)
A young actress hitch-hikes to Hollywood to break into pictures and also to see her estranged scriptwriter father.
Fairly agreeable comedy-drama in the Neil Simon manner, with the studio background an extra plus.
w Neil Simon *play* Neil Simon *d* Herbert Ross *ph* David M. Walsh *m* Marvin Hamlisch *pd* Albert Brenner
☆ Walter Matthau, Ann-Margret, Dinah Manoff, Lance Guest, Lewis Smith

IP5
France 1992 119m colour Panavision
Artificial Eye/Cargo/Gaumont (Jean-Jacques Beineix)
A black rap performer and a graffiti artist steal a car on a trip across France and discover an old man on the back seat.
A road movie that covers a lot of ground without getting anywhere; it attempts romance but achieves whimsy.
w Jean-Jacques Beineix, Jacques Forgeas *d* Jean-Jacques Beineix *ph* Jean-François Robin *m* Gabriel Yared *ad* Dan Weil *ed* Joëlle Hache
☆ Yves Montand, Olivier Martinez, Sekkou Sall, Géraldine Pailhas, Colette Renard, Sotigui Kouyate
'Beineix specialises in a grandiloquent glossiness that masquerades as art.' – *Nigel Andrews, Financial Times*
'A dismal French road movie.' – *Philip French, Observer*
† It was Yves Montand's last film.

I Passed for White
US 1960 92m bw
Allied Artists (Fred M. Wilcox)
A light-skinned Negress comes to New York but fails to achieve happiness by pretending to be white.
Earnest, rather dreary social drama which doesn't get anywhere.
d Fred M. Wilcox *ph* George J. Folsey *m* Johnny Williams
☆ Sonya Wilde, James Franciscus, Pat Michon, Elizabeth Council

I.Q.
US 1994 95m DeLuxe Super 35
UIP/Sandollar (Carol Baum, Fred Schepisi)
Albert Einstein encourages a garage mechanic to court his niece by pretending to be a physicist.
A downright peculiar romantic comedy that gains very little from its introduction of renowned scientists into a mundane situation comedy; what it really needed was for Einstein and his cronies to be played by the Three Stooges.
w Andy Breckman, Michael Leeson *d* Fred Schepisi *ph* Ian Baker *m* Jerry Goldsmith *pd* Stuart Wurtzel *ed* Jill Bilcock
☆ Tim Robbins, Meg Ryan, Walter Matthau (Einstein), Gene Saks, Lou Jacobi, Stephen Fry, Joseph Maher, Frank Whaley, Tony Shalhoub, Charles Durning, Keene Curtis (as Eisenhower)
'Disappointingly bland Capraesque comedy.' – *Philip French, Observer*

'The sweetest movie anyone would ever wish to see!'
I Remember Mama **
US 1948 134m bw
RKO (Harriet Parsons)
A novelist remembers some of the adventures of growing up with her Norwegian-American family.
Overlong, but well-upholstered nostalgia: warm-hearted, sentimental, nicely detailed, richly acted but just a little boring in spots.
w De Witt Bodeen *play* John Van Druten *book* *Mama's Bank Account* by *Kathryn Forbes* *d George Stevens ph* Nicholas Musuraca *m* Roy Webb
☆ *Irene Dunne, Barbara Bel Geddes, Oscar Homolka, Edgar Bergen, Philip Dorn, Ellen Corby*, Florence Bates, Cedric Hardwicke, Barbara O'Neil, Rudy Vallee
🏆 Nicholas Musuraca; Irene Dunne; Barbara Bel Geddes; Oscar Homolka; Ellen Corby

I Saw What You Did
US 1965 82m bw
Universal/William Castle
A murderer thinks that two playful teenagers have witnessed his deed, and sets out to kill them too.
Predictable and long-winded suspenser, very short of inventive detail.
w William McGivern *novel* Ursula Curtiss *d* William Castle *ph* Joseph Biroc *m* Van Alexander
☆ John Ireland, Joan Crawford, Leif Erickson

I See a Dark Stranger **
GB 1945 112m bw
GFD/Individual (Frank Launder, Sidney Gilliat)
US title: *The Adventuress*
An Irish colleen who hates the English comes to England to spy for the Germans but falls in love with a young English officer.
Slipshod plotting does not quite destroy the jolly atmosphere of this comedy-thriller which has the cheek to take an IRA member as its heroine. Good fun, very well staged.
w Frank Launder, Sidney Gilliat, Wolfgang Wilhelm d Frank Launder ph Wilkie Cooper *m* William Alwyn
☆ Deborah Kerr, Trevor Howard, Raymond Huntley, Norman Shelley, Michael Howard, Brenda Bruce, Liam Redmond, Brefni O'Rorke
'It is the cinematic equivalent of Irish blarney which inspires most of this picture.' – *MFB*
'There is some intelligence, grace and fun here, but essentially this seems to me a supercilious drama, as if it had been made by bright young men who had decided to package and toss a bone to the groundlings.' – *James Agee*

I Sent a Letter to My Love **
France 1981 102m colour
Cineproductions (Lise Fauyolles, Giorgio Silvagni)
original title: *Chère Inconnue*
A crippled brother unknowingly carries on a love affair by letter with his sister.
Gentle tale of two lonely people finding an unexpected release from each other.
w Moshe Mizrahi, Gérard Brach *novel* Bernice Rubens *d* Moshe Mizrahi *ph* Ghislain Cloquet *m* Philippe Sarde *ad* Bernard Evein *ed* Françoise Bonnot
☆ Simone Signoret, Jean Rochefort, Delphine Seyrig, Genevieve Fontanel, Dominique Labourier
'Insensitive direction and unconvincing performances ruin an interesting dramatic idea.' – *Variety*
'This muted, smouldering French film first teases and eventually clutches our emotions.' – *Judith Crist, Saturday Review*

I Shall Return: see *An American Guerilla in the Philippines*

'You only get one shot at fame.'
I Shot Andy Warhol *
GB 1996 106m Technicolor
Electric/Playhouse/Samuel Goldwyn/BBC Arena (Tom Kalin, Christine Vachon)
Frustrated by her failure to make an impact on the world, the lesbian founder of SCUM (the Society for Cutting Up Men) attempts to kill Andy Warhol.
Intriguing biopic, of interest not so much for its concentration on the inadequacies of its central character as for its recreation of New York's louche artistic community of the late 60s.
w Mary Harron, Daniel Minahan *d* Mary Harron *ph* Ellen Kuras *m* John Cale *pd* Therese Deprez *ed* Keith Reamer
☆ Lili Taylor, Jared Harris (Andy Warhol), Lothaire Bluteau, Martha Plimpton, Stephen Dorff (Candy Darling), Anna Thompson, Peter Friedman, Tahnee Welch
'An exemplary and dynamic work that goes about as far as a narrative film can on both analyzing a complex personality and portraying a cultural scene.' – *Todd McCarthy, Variety*

I Shot Jesse James *
US 1948 81m bw
Lippert/Screen Guild (Carl K. Hittleman)
The story of Bob Ford, who gunned down the famous outlaw.
Doubtfully historical but quite lively Western melodrama.
wd Samuel Fuller *story* Homer Croy *ph* Ernest Miller *m* Albert Glasser *ad* Frank Hotaling *ed* Paul Landres
☆ Preston Foster, John Ireland, Barbara Britton, Reed Hadley, J. Edward Bromberg, Victor Kilian, Tom Tyler

'Attitude meets espionage.'
I Spy
US 2002 96m DeLuxe
Columbia/Tall Trees/C-2/Sheldon Leonard (Jenno Topping, Betty Thomas)
A secret agent recruits a boxing champion to help him stop a terrorist attack on the United States.
Lacklustre action comedy and an attempt to create a new franchise from an old TV series; it has just a little spark between its two stars to give it an occasional semblance of life.
w Marianne Wibberley, Cormac Wibberley, Jay Scherick, David Ronn *based on characters created by* Morton Fine, David Friedkin *d* Betty Thomas *ph* Oliver Wood *m* Richard Gibbs *pd* Marcia Hinds-Johnson *ed* Peter Teschner
☆ Eddie Murphy (Kelly Robinson), Owen Wilson (Alex Scott), Famke Janssen (Rachael), Malcolm McDowell (Gundars), Gary Cole (Carlos), Phill Lewis (Jerry), Viv Leacock (T. J.)
'Stinker doesn't begin to describe this movie's character – both frenzied and dispiriting.' – *Joe Morgenstern, Wall Street Journal*
'Something lazy, slow, shallow, stupid, amateurish, unfunny, unsuspenseful, uninformed, unspeakably dull and witlessly written, directed and acted (the special effects suck, too).' – *Peter Travers, Rolling Stone*
† The film cost $70m and took $33m at the US box-office.
†† *I Spy* ran on television from 1965-68, starring Bill Cosby as an agent and Robert Culp as his partner, a tennis champion.

I Stand Alone: see *Seul contre Tous*

I Stand Condemned: see *Moscow Nights*

I Start Counting
GB 1969 105m DeLuxe
UA/Triumvirate (David Greene)
A young girl thinks her foster-brother may be the sex murderer known to be rampant in the locality. But after a great many red herrings, of course, he is not.
Strained psychological suspenser with good moments between the longueurs.
w Richard Harris *novel* Audrey Erskine Lindop *d* David Greene *ph* Alex Thomson *m* Basil Kirchin *pd* Brian Eatwell
☆ *Jenny Agutter*, Bryan Marshall, Clare Sutcliffe, Simon Ward, Lana Morris, Billy Russell, Fay Compton, Lally Bowers

I Still Know What You Did Last Summer
US 1998 101m CFI color Panavision
Columbia/Mandalay (Neal H. Moritz, Erik Feig, Stokely Chaffin, William S. Beasley)
Four teenagers are stalked by a hook-handed killer.
A sequel to a successful, self-referential horror movie that settles for more old-fashioned shocks; the gore flows, but predictability sets in early.
w Trey Callaway *d* Danny Cannon *ph* Vernon Layton *m* John Frizzell *pd* Doug Kraner *ed* Peck Prior
☆ Jennifer Love Hewitt, Freddie Prinze Jnr, Brandy, Mekhi Phifer, Muse Watson, Matthew Settl, Bill Cobbs, Jeffrey Combs, Jennifer Esposito, John Hawkes
'An empty, farcical blood bath that's virtually shock-free except for one preposterous plot twist.' – *Stephen Holden, New York Times*

I Stole a Million
US 1939 89m bw
Universal (Burt Kelly)
A cab driver cheated by a finance company becomes a criminal to support his family.
Ho-hum star melodrama.
w Nathanael West *story* Lester Cole *d* Frank Tuttle *ph* Milton Krasner
☆ George Raft, Claire Trevor, Dick Foran, Henry Armetta, Victor Jory, Joe Sawyer, Stanley Ridges
'Crime drama neatly packaged ... topper for key duals at normal b.o.' – *Variety*

I Take This Woman
US 1931 74m bw
Paramount (Hector Turnbull)
A reckless society girl falls for a cowhand and agrees to live in his ramshackle house.
Patchy romantic comedy-drama of little remaining interest.
w Vincent Lawrence *novel* *Lost Ecstasy* by Mary Roberts Rinehart *d* Marion Gering, Slavko Vorkapich *ph* Victor Milner
☆ Gary Cooper, Carole Lombard, Helen Ware, Lester Vail, Charles Trowbridge, Clara Blandick

I Take This Woman
US 1939 97m bw
MGM (Louis B. Mayer)
A doctor marries a beautiful European and decides too late that he does not love her.
Thin comedy-drama which Louis B. Mayer unaccountably took it into his head to produce personally. The results had to be re-shot so much and so often that Hollywood dubbed the film I Re-Take This Woman. It offers little in the way of entertainment.
w James Kevin McGuinness *story* Charles MacArthur *d* W. S. Van Dyke *ph* Harold Rosson *m* Bronislau Kaper
☆ Spencer Tracy, Hedy Lamarr, Verree Teasdale, Kent Taylor, Laraine Day, Mona Barrie, Jack Carson, Paul Cavanagh, Marjorie Main

I Thank a Fool
GB 1962 100m Metrocolor Cinemascope
MGM (Anatole de Grunwald)
A woman found guilty of the murder of her lover is offered a fresh start in the home of the prosecutor's family ... but another nightmare situation builds up.
Jane Eyre melodrama of the loonier type, with good actors struggling through a wild but unrewarding script.
w Karl Tunberg *novel* Audrey Erskine Lindop *d* Robert Stevens *ph* Harry Waxman *m* Ron Goodwin
☆ Peter Finch, Susan Hayward, Diane Cilento, Cyril Cusack, Kieron Moore, Athene Seyler

I Thank You
GB 1941 81m bw
Gainsborough
Actors seeking a backer become servants to a titled ex-star.
Acceptable comedy vehicle.
w Howard Irving Young, Val Guest, Marriott Edgar *d* Marcel Varnel
☆ Arthur Askey, Richard Murdoch, Lily Morris, Moore Marriott, Graham Moffatt, Kathleen Harrison

'Now! For the first time... that Mickey Spillane violence blasts the screen!'
I the Jury
US 1953 87m bw 3-D
Parklane (Victor Saville)
Private eye Mike Hammer avenges the murder of his friend.
Charmless toughie, roughly made and devoid of plot or character interest.
wd Harry Essex *novel* Mickey Spillane *ph* John Alton *m* Franz Waxman *ad* Wiard Ihnen *ed* Frederick Y. Smith
☆ Biff Elliott (Mike Hammer), Peggie Castle (Charlotte Manning), Preston Foster (Capt. Pat Chambers), Elisha Cook Jnr (Bobo), John Qualen (Dr Vickers), Margaret Sheridan (Velda), Alan Reed (George Kalecki), Frances Osborne (Myron)

I the Jury
US 1982 109m colour
American Cinema/Larco/Solofilm (Robert Solo)
An amoral private eye avenges the murder of his Vietnam buddy.
Hard, brutal thriller more in line than the previous version with the tone of the novel.
w Larry Cohen *d* Richard T. Heffron *ph* Andrew Laszlo *m* Bill Conti *pd* Robert Gundlach
☆ Armand Assante, Barbara Carrera, Laurene Landon, Alan King, Geoffrey Lewis, Paul Sorvino
'The repellent formula as usual, with the gun and the penis as interchangeable instruments of quick-fire tough-guy virility.' – *Sunday Times*

I, the Worst of All **
Argentina 1990 105m colour
Electric/Assai Communications/Screening 22/GEA (Lita Stantic)
original title: *Yo, la peor de todas*
In Mexico in the 17th century, the Church forces Sister Juana, a nun who is also a gifted poet and playwright, to forswear literature and the intellectual life.
An austere and moving account, based on fact and with an appeal wider than feminism, of a talent overwhelmed by religious and masculine prejudice and oppression.
w Maria Luisa Bemberg, Antonio Larreta *book* *Sor Juana: Her Life and Her World* (Sor Juana Ines de la Cruz o Las Trampas de la Fe) by Octavio Paz *d* Maria Luisa Bemberg *ph* Felix Monti *m* Luis Maria Serra *pd* Voytek *ed* Juan Carlos Macias
☆ Assumpta Serna, Dominique Sanda, Hector Alterio, Lautaro Murua, Alberto Segado, Franklin Caicedo, Graciela Araujo, Hugo Soto, Gerardo Romano

I Think I Do
US 1997 92m colour
Danger Filmworks/House of Pain/Robert Miller (Lane Janger)
When a group of old friends, all having doubts about their relationships, get together to celebrate a marriage, a gay TV writer discovers that his college room-mate, who once rejected his advances, now welcomes them.
Glossy sexual comedy that resembles an overstretched sitcom.
wd Brian Sloan *ph* Milton Kam *pd* Debbie Devilla *ed* François Keraudren
☆ Alexis Arquette, Christian Maelen, Maddie Corman, Guillermo Diaz, Lauren Velez, Jamie Harrold, Marianne Hagan, Tuc Watkins
'Just isn't funny enough or capable of providing enough food for thought about modern relationships.' – *Cosmo Landesman, Sunday Times*

I Wake Up Screaming **
US 1941 79m bw
TCF (Milton Sperling)
GB and alternative title: *Hot Spot*
A model is murdered and her sister joins forces with the chief suspect to find the real killer.
Moody thriller with plenty going for it including one memorable performance.
w Dwight Taylor *novel* Steve Fisher *d* H. Bruce Humberstone *ph* Edward Cronjager *m* Cyril Mockridge
☆ Betty Grable, Victor Mature, Carole Landis, *Laird Cregar*, William Gargan, Alan Mowbray, Allyn Joslyn, Elisha Cook Jnr
† Remade as *Vicki* (qv).

I Walk Alone *
US 1947 98m bw
Paramount (Hal B. Wallis)
An ex-smuggler comes out seeking vengeance after fourteen years in prison.
Dreary gangster drama unworthy of its stars.
w Charles Schnee *play* *Beggars Are Coming to Town* by Theodore Reeves *d* Byron Haskin *ph* Leo Tover *m* Victor Young
☆ Burt Lancaster, Kirk Douglas, Lizabeth Scott, Wendell Corey, Kristine Miller, George Rigaud, Marc Lawrence, Mike Mazurki
'The picture deserves, like four out of five other movies, to walk alone, tinkle a little bell, and cry Unclean, unclean.' – *James Agee*

I Walk the Line *
US 1970 97m Eastmancolor Panavision
Columbia/Frankenheimer/Lewis/Halcyon/Atticus (Harold D. Cohen)
A Tennessee sheriff protects moonshiners for the favours of their daughter; when an investigator arrives, bloodshed results.
Competent but uninteresting hothouse melodrama in which only the plot twists compel attention.
w Alvin Sargent *novel* *An Exile* by Madison Jones *d* John Frankenheimer *ph* *David M. Walsh* *md* Robert Johnson
☆ Gregory Peck, Tuesday Weld, Estelle Parsons, Ralph Meeker

'She's Alive ... Yet Dead! She's Dead ... Yet Alive!'
I Walked with a Zombie *
US 1943 68m bw
RKO (Val Lewton)
A nurse is retained by a Caribbean planter to care for his voodoo-sick wife.
Mild horror from the famous Lewton package; some style, but generally thin stuff, the plot having been mirthfully borrowed from Jane Eyre.
w Curt Siodmak, Ardel Wray *d* *Jacques Tourneur* *ph* J. Roy Hunt *m* Roy Webb
☆ Frances Dee, James Ellison, Tom Conway, Christine Gordon, Edith Barrett, James Bell, Sir Lancelot

I Wanna Hold Your Hand
US 1978 104m Technicolor
Universal/Steven Spielberg (Tamara Asseyev, Alex Rose)
A day in 1964 finds assorted New Jersey teenagers eagerly awaiting the Beatles' appearance on the Ed Sullivan Show.
Modest period comedy utilizing fresh young talent.
w Robert Zemeckis, Bob Gale *d* Robert Zemeckis *ph* Donald M. Morgan *m* The Beatles, Meredith Willson
☆ Nancy Allen, Bobby diCicco, Marc McClure, Susan Kendall Newman

I Want a Divorce
US 1940 74m bw
Paramount
A young law student marries rashly, but is prevented from doing anything about it by examples of the unhappiness brought by divorce.
Peculiar comedy-drama which never seems to make up its mind to any particular course.
w Frank Butler *story* Adela Rogers St Johns *d* Ralph Murphy *ph* Ted Tetzlaff *m* Victor Young
☆ Dick Powell, Joan Blondell, Frank Fay, Gloria Dickson, Jessie Ralph, Conrad Nagel, Harry Davenport, Sidney Blackmer, Louise Beavers

I Want to Live! *
US 1958 120m bw
UA/Walter Wanger
A vagrant prostitute is executed in the gas chamber despite growing doubt as to her guilt.
Sober, harrowing treatment of the Barbara Graham case, uneasily adapted to provide a star role amid the tirade against capital punishment.
w Nelson Gidding, Don Mankiewicz *d* Robert Wise *ph* Lionel Lindon *m* John Mandel *ed* William Hornbeck
☆ *Susan Hayward*, Simon Oakland, Virginia Vincent, Theodore Bikel, Wesley Lau, Philip Coolidge
'An inconclusive amalgam of variously unexplored themes.' – *Peter John Dyer*
Susan Hayward
Nelson Gidding, Don Mankiewicz; Robert Wise; Lionel Lindon; editing

I Want What I Want
GB 1971 105m Eastmancolor
Marayan (Raymond Stross)
Roy has a sex change operation and becomes Wendy.
Although based on an actual trans-sexual experience, this film confuses more than it informs, and provokes unintentional mirth when its glamorous star is playing a boy.
w Gillian Freeman *novel* Geoff Brown *d* John Dexter *ph* Gerry Turpin *m* Johnny Harris
☆ Anne Heywood, Paul Rogers, Harry Andrews, Jill Bennett

I Want You
US 1951 101m bw
Samuel Goldwyn
A family reacts to the Korean war.
Glossy small-town flagwaver; no Best Years of Our Lives.
w Irwin Shaw *stories* Edward Newhouse *d* Mark Robson *ph* Harry Stradling *m* Leigh Harline *ad* *Richard Day* *ed* Daniel Mandell
☆ Dorothy McGuire, Dana Andrews, Farley Granger, Peggy Dow, Robert Keith, Ray Collins, Mildred Dunnock, Martin Milner, Jim Backus
'A recruiting picture which seems to accept a third world war almost as a present reality.' – *Penelope Houston*
'Below the entertaining surface it has very little of value to offer.' – *Richard Mallett, Punch*

I Want You
GB 1998 87m Rank Colour 'Scope
Polygram/Revolution (Andrew Eaton)
A mute, voyeuristic youth observes the reunion of a hairdresser and her violent former lover, who has been released from prison after nine years.
An odd, disjointed, dingy drama of voyeurism, obsessive love and violent secrets that never comes to life.
w Eoin McNamee *d* Michael Winterbottom *ph* Slawomir Idziak *m* Adrian Johnston, Rare *pd* Mark Tildesley *ed* Trevor Waite
☆ Rachel Weisz, Alessandro Nivola, Labina Mitevska, Luka Petrusic, Graham Crowden, Ben Daniels, Carmen Ejogo, Geraldine O'Rawe
'An ambitious idea that succeeds more as a stylistic exercise than as an involving, fully realized drama.' – *Derek Elley, Variety*

I Wanted to See Angels *
Russia 1992 83m colour/bw
Screen Angel/12A Studio (Carolyn Cavallero)
original title: *Ya Hatiella Ooveedit Angelov*
After travelling to Moscow to menace a former associate, the 20-year-old bodyguard of a provincial gangster neglects his task when he becomes involved with a young prostitute.
A bleak, grainy, low-budget look at disaffected youth, interesting less for its desultory narrative than for what it shows of present-day Moscow, which is here a harsh environment of casual cruelty and crime, punk rock and bikers on ancient machines, obsessed with American culture.
w Sergei Bodrov, Carolyn Cavallero *d* Sergei Bodrov *ph* Alosha Radionov *m* Mongol Shoodan *ad* Valeri Kostrin *ed* Olga Grinspoon
☆ Alexei Baranov, Natasha Ginko, Lea Akeojakova, Evgeni Livovarov
'Feels like a late 1960s Yank disillusioned teen biker pic.' – *Variety*

'Blonde bomber – she flew them into the ground!'
I Wanted Wings *
US 1941 131m bw
Paramount (Arthur Hornblow Jnr)
The fortunes of three recruits to the American Air Force.
Cheerful, overlong recruiting poster with concessions to melodrama.
w Richard Maibaum, Beirne Lay Jnr, Sig Herzig *d* Mitchell Leisen *ph* Leo Tover, Elmer Dyer *m* Victor Young
☆ Ray Milland, William Holden, Brian Donlevy, Wayne Morris, Veronica Lake, Constance Moore, Harry Davenport, Phil Brown
'Far more a poster than a drama.' – *Howard Barnes, New York Herald Tribune*

'All the life and death moments a man can know!'
I Was a Communist for the FBI
US 1951 83m bw
Warner (Bryan Foy)
Matt Cvetic, a Pittsburgh steel worker, is actually an FBI agent working undercover to trap communists.
Crude and shoddy Red-baiting melodrama, a kind of updating of Confessions of a Nazi Spy but using a sadly deteriorated technique.
w Crane Wilbur, Matt Cvetic *d* Gordon Douglas *ph* Edwin DuPar *m* Max Steiner

☆ Frank Lovejoy, Dorothy Hart, Phil Carey, James Millican, Richard Webb, Paul Picerni, Konstantin Shayne

'It seems that this is a subject which Hollywood is incapable of tackling even at its customary level of journalistic efficiency.' – *Penelope Houston*

documentary feature

I Was a Fireman: see *Fires Were Started*

I Was a Male War Bride **

US 1949 105m bw

TCF (Sol C. Siegel)

GB title: *You Can't Sleep Here*

A WAC in Europe marries a French officer and can't get him home.

High-spirited farce against realistic backgrounds of war-torn Europe, which scarcely accord with Cary Grant's pretending to be a Frenchman (and later a Frenchwoman). Funny, though.

w Charles Lederer, Hagar Wilde, Leonard Spigelgass *d Howard Hawks ph* Norbert Brodine, Osmond Borradaile *m* Cyril Mockridge *md* Lionel Newman

☆ Cary Grant, *Ann Sheridan*, Marion Marshall, Randy Stuart

'It is excellent light entertainment but it is not likely to appeal to the prudish and some discretion should be exercised in booking it.' – *CEA Film Report*

I Was a Prisoner on Devil's Island

US 1941 71m bw

Columbia (Wallace MacDonald)

A young American seaman is involved in a brawl in which his captain dies; result, three years on Devil's Island.

Hokey but boring melodrama with production values at low level.

w Karl Brown *d* Lew Landers

☆ Donald Woods, Sally Eilers, Edward Ciannelli, Victor Kilian, Charles Halton

I Was a Spy **

GB 1933 89m bw

Gaumont (Michael Balcon)

In Belgium 1914, a nurse is trained as a spy.

Good standard war espionage melodrama.

w W. P. Lipscomb, Ian Hay *book* Marthe McKenna *d* Victor Saville *ph* Charles Van Enger *md* Louis Levy *ad* Alfred Junge *ed* Frederick Y. Smith

☆ Madeleine Carroll, Conrad Veidt, Herbert Marshall, Gerald du Maurier, Edmund Gwenn, Donald Calthrop, Nigel Bruce, Anthony Bushell, Martita Hunt

'Body of a boy! Mind of a monster! Soul of an unearthly thing!'

I Was a Teenage Frankenstein

US 1957 72m colour/bw

American International (Herman Cohen)

GB title: *Teenage Frankenstein*

Professor Frankenstein fashions a creature from selected morsels of old corpses, and kills a teenager to give it a more handsome head.

It seemed gruesome enough at the time, but by 1980 standards this is tame, cheap stuff, only notable for its occasional bravura.

w Kenneth Langtry *d* Herbert L. Strock *ph* Lothrop Worth *m* Paul Dunlap

☆ Whit Bissell, Phyllis Coates, Gary Conway, Robert Burton

PROFESSOR TO MONSTER: 'Answer me! I know you have a civil tongue in your head, because I sewed it in there!'

† In-joke: when the professor crates up the monster to send it to London, the address is 113 Wardour Street, which was Hammer House.

'The most amazing motion picture of our time!'

I Was a Teenage Werewolf

US 1957 76m bw

AIP/Sunset (Herman Cohen)

A scientist experiments on an aggressive student and turns him into a werewolf.

Hilarious farrago with a title which achieved a splendour of its own.

w Ralph Thornton *d* Gene Fowler Jnr *ph* Joseph LaShelle *m* Paul Dunlap

☆ Michael Landon, Whit Bissell, Yvonne Lime

I Was an Adventuress *

US 1940 81m bw

TCF (Darryl F. Zanuck)

A ballerina works as decoy for a pair of confidence tricksters.

Pleasing comedy drama with striking cast.

w Karl Tunberg, Don Ettlinger, John O'Hare *d* Gregory Ratoff *ph* Leon Shamroy, Edward Cronjager *md* David Buttolph

☆ Vera Zorina, Erich von Stroheim, Peter Lorre, Richard Greene, Sig Rumann, Fritz Feld, Cora Witherspoon

I Was Happy Here *

GB 1965 91m bw

Partisan (Roy Millichip)

US title: *Time Lost and Time Remembered*

A girl leaves her husband in London and returns to the little Irish port of her childhood.

Nicely made, over-mannered study in nostalgia and lost illusions.

w Edna O'Brien, Desmond Davis *d Desmond Davis ph Manny Wynn m* John Addison

☆ Sarah Miles, Cyril Cusack, Julian Glover, Sean Caffrey, Marie Kean

I Was Monty's Double **

GB 1958 100m bw

Film Traders/Maxwell Setton

US title: *Hell, Heaven and Hoboken*

To distract the Nazis in Africa, an actor is hired to pose as General Montgomery.

An amusing and intriguing first hour gives way to spy chases, but the overall provides solid entertainment.

w Bryan Forbes book M. E. Clifton-James *d John Guillermin ph* Basil Emmott *m* John Addison

☆ John Mills, Cecil Parker, M. E. Clifton-James, Patrick Allen, Leslie Phillips, Michael Hordern, Marius Goring

'Silva Is Alone In New York ... But Not For Long...'

I Was on Mars *

Germany/Switzerland/US 1991 87m Eastmancolor

Metro Tartan/Luna/Fama/Balthazar/Good Machine (Gudrun Ruzickova-Steiner)

A young Polish woman, alone and reduced to penury in New York, follows a con man who has stolen all her savings.

An entertainingly eccentric and baleful account, made on a small budget, of an innocent abroad, with the city seen in close-up as a threatening, decaying slum populated by hustlers of one kind or another.

w Dani Levy, Maria Schrader *d* Dani Levy *ph* Carl-F. Koschnick *m* Niki Reiser *pd* Dan Ouellette *ed* Susann Lahaye

☆ Maria Schrader, Dani Levy, Mario Giacalone, Antonia Rey

'There's no denying Levi's eye for comic detail, and the film abounds in resonant little scenes.' – *Sight and Sound*

'Dis-organised Crime.'

I Went Down *

GB/Ireland/Spain 1997 107m colour

Buena Vista/BBC/Irish Film Board/Treasure (Robert Walpole)

Two small-time crooks are given the task of finding the man who robbed the local gang boss.

A dark, comic road movie about outsiders moving with no great sense of purpose through a succession of dingy landscapes.

w Conor McPherson *d* Paddy Breathnach *ph* Cian de Buitlear *m* Dario Marianelli *pd* Zoe Macleod *ed* Emer Reynolds

☆ Brendan Gleeson, Peter McDonald, Peter Caffrey, Tony Doyle, Antoine Byrne, David Wilmot

'The film sustains its momentum, and its bad-taste scabrous humour, with likable aplomb.' – *Philip Kemp, Sight and Sound*

I Will ... I Will ... for Now

US 1975 108m Technicolor

Brut (C. O. Erickson)

Divorcees with sex problems eventually get together again.

Witless soft-core farrago of coy jokes, as clumsy and unappealing as its title.

w Norman Panama, Albert E. Lewin *d* Norman Panama *ph* John A. Alonzo *m* John Cameron *pd* Fernando Carrere

☆ Elliott Gould, Diane Keaton, Paul Sorvino, Victoria Principal, Warren Berlinger, Candy Clark, Robert Alda

I Wonder Who's Kissing Her Now *

US 1947 104m Technicolor

TCF (George Jessel)

The career of 1890s songwriter Joseph E. Howard.

Routine biopic, quite pleasantly handled.

w Lewis R. Foster *d* Lloyd Bacon *ph* Ernest Palmer *md* Alfred Newman *ch* Hermes Pan *ad* Richard Day, Boris Leven

☆ Mark Stevens, June Haver, Martha Stewart, Reginald Gardiner, Lenore Aubert, William Frawley, Gene Nelson

'The Coolest Event In 16,000 Years.'

Ice Age *

US 2002 81m DeLuxe

TCF/Blue Sky (Lori Forte)

As the ice age begins, a sloth, a sabre-toothed tiger and a mammoth combine to return a lost human child to his tribe.

Well-animated dinosaur of a story with some welcome moments of slapstick in the tradition of Chuck Jones.

w Michael Berg, Michael J. Wilson, Peter Ackerman *d* Chris Wedge, Carlos Saldanha *m* David Newman *pd* Brian McEntee *ed* John Carnochan

☆ voices of: Ray Romano (Manfred), John Leguizamo (Sid), Denis Leary (Diego), Goran Visnjic (Soto), Jack Black (Zeke), Tara Strong (Roshan)

'Eye-popping technique is employed in support of an entertaining story that, while not terribly original, is sufficiently arresting and often laugh-out-loud funny.' – *Joe Leydon, Variety*

animated feature

Ice Castles

US 1978 109m Metrocolor

Columbia/International Cinemedia Center (John Kemeny)

Nick and Lexie meet and fall in love at the ice rink. He goes into professional ice hockey; she becomes an Olympic champion but an accident leaves her blind.

Slick, empty, three-handkerchief wallow in the modern manner; well made but instantly forgettable.

w Donald Wrye, Gary L. Baim *d* Donald Wrye *ph* Bill Butler *m* Marvin Hamlisch *pd* Joel Schiller

☆ Robby Benson, Lynn-Holly Johnson, Colleen Dewhurst, Tom Skerritt, Jennifer Warren, David Huffman

song 'Through the Eyes of Love' (*m* Marvin Hamlisch, *ly* Carole Bayer Sager)

Ice Cold in Alex **

GB 1958 132m bw

ABP (W. A. Whittaker)

US title: *Desert Attack*

In 1942 Libya, the commander of a motor ambulance gets his vehicle and passengers to safety despite the hazards of minefields and a German spy.

Engrossing desert adventure with plenty of suspense sequences borrowed from The Wages of Fear; *long, but very well presented.*

w T. J. Morrison, Christopher Landon *d J. Lee-Thompson ph Gilbert Taylor m* Leighton Lucas

☆ John Mills, Sylvia Syms, Anthony Quayle, Harry Andrews

'Sparkling with Gaiety, Romance, Stars, Musical Thrills!'

Ice Follies of 1939

US 1939 82m bw (Technicolor sequence)

MGM (Harry Rapf)

A Hollywood star goes east to help her old ice-skating friends put on a show.

The downright peculiar sight of these particular stars on ice is backed by good turns and practically no story.

w Florence Ryerson, Edgar Allan Woolf *d* Reinhold Schünzel *ph* Joseph Ruttenberg, Oliver T. Marsh *m* Franz Waxman

☆ Joan Crawford, James Stewart, Lew Ayres, Lewis Stone, Lionel Stander, Bess Ehrhardt, Charles D. Brown, the International Ice Follies

Ice Palace

US 1960 143m Warnercolor

Warner (Henry Blanke)

After World War I, two men set up a fishery business in Alaska, and their subsequent lives are tied up with the political development of the state.

Tedious saga from a bestseller, with entertaining incidents but no real grip.

w Harry Kleiner *novel* Edna Ferber *d* Vincent Sherman *ph* Joseph Biroc *m* Max Steiner *ad* Malcolm Bert

☆ Richard Burton, Robert Ryan, Martha Hyer, Carolyn Jones, Jim Backus, Ray Danton, Diane McBain, Karl Swenson

The Ice Pirates

US 1984 94m Metrocolor

MGM-UA (John Foreman)

On a distant planet in the future, water has become precious, and the evil Templars have cornered it.

Extraordinarily talkative and unpersuasive space opera: pretentious hokum.

w Stewart Raffill, Stanford Sherman *d* Stewart Raffill *ph* Matthew F. Leonetti *m* Bruce Broughton *ad* David M. Haber, Ronald Kent Foreman *ed* Tom Walls

☆ Robert Urich, Mary Crosby, Michael D. Roberts, Anjelica Huston, Ron Perlman, John Carradine

Ice Station Zebra

US 1968 148m Metrocolor Super Panavision

MGM/Filmways (James C. Pratt)

Russian and American agents speed towards the North Pole to recover a lost capsule containing vital military information.

Talky and unconvincingly staged spy adventure with a disappointing lack of action and a great many cold war platitudes.

w Douglas Heyes, Harry Julian Fink *novel* Alistair MacLean *d* John Sturges *ph* Daniel L. Fapp *m* Michel Legrand

☆ Rock Hudson, Patrick McGoohan, Ernest Borgnine, Jim Brown, Tony Bill, Lloyd Nolan, Gerald S. O'Loughlin, Alf Kjellin

'It's terrible in such a familiar way that at some level it's pleasant. We learn to settle for so little, we moviegoers.' – *Pauline Kael*

Daniel L. Fapp; special effects (Hal Miller, J. McMillan Johnson)

'It was 1973, and the climate was changing.'

The Ice Storm **

US 1997 113m DeLuxe

Fox Searchlight/Good Machine (Ted Hope, James Schamus, Ang Lee)

In the 70s, a community of discontented middle-class families try to escape from their problems through sex: the adults with affairs and wife-swapping, the children with losing their virginity.

A cool and clever dissection of troubled people in confusing times, though its puritan connection between illicit sex and death seems forced.

w James Schamus *novel* Rick Moody *d* Ang Lee *ph* Frederick Elmes *m* Mychael Danna *pd* Mark Friedberg *ed* Tim Squyres

☆ Kevin Kline (Ben Hood), Joan Allen (Elena Hood), Henry Czerny (George Clair), Adam Hann-Byrd (Sandy Carver), Tobey Maguire (Paul Hood), Christina Ricci (Wendy Hood), Jamey Sheridan (Jim Carver), Elijah Wood (Mikey Carver), Sigourney Weaver (Janey Carver)

'Smug connect-the-dots evisceration of the American dream.' – *Joe Queenan*

'Pointed, witty and beautifully directed.' – *Geoff Brown, The Times*

Sigourney Weaver

Ice-Capades Revue

US 1942 79m bw

Republic (Robert North)

A New England farm girl inherits a bankrupt ice show.

Thin excuse for an ice revue, which is tolerable.

w Bradford Ropes, Gertrude Purcell *d* Bernard Vorhaus
☆ Ellen Drew, Richard Denning, Jerry Colonna, Barbara Jo Allen, Harold Huber, Vera Hruba, Joe Jackson Jnr

Iceland
US 1942 79m bw
TCF (William LeBaron)
GB title: *Katina*
A marine in Reykjavik falls for a local belle.
Superficial musical with a stage farce plot and unreal musical numbers.
w Robert Ellis, Helen Logan *d* H. Bruce Humberstone *ph* Arthur Miller *m/ly* Mack Gordon, Harry Warren *md* Emil Newman
☆ Sonja Henie, John Payne, Jack Oakie, Felix Bressart, Osa Massen

Iceman
US 1984 99m Technicolor Panavision
Universal (Patrick Palmer, Norman Jewison)
An oil-drilling team in the Arctic discovers the perfectly preserved body of a Neanderthal man, who having been returned to civilization wakes up and creates havoc.
All civilization's fault, of course: initial suspense gives way to boredom when morals are preached.
w Chip Proser, John Drimmer *d* Fred Schepisi *ph* Ian Baker *m* Bruce Smeaton *ad* Leon Ericksen, Josan Russo *ed* Billy Weber
☆ Timothy Hutton, Lindsay Crouse, John Lone, Josef Sommer, Danny Glover

The Iceman Cometh
Hong Kong 1989 120m colour 'Scope
Golden Harvest
aka: *Time Warriors*
The chief swordsman of a medieval Imperial Guard and his evil adversary, who has stolen a statue with occult powers, are trapped in ice and revived to continue their fight in modern-day Hong Kong.
Action-packed martial arts melodrama with a comic edge; it begins well, but its length is likely to deter all but addicts of the genre.
d Clarence Fok
☆ Yuen Biao, Yuen Wah, Maggie Cheung, Wong Jing
'Superb ... whether you're a fantasy fan, or you like some good old modern day kung fu fighting or both, then this film is a serious recommendation.' – *Rick Baker, Eastern Heroes*

Ich Will Doch Nur, Das Ihr Mich Liebt:
see *I Only Want You to Love Me*

Ichabod and Mr Toad **
US 1949 68m Technicolor
Walt Disney
aka: *The Adventures of Ichabod and Mr Toad*
Cartoon versions of stories by Washington Irving and Kenneth Grahame.
An uncomfortable double bill; the story of Ichabod, though well narrated by Bing Crosby, is macabre without being very interesting; The Wind in the Willows, *however, is charmingly pictured, and Mr Toad is splendidly voiced by Eric Blore.*
d Jack Kinney, Clyde Geronimi, James Algar *supervisor* Ben Sharpsteen

The Icicle Thief **
Italy 1989 85m colour
Metro/Bambú/Reitalia (Ernesto Di Sarro)
original title: *Ladri Di Saponette*
Watching the television screening of his new film, a director enters the movie when he discovers his characters are changing their lines and leaving the action to appear in commercials.
Witty parody of neo-realistic cinema (the title recalls de Sica's classic Bicycle Thieves*), commercialism and TV's treatment of films.*
w Maurizio Nichetti, Mauro Monti *d* Maurizio Nichetti *ph* Maria Battistoni *m* Manuel de Sica *pd* Ada Legori *ed* Rita Rossi, Anna Missoni
☆ Maurizio Nichetti, Caterina Sylos Labini, Federico Rizzo, Renato Scarpa, Heidi Komarex, Carlina Torta, Massimi Sacilotto, Claudio G. Fava
'An unqualified treat ... This sophisticated satire on the undifferentiated tap-flow of television is also a passionate declaration of love for the movies.' – *David Robinson, The Times*

I'd Climb the Highest Mountain *
US 1951 88m Technicolor
TCF (Lamar Trotti)
A Methodist preacher and his wife face the problems of life in a remote part of North Georgia.
Pleasant, rambling, adequately serious and old-fashioned family entertainment, well presented in Hollywood's medium style.
w Lamar Trotti *novel* Corra Harris *d* Henry King *ph* Edward Cronjager *m* Sol Kaplan *md* Lionel Newman
☆ Susan Hayward, William Lundigan, Rory Calhoun, Barbara Bates, Gene Lockhart, Lynn Bari, Ruth Donnelly, Alexander Knox

I'd Rather Be Rich *
US 1964 96m Eastmancolor
U-I/Ross Hunter
To comfort her dying grandfather, an heiress introduces an eligible stranger as her fiancé ... but the old man recovers and begins matchmaking.
Reasonably zesty remake of It Started with Eve, *kept afloat by Chevalier's performance.*
w Oscar Brodney, Leo Townsend, Norman Krasna *d* Jack Smight *ph* Russell Metty *m* Percy Faith *md* Joseph Gershenson *ad* Alexander Golitzen, George Webb *ed* Milton Carruth
☆ *Maurice Chevalier*, Sandra Dee, Robert Goulet, Andy Williams, Gene Raymond, Hermione Gingold, Charles Ruggles

An Ideal Husband *
GB 1947 96m Technicolor
British Lion/London Films (Alexander Korda)
In the 1890s, the career of a London diplomat is threatened by the reappearance of an old flame.
A slight, stiff play is swamped by the cast, the decor, and very garish colour, but there are moments of enjoyment along the way.
w Lajos Biro *play* Oscar Wilde *d* Alexander Korda *ph* Georges Périnal *m* Arthur Benjamin *ad* Vincent Korda, Cecil Beaton *ed* Oswald Hafenrichter
☆ Paulette Goddard, Hugh Williams, Michael Wilding, Diana Wynyard, C. *Aubrey Smith*, *Constance Collier*, Glynis Johns, Christine Norden
'The composing and cutting of this fine raw material is seldom above medium grade.' – *James Agee*

'He just doesn't know it yet.'
An Ideal Husband *
GB/USA 1999 98m colour
Pathé/Icon/Arts Council/Fragile/Miramax (Barnaby Thompson, Uri Fruchtmann, Bruce Davey)
An MP is saved from public disgrace at the hands of a scheming woman by his wife and his best friend.
Wilde's play has not gained from being opened up, though Everett's performance and Wilde's words keep the brittle comedy alive.
wd Oliver Parker *play* Oscar Wilde *ph* David Johnson *m* Charlie Mole *pd* Michael Howells *ed* Guy Bensley
☆ Cate Blanchett, Minnie Driver, Rupert Everett, Julianne Moore, Jeremy Northam, John Wood, Lindsay Duncan, Peter Vaughan, Jeroen Krabbé, Ben Pullen, Nickolas Grace
'It's on the film's determined stylishness that it loses the original's lightness of touch and somewhat downplays sparkling repartee in favour of a forced emotional element.' – *Angie Errigo, Empire*

Identification of a Woman
Italy 1982 130m Technicolor Technovision
Artificial Eye/Iter Film/Gaumont (Giorgio Nocella, Antonio Macri)
original title: *Identificazione di una Donna*
A film director searches for an ideal woman to spark off his new film.
A quest that the audience will tire of long before the end.
w Michelangelo Antonioni, Gérard Brach, Tonino Guerra *d* Michelangelo Antonioni *ph* Carlo di Palma *ad* Andrea Crisanti *ed* Michelangelo Antonioni
☆ Tomas Milian, Daniela Silverio, Christine Boisson, Sandra Monteleoni, Giampaolo Saccarola, Alessandro Ruspoli, Giada Gerini, Sergio Tardioli

Idiot Box
Australia 1996 83m Atlab Panavision
Central Park/AFFC (Glenys Rowe)
In a Sydney suburb two dim-witted, boozy, unemployed layabouts decide to rob a bank, and choose one under surveillance by the police, who are expecting a raid from professionals.
A slice of low-life among deadbeats that some found funny, though the company of its loud, foul-mouthed incompetents soon palls.
wd David Caesar *ph* Joseph Pickering *pd* Kerith Holmes *ed* Mark Perry
☆ Ben Mendelsohn, Jeremy Sims, John Polson, Graeme Blundell, Deborah Kennedy, Robyn Loau, Stephen Rae
'A wild ride, a fast, corrosive comedy.' – *Variety*

'Take a long ride on the short bus.'
The Idiots
Denmark 1998 115m colour
Zentropa/DRTV/DBC/Liberator/La Sept/ZDF/Arte/Argus/VPRO (Vibeke Windelov)
original title: *Idioterne*
In Copenhagen, friends form a commune in which they seek their 'inner idiot' by playing at being mentally and physically retarded.
A talented director pushes his art in the wrong direction: this is a scrappily filmed satire on family life, both conventional and communal, where the cult leader is far more parasitical and controlling than his abused suburban counterparts.
wd Lars von Trier *ph* Lars von Trier *ed* Molly Malene Stensgaard
☆ Bodil Jorgensen, Jens Albinus, Louise Hassing, Troels Lyby, Nikolaj Lie Kaas, Henrik Prip, Luis Mesonero, Louise Mieritz, Knud Romer Jorgensen, Trine Michelsen, Anne-Grethe Bjarup Riis
'Although some will find the jerky, shot-on-the-run style off-putting, this is real cinema: original, affecting, shattering.' – *Kim Newman, Empire*
'Weird and wonderful ... I cannot decide whether this film is courageous, offensive or plain idiotic.' – *Nigel Cliff, The Times*

Idiot's Delight *
US 1939 105m bw
MGM (Hunt Stromberg)
At the outbreak of World War II, in a hotel on the Swiss border, a hoofer with an all-girl troupe meets an old flame masquerading as a Russian countess.
Interesting but quite unsuccessful film version of a highly artificial play which had been carried off superbly by the Lunts but was now somewhat less well cast, though it did represent an early Hollywood challenge to Hitler. The flagwaving in fact made it more than a little boring.
w Robert E. Sherwood *play* Robert E. Sherwood *d* Clarence Brown *ph* William Daniels *m* Herbert Stothart
☆ Clark Gable, Norma Shearer, Edward Arnold, Charles Coburn, Burgess Meredith, Joseph Schildkraut, Laura Hope Crews, Skeets Gallagher, Pat Paterson, Fritz Feld
'Exceptionally entertaining comedy, a b.o. sock.' – *Variety*
'The fun and excitement are still there, however filtered it may be.' – *Film Daily*
'The mood of the whole thing is forced and cheap – the coming world war staged by Maurice Chevalier.' – *Otis Ferguson*
'Exactly the same pseudo-qualities as *The Petrified Forest*: a moral pretentiousness, a kind of cellophaned intellectuality.' – *Graham Greene*

The Idle Class *
US 1922 30m approx bw silent
First National/Charles Chaplin
A tramp dreams of the rich life and is mistaken for the husband of a lady.
Rather slight later Chaplin without the full-blooded farcical elements which made him so popular around 1917.
wd Charles Chaplin *ph* Rollie Totheroh
☆ Charles Chaplin, Edna Purviance, Mack Swain

The Idol
GB 1966 111m bw
Embassy (Leonard Lightstone)
A divorced woman falls in love with her son's friend.
Stupefyingly boring generation-gap sex drama.
w Millard Lampell *d* Daniel Petrie *ph* Ken Higgins *m* Johnny Dankworth
☆ Jennifer Jones, Michael Parks, John Leyton, Jennifer Hilary, Guy Doleman, Natasha Pyne
'Doesn't even qualify for worst picture of the year, missing the perfection and purity of that category by the sheer ineptness of script, direction, and performance.' – *Judith Crist*

Idol of Paris
GB 1948 105m bw
Premier (R. J. Minney)
In old Paris, a ragman's daughter becomes queen of the demi-mondaines.
Unintentionally hilarious copy of the Gainsborough period romances which had been so popular; much criticized because the leading ladies fight a duel with whips, but that's the least of its faults.
w Norman Lee, Stafford Dickens, Henry Ostrer *novel* Paiva Queen of Love by Alfred Shirkauer *d* Leslie Arliss *ph* Jack Cox *m* Mischa Spoliansky *ad* Albert Jullion *ed* A. H. Bates
☆ Beryl Baxter, Christine Norden, Michael Rennie, Margaretta Scott, Keneth Kent, Henry Oscar, Miles Malleson, Andrew Osborn, Andrew Cruickshank

The Idolmaker
US 1980 119m Technicolor
United Artists/Gene Kirkwood, Howard W. Koch
A songwriter accurately sums up his own limited talent and turns agent and starmarker.
Sharp but padded look behind the scenes of the pop industry; in the end of interest only to initiates.
w Edward Di Lorenzo *d* Taylor Hackford *ph* Adam Holender *m* Jeff Barry
☆ Ray Sharkey, Tovah Feldshuh, Peter Gallagher, Paul Land

Idols in the Dust:
see *Saturday's Hero*

If... ****
GB 1968 111m Eastmancolor
Paramount/Memorial (Lindsay Anderson, Michael Medwin)
Discontent at a boys' public school breaks out into rebellion.
Allegorical treatment of school life with much fashionable emphasis on obscure narrative, clever cutting, variety of pace, even an unaccountable changing from colour to monochrome and vice versa. It catches perfectly a mood of rebellion and dissatisfaction with the status quo.
w David Sherwin *d* Lindsay Anderson *ph* Miroslav Ondricek *m* Marc Wilkinson *pd* Jocelyn Herbert
☆ Malcolm McDowell, David Wood, Richard Warwick, Robert Swann, Christine Noonan, Peter Jeffrey, Arthur Lowe, Anthony Nicholls
'The school ... is the perfect metaphor for the established system all but a few of us continue to accept.' – *David Wilson*
'It's something like the Writing on the Wall.' – *Lindsay Anderson*
'Combines a cold and queasy view of youth with a romantic view of violence.' – *New Yorker*

If a Man Answers
US 1962 102m Technicolor
Universal/Ross Hunter
A wife decides to make her husband jealous.
Derivative second-team matrimonial comedy, all dressed up but with nowhere to go.
w Richard Morris *novel* Winifred Wolfe *d* Henry Levin *ph* Russell Metty *m* Hans Salter *ad* Alexander Golitzen *ed* Milton Carruth
☆ Sandra Dee, Bobby Darin, Micheline Presle, John Lund, Cesar Romero, Stefanie Powers

If Ever I See You Again
US 1978 105m colour
Columbia (Joe Brooks)
A songwriter attempts to win back the love of an old girlfriend.
Almost a one-man band of a movie that plays too long on one note and is better never seen at all.
w Joe Brooks, Martin Davidson *d* Joseph Brooks *ph* Adam Holender *m* Joe Brooks *ed* Rich Shaine
☆ Joe Brooks, Shelley Hack, Jimmy Breslin, Jerry Keller, George Plimpton, Michael Decker

If I Had a Million **
US 1932 88m bw
Paramount (Benjamin Glazer, Louis D. Lighton)
Various people each receive a million dollars from an eccentric who wants to test their reactions.
Interesting, dated multi-part comedy drama remembered chiefly for the brief sequence in which Laughton blows a raspberry to his boss and Fields chases road hogs. As an entertainment it's patchy, lacking an overall style.
w Claude Binyon, Whitney Bolton, Malcolm Stuart Boylan, John Bright, Sidney Buchman, Lester Cole, Isabel Dawn, Boyce DeGaw, Walter de Leon, Oliver H. P. Garrett, Harvey Gates, Grover Jones, Ernst Lubitsch, Lawton Mackaill, Joseph L. Mankiewicz, William Slavens McNutt, Seton I. Miller, Tiffany Thayer *story* Robert D. Andrews *d* Ernst Lubitsch, Norman Taurog, Stephen Roberts, Norman Z. McLeod, James Cruze, William A. Seiter, H. Bruce Humberstone
☆ W. C. Fields, *Charles Laughton, May Robson,* Richard Bennett, Alison Skipworth, Gary Cooper, Wynne Gibson, George Raft, Jack Oakie, Frances Dee, Charles Ruggles, Mary Boland, Roscoe Karns, Gene Raymond, Lucien Littlefield
'Not uninteresting, but spotty in retrospect … the cinematic porridge is naturally replete with a diversity of seasonings.' – *Variety*
'It develops an obvious idea in an obvious way.' – *Time*

If I Had My Way *
US 1940 82m bw
Universal (David Butler)
Two vaudevillians help an orphan girl and open a new night-club.
Quite likeable and very typical star vehicle of its period.
w William Conselman, James V. Kern *d* David Butler *ph* George Robinson *m* Frank Skinner
☆ Bing Crosby, Charles Winninger, Gloria Jean, El Brendel, Allyn Joslyn, Donald Woods, Eddie Leonard, Claire Dodd, Blanche Ring

If I Were Free
US 1933 65m bw
RKO
A man and woman, each unhappily married, try to get together.
Rather soppy drama which fails to develop.
w Dwight Taylor *play* *Behold We Live* by John Van Druten *d* Elliott Nugent
☆ Irene Dunne, Clive Brook, Nils Asther, Henry Stephenson, Laura Hope Crews
'Thin in texture, it never reaches a pace that really counts.' – *Variety*

'His love-making was as dangerous as his swordplay!'
If I Were King *
US 1938 101m bw
Paramount (Frank Lloyd)
The 14th-century poet and rascal François Villon matches wits with Louis XI and leads an uprising of the people.
A story which we have grown used to seeing with music as The Vagabond King *is here well presented but somehow rings hollow, with insufficient derring-do; it is the wrong kind of swashbuckling for its star, who is for once outacted by Rathbone in an unusual wily characterization.*
w Preston Sturges *d* Frank Lloyd *ph* Theodor Sparkuhl *m* Richard Hageman *ad* Hans Dreier, John Goodman
☆ Ronald Colman, *Basil Rathbone,* Frances Dee, Ellen Drew, C. V. France, Heather Thatcher, Henry Wilcoxon, Sidney Toler
'Healthy box office that will hit extended runs right down the line.' – *Variety*
'A well mounted and splendid production that carries along at a fascinating pace.' – *Daily Variety*
🏆 Richard Hageman; Basil Rathbone; art direction

If I'm Lucky
US 1945 79m bw
TCF (Brian Foy)
A singer runs for state governor and exposes corruption.
Lacklustre remake of Thanks a Million, *with decidedly dispirited elements.*
w Snag Werris, Robert Ellis, Helen Logan, George Bricker *d* Lewis Seiler *ph* Glen MacWilliams *m/ly* Edgar de Lange, Joseph Myrow *md* Emil Newman
☆ Vivian Blaine, Perry Como, Carmen Miranda, Harry James, Phil Silvers, Edgar Buchanan, Reed Hadley

If It's Tuesday, This Must Be Belgium *
US 1969 98m DeLuxe
UA/Wolper (Stan Margulies)
A group of American tourists have various adventures during a lightning tour of Europe.
Amusing comedy which does pretty well by a good idea.
w David Shaw *d* Mel Stuart *ph* Vilis Lapenieks *m* Walter Scharf
☆ Suzanne Pleshette, Ian McShane, Mildred Natwick, Murray Hamilton, Michael Constantine, Sandy Baron, Norman Fell, Peggy Cass, Marty Ingels, Pamela Britton, Luke Halpin, Aubrey Morris

If Looks Could Kill: see *Teen Agent*

If Lucy Fell
US 1996 94m Technicolor
Sony/TriStar/Motion Picture Corp (Brad Krevoy, Steve Stabler, Brad Jenkel)
Two flatmates make a pact to jump from Brooklyn Bridge if they fail to find the perfect mate before they reach 30.
Dim and charmless attempt at a romantic comedy.
wd Eric Schaeffer *ph* Ron Fortunato *m* Amanda Kravat, Charles Pettis *pd* Ginger Tougas *ed* Sue Graef
☆ Sarah Jessica Parker, Eric Schaeffer, Ben Stiller, Elle Macpherson, James Rebhorn, Dominic Luchese, Robert John Burke
'The sparks fly with some memorable verbal sparring and screen chemistry between the principals.' – *Leonard Klady, Variety*

'If men and women were emotionally, physically, biologically, astrologically, hormonally, psychologically, orgasmically the same … life would be easy.'
If Only
GB/France/Spain/Canada/Luxembourg 1998 95m colour
Pathé/HandMade/Paragon/Mandarin/Wild Rose/Parallel (Juan Gordon)
An actor, who lost the woman he loved when he told her of an affair, gets a chance to relive his life without repeating the mistake.
Curious little comedy about having to live with one's mistakes, which has a certain slight charm.
w Rafa Russo *d* Maria Ripoli *ph* Javier Salmones *m* Luis Mendo, Bernardo Fuster, Angel Illarramendi *pd* Grant Hicks *ed* Nacho Ruiz-Capillas
☆ Penelope Cruz, Douglas Henshall, Lena Headey, Gustavo Salmeron, Mark Strong, Eusebio Lazaro, Charlotte Coleman, Neil Stuke, Elizabeth McGovern
'Well-crafted and enjoyable.' – *Empire*

If This Be Sin: see *That Dangerous Age*

If Winter Comes
US 1948 97m bw
MGM (Victor Saville)
A sentimental idealist, unhappily married, finds himself at the mercy of village gossip when he takes in a pregnant girl.
Artificial romantic nonsense, unconvincingly staged and modernized from a very dated bestseller.
w Marguerite Roberts, Arthur Wimperis *novel* A. S. M. Hutchinson *d* Victor Saville *ph* George Folsey *m* Herbert Stothart
☆ Walter Pidgeon, Deborah Kerr, Janet Leigh, Angela Lansbury, Binnie Barnes, Dame May Whitty, Reginald Owen

If You Could Only Cook
US 1935 72m bw
Columbia
A young millionaire meets a poor girl and they get jobs as cook and butler.
Whimsical comedy-romance; thin but moderately beguiling.
w F. Hugh Herbert, Gertrude Purcell, Howard J. Green *d* William A. Seiter *ph* John Stumar *ad* Stephen Goosson *ed* Gene Havlick
☆ Jean Arthur, Herbert Marshall, Leo Carrillo, Lionel Stander, Frieda Inescort
'Plenty of chuckles … offers particularly strong promise for the nabes.' – *Variety*
† This was the film which enabled Frank Capra to get out of his Columbia contract, because they accidentally promoted it in Europe as being directed by him.

If You Feel Like Singing: see *Summer Stock*

If You Knew Susie *
US 1948 90m bw
RKO (Eddie Cantor)
A vaudeville couple retire to his ancestral home in New England.
Mild family comedy capitalizing on the team established in Show Business.
w Warren Wilson, Oscar Brodney *d* Gordon Douglas *ph* Frank Redman
☆ *Eddie Cantor, Joan Davis,* Allyn Joslyn, Bobby Driscoll, Charles Dingle

If You Live Shoot!: see *Django, Kill!*

Ikimono No Kiroku *
Japan 1955 113m bw
Toho (S. Motoki)
aka: *I Live in Fear*
A family attempts to have its father, a wealthy industrialist, declared of unsound mind because he wants them all to move to Brazil to escape the danger of radiation and the atom bomb.
Although the main theme has lost its topicality, the drama of the dynamics of family relationships still holds the interest, as does Mifune's uncharacteristic performance as an old man.
w Shinobu Hashimoto, Hideo Oguni, Akira Kurosawa *d* Akira Kurosawa *ph* Asakazu Nakai *m* Fumio Hayasaka
☆ Toshiro Mifune, Takashi Shimura, Minoru Chiaki, Masao Shimizu, Eiko Miyoshi, Haruko Togo, Yutaka Sada, Norkiro Sengoku

Ikiru **
Japan 1952 143m bw
Toho
aka: *Living*
aka: *Doomed*
A clerk learns that he is dying and spends his last months creating a children's playground.
A moving and beautifully made personal drama which also gives an interesting background of modern Japan.
w Hideo Oguni, Shinobu Hashimoto, Akira Kurosawa *d* *Akira Kurosawa* *ph* Asaishi Nakai *m* Fumio Hayasaka
☆ *Takashi Shimura,* Nobuo Kaneko, Kyoko Seki

Il était une fois un pays: see *Underground (1995)*

Il Faut Vivre Dangereusement
France 1975 100m colour
Fox/ORFT (Nelly Kaplan)
aka: *You've Got to Live Dangerously*
A private eye, hired to investigate a young woman, uncovers a plot to find a fabulous diamond.
Baroque thriller with more corpses than Hamlet, but one that fails to sustain interest, despite its recourse to naked flesh at every possible opportunity.
w Nelly Kaplan *d* Claude Makovsky *m* Claude Bolling *ad* Jacques Dugied *ed* Jocelyne Triquet
☆ Claude Brasseur, Annie Girardot

Il mio nome è Nessuno: see *My Name Is Nobody*

L'Ile au trésor: see *Treasure Island*

'Somewhere between L.A. and N.Y. Jake found the true meaning of Christmas.'
I'll Be Home for Christmas
US 1998 85m Technicolor
Buena Vista/Walt Disney/Mandeville (David Hoberman, Tracey Trench)
A spoilt, selfish student, abandoned in the Californian desert with no money, has 48 hours in which to get to New York so that he can get his Christmas present of a sports car.
Sentimental family comedy that runs along totally predictable lines; it is as bland as supermarket turkey.
w Tom Nursall, Harris Goldberg *story* Michael Allin *d* Arlene Sanford *ph* Hiro Narita *m* John Debney *pd* Cynthia Charette *ed* Anita Brandt-Burgoyne
☆ Jonathan Taylor Thomas, Jessica Biel, Adam LaVorgna, Sean O'Bryan, Gary Cole, Eve Gordon, Lauren Maltby, Andrew Lauer, Leslie Boone

'Both living a secret – each afraid to tell!'
I'll Be Seeing You **
US 1944 85m bw
David O. Selznick (Dore Schary)
A lady convict at home on parole for Christmas meets and falls for a shell-shocked soldier.
Schmaltzy, middle-American romantic drama with some nicely handled moments and plenty of talent on hand. In the Hollywood mainstream.
w Marion Parsonnet *novel* Charles Martin *d William Dieterle ph Tony Gaudio m* Daniele Amfitheatrof
☆ *Ginger Rogers, Joseph Cotten,* Shirley Temple, Spring Byington, Tom Tully, Chill Wills
'A sentimental, improbable picture, but unexpectedly rewarding in detail.' – *Richard Mallett, Punch*

I'll Be Your Sweetheart
GB 1945 104m bw
Gainsborough (Louis Levy)
In 1900, songwriters fight with copyright pirates.
Studio-bound musical romance without the necessary resonance.
w Val Guest, Val Valentine *d* Val Guest *ph* Phil Grindrod *md* Louis Levy
☆ Margaret Lockwood, Michael Rennie, Vic Oliver, Peter Graves, Moore Marriott, Frederick Burtwell, Maudie Edwards, Garry Marsh

I'll Be Yours
US 1947 90m bw
Universal (Felix Jackson)
A small-town girl tries to make good in the big city.
Slackly handled remake of The Good Fairy. *A doubtful 'A' production which did nothing for its star's ailing career.*
w Preston Sturges (adapted anonymously from his previous screenplay based on the Molnar original) *d* William A. Seiter *ph* Hal Mohr *m* Frank Skinner
☆ Deanna Durbin, Tom Drake, William Bendix, Adolphe Menjou, Walter Catlett, Franklin Pangborn

I'll Cry Tomorrow *
US 1955 119m bw
MGM (Lawrence Weingarten)
Lillian Roth, a Broadway/Hollywood star of the early thirties, becomes an alcoholic.
Fictionalized biopic, pretty well done of the True Confessions kind.
w Helen Deutsch, Jay Richard Kennedy *book* Lillian Roth, Gerold Frank *d* Daniel Mann *ph* Arthur E. Arling *m* Alex North *ad* Cedric Gibbons, Randall Duell
☆ *Susan Hayward,* Richard Conte, Eddie Albert, Jo Van Fleet, Don Taylor, Ray Danton, Margo
'By emphasizing physical degradation in almost every frame, the film makes her less an object of acutely personal concern than a street casualty seen remotely from the top of a bar.' – *Alexander Walker*
🏆 Arthur E. Arling; Susan Hayward; art direction

I'll Do Anything
US 1994 115m Technicolor
Columbia/Gracie (James L. Brooks, Polly Platt)
An out-of-work actor with a small daughter to support falls for a Hollywood executive while working as a chauffeur for an overbearing producer.
Moderate romantic comedy, more likely to interest those who work in Hollywood than a wider audience.
wd James L. Brooks *ph* Michael Ballhaus *m* Hans Zimmer *pd* Stephen J. Lineweaver *ed* Richard Marks
☆ Nick Nolte, Albert Brooks, Julie Kavner, Whittni Wright, Joely Richardson, Tracey Ullman, Joely Fisher, Jeb Brown
'Given its origins the movie is better than one might have anticipated yet has to be viewed as a

disappointment relative to Brooks' earlier features.' – *Variety*

† The film was originally intended as a musical. Eleven of the 12 songs were cut after some of the audience walked out at previews, and new footage was added.

I'll Get By
US 1950 86m Technicolor
TCF (William Perlberg)
Two songwriters meet success, then join the marines and are reunited with their former girlfriends.
Fair standard musical, a modernization of Tin Pan Alley.
w Mary Loos, Richard Sale *d* Richard Sale *ph* Charles G. Clarke *md* Lionel Newman *ch* Larry Ceballos *ad* Lyle Wheeler, Mary Loos *ed* J. Watson Webb
☆ June Haver, Gloria de Haven, William Lundigan, Dennis Day, Harry James, Thelma Ritter
Lionel Newman

I'll Give a Million *
US 1938 70m bw
TCF (Darryl F. Zanuck)
A millionaire becomes a tramp and disappears, letting it be known that he will give a fortune for genuine acts of kindness. Tramps are then royally entertained all over town.
Amusing Depression comedy with satirical touches.
w Boris Ingster, Milton Sperling *d* Walter Lang *ph* Lucien Andriot *md* Louis Silvers
☆ Warner Baxter, Peter Lorre, Marjorie Weaver, Jean Hersholt, John Carradine, J. Edward Bromberg, Lynn Bari, Fritz Feld, Sig Rumann
'Not worth that much ... the plot sags at the halfway mark and the wind-up is disappointing.' – *Variety*

Ill Met by Moonlight
GB 1956 104m bw Vistavision
Rank/Vega (Michael Powell, Emeric Pressburger)
US title: *Night Ambush*
In Crete during the German occupation, British agents work with partisans to capture a German general.
Disappointingly dreary war adventure with too many night locations, too little suspense and characterization, and photography which seems to be deliberately unattractive.
wd Michael Powell, Emeric Pressburger *book* W. Stanley Moss *ph* Christopher Challis *m* Mikis Theodorakis
☆ Dirk Bogarde, Marius Goring, David Oxley, Cyril Cusack, John Cairney, Laurence Payne, Wolfe Morris, Michael Gough

I'll Never Forget Whatshisname *
GB 1967 96m Technicolor
Universal/Scimitar (Michael Winner)
An advertising executive gives up power and money for integrity on a small literary magazine, but is won back by a mogul.
Vivid yet muddled tragi-comedy of the sixties, with splashes of sex and violence in trendy settings, a hero one really doesn't believe in, and a title which seems to have no meaning whatsoever.
w Peter Draper *d* Michael Winner *ph* Otto Heller *m* Francis Lai
☆ Oliver Reed, Orson Welles, Carol White, Harry Andrews, Michael Hordern, Wendy Craig, Marianne Faithfull

I'll Never Forget You: see *The House in the Square*

I'll See You in My Dreams *
US 1952 112m bw
Warner (Louis F. Edelman)
The domestic and professional life of songwriter Gus Kahn.
Quiet-toned, well made, quite forgettable musical.
w Melville Shavelson, Jack Rose *d* Michael Curtiz *ph* Ted McCord *md* Ray Heindorf *ch* Le Roy Prinz
☆ Doris Day, Danny Thomas, Frank Lovejoy, Patrice Wymore, James Gleason

I'll Take Romance
US 1937 85m bw
Columbia (Everett Riskin)
When an opera singer refuses to fulfil a South American contract, her impresario kidnaps her.
Moderate star vehicle.
w George Oppenheimer, Jane Murfin *d* Edward H. Griffith *ph* Lucien Andriot *m/ly* various
☆ Grace Moore, Melvyn Douglas, Helen Westley, Stuart Erwin, Margaret Hamilton, Walter Kingsford, Esther Muir

I'll Take Sweden
US 1965 96m Technicolor
UA/Edward Small
A widowed oil company executive accepts a Stockholm posting to remove his teenage daughter from an unsuitable attachment.
Feeble comedy which unwisely attempts to be with it, but is bogged down by amateurish handling and witwise is sadly without it.
w Nat Perrin, Bob Fisher, Arthur Marx *d* Frederick de Cordova *ph* Daniel L. Fapp *m* Jimmy Haskell
☆ Bob Hope, Tuesday Weld, Frankie Avalon, Dina Merrill, Jeremy Slate, John Qualen, Walter Sande

Illegal *
US 1955 88m bw
Warner (Frank P. Rosenberg)
A disillusioned District Attorney becomes a racketeer's lawyer but finally denounces him at the cost of his own life.
Competent remake of The Mouthpiece *(qv), a good star melodrama.*
w W. R. Burnett, James R. Webb *story* Frank J. Collins *d* Lewis Allen *ph* Peverell Marley *m* Max Steiner
☆ Edward G. Robinson, Nina Foch, Albert Dekker, Hugh Marlowe, Jayne Mansfield, Howard St John, Ellen Corby
'Hard-hitting stuff in the old gangster tradition.' – *MFB*

Illegal Entry
US 1949 84m bw
Universal-International
Undercover agents investigate a smuggling racket.
Routine, quite entertaining alleged exposé.
w Joel Malone *d* Frederick de Cordova *ph* William H. Daniels
☆ Howard Duff, George Brent, Marta Toren, Tom Tully, Paul Stewart, Gar Moore

Illegal Traffic
US 1938 67m bw
Paramount
The FBI tracks down an organization devoted to smuggling criminals away from danger.
Smart second feature based on J. Edgar Hoover's Persons in Hiding.
w Robert Yost, Lewis Foster, Stuart Anthony *d* Louis King
☆ J. Carrol Naish, Mary Carlisle, Robert Preston
'Good racketeer film ... should do better than average business.' – *Variety*

Illegally Yours
US 1988 102m Technicolor
UA/Crescent Moon/DEG (Peter Bogdanovich)
A juror sets out to prove the innocence of a woman he has loved from afar, who is accused of murder and blackmail.
Screwed-up attempt at a screwball comedy, painful to watch.
w M. A. Stewart, Max Dickens *d* Peter Bogdanovich *ph* Dante Spinotti *m* Phil Marshall *pd* Jane Musky *ed* Richard Fields, Ronald Krehel
☆ Rob Lowe, Colleen Camp, Kenneth Mars, Harry Carey Jnr, Kim Myers, Marshall Colt

Illicit
US 1931 81m bw
Warner
A disillusioned wife walks out on her husband and seeks solace elsewhere.
Undistinguished weepie, which later became Ex-Lady.
w Harvey Thew *d* Archie Mayo
☆ Barbara Stanwyck, Ricardo Cortez, Joan Blondell, Charles Butterworth
'Lacks a wallop and action.' – *Variety*

'Don't dare stare at...'
The Illustrated Man *
US 1969 103m Technicolor Panavision
Warner/SKM (Howard B. Kreitsek, Ted Mann)
A strange wanderer tells weird stories based on the tattooed pictures which cover him from tip to toe.
Oddball compendium based rather insecurely on Ray Bradbury stories; in this form they don't amount to much but the presentation is assured.
w Howard B. Kreitsek *d* Jack Smight *ph* Philip Lathrop *m* Jerry Goldsmith *ad* Joel Schiller
☆ Rod Steiger, Claire Bloom, Robert Drivas, Don Dubbins, Jason Evers
'A curiously passionless affair – efficient enough, meaty enough, but without poetry, without charm, without beauty.' – *Philip Strick*
'A pretentious comic strip of maudlin and muddled fantasies.' – *Judith Crist*

Illustrious Corpses *
Italy/France 1975 120m Technicolor
PEA/UA (Alberto Grimaldi)
original title: *Cadaveri Eccellenti*
A right-wing conspiracy to arouse feelings against dissidents is found to be behind the murders of public figures.
Elegant police melodrama on an unlikely political thesis.
w Francesco Rosi, Tonino Guerra, Lino Jannuzzi *novel Il Contesto* by Leonardo Sciascia *d* Francesco Rosi *ph* Pasqualino de Santis *m* Piero Piccioni
☆ Lino Ventura, Alain Cuny, Paolo Bonacelli, Marcel Bozzuffi, Max von Sydow, Fernando Rey, Charles Vanel, Tina Aumont
'Like watching layer after layer peeled off some diseased flower until the poisoned root is reached.' – *Michael Billington, Illustrated London News*

I'm All Right Jack ***
GB 1959 104m bw
British Lion/Charter (Roy Boulting)
A world-innocent graduate takes a job in industry; by starting at the bottom he provokes a national strike.
Satirical farce which manages to hit most of its widespread targets and finds corruption in high, low and middle places. A not inaccurate picture of aspects of British life in the fifties, and a presage of the satire boom to come with Beyond the Fringe *and* That Was the Week That Was.
w Frank Harvey, John Boulting, Alan Hackney novel Private Life *by Alan Hackney d* John Boulting *ph* Max Greene *m* Ken Hare
☆ *Ian Carmichael, Peter Sellers*, Irene Handl, Richard Attenborough, *Terry-Thomas*, Dennis Price, Margaret Rutherford, Liz Fraser, *John Le Mesurier*, Sam Kydd
Peter Sellers; screenplay

I'm Dancing as Fast as I Can
US 1982 106m Movielab
Paramount/Edgar J. Scherick/Scott Rudin
A documentary film-maker is rehabilitated after dependence on drugs.
Unabsorbing case history more suitable as a TV movie except that the acting for TV would not have been so far over the top.
w David Rabe *book* Barbara Gordon *d* Jack Hofsiss *ph* Jan de Bont *m* Stanley Silverman
☆ Jill Clayburgh, Nicol Williamson, Dianne Wiest, Joe Pesci, Geraldine Page, James Sutorius, Richard Masur, Kathleen Widdoes

I'm from Missouri
US 1939 77m bw
Paramount
The wife of a Missouri farmer and mule breeder has social aspirations.
Rural comedy patterned after the Will Rogers successes.
w John C. Moffitt, Duke Atterbury *d* Theodore Reed
☆ Bob Burns, Gladys George, Gene Lockhart, Judith Barrett, William Henry, Patricia Morison, E. E. Clive, Melville Cooper
'Moderate grosser for family trade.' – *Variety*

I'm Going Home **
Portugal/France 2000 90m colour
Artificial Eye/Madragoa/Gemini/France2 (Paulo Branco)
aka: *Vou Para Casa*
After the rest of his family is accidentally killed, leaving him to bring up his young grandson, an ageing actor reflects on his life and the increasingly poor roles offered to him.
Heartfelt meditation on old age from the oldest working director (he was 93 when he made this), with a dignified performance from Piccoli as a man who affirms the pleasures of life while acknowledging his own fading powers.
wd Manoel de Oliveira *ph* Sabine Lancelin *pd* Yves Fournier *ed* Valerie Loiseleux
☆ Michel Piccoli (Gilbert Valence), Antoine Chappey (Agent), Catherine Deneuve (Marguerite), John Malkovich (John Crawford), Leonor Baldaque (Sylvia), Leonor Silveira (Marie)
'The result is something as original as it is unlikely: a study in grief that is flooded with happiness.' – *Owen Gleiberman, Entertainment Weekly*
'This patient detailing of an actor's life – a portrait of the artist as an old man – has a fascination akin to watching a sun slowly disappear beneath the horizon.' – *Anthony Quinn, Independent*

I'm Gonna Git You, Sucka
US 1988 89m DeLuxe
UIP/United Artists/Ivory Way/Raymond Katz/Front Films (Peter McCarthy, Carl Craig)
Black heroes are recruited to overthrow a white gangster.
Good-natured parody of black action movies such as Shaft.
wd Keenen Ivory Wayans *ph* Tom Richmond *m* David Michael Frank *pd* Melba Farquhar, Catherine Hardwicke *ed* Michael R. Miller
☆ Keenen Ivory Wayans, Bernie Casey, Antonio Fargas, Steve James, Isaac Hayes, Jim Brown, Ja'Net DuBois, Dawn Lewis, John Vernon, Clu Gulager

Im Innern des Wals: see *In the Belly of the Whale*

Im Lauf der Zeit: see *Kings of the Road*

'Just a sensitive gal who climbed the ladder of success ... wrong by wrong! A story about a gal who lost her reputation – and never missed it!'
I'm No Angel ***
US 1933 88m bw
Paramount (William Le Baron)
A carnival dancer gets off a murder charge, moves into society and sues a man for breach of promise.
The star's most successful vehicle, credited with saving the fortunes of Paramount, remains a highly diverting side show with almost a laugh a minute. Released before the Legion of Decency was formed, it also contains some of Mae's fruitiest lines.
w Mae West d Wesley Ruggles *ph* Leo Tover *m/ly* Harvey Brooks, Gladys Dubois
☆ *Mae West*, Edward Arnold, Cary Grant, Gregory Ratoff, Ralf Harolde, Kent Taylor, Gertrude Michael
'The most freewheeling of all Mae's screen vehicles, and the most satisfying of the lot.' – *James Robert Parish*
'A quality of balance and proportion which only the finest films attain.' – *Views and Reviews*

I'm Not Rappaport
US 1996 135m DuArt
Gramercy/Greenstreet (John Penotti, John Starke)
Two 80-year-olds are determined not to go gentle into that good night.
Capable, sweetly comic performances from Matthau and Davis add a little humanity to what is a contrived and often implausible narrative.
wd Herb Gardner *play* Herb Gardner *ph* Adam Holender *m* Gerry Mulligan *pd* Mark Friedberg *ed* Wendey Stanzler, Emily Paine
☆ Walter Matthau, Ossie Davis, Amy Irving, Martha Plimpton, Craig T. Nelson, Boyd Gaines
'An uncomfortable mix of slap-shtick and social commentary, with the passage of time having

dulled the story's sense of humor.' – *Leonard Klady, Variety*

Images
Eire 1972 101m Technicolor Panavision
Lions Gate/Hemdale (Tommy Thompson)
A semi-hysterical woman is confronted by the images of her former lovers.
Pretentious psycho-drama which might have made a good half-hour.
wd Robert Altman *ph* Vilmos Zsigmond *m* John Williams
☆ Susannah York, René Auberjonois, Marcel Bozzuffi
John Williams

'When a father doesn't live up to his dreams ... a daughter has to stand up for hers.'
Imaginary Crimes *
US 1994 105m colour
Warner/Morgan Creek (James G. Robinson)
A con man, forever dreaming of riches around the corner, struggles to bring up his two daughters after their mother dies.
Nostalgic reminiscence, seen from the viewpoint of a teenager and embryonic writer, in which love conquers all.
w Kristine Johnson, Davia Nelson *book* Sheila Ballantyne *d* Anthony Drazan *ph* John J. Campbell *m* Stephen Endelman *pd* Joseph T. Garrity *ed* Elizabeth Kling
☆ Harvey Keitel, Fairuza Balk, Kelly Lynch, Vincent D'Onofrio, Diane Baker, Chris Penn, Amber Benson, Seymour Cassel, Annette O'Toole
'The script has stretches of pure corn and the plot mechanics get in the way of genuine feeling. The movie tries hard, but it's far too slight to click on the big screen.' – *Kim Newman, Empire*

Imaginary Sweetheart: see *Professional Sweetheart*

An Imaginary Tale
France 1990 100m colour
Mayfair/C. M. Luca/Téléscène/National Film Board of Canada (Claudio Luca, Robin Spry)
French title: *Une histoire inventée*
In Montreal, a jazz trumpeter falls in love with an actress, to the annoyance of her actor-lover.
Performances of Shakespeare's Othello *form a background to this tale of jealousy, treated as comic rather than tragic.*
w André Forcier, Jacques Marcotte *d* André Forcier *ph* George Dufaux *m* Serge Fiore *ad* Réal Ouellette *ed* François Gill
☆ Jean Lapointe, Louise Marleau, Charlotte Laurier, Marc Messier, Jean-François Pichette, France Castel, Tony Nardi
'Too hermetic to be much more than a light diversion.' – *Sight and Sound*

Imitation General
US 1958 88m bw
MGM (William Hawks)
France 1944: when a general is killed, a sergeant takes his place to preserve morale.
Odd, rather unpalatable war comedy-drama.
w William Bowers *d* George Marshall *ph* George Folsey
☆ Glenn Ford, Red Buttons, Taina Elg, Dean Jones, Kent Smith

Imitation of Life **
US 1934 109m bw
Universal (John M. Stahl)
A woman becomes rich through the pancake recipe of her black servant, but the latter has a tragic life because her daughter passes for white.
Monumentally efficient tearjerker, generally well done.
w William Hurlbut *novel* Fannie Hurst *d John Stahl* *ph* Merritt Gerstad *m* Heinz Roemheld
☆ *Claudette Colbert*, Warren William, *Louise Beavers*, Ned Sparks, Rochelle Hudson, Fredi Washington, Alan Hale, Henry Armetta
'Grim and harsh stuff ... its reception in the south cannot be judged or guessed by a northerner.' – *Variety*
'Classic, compulsively watchable rags-to-riches-and-heartbreak weeper.' – *New Yorker, 1977*
best picture

Imitation of Life *
US 1959 124m Eastmancolor
U-I (Ross Hunter)
Glossy remake of the above with its heroine now an actress; stunningly produced but dully acted, making its racially sensitive plot seem insincere.
w Eleanore Griffin, Allan Scott *d Douglas Sirk* *ph* Russell Metty *m* Frank Skinner
☆ Lana Turner, Juanita Moore, John Gavin, Susan Kohner, Dan O'Herlihy, Sandra Dee, Robert Alda
Juanita Moore; Susan Kohner

Immaculate Conception *
GB 1991 120m Metrocolor
Feature/Dehlavi Films/Film on Four (Jamil Dehlavi)
In Pakistan, a childless American woman is told that she will conceive if she returns to a shrine with her English husband, although she suspects him of having an affair with an Indian friend.
Tangled tale of adultery amid a clash of cultures, rendered exotic by its setting of a fertility cult administered by priestly eunuchs.
wd Jamil Dehlavi *ph* Nic Knowland *m* Richard Harvey *pd* Mike Porter *ed* Chris Barnes
☆ James Wilby, Melissa Leo, Shabana Azmi, Zia Mohyeddin, James Cossins, Shreeram Lagoo, Ronny Jhutti, Tim Choate

Immediate Family
US 1989 95m DeLuxe
Columbia (Sarah Pillsbury, Midge Sanford)
A rich but childless couple arrange to adopt the newborn baby of a poor, unmarried teenager.
Well-meaning, predictable problem movie that fails to involve an audience.
w Barbara Benedek *d* Jonathan Kaplan *ph* John W. Lindley *m* Brad Fiedel *ed* Jane Kurson
☆ Glenn Close, James Woods, Mary Stuart Masterson, Kevin Dillon, Linda Darlow, Jane Greer, Jessica James

The Immigrant **
US 1917 20m approx bw silent
Mutual
A penniless immigrant befriends a girl on the boat and later helps her in a café.
One of the most inventive early Chaplins, with touches of sentiment and social comment which for once only strengthen and do not antagonize.
wd Charles Chaplin *ph* William C. Foster, Rollie Totheroh
☆ Charles Chaplin, Edna Purviance, Albert Austin, Henry Bergman, Eric Campbell
'In its roughness and apparent simplicity it is as much a jewel as a story by O. Henry.' – *Photoplay*

Immoral Tales
France 1974 103m Eastmancolor
Argos (Anatole Dauman)
Four bawdy stories, ranging from 1498 to 1970.
The usual sex portmanteau with a little more strength in the detail and interest in human behaviour than usual.
wd Walerian Borowczyk *ph* Bernard Daillencourt, Guy Durban, Michel Zolat, Noel Véry *m* Maurice Le Roux
☆ Lise Danvers, Charlotte Alexandra, Paloma Picasso, Florence Bellamy
'You come out having learned something about the waywardness of life and love and having been taken on a mystery tour into the present, the past, and the enigmatic strangeness of womanhood.' – *Michael Billington, Illustrated London News*

Immortal Battalion: see *The Way Ahead*

'The genius behind the music. The madness behind the man. The untold love story of Ludwig Van Beethoven.'
Immortal Beloved
GB/US 1994 120m colour Panavision
Entertainment/Majestic/Icon (Bruce Davey)
Beethoven's secretary seeks to discover the identity of the mysterious woman that the unmarried Beethoven loved.
A narrative told in flashbacks to the women who played a part in Beethoven's life; the result is a standard and not particularly convincing portrait of the artist as a tortured genius.
wd Bernard Rose *ph* Peter Suschitzky *m* Beethoven *md* Sir Georg Solti *pd* Jiri Hlupy *ed* Dan Rae
☆ Gary Oldman, Jeroen Krabbe, Johanna Ter Steege, Isabella Rossellini, Marco Hofschneider, Valeria Golino, Matthew North, Miriam Margolyes
'Less than compelling due to the fragmentary telling of the story, off-putting nature of the main character and the failure of the filmmakers to make their investigation seem of any particular consequence.' – *Todd McCarthy, Variety*
'The whole thing is just this side of ludicrous.' – *Derek Malcolm, Guardian*

Immortal Sergeant *
US 1943 90m bw
TCF (Lamar Trotti)
In the North African campaign, a battle-toughened sergeant is killed after inspiring the raw recruits under his command.
'Inspirational' war adventure, quite neatly done but a shade embarrassed by its own poetic leanings.
w Lamar Trotti *novel* John Brophy *d* John Stahl *ph* Arthur Miller *m* David Buttolph
☆ Henry Fonda, Thomas Mitchell, Maureen O'Hara, Allyn Joslyn, Reginald Gardiner, Melville Cooper, Bramwell Fletcher, Morton Lowry
'By the time the first soldier has bit the sand, the film identifies itself: it is none other than Hollywood's old friend the Foreign Legion of Beau Geste vintage, jerked from the shelf and clothed in a new uniform.' – *Time*

The Immortal Story
France 1968 60m Eastmancolor
Albina/ORTF (Micheline Rozan)
In 19th-century Macao, a rich merchant tries to make an old seaman's story come true.
Muddled and stiltedly told fable which would have excited no attention if it had not been associated with the elusive Mr Welles.
wd Orson Welles *story* Isak Dinesen *ph* Willy Kurant *m* Erik Satie
☆ Orson Welles, Jeanne Moreau, Roger Coggio, Norman Eshley

Impact
US 1949 111m bw
(UA)
A woman and her lover plan the murder of her rich industrialist husband, but things go wrong and the husband survives under another name...
Curiously elongated but watchable melodrama, with the impression of a second team doing its best.
w Dorothy Reid *d* Arthur Lubin *ph* Ernest Laszlo
☆ Brian Donlevy, Ella Raines, Charles Coburn, Helen Walker, Anna May Wong

The Impatient Years
US 1944 91m bw
Columbia (Virginia Van Upp)
A soldier finds difficulty in adjusting to his civilian matrimonial state.
Thin star comedy.
w Virginia Van Upp *d* Irving Cummings *ph* Hal Mohr *m* Marlin Skiles
☆ Jean Arthur, Lee Bowman, Charles Coburn, Edgar Buchanan, Harry Davenport, Grant Mitchell, Jane Darwell

The Imperfect Lady: see *The Perfect Gentleman (1935)*

'Scandal seeks her out – even on her wedding night!'
The Imperfect Lady
US 1946 97m bw
Paramount (Karl Tunberg)
GB title: *Mrs Loring's Secret*
In 1890s London, an MP marries a lady with a past.
Dusty melodrama, adequately produced.
w Karl Tunberg *story* Ladislas Fodor *d* Lewis Allen *ph* John F. Seitz *m* Victor Young
☆ Ray Milland, Teresa Wright, Cedric Hardwicke, Virginia Field, Anthony Quinn, Reginald Owen, Melville Cooper, George Zucco, Rhys Williams, Charles Coleman, Miles Mander, Edmund Breon, Frederick Worlock
'To be avoided at any cost.' – *Graham Greene*

The Impersonator *
GB 1961 64m bw
Bryanston/Herald (Anthony Perry)
Americans at a British air base are suspected when a murderous prowler strikes.
Well made second-feature thriller with effective locations, suspense sequences and village atmosphere.
wd Alfred Shaughnessy *ph* John Coquillon *m* de Wolfe
☆ John Crawford, Jane Griffiths, Patricia Burke, John Salew

The Importance of Being Earnest **
GB 1952 95m Technicolor
Rank/Javelin/Two Cities (Teddy Baird)
Two wealthy and eligible bachelors of the 1890s have problems with their marriage prospects.
Disappointingly stagey rendering (when compared, say, with Occupe-toi d'Amélie*) of Britain's most wondrously witty lighter-than-air comedy of manners. As a record of a theatrical performance, however, it is valuable.*
w Anthony Asquith *play* Oscar Wilde
d Anthony Asquith *ph* Desmond Dickinson
m Benjamin Frankel *ad Carmen Dillon*
☆ *Michael Redgrave, Michael Denison, Edith Evans, Margaret Rutherford, Joan Greenwood, Miles* Malleson, Dorothy Tutin, Walter Hudd
'A more positive decision on style should have been taken. A film of this kind must be either an adaptation or a piece of filmed theatre. This one, being partially both, is not wholly either.' – *Gavin Lambert*

'Everybody Loves Ernest... But Nobody's Quite Sure Who He Really Is.'
The Importance of Being Earnest
US/GB 2001 98m Technicolor Panavision
Buena Vista/Miramax/Ealing/Fragile (Barnaby Thompson)
In London of the 1890s, two wealthy bachelors lead double lives, complicating their matrimonial prospects.
Disastrously heavy-handed adaptation of Wilde's classic comedy, ruining the rhythms of the original and opening it up to disastrous effect, losing its essential hothouse atmosphere.
wd Oliver Parker *ph* Tony Pierce-Roberts
m Charlie Mole *ch* Quinney Sachs *pd* Luciana Arrighi *ed* Guy Bensley
☆ Rupert Everett (Algy), Colin Firth (Jack), Frances O'Connor (Gwendolen), Reese Witherspoon (Cecily), Judi Dench (Lady Bracknell), Tom Wilkinson (Dr Chasuble), Anna Massey (Miss Prism), Edward Fox (Lane), Charles Kay (Gribsby)
'Utterly miscalculated... Wilde fans will turn away in dismay, with only costume drama diehards likely to support this on the big screen.' – *Robert Koehler, Variety*
'Oscar Lite, padded, primped and ceaselessly prettified with dream sequences and pop songs.' – *Peter Preston, Observer*

The Impossible Lover: see *Huddle*

Impossible Object: see *Story of a Love Story*

The Impossible Years
US 1968 98m Metrocolor Panavision
MGM/Marten (Lawrence Weingarten)
A university psychiatrist has trouble controlling his nubile 17-year-old daughter.
Wacky farce which veers between the tasteless and the ludicrous, and is never more than momentarily entertaining.
w George Wells *play* Bob Fisher, Arthur Marx
d Michael Gordon *ph* William H. Daniels
m Don Costa
☆ David Niven, Lola Albright, Chad Everett, Ozzie Nelson, Cristina Ferrare, Don Beddoe
'A comedy of the generation gap which didn't bridge it but fell right into it.' – *Gerald Garrett*

'In the future, not everyone is who they seem to be.'

Imposter

US 2001 96m Technicolor Panavision
Metrodome/Marty Katz/Mojo (Gary Fleder, Gary Sinise)

In 2079, when Earth is at war with Alpha Centauri, a government weapons scientist is suspected of being an alien replicant.
Low budget science-fiction of little interest: Philip K. Dick's themes of paranoia and identity have been better explored elsewhere, notably in Blade Runner.
w Caroline Case, Ehren Kruger, David Twohy *story* Philip K. Dick *adaptation* Scott Rosenberg *d* Gary Fleder *ph* Robert Elswit *m* Mark Isham *pd* Nelson Coates *ed* Armen Minasian, Bob Ducsay *sp* Jonathan Silver; ILM; Metrolight
☆ Gary Sinise (Spence Olham), Madeleine Stowe (Maya Olham), Vincent D'Onofrio (Hathaway), Tony Shalhoub (Dr Carone), Mekhi Phifer (Cale), Lindsay Crouse (Chancellor), Elizabeth Pena (Midwife)
'A stubbornly unexciting ride into the near future fronted by superb thesps in slumming mode.' – *Robert Koehler, Variety*
† The film was released after a two year delay.

'A musical, magical, cross-dressing, mistaken identity, cream puff-eating, hidden bomb kind of comedy!'

The Imposters *

US 1998 101m Technicolor
TCF/Fox Searchlight/First Cold Press (Beth Alexander, Stanley Tucci)

In the 30s, two out-of-work actors pretend to be stewards after they become inadvertent stowaways on an Atlantic liner.
An energetic farce of false identities and elaborate plots, which is enjoyable for as long as it lasts, though it hardly amounts to a successful revival of screwball comedy.
wd Stanley Tucci *ph* Ken Kelsch *m* Gary DeMichele *pd* Andrew Jackness *ed* Suzy Elmiger
☆ Oliver Platt, Stanley Tucci, Teagle F. Bougere, Elizabeth Bracco, Steve Buscemi, Billy Connolly, Allan Corduner, Hope Davis, Dana Ivey, Alfred Molina, Isabella Rossellini, Campbell Scott
'More than a dozen of New York's finest actors ham it up with such unrestrained glee ... that it hardly matters if this swirl of cotton candy disappears even before it touches the tip of your tongue.' – *Stephen Holden, New York Times*
† Woody Allen appears uncredited.

The Impostor

US 1944 92m bw
Universal
TV title: *Strange Confession*
A French convict escapes during a Nazi bombing raid, and in the guise of a dead man fights bravely for France.
Propagandist melodrama, more stiffly made than its talent would suggest.
wd Julien Duvivier
☆ Jean Gabin, Ellen Drew, Richard Whorf, Allyn Joslyn, Peter Van Eyck, Ralph Morgan

Impromptu *

GB 1989 107m colour
Rank/Sovereign/Governor/Les Films Ariane (Stuart Oken, Daniel A. Sherkow)

George Sand chases after Chopin to a country house-party and succeeds in seducing him later in Paris.
Lively re-telling of a well-known romance, but the modern, slangy dialogue makes it seem like a fancy-dress party, and it runs out of energy halfway through.
w Sarah Kernochan *d* James Lapine *ph* Bruno de Keyzer *md* Chris Walker *ad* Gérard Daoudal *ed* Michael Ellis
☆ Judy Davis, Hugh Grant, Mandy Patinkin, Bernadette Peters, Julian Sands, Ralph Brown, Georges Corraface, Anton Rodgers, Emma Thompson, Anna Massey
'Not wholly successful, this is nevertheless a surprisingly perky addition to the mainly dreary catalogue of films about the loves of deadweight famous names from the past.' – *Kim Newman, MFB*

Improper Channels

Canada 1979 91m colour

A father runs into administrative trouble when he takes his injured daughter to hospital.
Salutary but not very commanding tale for our times, with a leading performance that suffers from overfamiliarity.
w Morrie Rubinsky, Ian Sutherland, Adam Arkin *d* Eric Till *ph* Anthony Richmond *m* Maribeth Solomon, Micky Erbe
☆ Alan Arkin, Mariette Hartley, Monica Parker, Harry Ditson

Improper Conduct

US 1994 95m colour
Everest (Victor Bhalla/Jag Mundhra)

A woman decides to expose the sleazy married marketing man whose sexual harassment led to the death of her sister.
Uninteresting thriller, which exemplifies its theme of exploitation by including many scenes of voyeuristic and gratuitous sexual activity.
w Carl Austin *story* Jag Mundhra *d* Jag Mundhra *ph* James Michaels *m* Alan Dermarderosian *pd* Brian McCabe *ed* Wayne Schmidt, David Schulman
☆ Steven Bauer, Tahnee Welch, John Laughlin, Nia Peeples, Lee Anne Beaman, Stuart Whitman

An Impudent Girl **

France 1985 97m colour
Artificial Eye/Oliane/A2/Telema/Monthyon (Marie-Laure Reyre)

original title: *L'Effrontée*
An awkward 13-year-old girl begins to grow up.
Charming film of adolescent trauma, owing much to Carson McCuller's The Member of the Wedding *and superior to the US movie version.*
w Claude Miller, Luc Beraud, Bernard Stora, Annie Miller *d* Claude Miller *ph* Dominique Chapuis *m* Alain Jomy *pd* Jean-Pierre Kohut Svelko *ed* Albert Jurgenson
☆ Charlotte Gainsbourg, Bernadette Lafont, Jean-Claude Brialy, Raoul Billerey, Clothilde Baudon, Jean-Philippe Ecoffey

Impulse

US 1984 99m DeLuxe
Tim Zinnemann/ABC Motion Pictures

After an earthquake, a small farming community is menaced by a mysterious subterranean substance which makes people self-destructive.
Modest, mildly humorous sci-fi which has its fun without explaining anything at all.
w Bart Davis, Don Carlos Dunaway *d* Graham Baker
☆ Tim Matheson, Meg Tilly, Hume Cronyn, John Karlen, Amy Stryker

Impulse

US 1990 108m Technicolor
Warner (Albert S. Ruddy, André Morgan)

An undercover cop keeps quiet about the murder of a missing witness.
Implausible thriller.
w John de Marco, Leigh Chapman *d* Sondra Locke *ph* Dean Semler *m* Michel Colombier *pd* William A. Elliott *ed* John W. Wheeler
☆ Theresa Russell, Jeff Fahey, George Dzundza, Alan Rosenberg, Nicholas Mele, Eli Danker, Charles McCaughan, Lynne Thigpen, Shawn Elliott

In a Lonely Place *

US 1950 93m bw
Columbia/Santana (Robert Lord)
An embittered Hollywood scriptwriter escapes a murder charge but loses his girlfriend through his violent temperament.
Curious character melodrama which intrigues without satisfying.
w Andrew Solt *novel* Dorothy B. Hughes *d* Nicholas Ray *ph* Burnett Guffey *m* George Antheil
☆ Humphrey Bogart, Gloria Grahame, Frank Lovejoy, Carl Benton Reid, Art Smith, Jeff Donnell
'It remains better than average, but lacks the penetration which would make it really interesting.' – *Gavin Lambert*

In a Year with 13 Moons

West Germany 1978 124m colour
Tango/Project/Filmverlag der Autoren

original title: *In einem Jahr mit 13 Monden*
Ordeals of a man who undergoes a sex change.
Unattractive case history with expressionist decoration.
wd Rainer Werner Fassbinder *ph* Rainer Werner Fassbinder *m* Peter Raben
☆ Volker Spengler, Ingrid Caven, Gottfried John, Elisabeth Trissenaar, Eva Mattes

In All Innocence: see *En Plein Coeur*

'An Out-And-Out Comedy.'

In & Out *

US 1997 90m DeLuxe
Paramount/Spelling Films (Scott Rudin)

Just before his wedding, a small-town teacher is 'outed' as a homosexual during a speech by a former pupil, now a Hollywood star, as he accepts an Oscar.
Brisk, mildly amusing comedy that is careful not to offend.
w Paul Rudnick *d* Frank Oz *ph* Rob Hahn *m* Mark Shaiman *pd* Ken Adam *ed* Dan Hanley, John Jympson
☆ Kevin Kline, Joan Cusack, Matt Dillon, Debbie Reynolds, Wilford Brimley, Bob Newhart, Tom Selleck
'A screwball comedy that is always genial and often hilarious.' – *Stephen Amidon, Sunday Times*
† The inspiration for the comedy was a speech made by Tom Hanks when accepting an Oscar for *Philadelphia*.
†† Glenn Close, Whoopi Goldberg and Jay Leno appear as themselves.
Joan Cusack

In Bed with Madonna: see *Truth or Dare*

In Caliente

US 1935 85m bw
Warner
In a Mexican horse racing resort, a dancer falls for the magazine editor who criticized her act.
Very slim storyline fails to make this a major musical despite attractive numbers including 'The Lady in Red'.
w Jerry Wald, Julius Epstein *d* Lloyd Bacon *ph* Sol Polito, George Barnes *m/ly* various *ch* Busby Berkeley
☆ Dolores del Rio, Pat O'Brien, Edward Everett Horton, Leo Carrillo, Glenda Farrell, Judy Canova, Phil Regan, Wini Shaw, Herman Bing

In Celebration

GB 1974 131m Eastmancolor
Ely Landau/Cinevision
Three sons travel north for their miner father's fortieth wedding anniversary.
Sharply observant but fairly predictable dramatics, plainly filmed.
w David Storey *play* David Storey *d* Lindsay Anderson *ph* Dick Bush *m* Christopher Gunning
☆ Alan Bates, James Bolam, Brian Cox, Constance Chapman, Bill Owen

In Cold Blood ***

US 1967 134m bw Panavision
Columbia/Richard Brooks

An account of a real life crime in which an entire family was brutally murdered by wandering gunmen.
Unnecessarily complicated as narrative, and uncompromisingly brutal in treatment, this well-meaning film is hard to take in many ways.
wd Richard Brooks *book* Truman Capote *ph* Conrad Hall *m* Quincy Jones
☆ Robert Blake, Scott Wilson, John Forsythe, Paul Stewart, Gerald S. O'Loughlin, Jeff Corey
'It marks a slight step up for its director, best remembered for reducing *Lord Jim* to Pablum and *The Brothers Karamazov* to pulp.' – *John Simon*
† It was remade as an 180m TV mini-series in 1990, directed by Jonathan Kaplan and starring Anthony Edwards and Eric Roberts.
Richard Brooks (as writer); Richard Brooks (as director); Conrad Hall; Quincy Jones

In Country

US 1989 115m DuArt
Warner (Norman Jewison, Richard Roth)

A young girl attempts to discover more about her father, a soldier who died in Vietnam.
Mundane account of a child coming to terms with her life.
w Frank Pierson, Cynthia Cidre *novel* Bobbie Ann Mason *d* Norman Jewison *ph* Russell Boyd *m* James Horner *pd* Jackson DeGovia *ed* Antony Gibbs, Lou Lombardo
☆ Bruce Willis, Emily Lloyd, Joan Allen, Kevin Anderson, Richard Hamilton, Judith Ivey, Peggy Rea, John Terry, Dan Jenkins

'What would you do to get in?'

The In Crowd

US 2000 104m colour
Warner/Morgan Creek (James G. Robinson)

Released from a mental hospital to work in a country club, a girl is befriended by a wealthy psychopath and her friends.
Formulaic thriller with slight lesbian overtones but little to interest anyone.
w Mark Gibson, Philip Halprin *d* Mary Lambert *ph* Tom Priestley *m* Jeff Rona *pd* John D. Kretschmer *ed* Pasquale Buba
☆ Lori Heuring (Adrien Williams), Susan Ward (Brittany Foster), Daniel Hugh Kelly (Dr Thompson), Matthew Settle (Matt Curtis), Nathan Bexton (Bobby), Laurie Fortier (Kelly), Kim Murphy (Joanne), Ethan Erickson (Tom)
'Probably the only people who could be surprised at this movie will be those who wandered into the wrong multiplex theater by mistake.' – *Elvis Mitchell, New York Times*

In Custody

GB 1993 120m Technicolor
Merchant Ivory/Channel 4 (Walid Chowhan)
A teacher, sent to interview the greatest living poet of the dying Urdu language, finds that his hero is a broken-down drunk.
A stately, uninvolving examination of an urgent topic, that of tradition losing out to commerce and debased culture.
w Anita Desai, Shahrukh Husain *novel* Anita Desai *d* Ismail Merchant *ph* Larry Pizer *m* Zakir Hussain, Ustad Sultan Khan *pd* Suresh Sawant *ed* Roberto Silvi
☆ Shashi Kapoor, Om Puri, Shabana Azmi, Sushma Seth, Neena Gupta, Prayag Raj, Tinnu Anand
'As for Merchant, perhaps he should stick to producing.' – *Robin Brooks, Empire*

'What started as a dream, ended as a nightmare.'

In Dreams

US 1999 99m Technicolor 'Scope
DreamWorks (Stephen Woolley)

A mother finds that she can communicate in dreams with the serial killer who murdered her young daughter.
Unattractive psychological thriller that begins on a note of hysteria and remains on that high-pitched level throughout.
w Bruce Robinson, Neil Jordan *novel* *Doll's Eyes* by Bari Wood *d* Neil Jordan *ph* Darius Khondji *m* Elliot Goldenthal *pd* Nigel Phelps *ed* Tony Lawson
☆ Annette Bening, Aidan Quinn, Robert Downey Jnr, Paul Guilfoyle, Dennis Boutsikaris, Stephen Rea, Prudence Wright Holmes, Katie Sagona
'A silly and unpleasant psycho-chiller.' – *Peter Bradshaw, Guardian*
'A complete and utter mess from top to bottom.' – *Bruce Robinson*

In Enemy Country

US 1968 107m Techniscope
Universal (Harry Keller)
In 1939 Paris, the French secret service evolves an elaborate four-year undercover plan.
Standard, overlong espionage melodrama with no surprises.
w Edward Anhalt *story* Sy Bartlett *d* Harry Keller *ph* Loyal Griggs *m* William Lava
☆ Tony Franciosa, Anjanette Comer, Guy Stockwell, Paul Hubschmid, Tom Bell, Harry Townes, Michael Constantine, John Marley

'To Some, Losing Control Is ... Everything.'

In Excess

Italy 1991 94m Fotocinema
Metrofilm/PAC (Galliano Juso)

An English screenwriter grows increasingly jealous of his wife after she insists on spending her weekends with a sadistic lover.
Glossy, sterile, would-be erotic thriller that fails to satisfy on any level.
w Sergio Bazzini *novel* Alberto Moravia *d* Mauro Bolognini *ph* Giuseppe Lanci *m* Ennio Morricone *pd* Claudio Cinini *ed* Sergio Montanari
☆ Julian Sands, Joanna Pacula, Tcheky Karyo, Lara Wendel, Mario Di Stefano

'A pretentious Euro-production which shifts between haunting lyricism and self-indulgence.' – *Sight and Sound*

'Humourless tosh.' – *Empire*

In Gay Madrid

US 1930 78m bw
MGM

A Spanish blade is torn between two women.
Feeble star vehicle, presumably aimed at the Spanish market.
w Bess Meredyth, Edwin Justus Mayer, Salisbury Field *novel* Alejandro Perez Lugin *d* Robert Z. Leonard
☆ Ramon Novarro, Dorothy Jordan, Lottice Howell, Claude King, Eugenie Besserer

'Unreal story, poor acting, ditto direction and general lack of popular appeal.' – *Variety*

In God We Trust

US 1980 97m Technicolor
Universal

A monk leaves his monastery to raise some ready cash.
Dismal and tasteless attempt at religious satire.
w Marty Feldman, Chris Allen *d* Marty Feldman *ph* Charles Correll *m* John Morris
☆ Marty Feldman, Peter Boyle, Louise Lasser, Richard Pryor, Wilfrid Hyde-White

'A rare achievement – a comedy with no laughs. Its energy is prodigious. But only rarely is it matched by invention.' – *Variety*

In Harm's Way *

US 1965 167m bw Panavision
Paramount/Sigma (Otto Preminger)

The American navy retaliates after Pearl Harbor.
Odd mix of all-star action, spectacle (mostly models) and personal romances, with a few interesting scenes; shorn of colour it seems rather half-hearted.
w Wendell Mayes *novel* James Bassett *d* Otto Preminger *ph* Loyal Griggs *m* Jerry Goldsmith *titles* Saul Bass
☆ John Wayne, Kirk Douglas, Patricia Neal, Tom Tryon, Paula Prentiss, Brandon de Wilde, Stanley Holloway, Burgess Meredith, Henry Fonda, Dana Andrews, Franchot Tone, Jill Haworth, George Kennedy, Hugh O'Brian, Carroll O'Connor and also Patrick O'Neal, Slim Pickens, Bruce Cabot, Larry Hagman, James Mitchum

'Lacks even a touch of the touch.' – *Stanley Kauffmann*

Loyal Griggs
Patricia Neal

In Like Flint

US 1967 107m DeLuxe Cinemascope
TCF (Saul David)

Top agent Derek Flint unmasks a subversive female spy ring which has kidnapped the President.
This sequel to Our Man Flint *(qv) is silly rather than funny, a spy spoof which becomes irritatingly hard to take.*
w Hal Fimberg *d* Gordon Douglas *ph* William Daniels *m* Jerry Goldsmith
☆ James Coburn, Lee J. Cobb, Jean Hale, Andrew Duggan, Anna Lee

'It gently founders in yards of flat dialogue, lavishly uninteresting sets, fuzzy colour processing, and a supporting cast in which all the girls look alarmingly mass produced.' – *MFB*

In Love and War

US 1958 111m Eastmancolor
Cinemascope
TCF (Jerry Wald)

Three men from different backgrounds join the US Marines and see service in the Pacific.
Self-conscious propaganda concoction of bare routine interest.
w Edward Anhalt *novel* Anton Myrer *d* Philip Dunne *ph* Leo Tover *m* Hugo Friedhofer
☆ Jeffrey Hunter, Robert Wagner, Bradford Dillman, Dana Wynter, Hope Lange, Sheree North, France Nuyen

'In war they found each other ... In each other they found love...'

In Love and War *

US 1996 115m Rank Colour Panavision
Entertainment/New Line/Dimitri Villard

In Italy during the First World War, the 18-year-old Ernest Hemingway falls in love with a 26-year-old nurse.
Oddly stilted account of an experience that seems to have had a lasting effect on Hemingway; it's just a story of a sentimental interlude between a boy and a woman.
w Allan Scott, Clancy Sigal, Anna Hamilton Phelan *book* *Hemingway in Love and War* by Henry S. Villard, James Nagel *d* Richard Attenborough *ph* Roger Pratt *m* George Fenton *pd* Stuart Craig *ed* Lesley Walker
☆ Sandra Bullock (Agnes von Kurowsky), Chris O'Donnell (Ernest Hemingway), Mackenzie Astin (Henry Villard), Ingrid Lacey (Elsie MacDonald), Emilio Bonucci, Margot Steinberg, Colin Stinton, Ian Kelly

'Doesn't get under the skin of its protagonists, leaving the viewer unmoved and passably interested at best.' – *Todd McCarthy, Variety*

In Name Only *

US 1939 94m bw
RKO (Pandro S. Berman)

A rich man falls in love but his wife refuses a divorce.
The stars seem unhappy in this sombre matrimonial drama, but of its kind it's surprisingly well made.
w Richard Sherman *novel* *Memory of Love* by Bessie Brewer *d* John Cromwell *ph* J. Roy Hunt *m* Roy Webb
☆ Cary Grant, Carole Lombard, Kay Francis, Charles Coburn, Helen Vinson

'Sock romantic drama ... will get maximum playing time and the best dating the country offers.' – *Variety*

'Shot with a refined taste for interior decoration ... it is oversweetened with the material for tears.' – *Graham Greene*

'The talking picture reaches perfection!'

In Old Arizona **

US 1929 95m bw
Fox

Adventures of the Cisco Kid.
Primitive sound Western, a sensation in its day but now of purely historical interest.
w Tom Barry *stories* O. Henry *d* Raoul Walsh, Irving Cummings *ph* Arthur Edeson
☆ Warner Baxter, Edmund Lowe, Dorothy Burgess, J. Farrell MacDonald
† See also *The Cisco Kid.*
Warner Baxter
best picture; Tom Barry; Irving Cummings; Arthur Edeson

In Old California

US 1942 89m bw
Republic

A Boston pharmacist heads west towards gold rush California.
Moderate star Western with parsimonious budget.
w Gertrude Purcell, Frances Hyland *d* William McGann
☆ John Wayne, Binnie Barnes, Albert Dekker, Helen Parrish, Patsy Kelly, Edgar Kennedy, Dick Purcell, Charles Halton

In Old Chicago ***

US 1937 115m bw
TCF (Kenneth MacGowan)

Events leading up to the great Chicago fire include a torrid romance between a gambler and a café singer.
Spectacular melodrama which with its two-million-dollar budget was a deliberate attempt to outdo San Francisco, and only failed because the cast was less interesting. A splendid studio super-production.
w Lamar Trotti, Sonya Levien *novel* *We the O'Learys* by Niven Busch *d* Henry King *ph* Peverell Marley *md* Louis Silvers *ad* William Darling *ed* Barbara McLean *sp* H. Bruce Humberstone, Daniel B. Clark, Fred Sersen, Louis J. Witte, Ralph Hammeras
☆ Tyrone Power, Alice Faye, Don Ameche, *Alice Brady*, Andy Devine, Brian Donlevy, Phyllis Brooks, Tom Brown, Sidney Blackmer, Berton Churchill, Paul Hurst, Rondo Hatton, Eddie Collins

'Sock spectacle film ... an elaborate and liberally budgeted entertainment.' – *Variety*

Alice Brady
best picture; Niven Busch (original story); Louis Silvers

In Old Kentucky

US 1935 85m bw
TCF (Edward Butcher)

A family feud is settled by a horse race.
Warm-hearted, old-fashioned stuff, and the star's last film.
w Sam Hellman, Gladys Lehman *play* Charles T. Dazey *d* George Marshall
☆ Will Rogers, Bill Robinson, Dorothy Wilson, Russell Hardie

In Old Mexico

US 1938 62m bw
Paramount (Harry Sherman)

Hopalong Cassidy rides out in search of the outlaw who shot the son of a friend and is now trying to kill him.
Slow-moving Western, strictly for fans of our hero.
w Harrison Jacobs *d* Edward D. Venturini *ph* Russell Harlan *m* Gregory Stone *ad* Lewis J. Rachmil *ed* Robert Warwick
☆ William Boyd, George Hayes, Russell Hayden, Paul Sutton, Allan Garcia, Jane Clayton, Glenn Strange

In Old Montana

US 1942 61m bw
Equity (C. C. Burr)

In Montana in the 1880s, an army officer goes undercover to prevent a range war between cattlemen and sheep-herders.
Despite its theme, which is treated in a threadbare manner, the emphasis here is on songs and comedy, neither done with much style.
w Jackson Parks, Raymond K. Johnson, Homer King Gordon, Barney Hutchinson *d* Raymond K. Johnson *ph* Marcel Picard, Harvey Gould *ad* Ben Berk *ed* Charles Henkel
☆ Fred Scott, Jean Carmen, John Merton, Harry Harvey, Walter McGrail, Wheeler Oakman, Frank LaRue, Allen Cavan, Jane Keckley
† There is a continuity error early in the film, in which John Merton as the villain unbuttons his shirt, removes his gunbelt and then unbuttons his shirt again.

In Old Oklahoma: see *War of the Wildcats*

In Our Time *

US 1944 110m bw
Warner (Jerry Wald)

English girl marries Polish count and helps defy the Nazis.
Ambitious, would-be meaningful melodrama that doesn't quite come off.
w Ellis St Joseph, Howard Koch *d* Vincent Sherman *ph* Carl Guthrie *m* Franz Waxman
☆ Ida Lupino, Paul Henreid, Nancy Coleman, *Nazimova*, Mary Boland, Victor Francen, Michael Chekhov

'The story starts a good many hares but prudently refrains from following them.' – *Richard Mallett, Punch*

In Person

US 1935 85m bw
RKO (Pandro S. Berman)

A glamorous but exhausted film star tries to escape her public by fleeing incognito to the country.
Mild star comedy.
w Allan Scott *novel* Samuel Hopkins Adams *d* William A. Seiter *ph* Edward Cronjager *m* Roy Webb *songs* Oscar Levant, Dorothy Fields
☆ Ginger Rogers, George Brent, Alan Mowbray, Grant Mitchell, Samuel S. Hinds, Spencer Charters

'Inept starring debut for Ginger Rogers ... a very weak affair.' – *Variety*

In Praise of Love: see *Éloge De L'amour*

In Praise of Older Women

Canada 1978 108m colour
Warner/Canadian Film Development/Famous Players & TSM Investments (Robert Lantos, Claude Héroux)

A young Hungarian has affairs with older women in his homeland and, following the revolution, in Canada.
Episodic movie that soon becomes numbingly repetitious.
w Paul Gottlieb *novel* Stephen Vizinczey *d* George Kaczender *ph* Miklos Lente *m* Tibor Polgar *ad* Wolf Kroeger *ed* George Kaczender, Peter Wintonick
☆ Tom Berenger, Karen Black, Susan Strasberg, Helen Shaver, Marilyn Lightstone, Alexandra Stewart

In Rosie's Room: see *Rosie the Riveter*

In Search of Gregory

GB 1969 90m Technicolor
Universal/Vic Films/Vera Films (Joe Janni, Daniele Senatore)

A girl attends her father's wedding to meet a mysterious guest named Gregory, whom she never quite contacts.
Irritatingly pretentious Pinterish puzzle-drama with apparently no hidden depths except the urge to be clever.
w Tonino Guerra, Lucile Laks *d* Peter Wood *ph* Otto Heller, Giorgio Tonti *m* Ron Grainer
☆ Julie Christie, Michael Sarrazin, John Hurt, Adolfo Celi, Roland Culver, Tony Selby

'Moments in a vacuum: however lively the surface, the centre remains depressingly inert.' – *MFB*

'A thousand thrills ... and Hayley Mills'

In Search of the Castaways ***

GB 1961 100m Technicolor
Walt Disney (Hugh Attwooll)

With the aid of an eccentric professor, three children seek their lost explorer father in some geographically fantastic regions of South America.
Engaging Victorian fantasy which starts realistically but builds up to sequences in the manner of The Wizard of Oz *and concludes in* Treasure Island *vein. Jaunty juvenile fare.*
w Lowell S. Hawley *novel* *Captain Grant's Children* by Jules Verne *d* Robert Stevenson *ph* Paul Beeson *m* William Alwyn *ad* Michael Stringer
☆ *Maurice Chevalier, Hayley Mills*, George Sanders, Wilfrid Hyde-White, *Wilfrid Brambell*

In Society *

US 1944 74m bw
Universal (Edmund Hartmann)

Two incompetent plumbers ruin a mansion.
One of the better A & C romps, with little padding between the comedy highlights, though the trimmings are fearsomely dated.
w John Grant, Hal Fimberg, Edmund L. Hartmann *d* Jean Yarbrough *ph* Jerome Ash *m* Edgar Fairchild
☆ Bud Abbott, Lou Costello, Kirby Grant, Ann Gillis, Arthur Treacher, Steve Geray, George Dolenz, Marion Hutton

'A young man. An older woman. Her ex-husband. Things are about to explode...'

In The Bedroom **

US 2001 138m CFI
Buena Vista/GreeneStreet/Good Machine (Graham Leader, Ross Katz, Todd Field)

The marriage of a middle-aged doctor and his wife, a teacher, grows fractious when their son is killed.
Compelling drama of marital tensions at breaking point, of parents who have invested their future in their only child; but the violent ending vitiates all that has gone before.
w Rob Festinger, Todd Field *story* *Killings* by Andre Dubus *d* Todd Field *ph* Antonio Calvache *m* Thomas Newman *ad* Shannon Hart *ed* Frank Reynolds
☆ *Sissy Spacek* (Ruth Fowler), *Tom Wilkinson* (Matt Fowler), Nick Stahl (Frank Fowler), *Marisa*

Tomei (Natalie Strout), William Mapother (Richard Strout), William Wise (Willis Grinnel), Celia Weston (Katie Grinnel), Karen Allen (Marla Keyes)

'An intensely emotional family drama drenched by the earth's elements and outfitted with the myriad details of the stuff of life.' – *Todd McCarthy, Variety*

'There are scenes as true as movies can make them, and even when the story develops thriller elements, they are redeemed, because the movie isn't about what happens, but about why.' – *Roger Ebert, Chicago Sun-Times*

picture; Rob Festinger, Todd Field (screenplay);Tom Wilkinson; Sissy Spacek; Marisa Tomei

In the Belly of the Whale *

West Germany 1985 96m colour
DNS Film/Haro Senft/NDR
original title: *Im Innern des Wals*

Fleeing from her violent father, an adolescent girl goes in search of the mother she has not seen for ten years.

Teenage angst is set against adult violence and unhappy love affairs.

w Michael Junker, Doris Dörrie *d* Doris Dörrie *ph* Alex Block *m* Claus Bantzer *ad* Jörg Neuman *ed* Raimund Barthelmes

☆ Janna Marangosoff, Eisi Gulp, Peter Saltmann, Silvia Reize

'The drama. The passion. The intrigue. And rehearsals haven't even started.'

In the Bleak Midwinter *

GB 1995 98m bw
Rank/Midwinter (David Barron)

An out-of-work actor gathers together a motley crew of unemployed thespians to put on a production of *Hamlet* in a village church.

A sentimental comedy with amusing moments, although the script is too manipulative to achieve the required tear-jerking, and some of the performances shade into caricature.

wd Kenneth Branagh *ph* Roger Lanser *m* Jimmy Yuill *pd* Tim Harvey *ed* Neil Farrell

☆ Michael Maloney, Richard Briers, Mark Hadfield, Julia Sawalha, Nick Farrell, Gerard Horan, John Sessions, Celia Imrie, Hetta Charnley, Joan Collins, Jennifer Saunders

'Is only likely to end up as the answer to a riddle in a Christmas cracker: "What's broad and thin and weak and tired?"' – *Adam Mars-Jones, Independent*

'Both shrewdly written and well played.' – *Derek Malcolm, Guardian*

In the Company of Men **

US 1997 97m colour
Alliance/Stephen Pevner/Atlantis/Fair and Square (Mark Archer, Stephen Pevner)

Two corporate workers, unhappy at being ditched by their girlfriends, decide to get their revenge by dating and dumping on the first vulnerable woman they meet.

Effective but very manipulative piece of social drama, too diagrammatic to be dramatically convincing, but providing some biting dialogue and controversial subject-matter.

wd Neil LaBute *ph* Tony Hettinger *m* Ken Williams, Karel Roessing *pd* Julia Henkel *ed* Joel Plotch

☆ Aaron Eckhart, Stacy Edwards, Matt Malloy, Mark Rector, Jason Dixie, Emily Cline

'A serious, brainy and highly entertaining film – the best kind of popular cinema.' – *Richard Williams, Guardian*

'Passes itself off as an exposé of cynicism and manipulation but the movie itself is more cynical and manipulative than its subject. Like so many "issue" films, it's a talking point, not a movie.' – *Mark Steyn, Spectator*

In the Cool of the Day

GB 1962 91m Metrocolor Panavision
MGM (John Houseman)

The frail wife of a New York publisher dies in Greece after an affair with his colleague.

Travelogue with romantic asides; a pretty glum business.

w Meade Roberts *novel* Susan Ertz *d* Robert Stevens *ph* Peter Newbrook *m* Francis Chagrin *ad* Ken Adam

☆ Jane Fonda, Peter Finch, Arthur Hill, Angela Lansbury, Constance Cummings

In the Doghouse

GB 1961 93m bw
Rank (Hugh Stewart)

Misadventures of a newly qualified vet.

Easy-going farce with animal interest and a great many familiar faces.

w Michael Pertwee *novel It's a Vet's Life* by Alex Duncan *d* Darcy Conyers *ph* Alan Hume *m* Philip Green

☆ Leslie Phillips, Peggy Cummins, Hattie Jacques, James Booth, Dick Bentley, Colin Gordon, Joan Heal, Fenella Fielding, Esma Cannon, Richard Goolden, Joan Hickson, Vida Hope, Harry Locke, Kynaston Reeves

In the Folds of the Flesh (dubbed)

Italy/Spain 1970 90m Eastmancolor
MGB/Talia (Sergio Bergonzelli)

original title: *Nelle Pieghe della Carne*

A murder tips a family into madness.

Absurd and bloody thriller which, with its incestuous trio of vulture-keeping homicidal maniacs, tilted camera angles and optical effects, fails to live up to its Freudian pretentiousness.

w Fabio de Agostini, Sergio Bergonzelli *d* Sergio Bergonzelli *ph* Mario Pacheco *m* Jesus Villa Rojo *ad* Eduardo Torre de la Fuente *ed* Donatella Baglivo

☆ Eleonora Rossi Drago, Pier Angeli (Anna Maria Pierangeli), Fernando Sancho, Alfredo Majo, Emilio Gutierrez Caba, Maria Rosa Sclauzero

'Anywhere but Paris it would have been a scandal!'

In the French Style *

US/France 1962 105m bw
Columbia/Casanna/Orsay (Robert Parrish, Irwin Shaw)

An American girl in Paris has affairs with a young boy and with a divorced newspaperman.

Smooth, episodic, romantic character study, well made but with no perceptible dramatic point.

w Irwin Shaw *d* Robert Parrish *ph* Michel Kelber *m* Josef Kosma

☆ *Jean Seberg*, Stanley Baker, Philippe Fouquet

In the Good Old Summertime *

US 1949 102m Technicolor
MGM (Joe Pasternak)

In a Chicago music store in 1906, a salesgirl corresponds through a dating service with a man who turns out to be the manager she detests.

Cheerful remake of The Shop around the Corner *(qv), with agreeable music, garish colour and not much style.*

w Albert Hackett, Frances Goodrich, Ivan Tors *play The Shop Around the Corner* by Miklos Laszlo *d* Robert Z. Leonard *ph* Harry Stradling *md* George Stoll *ch* Robert Alton *ad* Randell Duell *ed* Adrienne Fazan

☆ Judy Garland, Van Johnson, S. Z. Sakall, Spring Byington, Clinton Sundberg, Buster Keaton, Lillian Bronson

♫ 'Merry Christmas'; 'In the Good Old Summertime'; 'Meet Me Tonight in Dreamland'; 'Put Your Arms Around Me, Honey'; 'Wait 'Till the Sun Shines Nellie'; 'In the Evening'; 'I Don't Care'

In the Heat of the Night ****

US 1967 109m DeLuxe
UA/Mirisch (Walter Mirisch)

In a small Southern town, the bigoted and bombastic sheriff on a murder hunt grudgingly accepts the help of a black detective.

A tense and exciting thriller that also explores racism through the explosive clash of two contrasting personalities.

w Stirling Silliphant *d Norman Jewison* *ph Haskell Wexler* *m* Quincy Jones *ad* Paul Groesse *ed* Hal Ashby

☆ *Sidney Poitier*, *Rod Steiger*, Warren Oates, Quentin Dean, William Schallert

'A very nice film and a very good film and yes, I think it's good to see a black man and a white man working together ... but it's not going to take the tension out of New York City; it's not going to stop the riots in Chicago.' – *Rod Steiger*

† Poitier subsequently starred in a couple of very inferior sequels, *They Call Me Mister Tibbs* and *The Organization* (both qv).

best picture; Stirling Silliphant; Rod Steiger; Hal Ashby; sound

Norman Jewison; sound effects (James A. Richard)

Rod Steiger

In the Line of Fire *

US 1993 129m Technicolor Panavision
Columbia (Jeff Apple)

A secret service agent, who is haunted by his failure to save President Kennedy, is taunted by a ruthless killer who announces he intends to assassinate the current US President.

An enjoyable thriller that provides Eastwood the opportunity to develop an unstereotypical character, but which also lets Malkovich go over the top as a carpet-chewing baddie, and lacks suspense.

w Jeff Maguire *d* Wolfgang Petersen *ph* John Bailey *m* Ennio Morricone *pd* Lilly Kilvert *ed* Anne V. Coates

☆ Clint Eastwood, John Malkovich, Rene Russo, Dylan McDermott, Gary Cole, Fred Dalton Thompson, John Mahoney, Greg Alan-Williams

'Meat-and-potatoes genre-picture entertainment: nothing fancy, nothing unusual.' – *Terrence Rafferty, New Yorker*

'The story is from recycled thrillersville, but it's snappy and appealing in its fast, tense treatment.' – *Angie Errigo, Empire*

John Malkovich; Jeff Maguire; Anne V. Coates

In the Mood: see *The Woo Woo Kid*

In the Mood for Love ***

Hong Kong 2000 97m colour
Metro Tartan/Block 2/Paradis/Jet Tone (Wong Kar-wai)

original title: *Huayang Nianhua*

In Hong Kong in the early 1960s, a newspaper editor and a secretary form a tentative relationship after they discover that their respective partners are having an affair.

Delicate, subdued study in unrequited love, in which the reluctant couple almost merge into the background of a life that is long gone; it has about it an affecting air of broken-hearted nostalgia.

wd Wong Kar-wai *ph* Christopher Doyle, Mark Li Ping-bing *m* Michael Galasso, Umebayashi Shigeru *pd William Chang* *ed* William Chang

☆ *Tony Leung Chiu-wai* (Chow Mo-wan), *Maggie Cheung* (Su Li-zhen), Lai Chin (Mr Ho), Rebecca Pan (Mrs Suen), Siu Ping-lam (Ah-ping)

'Dazzles with a heady atmosphere of romantic melancholy and ravishing visuals straight out of a '60s Vogue spread but neglects to construct the kind of dramatic complexity to provide any lasting emotional resonance.' – *David Rooney, Variety*

† Tony Leung won the Best Actor award at the Cannes Film Festival in 2000 for his performance.

In the Mouth of Madness

US 1995 95m Film House colour Panavision
New Line (Sandy King)

An insurance agent investigates the disappearance of a best-selling horror author, whose latest book is making its readers lose their sanity, and finds himself living in the author's fictional world.

An intriguing notion is abandoned after a while for a more conventional horror movie in the H. P. Lovecraft mould of monstrous beings striving to recapture the world.

w Michael de Luca *d* John Carpenter *ph* Gary B. Kibbe *m* John Carpenter, Jim Lang *pd* Jeff Steven Ginn *ed* Edward A. Warschilka *sp* Industrial Light and Magic

☆ Sam Neill, Julie Carmen, Jürgen Prochnow, Charlton Heston, David Warner, John Glover, Bernie Casey, Peter Jason, Frances Bay

'The plotline is so incoherent that in the end you don't much care what happens to whom and why.' – *Derek Malcolm, Guardian*

In the Name of the Father **

Eire/GB 1993 133m Technicolor
Universal/Hell's Kitchen/Gabriel Byrne (Jim Sheridan)

Four young Irish friends are framed by the police for planting an IRA bomb that blows up a Guildford pub.

A true story, filled with a righteous indignation and deftly told, but debasing its own authenticity with its final, hollow court-room scene which is not only completely invented and inaccurate in its portrayal of British procedure, but is played like the climax from a Perry Mason movie; it is at its best when exploring the relationship between father and son.

w Terry George, Jim Sheridan *d* Jim Sheridan *ph Peter Biziou* *m* Trevor Jones *pd* Caroline Amies *ed Gerry Hambling*

☆ *Daniel Day-Lewis*, *Pete Postlethwaite*, Emma Thompson, John Lynch, Mark Sheppard, Beatie Edney, Marie Jones, Britta Smith, Corin Redgrave

'Solid and well-crafted, with moments of great power.' – *Adam Mars-Jones, Independent*

'Unashamed Irish myth-making. But considering the sensitivity of the issues involved, it is a bit odd that Sheridan has taken quite such liberties with the truth. This is, after all, a film about a man who spent 14 years in prison because people made up stories about him.' – *Martin Bright, Sight and Sound*

Daniel Day-Lewis; Pete Postlethwaite; Emma Thompson; Jim Sheridan (as director); Terry George, Jim Sheridan; Gerry Hambling

In the Navy *

US 1941 86m bw
Universal (Alex Gottlieb)

Two incompetents and a singing heart-throb are naval recruits.

A basically feeble follow-up to Buck Privates *which outgrossed its predecessor and now stands as an interesting pointer to how mass entertainment has changed since 1941.*

w John Grant, Arthur T. Horman *d* Arthur Lubin *ph* Joseph Valentine *m/ly* Gene de Paul, Don Raye

☆ Bud Abbott, Lou Costello, Dick Powell, The Andrews Sisters, Claire Dodd, Dick Foran, Shemp Howard

In the Realm of Passion: see *Ai No Borei*

In the Shadow of the Wind

France/Canada 1987 107m colour
Cinevideo/Les Film Ariane/TFI Films (Justine Héroux)
original title: *Les Fous de Bassan*

A middle-aged artist recalls an earlier time when he disrupted the life of a small, puritannical fishing community.

Slow-moving movie that tries for, and misses, a tragic dimension.

w Sheldon Chad, Marcel Beaulieu, Yves Simoneau *novel* Anne Hébert *d* Yves Simoneau *ph* Alain Dostie *m* Richard Grégoire *ad* Michel Proulx *ed* Joele Van Effenterre

☆ Steve Banner, Charlotte Valandrey, Laure Marsac, Angèle Coutu, Paul Hébert, Marie Tifo, Bernard-Pierre Donnadieu, Lothaire Bluteau, Jean-Louis Millette

In the Soup **

US/Japan/Germany/France 1992 93m bw
Will Alliance/Pandora/Why Not/Odessa/Alta/Mikado (Jim Stark, Hank Blumenthal)

A con-man uses an independent film director trying to raise the money to finance his screenplay as a front for his schemes.

An amusing off-beat comedy about the education of an innocent.

w Alexandre Rockwell, Tim Kissell *d Alexandre Rockwell* *ph* Phil Parmet *m* Mader *pd* Mark Friedberg *ed* Dana Congdon

☆ Steve Buscemi, *Seymour Cassel*, Jennifer Beals, Pat Moya, Will Patton, Jim Jarmusch, Carol Kane

'Winning performances and gentle, self-deprecating humor put this across as an audience pleaser for the specialized film crowd.' – *Variety*

† Although the cinema release was in black and white, the film was issued on video in a colour print.

In the White City *
Portugal/Switzerland 1983 108m colour
Contemporary/Metro filme/Filmograph/WDR/Channel 4 (Paulo Branco, Alain Tanner, Antonio Vaz da Silver)
original title: *Dans La Ville Blanche*
Jumping ship in Lisbon, a married sailor falls in love with a local girl and sends home movies of the city to his wife.
A study in masculine alienation, dependent on its images to carry its message of distintegration and illusory freedom.
wd Alain Tanner *ph* Acacio de Almeida *m* Jean-Luc Barbier *ad* Maria Jose Branco *ed* Laurent Uhler
☆ Bruno Ganz, Teresa Madruga, Julia Vonderlinn, José Carvalho, Victor Costa, Francisco Baiao, José Wallenstein, Lidia Franco

In the Woods: see *Rashomon*

'No one is as good as Bette when she's bad!'
In This Our Life **
US 1942 101m bw
Warner (David Lewis)
A neurotic girl steals her sister's husband, leaves him in the lurch, dominates her hapless family and is killed while on the run from the police.
Splendid star melodrama with good supporting acting and background detail.
w Howard Koch novel Ellen Glasgow *d John Huston ph* Ernest Haller *m* Max Steiner
☆ *Bette Davis, Charles Coburn*, Olivia de Havilland, Frank Craven, George Brent, Dennis Morgan, Billie Burke, Hattie McDaniel, Lee Patrick, Walter Huston (uncredited)

In This World **
GB 2002 89m DeLuxe
ICA/Film Consortium/BBC/Film Council/The Works/ Revolution (Andrew Eaton, Anita Overland)
Two young Afghans living in Shamshatoo refugee camp in Pakistan decide to try to reach Britain.
Shot on digital video, this falls somewhere between documentary and drama, recreating the experience of the vast journey by bus, car, and lorry with its monotony and sudden flurries of action, its uncertainties and dangers. It is an untidy movie, with no easy resolution, just an underlying desperation.
w Tony Grisoni *d* Michael Winterbottom *ph* Marcel Zyskind *m* Dario Marianelli *ed* Peter Christelis
☆ Jamal Udin Torabi, Enayatullah, Imran Paracha, Hiddayatullah, Kerem Atabeyoglu, Erham Sekizcan, Nabil Elouahabi
'An audacious undertaking that some might dismiss because it feels unfinished, in the sense of ragged round the edges… a truly existential road movie, in which the characters are the road they travel.' – *Jonathan Romney, Independent*

'He didn't know how far he'd have to go.'
In Too Deep
US 1999 96m DeLuxe
Metrodome/Dimension/Suntaur (Paul Aaron, Michael Henry Brown)
An undercover cop infiltrates the operations of a Cincinnati crime boss and becomes confused about where his loyalties lie.
Gritty urban drama of moral corruption that was done rather better in Bill Duke's Deep Cover *(qv) a few years back.*
w Michael Henry Brown, Paul Aaron *d* Michael Rymer *ph* Ellery Ryan *m* Christopher Young *pd* Dan Leigh *ed* Dany Cooper *cos* Shawn Barton
☆ Omar Epps (Jeff Cole/J. Reid), LL Cool J (Dwayne Gittens ('God')), Nia Long (Myra), Stanley Tucci (Preston Boyd), Hill Harper (Breezy T.), Pam Grier (Det Angela Wilson), Jake Webber (Daniel Connolly), Richard Brooks (Wesley), David Patrick Kelly (Rick Scott)
'Its aura of made-for-television prosaicness fatally diminishes it.' – *Danny Leigh, Sight and Sound*

In Which We Serve ****
GB 1942 114m bw
Rank/Two Cities (Noël Coward)
Survivors from a torpedoed destroyer recall their life at sea and on leave.
Dated but splendid flagwaver; an archetypal British war film of almost limitless propaganda value.
w Noël Coward d Noël Coward, David Lean
ph Ronald Neame *m* Noël Coward
☆ *Noël Coward*, Bernard Miles, *John Mills*, Richard Attenborough, *Celia Johnson*, Kay Walsh, Joyce Carey, Michael Wilding, Penelope Dudley Ward, Kathleen Harrison, Philip Friend, George Carney, Geoffrey Hibbert, James Donald
COMMANDER (NOËL COWARD): 'The Torrin has been in one scrap after another, but even when we've had men killed, the majority survived and brought the old ship back. Now she lies in 1500 fathoms and with her more than half our shipmates. If they had to die, what a grand way to go! And now they lie all together with the ship we loved, and they're in very good company. We've lost her, but they're still with her. There may be less than half the Torrin left, but I feel that we'll all take up the battle with even stronger heart. Each of us knows twice as much about fighting, and each of us has twice as good a reason to fight. You will all be sent to replace men who've been killed in other ships, and the next time you're in action, remember the Torrin! I should like to add that there isn't one of you that I wouldn't be proud and honoured to serve with again.'
'One of the screen's proudest achievements at any time and in any country.' – *Newsweek*
'Never at any time has there been a reconstruction of human experience which could touch the savage grandeur and compassion of this production.' – *Howard Barnes, New York Herald Tribune*
† The story and the Coward character were based on the experiences of Louis Mountbatten, whose ship, HMS *Kelly*, was sunk under him.
Special Award to Noël Coward
best picture; Noël Coward (as writer)

The In-Laws
US 1979 103m Technicolor
Warner (Alan Arkin)
A timorous dentist and a CIA spy, whose children are to marry, find themselves unwillingly linked together in gunplay in a South American republic.
Two charismatic actors can't fail to get some laughs, but the extended script makes it a bumpy ride.
w Andrew Bergman *d* Arthur Hiller *ph* David M. Walsh *m* John Morris *pd* Pato Guzman
☆ Peter Falk, Alan Arkin, Richard Libertini, Penny Peyser, Nancy Dussault
'It seems incapable either of adhering to the conventions of a comedy-thriller plot or of mustering sufficient invention to abandon plot altogether for a farcical free-for-all.' – *Tim Pulleine, MFB*

Inadmissible Evidence **
GB 1968 96m bw
Paramount/Woodfall (Ronald Kinnoch)
A frustrated 40-year-old solicitor is on the verge of a nervous breakdown.
Interesting and surprisingly successful transcription of a difficult play which was virtually an anti-humanity soliloquy.
w John Osborne play John Osborne *d Anthony Page ph* Kenneth Hodges *m* Dudley Moore *ad* Seamus Flannery
☆ *Nicol Williamson*, Eleanor Fazan, Jill Bennett, Peter Sallis, Eileen Atkins, Isabel Dean
'A play that was conceived as an increasingly bad dream has been made into a grittily detailed, naturalistic film.' – *Stanley Kauffmann*

'A story of sex, drugs, nudity and gratuitous study.'
Inbetweeners
GB 2001 86m colour
Universal/Britpack (Darren Paul Fisher)
A group of first-year students experience life at the University of Great Britain.
Uninvolving romantic comedy about an undifferentiated group, recycling the tiredest clichés of undergraduate existence.
wd Darren Paul Fisher *ph* Matthew Woolf *pd* Henry Davis *ed* Darren Fisher, Kerrie Campbell, Allan Williams
☆ Finlay Robertson (David Marshall), Kate Loustau (Nicole Miles), Lynn Edmonstone (Steph Thornhill), Toby Walton (Jack Easterford), Sarah Vandenbergh (Cassie Sanderson), Katy Kennedy (Mel Reeves), Jane Peachey (Beth Morton), Gary Fannin (Clark Slater), Alex Harcourt-Smith (Marc Bailey-Piper)
'Competently done, but dull.' – *Sight and Sound*

'She was the biggest sucker of them all!'
Incendiary Blonde *
US 1945 112m Technicolor
Paramount (Joseph Sistrom)
The life of twenties night-club queen Texas Guinan.
Laundered biopic with guns, girls and gangsters as well as songs.
w Claude Binyon, Frank Butler *d* George Marshall *ph Ray Rennahan m* Robert Emmett Dolan
☆ *Betty Hutton*, Arturo de Cordova, Charles Ruggles, Albert Dekker, Barry Fitzgerald, Mary Philips, Bill Goodwin, Eduardo Ciannelli, Maurice Rocco
'It runs its noisy but high-minded course through steamy emotion, painful misunderstanding and dramatic self-sacrifice, winding up in the snow among the blood of dead gangsters. Have we ever seen gangsters in Technicolor before?' – *Richard Mallett, Punch*
'A brassy synthesis of colour, song and dance, spattered with laughs.' – *Daily Herald*
Robert Emmett Dolan

L'incendio di Roma: see *Fire over Rome*

'See The Terror! Feel The Pleasure! Taste The Pain!'
Incense for the Damned
GB 1970 87m Eastmancolor
Grand National/Lucinda/Titan (Graham Harris)
video title: *Blood Suckers*
An Oxford academic holidays in Greece and becomes a vampire.
A moderately successful attempt to create a modern-day vampire story, substituting sexual perversion for the usual occult approach.
w Julian More *novel Doctors Wear Scarlet* by Simon Raven *d* Michael Burrowes (Robert Hartford-Davis) *ph* Desmond Dickinson *m* Bobby Richards *pd* George Provis
☆ Patrick Macnee (Major Longbow), Peter Cushing (Dr Goodrich), Alex Davion (Tony Seymour), Johnny Sekka (Bob Kirby), Madeline Hinde (Penelope), Patrick Mower (Richard Fountain), Imogen Hassall (Chriseis), Edward Woodward (Holmstrom), William Mervyn (Honeydew), David Lodge (Colonel)
'Well enough constructed to amount to a richly subversive exercise in the genre.' – *David Pirie, MFB*
† The film was cut by four minutes for its British release and disowned by its director, who did not regard it as finished. It was given a trade show in 1972 but did not receive a London showing until 1976.

Inchon
US 1981 140m colour
One Way Productions (Mitsuharu Ishii)
General MacArthur is affected by divine guidance during a major battle of the Korean war.
A very curious enterprise apparently financed by the Moonies. The religious angle sits oddly with the war scenes, and the result is an unsatisfactory mess.
w Robin Moore, Laird Koenig *d* Terence Young *ph* Bruce Surtees *m* Jerry Goldsmith
☆ Laurence Olivier (MacArthur), Jacqueline Bisset, David Janssen, Ben Gazzara, Toshiro Mifune, Richard Roundtree, Gabriele Ferzetti, Rex Reed
'A near total loss as well as a laugh.' – *Bruce Williamson, Playboy*
'The worst movie ever made, a turkey the size of Godzilla.' – *Jack Kroll, Newsweek*
'Quite possibly the worst movie ever made … stupefyingly incompetent.' – *Peter Rainer, Los Angeles Herald Examiner*
'As military spectacles go, one of the sorriest in military history.' – *Richard Schickel, Time*

Incident at Owl Creek *
France 1961 27m bw
Marcel Ichac/Films de Centaure/Paul de Roubaix
original title: *La Rivière du Hibou*
US title: *An Occurrence At Owl Creek*
During the American Civil War a man is about to be hanged, and imagines how he might escape.
Intriguing but somewhat overpraised short with a rather obvious solution.
wd Robert Enrico *story* Ambrose Bierce *ph* Jean Boffety *m* Henri Lanoë
☆ Roger Jacquet, Anne Cornaly, Anker Larsen
'A powerful and remarkable film.' – *MFB*
best short film

Incident at Phantom Hill
US 1966 88m Technicolor Techniscope
Universal
Two men face desperate odds to reach one million dollars in gold.
Full-blooded Western programmer with useful performances.
w Frank Nugent *d* Earl Bellamy *ph* William Margulies *m* Hans J. Salter
☆ Robert Fuller, Dan Duryea, Jocelyn Lane, Claude Akins, Noah Beery Jnr

'Harry Donovan Is A Master In The Art Of Deception … Trapped In A Life So Perfect Even The Truth Can't Save Him.'
Incognito
US 1997 106m Technicolor Panavision
Warner/Morgan Creek (James G. Robinson)
An art forger is offered a fortune to fake a Rembrandt for crooked dealers.
Ridiculous thriller, the cinematic equivalent of painting by numbers.
w Jordan Katz *d* John Badham *ph* Denis Crossan *m* John Ottman *pd* Jamie Leonard *ed* Frank Morriss
☆ Jason Patric, Irène Jacob, Thomas Lockyer, Ian Richardson, Simon Chandler, Rod Steiger, Pip Torrens, Ian Holm
'Starts badly and gets even worse, giving it a special kind of entertainment value.' – *George Perry*

Les Inconnus dans la Maison *
France 1941 94m bw
Continental
An embittered ex-barrister saves his teenage daughter from a murder charge.
Unlikely melodrama remade as Stranger in the House; *this version has more compelling writing and acting.*
w Henri-Georges Clouzot novel Georges Simenon *d* Henri Decoin *ph* Jules Kruger *m* Roland Manuel
☆ *Raimu*, Juliette Fabre, Jacques Baumer, Jean Tissier

The Incredible Journey **
US 1963 80m Technicolor
Walt Disney (James Algar)
Two dogs and a cat, separated from their owners, escape and travel 250 miles home.
A novelty attraction which keeps going purely on its animal interest, which is considerable.
w James Algar *book* Sheila Burnford *d* Fletcher Markle *ph* Kenneth Peach, Jack Couffer, Lloyd Beebe *m* Oliver Wallace

The Incredible Melting Man
US 1977 84m Movielab
AIP/Quartet (Max J. Rosenberg)
The survivor of a space flight is rushed to hospital with radiation burns and an infection which causes his flesh to melt.
Unpleasant and nonsensical horror film with a few unintentional laughs and a plot borrowed from The Quatermass Experiment.
wd William Sachs *ph* Willy Curtis *m* Arlon Ober
☆ Alex Rebar, Burr DeBenning, Myron Healey, Michael Alldredge

The Incredible Mr Limpet
US 1964 102m Technicolor
Warner (John C. Rose)
A meek but patriotic clerk is turned down by the navy and turns into a fish. In this form he becomes a radar assistant to a warship.
Sentimental sub-Disney goo, part animated.
w Jameson Bewer, John C. Rose *novel* Theodore Pratt *d* Arthur Lubin *ph* Harold Stine *m* Frank Perkins
☆ Don Knotts, Andrew Duggan, Larry Keating, Jack Weston

The Incredible Sarah *
GB 1976 105m Technicolor Panavision
Readers Digest (Helen M. Strauss)

The career of French actress Sarah Bernhardt up to the age of thirty-five.
Mildly pleasing old-fashioned biopic with remarkably unreliable detail and a regrettably bland approach to its fascinating subject.
w Ruth Wolff *d* Richard Fleischer
ph Christopher Challis *m* Elmer Bernstein
pd Elliot Scott
☆ Glenda Jackson, Daniel Massey, Yvonne Mitchell, Douglas Wilmer, David Langton, Simon Williams, John Castle, Edward Judd, Peter Sallis
'An incredibly old-fashioned movie full of the most unforgettable moments you have ever tried to forget.' – *Andrew Sarris, Village Voice*
'A job lot of obligatory Hollywood platitudes strung together with all the skill of Captain Hook trying to thread a needle.' – *Benny Green, Punch*
'In the stupefying tradition of *Song of Norway*.' – *Pauline Kael*

'So incredible you'll talk about it for years to come!'
The Incredible Shrinking Man *
US 1957 81m bw
U-I (Albert Zugsmith)

After being caught in a radioactive mist, a man shrinks inexorably to micro-size.
Horrifyingly inevitable sci-fi with imaginative touches gracing a cheap production.
w Richard Matheson d Jack Arnold *ph* Ellis W. Carter *m* Hans Salter *sp Clifford Stine, Roswell A. Hoffman, Everett H. Bronssard*
☆ Grant Williams, Randy Stuart, April Kent, Paul Langton
'It opens up new vistas of cosmic terror.' – *Peter John Dyer*
'One hails a science fiction film which is both inventive and humane.' – *Sunday Times*
'Simple, ingenious, effective.' – *The Times*

The Incredible Shrinking Woman
US 1981 88m Technicolor
Universal/Lija (Hank Moonjean)

A housewife finds herself shrinking after using a new perfume…
Hamfisted spoof on The Incredible Shrinking Man, *with flat jokes and rather poor trick photography.*
w Jane Wagner *d* Joel Schumacher *ph* Bruce Logan *m* Suzanne Ciani
☆ Lily Tomlin, Charles Grodin, Ned Beatty, Henry Gibson, Elizabeth Wilson
'Leaden satire on consumerism … even the special effects are barely passable.' – *Time Out, 1984*

The Incredible Torture Show: see *Bloodsucking Freaks*

The Incredible Two-Headed Transplant
US 1970 88m DeLuxe
Mutual General/Trident/American International (John Lawrence)

A mad doctor grafts an extra head onto a homicidal maniac.
Full-blooded nonsense on a low budget; utterly repellent to some, but done with sufficient verve to be a minor cult title to others.
w James Gordon White, John Lawrence
d Anthony M. Lanza *ph* John Steely, Glen Gano, Paul Hipp *m* John Barber
☆ Bruce Dern, Pat Priest, Casey Kasem, Berry Kroeger

The Incredibly Strange Creatures who Stopped Living and Became Mixed-up Zombies
US 1963 82m colour
Morgan Steckler Productions

A gypsy fortune-teller keeps monsters of her own making at the back of her tent.
Murder and mayhem at the carnival: cheap exploitation item which for long was thought to be a fragment of someone's imagination, but turns out really to exist.
w Gene Pollock, Robert Silliphant *d* Cash Flagg (Ray Dennis Steckler) *ph* Joseph V. Mascelli
m Libby Quinn
☆ Cash Flagg, Carolyn Brandt, Brett O'Hara

The Incredibly True Adventure of 2 Girls in Love
US 1995 94m colour
Feature/Smash (Dolly Hall)

Two lesbian high-school students face rejection from friends and family when they fall in love.
Apart from the fact that its protagonists are of the same sex, this is otherwise a predictable movie of teenage angst and rebellion.
wd Maria Maggenti *ph* Tami Reiker *m* Terry Dame *pd* Ginger Tougas *ed* Susan Graef
☆ Laurel Holloman, Maggie Moore, Kate Stafford, Sabrina Artel, Toby Poser, Nelson Rodriguez
'A pacy, sweet and candid treat.' – *Empire*

Incubo Sulla Città Contaminata: see *Nightmare City*

'The Dreams. The Nightmares. The Desires. The Fears. The Mystery. The Revelation. The Warning.'
Incubus
Canada 1981 92m colour
Guardian Trust Company

Women are raped by a rampant demon.
Utterly distasteful horror film.
w George Franklin *novel* Ray Russell *d* John Hough
☆ John Cassavetes, Kerrie Keane, Helen Hughes, Erin Flannery, John Ireland

'A husband. A wife. A billionaire. A proposal.'
Indecent Proposal
US 1993 117m DeLuxe
Paramount (Sherry Lansing)

In Las Vegas, after her husband has lost the last of his money in a desperate gamble, a wealthy man offers a woman a million dollars to spend a night with him.
Glutinous problem drama of transcendent silliness; perhaps the dilemma would have seemed more interesting if the millionaire had been less personable than Redford, although it would still have remained a ridiculous enterprise.
w Amy Holden Jones *novel* Jack Engelhard
d Adrian Lyne *ph* Howard Atherton *m* John Barry *pd* Mel Bourne *ed* Joe Hutshing
☆ Robert Redford, Demi Moore, Woody Harrelson, Seymour Cassel, Oliver Platt, Billy Bob Thornton, Rip Taylor, Billy Connolly
'One of those high-concept pictures with a big windup and weak delivery.' – *Variety*
'Unredeemingly awful.' – *Philip French, Observer*

'Prepare for Impact!'
Independence Day *
US 1996 145m DeLuxe Super 35
TCF/Centropolis (Dean Devlin)

A plucky pilot and a computer expert defeat an alien invasion of hundreds of vastly destructive spaceships.
Enjoyably silly, jingoistic nonsense that found an appreciative audience for its sensational effects of blowing up the White House and most of the world; it sticks closely to the plot of The War of the Worlds, *offering a technological version of a biological virus to knock out the aliens.*
w Dean Devlin, Roland Emmerich *d* Roland Emmerich *ph* Karl Walter Lindenlaub *m* David Arnold *pd* Oliver Scholl, Patrick Tatopolous
ed David Brenner *sp* Patrick Tatopoulos, Volker Engel, Douglas Smith, Pacific Ocean Post Digital
☆ Will Smith, Bill Pullman, Jeff Goldblum, Mary McDonnell, Judd Hirsch, Margaret Colin, Randy Quaid, Robert Loggia, James Rebhorn, Harvey Fierstein, Adam Baldwin, Brent Spiner, Vivica A. Fox, Harry Connick Jnr
'Lavish in scale, cornball to a T and a wonderfully enthusiastic blend of fifties sci-fi and seventies disaster movies.' – *Derek Malcolm, Guardian*
'Apotheosis of the video zap games that kids play; but fun for folk with popcorn appetites.' – *Alexander Walker*
'The first futuristic disaster movie that's as cute as a button.' – *Lisa Schwarzbaum, Entertainment Weekly*
† The biggest box-office success of 1996, it grossed around $746m around the world, and $306m in the US.
🏆 visual effects (Volker Engel, Douglas Smith, Clay Pinney, Joseph Viskocil)
🎗 sound

'300,000 volts of horror!'
Indestructible Man
US 1956 70m bw
Allied Artists
The dead body of a vicious killer is given new life by a mad doctor.
Low-budget horror mayhem with no style at all.
w Vy Russell, Sue Bradford *d* Jack Pollexfen
☆ Lon Chaney Jnr, Robert Shayne, Casey Adams, Marian Carr

The Indian Fighter
US 1955 88m Technicolor Cinemascope
UA/Bryna (William Schorr)
An Indian fighter protects a wagon train from the Sioux.
Simple-minded Western with touches of philosophy and not much drive.
w Frank Davis, Ben Hecht *story* Robert L. Richards *d* André de Toth *ph* Wilfrid M. Cline
m Franz Waxman
☆ Kirk Douglas, Elsa Martinelli, Walter Abel, Walter Matthau, Diana Douglas, Eduard Franz, Lon Chaney Jnr, Alan Hale Jnr, Elisha Cook Jnr
† The film credited Ben Kadish as the writer of the original story because Richards was blacklisted.

The Indian in the Cupboard
US 1995 96m DeLuxe
Columbia/Scholastic (Kathleen Kennedy, Frank Marshall, Jane Startz)

A nine-year-old boy's toy Indian comes alive when put inside a magic cupboard.
A pleasant but unremarkable fairy story that makes limited use of its interesting central concept.
w Melissa Mathison *novel* Lynne Reid Banks
d Frank Oz *ph* Russell Carpenter *m* Randy Edelman *pd* Leslie McDonald *ed* Ian Crafford
sp Industrial Light and Magic
☆ Hal Scardino, Litefoot, Lindsay Crouse, Richard Jenkins, Rishi Bhat, David Keith, Steve Coogan
'Never comes to life as a movie. Earnest and well-intentioned, the promising concept feels stretched to feature length and should play best only with younger kids.' – *Variety*

The Indian Runner
US 1991 126m DeLuxe
Columbia TriStar/Mount Film Group/Mico/NHK Enterprises (Don Philips)

A small-town cop has a stormy relationship with his criminally inclined brother.
Glum and talky drama drawn out to an inordinate length, long after it has exhausted any interest.
wd Sean Penn *ph* Anthony B. Richmond *m* Jack Nitzsche *pd* Michael Haller *ed* Jay Cassidy, Phil Linson *song* 'Highway Patrolman' by Bruce Springsteen
☆ David Morse, Viggo Mortensen, Valeria Golino, Patricia Arquette, Charles Bronson, Sandy Dennis, Dennis Hopper, Jordan Rhodes
'More than two hours' worth of predictable characters and plot developments visible at a distance of some miles.' – *Kim Newman, Empire*

Indian Scout
US 1949 70m bw
Edward Small
Episodes in the life of Davy Crockett.
Minor Western which hit the spot with small-town audiences, and in the late fifties, after the success of the Disney film, was reissued as Davy Crockett, Indian Scout.
w Richard Schayer *d* Ford Beebe *ph* John Mescall *m* Paul Sawtell
☆ George Montgomery, Ellen Drew, Philip Reed, Noah Beery Jnr

Indian Summer: see *The Judge Steps Out (1947)*

Indian Summer
US 1993 97m Technicolor Panavision
Touchstone/Outlaw (Jeffrey Silver, Robert Newmyer)

aka: *Alive and Kicking*
Friends meet up for one last week at summer camp after a gap of 20 years.
Nostalgic, sentimental drama that suggests problems can be solved by reverting to childhood behaviour, but it does have moments of charm.
wd Mike Binder *ph* Tom Sigel *m* Miles Goodman *pd* Craig Stearns *ed* Adam Weiss
☆ Alan Arkin, Matt Craven, Diane Lane, Bill Paxton, Elizabeth Perkins, Kevin Pollak, Sam Raimi, Vincent Spano, Julie Warner, Kimberly Williams

Indian Summer: see *Alive and Kicking (1996)*

'The Man With The Hat Is Back. And This Time He's Bringing His Dad.'
Indiana Jones and the Last Crusade **
US 1989 127m DeLuxe Panavision
UIP/Paramount/Lucasfilm (Robert Watts)

Indiana Jones goes in search of his father who disappeared while looking for the Holy Grail.
The formula as before, which still works thanks to some splendid set-pieces and the genial interplay between Ford and Connery.
w Jeffrey Boam *story* George Lucas, Menno Meyjes *d* Steven Spielberg *ph* Douglas Slocombe
m John Williams *pd* Elliot Scott *ed* Michael Kahn
☆ Harrison Ford, Sean Connery, Denholm Elliott, Alison Doody, John Rhys-Davies, Julian Glover, River Phoenix, Michael Byrne, Kevork Malikyan, Robert Eddison, Richard Young, Alexei Sayle
🏆 sound
🎗 John Williams; sound effects editing

'The hero is back!'
Indiana Jones and the Temple of Doom **
US 1984 118m Rank Colour/DeLuxe Panavision
Paramount/Lucasfilm (Robert Watts)

A prequel to *Raiders of the Lost Ark*: Jones in 1935 finds the sacred Sankara stone.
Slow-starting adventure romp with much ingenuity and too much brutality and horror. In the US it caused the creation of a new censor certificate: PG(13).
w Willard Huyck, Gloria Katz *story* George Lucas *d Steven Spielberg ph* Douglas Slocombe, Allen Daviau *m* John Williams *pd Elliot Scott*
☆ Harrison Ford, Kate Capshaw, Ke Huy Quan, Philip Stone
'One of the most sheerly pleasurable physical comedies ever made.' – *Pauline Kael, New Yorker*
'A thin, arch, graceless affair.' – *Observer*
'A two-hour series of none too carefully linked chase sequences … sitting on the edge of your seat gives you a sore bum but also a numb brain.' – *Guardian*
🎗 music; visual effects

Indianapolis Speedway
US 1939 82m bw
Warner
A racetrack driver wants his kid brother to continue in college, but he has the racing fever.
Editor's-bench mélange of The Crowd Roars *(1932) and* Here Comes the Navy; *this doesn't star Cagney.*
w Sig Herzig, Wally Klein *d* Lloyd Bacon
☆ Pat O'Brien, Ann Sheridan, John Payne, Gale Page, Frank McHugh, Regis Toomey
'It contains just about every cliché such type melodrama can have.' – *Variety*
† Frank McHugh played the same role in the 1932 version.

Indio Black, Sai che ti Dico: Sei un Gran Figlio di…: see *The Bounty Hunters*

'Through one indiscretion … a woman with a future became a woman with a past!'
Indiscreet
US 1931 92m bw
Art Cinema Corporation (Joseph M. Schenck)
A socialite endangers her own romance when she tries to protect her younger sister.
Embarrassing and slow-moving farce which helped to kill its star's career.

d Leo McCarey *ph* Ray June, Gregg Toland *m* Alfred Newman *w/songs* Brown, de Sylva and Henderson
☆ Gloria Swanson, Ben Lyon, Monroe Owsley, Barbara Kent, Arthur Lake, Maude Eburne, Henry Kolker

'How dare he make love to me – and not be a married man!'

Indiscreet **
GB 1958 100m Technicolor
Grandon (Stanley Donen)
An American diplomat in London falls in love with an actress but protects himself by saying he is married.
Affairs among the ultra rich, amusing when played by these stars but with imperfect production values which the alarmingly thin plot allows one too much time to consider.
w Norman Krasna *play Kind Sir* by Norman Krasna *d* Stanley Donen *ph* Frederick A. Young *m* Richard Bennett, Ken Jones
☆ *Cary Grant, Ingrid Bergman,* Phyllis Calvert, Cecil Parker, David Kossoff, Megs Jenkins
'One is often on the point of being bored, but one never is, quite.' – *Richard Roud*
'A film to which you would not hesitate to take your jeweller, your architect, your home decorator, your dressmaker and your domestic staff.' – *Alexander Walker*

Indiscretion: see *Christmas in Connecticut (1945)*

Indiscretion: see *Indiscretion of an American Wife (1954)*

Indiscretion of an American Wife *
Italy/US 1954 75m bw
David O. Selznick (Vittorio de Sica)
aka: *Terminus Station*
aka: *Indiscretion*
An American woman and an Italian professor say goodbye in Rome's terminal station.
Strained attempt to re-do Brief Encounter *against the busy background of a great railway station; moments of interest, but artificiality prevails, and the plot never gets up enough steam.*
w Cesare Zavattini, Truman Capote, etc *d* Vittorio de Sica *ph* G. R. Aldo *m* Aldo Cicognini
☆ Jennifer Jones, Montgomery Clift, Gino Cervi, Richard Beymer

Indochine **
France 1992 158m colour
Paradis/La Générale d'Images/BAC/Orly/Ciné Cinq (Eric Heumann)
In the unsettled Indochina of the 1930s, the adopted Indochinese daughter of the female head of a rubber plantation runs away to be with the French naval officer loved by her and her mother.
A glossy romantic drama dominated by Deneuve's performance.
w Erik Orsenna, Louis Gardeal, Catherine Cohen, Régis Wargnier *d* Régis Wargnier *ph* François Catonne *m* Patrick Doyle *ed* Genevieve Winding
☆ *Catherine Deneuve,* Vincent Perez, Linh Dan Pham, Jean Yanne, Dominique Blanc, Henri Marteau, Mai Chau
'A riveting romantic saga.' – *Variety*
'It has the breadth and intelligence of the David Lean epics from whose plots it borrows so freely ... And in Deneuve the movie has a star of epic glamour and gravity. Her presence is like some handsome monument to the French spirit miraculously preserved on the streets of Vietnam.' – *Richard Corliss, Time*
🏆 foreign language film
🎖 Catherine Deneuve

Inferno: see *Desert Heat*

Inferno **
US 1953 83m Technicolor 3-D
TCF (William Bloom)
When a millionaire breaks his leg in the desert, his wife and her lover leave him to die; but he contrives to catch up with them.
An outdoor melodrama which made better use of 3-D than any other film, suggesting the lone handicapped figure in the vast spaces; but the lovers are dull and the fire climax perfunctory.
w Francis Cockrell *d* Roy Baker *ph* Lucien Ballard *m* Paul Sawtell
☆ *Robert Ryan,* William Lundigan, Rhonda Fleming
'Its chief merit is a strong and simple story.' – *C. A. Lejeune*

Inferno
Italy 1980 107m Technicolor
TCF (Claudio Argento)
A New York apartment house is occupied by satanists who murder those who learn their secret.
Absurdly overplotted and mainly incomprehensible shocker with some small pretensions to style.
wd Dario Argento *ph* Romano Albani *m* Keith Emerson *ad* Giuseppe Bassan *ed* Franco Fraticelli *sp* Mario Bava, Germano Natali, Pino Leone
☆ Leigh McCloskey (Mark Elliot), Irene Miracle (Rose Elliot), Eleonora Giorgi (Sara), Daria Nicolodi (Elise), Alida Valli (Carol), Feodor Chaliapin (Varelli), Sacha Pitoeff (Kazanian)

Infinity
US 1996 119m DeLuxe
First Look (Joel Soisson, Michael Leahy, Patricia Broderick, Matthew Broderick)
A Nobel Prize-winning scientist looks back on his early life and his marriage to a woman dying of tuberculosis.
A slight but charming biopic that concentrates on the private life of a brilliant man, Richard Feynman, and his doomed romance with Arline Greenbaum.
w Patricia Broderick *memoirs* Richard Feynman *d* Matthew Broderick *ph* Toyomichi Kurita *m* Bruce Broughton *pd* Bernt Capra *ed* Elena Maganini, Bill Johnson, Amy Young
☆ Matthew Broderick, Patricia Arquette, Peter Riegert, Dori Brenner, Peter Michael Goetz, Zeljko Ivanek, James LeGros, Jeffrey Force
'A static, old-fashioned film that only intermittently involves the viewer.' – *Emanuel Levy, Variety*

The Informer ***
US 1935 91m bw
RKO (Cliff Reid)
An IRA leader is betrayed by a simple-minded hanger-on who wants money to emigrate; he is hounded by fellow rebels and his own conscience.
A tedious plot is turned into brilliant cinema by full-blooded acting and a highly stylized yet brilliantly effective mise en scène which never attempts reality.
w Dudley Nichols *novel* Liam O'Flaherty *d John Ford ph Joseph H. August m Max Steiner ad Van Nest Polglase ed* George Hively
☆ *Victor McLaglen,* Heather Angel, Margot Grahame, Una O'Connor, Wallace Ford, Preston Foster, J. M. Kerrigan, Joe Sawyer, Donald Meek
'A tough subject, a sure critic's picture, but dubious box office.' – *Variety*
'As impressive as *Scarface*, or anything in the whole powerful literature redolent of fog and grime and dreariness which the Germans gave to the Americans.' – *Bardèche and Brasillach*
'Among the best five pictures since the coming of sound.' – *Baltimore Sun*
† An early British sound version was made in 1929 by Arthur Robison for BIP, with Lars Hansen and Lya de Putti. Dudley Nichols became the first person to refuse to accept an Oscar, due to a quarrel between the Academy and some industry organizations.
🏆 Dudley Nichols; John Ford; Max Steiner; Victor McLaglen
🎖 best picture; editing

The Informers
GB 1963 104m bw
Rank (William MacQuitty)
US title: *Underworld Informers*
A police informer is murdered and his brother takes revenge.
Basic police melodrama, with clumsy script and jaded direction.
w Alun Falconer *novel Death of a Snout* by Douglas Warner *d* Ken Annakin *ph* Reg Wyer *m* Clifton Parker
☆ Nigel Patrick, Colin Blakely, Derren Nesbitt

L'Ingénue Libertine
France 1950 88m approx bw
Codo-Cinéma (Jean Velter)
A romantic girl lives in an imaginary world of affairs, but can't bring herself to consummate her marriage.
Minor period sex comedy which has the distinction of being Britain's first 'X' film, though the naughtiness is more implied than stated.
w P. Laroche *novel* Colette *d* Jacqueline Audry *ph* Grignon *m* Vincent Scotto
☆ Daniele Delorme, Frank Villard, Jean Tissier

Inherit the Wind **
US 1960 127m bw
UA/Lomitas (Stanley Kramer)
A fictionalized account of the 1925 Scopes 'monkey trial', when a schoolmaster was accused of teaching the theory of evolution.
Splendid theatrics with fine performances, marred by boring subplots but enhanced by a realistic portrait of a sweltering Southern town.
w Nathan E. Douglas (Nedrick Young), Harold Jacob Smith *play* Jerome Lawrence, Robert E. Lee *d Stanley Kramer ph Ernest Laszlo m* Ernest Gold *ed* Frederic Knudtson
☆ Spencer Tracy, Fredric March, Florence Eldridge, Gene Kelly, Dick York, Donna Anderson, Harry Morgan, Elliott Reid, Claude Akins
† Screenwriter Nedrick Young used a pseudonym because he was blacklisted at the time.
🎖 script; Ernest Laszlo; Spencer Tracy; editing

The Inheritance: see *Uncle Silas (1947)*

The Inheritance
Italy 1976 121m Eastmancolor
Flag Productions (Gianni Hecht Lucari)
original title: *L'Eredità Ferramonti*
In Rome of the 1880s, a wealthy father disinherits his children but succumbs to the wiles of his daughter-in-law.
Sumptuous period soap opera, for which Sanda won a best actress award at the Cannes Film Festival.
w Ugo Pirro, Sergio Bazzini *novel* Gaetano Carlo Chelli *d* Mauro Bolognini *ph* Ennio Guarnieri *m* Ennio Morricone *ad* Luigi Scaccianoce *ed* Nino Baragli
☆ Anthony Quinn, Fabio Testi, Dominique Sanda, Luigi Proietti, Adriana Asti, Paolo Bonacelli, Rosella Rusconi, Harold Bromley

Injeong Sajeong Bolgeos Eobsda *
South Korea 1999 112m bw/colour
Metro Tartan/Taewon Entertainment/Kookmin/Samboo (Chung Tae-Won)
GB title: *Nowhere to Hide*
A slouching cop tracks down a hitman who is a master of disguise.
An over-elaborate style, full of fancy wipes, bullet-holed intertitles, freeze-frames and selfconciously arty shots, does little to hide the threadbare nature of the narrative; its exuberance carries it through.
wd Lee Myung-Se *ph* Jeong Kwang-Seok, Song Haeng-Ki *m* Cho Sung-Woo, Kim Dae-Hong *pd* Lee Myung-Se *ed* Go Im Pyo
☆ Park Joong-hoon (Detective Woo), Ahn Sung-Ki (Chang Sungmin), Jang Dong-Kun (Detective Kim), Choi Ji-Woo (Juyon), Do Yong-Ku (Detective Chang), Shim Cheol-Jong (Detective Chu)
'A wild devil-may-care demonstration of style that hits more targets than it misses.' – *Derek Elley, Variety*
† The UK release ran for 100m.

Inn for Trouble
GB 1960 90m bw
Film Locations/Eros
A suburban couple become country publicans.
Amiable extension of a popular TV series, The Larkins.
w Fred Robinson *d* C. M. Pennington-Richards *ph* Eric Cross *m* Philip Green
☆ Peggy Mount, David Kossoff, Leslie Phillips, Glyn Owen, Charles Hawtrey, A. E. Matthews, Yvonne Monlaur, Irene Handl

The Inn of the Sixth Happiness **
GB 1958 158m DeLuxe Cinemascope
TCF (Mark Robson)
An English servant girl becomes a missionary and spends many arduous years in China.
Romanticized biopic of Gladys Aylward, with lots of children, a happy ending, and everyone sensationally miscast. Somehow it all works, even North Wales standing in for China.
w Isobel Lennart *book The Small Woman* by Alan Burgess *d* Mark Robson *ph* Frederick A. Young *m* Malcolm Arnold *ed* Ernest Walter
☆ Ingrid Bergman, Curt Jurgens, Robert Donat, Athene Seyler, Ronald Squire, Richard Wattis, Moultrie Kelsall
🎖 Mark Robson

The Inner Circle
Italy 1991 137m Technicolor
Columbia TriStar/Numero Uno (Claudio Bonivento)
Italian title: *Il Proiezionista*
A cinema projectionist goes to work for Stalin, an act that has a devastating effect on his marriage.
A movie that attempts to explain the appeal to the Russian people of Stalin, but achieves only a trivialization of history.
w Andrei Konchalovsky, Anatoli Usov *d* Andrei Konchalovsky *ph* Ennio Guarnieri *m* Eduard Artemyev *pd* Ezio Frigerio *ed* Henry Richardson
☆ Tom Hulce, Lolita Davidovich, Bob Hoskins, Alexandre Zbruev, Feodor Chaliapin Jnr, Bess Meyer, Maria Baranova, Irina Kuptchenko
'A dramatically messy, momentarily compelling look at Stalin's tyranny.' – *Variety*
'The umpteenth film to turn truth-based political tragedy into dial-a-cliché melodrama. Overacted by almost everyone in sight and scripted for stark risibility ... it comes to life only when raiding history direct.' – *Nigel Andrews, Financial Times*

Inner Sanctum
The title was taken from a radio show featuring mystery stories with a last minute twist. The films were introduced rather oddly by a misshapen head in a crystal ball on the empty table of a boardroom. The head belonged to David Hoffman, and he introduced each film: 'This ... is the inner sanctum...' (The original reference was presumably to the innermost working of the human mind.) The films, made for Universal, all starred Lon Chaney Jnr (who alternated as hero and villain); they were among the most boring and badly made second feature thrillers of the forties.
1943 Calling Dr Death
1944 Weird Woman, Dead Man's Eyes
1945 Strange Confession (remake of The Man Who Reclaimed His Head), The Frozen Ghost
1946 Pillow of Death

Innerspace *
US 1987 120m Technicolor
Warner/Amblin/Steven Spielberg/Guber-Peters (Michael Finnell)
A miniaturized air force flyer is injected into the body of a grocery clerk.
Derivative comedy with clever twists; very tolerable of its kind, but no Back to the Future.
w Jeffrey Boam, Chip Proser *d* Joe Dante *ph* Andrew Laszlo *m* Jerry Goldsmith *pd* James H. Spencer
☆ Dennis Quaid, Martin Short, Meg Ryan, Kevin McCarthy, Fiona Lewis
🏆 special visual effects (Dennis Muren)

Innocence is Bliss: see *Miss Grant Takes Richmond*

Innocence Unprotected *
Yugoslavia 1968 78m Eastmancolor/bw
Avala
original title: *Nevinosti Bez Zastite*
Interviews with the actor-writer-director of, and those who worked on, *Innocence Unprotected*, the first Serbian talkie made in 1942, which was confiscated during the Nazi occupation, together with excerpts from the film and from contemporary newsreels.
A fascinating collage from Makavejev, providing a documentary frame to scenes from a primitive story of

true love triumphant, in style more like a silent than a talking picture, and glorifying the death-defying acrobatics of its strong-man hero and director, filmed hanging from an aeroplane by a rope held in his teeth; both the new film and the old have a simple charm.
wd Dusan Makavejev *ph* Branko Perak, Stevan Miskovic *m* Vojislav Dostic *ed* Alexsander Popovic
☆ Dragoljub Aleksic, Ana Milosavljevic, Vera Jovanovic, Bratoljub Gligorijevic, Ivan Zivkovic, Pera Milosavljevic

The Innocent ***
Italy 1976 125m colour Technovision
Rizzoli (Giovanni Bertolucci)
original title: *Innocente*
aka: *The Intruder*
In Rome in the 1890s, a Sicilian aristocrat who keeps his wife informed of his own affair takes a terrible revenge when he discovers she also has a lover.
An elegant account of decadence and sexual politics, one that subverts the intentions of the novel on which it is based.
w Suso Cecchi D'Amico, Luchino Visconti, Enrico Medioli *novel* Gabriele d'Annunzio *d* Luchino Visconti *ph* Pasqualino de Santis *m* Chopin, Liszt, Mozart, Gluck *ad* Mario Garbuglia *ed* Ruggero Mastroianni
☆ Giancarlo Giannini, Laura Antonelli, Jennifer O'Neill, Rina Morelli, Didier Haudepin, Massimo Girotti, Marie Dubois
'An outstanding example of what Hemingway would have called grace under pressure.' – *Sight and Sound*
'The protagonist is meant to be an atheist hero, a brave anarch who pays the price for his amorality. But he comes out only a sordid, spoiled sensualist swine, with no kind of depth, so this story has no involvement for the viewer.' – *Stanley Kauffmann*
† Visconti had wanted Alain Delon and Romy Schneider for the two leads. He directed the film from a wheelchair and died just before its release.

'A passion beyond love. A crime beyond murder.'
The Innocent *
GB/Germany 1993 107m Eastmancolor
Island Lakeheart/Sievernich/Defa (Norma Heyman, Chris Sievernich, Wieland Schulz-Keil)
As the Berlin Wall comes down, a bungling English engineer returns to Germany and recalls his time there during the Cold War of the 50s, when he was assigned to the CIA, fell in love with a local woman and became involved in murder.
Uninvolving drama for the most part, though it improves as it continues, intertwining horror and humour as a naïve man finds himself in a situation beyond his control or understanding.
w Ian McEwan *novel* Ian McEwan *d* John Schlesinger *ph* Dietrich Lohmann *m* Gerald Gouriet *pd* Luciana Arrighi *ed* Richard Marden
☆ Anthony Hopkins, Isabella Rossellini, Campbell Scott, Hart Bochner, Ronald Nitschke, Jeremy Sinden, James Grant, Richard Durden
'An interesting idea and characters are otherwise wasted on a thudding succession of obvious moments which topple over into bathos.' – *Kim Newman, Empire*
† Anthony Hopkins composed and performed the soundtrack piano étude.

'For generations, the Mafia preyed on the innocent. Tonight, someone's feasting on them.'
Innocent Blood
US 1992 113m Technicolor
Warner (Lee Rich, Leslie Belzberg)
aka: *A French Vampire in America*
A female vampire regrets turning a Mafia hoodlum into a vampire.
Haphazard and anaemic vampire movie with comic elements which never really works on any level.
w Michael Wolk *d* John Landis *ph* Mac Ahlberg *m* Ira Newborn *pd* Richard Sawyer *ed* Dale Beldin *sp* Steve Johnson, Syd Dutton, Bill Taylor
☆ Anne Parillaud, Robert Loggia, Anthony LaPaglia, Don Rickles, Elaine Kagan, David Proval, Chazz Palminteri
'Teens and genre fans should eat up John Landis' latest mix of horror and camp comedy.' – *Variety*
'A gloomy, almost oppressive film.' – *Geoff Brown, The Times*
† Directors who make brief appearances in the movie include Dario Argento, Frank Oz, Sam Raimi, Michael Ritchie and Tom Savini.

Innocent Bystanders *
GB 1972 110m Eastmancolor
Sagittarius (George H. Brown)
The British secret service sends three agents to trace a Russian traitor.
Confused and violent espionage thriller; rather a waste of good production.
w James Mitchell *d* Peter Collinson *ph* Brian Probyn *m* John Keating
☆ Stanley Baker, Geraldine Chaplin, Dana Andrews, Donald Pleasence

Innocent Lies
GB/France 1995 88m colour
Polygram/Red Umbrella/Septieme (Simon Perry, Philippe Guez)
In France in 1938, an English policeman tries to clear up the mystery of the apparent suicide of his mentor and finds himself involved with an odd and incestuous English upper-middle-class family.
The credits include an acknowledgement to 'the inspiration provided by Agatha Christie for the making of this film, which does not purport to be a faithful adaptation of any of her work', but this stew of overheated sex and underdeveloped narrative bears little resemblance to the deadly gentility of her world. It is a thriller that contains no red herrings, only dead ends and lots of loose threads.
w Kerry Crabbe, Patrick Dewolf *d* Patrick Dewolf *ph* Patrick Blossier *m* Alexandre Desplat *pd* Bernd Lepel *ed* Chris Wimble, Joelle Hache
☆ Stephen Dorff, Gabrielle Anwar, Adrian Dunbar, Sophie Aubry, Joanna Lumley, Melvil Poupaud, Bernard Haller, Alexis Denisof
'It's a disgrace that, in its present form, this script was allowed to see the light of day.' – *Sheila Johnston, Independent*
'Fails on every count.' – *Sight and Sound*

An Innocent Man
US 1989 113m Technicolor
Warner/Touchstone/Silver Screen Partners IV (Ted Field, Robert W. Cort)
Framed by crooked cops, an engineer learns lessons of survival in prison, which he applies to seeking vengeance on his release.
Undistinguished melodrama.
w Larry Brothers *d* Peter Yates *ph* William A. Fraker *m* Howard Shore *pd* Stuart Wurtzel *ed* Stephen A. Rotter, William S. Scharf
☆ Tom Selleck, F. Murray Abraham, Laila Robins, David Rasche, Richard Young, Badja Djola, Todd Graff, M. C. Gainey

Innocent Moves: see *Searching for Bobby Fischer*

Innocent Sinners **
GB 1957 95m bw
Rank (Hugh Stewart)
A 13-year-old London girl builds a garden in the rubble of a bombed church, and gets into trouble with the police.
Likeable, slightly unfinished, mildly astringent little human drama full of well-observed character sketches.
w Neil Paterson *novel* An Episode of Sparrows by Rumer Godden *d* Philip Leacock *ph* Harry Waxman *m* Philip Green
☆ Flora Robson, Catherine Lacey, David Kossoff, Barbara Mullen, June Archer

The Innocent Sleep
GB 1995 110m colour Super 35
Starlight/Timedial (Scott Michell, Matthew Vaughn)
A tramp witnesses a murder in which a senior policeman was one of the killers.
Moderately gripping low-voltage thriller of corruption and cover-up.
w Ray Villis *d* Scott Michell *ph* Alan Dunlop *m* Mark Ayres *pd* Eve Mavrakis *ed* Derek Trigg
☆ Rupert Graves, Annabella Sciorra, Michael Gambon, Franco Nero, Graham Crowden, Oliver Cotton
† The film is loosely based on a real-life event: the death of Italian banker Roberto Calvi, who was found hanged under London's Blackfriars Bridge in the 80s.

The Innocents **
GB 1961 99m bw Cinemascope
TCF/Achilles (Jack Clayton)
In Victorian times, a spinster governess in a lonely house finds her young charges possessed by evil demons of servants now dead.
Elaborate revamping of Henry James's The Turn of the Screw, *the ghosts being now (possibly) the figments of a frustrated woman's imagination. The frissons would have worked better on a normal-shaped screen, but the decor, lighting and general handling are exceptional.*
w William Archibald, Truman Capote *d* Jack Clayton *ph* Freddie Francis *m* Georges Auric *ad* Wilfrid Shingleton
☆ Deborah Kerr, Megs Jenkins, Pamela Franklin, Martin Stephens, Michael Redgrave, Peter Wyngarde

Les Innocents aux Mains Sales: see *Innocents with Dirty Hands*

Innocents in Paris
GB 1953 102m bw
Romulus (Anatole de Grunwald)
British tourists spend a weekend in the gay city.
Strained compendium of anecdotes which misses an easy target.
w Anatole de Grunwald *d* Gordon Parry *ph* Gordon Lang *m* Josef Kosma
☆ Alastair Sim, Margaret Rutherford, Jimmy Edwards, Claire Bloom, Laurence Harvey, Ronald Shiner

Innocents of Paris
US 1929 69m bw
Paramount/Jesse L. Lasky
A Parisian junk dealer saves a boy's life and falls for his aunt.
Heavygoing and dated musical comedy which introduced Chevalier to world audiences.
w Ethel Doherty, Ernest Vajda *play* Flea Market by Charles Andrews *d* Richard Wallace *ph* Charles Lang *m/ly* Leo Robin, Richard A. Whiting
☆ Maurice Chevalier, Sylvia Beecher, Russell Simpson, George Fawcett
'The most childish thing in invention which to my knowledge has yet proceeded from the childlike cinema mind.' – *James Agate, Tatler*

Innocents with Dirty Hands ***
France/West Germany/Italy 1975 125m Eastmancolor
Fox-Rank/Films la Boétie/Terra/Jupiter (André Génovès)
original title: *Les Innocents aux Mains Sales*
An unhappy wife and her new young lover decide to kill her alcoholic husband, but he is aware of their plan.
An enjoyable, teasing thriller that keeps its audience, as well as its characters, guessing as one double-cross quickly follows upon another.
wd Claude Chabrol *novel* The Damned Innocents by Richard Neely *ph* Jean Rabier *m* Pierre Jansen *ad* Guy Littaye *ed* Jacques Gaillard
☆ Romy Schneider, Rod Steiger, Paolo Giusti, Jean Rochefort, François Maistre, Pierre Santini, François Perrot
'One of cinema's most enjoyable charades.' – *Richard Combs, MFB*

Inquest *
GB 1939 60m bw
Charter (John Boulting)
A coroner has his suspicions as to who murdered the deceased.
Modest courtroom suspenser which marked the Boultings' first attempt (the second was Suspect) *to raise the standard of second features.*
w Francis Miller *play* Michael Barringer *d* Roy Boulting *ph* D. P. Cooper *ad* John Maxted *ed* Roy Boulting
☆ Elizabeth Allan, Herbert Lomas, Hay Petrie, Barbara Everest, Olive Sloane

The Inquisitor **
France 1981 90m Eastmancolor
Gala/Ariane/TFI (Georges Dancigers, Alexandre Mnouchikine)
original title: *Garde à Vu*
On New Year's Eve, a police inspector questions a rich lawyer suspected of killing a child.
Excellently acted, engrossing contest of wits.
w Claude Miller, Jean Herman, Michel Audiard *novel* Brainwash by John Wainwright *d* Claude Miller *ph* Bruno Nuytten *m* Georges Delerue *ad* Eric Moulard *ed* Albert Jurgenson
☆ Lino Ventura, Michel Serrault, Guy Marchand, Romy Schneider, Didier Agostini, Patrick Depeyrat, Pierre Maguelon, Serge Malik
'Not unlike a *Twelve Angry Men* from which all comfortable certainties have been withdrawn.' – *Tom Milne, MFB*

Inseminoid
GB 1980 92m colour J-D-C Scope
Brent Walker/Jupiter (Richard Gordon, David Speechley)
US title: *Horror Planet*
On a far-off planet a scientist is raped by an alien and gives birth to monsters.
Cheap and nasty rip-off of Alien *that is full of disgusting effects and violent deaths but lacks any suspense.*
w Nick Maley, Gloria Maley *d* Norman J. Warren *ph* John Metcalfe *m* John Scott *pd* Hayden Pearce
☆ Robin Clarke, Jennifer Ashley, Stephanie Beacham, Judy Geeson, Victoria Tennant, Steven Grives, Barry Houghton
† Six minutes were cut from the film on its US release.

'A degenerate film with dignity!'
Inserts
GB 1975 117m DeLuxe
UA/Film and General (Davina Belling, Clive Parsons)
In 1930 Hollywood, a fading silent queen and a has-been director take to drugs.
Curious, interesting semi-porno melodrama with Pinterish asides and an inaccurate but stimulating feel of the film city at its height.
wd John Byrum *ph* Denys Coop *md* Jessica Harper
☆ Richard Dreyfuss, Jessica Harper, Veronica Cartwright, Bob Hoskins, Stephen Davies
'The ludicrous plot and the painfully obvious symbolism make it tempting to interpret *Inserts* as a comedy. Yet to assume that a bad movie about the making of a bad movie is somehow good by virtue of its badness is to be guilty of a kind of mimetic fallacy.' – *Robert Asahina, New Leader*

'This is the story of Daisy Clover ... Love at 15. Married at 16. Divorced at 17.'
Inside Daisy Clover *
US 1965 128m Technicolor Panavision
Warner/Pakula-Mulligan (Alan J. Pakula)
Tribulations of an adolescent movie star in thirties Hollywood.
Amusing, rather hysterical variant on A Star Is Born; *agreeably wacky in spots, glum in others. Would have benefited from the greater permissiveness possible a few years later.*
w Gavin Lambert *novel* Gavin Lambert *d* Robert Mulligan *ph* Charles Lang Jnr *m* André Previn *ch* Herbert Ross *ad* Robert Clatworthy
☆ Natalie Wood, Robert Redford, Ruth Gordon, Christopher Plummer, Roddy MacDowall
'The movie is short on characters, detail, activity, dialogue, even music; it's as if it's so determined to be stylish and sophisticated that rather than risk vulgarity or banality, it eliminates almost everything.' – *Pauline Kael, 1968*
Ruth Gordon

Inside Moves
US 1980 113m colour
Goodmark (Mark M. Tanz, R. W. Goodwin)
A failed suicide makes friends in Max's bar with other handicapped people.
Curious tragi-comedy which generally settles for sentimentality but provides a few funny moments along the way.
w Valerie Curtin, Barry Levinson *novel* Todd Walton *d* Richard Donner *ph* Laszlo Kovacs *m* John Barry
☆ John Savage, David Morse, Diana Scarwid, Amy Wright, Tony Burton, Harold Russell
'A dismal contribution in the Year of the Disabled Person.' – *John Pym, MFB*

'If you imagine *The Iceman Cometh* rewritten by William Saroyan as a tribute to Frank Capra, that's about it.' – *Sunday Times*
Diana Scarwid (supporting actress)

Inside Out *
GB/West Germany 1975 97m Technicolor
Warner/Kettledrum (Judd Bernard)
TV title: *The Golden Heist*
aka: *Hitler's Gold*
A German ex-commandant of a POW camp enlists the aid of Americans in a daring plan to kidnap a Nazi war criminal from East Germany and find buried Nazi loot.
Entertaining but very silly actioner with too many changes of mood, though some sequences please.
w Judd Bernard, Stephen Schneck d Peter Duffell ph John Coquillon m Konrad Elfers
☆ Telly Savalas, James Mason, Robert Culp, Aldo Ray, Gunter Meisner, Adrian Hoven, Charles Korvin, Richard Warner

Inside Straight
US 1951 89m bw
MGM (Richard Goldstone)
The life of a 19th-century tycoon is revealed in flashbacks during a poker game.
Solid melodrama which doesn't quite have the required spark.
w Guy Trosper d Gerald Mayer ph Ray June m Lennie Hayton
☆ David Brian, Arlene Dahl, Barry Sullivan, Mercedes McCambridge, Paula Raymond, Claude Jarman Jnr, Lon Chaney Jnr, John Hoyt

'Ordinary Men Of Uncommon Courage Risk All To Speak Out... And Change Everything.'
'Two Angry Men Driven To Tell The Truth...Whatever The Cost'
The Insider ***
US 1999 158m Technicolor Super 35
Buena Vista/Touchstone/Forward Pass (Michael Mann, Pieter Jan Brugge)
A TV producer persuades a former tobacco company scientist to expose the official denials that cigarettes are injurious to health, only to discover that his investigation will not be broadcast.
A true-life, devastating exposé of the way corporations and the media respond to unwelcome facts, and a gripping drama of an ordinary, principled man caught up in events beyond his control; if the film has a fault, it is that it is too long.
w Eric Roth, Michael Mann *Vanity Fair article* The Man Who Knew Too Much by Marie Brenner d *Michael Mann* ph Dante Spinotti pd Brian Morris ed William Goldenberg, Paul Rubell, David Rosenbloom
☆ Al Pacino (Lowell Bergman), *Russell Crowe* (Jeffrey Wigand), *Christopher Plummer* (Mike Wallace), Diane Venora (Liane Wigand), Philip Baker Hall (Don Hewitt), Lindsay Crouse (Sharon Tiller), Debi Mazar (Debbie De Luca), Stephen Tobolowsky (Eric Kluster), Colm Feore (Richard Scruggs), Bruce McGill (Ron Motley), Gina Gershon (Helen Caperelli), Michael Gambon (Thomas Sandefur), Rip Torn (John Scanlon), Michael Moore (Himself), Wings Hauser (Tobacco Lawyer)
'An edge-of-your-sear, gut-churning thriller.' – *Newsweek*
'A brilliant nail-biter of a true-story conspiracy.' – *Adam Smith, Empire*
picture; Russell Crowe; Michael Mann; script (Eric Roth, Michael Mann); Dante Spinotti; William Goldenberg, Paul Rubell, David Rosenbloom; sound (Andy Nelson, Doug Hemphill, Lee Orloff)

Insignificance
GB 1985 108m colour
Zenith/Recorded Picture Company (Jeremy Thomas)
On a hot night in 1953, a professor, an actress, a senator and a ballplayer meet in a New York hotel room.
Presumably meaningful but very boring talk piece in which the audience is supposed to recognize not merely well-known figures but a cross-section of America at the time.
w Terry Johnson *play* Terry Johnson d Nicolas Roeg ph Peter Hannan m Stanley Myers
☆ Gary Busey, Tony Curtis, Theresa Russell, Michael Emil

Insomnia **
Norway 1997 99m colour
Norsk Film/Nordic Screen (Petter J. Borgli, Tomas Backstrom, Tom Remlov)
On the trail of a killer, a Swedish-born cop, working in Norway, accidentally shoots his partner and covers up his guilt.
Deft psychological thriller of a man on the edge, set in a time of continual sunlight.
w Nikolaj Frobenius, Erik Skjoldbjaerg d Erik Skjoldbjaerg ph Erling Thurmann-Andersen m Geir Jenssen pd Eli Bo ed Hakon Overas
☆ Stellan Skarsgard, Sverre Anker Ousdal, Bjorn Floberg, Gisken Armand, Maria Bonnevie
'Offers a complex and emotionally compelling tale that doesn't settle for mere quirkiness or the de rigueur cop-thriller gore currently in vogue.' – *Steven Gaydos, Variety*

'Don't close your eyes.'
Insomnia **
US 2002 118m DeLuxe Panavision
Buena Vista/Alcon (Paul Junger Witt, Edward L. McDonnell, Broderick Johnson, Andrew A. Kosove)
Two Los Angeles cops go to the town of Nightmute, where the summer sun never sets, to investigate a schoolgirl's murder.
Effective remake of a Norwegian thriller; despite its added star power, it is no improvement on the original.
w Hillary Seitz *film* Insomnia by d Erik Skjoldbjaerg, w Nikolaj Frobenius, Erik Skjoldbjaerg d Christopher Nolan ph Wally Pfister m David Julyan pd Nathan Crowley ed Dody Dorn
☆ Al Pacino (Will Dormer), Robin Williams (Walter Finch), Hilary Swank (Ellie Burr), Maura Tierney (Rachel Clement), Martin Donovan (Hap Eckhart), Nicky Katt (Fred Duggar), Paul Dooley (Chief Nyback), Randy Stetz (Jonathan Jackson)
'A gripping, highly dramatic thriller.' – *Todd McCarthy, Variety*
'About as good a movie as you could have hoped for. Really good. Hole-in-one good.' – *Shawn Levy, Oregonian*
'Serves up Hollywood stars, superfluous action sequences, moral sermons and tidy conclusions.' – *Cosmo Landesman, Sunday Times*

Inspecteur Lavardin
France 1986 100m colour
Artificial Eye/MK2/Antenne 2/Suisse Romande TV (Marin Karmitz)
A detective investigates the murder of a respected writer.
Sequel to Cop Au Vin, *featuring an unorthodox cop, but less effective this time around.*
w Claude Chabrol, Dominique Roulet d Claude Chabrol ph Jean Rabier m Matthieu Chabrol ed Monique Fardoulis, Angela Braga-Marmet
☆ Jean Poiret, Jean-Claude Brialy, Bernadette Lafont, Jean-Luc Bideau, Jacques Dacqmine, Hermine Clair

The Inspector *
GB 1961 111m DeLuxe Cinemascope
TCF (Mark Robson)
US title: *Lisa*
In 1946 a Dutch policeman rescues a Jewish girl from an ex-Nazi and helps smuggle her to Palestine.
Peripatetic melodrama with surface suspense and subdued thoughts of ideology and race. Moments of interest, but generally dully developed and acted.
w Nelson Gidding *novel* Jan de Hartog d Philip Dunne ph Arthur Ibbetson m Malcolm Arnold
☆ Stephen Boyd, Dolores Hart, Leo McKern, Hugh Griffith, Donald Pleasence, Harry Andrews, Robert Stephens, Marius Goring
'A sluggish mélange of melodrama, romance, mystery and what the inactive might call action.' – *Judith Crist*

An Inspector Calls **
GB 1954 79m bw
British Lion/Watergate (A. D. Peters)
In 1912 a prosperous Yorkshire family is visited by a mysterious inspector who proves that each of them was partly responsible for the death of a young girl.
Tactful, enjoyable record of a celebrated play in its author's most typical manner.
w Desmond Davis *play* J. B. Priestley d *Guy Hamilton* ph *Ted Scaife* m Francis Chagrin ad Joseph Bato
☆ *Alastair Sim* (Inspector Poole), Jane Wenham (Eva Smith), Arthur Young (Arthur Birling), Olga Lindo (Sybil Birling), Brian Worth (Gerald Croft), Eileen Moore (Sheila Birling), Bryan Forbes (Eric Birling)

Inspector Clouseau
GB 1968 105m Eastmancolor Panavision
UA/Mirisch (Lewis J. Rachmil)
An incompetent French policeman is brought to London to investigate the aftermath of the Great Train Robbery.
Tiresome charade with all the jokes well telegraphed, and a background of swinging London.
w Tom and Frank Waldman d Bud Yorkin ph Arthur Ibbetson m Ken Thorne
☆ Alan Arkin, Delia Boccardo, Frank Finlay, Patrick Cargill, Beryl Reid, Barry Foster

Inspector Gadget
US 1999 78m Technicolor
Buena Vista/Walt Disney/Caravan (Jordan Kerner, Roger Birnbaum, Andy Heyward)
A half-human, half-robotic cop, equipped with mechanical devices for every occasion, battles against his evil twin.
Lavish, gimmick-laden extravaganza resembling a live-action cartoon, but, lacking a convincing narrative, the knockabout action soon palls.
w Kerry Ehrin, Zak Penn, Dana Olsen *characters created by* Andy Heyward, Jean Chalopin, Bruno Bianchi d David Kellogg ph Adam Greenberg m John Debney pd Michael White, Leslie Dilley ed Thom Noble, Adam Cody
☆ Matthew Broderick (Inspector Gadget/RoboGadget/ John Brown), Rupert Everett (Sanford Scolex), Joely Fisher (Brenda/RoboBrenda), Michelle Trachtenberg (Penny), Andy Dick (Kramer), Cheri Oteri (Mayor Wilson), Michael G. Hagerty (Sikes), Dabney Coleman (Chief Quimby), D.L. Hughley (Gadgetmobile voice), Rene Auberjonois (Artemus Bradford), Frances Bay (Thelma), Don Adams (voice of Brain)
'Demonstrates how a movie with little more on its mind than tickling the eyeballs of 7-year-olds can feature spiffy, jack-in-the-box special effects and still end up a dud.' – *Owen Gleiberman, Entertainment Weekly*

The Inspector General **
US 1949 101m Technicolor
Warner (Jerry Wald)
aka: *Happy Times*
An assistant elixir salesman with a travelling fair is mistaken by villagers for the dreaded inspector general.
Well wrought but basically boring version of a basically boring classic farce full of rhubarbing Old Russians. Nice production and hilarious moments do not quite atone for the dull stretches.
w Philip Rapp, Harry Kurnitz *play* Nikolai Gogol d Henry Koster ph Elwood Bredell m John Green ad Robert Haas *songs* Sylvia Fine
☆ *Danny Kaye, Walter Slezak,* Barbara Bates, Elsa Lanchester, Gene Lockhart, Alan Hale, Benny Baker, Walter Catlett

Inspector Hornleigh *
GB 1938 87m bw
TCF (Robert T. Kane)
The Chancellor of the Exchequer's bag is stolen.
First of three police comedy-dramas based on a character created for the radio series Monday Night at Eight *by Hans Priwin. Not bad, but the thinnest of the trio.*
w Bryan Wallace, Gerald Elliott, Richard Llewellyn d Eugene Forde ph Derrick Williams, Phil Tannura md Bretton Byrd
☆ *Gordon Harker, Alastair Sim,* Miki Hood, Hugh Williams, Steve Geray, Wally Patch, Edward Underdown, Gibb McLaughlin, Ronald Adam
'The opening shots – the murder in the squalid lodging and the stamp auction with the rows of poker faces and the elaborately mute bids – are not only good cinema, they are good English cinema, as national as a shot, say, from a Feyder, a de Mille or a Pommer.' – *Graham Greene*
'Interest is well sustained from the exciting opening shots to the crescendo at the close.' – *MFB*

Inspector Hornleigh Goes to It *
GB 1940 87m bw
TCF (Edward Black)
US title: *Mail Train*
Hornleigh and Bingham track down a fifth columnist.
Zestful comedy thriller climaxing on an express train: good fun for addicts of the genre.
w *Val Guest,* J. O. C. *Orton, Frank Launder* d Walter Forde ph *John Cox* md Louis Levy
☆ *Gordon Harker, Alastair Sim,* Phyllis Calvert, Edward Chapman, Charles Oliver, Raymond Huntley, Percy Walsh, David Horne, Peter Gawthorne

Inspector Hornleigh on Holiday *
GB 1939 87m bw
TCF (Edward Black)
The inspector and his sergeant solve the death of a fellow boarder at a seaside hotel.
Lively Hitchcockian comedy-thriller romp with an excellent script and plenty of variety of location.
w *Frank Launder, Sidney Gilliat,* J. O. C. *Orton* d Walter Forde ph John Cox md Louis Levy
☆ *Gordon Harker, Alastair Sim,* Linden Travers, Wally Patch, Edward Chapman, Philip Leaver, Kynaston Reeves

Inspiration
US 1930 74m bw
MGM
A French artists' model renounces her lover in case she harms his career.
Inane romantic melodrama.
w Gene Markey d Clarence Brown ph William Daniels
☆ Greta Garbo, Robert Montgomery, Lewis Stone, Marjorie Rambeau, Beryl Mercer, John Miljan
'As an adult problem it holds and never offends ... box office certainly, and a cinch for women.' – *Variety*
'Camille without the cough.' – *Motion Picture*

'He Gave Up What He Believed In, For The Ones He Loved.'
Instinct
US 1999 124m Technicolor Panavision
Buena Vista/Touchstone/Spyglass (Michael Taylor, Barbara Boyle)
A psychiatrist evaluates the mental condition of an anthropologist, who has lived in isolation with apes for several years and is accused of killing members of the search party that came looking for him.
Ludicrous psycho-melodrama that sets out to show that human society is corrupt in contrast to the natural world; all it demonstrates is how easily actors, given an unsatisfactory script, can compensate with hammy performances.
w Gerald DiPego *novel* Ishmael by Daniel Quinn d Jon Turteltaub ph Philippe Rousselot m Danny Elfman pd Garreth Stover ed Richard Francis-Bruce
☆ Anthony Hopkins (Ethan Powell), Cuba Gooding Jnr (Theo Caulder), Donald Sutherland (Ben Hillard), Maura Tierney (Lyn Powell), George Dzundza (Dr John Murray), John Ashton (Guard Dacks), John Aylward (Warden Keefer), Thomas Q. Morris (Pete), Doug Spinuzza (Nicko), Paul Bates (Bluto)
'Awkward, sluggish, finally ludicrous mix of suspense, character drama and inspirational fodder is half-baked on all counts.' – *Dennis Harvey, Variety*
'A mess of sanctimonious eco-drivel.' – *Neil Norman, London Evening Standard*

Institute Benjamenta *
GB 1995 105m bw
ICA/British Screen/Channel 4/Image/Pandora (Keith Griffiths, Janine Marmot)
A new arrival at a school for servants becomes the favourite of its owners.
Dense, slow, visually interesting movie, the first to use actors by makers of disturbing, surrealist animated

films; there's not much animation in this feature, and the audience is left to tease out its meaning.
w Alan Passes, The Brothers Quay *novel Jakob von Gunten* by Robert Walser *d* The Brothers Quay *ph* Nic Knowland *m* Lech Jankowski *pd* Jennifer Kernke *ed* Larry Sider
☆ Mark Rylance, Alice Krige, Gottfried John, Daniel Smith, Joseph Alessi

'Powerful food for unrest, and the first half hour is certainly one of the most extraordinary stretches of cinema this year.' – *Jonathan Romney, Guardian*

'Meticulously conjures a visually interesting netherworld that commands attention until alienation and indifference to the film's rarefied pursuits take over.' – *David Rooney, Variety*

'Tedium and repetition have never been so thrillingly filmed before.' – *Sight and Sound*

'All bets are on.'
Intacto *
Spain 2001 108m colour
Momentum/Sogecine/Telecinco/Canal+

In a world where luck can be traded or absorbed from others, the luckiest man falls out with a protege, who vows revenge after his luck is taken away from him.
Curious fable that has some effective moments, including a blindfold race through a forest in which the unlucky run full tilt into trees, but its one notion is not enough to sustain the movie.
w Juan Carlos Fresnadillo, Andres Koppel *d* Juan Carlos Fresnadillo *ph* Xavier Jimenez *m* Lucio Godoy *ad* Cesar Macarron *ed* Nacho Ruiz Capillas
☆ Leonardo Sbaraglia (Tomas Sanz), Eusebio Poncela (Federico), Monica Lopez (Sara), Antonio Dechent (Alejandro), Max Von Sydow (Samuel Berg), Guillermo Toledo (Horacio), Paz Gomez (Ana)

'Imagine finding the will to get up every morning to do another day's work on this stale story tarted up with relevance.' – *Stanley Kauffmann, New Republic*

The Intelligence Men
GB 1965 104m Eastmancolor
Rank/Hugh Stewart
US title: *Spylarks*
Two incompetent spies blunder through a series of adventures.
Inept and rather embarrassing big-screen debut for two excellent television comedians.
w S. C. Green, R. M. Hills *d* Robert Asher *ph* Jack Asher *m* Phillip Green
☆ Eric Morecambe, Ernie Wise, William Franklyn, April Olrich, Richard Vernon, David Lodge, Warren Mitchell, Francis Matthews

Intent to Kill *
GB 1958 89m bw Cinemascope
TCF/Zonic (Adrian Worker)

In a Montreal hospital, attempts are made on the life of a South American dictator recovering from a brain operation.
Solidly entertaining suspenser.
w Jimmy Sangster *d* Jack Cardiff *ph* Desmond Dickinson *m* Kenneth V. Jones
☆ Richard Todd, Betsy Drake, Herbert Lom, Warren Stevens, Alexander Knox

Interceptor
US 1992 92m colour
Trimark (Oliver G. Hess, Kevin M. Kallberg)

A pilot is the only man who can foil a terrorist attempt to steal two experimental Stealth fighters while they are being transported by air.
Run-of-the-mill action movie with the usual indestructible hero.
w John Brancato, Michael Ferris *d* Michael Cohn *ph* Lee Redmond *m* Rick Marvin *pd* Gary T. New *ed* Glenn A. Morgan *visual effects* Richard Kerrigan
☆ Andrew Divoff (Capt. Christopher Winfield), Elizabeth Morehead (Maj. Janet Morgan), Jurgen Prochnow (Phillips), J. Kenneth Campbell (Engineer), Jon Cedar (Elliot), John Prosky (Collins), Rick Marzan (Martinez), Daniel Namath (Lt. Rheinbeck)

Interference
US 1929 75m bw
Paramount
To prevent his wife from being blackmailed, a dying man commits murder and turns himself in.
Dreary drama with the distinction of being Paramount's first talking picture.
w Ernest Pascal, Hope Loring *play* Roland Pertwee, Harold Dearden *d* Lothar Mendes, Roy Pomeroy
☆ William Powell, Evelyn Brent, Clive Brook, Doris Kenyon

Interiors *
US 1978 95m Technicolor
UA/Jack Rollins-Charles H. Joffe

Everybody in a well-heeled American family has problems.
Curious attempt by Woody Allen to make his own version of the Bergmanesque psycho-dramas he usually satirizes. Apparently this is the real Woody, and the comedian was a mask. Oh, well.
wd Woody Allen *ph* Gordon Willis *m* none
☆ Kristin Griffith, Mary Beth Hurt, Richard Jordan, Diane Keaton, E. G. Marshall, Geraldine Page, Maureen Stapleton, Sam Waterston

'As dull as toothache and as predictable as a metronome.' – *Barry Took, Punch*

script; direction; Geraldine Page; Maureen Stapleton
Geraldine Page

Interlude
US 1957 89m Technicolor Cinemascope
U-I (Ross Hunter)
An American girl in Munich falls in love with an orchestral conductor but leaves him because of his insane wife.
Dull remake of When Tomorrow Comes *(qv), with poor script and performances.*
w Daniel Fuchs, Franklin Coen *d* Douglas Sirk *ph* R. F. Schoengarth *m* Frank Skinner
☆ Rossano Brazzi, June Allyson, Françoise Rosay, Marianne Cook, Keith Andes, Jane Wyatt

'Contains every cliché known to romantic fiction.' – *MFB*

Interlude *
GB 1968 113m Technicolor
Columbia/Domino (David Deutsch, Jack Hanbury)
A girl reporter falls for a celebrated orchestral conductor; they have an affair but he finally goes back to his wife.
Intermezzo *remade for the swinging London set, quite agreeable in parts because of the acting but generally rather soggy.*
w Lee Langley, Hugh Leonard *d* Kevin Billington *ph Gerry Fisher* *m* Georges Delerue *pd* Tony Woollard
☆ *Oskar Werner*, Barbara Ferris, *Virginia Maskell*, *John Cleese*, Donald Sutherland, Nora Swinburne, Alan Webb

'If you laughed at *Brief Encounter* you will roar over this one.' – *Wilfrid Sheed*

'It's got all the schmaltz and none of the style of the tearjerkers of yesteryear.' – *Judith Crist, 1973*

'Wild longings ... fierce desires he could not name ... for an interlude of stolen love! To one woman he gave his memories – to another he gave his dreams!'
Intermezzo ***
US 1939 69m bw
David O. Selznick

GB title: *Escape to Happiness*
A renowned, married violinist has an affair with his musical protégée.
Archetypal cinema love story, Hollywoodized from a Swedish original but quite perfect in its brief, sentimental way.
w George O'Neil *original scenario* Gosta Stevens, Gustav Molander *d Gregory Ratoff* *ph* Gregg Toland *m* Lou Forbes *ad* Lyle Wheeler *ed* Hal C. Kern, Francis D. Lyon
☆ *Leslie Howard, Ingrid Bergman*, John Halliday, Edna Best, Cecil Kellaway
† William Wyler is said to have assisted in the direction.
Lou Forbes

'Trust me ... I'm a cop.'
Internal Affairs
US 1990 115m Technicolor Panavision
UIP/Paramount (Frank Mancuso Jnr)

A duel to the death develops between an honest and a corrupt cop.
Unconvincing melodrama in which loud voices substitute for passion and feeling.
w Henry Bean *d* Mike Figgis *ph* John A. Alonso *m* Mike Figgis, Anthony Marinelli, Brian Banks *pd* Waldemar Kalinowski *ed* Robert Estrin
☆ Richard Gere, Andy Garcia, Nancy Travis, Laurie Metcalf, Richard Bradford, William Baldwin, Michael Beach

'Where *Internal Affairs* really succeeds is in its cracking narrative drive, moody atmospherics, and excellent performances, even in the smallest roles.' – *MFB*

'Stars of stage, screen, radio and boudoir throw a party for your entertainment!'
International House *
US 1933 73m bw
Paramount

A weird variety of travellers are quarantined in a Shanghai hotel where a local doctor has perfected television.
Madcap farce which succeeds in hits and misses.
w Francis Martin, Walter de Leon, Lou Heifetz, Neil Brant *d* A. Edward Sutherland *ph* Ernest Haller *m/ly* Ralph Rainger, Leo Robin
☆ *W. C. Fields, George Burns, Gracie Allen*, Peggy Hopkins Joyce, Stuart Erwin, Sari Maritza, Bela Lugosi, Edmund Breese, Lumsden Hare, Rose Marie, Rudy Vallee, Sterling Holloway, Cab Calloway and his band, Colonel Stoopnagle and Budd

'Cast includes enough names to offset the effects of an otherwise second-rate picture.' – *Variety*

'Constructed along the lines of a mammoth vaudeville show, the motivating story often is sidetracked entirely to permit a lot of unrelated hokum comedy.' – *Motion Picture Herald*

'A thousand thrills as two men battle across a continent!'
International Lady *
US 1941 102m bw
Edward Small
An FBI man falls for the lady Axis agent he is chasing.
Cliché-ridden melodrama partially saved by light comedy touches.
w Howard Estabrook *d* Tim Whelan *ph* Hal Mohr *m* Lucien Moraweck
☆ George Brent, Basil Rathbone, Ilona Massey, Gene Lockhart, George Zucco, Francis Pierlot, Martin Kosleck, Marjorie Gateson

International Settlement
US 1938 75m bw
TCF (Darryl F. Zanuck)
An adventurer becomes involved in Shanghai gun-running during the war between China and Japan.
Brisk action romance with good technical credits.
w Lou Breslow, John Patrick *d* Eugene Forde *ph* Lucien Andriot *md* Samuel Kaylin
☆ George Sanders, Dolores del Rio, June Lang, Dick Baldwin, Ruth Terry, John Carradine, Keye Luke, Harold Huber, Pedro de Cordoba

'Strong supporting picture for double bills.' – *Variety*

International Squadron *
US 1941 87m bw
Warner (Edmund Grainger)
A playboy becomes a fighting air ace.
Standard war story, quite well done; remake of Ceiling Zero *(qv).*
w Barry Trivers, Kenneth Gamet *story* Frank Wead *d* Lothar Mendes *ph* James Van Trees, Ted McCord *ed* Frank McGee
☆ Ronald Reagan, James Stephenson, Julie Bishop, Cliff Edwards, Reginald Denny, Olympe Bradna, William Lundigan, John Ridgely

International Velvet
GB 1978 125m Metrocolor
MGM (Bryan Forbes)

A hostile orphan becomes an international horsewoman.
Disappointing attempt to produce a sequel to 1944's National Velvet*; none of it coheres, one is not clear to whom it is intended to appeal, and some of the dialogue is fearsome.*
wd Bryan Forbes *ph* Tony Imi *m* Francis Lai *pd* Keith Wilson
☆ Nanette Newman, Tatum O'Neal, Anthony Hopkins, Christopher Plummer, Peter Barkworth, Dinsdale Landen

The Internecine Project *
GB 1974 89m Eastmancolor
Maclean and Co/Lion International/Hemisphere (Barry Levinson, Andrew Donally)

A Harvard professor arranges the mutual extermination of four people who could spoil a politician's presidential chances.
Coldly murderous romp with plenty of style.
w Barry Levinson, Jonathan Lynn *novel* Mort W. Elkind *d Ken Hughes* *ph* Geoffrey Unsworth *m* Roy Budd *pd* Geoffrey Drake *ed* John Shirley
☆ James Coburn, Lee Grant, Harry Andrews, Ian Hendry, Michael Jayston, Keenan Wynn

'He risked his life to save a rat – and what did he get for it?'
Internes Can't Take Money *
US 1937 75m bw
Paramount (Benjamin Glazer)
GB title: *You Can't Take Money*
A hospital doctor persuades a gangster friend to help a woman find her missing child.
Quite interesting minor melodrama, first of the Dr Kildare series which was subsequently recast and restyled by MGM.
w Rian James, Theodore Reed *story* Max Brand *d Alfred Santell* *ph* Theodor Sparkuhl *m* Gregory Stone
☆ Joel McCrea, Barbara Stanwyck, Lloyd Nolan, Stanley Ridges, Lee Bowman, Irving Bacon

'Satisfactory melodrama with a tear ... better than average standing at the box office.' – *Variety*

Interno d'un Convento:
see *Behind Convent Walls*

'Their nights are as fast and frantic as their days! Don't miss the wildest party ever filmed!'
The Interns *
US 1962 130m bw
Columbia/Interns Co./Robert Cohn

In an American hospital, newly qualified doctors have personal and career problems.
*Birth, abortion, sudden death, drugs and women's lib all figure in this melodramatic compendium which succeeds well enough on its own level and spawned a sequel (*The New Interns*) and an unsuccessful TV series.*
w Walter Newman, David Swift *novel* Richard Frede *d* David Swift *ph* Russell Metty *m* Leith Stevens
☆ Cliff Robertson, Michael Callan, James MacArthur, Nick Adams, Suzy Parker, Buddy Ebsen, Telly Savalas

Interpol
GB 1957 92m bw Cinemascope
Columbia/Warwick (Irving Allen, Albert R. Broccoli)
US title: *Pickup Alley*
The US Anti-Narcotics Squad trails across Europe the insane and ruthless leader of a drug ring.
Drearily routine thick ear electrified by one performance but not helped by wide screen.
w John Paxton *d* John Gilling *ph* Ted Moore *m* Richard Bennett
☆ Victor Mature, Anita Ekberg, *Trevor Howard*, Bonar Colleano, Marne Maitland, Eric Pohlmann, Alec Mango, Peter Illing, Sydney Tafler

Interrogation ***
Poland 1982 120m colour
Gala/Zespol Filmowy 'X' (Tadeusz Drewno)
original title: *Przesluchanie*
In the 1950s, a fun-loving singer is arrested, questioned and tortured by the secret police.
Harrowing, but uplifting in its depiction of an unquenchable human spirit. The film was banned by the authorities, its director moving to work in North America, and not released until 1990.
wd Ryszard Bugajski *ph* Jacek Petrycki *pd* Janusz Sosnowski *ed* Katarzyna Maciejko

☆ Krystyna Janda, Adam Ferency, Janusz Gajos, Agnieszka Holland, Anna Romantowska, Bozena Dykiel, Olgierda Lukaszewicza, Tomasz Dedek

The Interrupted Journey
GB 1949 80m bw
Valiant (Anthony Havelock-Allan)

An author leaves his wife for another woman, changes his mind on the journey, pulls the communication cord and causes a train crash. Or does he?
Minor melodrama with expressionist tendencies and a dream explanation. Interesting for its parts rather than its whole.
w Michael Pertwee *d* Daniel Birt *ph* Erwin Hillier
☆ Richard Todd, Valerie Hobson, Christine Norden, Tom Walls, Ralph Truman, Vida Hope

Interrupted Melody
US 1955 106m Eastmancolor
Cinemascope
MGM (Jack Cummings)
The story of Marjorie Lawrence, an Australian opera singer who fell victim to polio.
Standard biopic which jells less well than some.
w William Ludwig, Sonya Levien *d* Curtis Bernhardt *ph* Joe Ruttenberg, Paul Vogel *music supervisor* Saul Chaplin
☆ Eleanor Parker, Glenn Ford, Roger Moore, Cecil Kellaway, Stephen Bekassy
† Eleanor Parker's singing was dubbed by Eileen Farrell.
script
Eleanor Parker

'Make every move as if it were your last.'
Intersection
US 1994 98m DeLuxe
Paramount (Bud Yorkin, Mark Rydell)
An architect's love-life goes awry after a car crash.
Dim and glossy melodrama about the meaning of life; if you value every moment, then don't waste time watching it.
w David Rayfiel, Marshall Brickman *novel* Paul Guimard *d* Mark Rydell *ph* Vilmos Zsigmond *m* James Newton Howard *pd* Harold Michelson *ed* Mark Warner
☆ Richard Gere, Sharon Stone, Lolita Davidovich, Martin Landau, David Selby, Jenny Morrison
'A misguided attempt to retool a French art film as a Hollywood big-star vehicle.' – *Variety*
† It is a remake of *Les Choses de la Vie* (qv), directed in 1969 by Claude Sautet and starring Michel Piccoli and Romy Schneider.

Interview with a Serial Killer: see *White Angel*

'Drink From Me And Live Forever.'
Interview with the Vampire: The Vampire Chronicles **
US 1994 122m Technicolor
Warner/Geffen (Stephen Woolley, David Geffen)
A vampire reminisces about his life over the past 200 years and his enduring relationship with an older vampire, who initiated him and whom he later tries to kill, and the young girl vampire they both created.
A brooding period piece on horror themes and the price paid for immortality, with a homoerotic subtext, but lacking the necessary emotional depth and narrative credibility as it skips through the centuries; what lingers in the mind are some of the more spectacular set-pieces.
w Anne Rice *novel* Anne Rice *d* Neil Jordan *ph* Philippe Rousselot *m* Elliot Goldenthal *pd* Dante Ferretti *ed* Mick Audsley *sp* make-up: Stan Winston
☆ Tom Cruise, Brad Pitt, Antonio Banderas, Christian Slater, Stephen Rea, Kirsten Dunst, Virgina McCollam, John McConnell, Mike Seelig, Roger Lloyd Pack
'An anaemic experience. It doesn't frighten; still less, shock. For fear, it substitutes disgust. It's such a dishonest, hypocritical film. Largely an exercise in sado-masochism, it uses the traditional trappings of vampire legend as licence for its own fixation on an array of modern perversions it would be hard to get permission to show if they were performed in modern dress and contemporary times.' – *Alexander Walker, London Evening Standard*
'It seems that Neil Jordan is better at capturing the eternal ennui of the vampire condition than the cheap thrills which are the lifeblood of the genre.' – *Adam Mars-Jones, Independent*
'Best thought of as a lycanthropic *The Odd Couple*.' – *Joe Queenan*
Dante Ferretti; Elliot Goldenthal
Philippe Rousselot; Dante Ferretti

Intervista *
Italy 1987 105m Eastmancolor
Aljosha/RAI Uno/Cinecittà (Ibrahim Moussa)
Part autobiographical reminiscence, part celebration of the fiftieth anniversary of Cinecittà, part interview by Japanese television.
Fascinating, though also self-indulgent, trip through Fellini's past.
w Federico Fellini, Gianfranco Angelucci *d* Federico Fellini *ph* Tonino Delli Colli *m* Nicola Piovani *ad* Danilo Donati, Paul Mazursky, Leon Capetanos *ed* Nino Baragli
☆ Federico Fellini, Marcello Mastroianni, Anita Ekberg, Sergio Rubini, Lara Wendel, Paola Liguori, Nadai Ottaviani, Tonino Delli Colli, Danilo Donati

Intimacy *
US 1965 87m bw
Goldstone (David Heilwell)
A businessman in need of a government contract tries to compromise the official concerned.
Unusual minor melodrama, interesting but not quite successful.
w Eva Wolas *d* Victor Stoloff *ph* Ted Saizis *m* Geordie Hormel
☆ Barry Sullivan, Nancy Malone, Jack Ging, Joan Blackman, Jackie Shannon

Intimacy *
GB/France 2000 120m colour Super 35
Pathé/Telema/Studio Canal/Arte/France2/Mikado/Azor (Patrick Cassavetti, Jacques Hinstin)
A barman, who has anonymous sex every Wednesday with a married woman, begins to want to know more about his lover.
Bleak, sexually explicit drama of a loveless affair in seedy surroundings; it promises more than it delivers.
w Anne-Louise Trividic, Patrice Chéreau *stories* Hanif Kureishi *d* Patrice Chéreau *ph* Eric Gautier *m* Eric Neveux *pd* Hayden Griffin *ed* Francois Gedigier
☆ Mark Rylance (Jay), Kerry Fox (Claire), Timothy Spall (Andy), Alastair Galbraith (Victor), Philippe Calvario (Ian), Marianne Faithful (Betty), Susannah Harker (Susan), Rebecca Palmer (Pam)
'A tortured reflection on the complex relationship between love, sex, desire and obsession, distinguished by courageously raw performances.' – *David Rooney, Variety*

Intimate Relations: see *Les Parents Terribles (1948)*

'In the Spring of 1956, in a quaint little town, a crime took place that shocked a nation ... This is the true story.'
Intimate Relations *
GB/Canada 1995 99m DeLuxe
TCF/Intimate Relations/Chandlertown/Handmade/Boxer/Paragon (Angela Hart, Lisa Hope, Jon Slan)
In the mid-50s, a young sailor finds lodgings in a northern town and is seduced by his sex-starved middle-aged landlady and her pubescent daughter.
A blackly comic take on a true-life murder, in which a lower-middle-class gentility masks rapacious emotions; in its not-always-successful stylized approach, it edges towards the territory that Joe Orton marked out as his own.
wd Philip Goodhew *ph* Andrés Garretón *m* Lawrence Shragge *pd* Caroline Greville-Morris *ed* Pia di Ciaula
☆ Julie Walters, Rupert Graves, Matthew Walker, Laura Sadler, Holly Aird, Les Dennis, Elizabeth McKechnie
'A razor-sharp condemnation not of the historical 50s but of the mythic 50s so mistily invoked by John Major in his calls for a return to "decency" and "family values".' – *Claire Monk, Sight and Sound*

The Intimate Stranger *
GB 1956 95m bw
Anglo-Guild (Alec Snowden)
US title: *Finger of Guilt*
An American film producer in England is plagued by a strange girl who claims to have been his mistress.
Acceptable mystery thriller which holds the interest and has good detail.
w Howard Koch *novel Pay the Piper* by Peter Howard *d* Joseph Walton (Joseph Losey) *ph* Gerald Gibbs *m* Trevor Duncan
☆ Richard Basehart, Mary Murphy, Mervyn Johns, Constance Cummings, Roger Livesey, Faith Brook
† The film credited Peter Howard as the screenwriter because Howard Koch was blacklisted.

Intimate with a Stranger
GB 1994 94m colour
Independent International (Roderick Mangin-Turner)
A former academic turned gigolo decides, after servicing a succession of women, that life would be better with his former girlfriend.
A series of vapid sexual encounters combined with a little psycho-babble make for a depressing movie, a throwback to the sexploitation cycle of the 70s but more pretentious and even less interesting.
w Mel Woods, Roderick Mangin-Turner *d* Mel Roberts *ph* Nicholas Tebbet *m* Ledsam & Pugh *pd* Graeme Story *ed* Brian Smedley-Ashton
☆ Roderick Mangin-Turner, Daphne Nayer, Amy Tolsky, Lorelei King, Ellenor Wilkinson, Janis Lee, Darcey Ferrer
'Jaw-droppingly, eye-bogglingly awful.' – *Sheila Johnston, Independent*

Into the Blue
GB 1950 83m bw
Imperadio
US title: *Man in the Dinghy*
A cheerful stowaway on a yacht helps the owners catch smugglers.
Emaciated comedy which never gets going.
w Pamela Wilcox Bower, Donald Taylor, Nicholas Phipps *d* Herbert Wilcox *ph* Max Greene *m* Mischa Spoliansky
☆ Michael Wilding, Odile Versois, Jack Hulbert, Constance Cummings, Edward Rigby

Into the Night
US 1985 115m Technicolor
Universal/George Folsey Jnr, Ron Koslow
A harassed husband becomes even more so when one night at the airport he meets a dizzy girl with six smuggled emeralds.
A kind of nocturnal road film into which for some reason the director has crammed a number of his colleagues. None of it really works, even as an in-joke.
w Ron Koslow *d* John Landis *ph* Robert Paynter *m* Ira Newborn *pd* John Lloyd
☆ Jeff Goldblum, Michelle Pfeiffer, Richard Farnsworth, Irene Papas, Paul Mazursky, Roger Vadim, David Bowie

Into the Sun
US 1991 100m Foto-Kem
Trimark (Kevin M. Kallberg, Oliver G. Hess)
A top pilot is assigned to demonstrate his skills for the benefit of a Hollywood star of action movies.
Pleasant but unmemorable movie that becomes ridiculous towards the end.
w John Brancato, Michael Ferris *d* Fritz Kiersch *ph* Steve Grass *m* Randy Miller *pd* Gary T. New *ed* Barry Zetlin
☆ Anthony Michael Hall, Michael Paré, Deborah Maria Moore, Terry Kiser, Brian Haley, Michael St Gerard, Linden Ashby

'Where myth and magic walk the earth.'
Into the West *
Eire 1992 102m Technicolor
Entertainment/Little Bird/Parallel/Majestic/Miramax/Film Four/Newcomm (Jonathan Cavendish, Tim Palmer)
A father, a former traveller, hunts for his two sons who have run away from their Dublin home with a magical white horse, Tir na nOg.
An odd, likeable film, despite its not always successful mythic overtones, and one that should have an appeal to the young.
w Jim Sheridan, David Keating *story* Michael Pearce *d* Mike Newell *ph* Tom Sigel *m* Patrick Doyle *pd* Jamie Leonard *ed* Peter Boyle
☆ Gabriel Byrne, Ellen Barkin, Ciarán Fitzgerald, Ruaidhri Conroy, David Kelly, Johnny Murphy, Colm Meaney, John Kavanagh, Brendan Gleeson, Jim Norton
'Its heady mix of Irish myth and gritty realism will effortlessly capture the imaginations of all ages.' – *Empire*

Intolerance ****
US 1916 115m approx (24 fps) bw silent
D. W. Griffith
Four stories – including Belshazzar's feast and the massacre of St Bartholomew – of intolerance through the ages are intercut and linked by the image of a mother and her baby: 'out of the cradle, endlessly rocking'.
A massive enterprise of which audiences at the time and after were quite intolerant. Hard to take in parts, it rises to a fine climax as all the stories come to a head, including a modern one with a race between a car and train, and has been called 'the only film fugue'. At the time, by far the most expensive film ever made.
wd D. W. Griffith *ph* Billy Bitzer, Karl Brown
☆ Mae Marsh, Lillian Gish, Constance Talmadge, Robert Harron, Elmo Lincoln, Eugene Pallette
'A mad, brilliant, silly extravaganza. Perhaps the greatest movie ever made. In it one can see the source of most of the major traditions of the screen: the methods of Eisenstein and von Stroheim, the Germans and the Scandinavians, and, when it's bad, de Mille.' – *New Yorker, 1980*

Intrigue
US 1947 90m bw
UA/Star (Sam Bischoff)
In Shanghai after the war, a civilian pilot becomes unwittingly involved in drug smuggling.
Tedious and flashy pot-boiler.
w Barry Trivers, George Slavin *d* Edwin L. Marin *ph* Lucien Andriot *m* Louis Forbes
☆ George Raft, June Havoc, Tom Tully, Helena Carter

Intrigue in Paris: see *Miss V from Moscow*

The Intruder *
GB 1953 84m bw
British Lion/Ivan Foxwell
An ex-army officer surprises a burglar and recognizes his old comrade who has been ill-served by society.
Watchable but rather mechanical compendium drama in which a series of cameos supposedly sum up the problems of life in post-war Britain.
w Robin Maugham, John Hunter *novel Line on Ginger* by Robin Maugham *d* Guy Hamilton *ph* Ted Scaife *m* Francis Chagrin
☆ *Jack Hawkins*, Michael Medwin, Hugh Williams, George Cole, Dennis Price, Dora Bryan

The Intruder *
US 1961 84m bw
Filmgroup (Roger Corman)
GB title: *The Stranger*
A mild-mannered stranger arrives in a Southern town and stirs up racist trouble.
Cheaply-made social melodrama with many effective moments.
w Charles Beaumont *novel* Charles Beaumont *d Roger Corman* *ph* Taylor Byars *m* Herman Stein
☆ William Shatner, Frank Maxwell, Beverly Lunsford, Robert Emhardt, Jeanne Cooper, Leo Gordon, Charles Beaumont

The Intruder: see *The Innocent (1976)*

Intruder in the Dust ***
US 1949 87m bw
MGM (Clarence Brown)
In a Southern town, a boy and an old lady solve a mystery and prevent a black man from being lynched.
Excellent character drama which also offers vivid local colour, a murder puzzle and social comment. A semi-classic.
w Ben Maddow *novel* William Faulkner *d Clarence Brown* *ph Robert Surtees* *m* Adolph Deutsch

☆ *Juano Hernandez, Elizabeth Patterson*, David Brian, Claude Jarman Jnr, *Porter Hall*, Will Geer

'It is surely the years of range and experience which have given him a control of the medium so calm, sure and – apparently – easy that he can make a complex story seem simple and straightforward.' – *Pauline Kael*

'A really good movie that is also and incidentally the first honestly worked out "racial" film I have seen.' – *Richard Winnington*

'An example of gripping film craftsmanship.' – *News of the World*

The Invaders: see *49th Parallel*

'From out of space – came hordes of green monsters!'

Invaders from Mars

US 1953 82m Cinecolor
Edward L. Alperson

Martian invaders use hypnotized humans as saboteurs.

Poverty Row sci-fi partly redeemed by its erratic but talented designer who provides flashes of visual imagination.

w Richard Blake *ph* John Seitz *m* Raoul Kraushaar *d/pd William Cameron Menzies*

☆ Helena Carter, Arthur Franz, Leif Erickson, Hillary Brooke

Invaders from Mars

US 1986 100m TVC Color Panavision
Cannon (Menahem Golan, Yoram Globus)

A boy one night sees a space ship land in his back yard.

Astonishingly witless remake of a show that was a cheap second feature in 1953.

w Dan O'Bannon, Don Jakoby *d* Tobe Hooper *ph* Daniel Pearl *m* Christopher Young

☆ Karen Black, Hunter Carson, Timothy Bottoms, Louise Fletcher, Bud Cort

Invasion *

GB 1966 82m bw
AA/Merton Park (Jack Greenwood)

An English village is beset one night by invaders from outer space.

Understated, effective little suspenser, well done in all departments.

w Roger Marshall *d Alan Bridges ph* James Wilson *m* Bernard Ebbinghouse

☆ Edward Judd, Valerie Gearon, Lyndon Brook, Yoko Tani, Tsai Chin, Barrie Ingham, Arthur Sharp

'A modest but highly intelligent science fiction thriller.' – *Financial Times*

Invasion of Planet X: see *Invasion of the Astro-Monsters*

Invasion of the Astro-Monsters

Japan 1967 90m colour Tohoscope
Toho/Henry G. Saperstein Enterprises (Tomoyuki Tanaka)

aka: *Monster Zero*
aka: *Invasion of Planet X; Godzilla vs Monster Zero*

Aliens program three monsters, Godzilla, Rodan and Ghidrah, to attack the Earth.

Dull monster movie, its only novelty being its American leading man.

w Shinichi Sekizawa *d* Inoshiro Honda *ph* Hajime Koizumi *m* Akira Ifukube *ad* Takeo Kita *ed* Rhyohei Fujii *sp* Eiji Tsuburaya

☆ Nick Adams, Akira Takarada, Kumi Mizuno, Keiki Sawai, Jun Tazaki, Yoshio Tsuchiya, Akira Kubo

'The world as they knew it was slipping away from them. Time was running out for the human race. And there was nothing to hold on to – except each other!'

Invasion of the Body Snatchers ****

US 1955 80m bw Superscope
Allied Artists/Walter Wanger

A small American town is imperceptibly taken over by an alien force.

Persuasive, thoroughly satisfying, low-budget science fiction, put across with subtlety and intelligence in every department.

w Daniel Mainwaring *novel Jack Finney d Don Siegel ph* Ellsworth Fredericks *m* Carmen Dragon

☆ *Kevin McCarthy, Dana Wynter*, Larry Gates, *King Donovan*, Carolyn Jones, Virginia Christine, Sam Peckinpah

Invasion of the Body Snatchers *

US 1978 115m Technicolor
UA/Robert H. Solo

Failing to get officials to listen to the fact that the population is being replaced by aliens, a San Francisco public health inspector imitates the emotionless pod people in order to infiltrate their organisation.

Flashy updating of the 1956 classic, mistakenly set in a big city and confusingly unravelled, with nobody for the audience to empathize with. Its nicest effect is to have Kevin McCarthy appear in a cameo.

w W. D. Richter *d* Philip Kaufman *ph* Michael Chapman *m* Denny Zeitlin *pd* Charles Rosen

☆ Donald Sutherland, Brooke Adams, Leonard Nimoy, Veronica Cartwright, Jeff Goldblum, Art Hindle, Lelia Goldoni, Kevin McCarthy, Don Siegel

† The film was remade in 1993 as *Body Snatchers*.

Invasion of the Saucermen

US 1957 90m bw
AIP/Malibu (James H. Nicholson, Robert J. Gurney Jnr)

Little green aliens who land on Earth in a flying saucer are defeated by teenagers.

Science fiction with comic overtones, though done with so little finesse that it is difficult to know what is intentionally funny and what is accidentally so.

w Robert J. Gurney Jnr, Al Martin *story* Paul Fairman *d* Edward L. Cahn *ph* Fred West *m* Ronald Stein *ad* Don Ament *ed* Ronald Sinclair

☆ Steve Terrell, Gloria Castillo, Frank Gorshin

Invasion Quartet

GB 1961 87m bw
MGM (Ronald Kinnoch)

An ill-assorted foursome of officers and a boffin take on the dangerous mission of silencing a Nazi gun trained on Dover.

A plot which could have been handled any way is played unsatisfactorily for farce, and all concerned are understandably uneasy.

w Jack Trevor Story, John Briley *story* Norman Collins *d* Jay Lewis *ph* Geoffrey Faithfull, Gerald Moss *m* Ron Goodwin

☆ Bill Travers, Spike Milligan, Grégoire Aslan, John Le Mesurier, Thorley Walters, Maurice Denham, Millicent Martin, Cyril Luckham

'America wasn't ready – but he was!'

Invasion USA

US 1952 70m bw
Columbia (Albert Zugsmith)

A hypnotist in a New York bar gives a group of people a foretaste of what might happen to them under atomic attack.

Ludicrous, dangerous, hilarious low-budget exploitationer composed mainly of rubber rocks and old newsreels.

w Robert Smith *d* Alfred E. Green *ph* John L. Russell *m* Albert Glasser

☆ Dan O'Herlihy, Gerald Mohr, Peggie Castle

Invasion USA

US 1985 107m TVC Color
Cannon (Menahem Golan, Yoram Globus)

Ruthless foreign mercenaries invade the southern US.

Brainless farrago of violence which goes out of its way to be unpleasant but ends up being rather funny.

w James Bruner, Chuck Norris *d* Joseph Zito *ph* Joao Fernandes *m* Jay Chattaway

☆ Chuck Norris, Richard Lynch, Melissa Prophet, Alexander Zale

'Love, beauty, happiness. If you don't have it ... invent it.'

Inventing the Abbots *

US 1997 110m DeLuxe
TCF/Imagine (Ron Howard, Brian Grazier, Janet Meyers)

A man remembers events in the 50s, when his working-class family became involved with the family of a wealthy neighbour.

A nostalgic, small-town soap opera, in which three brothers woo two sisters, which investigates the power of myths to warp reality.

w Ken Hixon *story* Sue Miller *d* Pat O'Connor *ph* Kenneth MacMillan *m* Michael Kamen *pd* Gary Frutkoff *ed* Ray Lovejoy

☆ Joaquin Phoenix, Billy Crudup, Liv Tyler, Will Patton, Kathy Baker, Jennifer Connelly, Joanna Going, Barbara Williams

'An emotionally powerful but extremely old-fashioned coming-of-age saga.' – *Variety*

Investigation of a Citizen above Suspicion *

Italy 1970 115m Technicolor
Vera (Daniele Senatore)

A successful police inspector kills his mistress and, paranoically considering himself above suspicion, plants clues leading to himself and even confesses the crime.

Fairly engrossing character study with political undertones; cinematically quite striking, too.

w Ugo Pirro, Elio Petri *d Elio Petri ph* Luigi Kuveiller *m* Ennio Morricone

☆ Gian Maria Volonte, Florinda Bolkan, Salvo Randone, Gianni Santuccio

best foreign film

script

An Investigation of Murder: see *The Laughing Policeman*

The Investigator

France/Italy/Spain/West Germany 1967 98m Technicolor Techniscope
Warner/Waterview/Criterion/Franca/CCM (Nat Waschsberger)

original title: *Le Vicomte Règle Ses Comptes*
US title: *The Viscount*

An investigator chases across Europe to expose a gang of drug dealers.

Dull and dreary thriller that should have done better by its cast.

w Clark Reynolds, Georges Farrel *novel Bonne Mesure* by Jean Bruce *d* Maurice Cloche *ph* Henri Raichi *m* Georges Garvarentz *ad* Jean Douarinou *ed* Raymond Leboursier

☆ Kerwin Matthews, Edmond O'Brien, Jean Yanne, Fernando Rey, Jane Fleming (Silvia Sorrente), Yvette Lebon

'Irredeemable gangster melodrama.' – *Clive Hirshhorn*

† Folco Lulli replaced Edmond O'Brien in the foreign-language versions of the film.

Invincible

Germany/Ireland/GB/US 2001 133m colour
Film4/Werner Herzog/Tatfilm/Little Bird/Jan Bart

In the early 1930s, a Jewish strongman becomes a star in Berlin and tries to warn his fellow Poles of the dangers of fascism.

Muddled, slow-moving drama: its genuine athlete – winner of the World's Strongest Man competition – in the lead is the nearest it comes to reflecting any sort of reality.

wd Werner Herzog *ph* Peter Zeitlinger *m* Hans Zimmer, Klaus Badelt *pd* Ulrich Bergfelder *ed* Joe Bini

☆ Tim Roth (Hanussen), Jouko Ahola (Zishe), Anna Gourari (Marta Farra), Max Raabe (MC), Jacob Wein (Benjamin), Gustav Peter Wohler (Landwehr), Udo Kier (Count Helldorf), Herbert Golder (Rabbi Edelman)

'The film is confusion throughout. Nothing is plausible; much, unintelligible.' – *Alexander Walker*

'The English dialogue is stilted, the performances hollow, the pace evenly leaden, the larger social context non-existent.' – *Philip French, Observer*

Invisible Adversaries

Austria 1977 109m colour
Valie Export

original title: *Unsichtbare Gegner*

A female photographer becomes convinced that aliens are taking over people's bodies and robbing them of their humanity.

Bizarre images of alienation – a man urinating on a woman's head, a fish head gasping after it has been severed from its body, a baby in a fridge – reinforce an attack on conformity. But Invasion of the Body Snatchers *it isn't.*

w Peter Weibel *d* Valie Export *ph* Wolfgang Simon

☆ Susanne Widl, Peter Weibel, Dr Josef Plavek, Monica Helfer-Friedrich, Helke Sander, Dominick Dusek, Herbert Schmid, Edward Neversal

Invisible Agent *

US 1942 84m bw
Universal (George Waggner)

Nazi and Japanese spies seek the secret of invisibility from its inventor.

Lively fantasy thriller with a cast more distinguished than it deserves.

w Curt Siodmak *d* Edwin L. Marin *m* Hans Salter *sp John P. Fulton*

☆ Cedric Hardwicke, Peter Lorre, Ilona Massey, Jon Hall, Albert Basserman, J. Edward Bromberg, John Litel

Invisible Boy

US 1957 89m bw
MGM/Pan (Nicholas Nayfack)

A scientist allows his 10-year-old son to repair a robot, which comes under the control of an alien force.

Minor sci-fi utilizing the robot from Forbidden Planet.

w Cyril Hume *d* Herman Hoffman *ph* Harold Wellman *m* Les Baxter

☆ Richard Eyer, Philip Abbott, Harold J. Stone, Diane Brewster

The Invisible Circus

US 2001 92m DeLuxe
Entertainment/Fine Line/Industry Entertainment (Julia Chasman, Nick Wechsler)

In the mid-1970s, a teenager travels to Europe to discover the circumstances behind the death of her sister, who was involved in radical politics.

Contrived and predictable drama with an awkward flashback structure and an unconvincing dénouement.

wd Adam Brooks *novel* Jennifer Egan *ph* Henry Braham *m* Nick Laird-Clowes *pd* Robin Standefer *ed* Elizabeth King

☆ Jordana Brewster (Phoebe), Christopher Eccleston (Wolf), Cameron Diaz (Faith), Blythe Danner (Gail), Patrick Bergin (Gene), Camilla Belle (Phoebe as a child), Moritz Bleibtreu (Eric), Isabelle Pasco (Claire)

'The film is too pretty and schematic, but it does envelop the viewer in rue for a wasted life.' – *Richard Schickel, Time*

The Invisible Ghost

US 1941 66m bw
Monogram/Banner (Sam Katzman)

Maddened by the death of his wife, a doctor develops murderous tendencies.

Dire and chaotic horror that makes no sense at all.

w Helen Martin, Al Martin *d* Joseph H. Lewis *ph* Marcel le Picard *ed* Robert Golden

☆ Bela Lugosi, Polly Ann Young, John Maguire, Betty Compson, Clarence Muse, Terry Walker, Ernie Adams

'Creaky but enjoyable.' – *Sight and Sound*

'Even the moon is frightened of me – frightened to death!'

The Invisible Man ****

US 1933 71m bw
Universal (Carl Laemmle Jnr)

A scientist discovers a means of making himself invisible, but in the process becomes a megalomaniac.

Superb blend of eccentric character comedy, melodrama and trick photography in a Hollywood English setting; remarkably faithful to the spirit of the book. It made a star of Claude Rains in his first film, even though he is seen for only a couple of seconds.

w R. C. Sherriff, Philip Wylie *novel* H. G. Wells *d* James Whale *ph* Arthur Edeson *m* W. Frank Harling *ed* Ted J. Kent *sp* John P. Fulton
☆ Claude Rains, Gloria Stuart, William Harrigan, Henry Travers, E. E. Clive, Una O'Connor, Forrester Harvey, Dudley Digges, Holmes Herbert
GRIFFIN (CLAUDE RAINS): 'We'll start with a few murders. Big men, little men – just to show we make no distinction.'
'Well made and full of intentional and unintentional laughs. Should do well.' – *Variety*
'Taken either as a technical exercise or as a sometimes profoundly moving retelling of the Frankenstein fable, it is one of the most rewarding of recent films.' – *William Troy*
† Sequels, successively less interesting, were (all qv) *The Invisible Man Returns* (1940), *Invisible Woman* (1941), *Invisible Agent* (1942), *The Invisible Man's Revenge* (1944), *Abbott and Costello Meet the Invisible Man* (1951) and *Memoirs of an Invisible Man* (1992). A TV series with an anonymous hero was made by ATV in 1955; a Universal one with David McCallum followed in 1975, and was restructured as *The Gemini Man* in 1976.
Boris Karloff had been first choice for the role, but he turned it down.

The Invisible Man Returns
US 1940 81m bw
Universal (Ken Goldsmith)
A man convicted of killing his brother uses the secret of invisibility to find the real culprit.
Second in the series takes itself too seriously: a slow starter which works its way to a strong climax.
w Curt Siodmak, Lester Cole, Cedric Belfrage *d* Joe May *ph* Milton Krasner *m* Hans Salter, Frank Skinner *sp* John P. Fulton
☆ Vincent Price, Cedric Hardwicke, John Sutton, Nan Grey, Cecil Kellaway, Alan Napier, Forrester Harvey
'Though the film has its bright moments, and some weird ones too, the first freshness is gone. Even the effects seem repetitive.' – *Pauline Kael, 70s*

The Invisible Man's Revenge
US 1944 77m bw
Universal (Ford Beebe)
A psychopathic killer on the run takes refuge with a doctor who has discovered the secret of invisibility.
Curious reversion to the original story in that the invisible man is now again the villain; but otherwise there's no flavour at all to this horror comic set in a phoney England.
w Bertram Millhauser *d* Ford Beebe *m* Hans Salter *sp* John P. Fulton
☆ Jon Hall, Leon Errol, John Carradine, Alan Curtis, Evelyn Ankers, Gale Sondergaard, Halliwell Hobbes

The Invisible Menace
US 1938 55m bw
Warner
Murder at an army base brings strange revelations of the past.
Standard mystery in which the star seems misplaced.
w Crane Wilbur *play* Ralph S. Zink *d* John Farrow *ph* L. William O'Connell *ed* Harold McLernan
☆ Boris Karloff, Regis Toomey, Marie Wilson, Henry Kolker
'Undistinguished mystery meller, for bottom-lining the duals.' – *Variety*
† It was remade in 1943 as *Murder at the Waterfront*.

'Destruction To All He Touched Or Looked Upon!'
The Invisible Ray *
US 1935 79m bw
Universal (Edmund Grainger)
A scientist discovers a superpowerful element which makes him homicidal.
Slow-moving science fiction with a touch of horror, and the pattern for its star's many later roles as a sympathetic man who turns into a monster. Interesting rather than stimulating.
w John Colton *story* Howard Higgin, Douglas Hodges *d* Lambert Hillyer *ph* George Robinson *m* Franz Waxman *sp* John P. Fulton
☆ Boris Karloff, Bela Lugosi, Frances Drake, Frank Lawton, Walter Kingsford, Beulah Bondi, Violet Kemble Cooper, Nydia Westman
'An easy number to sell, it should do pretty good business.' – *Variety*

Invisible Stripes
US 1939 82m bw
Warner (Hal B. Wallis)
An ex-con finds it difficult to go straight.
By 1940 Warner must have been able to make rip-offs of Angels with Dirty Faces *in their sleep, and this one, despite its cast, suggests that they did.*
w Warren Duff *book* Warden Lewis E. Lawes *d* Lloyd Bacon *ph* Ernest Haller *m* Heinz Roemheld
☆ George Raft, Humphrey Bogart, William Holden, Flora Robson, Jane Bryan, Paul Kelly, Lee Patrick, Henry O'Neill, Moroni Olsen
'It's a familiar cinematic yarn but strengthened by a zippy pace, excellent performances and direction.' – *Variety*

The Invisible Woman
US 1941 72m bw
Universal (Burt Kelly)
A mad scientist turns a model invisible.
Screwball comedy with a deteriorating star at his hammiest: generally very laboured, but with some funny moments.
w Robert Lees, Fred Rinaldo, Gertrude Purcell *d* A. Edward Sutherland *ph* Elwood Bredell *md* Charles Previn
☆ John Barrymore, Charles Ruggles, Virginia Bruce, John Howard, Oscar Homolka, Donald MacBride, Edward Brophy, Shemp Howard, Margaret Hamilton, Maria Montez

Invitation
US 1952 81m bw
MGM (Lawrence Weingarten)
When a millionaire's daughter believes she is dying, revelations ensue about her beloved husband's original intentions.
Competently idiotic weepie with a happy ending.
w Paul Osborn *story* Jerome Weidman *d* Gottfried Reinhardt *ph* Ray June *m* Bronislau Kaper
☆ Dorothy McGuire, Van Johnson, Ruth Roman, Louis Calhern, Ray Collins, Michael Chekhov
'The dialogue is stagey and the treatment indeterminate, with overmuch reliance on the dubious emotional reinforcement of loud background music.' – *Penelope Houston*

L'Invitation ***
Switzerland/France 1973 100m colour
Groupe 5/Television Suisse/Citel Films/Planfilm
Following his mother's death, a middle-aged bachelor buys a home in the country and invites his office colleagues to a garden party.
Delightful comedy of manners that won a Special Jury Prize at the Cannes Film Festival.
w Claude Goretta, Michel Viala *d* Claude Goretta *ph* Jean Zeller *m* Patrick Moraz *ad* Yanko Hodjis *ed* Joelle Van Effenterre
☆ Jean-Luc Bideau, Jean Champion, Corinne Coderey, Pierre Collet, Neige Dolsky, Jacques Rispal, Michel Robin, Rosine Rochette, François Simon, Cecile Vassort

Invitation to a Gunfighter *
US 1964 92m DeLuxe
UA/Stanley Kramer (Richard Wilson)
A small-town tyrant hires a smooth gunfighter to keep down the farmers he has cheated.
Predictable, rather self-satisfied little Western with a studio look. Smart script and performances.
w Elizabeth and Richard Wilson *d* Richard Wilson *ph* Joseph MacDonald *m* David Raksin
☆ Yul Brynner, George Segal, Janice Rule, Pat Hingle

Invitation to Die: see *Wild*

Invitation to Happiness
US 1939 95m bw
Paramount (Wesley Ruggles)
A society girl marries a prizefighter.
Routine star romantic drama.
w Claude Binyon *d* Wesley Ruggles *ph* Leo Tover *m* Frederick Hollander
☆ Irene Dunne, Fred MacMurray, Charles Ruggles, Billy Cook, William Collier Snr, Marion Martin
'Heartthrob drama, geared for good biz.' – *Variety*

Invitation to the Dance **
GB 1954 92m Technicolor
MGM (Arthur Freed)
Three stories in dance and mime.
Unsuccessful ballet film which closed its star's great period and virtually ended the heyday of the Hollywood musical. The simple fact emerged that European ballet styles were not Kelly's forte; yet there was much to enjoy in Circus, Ring around the Rosy *and* The Magic Lamp.
ph Frederick A. Young *m* Jacques Ibert, André Previn, Rimsky-Korsakov *ad* Alfred Junge *wd/ch* Gene Kelly
☆ Gene Kelly, Igor Youskevitch, Tommy Rall, Belita, Tamara Toumanova

Invitation to the Wedding
GB 1985 90m colour widescreen
Chancery Lane (Joseph Brooks)
An aristocratic wedding causes trouble when the bride's uncle, the bishop, marries her to the wrong man at rehearsal.
A situation which could have been mildly amusing in the Quiet Wedding *vein is botched by an unfunny script and wildly eccentric casting, including Gielgud as an American evangelist.*
w William Fairchild *d* Joseph Brooks *ph* Freddie Young *m* Joseph Brooks
☆ Ralph Richardson, John Gielgud, Paul Nicholas, Elizabeth Shepherd, Ronald Lacey, John Standing, Susan Brooks

The Ipcress File **
GB 1965 109m Techniscope
Rank/Steven/Lowndes (Harry Saltzman)
An intelligence man traces a missing scientist and finds that one of his own superiors is a spy.
The attempt to present a low-key James Bond (glasses, good at cookery, supermarket shopper) is frustrated by flashy direction and a confused plot. It did herald a new genre though the whole ambiance is now sadly dated, like an old copy of The Sunday Times Colour Supplement.
w Bill Canaway, James Doran *novel* Len Deighton *d* Sidney J. Furie *ph* Otto Heller *m* John Barry *ad* Ken Adam
☆ Michael Caine, Nigel Green, Guy Doleman, Sue Lloyd, Gordon Jackson
'The deglamorized espionage story, but with plenty of tingle and zest, both in plot and camerawork.' – *Judith Crist*
† Two sequels appeared starring 'Harry Palmer' (never named in the books): *Funeral in Berlin* and *Billion Dollar Brain* (both qv).
best British film; Ken Adam; Otto Heller

Irene
US 1940 101m bw (colour sequence)
RKO/Imperator (Herbert Wilcox)
A New York Irish shopgirl moves into society.
Fairly dim picturization of the old musical: the cast does its best.
w Alice Duer Miller *play* James H. Montgomery *d* Herbert Wilcox *ph* Russell Metty *m/ly* Harry Tierney, Joseph McCarthy *md* Anthony Collins
☆ Anna Neagle, Ray Milland, Roland Young, Alan Marshal, May Robson, Billie Burke, Arthur Treacher, Marsha Hunt, Isabel Jewell, Ethel Griffies
'This pre-camp version tries to be innocuously charming, and the effort is all too evident.' – *New Yorker, 1976*
† Previously filmed in 1926 with Colleen Moore.
Anthony Collins

'Her Greatest Talent Was For Life.'
Iris **
GB/US 2001 90m colour
Buena Vista/BBC/Intermedia/Mirage (Robert Fox, Scott Rudin)
Biopic of novelist and philosopher Iris Murdoch and her relationship with her husband, academic John Bayley, as a young woman and as an elderly sufferer from Alzheimer's disease.
Deftly switching back and forth from the young Iris to the diminished old, this somehow misses out on what made her a fascinating figure; some accomplished acting saves it from becoming merely a moderately intriguing drama of an unusual marriage.
w Richard Eyre, Charles Wood *books* Iris: A Memoir, Elegy for Iris by John Bayley *d* Richard Eyre *ph* Roger Pratt *m* James Horner (solo violin, Joshua Bell) *pd* Gemma Jackson *ed* Martin Walsh
☆ Judi Dench (Iris Murdoch), Jim Broadbent (John Bayley), Kate Winslet (Young Iris), Hugh Bonneville (Young John), Penelope Wilton (Janet Stone), Juliet Aubrey (Younger Janet), Samuel West (Young Maurice), Timothy West (Old Maurice), Eleanor Bron (College Principal), Joan Bakewell (TV Presenter)
'Intimate, frank and shattering without being maudlin or sudsy.' – *Rex Reed*
'The audience is transported between two very obvious stories and becomes slightly irritated by the grinding inevitability of both of them. As a result, Iris Murdoch gets lost in the shuffle.' – *Elvis Mitchell, New York Times*
Jim Broadbent
Judi Dench; Kate Winslet
Judi Dench

Irish Eyes Are Smiling **
US 1944 90m Technicolor
TCF (Damon Runyon)
The life and times of an 1890s songwriter, Ernest R. Ball.
Standard musical biopic, handsomely mounted.
w Earl Baldwin, John Tucker Battle *d* Gregory Ratoff *ph* Harry Jackson *md* Alfred Newman, Charles Henderson
☆ Dick Haymes, June Haver, Monty Woolley, Anthony Quinn, Beverly Whitney, Maxie Rosenbloom, Veda Ann Borg, Clarence Kolb
Alfred Newman, Charles Henderson

The Irish in Us
US 1935 84m bw
Warner (Samuel Bischoff)
Adventures of three New York brothers.
Routine, good-natured star action frolic.
w Earl Baldwin *d* Lloyd Bacon *ph* George Barnes *md* Leo F. Forbstein
☆ James Cagney, Pat O'Brien, Olivia de Havilland, Mary Gordon, Frank McHugh, Allen Jenkins, J. Farrell MacDonald, Thomas Jackson
'A hokey laugh ensemble that will be oke.' – *Variety*

The Irishman *
Australia 1978 110m Gevacolor
Forest Home/SAFC (Anthony Buckley)
In the 20s, a heavy-drinking, horse-loving Irish teamster finds it hard to come to terms with the arrival of motor-driven transport and the demands of his family.
Family drama acted out against spacious landscapes, good to look at but too predictable and with a score that emphasizes its sentimental aspects.
wd Donald Crombie *novel* Elizabeth O'Conner *ph* Peter James *m* Charles Marawood *pd* Owen Williams *ed* Tim Wellburn
☆ Michael Craig, Robyn Nevin, Simon Burke, Gerard Kennedy, Lou Brown, Tony Barry, Bryan Brown, John Bluthal

'A story of bloodshed, passion, desire and death ... everything in fact that makes life worth living!'
Irma La Douce *
US 1963 146m Technicolor Panavision
UA/Phalanx/Mirisch/Edward L. Alperson (Billy Wilder)
A Paris policeman falls for a prostitute and becomes her pimp.
A saucy yarn originally presented inventively as a small-scale stage musical becomes a tasteless yawn on the big screen, especially when presented at such length and without the songs. Minor compensations abound but are insufficient.
w Billy Wilder, I. A. L. Diamond *play* Alexandre Breffort *d* Billy Wilder *ph* Joseph LaShelle *m* Marguerite Monnot *md* André Previn *ad* Alexander Trauner *ed* Daniel Mandell *cos* Orry-Kelly
☆ Shirley MacLaine (Irma La Douce), Jack Lemmon (Nestor), Lou Jacobi (Moustache), Herschel Bernardi (Inspector LeFevre), Joan

Shawlee (Amazon Annie), Bruce Yarnell (Hippolyte)

'What hurts the film the most is its length. Two hours and 23 minutes is an awfully long haul for a frivolous farce.' – *Variety*

'It's false. It just doesn't work.' – *Billy Wilder*

André Previn

Joseph LaShelle; Shirley MacLaine

Irma Vep *

France 1996 98m colour

ICA/Dacia (Georges Benayoun)

A Hong Kong actress goes to Paris to star as a mysterious thief in a disastrous television remake of Louis Feuillade's silent French film *Les Vampires*.

Enjoyable mix of nostalgia for cinema's past and a celebration of the trials and triumphs of high-energy, low-budget film-making.

wd Olivier Assayas *ph* Eric Gautier *ad* François-Renaud Labarthe *ed* Luc Barnier

☆ Maggie Cheung, Jean-Pierre Leaud, Nathalie Richard, Antoine Basler, Nathalie Boutefeu, Bulle Ogier, Lou Castel, Arsinee Khanjian

'An inventive, often hilarious depiction of low-budget arthouse filmmaking.' – *Neon*

† The film was itself made in four weeks on a tiny budget.

Iron & Silk *

US 1990 92m DuArt

Sun/Tokyo Broadcasting (Shirley Sun)

A Chinese-speaking American graduate with a love of kung fu goes to China in the 80s to teach English and study martial arts.

Based on a true story, a film of great charm and good humour, as the representative of one culture tries to understand and appreciate another.

w Mark Salzman, Shirley Sun *book* Mark Salzman *d* Shirley Sun *ph* James Hayman *m* Michael Gibbs *pd* Calvin Tsao *ed* Geraldine Peroni, James V. Kwei

☆ Mark Salzman, Pan Qingfu, Jeanette Lin Tsui, Vivian Wu, Sun Xudong

The Iron Curtain

US 1948 87m bw

TCF (Sol C. Siegel)

A Russian official in Ottawa becomes disillusioned and reveals to the US authorities details of a spy ring.

Cold war biopic of Igor Gouzenko; not badly done in the semi-documentary mould.

w Milton Krims *d* William Wellman *ph* Charles G. Clarke *md* Alfred Newman, using Russian themes

☆ Dana Andrews, Gene Tierney, Berry Kroeger, Edna Best

The Iron Duke *

GB 1934 88m bw

Gaumont (Michael Balcon)

After Waterloo, the Duke of Wellington defeats a French scheme to discredit him.

A popular historical star vehicle of its time and a good example of British pre-war production in the Korda mould.

w Bess Meredyth *story* H. M. Harwood *d* Victor Saville *ph* Curt Courant *md* Louis Levy *ad* Alfred Junge *ed* Ian Dalrymple

☆ *George Arliss*, Gladys Cooper, Emlyn Williams, Ellaline Terriss, A. E. Matthews, Edmund Willard, Felix Aylmer

Iron Eagle

US 1986 119m Metrocolor

Tri-Star (Ron Samuels, Joe Wizan)

A young man rescues his hostage father from a Middle Eastern country.

Increasingly suspenseful adventure drama which suited America's mood.

w Kevin Elders, Sidney J. Furie *d* Sidney J. Furie *ph* Adam Greenberg *m* Basil Poledouris *pd* Robb Wilson King *ed* George Grenville

☆ Louis Gossett Jnr, Jason Gedrick, David Suchet, Tim Thomerson, Larry B. Scott

'Theaters may have to stay open from high noon to red dawn to handle the crowd.' – *Variety*

Iron Eagle II

Canada 1988 100m Bellevue-Pathé

Guild/Alliance Entertainment/Harkot Productions (Jacob Kotzky, Sharon Harel, John Kemeny)

American and Russian pilots co-operate to destroy a nuclear missile base in the Middle East.

Silly fantasy, made occasionally bearable by its airborne sequences.

w Kevin Elders, Sidney J. Furie *d* Sidney J. Furie *ph* Alain Dostie *m* Amin Bhatia *ad* Ariel Roshko *ed* Rit Wallis

☆ Louis Gossett Jnr, Mark Humphrey, Stuart Margolin, Alan Scarfe, Sharon H. Brandon, Maury Chaykin, Colm Feore, Clark Johnson, Jason Blicker

† There was a further sequel, *Aces: Iron Eagle III* (qv).

Iron Eagle IV

Canada 1995 95m colour

Norstar (Peter Simpson)

Delinquent teenagers training to be pilots uncover a high-level conspiracy involving toxic chemicals.

An action film aimed at an audience that can identify with its young heroes; they will also need to enjoy bad films.

w Michael Stokes *d* Sidney J. Furie *ph* Curtis Petersen *m* Paul Zaza *ad* Michael Parks *ed* Jeff Warren

☆ Louis Gossett Jnr, Al Waxman, Jason Cadieux, Joanne Vanicola

'Never manages to get off the runway.' – *Variety*

The Iron Giant ***

US 1999 86m Technicolor Celco Scope

Warner (Allison Abbate, Des McAnuff)

In 1957, a young boy tries to protect an iron giant from government officials who are convinced that it is an alien weapon and plan to destroy it.

Set at a time of Cold War and nuclear paranoia and the beginnings of space exploration, this is an engaging, well-animated fable of pacifism and self-realisation that should find a ready audience among adults as well as children.

w Tim McCanlies *book* *The Iron Man* by Ted Hughes *d* Brad Bird *ph* Mark Dinicola *m* Michael Kamen *pd* Mark Whiting *ed* Darren T. Holmes

☆ Featuring voices of: Jennifer Aniston, Eli Marienthal, Harry Connick Jnr, Vin Diesel, Christopher McDonald, James Gammon, Cloris Leachman, John Mahoney, M. Emmet Walsh

'An unalloyed success that works on several levels.' – *Variety*

'A modern classic.' – *Film Review*

† Despite critical plaudits, the movie did poorly at the box-office.

The Iron Hand: see *Fist of Fury*

The Iron Horse *

US 1924 119m (24 fps) bw silent

Fox

A man seeking to avenge his father's murder works on the first transcontinental railroad.

Archetypal Western, very slow to start but with an authentic cast of thousands.

w Charles Kenyon, John Russell *d* John Ford *ph* George Schneiderman

☆ George O'Brien (Davy Brandon), Madge Bellamy (Miriam Marsh), Cyril Chadwick (Peter Jesson), Fred Kohler (Deroux), Charles Edward Bull (Abraham Lincoln)

'At last a film has come from America which trusts the railroad, and sees magic in it, and power; which honours the railroad and holds it mightier than man; which loves the railroad and is content to follow it into the heart of romance.' – C. A. Lejeune

The Iron ladies: see *Satreelex*

The Iron Maiden

GB 1962 98m Eastmancolor

Anglo Amalgamated/GHW (Peter Rogers)

US title: *The Swinging Maiden*

An aircraft designer gets into trouble because of his affection for traction engines.

Feeble attempt to duplicate the success of Genevieve, *this time starring a steamroller. Very English.*

w Vivian Cox, Leslie Bricusse *d* Gerald Thomas *ph* Alan Hume *m* Eric Rogers

☆ Michael Craig, Alan Hale Jnr, Jeff Donnell, Cecil Parker, Noel Purcell, Roland Culver, the Duke of Bedford, Anne Helm

The Iron Major

US 1943 85m bw

RKO

The life of Frank Cavanaugh, football coach and hero of World War I.

Sub-standard biopic.

w Aben Kandel, Warren Duff *d* Ray Enright

☆ Pat O'Brien, Ruth Warrick, Robert Ryan, Leon Ames

'A respectful, rather dull picture ... all the talk is in words of less than one syllable.' – *James Agee*

The Iron Man

US 1931 73m bw

Universal (Carl Laemmle Jnr)

A prizefighter is spurred on by his money-hungry wife.

Competent, routine, ringside melodrama.

w Francis Edwards Faragoh *novel* W. R. Burnett *d* Tod Browning *ph* Percy Hilburn

☆ Lew Ayres, Jean Harlow, Robert Armstrong, John Miljan, Eddie Dillon, Ned Sparks

† Remade in 1937 as *Some Blondes Are Dangerous* and in 1951 under the original title.

Iron Man

US 1951 81m bw

Universal-International

A coal miner is persuaded to become a prizefighter, but success changes his character.

A somewhat changed version of the 1931 film; no better.

w George Zuckerman, Borden Chase *d* Joseph Pevney

☆ Jeff Chandler, Evelyn Keyes, Stephen McNally, Joyce Holden, Rock Hudson, Jim Backus, James Arness

The Iron Mask *

US 1929 97m bw talking sequences, sound and music score

UA/Douglas Fairbanks

The true prince of France is kidnapped and imprisoned, but the villains reckon without D'Artagnan and the three musketeers.

Spirited star rendition of Dumas, the last big silent costume drama of the twenties.

w Elton Thomas (Douglas Fairbanks) *novel* *Ten Years After* by Alexandre Dumas *d* Allan Dwan *ph* Henry Sharp *m* Hugo Riesenfeld *pd* Maurice Leloir

☆ Douglas Fairbanks, Nigel de Brulier, Belle Bennett, Marguerite de la Motte

'...a labyrinth of deception.'

Iron Maze

US/Japan 1991 102m CFI color

First Independent/Trans-Tokyo/J & M Entertainment (Ilona Herzberg, Hidenori Ueki)

A police-chief in a Pennsylvania steel town investigates the attempted murder of a Japanese businessman, who wants to build an amusement park on the site of the mill; the chief suspects are the man's American wife and her lover.

Based on the same story that Kurosawa used as an inspiration for Rashomon, *which was first filmed in Hollywood as* The Outrage, *this seems little more than a muddled protest at the Japanese takeover of US businesses (and, perhaps, of Hollywood studios).*

w Tim Metcalfe *story* *In A Grove* by Ryunosuke Akutagawa *d* Hiroaki Yoshida *ph* Morio Saequsa *m* Stanley Myers *pd* Toby Corbett, Toro Ueno *ed* Bonnie Koehler

☆ Jeff Fahey, Bridget Fonda, Hiroaki Murakami, J. T. Walsh, Gabriel Damon, John Randolph, Peter Allas, Carmen Filpi

'A mess from beginning to end, presenting three cardboard characters and a flashback-infested narrative which rivals *Passage to Marseille* and *Millennium* as one of the most inelegant ever committed to film.' – *Empire*

The Iron Mistress

US 1952 107m Technicolor

Warner (Henry Blanke)

The life of Westerner Jim Bowie and his famous knife.

Stolid actioner with uninspired script and performances.

w James R. Webb *novel* Paul I. Wellman *d* Gordon Douglas *ph* John Seitz *m* Max Steiner

☆ Alan Ladd, Virginia Mayo, Joseph Calleia, Phyllis Kirk, Alf Kjellin, Douglas Dick, Tony Caruso, George Voskovec

The Iron Petticoat

GB 1956 96m Technicolor Vistavision

Remus/Harry Saltzman (Betty E. Box)

An American air force officer persuades a Russian lady flyer of the advantages of the western way of life.

Feeble imitation of Ninotchka *with a saucy star team which simply doesn't jell.*

w Ben Hecht *d* Ralph Thomas *ph* Ernest Steward *m* Benjamin Frankel

☆ Bob Hope, Katharine Hepburn, James Robertson Justice, Robert Helpmann, David Kossoff, Alan Gifford, Paul Carpenter, Noelle Middleton

'They seem amazed to find themselves in a comedy that has no humour, and they go through the motions grimly, like children at dancing school, hoping it will all be over soon.' – *William K. Zinsser*

The Iron Triangle

US 1988 91m colour

Medusa/Eurobrothers/International Video Entertainment (Angela P. Schapiro, Tony Scotti)

An American officer is captured by two Vietcong, one idealistic, the other murderous.

War film more concerned with humanity than action, and effective enough in its small way.

w Eric Weston, John Bushelman, Lawrence Hilbrand *book* based on the diary of an unknown Vietcong soldier *d* Eric Weston *ph* Irv Goodnoff *m* Michael Lloyd, John D'Anrea, Nick Strimple *pd* Errol Kelly *ed* Roy Watts

☆ Beau Bridges, Haing S. Ngor, Liem Whatley, Johnny Hallyday, Jim Ishida, Ping Wu, Jack Ong, Sophie Trang

Iron Will

US 1994 109m Technicolor

Buena Vista/Disney (Patrick Palmer, Robert Schwartz)

In 1917, a youth enters a 500-mile dog-sled race and becomes an American hero.

Predictable, soft-centred drama of success against the odds.

w John Michael Hayes, Djordje Milicevic, Jeff Arch *d* Charles Haid *ph* William Wages *m* Joel McNeely *pd* Stephen Storer *ed* Andrew Doerfer

☆ Mackenzie Astin, Kevin Spacey, August Schellenberg, David Ogden Stiers, Brian Cox, George Gerdes, John Terry, Penelope Windust

Ironweed

US 1987 143m Technicolor

Taft Entertainment/Keith Barish/Home Box Office

An alcoholic down-and-out returns to his home town, where he is haunted by his violent past. Although forgiven by his family, he takes to the road again.

Relentlessly gloomy and ploddingly faithful re-creation of a Pulitzer prizewinner.

w William Kennedy *novel* William Kennedy *d* Hector Babenco *ph* Lauro Escorel *m* John Morris *pd* Jeannine C. Oppewall

☆ Jack Nicholson, Meryl Streep, Carroll Baker, Michael O'Keefe, Diane Venora, Tom Waits

Jack Nicholson; Meryl Streep

Irreconcilable Differences

US 1984 113m Technicolor

Lantana/Warner

Nine-year-old Casey interferes in her parents' planned divorce.

An ancient wheeze for a romantic comedy, here decked out with modern trimmings but no better intrinsically than it was in the thirties.

w Nancy Meyers, Charles Shyer *d* Charles Shyer

☆ Ryan O'Neal, Shelley Long, Drew Barrymore, Sam Wanamaker, Allen Garfield, Sharon Stone

The Irrefutable Truth About Demons
New Zealand 2000
First Sun/NZFC (Dave Gibson)
GB title: *The Truth About Demons*
An academic is targeted by a satanic cult.
Gruesome little shocker that manages a modicum of suspense.
wd Glenn Standring *ph* Simon Baumfield *m* Victoria Kelly, Joost Langeveld *pd* Clive Memmott *ed* Paul Sutorius *sp* Nigel Streeter
☆ Karl Urban (Harry Ballard), Katie Wolfe (Bennie), Jonathon Hendry (Le Valliant), Sally Stockwell (Celia), Tony MacIver (Johnny), Peter Daubé (Lawrence), Kelson Henderson (Wank), Mel Johnson (Alice)
'Packed with gore, elliptical CGI devils and numerous plot surprises.' – *Shivers*

Irrestistible Force
US 1993 74m colour
CBS/Davis (Michael Lake)
A suspended cop and his female partner combat a heavily armed group of white supremacists who take over a shopping mall.
Efficient, though ultimately silly, time-wasting action movie, designed mainly to display the high-kicking martial art skills of Rothrock.
w Carleton Eastlake *d* Kevin Hooks *ph* Kevan 'Loosey' Lind *m* David Michael Frank *pd* David R. Copping *ed* Andy Blumenthal
☆ Stacy Keach, Cynthia Rothrock, Christopher Neame, Kathleen Garrett, Michael Bacall, Nicholas Hammond, Paul Winfield

'Time destroys everything.'
Irreversible *
France 2002 97m colour
Metro Tartan/Nord-Ouest/Eskwad/Canal/120/De La Zone (Christophe Rossignon, Richard Grandpierre)
After a teacher's girlfriend is sexually assaulted, he and a friend visit a gay club to take revenge on the pimp who raped her.
There is something so brutalist and miserablist about Noé's view of the world that it can seem ludicrous, but not here: with a ferocious murder followed by a vicious rape, both shown in all their horror, this can be a shattering experience that offers no hope for humanity.
wd Gaspar Noé *ph* Gaspar Noé *m* Thomas Bangalter, Beethoven *ad* Alain Juteau *ed* Gaspar Noé
☆ Monica Bellucci (Alex), Vincent Cassel (Marcus), Albert Dupontel (Pierre), Philippe Nahon (Philippe), Jo Prestia (Le Ténia)
'A seductive and powerful film, but it is nevertheless steeped in sado-masochism, wherein lies its ability to repulse, shock and – lets be honest about this – *thrill*.' – *Leslie Felperin, Sight & Sound*
'An exploitation movie with a gimmick, not to mention a vacuous philosophy.' – *J. Hoberman, Village Voice*
'Even if you closed your eyes – a tempting option – you would still know that you were in the hollering presence of pain. The story is undiluted dread.' – *Anthony Lane, New Yorker*

Is Everybody Happy?
US 1929 80m bw
Warner
The life of a clarinettist who rises from poverty.
Or, The Ted Lewis Story, a primitive musical.
w Joseph Jackson, James A. Starr *d* Archie Mayo *m/ly* Harry Akst, Grant Clarke *ch* Larry Ceballos
☆ Ted Lewis, Alice Day, Ann Pennington, Lawrence Grant

Is Everybody Happy?
US 1943 73m bw
Columbia
A virtual remake of the 1929 biopic, with the star fourteen years older.
Low-budget filler with a few good numbers.
w Monte Brice *d* Charles Barton *ph* L. William O'Connell *md* Morris Stoloff
☆ Ted Lewis, Larry Parks, Michael Duane, Nan Wynn

Is Paris Burning?
France/US 1965 165m bw Panavision (colour sequence)
Paramount/Transcontinental/Marianne (Paul Graetz)
A multi-storied account of the 1944 liberation of Paris.
Muddled, scribbled, tedious and confusing attempt at a thinking man's all-star war epic.
w Francis Ford Coppola, Gore Vidal *book* Paris, *brûle-t-il?* by Larry Collins and Dominique Lapierre *d* René Clément *ph* Marcel Grignon *m* Maurice Jarre
☆ Leslie Caron, Gert Frobe, Charles Boyer, Yves Montand, Orson Welles, Alain Delon, Jean-Pierre Cassel, Jean-Paul Belmondo, Kirk Douglas, Glenn Ford, Claude Dauphin, Daniel Gélin, Anthony Perkins, Simone Signoret, Robert Stack and also George Chakiris
'An incoherent, ponderous and shallow tribute to one of the great experiences of our time, an insult to those with intimate knowledge of or experience with the liberation of Paris, an embarrassment for those interested in spectacular moviemaking.' – *Judith Crist*
Marcel Grignon

Isaac Littlefeathers
Canada 1985 90m colour
Lauron/Allarcom/King Motion Picture (Barry Pearson, William Johnson)
A hot-headed Indian boy, abandoned by his mother and his white father and adopted by a Jewish grocer, fights the prejudice he meets with violence.
A well-made drama about racial intolerance, with some nice touches but an over-reliance on cliché.
w Les Rose, Barry Pearson, John Katz *d* Les Rose *ph* Ed Higginson *m* Paul Zaza *ad* Richard Hudolin *ed* Mairin Wilkinson
☆ Lou Jacobi, William Korbut, Scott Hylands, Tom Heaton, Lynda Mason Green, Lorraine Behnan, George Clutesi, Vincent Gale, Robert Astle

Isadora *
GB 1968 138m Eastmancolor
Universal (Robert and Raymond Hakim)
US title: *The Loves of Isadora*
Eccentric character dancer Isadora Duncan reflects on her crowded and unconventional life.
Ambitious and expensive but finally unsatisfactory biopic of a controversial figure of the twenties.
w Melvyn Bragg, Clive Exton *d* Karel Reisz *ph* Larry Pizer *m* Maurice Jarre *pd* Jocelyn Herbert *ad* Michael Seymour, Ralph Brinton
☆ Vanessa Redgrave, Jason Robards Jnr, James Fox, Ivan Tchenko, John Fraser, Bessie Love
'A brave attempt at a daunting task.' – *Tom Milne*
Vanessa Redgrave

Ishtar
US 1987 107m Technicolor
Columbia/Delphi V (Warren Beatty)
Two untalented songwriters get involved with Middle Eastern turmoil.
Bitty rehash of old jokes and situations, vaguely resembling a Hope-Crosby Road picture of long ago, but far less funny despite costing 50 million dollars.
wd Elaine May *ph* Vittorio Storaro *pd* Paul Sylbert
☆ Dustin Hoffman, Warren Beatty, Isabelle Adjani, Charles Grodin, Jack Weston, Tess Harper
'One can't help but wonder whether the camel was the only blind creature who had something to do with this picture.' – *Daily Variety*

The Island *
Japan 1961 92m bw
Kindai Eiga Kyokai (Kaneto Shindo)
original title: *Hadaka no Shima*
The quiet tenor of life for the only family inhabiting a tiny island is eventually broken by illness and death.
Slow, controlled, beautiful film in which not a single word of dialogue is spoken. The artificiality of this concept eventually diminishes its stature.
wd Kaneto Shindo *ph* Kiyoshi Kuroda *m* Hikaru Hayashi
☆ Nobuko Otowa, Taiji Tonoyama, Shinji Tanaka, Masanori Horimoto
'A visual poem which mirrors tedium without ever inducing it.' – *MFB*

'For 300 years a terrifying secret has been kept from the outside world!'
The Island
US 1980 114m Technicolor Panavision
Universal (Richard Zanuck, David Brown)
A journalist is in fear of his life on a Caribbean island inhabited by the bloodthirsty descendants of 17th-century buccaneers.
Ridiculous shocker from the Jaws people; stupidly plotted and gruesome in detail.
w Peter Benchley *novel* Peter Benchley *d* Michael Ritchie *ph* Henri Decaë *m* Ennio Morricone
☆ Michael Caine, David Warner, Angela Punch McGregor, Frank Middlemass, Dudley Sutton, Colin Jeavons
'Suspense gives way to gut-level sadism aimed at the lowest common audience denominator.' – *Variety*

The Island at the Top of the World **
US 1974 93m Technicolor
Walt Disney (Winston Hibler)
In 1907, a rich Englishman commissions an airship to take him to a mythical arctic Shangri-La in search of his lost son.
Generally brisk and effective adventure fantasy whose trick effects are sufficiently splendid to redeem a sag in the middle and an overplus of Viking chatter which has to be laboriously translated.
w John Whedon *novel* The Lost Ones by Ian Cameron *d* Robert Stevenson *ph* Frank Phillips *m* Maurice Jarre *pd* Peter Ellenshaw *sp* Art Cruickshank, Danny Lee
☆ Donald Sinden, David Hartman, Jacques Marin, Mako

Island Escape: see *No Man Is an Island*

Island in the Sky *
US 1953 109m bw
Wayne-Fellows (Robert Fellows)
A transport plane makes a forced landing north of Greenland, and the crew must survive till help comes.
Well-made outdoor suspenser shot in the California Sierras.
w Ernest K. Gann *novel* Ernest K. Gann *d* William Wellman *ph* Archie Stout *m* Hugo Friedhofer *md* Emil Newman
☆ John Wayne, Lloyd Nolan, Walter Abel, Allyn Joslyn, Andy Devine, James Arness

Island in the Sun *
GB 1957 119m Technicolor Cinemascope
TCF (Darryl F. Zanuck)
Sexual and racial problems erupt on a West Indian island.
Portmanteau romantic melodrama which generally misfires, especially in an attempt to parallel Crime and Punishment; but the cast is interesting.
w Alfred Hayes *novel* Alec Waugh *d* Robert Rossen *ph* Frederick A. Young *m* Malcolm Arnold
☆ James Mason, Joan Fontaine, Harry Belafonte, John Williams, Dorothy Dandridge, Joan Collins, Michael Rennie, Patricia Owens, Stephen Boyd, Basil Sydney, Diana Wynyard, Ronald Squire, John Justin

Island of Desire: see *Saturday Island*

The Island of Dr Moreau *
US 1977 98m Movielab
AIP/Cinema 77 (Skip Steloff, John Temple-Smith)
In 1911, shipwrecked sailors land on a Pacific island where a mad doctor experiments with animal mutations.
A sprightly version of an old story; unfortunately it lacks any sense of the sinister, and the star is no match for Charles Laughton in Island of Lost Souls.
w John Herman Shaner, Al Ramrus *story* H. G. Wells *d* Don Taylor *ph* Gerry Fisher *m* Laurence Rosenthal
☆ Burt Lancaster, Michael York, Nigel Davenport, Barbara Carrera, Richard Basehart, Nick Cravat
'Cursed with lush colour photography instead of black and white atmospherics, and Lancaster's stolid mania instead of Laughton's manic zeal.' – *Sight and Sound*

The Island of Dr Moreau
US 1996 95m DeLuxe Panavision
Entertainment/New Line (Edward R. Pressman)
On a South Pacific island, genetically altered animals with human characteristics revolt against the mad scientist who created them.
Incoherent horror, notable for one of Brando's more eccentric performances, mercifully brief.
w Richard Stanley, Ron Hutchinson *d* John Frankenheimer *ph* William A. Fraker *m* Gary Chang *pd* Graham (Grace) Walker *ed* Paul Rubell
☆ Marlon Brando, Val Kilmer, David Thewlis, Fairuza Balk, Ron Perlman, Marco Hofschneider, Temuera Morrison, William Hootkins, Mark Dacascos, Nelson de la Rosa
'Astonishing four-fifths dreadful, one-fifth remarkable film.' – *Kim Newman, Sight and Sound*
† Director Richard Stanley was sacked after three days, though he returned incognito to play the part of a Dog-Man; David Thewlis replaced the originally cast Rob Morrow, and Walon Green worked uncredited on the script. The film cost $50m to make and grossed around $28m in the US.

Island of Lost Men
US 1939 64m bw
Paramount
An Oriental girl seeks her lost father in waterfront dives and finds him on a prison island.
Adequate action programmer.
w William R. Lipman, Horace McCoy *d* Kurt Neumann
☆ Anna May Wong, Broderick Crawford, Anthony Quinn, J. Carrol Naish
† A remake of *White Woman*.

'Out of the dark fantastic madness of his science he created her – the panther woman – throbbing to the hot flush of new-found love!'
Island of Lost Souls *
US 1932 74m bw
Paramount
On a remote South Sea island, mad Dr Moreau transforms animals into humans by vivisection.
Unchilling but interesting thriller with a rolling-eyed star performance.
w Waldemar Young, Philip Wylie *story* The Island of Dr Moreau by H. G. Wells *d* Erle C. Kenton *ph* Karl Struss
☆ Charles Laughton, Bela Lugosi, Richard Arlen, Kathleen Burke, Leila Hyams

Island of Lost Women
US 1958 72m bw
Jaguar/Warner
A newspaperman lands on a remote island where a scientist has retired from the world with his daughters.
Unexciting hokum with more talk than action.
w Ray Buffum *d* Frank Tuttle
☆ Jeff Richards, Venetia Stevenson, John Smith, Alan Napier

Island of Love
US 1963 101m Technicolor Panavision
Warner/Belgrave (Morton da Costa)
A gangster finances a film providing his girlfriend stars, but when it flops he chases the producers to a Greek island.
Dismally unfunny comedy wasting a talented cast.
w David R. Schwartz *d* Morton da Costa *ph* Harry Stradling *m* George Duning
☆ Robert Preston, Tony Randall, Walter Matthau, Giorgia Moll

Island of Terror
GB 1966 89m Eastmancolor
Planet (Tom Blakeley)
On an Irish island, a scientist makes monsters who thrive on bone.
Horror hokum, moderately done.
w Edward Andrew Mann, Alan Ramsen *d* Terence Fisher *ph* Reg Wyer *m* Malcolm Lockyer *sp* John St John Earl
☆ Peter Cushing, Edward Judd, Carole Gray, Eddie Byrne, Sam Kydd, Niall MacGinnis

Island of the Blue Dolphins
US 1964 93m Eastmancolor
U-I/Robert B. Radnitz
Two orphaned children grow up alone on a Californian island, protected by wild dogs.
Pleasant if unconvincing family film based on a true story.
w Ted Sherdeman, Jane Klove *novel* Scott O'Dell *d* James B. Clark *ph* Leo Tover *m* Paul Sawtell *ad* Alexander Golitzen, George Webb *ed* Ted J. Kent
☆ Celia Kaye, Larry Domasin, George Kennedy, Ann Daniel, Carlos Romero, Hal Jon Norman, Martin Garralaga

Island of The Living Dead: see *Zombie Flesh Eaters*

Island of the Lost
US 1968 92m colour
Ivan Tors
An anthropologist sets sail for an uncharted island and is shipwrecked on it.
Good-looking but singularly plotless action adventure.
w Richard Carlson, Ivan Tors *d* John Florea, Ricou Browning (underwater scenes)
☆ Richard Greene, Luke Halpin, Mark Hulswit

Island Rescue: see *Appointment with Venus*

Islands in the Stream
US 1977 105m Metrocolor Panavision
Paramount (Peter Bart, Max Palevsky)
On a Bahamian island in 1940, an expatriate American artist welcomes his three sons and reflects on the futility of life.
Shapeless semi-autobiographical fragments culminating unpersuasively in an action climax of heroic self-sacrifice. A film on which no expense has been spared and which doesn't work at all.
w Denne Bart Petitclerc *novel* Ernest Hemingway *d* Franklin Schaffner *ph* Fred J. Koenekamp *m* Jerry Goldsmith
☆ George C. Scott, David Hemmings, Gilbert Roland, Susan Tyrrell, Richard Evans, Claire Bloom, Hart Bochner, Julius Harris
'It is all too awful for words.' – *Benny Green, Punch*
photography

The Isle: see *Seom*

Isle of Forgotten Sins
US 1943 82m bw
PRC (Peter R. Van Duinen)
In the South Seas, villains congregate in search of sunken treasure.
Patchy tropical melodrama with a cast more interesting than the script.
w Raymond L. Schrock *story* Edgar G. Ulmer *d* Edgar G. Ulmer
☆ John Carradine, Gale Sondergaard, Sidney Toler, Frank Fenton, Rita Quigley, Veda Ann Borg

Isle of Fury
US 1936 60m bw
Warner
A fugitive from justice finds temporary peace on a South Sea island.
Limp remake of The Narrow Corner *(qv); its star later pretended he hadn't made it.*
w Robert Andrews, William Jacobs *novel* The Narrow Corner by W. Somerset Maugham *d* Frank McDonald
☆ Humphrey Bogart, Margaret Lindsay, Donald Woods

Isle of Sinners: see *Dieu a Besoin des Hommes*

Isle of the Dead **
US 1945 72m bw
RKO (Val Lewton)
On a Balkan island in 1912 a group of people shelter from the plague and fear that one of their number is a vampire.
Glum, ghoulish melodrama with some neatly handled shocks; quite different from any other horror film.
w Ardel Wray, Josef Mischel *d* Mark Robson *ph* Jack Mackenzie *m* Leigh Harline
☆ Boris Karloff, Ellen Drew, Helene Thimig, Marc Cramer, Katherine Emery, Alan Napier, Jason Robards

Isn't It Romantic *
US 1948 87m bw
Paramount (Daniel Dare)
Romance hits the household of an ex-Civil War colonel in Indiana.
Pleasant but forgettable period semi-musical.
w Theodore Strauss, Josef Mischel, Richard Breen *d* Norman Z. McLeod *ph* Lionel Lindon *m* Joseph J. Lilley
☆ Veronica Lake, Mona Freeman, Mary Hatcher, Roland Culver, Billy de Wolfe, Patric Knowles, Richard Webb, Kathryn Givney, Pearl Bailey

Isn't Life Wonderful? *
US 1924 99m (24 fps) bw silent
UA/David Wark Griffith
The life of a family in post-war Germany.
An unpopular subject, and a grey-looking film, but the director shows a lot of his strength in it.
wd D. W. Griffith *story* Geoffrey Moss *ph* Hendrik Sartov, Hal Sintzenich
☆ Carol Dempster, Neil Hamilton, Helen Lowell, Frank Puglia, Marcia Harris, Lupino Lane

Isn't Life Wonderful? *
GB 1952 83m Technicolor
ABP (Warwick Ward)
In 1902, drunken Uncle Willie runs a bicycle shop and manages to reconcile a lovers' quarrel.
Engaging, well-cast family comedy.
w Brock Williams *novel* Uncle Willie and the Bicycle Shop by Brock Williams *d* Harold French *ph* Erwin Hillier *m* Philip Green *ad* Terence Verity
☆ Donald Wolfit, Eileen Herlie, Cecil Parker, Eleanor Summerfield, Robert Urquhart, Cecil Trouncer

'Talent isn't everything.'
Isn't She Great *
US/GB/Germany/Japan 2000 95m colour
Universal/Mutual/Lobell/Bergman (Mike Lobell)
An ambitious but untalented actress becomes a best-selling novelist with the aid of her manager-husband.
Enjoyable biopic of publishing phenomenon Jacqueline Susann, an all-conquering icon of pop culture, who, in best melodramatic manner, kept her personal disasters hidden from her adoring readers.
w Paul Rudnick *article* Michael Korda *d* Andrew Bergman *ph* Karl Walter Lindenlaub *m* Burt Bacharach *pd* Stuart Wurtzel *ed* Barry Malkin *cos* Julie Weiss
☆ Bette Midler (Jacqueline Susann), Nathan Lane (Irving Mansfield), Stockard Channing (Florence Maybelle), David Hyde Pierce (Michael Hastings), John Cleese (Henry Marcus), John Larroquette (Maury Manning), Amanda Peet (Debbie), Christopher MacDonald (Brad Bradburn)
'Raucously funny and good-natured.' – *Sight and Sound*
'Veering from broad farce to sheer banality, pic isn't even unintentionally funny enough to qualify as guilty pleasure.' – *Emanuel Levy, Variety*

Istanbul
US 1956 84m Technicolor Cinemascope
U-I (Albert J. Cohen)
Various adventurers and an amnesiac girl seek stolen diamonds in Istanbul.
Dim remake of a flat-footed piece of thick ear called Singapore.
w Seton I. Miller, Barbara Gray, Richard Alan Simmons *d* Joseph Pevney *ph* William Daniels *m* Joseph Gershenson
☆ Errol Flynn, Cornell Borchers, John Bentley, Torin Thatcher, Leif Erickson, Martin Benson, Vladimir Sokoloff, Werner Klemperer, Nat King Cole, Peggy Knudsen

Istoria Asi Klyachinoi, kotoraya lyubila, da nie vshla zamuzh: see *Asya's Happiness*

It *
US 1927 72m (24 fps) bw silent
Famous Players-Lasky/Paramount (B. P. Schulberg)
A shopgirl tries to live by the tenets of Elinor Glyn's book, and finally marries her boss.
In its day a fast and funny spoof, and the years have not dealt too unkindly with it.
w Hope Loring, Louis D. Lighton *d* Clarence Badger *ph* H. Kinley Martin *adaptation* Elinor Glyn
☆ Clara Bow, Antonio Moreno, William Austin, Jacqueline Gadsdon, Gary Cooper, Elinor Glyn

It Ain't Hay
US 1943 79m bw
Universal (Alex Gottlieb)
GB title: *Money for Jam*
When a racehorse dies, a New York cabbie and his friend try to find a new one for the impecunious owners.
Formula Abbott and Costello with a small injection of sentiment and Runyonese. Not their best by a mile.
w Allen Boretz, John Grant *story* Princess O'Hara by Damon Runyon *d* Erle C. Kenton *ph* Charles von Enger *m/ly* Harry Revel, Paul Francis Webster
☆ Bud Abbott, Lou Costello, Grace McDonald, Cecil Kellaway, Patsy O'Connor, Eugene Pallette, Shemp Howard, Eddie Quillan

It All Came True *
US 1940 97m bw
Warner (Mark Hellinger)
A gangster hides out in a boarding house and puts it back on its feet.
Competent New York fairy story full of sweetness and light.
w Michael Fessier, Lawrence Kimble *story* Better Than Life by Louis Bromfield *d* Lewis Seiler *ph* Ernest Haller *m* Heinz Roemheld
☆ Humphrey Bogart, Ann Sheridan, Jeffrey Lynn, ZaSu Pitts, Una O'Connor, Jessie Busley, John Litel, Grant Mitchell, Felix Bressart

It All Starts Today **
France 1999 118m colour Super 35
Artificial Eye/Alain Sarde/Little Bear/TFI
original title: *Ca Commence Aujourd'hui*
In a deprived area, where unemployment is rife, an idealistic infant teacher tries to cope with inadequate aid from the local authorities and his own complicated private life.
Partly based on the experiences of his daughter's then-boyfriend (later her husband), Tavernier's film is suffused with a righteous anger, though he sweetens the pill with rather more glamour than one would expect.
w Dominique Sampiero, Tiffany Tavernier, Bertrand Tavernier *d* Bertrand Tavernier *ph* Alain Choquart *m* Louis Sclavis *ad* Thierry Francois *ed* Sophie Brunet
☆ Philippe Torreton (Daniel Lefebvre), Maria Pitarresi (Valeria), Nadia Kaci (Samia Damouni), Véronique Ataly (Mme Liénard), Nathalie Bécue (Cathy), Emmanuelle Bercot (Mme Tiévaux), Françoise Bette (Mme Delacourt), Christine Citti (Mme Baudoin)
'Every piece of grittiness in the film is undone by a corresponding bit of slickness.' – *Adam Mars-Jones, Times*

It Always Rains on Sunday ***
GB 1947 92m bw
Ealing (Henry Cornelius)
An escaped convict takes refuge in his married mistress's house in East London.
Influential slumland melodrama, now dated – the stuff of every other television play – but at the time electrifyingly vivid and very well done.
w Angus MacPhail, Robert Hamer, Henry Cornelius *novel* Arthur La Bern *d* Robert Hamer *ph* Douglas Slocombe *m* Georges Auric *ad* Duncan Sutherland *ed* Michael Truman
☆ Googie Withers, John McCallum, Jack Warner, Edward Chapman, Susan Shaw, Sydney Tafler
'Let me pay it the simplest of compliments and say that it has the persuasiveness of an exciting story professionally told.' – *Sunday Times*

It Came from beneath the Sea
US 1955 80m bw
Columbia/Sam Katzman (Charles Schneer)
A giant octopus half destroys San Francisco.
Tepid monster movie; special effects only fair.
w George Worthing Yates, Hal Smith *d* Robert Gordon *ph* Henry Freulich *md* Mischa Bakaleinikoff *ad* Paul Palmentola *ed* Jerome Thoms *sp* Ray Harryhausen
☆ Kenneth Tobey, Faith Domergue, Donald Curtis, Ian Keith

It Came from Outer Space **
US 1953 80m bw 3-D
U-I (William Alland)
A young astronomer sees a space ship land in the Arizona desert and tracks down the occupants who can adopt human appearance at will.
Quite bright science fiction, the first to use this theme of borrowing bodies and the first to utilize the Western desert locations. 3-D adds a shock moment or two.
w Harry Essex *story* Ray Bradbury *d* Jack Arnold *ph* Clifford Stine *m* Herman Stein *md* Joseph Gershenson
☆ Richard Carlson, Barbara Rush, Charles Drake, Kathleen Hughes
'A solid piece of eerie entertainment, replete with wild screams and bug-eyed monsters guaranteed to send scared customers out of this world.' – *Hollywood Reporter*
'Desert was Arnold's favourite location, and he used it consistently to create a sense of strangeness and menace otherwise much restricted by his budgets.' – *Time Out, 1982*

It Can't Be Winter, We Haven't Had Summer Yet
Canada 1980 84m colour
La Maison de Quatre (Louise Carré)
original title: *ça Peut Pas être l'Hiver, On n'a Même Pas Eu d'été*
A middle-aged woman, much to the apprehension of her children, enjoys a new lease of life after her husband's death.
Too pat and comfortable to be plausible, though it has some charm, apart from a dire excursion into a pop video halfway through.
wd Louise Carré *ph* Robert Vanherweghem *m* Marc O'Farrell *ed* André Théberge
☆ Charlotte Boisjoli, Jacques Galipeau, Céline Lomez, Serge Bélair, Mireille Thibault, Daniel Matte, Marie-Eve Doré, Martin Neufeld

It Conquered the World
US 1956 68m bw
AIP
Something from another planet is sheltered by a well-meaning scientist who discovers too late that its intentions are evil.
Tolerable horror comic on a risibly low budget.
w Lou Rusoff *d* Roger Corman *ph* Frederick E. West *m* Ronald Stein
☆ Peter Graves, Beverly Garland, Lee Van Cleef, Sally Fraser, Charles B. Griffith

It Could Happen to You
US 1939 73m bw
TCF
After a stag party, an advertising man finds a body in his car.
Neat second-feature mystery.
w Allen Rivkin, Lou Breslow *d* Alfred Werker
☆ Stuart Erwin, Gloria Stuart, Raymond Walburn, Douglas Fowley

'A Cop. A Waitress. A Lottery Ticket.'
'Life is full of surprises.'
It Could Happen to You
US 1994 101m Technicolor
Columbia TriStar/Adelson/Baumgarten/Lobell/Bergman (Mike Lobell)
A married cop makes good on his offer to a waitress of half the proceeds of a lottery ticket instead of a tip, even when he wins four million dollars.
A comedy of mild charm, but too calculating to be convincing in its belief that love conquers all.
w Jane Anderson *d* Andrew Bergman *ph* Caleb Deschanel *m* Carter Burwell *pd* Bill Groom *ed* Barry Malkin
☆ Nicolas Cage, Bridget Fonda, Wendell Pierce, Rosie Perez, Isaac Hayes, Seymour Cassel, Victor Rojas, Red Buttons
'A lame romantic comedy that is too calculating in its cornball sentimentality to tug effectively on the heartstrings.' – *Colin Brown, Screen International*
'It's good escapist fun for those who enjoy the anodine.' – *Marianne Gray, Film Review*

It Grows on Trees
US 1952 84m bw
U-I (Leonard Goldstein)
A housewife finds a money tree in her backyard.

Protracted fantasy comedy.
w Leonard Praskins, Barney Slater *d* Arthur Lubin *ph* Maury Gertsman *m* Frank Skinner *ad* Alexander Golitzen, Bernard Herzbrun *ed* Milton Carruth
☆ Irene Dunne, Dean Jagger, Joan Evans, Richard Crenna, Edith Meiser, Dee Pollock
† It was Irene Dunne's last film.

It Had to Be You
US 1947 98m bw
Columbia/Don Hartman
A dizzy dame runs out on three prospective husbands and is pursued by an Indian.
Weak sex farce without the courage of its lack of convictions.
w Norman Panama, Melvin Frank *d* Don Hartman, Rudolph Maté *ph* Rudolph Maté *m* Heinz Roemheld *md* Morris Stoloff
☆ Ginger Rogers, Cornel Wilde, Percy Waram, Spring Byington, Thurston Hall, Ron Randell

It Happened at the Inn: see *Goupi Mains Rouges*

It Happened at the World's Fair
US 1962 104m Metrocolor Panavision
MGM/Ted Richmond
At the Seattle World's Fair, two crop-dusting pilots have romantic intrigues.
Routine star vehicle.
w Si Rose, Seaman Jacobs *d* Norman Taurog *ph* Joseph Ruttenberg *m* Leith Stevens
☆ Elvis Presley, Gary Lockwood, Joan O'Brien, Yvonne Craig, Ginny Tiu

It Happened Here **
GB 1963 99m bw
UA/Kevin Brownlow, Andrew Mollo
What might have happened if the Germans had invaded England in 1940.
A remarkable semi-professional reconstruction which took seven years to film and is totally convincing in detail, but unfortunately rather confused and padded as drama.
wd Kevin Brownlow, Andrew Mollo ph Peter Suschitzky *m* Jack Beaver
☆ Sebastian Shaw, Pauline Murray, Fiona Leland, Honor Fehrson
'For a grain of artistic truth, we can forgive even the grainy photography and wavering sound with which part of it is afflicted.' – *John Simon*

It Happened in Athens
US 1961 100m DeLuxe Cinemascope
TCF (James S. Elliott)
At the first revival of the Olympic Games in 1896 a publicity-seeking actress announces that she will marry whoever wins the Marathon.
Witless extravagant romp, well mounted but adding up to zero.
w Laszlo Vadnay *d* Andrew Marton *ph* Curt Courant *m* Manos Hadjidakis
☆ Jayne Mansfield, Trax Colton, Bob Mathias

It Happened in Brooklyn *
US 1947 103m bw
MGM (Jack Cummings)
Young New Yorkers with musical talents find their way to fame.
Well-handled routine musical of its time.
w Isobel Lennart *d* Richard Whorf *ph* Robert Planck *m* Johnny Green *songs* Jule Styne, Sammy Cahn
☆ Frank Sinatra, Jimmy Durante, Kathryn Grayson, Peter Lawford, Gloria Grahame
'Aside from Sinatra and Durante the show amounts to practically nothing, but there is a general kindliness about it which I enjoyed.' – *James Agee*

It Happened in Hollywood
US 1937 67m bw
Columbia
A silent cowboy star is washed up when talkies come in.
Indifferent studio story.
w Ethel Hill, Harvey Ferguson, Sam Fuller, Myles Connolly *d* Harry Lachman
☆ Richard Dix, Fay Wray, Victor Kilian, Franklin Pangborn, Charles Arnt, Granville Bates
'It will have difficulty fitting in ... won't particularly satisfy 'em in the duals.' – *Variety*

It Happened on Fifth Avenue *
US 1947 115m bw
Allied Artists (Roy del Ruth)
A child of divorce finds amiable squatters in her millionaire father's house.
Curious, overlong, cheerful Capraesque comedy with the mildest of social pretensions.
w Everett Freeman, Frederick Stephani, Herbert Clyde Lewis *d* Roy del Ruth *ph* Henry Sharp
☆ Gale Storm, Ann Harding, Victor Moore, Charles Ruggles, Don Defore
original story

'Together For The First Time!'
It Happened One Night ***
US 1934 105m bw
Columbia (Frank Capra)
A runaway heiress falls in love with the reporter who is chasing her across America.
Highly successful and influential romantic comedy, the first to use buses and motels as background and still come up sparkling; it remains superlative in patches, but overall has a faded, dated air.
w Robert Riskin story Night Bus by Samuel Hopkins Adams *d Frank Capra ph* Joseph Walker *md* Louis Silvers *ad* Stephen Goosson *ed* Gene Havlick
☆ *Clark Gable, Claudette Colbert*, Walter Connolly, Roscoe Karns, Alan Hale, Ward Bond, Jameson Thomas, Arthur Hoyt
'A laughing hit that will mean important coin.' – *Variety*
'It will be a long day before we see so little made into so much.' – *Otis Ferguson*
'Something to revive your faith in a medium which could belong among the great arts.' – *Robert Forsythe*
'We may look askance at Capra's sententious notions about the miserable rich and the happy poor, but there's no doubting the chord he struck in depression audiences.' – *Time Out, 1980*
'It made audiences happy in a way that only a few films in each era do. In the mid-30s, the Colbert and Gable of this film became Americans' idealized view of themselves – breezy, likeable, sexy, gallant, and maybe just a little harebrained. It was the *Annie Hall* of its day – before the invention of anxiety.' – *Pauline Kael, 70s*
'One of the most entertaining films that has ever been offered to the public.' – *Observer*
† Remade 1956 (badly) as *You Can't Run Away From It.*
†† Robert Montgomery was the first choice for the Gable role, but he refused it because he had been on a bus in *Fugitive Lovers*. The Colbert role was first offered to Myrna Loy, Margaret Sullavan and Constance Bennett. Colbert was lured by a 40,000-dollar fee.
††† Steven Spielberg paid $607,500 at a 1996 auction for Clark Gable's Oscar, which he then presented to the Academy of Motion Picture Arts and Sciences.
best picture; Robert Riskin; Frank Capra; Clark Gable; Claudette Colbert

It Happened One Summer: see *State Fair (1945)*

It Happened One Sunday
GB 1943 99m bw
ABPC
In Liverpool, a Canadian seaman falls for an Irish maid.
Overlong romantic comedy with nowhere to go.
w Victor Skutezky, Frederic Gotfurt, Stephen Black *d* Karel Lamac
☆ Robert Beatty, Barbara White, Marjorie Rhodes, Ernest Butcher, Judy Kelly, Irene Vanbrugh

'A warm, wonderful movie that's stacked with joy for the whole family!'
It Happened to Jane
US 1959 98m Technicolor Cinemascope
Columbia/Arwin (Richard Quine)
A lady lobster dealer becomes involved in a battle with the railroad whose inefficiency affects her business.
Witless, wholesome farce which promises more than it delivers.
w Norman Katkov *d* Richard Quine *ph* Charles Lawton Jnr *m* George Duning
☆ Doris Day, Jack Lemmon, *Ernie Kovacs*, Steve Forrest
'Up to a point, this is a funny comedy. The point is reached about three-quarters of the way through when the film abruptly changes form and loses momentum.' – *Variety*

It Happened Tomorrow ***
US 1944 84m bw
UA/Arnold Pressburger
A reporter meets an old man with the power to show him tomorrow's newspaper headlines, so that he always gets scoops – including his own death...
Engaging fantasy, flawlessly made and quietly very entertaining.
w Dudley Nichols, René Clair d René Clair ph Archie Stout m Robert Stolz
☆ *Dick Powell*, Linda Darnell, *Jack Oakie, John Philliber*, Edgar Kennedy, Ed Brophy, George Cleveland, Sig Rumann
'Students of cinematic style will find many shrewdly polished bits to admire and enjoy.' – *James Agee*
'Diverting escapist entertainment for all audiences.' – *Variety*
Robert Stolz

It Happens Every Spring
US 1949 80m bw
TCF (William Perlberg)
A chemistry teacher discovers a formula that makes baseballs repellent to wood.
Smartly produced but rather desperate fantasy comedy.
w Valentine Davies *d* Lloyd Bacon *ph* Joe MacDonald *m* Leigh Harline
☆ Ray Milland, Jean Peters, Paul Douglas, Ed Begley, Ted de Corsia, Ray Collins, Jessie Royce Landis, Alan Hale Jnr
original story (Shirley W. Smith, Valentine Davies)

It Happens Every Thursday *
US 1953 80m bw
U-I (Anton Leader)
The new owner of a small-town newspaper becomes unpopular through his attempts to boost the circulation.
Pleasant comedy with amusing scenes.
w Dane Lussier *d* Joseph Pevney *ph* Russell Metty *m* Joseph Gershenson
☆ Loretta Young, John Forsythe, Jimmy Conlin, Frank McHugh, Edgar Buchanan, Jane Darwell

It Hurts Only When I Laugh: see *Only When I Laugh*

It Lives Again
US 1978 91m colour
Warner/Larco (Larry Cohen)
aka: *It's Alive II*
Three mutant killer babies are protected by a scientist from a cop determined to kill them.
A sequel to It's Alive *that is less effective because the babies are too visible for too much of the time.*
wd Larry Cohen *ph* Fenton Hamilton *m* Bernard Herrmann *ed* Curt Burch, Louis Friedman, Carol O'Blath
☆ Frederic Forrest, Kathleen Lloyd, John P. Ryan, John Marley, Andrew Duggan, Eddie Constantine, James Dixon
† It was followed by *It's Alive III* (qv).

It Rains on Our Love *
Sweden 1946 95m bw
Sveriges Folkbiografer (Lorens Marmstedt)
original title: *Det Regnar Pa Var Kärlek*
aka: *Man with an Umbrella*
A pregnant girl meets an ex-prisoner while waiting for a train and they decide to live together.
A mainly light-hearted movie about two irresponsible people making the best of the worst that life has to offer.
w Ingmar Bergman, Herbert Grevenius *play* Oscar Braathen *d* Ingmar Bergman *ph* Göran Strindberg, Hilding Bladh *m* Erland von Koch *ad* P. A. Lundgren *ed* Tage Holmberg
☆ Barbro Kollberg, Birger Malmsten, Gösta Cederlund, Ludde Gentzel, Douglas Hage, Hjördis Pettersson, Benkt-Ake Benktsson, Sture Ericson

It Should Happen to You **
US 1954 87m bw
Columbia (Fred Kohlmar)
A slightly daffy New York model with an urge to be famous rents a huge billboard and puts her name on it.
Likeable comedy which starts brightly and slowly falls apart, disappointing considering the credentials of the talents involved and the satiric possibilities of the plot.
w Ruth Gordon, Garson Kanin d George Cukor ph Charles Lang *m* Frederick Hollander
☆ *Judy Holliday, Jack Lemmon*, Peter Lawford, Michael O'Shea
'One of the funniest films to come out of Hollywood.' – *Life*

It Shouldn't Happen to a Vet
GB 1976 93m Technicolor
EMI/Talent Associates/Readers Digest
US title: *All Things Bright and Beautiful*
Adventures of a Yorkshire vet just before World War II.
Competent sequel to All Creatures Great and Small *(qv).*
w Alan Plater *books* James Herriot *d* Eric Till *ph* Arthur Ibbetson *m* Laurie Johnson
☆ John Alderton, Colin Blakely, Lisa Harrow, Bill Maynard, Richard Pearson, Raymond Francis, John Barrett, Paul Shelley

It Started in Naples *
US 1960 100m Technicolor Vistavision
Paramount/Capri (Jack Rose)
A Philadelphia lawyer goes to Naples to settle his dead brother's affairs, and falls for his nephew's aunt.
Nicely made, formula romantic comedy which started life as a vehicle for Gracie Fields.
w Melville Shavelson, Jack Rose, Suso Cecchi d'Amico *d* Melville Shavelson *ph* Robert Surtees *m* Alessandro Cicognini *ad* Hal Pereira, Roland Anderson
☆ Clark Gable, Sophia Loren, Vittorio de Sica, Marietto, Paulo Carlini
art direction

It Started in Paradise
GB 1952 94m Technicolor
GFD/British Film Makers (Leslie Parkyn, Sergei Nolbandov)
The career of an ambitious dress designer.
Stilted and garishly coloured but often amusing backstage melodrama of the fashion world: a Hollywood-style star vehicle which seems faintly surprising as a British product.
w Marghanita Laski *d* Compton Bennett *ph* Jack Cardiff *m* Malcolm Arnold *ad* Edward Carrick
☆ *Jane Hylton*, Ian Hunter, Terence Morgan, Muriel Pavlow, Brian Worth, *Martita Hunt, Ronald Squire, Harold Lang*, Joyce Barbour, Kay Kendall

It Started with a Kiss
US 1959 104m Metrocolor Cinemascope
MGM/Arcola (Aaron Rosenberg)
An army sergeant posted to Spain is embarrassed when his wife follows him.
Flabby comedy with the emphasis on sex and pratfalls.
w Charles Lederer *d* George Marshall *ph* Robert Bronner *m* Jeff Alexander
☆ Glenn Ford, Debbie Reynolds, Fred Clark, Edgar Buchanan, Eva Gabor

It Started with Eve **
US 1941 93m bw
Universal (Joe Pasternak)
A dying millionaire wants to see his grandson engaged, so a waitress obliges for an hour ... but the old man recovers.
Charming comedy which was probably the star's best film; remade as I'd Rather be Rich *(qv).*
w Norman Krasna, Leo Townsend *d* Henry Koster *ph* Rudolph Maté *md* Charles Previn, Hans Salter
☆ Deanna Durbin, Charles Laughton, Robert Cummings, Margaret Tallichet, Guy Kibbee, Walter Catlett, Catherine Doucet
'The perfect 8 to 80 picture.' – *Variety*
Charles Previn, Hans Salter

It Takes Two
US 1988 79m colour
United Artists (Robert Lawrence)

Three days before his wedding, a gullible 20-year-old Texan goes to the big city to buy a car and is taken for a ride.
A broad comedy that confuses energy and wit, leaving its audience tired rather than amused.
w Richard Christian Matheson, Thomas Szollosi *d* David Beaird *ph* Peter Deming *m* Carter Burwell *pd* Richard Hoover *ed* David Garfield
☆ George Newbern, Leslie Hope, Kimberly Foster, Barry Corbin, Anthony Geary, Frances Lee McCain

It Takes Two
US 1995 98m DeLuxe
Entertainment/Rysher/Dualstar (James Orr, Jim Cruickshank)

A 10-year-old orphan switches places with a rich girl who resembles her.
A modern, not very interesting, variation on The Prince and the Pauper, *which may keep those who can identify with its twee heroines moderately quiet on a rainy afternoon.*
w Deborah Dean Davis *d* Andy Tennant *ph* Kenneth D. Zunder *m* Sherman Foote, Ray Foote *pd* Ed Pisoni *ed* Roger Bondelli
☆ Kirstie Alley, Steve Guttenberg, Mary-Kate Olsen, Ashley Olsen, Philip Bosco, Jane Sibbett, Michelle Grisom, Desmond Roberts
'A predictable if not entirely charmless film, assembled from all the hoary clichés known to "B"-grade Hollywood.' – *Andy Richards, Sight and Sound*

It! The Terror from Beyond Space
US 1958 69m bw
Vogue/United Artists

A space ship returning from Mars is invaded by a worm-like monster.
Laughable but lively precursor of Alien; *rather more fun on the whole.*
w Jerome Bixby *d* Edward L. Cahn *ph* Kenneth Peach *m* Paul Sawtell, Bert Shefter *ad* William Glasgow
☆ Marshall Thompson, Shawn Smith, Kim Spaulding, Ann Doran, Dabbs Greer

It Was An Accident
GB/France 2000 96m Technicolor
Pathé/Arts Council/Canal+ (Paul Goodman)

An ex-convict who wants to go straight finds the odds stacked against him.
A jokey drama of petty crooks and thwarted romance, enjoyable enough but small-scale.
w Ol Parker *novel* Jeremy Cameron *d* Metin Huseyin *ph* Guy Defaux *m* Courtney Pine *pd* Joseph Bennett *ed* Annie Kocur *cos* Susannah Buxton
☆ Chiwetel Ejiofor (Nicky Burkett), Thandie Newton (Noreen Hurlock), Hugh Quarshie (George Hurlock), Max Beesley (Mickey Cousins), James Bolam (Fitch), Nicola Stapleton (Kelly), Neil Dudgeon (Holdsworth), Sidh Solanki (Rameez), Cavan Clerkin (Jimmy Foley), Jacqueline Williams (Sharon Burkett)
'A surprisingly genial London gangster comedy with its own distinct flavor and good ensemble chemistry among the multiethnic cast.' – *Derek Elley, Variety*

'Lessons in the language of love.'
Italian for Beginners **
Denmark 2000 112m colour
Pathé/Zentropa/DRTV/DFI (Ib Tardini)

original title: *Italiensk for Begyndere*
A young widowed minister moves to a new parish and joins an evening class filled wqith love-lorn locals.
Charming, but also sharply observant, comedy of suburban life and domestic traumas as shy and edgy individuals edge towards relationships with one another.
wd Lone Scherfig *ph* Jørgen Johansson *m* Puccini et al *ed* Gerd Tjur
☆ Anders W. Berthelsen (Andreas), Anette Støvelbaek (Olympia), Peter Gantzler (Jørgen Mortensen), Ann Eleonora Jørgensen (Karen), Lars Kaalund (Hal-Finn), Sara Indrio Jensen (Giulia), Elsbeth Steentoft (Verger), Rikke Wölck (Nurse)
'A delicious and delicately funny look at the residents of a Copenhagen neighborhood coping with the befuddling complications life tosses at them.' – *Kenneth Turan, Los Angeles Times*

The Italian Job **
GB 1969 100m Eastmancolor Panavision
Paramount/Oakhurst (Michael Deeley)

Crooks stage a traffic jam in Turin in order to pull off a bullion robbery.
Lively caper comedy which provides a good measure of entertainment.
w Troy Kennedy Martin *d* Peter Collinson *ph* Douglas Slocombe, Norman Warwick *m* Quincy Jones
☆ *Michael Caine, Noël Coward,* Benny Hill, Raf Vallone, Tony Beckley, Rossano Brazzi, Maggie Blye, Irene Handl, John Le Mesurier, Fred Emney

Italian Movie
US 1994 95m colour
DiLauro (Peter Guzzardo)

Desperate to pay off his gambling debts, a good-looking, married pizza restaurant owner finds work as a gigolo.
Dull domestic drama among an Italian-American community that seems to owe its video release to the involvement of newly popular James Gandolfini, even though he plays a minor and unattractive role.
w Angela Sciddurlo Rago, Eugenia Bone *story* *Broken Honor* by Marco Cristino *d* Roberto Monticello *ph* Ray Preziosi *m* Hayden Wayne *pd* Stephanie Carroll *ed* Janice Keuhnelian
☆ Michael Dellafemina (Leonardo), Caprice Benedetti (Anna), Janet Sarno (Nina), James Gandolfini (Angelo), Paul Carafotes (Philipo), Anthony Alessandro (Alfredo), Rita Moreno (Isabella)

An Italian Straw Hat ***
France 1927 74m (24 fps) bw silent
Albatross
original title: *Un Chapeau de Paille d'Italie*
The hero is prevented from getting to a wedding when his horse chews up a lady's straw hat and her escort demands that it be replaced.
Lively but gentle comedy of errors, a stage farce expanded for the screen and filled with visual gags. A very influential and still amusing piece.
wd René Clair *play* Eugène Labiche *ph* Maurice Desfassiaux, Nicolas Roudakoff *ad Lazare Meerson*
☆ Albert Préjean, Olga Tschekowa, Marise Maia, Alice Tissot
'The very springtime of screen comedy.' – *Tatler*
'One of the funniest films ever made.' – *Tribune, 1945*
'Still one of the funniest films in the world.' – *Sunday Times, 1948*

ItalianAmerican
US 1974 45m colour/bw
National Communications Foundation (Saul Rubin, Elaine Attias)

Martin Scorsese's affectionate portrait of his parents, as they talk about their upbringing, and their enjoyment of food, showing holiday snaps mainly of people at dinner.
A sophisticated home movie, rooting a family in their environment. The credits include the recipe for Mrs Scorsese's meatball sauce.
wd Martin Scorsese *ph* Alex Hirshfeld
☆ Catherine and Charles Scorsese
† It was released on video with three other shorts under the title *4 x Scorsese*.

Italiensk for Begyndere: see *Italian for Beginners*

It's a 2'6" above the Ground World
GB 1972 96m Eastmancolor
British Lion/Welbeck/Betty E. Box-Ralph Thomas
aka: *The Love Ban*
A Roman Catholic couple go on the pill.
Smutty, not very funny sex comedy.
w Kevin Laffan *play* Kevin Laffan *d* Ralph Thomas *ph* Tony Imi *m* Stanley Myers
☆ Nanette Newman, Hywel Bennett, Russell Lewis, Simon Henderson, Milo O'Shea
'Offering cheap thrills and easy laughs on the side by filling the screen with capering nudes.' – *Clyde Jeavons*

It's a Big Country
US 1952 89m bw
MGM (Robert Sisk)
Seven stories show the diversity of the US and the glory of being one of its citizens.
Stultifying flagwaver memorable chiefly as a waste of good actors.
w William Ludwig, Helen Deutsch, George Wells, Allen Rivkin, Dorothy Kingsley, Isobel Lennart *d* Richard Thorpe, Don Weis, John Sturges, Don Hartman, William Wellman, Charles Vidor, Clarence Brown *ph* John Alton, Ray June, William Mellor, Joseph Ruttenberg *m* Bronislau Kaper, Rudolph G. Kopp, David Raksin, David Rose
☆ Ethel Barrymore, Keefe Brasselle, Nancy Davis, Van Johnson, Gene Kelly, Janet Leigh, Marjorie Main, Fredric March, George Murphy, William Powell, S. Z. Sakall, Lewis Stone, James Whitmore

It's a Date *
US 1940 100m bw
Universal/Joe Pasternak

The daughter of a Broadway musical heroine has stage ambitions of her own, and chases an older man who is more interested in her mother.
Fairly pleasant but unduly elongated star comedy.
w Norman Krasna *d* William Seiter *ph* Joe Valentine *m* Charles Previn
☆ Deanna Durbin, Walter Pidgeon, Kay Francis, Eugene Pallette, Henry Stephenson, Cecilia Loftus, Samuel S. Hinds, S. Z. Sakall
'A natural which will roll grosses of upper bracket proportions.' – *Variety*

It's a Dog's Life: see *The Bar Sinister*

It's a Gift **
US 1934 73m bw
Paramount (William Le Baron)

A general store proprietor buys an orange ranch by mail and transports his family to California.
Roughly assembled comedy of disasters which happens to show the star more or less at his best, though the expected climax is lacking.
w Jack Cunningham *story* W. C. Fields, J. P. McEvoy *d* Norman Z. McLeod *ph* Henry Sharp
☆ *W. C. Fields,* Kathleen Howard, Jean Rouverol, Julian Madison, Tommy Bupp, Baby LeRoy
'An enormously amusing succession of rough and ready gags.' – *Literary Digest*

It's a Grand Life
GB 1953 102m bw
Mancunian/John E. Blakeley
A nitwit army private plays Cupid.
Senseless and under-rehearsed farce which has interest for fans of the usually drunken star.
w H. F. Maltby, Frank Randle *d* John E. Blakeley *ph* Ernest Palmer *ad* Alec Gray *ed* Dorothy Stimson
☆ Frank Randle, Diana Dors, Dan Young, Michael Brennan, Jennifer Jayne, John Blythe
† The film opens with the disclaimer: 'This film has been produced with the sole intention of providing Burlesque Comedy Entertainment, and is not meant in any way to be derogatory to any of the Services.'

It's a Great Day!
GB 1956 71m bw
Butchers/Grove (Victor Lyndon)
A jobbing builder is suspected of theft and, with his family, prevented from attending a royal event.
Film version of The Grove Family, *Britain's first TV soap opera, a mix of comedy and domestic drama; it is well enough done, but more of sociological interest than anything else.*
w Michael and Roland Pertwee *d* John Warrington *ph* Cedric Williams *m* Eric Spear *ad* Norman Arnold *ed* Joseph Sterling
☆ Ruth Dunning, Edward Evans, Peter Bryant, Nancy Roberts, Sheila Sweet, Margaret Downs, Christopher Beeny, Vera Day, Sidney James, Victor Maddern

It's a Great Feeling *
US 1949 85m Technicolor
Warner (Alex Gottlieb)

No one will direct a Jack Carson movie, so he has to do it himself.
Amiable studio farce with plenty of guest appearances.
w Jack Rose, Mel Shavelson *d* David Butler *ph* Wilfrid M. Cline *m* Ray Heindorf *songs* Jule Styne, Sammy Cahn
☆ Jack Carson, Doris Day, Dennis Morgan, Bill Goodwin, Gary Cooper, Joan Crawford, Errol Flynn, Sydney Greenstreet, Danny Kaye, Patricia Neal, Edward G. Robinson, Jane Wyman, Eleanor Parker, Ronald Reagan
title song

It's a Mad Mad Mad Mad World **
US 1963 192m Technicolor Ultra Panavision 70
UA/Stanley Kramer

An assortment of people including a frustrated cop are overcome by greed when they hear of buried loot.
Three hours of frantic chasing and violent slapstick is too much even when done on this scale and with this cast, but one must observe that scene for scene it is extremely well done and most of the players are in unusually good form though they all outstay their welcome and are upstaged by the stunt men.
w William and Tania Rose *d Stanley Kramer* *ph Ernest Laszlo* *m Ernest Gold* *stunts* Carey Loftin *titles Saul Bass*
☆ Spencer Tracy, Jimmy Durante, *Milton Berle,* Sid Caesar, Ethel Merman, Buddy Hackett, Mickey Rooney, Dick Shawn, *Phil Silvers, Terry-Thomas,* Jonathan Winters, Edie Adams, Dorothy Provine, Eddie Anderson, Jim Backus and also William Demarest, Peter Falk, Paul Ford, Leo Gorcey, Ben Blue, Edward Everett Horton, Buster Keaton, Joe E. Brown, Carl Reiner, the Three Stooges, ZaSu Pitts, Sterling Holloway, Jack Benny, Jerry Lewis
'To watch on a Cinerama screen in full colour a small army of actors inflict mayhem on each other with cars, planes, explosives and other devices for more than three hours with stereophonic sound effects is simply too much for the human eye and ear to respond to, let alone the funny bone.' – *Dwight MacDonald*
Ernest Laszlo; Ernest Gold; title song (*m* Ernest Gold, *ly* Mack David)

It's a Pleasure
US 1945 90m Technicolor
International/RKO
The career of an ice-skating couple is interrupted when he takes to drink.
Unimpressive vehicle from the star's waning years: the numbers are good but the rest very soggy.
w Lynn Starling, Elliot Paul *d* William A. Seiter
☆ Sonja Henie, Michael O'Shea, Marie McDonald

It's a Small World
US 1935 72m bw
Fox
A man and woman fall in love after being stranded by a car crash in a small Louisiana town.
Mildly amusing comedy.
w Sam Hellman, Gladys Lehman *d* Irving Cummings
☆ Spencer Tracy, Wendy Barrie, Raymond Walburn, Virginia Sale, Irving Bacon
'Very weak entertainment, strictly for double bills.' – *Variety*

It's a Wise Child
US 1931 73m bw
Cosmopolitan/MGM
When a girl is thought to be pregnant, her family hunts the father.
Tasteless comedy with too few laughs.
w Laurence E. Johnson *play* Laurence E. Johnson *d* Robert Z. Leonard
☆ Marion Davies, Sidney Blackmer, James Gleason, Polly Moran, Marie Prevost, Lester Vail
'No subject matter here for family audiences … it must prove embarrassing to young unmarried couples attending the theatre together.' – *Variety*

It's a Wonderful Life ****
US 1946 129m bw
RKO/Liberty Films (Frank Capra)

A man is prevented from committing suicide by an elderly angel, who takes him back through his life to show him what good he has done.
Superbly assembled small-town comedy drama in a fantasy framework; arguably Capra's best and most typical work.
w Frances Goodrich, Albert Hackett, Frank Capra *d* Frank Capra *ph* Joseph Walker, Joseph Biroc *m* Dimitri Tiomkin *ed* William Hornbeck
☆ *James Stewart, Henry Travers,* Donna Reed, Lionel Barrymore, Thomas Mitchell, Beulah Bondi, Frank Faylen, Ward Bond, Gloria Grahame, H. B. Warner, Frank Albertson, Samuel S. Hinds, Mary Treen
CLARENCE (HENRY TRAVERS): 'Every time you hear a bell ring, it means that some angel's just got his wings.'
'One of the most efficient sentimental pieces since *A Christmas Carol*.' – *James Agee*
'The most brilliantly made motion picture of the 1940s, so assured, so dazzling in its use of screen narrative.' – *Charles Higham*
'In its own icky, bittersweet way, it's terribly effective.' – *New Yorker, 1977*
'At its best all this seems to me insipid, and at its worst an embarrassment to both flesh and spirit.' – *Richard Winnington, News Chronicle*
best picture; Frank Capra; James Stewart; editing

It's a Wonderful World *
US 1939 86m bw
MGM (Frank Davis)
Kidnapped by a suspected murderer, a girl helps him track down the real criminal.
Madcap comedy mystery which now seems much fresher and funnier than it did at the time. A highlight of the crazy comedy cycle.
w Ben Hecht, Herman J. Mankiewicz *d* W. S. Van Dyke II *ph* Oliver Marsh *m* Edward Ward
☆ Claudette Colbert (Edwina Corday), James Stewart (Guy Johnson), Guy Kibbee (Capt Streeter), Nat Pendleton (Sgt Koretz), Frances Drake (Vivian Tarbel), Edgar Kennedy (Lt Meller), Ernest Truex (Willie Heyward), Richard Carle, Sidney Blackmer, Andy Clyde, Cliff Clark, Hans Conried
'It's right down the alley for general audiences.' – *Variety*
'One of the few genuinely comic pictures in a dog's age.' – *Otis Ferguson*

It's a Wonderful World
GB 1956 90m Technicolor Spectascope
Renown/George Minter
Two songwriters struggle to compose a hit song, until one discovers a way to be successful: by recording an old tune backwards.
Dull and uninspired musical, making fun of modern styles, but only offering in its stead some extremely dreary examples of 50s pop.
wd Val Guest *ph* Wilkie Cooper *md* Robert Farnon *ad* Elven Webb *ed* John Pomeroy
☆ Terence Morgan, George Cole, Kathleen Harrison, Mylene Nicole (aka Mylene Demongeot), James Hayter, Richard Wattis, Reginald Beckwith, Maurice Kaufmann, Harold Lang, Ted Heath and His Music

'Save your screams till you see its face!'
It's Alive
US 1974 91m Technicolor
Warner/Larco (Larry Cohen)

A new-born baby turns out to be a vicious monster.
Exploitation horror flick in the worst of taste, with a good central performance.
wd Larry Cohen *ph* Fenton Hamilton *m* Bernard Herrmann *ed* Peter Honess
☆ *John Ryan,* Sharon Farrell, Andrew Duggan, Guy Stockwell, James Dixon, Michael Ansara
'The best horror movie ever.' – *Quentin Crisp, Christopher Street*
† It was followed by *It Lives Again* and *It's Alive III: Island of The Alive* (qv).

It's Alive II: see *It Lives Again*

It's Alive III: Island of the Alive
US 1988 91m Technicolor
Warner/Larco (Paul Stader)

A mutant baby, whose father has gone to court to protect his right to live, swiftly grows to adulthood on a remote island with others of his kind and then heads back to America with his own child.
Wild, undisciplined horror film full of satirical thrusts at everything from attitudes to AIDS to media exploitation.
wd Larry Cohen *ph* Daniel Pearl *m* Laurie Johnson, Bernard Herrmann *ad* George Stoll *ed* David Kern *sp* Steve Neill, Rick Baker, William Hedge
☆ Michael Moriarty, Karen Black, Laurene Landon, James Dixon, Neal Israel, Art Lund, Ann Dane, Macdonald Carey, Gerrit Graham
'This is from the Cohen home-movie stable and non-aficionados should beware: production values and special effects are as hokey as ever.' – *Anne Billson, Shock Xpress*
† The film was shot in four weeks in Hawaii and Los Angeles.

It's All Happening
GB 1963 101m Eastmancolor
British Lion/Magna/KNP (Norman Williams)
US title: *The Dream Maker*
A talent scout for a recording agency helps to save an orphanage and makes himself a star in the process.
Unassuming, jolly little comedy with music; a better title would have made it more memorable.
w Leigh Vance *d* Don Sharp *ph* Ken Hodges *m* Philip Green
☆ Tommy Steele, Angela Douglas, Michael Medwin, Bernard Bresslaw, Walter Hudd, Jean Harvey, Richard Goolden

It's All Yours
US 1937 80m bw
Columbia
A millionaire leaves a fortune to his favourite secretary, hoping that it will make his nephew take notice of her.
Unpersuasive romantic comedy with slightly crazy touches.
w Mary C. McCall Jnr *d* Elliott Nugent
☆ Madeleine Carroll, Francis Lederer, Mischa Auer, Grace Bradley
'Of the whimsy, gay school currently in vogue ... too light to figure importantly at solo b.o.' – *Variety*

It's Always Fair Weather **
US 1955 101m Eastmancolor
Cinemascope
MGM (Arthur Freed)

In 1945 three army veterans vow to meet ten years on, but they find each other dull failures until they go on a wild spree.
Rather dejected New Yorkish comedy with musical sequences; some of it works very well, but the colour is crude and the wide screen doesn't help.
d Gene Kelly, Stanley Donen *ph* Robert Bronner *md* André Previn *w/m/ly* Betty Comden, Adolph Green
☆ *Gene Kelly,* Dan Dailey, Michael Kidd, Dolores Gray, Cyd Charisse
† Michael Kidd's vocals were dubbed by Jud Conlin.
Betty Comden, Adolph Green (as writers); André Previn

It's Great to Be Young *
GB 1956 93m Technicolor
AB-Pathé/Marble Arch (Victor Skutezky)
A popular teacher falls foul of the new headmaster who tries to disband the school orchestra.
Very acceptable but totally forgettable star comedy.
w Ted Willis *d* Cyril Frankel *ph* Gilbert Taylor *m* Ray Martin, Lester Powell, John Addison
☆ John Mills, Cecil Parker, Jeremy Spenser, Dorothy Bromiley, John Salew, Derek Blomfield, Eleanor Summerfield, Bryan Forbes

It's Hard to Be Good
GB 1948 93m bw
GFD/Two Cities (Jeffrey Dell)
A demobbed war hero determines to spread peace and goodwill, but comes one cropper after another.
Well intended but somehow unprofessional comedy which irritates more than it amuses.
wd Jeffrey Dell *ph* Laurie Friedman *m* Antony Hopkins
☆ Jimmy Hanley, Anne Crawford, Raymond Huntley

It's Hot in Hell: see *A Monkey in Winter*

It's in the Air *
GB 1938 86m bw
ATP (Basil Dean)
US title: *George Takes the Air*
Adventures of an accident-prone RAF recruit.
Amiable star comedy with good situations and songs.
wd Anthony Kimmins *ph* Gordon Dines, Ronald Neame
☆ *George Formby,* Garry Marsh, Polly Ward, Julien Mitchell, Jack Hobbs, Hal Gordon

It's in the Bag: see *L'Affaire est dans le Sac (1932)*

It's in the Bag **
US 1945 87m bw
(UA)
GB title: *The Fifth Chair*
The owner of a flea circus seeks a legacy hidden in one of five chairs which have been sold to a variety of people.
Patchily amusing, star-studded comedy which was also filmed as Keep Your Seats Please *and* The Twelve Chairs. *Full enjoyment requires some knowledge of American radio characters.*
w Jay Dratler, Alma Reville *d* Richard Wallace *ph* Russell Metty *m* Werner Heymann
☆ *Fred Allen,* Binnie Barnes, *Jack Benny,* Robert Benchley, Don Ameche, Victor Moore, Rudy Vallee, William Bendix, Jerry Colonna
'An untidy piece that doesn't make the most of itself but is full of fun.' – *Richard Mallett, Punch*

It's Love Again *
GB 1936 83m bw
Gaumont (Michael Balcon)

A chorus girl poses as a socialite who has hit the headlines without ever existing.
Delightfully dated comedy musical.
w Lesser Samuels, Marion Dix, Austin Melford *d Victor Saville* *ph* Glen MacWilliams *m* Louis Levy, Bretton Byrd *md* Louis Levy *ad* Alfred Junge *ed* A. L. Barnes *songs* Harry Woods, Sam Coslow
☆ *Jessie Matthews,* Robert Young, Sonnie Hale, Ernest Milton, Robb Wilton, Sara Allgood, Athene Seyler, Cyril Raymond
'Mr Saville has directed it with speed, efficiency and a real sense of the absurd.' – *Graham Greene*

'The tops in topsy-turvy romance!'
It's Love I'm After *
US 1937 90m bw
Warner (Harry Joe Brown)
A beloved stage star couple fight like cat and dog behind the scenes.
Amusing romantic farce which has worn rather less well than might have been expected but does present two stars at their peak.
w Casey Robinson *d* Archie Mayo *ph* James Van Trees *m* Heinz Roemheld
☆ *Bette Davis, Leslie Howard,* Olivia de Havilland, Patric Knowles, Eric Blore, George Barbier, Spring Byington, Bonita Granville, E. E. Clive
'Smash comedy hit. Arrange extra playing time for this one.' – *Variety*
'One of the most delightful and diverting comedies the madcap cinema has yet turned out.' – *New York World Telegram*
'Proceeds like a somewhat deranged *Taming of the Shrew* ... [BD and LH] are surrounded by that set of millionaires, valets and heiresses that were at one time as much of a convention in American comedy as the fops of Restoration theatre.' – *American Film Institute*

It's Magic: see *Romance on the High Seas*

It's My Party
US 1996 110m DeLuxe
UA/Opala (Joel Thurm, Randal Kleiser)

A handsome Los Angeles architect, who discovers that he is HIV-positive and facing imminent death, decides to end his life with a two-day party.
A sentimental comedy with the most prolonged death-bed scene since the departure of Little Nell; those who can identify with its protagonist will enjoy it most.
wd Randal Kleiser *ph* Bernd Heinl *m* Basil Poledouris *pd* Clark Hunter *ed* Ila von Hasperg
☆ Eric Roberts, Gregory Harrison, Margaret Cho, Bruce Davison, Lee Grant, Devon Gummersall, Marlee Matlin, Roddy McDowall, Olivia Newton-John, Bronson Pinchot, George Segal, Dennis Christopher, Sally Kellerman
'Not since Tom Sawyer attended his own funeral has there been such an orgy of weepy self-congratulation.' – *Stephen Farber, Movieline*

It's My Turn
US 1980 90m Metrocolor
Columbia/Rastar/Martin Elfand

A lady mathematics professor decides to seize her chances when she falls for the son of her father's new wife.
Unattractive and rather uninteresting comedy-drama with strong overtones of women's lib.
w Eleanor Bergstein *d* Claudia Weill *ph* Bill Butler *m* Patrick Williams
☆ Jill Clayburgh, Michael Douglas, Charles Grodin, Beverly Garland, Steven Hill

It's Never Too Late
GB 1956 95m Eastmancolor
Park Lane/ABP
A mother considered dull by her family starts a new career as a scriptwriter.
Acceptable but quite unexciting matinée comedy.
w Edward Dryhurst *play* Felicity Douglas *d* Michael McCarthy
☆ Phyllis Calvert, Guy Rolfe, Susan Stephen, Patrick Barr, Delphi Lawrence, Sarah Lawson, Peter Hammond

It's Never Too Late to Mend
GB 1937 67m bw
George King
An evil squire schemes for the hand of the farmer's beautiful daughter.
Archetypal melodrama of the 'Fie, Sir Jasper' school, mainly interesting in this version for the antics of its heavy-breathing star.
w H. F. Maltby *play* Charles Reade, Arthur Shirley *d* David MacDonald *ph* Hone Glendinning
☆ *Tod Slaughter,* Marjorie Taylor, Jack Livesey, Lawrence Hanray

It's Not Cricket
GB 1949 77m bw
GFD/Gainsborough (Betty Box)
Bowler-hatted officers catch a Nazi spy.
Over-spoofed comedy which barely allows the stars a real chance.
w Gerard Bryant, Lyn Lockwood, Bernard MacNab *d* Alfred Roome, Roy Rich *ph* Gordon Lang *m* Arthur Wilkinson
☆ Basil Radford, Naunton Wayne, Maurice Denham, Susan Shaw, Nigel Buchanan, Diana Dors

It's Not Just You Murray! *
US 1964 16m bw
New York University

A crook describes how he made it to the top.
An exuberant short, revealing Scorsese's interest in American low-life and European film directors, expressed here in a light-hearted style with an ironic voice-over that rarely matches the truth of what is shown on-screen.
w Martin Scorsese, Mardik Martin *d* Martin Scorsese *ph* Richard H. Coll *m* Richard H. Coll *ed* Eli F. Bleich
☆ Ira Rubin, Sam DeFazio, Andrea Martin, Catherine Scorsese
† It was released on video with three other shorts under the title *4 x Scorsese*.

It's Not the Size that Counts: see *Percy's Progress*

It's Only Money: see *Double Dynamite (1951)*

It's Only Money
US 1962 84m bw
Paramount/York/Jerry Lewis Productions (Paul Jones)
A TV repair mechanic hampers his detective friend in a search for a missing heir, which turns out to be himself.
Patchy mystery spoof with the star in rather better form than usual, and a memorable scene in which he is chased by an army of lawnmowers.
w John Fenton Murray *d* Frank Tashlin *ph* W. Wallace Kelley *m* Walter Scharf
☆ Jerry Lewis, Zachary Scott, Joan O'Brien, Jesse White, Jack Weston

It's That Man Again **
GB 1942 84m bw
GFD/Gainsborough (Edward Black)
The Mayor of Foaming-at-the-Mouth puts on a show to save a bombed theatre.
Smart, fast-moving comedy which no longer seems particularly funny in itself but is an invaluable record of the characters and wisecracks of a radio show which proved a prime morale booster during World War II.
w Howard Irving Young, Ted Kavanagh d Walter Forde ph Basil Emmott *m* Hans May *ad* W. Murton *ed* R. E. Dearing
☆ Tommy Handley, Jack Train, Greta Gynt, Dino Galvani, Dorothy Summers, Horace Percival, Sidney Keith, Clarence Wright

It's Tough to be Famous
US 1932 81m bw
First National
A young naval hero finds that fame destroys his private life.
Unco-ordinated comedy-drama.
w Robert Lord, Mary McCall Jnr *d* Alfred E. Green
☆ Douglas Fairbanks Jnr, Mary Brian, Walter Catlett, J. Carrol Naish
'Lightweight feature possessing sufficient entertainment value to give theatres a moderate week.' – *Variety*

Ivan Groznyi: see *Ivan the Terrible*

Ivan the Terrible **
USSR 1942 100m bw some Agfacolor in part two
Mosfilm
original title: *Ivan Groznyi*
The life of a 16th-century tsar.
A heavy-going film overflowing with grim, gloomy and superbly composed images: the plot is by the way, and part two (released in 1946 and also known as The Boyars' Plot*) is not up to the standard of part one, in which the coronation sequence alone is a masterpiece of cinema.*
ph Edouard Tissé (exteriors), Andrei Moskvin (interiors) *m Sergei Prokofiev ad Isaac Shpinel, L. Naumova wd/ed Sergei Eisenstein*
☆ Nikolai Cherkassov, Ludmilla Tselikovskaya, Serafima Birman
'A visual opera, with all of opera's proper disregard of prose-level reality … an extraordinarily bold experiment, fascinating and beautiful to look at.' – *James Agee*

Ivanhoe *
GB 1952 106m Technicolor
MGM (Pandro S. Berman)
Derring-do among the knights of medieval England.
Tolerable, big-budget spectacular based on Sir Walter Scott's novel.
w Noel Langley, Aeneas Mackenzie *d* Richard Thorpe *ph* F. A. Young *m* Miklos Rozsa
☆ Robert Taylor, Joan Fontaine, Elizabeth Taylor, Emlyn Williams, George Sanders, Robert Douglas, Finlay Currie, Felix Aylmer, Francis de Wolff, Guy Rolfe, Norman Wooland, Basil Sydney
† After refusing to co-operate with the House UnAmerican Activities Committee, screenwriter Marguerite Roberts was sacked by MGM and her name excluded from the credits.
best picture; F. A. Young; Miklos Rozsa

Ivanovo Detstvo: see *Ivan's Childhood*

Ivan's Childhood ***
USSR 1962 95m bw
Mosfilm (G. Kuznetsov)
original title: *Ivanovo Detstvo*
A vengeful 12-year-old escapes from a concentration camp and joins the partisans after his family is killed by the Nazis.
Probably Tarkovsky's most accessible film, a tragic tale beautifully told.
w Vladimir Bogomolov, Mikhail Papava *novel* Vladimir Bogomolov *d Andrei Tarkovsky ph* Vadim Yusov *m* Vyacheslav Ovchinnikov *ad* Evgeni Cherniaev *ed* G. Natanson
☆ Kolya Burlyaev, Irma Takovskaya, Valentin Zubkov, E. Zharikov, S. Krylov, Nikolai Grinko, L. Malyavina, Andrey Mikhalkov Konchalovsky
'The film is not disfigured by the unnaturally cheery or the conventionally hysterical. With one blow it annuls a whole cinémathèque of the war films of all lands.' – *Ivor Montagu, Sight and Sound*
† It won the Golden Lion for best film at the Venice Film Festival in 1962.

'There's a fine line between success and excess.'
Ivansxtc **
US 2000 93m DeLuxe
Metro Tartan/Rhino (Lisa Enos)
A successful agent with a large appetite for sex and drugs discovers that he has incurable cancer just as he pulls off an important deal.
A jaundiced look at Hollywood and its lack of soul, shot in murky video by its disillusioned director. It gains immeasurably from Houston's seductive performance as the agent.
w Bernard Rose, Lisa Enos *novella The Death of Ivan Illyich* by Leo Tolstoy *d* Bernard Rose *ph* Bernard Rose *m* Wagner *ed* Bernard Rose
☆ *Danny Huston* (Ivan Beckman), Peter Weller (Don West), Lisa Enos (Charlotte White), Joanne Duckman (Marcia Beckman), Angela Featherstone (Amanda Hill), Caroleen Feeney (Rosemary Kramer), Valeria Golino (Constanza Vero), James Merendino (Danny McTeague)
'Harrowing, astonishingly caustic, and nigh-on essential viewing.' – *Daily Telegraph*
'A darkly brilliant movie: tight and bunched and hostile as a fist.' – *Peter Bradshaw, Guardian*

I've Always Loved You
US 1946 116m Technicolor
Republic
GB title: *Concerto*
A brilliant pianist becomes jealous of his girl pupil, despite his love for her.
High-flown romantic tosh with music, an unusual departure for this studio; most notable for Arthur Rubinstein on the sound track.
w Borden Chase *d* Frank Borzage *ph* Tony Gaudio *m* Walter Scharf
☆ Philip Dorn, Catherine McLeod, Felix Bressart, Maria Ouspenskaya, William Carter

I've Got Your Number
US 1934 68m bw
Warner
Telephone service engineers help prove a girl innocent of burglary.
Cheerful, fast-moving programmer typical of its studio at the time.
w Warren Duff, Sidney Sutherland *d* Ray Enright *ph* Arthur Todd *ad* Esdras Hartley *ed* Clarence Kolster
☆ Joan Blondell, Pat O'Brien, Allen Jenkins, Glenda Farrell, Eugene Pallette

I've Gotta Horse
GB 1965 92m Technicolor Techniscope
Warner/Windmill (Larry Parnes, Kenneth Hume)
aka: *Wonderful Day*
An animal-loving pop singer becomes a racehorse owner.
A failed attempt to turn an English rocker into a family entertainer; the songs are trite and the script triter.
w Ronald Wolfe, Ronald Chesney *story* Kenneth Hume, Larry Parnes *d* Kenneth Hume *ph* Ernest Steward *m/ly* David Heneker, John Taylor *md* Michael Leander *ch* Ross Taylor *ad* Scott McGregor *ed* Ernest Hosler
☆ Billy Fury, Michael Medwin, Amanda Barrie, Bill Fraser, Jon Pertwee, Fred Emney, Leslie Dwyer, Peter Gilmore, Marjorie Rhodes, The Bachelors

I've Heard the Mermaids Singing *
Canada 1987 84m colour
Contemporary/Electric/Ontario Arts Council/Canada Council/National Film Board/Ontario Film Development Corp/Telefilm Canada (Patricia Rozema)
An untalented woman falls in love with the owner of the art gallery where she works.
Gentle, quirky and enjoyable romance.
wd Patricia Rozema *ph* Douglas Koch *m* Mark Korven *ad* Valanne Ridgeway *ed* Patricia Rozema
☆ Sheila McCarthy, Ann-Marie MacDonald, John Evans, Brenda Kamino, Richard Monette

I've Lived Before
US 1956 82m bw
U-I (Howard Christie)
After a plane crash, the pilot recovers but believes himself to be another airman who died in 1918.
Dullish, talky drama which wastes its interesting reincarnation theme.
w Norman Jolley, William Talman *d* Richard Bartlett *ph* Maury Gertsman *m* Herman Stein *ad* Alexander Golitzen, Richard H. Riedel, Alfred Sweeney *ed* Milton Carruth, Fred MacDowell
☆ Jock Mahoney, Leigh Snowden, Ann Harding, John McIntire, Raymond Bailey, Jerry Paris

Ivory Hunter: see *Where No Vultures Fly*

Ivy *
US 1947 99m bw
Universal (William Cameron Menzies)
In Edwardian society England, a lady poisoner gets her come-uppance.
Curiously ineffective period thriller in which the star is the elegant but artificial production design: the script is deadly dull.
w Charles Bennett *novel* Mrs Belloc Lowndes *d Sam Wood ph Russell Metty m* Daniele Amfitheatrof *pd William Cameron Menzies*
☆ Joan Fontaine, Herbert Marshall, Patric Knowles, Richard Ney, Cedric Hardwicke, Lucile Watson, Sara Allgood, Henry Stephenson, Rosalind Ivan, Lillian Fontaine, Una O'Connor, Isobel Elsom, Alan Napier, Paul Cavanagh, Gavin Muir and also Norma Varden
'The real star is whoever was responsible for the dressing, setting, lighting and shooting, and that, I infer from past performance, is the producer, William Cameron Menzies.' – *James Agee*

J

'He's a District Attorney. He will risk his life, the lives of his family, everything he holds dear for the one thing he holds sacred ... the truth.'

JFK **

US 1991 189m DuArt Panavision

Warner/Le Studio Canal/Regency Enterprises/Alcor (A. Kitman Ho, Oliver Stone)

New Orleans DA Jim Garrison investigates the assassination of President Kennedy and uncovers what amounts to a *coup d'état* to kill him because he wanted to pull out of Vietnam.

Bad history and a bullying, though engrossing, movie, mixing fact and dubious speculation indiscriminately.

w Oliver Stone, Zachary Sklar *book* On the Trail of the Assassins by Jim Garrison; *Crossfire: The Plot That Killed Kennedy* by Jim Marrs *d* Oliver Stone *ph* Robert Richardson *m* John Williams *pd* Victor Kempster *ed* Joe Hutshing, Pietro Scalia

☆ Kevin Costner, Sissy Spacek, Joe Pesci, Tommy Lee Jones, Gary Oldman, Jay O. Sanders, Michael Rooker, Laurie Metcalf, Gary Grubbs, John Candy, Jack Lemmon, Walter Matthau, Ed Asner, Donald Sutherland, Kevin Bacon and also Brian Doyle-Murray, Sally Kirkland, Jim Garrison

'A rebuke to official history and a challenge to continue investigating the crime of the century, Oliver Stone's *JFK* is electric muckraking filmmaking.' – *Variety*

'The first thing to be said about *JFK* is that it is a great movie, and the next is that it is one of the worst great movies ever made. It is great in spite of itself, and such greatness owes more to the moxie of the director than to his special talents.' – *Norman Mailer, Vanity Fair*

'Courageous, gripping, reckless ... the culmination or apotheosis of the paranoid political thriller.' – *Philip French, Observer*

'Shortchanges the audience and at the end plays like a bait-and-switch scam.' – *Vincent Canby, New York Times*

Robert Richardson; editing

film; Oliver Stone; Tommy Lee Jones; Oliver Stone, Zachary Sklar (screenplay adaptation); John Williams; sound

J. R.: see *Who's That Knocking at My Door*

J. W. Coop *

US 1971 112m Eastmancolor

Columbia/Robertson and Associates (Cliff Robertson)

After ten years in prison, a rodeo rider returns to his home town.

Well-made but rather inconsequential drama with attractive locations.

w Cliff Robertson, Gary Cartwright, Bud Shrake *d* Cliff Robertson *ph* Frank Stanley *m* Don Randi, Louie Shelton

☆ Cliff Robertson, Cristina Ferrare, Geraldine Page, R. G. Armstrong

Jabberwocky

GB 1977 101m Technicolor

Umbrella (John Goldstone, Sandy Lieberson)

A medieval cooper's apprentice is mistaken for a prince and slays the dragon which is terrorizing the neighbourhood.

An intellectual Carry On film, with very little more taste and a great deal more unpleasant imagery. Despite much re-editing, the laughs are very intermittent.

w Charles Alverson, Terry Gilliam *d* Terry Gilliam *ph* Terry Bedford *m* De Wolfe *pd* Roy Smith

☆ Michael Palin, Max Wall, Deborah Fallender, Warren Mitchell, John Le Mesurier, Harry H. Corbett, Rodney Bewes, Bernard Bresslaw

'The constant emphasis on blood, excrement, dismemberment and filth ultimately becomes rather wearing.' – *Michael Billington, Illustrated London News*

J'Accuse *

France 1939 95m bw

Forrester-Parant

A scientist intends his invention to end war; when it is put to a contrary purpose, he calls the war dead to rise from their graves and accuse humanity.

Stern, well acted, but (as it proved) ineffective propaganda.

wd Abel Gance

☆ Victor Francen, Jean Max, Renée Devillers

Jack

US 1996 113m Technicolor

Buena Vista/Hollywood/American Zoetrope/Great Oaks (Ricardo Mestres, Fred Fuchs, Francis Ford Coppola)

A 10-year-old boy, who has a rare condition that means he has the body of a 40-year-old, goes to school for the first time.

An unbelievably bad, totally risible movie played all out for sentimentality; it represents a regrettable infantile regression by its director and star.

w James DeMonaco, Gary Nadeau *d* Francis Ford Coppola *ph* John Toll *m* Michael Kamen *pd* Dean Tavoularis *ed* Barry Malkin

☆ Robin Williams, Diane Lane, Jennifer Lopez, Brian Kerwin, Fran Drescher, Bill Cosby, Michael McKean

'It's hard to shake the feeling that Coppola has become a hack in an artist's body.' – *Owen Gleiberman, Entertainment Weekly*

Jack Ahoy!

GB 1934 82m bw

Gaumont (Michael Balcon)

An accident-prone naval rating routs bandits and wins the girl.

Tailor-made star comedy with skilful moments.

w Jack Hulbert, Leslie Arliss, Gerard Fairlie, Austin Melford *story* Sidney Gilliat, J. O. C. Orton *d* Walter Forde *ph* Bernard Knowles *m* Bretton Byrd *ed* Ralph Kemplen

☆ Jack Hulbert, Nancy O'Neil, Alfred Drayton, Tamara Desni

'Mr Hulbert is equal to all his occasions ... his abounding energy and high spirits are never monotonous or wearisome.' – *E. V. Lucas, Punch*

'Sometimes ... It's The Little Things In Life That Bring People Together'

Jack & Sarah

GB/France 1995 110m colour

Polygram/British Screen/Canal/Granada TV/ Mainstream (Pippa Cross, Simon Channing-Williams, Janette Day)

A lawyer whose wife dies in childbirth tries to cope with bringing up his baby daughter.

Moderately entertaining, though unmemorable, comedy with romantic overtones, small in scope and ambition.

wd Tim Sullivan *ph* Jean Yves Escoffier *m* Simon Boswell *pd* Christopher J. Bradshaw *ed* Lesley Walker

☆ Richard E. Grant, Samantha Mathis, Judi Dench, Ian McKellen, Eileen Atkins, Cherie Lunghi, Imogen Stubbs, David Swift, Kate Hardie

'Good for an easy laugh and a warm glow, but it lacks the sharpness and dexterity of the best British comedies.' – *Geoff Brown, The Times*

Jack and the Beanstalk

US 1952 78m Supercinecolor

Warner/Alex Gottlieb

A babysitter dreams the story he is reading aloud.

Rather feeble star comedy aimed entirely at the kiddie set, and with none of the familiar routines. The 'bookends', as is customary, are in black and white.

w Nat Curtis *d* Jean Yarbrough *ph* George Robinson *m* Heinz Roemheld

☆ Bud Abbott, Lou Costello, Buddy Baer, Dorothy Ford, William Farnum

Jack Be Nimble

New Zealand 1992 95m colour

Metro Tartan/Essential/New Zealand Film Commission (Jonathan Dowling, Kelly Rogers)

An unhappy youth, separated from his psychic sister, invents a machine to hypnotize and kill his cruel, adopted parents, but their spirits seek revenge.

Ghoulish and disturbing horror, offering nothing in the way of comfort.

wd Garth Maxwell *ph* Donald Duncan *m* Chris Neal *pd* Grant Major *ed* John Gilbert *sp* Kevin Chisnall

☆ Alexis Arquette, Sarah Smuts-Kennedy, Bruno Lawrence, Tony Barry, Elizabeth Hawthorne, Brenda Simmons, Gilbert Goldie

'This deeply weird melodrama ... at once affecting, funny and horrifying.' – *Kim Newman, Empire*

'Miracles Can Happen.'

Jack Frost

US 1998 101m Technicolor Panavision

Warner (Irving Azoff, Mark Canton)

A dead rock singer comes back to life as a snowman built by his 12-year-old son.

Gruesomely sentimental tale of male bonding.

w Mark Steven Johnson, Steve Bloom, Jonathan Roberts, Jeff Cesario *d* Troy Miller *ph* Laszlo Kocacs *m* Trevor Rabin *pd* Mayne Berke *ed* Lawrence Jordan

☆ Michael Keaton, Kelly Preston, Mark Addy, Joseph Cross, Andy Lawrence, Eli Marienthal, Will Rothhaar

'Any adults in the audience will find themselves fighting for breath beneath the film's avalanche-weight of sentiment. Pure slush.' – *Tom Shone, Sunday Times*

Jack London

US 1943 93m bw

Samuel Bronston/United Artists

Jack London seeks various kinds of adventure, writes a book about the Klondike, and warns the world of the Japanese menace.

Occasionally bright but generally faltering biopic, obviously made on the cheap.

w Ernest Pascal *d* Alfred Santell

☆ Michael O'Shea, Susan Hayward, Osa Massen, Harry Davenport, Virginia Mayo, Jonathan Hale

Frederick E. Rich (music)

Jack of All Trades *

GB 1936 76m bw

Gainsborough (Michael Balcon)

A cheerful con man talks his way into a top job in an international firm.

Odd amalgam of star comedy, musical numbers of the Astaire/Rogers type, shafts of satire from the original play, and finally some flat-footed farce. Certainly worth a look.

w Jack Hulbert, Austin Melford, J. O. C. Orton *play* Youth at the Helm by Hubert Griffith, Paul Vulpuis *d* Jack Hulbert, Robert Stevenson *ph* Charles Van Enger *md* Louis Levy *ad* Vetchinsky *ed* T. R. Fisher

☆ Jack Hulbert, Gina Malo, Robertson Hare, Athole Stewart, Felix Aylmer, H. F. Maltby

'The film degenerates into nothing but the jutting jaw and the permanent grin, the same memory one takes away from all Mr Hulbert's films.' – *Graham Greene*

Jack of Diamonds

US/West Germany 1967 105m Metrocolor

MGM/Harris/Bavaria Atelier

A retired jewel thief introduces a brilliant pupil into society.

Repetitive and rather glum comedy-drama which perks up occasionally.

w Jack de Witt, Sandy Howard *d* Don Taylor *ph* Ernst Wild *m* Peter Thomas

☆ George Hamilton, Joseph Cotten, Marie Laforet, Maurice Evans, Wolfgang Preiss, Lilli Palmer, Carroll Baker, Zsa Zsa Gabor

Jack Slade

US 1953 90m bw

Allied Artists

GB title: *Slade*

A Western gunman becomes a psychopathic killer.

Cliché-ridden but rather brutish Western, thought sensationally violent at the time.

w Warren Douglas *d* Harold Schuster *ph* William Sickner *m* Paul Dunlap

☆ Mark Stevens, Dorothy Malone, Barton MacLane, John Litel, Paul Langton, Harry Shannon

'A Father. Two Sons. A Love Story.'

'Every Family Needs A Hero.'

Jack the Bear

US 1993 99m DeLuxe Super 35

TCF/American Filmworks/Lucky Dog (Bruce Gilbert)

In the 1970s, following the death of his wife, an actor begins to drink heavily as he tries to cope with his two young sons and unbalanced neighbour.

Family drama that veers towards melodrama without becoming very interesting.

w Steven Zaillian *novel* Dan McCall *d* Marshall Herskovitz *ph* Fred Murphy *m* James Horner *pd* Lilly Kilvert *ed* Steven Rosenblum

☆ Danny DeVito, Robert J. Steinmiller Jnr, Miko Hughes, Gary Sinise, Art LaFleur, Stefan Gierasch, Erica Yohn, Andrea Marcovicci

'Its effect is that of a TV series that has been telescoped and packed, with each of its rather glib resolutions, into an hour and a half. Despite a surfeit of material, nothing is thorny enough to sustain and the result is a long haul.' – *Amanda Lipman, Sight and Sound*

Jack the Giant Killer **

US 1961 94m Technicolor

Zenith/Edward Small (Robert E. Kent)

Demon Pendragon kidnaps the princess of Cornwall but she is rescued by a farmer's son.

Very creditable fairy tale, with the right style and atmosphere assisted by vigorous acting, good pace and excellent trick effects. Unfortunately it turned out rather scary for a child audience and so fell between two stools.

w Orville Hampton, Nathan Juran d Nathan Juran ph David S. Horsley m Paul Sawtell, Bert Shefter *ad Fernando Carere, Frank McCoy sp Howard Anderson*

☆ Kerwin Mathews, Judi Meredith, *Torin Thatcher, Don Beddoe*, Walter Burke, Barry Kelley

'He baffled the great Scotland Yard, the celebrated Arthur Conan Doyle, and Robert Louis Stevenson!'

Jack the Ripper

GB 1958 84m bw

Mid Century (Baker and Berman)

In Victorian London the Ripper murders are finally attributed to a demented surgeon.

film suitable for family viewing · VHS video-cassette for the British PAL system · VHS video-cassette for the British PAL system in wide screen-format · Video cassette in a computer-colourised version · American NTSC video-cassette · Laser disc

Flat and rather flabby treatment of a cause célèbre, saved by a reasonably convincing period look.
w Jimmy Sangster *m* Stanley Black *d/ph* Robert S. Baker, Monty Berman
☆ Ewen Solon, Lee Patterson, Eddie Byrne, Betty McDowall, John Le Mesurier

The Jackal
US 1997 124m DeLuxe Panavision
Universal/Mutual/Alphaville (James Jacks, Sean Daniel, Michael Caton-Jones, Kevin Jarre)
In revenge for his brother's death at the hands of the FBI, a Russian gangster hires a top assassin, a master of disguise, to kill a leading American.
Dull thriller, in which an audience is expected to care that someone appears to be planning to shoot the head of the FBI, while he is hunted by an IRA killer, a Basque terrorist and a former KGB agent.
w Chuck Pfarrer *screenplay The Day of the Jackal by Kenneth Ross* *d* Michael Caton-Jones *ph* Karl Walter Lindenlaub *m* Carter Burwell *pd* Michael White *ed* Jim Clark
☆ Bruce Willis, Richard Gere, Sidney Poitier, Diane Venora, Tess Harper, J. K. Simmons, Mathilda May, Stephen Spinella
'An involving high-tech thriller that occasionally hits peaks of pulsating excitement.' – *Variety*
'Such a banal and redundant blockbuster, one senses there was no reason to make it, other than the desire to cash in on the stars' names.' – *David Tse, Sight and Sound*

Jackass Mail
US 1942 80m bw
MGM (John Considine Jnr)
A horse thief marries the proprietress of a gambling saloon in the hope of hijacking her mail line, but she reforms him.
Boisterously conceived but anaemically scripted Western comedy with the stars in full throttle.
w Lawrence Hazard *d* Norman Z. McLeod *ph* Clyde de Vinna *m* David Snell, Earl Brent
☆ Wallace Beery, Marjorie Main, J. Carrol Naish, Darryl Hickman, William Haade, Hobart Cavanaugh
'This time at least they are repeating their variation on the Min-and-Bill routine among companions whose resemblance to burlesque is as unabashed as their own.' – *Bosley Crowther, New York Times*

'Do not attempt this at home'
Jackass The Movie
US 2002 85m DeLuxe
Paramount/MTV/Dickhouse/Lynch Siderow (Jeff Tremaine, Spike Jonze, Johnny Knoxville)
A group of young men indulge in a series of tasteless pranks and damgerous stunts.
A movie version of a TV series that is an outgrowth, or possibly a carbuncle, from so-called reality television. Those who like to watch grown men behaving badly while risking injury will love it.
d Jeff Tremaine *ph* Dimitry Elyashkevich *ed* Liz Ewart, Mark Hansen, Kristine Young
☆ Johnny Knoxville, Bam Margera, Chris Pontius, Steve-O, Dave England, Ryan Dunn, Jason Preston Lacyn 'Wee Man' Acuna
'Quite possibly the most exuberantly distasteful hodgepodge of beery anarchy and death-wishing irresponsibility ever unleashed by a major Hollywood distrib.' – *Joe Leydon, Variety*
'This plotless, crudely videotaped collection of moronic stunts is a movie in the same sense that those hideous, velvet depictions of Elvis are paintings.' – *Lou Lumenick, New York Post*

Jackboot Mutiny
Germany 1955 77m bw
Arca-Ariston
original title: *Es Geschah am 20 Juli*
An account of the army officers' plot to assassinate Hitler.
Documentary-like treatment without much attempt at characterization. An important historical document nevertheless.
w W. P. Zibaso, Gustav Machaty *d* G. W. Pabst *ph* Kurt Hasse *m* Johannes Weissenbach
☆ Bernhard Wicki, Karl Ludwig Diehl, Carl Wery

Jackie Brown **
US 1997 155m CFI color
Buena Vista/Miramax/A Band Apart (Lawrence Bender)
An air stewardess outsmarts a ruthless gun-runner and the FBI.
An absorbing, if overlong, thriller, successfully combining intrigue and character development to create a satisfying mix that updates the style of the blaxploitation movies of the 70s.
wd Quentin Tarantino *novel Rum Punch* by Elmore Leonard *ph* Guillermo Navarro *pd* David Wasco *ed* Sally Menke
☆ Pam Grier, Samuel L. Jackson, Robert Forster, Bridget Fonda, Michael Keaton, Robert de Niro, Michael Bowen, Chris Tucker
'Offers an abundance of pleasures, especially in the realm of characterization and atmosphere.' – *Variety*

'Jackie Chan Fights For The World In His Biggest Action Film Ever!'
Jackie Chan's First Strike (dubbed) *
Hong Kong/US 1996 84m DeLuxe 'Scope
Entertainment/Paragon/New Line/Golden Harvest (Barbie Tung)
original title: *Jingcha Gushi 4 Zhi Jiandan Renwu*
A Hong Kong policeman becomes involved with arms dealers in Russia and Australia.
A typical Jackie Chan action film, not to be taken seriously but to be enjoyed for the panache and daring of its stunts, which are many and spectacular.
w Stanley Tong, Nick Tramontane, Greg Mellott, Elliot Tong, Doris Wang *d* Stanley Tong *ph* Jingle Ma *m* J. Peter Robinson *pd* Oliver Wong *ed* Peter Cheung, Chi Wai Yau
☆ Jackie Chan, Chen Chun Wu, Jackson Lou, Bill Tung, Jouri Petrov, Grishajeva Nonna
'Just one death-defying deed after another. But it's a sight more entertaining than films that cost a fortune and deliver only confusion.' – *Alexander Walker, London Evening Standard*

Jacknife
US 1988 103m Technicolor
Vestron/Kings Road Entertainment (Robert Schaffel, Carol Baum)
A Vietnam veteran begins a relationship with the sister of an old army friend.
Well-acted but only occasionally interesting.
w Stephen Metcalfe *play Strange Snow* by Stephen Metcalfe *d* David Jones *ph* Brian West *pd* Edward Pisoni *ed* John Bloom
☆ Robert DeNiro, Ed Harris, Kathy Baker, Charles Dutton, Elizabeth Franz, Tom Isbell, Loudon Wainwright III, Sloane Shelton, Ivan Brogger

The Jackpot **
US 1950 85m bw
TCF (Samuel G. Engel)
A suburban husband finds that life becomes complicated when winning the jackpot on a radio quiz makes him a celebrity.
Modest, skilful comedy in Hollywood's best manner.
w Phoebe and Henry Ephron *d Walter Lang* *ph* Joseph LaShelle *md* Lionel Newman
☆ *James Stewart*, Barbara Hale, James Gleason, Fred Clark, Alan Mowbray, Patricia Medina, Natalie Wood, Tommy Rettig, Robert Gist, Lyle Talbot

Jack's the Boy *
GB 1932 91m bw
Gainsborough (Michael Balcon)
US title: *Night and Day*
The police commissioner's son proves his worth in rounding up a smash-and-grab gang.
Dated but lively farce which established its star as a British box-office attraction of the 30s.
w W. P. Lipscomb *story* Jack Hulbert, Douglas Furber *d* Walter Forde *ph* Leslie Rowson *m/ly* Vivian Ellis, Douglas Furber *md* Louis Levy *ad* Vetchinsky *ed* Ian Dalrymple, John Goldman
☆ *Jack Hulbert, Cicely Courtneidge*, Francis Lister, Winifred Shotter, Peter Gawthorne, Ben Field
'A riotously funny, good, clean, honest British picture.' – *Sydney Carroll, Sunday Times*
† The film in which Hulbert sang 'The Flies Crawled Up the Window'.

Jack's Wife: see *Season of the Witch*

Jackson County Jail
US 1976 84m Metrocolor
UA/New World (Roger Corman)
A lady driver is hijacked, attacked, disbelieved by the local police, thrown into jail and raped by the jailer, whom she brains with a stool.
An exploitation piece with social pretensions which it in no way justifies: it is however quite competently entertaining in its mindlessly violent way.
w Donald Stewart *d* Michael Miller *ph* Bruce Logan *m* Loren Newkirk
☆ Yvette Mimieux, Tommy Lee Jones, Robert Carradine, Frederic Cook, Severn Darden, Howard Hesseman

Jacob's Ladder
US 1990 113m Technicolor
Tri-Star/Carolco (Alan Marshall)
A Vietnam veteran is unwittingly the subject of secret experiments with chemical weapons.
Exceedingly silly on every level, particularly in its supernatural dabblings.
w Bruce Joel Rubin *d* Adrian Lyne *ph* Jeffrey L. Kimball *m* Maurice Jarre *pd* Brian Morris *ed* Tom Rolf
☆ Tim Robbins, Elizabeth Pena, Danny Aiello, Matt Craven, Pruitt Taylor Vince, Jason Alexander, Patricia Kalember
'Dull, unimaginative and pretentious.' – *Variety*

Jacqueline *
GB 1956 93m bw
Rank (George H. Brown)
A Belfast shipyard worker cannot stand heights, takes to drink, and is helped by his small daughter.
Convincing, well-made, realistically set domestic comedy-drama.
w Patrick Kirwan, Liam O'Flaherty *d* Roy Baker *ph Geoffrey Unsworth* *m* Cedric Thorpe Davie
☆ John Gregson, Kathleen Ryan, Jacqueline Ryan, Noel Purcell, Cyril Cusack, Marie Kean, Liam Redmond, Maureen Delany

Jacqueline Susann's Once Is Not Enough: see *Once Is Not Enough*

Jacquot de Nantes **
France 1991 119m bw/colour
Cine-Tamaris/Canal/La Sept/La Sofiarp (Agnes Varda, Perrine Baudin)
Biopic of the early years of the life of director Jacques Demy, combined with clips from his films and interviews with him, based on his own memoirs.
A labour of love from Demy's wife that is both moving as a tribute and fascinating in its exploration of a youthful obsession.
wd Agnès Varda *ph* Patrick Blossier, Agnes Godard, Georges Strouve *m* Joanna Bruzdowicz *pd* Robert Nardone, Olivier Radot *ed* Marie-Jo Audiard
☆ Philippe Maron, Edouard Joubeaud, Laurent Monnier, Brigitte de Villepoix, Daniel Dublet, Guillaume Navaud
'A delightful, if overlong, depiction of the formative years of a youngster determined to make films when he grows up.' – *Variety*

Jacula: see *Female Vampire*

'Some Fantasies Go Too Far.'
Jade
US 1995 95m DeLuxe
UIP/Paramount (Robert Evans, Craig Baumgarten, Gary Adelson)
In San Francisco, an assistant DA investigates the axe murder of a millionaire and discovers evidence that links it with a former girlfriend, now married to a successful lawyer, and the Governor of California.
A bungled attempt at an erotic thriller, in which the murder makes less sense the more we are told about it; the narrative is just an excuse for a little sleaze, including irrelevant scenes of sexual activity.
w Joe Eszterhas *d* William Friedkin *ph* Andrzej Bartkowiak *m* James Horner *pd* Alex Tavoularis *ed* Augie Hess
☆ David Caruso, Linda Fiorentino, Chazz Palminteri, Michael Biehn, Richard Crenna, Donna Murphy, Ken King
'Writer Joe Eszterhas's follow-up to his *Showgirls* fiasco is every bit as hopeless, and this time he takes some good actors down with him.' – *Bruce Diones, New Yorker*
'For sheer nastiness, allied to a lush, well-decorated camera style, William Friedkin's *Jade* … takes some beating.' – *Derek Malcolm, Guardian*

Jag är nyfiken – gul: see *I Am Curious – Yellow*

Jagged Edge **
US 1985 108m Metrocolor
Columbia/Martin Ransohoff
A lady lawyer defends a newspaper publisher who may or may not be guilty of murder.
Well-crafted courtroom mystery with fashionable violence and a few unexpected twists.
w Joe Eszterhas *d* Richard Marquand *ph* Matthew F. Leonetti *m* John Barry *pd* Gene Callahan *ed* Sean Barton, Conrad Buff
☆ Jeff Bridges, Glenn Close, Peter Coyote, Robert Loggia, Leigh Taylor-Young, John Dehner
Robert Loggia (supporting actor)

Jaguar Lives
US 1979 90m Eastmancolor
Jaguar (Sandy Howard)
Exploits of an international secret agent with skill in the martial arts.
Flashy, violent, James Bond rip-off, years behind its time.
w Yabo Yablonsky *d* Ernest Pintoff *ph* John Cabrera *m* Robert Ragland
☆ Joe Lewis, Christopher Lee, Donald Pleasence, Capucine, Barbara Bach, Joseph Wiseman, Woody Strode, John Huston

J'ai Épousé une Ombre: see *I Married a Dead Man*

Jailbirds: see *Pardon Us*

Jailhouse Rock *
US 1957 96m bw Cinemascope
MGM (Pandro S. Berman)
An ex-convict becomes a pop star.
Reasonably competent star vehicle, sourer in tone than most.
w Guy Trosper *story* Ned Young *d* Richard Thorpe *ph* Robert Bronner *md* Jeff Alexander
☆ Elvis Presley, Judy Tyler, Mickey Shaughnessy, Vaughn Taylor, Dean Jones

Jakarta
Indonesia/US 1988 95m colour Panavision
Medusa/Parkit Films/Troma
An ex-CIA agent is taken to Indonesia to put an end to a local big-time drug dealer.
Inconsequential thriller.
w Charles Kaufman, Ralph Soll *d* Charles Kaufman *ph* Robert Chappell, Kasiyo Hadiwijoyo *m* Jay Chattaway *pd* Susan Kaufman *ed* Michael Spence, Norman Benny
☆ Christopher Noth, Sue Francis Pai, Franz Tumbuan, Ronald Hunter, Zoraya Perucha, David Sharp, David Gale

Jake Speed
US 1986 100m Technicolor
Crawford/Lane/Foster/Balcor
A famous hero tracks down an American girl abducted in Paris.
Adventure hokum with spoof elements which don't come off.
w Wayne Crawford, Andrew Lane *d* Andrew Lane *ph* Bryan Loftus *m* Mark Snow *pd* Norman Baron
☆ Wayne Crawford, John Hurt, Dennis Christopher, Karen Kopins, Leon Ames

'When all hope was lost, he invented it.'

Jakob the Liar *

US 1999 114m DeLuxe

Columbia/Blue Wolf/Kasso (Marsha Garces Williams, Steven Haft)

In Nazi-occupied Poland, a Jewish café owner keeps hope in the ghetto high by pretending to own a radio and relaying news of a Russian advance.

Doggedly earnest drama with an ironic undertone, probably too restrained in its treatment to have a wide appeal.

w Peter Kassovitz, Didier Decoin *book* Jurek Becker *d* Peter Kassovitz *ph* Elemer Ragalyi *m* Edward Shearmur *pd* Luciana Arrighi *ed* Claire Simpson

☆ Robin Williams (Jakob Heym), Alan Arkin (Frankfurter), Bob Balaban (Kowalsky), Hannah Taylor Gordon (Lina), Michael Jeter (Avron), Armin Mueller-Stahl (Kirschbaum), Liev Schreiber (Mischa), Nina Siemaszko (Rosa), Mathieu Kassovitz (Herschel), Justus von Dohnanyi (Preuss), Mark Margolis (Fajngold), Gregg Bello (Blumenthal)

'A bitterly whimsical slice of mordant Yiddish-style humor that plays more like an Eastern European fable than a piece of emotional Hollywood pandering.' – *Todd McCarthy, Variety*

'A dreadful, enervated mess.' – *Glenn Kenny, Premiere*

† The film failed at the US box-office, grossing around $5m.

Jalna

US 1935 75m bw

RKO

Episodes in the life of the Whiteoaks family.

Flat adaptation of a Canadian bestseller.

w Anthony Veiller, Garrett Fort, Larry Bachmann *novel* Mazo de la Roche *d* John Cromwell

☆ Kay Johnson, Ian Hunter, C. Aubrey Smith, Jessie Ralph, Nigel Bruce, David Manners, Peggy Wood, Halliwell Hobbes

'Nice production of a not very good adaptation.' – *Variety*

Jalsaghar: see *The Music Room*

Jamaica Inn *

GB 1939 107m bw

Mayflower (Erich Pommer)

In old Cornwall, an orphan girl becomes involved with smugglers.

Stagey, stilted adventure story which never loses its studio feel or takes fire as a Hitchcock picture. The cast keeps it interesting.

w Sidney Gilliat, Joan Harrison, J. B. Priestley *novel* Daphne du Maurier *d Alfred Hitchcock* *ph* Harry Stradling, Bernard Knowles *m* Eric Fenby *ad* Tom Morahan *ed* Robert Hamer

☆ Charles Laughton, Maureen O'Hara, Leslie Banks, Robert Newton, Emlyn Williams, Wylie Watson, Marie Ney, Morland Graham

'Should get good but not outstanding b.o. Superb direction, excellent casting, expressive playing and fine production offset an uneven screenplay.' – *Variety*

'I was irresistibly reminded of an all-star charity matinee.' – *Graham Greene*

Jamaica Run

US 1953 92m Technicolor

Paramount/Pine-Thomas

A search for documents, which may apportion a great house to another branch of the family, leads to murder.

Plot-bound romantic mystery in period, with elements of a Caribbean Rebecca. *Watchable medium-budget hokum.*

wd Lewis R. Foster *novel* Max Murray *ph* Lionel Lindon *m* Lucien Cailliet

☆ Ray Milland, Arlene Dahl, Wendell Corey, Patric Knowles

James and the Giant Peach **

US 1996 79m Technicolor

Guild/Disney/Allied Filmmakers (Denise di Novi, Tim Burton)

An unhappy boy goes on a magical journey inside a giant peach, accompanied by six friendly insects.

Witty stop-motion animated feature, softer-centred than Dahl's original, but still ripe with delights.

w Karey Kirkpatrick, Jonathan Roberts, Steve Bloom *novel* Roald Dahl *d* Henry Selick *ph* Pete Kozachik, Hiro Narita *m* Randy Newman *pd* Harley Jessup *ed* Stan Webb

☆ Paul Terry, Joanna Lumley, Miriam Margolyes, Pete Postlethwaite and also the voices of: Simon Callow, Richard Dreyfuss, Jane Leeves, Susan Sarandon, David Thewlis

'Can be recommended to almost anyone. It's a peach.' – *Tom Shone, Sunday Times*

Randy Newman

The James Brothers: see *The True Story of Jesse James*

The James Gang

GB 1997 99m colour

Polygram/Paragon/HandMade/BBC/Revolution (Andrew Eaton)

After her home is burned down by a loan shark, a Scottish woman and her four children head for London to be reunited with her feckless husband; the family then drives round England committing a series of petty robberies.

An unhappy mix of gritty social realism and stylized comedy; its disparate elements never come together and the result, despite some effective acting, is a dispiriting road movie.

w Stuart Hepburn *story* Andrew Eaton, Paul Lee *d* Mike Barker *ph* Benjamin Seresin *m* Bernard Butler *pd* Alice Normington *ed* Guy Bensley

☆ John Hannah, Helen McCrory, Jason Flemyng, Toni Collette, Darren Brownlie, David Brownlie, Lauren McMurray, Lauren McCracken

'As with so many recent, mediocre British films, it's the quality of the performances which partly redeems *The James Gang*.' – *Leslie Felperin, Sight and Sound*

'A Film Where Women Eat Men And Men Eat Ham.'

Jamón Jamón *

Spain 1992 91m colour

Metro Tartan/Lolafilms/Ovideo/Sogepaq (Andrés Vicente Gómez)

A wealthy mother decides she wants a local stud for herself after hiring him to seduce her son's girlfriend.

Broad and enjoyable comedy of sex and male virility, not to be taken seriously despite its downbeat, partner-swapping finale.

w Cuca Canals, Bigas Luna, Quim Monzó *d* Bigas Luna *ph* José Luis Alcaine *m* Nicola Piovani *pd* Chu Uroz, Noemi Campano *ad* Julio Esteban *ed* Teresa Font

☆ Stefania Sandrelli, Anna Galiena, Juan Diego, Penélope Cruz, Javier Bardem, Jordi Molla

'Racy and surreal farce.' – *Empire*

'His storytelling wanders too arbitrarily between slapstick eroticism and an exaggerated neo-realism to achieve any clarity of focus.' – *Philip Strick, Sight and Sound*

Jana-Aranya: see *The Middle Man*

Jane and the Lost City

GB 1988 92m colour

Blue Dolphin/Marcel-Robertson (Harry Robertson)

A girl with a penchant for stripping becomes a British agent during the Second World War.

Based on a once-famous Daily Mirror *strip cartoon, a tatty, low-budget romp of no perceptible interest, other than to students of the decline of British cinema.*

w Mervyn Haisman *story* Mervyn Haisman, Terry Marcel, Harry Robertson *d* Terry Marcel *ph* Paul Beeson *m* Harry Robertson *pd* Michael Pickwoad *ed* Alan Jones

☆ Sam Jones, Maud Adams, Jasper Carrott, Kirsten Hughes, Graham Stark, Robin Bailey, Ian Roberts, Elsa O'Toole

Jane Eyre

US 1934 62m bw

Monogram

A Poverty Row transcription of the Charlotte Brontë novel: see below.

w Adele Comandini *d* Christy Cabanne

☆ Virginia Bruce, Colin Clive, Beryl Mercer, Jameson Thomas, Aileen Pringle

'The cast appear to have considered their tasks with considerable melancholy.' – *Variety*

'A love story every woman would die a thousand deaths to live!'

Jane Eyre ***

US 1943 96m bw

TCF (William Goetz)

In Victorian times, a harshly treated orphan girl becomes governess in a mysterious Yorkshire mansion with a brooding master.

Sharply paced, reasonably faithful and superbly staged Hollywood version of Charlotte Brontë's archetypal romantic novel which stimulated so many imitations, including Rebecca.

w Aldous Huxley, Robert Stevenson, John Houseman d Robert Stevenson ph George Barnes m Bernard Herrmann ad Wiard B. Ihnen, James Basevi sp Fred Sersen

☆ *Joan Fontaine, Orson Welles,* Margaret O'Brien, *Henry Daniell,* John Sutton, Agnes Moorehead, Elizabeth Taylor, Peggy Ann Garner, Sara Allgood, Aubrey Mather, Hillary Brooke, Edith Barrett, Ethel Griffies, Barbara Everest, *John Abbott*

'A careful and tame production, a sadly vanilla-flavoured Joan Fontaine, and Orson Welles treating himself to broad operatic sculpturings of body, cloak and diction, his eyes glinting in the Rembrandt gloom, at every chance, like side orders of jelly.' – *James Agee*

'The essentials are still there; and the non-essentials, such as the gloom, the shadows, the ground mist, the rain and the storms, have been expanded and redoubled and magnified to fill up the gaps.' – *Richard Mallett, Punch*

Jane Eyre

GB 1970 110m Eastmancolor

British Lion/Omnibus/Sagittarius (Frederick H. Brogger)

A Victorian governess discovers that the master she comes to love hides a secret in his attic.

A generally lacklustre version of a classic story, enlivened by Scott's performance.

w Jack Pulman *novel* Charlotte Brontë *d* Delbert Mann *ph* Paul Beeson *m* John Williams *ad* Alex Vetchinsky *ed* Peter Boita

☆ George C. Scott, Susannah York, Ian Bannen, Jack Hawkins, Nyree Dawn Porter, Rachel Kempson, Kenneth Griffith, Peter Copley, Michele Dotrice, Clive Morton, Constance Cummings

'A pleasant if unispired reminder of Charlotte's most successful novel.' – *David Pirie, MFB*

Jane Eyre

US 1996 112m colour

Miramax/Rochester (Dyson Lovell)

In the 1820s, a governess falls in love with her secretive employer, who keeps a mystery hidden in the attic.

Glum and emotionally stolid version that fails to evoke the necessary romance.

w Hugh Whitemore, Franco Zeffirelli *novel* Charlotte Brontë *d* Franco Zeffirelli *ph* David Watkin *m* Alessio Vlad, Claudio Capponi *pd* Roger Hall *ed* Richard Marden

☆ William Hurt, Charlotte Gainsbourg, Joan Plowright, Anna Paquin, Geraldine Chaplin, Billie Whitelaw, Maria Schneider, Fiona Shaw, Elle Macpherson, John Wood, Amanda Root

'Zeffirelli's approach to period drama – faithful, four-square and flat as a miniseries – itself feels like something of a period piece.' – *Tom Shone, Sunday Times*

Janice Beard 45 WPM

GB 1999 81m Technicolor

UIP/Film Consortium/Arts Council/WAVE/Channel4/Dakota (Judy Counihan)

A Scottish woman, who hopes to find a cure for her agoraphobic mother, gets a job in London as a temporary secretary.

Dreary would-be comedy, of industrial espionage and office mishaps, that is best avoided.

w Clare Kilner, Ben Hopkins *d* Clare Kilner *ph* Richard Greatrex, Peter Thwaites *m* Paul Carr *pd* Sophie Becher *ed* Mary Finlay

☆ Eileen Walsh (Janice Beard), Rhys Ifans (Sean), Patsy Kensit (Julia), David O'Hara (O'Brien), Sandra Voe (Mimi), Frances Gray (Violet), Zita Sattar (Jane), Amelia Curtis (June)

'An unsatisfying mess.' – *Film Review*

Janice Meredith

US 1924 153m bw silent

Metro-Goldwyn/Cosmopolitan

GB title: *The Beautiful Rebel*

Vicissitudes of the coquettish daughter of a New Jersey family through the War of Independence.

Marathon melodrama not unlike Gone with the Wind *in subject matter, but of no remaining interest.*

w Lillie Hayward *novel* Paul Leicester Ford *d* E. Mason Hopper *ph* Ira H. Morgan, George Barnes *m* Deems Taylor *ad* Joseph Urban

☆ Marion Davies, Harrison Ford, Macklyn Arbuckle, Joseph Kilgour, George Nash, Tyrone Power Snr, May Vokes, W. C. Fields, Olin Howland

Janie

US 1944 106m bw

Warner (Brock Pemberton)

The teenage daughter of a middle-class American household gets into innocent scrapes with the army.

Deafening tomboy farce.

w Agnes Christine Johnston, Charles Hoffman *play* Josephine Bentham, Herschel V. Williams Jnr *d* Michael Curtiz *ph* Carl Guthrie *m/ly* Lee David, Sammy Cahn, Jule Styne *ed* Owen Marks

☆ Joyce Reynolds, Robert Hutton, Ann Harding, Edward Arnold, Robert Benchley, Claire Foley, Hattie McDaniel

† *Janie Gets Married*, made the following year and running 89m, had almost identical credits except that Joan Leslie replaced Joyce Reynolds and Dorothy Malone joined the cast.

Owen Marks

The Janitor: see *Eye Witness (1981)*

The January Man

US 1989 97m DeLuxe

UIP/MGM (Norman Jewison, Ezra Swerdlow)

A disgraced policeman tracks down a serial killer.

Ludicrously implausible thriller.

w John Patrick Shanley *d* Pat O'Connor *ph* Jerzy Zielinksi *m* Marvin Hamlisch *pd* Philip Rosenberg *ed* Lou Lombardo

☆ Kevin Kline, Susan Sarandon, Mary Elizabeth Mastrantonio, Harvey Keitel, Danny Aiello, Rod Steiger, Alan Rickman, Faye Grant, Ken Welsh

'A damp sock of a movie.' – *Washington Post*

Japón

Mexico/Spain 2001 133m colour Cinemascope

Artificial Eye/No Dream/Mantarraya/Solaris (Carlos Reygadas)

An anonymous middle-aged man arrives at a remote village with the intention of killing himself; he changes his mind after making love to the elderly woman with whom he stays.

An old-fashioned art film with a grainy texture, much uneccessary movement of the camera, the accompaniment of classical music, a non-professional cast (one of whom complains on camera about the meanness of the film company), and a gloomy ending.

wd Carlos Reygadas *ph* Diego Martinez Vignatti *m* Shostakovich, Bach *ad* Alejandro Reygadas *ed* Daniel Melguizo

☆ Alejandro Ferretis (The man), Magdalena Flores (Ascen)

'An unusually tranquillizing experience.' – *Alexander Walker*

Jarrapellejos **

Spain 1987 108m colour

Penelope/Television Española (Jose G. Blanco Sola, Jose Joaquin Aguirre)

In the early 1900s, a corrupt landowner in a small town covers up the rape and murder of a mother and daughter.

Devastating exposé of social and sexual hypocrisy, shot in a stately fashion.

w Antonio Gimenez Rico, Manuel Gutierrez Aragon *novel* Felipe Trigo *d* Antonio Gimenez Rico *ph* Jose Luis Alcaine *m* Carmelo A. Bernaola *ad* Rafael Palmero *ed* Miguel Gonzalez Sinde

☆ Antonio Ferrandis, Juan Diego, Lydia Bosch, Amparo Larrañaga, Joaquin Hinojosa, Miguel A. Rellan, Aitana Sanchez-Gijon, Carlos Tristancho, Florinda Chico, Jose Coronado

Jason and the Argonauts ***

GB 1963 104m Technicolor

Columbia/Charles H. Schneer

With help and hindrance from the gods, Jason voyages in search of the Golden Fleece and meets all kinds of monsters.

Rambling semi-classic mythological fantasy which keeps its tongue firmly in its cheek and provides a framework for some splendid stop-frame animation.

w Jan Read, Beverley Cross *d Don Chaffey ph* Wilkie Cooper *m Bernard Herrmann sp Ray Harryhausen*

☆ Todd Armstrong, Honor Blackman, Niall MacGinnis, Andrew Faulds, Nancy Kovack

Jason Goes to Hell: The Final Friday

US 1993 88m DeLuxe

New Line (Sean S. Cunningham)

Jason attempts to kill his relatives so that he can live forever.

The series ends, but does not even manage a whimper on the way out; it simply fades away into witless, boring nonsense. The most frightening moment comes at the end, with the hint that he and Freddy, hero of the Nightmare on Elm Street *series, may be teamed in a new movie.*

w Dean Lorey, Jay Huguely *d* Adam Marcus *ph* William Dill *m* Harry Manfredini *pd* W. Brooke Wheeler *ed* David Handman

☆ Jon D. LeMay, Kari Keegan, Kane Hodder, Steve Williams, Steven Culp, Erin Gray, Rusty Schwimmer

'Jason goes to hell and not a moment too soon.' – *Variety*

† The film was the ninth and last film in the *Friday the 13th* series (qv).

'Evil Gets An Upgrade'

Jason X

US 2002 92m DeLuxe

New Line/Sean S. Cunningham (Noel J. Cunningham)

In the 25th century, students aboard a spaceship find the frozen body of a serial killer, and revive it.

Gory and uninmaginative rehash of Alien.

w Todd Farmer *d* James Isaac *ph* Derrick Underschultz *m* Harry Manfredini *pd* John Dondertman *ed* David Handman *cos* Maxyne Baker

☆ Lexa Doig (Rowan), Lisa Ryder (KAY-EM 14), Chuck Campbell (Tsunaron), Jonathan Potts (Professor Lowe), Peter Mensah (Sgt Brodski), Melyssa Ade (Janessa), Kane Hodder (Jason), David Cronenberg (Dr Wimmer)

'The look and feel of this film is lower rent than any of the space travel films Roger Corma made, while pic's cast has been outfitted in the most eye-poppingly atrocious costumes this side of Starfleet Academy.' – *Scott Foundas, Variety*

Jason's Lyric *

US 1994 119m colour

Polygram/Propaganda (Doug McHenry, George Jackson)

In Houston, a hard-working television salesman is drawn into the world of crime by his love for his crooked brother and for the sister of a local gangster.

Grim drama of characters trapped by circumstance and the ghetto, but one that recycles old themes without adding much to them.

w Bobby Smith Jnr *d* Doug McHenry *ph* Francis Kenny *m* Afrika, Matt Noble *pd* Simon Dobbin *ed* Andrew Mondshein

☆ Allen Payne, Jada Pinkett, Bokeem Woodbine, Anthony 'Treach' Criss, Lisa Carson, Forest Whitaker, Suzzanne Douglas

'The soundtrack CD may find an audience, but no one should relish the film itself, a horrid collison between *West Side Story, East of Eden* and a pile of junk.' – *Geoff Brown, The Times*

'A tough film, well shot and directed but paying strict attention, above all, to the performances. Even though made with music that's obviously sellable in record form, it never resorts to out and out cliché.' – *Derek Malcolm, Guardian*

Jassy

GB 1947 102m Technicolor

GFD/Gainsborough (Sydney Box)

A gypsy servant girl falls in love with her master but is accused of murder.

Period romantic melodrama of the Man in Grey *school; poor of its kind despite high production values.*

w Dorothy and Campbell Christie, Geoffrey Kerr *novel* Norah Lofts *d* Bernard Knowles *ph* Geoffrey Unsworth *m* Henry Geehl *md* Louis Levy *ad* George Provis *ed* Charles Knott *cos* Elizabeth Haffenden

☆ Margaret Lockwood (Jassy), Patricia Roc (Dilys), Dennis Price (Christopher Hatton), Basil Sydney (Nick Helmar), Dermot Walsh (Barney Hatton), Nora Swinburne (Mrs Hatton), Linden Travers (Mrs Helmar), Ernest Thesiger (Sir Edward Follesmark), Cathleen Nesbitt (Elizabeth Twisdale), John Laurie (Woodroffe), Jean Cadell (Meggie), Clive Morton (Sir William Fennell), Grace Arnold (Maid), Maurice Denham (Jim Stoner), Alan Wheatley (Sir Edward Walker)

'As a piece of unabashed romantic hokum, I found it more and more diverting as the plot thickened.' – *Evening Standard*

Jaws **

US 1975 125m Technicolor Panavision

Universal/Zanuck-Brown (William S. Gilmore Jnr)

A man-eating shark causes havoc off the Long Island coast.

In the exploitation-hungry seventies this film took more money than any other. In itself, despite genuinely suspenseful and frightening sequences, it is a slackly narrated and sometimes flatly handled thriller with an over-abundance of dialogue and, when it finally appears, a pretty unconvincing monster.

w Peter Benchley, Carl Gottlieb *novel* Peter Benchley *d Steven Spielberg ph* Bill Butler *m John Williams ad* Joseph Alves Jnr *ed* Verna Fields

☆ *Robert Shaw, Roy Scheider, Richard Dreyfuss,* Lorraine Gary, Murray Hamilton, Carl Gottlieb

'A mind-numbing repast for sense-sated gluttons. Shark stew for the stupefied.' – *William S. Pechter*

'The opening sequences have few parallels in modern cinema; like the shower scene in *Psycho* they will haunt a whole generation.' – *Les Keyser, Hollywood in the Seventies*

Academy Award: John Williams; Verna Fields; sound

Academy Award nomination: best picture

BAFTA: John Williams

'Just when you thought it was safe to go back in the water…'

Jaws 2

US 1978 117m Technicolor Panavision

Universal/Richard Zanuck, David Brown (Joe Alves)

Another man-eating shark menaces teenagers in the Long Island resort of Amity.

Repetitive and feeble sequel aimed directly at the popcorn market.

w Carl Gottlieb, Howard Sackler, Dorothy Tristan *d* Jeannot Szwarc *ph* Michael Butler, David Butler, Michael McGowan *m* John Williams

☆ Roy Scheider, Lorraine Gary, Murray Hamilton, Joseph Mascolo, Collin Wilcox

'A manipulation of the audience, in the best sense of the term' – *Jeannot Szwarc, director*

'The third dimension is terror!'

Jaws 3-D

US 1983 99m Technicolor ArriVision 3-D

Alan Landsburg/Universal (Rupert Hitzig)

A man-eating shark turns up in a Florida theme park.

Noisy additional chapter to this string of shocks.

w Richard Matheson, Carl Gottlieb *story* Guerdon Trueblood *d* Joe Alves *ph* James A. Contner *m* Alan Parker *pd* Woods Macintosh *ed* Randy Roberts, Corky Ehlers

☆ Dennis Quaid, Bess Armstrong, Simon MacCorkindale, Louis Gossett Jnr, John Putch, Lea Thompson

Jaws: The Revenge

US 1987 100m colour Super 35

UIP/Universal (Joseph Sargent)

Superfluous fourth story in the Jaws series, almost indistinguishable from the others once you accept that the sharks are after Brody's widow.

w Michael de Guzman *d* Joseph Sargent *ph* John McPherson *m* Michael Small *pd* John Lloyd *ed* Michael Brown

☆ Lorraine Gary, Lance Guest, Mario Van Peebles, Karen Young, Michael Caine

'Hollywood Had It Coming.'

Jay and Silent Bob Strike Back

US 2001 104m DeLuxe Super 35

Buena Vista/Dimension/View Askew (Scott Mosier)

Two slackers set out to sabotage a Hollywood movie featuring comic-book characters based on themselves.

Knockabout, self-indulgent, self-referential comedy that goes round in ever-decreasing circles.

wd Kevin Smith *ph* Jamie Anderson *m* James L. Venable *pd* Robert 'Ratface' Holtzman *ed* Kevin Smith, Scott Mosier

☆ Ben Affleck (Holden/Himself), Jeff Anderson (Randal), Diedrich Bader (Security Guard), Eliza Dushku (Sissy), Shannon Elizabeth (Justice), Will Ferrell (Willenholly), Mark Hammill (Cocknocker), Ali Larter (Chrissy), Jason Lee (Brodie/Banky), Jason Mewes (Jay), Chris Rock (Chaka), Seann William Scott (Brent), Kevin Smith (Silent Bob)

'Uneven and quite messily made.' – *Derek Malcolm, Guardian*

The Jayhawkers

US 1959 110m Technicolor Vistavision

Paramount/Panama and Frank

Before the Civil War, a farmer defeats a militant posse of private raiders.

Unconvincing but rather unusual Western, flat patches alternating with striking ones.

w Melvin Frank, Joseph Petracca, Frank Fenton, A. I. Bezzerides *d* Melvin Frank *ph* Loyal Griggs *m* Jerome Moross

☆ Fess Parker, Jeff Chandler, Nicole Maurey, Henry Silva, Herbert Rudley

Jazz Comedy *

USSR 1934 93m bw

Mosfilm

original title: *Vesolye Rebyata*

A shepherd is frequently mistaken for a famous conductor.

Peripatetic comedy with many sight gags and western slapstick: Russian comedy being still a rare thing, it seems something of a revelation.

w Grigori Alexandrov, Nikolai Erdman, V. Mass *d Grigori Alexandrov ph* Vladimir Nilsen *m* Isaac Dunayevsky

☆ Lubov Orlova, Leonid Utyosov, Maria Strelkova

'The best thing that has happened to the cinema since René Clair made *The Italian Straw Hat* … a picture of almost ecstatic happiness.' – *Graham Greene*

Jazz on a Summer's Day ***

US 1959 85m DeLuxe

Galaxy/Raven (Allan Green)

Exemplary documentary about the Newport Jazz Festival, incorporating many excellent performances from the musicians involved.

Made by a famous fashion photographer, this is visually as interesting as it is musically. With its witty juxtaposition of images and sound, it remains probably the best documentary of its kind so far.

w Arnold Pearl, Albert D'Annibale *d Bert Stern ph* Bert Stern, Courtney Hafela, Ray Phealan *md* George Avakian *ed* Aram Avakian

☆ Louis Armstrong, Mahalia Jackson, Gerry Mulligan, Dinah Washington, Chico Hamilton, Anita O'Day, George Shearing, Chuck Berry, Jack Teagarden, Thelonious Monk, Big Maybelle, Sonny Stitt

'New songs and old favourites sung by Mr Jolson during the action of the story on the Vitaphone!'

The Jazz Singer ****

US 1927 89m bw

Warner

A cantor's son makes it big in show business.

Archetypal Jewish weepie which became of absorbing interest as the first talkie film (songs and a few fragments of speech) and in its way, surprisingly, is not half bad.

w Alfred A. Cohn *play* Samson Raphaelson *d Alan Crosland ph* Hal Mohr *md* Louis Silvers

☆ *Al Jolson*, May McAvoy, Warner Oland, Eugenie Besserer, Otto Lederer

'A beautiful period piece, extravagantly sentimental … yet entirely compelling in its own conviction.' – *NFT, 1969*

'*The Jazz Singer* definitely establishes the fact that talking pictures are imminent. Everyone in Hollywood can rise up and declare that they are not, and it will not alter the fact. If I were an actor with a squeaky voice I would worry.' – *Welford Beaton, The Film Spectator*

Academy Award: Special Award to Warner for producing 'the pioneer outstanding talking picture'

Academy Award nomination: Alfred A. Cohn

The Jazz Singer

US 1953 107m Technicolor

Warner (Louis F. Edelman)

Ill-considered, schmaltzy remake of the above.

w Frank Davis, Leonard Stern, Lewis Meltzer *d* Michael Curtiz *ph* Carl Guthrie *m* Max Steiner *md* Ray Heindorf

☆ Danny Thomas, Peggy Lee, Mildred Dunnock, Eduard Franz

Academy Award nomination: Ray Heindorf; Max Steiner

The Jazz Singer

US 1980 115m DeLuxe

EMI/Jerry Leider

Oddly-timed reprise of the above, with doting mum replaced by patient wife.

A good basis for a best-selling album, otherwise a pointless enterprise.

w Herbert Baker, Stephen H. Foreman *d* Richard Fleischer *ph* Isidore Mankofsky *m* Leonard Rosenman *pd* Harry Horner

☆ Neil Diamond, Laurence Olivier, Lucie Arnaz, Catlin Adams, Sully Boyar

'What is jazz to Neil Diamond and what is Neil Diamond to jazz? Old title has nothing to do with music on display here and would seem meaningless to modern audiences.' – *Variety*

Jazzboat

GB 1959 96m bw Cinemascope

Warwick/Columbia

A jazz musician pretends to be a crook and leads the police to an important gang.

Flimsy comedy with a background of pop acts. Very dated.

w Ken Hughes, John Antrobus *d* Ken Hughes *ph* Ted Moore *m* Kenneth Jones *ch* Lionel Blair

☆ Anthony Newley, Anne Aubrey, David Lodge, Lionel Jeffries, Bernie Winters, James Booth, Al Mulock, Joyce Blair, Leo McKern, Ted Heath and his Music

Je T'Aime, Je T'Aime **

France 1967 94m Eastmancolor

TCF/Parc/Fox Europa (Mag Bodard)

During experiments with a time-machine, a suicidal man relives the experience of an unhappy love affair that led him to attempt to take his own life.

A fascinating, if sometimes confusing, speculation on the nature of time and the fact that there are no second chances in life.

w Jacques Sternberg *d* Alain Resnais *ph* Jean Boffety *m* Krzysztof Penderecki, Jean-Claude Pelletier, Jean Dandeny *ad* Jacques Dugied, Auguste Pace *ed* Albert Jurgenson, Colette Leloup

☆ Claude Rich, Olga Georges-Picot, Anouk Ferjac, Annie Fargue, Bernard Fresson, Yvette Etievant

'A work that deserves to be studied and discussed: to see it is essential.' – *Gordon Gow, Films and Filming*

Je T'Aime Moi Non Plus
France 1975 90m Eastmancolor
President/Renn (Jacques-Eric Strauss)
aka: *I Love You No More*
A gay truck driver begins an affair with a boyish girl which proves difficult to consummate and also upsets his jealous Italian boyfriend.
Rambling, inconsequential, intermittently entertaining tale that gives the impression that the actors made it up as they went along.
wd Serge Gainsbourg *ph* Willy Kurant *m* Serge Gainsbourg *ad* Theo Meurisse *ed* Kenout Peltier
☆ Jane Birkin, Joe Dallesandro, Hugues Quester, Rene Kolldehoff, Gérard Depardieu, Michel Blanc

Je Vous Aime
France 1981 105m Eastmancolor
Renn Productions/FR3 (Pierre Grunstein)
A woman changes husbands as if they were dresses.
Shallow depiction of an incurable romantic, or obsessive promiscuity, depending on your viewpoint. From either, it makes for a dull movie.
w Claude Berri, Michel Grisolia *d* Claude Berri *ph* Etienne Becker *m* Serge Gainsbourg *ad* Pierre Guffroy *ed* Arlette Langmann
☆ Catherine Deneuve, Jean-Louis Trintignant, Gérard Depardieu, Serge Gainsbourg, Alain Souchon, Christian Marquand

Jealousy *
US 1945 70m bw
Republic
A failed writer, jealous of his wife's friendship with another man, is found murdered.
Curious but interesting melodrama with much talent breaking through.
w Arnold Phillips, Gustav Machaty, Dalton Trumbo *d* Gustav Machaty *m* Hanns Eisler
☆ Nils Asther, John Loder, Jane Randolph, Karen Morley
'It is a sympathetic film, and in spite of its overall failure, contains enough sincerity and enough artistry to make most of the other films mentioned here look sick.' – *James Agee*

Jealousy Italian Style *
Italy/Spain 1970 106m Technicolor Panavision
Dean/Jupiter Generale/Midega (Pio Angeletti, Adriano de Micheli)
original title: *Dramma della Gelosia – Tutti i Particolari in Cronaca*
aka: *A Drama of Jealousy; The Pizza Triangle*
Two friends – a married bricklayer and a pizza cook – fall in love with the same woman, who cannot choose between them, resulting in disaster for all three.
Mildly amusing, if over-loud and vociferous, comedy that takes swipes at, among other targets, male–female relationships, modern Italian design, politics, and Fellini's liking for grotesques.
w Furio Scarpelli, Agenore Incrocci, Ettore Scola *d* Ettore Scola *ph* Carlo Di Palma *m* Armando Trovaioli *ad* Luciano Ricceri *ed* Alberto Gallitti
☆ Marcello Mastroianni, Giancarlo Giannini, Monica Vitti, Manolo Zarzo, Marisa Merlini, Hercules Cortes
† Mastroianni's performance won him the Best Actor award at the Cannes Film Festival in 1970.

Jean de Florette **
France 1986 121m Eastmancolor Technovision
Renn/Films A2/RAI2/DD
Elemental story of feuding over water supplies in rural France in the 20s.
Stunning performances and detailed depiction of Provençal farming life made it a wild success in France, repeated to a remarkable extent abroad.
w Claude Berri, Gérard Brach *novel* Marcel Pagnol *d* Claude Berri *ph* Bruno Nuytten *m* Jean-Claude Petit *pd* Bernard Vezat
☆ Yves Montand, Gérard Depardieu, Daniel Auteuil, Elisabeth Depardieu
† The saga continued in *Manon des Sources* (qv), from Pagnol's sequel *L'eau de collines*.
best picture; adapted screenplay; cinematography; Daniel Auteuil

Jeanne Eagels *
US 1957 114m bw
Columbia (George Sidney)
A sideshow dancer becomes a Broadway star of the twenties but dies of drugs.
Well-upholstered but basically too conventional showbiz biopic.
w Daniel Fuchs, Sonya Levien, John Fante *d* George Sidney *ph* Robert Planck *m* George Duning
☆ Kim Novak, Jeff Chandler, Agnes Moorehead, Charles Drake, Larry Gates, *Virginia Grey*

Jeanne la Pucelle: Part I, Les Batailles; Part II, Les Prisons **
France 1994 238m colour
Artificial Eye/Mayfair/La Sept/France 3/Pierre Grise
The story of the life and death at the stake of Joan of Arc. Part I deals with Joan persuading the French court that she has been sent by God to drive the English from France. Part II concentrates on the political machinations that followed her successes, her trial and death.
Absorbing, exhaustively detailed drama that follows Joan in close-up, ignoring opportunities for spectacle; its length, though, remains a problem.
w Christine Laurent, Pascal Bonitzer *d* Jacques Rivette *ph* William Lubtchansky *m* Jordi Savall *pd* Mau de Chauvigny *ed* Nicole Lubtchanksy
☆ Sandrine Bonnaire (Jeanne), André Marcon (Dauphin), Jean-Louis Richard, Marcel Bozonnet, Didier Sauvegrain, Patrick Le Mauff, Jean-Pierre Lorit, Jean-Pierre Becker, Mathieu Busson
'An original, prowling and restless film with an outstanding central performance.' – *Empire*
'Is certainly a sumptuous costume drama, but it's also as cold and as dry as any history lesson.' – *Film Review*
† Part I 117m, Part II 121m. The original running time for the film's French release was Part I 160m, Part II 176m.

Jeanne's House **
France 1987 94m colour
MDG/FR3 (Marie-Dominique Girodet)
original title: *La Maison de Jeanne*
A restaurateur, driven to the point of breakdown by her passive husband, demanding mother and noisy children, falls in love with her new landlord.
Witty movie of domestic conflict that comes to a surprising conclusion.
wd Magali Clement *ph* Pierre Novion *m* Raymond Alessandrini *ad* Bruno Bruneau *ed* Amina Mazani
☆ Christine Boisson, Benoit Regent, Jean-Pierre Bisson, Marie Trintignant, Michelle Goddet, Maxime Leroux, Pascale Audret, Jacques Richard

Jeannie *
GB 1941 101m bw
GFD/Tansa (Marcel Hellman)
US title: *Girl in Distress*
A Scots girl comes into money and takes a European holiday.
Mildly astringent, generally amusing comedy which overcomes shaky production. Remade as Let's Be Happy *in 1952.*
w Anatole de Grunwald, Roland Pertwee *play* Aimée Stuart *d* Harold French *ph* Bernard Knowles *m* Mischa Spoliansky
☆ *Barbara Mullen*, Michael Redgrave, *Albert Lieven*, Wilfrid Lawson, Kay Hammond, Edward Chapman, Googie Withers, Gus MacNaughton
'One of the easiest, sweetest of light comedies.' – *James Agee*
'As enchanting a bit of rue and nonsense as we've succumbed to in many a month.' – *New York Times*

Jeder für sich und Gott gegen alle: see *The Enigma of Kaspar Hauser*

'What's Eating You?'
Jeepers Creepers
US 2001 89m FotoKem
UA/American Zoetrope/Cinerenta-Cinebeta (Barry Opper, Tom Luse)
A brother and sister are terrorised by a demon.
Spooky little horror with a feel-bad ending that begins promisingly but quickly loses the plot.
wd Victor Salva *ph* Don E. Fauntleroy *m* Bennett Salvay *pd* Steven Legler *ed* Ed Marx *sp* Brad Parker; Make-up & Monster Studios; E=MC^2
☆ Gina Phillips (Trish), Justin Long (Darry), Jonathan Breck (The Creeper), Patricia Belcher (Jezelle Gay Hartman), Brandon Smith (Sgt Davis Tubbs), Eileen Brennan (Cat Lady)
'A clever thriller-chiller combining laughter with creepiness that should satisfy horror fans.' – *Kevin Thomas, Los Angeles Times*

Jefferson in Paris
US 1995 139m colour
Buena Vista/Merchant Ivory (Ismail Merchant)
In the 1780s, Thomas Jefferson becomes the US Ambassador to France, where he courts a married artist and fathers a child on a young, black slave in his household.
Glossily presented period drama that is all show and no substance.
w Ruth Prawer Jhabvala *d* James Ivory *ph* Pierre Lhomme *m* Richard Robbins *pd* Guy-Claude Françoise *ed* Andrew Marcus, Isabel Lorente
☆ Nick Nolte, Greta Scacchi, Jean-Pierre Aumont, Thandie Newton, Simon Callow, Seth Gilliam, James Earl Jones, Michel Lonsdale, Nancy Marchand, Gwyneth Paltrow
'A dreary, tedious, condescending film that, given its sexual subplot, is quite amazingly passionless.' – *Joe Queenan*
'The high-minded look of the film, combined with Jhabvala's uncharacteristically muddled handling of the story, makes for a distinctly queasy experience.'– *Adam Mars-Jones, Independent*
'Two-and-a-half hours of beautifully costumed inconsequence.' – *Tom Shone, Sunday Times*

Jeffrey *
US 1995 94m Technicolor
Film Four/Workin' Man/The Booking Office (Mark Balsam, Mitchell Maxwell, Victoria Maxwell)
A gay actor decides to give up sex and then meets the man of his dreams.
A slight and bitchy comedy of the strains and confusions that the arrival of AIDS has brought to matters of love and sex.
w Paul Rudnick *play* Paul Rudnick *d* Christopher Ashley *ph* Jeffrey Tufano *m* Stephen Endelman *pd* Michael Johnston *ed* Cara Silverman
☆ Steven Weber, Patrick Stewart, Bryan Batt, Sigourney Weaver, Nathan Lane, Olympia Dukakis
'Quite successfully walks the tightrope between utter sincerity and queenly silliness.' – *Derek Malcolm, Guardian*

J'Embrasse Pas *
France 1991 115m colour 'Scope
President/BAC/Salome/Ciné Cinq/Canal Plus (Maurice Benart, Jacques Eric-Strauss, Jean Labadie)
aka: *I Don't Kiss*
An ill-educated but ambitious youth from the country comes to Paris, finds success as a male prostitute and falls for a whore.
Dour moral tale of disillusioned youth that comes to no satisfactory conclusion.
w Jacques Nolot, André Téchiné, Michel Grisolia *d* André Téchiné *ph* Thierry Arbogast *m* Philippe Sarde *ed* Claudine Merlin, Edith Vassard
☆ Philippe Noiret, Emmanuelle Béart, Manuel Blanc, Hélène Vincent, Yvan Desni

Jennie: see *Portrait of Jennie*

Jennifer
US 1953 73m bw
AA (Berman Swartz)
The lady housekeeper of a California mansion broods on the mysterious disappearance of her predecessor.
Slight, quietly effective suspenser with a letdown ending.
w Virginia Myers *d* Joel Newton *ph* *James Wong Howe* *m* Ernest Gold
☆ Ida Lupino, Howard Duff, Robert Nichols, Mary Shipp

'On the trail of a serial killer, Detective John Berlin has no clues and no suspects. And no alibi.'
Jennifer Eight
US 1992 120m DeLuxe
Paramount (Gary Lucchesi, David Wimbury)
A burnt-out cop, moving to a new small-town job, faces local derision when he decides a murder has been committed by a serial killer who targets blind women.
A drawn-out, predictable thriller that becomes more ridiculous the longer it lasts; and it lasts a long time.
wd Bruce Robinson *ph* Conrad L. Hall *m* Christopher Young *pd* Richard Macdonald *ed* Conrad Buff
☆ Andy Garcia, Uma Thurman, John Malkovich, Lance Henriksen, Kathy Baker, Kevin Conway, Graham Beckel
'Although initially menacing, Robinson's addition to the serial killer genre falls back on clichés.' – *Sight and Sound*
'A sombre character-oriented suspense mystery, this is notable both for its stunningly atmospheric cinematography and the dark psychological undercurrents lurking beneath the surface.' – *Empire*
† The film was released direct to video in Britain.

Jenny Lind: see *A Lady's Morals*

Jeopardy
US 1952 69m bw
MGM (Sol Baer Fielding)
A man on a camping holiday falls off a jetty and gets stuck in the timbers while the water rises; his wife frantically seeks help from an escaped convict.
Panic melodrama enjoyable for its clichés.
w Mel Dinelli *d* John Sturges *ph* Victor Milner *m* Dimitri Tiomkin
☆ Barbara Stanwyck, Barry Sullivan, Ralph Meeker

'Some say he's dead ... some say he never will be!'
Jeremiah Johnson **
US 1972 107m Technicolor Panavision
Warner (Joe Wizan)
In the 1850s an ex-soldier becomes a mountain trapper.
Splendidly made if rather desultorily plotted adventure story with the feel of raw reality.
w John Milius, Edward Anhalt *d* *Sydney Pollack* *ph* Duke Callaghan *m* John Rubinstein, Tim McIntire
☆ Robert Redford, Will Geer, Allyn McLerie

Jeremy
US 1973 90m DeLuxe
UA/Kenasset (George Pappas)
A music student falls in love with a ballet dancer.
Sentimental love story with nothing positive to commend it, chiefly interesting because for commercial release it was blown up from 16mm.
wd Arthur Barron *ph* Paul Goldsmith *m* Lee Holdridge
☆ Robby Benson, Glynnis O'Connor, Len Bari, Leonardo Cimino

Jericho
GB 1937 77m bw
Buckingham (Walter Futter, Max Schach)
US title: *Dark Sands*
A court-martialled officer pursues a murderous deserter across Africa.
Lively star vehicle of its day.
w Frances Marion, George Barraud, Peter Ruric, Robert N. Lee *d* Thornton Freeland *ph* John W. Boyle
☆ Paul Robeson, Henry Wilcoxon, Wallace Ford, John Laurie, James Carew
'Can't fail to interest audiences throughout the world.' – *Variety*

The Jerk
US 1979 94m Technicolor
Universal/Aspen (Peter MacGregor-Scott)
An innocent white man brought up by black sharecroppers goes out into the world and first makes, then loses a fortune.
Hit-or-miss star vehicle with flashes of satire and fallen aspirations to be a modern Candide.
w Steve Martin, Carl Gottlieb, Michael Elias *d* Carl Reiner *ph* Victor J. Kemper *m* Jack Elliott

☆ Steve Martin, Bernadette Peters, Catlin Adams, Bill Macy, Maurice Evans
'Goofy, dumb, innocent, loud, uncoordinated, bashful and quite dirty.' – *Variety*

Jerry and Tom *
US 1998 106m DeLuxe
Miramax/Lions Gate (Elinor Reid, Vivienne Leebosh, Michael Paseornek, Saul Rubinek)
A hitman and his young apprentice have differing approaches to their job.
Deft, skilful, slow-burning, conversational thriller that breathes new vitality into over-familiar material.
w Rick Cleveland *d* Saul Rubinek *ph* Paul Sarossy *m* David Buchbinder *pd* David Hackl *ed* Sloane Klevin
☆ Joe Mantegna, Sam Rockwell, Maury Chaykin, Ted Danson, Charles Durning, William H. Macy, Peter Riegert
'Very well acted and beautifully directed.' – *Variety*

'Everybody loved him ... Everybody disappeared.'
'The rest of his life begins now...'
Jerry Maguire *
US 1996 139m Technicolor
Columbia TriStar/Gracie (James L. Brooks, Laurence Mark, Richard Sakai, Cameron Crowe)
A successful sports agent turns idealistic and loses his job but finds love and fulfilment.
An enjoyable movie that works best in its more intimate moments; its wider theme, of one man's redemption through learning to care for others, is vitiated by its feel-good ending, when the difference between agent-as-shark and agent-as-good-guy is obliterated.
wd Cameron Crowe *ph* Janusz Kaminski *m* Nancy Wilson *pd* Stephen Lineweaver *ed* Joe Hutshing
☆ *Tom Cruise, Cuba Gooding Jnr, Renee Zellweger,* Kelly Preston, Jerry O'Connell, Jay Mohr, Regina King
'If this is the best Hollywood can offer, you wonder what all the talent is doing.' – *Derek Malcolm, Guardian*
Cuba Gooding Jnr
best picture; Tom Cruise; Cameron Crowe (as writer); Joe Hutshing

Jersey Girl
US 1992 95m Technicolor
Entertainment/Electric/Interscope
A New Jersey teacher crashes her Volkswagen into a Mercedes belonging to the kind of person that she needs to improve her life: a successful and handsome man from Manhattan.
Amiable comedy of class differences with true love winning out in the end, to no one's surprise.
w Gina Wendkos *d* David Burton Morris *ph* Ron Fortunato *m* Misha Segal *pd* Lester Cohen *ed* Norman Hollyn
☆ Jami Gertz, Dylan McDermott, Molly Price, Aida Turturro, Star Jasper, Sheryl Lee, Joseph Bologna, Joseph Mazzello, Philip Casnoff
'Pic has the potential to warm the hearts of ancillary viewers, especially young women.' – *Variety*

The Jerusalem File
US/Israel 1971 96m Metrocolor
MGM/Sparta (Ram Ben Efraim)
American archaeologists in Jerusalem become involved in Arab/Israeli espionage.
Muddled mixture of action and politics.
w Troy Kennedy Martin *d* John Flynn *ph* Raoul Coutard *m* John Scott
☆ Bruce Davison, Nicol Williamson, Donald Pleasence, Ian Hendry

Jesse James **
US 1939 106m Technicolor
TCF (Nunnally Johnson)
After the Civil War, two brothers take to train robbing when railroad employees harass their family.
The life of an outlaw turns into family entertainment when Hollywood bathes it in sentiment, soft colour, family background and warm humour. It works dangerously well, and the action sequences are splendid.
w Nunnally Johnson d Henry King ph George Barnes md Louis Silvers *ad William Darling, George Dudley*
☆ Tyrone Power, Henry Fonda, Nancy Kelly, Jane Darwell, Randolph Scott, Henry Hull, Slim Summerville, Brian Donlevy, J. Edward Bromberg, John Carradine, Donald Meek
'Sock outdoors meller, vigorous and intensely dramatic in its unfolding ... box office smacko.' – *Variety*
'An authentic American panorama.' – *New York Times*
† Sequel 1940: *The Return of Frank James*. Remake 1957: *The True Story of Jesse James*.

Jesse James Meets Frankenstein's Daughter
US 1965 82m Pathécolor
Avco Embassy/Circle/Embassy (Carroll Case)
Baron Frankenstein's granddaughter moves to a Mexican village where she sets up in the family business and falls in love with Jesse James.
Low-budget nonsense, played and directed with little sense of style or purpose.
w Carl K. Hittleman *d* William Beaudine *ph* Lothrop Worth *m* Raoul Kraushaar *ad* Paul Sylos, Harry Reif *ed* Roy Livingston
☆ John Lupton, Estelita, Cal Bolder, Narda Onyx, Steven Geray, Raymond Barnes
'With script and direction proving equally frail, the film is only prevented from becoming the camper's delight promised by the title by the fact that the cast plod through it all with gravity hardly befitting the occasion.' – *Tom Milne, MFB*
† The same director was also responsible for *Billy the Kid vs Dracula* (qv).

Jessica
France/Italy/US 1962 105m Technicolor Panavision
UA/Ariane/Dear Film (Jean Negulesco)
The attractive midwife in a Sicilian village causes the women to go on a sex strike.
Synthetic rustic naughtiness showing several influences imperfectly assimilated.
w Edith Sommer *novel The Midwife of Pont Clery* by Flora Sundstrom *d* Jean Negulesco *ph* Piero Portalupi *m* Mario Nascimbene
☆ Angie Dickinson, Maurice Chevalier, Noel Noel, Gabriele Ferzetti, Sylva Koscina, Agnes Moorehead, Marcel Dalio

Jesus Christ Superstar *
US 1973 107m Technicolor Todd-AO 35
Universal (Norman Jewison, Robert Stigwood)
Young tourists in Israel re-enact episodes of the life of Christ.
Location-set fantasia based on the phenomenally successful rock opera; some of it works, but the original concept was a theatrical one.
w Melvyn Bragg, Norman Jewison *d* Norman Jewison *ph Douglas Slocombe m/ly Andrew Lloyd Webber, Tim Rice md* André Previn
☆ Ted Neeley, Carl Anderson, Yvonne Elliman, Barry Dennen
'One of the true fiascos of modern cinema.' – *Paul D. Zimmerman*
André Previn

Jesus of Montreal ***
Canada/France 1989 120m colour
Max Films/Gérard Mital Productions/NFB Canada (Roger Frappier, Pierre Gendron)
original title: *Jésus de Montréal*
An actor, chosen to play Christ in a religious play, finds himself in conflict with the church authorities.
A modern morality, surprisingly effective despite sometimes forced parallels between the actor's experiences and those of Jesus, and fuelled by a passionate irony.
wd Denys Arcand *ph* Guy Dufaux *m* Yves Laferrière, François Dompierre, Jean-Marie Benoît *ad* François Seguin *ed* Isabelle Dedieu
☆ Lothaire Bluteau, Catherine Wilkening, Johanne-Marie Tremblay, Rémy Girard, Robert Lepage, Gilles Pelletier, Yves Jacques
'Arcand is a master of tone, a sympathetic director of actors, and an unsanctimonious moralist, who locates his fable within a well-observed society.' – *Philip French, Observer*
best foreign film

Jesus' Son **
US/Canada 1999 108m Technicolor Super 35
Alliance/Lions Gate/Evenstar (Lydia Dean Pilcher, Elizabeth Cuthrell, David Urrutia)
An accident-prone drifter finds redemption despite his disaster-strewn relationship with a heroin-addicted woman.
Downbeat and often grim drama, set among layabouts and drug-addicts in the 70s, that manages to suggest a sweet sense of humanity.
w Elizabeth Cuthrell, David Urrutia, Oren Moverman *short stories* Denis Johnson *d* Alison Maclean *ph* Adam Kimmel *m* Joe Henry *pd* David Doernberg *ed* Geraldine Peroni, Stuart Levy
☆ Billy Crudup (FH), Samantha Morton (Michelle), Denis Leary (Wayne), Jack Black (Georgie), Will Patton (John Smith), Greg Germann (Dr Shanis), Holly Hunter (Mira), Dennis Hopper (Bill)
'An intermittently compelling and occasionally hilarious road movie.' – *Todd McCarthy, Variety*
'William Burroughs would love this stuff. Others will find it too nightmarish to stomach.' – *James Christopher, Times*

Jet: see *Ground Control*

Jet Li's The Enforcer: see *The Enforcer (1995)*

Jet over the Atlantic
US 1958 95m bw
Warner/Inter Continental (Benedict Bogeaus)
A noble British passenger on a plane from Madrid to New York has planted a gas bomb in the luggage compartment.
Mechanical airborne suspenser with the usual assortment of unconvincing types making unconvincing gestures.
w Irving H. Cooper *d* Byron Haskin *ph* George Stahl *m* Lou Forbes
☆ Guy Madison, Virginia Mayo, George Raft, George Macready, Ilona Massey, Anna Lee, Margaret Lindsay, Venetia Stevenson, Mary Anderson, Brett Halsey, Frederic Worlock

Jet Pilot
US 1957 112m Technicolor
Howard Hughes (Jules Furthman)
A Russian lady spy falls for an American pilot.
Lamentably dull and stupid romantic actioner of which all concerned should be thoroughly ashamed, especially as it took seven years to complete and is not even technically competent.
w Jules Furthman *d* Josef von Sternberg (and others) *ph* Winton C. Hoch *m* Bronislau Kaper
☆ John Wayne, Janet Leigh, Jay C. Flippen, Paul Fix, Richard Rober, Roland Winters, Ivan Triesault, Hans Conried
'One of the most childish, tedious and futile cold war spy dramas yet concocted by a Hollywood screenwriter.' – *John Gillett*

Jet Storm *
GB 1959 99m bw
British Lion/Britannia/Pendennis (Steven Pallos)
An airliner in flight from London to New York is discovered to have a bomb on board.
All-star slice-of-life suspenser with competently handled dialogue and situations.
w Cy Endfield, Sigmund Miller *d* Cy Endfield *ph* Jack Hildyard *m* Thomas Rajna
☆ Richard Attenborough, George Rose, Hermione Baddeley, Mai Zetterling, Diane Cilento, Stanley Baker, Harry Secombe, Virginia Maskell, Elizabeth Sellars, Sybil Thorndike, Bernard Braden, Cec Linder, David Kossoff

Jetsons: The Movie
US 1990 83m CFI color
UIP/Universal/Hanna-Berbera/Wang/Cuckoo's Nest Studios (Bruce David Johnson)
The Jetson family solve the problem of alien saboteurs who object to their asteroid being the site of a mining factory.
Poorly animated situation comedy that would be better suited to television and best suited to the nearest garbage disposal unit.
w Dennis Marks, Carl Sautter *d* William Hanna, Joseph Barbera *ph* Daniel Bunn *m* John Debney
☆ Featuring the voices of George O'Hanlon, Mel Blanc, Penny Singleton, Tiffany, Patric Zimmerman, Don Messick, Jean Vanderpyl
'This exercise in high-tech tedium might prove more bewildering than charming to its pre-teen audience.' – MFB

Jeu de Massacre *
France 1967 94m colour
Coficitel/A. J. Films/Films Modernes/Francinor (René Thevenet)
US title: *The Killing Game*
aka: *Comic Strip Hero*
An impoverished comic-book writer and his artist wife become involved with a wealthy young fantasist.
Witty games-playing on the themes of illusion and reality.
wd Alain Jessua *ph* Jacques Robin *m* Jacques Loussier *ad* Claire Forestier *ed* Nicole Marko
☆ Claudine Auger, Jean-Pierre Cassel, Michel Duchaussoy, Eleonore Hirt, Guy Saint-Jean, Anna Gaylor, Nancy Holloway

La Jeune Fille Assassinée: see *Charlotte*

Le Jeune Werther *
France 1992 90m colour
Home Made Movies/Canal/Alain Sarde
aka: *Young Werther*
Young teenagers try to discover why one of their friends killed himself.
An updated version of, and commentary on, Goethe's tale of impossibly romantic love, rather too doom-laden to be entirely convincing as a portrait of modern-day young.
wd Jacques Doillon *ph* Christophe Pollock *m* Philippe Sarde *ed* Nicole Lubtchansky
☆ Ismaël Jolé-Ménébhi, Thomas Brémond, Simon Clavière, Pierre Mézerette, Faye Anastasia, Miren Capello, Sunny Lebrati, Mirabelle Rousseau, Jessica Tharaud
'The writer-director does ask a lot of his audience to maintain interest in a feature film almost entirely devoted to 13-year-old talk sessions.' – *Variety*

Jeux Interdits ***
France 1952 84m bw
Robert Dorfmann (Paul Joly)
aka: *Forbidden Games*
aka: *The Secret Game*
In 1940, the little daughter of refugee parents sees her parents killed, and takes refuge with a peasant family, the small son of which helps her bury her dead puppy. They make a game of building a cemetery, which leads to a village feud...
Poignant anti-war tract which seemed a masterpiece at the time and is full of marvellous moments, but no longer holds up as a whole.
w Jean Aurenche, Pierre Bost novel François Boyer *d René Clément ph* Robert Julliard *m* Narciso Yepes
☆ *Brigitte Fossey, Georges Poujouly,* Amédée, Laurence Badie, Jacques Marin, Suzanne Courtal, Lucien Hubert
'A truly imposing achievement of blending several seemingly unrelated elements into a totally meaningful whole.' – *John Simon, 1967*
foreign film
François Boyer (original story)
picture

Les Jeux Sont Faits *
France 1947 91m bw
Films Gibe
Falling in love in Purgatory, two murdered people get a second chance to return to earth, but spend their time quarrelling.
Somewhat despondent romantic fantasy with morsels of wit.
w Jean-Paul Sartre *d* Jean Delannoy *ph* Christian Matras *m* Georges Auric
☆ Micheline Presle, Marcel Pagliero, Marguerite Moreno, Charles Dullin

Jew Suss **

GB 1934 109m bw

Gaumont (Michael Balcon)

US title: *Power*

In old Württemberg, a Jew gains power to help his people, then finds he is Gentile.

Interesting, heavy-handed historical satire on the pointlessness of race distinctions, made partly in answer to Nazi oppression in Germany.

w Dorothy Farnum, A. R. Rawlinson *novel* Lion Feuchtwanger *d* Lothar Mendes *ph* Bernard Knowles, Roy Kellino *md* Louis Levy *ad* Alfred Junge *ed* Otto Ludwig

☆ *Conrad Veidt*, Benita Hume, Frank Vosper, Cedric Hardwicke, Gerald du Maurier, Pamela Ostrer

'Powerful as an artistic film achievement ... but may have to struggle for commercial contentment.' – *Variety*

Jew Suss *

Germany 1940 85m bw

Terra

Celebrated travesty of the above, in which the Jew is wholly evil and rapes Aryan girls.

w Ludwig Metzger, Veit Harlan, Eberhard Wolfgang Möller *d* Veit Harlan *ph* Bruno Mondi *m* Wolfgang Zeller

☆ Ferdinand Marian, Werner Krauss, Heinrich George, Kristina Söderbaum

'The epitome of anti-semitic propaganda ... the most notorious film of the Third Reich and one which brought disgrace on almost everyone connected with it.' – *Georges Sadoul*

'Highly recommended for its artistic value and, to serve the politics of the State, recommended for young people.' – *Josef Goebbels*

'When the going gets tough, the tough get going!'

Jewel of the Nile *

US 1985 104m Technicolor J-D-C Scope

TCF/Michael Douglas

A lady novelist gets into trouble when she accepts an invitation from a Middle Eastern potentate.

Moderate sequel to Romancing the Stone; *plenty of action, but dull spots in between.*

w Mark Rosenthal, Lawrence Konner *d* Lewis Teague *ph* Jan DeBont *m* Jack Nitzsche *pd* Richard Dawking, Terry Knight

☆ Michael Douglas, Kathleen Turner, Danny DeVito, Spiros Focas

'Mass destruction, endless gunfire and a fiery finish ... the only box office question is whether the film comes late in the cycle for Saturday matinee revivals.' – *Variety*

Jewel Robbery *

US 1932 68m bw

Warner

A jewel thief and a millionaire's wife fall in love in Vienna.

Good sparkling fun in the shadow of Trouble in Paradise *(qv).*

w Erwin Gelsey *story* Ladislaus Fodor *d William Dieterle ph* Robert Kurrle *md* Leo B. Forbstein *ad* Robert Haas *ed* Ralph Dawson

☆ *William Powell*, Kay Francis, Hardie Albright, André Luguet, Henry Kolker, Spencer Charters, Alan Mowbray, Helen Vinson, Lee Kohlmar

'The Greatest Actress Of The Screen ... In The Greatest Romance Of The South!'

Jezebel ***

US 1938 104m bw

Warner (Henry Blanke)

Before the Civil War, a Southern belle stirs up trouble among the menfolk by her wilfulness and spite, but atones when a plague strikes.

Superb star melodrama, tossed to her in compensation for losing Gone with the Wind, *and dealt with in high style by all concerned.*

w Clements Ripley, Abem Finkel, John Huston *play* Owen Davis Snr *d William Wyler ph Ernest Haller m Max Steiner*

☆ *Bette Davis*, Henry Fonda, George Brent, Margaret Lindsay, Fay Bainter, Richard Cromwell, Donald Crisp, Henry O'Neill, John Litel, Spring Byington, Eddie Anderson, Gordon Oliver, Irving Pichel

'Good femme film, assured of okay results.' – *Variety*

'Its excellences come from many sources – good plotting and writing, a director and photographer who know how to make the thing flow along with dramatic pictorial effect, and a cast that makes its story a record of living people.' – *James Shelley Hamilton, National Board of Review*

'Without the zing Davis gave it, it would have looked very mossy indeed.' – *Pauline Kael, 1968*

Bette Davis; Fay Bainter

best picture; Ernest Haller; Max Steiner

The Jezebels: see *Switchblade Sisters*

Jigokumon: see *Gate of Hell*

Jigsaw

US 1949 72m bw

UA/Tower (The Danzigers)

An assistant District Attorney uncovers a mob stirring up racial hatred.

Undistinguished piece of do-goodery, curiously decorated by guest stars doing bit parts as a gesture of goodwill.

w Fletcher Markle, Vincent McConnor *d* Fletcher Markle *ph* Don Malkames *m* Robert Stringer

☆ Franchot Tone, Jean Wallace, Myron McCormick, Marc Lawrence, Marlene Dietrich, Henry Fonda, John Garfield, Marsha Hunt, Leonard Lyons, Burgess Meredith

Jigsaw **

GB 1962 107m bw Cinemascope

British Lion/Britannia/Figaro (Val Guest)

Brighton policemen track down the murderer of a woman found in a lonely house on the beach.

Absorbing and entertaining little murder mystery which sustains its considerable length with interesting detail and plays as fair as can be with the audience. Excellent unassuming entertainment.

wd Val Guest *play Sleep Long My Love* by Hilary Waugh *ph* Arthur Grant *m* none

☆ *Jack Warner*, Ronald Lewis, *Michael Goodliffe*, Yolande Donlan, John Barron

The Jigsaw Man

GB 1985 98m colour

J & M

A British traitor in Moscow is given a new face and sent back home, where he becomes a double agent.

Somewhat elementary cold war chicanery with an abundance of talk before a routine action finish. Production was interrupted by financial crises, and the final result is patchy to say the least.

w Jo Eisinger *d* Terence Young *ph* Freddie Francis *m* John Cameron

☆ Michael Caine, Laurence Olivier, Robert Powell, Susan George, Michael Medwin, Vladek Sheybal

Jim Buck

US 1977 86m colour

Wildfire (James Rokos, Andzrej Krakowski)

aka: *Portrait of a Hitman*

An artistic hitman discovers that the person he has been hired to shoot is an old friend who once saved his life.

An incoherent and never-less-than-silly thriller, directed without style and acted with little conviction.

w Yabo Yablonsky *d* Allan A. Buckhantz *ph* Charles Correll *m* Laurence Rosenthal *pd* Elayne Ceder *ed* Michael Ripps

☆ Jack Palance, Bo Svenson, Richard Roundtree, Ann Turkel, Rod Steiger, Herb Jeffries, Richard Ahn

Jim Thorpe, All-American

US 1951 105m bw

Warner (Everett Freeman)

GB title: *Man of Bronze*

A Red Indian becomes a star footballer, but later succumbs to drink.

Adequate sporting biopic.

w Douglas Morrow, Everett Freeman *d* Michael Curtiz *ph* Ernest Haller *m* Max Steiner

☆ Burt Lancaster, Charles Bickford, Steve Cochran, Phyllis Thaxter, Dick Wesson

Jimmy Hollywood

US 1994 113m DeLuxe

Paramount/Baltimore Pictures (Mark Johnson, Barry Levinson)

An obsessive would-be actor becomes a celebrity when he turns vigilante after his car radio is stolen.

Drama of the low life and underside of Hollywood which lacks bite; nor does it work as a character study.

wd Barry Levinson *ph* Peter Sova *m* Robbie Robertson *pd* Linda DeScenna *ed* Jay Rabinowitz

☆ Joe Pesci, Christian Slater, Victoria Abril, Jason Beghe, John Cothran Jnr

'Oddball attempt to mix offbeat comedy with social commentary and fringe-level character study. However well intentioned, the contrary elements just don't mesh.' – *Variety*

'Creeps out to please the completists and mildly irritate anyone else who happens to rent it.' – *Kim Newman, Empire*

† Harrison Ford plays a cameo role, and Barry Levinson also appears, in the film's final joke. It was released direct to video in Britain.

Jimmy Neutron: Boy Genius

US 2001 83m DeLuxe

Paramount/Nickelodeon/O Entertainment (Steve Oedekerk, John A. Davis, Albie Hecht)

A child genius and his friends rescue their parents, who have been kidnapped by egg-like aliens.

Lively cartoon for small children that is unlikely to interest any other age group; the animation is never more than adequate.

w John A. Davis, David N. Weiss, J. David Stem, Steve Oedekerk *d* John A. Davis *m* John Debney *pd* Fred Cline *ed* Jon Michael Price, Gregory Perler

☆ voices of: Megan Cavanagh, Mark DeCarlo, Debi Derryberry, Jeff Garcia, Bob Goen, Mary Hart, Carolyn Lawrence, Andrea Martin

'It has the bright Rube Goldberg energy of one of Jimmy's contraptions, and it resists the common kid-movie tendency to lecture its young audience about individuality, self-esteem or other stuff they hear enough about in school.' – *A. O. Scott, New York Times*

animated feature film

Jimmy Reardon

US 1988 92m colour

Island/Enterprise/Fox (Russell Schwartz)

original title: *A Night in the Life of Jimmy Reardon*

A romantic youth finds he has a rival for the girl he loves.

Teenage angst, deftly done but lacking a wider perspective.

wd William Richert *novel Aren't You Ever Gonna Kiss Me Goodbye* by William Richert *ph* John J. Connor *m* Bill Conti *pd* Norman Newberry *ed* Suzanne Fenn

☆ River Phoenix, Ann Magnuson, Meredith Salenger, Matthew Perry, Ione Skye, Jane Hallaren, Paul Koslo, Jason Court

Jimmy the Gent *

US 1934 67m bw

Warner (Robert Lord)

A racketeer supplies heirs for unclaimed estates.

Adequate star crime comedy.

w Bertram Millhauser *d* Michael Curtiz *ph* Ira Morgan *md* Leo F. Forbstein

☆ *James Cagney*, Bette Davis, Alice White, Allen Jenkins, Arthur Hohl, Mayo Methot, Alan Dinehart, Hobart Cavanaugh, Ralf Harolde, Philip Reed, Joe Sawyer

'Fast and flip, rough and rowdy.' – *New York American*

Jimmy the Kid

US 1982 85m CFI color

Zephyr (Ronald Jacobs)

An incompetent bunch of crooks kidnap a young boy, the precocious son of wealthy parents, who decides he does not want to go home.

An unendearing comedy that relies on contrived slapstick and features some charmless performances, especially from its teenage star.

w Sam Bobrick *novel* Donald E. Westlake *d* Gary Nelson *ph* Dennis Dalzell *m* John Cameron *ad* Bill Ross *ed* Richard C. Meyer

☆ Gary Coleman, Paul Le Mat, Ruth Gordon, Dee Wallace, Cleavon Little, Avery Schreiber, Pat Morita, Fay Hauser, Walter Olkewicz, Don Adams

Jing Ke Ci Qin Wang: see *The Emperor and the Assassin*

Jingcha Gushi: see *Police Story*

Jingcha Gushi 4 Zhi Jiandan Renwu: see *Jackie Chan's First Strike*

Jingle All the Way

US 1996 88m DeLuxe

TCF (Chris Columbus, Mark Radcliffe, Michael Barnathan)

On Christmas Eve, a salesman searches frantically for the special toy, sold out in all the shops, that his son wants.

Tedious action comedy with heavy-handed slapstick; it's undiluted humbug.

w Randy Kornfield *d* Brian Levant *ph* Victor J. Kemper *m* David Newman *pd* Leslie McDonald *ed* Kent Beyda, Wilton Henderson, Adam Weiss

☆ Arnold Schwarzenegger, Sinbad, Phil Hartman, Rita Wilson, Robert Conrad, Martin Mull, Jake Lloyd, James Belushi, Harvey Korman

'This ghastly, paper-thin piece of Yuletide rubble from the *Home Alone* stable is rather like that Christmas pudding you forgot to eat last year, which now lies on a kitchen shelf, soft in the centre with a hard-as-nails exterior.' – *Derek Malcolm, Guardian*

Jinxed!

US 1982 103m Technicolor

MGM-UA/Herb Jaffe

A frustrated blackjack dealer seduces the girl of a frequent winner.

Unfunny gambling comedy which never begins to cohere.

w Bert Blessing, David Newman *d* Don Siegel *ph* Vilmos Zsigmond *m* Bruce Roberts, Miles Goodman

☆ Bette Midler, Ken Wahl, Rip Torn, Val Avery, Jack Elam, Benson Fong, Jacqueline Scott

'*Jinxed* stinks.' – *Don Siegel*

Jit *

Zimbabwe 1990 92m bw

ICA/FilmAfrica/Makuvisi (Rory Kilalea)

A youth takes various jobs in order to raise the money he needs to buy the bride he wants.

Lively low-budget comedy, the first feature film to be made in Zimbabwe, with an engaging soundtrack of local popular music.

wd Michael Raeburn *ph* João Costa *m* Oliver Mtukudzi *pd* Lindie Pankiv *ed* Justin Krish

☆ Dominic Makuvachuma, Sibongile Nene, Farai Sevenzo, Winnie Ndemera, Oliver Mtukudzi, Lawrence Simbarashe

Jitsuroku Abe Sada: see *A Woman Called Abé Sada*

Jitterbugs *

US 1943 75m bw

TCF (Sol M. Wurtzel)

Laurel and Hardy help a night-club singer to fight off gangsters.

The last Laurel and Hardy film to contain any good scenes, and almost the only one of their TCF films that did.

w Scott Darling *d* Malcolm St Clair *ph* Lucien Andriot *m/ly* Charles Newman, Lew Pollack *md* Emil Newman *ed* James Bashevi, Chester Gore

☆ Stan Laurel, Oliver Hardy, Vivian Blaine, Bob Bailey, Douglas Fowley, Noel Madison, Lee Patrick

Jivaro

US 1953 91m Technicolor 3D

Paramount/William H. Pine, William C. Thomas

GB title: *Lost Treasure of the Amazon*

A mixed party of Americans follows a drunken treasure seeker into the jungle.

Elementary treasure hunt adventure, hampered by studio foliage, bad script and half-hearted acting.

w Winston Miller *novel* The Lost Treasure by David Duncan *d* Edward Ludwig *ph* Lionel Lindon *m* Gregory Stone *ad* Hal Pereira, Earl Hedrick *ed* Howard A. Smith *cos* Edith Head

☆ Fernando Lamas (Rio), Rhonda Fleming (Alice Parker), Brian Keith (Tony), Lon Chaney Jnr (Pedro), Marvin Miller (Kovanti), Richard Denning (Jerry Russell), Rita Moreno (Maroa), Morgan Farley (Vinny)

Joan Medford Is Missing: see *House of Horrors*

Joan of Arc
US 1948 145m Technicolor
RKO/Sierra/Walter Wanger
The last campaign of the Maid of Orleans.
Strictly from Dullsville; one studio set-piece follows another, and a group of talented people clearly thought that prestige would sell itself without the hard work that goes into more commercial productions.
w Maxwell Anderson, Andrew Solt *play Joan of Lorraine* by Maxwell Anderson *d* Victor Fleming *ph* Joe Valentine *m* Hugo Friedhofer *md* Emil Newman *ad* Richard Day *ed* Frank Sullivan
☆ Ingrid Bergman, José Ferrer, George Coulouris, Francis L. Sullivan, Gene Lockhart, Ward Bond, John Ireland, Hurd Hatfield, Cecil Kellaway, George Zucco, J. Carrol Naish
'A bad film with one or two good things. It is childishly oversimplified, its battles *papier mâché*, its heroine far too worldly, its spiritual content that of a chromo art calendar.' – *Herman G. Weinberg*
Joe Valentine; Walter Wanger (Special Award for 'adding to the moral stature' of the industry by his production)
Hugo Friedhofer; Ingrid Bergman; José Ferrer; art direction; editing

Joan of Ozark
US 1942 82m bw
Republic
GB title: *The Queen of Spies*
A hillbilly sharpshooter becomes a national spy heroine.
Scatty comedy of moderate liveliness.
w Robert Harari, Eve Greene and Jack Townley *d* Joseph Santley
☆ Judy Canova, Joe E. Brown, Eddie Foy Jnr, Jerome Cowan, Alexander Granach

Joan of Paris
US 1942 95m bw
RKO (David Hempstead)
A French resistance leader sacrifices herself so that Allied pilots can escape.
Well-made propaganda adventure dignified by excellent cast.
w Charles Bennett, Ellis St Joseph *story* Jacques Thery, Georges Kessel *d* Robert Stevenson *ph* Russell Metty *m* Roy Webb
☆ Michele Morgan, Paul Henreid, Thomas Mitchell, Laird Cregar, May Robson, Alexander Granach, Alan Ladd
Roy Webb

Joan the Woman **
US 1916 125m approx bw silent
Cardinal
The story of Joan of Arc.
An epic spectacle typical of its director.
w Jeanie Macpherson *d* Cecil B. de Mille
☆ Geraldine Farrar, Raymond Hatton, Wallace Reid, Hobart Bosworth, Theodore Roberts

Joanna
GB 1968 122m DeLuxe Panavision
TCF/Laughlin (Michael S. Laughlin)
A girl art student comes to London and quickly finds the road to ruin.
Antediluvian rubbish tarted up with swinging London settings.
wd Mike Sarne *ph* Walter Lassally *m* Rod McKuen
☆ Genevieve Waite, Christian Doermer, Calvin Lockhart, Donald Sutherland
'An unnecessarily protracted punishing of a very dead quadruped.' – *MFB*

The Job **
Italy 1961 90m bw
24 Horses Films (Alberto Soffientini)
original title: *Il Posto*
A teenage boy gets his first job, and progresses from office boy to clerk when a senior man dies.
Appealingly observant social comedy, very simple and extremely effective.
wd Ermanno Olmi *ph* Lamberto Caimi
☆ Sandro Panzeri, Loredana Detto
'Rueful and funny and honest … the players have been encouraged not so much to act as to behave. Olmi stalks them like a naturalist, and the result is a small, unique and perfect achievement in film-making.' – *Penelope Houston, MFB*

Jób Lázadása: see *The Revolt of Job*

Jobman *
South Africa 1990 97m Technicolor
Blue Rock/Three's Company (Christopher Coy)
In the 60s, the persecuted, deaf-mute son of a preacher is forced to fight to protect himself, his wife and child from attack by those who resent his strivings for an independent life.
A tense drama of persecution and retribution, much like a Western in style – and one that can be taken as a political allegory of the dispossessed, who are left with no voice in their country's concerns and no recourse to any means other than violence.
w Darrell Roodt, Greg Latter *story* Achmat Dangor *d* Darrell Roodt *ph* Paul Witte *m* Joel Goldsmith *pd* Dave Barkham *ed* Shelley Wells
☆ Kevin Smith (Jobman), Tertius Meintjes, Lynn Gaines, Marcel Van Heerden, Goliath Edwards, Josephine Liedeman, Bill Curry
'A simple, poetic tale with a powerful central image that hints at underlying social and political themes but fails to really activate them.' – *Variety*

Jock of the Bushveld
South Africa 1988 90m colour
Toron (Duncan MacNeillie)
The adventures of an ambitious Irishman and his hunting dog, which was once the runt of the litter, in South Africa in the 1880s.
Based on a true story, of the early life of a prominent South African politician and author, an episodic adventure that never quite holds the attention; it is colourful but bland.
w John Cundill *book* Sir Percy Fitzpatrick *d* Gray Hofmeyr *ph* Mike Buckley *m* Kenneth Hutchinson *ad* John Gerber *ed* Valma Muir
☆ Jonathan Rands, Gordon Mulholland, Jocelyn Broderick, Wilson Dunster, Olivier Ngwenya

Joe *
US 1970 107m DeLuxe
Cannon (David Gil)
A construction worker in a bar meets a businessman who has just killed his daughter's drug addicted lover; they become buddies in their hatred of hippies.
Highly successful in America as a backlash against permissiveness, this rough-hewn opportunistic melodrama is vivid enough but moves in fits and starts.
w Norman Wexler *m* Bobby Scott *d/ph* John G. Avildsen
☆ Peter Boyle, Dennis Patrick, Audrey Caire, Susan Sarandon
'A bad film disfigured by brute strokes of tendentiousness.' – *Penelope Gilliatt*
Norman Wexler

Joe Dakota
US 1957 90m Technicolor Cinemascope
U-I (Howard Christie)
A stranger appears in a Western town in search of his Indian friend, who turns out to have been murdered by the townspeople so that they can share the profits from his oil well.
Feeble rip-off of Bad Day at Black Rock.
w William Talman, Norman Jolley *d* Richard Bartlett *ph* George Robinson *m* Hans Salter *md* Joseph Gershenson
☆ Jock Mahoney, Luana Patten, Charles McGraw, Barbara Lawrence, Claude Akins, Lee Van Cleef

'Keep on Moppin' in the Free world.'
'Dig it.'
Joe Dirt
US 2001 90m DeLuxe
Columbia/Happy Madison (Robert Simonds)
A dim-witted man goes in search of the parents who abandoned him as a child at the Grand Canyon.
If only they had pushed him over the edge, and thrown this lamentable effort after him…
w David Spade, Fred Wolf *d* Dennie Gordon *ph* John R. Leonetti *m* Waddy Wachtel *pd* Perry Andelin Blake *ed* Peck Prior
☆ David Spade (Joe Dirt), Dennis Miller (Zander Kelly), Brittany Daniel (Brandy), Kid Rock (Robby), Adam Beach (Kicking Wing), Erik Per Sullivan (Little Joe Dirt), Christopher Walken (Clem), Caroline Aaron (Joe's Mom), Fred Ward (Joe's Dad), Jaime Pressly (Jill)
'Smells like uncollected garbage from Adam Sandler, who exec-produced this dead raccoon of a movie.' – *Peter Travers, Rolling Stone*

Joe Hill: see *The Ballad of Joe Hill*

Joe Kidd
US 1972 87m Technicolor Panavision
Universal/Malpaso (Sidney Beckerman)
A disreputable bounty hunter tracks down the leader of a tribe of Mexican bandits.
Rough-and-tumble star Western with untenable moral attitudes.
w Elmore Leonard *d* John Sturges *ph* Bruce Surtees *m* Lalo Schifrin
☆ Clint Eastwood, Robert Duvall, John Saxon, Don Stroud, James Wainwright

Joe Macbeth
GB 1955 90m bw
Film Locations/Frankovich (George Maynard)
A gangster is urged by his wife to rub out his boss.
Almost too bad to be funny, this effort to update Shakespeare has actors behaving as though they were stuck in treacle, and its gimmick quality is quickly dissipated by an indifferent production.
w Philip Yordan *d* Ken Hughes *ph* Basil Emmott *m* Trevor Duncan
☆ Paul Douglas, Ruth Roman, Grégoire Aslan, Bonar Colleano, Sidney James

Joe Palooka, Champ
US 1946 72m bw
Monogram (Hal E. Chester)
A boxing promoter grooms a young dope for the ring.
Modest series opener with plenty to be modest about.
w Cy Endfield, Albert de Pina *d* Reginald Le Borg
☆ Leon Errol, Joe Kirkwood, Elyse Knox, Eduardo Ciannelli, Joe Sawyer, Elisha Cook Jnr

'The Story Of A Boy's Journey To Manhood.'
Joe Panther
US 1976 110m
Artists Creation (Stewart H. Beveridge)
A Seminole youth experiences prejudice and tragedy when he tries to work in the white man's world.
Pleasant rites-of-passage drama about an adolescent and his dog that takes in alligator wrestling along the way, though it may now seem too tame for its intended youthtul audience.
w Dale Eunson *novel* Zachary Ball *d* Paul Krasny *ph* Robert L. Morrison *m* Fred Karlin *ad* Don K. Ivey *ed* Mike Vejar, Millie Moore
☆ Brian Keith (Captain Harper), Ricardo Montalban (Turtle George), Alan Feinstein (Rocky), Cliff Osmond (Rance), A Martinez (Billy Tiger), Ray Tracey (Joe Panther)

Joe Smith American *
US 1942 63m bw
MGM (Jack Chertok)
GB title: *Highway to Freedom*
An aircraft factory worker with special knowledge is kidnapped by Nazis but leads the FBI to his captors.
Watchable propaganda thriller credited with easing Americans into a war mood.
w Allen Rivkin *story* Paul Gallico *d* Richard Thorpe *ph* Charles Lawton Jnr *m* Daniele Amfitheatrof

☆ Robert Young, Marsha Hunt, Darryl Hickman, Harvey Stephens, Jonathan Hale, Noel Madison, Joseph Anthony
'Not a high-powered movie, it is a first rate die for the new propaganda models which Hollywood is readying for mass production.' – *Time*

'A Comedy About Somebody Everybody Can Believe In.'
Joe Somebody
US 2001 98m DeLuxe
TCF/Fox 2000/Regency (Arnold Kopelson, Anne Kopelson, Matthew Gross, Ken Atchity, Brian Reilly)
After he is humiliated by the office bully, a man has a breakdown and regains respect by challenging his tormentor to a fight.
Mild-mannered comedy of corporate life with a little romance thrown in, but it doesn't punch its weight.
w John Scott Shepherd *d* John Pasquin *ph* Daryn Okada *m* George S. Clinton *pd* Jackson De Govia *ed* David Finfer
☆ Tim Allen (Joe Scheffer), Julie Bowen (Meg Harper), Kelly Lynch (Callie Scheffer), Hayden Panettiere (Natalie Scheffer), Jim Belushi (Chuck Scarett), Greg Germann (Jeremy)
'A simple, wholesome parable, crashingly obvious, and we sit patiently while the characters and the screenplay slowly arrive at the inevitable conclusion.' – *Roger Ebert, Chicago Sun-Times*

Joe versus the Volcano
US 1990 102m Technicolor Panavision
Warner/Amblin Entertainment (Teri Schwartz)
Told that he has only a few months to live, a man agrees to jump into a volcano to prevent an eruption and save an island for an entrepreneur.
Weak whimsy, directed without flair.
wd John Patrick Shanley *ph* Stephen Goldblatt *m* Georges Delerue *pd* Bo Welch *ed* Richard Halsey
☆ Tom Hanks, Meg Ryan, Lloyd Bridges, Robert Stack, Abe Vigoda, Dan Hedaya, Barry McGovern, Amanda Plummer, Ossie Davis, Jayne Haynes

'Sex. Bugs. Rock 'n' Roll.'
Joe's Apartment
US 1996 80m colour
Warner/Geffen/MTV (Diana Phillips, Bonni Lee)
A youth having problems with his girlfriend and his evil landlord shares his apartment with hundreds of singing and dancing cockroaches.
A one-joke movie, stretched well beyond breaking point.
wd John Payson *ph* Peter Deming *m* Carter Burwell *pd* Carol Spier *ed* Peter Frank
☆ Jerry O'Connell, Megan Ward, Jim Turner, Jim Sterling, Sandra Denton, Robert Vaughn, Don Ho and also the voices of: Reginald Hudlin, Bill West
† It is based on a short film of the same name, made by Payson for MTV.

Joey Boy
GB 1965 91m bw
British Lion/Launder-Gilliat
In 1941, a group of petty crooks join the army.
Abysmal service comedy, incredibly cheap and tatty and the nadir of several of the talents involved.
wd Frank Launder *ph* Arthur Lavis *m* Philip Green
☆ Harry H. Corbett, Stanley Baxter, Bill Fraser, Reg Varney, Percy Herbert, Lance Percival
'As visually shoddy as it is unfunny … the final shot (Corbett pulling a lavatory chain) is all too crudely apt.' – *MFB*

Johann Mouse ***
US 1952 8m Technicolor
MGM (Fred Quimby)
Strauss's mouse dances to his master's music; the cat, to lure him out, learns to play the piano.
Splendid Tom and Jerry cartoon from the great period of this neglected art.
best cartoon

John and Julie
GB 1955 82m Eastmancolor
Group Three (Herbert Mason)
Two children run away to see the coronation.

Genial little family comedy full of stock comic characters.
wd William Fairchild *ph* Arthur Grant *m* Philip Green
☆ Colin Gibson, Leslie Dudley, Peter Sellers, Moira Lister, Wilfrid Hyde-White, Sidney James, Andrew Cruickshank

John and Mary *
US 1969 92m DeLuxe Panavision
TCF/Debrod (Ben Kadish)
Two New Yorkers have a one-night affair and cannot decide whether to continue.
Slight, disappointing sex comedy vehicle for two stars who were very hot at the time.
w John Mortimer *novel* Mervyn Jones *d* Peter Yates *ph* Gayne Rescher *m* Quincy Jones *pd* John Robert Lloyd
☆ Dustin Hoffman, Mia Farrow, Michael Tolan, Sunny Griffin, Tyne Daly
'The emphasis is not on action but on acting, which although skilful and subtly nuanced does not in this case amount to the same thing as character.' – *Jan Dawson*
'Despite all the "now" sets and surfaces, it's like an old comedy of the thirties – minus the comedy.' – *Judith Crist*
Dustin Hoffman

John Carpenter's Escape from LA: see *Escape from LA*

John Carpenter's Ghosts of Mars: see *Ghosts of Mars*

'Prepare For The Dawn.'
John Carpenter's Vampires *
US 1998 104m Foto-Kem Panavision
Largo/Film Office/Storm King (Sandy King)
aka: *Vampires*
A vampire killer and his gang of mercenaries are hired by the Vatican to destroy a 600-year-old vampire terrorizing the American Southwest.
Entertaining low-budget horror-cum-western that works up to a satisfying climax.
w John Carpenter, Don Jacoby, Dan Mazur *novel Vampire$* by John Steakley *d* John Carpenter *ph* Gary B. Kibbe *m* John Carpenter *pd* Thomas A. Walsh *ed* Edward A. Warschilka *sp* Darrell D. Pritchett; make-up fx: KNB EFX
☆ James Woods, Daniel Baldwin, Sheryl Lee, Thomas Ian Griffith, Tim Guinee, Maximilian Schell, Cary-Hiroyuki Tagawa
'Taps into an appealing mix of anti-clerical sentiment, unsentimental rebel codes and gung-ho gouging and splattering. Unlike garlic, Carpenter's humor-leavened handling of evil doesn't leave a bad taste in the mouth.' – *Lisa Nesselson, Variety*
† It was followed by a sequel *Vampires: Los Muertos* in 2002, directed by Tommy Lee Wallace.

John Goldfarb, Please Come Home
US 1965 96m DeLuxe Cinemascope
TCF/Steve Parker/J. Lee-Thompson
An American spy pilot crashlands near the palace of a Middle Eastern potentate at the same time as a girl reporter arrives for an interview.
Would-be satire on the cold war, anti-feminism, American football, American/Arab relations, etc. None of it works for a minute, and the actors' desperation can be plainly seen.
w William Peter Blatty *d* J. Lee-Thompson *ph* Leon Shamroy *m* Johnny Williams
☆ Shirley MacLaine, Richard Crenna, Peter Ustinov, Fred Clark, Wilfrid Hyde-White, Jim Backus

'They were totally unqualified to try the case of a lifetime ... but every underdog has his day.'
John Grisham's The Rainmaker **
Germany/US 1997 136m DeLuxe Panavision
UIP/Constellation/American Zoetrope (Michael Douglas, Steven Reuther, Fred Fuchs)
With the aid of a sleazy para-legal, an idealistic young lawyer sues a big insurance company, which refuses to pay benefits to a man dying of leukaemia.
A well-made, satisfying account of a David versus Goliath contest that makes effective use of all the suspenseful tricks of courtroom dramas.
wd Francis Ford Coppola *novel* John Grisham *ph* John Toll *m* Elmer Bernstein *pd* Howard Cummings *ed* Barry Malkin, Melissa Kent
☆ Matt Damon, Claire Danes, Jon Voight, Mary Kay Place, Mickey Rourke, Danny De Vito, Dean Stockwell, Teresa Wright, Virginia Madsen, Roy Scheider
'One of the few films that say something important about life and work in the US today. This is a populist movie made by a master.' – *Alexander Walker, London Evening Standard*

John Loves Mary
US 1948 87m bw
Warner (Jerry Wald)
A GI returns home to get married, but unfortunately, to help a friend, he has already entered into a marriage of convenience.
Moderately amusing comedy with an excess of complications.
w Phoebe and Henry Ephron *play* Norman Krasna *d* David Butler *ph* Peverell Marley *m* David Buttolph
☆ Ronald Reagan, Patricia Neal, Jack Carson, Virginia Field

John Meade's Woman
US 1937 82m bw
Paramount
A timber industrialist marries a farm girl.
Solemn star drama.
w Vincent Lawrence, Herman J. Mankiewicz *d* Richard Wallace
☆ Edward Arnold, Francine Larrimore, Gail Patrick, George Bancroft
'One more picture with a message. Edward Arnold's pictures are beginning to look alike.' – *Variety*

John Paul Jones
US 1959 126m Technirama
Warner/Samuel Bronston
At the time of the American revolution a young Scotsman rises to great heights in the American navy.
Fragmented biopic with a succession of guest stars which turn it into a charade almost as silly as The Story of Mankind. *On that level it is not unentertaining.*
wd John Farrow *ph* Michel Kelber *m* Max Steiner
☆ Robert Stack, Charles Coburn (Benjamin Franklin), Bette Davis (Catherine the Great), Marisa Pavan, Jean-Pierre Aumont, Peter Cushing, Bruce Cabot, Macdonald Carey

'Give a father no options and you leave him no choice.'
John Q
US 2002 116m DeLuxe
Entertainment/New Line (Mark Burg, Oren Koules)
A hard-up father takes people hostage at a hospital when his son is denied further treatment for a heart condition.
Hectoring drama in favour of a national health insurance: its heart may be in the right place, but it has misplaced its mind.
w James Kearns *d* Nick Cassavetes *ph* Rogier Stoffers *m* Aaron Zigman *pd* Stefania Cella *ed* Dede Allen
☆ Denzel Washington (John Q. Archibald), Robert Duvall (Grimes), James Woods (Dr Turner), Anne Heche (Rebecca Payne), Kimberly Elise (Denise Archibald), Shawn Hatosy (Mitch), Ray Liotta (Police Chief Monroe), Daniel E. Smith (Mike Archibald)
'Will leave most audiences in dire need of medical attention, though it would be hard to say if that need will come from the painful collection of plot clichés or Aaron Zigman's assaultive soundtrack.' – *Elvis Mitchell, New York Times*
'Truly awful – an "issue" movie which cheapens its issue with fatuous emotional grandstanding.' – *Peter Bradshaw, Guardian*

John Woo's Once a Thief
US 1995 96m colour
Alliance/WCG/NDG
GB video title: *John Woo's Violent Tradition*
After double-crossing his boss, an American member of a Hong Kong criminal gang goes to work in Vancouver on a covert police operation against his former associates.
Mindless, violent thriller, although tame by Woo's standards, since it was made as a pilot for a TV series; its central characters are unattractive and the narrative unoriginal.
w Glenn Davis, William Laurin *d* John Woo *ph* Bill Wong *m* Amin Bhatia *pd* Douglas Higgins *ed* David Wu
☆ Sandrine Holt, Ivan Sergei, Nicholas Lea, Robert Ito, Michael Wong, Alan Scarfe, Jennifer Dale
'Tailor-made for stupid American audiences.' – *Total Cinema*
† The film is an American variation on Woo's *Once a Thief* (qv), made in Hong Kong in 1991.

Johnny Allegro *
US 1949 81m bw
Columbia (Irving Starr)
GB title: *Hounded*
A private eye eliminates a counterfeiter and marries his wife.
Cheeky variation on the plot of Gilda, *with Macready repeating his role; later stages borrow from* The Most Dangerous Game. *All mildly diverting.*
w Karen de Wolf, Guy Endore, James Edward Grant *d* Ted Tetzlaff *ph* Joseph Biroc *m* George Duning
☆ George Raft, George Macready, Nina Foch, Will Geer, Ivan Triesault
'Without any particular distinction, but certainly not boring.' – *Richard Mallett, Punch*

Johnny Angel *
US 1945 79m bw
RKO (William L. Pereira)
A seaman solves the mystery of his father's ship, found empty and adrift in the Gulf of Mexico.
Very watchable mystery with plenty of plot twists and efficient presentation.
w Steve Fisher *d* Edwin L. Marin *ph* Harry J. Wild *m* Leigh Harline
☆ George Raft, Claire Trevor, Signe Hasso, Lowell Gilmore, Hoagy Carmichael, Marvin Miller

Johnny Apollo
US 1940 93m bw
TCF (Harry Joe Brown)
A well-heeled young man turns crook.
Moderate crime melo, impeccably turned out.
w Philip Dunne, Rowland Brown *d* Henry Hathaway *ph* Arthur Miller *m* Cyril Mockridge *md* Alfred Newman
☆ Tyrone Power, Dorothy Lamour, Edward Arnold, Lloyd Nolan, Charles Grapewin, Lionel Atwill, Marc Lawrence, Jonathan Hale

'There was temptation in her helpless silence – and then torment!'
Johnny Belinda **
US 1948 103m bw
Warner (Jerry Wald)
In a remote fishing community, a deaf mute girl is raped and the sympathetic local doctor is suspected of being the father of her baby.
Melodrama of the old school which in 1948 seemed oddly to mark a new permissiveness and made a big star of Jane Wyman; the production and locations were also persuasive.
w Irmgard von Cube, Allen Vincent *play* Elmer Harris *d Jean Negulesco ph Ted McCord m* Max Steiner *md* Leo F. Forbstein *ad* Robert Haas
☆ *Jane Wyman, Lew Ayres, Charles Bickford,* Agnes Moorehead, Stephen McNally, Jan Sterling, Rosalind Ivan, Mabel Paige
'Hollywood has tried something dangerously different here, and succeeded in making a powerful and sensitive job of it.' – *Observer*
'An atmosphere in which the hokey, tearjerking elements are used for more than mere pathos – an example of technique over subject matter.' – *Pauline Kael, 70s*
Jane Wyman
best picture; script; Jean Negulesco; Ted McCord; Max Steiner; Lew Ayres; Charles Bickford; Agnes Moorehead; art direction

Johnny Come Lately *
US 1943 97m bw
Cagney Productions (William Cagney)
GB title: *Johnny Vagabond*
A travelling newspaperman is jailed for vagrancy in a small town and stays to expose corrupt politicians.
A turn-of-the-century folksy drama seemed an odd choice for a Cagney independent production, and it was not very persuasively made, but the star produced moments of his old charisma.
w John Van Druten *novel McLeod's Folly* by Louis Bromfield *d* William K. Howard *ph* Theodor Sparkuhl *m* Leigh Harline
☆ James Cagney, *Grace George,* Marjorie Main, Marjorie Lord, Hattie McDaniel, Edward McNamara, Bill Henry, Robert Barrat, George Cleveland, Margaret Hamilton, Lucien Littlefield, Irving Bacon
'The kind of business that might result if Jimmy Cagney, the immortal Hollywood movie star, had returned to play the lead in the annual production of his old high school's Masque and Film Club.' – *John T. McManus*
'The film does show a fatal commercial uneasiness and, I half suspect, radical loss or atrophy of cinematic judgment. But ... there is a general ambience of hope and pleasure about the production which, regrettably, loses its glow.' – *James Agee*
Leigh Harline

Johnny Comes Flying Home
US 1946 65m bw
Aubrey Schenck/TCF
Three discharged flyers build an air freight company.
The Best Years of Our Lives *it isn't, not on this budget, but it clumsily expresses some of the same concerns.*
w Jack Andrews, George Bricker *d* Ben Stoloff
☆ Richard Crane, Faye Marlowe, Martha Stewart, Roy Roberts, Henry Morgan

Johnny Concho
US 1956 84m bw
UA/Kent (Frank Sinatra)
A coward runs Cripple Creek because he has a gunfighter brother, but when the latter is shot another gunman takes over.
Unexpected small-scale Western, pleasantly made but no High Noon.
w David P. Harmon, Don McGuire *d* Don McGuire *ph* William Mellor *m* Nelson Riddle
☆ Frank Sinatra, *William Conrad,* Phyllis Kirk, Wallace Ford, John Qualen

Johnny Cool *
US 1963 101m bw
UA/Chrislaw (William Asher)
A Sicilian bandit is sent to the US on a mission of vengeance.
Chilling gangster thriller, the callousness of which is apparently meant to be counterpointed by the humorous cameo appearances of several well-known faces. This does not work.
w Joseph Landon *novel* John McPartland *d* William Asher *ph* Sam Leavitt *m* Billy May
☆ *Henry Silva,* Elizabeth Montgomery, Jim Backus, Marc Lawrence, John McGiver, Sammy Davis Jnr, Mort Sahl, Telly Savalas, Joseph Calleia, Robert Armstrong, Douglass Dumbrille, Elisha Cook Jnr

'Organized crime has never been so disorganized!'
Johnny Dangerously
US 1984 90m DeLuxe
TCF/Edgewood (Michael Hertzberg)
A boy takes up crime to pay for an operation for his ailing mother.
1930s gangster send-up which fails to register, and is filled with unnecessary excesses.
w Norman Steinberg, Bernie Kukoff, Harry Colomby, Jeff Harris *d* Amy Heckerling *ph* David M. Walsh *m* John Morris *pd* Joseph R. Jennings *ed* Pembroke J. Herring
☆ Michael Keaton, Joe Piscopo, Marilu Henner, Maureen Stapleton, Peter Boyle, Griffin Dunne, Richard Dmitri, Glynnis O'Connor, Dom DeLuise, Ray Walston
'The material given all of them just gets worse and worse.' – *Variety*

Johnny Dark
US 1954 85m Technicolor
U-I (William Alland)
A motor company produces a new sports car designed by an employee, who drives it in a race.
Competent, unremarkable action melodrama tailor-made for its star.
w Franklin Coen *d* George Sherman *ph* Carl Guthrie *m* Hans Salter
☆ Tony Curtis, Piper Laurie, Don Taylor, Paul Kelly, Ilka Chase, Sidney Blackmer

Johnny Doughboy
US 1943 64m bw
Republic
A teenage girl star runs away, falls for a middle-aged playwright, and joins an acting troupe called The Hollywood Victory Caravan.
Curious attempt to make a child star grow up, with a supporting cast laced with others of her ilk.
w Lawrence Kimble *d* John H. Auer *m* Walter Scharf
☆ Jane Withers, Henry Wilcoxon, William Demarest, Ruth Donnelly; and Bobby Breen, Baby Sandy, Butch and Buddy, Spanky McFarland, etc
Walter Scharf

'The flaming drama of a high-born beauty who blindly loved the most icy-hearted big shot gangland ever knew!'
Johnny Eager *
US 1942 107m bw
MGM (John W. Considine)
A gangster makes a play for a society girl.
Well-made, rather unattractive gangster melodrama.
w John Lee Mahin, James Edward Grant *d* Mervyn Le Roy *ph* Harold Rosson *m* Bronislau Kaper
☆ Robert Taylor, Van Heflin, Lana Turner, Edward Arnold, Robert Sterling, Patricia Dane, Glenda Farrell, Henry O'Neill
Van Heflin

Johnny Frenchman
GB 1945 111m bw
Ealing (S. C. Balcon)
Rivalry between the fishermen of Cornwall and Brittany prevents the course of true love from running smooth.
Rhubarbing extras and studio sets make this an unreal and disappointing Ealing melodrama, and all the actors look helpless.
w T. E. B. Clarke *d* Charles Frend *ph* Roy Kellino *m* Clifton Parker
☆ Françoise Rosay, Tom Walls, Patricia Roc, Paul Dupuis, Ralph Michael, Frederick Piper, Arthur Hambling

Johnny Got His Gun
US 1971 111m colour
World Entertainments Ltd (Bruce Campbell)
In 1918 a soldier is so badly wounded as to lose arms, legs, eyes, ears, mouth and nose, and begs his doctors to kill him.
A horrifying and fascinating premise turns out to have nowhere to go, at least not in this talky treatment which the author has nurtured too long.
wd Dalton Trumbo *ph* Jules Brenner *m* Jerry Fielding
☆ Timothy Bottoms, Jason Robards Jnr, Marsha Hunt, Donald Sutherland, Kathy Fields, Diane Varsi

Johnny Guitar *
US 1953 110m Trucolor
Republic (Nicholas Ray)
In old Arizona, the proprietress of a gambling saloon stakes a claim to valuable land and incurs the enmity of a lady banker.
Weird Freudian Western notable for a running catfight between its lady protagonists; the title character is decidedly secondary. Not exactly a good movie, but memorable because it's almost always over the top.
w Philip Yordan *novel* Roy Chanslor *d* Nicholas Ray *ph* Harry Stradling *m* Victor Young
☆ *Joan Crawford, Mercedes McCambridge*, Sterling Hayden, Ernest Borgnine, Ward Bond, John Carradine, Scott Brady
'A very rum western, with cockeyed feminist attitudes.' – *New Yorker, 1975*

Johnny Handsome
US 1989 94m Technicolor
Guild/Carolco Pictures/Guber-Peters (Charles Roven)
A deformed petty criminal undergoes surgery to give him a new appearance.
A thriller of betrayal and double-cross that never fully engages the attention.
w Ken Friedman *novel* *The Three Worlds of Johnny Handsome* by John Godey *d* Walter Hill *ph* Matthew F. Leonetti *m* Ry Cooder *pd* Gene Rudolf *ed* Freeman Davies, Carmel Davies, Donn Aron
☆ Mickey Rourke, Ellen Barkin, Elizabeth McGovern, Morgan Freeman, Forest Whitaker, Lance Henriksen, Scott Wilson, David Schramm, Yvonne Bryceland
'A taut, violent, moody thriller.' – *Philip French, Observer*
'A faintly risible mess, torn between a dozen stools and never managing to settle squarely on any of them.' – *Tom Milne, MFB*

Johnny Holiday
US 1949 92m bw
United Artists (R. W. Alcorn)
A reform school boy becomes a goodie through devotion to his sergeant.
Sentimental mush.
w Jack Andrews, Willis Goldbeck, Frederick Stephani *d* Willis Goldbeck *ph* Hal Mohr *m* Franz Waxman
☆ William Bendix, Stanley Clements, Allen Martin Jnr, Herbert Newcomb, Hoagy Carmichael

Johnny in the Clouds: see *The Way to the Stars*

'Meet the ultimate hard drive.'
Johnny Mnemonic
Canada 1995 98m Film House colour
TCF/Alliance (Don Carmody)
In the future, ruthless killers hunt down a courier who will die unless he can quickly transfer important information implanted in a microchip in his brain.
A cyberpunk thriller that, like every other movie that has attempted to cash in on virtual reality, crashes and leaves only confusion behind.
w William Gibson *story* William Gibson *d* Robert Longo *ph* François Protat *m* Brad Fiedel *pd* Nilo Rodis Jamero *ed* Ronald Sanders *sp* Sony Pictures Imageworks, Fantasy II, CORE Digital Pictures
☆ Keanu Reeves, Dolph Lundgren, Takeshi Kitano, Ice T, Dina Meyer, Denis Akiyama, Henry Rollins, Barbara Sukowa, Udo Kier
'High-tech trash, film as video-game.' – *Variety*
'Colossally inept badaptation.' – *Premiere*

Johnny Nobody
GB 1960 88m bw Warwickscope
Columbia/Viceroy (Irving Allen, Albert Broccoli)
A drunken Irish author challenges God to strike him dead for blasphemy. When an amnesiac shoots him, a nationwide religious controversy begins, but the deed is found to have a mercenary motive.
A mysterious rigmarole which irritates more than it entertains.
w Patrick Kirwan *story* *The Trial of Johnny Nobody* by Albert Z. Carr *d* Nigel Patrick *ph* Ted Moore *m* Ron Goodwin
☆ Nigel Patrick, Aldo Ray, Yvonne Mitchell, William Bendix, Cyril Cusack, Niall MacGinnis, Bernie Winters, Noel Purcell, Jimmy O'Dea
'The more one thinks of it, the more one is amazed that anyone should have thought a plot and players as uniformly unlikely as these could have worked out satisfactorily.' – *Peter John Dyer, MFB*

Johnny O'Clock
US 1946 95m bw
Columbia
A gambler appears to be involved in the death of a crooked policeman, but a girl helps to clear him.
Tawdry material made palatable by surface slickness.
wd Robert Rossen *ph* Burnett Guffey
☆ Dick Powell, Ellen Drew, Lee J. Cobb, Evelyn Keyes

Johnny Rocco
US 1958 83m bw
Allied Artists
The small son of a gangster is affected by his father's notoriety.
Awful sentimental melodrama with tear-stained ending; for connoisseurs of cliché.
w James O'Hanlon, Samuel F. Roeca *d* Paul Landres *ph* William Margulies *m* Edward J. Kay
☆ Richard Eyer, Stephen McNally, Coleen Gray, Russ Conway

Johnny Stecchino **
Italy 1991 102m Technicolor
Tiger/Pentafilm (Mario and Vittorio Cecchi Gori)
The wife of a Sicilian gangster whom many people want dead discovers that a naive bus driver is her husband's double.
Relaxed comedy of mistaken identity that makes fun of the Mafia and displays Benigni's gifts as a sweet-natured clown.
w Vincenzo Cerami, Roberto Benigni *d* Roberto Benigni *ph* Giuseppe Lanci *m* Evan Lurie *pd* Paolo Biagetti *ed* Nino Baragli
☆ Roberto Benigni, Nicoletta Braschi, Paolo Bonacelli, Franco Volpi, Ivano Marescotti, Turi Scalia, Loredana Romito
† The film broke all box-office records in Italy.

'A Smooth Comedy...'
Johnny Suede *
US/Switzerland/France 1991 97m Fujicolour
Artificial Eye/Vega/Balthazar/Starr/Arena (Yoram Mandel, Ruth Waldburger)
After a pair of suede shoes drops on top of a phone booth he's using, an ineffectual young man with an exaggerated quiff puts them on and tries to become a rock star.
Stylish exploration of pop style, although a certain tedium sets in before the end.
wd Tom DiCillo *ph* Joe DeSalvo *m* Jim Farmer, Link Wray *pd* Patricia Woodbridge *ed* Geraldine Peroni
☆ Brad Pitt, Catherine Keener, Calvin Levels, Alison Moir, Nick Cave, Peter McRobbie, Ashley Gardner, Dennis Parlato, Ron Vawter, Tina Louise
'There are moments of quirky charm and humor in this odd, stylized fable.' – *Stephen Farber, Movieline*

Johnny Tiger
US 1966 102m colour
Nova Hook (John Hugh)
A repressed schoolteacher learns to trust his feelings after working on an Indian reservation and encouraging a wild young half-breed Seminole to study.
Formulaic confrontational drama of minimal interest.
w Paul Crabtree, John Hugh *d* Paul Wendkos *ph* Charles Straumer *m* John Green *ed* Harry Coswick
☆ Robert Taylor, Geraldine Brooks, Chad Everett, Brenda Scott, Marc Lawrence

Johnny Tremain
US 1957 81m Technicolor
Walt Disney
In 1773 Boston an apprentice silversmith joins the Sons of Liberty and helps start the War of Independence.
Schoolbook history with little vitality.
w Tom Blackburn *novel* Esther Forbes *d* Robert Stevenson *ph* Charles P. Boyle *m* George Bruns
☆ Hal Stalmaster, Luana Patten, Jeff York, Sebastian Cabot, Richard Beymer, Walter Sande

Johnny Trouble
US 1956 88m bw
Clarion (John H. Auer)
An elderly widow becomes involved with a boys' college and thinks she has found her lost grandson.
Sentimental, whimsical star vehicle.
w Charles O'Neal, David Lord *d* John H. Auer *ph* Peverell Marley *m* Frank de Vol
☆ *Ethel Barrymore*, Stuart Whitman, Cecil Kellaway, Carolyn Jones, Jesse White

Johnny Vagabond: see *Johnny Come Lately*

Johns
US 1995 96m CFI color
Metrodome/Bandeira (Beau Flynn, Stefan Simchowitz)
A male prostitute's attempt to help a fellow hustler pay off his debts goes wrong.
A downbeat chronicle of sex and violence, inadequate and unsatisfactory despite some earnest performances.
wd Scott Silver *ph* Tom Richmond *m* Charles Brown, Danny Caron *pd* Amy Beth Silver *ed* Dorian Harris
☆ David Arquette, Lukas Haas, Wilson Cruz, Keith David, Christopher Gartin, Elliott Gould, Terrence Dashon Howard, Richard Timothy Jones
'Works well as an MTV-style day in the life of LA rent boys, but its heart (which is in the right place) isn't quite substantial enough to support the emotional resonance the film needs.' – *Peter Griffiths, Film Review*

The Johnstown Flood *
US 1926 70m approx (24 fps) bw silent
Fox
A construction worker is warned by his girlfriend of an approaching flood, in which she dies.
Curious melodrama with mild spectacle.
w Edfrid Bingham, Robert Lord *d* Irving Cummings
☆ George O'Brien, Janet Gaynor, Paul Panzer, George Harris

The Joke **
Czechoslovakia 1968 78m bw
Studio Barrandov (Milos Stejskal)
original title: *Zert*
Fifteen years after being severely punished for making a joke about Trotsky, a man takes revenge on one of his judges and discovers that his action rebounds upon him.
Deft and deadly ironic political fable of the Stalinist era, with its seamless mix of past despair and present regret.
w Milan Kundera, Jaromil Jires *novel* Milan Kundera *d* Jaromil Jires *ph* Jan Curik *m* Zdenek Pololanik *ad* Leos Karen
☆ Josef Somr, Jana Ditetova, Ludek Munzar, Jaroslava Obermaierova
† The film was banned by the Czech authorities in the 70s.

The Joker Is Wild *
US 1957 126m bw Vistavision
Paramount/Charles Vidor
Joe E. Lewis, a twenties night-club singer, loses his voice after an attack by gangsters, and becomes a comedian.
Reasonably lively showbiz biopic in jaundiced vein; good atmosphere but far too long.
w Oscar Saul *book* Art Cohn *d* Charles Vidor *ph* Daniel L. Fapp *m* Walter Scharf
☆ *Frank Sinatra*, Mitzi Gaynor, Eddie Albert, Jeanne Crain, Beverly Garland, Jackie Coogan, Ted de Corsia
song 'All the Way' (*m*Jimmy Van Heusen, *ly*Sammy Cahn)

The Jokers **
GB 1967 94m Technicolor
Universal/Adastra/Gildor/Scimitar (Maurice Foster, Ben Arbeid)
Two young brothers in London society plan to create a sensation by borrowing (and replacing) the crown jewels.
Bright suspense comedy which sums up the swinging London era pretty well and is generally amusing though it finally lacks aplomb.
w *Dick Clement, Ian La Frenais* *d* *Michael Winner* *ph* Ken Hodges *m* Johnny Pearson
☆ Michael Crawford, Oliver Reed, Harry Andrews, *James Donald*, Daniel Massey, Michael Hordern, Gabriella Licudi, Frank Finlay, Warren Mitchell, Rachel Kempson, Peter Graves

A Jolly Bad Fellow *
GB 1964 95m bw
British Lion/Pax/Tower/Michael Balcon (Donald Taylor)
US title: *They All Died Laughing*
A brash chemistry don tries a new poison on his enemies.
Interesting but finally irritating comedy of murders with a punnish rather than a donnish script and only moments of genuine sub-Ealing hilarity.

w Robert Hamer, Donald Taylor *novel* *Don Among the Dead Men* by C. E. Vulliamy *d* Don Chaffey *ph* Gerald Gibbs *m* John Barry
☆ Leo McKern, Janet Munro, Maxine Audley, Duncan Macrae, Dennis Price, Miles Malleson, Leonard Rossiter

Jolson Sings Again **
US 1949 96m Technicolor
Columbia (Sidney Buchman)

Al Jolson's later career and second marriage to a nurse he met while entertaining troops in World War II.
Breezy, routine, rather empty sequel to the following.
w Sidney Buchman *d* Henry Levin *ph* William Snyder *md* Morris Stoloff, George Duning
☆ Larry Parks, Barbara Hale, William Demarest, Ludwig Donath, Bill Goodwin, Tamara Shayne, Myron McCormick

'Just relax and enjoy yourself.' – *Daily Express*

'I love it now – every last sentimental showbiz cliché, every oversung song.' – *Daily Telegraph, 1969*

Sidney Buchman; William Snyder; Morris Stoloff, George Duning

The Jolson Story ****
US 1946 129m Technicolor
Columbia (Sidney Skolsky)

Asa Yoelson, son of a cantor, becomes Al Jolson, the great entertainer of the twenties; but showbiz success brings marital difficulties.
Whitewashed biopic in impeccable Hollywood style, with everything working shamelessly right, a new star in the leading role, perfect if unambitious production values, and a deluge of the best songs ever written.
w Stephen Longstreet d Alfred E. Green, Joseph H. Lewis ph Joseph Walker *md* Morris Stoloff *ed* William Lyon
☆ *Larry Parks, William Demarest, Evelyn Keyes, Ludwig Donath, Tamara Shayne,* Bill Goodwin, *Scotty Beckett,* John Alexander

'I have nothing in the world against this picture except that at least half of it seemed to me enormously tiresome.' – *James Agee*

† 3rd biggest moneyspinner of 1946, after *The Best Years of Our Lives* and *Duel in the Sun*.
†† Jolson dubbed Larry Parks's singing of his songs.
Morris Stoloff
Joseph Walker; Larry Parks; William Demarest; William Lyon

'Everyone's book is now everyone's motion picture!'
Jonathan Livingston Seagull
US 1973 114m DeLuxe Panavision
Paramount/JLS Partnership/Hall Bartlett

The life of a seagull who aims to fly faster than any of his peers and eventually arrives in a perfect world.
Weird 'family' fantasy based on a phenomenally successful book which clearly could not translate easily to the screen. The bird photography is much more successful than the mysticism.
w Richard Bach *novel* Richard Bach *d* Hall Bartlett *ph* Boris Leven *m* Neil Diamond, Lee Holdridge

'A parable couched in the form of a nature film of overpowering beauty and strength in which, perhaps to our horror, we are forced to recognize ourselves in a seagull obsessed with the heights.' – *Michael Korda*

'It may be that the creature best qualified to review it is another seagull.' – *Benny Green, Punch*

'If one must spend two hours following the adventures of a bird, far better that the hero be Donald Duck.' – *Jay Cocks, Time*

'The sort of garbage that only a seagull could love.' – *Judith Crist*

Jack Couffer

The Jones Family
Less human, more farcical than the Hardy films (qv), this series was TCF's second feature answer to MGM's money-makers, and pleased a lot of people at the time. Pop was Jed Prouty, Mom was Spring Byington, Grandma was Florence Roberts, and the youngsters included Kenneth Howell, George Ernest, Billy Mahan, June Carlson and June Lang. The first script was from a play by Katharine Cavanaugh, and the principal director was Frank Strayer.
1936 Every Saturday Night, Educating Father, Back to Nature
1937 Off to the Races, Borrowing Trouble, Hot Water
1938 Love on a Budget, Trip to Paris, Safety in Numbers, Down on the Farm
1939 Everybody's Baby, Quick Millions, The Jones Family in Hollywood, Too Busy to Work
1940 On Their Own
† An earlier series with different actors was abandoned after two episodes: *Young as You Feel* (1931), *Business and Pleasure* (1932).

'The epic love story in which everybody has a great role and a big part.'
Joseph Andrews
GB 1977 104m Eastmancolor
UA/Woodfall (Neil Hartley)
Adventures of a naïve 18th-century footman.
Woebegone attempt to restage Tom Jones.
w Allan Scott, Chris Bryant *d* Tony Richardson *ph* David Watkin *m* John Addison *pd* Michael Annals
☆ Peter Firth, Ann-Margret, Michael Hordern, Beryl Reid, Jim Dale, Peter Bull, John Gielgud, Hugh Griffith, Timothy West, Wendy Craig, Peggy Ashcroft, James Villiers, Karen Dotrice, Ronald Pickup

'Even the incidental pleasures cannot offset the sense of *déjà vu* which pervades this musty enterprise.' – *John Pym, MFB*

Joseph Conrad's The Secret Agent: see *The Secret Agent*

Josephine and Men
GB 1955 98m Eastmancolor
Charter (John and Roy Boulting)
The three romances of a determined young woman.
Alarmingly thin, old-fashioned romantic comedy with all resolved in a country cottage. Nothing quite works, especially the colour.
w Nigel Balchin, Roy Boulting, Frank Harvey *d* Roy Boulting *ph* Gilbert Taylor *m* John Addison
☆ Glynis Johns, *Jack Buchanan*, Donald Sinden, Peter Finch, Heather Thatcher, Ronald Squire

Josette
US 1938 73m bw
TCF (Gene Markey)
A New Orleans coquette teases two men.
Very minor musical, well enough presented but adding up to almost nothing.
w James Edward Grant *d* Allan Dwan *ph* John Mescall *m/ly* Harry Revel, Mack Gordon
☆ Simone Simon, Don Ameche, Robert Young, Joan Davis, Bert Lahr, Paul Hurst, William Collier Snr, Lynn Bari, William Demarest

'Rollicking farce with music ... a corking good entertainment.' – *Variety*

'Why run away from home when you can drive?'
Josh and S.A.M.
US 1993 98m Technicolor
Rank/Castle Rock/New Line/City Lights (Martin Brest)

Two young brothers, unhappy at home with their father, run away.
An odd, sentimental drama of adolescent fantasy, which mainly shows how a 12-year-old can become a success by the use of deft lies and deceit.
w Frank Deese *d* Billy Weber *ph* Don Burgess *m* Thomas Newman *pd* Marcia Hinds-Johnson *ed* Chris Lebenzon
☆ Jacob Tierney, Noah Fleiss, Martha Plimpton, Stephen Tobolowsky, Chris Penn, Joan Allen, Maury Chaykin, Udo Kier

'A marvellous example of how uninspired and lacking in vision most American movie-making has become. Competent and reasonably entertaining, it's ultimately forgettable.' – *Nigel Robinson, Film Review*

'The hunted has become the hunter. And there will be no mercy.'
Joshua Tree
US 1993 94m Foto-Kem Super 35
Vision International (Illana Diamant, Andy Armstrong)

video title: *Army of One*
A trucker escapes from prison, takes a female cop as hostage and goes to seek revenge on those who killed his partner and framed him for murder.
An action film with a familiar plot but also possessing a slight sense of irony, with a little bow along the way to Bogart and a violent confrontation with Chinese crooks straight out of a Hong Kong movie.
w Steven Pressfield *d* Vic Armstrong *ph* Dan Turrett *m* Joel Goldsmith *pd* John J. Moore *ed* Paul Morton
☆ Dolph Lundgren (Santee), George Segal (Severence), Kristian Alfonso (Rita), Geoffrey Lewis (Capeda), Bert Remsen (Woody Engstrom), Michelle Phillips (Esther), Beau Starr (Rudisill)

'Serviceable action-suspense pic.' – *Sight and Sound*

'Here kitty, kitty, kitty...'
Josie and the Pussycats
US 2001 98m DeLuxe
TCF/MGM/Universal/Riverdale (Marc Platt, Tracey Edmonds, Chuck Grimes, Tony DeRosa-Grund)

An all-girl rock group top the hit parade and expose a government conspiracy to brainwash teenage audiences.
Badly acted, bubblegum pop fodder that pretends to preach an anti-consumerist message while being blatantly, slickly commercial and overloaded with product placements.
wd Deborah Kaplan, Harry Elfont *based on characters from* Archie comics *ph* Matthew Libatique *m* John Frizzell *pd* Jasna Stefanovich *ed* Peter Teschner, Gabriel Wrye *cos* Leesa Evans
☆ Rachael Leigh Cook (Josie McCoy), Tara Reid (Melody Valentine), Rosario Dawson (Valerie Brown), Alan Cumming (Wyatt Frame), Parker Posey (Fiona), Gabriel Mann (Alan M.), Paulo Costanzo (Alexander Cabot), Missi Pyle (Alexandra Cabot)

'Sensationally exuberant, imaginatively crafted and intoxicatingly clever.' – *Joe Leydon, Variety*

'Few people other than future airline passengers should be subjected to such misery.' – *Elvis Mitchell, New York Times*

Jour de Fête ***
France 1948 87m bw
Francinex (Fred Orain)

A village postman sees a film about the efficiency of the American postal service and decides to smarten himself up.
First, and some say best, of Tati's comedy vehicles: two-thirds superb local colour, one-third hilarious slapstick.
w Jacques Tati, Henri Marquet *d Jacques Tati* *ph* Jacques Mercanton *m* Jean Yatove
☆ *Jacques Tati*, Guy Decomble, Paul Fankeur, Santa Relli

'You could watch it with a bout of toothache and it would make you laugh.' – *Daily Express*

'It is not progressive; it won't be a landmark in the history of the cinema; but it gives me more pleasure than any film for the last five years.' – *Dilys Powell*

† A reissue version had colour items hand-painted in each frame, and proved quite effective.
†† A restored version in colour, made by Tati on experimental Thomsoncolour film but never printed at the time due to technical problems, was released in 1994 as part of France's celebration of the centenary of cinema. It has also been released on video-cassette.

Le Jour Se Lève ***
France 1939 95m bw
Sigma

aka: *Daybreak*
A murderer is besieged by police in his attic room, remembers his past through the night, and shoots himself.
A model of French poetic realism, and a much-praised film which was almost destroyed when it was bought for an American remake (The Long Night).
w Jacques Viot, Jacques Prévert d Marcel Carné *ph* Curt Courant, Philippe Agostini, André Bac *m* Maurice Jaubert *ad* Alexander Trauner
☆ *Jean Gabin*, Jules Berry, Arletty, Jacqueline Laurent

'The man walks about his room, moves a few things, lies on his bed, looks out of the window, chain-smokes ... and one is genuinely interested in him all the time (remembering afterwards that there exist directors who contrive to be boring even when they use fifteen characters in a motor car chase crackling with revolver shots).' – *Richard Mallett, Punch*

Le Journal de Lady M: see *The Diary of Lady M*

Journal d'un Curé de Campagne: see *The Diary of a Country Priest*

Le Journal d'une Femme de Chambre: see *The Diary of a Chambermaid*

Journal of a Crime
US 1934 65m bw
Warner
A woman shoots her husband's mistress and gets amnesia before she can confess.
Melodramatic farrago which entertains by its very excesses.
w F. Hugh Herbert, Charles Kenyon *play* Jacques Deval *d* William Keighley
☆ Ruth Chatterton, Adolphe Menjou, Claire Dodd, Douglass Dumbrille, George Barbier

'High in sympathetic interest and force.' – *Variety*

Une Journée Bien Remplie: see *A Full Day's Work*

The Journey
US 1959 125m Technicolor
MGM/Alby (Anatole Litvak)
During the 1956 Hungarian uprising, a busload of international passengers is detained overnight by a Russian major.
Pretentious, predictable and dull multi-melodrama peopled by uninteresting characters; different handling might have made a Casablanca *of it.*
w George Tabori *d* Anatole Litvak *ph* Jack Hildyard *m* Georges Auric
☆ Yul Brynner, Deborah Kerr, Jason Robards Jnr, Anouk Aimée, Robert Morley, E. G. Marshall, Anne Jackson, David Kossoff, Kurt Kasznar, Gerard Oury

'Ten minutes of this and we know where we are: we are back in the 1930s with Alfred Hitchcock and that glamorous band of international characters trapped in Mitteleuropa.' – *Steven Marcus*

Journey Back to Oz *
US 1974 90m colour
Norm Prescott and Lou Scheimer/Filmation

Dorothy makes a return journey over the rainbow to fight the wicked witch's sister.
Competent cartoon version of Frank Baum themes from The Wizard of Oz.
d Hal Sutherland
☆ Featuring the voices of Liza Minnelli, Milton Berle, Ethel Merman, Margaret Hamilton, Mickey Rooney, Paul Ford
† Made in 1964, but not released for a decade.

Journey Beneath the Desert
Italy/France 1961 195m Eastmancolor
CCM/Fidès

original title: *Antinea, l'Amante della Città Sepolta*
After a forced landing in the Sahara Desert, three engineers discover underground the lost continent of Atlantis, ruled over by a despotic queen.
Leisurely adventure of a familiar kind, the fourth version of the story, which was first filmed in 1921 as L'Atlantide *(qv). Here the actors seem unable to compete with the set design.*
w André Tabet, Ugo Liberatore, Remigio Del Grosso, Amedeo Nazzari *novel* *L'Atlantide* by Pierre Benoit *d* Edgar G. Ulmer, Giuseppe Masini *ph* Enzo Serafin *m* Carlo Rustichelli *pd* Piero Filippone *ed* Renato Cinquini
☆ Haya Harareet, Jean-Louis Trintignant, James Westmoreland, Amedeo Nazzari, Georges Riviere, Giulia Rubini, Gian Maria Volonte

† The uncredited Frank Borzage also directed some sequences.

Journey for Margaret *
US 1942 81m bw
MGM (B. P. Fineman)

An American correspondent brings home an orphan from the London blitz.
Efficient tearful propaganda which coincidentally made a star of little Margaret O'Brien.
w David Hertz, William Ludwig *book* William L. White *d* W. S. Van Dyke *ph* Ray June *m* Franz Waxman
☆ Robert Young, Laraine Day, *Margaret O'Brien*, Billy Severn, Fay Bainter, Signe Hasso, Nigel Bruce, Halliwell Hobbes

Journey into Autumn *
Sweden 1954 86m bw
Sandrews (Rune Waldekrantz)

original title: *Kvinnodrom*
Two business women visiting Gothenburg have difficult relationships to settle.
Moody, impressionist sex drama which succeeds by fits and starts.
wd Ingmar Bergman *ph* Hilding Bladh
☆ Eva Dahlbeck, Harriet Andersson, Gunnar Bjornstrand, Ulf Palme, Inga Landgre, Naima Wifstrand
'Scenes of austere anti-romanticism and painful irony.' – *Peter John Dyer, MFB*

Journey into Fear ***
US 1942 71m bw
RKO (Orson Welles)

A munitions expert finds himself in danger from assassins in Istanbul, and has to be smuggled home.
Highly enjoyable impressionist melodrama supervised by Orson Welles and full of his touches and excesses.
w Joseph Cotten, Orson Welles novel Eric Ambler d Norman Foster (and Orson Welles) ph Karl Struss *m* Roy Webb *md* Constantin Bakaleinikoff
☆ *Joseph Cotten*, Dolores del Rio, Jack Moss, Orson Welles, Ruth Warrick, Agnes Moorehead
'Brilliant atmosphere, the nightmare of pursuit, eccentric encounters on the way, and when the shock comes it leaps at eye and ear.' – *William Whitebait*
† A 1976 remake, much heralded, was for obscure legal reasons hardly seen. Directed by Daniel Mann for New World, it starred Zero Mostel, Shelley Winters, Stanley Holloway, Vincent Price, Donald Pleasence, Sam Waterston, Joseph Wiseman, Scott Marlowe and Yvette Mimieux.

Journey into Light
US 1951 87m bw
TCF/Joseph Bernhard
A minister loses his faith, becomes a derelict, and is reformed by a blind girl.
An old-fashioned tract in pictures. Has to be seen to be believed, but quite nicely made.
w Stephanie Nordli, Irving Shulman *d* Stuart Heisler *m* Paul Dunlap
☆ Sterling Hayden, Viveca Lindfors, Thomas Mitchell, H. B. Warner, Ludwig Donath, Jane Darwell, Charles Evans
'Slow, inept, and often extremely embarrassing.' – *MFB*

The Journey of August King
US 1995 92m Technicolor
Miramax (Nick Wechsler, Sam Waterston)

In 1815, a farmer protects a runaway slave girl, who has escaped from a rich and ruthless landowner.
Slow-moving drama that never sparks into life, despite the good intentions of those involved.
w John Ehle *novel* John Ehle *d* John Duigan *ph* Slawomir Idziak *m* Stephen Endelman *pd* Patricia Norris *ed* Humphrey Dixon
☆ Jason Patric, Thandie Newton, Larry Drake, Sam Waterston, Nesbitt Blaisdell, John Doman
'A strongly crafted, if unexcitingly simple drama of moral courage.' – *Variety*
† Directors George Roy Hill and Robert Mulligan earlier tried to set up productions of Ehle's novel, which was published in 1971.

Journey of Honor: see *Shogun Warrior*

Journey of Hope *
Switzerland 1990 110m colour
Mainline/Catpics/Condor/SRG/RTSI/Film Four (Alfi Sinniger, Peter Fueter)

original title: *Reise der Hoffnung*
A Turkish father and mother and their young son, part of a group of illegal immigrants abandoned by their guide, try to make their way across a mountain pass into Switzerland.
Moving, almost documentary account of refugees seeking a better life.
w Xavier Koller, Feride Çiçekoğlu, Heike Hubert *d* Xavier Koller *ph* Elemer Ragalyi *ad* Luigi Pelizzo, Kathrin Brunner *ed* Galip Iyitanir
☆ Necmettin Çobanoğlu, Nur Srer, Emin Sivas, Erdinç Akbas, Yaman Okay, Yasar Gner, Hseyin Mete, Yaman Tarcan
best foreign film

The Journey of Natty Gann
US 1985 105m colour Panavision
Walt Disney (Michael Lobell)

During the Chicago depression, a girl follows her father west and hitch-hikes across America.
A kind of human Lassie Come Home: doggedly watchable but not inspiring, especially since it was shot in Canada.
w Jeanne Rosenberg *d* Jeremy Kagan *ph* Richard Bush *m* James Horner
☆ Meredith Salenger, John Cusack, Ray Wise, Scatman Crothers
'Cut to an hour, it would make a fine Disney telepic.' – *Variety*
costumes (Albert Wolsky)

Journey to Italy: see *Voyage to Italy*

Journey to Shiloh
US 1967 101m Techniscope
Universal
Seven young Texans leave home to fight in the Civil War.
Episodic Western which failed in its ambition to reach epic stature.
w Gene Coon *novel* *Fields of Honour* by Will Henry *d* William Hale *ph* Enzo A. Martinelli *m* David Gates
☆ James Caan, Michael Sarrazin, Brenda Scott, Paul Petersen, Don Stroud, Michael Burns, Michael Vincent, Harrison Ford, John Doucette, Noah Beery Jnr

Journey to the Beginning of the World *
Portugal/France 1997 95m colour
Artificial Eye/Madragoa/Gemini (Paulo Branco)
An elderly film director goes on a journey into his past in the company of three actors.
Elegiac celebration of, and farewell to, the forces and places that form an individual; it was Mastroianni's last film.
wd Manoel de Oliveira *ph* Renato Berta *m* Emmanuel Nunes *pd* Maria José Branco *ed* Valérie Loiseleux
☆ Marcello Mastroianni, Jean-Yves Gautier, Leonor Silveira, Diogo Dória, Isabel de Castro, Cecile Sanz de Alba
'The star takes it like a sweet swansong that makes his performance feel like an unforced tribute to his own long career. An unusually touching obituary.' – *Alexander Walker, London Evening Standard*
'A more stupefyingly uncinematic film has probably never been made.' – *Gaby Wood, Guardian*

Journey to the Center of the Earth ***
US 1959 132m DeLuxe Cinemascope
TCF (Charles Brackett)

An Edinburgh professor and assorted colleagues follow an explorer's trail down an extinct Icelandic volcano to the Earth's centre.
Enjoyable hokum which gets more and more fantastic but only occasionally misses its footing; it ends splendidly with the team being catapulted out of Stromboli on a tide of lava.
w Walter Reisch, Charles Brackett novel Jules Verne *d Henry Levin ph* Leo Tover *m Bernard Herrmann ad* Lyle R. Wheeler, Franz Bachelin, Herman A. Blumenthal
☆ *James Mason, Arlene Dahl, Pat Boone*, Peter Ronson, Diane Baker, Thayer David
'The attraction of a Jules Verne fantasy … is in the endearing contrast between the wildest adventures and the staidest Victorian propriety on the part of those undergoing them … There is about the whole film a good-natured enjoyment of its own excesses.' – *Penelope Houston*
art direction

'Caught in a fantastic time trap.'
Journey to the Center of Time
US 1967 82m colour
Ember/Flamingo/Borealis-Dorad (Ray Dorn, David L. Hewitt)

Scientists inadvertently send themselves to the year 5000 AD, at a time of a war with aliens, and then travel to 1,000,000 BC where they are attacked by monsters.
Low-budget, unexciting sci-fi, with the prehistoric world represented by one medium-sized lizard, dry ice and coloured lights.
w David Prentiss *d* David L. Hewitt *ph* Robert Caramico *pd* Edward D. Engoron *ed* Bill Welburn *sp* Modern Film Effects
☆ Scott Brady, Gigi Perreau, Anthony Eisley, Abraham Sofaer, Poupee Gamin

Journey to the Far Side of the Sun *
GB 1969 99m DeLuxe Cinemascope
Universal/Century 21 Productions (Gerry Anderson)

aka: *Doppelgänger*
An astronaut on a mission to a hitherto undetected planet discovers it to be an exact duplicate of Earth, and his own double returns in his place.
Intriguing, impeccably produced, but rather dull science fiction.
w Gerry and Sylvia Anderson, Donald James *d* Robert Parrish *ph* John Read *m* Barry Gray *sp* Harry Oakes *models* Derek Meddings
☆ Ian Hendry, Roy Thinnes, Patrick Wymark, Lynn Loring, Herbert Lom, George Sewell, Ed Bishop

Journey to the South (dubbed)
Argentina/Yugoslavia 1988 90m colour
Art Film 80/Smart Egg/CFS (Jorge Estrada Mora, Aleksandar Stojanović)

original title: *El Camino del Sur*
In the 1920s, a young Yugoslavian girl thinks she is marrying a wealthy European who lives in Buenos Aires, but discovers instead that she has been sold to work in a brothel.
Episodic treatment of the once-flourishing white slave trade in East European women, a colourful but unconvincing melodrama.
w Juan Bautista Stagnaro, Elida Cecconi *story* Beda Docampo Feijoo *d* Juan Bautista Stagnaro *ph* Karpo A. Godina *m* Zoran Simjanović *ad* Nikola Lazarevski, Santijago Eider *ed* Enrique Muzio, Snezana Ivanović
☆ Mirjana Joković, Adrian Ghio, Zarko Lausević, Mira Furlan, Osvaldo Santoro

Journey Together *
GB 1944 95m bw
RAF Film Unit (John Boulting)

Trainee pilots receive instruction in England and America before going on their first bombing mission.
Modest wartime semi-documentary, pleasingly done.
w Terence Rattigan *d* John Boulting *ph* Harry Waxman *m* Gordon Jacob *pd* John Howell
☆ Richard Attenborough, Jack Watling, David Tomlinson, Edward G. Robinson, Hugh Wakefield, Sebastian Shaw, Ronald Adam, Bessie Love
'It has a natural dignity as well as a natural fun.' – *Listener*
'One of the most realistic and brilliant films of the war in the air.' – *News Chronicle*

Journey's End *
GB/US 1930 120m bw
Gainsborough/Welsh-Pearson/Tiffany-Stahl (George Pearson)
France 1917: personal tensions mount as men die in the trenches.
Primitive early sound version (made in Hollywood because of better equipment) of a justly celebrated play first performed a year earlier. Cinematically uninteresting, with acting generally over the top, but it kept Whale and Clive in Hollywood where they shortly collaborated on Frankenstein.
w Joseph Moncure March, Gareth Gundrey *play* R. C. Sherriff *d* James Whale *ph* Benjamin Kline *m* none *ad* Harvey Libbert *ed* Claude Berkeley
☆ Colin Clive, Ian MacLaren, David Manners, Billy Bevan, Anthony Bushell, Robert Adair
'No crystal gazing required to forecast a big measure of success.' – *Variety*
'It has been transferred to the screen with the greatest possible tact and discretion.' – *James Agate*
'Hollywood has produced its first sex-appeal-less film. Mr George Pearson is to be congratulated on his restraint.' – *Punch*
'Almost painfully English … I cannot believe that the strangulated emotions which resulted can have meant much to audiences outside the English-speaking world.' – *Basil Wright, 1972*
† It was the first Anglo-American co-production.

Jours Tranquilles à Clichy: see *Quiet Days in Clichy*

Joy House
France 1964 98m bw Franscope
MGM (Jacques Bar)

aka: *The Love Cage*
The husband of a wealthy American woman in France tries to kill her boyfriend.
Weird hothouse drama, an unsuccessful attempt to combine French and American styles.
w René Clément, Pascal Jardin, Charles Williams *novel* Day Keene *d* René Clément *ph* Henri Decae *m* Lalo Schifrin *ad* Jean Andre *ed* Fedora Zincone
☆ Jane Fonda, Alain Delon, Lola Albright

Joy in the Morning
US 1965 103m Metrocolor
MGM (Henry T. Weinstein)
Early episodes in the marriage of a poor teenage student.
Glutinous romantic drama, quite well made.
w Sally Benson, Alfred Hayes, Norman Lessing *novel* Betty Smith *d* Alex Segal *ph* Ellsworth Fredricks *m* Bernard Herrmann
☆ Richard Chamberlain, Yvette Mimieux, Arthur Kennedy, Oscar Homolka, Joan Tetzel, Sidney Blackmer

'Between every mother and daughter there is a story that must be told.'
The Joy Luck Club
US 1993 139m Technicolor
Buena Vista/Hollywood Pictures (Wayne Wang, Amy Tan, Ronald Bass, Patrick Markey)

The relationships of four Chinese-American daughters with their Chinese mothers are recalled.
A long, slick, mostly sentimental wallow in the past that fails to throw much light on the present or the future; it lacks the sense of culture clash and quirky humour evident in the director's earlier, low-budget films.
w Amy Tan, Ronald Bass *novel* Amy Tan *d* Wayne Wang *ph* Amir Mokri *m* Rachel Portman *pd* Donald Graham Burt *ed* Maysie Hoy
☆ Kieu Chinh, Tsai Chin, France Nuyen, Lisa Lu, Ming-Na Wen, Tamlyn Tomita, Lauren Tom, Victor Wong
'Beautifully made and acted and emotionally moving into the bargain.' – *Variety*
'Delivers neither subtlety nor heart-warming ebullience. Everything is shoe-horned into the fake conflicts and resolutions of soap opera … If you go to this film with a date whom you want to impress with your sensitivity, bring onions.' – *Adam Mars-Jones, Independent*

Joy of Living *
US 1938 90m bw
RKO (Felix Young)

A practical-minded Broadway songstress succumbs to the charms of an aristocratic freewheeler.
Zany romantic comedy, not quite zippy enough to make one forget its irritating archness, but socio-historically very interesting, in the mould of You Can't Take It With You.

w Gene Towne, Allan Scott, Graham Baker *story* Dorothy Fields, Herbert Fields *d* Tay Garnett *ph* Joseph Walker *m/ly* Jerome Kern, Dorothy Fields *md* Frank Tours
☆ Irene Dunne, Douglas Fairbanks Jnr, Alice Brady, Guy Kibbee, Lucille Ball, Eric Blore, Jean Dixon, Warren Hymer, Billy Gilbert
'Fair farce … bereft of sufficient novelty or comedy plot to sustain itself through an hour and a half of gags.' – *Variety*

'It started as a joke. Now the joke is on them.'
Joy Ride *
US 2001 97m DeLuxe Panavision
TCF/New Regency/Bad Robot/Liveplanet (J. J. Abrams, Chris Moore)
GB title: *Roadkill*
On a cross-country drive, three students are terrorised by a murderous trucker.
Spielberg did it rather better with Duel, but this is an undeniabky suspenseful thriller about callow youths going too far.
w Clay Tarver, J. Abrams *d* John Dahl *ph* Jeffrey Jur *m* Marco Beltrami *pd* Rob Pearson *ed* Eric L. Beason, Scott Chestnut, Todd E. Miller, Glen Scantlebury *cos* Terry Dresbach
☆ Steve Zahn (Fuller Thomas), Paul Walker (Lewis Thoma), Leelee Sobieski (Venna), Jessica Bowman (Charlotte), Stuart Stone (Danny), Basil Wallace (Car Salesman), Brian Leckner (Officer Keeney)
'Hot-wired, white-knuckle thriller…steadily gains momentum while speeding through familiar territory.' – *Joe Leydon, Variety*
'First-rate pure thriller, an exercise that depends on believable characters and the director's skill in putting the pieces together.' – *Roger Ebert, Chicago Sun-Times*

Joyless Street *
Germany 1925 139m (24 fps) bw silent
Sofar Film
original title: *Die Freudlose Gasse*
Problems of the inhabitants of a street in Vienna after World War I.
Realistic but studio-set melodrama which brought its director and Greta Garbo to international fame. In itself the film begins by stimulating and ends by boring.
w Willy Haas *novel* Hugo Bettauer *d* G. W. Pabst *ph* Guido Seeber, Curt Oertel, Robert Lach
☆ Asta Nielsen, Werner Krauss, *Greta Garbo*, Valeska Gert, Agnes Esterhazy
'Moments of searing pain, of mental anguish, of sheer unblemished beauty.' – *Paul Rotha, The Film Till Now*

Joyriders
GB 1988 96m Technicolor
Pathé/Granada/British Screen/Little Bird/Film Four (Emma Hayter)
A battered wife runs away with a petty criminal.
Road movie that, for all its squalor, never comes near to reality.
w Andy Smith *story* Aisling Walsh, Andy Smith *d* Aisling Walsh *ph* Gabriel Beristain *pd* Leigh Malone *ed* Thomas Schwalm
☆ Patricia Kerrigan, Andrew Connolly, Billie Whitelaw, David Kelly, John Kavanagh, Deirdre Donoghue, Tracy Peacock, Rolf Saxon, Otto Jarman

Ju Dou **
Japan/China 1990 94m Eastmancolor
ICA/Tokuma Shoten/China Film/X'ian Film Studio (Shigeru Mori, Hiroyuki Kato, Zhao Hangao)
An impotent old man succeeds in revenging himself on his adulterous wife and her lover, his nephew, through their son.
A tragic folk-tale, colourfully told.
w Liu Heng *story* *Fuxi Fuxi* by Liu Heng *d* Zhang Yimou, Yang Fengliang *ph* Gu Changwei, Yang Lun *m* Zhao Jiping *ad* Cao Jiuping, Xia Rujin *ed* Du Yuan
☆ Li Wei, Gong Li, Li Baotian, Zhang Yi, Zheng Jian
'A film where the images do the talking, and almost everything they have to say is deeply cautionary.' – *MFB*
† The film was banned in China.
best foreign film

'See it now! Remember it always!'
'A story so momentous it required six Academy Award stars and a cast of 1,186 players!'
Juarez **
US 1939 132m bw
Warner (Hal. B. Wallis, Henry Blanke)
A revolutionary leader causes the downfall of Emperor Maximilian of Mexico.
Spectacular historical drama with many fine moments which do not quite coalesce into a dramatic whole, chiefly owing to the lack of a single viewpoint.
w John Huston, Wolfgang Reinhardt, Aeneas Mackenzie *d William Dieterle ph Tony Gaudio m Erich Wolfgang Korngold*
☆ *Brian Aherne*, Bette Davis, Paul Muni, Claude Rains, John Garfield, Donald Crisp, Gale Sondergaard, Joseph Calleia, Gilbert Roland, Henry O'Neill, Pedro de Cordoba, Montagu Love, Harry Davenport
'With such potent box office values, its success at theatres seems assured.' – *Variety*
'A million dollars' worth of ballroom sets, regimentals, gauze shots and whiskers.' – *Otis Ferguson*
'Dramatically by far the most effective of Warners' biographical films of the thirties.' – *Graham Greene*
'Muni's big-star solemn righteousness is like a dose of medicine.' – *New Yorker, 1977*
† Based vaguely on two novels: *The Phantom Crown* by Bertita Harding, and *Maximilian and Carlotta* by Franz Werfel.
†† According to Brian Aherne the film was to have been called *The Phantom Crown*, but Muni's contract enabled him to insist that the name of his character should appear in the title.
Brian Aherne

'Remember his name … You'll remember his story!'
Jubal
US 1956 101m Technicolor Cinemascope
Columbia (William Fadiman)
A rancher's wife causes trouble when she falls in love with a wandering cowhand.
Solid sex Western, moderately interestingly done.
w Russell S. Hughes, Delmer Daves *novel Jubal Troop* by Paul Wellman *d* Delmer Daves *ph* Charles Lawton *m* David Raksin
☆ Glenn Ford, Ernest Borgnine, Felicia Farr, Rod Steiger, Valerie French, Charles Bronson, Noah Beery Jnr

Jubilee *
GB 1978 104m colour
Whaley-Malin/Megalovision
Queen Elizabeth I is transported by her astrologer into the latter part of the 20th century, and is appalled by what she sees.
Outrageous dissection of modern urban life, full of black jokes: it has the right attitudes but is not free of a determination to shock at all costs.
w Derek Jarman and others *d* Derek Jarman *ph* Peter Middleton *m* Brian Eno
☆ Jenny Runacre, Little Nell, Toyah Willcox, Jordan, Hermine Demoriane
'One of the most intelligent and interesting films to be made in Britain in a long time.' – *Scott Meek, MFB*

Jubilee Trail *
US 1954 103m Trucolor
Republic (Joseph Kane)
Jealousy and murder by covered wagon en route from New Orleans to the California gold fields.
Bumpy adventure melodrama, generally quite entertaining.
w Bruce Manning *novel* Gwen Bristow *d* Joseph Kane *ph* Jack Marta *m* Victor Young
☆ Vera Hruba Ralston, Forrest Tucker, Joan Leslie, Pat O'Brien, John Russell, Ray Middleton

Judas Was a Woman: see *La Bête Humaine*

'A time without pity. A society without mercy. A love without equal.'
Jude *
GB 1996 123m Technicolor Panavision
PolyGram/BBC Films/Revolution (Andrew Eaton)
After his wife leaves him, a rural labourer decides to revive his dream of becoming a teacher and moves to a university town, where he falls in love with his cousin.
An unhappy adaptation, with some jarringly anachronistic dialogue, which only occasionally gets to grips with Hardy's tragic story.
w Hossein Amini *novel* Thomas Hardy *d* Michael Winterbottom *ph* Eduardo Serra *m* Adrian Johnston *pd* Joseph Bennett *ed* Trevor Waite
☆ Christopher Eccleston, Kate Winslet, Liam Cunningham, Rachel Griffiths, June Whitfield, Ross Colvin Turnbull, James Daley
'A little triumph.' – *Adam Mars-Jones*
'An ambitious, sensitive, but ultimately uninvolving effort.' – *Geoff Andrew, Time Out*

Judex **
France 1916 300m approx bw silent
Gaumont
A Robin Hood type crimefighter destroys the empire of an evil banker.
Stylishly enjoyable serial from the maker of Les Vampires *and* Fantômas.
w Arthur Bernade, Louis Feuillade *d Louis Feuillade*
☆ René Creste, Musidora, Yvette Andreyor, Louis Leubas
† Another *Judex* serial was made in 1917, and in 1933 came a feature version directed by Maurice Champreux, with René Ferte. In 1963 Georges Franju directed another feature remake with Channing Pollock, and this was extremely well received.

The Judge and the Assassin **
France 1976 125m colour Panavision
Arrow/Lira (André Hoss)
original title: *Le Juge et L'Assassin*
In the 1890s, at a time of unrest, unemployment and poverty, a judge expends his energies in persuading a former sergeant, disappointed in love, to confess to raping and killing children as he tramped across France.
Gripping examination of the mind of a mass murderer and a passionate indictment of a society that uses justice as a means of oppression.
w Jean Aurenche, Bertrand Tavernier, Pierre Bost *d* Bertrand Tavernier *ph* Pierre William Glenn *m* Philippe Sarde *ad* Antoine Roman *ed* Armand Psenny
☆ *Philippe Noiret*, Michel Galabru, Isabelle Huppert, Jean-Claude Brialy, Renée Faure, Cecile Vassort, Yves Robert

'In The Future, One Man Is The Law.'
Judge Dredd
US 1995 96m Technicolor Panavision
Guild/Cinergi (Charles M. Lippincott, Beau E. L. Marks)
In Mega City One in AD 2139, Judge Dredd is exiled after being framed for a murder committed by his evil clone.
John Wagner and Carlos Ezquerra's comic-book creation of a shoot-first-ask-questions-later cop who is also judge and jury finds the ideal actor in Sylvester Stallone, but the film strands him without a decent script in which he can flex his muscles.
w William Wisher, Steven E. de Souza *d* Danny Cannon *ph* Adrian Biddle *m* Alan Silvestri *pd* Nigel Phelps *ed* Alex Mackie, Harry Keramidas
☆ Sylvester Stallone, Armand Assante, Diane Lane, Rob Schneider, Joan Chen, Jürgen Prochnow, Max von Sydow, Joanna Miles, Balthazar Getty, Maurice Roeves, Ian Dury
'What's worrying is that so much time and energy can be spent on such a crashingly stale chunk of genre hardware.' – *Jonathan Romney*
'With its routine story-line and unsurprising visuals, you feel as if you have already seen *Judge Dredd* before it is even 10 minutes old.' – *Stephen Amidon, Sunday Times*
'Thunderous, unoriginal futuristic hardware show for teenage boys.' – *Variety*
'Continuously beautiful and interesting from beginning to end … With its first-rate rumbling sound effects, its lavish, old-fashioned score and its exquisite palette of muted browns and pale blues, *Judge Dredd* offers a sophisticated aesthetic experience.' – *Camille Paglia, TLS*
† The film took around $34m at the US box-office and another $78m elsewhere during 1995.

'Enough laughs to make your head spin!'
Judge Priest *
US 1934 79m bw
Fox (Sol M. Wurtzel)
A political judge sees fair play through a criminal case.
Mainly effective star vehicle.
w Dudley Nichols, Lamar Trotti *stories* Irvin S. Cobb *d* John Ford *ph* George Schneiderman *m* Samuel Kaylin
☆ *Will Rogers*, Tom Brown, Anita Louise, *Henry B. Walthall*, David Landau, Rochelle Hudson
'A great part for Will Rogers and a box office bet.' – *Variety*

The Judge Steps Out *
US 1947 91m bw
RKO
GB title: *Indian Summer*
A middle-aged judge leaves his wife and sets off on an aimless journey in the course of which he falls in love with a café proprietress.
A pleasing human story, simply told in a manner which at the time seemed more French than American.
w Boris Ingster, Alexander Knox *d* Boris Ingster *ph* Robert de Grasse *m* Constantin Bakaleinikoff
☆ *Alexander Knox, Ann Sothern*, George Tobias, Sharyn Moffett

A Judgement in Stone: see *La Cérémonie*

'The things you'll see and the things you'll feel are the things that will be part of you as long as you live!'
Judgment at Nuremberg **
US 1961 190m bw
UA/Roxlom (Stanley Kramer)
A fictionalized version of the 1948 trial of the Nazi leaders for crimes against humanity.
Interminable, heavy-going dramatic documentary expanded from a succinct TV play into a courtroom marathon with philosophical asides. All good stuff, but too much of it.
w Abby Mann *play* Abby Mann *d* Stanley Kramer *ph* Ernest Laszlo *m* Ernest Gold *pd* Rudolph Sternad
☆ Spencer Tracy, Marlene Dietrich, Burt Lancaster, Richard Widmark, *Maximilian Schell*, Judy Garland, Montgomery Clift, William Shatner, Edward Binns, Werner Klemperer, Torben Meyer, Alan Baxter, Ray Teal
'Some believe that by tackling such themes Kramer earns at least partial remission from criticism. How much? 20 per cent off for effort?' – *Stanley Kauffmann*
† Burt Lancaster replaced Laurence Olivier, who was originally cast.
Abby Mann; Maximilian Schell
best picture; Stanley Kramer; Ernest Laszlo; Spencer Tracy; Judy Garland; Montgomery Clift

'Prepare for Impact.'
Judgment Day
US 1999 90m FotoKem
Cinetel
The only scientist who can save the world from collision with an asteroid is kidnapped by the leader of a religious cult.
Despite the slightly different narrative approach, this is low-budget action as usual, with the standard prolonged gun-battles along corridors and high-level walkways and stairs.
w William Carson *d* John Terlesky *ph* Maximo Munzi *m* Joseph Williams
☆ Ice T (Reese), Suzy Amis (Tyrell), Mario Van Peebles (Payne), Coolio (Luther), Linden Ashby (Corbett), Tommy 'Tiny' Lister Jnr (Clarence), Max Gail (Meech), Mark Deakins (McNally), James Eckhouse (Keller), David Wells (Dr Richard Keller), Shireen Crutchfield (Rachel)

Judgment Deferred
GB 1951 88m bw
Group Three (John Baxter)
A collection of Dorset eccentrics brings to book the head of a dope smuggling ring who has framed one of their associates.
An unusual story can't compensate for stagey handling in this first disappointing production of a company set up by the National Film Finance Corporation to make low budget films with top talent.

w Geoffrey Orme, Barbara Emary, Walter Meade *d* John Baxter *ph* Arthur Grant *m* Kennedy Russell
☆ Hugh Sinclair, Helen Shingler, Abraham Sofaer, Leslie Dwyer, Joan Collins, Harry Locke, Elwyn Brook Jones, Bransby Williams, Maire O'Neill, Harry Welchman
† This was an expanded remake of *Dosshouse*.

Judgment in Berlin
US 1988 96m Eastmancolor
Hobo/Bibo TV/January Enterprises/Sheen-Greenblatt (Joshua Sinclair, Ingrid Windisch)
An East German is tried by an American court in Berlin after hijacking a Polish airliner.
Despite being based on an actual incident, this courtroom drama lacks conviction.
w Joshua Sinclair, Leo Penn *book* Herbert J. Stern *d* Leo Penn *ph* Gabor Pogany *ad* Jan Schlubach, Peter Alteneder *ed* Teddy Darvas
☆ Martin Sheen, Sam Wanamaker, Max Gail, Juergen Heinrich, Heinz Hoenig, Carl Lumbly, Max Volkert Martens, Christine Rose, Sean Penn

Judgment Night
US 1993 110m colour Super 35
Universal/Largo/JVC (Gene Levy)
Four friends are pursued by killers after they get lost in a city slum and witness a gangland murder.
Violent and implausible chase thriller that requires only that its protagonists behave with great stupidity.
w Lewis Colick *d* Stephen Hopkins *ph* Peter Levy *m* Alan Silvestri *pd* Joseph Nemec III *ed* Timothy Wellburn
☆ Emilio Estevez, Cuba Gooding Jnr, Denis Leary, Stephen Dorff, Jeremy Piven, Peter Greene, Erik Schrody, Michael Wiseman
'Exceedingly well directed, cleverly filmed and edited, tension-filled affair. It is also a wholly preposterous, muddled, paranoid view of the inner-city nightmare.' – *Leonard Klady, Variety*

Judith
US 1965 109m Technicolor Panavision
Paramount/Cumulus/Command (Kurt Unger)
In 1947 Israel, loyalists rescue the wife of an escaped war criminal and ask her to identify him, but she takes her own revenge.
Glowering kibbutz adventures, well enough made but adding up to neither one thing nor the other, and rather confusing to non-Jews.
w John Michael Hayes *story* Lawrence Durrell *d* Daniel Mann *ph* John Wilcox *m* Sol Kaplan *pd* Wilfrid Shingleton
☆ *Sophia Loren*, Peter Finch, Jack Hawkins, Hans Verner, André Morell
'Tasteless and pretentious ... Here is tragedy and glory being used as window dressing for some cheap little undercover-agent episodes and fleshly exploitation.' – *Judith Crist*

Judith of Bethulia
US 1913 42m (24 fps) bw silent
Biograph (D. W. Griffith)
A widow in a city attacked by the Assyrians courts their leader and beheads him.
Semi-biblical melodrama in Griffith's most Victorian style.
w Frank Woods *d* D. W. Griffith *ph* Billy Bitzer
☆ Blanche Sweet, Henry B. Walthall, Lillian Gish, Dorothy Gish, Lionel Barrymore, Mae Marsh, Robert Harron

Judy Berlin *
US 1998 94m bw
Blue Light/Sundance (Rocco Caruso)
In Long Island, during an eclipse of the sun, a would-be actress says her goodbyes as she prepares to leave for Los Angeles.
Delicate, well-observed mood piece of frustrated lives and ill-judged hope.
wd Eric Mendelsohn *ph* Jeffrey Seckendorf *m* Michael Nicholas *pd* Charlie Kulsziski *ed* Eric Mendelsohn
☆ Barbara Barrie (Sue Berlin), Bob Dishy (Arthur Gold), Edie Falco (Judy Berlin), Carlin Glynn (Maddie), Aaron Harnick (David Gold), Bette Henritze (Dolores Engler), Madeline Kahn (Alice Gold), Julie Kavner (Marie), Anne Meara (Bea), Novella Nelson (Carol)
'An offbeat whimsy that may be just a tad too fragile for its own good.' – *Dennis Harvey, Variety*

Juggernaut
GB 1937 64m bw
Ambassador (Julius Hagen)
A scientist lacking funds for his experiments agrees to commit murder.
Tedious melodrama which wastes Karloff's time.
w Cyril Campion, H. Fowler Mear, H. Fraenkel *d* Henry Edwards *ph* Sidney Blythe
☆ Boris Karloff, Mona Goya, Joan Wyndham, Arthur Margetson, Anthony Ireland, Morton Selten
'It gets into motion slowly and reaches the meat of the plot after numerous distractions.' – *Variety*

Juggernaut **
GB 1974 110m DeLuxe Panavision
United Artists/David E. Picker (Richard Alan Simmons)
A transatlantic liner is threatened by a mad bomber.
Elaborate suspense spectacular, most of which works pretty well.
w Richard Alan Simmons *d* Richard Lester *ph* Gerry Fisher *m* Ken Thorne *pd* Terence Marsh
☆ Richard Harris, David Hemmings, Omar Sharif, Anthony Hopkins, Ian Holm, Shirley Knight, Roy Kinnear, Cyril Cusack, Freddie Jones
'However unoriginal its basic ingredients, it hardly ever slackens its pace or diverts attention from its central premise.' – *Jonathan Rosenbaum*
'Jaunty, cynical slapstick.' – *New Yorker*

The Juggler
US 1953 88m bw
Columbia/Stanley Kramer
A Jewish refugee in Palestine has a horror of being imprisoned, and runs away from a transit camp with a small wandering boy.
Well-meaning cheapie, a curiously aimless topical drama which fails to make any of its several points.
w Michael Blankfort *novel* Michael Blankfort *d* Edward Dmytryk *ph* Roy Hunt *m* Georges Antheil
☆ Kirk Douglas, Milly Vitale, Paul Stewart, Joey Walsh

'Power. Respect.'
Juice **
US 1992 91m Technicolor
Electric/Paramount/Island World (David Heyman, Neal H. Moritz, Peter Frankfurt)
Four young friends from Harlem find their relationship alters after they rob a store and kill its owner.
Gripping tale of inner-city despair and the dead end offered by violence.
w Gerard Brown, Ernest R. Dickerson *d* Ernest R. Dickerson *ph* Larry Banks *m* Hank Shocklee & The Bomb Squad *pd* Lester Cohen *ed* Sam Pollard, Brunilda Torres
☆ Omar Epps, Tupac Shakur, Jermaine Hopkins, Khalil Kain, Cindy Herron, Vincent Laresca, Samuel L. Jackson, George O. Gore, Grace Garland, Queen Latifah
'A vivid slice of everyday fun and mortal danger in young Harlem.' – *Joe Brown, Washington Post*
'Demonstrates the black community's untapped talent waiting for opportunities on both sides of the camera, but it also reflects the confined realm within which the filmmakers and performers are forced to operate.' – *Variety*

Jujiro: see *Crossroads*

Juke Girl
US 1942 90m bw
Warner (Jack Saper, Jerry Wald)
Fruit workers in Florida get involved in murder.
Hokum melodrama with all concerned treading water.
w A. I. Bezzerides *novel* Theodore Pratt *d* Curtis Bernhardt *ph* Bert Glennon *m* Adolph Deutsch
☆ Ann Sheridan, Ronald Reagan, Richard Whorf, Gene Lockhart, Faye Emerson, George Tobias, Alan Hale, Howard da Silva, Donald McBride, Fuzzy Knight, Willie Best

Jules et Jim ****
France 1962 105m bw Franscope
Films du Carrosse/SEDIF (Marcel Berbert)
Before World War I, in Paris, a girl alternates between a French and a German student, and after the war they meet again to form a constantly shifting triangle.
Charming, quintessentially French period romance, technically interesting, emotionally uplifting, and acted and directed with verve and feeling.
w *François Truffaut, Jean Gruault* *novel* Henri-Pierre Roche *d* *François Truffaut* *ph* Raoul Coutard *m* Georges Delerue
☆ *Oskar Werner, Jeanne Moreau*, Henri Serre
'The sense is of a director intoxicated with the pleasure of making films.' – *Penelope Houston, MFB*

Jules Verne's Rocket to the Moon
US 1967 95m colour Panavision
AIP (Harry Alan Towers)
aka: *Those Fantastic Flying Fools*
aka: *Blast-Off*
Escaping from his creditors to England, Phineas T. Barnum finances a trip to the moon in an attempt to recoup his fortunes.
Farcical Victoriana that owes little to Jules Verne and more to the Carry On films, though it leans more to genteel slapstick than genial vulgarity. Some skilled character actors provide moments of amusement.
w Dave Freeman *story* Peter Welbeck (Harry Alan Towers), 'inspired by the writings of Jules Verne' *d* Don Sharp *ph* Reg Wyer *m* Patrick John Scott *ad* Frank White *ed* Ann Chegwidden
☆ Burl Ives, Troy Donahue, Gert Frobe, Hermione Gingold, Lionel Jeffries, Dennis Price, Terry-Thomas, Daliah Lavi, Stratford Johns, Graham Stark, Jimmy Clitheroe
† Jules Verne's novel was filmed more seriously, but no more successfully, in 1958 as *From the Earth to the Moon* (qv).

Jules Verne's Sea Devils (dubbed)
Spain 1981 87m Eastmancolor Dinavision
Almena/Cinevision (Alfredo Casado)
original title: *Los Diablos del Mar*
A group of youthful immigrants, on their way to Australia, escape from pirates only to be shipwrecked in Africa, where they fall foul of slave traders.
Vapid, politically incorrect action movie, particularly unconvincing in scenes involving attacks by wild animals and in its heavy-handed moments of comedy.
w Joaquin Grau, Juan Piquer *story* *Fifteen years old Captain* by Jules Verne *d* J. Piquer Simon *ph* Juan Marine *m* Alfonso Agullo, Carlos Villa *pd* Gumer Andres *ed* Antonio Gimeno
☆ Ian Sera, Frank Brana, Patty Shepard, Flavia Zarzo, Gaby Gimenez, Aldo Sambrell

'A story of turmoil, of courage, of love!'
Julia ***
US 1977 117m Technicolor
TCF (Richard Roth)
Lillian Hellman reflects on the fortunes of her friend Julia, filled with enthusiasm for European causes and finally killed by the Nazis.
Thoughtful, elegant patchwork of thirties memories, a vehicle for actors and a subtle, self-effacing director.
w Alvin Sargent *book* *Pentimento* by Lillian Hellman *d* *Fred Zinnemann* *ph* Douglas Slocombe *m* Georges Delerue *pd* Carmen Dillon, Gene Callahan, Willy Holt *ed* Walter Murch
☆ Jane Fonda, Vanessa Redgrave, Jason Robards Jnr, Maximilian Schell, Hal Holbrook, Meryl Streep, Rosemary Murphy, Cathleen Nesbitt, Maurice Denham
'After a while it becomes apparent that Zinnemann and Sargent are trafficking in too many quotations and flashbacks because they can't find the core of the material.' – *Pauline Kael*
Academy Award: script; Vanessa Redgrave; Jason Robards Jnr
Academy Award nomination: best picture; Fred Zinnemann; Douglas Slocombe; Georges Delerue; Jane Fonda; Maximilian Schell
BAFTA: best picture; Alvin Sargent; Douglas Slocombe; Jane Fonda

'An erotic comedy about life on the line.'
Julia Has Two Lovers
US 1990 85m colour
Oneira (Bashar Shbib)
A woman, who has ambivalent feelings about her current lover, begins a romance with a man who dials her number by mistake.
Low-budget romance that fails to ring bells.
w Daphna Kastner, Bashar Shbib *d* Bashar Shbib *ph* Stephen Reizes *m* Emilio Kauderer *ed* Dan Foegelle, Bashar Shbib
☆ Daphna Kastner, David Duchovny, David Charles, Tim Ray

Julia Misbehaves
US 1948 99m bw
MGM (Everett Riskin)
An actress returns to her stuffy husband when her daughter is about to marry.
Desperate attempt to find a vehicle for a fading star team.
w William Ludwig, Arthur Wimperis, Harry Ruskin *novel* *The Nutmeg Tree* by Margery Sharp *d* Jack Conway *ph* Joseph Ruttenberg *m* Adolph Deutsch
☆ Greer Garson, Walter Pidgeon, Elizabeth Taylor, Peter Lawford, Cesar Romero, Lucile Watson, Nigel Bruce, Mary Boland, Reginald Owen, Ian Wolfe, Edmund Breon, Fritz Feld, Aubrey Mather, Henry Stephenson

Julian Po
US 1997 78m Technicolor
Entertainment/Fine Line/Cypress/Mindel/Shaw (Joseph Pierson, Jon Glascoe)
Small townspeople make a hero out of stranger who claims that he has come to their town to kill himself.
Bland mystery of a movie that never quite explains itself.
wd Alan Wade *novella* *La Mort de Monsieur Golouga* by Branimir Scepanovic *ph* Bernd Heinl *m* Patrick Williams *pd* Stephen McCabe *ed* Jeffrey Wolf
☆ Christian Slater (Julian Po), Robin Tunney (Sarah), Michael Parks (Vern), Cherry Jones (Lucy), Frankie R. Faison (Sheriff), Harve Presnell (Mayor), Allison Janney (Lilah)
'A dull, faintly puzzling nullity of a movie.' – *Peter Bradshaw, Guardian*

Julie *
US 1956 97m bw
MGM/Arwin (Marty Melcher)
A concert pianist plans to murder his wife.
Wildly improbable but entertaining suspenser in which the lady finally has to assume control of an airplane.
wd Andrew Stone *ph* Fred Jackman Jnr *m* Leith Stevens
☆ Doris Day, Louis Jourdan, Barry Sullivan, Frank Lovejoy, John Gallaudet
'Some of the dialogue reaches a fine pitch of banality.' – *MFB*
Academy Award nomination: Andrew Stone (as writer); title song (*m* Leith Stevens, *ly* Tom Adair)

'You've got to risk it all to get your first hit.'
Julie and the Cadillacs
GB 1997 107m colour
Capricorn/Parker Mead (John Dean, Sean O'Mahony)
In the mid 60s, a girl singer and her band move from Liverpool to London in search of stardom.
Bland 'B' movie of British pop that arrived 30 years too late to find an audience.
w John Dean *d* Bryan Izzard *ph* Les Young *m/ly* John Dean *pd* Jeremy Bear *ed* James Thomas
☆ Toyah Willcox (Barbara Gifford), Victor Spinetti (Cyril Wise), Peter Polycarpou (Phil Green), Thora Hird (Julie's grandmother), James Grout (Mr Watkins), Mike Berry (Mac MacDonald), Tina Russell (Julie Carr), Ben Richards (Mike Williams), Billy Boyd (Jimmy Campbell), David Habbin (John Wood), Chris O'Neill (Tony Henderson), Matt Rayner (Roy Holgate)
'Starry-eyed, amateurish and endearingly bouncy.' – *Philip Kemp, Sight and Sound*

Julien Donkey-Boy *
US 1999 100m colour
Fine Line/Independent Pictures (Cary Woods, Scott Macaulay, Robin O'Hara)

A schizophrenic youth, capable of violence to others, shares his New York home with his equally dysfunctional father, brother and pregnant sister.
An intermittently interesting attempt to provide a visual equivalent to the central character's unbalanced view of the world; it has its moments, but the effect of the fuzzily lurid colours, the lurchings of the hand-held camera and the often muddy sound is a diminishing one, as is the shock of incest, death and general weirdness.
wd Harmony Korine *ph* Anthony Dod Mantle *ed* Valdis Oskarsdottir
☆ Ewen Bremner (Julien), Chloe Sevigny (Pearl), Werner Herzog (Father), Evan Neumann (Chris), Joyce Korine (Grandma), Chrissy Kobylak (Chrissy), Alvin Law (Neighbor)
'A pointless attempt to give a semblance of realism to what is patently fiction. And very tedious, shallow fiction it is, too.' – *Ed Porter, Sunday Times*

Juliet of the Spirits *
Italy/France 1965 145m Technicolor
Federiz/Francoriz (Clemente Fracassi)
original title: *Giulietta degli Spiriti*
A bored middle-aged woman finds she can conjure up spirits who lead her into a life of sensual gratification.
A fascinating patchwork of autobiographical flashbacks, the distaff side of Eight and a Half.
w Federico Fellini, Tullio Pinnelli, Brunello Rondi, Ennio Flaiano *d Federico Fellini ph Gianni di Venanzo m* Nino Rota
☆ *Giulietta Masina*, Mario Pisu, Sandra Milo, Valentina Cortese, Sylva Koscina
'A kaleidoscope of fantasy, a series of artistically inventions, of which only a few are artistically justified ... an extravagant illusion, a huge confidence trick, with little new to say and an often pedantic way of saying it.' – *David Wilson, MFB*

'Greater than Ivanhoe!'
'Thrill to ruthless men and their goddess-like women in a sin-swept age!'
'Thrill to traitors and heroes, killings and conspiracies, passions and violence in Rome's most exciting age!'
Julius Caesar **
US 1953 121m bw
MGM (John Houseman)
Cassius and Brutus lead the conspirators who murder Caesar, but are themselves routed by Mark Antony.
Straightforward, rather leaden presentation of Shakespeare's play, lit by effective moments in the acting, but the sudden change from talk to battle is not smoothed over.
wd Joseph L. Mankiewicz *ph* Joseph Ruttenberg *m* Miklos Rozsa *ad* Cedric Gibbons, Edward Carfagno
☆ *John Gielgud, James Mason*, Marlon Brando, Greer Garson, Deborah Kerr, Louis Calhern, Edmond O'Brien, George Macready, Michael Pate, John Hoyt, Alan Napier
art direction
best picture; Joseph Ruttenberg; Miklos Rozsa; Marlon Brando
John Gielgud; Marlon Brando

Julius Caesar
GB 1969 116m Technicolor Panavision
Commonwealth United (Peter Snell)
Elementary production with a surprising number of faults and very few merits.
w Robert Furnival *d* Stuart Burge *ph* Ken Higgins *m* Michael Lewis *pd* Julia Trevelyan Oman
☆ Richard Johnson, Jason Robards Jnr, *John Gielgud*, Charlton Heston, Robert Vaughn, Richard Chamberlain, Diana Rigg, Jill Bennett, Christopher Lee, Alan Browning, Andrew Crawford
'Ugly, ill-spoken, ham-fisted.' – *Sight and Sound*

Jumanji *
US 1995 104m Technicolor
Columbia TriStar/Interscope/Teitler (Scott Kroopf, William Teitler)
Two children play a mysterious board game that releases after 25 years a child, now grown to be a man, who was trapped within it, together with an invasion of jungle animals.
Unsuccessful, convoluted fantasy that surprises only with its special effects of wild animals rampaging through a house and the streets of an American town.
w Jonathan Hensleigh, Greg Taylor, Jim Strain *book* Chris Van Allsburg *d* Joe Johnston *ph* Thomas Ackerman *m* James Horner *pd* James Bissell *ed* Robert Dalva *sp* Industrial Light and Magic
☆ Robin Williams, Bonnie Hunt, Kirsten Dunst, Bradley Pierce, Bebe Neuwirth, Jonathan Hyde, David Alan Grier, Patricia Clarkson, Adam Hann-Byrd
'The filmmakers re-create safari beasts with wizardly finesse but can't think of anything to do with them but zap you. The plot is cardboard Spielberg.' – *Entertainment Weekly*

Jumbo *
US 1962 124m Metrocolor Panavision
MGM (Joe Pasternak, Martin Melcher)
aka: *Billy Rose's Jumbo*
In 1910, the daughter of the owner of a shaky circus prevents a take-over bid.
Hoary circus story with music. General effect disappointing: the elephant steals the show.
w Sidney Sheldon *play* Ben Hecht, Charles MacArthur *d* Charles Walters *ph* William H. Daniels *m/ly* Richard Rodgers, Lorenz Hart *md* George Stoll *ch* Busby Berkeley
☆ *Doris Day, Jimmy Durante*, Stephen Boyd, Martha Raye, Dean Jagger
† Stephen Boyd's singing was dubbed by James Joyce.
George Stoll

Jump for Glory
GB 1937 89m bw
Criterion (Douglas Fairbanks Jnr, Marcel Hellman)
US title: *When Thief Meets Thief*
Adventures of a cat burglar who accidentally kills his ex-partner.
Curious star comedy drama with pleasing scenes.
w John Meehan Jnr, Harold French *novel* Gordon MacDonnell *d* Raoul Walsh *ph* Cedric Williams
☆ Douglas Fairbanks Jnr, Valerie Hobson, Alan Hale, Edward Rigby, Barbara Everest, Jack Melford, Anthony Ireland
'Starts off at a commendable pace but doesn't carry through.' – *Variety*

Jump into Hell
US 1955 93m bw
Warner (David Weisbart)
Paratroops relieve a fort in Indo-China.
Mediocre semi-documentary war heroics.
w Irving Wallace *d* David Butler *ph* Peverell Marley *m* David Buttolph
☆ Jacques Sernas, Kurt Kasznar, Arnold Moss, Peter Van Eyck, Pat Blake

'Living in Hell and Loving It!'
Jump the Gun *
GB/South Africa 1996 124m Metrocolor
Film Four/Parallax/Xencat (Indra de Lanerolle)
Johannesburg is the destination of an oil-rig worker looking for fun and a singer hoping for work.
Slight but engaging movie of a city undergoing change, seen from the perspective of the streets.
wd Les Blair *ph* Seamus McGarvey *m* Joe Nina *pd* David Barkham *ed* Oral Norrie Ottey
☆ Baby Cele, Lionel Newton, Thulani Nyembe, Rapulana Seiphemo, Danny Keogh, Joe Nina
'Despite unevenness and not much dramatic structure, the partly improvised screenplay works well.' – *Derek Malcolm, Guardian*

'Live a little first.'
Jump Tomorrow *
GB/US 2001 96m Technicolor
Film4/Eureka/Jorge (Nicola Usborne)
Encouraged by a love-lorn Frenchman, an office worker abandons his plans for an arranged marriage to pursue a woman he meets at the airport.
A would-be romantic comedy that turns out to be more a buddy movie about an odd couple of near-strangers; it has an enjoyably quirky quality.
wd Joel Hopkins *ph* Patrick Cady *m* John Kimbrough *pd* John Panno *ed* Susan Littenberg
☆ Tunde Adebimpe (George), Hippolyte Girardot (Gerard), Natalia Verbeke (Alicia), James Wilby (Nathan), Patricia Mauceri (Consuelo), Isiah Whitlock Jnr (George's Uncle), Kaili Vernoff (Heather Leather), Abiola Wendy Abrams (Sophie)
'The whole movie is diagrammed. It's a just-add-water trifle.' – *Owen Gleiberman, Entertainment Weekly*
'Slightly screwy romantic comedy... becomes increasingly charming as it goes along.' – *Amy Taubin, Village Voice*

Jumpin' Jack Flash
US 1986 100m DeLuxe
TCF (Lawrence Gordon-Joel Silver)
A black office worker finds herself plunged into espionage.
Tiresome, dirty-talking, would-be wild and woolly comedy which fails to establish itself.
w David H. Franzoni, J. W. Melville, Patricia Irving, Christopher Thompson *d* Penny Marshall *ph* Matthew F. Leonetti *m* Thomas Newman *pd* Robert Boyle *ed* Mark Goldblatt
☆ Whoopi Goldberg, Stephen Collins, John Wood, Carol Kane, Annie Potts, Roscoe Lee Browne

Jumping for Joy
GB 1955 88m bw
Rank/Raymond Stross
A track attendant acquires a winning greyhound and exposes a group of crooks.
Totally predictable star comedy which needs livening up.
w Jack Davies, Henry E. Blyth *d* John Paddy Carstairs *ph* Jack Cox *m* Larry Adler
☆ Frankie Howerd, Stanley Holloway, A. E. Matthews, Tony Wright, Alfie Bass, Joan Hickson, Lionel Jeffries

Jumping Jacks *
US 1952 96m bw
Paramount/Hal B. Wallis
Two cabaret comedians join the paratroops.
Standard star farce, one of Martin and Lewis's best.
w Robert Lees, Fred Rinaldo, Herbert Baker *d* Norman Taurog *ph* Daniel L. Fapp *m* Joseph J. Lilley
☆ Dean Martin, *Jerry Lewis*, Mona Freeman, Robert Strauss, Don Defore

June Bride
US 1948 97m bw
Warner (Henry Blanke)
Two bickering reporters are sent to cover a small-town wedding.
Sloppily structured romantic farce in which nothing ever comes together.
w Ranald MacDougall *play Feature for June* by Eileen Tighe, Graeme Lorimer *d* Bretaigne Windust *ph* Ted McCord *m* David Buttolph
☆ Bette Davis, Robert Montgomery, Fay Bainter, Tom Tully, Betty Lynn, Barbara Bates, Jerome Cowan, Mary Wickes, Debbie Reynolds

June Night *
Sweden 1940 90m bw
AB Svensk Filmindustri
original title: *Juninatten*
Recovering from being shot by her lover, a shop assistant moves to Stockholm but cannot escape her past.
A complex examination of the power of passion and the public fascination with scandal, even though its resolution is bungled.
w Ragnar Hyltén-Cavallius *story* Tora Nordstrom-Bonnier *d* Per Lindberg *ph* Åke Dahlquist *m* Jules Sylvain, Gunnar Johansson
☆ Ingrid Bergman, Marianne Löfgren, Lill-Tollie Zellman, Marianne Aminoff, Olof Widgren, Gunnar Sjöberg

Jungfrukällan: see *The Virgin Spring*

Jungle 2 Jungle *
US 1997 105m colour
Buena Vista/Walt Disney/TF1 (Brian Reilly)
A New York businessman brings back to the city his 13-year-old son, who has lived all his life in the Amazon jungle.
Mildly entertaining comedy of a father–son relationship in two differing cultures, so that each has a turn at getting things wrong.
w Bruce A. Evans, Raynold Gideon *d* John Pasquin *ph* Tony Pierce-Roberts *m* Michael Convertino *pd* Stuart Wurtzel *ed* Michael A. Stevenson *film Un Indien dans la ville by Hervé Palud, Thierry Lhermitte, Igor Aptekman, Philippe Bruneau de la Salle*
☆ Tim Allen, Martin Short, JoBeth Williams, Lolita Davidovich, Sam Huntington, David Ogden Stiers, Bob Dishy
'A warm-hearted family outing.' – *Variety*

'More thrilling than the deeds of man ... more beautiful than the love of woman ... more wonderful than the dreams of children!'
The Jungle Book *
US 1942 109m Technicolor
Alexander Korda
aka: *Rudyard Kipling's Jungle Book*
Growing up with animals in an Indian forest, a boy forestalls the getaway of three thieves.
High-budgeted but rather boring live action version with stiff-jointed model animals.
w Laurence Stallings *stories* Rudyard Kipling *d* Zoltan Korda, André de Toth *ph* Lee Garmes, W. Howard Greene *m* Miklos Rozsa *ad* Vincent Korda
☆ Sabu, Joseph Calleia, John Qualen, Frank Puglia, Rosemary de Camp
cinematography; Miklos Rozsa; Vincent Korda

'The Jungle is Jumpin'.'
Jungle Book *
US 1967 78m Technicolor
Walt Disney
An Indian orphan is raised by very vocal jungle animals.
Cartoon version relying less on action than on songs and voices; patchily successful but no classic.
w Larry Clemmons, Ralph Wright, Ken Anderson, Vance Gerry *d* Wolfgang Reitherman *m* George Bruns *m/ly* Richard and Robert Sherman, Terry Gilkyson *ed* Tom Acosta, Norman Carlisle
☆ voices of: Phil Harris (Baloo), Sebastian Cabot (Bagheera), Louis Prima (King Louie of the Apes), George Sanders (Shere Khan), Sterling Holloway (Kaa), J. Pat O'Malley (Colonel Hathi/Buzzie), Bruce Reitherman (Mowgli)
† It was the last animated movie to be personally supervised by Walt Disney.
♫ 'The Bare Necessities'; 'Colonel Hathi's March'; 'I Wanna Be Like You'; 'My Own Home'; 'That's What Friends Are For'; 'Trust In Me'
song 'The Bare Necessities' (m/ly Terry Gilkyson)

Jungle Book: see *Rudyard Kipling's Jungle Book (1994)*

'Feel the jungle beat.'
The Jungle Book 2
US 2003 72m Technicolor
Buena Vista/Walt Disney (Mary Thorne, Chris Chase)
Mowgli, now living with other humans, pines for his jungle friends.
A belated sequel that isn't much fun, content to recycle the hit songs from the first film, and to display poorer animation.
w Karl Geurs *d* Steve Trenbirth *m* Joel McNeely *m/ly* Lorraine Feather, Paul Grabowsky *ad* Michael Peraza *ed* Peter N. Lonsdale, Christopher Gee
☆ voices of: John Goodman (Baloo), Haley Joel Osment (Mowgli), Mae Whitman (Shanti), Connor Funk (Ranjan), Bob Joles (Bagheera), Tony Jay (Shere Khan), John Rhys-Davies (Ranjan's Father), Phil Collins (Lucky)
'Less a film than an ersatz simulation, reducing the wit and charm of the original film to the level of a bog-standard TV special.' – *Andrew Osmond, Sight & Sound*

♫ 'I Wanna Be Like You'; 'Jungle Rhythm'; 'Bare Necessities'; 'Colonel Hathi's March'; 'W-I-L-D'; 'Right Where I Belong'

Jungle Book 2: Mowgli and Baloo: see *Rudyard Kipling's The Second Jungle Book: Mowgli and Baloo*

Jungle Captive
US 1945 63m bw
Universal
A mad doctor steals the body of Paula the ape woman and restores it to life.
Arrant rubbish, a sequel to Captive Wild Woman *and* Jungle Woman.
w M. Coates Webster, Dwight V. Babcock
d Harold Young
☆ Otto Kruger, Phil Brown, Rondo Hatton, Jerome Cowan, Amelita Ward

Jungle Fever **
US 1991 132m DuArt
UIP/Universal/Forty Acres and A Mule Filmworks (Spike Lee)
A black architect leaves his wife and child to live with his Italian-American secretary.
Sharply observed drama of racism and prejudice that raises more questions than it attempts to answer.
wd Spike Lee *ph* Ernest Dickerson *m* Terence Blanchard, Stevie Wonder *pd* Wynn Thomas *ed* Sam Pollard, Brunilda Torres
☆ Wesley Snipes, Annabella Sciorra, Spike Lee, Ossie Davis, Ruby Dee, Samuel L. Jackson, Lonette McKee, John Turturro, Frank Vincent, Anthony Quinn, Tim Robbins, Brad Dourif
'An inspired and very welcome return to form.' – *Empire*

Jungle Fighters: see *The Long and the Short and the Tall*

Jungle Jim
When Johnny Weissmuller began to show his middle-age spread, Columbia put him in a jacket and more or less redid his Tarzan thing in a series of second features which appeared to be shot in producer Sam Katzman's back garden and gradually indulged in wilder and wilder plots. None of them has more than curiosity value.
1948 Jungle Jim
1949 The Lost Tribe
1950 Captive Girl, Mark of the Gorilla, Pygmy Island
1951 Fury of the Congo, Jungle Manhunt
1952 Jungle Jim in the Forbidden Land, Voodoo Tiger
1953 Savage Mutiny, Valley of the Headhunters, Killer Ape
1954 Jungle Maneaters, Cannibal Attack
1955 Jungle Moon Men, Devil Goddess
w main scriptwriters were Carroll Young, Dwight Babcock, Sam Newman *d* main directors William Berke, Lee Sholem, Spencer G. Bennet

'Men staked their lives for just one look at the thrilling beauty of this tiger woman!'
The Jungle Princess *
US 1936 84m bw
Paramount (E. Lloyd Sheldon)
A British hunter is injured on a tropical island and rescued by a native girl and her animal retinue.
Dorothy Lamour's first film role cast her as the female Tarzan she was to play (in a sarong, of course) a dozen times again. This is strictly a programmer, but after its success it was all done again, rather better, as Her Jungle Love.
w Cyril Hume, Gerald Geraghty, Gouverneur Morris *d* William Thiele *ph* Harry Fischbeck *md* Boris Morros
☆ *Dorothy Lamour, Ray Milland*, Akim Tamiroff, Lynne Overman, Molly Lamont, Hugh Buckler
'Fairly palatable entertainment most of the way.' – *Variety*
'Poor Mr Lynne Overman is expected to lend humorous relief to a film already richly comic.' – *Graham Greene*
† On this trip the tiger was Liamu and the chimp Bogo.

Jungle Woman
US 1944 54m bw
Universal
A mad doctor restores an ape to life. It turns into a beautiful woman.
Middle section of a talentless trio of which the first is Captive Wild Woman *and the third* Jungle Captive.
w Bernard Schubert, Henry Sucher, Edward Dein
d Reginald LeBorg
☆ J. Carrol Naish, Acquanetta, Evelyn Ankers, Milburn Stone, Richard Davis, Lois Collier

'Nothing is inconceivable.'
Junior
US 1994 109m Eastmancolor
UIP/Northern Lights (Ivan Reitman)
A scientist tests a fertility drug on a male colleague, with the result that he becomes pregnant.
A less amusing reunion of the team that produced Twins, *a still-born, surprisingly old-fashioned comedy with its belief that the essence of femininity resides in being helpless and hopeless, nagging and clinging; the old jokes are not always the best.*
w Kevin Wade, Chris Conrad *d* Ivan Reitman *ph* Adam Greenberg *m* James Newton Howard *pd* Stephen Lineweaver *ed* Sheldon Kahn, Wendy Greene Bricmont
☆ Arnold Schwarzenegger, Danny DeVito, Emma Thompson, Frank Langella, Judy Collins, Pamela Reed, Aida Turturro, James Eckhouse
'What separates this straightforward chuckler from the pack is its shrewd reliance on character rather than plot, and that human dimension proves surprisingly poignant.' – *Leonard Klady*
song 'Look What Love Has Done'

Junior Army
US 1943 70m bw
Columbia (Colbert Clark)
An English boy goes to an American military academy.
Routine propaganda item which might almost have been titled David Copperfield Meets the Dead End Kids.
w Albert Bein, Paul Gangelin *d* Lew Landers
☆ Freddie Bartholomew, Billy Halop, Huntz Hall, Bobby Jordan, Don Beddoe, Peter Lawford, Boyd Davis

Junior Bonner *
US 1972 105m Movielab Todd-AO 35
ABC/Booth-Gardner/Joe Wizan/Solar
An ageing rodeo star returns to his home town and finds his family in trouble.
Well-made, rather downcast and not very interesting drama, remarkably gentle from this director.
w Jeb Rosebrook *d* Sam Peckinpah *ph* Lucien Ballard *m* Jerry Fielding
☆ Steve McQueen, Ida Lupino, Robert Preston, Joe Don Baker, Ben Johnson

Junior Miss *
US 1945 94m bw
TCF (William Perlberg)
A teenager causes trouble by meddling in the lives of her family.
Amusing family comedy from a hit play.
w George Seaton *play* Jerome Chodorov, Joseph Fields *stories* Sally Benson *d* George Seaton *ph* Charles Clarke *m* David Buttolph
☆ *Peggy Ann Garner*, Allyn Joslyn, Faye Marlowe, Mona Freeman, Michael Dunne, John Alexander

'A black comedy about love, money, cold canned spaghetti, karaoke, involuntary good deeds and the joy of being comatose.'
Junk Mail *
Norway 1997 79m colour
MovieMakers/Norsk Film/Atlas (Dag Nordahl, Peter Boe)
original title: *Budbringeren*
An inquistive postman becomes involved in the complicated life of a young woman.
An edgy and glumly enjoyable semi-thriller, about a hapless individual out of his depth.
w Pal Sletaune, Jonny Halberg *d* Pal Sletaune *ph* Kjell Vassdal *m* Joachim Holbek *pd* Karl Juliusson *ed* Pal Gengenbach
☆ Robert Skjaerstad (Roy Amundsen), Andrine Saether (Line Groberg), Per Egil Aske (Georg Rheinhardsen), Eli Anne Linnestad (Betsy), Trond Hovik (Saether), Henriette Steenstrup (Gina), Trond Fausa Aurvag (Espen), Adne Olav Sekkelsten (Per)
'An offbeat, blackly humorous love story with a grotesque edge.' – *Derek Elley, Variety*

Juno and the Paycock
GB 1930 85m bw
British International (John Maxwell)
US title: *The Shame of Mary Boyle*
During the Irish troubles of the early twenties, tragedy comes to a poor Dublin family.
A plainly done film version of a modern classic whose changes of mood would not in any case have worked well on the screen.
w Alfred Hitchcock, Alma Reville *play* Sean O'Casey *d* Alfred Hitchcock *ph* Jack Cox *ad* Norman Arnold *ed* émile de Ruelle
☆ Sara Allgood, Edward Chapman, Maire O'Neill, Sidney Morgan, John Longden
'A film which completely justifies the talkies.' – *James Agate*
'Just a photograph of a stage play.' – *Alfred Hitchcock*

Jupiter's Darling *
US 1954 96m Eastmancolor Cinemascope
MGM (George Wells)
Advancing on Rome, Hannibal falls in love with the dictator's fiancée.
A splendid example of the higher lunacy, with coloured elephants decorating an MGM musical about the fall of the Roman Empire. Small elements can be salvaged, and the gall is enough to be divided into three parts.
w Dorothy Kingsley *play* The Road to Rome by Robert E. Sherwood *d* George Sidney *ph* Paul C. Vogel, Charles Rosher *m* David Rose *m/ly* Burton Lane, Harold Adamson *ch* Hermes Pan *ad* Cedric Gibbons, Uric McCleary
☆ Esther Williams, Howard Keel, George Sanders, Marge and Gower Champion, Richard Haydn, William Demarest
'If it had been my first picture, there wouldn't have been a second.' – *Esther Williams*

'An adventure 65 million years in the making.'
Jurassic Park **
US 1993 127m colour
UIP/Universal/Amblin (Kathleen Kennedy, Gerald R. Molen)
Genetically re-created from blood taken from ancient mosquitoes, dinosaurs run amok in a theme park.
The dinosaurs are amazing: living, breathing, believable creatures, which is more than you can say for the actors in this otherwise cardboard creation, hung up on toilet jokes and often seeming no more than an elongated commercial for all the merchandise associated with the movie, which includes a long, shameless pan along shelves of the toys and books available. The film was distributed with a warning that it might upset sensitive children. Sensitive adults are likely to be disappointed, too.
w Michael Crichton, David Koepp *novel* Michael Crichton *d* Steven Spielberg *ph* Dean Cundey *m* John Williams *pd* Rick Carter *ed* Michael Kahn *sp* Dennis Muren, Stan Winston, Phil Tippett, Pamela Easley
☆ Sam Neill, Laura Dern, Jeff Goldblum, Richard Attenborough, Bob Peck, Martin Ferrero, B. D. Wong, Joseph Mazello, Ariana Richards, Samuel L. Jackson
'Doesn't have the imagination – or the courage – to take us any place we haven't been a thousand times before. It's just a creature feature on amphetamines.' – *Terrence Rafferty, New Yorker*
'The dinosaurs are wonderful, but they aren't on the set enough of the time (yes, I know how much more they cost than human actors). Unfortunately, the plot line for the human actors reduces to pap and romantic drivel of the worst kind, the very antithesis of the book's grappling with serious themes.' – *Stephen Jay Gould*
† Among the many inconsistencies in the narrative, Sam Neill warns that the Tyrannosaurus Rex reacts to movement when he can have no knowledge or experience of this fact.
†† It was followed by two sequels: *The Lost World: Jurassic Park* and *Jurassic Park III*.
sound; sound effects editing; visual effects

'This Time It's Not Just A Walk In The Park!'
Jurassic Park III
US 2001 92m DeLuxe
UIP/Amblin (Kathleen Kennedy, Larry Franco)
A palaeontologist is tricked into returning to an island inhabited by intelligent dinosaurs.
Hectic chase movie that, jettisoning the slight intellectual content of the first two movies, concentrates on shocks and thrills, which it delivers efficiently.
w Peter Buchman, Alexander Payne, Jim Taylor *d* Joe Johnston *ph* Shelly Johnson *m* Don Davis *pd* Ed Verreaux *ed* Robert Dalva *sp* Stan Winston
☆ Sam Neill (Dr Alan Grant), William H. Macy (Paul Kirby), Tea Leoni (Amanda Kirby), Alessandro Nivola (Billy Brennan), Trevor Morgan (Eric Kirby), Michael Jeter (Udesky), John Diehl (Cooper), Bruce A. Young (Nash), Laura Dern (Ellie)
'An all-action, helter-skelter, don't-forget-to-buy-the-computer-game ride that makes the two previous installments look like models of classic filmmaking.' – *Derek Elley, Variety*

'There Is No Defence.'
The Juror
US 1996 118m Technicolor Panavision
Columbia (Irwin Winkler, Rob Cowan)
A sculptor, intimidated by a gangster to free a killer when serving on a jury, finds herself caught between the Mob and the law.
Routine woman-in-jeopardy movie that does not even maintain a sense of suspense.
w Ted Tally *book* George Dawes Green *d* Brian Gibson *ph* Jamie Anderson *m* James Newton Howard *pd* Jan Roelfs *ed* Robert Reitano
☆ Demi Moore, Alec Baldwin, Joseph Gordon-Levitt, Anne Heche, James Gandolfini, Lindsay Crouse, Tony Lo Bianco
'Has only a transitory impact – once seen, soon forgotten – though it does have its moments of inevitable chill.' – *Tom Hutchinson, Film Review*

Jury Duty
US 1995 86m Technicolor
TriStar/Triumph/Weasel (Yoran Ben-Ami, Peter M. Lenkov)
A layabout member of a jury attempts to prolong the trial of a serial killer so that he can continue to enjoy being sequestered in a luxury hotel.
Ineffably terrible comedy, a celebration of stupidity and tasteless jokes.
w Neil Tolkin, Barbara Williams, Samantha Adams *d* John Fortenberry *ph* Avi Karpick *m* David Kitay *pd* Deborah Raymond *ed* Stephen Semel
☆ Pauly Shore, Tia Carrere, Stanley Tucci, Brian Doyle-Murray, Abe Vigoda, Charles Napier, Richard Edson, Shelley Winters, Andrew Dice Clay (uncredited)
'Not only has the distinction of being one of the worst major studio releases of recent memory, it's also one of the most morally dubious.' – *Brian Lowry, Variety*

Jury's Evidence
GB 1935 71m bw
British Lion (Herbert Smith)
The jury in a murder trial disagrees.
Courtroom drama with an unsatisfactory finish.
w Ian Dalrymple *play* Jack de Leon, Jack Celestin *d* Ralph Ince *ph* George Stretton
☆ Hartley Power, Margaret Lockwood, Nora Swinburne, Sebastian Shaw

The Jury's Secret
US 1937 64m bw
Universal
The guilty man in a murder case is on the jury.
Slow-moving courtroom drama with an unsatisfactory twist.
w Lester Cole, Newman Levy *d* Edward Sloman
☆ Kent Taylor, Fay Wray, Jane Darwell, Nan Grey, Larry Blake, Fritz Leiber
'Doomed for no honours such as b.o.' – *Variety*

Just a Gigolo
US 1931 71m bw
MGM
A young lord masquerades as a gigolo to avoid being the prey of gold diggers.

Slackly handled comedy which doesn't come off.
w Hans Kraly, Richard Schayer, Claudine West *d* Jack Conway
☆ William Haines, Irene Purcell, C. Aubrey Smith, Lillian Bond

'Too much talk, too little action.' – *Variety*

Just a Gigolo
West Germany 1978 147m colour
Leguan (Rolf Thiele)

A young Prussian veteran of World War I intends to succeed, but stumbles through the Berlin underworld and is accidentally shot in a street skirmish.
An international misadventure whose English version is not only interminable and badly dubbed but extremely clumsily made.
w Ennio de Concini, Joshua Sinclair *d* David Hemmings *ph* Charly Steinberger *m* Gunther Fischer *pd* Peter Rothe
☆ David Bowie, Sydne Rome, Kim Novak, Marlene Dietrich, David Hemmings, Maria Schell, Curt Jurgens, Erika Pluhar

'It often goes for laughs it hasn't a hope of getting; sometimes it aspires to tragic dignity and looks truly inept. It would be kinder to yourself and to everybody involved to overlook it.' – *Time Out*

Just Across the Street
US 1952 78m bw
Universal-International/Leonard Goldstein
Complications arise when a plumber's secretary pretends to be rich.
Silly and pointless comedy which provides its talent with nothing to do.
w Roswell Rogers, Joel Malone *d* Joseph Pevney *ph* Maury Gertsman *ed* Virgil Vogel
☆ Ann Sheridan, John Lund, Robert Keith, Cecil Kellaway, Harvey Lembeck, Natalie Schafer, Alan Mowbray

'If you think you know her, think again.'
Just Another Girl on the I.R.T.
US 1992 97m colour
Metro Tartan/Miramax/Truth 24 F.P.S. (Erwin Wilson)

A 17-year-old rebellious black Brooklyn girl with aspirations to be a doctor becomes pregnant by a boy she meets at a party.
A sympathetic portrait of a teenager refusing to come to terms with reality, brightly performed but hampered by a script that sticks to the obvious and settles for an easy resolution.
wd Leslie Harris *ph* Richard Connors *m* Eric Sadler, Willie Bruno II *pd* Michael O'Dell Green *ed* Jack Haigis
☆ Ariyan A. Johnson, Kevin Thigpen, Ebony Jerido, Jerard Washington, Chequita Jackson

'A crude but disturbing exposé of teenage ignorance and denial about the facts of life on the streets and in the bedroom.' – *Variety*

'The movie's only strong point is its sharp and zappy cast. But hazy vision finally saps even their energy – just as the pasted-on happy ending mocks their efforts to keep things real.' – *Cynthia Rose, Sight and Sound*

Just Around the Corner
US 1938 70m bw
TCF (David Hempstead)

A little girl helps her dad to get on in business.
Tedious Little Miss Fixit tale from the period when Shirley's star was sliding.
w Ethel Hill, J. P. McEvoy, Darrell Ware *d* Irving Cummings *ph* Arthur Miller *md* Louis Silvers
☆ Shirley Temple, Charles Farrell, Bert Lahr, Joan Davis, Amanda Duff, Bill Robinson, Franklin Pangborn, Cora Witherspoon

'Top flight for general all-round entertainment.' – *Variety*

Just Before Dawn
US 1980 90m Movielab
Oakland
Visitors to a mountain area are terrorized by a cleaver-wielding killer.
Teenage shocker with just a little more style than most.
w Mark Arywitz, Gregg Irving *d* Jeff Lieberman
☆ George Kennedy, Mike Kellin, Chris Lemmon, Gregg Henry, Deborah Benson

Just Between Friends
US 1986 120m DeLuxe
Orion/MTM (Edward Teets, Allan Burns)

A middle-aged woman finds little excitement in her household, and fancies a lesbian relationship; but her husband dies and she finds herself pregnant.
Ho-hum melodrama of our time.
wd Allan Burns *ph* Jordan Cronenweth *m* Patrick Williams *pd* Sydney Z. Litwack
☆ Mary Tyler Moore, Ted Danson, Christine Lahti, Sam Waterston, Salome Jens

'The main difference between this and a TV movie is that this doesn't have commercials.' – *Variety*

'Buried deep in the Florida Everglades is a secret that can save an innocent man or let a killer kill again.'
Just Cause
US 1995 colour Panavision
Warner/Fountainbridge (Lee Rich, Arne Glimcher, Steve Perry)

A Harvard law professor goes to Florida to prove that a black youth awaiting execution for murder is innocent, accompanied by the detective who he claims beat him into confessing to the crime.
Lacklustre thriller that becomes increasingly silly and derivative the longer it lasts, so that it exhausts patience and credibility long before the end.
w Jeb Stuart, Peter Stone *novel* John Katzenbach *d* Arne Glimcher *ph* Lajos Koltai *m* James Newton Howard *pd* Patrizia von Brandenstein *ed* William Anderson
☆ Sean Connery, Laurence Fishburne, Kate Capshaw, Blair Underwood, Ruby Dee, Ed Harris, Christopher Murray, Daniel J. Travanti, Ned Beatty, Scarlett Johansson

'We watch a passable investigative thriller spiral into an absurd, ineffectual melodrama.' – *Geoff Brown, The Times*

Just for You
US 1952 104m Technicolor
Paramount (Pat Duggan)
A successful songwriter finds that his troublesome teenage son is in love with his own fiancée.
Tiresomely scripted, pleasantly played romantic comedy with music.
w Robert Carson *novel* *Famous* by Stephen Vincent Benet *d* Elliott Nugent *ph* George Barnes *m* Hugo Friedhofer *m/ly* Harry Warren, Leo Robin *md* Emil Newman
☆ Bing Crosby, Jane Wyman, Bob Arthur, Ethel Barrymore, Natalie Wood, Cora Witherspoon, Regis Toomey
song 'Zing a Little Zong'

Just Heroes
Hong Kong 1989 96m colour
Magnum (Tsui Hark)

When a gang leader is assassinated, a power struggle begins among surviving members to succeed him and discover the identity of his killer.
A movie that grows misty-eyed and sentimental about ruthless killers; admirers of John Woo may enjoy the final shoot-out, with its jokey references to A Better Tomorrow *(a film that all the best gangsters have evidently seen).*
w Nieh Kuang, Tommy Hau *d* John Woo, Wu Ma *ph* Chu Wai Ki, Yee Tung Lung *m* Romeo Diaz, James Wong *ad* Ringo Cheung, Andy Lee *ed* Choi Hung
☆ John Chiang, Danny Lee, Chan Kwon Tai, Kelly Chu, Cally Kwong, Wu Ma, Ti Lung, Chiu Lui

Just Imagine
US 1930 102m bw
Fox
A man who dies in 1930 is revived in 1980 and can't get used to the pace of life.
Famous fantasy which doesn't live up to its reputation and can now be seen as hampered by poor sets, script and acting. Futuristic sets are few but choice.
d David Butler *ph* Ernest Palmer *m* Hugo Friedhofer *md* Arthur Kay *ch* Seymour Felix *ad* Stephen Goosson, Ralph Hammeras *w/songs* De Sylva, Brown, Henderson
☆ El Brendel, Maureen O'Sullivan, John Garrick, Frank Albertson, Marjorie White, Hobart Bosworth, Mischa Auer, Wilfred Lucas

'Needs to be sold in advance on its novelty angle … it seems essential that something be done to make them say "Go down and take a look at that crazy picture".' – *Variety*
art direction

'She stole his heart. He stole her clothes.'
Just Like a Woman
GB 1992 106m Eastmancolor
Rank/Zenith/LWT/British Screen (Nick Evans)

An American living in London moves into lodgings after his wife throws him out, and reveals to his landlady that he is a transvestite.
Tedious comedy of minimal interest, even to cross-dressers.
w Nick Evans *novel* *Geraldine, for the Love of a Transvestite* by Monica Jay *d* Christopher Monger *ph* Alan Hume *m* Michael Storey *pd* John Box *ed* Nicolas Gaster
☆ Julie Walters, Adrian Pasdar, Paul Freeman, Susan Wooldridge, Gordon Kennedy, Ian Redford, Shelley Thompson

'The film remains poky, parochial, and its message is clear – no sex, please, we're British.' – *Geoff Brown, The Times*

'A tepid comedy of Anglo-Saxon inhibition.' – *Philip French, Observer*

Just My Luck
GB 1957 86m bw
Rank (Hugh Stewart)
A jeweller's assistant becomes involved in horse racing.
Flat star vehicle.
w Alfred Shaughnessy *d* John Paddy Carstairs *ph* Jack Cox *m* Philip Green
☆ Norman Wisdom, Jill Dixon, Leslie Phillips, Margaret Rutherford, Delphi Lawrence

Just Off Broadway
US 1942 66m bw
TCF/Sol M. Wurtzel
Michael Shayne investigates a court case on which he is sitting as a juror.
Standard second feature mystery, reasonably well made.
w Arnaud D'Usseau *d* Herbert I. Leeds
☆ Lloyd Nolan, Marjorie Weaver, Phil Silvers, Janis Carter, Richard Derr, Chester Clute

Just Tell Me What You Want
US 1980 112m Technicolor
Warner/Jay Presson Allen, Sidney Lumet

A powerful tycoon starts to weave plots when one of his harem wants to go independent.
Thoroughly silly melodrama with a few incidental humours.
w Jay Presson Allen *novel* Jay Presson Allen *d* Sidney Lumet *ph* Oswald Morris *m* Charles Strouse *pd* Tony Walton
☆ Ali MacGraw, Alan King, Myrna Loy, Keenan Wynn, Tony Roberts, Dina Merrill, Peter Weller

'Jay Presson Allen has adapted her trashy novel into a trashy picture … Myrna Loy looks as if she's constantly amazed at the kinds of films getting made these days, and she's absolutely right.' – *Variety*

'In love, you can't accept anything at face value.'
Just the Ticket
US 1998 115m DeLuxe
Entertainment/CineSon (Gary Lucchesi, Andy Garcia)

In order to impress his girfriend, a tout tries to corner the market in tickets for the Pope's Mass at Yankee Stadium.
Gritty romantic comedy with no spark between its stars, and not much comedy either.
wd Richard Wenk *ph* Ellen Kuras *m* Rick Marotta *pd* Franckie Diago *ed* Christopher Cibelli
☆ Andy Garcia, Andie MacDowell, Richard Bradford, Laura Harris, Andre Blake, Elizabeth Ashley, Patrick Breen, Fred Asparagus, Louis Mustillo, Ron Leibman, Chris Lemmon, Don Novello, Abe Vigoda, Irene Worth

'Even though his performance is passable, the only real romance on show in this vanity vehicle is Garcia's love affair with himself.' – *Total Film*

Just the Way You Are
US 1984 95m Metrocolor
MGM-UA (Leo L. Fuchs)

A young fluteplayer tries to carve a career for herself while overcoming a physical disability.
Odd little comedy-drama with little plot beyond the central character's crippled leg; not likely to make much headway.
w Allan Burns *d* Edouard Molinaro *ph* Claude Lecomte *m* Vladimir Cosmar *ad* François de Lamotte *ed* Claudio Ventura, Georges Klotz
☆ Kristy McNichol, Michael Ontkean, Kaki Hunter, André Dussolier, Robert Carradine

'They're Not Just From Another Time, They're From France.'
Just Visiting
US/France 2001 89m Technicolor Super 35
Buena Vista/Hollywood (Patrice Ledoux, Ricardo Mestres)

A wizard sends a French knight and his servant forward in time from the 12th century to Chicago in 2000.
A remake of the 1993 French movie Les Visiteurs *that does not live up to the boisterous comedy of the original.*
w Christian Clavier, Jean-Marie Poiré, John Hughes *based on* *Les Visiteurs* by Christian Clavier, Jean-Marié Poire *d* Jean-Marie Gaubert *ph* Ueli Steiger *m* John Powell *pd* Doug Kraner *ed* Michael A. Stevenson
☆ Jean Reno (Thibault), Christina Applegate (Rosalind/Julia), Christian Clavier (Andre), Matthew Ross (Hunter), Tara Reid (Angelique), Bridgette Wilson-Sampras (Amber), John Aylward (Byron), George Plimpton (Dr Brady), Malcolm McDowell (Wizard)

'One of those rare American remakes of a French film that preserves the flavor of the original and even improves upon it.' – *Roger Ebert, Chicago Sun-Times*

'If you have a barge pole, do not use it to touch this mirthless film.' – *Philip French, Observer*

Just William
GB 1939 94m bw
Associated British (Walter C. Mycroft)
William, hunting for bomb-carrying spies, foils a con man and helps his father in his campaign to become a local councillor.
The first and best of the William series, with a good cast and a genuine feeling for children's fantasy and anarchy.
w Graham Cutts, Doreen Montgomery, Ireland Wood *novel* Richmal Crompton *d* Graham Cutts *ph* Walter Harvey *ad* Cedric Dawe *ed* E. B. Jarvis
☆ Fred Emney, Basil Radford, Iris Hoey, Amy Veness, Dicky Lupino, Roddy McDowall, Norman Robinson, Peter Miles, Jenny Laird, David Tree

Just William's Luck
GB 1947 85m bw
Alliance (James Carter)
William tries to marry off his brother so that he can inherit his bicycle, and succeeds in foiling a gang of smugglers.
Limp comedy that fails to translate to the screen the verbal exuberance and mayhem of the novels.
wd Val Guest *novel* Richmal Crompton *ph* Bert Mason *m* Robert Farnon *ad* Harry Moore *ed* Anne Barker
☆ William Graham (William), Leslie Bradley (The Boss), Garry Marsh (Mr Brown), Jane Walsh (Mrs Brown), Hugh Cross (Robert), Kathleen Stuart (Ethel), Muriel Aked (Emily), Joan Hickson (Hubert's Mother), A. E. Matthews (The Tramp), Michael Medwin (Boss Gang Member), Michael Balfour (Jenks)
† It was followed by a sequel, *William at the Circus* (qv).

Just You and Me, Kid
US 1979 93m Metrocolor
Columbia/Irving Fein-Jerome M. Zeitman
An elderly comedian reluctantly takes care of a naked teenager on the run from a dope pusher.
Virtually a one-set comedy which quickly tires the eye and ear; not a good idea despite the veteran star.
w Oliver Hailey, Leonard Stern *d* Leonard Stern *ph* David Walsh *m* Jack Elliott
☆ George Burns, Brooke Shields, Burl Ives, Lorraine Gary, John Schuck, Keye Luke, Leon Ames, Ray Bolger, Carl Ballantine

Justice Est Faite ★
France 1950 105m bw
Silver Films
The personal lives of jurors in a mercy killing case affect their verdict.
Absorbing courtroom drama with a message.
w Charles Spaak, André Cayatte *d* André Cayatte
ph Jean Bourgoin *m* Raymond Legrand
☆ Valentine Tessier, Claude Nollier, Jacques Castelot, Michel Auclair

Justice for Sale: see *Night Court*

Justine
US 1969 116m DeLuxe Panavision
TCF/Pandro S. Berman
In Alexandria in the thirties, the beautiful wife of a wealthy banker influences the lives of all who meet her.
Disastrous condensed version of a very unusual set of novels whose atmosphere has not translated at all well. The result is like a bad rehearsal for a film, which is not surprising in view of the number of producers variously involved. The author feared 'a sort of Peyton Place *with camels', and got it.*
w Lawrence B. Marcus *novels The Alexandria Quartet* by *Lawrence Durrell* *d* George Cukor
ph Leon Shamroy *m* Jerry Goldsmith
☆ Anouk Aimée, Michael York, Dirk Bogarde, Anna Karina, John Vernon, George Baker, Philippe Noiret, Robert Forster, Jack Albertson, Michael Dunn, Barry Morse, Cliff Gorman, Severn Darden
'Could well stand as a model of what can happen when Hollywood gets to grips with a celebrated literary property.' – *David Wilson*
'Despite leaden forays into homosexuality, transvestitism, incest, and child prostitution, it remains as naively old-fashioned in its emotional and intellectual vocabulary as in its actual verbiage and cinematic technique.' – *John Simon*
† The film is said to have been eight years in preparation. Joseph Strick was fired as director when the cast and crew returned to Los Angeles after shooting exteriors in Tunisia. Cukor, reported Michael York, 'made his disapproval of some of his inherited cast quite unambiguous. At the mention of our leading lady his face would flush.'

Justine and Julia: see *Marquis de Sade: Justine*

'The only way he can stay pro, is to play (like) a girl.'
Juwanna Mann
US 2001 91m Technicolor
Warner/Morgan Creek (James G. Robinson, Steve Oedekerk, Bill Gerber)
A disgraced basketball player turns transvestite so that he can join a woman's team.
Mildly amusing cross-dressing comedy that cannot compare to either Tootsie or Some Like It Hot.
w Bradley Allenstein *d* Jesse Vaughan
ph Reynaldo Villalobos *m* Wendy Melvoin, Lisa Coleman *pd* Eve Cauley Turner *ed* Seth Flaum
☆ Miguel A. Nunez Jnr (Jamal Jefferies/Juwanna Mann), Vivica A. Fox (Michelle Langford), Kevin Pollak (Lorne Daniels), Tommy Davidson (Puff Smokey Smoke), Kim Wayans (Latisha Jansen), Jenifer Lewis (Aunt Ruby), Ginuwine (Romeo), Kimberly 'Lil' Kim' Jones (Tina Parker)
'Sloppy, amusing comedy that proceeds from a stunningly unoriginal premise.' – *A. O. Scott, New York Times*
'Hilarity does not ensue.' – *Anthony Quinn, Independent*

K2
US 1991 111m Technicolor
Entertainment/TransPacific/Majestic (Jonathan Taplin, Marilyn Weiner, Tim Van Rellim)

Two friends join an ill-assorted expedition to climb the Himalayan mountain K2.
A tame buddy-buddy movie that has nowhere to go but down.
w Patrick Myers, Scott Roberts *play* Patrick Myers *d* Franc Roddam *ph* Gabriel Beristain *m* Chaz Jankel *pd* Andrew Sanders *ed* Sean Barton
☆ Michael Biehn, Matt Craven, Raymond J. Barry, Hiroshi Fujioka, Luca Bercovici, Patricia Charbonneau, Julia Nickson-Soul, Jamal Shah
‘Begins as mindlessly as it means to – and does – go on.’ – *Sight and Sound*
‘On this evidence, climbing K2 can’t be any harder than sitting through it.’ – *Kim Newman, Empire*

K9000
US 1989 90m colour
Fries Entertainment (J. Rickley Dunn)

A cop teams up with a cybernetic dog to bust a crime syndicate.
Witless compendium of action picture clichés.
w Steven E. de Souza, Michael Part *d* Kim Manners *ph* Frank Raymond *m* Jan Hammer *pd* Elliott Gilbert *ed* J. P. Farrell
☆ Chris Mulkey, Catherine Oxenberg, Dennis Haysbert, Dana Gladstone, Jerry Houser, Judson Scott, Anne Haney, Thom McFadden

‘Fate has found its hero.’
K-19: The Widowmaker *
US/Germany/GB 138m DeLuxe Panavision
Paramount/IntermediaNational Geographic/Palomar/First Light/IMF (Kathryn Bigelow, Joni Sighvatsson, Christine Whitaker, Edward S. Feldman)

Thre crew of a Russian nuclear submarine face disaster when it malfunctions on its maiden voyage.
Much like many other submarine adventures in its slick but shallow way, this still provides enough suspense to keep its audience watching.
w Christopher Kyle *story* Louis Nowra *d* Kathryn Bigelow *ph* Jeff Cronenweth *m* Klaus Badelt *pd* Karl Juliusson , Michael Novotny *ed* Walter Murch *sp* Bruce Jones, John Nelson; ILM
☆ Harrison Ford (Alexei Vostrikov), Liam Neeson (Mikhail Polenin), Peter Sarsgaard (Vadim Radtchenko), Joss Ackland (Marshal Zelentstov), John Shrapnel (Admiral Bratyeev), Donald Sumpter (Dr Savran), Tim Woodward (Partonov), Steve Nicholson (Demichev)
‘The movie is efficient enough, but its dramatic freight includes every submarine cliché in the ship’s manifesto.’ – *Philip French, Observer*
‘Piles up one nerve-racking crisis after another, interspersed with moments of ethereal, almost otherworldly beauty.’ – *A.O. Scott, New York Times*

‘Meet the two toughest cops in town. One’s just a little smarter than the other.’
K-9
US 1988 102m DeLuxe
UIP/Universal (Lawrence Gordon, Charles Gordon)

A narcotics cop teams up with an Alsatian.
A not-so-shaggy dog story with a couple of laughs.
w Steven Siegel, Scott Myers *d* Rod Daniel *ph* Dean Semler *m* Miles Goodman *pd* George Costello *ed* Lois Freeman-Fox
☆ James Belushi, Mel Harris, Kevin Tighe, Ed O’Neill, Jerry Lee, James Handy, Daniel Davis, Cotter Smith, John Snyder, Pruitt Taylor Vince

‘Change The Way You Look At The World.’
‘Celebrate The Possibilities.’
K-Pax
US 2001 121m Technicolor Panavision
Universal/Intermedia/IMF (Lawrence Gordon, Lloyd Levin, Robert F. Colesberry)

A psychiatrist examines a man who claims to be an alien from the planet K-Pax.
Watchable performances from the two leads save this shaggy dog story from seeming quite as pointless as it is.
w Charles Leavitt *novel* Gene Brewer *d* Iain Softley *ph* John Mathieson *pd* John Beard *ed* Craig McKay *sp* Centropolis Effects *cos* Louise Mingenbach
☆ Kevin Spacey (Prot), Jeff Bridges (Dr Mark Powell), Mary McCormack (Rachel Powell), Alfre Woodard (Claudia Villars), David Patrick Kelly (Howie), Saul Williams (Ernie), Peter Gerety (Sal), Celia Weston (Mrs Archer)
‘Gives off a great deal of light but generates little heat in a drama that aspires to cosmic themes but ends up with plain, comforting homilies.’ – *Robert Koehler, Variety*
‘As a brainless laugh riot, it’s as funny as a flu epidemic. As a drama, it’s an unintentional Robin Williams vehicle sour beyond its shelf life.’ – *Rex Reed, New York Observer*

Kàdisbellan: see *The Slingshot*

‘In A World Of Ancient Traditions’
Kadosh *
Israel/France/Italy 1999 117m colour
Downtown/Agav Hafakot/MP/Canal+/Mikado (Amos Gitai, Michel Propper)

Despite being in love with his wife of ten years, an ultra-orthodox Jew follows his rabbi’s advice and divorces her so that he can have children.
Set in modern-day Jerusalem, this is a tragic, well-told story of conflicting demands and religious orthodoxy, but one that secular audiences will find easy to ignore.
w Eliette Abecassis, Amos Gitai *d* Amos Gitai *ph* Renato Berta *m* Louis Sclavis *pd* Miguel Markin *ed* Monica Coleman, Kobi Netanel *cos* Laura Dinolesko
☆ Yoram Hattab (Meir), Yael Abecassis (Rivka), Meital Barda (Malka), Uri Klauzner (Yossef), Yussuf Abu-Warda (Rav Shimon), Lea Koenig (Elisheva), Sami Hori (Yaakov), Rivka Michaeli (Gynaecologist), Samuel Calderon (Uncle Shmouel), David Cohen (Shlomo)
‘A surprisingly affecting love story.’ – *Patrick Peters, Empire*
‘Slow, stifling and beautifully shot.’ – *James Christopher, Times*

Kafka *
US/France 1991 98m bw/colour
Guild/Renn/Baltimore/Pricel (Stuart Cornfeld, Harry Benn)

A timid insurance clerk finds himself drawn into an anarchist plot when he investigates the disappearance of a friend.
An intriguing attempt to create a paranoid fiction combining elements of Kafka’s life and his stories; it is stylish though not entirely successful, closer to the basics of a horror movie than to its author’s works.
w Lem Dobbs *d* Steven Soderbergh *ph* Walt Lloyd *m* Cliff Martinez *pd* Gavin Bocquet *ed* Steven Soderbergh
☆ Jeremy Irons, Theresa Russell, Joel Grey, Ian Holm, Jeroen Krabbé, Armin Mueller-Stahl, Alec Guinness, Brian Glover, Robert Flemyng
‘Soderbergh’s film has few surprises because he sticks too matter-of-factly to Kakfa basics, where others have spun out their own distinctive take.’ – *Nick James, Sight and Sound*
‘Soderbergh’s most entertaining, least pretentious film to date, this is weirdly recommended.’ – *Kim Newman, Empire*

Kagemusha ***
Japan 1980 179m Eastmancolor
TCF/Toho (Akira Kurosawa)

aka: *The Double*
aka: *Shadow Warrior*
On the death of a clan chief his place is taken by the lookalike hired to overlook battlefields while the chief is really busy elsewhere.
Fascinating Japanese epic centring on stately ritual and court intrigue, with the occasional battle for spectacular action; one of the director’s most impressive works.
w Akira Kurosawa, Masato Ide *d* *Akira Kurosawa* *ph* *Kazuo Miyagawa, Asakazu Nakai* *m* Shinichiro Ikebe *ad* Yoshiro Muraki
☆ Tatsuya Nakadai (Shingen Takeda/Thief), Tsutomu Yamazaki (Nobukado Takeda), Kenichi Hagiwara (Katsuyori Takeda), Kota Yui (Takemaru Takeda), Hideo Murata (Nobuharu Baba), Takayuki Shiho (Masatoyo Natio), Shuhei Sugimori (Masanobu Kosaka), Noboru Shimizu (Masatane Hara)
‘Probably the director’s most physically elaborate, most awesome film, full of magnificent views of lines of mounted soldiers slowly crossing grand landscapes.’ – *Vincent Canby, New York Times*
best foreign film; art direction
direction; costume design

Kakushi Toride No San-Akunin: see *The Hidden Fortress*

El Kalaa *
Algeria 1988 98m Eastmancolor
Metro/Le Centre Algérien de l’Art et l’Industrie Cinématographique (Tahar Harhoura)
aka: *The Citadel*
A merchant runs into opposition when he decides to take a fourth wife.
Successful on the level of a village soap opera.
wd Mohamed Chouikh *ph* Allel Yahyaoui *ad* Zerrouki Boukhari, Ahmed Kobbi *ed* Yamina Chouikh
☆ Khaled Barkat, Djillali Ain Tedelles, Fettouma Ousliha, Fatima Belhadj, Momo

‘The switched-on thriller!!!’
Kaleidoscope *
GB 1966 103m Technicolor
Warner/Winkast (Elliott Kastner)
reissue title: *The Bank Breaker*
An American playboy breaks into a playing card factory and marks the designs so that he can win in every European casino.
Would-be swinging comedy-thriller which in fact is entertaining only when it stops trying to dazzle.
w Robert and Jane Howard-Carrington *d* Jack Smight *ph* *Christopher Challis* *m* Stanley Myers *ad* Maurice Carter
☆ Warren Beatty, Susannah York, Clive Revill, Eric Porter, Murray Melvin
‘A “groovie movie” it certainly is, with a battery of fashionable camera tricks, kaleidoscopic dissolves, and virtually every scene introduced from behind an irrelevant piece of furniture.’ – *David Wilson*

‘Fear Never Travels Alone.’
Kalifornia
US 1993 118m DeLuxe Cinemascope
Rank/Propaganda/Polygram/Viacom (Tim Clawson)

A couple driving across America to write about and photograph sites of murders unwittingly have as travelling companions a killer and his girlfriend.
An unlovely road movie, simultaneously violent and smug – and too knowing for its own good.
w Tim Metcalfe *d* Dominic Sena *ph* Bojan Bazelli *m* Carter Burwell *pd* Michael White *ed* Martin Hunter
☆ Brad Pitt, Juliette Lewis, David Duchovny, Michelle Forbes, Sierra Pecheur, Gregory Mars Martin
‘An extremely handsome production imbued with a chilling surrealistic sensibility.’ – *Variety*
‘Looks a treat, tells what ought to be a fascinating story but ends up wallowing in its own pretensions.’ – *Derek Malcolm, Guardian*

‘Submit to love and feel the pain of too much tenderness.’
Kama Sutra
India/GB/Japan/Germany 1996 114m Technicolor
Film Four/Rasa/NDF/Pony Canyon/Pandora/Mirabai (Mira Nair, Lydia Dean Pilcher)

In 16th-century India, a servant girl seeks sexual freedom after she is cast out of the court for seducing the king just before his marriage to her childhood friend.
Exotic settings and beautiful women fail to enliven a dull movie, peopled by cardboard characters mouthing romantic clichés.
w Helena Kriel, Mira Nair *d* Mira Nair *ph* Declan Quinn *m* Mark Friedberg *ed* Kristina Boden
☆ Naveen Andrews, Sarita Choudhury, Ramon Tikaram, Rekha, Indira Varma, Pearl Padamsee, Arundhati Rao
‘Reactionary soft-core erotica that could be sold as “Emmanuelle Goes to Bollywood”.’ – *Philip French, Observer*

Kameradschaft *
Germany 1931 92m bw
Nerofilm
aka: *Comradeship*
On the Franco-German border French miners are imprisoned below ground and Germans burrow to free them.
Salutary message film with good dramatic pointing.
w Laszlo Vajda, Karl Otten, Peter Martin Lampel *d* G. W. Pabst *ph* Fritz Arno Wagner, Robert Baberski
☆ Ernst Busch, Alexander Granach, Fritz Kampers, Gustav Puttjer

Kamikaze
France 1986 89m Eastmancolor Cinemascope
Blue Dolphin/Les Films du Loup/ARP/Gaumont (Luc Besson)
An electronics engineer develops a deadly weapon that can kill anyone appearing live on television.
Weak thriller that fails to make anything of its silly central concept.
w Luc Besson, Didier Grousset *d* Didier Grousset *ph* Jean-François Robin *m* Eric Serra *ed* Olivier Mauffroy
☆ Richard Bohringer, Michel Galabru, Dominique Lavanant, Riton Leibman, Kim Massee, Harry Cleven, Romane Bohringer, Etienne Chicot, Philippe Girard
‘When the action stops and the talking starts, the amiable triviality of the whole exercise becomes tediously apparent.’ – *Philip Strick, MFB*

Kanal *
Poland 1956 97m bw
Film Polski (Stanislaw Adler)

aka: *They Loved Life*
In 1944, an anti-Nazi resistance group is trapped in a sewer.
A suffocatingly unpleasant film to watch; its message and technical excellence are undoubted.

w Jerzy Stawinski *novel* Kloakerne by Jerzy Stawinski *d* Andrzej Wajda *ph* Jerzy Lipman *m* Jan Krenz
☆ Teresa Izewska, Tadeusz Janczar, Emil Kariewicz, Wienczylaw Glinski

Kanchenjungha **
India 1962 102m colour
NCA Productions
During an afternoon on holiday in Darjeeling, a domineering father tries to arrange his daughter's marriage to an older, eligible bachelor.
Leisurely examination of attitudes to love and marriage and of the relationship between the sexes. It was Ray's first film in colour.
wd Satyajit Ray *ph* Subrata Mitra *m* Satyajit Ray *ad* Bansi Chandragupta *ed* Dulal Dutta
☆ Chhabi Biswas, Anil Chatterjee, Karuna Banerjee, Anubha Gupta, Subrata Sen, Sibani Singh, Alaknanda Roy, Arun Mukherjee, N. Viswanathan
'Under the primitive working circumstances, the story about love and ambition and the collision of cultures was perhaps too complex, but the setting and the beautiful women help to compensate for the awkwardness and naiveté.' – *Pauline Kael*

Kandahar: see *Safar é Ghandehar*

Kangaroo
US 1952 84m Technicolor
TCF (Robert Bassler)
In old Australia, a con man pretends to be a rancher's long-lost heir, then complicates things by falling in love with the rancher's daughter.
Standard romantic action hokum.
w Harry Kleiner *d* Lewis Milestone *ph* Charles G. Clarke *m* Sol Kaplan
☆ Maureen O'Hara, Peter Lawford, Finlay Currie, Richard Boone, Chips Rafferty, Charles Tingwell

Kangaroo *
Australia 1987 110m colour Panavision
Ross Dimsey
After the First World War, an English writer and his German-born wife decide to settle in Australia, where they become involved with the leader of a secret fascist organization, who plans to become the country's dictator.
Effective treatment of Lawrence's semi-autobiographical novel, attacking what he saw as England's cultural decline, with Friels's performance based firmly upon the personality of its author.
w Evan Jones *novel* D. H. Lawrence *d* Tim Burstall *ph* Dan Burstall *m* Nathan Waks *pd* Tracy Watt *ed* Edward McQueen-Mason
☆ Colin Friels, Judy Davis, Hugh Keays-Byrne, John Walton, Julie Nihill, Peter Hehir, Peter Cummins
† The film was made in 1985 and not released for two years.

'He stole the money... and he's not giving it back.'
Kangaroo Jack
US 2003 89m Technicolor Panavision
Warner/Castle Rock (Jerry Bruckheimer)
A Brooklyn hairdresser and his friend, a petty crook, chase around Australia after a kangaroo that hops off with a package they were meant to deliver to an associate of his gangster stepfather.
Simple-minded farce about stupid people that is a familiar mixture of crass and tasteless jokes and broad slapstick; it has all the subtlety and humour of a punch on the nose.
w Steve Bing, Scott Rosenberg *d* David McNally *ph* Peter Menzies Jnr *pd* George Liddle *ed* John Murray, William Goldenberg *sp* Secret Lab
☆ Jerry O'Connell (Charlie Carbone), Anthony Anderson (Louis Booker), Estella Warren (Jessie), Michael Shannon (Frankie), Christopher Walken (Sal Maggio), Bill Hunter (Blue), Marton Csokas (Mr Smith), David Ngoombujarra (Mr Jimmy)
'Shrill and silly farce in which a CGI marsupial seems more lifelike than most of its flesh-and-blood co-stars.' – *Joe Leydon, Variety*

'I'll make this town keep the peace – if I have to blow it to pieces!'
The Kansan
US 1943 79m bw
UA (Harry Sherman)
A wandering marksman stops off to become marshal of a frontier town.
Solid routine Western with good performances.
w Harold Shumate *book* Frank Gruber *d* George Archainbaud *m* Gerard Carbonara
☆ Richard Dix, Albert Dekker, Jane Wyatt, Eugene Pallette, Victor Jory, Robert Armstrong, Clem Bevans, Hobart Cavanaugh, Willie Best
Gerard Carbonara

Kansas
US 1988 106m colour
Cannon/Trans World Entertainment (George Litto)
A drifter falls foul of a crook and in love with a farmer's daughter.
Well-photographed wide open spaces that are empty of interest.
w Spencer Eastman *d* David Stevens *ph* David Eggby *m* Pino Donaggio *pd* Matthew Jacobs *ed* Robert Barrere
☆ Andrew McCarthy, Matt Dillon, Leslie Hope, Brent Jennings, Kyra Sedgwick, Harry Northup, Arlen Dean Snyder

Kansas City *
US 1996 115m CFI color
Electric/Sandcastle 5/CiBy 2000 (Robert Altman)
The wife of a petty thief, who is being held captive by a powerful gangster, kidnaps a politician's drug-addicted wife in a bid to get her husband released.
Muddled story of power and corruption in Kansas City of the 30s, though admirers of the blues-tinged jazz of the period will appreciate the wonderful music on display.
w Robert Altman, Frank Barhydt *d* Robert Altman *ph* Oliver Stapleton *m* John Cale *pd* Stephen Altman *ed* Geraldine Peroni
☆ Jennifer Jason Leigh, Miranda Richardson, Harry Belafonte, Michael Murphy, Dermot Mulroney, Steve Buscemi
'The film-making seems almost careless, and often perfunctory, as if Altman's memories – a mixture of fond nostalgia and his usual acerbic irony – aren't quite clear enough for the deal in hand.' – *Derek Malcolm, Guardian*

Kansas City Bomber
US 1972 99m Metrocolor
MGM/Levy-Gardner-Laven/Raquel Welch (Marty Elfand)
A roller skating star finds time between affairs to beat her rival in a big match.
Vulgar melodrama with good action scenes.
w Thomas Rickman, Calvin Clements *d* Jerrold Freedman *ph* Fred Koenekamp *m* Don Ellis
☆ Raquel Welch, Kevin McCarthy, Norman Alden, Jeanne Cooper

Kansas City Confidential
US 1952 98m bw
United Artists/Edward Small
GB title: *The Secret Four*
An ex-detective plans a perfect crime, and recruits three confederates who all remain unknown to each other by wearing masks.
Moderately lively if violent thriller which gets less inventive as it goes along but satisfies the action buffs.
w George Bruce, Harry Essex *d* Phil Karlson *ph* George Diskant *m* Paul Sawtell
☆ Preston Foster, John Payne, Coleen Gray, Lee Van Cleef, Neville Brand, Jack Elam, Dona Drake

Kansas City Princess
US 1934 64m bw
Warner (Lou Edelman)
Gold diggers go to Paris.
Light farce comedy, somewhat lacking in punch.
w Sy Bartlett, Manuel Seff *d* William Keighley
☆ Joan Blondell, Glenda Farrell, Hugh Herbert, Robert Armstrong, Osgood Perkins, Hobart Cavanaugh
'Just a comedy, good for better than moderate biz.' – *Variety*

Kansas Raiders
US 1951 80m Technicolor
Universal-International
During the Civil War, Jesse James joins Quantrill's Raiders.
Fast-moving, fairly violent Western only remotely based on fact.
w Robert L. Richards *d* Ray Enright *ph* Irving Glassberg *m* Joseph Gershenson *ad* Bernard Herzbrun, Emrich Nicholson *ed* Milton Carruth
☆ Audie Murphy, Brian Donlevy, Marguerite Chapman, Scott Brady, Tony Curtis, Richard Arlen, James Best, Richard Long

Kaos **
Italy 1984 188m Eastmancolor
RAI-TV/Filmtre (Giuliano de Negri)
Five stories by Pirandello are combined in settings near his birthplace.
Generally fascinating mixture of tales which range from comedy to horror, styled by master film-makers.
wd Paolo and Vittorio Taviani *ph* Giuseppe Lanci *m* Nicola Piovani *ed* Roberto Perignani
☆ Margarita Lozano, Claudio Bigagli, Enrica Maria Modugno, Ciccio Ingrassia, Franco Franchi, Biagio Barone, Omero Antonutti

Kapo
Italy/France 1960 115m bw
Vides/Zebra/Francinex
A French Jewess survives the horrors of a Nazi concentration camp and becomes camp guard.
Curious exploitation piece which turns tragedy into melodrama, and doesn't even do that with much flair.
w Franco Solinas, Gillo Pontecorvo *d* Gillo Pontecorvo *ph* Goffredo Bellisario, Alexander Sekulovic *m* Carlo Rustichelli
☆ Susan Strasberg, Laurent Terzieff, Emmanuelle Riva
best foreign film

Karakter: see *Character*

The Karate Kid *
US 1984 127m Metrocolor
Columbia/Delphi II (Jerry Weintraub)
A teenage boy, new to California, joins a karate club and defeats the local bullies.
A kind of amateur Rocky*, not bad in its way, but its huge commercial success in the US remains mystifying.*
w Robert Mark Kamen *d* John G. Avildsen *ph* James Crabe *m* Bill Conti *pd* William J. Cassidy *ed* Bud Smith, Walt Mulconery
☆ Ralph Macchio, Noriyuki 'Pat' Morita, Elisabeth Shue, Martin Kove, Randee Heller, William Zabka
Pat Morita (supporting actor)

Karate Kid III
US 1989 112m DeLuxe
Columbia TriStar (Jerry Weintraub)
The karate kid defeats villains who attempt to humiliate him.
Even less interesting than Part II.
w Robert Mark Kamen *d* John G. Avildsen *ph* Stephen Yaconelli *m* Bill Conti *pd* William F. Matthews *ed* John Carter, John G. Avildsen
☆ Ralph Macchio, Noriyuki 'Pat' Morita, Robyn Lively, Thomas Ian Griffith, Martin L. Kove, Sean Kanan, Jonathan Avildsen
'Young love, meanwhile, has rarely been shown so boringly on screen.' – *MFB*

The Karate Kid Part II
US 1986 113m DeLuxe
Columbia/Delphi II (Jerry Weintraub)
Daniel's teacher heads back to Okinawa where his father is gravely ill.
Tedious attempt to spin out a surprise hit; no surprises this time.
w Robert Mark Kamen *d* John G. Avildsen *ph* James Crabe *m* Bill Conti *pd* William J. Cassidy *ed* David Garfield, Jane Kurson, John G. Avildsen
☆ Pat Morita, Ralph Macchio, Nobu McCarthy, Danny Kamekona
song 'Glory of Love'

The Karate Killers
US 1967 90m Metrocolor
MGM/Arena (Boris Ingster)
The men from U.N.C.L.E. foil enemy agents who steal a formula for making gold out of sea water.
Comic-strip spy spoof, featuring two incompetent agents who are forever being knocked out by the opposition, even when it's no stronger than geisha girls; a starry cast is given very little to do.
w Norman Hudis *story* Boris Ingster *d* Barry Shear *ph* Fred Koenekamp *m* Richard Shores *ad* George W. Davis
☆ Robert Vaughn, David McCallum, Joan Crawford, Curt Jurgens, Telly Savalas, Herbert Lom, Terry Thomas, Leo G. Carroll, Kim Darby, Diane McBain
† The film was edited from episodes of the television series *The Man from U.N.C.L.E.*

Käre John: see *Dear John*

Kaspar Hauser
Germany 1993 139m colour
Arrow/Multimedia München/WDR/ORF/SVT/ARTE/Telepool/LFA (Andreas Meyer)
original title: *Verbrechen am Seelenleben eines Menschens*
The heir to the throne of Baden becomes a pawn in a European power struggle; he is imprisoned for years, set free when he is unable to talk, but is still unable to escape his enemies.
A complex political drama that overwhelms the human interest of its story; it pales in comparison with Werner Herzog's The Enigma of Kaspar Hauser *(qv).*
wd Peter Sehr *ph* Gernot Roll *m* Nikos Mamangakis *ad* O. Jochen Schmidt, Karel Vacek *ed* Heidi Handorf, Susanne Hartmann
☆ André Eisermann, Udo Samel, Jeremy Clyde, Katharina Thalbach, Cécile Paoli, Hansa Czypionka, Dieter Mann
'It ends up as *Dynasty* in funny wigs, although much cruder, submerging the fascinating story at its core with coarse couplings and obscure plot points.' – *Tom Shone, Sunday Times*
† It was originally shown in a version that ran for 182m.

'If they lived in the same century they'd be perfect for each other.'
Kate and Leopold
US 2001 121m DeLuxe
Buena Vista/Miramax (Cathy Konrad)
An English duke is transported from 1876 to the present day, where he falls in love with a market researcher.
Vapid romantic comedy, with its endorsement of the past as a time when men were men and women did as they were told.
w Steven Rogers, James Mangold *d* James Mangold *ph* Stuart Dryburgh *m* Rolfe Kent *pd* Mark Friedberg *ed* David Brenner
☆ Meg Ryan (Kate McKay), Hugh Jackman (Leopold), Liev Schreiber (Stuart Bessler), Breckin Meyer (Charlie McKay), Natasha Lyonne (Darci), Bradley Whitford (J. J. Camden), Paxton Whitehead (Uncle Millard), Spalding Gray (Dr Geisler), Philip Bosco (Otis)
'Thoroughly predictable but surprisingly pleasant.' – *San Francisco Examiner*
song 'Until' (m/l Sting)

Kate Plus Ten
GB 1938 81m bw
Wainwright (Richard Wainwright)
A police inspector falls for the attractive female leader of a bullion gang.
Curious comedy thriller with insufficient of either commodity.
w Jack Hulbert, Jeffrey Dell *novel* Edgar Wallace *d* Reginald Denham *ph* Roy Kellino *m* Allan Gray *ad* D. L. W. Daniels *ed* E. M. Hunter
☆ Jack Hulbert, Genevieve Tobin, Noel Madison, Francis L. Sullivan, Arthur Wontner, Frank Cellier, Googie Withers, Peter Haddon, Felix Aylmer, Leo Genn, Edward Lexy

Kathleen
US 1941 88m bw MGM (George Haight)
A neglected daughter finds a new wife for her widowed father.
One of the reasons for Shirley Temple's early retirement.

w Mary McCall Jnr *story* Kay Van Riper *d* Harold S. Bucquet *ph* Sidney Wagner *m* Franz Waxman
☆ Shirley Temple, Herbert Marshall, Laraine Day, Gail Patrick, Felix Bressart, Nella Walker, Lloyd Corrigan

Kathy O
US 1958 99m Eastmancolor Cinemascope
U-I (Sy Gomberg)
A temperamental child star befriends a lonely columnist.
Overlong Hollywood comedy drama with amusing moments.
w Jack Sher, Sy Gomberg *d* Jack Sher *ph* Arthur E. Arling *m* Frank Skinner *m/ly* Charles Tobias, Ray Joseph
☆ Patty McCormack, Dan Duryea, Jan Sterling, Sam Levene

Katia Ismailova *
France/Russia 1994 94m colour
Films du Rivage/Studio TTL/Lumière/CNC/Gorki Studios (Marc Ruscart, Igor Tolstunov)
original title: *Podmoskovnye vechera*
A woman who acts as secretary to her husband's mother, a romantic novelist, begins an affair with a carpenter during a stay at her mother-in-law's rural retreat.
An updated version of Nikolai Leskov's story of passion, murder and class conflict, with the passion downplayed; it has a certain fascination, though.
w Alla Krinitsyna, François Gérif, Cécile Vargaftig *novella Maria Sheptunova, Stanislav Govorukhin* *d* Valerii Todorovsky *ph* Sergei Koslov *m* Leonid Dessiatnikov *ad* Aleksandr Osipov *ed* Hélène Gargarin, Alla Streinikova
☆ Ingeborga Dapkunaite, Vladmir Mashkov, Alisa Freindlikh, Aleksandr Feklistov, Yuri Kuznetsov

'Slyly sustained *noir* atmosphere puts across the classic murder-without-remorse narrative.' – *Variety*

† Leskov's story *Katarina Ismailova* was also the basis for Shostakovich's opera *Lady Macbeth of the Mtsensk District*, which was filmed in 1966 by Mikhail Shapiro, starring Galina Vishnevskaya.

Katie Did It
US 1951 81m bw
Universal-International (Leonard Goldstein)
A small town is shocked when young Katie comes back having posed in scanty attire for a commercial artist.
Feeble comedy which totters to a lame conclusion.
w Jack Henley *d* Frederick de Cordova *ph* Russell Metty *m* Frank Skinner
☆ Ann Blyth, Mark Stevens, Cecil Kellaway, Elizabeth Patterson, Jesse White, Harold Vermilyea, Craig Stevens

Katie's Passion: see *Keetje Tippel*

Katina: see *Iceland*

Katinka *
Denmark/Sweden 1988 96m colour
Nordisk Film/AB Svensk Filmindustri (Bo Christensen)
The wife of a village station master and a new farm foreman fall in love.
Intense domestic tragedy, in the manner of Ingmar Bergman.
w Klaus Rifberg *novel Ved Vejen* by Herman Bang *d* Max von Sydow *ph* Sven Nykvist *m* Georg Riedel *ed* Janus Billeskov Jansen
☆ Tammi ìst, Ole Ernest, Kurt Ravn

Kavkazskii Plennik: see *Prisoner of the Mountains*

Kazaam
US 1996 93m Technicolor
Buena Vista/Touchstone/Interscope/PolyGram (Scott Kroopf, Paul M. Glaser, Bob Engelman)
An unhappy boy, searching for his father, a petty criminal, finds a genie who grants him three wishes.
Grim fantasy of minimal interest, other than to watch an attempt to turn a sporting baseball hero into a film star.
w Christian Ford, Roger Soffer *story* Paul Michael Glaser *d* Paul Michael Glaser *ph* Charles Minsky *m* Christopher Tyng *pd* Donald Burt *ed* Michael E. Polokow
☆ Shaquille O'Neal, Francis Capra, Ally Walker, James Acheson, Marshall Manesh, Fawn Reed, John Costelloe, JoAnne Hart

'Too gritty, violent and downbeat for tykes, it's also a bit juvenile and fairy tale-like for teens and older auds.' – *Godfrey Cheshire, Variety*

The Keep
US 1983 93m Metrocolor Scope
Paramount (Gene Kirkwood, Howard W. Koch Jnr)
German troops in 1941 occupy a castle in the Carpathian Alps, and discover that it contains an evil force.
Extraordinary combination of war and fantasy fiction, not entirely dissimilar from Castle Keep *which had a similar exposition.*
wd Michael Mann *novel* F. Paul Wilson *ph* Alex Thomson *m* Tangerine Dream
☆ Scott Glenn, Alberta Watson, Jurgen Prochnow, Robert Prosky, Gabriel Byrne, Ian McKellen

Keep an Eye on Amelia: see *Occupe-Toi d'Amélie*

Keep 'Em Flying
US 1941 86m bw
Universal (Glenn Tryon)
Two incompetents in the Army Air Corps get mixed up with identical twin girls.
A big moneymaker of its day, this comedy now seems especially resistible.
w True Boardman, Nat Perrin, John Grant *d* Arthur Lubin *ph* Joseph Valentine *m* Frank Skinner
☆ Bud Abbott, Lou Costello, Martha Raye, Carol Bruce, William Gargan, Dick Foran, Charles Lang
song 'Pig Foot Pete' (*m* Gene de Paul, *ly* Don Raye)

Keep Fit *
GB 1937 82m bw
ATP (Basil Dean)
A barber mistaken for an athlete finally excels at sport and also catches a thief.
Good star vehicle with snappy songs and fast comedy scenes.
w Anthony Kimmins, Austin Melford *d Anthony Kimmins* *ph* Ronald Neame, Gordon Dines *m/ly* Harry Gifford, Fred E. Cliffe *ad* Wilfred Shingleton *ed* Ernest Aldridge
☆ *George Formby*, Kay Walsh, Guy Middleton, Gus McNaughton, Edmund Breon, George Benson, C. Denier Warren, Hal Gordon, Hal Walters, Leo Franklyn

Keep It Up Downstairs
GB 1976 94m Technicolor
EMI/Pyramid (Hazel Adair)
A bed-hopping aristocratic family are faced with losing their ancestral home.
Dire sex farce that apes but fails to emulate the low style of the Carry On *movies.*
w Hazel Adair *d* Robert Young *ph* Alan Pudney *m* Michael Nyman *ad* Jacqueline Charrott-Lodwige *ed* Mike Campbell
☆ Diana Dors, Jack Wild, William Rushton, Aimi MacDonald, Françoise Pascal, Neil Hallett, Julian Orchard

'The cast, required to bare breasts and buttocks at regular intervals, is able to make no headway against the inane script and consistently mistimed direction.' – *Verina Glaessner, MFB*

Keep Smiling *
GB 1938 91m bw
TCF (Robert T. Kane)
US title: *Smiling Along*
Problems of a touring concert party.
Pretty good star vehicle, though with unfortunate signs of an attempt to glamorize Our Gracie.
w Val Valentine, Rodney Ackland *story* Sandor Farago, Alexander G. Kemedi *d* Monty Banks *ph* Max Greene *md* Bretton Byrd *ad* Oscar Werndorff *ed* James B. Clark
☆ Gracie Fields, Roger Livesey, Mary Maguire, Peter Coke, Jack Donohue, Tommy Fields, Eddie Gray, Edward Rigby, Hay Petrie

Keep Smiling
US 1938 77m bw
TCF (John Stone)
The niece of a Hollywood director finds him on the skids.
More than usually substantial star comedy-drama.
w Frances Hyland, Albert Ray *story* Frank Fenton, Lynn Root *d* Herbert I. Leeds *ph* Edward Cronjager *md* Samuel Kaylin
☆ Jane Withers, Henry Wilcoxon, Gloria Stuart, Helen Westley, Jed Prouty, Pedro de Cordoba, Douglas Fowley

'A kids' picture with an adult punch.' – *Variety*

Keep the Aspidistra Flying
GB 1997 100m Rank Colour
First Independent/Overseas/Arts Council/Bonaparte/UBA/Sentinel (Peter Shaw)
US title: *A Merry War*
A copywriter gives up his job to become a poet, but, after he makes his girlfriend pregnant, embraces the middle-class, suburban life.
A misguided, glossy production that emasculates all the passion and vitality of the original.
w Alan Plater *novel* George Orwell *d* Robert Bierman *ph* Giles Nuttgens *m* Mike Batt *pd* Sarah Greenwood *ed* Bill Wright
☆ Richard E. Grant, Helena Bonham Carter, Julian Wadham, Jim Carter, Harriet Walter, Lesley Vickerage, Liz Smith, Barbara Leigh Hunt, Bill Wallis

'Drains the novel of its class anger and turns it into a celebration of the joys of capitalism.' – *Richard Williams, Guardian*
'A betrayal of art.' – *Alexander Walker*

Keep Your Powder Dry
US 1945 93m bw
MGM (George Haight)
Three girls from different backgrounds join the WACS.
Totally uninteresting and unconvincing female flagwaver.
w Mary C. McCall Jnr, George Bruce *d* Edward Buzzell *ph* Ray June *m* David Snell
☆ Lana Turner, Laraine Day, Susan Peters, Agnes Moorehead, Bill Johnson, Natalie Schafer, June Lockhart, Lee Patrick

Keep Your Seats Please *
GB 1936 82m bw
ATP (Basil Dean)
A prospective heir seeks a fortune hidden in one of six chairs.
Good star comedy on a theme later reworked in It's in the Bag *(qv) and* The Twelve Chairs *(qv).*
w Tom Geraghty, Ian Hay, Anthony Kimmins *play Twelve Chairs* by Elie Ilf, Eugene Petrov *d* Monty Banks *ph* John W. Boyle *m/ly* Harry Parr-Davies, Harry Gifford, Fred E. Cliffe *ad* R. Holmes Paul *ed* Jack Kitchin
☆ *George Formby*, Florence Desmond, Alastair Sim, Gus McNaughton, Harry Tate

Keeper of the Bees
US 1935 76m bw
Monogram (Trem Carr)
A country boy makes good.
Victorian-style fable for rural audiences.
w Adele Buffington *novel* Gene Stratton Porter *d* Christy Cabanne
☆ Neil Hamilton, Betty Furness, Emma Dunn, Edith Fellows, Hobart Bosworth

'For discriminating patronage, a washout … a calico narrative for the crossroads.' – *Variety*

Keeper of the Flame *
US 1942 100m bw
MGM (Victor Saville)
A reporter befriends the widow of a politician and forces her to disclose her husband's guilty secret.
Well-acted but over-solemn melodrama which badly needs a sting in the tail.
w Donald Ogden Stewart *novel* I. A. R. Wylie *d* George Cukor *ph* William Daniels *m* Bronislau Kaper
☆ *Spencer Tracy*, Katharine Hepburn, Richard Whorf, Margaret Wycherly, Donald Meek, Stephen McNally, Audrey Christie, Frank Craven

'An expensive testimonial to Hollywood's inability to face a significant theme.' – *Time*
'Unorthodox and on the whole absorbing drama. Ominous portents and overtones take the place of physical action.' – *Christian Science Monitor*
'A gothic wet blanket of a movie.' – *Pauline Kael, 70s*

Keepers of Youth
GB 1931 70m bw
BIP (John Maxwell)
A young schoolmaster finds his fresh ideas make him unpopular, especially when he is found in a compromising position with the assistant matron.
Old-fashioned drama with a few lively scenes.
w Frank Launder, Thomas Bentley, Walter Mycroft *play* Arnold Ridley *d* Thomas Bentley *ph* James Wilson, Bert Ford
☆ Garry Marsh, Ann Todd, Robin Irvine, John Turnbull, O. B. Clarence, Mary Clare

'If you have to believe in something, you might as well believe in love.'

Keeping the Faith
US 2000 129m Technicolor
Buena Vista/Touchstone/Spyglass (Howard Koch, Edward Norton, Stuart Blumberg)
Two close friends, a Catholic priest and a rabbi, experience jealousies when they both fall for the same woman, an old schoolfriend who re-enters their lives.
A romantic drama that tries too hard to be cute and lovable.
w Stuart Blumberg *d* Edward Norton *ph* Anastas Michos *m* Elmer Bernstein *pd* Wynn P. Thomas *ed* Malcolm Campbell
☆ Ben Stiller (Jake), Edward Norton (Brian), Jenna Elfman (Anna), Anne Bancroft (Ruth), Eli Wallach (Rabbi Lewis), Ron Rifkin (Larry Friedman), Milos Forman (Father Havel), Holland Taylor (Bonnie Rose), Lisa Edelstein (Ali Decker), Rena Sofer (Rachel Rose), Brian George (Indian bartender), Ken Leung (Don)

'Gossamer-light confection is a surefire winner to lift the heaviest heart.' – *Ian Freer, Empire*

Keetje Tippel *
Netherlands 1975 104m Technicolor
Rob Houwer Film
aka: *Katie's Passion*
aka: *A Girl Called Katy Tippel; Cathy Tippel; Hot Sweat*
In the 1880s, a young woman moves with her poverty-stricken family from the country to Amsterdam, where she rises from reluctant prostitution to a life in high society.
Pleasant period piece, although too episodic to give much insight into its central character, despite a fine performance from van de Ven.
w Gerard Soeteman *book* Neel Doff *d* Paul Verhoeven *ph* Jan de Bont *m* Rogier van Otterloo *ad* Roland de Groot, Dik Schillemans *ed* Jane Sperr
☆ *Monique van de Ven*, Rutger Hauer, Andrea Domburg, Hannah de Leeuwe, Peter Faber, Eddy Brugman, Fons Rademakers

† The film is based on the autobiography of Katy Neel Doff. It was released on video in Britain in a dubbed version under the title *Katie's Passion*.

Kelly and Me
US 1956 86m Technicolor Cinemascope
U-I (Robert Arthur)
The ups and downs of a song and dance man and the dog who shares his act.
Mild vaudeville saga with totally predictable twists.
w Everett Freeman *d* Robert Z. Leonard *ph* Maury Gertsman *m* Joseph Gershenson *ad* Alexander Golitzen, William Newberry *ed* Ted J. Kent
☆ Van Johnson, Piper Laurie, Martha Hyer, Onslow Stevens, Herbert Anderson, Gregory Gaye, Dan Riss

Kelly the Second
US 1936 71m bw
MGM
A determined lady trains a dimwitted prizefighter.
Easy-going farce from a studio which knew how to make them; but this wasn't one of the best.
w Jack Jevne, Gordon Douglas *d* Hal Roach
☆ Patsy Kelly, Guinn Williams, Charley Chase, Pert Kelton, Harold Huber

Kelly's Heroes
US/Yugoslavia 1970 143m Metrocolor Panavision
MGM/The Warriors/Avala (Gabriel Kotzka, Sidney Beckerman)

During World War II, an American platoon abducts a German general and accidentally discovers the whereabouts of a fortune in gold.
Crude slam-bang actioner for the obvious market.
w Troy Kennedy Martin *d* Brian G. Hutton *ph* Gabriel Figueroa *m* Lalo Schifrin *pd* Jonathan Barry *ed* John Jympson *second unit* Andrew Marton
☆ Clint Eastwood (Lt Kelly), Telly Savalas (Big Joe), Don Rickles (Crapgame), Donald Sutherland (Oddball), Carroll O'Connor (General Colt), Stuart Margolin (Little Joe), Dick Davalos (Gutowski), Perry Lopez (Petuko), Dee Pollock (Jonesy), Michael Clark (Grace), Gene Collins (Babra), Harry Dean Stanton (Willard)
'Over two hours of consistently devastating explosions, pyrotechnics and demolition.' – *MFB*
'Made for no possible reason other than a chance to use the Yugoslav army at cut rates.' – *Judith Crist, 1973*

The Kennel Murder Case **
US 1933 73m bw
Warner (Robert Presnell)

Philo Vance proves that an apparent suicide is really murder.
Complex murder mystery, very smartly handled and often cited as a classic of the genre; later remade as Calling Philo Vance.
w Robert N. Lee, Peter Milner *novel* S. S. Van Dine *d* Michael Curtiz *ph* William Reese *ad* Jack Okey *ed* Ed N. McLarnin
☆ William Powell, Mary Astor, Eugene Pallette, Ralph Morgan, Helen Vinson, Jack La Rue, Paul Cavanagh, Robert Barrat
'Entertaining all the way.' – *Variety*
'Players are cast so inevitably to type that the film is like a demonstration of the principles of running a stock company.' – *New Yorker, 1978*
'Stylistically a little gem.' – *Clive Hirschhorn*
† See also *Philo Vance*.

The Kentuckian
US 1955 104m Technicolor Cinemascope
UA/Hecht-Lancaster (Howard Hecht)

A Kentucky backwoodsman takes his small son to settle in Texas.
Ambling mid-Western with moments of interest.
w A. B. Guthrie Jnr *novel The Gabriel Horn* by Felix Holt *d* Burt Lancaster *ph* Ernest Laszlo *m* Bernard Herrmann
☆ Burt Lancaster, Dianne Foster, Diana Lynn, *Walter Matthau*, John McIntire, Una Merkel, John Carradine

Kentucky *
US 1938 95m Technicolor
TCF (Gene Markey)
Horse-breeding rivalry prevents the smooth running of true love.
Harmless family entertainment, more professionally handled than its innumerable later imitations. Remade as April Love.
w Lamar Trotti *novel The Look of Eagles* by John Taintor Foote *d* David Butler *ph* Ernest Palmer *md* Louis Silvers
☆ Loretta Young, Richard Greene, Walter Brennan, Douglass Dumbrille, Karen Morley, Moroni Olsen, Russell Hicks
'An outstanding effort, geared for top money.' – *Variety*
Walter Brennan

The Kentucky Fried Movie
US 1977 90m colour
Alpha/Kentucky Fried Theatre (Robert K. Weiss)

Comedy sketches from the University of Wisconsin parodying television programmes and commercials.
The writers later gave us Airplane. *Enough said?*
w David and Jerry Zucker, Jim Abrahams *d* John Landis *ph* Stephen M. Katz *ad* Rick Harvel *ed* George Folsey Jnr
☆ Marilyn Joi, Saul Kahan, Marcy Goldman, Joe Medalis

Kentucky Kernels
US 1934 74m bw
RKO

GB title: *Triple Trouble*
An orphan left with two musicians proves to be the heir to a fortune, but the way to it is through feuding hillbilly country.
Fairly funny Wheeler and Woolsey comedy, in other words one of their better efforts.
w Bert Kalmar, Harry Ruby and Fred Guiol *d* George Stevens
☆ Bert Wheeler, Robert Woolsey, Mary Carlisle, Spanky McFarland, Noah Beery, Willie Best

'It's Fun O'Clock, Mountain Time! And How The Fun Keeps Mountin' Up!'
Kentucky Moonshine *
US 1938 87m bw
TCF (Darryl F. Zanuck)
In the hope of a radio contract, the Ritz Brothers masquerade as hillbillies and find themselves in the middle of a feud.
One of the trio's best solo vehicles.
w Art Arthur, M. M. Musselman *d* David Butler *ph* Robert Planck *m/ly* Lew Pollack, Sidney Mitchell *md* Louis Silvers
☆ *The Ritz Brothers*, Tony Martin, Marjorie Weaver, Slim Summerville, John Carradine, Wally Vernon, Berton Churchill, Eddie Collins
'It's crazy and it's wild, but it's funny and grand entertainment.' – *Variety*

Keoma (dubbed) *
Italy 1976 101m Eastmancolor 'Scope
Uranos (Manolo Bolognini)

aka: *Keoma – Violent Breed*
aka: *The Violent Breed*
A half-breed Indian returns to his home to save the town from a ruthless landowner who is letting the people die from a plague.
Melodramatic spaghetti Western with metaphysical overtones, including a Mother Courage-like figure wandering through desolate landscapes; with its themes of revenge and family feuds, it plays like a Greek tragedy and is stylishly done, apart from the abysmal musical accompaniment, featuring Nero singing like an out-of-tune Lee Marvin.
w Mino Roli, Nico Ducci, Luigi Montefiori, Enzo G. Castellari *d* Enzo G. Castellari *ph* Aiace Parolin *m* Guido and Maurizio de Angelis *ad* Carlo Simi *ed* Gianfranco Amicucci
☆ Franco Nero, William Berger, Woody Strode, Olga Karlatos, Orso Maria Guerrini, Gabriella Giacobbe, Antonio Marsina, John Loffredo

La Kermesse Héroïque **
France 1935 115m bw
Tobis
aka: *Carnival in Flanders*
When Spaniards invade a Flemish town in 1616, the men make themselves scarce and the women find other ways of conquering.
Sprightly though overlong comedy which seemed risqué at the time and therefore enjoyed international success.
w Charles Spaak, Jacques Feyder novel Charles Spaak *d Jacques Feyder ph* Harry Stradling *m* Louis Beydts *ad* Lazare Meerson
☆ *Françoise Rosay, Louis Jouvet*, Jean Murat, Alfred Adam, André Alerme
'A mixture of gay absurdity and shrewd comment, selecting its own pitch and holding it – comedy, you might say, self-contained.' – *Otis Ferguson*
'Everything fits perfectly into the pattern of cultured and sophisticated entertainment. Nowhere is there a false touch.' – *The Times, 1952*

The Kerosene Seller's Wife
USSR 1989 104m colour
Circle Film Unit
A former surgeon, reduced to selling kerosene in the street, is betrayed by his bureaucratic twin brother while his wife begins an affair with a young musician.
A bleak, disjointed, absurdist comedy of life among the dispossessed.
wd Alexander Kaidanovsky *ph* Alexei Rodionov *m* Bach, Beethoven, Mozart, Schubert *ad* Teador Tezhik, Viktor Zenkov
☆ Anna Myasoedova, Alexander Baluev, Vitautas Paukshte

Kes ****
GB 1969 109m Technicolor
UA/Woodfall (Tony Garnett)

In a northern industrial town, a boy learns about life from the fate of his pet bird.
Realistic family drama that is one of the key British films of its period.
w Barry Hines, Ken Loach, Tony Garnett *novel A Kestrel for a Knave* by Barry Hines *d Ken Loach ph* Chris Menges *m* John Cameron
☆ David Bradley, Lynne Perrie, Colin Welland, Freddie Fletcher, Brian Glover
'There emerges a most discouraging picture of life in the industrial north ... infinitely sad in its total implications, it is also immensely funny in much of its detail.' – *Brenda Davies*
'Particularly to be admired is the way in which the dialogue has been kept flowing, as if it were always spontaneous, something proceeding from the moment.' – *Dilys Powell*
Colin Welland; David Bradley

The Kettles
The rustic couple evolved from characters in *The Egg and I* (qv); Marjorie Main and Percy Kilbride went on to play them in a cheap but very popular series for Universal, variously scripted and directed.
1949 Ma and Pa Kettle
1950 Ma and Pa Kettle Go to Town
1951 Ma and Pa Kettle Back on the Farm
1952 Ma and Pa Kettle at the Fair
1953 Ma and Pa Kettle on Vacation
1954 Ma and Pa Kettle at Home
1955 Ma and Pa Kettle at Waikiki
1956 The Kettles in the Ozarks (Arthur Hunnicutt instead of Kilbride)
1957 The Kettles on Old Macdonald's Farm (Parker Fennelly instead of Kilbride)

'All They Want To Do Is...Do It!!!'
Kevin & Perry Go Large
GB/US 2000 83m DeLuxe
Icon/Tiger Aspect/Fragile (Peter Bennett-Jones, Jolyon Symonds, Harry Enfield)

Two teenage boys go to Ibiza in the hope of losing their virginity.
Coarse and smutty comedy, using characters familiar from TV comedy sketches, where they did not so quickly wear out their welcome.
w Harry Enfield, David Cummings *d* Ed Bye *ph* Alan Almond *pd* Tom Brown *ed* Mark Wybourn
☆ Harry Enfield (Kevin), Kathy Burke (Perry), Rhys Ifans (Eye Ball Paul), Laura Fraser (Candice), James Fleet (Dad), Louisa Rix (Mum), Tabitha Waddy (Gemma), Paul Whitehouse (Bouncer), Ken Cranham (Vicar), Patsy Byrne (Old lady)
'Just one overlong middle-aged sneer at teen life.' – *Cosmo Landesman, Sunday Times*
'As a British answer to the wave of American gross-out comedies, it falls woefully short.' – *Andrew Pulver, Guardian*
'Connoisseurs of bodily fluids on screen will doubtless appreciate how the makeover sequence climaxes with a multiple zit-squeezing money-shot.' – *Mark Sinker, Sight and Sound*

The Key *
US 1934 71m bw
Warner
In Ireland in the twenties, a British army captain falls for the wife of an intelligence officer.
Heroics among the black and tans; interesting but dated drama.
w Laird Doyle *play* R. Gore-Brown, J. L. Hardy *d* Michael Curtiz *ph* Ernest Haller
☆ William Powell, Edna Best, Colin Clive, Hobart Cavanaugh, Halliwell Hobbes, Henry O'Neill, Arthur Treacher, Donald Crisp

'The door opened into a haven from hell ... and the girl came with the key!'
The Key *
GB 1958 134m bw Cinemascope
Columbia/Open Road (Carl Foreman)

World War II tugboat skippers, about to embark on dangerous missions, pass on the key to an apartment and a girl to go with it.
Rather foolish symbolic melodrama which never makes its purpose clear but along the way provides fragments of love story, chunks of the supernatural and dollops of war action, rather languidly assembled with great technical competence but little real feeling. The talent occasionally shows through.
w Carl Foreman *novel Stella* by Jan de Hartog *d* Carol Reed *ph* Oswald Morris *m* Malcolm Arnold
☆ William Holden, Sophia Loren, *Trevor Howard*, Oscar Homolka, Kieron Moore
Trevor Howard

The Key
Italy 1984 116m Technicolor
Enterprise/San Francisco Film (Giovanni Bertolucci)

As Mussolini begins his rise to power, an art professor keeps a diary concerning his frustration over his wife's prudery; in turn she begins a diary of her affair with her daughter's boyfriend.
Atrocious soft-core porn that takes in transvestism, necrophilia and urolagnia and includes Finlay dressed in bra, panties, suspenders and stockings having a heart attack while making love. Avoid.
wd Tinto Brass *novel Kagi* by Junichiro Tanizaki *ph* Silvano Ippoliti *m* Ennio Morricone *ad* Paolo Biagetti *ed* Tinto Brass
☆ Frank Finlay, Stefania Sandrelli, Franco Branciaroli, Barbara Cupisti, Armando Marra, Maria Grazia Bon, Gino Cavalieri
'Where there's muck, there's brass; and where there's cinematic muck, there's Tinto Brass.' – *Virgin Film Yearbook*

'A storm of fear and fury in the sizzling Florida keys!'
Key Largo ***
US 1948 101m bw
Warner (Jerry Wald)

A returning war veteran fights gangsters on the Florida keys.
Moody melodrama on similar lines to To Have and Have Not: *it sums up the post-war mood of despair, allows several good acting performances, and builds up to a pretty good action climax.*
w Richard Brooks, John Huston play Maxwell Anderson *d John Huston ph Karl Freund m* Max Steiner
☆ *Humphrey Bogart*, Lauren Bacall, *Claire Trevor, Edward G. Robinson, Lionel Barrymore*, Thomas Gomez, Marc Lawrence
'It's a confidently directed, handsomely shot movie, and the cast go at it as if the nonsense about gangsters and human dignity were high drama.' – *New Yorker, 1977*
'A completely empty, synthetic work.' – *Gavin Lambert*
Claire Trevor

Key to the City
US 1950 101m bw
MGM (Z. Wayne Griffin)
At a San Francisco convention, two mayors get involved in several escapades and fall in love.
Routine romantic comedy.
w Robert Riley Crutcher *d* George Sidney *ph* Harold Rosson *m* Bronislau Kaper
☆ Clark Gable, Loretta Young, Frank Morgan, James Gleason, Marilyn Maxwell, Raymond Burr, Lewis Stone, Raymond Walburn, Pamela Britton
'A comedy made to measure ... the script concerns itself with wringing every possible laugh from a number of stock situations.' – *Variety*

'Don't come if you're afraid to see what's on the other side of...'
The Keyhole *
US 1933 70m bw
Warner (Hal Wallis)
A divorce investigator falls for the wife he is commissioned to frame.
Unsavoury little drama, unusual enough to be interesting.
w Robert Presnell *novel Adventures* by Alice Duer Miller *d* Michael Curtiz
☆ Kay Francis, George Brent, Glenda Farrell, Allen Jenkins, Monroe Owsley

The Keys of the Kingdom *
US 1944 137m bw
TCF (Joseph L. Mankiewicz)

The life of a 19th-century Scottish priest in China.
Studio-made missionary melodrama, a big hit for its new star but otherwise an undistinguished piece of work with a shuffling pace and not much by way of climax.

w Joseph L. Mankiewicz, Nunnally Johnson *novel* A. J. Cronin *d* John M. Stahl *ph* Arthur Miller *m* Alfred Newman *ad* James Basevi, William Darling
☆ *Gregory Peck*, Thomas Mitchell, Vincent Price, Rose Stradner, Roddy McDowall, Edmund Gwenn, Cedric Hardwicke, Peggy Ann Garner, James Gleason, Anne Revere

'Long, earnest, long, worthy, interesting and long.' – *Richard Mallett, Punch*

Arthur Miller; Alfred Newman; Gregory Peck; art direction

Keys to Tulsa
US 1997 113m CFI color
Polygram/ITC/Peyton/Empire (Leslie Greif, Harley Peyton)

The prodigal son of a wealthy family falls among blackmailers and murderers.
Barnstorming, scenery-chewing performances help stave off apathy for a while, but this thriller runs short of excitement long before its end.
w Harley Peyton *novel* Brian Fair Berkey *d* Leslie Greif *ph* Robert Fraisse *m* Stephen Endelman *pd* Derek R. Hill *ed* Eric L. Beason, Louis F. Cioffi, Michael R. Miller
☆ Eric Stoltz, Cameron Diaz, Randy Graff, Mary Tyler Moore, James Coburn, Deborah Kara Unger, Michael Rooker, Peter Strauss, James Spader

'A wonderfully written and performed comic crime meller.' – *Variety*

'Where the Nile divides, their mighty conflict begins!'
Khartoum *
GB 1966 134m Technicolor Ultra Panavision
UA/Julian Blaustein

The last years of General Gordon.
Dullish history book stuff which fails to explain Gordon the man but occasionally erupts into glowing action.
w Robert Ardrey *d* Basil Dearden *ph* Edward Scaife, Harry Waxman *m* Frank Cordell
☆ *Charlton Heston*, Laurence Olivier, Ralph Richardson, Richard Johnson, Hugh Williams, Alexander Knox, Johnny Sekka, Nigel Green, Michael Hordern

'Academic accuracy and spectacular battles are unhappy partners.' – *MFB*

'Beautifully photographed, lavishly mounted, intelligently acted, but ultimately dull.' – *Sight and Sound*

Robert Ardrey

Kick!
US 1978 90m Movielab
Sean S. Cunningham Films (Sean S. Cunningham, Stephen Miner)
A soccer team of orphans decide to bet on themselves with stolen money to win a championship game so that they can pay off their coach's gambling debts.
A dull and clumsy comedy that offers the messages that theft is good and obsessive gambling is endearing, though few will stay awake long enough to discover them.
w Victor Miller *story* Stephen Miner *d* Sean S. Cunningham *ph* Barry Abrams *m* Harry Manfredini *ad* Virginia Field *ed* Stephen Miner
☆ Jim Baker, Malachy McCourt, Chet Doherty, Sel Skolnick

Kickboxer
US 1989 103m Technicolor
Entertainment/Kings Road Entertainment (Mark DiSalle)

After his brother is crippled in a fight, an American kickboxer seeks revenge.
Standard martial arts adventure.
w Glenn Bruce *story* Mark DiSalle, Jean Claude Van Damme *d* Mark DiSalle, David Worth *ph* Jon Kranhouse *m* Paul Hertzog *pd* Shay Austin *ed* Wayne Wahrman
☆ Jean Claude Van Damme, Dennis Alexio, Dennis Chan, Tong Po (Michel Qissi), Haskell Anderson, Rochelle Ashana, Steve Lee, Richard Foo, Ricky Lui

Kickboxer II: The Road Back
US 1990 89m colour
Entertainment/Kings Road (Tom Karnowski)

A retired kickboxer is forced back into the ring to defeat a Thai gangster's champion.
Direly inept sequel.
w David S. Goyer *d* Albert Pyun *ph* Mark Emery Moore *m* Tony Riparetti, James Saad *ad* Nicholas T. Prevost *ed* Alan E. Baumgarten
☆ Sasha Mitchell, Peter Boyle, Dennis Chan, Cary-Hiroyuki Tagawa, John Diehl, Michel Qissi, Heather McComb, Vince Murducco, Matthias Hues

'Has all the faults of many Stateside chop-socky carbons: slow pacing, fortune-cookie philosophy and fight sequences shot from all the wrong angles.' – *Variety*

Kickboxer III: The Art of War
US 1992 92m DeLuxe
Vision International (Michael Pariser)

In Rio de Janeiro, an American kick-boxer takes revenge on a fight promoter who is also a white slaver.
Only a slight variation here on the single plot that seems to serve for every martial arts movie, and there is no variation at all on the usual high-kicking and predictable action.
w Dennis Pratt *d* Rick King *ph* Edgar Moura *m* Harry Manfredini *pd* Clovis Bueno *ed* Dan Lowenthal
☆ Sasha Mitchell, Dennis Chan, Richard Comar, Noah Verduzco, Milton Goncalves, Alethea Miranda, Miguel Orniga

'A routine martial arts pic that benefits from attractive Brazilian location photography.' – *Variety*

Kicking and Screaming *
US 1995 96m Foto-Kem
Trimark/Sandollar/Joel Castleberg

Newly graduated students find that they cannot tear themselves away from their university campus.
Slick and witty comedy of young men and women postponing adult life for as long as they can.
wd Noah Baumbach *story* Noah Baumbach, Oliver Berkman *ph* Steven Bernstein *m* Phil Marshall *pd* Dan Whifler *ed* J. Kathleen Gibson
☆ Josh Hamilton, Olivia D'Abo, Chris Eigeman, Parker Posey, Jason Wiles, Cara Buono, Carlos Jacott, Elliott Gould, Eric Stoltz

'Mildly amusing and occasionally exasperating – a self-analysis of the self-analysis of a self-analytical generation.' – *Variety*

Kicking the Moon Around
GB 1938 78m bw
Vogue (Howard Welsch)
US title: *The Playboy*
aka: *Millionaire Merry Go Round*
A millionaire goes into show business to establish a career for his singing protégée.
Mild, frothy comedy, dated but quite fluent.
w Angus MacPhail, Roland Pertwee, Michael Hogan, Harry Fowler Mear *story* Tom Geraghty *d* Walter Forde *ph* Francis Carver *ad* John Bryan *ed* Derek Twist
☆ Ambrose and his Orchestra, Evelyn Dall, Hal Thompson, Florence Desmond, Harry Richman, C. Denier Warren, Max Bacon

'6 Reels of Joy.'
The Kid ***
US 1921 52m approx (24 fps) bw silent
First National/Charles Chaplin

A tramp brings up an abandoned baby, and later loses him to his mother; but there is a happy ending.
Sentimental comedy set in the slums. The comedy is very sparingly laid on, but the effect of the whole is much less painful than the synopsis would suggest, the production is comparatively smooth, the child actor is sensational, and the film contains much of the quintessential Chaplin.
wd Charles Chaplin ph Rollie Totheroh
☆ *Charles Chaplin, Jackie Coogan*, Edna Purviance

Kid
US 1990 91m Alpha Cine
Entertainment/Tapestry Films (Robert L. Levy, Peter Abrams, Nathan Zahavi)

A teenager returns to his home town for revenge on the locals who killed his parents.
Dull, morally confused modern Western.
w Leslie Bohem *d* John Mark Robinson *ph* Robert Yeoman *m* Tim Truman *pd* Sharon Seymour *ed* Nathan Zahavi
☆ C. Thomas Howell, Sarah Trigger, Brian Austin Green, R. Lee Ermey, Dale Dye, Michael Bowen, Damon Bowen, Lenore Kasdorf

'Ludicrously recasts a barely stubbled youth in the role of the outsider-avenger.' – *MFB*

Kid Auto Races at Venice
US 1914 6m approx bw silent
Keystone/Mack Sennett
This much-mentioned film is no more than a few candid camera shots of a children's car race on the California beach. It so happened that the young Charles Chaplin was called upon to liven up proceedings by causing a nuisance, and hastily conceived his tramp costume to do so. His fragments of comedy, primitive though they now seem, made him a star.
wd Henry Lehrman *ph* Frank D. Williams

Kid Blue
US 1973 100m DeLuxe Panavision
TCF/Marvin Schwarz Productions
In 1902 Texas a young outlaw tries to go straight.
Deliberately myth-deflating Western with agreeably rich detail.
w Edwin Shrake *d* James Frawley *ph* Billy Williams *m* Tim McIntire, John Rubinstein *pd* Joel Schiller
☆ Dennis Hopper, Warren Oates, Peter Boyle, Ben Johnson, Lee Purcell, Janice Rule, Clifton James

The Kid Brother ****
US 1927 83m bw silent
Paramount/Lloyd (Harold Lloyd)
The youngest son in the family proves that he is more than the household drudge.
Lively, slapstick comedy with the star at his best.
w John Grey, Tom Crizer, Ted Wilde *d* Ted Wilde, J. A. Howe, Lewis Milestone *ph* Walter Lundin, Henry N. Kohler *ad* Liell K. Vedder *ed* Allen McNeil
☆ *Harold Lloyd*, Jobyna Ralston, Walter James, Leo Willis, Olin Francis, Constantine Romanoff

'As gaggy a gag picture as he has ever done.' – *Variety*

The Kid Comes Back
US 1937 61m bw
Warner (Bryan Foy)
A tenderfoot from Texas is trained by an ex-champion prizefighter.
Not really a sequel to Kid Galahad, *but a second feature in its wake; as such, fair.*
w George Bricker, E. J. Flanagan *d* B. Reeves Eason
☆ Wayne Morris, Barton MacLane, June Travis, Maxie Rosenbloom

'Brisk, fast, strong dualler.' – *Variety*

A Kid for Two Farthings *
GB 1955 96m Eastmancolor
London Films (Carol Reed)

Among the colourful characters of London's Petticoat Lane market moves a boy whose pet goat seems to have the magical power of a unicorn.
Whimsical character comedy-drama made with some style but too insubstantial and unconvincing to be affectionately remembered.
w Wolf Mankowitz *d* Carol Reed *ph* Ted Scaife *m* Benjamin Frankel
☆ Celia Johnson, Diana Dors, David Kossoff, Brenda de Banzie, Sydney Tafler, Primo Carnera, Joe Robinson, Jonathan Ashmore

The Kid from Brooklyn
US 1946 114m Technicolor
Samuel Goldwyn

A timid milkman becomes a prizefighter.
Yawn-provoking comedy, a remake of Harold Lloyd's The Milky Way; *the first indication that Danny Kaye could be a bore.*
w Grover Jones, Frank Butler, Richard Connell *d* Norman Z. McLeod *ph* Gregg Toland *m/ly* Jule Styne, Sammy Cahn *md* Carmen Dragon
☆ Danny Kaye, Virginia Mayo, Vera-Ellen, Steve Cochran, Eve Arden, Walter Abel, Lionel Stander, Fay Bainter, Clarence Kolb
† Lionel Stander played the same role in *The Milky Way*.

The Kid from Kokomo
US 1939 92m bw
Warner (Sam Bischoff)
A farm boy's fight manager decides that for publicity purposes he must acquire a family.
Yet another follow-up to Kid Galahad, *this time on the farcical side. Not bad, but too long.*
w Jerry Wald, Richard Macaulay, Dalton Trumbo *d* Lewis Seiler
☆ Pat O'Brien, Wayne Morris, Joan Blondell, May Robson, Jane Wyman, Stanley Fields, Maxie Rosenbloom, Sidney Toler, Ed Brophy

'Full of laughs, and a very probable money-getter.' – *Variety*

The Kid from Left Field
US 1953 80m bw
TCF (Leonard Goldstein)
A big league basketball player is reduced to selling peanuts at the games, but passes on advice through his small son, who is appointed team manager.
Half-hearted whimsy for addicts.
w Jack Sher *d* Harmon Jones *ph* Harry Jackson *m* Lionel Newman
☆ Dan Dailey, Billy Chapin, Anne Bancroft, Lloyd Bridges, Ray Collins, Richard Egan

The Kid from Spain **
US 1932 90m bw
Samuel Goldwyn
A simpleton is mistaken for a celebrated bullfighter.
Charmingly dated star musical which, though primitive in some respects, is a splendid reminder of its period.
w William Anthony McGuire, Bert Kalmar, Harry Ruby *d* Leo McCarey *ph* Gregg Toland *m/ly* Bert Kalmar, Harry Ruby *ch Busby Berkeley*
☆ *Eddie Cantor*, Lyda Roberti, Robert Young, Ruth Hall, John Miljan, Noah Beery, J. Carrol Naish, Stanley Fields, Betty Grable, Paulette Goddard

'A corking comedy ... it'll get a lot of money.' – *Variety*

The Kid from Texas
US 1950 85m Technicolor
Universal-International
GB title: *Texas Kid, Outlaw*
The last rampage of Billy the Kid.
Surprisingly violent Western for its time; otherwise unremarkable.
w Robert Hardy Andrews, Karl Kamb *d* Kurt Neumann
☆ Audie Murphy, Gale Storm, Albert Dekker, Shepperd Strudwick, Will Geer, William Talman

Kid Galahad *
US 1937 101m bw
Warner (Samuel Bischoff)

TV title: *Battling Bellhop*
A bellhop is groomed as a prizefighter, and his trainer grows jealous.
Good standard prizefight melodrama, remade as The Wagons Roll at Night *and later as* Kid Galahad *with Elvis Presley (see below).*
w Seton I. Miller *novel* Francis Wallace *d* Michael Curtiz *ph* Tony Gaudio *m* Heinz Roemheld, Max Steiner
☆ Edward G. Robinson, Bette Davis, Wayne Morris, Jane Bryan, Humphrey Bogart, Harry Carey

'Good prizefight picture with action, melodrama and names. Unusual in that women will like it.' – *Variety*

Kid Galahad
US 1962 96m DeLuxe Panavision
UA/Mirisch (David Weisbart)

Tolerable light-hearted musical remake of the above.
w William Fay *d* Phil Karlson *ph* Burnett Guffey *m* Jeff Alexander
☆ Elvis Presley, Lola Albright, Gig Young, Joan Blackman, Charles Bronson, Ned Glass, David Lewis, Robert Emhardt

Kid Glove Killer *
US 1942 73m bw
MGM (Jack Chertok)
A police laboratory scientist tracks down the murderer of the mayor and finds his best friend is the culprit.
Professional police suspenser of the kind now tackled by television.
w John Higgins, Allen Rivkin *d* Fred Zinnemann *ph* Paul C. Vogel *m* David Snell
☆ Van Heflin, Lee Bowman, Marsha Hunt, Samuel S. Hinds, Eddie Quillan

A Kid in King Arthur's Court
US 1995 89m Technicolor
Buena Vista/Trimark/Tapestry (Robert L. Levy, Peter Abrams, J. P. Guerin)
During an earthquake, a teenager is transported back to the sixth century and helps an aged King Arthur defeat his enemies.
A youthful twist to Mark Twain's fantasy does nothing to persuade an audience that it was worth doing.
w Michael Part, Robert L. Levy *d* Michael Gottlieb *ph* Elemer Ragalyi *m* J. A. C. Redford *pd* Laszlo Gardonyi *ed* Michael Ripps, Anita Brandt-Burgoyne
☆ Thomas Ian Nicholas, Joss Ackland, Art Malik, Paloma Baeza, Kate Winslet, Ron Moody, Daniel Craig, David Tysall
'Run-of-the-mill.' – *Variety*

Kid Millions *
US 1934 90m bw (Technicolor sequence)
Samuel Goldwyn
An East Side kid inherits a fortune and has the time of his life.
Dated star musical with moments which still please.
w Arthur Sheekman, Nat Perrin, Nunnally Johnson *d* Roy del Ruth *ph* Ray June *m/ly* Walter Donaldson and Gus Kahn, Burton Lane and Harold Adamson, Irving Berlin *md* Alfred Newman *ad* Richard Day *ed* Stuart Heisler
☆ Eddie Cantor, Ethel Merman, Ann Sothern, George Murphy, Warren Hymer
'Goldwyn-Cantor girl-and-gag socko.' – *Variety*

Kid Nightingale
US 1939 56m bw
Warner
A waiter is promoted into a prizefighter, and sings as he knocks out each opponent.
Self-spoofing comedy with some laughs.
w Charles Belden, Raymond Schrock, Lee Katz *d* George Amy
☆ John Payne, Jane Wyman, Walter Catlett, Ed Brophy, Charles D. Brown
'It's so absolutely silly it's almost good.' – *Variety*

'One man had been like any other to Nora. Then she met the kid.'
Kid Rodelo
US/Spain 1966 91m bw
Trident/Fenix/Paramount
An outlaw fresh from prison races his former partners for the hidden loot.
Dull Western.
w Jack Natteford *story* Louis L'Amour *d* Richard Carlson
☆ Don Murray, Janet Leigh, Richard Carlson, Broderick Crawford, Jose Nieto

'The Story Of A Man Who Seduced Hollywood.'
The Kid Stays in the Picture **
US 2002 93m Technicolor
Momentum/Highway/Ministry of Propaganda (Graydon Carter, Brett Morgen, Nanette Burstein)
Documentary about the rise of film producer Robert Evans, who became head of Paramount, and his subsequent fall from grace and re-emergence.
Based on Evans' autobiography, this is both an entertaining and self-aggrandising account of Hollywood life, revealing in its glimpse into a tinselled world where self-importance is a virtue.
w Brett Morgen *book* Robert Evans *d* Brett Morgen, Nanette Burstein *ph* John Bailey *m* Jeff Danna *ed* Jun Diaz
☆ Robert Evans (Narrator)
'Half-fact, half-fanciful and all riveting… great fun and compulsively watchable.' – *Peter Travers, Rolling Stone*
'An admitted egomaniac, Evans is no Hollywood villain, and yet this grating showcase almost makes you wish he'd gone the way of Don Simpson.' – *Michael Atkinson, Village Voice*

Kidco
US 1984 105m colour
TCF (Frank Yablans, David Niven Jnr)
A boy who thinks up a series of money-making schemes in the hope of getting rich while young finds himself in trouble with the law.
Mildly amusing comedy, said to be based on a true story, but one without a natural audience: its concerns are too old for kids, and too silly for adults.
w Bennett Tramer *d* Ronald F. Maxwell *ph* Paul Lohmann *m* Michael Small *pd* Fred Price *ed* David E. McKenna
☆ Scott Schwartz, Clifton James, Charles Hallahan, Maggie Blye, Basil Hoffman, Phil Rubenstein, Cinnamon Idles, Tristine Skyler, Elizabeth Gorcey

Kidnapped: see *Miss Fane's Baby Is Stolen (1933)*

'Strangely they met … gallantly they risked their lives for each other … a valiant three against a nation's vengeful might!'
Kidnapped *
US 1938 93m bw
TCF (Kenneth MacGowan)
During the Jacobite rebellion a young boy is sold by his wicked uncle as a slave, and is helped by an outlaw.
Much altered version of a classic adventure story, exciting enough in its own right, and well made in the thirties tradition.
w Sonya Levien, Richard Sherman, Walter Ferris *novel* Robert Louis Stevenson *d* Alfred L. Werker *ph* Bert Glennon *m* Arthur Lange
☆ Warner Baxter, Freddie Bartholomew, Arleen Whelan, John Carradine, C. Aubrey Smith, Nigel Bruce, Reginald Owen
'Strange modifications have been wrought … ambitious effort which misses top rating.' – *Variety*

Kidnapped *
GB 1959 95m Technicolor
Walt Disney (Hugh Attwooll)
A remake fairly faithful to the book, which results in a few *longueurs*; but in general the action is spirited.
wd Robert Stevenson *ph* Paul Beeson *m* Cedric Thorpe Davie
☆ Peter Finch, James MacArthur, Bernard Lee, John Laurie, Finlay Currie, Niall MacGinnis, Peter O'Toole, Miles Malleson, Oliver Johnston, Duncan Macrae, Andrew Cruickshank

Kidnapped *
GB 1971 107m Movielab
Panavision
Omnibus (Frederick H. Brogger)
Remake incorporating sections of *Catriona*. Not particularly exciting, but the acting helps.
w Jack Pulman *d* Delbert Mann *ph* Paul Beeson *m* Roy Budd
☆ Michael Caine, Lawrence Douglas, Trevor Howard, Jack Hawkins, Donald Pleasence, Gordon Jackson, Freddie Jones, Jack Watson

The Kidnappers *
GB 1953 95m bw
Rank/Nolbandov-Parkyn
US title: *The Little Kidnappers*
In a Nova Scotian village at the turn of the century a stern old man denies his young grandchildren a pet, so they borrow a baby and hide it in the woods.
Fairly pleasing and popular whimsy for family audiences.
w Neil Paterson *d* Philip Leacock *ph* Eric Cross *m* Bruce Montgomery
☆ *Duncan Macrae, Vincent Winter, Jon Whiteley*, Theodore Bikel, Jean Anderson
† Vincent Winter and Jon Whiteley were given honorary Oscars for their 'outstanding' performances.

The Kidnapping of the President *
Canada 1980 113m DeLuxe
Sefel (George Mendeluk, John Ryan)
Third-world terrorists devise a plot to bring America to its knees by kidnapping the president.
Spirited political thriller which suffers chiefly from overlength.
w Richard Murphy *novel* Charles Templeton *d* George Mendeluk *ph* Mike Malloy *m* Paul J. Zaza
☆ Hal Holbrook, William Shatner, Van Johnson, Ava Gardner, Miguel Fernandez, Cindy Girling, Elizabeth Shepherd

Kids **
US 1995 90m colour
Electric/Shining Excalibur/Independent/The Guys Upstairs (Cary Woods)
A day in the life of a group of teenagers, involved in their favourite pastimes of skateboarding, drugs and sex; one boy seeks out virgins for sex, while one of the girls he has deflowered discovers that she is HIV-positive.
A gritty, documentary-style drama of street life among the middle-class young, one that caused much controversy on its release; it has a feel of truth about it, together with a desire to shock and indulge in fantasies. In a few years' time, it may seem no more than a skilful variation on the themes of 50s youth exploitation movies like High School Confidential.
w Harmony Korine *d* Larry Clark *ph* Eric Edwards *m* Lou Barlow, John Davis *pd* Kevin Thompson *ed* Christopher Tellefsen
☆ Lee Fitzpatrick, Sarah Henderson, Justin Pierce, Jonathan S. Kim, Adriane Brown, Sajam Bhagat, Billy Valdes
'Personally, this film has left flash-frames and memory triggers in my mind that won't quite shift, and there has to be something said for any work of art that's that powerful.' – *Leslie Felperin, Sight and Sound*
'That the end product is an *experience* can hardly be denied. Whether it is an experience that anyone would wish to endure on a Saturday night, though, is another question altogether.' – *Clark Collis, Empire*
† The version shown in Britain was cut by one minute. The film was banned from its cinemas in Britain by Warner Bros Theatres.

Kids in the Hall: Brain Candy
US 1996 89m DeLuxe
Starlight/Paramount/Lake Shore (Lorne Michaels)
A pharmaceutical company markets a new drug that makes everyone happy, ignoring its side effects.
Ineffectual satire, performed with more enthusiasm than skill.
w Norm Hiscock, Bruce McCullough, Kevin McDonald, Mark McKinney, Scott Thompson *d* Kelly Makin *ph* David A. Makin *m* Craig Northey *pd* Gregory P. Keen *ed* Christopher Cooper
☆ David Foley, Bruce McCulloch, Kevin McDonald, Mark McKinney, Scott Thompson, Kathryn Greenwood, Amy Smith
'Both screenplay and jokes leave a lot to be desired.' – *Derek Malcolm, Guardian*

The Kid's Last Fight: see *The Life of Jimmy Dolan*

Kids Return *
Japan 1996 107m Fujicolour
ICA/Office Kitano (Masayuki Mori, Yasushi Tsuge, Takio Yoshida)
Two young friends meet up after a long absence and recall their delinquent past, when both failed in their ambitions: one to become a successful boxer, the other a gangster.
A meandering portrait of two losers, observed with a compassionate detachment.
wd Takeshi Kitano *ph* Katsumi Yanagishima *m* Joe Hisaishi *md* Yukio Yamashita *pd* Norishiro Isoda *ed* Takeshi Kitano, Yoshinori Ota
☆ Masanobu Ando, Ken Kaneko, Leo Morimoto, Hatsuo Yamaya, Mitsuko Oka, Ryo Ishibashi, Susumu Terajima
'It goes further and deeper than earlier Kitano films, which means that it is the most interesting Japanese film in some time.' – *Tony Rayns, Sight and Sound*
'Ultimately it's just plain depressing and somewhat pointless.' – *Nick Briggs, Film Review*

Kika
Spain 1993 114m colour
Electric Pictures/El Deseo/Ciby 2000 (Esther Garcia)
The overlapping lives of a psychologist turned reporter, who videotapes sexual scandals and murders for a TV show, and a beautician, who lives with a depressed photographer mourning his mother's suicide, after she is raped by a pornographic movie star on the run from the police.
A chic and glossy look at voyeurism, a sort of Spanish Peeping Tom that is also partly a satire on television's habit of serving up 'reality' as entertainment, but is mainly a recycling of the themes of Almodóvar's previous movies. The director's shock tactics are beginning to lose their impact, especially when combined with an ill-constructed narrative.
wd Pedro Almodóvar *ph* Alfredo Mayo *ad* Javier Fernandez, Alain Bainée *ed* José Salcedo
☆ Veronica Forqué, Peter Coyote, Victoria Abril, Alex Casanova, Charo Lopez, Rossy de Palma, Santiago Lajusticia, Anabel Alonso, Bibi Andersen, Manuel Bandera
'What use is style when the content is all over the place, and a genuine attempt to say something that matters simply gets lost in the making.' – *Philippa Bloom, Empire*

Kiki
US 1931 96m bw
UA/Mary Pickford (Joseph M. Schenck)
A tomboyish chorus girl sets her cap at her divorced producer.
Long unseen star musical.
w Sam Taylor *play* David Belasco *d* Sam Taylor *ph* Karl Struss *m* Alfred Newman
☆ Mary Pickford, Reginald Denny, Joseph Cawthorn, Margaret Livingston
'Too long and too light … what was to have been a cocktail has turned out to have been a soda.' – *Variety*

Kikuchi
Japan 1990 68m colour
ICA/Vortex Japan (Shuichi Ohi)
A laundry worker, who leads an aimless life, becomes obsessed with a check-out girl at a supermarket.
Quirky small film, with little in the way of action or dialogue.
wd Kenchi Iwamoto *ph* Hideo Fukuda *pd* Takashi Iwai *ed* Keiichi Okada
☆ Jiro Yoshimura, Yasuhiro Oka, Misa Kukuma, Papa Akiyama, Mama Akiyama, Masaya Yasumura

'A journey to friendship.'
Kikujiro
Japanese 1999 122m colour
Pathé/Bandai Visual/Tokyo FM/Nippon Herald/Office Kitano (Masuyuki Mori, Takio Yoshida)
A lonely 9-year-old boy is taken on a journey to see the mother he has never known by a morose middle-aged man.
Broad, episodic, slapstick comedy of a shiftless ne'er-do-well learning to care for someone other than himself; but the action grows ever more manipulative and sentimental, and is interspersed with clumsy dream sequences.
wd Takeshi Kitano *ph* Katsumi Yanagishima *m* Joe Hisaishi *ad* Norihiro Isoda *ed* Takeshi Kitano, Yoshinori Ota *cos* Fumio Iwasaki
☆ Beat Takeshi (Kikujiro), Yusuke Sekiguchi (Masao), Kayoko Kishimoto (Kikujiro's wife), Gidayu Great (Biker/Fatso), Rakkyo Ide (Biker/Baldy), Akaji Maro (Scary Man), Yuko Daike (Masao's Mother), Fumie Hosokawa (Juggling Girl), Daigaku Sekine (Yakuza boss), Beat Kiyoshi (Bus-stop man)
'Its treacly mix of emotional manipulation and klutzy comedy will make it hard to digest for most audiences.' – *David Rooney, Variety*

Kill
France/Spain/Italy/West Germany 1971 102m Eastmancolor
Procinex-Barnabe/Este/ICAR/Dieter Geissler (Alexander Salkind)
aka: *Kill, Kill, Kill*
The International Narcotics Bureau's best agent goes to Pakistan to catch the boss of a worldwide drugs syndicate, whose dealers are being killed by a vigilante.
Risible and amateurish thriller, occasionally almost engagingly silly – as when blues pianist Memphis Slim performs in a room occupied by naked, manacled women, dismembered mannequins and a worried man wearing a monocle, or when the dead bounce on trampolines – but more often merely very, very bad. An unshaven Boyd postures in brown leather, Mason frowns, and Seberg's vacuous role is the worst in a career notable for poor performances.
wd Romain Gary *ph* Edmond Richard *m* Berto Pisano, Jacques Chaumont *ad* Enrique Alarcon *ed* Roger Dwyre
☆ James Mason, Jean Seberg, Stephen Boyd, Curt Jurgens, Daniel Emilfork, Mauro Parenti, Carlos Montoya, Henri Garcin

Kill and Pray (dubbed) *
Italy/W. Germany 1967 102m colour
Castor/Mancor Chretien/Luce/Tefi (Carlo Lizzani)
original title: *Requiescant*
The adopted son of a preacher discovers that he is the sole survivor of a massacre, instigated by an American in order to steal land promised to the Mexican peasants.
Stylish Marxist spaghetti Western, though the politics are subsumed in the usual ingredients of plangent music, over-the-top confrontations, bizarre happenings and multiple deaths. Pasolini pops up unexpectedly as a revolutionary priest.
w Andrew Baxter, Denis Greene, Edward Williams *story* Arnold Elias, Frank Mills *d* Carlo Lizzani *ph* Alexander Clark *m* Roger Higgins *ad* Geoffrey Bailey *ed* Frank Rubien
☆ Lou Castel, Mark Damon, Pier Paolo Pasolini, Barbara Frey, Rossana Krisman, Mary Ellen Maxwell

Kill Her Gently
GB 1958 75m bw
Fortress/Columbia
A madman hires two convicts to murder his wife.
Very mild and unmemorable thriller.
w Paul Erickson *d* Charles Saunders *ph* Walter Harvey *m* Edwin Astley
☆ Griffith Jones, Maureen Connell, Marc Lawrence, George Mikell

Kill Me Again
US 1989 96m DeLuxe
Palace/Propaganda Films/ITC (David W. Warfield, Sigurjon Sighvatsson, Steve Golin)
On the run from her boyfriend, whom she robbed, a woman pays a private eye to fake her death.
Not very successful attempt to recreate the style of 1940s film noir.
w John R. Dahl, David W. Warfield *d* John R. Dahl *ph* Jacques Steyn *m* William Olvis *pd* Michelle Minch *ed* Frank Jiminez, Jonathan Shaw, Eric Beason
☆ Val Kilmer, Joanne Whalley-Kilmer, Michael Madsen, Jonathan Gries, Pat Mulligan, Nick Dimitri

Kill or Cure
GB 1962 88m bw
MGM (George H. Brown)
A series of murders at a nature clinic are solved by a bumbling private detective.
Flatfooted and unprofessional murder farce whose only pace is slow.
w David Pursall, Jack Seddon *d* George Pollock *ph* Geoffrey Faithfull *m* Ron Goodwin
☆ Terry-Thomas, Eric Sykes, Dennis Price, Lionel Jeffries, Moira Redmond, David Lodge, Ronnie Barker

The Kill-Off *
US 1989 97m Technicolor
Palace/Filmworld International (Lydia Dean Pilcher)
Three men set out to kill a vindictive, bed-ridden town gossip.
Low-life thriller that manages an authentic sleaziness.
wd Maggie Greenwald *novel* Jim Thompson *d* Maggie Greenwald *ph* Declan Quinn *m* Evan Lurie *pd* Pamela Woodbridge *ed* James Y. Kwei
☆ Loretta Gross, Andrew Lee Barrett, Jackson Sims, Steve Monroe, Cath Haase, William Russell, Jorjan Fox, Sean O'Sullivan, Ellen Kelly

En Kille Och En Tjej: see *A Lover and His Lass*

Killer!: see *Que la Bête Meure*

The Killer *
Hong Kong 1989 111m colour
Palace/Film Workshop/Golden Princess/Magnum (Tsui Hark)
original title: *Diexue Shuang Xiong*
A hired killer is double-crossed by his employer.
Excessively violent imitation of Hollywood gangster movies.
wd John Woo *ph* Wong Wing-Hang, Peter Pao *m* Lowell Lowe *ad* Luk Man-Wah *ed* Fan Kung-Ming
☆ Chow Yun-Fat, Danny Lee, Sally Yeh, Chu Kong, Kenneth Tsang, Lam Chung, Shing Fui-On
'In its serenely overstated way, it is as resonant and emotive as the "classics" it refers to.' – *Tony Rayns, MFB*

Killer: see *Bulletproof Heart (1995)*

Killer: a Journal of Murder *
US 1995 92m Technicolor
First Independent/Spelling/Ixtlan (Janet Yang, Mark Levinson)
In the 20s, a prisoner is befriended by a guard who persuades him to write the story of his life; it turns out to be a confession to 21 murders, and he soon increases the number by beating to death a brutal guard.
A portrait of a self-destructive, cold-blooded killer, based on a true story, but turned into familiar Hollywood fare, notable only for Woods' chilling performance in the title role.
wd Tim Metcalfe *book* Thomas E. Gaddis, James O. Long *ph* Ken Kelsch *m* Graeme Revell *pd* Sherman Williams *ed* Richard Gentner
☆ James Woods, Robert Sean Leonard, Ellen Greene, Cara Buono, Robert John Burke, Richard Riehle, Harold Gould

Killer Calibre 32 (dubbed)
Italy 1967 95m Eastmancolor 'Scope
Explorer '58 (Bruno Turchetto)
US title: *32 Caliber Killer*
A gunman, who hires himself out to kill criminals at $1000 a time, eliminates a ruthless gang of bank robbers.
Deservedly obscure, slow-moving spaghetti Western, directed in an exaggerated comic-book style and concentrating on the familiar ingredients of gunfights and bar-room brawls; it has most of the clichés of the genre.
w Enzo Gicca *d* Al Bradley (Alfonso Brescia) *ph* Bob Roberts *m* Robby Poitevin *ad* Lambert Walker *ed* Edwin Zimmerman
☆ Peter Lee Lawrence (Silver), Sherill Morgan (Doll), Agnès Spaak (Beth), Cole Kitosch (Spot), Lucy Slade (Janet), Andrew Bosich (Averell), Mirko Ellis (Sheriff), Max Dean (Judd), John Barth (Parker)

The Killer Elite
US 1975 120m DeLuxe Panavision
UA/Exeter-Persky Bright (Martin Baum, Arthur Lewis)
A private crime fighting organization handles cases which the CIA prefers not to.
Smooth, fashionable violence which seems to proclaim the end of a cycle.
w Marc Norman, Stirling Silliphant *novel* *Monkey in the Middle* by Robert Rostand *d* Sam Peckinpah *ph* Philip Lathrop *m* Jerry Fielding
☆ James Caan, Robert Duvall, Arthur Hill, Gig Young, Mako, Bo Hopkins, Burt Young, Tom Clancy
'Merely a commercial chore.' – *Tom Milne*
'A mysterious, elliptical, visually triumphant film about personal survival in a world of mean-minded machination.' – *Michael Billington, Illustrated London News*

Killer Fish
France/Brazil 1978 101m colour
Victoria/Filmar do Brasil/Fawcett-Majors (Alex Ponti)
The leader of a burglary gang hides their haul in a dammed reservoir which he stocks with piranha fish.
Heavy-going underwater shocker, with no fun while the fish are off-screen.
w Michael Rogers *d* Antonio Margheriti
☆ Lee Majors, Karen Black, Margaux Hemingway, Marisa Berenson, James Franciscus
'A slapdash actioner which casts its rod in water so overfished of late that it's amazing there's still anything down there biting.' – *Variety*

Killer Force: see *The Diamond Mercenaries*

Killer Grizzly: see *Grizzly*

The Killer Inside Me
US 1976 99m Metrocolor Panavision
Devi (Michael W. Leighton)
A well-respected small-town deputy sheriff in Montana, seriously disturbed by memories of his violent childhood, finds that his life is out of control.
Unimpressive and implausible psychological study of a man's disintegration, lacking the sleazy authenticity of the novel.
w Edward Mann, Robert Chamblee *novel* Jim Thompson *d* Burt Kennedy *ph* William A. Fraker *m* Tim McIntire, John Rubinstein *ed* Danford B. Greene, Aaron Stell
☆ Stacy Keach, Susan Tyrrell, Tisha Sterling, Keenan Wynn, John Carradine, Don Stroud, Charles McGraw, John Dehner, Pepe Serna, Royal Dano, Julie Adams

The Killer Is on the Phone
Italy 1972 102m Eastmancolor Cinescope
Cathay/Difnei (Vittorio Bartattolo, Aldo Scavarda)
original title: *Assassino ... è al telefono*
An unstable actress is stalked by a killer.
A dull and unimaginative thriller.
w Alberto de Martino, Vincenzo Mannino, Adriano Bolzoni, Renato Izzo *d* Alberto de Martino *ph* Aristide Massaccesi *m* Stelvio Cipriani *ad* Antonio Visone *ed* Otello Colangeli
☆ Anne Heywood, Telly Savalas, Rossella Falk
† The film was cut to 83m for its British release.

Killer McCoy
US 1947 104m bw
MGM (Sam Zimbalist)
A prizefighter becomes involved in a murder.
Grade A production applied to a grade B script.
w Frederick Hazlitt Brennan, Thomas Lennon, George Bruce, George Oppenheimer *d* Roy Rowland *ph* Joseph Ruttenberg *m* David Snell
☆ Mickey Rooney, Ann Blyth, Brian Donlevy, James Dunn, Tom Tully, Sam Levene, James Bell, Gloria Holden

Killer Meets Killer: see *Each Dawn I Die*

'From the secret archives of the Vatican.'
Killer Nun (dubbed)
Italy 1979 86m colour
Cinesud/Calliope (Enzo Gallo)
original title: *Suor Omicidi*
In a lunatic asylum, a nun kills the male patients while framing another nun for the murders.
An over-the-top melodramatic horror, given matching histrionics by the cast.
w Giulio Berruti, Alberto Tarallo *d* Giulio Berruti *ph* Tonino Maccoppi *m* Alessandro Alessandroni *pd* Franco Vanorio *ed* Mario Giacco
☆ Anita Ekberg (Sister Gertrude), Alida Valli (Mother Superior), Massimo Serato, Daniele Dublino, Laura Nucci, Alice Gerhardi, Ileana Fraja, Lee De Barriault, Paola Morra, Lou Castel, Joe Dallesandro (Patrick)
'This hits all the proper lurid notes. But like many Italian exploitation movies, it's torn between sleaze and artiness.' – *Empire*

Killer of Killers: see *The Mechanic*

Killer on a Horse: see *Welcome to Hard Times*

Killer Tongue
GB/Spain 1996 99m colour 'Scope
Entertainment/Lolafilms/Sogatel/Spice Factory/Noel Gay (Christopher Figg, Andrés Vicente Gómez)
A Martian meteor transforms a bank robber, waiting for her boyfriend, into a creature with a killer tongue, and her pet poodles become drag queens.
Direly stupid comic horror, nasty and tasteless and displaying neither wit nor imagination.
wd Alberto Sciamma *ph* Denis Crossan *m* Fangoria *pd* José Luis del Barco, Cath Pater Lancucki *ed* Jeremy Gibbs
☆ Melinda Clarke, Jason Dar, Mapi Galán, Mabel Karr, Robert Englund, Alicia Borrachero, Doug Bradley
'Just trash.' – *Sight and Sound*
'Never sharp or funny enough to engage even passing interest.' – *Alan Jones, Empire*

The Killers ***
US 1946 105m bw
U-I (Mark Hellinger)
TV title: *A Man Alone*
In a small sleazy town a gangster waits for two assassins to kill him, and we later find out why.
Elaborate tale of cross and double-cross, stunningly executed.
w Anthony Veiller *story* Ernest Hemingway *d* Robert Siodmak *ph* Elwood Bredell *m* Miklos Rozsa *ed* Arthur Hilton
☆ Burt Lancaster, Edmond O'Brien, Ava Gardner, Albert Dekker, Sam Levene, John Miljan, Virginia Christine, Vince Barnett, Charles D. Brown, Donald MacBride, Phil Brown, Charles McGraw, William Conrad
'About one tenth is Hemingway's, the rest is Universal-International's.' – *Richard Winnington*
'Seldom does a melodrama maintain the high tension that distinguishes this one.' – *Variety*
'There is nothing unique or even valuable about the picture, but energy combined with attention to form and detail doesn't turn up every day; neither does good entertainment.' – *James Agee*
† John Huston contributed to the script but is not credited.
Anthony Veiller; Robert Siodmak; Miklos Rozsa; Arthur Hilton

The Killers ***
US 1964 95m Pathécolor
U-I (Don Siegel)
A man waits to be killed.
Zesty, brutal remake of the 1946 movie intended for TV, but released theatrically because of its violence.
w Gene L. Coon *story* Ernest Hemingway *d* Don Siegel *ph* Richard L. Rawlings *m* Johnny Williams *ad* Frank Arrigo, George Chan *ed* Richard Belding
☆ John Cassavetes, *Lee Marvin*, Clu Gulager, Angie Dickinson, Ronald Reagan, Claude Akins
† This was Ronald Reagan's last feature film and the first in which he played a bad guy.
Lee Marvin

'Her soft mouth was the road to sin-smeared violence!'
Killer's Kiss
US 1955 64m bw
UA/Stanley Kubrick
A prizefighter rescues a girl from her gangster lover, and is marked for death.
Tedious low-budget indie which first brought its director into notice.
m Gerald Fried *wd/ph* Stanley Kubrick
☆ Frank Silvera, Irene Kane, Jamie Smith

The Killers of Kilimanjaro
GB 1959 91m Technicolor Cinemascope
Columbia/Warwick (John R. Sloan)
US title: *Adamson of Africa*
A railroad engineer helps a girl find her lost father and fiancé.
Old-fashioned safari adventure full of action and animals.
w Richard Maibaum, Cyril Hume *d* Richard Thorpe *ph* Ted Moore *m* William Alwyn
☆ Robert Taylor, Anne Aubrey, Grégoire Aslan, Anthony Newley

The Killing **
US 1956 83m bw
UA/Harris-Kubrick (J. B. Harris)

An ex-convict recruits helpers to steal two million dollars from a racetrack.
Incisive, entertaining, downbeat caper movie clearly influenced by The Asphalt Jungle *and* Rififi.
wd Stanley Kubrick *novel* Clean Break by Lionel White *ph* Lucien Ballard *m* Gerald Fried
☆ Sterling Hayden, *Marie Windsor*, Jay C. Flippen, Elisha Cook Jnr, Coleen Gray, Vince Edwards, Ted de Corsia, Joe Sawyer, Tim Carey
'The visual authority constantly dominates a flawed script.' – *Arlene Croce*
'The camera watches the whole shoddy show with the keen eye of a terrier stalking a pack of rats.' – *Time*

'It was a war unlike any other war ... Against an enemy unlike any other enemy.'
The Killing Box *
US 1992 92m colour
Motion Picture Corporation/Fred Kuehnert (Brad Krevoy, Steve Stabler)

In the 1860s, a Confederate regiment wiped out in a massacre in Tennessee becomes possessed by inhuman forces from Africa, brought to America by slavers, and forms an army of vampiric zombies.
Quirky, atmospheric horror movie with overtones of voodoo and Lovecraft; it can be taken as an allegory of racism or some other plague, or enjoyed as an intelligent essay in creepiness, although its lack of gore may disappoint fans of the more visceral horrors.
w Matt Greenberg *d* George Hickenlooper *ph* Kent Wakeford *m* Cory Lerios, John D'Andrea *pd* Mick Strawn *ed* Monte Hellman *sp* make-up effects: KNB EFX Group
☆ Corbin Bernsen, Adrian Pasdar, Ray Wise, Cynda Williams, Roger Wilson, Alexis Arquette, Martin Sheen, Josh Evans, Billy Bob Thornton, Jefferson Mays
'An eerie blend of bleak war movie and mainstream horror ... an outstanding debut.' – *Sight and Sound*
† Hickenlooper has said that the available version was cut by the producers. He also appears in a small role as an artist.

Killing Cars (dubbed)
West Germany 1985 94m colour
Sentana (Mario Krebs)
The designer of a car that runs without petrol finds himself enmeshed in an international conspiracy to bury his invention.
Heavy-handed ecological thriller, more interested in slick surfaces and fashionable posturing than in its ostensible message.
wd Michael Verhoeven *ph* Jacques Steyn *ad* Norbert Scherer *ed* Fred Srp
☆ Jurgen Prochnow, Senta Berger, Agnes Soral, Daniel Gélin, Bernhard Wicki, William Conrad

Killing Dad
GB 1989 93m Technicolor Panavision
Palace/Scottish TV Film Enterprises/British Screen/Applecross (Iain Smith)

When a down-at-heel father tries to return to the family he abandoned more than twenty years before, his ineffectual son decides to kill him.
Limp, forced and unfunny attempt at a black comedy.
wd Michael Austin *novel* Berg by Anna Quinn *d* Michael Austin *ph* Gabriel Beristain *m* Chaz Jankel, David Storrs *pd* Adrienne Atkinson *ed* Edward Marner, Derek Trigg
☆ Denholm Elliott, Julie Walters, Richard E. Grant, Anna Massey, Laura del Sol
'Signally fails to amuse.' – *MFB*

The Killing Fields ***
GB 1984 141m colour
Goldcrest/Enigma (*David Puttnam*)

An American journalist is engulfed in the horror of Cambodia, and his native adviser disappears and is thought to be dead.
Brilliantly filmed, but probably too strong for a commercial audience to stomach, this true adventure tosses one into the horror of modern war and leaves one reeling despite its comparatively happy ending.
w Bruce Robinson, from the article 'The Death and Life of Dith Pran' by Sidney Schanberg *d Roland Joffé ph Chris Menges m* Mike Oldfield *pd* Roy Walker *ed* Jim Clark
☆ *Sam Waterston* (Sidney Schanberg), *Haing S. Ngor* (Dith Pran), John Malkovich, Julian Sands, Craig T. Nelson
Academy Award: Haing S. Ngor (supporting actor); photography; editing
Academy Award nomination: best picture; Sam Waterston; adapted screenplay; Roland Joffe
BAFTA: best picture; adapted screenplay; Haing S. Ngor (supporting actor)

The Killing Game: see *Jeu de Massacre*

Killing Machine
Spain 1984 96m colour
Golden Sun/Esme (Carlos Vasallo)

A Spanish lorry driver and explosives expert, on his final journey to Germany, takes revenge on the French gangsters who burned his truck and killed his pregnant wife.
Uninvolving and violent thriller which, despite its transcontinental setting, lacks much sense of place or purpose; the conflict of accents and styles of acting does not aid enjoyment.
wd J. Antony Loma *ph* Alexander Ulloa *m* Guido and Maurizio de Angelis *ed* Nicholas Wentworth
☆ Jorge Rivero, Margaux Hemingway, Lee Van Cleef, Willie Aames, Hugo Stiglitz, Ana Obregon, Richard Jaeckel

Killing Me Softly
US 2002 100m DeLuxe
MGM/Montecito (Lynda Myles, Joe Medjuck, Michael Chinich)

In London, an American woman falls instantly in love with a famous English mountaineer, marries him and then has doubts about the relationship.
Risible romantic twaddle, an overheated clichéd melodrama with its two stars at their most lugubrious.
w Kara Lindstrom *novel* Nicci French *d* Chen Kaige *ph* Michael Coulter *m* Patrick Doyle *pd* Gemma Jackson *ed* Jon Gregory
☆ Heather Graham (Alice), Joseph Fiennes (Adam Tallis), Natascha McElhone (Deborah Tallis), Ulrich Thomsen (Klaus), Ian Hart (Daniel), Jason Hughes (Jake), Helen Grace (Lucy)
'Turkeys don't come plumper than this. It's a jaw-dropping catastrophe of a movie, a gruesome multiple pile-up of reputations.' – *Peter Bradshaw, Guardian*

The Killing of a Chinese Bookie
US 1976 113m colour
John Cassavetes

A Los Angeles night-club owner is prevailed upon by gangsters to pay off his debt by eliminating a troublesome Chinese.
Another unendurable slab of Cassavetes pretentiousness; why he went on trying, in the face of twenty years of public indifference, is beyond imagining.
wd John Cassavetes
☆ Ben Gazzara, Timothy Carey, Seymour Cassel, Morgan Woodward

The Killing of Angel Street
Australia 1981 100m colour
Forest Home Films (Anthony Buckley)

Residents fight to save old terraced houses from demolition.
Rather routine light drama, like an Ealing comedy without laughs.
w Michael Craig, Cecil Holmes, Evan Jones *d* Donald Crombie *ph* Peter James *m* Brian May
☆ Elizabeth Alexander, John Hargreaves, Reg Lye, David Downer

'What Power Should A Man Possess To Challenge The Prince Of Darkness?'
The Killing of Satan (dubbed)
Philippines 1983 95m colour
Cinex (Pio C. Lee)

On a small island, the new village headman uses magic powers against the Prince of Magic who has kidnapped his daughter to sacrifice to the devil.
Risible, cheaply made, quasi-religious horror with low-rent special effects and occasional moments of shock and gore.
w Jose Mari Avellana *d* Efren C. Piñon *ph* Ricardo Herrera *md* Ernani Cuenco *ad* Cornelio Ramirez *ed* Boy Vinarao
☆ Ramon Revilla (Lando San Miguel), Elizabeth Oropesa, George Estregan, Paquito Diaz, Cecille Castillo (Luisa), Erlyn Umali, Charlie Davao (Satan)

The Killing of Sister George *
US 1969 138m Metrocolor
Associates and Aldrich/Palomar

An ageing lesbian actress is fired from a TV serial and her life collapses around her.
Heavily handled film version of an amusing and moving play; everything is clumsily spelt out, including the love scenes, and the actresses are forced to repeat themselves.
w Lukas Heller *play Frank Marcus d* Robert Aldrich *ph* Joseph Biroc *m* Gerald Fried
☆ Beryl Reid, Susannah York, *Coral Browne*, Ronald Fraser, Patricia Medina, Hugh Paddick, Cyril Delevanti
'The play was second-rate, but with its nice blend of the homely and the chilling, the absurdist and the perverse, it had the quality of a Kraft-Ebbing comic book. Aldrich and Heller have turned this material into a crawling tear-jerker, the lines spoken at a speed adjusted to non-English or non-language-speaking audiences.' – *John Simon*
'A clumpingly archaic piece of film-making.' – *New Yorker, 1982*

The Killing Time
US 1987 95m Foto-Kem
New World/Tapestry (Peter Abrams, Robert L. Levy)

Corruption thrives in a small Californian town, where the sheriff agrees to help his former lover kill her husband, a ruthless businessman, and a murderer has assumed the identity of his new deputy.
Unconvincing thriller with stereotyped characters and a basic plot that has been recycled too often; there's no tension in the tale.
w Don Bohlinger, James Nathan, Bruce Franklin Singer *ph* Paul H. Goldsmith *m* Paul Chihara *pd* Bernt Amadeus Capra *ed* Lorenzo Destefano
☆ Beau Bridges, Kiefer Sutherland, Joe Don Baker, Wayne Rogers, Camelia Kath, Janet Carroll, Michael Madsen

Killing Zoe *
US 1993 96m CFI color
Rank/Davis (Samuel Hadida)

An American joins a Parisian gang planning a bank raid on Bastille Day.
Violent, blood-soaked thriller, filmed in a consciously arty manner and borrowing moments from other films on similar themes; there is talent on show, but not a great deal of originality.
wd Roger Avary *ph* Tom Richmond *m* Tomandandy *pd* David Wasco *ed* Kathryn Himoff
☆ Eric Stoltz, Julie Delpy, Jean-Hugues Anglade, Gary Kemp, Bruce Ramsay, Tai Thai, Kario Salem
'Has not much in its head and less in its heart.' – *Jonathan Romney, Guardian*

Kilroy Was Here
US 1947 68m bw
Monogram (Sid Luft)
A hellraiser of the Pacific war goes to college.
Mild comedy reuniting two former child stars, but without many other ideas.
w Dick Irving Hyland *d* Phil Karlson *ph* William Sickner
☆ Jackie Cooper, Jackie Coogan, Wanda McKay, Frank Jenks

Kim *
US 1950 112m Technicolor
MGM (Leon Gordon)

The orphaned son of a British soldier in India has adventures with his horseman friend who belongs to the British secret service.
Colourful Boys' Own Paper high jinks, quite lively but never convincing.
w Leon Gordon, Helen Deutsch, Richard Schayer *novel* Rudyard Kipling *d* Victor Saville *ph* William Skall *m* André Previn
☆ Errol Flynn, Dean Stockwell, Paul Lukas, Robert Douglas, Thomas Gomez, Cecil Kellaway, Arnold Moss, Reginald Owen
'Ornate, lavish, but curiously lacking in genuine atmosphere, vitality or period sense.' – *Penelope Houston*

Kin
GB 2000 89m DeLuxe Panavision
Bard/BSkyB/British Screen/Arts Council/M-Net (Margaret Matheson)
In Namibia, a white woman who works to save endangered elephants, causes family ructions when she falls for a black American lawyer.
Muted story of fractured relationships that sat on the shelf for three years before limping into the light.
wd Elaine Proctor *ph* Amelia Vincent *m* Justin Adams *pd* Mark Wilby *ed* Nicholas Gaster
☆ Miranda Otto (Anna), Isaiah Washington (Stone), Chris Chameleon (Marius), Moses Kandjoze (Naniserri), Ndondoro Hevita (Old Man), Susan Coetzer (Katinka), Martin Stefanus (Pahere), Cornelius Tjiuma (Chohorerwa)
'A veritable rainbow of cinematic cliché, poor acting and lame dialogue.' – *Steve Grant, Sunday Times*

Kind Hearts and Coronets ***
GB 1949 106m bw
Ealing (Michael Relph)

An impecunious heir eliminates eight D'Ascoynes who stand between him and the family fortune.
Witty, genteel black comedy well set in the stately Edwardian era and quite deserving of its reputation for wit and style; yet the effect is curiously muffled and several opportunities are missed.
w Robert Hamer, John Dighton novel Israel Rank by Roy Horniman *d Robert Hamer ph* Douglas Slocombe *md* Ernest Irving *ad* William Kellner *ed* Peter Tanner
☆ *Dennis Price* (Louis Mazzini), *Alec Guinness* (Lord D'Ascoyne/Henry D'Ascoyne/Canon D'Ascoyne/General D'Ascoyne/Admiral D'Ascoyne/Ascoyne D'Ascoyne/Lady Agatha D'Ascoyne/Duke of Chalfont), *Valerie Hobson* (Edith), *Joan Greenwood* (Sibella), Miles Malleson (Hangman), Arthur Lowe (Reporter), Audrey Fildes (Mrs Mazzini), John Penrose (Lionel), Hugh Griffith (Lord High Steward), Clive Morton (Prison Governor)
'A brilliant misfire for the reason that its plentiful wit is literary and practically never pictorial.' – *Richard Winnington*
'Enlivened with cynicism, loaded with dramatic irony and shot through with a suspicion of social satire.' – *Daily Telegraph*
'The film in general lacks a visual style equal to its script ... All the same, *Kind Hearts and Coronets* is a very funny film and it gets away with a great deal. With so much, in fact, that its makers deserve salutation as pioneers in the little-explored territory of adult British cinema.' – *Lindsay Anderson*
'A film which can be seen and seen again with undiminished pleasure.' – *Basil Wright, 1972*

Kind Lady *
US 1935 76m bw
MGM/Lucien Hubbard
aka: *House of Menace*
A confidence trickster insinuates himself and his criminal friends into the house of an invalid lady.
Unusual but unconvincing melodrama with overwrought leading performances.
w Bernard Schubert *play* Edward Chodorov *story* Hugh Walpole *d* George B. Seitz *ph* George Folsey *m* Edward Ward
☆ Basil Rathbone, Aline MacMahon, Mary Carlisle, Frank Albertson, Dudley Digges, Doris Lloyd
'Leisurely pace cramps effectiveness.' – *Variety*

Kind Lady *
US 1951 78m bw
MGM (Armand Deutsch)
Edwardian-set remake of the above, rather more subtly acted but failing to extract all possible *frissons*.
w Jerry Davis, Edward Chodorov, Charles Bennett *d* John Sturges *ph* Joseph Ruttenberg *m* David Raksin

☆ Maurice Evans, Ethel Barrymore, Angela Lansbury, Keenan Wynn, Betsy Blair, John Williams

'A curiously tame melodrama whose shocks, when they do come, are muffled and ineffectual.' – *Penelope Houston*

'Get even... or go under?'

A Kind of Hush

GB 1998 95m Technicolor
Metrodome/First Film/British Screen (Roger Randall-Cutler)

A gang of rent boys, sexually abused as children, take their revenge by beating up and robbing customers and attempting to blackmail a pimp.
Unlovely revenge drama, in which being abused in the past is shown as excusing abusive behaviour in the present; despite the efforts of a likable cast, it fails to make a convincing case for vengeance.
wd Brian Stirner *novel* *Getting Even* by Richard Johnson *ph* Jack Petrycki *m* Arvo Part *pd* Mark Stevenson *ed* David Martin
☆ Harley Smith (Stu), Marcella Plunkett (Kathleen), Nathan Constance (Tony), Ben Roberts (Simon), Paul Williams (Mick), Peter Saunders (Wivva), Mike Fibbens (Fish), Roy Hudd (Chef)

'Provides a welcome reminder that contemporary British drama can be moving and gritty without relying on constant blaring rock anthems and camera tricks. It is certainly one to make a noise about.' – *Screen International*

'A Kind Of Loving that knew no wrong until it was too late!'

A Kind of Loving ****

GB 1962 112m bw
Anglo-Amalgamated/Waterhall/Vic Films (Joe Janni)

A young north country draughtsman is forced into marriage, has to live with his dragon-like mother-in-law, and finally sorts out a relationship with his unhappy wife.
Blunt melodrama with strong kinship to Saturday Night and Sunday Morning, *strikingly directed and photographed amid urban grime and suburban conformity.*
w Keith Waterhouse, Willis Hall novel Stan Barstow d John Schlesinger ph Denys Coop m Ron Grainer
☆ *Alan Bates, June Ritchie, Thora Hird, Bert Palmer, Gwen Nelson*

'You will be shocked by this highly moral film only if you are shocked by life.' – *Evening News*

Kindergarten Cop

US 1990 110m colour
Universal (Ivan Reitman, Brian Grazer)

A cop, attempting to catch a drug dealer, works undercover as a teacher.
Muscle-bound would-be comedy, with an undercurrent of brutality and objectionable morality.
w Murray Salem, Herschel Weingrod, Timothy Harris *d* Ivan Reitman *ph* Michael Chapman *m* Randy Edelman *pd* Bruno Rubeo *ed* Sheldon Kahn, Wendy Bricmont
☆ Arnold Schwarzenegger, Penelope Ann Miller, Pamela Reed, Linda Hunt, Richard Tyson, Carroll Baker, Joseph Cousins, Christian Cousins

The Kindred

US 1987 97m Technicolor
Norkat/F-M Entertainment (Jeffrey Obrow)

Young scientists fall foul of a genetically engineered monster.
Unoriginal and uninteresting.
w Jeffrey Obrow, Stephen Carpenter, John Penney, Earl Ghaffari, Joseph Stefano *d* Jeffrey Obrow, Stephen Carpenter *ph* Stephen Carpenter *m* David Newman *pd* Chris Hopkins *ed* John Penney, Earl Ghaffari
☆ David Allen Brooks, Rod Steiger, Amanda Pays, Talia Balsam, Kim Hunter, Timothy Gibbs, Peter Frechette, Julia Montgomery

King and Country *

GB 1964 86m bw
BHE (Norman Priggen, Joseph Losey)

In the trenches during World War I, a private is court-martialled and shot for desertion.
Neat cinematic treatment of a very downbeat play.
w Evan Jones *play* *Hamp* by John Wilson *d* Joseph Losey *ph* *Denys Coop* *m* Larry Adler *pd* Richard Macdonald
☆ Tom Courtenay, *Dirk Bogarde*, Leo McKern, Barry Foster, James Villiers, Peter Copley

The King and Four Queens

US 1956 86m DeLuxe Cinemascope
UA/Russ/Field/Gabco (David Hempstead)

A cowboy braves the wrath of a lady sharpshooter to gain gold and the hand of one of her four daughters.
Tawdry sex Western sporadically enlivened by good-humoured playing.
w Margaret Fitts, Richard Alan Simmons *d* Raoul Walsh *ph* Lucien Ballard *m* Alex North
☆ Clark Gable, Eleanor Parker, Jo Van Fleet, Jean Willes, Barbara Nichols, Sara Shane, Roy Roberts

'A superficially cynical exercise in the rival attractions of sex and money.' – *MFB*

The King and I *

US 1956 133m Eastmancolor Cinemascope 55
TCF (Charles Brackett)

Musical remake of *Anna and the King of Siam* (qv), from the highly successful stage production.
The film is opulent in lush detail but quite lacking in style.
w Ernest Lehman *book/ly* *Oscar Hammerstein II* *d* Walter Lang *ph* Leon Shamroy *m* *Richard Rodgers* *md* Alfred Newman, Ken Darby *ad* Lyle Wheeler, John DeCuir
☆ *Deborah Kerr, Yul Brynner*, Rita Moreno, Martin Benson, Alan Mowbray, Geoffrey Toone, Terry Saunders

'Gaiety has something of a struggle to survive.' – *Penelope Houston*

† Deborah Kerr's singing was dubbed by Marni Nixon, and Rita Moreno's by Leona Gordon.
Yul Brynner; Alfred Newman, Ken Darby; art direction
best picture; Walter Lang; Leon Shamroy; Deborah Kerr

The King and I

US 1999 87m colour 'Scope
Warner/Morgan Creek/Rankin/Bass/Nest (James G. Robinson, Arthur Rankin, Peter Bakalian)

An English governess helps foil a palace coup against the King of Siam.
An animated, cut-down version of the Broadway musical, now aimed at a youthful audience, with only a handful of the original 20 songs surviving; it may suffice for a wet afternoon.
w Peter Bakalian, Jacqueline Feather, David Seidler; Brian Nissen (additional dialogue) *musical* Richard Rodgers, Oscar Hammerstein II *adaptor* Arthur Rankin *d* Richard Rich *md* William Kidd *ed* James D. Koford
☆ Featuring the voices of: Miranda Richardson (sung by Christiane Noll), Martin Vidnovic, Ian Richardson, Darrell Hammond, Allen D. Hong (sung by David Burnham), Armi Arabe (sung by Tracy Venner Warren), Adam Wylie, Sean Smith

'Broadway musical purists will shudder in horror, but parents will be whistling a happy tune that there's at least one acceptable pic out there for their kids.' – *Robert Koehler, Variety*

♫ I Whistle a Happy Tune; Hello Young Lovers; Shall I Tell You What I Think of You?; The March of the Siamese Children; Getting to Know You; A Puzzlement; I Have Dreamed; Shall We Dance?

The King and the Chorus Girl

US 1937 94m bw
Warner (Mervyn Le Roy)
GB title: *Romance Is Sacred*

A European prince on the spree falls for a New York chorine.
Reasonably lively romantic comedy.
w Norman Krasna, Groucho Marx *story* *Grand Passion* by Norman Krasna, Groucho Marx *d* Mervyn Le Roy *ph* Tony Gaudio *m* Werner Heymann
☆ Joan Blondell, Fernand Gravet, Edward Everett Horton, Jane Wyman, Alan Mowbray, Mary Nash, Kenny Baker

'Sure word of mouth and a shoo-in for dough.' – *Variety*

King Arthur Was a Gentleman

GB 1942 99m bw
GFD/Gainsborough (Edward Black)

A soldier becomes a hero when he believes he has King Arthur's sword.
Not-too-successful attempt to turn a music hall comedian into a figure of Chaplinesque pathos.
w Val Guest, Marriott Edgar *d* Marcel Varnel *ph* Arthur Crabtree
☆ Arthur Askey, Evelyn Dall, Anne Shelton, Max Bacon, Jack Train, Peter Graves, Vera Frances, Ronald Shiner, Brefni O'Rorke

'Don't Mess With Mother Nature!'

King Cobra

US 1998 105m CFI
Trimark/Hill & Brand (David Hillenbrand, Scott Hillenbrand)

After a scientific experiment goes wrong, a giant snake, which is a cross between a cobra and a rattlesnake, threatens a small town.
This might have been called Fangs *so closely does it stick to the narrative format of* Jaws, *with a monster on the loose, a mayor who ignores warnings, and an expert who is brought in for a battle to the death; it is competently done.*
wd David Hillenbrand, Scott Hillenbrand *ph* Philip D. Schwartz *m* David Berrel *pd* Jack Cloud *ed* Guy W. Cearley *sp* CBFX: Charles Chiodo, Stephen Chiodo, Edward Chiodo
☆ Pat Morita (Nick Hashimoto), Scott Brandon (Dr Brad Kagen), Kasey Fallo (Jo Biddle), Joseph Ruskin (Dr Irwin Burns), Courtney Gains (Dr Joseph McConnell), Eric Lawson (Sheriff Ben Lowry), Arell Blanton (Jesse), Jerry Kernion (Conrad), Michael Leopard (Buck), Erik Estrada (Bernie Alvarez), Hoyt Axton (Mayor Ed Biddle)

'The resultant hokum even manages to make 1997's *Anaconda* look like a genre triumph. And if that isn't a telling indictment, nothing is.' – *Empire*

King Creole

US 1958 116m bw Vistavision
Paramount/Hal B. Wallis

A failed graduate becomes a singer in a New Orleans night-club, and gets involved with gangsters.
Disagreeable crook melodrama turned into a musical star vehicle.
w Herbert Baker, Michael V. Gazzo *novel* *A Stone for Danny Fisher* by Harold Robbins *d* Michael Curtiz *ph* Russell Harlan *m* Walter Scharf
☆ Elvis Presley, Carolyn Jones, Dean Jagger, Walter Matthau, Dolores Hart, Paul Stewart

King David

GB/US 1985 114m Rank Colour Panavision
Paramount/Martin Elfand

The biblical story of David's involvements with Saul, Goliath and Bathsheba.
Astonishingly tedious, confused and inept retelling of familiar tales, especially so for an audience which needs to be lured back to them.
w Andrew Birkin, James Costigan *d* Bruce Beresford *ph* Donald McAlpine *m* Carl Davis *pd* Ken Adam *ed* William Anderson
☆ Richard Gere, Edward Woodward, Denis Quilley, Jack Klaff, Cherie Lunghi, Alice Krige, Hurd Hatfield, John Castle, Niall Buggy

A King in New York *

GB 1957 109m bw
Attica (Charles Chaplin)

A penniless European king finds himself at odds with the American way of life.
Feeble Chaplin comedy from his anti-American period; tedious dialogue and poor physical production allow only momentary flashes of the satire intended.
ph Georges Périnal *wd/m* Charles Chaplin
☆ Charles Chaplin, Michael Chaplin, *Oliver Johnston*, Dawn Addams, Jerry Desmonde, Harry Green, Maxine Audley, Sid James

'Unhappily he is a sadder and an older man; the real punch is gone. His dethroned king is an ironically apt image.' – *Marvin Felheim*

'Maybe the worst film ever made by a celebrated film artist.' – *New Yorker, 1977*

'It shows how the coming of sound was a curse to Chaplin; how its freedoms dissipated his strengths; how his attempts to exploit it intellectually and ideologically played to his weaknesses; how, in short, he was much more grievously hurt by history in art than by history in politics.' – *Stanley Kauffmann*

'An overblown, self-piteous excursion into autobiography.' – *Time Out, 1984*

The King is Alive *

Denmark/Sweden/Norway/Finland 2000 110m colour
Pathé/Newmarket/Good MachineZentropa (Patricia Kruijer, Vibeke Windelov)

Watched by an elderly black man who is its only resident, a group of tourists are stranded in a ghost town in the Namibian desert when their coach runs out of petrol. While waiting for rescue, they pass the time by acting *King Lear*, as it is remembered by one of their number, an actor.
Intriguing psychological drama that shades into melodrama as it uses Shakespeare as a source for the intense soul-searching of its characters, who look for love and find desolation.
w Kristian Levring, Anders Thomas Jensen *inspired by* *King Lear* by William Shakespeare *d* Kristian Levring *ph* Jens Schlosser *ed* Nicholas Wayman-Harris
☆ Miles Anderson (Jack), Romane Bohringer (Catherine), David Bradley (Henry), David Calder (Charles), Bruce Davison (Ray), Brion James (Ashley), Peter Kubheka (Kanana), Vusi Kunene (Moses), Jennifer Jason Leigh (Gina), Janet McTeer (Liz), Chris Walker (Paul), Lia Williams (Amanda)

'Stylish and gritty, *The King Is Alive* lacks the impact of revelation that might have made the journey worth taking.' – *Kevin Thomas, Los Angeles Times*

† The film was the fourth to be made under the rules of the Dogme declaration.

The King is Dancing: see *Le Roi Danse*

King Kong ****

US 1933 100m bw
RKO (Merian C. Cooper)

A film producer on safari brings back a giant ape which terrorizes New York.
The greatest monster movie of all, a miracle of trick work and suspense, with some of the most memorable moments in film history.
w James Creelman, Ruth Rose *story* Edgar Wallace *d* *Merian C. Cooper, Ernest Schoedsack* *ph* Edward Linden, Vernon Walker, L. O. Taylor *m* Max Steiner *sound effects* Murray Spivak *chief technician* Willis J. O'Brien
☆ *Robert Armstrong, Fay Wray*, Bruce Cabot, Frank Reicher

CARL DENHAM (ROBERT ARMSTRONG): 'It wasn't the airplanes. It was beauty killed the beast.'

'If properly handled, should gather good grosses in a walk ... and may open up a new medium for scaring babies via the screen.' – *Variety*

'Just amusing nonsense punctuated by such reflections as why, if the natives wanted to keep the monster on the other side of the wall, they should have built a door big enough to let him through.' – *James Agate*

'The most exciting motion picture event of all time!'

King Kong

US 1976 135m Metrocolor Panavision
Dino de Laurentiis

Semi-spoof remake with added sexual overtones; though launched on a massive wave of publicity, it lacks both the charm and the technical resources of its predecessor.
w Lorenzo Semple Jnr *d* John Guillermin *ph* Richard H. Kline *m* John Barry *pd* Dale Hennesy, Mario Chiari
☆ Jeff Bridges, Charles Grodin, Jessica Lange, John Randolph, René Auberjonois, Julius Harris, Ed Lauter

'The one and original lovable monster is lost amid all the hydraulic manipulations in what now emerges as the story of a dumb blonde who falls for a huge plastic finger.' – *Judith Crist, Saturday Review*

'Even with colour, the settings of Kong II are no match for the rich black-and-white chiaroscuro of Kong I, with its echoes of artists like Gustave

Doré and Max Ernst and its sensitivity to the emotional values of tone and texture.' – *Jack Kroll, Newsweek*
† *King Kong Lives* (L) crept out minimally in 1986.
visual effects (Carlo Rambaldi, Glen Robinson, Frank Van Der Veer)
Richard H. Kline

King Lear *
GB/Denmark 1970 137m bw
Columbia/Filmways-Laterna (Michael Birkett)
Tragedy ensues when an old king prematurely divides his kingdom between his daughters.
Miserably photographed in freezing Jutland, this is a deliberately downbeat version which despite its varied points of interest is extremely hard to sit through.
wd Peter Brook *play* William Shakespeare *ph* Henning Kristiansen *m* none *pd* Georges Wakhevitch
☆ Paul Scofield, Irene Worth, Alan Webb, Tom Fleming, Susan Engel, Cyril Cusack, Patrick Magee, Jack MacGowran

King Lear
US 1987 90m colour
Cannon (Menahem Globus, Yoram Golan)
A culture expert travelling in France thinks of a mad old man and his daughter as subjects for a film.
Sheer nonsense doodled by the director with someone else's money.
wd Jean-Luc Godard *play* William Shakespeare *ph* Sophie Maintigneux *ed* Jean-Luc Godard
☆ Burgess Meredith, Peter Sellars, Molly Ringwald, Jean-Luc Godard, Norman Mailer, Kate Mailer, Woody Allen

King of Alcatraz *
US 1938 56m bw
Paramount (William C. Thomas)
Convicts escape on a freighter, but one needs surgery.
Pacy programmer with a stalwart cast.
w Irving Reis *d* Robert Florey *ph* Harry Fischbeck *md* Boris Morros
☆ Gail Patrick, J. Carrol Naish, Lloyd Nolan, Harry Carey, Robert Preston, Anthony Quinn, Dennis Morgan, Porter Hall
'Good gangster actioner … will please those liking crime cinematics.' – *Variety*

King of Burlesque *
US 1935 88m bw
TCF (Kenneth MacGowan)
A vaudeville impresario overcomes his troubles.
Well-written musical with plenty of variety talent.
w James Seymour, Gene Markey, Harry Tugend *d* Sidney Lanfield *ph* Peverell Marley *m/ly* various *ch* Sammy Lee
☆ Warner Baxter, Alice Faye, Jack Oakie, Mona Barrie, Arline Judge, Dixie Dunbar, Gregory Ratoff, Herbert Mundin, *Fats Waller*, Kenny Baker
'Big-time musical, with production, material and cast making up for story shortcomings.' – *Variety*
† It was remade as *Hello Frisco Hello*
♫ 'I've Got My Fingers Crossed'; 'Lovely Lady'; 'Spreadin' Rhythm Around'; 'Whose Big Baby Are You?'; 'I'm Shooting High'; 'I Love to Ride the Horses'
Sammy Lee

King of Chinatown
US 1939 56m bw
Paramount (Stuart Walker)
A top racketeer is double-crossed by his henchman.
Smartly paced underworld melodrama.
w Lillie Hayward, Irving Reis, Herbert Biberman *d* Nick Grinde
☆ Anna May Wong, Akim Tamiroff, Sidney Toler, J. Carrol Naish, Philip Ahn, Anthony Quinn
'Good support for key duals.' – *Variety*

King of Comedy ****
US 1983 109m Technicolor
TCF/Embassy International (Arnon Milchan)
Obsessed with becoming a chat show host, an aspiring comedian kidnaps his idol and ransoms him for a spot in the show.
Amusing, underplayed farce with a tragic lining: a very convincing picture of the media today.
w Paul D. Zimmerman *d* Martin Scorsese *ph* Fred Shuler *m* various *md* Robbie Robertson *pd* Boris Leven
☆ *Robert DeNiro, Jerry Lewis*, Diahnne Abbott, Sandra Bernhard
'This is a very frightening film, and in retrospect nothing about it seems funny at all.' – *Variety*
'Unquestionably one of the films of the year.' – *Guardian*
'A most eerie and memorable picture.' – *Spectator*
best original screenplay

King of Gamblers
US 1937 79m bw
Paramount
aka: *Czar of the Slot Machines*
A ruthless gangster loves a singer who loves a reporter who is out to expose him.
A muddled script mars this pacy lower-birth item.
w Doris Anderson *d* Robert Florey *ph* Harry Fischbeck *m* Boris Morros
☆ Akim Tamiroff, Claire Trevor, Lloyd Nolan, Buster Crabbe, Porter Hall
'Well enough done to rate okay in the smaller spots solo.' – *Variety*

King of Hearts
France/Italy 1966 110m Eastmancolor Techniscope
UA/Fildebroc/Montoro (Philippe de Broca)
original title: *Le Roi de Coeur*
In World War I, a Scottish soldier finds a war-torn town occupied only by lunatics who have escaped from the asylum and who want to make him their king.
Heavy-handed whimsy which never catches fire despite the talents involved.
w Daniel Boulanger *d* Philippe de Broca *ph* Pierre Lhomme *m* Georges Delerue
☆ Alan Bates, Geneviève Bujold, Jean-Claude Brialy, Françoise Christophe, Pierre Brasseur, Micheline Presle, Adolfo Celi, Julien Guiomar

King of Jazz ***
US 1930 101m Technicolor
Universal (Carl Laemmle Jnr)
Musical revue.
Stylish, spectacular, revelatory early musical: a treasure trove.
w Harry Ruskin, Charles MacArthur *ph* Hal Mohr, Ray Rennahan, Jerome Ash *ad Herman Rose devised/d John Murray Anderson*
☆ *Paul Whiteman and his orchestra*, John Boles, Bing Crosby (with the Rhythm Boys), Laura la Plante, Glenn Tryon, Slim Summerville, Walter Brennan
'A box office picture anywhere for one week.' – *Variety*
♫ 'Happy Feet'; 'A Bench in the Park'; 'My Bridal Veil'; 'Song of the Dawn'; 'I Like to Do Things for You'; 'Music Has Charms'; 'My Lover'; 'It Happened in Monterey'; 'Ragamuffin Romeo'; 'So the Bluebirds and the Blackbirds Got Together'
Herman Rose

'Under a master director and the reverent genius of great players, the story of Christ has taken human form and greater understanding!'
'Dramatic magnificence, spectacular splendour, riotous joy, tigerish rage, undying love, terrifying tempests, appalling earthquakes!'
King of Kings **
US 1927 155m approx (24 fps) bw silent
Pathé/Cecil B. de Mille
The life of Jesus, seen more or less from the viewpoint of Mary Magdalene.
A patchy but frequently moving and pictorially effective work, ranging from the sublime (the first view of Jesus as a blind man regains his sight) to the ridiculous ('Harness my zebras, gift of the Nubian king!' says the Queen of Sheba in a sub-title).
w Jeanie Macpherson *d Cecil B. de Mille ph J. Peverell Marley ed* Anne Bauchens, Harold McLernon
☆ H. B. *Warner* (Jesus), Jacqueline Logan (Mary Magdalene), Joseph Schildkraut (Judas), Ernest Torrence (Peter), Victor Varconi (Pilate), Dorothy Cumming (Mary, mother of Jesus), Rudolph Schildkraut (Caiaphas), Alan Brooks (Satan)
'The most impressive of all motion pictures.' – *Mordaunt Hall, New York Times*
'A picture which will tend to standardize the world's conception of the New Testament … de Mille has one of the best business minds in pictures and making King of Kings was the most brilliant stroke of his successful business career.' – *Welford Beaton, The Film Spectator*

'A story of the Christ! The glory of his spoken words!'
King of Kings *
US 1961 161m Super Technirama
MGM/Samuel Bronston
The life of Jesus Christ.
Known in the trade as I Was a Teenage Jesus, *this good-looking but rather tedious film is neither vulgar nor very interesting; a solemn, decent, bible-in-pictures pageant.*
w Philip Yordan *d* Nicholas Ray *ph* Franz Planer, Manuel Berenger *m* Miklos Rozsa *ad* Georges Wakhevitch
☆ Jeffrey Hunter, Robert Ryan, Siobhan McKenna, Frank Thring, Hurd Hatfield, Rip Torn, Harry Guardino, Viveca Lindfors, Rita Gam
'I have decided to confer on *King of Kings* both my 1961 Scripture Prizes: (1) Dullest; (2) Most Undenominational.' – *Dilys Powell*
† Nicholas Ray's reaction to film critics who attacked the film was, 'They are not hip enough with the times of Christ.'

The King of Marvin Gardens *
US 1972 104m Eastmancolor
Columbia/BBS (Bob Rafelson)
The host of a late night radio talk show gets embroiled in his brother's schemes.
Thoughtful tragi-comedy overweighted by talk, but with good performances.
w Jacob Brackman *d* Bob Rafelson *ph* Laszlo Kovacs
☆ Jack Nicholson, Bruce Dern, Ellen Burstyn, Julia Anne Robinson
'Indecipherable dark nonsense about brothers and goals and the American dream. An unqualified disaster.' – *New Yorker*
'Glum news from the people who made *Five Easy Pieces*, which had a lot of good work in it along with some pretentious flab. In their new picture the flab has taken over.' – *Stanley Kauffmann*

King of New York
US 1990 103m colour
Rank/Reteitalia/Scena/Caminito (Mary Kane)
Released from prison, a New York gangster takes over the city's drug trafficking by murdering his rivals.
Excessively violent and sadistic fantasy, with a mannered leading performance.
w Nicholas St John *d* Abel Ferrara *ph* Bojan Bazelli *m* Joe Delia *pd* Alex Tavoularis *ed* Anthony Redman
☆ Christopher Walken, David Caruso, Larry Fishburne, Victor Argo, Wesley Snipes, Janet Julian, Joey Chin, Giancarlo Esposito
'Executed with the mix of splatter and gallows humour that Ferrara has made his own.' – *Sight and Sound*
'A nihilistic exercise in designer pessimism stating that the American system is corrupt from top to bottom.' – *Philip French, Observer*

King of Paris
GB 1935 75m bw
British and Dominions (Herbert Wilcox)
The story of a French stage impresario, supposedly based on Sacha Guitry.
Interesting try for a minority audience.
w W. P. Lipscomb, John Drinkwater, Paul Gangelin *play La Voie Lactée* by Alfred Savoir, John van Druten *d* Jack Raymond *ph* Freddie Young *ad* L. P. Williams
☆ Cedric Hardwicke, Marie Glory, Ralph Richardson, Phyllis Monkman
'Nothing much to be desired in this picture, excepting a story.' – *Variety*

King of the Children *
China 1988 107m colour
ICA/Xi'an Film Studio (Wu Tianming)
A youth, first sent from the city to work on a farm during the Cultural Revolution, is transferred to teach at a remote school where he uses unconventional methods which soon cause trouble.
Pleasant film with much of interest, though its deeper implications are likely to be understood only by a Chinese audience.
w Chen Kaige, Wan Zhi *story Haizi Wang* by Ah Cheng *d* Chen Kaige *ph* Gu Changwei *m* Qu Xiaosong *ad* Chen Shaohua *ed* Liu Miaomiao
☆ Xie Yuan, Yank Xuewen, Chen Shaohua, Zhang Camimei, Xu Guoqing

King of the Damned *
GB 1935 76m bw
Gaumont (Michael Balcon)
On a tropical island convict settlement, harsh treatment leads to mutiny.
A downright peculiar project for a British studio at this time, but technically very competent for those who like this kind of thing.
w Charles Bennett, Sidney Gilliat, Noel Langley *play* John Chancellor *d* Walter Forde *ph* Bernard Knowles *md* Louis Levy *ad* Oscar Werndorff *ed* C. Randell
☆ Conrad Veidt, Helen Vinson, Noah Beery, Cecil Ramage, Edmund Willard, Raymond Lovell, Allan Jeayes, Percy Parsons
'Goes so far overboard on gloom that it defeats its own end.' – *Variety*

King of the Gypsies
US 1978 112m Technicolor
Paramount/Dino de Laurentiis (Anna Gross)
A gypsy leader is denied the hand in marriage of the daughter of a rival, so he kidnaps her.
Ethnic melodrama which despite its vigorous insistence on tradition – or perhaps because of it – plays like a mad musical without any songs.
w Frank Pierson *novel* Peter Maas *d* Frank Pierson *ph* Sven Nykvist, Edward Lachman *m* David Grisman *pd* Gene Callahan
☆ Sterling Hayden, Brooke Shields, Shelley Winters, Susan Sarandon, Judd Hirsch, Eric Roberts

King of the Hill *
US 1993 102m DeLuxe Panavision
Wildwood/Bona Fide/Gramercy (Albert Berger, Barbara Maltby, Ron Yerxa)
A 10-year-old boy grows up in St Louis during the Depression of the 30s.
A gentle, sometimes touching drama of an observant boy trying to make the best of life, but steeped in a somewhat rosy nostalgia.
wd Steven Soderbergh *book* A. E. Hotchner *ph* Elliot Davis *m* Cliff Martinez *pd* Gary Frutkoff *ed* Steven Soderbergh
☆ Jesse Bradford, Jeroen Krabbé, Lisa Eichhorn, Karen Allen, Spalding Gray, Elizabeth McGovern, Joseph Krest, Cameron Boyd
'This densely detailed, superbly acted evocation of a resourceful boy's life during the depths of the Depression animates another time and place, while quietly underlining the parallels to contemporary problems.' – *Variety*

'Body of a Greek god! Strength of a Hercules!'
King of the Jungle
US 1933 73m bw
Paramount
A small boy grows up with lions; he is captured with them and sold to an American circus.
Sub-Tarzan hokum which cheered up the kids.
w Philip Wylie, Fred Niblo Jnr, C. T. Stoneham *d* H. Bruce Humberstone, Max Marcin
☆ Buster Crabbe, Frances Dee, Douglass Dumbrille, Robert Adair, Robert Barrat
'Minus any help from the marquee it will have to attract on merit alone, and on merit it rates fair business.' – *Variety*

King of the Khyber Rifles
US 1953 100m Technicolor Cinemascope
TCF (Samuel Bischoff, David Diamond)
In 1857 a British garrison in India is threatened by the forces of Kuuram Khan but saved by a half-caste officer.
Standard North-West Frontier adventure, old-fashioned and rather dull.
w Ivan Goff, Ben Roberts *d* Henry King *ph* Leon Shamroy *m* Bernard Herrmann *ad* Lyle Wheeler

☆ Tyrone Power, Terry Moore, Michael Rennie, Guy Rolfe, John Justin

King of the Roaring Twenties
US 1961 106m bw
Warner/AA/Bischoff-Diamond
GB title: *The Big Bankroll*
A gambler, Arnold Rothstein, becomes powerful among twenties gangsters.
Routine crime drama, shoddily made.
w Jo Swerling *book* The Big Bankroll by Leo Katcher *d* Joseph M. Newman *ph* Carl Guthrie *m* Franz Waxman
☆ David Janssen, Dianne Foster, Mickey Rooney, Mickey Shaughnessy, Diana Dors, Dan O'Herlihy, Jack Carson, Keenan Wynn, William Demarest, Joseph Schildkraut, Regis Toomey, Murvyn Vye
'Superficial, shopworn biography of an infamous bookie.' – *MFB*

King of the Turf
US 1939 88m bw
Edward Small
A gambler out of luck befriends a small boy who turns out to be his own son.
Hard to take even at the time, this sentimental tarididdle does not bear later scrutiny.
wd George Bruce
☆ Adolphe Menjou, Dolores Costello, Walter Abel, Roger Daniel
'Dandy racetrack yarn ... it has a refreshing appeal and the dialogue is excellent.' – *Variety*

King of the Underworld
US 1938 69m bw
Warner (Bryan Foy)
When her husband is killed by gangsters, a doctor takes her own steps to round them up.
Sex-change remake of Dr Socrates; *certainly no better.*
w George Bricker, Vincent Sherman *d* Lewis Seiler
☆ Kay Francis, Humphrey Bogart, James Stephenson, John Eldredge
'It will have trouble even in the duals.' – *Variety*

King of the Wind
US 1989 102m Technicolor
Enterprise/Davis Panzer/HTV International (Michael Guest, Paul Sarony, Peter S. Davis, William Panzer)
Adventures in France and England of a young Arab groom and his horse.
Lamely told and a waste of everyone's time.
w Phil Frey *novel* Marguerite Henry *d* Peter Duffell *ph* Brian Morgan *m* John Scott *pd* Ken Sharp *ed* Lyndon Matthews
☆ Frank Finlay, Jenny Agutter, Nigel Hawthorne, Navin Chowdhry, Ralph Bates, Neil Dickson, Barry Foster, Jill Gascoine, Joan Hickson, Anthony Quayle, Ian Richardson, Norman Rodway, Peter Vaughan, Richard Harris, Glenda Jackson

King, Queen, Knave *
US/West Germany 1972 92m Eastmancolor
Wolper/Maran (Lutz Hengst)
The wife of a Munich bookseller falls for his adolescent nephew.
Amusing, capriciously directed sex comedy.
w David Shaw, David Seltzer *novel* Vladimir Nabokov *d* Jerzy Skolimowski *ph* Charly Steinberger *m* Stanley Myers
☆ Gina Lollobrigida, David Niven, John Moulder-Brown, Mario Adorf, Carl Fox-Duering

King Ralph
US 1991 97m Eastmancolor
UIP/Universal/Mirage/Ibro (Jack Brodsky)
A Las Vegas entertainer becomes King of England when the Royal Family is electrocuted.
Witless farce, set in an England that even P.G. Wodehouse would have found quaintly old hat.
wd David S. Ward *novel* Headlong by Emlyn Williams *ph* Kenneth MacMillan *m* James Newton Howard *pd* Simon Holland *ed* John Jympson
☆ John Goodman, Peter O'Toole, John Hurt, Camille Coduri, Richard Griffiths, Leslie Phillips, James Villiers, Joely Richardson, Niall O'Brian, Julian Glover, Judy Parfitt
'As the man who wouldn't be King if he could help it, Goodman redeems what might have been just another high-concept comedy for the party of humanity.' – *Richard Schickel, Time*

'Even Hell had to have a monarch!'
King Rat **
US 1965 134m bw
Columbia/Coleytown (James Woolf)
In Singapore's Changi Gaol during World War II an American corporal lives more comfortably than the other prisoners by shabby dealings with the camp guards.
Overlong but generally gripping character melodrama – 'not a story of escape but a story of survival'.
wd Bryan Forbes *novel* James Clavell *ph* Burnett Guffey *m* John Barry
☆ *George Segal*, Tom Courtenay, John Mills, James Fox, Denholm Elliott, Todd Armstrong, Patrick O'Neal, James Donald, Alan Webb, Leonard Rossiter, Geoffrey Bayldon
Burnett Guffey

King Richard and the Crusaders
US 1954 113m Warnercolor Cinemascope
Warner (Henry Blanke)
During the Crusades, the dreaded Saladin arrives in England in disguise and falls in love with Lady Edith...
Crudely confected comic strip version of Sir Walter Scott's The Talisman, *ineptly written and cast, with poor production values.*
w John Twist *d* David Butler *ph* Peverell Marley *m* Max Steiner
☆ Rex Harrison (Saladin), Virginia Mayo, George Sanders, Laurence Harvey, Robert Douglas
LADY EDITH (VIRGINIA MAYO): 'Fight, fight, fight! That's all you think of, Dick Plantagenet!'
'Do not adjust your set – the sound you hear is Sir Walter Scott turning in his grave.' – *Sunday Express*
'It shows why the Crusades never really amounted to much.' – *Time*

King Solomon of Broadway
US 1935 72m bw
Universal
A night-club owner gambles away money he has borrowed from the mob.
Stale underworld melodrama.
w Harry Clork, Doris Malloy *d* Alan Crosland
☆ Edmund Lowe, Dorothy Page, Pinky Tomlin, Louise Henry, Charles Grapewin
'Won't go very far; mostly for doubles.' – *Variety*

King Solomon's Mines *
GB 1937 80m bw
Gainsborough (Geoffrey Barkas)
Explorers in Africa persuade an exiled chief to help them find a diamond mine.
Rather somnolent though well-cast version of a favourite adventure novel, with a splendid final reel.
w Michael Hogan, A. R. Rawlinson, Roland Pertwee, Ralph Spence, Charles Bennett *novel* H. Rider Haggard *d* *Robert Stevenson* *ph* Glen MacWilliams *m* Mischa Spoliansky
☆ Cedric Hardwicke, *Paul Robeson*, Roland Young, John Loder, Anna Lee, Sydney Fairbrother, Robert Adams
'If the pop houses can accept its half-throttle speed, they'll get all the thrills and entertainment they want.' – *Variety*
'They kept the eye of the camera open for every form of wild and savage life and crammed it all into the picture, so one gets the impression that Allan Quartermain is delivering a lecture with illustrations rather than taking part in an adventure.' – *Richard Mallett, Punch*

King Solomon's Mines *
US 1950 102m Technicolor
MGM (Sam Zimbalist)
A woman goes in search of her husband, who disappeared in Africa while seeking the diamond mines of King Solomon.
A remake of Rider Haggard's novel which is largely travelogue with the merest trimmings of story.
w Helen Deutsch *novel* H. Rider Haggard *d* Compton Bennett *ph* Robert Surtees *ed* Ralph E. Winters, Conrad A. Nervig
☆ Stewart Granger, Deborah Kerr, Richard Carlson, Hugo Haas, Lowell Gilmore
† Andrew Marton directed the second unit sequences.
Robert Surtees; editing
best picture

King Solomon's Mines
US 1985 100m colour Cinemascope
Cannon
Quatermain is hired by a girl who wants to find her kidnapped father.
Adaptation in the vein of Indiana Jones and then some: the leading characters are almost boiled in a pot. Enjoyment depends on your sense of humour.
w Gene Quintano, James R. Silke *novel* H. Rider Haggard *d* J. Lee-Thompson *ph* Alex Phillips *m* Jerry Goldsmith *pd* Luciano Spadoni *ed* John Shirley
☆ Richard Chamberlain (Quatermain), Sharon Stone (Jessie), Herbert Lom (Colonel Bockner), John Rhys-Davies (Dogati), Ken Gampu (Umbopo), June Buthelezi (Gagoola), Sam Williams (Scragga)
'The cinema's equivalent to junk food.' – *Sunday Mail*

The King Steps Out *
US 1936 85m bw
Columbia (William Perlberg)
Emperor Franz Josef falls in love with the sister of the princess to whom he is betrothed.
Rather heavy-handed romance with music, not in its director's best style but showing flashes of his decorative talent.
w Sidney Buchman *operetta* Cissy *by Herbert and Ernst Marischka* *d* Josef von Sternberg *ph* Lucien Ballard *m/ly* Fritz Kreisler, Dorothy Fields *ad* Stephen Goosson
☆ Grace Moore, Franchot Tone, Walter Connolly, Raymond Walburn, Herman Bing, Victor Jory, Elizabeth Risdon, Nana Bryant, Frieda Inescort, Thurston Hall
'Josef von Sternberg asked that it not be included in retrospectives of his work, but he really did make the damned thing.' – *New Yorker, 1977*

The Kingdom **
Denmark 1994 279m colour
ICA/Zentropa/Denmark Radio TV/Swedish TV/WDR/Arte (Ole Reim)
original title: *Riget*
Ghosts stalk a large Copenhagen hospital, staffed by unbalanced doctors and nurses.
Bizarre drama, originally made for television, that resembles a patient's worst nightmares, where one doctor abandons his charges to practise voodoo and another is impregnated by the ghost of a malignant murderer; it is the obverse of your average soap opera and compulsive viewing.
w Tómas Gislason, Lars von Trier, Nils Vorsel *d* Lars von Trier *ph* Eric Kress *m* Joachim Holbek *ad* Jett Lehmann *ed* Jacob Thuesen, Molly Marlene Stensgaard
☆ Ernst Hugo Järegard, Kirsten Rolffes, Ghita Norby, Soren Pilmark, Udo Kier, Otto Brandenburg, Jens Okking, Holger Juul Hansen
'Meld of black-comedy soap and Z-grade horror flick that looks like an instant cult item among auds willing to go the stretch.' – *Variety*

Kingdom of the Spiders
US 1977 95m colour
Arachnid/Dimension (Henry Fownes)
In an Arizona valley the death rate soars when tarantulas begin preying in groups on humans instead of singly on each other.
The spiders is coming, as Hitch might have remarked, and not even giant-size. Standard shudders, efficiently presented.
w Richard Robinson, Alan Caillou *d* John Cardos *ph* John Morrill, John Wheeler *md* Igo Kantor
☆ William Shatner, Tiffany Bolling, Woody Strode, David MacLean

'From the idiots what brung you *Dumb and Dumber*.'
Kingpin
US 1996 113m DeLuxe Super 35
Entertainment/Rysher/Motion Picture Corp (Brad Krevoy, Steve Stabler, Bradley Thomas)
A sleazy tenpin bowling champion is matched against one of his former victims, a one-armed alcoholic.
Dismal, rotten comedy, peopled by grotesques and driven by disgust.
w Barry Fanaro, Mort Nathan *d* Peter Farrelly, Bobby Farrelly *ph* Mark Irwin *m* Freedy Johnston *pd* Sidney J. Bartholomew Jnr *ed* Christopher Greenbury
☆ Woody Harrelson, Randy Quaid, Vanessa Angel, Bill Murray, Chris Elliott, William Jordan, Richard Tyson
'Another unsubtle, ugly farce featuring people to whom even the dimmest audience can feel intellectually superior.' – *George Perry*

Kings and Desperate Men
Canada 1983 118m colour
Alexis Kanner
A radio talk show host is held hostage by a group of unpredictable, idealistic terrorists.
Indulgently scripted, directed and acted, and dreary to watch.
w Edmund Ward, Alexis Kanner *d* Alexis Kanner *ph* Henry Lucas, Paul Van der Linden *m* Michel Robidoux, Pierre F. Brault *ad* Will McCrow *ed* Henry Lucas
☆ Patrick McGoohan, Alexis Kanner, Andrea Marcovicci, Margaret Trudeau

Kings Go Forth
US 1958 109m bw
UA/Ross-Eton (Frank Ross)
August 1944: two American soldiers fall out over a black French woman who is torn between them.
Heavy-going war melodrama, well enough done for those who can take it.
w Merle Miller *novel* Joe David Brown *d* Delmer Daves *ph* Daniel Fapp *m* Elmer Bernstein
☆ Frank Sinatra, Tony Curtis, Natalie Wood, Leora Dana, Karl Swenson

Kings of the Road
Germany 1975 176m bw
Wim Wenders Productions
original title: *Im Lauf der Zeit*
Two men on a bus talk of their past lives, their problems, their hopes and their fears.
Impossibly tedious two-hander which doubtless says something about life for those with the patience to sit it out.
wd Wim Wenders *ph* Robby Müller, Martin Schäfer *m* Alex Linstädt *ed* Peter Pryzgodda
☆ Rüdiger Vogler, Hanns Zischler, Lisa Kreuzer

Kings of the Sun
US 1963 108m DeLuxe Panavision
UA/Mirisch (Lewis J. Rachmil)
A Mayan tribe emigrates from Mexico to Texas and makes peace with the local Indian chief.
Ponderous dark age epic replete with human sacrifice, high-mindedness and solemn pauses. The actors and sets carry it as far as it will go.
w Elliott Arnold, James R. Webb *d* J.Lee-Thompson *ph* Joe MacDonald *m* Elmer Bernstein *ad* Alfred Ybarra
☆ Yul Brynner, George Chakiris, Shirley Anne Field, Richard Basehart, Brad Dexter, Barry Morse

'The king's ships ... the king's gold ... the king's girls ... were the treasure!'
The King's Pirate
US 1967 100m Technicolor
Universal (Robert Arthur)
An American in the 18th-century British navy infiltrates a pirate stronghold in Madagascar.
Tatty remake of Against All Flags, *rising to a few minor heights of swashbuckling.*
w Paul Wayne *d* Don Weis *ph* Clifford Stine *m* Ralph Ferraro
☆ Doug McClure, Jill St John, Guy Stockwell, Kurt Kasznar, Torin Thatcher, Richard Deacon, Sean McClory

King's Rhapsody
GB 1955 93m Eastmancolor Cinemascope
Everest (Herbert Wilcox)
An exiled Ruritanian king leaves his mistress to return home to a political marriage.
Love versus duty in a ludicrously inept film of Ivor Novello's highly theatrical musical drama, cheaply made and killed stone dead by casting and wide screen.
w Pamela Bower, Christopher Hassall, A. P. Herbert *d* Herbert Wilcox *ph* Max Greene
☆ Errol Flynn, Anna Neagle, Patrice Wymore, Martita Hunt, Finlay Currie

'Out of the hushed strangeness of these lives, and out of the shadows that hid their shame, filmdom has fashioned a drama most unusual, most touching and most wonderful!'
'The town they talk of in whispers!'
Kings Row ★★★★
US 1942 127m bw
Warner (Hal B. Wallis)
In a small American town during the early years of the century, three children grow up into a world of cruelty and madness.
Superb Hollywood melodrama, a Peyton Place with great visual strength, haunting music and a wholly absorbing if incredible plot.
w Casey Robinson novel Henry Bellamann *d Sam Wood ph James Wong Howe m Erich Wolfgang Korngold pd William Cameron Menzies*
☆ *Ann Sheridan, Robert Cummings,* Ronald Reagan, *Claude Rains,* Betty Field, Charles Coburn, Nancy Coleman, *Maria Ouspenskaya,* Harry Davenport, Judith Anderson, Karen Verne
DRAKE (RONALD REAGAN): 'Where's the rest of me?'
'Half masterpiece and half junk.' – *James Agate*
'Tranquilly accepting many varieties of psychopathic behaviour as the simple facts of life, this film has its own kind of sentimental glow, yet the melodramatic incidents are surprisingly compelling.' – *New Yorker, 1982*
'One of the great melodramas, a veritable Mount Rushmore of physical and emotional cripples.' – *Time Out, 1981*
† The film was made in 1941, but its release was delayed for a year because the studio thought it too downbeat. It was not a great box-office success.
best picture; Sam Wood; James Wong Howe

A King's Story ★
GB 1965 102m Technicolor
Le Vien Films (Jack Le Vien)
Interviews with the Duke and Duchess of Windsor are interspersed with newsreels of the abdication crisis.
Earnest popular documentary with many points in its favour, including a resounding commentary by Orson Welles.
w Glyn Jones *d* Harry Booth *m* Ivor Slaney
best documentary

The King's Thief
US 1955 79m Eastmancolor Cinemascope
MGM (Edwin H. Knopf)
The Duke of Brampton plots treason against Charles II but a highwayman robs him of an incriminating notebook.
Dismal swashbuckler with neither zest nor style, just a cast of unhappy-looking actors.
w Christopher Knopf *story* Robert Hardy Andrews *d* Robert Z. Leonard *ph* Robert Planck *m* Miklos Rozsa
☆ David Niven, Edmund Purdom, Ann Blyth, George Sanders, Roger Moore

The King's Vacation
US 1933 62m bw
Warner
A king abdicates to seek the simple life.
Pleasing fable with a few theatrical ironies.
w Ernest Pascal, Maude T. Howell *d* John Adolfi
☆ George Arliss, Florence Arliss, Dick Powell, Marjorie Gateson, Dudley Digges

The King's Whore ★
France/GB/Austria/Italy 1990 138m colour
ASC/FR3/Cinema e Cinema/Umbrella (Maurice Benart, Wieland Schullz-Keil, Paolo Zaccaria)
The beautiful wife of a courtier is forced to become a king's mistress.
Sumptuously romantic drama, conceived on a grand scale, but ultimately failing to live up to it.
w Daniel Vigne, Frederic Raphael, Axel Corti, Derek Marlowe *novel Jeanne, Putain du Roi* by Jacques Tournier *d* Axel Corti *ph* Gernot Roll *m* Gabriel Yared *pd* Francesco Frigeri *ed* Joelle Van Effenterre
☆ Timothy Dalton, Valeria Golino, Stephane Freiss, Robin Renucci, Feodor Chaliapin, Eleanor David, Margaret Tyzack, Paul Crauchet
'The 17th century melodrama is less magnificent than it first appears, as it proves to be built around the small and inflexible obsessions of less-than-heroic characters.' – *Variety*
'A movie that makes one glad to have missed the 17th century.' – *Derek Malcolm, Guardian*

Kini and Adams ★
France 1997 93m colour 'Scope
Noe/Les Films de la Plaine/Polar/Framework (Cedomir Kola, Sophie Salbot, Frédérique Dumas)
Two impoverished farmers, who dream of starting a new life in the city, fall out when one of them gets a better job than the other.
Ambitious, but not always successful, drama of male rivalry, where the landscapes come near to overwhelming the characters.
w Idrissa Ouédraogo, Olivier Lorelle, Santiago Amigorena *d* Idrissa Ouédraogo *ph* Jean-Paul Meurisse *m* Wally Badarou *ad* Heather Cameron *ed* Monica Coleman
☆ Vusi Kunene, David Mohloki, Nthati Moshesh, John Kani, Netsayi Chigwendere, Fidelis Cheza

Kinjite: Forbidden Subjects
US 1989 97m TVC Color
Cannon/Golan Globus (Pancho Kohner)
A cop goes after a pimp specializing in child prostitutes.
Depressingly violent and nasty thriller, little more than a rerun of the star's Death Wish *vigilante series.*
w Harold Nebenzal *d* J. Lee-Thompson *ph* Gideon Porath *ed* Peter Lee-Thompson, Mary E. Jochem
☆ Charles Bronson, Perry Lopez, Juan Fernandez, Peggy Lipton, James Pax, Sy Richardson, Marion Kodama Yue, Bill McKinney

Kipps ★★★
GB 1941 112m bw
TCF (Edward Black)
US title: *The Remarkable Mr Kipps*
In 1906, a draper's assistant comes into money and tries to crash society.
Charming, unassuming film of a well-loved novel, later musicalized as Half a Sixpence.
w Sidney Gilliat *novel* H. G. Wells *d Carol Reed ph* Arthur Crabtree *m* Charles Williams
☆ Michael Redgrave, Phyllis Calvert, Diana Wynyard, *Arthur Riscoe,* Max Adrian, Helen Haye, Michael Wilding, Lloyd Pearson, Edward Rigby, Hermione Baddeley, Frank Pettingell, Beatrice Varley, Kathleen Harrison, Felix Aylmer
'It has the old fashioned charm of wax roses under a glass bell.' – *New York Times*

Kisenga, Man of Africa: see *Men of Two Worlds*

Kismet
US 1930 90m bw 65mm Vitascope
Warner
An Oriental magician overcomes a wicked vizier.
Rather tame filming of a spectacular which belongs on the stage.
w Howard Estabrook *play* Edward Knoblock *d* John Francis Dillon *ph* John Seitz
☆ Otis Skinner, Loretta Young, David Manners, Mary Duncan, Sidney Blackmer, Ford Sterling, Edmund Breese, Montagu Love

Kismet ★
US 1944 100m Technicolor
MGM (Everett Riskin)
TV title: *Oriental Dream*
Hollow and humourless but striking-looking remake of the above.
w John Meehan *d William Dieterle ph Charles Rosher m* Herbert Stothart *ad* Cedric Gibbons, Daniel B. Cathcart
☆ Ronald Colman, Marlene Dietrich, James Craig, Edward Arnold, Hugh Herbert, Joy Ann Page, Florence Bates, Harry Davenport, Hobart Cavanaugh, Robert Warwick
'Enormous sets and crowding players are handled with such a clarity of line and colour that their gorgeousness never becomes untidy.' – *MFB*
Charles Rosher; Herbert Stothart; art direction

Kismet
US 1955 113m Eastmancolor Cinemascope
MGM (Arthur Freed)
Unlucky musical remake from the stage show with Borodin music.
w Charles Lederer, Luther Davis *musical play Charles Lederer, Luther Davis d* Vincente Minnelli *ph* Joseph Ruttenberg *ch* Jack Cole *ad* Cedric Gibbons, Preston Ames
☆ Howard Keel, Ann Blyth, Dolores Gray, Vic Damone, Monty Woolley, Sebastian Cabot, Jay C. Flippen, Mike Mazurki, Jack Elam
'The whole thing was done with too heavy a hand.' – *Howard Keel*

The Kiss ★
US 1929 64m approx (24 fps) bw silent
MGM (Albert Lewin)
A woman is accused of the murder of her jealous husband.
A wisp of a melodrama, enlivened by its star; otherwise only notable as MGM's last silent picture.
w Hans Kraly *d* Jacques Feyder *ph* William Daniels
☆ Greta Garbo, Lew Ayres, Conrad Nagel, Holmes Herbert, Anders Randolf

The Kiss
US 1988 98m colour
Columbia TriStar/Trilogy Entertainment/Astral Film Enterprises (Pen Densham, John Watson)
A glamorous model is possessed by a demonic snake-like creature.
Unimaginative horror movie.
w Stephen Volk, Tom Ropelewski *d* Pen Densham *ph* François Protat *m* J. Peter Robinson *pd* Roy Forge Smith *ed* Stan Cole *sp* Chris Walas
☆ Pamela Collyer, Peter Dvorsky, Joanna Pacula, Meredith Salenger, Mimi Kuzyk, Nicholas Kilbertus, Sabrina Boudot, Shawn Levy, Jan Rubes, Celine Lomez

Kiss and Kill: see *Sax Rohmer's The Blood of Fu Manchu*

'Women were putty in his hands!'
Kiss and Make Up
US 1934 80m bw
Paramount (B. P. Schulberg)
A Parisian beauty specialist forsakes a rich client for his loyal secretary.
Forgettable romantic comedy.
w Harlan Thompson, George Marion Jnr *play* Stephen Bekeffi *d* Harlan Thompson *ph* Leon Shamroy
☆ Cary Grant, Genevieve Tobin, Helen Mack, Edward Everett Horton, Lucien Littlefield, Mona Maris
'More gags than romance … a nice picture lacking sufficient strength to wow, but should do all right.' – *Variety*

Kiss and Tell ★
US 1945 92m bw
Columbia (Sol C. Siegel)
To protect another girl, an irrepressible teenager pretends to be pregnant.
Good-humoured farcical comedy which at the time was thought pretty shocking, especially with the infant darling of the thirties in the lead.
w F. Hugh Herbert play F. Hugh Herbert *d* Richard Wallace *ph* Charles Lawton *m* Werner Heymann
☆ *Shirley Temple,* Robert Benchley, Walter Abel, Jerome Courtland, Katherine Alexander, Porter Hall, Tom Tully
'All brilliantly characteristic of the worst anyone could think of American life.' – *James Agee*

A Kiss before Dying ★
US 1956 94m DeLuxe Cinemascope
UA/Crown (Robert Jacks)
A college boy kills women who get in his way.
Reasonably absorbing exercise in psychopathology which would have been more effective on a smaller screen.
w Lawrence Roman *novel* Ira Levin *d* Gerd Oswald *ph* Lucien Ballard *m* Lionel Newman
☆ Jeffrey Hunter, Joanne Woodward, Robert Wagner, Virginia Leith, Mary Astor, George Macready

A Kiss before Dying ★
US 1991 93m Eastmancolor
UIP/Universal/Initial (Robert Lawrence)
A woman discovers that the man she married is a multiple murderer.
Moderately effective thriller, though it offers a considerable simplification of the novel on which it is based.
wd James Dearden *novel* Ira Levin *ph* Mike Southon *m* Howard Shore *pd* Jim Clay *ed* Michael Bradsell
☆ Matt Dillon, Sean Young, Max von Sydow, Jim Fyfe, Ben Browder, Diane Ladd, James Bonfanti
'As exciting as watching someone go bald.' – *Anthony Lane, Independent on Sunday*

The Kiss before the Mirror
US 1933 66m bw
Universal
A lawyer defends a man who killed his wife from jealousy, then finds that the same thing is happening to him.
Stilted drama which was thought stylish at the time but is now a disappointment from this director; miscast, too.
w William Anthony McGuire *play* Lazslo Fodor *d* James Whale *ph* Karl Freund *ed* Ted J. Kent
☆ Frank Morgan, Nancy Carroll, Gloria Stuart, Paul Lukas, Charles Grapewin
'Direction and adaptation lift this one into passable entertainment.' – *Variety*
† It was remade in 1938 as *Wives Under Suspicion.*

A Kiss for Corliss
US 1949 88m bw
UA/Strand/James Nasser (Colin Miller)
aka: *Almost a Bride*
A teenager develops a crush on a middle-aged roué.
Dismal sequel to Kiss and Tell *in the shadow of* The Bachelor and the Bobby Soxer.
w Howard Dimsdale *d* Richard Wallace *ph* Robert de Grasse *m* Werner Heymann
☆ David Niven, Shirley Temple, Tom Tully, Darryl Hickman, Virginia Welles
'A disastrous teenage potboiler.' – *David Niven*
'I sometimes think that David Niven/Should not take all the parts he's given;/While of the art of Shirley Temple/I, for the moment, have had ample.' – *C. A. Lejeune*

A Kiss in the Dark
US 1949 87m bw
Warner (Harry Kurnitz)
A concert pianist finds romance in a boarding house peopled with zany characters.
Paper-thin romantic comedy.
w Harry Kurnitz *d* Delmer Daves *ph* Robert Burks *m* Max Steiner
☆ David Niven, Jane Wyman, Broderick Crawford, Maria Ouspenskaya, Victor Moore, Wayne Morris, Joseph Buloff, Curt Bois

Kiss Me Again ★★
US 1925 77m approx (24 fps) bw silent
Warner
A bored wife is tempted to stray, but doesn't.
Excellent silent comedy from an old boulevard farce, remade to less effect in the forties as That Uncertain Feeling.
w Hans Kraly *play Divorçons* by Victorien Sardou, Emile de Najac *d Ernst Lubitsch ph* Charles von Enger
☆ Marie Prévost, Monte Blue, John Roche, Willard Louis, Clara Bow
'Another sex masterpiece from the Attila of Hollywood … Continental high comedy done in the central European manner with Germanic harshness and irony of attack.' – *Ted Shane, New Yorker*
'Perhaps the most exquisite light screen comedy ever made on the subject of l'amour.' – *Herman G. Weinberg*

Kiss Me Again
US 1931 74m Technicolor
Warner
GB title: *Toast of the Legion*
A French lieutenant and a cabaret singer chase each other half across the world.
Modest musical from Victor Herbert's Mademoiselle Modiste; *popular at the time as a vehicle for two-colour Technicolor.*
w Julien Josephson, Paul Perez *d* William A. Seiter
☆ Walter Pidgeon, Bernice Claire, Frank McHugh, Edward Everett Horton
'Doubtful as strong b.o. but clean, deserving, and may get a break.' – *Variety*

'I don't care what you do to me, Mike – just do it fast!'
Kiss Me Deadly ***
US 1955 105m bw
UA/Parklane (Robert Aldrich)
By helping a girl who is nevertheless murdered, Mike Hammer prevents crooks from stealing a case of radio-active material.
Exuberant and harsh thriller set in an unlovely world and shot with brutal close-ups and unusual camera angles that create a disquieting effect. It is as unremittingly tough as its thuggish hero.
w A. I. Bezzerides *novel* Mickey Spillane *d* Robert Aldrich *ph* Ernest Laszlo *m* Frank de Vol
☆ Ralph Meeker, Albert Dekker, Cloris Leachman, Paul Stewart, Juano Hernandez, Wesley Addy, Maxene Cooper
'This meeting of "art" and pulp literature is, to say the least, curious.' – *MFB*

Kiss Me Goodbye
US 1982 101m DeLuxe
TCF/Boardwalk/Burt Sugarman/Keith Barish (Robert Mulligan)
A widow planning to marry again is harassed by the ghost of her first husband.
It worked in Blithe Spirit, *but this is on a different level, a toned-down rendering of the heavy-breathing Brazilian farce* Donna Flor and Her Two Husbands, *and it doesn't work on any level.*
w Charlie Peters *d* Robert Mulligan *ph* Donald Peterman *m* Ralph Burns *pd* Philip M. Jefferies *ed* Sheldon Kahn
☆ James Caan, Sally Field, Jeff Bridges, Paul Dooley, Claire Trevor, Mildred Natwick, William Prince

Kiss Me Guido
US/GB 1997 86m colour
Paramount/Capitol/Kardana/Swinsky/Redeemable (Ira Deutchman, Christine Vachon)
A hopeful heterosexual actor leaves home for a flat-share and discovers that his fellow-tenant is gay.
Feeble sitcom with few laughs and nothing else to recommend it, whatever your sexual predilections.
wd Tony Vitale *ph* Claudia Raschke *pd* Jeffrey Rathaus *ed* Alexander Hall
☆ Nick Scotti, Anthony Barrile, Anthony DeSando, Craig Chester, Dominick Lombardozzi, Molly Price, Christopher Lawford
'A bright, snappy culture-clash farce.' – *Variety*

'Bigger, Better, Blushing-er Than The Famed Broadway Smash Hit!'
Kiss Me Kate **
US 1953 111m Anscocolor 3-D
MGM (Jack Cummings)
The married leading players of a musical version of *The Taming of the Shrew* lead an equally tempestuous life backstage.
Brisk, bright screen version of the Broadway musical hit.
w Dorothy Kingsley *play* Samuel and Bella Spewack *d George Sidney ph* Charles Rosher *m/ly Cole Porter md* André Previn, Saul Chaplin *ch Hermes Pan ad* Cedric Gibbons, Urie McCleary *ed* Ralph E. Winters
☆ *Howard Keel* (Fred Graham/Petruchio), *Kathryn Grayson* (Lilli Vanessi/Katherine), *Ann Miller* (Lois Lane/Bianca), Keenan Wynn (Lippy), Bobby Van (Gremio), Tommy Rall (Bill Calhoun/Lucentio), James Whitmore (Slug), Bob Fosse (Hortentio), Kurt Kasznar (Baptista)
♫ So in Love; Too Darn Hot; So Kiss Me Kate; Why Can't You Behave; Wunderbar; We Open in Venice; Tom, Dick or Harry; I've Come to Wive it Wealthily in Padua; I Hate Men; Were Thine That Special Face; Where is the Life That Late I Led?; Always True to You in My Fashion; Brush Up Your Shakespeare; From This Moment On
André Previn, Saul Chaplin

Kiss Me Stupid *
US 1964 124m bw Panavision
UA/Mirisch/Phalanx/ (Billy Wilder)
A womanizing pop singer stops overnight in a small California desert town and shows interest in an unsuccessful songwriter in order to get at his wife.
Draggy, tasteless, surprisingly unamusing smoking room story, with the actors behaving as though driven against their will (apart from Dean Martin, ideally cast as the idol who gets a headache if he doesn't have sex every night). Some good wisecracks, but it should have been much faster and funnier.
w Billy Wilder, I. A. L. Diamond *play L'oro della fantasia* by Anna Bonacci *d* Billy Wilder *ph* Joseph LaShelle *m* André Previn *m/ly* George and Ira Gershwin *pd* Alexander Trauner
☆ Dean Martin, Kim Novak, Ray Walston, Cliff Osmond
'A work of ferocious tastelessness ... Swiftian in its relentless disgust.' – *Peter Barnes*

'You know what I do to squealers? I let them have it in the belly. So they can roll around for a long time thinking it over!'
Kiss of Death **
US 1947 98m bw
TCF (Fred Kohlmar)
A captured thief informs on his own gang, and a psychopathic killer is sent to extract vengeance.
Gloomy, well-made semi-location thriller which descends into heavy melodrama. Remade as The Fiend Who Walked the West.
w Ben Hecht, Charles Lederer *d* Henry Hathaway *ph* Norbert Brodine *m* David Buttolph
☆ *Victor Mature, Richard Widmark,* Brian Donlevy, Coleen Gray, Karl Malden, Taylor Holmes
'A tense, terrifying crime melodrama with an unusually authentic seamy atmosphere.' – *New Yorker, 1980*
'Economy of narration enhances the compactness and tautness of the whole and achieves that rarity, a picture minus unnecessary footage.' – *National Board of Review*
'It illustrates a new and vigorous trend in US moviemaking. One of the best things that is happening in Hollywood is the tendency to move out of the studio – to base fictional pictures on fact, and to shoot them not in painted studio sets but in actual places.' – *James Agee*
original story (E. Lipsky); Richard Widmark

'Whatever doesn't kill you ... makes you stronger.'
Kiss of Death *
US 1995 101m DeLuxe
TCF (Barbet Schroeder, Susan Hoffman)
A former car thief finds himself locked in a battle of survival with a vicious criminal.
A heavily rewritten remake of the above, which was intended to launch Caruso, from TV's NYPD Blue, *as a film star, but his performance seemed wan when confronted by the scenery-chewing Cage as a quirky psychopath, unbalancing the narrative and reducing interest in the story's outcome.*
w Richard Price *story* Eleazar Lipsky *d* Barbet Schroeder *ph* Luciano Tovoli *m* Trevor Jones *pd* Mel Bourne *ed* Lee Percy
☆ David Caruso, Nicolas Cage, Samuel L. Jackson, Helen Hunt, Kathryn Erbe, Stanley Tucci, Michael Rapaport, Ving Rhames, Philip Baker Hall, Anthony Head
'Far too loud and silly, but quite entertaining should you wish to suspend your disbelief.' – *Derek Malcolm, Guardian*

Kiss of Evil: see *Kiss of the Vampire*

Kiss of Fire
US 1955 86m Technicolor
Universal-International (Samuel Marx)
An ex-soldier escorts an exiled princess on a dangerous journey through Mexico.
Slightly unusual but rather clumsy swashbuckler of no especial merit.
w Franklin Coen, Richard Collins *novel The Rose and the Flame* by Jonreed Lauritzen *d* Joseph M. Newman *ph* Carl Guthrie *m* Hans Salter *md* Joseph Gershenson
☆ Jack Palance, Barbara Rush, Martha Hyer

'Kiss Fear Goodbye.'
Kiss of the Dragon
France/US 2001 98m colour Technovision
TCF/Europa/Quality Growth/Current & Immortal/ Canal+ (Luc Besson, Jet Li, Steven Chasman, Happy Walters)
In Paris, a Chinese government agent is framed for murder by a crooked cop.
Some spectacular fights enliven an otherwise unexceptional action movie, in which Jet Li demonstrates his prowess in hand-to-hand combat.
w Luc Besson, Robert Mark Kamen *story* Jet Li *ph* Thierry Arbogast *m* Craig Armstrong *pd* Jacques Bufnoir *ed* Marco Cave *cos* Pierre Bechir, Annie Thiellement *action director* Cory Yuen
☆ Jet Li (Liu Jiuan), Bridget Fonda (Jessica), Tcheky Karyo (Jean-Pierre Richard), Laurence Ashley (Aja), Burt Kwouk (Uncle Tai), Cyril Raffaelli (Twin No. 1), Didier Azoulay (Twin No. 2), John Forgeham (Max), Max Ryan (Lupo)
'Old-fashioned martial arts programmer, a hard-core action film for hard-core action junkies.' – *Kenneth Turan, Los Angeles Times*

Kiss of the Spider Woman **
US/Brazil 1985 119m MGM Color
HB/Sugarloaf (David Weisman)
Fantasies of two prisoners in a South American jail.
One of those lucky flukes, an opening up of a fringe novel about the relationship between a flagrant homosexual and a political prisoner; the former entertains the latter with accounts of his favourite pulp movies. Not for Aunt Edna.
w Leonard Schrader *novel* Manuel Puig *d* Hector Babenco *ph* Rodolfo Sanchez *m* John Neschling *pd* Clovis Bueno
☆ *William Hurt, Raul Julia,* Sonia Braga
William Hurt
best picture; direction; adapted screenplay
William Hurt

Kiss of the Tarantula
US 1976 84m Eastmancolor
New Realm/Manson (Daniel B. Cady)
GB title: *Shudder*
A young girl kills those she does not like with her pet spiders.
Excessively dim horror movie without thrills or shudders.
w Warren Hamilton Jnr *story* Daniel B. Cady *d* Chris Munger *ph* Henning Schellerup *m* Phillan Bishop *ed* Warren Hamilton Jnr
☆ Suzanne Ling, Eric Mason, Herman Wallner, Patricia Landon, Beverly Eddins, Jay Scott Neal, Rebecca Eddins, Rita French
'The spiders are good for one or two mild sensations as they crawl lovingly over their initial victims, but even they are gradually overcome by the appalling banality of the script and the general lethargy of the direction.' – *Tom Milne*

Kiss of the Vampire *
GB 1964 88m Eastmancolor
Rank/Hammer (Anthony Hinds)
US title: *Kiss of Evil*
In 1910 a Bavarian disciple of Dracula lures a British honeymoon couple.
This unsubtle variation on Dracula is handled in lively fashion, with a splendid climax in which assorted white-robed vampires are destroyed by bats.
w John Elder (Anthony Hinds) *d Don Sharp ph* Alan Hume *m* James Bernard *pd* Bernard Robinson *ed* James Needs
☆ *Noel Willman,* Clifford Evans, Edward de Souza, Jennifer Daniel, Isobel Black
PROF. ZIMMER (NOEL WILLMAN): 'You must not expect your Queensberry rules here, Mr Harcourt.'

Kiss or Kill **
Australia 1997 95m Atlab
AFFC/Bill Bennett
Two edgy petty thieves go on the run with a video of child pornography, chased by a murderous famous footballer who features on the tape, and the police.
A tense road movie that resembles an Australian variation on Badlands, with an amoral young couple on the run across wide-open spaces; it adds a few original twists of its own to the familiar genre, and dispenses with a musical soundtrack.
wd Bill Bennett *ph* Malcolm McCulloch *pd* Andrew Plumer *ed* Henry Dangar
☆ Frances O'Connor, Matt Day, Chris Haywood, Barry Otto, Max Cullen, Andrew S. Gilbert, Barry Langrishe
'Solid scripting, intelligent thesping and a bold sense of humor.' – *David Stratton, Variety*

'They won't stop us – nobody can stop us!'
Kiss the Blood Off My Hands
US 1948 80m bw
Universal/Hecht-Norma (Harold Hecht)
GB title: *Blood on My Hands*
A nurse helps a seaman on the run for murder.
Risible romantic melodrama in never-was London docks setting, with Newton large as life and twice as villainous.
w Leonardo Bercovici *novel* Gerald Butler *d* Norman Foster *ph* Russell Metty *m* Miklos Rozsa *ad* Bernard Herzbrun, Nathan Juran *ed* Milton Carruth
☆ Joan Fontaine, Burt Lancaster, Robert Newton, Lewis Russell, Aminta Dyne

Kiss the Boys Goodbye *
US 1941 85m bw
Paramount (Paul Jones)
A Broadway producer falls for one of his chorines.
Moderately smart musical entertainment of its time.
w Harry Tugend, Dwight Taylor *play* Clare Boothe *d* Victor Schertzinger *ph* Ted Tetzlaff *m/ly* Victor Schertzinger, Frank Loesser
☆ Don Ameche, Mary Martin, Oscar Levant, Rochester, Raymond Walburn, Connee Boswell, Virginia Dale, Barbara Jo Allen, Elizabeth Patterson

Kiss the Bride Goodbye
GB 1944 89m bw
Butcher
A runaway couple are unwittingly abetted by her uncle.
Unsubtle family farce.
w Jack Whittingham *d* Paul Stein
☆ Patricia Medina, Jimmy Hanley, Frederick Leister, Marie Lohr, Claud Allister, Ellen Pollock, Wylie Watson

'There's only one way Det. Alex Cross can get close to a deadly collector ... with the help of the only woman who got away.'
Kiss the Girls
US 1997 120m DeLuxe Panavision
Paramount/Rysher (David Brown, Joe Wizan)
A forensic psychologist goes on the track of a psychopath who is kidnapping and killing women.
Unpleasant thriller which expects its audience to get its pleasures from watching women being stalked and threatened.
w David Klass *novel* James Patterson *d* Gary Fleder *ph* Aaron Schneider *m* Mark Isham *pd* Nelson Coates *ed* William Steinkamp, Harvey Rosenstock
☆ Morgan Freeman (Alex Cross), Ashley Judd (Kate McTiernan), Cary Elwes (Nick Ruskin), Tony Goldwyn (Will Rudolph), Jay O. Sanders (Kyle Craig), Bill Nunn (Sampson), Brian Cox (Chief Hatfield), Alex McArthur (Sikes), Richard T. Jones (Seth Samuel), Jeremy Piven (Henry Castillo)
'Devotes itself to exploiting every fear and phobia about men to which women are prey. It's a flagrantly dangerous picture ... a grossly indecent product.' – *Alexander Walker, London Evening Standard*
† Morgan Freeman again played the role of detective Alex Cross in the 2001 movie *Along Came a Spider* (qv).

Kiss the Girls and Make Them Die

Italy 1966 106m Technicolor
Dino de Laurentiis
original title: *Si Tutte le Donne del Mondo...*
A rich industrialist has a plan to sterilize the whole male population of the world and restock it with his own mistresses, whom he keeps in suspended animation.
Patchy James Bond spoof.
w Jack Pulman, Dino Maiuri *d* Henry Levin, Dino Maiuri *ph* Aldo Tonti *m* Mario Nascimbene
☆ Michael Connors, Dorothy Provine, Raf Vallone, Terry-Thomas

Kiss Them for Me

US 1957 105m Eastmancolor
Cinemascope
TCF (Jerry Wald)
Three navy pilots spend a weekend's unofficial leave in San Francisco, and get into various kinds of trouble.
Based on a novel which also served as source for the musical Hit the Deck, *this very heavy-footed comedy with serious asides is most unsuitably cast and generally ill-timed and unattractive.*
w Julius Epstein *novel* Shore Leave by Frederic Wakeman *d* Stanley Donen *ph* Milton Krasner *m* Lionel Newman
☆ Cary Grant, Jayne Mansfield, Suzy Parker, Ray Walston, Larry Blyden, Leif Erickson, Werner Klemperer

Kiss Tomorrow Goodbye

US 1950 102m bw
Cagney Productions (William Cagney)
A violent criminal breaks jail and plans several daring robberies.
Surprisingly brutal star melodrama which failed to repeat the success of White Heat.
w Harry Brown *novel* Horace McCoy *d* Gordon Douglas *ph* Peverell Marley *m* Carmen Dragon
☆ James Cagney, Barbara Payton, Ward Bond, Luther Adler, Helena Carter, Steve Brodie, Rhys Williams, Barton MacLane, Frank Reicher, John Litel

'The mixture as before without an ingredient changed.' – *Otis Guernsey Jnr*

Kissed *

Canada 1996 78m colour
Metro/Tartan/Boneyard (Dean English, Lynne Stopkewich)
A young woman working in a funeral home makes love to the more attractive male corpses.
A dreamy evocation of the taboo subject of necrophilia which borders on the lifeless.
w Angus Fraser, Lynne Stopkewich *story* Barbara Gowdy *d* Lynne Stopkewich *ph* Gregory Middleton *m* Don MacDonald *pd* Eric McNab *ed* John Pozer, Peter Roeck, Lynne Stopkewich
☆ Molly Parker, Peter Outerbridge, Jay Brazeau, Natasha Morley, Jessie Winter Mudie, James Timmons

'This gently humorous film manages to present its disturbing psychology with understanding.' – *George Perry, Sunday Times*

'It's far too insultingly simplistic and naive on both the psychological and narrative levels to be taken that seriously.' – *Alan Jones, Film Review*

Kisses for My President

US 1964 113m bw
Warner/Pearlayne (Curtis Bernhardt)
America's first woman president causes problems for her husband.
Solidly-carpentered comedy with too few ideas for its length.
w Claude Binyon, Robert G. Kane *d* Curtis Bernhardt *ph* Robert Surtees *m* Bronislau Kaper
☆ Polly Bergen, Fred MacMurray, Arlene Dahl, Eli Wallach, Edward Andrews

Kissin' Cousins

US 1963 96m Metrocolor Panavision
MGM/Four Leaf (Sam Katzman)
The USAF wants to build a missile base on Smokey Mountain, and their PR man discovers that one of the hillbillies is his double.
A feeble production in every sense, even below its star's usual standard.
w Gerald Drayson Adams, Gene Nelson *d* Gene Nelson *ph* Ellis W. Carter *md* Fred Karger
☆ Elvis Presley, Arthur O'Connell, Glenda Farrell, Jack Albertson

Kissing a Fool

US 1998 94m DeLuxe
Universal/Largo/RL (Tag Mendillo, Andrew Form, Rick Lashbrook)
A sportswriter asks his best friend to attempt to seduce his girlfriend, in order to test her fidelity.
Contrived comedy that needs a lightness of touch, rather than the clumping treatment it gets here.
w James Frey, Doug Ellin *d* Doug Ellin *ph* Thomas Del Ruth *m* Joseph Vitarelli *pd* Charles Breen *ed* David Finfer
☆ David Schwimmer, Jason Lee, Mili Avital, Bonnie Hunt, Vanessa Angel, Kari Wuhrer, Frank Medrano, Bitty Schram

'Tries too hard to shake things up just a little, but falls between rather too many stools.' – *Bob McCabe, Empire*

The Kissing Bandit

US 1948 102m Technicolor
MGM (Joe Pasternak)
In old California, a young businessman finds he is expected to keep up his bandit father's criminal and romantic reputation.
Silly, witless musical which never settles into gear; mocked by its star as Benny mocked The Horn Blows at Midnight.
w Isobel Lennart, John Briard Harding *d* Laslo Benedek *ph* Robert Surtees *m* Georgie Stoll *m/ly* Nacio Herb Brown, Earl Brent, Edward Heyman
☆ Frank Sinatra, Kathryn Grayson, J. Carrol Naish, Mildred Natwick, Mikhail Rasumny, Billy Gilbert, Clinton Sundberg

'Was *Kissing Bandit* the nadir of my career? Hell, it was the *nadir* of anybody's career.' – *Frank Sinatra*

'When it comes to love, sometimes she just can't think straight.'

Kissing Jessica Stein *

US 2001 97m Duart
TCF/Eden Wurmfeld/Brad Zions/Cineric/Michael Alden
A Manhattan copy-editor looks for romance and finds it where she would least expect to.
A romance involving a seemingly heterosexual woman who falls in love with an occasional lesbian; otherwise a typical New York comedy, full of smart remarks, angst-ridden inhabitants and a match-making Jewish mother.
w Heather Juergensen, Jennifer Westfelt *play* Lipschtick by Heather Juergensen, Jennifer Westfelt *d* Charles Herman-Wurmfeld *ph* Lawrence Sher *m* Marcelo Zarvos *pd* Charlotte Bourke *ed* Kristy Jacobs Maslin, Gregory Tillman
☆ Jennifer Westfeldt (Jessica Stein), Heather Juergensen (Helen Cooper), Scott Cohen (Josh Meyers), Tovah Feldshuh (Judy Stein), Jackie Hoffman (Joan), Michael Mastro (Martin), Carson Elrod (Sebastian), David Aaron Baker (Dan Stein)

'One of the most highly entertaining films around, and – better still – one of the greatest romantic comedies of the past decade.' – *Jeffrey M. Anderson, San Francisco Examiner*

Kit Carson

US 1940 95m bw
Edward Small
Adventures of the pioneer Indian scout.
Thinly scripted Western imaginings with a sturdy but not alluring cast.
w George Bruce *d* George B. Seitz
☆ Jon Hall, Lynn Bari, Dana Andrews, Harold Huber, Ward Bond, Renie Riano, Raymond Hatton

Kitchen

Hong Kong/Japan 1997 112m colour
Alliance/Golden Harvest Crown/Amuse (Yim-Ho, Akira Morishige)
original title: *Wo Ai Chufang*
Homeless after her grandmother's death, a grieving woman goes to live with a hairdresser and his transsexual father.
A strange, muted tale of love and loss among eccentric misfits, filmed in an expressionist style among dated artefacts; definitely an acquired taste.
wd Yim Ho *novel* Banana Yoshimoto *ph* Poon Hang-Sang *m* Otomo Yoshihide, Uchihashi Kazuhisa *ad* James Leung, Jason Mok *ed* Poon Hung-Yiu
☆ Jordan Chan, Yasuko Tomita, Law Kar-Ying, Karen Mok, Lau Siu-Ming, Lo Koon Lan

The Kitchen Toto *

GB 1987 95m colour
Cannon/Skreba/British Screen/Film Four (Ann Skinner)
1950: in Kenya, a police officer agrees to take in the son of a black priest murdered by the Mau Mau.
Rather lumpy but well-meaning drama with a tragic ending.
wd Harry Hook *ph* Roger Deakins *m* John Keane *pd* Jamie Leonard *ed* Tom Priestley
☆ Bob Peck, Phyllis Logan, Edwin Mahinda, Robert Urquhart

Kitten with a Whip

US 1964 83m bw
Universal
A girl escaped from reform school takes refuge with a politician whose wife is away.
Over-the-top melodrama thought bannable at the time.
wd Douglas Heyes *book* Wade Miller
☆ Ann-Margret, John Forsythe, Patricia Barry, Ann Doran, Audrey Dalton

Kitty

GB 1928 90m (24 fps) bw silent
BIP/Burlington (Victor Saville)
A shopgirl loves a paralysed amnesiac, but his mother interferes.
Uninteresting romantic melodrama, notable only as Britain's first sound film: a few dialogue sequences were quickly added (in New York).
w Violet Powell, Benn W. Levy *novel* Warwick Deeping *d* Victor Saville *ph* Karl Puth
☆ John Stuart, Estelle Brody, Dorothy Cumming, Marie Ault, Olaf Hytten

'She had all London on a MARRY-go-round!'

Kitty ***

US 1945 103m bw
Paramount (Karl Tunberg)
In 18th-century London, an aristocrat makes a duchess of a guttersnipe.
Well-detailed period Pygmalion *which works much better than one would expect.*
w Darrell Ware, Karl Tunberg *novel* Rosamund Marshall *d* Mitchell Leisen *ph* Daniel L. Fapp *m* Victor Young *ad* Hans Dreier, Walter Tyler
☆ Paulette Goddard, Ray Milland, Cecil Kellaway, Constance Collier, Reginald Owen, Patric Knowles, Dennis Hoey, Sara Allgood, Eric Blore, Gordon Richards, Michael Dyne

'Enough sex, wit and urbane cynicism to make one forget a footling ending.' – *Peter John Dyer, MFB*

'It is excellently cast, delightfully acted, and the rather sordid story is told with subtlety and skill.' – *Picture Show*

'The most glamorous study of unrelieved sordidness that the screen has presented.' – *Motion Picture Herald*

Academy Award nomination: art direction

'The most daring novel ever written by a man about a woman!'

Kitty Foyle **

US 1940 108m bw
RKO (Harry E. Edgington, David Hempstead)
A white-collar girl has a troubled love life.
Solid entertainment of its time, especially aimed at ambitious young ladies.
w Dalton Trumbo, Donald Ogden Stewart *novel* Christopher Morley *d* Sam Wood *ph* Robert de Grasse *m* Roy Webb
☆ Ginger Rogers, Dennis Morgan, James Craig, Eduardo Ciannelli, Ernest Cossart, Gladys Cooper, Mary Treen

Academy Award: Ginger Rogers
Academy Award nomination: best picture; Dalton Trumbo; Sam Wood

The Klansman

US 1974 112m Technicolor
Paramount/Atlanta (William Alexander)
An Alabama sheriff confronts the Ku Klux Klan.
Violent melodrama, all noise, brutality and bad acting.
w Millard Kaufman, Samuel Fuller *novel* William Bradford Huie *d* Terence Young *ph* Lloyd Ahern, Aldo Tonti *m* Stax Organization
☆ Lee Marvin, Richard Burton, Cameron Mitchell, O. J. Simpson, Lola Falana, David Huddleston, Luciana Paluzzi, Linda Evans

'There's not a shred of quality, dignity, relevance or impact in this yahoo-oriented bunk.' – *Variety*

'Mae goes north and Alaska goes west!'

Klondike Annie

US 1936 83m bw
Paramount (William Le Baron)
A torch singer on the run disguises herself as a missionary and revivifies a Klondike mission.
Laundered Mae West vehicle, from her fading period but not too bad.
w Mae West, Marion Morgan, George B. Dowell *d* Raoul Walsh *ph* George Clemens
☆ Mae West, Victor McLaglen, Philip Reed, Helen Jerome Eddy, Harry Beresford, Harold Huber, Esther Howard

'I found the whole film fun, more fun than any other of Miss West's since the superb period piece, *She Done Him Wrong*.' – *Graham Greene*

Klute ***

US 1971 114m Technicolor Panavision
Warner (Alan J. Pakula)
A policeman leaves the force to investigate the disappearance of a research scientist, and takes up with a call girl who is involved.
Excellent adult thriller with attention to detail and emphasis on character.
w Andy K. Lewis, Dave Lewis *d* Alan J. Pakula *ph* Gordon Willis *m* Michael Small
☆ Jane Fonda, Donald Sutherland, Charles Cioffi, Roy Scheider, Rita Gam

Academy Award: Jane Fonda
Academy Award nomination: Andy K. Lewis, Dave Lewis

The Knack ****

GB 1965 84m bw
UA/Woodfall (Oscar Lewenstein)
A sex-starved young teacher lets one room of his house to a successful womanizer, another to an innocent girl from the north.
An excuse for an anarchic series of visual gags, a kaleidoscope of swinging London in which anything goes. Brilliantly done in the style of A Hard Day's Night.
w Charles Wood *play* Ann Jellicoe *d* Richard Lester *ph* David Watkin *m* John Barry
☆ Michael Crawford, Ray Brooks, Rita Tushingham, Donal Donnelly

'The whole film has the anarchic quality modish today and at all times appealing to a new generation understandably bent on overturning the ideas which have hardened in the minds of their elders.' – *Dilys Powell*

'The running jokes and gags never come off.' – *Pauline Kael*

Knave of Hearts *

GB 1954 103m bw
Transcontinental (Paul Graetz)
aka: *Monsieur Ripois et Son Nemesis*
US title: *Lover Boy*
A born philanderer confesses all his affairs to his wife.
Well-observed though strangely flat and disappointing sex comedy, something of a pioneer in its time and therefore perhaps too diffident in its approach.
w René Clément, Hugh Mills *d* René Clément *ph* Oswald Morris *m* Roman Vlad
☆ Gérard Philipe, Margaret Johnston, Joan Greenwood, Natasha Parry, Valerie Hobson

Knickerbocker Holiday *

US 1944 84m bw
UA/PCA/Harry Joe Brown
In old New Amsterdam, a one-legged tyrant finally sees the light.

Artificial musical from a famous Broadway original, staged in 1938, with engaging moments including Charles Coburn singing 'September Song'.
w David Boehm, Harry Goldman, Rowland Leigh, Thomas Lennon *novel* *Father Knickerbocker's History of New York* by Washington Irving *d* Harry Joe Brown *ph* Phil Tannura *m* Werner Heymann *m/ly* Kurt Weill, Maxwell Anderson
☆ Charles Coburn, Nelson Eddy, Constance Dowling, Ernest Cossart, Shelley Winters, Otto Kruger
Werner Heymann, Kurt Weill

Knife in the Water *
Poland 1962 94m bw
ZRF Kamera (Stanislaw Zylewicz)
original title: *Noz w Wodzie*
A young couple ask a hitchhiker to spend a weekend on their yacht, and regret it.
Detached little melodrama in which the sex and violence hover beneath the surface. All very watchable, but in a minor key.
w Jerzy Skolimowski, Roman Polanski, Jakub Goldberg *d* *Roman Polanski* *ph* Jerzy Lipman *m* Krzystof Komeda
☆ Leon Niemczyk, Jolanta Umecka, Zygmunt Malanowicz
'Has all the virtues of an intensely psychological, sardonically probing modern novel.' – *John Simon*
best foreign film

Knight Moves
US/Germany 1992 116m Eastmancolor Super 35
Columbia TriStar/Knight Moves/Cine Vox (Ziad El Khoury, Jean-Luc Defait)
A chess champion is suspected of being a serial killer.
Lacklustre thriller with little suspense or sense of reality.
w Brad Mirman *d* Carl Schenkel *ph* Dietrich Lohmann *md* Anne Dudley *pd* Graeme Murray *ed* Norbert Herzner
☆ Christopher Lambert, Diane Lane, Tom Skerritt, Daniel Baldwin, Ferdinand Mayne, Katherine Isobel, Charles Bailey-Gates, Arthur Strauss
'Mannered, heavy-handed and rather ridiculous.' – *Philip French, Observer*

Knight of the Plains
US 1938 57m bw
Equity/Spectrum/Stan Laurel (Jed Buell)
A cowboy defeats a confidence trickster who tries to cheat settlers out of their land.
Amiable Western, starring one of the many singing cowboys of the time; although it sticks to all the conventions – bearded comic sidekick, a hero who puts away his gun to fight the villain with his fists – it has more sprightly narrative than most of its kind.
w Fred Myton *d* Sam Newfield *ph* Mack Stengler *md* Lew Porter *ed* Robert Jahns
☆ Fred Scott, Al St John, Marion Weldon, John Merton, Richard Kramer, Frank La Rue, Lafe McKee

Knight without Armour **
GB 1937 107m bw
London Films (Alexander Korda)
During the Russian Revolution of 1917, a widowed countess is helped to safety by a British translator.
Underrated romantic adventure with big production values and some splendid moments.
w Lajos Biro, Arthur Wimperis, Frances Marion *novel* James Hilton *d* *Jacques Feyder* *ph* *Harry Stradling, Bernard Browne, Jack Cardiff* *m* Miklos Rozsa *md* Muir Mathieson *ad* Lazare Meerson *ed* William Hornbeck, Francis Lyon
☆ *Robert Donat, Marlene Dietrich,* Irene Vanbrugh, Herbert Lomas, Austin Trevor, Basil Gill, David Tree, John Clements, Lawrence Hanray
'Another feather in the cap of Alexander Korda for his series of artistic film productions. There is relatively little to find fault with and much to praise.' – *Variety*
'A first-class thriller, beautifully directed, with spare and convincing dialogue and a nearly watertight scenario.' – *Graham Greene*

Knightriders
US 1981 155m colour
United (Richard P. Rubinstein)
A group of wandering hippies, led by a man obsessed with notions of chivalry, re-enact medieval tournaments on motor-bikes.
A glum and wordy movie, revealing little point or purpose.
wd George A. Romero *ph* Michael Gornick *m* Donald Rubinstein *pd* Cletus Anderson *ed* George A. Romero, Pasquale Buba
☆ Ed Harris, Gary Lahti, Tom Savini, Amy Ingersoll, Patricia Tallman, Christine Forrest

Knights and Emeralds
GB 1986 94m colour
Warner/Goldcrest/Enigma (Susan Richards, Raymond Day)
A young white drummer joins a rival black band for the national marching bands championship.
Dull teen drama of racial relationships, accompanied by a great deal of uninteresting music.
wd Ian Emes *ph* Richard Greatrex *m* Colin Towns *ad* Deborah Gillingham *ed* John Victor-Smith
☆ Christopher Wild, Beverley Hills, Warren Mitchell, Bill Leadbitter, Rachel Davies

Knights of the Round Table *
GB 1953 115m Eastmancolor Cinemascope
MGM (Pandro S. Berman)
Lancelot, banished from King Arthur's court for loving Guinevere, returns to defeat the evil Modred.
Disappointingly flat, pageant-like adaptation of the legends, with a few lively strands insufficiently firmly drawn together.
w Talbot Jennings, Jan Lustig, Noel Langley *d* Richard Thorpe *ph* Frederick A. Young, Stephen Dade *m* Miklos Rozsa *ad* Alfred Junge, Hans Peters
☆ Robert Taylor, Mel Ferrer, Ava Gardner, Anne Crawford, Stanley Baker, Felix Aylmer, Robert Urquhart, Niall MacGinnis
art direction

Knights of the Teutonic Order *
Poland 1960 180m Eastmancolor Dyaliscope
Studio Unit (Zygmunt Krol)
original title: *Krzyzacy*
Teutonic knights pillage Poland on the pretext of converting the inhabitants to Christianity; when they kill a noblewoman, her daughter swears revenge.
Medieval epic differing little from those of Hollywood, but splendid to look at.
w Jerzy Stefan Stawinski, Aleksander Ford *novel* Henryk Sienkiewicz *d* Aleksander Ford *ph* Mieczyslaw Jahoda *m* Kazimierz Serocki
☆ Urszula Modrzynska, Grazyna Staniszewska, Andrzej Szalawski

'He Will Rock You.'
A Knight's Tale
US 2001 132m DeLuxe Super 35
Columbia TriStar/Escape Artists/Finestkind (Tim Van Rellim, Todd Black, Brian Helgeland)
A young peasant boy realises the American dream a few centuries too early by breaking class barriers to become a champion knight.
Deliberately anachronistic romp that tries to persuade its audience that jousting was the Olde English rock'n'roll and that the medieval era was a time of proto-hippies; it's difficult to see why its makers bothered, or what they thought they were achieving by this pop-saturated history.
wd Brian Helgeland *ph* Richard Greatrex *m* Carter Burwell *pd* Tony Burrough *ed* Kevin Stitt *sp* Mill Film *cos* Caroline Harris
☆ Heath Ledger (William Thatcher), Mark Addy (Roland), Rufus Sewell (Count Adhemar), Paul Bettany (Chaucer), Shanynn Sossamon (Jocelyn), Alan Tudyk (Wat), Laura Fraser (Kate), Christopher Cazenove (John Thatcher), Berenice Beso (Christiana), James Purefoy (Colville)
PAUL BETTANY: 'Geoffrey Chaucer's the name, writing's the game'
'Rarely has a period costume picture been quite so craven in courting a young audience.' – *Todd McCarthy, Variety*
'Half Python, half Ivanhoe—and not as much fun as either.' – *Richard Schickel, Time*

Knock Off
US 1998 91m DeLuxe Super 35
Knock/MDP/Film Workshop/Val D'Oro (Nansun Shi)
In Hong Kong, a former forger of designer clothes and his partner, a CIA agent, foil the activities of violent smugglers.
Hectic action movie with a confusing plot and frantic fights, which is to say the mixture as usual for its star.
w Steven E. de Souza *d* Tsui Hark *ph* Arthur Wong *m* Ron Mael, Russell Mael *pd* James Leung, Bill Lui *ed* Mak Chi Sin
☆ Jean-Claude Van Damme (Marcus Ray), Rob Schneider (Tommy Hendricks), Lela Rochon (Karen Leigh), Paul Sorvino (Harry Johansson), Michael Fitzgerald Wong (Han), Carmen Lee (Ling Ho), Glen Chin (Skinny), Jeff Joseph Wolfe (Skaar), Wyman Wong (Eddie Wang)
'Much of the movie simply consists of the gung-ho heroes doing the standard acrobatic butt-kicking that passes for action in the undemanding Far East market.' – *Alexander Walker*

Knock on Any Door *
US 1949 100m bw
Columbia/Santana (Robert Lord)
A defence lawyer pleads with the jury for the life of a slum boy on a murder charge.
Smartly-made but empty melodrama making facile social points.
w Daniel Taradash, John Monks Jnr *novel* Willard Motley *d* Nicholas Ray *ph* Burnett Guffey *m* George Antheil
☆ Humphrey Bogart, John Derek, George Macready, Allene Roberts

Knock on Wood **
US 1954 103m Technicolor
Paramount (Norman Panama, Melvin Frank)
Stolen plans are hidden inside the dummy of an unsuspecting ventriloquist.
Excellent star comedy with good script and production (but some strange ideas of London's geography).
wd *Norman Panama, Melvin Frank* *ph* Daniel Fapp *m* Leith Stevens *m/ly* Sylvia Fine *ch* Michael Kidd
☆ *Danny Kaye, Mai Zetterling,* David Burns, Torin Thatcher, Leon Askin, Abner Biberman, Steve Geray
Norman Panama, Melvin Frank (script)

Knockout: see *Knute Rockne, All American*

Knocks at My Door **
Venezuela/Cuba/Argentina 1993 106m Agfacolor
Foncine/CONAC/ASP/ICAIC/Channel 4 (Alejandro Saderman)
original title: *Golpes a Mi Puerta*
Two nuns face execution for sheltering a young radical being hunted by a military death-squad.
Gripping and timely drama of courage and obduracy, political expediency and state brutality.
w Juan Carlos Gene, Alejandro Saderman *play* Juan Carlos Gene *d* Alejandro Saderman *ph* Jonny Semeco, Adriano Moreno *m* Julio D'Escrivan *ad* Marietta Perroni *ed* Claudia Uribe
☆ Verónica Oddó, Elba Escobar, Juan Carlos Gené, José Antonio Rodriguez, Ana Castell, Mirta Ibarra, Frank Spano

Knute Rockne, All American
US 1940 98m bw
Warner (Robert Fellows)
GB title: *Knockout*
aka: *A Modern Hero*
The career of a famous Notre Dame football coach.
Standard sporting biopic.
w Robert Buckner *d* Lloyd Bacon *ph* Tony Gaudio *m* Ferde Grofé
☆ Pat O'Brien, Ronald Reagan, Gale Page, Donald Crisp, Albert Basserman, John Qualen, John Sheffield

Koenigsmark
France 1935 114m bw
Roger Richebé/Capitol
A princess falls for a commoner.
Rather elementary royal romance in a Ruritanian background, filmed simultaneously in French and English by the same principals.
novel Pierre Benoit *d* Maurice Tourneur *ph* Victor Armenise *m* Jacques Ibert
☆ Elissa Landi, Pierre Fresnay, John Lodge

'Pain Is Their Pleasure.'
Kojitmal *
South Korea 1999 111m colour
Alliance/Shincine/Korea Films (Shin Chul)
aka: *Lies*
An 18-year-old schoolgirl enjoys an obsessive affair with a married middle-aged sculptor.
Deft account of a sado-masochistic relationship, in which control passes from the apparently stronger to the seemingly weaker partner. The sexual scenes are often brutal and, when the two choose poles with which to beat one another, even absurd.
wd Jang Sun Woo *novel* *Tell Me a Lie* by Jang Jung Il *ph* Kim Woo Hyung *m* Dal Palan *pd* Kim Myeong Kyeong *ed* Park Gok Ji
☆ Lee Sang Hyun (J), Kim Tae Yeon (Y), Jeon Hye Jin (Woori), Choi Hyun Joo (G), Han Kwon Taek (Y's brother)
'Although for a certain amount of time the boldness and frankness of the film impresses, ultimately it outstays its welcome.' – *David Stratton, Variety*
'Deliciously witty.' – *Tony Rayns*
† Jang Jung-Il's novel was banned as pornographic in Korea and withdrawn a month after publication, and he was sent to prison for two months.

Kokaku Kidotai: see *Ghost in the Shell*

Kokoda Crescent
Australia 1988 83m colour
Phillip Emanuel
When a youth dies from an overdose of heroin, his grandfather decides to take action against the drug dealer involved.
Ponderous tale of old soldiers finding a new campaign to fight.
w Patrick Cook *d* Ted Robinson *ph* Dan Burstall *m* Peter Best *pd* Leslie Binns *ed* Robert Gibson
☆ Warren Mitchell (Stan), Ruth Cracknell (Alice), Bill Kerr (Russ), Madge Ryan (Margaret), Martin Vaughan (Eric), Steve Jacobs (Detective), Penne Hackforth-Jones (Carol)

Koks I Kulissen: see *Ladies on the Rocks*

Kolobos
US 1999 83m FotoKem
Armitage (Nne Ebong, Dana Altman)
Five young people answer an advert to appear in an experimental film and find themselves trapped in an old dark house with doors and windows sealed.
Cheap and nasty horror movie, low on imagination and high on gruesome effects; it finally leaves its audience as much in the dark as its characters.
w Nne Ebong, Daniel Liatowitsch, David Todd Ocvirk *d* Daniel Liatowitsch, David Todd Ocvirk *ph* Yoram Astrakhan *m* William Kidd *pd* Preston Fisher *ed* Brian Olson
☆ Amy Weber (Kyra), Donny Terranova (Tom), Nichole Pelerine (Erica), John Fairlie (Gary), Promise LaMarco (Tina), Ilia Volok (Faceless), Linnea Quigley (Dorothy)
'Wholly baffling horror farrago.' – *Sight and Sound*

'The Ultimate Bachelor Has Finally Met His Match!'
Kolya ***
Czech Republic/France/GB 1996 105m colour
Buena Vista/Portobello/Ceska Televize/Biograf Jan Sverák
In Prague, a penniless musician marries for cash a Russian woman who needs Czech papers and finds that the transaction leaves him with her five-year-old son.
Charming, tough-minded drama of people trying to get by within a system that leaves them little room for manoeuvre.
w Zdenek Sverák *idea* Pavel Taussig *d* Jan Sverák *ph* Vladimir Smutny *m* Ondrej Soukup *ed* Alois Visárek
☆ Zdenek Sverák, Andrej Chalimon, Libuse Safránková, Ondrej Vetchy, Stella Zázvorková, Ladislav Smoljak, Irina Livanova

'Balances heart-warming sentiment with gentle humor and observations that strike universal chords.' – *David Rooney, Variety*
foreign film

Komissar **
USSR 1967 108m colour Cinemascope
Artificial Eye/Gorky Studios (V. Levin, L. Prilutzkaya)
aka: *The Commissar*
During the Civil War of the 1920s, a pregnant soldier of the Red Army moves in with a poor Jewish family to have her child.
First publicly shown twenty years after it was made, the film's events indict anti-Semitism and foreshadow the later treatment of the Jews within the context of a simple domestic story.
wd Alexander Askoldov *novel In the Town of Berdichev* by Vasily Grossman *ph* Valery Ginsburg *m* Alfred Schnittke *ad* Sergei Serebrennikov *ed* V. Isayeva, N. Loginova, S. Lyashinskaya
☆ Nonna Mordyukova, Rolan Bykov, Raisa Niedashkovskaya, Vasily Shukshin

Komitas
West Germany 1988 106m colour
ICA/Margarita Woskanjan Filmproduction/WDR/SFB/Channel 4
Visually striking meditation on an Armenian monk and composer traumatized into silence by the Turkish massacre of his countrymen in 1915.
Limited in its appeal.
wd Don Askarjan *ph* Jorgos Arvanitis, Martin Gressmann, Eberhard Geik *m* Komitas and others *ad* Jurgen Kiebach, Michael Poladian *ed* Rene Perraudin, Marion Regentrop
☆ Samvel Ovasapain, Margarita Woskanjan, Onig Saadetian, Yeghishe Mougikian

'Welcome to the bottom of the food chain.'
Komodo
Australia 1999 90m colour
Scanbox Asia Pacific (Alan Riche, Tony Ludwig)
A youth returns to an island where his parents were slaughtered to discover it is inhabited by carnivorous Komodo lizards.
Feeble low-budget horror with no scares and little suspense.
w Hans Bauer, Craig Mitchell *d* Michael Lantieri *ph* David Burr *m* John Debney *pd* George Liddle *ed* Michael Fallavollita *sp* John Cox Creature Workshop; Tippet Studios
☆ Jill Hennessy (Victoria), Billy Burke (Oates), Kevin Zegers (Patrick Connelly), Paul Gleeson (Denby), Nina Landis (Annie), Simon Westaway (Bracken)

Koneko Monogatari: see *The Adventures of Milo and Otis*

Konga
GB 1960 90m Eastmancolor Spectamation
Anglo Amalgamated/Merton Studios (Nat Cohen, Stuart Levy)
A scientist's experiments on a chimpanzee turn it into a monstrous killer ape.
Ridiculous mad-scientist movie, with some over-the-top acting in an attempt to distract attention from the risible script.
w Aben Kandel, Herman Cohen *d* John Lemont *ph* Desmond Dickinson *m* Gerard Schurmann *md* Muir Mathieson *ad* Wilfred Arnold *ed* Jack Slade
☆ Michael Gough, Margo Johns, Jess Conrad, Claire Gordon, Jack Watson, Austin Trevor, George Pastell, Leonard Sachs

Kongbufenzi: see *The Terrorizer*

Kongo
US 1932 86m bw
MGM
An embittered African recluse takes revenge on the daughter of his former enemy.
No-holds-barred melodrama which never really exerts the right grip; a remake of the Lon Chaney silent West of Zanzibar.
w Leon Gordon *play* Chester de Vonde, Kilbourn Gordon *d* William Cowen *ph* Harold Rosson
☆ Walter Huston, Lupe Velez, Virginia Bruce, Conrad Nagel, C. Henry Gordon
'Horror and tropical stuff combined ... chiefly for the daily grinds.' – *Variety*

Der Kongress Tanzt: see *Congress Dances*

Kontrakt: see *The Contract*

Konyets Sankt-Peterburga: see *The End of St Petersburg*

Kopek and Broom: see *Find the Lady*

Korczak
Poland/Germany/France/GB 1990 118m colour
Artificial Eye/Filmstudio 'Perspektywa'/Regina Ziegler Filmproduktion/Erato Films/BBC Films/Telmar Film International (Regina Ziegler, Janusz Morgenstern, Daniel Tocsan du Plantier)
The director of a Polish orphanage attempts to protect his charges from the Nazis.
Despite, or perhaps because of, being based on reality, the film fails to engage satisfactorily with its subject matter.
w Agnieszka Holland *d* Andrzej Wajda *ph* Robby Müller *m* Wojciech Kilar *pd* Allan Starski *ed* Ewa Smal
☆ Wojtek Pszoniak, Ewa Dalkowska, Piotr Kozlowski, Marzena Trybala, Wojciech Klata, Adam Siemion, Karolina Czernicka, Agnieszka Kruk

To Koritsi me ta Mavra: see *The Girl in Black*

Korkalen: see *Thy Soul Shall Bear Witness*

Koroshi No Rakuin **
Japan 1967 91m colour Nikkatsu-scope
Nikkatsu (Iwai Kaneo)
aka: *Branded to Kill*
The number three hitman in Tokyo, whose fetish is smelling boiled rice, finds himself the target of the top killer.
A strange but enjoyable thriller, with its quirky originality, odd angles and odder hero as well as some effective suspense.
w Guryu Hachiro *d* Suzuki Seijun *ph* Nagatsuka Kazue *m* Yamamoto Naozumi *ad* Kawahara Sukezo *ed* Tanji Mutsuo
☆ Shishido Jo, Ogawa Mariko, Mari Annu, Nanbara Koji, Tamagawa Isao, Minami Hiroshi
'His film-making remains a wonderful subversion of commercial genres, wildly over-the-top, stylistically imaginative and totally watchable for its sheer (possibly ironic) audacity.' – *Derek Malcolm, Guardian*
'One of Suzuki's greatest, and it stands as his last word to date on the yakuza genre.' – *Tony Rayne*
† The film caused Suzuki's sacking from the Nikkatsu studios, when he became a scapegoat for a change in policy.

Korotkie Vstrechi: see *Short Encounters*

Koshikei: see *Death by Hanging*

Kotch *
US 1971 114m Metrocolor
ABC/Kotch Company (Richard Carter)
An eccentric 72-year-old widower is at odds with his family and helps a pregnant babysitter.
Variously amusing, moving and sentimental, this generally likeable film about a crotchety grandpa is sustained by its star performance.
w John Paxton *novel* Katherine Topkins *d* Jack Lemmon *ph* Richard H. Kline *m* Marvin Hamlisch
☆ *Walter Matthau*, Deborah Winters, Felicia Farr, Charles Aidman
'A nice, sentimental, Life-Can-Be-Beautiful comedy of the second order.' – *Judith Crist*
Walter Matthau; song 'Life Is What You Make It' (*m*Marvin Hamlisch, *ly*Johnny Mercer)

Koyaanisqatsi *
US 1983 86m DeLuxe
Island Alive/Blue Dolphin/Institute for Regional Education (Godfrey Reggio)
A panoramic view of contemporary America without commentary or narrative, using time-lapse photography. The title is an Indian word meaning 'a state of life that calls for another way of living'.
A rather pointless, very beautiful, and finally rather boring experience.
w Ron Fricke, Godfrey Reggio, Michael Hoenig, Alton Walpole *d* Godfrey Reggio *ph* Ron Fricke *m* Philip Glass *ed* Anton Walpole, Ron Fricke
'Arrogant bombast, provoking no response except "wow".' – *Sight & Sound*
† It was followed by *Powaqqatsi* (qv), which gave a similar treatment to the Third World.

Krakatoa, East of Java
US 1968 136m Technicolor Cinerama
ABC/Cinerama (Lester A. Sansom)
In 1883 the SS *Batavia Queen* leaves Singapore and is engulfed by the Krakatoa eruption.
Mindless spectacular, technically quite impressive but with no dramatic interest whatsoever. (Krakatoa is actually west of Java.)
w Clifford Newton Gould, Bernard Gordon *d* Bernard Kowalski *ph* Manuel Berenguer *m* Frank de Vol *pd/sp* Eugene Lourié
☆ Maximilian Schell, Diane Baker, Brian Keith, Rossano Brazzi, Barbara Werle, John Leyton, Sal Mineo, J. D. Cannon, Marc Lawrence
'Apparently designed to disprove the old adage, "they don't make them like that any more". At a conservative count it includes such sure-fire cinematic ingredients as hidden treasure, deep-sea divers with shattered lungs and claustrophobia, mutiny and fire on board ship, nuns, convicts, a lost orphan boy, girl divers and even a little striptease, climaxing in the biggest explosion and the greatest tidal wave known to history.' – *MFB*
special visual effects

'There are three sides to this love story!'
Kramer versus Kramer ***
US 1979 105m Technicolor
Columbia/Stanley Jaffe (Richard C. Fischoff)
A divorced advertising executive gets temporary custody of his seven-year-old son.
New-fashioned tearjerker, as slick as a colour supplement and catnip to the emotion-starved masses.
wd Robert Benton novel Avery Corman *ph* Nestor Almendros *md* Erma E. Levin *pd* Paul Sylbert *ed* Jerry Greenberg
☆ *Dustin Hoffman, Justin Henry*, Meryl Streep, Jane Alexander, Howard Duff
'Pastel colours, a cute kid and a good script made this one of the most undeserved successes of the year: wall-to-wall sentiment.' – *Time Out*
best picture; Robert Benton (as director); Dustin Hoffman; Meryl Streep; screenplay adapted from another medium
Justin Henry; Jane Alexander; Nestor Almendros; editing

'When people are afraid of you ... You can do everything. Remember that.'
The Krays **
GB 1990 119m colour
Rank/Parkfield (Dominic Anciano, Ray Burdis)
Twins, who grow up in a mother-dominated household, become feared and fearsome East End thugs.
Made with the cooperation of its real-life protagonists, it stays within a gangster milieu and comes close to glamorizing them both.
w Philip Ridley *d* Peter Medak *ph* Alex Thomson *m* Michael Kamen *pd* Michael Pickwoad *ed* Martin Walsh
☆ Billie Whitelaw, Gary Kemp, Martin Kemp, Susan Fleetwood, Charlotte Cornwell, Jimmy Jewel, Avis Bunnage, Kate Hardie, Alfred Lynch, Tom Bell, Steven Berkoff
'The direction does not flinch, as do most other British crime-class-nostalgia movies, from graphic violence.' – *MFB*
'The movie comes over like a collaboration between Joan Littlewood's Theatre Workshop, an ungifted follower of Sigmund Freud and the postcard artist Donald McGill.' – *Philip French, Observer*

Kreitzerova Sonata
USSR 1987 135m colour
Cannon/Mosfilm (Maria Zakharova)
aka: *The Kreutzer Sonata*
A jealous husband tells a fellow traveller how he came to kill his wife.
Restlessly faithful to the book, but failing to engage its audience.
w Mikhail Schweitzer *novel* Leo Tolstoy *d* Mikhail Schweitzer, Sofia Milkina *ph* Mikhail Agraovich *m* Sofia Gubaidulina *pd* Igor Lemeshev, Vladimir Fabrikov *ed* Lyudmila Feiginova
☆ Oleg Yankovsky, Aleksandr Trofimov, Irina Seleznyova, Dmitri Pokrovsky

'If you miss the first five minutes you miss one suicide, two executions, one seduction and the key to the plot!'
The Kremlin Letter
US 1970 122m DeLuxe Panavision
TCF (Carter de Haven, Sam Wiesenthal)
An American intelligence team is sent undercover to Moscow to retrieve an arms treaty mistakenly signed.
Tediously violent cold war mystifier: a few good performances do not make it worth unravelling.
w John Huston, Gladys Hill *novel* Noel Behn *d* John Huston *ph* Ted Scaife *m* Robert Drasnin *pd* Ted Haworth
☆ Richard Boone, Orson Welles, Bibi Andersson, Max von Sydow, Patrick O'Neal, Ronald Radd, George Sanders, Dean Jagger, Nigel Green, Barbara Parkins, Lila Kedrova, Michael MacLiammoir, Sandor Eles, Niall MacGinnis, John Huston
'One of those all-star international spy sagas that trick out an indecipherably tortuous plot with a series of vignettes in which the pleasures of star-spotting are expected to compensate for any narrative longueurs.' – *Nigel Andrews*

Der Krieger und die Kaiserin
Germany 2000 135m colour Super 35
Pathé/X Filme (Stefan Arndt, Maria Kopf)
aka: *The Princess and the Warrior*
A nurse tracks down the man who saved her life and becomes involved in crime.
A gritty and unconvincing romance, taken at a slow tempo, and with mystic sequences that only add to the air of confusion.
wd Tom Tykwer *ph* Frank Griebe *m* Tom Tykwer, Johnny Kilmek, Reinhold Heil *pd* Uli Hanisch *ed* Mathilde Bonnefoy *cos* Monika Jacobs
☆ Franka Potente (Sissi), Benno Furmann (Bodo), Joachim Krol (Walter), Marita Breuer (Sissi's mother), Jurgen Tarrach (Schmatt), Lars Rudolph (Steini), Melchior Beslon (Otto), Ludger Pistor (Werner Durr)
'A botch, but it's the kind of bad movie that can only happen to a good – and potentially great – filmmaker.' – *Gene Seymour, Newsday*

Krippendorf's Tribe
US 1998 94m Technicolor
Buena Vista/Touchstone/Mora-Brezner-Steinberg-Tenenbaum/Dreyfuss-James (Larry Brezner)
A widowed anthropologist, who has spent his research grant on his children, invents a lost New Guinea tribe, faking film of them in his back yard.
Energetic comedy, though lacking in wit or humour; its sexual jokes are likely to alienate a family audience, for which it was presumably intended.
w Charlie Peters *book* Frank Parkin *d* Todd Holland *ph* Dean Cundey *m* Bruce Broughton *pd* Scott Chambliss *ed* Jon Poll
☆ Richard Dreyfuss, Jenna Elfman, Natasha Lyonne, Gregory Smith, Carl Michael Lindner, Stephen Root, Elaine Stritch, Tom Poston, David Ogden Stiers, Lily Tomlin, Zakes Mokae
'Frenetic, formulaic and instantly forgettable.' – *Joe Leydon, Variety*
† The film was released direct to video in Britain.

Krótki Film o Miłości: see *A Short Film about Love*

Krótki Film o Zabijaniu: see *A Short Film about Killing*

Krull
GB 1983 121m Metrocolor Panavision
Columbia/Ted Mann-Ron Silverman
Prince Colwyn's bride-to-be is abducted by the Beast of the Black Fortress.

Old-fashioned derring-do taking place on a somewhat unattractive planet; nevertheless fairly lively in its action and trick effects.
w Stanford Sherman *d* Peter Yates *ph* Peter Suschitzky *m* James Horner *pd* Stephen Grimes
☆ Ken Marshall, Lysette Anthony, Freddie Jones, Francesca Annis, Alun Armstrong, David Battley, Bernard Bresslaw, John Welsh, Tony Church, Bernard Archard

'Nearly everything in it has been done before, in some cases rather better, but rarely quite so likeably.' – *Nick Roddick, MFB*

'Not really thrilling enough to be a blockbuster and not light enough to be anything else.' – *Sight and Sound*

Krzyzacy: see *Knights of the Teutonic Order*

Kuang Ye San Qian Jing: see *Wild*

'When you have attitude, who needs experience?'
Kuffs
US 1992 101m Technicolor
Universal/EvansGideon (Raynold Gideon)
A high-school dropout inherits his murdered brother's private police business and sets out to avenge his death.
Messily coarse comedy not helped by the star's direct addresses to the camera.
w Bruce A. Evans, Raynold Gideon *d* Bruce A. Evans *ph* Thomas Del Ruth *m* Harold Faltermeyer *pd* Victoria Paul, Armin Ganz *ed* Stephen Semel
☆ Christian Slater, Tony Goldwyn, Milla Jovovich, Bruce Boxleitner, Troy Evans, George de la Pena, Leon Rippy

'Film veers from ultra-violence to slapstick comedy in an arbitrary and irritating fashion. Hokey camera angles and flashy dissolves fail to pump up the action.' – *Variety*

'The film comes to resemble the bastard child of *Miami Vice* and an especially bad movie-of-the-week.' – *New York Times*

Kühle Wampe ★★★
Germany 1932 73m bw
Prometheus/Praesens (George Hoellering)
aka: *Whither Germany?*
During the Depression in Berlin, a working-class family is forced to move to a shantytown on the outskirts of the city.
A powerful attack on capitalist brutality and working-class apathy, which also suggested that the hope of the future lay with the revolutionary young, an optimism that was sadly misplaced. It is the only film in which Brecht was in control, working with a collective of like-minded collaborators.
w Bertold Brecht, Ernst Ottwald *d* Slaten Dodow *ph* Günther Krampf *m* Hanns Eisler, Josef Schmidt
☆ Hertha Thiele, Ernst Busch, Martha Wolter, Adolf Fischer, Lili Schönborn, Max Sablotzki, Alfred Schaefer
† German authorities banned the film on its release as offending 'against the vital interests of the state' and as being 'a summons to violence and subversion'. Brecht, by lying, persuaded the censor to release it with a few minor cuts. He later wrote, 'Leaving the building we did not conceal our high opinion of the censor. He had penetrated the essence of our artistic intentions with far greater sagacity than our most benevolent critics.'

'Courage conquers all.'
Kull the Conqueror
US 1997 95m DeLuxe Panavision
Universal (Raffaella de Laurentiis)
The ancient evil spirit is summoned up to prevent a lowly born barbarian inheriting the throne of Valusia.
Routine sword-and-sorcery stuff that lacks any panache or visual magic.
w Charles Edward Pogue *characters created by* Robert E. Howard *d* John Nicolella *ph* Rodney Charters *m* Joel Goldsmith *pd* Benjamin Fernandez *ed* Dallas Puett *sp* Kit West; Richard Malzahn; make-up fx: Gianetto de Rossi
☆ Kevin Sorbo, Tia Carrere, Thomas Ian Griffith, Litefoot, Karina Lombard, Roy Brocksmith, Harvey Fierstein, Edward Tudor-Pole, Douglas Henshall

'No more than a well-crafted, diverting romp.' – *Variety*

Kumonosu-Jo: see *Throne of Blood*

Kundun ★
US 1997 134m Technicolor 'Scope
Buena Vista/Touchstone (Barbara de Fina)
Biopic of the Dalai Lama, from his discovery as a baby to his exile from Tibet after the Chinese invasion of his country.
A visually splendid, but intellectually flabby, hagiography: by concentrating on a child's-eye view of events, its makers deliberately evade any attempt to provide a political or social context for what is shown.
w Melissa Mathison *d* Martin Scorsese *ph* Roger Deakins *m* Philip Glass *pd* *Dante Ferretti* *ed* Thelma Schoonmaker
☆ Tenzin Thuthob Tsarong, Sonam Phunstok, Gyatso Lukhang, Robert Lin, Tencho Gyalpo, Tsewang Migyur Khangsa

'One from the heart, a majestic spectacle of images and sounds. But pic is bogged down by a routine screenplay.' – *Variety*

🏆 Dante Ferretti (art direction; costume design)

Kung Fu Street Fighter (dubbed)
Japan 1974 74m Eastmancolor Actionscope
Eural/Toei-Kyoto Eiga/Titan (Norimichi Matsudaira)
original title: *Gekitotsu! Satsujinken*
A Japanese hitman offers his services to protect an oil heiress, who is threatened by Chinese businessmen with Mafia connections.
An unsavoury martial arts movie with a thuggish hero, whose behaviour is excused because his father was killed by a Chinese firing squad.
w Koji Yakada, Motohiro Torii *d* Shigehiro Ozawa *ph* Kenji Horikoshi *m* Tony Tsushima *ad* Takatoshi Suzuki *ed* Kozo Horiike
☆ Sonny Chiba, Gerald Yamada, Doris Nakajima, Tony Cetera, Tatsuro Endo, Masashi Ishibashi

'The plentiful fight scenes are choreographed and stage-managed with unusual vigour, rising to operatic delirium for the climax.' – *Tony Rayns, MFB*

† It was followed by a sequel, *Blood of the Dragon* (qv).

Kung Pow: Enter the Fist
US 2001 81m DeLuxe Panavision
TCF/O Entertainment (Paul Marshal, Tom Koranda, Steve Oedekerk)
The adventures of The Chosen one, a master in martial arts who must do battle with a bad-tempered cow.
A parody of kung-fu movies, using an old example of the genre Tiger & Crane Fists/Hu He Shuangxing, to which Oedekerk has added new scenes and dubbed new dialogue. It's silliness is infectious.
wd Steve Oedekerk *ph* John J. Connor *pd* Hector Velez *ed* Paul Marshal
☆ Steve Oedekerk (Chosen One), Lung Fai (Master Pain), Leo Lee (Young Master Pain)

'Consistently silly and intermittently laugh-out-loud funny spoof.' – *Eddie Cockrell, Variety*

Kuroi Ame: see *Black Rain*

'Beware the haunted women who lurk in the bamboo forest as black cats craving the blood of men!'
Kuroneko ★★
Japan 1968 99m bw Tohoscope
Toho/Indai Eiga/Nihon Eiga Shinsha
aka: *Black Cat*
Raped and murdered by a wandering gang of soldiers, a woman and her daughter-in-law return as vengeful spirits, haunting a city gate and killing the samurai they meet.
A bleak and impassively elegant fable of the casual slaughters of war and the suffering of women.
wd Kaneto Shindo *ph* Kiyomi Kuroda *m* Hikaru Hayashi *ed* Hisao Enoki
☆ Kichiemon Nakamura, Nobuko Otowa, Kei Sato, Rokko Toura, Kiwako Taichi, Taiji Tonoyama, Takao Kanze

'The Film Courtney Doesn't Want You To See!'
Kurt and Courtney
GB 1998 100m colour
Downtown/Strength (Nick Broomfield)
A documentary on rock singer Kurt Cobain's suicide, in which various interested parties advance their own paranoid theories, claiming he was murdered.
Courtney Love, Cobain's widow, refused to participate in the movie or to allow his music to be played, which is here treated as an assault on civil liberties rather than the good sense it was.
d Nick Broomfield *ph* Joan Churchill *ed* Mark Atkins

'Seems a labour of hate, full of feeble excuses and sluggish charisma. It's just another way of saying "the dog ate my homework".' – *Gaby Wood, Guardian*

Kvinnodrom: see *Journey into Autumn*

Kvinnors Väntan: see *Waiting Women*

Kwaidan ★★★★
Japan 1964 164m Eastmancolor Tohoscope
Ninjin Club/Bungei
Four elegant ghost stories by Laadio Hearn.
A literally haunting film that is among the most beautiful ever made, with its succession of exotic, perfectly composed images and strange narratives.
w Yoko Mizuki *d* *Masaki Kobayashi* *ph* *Yoshio Miyajima* *m* Toru Takemitsu *ad* *Shigemasa Toda*
☆ Rentaro Mikuni, Ganjiro Nakamura, Katsuo Nakamura
🏆 best foreign film

L

L.627 ★★
France 1992 146m colour
Artificial Eye/Little Bear (Alain Sarde)

A dedicated Paris cop joins a newly established team set up to deal with drug dealers.
A documentary-style film of police at work that inevitably reveals the grim underside of urban life, and problems that defy solution.
w Michel Alexandre *d Bertrand Tavernier*
ph Alain Choquart *m* Philippe Sarde *pd* Guy-Claude François *ed* Ariane Boeglin
☆ Didier Bezace, Charlotte Kady, Philippe Torreton, Nils Tavernier, Jean-Paul Comart, Jean-Roger Milo, Lara Guirao, Cécile Garcia-Fogel, Claude Brosset
'With extraordinary documentary realism, the director has produced one of his best and most challenging films.' – *Variety*
† The title refers to the legislation against the possession and use of narcotics.

'Everything Is Suspect ... Everyone Is For Sale ... And Nothing Is What It Seems.'
LA Confidential ★★★★
US 1997 136m Technicolor Panavision
Warner/Regency (Arnon Milchan, Curtis Hanson, Michael Nathanson)

In Los Angeles in the early 50s, an incorruptible cop learns that you cannot always play by the rules.
Exemplary, excellently acted thriller of creeping corruption, full of surprises; only the coda disappoints.
w Brian Helgeland, Curtis Hanson novel James Ellroy *d Curtis Hanson ph Dante Spinotti m* Jerry Goldsmith *pd* Jeannine Oppewall *ed* Peter Honess
☆ *Kevin Spacey, Russell Crowe, Guy Pearce*, James Cromwell, David Strathairn, *Kim Basinger*, Danny DeVito, Graham Beckel
'It's not quite the full-strength java Ellroy writes, but it's about as hard as a 1990s studio picture can be.' – *Kim Newman, Empire*
'An irresistible treat with enough narrative twists and memorable characters for a half-dozen films.' – *Variety*
† It grossed around $38m in the US, and another $30m elsewhere.
Kim Basinger; Curtis Hanson, Brian Helgeland
best picture; Curtis Hanson (as director); Dante Spinotti; Jerry Goldsmith; Jeannine Oppewall; Peter Honess; sound
Peter Honess

'Something Funny Is Happening in L.A.'
L.A. Story ★
US 1991 95m Technicolor
Guild/Rastar (Daniel Melnick, Michael Rachmil)

A TV weather forecaster in Los Angeles falls for a visiting English journalist.
A pleasant romantic comedy, though the love affair is mainly with Los Angeles itself.
w Steve Martin *d* Mick Jackson *ph* Andrew Dunn *m* Peter Melnick *pd* Lawrence Miller *ed* Richard A. Harris
☆ Steve Martin, Victoria Tennant, Richard E. Grant, Marilu Henner, Sarah Jessica Parker, Susan Forristal, Kevin Pollak, Patrick Stewart
'A light-headed joyride for an audience.' – *Pauline Kael, New Yorker*

L.A. Takedown ★
US 1989 95m CFI color
Ajar/WIN (Patrick Markey)

A dedicated cop with marital problems pits his wits against a highly professional and ruthless gang.
Slick, melodramatic thriller, made for TV, which its director remade as the big-budget Heat, *starring Robert DeNiro and Al Pacino; this version is less strenuous and emphatic, and plays down the male bonding between its two protagonists.*
wd Michael Mann *ph* Ron Garcia *m* Tim Truman *pd* Dean Taucher *ed* Dov Hoenig
☆ Scott Plank, Michael Rooker, Ely Pouget, Vincent Guastaferro, Richard Chaves, Victor Rivers, Laura Harrington, Daniel Baldwin, Juan Fernandez
'A brisk little thriller, enjoyable in its own right, but fascinating as a trial run for the real thing.' – *Sight and Sound*

LA Without a Map
GB/France/Finland/Luxembourg 1998 107m
DeLuxe Technovision
United Media/Dan/Euro American/Marianna (Julie Baines, Sarah Daniel, Pierre Assouline)
An English aspiring writer falls for an American actress and follows her to Los Angeles.
Dreary, ambling narrative of uninteresting people passing the time in a futile manner.
w Mika Kaurismaki, Richard Rayner *novel* Richard Rayner *d* Mika Kaurismaki *ph* Michel Amathieu *m* Sebastien Cortella *pd* Caroline Hanania *ed* Ewa J. Lind
☆ David Tennant (Richard Tennant), Vinessa Shaw (Barbara), Julie Delpy (Julie), Vincent Gallo (Moss), Cameron Bancroft (Patterson), Joe Dallesandro (Michael), Anouk Aimée (Herself), Saskia Reeves (Joy), Margi Clarke (Bradford woman), Monte Hellman (Himself)
'A pointless, directionless film.' – *Guardian*
'Dire.' – *Alexander Walker*

'On the Long Island Expressway there are lanes going east, lanes going west, and lanes going straight to hell.'
L.I.E. ★★
US 2001 101m colour
Metro Tartan/Alter Ego/Belladonna (Linda Moran, Rene Bastian, Michael Cuesta)

In Long Island, a 15 year-old delinquent boy begins to form a relationship with a wealthy, middle-aged pederast.
Delicate account of a taboo subject, notable for Brian Cox's performance that brings humanity to the character of an ageing predator.
w Stephen M. Ryder, Michael Cuesta, Gerald Cuesta *d* Michael Cuesta *ph* Romeo Tirone *m* Pierre Foldes *pd* Elise Bennett *ed* Eric Carlson, Kane Platt
☆ *Brian Cox* (Big John Harrigan), Paul Franklin Dano (Howie Blitzer), Billy Kay (Gary Terrio), Bruce Altman (Marty Blitzer), James Costa (Kevin Cole), Tony Donnelly (Brian), Walter Masterson (Scott)
'A deeply nuanced drama full of original angles.' – *David Rooney, Variety*
'Offers a rich, dark, bitter slice of contemporary life. But the film's arty embellishments undermine its bleak vision.' – *A. O. Scott, New York Times*

The L-Shaped Room ★
GB 1962 142m bw
British Lion/Romulus (James Woolf, Richard Attenborough)

A girl intending to have an abortion takes a room in a London suburban house which is none too clean but full of characters.
Watchable, mildly sensational low-life melodrama of the pre-swinging London era when well-to-dos thought it amusing to live in garrets. Hellishly overlong but enjoyable in patches because of the professionalism with which it is made.
w Bryan Forbes novel Lynne Reid Banks *d Bryan Forbes ph* Douglas Slocombe *m* Brahms, John Barry
☆ *Leslie Caron*, Tom Bell, *Brock Peters, Cicely Courtneidge*, Bernard Lee, *Avis Bunnage, Patricia Phoenix, Emlyn Williams*
'It would be hard to imagine a more unlikely, or commercially more sure-fire group of lodgers living under a single roof than this pregnant French girl, maladjusted negro, lesbian actress, couple of prostitutes, and unpublished writer who finally commits it all to paper – shades of *I Am a Camera* as well as *A Taste of Honey*.' – *MFB*
Leslie Caron
Leslie Caron

La Bamba ★
US 1987 108m colour
New Visions/Columbia (Taylor Hackford, Bill Borden)

The brief life of 1950s rock-and-roller Ritchie Valens, who at 17 was killed in the Buddy Holly plane crash.
Palatable biopic, for those who can stand this kind of music.
wd Luis Valdez *ph* Adam Greenberg *m* Carlos Santana, Miles Goodman *pd* Vince Cresciman *ed* Sheldon Kahn, Don Brochu
☆ Lou Diamond Phillips (Ritchie Valens), Esai Morales, Rosana de Soto, Elizabeth Pena, Danielle von Zerneck, Marshall Crenshaw (Buddy Holly)

La Conga Nights
US 1940 59m bw
Universal
An elderly music moron helps to found a night-club.
Flimsy excuse for a musical, with the star playing himself, four sisters and his mother.
w Jay Dratler, Harry Clork, Paul Smith *d* Lew Landers *ph* Elwood Bredell *ad* Jack Otterson *ed* Ted J. Kent
☆ Hugh Herbert, Dennis O'Keefe, Constance Moore, Eddie Quillan

La Spagnola ★
Australia 2001 90m Atlab
Metro Tartan/AFFC/SBSIWild Strawberries (Anna-Maria Monticelli)

In a poor Spanish and Italian immigrant community in Australia in 1960, a fiery Spanish mother finds herself at odds with her teenage daughter.
Exuberant drama of frustrated love and loss, given a sometimes unsettling comic treatment.
w Anna-Maria Monticelli *d* Steve Jacobs *ph* Steve Arnold *m* Cezary Skubiszewski *pd* Dee Molineaux *ed* Alexandre de Franceshi
☆ Lola Marceli (Lola), Alice Ansara (Lucia), Lourdes Bartolome (Manola), Alex Dimitriades (Stefano), Simon Palomare (Ricardo), Silvio Ofria (Bruno), Gabrielle Marsella (Maria), Helen Thomson (Wendy)
'A portrait of loneliness and sexual longing, mixed with hatred and desperation.' – *Peter Bradhsaw, Guardian*

Laberinto de Pasiones: see *Labyrinth of Passion*

Laburnum Grove ★★
GB 1936 73m bw
ATP (Basil Dean)
A suburban father reveals he is a forger.
Agreeable worm-turns comedy melodrama, much copied since.
w Gordon Wellesley, Anthony Kimmins *play* J. B. Priestley *d Carol Reed ph* John W. Boyle
☆ Cedric Hardwicke, Edmund Gwenn, Victoria Hopper, Ethel Coleridge, Katie Johnson, Francis James
'Here at last is an English film one can unreservedly praise.' – *Graham Greene*

Labyrinth
US 1986 101m colour J-D-C Scope
Tri-Star/Eric Rattray, George Lucas

A young girl embarks on a fantasy adventure to save her stepbrother from the clutches of the Goblin King.
Bizarre but tedious attempt to create a new Alice in Wonderland, *with the inventor of the Muppets in charge. Unfortunately his creatures become less attractive with each attempt, and the script is emaciated.*
w Terry Jones, from script by Dennis Less and Jim Henson *d* Jim Henson *ph* Alex Thomson *m* Trevor Jones *pd* Elliot Scott *conceptual designer* Brian Froud
☆ David Bowie, Jennifer Connelly, Toby Froud, Shelley Thompson
'A crashing bore ... no real charm or texture to capture the imagination.' – *Variety*

Labyrinth of Passion
Spain 1982 99m colour
Metro/Alphaville/Ha Sido Producida (Andrés Santana)

original title: *Laberinto de Pasiones*
The sexual adventures of a nymphomaniac and the gay son of an emperor.
The Spanish equivalent of an Andy Warhol movie: a delirious farrago of sex and psychobabble intended to shock and amuse.
wd Pedro Almodóvar *ph* Angel L. Fernandez *pd* Pedro Almodóvar *ed* José Salcedo
☆ Cecilia Roth, Imanol Arias, Helga Liné, Marta Fernandez-Muro, Angel Alcazar, Antonio Banderas, Agustin Almodóvar
'The quintessential Spanish cult movie.' – *Sight and Sound*

The Lacemaker
France/Switzerland/West Germany 1977 107m
Eastmancolor
Action/FR3/Citel/Janus (Yves Gasser)

original title: *La Dentellière*
An 18-year-old girl becomes ill and withdrawn when her first affair breaks up.
Careful social character study, witty and observant but in memory insufficiently differentiated from numerous exploitation pieces with similar plots.
w Pascal Lainé, Claude Goretta *novel* Pascal Lainé *d* Claude Goretta *ph* Jean Boffety *m* Pierre Jansen *ad* Serge Etter, Claude Chevant *ed* Joelle van Henterre, Nelly Meunier, Martine Charasson
☆ Isabelle Huppert, Yves Beneyton, Florence Giorgetti, Anne-Marie Düringer
Isabelle Huppert

Lacombe, Lucien ★★★★
France 1974 141m Eastmancolor
Rank/NEF/UPF/Vides/Hallelujah Films (Louis Malle)

A boy is rejected for the French resistance and joins the Gestapo instead.
Tragic fable, a mite overlong, which caused its creator to migrate to America because of criticism received in France.
w Louis Malle, Patrick Modiano *d Louis Malle ph* Tonino Delli Colli *m Django Reinhardt*
☆ Pierre Blaise, Aurore Clement, Holger Lowenadler, Thérèse Gieshe
'Malle's film is a long, close look at the banality of evil; it is – not incidentally – one of the least banal movies ever made.' – *Pauline Kael, New Yorker*
best foreign film
best film

The Lad
GB 1935 74m bw
Univeral (Julius Hagen)
A good-natured con man discovers that the inhabitants of a stately home have all got secrets to hide.
Old-fashioned, stagey but neatly plotted and quite watchable comedy thriller.
w Gerard Fairlie *play* Edgar Wallace *d* Henry Edwards *ph* Sydney Blythe *md* William L. Trytel *ad* James A. Carter *ed* Lister Laurance
☆ Gordon Harker, Betty Stockfeld, Jane Carr, Gerald Barry, Michael Shepley, Geraldine Fitzgerald, Sebastian Shaw, Barbara Everest

Ladder of Swords *
GB 1988 98m
Hobo/Film Four International/British Screen/Arden (Jennifer Howarth)
A circus performer is investigated by a policeman convinced that he has murdered his wife.
Well acted but rarely believable with its contrivances of a convenient death and a dim cop.
w Neil Clarke *story* Norman Hull, Neil Clarke *d* Norman Hull *ph* Thaddeus O'Sullivan *m* Stanley Myers *pd* Caroline Hanania *ed* Scott Thomas
☆ Martin Shaw, Eleanor David, Juliet Stevenson, Bob Peck, Simon Molloy, Pearce Quigley, Anthony Benson, Graham Rigby
'The whole enterprise is marked by a nimble, self-confident energy.' – *MFB*

Laddie
US 1935 70m bw
RKO (Pandro S. Berman)
A young farmer loves the squire's daughter, but the squire says no.
Rather dim old-fashioned rural romance.
w Ray Harris, Dorothy Yost *play* Gene Stratton Porter *novel* Gene Stratton Porter *d* George Stevens
☆ John Beal, Gloria Stuart, Virginia Weidler, Charlotte Henry, Donald Crisp
† Remade in 1940 by Cliff Reid for RKO, with Tim Holt, Virginia Gilmore.

Ladies Courageous
US 1944 88m bw
Universal (Walter Wanger)
Girls ferry war planes from base for the USAF.
Absolutely predictable propaganda potboiler.
w Norman Reilly Raine, Doris Gilbert *d* John Rawlins *ph* Hal Mohr *m* Dimitri Tiomkin
☆ Loretta Young, Geraldine Fitzgerald, Diana Barrymore, Evelyn Ankers, Anne Gwynne, Philip Terry, David Bruce, Lois Collier, Samuel S. Hinds
'Needs exploitation hype to catch nominal biz ... wandering continuity fails to generate much punch.' – *Variety*

Ladies' Day
US 1943 62m bw
Bert Gilroy/RKO
A baseball pitcher loses his touch when he falls in love, so has to be kept away from his latest girl.
Mildly wacky comedy with a fairly nimble touch.
w Charles E. Roberts, Dane Lussier *play* Robert Considine, Edward C. Lilley and Bertrand Robinson *d* Leslie Goodwins
☆ Lupe Velez, Eddie Albert, Patsy Kelly, Max Baer, Jerome Cowan, Iris Adrian

Ladies in Love *
US 1936 97m bw
TCF (B. G. de Sylva)
Man-hunting girls in Budapest form a joint plan.
Amusing romantic nonsense.
w Melville Baker *play* Ladislaus Bus-Fekete *d* Edward H. Griffith *ph* Hal Mohr *md* Louis Silvers
☆ Janet Gaynor, Loretta Young, Constance Bennett, Simone Simon, Don Ameche, Paul Lukas, Tyrone Power, Alan Mowbray, Wilfrid Lawson, J. Edward Bromberg, Virginia Field

Ladies in Retirement **
US 1941 92m bw
Columbia (Lester Cowan)
A housekeeper murders her employer for the sake of her two mentally disturbed sisters.
Splendidly effective Grand Guignol, from a well-written play but filmically quite interesting. Remade with lots of gore as The Mad Room *(qv).*
w Reginald Denham, Edward Percy, Garrett Fort *play* Reginald Denham, Edward Percy *d* Charles Vidor *ph* George Barnes *m* Ernst Toch, Morris Stoloff *ad* Lionel Banks
☆ *Ida Lupino, Louis Hayward, Isobel Elsom, Edith Barrett, Elsa Lanchester,* Emma Dunn
'General excellence of script, direction, acting and mounting ... but too strong to catch general audience reaction on favourable plane.' – *Variety*
Ernst Toch, Morris Stoloff; Lionel Banks

Ladies Love Brutes
US 1930 83m bw
Paramount
A gangster tries to improve himself to marry a socialite.
Uneasy comedy-drama with good moments.
w Waldemar Young, Herman J. Mankiewicz *play* Pardon My Glove by Zoë Akins *d* Rowland V. Lee *ph* Harry Fischbeck
☆ George Bancroft, Mary Astor, Fredric March, Margaret Quimby, Stanley Fields

Ladies Love Danger
US 1935 69m bw
Fox
A playwright and amateur sleuth solves a series of murders.
Light, bright whodunnit.
w Samson Raphaelson *story* Ilya Zorn *d* H. Bruce Humberstone
☆ Gilbert Roland, Mona Barrie, Donald Cook, Adrienne Ames, Hardie Albright, Herbert Mundin
'Stronger marquee strength would have sent it into ace spots. As is, looks best for secondaries.' – *Variety*

Ladies' Man *
US 1931 70m bw
Paramount
A man of the world preys successfully on rich women until one grows jealous when her daughter falls for him.
Vivid, hard melodrama showing the blacker side of early thirties high society living.
w Herman J. Mankiewicz *d* Lothar Mendes *ph* Victor Milner
☆ William Powell, Kay Francis, Carole Lombard, Gilbert Emery, Olive Tell

'He's a hit with the misses, they go for his kisses!'
Ladies' Man
US 1947 90m bw
Paramount
A poor farmer strikes oil, becomes a millionaire, and finds himself a prize for the ladies.
Below-par comedy which wastes an agreeable cast.
w Edmund Beloin, Jack Rose and Lewis Meltzer *d* William D. Russell
☆ Eddie Bracken, Cass Daley, Virginia Welles, Spike Jones and his City Slickers

The Ladies Man
US 1961 106m Technicolor
Paramount/York (Jerry Lewis)
The adventures of an accident-prone houseboy at a Hollywood hotel for aspiring actresses.
Hit-or-miss collection of comic scraps which might have benefited from being put together on a less grandiose scale.
w Jerry Lewis, Bill Richmond *d* Jerry Lewis *ph* W. Wallace Kelley *m* Walter Scharf *ad* Hal Pereira, Ross Bellar *ed* Stanley Johnson
☆ Jerry Lewis, Helen Traubel, Jack Kruschen, Doodles Weaver, Gloria Jean, Kathleen Freeman, Hope Holiday, Pat Stanley, George Raft, Harry James and his band
'Regression into infantilism cannot be carried much further than this.' – *MFB*

'He's cool. He's clean. He's a love machine.'
The Ladies Man
US 2000 84m DeLuxe
Paramount/SNL (Lorne Michaels)
A radio sex therapist and compulsive seducer loses his job but finds true love.
Tedious, mercifully brief, comedy based on a Saturday Night Live sketch.
w Tim Meadows, Dennis McNicholas, Andrew Steele *d* Reginald Hudlin *ph* Johnny E. Jensen *m* Marcus Miller *pd* Franco De Cotiis *ed* Earl Watson
☆ Tim Meadows (Leon), Karyn Parsons (Julie), Billy Dee Williams (Lester), Will Ferrell (Lance), Lee Evans (Barney), Tiffani-Amber Thiessen (Honey DeLune), John Witherspoon (Scrap Iron), Jill Talley (Candy), Julianne Moore (Audrey)
'Where are the laughs?' – *Variety*

Ladies Must Live: see *The Home Towners*

Ladies of Leisure
US 1930 98m bw
Columbia
A gold digger gets an attack of conscience and gives up her rich fiancé.
Only fitfully interesting early Capra, with little sparkle in any department.
w Jo Swerling *play* Ladies of the Evening by Milton Herbert Gropper *d* Frank Capra *ph* Joseph Walker
☆ Barbara Stanwyck, Lowell Sherman, Ralph Graves, Marie Prevost
† The film was also released in a silent version for cinemas which had not yet been equipped for sound.

Ladies of the Big House
US 1931 77m bw
Paramount
A married couple are framed on a murder charge and sent to prison.
Melodramatic nonsense in the wake of The Big House.
w Louis Weitzenkorn *d* Marion Gering *ph* David Abel
☆ Sylvia Sidney, Gene Raymond, Wynne Gibson, Rockcliffe Fellowes, Earle Foxe
'Powerful in heart appeal and should do very well.' – *Variety*

Ladies of the Chorus
US 1948 61m bw
Columbia
A Broadway burlesque queen falls for a socialite.
Threadbare backstage support, notable only for the first leading performance of Marilyn Monroe.
w Harry Sauber and Joseph Carole *d* Phil Karlson *ph* Frank Redman *md* Mischa Bakaleinikoff
☆ Adele Jergens, Rand Brooks, Marilyn Monroe

Ladies of the Jury
US 1932 64m bw
RKO
A lady changes the minds of a murder jury to 'not guilty'.
Light-hearted early variation on Twelve Angry Men.
play Frederick Ballard *d* Lowell Sherman
☆ *Edna May Oliver,* Ken Murray, Roscoe Ates, Kitty Kelly, Guinn Williams, Cora Witherspoon
'A highly satisfying B house release.' – *Variety*

Ladies of the Park: see *Les Dames du Bois de Boulogne*

Ladies on the Rocks *
Denmark 1983 110m colour
Artificial Eye/Komme Films/Danish Film Institute
original title: *Koks I Kulissen*
Two women take their cabaret act on the road.
Small but well-observed film, with good performances.
w Christian Braad Thomsen, Helle Ryslinge, Annemarie Helger *d* Christian Braad Thomsen *ph* Dirk Bruel *m* Helle Ryslinge, Pernille Grumme, Annemarie Helger *ed* Grete Moldrup
☆ Helle Ryslinge, Annemarie Helger, Flemming Quist Moller, Hans Henrick Clemmensen, Gyda Hansen, Aksel Erhardsen

Ladies They Talk About *
US 1933 69m bw
Warner
Trouble in a women's prison.
Entertaining comedy-melodrama which had some brushes with the Hays Office because of its frankly man-hungry characters.
w Sidney Sutherland, Brown Holmes *play* Women in Prison by Dorothy Mackaye, Carlton Miles *d* Howard Bretherton, William Keighley *ph* John Seitz
☆ Barbara Stanwyck, Lyle Talbot, Preston Foster, Dorothy Burgess, Lillian Roth, Maude Eburne, Ruth Donnelly, Harold Huber
'Will get average business if sold to the hilt.' – *Variety*

Ladies Who Do
GB 1963 85m bw
British Lion/Bryanston/Fanfare (George H. Brown)
Charladies form a successful company from tips they salvage from wastepaper baskets.
Mild farce sustained by familiar actors.
w Michael Pertwee *d* C. M. Pennington-Richards *ph* Geoffrey Faithfull *m* Ron Goodwin
☆ Peggy Mount, Miriam Karlin, Robert Morley, Harry H. Corbett, Dandy Nichols

Ladri di Biciclette: see *Bicycle Thieves*

Ladri di Saponette: see *The Icicle Thief*

Il Ladro di Bambini: see *The Stolen Children*

The Lady and the Bandit
US 1951 78m bw
Columbia (Harry Joe Brown)
GB title: *Dick Turpin's Ride*
A highwayman sacrifices his own life to avenge his father and protect his wife.
Fairly pathetic example of historical whitewashing to provide minor excitements.
w Robert Libbott, Frank Burt *story* Duncan Renaldo from the poem by Alfred Noyes *d* Ralph Murphy *ph* Henry Freulich, Harry Waxman *m* George Duning
☆ Louis Hayward, Patricia Medina, Suzanne Dalbert, Tom Tully, John Williams, Alan Mowbray

The Lady and the Doctor: see *The Lady and the Monster*

The Lady and the Duke: see *L'Anglaise et Le Duc (2001)*

The Lady and the Mob
US 1939 65m bw
Columbia (Fred Kohlmar)
A lady bank owner menaced by gangsters forms her own mob.
Weak comedy.
w Richard Maibaum, Gertrude Purcell *d* Ben Stoloff *ph* John Stumar
☆ Fay Bainter, Ida Lupino, Lee Bowman, Henry Armetta, Warren Hymer, Harold Huber
'Neat, entertaining farce; rates exploitation.' – *Variety*

The Lady and the Monster
US 1944 86m bw
Republic (George Sherman)
aka: *Tiger Man*
GB title: *The Lady and the Doctor*
A scientist keeps alive the brain of a mortally injured financier, and it comes to dominate him.
Fair, over-padded version of a much filmed thriller (see also Donovan's Brain, Vengeance).
w Dane Lussier, Frederick Kohner *novel* Donovan's Brain by Curt Siodmak *d* George Sherman *ph* John Alton *m* Walter Scharf
☆ Erich von Stroheim, Richard Arlen, Vera Hruba Ralston, Mary Nash, Sidney Blackmer, Helen Vinson

The Lady and the Outlaw: see *Billy Two Hats*

Lady and the Tramp **
US 1955 76m Technicolor Cinemascope
Walt Disney (Erdmann Penner)
A pedigree spaniel falls foul of two Siamese cats and has a romantic adventure with a mongrel who helps her.
Pleasant cartoon feature in Disney's cutest and most anthropomorphic vein.
d Hamilton Luske, Clyde Geronimi, Wilfred Jackson *m* Oliver Wallace *m/ly* Peggy Lee, Sonny Burke
☆ Featuring the voices of Peggy Lee, Barbara Luddy, Bill Thompson, Bill Baucon, Stan Freberg
† *Lady and the Tramp II: Scamp's Adventure*, a direct-to-video sequel, was released in 2001.

Lady Be Good
US 1941 111m bw
MGM (Arthur Freed)

Married songwriters produce a musical.
Thin musical with good talent and tunes; very little connection with the 1924 musical show.
w Jack McGowan, Kay Van Riper, John McClain *d* Norman Z. McLeod *ph* George J. Folsey, Oliver T. Marsh *md* George Stoll *songs* various
☆ *Eleanor Powell*, Robert Young, Ann Sothern, Red Skelton, Dan Dailey, Virginia O'Brien, Reginald Owen, John Carroll, Lionel Barrymore, Jimmy Dorsey and his Orchestra
'A molasses-paced picture that extravagantly wastes talent and time ... poor direction, unimaginative story-telling and slipshod photography.' – *Variety*
♫ Songs include: 'Hang on to Me'; 'Fascinating Rhythm'; 'Lady Be Good'; 'You'll Never Know'; 'Your Words and My Music'.
song 'The Last Time I Saw Paris' (*m* Jerome Kern, *ly* Oscar Hammerstein II)

Lady By Choice *
US 1934 78m bw
Columbia
A publicity-mad dancer adopts an old rummy as a Mother's Day stunt.
Amusing sentimental comedy in the wake of Lady for A Day.
w Jo Swerling, Dwight Taylor *d* David Burton *ph* Ted Tetzlaff
☆ *Carole Lombard, May Robson*, Walter Connolly, Roger Pryor, Arthur Hohl, Raymond Walburn, James Burke, Henry Kolker
'Can very well stand on its own outside the deluxers if properly sold.' – *Variety*

Lady Caroline Lamb *
GB 1972 123m Eastmancolor Panavision
EMI/GEC/Pulsar/Video Cinematographica (Fernando Ghia)

In 1805, impulsive Lady Caroline Ponsonby marries William Lamb, later Lord Melbourne, and then disgraces him by her wildness.
Pale, disappointing historical fiction with good spots but no reverence for fact; slackly written and handled, and not helped by the wide screen.
wd Robert Bolt *ph* Oswald Morris *m* Richard Rodney Bennett *ad* Carmen Dillon
☆ Sarah Miles, Jon Finch, Richard Chamberlain (Byron), Margaret Leighton, John Mills (Canning), *Ralph Richardson* (George III), *Laurence Olivier* (Wellington)
'A period piece which rings a number of contemporary bells, both emotional and intellectual.' – *Variety*
'The film seems to have been made by a square Ken Russell.' – *Pauline Kael*

Lady Chatterley's Lover
France 1955 101m bw
Regie du Film/Orsay Film (Gilbert Cohen-Séat)
The wife of a crippled and impotent mine-owner has an affair with a coarse gamekeeper and enjoys it.
Hilariously po-faced transcription of a notorious novel, of no cinematic interest whatever.
w Gaston Bonheur, Philippe de Rothschild, Marc Allégret *novel* D. H. Lawrence *d* Marc Allégret *ph* Georges Périnal *m* Joseph Kosma
☆ Danielle Darrieux, Leo Genn, Erno Crisa

'The classic of erotic literature!'
Lady Chatterley's Lover
GB/France 1981 104m colour
Cannon/Producteurs Associés

A 'period' remake, lovingly photographed but with some risible soft porn episodes and no great interest in the acting.
w Christopher Wicking, Just Jaeckin *d* Just Jaeckin *ph* Robert Fraisse *m* Stanley Myers, Richard Harvey *pd* Anton Furst *ed* Eunice Mountjoy
☆ Sylvia Kristel, Nicholas Clay, Shane Briant, Ann Mitchell, Elizabeth Spriggs

The Lady Cop: see *La Femme-flic*

'Eve Sure Knows Her Apples!'
The Lady Eve ***
US 1941 97m bw
Paramount (Paul Jones)

A lady cardsharper and her father are outsmarted on a transatlantic liner by a millionaire simpleton; she plans an elaborate revenge.
Hectic romantic farce, the first to show its director's penchant for mixing up sexual innuendo, funny men and pratfalls. There are moments when the pace drops, but in general it's scintillating entertainment, especially after viewing its weak remake The Birds and the Bees *(qv).*
wd Preston Sturges *play* Monckton Hoffe *ph* Victor Milner *m* Leo Shuken, Charles Bradshaw *ad* Hans Dreier, Ernst Fegte *ed* Stuart Gilmore
☆ *Barbara Stanwyck, Henry Fonda, Charles Coburn, Eugène Pallette*, William Demarest, Eric Blore, Melville Cooper, Martha O'Driscoll, Janet Beecher, Robert Greig, Luis Alberni, Jimmy Conlin
'The whole theme, with all its variations of keys, is played to one end, to get laughs, and at several different levels it gets them.' – *National Board of Review*
'Preston Sturges, they tell me, is known in Hollywood as "the streamlined Lubitsch". This needn't put you off, because if he goes on producing films as lively as this one he will one day come to be known as Preston Sturges.' – *William Whitebait*
'This time Preston Sturges has wrapped you up another package that is neither very big nor very flashy, but the best fun in months.' – *Otis Ferguson*
'A mixture of visual and verbal slapstick, of high artifice and pratfalls ... it represents the dizzy high point of Sturges' writing.' – *New Yorker, 1977*
'The brightest sort of nonsense, on which Preston Sturges' signature is written large. The result has a sustained comic flavour and an individual treatment that are rarely found in Hollywood's antic concoctions.' – *New York Herald Tribune*
'A more charming or distinguished gem of nonsense has not occurred since It Happened One Night.' – *New York Times*
Monckton Hoffe (original story)

Lady for a Day ***
US 1933 95m bw
Columbia (Frank Capra)

Gangsters help an old apple seller to pose as a rich woman when her daughter visits.
Splendid sentimental comedy full of cinematic resource; the best translation of Runyon to the screen.
w Robert Riskin *story Madame La Gimp* by Damon Runyon *d* Frank Capra *ph* Joseph Walker
☆ *May Robson*, Warren William, Guy Kibbee, Glenda Farrell, Ned Sparks, Jean Parker, Walter Connolly, Nat Pendleton
'Exceptionally adroit direction and scenario ... sell it with plenty of adjectives as it will please everybody.' – *Variety*
best picture; Robert Riskin; Frank Capra; May Robson

Lady for a Night
US 1942 87m bw
Republic (Albert J. Cohen)

The lady owner of a gambling boat determines to break into society.
Moderate period comedy with a belated murder plot.
w Isabel Dawn, Boyce DeGaw *d* Leigh Jason *ph* Norbert Brodine *m* David Buttolph
☆ Joan Blondell, John Wayne, Ray Middleton, Philip Merivale, Blanche Yurka, Edith Barrett, Leonid Kinskey, Montagu Love

The Lady from Cheyenne
US 1941 87m bw
Universal (Frank Lloyd)
In 1860 Wyoming, a schoolmistress fights for women's rights.
Mild Western star romance.
w Kathryn Scola, Warren Duff *d* Frank Lloyd *ph* Milton Krasner *m* Frank Skinner
☆ Loretta Young, Robert Preston, Gladys George, Edward Arnold, Frank Craven, Jessie Ralph, Spencer Charters, Alan Bridge

Lady from Louisiana
US 1941 84m bw
Republic (Bernard Vorhaus)

In old Mississippi, a lottery-owner's daughter falls in love with a lawyer employed to make her father's business illegal.
Curious pot-boiler containing everything but the kitchen stove, including murder and a raging storm.
w Vera Caspary, Guy Endore, Michael Hogan *d* Bernard Vorhaus *ph* Jack Marta *m* Cy Feuer
☆ John Wayne, Ona Munson, Ray Middleton, Henry Stephenson, Helen Westley, Dorothy Dandridge, Jack Pennick

The Lady from Shanghai **
US 1948 87m bw
Columbia (Richard Wilson, William Castle)

A seaman becomes involved in the maritime wanderings of a crippled lawyer and his homicidal frustrated wife.
Absurd, unintelligible, plainly much cut and rearranged, this thriller was obviously left too much in Welles's hands and then just as unfairly taken out of them; but whole sequences of sheer brilliance remain, notably the final shoot-out in the hall of mirrors.
wd Orson Welles *novel If I Die Before I Wake* by Sherwood King *ph* Charles Lawton Jnr *m* Heinz Roemheld
☆ Orson Welles, Rita Hayworth, *Everett Sloane, Glenn Anders*, Ted de Corsia, Erskine Sanford, Gus Schilling
'The slurred social conscience of the hero leads him to some murky philosophizing, all of which with many individualities of diction clog the issue and the sound track. Sub-titles, I fear, would have helped.' – *Richard Winnington*

The Lady from Texas
US 1951 78m Technicolor
Universal-International (Leonard Goldstein)
A Civil War widow is thought to be committable.
Mild comedy of insanity, a pale shadow of Harvey *whose star it borrows.*
w Gerald Drayson Adams and Connie Lee Bennett *d* Joseph Pevney
☆ Josephine Hull, Mona Freeman, Howard Duff, Gene Lockhart, Craig Stevens, Ed Begley

The Lady from the Shanghai Cinema
Spain 1988 117m colour
Metro/Star/Raiz/Embrafilme/Chroma (Assunção Hernandes)
original title: *A dama do cine Shanghai*
After becoming obsessed with the wife of a lawyer who may also be a criminal, a cinema-going estate agent contemplates murder.
Murky pastiche of film noir *that deliberately confuses fantasy and reality; the central character might have been spared a great deal of misery if he had been better acquainted with Welles's* The Lady from Shanghai.
wd Guilherme Del Almeida Prado *ph* Cláudio Portioli, José Roberto Eliezer *m* Hermelino Neder *pd* Hector Gomez
☆ Maite Proença, Antonio Fagundes, José Lewgoy, Jorge Doria, José Mayer, Miguel Falabella, Paulo Villaca

'The relentless drama of a woman driven to the depths of emotion by a craving beyond control!'
The Lady Gambles
US 1949 99m bw
U-I (Michael Kraike)
A happy woman destroys her marriage when she becomes addicted to gambling.
Boring, overwrought, underplotted fiction for women.
w Roy Huggins *story* Lewis Meltzer, Oscar Saul *d* Michael Gordon *ph* Russell Metty *m* Frank Skinner *ad* Alexander Golitzen *ed* Milton Carruth
☆ Barbara Stanwyck, Robert Preston, Stephen McNally, Edith Barrett, John Hoyt
'A kind of Lost Weekend of the gaming tables.' – *Ella Smith*

Lady Godiva
US 1955 89m Technicolor
U-I (Robert Arthur)
GB title: *Lady Godiva of Coventry*
Lord Leofric tames a Saxon shrew but she suspects his motives and rides naked through the streets of Coventry to prove the loyalty of the Saxons.
Comic strip historical legend, reliably turned out for midwestern family audiences.
w Oscar Brodney, Harry Ruskin *d* Arthur Lubin *ph* Carl Guthrie *m* Hans Salter
☆ George Nader, Maureen O'Hara, Victor McLaglen, Eduard Franz, Torin Thatcher

Lady Godiva of Coventry: see *Lady Godiva*

Lady Godiva Rides Again
GB 1951 90m bw
British Lion/London Films/Sidney Gilliat, Frank Launder
A waitress wins a local beauty contest and becomes a charm school starlet and later a stripteaser.
Disappointing satirical comedy with good credentials.
w Frank Launder, Val Valentine *d* Frank Launder *ph* Wilkie Cooper *m* William Alwyn
☆ Pauline Stroud, Stanley Holloway, Diana Dors, Alastair Sim, George Cole, Dennis Price, John McCallum, Bernadette O'Farrell, Kay Kendall, Dora Bryan

Lady Hamilton: see *That Hamilton Woman*

The Lady Has Plans
US 1942 77m bw
Paramount (Fred Kohlmar)
A lady reporter in Lisbon is mistaken for a Nazi spy.
Competent fluff which veers between comedy and melodrama.
w Harry Tugend *d* Sidney Lanfield *ph* Charles Lang *m* Leo Shuken, Leigh Harline
☆ Paulette Goddard, Ray Milland, Albert Dekker, Roland Young, Margaret Hayes, Cecil Kellaway, Addison Richards, Edward Norris

Lady Ice
US 1973 92m Technicolor Panavision
Tomorrow Entertainment (Harrison Starr)

An insurance investigator steals a diamond and goes into partnership with a gangster's daughter.
Unamusing Miami-based thriller.
w Alan Trustman, Harold Clemins *d* Tom Gries *ph* Lucien Ballard *m* Perry Botkin Jnr
☆ Donald Sutherland, Jennifer O'Neil, Robert Duvall, Patrick Magee

'Because of its frank nature, we urge you – do not see it alone!'
Lady in a Cage
US 1964 97m bw
American Entertainments Corp. (Luther Davis)

A rich widow is trapped by roving marauders in her private elevator.
Unpleasant and boring suspenser with nasty details.
w Luther Davis *d* Walter Grauman *ph* Lee Garmes *m* Paul Glass *pd* Rudolf Sternad
☆ Olivia de Havilland, James Caan, Ann Sothern, Jeff Corey
'The film parades its pretensions on a note of high-pitched hysteria.' – *MFB*

Lady in a Jam
US 1942 78m bw
Universal (Gregory La Cava)
A scatterbrained socialite loses her money and inherits an Arizona farm.
A very thin vehicle for a star who deserved better.
w Eugene Thackrey, Frank Cockrell, Otho Lovering *d* Gregory La Cava *ph* Hal Mohr *m* Frank Skinner
☆ Irene Dunne, Patric Knowles, Ralph Bellamy, Eugene Pallette, Robert Homans, Samuel S. Hinds

Lady in Cement
US 1968 93m DeLuxe Panavision
TCF/Arcola/Millfield (Aaron Rosenberg)

A Florida private eye on his morning swim finds a dead blonde.
Routine private eye stuff with fashionable sex and violence added.
w Marvin H. Albert, Jack Guss *d* Gordon Douglas *ph* Joseph Biroc *m* Hugo Montenegro
☆ Frank Sinatra, Raquel Welch, Richard Conte, Martin Gabel, Lainie Kazan, Pat Henry, Steve Peck
'While Tony Rome seemed to herald a return to the forties thriller, Lady in Cement marks nothing more exciting than a return to Tony Rome.' – *MFB*

Lady in Distress: see *A Window in London*

The Lady in Question *
US 1940 81m bw
Columbia
A Parisian shopkeeper on a jury is responsible for getting a girl acquitted of a murder charge, but begins to worry when his son falls in love with her.
Stagey but quite satisfying Hollywood remake of the French drama Gribouille, *with Raimu and Michele Morgan.*
w Lewis Meltzer *story* Marcel Achard *d* Charles Vidor *ph* Lucien Andriot *m* Lucien Moraweck
☆ Brian Aherne, Rita Hayworth, Glenn Ford, Irene Rich, George Coulouris, Lloyd Corrigan, Evelyn Keyes, Edward Norris, Curt Bois, Frank Reicher

The Lady in Red
US 1979 93m Metrocolor
New World
The story of Dillinger's mistress.
Okay but uninspired gangster drama from a fresh angle.
w John Sayles *d* Lewis Teague
☆ Pamela Sue Martin, Robert Conrad, Louise Fletcher, Robert Hogan, Rod Gist

The Lady in the Car with Glasses and a Gun
France/US 1969 105m Eastmancolor
Panavision
Lira Film/Columbia (Anatole Litvak)
An English secretary in Paris decides to drive to the coast but has various adventures which make her believe she is either mad or amnesiac.
Muddled, tedious suspenser with a totally implausible 'explanation'.
w Richard Harris, Eleanor Perry *novel* Sebastien Japrisot *d* Anatole Litvak *ph* Claude Renoir *m* Michel Legrand
☆ Samantha Eggar, Oliver Reed, John McEnery, Stéphane Audran

'The minx in mink with a yen for men!'
Lady in the Dark **
US 1944 100m Technicolor
Paramount (Richard Blumenthal)
The editress of a fashion magazine is torn between three men, has worrying dreams, and takes herself to a psychoanalyst.
Lush, stylish and frequently amusing version of a Broadway musical, lacking most of the songs; despite its faults, an excellent example of studio spectacle and a very typical forties romantic comedy.
w Frances Goodrich, Albert Hackett *play* Moss Hart *d Mitchell Leisen ph Ray Rennahan m Kurt Weill md* Robert Emmett Dolan *ad Hans Dreier, Raoul Pene du Bois sp* Gordon Jennings *ly* Ira Gershwin
☆ *Ginger Rogers, Warner Baxter, Ray Milland,* Jon Hall, *Mischa Auer,* Mary Philips, Barry Sullivan
† The film was completed in 1942 but held up because of overstock.
†† Paramount chief Buddy de Sylva is credited with ruining the film by cutting the theme song, 'My Ship', which is the key to the psychoanalysis.
Ray Rennahan; Robert Emmett Dolan; art direction

Lady in the Iron Mask
US 1952 78m Natural Color
Wanger-Frenke/TCF
Princess Anne's twin sister is kept in an iron mask to prevent dispute about the succession.
Naïve twist on a well-worn legend; production values below par.
w Jack Pollexfen, Aubrey Wisberg *d* Ralph Murphy *ph* Ernest Laszlo *m* Dimitri Tiomkin
☆ Louis Hayward, Patricia Medina, Alan Hale Jnr, Judd Holdren, Steve Brodie, John Sutton

The Lady in the Lake *
US 1946 103m bw
MGM (George Haight)
A private eye is assigned to find a missing wife...
Complex private eye yarn which makes the original Chandler dialogue sound childish by over-reliance on the subjective camera method: we see the hero's face only when he looks in a mirror. An experiment that failed because it was not really understood.
w Steve Fisher *novel* Raymond Chandler *d* Robert Montgomery *ph* Paul C. Vogel *m* David Snell
☆ Robert Montgomery, Audrey Totter, Lloyd Nolan, Tom Tully, Leon Ames

Lady in the Morgue *
US 1938 70m bw
Universal
GB title: *The Case of the Missing Blonde*
A private eye investigates a suicide and uncovers three murders.
Smart 'B' feature frequently cited as a model of its kind.
w Eric Taylor, Robertson White *novel* Jonathan Latimer *d* Otis Garrett *ph* Stanley Cortez *ed* Ted J. Kent
☆ Preston Foster, Frank Jenks, Patricia Ellis, Thomas Jackson
† A previous film with the same characters and actors was *The Westland Case,* directed by Christy Cabanne in 1937.

Lady in White *
US 1988 113m DeLuxe
Virgin/New Sky Productions/Samuel Goldwyn Company (Andrew G. La Marca, Frank LaLoggia)
After seeing the ghost of a murdered girl, a young boy discovers the identity of her killer.
Modest, but rewarding, movie in its depiction of childhood traumas.
wd Frank LaLoggia *ph* Russell Carpenter *m* Frank LaLoggia *pd* Richard K. Hummel *ed* Steve Mann
☆ Lukas Haas, Len Cariou, Alex Rocco, Katherine Helmond, Jason Presson, Renata Vanni, Angelo Bertolini, Joelle Jacobi, Jared Rushton
'A ghost movie with an overcomplicated plot, but it has a poetic feeling that makes up for much of the clutter.' – *Pauline Kael, New Yorker*

The Lady Is a Square
GB 1958 99m bw
ABP/Wilcox-Neagle
An impoverished socialite widow tries to keep her husband's symphony orchestra going and is helped by a pop singer.
Strained attempt to carry on the Spring in Park Lane *tradition, with a few inspirations from Joe Pasternak and* One Hundred Men and a Girl. *Earnest performances, obvious jokes.*
w Harold Purcell, Pamela Bower, Nicholas Phipps *d* Herbert Wilcox *ph* Gordon Dines *md* Wally Stott
☆ Anna Neagle, Frankie Vaughan, Anthony Newley, Janette Scott, Wilfrid Hyde-White

The Lady Is Willing
GB 1933 74m bw
Columbia British
An ex-officer becomes a detective and takes his revenge on the financier who ruined him.
Interesting comedy-melodrama with strong cast.
w Guy Bolton *play* Louis Verneuil *d* Gilbert Miller
☆ Leslie Howard, Cedric Hardwicke, Binnie Barnes, Nigel Playfair, Nigel Bruce

The Lady Is Willing
US 1942 91m bw
Columbia (Mitchell Leisen)
A musical comedy star adopts a baby and falls in love with its pediatrician.
Dull mixture of light drama and heavy comedy, with all concerned ill at ease.
w James Edward Grant, Albert McCleery *d* Mitchell Leisen *ph* Ted Tetzlaff *m* W. Franke Harling
☆ Marlene Dietrich, Fred MacMurray, Aline MacMahon, Stanley Ridges, Arline Judge, Marietta Canty

Lady Jane
GB 1986 142m Technicolor
Paramount/Peter Snell
After the death in 1553 of Edward VI, a faction pushes into power his second cousin Lady Jane Grey.
The puzzle is why this dreary and overlong historical piece was made in an unsympathetic age; and why such an unsuitable leading lady was cast.
w David Edgar, Chris Bryant *d* Trevor Nunn *ph* Douglas Slocombe *m* Stephen Oliver *pd* Allan Cameron *ed* Anne V. Coates
☆ Helena Bonham Carter, Cary Elwes, John Wood, Michael Hordern, Jill Bennett, Jane Lapotaire, Sara Kestelman, Joss Ackland, Patrick Stewart, Richard Vernon
† The story was previously told in 1936 as *Tudor Rose.*

Lady Killer ***
US 1933 76m bw
Warner (Henry Blanke)
A cinema usher turns to crime, flees to Hollywood, and becomes a movie star.
Hectic slam-bang action comedy with melodramatic moments. Great fun.
w Ben Markson *novel* The Finger Man by Rosalind Keating Shaffer *d Roy del Ruth ph* Tony Gaudio *md* Leo F. Forbstein
☆ *James Cagney,* Mae Clarke, Leslie Fenton, Margaret Lindsay, Henry O'Neill, Willard Robertson, Raymond Hatton, Russell Hopton
'An all-time high in roughneck character work even for this rough-and-tumble star.' – *Variety*
'A kind of résumé of everything he has done to date in the movies.' – *New York Evening Post*
'Sprightly, more or less daring, thoroughly entertaining.' – *New York World Telegram*

The Lady Killers: see *The Ladykillers*

Lady L
France/Italy/US 1965 124m Eastmancolor
Panavision
Concordia/Champion/MGM (Carlo Ponti)
An 80-year-old lady recalls her romantic life from her youth as a Paris laundress.
Unhappy, lumbering, styleless attempt to recapture several old forms, indifferently though expensively made and acted.
wd Peter Ustinov *novel* Romain Gary *ph* Henri Alekan *m* Jean Françaix *ad* Jean D'Eaubonne, Auguste Capelier
☆ Sophia Loren, David Niven, Paul Newman, Peter Ustinov, Claude Dauphin, Philippe Noiret, Michel Piccoli, Marcel Dalio, Cecil Parker, Eugène Deckers

Lady, Let's Dance
US 1944 86m bw
Scott R. Dunlap/Monogram
An entertainment director for a California resort needs a new star.
Thin musical with production values ambitious for its source.
w Peter Milne and Paul Gerard Smith *d* Frank Woodruff
☆ Belita, James Ellison, Frick and Frack, Walter Catlett, Lucien Littlefield
Edward Kay (music); song 'Silver Shadows and Golden Dreams' (mLew Pollack, lyCharles Newman)

The Lady Lies
US 1929 75m bw
Paramount
A wealthy widowed attorney courts a working-class girl and offends his children.
Dated melodrama in primitive talkie technique.
w John Meehan, Garrett Fort *d* Hobart Henley
☆ Walter Huston, Claudette Colbert, Charles Ruggles, Tom Brown

Lady Luck
US 1946 97m bw
RKO (Warren Duff)
The daughter of a long line of ill-fated gamblers marries one and tries to reform him, but the reverse happens.
Tedious comedy drama.
w Lynn Root, Frank Fenton *d* Edwin L. Marin *ph* Lucien Andriot *m* Leigh Harline
☆ Robert Young, Barbara Hale, Frank Morgan, James Gleason, Don Rice, Harry Davenport, Lloyd Corrigan

'Music...Mystery...Murder...!'
Lady of Burlesque *
US 1943 91m bw
Hunt Stromberg
GB title: *Striptease Lady*
A burlesque dancer solves a number of backstage murders.
Agreeable murder mystery with strong injections of comedy.
w James Gunn *novel The G-String Murders* by Gypsy Rose Lee *d* William A. Wellman *ph* Robert de Grasse *m* Arthur Lange
☆ Barbara Stanwyck, Michael O'Shea, J. Edward Bromberg, Iris Adrian, Gloria Dickson, Charles Dingle
Arthur Lange

Lady of Deceit: see *Born to Kill*

Lady of Scandal
US 1930 67m bw
MGM
The son of a noble house wants to marry an actress, but the family is nasty to her.
Dated melodrama with sophisticated comedy asides.
w Hans Kraly *play The High Road* by Frederick Lonsdale *d* Sidney Franklin
☆ Ruth Chatterton, Basil Rathbone, Ralph Forbes, Nance O'Neil, Frederick Kerr, Herbert Bunston
'Should register well in any but the lowest grind.' – *Variety*

Lady of Secrets
US 1936 73m bw
B. P. Schulberg/Columbia
A rich girl's father prevents her marriage without knowing that she is pregnant.
Complicated and very boring mother-love yarn with the faint perfume of a bygone age.
w Joseph Anthony, Zoe Akins, Katherine Brush *d* Marion Gering
☆ Ruth Chatterton, Otto Kruger, Lionel Atwill, Lloyd Nolan, Marian Marsh, Elizabeth Risdon
'Chatterton, back to the screen after a long absence, is still having trouble with her offspring. This time she is also having trouble with the play, the direction, and the photography.' – *Variety*

Lady of the Boulevards: see *Nana*

The Lady of the Camelias (dubbed)
France/Italy/Germany 1981 121m Technicolor
Gaumont/Films du Losange/FR3/Opera/Tele-München (Margaret Menegoz, Monolo Bolognini)
original title: *La Dame aux Camélias*
As Alexandre Dumas rehearses his play *La Dame aux Camélias,* he recalls the tragic life of Alphonsine Plessis, the courtesan who was the model for its central character.
Uninspired and ponderous period drama, lacking in any sign of passion; what little life it might have had has been flattened by the dubbing.
w Enrico Medioli, Lucien Jean Aurenche, Vladimir Pozner *d* Mauro Bolognini *ph* Ennio Guarnieri *m* Ennio Morricone *ad* Mario Garbuglia *ed* Nino Baragli
☆ Isabelle Huppert, Gian Maria Volonte, Bruno Ganz, Fabrizio Bentivoglio, Fernando Rey, Clio Goldsmith, Mario Maranzana, Carla Fracci

Lady of the Night (dubbed)
Italy 1986 100m Telecolor
San Francisco/Metrofilm (Giovanni Bertolucci)
original title: *La Signora della Notte*
After three years of marriage, a wife decides she wants to have sex with strangers.
Risible and sleazy sexploitation movie, full of violence towards women.
w Galliano Juso, Piero Schivazappa *d* Piero Schivazappa *ph* Giuseppe Ruzzolini *m* Guido and Maurizio de Angelis *ad* Bruno Amalfitano *ed* Daniele Alabiso
☆ Serena Grandi, Fabio Sartor, Francesca Topi, Alberto di Stasio, Emanuela Taschini, Stanko Molnar

Lady of the Tropics
US 1939 92m bw
MGM (Sam Zimbalist)
An American playboy in Saigon marries a half-caste girl but her former admirer prevents her from getting a passport.
Interminable romantic melodrama with stars apparently straight from the taxidermist.
w Ben Hecht *d* Jack Conway *ph* George Folsey *m* Franz Waxman
☆ Robert Taylor, Hedy Lamarr, Joseph Schildkraut, Gloria Franklin, Ernest Cossart

'Mediocre and stagey romance, but stars should pull it through.' – *Variety*

Lady on a Train *
US 1945 84m bw
Universal (Felix Jackson)
A girl arriving in New York by train sees a murder committed and can't make anyone believe her.
Cheerful mystery which starts in the right spirit but does not progress too satisfactorily.
w Edmund Beloin, Robert O'Brien *novel* Leslie Charteris *d* Charles David *ph* Elwood Bredell *m* Miklos Rozsa *ad* John B. Goodman, Abraham Grossman *ed* Ted J. Kent
☆ Deanna Durbin, Ralph Bellamy, David Bruce, Edward Everett Horton, George Coulouris, Allen Jenkins, Dan Duryea, Patricia Morison

The Lady Pays Off
US 1951 80m bw
Universal-International (Albert J. Cohen)
A gambling schoolteacher agrees to pay off her debts by tutoring the casino owner's daughter.
Flat and unprofitable romantic comedy-drama.
w Frank Gill Jnr, Albert J. Cohen *d* Douglas Sirk *ph* William H. Daniels *m* Frank Skinner
☆ Linda Darnell, Stephen McNally, Gigi Perreau, Virginia Field, Ann Codee
'The sort of thing that people who shun the cinema imagine all films to be.' – C. A. *Lejeune*

Lady Possessed
US 1952 86m bw
Republic/Portland (James Mason)
An unbalanced woman imagines she is destined to take the place of a pianist's dead wife.
Weary melodramatic nonsense dating from Hollywood's first obsession with psychiatry.
w Pamela Kellino, James Mason *novel* Del Palma by Pamela Kellino *d* William Spier, Roy Kellino *ph* Karl Struss *m* Nathan Scott
☆ James Mason, June Havoc, Stephen Dunne, Fay Compton, Pamela Kellino, Steven Geray

The Lady Says No
US 1951 83m bw
UA/Stillman (Frank Ross, John Stillman Jnr)
A magazine photographer tames a female chauvinist author.
Very silly comedy with neither wit nor style.
w Robert Russell *d* Frank Ross *ph* James Wong Howe *m* Emil Newman
☆ Joan Caulfield, David Niven, James Robertson Justice, Lenore Lonergan, Henry Jones

Lady Scarface
US 1941 69m bw
RKO (Cliff Reid)
A police lieutenant captures a dangerous female gangster.
Weird gangster second feature with too many domestic comedy asides; notable only for the appearance in it of its dignified lead, fresh from Rebecca.
w Arnaud D'Usseau, Richard Collins *d* Frank Woodruff *ph* Nicholas Musuraca
☆ Judith Anderson, Dennis O'Keefe, Frances Neal, Mildred Coles, Eric Blore, Marc Lawrence

Lady Sings the Blues *
US 1972 144m Eastmancolor Panavision
Paramount/Motown/Weston/Furie (Jay Weston, James S. White)
The disastrous private life of jazz singer Billie Holiday.
Old-fashioned showbiz biopic with new-fashioned drugs, sex and squalor.
w Terence McCloy, Chris Clark, Suzanne de Passe *d* Sidney J. Furie *ph* John Alonzo *m* Michel Legrand *md* Gil Askey
☆ *Diana Ross*, Billy Dee Williams, Richard Pryor, James Callahan, Sid Melton
script; Gil Askey; Diana Ross

A Lady Surrenders
US 1930 95m bw
Universal
A misunderstanding turns an innocent husband into a bigamist after his wife has supposedly divorced him.
Totally effete romantic drama with no comedy relief.
w Gladys Lehman *novel* Sincerity by John Erskine *d* John Stahl
☆ Conrad Nagel, Genevieve Tobin, Basil Rathbone, Rose Hobart, Carmel Myers
'It fails from all angles: too stilted, slow, talky and punchless.' – *Variety*

A Lady Surrenders: see *Love Story (1944)*

A Lady Takes a Chance
US 1943 86m bw
RKO (Frank Ross)
aka: *The Cowboy and the Girl*
A New York office girl on holiday in Oregon falls for a rodeo rider.
Slender star action romance.
w Robert Ardrey *d* William A. Seiter *ph* Frank Redman *m* Roy Webb
☆ Jean Arthur, John Wayne, Charles Winninger, Phil Silvers, Mary Field, Don Costello, John Philliber, Grady Sutton, Hans Conried

The Lady Takes a Flyer
US 1958 95m Eastmancolor Cinemascope
Universal-International (William Alland)
A pilot's wife finds that life at home is not easy, especially with a baby.
Heavy comedy or light drama; on either count a bore.
w Danny Arnold *d* Jack Arnold
☆ Lana Turner, Jeff Chandler, Richard Denning, Chuck Connors, Andra Martin

The Lady Takes a Sailor *
US 1949 99m bw
Warner
A girl devoted to telling the truth insists on proving her story of a mysterious submarine which saved her after a sailing accident.
Curious romantic farce with echoes of the old slapstick tradition.
w Everett Freeman *d* Michael Curtiz *ph* Ted McCord *m* Max Steiner
☆ Jane Wyman, Dennis Morgan, Eve Arden, Allyn Joslyn, Robert Douglas, William Frawley

A Lady to Love
US 1930 92m bw
MGM
An ageing grape grower spots an attractive waitress, sends her a marriage proposal by mail, but encloses a photo of his handsome foreman.
Rather primitive but well-acted version of a subject later filmed more fluently under the title of the original play.
w Sidney Howard *play* They Knew What They Wanted by Sidney Howard *d* Victor Seastrom *ph* Merritt B. Gerstad
☆ Edward G. Robinson, Vilma Banky, Robert Ames, Richard Carle
'A hit as a talker: well directed, acted and treated.' – *Variety*

Lady Tubbs
US 1935 69m bw
Universal
An ex-cook crashes society and shows up the pretenders.
Mildly agreeable sentimental farce.
w Barry Trivers *novel* Homer Croy *d* Alan Crosland
☆ Alice Brady, Douglass Montgomery, Anita Louise, Alan Mowbray, Minor Watson, Russell Hicks, Hedda Hopper
'Solid laugh fare for the nabes.' – *Variety*

'Spies! Playing the game of love – and sudden death!'
The Lady Vanishes ****
GB 1938 97m bw
Gaumont British/Gainsborough (Edward Black)
En route back to England by train from Switzerland, an old lady disappears and two young people investigate.
The disappearing lady trick brilliantly refurbished by Hitchcock and his screenwriters, who even get away with a horrid model shot at the beginning. Superb, suspenseful, brilliantly funny, meticulously detailed entertainment.
w Sidney Gilliat, Frank Launder novel The Wheel Spins by Ethel Lina White *d Alfred Hitchcock ph* Jack Cox *md* Louis Levy
☆ *Margaret Lockwood, Michael Redgrave, Dame May Whitty, Paul Lukas, Basil Radford, Naunton Wayne, Catherine Lacey, Cecil Parker, Linden Travers*, Googie Withers, *Mary Clare*, Philip Leaver
'If it were not so brilliant a melodrama, we should class it as a brilliant comedy.' – *Frank S. Nugent*
'No one can study the deceptive effortlessness with which one thing leads to another without learning where the true beauty of this medium is to be mined.' – *Otis Ferguson*
'Directed with such skill and velocity that it has come to represent the very quintessence of screen suspense.' – *Pauline Kael, 70s*
† Hitchcock was actually second choice as director. The production was ready to roll as *Lost Lady*, directed by Roy William Neill, with Charters and Caldicott already in place, when Neill became unavailable and Hitch stepped in.

The Lady Vanishes
GB 1979 97m Eastmancolor
Panavision
Rank/Hammer (Michael Carreras, Tom Sachs)
A remake of the above in which everything goes wrong: wrong shape, wrong actors, wrong style (or lack of it).
Reasonable adherence to the original script can't save it.
w George Axelrod *d* Anthony Page *ph* Douglas Slocombe *m* Richard Hartley *pd* Wilfred Shingleton
☆ Cybill Shepherd, Elliott Gould, Angela Lansbury, Herbert Lom, Arthur Lowe, Ian Carmichael, Gerald Harper, Jenny Runacre, Jean Anderson

The Lady Wants Mink
US 1953 92m Trucolor
Republic (Herbert J. Yates)
A wife causes domestic upsets when she decides to start a mink farm in order to get the fur coat that she has always wanted.
A by-the-numbers comedy which comes to the predictable conclusions that the rural life is better than an urban existence and that money can't buy happiness; it fails to convince or even amuse.
w Dane Lussier, Richard Alan Simmons *story* Leonard Neubauer, Lou Schor *d* William A. Seiter *ph* Reggie Lanning *m* Stanley Wilson *ad* Martin Obzina *ed* Fred Allen
☆ Dennis O'Keefe, Ruth Hussey, Eve Arden, William Demarest, Gene Lockhart, Hope Emerson, Hillary Brooke, Tommy Rettig

Lady Windermere's Fan *
US 1925 80m (24 fps) bw silent
Warner
The mysterious Mrs Erlynne almost causes a scandal in London society.
Oscar Wilde's play transposed to the twenties, with the Lubitsch touch daringly displacing Wildean epigrams. Still more amusing than the sound remake, The Fan.
w Julien Josephson d Ernst Lubitsch ph Charles Van Enger
☆ *Ronald Colman*, May McAvoy, Irene Rich, Bert Lytell, Edward Martindel
'Lubitsch's best silent film, full of incisive details, discreet touches, nuances of gestures, where behaviour betrays the character and discloses the sentiment of the personages.' – *Georges Sadoul*

Lady Windermere's Fan: see *The Fan (1949)*

The Lady with a Lamp *
GB 1951 110m bw
British Lion/Imperadio (Herbert Wilcox)
The life of Florence Nightingale and her work in reforming the nursing service in 19th-century England.
Solid biopic, not quite in accord with history.
w Warren Chetham Strode *play* Reginald Berkeley *d* Herbert Wilcox *ph* Max Greene *m* Anthony Collins *ad* William C. Andrews
☆ Anna Neagle, Michael Wilding, Gladys Young, Felix Aylmer, Julian D'Albie, Arthur Young, Edwin Styles, Barbara Couper, Cecil Trouncer, Rosalie Crutchley
'A slow, sedate, refined chronicle ... Herbert Wilcox is a good deal more at ease with the balls and dinners, than with anything that happens later.' – *Penelope Houston*
'It may please fans of Anna Neagle and Michael Wilding, but not fans of Florence Nightingale.' – *Richard Mallett, Punch*

Lady with a Past *
US 1932 80m bw
RKO (Charles R. Rogers)
GB title: *Reputation*
A wealthy but shy girl almost accidentally finds herself with a reputation as a scarlet woman, and the men flock around her.
Moderately enjoyable star comedy drama.
w Horace Jackson *novel* Harriet Henry *d* Edward H. Griffith *ph* Hal Mohr *m* Max Steiner
☆ Constance Bennett, Ben Lyon, David Manners, Astrid Allwyn, Merna Kennedy, Blanche Frederici, Nella Walker
'Light and satisfying material for the women.' – *Variety*

The Lady with Red Boots (dubbed) *
France/Spain 1974 98m colour
UGC/CFDC (Claude Jaeger, Daniel Carrillo)
original title: *La Femme aux Bottes Rouges*
A poor and glamorous avant-garde novelist is attracted to a married publisher, and attracts in turn the attentions of a mysterious financier.
Enjoyably quirky study in obsession, with surrealist overtones.
w Pierre Jean Maintigneux, Jean-Claude Carrière, Clem Wood, Juan Buñuel *d* Juan Buñuel *ph* Leopold Villasenor *ad* Adolfe Cofino *ed* Genevieve Vaury, Maryse Siclier
☆ Catherine Deneuve, Fernando Rey, Adalberto Maria Merli, Jacques Weber, Jose Sacristan, Emma Cohen, Laura Betti

Lady with Red Hair *
US 1940 78m bw
Warner (Edmund Grainger)
The life of actress Mrs Leslie Carter and her association with impresario David Belasco.
Mildly interesting but unsatisfying biopic of a lady scarcely remembered.
w Charles Kenyon, Milton Krims, N. Brewster Morse, Norbert Faulkner *d* Curtis Bernhardt *ph* Arthur Edeson *m* Heinz Roemheld
☆ Miriam Hopkins, Claude Rains, Richard Ainley, John Litel, Laura Hope Crews, Helen Westley, Mona Barrie, Victor Jory, Cecil Kellaway, Fritz Leiber, Halliwell Hobbes

The Lady with the Little Dog *
USSR 1959 90m bw
Lenfilm
original title: *Dama s Sobachkoi*
In Yalta at the turn of the century, an unhappily married woman and a married man start an affair which lasts secretly over the years.
Modestly pleasing, subtly acted anecdote.
wd Josef Heifits story Anton Chekhov *ph* Andrei Moskvin *m* Jiri Sternwald *ed* D. Meschiev
☆ Iya Savvina, Alexei Batalov, Ala Chostakova

A Lady without Passport *
US 1950 84m bw
MGM (Samuel Marx)
A secret service undercover man tracks down aliens being smuggled into the US, and falls in love with one of them.
Routine material, very well handled.
w Howard Dimsdale *story* Lawrence Taylor *d Joseph H. Lewis ph* Paul C. Vogel *m* David Raksin
☆ Hedy Lamarr, John Hodiak, James Craig, George Macready, Steve Geray

Ladybird Ladybird **
GB 1994 101m colour
UIP/Parallax/Film Four (Sally Hibbin)
An unmarried mother whose four children have been taken into care also loses her next two to the social services, despite a stable relationship with a Paraguayan refugee.
A fierce and passionate attack on official attitudes to the unconforming, based on a true story – although the facts, or the interpretation of them here, have been questioned since the film's release. It gains from its powerful performance by Crissy Rock.
w Rona Munro *d* Ken Loach *ph* Barry Ackroyd *m* George Fenton, Mauricio Venegas *pd* Martin Johnson *ed* Jonathan Morris
☆ *Crissy Rock*, Vladimir Vega, Sandie Lavelle, Mauricio Venegas, Ray Winstone, Clare Perkins, Luke Brown, Lilly Farrell, Jason Strachey

'A Comedy With Balls.'

Ladybugs

US 1992 90m DeLuxe
Warner/Morgan Creek (Albert S. Ruddy, Andre E. Morgan)

A salesman takes over managership of a women's soccer team and has his son join it in drag.
Dismayingly stupid comedy that is embarrassing to watch.
w Curtis Burch *d* Sidney J. Furie *m* Richard Gibbs *pd* Robb Wilson King *ed* John W. Wheeler, Timothy N. Board
☆ Rodney Dangerfield, Jackée, Jonathan Brandis, Ilene Graff, Vinessa Shaw, Tom Parks
'This picture doesn't deserve any respect. Sexist, homophobic and woefully unfunny to boot, Rodney Dangerfield's latest starring effort is a waste of comic talent.' – *Variety*
'This week's candidate for the worst film in history.' – *Geoff Brown, The Times*

'Cursed for eternity! No force in heaven will release them ... no power on earth can save them!'

Ladyhawke

US 1985 124m Technicolor
Technovision
Warner/Richard Donner, Lauren Schuler

Medieval boy and girl lovers have been changed respectively into a wolf and a hawk, never simultaneously to resume their true forms.
Unpersuasive legend, dolefully told at excessive length.
w Edward Khmara, Michael Thomas, Tom Mankiewicz *d* Richard Donner *ph* Vittorio Storaro *m* Andrew Powell *pd* Wolf Kroeger *ed* Stuart Baird
☆ Matthew Broderick, Rutger Hauer, Michelle Pfeiffer, Leo McKern, John Wood

The Ladykillers ***

GB 1955 97m Technicolor
Ealing (Michael Balcon)

An old lady takes in a sinister lodger, who with his four friends commits a robbery. When she finds out, they plot to kill her, but are hoist with their own petards.
Witty black comedy, shot in muted colours, which approaches the grotesque without damaging its acerbic humour or sense of fantasy; it is one of the few films where death is both shocking and funny.
w William Rose d Alexander Mackendrick ph Otto Heller *m* Tristram Cary *ad* Jim Morahan *ed* Jack Harris
☆ Alec Guinness, *Katie Johnson*, Peter Sellers, Cecil Parker, Herbert Lom, Danny Green, Jack Warner, Frankie Howerd, Kenneth Connor
'To be frivolous about frivolous matters, that's merely boring. To be frivolous about something that's in some way deadly serious, that's true comedy.' – *Alexander Mackendrick*
'The acting is triumphant ... Artistically, I suspect, *The Ladykillers* needs a shade more of the macabre; it would be a better film if it were blacker. But I am beginning to find that I can see a joke better in twilight than midnight.' – *Dilys Powell*
'This sinister black comedy of murder accelerates until it becomes a grotesque fantasy of murder. The actors seem to be having a boisterous good time getting themselves knocked off.' – *Pauline Kael*
'One of the neatest blends of the mirthful and macabre I can remember.' – *Fred Majdalany, Time and Tide*
'Undoubtedly the most stylish, inventive and funniest British comedy of the year.' – *Alan Brien, London Evening Standard*
† The role of Professor Marcus, played by Alec Guinness, was originally intended for Alistair Sim. It has been claimed, though Guinness has denied it, that his toothy appearance was based on the critic Kenneth Tynan who worked for Ealing as a script editor.
William Rose
Katie Johnson; William Rose

The Lady's from Kentucky

US 1939 75m bw
Jeff Lazarus/Paramount
A crooked bookie is reformed by a lady horse breeder.
Yawnworthy drama with an unattractive hero.
w Malcolm Stuart Boylan *d* Alexander Hall
☆ George Raft, Ellen Drew, Hugh Herbert, ZaSu Pitts, Louise Beavers, Forrester Harvey
'It starts with promise, stumbles in the middle section, and drags itself across the line for the finish.' – *Variety*

A Lady's Morals

US 1930 86m bw
MGM
GB title: *Jenny Lind*
aka: *The Soul Kiss*
The 'Swedish nightingale' learns that love is more important than a singing career.
Cliché-strewn romance with music.
w Hans Kraly, Claudine West, John Meehan, Arthur Richman *d* Sidney Franklin *m* Herbert Stothart
☆ Grace Moore, Reginald Denny, Wallace Beery, Jobyna Howland
'Class production of money potentialities.' – *Variety*
† Wallace Beery played P. T. Barnum, a role he was to repeat four years later in *The Mighty Barnum*.

Lafayette

France/Italy 1961 158m Super Technirama 70
Copernic/Cosmos (Maurice Jacquin)
French officers help America in the revolutionary war of 1776.
Nerveless international epic, interesting only for its star cameos.
w Jean-Bernard Luc, Suzanne Arduini, Jacques Sigurd, François Ponthier, Jean Dréville, Maurice Jacquin *d* Jean Dréville *ph* Claude Renoir, Roger Hubert *m* Steve Laurent, Pierre Duclos
☆ Michel Le Royer, Jack Hawkins, Orson Welles, Howard St John, Vittorio de Sica, Edmund Purdom, Jacques Castelot, Folco Lulli
'It looks, sounds and smells like nothing so much as the same old indigestible, ill-dubbed, co-produced continental spectaculars which have already turned the stomach in a whole range of lesser screen ratios.' – *MFB*
'A totally forgettable film... the only bit of acting I have ever done soley for money.' – *Jack Hawkins*

Lafayette Escadrille

US 1957 93m bw
Warner (William Wellman)
GB title: *Hell Bent for Glory*
Early in World War I, a young American joins the French air force.
The director's valedictory film, on a subject close to his heart, is a curiously disappointing, flat and disjointed affair, partly salvaged by a good period feel.
w A. S. Fleischman *d* William A. Wellman *ph William Clothier m* Leonard Rosenman
☆ Tab Hunter, Etchika Choreau, David Janssen, Clint Eastwood, Will Hutchins, Paul Fix

'Once Upon A Time In India'

Lagaan **

India 2001 224m colour 'Scope
SET/Jhamu Sughand (Aamir Khan)

In 1893, Indian villagers play a cricket match against the ruling British to determine whether they will have to pay an agricultural tax.
Accomplished, well-acted Bollywood epic, with at its centre a three-day cricket match that seems almost as long on-screen as it would be in real life.
w Ashutosh Gowariker, Kumar Dave, Sanjay Dayma, K. P. Saxena *d Ashutosh Gowariker ph Anil Mehta m/ly* A. R. Rahman, Javed Akhtar *pd* Nitin Chandrakant Desai *ed* Ballu Saluja *cos* Bhanu Athaiya
☆ Aamir Khan (Bhuvan), Gracy Singh (Gauri), Rachel Shelley (Elizabeth Russell), Paul Blackthorne (Capt. Andew Russell), Suhasini Mulay (Yashodamai), Kulbhushan Kharbanda (Rajah Puran Singh), Raghuveer Yadav (Bhura), Rajendra Gupta (Mukhiya), Jeremy Child (Major Cotton)
'Lagaan employs all the established narrative devices of commercial Hindi cinema – songs and dances, dramatic flashpoints, love stories, et al – but it is anything but a formula film.' – *Hindustan Times*
'Larger than life and outrageously enjoyable, it's got a dash of spaghetti western, a hint of Kurosawa, with a bracing shot of Kipling.' – *Peter Bradshaw, Guardian*
foreign language film

The Lair of the White Worm

GB 1988 93m Technicolor
Vestron (Ken Russell)

A female vampire attempts to make human sacrifices to an ancient snake god.
Grotesque horror done without finesse or subtlety.
wd Ken Russell *novel* Bram Stoker *ph* Dick Bush *m* Stanlislas Syrewicz *ed* Peter Davies *sp* Geoff Portass
☆ Amanda Donohoe, Hugh Grant, Catherine Oxenberg, Peter Capaldi, Sammi Davis, Stratford Johns, Paul Brooke, Imogen Claire, Christopher Gable
'He proves incapable of handling straight suspense, horror, or supernatural sequences.' – *MFB*
'How on earth can you take seriously the vision of Catherine Oxenberg, dressed in Marks & Spencer's underwear, being sacrificed to a fake, phallic worm two hundred feet long?' – *Ken Russell*

Laissez-Passer **

France/Germany/Spain 2001 170m colour
'Scope
Artificial Eye/Alain Sarde/Little Bear/France 3/France 2/KC Medien/Vertigo

aka: *Safe Conduct*
In occupied France in the early 40s, a womanising screenwriter and an assistant director, who is also a Resistance fighter, go to work for a production company controlled by the Nazis.
Fascinating true story of the wartime experiences of two actual French filmmakers, Jean Aurenche and Jean Devaivre, that raises still vital questions about compromise, survival and artistic integrity.
w Jean Cosmos, Bertrand Tavernier *d* Bertrand Tavernier *ph* Alain Choquart *pd* Emile Ghigo *ed* Sophie Brunet
☆ Jacques Gamblin (Jean Devaivre), Denis Podalydes (Jean Aurenche), Christian Berkel (Dr Greven), Marie Gillain (Olga), Charlotte Kady (Suzanne Raymond), Marie Desgranges (Simone Devaivre), Thierry Gibault (Paul Maillebuau), Christophe Odent (Pierre Bost)
'An extended chamber piece, full of secrecy, agony, domestic comedy and rolled out at great, if indulgent length: a Bayeux tapestry of personal tension.' – *Peter Bradshaw, Guardian*
'Entrancing, rueful inquiry into movies as historical cross-examination.' – *Michael Atkinson, Village Voice*

Lake Consequence

US 1992 90m colour
Rank/10dB/Zalman King (Avram Butch Kaplan)

A housewife who was gang-raped by a rock band wants more of the same.
Glossy, cliché-ridden would-be erotica for the easily pleased.
w Zalman King, Melanie Finn, Henry Cobbold *story* MacGregor Douglas *d* Rafael Eisenman *ph* Harris Savides *m* George S. Clinton *pd* Dominic Watkins *ed* James Gavin Bedford, Curtis Edge
☆ Billy Zane, Joan Severance, May Karasun, Whip Hubley, Courtland Mead, Dan Reed, Christi Allen
'Slickly shot, but over dramatised (some of the editing is positively epileptic) at the expense of any remotely believable dialogue or acting, this, given its pedigree, is high on sauce but low on just about everything else.' – *Empire*

'You'll never know what bit you.'

Lake Placid

US 1999 82m Technicolor Panavision
TCF/Fox 2000/Phoenix/Rocking Chair (David E. Kelley, Michael Pressman)

A New York expert investigates reports of giant crocodiles inhabiting a lake in northern Maine.
A cheapjack horror movie that puts the emphasis on jokes, but a few good one-liners are not enough to enliven so much predictability.
w David E. Kelley *d* Steve Miner *ph* Daryn Okada *m* John Ottman *pd* John Willett *ed* Marshall Harvey, Paul Hirsch *sp* Stan Winston
☆ Bill Pullman (Jack Wells), Bridget Fonda (Kelly Scott), Oliver Platt (Hector Cyr), Brendan Gleeson (Sheriff Hank Keough), Betty White (Mrs Delores Bickerman), David Lewis (Walt Lawson), Tim Dixon (Stephen Daniel), Natassia Malthe (Janine), Mariska Hargitay (Myra Okubo), Meredith Salenger (Deputy Sharon Gare)
'A B-movie dud.' – *Entertainment Weekly*

Lake Placid Serenade

US 1944 85m bw
Republic (Harry Grey)
A Czech girl skater is sent to America to represent her country.
Simple-minded entertainment overloaded with musical numbers.
w Dick Irving Hyland, Doris Gilbert *book* Frederick Kohner *d* Steve Sekely
☆ Vera Hruba Ralston, Robert Livingston, Eugene Pallette, Vera Vague, Walter Catlett, Lloyd Corrigan, William Frawley

Lamb

GB 1986 110m Eastmancolor
Cannon/Flickers/Limehouse/Channel 4 (Neil Zeiger)

A young priest at a harsh Irish reform school absconds with a 14-year-old pupil, an act with tragic consequences for them both.
Rather wearisome transcription of religious thesis into makeshift drama: disturbing but not satisfying.
w Bernard MacLaverty *novel* Bernard MacLaverty *d* Colin Gregg *ph* Mike Garfath *m* Van Morrison *pd* Austen Spriggs *ad* Peter Delfgou
☆ Liam Neeson, Hugh O'Conor, Harry Towb, Frances Tomelty, Ian Bannen

Lambada

US 1990 98m Alpha Cine Panavision
Warner/Cannon/Film and Television Company (Peter Shepherd)

A teacher spends his nights as a lambada dancer so that he can give lessons to a gang of dropouts.
Dismal attempt to cash in on a short-lived American dance craze.
w Joel Silberg, Sheldon Renan *d* Joel Silberg *ph* Roberto D'Ettore Piazzoli *m* Greg DeBelles *pd* Bill Cornfield *ed* Marcus Manton
☆ J. Eddie Peck, Melora Hardin, Shabba-Doo, Ricky Paul Goldin, Basil Hoffman, Dennis Burkley, Keene Curtis

Lambada: Forbidden Dance

US 1990 97m Foto-Kem
Columbia/21st Century (Richard L. Albert, Marc S. Fischer)

aka: *The Forbidden Dance*
aka: *Lambada: Baile Prohibido*
A Brazilian princess travels to Los Angeles to try to save her rain-forest from being destroyed by American developers – and becomes a lambada dancer so she can make a public appeal on television.
Risibly clumsy attempt to exploit both a short-lived dance craze and ecological concern; after watching Laura Herring dance, you will understand why it should be forbidden.
w Roy Langsdon, John Platt *story* Joseph Goldman *d* Greydon Clark *ph* R. Michael Stringer *m* Vladimir Horunzhy *ed* Robert Edwards, Earl Watson
☆ Laura Herring, Jeff James, Richard Lynch, Sid Haig, Kid Creole and the Coconuts, Barbra Brighton

The Lambeth Walk

GB 1939 84m bw
CAPAD/Pinebrook (Anthony Havelock-Allan)
A Cockney bloke inherits a dukedom.
Mild screen version of a popular musical play and a song which became a nationwide hit.
w Clifford Grey, John Paddy Carstairs, Robert Edmunds *play Me and My Girl* by Louis Rose, Douglas Furber, Noel Gay *d* Albert de Courville *ph* Francis Carver
☆ Lupino Lane, Sally Gray, Seymour Hicks, Enid Stamp Taylor, Wilfrid Hyde-White, Charles Heslop, Norah Howard

Lamerica ***

Italy/France 1994 125m colour
Cinemascope
CGG Tiger/Arena (Mario and Vittorio Cecchi Gori)

Two Italian con men come unstuck when they go to Albania to get rich quick.

Powerful and bleak drama of appalling poverty and despair, and of the humanity that somehow survives in the direst situations.
w Gianni Amelio, Andrea Porporati, Alessandro Sermoneta *d Gianni Amelio ph Luca Bigazzi*
m Franco Piersanti *ad* Giuseppe M. Gaudino
ed Simona Paggi
☆ *Enrico Lo Verso*, Michele Placido, Carmelo di Mazzarelli, Piro Milkani

'Its evangelical sincerity and the sweeping emotion of its finale could win the director new admirers abroad.' – *Variety*

† The film won a Felix as European film of the year in 1994.

The Lamp Still Burns

GB 1943 90m bw
GFD/Two Cities (Leslie Howard)
Adventures of wartime probationary nurses.
Understated wartime morale-builder, no longer very interesting.
w Elizabeth Baron, Roland Pertwee *novel* One Pair of Feet by Monica Dickens *d* Maurice Elvey
ph Robert Krasker
☆ Rosamund John, Stewart Granger, Godfrey Tearle, Sophie Stewart, John Laurie, Margaret Vyner, Cathleen Nesbitt, Joyce Grenfell

Lan Fengzheng: see *The Blue Kite*

Lancashire Luck

GB 1937 74m bw
Paramount British
A poor girl's life is changed when her father wins the pools.
Modest comedy which started its star's career.
w A. R. Rawlinson *story* Ronald Gow *d* Henry Cass
☆ Wendy Hiller, George Carney, Muriel George, Nigel Stock, George Galleon

Lancelot and Guinevere *

GB 1962 117m Eastmancolor
Panavision
Emblem (Cornel Wilde)
US title: *Sword of Lancelot*
Sir Lancelot covets the wife of his beloved King Arthur, but after Arthur's death she takes the veil.
Decently made, rather tame transcription of the legends, with all concerned doing quite creditably but not brilliantly.
w Richard Schayer, Jefferson Pascal *d* Cornel Wilde *ph* Harry Waxman *m* Ron Goodwin
☆ Cornel Wilde, Jean Wallace, Brian Aherne, George Baker, John Barrie

Lancelot du Lac ***

France/Italy 1974 85m Eastmancolor
Mara/Laser/ORTF/Gerico Sound (Jean Yanne, Jean-Pierre Rassam)
aka: *Le Graal*
aka: *The Grail*
The high ideals of chivalry wither as Lancelot, with the few remaining Knights of the Round Table, returns disillusioned from the failed quest to find the Holy Grail and resumes his love affair with Guinevere, wife of King Arthur.
Austerely impressive drama of the loss of faith, conjuring up a medieval world with great economy of means.
wd Robert Bresson ph Pasqualino de Santis
m Philippe Sarde *ad* Pierre Charbonnier
ed Germaine Lamy
☆ Luc Simon, Laura Duke Condominas, Humbert Balsan, Vladimir Antolek-Oresek, Patrick Bernard, Arthur de Montalembert

'Like so much of Bresson's work this is not so much a movie more a religious experience, but you don't have to be religious to enjoy it.' – *Tom Hutchinson, Film Review*

Lancer Spy *

US 1937 80m bw
TCF
A German spy is captured and his English double is sent back to replace him.
World War I yarn on the lines of The Great Impersonation *(qv). Excellent production and a good beginning and end, but a slow middle.*
w Philip Dunne *novel* Marthe McKenna
d Gregory Ratoff *ph* Barney McGill *m* Arthur Lange
☆ *George Sanders*, Dolores del Rio, Peter Lorre, Joseph Schildkraut, Virginia Field, Sig Rumann, Fritz Feld

'Sometimes exciting, always absorbing, and played with serious intensity.' – *Variety*

'A Story from the Spanish Civil War'

Land and Freedom ***

GB/Germany/Spain 1995 110m colour
Artificial Eye/Parallax/Messidor/Road Movies (Rebecca O'Brien)
An unemployed Liverpudlian Communist goes to fight in the Spanish Civil War on the side of the socialist POUM, but comes to discover that the activities of the Stalinist Republican forces and Communists in suppressing other left-wing groups will give victory to the Fascists.
An engrossing and passionate Orwellian account of the Spanish Civil War, as experienced on an individual level, which is framed by a death in present-day Liverpool in an attempt to point up the contemporary relevance of its story of a revolution betrayed.
w Jim Allen d Ken Loach ph Barry Ackroyd
m George Fenton *pd* Martin Johnson
ed Jonathan Morris
☆ *Ian Hart, Rosana Pastor*, Iciar Bollain, Tom Gilroy, Marc Martinez, Frederic Pierrot, Suzanne Maddock

'Direct, passionate and formidably informed by political conviction.' – *Derek Malcolm, Guardian*

'Ken Loach's real triumph is to get the viewer rooting for characters in a conflict that, for most, is as remote as the Trojan War.' – *John Hopewell, Variety*

The Land before Time

US 1988 69m Technicolor
UIP/Universal/Amblin (Don Bluth, Gary Goldman, John Pomeroy)
An orphaned dinosaur sets out with friends to find the way to a valley of plenty.
Over-cute, immensely sentimental animated feature.
w Stu Krieger *story* Judy Freudberg, Tony Geiss
d Don Bluth *ph* Jim Mann *m* James Horner
☆ Featuring Voices of Gabriel Damon, Helen Shaver, Bill Erwin, Candice Houston, Pat Hingle, Burke Barnes, Judith Barsi, Will Ryan

Land of Desire: see *A Ship to India*

Land of Fury: see *The Seekers*

Land of Liberty *

US 1939 137m bw
Motion Picture Producers and Distributors of America
A compilation of footage from American historical films, amounting hopefully to a history of America as seen by Hollywood.
A pretty impressive job of selection and editing, compiled for the New York World's Fair.
w Jeannie Macpherson, Jesse Lasky Jnr *ed* Cecil B. de Mille and others

'Her treachery stained every stone of the pyramid!' '20,000 workers and technicians! 1,600 camels! 104 specially built barges! 9,753 players in one scene alone!'

Land of the Pharaohs *

US 1955 105m Warnercolor Cinemascope
Warner/Continental (Howard Hawks)
Pharaoh is obsessed with life after death and builds a great pyramid for himself and his treasures … but his wife is ambitious…
Unexpected, interesting excursion into Ancient Egypt, distended by Cinemascope; basically a macabre melodrama with a final spectacular twist. The engineering details would make a fascinating documentary.
w William Faulkner, Harry Kurnitz, H. Jack Bloom
d Howard Hawks *ph Lee Garmes, Russell Harlan*
m Dimitri Tiomkin ad Alexander Trauner
☆ Jack Hawkins, Joan Collins, Alexis Minotis, James Robertson Justice, Sydney Chaplin

'A perfectly ridiculous film.' – *Jack Hawkins*

Land Raiders

US 1969 100m Technicolor
Columbia (Charles H. Schneer)
Two brothers quarrel when one attempts to exterminate neighbouring Apaches so that he can take over their lands.
Routine Western of jealousy and greed, not helped by the miscasting of its two protagonists.
w Ken Pettus *d* Nathan H. Duran *ph* Wilkie Cooper *m* Bruno Nicolai *ad* Jose Alguero
ed Archie Ludski
☆ Telly Savalas, George Maharis, Arlene Dahl, Janet Landgard, Phil Brown, Paul Picerni, George Coulouris, Guy Rolfe, Jocelyn Lane

The Land that Time Forgot *

GB 1974 91m Technicolor
Amicus (John Dark)
In 1916, survivors from a torpedoed supply ship find themselves on a legendary island full of prehistoric monsters.
Lively old-fashioned adventure fantasy with good technical credits.
w James Cawthorne, Michael Moorcock
novel Edgar Rice Burroughs *d* Kevin Connor
ph Alan Hume *m* Douglas Gamley *pd Maurice Carter sp* Derek Meddings, Roger Dicken
☆ Doug McClure, John McEnery, Susan Penhaligon, Keith Barron, Anthony Ainley

The Land Unknown *

US 1957 78m bw Cinemascope
U-I (William Alland)
A plane is forced down into a strange Antarctic valley where dinosaurs still roam.
Efficient adventure fantasy on King Kong lines but without any of that film's panache.
w Laszlo Gorog *d* Virgil Vogel *ph* Ellis Carter
m Hans Salter *sp* Roswell Hoffman, Fred Knoth, Orien Ernest, Jack Kevan
☆ Jock Mahoney, Shawn Smith, William Reynolds, Henry Brandon

Land without Bread *

Spain 1932 27m bw
Ramon Acin
aka: *Las Hurdes*
A famous documentary showing the poorest region of northern Spain, notable for some stunningly unpleasant images impeccably staged.
ph Eli Lotar *wd/ed* Luis Buñuel

'An honest and hideous picture.' – *Graham Greene*

Land without Music *

GB 1936 80m bw
Capitol Films (Max Schach)
US title: *Forbidden Music*
The ruler of a Ruritanian country bans music because her subjects are too busy singing to make money. A revolutionary singer however wins the duchess's hand and reverses her decision.
Artless but attractively played operetta with the star in excellent form.
w Marion Dix, L. Du Garde Peach *story* Fritz Koselka, Armin Robinson *d* Walter Forde
ph John Boyle *m* Oscar Straus
☆ Richard Tauber, Jimmy Durante, Diana Napier, June Clyde, Derrick de Marney, Esme Percy, George Hayes, Edward Rigby

Landfall

GB 1949 88m bw
ABPC (Victor Skuzetzky)
A test pilot mistakenly believes that he accidentally sank a British submarine.
Second-rate transcription of a popular novel.
w Talbot Jennings, Gilbert Gunn, Anne Burnaby
novel Nevil Shute *d* Ken Annakin *ph* Wilkie Cooper
☆ Michael Denison, Patricia Plunkett, Kathleen Harrison, David Tomlinson, Joan Dowling, Maurice Denham, A. E. Matthews, Margaretta Scott, Sebastian Shaw, Laurence Harvey

The Landgirls *

GB/France 1997 111m colour Panavision
Film Four/InterMedia/Greenpoint/West Eleven (Simon Relph)
During the Second World War, three young women go to work as labourers on an isolated Dorset farm, and are attracted to the farmer's son.
Pleasant nostalgic wallow, which eschews class conflicts for gentler romance.
w David Leland, Keith Dewhurst *novel* Angela Huth *d* David Leland *ph* Henry Braham
m Brian Lock *pd* Caroline Amies *ed* Nick Moore
☆ Catherine McCormack, Rachel Weisz, Anna Friel, Steven Mackintosh, Tom Georgeson, Maureen O'Brien, Lucy Akhurst

'The period is created in such loving detail that the film risks looking like a museum piece, complete with old planes, Hovis ad-like farm workers in breeches and braces, and even fun-loving GIs.' – *Geoffrey Macnab, Sight and Sound*

The Landlord *

US 1970 110m DeLuxe
United Artists/Mirisch/Carter (Norman Jewison)
A tycoon's son buys a tenement in Brooklyn's black ghetto, and conscience diverts him into improving the lot of his tenants.
Overlong satirical comedy, good on detail but short on structure.
w Bill Gunn *novel* Kristin Hunter *d Hal Ashby*
ph Gordon Willis *m* Al Kooper *pd* Robert Boyle
☆ *Beau Bridges, Lee Grant*, Pearl Bailey, Diana Sands

'Bad taste from start to finish … not an avenue of offensiveness to any race is left unexplored.' – *Judith Crist*

Lee Grant

Landru

France/Italy 1962 115m Eastmancolor
Rome-Paris/CC Champion (Carlo Ponti, Georges de Beauregard)
aka: *Bluebeard*
The true story of a furniture dealer who murdered women for financial gain, also treated by Chaplin in *Monsieur Verdoux*.
A curious artificial style has been adopted, making a tragi-comedy look like a farce which isn't very funny, and falls on very stony ground indeed despite the all star cast.
w Françoise Sagan *d* Claude Chabrol *ph* Jean Rabier *m* Pierre Jansen
☆ Charles Denner, Michèle Morgan, Danielle Darrieux, Hildegarde Knef, Stéphane Audran, Catherine Rouvel

Landscape in a Mist *

Greece/France/Italy 1988 125m colour
Artificial Eye/Paradis Films/ET-1/Basicinematografica/Channel 4 (Theo Angelopoulos)
original title: *Topio Stin Omichli*
Two children, an eleven-year-old girl and her five-year-old brother, travel through Greece in an attempt to reach Germany and the father they have never known.
Lyrical, but slow-moving account of a child's discovery of the world that would have been as meaningful at half its length.
w Theo Angelopoulos, Tonino Guerra, Thanassis Valtinos *d* Theo Angelopoulos *ph* Giorgos Arvanitis *m* Eleni Karaindrou *ad* Mikes Karapiperis *ed* Yannis Tsitsopoulos
☆ Michalis Zeke, Tania Palaiologou, Stratis Tzortzoglou

'Sometimes love isn't enough.'

Lantana ***

Australia/Germany 2001 121m Technicolor
Panavision
Winchester/AFFC/MPB (Jan Chapman)
In Sydney, an unhappily married policeman investigates the disappearance of a psychiatrist and uncovers guilty secrets in several lives.
An intense exploration of prickly relationships rather than a whodunnit, this well-crafted and -acted movie provides both suspense and insight.
w Andrew Bovell play Speaking in Tongues by Andrew Bovell *d Ray Lawrence ph* Mandy Walker *m* Paul Kelly *pd* Kim Buddee *ed* Karl Sodersten
☆ Anthony LaPaglia (Leon Zat), Geoffrey Rush (John Knox), Barbara Hershey (Dr Valerie Somers), Kerry Armstrong (Sonja Zat), Rachael Blake (Jane O'May), Vince Colosimo (Nik D'Amato), Daniela Farinacci (Paula D'Amato), Peter Phelps (Patrick Phelan)

'Elegant but never overstated, sinister but never coldhearted, this is a note-perfect masterwork on a modest, human scale.' – *Andrew O'Hehir, Salon.com*

'It was subtle, really interesting, and it also possessed a word I would use with great care: integrity.' – *Harold Pinter*

Lapse of Memory
Canada/France 1992 90m colour
Rank/Max/Gérard Mital/FR3/SGGC/Jean-Bernard Fetoux
aka: *Mémoire Traquée*
With the help of a psychiatrist, a teenage boy attempts to relive the shocking events that caused him to lose his memory.
Dull thriller, done with plodding flashbacks, which fails to come to a satisfactory conclusion.
w Patrick Dewolf, Philippe Le Guay, John Frizzell *novel I Am the Cheese* by Robert Cormier *d* Patrick Dewolf *ph* Eduardo Serra *m* Alexandre Desplat *pd* François Seguin *ed* Fabienne Alvarez-Giro
☆ John Hurt, Marthe Keller, Matthew Mackay, Kathleen Robertson, Marion Peterson
'Fine direction, acting and editing should add up to a strong commercial potential.' – *Variety*
† The novel was first filmed in 1983 as *I Am the Cheese* (qv).

'Born into wealth. Groomed by the elite. Trained for combat.'
Lara Croft: Tomb Raider
US/Germany/GB/Japan 2001 100m DeLuxe Super 35
Paramount/Mutual/Eidos (Lawrence Gordon, Lloyd Levin, Colin Wilson)
An aristocratic adventurer saves the world from an evil organisation that plans to turn back time.
Trivial nonsense, a worthless farrago of stupefying boredom, based on best-selling videogames; Jolie, though, does seem like the creation of a masculine cyber-fantasy.
w Patrick Massett, John Zinman, Simon West *story* Mike Werb, Michael Colleary *d* Simon West *ph* Peter Menzies Jnr *m* Graeme Revell *pd* Kirk M. Petruccelli *ed* Dallas S. Puett, Glen Scantlebury
☆ Angelina Jolie (Lara Croft), Jon Voight (Lord Croft), Noah Taylor (Bryce), Iain Glen (Manfred Powell), Daniel Craig (Alex West), Christopher Barrie (Hillary), Julian Rhind-Tutt (Mr Pimms), Richard Johnson (Distinguished Gentleman), Leslie Phillips (Wilson)
'Has the distinction of being a major motion picture that's far less imaginative, and quite a bit more stupid, than the interactive game it's based on.' – *Todd McCarthy, Variety*
'Elevates goofiness to an art form. Here is a movie so monumentally silly, yet so wondrous to look at, that only a churl could find fault.' – *Roger Ebert, Chicago Sun-Times*

Larceny
US 1948 89m bw
Universal (Aaron Rosenberg)
A con man fleeces a war widow into paying for a memorial to her husband, but falls in love with her.
Drearily predictable melodrama.
w Herbert F. Margolis, Louis Markein, William Bowers *novel The Velvet Fleece* by Lois Ely, John Fleming *d* George Sherman *ph* Irving Glassberg *m* Leith Stevens
☆ Joan Caulfield, John Payne, Dan Duryea, Shelley Winters, Dorothy Hart, Richard Rober, Dan O'Herlihy

Larceny, Inc
US 1942 95m bw
Warner (Jack Saper, Jerry Wald)
An ex-convict tries to rob a bank but finds that honesty pays best.
Tepid comedy-drama from the period when Warner were taming their gangster image.
w Everett Freeman, Edwin Gilbert *play The Night before Christmas* by Laura and S. J. Perelman *d* Lloyd Bacon *ph* Tony Gaudio
☆ Edward G. Robinson, Jane Wyman, Broderick Crawford, Anthony Quinn, Jack Carson, Edward Brophy, Harry Davenport, John Qualen, Barbara Jo Allen, Jackie Gleason, Grant Mitchell, Andrew Tombes
'The dialogue is brilliantly economical: this sort of Hollywood wit has the crackle of stage-thunder. And the acting is superb.' – *James Agate*

Larceny Lane: see *Blonde Crazy*

Large
GB 2001 80m colour
UIP/Film Consortium/Film4 (Alex Usborne)
Friends of a rock star's son attempt to sabotage his chances of inheriting a fortune.
British attempt at a gross teen comedy, very tasteless but rarely funny.
w Justin Edgar, Mike Dent *d* Justin Edgar *ph* Robbie Ryan *m* David A. Hughes *pd* Julian Fullalove *ed* Eddie Hamilton
☆ Luke de Woolfson (Jason), Melanie Gutteridge (Sophie), Simon Lowe (Rob), Lee Oakes (Ian), Mirren Delaney (Lisa Gates), Emma Catherwood (Rachel 'Measley' Beasley), Zita Sattar (Kylie), Tim Harris (Malcolm Tuttle)
'Absolutely terrible… a manic, charmless, utterly unfunny would-be Farrellyesque comedy about sex and clubbing.' – *Peter Bradshaw, Guardian*

Larger than Life
1996 93m DeLuxe
MGM/UA/Trilogy/RCS/Majestic/Trilogy (Richard B. Lewis, John Watson, Pen Densham)
A motivational speaker takes an elephant, left to him by his father, a circus clown, on a journey across America.
Bland comedy, from which its star seems to be distancing himself as fast as he can; in that, he has my sympathy.
w Roy Blount Jnr *story* Pen Densham, Garry Williams *d* Howard Franklin *ph* Elliot Davis *m* Miles Goodman *pd* Marcia Hinds-Johnson *ed* Sidney Levin
☆ Bill Murray, Janeane Garofalo, Matthew McConaughey, Keith David, Pat Hingle, Jeremy Piven, Lois Smith, Harve Presnell, Linda Fiorentino
'An enjoyably daft comedy with high production values and a watertight script that combines a feelgood message concerning personal growth with all the slapstick one would expect from an elephant road movie.' – *Liese Spencer, Sight and Sound*

Larks on a String **
Czechoslovakia 1969 94m colour
Barrandov Filmstudio (Karel Kochman)
original title: *Skrivanci Na Niti*
Intellectuals and the displaced middle class prove resistant to change when they are punished by being forced to work on an industrial scrapheap.
Witty, blackly humorous satire on the Communist re-education of the bourgeoisie, marked by humanity, well-aimed barbs – a trade union executive gets out of his chauffeur-driven car and puts on a cloth cap before addressing the workers – and a scathing contempt for ideologically blinkered bureaucrats.
w Bohumil Hrabal, Jiri Menzel *d* Jiri Menzel *ph* Jaromir Sofr *m* Jiri Sust *ed* Josef Lojik
☆ Rudolf Hrusinsky, Vlastimil Brodsky, Vaclav Neckar, Jitka Zelenohorska, Jaroslav Satoransky, Vladmir Smeral, Ferdinand Kruta
'A courageous, bittersweet comedy of considerable charm and invention.' – *Variety*
† The film was banned for 21 years and not seen publicly until the 1990 Berlin Film Festival, where it shared the Golden Bear award as best film.

The Las Vegas Story
US 1952 88m bw
RKO (Robert Sparks)
When an investment broker and his new wife stop at Las Vegas, her shady past begins to emerge.
So-so programmer with some eccentric talents in average form, capped by a desert helicopter chase.
w Paul Jarrico, Earl Felton, Harry Essex *d* Robert Stevenson *ph* Harry J. Wild *m* Leigh Harline *md* Constantin Bakaleinikoff
☆ Jane Russell, Victor Mature, Vincent Price, Hoagy Carmichael, Colleen Miller, Brad Dexter, Jay C. Flippen
† Paul Jarrico's name was omitted from the film's credits at the time because he was blacklisted.

The Laser Man
Hong Kong 1988 90m colour
Peter Wang Films/Hong Kong Film Workshop (Peter Wang)
An out-of-work laser scientist is hired by a mysterious corporation to develop a deadly weapon.
Quirky thriller – the Chinese hero has a Jewish mother – but lacking anything other than its deliberate eccentricity.
wd Peter Wang *ph* Ernest Dickerson *m* Mason Daring *pd* Lester Cohen *ed* Graham Weinbren
☆ Marc Hayashi, Maryann Urbano, Joan Copeland, Tony Ka-Fei Leung, Neva Small, David Chan, Sally Yeh, Peter Wang

The Lash
US 1930 76m bw
First National
Adventures of a Spanish-Californian Robin Hood.
Or, The Mark of Zorro in all but name: a stalwart early talkie.
w Bradley King *story Adios* by Lanier and Virginia Bartlett *d* Frank Lloyd
☆ Richard Barthelmess, Mary Astor, James Rennie, Marian Nixon
'A good action talker in the western romantic strain.' – *Variety*
† Filmed in VitaScope (65mm).

Lashou Shentan: see *Hard Boiled*

Lasky Jedne Plavovlasky: see *Loves of a Blonde*

Lassie
The official Lassie series, made by MGM, was as follows:
1943 Lassie Come Home (qv)
1945 Son of Lassie *d* S. Sylvan Simon with Peter Lawford, Donald Crisp, Nigel Bruce
1946 Courage of Lassie *d* Fred M. Wilcox with Elizabeth Taylor, Frank Morgan, Tom Drake
1948 The Hills of Home (GB: Master of Lassie) *d* Fred M. Wilcox with Edmund Gwenn, Donald Crisp, Tom Drake
1949 The Sun Comes Up *d* Richard Thorpe with Jeanette MacDonald, Lloyd Nolan
1949 Challenge to Lassie *d* Richard Thorpe with Edmund Gwenn, Donald Crisp
1951 The Painted Hills *d* Harold F. Kress with Paul Kelly, Bruce Cowling
† Later 'Lassie' features were taken from episodes of the long-running TV series.

Lassie
US 1994 92m DeLuxe
Paramount/Broadway Pictures (Lorne Michaels)
aka: *Lassie: A New Generation*
A city boy is captivated by a sheepdog when he moves with his family to the country.
Glossy updating of the old story, but the magic has worn rather thin by now.
w Matthew Jacobs, Gary Ross, Elizabeth Anderson *d* Daniel Petrie *ph* Kenneth MacMillan *m* Basil Poledouris *pd* Paul Peters *ed* Steve Mirkovich
☆ Helen Slater, Thomas Guiry, Jon Tenney, Frederic Forrest, Richard Farnsworth, Brittany Boyd, Michelle Williams
'A hollow, post-yuppie update … Everything in the movie smacks of trend-surfing.' – *Michael Sragow, New Yorker*

Lassie: A New Generation: see *Lassie (1994)*

Lassie Come Home *
US 1943 88m Technicolor
MGM (Samuel Marx)
A poor family is forced to sell its beloved dog, but she makes a remarkable journey to return to them.
First of the Lassie films and certainly the best: an old-fashioned heartwarmer.
w Hugo Butler *novel* Eric Knight *d* Fred M. Wilcox *ph* Leonard Smith *m* Daniele Amfitheatrof
☆ Roddy McDowall, Elizabeth Taylor, Donald Crisp, Edmund Gwenn, Dame May Whitty, Nigel Bruce, Elsa Lanchester, J. Pat O'Malley
'The late Eric Knight wrote this immortal essay in Doggery-Woggery. MGM finished it off.' – *Richard Winnington*
Leonard Smith

Lassiter
US 1984 100m Technicolor
Pan Pacific/Golden Harvest (Albert S. Ruddy)
An American detective in pre-war London is forced by Scotland Yard to steal papers from the German Embassy.
Flat to the point of stultification, this marks yet another failure to make a big screen star of Tom Selleck.
w David Taylor *d* Roger Young *ph* Gil Taylor *m* Ken Thorne *pd* Peter Mullins *ed* Benjamin Weissman, Richard Hiscott
☆ Tom Selleck, Jane Seymour, Lauren Hutton, Bob Hoskins, Joe Regalbuto, Ed Lauter, Warren Clarke

Last Action Hero
US 1993 131m Technicolor Panavision
Columbia TriStar/Columbia (Steve Roth, John McTiernan)
A magic ticket enables a boy to enter the world of an action movie, but it also allows the villain to escape into the real world, where he is followed by the boy and the film's muscular hero.
A film that tries to have it both ways, simultaneously mocking and celebrating the conventions of action movies, which leaves audiences, as well as the actors and director, in a state of bewildered confusion.
w Shane Black, David Arnott *story* Zack Penn, Adam Leff *d* John McTiernan *ph* Dean Semler *m* Michael Kamen *pd* Eugenio Zanetti *ed* John Wright
☆ Arnold Schwarzenegger, F. Murray Abraham, Art Carney, Charles Dance, Frank McRae, Tom Noonan, Robert Prosky, Anthony Quinn, Mercedes Ruehl, Ian McKellen, Joan Plowright, Tina Turner
'A joyless, soulless machine of a movie.' – *Variety*
'A perfect example of cinematic self-hatred.' – *Sight and Sound*
† The film's production costs were reportedly $100 million. It took around $28 million at the US box-office, though better results elsewhere meant that its final loss was reckoned to be some $20 million, although some estimates put it much higher.

The Last Adventurers
GB 1937 77m bw
Conway (H. Fraser Passmore)
Adventures on board a fishing trawler.
Acceptable low-budget outdoor drama.
w Denison Clift *d* Roy Kellino *ph* Eric Cross *m* Eric Ansell *ad* W. R. Brinton *ed* David Lean
☆ Niall MacGinnis, Linden Travers, Roy Emerton, Kay Walsh, Peter Gawthorne, Katie Johnson

The Last American Hero *
US 1973 95m DeLuxe Panavision
TCF/Wizan/Rojo (John Cutts, William Roberts)
The adventures of an illicit whisky distiller with a passion for fast cars.
Observant, amusing hillbilly comedy drama based on the early life of racing driver Junior Johnson.
w William Roberts *d Lamont Johnson ph* George Silano *m* Charles Fox
☆ *Jeff Bridges, Valerie Perrine*, Geraldine Fitzgerald, Ned Beatty, Art Lund, Gary Busey
'A pop saga phrased with rough vernacular authenticity.' – *Bruce Williamson, Playboy*
† Reissue title: *Hard Driver.*

The Last Angry Man *
US 1959 100m bw
Columbia (Fred Kohlmar)
An old doctor in a Brooklyn slum is made the subject of a TV documentary.
Self-confidently sentimental wallow which just about works.
w Gerald Green *novel* Gerald Green *d* Daniel Mann *ph* James Wong Howe *m* George Duning *ad* Carl Anderson
☆ *Paul Muni*, David Wayne, Betsy Palmer, Luther Adler, Dan Tobin, Robert F. Simon
Paul Muni; art direction

The Last Battle
France 1983 92m bw Cinemascope
ICA/Les Films du Loup (Luc Besson)
original title: *Le Dernier Combat*
A samurai swordsman runs amok in a world destroyed by nuclear war.
Chic, virtually silent film that borrows from dozens of other works on the same theme.
wd Luc Besson *ph* Carlo Varini *m* Eric Serra *ed* Sophie Schmit

☆ Pierre Jolivet, Jean Bouise, Fritz Wepper, Jean Reno, Maurice Lany, Pierre Carrive, Jean-Michel Castanie, Michel Doset

The Last Blitzkrieg
US 1959 84m bw
Columbia/Sam Katzman
During the Battle of the Bulge a German leads a squad of American saboteurs.
Weakly pacifist, technically incompetent war adventure.
w Lou Morheim *d* Arthur Dreifuss *ph* Ted Scaife *m* Hugo de Groot
☆ Van Johnson, Kerwin Mathews, Dick York, Larry Storch

'They're two fallen heroes up against the gambling syndicate in pro sports. Everyone had counted them out. But they're about to get back into the game.'
The Last Boy Scout
US 1991 105m Technicolor Panavision
Warner/Geffen/Silver (Joel Silver, Michael Levy)
A too-honest secret agent turned private eye is hired by a former football player to protect his girlfriend, a stripper.
Standard buddy-buddy action movie with high-budget special effects and non-stop violence.
w Shane Black *story* Shane Black, Greg Hicks *d* Tony Scott *ph* Ward Russell *m* Michael Kamen *pd* Brian Morris *ed* Mark Goldblatt, Mark Helfrich
☆ Bruce Willis, Damon Wayans, Chelsea Field, Noble Willingham, Taylor Negron, Danielle Harris, Halle Berry, Bruce McGill
'Entertaining if mindless shoot-'em-up … the Boy Scouts' "Be Prepared" motto could be taken as a warning to check one's brain at the door.' – *Variety*
'To give it a negative review would be dishonest. To be positive is to seem to approve its sickness.' – *Roger Ebert*
† Shane Black was reportedly paid $1.75 million for his screenplay.

The Last Bridge
Austria/Yugoslavia 1953 95m bw
Cosmopol/UFUS (Carl Szokoll)
During World War II, a German nurse in Yugoslavia is captured by partisans and turns to their point of view.
Message melodrama, very ably put together with a bleakly tragic climax; but nothing at all new.
w Helmut Kautner, Norbert Kunze *d* Helmut Kautner *ph* Elio Carniel *m* Carl de Groof
☆ Maria Schell, Bernhard Wicki, Barbara Rütting, Carl Möhner

The Last Broadcast *
US 1998 86m colour
Metrodome/FFM (Stefan Avalos, Lance Weiler)
An amateur film-maker investigates the 'Jersey Devil' murder of 1996, in which cable TV presenters died while presenting a live show from a remote forest where they were attempting a contact with the supernatural.
Clever, inventive low-budget horror that predates The Blair Witch Project *(qv), with which it has some similarities.*
wd Stefan Avalos, Lance Weiler *ph* Lance Weiler *m* A. D. Roso, Stefan Avalos *ed* Stefan Avalos
☆ David Beard (David Leigh), Jim Seward (Jim Suerd), Stefan Avalos (Steven Avkast), Lance Weiler (Locus Wheeler), Rein Clabbers (Rein Clackin), Michele Pulaski (Michelle Monarch), Tom Brunt (Video engineer), Mark Rublee (Video editor), A. D. Roso (Lead investigator), Dale Worstall (Psychologist)
'All dull film… Don't expect to be scared or shocked. Or in any way entertained.' – *Rupert Laight, Film Review*

'No Castle Can Have Two Kings.'
The Last Castle
US 2001 131m Technicolor Panavision
UIP/DreamWorks (Robert Lawrence)
A disgraced general organises a revolt among his fellow-prisoners against a corrupt and ruthless warden.
Stale drama of redemption and discipline that recycles most of the clichés familiar from other prison and gung-ho war movies, and miscasts Redford as an action hero.
w David Scarpa, Graham Yost *d* Rod Lurie *ph* Shelly Johnson *m* Jerry Goldsmith *pd* Kirk M. Petruccelli *ed* Michael Jablow, Kevin Stitt
☆ Robert Redford (Gen. Eugene Irwin), James Gandolfini (Col Winter), Mark Ruffalo (Yates), Delroy Lindo (Gen. Jim Wheeler), Clifton Collins Jnr (Aguilar), Steve Burton (Capt. Peretz), Brian Goodman (Beaupre), Paul Calderon (Dellwo), Jeremy Childs (Cutbush), Robin Wright Penn (uncredited) (Rosalie)
'Disappointingly pedestrian prison meller.' – *Variety*

The Last Chance *
Switzerland 1945 105m bw
Praesens Film
In 1943 an Englishman and an American escape from a fascist camp in northern Italy and with the help of refugees cross the mountains into Switzerland.
Earnest propaganda piece which struck the spot at the time: cinematically rather plodding, but with some exciting scenes.
w Richard Schweitzer *d* Leopold Lindtberg *ph* Emil Berna *m* Robert Blum
☆ E. G. Morrison, Ray Reagan, John Hoy, Luisa Rossi

The Last Command **
US 1928 100m approx (24 fps) bw silent
Paramount
An exiled Russian general goes berserk when given a role in a movie which virtually involves playing himself.
Fascinating ironic comedy tailored for an international star who was not to survive the talkies.
w John F. Goodrich *story* Lajos Biro *d* Josef von Sternberg *ph* Bert Glennon *ad* Hans Dreier
☆ *Emil Jannings*, William Powell, Evelyn Brent, Nicholas Soussanin
🏆 Emil Jannings
🏆 best picture; Lajos Biro

The Last Command *
US 1955 110m Trucolor
Republic (Frank Lloyd)
Jim Bowie returns to Texas in the 1830s and dies at the Alamo alongside other famous men.
Reasonably interesting Western on a subject which has often figured but seldom worked.
w Warren Duff *d* Frank Lloyd *ph* Jack Marta *m* Max Steiner
☆ Ernest Borgnine, Sterling Hayden, Anna Maria Alberghetti, Arthur Hunnicutt, Richard Carlson, J. Carrol Naish

'Sometimes justice is a crime.'
Last Dance
US 1996 103m Technicolor
Buena Vista/Touchstone (Steven Haft)
An idealistic lawyer fights to have a death sentence on a murderess commuted to life imprisonment, after she has spent 12 years on Death Row.
Earnest, old-fashioned melodrama, aimed at the tear ducts of the susceptible.
w Ron Koslow *d* Bruce Beresford *ph* Peter James *m* Mark Isham *pd* John Stoddart *ed* John Bloom
☆ Sharon Stone, Rob Morrow, Randy Quaid, Peter Gallagher, Jack Thompson, Don Harvey, Jayne Brook, Pamela Tyson, Skeet Ulrich
'That most joyless of beasts: melodrama without the guts, a weepie with its plumbing pulled out.' – *Tom Shone, Sunday Times*

Last Days of Chez Nous *
Australia 1992 96m Eastmancolor
Metro/Jan Chapman/Australian Film Finance Corp.
In Sydney, while a wife is away on holiday, her sister has an affair with her French husband and her daughter goes to bed with the lodger.
A slight but perceptive domestic drama.
w Helen Garner *d* Gillian Armstrong *ph* Geoffrey Simpson *m* Paul Grabowsky *pd* Janet Patterson *ed* Nicholas Beauman
☆ Lisa Harrow, Bruno Ganz, Kerry Fox, Miranda Otto, Kiri Paramore, Bill Hunter
'Beautifully acted and crafted.' – *Variety*
'Poignantly observed and dry-humoured account of emotional blundering and bruising.' – *Lizzie Franke, Sight and Sound*

'History is made at night.'
The Last Days of Disco *
US 1998 113m Technicolor
Warner/Castle Rock/Westerly (Whit Stillman)
A loquacious group of friends congregate in a New York night-club that is under investigation by the police.
A smart comedy of sexual manners in an incongruous setting.
wd Whit Stillman *ph* John Thomas *m* Mark Suozzo *ch* John Carrafa *pd* Ginger Tougas *ed* Andrew Hafitz, Jay Pires
☆ Chloe Sevigny, Kate Beckinsale, Chris Eigeman, Matt Keeslar, Mackenzie Astin, Matthew Ross, Tara Subkoff, Burr Steers, David Thornton, Jaid Barrymore, Michael Weatherly, Robert Sean Leonard, Jennifer Beals
'Is as interesting to watch for its serious disjuncture between style and content as for its cute cast and fabulous soundtrack.' – *Todd McCarthy, Variety*

The Last Days of Dolwyn *
GB 1949 95m bw
London/BLPA (Anatole de Grunwald)
US title: *Woman of Dolwyn*
A Welsh valley is flooded to make a reservoir and a village has to be evacuated.
Interesting but rather stagey drama based on an actual 19th-century event, with personal melodrama added.
wd Emlyn Williams ph Otto Heller *m* John Greenwood
☆ *Edith Evans*, Emlyn Williams, Richard Burton, Hugh Griffith, Barbara Couper, Allan Aynesworth
'The conventionally picturesque Welsh flavour and mounting probabilities apart, the treatment is stiff and episodic.' – *MFB*

The Last Days of Man on Earth: see *The Final Programme*

'Pompeii … drunk with wealth and power … rotten with pagan pleasures … doomed to fiery death from the skies!'
The Last Days of Pompeii *
US 1935 96m bw
RKO (Merian C. Cooper)
In ancient Pompeii, various personal dramas are submerged in the eruption of Vesuvius.
Starchy melodrama capped by a reel of spectacular disaster.
w Ruth Rose, Boris Ingster *novel* Lord Lytton *d* Merian C. Cooper, Ernest Schoedsack *ph* Eddie Linden Jnr, J. Roy Hunt *m* Roy Webb *sp Vernon Walker, Harry Redmond*
☆ Preston Foster, Basil Rathbone, Alan Hale, Dorothy Wilson
'Well-done spectacle minus romance and cast names. Should do all right generally.' – *Variety*

The Last Detail **
US 1973 104m Metrocolor
Columbia/Acrobat/Persky-Bright (Gerald Ayres)
Two hardened naval petty officers escort a young recruit, sentenced for thieving, from Virginia to a New Hampshire jail, and give him a wild last night.
Foul-mouthed weekend odyssey, with a few well-observed moments for non-prudes. Technically the epitome of Hollywood's most irritating seventies fashion, with fuzzy sound recording, dim against-the-light photography, and a general determination to show up the ugliness of everything around us.
w Robert Towne *novel* Darryl Ponicsan *d* Hal Ashby *ph* Michael Chapman *m* Johnny Mandel
☆ *Jack Nicholson*, Otis Young, Randy Quaid, Clifton James, Carol Kane
'Visually it is relentlessly lower-depths gloomy, and the material, though often very funny, is programmed to wrench your heart.' – *New Yorker*
🏆 Robert Towne; Jack Nicholson; Randy Quaid
BAFTA: Jack Nicholson; Robert Towne

The Last Dinosaur
US 1977 100m colour
Rankin-Bass Productions
An oil-drilling team discovers a *tyrannosaurus rex* while probing the polar oil-cap.
Inept monster saga with poorish special effects from a Japanese team.
w William Overgard *d* Alex Grasshoff, Tom Kotani *ph* Shoshi Ueda *m* Maury Laws
☆ Richard Boone, Joan Van Ark, Steven Keats

The Last Dragon
US 1985 109m colour
TriStar/Motown (Rupert Hitzig)
aka: *Berry Gordy's The Last Dragon*
A martial arts expert returns to Harlem and saves a video disc jockey from gangsters and the neighbourhood from a self-styled shogun and his high-kicking gang.
A camp mix of kung-fu and music, directed in a broad and unsubtle manner and aimed at a young and undiscriminating audience; it is more an extended rock video than a conventional movie.
w Louis Venosta *d* Michael Schultz *ph* James A. Contner *m* Misha Segal, Willie Hutch, Norman Whitfield *pd* Peter Larkin *ed* Christopher Holmes
☆ Taimak, Vanity, Julius J. Carry III, Chris Murney, Leo O'Brien, Faith Prince, Glen Eaton, Mike Starr, Jim Moody

'He thinks someone is trying to kill him. He's dead right!'
Last Embrace
US 1979 101m Technicolor
UA (Michael Taylor, Dan Wigutow)
An investigator survives a number of attacks on his life, though his wife is killed in the first of them.
Hitchcockian mystery without the master's zest or humour, though it leads to a pretty exciting climax at Niagara Falls.
w David Shaber *novel The 13th Man* by Murray Teigh Bloom *d* Jonathan Demme *ph* Tak Fujimoto *m* Miklos Rozsa
☆ Roy Scheider, Janet Margolin, Sam Levene, John Glover, Charles Napier, Christopher Walken, Jacqueline Brookes
'A case study of late seventies movie-making which does everything in its power to avoid taking risks.' – *John Pym, MFB*

The Last Emperor **
Italy/Hong Kong/GB 1987 160m approx
Technicolor Technovision
Columbia/Yanco Films/Tao Films/Recorded Picture Company/Screenframe/AAA Soprofilm (Jeremy Thomas)
The life of China's last imperial ruler, from ascending the throne as a puppet-like 3-year-old, to serene old age as a gardener in Mao's People's Republic.
A lavish spectacle which caught the imagination of audiences, though many found the compression of 60 years of Chinese politics baffling.
w Mark Peploe, Bernardo Bertolucci *d Bernardo Bertolucci ph* Vittorio Storaro *m* Ryuichi Sakamoto, David Byrne, Cong Su *pd* Ferdinando Scarfiotti *ad* Bruno Cesari *ed* Gabriella Cristiani
☆ John Lone, Joan Chen, Peter O'Toole, Ying Ruocheng
† A director's cut, a version running for 219m, was released in December 1998, and is also available Reviewing it for the *New York Times*, director-writer Oliver Stone called it 'a masterpiece – a fully shaped historical epic'.
🏆 picture; Bernardo Bertolucci; script (Mark Peploe, Bernardo Bertolucci); Vittorio Storaro; Ryuichi Sakamoto, David Byrne, Cong Su; Gabriella Cristiani; Bruno Cesari; costume design; sound
BAFTA: film

The Last Escape
GB 1970 90m DeLuxe
Oakmont/UA
An American officer in Munich tries to rescue a German scientist from the Nazis.
Standard World War II actioner.
w Herman Hoffman *d* Walter Grauman *ph* Gernot Roll *ad* Rolf Zehetbauer

☆ Stuart Whitman, John Collin, Martin Jarvis, Pinkas Braun

Last Exit to Brooklyn ***
West Germany 1989 98m colour
Guild/Neue Constantin Film Produktion/Bavaria Film/ Allied Filmmakers (Bernd Eichinger)

Striking workers and their families and a prostitute lead thwarted lives in Brooklyn in the early 1950s.
True to the spirit of Selby's grim, but compassionate, low-life novel, with some brilliant ensemble acting.
w Desmond Nakano *novel* Hubert Selby Jnr *d* *Uli Edel* *ph* Stefan Czapsky *m* *Mark Knopfler* *pd* David Chapman *ad* Mark Haak *ed* Peter Przygodda
☆ Stephen Lang, Jennifer Jason Leigh, Burt Young, Peter Dobson, Christopher Murney, Jerry Orbach, Alexis Arquette
'Edel surprisingly has managed to capture exactly the horrified yet tender tone of Selby's book.' – *MFB*

The Last Flight ***
US 1931 80m bw
Warner
In 1919, four veteran American flyers stay on in Paris in the hope of calming their shattered physical and emotional states.
Fascinatingly offhand study on post-war cynicism and the faint hope of a better world, beautifully written and directed in a manner more effective than The Sun Also Rises.
w *John Monk Saunders* *novel* *Single Lady* by John Monk Saunders *d* *William Dieterle* *ph* Sid Hickox
☆ *Richard Barthelmess*, *Helen Chandler*, David Manners, John Mack Brown, *Elliott Nugent*, Walter Byron
'If the crowd can understand that girl character in this picture the film is an undoubted grosser.' – *Variety*
'A narrative as tight and spare as a Racine tragedy ... unique in Hollywood of that time in its persistent, calculated understatement.' – *Tom Milne, 1975*
† In magazine form the story was known as 'Nikki and her War Birds'.

The Last Flight of Noah's Ark
US 1980 98m Technicolor
Walt Disney

An impecunious pilot reluctantly flies an orphanage worker and a cargo of animals across the Pacific, only to be stranded with them on a desert island.
It must have sounded like a good idea, but if it was to work at all it needed much sharper handling.
w Steven W. Carabatsos, Sandy Glass, George Arthur Bloom *story* *The Gremlin's Castle* by Ernest K. Gann *d* Charles Jarrott *ph* Charles F. Wheeler *m* Maurice Jarre
☆ Elliott Gould, Geneviève Bujold, Ricky Schroder, Tammy Lauren, Vincent Gardenia

The Last Frontier: see *Savage Wilderness (1956)*

'The big fellow is out of Alcatraz – ready to show them no mercy!'
The Last Gangster *
US 1937 81m bw
MGM (J. J. Cohn)
A gangster is released from Alcatraz and plans vengeance on his wife for deserting him.
Clean-cut star melodrama which suddenly turns sentimental.
w John Lee Mahin *d* Edward Ludwig *ph* William Daniels *m* Edward Ward *montage* *Slavko Vorkapich*
☆ Edward G. Robinson, Rose Stradner, James Stewart, Lionel Stander, Douglas Scott, John Carradine, Sidney Blackmer, Edward Brophy
'May indeed be the last gangster movie ... a good film which will blossom at the b.o.' – *Variety*
'A lot of water has flowed under the bridge since *Little Caesar*, but Mr Robinson has breasted the tides to make his impersonation of a 1937 thug as persuasive as was his portrait of a killer in that earlier classic of rats and rackets.' – *Frank Nugent*

The Last Gangster: see *Roger Touhy, Gangster (1944)*

The Last Gentleman
US 1934 80m bw
Fox
The career of a New England millionaire.
Pleasing star family drama.
w Leonard Praskins *d* Sidney Lanfield
☆ George Arliss, Edna May Oliver, Ralph Morgan, Janet Beecher, Charlotte Henry
'A prolonged monologue ... mediocre film which must depend on the star's rep.' – *Variety*

The Last Grenade
GB 1969 93m Eastmancolor Panavision
Cinerama/Dimitri de Grunwald/Josef Shaftel
An army mercenary is betrayed by an ex-friend in the Congo and pursues him to Hong Kong.
Violent action melodrama with few redeeming qualities.
w Kenneth Ware *novel* *The Ordeal of Major Grigsby* by John Sherlock *d* Gordon Flemyng *ph* Alan Hume *m* Johnny Dankworth
☆ Stanley Baker, Alex Cord, Honor Blackman, Richard Attenborough, Rafer Johnson, Andrew Keir, Ray Brooks, Julian Glover, John Thaw

The Last Hard Men
US 1976 97m DeLuxe Panavision
TCF/Belasco-Seltzer-Thatcher
A train robber breaks jail and sets out to revenge himself on the now-retired lawman who committed him.
Tough action adventure without much sense except to paint the end of the golden days of the west.
w Guerdon Trueblood *novel* *Gun Down* by Brian Garfield *d* Andrew V. McLaglen *ph* Duke Callaghan *m* Jerry Goldsmith
☆ Charlton Heston, James Coburn, Barbara Hershey, Christopher Mitchum, Michael Parks, Jorge Rivero, Thalmus Rasulala
'Script and direction seem equally tired.' – *Sight and Sound*
'The action proceeds slackly from one setpiece shoot-up to the next, barely providing the voltage for the two leads to expand their stereotyped roles into displays of star power.' – *Richard Combs, MFB*

The Last Harvest *
Argentina 1992 91m colour
Arenas/Jorge Estrada Mora (Julio Lencina, Ricardo Freixa)
original title: *La Ultima Siembra*
On an Argentinian ranch, conflict grows between an Indian miner turned maize farmer and the American-educated son of the landowner who wants to replace the cattle with a tobacco plantation.
Leisurely examination of a clash between races, classes and entrenched attitudes, coming heavily down on the side of conservatism.
wd Miguel Pereira *novel* *Los Humilides* by Miguel Angel Pereira *ph* Pablo Esteban Courtalón *m* Ariel Petrocelli, Tukuta Gordillo Isamara *ad* Mirta Spagarino *ed* Miguel Perez
☆ Patricio Contreras, Leonor Manso, Mario Pasik, Alberto Benegas, Gonzalo Morales, Antonio Paleari

Last Holiday *
GB 1950 88m bw
ABPC/Watergate (Stephen Mitchell, A. D. Peters, J. B. Priestley)

A man with a short time to live has a thoroughly enjoyable and useful final fling.
Slight, amusing and moving comedy drama spoiled by an unnecessary double twist.
w J. B. Priestley *d* Henry Cass *ph* Ray Elton *m* Francis Chagrin
☆ *Alec Guinness*, *Kay Walsh*, Beatrice Campbell, Grégoire Aslan, Bernard Lee, Wilfrid Hyde-White, Helen Cherry, Sidney James, Muriel George

'To Avoid Fainting Keep Repeating, It's Only A Movie ... Only A Movie ... Only A Movie ... Only A Movie.'
Last House on the Left
US 1972 91m colour
Hallmark (Sean S. Cunningham)

Parents seek revenge after their daughter is raped and killed by a gang of escaped convicts.
Low-budget shocker, updating and debasing Ingmar Bergman's Virgin Spring.
wd Wes Craven *ph* Victor Hurwitz *m* Steve Chapin, David Hess *ed* Wes Craven
☆ David Hess, Lucy Grantham, Sandra Cassel, Marc Sheffler, Jeramie Rain, Fred Lincoln

Last House on the Left Part II: see *A Bay of Blood*

The Last Hunt *
US 1956 103m Eastmancolor
Cinemascope
MGM (Dore Schary)
Buffalo hunters fall out with each other.
Terse, brutish outdoor Western with something to say about old Western myths and a famous ending in which the bad guy freezes to death while waiting to gun down the hero.
wd *Richard Brooks* *ph* Russell Harlan *m* Daniele Amfitheatrof
☆ Stewart Granger, Robert Taylor, Debra Paget, Lloyd Nolan, Russ Tamblyn, Constance Ford

The Last Hurrah **
US 1958 125m bw
Columbia (John Ford)

The political boss of a New England town fights his last campaign.
Enjoyable if disjointed melodrama, an old man's film crammed with cameo performances from familiar faces: important as one of Hollywood's great sentimental reunions.
w *Frank Nugent* *novel* Edwin O'Connor *d* *John Ford* *ph* Charles Lawton Jnr
☆ *Spencer Tracy*, Jeffrey Hunter, Dianne Foster, *Pat O'Brien*, *Basil Rathbone*, *Edward Brophy*, *Donald Crisp*, *James Gleason*, *John Carradine*, *Ricardo Cortez*, *Wallace Ford*, *Frank McHugh*, Frank Albertson, Anna Lee, Jane Darwell and also Willis Bouchey, Basil Ruysdael
† A TV version was subsequently made with Carroll O'Connor.

Last Images of the Shipwreck
Argentina/Spain 1989 129m colour
Palace/Cinequanon/TVE (Hugo Lauria)

original title: *Ultimas Imagenes del Naufragio*
A would-be writer befriends a prostitute and her crooked brother in order to gather material for a novel.
Playing rather unsuccessful games with illusion and reality, this odd movie soon loses its way.
wd Eliseo Subiela *ph* Alberto Basail *m* Pedro Aznar *pd* Abel Facello *ed* Mercela Saenz
☆ Lorenzo Quniteros, Noemi Frenkel, Hugo Soto, Pablo Brichta, Sara Benitez, Andres Tiengo, Alicia Aller, Alfredo Stuart

The Last Island
Netherlands 1990 109m colour
First Floor (Laurens Geels, Dick Maas)
Four men and two women, the only survivors of an air crash on an uninhabited island who also believe that they are the last people left alive in the world, find that their lives are dominated by an increasingly unbalanced military and religious bigot.
A feminist retelling of a familiar scenario, watchable, but too schematic to be entirely successful.
wd Marleen Gorris *ph* Marc Felperlaan *m* Boudewijn Tarenskeen *ad* Harry Ammerlaan *ed* Hans van Dongen
☆ Paul Freeman, Shelagh McLeod, Patricia Hayes, Kenneth Colley, Mark Hembrow, Marc Berman, Ian Tracey

The Last Journey *
GB 1935 66m bw
Twickenham (Julius Hagen)

The driver of an express train, driven mad with jealousy, goes berserk.
Workmanlike little train suspenser with an exciting climax.
w John Soutar, H. Fowler Mear *story* J. Jefferson Farjeon *d* Bernard Vorhaus *ph* Percival Strong, Billy Luff *ad* James Carter
☆ Godfrey Tearle, Hugh Williams, Julien Mitchell, Judy Gunn, Nelson Keys, Frank Pettingell, Olga Lindo, Sydney Fairbrother

The Last Laugh ***
Germany 1924 73m approx (24 fps) bw
silent
UFA

original title: *Der Letzte Mann*
The old doorman of a luxury hotel is given the job of lavatory attendant but comes into a fortune and gets his revenge.
Ironic anecdote made important by its virtual abandonment of dialogue and whole-hearted adoption of the camera eye technique which gives some thrilling dramatic effects.
w *Carl Mayer* *d* *F. W. Murnau* *ph* Karl Freund
☆ *Emil Jannings*, Max Hiller, Maly Delschaft, Hans Unterkirchen
'A marvellous picture – marvellous in its simplicity, its economy of effect, its expressiveness, and its dramatic power.' – *Life*
† A German remake of 1955 had Hans Albers in the lead and was of no interest.

Last Man Standing *
US 1996 101m CFI color Panavision
New Line (Walter Hill, Arthur Sarkissian)

In the 30s, a gunman on the run finds himself in a small Texas town ruled by two rival gangs of bootleggers.
A Hollywood Western influenced by other schools of film-making. The wit and charm of Kurosawa's original, Yojimbo, *has been replaced by a raw energy and gunfights in the style of John Woo; but its glum, conscienceless protagonist lacks the style of Toshiro Mifune or even Clint Eastwood in the spaghetti Western version,* A Fistful of Dollars.
wd Walter Hill *story* Ryuzo Kikushima, Akira Kurosawa *ph* Lloyd Ahern *m* Ry Cooder *pd* Gary Wissner *ed* Freeman Davies
☆ Bruce Willis, Christopher Walken, Bruce Dern, Alexandra Powers, David Patrick Kelly, William Sanderson, Karina Lombard, Ned Eisenberg, Michael Imperioli
'Goes wholly down the comic book route Hill marked out as early as *The Warriors*, offering wham-bang style but nothing else.' – *Kim Newman, Sight and Sound*
† The film cost \$57m to make, including \$16m to Bruce Willis, and took \$18m at the US box-office.
†† Elmer Bernstein's original score, which was rejected by Hill, has also been released on CD.

The Last Man to Hang?
GB 1956 75m bw
ACT Films/Columbia
Sir Roderick Strood is on trial for the murder of his neurotic wife.
Reasonably interesting co-feature based on Gerald Bullett's The Jury; *the title refers to the no-hanging bill then passing through Parliament.*
w Gerald Bullett and others *d* Terence Fisher
☆ Tom Conway, Elizabeth Sellars, Eunice Gayson, Freda Jackson, Hugh Latimer, Anthony Newley, Margaretta Scott

The Last Married Couple in America
US 1979 102m Technicolor
Universal/Cates Brothers (John Shaner)

A Los Angeles couple resist the efforts of their friends to involve them in the swinging life.
Tolerable sex comedy of modern mores, a shade too long delayed after Bob and Carol and Ted and Alice.
w John Herman Shaner *d* Gilbert Cates *ph* Ralph Woolsey *m* Charles Fox *pd* Gene Callahan
☆ Natalie Wood, George Segal, Richard Benjamin, Arlene Golonka, Alan Arbus, Marilyn Sokol, Dom DeLuise, Valerie Harper

The Last Metro ****
France 1980 131m Fujicolour
Les Films du Carrosse/Andrea/SEDIF/TF1/SFP (Jean-José Richer)

original title: *Le Dernier Métro*
In occupied Paris, the Jewish manager of a theatre hides in the cellar of the building.
Tightly enclosed symbolic melodrama of oppression and release that concentrates on individual lives caught up in a moment of mass madness and seeking refuge in their dedication to their art.
w François Truffaut, Suzanne Schiffman *d* *François Truffaut* *ph* Nestor Almendros

m Georges Delerue *ad* Jean-Pierre Kohut Svelko *ed* Martine Barraque
☆ *Catherine Deneuve, Gérard Depardieu,* Jean Poiret, Heinz Bennent
best foreign film

The Last Mile *
US 1932 84m bw
World Wide (E. W. Hammons)
Tensions mount in jail as the execution of Killer Mears approaches.
Strident melodrama which works up quite a head of hysteria.
w Seton I. Miller *play* John Wexley *d* Sam Bischoff *ph* Arthur Edeson
☆ Preston Foster, Howard Phillips, George E. Stone, Noel Madison
'Subject's lure is confined to the morbid-minded sensation seeker ... without feminine interest.' – *Variety*

The Last Mile
US 1959 81m bw
UA/Vanguard (Milton Subotsky)
Even more hysterical remake, retaining the original period.
A cheerless, though literally electrifying, entertainment.
w Milton Subotsky, Seton I. Miller *d* Howard W. Koch *ph* Joseph Brun *m* Van Alexander
☆ Mickey Rooney, Clifford David, Frank Conroy, Frank Overton, Leon Janney

The Last Movie
US 1971 108m Technicolor
Universal
Moviemakers go to Peru to film a Western.
Muddled and pretentious melodrama following the success of Easy Rider.
w Stewart Stern *d* Dennis Hopper *m* Kris Kristofferson
☆ Dennis Hopper, Julie Adams, Peter Fonda, Kris Kristofferson, Rod Cameron, Daniel Ades, Michael Anderson Jnr, Sam Fuller

Last Night *
Canada 1998 94m colour
Rhombus/CBC/La Seot Arte/Haut Et Court (Niv Fichman, Daniel Iron)
With the world ending at midnight, a man who decides to spend his last hours alone finds himself trying instead to help a stranded woman get home to her husband.
Genial comedy of the death of the world, which ends not with an apocalypse but a few hapless, genteel gestures of regret.
wd Don McKellar *ph* Douglas Koch *m* Alexina Louie, Alex Pauk *pd* John Dondertman *ed* Reginald Harkema
☆ Don McKellar (Patrick Wheeler), Sandrah Oh (Sandra), Callum Keith Rennie (Craig Zwiller), Sarah Polley (Jennifer Wheeler), Trent McMullen (Alex), David Cronenberg (Duncan), Robin Gammell (Mr Wheeler), Roberta Maxwell (Mrs Wheeler), Tracy Wright (Donna), Michael McMurtry (Menzies), Geneviève Bujold (Mrs Carlton)
'Bittersweet pic is funny, heart-wrenching and life-affirming. The modestly produced first feature has offbeat appeal.' – *Leonard Klady, Variety*

The Last of England
GB 1987 87m bw/colour
Blue Dolphin/Anglo International/British Screen/ Channel 4/ZDF-Tartan Films (James Mackay, Don Boyd)
Impressionistic mix of home movies and images of urban disintegration.
Too personal to communicate much, even to a sympathetic audience.
d Derek Jarman *ph* Derek Jarman, Christopher Hughes, Cerith Wyn Evans, Richard Heslop *m* Simon Turner, Andy Gill, Mayo Thompson, Albert Oehlen, Barry Adamson, El Tito *pd* Christopher Hobbs *ed* Peter Cartwright, Angus Cook, Sally Yeadon, John Maybury
☆ Spring, John Phillips, Gay Gaynor, Gerrard McArthur, Matthew Hawkins, Tilda Swinton, Spencer Leigh

The Last of His Tribe
US 1992 90m CFI color
HBO Pictures/River City (John Levoff, Robert Lovenheim)
In the early 1900s a Californian anthropologist forms a friendship with Ishi, the last surviving Yahi Indian who still lives in the traditional way.
Well-meaning but dull re-telling of a fascinating true story.
w Stephen Harrigan *d* Harry Hook *ph* Martin Fuhrer *m* John E. Keane *pd* Michael Baugh *ed* Bill Yahraus
☆ Jon Voight, Graham Greene, David Ogden Stiers, Jack Blessing, Anne Archer
† The film was made for cable television in the States and released direct to video in Britain.

The Last of Mrs Cheyney
US 1929 94m bw
MGM
A confidence woman in British high society falls in love.
Old theatrical warhorse, much filmed but never very satisfactorily. (See below.)
w Hans Kraly, Claudine West *play* Frederick Lonsdale *d* Sidney Franklin *ph* William Daniels
☆ Norma Shearer, Basil Rathbone, George Barraud, Hedda Hopper, Maude Turner Gordon, Herbert Bunston
Hans Kraly

The Last of Mrs Cheyney
US 1937 98m bw
MGM (Lawrence Weingarten)
Adequate, unexciting remake.
w Leon Gordon, Samson Raphaelson, Monckton Hoffe *d* Richard Boleslawski *ph* George Folsey *m* William Axt
☆ Joan Crawford, Robert Montgomery, William Powell, Frank Morgan, Jessie Ralph, Nigel Bruce, Benita Hume, Melville Cooper, Sara Haden
'Good film fodder, although not particularly socko.' – *Variety*
† A further remake was *The Law and the Lady* (qv).

'Any number can play; any number can die!'
The Last of Sheila *
US 1973 123m Technicolor
Warner (Herbert Ross)
A Hollywood star is killed by a hit-and-run driver; a year later her husband invites six friends to his yacht, and murders begin.
Confused, in-jokey showbiz whodunnit with flashes of interest.
w Stephen Sondheim, Anthony Perkins *d* Herbert Ross *ph* Gerry Turpin *m* Billy Goldenberg *ad* Ken Adam
☆ Richard Benjamin, Dyan Cannon, James Coburn, James Mason, Joan Hackett, Ian MacShane, Raquel Welch
'The most teasing riddles for an audience are likely to be the real identities of the personalities being satirized.' – *MFB*

Last of the Bad Men
US 1957 79m DeLuxe Cinemascope
Allied Artists (Vincent M. Fennelly)
In the 1870s, a Chicago detective poses as a wanted man in order to infiltrate a gang of outlaws in Colorado.
A mediocre Western in which much of the narrative consists of a portentous voice-over in the documentary style of Dragnet, *turning it into more of an illustrated lecture than a movie.*
w Daniel B. Ullman, David Chantler *d* Paul Landres *ph* Ellsworth Fredricks *m* Paul Sawtell *ad* David Milton *ed* William Austin
☆ George Montgomery, James Best, Douglas Kennedy, Keith Larsen, Robert Foulk, Willis Bouchey, Michael Ansara

The Last of the Buccaneers
US 1950 79m Technicolor
Columbia (Sam Katzman)
The story of Jean Lafitte, French privateer in the war of 1812.
Cheerful low-budget swashbuckler.
w Robert E. Kent *d* Lew Landers *ph* Vincent Farrar *m* Mischa Bakaleinikoff
☆ Paul Henreid, Jack Oakie, Karin Booth, Edgar Barrier, Mary Anderson, John Dehner

The Last of the Comanches *
US 1953 85m Technicolor
Columbia (Buddy Adler)
GB title: *The Sabre and the Arrow*
Survivors of an Indian raid take refuge in an abandoned mission until help arrives.
Competent Western remake of Sahara *(which was a remake of* The Lost Patrol*).*
w Kenneth Gamet *d* André de Toth *ph* Charles Lawton Jnr *m* George Duning
☆ Broderick Crawford, Barbara Hale, Lloyd Bridges, Martin Milner

'A Secret Lost In Time For Over 130 Years Is About To Be Discovered.'
Last of the Dogmen
US 1995 117m DeLuxe Panavision
Guild/Last of the Dogmen/Carolco/Savoy (Joel B. Michaels)
A bounty hunter, searching for escaped convicts, discovers instead a group of Cheyenne still following their old way of life in an isolated part of Montana.
Confused tale that aims for some spiritual meaning but misses, ending queasily as a celebration of noble savages.
wd Tab Murphy *ph* Karl Walter Lindenlaub *m* David Arnold *pd* Trevor Williams *ed* Richard Halsey
☆ Tom Berenger, Barbara Hershey, Kurtwood Smith, Steve Reevis, Andrew Miller, Gregory Scott Cummins, Mark Boone Jnr
'Thick with implausibilities and sentimental twaddle, and even the breathtaking scenery of the Rockies cannot excuse it.' – *George Perry*

Last of the Fast Guns
US 1959 82m Eastmancolor Cinemascope
Universal-International
Rival gunfighters form a friendship but fall out over their mission.
Mildly unusual Western programmer.
w David P. Harmon *d* George Sherman *ph* Alex Phillips *ad* Alexander Golitzen
☆ Gilbert Roland, Jock Mahoney, Linda Cristal, Eduard Franz, Lorne Greene, Carl Benton Reid

The Last of the Finest: see *Blue Heat*

'When School Ends ... And Life Begins.'
Last of the High Kings
Ireland/GB/Denmark 1996 104m colour
First Independent/Parallel/Northolme/Nordisk (Tim Palmer)
In the mid-70s, an Irish teenager enjoys an event-filled summer holiday in which he discovers sex.
Pleasant but very predictable family drama of the dawning of maturity, offering nothing that hasn't been seen many times before.
w David Keating, Gabriel Byrne *novel* Ferdia Mac Anna *d* David Keating *ph* Bernd Heinl *m* Michael Convertino *pd* Frank Conway *ed* Ray Lovejoy
☆ Catherine O'Hara, Jared Leto, Christina Ricci, Gabriel Byrne, Stephen Rea, Colm Meaney
'Ambles along with a twinkle in its eye for most of the time.' – *Variety*

The Last of the Mohicans
US 1936 91m bw
Edward Small
Incidents during colonial America's French-Indian war.
Vigorous if rough-and-ready Western, later remade (poorly) as Last of the Redmen *and as a Canadian TV series.*
w Philip Dunne, John Balderston, Paul Perez, Daniel Moore *novel* James Fenimore Cooper *d* George B. Seitz *ph* Robert Planck *m* Roy Webb
☆ Randolph Scott, Binnie Barnes, Bruce Cabot, Henry Wilcoxon, Heather Angel, Hugh Buckler

The Last of the Mohicans *
US 1992 122m colour 'Scope
Warner/Morgan Creek (Michael Mann, Hunt Lowry)
The white, adopted son of an Indian rescues a British officer's two daughters from hostile Indians and falls in love with one of them.
An ambitious but flawed epic adventure: the characterization is as shallow as the photography, the action is repetitious, the narrative lacks suspense and the romance is unconvincing, with Cooper's self-reliant woodsman here tamed into domesticity.
w Michael Mann, Christopher Crowe *novel* James Fenimore Cooper *screenplay* Philip Dunne *d* Michael Mann *ph* Dante Spinotti *m* Trevor Jones, Randy Edelman *pd* Wolf Kroeger *ed* Dov Hoenig, Arthur Schmidt
☆ Daniel Day-Lewis (Nathaniel Poe/Hawkeye), Madeleine Stowe (Cora Munro), Russell Means (Chingachgook), Eric Schweig (Uncas), Jodhi May (Alice Munro), Steven Waddington (Major Duncan Heyward), Wes Studi (Magua), Maurice Roeves (Colonel Munro), Patrice Chereau (General Montcalm)
'Whether it was because we were young or the movies were young or the world was at least youngish, old-fashioned Hollywood history was exhilarating. In retrospect there is something alarming about its simplicities and the enthusiasm we brought to it. It is the great virtue of this grandly scaled yet deliriously energetic movie that it reanimates that long-ago feeling without patronizing it – and without making us think we will wake up some day once again embarrassed by it.' – *Richard Schickel, Time*
'Michael Mann has been aiming all along at two very different targets, trying to turn an adventure story into a responsible account of Native American life, while also making it lovey-dovey enough for the market place.' – *Adam Mars-Jones, Independent*
sound
Dante Spinotti

Last of the Red Hot Lovers *
US 1972 98m Technicolor
Paramount (Howard W. Koch)
A middle-aged fish restaurateur feels the need for an extra-marital spree.
Modest, plainly-filmed sex comedy from a reliable stable.
w Neil Simon *play* Neil Simon *d* Gene Saks *ph* Victor J. Kemper *m* Neal Hefti
☆ Alan Arkin, Paula Prentiss, Sally Kellerman, Renée Taylor

Last of the Redmen
US 1947 78m Vitacolor
Sam Katzman/Columbia
GB title: *Last of the Redskins*
British soldiers escort a general's children through Indian country.
Tinpot rendition of The Last of the Mohicans.
w Herbert Dalmas, George H. Plympton *d* George Sherman
☆ Jon Hall, Michael O'Shea, Evelyn Ankers, Julie Bishop, Buster Crabbe

Last of the Secret Agents
US 1966 90m Technicolor
Paramount
Two odd job men are recruited as spies.
Pratfall comedy featuring a briefly existing comedy double act.
w Mel Tolkin *d* Norman Abbott
☆ Marty Allen, Steve Rossi, John Williams, Nancy Sinatra, Lou Jacobi, Theo Marcuse, Sig Rumann

Last Orders ***
GB/Germany 2001 110m DeLuxe
Metrodome/Winchester/MBP/Scala (Fred Schepisi, Elisabeth Robinson)
Three elderly Londoners look back on their lives and loves as they gather for a trip to the seaside to scatter the ashes of a mutual friend.
A deft, working-class remembrance of things past, a gently humorous, unsentimental account, tinged with melancholy, of the pleasures and pains of ordinary life; it gets excellent ensemble acting from its cast.
wd Fred Schepisi *ph* Brian Tufano *m* Paul Grabowsky *pd* Tim Harvey *ed* Kate Williams *cos* Jill Taylor
☆ *Michael Caine* (Jack), *Bob Hoskins* (Ray), *Tom Courtenay* (Vic), *David Hemmings* (Lenny), Ray Winstone (Vince), Helen Mirren (Amy), JJ Feild (Young Jack), Anatol Yusef (Young Ray), Cameron Fitch (Young Vic), Nolan Hemmings (Young Lenny), Kelly Reilly (Young Amy), Laura Morelli (June)

'A moving study of the pleasures and obligations of friendship.' – *Philip French, Observer*
'A subtly powerful drama that finally tells us that not only is death not the end, sometimes it makes for new beginnings.' – *Kevin Courrier, Boxoffice*
'*Last Orders* is low-grade plot engineering but is endurable because we wait for some revelation that will justify the mechanics. But nothing of the kind comes our way.' – *Stanley Kaufmann*

'Open war between a handful of English and swarming tribesmen! Hidden war between fellow-officers who love the same woman!'

The Last Outpost *
US 1935 75m bw
Paramount (E. Lloyd Sheldon)
A British officer is captured by the Kurds and freed by an adventurer whose wife he covets.
Patchy, unusual adventure story with good moments.
w Philip MacDonald *story* F. Britten Austin *d* Charles Barton, Louis Gasnier *ph* Theodor Sparkuhl
☆ Cary Grant, Claude Rains, Gertrude Michael, Kathleen Burke, Colin Tapley, Akim Tamiroff, Billy Bevan, Jameson Thomas
'Loosely-woven melodramatic mélange.' – *Variety*
'Half of it is remarkably good and half of it quite abysmally bad. One can even put one's finger on the joins.' – *Graham Greene*

The Last Outpost
US 1951 89m Technicolor
Paramount/Pine-Thomas
A Civil War colonel finds his brother fighting on the other side.
Routine historical action romance.
w Geoffrey Homes, G. Worthing Yates, Winston Miller *d* Lewis R. Foster *ph* Loyal Griggs *m* Lucien Cailliet
☆ Ronald Reagan, Bruce Bennett, Rhonda Fleming, Noah Beery Jnr

The Last Page
GB 1952 84m bw
Exclusive/Hammer-Lippert
US title: *Manbait*
A bookseller is framed for the death of a blackmailer.
Curious English mystery with American stars.
w Frederick Knott *play* James Hadley Chase *d* Terence Fisher *ph* Walter J. Harvey *md* Frank Spencer
☆ George Brent, Marguerite Chapman, Diana Dors, Raymond Huntley, Peter Reynolds, Eleanor Summerfield

The Last Parade
US 1931 82m bw
Columbia
A detective and a racketeer are buddies in the war, but not afterwards.
Predictable character melodrama with no remaining interest.
w Dorothy Howell, Casey Robinson *d* Erle C. Kenton
☆ Jack Holt, Constance Cummings, Tom Moore, Gaylord Pendleton
'In for money, but not that strong for a holdover.' – *Variety*

The Last Picture Show ****
US 1971 118m bw
Columbia/LPS/BBS (Stephen J. Friedman)
Teenage affairs in a small Texas town in 1951, ending with the hero's embarkation for Korea and the closing of the tatty cinema.
Penetrating nostalgia with over-emphasis on sex; the detail is the attraction.
w Larry McMurtry, Peter Bogdanovich *d* Peter Bogdanovich *ph* Robert Surtees *m* original recordings *pd* Polly Platt
☆ Timothy Bottoms, Jeff Bridges, Cybill Shepherd, *Ben Johnson*, *Cloris Leachman*, Ellen Burstyn
'The most important work by a young American director since Citizen Kane.' – *Paul D. Zimmerman*
'So many things in it are so good that I wish I liked it more.' – *Stanley Kauffmann*
'Colour always had a tendency to prettify, and I didn't want that. I didn't want it to be a nostalgic piece.' – *Peter Bogdanovich*
† *Texasville* (qv), a sequel featuring many of the same actors, was filmed by Bogdanovich in 1990.
Ben Johnson; Cloris Leachman
best picture; script; Peter Bogdanovich (as director); Robert Surtees; Jeff Bridges; Ellen Burstyn
script; Ben Johnson; Cloris Leachman

The Last Posse
US 1953 73m bw
Columbia
Members of a thief-catching posse fall out on the way and return in disgrace.
Stumbling little Western, a poor return to the star after All the King's Men.
w Seymour and Connie Lee Bennett, Kenneth Gamet *d* Alfred Werker
☆ Broderick Crawford, John Derek, Wanda Hendrix, Charles Bickford

'A different kind of love story!'

The Last Remake of Beau Geste
US 1977 85m Technicolor
Universal (William S. Gilmore Jnr)
The Geste brothers find themselves in the Foreign Legion after the theft of the Blue Water sapphire.
Woebegone spoof of a romantic original, with most of the jokes totally irrelevant to the purpose and seldom at all funny.
w Marty Feldman, Chris J. Allen *d* Marty Feldman *ph* Gerry Fisher *m* John Morris
☆ Marty Feldman, Michael York, Ann-Margret, Peter Ustinov, Trevor Howard, James Earl Jones, Henry Gibson, Terry-Thomas, Roy Kinnear, Spike Milligan, Hugh Griffith, Irene Handl
'A ragbag of a film which looks like nothing so much as a Monty Python extravaganza in which inspiration has run dry and the comic timing gone sadly awry.' – *Tom Milne, MFB*

Last Resort **
GB 2000 73m colour
Artificial Eye/BBC (Ruth Caleb)
Jilted by her English fiancé, a young Russian women and her son seek political asylum and are sent to a seaside detention centre, where she finds work with a pornographer and is courted by a local man.
Small-scale but affecting drama, detailing the personal, rather than the political, effects of being stranded in a strange and unfriendly country given to a labyrinthine bureaucracy.
w Paul Pawlikowski, Rowan Joffe *d* Paul Pawlikowski *ph* Ryszard Lenczewski *m* Max de Wardener *pd* Tom Bowyer *ed* David Charrup
☆ Dina Korzun (Tanya), Artiom Strelnikov (Artiom), Paddy Considine (Alfie), Lindsey Honey (Les), Dave Bean (Frank), Perry Benson (Immigration officer), Adrian Scarborough (Council official)
'A slight but affectionately felt story, with loneliness at its heart, not asylum.' – *Alexander Walker*
'A bracing breath of fresh air for British cinema.' – *Lizzie Franke, Sight and Sound*

Last Rites
US 1988 103m DeLuxe
MGM (Donald P. Bellisario, Patrick McCormick)
A Catholic priest falls in love with a woman whom his gangster father wishes to kill.
Turgid thriller, slow-paced and uninteresting despite its hints of incest and emphasis on sex.
wd Donald P. Bellisario *ph* David Watkin *m* Bruce Broughton *ed* Pembroke J. Herring
☆ Tom Berenger, Daphne Zuniga, Chick Vennera, Anne Twomey, Paul Dooley, Dane Clark, Vassili Lambrinos

The Last Run *
US 1971 92m Metrocolor Panavision
MGM (Carter de Haven)
An ex-Chicago gangster retired to a Portuguese fishing village undertakes one last fatal job.
Well-made, rather uninteresting downbeat melodrama.
w Alan Sharp *d* Richard Fleischer *ph* Sven Nykvist *m* Jerry Goldsmith
☆ *George C. Scott*, Tony Musante, Trish Van Devere

The Last Safari
GB 1967 110m Technicolor
Paramount (Henry Hathaway)
A disillusioned white hunter takes on one last safari.
Dullsville adventure story with good animal photography redeeming some of the clichés.
w John Gay *novel Gilligan's Last Elephant* by Gerald Hanley *d* Henry Hathaway *ph* Ted Moore *m* Johnny Dankworth
☆ Stewart Granger, Kaz Garas, Gabriella Licudi, Johnny Sekka, Liam Redmond, Eugene Deckers

The Last Seduction ***
US 1994 110m CFI color
ITC (Jonathan Shestack)
A tough, manipulative New York woman leaves her husband, taking with her a million dollars he made on a drug deal.
Virtuoso revamping of the film noir genre, with a clever, tightly written, witty script, taut direction and a splendidly tart performance from Fiorentino.
w Steve Barancik d John Dahl ph Jeffrey Jur *m* Joseph Vitarelli *pd* Linda Pearl *ed* Eric L. Beason
☆ *Linda Fiorentino*, Peter Berg, J. T. Walsh, Bill Nunn, Bill Pullman
'Funny, sexy and so intricately plotted that you are never quite sure what is going to happen next.' – *Derek Malcolm, Guardian*
'Erotically ravenous, exceptionally witty, and impressively knowledgeable about all the dirty deals and low maneuvers that keep a corrupt world going.' – *David Denby, New York*

'In the heart of a young woman lies a secret that divides a nation.'

The Last September
GB/France/Ireland 1999 103m colour
Matrix /Scala/IFB (Yvonne Thunder)
In 1920, the Anglo-Irish aristocracy enjoy a weekend party on a Cork estate, while an IRA gunman hides nearby.
Elegant but empty drama of the beginning of the Irish troubles.
w John Banville *novel* Elizabeth Bowen *d* Deborah Warner *ph* Slawomir Idziak *m* Zbigniew Preisner *pd* Caroline Amies *ed* Kate Evans *cos* John Bright
☆ Maggie Smith (Lady Myra), Michael Gambon (Sir Richard Naylor), Jane Birkin (Francie Montmorency), Fiona Shaw (Marda Norton), Lambert Wilson (Hugo Montmorency), David Tennant (Capt Gerald Colthurst), Richard Roxburgh (Daventry), Keeley Hawes (Lois Farquar), Gary Lydon (Peter Connolly), Jonathan Slinger (Laurence Carstairs)
'A carefully fashioned but gloom-cloaked expression of familiar themes about a dying class of people during changing times.' – *Todd McCarthy, Variety*

The Last Shot You Hear
GB 1970 90m bw
Lippert-TCF (Jack Parsons)
Lovers plot murder, but the scheme backfires.
Unassuming mystery programmer from a West End success.
w Tim Shields *play The Sound of Murder* by William Fairchild *d* Gordon Hessler
☆ Hugh Marlowe, Zena Walker, Patricia Haines, William Dysart, Thorley Walters

The Last Stage *
Poland 1947 110m bw
Film Polski
original title: *Ostatni Etap*
Women suffer but one is finally rescued from the Nazi concentration camp at Auschwitz.
A dour, obsessive, horrifying record of human inhumanity, set in the actual camp and made by two former inmates.
w Wanda Jakubowska, Gerda Schneider *d* Wanda Jakubowska *ph* Borys Monastyrski *m* R. Palester
☆ Huguette Faget, W. Bartowna, T. Gorecka

The Last Starfighter *
US 1984 101m Technicolor Panavision
Lorimar/Universal (Gary Adelson, Edward O. Denault)
A teenage whiz at video games is abducted by the survivors of a distant planet who need his skills if they are to outwit their enemies.
A surprisingly pleasant variation on the Star Wars *boom, with sharp and witty performances from two reliable character actors and some elegant gadgetry to offset the teenage mooning.*
w Jonathan Betuel d Nick Castle *ph* King Baggot *m* Craig Safan *pd* Ron Cobb *ed* C. Timothy O'Meara
☆ Lance Guest, *Robert Preston*, *Dan O'Herlihy*, Catherine Mary Stewart, Barbara Bosson, Norman Snow

Last Summer *
US 1969 97m Eastmancolor
Alsid/Francis (Alfred Crown, Sidney Beckerman)
Well-to-do teenagers have sexual adventures on a summer seaside holiday.
Striking off-beat melodrama with vividly sketched characters.
w Eleanor Perry novel Evan Hunter *d Frank Perry ph* Gerald Hirschfeld *m* John Simon
☆ Barbara Hershey, Richard Thomas, Bruce Davison, Cathy Burns, Ernesto Gonzales, Ralph Waite
Cathy Burns

Last Summer in the Hamptons
US 1995 105m Technicolor
Revere/Rainbow/Jagtoria (Judith Wolinsky)
Family, friends and hangers-on gather for a final weekend at the home of an ageing Hollywood actress.
A tame comedy of theatrical chit-chat and tantrums, in which self-absorbed people fail to communicate with an audience.
w Henry Jaglom, Victoria Foyt *d* Henry Jaglom *ph* Hanania Baer *ad* Bruce Postman, Jeff Monte *ed* Henry Jaglom
☆ Victoria Foyt, Viveca Lindfors, Jon Robin Baitz, Savannah Boucher, Roscoe Lee Browne, André Gregory, Roddy McDowall, Martha Plimpton
'One has the uneasy feeling that Jaglom actually admires this pretentious, narcissistic circle of pseuds, which, of course, nullifies its satiric thrust.' – *George Perry*

The Last Sunset
US 1961 112m Eastmancolor
U-I (Brynaprod) (Eugene Frenke, Edward Lewis)
A killer and his hunter learn a lot about each other before the final showdown.
Slow psycho-Western with pretensions to tragedy.
w Dalton Trumbo *novel Showdown at Crazy Horse* by Howard Rigsby *d* Robert Aldrich *ph* Ernest Laszlo *m* Ernest Gold
☆ Rock Hudson, Kirk Douglas, Dorothy Malone, Carol Lynley, Joseph Cotten, Regis Toomey, Neville Brand

The Last Supper *
Cuba 1976 125m colour
Cuban Film Institute (Santiago Llapin, Camilo Vives)
original title: *La Ultima Cena*
In 18th-century Cuba, an aristocratic plantation owner attempts to get on better terms with his slaves.
Intermittently powerful, if overlong, political drama on the corruption of power and the acquiesence of the Church in the requirements of the State.
w Tomás Gonzalez, Maria Eugenia Haya, T. G. Alea *d* T. G. Alea *ph* Mario García Joya *m* Leo Brouwer *ad* Carlos Arditi *ed* Nelson Rodriguez
☆ Nelson Villagra, Silvano Rey, Luis Alberto García, José Antonio Rodriguez, Mario Balmaseda
'A laborious historical analogy, clumsy in the making and in implication, ineffectual esthetically and, for that matter, politically.' – *Stanley Kauffmann*

'Eat ... drink ... and be buried...'
The Last Supper
US 1996 100m CFI color
Electric/Vault (Matt Cooper, Larry Weinberg)
A group of graduate students, who share a house, invite illiberal people to dinner and poison them.
A slight black comedy that skirts around the matter of the end justifying the means, but which fails to develop its theme in an interesting way.
w Dan Rosen *d* Stacy Title *ph* Paul Cameron *m* Mark Mothersbaugh *pd* Linda Burton *ed* Luis Colina
☆ Annabeth Gish, Cameron Diaz, Jonathan Penner, Courtney B. Vance, Ron Eldard, Jason Alexander, Nora Dunn, Charles Durning, Bryn Erin, Mark Harmon, Bill Paxton, Ron Perlman
'It may be too clever for immediate cultdom – it would make a great stage play, which means there's little showy film business – but it's one of those films you'll remember.' – *Kim Newman, Empire*

Last Tango in Paris *
France/Italy/US 1972 129m Technicolor
Les Artistes Associés/PEA/UA (Alberto Grimaldi)
A middle-aged man and a young French girl have a doomed love affair.
Pretentious sex melodrama mainly notable for being banned.
w Bernardo Bertolucci, Franco Arcalli *d* Bernardo Bertolucci *ph* Vittorio Storaro *m* Gato Barbieri *ad* Ferdinando Scarfiotti *ed* Franco Arcalli, Roberto Perpignani
☆ Marlon Brando (Paul), Maria Schneider (Jeanne), Jean-Pierre Léaud (Tom), Massimo Girotti (Marcel), Veronica Lazare (Rosa), Maria Michi (Rosa's mother), Gitt Magrini (Jeanne's mother)
'An intense meditation on the realization of mortality.' – *Sight and Sound*
Bernardo Bertolucci (as director); Marlon Brando

The Last Temptation of Christ *
US/Canada 1988 163m Technicolor
Universal/Cineplex Odeon (Harry Ufland)
On the cross, Jesus dreams of escaping his destiny and living the life of an ordinary man.
Beautifully shot and strikingly acted, but wordy and too long; pre-release notoriety muffled consideration of the film's intentions.
w Paul Schrader *novel* Nikos Kazantzakis *d* Martin Scorsese *ph* Michael Ballhaus *m* Peter Gabriel *pd* John Beard *ed* Thelma Schoonmaker
☆ Willem Dafoe (Jesus), Harvey Keitel (Judus), Barbara Hershey (Mary Magdalene), Harry Dean Stanton (Paul), David Bowie (Pontius Pilate), Verna Bloom (Mary, mother of Jesus), Andre Gregory (John the Baptist), Juliette Caton, Roberts Blossom, Irvin Kershner
'A film of challenging ideas and not salacious provocations.' – *Variety*
Martin Scorsese

The Last Thrill: see *Female Vampire*

The Last Time I Committed Suicide
US 1997 92m colour/bw
Feature Film/Kushner-Locke/Tapestry (Edward Bates, Louise Rosner)
Beat writer Neal Cassady loses his girlfriend and his chance of employment.
Meandering tale of minimal interest, totally dependent on an audience's knowledge that Cassady was said to be the inspiration behind Jack Kerouac's novel On the Road.
wd Stephen Kay *letter* Neal Cassady *ph* Bobby Bukowski *pd* Amy Ancona *ed* Dorian Harris
☆ Thomas Jane, Keanu Reeves, Adrien Brody, Joe Doe, Claire Forlani, Marg Helgenberger, Gretchen Mol, Tom Bower (uncredited)
'If, halfway through you feel you can't take any more, it's not because it's immoral or chauvinist, it's because it's boring.' – *Gaby Wood, Guardian*

The Last Time I Saw Archie
US 1961 98m bw
UA/Mark VII/Manzanita/Talbot (Jack Webb)
Adventures of a con man amid overage civilian pilots at an army/air force base.
Patchy service comedy.
w William Bowers *d* Jack Webb *ph* Joe MacDonald *m* Frank Comstock
☆ Jack Webb, Robert Mitchum, Martha Hyer, France Nuyen, Louis Nye, Jimmy Lydon, Richard Arlen, Don Knotts, Robert Strauss, Joe Flynn

The Last Time I Saw Paris
US 1954 116m Technicolor
MGM (Jack Cummings)
A writer recalls his romance with a wealthy American girl in Paris.
Dull romantic drama which very deadeningly and predictably updates F. Scott Fitzgerald's Babylon Revisited.
w Julius J. and Philip G. Epstein, Richard Brooks *d* Richard Brooks *ph* Joseph Ruttenberg *m* Conrad Salinger
☆ Elizabeth Taylor, Van Johnson, Walter Pidgeon, Donna Reed, Eva Gabor

Last Train (dubbed)
France/Italy 1973 100m Eastmancolor/bw Panavision
Lira/Capitolina (Raymond Danon)
original title: *Le Train*
In 1941, on a train fleeing from the Germans, a Frenchman becomes separated from his pregnant wife and young daughter and begins an affair with a German Jewish refugee.
Somewhat glum romance, set against a background of war and casual death, with a downbeat ending.
w Pascal Jardin, Pierre Granier-Deferre *novel* Georges Simenon *d* Pierre Granier-Deferre *ph* Walter Wottitz *m* Philippe Sarde *ad* Jacques Saulnier *ed* Jean Ravel
☆ Jean-Louis Trintignant, Romy Schneider, Maurice Biraud, Regine, Serge Marquand, Anne Wiazemsky, Nike Arrighi

Last Train from Gun Hill *
US 1959 98m Technicolor Vistavision (Paramount)
A marshal tracks down the man who raped and murdered his wife; it turns out to be the son of an old friend.
Good suspense and action Western culminating in a High Noon *situation.*
w James Poe *story* Les Crutchfield *d* John Sturges *ph* Charles Lang Jnr *m* Dimitri Tiomkin
☆ Kirk Douglas, Anthony Quinn, Earl Holliman, Carolyn Jones, Brian Hutton

'Flaming love drama set against the background of Spain's Civil War!'
The Last Train from Madrid
US 1937 85m bw
Paramount (George M. Arthur)
A variety of people escape the fighting in the Spanish Civil War.
Tawdry topical melodrama with cliché characters and situations.
w Louis Stevens, Robert Wyler *d* James Hogan *ph* Harry Fischbeck *md* Boris Morros
☆ Dorothy Lamour, Lew Ayres, Gilbert Roland, Karen Morley, Lionel Atwill, Helen Mack, Robert Cummings, Olympe Bradna, Anthony Quinn, Lee Bowman, George Lloyd
'It is probably the worst film of the decade and should have been the funniest.' – *Graham Greene*
'Simply a topical and different background for a glib little fiction.' – *Frank S. Nugent*

The Last Tycoon
US 1976 124m Technicolor
Paramount/Academy/Sam Spiegel
The production head of a Hollywood studio in the thirties has his troubles complicated when he falls in love with a girl who reminds him of his dead wife.
Astonishingly inept and boring big budget all-star melodrama which doesn't even begin promisingly (the scenes from supposed thirties films are woefully inaccurate in style); it then bogs down in interminable dialogue scenes, leaving its famous cast all at sea.
w Harold Pinter *novel* F. Scott Fitzgerald *d* Elia Kazan *ph* Victor Kemper *m* Maurice Jarre *pd* Eugene F. Callahan
☆ Robert DeNiro, Robert Mitchum, Tony Curtis, Jeanne Moreau, Jack Nicholson, Ingrid Boulting, Donald Pleasence, Ray Milland, Dana Andrews, John Carradine
'So enervated it's like a vampire movie after the vampires have left.' – *New Yorker*
'That the result is incoherent is no surprise; that it is so hollow and visually graceless adds a kind of wonder to the disappointment.' – *Sight and Sound*
'The breathless reverence that informs the movie kills it stone dead.' – *Michael Billington, Illustrated London News*
'It seems to me that Kazan and Pinter have failed disastrously, but then perhaps the task is impossible anyway.' – *Benny Green, Punch*

The Last Valley
GB 1970 128m Eastmancolor Todd-AO
ABC/Season/Seamaster (James Clavell)
In 1641 during the Thirty Years War a scholar tries to defend a remote and prosperous Swiss valley against a horde of mercenaries.
Big-scale historical action picture crammed with pillage, torture, rape, death at the stake, throat cutting and general carnage; reasonably literate for all that, and convincingly set.
wd James Clavell *novel* J. B. Pick *ph* Norman Warwick *m* John Barry *ad* Peter Mullins
☆ Michael Caine, Omar Sharif, Florinda Bolkan, Nigel Davenport, Per Oscarsson, Arthur O'Connell, Brian Blessed

The Last Voyage *
US 1960 91m Metrocolor
MGM/Andrew and Virginia Stone
A boiler room explosion causes an old passenger liner to sink.
Spectacular if dramatically deficient actioner for which a genuine liner (awaiting scrapping) was sunk.
wd Andrew L. Stone *ph* Hal Mohr *m* Rudy Schrager
☆ Robert Stack, Dorothy Malone, Edmond O'Brien, George Sanders, Woody Strode, Jack Kruschen
'A prolonged nerve stretcher.' – *MFB*

'They pitted the fire of their youth against the flame of the frontier – when America was moving west!'
The Last Wagon
US 1956 99m Eastmancolor Cinemascope
TCF (William B. Hawks)
A half-breed wanted for murder joins an 1875 wagon train.
Heavy-going big-scale Western.
w James Edward Grant, Delmer Daves, Gwen Bagni *d* Delmer Daves *ph* Wilfrid Cline *m* Lionel Newman
☆ Richard Widmark, Felicia Farr, Tommy Rettig, Susan Kohner, Ray Stricklyn, Nick Adams, Carl Benton Reid

The Last Waltz ***
US 1978 115m DeLuxe
UA/Martin Scorsese, Jonathan Taplin (Robbie Robertson)
Documentary featuring the last concert of the rock group The Band at the Winterland, San Francisco, on Thanksgiving Day, 1976, after 16 years on the road.
Perhaps the best movie so far of a rock concert, one that also features many of the most influential performers of the era, together with some brief but revealing interviews with the band members.
d Martin Scorsese *ph* Michael Chapman, Laszlo Kovacs, Vilmos Zsigmond, David Myers, Bobby Byrne, Michael Watkins, Hiro Narita *pd* Boris Leven *ed* Yeu-Bun Yee, Jan Roblee
☆ Robbie Robertson, Rick Danko, Richard Manuel, Levon Helm, Garth Hudson, Eric Clapton, Neil Diamond, Bob Dylan, Joni Mitchell, Neil Young, Emmylou Harris, Ringo Starr, Paul Butterfield, Dr John, Van Morrison and also Ronnie Hawkins, The Staples, Muddy Waters, Ron Wood

The Last Warning *
US 1929 88m bw
Universal
Murder backstage.
Shot as a silent film, with sound hurriedly added, this remains a stylish comedy-thriller with all the familiar ingredients of the whodunnit.
w Alfred A. Cohn *d* Paul Leni *ph* Hal Mohr
☆ Laura La Plante, Montagu Love, Roy D'Arcy, John Boles, Mack Swain, Slim Summerville, Margaret Livingston
† Remade in 1938 as *The House of Fear*, a William Gargan second feature.

The Last Warning
US 1938 62m bw
Universal (Irving Starr)
A private eye mystery.
Better-than-average second feature.
w Edmund L. Hartmann *novel* *The Dead Don't Care* by Jonathan Latimer *d* Albert S. Rogell
☆ Preston Foster, Joyce Compton, Frank Jenks

The Last Warrior: see *Flap*

The Last Wave *
Australia 1977 106m Atlab (UA)
During a spell of freak weather, a lawyer has recurrent dreams which give him the key to an Aborigine prophecy about the world being destroyed by flood...
Curious supernatural drama successfully played as a mystery, with excellent atmosphere and special effects.
w Peter Weir, Tony Morphett, Petru Popescu *d* Peter Weir *ph* Russell Boyd *m* Charles Wain *pd* Goran Warff
☆ Richard Chamberlain, Olivia Hamnet, Frederick Parslow
'A Hitchcockian sense of minatory dislocation.' – *Tim Pulleine, MFB*

The Last Winter
Canada 1989 103m colour
Telefilm Canada/CIDO/Rode/John Aaron/NFBC (Jack Clements, Ken Rodeck)
A young boy is upset to discover that his father is planning to move the family from their farm to work in the city.
Pleasant, nostalgic, forgettable drama of childhood, with too little action and too much talk to interest the young.
wd Aaron Kim Johnston *ph* Ian Elkin *m* Victor Davies *pd* Perri Gorrara *ed* Lara Mazur
☆ Gerard Parkes, David Ferry, Wanda Cannon, Marsha Moreau, Nathaniel Moreau, Katie Murray, Joshua Murray

The Last Word
US 1979 105m colour
Variety International Pictures
An Irish inventor by wily stratagems prevents the demolition of the apartment block he occupies.
Oddly old-fashioned comedy drama of little obvious appeal.
w Michael Varhol, Greg Smith, Kit Carson *d* Roy Boulting
☆ Richard Harris, Karen Black, Martin Landau, Biff McGuire, Dennis Christopher

Last Year at Marienbad ***
France/Italy 1961 94m bw Dyaliscope
Terra/Tamara/Cormoran/Precitel/Como/Argos/Cinetel/Silver/Cineriz (Raymond Froment)
original title: *L'Année Dernière à Marienbad*
In a vast old-fashioned hotel, a man meets a woman who may or may not have had an affair with him the previous year in Marienbad – or was it Frederiksbad?
A dreamy, elegant film which presents a puzzle with no solution. It has its attractions for film buffs and cryptogram addicts, but is not for anyone who simply wants to be told a story.
w Alain Robbe-Grillet *d* Alain Resnais *ph* Sacha Vierny *m* Francis Seyrig *ad* Jacques Saulnier
☆ Delphine Seyrig, Giorgio Albertazzi, Sacha Pitoeff
'Elaborate, ponderous and meaningless.' – *Newsweek*
'Clearly the film's creators know exactly what they want to do and have done it with complete success. Whether one responds to the result is entirely a matter of temperament.' – *John Russell Taylor, MFB*
Alain Robbe-Grillet

The Last Yellow
GB/Germany 1999 94m colour
Capitol/Scala/Hollywood Partners/Arts Council/BBC (Jolyon Symonds)

A dim-witted youth pays £500 to an overweight fantasist to go to London to kill the thug who left his brother brain-damaged.
Low-key, small-scale drama of two losers unable to deal with life's little difficulties; it looks misplaced on the big screen.
w Paul Tucker *play* Paul Tucker *d* Julian Farino *ph* David Odd *m* Adrian Johnston *pd* John Paul Kelly *ed* Pia di Ciaula
☆ Mark Addy (Frank), Charlie Creed-Miles (Kenny), Samantha Morton (Jackie), Kenneth Cranham (Len), Alan Atherall (Donut)
'Well-made, but unremarkable and depressingly unappealing at times.' – *Nick Briggs, Film Review*

Late August, Early September
France 1999 111m colour
Artificial Eye/Dacia/Cinéa (Georges Benayoun, Philippe Carcassonne)

original title: *Fin Août, Début Septembre*
A dying writer influences the lives of a close-knit group of friends.
Restless drama of changing partners and emotional crises that is so intensely focused as to exclude spectators.
wd Olivier Assayas *ph* Denis Lenoir *pd* François-Renaud Labarthe *ed* Luc Barnier
☆ Mathieu Amalric (Gabriel Deshayes), Virginie Ledoyen (Anne Rosenwald), François Cluzet (Adrien Willer), Jeanne Balibar (Jenny), Alex Descas (Jérémie), Arsinée Khanjian (Lucie), Nathalie Richard (Maryelle Deshayes), Mia Hanson-Love (Vera)
'I understand Assayas's wish is to lower daily reality to the point of ordinariness. I think he's lowered it to the point of dullness.' – *Alexander Walker, London Evening Standard*

The Late Edwina Black *
GB 1951 78m bw
IFD/Elvey-Gartside (Ernest Gartside)

US title: *Obsessed*
When a schoolteacher's wife is found dead, the police have three suspects.
Adequately suspenseful Victorian thriller from a successful play.
w Charles Frank, David Evans *play* William Dinner, William Morum *d* Maurice Elvey *ph* Stephen Dade *m* Allan Gray
☆ Geraldine Fitzgerald, David Farrar, *Roland Culver*, Jean Cadell, Mary Merrall, Harcourt Williams, Charles Heslop, Ronald Adam

'Tomorrow wasn't just another day.'
Late for Dinner
US 1991 93m DeLuxe
First Independent/New Line/Castle Rock (Dan Lupovitz, W. D. Richter)

After being unwittingly frozen for 19 years, a man and his retarded brother-in-law wake up to discover that the world has moved on to 1991.
Rip van Winkle without a twinkle.
w Mark Andrus *d* W. D. Richter *ph* Peter Sova *m* David Mansfield *pd* Lilly Kilvert *ed* Richard Chew, Robert Leighton
☆ Brian Wimmer, Peter Berg, Marcia Gay Harden, Peter Gallagher, Colleen Flynn, Kyle Secor, Michael Beach

The Late George Apley *
US 1946 96m bw
TCF (Fred Kohlmar)
The uneventful family life of a Boston blueblood.
Pleasant but tame family comedy-drama, solidly carpentered.
w Philip Dunne *novel* John P. Marquand *d* Joseph L. Mankiewicz *ph* Joseph LaShelle *m* Cyril Mockridge
☆ *Ronald Colman*, Edna Best, Vanessa Brown, Richard Haydn, Peggy Cummins, Charles Russell

Late Marriage: see *Hatuna Meuheret*

'Let's not go to work.'
Late Night Shopping
GB/Germany 2001 91m DeLuxe
FilmFour/GFO/Scottish Screen/NLF//Senator/Ideal (Angus Lamont)

Four friends, who work on the night shift in dead-end jobs, try to improve their love-lives.
Slight, pawky comedy that outstays its welcome.
w Jack Lothian *d* Saul Metzstein *ph* Brian Tufano *m* Alex Heffes *pd* Mike Gunn *ed* Justine Wright
☆ Luke de Woolfson (Sean), James Lance (Vincent), Kate Ashfield (Jody), Enzo Cilenti (Lenny), Heike Makatsch (Madeline Zozzocolovich), Shauna MacDonald (Gail), Sienna Guillory (Susie), Laurie Ventry (Joe)
'A wonderfully out-there slacker comedy that's as tight as a drum in script, direction and performances.' – *Derek Elley, Variety*

The Late Show *
US 1977 93m Metrocolor
Warner (Robert Altman)

An ageing private eye in Los Angeles finds that his ex-partner's death and a lost cat have a complex connection.
A more-or-less engaging spoof of, or perhaps a valediction to, the private eye genre, with engaging scenes marred by poor colour and occasional excesses of violent action.
wd Robert Benton *ph* Chuck Rosher *m* Ken Wannberg *ed* Lou Lombardo, Peter Appleton
☆ *Art Carney*, Lily Tomlin, Bill Macy, Ruth Nelson, Howard Duff, Joanna Cassidy, Eugene Roche
'On its own terms, it's perfectly executed. The squalid settings stink of decay; the spare pacing captures the tough style of Hammett prose; and the stylized use of blood puts some sting into murder.' – *Frank Rich, New York Post*
Robert Benton (for script)

Latin Lovers
US 1953 104m Technicolor
MGM (Joe Pasternak)

An heiress on holiday in Brazil looks for a man who will love her for herself alone.
Barren romantic drama, flatfooted and drawn out.
w Isobel Lennart *d* Mervyn Le Roy *ph* Joseph Ruttenberg *m* George Stoll
☆ Lana Turner, Ricardo Montalban, John Lund, Louis Calhern, Jean Hagen

Latin Quarter *
GB 1945 80m bw
British National (Louis H. Jackson, Derrick de Marney)
US title: *Frenzy*
In 1890s Paris a mad sculptor murders his fiancée and hides her inside his latest exhibit.
Artificial-looking but melodramatically effective thriller with a chilling climax and a detailed Degas-period background.
wd Vernon Sewell play L'Angoisse by Pierre Mills, Charles Vylars *ph* Gunther Krampf
☆ Derrick de Marney, Joan Greenwood, Beresford Egan, Frederick Valk, Lily Kann, Martin Miller

Laugh and Get Rich
US 1931 72m bw
RKO (William Le Baron)
A man invests his wife's money in a tyre with a whistling valve.
Inconsequential comedy with ancient jokes.
w Ralph Spence, Gregory La Cava *d* Gregory La Cava *ph* Jack MacKenzie *ad* Max Ree
☆ Hugh Herbert, Edna May Oliver, Dorothy Lee, Robert Emmett Keane
'Entertainment for the willing.' – *Variety*

Laugh with Max Linder **
France 1963 88m bw
Films Max Linder
original title: *En Compagnie de Max Linder*
Excerpts from three of the dapper comedian's most famous American comedies: *Be My Wife* (1921), *The Three Must-Get-Theres* (1922), *Seven Years' Bad Luck* (1923).
A compilation which must serve as a consensus of this almost forgotten comedian's work. The gag with a broken mirror in particular was borrowed by innumerable other comedians, notably the Marx Brothers in Duck Soup. *Audiences new to Linder's work will find him not especially sympathetic but capable of many felicities. He wrote, produced and directed all three films.*
compiler Maud Max Linder

Laughing Anne
GB 1953 90m Technicolor
Republic/Wilcox-Neagle
French Anne and her boxing lover are characters of the Javanese waterfront; he kills her after she has fallen for a sea captain.
Cheap and turgid adaptation of a Joseph Conrad story; the author would not recognize it. Studio settings put the lid on hilariously bad work all round.
w Pamela Bower *d* Herbert Wilcox *ph* Max Greene *m* Anthony Collins
☆ Margaret Lockwood, Forrest Tucker, Ronald Shiner, Wendell Corey, Robert Harris

Laughing at Trouble
US 1937 60m bw
Max Golden/TCF
A small town newspaper editress untangles personal problems.
Acceptable second feature which almost became a series.
w Robert Ellis and Helen Logan *d* Frank R. Strayer
☆ Jane Darwell, Sara Haden, Lois Wilson, Margaret Hamilton, Allan Lane, John Carradine

Laughing Gravy ***
US 1931 20m bw
Hal Roach

Stan and Ollie retrieve their dog when the landlord throws it out into the snow.
One of the most endearing comedies of these stars, and one of the simplest.
w H. M. Walker *d* James W. Horne *ph* Art Lloyd *ed* Richard Currier
☆ Stan Laurel, Oliver Hardy, Charlie Hall, Harry Bernard

The Laughing Lady
GB 1946 93m Technicolor
Louis H. Jackson/British National
During the French revolution, an artist under sentence is required to steal an English lady's pearls.
Heavy-going operetta with the sense that all concerned have bitten off more than they can chew.
w Jack Whittingham *play* Ingram d'Abbes *d* Paul Stein *ph* Geoffrey Unsworth *m* Hans May *ch* Eileen Baker *ad* R. Holmes Paul *ed* Alan Osbiston
☆ Anne Ziegler (Denise), Webster Booth (Andre), Peter Graves (Prince of Wales), Felix Aylmer (Sir Felix Mountroyal), Francis L. Sullivan (Sir William Tremayne), Paul Dupuis (Pierre), Ralph Truman (Lord Mandeville), Chili Bouchier (Louise), Charles Goldner (Robespierre), Anthony Nicholls (Mr Pitt)

'Eight people know who the killer is – and they're all dead!'
The Laughing Policeman *
US 1973 112m DeLuxe
TCF (Stuart Rosenberg)

GB title: *An Investigation of Murder*
A mad machine-gunner eludes the San Francisco police.
Downbeat, semi-documentary police thriller with pretensions. Too complex by half, with an overplus of characterization, but the location work is excellent.
w Thomas Rickman *novel* Maj Sjowall, Per Wahloo *d* Stuart Rosenberg *ph* David Walsh *m* Charles Fox
☆ Walter Matthau, Bruce Dern, Lou Gossett, Albert Paulsen, Anthony Zerbe

Laughing Sinners
US 1931 71m bw
MGM
A girl with a past joins the Salvation Army.
Glum romance which however started an effective star combination.
w Bess Meredyth and Martin Flavin *d* Harry Beaumont
☆ Joan Crawford, Clark Gable, Neil Hamilton, Marjorie Rambeau, Guy Kibbee

Laughter **
US 1930 99m bw
Paramount (Herman J. Mankiewicz)
An ex-Follies girl marries a millionaire but later goes on a spree with the composer she once loved.
Sharply observed, before its time romantic comedy reminiscent now of the later Philadelphia Story *in its attitudes to wealth and love. A precursor of the smart crazy comedies of the mid-thirties.*
w Donald Ogden Stewart d Harry d'Abbadie d'Arrast ph George Folsey
☆ Fredric March, Nancy Carroll, Frank Morgan, Glenn Anders, Diane Ellis
'One of the best talking pictures I have ever seen.' – *James Agate*
'A talkie with so fast a pace that it crowds the comprehension of half the customers ... marked at intervals by superb dialogue and the quick hand of a smart director.' – *Pare Lorentz*
'A lovely sophisticated comedy.' – *New Yorker, 1977*
original story (Donald Ogden Stewart, Harry d'Abbadie d'Arrast, Douglas Doty)

Laughter in Paradise *
GB 1951 93m bw
Transocean (Mario Zampi)
An eccentric leaves in his will a fortune for each of his relations providing they will perform certain embarrassing or criminal acts.
A funny idea gets half-hearted treatment, but the good bits are hilarious.
w Michael Pertwee, Jack Davies *d* Mario Zampi *ph* William McLeod *m* Stanley Black
☆ *Alastair Sim, Joyce Grenfell*, Hugh Griffith, Fay Compton, John Laurie, George Cole, Guy Middleton, Ronald Adam, Leslie Dwyer, A. E. Matthews, Beatrice Campbell
† Remade 1972 as *Some Will, Some Won't*.

Laughter in the Dark *
GB/France 1969 104m DeLuxe
UA/Woodfall/Winkast/Marceau (Neil Hartley)
A wealthy art dealer is taken in by an ambitious usherette and her lover, and after being blinded in a car accident tries to kill them.
Unsatisfactory adaptation of a novel with a very specialized appeal: conventional swinging London and Riviera settings only confuse the spectator. Moments do work, though.
w Edward Bond *novel* Vladimir Nabokov *d* Tony Richardson *ph* Dick Bush *m* Raymond Leppard *ad* Julia Trevelyan Oman
☆ Nicol Williamson, Anna Karina, Jean-Claude Drouot, Peter Bowles, Sian Phillips
'It fails to create the slightest interest in its trio of repulsive characters.' – *Philip Strick*

Laughterhouse *
GB 1984 93m colour
Greenpoint/Film Four International (Ann Scott)
aka: *Singleton's Pluck*
A Norfolk farmer decides to walk his fattened geese to market.
An attempt to revive the tradition of Ealing comedy lands up somewhere on the wrong side of Group Three. Not enough plot, almost no jokes, and the geese are almost the only pleasant creatures.
w Brian Glover *d* Richard Eyre *ph* Clive Tickner *m* Dominic Muldowney
☆ Ian Holm, Penelope Wilton, Bill Owen, Richard Hope, Stephen Moore, Rosemary Martin

Laura ***
US 1944 85m bw
TCF (Otto Preminger)

A beautiful girl is murdered ... or is she? A cynical detective investigates.
A quiet, streamlined little murder mystery that brought a new adult approach to the genre and heralded the mature film noir of the later forties. A small cast responds perfectly to a classically spare script, and in Clifton Webb a new star is born.
w Jay Dratler, Samuel Hoffenstein, Betty Reinhardt novel Vera Caspary *d* Otto Preminger *ph Joseph LaShelle m David Raksin ad* Lyle Wheeler, Leland Fuller
☆ *Dana Andrews, Clifton Webb*, Gene Tierney, Judith Anderson, *Vincent Price*, Dorothy Adams, James Flavin
WALDO LYDECKER (CLIFTON WEBB): 'It's lavish, but I call it home.'
WALDO: 'I shall never forget the weekend Laura

died. A silver sun burned through the sky like a huge magnifying glass. It was the hottest Sunday in my recollection. I felt as if I were the only human being left in New York … I had just begun Laura's story when another of those detectives came to see me. I had him wait.'

WALDO: 'In my case, self-absorption is completely justified. I have never discovered any other subject quite so worthy of my attention.'

'Everybody's favourite chic murder mystery.' – *New Yorker, 1977*

† Rouben Mamoulian directed some scenes before handing over to Preminger.

Academy Award: Joseph LaShelle

Academy Award nomination: script; Otto Preminger; Clifton Webb; art direction

Laurel and Hardy in Toyland: see *Babes in Toyland (1934)*

The Laurel and Hardy Murder Case

US 1930 30m bw

Hal Roach

Heirs to a fortune are menaced by a mad murderer.

Empty spoof on The Cat and the Canary *which affords little scope.*

w H. M. Walker *d* James Parrott *ph* George Stevens, Walter Lundin

☆ Stan Laurel, Oliver Hardy, Fred Kelsey, Del Henderson, Dorothy Granger, Frank Austin, Tiny Sandford

Laurel and Hardy's Laughing Twenties **

US 1965 90m bw

MGM/Robert Youngson

Excerpts from lesser comedians of the period – Max Davidson, Charlie Chase – are interspersed with highlights from Laurel and Hardy's silent two-reelers.

A hilarious and craftsmanlike compilation, perhaps a little too long for its own good.

m Skeets Alquist *w/ed* Robert Youngson *commentator* Jay Jackson

† Films extracted include *Putting Pants on Philip, From Soup to Nuts, Wrong Again, The Finishing Touch, Liberty, Double Whoopee, Leave 'Em Laughing, You're Darn Tooting* and the custard pie climax from *The Battle of the Century*.

Laurin (dubbed)

Germany 1985 80m colour

Salinas/TS-Film/Dialog/Südwestfunk (Bernhardt Stampfer, Andreas Bareiss)

In a small village, a young girl outwits a child murderer.

Confused attempt at a spooky narrative; its length and the great many loose ends suggest it has been heavily cut. All that remains is a little queasy atmosphere.

w Robert Sigl, Adam Rozgonyi *d* Robert Sigl *ph* Nyika Jancso *m* Jacques Zwart, Hans Jansen *ed* Teri Losonci

☆ Dora Szinetar, Brigitte Karner, Karoly Eperjes, Hedi Temessy

'Two men. One mission. Twice the mess...'

Lava

GB 2001 100m Soho Images

Winchester/Walking Point/Sterling (Michael Riley, Gregor Truter)

A drifter offers to help a friend take revenge on the man who beat his brother and left him brain-damaged.

Odd, edgy, black comedy that promises more than it delivers.

wd Joe Tucker *ph* Ian Liggett *m* Simon Fisher-Turner *pd* Philip Robinson *ed* St John O'Rorke

☆ Joe Tucker (Smiggy), James Holmes (Philip), Nicola Stapleton (Julie), Tameka Empson (Maxine), Johann Myers (Curtis), Dennis Titus (Claude), Grahame Fox (Darrel), Mark Leadbetter (Neville), Tom Bell (Eric), Leslie Grantham (Mr Aladdin)

'A profane and uncompromising comedy, several shades darker than the majority of recent British movies.' – *Ryan Gilbey, Sight and Sound*

† It has a virtually identical plot to the 1999 movie, *The Last Yellow* (qv), which was scripted by Paul Tucker, brother of Joe Tucker.

The Lavender Hill Mob ****

GB 1951 78m bw

Ealing (Michael Truman)

A timid bank clerk conceives and executes a bullion robbery.

Superbly characterized and inventively detailed comedy, one of the best ever made at Ealing or in Britain.

w T. E. B. Clarke d Charles Crichton ph Douglas Slocombe m Georges Auric *ad* William Kellner *ed* Seth Holt

☆ *Alec Guinness, Stanley Holloway*, Sidney James, Alfie Bass, Marjorie Fielding, Edie Martin, John Gregson, Gibb McLaughlin, Sydney Tafler, Audrey Hepburn

'Amusing situations and dialogue are well paced and sustained throughout: the climax is delightful.' – *MFB*

'An outrageous comedy, of course, but the observations of detail and character are so true, the sense of a familiar place so sharp, that few will resent the gusto with which the outrage is perpetrated.' – C. A. *Lejeune*

Academy Award: T. E. B. Clarke

Academy Award nomination: Alec Guinness

BAFTA: British film

The Law: see *Where the Hot Wind Blows*

Law and Disorder: see *Spies of the Air (1939)*

Law and Disorder *

GB 1958 76m bw

British Lion/Hotspur (Paul Soskin)

Crooks rally round a confederate about to be arrested, to prevent his son from learning of his father's real career.

Amusing, well-pointed caper on sub-Ealing lines.

w T. E. B. Clarke *novel Smuggler's Circuit* by Denys Roberts *d* Charles Crichton *ph* Ted Scaife *m* Humphrey Searle

☆ Michael Redgrave, Robert Morley, Joan Hickson, Lionel Jeffries, Ronald Squire, Elizabeth Sellars

Law and Disorder *

US 1974 102m Technicolor Panavision

Memorial/Leroy Street/Ugo Fadsin (William Richert)

New York suburbanites aghast at escalating violence form themselves into a vigilante patrol.

Bewilderingly uneven comedy drama which starts as satirical comedy and ends with one of the heroes dead and the other moralizing. Sporadically interesting, and certainly topical.

w Ivan Passer, William Richert, Kenneth Harris Fishman *d* Ivan Passer *ph* Arthur J. Ornitz *m* Andy Badale

☆ Ernest Borgnine, Carroll O'Connor, Karen Black, Ann Wedgeworth, Leslie Ackerman, David Spielberg

The Law and Jake Wade *

US 1958 86m Metrocolor Cinemascope

MGM (William Hawks)

A marshal helps an old outlaw friend to escape from jail, and lives to regret it.

Good standard Western, enjoyable throughout but with no outstanding merits.

w William Bowers *novel* Marvin H. Albert *d* John Sturges *ph* Robert Surtees *ad* William Horning, Daniel B. Cathcart *ed* Ferris Webster

☆ Robert Taylor (Jake Wade), Richard Widmark (Clint Hollister), Patricia Owens (Peggy Carter), Robert Middleton (Ortero), Henry Silva (Rennie), De Forest Kelley (Wexler), Burt Douglas (Lieutenant), Eddie Firestone (Burke)

Law and Order *

US 1932 80m bw

Universal

A cowboy becomes marshal and cleans up Tombstone.

Drily effective fictionalization of Wyatt Earp's exploits, with a good star performance.

w John Huston story Saint Johnson by W. R. Burnett *d* Edward L. Cahn *ph* Jackson Rose *ed* Milton Carruth

☆ *Walter Huston*, Harry Carey, Raymond Hatton, Russell Simpson, Russell Hopton

Law and Order

US 1953 80m Technicolor

Universal-International

Curious belated sequel to the above with Johnson moving on to tame Cottonwood; actual presentation rather dull.

w John and Gwen Bagni, D. D. Beauchamp *story Saint Johnson* by W.R. Burnett *d* Nathan Juran *ph* Clifford Stine *ad* Robert Clatworthy, Alexander Golitzen *ed* Ted J. Kent

☆ Ronald Reagan, Dorothy Malone, Preston Foster, Alex Nicol, Russell Johnson, Ruth Hampton, Barry Kelley, Dennis Weaver

The Law and the Lady

US 1951 104m bw

MGM (Edwin H. Knopf)

A couple of confidence tricksters inveigle themselves into the house of a vulgar millionairess, but one of them has an attack of conscience.

Dreary remake of The Last of Mrs Cheyney *(qv) with the locale altered, the plot simplified, and the level of wit diluted.*

w Leonard Spigelgass, Karl Tunberg *d* Edwin H. Knopf *ph* George Folsey *m* Carmen Dragon

☆ Greer Garson, Michael Wilding, Fernando Lamas, Marjorie Main, Hayden Rorke, Margalo Gillmore, Ralph Dumke

Law of Desire *

Spain 1987 101m colour

Other Cinema/El Deseo/Laurenfilm (Ester Garcia)

original title: *La Ley del Deseo*

A glamorous homosexual film director is pursued by a male would-be lover while sharing his apartment with his former brother, who has undergone a sex change, and her transvestite lover's daughter.

Delirious, stylish mix of sex and passion, though many may regard it as too camp and overdone.

wd Pedro Almodóvar *ph* Angel Luis Fernandez *pd* Javier Fernandez *ed* Jose Salcedo

☆ Eusebio Poncela, Carmen Maura, Antonio Banderas, Miguel Molina, Manuela Velasco, Bibi Andersen, Fernando Guillen

'Almodovar's tone is not like anyone else's; the film has the exaggerated plot of an absurdist Hollywood romance … The film is festive. It doesn't disguise its narcissism; it turns it into bright-coloured tragi-comedy.' – *Pauline Kael, New Yorker*

The Law of the Lawless

US 1963 87m Techniscope

Paramount/A. C. Lyles

A judge arrives in a small Western town to conduct the murder trial of a former friend.

Jaded Western of interest only for the producer's custom of packing the bit roles with former stars.

w Steve Fisher *d* William F. Claxton *ph* Lester Shorr

☆ Dale Robertson, Yvonne de Carlo, William Bendix, Bruce Cabot, Barton MacLane, John Agar, Richard Arlen, Kent Taylor, Lon Chaney Jnr

Law of the Tropics

US 1941 76m bw

Warner (Ben Stoloff)

A café singer on the run from a murder charge marries a South American rubber plantation owner.

Hackneyed melodrama born from a mating of Oil for the Lamps of China *and* Tropic Zone.

w Charles Grayson *d* Ray Enright *ph* Sid Hickox *m* Howard Jackson

☆ Constance Bennett, Jeffrey Lynn, Regis Toomey, Mona Maris, Frank Puglia, Thomas Jackson, Craig Stevens

'Out of the most exciting pages of frontier history!'

The Law Versus Billy the Kid

US 1954 73m Technicolor

Sam Katzman/Columbia

Billy the Kid is driven into crime to avenge a friend.

Technicolor seems wasted on this two-bit Western which can't even manage to tell a clear story.

w John T. Williams *d* William Castle

☆ Scott Brady, Betta St John, James Griffith, Alan Hale Jnr, Paul Cavanagh

The Lawless

US 1949 83m bw

Paramount/Pine-Thomas

GB title: *The Dividing Line*

The editor of a California small-town newspaper defends a Spanish boy who is being victimized by the racist element.

Well-meaning 'realistic' melodrama, unfortunately among the dullest of the socially conscious movies of this period.

w Geoffrey Homes *d* Joseph Losey *ph* Roy Hunt *m* Mahlon Merrick

☆ Macdonald Carey, Gail Russell, John Sands, John Hoyt, Lee Patrick, Lalo Rios

The Lawless Breed

US 1952 83m Technicolor

U-I (William Alland)

The adventures and repentance of badman John Wesley Hardin.

Standard Western programmer with the star in an unlikely role.

w Bernard Gordon *d* Raoul Walsh *ph* Irving Glassberg *m* Joseph Gershenson

☆ Rock Hudson, Julie Adams, John McIntire, Dennis Weaver, Hugh O'Brian

The Lawless Frontier

US 1934 53m bw

Lone Star/Malvern

A cowboy comes to the rescue when a ruthless renegade takes a fancy to a gold prospector's granddaughter.

Rudimentary Western with stilted, melodramatic acting and not much action other than a couple of examples of Canutt's stunt riding.

wd Robert North Bradbury *ph* Archie Stout *ad* E. R. Hickson *ed* Charles Hunt

☆ John Wayne, Sheila Terry, Jack Rockwell, George Hayes, Buffalo Bill Jnr, Yakima Canutt, Earl Dwire

'We think we live in a rational world... then we screw it up.'

Lawless Heart *

GB 2001 100m colour

Optimum/IoMFC/British Screen/FC/October (Martin Pope)

Lives and relationships of old friends intertwine and overlap after they are reunited at the funeral of a gay restaurateur.

A film that revisits the same events three times, as seen from the varying viewpoints of the people involved; the method loses its interest the second time around.

wd Neil Hunter, Tom Hunsinger *ph* Sean Bobbit *m* Adrian Johnston *pd* Lynne Whiteread *ed* Scott Thomas

☆ Douglas Henshall (Tim), Tom Hollander (Nick), Bill Nighy (Dan), Clementine Celarie (Corinne), Josephine Butler (Leah), Ellie Haddington (Judy), Stuart Laing (David), Sukie Smith (Charlie)

'A thoughtful, funny and melancholic meditation on the notion that all hearts are lawless and out of control when under emotional stress.' – *Kenneth Turan, Los Angeles Times*

'A consistently witty and heartfelt portrait of contemporary British lives.' – *John Mount, Sight and Sound*

A Lawless Street

US 1955 78m Technicolor

Columbia (Harry Joe Brown)

A marshal marries a dance hall entertainer, and loses interest in his job when she leaves him.

Enjoyable minor Western.

w Kenneth Gamet *novel Marshal of Medicine Bend* by Brad Ward *d* Joseph H. Lewis *ph* Ray Rennahan *m* Paul Sawtell

☆ Randolph Scott, Angela Lansbury, Warner Anderson, Jean Parker, Wallace Ford, John Emery, James Bell, Ruth Donnelly, Michael Pate, Jeanette Nolan, Don Megowan

Lawman *

US 1970 99m Technicolor

UA/Scimitar (Michael Winner)

When a marshal tracks down drunken cowboys who have killed an old man, the townsfolk's resistance leads to a bloodbath.

Terse, violent Western with a good cast.

w Gerald Wilson *d* Michael Winner *ph* Bob Paynter *m* Jerry Fielding
☆ Burt Lancaster, Robert Ryan, Lee J. Cobb, Sheree North, Robert Duvall, Joseph Wiseman, John McGiver, Albert Salmi, J. D. Cannon

Lawn Dogs **
GB 1997 101m Rank Colour
Carlton/Rank/Toledo (Duncan Kenworthy)
A young girl, whose parents live in a secure community behind protected gates, forms a friendship with the tough youth who cuts the grass.
A fable, both charming and dark, of the dangers of civilizing the environment.
w Naomi Wallace *d* John Duigan *ph* Elliot Davis *pd* John Myhre *ed* Humphrey Dixon
☆ Sam Rockwell, Christopher McDonald, Kathleen Quinlan, Bruce McGill, Mischa Barton, David Barry Gray
'A true and compelling portrait of a so-called "secure community" which proves instead to be imprisoned by its own paranoia. A gem.' – *Mark Steyn, Spectator*

'God Made Him Simple. Science Made Him A God.'
The Lawnmower Man *
GB/US 1992 108m DeLuxe
First Independent/Allied Vision/Lane Pringle/Fuji Eight (Gimel Everett)
aka: *Stephen King's The Lawnmower Man*
A doctor experiments with drugs and computer technology to improve the mind of his retarded gardener, with startling and unforeseen results.
Some impressive special effects, simulating 'virtual reality' – a computer-created world – enliven an otherwise drab and predictable science fiction movie.
w Brett Leonard, Gimel Everett *story* Stephen King *d* Brett Leonard *ph* Russell Carpenter *m* Dan Wyman *pd* Alex McDowell *ed* Alan Baumgarten *sp* Angel Studios, Xaos Inc.
☆ Jeff Fahey, Pierce Brosnan, Jenny Wright, Geoffrey Lewis, Mark Bringleson, Jeremy Slate, Dean Norris
'It all works surprisingly well, with interesting and well-integrated visual effects, some nice humour and a few genuinely visionary effects.' – *Kim Newman, Empire*
† Stephen King was granted an injunction forbidding the film's producers from using his name in connection with the film.
†† A director's cut of the film was also released on video with a running time of 142m.

Lawnmower Man 2: Beyond Cyberspace
US 1995 92m colour Panavision
First Independent/Allied Entertainments/Fuji Eight (Edward Simons, Keith Fox)
A legless former imbecile attempts to create the city of the future in cyberspace, where he can control the world.
An incoherent and incompetent fantasy aimed at the young.
wd Farhad Mann *ph* Ward Russell *m* Robert Folk *pd* Ernest Roth *ed* Peter Berger, Joel Goodman *sp* Cinesite
☆ Patrick Bergin, Matt Frewer, Austin O'Brien, Ely Pouget, Camille Cooper, Kevin Conway, Patrick La Breque, Crystal Celeste Grant
'Stumbles from one unconnected moment to the next unexciting one.' – *Alan Jones, Film Review*

Lawrence of Arabia ****
GB 1962 221m Technicolor Super Panavision 70
Columbia/Horizon (Sam Spiegel)
An adventurer's life with the Arabs, told in flashbacks after his accidental death in the thirties.
Sprawling epic which manages after four hours to give no insight whatever into the complexities of character of this mysterious historic figure, but is often spectacularly beautiful and exciting along the way.
w Robert Bolt, Michael Wilson *d David Lean* *ph Frederick A. Young* *m Maurice Jarre* *pd John Box* *ad John Stoll*
☆ *Peter O'Toole, Omar Sharif, Arthur Kennedy,* Jack Hawkins, Donald Wolfit, Claude Rains, Anthony Quayle, *Alec Guinness*, Anthony Quinn, José Ferrer, Michel Ray, Zia Mohyeddin
'Grandeur of conception is not up to grandeur of setting.' – *Penelope Houston*
'Lean has managed to market epics as serious entertainment rather than as the spectacles they are.' – *Time Out, 1980*
† Albert Finney turned down the role before O'Toole was offered it.
†† Michael Wilson was uncredited at the time for his work on the script because he had been blacklisted.
best picture; David Lean; Frederick A. Young; Maurice Jarre
Robert Bolt; Peter O'Toole; Omar Sharif
best picture; best British picture; Robert Bolt; Peter O'Toole

Laws of Gravity *
US 1992 98m colour
Oasis/The Shooting Gallery (Bob Gosse, Larry Meistrich)
In Brooklyn, friendship between two young, petty crooks is strained when they become involved with a gangster who is trying to sell guns.
Down-beat drama of losers, effectively filmed and acted in a documentary style although it does cover familiar territory.
wd Nick Gomez *ph* Jean de Segonzac *m* Douglas Cuomo *pd* Monica Bretherton *ed* Tom McArdle
☆ Peter Greene, Edie Falco, Adam Trese, Arabella Field, Paul Schulze, Saul Stein, James McCauley
'Reasonably acted with some funny, protracted conversations.' – *Empire*

The Lawyer *
US 1970 120m Technicolor
Paramount (Brad Dexter)
An ambitious young Italian-American defence lawyer takes on a murder case.
Smartly scripted, perfectly ordinary courtroom drama in a well-detailed Western setting. The star subsequently played the same character in a TV series, Petrocelli.
w Sidney J. Furie, Harold Buchman *d Sidney J. Furie* *ph* Ralph Woolsey *m* Malcolm Dodds
☆ Barry Newman, Harold Gould, Diana Muldaur, Robert Colbert, Kathleen Crowley, Booth Colman

Lawyer Man
US 1932 68m bw
Warner
An honest lawyer becomes corrupted by success.
Smart, cynical melodrama, dated but sufficiently fast-paced to remain interesting.
w Rian James, James Seymour *novel* Max Trell *d* William Dieterle *ph* Robert Kurrle
☆ William Powell, Joan Blondell, Helen Vinson, Alan Dinehart, Allen Jenkins, David Landau, Claire Dodd
'Good picture in the lawyer cycle.' – *Variety*

Laxdale Hall
GB 1952 77m bw
Group Three (Alfred Shaughnessy)
US title: *Scotch on the Rocks*
MPs are sent to investigate a tiny Hebridean island which refuses to pay road tax.
Thin rehash of Whisky Galore *put together without the Ealing style. Minor compensations can be found.*
w John Eldridge, Alfred Shaughnessy *d* John Eldridge *ph* Arthur Grant *m* Frank Spencer
☆ Raymond Huntley, Ronald Squire, Sebastian Shaw, Fulton Mackay, Kathleen Ryan, Kynaston Reeves
'Constantly amusing in its quiet and wry fashion.' – *Cinema*

Lazy Bones: see *Hallelujah I'm a Bum*

Le Fils ***
Belgium/France 2002 103m colour
Artificial Eye/Films du Fleuve/Archipel35/RTBF (Jean-Pierre and Luc Dardenne, Denis Freyd)
aka: *The Son*
A carpentry teacher at a vocational training school for delinquent boys takes as a pupil the youth who killed his young son.
A simple, deeply affecting drama of loss and forgiveness, involving individuals who are defined by their work and the respect they bring to it.
wd Jean-Pierre Dardenne, Luc Dardenne *ph* Alain Marcoen *pd* Igor Gabriel *ed* Marie-Helene Dozo
☆ Olivier Gourmet (Olivier), Morgan Marinne (Francis), Isabella Soupart (Magali)
'The ability to conceive a compact drama on this huge subject and to embody it as perfectly as they have done, added to what they have already accomplished, puts Jean-Pierre and Luc Dardenne among the premier film artists of our time.' – *Stanley Kaufmann, New Republic*
'It is as assured and flawless a telling of sadness and joy as I have ever seen.' – *Roger Ebert, Chicago Sun-Times*

Le Mans *
US 1971 108m DeLuxe Panavision
Solar/Cinema Center (Jack N. Reddish)
A sullen American enters for the 24-hour race.
Almost no plot and little documentary examination; what's left is a multitude of racing shots with Steve McQueen at the wheel. For some this may be enough.
w Harry Kleiner *d* Lee H. Katzin *ph* Robert B. Hauser, René Gruissart Jnr *m* Michel Legrand
☆ Steve McQueen, Siegfried Rauch, Elga Anderson, Ronald Leigh-Hunt

Le Placard *
France 2000 80m colour 'Scope
Optimum/Gaumont/EFVE/TF1 (Alain Poire)
aka: *The Closet*
About to be fired, a heterosexual office-worker keeps his job by pretending to be gay.
One joke comedy that has a couple of hilarious moments.
d Francis Veber *ph* Luciano Tovoli *m* Vladimir Cosma *ad* Hugues Tissandier *ed* Georges Klotz
☆ Daniel Auteuil (Francois Pignon), Gerard Depardieu (Felix Santini), Thierry Lhermitte (Guillaume), Michele Laroque (Miss Bertrand), Michel Aumont (Belone), Jean Rochefort (Kopel), Alexandra Vandernoot (Christine)
'Worth a look, but not a detour or a journey.' – *Roger Ebert, Chicago Sun-Times*

Le Roi Danse
France/Germany/Belgium 2000 114m colour
Cinéfrance/K-Star/France2/MMC/RTL-1/K-Dance/K2 (Dominique Janne)
aka: *The King is Dancing*
On his deathbed Lully, court composer and ballet master to Louis XIV, recalls the king's love of dancing in his spectacular productions.
Ludicrously overblown melodrama of the rivalry between Lully and Molière, with much pouting and petulance by its cast. Pretty sets and costumes, though.
w Eve de Castro, Andrée Corbiau, Gérard Corbiau, Didier Decoin *novel Lully ou le musicien du soleil* by Philippe Beaussant *d* Gérard Corbiau *ph* Gérard Simon *md* Reinhard Goebel *pd* Hubert Pouillé *ed* Ludo Troch, Philippe Ravoet *cos* Olivier Beriot
☆ Benoit Magimel (Louis XIV), Boris Terral (Jean-Baptiste Lully), Tchéky Karyo (Molière), Colette Emmanuelle (Anne of Austria), Cécile Bois (Madeleine), Claire Keim (Julie), Johan Leysen (Cambert), Idwig Stéphane (Prince de Conti)
'Watching this... is like inhaling pomade.' – *Peter Bradshaw, Guardian*

Leadbelly *
US 1976 126m Eastmancolor
CIC/Brownstone/David Paradine (Marc Merson)
Biopic of the tough folk and blues singer and guitarist Huddie Ledbetter, concentrating on his earlier years and his times in chain gangs.
Pleasing, if stolid, account of a fascinating performer who sang his way out of prison.
w Ernest Kinoy *d* Gordon Parks *ph* Bruce Surtees *m* Fred Karlin *m/ly* Huddie Ledbetter *pd* Robert Boyle *ed* Harry Howard
☆ Roger E. Mosley, Paul Benjamin, Madge Sinclair, Alan Manson, Albert P. Hall, Art Evans, James E. Brodhead, John Henry Faulk
'Little more than the traditional biopic molasses.' – *MFB*
† Leadbelly's songs are sung by HiTide Harris.

'Indecent. Immoral. Irresistible. It's the role he was born to play.'
The Leading Man
GB 1996 99m Metrocolor
Guild/J&M (Bertil Ohlsson, Paul Raphael)
An English playwright permits his star, a Hollywood actor, to seduce his wife so that he can continue his affair with his play's leading actress.
Drab domestic drama of cultural differences, treated like a soap opera.
w Virginia Duigan *d* John Duigan *ph* Jean-François Robin *m* Edward Shearmur *pd* Caroline Hanania *ed* Humphrey Dixon
☆ Jon Bon Jovi, Lambert Wilson, Anna Galiena, Thandie Newton, Barry Humphries, David Warner, Patricia Hodge, Diana Quick, Harriet Walter
'It's all predictable, artificial and long past its sell-by date.' – *Alexander Walker, London Evening Standard*

League of Frightened Men
US 1937 71m bw
Columbia
Nero Wolfe solves another murder case from his armchair.
Fair dectective story, but a negation of film.
w Eugene Solow, Guy Endore *novel* Rex Stout *d* Alfred E. Green
☆ Walter Connolly, Lionel Stander, Eduardo Ciannelli, Irene Hervey, Victor Kilian, Nana Bryant
'Hardly any audience likes to watch a character who just sits and thinks.' – *Variety*

The League of Gentlemen ***
GB 1960 112m bw
Rank/Allied Film Makers (Michael Relph)
An ex-army officer recruits high-class misfits with guilty secrets to help him in a bank robbery.
Delightfully handled comedy adventure, from the days (alas) when crime did not pay; a lighter ending would have made it a classic.
w Bryan Forbes *novel* John Boland *d Basil Dearden* *ph* Arthur Ibbetson *m* Philip Green
☆ *Jack Hawkins*, Richard Attenborough, *Roger Livesey, Nigel Patrick*, Bryan Forbes, Kieron Moore, Terence Alexander, *Norman Bird*, Robert Coote, Melissa Stribling, Nanette Newman, Gerald Harper, Patrick Wymark, David Lodge, Doris Hare and also Lydia Sherwood

'Once in a lifetime you get a chance to do something different.'
A League of Their Own *
US 1992 128m Technicolor Panavision
Columbia/Parkway
During the Second World War, women are recruited to play in an all-female baseball league.
A comedy that trundles along in a predictable fashion, settling for sentimentality rather than humour.
w Lowell Ganz, Babaloo Mandel *story* Kim Wilson, Kelly Candaele *d* Penny Marshall *ph* Miroslav Ondricek *m* Hans Zimmer *pd* Bill Groom *ed* George Bowers
☆ Tom Hanks, Geena Davis, Madonna, Lori Petty, Jon Lovitz, David Strathairn, Garry Marshall, Bill Pullman, Megan Cavanagh, Tracy Reiner, Rosie O'Donnell, Ann Cusack
'This movie aims for the tear ducts and the funny bone as ruthlessly as the summer's big action-fantasy hits go after the viscera. It unfolds in field-of-dreams land – complete with cornstalks.' – *Michael Sragow, New Yorker*
'Awash in sentimentality and manic energy but only occasionally bubbling over with high humor.' – *Variety*

Lean on Me
US 1989 108m Technicolor
Warner (Norman Twain)
A stern teacher tames the pupils at New Jersey's toughest school.
Given its subject matter, a surprisingly soft-centred drama, based on a true story.
w Michael Schiffer, Douglas Seelig *d* John G. Avildsen *ph* Victor Hammer *m* Bill Conti *pd* Doug Kraner *ed* John Carter, John G. Avildsen
☆ Morgan Freeman, Beverly Todd, Robert Guillaume, Alan North, Lynne Thigpen, Robin Bartlett, Ethan Phillips

Leap of Faith
US 1992 108m colour
Paramount (Michael Manheim, David V. Picker)
A fraudulent preacher works a miracle.
Unsatisfactory drama that begins as an exposé of cheapjack evangelists and their tricks and ends as something even more exploitative and crass.
w Janus Cercone *d* Richard Pearce *ph* Matthew F. Leonetti *m* Cliff Eidelman *pd* Patrizia von

Brandenstein *ed* Don Zimmerman, Mark Warner, John F. Burnett
☆ Steve Martin, Debra Winger, Lolita Davidovich, Liam Neeson, Lukas Haas, Meat Loaf
'One finds oneself just thanking God the movie's ended.' – *Film Review*

The Learning Tree *
US 1969 107m Technicolor Panavision
Warner
A black youth comes to maturity in Kansas, as he experiences the good and the bad in the society around him.
Despite its semi-autobiographical nature, the prevailing tone is nostalgic and almost elegiac; the past, despite its racism, is recollected with affection.
wd Gordon Parks *novel* Gordon Parks *ph* Burnett Guffey *m* Gordon Parks *ad* Ed Engoron
ed George R. Rohrs
☆ Kyle Johnson, Alex Clarke, Estelle Evans, Dana Elcar, Mita Waters, Joel Fluellen, Malcolm Atterbury, James Rushing

Lease of Life *
GB 1954 94m Eastmancolor
Ealing (Jack Rix)
A poor clergyman is given a year to live, and puts it to good use.
Somewhat depressing but well-acted drama with excellent village atmosphere.
w Eric Ambler *d* Charles Frend *ph* Douglas Slocombe *m* Alan Rawsthorne
☆ *Robert Donat*, Kay Walsh, Adrienne Corri, Denholm Elliott

The Leather Boys *
GB 1963 108m bw Cinemascope
British Lion/Garrick (Raymond Stross)
Two working-class teenagers marry for sex; she becomes a drudge and he develops a relationship with a homosexual motorcyclist.
Sharply-observed slice of low life which now seems quite dated, the central figures no longer being of the 'heroic' interest given them at the time. Technically the film is tediously and fashionably flashy.
w Gillian Freeman *novel* Elliot George *d* Sidney J. Furie *ph* Gerald Gibbs *m* Bill McGuffie
☆ Rita Tushingham, Dudley Sutton, Colin Campbell, Gladys Henson

The Leather Saint
US 1955 86m bw Vistavision
Paramount (Norman Retchin)
To provide his parish hospital with medical equipment, a Catholic priest becomes a commercial prizefighter.
Unlikely piece of religiosity, not too badly done.
w Norman Retchin, Alvin Ganzer *d* Alvin Ganzer *ph* Haskell Boggs *md* Irvin Talbot
☆ Paul Douglas, John Derek, Cesar Romero, Ernest Truex, Jody Lawrance

Leathernecking
US 1930 80m bw (colour sequence)
RKO (Louis Sarecky)
GB title: *Present Arms*
A Honolulu socialite falls for a marine, but grows cool when she discovers that he is a private and not an officer as he pretended.
Curiously cast, spasmodically funny non-musical version of a Rodgers and Hart Broadway hit.
w Alfred Jackson, Jane Murfin *play* *Present Arms* by Herbert Fields, Rodgers and Hart *d* Edward F. Cline *ph* J. Roy Hunt *m* Oscar Levant
☆ Irene Dunne, Ken Murray, Eddie Foy Jnr, Louise Fazenda, Ned Sparks, Lilyan Tashman
'Weak medley of horseplay and romantic musical, and both poor.' – *Variety*

Leave All Fair *
New Zealand 1984 88m colour
Pacific Films (John O'Shea)
At the end of his life, John Middleton Murry recalls his relationship with his first wife, the writer Katherine Mansfield.
Intelligent and ambivalent drama, leaving open the question of whether Murry was the betrayer or saviour of his wife's reputation.
w Stanley Harper, Maurice Pons, Jean Betts, John Reid *d* John Reid *ph* Bernard Lutic *m* Stephen McCurdy *ad* Joe Bleakley *ed* Ian John
☆ John Gielgud, Jane Birkin, Feodor Atkine, Simon Ward

Leave 'Em Laughing *
US 1928 20m bw silent
Hal Roach
Stan has toothache, visits the dentist, and accidentally causes all concerned to inhale an overdose of laughing gas.
The earlier sequences are only mildly funny, but the laughing finale is irresistible.
w Hal Roach, Reed Heustis *d* Clyde Bruckman *ph* George Stevens *ed* Richard Currier *supervisor* Leo McCarey
☆ Stan Laurel, Oliver Hardy, Edgar Kennedy, Charlie Hall

'The sum total of all human emotion!'
Leave Her to Heaven
US 1946 111m Technicolor
TCF (William A. Bacher)
A selfish, jealous woman causes unhappiness for those around her, even in her suicide.
No-holds-barred melodrama of the old school; what seemed lush production at the time now looks tatty.
w Jo Swerling *novel* Ben Ames Williams *d* John M. Stahl *ph* Leon Shamroy *m* Alfred Newman *ad* Lyle Wheeler, Maurice Ransford
☆ Gene Tierney, Cornel Wilde, Jeanne Crain, Vincent Price, Mary Philips, Ray Collins, Gene Lockhart, Reed Hadley, Chill Wills
'The story's central idea might be plausible enough in a dramatically lighted black and white picture ... but in the rich glare of Technicolor, all its rental library characteristics are doubly glaring.' – *James Agee*
Academy Award: Leon Shamroy
Academy Award nomination: Gene Tierney; art direction

'The Beav is back.'
Leave It to Beaver
US 1997 88m DeLuxe
Universal (Robert Simmonds)
Two young brothers in an all-American family overcome the problems in their lives.
Those never exposed to the nostalgic TV sitcom of minor domestic happenings are likely to find this deadening entertainment; those who were may come to the same conclusion.
w Brian Levant and Lon Diamond *TV serial* Bob Mosher and Joe Connelly *d* Andy Cardiff *ph* Thomas Del Ruth *m* Randy Edelman *pd* Perry Andelin Blake
☆ Christopher McDonald, Janine Turner, Cameron Finley, Erik von Detten, Adam Zolotin, Barbara Billingsley, Ken Osmond, Erika Christensen
'Mildly subversive touches are separated by long stretches of unremarkable tedium.' – *Variety*
† Barbara Billingsley and Ken Osmond both appeared in the original TV sitcom, which ran from 1957 to 1963.

The Leavenworth Case
US 1935 66m bw
Republic
Police investigate the murder of a wealthy man.
Sluggish transcription of what claims to be the first American detective story.
w Albert DeMond, Sidney Sutherland *novel* Anna Katherine Green
☆ Donald Cook, Jean Rouverol, Norman Foster, Erin O'Brien-Moore, Maude Eburne, Warren Hymer
'Just another detective meller.' – *Variety*

Leaves from Satan's Book *
Denmark 1919 80m approx (24 fps) bw silent
Nordisk
Episodes from the activities of Satan through the ages: with Christ, the Inquisition, the French Revolution and the Russian Revolution.
Vaguely propagandist short-story compilation with effective moments.
w Edgar Hoyer, Carl Dreyer *novel* *The Sorrows of Satan* by Marie Corelli *d* Carl Dreyer *ph* George Schneevoigt

Leaving Las Vegas **
US 1995 112m Foto-Kem
Entertainment/Initial (Lila Cazes, Annie Stewart)
An alcoholic writer goes to Las Vegas to drink himself to death and meets a prostitute who invites him to live with her.
A tragic drama that leaves unexplained the self-destructive motives of its protagonists; at times Cage's performance recalls James Stewart's in Harvey*, and Shue's kindly tart amid the Vegas glitz seems as much an alcoholic's fantasy as a large white rabbit. The movie's emotional force is undercut by the maudlin ballads that swell on the soundtrack at climactic moments.*
wd *Mike Figgis* *novel* John O'Brien *ph* Declan Quinn *m* Mike Figgis *pd* Waldemar Kalinowski *ed* John Smith
☆ *Nicolas Cage, Elisabeth Shue*, Julian Sands, Richard Lewis, Valeria Golino, Graham Beckel, Laurie Metcalf, Lou Rawls, Carey Lowell
'Although the movie is terribly, crushingly sad, its honesty is invigorating: it names its poison and downs it, neat.' – *Terrence Rafferty, New Yorker*
'Jazzy, soulfully florid fairy tale – as affecting and sublimely irresponsible as its doomed protagonist.' – *J. Hoberman, Premiere*
† Author John O'Brien committed suicide just before the film went into production.
Academy Award: Nicolas Cage
Academy Award nomination: Elisabeth Shue; Mike Figgis (as director and as writer)

Leaving Lenin **
GB 1993 93m colour
Feature/Gaucho/SC4 (Pauline Williams)
original title: *Gadael Lenin*
On a school trip to St Petersburg, the three teachers in charge become separated from the sixth-formers they are accompanying.
A slight but enjoyable Welsh comedy about the pains and pleasures of adolescence.
w Endaf Emlyn, Sion Eirian *d* Endaf Emlyn *ph* Ray Orton *m* John Hardy *ad* Vera Zelenkskaya *ed* Chris Lawrence
☆ Sharon Morgan, Ifan Huw Dafydd, Wyn Bowen Harris, Steffan Trevor, Ivan Shvedov, Catrin Mai, Richard Harrington, Shelley Rees
'The joy of this captivating comedy is that in spite of the ludicrousness of its situations, it is totally credible.' – *James Cameron-Wilson, Film Review*

Leaving Normal
Canada/US 1992 110m colour
Universal (Lindsay Doran)
An abrasive cocktail waitress and a young wife running from her second husband leave the small Western town of Normal and head for Alaska and freedom, which does not entirely live up to their expectations.
Loud and unsubtle road movie of female bonding, with a little male–female bonding on the side.
w Edward Solomon *d* Edward Zwick *ph* Ralf Bode *m* W. G. Snuffy Walden *pd* Patricia Morris *ed* Victor DuBois
☆ Christine Lahti, Meg Tilly, Lenny von Dohlen, Maury Chaykin, Patrika Darbo, Eve Gordon, James Eckhouse, Brett Cullen, James Gammon
'Not for all tastes ... has a serious undertone in its depiction of losers who keep struggling to assert themselves in an unfeeling and male-dominated world.' – *Variety*
† Cher and Demi Moore were originally cast in the leading roles.

Lebenszeichen: see *Signs of Life*

La Lectrice **
France 1988 98m colour
Curzon Films/Elefilm/AAA/TSF/Ciné 5/Sofimage (Rosalinde Deville)
A beautiful young woman, hired to read books out loud to people who are disabled in some way, has unexpected effects on her customers.
Witty games-playing comedy.
w Michel Déville, Rosalinde Déville *novel* Raymond Jean *d* Michel Déville *ph* Dominique Le Rigoleur *m* Beethoven *pd* Thierry Leproust *ed* Raymonde Guyot
☆ *Miou-Miou*, Régis Royer, Christian Ruché, Maria Cesars, Patrick Chesnais, Marianne Denicourt, Pierre Dux
'A frothy conceit, a true jeu d'esprit, but when it has said all that it has to say, albeit with panache, it has said nothing.' – *MFB*

'You can count the truly daring concepts in the making of motion pictures on the fingers of your right hand. Now add...'
The Left Hand of God
US 1955 87m DeLuxe Cinemascope
TCF (Buddy Adler)
China, 1947: a Catholic priest newly arrived in a small village proves to be an American flyer on the run from a warlord; but he contrives to work a small 'miracle'.
Hollywood religiosity at its most contrived, put together without distinction; the players have a wary look.
w Alfred Hayes *novel* William E. Barrett *d* Edward Dmytryk *ph* Franz Planer *m* Victor Young
☆ Humphrey Bogart, Gene Tierney, Lee J. Cobb, E. G. Marshall, Agnes Moorehead

The Left Handed Gun *
US 1958 102m bw
Warner/Haroll (Fred Coe)
Billy the Kid sets out to shoot four men who have killed his friend.
'Method'-oriented Western, efficiently made but somewhat downcast.
w *Leslie Stevens*, *TV play* Gore Vidal *d* Arthur Penn *ph* Peverell Marley *m* Alexander Courage
☆ Paul Newman, John Dehner, Lita Milan, Hurd Hatfield

Left Luggage
Netherlands/Belgium/USA 1997 100m colour
Downtown/Shooting Star/Flying Dutchman (Ate de Jong, Hans Pos, David Schram)
In Antwerp, a philosophy student becomes the nanny of a four-year-old boy, whose parents are Hassidic Jews.
A study in contrasts, between modern attitudes and non-materialistic traditional ones, that is unfortunately overwhelmed by its sentimentality.
w Edwin de Vries *novel* *The Shovel and the Loom* by Carl Friedman *d* Jeroen Krabbé *ph* Walther Vanden Ende *m* Henny Vrienten *ad* Hemmo Sportal *ed* Edgar Burcksen
☆ Isabella Rossellini, Maximilian Schell, Laura Fraser, Jeroen Krabbé, Marianne Saegebrecht, David Bradley, Adam Monty, Chaim Topol
'It's a pity that a film which otherwise has a great deal going for it ultimately winds up as ghettoised as the community it portrays.' – *Caroline Westbrook, Empire*

'Top of the poll for laughs!'
Left Right and Centre *
GB 1959 95m bw
Vale/Launder and Gilliat
A TV personality becomes Tory candidate at a by-election.
Scrappy political comedy with the saving grace of a large number of comic talents.
w Sidney Gilliat, Val Valentine *d* Sidney Gilliat *ph* Gerald Gibbs *m* Humphrey Searle
☆ Ian Carmichael, Alastair Sim, Patricia Bredin, Richard Wattis, Eric Barker, Gordon Harker, George Benson, Frederick Leister

The Legacy
GB 1978 102m colour
Columbia/Pethurst/Turman-Foster (David Foster)
An American designer goes to stay with her employer and finds herself in the middle of an occult murder plot.
Cliché-ridden screamer which will please the easily pleased.
w Jimmy Sangster, Patrick Tilley, Paul Wheeler *d* Richard Marquand *ph* Dick Bush, Alan Hume *m* Michael J. Lewis *pd* Disley Jones *ed* Anne Coates
☆ Katharine Ross, Sam Elliott, Roger Daltrey, John Standing, Ian Hogg, Margaret Tyzack, Charles Gray, Lee Montague, Hildegard Neil

'Like father, like son...'
Legacy of Rage (dubbed)
Hong Kong 1987 82m colour
Imperial (John Sham, Linda Kuk)

After six years in jail for a crime he did not commit, a former waiter teams up with a cell-mate to seek revenge on the gangster who framed him.
Standard martial arts adventure, notable only for Brandon Lee's debut.
wd Ronny Yu
☆ Brandon Lee, Onno Boelee (Bolo Yeung), Michael Wong, Regina Kent, Tanya George
'Offers too few thrills to satisfy hard-core action fans.' – *Film Review*

Legal Eagles
US 1986 114m Technicolor Panavision
Universal/Northern Lights (Ivan Reitman)

An assistant DA becomes involved for the defence in an arson case.
Sophisticated but messy comedy with odd unrelated asides, reminiscent of the TV series Moonlighting *but with top production values.*
w Jim Cash, Jack Epps Jnr *d* Ivan Reitman *ph* Laszlo Kovacs *m* Elmer Bernstein
☆ Robert Redford, Debra Winger, Daryl Hannah, Brian Dennehy, Terence Stamp, Steven Hill

'Boldly going where no blonde has gone.'
Legally Blonde
US 2001 96m DeLuxe Super 35
TCF/MGM (Marc Platt, Ric Kidney)

Dumped by her ambitious boy friend, a blonde proves that a knowledge of designer labels can take you to the top at Harvard Law School.
Fluffy comedy made watchable by Reese Witherspoon's engaging performance.
w Karen McCullah Lutz, Kirsten Smith *book* Amanda Brown *d* Robert Luketic *ph* Anthony B. Richmond *m* Rolfe Kent *pd* Melissa Stewart *ed* Anita Brandt Burgoyne, Garth Craven
☆ *Reese Witherspoon* (Elle Woods), Luke Wilson (Emmett Richmond), Selma Blair (Vivian Kensington), Matthew Davis (Warner), Victor Garber (Professor Callahan), Jennifer Coolidge (Paulette), Holland Taylor (Professor Stromwell), Ali Larter (Brooke Taylor Windham), Raquel Welch (Mrs Windham Vandermark)
'A featherweight comedy balanced between silliness and charm. It is impossible to dislike.' – *Roger Ebert, Chicago Sun-Times*
'Smug yet clueless... a junk-food movie striving to be nutritious.' – *Jessica Winter, Village Voice*

The Legend: see *Fong Sai Yuk*

'There May Never Be Another Dawn.'
Legend ★
GB 1985 94m Fujicolour Panavision
TCF/Universal/Legend Productions (Arnon Milchan)

Young peasant Jack takes his sweetheart on a quest to see the last surviving unicorns, but Satan uses them as pawns in his own game.
Elegant fairy tale for the few grown-ups who have use for such a thing. More to look at than to listen to.
w William Hjortsberg *d* Ridley Scott *ph* Alex Thomson *m* Tangerine Dream, Jerry Goldsmith *pd* Assheton Gorton *ed* Terry Rawlings
☆ *Tim Curry* (Darkness), Mia Sara (Lili), Tom Cruise (Jack), David Bennent (Gump), Alice Playten (Blix), Billy Barty (Screwball), Cork Hubbert (Brown Tom), Peter O'Farrell (Pox)
'The dying gasp of the sword and sorcery cycle.' – *Philip French, Observer*
'The enchanted forests constantly threaten to sell us something – most frequently soft toilet paper.' – *Ibid.*
† The film was reissued in a "director's cut" that runs for 114m.
make-up (Rob Bottin, Peter Robb-King)

'An Epic Story Of A Man Who Could Do Anything... Except Be Ordinary.'
The Legend of 1900 ★
Italy 1998 125m Cinecittà colour Technovision
Fine Line/Medusa/Sciarlo

original title: *La Leggenda Del Pianista Sull'Oceano*
US title: *The Legend of the Pianist on the Ocean*
An abandoned child, named 1900 after the year of his birth, spends his entire life as a virtuoso pianist aboard the trans-Atlantic liner on which he was born.
Lavish, good-looking but curious fable that suggests significance without ever revealing it.
wd Giuseppe Tornatore *monologue* *Novecento* by Alessandro Baricco *ph* Lajos Koltai *m* Ennio Morricone *pd* Francesco Frigeri *ed* Massimo Quaglia *cos* Maurizio Millenotti
☆ Tim Roth (Danny Boodman T. D. Lemon Novecento), Pruitt Taylor Vince (Max), Melanie Thierry (The Girl), Bill Nunn (Danny Boodmann), Peter Vaughan (Music store owner), Niall O'Brien (Harbour master), Alberto Vasquez (Mexican machinist), Clarence Williams III ('Jelly Roll' Morton), Gabrielle Lavia (Farmer)
'A darn good yarn told in classic style, but invigorated by inventiveness and imagination. Truly magnificent.' – *Nick Briggs, Film Review*
† The film ran for 170m when first shown at the Cannes Film Festival.

'It Was Just A Moment Ago.'
The Legend of Bagger Vance
US 2000 127m Technicolor
TCF/DreamWorks/Wildwood/Allied (Robert Redford, Michael Nozik, Jake Eberts)

In the late 20s, a mysterious black caddy helps a once promising golfer, who returned from the war in bad shape, to win a tournament against top players.
Golf is treated as a viable substitute for religion in this insufferably mystic and torpid movie, which is given to nostalgia for a past that never was; it also reduces dialogue to an exchange of sentimental banalities.
w Jeremy Leven *novel* Steven Pressfield *d* Robert Redford *ph* Michael Ballhaus *m* Rachel Portman *pd* Stuart Craig *ed* Hank Corwin
☆ Will Smith (Bagger Vance), Matt Damon (Rannulph Junuh), Charlize Theron (Adele Invergordon), Bruce McGill (Walter Hagen), Joel Gretsch (Bobby Jones), Lane Smith (Grantland Rice), Harve Presnell (John Invergordon), J. Michael Moncrief (Hardy Greaves), Peter Gerety (Neskaloosa), Michael O'Neill (O.B. Keeler), Thomas Jay Ryan (Spec Hammond), Jack Lemmon (Old Hardy Greaves/Narrator)
'A lightweight, modestly engaging yarn sporting reductive mystical and philosophical elements that are both valid and borderline silly.' – *Todd McCarthy, Variety*
'Might charitably be described as an inspirational poster blown up into a feature film.' – *A.O. Scott, New York Times*

The Legend of Billie Jean
US 1985 96m Metrocolor
Tri-Star/Rob Cohen (Jon Peters, Peter Guber)

While protecting her brother, a girl becomes an outlaw by accident.
Unattractive and even distasteful farrago which is presumably intended to teach kids, so far as the law is concerned, how to eat their cake and have it.
w Mark Rosenthal, Lawrence Konner *d* Matthew Robbins *ph* Jeffrey L. Kimball *m* Craig Safan *pd* Ted Haworth *ed* Cynthia Scheider
☆ Helen Slater, Keith Gordon, Christian Slater, Richard Bradford, Peter Coyote
'The germ of an idea, but hardly a reason for a film.' – *Variety*

The Legend of Fong Sai Yuk: see *Fong Sai Yuk*

The Legend of Fong Sai Yuk II: see *Fong Sai Yuk II*

'For the sake of your sanity, pray it isn't true!'
The Legend of Hell House ★
GB 1973 94m DeLuxe
TCF/Academy (Albert Fennell, Norman T. Herman)

Four people arrive at a haunted house in which several psychic investigators have been killed.
Harrowing thriller, a less solemn but more frightening version of The Haunting.
w Richard Matheson *novel* Richard Matheson *d* John Hough *ph* Alan Hume *m* Brian Hodgson, Delia Derbyshire
☆ Pamela Franklin, Roddy McDowall, Clive Revill, Gayle Hunnicutt, Roland Culver, Peter Bowles, Michael Gough
'One of the most absorbing, goose-fleshing and mind-pleasing ghost breaker yarns on film.' – *Judith Crist, 1977*

The Legend of Lobo ★
US 1962 67m Technicolor
Walt Disney (James Algar)

The life of a forest wolf.
Anthropomorphic entertainment in which a dreaded animal becomes something of a hero and finally saves his mate from bounty hunters. Impeccably contrived, like a live-action Bambi.
w Dwight Hauser, James Algar *story* Ernest Thompson Seton *d* James Algar *ph* Jack Couffer, Lloyd Beebe *m* Oliver Wallace

The Legend of Lylah Clare ★
US 1968 130m Metrocolor Panavision
MGM/Robert Aldrich
A mad director brings an unknown actress to Hollywood because of her resemblance to a former star, his creation, who had died mysteriously.
Unintentionally risible melodrama with echoes of Svengali *and* Sunset Boulevard; *not to the public's taste, or anyone else's, in the late sixties.*
w Hugo Butler, Jean Rouverol *TV play* Robert Thom, Edward de Blasio *d* Robert Aldrich *ph* Joseph Biroc *m* Frank de Vol
☆ Peter Finch, Kim Novak, Ernest Borgnine, Coral Browne, Milton Seltzer, Rossella Falk, Gabriele Tinti, Valentina Cortesa, George Kennedy

Legend of the Demon Womb
Japan 1990 84m colour
Toshio Maeda/West Cape
original title: *Urotsukidoji II*
Demons and man-beasts fight to prevent the son of a mad Nazi from gaining ultimate power by killing the boy who is destined to be the over-fiend, the god of gods.
Extremely gruesome animated fantasy, concentrating on graphic sex, from masturbation, fellatio and lesbianism to rape, and much violence, including decapitations, multiple murders and human sacrifice.
w Noboru Aikawa *story* Toshio Maeda *d* Hideki Takayama *ph* Hideo Okazaki *m* Masamichi Amano *ad* Hitoshi Nagao *ed* Shigeru Nishiyama
☆ Featuring the voices of Christopher Courage, Rebel Joy, Danny Bush, Lucy Morales, Rose Palmer
† A sequel to the equally gruesome *Legend of the Overfiend* (qv). It was followed by the video releases of *Urotsukidoji III: Episode 1* and *Urotsukidoji III: Episode 2*, which both continue the mixture as before with an unintelligible narrative, an impenetrable mythology, a comic-book style of animation, and much sex and violence.

Legend of the Holy Drinker ★★
Italy 1988 128m colour
Artificial Eye/Aura Film/Cecchi Gori Group/Tiger Cinematografica/RAI Uno (Roberto Cicutto, Vincenzo de Leo)

original title: *La Leggenda del Santo Bevitore*
An alcoholic tramp is repeatedly frustrated in his attempts to repay money to the shrine of a saint.
An odd fable, beautifully presented.
w Tullio Kezich, Ermanno Olmi *novel* *Die Legende des Heiligen Trinkers* by Joseph Roth *d* Ermanno Olmi *ph* Dante Spinotti *m* Stravinsky *pd* Gianni Quaranta *ed* Ermanno Olmi
☆ Rutger Hauer, Anthony Quayle, Sandrine Dumas, Dominique Pinon, Sophie Segalen, Jean Maurice Chanet, Cecile Paoli, Joseph de Medina

'The film where you hiss the villain and cheer the hero!'
The Legend of the Lone Ranger
US 1981 98m Technicolor Panavision
ITC/Jack Wrather (Walter Coblenz)

A much-betrayed young Texan, almost killed in an ambush, is nursed back to health by an Indian and becomes a masked avenger.
Extremely ill-constructed and moody Western, apparently photographed through brown Windsor soup, which doesn't slip into the right gear until twenty minutes before the end.
w Ivan Goff, Ben Roberts, Michael Kane, William Roberts *d* William A. Fraker *ph* Laszlo Kovacs *m* John Barry
☆ Klinton Spilsbury, Michael Horse, Christopher Lloyd, Matt Clark
'Wallows in endless sentiment before switching to what may possibly have been intended as parody.' – *Sight and Sound*
'Tedious hokum ... the kind of film that closes cinemas.' – *Sunday Times*

Legend of the Lost
US 1957 107m Technirama
UA/Batjac/Robert Haggiag/Dear (Henry Hathaway)
Two adventurers and a slave girl seek a lost city in the Sahara.
Tediously vague and underplotted desert adventure with a few attractive moments.
w Robert Presnell Jnr, Ben Hecht *d* Henry Hathaway *ph* Jack Cardiff *m* A. F. Lavagnino
☆ John Wayne, Sophia Loren, Rossano Brazzi

Legend of the Overfiend (dubbed)
Japan 1989 96m colour
West Cape Corp (Yasuhito Yamaki)

original title: *Urotsukidōji*
Creatures from two parallel universes battle to become supreme rulers of the Earth.
Revolting and thoroughly nasty animated feature, full of rape, masturbation, mutilation and grotesque mutations, with heads exploding and eyeballs popping. What narrative there is amid the sex and violence makes little sense.
w Noboru Aikawa *story* Toshio Maeda *d* Hideki Takayama *m* Masamichi Amano *ad* Shigemi Ikeda *ed* Shigeru Nishiyama
☆ Featuring the voices of Christopher Courage, Rebel Joy, Danny Bush, Lucy Morales, Rose Palmer
'Formula heroics, facile science fiction futurism, slavering monsters and tediously repetitive violence – the animated fantasies of the Manga school have everything to satisfy the adolescent mind.' – *Sight and Sound*

The Legend of the Pianist on the Ocean: see *The Legend of 1900*

The Legend of the Seven Golden Vampires
GB/Hong Kong 1974 89m Eastmancolor Panavision
Hammer-Shaw (Don Houghton, Vee King Shaw)

US title: *The Seven Brothers Meet Dracula*
In 1904 Chungking, Professor Van Helsing finds his old enemy Dracula behind a Chinese vampire cult.
Hectic, outlandish mix of Hammer horror and Kung Fu; plenty of gusto but not much sense.
w Don Houghton *d* Roy Ward Baker *ph* John Wilcox, Roy Ford *m* James Bernard
☆ Peter Cushing, David Chiang, Julie Ege, Robin Stewart, John Forbes Robertson

Legend of the Suram Fortress ★
USSR 1984 87m colour
Poseidon/Georgianfilm Studio (X. Gogiladze, M. Simxaev)

original title: *Legenda Suramskoi Kreposti*
A youth lets himself be immured in the walls of a fortress to stop it from crumbling.
Colourful re-enactment of a folk tale, though not up to the director's best work.
w Vazha Gigashvili *book* D. Tchonghadze *d* Sergo Paradjanov, Dodo Abashidze *ph* Sergo Sixarulidze *m* Dzhansugh K'axidze *ad* Alexandr Dzhanishiev *ed* K'ora Ts'ereteli

☆ Venerik'o Andzhaparidze, Dodo Abashidze, Sopik'o Ch'iaureli, Duduxana Ts'erodze, Tamar Tsitsishuili

Legend of the Werewolf
GB 1974 90m Eastmancolor
Tyburn (Kevin Francis)

In the 1860s, a boy brought up by wolves changes into one at the full moon.
Cheap and cheerful horror movie, much in the Hammer style, bright but unsubtle.
w Anthony Hinds *d* Freddie Francis *ph* John Wilcox *m* Harry Robinson *ad* Jack Shampan *ed* Henry Richardson
☆ Peter Cushing, David Rintoul, Ron Moody, Hugh Griffith, Roy Castle, Stefan Gryff, Lynn Dalby, Renee Houston, Marjorie Yates

The Legend of Tom Dooley
US 1959 77m bw
Columbia/Shpetner
At the end of the Civil War, Confederate youths take the law into their own hands and attack Unionists.
Youthful rebellion in historical mould, decently but rather dully delivered, based on a folk ballad.
w Stan Shpetner *d* Ted Post *ph* Gilbert Warrenton *m* Ronald Stein
☆ Michael Landon, Richard Rust, Jo Morrow

'The men of the Ludlow family. A woman's grace brought them together. Then her passion tore them apart.'
Legends of the Fall
US 1994 134m Technicolor
TriStar/Bedford Falls/Pangaea (Edward Zwick, Bill Wittliff)

An army officer retires to a ranch with his three sons: one is killed in the First World War, the surviving two fall in love with the same woman; one goes on to become a successful politician, and the other a bootlegger and outcast.
Period family saga, reminiscent of East of Eden, *with Brad Pitt glowering as a latter-day James Dean; enjoyable as a soap opera but its aspirations to be something more come to nothing.*
w Susan Shilliday, Bill Wittliff *novel* Jim Harrison *d* Edward Zwick *ph* John Toll *m* James Horner *pd* Lilly Kilvert *ed* Steven Rosenblum
☆ Anthony Hopkins, Brad Pitt, Aidan Quinn, Henry Thomas, Julia Ormond, Karina Lombard, Gordon Tootoosis, Tantoo Cardinal, Paul Desmond

'A silly melodrama trying to be an epic.' – *Time*
'A visceral, thoughtful and emotionally exhausting saga.' – *Variety*

John Toll
Lilly Kilvert

La Leggenda Del Pianista Sull'Oceano: see *The Legend of 1900*

The Lemon Drop Kid *
US 1951 91m bw
Paramount (Robert A. Welch)

A gangster forces a bookie to find the money which he has lost on a horse through the bookie's incompetence.
Amusing Bob Hope/Runyon vehicle despite heavy sentiment about an old folks' home. The Santa Claus sequences are memorable.
w Edmund Hartmann, Frank Tashlin, Robert O'Brien *story* Damon Runyon *d* Sidney Lanfield *ph* Daniel L. Fapp *m* Victor Young
☆ *Bob Hope*, Marilyn Maxwell, Lloyd Nolan, Jane Darwell, Andrea King, Fred Clark, Jay C. Flippen, William Frawley, Harry Bellaver
† The previous 1934 version starred Lee Tracy, Helen Mack and William Frawley; ran 60m; and was directed by Marshall Neilan for Paramount

The Lemon Sisters
US 1990 93m Technicolor
Miramax/Lightyear (Joe Kelly)

In Atlantic City, three childhood friends with dreams of becoming stars grow up to face the realities of life and love.
Drearily witless comedy, in which most of the narrative thrust is confined to a voice-over; the inert direction only emphasizes that this is a bland movie about the dull lives of people of limited talent.
w Jeremy Pikser *d* Joyce Chopra *ph* Bobby Byrne *m* Dick Hyman *pd* Patrizia von Brandenstein *ed* Joe Weintraub, Michael R. Miller
☆ Diane Keaton, Carol Kane, Kathryn Grody, Elliott Gould, Ruben Blades, Estelle Parsons, Richard Libertini, Aidan Quinn

Lena's Holiday
US 1991 97m colour
Crown International/Marimark (Marilyn Jacobs Tenser)

A young East German girl goes on holiday to Los Angeles.
Mildly agreeable comedy of a culture clash.
w Deborah Tilton, Michael Keusch *d* Michael Keusch *ph* Louis DiCesare *m* Steve Schiff *pd* Milo *ed* Bill Swenson
☆ Chris Lemmon, Nick Mancuso, Michael Sarrazin, Felicity Waterman, Pat Morita, Bill Dana, Liz Torres, Susan Anton

Lenin in October *
USSR 1937 111m bw
Mosfilm
original title: *Lenin v Octiabrye*
The activities of Lenin during the revolution.
Stalwart propaganda piece, of solid but not outstanding cinematic interest.
w Alexei Kapler *d* *Mikhail Romm* *ph* Boris Volchok *m* Anatoli Alexandrov
☆ Boris Shchukin

'We have reached the end of the Communist film. It is to be all "Heroes and Hero-Worship" now: the old films are to be remade for the new leaders: no more anonymous mothers will run in the van of the workers against the Winter Palace. The USSR is to produce Fascist films from now on.' – *Graham Greene*

† The success of this film provoked *Lenin in 1918*, made in the following year (132m) by the same talents, with Cherkassov as Gorky. Many other Russian films on Lenin have followed.

Lenin v Octiabrye: see *Lenin in October*

'Somewhere in the tundra lived the worst rock'n'roll band in the world...'
Leningrad Cowboys Go America **
Finland/Sweden 1989 78m
Artificial Eye/Villealfa/Swedish Film Institute/Finnish Film Foundation (Aki Kaurismäki, Klas Olofsson, Katinka Farago)

An inept rock band travels through America in search of fame and fortune, which prove elusive.
Engagingly ramshackle comedy, with keen observation of the underside of the American dream
wd Aki Kaurismäki *story* Sakke Järvenpää, Aki Kaurismäki, Mato Valtonen *ph* Timo Salminen *m* Mauri Sumén *ed* Raija Talvio
☆ Matti Pellonpää, Kari Väänänen, Sakke Jarvenpää, Hiekki Keskinen, Pimme Oinonen, Silu Seppälä, Mauri Sumén, Mato Valtonen, Pekka Virtanen, Jim Jarmusch

Lenny ***
US 1974 111m bw
UA (Marvin Worth)

The career of obscene comedian Lenny Bruce and his struggles with the law.
Old-fashioned rags-to-riches-to-rags story, rampant with the new permissiveness. Filmically extremely clever, emotionally hollow.
w Julian Barry *play* Julian Barry *d* *Bob Fosse* *ph* Bruce Surtees *md* Ralph Burns *pd* Joel Schiller
☆ *Dustin Hoffman*, Valerie Perrine, Jan Miner, Stanley Beck, Gary Morton

'For audiences who want to believe that Lenny Bruce was a saintly gadfly who was martyred for having lived before his time.' – *New Yorker*

best picture; Julian Barry; Bob Fosse; Bruce Surtees; Dustin Hoffman; Valerie Perrine
Valerie Perrine

Leo the Last
GB 1969 104m DeLuxe
UA/Char/Wink/Boor (Irwin Winkler, Robert Chartoff)
An alienated aristocrat brings his retinue to a London slum and has an effect on most of the inhabitants.
Infuriating symbolic fantasy; only the writer-director (presumably) has any idea what it is about.
w William Stair, John Boorman *d* John Boorman *ph* Peter Suschitsky *m* Fred Myrow *pd* Tony Woollard
☆ Marcello Mastroianni, Billie Whitelaw, Calvin Lockhart, Glenna Forster Jones, Graham Crowden, Gwen Ffrangcon Davies, David de Keyser, Vladek Sheybal, Kenneth J. Warren

'One must be grateful for the bold, high-spirited experiments and surprises ... They are never boring.' – *Dilys Powell*

'The Classic Novel. The Timeless Love Story.'
Leo Tolstoy's Anna Karenina
US 1997 108m Technicolor Panavision
Warner/Icon (Bruce Davey)

In Russia, a married woman begins a doomed affair with a gallant and infatuated cavalry officer.
A clumsy, by-the-numbers treatment, often opulent to look at, well enough acted, but lacking in any depth or feeling.
wd Bernard Rose *novel* Leo Tolstoy *ph* Daryn Okada *m* *Tchaikovsky et al* *md* Sir Georg Solti *pd* John Myhre *ed* Victor Du Bois
☆ Sophie Marceau, Sean Bean, Alfred Molina, Mia Kirshner, James Fox, Fiona Shaw, Danny Huston, Phyllida Law, David Scofield, Saskia Wickham, Jennifer Hall

'This passionless Classics Illustrated-style rendition possesses no distinction to attract an audience.' – *Todd McCarthy, Variety*

'Léolo's fantasy is of Bianca and Sicily. His reality is Murder and Madness.'
Léolo *
Canada/France 1992 103m colour
Alliance/Verseau/Flach/Canal (Lyse Lafontaine, Aimée Danis)

In a poor part of Montreal, a dreamy small boy, growing up at odds with his mainly demented family, retreats from reality.
A dark tragi-comic account of the flowering and the failure of an imagination.
wd Jean-Claude Lauzon *ph* Guy Dufaux *ad* François Séguin *ed* Michel Arcand
☆ Ginette Reno, Pierre Bourgault, Maxime Collin, Giuditta Del Vecchio, Julien Guiomar

'A semi-autobiographical phantasmagoria about growing up in a 1960s East-Montreal French-Canadian tenement populated by Fellini-esque grotesques.' – *Philip French, Observer*

'He Moves Without Sound, Kills Without Emotion, Disappears Without Trace.'
'If you want the job done right, hire a professional.'
Leon **
France 1994 110m Technicolor Technovision
Buena Vista/Gaumont/Dauphin (Luc Besson)

US title: *The Professional*
A hitman makes the mistake of befriending a 12-year-old girl whose family is murdered by a crooked policeman and his thugs.
Tense and involving thriller, dealing in heightened fantasy rather than reality, about a killer with a weakness.
wd Luc Besson *ph* Thierry Arbogast *m* Eric Serra *pd* Dan Weil *ed* Sylvie Landra
☆ *Jean Reno*, Gary Oldman, Natalie Portman, Danny Aiello, Peter Appel, Michael Badalucco, Ellen Greene, Elizabeth Regen

'The most satisfactory blend of brilliance and not quite original thought. It's a well-orchestrated thriller that never treats itself too seriously, skates on fairly thin ice but comes out smelling mainly of roses.' – *Derek Malcolm, Guardian*
'A naïve fairy tale splattered with blood. Mix of cynicism and sentiment will ring hollow to cine-literate sophisticates but may play well to the gallery.' – *Lisa Nesselson, Variety*

Léon Morin, Priest *
France/Italy 1961 117m bw
Rome – Paris Films (Georges de Beauregard)
During the German occupation of France a young widow finds herself falling in love with the young priest who is converting her to religion.
An intellectual romance, sharp and witty for the most part, with vivid wartime backgrounds.
wd Jean-Pierre Melville *novel* Béatrix Beck *ph* Henri Decaë *m* Martial Solal, Albert Raisner
☆ Jean-Paul Belmondo, Emmanuele Riva, Irène Tunc, Marielle Gozzi

Leon the Pig Farmer
GB 1992 104m colour
Electric/Leon the Pig Farmer Production (Gary Sinyor, Vadim Jean)

A Jewish estate agent discovers that his real father is a Yorkshire pig farmer.
Laboured low-budget comedy of racial stereotypes.
w Gary Sinyor, Michael Norman *d* Vadim Jean, Gary Sinyor *ph* Gordon Hickie *m* John Murphy *pd* Simon Hicks *ed* Ewa Lind
☆ Mark Frankel, Gina Bellman, Janet Suzman, Brian Glover, Connie Booth, Maryam D'Abo

'Overall, flashes of inspiration are outweighed by laboured skits that fall somewhat flat, but this is a worthy and promising effort.' – *Empire*
'The comedy has wit and pace. It has originality that Mel Brooks might envy.' – *Alexander Walker, London Evening Standard*

† The film was made on a budget of £160,000. It won the International Critics' Prize at the Venice Film Festival and an award for best first film at the Edinburgh Film Festival.

The Leopard ****
US/Italy 1963 205m Technirama
TCF/Titanus/SNPC/GPC (Goffredo Lombardo)

original title: *Il Gattopardo*
The family life of an Italian nobleman at the time of Garibaldi.
Elaborate, complex family saga, painted like an old master with great care and attention to detail, but with not much chance outside Italy of delivering its original dramatic force. Visconti had asked for Lancaster, so TCF picked up the international release but couldn't make head or tail of it commercially; they even ruined its high quality by releasing a dubbed, shortened version in Cinemascope and DeLuxe colour of poor standard.
wd *Luchino Visconti* *novel* Giuseppe de Lampedusa *ph* *Giuseppe Rotunno* *m* Nino Rota *ad* *Mario Garbuglia*
☆ Burt Lancaster, Claudia Cardinale, Alain Delon, Paolo Stoppa, Serge Reggiani, Leslie French

Leopard in the Snow
GB/Canada 1977 94m Technicolor
Seastone/Leopard in the Snow (W. Laurence Heisey)

A girl caught in a Cumberland blizzard is rescued by a mysterious stranger with a pet leopard. He turns out to be a disfigured racing driver, and she falls in love with him.
A deliberate cross between Jane Eyre and a shopgirl's romance, adequately produced for its intended audience.
w Anne Mather, Jill Hyem *novel* Anne Mather *d* Gerry O'Hara *ph* Alfie Hicks *m* Kenneth V. Jones
☆ Keir Dullea, Susan Penhaligon, Jeremy Kemp, Kenneth More, Billie Whitelaw

The Leopard Man **
US 1943 59m bw
RKO (*Val Lewton*)

Murders in a Mexican border town are attributed to an escaped leopard.
Effective minor piece in the Lewton horror gallery; poor plot countered by highly effective suspense sequences.
w Ardel Wray, Edward Dein *novel* *Black Alibi* by Cornell Woolrich *d* *Jacques Tourneur* *ph* Robert de Grasse *m* Roy Webb
☆ Dennis O'Keefe, Jean Brooks, Margo, James Bell, Isabel Jewell

'It's all confusion, too much for an audience to follow.' – *Variety*

Lepa Sela Lepo Gore: see *Pretty Village Pretty Flame*

Lepke
US 1974 110m DeLuxe Panavision
Warner/AmeriEuro Pictures (Menahem Golan)

After World War I a small-time crook becomes head of Murder Incorporated.
Violent but totally uninteresting gangster melodrama; fidelity to fact is not enough.

w Wesley Lau, Tamar Hoffs *d* Menahem Golan *ph* Andrew Davis *m* Ken Wannberg *pd* Jack Degovia
☆ Tony Curtis, Anjanette Comer, Michael Callan, Warren Berlinger, Milton Berle, Gianni Russo
'A kosher version of The Godfather.' – *Verina Glaessner*

Leprechaun
US 1992 92m CFI color
Trimark (Jeffrey B. Mallian)
A leprechaun terrorizes a household while searching for gold that was stolen from him.
Lugubrious, trivial horror with some nasty moments of violence.
wd Mark Jones *ph* Levie Isaacs *m* Kevin Kiner *pd* Naomi Slodki *ed* Christopher Roth
☆ Warwick Davis, Jennifer Aniston, Mark Holton, Ken Olandt, Robert Gorman, John Sanderford
'A dull, unscary horror movie whose sole selling point is some extraneous gore footage.' – *Variety*

'The Gold, the Bride and the Ugly...'
Leprechaun 2
US 1994 85m CFI color
Trimark (Donald Borchers)
GB title: *One Wedding and Lots of Funerals*
A leprechaun returns after a thousand years to claim as his bride a girl who sneezes three times.
A sequel that bears little resemblance to the original in its narrative, apart from the accumulation of dead bodies to the accompaniment of jokey violence.
w Turi Meyer, Al Septien *d* Rodman Flender *m* Jonathan Elias *pd* Anthony Tremblay *ed* Christopher Roth, Richard Gentner
☆ Warwick Davis, Charlie Heath, Sandy Baron, Shevonne Durkin, Adam Biesk, James Lancaster
'This malevolent little horror item is a nasty bit of business that revels in chicanery and gore.' – *Leonard Klady, Variety*

Les Girls: see *Girls*

Les Misérables: see *Misérables*

Les Patterson Saves the World
Australia 1987 90m colour Panavision
Recorded Releasing/Humpstead (Sue Milliken)
A coarse and slobbish Australian diplomat foils a dastardly plot to unleash a deadly virus.
Gross and tasteless comedy, without wit or style.
w Barry Humphries, Diane Milstead *d* George Miller *ph* David Connell *m* Tim Finn *pd* Graham 'Grace' Walker *ed* Tim Wellburn
☆ Barry Humphries, Pamela Stephenson, Thaao Penghlis, Andrew Clarke, Henri Szeps, Hugh Keays-Byrne

Lesbian Vampires: see *Vampyros Lesbos*

Less than Zero
US 1987 98m DeLuxe
TCF (Jon Avnet, Jordan Kerner)
A group of the rich young and upwardly mobile in Los Angeles become hooked on a meaningless round of drugs, parties and sex.
Limp attempt to film a best-selling novel of the blank generation, concentrating not so much on the despair and self-pity of the participants as on their enviable life-style.
w Harley Peyton *novel* Bret Easton Ellis *d* Marek Kanievska *ph* Edward Lachman *m* Thomas Newman *pd* Barbara Ling *ed* Peter E. Berger, Michael Tronick
☆ Andrew McCarthy, Jami Gertz, Robert Downey Jnr, James Spader, Tony Bill, Nicholas Pryor, Donna Mitchell

A Lesson in Love
Sweden 1954 95m bw
Svensk Filmindustri (Allan Ekelund)
original title: *En Lektion I Kärlek*
A gynaecologist and his wife grow bored and turn to other partners, but are reconciled.
Slight comedy, surprisingly unsubtle for its creator, but passable.
wd Ingmar Bergman *ph* Martin Bodin, Bengt Nordwal *m* Dag Wirén *ad* P. A. Lundgren *ed* Oscar Rosander
☆ Gunnar Björnstrand, Eva Dahlbeck, Harriet Andersson, Yvonne Lombard, Ake Grönberg

Lest We Forget: see *Hangmen Also Die*

Let 'Em Have It *
US 1935 90m bw
Edward Small
GB title: *False Faces*
The FBI go after criminals on a terror spree.
Lively cops and robbers with some starkly effective moments.
w Joseph Moncure March, Elmer Harris *d* Sam Wood *ph* J. Peverell Marley, Robert Planck
☆ Richard Arlen, Virginia Bruce, Alice Brady, Bruce Cabot, Harvey Stephens, Eric Linden, Joyce Compton, J. Farrell MacDonald

Let Freedom Ring
US 1939 100m sepia
MGM (Harry Rapf)
A Westerner returns to his home town and clears it of corruption.
Elementary Hollywood actioner with curious credits, climaxed by Eddy singing The Star Spangled Banner.
w Ben Hecht *d* Jack Conway *ph* Sidney Wagner *m* Arthur Lange
☆ Nelson Eddy, Victor McLaglen, Virginia Bruce, Lionel Barrymore, H. B. Warner, Raymond Walburn, Edward Arnold, Guy Kibbee, Charles Butterworth, Billy Bevan
'Big box office ... lusty patriotic meller. Cinch for exploitation.' – *Variety*

Let George Do It **
GB 1940 82m bw
Ealing (Basil Dearden)
A ukelele player accidentally goes to Bergen instead of Blackpool and is mistaken for a spy.
Generally thought to be the best George Formby vehicle, with plenty of pace, good situations and catchy tunes.
w John Dighton, Austin Melford, Angus MacPhail, Basil Dearden *d* Marcel Varnel *ph* Gordon Dines, Ronald Neame
☆ *George Formby*, Phyllis Calvert, Garry Marsh, Romney Brent, Bernard Lee, Coral Browne, Torin Thatcher, Hal Gordon

'The shocking true story of an unbelievable miscarriage of justice.'
Let Him Have It **
GB 1991 115m colour
First Independent/Vivid/Le Studio Canal Plus/British Screen (Luc Roeg, Robert Warr)
Derek Bentley, an 18-year-old with a low IQ, is hanged for a murder committed by another.
Affecting drama that keeps its focus on its central character.
w Neal Purvis, Robert Wade *d* Peter Medak *ph* Oliver Stapleton *m* Michael Kamen *pd* Michael Pickwoad *ed* Ray Lovejoy
☆ Christopher Eccleston, Paul Reynolds, Tom Bell, Eileen Atkins, Clare Holman, Michael Elphick, Mark McGann, Tom Courtenay, Michael Gough
'A powerful mix of social conscience and solid entertainment.' – *Variety*
'The straightforward, chronological narrative of this often moving naturalistic drama is both its major emotional strength and its chief dramatic weakness.' – *Nigel Floyd, Sight and Sound*
'Woolly liberal armchair bollocks. And I was crap in it.' – *Christopher Eccleston*

Let It Be Me
US 1995 100m colour
Rysher (David Kirkpatrick, Keith Samples)
GB title: *Love Dance*
An engaged man faces the loss of his fiancée when he persuades her to take dancing lessons.
Tired romantic comedy centred on dance, but never less than flat-footed.
wd Eleanor Bergstein *ph* Miroslav Ondrícek *m* Joseph Vitarelli *ch* Miranda Garrison *pd* David Chapman *ed* Bill Pankow
☆ Campbell Scott (Gabriel), Jennifer Beals (Emily), Yancy Butler (Corinne), Patrick Stewart (John), Jamie Goodwin (Bud), Josh Mostel (Jordan), Elise Neal (Carlita), Heather Graham (Perfumery Saleswoman), Daniel McDonald (Fred), Leslie Caron (Marguerite)

Let It Ride
US 1989 86m Technicolor
Paramount (David Giler)
A compulsive and unsuccessful gambler comes good at the race-track.
A comedy that limps along for most of its length.
w Ernest Morton (Nancy Dowd) *book* Good Vibes by Jay Cronley *d* Joe Pykta *ph* Curtis J. Wehr *m* Giorgio Moroder *pd* Wolf Kroeger *ed* Dede Allen
☆ Richard Dreyfuss, David Johansen, Teri Garr, Allen Garfield, Jennifer Tilly, Michelle Phillips, Mary Woronov, Robbie Coltrane

Let No Man Write My Epitaph
US 1960 106m bw
Columbia/Boris D. Kaplan
A slum boy wants to become a concert pianist but falls in with gangsters.
Squalid, predictable melodrama without many redeeming features.
w Robert Presnell Jnr *novel* Willard Motley *d* Philip Leacock *ph* Burnett Guffey *m* George Duning
☆ James Darren, Shelley Winters, Burl Ives, Jean Seberg, Jeanne Cooper, Ricardo Montalban, Ella Fitzgerald

'Something is rotten in the City of the Angels.'
Let the Devil Wear Black
US 1998 89m DeLuxe
New Moon/Trimark (Matt Salinger)
After his father dies of a heart attack, his son believes that he was murdered by his uncle, who plans to marry his mother.
A modern variation on Hamlet, set among the low life of Los Angeles. It keeps the bare bones of the narrative but misses out on the tragedy in favour of a more conventional thriller of betrayal, one where the Hamlet-figure makes love in a bathroom to his addled and pregnant Ophelia-like girlfriend.
w Jonathan Penner, Stacy Title *d* Stacy Title *ph* Jim Whitaker *m* Christophe Beck *pd* Alec Hammond *ed* Luis Colina *cos* Leesa Evans
☆ Jonathan Penner (Jack Lyne), Jacqueline Bisset (Helen Lyne), Mary-Louise Parker (Julia Hirsch), Jamey Sheridan (Carl Lyne), Jonathan Banks (Satch), Philip Baker Hall (Saul Hirsch), Maury Chaykin (Bruce), Chris Sarandon (Jack's Father), Jeffrey Schoeny (Young Jack), Randall Batinkoff (T.B. Bradbury), Norman Reedus (Brautigan), Thomas Duffy (Bartender), Tony Plana (Tall), Lobo Sebastian (Ugly), Kevin West (Pharmacist)
'A first-rate ensemble cast and genuinely clever reworkings of Shakespearean plot devices are the major selling points.' – *Joe Leydon, Variety*

Let the People Sing *
GB 1942 105m bw
British National (John Baxter)
An out-of-work comedian persuades a drunken nobleman to join a protest against the closing of a village hall.
A development of The Good Companions *which compares quite nicely with the Capra films from across the water: naïve but entertaining, with good star performances.*
w John Baxter, Barbara K. Emery, Geoffrey Orme *novel* J. B. Priestley *d* John Baxter *ph* James Wilson
☆ *Alastair Sim, Fred Emney, Edward Rigby*, Patricia Roc, Oliver Wakefield, Marian Spencer, Olive Sloane, Gus McNaughton, Charles Hawtrey

Let Them Live
US 1937 71m bw
Universal
A young man matches wits with a crooked town boss.
Tepid second-feature drama.
w Bruce Manning, Lionel Houser *d* Harold Young
☆ John Howard, Nan Grey, Edward Ellis, Judith Barrett
'Better than many of its kind ... should please in nabes.' – *Variety*

Let Us Be Gay
US 1930 79m bw
MGM
Divorcees meet again, many years later, in Paris.
Predictable star romance, now very dated, like its title.
w Frances Marion *play* Rachel Crothers *d* Robert Z. Leonard
☆ Norma Shearer, Rod La Rocque, Marie Dressler, Sally Eilers, Raymond Hackett, Hedda Hopper
'Strong on all counts, romance, comedy, human sympathy and gorgeous clothes against a glamorous setting.' – *Variety*

Let Us Live
US 1937 67m bw
Columbia
An innocent taxi driver is convicted of murder.
Intense little melodrama which served its purpose.
w Joseph F. Dineen, Anthony Veiller and Allen Rivkin *d* John Brahm
☆ Maureen O'Sullivan, Henry Fonda, Ralph Bellamy
'Heavy dramatic preachment with limited appeal.' – *Variety*

Lethal Tender
Canada 1996 93m colour
Le Monde (Julian Grant)
A Chicago cop is the only one who can save the city's water supply when gangsters take over the filtration plant as part of an elaborate multi-million dollar robbery.
A standard action movie that gains a little from its unusual setting, though otherwise it sticks to the usual genre conventions, with otherwise ruthless killers suddenly becoming squeamish when they have a chance to shoot the hero.
w Tony Johnston *d* John Bradshaw *ph* Gerald R. Goozee *m* Lou Natale *pd* John Gillespie *ed* Paul Day
☆ Jeff Fahey (David Chase), Kim Coates (Montesi), Carrie-Ann Moss (Melissa Wilkins), Gary Busey (Mr Turner), Denis Akiyama (Detective Peter Ota), David Mucci (Wally), David Fraser (Ed Williams), Martin Roach (Sammy)

Lethal Weapon *
US 1987 110m Technicolor
Warner/ Richard Donner, Joel Silver
A slightly unhinged cop uncovers a drug smuggling operation.
Extremely violent policier which caters to the Rambo crowd but has enough pizazz to recommend it to most classes.
w Shane Black *d* Richard Donner *ph* Stephen Goldblatt *m* Michael Kamen, Eric Clapton
☆ Mel Gibson, Danny Glover, Gary Busey, Mitchell Ryan, Tom Atkins, Darlene Love
'Style masquerading as content.' – *Daily Variety*

Lethal Weapon 2
US 1989 111m colour Panavision
Warner/Silver Pictures (Richard Donner, Joel Silver)
Two cops hunt down drug smugglers protected by diplomatic immunity.
Slick action film with South Africans as the villains, fast-paced enough for the many implausibilities of plot and character to flash by.
w Jeffrey Boam *story* Shane Black, Warren Murphy *d* Richard Donner *ph* Stephen Goldblatt *m* Michael Kamen, Eric Clapton, David Sanborn *pd* J. Michael Riva *ed* Stuart Baird
☆ Mel Gibson, Danny Glover, Joe Pesci, Joss Ackland, Derrick O'Connor, Patsy Kensit

'The magic is back again.'
Lethal Weapon 3
US 1992 118m Technicolor Panavision
Warner/Silver Pictures (Richard Donner, Joel Silver)
Two detectives expose a former cop who is running an arms racket.
A succession of violent set pieces substitutes for narrative and character in this increasingly cynical series.
w Jeffrey Boam, Robert Mark Kamen *d* Richard Donner *ph* Jan de Bont *m* Michael Kamen, Eric Clapton, David Sanborn *pd* James Spencer *ed* Robert Brown, Battle Davis
☆ Mel Gibson, Danny Glover, Joe Pesci, Rene Russo, Stuart Wilson, Steve Kahan, Darlene Love, Traci Wolfe
'A pic that's really more about moments – comic or thrilling – than any sort of cohesive whole.' – *Variety*

'It celebrates a luxurious kind of destruction and disorder that can only appear mindless amid today's realities.' – *Vincent Canby, New York Times*

'The action you expect, the faces you love.'

Lethal Weapon 4
US 1998 127m Technicolor Panavision
Warner/Silver/Doshudo (Joel Silver, Richard Donner)

Two LA cops tangle with Chinese gangsters smuggling illegal immigrants into the country.
When even the publicity tag stresses the predictability of what's on offer, then it's no surprise to discover that the usual fare is on offer: noisy explosions, noisy dialogue, and effusive male bonding.
w Channing Gibson *story* Jonathan Lemkin, Alfred Gough, Miles Millar *d* Richard Donner *ph* Andrzej Bartkowiak *m* Michael Kamen, Eric Clapton, David Sanborn *ch* martial arts: Cory Yuen, Huen Chiu Ku, Chi Wah Ling *pd* J. Michael Riva *ed* Frank J. Urioste, Dallas Puett
☆ Mel Gibson, Danny Glover, Joe Pesci, Rene Russo, Chris Rock, Jet Li, Steve Kahan, Kim Chan, Darlene Love, Traci Wolfe, Eddy Ko, Steven Lam, Richard Libertini
'Hollywood cinema that justifies big bucks and bigger bangs.' – *Richard Williams, Guardian*
'I almost fell asleep during one explosion, only to be rudely awoken by the din of comic business going on in the foreground. Hard to believe, I know, but then you haven't heard the noise levels that the director, Richard Donner, appears to believe are essential to great comedy – levels equalled only by the shrill creak of contrivance as he cranks up each comic situation.' – *Tom Shone, Sunday Times*

Let's Be Famous
GB 1939 83m bw
Ealing (Michael Balcon)
A stage-struck Irish lad and Lancashire lass have various adventures in London.
Easy-going comedy introducing radio personalities of the day.
w Roger MacDougall, Allan MacKinnon *d* Walter Forde *ph* Ronald Neame, Gordon Dines *md* Ernest Irving
☆ Jimmy O'Dea, Betty Driver, Sonnie Hale, Patrick Barr, Basil Radford, Milton Rosmer, Garry Marsh

Let's Be Happy
GB 1957 107m Technicolor Cinemascope
ABP/ Marcel Hellman
Footling musical remake of *Jeannie* (qv).
w Diana Morgan *d* Henry Levin *ph* Erwin Hillier *m* Nicholas Brodszky *md* Louis Levy *songs* Nicholas Brodszky, Paul Francis Webster
☆ Vera-Ellen, Tony Martin, Robert Flemyng, Zena Marshall, Guy Middleton, Katherine Kath, Jean Cadell, Gordon Jackson
'Success still eludes the Anglo-American musical.' – *MFB*

Let's Dance
US 1950 112m Technicolor
Paramount (Robert Fellows)

Show business partners reunite after five years of private life.
Tediously plotted musical with a couple of good numbers.
w Allan Scott *story* Maurice Zolotow *d* Norman Z. McLeod *ph* George Barnes *m* Robert Emmett Dolan *songs* Frank Loesser
☆ Fred Astaire, Betty Hutton, Roland Young, Ruth Warrick, Lucile Watson, Barton MacLane, Shepperd Strudwick, Melville Cooper, Harold Huber, George Zucco

Let's Do It Again
US 1953 95m Technicolor
Columbia (Oscar Saul)
A songwriter and his wife plan a divorce but call it off in the nick of time.
Tame musical remake of The Awful Truth *(qv), pleasant enough but lacking style and punch.*
w Mary Loos, Richard Sale *d* Alexander Hall *ph* Charles Lawton Jnr *m* George Duning *md* Morris Stoloff *songs* Lester Lee, Ned Washington
☆ Jane Wyman, Ray Milland, Aldo Ray, Leon Ames

Let's Do It Again
US 1975 113m Technicolor
Warner/First Artists/Verdon (Melville Tucker, Pembroke J. Herring)

Three Atlanta workers conceive a zany plan to raise money for their church by hypnotizing a boxer into winning a big fight.
Lively but overlong farce reassembling the black talents of Uptown Saturday Night.
w Richard Wesley *d* Sidney Poitier *ph* Donald M. Morgan *m* Curtis Mayfield
☆ Sidney Poitier, Bill Cosby, Calvin Lockhart, John Amos, Denise Nicholas, Ossie Davis, Jimmy Walker

Let's Face It
US 1943 76m bw
Paramount (Fred Kohlmar)
A smart-alec soldier has a plot involving a ladies' health camp, but finds himself up to his neck in spies.
Tepid star comedy which unaccountably ditches almost all the numbers from the musical on which it was based.
w Harry Tugend *play* Cradle Snatchers by Norma Mitchell, Russell Medcraft *musical play* Dorothy and Herbert Fields, Cole Porter *d* Sidney Lanfield *ph* Lionel Lindon *songs* Cole Porter
☆ Bob Hope, Betty Hutton, Eve Arden, Phyllis Povah, Dona Drake, ZaSu Pitts, Marjorie Weaver, Raymond Walburn, Joe Sawyer

Let's Fall in Love
US 1933 67m bw
Columbia
A film director passes off a circus attendant as a glamorous foreign star.
Lightweight comedy with music which did okay.
w Herbert Fields *d* David Burton
☆ Edmund Lowe, Ann Sothern, Miriam Jordan, Gregory Ratoff
'No chorus, no legs, no undressing for a change ... moderately geared for moderate income.' – *Variety*

Let's Get Laid
GB 1977 96m Technicolor
Norfolk International (Brian Smedley-Aston)
In 1947, a dimwitted demobbed soldier is chased by police and secret agents after he inadvertently acquires a secret weapon hidden inside a cigarette lighter.
Tiresome and tasteless farcial thriller, not helped by Askwith's gormless act. Its main aim is to get Fiona Richmond to discard her clothes, and even to achieve this, the feeble script has to resort to frequent dream sequences, including one in which she is dressed as a Nazi officer.
w Michael Robson *d* James Kenelm Clarke *ph* Phil Meheux *m* James Kenelm Clarke *md* Johnny Pearson *ad* Ken Bridgeman *ed* Jim Connock
☆ Fiona Richmond (Maxine Lupercal), Robin Askwith (Gordon Laid/Jimsy Deveroo), Anthony Steel (Moncrieff Dovecraft), Linda Hayden (Gloria), Graham Stark (Inspector Nugent), Roland Curram (Rupert Dorchester), Tony Haygarth (Sgt Costello), Patrick Holt (Commissioner)
'Remains fatally undecided whether to go for parody or pastiche, and duly fails as either.' – *Tim Pulleine, MFB*

Let's Get Lost *
US 1988 120m bw
Mainline/Little Bear (Bruce Weber)

Documentary on the life of jazz trumpeter and drug addict Chet Baker.
Fascinating series of interviews with friends, associates and lovers, interspersed with film from Baker's earlier life and some modern-day performances.
w Susan Stribling *d* Bruce Weber *ph* Jeff Preiss *m* Chet Baker *ad* Sam Shahid, Donald Sterzin, Rise Daniels *ed* Angelo Corrao

Let's Get Married
US 1937 68m bw
Columbia
A politician's daughter falls for the weather bureau chief.
Aimless romantic comedy which gets by on its performers.
w Ethel Hill *story* A. H. Z. Carr *d* Alfred E. Green
☆ Ida Lupino, Walter Connolly, Ralph Bellamy, Reginald Denny, Raymond Walburn
'Mediocre dualler.' – *Variety*

Let's Go Native
US 1930 75m bw
Paramount
Various people are shipwrecked on a South Sea island.
Easy-going farce comedy with music.
w George Marion Jnr, Percy Heath *d* Leo McCarey
☆ Jack Oakie, Jeanette MacDonald, Skeets Gallagher, James Hall, Kay Francis
'Hokum laughs with songs and dances.' – *Variety*

Let's Go Places
US 1930 70m bw
Fox
A young tenor goes to Hollywood, is mistaken for someone more famous and becomes a star.
Lightweight comedy with mildly interesting studio scenes.
w William K. Wells *d* Frank Strayer
☆ Joseph Wagstaff, Lola Lane, Sharon Lynn, Ilka Chase, Walter Catlett, Dixie Lee
'Plenty of music, no drawing names. Rates moderate for the big houses.' – *Variety*

Let's Hope It's a Girl *
Italy/France 1985 119m colour
Artificial Eye/Clemi Cinematografica/Producteurs Associes/Soprofilms/A2 (Raimondo Castelli, Bruno Ridolfi)
original title: *Speriamo Che Sia Femmina*
A countess strives, with the help of other women of the household, to keep running the family farm.
Gently amusing, rambling comedy.
w Leo Benvenuti, Tullio Pinelli, Suso Cecchi D'Amico, Piero de Bernardi, Mario Monicelli *d* Mario Monicelli *ph* Camillo Bazzoni *m* Nicola Piovani *ad* Enrico Fiorentini *ed* Ruggero Mastroianni
☆ Liv Ullmann, Catherine Deneuve, Philippe Noiret, Bernard Blier, Giuliana de Sio, Stefania Sandrelli, Athina Cenci, Lucrezia Lante Della Rovere

Let's Kill Uncle
US 1966 92m colour
Universal/William Castle
A boy is threatened by his wicked uncle, and retaliates.
Mildly intriguing black comedy, leadenly handled.
w Mark Rodgers *novel* Rohan O'Grady *d* William Castle *ph* Harold Lipstein *m* Herman Stein
☆ Nigel Green, Mary Badham, Pat Cardi, Robert Pickering

Let's Live a Little
US 1948 85m bw
Eagle-Lion/United California Productions
An advertising agent falls for his lady psychiatrist, and after many vicissitudes they and their former partners make it to the altar.
Mild comedy which just about bubbles along despite a rather uncomfortable cast.
w Albert J. Cohen, Jack Harvey *d* Richard Wallace *ph* Ernest Laszlo *m* Werner Heymann
☆ Hedy Lamarr, Robert Cummings, Anna Sten, Robert Shayne, Mary Treen

Let's Live Tonight
US 1935 75m bw
Columbia
Two millionaire brothers in Monte Carlo love the same girl.
Flimsy romantic comedy which gets by on its music.
w Gene Markey, Bradley King *d* Victor Schertzinger
☆ Lilian Harvey, Tullio Carminati, Hugh Williams, Janet Beecher, Tala Birell, Luis Alberni
'A parrot gets most of the laughs, which tips off the script.' – *Variety*

Let's Make a Night of It
GB 1937 92m bw
Associated British
In Nice, a husband and wife own rival night-clubs.
Slim musical with rather too many interpolated turns.
w Hugh Brooke *radio play* The Silver Spoon by Henrik Ege *d* Graham Cutts *ph* Otto Kanturek *m/ly* Jimmie Kennedy, Michael Carr
☆ Buddy Rogers, June Clyde, Claire Luce, Fred Emney, Iris Hoey, Steve Geray, Syd Walker, Afrique, Oliver Wakefield, Brian Michie, Joe Loss and his Band, Sidney Lipton and his Band
'Definitely no appeal for the US.' – *Variety*

Let's Make It Legal
US 1951 77m bw
TCF
An attractive grandmother divorces her gambler husband and takes up with an old boyfriend.
Unremarkable but competent star comedy.
w F. Hugh Herbert, I. A. L. Diamond *d* Richard Sale *ph* Lucien Ballard *m* Cyril Mockridge
☆ Claudette Colbert, Zachary Scott, Macdonald Carey, Barbara Bates, Robert Wagner, Marilyn Monroe

Let's Make Love *
US 1960 118m DeLuxe Cinemascope
TCF (Jerry Wald)

A multi-millionaire, learning that he is to be burlesqued in a Broadway show, joins the cast as an actor.
Complex, moderately sophisticated, occasionally funny musical inspired by On The Avenue *(qv); lively characterizations but poor numbers.*
w Norman Krasna *d* George Cukor *ph* Daniel L. Fapp *md* Lionel Newman, Earl H. Hagen *ch* Jack Cole *songs* Sammy Cahn, Jimmy Van Heusen
☆ Yves Montand, Marilyn Monroe, Tony Randall, Wilfrid Hyde-White, Frankie Vaughan, David Burns, and guests Bing Crosby, Gene Kelly, Milton Berle
Academy Award nomination: Lionel Newman, Earl H. Hagen

Let's Make Music
US 1940 85m bw
RKO (Howard Benedict)
An old maid of a teacher writes a school song that unexpectedly becomes a novelty hit.
Slight but pleasant time-filler that includes a performance of Crosby's hit 'Big Noise from Winnetka'. Its only surprise is that it was written by the acerbic novelist Nathanael West during his time as an ill-paid Hollywood hack.
w Nathanael West; special dialogue for Bob Crosby by Helen Phillips, Bernard Dougall *d* Leslie Goodwins *ph* Jack Mackenzie *ad* Van Nest Polglase *ed* Desmond Marquette
☆ Bob Crosby, Jean Rogers, Elisabeth Risdon, Joseph Buloff, Joyce Compton, Bob Crosby's Orchestra featuring The Bobcats

Let's Make Up: see *Lilacs in the Spring*

Let's Scare Jessica to Death
US 1971 89m colour
Paramount/Jessica Co (Charles B. Moss Jnr)

Back home after a nervous breakdown, our heroine is troubled by voices and visions, not to mention an ambulant corpse and a vampire or two.
Competent screamie.
w Norman Jonas, Ralph Rose *d* John Hancock *ph* Bob Baldwin *m* Orville Stoeber
☆ Zohra Lampert, Barton Heyman, Kevin O'Connor

Let's Spend the Night Together
US 1982 94m Technicolor
Embassy (Ronald L. Schwary)

A concert film shot on the Rolling Stones' tour of America in 1981, including performances from the Sun Devil Stadium in Tempe, Arizona and the Brendan Byrne Arena in Rutherford, New Jersey.
Fan material, providing nothing of backstage interest, and performances, in the large and impersonal arenas favoured by rock stars, which seem strictly by rote despite their energy.
d Hal Ashby *ph* Caleb Deschanel, Gerald Feil *m/ly* Mick Jagger, Keith Richards and others *ed* Lisa Day, Sonya Sones, Lorinda Hollingshead
♫ Songs performed include 'All Down the Line', 'Beast of Burden', 'Black Limousine', 'Brown Sugar', 'Hang Fire', 'Honky Tonk Woman', 'Jumpin' Jack Flash', 'Let It Bleed', 'Let's Spend the Night Together', 'Satisfaction', 'Under My Thumb' and 'You Can't Always Get What You Want'.

The Letter *
US 1929 61m bw
Paramount
Early talkie version of a solid piece of theatre.
See below.
play W. Somerset Maugham *story* W. Somerset Maugham *d* Jean de Limur
☆ Jeanne Eagels, O. P. Heggie, Reginald Owen, Herbert Marshall, Irene Browne
AA Jeanne Eagels

'With all my heart, I still love the man I killed!'
The Letter ****
US 1940 95m bw
Warner (Robert Lord)
A rubber plantation owner's wife kills a man in what seems to have been self-defence; but a letter from her proves it to have been a crime of passion, and becomes an instrument of blackmail.
Excellent performances and presentation make this the closest approximation on film to reading a Maugham story of the Far East, though censorship forced the addition of an infuriating moral ending.
w Howard Koch *story* W. Somerset Maugham *d* William Wyler *ph* Tony Gaudio *m* Max Steiner *ed* Warren Low
☆ Bette Davis, Herbert Marshall, James Stephenson, Sen Yung, Frieda Inescort, Gale Sondergaard, Bruce Lester, Tetsu Komai
'The writing is taut and spare throughout ... the unravelling of Maugham's story is masterly and the presentation visual and cinematic ... the audience at the trade show did not move a finger.' – *James Agate*
† Herbert Marshall played the lover in the first version and the husband in the second.
AA best picture; William Wyler; Tony Gaudio; Max Steiner; Bette Davis; James Stephenson; Warren Low

A Letter for Evie
US 1945 88m bw
William H. Wright/MGM
A girl starts confusion when she writes a letter to an unknown soldier; a wimp writes back but sends his he-man buddy's photograph.
Predictable comedy with longueurs.
w De Vallon Scott, Alan Friedman *d* Jules Dassin
☆ Marsha Hunt, John Carroll, Hume Cronyn, Spring Byington, Pamela Britton, Norman Lloyd

'The story that will live ... as long as there is love!'
Letter from an Unknown Woman ***
US 1948 89m bw
Universal/Rampart (John Houseman)
A woman wastes her life in unrequited love for a rakish pianist.
Superior 'woman's picture' which gave its director his best chance in America to recreate his beloved Vienna of long ago. Hollywood production magic at its best.
w Howard Koch *novel* Stefan Zweig *d* Max Ophüls *ph* Franz Planer *m* Daniele Amfitheatrof *ad* Alexander Golitzen *ed* Ted J. Kent
☆ Joan Fontaine, Louis Jourdan, Mady Christians, Art Smith, Marcel Journet
'A film full of snow, sleigh bells, lights gleaming in ornamental gardens and trysts at night.' – *Charles Higham, 1972*
'It is fascinating to watch the sure deft means by which Ophuls sidetracks seemingly inevitable clichés and holds on to a shadowy, tender mood, half buried in the past. Here is a fragile filmic charm that is not often or easily accomplished.' – *Richard Winnington*
'Film narrative of a most skilled order.' – *William Whitebait*
'Probably the toniest "woman's picture" ever made.' – *Pauline Kael, 70s*

Letter of Introduction *
US 1938 100m bw
Universal (John M. Stahl)
A young actress is encouraged by an ageing star whom she does not know is her father.
Commercial melodrama with luxury trimmings, all very neatly packaged.
w Sheridan Gibney, Leonard Spigelgass *d* John M. Stahl *ph* Karl Freund *m* Charles Previn *ed* Ted J. Kent
☆ Adolphe Menjou, Andrea Leeds, Edgar Bergen and Charlie McCarthy, George Murphy, Eve Arden, Rita Johnson, Ernest Cossart, Ann Sheridan
'Headed for big business everywhere.' – *Variety*

A Letter to Brezhnev **
GB 1985 95m colour
Yeardream/Film Four International/Palace Productions (Janet Goddard)
Two girls from Liverpool spend a busy night with Russian sailors; when one of them receives no subsequent letters, she writes to Brezhnev and is invited to Moscow.
Vivid it is, but also raucous and seedy until true love enters as a redeeming factor. The critics loved it, thinking it about unemployment and urban decline; it certainly paints a low picture of Liverpool.
w Frank Clarke *d* Chris Bernard *ph* Bruce McGowan *m* Alan Gill *ed* Lesley Walker
☆ Alfred Molina, Peter Firth, Margi Clarke, Tracy Lea, Alexandra Pigg
'Fast-moving, funny, entertaining and poignant ... in short how to make a British film.' – *Jill Forbes, MFB*

'A peek into the other woman's male!'
A Letter to Three Wives **
US 1949 102m bw
TCF (Sol C. Siegel)
Three wives on a picnic receive word from a friend that she has run off with one of their husbands.
Amusing short-story compendium which seemed more revelatory at the time than it does now, and paved the way for its writer-director's heyday.
wd Joseph L. Mankiewicz *novel* John Klempner *ph* Arthur Miller *m* Alfred Newman
☆ Jeanne Crain, Ann Sothern, Linda Darnell, Jeffrey Lynn, Kirk Douglas, *Paul Douglas*, Barbara Lawrence, Connie Gilchrist, Florence Bates, Hobart Cavanaugh, and the voice of Celeste Holm
'A mere shadow of those acid Hollywood comedies of the thirties ... over-written and under-directed ... but it has a supply of ironies and makes a certain alkaline comment on present-day American customs and manners.' – *Richard Winnington*
'Replete with sharp dialogue. He aims barbed darts at the country's favourite institutions, and makes them score with telling effect.' – *Variety*
AA Joseph L. Mankiewicz (as writer); Joseph L. Mankiewicz (as director)
AA best picture

Letters from a Dead Man *
USSR 1986 87m colour/bw
Artificial Eye/Lenfilm/Sovexportfilm
original title: *Pisma Myortvovo Cheloveka*
After a nuclear holocaust, a scientist composes letters to his missing son while trying to rescue young survivors thrown out of the central shelter.
Grim and powerful for the most part, although not always easy to watch.
w Konstantin Lopushansky, Vyacheslav Rybakov, Boris Strugatsky *d* Konstantin Lopushansky *ph* Nikolai Pokoptsev *m* Alexander Zhurbin, Faure *ad* Yelema Amshinskaya, Viktor Ivanov
☆ Rolan Bykov, I. Ryklin, V. Mikailov, A. Sabinin, V. Lobanov, N. Gryakalova, V. Mayorova, V. Dvorzhetski

Letty Lynton
US 1932 84m bw
MGM
When one lover is murdered, Letty turns to another to prove her innocent.
Bad girl drama which established the star's box-office appeal.
w John Meehan and Wanda Tuchock *d* Clarence Brown
☆ Joan Crawford, Robert Montgomery, Nils Asther, May Robson, Lewis Stone
'Big grosses are written all over this one.' – *Variety*

Letyat Zhuravli: see *The Cranes are Flying*

Der Letzte Mann: see *The Last Laugh*

Leviathan
US/Italy 1989 98m Technicolor J-D-C Scope
Fox/Gordon Company/Filmauro (Luigi de Laurentiis, Aurelio de Laurentiis)
Deep sea miners are the victims of a monstrous genetic experiment gone wrong.
An underwater variation on Alien, *lacking originality and suspense.*
w David Peoples, Jeb Stuart *d* George P. Cosmatos *ph* Alex Thomson *m* Jerry Goldsmith *pd* Ron Cobb *ed* Roberto Silvi, John F. Burnett *sp* Perpetual Motion Pictures, Stan Winston Studios
☆ Peter Weller, Richard Crenna, Amanda Pays, Daniel Stern, Ernie Hudson, Michael Carmine, Meg Foster, Lisa Eilbacher, Hector Elizondo
'Given the familiarity of it all, Leviathan is at least an enjoyable rip-off.' – *MFB*

Les Lèvres Rouges: see *Daughters of Darkness*

Lewis & Clark & George
US 1997 84m CFI color
Davis/Dark Matter (J. Todd Harris, Dan Gunther)
Two escaped convicts team up with a cigar-smoking woman to search for a gold mine.
A tongue-in-cheek, offbeat cowboy road movie, a tale of double- and triple-cross, which rounds up the usual situations and violently recycles them.
wd Rod McCall *ph* Michael Mayers *m* Ben Vaughn *pd* John Huke *ed* Ed Marx
☆ Rose McGowan, Salvator Xuereb, Dan Gunther, Art LaFleur, James Brolin, Paul Bartel
'This self-consciously quirky offering is unashamed of regurgitating most of the genre's clichés.' – *Independent*

La Ley del Deseo: see *Law of Desire*

L'Homme du Train: see *The Man on the Train*

L'Humanité **
France 1999 148m colour Panavision
Artificial Eye/3B/Arte/CRRAV (Jean Brehat, Rachid Bouchareb)
In a small Flanders town, a lonely, emotionally unstable cop investigates the rape and murder of a schoolgirl.
Slow-paced, plodding movie of the dull, dour and inarticulate; its length will come near to defeating even those who respond to its slow rhythms and gradual, uncompromising unfolding of individual lives in a particular place.
wd Bruno Dumont *ph* Yves Cape *m* Richard Cuvillier *ad* Marc-Philippe Guerig *ed* Guy Lecorne *cos* Nathalie Raoul
☆ Emmanuel Schotte (Pharaon De Winter), Severine Caneele (Domino), Philippe Tullier (Joseph), Ghislain Ghesquiere (Police Chief), Ginette Allegre (Eliane)
'A tale of compassion and empathy that will trigger impatience and intolerance in many viewers.' – *Lisa Nesselson, Variety*

Les Liaisons Dangereuses *
France 1959 106m bw
Films Marceau
Valmont and his wife compare notes on each other's affairs.
Showy modernization of a notorious minor classic.
w Roger Vailland, Roger Vadim, Claude Brulé *novel* Choderlos de Laclos *d* Roger Vadim *ph* Marcel Grignon *m* Jack Murray, Thelonius Monk
☆ Gérard Philipe, Jeanne Moreau, Annette Vadim, Jeanne Valerie, Simone Renant, Jean-Louis Trintignant
'A woman's picture par excellence.' – *John Russell Taylor, MFB*

Liam **
GB/Germany 2000 91m colour
Artificial Eye/BBC/Liam/Road Movies/Mida/Diaphana/Bim/ WDR/Arte/ARD/Degeto (Colin McKeown, Martin Tempia)
In Liverpool in the early 30s, a young, stammering Catholic boy undergoes a harsh education and watches his father turning to fascism and violence after he loses his job.
Raw and emotional account of life during the Depression, recalled with a powerful immediacy.
w Jimmy McGovern *d* Stephen Frears *ph* Andrew Dunn *m* John Murphy *pd* Stephen Fineren *ed* Kristina Hetherington
☆ Ian Hart (Dad), Claire Hackett (Mam), Anthony Borrows (Liam), David Hart (Con), *Megan Burns* (Teresa), Anne Reid (Mrs Abernathy), Russell Dixon (Father Ryan), Julia Deakin (Auntie Aggie), Andrew Schofield (Uncle Tom), Bernadette Shortt (Lizzie)
'A passionate drama bursting with humor and affection, and Frears handles the material with his customary skill and intelligence.' – *David Stratton, Variety*

Lianlian Feng Chen: see *Dust in the Wind*

Lianna
US 1983 112m DuArt
Winwood
A wife and mother becomes a lesbian.
That's all there is, folks, not much in the way of plot, and barely enough for a TV movie; but some good observation and acting come through.
ph Austin de Besche *m* Mason Daring
wd/ed John Sayles
☆ Linda Griffiths, Jane Hallaren, Jon de Vries, Jo Henderson

'You come looking, you might not like what you find.'
Liar *
US 1997 102m Foto-Kem 'Scope
First Independent/MDP (Peter Glatzer)
aka: *Deceiver*
A wealthy alcoholic playboy investigates the cops who questioned him over the murder of a prostitute.
Tricksy, over-elaborate thriller, intent on confusing its audience; but its makers show promise of better things to come.
wd Jonas and Joshua Pate *ph* Bill Butler *m* Harry Gregson-Williams *pd* John Kretschmer *ed* Dan Lebental
☆ Tim Roth, Chris Penn, Michael Rooker, Renee Zellweger, Ellen Burstyn, Rosanna Arquette
'Flashy exercise in style and obfuscation.' – *Variety*

'Trust Me.'
Liar, Liar
US 1997 87m DeLuxe
Universal/Imagine (Brian Grazer)
A young boy's wish becomes true – and his father, an unscrupulous lawyer, is forced to tell the truth for 24 hours.
A comedy that merges Carrey's now familiar frenetic mugging with some gruesome sentimentality; soft-centred slapstick is not a pretty sight.
w Paul Guay, Stephen Mazur *d* Tom Shadyac *ph* Russell Boyd *m* John Debney *pd* Linda de Scenna *ed* Don Zimmerman
☆ Jim Carrey, Maura Tierney, Jennifer Tilly, Swoosie Kurtz, Amanda Donohoe, Cary Elwes
'Isn't designed to win Carrey any converts, but is shrewdly calculated to include enough lightly lewd humor to keep adults amused while the kids enjoy the slapstick shenanigans.' – *Todd McCarthy, Variety*
† A similar notion was used in the Bob Hope comedy *Nothing but the Truth* (qv).

Libel *
GB 1959 100m bw
MGM/Comet (Anatole de Grunwald)
An ex-POW baronet is accused of being an impostor.
Old-fashioned courtroom spellbinder, quite adequately done though occasionally creaky.
w Anatole de Grunwald, Karl Tunberg *play* Edward Wooll *d* Anthony Asquith *ph* Robert Krasker *m* Benjamin Frankel *ad* Paul Sheriff
☆ Dirk Bogarde, Olivia de Havilland, Paul Massie, Wilfrid Hyde-White, Robert Morley, Anthony Dawson, Richard Wattis, Martin Miller, Millicent Martin

Libeled Lady **

US 1936 98m bw

MGM (Lawrence Weingarten)

An heiress sues a newspaper, and the editor hires a friend to compromise her.

Lively four-star romantic comedy which sums up its era as well as any.

w Maurine Watkins, Howard Emmett Rogers, George Oppenheimer d Jack Conway ph Norbert Brodine *m* William Axt

☆ *Jean Harlow, Myrna Loy, Spencer Tracy, William Powell, Walter Connolly, Charley Grapewin,* Cora Witherspoon, E. E. Clive, Charles Trowbridge

'Handsomely mounted and produced, lavishly costumed, cleverly written and artfully directed, *Libeled Lady* is entirely worthy of the noble comedians who head its cast.' – *Bland Johaneson, New York Daily Mirror*

† Remade as *Easy to Wed* (qv); central situation borrowed for *Man's Favorite Sport* (qv).

best picture

'All she wanted was her black man's money and her white man's love!'

The Liberation of L. B. Jones *

US 1970 102m Technicolor

Columbia/Liberation Co (Ronald Lubin)

Racial murder is the result when a black undertaker wants a divorce in a small Tennessee town.

Violent, pointless but well-made melodrama which really does not take matters much further than Intruder in the Dust.

w Stirling Silliphant, Jesse Hill Ford, from Ford's novel *d William Wyler ph* Robert Surtees *m* Elmer Bernstein

☆ Lee J. Cobb, Anthony Zerbe, Roscoe Lee Browne, Lola Falana, Lee Majors, Barbara Hershey, Yaphet Kotto, Arch Johnson, Chill Wills

'With its genuinely ferocious climax it adds up to probably the most powerful, if not the most sophisticated, race-war film the commercial studios have yet produced.' – *Nigel Andrews*

Liberty **

US 1929 20m bw silent

Hal Roach

Two convicts escape and have adventures high on a construction site.

Amusing gags are succeeded by breathtaking thrills in the Harold Lloyd style.

w Leo McCarey, H. M. Walker *d* Leo McCarey *ph* George Stevens *ed* Richard Currier, William Terhune

☆ Stan Laurel, Oliver Hardy, James Finlayson, Jean Harlow, Tom Kennedy

† Lloyd French and James Horne also directed some sequences.

'You're only young once, but you remember forever.'

Liberty Heights *

US 1999 127m Technicolor

Warner/Baltimore/Spring Creek (Barry Levinson, Paula Weinstein)

In Baltimore in the 1950s, the adolescent sons of a Jewish family cope with the problems of growing up.

Over-long and heavy-handed recreation of social change that comes to life only fitfully.

wd Barry Levinson *ph* Chris Doyle *m* Andrea Morricone *pd* Vincent Peranio *ed* Stu Linder *cos* Gloria Gresham

☆ Adrien Brody (Van Kurtzman), Ben Foster (Ben Kurtzman), Orlando Jones (Little Melvin), Bebe Neuwirth (Ada Kurtzman), Joe Mantegna (Nate Kurtzman), Rebekah Johnson (Sylvia), David Krumholtz (Yussel), Richard Kline (Charlie), Vincent Guastaferro (Pete), Justin Chambers (Trey)

'This exceptionally successful director seems to be rediscovering his voice as a writer, and in the process has made his best film.' – *Todd McCarthy, Variety*

'The screenplay and performances are too muted for the movie to come to terms with growing pains cushioned in the nostalgic haze.' – *Stephen Holden, New York Times*

Licence to Kill *

US 1989 133m Technicolor Panavision

UIP/United Artists/Danjaq (Albert R. Broccoli, Michael G. Wilson)

James Bond goes after a drug dealer who has injured his best friend.

The mixture is much as usual, though the action is more violent and Bond has become more of a free agent.

w Michael G. Wilson, Richard Maibaum *d* John Glen *ph* Alec Mills *m* Michael Kamen *pd* Peter Lamont *ed* John Grover

☆ Timothy Dalton, Carey Lowell, Robert Davi, Talisa Soto, Anthony Zerbe, Frank McRae, Everett McGill, Wayne Newton, Benicio del Toro

License to Drive

US 1988 88m DeLuxe

TCF/Davis/Licht/Mueller

A 16-year-old, unable to tell his friends that he has failed his driving test, borrows his grandfather's car for a date with the girlfriend of his dreams.

Heavy-handed and tiresome teenage farce; it works on a mechanical level, managing to maintain an accelerating momentum of incident, but rarely produces even a smile.

w Neil Tolkin *d* Greg Beeman *ph* Bruce Surtees *m* Jay Ferguson *pd* Lawrence G. Paull *ed* Wendy Greene Bricmont

☆ Corey Haim, Corey Feldman, Carol Kane, Richard Masur, Heather Graham, Michael Manasseri, Harvey Miller, M. A. Nickles, Nina Siemaszko

Licensed to Kill

GB 1965 97m Eastmancolor

Alistair Films (Estelle E. Richmond)

US title: *The Second Best Secret Agent in the Whole Wide World*

The Foreign Office calls in agent Charles Vine to protect a top international scientist.

Cheap copy of James Bond which wins no laurels but produces a few efficient routine thrills.

w Howard Griffiths, Lindsay Shonteff *d* Lindsay Shonteff *ph* Terry Maher *m* Bertram Chappell

☆ Tom Adams, Veronica Hurst, Karel Stepanek, Felix Felton, Peter Bull

The Lie: see *Mensonge*

Eine Liebe in Deutschland: see *A Love in Germany*

Liebelei *

Austria 1932 85m bw

Fred Lissa

A young army officer falls in love; but he is killed in a duel and his girl commits suicide.

Semi-classic romantic novelette, like a warm-up for Letter from an Unknown Woman.

w Hans Wilhelm, Kurt Alexander *story* Arthur Schnitzler *d Max Ophüls ph* Franz Planer *m* Theo Macheber

☆ Magda Schneider, Wolfgang Liebeneiner, Luise Ullrich, Willy Eichberger, Gustaf Gruendgens, Paul Hoerbiger

† A revised French version played as *Une Histoire d'Amour*. The story had previously been shot under the same title in Germany in 1927; and in the sixties Romy Schneider and Alain Delon appeared in a French remake called *Christine*.

Liebestraum

US 1991 113m DuArt

UIP/MGM/Initial (Eric Fellner)

An architectural writer, returning home to visit his dying mother, unwittingly uncovers her violent past which has repercussions in the present.

Involved thriller that leaves a lot of questions unanswered.

wd Mike Figgis *ph* Juan Ruiz Anchia *m* Mike Figgis *pd* Waldemar Kalinowski *ed* Martin Hunter

☆ Kevin Anderson, Pamela Gidley, Bill Pullman, Kim Novak, Graham Beckel, Zach Grenier, Thomas Kopache

'Seldom has the gulf between artistic intentions and end result yawned so protractedly.' – *Empire*

† A central scene, set in a brothel and lasting eleven minutes, was cut from the film before its release in America.

Lien-lien feng-ch'en: see *Dust in the Wind*

Les Liens du Sang: see *Blood Relatives*

Lies: see *Kojitmal*

Lies My Father Told Me

Canada 1975 102m colour

Columbia/Pentimento/Pentacle (Anthony Bedrich, Harry Gulkin)

Adventures of a poor Jewish boy and his grandfather in Montreal in the twenties.

Effectively if rather dishonestly sentimental, this is the kind of family picture for which critics are always clamouring but which few people in the seventies would pay to see.

w Ted Allan *book* Ted Allan *d* Jan Kadar *ph* Paul Van der Linden *m* Sol Kaplan

☆ Yossi Yadin, Len Birman, Marilyn Lightstone, Jeffrey Lynas

'Sentiment by numbers ... a lovable child awakening to discovery of the world; a lovable, whimsical old grandfather; a lovable, ne'er-do-well father; a lovable, long-suffering mother; a lovable, broken-down horse; lovable neighbours; a lovable whore across the way. It all strives so hard to be lovable that you want to scream.' – *David Robinson, The Times*

† A British low-budget film was made from the same material in 1960, changing the venue to Ireland and the race to Irish.

Ted Allan

Lt Robin Crusoe USN

US 1966 114m Technicolor

Walt Disney (Bill Walsh, Ron Miller)

A navy pilot parachutes on to a Pacific island and gets involved in the local women's lib movement.

Slow-paced family comedy with very few laughs.

w Bill Walsh, Don da Gradi *d* Byron Paul *ph* William Snyder *m* Bob Brunner

☆ Dick Van Dyke, Nancy Kwan, Akim Tamiroff

The Lieutenant Wore Skirts

US 1955 99m Eastmancolor Cinemascope

TCF (Buddy Adler)

When a TV writer joins the service, his wife enlists to be near him; but he is rejected on medical grounds.

Raucous, tasteless farce which tries far too hard to raise laughs.

w Albert Beich, Frank Tashlin *d* Frank Tashlin *ph* Leo Tover *m* Cyril Mockridge

☆ Tom Ewell, Sheree North, Rita Moreno, Rick Jason, Les Tremayne

'Share It With Someone You Love.'

Life *

US 1999 109m DeLuxe

Universal/Imagine (Brian Grazer, Eddie Murphy)

A conman and a bank clerk, both framed for murder, spend a lifetime together in prison.

Amiable prison variation on The Odd Couple, *which gets by on the interplay between its two stars, though reality never intrudes.*

w Robert Ramsey, Matthew Stone *d* Ted Demme *ph* Geoffrey Simpson *m* Wyclef Jean *pd* Dan Bishop *ed* Jeffrey Wolf *sp* make-up fx: Rick Baker *cos* Lucy Corrigan

☆ Eddie Murphy (Rayford Gibson), Martin Lawrence (Claude Banks), Obba Babatunde (Willie Long), Ned Beatty (Dexter Wilkins), Bernie Mac (Jangle Leg), Miguel A. Nunez Jnr (Biscuit), Clarence Williams III (Winston Hancock), Bokeem Woodbine (Can't Get Right), Michael 'Bear' Taliferro (Goldmouth), Barry Shabaka Henley (Pokerface), R. Lee Ermey (Older Sheriff Pike), Nick Cassavetes (Sgt Dillard), Noah Emmerich (Stan Blocker), Rick James (Spanky)

'Careens from decade to decade, and from relative dramatic realism to frequent hilarity, in often-winning fashion.' – *Todd McCarthy, Variety*

'It's unfunny, it lacks excitement, tension or even a sense of oppression, and it never involves us for a moment with its characters.' – *Philip Kemp, Sight and Sound*

make-up (Rick Baker)

Life After Dark: see *Girls in the Night*

The Life and Death of a Hollywood Extra *

US 1927 11m (24 fps) bw silent

(Robert Florey and Slavko Vorkapich)

A nonentity arrives in Hollywood and dreams of becoming a star.

Avant-garde short, still interesting if less revolutionary than it seemed at the time.

wd Robert Florey and Slavko Vorkapich ph Slavko Vorkapich and Gregg Toland *ad/ed Slavko Vorkapich*

☆ Jules Raucort, Georges Voya

The Life and Death of Colonel Blimp ***

GB 1943 163m Technicolor

GFD/Archers (Michael Powell, Emeric Pressburger)

US title: *Colonel Blimp*

A British soldier survives three wars and falls in love with three women.

Not the Blimp of the cartoon strip, but a sympathetic figure in a warm, consistently interesting if idiosyncratic love story against a background of war. The Archers as usual provide a sympathetic German lead (friend of the hero); quite a coup in wartime.

wd Michael Powell, Emeric Pressburger ph Georges Perinal *m* Allan Gray *ad* Alfred Junge *ed* John Seabourne

☆ Roger Livesey, Anton Walbrook, Deborah Kerr, Roland Culver, James McKechnie, Albert Lieven, Arthur Wontner, A. E. Matthews, David Hutcheson, Ursula Jeans, John Laurie, Harry Welchman

'There is nothing brilliant about the picture, but it is perceptive, witty and sweet-tempered.' – *James Agee*

'No one else has so well captured English romanticism banked down beneath emotional reticence.' – *Time Out, 1985*

The Life and Extraordinary Adventures of Private Ivan Chonkin *

GB/France/Italy/Czechoslovakia/Russia 1994 111m colour

Portbello/MK2/Canal/La Sept/CNC/Channel 4/ Fandango/Domenico Procacci/Studio 89/Studio Trite (Eric Abraham)

An army private, sent to an isolated village to guard a plane crash, begins an affair with the local postmistress and attracts the attention of the secret police.

Interesting, slightly ramshackle comedy, championing simple virtues in the face of repressive bureaucracy.

w Zdenek Sverák, Vladimir Voinovich *novel* Vladimir Voinovich *d* Jiri Menzel *ph* Jaromir Sofr *m* Jiri Sust *pd* Milan Bycek *ed* Jiri Brozek, Elisabeth Guido

☆ Gennadiy Nazarov, Zoya Buryak, Vladimir Ilyin, Valeriy Dubrovin, Alexei Zharkov, Zinovil Gerdt

† Vladimir Voinovich turned his original film script, written in the mid-60s, into a novel which was banned in the Soviet Union and published in Paris; it led to his exile in 1980, after he lost his citizenship, which was not restored to him until 1990.

Life and Nothing But **

France 1989 134m colour Panavision

Artificial Eye/Hachette Première et Cie/AB Films/Little Bear/A2 (René Cleitman)

original title: *La Vie Et Rien D'Autre*

Two women, one searching for her missing husband, the other for her lover among the patients at a military hospital, discover that they are looking for the same man.

Complex and affecting movie of love and disillusion, of individual tragedy and national pride, set at the end of the First World War.

w Jean Cosmos, Bertrand Tavernier *d* Bertrand Tavernier *ph* Bruno de Keyzer *m* Oswald d'Andrea *pd* Guy-Claude François *ed* Armand Psenny

☆ Philippe Noiret, Sabine Azéma, Pascale Vignal, Maurice Barrier, François Perrot, Jean-Pol Dubois, Daniel Russo, Michel Duchaussoy, Arlette Gilbert

best foreign picture

'I want peace – and I don't care who I kill to get it!'

The Life and Times of Judge Roy Bean *

US 1972 124m Technicolor Panavision
National General/First Artists (John Foreman)

A fantasia on the famous outlaw judge of the old west.

Sporadically entertaining but schematically messy mixture of burlesqued folklore and violent action, not in the same league as Butch Cassidy.

w John Milius *d* John Huston *ph* Richard Moore *m* Maurice Jarre

☆ Paul Newman, Ava Gardner, Jacqueline Bisset, Tab Hunter, Stacy Keach, Roddy McDowall, Anthony Perkins, John Huston

song 'Marmalade, Molasses and Honey' (*m* Maurice Jarre, *ly* A. and M. Bergman)

'Seen from a distance, it's perfect.'

Life as a House

US/Germany 2001 125m DeLuxe Panavision

A dying architect tries to connect with his troubled teenage son while rebuilding the house in which he lives.

Slick lachrymose drama of male bonding that is contrived and unconvincing..

'May satisfy those who like their movies to offer life lessons and provide role models.' – *Bob Graham, San Francisco Chronicle*

Life at the Top *

GB 1965 117m bw
Columbia/Romulus (James Woolf)

Ten years after marrying into money, Joe Lampton is dissatisfied, and he and his wife both have affairs.

Rough-talking but basically predictable and old-fashioned sequel to Room at the Top, *a bit compromised by having to reflect the sixties London scene; the early Yorkshire sequences are the best.*

w Mordecai Richler *d* Ted Kotcheff *ph* Oswald Morris *m* Richard Addinsell

☆ Laurence Harvey, Jean Simmons, Honor Blackman, Michael Craig, Donald Wolfit, *Margaret Johnston*, Allan Cuthbertson, Ambrosine Philpotts, Robert Morley, Nigel Davenport, George A. Cooper

'Another thoroughly mean-spirited film of a kind which has been taking root in the British cinema.' – *Tom Milne*

† The character of Joe Lampton was later used in a long-running TV series called *Man at the Top*, which sprouted a film of its own under that title.

Life Begins

US 1932 72m bw
Warner (Ray Griffith)
GB title: *Dream of Life*

A night in a maternity hospital.

Multi-melodrama later remade as A Child Is Born. *Passable.*

w Earl Baldwin *play* Mary McDougal Axelson *d* James Flood *ph* James Van Trees

☆ Loretta Young, Eric Linden, Aline MacMahon, Preston Foster, Glenda Farrell, Frank McHugh, Clara Blandick, Elizabeth Patterson, Gilbert Roland

'Splendid women's picture promising at least solid matinée business.' – *Variety*

Life Begins at 40

US 1935 85m bw
TCF (Sol M. Wurtzel)

A small-town editor, whose paper is repossessed by the bank manager, starts a rival publication and investigates the conviction for robbery of a bank clerk.

Mildly entertaining rustic humour, aimed at giving Rogers the opportunity to spout his cracker-barrel philosophy.

w Lamar Trotti, Robert Quillen *book* Walter B. Pitkin *d* George Marshall *ph* Harry Jackson *md* Samuel Kaylin *ad* Duncan Cramer, Albert Hogsett

☆ Will Rogers, Richard Cromwell, George Barbier, Rochelle Hudson, Jane Darwell, Slim Summerville, Sterling Holloway

Life Begins at Eight-Thirty *

US 1942 85m bw
TCF (Nunnally Johnson)
GB title: *The Light of Heart*

A distinguished actor is reduced through drink to being a street corner Santa Claus.

Diluted and sentimentalized version of an agreeable play.

w Nunnally Johnson *play* The Light of Heart by Emlyn Williams *d* Irving Pichel *ph* Edward Cronjager *m* Alfred Newman

☆ *Monty Woolley*, Ida Lupino, Cornel Wilde, Sara Allgood, Melville Cooper, J. Edward Bromberg

Life Begins in College *

US 1937 80m bw
TCF
GB title: *The Joy Parade*

Three zanies save the honour of the college football team.

Another of the myriad college football stories of the thirties, but this time enlivened by comedians in the leads.

w Karl Tunberg, Don Ettlinger *d* William A. Seiter

☆ The Ritz Brothers, Joan Davis, Tony Martin, Gloria Stuart, Fred Stone, Nat Pendleton

'The Ritzes soar to stardom; a box office touchdown.' – *Variety*

Life Dances On: see *Un Carnet de Bal*

Life for Ruth *

GB 1962 91m bw
Rank/Allied Film Makers (Michael Relph, Basil Dearden)
US title: *Condemned to Life*

A little girl dies because her parents' religion forbids blood transfusions.

Dramatized from the headlines, this little case history is small beer as film-making, and not exactly entertainment, but absorbing as a comment on human behaviour.

w Janet Green, John McCormick *d* Basil Dearden *ph* Otto Heller *m* William Alwyn *md* Muir Mathieson

☆ Michael Craig, Patrick McGoohan, Janet Munro, Paul Rogers, Megs Jenkins, Frank Finlay, Maureen Pryor

Life in Danger

GB 1959 63m bw
Butchers/Parroch (Jack Parsons)

Angry villagers hunt for a murderer who has escaped from a nearby mental hospital.

Competent thriller with a twist in its tail.

w Malcolm Hulke, Eric Paice *d* Terry Bishop *ph* Peter Hennessy *m* William Davies *ad* Peter Proud *ed* John Trumper

☆ Derren Nesbitt, Julie Hopkins, Howard Marion Crawford, Victor Brooks, Jack Allen, Christopher Witty, Carmel McSharry, Bruce Seton

Life in Emergency Ward 10

GB 1958 84m bw
Eros Films (Ted Lloyd)

A new consultant at the hospital causes controversy by introducing an experimental modification to heart surgery techniques and becoming involved with a colleague's wife.

A spin-off from a popular TV series, though still looking as if it were made for the small screen and scripted as a series of anecdotal episodes that mix comedy and sentimentality in predictable ways.

w Tessa Diamond, Hazel Adair *d* Robert Day *ph* Geoffrey Faithfull *m* Philip Green *ad* George Beech *ed* Lito Carruthers

☆ Michael Craig, Wilfrid Hyde-White, Dorothy Alison, Glyn Owen, Charles Tingwell, Frederick Bartman, Rosemary Miller, Joan Sims

A Life in the Balance *

US 1954 75m bw
TCF/Panoramic (Leonard Goldstein)

A Mexican widower springs into action when his young son is kidnapped by a murderer.

Taut little melodrama taking place during one night in Mexico City; made with vigour on a low budget.

w Robert Presnell Jnr, Leo Townsend *d* Harry Horner *ph* J. Gomez Urquiza *m* Raul Lavista

☆ Ricardo Montalban, Anne Bancroft, Lee Marvin

Life Is a Bed of Roses *

France 1983 111m Eastmancolor
Philippe Dusart/Soprofilms/Films A2/Fideline/Ariane/Filmedis/Ministry of Culture (Philippe Dusart)
original title: *La Vie est un Roman*

A count opens a temple of happiness and starts to re-educate his friends.

Dense fantasy which never really explains itself but provides pleasant moments along the way.

w Jean Gruault *d* Alain Resnais *ph* Bruno Nuytten *m* M. Philippe-Gerard

☆ Vittorio Gassman, Ruggero Raimondi, Geraldine Chaplin, Fanny Ardant, Pierre Arditi

Life Is a Circus

GB 1958 84m bw
Vale Film (M. Smedley Aston)

An odd-job man in a rundown circus finds Aladdin's lamp.

Feeble comedy by the Crazy Gang in a state of geriatric disrepair, simply going through the motions, which is an understandable reaction given the script. Chesney Allen makes a brief appearance to sing 'Underneath the Arches' with his old partner, Bud Flanagan.

wd Val Guest *ph* Arthur Graham *m* Philip Green *ad* Tony Masters *ed* Bill Lenny

☆ Bud Flanagan, Jimmy Nervo, Teddy Knox, Cahrlie Naughton, Jimmy Gold, Monsewer Eddie Gray, Shirley Eaton, Michael Holliday, Joseph Tomelty, Lionel Jeffries

Life Is a Long Quiet River: see *La Vie Est un Long Fleuve Tranquille*

'The unforgettable film that proves love, family and imagination conquer all.'

Life Is Beautiful ***

Italy 1997 122m colour
Buena Vista/Melampo (Elda Ferri, Gianluigi Braschi)
original title: *La Vita è Bella*

During the Second World War, a Jewish bookshop owner, sent with his family to a concentration camp, protects his young son by pretending that they are in a holiday camp.

A bold and brave film, and one well worth seeing, despite some rather contrived slapstick in the early sequences; yet, in the end, clowning does not merely seem an inappropriate response to the realities of a concentration camp, but the wrong response.

w Vincenzo Cerami, Roberto Benigni *d Roberto Benigni ph* Tonino Delli Colli *m Nicola Piovani pd* Danilo Donati *ed* Simona Paggi

☆ *Roberto Benigni*, Nicoletta Braschi, Giustino Durano, Sergio Bustric, Marisa Paredes, Horst Buchholz, Lydia Alfonsi, Giuliana Lojodice, Giorgio Cantarini

'Sluggish, uneven and lacking in rhythm, it nonetheless has enough pathos and winning humor to ensure national success.' – *David Rooney, Variety*

'What he has made is not, in fact, a comedy about the Holocaust – a project that would have required a sinewy nerve and a black spluttering wit. He has made an allegory about comedy's redemptive power – a softer, more fogbound beast.' – *Tom Shone, Sunday Times*

'One of the most unconvincing and self-congratulatory movies ever made.' – *David Denby, New Yorker*

† The film took in excess of $40m at the US box-office, more than any other foreign-language film, and also grossed more than $152m around the world.

†† Benigni's concentration-camp number, 7397, was chosen as a tribute to Charlie Chaplin, who wore the same number in *The Great Dictator*.

foreign-language film; Roberto Benigni (actor); Nicola Piovani

best picture; Roberto Benigni (director); Vincenzo Cerami, Roberto Benigni (script); Simona Paggi

Roberto Benigni (actor)

Life Is Cheap ... But Toilet Paper Is Expensive *

US 1990 88m colour
ICA/Forever Profit Investments/Far East Stars (Winnie Fredriksz)

Travelling from San Francisco to Hong Kong to deliver a gift to a local gangster, an Asian-American is plunged into a society he fails to understand and circumstances that lead to his humiliation.

Inventive, low-budget thriller of cultural bewilderment, mixed in with documentary-style monologues from the locals.

w Spencer Nakasako *story* Amir Mokri, Spencer Nakasako, Wayne Wang *d* Wayne Wang *ph* Amir Mokri *m* Mark Adler *ad* Colette Koo *ed* Chris Sanderson, Sandy Nervig

☆ Chan Kim Wan, Spencer Nakasako, Victor Wong, Cheng Kwan Min, Cora Miao, Lam Chung

'Audaciously stylish and visually mesmerizing ... Wayne Wang's take on the conundrum of Chinese identity has all the narrative logic of a tilted pinball machine.' – *Variety*

Life Is Sweet

GB 1990 103m Metrocolor
Palace/Thin Man/Film Four International/British Screen (Simon Channing-Williams)

An unexceptional couple and their grown-up children survive minor disasters.

Mildly amusing suburban comedy, though the actors' attitude to their characters ranges from condescension to caricature.

wd Mike Leigh *ph* Dick Pope *m* Rachel Portman *pd* Alison Chitty *ed* Jon Gregory

☆ Alison Steadman, Jim Broadbent, Claire Skinner, Jane Horrocks, Stephen Rea, Timothy Spall

A Life Less Ordinary *

GB 1997 103m Rank Colour Super 35
Polygram/Figment (Andrew Macdonald)

Two angels are given the task of making a wealthy, spoilt young woman and a janitor fall in love.

A surreal romantic comedy where fantasy and reality fail to cohere into a satisfactory whole.

w John Hodge *d* Danny Boyle *ph* Brian Tufano *m* David Arnold *pd* Kave Quinn *ed* Masahiro Hirakubo

☆ Ewan McGregor, Cameron Diaz, Holly Hunter, Delroy Lindo, Ian Holm, Ian McNeice, Stanley Tucci, Dan Hedaya, Maury Chaykin

'A pleasant enough ride in parts, but has too many half-realised ideas in the script to satisfy at any emotional level.' – *Derek Elley, Variety*

† The film cost $12m and took $4.3m at the US box-office.

The Life of Adolf Hitler *

West Germany 1961 102m bw
Real Film

A documentary culled from newsreel material; somehow less arresting than one would have hoped, though undoubtedly worthy.

w Helga Koppel *d* Paul Rotha *ed* Paul Rotha

The Life of Brian: see *Monty Python's Life of Brian*

'The crime is clear. The truth is not.'

The Life of David Gale

US/GB/Germany 2002 130m DeLuxe 'Scope
Universal/Intermedia/Saturn/Dirty Hands (Alan Parker, Nicolas Cage)

A journalist attempts to save a campaigner against capital punishment who is found guilty of rape and murder and sentenced to death.

Glib, bombastic and muddled drama, anti-intellectual in tone, that takes itself, but not its subject-matter, very seriously.

w Charles Randolph *d* Alan Parker *ph* Michael Seresin *m* Alex Parker, Jake Parker *pd* Geoffrey Kirkland *ed* Gerry Hambling

☆ Kevin Spacey (David Gale), Kate Winslet (Bitsey Bloom), Laura Linney (Constance Harraway), Gabriel Mann (Zack Stemmons), Matt Craven (Dusty Wright), Rhona Mitra (Berlin), Leon Rippy (Braxton Belyeu)

'Heavy-handed, ponderous and simplistic polemic against the death penalty pretending to be a film.' – *Cosmo Landesman, Sunday Times*

'Has nothing coherent to say about capital punishment, or anything else. It's a dead film lurching.' – *Joe Morgenstern, Wall Street Journal*

'He plucked from the gutter a faded rose and made an immortal masterpiece!'

The Life of Emile Zola ***

US 1937 116m bw
Warner (Henry Blanke)

The French writer intervenes in the case of Alfred Dreyfus, condemned unjustly to Devil's Island.

The box-office success of this solidly-carpentered piece of Hollywood history was compounded in equal parts of star power and the sheer novelty of having such a thing turn up at the local Odeon.

w Norman Reilly Raine *story* Heinz Herald and Geza Herczeg *d William Dieterle ph Tony Gaudio* *m* Max Steiner *ad Anton Grot*
☆ *Paul Muni, Joseph Schildkraut,* Gale Sondergaard, Gloria Holden, Donald Crisp, Erin O'Brien Moore, John Litel, Henry O'Neill, Morris Carnovsky, Ralph Morgan, Louis Calhern, Robert Barrat, Vladimir Sokoloff, Harry Davenport, Robert Warwick and also Walter Kingsford

'Destined to box office approval of the most substantial character. It is finely made and merits high rating as cinema art and significant recognition as major showmanship.' – *Variety*

'Along with Louis Pasteur, it ought to start a new category – the Warner crusading films, costume division.' – *Otis Ferguson*

'A grave story told with great dignity and superbly played and produced.' – *Pare Lorentz*

'One of the fine ones which begin as a film and end as an experience.' – *John Grierson*

'Rich, dignified, honest and strong, it is at once the finest historical film ever made and the greatest screen biography.' – *New York Times*

best picture; script; Joseph Schildkraut

original story; William Dieterle; Max Steiner; Paul Muni; Anton Grot

A Life of Her Own

US 1950 108m bw
MGM (Voldemar Vetluguin)

An innocent girl from Kansas becomes one of New York's top models.
Road to ruin, American style, from the pages of a women's magazine.
w Isobel Lennart *d* George Cukor *ph* George Folsey *m* Bronislau Kaper
☆ Lana Turner, Ray Milland, Tom Ewell, Louis Calhern, Ann Dvorak, Barry Sullivan, Jean Hagen

'This story belongs to the realms of soap opera – extremely artificial, highly moral in tone, and deliberately concocted to combine luxurious settings with an elementary assault on the audience's emotions.' – *MFB*

The Life of Jimmy Dolan

US 1933 85m bw
Warner (Hal B. Wallis)
GB title: *The Kid's Last Fight*

An amiable wanderer is mistaken for a prize fighter wanted for murder.
Modest character romance, later remade as They Made Me a Criminal.
w David Boehm, Erwin Gelsey *play* Bertram Millhauser, Beulah Marie Dix *d* Archie Mayo *ph* Arthur Edeson
☆ Douglas Fairbanks Jnr, Loretta Young, Aline MacMahon, Guy Kibbee, Lyle Talbot, Fifi D'Orsay, Harold Huber, George Meeker

The Life of Oharu ***

Japan 1952 110m bw
Shin Toho
original title: *Saikaku Ichidai Onna*

In the 1680s the daughter of a samurai recalls her descent to prostitution through her love for a servant.
Superbly photographed and acted tragedy of a woman trapped by a remorseless fate.
w Yoshikata Yoda, Kenji Mizoguchi *novel* Saikaku Ihara *d Kenji Mizoguchi ph Yoshima Kono, Yoshimi Hirano* *m* Ichiro Saito
☆ *Kinuyo Tanaka,* Hisako Yamane, Toshiro Mifune, Yuriko Hamada

The Life of Riley

US 1948 87m bw
Universal-International (Irving Brecher)

The trials of a family man in a low-paid job.
Adequate transcription from a radio series.
wd Irving Brecher *ph* William H. Daniels *m* Frank Skinner *ad* John De Cuir, Bernard Herzbrun *ed* Milton Carruth
☆ William Bendix, James Gleason, Rosemary de Camp, Bill Goodwin, Beulah Bondi, Richard Long

Life of the Party

US 1930 78m Technicolor
Warner

Two gold-digging shop girls operate from a modiste's.
Half-hearted vulgar comedy, rather oddly given colour status.
w Arthur Caesar *story* Melville Crossman (Darryl F. Zanuck) *d* Roy del Ruth
☆ Winnie Lightner, Irene Delroy, Charles Butterworth, Jack Whiting

'Spotty for laughs and business.' – *Variety*

Life of the Party

US 1937 86m bw
RKO

A girl tries to evade suitors arranged by her mother.
Very thin comedy with several second-bracket names; not at all memorable.
w Bert Kalmar, Harry Ruby, Viola Brothers Shore *d* William A. Seiter *ph* J. Roy Hunt *md* Roy Webb
☆ Joe Penner, Harriet Hilliard, Gene Raymond, Parkyakarkus, Victor Moore, Helen Broderick, Billy Gilbert, Ann Miller

'Should prove fairish entertainment and do fairly at the b.o.' – *Variety*

The Life of Vergie Winters

US 1934 82m bw
RKO (Pandro S. Berman)

A rising politician marries for position but keeps watch over his mistress and their child.
Archetypal soap opera, a cross between Stella Dallas *and* Back Street.
w Jane Murfin *novel* Louis Bromfield *d* Alfred Santell *ph* Lucien Andriot *m* Max Steiner
☆ Ann Harding, John Boles, Helen Vinson, Frank Albertson, Lon Chaney Jnr, Sara Haden, Ben Alexander, Donald Crisp

Life on a String **

GB/Germany/China 1991 120m Eastmancolor
Serene/Pandora/Beijing Film Studio/Herald Ace/Film Four/Berlin Filmforderung (Don Ranvaud)
original title: *Bian Zhou Bian Chang*

Accompanied by a blind youth, an elderly blind musician wanders the countryside waiting for a cure for his affliction which will come when he has broken a thousand strings while playing his three-stringed guitar.
Beautiful to look at, full of spectacular and striking images, this sedately-paced movie remains obscure to the end.
wd Chen Kaige *story* Shi Tiesheng *ph* Gu Changwei *m* Qu Xiaosong *pd* Shao Ruigang *ed* Pei Xiaonan
☆ Li Zhongyuan, Huang Lei, Xu Qing, Ma Ling, Zhang Zhengyuan

'A rich film experience, but its length and lack of conventional narrative will be factors to overcome in getting the film across to arthouse audiences.' – *Variety*

'What if you got a chance to discover who you really are?'

Life or Something Like It

US 2002 103m DeLuxe Panavision
TCF/Regency/Epsilon Motion (Arnon Milchan, John Davis, Chi-Li Wong, Toby Jaffe)

Believing she is going to die in a week, a Seattle TV news reporter, who is involved with two men and is about to land a top job, examines her life and finds it wanting.
Deeply silly romantic comedy, a genre for which its stars have little talent, but no actor or director could have made this particular script sound good.
w John Scott Shepherd, Dana Stevens *d* Stephen Herek *ph* Stephen H. Burum *m* David Newman *pd* Bill Groom *ed* Trudy Ship
☆ Angelina Jolie (Lanie Kerrigan), Edward Burns (Pete), Tony Shalhoub (Prophet Jack), Christian Kane (Cal), Melissa Errico (Andrea), James Gammo (Lanie's Father), Stockard Channing (Deborah Connors)

'This middlebrow trifle may engage the emotions of a certain tier of young professional women torn by the perceived conflicting desires of realizing career fantasies and settling down with a Regular Joe.' – *Todd McCarthy, Variety*

Life Returns

US 1938 62m bw
Scienart

A fictional story leads up to the actual experiment performed in 1934 by Dr Robert E. Cornish when he brought a dead dog back to life.
Weird mélange of fact and fiction; despite the achievement, the presentation never catches fire. The film was banned in Britain.
w Arthur Horman, John F. Goodrich *d* Eugene Frenke
☆ Onslow Stevens, George Breakston, Valerie Hobson, Lois Wilson

'A picture much longer to the audience than its accredited running time would indicate.' – *Variety*

Life Stinks

US 1991 95m DeLuxe
TCF/Brooks Films/Le Studio Canal Plus (Mel Brooks)

A rich property developer takes a bet that he can survive on his own on the streets of a slum for thirty days.
Crass, tasteless comedy in which the jokes are poor.
w Mel Brooks, Rudy de Luca, Steve Haberman *story* Mel Brooks, Ron Clark, Rudy de Luca, Steve Haberman *d* Mel Brooks *ph* Steven Poster *m* John Morris *pd* Peter Larkin *ed* David Rawlins
☆ Mel Brooks, Lesley Ann Warren, Jeffrey Tambor, Stuart Pankin, Howard Morris, Rudy de Luca, Teddy Wilson, Billy Barty

'Antic comedy has more laughs than the filmmaker's last couple of efforts, and presents an amiably sympathetic, if unreliable, look at the homeless.' – *Variety*

Life Upside Down *

France 1964 92m bw
A.J. Films
original title: *La Vie à l'Envers*

A pleasant, ordinary young man discovers the joy of being absolutely alone, and begins to detach himself from his surroundings, ending up in a barren flat and a private hospital ward.
Engaging semi-comic case history which generates much sympathy for its eccentric hero.
wd Alain Jessua ph Jacques Robin *m* Jacques Loussier
☆ Charles Denner, Anna Gaylor, Guy Saint-Jean, Nicole Gueden

'The tone is civilized, quiet, infinitely peaceful and often brilliantly funny.' – *Brenda Davies, MFB*

'Amusing or disturbing depending on whether it is viewed from the outside or the inside, but perceptive and artistic whichever way one views it.' – *John Simon*

'Take your cookie to see the picture that takes the cake for laughs!'

Life with Father *

US 1947 118m Technicolor
Warner (Robert Buckner)

Turn-of-the-century anecdotes of an irascible well-to-do paterfamilias who won't be baptized.
Well-upholstered screen version of a long-running play; oddly tedious considering the talent involved.
w Donald Ogden Stewart *play* Howard Lindsay, Russel Crouse *d* Michael Curtiz *ph* Peverell Marley, William V. Skall *m* Max Steiner *ad* Robert Haas
☆ William Powell, Irene Dunne, Edmund Gwenn, ZaSu Pitts, Elizabeth Taylor, Martin Milner, Jimmy Lydon, Emma Dunn, Moroni Olsen, Elizabeth Risdon

'Everybody seems to be trying too hard … the director is totally out of his element in this careful, deadly version.' – *New Yorker, 1978*

† Censorship of the day absurdly clipped Father's famous last line: 'I'm going to be baptized, damn it!'

Peverell Marley, William V. Skall; Max Steiner; William Powell; Robert Haas

Life with Mikey

US 1993 91m Technicolor
Buena Vista/Touchstone (Scott Rudin, Teri Schwartz)
GB title: *Give Me a Break*

A former child star turned agent discovers a new talent when a 10-year-old girl tries to steal his wallet.
Pleasant, undemanding, unmemorable comedy.
w Marc Lawrence *d* James Lapine *ph* Rob Hahn *m* Alan Menken *pd* Adrianne Lobel *ed* Robert Leighton
☆ Michael J. Fox, Christina Vidal, Nathan Lane, Cyndi Lauper, David Huddleston, David Krumholtz

'Screams "cute" from every pore but should play well with kids and won't insult the intelligence of adults.' – *Variety*

† It was released direct to video in Britain.

'Doggie's got a bone … Whose bone?'

Life with the Cannibals

US 1996 95m Foto-Kem
Dorian (Harry Bromley-Davenport)

A wimp finds a new life, living next to the neighbourhood serial killer.
A weak and witless black comedy; all that can be said in its favour is that, considering its theme of multiple murder, it downplays any depiction of violence.
w Daryl Haney *d* Harry Bromley-Davenport *ph* Marco Cappetta, Ricardo Gale, Hector Rivera *m* Mark Hart *pd* Kate Perotti, Yvette Taylor *ed* Van Rieben
☆ Kieran Mulroney, Juliet Landau, Mason Adams, Bette Ford, Daryl Haney, Wings Hauser

Life with the Lyons

GB 1954 81m bw
Exclusive/Hammer (Robert Dunbar)

The Lyon family have problems with their landlord when they move into a fashionable house by London's Marble Arch.
An extended low-budget situation comedy, based on a popular radio series, given rather more skilled playing than it deserves.
w Val Guest, Robert Dunbar *d* Val Guest *ph* Walter Harvey *m* Arthur Wilkinson *ad* Wilfred Arnold *ed* Douglas Myers
☆ Ben Lyon, Bebe Daniels Lyon, Richard Lyon, Barbara Lyon, Horace Percival, Molly Weir, Hugh Morton, Arthur Hill, Doris Rogers, Gwen Lewis, Belinda Lee

Lifeboat **

US 1944 96m bw
TCF (Kenneth MacGowan)

Survivors from a torpedoed passenger ship include the U-Boat commander responsible.
Propaganda gimmick melodrama interesting for the casting and for Hitchcock's response to the challenge of filming in one cramped set.
w Jo Swerling *story* John Steinbeck *d* Alfred Hitchcock *ph* Glen MacWilliams *m* Hugo Friedhofer
☆ *Tallulah Bankhead, Walter Slezak,* Henry Hull, John Hodiak, Canada Lee, William Bendix, Mary Anderson, Heather Angel, Hume Cronyn

'The initial idea – a derelict boat and its passengers as microcosm – is itself so artificial that … it sets the whole pride and brain too sharply to work on a tour de force for its own sake.' – *James Agee*

John Steinbeck; Alfred Hitchcock; Glen MacWilliams

Lifeforce

US 1985 101m Eastmancolor Super 35
Cannon (Menahem Golan, Yoram Globus)

An Anglo-American space expedition investigating Halley's Comet discovers that it hides a two-mile-high alien spaceship containing the bodies of giant, bat-like creatures and three humanoids in suspended animation.
Extraordinarily bizarre mix of science fiction and vampire movie, more likely to provoke derision than any other emotion.
w Dan O'Bannon, Don Jakoby *novel Space Vampires* by Colin Wilson *d* Tobe Hooper *ph* Alan Hume *m* Henry Mancini, Michael Kamen, James Guthrie *pd* John Graysmark *ed* John Grover *sp* John Dykstra, Nick Maley, John Gant
☆ Steve Railsback, Peter Firth, Frank Finlay, Patrick Stewart, Michael Gothard, Nicholas Ball, Mathilda May, Aubrey Morris

Lifeguard

US 1976 96m CFI color
Paramount (Ron Silverman)

A beach guard at 30 reviews his life and his future.
Odd but not unlikeable little personal drama which barely got released.
w Ron Koslow *d* Daniel Petrie *ph* Ralph Woolsey *md* Dale Menten
☆ Sam Elliott, Anne Archer, Stephen Young, Parker Stevenson, Kathleen Quinlan

Lifespan
US/Netherlands 1975 85m Eastmancolor
Respectable/Whitepal (Alexander Whitelaw)

An American expert on ageing discovers that a Dutch colleague who killed himself was conducting successful experiments in prolonging life.
Mundane drama that promises more than it finally delivers; it strains for significance without achieving it.
w Alexander Whitelaw, Judith Roscoe, Alva Ruben *d* Alexander Whitelaw *ph* Eddie van der Enden *m* Terry Riley *ad* Dick Schillemans *ed* Guust Verschuuren, Jann Dopp, Hetty Konig
☆ Hiram Keller, Tina Aumont, Klaus Kinski, Fons Rademakers, Eric Schneider, Frans Mulders

The Lift
Netherlands 1983 99m Eastmancolor
Warner/Sigma Films (Matthijs Van Heijningen)

An office block elevator seems to assume deadly powers. After a murderous car, a murderous lift.
Slick but rather empty semi-horror.
wd Dick Maas *ph* Marc Felperlaan *m* Dick Maas *ad* Harry Ammerlaan *ed* Hans Van Dongen
☆ Huub Stapel, Willeke Van Ammelrooy, Josine Van Dalsum

Lift to the Scaffold *
France 1957 89m bw
Nouvelles Editions de Films (Jean Thuillier)

original title: *Ascenseur pour l'Echafaud*
US title: *Frantic*
An executive murders his employer but is trapped in the building all night; meanwhile his car is stolen and he is arrested for a murder committed by the thief.
Complex, watchable suspenser with pretensions.
w Roger Nimier, Louis Malle *novel* Noel Calef *d* Louis Malle *ph* Henri Decaë *m* Miles Davis
☆ Maurice Ronet, Jeanne Moreau, Georges Poujouly, Yori Bertin, Lino Ventura
'Cold, clever and rather elegant.' – *Penelope Houston, MFB*

The Light across the Street
France 1955 99m bw
EGC/Fernand Rivers (Jacques Gauthier)
original title: *La Lumière d'en Face*
A lorry driver, injured in an accident, becomes insanely jealous of his young wife.
Low-life melodrama tailored for the sultry attractions of its new star.
w Louis Cahavance, René Masson, René Lefèvre *d* Georges Lacombe *ph* Louis Page *m* Norbert Glanzberg
☆ Brigitte Bardot, Raymond Pellégrin, Roger Pigaut, Claude Romain

The Light at the Edge of the World
US/Spain/Liechtenstein 1971 120m Eastmancolor Panavision
Bryna/Jet/Triumfilm (Kirk Douglas, Ilya Salkind)

A lighthouse keeper near Cape Horn resists a band of wreckers.
Pretentious, disaster-prone version of a simple adventure story; one wonders not so much what went wrong as whether anything went right in this international venture.
w Tom Rowe *novel* Jules Verne *d* Kevin Billington *ph* Henri Decaë *m* Piero Piccioni
☆ Kirk Douglas, Yul Brynner, Samantha Eggar, Jean-Claude Drouot, Fernando Rey, Renato Salvatori

The Light Fantastic: see *Love Is Better Than Ever*

The Light in the Forest
US 1958 92m Technicolor
Walt Disney

Kidnapped by Indians as an infant, a teenager is returned to his parents but finds the white man's ways disturbing.
Modest frontier drama with a moral.
w Lawrence Edward Watkin *novel* Conrad Richter *d* Herschel Daugherty *ph* Ellsworth Fredericks *m* Paul Smith
☆ James MacArthur, Carol Lynley, Jessica Tandy, Wendell Corey, Fess Parker, Joanne Dru, Joseph Calleia

The Light in the Piazza
GB 1962 101m Metrocolor Cinemascope
MGM (Arthur Freed)
An American matron in Florence tries to marry off her mentally retarded daughter to a wealthy Italian.
Puzzling romantic drama in which one is never quite sure why the characters behave as they do; in the end all one appreciates is the tour of northern Italy.
w Julius J. Epstein *novel* Elizabeth Spencer *d* Guy Green *ph* Otto Heller *m* Mario Nascimbene
☆ Olivia de Havilland, Yvette Mimieux, George Hamilton, Rossano Brazzi, Barry Sullivan

Light of Day
US 1987 107m Astrocolor
Taft/Keith Barish/Tri-Star

A Cleveland family is upset by illness and rock'n'roll.
Drab musical wallow which seems to have little point.
wd Paul Schrader *ph* John Bailey *m* Thomas Newman *pd* Jeannine Claudia Oppewall *ed* Jacqueline Cambas
☆ Michael J. Fox, Joan Jett, Gena Rowlands, Michael McKean

The Light of Heart: see *Life Begins at Eight-Thirty*

Light Sleeper *
US 1991 103m DuArt
Guild/Grain of Sand (Linda Reisman)

A drug delivery man and former addict contemplates his future as his employer decides to give up the business and go straight.
An intelligent and occasionally gripping thriller.
wd Paul Schrader *ph* Ed Lachman *m* Michael Been *pd* Richard Hornung *ed* Kristina Boden
☆ Willem Dafoe, Susan Sarandon, Mary Beth Hurt, Dana Delany, David Clennon, Victor Garber, Jane Adams, Paul Jabara
'Contemplative and violent by turns, this quasi-thriller about a long-time drug dealer leaving the business has a great deal to recommend it but could have been significantly better had Schrader done some fresh plotting and not relied on his standby gunplay to resolve issues.' – *Variety*

'Laugh, you little fool, laugh ... for I'm giving you something you never had before – a soul ... on canvas!'
The Light that Failed *
US 1939 97m bw
Paramount (William A. Wellman)
A London artist is going blind as the result of a war wound, and must finish the portrait of the little Cockney whom he loves.
Nicely-made but rather boring star romance; no surprises in plot or performance.
w Robert Carson *story* Rudyard Kipling *d* William Wellman *ph* Theodor Sparkuhl *m* Victor Young
☆ Ronald Colman, Walter Huston, Ida Lupino, Dudley Digges, Muriel Angelus, Fay Helm
'Production fine for moderate b.o. Will catch attention of the carriage trade, the literati crowd and the critics.' – *Variety*
† Previously filmed in 1916 and 1923.

The Light Touch
US 1951 107m bw
MGM (Pandro S. Berman)
An elegant art thief tries to doublecross the gangster who employs him.
Elongated and witless romantic charade on European locations.
wd Richard Brooks *story* Jed Harris, Tom Reed *ph* Robert Surtees *m* Miklos Rozsa
☆ Stewart Granger, George Sanders, Pier Angeli, Kurt Kasznar, Larry Keating, Rhys Williams, Norman Lloyd, Mike Mazurki
'A comedy thriller which moves far too slowly for its imperfections to be overlooked.' – *Penelope Houston, MFB*

The Light Touch: see *Touch and Go (1955)*

Light Up the Sky
GB 1960 90m bw
British Lion/Bryanston (Lewis Gilbert)

Life on a searchlight battery during World War II.
Wartime comedy-drama with accent on the laughs but adding dollops of tragedy and sentiment. A very patchy entertainment.
w Vernon Harris *play* Touch It Light by Robert Storey *d* Lewis Gilbert *ph* John Wilcox *m* Douglas Gamley
☆ Ian Carmichael (Lt Ogleby), Tommy Steele (Eric McCaffey), Benny Hill (Syd McCaffey), Sydney Tafler (Ted Green), Victor Maddern (Lance Bombardier Tomlinson), Harry Locke (Roland Kenyon), Johnny Briggs (Leslie Smith), Dick Emery (Harry), Cyril Smith ('Spinner' Rice), Cardew Robinson (Compere), Susan Burnet (Jean), Sheila Hancock (Theatre Act), Fred Griffiths (Mr Jennings)

The Lighthorsemen *
Australia 1988 110m colour Super 35
Medusa/RKO (Simon Wincer, Ian Jones)

Comrades take part in the cavalry charge on the fortified city of Beersheba in the First World War.
Intermittently exciting re-creation of a historic event, at its best in the battle scenes.
w Ian Jones *d* Simon Wincer *ph* Dean Semler *m* Mario Millo *pd* Bernard Hides *ed* Adrian Carr
☆ Jon Blake, Peter Phelps, Tony Bonner, Bill Kerr, John Walton, Gary Sweet, Tim McKenzie, Sigrid Thornton, Anthony Andrews

'The brightest light hides your darkest fear'
Lighthouse
GB 1999 95m colour
Winchester/Arts Council/British Screen/BSkyB (Mark Leake, Tim Dennuson)

US title: *Dead of Night*
A serial killer stalks the survivors of a wrecked prison ship.
Old-fashioned low budget horror in the slasher genre, providing nothing that hasn't been seen too many times before.
wd Simon Hunter *ph* Tony Imi *m* Debbie Wiseman *pd* Simon Bowles *ed* Paul Green
☆ James Purefoy (Richard Spader), Rachel Shelley (Dr Kirsty McCloud), Christopher Adamson (Leo Rook), Paul Brooke (Captain Campbell), Don Warrington (Prison Officer Ian Goslet), Chris Dunne (Chief Prison Officer O'Neil), Bob Goody (Weevil), Pat Kelman (Spoons)
'Even by the rock-bottom standard of Lottery-funded losers, this is pitiful.' – *Christopher Tookey, Daily Mail*

Lightnin' *
US 1930 94m bw
Fox
A country fellow is wiser than he seems, and in between setting other folks' lives right, persuades his own wife not to divorce him.
Archetypal Will Rogers star part which he played on the stage; now his first big talkie hit.
play Frank Bacon, Winchell Smith *d* Henry King
☆ *Will Rogers*, Louise Dresser, Joel McCrea, Sharon Lynn, J. M. Kerrigan
'A production of the highest quality in all its phases.' – *Variety*

Lightning Jack
Australia 1994 93m colour Panavision
Buena Vista/Lightning Ridge/Village Roadshow (Paul Hogan, Greg Coote, Simon Wincer)

The adventures of a bungling, near-sighted outlaw and his mute companion.
A spoof Western a few bullets short of a six-shooter, with its few tired jokes milked relentlessly for laughs.
w Paul Hogan *d* Simon Wincer *ph* David Eggby *m* Bruce Rowland *pd* Bernard Hides *ed* O. Nicholas Brown
☆ Paul Hogan, Cuba Gooding Jnr, Beverly D'Angelo, Pat Hingle, Kamala Dawson, Roger Daltrey, L. Q. Jones, Richard Riehle, Frank McRae
'A good natured, if laconic, oater that rides along nicely.' – *Variety*

Lightning over Water
West Germany/Sweden 1980 91m Movielab
Road Movies/Viking Film (Renée Gunde-Lach, Pierre Cottrell, Chris Sievernich)
aka: *Nick's Movie*
A record of the last months of Nicholas Ray's life, when he was hoping to revive his career while visibly dying from cancer.
Unique and uneasy, something for film buffs to chew over.
wd Nicholas Ray, Wim Wenders *m* Ronee Blakley *ed* Wim Wenders, Peter Przygodda

Lightning Strikes Twice
US 1951 91m bw
Warner (Henry Blanke)
A woman decides to clear her lover of suspicion of murder, but later has her own doubts.
Silly melodrama with no credibility, little suspense, and too much talk.
w Lenore Coffee *novel* Margaret Echard *d* King Vidor *ph* Sid Hickox *m* Max Steiner
☆ Richard Todd, Ruth Roman, Mercedes McCambridge, Zachary Scott, Darryl Hickman, Frank Conroy, Kathryn Givney

Lights of New York ***
US 1928 57m bw
Warner
A chorus girl becomes involved with gangsters.
The first '100 per cent all-talking' film, dramatically primitive but historically important.
w F. Hugh Herbert, Murray Roth *d* Bryan Foy *ph* E. B. DuPar
☆ Helene Costello, Cullen Landis, Wheeler Oakman, Eugene Pallette, Tom Dugan, Gladys Brockwell, Mary Carr
'100 per cent crude.' – *Variety*

Lights of Old Broadway
US 1925 80m approx (24 fps) bw silent
MGM
Twin orphan girls find very different routes to happiness.
One of the star's most popular vehicles.
w Carey Wilson *d* Monta Bell
☆ Marion Davies, Conrad Nagel, George K. Arthur, Julia Swayne Gordon

Lights of Variety *
Italy 1950 94m bw
Film Capitolium (Alberto Lattuada)

original title: *Luci del Varieta*
aka: *Variety Lights*
A stage-struck young girl forsakes the manager of the troupe in which she found stardom for the bright lights of the city.
Tragi-comical backstage story in which the bits of detail are more entertaining than the plot.
w Federico Fellini *d* Alberto Lattuada *ph* Otello Martelli *m* Felice Lattuada *ad* Aldo Buzzi
☆ Peppino de Filippo (Checco Dalmonte), Carla del Poggio (Liliana), Giulietta Masina (Melina Amour), John Kitzmiller (Johnny), Folco Lulli (Liliana's lover), Dante Maggio (Comedian)
'Told with the humor and compassion, the subtlety and sensitivity, and marked by the satiric eye, the keenness of insight, the appreciation of human frailty, that are Fellini's strong points.' – *Judith Crist*

Lights Out: see *Bright Victory*

The Lightship
US 1985 89m colour
Rank/CBS (Moritz Borman, Bill Benenson)
A lightship is taken over by a gang of psychopathic crooks on the run.
Echoes of Key Largo abound in this dreary suspense melodrama which aspires to more meaning than is evident.
w William Mai, David Taylor *novel* Siegfried Lenz *d* Jerzy Skolimowski *ph* Charly Steinberger *m* Stanley Myers *ad* Holger Gross *ed* Barry Vince, Scott Hancock
☆ Robert Duvall, Klaus Maria Brandauer, Tom Bower, Robert Constanzo

Like Father Like Son
US 1987 98m Technicolor
Grazer-Valdes/Tri-Star

A surgeon and his son find themselves in each other's bodies.

Role-reversal comedy at the beginning of a trend; in itself a bore.
w Lorne Cameron, Steven L. Bloom *d* Rod Daniel *ph* Jack N. Green *m* Miles Goodman *pd* Dennis Gassner *ed* Lois Freeman-Fox
☆ Dudley Moore, Kirk Cameron, Sean Astin, Patrick O'Neal, Margaret Colin

Like Grains of Sand *
Japan 1995 129m Fujicolour
ICA/Toho/Pia/YES (Yoshishige Shimatani, Kazuo Hayashi, Kiyomi Kanazawa, Yuuka Nakazawa)
original title: *Nagisa no Sindbad*
A teenage boy discovers that he is gay.
Sensitive and provocative account of the emotional confusions and self-imposed repressions of a growing sexual awareness.
wd Ryosuke Hashiguchi *ph* Shogo Ueno *m* Kazuya Takahashi *ed* Miho Yoneda
☆ Yoshinori Okada, Kota Kusano, Ayumi Hamazaki, Koji Yamaguchi, Kumi Takada, Shizuka Isami
'Very probably the best film ever made about problems faced by a gay kid in his teens ... It gets inside adolescent emotions and insecurities with piercing accuracy.' – *Tony Rayns, Sight and Sound*

Like Mike
US 2002 100m DeLuxe
TCF/NBA (Barry Josephson, Peter Heller)
A young orphan becomes a basketball star with the aid of some magic sneakers.
A sports fantasy for the young and easily amused, who may not notice its recycling of familiar moments from other movies.
w Michael Elliot, Jordan Moffet *d* John Schultz *ph* Shawn Maurer *m* Richard Gibbs *pd* Arlan Jay Vetter *ed* Peter Berger, John Pace
☆ Lil' Bow Wow (Calvin), Morris Chestnut (Tracey Reynolds), Jonathan Lipnicki (Murph), Robert Forster (Coach Wagner), Crispin Glover (Stan Bittleman), Eugene Levy (Frank Bernard), Brenda Song (Reg), Jesse Plemons (Ox)
'This irritatingly feeble basketball movie for kids is co-produced by the NBA, for whom it is pretty candidly designed as a giant feature-length commercial.' – *Peter Bradshaw, Guardian*
'A valueless kiddie paean to pro basketball.' – *Mark Holcomb, Village Voice*

'A Delicious Love Story.'
Like Water for Chocolate **
Mexico 1991 114m colour
Electric/Cinevista/NCCA/NTDF/Alfonso Arau
original title: *Como agua para chocolate*
In Mexico in the early 1900s, forced to stay at home to look after her mother and to see the man she loves marry her sister, the youngest of three daughters puts all her emotions into her cooking.
Part soap opera, part delightful fable and wholly enjoyable, this is a sweet, rich but not indigestible romantic drama.
w Laura Esquivel *novel* Laura Esquivel *d* Alfonso Arau *ph* Emmanuel Lubezki, Steve Bernstein *m* Leo Brower *pd* Marco Antonio Arteaga, Mauricio de Aguinaci, Denise Pizzini *ed* Carlos Bolado, Francisco Chiu
☆ Marco Leonardi, Lumi Cavazos, Regina Torne, Mario Ivan Martinez, Ada Carrasco, Yareli Arizmendi, Claudette Maille, Pilar Aranda
'This classic love story bridging generations is so compelling and splendidly expressed in the script that the frustrated filmgoer can only shake his head at the incompetent handling.' – *Variety*
'The film acts as a kind of palliative for the middle-class audiences with which it has been so successful. Despite all the changes brought about in Mexican society by the Revolution and its aftermath, they can still feel comfortable with those things that have remained the same: the servants in their kitchens.' – *John Kraniauskas, Sight and Sound*
† The title refers to the heroine's temper, kept just below boiling point – like water for chocolate.

The Likely Lads *
GB 1976 90m bw
EMI (Aida Young)
Two Geordie friends, with wife and mistress, go on a touring holiday.
Valuable as a record of an excellent and long-running TV series, this big-screen version finds most of the humour regrettably broadened.
w Dick Clement, Ian La Frenais *d* Michael Tuchner *ph* Tony Imi *m* Mike Hugg
☆ *Rodney Bewes, James Bolam*, Brigit Forsyth, Mary Tamm, Sheila Fearn, Zena Walker

A Likely Story
US 1947 88m bw
RKO (Richard H. Berger)
A man thinks he has only a short time to live, and in trying to do his best for a girlfriend gets mixed up with gangsters.
Even a star cast could not have made much of this zany comedy script.
w Bess Taffel *d* H. C. Potter *ph* Roy Hunt *m* Leigh Harline *md* Constantin Bakaleinikoff
☆ Barbara Hale, Bill Williams, Lanny Rees, Sam Levene, Dan Tobin, Nestor Paiva

Li'l Abner *
US 1959 113m Technicolor Vistavision
Paramount/Panama-Frank (Norman Panama)
The hillbilly town of Dogpatch, tagged the most useless community in America, fights being used as a test site for A-bombs.
Set-bound, intrinsically American, but bright and cheerful film of a stage show about Al Capp's famous comic strip characters.
wd Norman Panama, Melvin Frank from the musical show (ly Johnny Mercer, words Gene de Paul)
ph Daniel L. Fapp *m* Gene de Paul *md* Joseph Lilley, Nelson Riddle *ch Dee Dee Wood, Michael Kidd*
☆ Peter Palmer, Leslie Parrish, Billie Hayes, Howard St John, Stubby Kaye, Stella Stevens, Julie Newmar, Robert Strauss
'As joyous, screwy, dancin' and jokin' a musical show as Hollywood has sent us for a long time.' – *Sunday Dispatch*
Joseph Lilley, Nelson Riddle

The Lilac Domino
GB 1937 79m bw
Grafton-Capitol-Cecil
A Hungarian count is attracted at the gambling tables by a masked girl.
Surprisingly undercast version of a popular operetta.
w Basil Mason, Neil Gow, R. Hutter and Derek Neame *play* Rudolf Bernauer, E. Gatti and B. Jenbach *d* Fred Zelnik
☆ June Knight, Michael Bartlett, Athene Seyler, Richard Dolman, S. Z. Sakall, Fred Emney, Jane Carr

Lilac Time *
US 1928 90m approx bw silent with sound effects
First National
GB title: *Love Never Dies*
A French girl promises to wait for an American flyer, but his stern father tells her he is dead.
Popular war romance which retains moments of interest.
w Carey Wilson *play* Jane Cowl, Jane Murfin *ph* Sid Hickox *m* Nathaniel Shilkret *d/p* George Fitzmaurice
☆ Colleen Moore, Gary Cooper, Eugenie Besserer, Burr McIntosh, Arthur Lake

Lilacs in the Spring
GB 1954 94m Trucolor
Republic/Everest (Herbert Wilcox)
US title: *Let's Make Up*
During the London blitz a young actress is knocked unconscious and dreams of herself as Nell Gwyn, Queen Victoria and her own mother before waking up to deal with her personal problems.
Good-humoured theatrical charade deadened by poorish production and colour, strengthened by the star's game run-through of her staple characters. How Mr Flynn came to be involved is anybody's guess.
w Miles Malleson (uncredited) *play The Glorious Days* by Harold Purcell *d* Herbert Wilcox *ph* Max Greene *m* Robert Farnon
☆ *Anna Neagle*, Errol Flynn, Peter Graves, David Farrar, Kathleen Harrison

Lili *
US 1953 81m Technicolor
MGM (Edwin H. Knopf)
A 16-year-old orphan girl joins a carnival and falls in love with the magician.
Romantic whimsy dependent entirely on treatment, which is sometimes heavy-handed. Charm, ballet and puppets are provided, but a little cheerful song and dance would not have been amiss.
w Helen Deutsch *novel* Paul Gallico *ph* Robert Planck *m* Bronislau Kaper *ad* Cedric Gibbons, Paul Groesse *d/ch* Charles Walters
☆ *Leslie Caron*, Jean-Pierre Aumont, Mel Ferrer, Kurt Kasznar
'A lovely and beguiling little film, touched with the magic of romance.' – *Bosley Crowther*
Bronislau Kaper
Helen Deutsch; Charles Walters; Robert Planck; Leslie Caron; art direction
Leslie Caron

Lili Marleen *
West Germany 1980 116m colour
Roxy/CIP/Rialto/Bayerische Rundfunk (Luggi Waldleitner)
A German girl singer becomes famous and notorious during World War II by her rendition of an old song.
Curious mixture of melodrama and satire which doesn't really work but is always lively to watch.
w Manfred Purzer, Joshua Sinclair, Rainer Werner Fassbinder *novel The Sky Has Many Colours* by Lale Andersen *d* Rainer Werner Fassbinder *ph* Xaver Schwarzenberger *m* Peer Raben *ed* Juliane Lorenz, Rainer Werner Fassbinder
☆ Hanna Schygulla, Giancarlo Giannini, Mel Ferrer, Karl Heinz

Lilies *
Canada 1996 95m colour
Alliance/Triptych (Anna Stratton, Arnie Gelbart, Robin Cass)
In Quebec, a bishop who visits a prison to hear an inmate's confession is taken hostage and forced to watch a play about his homosexual past.
Complex drama on the theme of obsessive love and betrayal; its setting provides a reason for its extreme theatricality, with female roles played by men in drag.
w Michel Marc Bouchard *play Les Feluettes ou La Répétition d'un Drame Romantique* by Michel Marc Bouchard *d* John Greyson *ph* Daniel John *m* Myschael Danna *pd* Sandra Kybartas *ed* Andre Corriveau
☆ Brent Carver, Marcel Sabourin, Albert Pallascio, Jason Cadieux, Danny Gilmore, Matthew Ferguson, Alexander Chapman, Ian D. Clark
'Aesthetically and conceptually very impressive, but it is less than the sum of its parts, its intelligence not sufficiently balanced and buttressed by the careful observation of character.' – *Rob White, Sight and Sound*

Lilies of the Field
US 1930 60m bw
First National
A chorus girl has been robbed of her child by framed divorce court evidence.
Backstage melodrama with music, very dated now but with interesting credits.
w John Goodrich *play* William Hurlbut *d* Alexander Korda *ph* Lee Garmes
☆ Corinne Griffith, Ralph Forbes, John Loder, Patsy Paige, Freeman Wood, Virginia Bruce
'Big revue sequences in backstage locale. Better than average programmer.' – *Variety*
† It was a remake of a 1924 film directed by John Francis Dillon and starring Corinne Griffith.

Lilies of the Field *
US 1963 94m bw
UA/Rainbow/Ralph Nelson
An itinerant black workman in New Mexico helps a group of German nuns to build a chapel.
Liberal, sentimental, under-dramatized little comedy with everyone coming to understand each other's point of view, so that the audience feels improved if not especially entertained.
w James Poe *novel* William E. Barrett *d* Ralph Nelson *ph* Ernest Haller *m* Jerry Goldsmith
☆ *Sidney Poitier*, Lilia Skala, Lisa Mann
Sidney Poitier
best picture; James Poe; Ernest Haller; Lilia Skala

Liliom *
US 1930 94m bw
Fox
A Budapest carnival man is killed in a fight but later comes back from heaven to see how his family is doing.
Ingeniously-staged fantasy, very dated but a lot more interesting than its musical remake Carousel (qv).
w S. N. Behrman *play* Ferenc Molnar *d* Frank Borzage *ph* Chester Lyons *m* Richard Fall
☆ Charles Farrell, Rose Hobart, Estelle Taylor, Lee Tracy, Walter Abel, Guinn Williams, H. B. Warner, Dawn O'Day (Anne Shirley)
'Beyond the depth of Farrell's dramatic ability ... shapes up as passable for a week-stand in the keys.' – *Variety*

'Before Eve there was Evil ... and her name was Lilith!'
Lilith *
US 1964 126m bw
Columbia/Centaur (Robert Rossen)
A trainee therapist at an asylum falls in love with a patient.
Strange, wistful, poetic and rather soporific character melodrama.
wd Robert Rossen *novel* J. R. Salamanca *ph* Eugene Schufftan *m* Kenyon Hopkins *pd* Richard Sylbert
☆ Warren Beatty, Jean Seberg, Peter Fonda, Kim Hunter, Anne Meacham, James Patterson, Jessica Walter, Gene Hackman
'A remarkable attempt to dig a little deeper in an almost untilled field, and to throw some light on the relationship between madness and the creative imagination.' – *Tom Milne*

Lilja 4-ever: see *Lilya 4-Ever*

Lillian Russell *
US 1940 130m bw
TCF (Gene Markey)
The life and loves of the famous 1890s entertainer.
Flabby and inaccurate biopic, worth seeing for its highlights but flatly and incompetently written.
w William Anthony McGuire *d* Irving Cummings *ph* Leon Shamroy *md* Alfred Newman *ad* Richard Day, Joseph C. Wright
☆ Alice Faye, Don Ameche, Edward Arnold, Warren William, Henry Fonda, Leo Carrillo, Helen Westley, Dorothy Peterson, Ernest Truex, Nigel Bruce, Claud Allister, Lynn Bari, Weber and Fields, Eddie Foy Jnr, Una O'Connor
art direction

Lilly Turner
US 1933 65m bw
Warner
A girl unwittingly marries a bigamist, then a drunk who will give her baby a name.
Turgid mother-love saga.
w Gene Markey, Kathryn Scola *play* Philip Dunning, George Abbott *d* William A. Wellman
☆ Ruth Chatterton, George Brent, Frank McHugh, Ruth Donnelly, Guy Kibbee, Robert Barrat
'Spotty returns most probable.' – *Variety*

'There's one in every family.'
Lilo & Stitch *
US 2002 85m Technicolor
Buena Vista/Walt Disney (Clark Spencer)
A Hawaiian orphan befriends a curious creature who is an alien outlaw.
Lively, colourful, short and sweet animated feature that should amuse young children, though probably not their parents.
wd Chris Sanders, Dean Dubois *m* Alan Silvestri *pd* Paul Felix *ed* Darren Holmes
☆ voices of: Daveigh Chase (Lilo), Christopher Michael Sanders (Stitch), Tia Carrere (Nani), David Ogden Stiers (Jumba), Kevin McDonald (Pleakley), Ving Rhames (Cobra Bubbles), Zoe Caldwell (Grand Councilwoman), Jason Scott Lee (David Kawena)
'The story's holes and conventions grow ever wider and the humor diminishes as the film

progresses, and it finishes up as a lesser Disney effort.' – *Jeffrey M. Anderson, San Francisco Examiner*
'Funny, sassy, startling, original.' – *Roger Ebert*
animated feature

Lily in Love
US/Hungary 1985 103m colour
Robert Halmi
Denied the lead in a film scripted by his wife, an actor disguises himself as an Italian in order to get the part.
A weak comedy, done with some style.
w Frank Cucci *d* Karoly Makk *ph* John Lindley *m* Szaboks Fenyes *ad* Tamas Vayer *ed* Norman Gay
☆ Christopher Plummer, Maggie Smith, Elke Sommer, Adolph Green

Lilya 4-Ever **
Sweden/Denmark 2002 109m colour
Metrodome/Memfis/Zentropa/i Vast/SVT/Nordisk (Lars Jönsson)
original title: *Lilja 4-ever*
Abandoned by her mother, who leaves the Soviet Union to start a new life in America with her boyfriend, a 16 -year-old girl takes to glue-sniffing and prostitution; then she meets a man who promises to find her a job in Sweden.
A dour tale of betrayal, given what uplift it has by Akinshina's radiant performance as the amoral Lilya, a girl with no insight into her own or her friends' troubles. Moodysson's attempt to lift the tragic mood at the very end fails to take wing.
wd Lukas Moodysson *ph* Ulf Brantas *m* Nathan Larson *ad* Josefin Asberg *ed* Michal Leszczylowski
☆ *Oksana Akinshina* (Lilya), Artiom Bogucharski (Volodya), Liliya Shinkaryova (Aunt Anna), Pavel Ponomaryov (Andrei), Tomas Neumann (Witek), Lyubov Agapova (Lilya's Mother), Tonu Kark (Sergei)
'It is Akinshina's presence and performance that make the pedestrian story heart-wrenching. She is pretty, responsive, reflective.' – *Stanley Kaufmann, New Republic*
'A haunting and incandescent work of art.' – *Owen Gleiberman, Entertainment Weekly*

Limbo *
US 1972 111m Technicolor
Universal (Linda Gottlieb)
aka: *Chained to Yesterday*
Women wait for their husbands to return from Vietnam.
Worthy but dramatically uninteresting multi-storied semi-propaganda piece with an untried cast.
w Joan Silver, James Bridges *d* Mark Robson *ph* Charles Wheeler *m* Anita Kerr *pd* *Gemma Jackson*
☆ Kate Jackson, Katherine Justice, Stuart Margolin, Hazel Medina, Kathleen Nolan

'A condition of unknowable outcome.'
Limbo
US/Germany 1999 127m CFI
Columbia TriStar/Global/Screen Gems (Maggie Renzi)
Fleeing from murderous drug dealers, a former fisherman, a nightclub singer and her teenage daughter are stranded on a remote, uninhabited island.
This odd, broken-backed story begins as a portrait of life in a small Alaskan community, with a tentative romance on the side, and then changes into a survival story. The ending is calculated to infuriate all who make it through the rest of the movie.
wd John Sayles *ph* Haskell Wexler *ad* Keith Neely *ed* John Sayles
☆ Mary Elizabeth Mastrantonio (Donna De Angelo), David Strathairn (Joe Gastineau), Vanessa Martinez (Noelle De Angelo), Kris Kristofferson (Smilin' Jack), Casey Siemaszko (Bobby Gastineau), Kathryn Grody (Franki), Rita Taggart (Lou), Leo Burmester (Harmon King), Michael Laskin (Albright)
'A thinly realized survival tale that falls flat dramatically and cinematically.' – *Todd McCarthy, Variety*

'Romantic ruler of London's half-world!'
Limehouse Blues *
US 1934 65m bw
Paramount
aka: *East End Chant*
In London's shady quarter, an oriental roustabout tries to leave his jealous mistress for a girl with a shady past.
Artificial, atmospheric melodrama set in a never-never Limehouse redolent of Broken Blossoms. *Interesting for its very excesses.*
w Arthur Phillips, Cyril Hume, Grover Jones *d* Alexander Hall *ph* Harry Fischbeck
☆ George Raft, Anna May Wong, Jean Parker, Kent Taylor, Billy Bevan
'Weak and slow-moving ... won't satisfy the average fan.' – *Variety*

Limelight
GB 1935 80m bw
GFD/Herbert Wilcox
US title: *Backstage*
A chorus girl helps a street singer to become a star.
Highly predictable backstage musical drama which made a nine days wonder of 'The Street Singer'.
w Laura Whetter *d* Herbert Wilcox *ph* Henry Harris
☆ Anna Neagle, *Arthur Tracy*, Jane Winton, Ellis Jeffreys, Muriel George
'A syrupy concatenation to win all British hearts.' – *James Agate*

Limelight ***
US 1952 144m bw
Charles Chaplin
A broken-down music hall comedian is stimulated by a young ballerina to a final hour of triumph.
Sentimental drama in a highly theatrical London East End setting. In other hands it would be very hokey, but Chaplin's best qualities, as well as his worst, are in evidence, and in a way the film sums up his own career.
wd Charles Chaplin ph Karl Struss m Charles Chaplin, Raymond Rasch, Larry Russell ad Eugene Lourié photographic consultant Rollie Totheroh
☆ *Charles Chaplin, Claire Bloom, Buster Keaton*, Sydney Chaplin, Nigel Bruce, Norman Lloyd
'From the first reel it is clear that he now wants to talk, that he loves to talk ... where a development in the story line might easily be conveyed by a small visual effect, he prefers to make a speech about it ... it is a disturbing rejection of the nature of the medium itself.' – *Walter Kerr*
'Surely the richest hunk of self-gratification since Huck and Tom attended their own funeral.' – *New Yorker, 1982*
'His exhortations about life, courage, consciousness and "truth" are set in a self-pitying, self-glorifying story.' – *Pauline Kael, 70s*
Charles Chaplin, Raymond Rasch, Larry Russell
Claire Bloom (newcomer)

'Tell Them I'm Coming.'
The Limey *
US 1999 90m CFI
Artisan (John Hardy, Scott Kramer)
After he leaves prison, an English criminal goes to Los Angeles to discover how his daughter died.
A revenge thriller told in an elliptical manner that does not quite conceal the familiarity and predictability of its story.
w Lem Dobbs *d* Steven Soderbergh *ph* Ed Lachman *m* Cliff Martinez *pd* Gary Frutkoff *ed* Sarah Flack
☆ Terence Stamp (Wilson), Peter Fonda (Valentine), Lesley Ann Warren (Elaine), Luis Guzman (Ed), Barry Newman (Avery), Joe Dallesandro (Uncle John), Nicky Katt (Stacy), Amelia Heinle (Adhara), Melissa George (Jennifer)
'A contemplative, character-driven drama that underplays the familiar crime genre and underworld milieu in favor of a more resonant story about family and intergenerational issues.' – *Emanuel Levy, Variety*
† The scenes showing Stamp as a young man are taken from Ken Loach's *Poor Cow* (qv), made in 1967.

Limit Up
US 1989 88m colour
Medusa/Management Company Entertainment (Jonathan D. Krane)
A woman sells her soul to an apparent demon in exchange for a successful career on the stock exchange.
A dull fantasy, dimly directed.
w Richard Martini, Luana Anders *d* Richard Martini *ph* Peter Lyons Collister *m* John Tesh *pd* R. Clifford Searcy *ed* Sonny Baskin
☆ Nancy Allen, Dean Stockwell, Brad Hall, Danitra Vance, Ray Charles, Rance Howard, Sandra Bogan

The Limping Man
GB 1953 74m bw
Banner/Eros (Donald Ginsberg)
An American leaving his plane at Heathrow sees another passenger shot by a limping man.
Initially intriguing thriller which gives up the ghost and tacks on a dream ending.
w Reginald Long, Alistair MacLean *d* Charles de Lautour *ph* Jonah Jones *m* Arthur Wilkinson
☆ Lloyd Bridges, Moira Lister, Helene Cordet, Bruce Beeby, Alan Wheatley, Leslie Phillips

Linda *
GB 1960 61m bw
Independent Artists
A teenage girl falls for a member of a street gang.
Nicely atmospheric low-life romance; no real content but plenty of raw style.
w Bill MacIlwraith *d* Don Sharp *ph* Michael Reed *m* Garry Hughes
☆ Carol White, Alan Rothwell, Cavan Malone, Lois Dane, Edward Cast

The Lineup *
US 1958 86m bw
Columbia (Frank Cooper)
San Francisco police trap a gunman who is also a drug contact.
Energetic, polished movie version of a popular TV series, San Francisco Beat.
w Stirling Silliphant *d Don Siegel ph* Hal Mohr *m* Mischa Bakaleinikoff
☆ Warner Anderson, Robert Keith, Eli Wallach

'He wants to be tied down. She wants to be tied up. It's not what you think.'
The Linguini Incident
US 1992 98m CFI color
Rank/Isolar (Arnold Orgolini)
A waitress who wants to be an escape artist and a barman seeking a wife set out to rob an antique shop of a ring that once belonged to Houdini.
No escape from boredom in this trivial and lacklustre comedy.
w Richard Shepard, Tamar Brott *d* Richard Shepard *ph* Robert Yeoman *m* Thomas Newman *pd* Marcia Hinds-Johnson *ed* Sonya Polonsky
☆ Rosanna Arquette, David Bowie, Eszter Balint, André Gregory, Buck Henry, Viveca Lindfors, Marlee Matlin
'Energetic actors can't overcome the uninspired, poverty-row production values.' – *Variety*

Link
GB 1986 103m Technicolor
Cannon/EMI (Richard Franklin)
A scientist in a lonely house educates chimpanzees, but one proves malevolent.
Not much plot for a long film, and no suspense either.
w Everett DeRoche *d* Richard Franklin *ph* Mike Malloy *m* Jerry Goldsmith
☆ Terence Stamp, Elisabeth Shue, Steven Pinner, Richard Garnett
'What is missing from Link is a reason to see it.' – *Variety*

The Lion
GB 1962 96m DeLuxe Cinemascope
TCF (Samuel G. Engel)
An American lawyer goes to Africa to visit his ex-wife and their child.
Unabsorbing marital drama with child and animal interest.
w Irene and Louis Kamp *novel* Joseph Kessel *d* Jack Cardiff *ph* Ted Scaife *m* Malcolm Arnold
☆ William Holden, Trevor Howard, Capucine, Pamela Franklin
'The main fault must be attributed to the spiritless direction of Jack Cardiff, whose recent change of métier has resulted in the industry losing a great lighting cameraman.' – *John Gillett*

The Lion Has Wings *
GB 1939 76m bw
London Films (Alexander Korda)
A documentary drama tracing the steps leading up to the outbreak of war.
Once-inspiring propaganda piece, now regrettably hilarious. Valuable social history, though.
w Adrian Brunel, E. V. H. Emmett *d* Michael Powell, Brian Desmond Hurst, Adrian Brunel *ph* Harry Stradling *m* Richard Addinsell
☆ Merle Oberon, Ralph Richardson, June Duprez, Robert Douglas, Anthony Bushell, Derrick de Marney, Brian Worth, Austin Trevor
'As a statement of war aims, one feels, this leaves the world beyond Roedean still expectant.' – *Graham Greene*

The Lion in Winter *
GB 1968 134m Eastmancolor Panavision
Avco Embassy/Haworth (Martin Poll)
Henry II and Eleanor of Aquitaine celebrate Christmas together and have a family row.
An acting feast for two principals and assorted supports, a talking marathon in which not all the talk is good, a smart comedy with sudden lapses into melodrama; stimulating in parts but all rather tiresome by the end, especially as there is not much medieval splendour.
w James Goldman *play* James Goldman *d* Anthony Harvey *ph* Douglas Slocombe *m* John Barry
☆ *Katharine Hepburn, Peter O'Toole*, Jane Merrow, John Castle, Anthony Hopkins, Nigel Terry, Timothy Dalton
'He is not writing a factual movie about the Plantagenets but an interpretation in which he combines their language and ours.' – *Philip T. Hartung*
James Goldman; John Barry; Katharine Hepburn
best picture; Anthony Harvey; Peter O'Toole
John Barry

A Lion Is in the Streets *
US 1953 88m Technicolor
Warner/Cagney Productions (William Cagney)
An itinerant confidence trickster becomes a defender of the people, is nominated for governor, and becomes corrupt.
Busy melodrama which came a bit soon after All the King's Men.
w Luther Davis *novel* Adria Locke Langley *d* Raoul Walsh *ph* Harry Stradling *m* Franz Waxman *pd* Wiard Ihnen
☆ *James Cagney*, Barbara Hale, Anne Francis, Warner Anderson, John McIntire, Jeanne Cagney, Lon Chaney Jnr, Frank McHugh, Larry Keating, Onslow Stevens, James Millican, Sara Haden
'A headlong and dynamic drama which offers Mr Cagney one of his most colourful and meaningful roles.' – *Bosley Crowther*

The Lion King ***
US 1994 88m Technicolor
Buena Vista/Walt Disney (Don Hahn)
A lion cub, exiled by his evil uncle, grows up enjoying the easy life, but is persuaded that he must fight to restore himself to his rightful place as king.
An entertaining animated drama with some stunning moments, but a somewhat preachy tone; it isn't as much fun as the recent Disney features, although it found great favour with the public.
w Irene Mecchi, Jonathan Roberts, Linda Woolverton *d* Roger Allers, Rob Minkoff *m* Hans Zimmer, Lebo M *m/ly* Elton John, Tim Rice *pd* Chris Sanders
☆ Featuring the voices of Matthew Broderick, Rowan Atkinson, Niketa Calame, Jim Cummings, Whoopi Goldberg, Jeremy Irons, Robert Guillaume, James Earl Jones, Cheech Marin, Jonathan Taylor Thomas
'Bambi, but with carnivores ... The animation, computer-assisted in some of the more elaborate

sequences, is sometimes impressive, but rarely impressive enough to overcome a certain impersonality – a stubborn mechanical coldness.' – *Terrence Rafferty, New Yorker*

'Its true glories are in storytelling, voicemanship and scenic splendour – virtues that would be familiar by now from earlier Disney cartoons if they weren't, each time, so wonderfully fresh.' – *Time*

† The film was the biggest earner of 1994 in the US, taking $298.9m at the box-office. Its plot reportedly resembles that of *Jungle Taitei* (aka *Jungle Emperor*), a Japanese animated series made in the 60s.

Hans Zimmer; song 'Can You Feel the Love Tonight' (*m* Elton John, *ly* Tim Rice)

songs 'Circle of Life', 'Hakuna Matata'

Lion of the Desert

US 1980 163m Eastmancolor Panavision

Falcon International (Moustapha Akkad)

In 1929 an Italian general in Libya withstands the attacks of rebel leader Omar Mukhtar.

Whitewashed account of the activities of a patriarchal partisan who was hanged in 1931. Of interest primarily to Arab zealots.

w H. A. L. Craig *d* Moustapha Akkad *ph* Jack Hildyard *m* Maurice Jarre *pd* Mario Garbuglia, Syd Cain

☆ Anthony Quinn, Oliver Reed, Irene Papas, Raf Vallone, Rod Steiger, John Gielgud, Andrew Keir

Lionheart

US 1987 104m colour

Orion (Stanley O'Toole, Talia Shire)

On his way to join King Richard the Lionheart's crusade, a young knight rescues a band of children from a slave trader.

Aimed at a family audience, it lacks excitement and pace and is best treated as a soporific.

w Menno Meyjes, Richard Outten *d* Franklin J. Schaffner *ph* Alec Mills *m* Jerry Goldsmith *pd* Gil Parrondo *ed* David Bretherton, Richard Haines

☆ Eric Stoltz, Gabriel Byrne, Nicola Cowper, Dexter Fletcher, Deborah Barrymore, Nicholas Clay, Bruce Purchase, Neil Dickson, Chris Pitt

'High on heart-warming ideals, but low in every other department.' – *Empire*

Lionheart: see *AWOL (1990)*

The Lion's Den: see *La Boca del Lobo*

'Rape was only the beginning!'

Lipstick

US 1976 90m Technicolor

Paramount/Dino de Laurentiis (Freddie Fields)

A girl is raped but gets nowhere in court until her sister lures the man to rape her too.

Franker but not very interesting extension of a fifties co-feature, with all the developments well telegraphed.

w David Rayfiel *d* Lamont Johnson *ph* Bill Butler *m* Michel Polnareff

☆ Margaux Hemingway, Perry King, Anne Bancroft, Chris Sarandon, Mariel Hemingway, Robin Gammell

'One of Lipstick's points is that voyeurism encourages senseless crime, but it unfortunately ignores its own lesson.' – *Marsha McCreadie, Films in Review*

Liquid Sky

US 1982 118m TVC Color

Z Films (Slava Tsukerman)

Aliens in a flying saucer land on the roof of a New York skyscraper in search of a heroin-like drug, which they obtain by killing people during orgasm.

A film with an undeserved cult reputation, presumably because it is set among punks and junkies; otherwise it is tediously plotted and poorly written and acted, dealing with unattractive characters in an unpleasant environment.

w Slava Tsukerman, Anne Carlisle, Nina V. Kerova *d* Slava Tsukerman *ph* Yuri Neyman *m* Slava Tsukerman, Brenda L. Hutchinson, Clive Smith *pd* Marina Levikova-Neyman *ed* Sharyn Leslie Ross

☆ Anne Carlisle, Paula E. Sheppard, Bob Brady, Susan Doukas, Elaine C. Grove, Stanley Knap, Jack Adalist, Otto von Wernherr

'By turns self-consciously bizarre and beautiful.' – *Sight and Sound*

The Liquidator *

GB 1965 104m Metrocolor Panavision

MGM/Leslie Elliott (Jon Pennington)

An ex-war hero is recruited by the secret service as an eliminator of security risks.

Fairly lively James Bond spoof which is never quite as funny as it imagines.

w Peter Yeldham *novel* John Gardner *d* Jack Cardiff *ph* Ted Scaife *m* Lalo Schifrin

☆ Rod Taylor, Trevor Howard, *David Tomlinson*, Jill St John, Wilfrid Hyde-White, Derek Nimmo, Eric Sykes, Akim Tamiroff

Lisa: see *The Inspector*

Lisa and the Devil

Italy 1974 93m Technicolor

Leone International (Alfred Leone)

original title: *Il Diavolo e il Morto*

A tourist stranded in a small town takes refuge in an old, dark villa.

Baroque thriller that constantly teeters on the edge of absurdity before finally falling.

w Mario Bava, Alfred Leone *d* Mario Bava *ph* Cecilio Paniagua *m* Carlo Savina *ad* Nedo Azzini *ed* Carlo Reali

☆ Telly Savalas, Elke Sommer, Sylva Koscina, Alessio Orano, Alida Valli, Gabriele Tinti, Kathy Leone

'Not quite in the first rank of the director's work, it's still a bizarre gem.' – *Empire*

Lisbon

US 1956 90m Trucolor Naturama

Republic (Ray Milland)

An international crook negotiates an Iron Curtain prisoner's release, but the man's wife has other ideas.

Glossy international intriguer with smart performances.

w John Tucker Battle *d* Ray Milland *ph* Jack Marta *m* Nelson Riddle

☆ Ray Milland, *Claude Rains*, Maureen O'Hara, Yvonne Furneaux, Francis Lederer, Percy Marmont, Edward Chapman

The Lisbon Story

GB 1946 103m bw

British National

Spies in 1940 Lisbon rescue a French atom scientist.

Flat filming of a musical show which kept Britons humming 'Pedro the Fisherman' throughout World War II.

w Jack Whittingham *play* Harold Purcell, Harry Parr-Davies *d* Paul Stein *ph* Ernest Palmer *m/ly* Harold Purcell, Harry Parr-Davies

☆ Patricia Burke, David Farrar, Walter Rilla, *Richard Tauber*, Austin Trevor, Harry Welchman

The List of Adrian Messenger **

US 1963 98m bw

U-I/Joel (Edward Lewis)

An intelligence officer traps a mass murderer with a penchant for disguise.

Old-fashioned mystery thriller, as though Holmes and Watson were combating a modern Moriarty (and a rough-hewn production). The whole thing is camped up like an end-of-term treat, and as a further gimmick four guest stars allegedly appear under heavy disguise in cameo parts.

w Anthony Veiller *novel* Philip MacDonald *d* John Huston *ph* Joe MacDonald *m* Jerry Goldsmith

☆ *George C. Scott, Kirk Douglas, Clive Brook*, Dana Wynter, Jacques Roux, Walter Tony Huston, Herbert Marshall, Bernard Archard, Gladys Cooper; and Robert Mitchum, Frank Sinatra, Burt Lancaster, Tony Curtis

'A leisurely, underplayed thriller with some good performances and a gimmick which turns it into a guessing contest.' – *L.A. Times*

Listen

US 1996 101m Eastmancolor Panavision

Orion/Greg H. Sims/Devin/Rampage (Diane Patrick-O'Connor)

A San Francisco advertising executive overhears some telephone conversations and realizes that a serial killer lives in the same apartment block as her.

Convoluted and derivative thriller that requires more attention than it deserves to follow the improbabilities of its narrative.

w Jonas Quastel, Michael Bafaro *d* Gavin Wilding *ph* Brian Pearson *m* David Davidson *pd* Cathy Robertson *ed* Melinda Seabrook

☆ Brooke Langton, Gordon Currie, Sarah Buxton, Joel Wyner, Evan Taylor, Andy Romano, Jeff Burnett

'A stylish, and extremely empty-headed, film.' – *Variety*

Listen Darling

US 1938 70m bw

MGM (Jack Cummings)

Children try to find their widowed mother a new husband.

Slight domestic comedy chiefly notable for its young talent.

w Elaine Ryan, Anne Morrison Chapin *story* Katherine Brush *d* Edwin L. Marin *ph* Charles Lawton Jnr *m* George Axt *md* George Stoll

☆ Mary Astor, Judy Garland, Freddie Bartholomew, Walter Pidgeon, Alan Hale, Scotty Beckett, Charley Grapewin, Barnett Parker, Gene Lockhart

'Inauspicious start for the Garland- Bartholomew team ... mediocre story hurts.' – *Variety*

Listen to Britain ****

GB 1941 20m bw

Ministry of Information (Crown Film Unit)

Images of Britain at war.

A brilliant compilation of almost poetic sights and sounds which distil the essence of a year.

ph H. E. Fowle *d/ed* *Humphrey Jennings*

Listen to Me

US 1989 110m CFI color

Columbia TriStar/Weintraub Entertainment/Martin Bregman (Marykay Powell)

Two students fall in love while being members of their college debating team.

Of limited interest, unless you happen to be a member of a debating team, and even then it is unlikely to hold your attention for long.

wd Douglas Day Stewart *ph* Fred J. Koenekamp *m* David Foster *pd* Gregory Pickrell *ed* Anne V. Coates

☆ Kirk Cameron, Jami Gertz, Roy Scheider, Amanda Peterson, Tim Quill, George Wyner, Anthony Zerbe, Christopher Atkins

Listen Up: The Lives of Quincy Jones

US 1990 115m Technicolor

Warner/Cort (Courtney Sale Ross)

Documentary on the life of the influential record producer, arranger and composer who began as a big-band trumpeter.

Distractingly edited, as if intended for an audience with a very short attention span, and mainly given over to performances and uninformative interviews with those with whom Jones has worked, from jazz musicians such as Lionel Hampton, Miles Davis and Ella Fitzgerald to rock singer Michael Jackson and rapper Big Daddy Kane.

d Ellen Weissbrod *ph* Stephen Kazmierski *m* Quincy Jones *ed* Milton Moses

Lisztomania

GB 1975 104m colour Panavision

Warner/VPS/Goodtimes (Roy Baird, David Puttnam)

The life of Liszt seen in terms of a modern pop performer.

The most excessive and obscene of all this director's controversial works, incapable of criticism on normal terms except that it seems unusually poor in production values.

wd Ken Russell *ph* Peter Suschitzky *md* John Forsyth

☆ Roger Daltrey, Sara Kestelman, Paul Nicholas, Fiona Lewis, John Justin, Ringo Starr

'ample dialogue: 'Piss off, Brahms!'

'Ken Russell's first completely unmitigated catastrophe in several years ... a welter of arbitrary gags, manic self-references and frantic exploitation-movie clichés.' – *Tony Rayns*

'Oscar Wilde once said "Each man kills the thing he loves", and the remark perfectly suits Ken Russell's film treatments of classical composers ... he has bludgeoned into pulp some of the finest music civilization has produced.' – *Patrick Snyder*

'This gaudy compendium of camp, second-hand Freud and third-rate pastiche is like a bad song without end.' – *Sight and Sound*

Liten Ida: see *Little Ida*

Little Accident

US 1930 82m bw

Universal

A man is about to marry again when he finds that his first wife is having his baby.

Stretched-out comedy which fumbles its way along.

w Gladys Lehman *play* Floyd Dell, Thomas Mitchell *d* William James Craft

☆ Douglas Fairbanks Jnr, Anita Page, Sally Blane, ZaSu Pitts, Joan Marsh, Roscoe Karns, Slim Summerville

'If anybody thinks 82 minutes is the proper time for this film, they should be made to sit through it twice.' – *Variety*

Little Accident

US 1939 65m bw

Universal

A baby is passed from hand to hand after her father abandons her.

Simple-minded comedy bearing little relation to the above; it's now a vehicle for the baby.

w Paul Yawitz, Eve Greene *d* Charles Lamont

☆ Baby Sandy, Hugh Herbert, Richard Carlson, Florence Rice, Ernest Truex, Fritz Feld, Edgar Kennedy

'Elemental comedy for supporting attraction in nabes.' – *Variety*

Little Annie Rooney *

US 1925 99m (24 fps) bw silent

United Artists/Mary Pickford

A 12-year-old tomboy in a New York slum rounds up the killer of her policeman father.

Sentimental melodrama tailored for a 32-year-old star who liked playing kids. Of minor historical interest.

w Hope Loring, Louis D. Lighton *d* William Beaudine *ph* Charles Rosher, Hal Mohr *m* Joseph Plunkett

☆ *Mary Pickford*, William Haines, Walter James, Gordon Griffith

The Little Ark

US 1971 86m DeLuxe Panavision

Cinema Center/Robert B. Radnitz

Two war orphans and their pets, trapped in a flood, sail to safety in a houseboat.

Well-meaning, somewhat allegorical family film, too desultory to maintain interest and rather too frightening for children.

w Joanna Crawford *novel* Jan de Hartog *d* James B. Clark *ph* Austin Dempster, Denys Coop *m* Fred Karlin

☆ Theodore Bikel, Philip Frame, Genevieve Ambas

song 'Come Follow Follow Me' (*m*Fred Karlin, *ly*Marsha Karlin)

Little Big Horn *

US 1951 86m bw

Lippert (Carl K. Hittleman)

GB title: *The Fighting Seventh*

A cavalry squad sets out to warn Custer about Little Big Horn, but all the men are massacred before Custer arrives.

Dour, impressive low-budget Western.

wd Charles Marquis Warren *ph* Ernest Miller *m* Paul Dunlap

☆ Lloyd Bridges, John Ireland, Marie Windsor, Reed Hadley, Hugh O'Brian, Wally Cassell, King Donovan

Little Big League

US 1994 119m Technicolor

Rank/Castle Rock/Lobell/Bergman

A 12-year-old boy is left a baseball team by his grandfather and decides to take over as manager.

Amiable but uninvolving entertainment for sports-struck kids.

w Gregory K. Pincus, Adam Scheinman *d* Andrew Scheinman *ph* Donald E. Thorin *m* Stanley Clarke *pd* Jeffrey Howard *ed* Michael Jablow
☆ Luke Edwards, Timothy Busfield, John Ashton, Ashley Crow, Kevin Dunn, Jason Robards, Billy L. Sullivan

'Has its heart in the right place but never makes it out of the infield in terms of laughs or excitement.' – *Variety*

'The Cavalry Against The Indians And Dustin Hoffman Is On Both Sides!'

Little Big Man *
US 1970 147m Technicolor Panavision
Stockbridge/Hiller/Cinema Center (Stuart Millar)

An aged veteran of the old west recounts his life story – with elaborations.
A number of episodes varying from stark tragedy to satirical farce are framed for no good reason by the star in heavy disguise; the intention is hard to guess but there are goodies along the way.
w Calder Willingham *novel* Thomas Berger *d* Arthur Penn *ph* Harry Stradling *m* John Hammond *pd* Dean Tavoularis
☆ Dustin Hoffman, Martin Balsam, Faye Dunaway, *Chief Dan George*, Richard Mulligan, Jeff Corey

'A hip epic, with an amiable first hour. Then the massacres and messages take over.' – *New Yorker, 1976*

'A tangy and, I think, unique film with American verve, about some of the things American verve has done.' – *Stanley Kauffmann*

Chief Dan George

Little Big Shot
US 1935 80m bw
Warner
A gangster's child is orphaned and cared for by two con men.
Reasonably lively vehicle for a new child star who didn't last.
w Jerry Wald, Julius J. Epstein, Robert Andrews *d* Michael Curtiz
☆ Sybil Jason, Glenda Farrell, Robert Armstrong, Edward Everett Horton, Jack La Rue, J. Carrol Naish, Edgar Kennedy

'Should pave the way handily for young Miss Jason's future.' – *Variety*

A Little Bit of Heaven
US 1940 87m bw
Universal (Joe Pasternak)
A 12-year-old girl becomes a singing sensation but runs into family opposition.
Predictable vehicle for a young star being built up as a stop-gap Deanna Durbin.
w Daniel Taradash, Gertrude Purcell, Harold Goldman *story* Grover Jones *d* Andrew Marton *ph* John Seitz *m* Charles Previn
☆ Gloria Jean, Robert Stack, Hugh Herbert, C. Aubrey Smith, Stuart Erwin, Nan Grey, Eugene Pallette, Billy Gilbert, Butch and Buddy

Little Boy Lost
US 1953 95m bw
Paramount (William Perlberg)
An American returns to Paris after the war to find his wife dead and his small son missing.
Rather dull tearjerker.
wd George Seaton *novel* Marghanita Laski *ph* George Barnes *m* Victor Young
☆ Bing Crosby, Claude Dauphin, Christian Fourcade, Gabrielle Dorziat, Nicole Maurey

Little Buddha *
France/GB 1993 123m Technicolor Technovision
Buena Vista/Ciby 2000/Recorded Picture (Jeremy Thomas)

A lama, who leaves his monastery in Bhutan to find the reincarnation of his own teacher, discovers three candidates, including a young American boy.
Two themes – a childlike retelling of the story of how Siddharta becomes the Buddha and the drama of an American family's immersion in an unfamiliar culture – exist uneasily together, despite their symmetry. There is a naïvety in both; but the photography – predominantly a cool blue in its American settings, glowing golden in its eastern scenes – and composition provide a constant visual fascination.
w Rudy Wurlitzer, Mark Peploe *story* Bernardo Bertolucci *d* Bernardo Bertolucci *ph* Vittorio Storaro *m* Ryuichi Sakamoto *pd* James Acheson *ed* Pietro Scalia
☆ Keanu Reeves, Ying Ruocheng, Chris Isaak, Bridget Fonda, Alex Wiesendanger, Raju Lal, Greishma Makar Singh

'After 30 years of making passionately skeptical movies, Bertolucci has made a film of the most sophisticated simplicity. His triumph is to make you see the Buddhist world through his eyes. It shines like innocence reincarnated.' – *Richard Corliss, Time*

'Long, solemn and humourless, this isn't going to win many converts to the cinema, let alone Buddhism.' – *Kim Newman, Empire*

Little Caesar ****
US 1931 77m bw
Warner

The rise and fall of a vicious gangster.
Its central character clearly modelled on Al Capone, this also has historical interest as vanguard of a spate of noisy gangster films. The star was forever identified with his role, and the film, though technically dated, moves fast enough to maintain interest over sixty years later.
w Francis Faragoh, Robert N. Lee *novel* W. R. Burnett *d Mervyn Le Roy ph* Tony Gaudio *m* Erno Rapee
☆ *Edward G. Robinson*, Douglas Fairbanks Jnr, Glenda Farrell, William Collier Jnr, Ralph Ince, George E. Stone, Thomas Jackson, Stanley Fields, Sidney Blackmer

'It has irony and grim humour and a real sense of excitement and its significance does not get in the way of the melodrama.' – *Richard Dana Skinner*

'One of the best gangster talkers yet turned out ... a swell picture.' – *Variety*

Francis Faragoh, Robert N. Lee

The Little Colonel **
US 1935 80m bw (colour sequence)
Fox (B. G. de Sylva)

In a Southern household after the Civil War, a little girl ends a family feud, plays Cupid to her sister, routs a few villains and mollifies her cantankerous grandfather.
First-class Temple vehicle, the first to boast an expensive production.
w William Conselman *novel* Annie Fellows Johnston *d* David Butler *ph* Arthur Miller *md* Arthur Lange
☆ *Shirley Temple, Lionel Barrymore*, Evelyn Venable, John Lodge, Bill Robinson, Hattie McDaniel, Sidney Blackmer

The Little Damozel
GB 1933 73m bw
British and Dominions
A gambler marries a young singer for a bribe, but falls in love with her.
Lavender-tinted romance with music; notable as its star's first major role.
w Donovan Pedelty *play* Monckton Hoffe *d* Herbert Wilcox *m* Ray Noble, Noël Coward
☆ Anna Neagle, James Rennie, Benita Hume, Athole Stewart, Alfred Drayton

Little Darlings
US 1980 92m Metrocolor Panavision
Paramount/Stephen J. Friedman

Teenage girls at a summer camp take bets on who will lose her virginity first.
Crass and tasteless comedy with only prurient appeal.
w Kimi Peck, Dalene Young *d* Ronald F. Maxwell *ph* Fred Batka *m* Charles Fox *pd* William Hiney *ed* Pembroke J. Herring
☆ Tatum O'Neal, Kristy McNichol, Krista Errickson, Armand Assante

Little Dorrit **
GB 1987 357m Technicolor
Sands/Cannon (John Brabourne)

Faithful adaptation of classic novel.
Lovingly made by a large team, economically and authentically re-creating Dickens's London, with a starry cast giving their all. Adored by audiences who could take the length.
wd Christine Edzard novel Charles Dickens *ph* Bruno de Keyzer *m* Giuseppe Verdi
☆ Derek Jacobi, Joan Greenwood, Max Wall, *Alec Guinness*, Cyril Cusack, Sarah Pickering, Eleanor Bron, Robert Morley
† Part 1 is 176m, Part 2 runs to 181m.
Alec Guinness; best adapted screenplay

The Little Drummer Girl *
US 1984 130m Technicolor
Warner/Pan Arts (Robert L. Crawford)

An American actress in Britain is persuaded by Israeli agents to lose her Arab sympathies and spy for them.
Tediously protracted and unexciting version of a novel which was generally agreed to have been based on Vanessa Redgrave. Interesting for its quality look and surface style only: the intricate plotting of the Le Carré manner is surely no longer fashionable.
w Loring Mandel *novel* John Le Carré *d* George Roy Hill *ph* Wolfgang Treu *m* Dave Grusin *pd* Henry Bumstead *ed* William Reynolds
☆ Diane Keaton, Yorgo Voyagis, Klaus Kinski, Sami Frey, Michael Cristofer, David Suchet, Eli Danker, Thorley Walters, Anna Massey
† Author Le Carré appears in a small role under his real name of David Cornwell.

Little Egypt
US 1951 81m Technicolor
Universal-International (Jack Gross)
GB title: *Chicago Masquerade*
An American girl poses as an Egyptian princess at the Chicago World's Fair.
Sluggish turn-of-the-century romantic melodrama based on a factual swindle involving a phoney Nile reclamation project.
w Oscar Brodney, Doris Gilbert *d* Frederick de Cordova *ph* Russell Metty *md* Joseph Gershenson
☆ Rhonda Fleming, Mark Stevens, Nancy Guild, Charles Drake, Tom D'Andrea, Minor Watson, Steve Geray

Little Fauss and Big Halsy
US 1970 99m Movielab Panavision
Paramount/Alfran/Furie (Albert S. Ruddy)
Two motor cycle track racers team up and have violent adventures round the country.
Rather pointless capers in the wake of Easy Rider, neither interesting nor well done.
w Charles Eastman *d* Sidney J. Furie *ph* Ralph Woolsey *m* Johnny Cash, Bob Dylan, Carl Perkins
☆ Robert Redford, Michael J. Pollard, *Noah Beery Jnr*, Lauren Hutton

'A sort of Batman and Robin on wheels.' – *Rex Reed*

The Little Foxes ***
US 1941 116m bw
Samuel Goldwyn

A family of schemers in post-Civil War days will stop at nothing to outwit each other.
Superb film of a brilliant play; excellent to look at and listen to, with a compelling narrative line and memorable characters.
w Lillian Hellman play Lillian Hellman *d William Wyler ph Gregg Toland m* Meredith Willson *ad* Stephen Goosson *ed* Daniel Mandell
☆ *Bette Davis, Herbert Marshall, Teresa Wright*, Richard Carlson, *Charles Dingle, Dan Duryea, Carl Benton Reid, Patricia Collinge*, Jessica Grayson, Russell Hicks

HORACE GIDDENS (HERBERT MARSHALL): 'Maybe it's easy for the dying to be honest. I'm sick of you, sick of this house, sick of my unhappy life with you. I'm sick of your brothers and their dirty tricks to make a dime. There must be better ways of getting rich than building sweatshops and pounding the bones of the town to make dividends for you to spend. You'll wreck the town, you and your brothers. You'll wreck the country, you and your kind, if they let you. But not me, I'll die my own way, and I'll do it without making the world any worse. I leave that to you.'

'One of the really beautiful jobs in the whole range of movie making.' – *Otis Ferguson*

'No one knows better than Wyler when to shift the camera's point of view, when to cut, or how to relate the characters in one shot to those in the next ... you never have to wonder where you are in a Wyler picture.' – *Arthur Knight*

best picture; Lillian Hellman; William Wyler; Meredith Willson; Bette Davis; Teresa Wright; Patricia Collinge; Stephen Goosson; Daniel Mandell

Little Friend
GB 1934 85m bw
Gaumont
A girl is driven to attempt suicide by her parents' proposed divorce.
Fairly well written but rather stilted domestic drama which maintained a small reputation.
w Margaret Kennedy, Christopher Isherwood and Berthold Viertel *novel* Ernst Lothar *d* Berthold Viertel
☆ Nova Pilbeam, Matheson Lang, Lydia Sherwood, Arthur Margetson, Allan Aynesworth, Jean Cadell, Jimmy Hanley

The Little Giant
US 1933 74m bw
Warner

At the end of Prohibition, a beer baron moves to California and tries to break into society.
Disappointingly unfunny gangster comedy which never really gets going.
w Robert Lord, Wilson Mizner *d* Roy del Ruth *ph* Sid Hickox *md* Leo F. Forbstein
☆ Edward G. Robinson, Mary Astor, Helen Vinson, Kenneth Thomson, Russell Hopton, Donald Dillaway

'It makes Robinson a comedy character surrounded by semi-travesty and the fans are likely to resent it.' – *Variety*

'From homicide to house parties – from dames to debutantes!'

Little Giant
US 1946 91m bw
Universal (Joseph Gershenson)
GB title: *On the Carpet*
Misadventures of a vacuum cleaner salesman.
Curious, unsatisfactory Abbott and Costello comedy in which the boys play separate characters instead of working as a team. They should have waited for a better script before experimenting.
w Paul Jarrico, Richard Collins, Walter de Leon *d* William A. Seiter *ph* Charles van Enger *m* Edgar Fairchild
☆ Bud Abbott, Lou Costello, Brenda Joyce, George Cleveland, Elena Verdugo

Little Giants *
US 1994 105m colour
Warner/Amblin (Arne L. Schmidt)

When his sporting hero of a brother rejects his daughter as not good enough to play in a junior football team, a wimp decides to create his own team featuring her and other rejects.
Amiable and amusing sporting comedy, despite its predictability.
w James Ferguson, Robert Shallcross, Tommy Swerdlow, Michael Goldberg *d* Duwayne Dunham *ph* Janusz Kaminski *m* John Debney *pd* Bill Kenney *ed* Donn Cambern
☆ Rick Moranis, Ed O'Neill, John Madden, Shawna Waldron, Mary Ellen Trainor, Matthew McCurley, Susanna Thompson, Brian Haley

The Little Girl Who Lives Down the Lane
US/Canada/France 1976 94m colour
Zev Braun/ICL/Filmedis-Filmel (Zev Braun)

A 13-year-old girl, when her father dies, is discovered to be keeping her mother's corpse in the cellar, and doesn't stop at more murders to keep her secret.
Tasteless piece of grand guignol, badly directed and over-acted.
w Laird Koenig *novel* Laird Koenig *d* Nicolas Gessner *ph* Rene Verzier *m* Christian Gaubert
☆ Jodie Foster, Alexis Smith, Martin Sheen, Scott Jacoby
† Originally intended as a TV movie.

The Little Hut
US 1957 90m Eastmancolor
MGM/Herbson SA (F. Hugh Herbert, Mark Robson)
A man, his wife and her lover are shipwrecked on a desert island.
Sophisticated French farce which falls resoundingly flat in this bowdlerized Hollywood version in bilious colour,

fatally compromising itself at the beginning with a 'realistic' London prologue.
w F. Hugh Herbert *play* André Roussin and Nancy Mitford *d* Mark Robson *ph* Frederick A. Young *m* Robert Farnon *ad* Elliot Scott *ed* Ernest Walter
☆ Stewart Granger, David Niven, Ava Gardner, Walter Chiari, Finlay Currie, Jean Cadell

Little Ida **
Norway 1981 79m Eastmancolor
Minema/Norsk Film/Svenska Filminstituten (Harald Ohrvik, Sven Johansen)
original title: *Liten Ida*
A seven-year-old girl is ostracized because of her mother's relationship with a Nazi soldier.
Unsentimental, excellently acted account of childhood suffering.
w Marit Paulsen, Laila Mikkelsen *novel* Marit Paulsen *d* Laila Mikkelsen *ph* Hans Welin, Kjell Vassdal *m* Eyvind Solas *ad* Anders Barreus *ed* Peter Falck
☆ Sunniva Lindekleiv, Howard Halvorsen, Lise Fjeldstad, Arne Lindtner Ness, Ellen Westerfjell, Roennaug Alten

Little Johnny Jones
US 1929 73m bw
First National
An American jockey wins the Derby.
Mild comedy with music from the old George M. Cohan play.
w Adelaide Heilbron and Edward Buzzell *d* Mervyn Le Roy
☆ Eddie Buzzell, Alice Day, Edna Murphy, Robert Edeson
'Familiar formula but done nicely.' – *Variety*

The Little Kidnappers: see *The Kidnappers*

Little Lord Fauntleroy *
US 1921 11m (24 fps) bw silent
United Artists/Mary Pickford
An American boy who lives with his widowed mother discovers he is heir to an English dukedom.
Over-upholstered sentimental extravaganza tailored for a star in her twenties playing both young Cedric and his mother, a curious double. One can now only wonder at the immense appeal this film had in its own time; but that is not to diminish the vitality of its star.
w Bernard McConville *novel* Frances Hodgson Burnett *d* Jack Pickford, Alfred E. Green *ph* Charles Rosher *m* Louis F. Gottschalk
☆ Mary Pickford, Claude Gillingwater, Kate Price, James A. Marcus, Emmett King

Little Lord Fauntleroy *
US 1936 98m bw
David O. Selznick
A sound remake which did surprisingly well at the box-office and is still very watchable.
w Richard Schayer, Hugh Walpole, David O. Selznick *d* John Cromwell *ph* Charles Rosher *m* Max Steiner
☆ *Freddie Bartholomew, C. Aubrey Smith*, Mickey Rooney, Dolores Costello, Jessie Ralph, Guy Kibbee
† A TV movie version appeared in 1980, with Ricky Schroder and Alec Guinness.

Little Man Tate *
US 1991 99m DeLuxe
Columbia TriStar/Orion (Scott Rudin, Peggy Rajski)
A battle develops over the future of a precociously bright child between his working-class mother and a teacher of gifted children.
A drama of family tensions that might have worked better on television.
w Scott Frank *d* Jodie Foster *ph* Mike Southon *m* Mark Isham *pd* Jon Hutman *ed* Lynzee Klingman
☆ Jodie Foster, Dianne Wiest, Adam Hann-Byrd, Harry Connick Jnr, David Pierce, Debi Mazar, P. J. Ochian
'A nice little film, but what audience it is meant to appeal to is, frankly, something of a mystery.' – *Angie Errigo, Empire*

Little Man, What Now? *
US 1934 95m bw
Universal
Problems of Germany in the grip of unemployment.
One of the studio's several 'sequels' to All Quiet on the Western Front, *poignant at the time but now very dated.*
w William Anthony McGuire *novel* Hans Fallada *d* Frank Borzage *ph* Norbert Brodine *ed* Milton Carruth
☆ Margaret Sullavan, Douglass Montgomery, Alan Hale, Muriel Kirkland, Alan Mowbray, Mae Marsh
'Human, homely and romantic ... should get ample b.o. attention.' – *Variety*

Little Men
US 1935 77m bw
Mascot
Joe and her professor run a school for boys.
Slapdash sequel to Little Women; *not an ambitious production.*
w Gertrude Orr *novel* Louisa M. Alcott *d* Phil Rosen
☆ Ralph Morgan, Erin O'Brien-Moore, Junior Durkin, Cora Sue Collins, Frankie Darro, Dickie Moore
'Goes overboard on pathos ... tears flow over the most insignificant matters.' – *Variety*
† A remake emerged from RKO in 1940, but was ill received. Running 84 minutes, it starred Kay Francis, Jack Oakie, James Lydon, and Ann Gillis, not to mention Elsie the cow. Mark Kelly and Arthur Caesar wrote it, Norman Z. McLeod directed; for Graham Towne and Gene Baker.

The Little Mermaid **
US 1989 83m
Warner/Walt Disney/Silver Screen Partners IV (Howard Ashman, John Musker)
A mermaid falls in love with a prince and longs to be human.
A return to Disney's classic manner, with some excellent animation, though sentimentality is rampant.
wd John Musker, Ron Clements *story* Hans Christian Andersen *m* Alan Menken *m/ly* Howard Ashman, Alan Menken
☆ Featuring Voices of Rene Auberjonois, Christopher Daniel Barnes, Jodi Benson, Pat Carroll, Paddi Edwards, Buddy Hackett, Jason Marin, Kenneth Mars, Edie McClurg, Will Ryan, Ben Wright, Samuel E. Wright
best original score; best song 'Under the Sea' (m/l Alan Menken; Howard Ashman)
song 'Kiss the Girl' (m/l Alan Menken; Howard Ashman)

The Little Minister
US 1934 110m bw
RKO (Pandro S. Berman)
In 1840 Scotland, the gypsy girl with whom the new pastor falls unsuitably in love is really the local earl's wayward ward.
Tedious film version of a cloyingly whimsical play.
w Jane Murfin, Sarah Y. Mason, Victor Heerman *play* J. M. Barrie *d* Richard Wallace *ph* Henry Gerrard *m* Max Steiner
☆ *Katharine Hepburn*, John Beal, Alan Hale, Donald Crisp, Lumsden Hare, Andy Clyde, Beryl Mercer, Dorothy Stickney, Frank Conroy, Reginald Denny
'Fine production of an old favourite.' – *Variety*
'Although dear Barrie's elfin whimsies are likely to cause teeth-gnashing among unsympathetic moderns, Miss Hepburn plays the part with likeable sprightliness and charm.' – *André Sennwald, New York Times*

Little Miss Broadway
US 1938 70m bw
TCF (David Hempstead)
A small girl is adopted by the owner of a hotel for vaudeville artistes.
One of the child star's more casual vehicles, but quite pleasing.
w Harry Tugend, Jack Yellen *d* Irving Cummings *ph* Arthur Miller *md* Louis Silvers
☆ Shirley Temple, George Murphy, Jimmy Durante, Edna May Oliver, Phyllis Brooks, George Barbier, Edward Ellis, Jane Darwell, El Brendel, Donald Meek, Claude Gillingwater, Russell Hicks
'It can't be old age, but it does look like weariness.' – *New York Times*
'Shirley is better than her new vehicle, which in turn is better than her last one.' – *Variety*

Little Miss Marker **
US 1934 80m bw
Paramount (B. P. Schulberg)
GB title: *The Girl in Pawn*
A cynical racetrack gambler is forced to adopt a little girl, who not only softens him but saves him from his enemies.
The twin appeals of Temple (a new hot property) and Runyon made this a big hit of its time.
w William R. Lipman, Sam Hellman, Gladys Lehman *story* Damon Runyon *d* Alexander Hall *ph* Alfred Gilks *songs* Leo Robin, Ralph Rainger
☆ *Shirley Temple, Adolphe Menjou*, Dorothy Dell, Charles Bickford, Lynne Overman, Frank McGlynn Snr, Willie Best
'A good response to that element which claims there is nothing good in pictures. Clean, funny, with thrills and heart appeal all nicely blended.' – *Variety*
'No one can deny that the infant was a trouper: she delivers her lines with a killer instinct.' – *Pauline Kael, 70s*
† Remade as *Sorrowful Jones* (qv).

Little Miss Marker
US 1980 103m Technicolor
Universal (Jennings Lang)
Mainly glutinous remake of the above, with acerbic asides from the star.
wd Walter Bernstein *ph* Philip Lathrop *m* Henry Mancini
☆ Walter Matthau, Julie Andrews, Tony Curtis, Bob Newhart, Sara Stimson, Lee Grant, Brian Dennehy

Little Mr Jim
US 1946 92m bw
Orville O. Dull/MGM
The plight of a youngster when mother dies and father takes to drink.
Unabashed tearjerker with a fairly resistible child star.
w George Bruce *novel* *Army Brat* by Tommy Wadelton *d* Fred Zinnemann
☆ Jackie 'Butch' Jenkins, James Craig, Frances Gifford, Luana Patten, Spring Byington

Little Murders
US 1971 108m DeLuxe
TCF/Brodsky-Gould (Jack Brodsky)
A young photographer rises above all the urban horror of New York life, but when his wife is killed by a sniper he takes to violence.
This adaptation of an ultrablack comedy would have worked better as a comic strip, for its characters are satirical puppets, and when played by human beings the whole thing seems violently silly.
w Jules Feiffer *play* Jules Feiffer *d* Alan Arkin *ph* Gordon Willis *m* Fred Kaz
☆ Elliott Gould, Marcia Rodd, Elizabeth Wilson, Vincent Gardenia, Alan Arkin

Little Nellie Kelly *
US 1940 100m bw
MGM (Arthur Freed)
The daughter of a New York Irish cop patches up a family feud.
Sentimental nostalgic vehicle for young Judy Garland, who plays both wife and daughter and sings plenty of standard melodies.
w Jack McGowan *play* George M. Cohan *d* Norman Taurog *ph* Ray June *m/ly* George M. Cohan, Roger Edens, Nacio Herb Brown, Arthur Freed
☆ *Judy Garland*, George Murphy, Charles Winninger, Douglas McPhail, Arthur Shields, Forrester Harvey
♫ 'Nellie is a Darlin''; 'It's a Great Day for the Irish'; 'Singin' in the Rain'; 'Nellie Kelly I Love You'

'Be Unafraid, Be Very Unafraid.'
Little Nicky
US 2000 90m DeLuxe
Entertainment/New Line/Happy Madison/RSC Media (Robert Simonds, Jack Giarraputo)
The devil's slacker son goes to Earth to bring back his two wicked brothers who are intent on turning it into another Hell.
Sandler's persona of simple-minded man-child wearies more than usual in a cheap, crude, tasteless comedy that is woefully short on laughs.
w Tim Herlihy, Adam Sandler, Steven Brill *d* Steven Brill *ph* Theo Van De Sande *m* Teddy Castellucci *pd* Perry Andelin Blake *ed* Jeff Gourson *sp* makeup and creature fx: Howard Berger, Robert Kurtzman, Greg Nicotero *cos* Ellen Lutter
☆ Adam Sandler (Nicky), Patricia Arquette (Valerie), Harvey Keitel (Dad), Rhys Ifans (Adrian), Tommy 'Tiny' Lister Jnr (Cassius), Robert Smigel (Beefy), Allen Covert (Todd), Peter Dante (Peter), Jonathan Loughran (John), Blake Clark (Jimmy the Demon), Rodney Dangerfield (Lucifer), Kevin Nealon (Gatekeeper), Reese Witherspoon (Holly)
'A devilishly energetic vehicle that contains about as many laughs as his previous features combined.' – *Robert Koehler, Variety*
'Sandler delivers his first drop-dead dud with a jumble of sentimentality, vulgarity and inanity.' – *Total Film*

A Little Night Music *
Austria/West Germany 1977 125m Eastmancolor
Sascha Film/S & T (Elliott Kastner)
In Vienna at the turn of the century, a middle-aged lawyer, frustrated by the virginity of his young wife, turns to an old actress flame.
Fumbled version of a rather splendid Broadway musical based on Ingmar Bergman's Smiles of a Summer Night. *The locale is changed, several of the songs are cut, and the leads are miscast.*
w Hugh Wheeler *play* Hugh Wheeler *d* Harold Prince *ph* Arthur Ibbetson *m/ly* *Stephen Sondheim*
☆ Elizabeth Taylor, Diana Rigg, Len Cariou, Lesley-Anne Down, Hermione Gingold, Christopher Guard, Laurence Guittard
Jonathan Tunick (music adaptation)

Little Nikita
US 1988 98m DeLuxe
Columbia (Harry Gittes)
aka: *The Sleepers*
An all-American boy discovers from an FBI agent that his parents are not the average couple they seem, but Soviet spies.
Ineptly plotted thriller that piles on complexity at the cost of credibility; the acting is better than the script or direction deserve.
w John Hill, Bo Goldman *story* Tom Musca, Terry Schwartz *d* Richard Benjamin *ph* Laszlo Kovacs *m* Marvin Hamlisch, Joe Curiale *pd* Gene Callahan *ed* Jacqueline Cambas
☆ *Sidney Poitier*, River Phoenix, Richard Jenkins, Caroline Kava, Richard Bradford, Loretta Devine, Richard Lynch, Lucy Deakins

'Between good and evil and heaven and hell is...'
Little Odessa *
US 1994 98m Foto-Kem Super 35
First Independent/New Line (Paul Webster)
An exiled, edgy, hired killer returns to his Russian-Jewish community in Brighton Beach on an assignment and to see his family: heavy-handed father, dying mother and mixed-up younger brother.
Downbeat tale of melancholy lives, in which death and violence loom large; it compels almost as much as it repels.
wd James Gray *ph* Tom Richmond *pd* Kevin Thompson *ed* Dorian Harris
☆ Tim Roth, Edward Furlong, Moira Kelly, Vanessa Redgrave, Paul Guilfoyle, Natasha Andreichenko, Maximilian Schell
'A sparse, unforgiving work – part Oedipal drama, part thriller, bound together by a dense web of threat.' – *Tom Shone, Sunday Times*

Little Old New York
US 1940 100m bw
TCF (Raymond Griffith)
The story of Robert Fulton and his invention of the steamboat.
Romantic hokum with a veneer of fact; good production.
w Harry Tugend *play* Rida Johnson Young *d* Henry King *ph* Leon Shamroy *m* Alfred Newman

☆ Alice Faye, Richard Greene, Fred MacMurray, Henry Stephenson, Brenda Joyce, Andy Devine, Fritz Feld, Ward Bond

Little Orphan Annie
US 1932 60m bw
RKO
A girl orphan charms a millionaire.
Ineffective early version of the comic strip used many years later (equally ineffectively) as the basis for Annie.
w Wanda Tuchock, Tom McNamara *d* John Robertson *ph* Jack MacKenzie *ad* Carroll Clark
☆ Mitzi Green, Edgar Kennedy, May Robson, Buster Phelps

Little Otik: see *Otesanek*

The Little Prince
US 1974 89m Technicolor
Paramount/Stanley Donen
A small boy leaves the asteroid he rules to learn of life on Earth.
A whimsical bestseller turns into an arch musical which falls over itself early on and never recovers; in any case it fatally lacks the common touch, though it has pleasing moments.
w Alan Jay Lerner *novel* Antoine de St-Exupery *d* Stanley Donen *ph* *Christopher Challis* *m/ly* Frederick Loewe, Alan Jay Lerner *pd* John Barry
☆ Richard Kiley, Steven Warner, *Bob Fosse*, Gene Wilder, Joss Ackland, Clive Revill, Victor Spinetti, Graham Crowden
'Handsome production cannot obscure limited artistic achievement.' – *Variety*
† Kiley replaced Frank Sinatra, who backed out.
title song; musical adaptation (Angela Morley, Douglas Gamley)

The Little Princess **
US 1939 93m Technicolor
TCF (Gene Markey)
In Victorian London a little girl is left at a harsh school when her father goes abroad.
One of the child star's plushest vehicles, a charming early colour film complete with dream sequence and happy ending.
w Ethel Hill, Walter Ferris *novel* Frances Hodgson Burnett *d* Walter Lang *ph* *Arthur Miller, William Skall* *md* Louis Silvers
☆ *Shirley Temple*, Richard Greene, Anita Louise, Ian Hunter, Cesar Romero, Arthur Treacher, Mary Nash, Sybil Jason, Miles Mander, Marcia Mae Jones, Beryl Mercer, E. E. Clive

A Little Princess **
US 1995 97m Technicolor
Warner/Baltimore (Mark Johnson)
An English girl is sent by her father to an exclusive New York boarding school; when he is killed in the First World War, she is reduced to working as a servant.
A charming, highly coloured version of a familiar tale, done with a touch of magic.
w Richard LaGravenese, Elizabeth Chandler *novel* Frances Hodgson Burnett *d* *Alfonso Cuaron* *ph* *Emmanuel Lubezki* *m* Patrick Doyle *pd* *Bo Welch* *ed* Steven Weisberg
☆ Eleanor Bron, Liam Cunningham, Liesel Matthews, Rusty Schwimmer, Arthur Malet, Vanessa Lee Chester, Errol Sitahal, Heather DeLoach, Taylor Fry
'An exquisite, perfectly played serious fantasy that movingly stresses the importance of magic and the imagination in the scheme of things. A classic the moment it hits the screen, this should delight audiences of all persuasions.' – *Todd McCarthy, Variety*
Emmanuel Lubezki; Bo Welch

Little Rascals
US 1994 82m DeLuxe
UIP/Amblin (Michael King, Bill Oakes)
It takes the loss of their clubhouse and go-cart for members of the He-Man Woman Haters Club to discover that girls are not so bad after all.
Redundant, cloying and long-winded revival of a series of shorts starring small kids that belonged to the early, more innocent era of cinema by a director once noted for her sharpness in dealing with today's youth; this, in contrast, is soft and fuzzy and has nothing to offer other than precociousness.
w Paul Guay, Stephen Mazur, Penelope Spheeris, Robert Wolterstorff, Mike Scott *d* Penelope Spheeris *ph* Richard Bowen *m* William Ross *pd* Larry Fulton *ed* Ross Albert
☆ Travis Tedford, Bug Hall, Brittany Ashton Holmes, Kevin Jamal Woods, Zachary Mabry, Ross Elliot Bagley, Sam Saletta, Mel Brooks, Whoopi Goldberg, Daryl Hannah, Reba McEntire
'A brainless exercise in exploitation that boasts the worst ensemble acting I have ever seen.' – *James Cameron-Wilson, Film Review*

Little Red Monkey
GB 1954 74m bw
Anglo Amalgamated/Merton Park (Alec C. Snowden)
Police and an American secret service agent protect a defecting missile expert from an assassin who has already murdered four scientists.
Based on a television serial, a soft-paced spy thriller that provides only a modicum of entertainment.
w James Eastwood, Ken Hughes *story* Eric Maschwitz *d* Ken Hughes *ph* Joseph Ambor *m* Trevor Duncan, Jack Jordan *ad* George Haslam *ed* Geoffrey Muller, Inman Hunter
☆ Richard Conte, Rona Anderson, Russell Napier, Colin Gordon, Arnold Marlé, Sylva Langova, Noel Johnson, Donald Bisset

A Little Romance
US 1979 108m Technicolor
Warner/Orion (Patrick Kelley)
A French teenager elopes with an American girl, encouraged by a garrulous old pickpocket.
Treacly juvenile romance enriched by in-jokes and an enjoyably over-the-top star performance.
w Allan Burns *novel* Patrick Cauvin *d* George Roy Hill *ph* Pierre William Glenn *m* Georges Delerue *pd* Henry Bumstead
☆ *Laurence Olivier*, Diane Lane, Thelonious Bernard, Arthur Hill, Sally Kellerman, Broderick Crawford, David Dukes
Georges Delerue
Allan Burns

A Little Sex
US 1982 94m Technicolor
Universal/MTM (Robert de Laurentiis, Bruce Paltrow)
A young husband has a wandering eye.
Very thin comedy drama more suitable for TV if it were a little less outspoken.
w Robert de Laurentiis *d* Bruce Paltrow *ph* Ralf D. Bode *m* Georges Delerue
☆ Tim Matheson, Kate Capshaw, Edward Herrmann, John Glover

Little Shop of Horrors **
US 1960 70m bw
Santa Clara (Roger Corman)
A dim flower-shop assistant nurtures a man-eating plant.
A Corman quickie, allegedly shot in two days, that is a lively, if occasionally ramshackle, comic delight with a notable cameo from Nicholson as a masochist.
w Charles B. Griffith *d* *Roger Corman* *ph* Arch Dalzell *m* Fred Katz *ad* Daniel Haller *ed* Marshall Neilan Jnr
☆ Jonathan Haze, Jack Nicholson, Jackie Joseph, Mel Welles, Myrtle Vail, Dick Miller, Leola Wendorff
'One big sick joke, but it's essentially harmless and good-natured.' – *Variety*

Little Shop of Horrors *
US 1986 88m Technicolor
Warner (David Geffen)
Workers in a flower shop are menaced by a plant with sinister intent.
Transcript of the off-Broadway musical curiously inspired by a 1960 Roger Corman horror flick which few people saw. A strange item with occasional effective moments.
w Howard Ashman *play* Howard Ashman *d* Frank Oz *ph* Robert Paynter *m* Alan Menken *pd* *Roy Walker* *ed* John Jympson, Derek Trigg, Bob Gavin
☆ Rick Moranis, Ellen Greene, Vincent Gardenia, Steve Martin
'The best movie ever made about a man-eating plant.' – *People*
song 'Mean Green Mother from Outer Space'

Little Tough Guy
US 1938 83m bw
Universal
A New York slum boy gets involved with a gang and is sent to reform school.
A development of the Dead End Kids, with attitudes not yet crystallized, the overall tone being heavy.
w Gilson Brown, Brenda Weisberg *d* Harold Young
☆ Billy Halop, Helen Parrish, Marjorie Main, Huntz Hall, Gabriel Dell, Bernard Punsley, Jackie Searl, Hally Chester
'One of the best melodramas in recent years – very nearly as good as *Dead End*, and with the same cast of boys.' – *Graham Greene*

Little Tough Guys in Society
US 1938 75m bw
Universal
A society matron invites slum boys to her mansion as a corrective for her stuffy son.
The cast makes it plain that the Dead End Kids/Little Tough Guys are now headed for comedy, the reason being that their 'serious' films were thought to set a bad example.
w Edward Eliscu, Mortimer Offner *d* Erle C. Kenton
☆ Mary Boland, Mischa Auer, Edward Everett Horton, Helen Parrish, Jackie Searl, Frankie Thomas, Billy Benedict, Hally Chester, David Gorcey

'They're not just best friends. They're blood brothers.'
The Little Vampire
GB/Germany/Netherlands 2000 95m colour
Icon/Comet/Stonewood/Avrora/Propaganda (Richard Claus)
An American boy moves to Scotland where he befriends a young vampire and his family.
Kids' film given to preaching the virtues of tolerance to misfits.
w Karey Kirkpatrick, Larry Wilson *novels* Angela Sommer-Bodenburg *d* Uli Edel *ph* Bernd Heinl *m* Nigel Clarke, Michael Csanyi-Wills *pd* Joseph Nemec III *ed* Peter R. Adam *sp* Digital Renaissance
☆ Jonathan Lipnicki (Tony Thompson), Richard E. Grant (Frederick), Jim Carter (Rookery), Alice Krige (Freda), Rollo Weeks (Rudolph), John Wood (Lord McAshton), Pamela Gidley (Dottie Thompson), Tommy Hinkley (Bob Thompson), Anna Popplewell (Anna), Dean Cook (Gregory)
'It's refreshing to see a kids' film taking on such sinister subject matter. Solid entertainment for the Goosebumps generation.' – *Lizo Mzimba, Empire*

Little Vera *
USSR 1988 134m colour
Mainline/Gorky Studios (Yuri Prober)
original title: *Malenkaya Vera*
A young woman in a grim Russian town leads a disaffected life.
With its drunken father, promiscuous daughter and nagging mother, it will bring a sense of déjà vu to anyone familiar with the British kitchen sink dramas of the 1960s.
w Mariya Khmelik *d* Vasili Pichul *ph* Yefim Reznikov *m* Vladimir Matetski *ad* Vladimir Pasternak *ed* Yelena Zabolotskaya
☆ Natalya Negoda, Ludmilla Zaitseva, Andrei Sokolov, Yuri Nazarov, Alexander Alexeyev-Negreba, Alexandra Tabakova

'Finding Your Own Voice Can Be Magic.'
Little Voice *
GB 1998 96m DeLuxe
Miramax/Scala (Elizabeth Karlsen)
A sleazy agent spots star potential in an almost mute young woman who can impersonate singers such as Judy Garland and Marlene Dietrich.
About six plots are squeezed together here – including an unlikely romance, a daughter's queasy worship of her dead father – to the benefit of none; where the film comes to life is in the scenes between Horrocks and Caine, and the finale in a tawdry club. But to enjoy that, you also have to endure the grotesqueries of Brenda Blethyn's screeching performance.
wd Mark Herman *play* *The Rise and Fall of Little Voice* by Jim Cartwright *ph* Andy Collins *m* John Altman *pd* Don Taylor *ed* Michael Ellis
☆ *Jane Horrocks, Michael Caine*, Ewan McGregor, Jim Broadbent, Brenda Blethyn, Annette Badland, Philip Jackson
'There's a full-bloodedness about the film which bludgeons you into admiration. It slaps you on the back, kicks you in the gut, dares you not to laugh and cry and leaves your subconscious reeling.' – *Andy Medhurst, Sight and Sound*
Brenda Blethyn

'They leap from the book and live!'
Little Women ***
US 1933 115m bw
RKO (David O. Selznick, Merian C. Cooper, Kenneth MacGowan)
The growing up of four sisters in pre-Civil War America.
Charming 'big picture' of its day, with excellent production and performances.
w Sarah Y. Mason, Victor Heerman *novel* Louisa May Alcott *d* *George Cukor* *ph* Henry Gerrard *m* Max Steiner
☆ *Katharine Hepburn*, Paul Lukas, Joan Bennett, Frances Dee, Jean Parker, *Spring Byington*, Edna May Oliver, Douglass Montgomery, Henry Stephenson, Samuel S. Hinds, John Lodge, Nydia Westman
'If to put a book on the screen with all the effectiveness that sympathy and good taste and careful artifice can devise is to make a fine motion picture, then *Little Women* is a fine picture.' – *James Shelley Hamilton*
'One of the most satisfactory pictures I have ever seen.' – *E. V. Lucas, Punch*
'A reminder that emotions and vitality and truth can be evoked from lavender and lace as well as from machine guns and precision dances.' – *Thornton Delehanty, New York Post*
script
best picture; George Cukor

Little Women *
US 1949 122m Technicolor
MGM (Mervyn Le Roy)
Syrupy Christmas-card remake, notably lacking the light touch.
w Andrew Solt, Sarah Y. Mason, Victor Heerman *d* Mervyn Le Roy *ph* Robert Planck, Charles Schoenbaum *m* Adolph Deutsch (after Max Steiner) *ad* Cedric Gibbons, Paul Groesse
☆ June Allyson, Elizabeth Taylor, Peter Lawford, Margaret O'Brien, Janet Leigh, Mary Astor
'It will raise a smile and draw a tear from the sentimental.' – *MFB*
art direction
cinematography

Little Women **
US 1994 118m colour
Columbia TriStar/Di Novi Pictures
Four girls grow to womanhood in 19th-century New England.
A pleasing remake with a decidedly feminist tone that occasionally lapses into oversweetness.
w Robin Swicord *novel* Louisa May Alcott *d* Gillian Armstrong *ph* Geoffrey Simpson *m* Thomas Newman *pd* Jan Roelfs *ed* Nicholas Beauman
☆ Winona Ryder, Gabriel Byrne, Trini Alvarado, Samantha Mathis, Kirsten Dunst, Claire Danes, Susan Sarandon, Eric Stoltz, John Neville, Mary Wickes
'The kind of film which, even when overlaid by the emotional goo of an often too insistent score, succeeds in preventing nausea by its sensible attention to the detail of Alcott's story.' – *Derek Malcolm, Guardian*
Winona Ryder; costume design; Thomas Newman

The Little World of Don Camillo *
France/Italy 1952 106m bw
Rizzoli-Amato-Francinex (Giuseppe Amato)
In a small Italian village the parish priest and the communist mayor are in a constant state of amiable feud.

Slightly lethargic character comedy with a mild message for its times, popular enough to warrant several sequels.
w Julien Duvivier, René Barjavel *novel* Giovanni Guareschi *d* Julien Duvivier *ph* Nicolas Hayer *m* Alessandro Cicognini
☆ Fernandel, Gino Cervi, Sylvie, Manara, Vera Talqui, Franco Interlenghi
'Cute and cosy.' – *MFB*

The Littlest Horse Thieves: see *Escape from the Dark*

The Littlest Rebel *
US 1935 70m bw
TCF (B. G. de Sylva)
A small Southern girl persuades President Lincoln to release her father.
Charming, archetypal early Temple vehicle, very well produced.
w Edwin Burke *play* Edward Peple *d* David Butler *ph* John Seitz *m* Cyril Mockridge
☆ *Shirley Temple*, John Boles, Jack Holt, Karen Morley, *Bill Robinson*, Guinn Williams, Willie Best, Frank McGlynn Snr
'Shirley Temple as the public likes her ... which means money.' – *Variety*

Live a Little, Steal a Lot
US 1974 102m CFI color
American International (Dominick Galate)
aka: *Murph the Surf*
Jewel thieves go from success to success, but the police finally force them to strike a bargain and return the gems.
Elaborate but rather unattractive caper story based on the exploits of two real criminals.
w E. Arthur Kean *story* Allan Dale Kuhn *d* Marvin Chomsky *ph* Michel Hugo *m* Philip Lambro
☆ Robert Conrad, Don Stroud, Donna Mills, Robyn Miller, Luther Adler, Paul Stewart

Live and Let Die *
GB 1973 121m Eastmancolor
UA/Eon (Harry Saltzman)
James Bond chases a black master criminal and becomes involved in West Indian Voodoo.
Standard tongue-in-cheek spy adventure with a new lightweight star and an air of déjà vu. *Professional standards high.*
w Tom Mankiewicz *novel* Ian Fleming *d* Guy Hamilton *ph* Ted Moore *m* George Martin *titles* Maurice Binder
☆ Roger Moore, Yaphet Kotto, Jane Seymour, Clifton James, David Hedison, Bernard Lee, Lois Maxwell
'Plot lines have descended further to the level of the old Saturday afternoon serial, and the treatment is more than ever like a cartoon.' – *Variety*
'A Bond movie is not made. It is packaged. Like an Almond Joy. So much coconut to this much chocolate and a dash of raisins.' – *Joseph Gelmis*
title song (m/ly Paul and Linda McCartney)

Live Flesh **
France/Spain 1997 100m colour 'Scope
El Deseo/CiBy 2000/France 3 (Agustín Almodóvar)
original title: *Carne Trémula*
In Madrid, the lives and loves of two policemen, their wives and an ex-convict, the son of a prostitute, intertwine.
Colourful, intricate, entertaining drama of love and loss, revenge and passion, moving from a time of repression to freedom.
w Pedro Almodóvar, Ray Loriga, Jorge Guerricaechevarria *novel* Ruth Rendell *d* *Pedro Almodóvar* *ph* Affonso Beato *m* Alberto Iglesias *ad* Antxon Gómez *ed* José Salcedo
☆ Javier Bardem, Francesca Neri, Liberto Rabal, Angela Molina, José Sancho, Penelope Cruz, Pilar Bardem
'Discerning viewers internationally should be impressed and entertained by the mature flow of the twisty narrative, in which earned emotion takes precedence over shock value.' – *Lisa Nesselson, Variety*

Live for Life
France/Italy 1967 130m Eastmancolor
UA/Ariane/Vides
original title: *Vivre pour Vivre*
A news reporter forsakes his wife for a fashion model.
Interminable and unoriginal romantic drama against Sunday supplement backgrounds.
w Pierre Uytterhoeven, Claude Lelouch *m* Francis Lai *d/ph* Claude Lelouch
☆ Yves Montand, Candice Bergen, Annie Girardot, Irene Tunc
'The overall effect is of *Gone with the Wind* remade by Jacopetti.' – *New Yorker*
best foreign film

The Live Ghost
US 1934 20m bw
Hal Roach
Two reluctant sailors think they have murdered one of their mates.
Somewhat unyielding material for Stan and Ollie, but still funnier than any of their rivals at the time.
w H. M. Walker *d* Charles Rogers
☆ Laurel and Hardy, Walter Long, Arthur Housman

Live, Love and Learn
US 1937 78m bw
MGM (Harry Rapf)
A bohemian painter is tamed by marriage.
Tiresome romantic trifle.
w Charles Brackett, Cyril Hume, Richard Maibaum *d* George Fitzmaurice *ph* Ray June *m* Edward Ward
☆ Robert Montgomery, Rosalind Russell, Robert Benchley, Helen Vinson, Mickey Rooney, Monty Woolley, E. E. Clive, Maude Eburne
'Mildly entertaining mixture of slapstick and drama around the theme of art vs material success.' – *Variety*

Live Now, Pay Later
GB 1962 104m bw
(Regal) Woodlands/Jay Lewis (Jack Hanbury)
A credit store salesman is himself heavily in debt, and his private life is in ruins; but even after a chapter of unexpected and tragic events he remains irrepressibly optimistic.
A satirical farce melodrama which lets fly in too many directions at once and has a cumulatively cheerless effect despite funny moments.
w Jack Trevor Story *d* Jay Lewis *ph* Jack Hildyard *m* Ron Grainer
☆ Ian Hendry, John Gregson, June Ritchie, Geoffrey Keen, Liz Fraser

Live Nude Girls
US 1995 92m colour
Republic (Cara Tapper, Steve White, Barry Bernardi)
Six women gather for the female equivalent of a stag party, and consider their various relationships.
Unenlightening drama of small talk about tiny events by an uninteresting ensemble.
wd Julianna Lavin *ph* Christopher Taylor *m* Anton Sanko *pd* Jerry Fleming *ed* Kathryn Himoff
☆ Dana Delany, Kim Cattrall, Cynthia Stevenson, Laila Robins, Lora Zane, Olivia D'Abo, Glenn Quinn, Tim Choate, Jeremy Jordan

Live Today for Tomorrow: see *An Act of Murder (1964)*

'1750 to 1! Always outnumbered! Never outfought!'
Lives of a Bengal Lancer **
US 1934 119m bw
Paramount (Louis D. Lighton)
Adventures on the North-West Frontier.
British army heroics are here taken rather solemnly, but the film is efficient and fondly remembered.
w Waldemar Young, John L. Balderston, Achmed Abdullah, Grover Jones, William Slavens McNutt *book* Francis Yeats-Brown *d* Henry Hathaway *ph* Charles Lang *m* Milan Roder *ad* Hans Dreier, Roland Anderson *ed* Ellsworth Hoagland
☆ Gary Cooper, *Franchot Tone*, *Richard Cromwell*, *Sir Guy Standing*, C. Aubrey Smith, Monte Blue, Kathleen Burke, Colin Tapley, *Douglass Dumbrille*, Akim Tamiroff, Noble Johnson
'The best army picture ever made.' – *Daily Telegraph*
best picture; script; Henry Hathaway; art direction; editing

Living: see *Ikiru*

The Living Corpse *
Germany/USSR 1928 108m (24 fps) bw silent
Prometheus/Mezhrabpomfilm
original title: *Zhivoi Trup*
An unhappy husband, whose wife loves another, tries all manner of means to give her a divorce. Refused by both church and state, he kills himself.
Heavy-going dramatic tract, photographed and directed with stirring style.
w B. Gusman, Anatoly Marienhof *play* Leo Tolstoy *d* *Fedor Ozep* *ph* *Anatoly Golovnya*
☆ *Vsevolod Pudovkin*, Maria Jacobini, V. Garden, Gustav Diessl
'One of the really few achievements of the Russian industry: a picture so gripping that it will hold any audience.' – *Variety*

The Living Daylights **
GB 1987 130m Technicolor Panavision
MGM-UA/Eon (Albert R. Broccoli, Michael G. Wilson)
James Bond helps the Soviets chase a KGB defector with sinister intent.
25th-anniversary Bond heroics with more adult style than usual, and all technical aspects up to par.
w Richard Maibaum, Michael G. Wilson *d* John Glen *ph* Alec Mills *m* John Barry *pd* Peter Lamont
☆ *Timothy Dalton*, Maryam d'Abo, Jeroen Krabbe, Joe Don Baker, John Rhys-Davies, Art Malik, Robert Brown

The Living Dead at the Manchester Morgue (dubbed) *
Spain/Italy 1974 93m Eastmancolor
Miracle/Star/Flaminia (Edmundo Amati)
original title: *Fin de Semana para los Muertos*
aka: *Don't Open the Window*
The dead are brought back to life as flesh-eating zombies by insects infected by an experimental crop-dusting machine.
An effectively creepy variation on The Night of the Living Dead, *filmed in England.*
w Sandro Continenza, Marcello Coscia *d* Jorge Grau *ph* Francisco Sempere *m* Giuliano Sorgini *pd* Carlo Leva *ed* Vincenzo Tomassi *sp* Giannetto de Rossi, Luciano Bird
☆ Ray Lovelock, Christine Galbo, Arthur Kennedy, Aldo Massasso, Giorgio Trestini, Roberto Posse
'A director with a genuine talent for the macabre mood and unsettling detail.' – *Verina Glaessner*

The Living Dead Girl *
France 1982 98m colour
ABC/Aleriaz/Du Yaka/Sam Selsky
original title: *La Morte Vivante*
Toxic waste, released by an earthquake, revives the corpse of a young woman who needs blood to survive.
Spooky movie with some original touches, including a reluctant zombie, but containing rather too much gore for most tastes.
w Jean Rollin, Jacques Ralf *d* Jean Rollin *ph* Max Monteillet *m* Philippe d'Aram *ed* Janette Kronegger *sp* Benoit Lestang
☆ Marina Pierro, Françoise Blanchard, Mike Marshall, Carina Barone, Fanny Magieri, Patricia Besnard-Rousseau, Veronique Pinson
'This has a weird feel achieved by combining pastoral visions of an idyllic French countryside with oddly-staged tableaux of blood sacrifice and monstrous innocence. Very violent but not really scary.' – *Empire*
† The British video release runs for 86m.

The Living Desert ***
US 1953 72m Technicolor
Walt Disney (James Algar)
A light-hearted documentary showing the animals and insects which live in American desert areas.
The aim is entertainment and Disney is not above faking, e.g. the famous sequence in which scorpions appear to do a square dance, but on its level the thing is brilliantly done.
w James Algar, Winston Hibler, Ted Sears *d* *James Algar* *ph* N. Paul Kenworthy Jnr, Robert H. Grandall *m* Paul Smith *special processes* Ub Iwerks
'The film has the same cosy anthropomorphism as a Disney cartoon and its facetious commentary and vulgar music score are typical of others in the series.' – *Georges Sadoul*
† The other 'True Life Adventures' were: *Seal Island* 49 (2 reels), *Beaver Valley* 50 (2 reels), *Nature's Half Acre* 51 (2 reels), *Water Birds* 52 (2 reels), *Bear Country* 53, *Prowlers of the Everglades* 53, *The Vanishing Prairie* 54, *The African Lion* 55, *Secrets of Life* 56, *White Wilderness* 58, *Jungle Cat* 60.
Documentary

'A gleeful journey of sex and violence.'
The Living End
US 1992 84m colour
Mainline/Strand Releasing/Desperate Pictures (Marcus Hu, Jon Gerrans)
Two HIV-positive homosexuals – one a drifter, the other a film critic – head for San Francisco, indulging in casual sex and slaughter along the way.
A movie that its director has defined as 'irresponsible', although deliberately unpleasant and self-pitying would seem a more accurate description.
wd Gregg Araki *ph* Gregg Araki *m* Cole Coonce *ed* Gregg Araki
☆ Mike Dytri, Craig Gilmore, Mark Finch, Mary Woronov, Johanna Went, Darcy Marta, Paul Bartel
'Mark this down as the first, worst film of a director who may improve when he empties his system of gay special pleading and camp melodramatics.' – *Nigel Andrews, Financial Times*

Living Free
GB 1972 92m colour
Columbia/Open Road/High Road (Paul Radin)
On the death of Elsa the lioness, George and Joy Adamson capture her three cubs and transfer them for their own safety to Serengeti.
Sloppy sequel to Born Free, *depending very heavily on the appeal of the cubs.*
w Millard Kaufman *d* Jack Couffer *ph* Wolfgang Suschitzky *m* Sol Kaplan
☆ Susan Hampshire, Nigel Davenport, Geoffrey Keen
† It was followed in 1999 by *To Walk With Lions*, a film about the last days of George Adamson and his wildlife preserve.

'Amazing adventures beneath the curse of the jaguar god!'
The Living Idol
Mexico/US 1956 100m Eastmancolor Cinemascope
MGM (Albert Lewin)
A Mexican girl becomes possessed by the spirit of the jaguar to whom local maidens were once sacrificed.
Pretentious but rather enjoyable highbrow hokum of the heady kind expected from this producer.
wd Albert Lewin *ph* Jack Hildyard *m* Rodolpho Halffter
☆ James Robertson Justice, Steve Forrest, Liliane Montevecchi

Living in a Big Way
US 1947 103m bw
MGM (Pandro S. Berman)
A demobbed GI finds he can't get on with his rich selfish wife and opens up a charity home for the families of war casualties.
Odd mixture of comedy, drama and a few songs and dances, not forgetting a message or two. It mostly falls flat on its face.
w Gregory La Cava, Irving Ravetch *d* Gregory La Cava *ph* Harold Rosson *m* Lennie Hayton
☆ Gene Kelly, Marie McDonald, Charles Winninger, Phyllis Thaxter, Spring Byington, Clinton Sundberg

'Meet The Film Crew From Hell! In The Looniest Movie About The Movies'
'Warning. This Film Contains Explicit Scenes of Sex, Violence And People Being Perfectly Horrid To One Another.'
'This Is No Place For Luvvies'

Living in Oblivion **
US 1995 90m colour/bw
Entertainment/JDI/Lemon Sky (Michael Griffiths, Marcus Viscidi)

A low-budget film-maker has nightmares about his current project, while dealing with an egomaniacal leading man, a temperamental cinematographer and a dwarf who objects to appearing in dream sequences.
Energetic and entertaining joke at the expense of wannabe film-makers, skewering pretentiousness while demonstrating that what happens behind the camera can be more interesting than what takes place in front of it; James LeGros provides a nice turn as an impossibly vain star – any resemblance between him and Brad Pitt, who appeared in the director's Johnny Suede *(qv), is presumably coincidental.*
wd Tom DiCillo *ph* Frank Prinzi *m* Jim Farmer *pd* Thérèse DePrez *ed* Camilla Toniolo
☆ *Steve Buscemi*, Catherine Keener, Dermot Mulroney, Danielle von Zerneck, James LeGros, Peter Dinklage
'It has a sharp, fresh feel to it: a joke that'll please not only insiders, but any movie lover.' – *Alexander Walker*

Living It Up *
US 1954 95m Technicolor
Paramount/Hal B. Wallis (Paul Jones)
A suspected victim of radium poisoning is played up by the press into a national hero.
Remake of Nothing Sacred *with Lewis as Carole Lombard; deserves a mark for cheek.*
w Jack Rose, Mel Shavelson *d* Norman Taurog *ph* Daniel Fapp *m* Walter Scharf
☆ Dean Martin, Jerry Lewis, Janet Leigh, Edward Arnold, Fred Clark, Sheree North, Sig Rumann

Living on Velvet *
US 1935 77m bw
Warner (Edward Chodorov)
A happy-go-lucky aviator changes his life style when he narrowly escapes death in a crash.
Reasonably interesting 'serious' drama of its period.
w Jerry Wald, Julius Epstein *d* Frank Borzage *ph* Sid Hickox *md* Leo F. Forbstein
☆ George Brent, Kay Francis, Warren William, Helen Lowell, Henry O'Neill, Samuel S. Hinds, Russell Hicks, Edgar Kennedy
'Three good names but doubtful of pulling above ordinary business.' – *Variety*

Living Out Loud
US 1998 93m Technicolor Panavision
Entertainment/New Line/Jersey (Danny de Vito, Michael Shamberg, Stacey Sher)

An abandoned wife makes a friend of her building's lift operator, whose wife has thrown him out.
Romantic drama about an odd couple's failure to get together, mainly because the script raises issues only to avoid working them out.
wd Richard LaGravenese *ph* John Bailey *m* George Fenton *pd* Nelson Coates *ed* Jon Gregory, Lynzee Klingman
☆ Holly Hunter, Danny de Vito, Queen Latifah, Martin Donovan, Richard Schiff, Elias Koteas
'A talky, introspective character study laced with flights of musical fantasy.' – *Janet Maslin, New York Times*
'A movie that looks as if it wants to have its cake and eat it, preferably from a highly gilded plate.' – *Derek Malcolm, Guardian*

Ljubavni Slucaj: see *The Switchboard Operator*

The Llano Kid
US 1939 70m bw
Paramount
A bandit is persuaded to impersonate the long-lost son of a wealthy Mexican family.
Uninteresting minor Western, indifferently directed.
w Wanda Tuchock *story Double-Dyed Deceiver* by O. Henry *d* Edward D. Venturini *ph* Russell Harlan *m* Victor Young *ad* Lewis J. Rachmil *ed* Sherman A. Rose
☆ Tito Guizar, Gale Sondergaard, Alan Mowbray, Jane Clayton, Emma Dunn, Minor Watson, Glenn Strange
† It was a remake of *The Texan* (qv).

'The Love Story Which Changed The Story Of An Empire!'
'The Picture The World Is Waiting For!'

Lloyd's of London **
US 1936 115m bw
TCF (Kenneth MacGowan)
A young messenger boy in the 18th century grows up to found a great insurance company.
Thoroughly well mounted, if unconvincing and slightly boring, historical charade in which the Prince of Wales, Lord Nelson, Dr Johnson and other personages make guest appearances. An archetypal prestige film of its time which also turned out to be box-office.
w Ernest Pascal, Walter Ferris *book* Curtis Kenyon *d Henry King ph Bert Glennon md* Louis Silvers *ad* William S. Darling
☆ Tyrone Power, Madeleine Carroll, George Sanders, Freddie Bartholomew, C. Aubrey Smith, Guy Standing, Virginia Field, Montagu Love, Gavin Muir, Miles Mander, Una O'Connor, E. E. Clive
'Fictional history with fine production but weak from marquee standpoint ... basically it's the story of the beginning and rise of an insurance company, and how can average audiences be asked to get excited about that?' – *Variety*
'The name of England is so freely on the characters' lips that we recognize at once an American picture. These people live, make love, bear children all from the most patriotic motives, and it's all rather like London in coronation week.' – *Graham Greene*
art direction

Lo Chiamavano Trinità: see *They Call Me Trinity*

Loaded
GB/New Zealand 1994 96m colour
Blue Dolphin/NFTC/British Screen/NZFC (David Hazlett, Caroline Hewitt, Bridget Ikin, John Maynard)

A group of schoolfriends, who travel to the country to make a horror video, panic when, after taking drugs, one of them is killed in a motorcycle accident.
Ambitious but muddled and disjointed movie of adolescent longings and power games; its point gets lost among its video voyeurisms.
wd Anna Campion *ph* Alan Almond *m* Simon Fisher Turner *pd* Alistair Kay *ed* John Gilbert
☆ Oliver Milburn, Catherine McCormack, Thandie Newton, Dearbhla Molloy, Danny Cunningham, Nick Patrick
'Talky and embarrassingly pretentious bore about 20-something angst.' – *Film Review*
† The film was shown at the 1994 Venice Film Festival as *Bloody Weekend* and given a release two years later.

Loan Shark *
US 1952 79m bw
Lippert

A detective goes undercover as a tyre worker in order to undermine a loan shark operation.
Competent co-feature with technical aspects in good shape.
w Martin Rackin, Eugene Ling *d* Seymour Friedman *ph* Joseph Biroc
☆ George Raft, Dorothy Hart, Paul Stewart, Helen Westcott, John Hoyt

Local Hero **
GB 1983 111m colour
Enigma/Goldcrest (David Puttnam)

A young American executive meets various difficulties when he is sent to a Scottish coastal village to arrange for the building of a new refinery.
Reminiscent of various Ealing comedies, especially Whisky Galore *and* The Maggie, *this ambitious comedy is really not funny enough for its great length.*
wd Bill Forsyth ph Chris Menges *m* Mark Knopfler
☆ Burt Lancaster, Peter Riegert, *Denis Lawson*, Peter Capaldi, Fulton Mackay, Jenny Seagrove
'Little in the way of obvious commercial hooks ... dominated by a constantly surprising sense of whimsicality.' – *Variety*
direction

Le Locataire: see *The Tenant*

Loch Ness
GB 1995 101m Metrocolor Panavision
Polygram/Working Title/Stephen Ujlaki (Tim Bevan)

An American scientist goes to Scotland to debunk the myth of the Loch Ness monster.
A romantic comedy that tries to get by on charm, and cannot quite manage it.
w John Fusco *d* John Henderson *ph* Clive Tickner *m* Trevor Jones *pd* Sophie Becher *ed* Jon Gregory
☆ Ted Danson, Joely Richardson, Ian Holm, Harris Yulin, James Frain, Keith Allen, Nick Brimble, Kirsty Graham, John Savident, Richard Vernon
'At its best a pleasant enough movie that more subdued, narcoleptic children might well enjoy. At its worst, it's really rather dull.' – *Bob McCabe, Empire*

'A Disgrace To Criminals Everywhere.'

Lock, Stock and Two Smoking Barrels **
GB 1998 95m colour
Polygram/Steve Tisch/SKA Films (Matthew Vaughan)

Four friends who lose everything in a rigged poker game resort to robbery in order to pay their debts.
Clever, stylish, intricately plotted black farce, enjoyable if you can surrender to its gleeful delight in murder and mayhem.
wd Guy Ritchie *ph* Tim Maurice-Jones *m* David A. Hughes, John Murphy *pd* Iain Andrews, Eve Mavrakis *ed* Niven Howie
☆ Jason Flemyng, Dexter Fletcher, Nick Moran, Jason Statham, Steven Mackintosh, Vinnie Jones, Sting, Lenny McLean, P. H. Moriarty, Steve Sweeney, Frank Harper, Stephen Marcus, Peter McNicholl
'The film has a pounding, free energy, and the swift slang of the script gives it a lightness of touch amid the threats and the bloodbaths.' – *Gaby Wood, Guardian*
† It was also released on video in 'The director's cut', which adds an extra 10 minutes of footage.
audience award

Lock Up
US 1989 109m Technicolor
Guild/White Eagle/Carolco/Gordon Company (Lawrence Gordon, Charles Gordon)

A tough prison warden tries to break the spirit of a tougher prisoner.
Nasty and sadistic, with no redeeming qualities.
w Richard Smith, Jeb Stuart, Henry Rosenbaum *d* John Flynn *ph* Donald E. Thorin *m* Bill Conti *pd* Bill Kenney *ed* Michael N. Knue, Donald Brochu
☆ Sylvester Stallone, Donald Sutherland, John Amos, Sonny Landham, Tom Sizemore, Frank McRae, Darlanne Fluegel, William Allen Young

'The restoration comedy about what cannot be restored!'

Lock Up Your Daughters
GB 1969 103m Technicolor
Columbia/Domino (David Deutsch)
In 18th-century London an aristocratic rake and various lower orders are all in search of female companionship and get their wires crossed.
Noisy, vulgar, ill-acted version (without music) of a successful musical based on two old theatrical warhorses.
w Keith Waterhouse, Willis Hall *play Rape upon Rape* by Henry Fielding and *The Relapse* by John Vanbrugh *d* Peter Coe *ph* Peter Suschitzky *m* Ron Grainer *pd* Tony Woollard
☆ Christopher Plummer, Roy Kinnear, Georgia Brown, Susannah York, Glynis Johns, Ian Bannen, Tom Bell, Elaine Taylor, Jim Dale, Kathleen Harrison, Roy Dotrice, Vanessa Howard, Fenella Fielding, Peter Bayliss, *Richard Wordsworth* and also Peter Bull, Fred Emney
'Subtlety is neither required nor displayed.' – *Jack Ibberson*

Lock Your Doors: see *The Ape Man*

The Locket
US 1946 85m bw
RKO (Bert Granet)

A *femme fatale* is bent on destroying men, and eventually we discover why.
Dark, confusing melodrama very typical of the immediate post-war years; it has little to say but says it dourly, even achieving flashbacks within flashbacks within flashbacks.
w Sheridan Gibney *d* John Brahm *ph* Nicholas Musuraca *m* Roy Webb
☆ Laraine Day, Robert Mitchum, Brian Aherne, Gene Raymond, Ricardo Cortez

'The past never lies.'

The Locusts
US 1997 124m FotoKem Panavision
Orion/MPC (Brad Krevoy, Steve Stabler, Bradley Thomas)

video title: *A Secret Sin*
In Kansas in the early 60s, a man trying to escape his past takes a job on a feed lot run by a vindictive, hard-drinking widow and her withdrawn son, who has never recovered from the suicide of his father.
Overlong, over-heated melodrama in the Southern Gothic tradition, given to obtrusive symbolism in its heady mix of sex, death, castration, impotence and incest.
wd John Patrick Kelley *ph* Phedon Papamichael *m* Carter Burwell *pd* Sherman Williams *ed* Kathryn Himoff, Erica Flaum
☆ Kate Capshaw (Delilah Ashford Potts), Jeremy Davies (Flyboy), Vince Vaughn (Clay Hewitt), Ashley Judd (Kitty), Paul Rudd (Earl), Daniel Meyer (Joel), Jessica Capshaw (Patsy)
'While this good-looking production lacks narrative economy and tends toward literary heavy-handedness, it nonetheless reps an entertaining debut driven by strongly drawn characters.' – *David Stratton, Variety*

The Lodger ***
GB 1926 84m approx (24 fps) bw silent
Gainsborough (Michael Balcon)

Subtitle: *A Story of the London Fog*
US title: *The Case of Jonathan Drew*
A modern version of the novel about a stranger who is (in this case) wrongly thought to be Jack the Ripper.
The first true Hitchcock film, full of his familiar dramatic visual touches. Oddly enough it was followed by three years during which he seemed to forget them.
w Eliot Stannard, Alfred Hitchcock *novel* Mrs Belloc Lowndes *d Alfred Hitchcock ph* Baron Ventimiglia *ed* Ivor Montagu
☆ Ivor Novello, June, Marie Ault, Arthur Chesney, Malcolm Keen
'It was the first time I exercised my style ... you might almost say it was my first picture.' – *Alfred Hitchcock, 1966*

The Lodger *
GB 1932 85m bw
Twickenham (Julius Hagen)
US title: *The Phantom Fiend*
The upstairs lodger is suspected of being Jack the Ripper...
Modernized version of a story already tackled by Hitchcock as a silent and to be done again in costume in 1944. Not bad, for a minor British film of the time.
w Ivor Novello, Miles Mander, Paul Rotha, H. Fowler Mear *novel* Mrs Belloc Lowndes *d* Maurice Elvey *ph* Stanley Blythe, Basil Emmott
☆ Ivor Novello, Elizabeth Allan, A. W. Baskcomb, Jack Hawkins, Barbara Everest, Peter Gawthorne, Kynaston Reeves
'They can make pictures in England ... the only point for discussion is why they do not make them oftener.' – *Variety*

The Lodger *
US 1944 84m bw
TCF (Robert Bassler)
1880s version of the above in which the lodger is Jack the Ripper.
Nicely mounted apart from some anachronisms, but a little dull.
w Barre Lyndon *d John Brahm ph Lucien Ballard m* Hugo Friedhofer
☆ Laird Cregar, Merle Oberon, George Sanders, Cedric Hardwicke, Sara Allgood, Aubrey Mather,

Queenie Leonard, Helena Pickard, Lumsden Hare, Frederick Worlock

'The only thing you can't have in this perfect world of total pleasure is your 30th birthday ... Logan is 29.'

Logan's Run *
US 1976 118m Metrocolor Todd-AO
MGM (Saul David)

In the future, people try to escape from a society which dooms everyone to death at thirty.
Interesting and quite exciting fantasy melodrama which mercifully moves instead of preaching.
w David Zelag Goodman novel William F. Nolan *d* Michael Anderson *ph* Ernest Laszlo *m* Jerry Goldsmith *pd* Dale Hennesy
☆ Michael York, Richard Jordan, Jenny Agutter, Roscoe Lee Browne, Farrah Fawcett-Majors, Peter Ustinov, Michael Anderson Jnr
'A science fiction film made by people who don't understand science fiction for the amusement of people who don't care one way or the other.' – *S. Frank, L. A. Panorama*
'It puts the future back two thousand years.' – *Benny Green, Punch*
Ernest Laszlo

La Loi: see *Where the Hot Wind Blows*

Lola *
France/Italy 1960 91m bw Franscope
Rome-Paris/Euro-International

A cabaret dancer in Nantes chooses between three men.
A slight romance which was much admired for its decoration and visual style, which reminded many of Max Ophuls.
wd Jacques Demy ph Raoul Coutard *m* Michel Legrand
☆ *Anouk Aimée*, Jacques Harden, Marc Michel, Elina Labourdette
'Like an adolescent's dream of romance, formed from old movies.' – *Pauline Kael, 70s*

Lola: see *Twinky (1969)*

Lola *
West Germany 1982 113m colour
Rialto-Trio (Horst Wendlandt)

A cabaret singer leads a double life.
Blue Angel country is the setting for this over-predictable fable from a director whose films always have interest.
w Peter Marthesheimer, Pea Froelich, Rainer Werner Fassbinder *d* Rainer Werner Fassbinder *ph* Xaver Schwarzenberger *m* Peer Raben *ed* Juliane Lorenz, Rainer Werner Fassbinder
☆ Barbara Sukowa, Mario Adorf, Armin Mueller-Stahl, Matthias Fuchs

Lola + Bilidikid *
Germany 1998 95m colour
Millivres/Zero/WDR/Arte (Martin Hagemann)

aka: *Lola and Billy the Kid*
In Berlin, a teenaged Turkish youth acknowledges his own homosexuality after discovering that his brother, who has been thrown out of home, has become a transvestite dancer.
A melodramatic tale of homophobia, revenge, and repression within gay culture and in the wider world, lightened by a camp sense of humour.
wd E. Kutlug Ataman *ph* Chris Squires *m* Arpad Bondy *ad* Mona Kino *ed* Ewa J. Lind
☆ Gandi Mukli (Lola), Baki Davrak (Murat), Erdal Yildiz (Bilidikid), Inge Keller (Ute), Michael Gerber (Friedrich), Hasan Ali Mete (Osman)
'By no means a cosy family film, but it is well worth watching.' – *Nick Briggs, Film Review*
† The director received death threats after the film was shown in Turkey.

Lola Montes *
France/Germany 1955 140m Eastmancolor Cinemascope
Gamma/Florida/Oska

The life of the famous courtesan and her romance with the King of Bavaria, told in diverting fragments by a circus ringmaster.
An elaborate, expensive and trickily presented historical charade which confused the public and bankrupted its production company; but the various shorter versions released didn't help.
w Max Ophüls, Annette Wademant, Franz Geiger *novel* Cécil Saint-Laurent *d Max Ophüls ph* Christian Matras *m* Georges Auric *ad* Jean d'Aubonne, Willy Schatz
☆ Martine Carol, Anton Walbrook, Peter Ustinov, Ivan Desny, Oskar Werner, Will Quadflieg
'If you want to know what form can really do for content, rush along.' – *Derek Malcolm, Guardian*

Lola Rennt: see *Run Lola Run*

Lolita **
GB 1962 152m bw
MGM/Seven Arts/AA/Anya/Transworld (James B. Harris)

A middle-aged lecturer falls for a 14-year-old girl and marries her mother to be near her.
Fitfully amusing but slightly plotted and very lengthy screen version of a sensational novel in which the heroine is only twelve, which makes a difference. The flashback introduction and various comic asides are pretentious and alienating.
w Vladimir Nabokov *novel* Vladimir Nabokov *d* Stanley Kubrick *ph* Oswald Morris *m* Nelson Riddle
☆ *James Mason, Shelley Winters*, Sue Lyon, Peter Sellers
'The director's heart is apparently elsewhere. Consequently, we face the problem without the passion, the badness without the beauty, the agony without the ecstasy.' – *Andrew Sarris*
'A diluted Blue Angel with a teenage temptress instead of a tart.' – *Stanley Kauffmann*
'So clumsily structured that you begin to wonder what was shot and then cut out, whether the beginning was intended to be the end; and it is edited in so dilatory a fashion that after the first hour, almost every scene seems to go on too long.' – *Pauline Kael*
† Before Mason was cast, Noël Coward and Laurence Olivier were sought for the role of Humbert Humbert.
Vladimir Nabokov

Lolita *
US/France 1997 137m colour
Pathé (Mario Kassar, Joel B. Michaels)

A college lecturer loves and loses a 12-year-old girl.
An unexpectedly bland remake, though it is, in outline, faithful to Nabokov's original; it fails in its depiction of the forbidden, lacking any sense of obsessional passion.
w Stephen Schiff *novel* Vladimir Nabokov *d* Adrian Lyne *ph* Howard Atherton *m* Ennio Morricone *pd* Jon Hutman *ed* Julie Monroe, David Bremner, F. Paul Benz
☆ Jeremy Irons, Melanie Griffith, Frank Langella, Dominique Swain, Suzanne Shepherd, Keith Reddin, Erin J. Dean
'Almost everything about the film testifies to Lyne's empty craftsmanship ... The truly shocking thing about his *Lolita* is its banality.' – *Richard Williams, Guardian*
'The crunch is, does this transgressive movie portray a sympathetic paedophile? The answer has to be yes.' – *Alexander Walker, London Evening Standard*
'Quite innocuous, and Lyne's finest film, for what it's worth.' – *Geoff Andrew, Time Out*
† The film failed to find a distributor in the United States; after some controversy, it was released uncut in Britain.

The Lolly Madonna War: see *Lolly Madonna XXX*

Lolly Madonna XXX
US 1973 105m Metrocolor
MGM (Rodney Carr-Smith)
GB title: *The Lolly Madonna War*
Tennessee hillbilly farmers fight over a meadow.
Violent feudin' melodrama, technically accomplished but of limited interest to non hillbillies.
w Rodney Carr-Smith, Sue Grafton *novel* Sue Grafton *d* Richard C. Sarafian *ph* Philip Lathrop *m* Fred Myrow
☆ Rod Steiger, Robert Ryan, Scott Wilson, Jeff Bridges, Season Hubley

London **
GB 1994 85m colour
BFI/Channel 4 (Keith Griffiths)

A traveller reluctantly returns to London at the urgent summons of a friend and former lover, a part-time teacher, and they explore the city, contrasting its present with its past and its missed potentialities.
An intriguing and original semi-documentary that is a voice-over narration by a sceptical, fictional observer together with an all-too-accurate portrait of a decaying and embattled place, with its freedoms restricted by the government's deliberate neglect and its dismantling of local power.
wd Patrick Keiller ph Patrick Keiller *ed* Larry Sider
☆ Paul Scofield (narrator)

London after Midnight *
US 1927 75m approx bw silent
MGM (Tod Browning)
GB title: *The Hypnotist*
A creepy house murder is solved by hypnotism, and a grinning monster proves to be a red herring.
Famous star thriller of which lamentably no prints survive; remade as Mark of the Vampire.
w Tod Browning, Waldemar Young *d* Tod Browning *ph* Merritt Gerstad
☆ *Lon Chaney*, Marceline Day, Conrad Nagel, Henry B. Walthall, Polly Moran

London Belongs to Me **
GB 1948 112m bw
GFD/Individual (Frank Launder, Sidney Gilliat)
US title: *Dulcimer Street*
A young boy is arrested on a murder charge and his boarding-house friends rally to his defence.
Unconvincing but highly entertaining sub-Dickensian comedy-drama with a rousing finish and an abundance of character roles.
w Sidney Gilliat, J. B. Williams *novel* Norman Collins *d Sidney Gilliat ph* Wilkie Cooper *m* Benjamin Frankel
☆ *Alastair Sim, Stephen Murray*, Richard Attenborough, Fay Compton, Wylie Watson, Susan Shaw, Ivy St Helier, Joyce Carey, Andrew Crawford, Eleanor Summerfield, Hugh Griffith, Gladys Henson
'Memorable for its character-drawing and for the excellence of its writing and acting.' – *Dilys Powell*

The London Blackout Murders
US 1942 58m bw
Republic
GB title: *Secret Motive*
A mild tobacconist murders people who are sabotaging the war effort.
Curious, set-bound little melodrama with an interesting lead performance.
w Curt Siodmak *d* George Sherman
☆ *John Abbott*, Mary McLeod, Lloyd Corrigan, Lester Matthews, Anita Bolster, Billy Bevan, Frederick Worlock

London by Night *
US 1937 70m bw
MGM
Apparent murders are really part of a blackmail scheme.
Reasonably intriguing mystery with good cast and atmosphere.
w George Oppenheimer *play* The Umbrella Man by Will Scott *d* William Thiele
☆ George Murphy, Rita Johnson, Leo G. Carroll, George Zucco, Virginia Field, Montagu Love, Eddie Quillan, Leonard Mudie
'Quality is there, but drawing power isn't.' – *Variety*

London Can Take It ****
GB 1940 9m bw
The Ministry of Information
Quentin Reynolds, an American war correspondent, shows Americans what the London blitz was like.
Historically significant short, credited with inclining Americans towards participation. In its own right, a brilliant job of editing and presentation.
w Quentin Reynolds *d* Harry Watt *ph* Jonah Jones, H. E. Fowle

London Kills Me
GB 1991 107m colour
Rank/Working Title/Polygram/Film Four (Tim Bevan)

A drug pusher, down on his luck, is told that he can have a job as a waiter providing he acquires a good pair of shoes.
Aimless drama of young drug addicts and hangers-on that goes nowhere slowly.
wd Hanif Kureishi *ph* Ed Lachman *m* Mark Springer, Sarah Sarhandi *pd* Stuart Walker *ed* Jon Gregory
☆ Justin Chadwick, Steven Mackintosh, Emer McCourt, Roshan Seth, Fiona Shaw, Brad Dourif, Tony Haygarth, Alun Armstrong
'The motivation is often obscure, the action is sometimes lacking in simple credibility, which is not to be blamed on the performers, and ultimately Kureishi fails to make his people interesting either as individuals or as social types. Nevertheless, he has attempted to take us into an unfamiliar subculture without making us feel that we are slumming.' – *Philip French, Observer*
'An amazing, hypnotizing, mind-bending shambles ... Photographed like a home video that has been savaged by the cat, the film is earnestly ugly and passionately shapeless.' – *Nigel Andrews, Financial Times*

London Melody
GB 1937 75m bw
GFD/Herbert Wilcox

US title: *Girls in the Street*
A diplomat falls for a dancer.
Light but rather humourless musical drama.
w Florence Tranter, Monckton Hoffe *d* Herbert Wilcox *ph* F. A. Young
☆ Anna Neagle, Tullio Carminati, Robert Douglas, Horace Hodges
'Excellent compilation of bromidial mush, beautifully produced and directed, which should satisfy.' – *Variety*

The London Nobody Knows *
GB 1967 53m Eastmancolor
Norcon/British Lion
James Mason wanders round the capital's by-ways in search of relics from former ages.
Unhurried but generally delightful documentary.
w Geoffrey Fletcher *book* Geoffrey Fletcher *d* Norman Cohen

London Town *
GB 1946 126m Technicolor
GFD/Wesley Ruggles
US title: *My Heart Goes Crazy*
An understudy finally achieves stardom thanks to his daughter's schemes.
Disastrous and expensive attempt to make a major British musical without a single new idea. Tasteless, tawdry and sluggish, but it does record for posterity four of the star's sketches.
w Elliot Paul, Siegfried Herzig, Val Guest *d* Wesley Ruggles *ph* Erwin Hillier
☆ *Sid Field*, Greta Gynt, Kay Kendall, Tessie O'Shea, Claude Hulbert, Sonnie Hale, Mary Clare, Petula Clark, Jerry Desmonde
'I can't see the point of importing an American director and giving him all the time and money in the world to play with when we can make bad musicals on our own, and quicker.' – *Richard Winnington*

The Lone Hand
US 1953 80m Technicolor
Universal-International
A quiet Western farmer is really a Pinkerton detective.
Slightly unusual Western in which the happy ending is not however in doubt.
w Joseph Hoffman *d* George Sherman *ph* Maury Gertsman *md* Joseph Gershenson
☆ Joel McCrea, Barbara Hale, Alex Nicol, Charles Drake, James Arness

The Lone Ranger
This high-minded Western character, with his black mask, his horse Silver and his Indian friend Tonto, originated (complete with 'William Tell' overture) as a 1933 radio serial in which he was played by George Seaton.
In 1938 he came to film via a Republic serial with a sequel in 1939 (see below). In 1949 Clayton

Moore brought him to TV in innumerable half-hour adventures. These eventually encouraged two feature versions; see below. Also, *The Legend of the Lone Ranger* (qv).

The Lone Ranger
US 1956 85m Warnercolor
Jack Wrather
The masked do-gooder foils a ranchers' plot to destroy an Indian reservation.
Tolerably watchable adventures.
w Herb Meadow *d* Stuart Heisler *ph* Edwin DuPar *m* David Buttolph *ed* Clarence Kolster
☆ Clayton Moore, Jay Silverheels, Lyle Bettger, Bonita Granville, Perry Lopez

The Lone Ranger and the Lost City of Gold
US 1958 81m colour
Jack Wrather
The masked rider solves murders which have been committed for a mysterious medallion.
Lively Western for kids.
w Robert Schaefer and Eric Freiwald *d* Lesley Selander *ph* Kenneth Peach *m* Les Baxter
☆ Clayton Moore, Jay Silverheels, Douglas Kennedy, Charles Watts

The Lone Rider Ambushed
US 1941 67m bw
Equity/PRC (Sigmund Neufeld)
A cowboy impersonates an outlaw in order to recover stolen bank money.
The best of the Lone Rider series, mainly owing to the gimmick of having Houston play the villain as well as the hero.
w Oliver Drake *d* Sam Newfield *ph* Jack Greenhalgh *m* Johnny Lang, Lew Porter *ad* Vin Taylor *ed* Holbrook N. Todd
☆ George Houston, Al St John, Maxine Leslie, Frank Hagney, Jack Ingham, Hal Price, Ted Adams, George Chesebro

The Lone Rider Fights Back
US 1941 64m bw
Equity/PRC (Sigmund Neufeld)
A wandering cowboy helps a rancher's niece solve the murder of her uncle.
Standard second-feature Western, with songs, fist- and gunfights and a little comedy between the action.
w Joseph O'Donnell *d* Sam Newfield *ph* Jack Greenhalgh *m* Johnny Lange, Lew Porter *ad* Vin Taylor *ed* Holbrook N. Todd
☆ George Houston, Al St John, Dorothy Short, Dennis Moore, Frank Hagney, Charles King, Frank Ellis

The Lone Rider in Ghost Town
US 1941 64m bw
PRC (Sigmund Neufeld)
A wandering cowboy rescues a mine engineer who has been kidnapped and hidden in a deserted town.
A mix of comedy, songs and a little action following the usual pattern of the Lone Rider series, in which our hero is suspected to be the bad guy, but proves his innocence by beating a confession out of the villains.
w Joe O'Donnell *d* Sam Newfield *ph* Jack Greenhalgh *m* Johnny Lange, Lew Porter *ed* Holbrook N. Todd
☆ George Houston, Al St John, Alaine Brandes, Budd Buster, Frank Hagney, Alden Chase, Reed Howes

Lone Star
US 1952 90m bw
MGM (Z. Wayne Griffin)
Andrew Jackson enlists the aid of a Texas adventurer to persuade Sam Houston to change his mind about an agreement with Mexico.
Slow-moving semi-Western, hard to follow for non-Americans. Production values quite high.
w Borden Chase, Howard Estabrook *d* Vincent Sherman *ph* Harold Rosson *m* David Buttolph
☆ Clark Gable, Ava Gardner, Lionel Barrymore, Broderick Crawford, Ed Begley, Beulah Bondi, James Burke, William Farnum, Lowell Gilmore, Moroni Olsen, Russell Simpson, William Conrad

'John Sayles invites you to return to the scene of the crime.'
Lone Star **
US 1996 135m colour Super 35
Rank/Castle Rock/Turner/Rio Dulce (R. Paul Miller, Maggie Renzi)
In a Texan border town a sheriff investigates the murder of one of his predecessors, who vanished in the mid-50s.
Engrossing, wide-ranging tale of the way in which the past and the present impinge upon the lives of a small community.
wd John Sayles *ph* Stuart Dryburgh *m* Mason Daring *pd* Dan Bishop *ed* John Sayles
☆ Chris Cooper, Elizabeth Peña, Kris Kristofferson, Matthew McConaughey, Jesse Borrego, Ron Canada, Frances McDormand, Joe Morton
'Never quites lives up, in its storytelling, to its incidental observations.' – *Adam Mars-Jones, Independent*
John Sayles (as writer)

The Lone Wolf
The jewel thief turned sleuth was created by Louis Joseph Vance and turned up in several silent films. During the talkie period several actors played Michael Lanyard; the role of his valet passed from Raymond Walburn to Eric Blore to Alan Mowbray. All the films were made for Columbia, but only the first was anything like a main feature.
1935 The Lone Wolf Returns *d* Roy William Neill with Melvyn Douglas
1938 The Lone Wolf in Paris *d* Albert S. Rogell with Francis Lederer
1939 The Lone Wolf Spy Hunt *d* Peter Godfrey with Warren William
1940 The Lone Wolf Strikes (qv)
1941 The Lone Wolf Meets a Lady (qv), The Lone Wolf Takes a Chance (qv), The Lone Wolf Keeps a Date (qv)
1941 Secrets of the Lone Wolf *d* Edward Dmytryk; WW
1943 One Dangerous Night (qv)
1943 Passport to Suez (qv)
1946 The Notorious Lone Wolf *d* D. Ross Lederman; with Gerald Mohr
1947 The Lone Wolf in London *d* Leslie Goodwins; GM
1947 The Lone Wolf in Mexico *d* D. Ross Lederman; GM
1949 The Lone Wolf and His Lady *d* John Hoffman; Ron Randell

The Lone Wolf Keeps a Date
US 1941 65m bw
Columbia
The Lone Wolf saves his stamp collection from villains and foils a kidnap plot.
Dull thriller, hampered by an overcomplex plot and rather too much broad comedy to be at all effective.
w Earl Felton, Sidney Salkow *novel* Louis Joseph Vance *d* Sidney Salkow *ph* Barney McGill *md* M. W. Stoloff *ad* Lionel Banks *ed* Richard Fantl
☆ Warren William, Frances Robinson, Bruce Bennett, Eric Blore, Thurston Hall, Jed Prouty, Fred Kelsey, Don Beddoe

Lone Wolf McQuade
US 1983 107m DeLuxe
1818/Top Kick/Orion (Yoram Ben-Ami, Steve Carver)
A tough Texas Ranger takes on horse rustlers and hijackers.
Adults-only action rubbish, disarmingly competently made.
w B. J. Nelson *d* Steve Carver *ph* Roger Shearman *m* Francesco de Masi *pd* Norm Baron *ed* Anthony Redman
☆ Chuck Norris, David Carradine, Barbara Carrera, Leon Isaac Kennedy
'A winningly ludicrous mish-mash of mayhem-movie rudiments and action-man reputations.' – *Paul Taylor, MFB*

The Lone Wolf Meets a Lady
US 1941 71m bw
Columbia
The Lone Wolf offers to help a bride when, on the eve of her society marriage, her ex-husband helps a thief steal her wedding present, a priceless diamond necklace.
Routine programmer, enlivened by the occasional line of smart dialogue.
w John Larkin, Wolfe Kaufman *story* Louis Joseph Vance *d* Sidney Salkow *ph* Henry Freulich *md* M. W. Stoloff *ad* Lionel Banks *ed* Al Clark
☆ Warren William, Eric Blore, Jean Muir, Victor Jory, Roger Pryor, Warren Hull, Thurston Hall, Georgia Caine

The Lone Wolf Strikes
US 1940 57m bw
Columbia (Fred Kohlmar)
The Lone Wolf impersonates a fence in order to recover a heiress's priceless pearl necklace and solve the murder of a friend.
One of the best of the series: a brisk and enjoyable thriller, with comic relief cut to the minimum.
w Harry Segall, Albert Duffy *story* Dalton Trumbo *d* Sidney Salkow *ph* Henry Freulich *md* M. W. Stoloff *ad* Lionel Banks *ed* Al Clark
☆ Warren William, Eric Blore, Joan Perry, Alan Baxter, Montagu Love, Robert Wilcox, Astrid Allwyn, Don Beddoe, Fred A. Kelsey

The Lone Wolf Takes a Chance
US 1941 76m bw
Columbia
Michael Lanyard, the Lone Wolf, bets a police inspector that he can stay out of trouble for 24 hours, and finds himself accused of murder and searching for a kidnapped inventor a few minutes later.
Watchable 'B' feature comedy-thriller that keeps the action and fun moving fast.
w Earl Fenton, Sidney Salkow *novel* Louis Joseph Vance *d* Sidney Salkow *ph* John Stumar *md* M. W. Stoloff *ad* Lionel Banks *ed* Viola Lawrence
☆ Warren William, Eric Blore, June Storey, Henry Wilcoxon, Don Beddoe, Thurston Hall, Lloyd Bridges

The Loneliness of the Long Distance Runner ***
GB 1962 104m bw
British Lion/Bryanston/Woodfall (Tony Richardson)
The only thing a Borstal boy does well is run, and as he trains he thinks back to his depressing life.
An unusual take on class war as a rebellious working-class delinquent takes part in a climactic race against a team of public schoolboys; interesting scenes, though, do not quite form a compelling whole.
w *Alan Sillitoe* *story* Alan Sillitoe *d* Tony Richardson *ph* Walter Lassally *m* John Addison
☆ *Tom Courtenay*, Michael Redgrave, James Bolam, Avis Bunnage, Alec McCowen, Joe Robinson, Julia Foster
Tom Courtenay

'In The Tradition Of The Great Ones!'
Lonely Are the Brave *
US 1962 107m bw Panavision
U-I/Joel (Edward Lewis)
The last of the cowboy rebels is no match for pursuit by jeep and helicopter.
A strange, sad, rather moving fable, with very good performances and action scenes, but a shade too unrelenting in its downbeat tone to become a popular classic.
w Dalton Trumbo *novel* *Brave Cowboy* by Edward Abbey *d* David Miller *ph* Philip Lathrop *m* Jerry Goldsmith
☆ *Kirk Douglas*, Walter Matthau, Gena Rowlands, Michael Kane, Carroll O'Connor, Karl Swenson, George Kennedy, Bill Raisch
'Above all a portrait to remember and cherish, alive, doomed, tragic, by Kirk Douglas.' – *Dilys Powell*

The Lonely Guy
US 1984 90m Technicolor
Universal (Arthur Hiller)
After being thrown out by his girlfriend, a writer discovers a secret society of single men.
Glossy but heavy-handed comedy, attempting satire but not succeeding in its aim.
w Ed Weinberger, Stan Daniels, Neil Simon *book* *The Lonely Guy's Book of Life* by Bruce J. Friedman *d* Arthur Hiller *ph* Victor J. Kemper *m* Jerry Goldsmith *pd* James D. Vance *ed* William Reynolds
☆ Steve Martin, Charles Grodin, Judith Ivey, Steve Lawrence, Robyn Douglass, Merv Griffin, Dr Joyce Brothers
'Generally likeable, but it makes you feel as though you were watching television.' – *Pauline Kael, New Yorker*

Lonely Hearts *
Australia 1981 95m Eastmancolor
Adams Packer Films (John B. Murray)
When his mother dies, a 50-year-old attempts to go on a belated romantic spree.
Unexpectedly amusing comedy reminiscent of a New Yorker cartoon.
w *Paul Cox, John Clarke* *d* *Paul Cox* *ph* Yuri Sokol *m* Norman Kaye
☆ Wendy Hughes, *Norman Kaye*, John Finlayson, Julia Blake, Jonathan Hardy

Lonely in America *
US 1990 96m DuArt
Arista/Apple (Tirlok Malik, Phil Katzman)
A young Indian arrives in New York to work for his uncle, and decides to strike out on his own.
Engaging comedy of an innocent abroad, with an eye for the foibles of both nationalities.
w Satyajit Joy Palit, Barry Alexander Brown, Nicholas Spencer *story* Tirlok Malik *d* Barry Alexander Brown *ph* Phil Katzman *m* Gregory Arnold *ad* Eduardo Capilla *ed* Tula Goenka
☆ Ranjit Chowdhry, Adelaide Miller, Robert Kessler, Melissa Christopher, David Toney, Franke Hughes, Anila Singh, R. Ganesh, Tirlok Malik

The Lonely Lady
US 1982 92m Technicolor
KGA Industries/Harold Robbins International
A girl graduate in Los Angeles suffers various setbacks and assaults on her way to being a film star.
Risible concoction designed to show off the non-talents of a non-star in a film financed by her husband.
w John Kershaw, Shawn Randall *novel* Harold Robbins *d* Peter Sasdy *ph* Brian West *m* Charles Calello
☆ Pia Zadora, Lloyd Bochner, Bibi Besch, Joseph Cali, Anthony Holland, Jared Martin

The Lonely Man
US 1957 87m bw Vistavision
Paramount (Pat Duggan)
An outlaw hopes to regain social recognition and contacts the son who abhors him.
Dullish psycho Western.
w Harry Essex, Robert Smith *d* Henry Levin *ph* Lionel Lindon *m* Van Cleave
☆ Jack Palance, Anthony Perkins, Elaine Aiken, Neville Brand, Lee Van Cleef, Elisha Cook Jnr, Robert Middleton

The Lonely Passion of Judith Hearne **
GB 1987 116m Fujicolour
HandMade (George Harrison, Denis O'Brien)
A middle-aged piano teacher's hopeless life in Dublin boarding houses.
Inevitably gloomy tale, intelligently crafted and with wonderfully detailed performances.
w Peter Nelson *novel* Brian Moore *d* Jack Clayton *ph* Peter Hannan *m* Georges Delerue *pd* Michael Pickwoad
☆ *Maggie Smith*, Bob Hoskins, Wendy Hiller, Marie Kean, Prunella Scales
Maggie Smith

The Lonely Woman: see *Voyage to Italy*

Lonelyhearts *
US 1958 103m bw
UA/Dore Schary
A young journalist finds himself engrossed, appalled and sickened by his work on the agony column.
Episodic, occasionally interesting but generally too vaguely liberal; an intellectual reshaping of a despairing novel. The producer as usual is well meaning but doesn't quite make it.
w Dore Schary *novel* Nathanael West *d* Vincent J. Donehue *ph* John Alton *m* Conrad Salinger

☆ Montgomery Clift, Robert Ryan, Myrna Loy, Dolores Hart, Maureen Stapleton
Maureen Stapleton

Lonesome *
US 1928 69m (24 fps) bw silent
Universal (Carl Laemmle Jnr)
Young lovers lose each other at Luna Park but later discover that they are neighbours.
Amiable exploration of the life of city workers, comparable with The Crowd *but showing a lighter touch.*
w Edward T. Lowe *d* Paul Fejos *ph* Gilbert Warrenton
☆ Glenn Tryon, Barbara Kent
† Had sound effects and some talking sequences.

Lonesome Cowboys
US 1968 105m colour
Andy Warhol Films
aka: *Andy Warhol's Lonesome Cowboys*
A gang of outlaws rides into town, where the only inhabitants are a wealthy woman, her male nurse and a transvestite sheriff.
A sort of improvised and inspired home movie, a gay Western made by city lovers who regard wide-open spaces and horses with great suspicion.
wd Paul Morrissey
☆ Viva, Taylor Mead, Tom Hompertz, Louis Waldron, Joe Dallesandro, Eric Emerson

The Long Absence: see *Une Aussi Longue Absence*

Long Ago Tomorrow: see *The Raging Moon*

The Long and the Short and the Tall *
GB 1960 105m bw
ABP/Michael Balcon
US title: *Jungle Fighters*
In Malaya during World War II a Japanese scout is captured by a British patrol.
Stark war melodrama with the emphasis on character. Vivid at the time, it now seems very routine.
w Wolf Mankowitz *play* Willis Hall *d* Leslie Norman *ph* Erwin Hillier *m* Stanley Black
☆ Laurence Harvey, Richard Todd, David McCallum, Richard Harris, Ronald Fraser, John Meillon, John Rees, Kenji Takaki

The Long Arm **
GB 1956 96m bw
Ealing (Tom Morahan)
US title: *The Third Key*
A Scotland Yard superintendent solves a series of robberies.
Good straightforward police thriller with careful detail.
w Janet Green, Robert Barr d Charles Frend *ph* Gordon Dines *m* Gerbrand Schurmann
☆ *Jack Hawkins*, Dorothy Alison, John Stratton, Michael Brooke, Geoffrey Keen, Sydney Tafler, Meredith Edwards, Ralph Truman, Ursula Howells
'A generally efficient example of popular British film-making.' – *MFB*

The Long Dark Hall
GB 1951 86m bw
British Lion/Five Oceans (Anthony Bushell)
A chorus girl is murdered and her married lover is accused.
Miserable mystery with a trick ending, most inappropriately cast.
w Nunnally Johnson, W. E. C. Fairchild *d* Anthony Bushell, Reginald Beck *ph* Wilkie Cooper *m* Benjamin Frankel
☆ Rex Harrison, Lilli Palmer, Raymond Huntley, Denis O'Dea, Anthony Bushell, Henry Longhurst, Patricia Wayne, Meriel Forbes, Brenda de Banzie, Anthony Dawson

The Long Day Closes ***
GB 1992 85m colour
Mayfair/Palace/Film Four/BFI (Olivia Stewart)
A man remembers growing up in working-class Liverpool of the mid-1950s as a solitary, movie-obsessed 11-year-old.
Remarkable, atmospheric, understated, nostalgic movie, dealing with emotional repression and the release offered by the cinema.
wd Terence Davies ph Michael Coulter md Robert Lockhart *pd Christopher Hobbs ed* William Diver
☆ Marjorie Yates, Leigh McCormack, Anthony Watson, Nicholas Lamont, Ayse Owens, Tina Malone, Jimmy Wilde, Robin Polley
'A technically elaborate, dryly witty mood piece.' – *Variety*
'A warm and oddly moving experience.' – *Empire*
'Davies' best film yet testifies to the vigour and flexibility of cinematic realisms.' – *Raymond Durgnat, Sight and Sound*

The Long Day's Dying
GB 1968 95m Techniscope
Paramount/Junction Films (Harry Fine)
Three British paratroopers in Europe are cut off from their unit and die pointlessly.
Violent, irritating anti-war film which resurrects all the clichés and makes itself unpleasant into the bargain.
w Charles Wood *novel* Alan White *d* Peter Collinson *ph* Brian Probyn *m* Malcolm Lockyer *pd* Disley Jones
☆ David Hemmings, Tom Bell, Tony Beckley, Alan Dobie
'It is typical of all that is wrong with the film that it should end on a frozen frame of a soldier in the act of dying while heavily ironic patriotic music swells on the sound track.' – *David Wilson*

Long Day's Journey into Night **
US 1962 174m bw
Ely Landau
Connecticut 1912: days in the life of an ageing actor, his drug addicted wife and their sons, one of whom is an alcoholic and the other Eugene O'Neill.
Heavy going, nicely handled, superbly acted version of a play which can be a player's triumph and certainly is here; but it still has more effect in the theatre.
w Eugene O'Neill *d Sidney Lumet ph Boris Kaufman m* André Previn *pd Richard Sylbert*
☆ *Ralph Richardson, Katharine Hepburn,* Jason Robards Jnr, *Dean Stockwell*
'Letting his players have their head, lighted miraculously so that every flicker of emotion is preserved, and pursuing them with Kaufman's unobtrusive camera, Lumet illuminates the play, line by line, and gives it all the impact of a live performance.' – *Brenda Davies*
'A very great play has been not translated to the screen but reverently put behind glass.' – *John Simon*
Katharine Hepburn

The Long Duel
GB 1967 115m Technicolor Panavision
Rank (Ken Annakin)
On the North-West Frontier in the twenties, British officers disagree about handling the natives, and one of them forms a strong regard for the native leader.
Unconvincing cut-price Indian adventure with little cohesion and less entertainment value.
w Peter Yeldham *d* Ken Annakin *ph* Jack Hildyard *m* Patrick John Scott
☆ Trevor Howard, Yul Brynner, Harry Andrews, Charlotte Rampling, Virginia North, Andrew Keir, Laurence Naismith, Maurice Denham
'The dialogue seems to have been written by a computer fed a programme of execrable films on the same theme.' – *MFB*

The Long Good Friday **
GB 1980 105m colour
Black Lion/Calendar (Barry Hanson)
A gangland boss faces violent reprisals from the competition.
Heavily melodramatic stylish updating of Scarface *in a London East End setting. A critical success despite vicious detail and IRA plot involvement.*
w Barrie Keefe d John Mackenzie *ph* Phil Meheux *m* Francis Monkman *ad* Vic Symonds *ed* Mike Taylor
☆ *Bob Hoskins* (Harold), Helen Mirren (Victoria), Dave King (Parky), Bryan Marshall (Harris), Eddie Constantine (Charlie), Stephen Davis (Tony), Paul Freeman (Colin), George Coulouris (Gus), Pierce Brosnan (First Irishman)
'Much more densely plotted and intelligently scripted than most such yarns.' – *Variety*

'Nothing says goodbye like a bullet!'
The Long Goodbye
US 1973 111m Technicolor Panavision
UA/Lions Gate (Jerry Bick)
Philip Marlowe helps an eccentric friend who is suspected of murdering his wife.
Ugly, boring travesty of a well-respected detective novel, the apparent intention being to reverse the author's attitudes completely and to substitute dullness and incomprehensibility.
w Leigh Brackett *novel* Raymond Chandler *d* Robert Altman *ph* Vilmos Zsigmond *m* John T. Williams
☆ Elliott Gould, Nina Van Pallandt, Sterling Hayden, Mark Rydell, Henry Gibson
'Altman's fragmentation bomb blows up itself rather than the myths he has said he wants to lay to rest.' – *Sight and Sound*
'The trouble is that this Marlowe is an untidy, unshaven, semi-literate dimwit slob who could not locate a missing skyscraper and who would be refused service at a hot dog stand.' – *Charles Champlin*
'A spit in the eye to a great writer.' – *Michael Billington, Illustrated London News*

The Long Gray Line *
US 1955 138m Technicolor Cinemascope
Columbia (Robert Arthur)
The career of an athletics trainer at West Point.
Dim biopic, the kind of true life yarn that Americans like, produced in the cheerful, sentimental, sparring way that John Ford likes.
w Edward Hope *book Bringing Up the Brass* by Marty Maher *d* John Ford *ph* Charles Lawton Jnr *m* George Duning *md* Morris Stoloff
☆ Tyrone Power, Maureen O'Hara, Donald Crisp, Ward Bond, Robert Francis, Betsy Palmer, Phil Carey, Harry Carey Jnr, Patrick Wayne, Sean McClory
'Its celebration of the codes and ideals of West Point vexatiously combines sentimental cosiness and a kind of religious awe.' – *Gavin Lambert*

The Long Hot Summer *
US 1958 118m Eastmancolor
Cinemascope
TCF (Jerry Wald)
Conflict arises between a Mississippi town boss and a tenant farmer.
Busy Peyton Place*-style family brawling saga with sex on the side, flabby as narrative but compulsive as character study.*
w Irving Ravetch, Harriet Frank *stories* William Faulkner *d* Martin Ritt *ph* Joseph LaShelle *m* Alex North
☆ *Orson Welles, Paul Newman,* Joanne Woodward, Tony Franciosa, Lee Remick, Angela Lansbury

Long John Silver
Australia 1953 106m Eastmancolor
Cinemascope
TI Pictures (Joseph Kaufman)
Back from Treasure Island, Silver and Hawkins plan a return visit with fresh clues to the treasure.
Cheaply produced, bitsy-piecy adventure fragments with no one to restrain the star from eye-rolling.
w Martin Rackin *d* Byron Haskin *ph* Carl Guthrie *m* David Buttolph *ed* Manuel Del Campo
☆ Robert Newton (Long John Silver), Connie Gilchrist (Purity Pinker), Kit Taylor (Jim Hawkins), Rod Taylor (Israel Hand), Eric Reiman (Trip Fenner), Syd Chambers (Ned Shill), Grant Taylor (Patch), John Brunskill (Old Stingley)

The Long Kiss Goodnight
US 1996 120m CFI color
Entertainment/New Line/Forge/Steve Tisch (Renny Harlin, Stephanie Austin, Shane Black)
With the help of a private eye, an amnesiac teacher discovers that she was once a CIA assassin and so puts her life at risk.
Daft, fast-paced thriller with the usual paranoia about government double-dealing, with only its extreme silliness to differentiate it from others of its genre.
w Shane Black *d* Renny Harlin *ph* Guillermo Navarro *m* Alan Silvestri *pd* Howard Cummings *ed* William Goldenberg
☆ Geena Davis, Samuel L. Jackson, Patrick Malahide, Craig Bierko, Brian Cox, David Morse, G. D. Spradlin
'A superbly entertaining action movie, perhaps the best of this year's many shoot-'em-ups.' – *Sight and Sound*
† The film cost around $70m, including $4m to its screenwriter, with another $25m being spent on marketing. It took some $33.8m at the US box-office.
†† Samuel L. Jackson's character originally died at the end of the film, which upset preview audiences. As a result, the ending was reshot so that he lived.

Long Live Life **
France 1984 Eastmancolor
UGC/Les Films 13/Top No. 1 (Eugene Bellin)
Police and scientists investigate after a businessman and an actress are both unable to account for a three-day absence from their homes.
Tricksy whodunnit in the shadow of the nuclear holocaust, mixing dreams and reality and with several twists in its tale.
wd Claude Lelouch ph Bernard Lutic *m* Didier Barbelivien *pd* Jacques Bufnoir *ed* Hugues Darmois, Pauline Leroy
☆ Charlotte Rampling, Michel Piccoli, Jean-Louis Trintignant, Evelyne Bouix, Charles Aznavour, Laurent Malet, Tanya Lopert, Anouk Aimee

Long Live the Lady! **
Italy 1987 106m colour
Artificial Eye/Rai Channel 1 Cinemaundici (Giampietro Bonamigo)
original title: *Lunga Vita Alla Signora!*
Six catering students go to a hotel converted from a mysterious castle to help prepare a grand banquet presided over by a spectral old lady.
Innocence and inexperience meet sophistication and tradition in a witty, deliberately ambiguous film.
wd Ermanno Olmi *ph* Maurizio Zaccaro, Ermanno Olmi *m* George Philip Telemann *ed* Giulia Ciniselli, Ermanno Olmi
☆ Marco Esposito, Simona Brandalise, Stefania Busarello, Simone Dalla Rosa, Lorenzo Paolini, Tarcisio Tosi, Marisa Abbate

The Long Long Trailer *
US 1954 96m Anscocolor
MGM (Pandro S. Berman)
A construction engineer and his bride buy a trailer for their honeymoon, and wish they hadn't.
Disaster comedy with long bright periods and the inevitable saggy bits.
w Frances Goodrich, Albert Hackett *novel* Clinton Twiss *d* Vincente Minnelli *ph* Robert Surtees *m* Adolph Deutsch
☆ Lucille Ball, Desi Arnaz, Marjorie Main, Keenan Wynn, Moroni Olsen

The Long Memory
GB 1952 96m bw
Rank/Europa (Hugh Stewart)
An ex-con, framed for a murder he did not commit, plots revenge but instead uncovers a fresh crime.
Slow and dreary melodrama set largely on a barge, never rising to anything like excitement.
w Robert Hamer, Frank Harvey *novel* Winston Clewes *d* Robert Hamer *ph* Harry Waxman *m* William Alwyn
☆ John Mills, John McCallum, Elizabeth Sellars, Geoffrey Keen

'Love that promised the world – and paid off in bullets!'
The Long Night *
US 1947 97m bw
(RKO)
A young man shoots the seducer of his sweetheart and barricades himself in a room against the police.
Good-looking but empty remake of Le Jour se Lève.
w John Wexley *story* Jacques Viot *d* Anatole Litvak *ph* Sol Polito *m* Dimitri Tiomkin
☆ Henry Fonda, Barbara Bel Geddes, Vincent Price, Ann Dvorak, Queenie Smith
'This film faithfully reproduces the letter while altering the spirit of the original almost beyond recognition.' – *MFB*
'It would be interesting to see it on a double bill with its French original. Both films clearly rate themselves as tragedies; they are merely intelligent trash. But the old one is much more

discreet with its self-pity and much more sharply edged.' – *James Agee*

'A classic of the bashful age!'
Long Pants *
US 1927 58m (24 fps) bw silent
First National/Harry Langdon
A country bumpkin has trouble in the city.
Far from the best Langdon comedy, but funny in flashes.
w Arthur Ripley *d* Frank Capra *ph* Elgin Lesley
☆ *Harry Langdon*, Gladys Brockwell, Alan Roscoe, Alma Bennett

The Long Ride Home: see *A Time for Killing*

'All the world loves an outlaw. For some damn reason they remember 'em!'
The Long Riders
US 1980 99m Technicolor
UA/Huka (Tim Zinnemann)
The story of Western outlaw brothers named Younger, Miller and James.
Well-worn territory with new-fangled violent detail. Not much of an attraction despite the gimmick of having the various anti-heroes played by real brothers.
w Bill Bryden, Steven Phillip Smith, Stacy Keach, James Keach *d* Walter Hill *ph* Ric Waite *m* Ry Cooder *pd* Jack T. Collis
☆ Stacy Keach, James Keach, David Carradine, Keith Carradine, Robert Carradine, Dennis Quaid, Randy Quaid
'A satisfying, intelligently worked-out retelling of the classic movie-Western folk romance about the James brothers.' – *New Yorker*

The Long Ships
GB/Yugoslavia 1963 126m Technirama
Columbia/Warwick/Avila (Irving Allen)
A Viking adventurer and a Moorish prince fall out over a golden bell.
Stilted medieval epic with some visual compensations but more chat than action.
w Berkely Mather, Beverley Cross *novel* Frans T. Bengtsson *d* Jack Cardiff *ph* Christopher Challis *m* Dusan Radic
☆ Richard Widmark, Sidney Poitier, Russ Tamblyn, Rosanna Schiaffino, Oscar Homolka, Colin Blakely
'To say it was disastrous is a compliment.' – *Sidney Poitier*

The Long, the Short and the Tall: see *The Long and the Short and the Tall*

'Play It to Death.'
Long Time Dead
GB 2001 93m Technicolor
UIP/Working Title/Film Council/WT◊/Midfield (James Gay-Rees)
Students, who use a ouija board at a party, summon up a fire demon, who begins to slaughter them.
Risible 'teen slasher movie, in which uninteresting people are killed by a forgettable monster.
w Eitan Arrusi, Daniel Bronzite, Chris Baker, Andy Day *d* Marcus Adams *ph* Nic Morris *m* Don Davis *pd* Alison Riva *ed* Lucia Zucchetti, Niven Howie
☆ Joe Absolom (Rob), Lara Belmon (Stella), Melanie Gutteridge (Annie), Lukas Haas (Webster), James Hillier (Spence), Alec Newman (Liam), Mel Raido (Joe), Marsha Thomason (Lucy), Tom Bell (Becker), Michael Feast (Paul Brennan)
'An unintentionally hilarious romp that makes the Hammer horror cycle look like high art.' – *Uncut*

'The love of woman in their eyes – the salt of the sea in their blood!'
The Long Voyage Home **
US 1940 104m bw
Walter Wanger
Merchant seamen on shore leave get drunk, philosophize and have adventures.
Stagey-looking but dramatically interesting amalgam of four one-act plays by Eugene O'Neill, with talent abounding.
w Dudley Nichols *d* *John Ford* *ph* Gregg Toland *m* Richard Hageman *ed* Sherman Todd
☆ John Wayne, Thomas Mitchell, Ian Hunter, Ward Bond, Barry Fitzgerald, Wilfrid Lawson, *Mildred Natwick*, John Qualen, Arthur Shields, Joe Sawyer
'One of the finest of all movies that deal with life at sea.' – *Pauline Kael, 70s*
best picture; Dudley Nichols; Gregg Toland; Richard Hageman; Sherman Todd

The Long Wait
US 1954 93m bw
UA/Parklane (Lesser Samuels)
An amnesia victim returns home to solve a murder in which he was involved.
Flatulent version of a Mickey Spillane novel, over-plotted and inadequately motivated.
w Alan Green, Lesser Samuels *d* Victor Saville *ph* Franz Planer *m* Mario Castelnuovo Tedesco
☆ Anthony Quinn, Charles Coburn, Gene Evans, Peggie Castle, Dolores Donlan

Long Weekend
Australia 1977 100m colour Panavision
Dugong Films (Colin Eggleston)
Wild life appears to gang up on a couple with marital problems who go for a camping trip to an isolated beach.
Didactic thriller, too predictable to hold anyone's interest for long.
w Everett de Roche *d* Colin Eggleston *ph* Vincent Monton *m* Michael Carlos *pd* Larry Eastwood *ed* Brian Kavanagh
☆ John Hargreaves, Briony Behets

Long Zhi Ren Zhe (dubbed) *
Hong Kong 1982 95m colour
Seasonal (Ng See Yuen)
US title: *Ninja in the Dragon's Den*
A Chinese martial-arts student defends an elderly Japanese, a former ninja, against a would-be assassin.
Narrative coherence is sacrificed for sensational fight sequences, beginning with a battle on stilts, that will excite fans of the genre, providing they can endure other moments of broad comedy.
w Ng See Yuen, Corey Yuen *d* Corey Yuen (Yuen Kwei) *ph* Ng Kwok Hao
☆ Conan Lee, Hiroyuki Sanada, Hwang Jang Lee, Tai Po, Kam Lung, Tin Chung Ho, Tin Fung

The Longest Day **
US 1962 169m bw Cinemascope
TCF (*Darryl F. Zanuck, Elmo Williams*)
A multi-faceted account of the landings in Normandy in June 1944.
Extraordinarily noisy war spectacular, enjoyable as a violent entertainment once one has caught all the threads, but emotionally unaffecting because every part is played by a star.
w Cornelius Ryan, Romain Gary, James Jones, David Pursall, Jack Seddon *book* Cornelius Ryan *d* Andrew Marton, Ken Annakin, Bernhard Wicki *ph* Henri Persin, Walter Wottitz, Pierre Levent, Jean Bourgoin *m* Maurice Jarre, Paul Anka
☆ John Wayne, Robert Mitchum, Henry Fonda, Robert Ryan, Rod Steiger, Robert Wagner, Paul Anka, Fabian, Tommy Sands, Richard Beymer, Mel Ferrer, Jeffrey Hunter, Sal Mineo, Roddy McDowall, Stuart Whitman and also Steve Forrest, Eddie Albert, Edmond O'Brien, Red Buttons, Tom Tryon, Alexander Knox, Ray Danton, Ron Randell, Richard Burton, Donald Houston, Kenneth More, Peter Lawford, Richard Todd, Leo Genn, John Gregson, Sean Connery, Michael Medwin, Leslie Phillips, Irina Demich, Bourvil, Jean-Louis Barrault, Christian Marquand, Arletty, Curt Jurgens, Paul Hartmann, Gert Frobe, Wolfgang Preiss, Peter Van Eyck, Christopher Lee, Eugene Deckers, Richard Wattis
photography
best picture

The Longest Yard
US 1974 122m Technicolor
Paramount/Long Road (Albert S. Ruddy)
GB title: *The Mean Machine*
Imprisoned for drunkenness and car theft, a football star is blackmailed into training a prison football team of hulking misfits.
Violent, meandering comedy-drama with murderous jokes but no narrative grip.
w Tracy Keenan Wynn *d* Robert Aldrich *ph* Joseph Biroc *m* Frank de Vol
☆ Burt Reynolds, Eddie Albert, Ed Lauter, Michael Conrad, Jim Hampton

The Longshot
US 1986 89m DeLuxe
Orion/Longshot (Lang Elliott)
Four disgruntled punters borrow money from a local gangster to bet on a horse that a con man has told them is a certain winner.
An also-ran of a comedy, inconsequential and witless.
w Tim Conway *d* Paul Bartel *ph* Robby Muller *m* Charles Fox *ad* Joseph M. Altadonna *ed* Adam Toomayan
☆ Tim Conway, Harvey Korman, Jack Weston, Ted Wass, Stella Stevens, Jonathan Winters, Anne Meara, George DiCenzo, Jorge Cervera

Longtime Companion *
US 1990 99m colour
Palace/Companion Productions/American Playhouse (Stan Wlodkowski)
A group of homosexuals, watching their lovers and friends dying of AIDS, decide to become actively involved in fighting the disease.
While tracing its characters' lives from the beginning to the end of the 1980s, the film avoids easy emotion and sentimentality, though it stays with the somewhat sexless affluent middle-classes who are able to articulate their concerns.
w Craig Lucas *d* Norman René *ph* Tony Jannelli *m* Greg DeBelles *pd* Andrew Jackness *ed* Katherine Wenning
☆ Stephen Caffrey, Patrick Cassidy, Brian Cousins, Bruce Davison, John Dossett, Mark Lamos, Dermot Mulroney, Mary-Louise Parker
Bruce Davison

Look Back in Anger *
GB 1959 99m bw
ABP/Woodfall (Gordon L. T. Scott)
A bad-tempered young man with a grudge against life and the government runs a market stall, lives in a squalid flat, and has an affair with his wife's best friend.
Well-made version of a play whose sheer dreariness was theatrically stimulating but in terms of film realism becomes only depressing and stupid despite competence all round. It also set shoddy standards for its many less proficient imitators.
w Nigel Kneale *play* *John Osborne* *d* Tony Richardson *ph* *Oswald Morris* *m* Chris Barber
☆ *Richard Burton*, *Mary Ure*, *Claire Bloom*, *Edith Evans*, *Gary Raymond*, Glen Byam Shaw, Phyllis Neilson-Terry, Donald Pleasence, George Devine

Look Before You Love
GB 1948 96m bw
Burnham/Rank
Romance in Rio for a girl of the embassy staff.
Abysmal romantic comedy with little of either commodity in evidence.
w Reginald Long *d* Harold Huth
☆ Margaret Lockwood, Griffith Jones, Norman Wooland, Phyllis Stanley, Michael Medwin, Maurice Denham

'The sunshine story of Broadway's glory girl!'
Look for the Silver Lining *
US 1949 106m Technicolor
Warner (William Jacobs)
The life story of twenties stage star Marilyn Miller.
Harmless musical biopic with a sense of humour.
w Phoebe and Henry Ephron, Marian Spitzer *story* Bert Kalmar, Harry Ruby *d* David Butler *ph* Peverell Marley *md* Ray Heindorf
☆ June Haver, *Ray Bolger*, *Charles Ruggles*, Gordon MacRae, Rosemary de Camp, S. Z. Sakall, Walter Catlett
Ray Heindorf

Look Up and Laugh *
GB 1935 82m bw
ATP (Basil Dean)
Market stallholders defy a big chain store.
Good star comedy with music.
w Gordon Wellesley *story* J. B. Priestley *d* Basil Dean *ph* Robert G. Martin *md* Ernest Irving
☆ Gracie Fields, Douglas Wakefield, Harry Tate, Alfred Drayton, Morris Harvey, Vivien Leigh, Robb Wilton

Look Who's Laughing
US 1941 75m bw
RKO (Allan Dwan)
See also: *Here We Go Again*
Fibber McGee and Molly act as unexpected hosts to Edgar Bergen and Charlie McCarthy.
Exploitation of radio sitcoms, acceptable at the time. With Lucille Ball.
w James V. Kern and others *d* Allan Dwan *ph* Frank Redman *m* Roy Webb

Look Who's Talking
US 1989 96m Technicolor
Columbia TriStar (Jonathan D. Krane)
A baby comments on the growing relationship between his unmarried mother and a taxi driver.
Indifferent comedy that enjoyed a great success through the novelty of adult speech and attitudes issuing from the mouth of a baby.
wd Amy Heckerling *ph* Thomas Del Ruth *m* David Kitay *ad* Reuben Freed, Graeme Murray *ed* Debra Chiate
☆ John Travolta, Kirstie Alley, Olympia Dukakis, George Segal, Abe Vigoda, Bruce Willis, Twink Caplan, Joy Boushel, Don S. Davis
'Carelessly put together, ugly to look at and mawkish and stupid in turn.' – *Derek Malcolm, Guardian*

Look Who's Talking Now
US 1993 97m colour
Columbia TriStar (Jonathan D. Krane)
A mongrel and a spoilt poodle comment on family tribulations when they are not snapping insults at each other.
Direly unamusing sequel in a series that ran out of momentum halfway through the first film; the dogs get the best lines, but even they should complain to their agents.
w Tom Ropelewski, Leslie Dixon *d* Tom Ropelewski *ph* Oliver Stapleton *m* William Ross *pd* Michael Bolton *ed* Michael A. Stevenson, Harry Hitner
☆ John Travolta, Kirstie Alley, Lysette Anthony, Olympia Dukakis, David Gallagher, Tabitha Lupien, George Segal and also the voices of Danny DeVito, Diane Keaton
'There is clearly still a collection of folk in Tinseltown insisting that a third instalment of an enjoyable one-joke movie made with no imagination, irony or flair is a really good idea ... it isn't.' – *Philip Thomas, Empire*

Look Who's Talking Too
US 1990 81m Technicolor
Columbia TriStar (Jonathan D. Krane)
Small babies comment on the disagreements between a husband and wife.
All that this sad comedy has to recommend it is the novelty of adult voices issuing from the mouths of babes, a joke that quickly outstays its welcome.
w Amy Heckerling, Neal Israel *d* Amy Heckerling *ph* Thomas Del Ruth *m* David Kitay *pd* Reuben Freed *ed* Debra Chiate
☆ John Travolta, Kirstie Alley, Olympia Dukakis, Elias Koteas, Twink Caplan and also the voices of Bruce Willis, Roseanne Barr, Damon Wayans, Mel Brooks
'Whenever Heckerling runs out of inspiration, which is every couple of minutes, she slaps an old rock 'n' roll record on the turntable and transforms the film into a music-video.' – *Philip French, Observer*

Looker
US 1981 94m colour
Warner/The Ladd Company (Howard Jeffrey)
A plastic surgeon investigates the murders of beautiful models who were his clients.
Unconvincing, paranoid science-fiction thriller about advertising.
wd Michael Crichton *ph* Paul Lohmann *m* Barry DeVorzon *pd* Dean Edward Mitzner *ed* Carl Kress
☆ Albert Finney, James Coburn, Susan Dey, Leigh Taylor-Young, Dorian Harewood, Tim Rossovich

Lookin' to Get Out
US 1982 105m colour
Lorimar/North Star/Voight-Schaffel (Robert Schaffel)
A couple of inveterate gamblers take on the Las Vegas establishment.
Fairly pleasant, mindless, quite forgettable comedy.
w Al Schwartz, Jon Voight *d* Hal Ashby *ph* Haskell Wexler *m* Johnny Mandel *pd* Robert Boyle
☆ Jon Voight, Ann-Margret, Burt Young, Bert Remsen, Jude Farese, Richard Bradford

Looking for Love
US 1964 83m Metrocolor Panavision
Joe Pasternak/MGM
A talented girl can't decide between show business and marriage.
Limp, would-be-cute romantic nonsense with poor musical numbers.
w Ruth Brooks Flippen *d* Don Weis *ph* Milton Krasner *m* George Stoll
☆ Connie Francis, Jim Hutton, Susan Oliver, Joby Baker, Barbara Nichols, Jay C. Flippen, Jesse White, Charles Lane

Looking for Mr Goodbar
US 1977 136m Metrocolor Panavision
Paramount (Freddie Fields)
A teacher of deaf children leads a sordid secret night life.
Exploitative and very boring sex melodrama which doesn't even make one believe in its central character.
wd Richard Brooks *novel* Judith Rossner *ph* William A. Fraker *m* Artie Kane *ad* Edward Carfagno
☆ Diane Keaton, Tuesday Weld, William Atherton, Richard Kiley
'Brooks has laid a windy jeremiad about permissive sex on top of fractured film syntax.' – *Judith Crist*
William A. Fraker; Tuesday Weld

'A four hundred year old work-in-progress.'
Looking for Richard **
US 1996 109m DuArt
TCF (Michael Hadge, Al Pacino)
Al Pacino investigates the problems of playing Shakespeare's Richard III with American actors, rehearses the play and films parts of it in costume.
Fascinating glimpse into an actor's preparation for a classic role, done without pretentiousness.
w Al Pacino, Frederic Kimball *play* *Richard III* by William Shakespeare *d* Al Pacino *ph* Robert Leacock, Nina Kedrem, John Kranhouse, Steve Confer *m* Howard Shore *ad* Kevin Ritter *ed* Pasquale Buba, William A. Anderson, Ned Bastille, Andre Betz
☆ Al Pacino, Penelope Allen, Harris Yulin, Alec Baldwin, Kevin Spacey, Estelle Parsons, Winona Ryder, Aidan Quinn
'This is not just a film about Shakespeare's *Richard III* – it is also a lucid and compelling adaptation of the play.' – *Geoffrey Macnab, Sight and Sound*

Looking Forward
US 1933 76m bw
MGM
A shop owner finds he must sell his property and fire valued staff.
Depression fable from Dodie Smith's play Service, *adequately mounted.*
w Bess Meredyth, H. M. Harwood *d* Clarence Brown
☆ Lewis Stone, Lionel Barrymore, Benita Hume, Elizabeth Allan, Phillips Holmes, Colin Clive

The Looking Glass War
GB 1969 107m Technicolor Panavision
Columbia/M. J. Frankovich (John Box)
The British secret service sends a young Pole into East Germany to find a top secret film.
Jaundiced spy story which aims for irony and tragedy but becomes merely verbose and irritating.
wd Frank R. Pierson *novel* John Le Carré *ph* Austin Dempster *m* Wally Stott
☆ Christopher Jones, Pia Degermark, Ralph Richardson, Anthony Hopkins, Paul Rogers, Susan George, Ray McAnally, Robert Urquhart, Maxine Audley, Anna Massey

'There are a lot of incidental pleasures, but in the final analysis they only add up to half a film.' – *Nigel Andrews*

Looking on the Bright Side *
GB 1931 81m bw
ATP (Basil Dean)
A songwriter gets ideas above his station but eventually returns to the manicurist who loves him.
Dated but lively musical which helped confirm Gracie's stardom.
w Basil Dean, Archie Pitt, Brock Williams *d* Basil Dean, Graham Cutts *ph* Robert G. Martin *md* Carroll Gibbons
☆ Gracie Fields, Richard Dolman, Julian Rose, Wyn Richmond

Loophole
GB 1980 105m colour
Brent Walker (Julian Holloway, David Korda)
A safecracker plans to rob the vault of a London bank.
Dim caper yarn which can't make its mind up how serious it means to be. As it stands, it is all very old hat and has a cop-out finish.
w Jonathan Hales *novel* Robert Pollock *d* John Quested *ph* Michael Reed *m* Lalo Schifrin
☆ Albert Finney, Martin Sheen, Susannah York, Colin Blakely, Jonathan Pryce, Robert Morley, Alfred Lynch

Loose Ankles
US 1930 66m bw
First National
A girl's inheritance will be cancelled if she is involved in scandal. Rival claimants try to ensure that she is.
Thin, amiable comedy based on a Broadway success.
w Gene Towne *play* Sam Janney *d* Ted Wilde
☆ Loretta Young, Douglas Fairbanks Jnr, Louise Fazenda, Otis Harlan, Daphne Pollard, Inez Courtney
'Will bring a chuckle to the most hard-boiled metropolite.' – *Variety*

Loose Cannons
US 1990 94m colour Panavision
TriStar (Aaron Spelling, Alan Griesman)
Two misfit cops track down a gang of killers who are attempting to recover a pornographic movie of Hitler and friends, which is to be used to discredit a German politician.
Poor, coarse-toned comedy thriller, one of the worst movies of the decade; the jokes are based on madness and violence, and Aykroyd's lunatic turns are embarrassing.
w Richard Christian Matheson, Richard Matheson, Bob Clark *d* Bob Clark *ph* Reginald H. Morris *m* Paul Zaza *pd* Harry Pottle *ed* Stan Cole
☆ Dan Aykroyd, Gene Hackman, Dom DeLuise, Ronny Cox, Nancy Travis, Paul Koslo, Dick O'Neill, Robert Prosky

Loose Connections *
GB 1983 96m colour
Umbrella/Greenpoint (Simon Perry)
Adventures on a drive to Munich.
Thin, easy-going road comedy. Pleasant enough, but no Genevieve.
w Maggie Brooks *d* Richard Eyre *ph* Clive Tickner *m* Dominic Muldowney
☆ Lindsay Duncan, Stephen Rea, Carole Harrison, Frances Low

Loot *
GB 1970 101m Eastmancolor
Performing Arts Ltd (Arthur Lewis)
A crook hides his mother's body and uses the coffin to carry the proceeds of a robbery.
Breakneck black farce which still can't move quite fast enough to cover up its bad taste, though well done by all concerned.
w Ray Galton, Alan Simpson *play* Joe Orton *d* Silvio Narizzano *ph* Austin Dempster *m* Keith Mansfield, Richard Willing-Denton *ad* Anthony Pratt
☆ Richard Attenborough, Lee Remick, Hywel Bennett, Milo O'Shea, Dick Emery

The Looters
US 1955 87m bw
Universal
A plane crashes on Pike's Peak, and rescuers fall out about whether to loot the wreckage.
Competent co-feature of its period and style.
w Richard Alan Simmons *d* Abner Biberman
☆ Rory Calhoun, Ray Danton, Thomas Gomez, Julie Adams, Frank Faylen, Rod Williams

Lord Camber's Ladies
GB 1932 80m bw
BIP
A nobleman tries to murder his way out of a romantic tangle.
Rather dull suspenser notable only for its stagey cast and the fact that Alfred Hitchcock produced it.
w Benn W. Levy, Edwin Greenwood and Gilbert Wakefield *novel* *The Case of Lady Camber* by Horace Annesley Vachell *d* Benn W. Levy
☆ Gerald du Maurier, Gertrude Lawrence, Benita Hume, Nigel Bruce, Clare Greet, A. Bromley Davenport

Lord Edgware Dies
GB 1934 81m bw
Real Art
Hercule Poirot proves that an elderly nobleman was not killed by his young wife.
Modest whodunnit: the intended series did not catch on.
w H. Fowler Mear *novel* Agatha Christie *d* Henry Edwards
☆ Austin Trevor, Jane Carr, Richard Cooper, John Turnbull, Michael Shepley

Lord Jeff
US 1938 78m bw
MGM (Frank Davis)
GB title: *The Boy from Barnardo's*
A well-brought-up boy gets into trouble and is sent under supervision to a naval school.
Adequate family film with absolutely no surprises.
w James K. McGuinness *story* Bradford Ropes, Val Burton, Endré Bohem *d* Sam Wood *ph* John Seitz *m* Edward Ward
☆ Freddie Bartholomew, Mickey Rooney, Charles Coburn, Herbert Mundin, Terry Kilburn, Gale Sondergaard, Peter Lawford

Lord Jim *
GB 1964 154m Technicolor Super Panavision
Columbia/Keep (René Dupont)
Adventures of a sailor who prowls the Far East looking for truth; he helps enslaved natives, is raped by a tribal chief, and finally sacrifices his life.
Lush and very boring farrago of miscellaneous incident, with a central character about whose fate no one can care. However, an expensive production must have its points of interest, and the belated introduction of a gentleman villain gives a little edge.
wd Richard Brooks *novel* Joseph Conrad *ph* Frederick A. Young *m* Bronislau Kaper *pd* Geoffrey Drake
☆ Peter O'Toole, *James Mason*, Eli Wallach, Paul Lukas, Jack Hawkins, Daliah Lavi, Curt Jurgens, Akim Tamiroff

Lord Love a Duck *
US 1966 105m bw
UA/Charleston (George Axelrod)
A senior Los Angeles student practises hypnotism on his girlfriend.
Rather sloppy satire on American culture and fancies, dressed up as crazy comedy; occasional laughs.
w Larry H. Johnson, George Axelrod *novel* Al Hine *d* George Axelrod *ph* Daniel Fapp *m* Neal Hefti
☆ Roddy McDowall, Tuesday Weld, Lola Albright, Ruth Gordon, Harvey Korman, Max Showalter
'The ne plus ultra of cinematic bad taste, blending in equal and unsurpassable measure vulgarity, pretentiousness, inept imitation (usually posing as parody), stupidity and such a proliferation of stomach-turning jokes as would take your average smut pedlar a lifetime to assemble.' – *John Simon*

Lord of the Flies
GB 1963 91m bw
Allen-Hogdon Productions/Two Arts (Lewis M. Allen)
After a plane crash, a party of English schoolboys are stranded on an uncharted tropical island and gradually turn savage.
Semi-professional production of a semi-poetic novel which worked well on the printed page but on screen seems crude and unconvincing.
wd Peter Brook *novel* William Golding *ph* Tom Hollyman, Gerald Feil *m* Raymond Leppard
☆ James Aubrey, Tom Chapin, Hugh Edwards, Roger Elwin, Tom Gaman

'A Classic Story of Conflict and Survival'
Lord of the Flies
US 1990 90m DeLuxe Panavision
Columbia/Castle Rock/Nelson/Jack's Camp/Signal Hill (Ross Milloy)
Boys from a US military school, survivors of an air crash on an uninhabited tropical island, revert to savagery.
Dull remake, with crude melodrama substituting for the subtle social disintegration of the original.
w Sara Schiff *novel* William Golding *d* Harry Hook *ph* Martin Fuhrer *m* Philippe Sarde *pd* Jamie Leonard *ed* Harry Hook
☆ Balthazar Getty, Chris Furth, Danuel Pipoly, Badgett Dale, Edward Taft, Andrew Taft, Bob Peck, Bill Schoppert, Michael Greene
'Individual performances mostly never rise above the semi-amateur level.' – *Variety*
'A Technicolor travel brochure in which a pack of already uncivilized kids act rough and talk dirty like children temporarily freed from the vigilance of their parents.' – *Alexander Walker, London Evening Standard*

Lord of the Rings *
US 1978 133m DeLuxe
UA/Fantasy (Saul Zaentz)
In Middle Earth the Dark Lord loses a powerful ring, and a Hobbit tries to prevent him from getting it back.
Disappointingly stolid, overlong and confused cartoon version of a modern classic which may well deserve all those adjectives. Parts of it are charming, and the method of making cartoons from film of actors photographed in the ordinary way is certainly ingenious though it denies the cartoon characters their own full richness.
w Chris Conkling, Peter S. Beagle *books* J. R. R. Tolkien *d* Ralph Bakshi *ph* Timothy Galfas *m* Leonard Rosenman
☆ Featuring the voices of Christopher Guard, John Hurt, William Squire, Michael Scholes

'The Legend Comes To Life'
The Lord of the Rings: The Fellowship Of The Ring ***
US/New Zealand 2001 178m DeLuxe Super35
Entertainment/New Line/Wingnut (Barrie M. Osborne, Peter Jackson, Fran Walsh, Tim Sanders)
A Hobbit inherits a magic ring that could enslave all the races of Middle Earth unless it is destroyed.
Epic, ambitious account that captures the essence of the first volume of Tolkien's cult novel; it is one of the few fantasy movies that powerfully conveys the conviction that it is dealing with matters of life and death.
w Fran Walsh, Philippa Boyens, Peter Jackson *d* *Peter Jackson* *ph* *Andrew Lesnie* *m* Howard Shore *pd* Grant Major *ed* *John Gilbert* *sp* Taylor/WETA Workshop *cos* Ngila Dickson, Richard Taylor
☆ Elijah Wood (Frodo Baggins), Ian McKellen (Gandalf), Liv Tyler (Arwen), Viggo Mortensen (Aragorn), Sean Astin (Sam), Cate Blanchett (Galadriel), John Rhys-Davies (Gimli), Billy Boyd (Pippin), Dominic Monaghan (Merry), Orlando Bloom (Legolas), Christopher Lee (Saruman), Hugo Weaving (Elrond), Sean Bean (Boromir), Ian Holm (Bilbo Baggins), Andy Serkis (Gollum)
'A grand, even visionary entertainment.' – *Sight & Sound*
'Looks to please the book's legions of fans with its imaginatively scrupulous rendering of the tome's characters and worlds on the screen, as well as the uninitiated with its uninterrupted flow of incident and spectacle.' – *Todd McCarthy, Variety*

Andrew Lesnie; Howard Shore; Peter Owen, Richard Taylor; visual effects (Jim Rygiel, Randall William Cook, Richard Taylor, Mark Stetson)
picture; Peter Jackson; Ian McKellen; Grant Major; Ngila Dickson, Richard Taylor; John Gilbert; sound (Christopher Boyes, Michael Semanick, Gethin Creagh, Hammond Peek); song 'May It Be' (m/l Enya, Nicky Ryan, Roma Ryan)
film; Peter Jackson; visual effects; make up/hair

'A New Power Is Rising.'

The Lord of the Rings: The Two Towers ***
US/New Zealand/Germany 2002 179m
DeLuxe 'Scope
Entertainment/New Line/Wingnut (Barrie M. Osborne, Fran Walsh, Peter Jackson)

The Fellowship of the Ring is split into three groups, each facing different dangers, as the evil Saruman launches his armies in a bid to control Middle Earth.
The narrative force slackens and fragments in this middle section of the trilogy, but the thrill of the action sequences and the sense that a world is in deadly peril make it as absorbing as the first film.
ph Andrew Lesnie *m* Howard Shore *pd* Grant Major *ed* Michael Horton, Jabez Olssen
sp Richard Taylor *cos* Ngila Dickson, Richard Taylor
☆ Elijah Wood (Frodo), Ian McKellen (Gandalf), Liv Tyler (Arwen), Viggo Mortensen (Aragorn), Sean Astin (Sam), Cate Blanchett (Galadriel), John Rhys-Davies (Gimli), Bernard Hill (Theoden), Christopher Lee (Saruman), Billy Boyd (Pippin), Dominic Monaghan (Merry), Orlando Bloom (Legolas), Hugo Weaving (Elrond), Miranda Otto (Eowyn), Brad Dourif (Wormtongue) and also Andy Serkis (Gollum)
'The most incredible accomplishment of "Towers" is that at its heart it is a transition film that lasts nearly three hours and holds the viewer's attention.' – *Elvis Mitchell, New York Times*
'Contains intense combat and fantasy horror scenes, long-haired men smoking unfeasibly long pipes, women with pointy ears, and lots and lots of interminable nerdish nonsense.' – *Peter Bradshaw, Guardian*
visual effects (Jim Rygiel, Joe Letteri, Randall William Cook, Alex Funke); sound editing (Ethan Van der Ryn, Mike Hopkins)
picture; Michael Horton; Grant Major (with Dan Hennah, Alan Lee); sound (Christopher Boyes, Michael Semanick, Michael Hedges, Hammond Peek)
Ngila Dickson, Richard Taylor; visual effects (Jim Rygiel, Joe Letteri, Randall William Cook, Alex Funke)

The Lords of Discipline
US 1982 103m Eastmancolor
Paramount (Herb Jaffe, Gabriel Katzka)

Murky goings-on at the Carolina Military Institute.
Strictly for those interested in army cadets being unpleasant to each other.
w Thomas Pope, Lloyd Fonvielle *novel* Pat Conroy *d* Franc Roddam *ph* Brian Tufano *m* Howard Blake *pd* John Graysmark *ed* Michael Ellis
☆ David Keith, Robert Prosky, G. D. Spradlin, Barbara Babcock, Michael Biehn, Rick Rossovich

The Lords of Flatbush *
US 1974 86m Technicolor
Columbia (Stephen F. Verona)

Adventures of Brooklyn street gangs.
Not quite the violent movie one might think, and interesting for its cast as well as some thoughtful passages.
w Stephen F. Verona, Martin Davidson, Gayle Glecker, Sylvester Stallone *d* Stephen F. Verona, Martin Davidson
☆ Perry King, Henry Winkler, Sylvester Stallone, Paul Mace, Susan Blakely, Maria Smith

Lorenzo's Oil **
US 1992 135m Technicolor
UIP/Universal/Kennedy Miller (Doug Mitchell, George Miller)

After they are told their young son has a fatal disease, his parents defy medical opinion to find a cure.
An inspiring true story of faith and determination, but acted and directed as an all-out emotional assault that some will find wearying before the end.
w George Miller, Nick Enright *d* George Miller *ph* John Seale *pd* Kristi Zea *ed* Richard Francis-Bruce, Marcus D'Arcy, Lee Smith
☆ Nick Nolte, *Susan Sarandon*, Peter Ustinov, Kathleen Wilhoite, Gerry Bamman, Margo Martindale, James Rebhorn, Ann Hearn, Maduka Steady, Zack O'Malley Greenburg
'As gruelling a medical case study as any audience would ever want to sit through … A one-of-a-kind film that will devastate some viewers and prove too overbearing and clinical for others, it is as obsessive and relentless as its leading characters.' – *Variety*
† Medical research released in 1993 claimed that the oil produced 'no detectable clinical improvement' in sufferers from the brain disease.
Susan Sarandon; George Miller (as writer), Nick Enright

Lorna Doone **
GB 1934 90m bw
ATP (Basil Dean)
In 1625 on Exmoor, a farmer comes to love an outlaw's daughter who proves to be in reality a kidnapped heiress.
Simple, straightforward, effective version of the famous romance, with refreshing use of exteriors.
w Dorothy Farnum, Miles Malleson, Gordon Wellesley *novel* R. D. Blackmore *d Basil Dean* *ph* Robert Martin
☆ Victoria Hopper, John Loder, Margaret Lockwood, *Roy Emerton*, Edward Rigby, Mary Clare, Roger Livesey, George Curzon, D. A. Clarke-Smith, Lawrence Hanray, Amy Veness, Eliot Makeham
'It has polish, but it lacks drama and grip.' – *Variety*

Lorna Doone
US 1951 89m Technicolor
Columbia (Edward Small)
A farmer's son falls in love with the daughter of an outlawed family who defy King Charles II by continuing to rule Exmoor from their impregnable castle..
Living up to the credits, which read 'Freely adapted from R.D. Blackmore's immortal classic of Old England', this grotesque remake treats the story like a cheap Western.
w Jesse L. Lasky Jnr, Richard Schayer *adaptation* George Bruce *d* Phil Karlson *ph* Charles Van Enger *m* George Duning *ad* Harold MacArthur *ed* Al Clark *cos* Jean Louis
☆ Barbara Hale (Lorna Doone), Richard Greene (John Ridd), Anne Howard (Annie Ridd), William Bishop (Carver Doone), Carl Benton Reid (Sir Ensor Doone), Ron Randell (Tom Faggus), Sean McClory (Charleworth Doone), Onslow Stevens (Counsellor Doone), Lester Matthews (King Charles II), John Dehner (Baron de Wichehalse), Gloria Petroff (Lorna Doone as a child)

Los Amantes del Circulo Polar: see *Lovers of the Arctic Circle*

'Dare to be different.'

Loser
US 2000 95m DeLuxe
Columbia (Amy Heckerling, Twink Caplan)

A farm boy from the MidWest finds himself ostracized at New York University.
Clumsy teen comedy that veers haphazardly between sentimentality and broad humour.
wd Amy Heckerling *ph* Rob Hahn *m* David Kitay *pd* Steven Jordan *ed* Debra Chiate
☆ Jason Biggs (Paul Tannek), Mena Suvari (Dora Diamond), Zak Orth (Adam), Tom Sadoski (Chris), Jimmi Simpson (Noah), Greg Kinnear (Prof. Edward Alcott), Dan Aykroyd (Dad)
'This tepid comedy-drama is, lamentably, aptly titled.' – *Dennis Harvey, Variety*

Loser Takes All
GB 1956 88m Eastmancolor Cinemascope
British Lion/John Stafford
An accountant and his wife are invited to Monte Carlo but the high life estranges them.
Tedious taradiddle from an unexpected quarter; not a success by any standard.
w Graham Greene *novel* Graham Greene *d* Ken Annakin *ph* Georges Périnal *m* Alessandro Cicognini
☆ Glynis Johns, Rossano Brazzi, Robert Morley, Joyce Carey, A. E. Matthews, Tony Britton, Felix Aylmer, Albert Lieven, Geoffrey Keen

Loser Takes All
GB 1990 87m Technicolor
Miramax/British Screen/Ideal Communications/BBC/Flamingo (Christine Oestreicher, Graham Easton)

aka: *Strike It Rich*
A poor accountant discovers that his gift for winning at roulette causes problems on his honeymoon.
Slick, glossy and dull drama, with none of the needed sense of romance and irony.
wd James Scott *novel* Graham Greene *ph* Robert Paynter *m* Cliff Eidelman, Shirley Walker *pd* Christopher Hobbs
☆ Robert Lindsay, Molly Ringwald, John Gielgud, Michel Blanc, Frances de la Tour, Vladek Sheybal, Marius Goring, Max Wall, Margi Clarke, Simon de la Brosse

Losing Isaiah
US 1995 106m DeLuxe
Paramount (Howard W. Koch Jnr, Naomi Foner)

A black single mother, a former drug addict, goes to the law to get back the baby she abandoned, which has been adopted by a white, middle-class couple.
A contrived drama, concentrating on racism, in which the characters are little more than cardboard cut-outs, representing a particular viewpoint; it rarely convinces.
w Naomi Foner *novel* Seth Margolis *d* Stephen Gyllenhaal *ph* Andrzej Bartkowiak *m* Mark Isham *pd* Jeannine C. Oppewall *ed* Harvey Rosenstock
☆ Jessica Lange, Halle Berry, David Strathairn, Cuba Gooding Jnr, Samuel L. Jackson, Daisy Egan, Marc John Jefferies
'Audiences will assuredly get worked up by this grimly serious, issue-oriented drama.' – *Variety*
† It was released direct to video in Britain.

Loss of Innocence: see *The Greengage Summer*

The Loss of Sexual Innocence *
GB/US 1998 106m colour
Columbia TriStar/Summit/Newmarket/Red Mullet (Mike Figgis, Annie Stewart)
A film director's childhood in Africa, his adolescence and his experiences filming in Tunisia are contrasted with the story of Adam and Eve and their expulsion from paradise.
A very personal film that does not always connect with a wider audience, though it has its moments; the links between the episodic events and the clumsily handled Bible story are tenuous at best.
wd Mike Figgis *ph* Benoit Delhomme *m* Mike Figgis *pd* Giorgio Desideri *ed* Matthew Wood
☆ Julian Sands (Nic), Saffron Burrows (Twins), Stefano Dionisi (Lucca), Jonathan Rhys Meyers (Nic, aged 16), Kelly Macdonald (Susan), Femi Ogumbanjo (Adam), Hanne Klintoe (Eve), Johanna Torrel (Nic's wife), George Moktar (Nic aged 12), John Cowey (Nic aged 5), Bernard Hill (Susan's father), Rossy de Palma (Blind woman)
'Visually exquisite, intensely personal meditation on the story of Adam and Eve.' – *Stephen Holden, New York Times*

Lost *
GB 1955 89m Technicolor
Rank (Vivian A. Cox)
US title: *Tears for Simon*
The police go on the trail of a stolen child.
Mildly effective semi-documentary police story, with good use of locations.
w Janet Green *d* Guy Green *ph* Harry Waxman *m* Benjamin Frankel
☆ David Farrar, David Knight, Julia Arnall, Anthony Oliver, Thora Hird, Eleanor Summerfield, Marjorie Rhodes, Joan Sims

Lost and Found
US 1979 105m Technicolor Panavision
Columbia/Gordon (Melvin Frank)

A widowed American professor meets an English divorcee on a skiing holiday, but after marriage they prove to be incompatible.
Unattractive romantic comedy-drama which despite capable stars degenerates into a series of wounding slanging matches.
w Melvin Frank, Jack Rose *d* Melvin Frank *ph* Douglas Slocombe *m* John Cameron *pd* Trevor Williams
☆ Glenda Jackson, George Segal, Maureen Stapleton, Paul Sorvino, John Cunningham, Hollis McLaren

Lost Angel *
US 1943 91m bw
MGM (Robert Sisk)
A lost little girl is adopted by a reporter.
Good star vehicle for the sentimentally-inclined, with solid production and casting back-up.
w Isobel Lennart *d* Roy Rowland *ph* Robert Surtees *m* Daniele Amfitheatrof
☆ *Margaret O'Brien*, James Craig, Marsha Hunt, Philip Merivale, Henry O'Neill, Donald Meek, Keenan Wynn
'A beautiful opportunity for true satire is offered and, I regret to say, thrown away. For our little Gulliver is rapidly decivilized by all the familiar bromidic palliatives: love, crooning, fairies and night clubs.' – *Richard Winnington*

Lost Angels: see *The Road Home*

Lost Boundaries *
US 1949 105m bw
Film Classics (Louis de Rochemont)
In a New Hampshire town in the forties, a beloved doctor and his wife are found to have negro blood.
Well-meaning but dramatically ineffective racial drama which meanders along allowing an occasional burst of genuine feeling to come through.
w Virginia Shaler, Eugene Ling *d* Alfred Werker *ph* William J. Miller *m* Louis Applebaum
☆ Mel Ferrer, Beatrice Pearson, Richard Hylton, Susan Douglas, Canada Lee, Grace Coppin
'It cannot be said to betray its subject, but is, rather, unequal to it.' – *Gavin Lambert*

The Lost Boys
US 1987 92m Technicolor Panavision
Warner (Harvey Bernhard)

Vampiric bikers corrupt innocent teenagers.
Wild nonsense which affronts all classes by its sheer excesses.
w Janice Fischer, James Jeremias, Jeffrey Boam *d* Joel Schumacher *ph* Michael Chapman *m* Thomas Newman *pd* Bo Welch *ed* Robert Brown
☆ Jason Patric, Corey Haim, Dianne Wiest, Barnard Hughes, Kiefer Sutherland

'Wherever their feet touched ground, a new adventure was born!'

Lost Command
US 1966 128m Technicolor Panavision
Columbia/Red Lion (Mark Robson)

Adventures of a French paratroop regiment in Indo-China and Algeria.
Anti-war war adventure; noisy but scarcely inspired.
w Nelson Gidding *novel The Centurions* by Jean Larteguy *d* Mark Robson *ph* Robert Surtees *m* Franz Waxman
☆ Anthony Quinn, Alain Delon, George Segal, Michèle Morgan, Maurice Ronet, Claudia Cardinale, Grégoire Aslan, Jean Servais

The Lost Continent *
GB 1968 98m Technicolor
Hammer (Michael Carreras)

The captain of a tramp steamer illegally carries dynamite, and he and his passengers are stranded in a weird Sargasso Sea colony run by the Spanish Inquisition.

Hilariously imaginative hokum with splendid art direction and some of the grottiest monsters on film; but memorable moments do not quite add up to a classic of the genre.
w Michael Nash *novel Uncharted Seas* by Dennis Wheatley *d* Michael Carreras *ph* Paul Beeson *m* Gerard Schurmann *ad Arthur Lawson* *sp* Robert A. Mattey, Cliff Richardson
☆ Eric Porter, Hildegarde Neff, Suzanna Leigh, Tony Beckley, Nigel Stock, Neil McCallum, Jimmy Hanley, James Cossins, Victor Maddern
'One of the most ludicrously enjoyable bad films since Salome Where She Danced.' – *MFB*

Lost Highway *
US 1996 134m CFI color
Polygram/CiBy 2000/Asymmetrical (Deepak Nayar, Tom Sternberg, Mary Sweeney)
The character of a man found guilty of murdering his wife melds with that of a garage mechanic involved with a gangster's girlfriend.
An exploration of four characters in search of each other that leaves them, and the audience, too often stranded in limbo.
w David Lynch, Barry Gifford *d* David Lynch *ph* Peter Deming *m* Angelo Badalamenti *pd* Patricia Norris *ed* Mary Sweeney
☆ Bill Pullman, Patricia Arquette, Balthazar Getty, Robert Blake, Natasha Gregson Wagner, Richard Pryor, Gary Busey, Jack Nance, Henry Rollins
'The most radical, dreamlike and complicated movie David Lynch has made.' – *Derek Malcolm, Guardian*
'Asserts an all American, suburban-Puritan belief in the idiosyncratic eyewitness and the visionary, the truth of an individual viewpoint and even of messianic derangement, while all the while conveying almost wearily that such subjectivity as idealised elsewhere has entered terminal decline.' – *Marina Warner, Sight and Sound*

Lost Honeymoon
US 1947 70m bw
Eagle-Lion
An amnesiac GI fails to remember either his wife or his young family.
Artificial comedy which the actors can't carry off.
w Joseph Fields *d* Leigh Jason
☆ Franchot Tone, Ann Richards, Tom Conway

Lost Horizon ****
US 1937 130m bw
Columbia (Frank Capra)
Escaping from a Chinese revolution, four people are kidnapped by plane and taken to an idyllic civilization in a Tibetan valley, where the weather is always kind and men are not only gentle to each other but live to a very advanced age.
Much re-cut romantic adventure which leaves out some of the emphasis of a favourite Utopian novel but stands up pretty well on its own, at least as a supreme example of Hollywood moonshine, with perfect casting, direction and music. If the design has a touch of Ziegfeld, that's Hollywood.
w Robert Riskin novel James Hilton d Frank Capra ph Joseph Walker *m Dimitri Tiomkin ad* Stephen Goosson
☆ *Ronald Colman, H. B. Warner, Thomas Mitchell, Edward Everett Horton, Sam Jaffe,* Isabel Jewell, Jane Wyatt, Margo, John Howard
'One of the most impressive of all thirties films, a splendid fantasy which, physically and emotionally, lets out all the stops.' – *John Baxter, 1968*
'One is reminded of a British critic's comment on Mary of Scotland, "the inaccuracies must have involved tremendous research".' – *Robert Stebbins*
'The best film I've seen for ages, but will somebody please tell me how they got the grand piano along a footpath on which only one person can walk at a time with rope and pickaxe and with a sheer drop of three thousand feet or so?' – *James Agate*
'If the long dull ethical sequences had been cut to the bone there would have been plenty of room for the real story: the shock of western crudity and injustice on a man returned from a more gentle and beautiful way of life.' – *Graham Greene*
† A 1943 reissue trimmed down the negative still further, to 109 minutes; but in 1979 the American Film Institute restored a print of the original length.
Stephen Goosson
best picture; Dimitri Tiomkin; H. B. Warner

'The adventure that will live forever has been transformed into spectacular musical drama!'
'Come to Shangri-La and a new world of love!'
Lost Horizon *
US 1973 143m Technicolor Panavision
Columbia/Ross Hunter
Torpid remake with a good opening followed by slabs of philosophizing dialogue and an unbroken series of tedious songs.
w Larry Kramer *d* Charles Jarrott *ph Robert Surtees m* Burt Bacharach *ad* Preston Ames *songs* Burt Bacharach, Hal David
☆ *Peter Finch,* Liv Ullmann, Sally Kellerman, *Bobby Van,* George Kennedy, Michael York, Olivia Hussey, James Shigeta, John Gielgud, Charles Boyer
'It will never play again outside of Shangri-La.' – *Les Keyser, Hollywood in the Seventies*
'Only Ross Hunter would remake a 1937 movie into a 1932 one.' – *Judith Crist*
'It can't even be enjoyed as camp.' – *Newsweek*
'The narrative has no energy, and the pauses for the pedagogic songs are so awkward that you feel the director's wheelchair needs oiling.' – *Pauline Kael*

The Lost Illusion: see *The Fallen Idol*

Lost in a Harem **
US 1944 89m bw
MGM (George Haight)
Two travelling entertainers in the Middle East get mixed up with a conniving sultan, who hypnotizes them.
Lively, well-staged romp which shows the comedians at their best and uses astute borrowings from burlesque, pantomime, and Hollywood traditions of fantasy and running jokes.
w Harry Ruskin, John Grant, Harry Crane d Charles Reisner ph Lester White *m* David Snell
☆ *Bud Abbott, Lou Costello, Douglass Dumbrille,* Marilyn Maxwell, John Conte, Jimmy Dorsey and his Orchestra

Lost in Alaska: see *Abbott and Costello Lost in Alaska*

Lost in America *
US 1985 91m Technicolor Panavision
Warner/Geffen Company (Marty Katz)
A successful couple drop out of their expensive life-style to discover that poverty has its disadvantages.
Witty demolition of yuppie attitudes to the simple life.
w Albert Brooks, Monica Johnson *d* Albert Brooks *ph* Eric Saarinen *m* Arthur B. Rubinstein *pd* Richard Sawyer *ed* David Finfer
☆ Albert Brooks, Julie Hagerty, Michael Greene, Garry K. Marshall, Maggie Roswell, Tom Tarpey

Lost in La Mancha **
GB 2002 93m colour
Optimum/Quixote Films/Low Key (Lucy Darwin)
Documentary on the disasters that beset director Terry Gilliam when attempting to make *The Man Who Killed Don Quixote.*
With a leading actor taken ill, a storm destroying the sets and jet fighters screaming overhead, this is an object lesson in how not to make a big budget feature. For those not involved the six days before the project was abandoned resemble a surreal comedy that belongs in the Monty Python canon.
wd Keith Fulton, Louis Pepe *ph* Louis Pepe *m* Miriam Cutler *ed* Jacob Bricca *animation* Chaim Bianco
☆ Jeff Bridges (Narrator), Terry Gilliam, Johnny Depp, Jean Rochefort, Bernard Bouix, Rene Cleitman, Phil Patterson, Benjamin Fernandez
'A hilarious comedy of catastrophe.' – *Alexander Walker*

Lost in Siberia *
GB/USSR 1992 108m Eastmancolor
Winstone/Spectator/Mosfilm
aka: *Zateriannyi v Sibiri*
In the late 40s an English archaeologist working on the border between Persia and Russia is accused of being a spy and sent to Siberia.
One of an unsuccessful series of co-productions with the West; this has the effect of diminishing the Russian experience of the gulags in favour of a thriller-like movie, but it has its moments.
w James Brabazon, Alexander Mitta, Valery Fried, Yuri Korotkov *d* Alexander Mitta *ph* Vladimir Shevtsik *m* Leonid Desyatnikov *ad* Valery Yurkevitch, Vatali Klimenkov *ed* Anthony Sloman, Nadezhda Veselovskaya
☆ Anthony Andrews, Yelena Mayorova, Vladimir Ilyin, Ira Mikhalyova, Yevgeni Mironov, Alexei Zharkov, Valentin Gaft, Alexander Bureyev

Lost in Space
US 1998 131m colour Panavision
New Line/Prelude/Irwin Allen (Mark W. Koch, Stephen Hopkins, Akiva Goldsman, Carla Fry)
In 2058, a family journey to another planet is sabotaged and they become lost.
Yet another doomed attempt to transfer a creaking 60s TV series to the big screen; its makers might have found a better script than the tired specimen on offer.
w Akiva Goldsman *d* Stephen Hopkins *ph* Peter Levy *m* Bruce Broughton *pd* Norman Garwood *ed* Ray Lovejoy
☆ William Hurt, Mimi Rogers, Heather Graham, Lacey Chabert, Jack Johnson, Gary Oldman, Matt LeBlanc, Jared Harris, Mark Goddard, Lennie James, Marta Kristen, June Lockhart, Edward Fox, Dick Tufeld (robot's voice)
'Plays more towards the serious with hi-tech gloomier sets and lighting and an examination of the disintegration of the family. At its core, however, the movie is stupid.' – *James E. Brooks, Film Review*
† June Lockhart played Maureen Robinson, Mark Goddard was pilot Don West, and Dick Tufeld was the robot's voice in the TV series, which ran from 1965 to 1968.

Lost in the Stars *
US 1974 114m colour
American Express/Cinevision/Ely Landua
A country priest goes to Johannesburg in search of his son, and discovers him in prison, awaiting trial for murder.
Effective treatment of a bestselling book, though it does incline towards over-earnestness.
w Alfred Hayes *novel Cry the Beloved Country* by Alan Paton *d* Daniel Mann *ph* Robert Hauser *m/ly* Kurt Weill, Maxwell Anderson *md* Alex North *pd* Jack Martin Smith *ed* Walter Hannemann
☆ Brock Peters, Melba Moore, Raymond St Jacques, Clifton Davis, Paul Rogers, Paula Kelly, John Williams

Lost in Time: see *Waxwork II: Lost in Time*

Lost in Yonkers *
US 1993 114m colour
Columbia TriStar/Rastar (Ray Stark)
aka: *Neil Simon's Lost in Yonkers*
In the early 40s, two youths go to stay with their formidable grandmother and her handicapped daughter.
Often charming version of a nostalgic Simon play, crisply acted but rather bland.
w Neil Simon *d* Martha Coolidge *ph* Johnny E. Jensen *m* Elmer Bernstein *pd* David Chapman *ed* Steven Cohen
☆ Richard Dreyfuss, Mercedes Ruehl, Irene Worth, Mike Damus, Brad Stoll, Robert Guy Miranda, Jack Laufer
'You laugh a little, you cry a little, you admire the skill with which everything is put together.' – *Caren Myers, Sight and Sound*

A Lost Lady
US 1934 71m bw
Warner
A girl falls in love with a much older man.
Empty-headed and over-familiar romantic melodrama.
w Gene Markey, Kathryn Scola *novel* Willa Cather *d* Alfred E. Green
☆ Barbara Stanwyck, Frank Morgan, Ricardo Cortez, Lyle Talbot, Philip Reed, Hobart Cavanaugh, Henry Kolker
'Lightweight in story and interesting only as a femme style display.' – *Variety*

'He crowded a lifetime into 37 suspenseful hours!'
The Lost Man
US 1969 113m Technicolor Panavision
Universal (Ernest B. Wehmeyer)
After a robbery, a crook is pursued by the police and goes into hiding.
Odd Man Out *made over as a vehicle for polemics about civil rights for blacks: too shiny, too long, too talky to have any grip.*
wd Robert Alan Aurthur *ph* Jerry Finnerman *m* Quincy Jones
☆ Sidney Poitier, Joanna Shimkus, Al Freeman Jnr, Michael Tolan, Leon Bibb, Richard Dysart, David Steinberg, Paul Winfield

'In a strange house of hate – they loved where love had never dared to live before!'
The Lost Moment *
US 1947 89m bw
Universal/Walter Wanger (Martin Gabel)
An American publisher goes to Venice to recover love letters written by a famous poet to a lady now aged 105.
Slightly absurd but memorable period drama with a guilty secret eventually coming to light, all put across with apparently deliberate artificiality.
w Leonardo Bercovici *novel The Aspern Papers* by Henry James *d* Martin Gabel *ph* Hal Mohr *m* Daniele Amfitheatrof *ad* Alexander Golitzen *ed* Milton Carruth
☆ Robert Cummings, Susan Hayward, *Agnes Moorehead,* Joan Lorring, Eduardo Ciannelli
'A compelling piece, highly stylized and very personal, with a beautifully photographed studio recreation of Venice.' – *NFT, 1973*

'Boiling passions in the burning sands!'
The Lost Patrol *
US 1934 74m bw
RKO (Cliff Reid)
A small British army group is lost in the Mesopotamian desert under Arab attack.
Much-copied adventure story of a small patrol under attack (compare Sahara, Bataan *and* The Last of the Comanches *for a start). The original now seems pretty starchy but retains moments of power.*
w Dudley Nichols story Patrol by Philip MacDonald *d John Ford ph Harold Wenstrom m* Max Steiner
☆ *Victor McLaglen, Boris Karloff,* Wallace Ford, Reginald Denny, J. M. Kerrigan, Billy Bevan, Alan Hale
'Although the running time is long, there's nothing draggy about it.' – *Variety*
† A silent British version was released in 1929, written and directed by Walter Summers for British Instructional, with Cyril McLaglen, Sam Wilkinson and Terence Collier.
Max Steiner

The Lost People
GB 1949 89m bw
GFD/Gainsborough (Gordon Wellesley)
Displaced persons gather for comfort in a disused German theatre.
Once again a very flat film has been unsuitably made from an effective piece of theatre, with all possible types present and all views represented. Not on.
w Bridget Boland *play Cockpit* by Bridget Boland *d* Bernard Knowles *ph* Jack Asher *m* John Greenwood
☆ Richard Attenborough, Mai Zetterling, Siobhan McKenna, Dennis Price, Maxwell Reed, William Hartnell, Gerard Heinz, Harcourt Williams, Marcel Poncin

'Innocence Isn't Lost. It's Taken...'
The Lost Son *
GB/France 1999 102m colour
UIP/Film Consortium/Le Studio Canal+/Scala/Ima Films (Finola Dwyer)
A French private eye, working in London, is hired to find a drug-addicted photographer, the son of a

wealthy couple, and finds himself investigating an international paedophile ring.
Tense, violent thriller that leaves too much unexplained in the motivation of its protagonist and has a final revelation that will surprise no-one.
w Eric and Margaret Leclere, Mark Mills *d* Chris Menges *ph* Barry Ackroyd *m* Goran Bregovic *pd* John Beard *ed* Pamela Power, Luc Barnier
☆ Daniel Auteuil (Xavier Lombard), Nastassja Kinski (Deborah Spitz), Katrin Cartlidge (Emily), Ciaran Hinds (Carlos), Marianne Denicourt (Nathalie), Bruce Greenwood (Friedman), Billie Whitelaw (Mrs Spitz), Cyril Shaps (Mr Spitz)

'Has all the makings of a powerful thriller. But the drama never really clicks into gear, and the thrills are fleeting.' – *Derek Elley, Variety*

'Deliver us from evil.'
Lost Souls
US 2000 97m DeLuxe
New Line/Prufrock (Nina R. Sadowsky, Meg Ryan)

A Catholic schoolteacher realises that a best-selling author is about to be possessed by the devil.
Visually interesting, but dramatically dull and predictable movie, no more than The Exorcist-lite.
w Pierce Gardner, Betsy Stahl *d* Janusz Kaminski *ph* Mauro Fiore *m* Jan Kaczmarek *pd* Garreth Stover *ed* Anne Goursaud, Andrew Mondshein *sp* Jay Riddle, Cinesite *cos* Jill Ohanneson
☆ Winona Ryder (Maya Larkin), Ben Chaplin (Peter Kelson), Sarah Wynter (Claire Van Owen), Philip Baker Hall (Father James), John Hurt (Father Lareaux), Elias Koteas (John Townsend), Brian Reddy (Father Frank), John Beasley (Mike Smythe), John Diehl (Henry Birdson), Victor Slezak (Father Thomas), Brad Greenquist (George Viznik), W. Earl Brown (William Kelson)

'He might have the best tunes, but the Devil's got the worst movie.' – *Film Review*

'Shot at only by cameras – yet falling in flames!'
The Lost Squadron *
US 1932 79m bw
RKO (David O. Selznick)

World War I pilots find work stunting for a movie studio.
Unusual comedy-drama with several points of interest.
w Herman J. Mankiewicz, Wallace Smith *d* George Archainbaud *ph* Leo Tover, Edward Cronjager *m* Max Steiner
☆ Richard Dix, Mary Astor, Erich von Stroheim, Joel McCrea, Dorothy Jordan, Hugh Herbert, Robert Armstrong

'A pretty good show ... whether it will get back what it cost is something else again.' – *Variety*

Lost Treasure of the Amazon: see *Jivaro*

'From the best-seller that was talked about in whispers!'
'The picture that dares to bare a man's soul!'
The Lost Weekend ****
US 1945 101m bw
Paramount (*Charles Brackett*)

Two days in the life of a young dipsomaniac writer.
Startlingly original on its release, this stark little drama keeps its power, especially in the scenes on New York streets and in a dipso ward. It could scarcely have been more effectively filmed.
w Charles Brackett, Billy Wilder novel Charles Jackson *d Billy Wilder ph John F. Seitz m* Miklos Rozsa *ed* Doane Harrison
☆ *Ray Milland*, Jane Wyman, Philip Terry, *Howard da Silva, Frank Faylen*

DON BIRNAM (RAY MILLAND): 'It shrinks my liver, doesn't it, Nat? It pickles my kidneys, yeah. But what does it do to my mind? It tosses the sandbags overboard so the balloon can soar. Suddenly I'm above the ordinary. I'm competent, supremely competent. I'm walking a tightrope over Niagara Falls. I'm one of the great ones. I'm Michelangelo, moulding the beard of Moses. I'm Van Gogh, painting pure sunlight. I'm Horowitz, playing the Emperor Concerto. I'm John Barrymore before the movies got him by the throat. I'm Jesse James and his two brothers – all three of 'em. I'm W. Shakespeare. And out there it's not Third Avenue any longer – it's the Nile, Nat, the Nile – and down it moves the barge of Cleopatra.'

'A reminder of what celluloid is capable of achieving when used by a good director.' – *Spectator*

'I undershtand that liquor interesh; innerish; intereshtsh are rather worried about thish film. Thatsh tough.' – *James Agee*

'Most to be admired are its impressions of bare dreadful truth: the real crowds in the real streets as the hero-victim lugs his typewriter to the pawnshop, the trains screaming overhead, the awful night as he makes his escape from the alcoholics' ward.' – *Dilys Powell*

'A distinguished film, rich in cinematic ingenuity.' – *The Times*

🏆 best picture; script; Billy Wilder (as director); Ray Milland
🎗 John F. Seitz; Miklos Rozsa; editing

'Sir Arthur Conan Doyle's Stupendous Story of Adventure and Romance.'
The Lost World **
US 1925 60m bw
First National

The irascible Professor Challenger leads an expedition to prove his claim that prehistoric creatures are still living on a remote plateau in South America.
A sensational film of its time, complete with dinosaurs, an apeman, a volcanic eruption, a forest fire and a brontosaurus running wild in the streets of London, destroying Tower Bridge. It still retains a naïve charm, as well as providing a narrative that has served as a prototype for dozens of similar films since.
novel Arthur Conan Doyle *d* Harry O. Hoyt *ph* Arthur Edeson *sp* Willis O'Brien, Ralph Hammeras, Fred Jackman
☆ Wallace Beery, Lewis Stone, Bessie Love, Lloyd Hughes, Alma Bennett, Arthur Hoyt, Margaret McWade, Bull Montana

'This has precious few touches to visual imagination to complement its wonderful monsters and stirring romance.' – *Empire*

'In the middle of the twentieth century you fall off the brink of time!'
The Lost World
US 1960 98m DeLuxe Cinemascope
TCF/Saratoga (Irwin Allen)
Professor Challenger is financed by a newspaper to confirm the report of prehistoric life on a South African plateau.
Pitiful attempt to continue the success of Journey to the Center of the Earth, *with the story idiotically modernized, unconvincing monsters, a script which inserts conventional romance and villainy, and fatal miscasting of the central part.*
w Irwin Allen, Charles Bennett *novel* Sir Arthur Conan Doyle *d* Irwin Allen *ph* Winton C. Hoch *m* Bert Shefter, Paul Sawtell
☆ Claude Rains, *Michael Rennie*, David Hedison, *Richard Haydn*, Fernando Lamas, Jill St. John, Ray Stricklyn

'Resembles nothing so much as a ride on a rundown fairground Ghost Train.' – *MFB*

The Lost World: Jurassic Park *
US 1997 134m DeLuxe
Universal/Amblin (Gerald R. Molen, Colin Wilson)

A team of experts goes to investigate how an island used as a breeding ground for the recreated dinosaurs of Jurassic Park has become a self-supporting eco-system.
The special effects are to be wondered at, as is the fact that the script is cloned from the oldest and most familiar elements of monster movies; this is a dinosaur about dinosaurs.
w David Koepp *novel* Michael Crichton *d* Steven Spielberg *ph* Janusz Kaminski *m* John Williams *pd* Rick Carter *ed* Michael Kahn *sp* Dennis Muren, Stan Winston, Randal M. Dutra, Michael Lantieri
☆ Jeff Goldblum, Julianne Moore, Pete Postlethwaite, Vince Vaughn, Vanessa Lee Chester, Arliss Howard, Richard Attenborough, Peter Stormare, Harvey Jason, Richard Schiff

'The dinosaur creations are even better than those in the first film. But underneath the technical virtuosity is a standard chase film.' – *Variety*

'This feels like the kind of sequel a master hands over to an apprentice, and you sense that although much effort was lavished on the special effects, Spielberg's interest in the story was perfunctory.' – *Roger Ebert, Chicago Sun-Times*

† The film had the biggest worldwide gross of 1997, of more than $611m. It also holds the record for the biggest opening weekend in cinema history, taking $72m at the US box-office.
🎗 visual effects

The Lottery Bride
US 1930 85m bw
Arthur Hammerstein/United Artists

A girl goes on the run when she finds herself first prize in a lottery.
Dismal operetta from the period when silent techniques were still giving way to sound.
w Horace Jackson, Howard Emmett Rogers *story* Herbert Stothart *d* Paul Stein
☆ Jeanette MacDonald, Joe E. Brown, John Garrick, ZaSu Pitts

'One of the worst of the really very bad features released since sound.' – *Variety*

Lottery Lover
US 1935 80m bw
Fox
A shy sailor wins a lottery prize, an introduction to a Folies Bergère star, but falls in love with the public relations girl organizing the stunt.
Faded romantic comedy of little surviving interest.
w Sig Herzig *d* William Thiele
☆ Lew Ayres, Reginald Denny, Pat Paterson, Sterling Holloway

The Loudest Whisper: see *The Children's Hour*

Louisa *
US 1950 90m bw
Universal-International
A much-married man finds that both his daughter and his mother have boyfriend trouble.
Friendly generation gap comedy with practised talent.
w Stanley Roberts *d* Alexander Hall *ph* Maury Gertsman *m* Frank Skinner *ad* Robert Boyle, Bernard Herzbrun *ed* Milton Carruth
☆ Ronald Reagan, Spring Byington, Charles Coburn, Ruth Hussey, Edmund Gwenn, Piper Laurie, Scotty Beckett

Louise *
France 1939 99m bw
European Film Distributors
A seamstress is rescued from a life of shame.
Ill-advised venture into film opera for an American star.
w Steve Passeur *opera* Gustave Charpentier *d* Abel Gance
☆ Grace Moore, Georges Thill, André Pernet

'Tedious and unconvincing.' – *Variety*

'Visually and dramatically it is one of the funniest films to be seen in London. It is all bacchanalia among the blossoms and situations whose grotesqueness is deliciously enhanced by the personality of the distinguished singer. Oh, the tiptoeings of Miss Moore, the sedate coquetry, the little trills and carollings, and the great stony teeth.' – *Graham Greene*

Louisiana
US 1947 82m bw
Lindsley Parsons/Monogram
A poor singing farmer becomes governor.
Musical biopic of only historical interest.
w Jack de Witt *d* Phil Karlson
☆ Jimmie Davis, Margaret Lindsay, John Gallaudet, Freddie Stewart

Louisiana Purchase *
US 1941 98m Technicolor
Paramount (Harold Wilson)
Efforts are made to compromise a politician.
Quite lively transcription of a Broadway musical success with elements of political satire including a climactic filibuster scene.
w Jerome Chodorov, Joseph Fields *play* Morrie Ryskind *d* Irving Cummings *ph* Harry Hallenberger, Ray Rennahan *ad* Raoul Pene du Bois *songs* Irving Berlin
☆ *Bob Hope*, Vera Zorina, *Victor Moore*, Irene Bordoni, Dona Drake, Raymond Walburn, Maxie Rosenbloom, Frank Albertson, Donald MacBride, Andrew Tombes
🎗 Harry Hallenberger, Ray Rennahan; Raoul Pene du Bois

Louisiana Story *
US 1948 77m bw
Standard Oil Company (Robert Flaherty)

In the Louisiana bayous a young native boy watches as oil drillers make a strike.
Quite beautiful but over-extended semi-documentary.
w Robert and Frances Flaherty *d* Robert Flaherty *ph* Richard Leacock *m* Virgil Thomson *ed* Helen Van Dongen
☆ Joseph Boudreaux, Lionel Leblanc, Frank Hardy

'The film will be remembered, not for its content, but for the sustained beauty of photography and music, harmonised in shots recalling the delicacy of Chinese landscape painting.' – *Campbell Dixon*

🎗 original story

Loulou
France 1980 105m Eastmancolor
Gaumont/Action Films

A smart young business woman sets up an uneasy menage with a working-class layabout.
Curious but not particularly interesting character study, watchable mainly for its detail.
w Arlette Langmann *d* Maurice Pialat *ph* Pierre-William Glenn, Jacques Loiseleux *md* Philippe Sarde
☆ Isabelle Huppert, Gérard Depardieu, Guy Marchand, Humbert Balsan

The Lovable Cheat
US 1949 79m bw
Film Classics/Skyline (Edward Lewis, Richard Oswald)

A bankrupt merchant tries to keep the bailiffs at bay by hurriedly finding a rich husband for his daughter.
A stolid, stagey treatment that lacks cinematic flair and humour.
w Edward Lewis, Richard Oswald *play* Mercadet Le Faiseur by Honoré de Balzac *d* Richard Oswald *ph* Paul Wano *m* Karl Hajos *ad* Boris Leven *ed* Douglas Bagier
☆ Charlie Ruggles, Peggy Ann Garner, Buster Keaton, Curt Bois, Richard Ney, Alan Mowbray, Iris Adrian, Fritz Feld, Ludwig Donath

'Caught in the swirl of passions and sacrifice!'
Love *
US 1927 82m (24 fps) bw silent
MGM (Edmund Goulding)

Anna Karenina leaves her husband and child for Count Vronsky.
Marginally interesting first shot at a famous subject by a star who came back to it in 1935.
w Frances Marion, Lorna Moon *novel* Leo Tolstoy *d* Edmund Goulding *ph* William Daniels *m* Ernst Luz *ad* Cedric Gibbons, Alexander Toluboff
☆ Greta Garbo, John Gilbert, Brandon Hurst, Philippe de Lacy, George Fawcett, Emily Fitzroy
† An alternative happy ending was provided for exhibitors who wanted it.

Love Affair
US 1932 68m bw
Columbia
An heiress falls for a flying instructor.
Mild romantic comedy drama.
w Jo Swerling *story* Ursula Parrott *d* Thornton Freeland *ph* Ted Tetzlaff
☆ Dorothy Mackaill, Humphrey Bogart, Jack Kennedy, Astrid Allwyn, Halliwell Hobbes, Barbara Leonard

'A neighbourhood operation, that's about its worth.' – *Variety*

Love Affair ***
US 1939 89m bw
RKO (Leo McCarey)

On a transatlantic crossing, a European man of the world meets a New York girl, but their romance is flawed by misunderstanding and physical accident.
The essence of Hollywood romance, and one of the most fondly remembered films of the thirties, perhaps because of the easy comedy sense of the first half.
w Delmer Daves, Donald Ogden Stewart story Mildred Cram, Leo McCarey *d Leo McCarey ph* Rudolph Maté *m* Roy Webb *ad* Van Nest Polglase, Al Herman

☆ *Charles Boyer, Irene Dunne, Maria Ouspenskaya,* Lee Bowman, Astrid Allwyn, Maurice Moscovich

'Production is of grade A quality ... its b.o. chances look good.' – *Variety*

'Those excited over the mastery of form already achieved in pictures, will like to follow this demonstration of the qualities of technique and imagination the films must always have and keep on recruiting to their service ... Clichés of situation and attitude are lifted almost beyond recognition by a morning freshness of eye for each small thing around.' – *Otis Ferguson*

'McCarey brought off one of the most difficult things you can attempt with film. He created a mood, rather than a story; he kept it alive by expert interpolations; he provided comedy when he needed comedy and poignancy when he needed substance; and he did it with the minimum of effort.' – *Pare Lorentz*

† Remade as *An Affair to Remember* (qv).

best picture; original story; Irene Dunne; Maria Ouspenskaya; art direction; song 'Wishing' (*m/ly* Buddy de Sylva)

Love Affair

US 1994 108m Technicolor
Warner/Mulholland (Warren Beatty)

A couple find that the course of true love does not run smooth and similar clichés.

An inexplicable remake of a sentimental weepie, predicated on the fact that its stars are married to one another, which is hardly reason enough to disinter something done with much more style a generation ago; an affair to forget.

w Robert Towne, Warren Beatty *story* Mildred Cram, Leo McCarey *screenplay Delmer Daves, Donald Ogden Stewart d* Glenn Gordon Caron *m* Ennio Morricone *pd* Fernando Scarfiotti *ed* Robert C. Jones

☆ Warren Beatty, Annette Bening, Katharine Hepburn, Garry Shandling, Pierce Brosnan, Kate Capshaw, Chloe Webb

'Not a disaster, but it's not good either; its kitsch derives from old "woman's film" formulas but put together without the conviction or the moral urgency that once made such stuff irresistible.' – *David Denby, New York*

'Marks the nadir of Hollywood's obsession with re-makes to date.' – *Denis Seguin, Screen International*

† The film was first made by Leo McCarey in 1939 starring Charles Boyer and Irene Dunne and remade as *An Affair to Remember* in 1957, again directed by Leo McCarey and starring Cary Grant and Deborah Kerr.

Love Affair, or the Case of the Missing Switchboard Operator: see *The Switchboard Operator*

Love After Love: see *Après l'Amour*

Love among the Millionaires

US 1930 70m bw
Paramount

A waitress falls for the son of a railroad president.

Ho-hum star vehicle without much get-up-and-go.

w Grover Jones, William Conselman, Joseph L. Mankiewicz *d* Frank Tuttle

☆ Clara Bow, Stanley Smith, Mitzi Green, Skeets Gallagher, Stuart Erwin

'It will call for a lot of faith from the Clara Bow admirers to accept her in this kind of a part, the sweet wishy-washy thing, after the bum publicity she's been getting.' – *Variety*

Love and a .45 *

US 1994 101m colour
Trimark (Darin Scott)

A petty crook, who shoots his psychotic partner for killing a checkout girl during a robbery, takes to the road with his girl pursued by the law and assorted low-life.

Slick, enjoyably trashy exploitation movie that updates a familiar theme.

wd C. M. Talkington *ph* Tom Richmond *m* Tom Verlaine *pd* Deborah Pastor *ed* Bob Ducsay

☆ Gil Bellows, Renee Zellweger, Rory Cochrane, Jeffrey Combs, Jace Alexander, Jack Nance, Michael Bowen, Peter Fonda

'The fact that *Love and a 45* is so unapologetically irresponsible (the lingering tattoo torture scene is lip-smackingly sadistic) only makes it more endearing.' – *Sight and Sound*

'All's fair in love and basketball.'

Love & Basketball

US 2000 124m DeLuxe
New Line/40 Acres and a Mule (Spike Lee, Sam Kitt)

Two school friends with a talent for basketball begin dating when they go to University, then go their separate ways only to meet again...

A movie that questions some masculine assumptions about feminine roles, but mainly is content to get by on its slight charm.

wd Gina Prince-Bythewood *ph* Reynaldo Villalobos *m* Terence Blanchard *pd* Jeff Howard *ed* Terilyn Shropshire *cos* Ruth Carter

☆ Sanaa Lathan (Monica Wright), Omar Epps (Quincy McCall), Alfre Woodard (Camille Wright), Dennis Haysbert (Zeke McCall), Debbie Morgan (Mona McCall), Harry J. Lennix (Nathan Wright), Kyla Pratt (Young Monica), Glenndon Chatman (Young Quincy)

'An easy feel-good movie, but falls far short of the challenging film it aspires to be.' – *Emma Cochrane, Empire*

Love and Bullets

US 1978 103m Metrocolor
ITC (Pancho Kohner)

A gangster's mistress is brought back from Switzerland by a revengeful Phoenix cop.

Downbeat bang-bang with a high death rate and a glum finale; generally low-grade stuff.

w Wendell Mayes, John Melson *d* Stuart Rosenberg *ph* Fred Koenekamp *m* Lalo Schifrin *pd* John DeCuir

☆ Charles Bronson, Jill Ireland, Rod Steiger, Henry Silva, Strother Martin, Bradford Dillman, Michael V. Gazzo

'A relatively dismaying example of the Lew Grade entertainment formula: as locations, production values and clichéd set-pieces proliferate, scripts increasingly look like shaggy dog stories desperately in search of a point, and actors are left to do their own thing as characters disintegrate.' – *Richard Combs, MFB*

'Love and bullets my eye: embarrassment and tedium would be more like it.' – *Time Out*

Love and Death *

US 1975 85m DeLuxe Panavision
UA/Jack Rollins, Charles H. Joffe

In 1812 Russia, a man condemned reviews the follies of his life.

Personalized comedy fantasia inspired by War and Peace, *Ingmar Bergman and S. J. Perelman. Basically only for star fans.*

wd Woody Allen *ph* Ghislain Cloquet *m* Prokofiev

☆ Woody Allen, Diane Keaton, Georges Adel, Despo, Frank Adu

'I have a feeling that one of these days Allen will get it most dreadfully together and make a film which is more than a string of funny one-liners and set-pieces. He hasn't quite done it here.' – *Benny Green, Punch*

Love and Death on Long Island **

GB/Canada 1996 93m Technicolor
Guild/Skyline/Imagex/British Screen/Telefilm Canada/ Arts Council/NSFDC (Steve Clark-Hall, Christopher Zimmer)

A reclusive, intellectual British novelist becomes obsessed with a good-looking American actor, who appears in trashy movies, and goes to America to try to seduce him.

Engaging, witty, slender movie that extracts much amusement from a clash between two cultures and vastly differing sensibilities.

wd Richard Kwietniowski *novel* Gilbert Adair *ph* Oliver Curtis *m* The Insects, Richard Grassby-Lewis *pd* David McHenry *ed* Susan Shipton

☆ *John Hurt,* Jason Priestley, Fiona Loewi, Sheila Hancock, Maury Chaykin, Gawn Grainger, Elizabeth Quinn

'Bittersweet blend of *Death in Venice* and *Porky's*.' – *David Parkinson, Empire*

Richard Kwietniowski (best newcomer)

Love and Hisses *

US 1937 84m bw
TCF (Kenneth MacGowan)

A gossip columnist and a bandleader continue their feud.

Moderate sequel to Wake Up and Live *(qv); it got by.*

w Art Arthur, Curtis Kenyon *d* Sidney Lanfield *ph* Robert Planck *m* Louis Silvers

☆ Walter Winchell, Ben Bernie and his orchestra, Joan Davis, Bert Lahr, Simone Simon, Ruth Terry

Love and Human Remains *

Canada 1993 100m colour
Rank/Max/Atlantis (Roger Frappier)

A gay actor turned waiter searches for sex while his flatmate, a female book reviewer, looks for love among people with hang-ups of their own.

A modern romance in a world of AIDS and serial killers, often witty and sceptical but also increasingly unbelievable and hysterical.

w Brad Fraser *play Unidentified Human Remains and the Nature of Love* by Brad Fraser *d* Denys Arcand *ph* Paul Sarossy *m* John McCarthy *pd* François Seguin *ed* Alain Baril

☆ Thomas Gibson, Ruth Marshall, Cameron Bancroft, Mia Kirshner, Joanne Vannicola, Matthew Ferguson, Rick Roberts

'A bawdy and spirited comedy about a group of mostly 30ish urbanites trying to get a grip on their sexuality and place in the world.' – *Todd McCarthy, Variety*

'The more it progresses, the more it falls into banality and melodrama.' – *Derek Malcolm, Guardian*

Love and Money

US 1980 95m Metrocolor
Lorimar

A banker kidnaps a financier's wife, and finds himself in dead trouble.

Incoherent light melodrama which barely got released.

wd James Toback *ph* Fred Schuler *ad* Lee Fischer

☆ Ray Sharkey, Ornella Muti, Klaus Kinski, Armand Assante, King Vidor (as the hero's senile grandfather), William Prince

'The trouble with love is, you never know where it's going to strike next.'

Love and Other Catastrophes **

Australia 1996 79m Cinevex
TCF/Screwball Five/AFC (Stavros Andonis Efthymiou)

In Melbourne, five university students cope with the problems of life, learning and love.

High-spirited, episodic account of the young enjoying the little dramas of everyday experience, which skates on the surface of life without putting a foot wrong.

w Yael Bergman, Emma-Kate Croghan, Helen Bandis *d* Emma-Kate Croghan *ph* Justin Brickle *m* Oleh Witer *ad* Lisa Collins *ed* Ken Sallows

☆ Matt Day (Michael), Frances O'Connor (Mia), Alice Garner (Alice), Radha Mitchell (Danni), Matthew Dyktynski (Ari), Kim Gyngell (Professor Leach), Suzi Dougherty, Suzanne Dowling (Dr Russell), Torquil Neilson

'A sharp, short, excellent little movie that comes in looking suspiciously like an Andy Warhol home movie and grows into a truly rewarding, original and spontaneous piece of entertainment.' – *Marianne Gray, Film Review*

Love and Pain and the Whole Damn Thing

US 1972 113m Eastmancolor
Columbia/Gus (Alan J. Pakula)

An asthmatic young American on holiday in Spain has an affair with an older woman suffering from an incurable disease.

Dreary doomed romance studiously treated as tourist comedy.

w Alvin Sargent *d* Alan J. Pakula *ph* Geoffrey Unsworth *m* Michael Small

☆ Maggie Smith, Timothy Bottoms

Love and Sacrifice: see *America*

'Get A Love Life!'

Love & Sex

US 2000 80m FotoKem
Behaviour Worldwide (Timothy Scott Bogart, Martin J. Barab, Brad Wyman)

A female journalist, given to reminiscing about her various relationships, has an off-and-on affair with an artist.

Slick but bland romantic comedy in which couples analyse their attitudes to one another ad nauseam.

wd Valerie Breiman *ph* Adam Kane *pd* Sara Sprawls *ed* Martin Applebaum *cos* Sara Jane Slotnick

☆ Famke Janssen (Kate Welles), Jon Favreau (Adam Levy), Noah Emmerich (Eric), Ann Magnuson (Ms Steinbacher), Cheri Oteri (Joey Santino), Robert Knepper (Gerard), Vincent Ventresca (Richard), David Schwimmer (Jehovah's Witness (uncredited))

'Serves up the kind of cutesy-wootsy sentiment that makes me pukesy.' – *Cosmo Landesman, Sunday Times*

Love at First Bite *

US 1979 96m colour
Simon (Joel Freeman)

Count Dracula flees from the communists and settles in New York.

Energetic spoof, with jokes on the sexy side; good work all round.

w Robert Kaufman *d* Stan Dragoti *ph* Edward Rosson *m* Charles Bernstein *pd* Serge Krizman

☆ *George Hamilton,* Susan St James, Richard Benjamin, Dick Shawn, Arte Johnson

'Love is so hard to find you have to hire a detective'

Love at Large *

US 1990 97m DeLuxe
Rank/Orion (David Blocker)

A private eye checks on the wrong man, while a female detective is hired by his girlfriend to check on him.

Enjoyably light-hearted treatment of an intricate plot of double-cross and double lives.

wd Alan Rudolph *ph* Elliot Davis *m* Mark Isham *pd* Stephen Legler *ed* Lisa Churgin

☆ Tom Berenger, Elizabeth Perkins, Anne Archer, Kate Capshaw, Annette O'Toole, Ted Levine, Ann Magnuson, Kevin J. O'Connor, Ruby Dee, Barry Miller, Neil Young

The Love Ban: see *It's a 2' 6" Above the Ground World*

A Love Bewitched

Spain 1985 98m colour
Emilian Piedra
original title: *El Amor Brujo*

The future marriage of two children is arranged by their gypsy fathers with tragic results.

A dance drama likely to appeal only to aficionados of the genre.

w Carlos Saura, Antonio Gades *d* Carlos Saura *ph* Teo Escamilla *m* Manuel de Falla *pd* Gerardo Vera *ed* Pedro Del Rey

☆ Antonio Gades, Cristina Hoyos, Laura Del Sol, Juan Antonio Jiminez, Emma Penella, La Polaca, Gomez de Jerez

The Love Bug **

US 1968 107m Technicolor
Walt Disney (Bill Walsh)

An unsuccessful racing driver finds that his small private Volkswagen has a mind of its own.

Amusing, pacy period fantasy in the best Disney style.

w Bill Walsh, Don da Gradi *d Robert Stevenson* *ph* Edward Colman *m* George Bruns *sp Eustace Lycett*

☆ David Tomlinson, Dean Jones, Michele Lee, Buddy Hackett, Joe Flynn, Benson Fong, Joe E. Ross

The Love Cage: see *Joy House*

'He promised to love, honor and protect. She promised to love, cheat and steal.'

Love, Cheat & Steal
US 1994 96m Foto-Kem
ITC/Showtime Network/MPCA (Brad Kevoy, Steve Stabler)

A killer escapes from prison and forces his former wife to help him to rob her new husband's bank.
Formula thriller of betrayal and double-cross that early promises more than it ultimately delivers.
wd William Curran *ph* Kent Wakeford *pd* Jane Ann Stewart *ed* Carole Kravetz
☆ John Lithgow, Eric Roberts, Madchen Amick, Donald Moffat, Richard Edson, Dan O'Herlihy, David Ackroyd
'A desperate wannabe *film noir* that lacks the form's crucial elements of suapenseful ambience and steamy sexuality.' – *Emanuel Levy, Variety*

The Love Child
GB 1987 101m colour
BFI/Frontroom Pro/Channel 4/VPRO TV (Angela Topping)
An orphaned South London youth falls in love with an artist living in a squat.
Weak whimsy of working-class life.
w Gordon Hann *d* Robert Smith *ph* Thaddeus O'Sullivan *m* Colin Gibson, Kenny Craddock *pd* Caroline Hanania *ed* John Davies
☆ Sheila Hancock, Peter Capaldi, Percy Herbert, Lesley Sharp, Alexei Sayle, Arthur Hewlett, Cleo Sylvestre, Stephen Lind

Love Crazy *
US 1941 100m bw
MGM (Pandro S. Berman)
When his wife threatens to divorce him, a businessman hatches all manner of crazy schemes, including disguising himself as his own sister.
Zany romantic comedy, over-stretched but with a fair share of hilarity.
w William Ludwig, Charles Lederer, David Hertz *d* Jack Conway *ph* Ray June *m* David Snell
☆ *William Powell, Myrna Loy*, Gail Patrick, Jack Carson, Florence Bates, Sidney Blackmer, Vladimir Sokoloff, Donald MacBride, Sig Rumann, Sara Haden, Elisha Cook Jnr, Kathleen Lockhart

Love Crimes
US 1991 90m DeLuxe
Rank/Sovereign/Miramax (Lizzie Borden, Rudy Langlais)

An assistant DA goes undercover so that she can trap a photographer who is raping the women who pose for him.
Confused thriller that seems uncertain as to what kind of film it wants to be; it finally settles for mediocrity.
w Allan Moyle, Laurie Frank *d* Lizzie Borden *ph* Jack N. Green *m* Graeme Revell, Roger Mason *pd* Armin Ganz *ed* Nicholas C. Smith, Mike Jackson
☆ Sean Young, Patrick Bergin, Arnetia Walker, James Read, Ron Orbach, Fern Dorsey, Tina Hightower, Donna Biscoe

Love Dance: see *Let It Be Me (1999)*

A Love Divided *
Ireland 1999 100m colour
RTE/BBC/IFB/Parallel (Alan Moloney, Tim Palmer, Gerry Gregg)
In Ireland in the 1950s, a Protestant woman marries a Catholic farmer; but she leaves him when the local priest insists that their daughters must be educated at the village Catholic school.
Based on a true story, an effective narrative of a domestic disagreement that escalates into a bigoted religious controversy that destroys a community.
w Stuart Hepburn *screenplay* Deirdre Dowling, Gerry Gregg *d* Sydney Macartney *ph* Cedric Culliton *m* Fiachra Trench *pd* Alan Farquharson *ed* Ray Roantree
☆ Liam Cunningham (Sean Cloney), Orla Brady (Sheila Cloney), Tony Doyle (Fr. Stafford), Peter Caffrey (Andy Bailey), John Kavanagh (Bishop Staunton), Brian McGrath (Tom Kelly), Jim Norton (Rev. Fisher), Ali White (Dorothy Kelly)
† In 1998, the Catholic church formally apologised for its role in the affair.

Love etc.
France 1996 104m colour Panavision
Pathé/Aliceléo/France3/Canal+ (Patrick Godeau)

Two friends, one shy, the other flamboyant, compete for the love of the same woman.
Slight, playful treatment of a triangular romance.
w Marion Vernoux, Dodine Herry *novel Talking It Over* by Julian Barnes *d* Marion Vernoux *ph* Eric Gautier *m* Alexandre Desplat *pd* François Emmanuelli *ed* Jennifer Auge
☆ Charlotte Gainsbourg, Yvan Attal, Charles Berling, Thibault de Montalembert, Elodie Navarre, Marie Adam

Love Eternal *
France 1943 111m bw
André Paulvé

original title: *L'Eternel Retour*
The love story of Tristan and Isolde.
This modernized version had a Teutonic look and was respected rather than admired.
w Jean Cocteau *d* Jean Delannoy *ph* Roger Hubert *m* Georges Auric *ad* Wakhevitch
☆ Jean Marais, Madeleine Sologne, Jean Murat, Yvonne de Bray
'There it is, the whole dolorous bag of tricks, the island, the love potion, the scarf on the mast, the dark tower, the aching rejection of life, valid according to its intentions, often superbly beautiful in its execution, but rotted.' – *Richard Winnington*

Love Field
US 1992 104m DeLuxe
Orion (Sarah Pillsbury, Midge Sanford)

A hairdresser in Dallas who identifies with Jacqueline Kennedy goes to attend President Kennedy's funeral and is attracted to a black man she meets on the way.
Intensely American movie that is too parochial to be rewarding.
w Don Roos *d* Jonathan Kaplan *ph* Ralf Bode *m* Jerry Goldsmith *pd* Mark Freeborn *ed* Jane Kurson
☆ Michelle Pfeiffer, Dennis Haysbert, Stephanie McFadden, Brian Kerwin, Louise Latham, Peggy Rea, Beth Grant
Michelle Pfeiffer

Love from a Stranger *
GB 1936 90m bw
Trafalgar (Max Schach)

A young woman realizes she may have married a maniac.
Stalwart suspenser from a popular novel and play.
w Frances Marion *play* Frank Vosper *story Philomel Cottage* by Agatha Christie *d* Rowland V. Lee *ph* Philip Tannura *m* Benjamin Britten
☆ *Ann Harding, Basil Rathbone*, Binnie Hale, Bruce Seton, Jean Cadell, Bryan Powley, Joan Hickson, Donald Calthrop
'Gorgeously photographed and splendidly cut ... takes front rank with the long list of gruesome films produced in recent years.' – *Variety*

Love from a Stranger
US 1947 81m bw
Eagle Lion (James J. Geller)

GB title: *A Stranger Walked In*
Stilted period remake.
w Philip MacDonald *d* Richard Whorf *ph* Tony Gaudio *m* Hans Salter
☆ Sylvia Sidney, John Hodiak, Ann Richards, John Howard, Isobel Elsom, Frederick Worlock

The Love God?
US 1969 103m Techniscope
Universal (Edward J. Montagne)
A meek ornithologist is thought to be the brains behind a girlie magazine, and becomes a national sex symbol.
Dispiriting and very talkative star farce which would have been long at half the time.
wd Nat Hiken *ph* William Margulies *m* Vic Mizzy
☆ Don Knotts, Edmond O'Brien, Anne Francis, James Gregory, Maureen Arthur
'Strictly for admirers of Don Knotts. Can there really be many?' – *MFB*

The Love Goddesses **
US 1965 87m bw
Paramount/Walter Reade/Sterling

A light-hearted account of female sexuality on the Hollywood screen.
Sharp-eyed compilation film which is worth a dozen books on the subject.
w Saul J. Turell, Graeme Ferguson m Percy Faith *narrator* Carl King
'A compilation of shrapnel from old sex-bomb movies, full of deliciously improbable moments.' – *Newsweek*
† Clips include *Blonde Venus, Morocco, True Heart Susie, Cleopatra* (1934), *Intolerance, The Cheat, The Sheik, Blood and Sand, The Sorrows of Satan, The Love of Sunya, Diary of a Lost Girl, Ecstasy, L'Atlantide, Peter the Tramp, Cabin in the Cotton, Platinum Blonde, Gold Diggers of 1933, No Man of Her Own, Professional Sweetheart, Love Me Tonight, I'm No Angel, Baby Face, They Won't Forget, College Swing, Her Jungle Love, Gilda, A Place in the Sun, Some Like it Hot.*

Love Happy *
US 1949 85m bw
Lester Cowan/Mary Pickford

A group of impoverished actors accidentally gets possession of the Romanov diamonds.
The last dismaying Marx Brothers film, with Harpo taking the limelight and Groucho loping in for a couple of brief, tired appearances. A roof chase works, but Harpo tries too hard for sentiment, and the production looks shoddy.
w Ben Hecht, Frank Tashlin, Mac Benoff *d* David Miller *ph* William Mellor *m* Ann Ronell
☆ Groucho Marx, Harpo Marx, Chico Marx, Eric Blore, Ilona Massey, Marilyn Monroe, Vera-Ellen

Love Has Many Faces
US 1964 104m Eastmancolor
Columbia/Jerry Bresler

A rich woman marries a beach boy and has an affair with another, who is murdered.
Hilarious but unentertaining sex melodrama built around an overage star.
w Marguerite Roberts *d* Alexander Singer *ph* Joseph Ruttenberg *m* David Raksin
☆ Lana Turner, Cliff Robertson, Hugh O'Brian, Stefanie Powers, Ruth Roman, Virginia Grey
'For connoisseurs of perfectly awful movies.' – *Judith Crist*

Love Hate: see *L'Albatross*

'Till Death Us Do Part.'

Love, Honour and Obey
GB 1999 98m DeLuxe
UIP/BBC/Fugitive (Dominic Anciano, Ray Burdis)

Trouble erupts when a North London gangster admits a new member to his gang.
Dreary would-be thriller, in which actors who ought to know better play at being criminals.
wd Dominic Anciano, Ray Burdis *ph* John Ward *pd* Nick Burnell *ed* Rachel Meyrick
☆ Sadie Frost (Sadie), Jonny Lee Miller (Jonny), Jude Law (Jude), Ray Winstone (Ray), Kathy Burke (Kathy), Sean Pertwee (Sean), Denise Van Outen (Maureen), Rhys Ifans (Matthew), Dominic Anciano (Dominic), Ray Burdis (Ray)
'Another strong contender for the worst Britflick of the year.' – *Sight and Sound*
'What's more unforgivable than the raggedness and puerility is the pervasive smugness.' – *Angie Errigo, Empire*
† The same writer-directors, together with many of the same cast, made the equally dire *The Final Cut* (v).

'A big comedy about life's little heartaches'

Love Hurts
US 1990 115m CFI color
Vestron/Love Hurts Production (Bud Yorkin, Doro Bachrach)

Returning home for his sister's wedding, a philanderer puts his past behind him.
A botched attempt, with unsympathetic characters, to return to comic style of Capra.
w Ron Nyswaner *d* Bud Yorkin *ph* Adam Greenberg *m* Frank DeCaro *pd* Armin Ganz *ed* John C. Horger
☆ Jeff Daniels, Judith Ivey, John Mahoney, Cynthia Sikes, Amy Wright, Cloris Leachman, Mary Griffin, Thomas Allen

Love in Ambush
Australia/France 1997 110m colour
Becker/Fit (Jean-Pierre Ramsay Levi, David Hannay)
An Australian woman goes to Cambodia in search of her brother, who has gone missing in action, and seeks help from her former husband.
A mix of romantic and political drama, set against the rise of the Khmer Rouge and CIA deviousness, but uninvolving for all that.
w Loup Durand, David Ambrose, Christine Miller, Carl Schultz *d* Carl Schultz *ph* John Stokes *m* Olivier Lliboutry *pd* Georgina Greenhill *ed* Minh-Tam Nguyen
☆ Jacques Perrin (Pascal Lasalle), Sigrid Thornton (Shelley Kincaird), Gary Sweet (Eddie Norton), Bernadette Lafont (Madeleine Carver), David Clendenning (Charles Carver), Grant Piro (Jon Kincaird), James Tolkan (Price)

Love in Black and White *
France 1920 23m bw
Saturnfilm

The cast of a travelling show fall in love with a sleeping beauty.
One of the director's lesser efforts, with a less coherent story than usual and less inspired stop-motion animation; the characters include a Charlie Chaplin doll.
wd Ladislaw Starewicz *story* René Buzelin *m* Roger White
† The film has been released on video with the feature-length *The Tale of the Fox* (qv) and four other shorts under the title *Ladislaw Starewicz: Selected Films.*

Love in Bloom
US 1934 76m bw
Paramount
A carnival owner's daughter marries a songwriter.
Lame little romance broken up by crosstalk from Burns and Allen; an ill-considered entertainment.
w J. P. McEvoy, Keene Thompson *d* Elliott Nugent
☆ George Burns, Gracie Allen, Dixie Lee, Joe Morrison
'Radio pair may save their latest celluloid effort, but it won't help their future on the screen.' – *Variety*
song 'She Loves Me Not' (*m*Ralph Rainger, *ly*Leo Robin)

A Love in Germany *
West Germany/France 1983 107m colour
Artificial Eye/CCC Filmkunst/Gaumont/TFL/Stand'Art (Arthur Brauner)

original title: *Eine Liebe in Deutschland*
A German woman and a Jewish prisoner-of-war fall in love during the Second World War.
Powerful drama, though it lacks a tragic dimension.
w Boleslaw Michalek, Agnieszka Holland *novel* Rolf Hochhuth *d* Andrzej Wajda *ph* Igor Luther *m* Michel Legrand *ad* Allan Starski, Gotz Heymann, Jurgen Henze *ed* Halina Prugar-Ketling
☆ Hanna Schygulla, Marie-Christine Barrault, Armin Mueller-Stahl, Elisabeth Trissenaar, Daniel Olbrychski, Piotr Lysak

Love in Las Vegas: see *Viva Las Vegas*

Love in the Afternoon: see *L'Amour, L'Après-midi*

Love in the Afternoon
US 1957 126m bw
AA (Billy Wilder)

The daughter of a private detective warns an American philanderer in Paris that an enraged husband is en route to shoot him.
Tired and dreary romantic sex comedy, miscast and far too long. With the talent around, there are of course a few compensations.
w Billy Wilder, I. A. L. Diamond *novel Ariane* by Claude Anet *d* Billy Wilder *ph* William Mellor *m* Franz Waxman *ad* Alexander Trauner

☆ Gary Cooper, Audrey Hepburn, Maurice Chevalier, John McGiver

Love in the Strangest Way **

France 1994 107m colour
Gala/Fildebroc/TF1/Capac/Ice (Michelle de Broca)

original title: *Elles n'oublient pas*

A woman takes her revenge on the married businessman who picked her up for a one-night stand.

Icy, gripping drama that follows a familiar pattern – the plot resembles that of Fatal Attraction *– but spins some original and unexpected variations.*

wd Christopher Frank *ph* Bertrand Chatry *m* Jean-Marie Senia *ad* Dominique Andre *ed* Catherine Dubeau

☆ Thierry L'hermitte, Maruschka Detmers, Nadia Fares

'Those who like French films, even when not sufficiently French, may well enjoy the thought of a swine slowly but surely twisting on the spit of fate.' – *Derek Malcolm, Guardian*

† Christopher Frank died before the film was edited.

Love Is a Ball

US 1962 112m Technicolor Panavision
UA/Oxford/Gold Medal (Martin H. Poll)
GB title: *All This and Money Too*

A Riviera matchmaker recruits instructors to train his star pupil, but one of them walks away with the lady.

Forgettable comedy in which more effort goes into the glamorous background than the script.

w David Swift, Tom and Frank Waldman *novel* *The Grand Duke and Mr Pimm* by Lindsay Hardy *d* David Swift *ph* Edmond Séchan *m* Michel Legrand

☆ Glenn Ford, Charles Boyer, Hope Lange, Ricardo Montalban, Telly Savalas, Ruth McDevitt, Ulla Jacobsson

Love Is a Headache

US 1938 73m bw
MGM

An actress on hard times gets a break through freak publicity.

Wholly artificial comedy, hammed up to little avail.

w Marion Parsonnet, Harry Ruskin, William Lipman, Lou Heifetz, Herbert Klein *d* Richard Thorpe

☆ Franchot Tone, Gladys George, Mickey Rooney, Ralph Morgan, Jessie Ralph, Ted Healy, Barnett Parker, Frank Jenks, Virginia Weidler, Fay Holden

'Dialogue is pungent, but fails to cover up slap-happy situations.' – *Variety*

'A love that defied five thousand years of tradition!'

Love Is a Many Splendored Thing *

US 1955 102m DeLuxe Cinemascope
TCF (Buddy Adler)

During the Korean War, a Eurasian lady doctor in Hong Kong falls in love with a war correspondent.

Self-admittedly sentimental soaper with a tragic ending; the theme tune kept it popular for years.

w John Patrick *novel* Han Suyin *d* Henry King *ph* Leon Shamroy *m* Alfred Newman *ad* Lyle Wheeler, George W. Davis

☆ Jennifer Jones, William Holden, Torin Thatcher, Isobel Elsom, Murray Matheson, Virginia Gregg, Richard Loo

Alfred Newman; title song (*m*Sammy Fain, *ly*Paul Francis Webster)

best picture; Leon Shamroy; Jennifer Jones; art direction

Love Is a Racket

US 1932 72m bw
Warner
GB title: *Such Things Happen*

A newspaperman covers up for a girl suspected of murder, but she lets him down.

Jaundiced comedy-drama of Broadway night life; quite effective.

w Courteney Terrett *d* William Wellman

☆ Douglas Fairbanks Jnr, Frances Dee, Ann Dvorak, Lee Tracy, Lyle Talbot, Warren Hymer

Love Is Better Than Ever

US 1951 81m bw
MGM (William H. Wright)

GB title: *The Light Fantastic*

A small-town girl falls for a New York theatrical agent.

Only moderate production values are brought to bear on this wispy plot which shows no signs of development.

w Ruth Brooks Flippen *d* Stanley Donen *ph* Harold Rosson *md* Lennie Hayton

☆ Larry Parks, Elizabeth Taylor, Josephine Hutchinson, Tom Tully, Ann Doran

Love Is My Profession: see *En Cas de Malheur*

Love Is News *

US 1937 78m bw
TCF (Earl Carroll, Harold Wilson)

An heiress marries a scoop-hunting reporter just to show him how embarrassing publicity can be.

Silly romantic comedy with plenty of laughs.

w Harry Tugend, Jack Yellen *d* Tay Garnett *ph* Ernest Palmer

☆ Tyrone Power, Loretta Young, Don Ameche, Slim Summerville, Dudley Digges, Walter Catlett, Jane Darwell, Stepin Fetchit, George Sanders, Frank Conroy, Elisha Cook Jnr

'Fast-moving comedy and good star names. Surefire.' – *Variety*

† Remade as *Sweet Rosie O'Grady* and *That Wonderful Urge*.

'Study for a portrait of Francis Bacon.'

Love Is the Devil **

GB 1998 91m colour
Artificial Eye/BBC/BFI/Première Heure/Uplink/Arts Council/Partners in Crime (Chiara Menage)

A homosexual artist begins a doomed love affair with a petty crook he discovers trying to burgle his home.

A wittily artificial biopic of Francis Bacon, which, in the absence of any of Bacon's paintings, contrives to imitate their style; it is blessed with a brilliant performance from Jacobi as the self-absorbed artist.

wd John Maybury ph John Mathieson *m* Ryuichi Sakamoto *pd* Alan Macdonald *ed* Daniel Goddard

☆ *Derek Jacobi* (Francis Bacon), Daniel Craig (George Dyer), Tilda Swinton (Muriel Belcher), Anne Lambton (Isabel Hawesthorne), Adrian Scarborough (Daniel Farson), Karl Johnson (John Deakin), Annabel Brooks (Henrietta Moraes), Richard Newbold (Blonde Billy)

'Unconventional, audacious and uncompromising in every sense.' – *David Rooney, Variety*

Love Jones *

US 1997 108m DeLuxe
Entertainment/New Line (Nick Wechsler, Jeremiah Samuels)

A poet who performs in a night-club becomes involved in an on-and-off affair with a photographer who has given up on love.

A small-scale romantic drama among the arty that has charm and wit, though a little too much gloss and contrivance for its own good.

wd Theodore Witcher *ph* Ernest Holzman *m* Darryl Jones *pd* Roger Fortune *ed* Maysie Hoy

☆ Larenz Tate, Nia Long, Isaiah Washington, Lisa Nicole Carson, Khalili Kain, Leonard Roberts, Bernadette L. Clarke

'A sexy and appealing love story set in the flavorsome world of black bohemians in contemporary Chicago.' – *Variety*

Love Lessons **

Sweden/Denmark 1995 128m colour
Gala/Per Holst Film

original title: *Lust och Fägring Stor*
aka: *All Things Fair*

In Sweden in the early 40s, a sexually curious 15-year-old boy begins an affair with his teacher, who is married to an alcoholic salesman.

Sprightly domestic drama of inexperience and maturity, hope and despair, affectionately acted and directed.

wd Bo Widerberg *ph* Morten Bruus *m* *Mahler, Beethoven et al* *pd* Palle Arestrup *ed* Bo Widerberg

☆ Johan Widerberg, Marika Lagercrantz, Tomas von Brömssen, Karin Huldt, Björn Kjellman

'A highly likeable film ... has a constant sense of sexuality and sensuality.' – *Gunnar Rehlin, Variety*

The Love Letter

US 1999 87m Technicolor
DreamWorks (Sarah Pillsbury, Midge Sanford, Kate Capshaw)

In a small, seaside town several people imagine that an unsigned love letter is addressed to them.

Amiable, and forgettable, small-scale romantic comedy that springs no surprises.

w Maria Maggenti *novel* Cathleen Schine *d* Peter Ho-Sun Chan *ph* Tami Reiker *m* Luis Bacalov *pd* Andrew Jackness *ed* Jacqueline Cambas

☆ Kate Capshaw (Helen), Blythe Danner (Lillian), Ellen DeGeneres (Janet), Geraldine McEwan (Miss Scattergoods), Julianne Nicholson (Jennifer), Tom Everett Scott (Johnny), Tom Selleck (George), Gloria Stuart (Eleanor), Bill Buell (Officer Dan), Alice Drummond (Postal clerk)

'It's a flimsy excuse for a movie and therefore no surprise that the end result is as charmless and cloying as it is.' – *James Cameron-Wilson, Film Review*

'Blood on her hands ... love in her heart!'

Love Letters *

US 1945 101m bw
Paramount (Hal B. Wallis)

A girl who has lost her memory through war shock is threatened by more physical danger.

Oddly unexciting romantic melodrama directed and designed in heavy but satisfying style. Typical post-war depressive fare.

w Ayn Rand *novel* *Pity My Simplicity* by Chris Massie *d* *William Dieterle* *ph* Lee Garmes *m* *Victor Young* *ad* Hans Dreier, Roland Anderson

☆ Jennifer Jones, Joseph Cotten, Ann Richards, Gladys Cooper, Anita Louise, Cecil Kellaway, Robert Sully, Byron Barr, Reginald Denny, Lumsden Hare

Jennifer Jones; title song (*m*Victor Young, *ly*Edward Heyman); Victor Young; art direction

Love Letters *

US 1983 89m DeLuxe
Roger Corman/Millennium

Affected by her mother's old letters revealing an unconsummated love, a twenty-two-year-old girl begins an affair with an older man.

Low-budget drama which might have worked better as a television play; but it has its memorable aspects.

wd Amy Jones *ph* Alec Hirschfeld *m* Ralph Jones

☆ Jamie Lee Curtis, James Keach, Matt Clark, Bonnie Bartlett, Bud Cort, Amy Madigan

Love Letters of a Star

US 1936 66m bw
Universal

A blackmailed rich girl takes poison.

Complicated but efficient murder mystery.

w Lewis R. Foster, Milton Carruth, James Mulhauser *novel* *The Case of the Constant God* by Rufus King *d* Lewis R. Foster, Milton Carruth *ph* Milton Krasner *ed* Frank Gross

☆ Henry Hunter, Polly Rowles, C. Henry Gordon, Walter Coy, Hobart Cavanaugh, Mary Alice Rice

'Good family entertainment ... ought to do all right.' – *Variety*

Love, Life and Laughter *

GB 1934 83m bw
ATP (Basil Dean)

A film actress catches the eye of a Ruritanian prince.

Lively star vehicle ranging from sentiment to slapstick.

w Robert Edmunds *d* Maurice Elvey

☆ Gracie Fields, John Loder, Norah Howard, Allan Aynesworth, Esme Percy, Robb Wilton, Fred Duprez, Horace Kenney, Veronica Brady

'A Comic Tragedy.'

Love Liza *

Germany/US/France 2002 89m colour
Columbia-TriStar/Kinowelt/Wild Bunch/Canal+/Muse/Blacklist (Chris Hanley, Fernando Sulichin, Ruth Charny, Jeff Rota)

After the unexpected suicide of his wife, a website designer slowly goes to pieces.

Melancholy, quirky movie graced with a good central performance but otherwise hard going and frequently baffling.

w Gordy Hoffman *d* Todd Louiso *ph* Lisa Rinzler *m* Jim O'Rourke *pd* Stephen Beatrice *ed* Anne Stein, Katz

☆ Philip Seymour Hoffman (Wilson Joel), Kathy Bates (Mary Ann Bankhead), Jack Kehler (Denny), Sarah Koskoff (Maura Haas), Stephen Tobolowsky (Tom Bailey), Erika Alexander (Brenda)

'May frustrate as many viewers as it delights (if not more) and it is almost relentlessly depressing, but it's also a principled, sharply realistic film that captures a highly convincing vision of Middle America.' – *Andrew O'Hehir*

The Love Lottery

GB 1953 83m Technicolor
Ealing (Monja Danischewsky)

A British film star is persuaded to offer himself as first prize in a lottery.

Satirical farce which doesn't come off, mainly owing to paucity of comedy ideas.

w Harry Kurnitz *d* Charles Crichton *ph* Douglas Slocombe *m* Benjamin Frankel *pd* Tom Morahan

☆ David Niven, Herbert Lom, Peggy Cummins, Anne Vernon, Charles Victor, Gordon Jackson, Felix Aylmer, Hugh McDermott

The Love Machine

US 1971 110m Eastmancolor
Columbia/Mike Frankovich

Megalomaniac TV reporter progresses to network programme controller but is finally undone by his vivid sex life.

Stodgy, silly melodrama from a bestseller whose inspiration was well known in TV circles.

w Samuel Taylor *novel* Jacqueline Susann *d* Jack Haley Jnr *ph* Charles Lang Jnr *m* Artie Butler

☆ John Phillip Law, Dyan Cannon, Robert Ryan, Jackie Cooper, David Hemmings, Shecky Greene

The Love Match *

GB 1955 85m bw
British Lion/Beaconsfield (Maclean Rogers)

A North Country train driver's enthusiasm for his local football team lands him in trouble at home and work.

A regional farce, full of stock characters and situations, but given some individuality by the likeable performances of its cast.

w Geoffrey Orme, Glenn Melvyn *play* Glenn Melvyn *d* David Paltenghi *ph* Arthur Grant *m* Wilfred Burns *ad* Bernard Robinson *ed* J. M. Sterling

☆ Arthur Askey, Thora Hird, Glenn Melvyn, Robb Wilton, Shirley Eaton, Edward Chapman, William Franklyn, Patricia Hayes, Maurice Kaufmann

Love Me Darling

Denmark 1971 88m Eastmancolor
Cinecenta/Gabriel Axel
original title: *Med Kaerlig Hilsen*

Two lovers journey through time, enjoying themselves from the Garden of Eden onwards.

A series of farcical sketches on the subject of sex, without any evidence of humour or eroticism.

wd Gabriel Axel *ph* Rolf Rînne *m* B. Fabricius Bjerre *ad* Erik Bjoric *ed* Anders Refn

☆ Buster Larsen, Birte Tove, Christian Sarvig, Lone Helmer

'Completely lacking in style or originality, the film also fails to titillate, since its actors project about as much sex-appeal as damp cardboard.' – *Carol Howard, MFB*

Love Me Forever

US 1935 92m bw
Columbia
GB title: *On Wings of Song*

A down and out singer makes good.

Fair star vehicle.

w Jo Swerling, Sidney Buchman *d* Victor Schertzinger *ph* Joe Walker *md* Louis Silvers

☆ Grace Moore, Leo Carrillo, Robert Allen, Spring Byington, Michael Bartlett, Thurston Hall, Douglas Dumbrille, Luis Alberni

'Gangsters and grand opera are tough to mix, but … should be all right in major towns.' – *Variety*

Love Me or Leave Me **

US 1955 122m Eastmancolor
Cinemascope
MGM (Joe Pasternak)

Twenty singer Ruth Etting is befriended by a racketeer who pushes her to the top but drives her to drink and despair in the process.

Agreeably bitter showbiz biopic which gives the impression of being not too far from the truth.

w Daniel Fuchs, Isobel Lennart *d Charles Vidor ph* Arthur E. Arling *md* Percy Faith, George Stoll *ad* Cedric Gibbons, Urie McCleary

☆ *Doris Day, James Cagney, Cameron Mitchell,* Robert Keith, Tom Tully, Harry Bellaver, Richard Gaines

original story (Daniel Fuchs)

script; Percy Faith, George Stoll; James Cagney; song 'I'll Never Stop Loving You' (*m* Nicholas Brodszky, *ly* Sammy Cahn)

Love Me Tender

US 1956 95m bw Cinemascope
TCF (David Weisbart)

Three brothers fall out over loot they have brought home from the Civil War.

Odd Western designed (perhaps after shooting began) as Presley's introductory vehicle; he sings four songs before getting shot, and reappears in ghostly form at the end.

w Robert Buckner *d* Robert D. Webb *ph* Leo Tover *m* Lionel Newman

☆ Richard Egan, Debra Paget, Elvis Presley, Robert Middleton, William Campbell, Neville Brand, Mildred Dunnock, Bruce Bennett, James Drury, Ken Clark, Barry Coe

'I understand this performance is tame compared with the one Mr Presley can put up when not handicapped by a motion picture. My concern is with a moving picture made nonsense of by him.' – *C. A. Lejeune*

Love Me Tonight ****

US 1932 104m bw
Paramount (Rouben Mamoulian)

A Parisian tailor accidentally moves into the aristocracy.

The most fluently cinematic comedy musical ever made, with sounds and words, lyrics and music, deftly blended into a compulsively and consistently laughable mosaic of sophisticated nonsense; one better than the best of Lubitsch and Clair.

w Samuel Hoffenstein, Waldemar Young, George Marion Jnr play Tailor in the Château by Leopold Marchand and Paul Armont *d Rouben Mamoulian ph Victor Milner songs Rodgers and Hart*

☆ *Maurice Chevalier, Jeanette MacDonald, Charles Butterworth, Charles Ruggles, Myrna Loy, C. Aubrey Smith,* Elizabeth Patterson, Ethel Griffies, Blanche Frederici, Robert Greig

'A musical frolic, whimsical in its aim and delicately carried out in its pattern.' – *Variety*

'Gay, charming, witty, it is everything that the Lubitsch musicals should have been but never were.' – *John Baxter, 1968*

'With the aid of a pleasant story, a good musician, a talented cast and about a million dollars, he has done what someone in Hollywood should have done long ago – he has illustrated a musical score.' – *Pare Lorentz*

'It has that infectious spontaneity which distinguishes the American musical at its best.' – *Peter Cowie, 1970*

'A rich amalgam of filmic invention, witty decoration and wonderful songs.' – *NFT, 1974*

'What a picture! First you have Chevalier, and last you have Chevalier!' – *Photoplay*

Love, Mother **

Hungary 1987 102m colour
Mafilm/Objektiv
original title: *Csok, Anyu*

A small boy plays truant from school and, using a home-made periscope and binoculars, spies on the life of his preoccupied parents and their neighbours, discovering more than it is good for him to know.

A charming and quirky comedy of the little mishaps, misbehaviours and pressures of everyday life which gradually moves into darker territory, analysing a family that is falling apart.

w Istvan Kardos *d* Janos Rozsa *ph* Elemer Ragalyi *m* Janos Brody

☆ Dorottya Udvaros, Robert Koltai, Sandor Gaspar, Kati Lajtai, Simon G. Gevai, Peter Andorai

The Love Nest

US 1923 22m (24 fps) bw silent
Buster Keaton Productions

Buster dreams of a solitary voyage in a small boat. Long lost but ultimately disappointing Keaton short.

wd Buster Keaton, Edward F. Cline

☆ Buster Keaton, Joe Roberts, Virginia Fox

Love Nest

US 1951 84m bw
TCF

A writer and his wife invest in an apartment building but find their tenants time-consuming.

Fairly lively comedy with varied talent.

w I. A. L. Diamond *novel* Scott Corbett *d* Joseph Newman *ph* Lloyd Ahern *m* Cyril Mockridge

☆ William Lundigan, June Haver, Frank Fay, Marilyn Monroe, Jack Paar, Leatrice Joy

Love Never Dies: see *Lilac Time*

The Love of Jeanne Ney *

Germany 1927 98m (24 fps) bw silent
UFA

In the Crimea during the Russian Revolution, a political observer is accidentally killed by his daughter's lover.

Inconsistently-styled contemporary melodrama. The abiding interest is in the detailed treatment rather than the story or acting.

w Ladislas Vajda, Rudolf Leonhardt, Ilya Ehrenberg *d* G. W. Pabst *ph* Fritz Arno Wagner, Walter Robert Lach

☆ Edith Jehane, Uno Henning, Fritz Rasp, Brigitte Helm

The Love of Sunya

US 1927 80m (24 fps) bw silent
Swanson Producing Corporation

A yogi recognizes two young lovers as people he wronged in a previous existence, and warns them of impending disaster.

Star tosh of its period, unthinkable now as a screen attraction.

w Earle Brown *play The Eyes of Youth* by Max Marcin, Charles Guernon *d* Albert Parker *ph* Robert Martin *ad* Hugo Ballin

☆ Gloria Swanson, John Boles, Anders Randolf, Hugh Miller, Flobelle Fairbanks, Raymond Hackett

† Previously filmed as *Eyes of Youth* with Clara Kimball Young.

Love on the Dole ***

GB 1941 100m bw
British National (John Baxter)

Life among unemployed cotton workers in industrial Lancashire between the wars.

Vividly characterized, old-fashioned social melodrama, well made on a low budget; a rare problem picture for Britain at this time.

w Walter Greenwood, Barbara K. Emery, Rollo Gamble *novel Walter Greenwood d John Baxter ph* James Wilson *m* Richard Addinsell

☆ *Deborah Kerr,* Clifford Evans, *George Carney,* Joyce Howard, Frank Cellier, Geoffrey Hibbert, *Mary Merrall,* Maire O'Neill, *Marjorie Rhodes,* A. Bromley Davenport, Marie Ault, Iris Vandeleur, Kenneth Griffith

'Kissing and kidding their way from Mayfair to the Mediterranean in a transcontinental caravan of jollity!'

Love on the Run *

US 1936 81m bw
MGM (Joseph L. Mankiewicz)

Rival newspapermen help an heiress to escape an unwanted wedding and in the process uncover a ring of spies.

Harebrained star farce, smoothly assembled and still fairly funny.

w John Lee Mahin, Manuel Seff, Gladys Hurlbut *d* W. S. Van Dyke *ph* Oliver T. Marsh *m* Franz Waxman

☆ Clark Gable, Joan Crawford, Franchot Tone, Reginald Owen, Mona Barrie, Ivan Lebedeff, William Demarest

'Should collect its share at the gate through the sheer momentum of the Gable-Crawford combo.' – *Variety*

'A slightly daffy cinematic item of absolutely no importance.' – *New York Times*

Love on the Run *

France 1979 95m Eastmancolor
Les Films du Carrosse (François Truffaut)

Antoine Doinel, separated from his family, is still having girl trouble.

Amorous adventure of the character first glimpsed in Les Quatre Cent Coups *and presumably based on the director; fair sophisticated fun for those who appreciate the joke.*

w François Truffaut, Marie-France Pisier, Jean Aurel, Suzanne Schiffman *d* François Truffaut *ph* Nestor Almendros *m* Georges Delerue *pd* Jean-Pierre Kohut Svelko *ed* Martine Barraqué

☆ Jean-Pierre Léaud, Marie-France Pisier, Claude Jade, Rosy Varte

Love on Wheels

GB 1932 87m bw
Gainsborough

A department store assistant becomes publicity-conscious.

Zippy little comedy of its day.

w Victor Saville, Angus MacPhail, Robert Stevenson and Douglas Furber *d* Victor Saville

☆ Jack Hulbert, Edmund Gwenn, Leonora Corbett, Gordon Harker, Percy Parsons, Roland Culver, Miles Malleson

The Love Parade **

US 1929 112m bw
Paramount (Ernst Lubitsch)

The prince of Sylvania marries.

Primitive sound operetta set among the idle European rich, with clear but faded instances of the Lubitsch touch.

w Ernest Vajda, Guy Bolton *play The Prince Consort* by Leon Xanrof and Jules Chancel *d Ernst Lubitsch ph* Victor Milner *ad* Hans Dreier *songs* Victor Schertzinger, Clifford Grey

☆ Maurice Chevalier, Jeanette MacDonald, Lupino Lane, Lillian Roth, Edgar Norton, Lionel Belmore, Eugene Pallette

'The first truly cinematic screen musical in America.' – *Theodore Huff*

best picture; Ernst Lubitsch; Victor Milner; Maurice Chevalier; Hans Dreier

'Imagine if sex appeal came in a bottle.'
'If you've got it – you get it!'

Love Potion No. 9

US 1992 97m CFI color
TCF (Dale Launer)

Unattractive scientists discover a chemical that makes the user irresistible to the opposite sex.

Occasionally amusing teen comedy, but one that fails to develop its central idea to any effect.

wd Dale Launer *ph* William Wages *m* Jed Leiber *pd* Linda Pearl *ed* Suzanne Petit

☆ Tate Donovan, Sandra Bullock, Mary Mara, Dale Midkiff, Hillary Bailey Smith, Dylan Baker, Anne Bancroft

'A light-hearted one-joke romantic comedy that tries too hard to be cute.' – *Variety*

Love, Soldiers and Women

France/Italy 1953 96m bw
Franco-London/Continental
original title: *Destinées*
US title: *Daughters of Destiny*

Three stories of women in war: Joan of Arc, Lysistrata, and a modern American war widow visiting her husband's grave.

Uninteresting patchwork with Lysistrata predictably stealing the show.

Jeanne

w Jean Aurenche, Pierre Bost *d* Jean Delannoy with Michèle Morgan

Elizabeth

w Sergio Amedei *d* Marcel Pagliero with Claudette Colbert, Eleanora Rossi Drago

Lysistrata

w Jean Ferry, Henri Jeanson, Carlo Rim *play* Aristophanes *d* Christian-Jaque with Martine Carol, Raf Vallone, Paolo Stoppa

Love Story

GB 1944 112m bw
GFD/Gainsborough (Harold Huth)
US title: *A Lady Surrenders*

In Cornwall during World War II, a half-blind airman falls for a pianist with a weak heart.

Novelettish love story which became popular because of its Cornish Rhapsody.

w Leslie Arliss, Doreen Montgomery, Rodney Ackland *novel* J. W. Drawbell *d* Leslie Arliss *ph* Bernard Knowles *m Hubert Bath*

☆ Margaret Lockwood, Stewart Granger, Patricia Roc, Tom Walls, Reginald Purdell, Moira Lister

'A splendid, noble and fatuous piece.' – *C. A. Lejeune*

'In psychology and dialogue this is straight out of Mabel's Weekly.' – *Richard Winnington*

Love Story: see *Une Histoire d'Amour (1951)*

Love Story *

US 1970 100m Movielab
Paramount (David Golden)

Two students marry; she dies.

A barrage of ripe old Hollywood clichés spiced with new-fangled bad language. In the circumstances, well enough made, and certainly astonishingly popular.

w Erich Segal *novelette Erich Segal d* Arthur Hiller *ph* Dick Kratina *m* Bach, Mozart, Handel *md* Francis Lai

☆ Ali MacGraw, Ryan O'Neal, Ray Milland, John Marley

'Camille with bullshit.' – *Alexander Walker*

Francis Lai

best picture; Erich Segal; Arthur Hiller; Ali MacGraw; Ryan O'Neal; John Marley

Love Streams

US 1984 141m Metrocolor
Cannon (Menahem Golan, Yoram Globus)

A distraught woman whose marriage has gone sour moves in with her philandering brother.

Elongated study of two life styles, not so shapeless as most Cassavetes films, but not exactly dramatic or endearing either.

w Ted Allan, John Cassavetes *play* Ted Allan *d* John Cassavetes *ph* Al Ruban *m* Bo Harwood *ad* Phedon Papamichael *ed* George C. Villasenor

☆ Gena Rowlands, John Cassavetes, Diahnne Abbott, Seymour Cassel, Margaret Abbott

The Love Test

GB 1935 63m bw
Fox British (Leslie L. Landau)

Research scientists plot to prevent a woman from taking over as head of the laboratory by selecting one of their number to seduce her.

Competent, if unoriginal, comedy with an occasional directorial touch that lifts it out of the very ordinary.

w Selwyn Jepson *story* Jack Celestin *d* Michael Powell *ph* Arthur Crabtree

☆ Judy Gunn, Louis Hayward, David Hutcheson, Googie Withers, Morris Harvey, Aubrey Dexter, Gilbert Davis, Bernard Miles

'A light, bright romantic comedy.' – *Variety*

Love That Brute

US 1950 85m bw
TCF (Fred Kohlmar)

A ruthless Chicago gangleader is actually a softy, leaving his supposedly rubbed-out enemies in a comfortable cellar; a young governess persuades him to reform.

Rickety, dully-scripted gangster farce.

w Darrell Ware, John Lee Mahin, Karl Tunberg *d* Alexander Hall *ph* Lloyd Ahern *m* Cyril Mockridge

☆ Paul Douglas, Jean Peters, Cesar Romero, Joan Davis, Arthur Treacher

Love Thy Neighbour *

US 1940 81m bw
Paramount

Two radio comics fall out.

Curious mixture of fact and fiction, basing its plot on the publicity feud between Benny and Allen, who appear 'in character' as themselves.

w William Morrow, Edmund Beloin, Ernest Pagano, Z. Myers *pd* Mark Sandrich

☆ Jack Benny, Fred Allen, Mary Martin, Eddie Anderson, Verree Teasdale, Virginia Dale, Richard Denning

Love Thy Neighbour
GB 1973 85m Technicolor
EMI/Hammer (Roy Skeggs)
A prejudiced white worker has coloured neighbours.
Elongated screen version of the popular TV series in which the West Indians smile through all the insults and come out top in the end. It might have been worse, but not much.
w Vince Powell, Harry Driver *d* John Robins *ph* Moray Grant *m* Albert Elms
☆ Jack Smethurst, Kate Williams, Rudolph Walker, Nina Baden-Semper, Bill Fraser, Charles Hyatt, Keith Marsh, Patricia Hayes, Arthur English

Love under Fire
US 1937 75m bw
TCF (Nunnally Johnson)
A detective catches up with a lady jewel thief in Madrid during the Spanish Civil War.
Adequately entertaining but rather tasteless adventure comedy.
w Gene Fowler, Allen Rivkin, Ernest Pascal *play* Walter Hackett *d* George Marshall *ph* Ernest Palmer *m* Arthur Lange
☆ Loretta Young, Don Ameche, Frances Drake, Walter Catlett, John Carradine, Borrah Minevitch and his Rascals, Sig Rumann, Harold Huber, E. E. Clive, Katherine de Mille
'Melodrama with music cooked up for the duals.' – *Variety*

Love! Valour! Compassion! *
US 1997 110m DeLuxe
Entertainment/New Line/Fine Line (Doug Chapin, Barry Krost)
Eight homosexual friends and lovers get together for three weekend house parties.
Witty, occasionally poignant, account of shifting relationships in the shadow of AIDS.
w Terrence McNally *play* Terrence McNally *d* Joe Mantello *ph* Alik Sakharov *m* Harold Wheeler *pd* François Séguin *ed* Colleen Sharp
☆ Jason Alexander, Randy Becker, Stephen Bogardus, John Glover, John Benjamin Hickey, Justin Kirk, Stephen Spinella
'A perceptive, often hilarious look at life in the AIDS era.' – *Variety*

'There is a moment ... a long moment ... when everything is risked with the proper stranger!'
Love with the Proper Stranger **
US 1964 100m bw
Paramount/Boardwalk (Alan J. Pakula)
A musician tries to help his pregnant shopgirl friend get an abortion, but they decide to get married instead.
Oddly likeable comedy drama set on New York's Italian East Side, with an excellent location sense.
w Arnold Schulman *d* *Robert Mulligan* *ph* Milton Krasner *m* Elmer Bernstein
☆ *Steve McQueen, Natalie Wood, Tom Bosley*, Edie Adams, Herschel Bernardi
Arnold Schulman; Milton Krasner; Natalie Wood

'In her heart she embraced it. In her soul she feared it.'
Loved
US 1996 103m DeLuxe
Downtown/Crosslight/MDP/Clyde Is Hungry/Palisades (Philippe Caland, Sean Penn)
A woman testifies against her former boyfriend, a serial abuser of women.
Enigmatic exploration of obsessive female–male relationships, which never quite clarifies the issues, despite a strong central performance.
wd Erin Dignam *ph* Reynaldo Villalobos *m* David Baerwald *pd* Barry Robison *ed* Gillian Hutchings, David Rogow, Ann Trulove
☆ William Hurt, *Robin Wright Penn*, Amy Madigan, Lucinda Jenny, Joanna Cassidy, Paul Dooley, Anthony Lucero, Jennifer Rubin, Sean Penn
'Deserves kudos for eschewing standard entertainment values.' – *Ken Eisner, Variety*

The Loved One *
US 1965 118m bw
MGM/Filmways (Neil Hartley)
A young English poet in California gets a job at a very select burial ground.
A pointed satire on the American way of death has been allowed to get out of hand, with writer and actors alike laying it on too thick; but there are pleasantly waspish moments in a movie advertised as 'the motion picture with something to offend everybody'.
w Terry Southern, Christopher Isherwood *novel* Evelyn Waugh *d* Tony Richardson *ph* *Haskell Wexler* *m* John Addison *pd* Rouben Ter-Arutunian
☆ *Robert Morse*, John Gielgud, Rod Steiger, *Liberace*, Anjanette Comer, Jonathan Winters, Dana Andrews, Milton Berle, James Coburn, Tab Hunter, Margaret Leighton, Roddy McDowall, Robert Morley, Lionel Stander
'Even a chaotic satire like this is cleansing, and it's embarrassing to pan even a bad movie that comes out against God, mother and country.' – *Pauline Kael, 1968*
'A spineless farrago of collegiate gags.' – *Stanley Kauffmann*
'A sinking ship that makes it to port because everyone on board is too giddy to panic.' – *New Yorker, 1978*

'The Meanest ... Roughest ... Toughest ... Gang Ever To Hit The Screen! Muscles Clad In Black Leather ... Incest ... And Murder!'
'Sworn To Fun ... Loyal To None!!!'
The Loveless
US 1983 83m colour
Mainline/Pioneer Films (Grafton Nunes, A. Kitman Ho)
In the 1950s, a gang of bikers cause problems in a small Southern town.
Arty (the settings are reminiscent of the paintings of Edward Hopper), derivative and inconsequential drama.
wd Kathryn Bigelow, Monty Montgomery *ph* Doyle Smith *m* Robert Gordon *pd* Lilly Kivert *ed* Nancy Kantner
☆ Willem Dafoe, Robert Gordon, Marin Kanter, J. Don Ferguson, Tina L'Hotsky

'Lf you're hoping for the perfect family, don't hold your breath...'
Lovely & Amazing *
US 2001 89m colour
Metro Tartan/Blow Up/Good Machine/Roadside Attractions (Anthony Bregman, Eric d'Arbeloff, Ted Hope)
A self-absorbed mother with two grown-up, discontented daughters adopts a young black girl.
Brisk and engaging comedy about women's insecurities, particularly in their dealings with men and each other.
wd Nicole Holofcener *ph* Harlan Bosmajian *m* Craig Richey *pd* Devorah Herbert *ed* Rob Frazen
☆ Catherine Keener (Michelle Marks), Brenda Blethyn (Jane Marks), Emily Mortimer (Elizabeth Marks), Raven Goodwin (Annie Marks), Aunjaue Ellis (Lorraine), Clark Gregg (Bill), Jake Gyllenhaal (Jordan), James LeGros (Paul), Michael Nouri (Dr Crane), Dermot Mulroney (Kevin McCabe)
'Intelligent and funny but a little unfocussed.' – *David Denby, New Yorker*
'A frustrating and disappointing film.' – *Peter Bradshaw, Guardian*
† The film was shot on high definition video.

Lovely Rita *
Austria/Germany 2001 80m colour
ICA/Coop 99/Essential/Prisma (Antonin Svoboda, Philippe Bober, Heinz Stussak)
In the suburbs of Vienna, a confused teenage girl experiments with sex before turning her anger on to preoccupied parents.
Chilling, small-scale study of suburban teenage angst and anomie, and the discovery that freedom can be more frightening than convention.
wd Jessica Hausner *ph* Martin Gschlacht *ad* Katharina Woeppermann *ed* Karin Hartusch
☆ Barbara Osika (Rita), Christoph Bauer (Fexi), Peter Fiala (Bus driver), Wolfgang Kostal (Rita's father), Karina Brandlmayer (Rita's mother)
'A deliciously observed, ironic take on middle-class Austrian life.' – *Derek Elley, Variety*

Lovely to Look At: see *Thin Ice (1937)*

Lovely to Look At *
US 1952 102m Technicolor
MGM (Jack Cummings)
Three Broadway producers inherit a Paris fashion house.
Lavish but dullish remake of Roberta (qv)*, in itself no great shakes as a storyline; again the fashions and the numbers are the thing.*
w George Wells, Harry Ruby *d* Mervyn Le Roy *ph* George J. Folsey *m* Jerome Kern *ad* Cedric Gibbons, Gabriel Scognamillo
☆ Howard Keel, Kathryn Grayson, Ann Miller, Red Skelton, Marge and Gower Champion, Zsa Zsa Gabor, Kurt Kasznar
♫ 'Lovely to Look At'; 'I'll Be Hard to Handle'; 'Yesterdays'; 'The Most Exciting Night'; 'You're Devastating'; 'I Won't Dance'; 'Smoke Gets in Your Eyes'; 'The Touch of Your Hand'.

A Lovely Way to Die
US 1968 98m Techniscope
Universal (Richard Lewis)
GB title: *A Lovely Way to Go*
An ex-cop becomes bodyguard to a suspected murderess, but proves her innocent.
Offbeat mélange of caper comedy, black farce, private eye detection, courtroom drama, spectacular action and routine thick ear. Doesn't work.
w A. J. Russell *d* David Lowell Rich *ph* Morris Hartzband *m* Kenyon Hopkins
☆ Kirk Douglas, Sylva Koscina, Eli Wallach, *Martyn Green*, Kenneth Haigh, Sharon Farrell
'The net result is rather as though Philip Marlowe had met Doris Day on his not very inspiring way to the forum.' – *MFB*

A Lovely Way to Go: see *A Lovely Way to Die*

The Lover: see *L'Amant*

A Lover and His Lass *
Sweden 1975 90m Eastmancolor
SF/SFI (Bengt Forslund, Olle Hellbom, Olle Nordemar)
original title: *En Kille Och En Tjej*
aka: *Boy Meets Girl*
The amorous adventures of a hypochrondriac unemployed journalist.
Pleasant comedy about the slow maturing of a young drifter.
w Lasse Hallström, Lasse Brännström *d* Lasse Hallström *ph* Eddie Akberg, Lasse Ulander *m* Berndt Egerbladh *ad* Stig Limer *ed* Lasse Hallström
☆ Lasse Brännström, Mariann Rudberg, Christer 'Bonzo' Jonsson, Börje Ahlstedt, Roland Hedlund, Chatarina Larsson, Anna Godenus, Gun Jönsson

Lover Boy: see *Knave of Hearts*

Lover Come Back
US 1946 90m bw
Universal (Howard Benedict)
When a war correspondent returns, his wife discovers that he hasn't been so lonely overseas as he might have been.
Very tolerable star comedy which at the time seemed quite fresh.
w Michael Fessier, Ernest Pagano *d* William A. Seiter *ph* Joseph Valentine *m* Hans J. Salter
☆ George Brent, Lucille Ball, Vera Zorina, Charles Winninger, Carl Esmond, Raymond Walburn, Franklin Pangborn, Louise Beavers
'Should chalk up good grosses in most situations.' – *Variety*

Lover Come Back **
US 1961 107m Eastmancolor
U-I/Seven Pictures/Nob Hill/Arwin (Stanley Shapiro, Marty Melcher)
Rival executives find themselves advertising a non-existent product.
Fairly sharp advertising satire disguised as a romantic comedy; the most entertaining of the Day-Hudson charmers.
w *Stanley Shapiro, Paul Henning* *d* Delbert Mann *ph* Arthur E. Arling *m* Frank de Vol
☆ Doris Day, Rock Hudson, *Tony Randall*, Jack Oakie, Edie Adams
Stanley Shapiro, Paul Henning

Loverboy
US 1989 99m Technicolor
Columbia TriStar/Crescent Film Enterprises (Gary Foster, Willie Hunt)
A pizza delivery boy pays his way through college by becoming a lover to his female customers.
Feeble comedy with little wit or sense.
w Robin Schiff, Tom Ropelewski, Leslie Dixon *d* Joan Micklin Silver *ph* John Davis *m* Michel Colombier *pd* Dan Leigh *ed* Rick Shaine
☆ Patrick Dempsey, Kate Jackson, Kirstie Alley, Carrie Fisher, Robert Ginty, Nancy Valen, Charles Hunter Walsh, Barbara Carrera
'The material often suggests a crude and juvenile variation on The Graduate.' – *MFB*

The Lovers: see *Les Amants (1958)*

The Lovers
GB 1972 89m Eastmancolor
British Lion/Gildor (Maurice Foster)
A Manchester bank clerk with a prim girlfriend finds it difficult to lose his virginity.
Well-written but rather arch comedy which seemed much funnier and fresher as a TV series.
w Jack Rosenthal *d* Herbert Wise *ph* Bob Huke *m* Carl Davis
☆ Richard Beckinsale, Paula Wilcox, Joan Scott, Susan Littler, John Comer, Stella Moray, Nikolas Simmonds

'This landlady has more than just rent on her mind.'
Lovers *
Spain 1991 103m colour
Mainline/TVE/Pedro Costa
original title: *Amantes*
In the 1950s, a young Spanish man finds himself torn between his virginal fiancée and the sexy, sophisticated widow with whom he lodges.
Overheated and old-fashioned drama that becomes increasingly melodramatic as it continues.
w Carlos Perez, Alvaro Del Amo, Vicente Aranda *d* Vicente Aranda *ph* José Luis Alcaine *m* José Nieto *ad* Josep Rosell *ed* Teresa Font
☆ Victoria Abril, Jorge Sanz, Maribel Verdu, Enrique Cerro, Mabel Escano, José Cerro, Gabriel Latorre
'A nicely photographed, well-dressed, at times distinctly tedious love triangle thriller.' – *Empire*

Lovers
France/GB 1999 100m colour
Toloda/Bar-Nothing/TF1/Canal+/Film4 (Pascal Arnold, Jean-Marc Barr)
In Paris, a bookshop assistant falls in love with a Yugoslavian artist.
Intense romantic drama that becomes too claustrophobic in its concentration on the momentary moods of its lovers; it provides so little information about either that their relationship and predicaments fail to interest.
w Pascal Arnold, Jean-Marc Barr *d* Jean-Marc Barr *ad* Francoise Rabut *ed* Brian Schmitt
☆ Elodie Bouchez (Jeanne), Serguci Trifunovic (Dragan), Genevieve Page (Alice), Dragan Nicolic (Zlatan), Thibault de Montalembest (Jean-Michel)
† It was filmed with handheld cameras using available light, under the rules of Dogme 95.

Lovers and Other Strangers ***
US 1970 104m Metrocolor
ABC/David Susskind
After living together for eighteen months, Susan and Mike decide to get married, and find their parents have sex problems of their own.
Wise, witty and well-acted sex farce, with many actors making the most of ample chances under firm directorial control.
w *Renée Taylor, Joseph Bologna, David Zelag Goodman* *d* *Cy Howard* *ph* *Andrew Laszlo* *m* Fred Karlin
☆ *Gig Young, Anne Jackson, Richard Castellano*, Bonnie Bedelia, Michael Brandon, *Beatrice Arthur*, Robert Dishy, Harry Guardino, Diane Keaton, Cloris Leachman, Anne Meara, Marian Hailey
'An extremely engaging comedy.' – *Gillian Hartnoll*
song 'For All We Know' (*m*Fred Karlin, *ly*Robb Wilson, Arthur James)
script, Richard Castellano

Lovers Courageous
US 1932 78m bw
MGM
An unsuccessful playwright covets the admiral's daughter.
Heavily-titled comedy with good performances of the period.
w Frederick Lonsdale *d* Robert Z. Leonard
☆ Robert Montgomery, Madge Evans, Roland Young, Frederick Kerr, Reginald Owen, Halliwell Hobbes, Alan Mowbray

Lovers Like Us: see *Call Him Savage*

Lovers Must Learn: see *Rome Adventure*

The Lovers of Lisbon *
France 1954 112m bw
EGC/Hoche/Fides (Jacques Gauthier)
original title: *Les Amants du Tage*
A man who has killed his unfaithful wife is acquitted of murder, gets a job as a taxi driver in Lisbon, and falls for a rich Englishwoman who has killed her husband and is being pursued by a police inspector.
Pretentious tosh with a few compensations.
w Marcel Rivet *novel* Joseph Kessel *d* Henri Verneuil *ph* Roger Hubert *m* Lucien Legrand
☆ Daniel Gélin, Françoise Arnoul, Trevor Howard, Ginette Leclerc, Marcel Dalio

Lovers of Montparnasse *
France 1958 110m bw
Franco London Films (Ralph Baum)
original title: *Les Amants de Montparnasse*
US title: *Modigliani of Montparnasse*
Alcoholic and ill, Modigliani pursues his art and the young woman who inspires him to paint.
Moderate biopic, though with an unconvincing performance from Philipe.
w Jacques Becker, Max Ophuls, Henri Jeanson *novel* *Les Montparnos* by Michel Georges Michel *d* Jacques Becker *ph* Christian Matras *m* Paul Misraki *pd* J. A. d'Eaubonne *ed* Marguerite Renoir
☆ Gérard Philipe, Lilli Palmer, Léa Padovani, Lino Ventura, Anouk Aimée

'Destiny cannot be denied.'
Lovers of the Arctic Circle ***
Spain/France 1998 108m colour Super 35
Metro Tartan/Alicia/Bailando en la Luna/Sogetel (Fernando Bovaira, Enrique Lopez Lavinge)
original title: *Los Amantes del Circulo Polar*
The lives of a man and a woman interlock from their first meeting in childhood, but their later attempts to meet one another are frustrated.
A unusual, lyrical movie about predestination, and the way one life links unexpectedly with another; it is also a charmingly romantic tale of loves lost and won.
d Julio Medem *ph* Gonzalo F. Berridi *m* Alberto Iglesias *pd* Satur Udarreta, Karmele Soler, Estibaliz Markiegi, Itziar Arrieta *ed* Ivan Aledo
☆ Najwa Nimri (Ana), Fele Martinez (Otto), Nancho Nova (Alvaro), Maru Valdivieslo (Olga), Peru Medem (Otto as a child), Sara Valiente (Ana as a child), Victor Hugo Oliveira (Adolescent Otto), Kristel Diaz (Adolescent Ana), Pep Munné (Javier)
'It never loses the air of a dispassionate exercise, arranged by its creator according to an oppressively rigid pattern of his own.' – *Edward Porter, Sunday Times*

The Lovers of Toledo
Italy/France/Spain 1952 82m bw
EGE/Lux/Athenea (Raymond Eger)
In 1825 a cruel police chief releases a political prisoner in return for the hand in marriage of his mistress.
Curiously unpersuasive period melodrama with good credits but too many international cooks.
w Claude Vermorel *story* *Le Coffre et le Revenant* by Stendhal *d* Henri Decoin *ph* Michel Kelber *m* Jean-Jacques Grunenwald
☆ Pedro Armendariz, Alida Valli, Gérard Landry, Françoise Arnoul

The Lovers of Verona: see *Les Amants de Vérone*

Lovers on the Pont-Neuf: see *Les Amants du Pont-Neuf*

Love's a Bitch: see *Amores Perros*

'A New Spin On The Old Song and Dance.'
Love's Labours Lost *
GB/France/US 2000 94m colour Super 35
Pathé/Intermedia/Shakespeare/Arts Council/Canal+/Miramax (David Barron, Kenneth Branagh)
In 1939, the King of Navarre goes on a celibate retreat into the woods with three friends; then the Princess of France arrives with three female companions.
Lively attempt to revive the Hollywood musical, though why the 30s melodies were hung upon the bare bones of Shakespeare's comedy is hard to understand; the result is a lightweight romantic romp with songs that have been better sung elsewhere.
wd Kenneth Branagh *play* William Shakespeare *ph* Alex Thomson *m* Patrick Doyle *m/ly* Irving Berlin, George Gershwin, Jerome Kern, Cole Porter *ch* Stuart Hopps *pd* Tim Harvey *ed* Neil Farrell, Dan Farrell *cos* Anna Buruma
☆ Alessandro Nivola (King), Alicia Silverstone (Princess), Natascha McElhone (Rosaline), Kenneth Branagh (Berowne), Carmen Ejogo (Maria), Matthew Lillard (Longaville), Adrian Lester (Dumaine), Emily Mortimer (Katherine), Richard Briers (Nathaniel), Geraldine McEwan (Holofernia), Stefania Rocca (Jaquenetta), Jimmy Yuill (Costard), Timothy Spall (Don Armado), Anthony O'Donnell (Moth)
'The result is not a classic, but it is fun: short, sharp and fast-paced.' – *Derek Malcolm, Screen International*
♫ I'd Rather Charleston; I Get a Kick Out of You; I Won't Dance; No Strings; Cheek to Cheek; The Way You Look Tonight; I've Got a Crush on You; Let's Face the Music and Dance; There's No Business Like Show Business; They Can't Take That Away From Me

Loves of a Blonde *
Czechoslovakia 1965 82m bw
Barrandov Studios
original title: *Lasky Jedne Plavovlasky*
aka: *A Blonde in Love*
A factory girl falls for a visiting musician but meets suspicion from his family when she pursues him.
Mild anecdote with excellent humorous detail which endeared it to international critics.
w Milos Forman, Jaroslav Papousek, Ivan Passer *d* Milos Forman *ph* Miroslav Ondricek *m* Evzen Illin
☆ Hanna Brejchova, Vladimir Pucholt
'It depends on an instinctive sense of timing and a consistent vision of life and people.' – *Georges Sadoul*
best foreign film

The Loves of Carmen
US 1948 99m Technicolor
Columbia (Charles Vidor)
In 1820s Seville, a dragoon corporal is enslaved by a gypsy, kills her husband and becomes an outlaw.
Unrewarding version of the original much-filmed story, with both stars plainly wishing they were elsewhere.
w Helen Deutsch *novel* Prosper Mérimée *d* Charles Vidor *ph* William Snyder *m* Mario Castelnuovo-Tedesco
☆ Rita Hayworth, Glenn Ford, Victor Jory, Ron Randell, Luther Adler, Arnold Moss, Margaret Wycherly, Bernard Nedell
William Snyder

The Loves of Count Iorga, Vampire: see *Count Yorga Vampire*

The Loves of Edgar Allan Poe
US 1942 67m bw
TCF (Bryan Foy)
The famous writer marries his childhood sweetheart but becomes an alcoholic.
A curiosity which fails to bring out the bizarre truth and emerges as a stilted charade.
w Samuel Hoffenstein, Tom Reed *d* Harry Lachman *ph* Lucien Andriot *m* Emil Newman
☆ John Shepperd, Linda Darnell, Virginia Gilmore, Jane Darwell, Frank Conroy, Henry Morgan

The Loves of Isadora: see *Isadora*

The Loves of Joanna Godden
GB 1947 89m bw
Ealing (Sidney Cole)
On Romney Marsh at the turn of the century, a woman farmer has three suitors.
Dullish 'woman's picture'.
w H. E. Bates, Angus Macphail *novel* Sheila Kaye-Smith *d* Charles Frend *ph* Douglas Slocombe *m* Ralph Vaughan Williams *md* Ernest Irving *ad* Duncan Sutherland *ed* Michael Truman *cos* Mark Luker
☆ Googie Withers (Joanna Godden), John McCallum (Arthur Alce), Jean Kent (Ellen Godden), Derek Bond (Martin Trevor), Chips Rafferty (Collard), Henry Mollison (Harry Trevor), Sonia Holm (Louise), Edward Rigby (Stuppen), Josephine Stuart (Grace Wickens)
'Made with sincerity, and its outdoor backgrounds abound in freshness and beauty, but I felt that it faltered because the script writers and the director permitted themselves to become so obsessed by the landscape and local colour that they regarded the plot as somewhat of a hindrance to their documentary explorations.' – *Ewart Hodgson, News of the World*
† Robert Hamer directed some scenes.

The Loves of Salammbo: see *Salambo*

Lovesick
US 1983 96m Technicolor
Warner/Ladd (Charles Okun)
A New York psychiatrist in love with a patient is guided by the ghost of Sigmund Freud.
Depressing comedy with a non-star and supporting players who must have been embarrassed.
wd Marshall Brickman *ph* Gerry Fisher *m* Philippe Sarde *pd* Philip Rosenberg
☆ Dudley Moore (Saul Benjamin), Elizabeth McGovern (Chloe Allen), Alec Guinness (Sigmund Freud), John Huston, Larry Rivers, Gene Saks, Renee Taylor, Alan King
'Flat, lamebrained and indigestible.' – *Geoff Brown, MFB*

Lovin' Molly *
US 1973 98m Movielab
Stephen Friedman (David Golden)
In Texas between 1925 and 1945, two men friends and an accommodating lady have a shifting relationship.
Odd little drama compendium, with fragments told by each in turn; too slight in structure and substance for complete success, but interesting most of the way.
w Stephen Friedman *novel* *Leaving Cheyenne* by Larry McMurtry *d* Sidney Lumet *ph* Edward Brown *m* Fred Hellerman
☆ Blythe Danner, Anthony Perkins, Beau Bridges, Edward Binns, Susan Sarandon

Loving **
US 1970 90m Eastmancolor
Columbia/Brooks Ltd (Don Devlin)
A commercial artist reaches crisis point with both his wife and his mistress.
Smart New Yorkish sex comedy, typical of many but better than most.
w Don Devlin *novel* Brooks Wilson Ltd by J. M. Ryan *d* Irvin Kershner *ph* Gordon Willis *m* Bernardo Segall *pd* Walter Scott Herndon
☆ George Segal, Eva Marie Saint, Sterling Hayden, Keenan Wynn, Nancie Phillips, Janis Young, David Doyle

Loving Couples *
Sweden 1964 118m bw
Sandrew (Rune Waldekranz)
original title: *älskande Par*
Three expectant mothers think back over their sex lives.
Superbly made, rather hollow diatribe against sex, presented as a series of intricate flashbacks. Along the way, there is much to enjoy, but the result is not really a film of importance.
w Mai Zetterling, David Hughes *novel* *Froknarna von Pahlen* by Agnes von Krusenstjerna *d* Mai Zetterling *ph* Sven Nykvist *m* Rodger Wallis
☆ Harriet Andersson, Gunnel Lindblom, Anita Bjork, Gunnar Bjornstrand, Eva Dahlbeck, Frank Sundstrom, Inga Landgre
'...that air of packaged neurosis so peculiar to the Swedish cinema.' – *Tom Milne, MFB*

Loving Couples
US 1980 98m Metrocolor
Time Life (Renee Valente)
Man-and-wife doctors decide to liven up their lives by having affairs.
Embarrassingly with-it romantic charade.
w Martin Donovan *d* Jack Smight *ph* Philip Lathrop *m* Fred Karlin
☆ Shirley MacLaine, James Coburn, Susan Sarandon, Stephen Collins, Sally Kellerman

Loving in the Rain
France/Italy/West Germany 1973 90m Eastmancolor
Lira Films/Terra Film (Raymond Danon)
original title: *Un Amour de Pluie*
A mother and her teenage daughter both experience a holiday love affair.
An inconsequential romance involving inconsequential people.
w Jean-Claude Brialy, Yves Simon *d* Jean-Claude Brialy *ph* Andreas Winding *m* Francis Lai *ed* Eva Zorn
☆ Romy Schneider, Nino Castelnuovo, Mehdi, Benedicte Bucher, Suzanne Flon

Loving You
US 1957 101m Technicolor Vistavision
Paramount/Hal B. Wallis
A press agent signs a young hillbilly singer to give zest to her husband's band.
Empty-headed, glossy star vehicle.
w Herbert Baker, Hal Kanter *d* Hal Kanter *ph* Charles Lang Jnr *m* Walter Scharf
☆ Elvis Presley, Lizabeth Scott, Wendell Corey, Dolores Hart, James Gleason

A Low Down Dirty Shame
US 1994 100m Technicolor
Buena Vista/Hollywood (Joe Roth, Roger Birnbaum)
A private eye investigates the South American drug dealer who cost him his job as a Los Angeles cop.
An action comedy that fails on both counts, unless you find men with guns inherently amusing.
wd Keenen Ivory Wayans *ph* Matthew F. Leonetti *m* Marcus Miller *pd* Robb Wilson King *ed* John F. Link
☆ Keenen Ivory Wayans, Charles S. Dutton, Jada Pinkett, Salli Richardson, Andrew Divoff, Corwin Hawkins, Gary Cervantes, Gregory Sierra
'A predictable and sluggishly paced plot with obligatory car chases and shoot-outs.' – *Lizzie Francke*

The Lower Depths: see *Les Bas-fonds (1936)*

The Lower Depths **
Japan 1957 124m bw
Toho
original title: *Donzoko*
An elderly pilgrim moves into a hovel and changes the lives of the derelicts who live there.
Effectively unsentimental, claustrophobic version of life at the bottom, although it betrays its theatrical origins, with more talk than action.
w Akira Kurosawa, Hideo Oguni *play* Maxim Gorky *d* Akira Kurosawa *ph* Ichio Yamazaki *m* Masaru Sato
☆ Isuzu Yamada, Toshiro Mifune, Bokuzen Hidari, Kyoko Kagawa, Akemi Nigishi, Nijiko Kiyokawa
'Lesser Kurosawa, but still high-quality cinema.' – *Empire*

Lucas
US 1986 100m DeLuxe
TCF (David Nicksay)
A studious 14-year-old boy tries for the football team after falling for a new 16-year-old girl at school.
Pleasant little movie about the problems of growing up, though it steers clear of reality and tries too hard to be charming.
wd David Seltzer *ph* Reynaldo Villalobos *m* Dave Grusin *ad* James Murakami *ed* Priscilla Nedd
☆ Corey Haim, Kerri Green, Charlie Sheen, Courtney Thorne-Smith, Winona Ryder, Guy Boyd

Luci del Varieta: see *Lights of Variety*

Lucia y El Sexo: see *Sex and Lucia*

Lucie Aubrac **
France 1997 116m colour Technovision
Pathé/Renn/TF1/DA/Pricel (Patrick Bordier)
A French woman is determined to liberate from prison her husband, a leading member of the Resistance, who has been sentenced to death by the Gestapo.
An emotional romance set against wartime privations and tribulations, all the more moving because it is based on a true story.
wd Claude Berri *book* Outwitting the Gestapo by Lucie Aubrac *ph* Vincenzo Marano *m* Philippe Sarde *ad* Olivier Radot *ed* Hervé de Luze
☆ Carole Bouquet, Daniel Auteuil, Patrice Chéreau, Eric Boucher, Jean-Roger Milo, Heino Ferch
'Tethered by a detached tone and directorial restraint, ultimately rendering a potential heart-wrenching yarn decidedly lacklustre.' – *Ian Freer, Empire*
† Juliette Binoche was replaced in the title role after several weeks' shooting.

The Luck of Ginger Coffey *
Canada/US 1964 100m bw
Crawley/Roth-Kershner (Leon Roth)
An Irish layabout in Canada finds it difficult to keep a job or protect his family.
Mildly interesting character study with good background detail of Montreal.
w Brian Moore *novel* Brian Moore *d* Irvin Kershner *ph* Manny Wynn *m* Bernardo Segall
☆ Robert Shaw, Mary Ure, Liam Redmond

The Luck of the Irish *
US 1948 99m bw
TCF (Fred Kohlmar)
A New York newsman's love life is complicated by a helpful leprechaun he meets in Ireland.
Hollywood moonshine, second class: the will and the players are there, but the script is not funny enough.
w Philip Dunne *novel* There Was a Little Man by Constance and Guy Jones *d* Henry Koster *ph* Joseph LaShelle *m* Cyril Mockridge
☆ Tyrone Power, *Cecil Kellaway*, Anne Baxter, Lee J. Cobb, James Todd, Jayne Meadows, J. M. Kerrigan, Phil Brown
Cecil Kellaway

The Luckiest Girl in the World
US 1936 75m bw
Charles R. Rogers/Universal
A rich girl bets her father that she can live in New York for a month on 150 dollars.
Lighthearted comedy with farcical trimmings.
w Herbert Fields, Henry Myers, Anne Jordan *d* Edward Buzzell
☆ Jane Wyatt, Louis Hayward, Eugene Pallette, Nat Pendleton, Catherine Doucet, Philip Reed
'Speed and gags offset story absurdity.' – *Variety*

Lucky Boy
US 1929 97m bw part silent
Tiffany-Stahl
A young Jewish boy makes it big on Broadway.
Simple-minded fable inspired by The Jazz Singer *(which Jessel is said to have turned down).*
w George Jessel *d* Norman Taurog, Charles C. Wilson
☆ George Jessel, Rosa Rosanova, William K. Strauss, Margaret Quimby

Lucky Break
GB/Germany/US 2001 107m colour
Film Four/Senator/Paramount/Miramax/Fragile/Lucky Break (Barnaby Thompson, Peter Cattaneo)
A jailed bank robber persuades other inmates to stage a musical to cover his escape from prison.
Slight, predictable comedy with a little charm and too much reliance on familiar stereotypes.
w Ronan Bennett *d* Peter Cattaneo *ph* Alwin Kuchler *m* Anne Dudley *pd* Max Gottlieb *ed* David Gamble *cos* Ffion Elinor
☆ James Nesbitt (Jimmy), Olivia Williams (Annabel), Timothy Spall (Cliff), Bill Nighy (Roger), Lennie James (Rudy), Ron Cook (Perry), Frank Harper (John Toombes), Raymond Waring (Darren), Christopher Plummer (Graham Mortimer), Julian Barratt (Paul), Peter Wight (Officer George Barratt), Celia Imrie (Amy)
'A thoroughly competent and disarmingly daft piece of work.' – *Nigel Cliff, Times*

Lucky Devils
US 1933 63m bw
David O. Selznick/RKO
Hollywood stuntmen rescue an actress from a suicide attempt.
Tolerable action special with interesting sidelights.
w Agnes Christine Johnston, Ben Markson *story* Casey Robinson, Bob Rose *d* Ralph Ince *ph* J. Roy Hunt
☆ William Boyd, Dorothy Wilson, William Gargan, Robert Rose, Roscoe Ates, Bruce Cabot

Lucky Jim **
GB 1957 95m bw
British Lion/Charter (Roy Boulting)
At a provincial university, an accident-prone junior lecturer has a disastrous weekend with his girlfriend and his professor.
Quite funny in its own right, this is a vulgarization of a famous comic novel which got its effects more subtly, with more sense of place, time and character.
w Jeffrey Dell, Patrick Campbell *novel* Kingsley Amis *d* John Boulting *ph* Max Greene *m* John Addison
☆ *Ian Carmichael, Hugh Griffith, Terry-Thomas*, Sharon Acker, Jean Anderson, Maureen Connell, Clive Morton, John Welsh, Reginald Beckwith, Kenneth Griffith
'An almost endless ripple of comfortable laughter.' – *News Chronicle*

'When he smiles, it's not because he likes you – it's because he likes what he's going to do to you!'
Lucky Jordan
US 1942 83m bw
Paramount (Fred Kohlmar)
A con man is drafted and overcomes Nazi agents.
Forgettable star cheapie.
w Darrell Ware, Karl Tunberg *d* Frank Tuttle *ph* John F. Seitz *m* Adolph Deutsch
☆ *Alan Ladd*, Helen Walker, Sheldon Leonard, Marie McDonald, Mabel Paige, Lloyd Corrigan, Dave Willock, Miles Mander
'It's still cops and robbers, no matter how you slice it ... Mr Ware and Mr Tunberg are not above dragging in mother love as the reason the gangster changes from a selfish killer to a patriot.' – *Joseph Pihodna, New York Herald Tribune*

Lucky Lady
US 1975 118m DeLuxe
TCF/Gruskoff/Venture (Michael Gruskoff)
A cabaret girl in 1930 Tijuana joins two adventurers in smuggling liquor into the US by boat.
Whatever can be done wrong with such a story has been done, including irritatingly washed out photography, kinky sex, and sudden switches from farce to gore. None of it holds the interest for a single moment.
w Willard Huyck, Gloria Katz *d* Stanley Donen *ph* Geoffrey Unsworth *m* Ralph Burns *pd* John Barry
☆ Liza Minnelli, Gene Hackman, Burt Reynolds, Michael Hordern, Geoffrey Lewis, Robby Benson
'A manic mess that tries to be all things to all people and ends up offering nothing to anyone.' – *Frank Rich*
'It sports its calculations on its sleeve like rhinestones.' – *Sight and Sound*
'They're all rumrunners in the early 30s, and they're meant to be adorable. This is a big expensive movie for people who don't mind being treated like hicks: the audience is expected to shudder with delight every time it hears an obscenity or sees a big movie star grin.' – *Pauline Kael, New Yorker*

Lucky Mascot: see *The Brass Monkey*

Lucky Me *
US 1954 100m Warnercolor Cinemascope
Warner (Henry Blanke)
Theatrical entertainers stranded in Florida get a lucky break.
Watchable, forgettable musical.
w James O'Hanlon, Robert O'Brien, Irving Elinson *d* Jack Donohue *ph* Wilfrid M. Cline *md* Ray Heindorf
☆ Doris Day, Robert Cummings, Phil Silvers, Eddie Foy Jnr, Nancy Walker, Martha Hyer, Bill Goodwin, Marcel Dalio
'The first Cinemascope musical ... pleasant, light-hearted, frothy entertainment.' – *MFB*

Lucky Nick Cain: see *I'll Get You for This*

Lucky Night
US 1939 90m bw
MGM (Louis D. Lighton)
An heiress goes out into the world to make a life for herself, and falls for a man she finds on a park bench.
Tedious pattern romance which did neither of its stars any good.
w Vincent Lawrence, Grover Jones *d* Norman Taurog *ph* Ray June *m* Franz Waxman
☆ Myrna Loy, Robert Taylor, Joseph Allen, Henry O'Neill, Douglas Fowley, Marjorie Main, Charles Lane, Bernard Nedell
'Light romantic comedy, okay for box office ... but certain sections might object to so much liquor-imbibing.' – *Variety*

Lucky Partners *
US 1940 101m bw
RKO (George Haight)
Two strangers share a sweepstake ticket and fall in love.
A very thin comedy kept afloat by its stars.
w Allan Scott, John Van Druten *story* Bonne Chance by Sacha Guitry *d* Lewis Milestone *ph* Robert de Grasse *m* Dimitri Tiomkin
☆ *Ronald Colman*, Ginger Rogers, Jack Carson, Spring Byington, Cecilia Loftus, Harry Davenport

The Lucky Star *
Canada 1980 110m colour
Tele Metropole International/Claude Leger
During World War II a Dutch Jewish boy studies wild west films and captures a German colonel.
Unusual and likeable family adventure story with an unnecessary downbeat ending.
w Max Fischer, Jack Rosenthal *d* Max Fischer *ph* Frank Tidy *m* Art Philipps
☆ Rod Steiger, Louise Fletcher, Brett Marx, Lou Jacobi, Helen Hughes

The Lucky Stiff
US 1949 101m bw
Amusement Enterprises/UA
A cabaret singer sentenced to death for murder is secretly reprieved but comes back as a 'ghost' to scare the real culprit into confession.
Weird comedy-melodrama which seems to embarrass all concerned.
wd Lewis R. Foster *novel* Craig Rice *ph* Ernest Laszlo
☆ Dorothy Lamour, Brian Donlevy, Claire Trevor, Irene Hervey

The Lucky Texan
US 1933 56m bw
Monogram/Lone Star (Paul Malvern)
Two crooked assayers try to cheat an old man out of his ranch and gold mine, but the son of his former partner saves the day.
Brisk programmer, with some novel stunts, including Wayne almost walking on water, 'Gabby' Hayes beginning to perfect the comic role of a whiskery and garrulous sidekick which he was to play for the next 18 years, and an unusual final chase involving horses, an automobile and a railcar.
wd Robert N. Bradbury *ph* Archie Stout *ed* Carl Pierson
☆ John Wayne, Barbara Sheldon, Lloyd Whitlock, George Hayes, Yakima Canutt, Ed Parker, Gordon Demaine, Earl Dwire

Lucretia Borgia
France/Italy 1952 105m approx Technicolor
Ariane/Filmsonor/Rizzoli
Cesare Borgia uses his beautiful sister as a political pawn.
Well-mounted but rather boring period barnstormer.
w Cécil Saint-Laurent, Jacques Sigurd, Christian-Jaque *d* Christian-Jaque *ph* Christian Matras *m* Maurice Thiriet
☆ Martine Carol, Pedro Armendariz, Massimo Serato, Valentine Tessier

Lucy Gallant *
US 1955 104m Technicolor Vistavision
Paramount/Pine-Thomas
The success story of a dressmaker who comes to run a group of fashion shops but neglects her love life.
Efficient, smartly-handled woman's picture.
w John Lee Mahin, Winston Miller *novel* The Life of Lucy Gallant by Margaret Cousins *d* Robert Parrish *ph* Lionel Lindon *m* Van Cleave
☆ Jane Wyman, Charlton Heston, Claire Trevor, Thelma Ritter, William Demarest, Wallace Ford, Tom Helmore, Mary Field

Ludwig *
Italy/France/West Germany 1972 186m Technicolor Panavision
Mega/Cinetel/Dieter Gessler/Divina (Robert Gordon Edwards)
The 19th-century King of Bavaria becomes involved in scandal and goes mad.
A stylish but historically questionable and highly coloured view of events; it drags its heels long before history did.
w Luchino Visconti, Enrico Medioli *d* Luchino Visconti *ph* Armando Nannuzzi *md* Franco Nannino
☆ Helmut Berger, Romy Schneider, Trevor Howard, Silvana Mangano, Helmut Griem, Nora Ricci, Gert Frobe, John Moulder Brown

The Lullaby: see *The Sin of Madelon Claudet*

'Happiness is busting out all over!'
Lullaby of Broadway *
US 1951 92m Technicolor
Warner (William Jacobs)
The daughter of a faded Broadway star becomes the new toast of the town.
Reasonably lively musical with solid production values but little style or wit.
w Earl Baldwin *d* David Butler *ph* Wilfrid Cline *md* Ray Heindorf *ad* Douglas Bacon *ed* Irene Morra *musical numbers staged by* Al White, Eddie Prinz
☆ Doris Day, Gene Nelson, S. Z. Sakall, Billy De Wolfe, Gladys George, Florence Bates, Anne Triola, Hanley Stafford, Page Cavanaugh Trio, Carlo and Constance De Mattiazzi
♫ In a Shanty in Old Shanty Town; The Lullaby of Broadway; Please Don't Talk About Me when I'm Gone; Somebody Loves Me; You're Dependable; You're Getting To Be a Habit With Me; Just One of Those Things; Zing! Went the Strings of My Heart; I Love the Way You Say Goodnight

Lulu: see *Pandora's Box*

Lulu Belle
US 1948 87m bw
Benedict Bogeaus/Columbia
A selfish singer has a bad effect on one man after another.
Dreary melodrama with a miscast star.
w Everett Freeman *play* Charles MacArthur, Edward Sheldon *d* Leslie Fenton
☆ Dorothy Lamour, George Montgomery, Otto Kruger, Albert Dekker, Glenda Farrell

La Lumière d'en Face: see *The Light Across the Street*

Lumière d'Eté *
France 1943 112m bw
Discina (André Paulvé)
The idle and decadent rich in a mountain hotel are affected in various ways by workmen in the valley below.
Unusual and generally interesting character melodrama.
w Jacques Prévert, Pierre Laroche *d* Jean Grémillon *ph* Louis Page *m* Roland Manuel
☆ Madeleine Renaud, Pierre Brasseur, Madeleine Robinson, Paul Bernard, Jane Marken, Georges Marchal

La Luna
Italy 1979 142m Eastmancolor
TCF/Fiction Cinematografica (Giovanni Bertolucci)
A singer has an incestuous relationship with her teenage son.
Interminable catalogue of events few people wanted to experience; the kindest description would be 'pretentious claptrap'.
w Giuseppe and Bernardo Bertolucci, Clare Peploe *d* Bernardo Bertolucci *ph* Vittorio Storaro *m* operatic excerpts
☆ Jill Clayburgh, Matthew Barry, Laura Betti, Renato Salvatori, Fred Gwynne

Luna de Miel: see *Honeymoon*

'A seriously wicked comedy hot from Jamaica'
The Lunatic
US 1992 93m CFI color
Island (Paul Heller, John Pringle)
A German photographer visiting Jamaica falls for a local butcher and a boy who talks to the trees.
Whimsical fable that passes an idle hour or so.
w Anthony C. Winkler *novel* Anthony C. Winkler *d* Lol Creme *ph* Richard Greatrex *m* Wally Badarou *ad* Giorgio Ferrarri *ed* Michael Connell
☆ Julie T. Wallace, Paul Campbell, Reggie Carter, Carl Bradshaw, Winston Stona, Linda Gambrill, Rosemary Murray, Lloyd Reckord
'An annoyingly cute fable.' – *Variety*

Lunch on the Grass **
France 1959 91m Eastmancolor
Compagnie Jean Renoir
original title: *Déjeuner sur l'Herbe*
An international scientist hears the pipes of Pan, embarks on a country idyll and impregnates a housemaid whom he later marries.
Charming if overlong frolic with ideas, a harking back to earlier Renoir themes such as in Boudu Sauvé des Eaux.
wd Jean Renoir ph Georges Leclerc *m* Joseph Kosma
☆ Paul Meurisse, Catherine Rouvel, Fernand Sardou, Ingrid Nordine
'A warm, loving, garrulous, undisciplined film.' – *Penelope Houston, MFB*

Lundi Matin: see *Monday Morning*

La Lune dans le Caniveau: see *The Moon in the Gutter*

Lunes de fiel: see *Bitter Moon*

Lunga Vita All Signora!: see *Long Live the Lady*

Lure of the Wilderness
US 1952 92m Technicolor
TCF (Robert L. Jacks)
A man falsely accused of murder hides for eight years in Georgia's Okefenokee swamp.
Remake of Swamp Water, *with Walter Brennan playing the same part. The plot works fairly well still, but colour doesn't suit the scenery.*
w Louis Lantz *story* Vereen Bell *d* Jean Negulesco *ph* Edward Cronjager *m* Franz Waxman
☆ Jeffrey Hunter, Jean Peters, Walter Brennan, Constance Smith, Jack Elam

Lured *
US 1947 102m bw
(UA) Hunt Stromberg (James Nasser)
GB title: *Personal Column*
An American dancer stranded in London helps Scotland Yard catch a killer.
Minor murder mystery with a pleasing cast.
w Leo Rosten, from the French film Pièges
d Douglas Sirk *ph* William Daniels *m* Michel Michelet *pd* Nicolai Remisoff
☆ Lucille Ball, George Sanders, Charles Coburn, Boris Karloff, Cedric Hardwicke, Alan Mowbray, George Zucco, Joseph Calleia, Robert Coote, Alan Napier

'Devils In Female Bodies Whose Embrace Is The Kiss Of Death For Man Or Woman!'
Lust for a Vampire
GB 1970 95m Technicolor
Hammer (Harry Fine, Michael Style)
In 1830 an English writer discerns that a pupil in an exclusive mid-European girls' school is a reincarnated vampire.
Dull Hammer horror, with the emphasis on lesbianism and nudity.
w Tudor Gates *novel Carmilla* by J. Sheridan Le Fanu *d* Jimmy Sangster *ph* David Muir *m* Harry Robinson
☆ Ralph Bates, Michael Johnson, Barbara Jefford, Suzanna Leigh, Yutte Stensgaard, Mike Raven, Helen Christie
'An embarrassment.' – *Jimmy Sangster*

Lust for Evil: see *Plein Soleil*

Lust for Gold
US 1949 90m bw
Columbia (S. Sylvan Simon)
A young man goes to Arizona to search for a lost gold mine discovered by his grandfather.
Moderate Western drama consisting largely of flashback.
w Ted Sherdeman, Richard English *novel Thunder God's Gold* by Barry Storm *d* S. Sylvan Simon *ph* Archie Stout *m* George Duning
☆ Ida Lupino, Glenn Ford, Gig Young, William Prince, Edgar Buchanan, Will Geer, Paul Ford

Lust for Life **
US 1956 122m Metrocolor Cinemascope
MGM (John Houseman)
The life of Vincent Van Gogh.
Fairly absorbing, not inaccurate, but somehow uninspiring biopic, probably marred by poor colour and wide screen; despite good work all round, it simply doesn't fall into a classic category.
w Norman Corwin *book* Irving Stone *d* Vincente Minnelli *ph* Freddie Young, Russell Harlan *m* Miklos Rozsa *ad* Cedric Gibbons, Hans Peters, Preston Ames *ed* Adrienne Fazan *cos* Walter Plunkett
☆ *Kirk Douglas* (Vincent Van Gogh), Anthony Quinn (Paul Gauguin), James Donald (Theo Van Gogh), Pamela Brown (Christine), Everett Sloane (Dr Gachet), Niall MacGinnis (Roulin), Noel Purcell (Anton Mauve), Henry Daniell (Theodrus Van Gogh), Lionel Jeffries, Madge Kennedy, Jill Bennett, Laurence Naismith
'Two hours of quite shattering and exciting entertainment.' – *Alan Dent, Illustrated London News*
† Anthony Quinn was on the screen for a total of eight minutes in his Oscar-winning role.
Anthony Quinn
Norman Corwin; Kirk Douglas; art direction

Lust in the Dust
US 1984 87m CFI color
Fox Run (Allan Glaser, Tab Hunter)
In the old west, a strong silent man and a drag queen beat the baddies to the gold.
Fitfully funny spoof for adults.
w Philip Taylor *d* Paul Bartel *ph* Paul Lohmann *m* Peter Matz *ed* Alan Toomayan
☆ Tab Hunter, Divine, Lainie Kazan, Geoffrey Lewis, Henry Silva, Cesar Romero, Woody Strode

Lust in the Sun (dubbed)
France/Spain 1971 84m Eastmancolor
Golden Era/Kerfrance/IMF
original title: *Dans la Poussiére du Soleil*
A son, who is regarded by many as a coward, revenges his father's death by killing his uncle.
Enjoyably bizarre updating of Hamlet *to a cowboy setting, with Polonius becoming the town's sheriff, and faithful enough to the original to include the 'play within the play'.*
wd Richard Balducci *play Hamlet* by William Shakespeare *ph* Tadusu G. Suzuki *m* Francis Lai *pd* Santiago Ontanon *ed* Liliane Fattori
☆ Maria Schell, Bob Cunningham, Daniel Beretta, Karin Meier, Pépé Calvo, Colin Drake
'The inherent silliness of the conception ... quickly converts the film into a variety skit.' – *MFB*

Lust och Fägring Stor: see *Love Lessons*

The Lusty Men *
US 1952 113m bw
RKO/Wald-Krasna (Jerry Wald)
Tensions lead to the death of one of a pair of rider friends on a rodeo tour.
Standard melodrama with semi-documentary detail and star performances.
w Horace McCoy, David Dortort *d* Nicholas Ray *ph Lee Garmes m* Roy Webb
☆ Robert Mitchum, Arthur Kennedy, Susan Hayward, Arthur Hunnicutt

Luther *
GB 1973 112m Eastmancolor
American Express/Ely Landau/Cinevision
In 1525, the teachings of Luther culminate in the Peasants' Revolt.
Hard-to-watch filming by the American Film Theatre of a singularly theatrical play, and not a very good one at that. Some good acting.
w Edward Anhalt *play* John Osborne *d* Guy Green *ph* Freddie Young *m* John Addison *pd* Peter Mullins
☆ Stacy Keach, Patrick Magee, Hugh Griffith, Robert Stephens, Alan Badel, Julian Glover, Judi Dench, Leonard Rossiter, Maurice Denham

Luv
US 1967 95m Technicolor Panavision
Columbia/Jalem (Martin Manulis)
When a man prevents an old friend from jumping off the Brooklyn Bridge and brings him home, a sexual square dance develops.
A modern comedy that should have stayed in the theatre.
w Elliott Baker *play* Murray Schisgal *d* Clive Donner *ph* Ernest Laszlo *m* Gerry Mulligan
☆ Jack Lemmon, Peter Falk, Elaine May, Nina Wayne, Eddie Mayehoff, Paul Hartman, Severn Darden
'A light but incisive comedy about the patterns and language of love in a Freud-ridden society has become an inept and lethally unamusing film farce.' – *MFB*

Luxury Liner
US 1933 72m bw
Paramount
Stories of various passengers on a liner bound from New York to Bremerhaven.
Interesting minor multi-drama, like a rough sketch for Ship of Fools *(qv).*
w Gene Markey, Kathryn Scola *novel* Gina Kaus *d* Lothar Mendes *ph* Victor Milner
☆ George Brent, Zita Johann, Vivienne Osborne, Alice White, Verree Teasdale, C. Aubrey Smith, Frank Morgan, Henry Wadsworth, Billy Bevan
'Not even the frank hook-up with Grand Hotel will help this entry much ... a loose and thin catch-as-catch-can affair.' – *Variety*

Luxury Liner
US 1948 98m Technicolor
MGM (Joe Pasternak)
The captain of a liner has trouble with his teenage daughter.
Minor shipboard musical with pleasing talents applied.
w Gladys Lehman, Richard Connell *d* Richard Whorf *ph* Ernest Laszlo *md* George Stoll
☆ George Brent, Jane Powell, Lauritz Melchior, Frances Gifford, Marina Koshetz, Xavier Cugat, Richard Derr, Connie Gilchrist

'His love dictates every move.'
The Luzhin Defence *
GB/France 2000 108m Technicolor
Entertainment/Renaissance/Clear Blue Sky/ICE3 (Caroline Wood, Stephen Evans, Louis Becker, Philippe Guez)
In Italy for a chess tournament, an obsessive Russian grandmaster has to choose between the game and love and marriage.
Good-looking but glum romantic drama about a prodigy who cannot escape his talent; its merits lie mainly in the performances of its protagonists.
w Peter Berry *novel* Vladimir Nabokov *d* Marleen Gorris *ph* Bernard Lutic *m* Alexandre Desplat *pd* Tony Burrough *ed* Michael Reichwein *cos* Jany Temime
☆ *John Turturro* (Alexander Luzhin), Emily Watson (Natalia), Geraldine James (Vera), Stuart Wilson (Valentinov), Christopher Thompson (Jean de Stassard), Fabio Sartor (Turati), Peter Blythe (Ilya), Orla Brady (Anna), Mark Tandy (Luzhin's father), Kelly Hunter (Luzhin's mother), Alexander Huntin (Young Luzhin)
'A smoothly made period romancer that's elevated by strong playing from its whole cast.' – *Derek Elley, Variety*

'The girl who thought she knew all about love!'
Lydia *
US 1941 104m bw
Alexander Korda (Lee Garmes)
An ageing lady recalls her former beaux.
Pleasing remake of Carnet du Bal, *with excellent production values.*
w Ben Hecht, Samuel Hoffenstein *story* Julien Duvivier, Laszlo Bus-Fekete *d Julien Duvivier ph Lee Garmes m* Miklos Rozsa *pd Vincent Korda*
☆ Merle Oberon, Joseph Cotten, Alan Marshal, Edna May Oliver, Hans Yaray, George Reeves, John Halliday, Sara Allgood
Miklos Rozsa

Lydia Bailey
US 1952 89m Technicolor
TCF (Jules Schermer)
In 1802 a Boston lawyer visits Haiti to obtain the signature of a wayward heiress, and becomes involved in the negro fight against the French.
Standard adventure romance with plenty of excitements.
w Michael Blankfort, Philip Dunne *novel* Kenneth Roberts *d* Jean Negulesco *ph* Harry Jackson *m* Hugo Friedhofer
☆ Dale Robertson, Anne Francis, Charles Korvin, William Marshall, Adeline de Walt Reynolds

M ★★★
Germany 1931 118m bw
Nero Film (Seymour Nebenzal)

A psychopathic murderer of children evades the police but is caught by the city's criminals who find his activities getting them a bad name.
An unmistakable classic whose oddities are hardly worth criticizing, this is part social melodrama and part satire, but entirely unforgettable, with most of its sequences brilliantly staged.
w Thea von Harbou, Paul Falkenberg, Adolf Jansen, Karl Vash *d* Fritz Lang *ph* Fritz Arno Wagner *m* Adolf Jansen *ad* Karl Vollbrecht, Emil Hasler
☆ Peter Lorre, Otto Wernicke, Gustav Gründgens
'Visual excitement, pace, brilliance of surface and feeling for detail.' – *New Yorker, 1977*
† Of Lang's later work, *Fury* comes closest to the feeling and style of M.

M ★
US 1951 82m bw
Columbia (Seymour Nebenzal)
Faithful but fated remake; without the heavy expressionist techniques, the story seems merely silly and the atmosphere is all wrong.
w Norman Reilly Raine, Leo Katcher *d* Joseph Losey *ph* Ernest Laszlo *m* Michel Michelet *pd* John Hubley *ed* Edward Mann
☆ David Wayne, Howard Da Silva, Luther Adler, Martin Gabel, Glenn Anders, Karen Morley, Norman Lloyd, Walter Burke
'I consciously repeated only one shot … essentially Lang's villain was my hero.' – *Joseph Losey*

M. Butterfly
US 1993 101m colour
Warner/Geffen (Gabriella Martinelli)

A French diplomat begins an affair with a Chinese performer in the Beijing Opera, unaware that he is being deceived.
Based on an actual scandal, which became a successful play, this is an unsuccessful movie, one that never convinces as to the truth or likelihood of its central relationship.
w David Henry Hwang *play* David Henry Hwang *d* David Cronenberg *ph* Peter Suschitzky *m* Howard Shore *pd* Carol Spier *ed* Ronald Sanders
☆ Jeremy Irons, John Lone, Barbara Sukowa, Ian Richardson, Shizuko Hoshi, Annabel Leventon, Vernon Dobtcheff, Richard McMillan
'Gets all dressed up in fancy threads but goes nowhere, due to a lack of chemistry and heat on the part of the two leads.' – *Todd McCarthy, Variety*
'The end result, while not entirely unrewarding, is another step away from the singular vision Cronenberg once expressed even in his marginal work.' – *Kim Newman, Empire*

Ma and Pa Kettle ★
US 1949 75m bw
U-I (Leonard Goldstein)

Pa Kettle wins a house in a contest and is accused of cheating.
First of a series of low-budget comedies which, based on characters from The Egg and I *(qv), had astonishing commercial success in America. The standard varied from adequate to painful.*
w Herbert Margolis, Louis Morheim, Al Lewis *d* Charles Lamont *ph* Maury Gertsman *m* Milton Schwarzwald
☆ Marjorie Main, Percy Kilbride, Richard Long, Meg Randall
'Not exactly Noël Coward.' – *Leonard Maltin*
† For others in the series, see under *The Kettles*.

Ma Nuit Chez Maud ★
France 1969 110m bw
Films du Losange (Pierre Cottreill)

aka: *My Night at Maud's*
A Catholic clerk in a small town falls in love with an elegant divorcee but can't bring himself to court her openly and marries someone else.
Subdued, literate talk-piece which finally exhausts rather than stimulates.
wd Eric Rohmer *ph* Nestor Almendros *ad* Nicole Rachline *ed* Cécile Decugis
☆ Jean-Louis Trintignant, Françoise Fabian, Marie-Christine Barrault
best foreign film; Eric Rohmer (as writer)

Ma Saison Préférée ★★
France 1993 127m colour Panavision
Arrow/TF1/DA/Alain Sarde

aka: *My Favourite Season*
An estranged brother and his married sister meet for some uneasy reunions as their mother becomes ill and increasingly frail.
Emotionally true, devastatingly accurate portrait of the subterranean tensions, guilt and anguish that exist within a conventional middle-class family, told in four chapters, each corresponding to a season.
w André Téchiné, Pascal Bonitzer *d* André Téchiné *ph* Thierry Arbogast *m* Philippe Sarde *pd* Carlos Conti *ed* Martine Giordano
☆ Catherine Deneuve, Daniel Auteuil, Marthe Villalonga, Jean-Pierre Bouvier, Chiara Mastroianni, Carmen Chaplin, Anthony Prada, Ingrid Caven
'A dull exposition of the glacial shifts in the emotional alignments within a dysfunctional middle-class family.' – *Variety*

Ma Vie en Rose ★★
France/Belgium/Switzerland/GB 1997 89m colour
Buena Vista/Haut et Court/WFE/Freeway/CAB/La Sept/RTBF/TF1 (Carole Scotta)

To the surprise of his parents and the horror of their neighbours, a seven-year-old boy insists that he is really a girl.
A strange but compelling movie about gender and identity, with a remarkable performance from its young protagonist.
w Chris Vander Stappen, Alain Berliner *d* Alain Berliner *ph* Yves Cape *m* Dominique Dalcan *pd* Véronique Melery *ed* Sandrine Deegan
☆ Michèle Laroque, Jean-Philippe Ecoffey, Hélène Vincent, Georges du Fresne, Daniel Hanssens, Laurence Bibot
'A generous and at times gorgeous instance of cinema's true powers and promise.' – *Sight and Sound*

Ma Vie Sexuelle ★★
France 1996 180m colour
BAC/Why Not/La Sept/France2/Canal+

original title: *Comment je me suis disputé … ('ma vie sexuelle')*
An unhappy 29-year-old academic with an unsatisfactory 10-year relationship and a desire for his best friend's girlfriend begins an affair with the girlfriend of a friend.
Complex and talkative disquisition on love, responsibility and the pleasures and pains of adultery; its tone is intellectual but not solemn: one character has a religious revelation while a girl dances in her underwear, while another says, 'I think I'm incredibly depressed,' as the woman he wants takes off her clothes.
w Arnaud Desplechin, Emmanuel Bourdieu *d* Arnaud Desplechin *ph* Eric Gautier *m* Krishna Lévy *pd* Antoine Platteau *ed* François Gédigier
☆ Mathieu Amalric, Emmanuelle Devos, Emmanuel Salinger, Marianne Denicourt, Thibault de Montalembert, Chiara Mastroianni
'Has its moments, but there are too few of them to justify the running time.' – *Empire*

Maborosi ★
Japan 1995 109m colour
ICA/TV Man Union (Naoe Gozu)

A wife, who has continued to mourn the death of her husband, a suicide, remarries a widower.
Austerely moving account of a twilight existence, of people trapped within a bleakly implacable landscape.
w Yoshihisa Ogita *story* Teru Miyamoto *d* Hirokazu Kore-Eda *ph* Masao Nakabori *m* Cheng Ming-Chang *ad* Kyoko Heya *ed* Tomoya Oshima
☆ Makiko Esumi, Takeshi Naito, Tadanobu Asano, Goki Kashiyama, Naomi Watanabe
'A powerful insight into the disabling force of grief.' – *George Perry*

'Every success has its story. And its price.'
Mac ★
US 1992 118m Technicolor
Entertainment/Macfilm (Nancy Tenenbaum, Brenda Goodman)

A construction worker, irritated by the sloppy standards of his foreman, decides to start his own business, working to the best of his ability; his two brothers join him but then leave.
A drama of obsession and integrity, with splendid ensemble acting and a gritty reality.
w John Turturro, Brandon Cole *d* John Turturro *ph* Ron Fortunato *m* Richard Termini, Vin Tese *pd* Robert Standefer *ed* Michael Berenbaum
☆ John Turturro, Katherine Borowitz, Michael Badalucco, Carl Capotorto, Ellen Barkin, John Amos, Dennis Farina
'Obviously made as a labour of love. But it is a bit of a labour to sit through.' – *Alexander Walker, London Evening Standard*
'A film of old-fashioned virtues – sincerity, worthiness, and probity – used in an unpatronising way.' – *Philip French*

Mac and Me
US 1988 99m
Guild/R. J. Louis

A family of aliens is inadvertently dumped in California.
A cardboard confection, copying much of the plot of E.T.*, that is little more than a dull and extended commercial for fast foods.*
w Steven Feke, Stewart Raffill *d* Stewart Raffill *ph* Nick McLean *m* Alan Silvestri *pd* W. Stewart Campbell *ed* Tom Walls
☆ Christine Ebersole, Jonathan Ward, Tina Caspary, Lauren Stanley, Jade Calegory, Vinnie Torrente, Martin West

'See it with someone who can carry you home!'
'So terrifying we have to insure your life!'
Macabre
US 1958 73m bw
AA (William Castle)
When a small-town doctor's daughter is kidnapped, he fears she may have been buried alive in the cemetery.
Genuine but unsuccessful attempt to film a horror comic; incredibly stodgy writing, acting and direction put the lid on it.
w Robb White *d* William Castle *ph* Carl Guthrie *m* Les Baxter
☆ William Prince, Jim Backus, Jacqueline Scott, Philip Tonge, Ellen Corby
'A ghoulish but totally ineffective horror piece, set mainly in undertakers' offices and an atmosphere of graveyards and swirling fog.' – *MFB*
† When first released, admission carried insurance against death by fright. Some said it should have been death by boredom.

'Keep A Cool Head!'
Macabre (dubbed)
Italy 1980 90m Telecolor
Medusa/AMA (Gianni Minervini, Antonio Avati)

original title: *Macabro*
A blind man becomes curious about his neighbour, a demented woman who, unknown to him, takes to bed every night the head of her dead lover, which she keeps in the refrigerator during the day.
Gruesome, though stylish, horror movie, which marked the debut of director Lamberto Bava.
w Lamberto Bava, Pupi Avati, Antonio Avati, Roberto Gandus *d* Lamberto Bava *ph* Francesco delli Colli *m* Ubaldo Continiello *ad* Katia Dottori *ed* Piera Gabutti *sp* Tonino Corridori, Angelo Mattei
☆ Bernice Stegers, Stanko Molnar, Roberto Posse, Veronica Zinny, Ferdinando Orlandi

Macao
US 1952 81m bw
RKO (Alex Gottlieb)

A wandering American in the Far East helps a detective catch a gangster.
A few flashy decorative touches show the director's hand, otherwise this is routine, murky thick ear.
w Bernard C. Schoenfeld, Stanley Rubin *d* Josef von Sternberg (and Nicholas Ray) *ph* Harry J. Wild *m* Anthony Collins
☆ Robert Mitchum, Jane Russell, William Bendix, Gloria Grahame, Thomas Gomez

Macaroni (dubbed) ★
Italy 1985 104m Eastmancolor
Massfilm/Filmauro (Luigi and Aurelio de Laurentiis, Franco Committeri)

An American engineer returns to Naples, where he fought 40 years earlier in the Second World War, and begins to relive a past he never had.
Gentle, nostalgic, bitter-sweet comedy of middle-aged frustrations, helped by the charm of the leading performances.
w Ruggero Maccari, Furio Scarpelli, Ettore Scola *d* Ettore Scola *ph* Claudio Ragona *m* Armando Trovaioli *pd* Luciano Ricceri *ed* Carla Simoncelli
☆ Jack Lemmon, Marcello Mastroianni, Daria Nicolodi, Isa Danieli, Maria Luisa Santella, Fabio Tenore, Patrizia Sacchi, Bruno Esposito
'A star vehicle, but it seems awfully out of date and joyless.' – *Vincent Canby, New York Times*

MacArthur the Rebel General ★
US 1977 130m Technicolor
Universal/Richard D. Zanuck, David Brown (Frank McCarthy)

The exploits of General MacArthur during the Pacific wars and his strained relationships with two presidents.
Sober, earnest political biography with war sequences; very well done but somehow unsympathetic.
w Hal Barwood, Matthew Robbins *d* Joseph Sargent *ph* Mario Tosi *m* Jerry Goldsmith *pd* John J. Lloyd *ed* George Nicholson *sp* Albert Whitlock
☆ Gregory Peck (General MacArthur), Dan O'Herlihy (President Roosevelt), Ed Flanders (President Truman), Ward Costello (General Marshall), Marj Dusay (Mrs MacArthur), Ivan Bonar (General Sutherland)
'A biopic that begins when its subject is sixty lacks roots – and in this case revelation.' – *Judith Crist*

'Taking on the drug lords is impossible. Taking on a country is insane.'

McBain
US 1991 102m TVC Color
Shapiro Glickenhaus (J. Boyce Harman Jnr)
A former soldier agrees to help the sister of a friend overthrow the corrupt government in Colombia.
Predictable and interminable, lacking any sense of reality.
wd James Glickenhaus *ph* Robert M. Baldwin Jnr *m* Christopher Franke *pd* Charles C. Bennett *ed* Jeffrey Wolf
☆ Christopher Walken, Maria Conchita Alonso, Michael Ironside, Steve James, Jay Patterson, T. G. Waites, Victor Argo, Hechter Ubarry, Russell Dennis Baker, Chick Vennera
'A silly action film geared mainly to overseas audiences.' – *Variety*

Macbeth *
US 1948 89m bw
Republic/Mercury (Orson Welles)
A famous – or infamous – attempt to film Shakespeare in twenty-one days in papier mâché settings running with damp; further hampered by the use of a form of unintelligible bastard Scots.
A few striking moments at the beginning remain; the rest should be silence.
w Orson Welles *play* William Shakespeare *d* Orson Welles *ph* John L. Russell *m* Jacques Ibert *ad* Fred Ritter *ed* Louis Lindsay
☆ Orson Welles, Jeanette Nolan, Dan O'Herlihy, Roddy McDowall, Edgar Barrier, Erskine Sanford

Macbeth
GB 1972 140m Technicolor Todd-AO 35
Playboy/Caliban (Andrew Braunsberg)
A sharpened and brutalized version; the blood swamps most of the cleverness and most of the poetry.
w Roman Polanski, Kenneth Tynan *play* William Shakespeare *d* Roman Polanski *ph* Gilbert Taylor *m* the Third Ear Band *pd* Wilfrid Shingleton *ed* Alastair MacIntyre
☆ Jon Finch (Macbeth), Francesca Annis (Lady Macbeth), Martin Shaw (Banquo), Nicholas Selby (Duncan), John Stride (Ross), Stephan Chase (Malcolm), Paul Shelley (Donalbain), Terence Bayler (Macduff), Keith Chegwin

Macbeth
Scotland 1997 129m colour
CJP/Cromwell/Lamancha/Grampian (Shona Donaldson)
In Scotland in the 11th century, Macbeth pays the price for murdering the king and seizing the throne.
Low-budget approach to Shakespeare's Scottish play, emphasizing the fact that it comes from north of the border, and by far the least interesting version so far.
w Bob Carruthers, Jeremy Freeston *play* William Shakespeare *d* Jeremy Freeston *ph* Dave Miller *m* Richard Cherns *ed* Owen Parker, Chris Gormlie
☆ Jason Connery (Macbeth), Helen Baxendale (Lady Macbeth), Graham McTavish, Kenny Bryans, Kern Falconer, Hildegard Neil, Chris Gormlie, John Corvin, Brian Blessed
'What do we get? A cross between a 1970s schools programme and a Scottish Tourist Board video. This is indeed a tragic Macbeth.' – *Giala Murray, Empire*
† Brian Blessed was credited as artistic adviser and for 'special direction of witches scenes'.

McCabe and Mrs Miller
US 1971 120m Technicolor Panavision
Warner (David Foster, Mitchell Brower)
At the turn of the century a gambling gunfighter comes to a northwest mining town and uses his money to set up lavish brothels.
Obscurely scripted, muddy-coloured and harshly recorded Western melodrama whose squalid 'realism' comes as close to fantasy as does The Wizard of Oz.
w Robert Altman, Brian McKay *novel* McCabe by Edmund Naughton *d* Robert Altman *ph* Vilmos Zsigmond *pd* Leon Ericksen
☆ Warren Beatty, Julie Christie, René Auberjonois, Shelley Duvall, John Schuck
'A fleeting, diaphanous vision of what frontier life might have been.' – *Pauline Kael*
'Altman directed *M*A*S*H*, which wandered and was often funny; then *Brewster McCloud*, which wandered and was not funny; now this, which wanders and is repulsive. The thesis seems to be that if you take a corny story, fuzz up the exposition, vitiate the action, use a childishly ironic ending, and put in lots of profanity and nudity, you have Marched On with Time.' – *Stanley Kauffmann*
Julie Christie

The McConnell Story
US 1955 107m Warnercolor Cinemascope
Warner (Henry Blanke)
GB title: *Tiger in the Sky*
The career and accidental death of a jet ace of the Korean war.
Crude, obvious and saccharine biopic.
w Ted Sherdeman, Sam Rolfe *d* Gordon Douglas *ph* John Seitz, Ted McCord *m* Max Steiner
☆ Alan Ladd, June Allyson, James Whitmore, Frank Faylen, Willis Bouchey

MacDonald of the Canadian Mounties: see *Pony Soldier*

McFadden's Flats
US 1935 65m bw
Paramount
The quarrel between a bricklayer and a barber affects their children.
Modest working-class comedy from a well-worn play.
w Arthur Caesar, Edward Kaufman, Casey Robinson, Andy Rice *play* Gus Hill *d* Ralph Murphy
☆ Walter C. Kelly, Andy Clyde, Richard Cromwell, Jane Darwell, Betty Furness, George Barbier
'Better-than-average family picture.' – *Variety*

McGuire Go Home: see *The High Bright Sun*

McHale's Navy
US 1997 108m DeLuxe
Universal/Bubble Factory (Sid, Bill and Jon Sheinberg)
On a Caribbean island, an ex-naval officer, who uses his ill-gotten money to finance good causes, finds his schemes thwarted when a tough new commander tightens up discipline on the naval base.
A misfiring comedy, ridiculous for all the wrong reasons, which suddenly veers into frenetic action, and finally sinks with all hands lost.
w Peter Crabbe *d* Bryan Spicer *ph* Buzz Feitshans *m* Dennis McCarthy *pd* Gene Rudolf *ed* Russel Denove
☆ Tom Arnold, Tim Curry, Dean Stockwell, David Alan Grier, Debra Messing, Ernest Borgnine, Thomas Chong, Bruce Campbell
'A ham-fisted, fitfully amusing lark that quickly runs aground.' – *Variety*
† The film is based on the TV sitcom, a waterlogged copy of Phil Silver's Sgt Bilko, that ran from 1962 to 1966 and starred Ernest Borgnine as McHale, the role played by Tom Arnold in the film.

The Machine (dubbed) *
France/Germany 1994 96m colour
Hachette Première/DD/Prima/M6/France 2/Studio Babelsberg (Patrick Bordier)
original title: *La Machine*
A brain specialist working with the criminally insane builds a machine to enable him to get inside the mind of a serial killer; but the experiment goes wrong, and the two switch bodies.
A deft psychological thriller, a variation on Frankenstein, *which creates an atmosphere of unease that is maintained until its horrific climax.*
wd François Dupeyron *novel* La Machine by René Belletto *ph* Dietrich Lohmann *m* Michel Portal *pd* Carlos Conti *ed* Noelle Boisson
☆ Gérard Depardieu, Nathalie Baye, Didier Bourdon, Natalia Woerner, Erwan Baynaud
'A cleverly choreographed roller-coaster ride of identity and appearances – with a stomach-churning dip yet to come.' – *Lisa Nesselson, Variety*
† There is an error in the video release. After an opening sequence, a caption reads 'eighteen months later'; it should read 'eighteen months earlier'.

'Even the Mafia calls him Mister!'

Machine Gun McCain
Italy 1970 94m Techniscope
Euroatlantica/Columbia
The Mafia springs a hardened criminal from jail and puts him to use.
Dull but violent Las Vegas-set mobster story with some echoes of Bonnie and Clyde.
w Giuliano Montaldo, Mino Roli *d* Giuliano Montaldo *m* Ennio Morricone
☆ John Cassavetes, Peter Falk, Britt Ekland, Gabriele Ferzetti

Macho Callahan
US 1970 100m Movielab Panavision
Avco/Felicidad (Bernard Kowalski, Martin C. Schute)
A vengeful cowboy annihilates all who stand in his way.
Squalid Mexican-made Western with unremitting emphasis on violence.
w Clifford Newton Gould *d* Bernard Kowalski *ph* Gerry Fisher *m* Pat Williams
☆ David Janssen, Lee J. Cobb, David Carradine, James Booth, Jean Seberg

MacKenna's Gold *
US 1969 136m Technicolor Super Panavision
Columbia/Highroad (Carl Foreman, Dimitri Tiomkin)
A dying Indian entrusts a sheriff with a map of the legendary Valley of Gold, and when the news breaks the map is in demand.
Curious serial-like Western melodrama packed with stars and pretensions above its station. On a lower level, it is quite enjoyable.
w Carl Foreman *novel* Will Henry *d* J. Lee-Thompson *ph* Joseph MacDonald, Harold Wellman *m* Quincy Jones *pd* Geoffrey Drake
☆ Gregory Peck, Omar Sharif, Telly Savalas, Camilla Sparv, Keenan Wynn, Julie Newmar, Ted Cassidy, Eduardo Ciannelli, Eli Wallach, Edward G. Robinson, Raymond Massey, Burgess Meredith, Anthony Quayle, Lee J. Cobb
'Preposterous hotch-potch of every cliché known to the gold lust book.' – *MFB*
'Twelve-year-olds of all ages might tolerate it.' – *Judith Crist*
'A western of truly stunning absurdity, a thriving example of the old Hollywood maxim about how to succeed by failing big.' – *Vincent Canby*

The McKenzie Break *
GB 1970 106m DeLuxe
UA/Levy-Gardner-Laven
During World War II, German prisoners at a Scottish camp stage an escape.
Effective little action suspenser.
w William Norton *d* Lamont Johnson *ph* Michael Reed *m* Riz Ortolani
☆ Brian Keith, Helmut Griem, Ian Hendry, Jack Watson, Patrick O'Connell, Horst Janson

'Only Mackintosh can save them now – and Mackintosh is dead!'

The Mackintosh Man *
GB 1973 99m Technicolor
Warner/Newman-Foreman/John Huston
A government agent is sent to prison to contact a criminal gang.
Convoluted but entertaining spy thriller with good performances and action sequences.
w Walter Hill *novel* The Freedom Trap by Desmond Bagley *d* John Huston *ph* Oswald Morris *m* Maurice Jarre *pd* Terry Marsh *ed* Russell Lloyd
☆ Paul Newman (Joseph Rearden), James Mason (Sir George Wheeler), Dominique Sanda (Mrs Smith), Nigel Patrick (Soames-Trevelyan), Harry Andrews (Angus Mackintosh), Michael Hordern (Brown), Ian Bannen (Slade), Peter Vaughan (Brunskill), Roland Culver (Judge), Percy Herbert (Taafe), Robert Lang (Jack Summers), Leo Genn (Rollins), Jenny Runacre (Gerda), John Bindon (Buster), Hugh Manning (Prosector)

McLintock *
US 1963 127m Technicolor Panavision
UA/Batjac (Michael Wayne)
A cattle baron can control a whole town but not his termagant wife.
Sub-Ford Western farce borrowed from The Taming of the Shrew, *with much fist-fighting and mud-splattering, and rather too much chat in between.*
w James Edward Grant *d* Andrew V. McLaglen *ph* William H. Clothier *m* Frank de Vol
☆ John Wayne, Maureen O'Hara, Yvonne de Carlo, Patrick Wayne, Stefanie Powers, Chill Wills, Bruce Cabot, Jack Kruschen

The McMasters
US 1969 90m Technicolor
JayJen (Dimitri de Grunwald)
A black man returning home from the Civil War gets unexpected help from a tough landowner.
Racial Western with black, white and red points of view, all very violently expressed.
w Harold Jacob Smith *d* Alf Kjellin *ph* Lester Shorr *m* Coleridge-Taylor Parkinson
☆ Brock Peters, Burl Ives, David Carradine, Nancy Kwan, Jack Palance, Dane Clark, John Carradine, L. Q. Jones, R. G. Armstrong

The Macomber Affair *
US 1946 89m bw
(UA) Benedict Bogeaus (Casey Robinson)
The wife of a bullying big game hunter falls for their guide.
Safari melodrama with a plot which has become a cliché but seemed fresh enough at the time. Goodish writing and acting.
w Casey Robinson *story* The Short Happy Life of Francis Macomber by Ernest Hemingway *d* Zoltan Korda *ph* Karl Struss *m* Miklos Rozsa
☆ Gregory Peck, Joan Bennett, Robert Preston, Reginald Denny, Carl Harbord, Jean Gillie
'The best movie job on Hemingway to date.' – *James Agee*
'It has survived the hazardous crossing from brilliant short story to film with practically no casualties.' – *Daily Mail*

Macon County Line
US 1973 89m Eastmancolor
Sam Arkoff/Max Baer
In mid-fifties Louisiana, a couple of hell-raisers are harassed by a local sheriff, and much bloodshed results.
Shapeless melodrama more or less in the wake of Easy Rider; *an unattractive film which unaccountably had great box-office success.*
w Max Baer, Richard Compton *d* Richard Compton *ph* Daniel Lacambre *m* Stu Phillips
☆ Alan Vint, Cheryl Waters, Geoffrey Lewis, Joan Blackman, Jesse Vint, Max Baer

'He's a busted cop, his gun is unlicensed, his methods unlawful, his story incredible!'

McQ
US 1974 111m Technicolor Panavision
Warner/Batjac/Levy-Gardner
A Seattle police detective goes after the gangster who killed his friend.
Rambling, violent thriller with good sequences but no cohesion.
w Lawrence Roman *d* John Sturges *ph* Harry Stradling Jnr *m* Elmer Bernstein
☆ John Wayne, Eddie Albert, Diana Muldaur, Colleen Dewhurst, Clu Gulager, David Huddleston, Julie Adams

Macu, the Policeman's Wife
Venezuela 1987 102m colour
Macu Films/Cinearte (Olegario Barrera)
original title: *Macu*
The young wife of a policeman suspects her husband of having murdered her lover and his friends.
Slice-of-life drama that was a big hit in its own country, but does not travel well.
w Solveig Hoogesteijn, Milagros Rodriguez *d* Solveig Hoogesteijn *ph* Andrés Agusti *m* Victor Cuica *ed* José Alcalde
☆ Maria Luisa Mosquera, Daniel Alvarado, Frank Hernández, Tito Aponte, Ana Castell, Carmen Palma, Iván Feo

McVicar
GB 1980 112m Eastmancolor
The Who Films/Brent-Walker (Bill Curbishley, Roy Baird, Roger Daltrey)
The true story of the escapes from prison of a violent criminal who was subsequently reformed and rehabilitated.
Some smart sequences don't prevent this from being an exploitation item.
w John McVicar and Tom Clegg *d* Tom Clegg *ph* Vernon Layton *m* Jeff Wayne *ad* Fred Carter *ed* Peter Boyle
☆ Roger Daltrey, Adam Faith, Cheryl Campbell, Billy Murray, Georgina Hale, Steven Berkoff

'Fall in love... With the beat.'
Mad About Mambo *
Ireland/GB 2000 92m colour
GramercyPhoenixFirst CityPlurabelle (David P. Kelly)
In Belfast, a would-be professional footballer joins a dance class to improve the way he moves and falls for the star pupil, a rich girl.
Oddly titled corny romance – it has nothing to do with the mambo – that is frequently implausible but gets by on the charm of its two stars.
wd John Forte *ph* Ashley Rowe *m* Richard Hartley *pd* Fiona Daly *ed* David Martin
☆ William Ash (Danny Mitchell), Keri Russell (Lucy McLoughlin), Brian Cox (Sidney McLoughlin), Theo Fraser Steele (Oliver Parr), Rosaleen Linehan (Mrs Burns), Maclean Stewart (Mickey), Tim Loane (Brother McBride), Julian Littman (Rudi Morelli)
'The movie is lightweight but irresistibly entertaining.' – *Stephen Farber, Movieline*

Mad about Men
GB 1954 90m Technicolor
GFD/Group Films (Betty Box)
By mutual agreement, a sports mistress and a mermaid change places for a while.
Laborious rehash of Miranda *with familiar jokes.*
w Peter Blackmore *d* Ralph Thomas *ph* Ernest Steward *m* Benjamin Frankel
☆ Glynis Johns, Donald Sinden, Anne Crawford, Margaret Rutherford, Dora Bryan, Nicholas Phipps, Irene Handl

Mad about Music *
US 1938 98m bw
Universal (Joe Pasternak)
A girl at a Swiss school adopts a personable visitor as her father.
Pleasing star vehicle with charm and humour; badly remade as Toy Tiger *(qv).*
w Bruce Manning, Felix Jackson *d* Norman Taurog *ph* Joseph Valentine *m* Frank Skinner, Charles Previn *m/ly* Harold Adamson, Jimmy McHugh
☆ *Deanna Durbin*, Herbert Marshall, Gail Patrick, Arthur Treacher, Helen Parrish, Marcia Mae Jones, William Frawley
'Another Durbin smash ... will mop up at the b.o.' – *Variety*
original story (Marcella Burke, Frederick Kohner); Joseph Valentine; Frank Skinner, Charles Previn

The Mad Adventures of 'Rabbi' Jacob: see *Les Aventures de Rabbi Jacob*

The Mad Bomber *
US 1972 91m Movielab
Scotia-Barber/College (Bert I. Gordon)
A detective tries to track down a bomber who is killing people by dynamiting buildings in Los Angeles in order to punish society.
Low-budget thriller, effective in a harsh and unpolished way.
wd Bert I. Gordon *story* Marc Behm *m* Michel Mention *ed* Gene Ruggiero
☆ Vince Edwards, Chuck Connors, Neville Brand, Christina Hart, Faith Quabius
'An attempt not to be sneezed at.' – *Tom Milne, MFB*
† The film was cut to 87m for its British release.

'A Desperate Man. An Ambitious Reporter. A Situation Gone Mad.'
Mad City **
US 1997 114m Technicolor Super 35
Warner/Punch (Arnold and Anne Kopelson)
To aid his slipping career, a reporter attempts to manipulate the accidental shooting of a museum security guard into an attention-grabbing television event.
Deft satire on the live television media circus that accompanies modern-day crime and terrorism; in part, it was suggested by the Waco siege in 1993, and is also an updating of Billy Wilder's Ace in the Hole *(qv).*
w Tom Matthews *d* Costa-Gavras *ph* Patrick Blossier *m* Thomas Newman *pd* Catherine Hardwicke *ed* Françoise Bonnot
☆ John Travolta (Sam Baily), Dustin Hoffman (Max Brackett), Mia Kirshner (Laurie Callahan), Alan Alda (Kevin Hollander), Robert Prosky (Lou Potts), Blythe Danner (Mrs Banks), William Atherton (Dohlen), Ted Levine (Alvin Lemke)
'Despite its easy social conscience, the movie is often hilarious and zeroes in on an essential, heartless truth about journalism.' – *David Tse, Sight and Sound*
† The film did poorly at the US box-office, taking around $10.4m.

'They don't take no bull.'
Mad Cows
GB 1999 90m Technicolor
Entertainment/Capitol/Newmarket/Flashlight (Frank Mannion, Aaron Simpson)
Jailed for shoplifting, an Australian woman breaks out of prison in order to get even with the uncaring, aristocratic father of her child and to stop the baby being adopted.
A failed farce that tempts its cast into overacting whenever possible, which is made worse by the clichéd directorial style, full of meaningless flourishes.
w Sara Sugarman, Sasha Hails *novel* Kathy Lette *d* Sara Sugarman *ph* Pierre Aim *m* Mark Thomas *pd* Joseph Nemec III *ed* John Jympson
☆ Anna Friel (Maddy), Joanna Lumley (Gillian), Anna Massey (Dwina Phelps), Greg Wise (Alex), Phyllida Law (Alex's mother), John Standing (Politician), Nicholas Woodeson (Slynne), Prunella Scales (Dr Minny Stinkler), Jodie Kidd (Tracey), Sophie Dahl (Prisoner)
'So astonishingly bad it made me break out in a thin film of cold sweat.' – *Peter Bradshaw, Guardian*
'A third-rate *Carry On* farce that will only make you weep and wonder: how did they ever get the money to make a film as bad as this?' – *Cosmo Landesman, Sunday Times*

'She knew the ecstasy and terror of loving him!'
The Mad Doctor
US 1941 90m bw
Paramount (George Arthur)
GB title: *A Date with Destiny*
A doctor marries wealthy women and then murders them.
Naïve melodrama of little interest except as a vehicle for its star.
w Howard J. Green *d* Tim Whelan *ph* Ted Tetzlaff *m* Victor Young
☆ *Basil Rathbone*, Ellen Drew, John Howard, Barbara Jo Allen, Ralph Morgan, Martin Kosleck

The Mad Doctor of Blood Island
Philippines/USA 1969 86m colour
Westland/Hemisphere (Eddie Romero)
aka: *Tomb of the Living Dead*
Visitors to a Pacific island discover that a scientist searching for the secret of eternal life has created a vegetable monster.
Dreary horror that receives the inept treatment it deserves from all those concerned in its making.
w Reuben Candy *d* Gerardo de Leon, Eddie Romero *ph* Justo Paulino *m* Tito Arevalo
☆ John Ashley, Angelique Pettyjohn, Ronald Remy, Alicia Alonso
'The script is trite, the dramatic structure slack and the violence unconvincing.' – *Paul Joannides, MFB*

Mad Dog and Glory
US 1992 97m Technicolor
UIP/Universal (Barbara DeFina, Martin Scorsese)
A timid and conventional Chicago cop is embarrassed when a gangster he inadvertently helps gives him a present of a beautiful woman for a week.
A movie that promises much but fails to deliver, quickly dwindling into something inconsequential, though it occasionally amuses; the problem lies in the passivity of its two central characters, including a female role that is totally inert.
w Richard Price *d* John McNaughton *ph* Robby Müller *m* Elmer Bernstein *pd* David Chapman *ed* Craig McKay, Elena Maganini
☆ Robert DeNiro, Uma Thurman, Bill Murray, David Caruso, Mike Starr, Tom Towles, Kathy Baker
'A pleasurably offbeat picture that manages the rare trick of being both charming and edgy.' – *Variety*
'Price's macho fantasy smells way past its dwell-by date.' – *Ian Penman, Sight and Sound*

Mad Dog Coll
US 1961 87m bw
Columbia-Warner/Thalia (Edward Schreiber)
Biopic about a violent gangster of the 1930s.
Predictable low-budget exploitation movie, offering no new insights into the times and the vicious mobsters it bred.
w Edward Schreiber *story* Leo Lieberman *d* Burt Balaban *ph* Gayne Reschner *m* Stu Phillips *ad* Richard Sylbert *ed* Ralph Rosenblum
☆ John Davis Chandler, Neil Nephew, Brooke Hayward, Jerry Orbach, Telly Savalas, Vincent Gardenia, Gene Hackman

Mad Dog Time: see *Trigger Happy*

Mad Dogs and Englishmen
GB 1995 97m Technicolor
Entertainment/Movie Screen/Moor Street (Peter Watson-Wood, Nigel Thomas)
An aristocratic drug addict is targeted by a corrupt cop who wants her dead.
Dim, daft thriller that becomes ever-more risible as it continues.
w Tim Sewell *d* Henry Cole *ph* John Peters *m* Barrie Guard *pd* Tony Stringer *ed* Lionel Selwyn, Simon Hilton
☆ Elizabeth Hurley, C. Thomas Howell, Joss Ackland, Claire Bloom, Frederick Treves, Andrew Connolly, Jeremy Brett, Louise Delamere
'Baffling to the point of boredom, this British thriller is as gripping as KY Jelly.' – *Empire*
'God-awful and quite rightly torn to shreds.' – *Joss Ackland*

'Adults Only! Censor's orders!'
The Mad Genius
US 1931 81m bw
Warner
A crippled puppeteer adopts a boy and makes him into a great dancer.
Curious variation on Trilby, *filmed as* Svengali *the previous year with much the same cast. Not a great success: the script is dreadful.*
w J. Grubb Alexander, Harvey Thew *play* The Idol by Martin Brown *d* Michael Curtiz *ph* Barney McGill *ad* Anton Grot
☆ John Barrymore, Marian Marsh, Donald Cook, Luis Alberni, Carmel Myers, Charles Butterworth, Boris Karloff, Frankie Darro
'Magnificent acting, but not the sort of thing that will panic the fans.' – *Variety*
† Many of the sets in this production had ceilings, ten years before the idea was supposed to have been invented for *Citizen Kane*.

The Mad Ghoul
US 1943 65m bw
Universal (Ben Pivar)
A mad scientist needs fresh hearts to keep alive the victims of his experiments with a poison vapour.
Stagey, tasteless horror melodrama.
w Brenda Weisberg, Paul Gangelin *story* Hans Kraly *d* James Hogan *ph* Milton Krasner *md* Hans Salter *ad* John B. Goodman *ed* Milton Carruth
☆ George Zucco, David Bruce, Evelyn Ankers, Turhan Bey, Robert Armstrong, Charles McGraw, Milburn Stone

Mad Little Island: see *Rockets Galore*

Mad Love **
US 1935 83m bw
MGM (John Considine Jnr)
GB title: *The Hands of Orlac*
A pianist loses his hands in an accident; a mad surgeon, in love with the pianist's wife, grafts on the hands of a murderer.
Absurd Grand Guignol done with great style which somehow does not communicate itself in viewer interest, only in cold admiration.
w Guy Endore, P. J. Wolfson, John Balderston *novel* The Hands of Orlac by Maurice Renard *d* *Karl Freund* *ph* Chester Lyons, Gregg Toland *m* Dmitri Tiomkin
☆ Colin Clive, Peter Lorre, Frances Drake, Ted Healy, Edward Brophy, Isabel Jewell, Sara Haden
'The results in screen potency are disappointing ... will probably do fair biz.' – *Variety*
'Mr Lorre cuts deeply into the darkness of the morbid brain.' – *New York Times*

Mad Love
US 1995 95m Technicolor
Buena Vista (David Manson)
An inhibited youth runs off with a lively girl whose behaviour soon becomes unbalanced.
A road movie about a manic depressive that is only occasionally interesting; neither of its main characters attains any individuality.
w Paula Milne *d* Antonia Bird *ph* Fred Tammes *m* Andy Roberts *pd* David Brisbin *ed* Jeff Freeman
☆ Chris O'Donnell, Drew Barrymore, Matthew Lillard, Richard Chaim, Robert Nadir, Joan Allen, Jude Ciccolella, Amy Sakasitz
'There's a half-decent road movie desperate to break free, but it gets stuck in a mire of fatuous slush.' – *Empire*

'Was it a hoax or horror? Magic or Murder!'
The Mad Magician
US 1954 72m bw
Columbia (Bryan Foy)
A magician's star-struck inventor murders his employer and several others who stand between him and the big time.
Hokey horror flick set in the eighties and originally shown in 3-D.
w Crane Wilbur *d* John Brahm *ph* Bert Glennon *m* Emil Newman, Arthur Lange *ad* P. Frank Sylos *ed* Grant Whytock
☆ Vincent Price (Don Gallico), Mary Murphy (Karen Lee), Eva Gabor (Claire Gallico Ormond), John Emery (Rinaldi), Patrick O'Neal (Det Bruce Allen), Donald Randolph (Ross Ormond), Lenita Lane (Alice Prentice), Jay Novello (Frank Prentice), Lyle Talbot (Barker)

The Mad Martindales
US 1942 55m bw
Walter Morosco/TCF
In 1900 San Francisco, an eccentric family gets out of debt.
The star's last film for a major studio is a filler of unrelieved tedium.
w Francis Edward Faragoh *d* Alfred Werker
☆ Jane Withers, Alan Mowbray, Marjorie Weaver, Jimmy Lydon, Byron Barr, George Reeves

Mad Masquerade: see *Washington Masquerade*

Mad Max *
Australia 1979 100m Eastmancolor Todd-AO 35
Warner/Mad Max Pty (Byron Kennedy)
In the future, motor cycle gangs combat the police.
Violent extravaganza with no real merit save its enthusiasm for destruction of both bikes and bodies.
w James McCausland, George Miller *d* George Miller *ph* David Eggby *m* Brian May *ad* Jon Dowding *ed* Tony Paterson, Cliff Hayes
☆ Mel Gibson, Joanne Samuel, Hugh Keays-Byrne, Steve Bisley

'Ruthless ... Savage ... Spectacular'

Mad Max 2 *

Australia 1981 96m colour Panavision
Warner/Kennedy Miller Entertainment (Byron Kennedy)

US title: *The Road Warrior*

A shortage of petrol causes all-out war between police and bikers.

Not much more than a retread of the above, but a more expensive, spectacular and violent one.

w Terry Hayes, George Miller, Brian Hannant *d* George Miller *ph* Dean Semler *m* Brian May *ad* Graham Walker *ed* David Stiven, Tim Wellburn, Michael Chirgwin

☆ Mel Gibson, Bruce Spence, Vernon Wells, Emil Minty

'Essentially just another display of vehicles smashing into each other.' – *David McGillivray, MFB*

Mad Max Beyond Thunderdome

Australia 1985 106m colour Panavision
Warner/Kennedy Miller (George Miller)

A drifter arrives in a desert town ruled by a ruthless woman.

More violent futuristic rubbish in similar vein to its predecessors.

w Terry Hayes, George Miller *d* George Miller and George Ogilvie *ph* Dean Semler *m* Maurice Jarre *pd* Graham Walker *ed* Richard Francis-Bruce

☆ Mel Gibson, Tina Turner, Angelo Rossitto, Helen Buday

The Mad Miss Manton *

US 1938 80m bw
RKO (Pandro S. Berman)

A zany socialite involves her friends in a murder mystery.

Mildly funny comedy-thriller without too much of either, but a good example of the style of thirties craziness at its zenith.

w Philip G. Epstein *d* Leigh Jason *ph* Nicholas Musuraca *m* Roy Webb

☆ Barbara Stanwyck, Henry Fonda, Sam Levene, Frances Mercer, Stanley Ridges, Whitney Bourne, Hattie McDaniel, Miles Mander

'Something ground out by people in a desperate mood.' – *Pauline Kael, 70s*

The Mad Monkey

Spain 1990 108m Eastmancolor Panavision
Hobo/Iberoamericana Films/Emmanuel Schlumberger (Andres Vincente Gomez)

original title: *El Mono Loco*

A screenwriter becomes involved with a young, incestuous brother and sister.

Ridiculous farrago of sex and drugs, devoid of sense and sensuality.

w Fernando Trueba, Manolo Matji *novel The Dream of the Mad Monkey* by Christopher Frank *d* Fernando Trueba *ph* Jose Luis Alcaine *m* Antoine Duhamel *ad* Pierre-Louis Thevenet *ed* Carmen Frias

☆ Jeff Goldblum, Miranda Richardson, Anemone, Dexter Fletcher, Daniel Ceccaldi, Liza Walker, Jerome Natali, Arielle Dombasle, Micaela Sebastian

The Mad Monster

US 1942 77m bw
Sigmund Neufeld/PRC

A mad scientist injects wolf blood into a man, who goes around at night killing people.

Inept and uncontrolled shocker, the kind of thing that gives horror films a bad name.

w Fred Myton *d* Sam Newfield

☆ George Zucco, Johnny Downs, Glenn Strange, Anne Nagel

Mad Monster Party

US 1967 94m Eastmancolor
Animagic
Embassy/Videocraft (Arthur Rankin Jnr)

Baron von Frankenstein invites Dracula, the Mummy, the Werewolf, the Hunchback of Notre Dame and other monsters to a party to celebrate his new invention.

A children's film that uses stop-motion animated figures, it is harmless but trivial entertainment.

w Len Korobkin, Harvey Kurtzman *story* Arthur Rankin Jnr *d* Jules Bass *m* Maury Laws *m/ly* Maury Laws, Jules Bass *sp* character design: Jack Davis

☆ Featuring the voices of Boris Karloff, Phyllis Diller, Alan Swift, Gale Garnett

The Mad Parade

US 1931 62m bw
Liberty/Paramount

A story told by women about the effect of the war on their sex.

Not really strong enough to be taken seriously, this was played as a novelty.

w Henry McCarthy and Frank R. Conkin *story* Gertrude Orr and Doris Malloy *d* William Beaudine

☆ Evelyn Brent, Irene Rich, Louise Fazenda, Lilyan Tashman, Marceline Day

'Chances for disappointing business greater than the opposite.' – *Variety*

The Mad Room

US 1969 92m Berkeley-Pathé
Columbia/Norman Mauer

A companion kills her wealthy employer so that her mentally retarded brother and sister will have a home.

Tasteless remake of Ladies in Retirement, *in the brutalized vein which audiences are supposed by producers to want. In modern dress and sharp locations, it succeeds only in being nauseating.*

w Bernard Girard, A. Z. Martin *d* Bernard Girard *ph* Harry Stradling Jnr *m* Dave Grusin

☆ Stella Stevens, Shelley Winters, Skip Ward, Carol Cole, Severn Darden

Mad Wednesday *

US 1947 79m bw
Howard Hughes

aka: *The Sin of Harold Diddlebock*

A middle-aged book-keeper is sacked and goes on the town.

Woolly and unattractive farce which proved something of a disaster for all the talents concerned but historically is of considerable interest. It begins with an excerpt from The Freshman *and continues to comic adventures with a lion.*

ph Robert Pittack *m* Werner Richard Heymann *wd/pd Preston Sturges (re-edited by others)*

☆ *Harold Lloyd, Jimmy Conlin,* Raymond Walburn, Franklin Pangborn, Al Bridge, Margaret Hamilton, Edgar Kennedy

† It has been released on video in Sturges' original 90m version, which was later cut to 79m by Howard Hughes.

Madagascar Skin

GB 1995 93m colour
BFI/Channel 4/Dan (Julie Baines)

A shy young homosexual, whose face bears a large birthmark in the shape of Madagascar, forms an uneasy relationship with a burly older man, whom he finds on a lonely beach buried up to his neck in sand.

A thin, almost arid tale of an unlikely love, well acted, but directed with a greater interest in visual compositions than in people.

wd Chris Newby *ph* Oliver Curtis *pd* Paul Cross *ed* Chris Newby, Annabel Ware

☆ Bernard Hill, John Hannah, Mark Anthony, Mark Petit, Danny Earl

'An eccentric and unselfconscious comedy which will surprise as much as it satisfies.' – *Empire*

Madam Satan *

US 1930 105m bw
MGM (C. B. de Mille)

When her husband strays, a socialite disguises herself as a mysterious *femme fatale* and wins him back.

Abysmal comedy in which both director and principals appear frozen until the closing reels present a crazy, spectacular party on a dirigible which crashes but allows a happy ending.

w Jeanie Macpherson, Gladys Unger, Elsie Janis *d* C. B. de Mille *ph* Harold Rosson *m* Herbert Stothart *m/ly* Clifford Grey, Herbert Stothart, Elsie Janis, Jack King *ad* Cedric Gibbons, Mitchell Leisen *ed* Anne Bauchens

☆ Kay Johnson, Reginald Denny, Lillian Roth, Roland Young

'A strange conglomeration of unreal incidents that are sometimes set forth with no little technical skill.' – *Mordaunt Hall, New York Times*

Madame: see *Madame Sans-Gêne (1962)*

Madame Bovary *

France 1933 120m bw
NSF (Robert Aron)

The bored wife of a provincial doctor seeks excitement and finds only disappointment and death.

A flawed version of Flaubert's novel, not helped by having had an hour cut from it before its original release, so that it has lost some of its characterization and continuity; the stylized acting by a cast drawn largely from the theatre, in contrast to the reality of the settings, adds to a feeling of dislocation.

wd Jean Renoir *novel* Gustave Flaubert *ph* Jean Bachelet *m* Darius Milhaud *ad* Robert Bys *ed* Marguerite Renoir

☆ Max Dearly, Valentine Tessier, Pierre Renoir, Daniel Lecourtois, Fernand Fabre

'Whatever it is that French women have – Madame Bovary had more of it!'

Madame Bovary

US 1949 114m bw
MGM (Pandro S. Berman)

A passionate girl marries a dull husband, takes a lover, and commits suicide.

Dull, emasculated version of a classic.

w Robert Ardrey *novel* Gustave Flaubert *d* Vincente Minnelli *ph* Robert Planck *m* Miklos Rozsa *ad* Cedric Gibbons, Jack Martin Smith

☆ Jennifer Jones, Van Heflin, James Mason, Louis Jourdan, Christopher Kent, Gene Lockhart, Gladys Cooper, John Abbott, George Zucco

'If you hadn't read the book, you wouldn't guess what it was about from this film.' – *Pauline Kael, 70s*

† Previously filmed in 1932 as *Unholy Love*.

🏆 art direction

Madame Bovary

France 1991 120m colour
Arrow/MK2/CED/FR3 (Marin Karmitz)

A bored housewife with social pretensions, married to a doctor, indulges in self-destructive behaviour.

A reasonably faithful, but lifeless, adaptation, which seems as stultifying as the middle-class existence it portrays.

wd Claude Chabrol *novel* Gustave Flaubert *ph* Jean Rabier *m* Matthieu Chabrol *ad* Michèle Abbé *ed* Monique Fardoulis

☆ Isabelle Huppert, Jean-François Balmer, Christophe Malavoy, Jean Yanne, Lucas Belvaux, Christiane Minazzoli

'Respectful, luxurious and eminently forgettable.' – *Sight and Sound*

'One of the world's magnificent romances of great, unselfish love!'

Madame Butterfly

US 1932 88m bw
Paramount (B. P. Schulberg)

A Japanese geisha commits hara kiri when an American lieutenant passes her up for a western girl.

Drearily modernized version of the opera without its music; an odd idea to say the least.

w Josephine Lovett, Joseph M. March *story* John Luther Long *play David Belasco d* Marion Gering *ph* David Abel *md* W. Franke Harling

☆ Sylvia Sidney, Cary Grant, Charlie Ruggles, Sandor Kallay, Irving Pichel, Helen Jerome Eddy

'The long-drawn tragedy might be bearable if it were expressed in music or poetry, without any such embellishment it is apt to be painfully pathetic.' – *The Times*

'Travels slow and makes for only fair entertainment.' – *Variety*

Madame Butterfly **

France/Japan/Germany/GB 1995 134m colour 'Scope
Blue Dolphin/Erato/Idéale/France3/Imalyre/VTCOM/Sony Classical (Daniel Toscan du Plantier, Pierre-Olivier Bardet)

In Japan in the early 1900s, an American naval officer casually marries and abandons a Japanese girl.

An effective and authentic-looking staging of the opera, acted and sung with conviction.

wd Frédéric Mitterrand *opera* Giacomo Puccini *libretto Giuseppe Giacosa, Luigi Illica ph* Philippe Welt *md* James Conlon *ad* Michel Glotz, Daniel Zalay, Michèle Abbe-Vannier, Taïeb Jellouli *ed* Luc Barnier

☆ Ying Huang, Richard Troxell, Ning Liang, Richard Cowan, Jing Ma Fan, Christopheren Nomura, Constance Hauman

'Mr and Mrs Miniver together again!'

Madame Curie *

US 1943 124m bw
MGM (Sidney Franklin)

The life and marriage of the woman who discovered radium.

Dignified and rather dull biopic which well exemplifies MGM's best production style of the forties.

w Paul Osborn, Paul H. Rameau *book* Eve Curie *d* Mervyn Le Roy *ph* Joseph Ruttenberg *m* Herbert Stothart *ad* Cedric Gibbons, Paul Groesse

☆ Greer Garson, Walter Pidgeon, Henry Travers, Albert Basserman, Robert Walker, C. Aubrey Smith, Dame May Whitty, Victor Francen, Elsa Basserman, Reginald Owen, Van Johnson

'It achieves a notable triumph in making the discovery of a new element seem almost as glamorous as an encounter with Hedy Lamarr.' – *C. A. Lejeune*

🏆 best picture; Joseph Ruttenberg; Herbert Stothart; Greer Garson; Walter Pidgeon; art direction

Madame De... *

France/Italy 1953 102m bw
Franco-London/Indus/Rizzoli

US title: *The Earrings of Madame de...*

Tragic misunderstandings arise when a society wife sells her earrings and tells her husband she has lost them.

Elegant, rather heavy-handed but superbly glossy extension of a fashionable novelette.

w Marcel Achard, Max Ophüls, Annette Wademant *novel* Louise de Vilmorin *d Max Ophüls ph* Christian Matras *m* Oscar Straus, Georges Van Parys *ad* Jean d'Eaubonne

☆ Charles Boyer, Danielle Darrieux, Vittorio de Sica, Lea di Lea, Jean Debucourt

Madame Dubarry **

Germany 1919 85m (24 fps) bw silent
Union-UFA

US title: *Passion*

The life and times of the glamorous courtesan of Louis XV.

Milestone silent film which introduced to the cinemas of America and Britain not only the subtleties of the European cinema but the more adaptable subtleties of a key director, here dealing rather heavy-handedly with material which he should later have re-used.

w Fred Orbing, Hans Kraly *d* Ernst Lubitsch *ph* Theodor Sparkuhl

☆ Pola Negri, Emil Jannings, Harry Liedtke, Reinhold Schünzel

Madame Dubarry

US 1934 77m bw
Warner

The life of the legendary courtesan at Versailles.

Utterly unpersuasive but sometimes decorative historical charade.

w Edward Chodorov *d* William Dieterle

☆ Dolores del Rio, Reginald Owen, Victor Jory, Anita Louise, Osgood Perkins, Verree Teasdale

'A lavish but not particularly distinguished production.' – *Variety*

Madame Pimpernel: see *Paris Underground*

Madame Rosa
France 1977 120m Eastmancolor
Lira Films
original title: *La Vie Devant Soi*
An elderly Jewish prostitute runs an unofficial nursery school and cares especially for a fourteen-year-old Arab.
Splendidly acted but basically dreary fable twisted from a novel which took the child's point of view.
wd Moshe Mizrahi *novel* Emile Ajar *ph* Nestor Almendros *m* Philippe Sarde
☆ *Simone Signoret*, Claude Dauphin, Samy Ben Youb
best foreign film

Madame Sans-Gêne
US 1925 110m (24 fps) bw silent
Paramount
During the French Revolution, Napoleon plays Cupid to a laundry-maid and her lover.
The story formed the basis of one of Gloria Swanson's last successes; but it was made in France and did not have the zip of her Hollywood productions.
w Forrest Halsey *d* Léonce Perret
☆ Charles de Roche, Emile Drain, Gloria Swanson

Madame Sans-Gêne
France/Italy/Spain 1962 100m Technirama
TCF/Cine Alliance/Gesi/Champion/Agata (Maleno Malenotti)
GB and US title: *Madame*
Historical romp based on an old theatrical warhorse.
Pretty stilted in this version; especially when dubbed.
w Henri Jeanson and others *play* Victorien Sardou *d* Christian-Jaque *ph* Roberto Gerardi *m* Francesco Lavagnino
☆ Sophia Loren, Robert Hossein, Julien Bertheau, Marina Berti

Madame Sousatzka
GB 1988 122m Eastmancolor
Curzon/Sousatzka Productions (Robin Dalton)
A piano teacher is reluctant to let go of her star pupil.
A parade of eccentrics is mixed with a little domestic drama, but it all remains inert and uninteresting.
w Ruth Prawer Jhabvala, John Schlesinger *novel* Bernice Rubens *d* John Schlesinger *ph* Nat Crosby *m* Gerald Gouriet *pd* Luciana Arrighi *ed* Peter Honess
☆ Shirley MacLaine, Peggy Ashcroft, Twiggy, Shabana Azmi, Leigh Lawson, Geoffrey Bayldon, Lee Montague, Robert Rietty, Navin Chowdhry

'No amount of technical finesse, or polite musical trappings, can make the film seem other than an unswallowable, old-fashioned, overlong slab of confectionery.' – *Geoff Brown, MFB*

Madame Spy
US 1942 63m bw
Universal
A glamorous Nazi spy turns out to be an American secret agent.
Elementary espionage stuff without much in the way of plot development.
w Lynn Riggs, Clarence Upson Young *d* Roy William Neill *ph* George Robinson *ed* Ted J. Kent
☆ Constance Bennett, Don Porter, John Litel, Edward Brophy, John Eldredge

Madame X *
US 1929 95m bw
MGM
TV title: *Absinthe*
After an accidental death, a wealthy woman disappears and goes down in the world; at a subsequent murder trial she is defended by her unrecognizing son.
Two silent versions (with Dorothy Donnelly and Pauline Frederick) had been made of this old theatrical warhorse; two sound versions followed this one. The thing defies criticism.
w Willard Mack *play* Alexandre Bisson *d* Lionel Barrymore
☆ Ruth Chatterton, Raymond Hackett, Mitchell Lewis, Sidney Toler, Carroll Nye, Lewis Stone, Richard Carle

'Works like this confound the reformers, elevate the name of pictures, and tell the world that there is an art in film making.' – *Variety*
Lionel Barrymore; Ruth Chatterton

Madame X *
US 1937 72m bw
MGM (James K. McGuinness)
Competent remake with an excellent cast.
w John Meehan *d* Sam Wood *ph* John B. Seitz *m* David Snell *ad* Cedric Gibbons *ed* Frank Hull
☆ *Gladys George*, John Beal, Warren William, Reginald Owen, Lynne Carver, Henry Daniell, Emma Dunn, Ruth Hussey, George Zucco, William Henry

'An upper bracketer when played with a strong companion.' – *Variety*

'A fine old play, dated and outmoded. Audiences will leave the theatre expecting to find the coachman with horse and buggy.' – *Variety*

'One man drove her to it – one man tempted her – one man degraded her – one man defended her!'
Madame X
US 1965 100m Technicolor
Universal/Ross Hunter/Eltee
An elaborately dressed remake which suffered from a wooden lead; the more expensive the production, the more obvious the holes in the plot and the psychology.
w Jean Holloway *play* Alexandre Bisson *d* David Lowell Rich *ph* Russell Metty *m* Frank Skinner *ad* Alexander Golitzen, George Webb *ed* Milton Carruth *cos* Jean Louis
☆ Lana Turner, John Forsythe, Ricardo Montalban, *Constance Bennett*, Burgess Meredith, Keir Dullea, Virginia Grey, Warren Stevens

'One is free to enjoy a luxurious wallow in emotions that are all the more enjoyable for having no connection whatever with reality.' – *Brenda Davies*

The Madcap Adventures of Mr Toad: see *Ichabod and Mr Toad*

Das Mädchen Rosemarie: see *The Girl Rosemarie*

Made
US 2001 94m DeLuxe
Momentum/Artisan (Vince Vaughn, Jon Favreau)
Two friends muddle through when they run an errand for a Los Angeles gangster.
Lumbering buddy movie with a few likeable moments.
wd Jon Favreau *ph* Chris Doyle *m* John O'Brien, Lyle Workman *pd* Anne Stuhler *ed* Curtiss Clayton
☆ Jon Favreau (Bobby), Vince Vaughn (Ricky), Sean Combs (Ruiz), Famke Janssen (Jessica), Faizon Love (Horrace), David O'Hara (Welshman), Vincent Pastore (Jimmy), Peter Falk (Max)

'The kind of crime comedy that you root for even as it grows progressively more irritating.' – *Peter Travers, Rolling Stone*

Made for Each Other *
US 1938 90m bw
David O. Selznick
Problems of a lawyer and his new wife culminate in the near-death of their infant son.
Smooth star tearjerker.
w Jo Swerling *d* John Cromwell *ph* Leon Shamroy *m* Hugo Friedhofer, David Buttolph *pd* William Cameron Menzies *theme* Oscar Levant
☆ Carole Lombard, James Stewart, Charles Coburn, Lucile Watson, Harry Davenport, Eddie Quillan, Esther Dale, Louise Beavers

'Made to order for strong box office.' – *Variety*

Made for Each Other *
US 1971 107m DeLuxe
TCF/Wylde Films (Roy Townshend)
Romance between two New Yorkers with inferiority complexes.
Elongated cabaret sketch, a Brooklynesque comedy of flashy brilliance but limited general interest.
w Renée Taylor, Joe Bologna *d* Robert B. Bean *ph* William Storz
☆ Renée Taylor, Joe Bologna

'At the sperm-bank, she asked for a tall, intelligent, black man. One out of three ain't bad.'
Made in America
US 1993 110m Technicolor
Warner/Stonebridge/Kalola/Regency/Canal (Arnon Milchan, Michael Douglas, Rick Bieber)
A black teenager, born by artificial insemination, discovers that her father is a white car-salesman with a crass manner.
An occasionally amusing comedy, owing more to the performances than the script, which skirts all the racial issues it raises to settle for a comforting situation comedy.
w Holly Goldberg Sloan *story* Marcia Brandwynne, Nadine Schiff *d* Richard Benjamin *ph* Ralf Bode *m* Mark Isham *pd* Evelyn Sakash *ed* Jacqueline Cambas
☆ Whoopi Goldberg, Ted Danson, Will Smith, Nia Long, Paul Rodriguez, Jennifer Tilly, Peggy Rea, Clyde Kusatsu

'It's a likeable effort, good enough for a sultry summer evening at the multiplex when the film you came to see is sold out.' – *Sight and Sound*

Made in Heaven
GB 1952 81m Technicolor
Rank/Fanfare
Married couples compete for the Dunmow Flitch.
Easy-going family comedy which aims to be liked.
w William Douglas Home *d* John Paddy Carstairs *ph* Geoffrey Unsworth *m* Ronald Hanmer
☆ David Tomlinson, Petula Clark, Sonja Ziemann, A. E. Matthews, Charles Victor, Sophie Stewart, Richard Wattis, Athene Seyler

Made in Heaven
US 1987 103m colour
Rudolph-Blocker/Lorimar (Raynold Gideon, Bruce A. Evans, David Blocker)
A boy is sent back from heaven to find his lost love.
Droopy fantasy on the lines of Here Comes Mr Jordan *but without the wit.*
w Bruce A. Evans, Raynold Gideon *d* Alan Rudolph *ph* Jan Kiesser *m* Mark Isham *pd* Paul Peters *ed* Tom Walls
☆ Timothy Hutton, Kelly McGillis, Maureen Stapleton, Don Murray, Marj Dusay, Debra Winger

Made in Hong Kong *
Hong Kong 1997 109m colour
ICA/Shu Kei's Creative Workshop/Nicetop/Team Work (Andy Lau, Doris Yang)
original title: *Xianggang Zhizao*
A gangster's debt collector believes he is haunted by the spirit of a dead schoolgirl, as he tries to raise money for a kidney transplant for the teenager he loves.
Nihilistic thriller of rootless young people on the edge; it de-glamorises violence and crime and doesn't leave its audience feeling good about life.
wd Fruit Chan *ph* O Sing-pui, Lam Wah-chuen *m* Lam Wah-chuen *ad* Ma Ka-kwan *ed* Tin Sam-fat *cos* Tin Muk
☆ Sam Lee Chan-Sam (To Chung-chau, 'August Moon'), Wenbers Li Tung-Chuen (Ah-Lung, 'Sylvester'), Neiky Yim (Lam Yuk-ping), Amy Tam (Susan), Chan Tat-Yee (Fat Chan), Doris Chow (Mrs To), Chang Sang (Cheung Siu-Wing)

'A portrait of angry youth that's as hypnotic as it's often maddeningly kinetic.' – *Derek Elley, Variety*

† The film was made for $80,000, using non-professional actors, and utilising the short-ends of film stock from movies that Chan had worked on over the years as an assistant director.

Madeleine *
GB 1949 114m bw
GFD/David Lean/Cineguild (Stanley Haynes)
In Victorian Glasgow a well-to-do young woman is accused of murdering her lover, but the verdict is 'not proven'.
Dramatically dead because of its ambiguous ending, this lavish and good-looking treatment of a cause célèbre was a mistake for all concerned, but its incidental pleasures are considerable.
w Nicholas Phipps, Stanley Haynes *d* *David Lean* *ph* *Guy Green* *m* William Alwyn *pd* *John Bryan* *cos* Margaret Furse
☆ Ann Todd, Leslie Banks, Elizabeth Sellars, Ivor Barnard, Ivan Desny, Norman Wooland, Edward Chapman, Barbara Everest, André Morell, Barry Jones, Jean Cadell, John Laurie, Eugene Deckers

'In an old house in Paris that was covered in vines, lived twelve little girls in two straight lines.'
Madeline *
US 1998 90m Technicolor
Sony Pictures/TriStar Pictures/Jaffilms/Pancho Kohner/Saul Cooper
In Paris, a girl rescues the son of an ambassador and ensures that the orphanage in which she lives is not shut down.
Energetic children's film of resourceful and plucky girls; adults may find it a little trying before the end.
w Mark Levin, Jennifer Flackett *book* Ludwig Bemelmans *d* Daisy von Scherler Mayer *ph* Pierre Aim *m* Michel Legrand *pd* Hugo Luczyc-Wyhowski *ed* Jeffrey Wolf
☆ Frances McDormand, Nigel Hawthorne, Hatty Jones, Stéphane Audran, Ben Daniels, Arturo Venegas, Katia Caballero, Chantal Neuwirth, Kristian de la Osa

'Witless and dramatically inept.' – *Cosmo Landesman, Sunday Times*

Mademoiselle Docteur *
GB 1937 84m bw
Grafton/Trafalgar (Max Schach)
A German lady spy falls for a British agent.
War melodrama vaguely based on fact and later remade as Fräulein Doktor.
w Jacques Natanson, Marcel Achard, Ernest Betts *d* Edmond T. Gréville *ph* Otto Heller
☆ Dita Parlo, John Loder, Erich von Stroheim, Claire Luce, Gyles Isham, Clifford Evans, John Abbott

'Even a thriller cannot thrill unless the characters are established in our imaginations, and the packed plot of this film allows them no chance.' – *Graham Greene*

Mademoiselle Fifi *
US 1944 69m bw
RKO (Val Lewton)
During the Franco-Prussian war a stagecoach is held up because a prostitute, despite the urging of her fellow passengers, refuses to sleep with a Prussian officer. When she gives in, they shun her, and she kills him.
Interesting low budget version of a story which inspired many films.
w Josef Mischel, Peter Ruric *stories* Boule de Suif/Mademoiselle Fifi by Guy de Maupassant *d* Robert Wise *ph* Harry Wild *m* Werner Heymann
☆ Simone Simon, Kurt Kreuger, John Emery, Alan Napier, Jason Robards Sr, Norma Varden, Helen Freeman, Fay Helm

'There is a gallant, fervent quality about the whole picture, faults and all, which gives it a peculiar kind of life and likeableness, and which signifies that there is one group of men working in Hollywood who have neither lost nor taken care to conceal the purity of their hope and intention.' – *James Agee*

Mademoiselle France: see *Reunion in France*

Madhouse *
GB 1974 92m Eastmancolor
AIP/Amicus (Milton Subotsky)
A reluctant horror actor makes a comeback and finds himself involved in a series of grisly murders.
In-jokey horror piece with clips from old AIP chillers; quite likeable.
w Greg Morrison *novel* Devilday by Angus Hall *d* Jim Clark *ph* Ray Parslow *m* Douglas Gamley
☆ Vincent Price, Peter Cushing, Robert Quarry, Adrienne Corri, Natasha Pyne, Linda Hayden, Barry Dennen

Madhouse
US 1990 90m colour
Rank/Orion/A Boy of the Year (Leslie Dixon)
Unwanted friends and neighbours move in as house guests of a young couple.
Remarkably unfunny domestic comedy, directed with a heavy hand.

wd Tom Ropelewski *ph* Denis Lewiston *m* David Newman *pd* Dan Leigh *ed* Michael Jablow
☆ John Larroquette, Kirstie Alley, Alison LaPlaca, John Diehl, Jessica Lundy, Bradley Gregg, Dennis Miller, Robert Ginty, Wayne Tippit

Madigan *
US 1968 100m Techniscope
Universal (Frank P. Rosenberg)

A Brooklyn police detective brings in a dangerous escaped criminal at the cost of his own life.
Lively, well-characterized police thriller with excellent locations.
w Henri Simoun, Abraham Polonsky *novel The Commissioner* by Richard Dougherty *d Don Siegel* *ph* Russell Metty *m* Don Costa
☆ *Richard Widmark, Henry Fonda,* Michael Dunn, Inger Stevens, Harry Guardino, James Whitmore, Susan Clark, Steve Ihnat, Don Stroud, Sheree North, Warren Stevens, Raymond St Jacques
† The character was later resurrected for a TV series also starring Richard Widmark.

Madison Avenue
US 1961 94m bw Cinemascope
TCF (Bruce Humberstone)
An advertising executive plans to revenge himself on his treacherous boss.
Predictable melodrama with an adequate plot but dismal acting and presentation.
w Norman Corwin *novel The Build-Up Boys* by Jeremy Kirk *d* H. Bruce Humberstone *ph* Charles G. Clarke *m* Harry Sukman
☆ Dana Andrews, Jeanne Crain, Eleanor Parker, Eddie Albert, Howard St John, Henry Daniell, Kathleen Freeman
'Simply nowhere near grand enough.' – *MFB*

Madman
US 1982 88m Cineffects colour
The Legend Lives (Gary Sales)

Young counsellors at a rundown summer camp discover that the nearby woods are the home of a mad axeman.
Deliberately formulaic slasher movie, in the mould of Friday the 13th, but much mouldier.
wd Joe Giannone *ph* James Momel *m* Stephen Horelick *md* Gary Sales *ed* Daniel Loewenthal
☆ Alexis Dubin (Betsy), Tony Fish (T. P.), Harriet Bass (Stacey), Seth Jones (Dave), Jan Claire (Ellie), Alex Murphy (Bill), Jimmy Steele (Richie), Paul Ehlers (Madman Marz)

'His Majesty was all powerful and all knowing. But he wasn't quite all there.'
'First he lost America. Now he's losing his mind.'

The Madness of King George ***
GB 1994 107m Technicolor
Rank/Samuel Goldwyn/Channel 4/Close Call (Stephen Evans, David Parfitt)

In the 1780s, King George III's behaviour becomes more and more eccentric and unbalanced until he is diagnosed as mad and comes close to losing his power.
Entertaining drama of the eccentricities of royalty, speculating that the King's problem may have been caused by the illness porphyria, and which also obliquely questions the point of the monarchy. Directed with a sense of pace and an excellent eye for the inequalities of society, even within palaces, it gains immeasurably by the superb performance of Hawthorne in the title role, honed by his having played it so often on stage.
w Alan Bennett *play The Madness of George III* by Alan Bennett *d Nicholas Hytner* *ph* Andrew Dunn *m* George Fenton, Handel *pd Ken Adam* *ed* Tariq Anwar
☆ *Nigel Hawthorne, Helen Mirren,* Ian Holm, Amanda Donohoe, Rupert Graves, Rupert Everett, Jim Carter, Geoffrey Palmer, John Wood, Jeremy Child, Cyril Shaps
'Essentially it is Hawthorne's triumph and no one else's, since he provides the holding centre without which the rest might have seemed an ephemeral romp, uncertain as to whether to comment on its own times or ours and drifting towards parody in both instances.' – *Derek Malcolm, Guardian*
† The title of the play, *The Madness of George III*, was not used in case audiences thought it was the third film in a series (just as audiences are said to have come out of *Henry V* regretting that they had missed the first four films).
Ken Adam
Nigel Hawthorne; Helen Mirren; Alan Bennett
best British picture; Nigel Hawthorne

Madness of the Heart
GB 1949 105m bw
GFD/Two Cities (Richard Wainwright)
A blind girl marries a French aristocrat and has to cope with a jealous neighbour.
Heavily disguised version of the Rebecca theme, with a happy ending after many alarums and excursions, most of them irrelevant. As film-making, very thin.
wd Charles Bennett *novel* Flora Sandstrom *ph* Desmond Dickinson *m* Allan Gray
☆ Margaret Lockwood, Paul Dupuis, Kathleen Byron, Maxwell Reed

Madonna of the Seven Moons
GB 1944 110m bw
GFD/Gainsborough (R. J. Minney)

Affected by childhood rape, a demure lady has a second life as a daring gypsy.
Novelettish balderdash killed stone dead by stilted presentation; but highly successful in its day.
w Roland Pertwee, Brock Williams *novel* Margery Lawrence *d* Arthur Crabtree *ph* Jack Cox
☆ Phyllis Calvert, Stewart Granger, Patricia Roc, Peter Glenville, John Stuart, Jean Kent, Nancy Price, Peter Murray Hill, Reginald Tate
'One of the most diverting British films of the forties.' – *Richard Roud*
'The purplest production English cinema has yet achieved.' – *Time and Tide*

The Madonna's Secret
US 1946 79m bw
Stephen Auer/Republic
Women attracted to a Parisian painter are all found dead.
Slow-moving mystery which manages to remain suspenseful.
w Bradbury Foote, William Thiele *d* William Thiele
☆ Francis Lederer, Gail Patrick, Ann Rutherford, Edward Ashley, Linda Stirling, John Litel

'Killing Is As Easy As Stealing Candy From A Baby'

La Madre Muerta
Spain 1993 107m colour Panavision
Metro Tartan/Gasteizko Zinema (Juanma Bajo Ulloa)
A petty crook kidnaps a mentally retarded woman whom he recognizes as the witness to his murder of her mother a decade earlier, but is unable to bring himself to kill her.
An oddly disturbing drama, of casual deaths and murky happenings suffused with a melodramatic religiosity; no doubt its director will go on to better films.
w Juanma Bajo Ulloa, Eduardo Bajo Ulloa *d* Juanma Bajo Ulloa *ph* Javier Aguirresarobe *m* Bingen Mendizabal *ad* Satur Idaretta *ed* Pablo Blanco
☆ Karra Elejalde, Lio, Ana Alvarez, Silvia Marsó
'As a dark thriller it is remarkably unpleasant.' – *George Perry*

Madron
US/Israel 1970 93m colour
Four Star Excelsior/GBC/Edric/Isracine/Zev Braun (Emanuel Henigman, Eric Weaver)

A nun, the only survivor of a massacre, attempts to escape the attentions of Apache warriors with the aid of a passing gunfighter.
A downbeat Western that concentrates on the contrasting characters of its two protagonists, but which fails to make the clash of personalities interesting. It was mostly filmed in the Negev Desert, which accounts for the uninteresting scenery.
w Edward Chappell, Leo McMahon *d* Jerry Hopper *ph* Marcel Grignon, Adam Greenberg *m* Riz Ortolani *ad* Robert Ramsey *ed* Renzo Lucidi
☆ Richard Boone, Leslie Caron, Gabi Amrani

The Madwoman of Chaillot *
GB 1969 142m Technicolor
Warner/Commonwealth United (Ely Landau)

An eccentric Parisian lady has equally eccentric friends, but her real life is in the past.
A highly theatrical whimsy which somewhat lacks humour, this should never have been considered as a film, certainly not as an all-star extravaganza; but it was, and it falls flat on its face in the first reel of tedious conversation.
w Edward Anhalt *play* Jean Giraudoux *d* Bryan Forbes *ph* Claude Renoir, Burnett Guffey *m* Michael J. Lewis *pd* Ray Simm
☆ Katharine Hepburn, Yul Brynner, Danny Kaye, Edith Evans, Charles Boyer, Claude Dauphin, John Gavin, Paul Henreid, Nanette Newman, Oscar Homolka, Margaret Leighton, Giulietta Masina, Richard Chamberlain, Donald Pleasence, Fernand Gravet
'One finds oneself too often longing for the drop of the curtain.' – *Brenda Davies*
'The intentions are honourable – defeat is inevitable.' – *Rex Reed*
'One of Giraudoux's less good and most fragile plays has been rewritten, bloated with inept contemporary references, drawn out to gigantic proportions of humourless vacuity, and peopled with a barrelful of nonacting stars.' – *John Simon*
'The remnants of Giraudoux' slight, whimsical play can still be perceived in Edward Anhalt's vile modernization, and a lot of famous actors can be recognized even in the performances they give here.' – *Pauline Kael, New Yorker*

Maedchen in Uniform *
Germany 1931 90m bw
Deutsche Film-Gemeinschaft

aka: *Girls in Uniform*
A girl at a strict boarding school falls in love with one of the teachers and commits suicide.
Famous early stab at lesbianism, remade in 1958 with Romy Schneider and Lilli Palmer. Interesting for content, not style.
w F. D. Andam, Christa Winsloe *play Gestern und Heute* by Christa Winsloe *d* Leontine Sagan *ph* Reimar Kuntze *m* Hansen Milde-Meissner
☆ Dorothea Wieck, Ellen Schwannecke, Hertha Thiele, Emilie Lunde
'At once a strident warning against the consequences of Hitler's regime and the first truly radical lesbian film.' – *Time Out, 1981*

Il Maestro
Belgium/France 1989 92m Fujicolour
Man's Films/Flach Film/RTBF/BTR (Marion Hänsel, François Lepetit)
aka: *The Maestro*
Returning to Italy to conduct *Madame Butterfly*, a Jewish conductor reveals a wartime betrayal that brings on a breakdown.
Small-scale, overstretched drama.
wd Marion Hänsel *story La Giacca Verde* by Mario Soldati *ph* Acacio de Almeida *m* Frederick Devreese *ad* Ernita Frigato, Antonello Geleng
☆ Malcolm McDowell, Charles Aznavour, Andréa Ferréol, Francis Lemaire

El Maestro de Esgrima: see *The Fencing Master*

Il Maestro di Don Giovanni: see *Crossed Swords*

Maestro – Ma Non Troppo
France 1985 90m colour
Antenne 2
A provincial orchestral conductor is kidnapped to prevent him from performing at a concert for world peace.
Farcical attempt at political satire.
w Christian Watton, Serge Korber *d* Serge Korber *ph* André Dumaître, Bernard Dumont *m* Greco Casadesus *ed* Claude Dufour
☆ Alain Doutey, Sophie Barjac, Claude Villers, Joelle Guillaud, Jean Gaven, Jacques Spiesser, Jess Hahn, Clément Harari

Mafia!
US 1998 84m Technicolor
Buena Vista/Touchstone/Tapestry (Bill Badalato)

aka: *Jane Austen's Mafia*
Two brothers vie with one another to take over the leadership of a Mafia family from their ageing father.
A tired send-up of The Godfather *trilogy and similar gangster movies; a few jokes might have helped.*
w Jim Abrahams, Greg Norberg, Michael McManus *d* Jim Abrahams *ph* Pierre Letarte *m* Gianni Frizzelli *pd* William Elliott *ed* Terry Stokes
☆ Jay Mohr, Billy Burke, Christina Applegate, Pamela Gidley, Olympia Dukakis, Lloyd Bridges, Jason Fuchs, Joe Viterelli, Tony Lo Bianco
'Has far more fart jokes than laughs.' – *Rob Mackie, Guardian*

The Magdalene Sisters **
GB/Ireland 2002 119m colour
Momentum/Scottish Screen/Film Council/Irish Film/PFP/Temple (Frances Higson)
In Ireland in the 1960s, three young women – one raped at a family wedding, one attracting the attention of boys, and one who had an illegitimate child – are all forced to work unpaid in the Magdalene Laundries, which were run by Catholic nuns for women judged to be in moral danger.
Fiercely angry film, based on true stories, that takes the lives of three women as representative of the many thousands who suffered. It is a powerful polemic, well acted and with moments of black humour among the futility and waste of lives.
wd Peter Mullan *ph* Nigel Willoughby *m* Craig Armstrong *pd* Mark Leese *ed* Colin Monie
☆ *Geraldine McEwan* (Sister Bridget), Anne-Marie Duff (Margaret), Nora-Jane Noone (Bernadette), Dorothy Duffy (Rose/Patricia), Eileen Walsh (Crispina), Mary Murray (Una), Britta Smith (Katy)
'A deliberately provocative film that triggers the audience's emotions in order to highlight important issues of personal freedom. Amen to that.' – *Alan Morrison, Empire*
'A sustained and all-but-deafening howl of rage on behalf of vulnerable women.' – *Peter Bradsahw, Guardian*
† The film won The Golden Lion at the Venice Film Festival.

The Maggie **
GB 1953 93m bw
Ealing (Michael Truman)
US title: *High and Dry*
An American businessman is tricked into sending his private cargo to a Scottish island on an old puffer in need of repair.
Mildly amusing comedy about the wily Scots; not the studio at its best, but pretty fair.
w William Rose d Alexander Mackendrick
ph Gordon Dines *m* John Addison
☆ Paul Douglas, *Alex Mackenzie*, James Copeland, Abe Barker, Dorothy Alison, Hubert Gregg, Geoffrey Keen, Andrew Keir, Tommy Kearins

Magic
US 1978 107m Technicolor
TCF/Joseph E. Levine

A ventriloquist obsessed by his dummy is impelled to murder.
Pretentious and occasionally unpleasant version of an oft-told tale.
w William Goldman *novel* William Goldman *d* Richard Attenborough *ph* Victor J. Kemper *m* Jerry Goldsmith *pd* Terence Marsh
☆ Anthony Hopkins, Ann-Margret, Burgess Meredith, Ed Lauter, E. J. Andre, David Ogden Stiers
'The gloomily withdrawn Hopkins has no vulgarity in his soul – nothing that suggests any connection with the world of entertainment – and the picture grinds along.' – *New Yorker*

The Magic Bow
GB 1946 106m bw
GFD/Gainsborough (R. J. Minney)
Episodes in the life of the violin virtuoso Paganini.
Poor costumer, dramatically and historically unpersuasive.
w Norman Ginsburg, Roland Pertwee *novel* Manuel Komroff *d* Bernard Knowles *ph* Jack Cox *m* Paganini, Beethoven, Tartini, Phil Green, Henry Geehl *md* Louis Levy *ad* Andrew Mazzei *ed* Alfred Roome *violin solos Yehudi Menuhin*
☆ Stewart Granger, Jean Kent, Phyllis Calvert, Dennis Price, Cecil Parker, Felix Aylmer, Frank Cellier, Marie Lohr, Henry Edwards

The Magic Box *
GB 1951 118m Technicolor
Festival Films (Ronald Neame)

The life of William Friese-Greene, a British cinema pioneer who died in poverty.
A joint British film industry venture to celebrate the Festival of Britain, this rather downbeat and uneventful story takes on the nature of a pageant or a series of charades, with well-known people appearing to no good purpose. But it means well.
w Eric Ambler *d* John Boulting *ph* Jack Cardiff *m* William Alwyn *pd* John Bryan
☆ Robert Donat, Margaret Johnson, Maria Schell, John Howard Davies, Renée Asherson, Richard Attenborough, Robert Beatty, Michael Denison, Leo Genn, Marius Goring, Joyce Grenfell, Robertson Hare, Kathleen Harrison, Jack Hulbert, Stanley Holloway and also Glynis Johns, Mervyn Johns, Barry Jones, Miles Malleson, Muir Mathieson, A. E. Matthews, John McCallum, Bernard Miles, Laurence Olivier, Cecil Parker, Eric Portman, Dennis Price, Michael Redgrave, Margaret Rutherford, Ronald Shiner, Sybil Thorndike, David Tomlinson, Cecil Trouncer, Peter Ustinov, Kay Walsh, Emlyn Williams, Harcourt Williams, Googie Withers
'An honest and often a very moving film.' – *Daily Express*
'Patriotic, sentimental, overlong and faintly embarrassing.' – *Time Out, 1984*

The Magic Carpet
US 1951 84m Supercinecolor
Sam Katzman/Columbia
The caliph's son returns as the Scarlet Falcon to rout the usurper.
Hopeless kid's matinée rubbish, not even performed with verve.
w David Matthews *d* Lew Landers *ph* Ellis Carter *ad* Paul Palmentola
☆ Lucille Ball, Raymond Burr, John Agar, Patricia Medina, George Tobias

The Magic Christian
GB 1969 95m Technicolor
Commonwealth United/Grand Films (Dennis O'Dell)

An eccentric millionaire spends his wealth deflating those who pursue money or power.
A series of variably funny but always unpleasant sketches, climaxing with citizens delving for spoils in a vat of blood and manure. In its aim to be satirical, very typical of its time.
w Terry Southern, Joe McGrath, Peter Sellers *novel* Terry Southern *d* Joe McGrath *ph* Geoffrey Unsworth *m* Ken Thorne *pd* Assheton Gorton
☆ Peter Sellers, Ringo Starr, Richard Attenborough, Laurence Harvey, Christopher Lee, Spike Milligan, Yul Brynner, Roman Polanski, Raquel Welch, Wilfrid Hyde-White, Fred Emney, John Le Mesurier, Dennis Price, Patrick Cargill, John Cleese and also Graham Chapman

The Magic Face
US 1951 90m bw
Columbia (Mort Briskin, Robert Smith)
A brilliant German impersonator kills Hitler, takes his place, and leads Germany deliberately into defeat.
Hilariously unlikely anecdote 'as told to William Shirer', performed with vigour but handicapped by a shoddy production.
w Mort Briskin, Robert Smith *d* Frank Tuttle *ph* Tony Braun *m* Herschel Burke Gilbert
☆ *Luther Adler*, Patricia Knight, Ilka Windish, William L. Shirer
'If Shirer believed this story, then he must be the only person in the world to do so.' – *Gavin Lambert*

Magic Fire
US 1954 94m Trucolor
Republic (William Dieterle)
The life and loves of Richard Wagner.
Remarkably boring biopic with much music but little story or characterization. Ugly colour minimizes German locations.
w Bertita Harding, E. A. Dupont, David Chantler *d* William Dieterle *ph* Ernest Haller *md* Erich Wolfgang Korngold
☆ Alan Badel, Yvonne de Carlo, Peter Cushing, Frederick Valk, Carlos Thompson, Valentina Cortesa

Magic Night: see *Goodnight Vienna*

The Magic of Lassie
US 1978 99m colour
Lassie Productions (Bonita Granville Wrather, William Beaudine Jnr)
A collie dog is sold but makes its way back home.
Downright peculiar revamp of Lassie Come Home *with music and an ageing all-star cast.*
w Jean Holloway, Richard M. Sherman, Robert B. Sherman *d* Don Chaffey *m* Irwin Kostal *songs* Richard and Robert Sherman
☆ James Stewart, Alice Faye, Mickey Rooney, Pernell Roberts, Stephanie Zimbalist, Gene Evans
song 'When You're Loved'

The Magic Sword
US 1962 80m Eastmancolor
UA/Bert I. Gordon

The son of a well-meaning witch rescues a princess from the clutches of an evil sorcerer.
Shaky medieval fantasy on too low a budget.
w Bernard Schoenfeld *d* Bert I. Gordon *ph* Paul Vogel *m* Richard Markowitz *sp* Milt Rice
☆ Basil Rathbone, Estelle Winwood, Gary Lockwood, Anne Helm

The Magic Sword: Quest for Camelot: see *Quest for Camelot*

'The guy with the dynamite heart meets the girl with the firecracker eyes!'
Magic Town
US 1947 103m bw
Robert Riskin Productions

An opinion pollster discovers a small town which exactly mirrors the views of the USA at large.
A bright Capraesque idea is extraordinarily dully scripted, the production looks dim, and all concerned are operating one degree under.
w Robert Riskin *d* William A. Wellman *ph* Joseph Biroc *m* Roy Webb
☆ James Stewart, Jane Wyman, Kent Smith, Regis Toomey, Donald Meek, Ned Sparks, Wallace Ford

The Magic Toyshop *
GB 1986 107m colour
Granada (Steve Morrison)
Three children are left in the care of their uncle, a puppet-maker.
Weird, sometimes grotesque fantasy focusing on an adolescent girl's sexual awakening.
w Angela Carter *novel* Angela Carter *d* David Wheatley *ph* Ken Morgan *m* Bill Connor *pd* Stephen Fineren *ed* Anthony Ham
☆ Tom Bell, Caroline Milmoe, Kilian McKenna

The Magician: see *The Face (1958)*

The Magician of Lublin
West Germany/Israel 1979 114m colour
Geria-Golan-Globus (Harry N. Blum)
In 1901 an itinerant magician with an active sex life dreams of being able really to fly.
Curious muddled fable with apparent correspondences to the Christ story, like Bergman's The Face. *In the end it does not confidently address itself to any audience, despite clever moments.*
w Irving S. White, Menahem Golan *novel* Isaac Bashevis Singer *d* Menahem Golan *ph* David Gurfinkel *m* Maurice Jarre *pd* Jürgen Kiebach
☆ Alan Arkin, Louise Fletcher, Valerie Perrine, Shelley Winters, Lou Jacobi, Warren Berlinger
'California Polish accents grapple with hamfisted direction and a script of surpassing banality.' – *Sight and Sound*

The Magnet
GB 1950 79m bw
Ealing (Sidney Cole)

A small boy steals a magnet and accidentally becomes a hero.
Very mild Ealing comedy, not really up to snuff.
w T. E. B. Clarke *d* Charles Frend *ph* Lionel Banes *m* William Alwyn
☆ Stephen Murray, Kay Walsh, William Fox, Meredith Edwards, Gladys Henson, Thora Hird, Wylie Watson

The Magnetic Monster *
US 1953 75m bw
UA/Ivan Tors
A new radio-active element causes 'implosions' of increasing size by drawing energy from the area around it.
Well-told low-budget sci-fi with the audience kept abreast of all developments; the undersea lab scenes are borrowed from an old German film, Gold.
w Curt Siodmak, Ivan Tors d Curt Siodmak ph Charles Van Enger *m* Blaine Sanford *pd* George Van Marter
☆ Richard Carlson, King Donovan, Jean Byron, Byron Foulger
'A crackling mixture of science and fiction.' – *Time*

'Real life screened more daringly than it's ever been before!'
The Magnificent Ambersons ****
US 1942 88m bw
RKO/Mercury (Orson Welles)

A proud family loses its wealth and its control of the neighbourhood, and its youngest male member gets his come-uppance.
Fascinating period drama told in brilliant cinematic snippets; owing to studio interference the last reels are weak, but the whole is a treat for connoisseurs, and a delight in its fast-moving control of cinematic narrative.
wd Orson Welles novel Booth Tarkington *ph Stanley Cortez m Bernard Herrmann ad Mark-Lee Kirk ed* Robert Wise, Mark Robson
☆ *Joseph Cotten, Dolores Costello, Agnes Moorehead, Tim Holt, Anne Baxter, Ray Collins, Richard Bennett,* Erskine Sanford, Donald Dillaway
NARRATOR (WELLES): 'And now Major Amberson was engaged in the profoundest thinking of his life, and he realized that everything which had worried him or delighted him during his lifetime – all his buying and building and trading and banking – that it was all a trifle and a waste beside what concerned him now, for the Major knew now that he had to plan how to enter an unknown country where he was not even sure of being recognized as an Amberson.'
NARRATOR: 'Something had happened. A thing which years ago had been the eagerest hope of many, many good citizens of the town. And now it had come at last: George Amberson Minafer had got his come-uppance. He got it three times filled and running over. But those who had so longed for it were not there to see it, and they never knew it. Those who were still living had forgotten all about it and all about him.'
'Rich in ideas that many will want to copy, combined in the service of a story that few will care to imitate.' – C. A. *Lejeune*
'Nearly every scene is played with a casual perfection which could only come from endless painstaking planning and rehearsals, and from a wonderful sense of timing.' – *Basil Wright, 1972*
'Even in this truncated form it's amazing and memorable.' – *Pauline Kael, 70s*
† Previously filmed in 1925 as *Pampered Youth.*
†† The credits are all at the end and all spoken, ending with: 'I wrote and directed the picture. My name is Orson Welles.'
best picture; Stanley Cortez; Agnes Moorehead

The Magnificent Brute
US 1936 77m bw
Universal
A blast furnace boss becomes involved with stolen money.
Star character drama; very predictable.
w Owen Francis, Lewis R. Foster, Bertram Millhauser *d* John G. Blystone *ph* Merritt Gerstad *ad* Albert S. Agostino, Jack Otterson *ed* Ted J. Kent
☆ Victor McLaglen, Binnie Barnes, Billy Burrud, William Hall, Jean Dixon
art direction

'The whisper of every woman – the toast of every man!'
Magnificent Doll
US 1946 95m bw
Universal/Hallmark (Jack H. Skirball, Bruce Manning)
Dolly Madison, wife of the President, finds that traitor Aaron Burr is a memory from her own past.
Uneasy historical semi-fiction, badly cast and rather boring, yet with some sense of period style.
w Irving Stone *d* Frank Borzage *ph* Joseph Valentine *m* Hans Salter *ad* Alexander Golitzen *ed* Ted J. Kent
☆ Ginger Rogers, David Niven, Burgess Meredith, Stephen McNally, Peggy Wood, Robert Barrat
'No duller case has ever been made out for liberty.' – *Daily Mail*
'Some day the moviemakers will discover that they can make history wonderfully believable and exciting by just sticking roughly to the facts.' – *The Times*

The Magnificent Dope
US 1942 83m bw
TCF (William Perlberg)

As a publicity stunt a success school brings the nation's most complete failure to New York, and he outsmarts them all.
Dim sub-Capra comedy.
w George Seaton *d* Walter Lang *ph* Peverell Marley *m* David Raksin and others *md* Emil Newman
☆ Henry Fonda, Lynn Bari, Don Ameche, Edward Everett Horton, George Barbier, Frank Orth, Hobart Cavanaugh

The Magnificent Fraud
US 1939 78m bw
Paramount
The president of a Latin American republic is murdered, and an impersonator takes his place.
Sharply played dramatic hokum.
w Gilbert Gabriel and Walter Ferris *d* Robert Florey
☆ Akim Tamiroff, Lloyd Nolan, Patricia Morison, Mary Boland
'Dull drama; no marquee names; filler fodder for duals.' – *Variety*

The Magnificent Matador
US 1955 94m Eastmancolor Cinemascope
Edward L. Alperson

GB title: *The Brave and the Beautiful*
A matador trains his illegitimate son to follow in his footsteps but has a premonition of his death in the ring.
Dreary bullfighting drama with romantic interludes.
w Charles Lang *d* Budd Boetticher *ph* Lucien Ballard *m* Raoul Kraushaar
☆ Anthony Quinn, Maureen O'Hara, Manuel Rojas, Richard Denning, Thomas Gomez, Lola Albright

Magnificent Obsession **
US 1935 112m bw
Universal (John M. Stahl)
The playboy who is half-responsible for the death of a woman's husband and for her own blindness becomes a surgeon and cures her.
Absurd soaper which was phenomenally popular and is certainly well done.
w George O'Neil, Sarah Y. Mason, Victor Heerman *novel Lloyd C. Douglas d John M. Stahl ph* Russell Metty *m* Franz Waxman *ad* Bernard Herzbrun, Emrich Nicholson *ed* Milton Carruth
☆ Irene Dunne, Robert Taylor, Ralph Morgan, Sara Haden, Charles Butterworth, Betty Furness, Arthur Hoyt, Gilbert Emery, Arthur Treacher
'Capital romance, a cinch for the femme trade.' – *Variety*

Magnificent Obsession **
US 1954 108m Technicolor
Universal (Ross Hunter)

Glossy remake which sent Ross Hunter to the commercial heights as a remaker of thirties weepies.
This one worked best.
w Robert Blees *d Douglas Sirk ph* Russell Metty *m* Frank Skinner
☆ Jane Wyman, Rock Hudson, Agnes Moorehead, Barbara Rush, Otto Kruger, Gregg Palmer, Paul Cavanagh, Sara Shane
Jane Wyman

The Magnificent Rebel
US 1960 94m Technicolor
Walt Disney (Peter V. Herald)
Episodes in the life of the young Beethoven.
Solid Disney biopic, shot in Vienna with good period detail.

w Joanne Court *d* Georg Tressler *ph* Göran Strindberg *md* Frederick Stark
☆ Karl Boehm, Ernst Nadhering, Ivan Desny, Gabriele Porks

'They were seven – and they fought like seven hundred!'
The Magnificent Seven **
US 1960 138m DeLuxe Panavision
UA/Mirisch-Alpha (John Sturges)

A Mexican village hires seven American gunmen for protection against bandits.
Popular Western based on the Japanese Seven Samurai; *good action scenes, but the rest is verbose and often pretentious.*
w William Roberts *d* John Sturges *ph* Charles Lang Jnr *m Elmer Bernstein*
☆ *Yul Brynner, Steve McQueen,* Robert Vaughn, *James Coburn, Charles Bronson,* Horst Buchholz, Eli Wallach, Brad Dexter, Vladimir Sokoloff, Rosenda Monteros
🏆 Elmer Bernstein

The Magnificent Seven Deadly Sins
GB 1971 107m colour
Tigon (Graham Stark)

Compendium of comedy sketches, a very variable ragbag of old jokes.
w Bob Larbey, John Esmonde, Dave Freeman, Barry Cryer, Graham Chapman, Graham Stark, Marty Feldman, Alan Simpson, Ray Galton, Spike Milligan *d* Graham Stark *ph* Harvey Harrison Jnr *m* Roy Budd
☆ Bruce Forsyth, Joan Sims, Roy Hudd, Harry Secombe, Leslie Phillips, Julie Ege, Harry H. Corbett, Ian Carmichael, Alfie Bass, Spike Milligan, Ronald Fraser

'A Brand New Seven — Doing Their Number! They put their lives on the line and let it ride!'
The Magnificent Seven Ride!
US 1972 100m DeLuxe
UA/Mirisch (William A. Calihan)

After his wife is killed, a marshall recruits a gang of convicts to save a Mexican village once again from bandits.
*Tired and very modest finale to a patchy series (*Return of the Seven, Guns of the Magnificent Seven*).*
w Arthur Rowe *d* George McCowan *ph* Fred Koenekamp *m* Elmer Bernstein *ad* John T. McCormack *ed* Walter Thompson
☆ Lee Van Cleef (Chris), Stefanie Powers (Laurie Gunn), Mariette Hartley (Arilla), Pedro Armendariz Jnr (Pepe Carral), Luke Askew (Skinner), Michael Callan (Noah Forbes), Bill Lucking (Walt Drummond), James B. Sikking (Hayes), Ed Lauter (Scott Elliott), Melissa Murphy (Madge Buchanan), Gary Busey (Hank Allan)

The Magnificent Showman: see *Circus World*

The Magnificent Two
GB 1967 100m Eastmancolor
Rank (Hugh Stewart)
One of two incompetent travelling salesmen in a Latin American banana republic is persuaded to pose as a dead rebel leader.
More or less a Bob Hope vehicle, adapted for the less realistic Morecambe and Wise with unhappy results: too few sight gags and a curious emphasis on violence. The third and last of their attempts to find film vehicles.
w S. C. Green, R. M. Hills, Michael Pertwee, Peter Blackmore *d* Cliff Owen *ph* Ernest Steward *m* Ron Goodwin
☆ Eric Morecambe, Ernie Wise, Margit Saad, Cecil Parker, Virgilio Teixeira, Isobel Black, Martin Benson

The Magnificent Yankee *
US 1950 88m bw
MGM (Armand Deutsch)
GB title: *The Man with Thirty Sons*
Episodes in the later life of Judge Oliver Wendell Holmes.
Vaguely well-meaning biopic without much dramatic sense.
w Emmet Lavery *play* Emmet Lavery *d* John Sturges *ph* Joseph Ruttenberg *m* David Raksin
☆ Louis Calhern, Ann Harding, Eduard Franz, Philip Ober, Richard Anderson, Edith Evanson
🏆 Louis Calhern

'Things fall down. People look up. And when it rains, it pours.'
Magnolia **
US 1999 188m DeLuxe Panavision
New Line/Ghoulardi (Joanne Sellar)

In Los Angeles, the lives of various dysfunctional people coincidentally intertwine and interact.
A sprawling, episodic drama which examines unhappy people: a dying father, suffused with guilt, his hysterical wife, an estranged, misogynistic son, an unloved cop, a bullying father and his clever, timid son, a dying games show host and his estranged daughter. It is a clever, intense film about relationships and the need for love, but ultimately seems so contrived and manipulative that much of its emotional power is dissipated.
wd Paul Thomas Anderson *ph* Robert Elswit *m* John Brion *m/ly* Aimee Mann *pd* William Arnold, Mark Bridges *ed* Dylan Tichenor
☆ Jason Robards (Earl Partridge), Julianne Moore (Linda Partridge), *Tom Cruise* (Frank Mackey), Philip Seymour Hoffman (Phil Parma), *John C. Reilly* (Officer Jim Kurring), Melora Walters (Claudia Gator), Philip Baker Hall (Jimmy Gator), Melinda Dillon (Rose Gator), Jeremy Blackman (Stanley Spector), Michael Bowen (Rick Spector), William H. Macy (Donnie Smith), Emmanuel Johnson (Dixon)
'May be self-regarding and pretentious, but there are some fiendishly clever moments.' – *James Christopher, Times*
'A remarkably inventive and audacious film that almost overcomes its flaws.' – *Emanuel Levy, Variety*
🏆 Tom Cruise; Paul Thomas Anderson; song 'Save Me' (m/l Aimee Mann)

Magnum Force
US 1973 124m Technicolor Panavision
Warner/Malpaso (Robert Daley)

Inspector Harry Callahan has to track down the cops who are slaughtering gangsters in cold blood.
Toned-down sequel to Dirty Harry; *the violence is still there but the hero no longer commits it.*
w John Milius, Michael Cimino *d* Ted Post *ph* Frank Stanley *m* Lalo Schifrin
☆ Clint Eastwood, Hal Holbrook, Mitch Ryan, Felton Perry, David Soul
'A ragbag of western mythology and head-on thuggery.' – *Sight and Sound*

The Magus
GB 1968 116m DeLuxe Panavision
TCF/Blazer (John Kohn, Jud Kinberg)
An English schoolmaster on a Greek island is influenced by the local magician.
Fashionable philosophical nonsense, an elaborate mystery with no solution; the kind of film that all concerned begin to wish they had never thought of, especially as the presentation has nothing like the panache required, so that not even the critics liked it.
w John Fowles *novel* John Fowles *d* Guy Green *ph* Billy Williams *m* Johnny Dankworth *pd* Don Ashton
☆ Michael Caine, Anthony Quinn, Candice Bergen, Anna Karina, Paul Stassino, Julian Glover, George Pastell
'Faintly ludicrous some of the time and painfully unexciting all of the time.' – *MFB*
'This may not be the most misguided movie ever made, but it's in there pitching.' – *Rex Reed*
'There's enough incoherence pretending to be enigma, sex play and chat about existentialism and self-discovery to make teenagers think they're having an experience; for grown-ups it's an ordeal.' – *Judith Crist*
'It has much of the fascination of a Chinese puzzle, but it would have been infinitely more enthralling if it hadn't been quite so flatly acted and directed.' – *Michael Billington, Illustrated London News*
'Probably the only movie in which one will ever see a copy of Empson's Seven Types of Ambiguity.' – *Pauline Kael, New Yorker*

The Mahabharata *
France 1989 171m colour
Virgin/Les Productions du 3ème Etage (Michel Propper)

A boy listens to the story of a great war between competing tribes.
The vast Indian epic poem of 100,000 couplets in this condensed cinematic form results in a complex incident-crammed narrative, in which the significance of specific events can be hard to comprehend.
w Peter Brook, Jean-Claude Carrière, Marie-Hélène Estienne *play* Jean-Claude Carrière *d* Peter Brook *ph* William Lubtchansky *m* Toshi Tsuchitori, Djamchid Cherirani, Kudsi Erguner, Kim Menzer, Mahmoud Tabrizi-Zadeh *pd* Chloe Obolensky *ed* Nicholas Gaster
☆ Urs Biher, Ryszard Cieslak, Georges Corraface, Mamadou Dioumé, Miriam Goldschmidt, Jeffrey Kissoon, Sotigui Kouyate, Tuncel Kurtiz, Robert Langdon Lloyd

Mahanagar: see *The Big City (1963)*

Mahler *
GB 1974 115m Technicolor
Goodtimes Enterprises (Roy Baird)

Fantasia on the life and times of the Jewish composer.
Fairly successful Ken Russell musical biopic on the lines of his early BBC specials.
wd Ken Russell ph Dick Bush *ad* Ian Whittaker *ed* Michael Bradsell
☆ Robert Powell, Georgina Hale, Richard Morant, Lee Montague, Rosalie Crutchley, Benny Lee, David Collings
'A piece of movie making that sets my pulses racing.' – *Michael Billington, Illustrated London News*
'Whether the title of the opus happens to be *Strauss* or *Tchaikovsky* or *Elgar* or *Brubeck*, the real title is always Russell.' – *Benny Green, Punch*
🏆 Georgina Hale

Mahogany
US 1975 109m colour Panavision
Paramount/Nikor (Rob Cohen, Jack Ballard)

The love life of a model and fashion designer.
Virtually a Joan Crawford vehicle redesigned for a black heroine who creates her own clothes. Fairly hilarious.
w John Byrum *d* Berry Gordy *ph* David Watkin *m* Michael Masser *ly* Gerry Goffin
☆ *Diana Ross*, Billy Dee Williams, Anthony Perkins, Jean-Pierre Aumont, Nina Foch, Beah Richards, Marisa Mell
'The level of silliness rises steadily.' – *Geoff Brown*
'Movies as frantically bad as Mahogany can be enjoyed on at least one level; the spectacle of a lot of people making fools of themselves.' – *Time*
'What *Mahogany* does so fascinatingly and sometimes hilariously is to pilfer certain stock clichés of 50's Hollywood and adapt them to a black milieu.' – *Molly Haskell*
🏆 song 'Do You Know Where You're Going To?' (*m* Michael Masser, *ly* Gerry Goffin)

Maid in Manhattan
US 2002 105m DeLuxe Panavision
Columbia/Revolution/Red Om (Elaine Goldsmith-Thomas, Deborah Schindler, Paul Schiff)

An ambitious politician mistakes a hotel maid for a socialite when he sees her wearing a guest's clothes and asks her out.
Trite, sickly, Cinderella romance with a miscast Fiennes, who, like his co-star, shows little talent for comedy.
w Kevin Wade *story* Edmond Dantes *d* Wayne Wang *ph* Karl Walter Lindenlaub *m* Alan Silvestri *pd* Jane Musky *ed* Craig McKay
☆ Jennifer Lopez (Marisa Ventura), Ralph Fiennes (Christopher Marshall), Natasha Richardson (Caroline Lane), Stanley Tucci (Jerry Siegel), Bob Hoskins (Lionel Bloch), Tyler Garcia Posey (Ty Ventura), Frances Conroy (Paula Burns)
'There won't be a person in the audience who can't guess exactly how it will turn out. Yet it goes through its paces with such skill and charm that, yes, I enjoyed it.' – *Roger Ebert, Chicago Sun-Times*
'Not so much a movie as a collection of career moves. J. Lo needs a comedy hit to support her principal activity, adorning magazine covers. Fiennes needs to warm his austere British image if he hopes to become a true international star.' – *Richard Schickel, Time*

'Love so glorious it was denounced as sin!'
Maid of Salem *
US 1937 86m bw
Paramount (Frank Lloyd)
In 1692 Salem, a young girl is accused of witchcraft but saved by her lover.
Remarkably solemn period melodrama, unfortunately betrayed by amiable but miscast leads.
w Bradley King, Walter Ferris, Durward Grinstead *d* Frank Lloyd *ph* Leo Tover *m* Victor Young
☆ Claudette Colbert, Fred MacMurray, Harvey Stephens, Gale Sondergaard, Louise Dresser, Edward Ellis, Beulah Bondi, Bonita Granville
'Weak and slow saga of witchcraft: stars the only hope.' – *Variety*
'Once the panic of witchcraft starts you are carried along on a vicious crescendo of madness and terror.' – *Stage*

Maid to Order
US 1987 96m DeLuxe
Vista/New Century (Herb Jaffe, Mort Engelberg)

A spoiled rich girl takes work as a maid but finds she has a fairy godmother.
Weird semi-fantasy which wasn't wanted in the 80s, Cinderella being out of fashion.
wd Amy Jones (co-writers Perry and Randy Howze) *ph* Shelly Johnson *m* Georges Delerue *pd* Jeffrey Townsend *ed* Sidney Wolinski
☆ Ally Sheedy, Michael Ontkean, Beverly D'Angelo, Valerie Perrine, Dick Shawn, Tom Skerritt

Maiden Voyage: see *Bridal Suite*

The Maids
GB 1974 95m Technicolor
Ely Landau/Cinevision

Two Paris maids evolve a sado-masochistic ritual involving the death of their employer, but never go through with it.
Unbalanced and dreary film version of an essentially theatrical play.
w Robert Enders, Christopher Miles *play* Jean Genet *d* Christopher Miles *ph* Douglas Slocombe *m* Laurie Johnson
☆ Glenda Jackson, Susannah York, Vivien Merchant, Mark Burns
'In view of the huge technical, stylistic and even metaphysical difficulties, I think it succeeds very well.' – *Stanley Kauffmann*

Maid's Night Out
US 1938 65m bw
RKO
A wealthy girl falls for the milkman, who is really a rich man who thinks she's the maid.
Skittish second-feature comedy which helped to build a new star.
w Bert Granet *d* Ben Holmes
☆ Joan Fontaine, Allan Lane, Billy Gilbert, Cecil Kellaway, Hedda Hopper

Maigret Sets a Trap *
France/Italy 1957 119m bw
Intermondia/J. P. Guibert/Jolly Film
Maigret sets a policewoman as decoy for a knife murderer…
Probably the best Maigret film, with excellent Parisian atmosphere and excellent acting.
w Michel Audiard *novel* Georges Simenon *d* Jean Delannoy *ph* Louis Page *m* Paul Misraki *ad René Renoux*
☆ *Jean Gabin*, Annie Girardot, Jean Desailly, Olivier Hussenot, Alfred Adam, Lino Ventura
'It is puzzling, it is intermittently exciting, it is not offensive to a modest intelligence, not at any rate a modest intelligence used to crime stories.' – *Dilys Powell*

Mail Order Bride
US 1963 83m Metrocolor Panavision
MGM (Richard E. Lyons)
GB title: *West of Montana*
An old Westerner tries to find a bride for a wild young man in his charge.
Mild Western comedy drama; quite tolerable.
wd Burt Kennedy *ph* Paul C. Vogel *m* George Bassman
☆ Buddy Ebsen, Lois Nettleton, Keir Dullea, Warren Oates, Marie Windsor

Mail Train: see *Inspector Hornleigh Goes To It*

The Main Attraction
GB 1962 90m Metrocolor
Seven Arts (John Patrick)
A wandering singer causes emotional problems backstage at a circus.
Limp melodrama with the star miscast as a fatal charmer.
w John Patrick *d* Daniel Petrie *ph* Geoffrey Unsworth *m* Andrew Adorian
☆ Pat Boone, Mai Zetterling, Nancy Kwan, Yvonne Mitchell, John Le Mesurier

The Main Event
US 1979 112m Technicolor
Warner/First Artists/Barwood (Jon Peters, Barbra Streisand)
A lady entrepreneur takes on a prizefighter.
Thin and very patchy comedy for confirmed addicts of its star.
w Gail Parent, Andrew Smith *d* Howard Zieff *ph* Mario Tosi *m* Michael Melvoin *pd* Charles Rosen
☆ Barbra Streisand, Ryan O'Neal, Paul Sand, Whitman Mayo, James Gregory

Main Street: see *I Married a Doctor*

Main Street to Broadway *
US 1953 102m bw
Lester Cowan Productions
After several reverses a young playwright sees his work through to a Broadway opening night; it fails, but he has learned several lessons.
Curious, flat attempt to show the public how Broadway works, with big stars playing themselves in cameo roles.
w Samson Raphaelson *d* Tay Garnett *ph* James Wong Howe
☆ Tom Morton, Mary Murphy, Ethel Barrymore, Lionel Barrymore, Shirley Booth, Rex Harrison, Lilli Palmer, Helen Hayes, Henry Fonda, Tallulah Bankhead, Mary Martin, Louis Calhern, John Van Druten, Cornel Wilde, Joshua Logan and also Agnes Moorehead, Gertrude Berg

Les Mains Sales
France 1951 103m bw
Fernand Rivers
aka: *Dirty Hands*
A young communist intellectual, required to kill a traitor, finds he can do so only when he suspects the man of making love to his wife.
Verbose and dull version of a play which had some international success as Crime Passionel.
wd Fernand Rivers *play* Jean-Paul Sartre *ph* Jean Bachelet
☆ Pierre Brasseur, Daniel Gélin, Claude Nollier

Maisie
US 1939 74m bw
MGM (J. Walter Ruben)
Adventures of a Brooklyn showgirl.
Acceptable programmer which led to a series, all quite watchable and absolutely forgettable.
The succeeding titles, mostly written by Mary McCall and directed by Marin or Harry Beaumont or Roy del Ruth, were:
1940 Congo Maisie (with John Carroll; a remake of Red Dust), Gold Rush Maisie (with Lee Bowman), Maisie Was a Lady (with Lew Ayres, Maureen O'Sullivan)
1941 Ringside Maisie (qv) (with George Murphy; GB title Cash and Carry)
1942 Maisie Gets Her Man (with Red Skelton; GB title She Got Her Man)
1943 Swing Shift Maisie (with James Craig; GB title The Girl in Overalls)
1944 Maisie Goes to Reno (qv) (with John Hodiak; GB title You Can't Do That to Me)
1946 Up Goes Maisie (with George Murphy; GB title Up She Goes)
1947 Undercover Maisie (with Barry Nelson; GB title Undercover Girl)
w Mary McCall Jnr *novel* *Dark Dame* by Wilson Collison *d* Edwin L. Marin *ph* Leonard Smith
☆ *Ann Sothern*, Robert Young, Ian Hunter, Ruth Hussey, Anthony Allan (John Hubbard), Cliff Edwards

Maisie Goes to Reno
US 1944 90m bw
MGM (George Haight)
GB title: *You Can't Do That to Me*
Maisie saves a rich wife from divorcing her soldier-husband.
Pleasant light-hearted programmer with a few comic moments.
w Mary C. McCall Jnr *story* Harry Ruby, James O'Hanlon *d* Harry Beaumont *ph* Robert Planck *m* David Snell *ad* Cedric Gibbons, Howard Campbell *ed* Frank E. Hull
☆ Ann Sothern, John Hodiak, Tom Drake, Marta Linden, Paul Cavanagh, Ava Gardner, Donald Meek

La Maison de Jeanne: see *Jeanne's House*

Le Maître de Musique: see *The Music Teacher*

Maitresse *
France 1976 112m Eastmancolor
Films du Losange/Jean Pierre Rassam (Pierre Andrieux)
A young man, newly arrived in Paris, begins an affair with a woman who earns her living as a dominatrix, but he becomes concerned about the difference between her relationship with him and her sado-masochistic professional life.
Love is seen as akin to a Venus fly-trap, a painful and devouring business, in this elegant, icy romantic drama that, with its emphasis on bizarre, masochistic activities, is not for the squeamish. It forces audiences to acknowledge that the behaviour on show is merely an extreme form of everyday relationships and games-playing.
w Barbet Schroeder, Paul Voujargol *d* Barbet Schroeder *ph* Nestor Almendros *m* Carlos D'Alessio *ad* Roberto Plate *ed* Denise de Casabianca *cos* Karl Lagerfeld
☆ Gérard Depardieu (Olivier), Bulle Ogier (Arian), André Rouver (Mario), Nathalie Keryan (Lucienne), Roland Bertin (Man in cage), Tony Taffin (Emile), Holger Lowenadler (Gautier)

'Sometimes your life comes into focus one frame at a time.'
The Majestic
US/Australia 2001 153m Technicolor
Warner/Castle Rock/Village Roadshow/NPV/ Darkwoods (Frank Darabont)
In 1951, an amnesiac blacklisted Hollywood screenwriter assumes the identity of the missing son of the owner of a rundown movie theatre.
Cliché-ridden drama of the triumph of small-town values that is in stark contrast to the realities of Hollywood's blacklisting.
w Michael Sloane *d* Frank Darabont *ph* David Tattersall *m* Mark Isham *pd* Gregory Melton *ed* Jim Page
☆ Jim Carrey (Peter Appleton), Martin Landau (Harry Trimble), Laurie Holden (Adele Stanton), David Ogden Stiers (Doc Stanton), James Whitmore (Stan Keller), Jeffrey DeMunn (Ernie Cole), Ron Rifkin (Kevin Bannerman), Hal Holbrook (Congressman Doyle), Bob Balaban (Majority Counsel Elvin Clyde), Brent Briscoe (Sheriff Cecil Coleman)
'A thick slice of bogus inspirational cheese that only makes itself look bad by recycling so many golden movie memories.' – *Todd McCarthy, Variety*
'A derivative, self-satisfied fable that couldn't be more treacly and simple-minded if it tried.' – *Kenneth Turan, Los Angeles Times*

'Is she a kid – or is she kidding?'
The Major and the Minor **
US 1942 100m bw
Paramount (Arthur Hornblow Jnr)
A girl poses as a child in order to travel half fare on a train, and is helped by an officer who falls for her.
Moderately smart comedy showing the writer-director's emergent style. Remade as You're Never Too Young *(qv).*
w Charles Brackett, Billy Wilder *d* *Billy Wilder* *ph* Leo Tover *m* Robert Emmett Dolan
☆ Ginger Rogers, Ray Milland, Rita Johnson, Robert Benchley, Diana Lynn, Edward Fielding, Frankie Thomas, Charles Smith
OSBORNE (ROBERT BENCHLEY): 'Why don't you get out of that wet coat and into a dry martini?'
'The script seems to have been concocted after the title.' – *New Yorker, 1977*

Major Barbara ***
GB 1941 121m bw
Gabriel Pascal
The daughter of an armaments millionaire joins the Salvation Army but resigns when it accepts her father's donation.
Stagey but compulsive version of a play in which the author takes typical side swipes at anything and everything within reach, allowing for some gorgeous acting (and overacting) by an impeccable cast.
w Anatole de Grunwald, Gabriel Pascal *play* Bernard Shaw *d* Gabriel Pascal, Harold French, David Lean *ph* Ronald Neame *m* William Walton *ad* Vincent Korda, John Bryan *ed* Charles Frend *cos* Cecil Beaton
☆ *Wendy Hiller, Rex Harrison, Robert Morley, Robert Newton, Marie Lohr*, Emlyn Williams, Sybil Thorndike, Deborah Kerr, David Tree, Felix Aylmer, Penelope Dudley Ward, Walter Hudd, Marie Ault, Donald Calthrop
'Shaw's ebullience provides an unslackening fount of energy ... his all-star cast of characters are outspoken as no one else is in films except the Marx Brothers.' – *William Whitebait*
'To call it a manifest triumph would be an arrant stinginess with words.' – *New York Times*

Major Dundee *
US 1964 134m Eastmancolor Panavision
Columbia (Jerry Bresler)
A small group of men from a US cavalry post sets out to annihilate marauding Indians.
Large-scale, rough-and-ready Western which rambles along in humourless vein but rises to some spectacularly bloodthirsty climaxes.
w Harry Julian Fink, Oscar Saul, Sam Peckinpah *d* Sam Peckinpah *ph* Sam Leavitt *m* Daniele Amfitheatrof
☆ Charlton Heston, Richard Harris, Jim Hutton, James Coburn, Michael Anderson Jnr, Warren Oates, Senta Berger, Slim Pickens

Major League
US 1989 106m Technicolor
Braveworld/Fox (Mark Rosenberg)
A hopeless baseball team turn winners when they learn their owner wants them to lose.
Broad and often tasteless comedy, too predictable to be funny.
wd David S. Ward *ph* Reynaldo Villalobos *m* James Newton Howard *pd* Jeffrey Howard *ed* Dennis M. Hill, Tony Lombardo
☆ Tom Berenger, Charlie Sheen, Corbin Bernsen, Margaret Whitton, James Gammon, Rene Russo, Wesley Snipes, Charles Cyphers

Major League II
US 1994 104m Technicolor
Warner/Morgan Creek (James G. Robinson, David S. Ward)
A baseball team reverts to its losing ways before the players pull themselves together and begin winning.
A smudged copy of the original, recycling the same narrative and failing to produce a moment of wit or originality.
w R. J. Stewart, Tom S. Parker, Jim Jennewein *d* David S. Ward *ph* Victor Hammer *m* Michel Colombier *pd* Stephen Hendrickson *ed* Paul Seydor, Donn Cambern
☆ Charlie Sheen, Tom Berenger, Corbin Bernsen, Dennis Haysbert, Eric Bruskotter, Omar Epps, David Keith, Randy Quaid
'A singularly unfunny, dramatically tepid follow-up.' – *Variety*

Major Payne
US 1995 97m DeLuxe
Universal/Wife 'n' Kids (Eric L. Gold, Michael Rachmil)
A tough military martinet is put in charge of a school cadet troop.
Soft-centred drama about a hard man learning that killing isn't everything in life, but the comedy is strictly by the numbers.
w Dean Lorey, Damon Wayans, Gary Rosen *d* Nick Castle *ph* Richard Bowen *m* Craig Safan *pd* Peter Larkin *ed* Patrick Kennedy
☆ Damon Wayans, Karyn Parsons, Bill Hickey, Michael Ironside, Albert Hall, Steven Martini, Andrew Harrison Leeds, Joda Blare-Hershman, Damien Wayans
'It's what is sometimes called a "warmedy", a cuddly comedy in which a crotchety hero sees the light by rubbing shoulders with humanity.' – *Leonard Klady, Variety*
† It is a remake of *The Private War of Major Benson* (qv).

A Majority of One
US 1961 156m Technicolor
Warner (Mervyn Le Roy)
A Jewish widow has a shipboard romance with a Japanese businessman.
Interminable stage-bound comedy-drama, boringly assembled and fatally compromised by the casting of stars who are neither Jewish nor Japanese.
w Leonard Spigelgass *play* Leonard Spigelgass *d* Mervyn Le Roy *ph* Harry Stradling *m* Max Steiner
☆ Rosalind Russell, Alec Guinness, Ray Danton, Madlyn Rhue
Academy Award nomination: Harry Stradling

Make a Wish
US 1937 75m bw
(RKO)
A composer discovers a boy singer at a summer camp.
Acceptable family entertainment.
w Gertrude Berg, Bernard Schubert, Earle Snell *d* Kurt Neumann *ph* John Mescall *m* Hugo Riesenfeld *songs* Oscar Straus
☆ Basil Rathbone, Bobby Breen, Marion Claire, Leon Errol, Henry Armetta, Ralph Forbes, Donald Meek
Academy Award nomination: Hugo Riesenfeld

Make Haste to Live
US 1954 89m bw
Republic (William A. Seiter)
A lady newspaper owner is embarrassed, to say the least, by the reappearance of her murderer husband, long thought dead.
Competent but rather dull programmer.
w Warren Duff *novel* The Gordons *d* William A. Seiter *ph* John L. Russell *m* Elmer Bernstein
☆ Dorothy McGuire, Stephen McNally, Mary Murphy, Edgar Buchanan, John Howard

Make Me a Star
US 1932 80m bw
Paramount (Lloyd Sheldon)
A grocery clerk goes to Hollywood and becomes a film star.
Modest remake of a silent success; see also Merton of the Movies.
w Sam Mintz, Walter de Leon, Arthur Kober *novel* *Merton of the Movies* by Harry Leon Wilson *d* William Beaudine *ph* Allen Siegler
☆ Stuart Erwin, Joan Blondell, ZaSu Pitts, Ben Turpin, Florence Roberts, Tallulah Bankhead, Clive Brook, Gary Cooper, Maurice Chevalier, Claudette Colbert, Fredric March, Jack Oakie, Charlie Ruggles, Sylvia Sidney
'Packed with laughs which offsets the longish running time.' – *Variety*

Make Me an Offer *
GB 1954 88m Eastmancolor
Group Three (W. P. Lipscomb)
An antique dealer has an ambition to own a famous vase.
Mildly pleasant Jewish comedy with interesting sidelights on the antique business.
w W. P. Lipscomb *novel* Wolf Mankowitz *d* Cyril Frankel *ph* Denny Densham *m* John Addison
☆ *Peter Finch*, Adrienne Corri, *Meier Tzelniker*, Rosalie Crutchley, Finlay Currie, *Ernest Thesiger*, Wilfrid Lawson, Alfie Bass

Make Mine a Million
GB 1959 82m bw
British Lion/Elstree Independent/Jack Hylton (John Baxter)
A TV make-up man strikes it rich by showing advertisements on non-commercial television.
Amiable, low-key comedy, relying heavily on the personality of its star.

w Peter Blackmore, Arthur Askey, Talbot Rothwell *story* Jack Francis *d* Lance Comfort *ph* Arthur Grant *m* Stanley Black *ad* Dennis Wreford *ed* Peter Pitt
☆ Arthur Askey, Sidney James, Dermot Walsh, Olga Lindo, Clive Morton, Sally Barnes, Leigh Madison, Bernard Cribbins, Gillian Lynee, The Penge Formation Dancers

Make Mine Mink **
GB 1960 101m bw
Rank (Hugh Stewart)
Members of a high-class boarding establishment steal furs to give the proceeds to charity.
Enjoyable comedy, expertly performed.
w Michael Pertwee, Peter Blackmore *play* *Breath of Spring* by Peter Coke *d* Robert Asher *ph* Reginald Wyer *m* Philip Green *ad* Carmen Dillon *ed* Roger Cherrill
☆ Terry-Thomas, Athene Seyler, Hattie Jacques, Billie Whitelaw, Raymond Huntley, Irene Handl, Kenneth Williams, Noel Purcell, Sydney Tafler
† The film was reissued with 21m cut.

Make Mine Music **
US 1946 74m Technicolor
Walt Disney (Joe Grant)
A programme of cartoon shorts: Johnny Fedora, All the Cats Join in, Without You, Two Silhouettes, Casey at the Bat, The Martins and the Coys, Blue Bayou, After You've Gone, Willie the Singing Whale, Peter and the Wolf
An insubstantial banquet, sometimes arty and sometimes chocolate boxy, which occasionally rises to the expected heights.
w various *d* various
'There is enough genuine charm and imagination and humour to make up perhaps one good average Disney short.' – *James Agee*

Make Way for a Lady
US 1936 63m bw
Zion Myers/RKO
A girl determines to find a mate for her widowed father.
Rather irritating comedy of embarrassment.
w Gertrude Purcell *novel* *Daddy and I* by Elizabeth Jordan *d* David Burton
☆ Herbert Marshall, Anne Shirley, Gertrude Michael, Margot Grahame, Clara Blandick, Taylor Holmes, Willie Best
'It lacks suspense, surprise, and plausibility.' – *Variety*

'Grandpa moves in! Daughter moves out! And the riot starts!'
Make Way for Tomorrow **
US 1937 94m bw
Paramount (Leo McCarey)
An elderly couple are in financial difficulty and have to be parted because their children will not help.
Sentimental drama which had a devastating effect at the time but now seems oversimplified and exaggerated.
w Vina Delmar *novel* *The Years Are So Long* by Josephine Lawrence *d* *Leo McCarey* *ph* William C. Mellor *m* George Antheil
☆ *Victor Moore*, *Beulah Bondi*, Thomas Mitchell, Fay Bainter, Porter Hall, Barbara Read, Maurice Moscovich, Elizabeth Risdon, Gene Lockhart
'Needs special exploitation: even so, business is apt to be spotty where played solo.' – *Variety*
'The most brilliantly directed and acted film of the year.' – *John Grierson*
'A sense of misery and inhumanity is left vibrating in the nerves.' – *Graham Greene*

The Maker *
US 1997 98m colour Panavision
Midsummer/New Image (Andrew Lazar, Demitri Samaha)
A suburban high-school youth becomes involved in criminal activities when his elder brother returns home after ten years away.
An enjoyable thriller that centres on the confusions and mixed loyalties of teenage life, avoiding both sentimentality and melodrama.
w Rand Ravich *d* Tim Hunter *ph* Hubert Taczanowski *m* Paul Buckmaster *pd* Jane Ann Stewart *ed* Scott Chestnut
☆ Matthew Modine, Jonathan Rhys Myers, Mary-Louise Parker, Michael Madsen, Fairuza Balk, Jesse Borrego
'Satisfies as both a clever suspenser and fairly believable drama.' – *Dennis Harvey, Variety*
† The film was released direct to video in Britain.

Making It: see *Les Valseuses*

Making Love
US 1982 111m DeLuxe
TCF/IndieProd (Allen Adler, Danny Melnick)
A young married doctor declares that he is gay and moves in with a friend.
Would-be daring melodrama whose producers quickly found that nobody was interested.
w Barry Sandler *story* A. Scott Berg *d* Arthur Hiller *ph* David M. Walsh *m* Leonard Rosenman *pd* James D. Vance *ed* William H. Reynolds
☆ Michael Ontkean, Kate Jackson, Harry Hamlin, Wendy Hiller, Arthur Hill, Nancy Olson

Making Mr Right
US 1987 98m colour
Rank/Orion (Mike Wise, Joel Tuber)
An android falls in love with a public relations consultant.
Slight comedy that soon runs out of anywhere to go.
w Floyd Byars, Laurie Frank *d* Susan Seidelman *ph* Edward Lachman *m* Chaz Jankel *pd* Barbara Ling *ed* Andrew Mondshein
☆ Ann Magnuson, John Malkovich, Glenne Headly, Ben Masters, Laurie Metcalf, Polly Bergen, Harsh Nayyar, Hart Bochner

Making Up *
Germany 1993 55m colour
Electric Pictures/Vela-X/Bayerischer Rundfunk (Ewa Karlström)
original title: *Abgeschminkt!*
Two single women fall in and out of love with unsuitable men.
A film-school graduation project that was a hit in its home country, this is an enjoyable comedy, mocking the over-enthusiastic pursuit of the opposite sex.
w Benjamin Taylor, Katja von Garnier, Hannes Jaenicke *d* Katja von Garnier *ph* Torsten Breuer *m* Peter Wenke, Tillmann Höhn *ad* Irene Edenhofer, Nikolai Ritter *ed* Katja von Garnier
☆ Katja Riemann, Nina Kronjäger, Gedeon Burkhard, Max Tidof, Daniela Lunkewitz, Peter Sattmann, Jochen Nickel
'An above-average single-woman's date comedy.' – *Variety*

Mala Noche *
US 1988 78m bw
The Other Cinema/Northern Film/Respectable (Gus Van Sant)
A homosexual store worker falls for a heterosexual illegal Mexican immigrant.
Interesting first feature, a study in obsession, shot on a minimal budget.
wd Gus Van Sant *story* Walt Curtis *ph* John Campbell *m* Creighton Lindsay
☆ Tim Streeter, Doug Cooeyate, Ray Monge, Nyla McCarthy
'Reminds you how exciting independent film-making can be ... has a sure feel for the more awkward corners of sexual exchange which we might prefer to forget.' – *Judith Williamson, New Statesman*

Malachi's Cove
GB 1973 75m Technicolor
Penrith/Impact Quadrant Films (Andrew Sinclair, Kent Walwin)
aka: *The Seaweed Children*
In 1880 Cornwall, a 14-year-old girl lives by selling seaweed.
Slimly-plotted film for the family, pleasant without being very interesting.
wd Henry Herbert *story* Anthony Trollope *ph* Walter Lassally *m* Brian Gascoigne
☆ Donald Pleasence, Dai Bradley, Veronica Quilligan, Arthur English, David Howe

Malaga
GB 1954 84m Technicolor
M. J. Frankovich/Film Locations
US title: *Fire Over Africa*
An American woman agent catches drug smugglers in Tangier.
Routine international thick ear.
w Robert Westerby *d* Richard Sale *ph* Christopher Challis *m* Benjamin Frankel
☆ Maureen O'Hara, Macdonald Carey, Binnie Barnes, Guy Middleton, Leonard Sachs

Malaga: see *Moment of Danger (1962)*

Malarek
Canada 1989 100m colour
Telescene (Jamie Brown, Robin Spry)
In Montreal in the early 70s, an aggressive would-be journalist, investigating the police cover-up of a killing, exposes widespread abuse at a juvenile detention centre.
A true story is forced into a familiar thriller format, but given some life by the intensity of Koteas's performance.
w Avrum Jacobson *autobiography* *Hey Malarek* by Victor Malarek *d* Roger Cardinal *ph* Karol Ike *m* Alexandre Stanké *ad* Claude Paré *ed* Yves Langlois
☆ Elias Koteas, Kerrie Keane, Al Waxman, Michael Sarrazin, Daniel Pilon, Kahil Karn

Malaya *
US 1949 95m bw
MGM (Edwin H. Knopf)
GB title: *East of the Rising Sun*
An adventurer attempts to smuggle rubber out of Japanese-occupied Malaya.
Dour action melodrama, unworthy of its considerable cast but watchable.
w Frank Fenton *d* Richard Thorpe *ph* George Folsey *m* Bronislau Kaper
☆ Spencer Tracy, James Stewart, Sydney Greenstreet, John Hodiak, Valentina Cortesa, Lionel Barrymore, Gilbert Roland

Malcolm
Australia 1986 86m colour
Enterprise/Cascade (David Parker, Nadia Tass)
A retarded but mechanically talented youth lives alone in a Melbourne suburb and takes in a petty criminal and his girlfriend.
Initially interesting but mishandled character study which never settles into a comfortable groove.
w David Parker *d* Nadia Tass *ph* David Parker *m* Simon Jeffes *ed* Ken Sallows
☆ Colin Friels, John Hargreaves, Lindy Davies, Chris Haywood, Charles Tingwell

Malcolm X **
US 1992 201m DuArt
Warner/Largo/Forty Acres and a Mule (Marvin Worth, Spike Lee)
Biopic of the turbulent life and violent death of the black revolutionary leader.
Despite Washington's powerful performance in the title role, an overlong and somewhat subdued treatment that seems anxious not to offend.
w Arnold Perl, Spike Lee *book* *The Autobiography of Malcolm X* as told to Alex Haley *d* Spike Lee *ph* Ernest Dickerson *m* Terence Blanchard *pd* Wynn Thomas *ed* Barry Alexander Brown
☆ *Denzel Washington*, Angela Bassett, Albert Hall, Al Freeman Jnr, Delroy Lindo, Spike Lee, Theresa Randle, Kate Vernon, Lonette McKee, Tommy Hollis
'A disappointingly sluggish and conventional film.' – *Variety*
'Always watchable even if one can't call it memorable.' – *Derek Malcolm, Guardian*
Denzel Washington; Ruth Carter (costume design)

The Male Animal *
US 1942 101m bw
Warner (Wolfgang Reinhardt)
A dry college professor emancipates himself when his wife becomes attracted to a football star.
Stagebound but amusing college comedy with pleasant humour and good performances. Remade as She's Working Her Way through College *(qv).*
w Julius J. and Philip G. Epstein, Stephen Morehouse Avery *play* James Thurber and Elliott Nugent *d* Elliott Nugent *ph* Arthur Edeson *m* Heinz Roemheld
☆ Henry Fonda, Olivia de Havilland, Jack Carson, Joan Leslie, Eugene Pallette, Don Defore, Herbert Anderson, Hattie McDaniel

'A world at war. A young man coming of age. And the woman who changed his life forever.'
Malèna *
Italy/US 2000 92m colour Panavision
Buena Vista/Medusa/Miramax (Carlo Bernasconi, Harvey Weinstein)
In Sicily in the early 1940s, a beautiful woman, who loses her husband in the war, is the object of an adolescent's day dreams.
Teenage fantasies of sexual success conflict with the realities of political failure and personal humiliation in this engaging fable that shows the influence of Fellini.
wd Giuseppe Tornatore *story* Luciano Vincenzoni *ph* Lajos Koltai *m* Ennio Morricone *pd* Francesco Frigeri *ed* Massimo Quaglia *cos* Maurizio Millenotti
☆ *Monica Bellucci* (Malena Scordia), Giuseppe Sulfaro (Renato Amoroso), Luciano Federico (Renato's father), Matilde Piana (Renato's mother), Pietro Notarianni (Professor Bonsignore), Gaetano Aronica (Nino Scordia), Gilberto Idonea (Centorbi), Angelo Pellegrino (Political secretary)
'A nudging, winking, leering pantomime about another small boy's affair with the local whore.' – *Alexander Walker, London Evening Standard*
Lajos Koltai; Ennio Morricone

Malenkaya Vera: see *Little Vera*

'Deception. Betrayal. Murder. Some Things You Never See Coming.'
Malice
US 1993 107m Technicolor
Rank/Castle Rock/New Line (Rachel Pfeffer, Charles Mulvehill, Harold Becker)
An academic finds that he is the victim of a confidence trick.
Elaborate, involved, over-heated thriller that makes little sense and provides less enjoyment.
w Aaron Sorkin, Scott Frank, Jonas McCord *d* Harold Becker *ph* Gordon Willis *m* Jerry Goldsmith *pd* Philip Harrison *ed* David Bretherton
☆ Alec Baldwin, Nicole Kidman, Bill Pullman, Bebe Neuwirth, George C. Scott, Anne Bancroft, Peter Gallagher, Josef Sommer, Tobin Bell
'A virtual scrapbook of elements borrowed from other suspense pics, but no less enjoyable for being so familiar.' – *Variety*
'One of the most shameless pieces of unadultered trash.' – *Alexander Walker, London Evening Standard*

'Ignore her, and she'll never go away.'
Malicious
US 1995 92m colour
Republic/Keystone (Robert Vince, William Vince)
After a one night stand with a college baseball hero, a discarded girl decides to take revenge on him and his girlfriend..
A youthful copy of the theme of Fatal Attraction, *done without suspense or interest; it is notable only for marking another downward slide in the career of Molly Ringwald.*
w George Saunders *d* Ian Corson *ph* Michael Slovis *m* Graeme Coleman *pd* Marian Witlak *ed* Richard Martin
☆ Molly Ringwald (Melissa), Patrick McGaw (Doug Gordon), Sarah Lassez (Laura), Ryan Michael (Mitch), Mimi Kuzyk (Mrs Gordon), John Vernon (Detective Pronzini), Rick Henrickson (Rich), Jennifer Copping (Judy)

Mallrats
US 1995 108m DeLuxe
Gramercy/Alphaville/View Askew (James Jacks, Sean Daniel, Scott Mosier)
A group of teenagers hang out in a shopping mall.
The laid-back, inconsequential humour of Smith's first film, Clerks, *wears thin here in a similar, but much more conventional, outing.*
wd Kevin Smith *ph* David Klein *m* Ira Newborn *pd* Dina Lipton *ed* Paul Dixon
☆ Shannen Doherty, Jeremy London, Jason Lee, Claire Forlani, Michael Rooker, Priscilla Barnes, Ben Affleck, Joey Lauren Adams, Renee Humphrey, Jason Mewes, Kevin Smith
'While admittedly ragged and ribald, it's a picture with an innate charm and honesty that should win over audiences.' – *Leonard Klady, Variety*

Malone
US 1987 92m DeLuxe
Orion (Leo L. Fuchs)

A disillusioned CIA hit man is not allowed to go 'straight'.
Moody but not unwatchable thriller largely set in Oregon.
w Christopher Frank *novel Shotgun* by William Wingate *d* Harley Cokliss *ph* Gerald Hirschfeld *m* David Newman *pd* Graeme Murray *ed* Todd Ramsay
☆ Burt Reynolds, Cliff Robertson, Kenneth McMillan, Cynthia Gibb, Scott Wilson, Lauren Hutton

Malou *
West Germany 1980 93m colour
Regina Ziegler
A teacher goes on a journey to discover more about her dead mother and, ultimately, herself.
This simple story of a woman trying to come to terms with the past and the present is sometimes too didactic, but often rewarding.
wd Jeanine Meerapfel *ph* Michael Ballhaus *m* Peer Raben *ad* Rainer Schaper *ed* Dagmar Hirtz
☆ Ingrid Caven, Grischa Huber, Helmut Griem, Ivan Desny, Marie Colbin, Peter Chatel, Margarita Calahorra

The Malta Story
GB 1953 103m bw
GFD/British Film Makers (Peter de Sarigny)

An English flyer is involved in the defence of Malta during World War II.
Glib propaganda piece which is not very excitingly written or characterized, and fails to convince on any but the most elementary level.
w William Fairchild, Nigel Balchin *d* Brian Desmond Hurst *ph* Robert Krasker *m* William Alwyn
☆ Alec Guinness, Anthony Steel, Muriel Pavlow, Jack Hawkins, Flora Robson, Renée Asherson, Ralph Truman, Reginald Tate, Hugh Burden

The Maltese Bippy
US 1969 92m Metrocolor Panavision
MGM
A skin flick star thinks he is turning into a werewolf.
Failed attempt to construct a crazy comedy for the stars of Laugh-In; even the spooky house sequences don't go.
w Everett Freeman, Ray Singer *d* Norman Panama
☆ Dan Rowan, Dick Martin, Carol Lynley, Julie Newmar, Mildred Natwick, Fritz Weaver, Robert Reed

The Maltese Falcon **
US 1931 80m bw
Warner

TV title: *Dangerous Female*
After the death of his partner, private eye Sam Spade is dragged into a quest for a priceless statuette.
Excellent crime melodrama with smart pace and performances. Remade as Satan Met a Lady *(1936); and see below.*
w Maude Fulton, Lucien Hubbard, Brown Holmes *novel Dashiell Hammett d Roy del Ruth*
ph William Rees
☆ *Ricardo Cortez*, Bebe Daniels, *Dudley Digges*, Dwight Frye, Robert Elliott, Thelma Todd, Oscar Apfel
'Any type of audience will enjoy it.' – *Variety*
'The best mystery thriller of the year.' – *New York Times*
'A nice blend of humour, intelligence and suspense.' – *Clive Hirschhorn, 1979*

'A guy without a conscience! A dame without a heart!'
'He's as fast on the draw as he is in the drawing room!'
The Maltese Falcon ****
US 1941 101m bw
Warner (Henry Blanke)

A private eye is hired to find a black sculpture of a bird.
A remake which shows the difference between excellence and brilliance; here every nuance is subtly stressed, and the cast is perfection.
wd John Huston ph Arthur Edeson m Adolph Deutsch
☆ *Humphrey Bogart, Mary Astor, Sydney Greenstreet, Elisha Cook Jnr, Barton MacLane*, Lee Patrick, *Peter Lorre*, Gladys George, *Ward Bond, Jerome Cowan*
GUTMAN (SYDNEY GREENSTREET): 'I distrust a close-mouthed man. He generally picks the wrong time to talk and says the wrong things. Talking's something you can't do judiciously, unless you keep in practice. Now, sir, we'll talk if you like. I'll tell you right out, I'm a man who likes talking to a man who likes to talk.'
SPADE (HUMPHREY BOGART) TO CAIRO (PETER LORRE): 'When you're slapped, you'll take it and like it!'
SPADE TO BRIGID (MARY ASTOR): 'Don't be too sure I'm as crooked as I'm supposed to be.'
GUTMAN: 'I distrust a man who says when. If he's got to be careful not to drink too much, it's because he's not to be trusted when he does.'
'The first crime melodrama with finish, speed and bang to come along in what seems like ages.' – *Otis Ferguson*
'A work of entertainment that is yet so skilfully constructed that after many years and many viewings, it has the same brittle explosiveness – and some of the same surprise – that it had in 1941.' – *Pauline Kael, 1968*
'The trick which Mr Huston has pulled is a combination of American ruggedness with the suavity of the English crime school – a blend of mind and muscle – plus a slight touch of pathos.' – *Bosley Crowther, New York Times*
'Admirable photography of the sort in which black and white gives full value to every detail, every flicker of panic.' – *Francis Wyndham*
best picture; John Huston (as writer); Sydney Greenstreet

Mama Loves Papa *
US 1933 70m bw
Paramount
A middle-class wife decides to do some social climbing.
Slight but amusing comedy which put together a useful team.
w Arthur Kober, Nunnally Johnson, Douglas MacLean, Keene Thompson *d* Norman Z. McLeod
☆ *Charles Ruggles, Mary Boland*, Lilyan Tashman, George Barbier, Morgan Wallace
'Exceptionally funny comedy ... a cinch builder.' – *Variety*
† A second film under this title was a Leon Errol vehicle of 1945.

La Maman et la Putain: see *The Mother and the Whore*

Mamba
US 1930 76m Technicolor
Tiffany
Germans in East Africa go to the bad during World War I.
Absurd melodrama climaxing with a Zulu uprising.
w Tom Miranda, Winifred Dunn *story* F. Schumann-Heink and John Reinhardt *d* Albert S. Rogell
☆ Jean Hersholt, Eleanor Boardman, Ralph Forbes, Josef Swickard
'It has its lowlights and highlights; in between it's not a bad programmer.' – *Variety*

Mamba
Italy 1988 81m colour
Medusa/Eidoscope/Reteitalia (Mario Orfini)

aka: *Fair Game*
A woman is locked in a room with a deadly snake by her murderous ex-boyfriend.
Modest, moderately suspenseful thriller that just manages to eke out its length.
w Lidia Ravera, Mario Orfini *d* Mario Orfini *ph* Dante Spinotti *m* Giorgio Moroder *pd* Ferdinando Scarfiotti *ed* Claudio Cutry
☆ Trudie Styler, Gregg Henry, Bill Moseley

Mambo
Italy/USA 1954 92m bw
Paramount/Ponti/De Laurentiis

A Venetian shopgirl loves a worthless gambler, is romanced by a haemophiliac count, and joins a dance troupe.
Patchy melodrama with plenty going on but no grip.
w Guido Piovene, Ivo Perelli, Ennio de Concini, Robert Rossen *d* Robert Rossen *ph* Harold Rosson *m* Nino Rota, Francesco Lavagnino *ch* Katherine Dunham *sets* Andrei Andrejew
☆ Silvana Mangano, Michael Rennie, Shelley Winters, Vittorio Gassman, Eduardo Ciannelli, Mary Clare, Katherine Dunham and her troupe

The Mambo Kings *
US 1992 104m DeLuxe
Warner/Canal/Regency/Alcor (Arnon Milchan, Arne Glimcher)

In the 1950s, a Cuban trumpeter and his brother, a singer, leave home to seek their fortunes in New York.
Energetic but dull version of a best-selling novel.
w Cynthia Cidre *novel The Mambo Kings Play Songs of Love* by Oscar Hijuelos *d* Arne Glimcher *ph* Michael Ballhaus *m* Robert Kraft, Carlos Franzetti *pd* Stuart Wurtzel *ed* Claire Simpson
☆ Armand Assante, Antonio Banderas, Cathy Moriarty, Maruschka Detmers, Pablo Calogero, Scott Cohen, Mario Grillo, Desi Arnaz Jnr, Roscoe Lee Browne, Tito Puente
'An ambitious, old-fashioned Hollywood film ... is bound to win converts to the intoxicating rhythms of Latino music.' – *Variety*
Song: 'Beautiful Maria of My Soul' (*m* Robert Kraft, *ly* Arne Glimcher)

'She'll coax the blues right out of your heart'
Mame *
US 1974 131m Technicolor Panavision
Warner/ABC (Robert Fryer, James Cresson)

In 1928, a 10-year-old boy goes to live with his eccentric, sophisticated aunt.
Old-fashioned and rather bad film of a much overrated Broadway musical, inept in most departments but with occasional show-stopping moments.
w Paul Zindel *play* Jerome Lawrence, Robert E. Lee *book Patrick Dennis d* Gene Saks *ph* Philip Lathrop *m/ly* Jerry Herman *pd* Robert F. Boyle
☆ *Lucille Ball, Beatrice Arthur*, Robert Preston, Bruce Davison, Jane Connell, Joyce Van Patten, John McGiver
'It makes one realize afresh the parlous state of the Hollywood musical, fighting to survive against misplaced superstars and elephantine budgets matched with minuscule imagination.' – *Geoff Brown*
'The cast seem to have been handpicked for their tone-deafness, and Lucille Ball's close-ups are shot blatantly out of focus.' – *Sight and Sound*
'So terrible it isn't boring; you can get fixated staring at it and wondering what Lucille Ball thought she was doing.' – *New Yorker, 1977*

Mamma Roma *
Italy 1962 114m bw
Arco/Cineriz (Alfredo Bini)

A pimp tries to blackmail a former prostitute into resuming her old profession by threatening to tell her teenage son about her past.
Ravishing photography is allied with over-emphatic moralizing in a film sympathetic to the deprivations of an underclass and overawed by the presence of Magnani among its otherwise non-professional cast.
wd Pier Paolo Pasolini *ph* Tonino delli Colli *m* Antonio Vivaldi *md* Carlo Rustichelli *ad* Flavio Mogherini *ed* Nino Baragli
☆ Anna Magnani, Franco Citti, Ettore Garofolo, Silvana Corsini, Luisa Loiano, Paolo Volponi, Luciano Gonini

Mammy *
US 1930 84m bw
Warner (Walter Morosco)

Murder backstage at a minstrel show.
One of the star's better musicals.
w L. G. Rigby, Joseph Jackson *d* Michael Curtiz *ph* Barney McGill *m* Irving Berlin
☆ *Al Jolson*, Lowell Sherman, Hobart Bosworth, Louise Dresser, Lee Moran

'Looks like money ... a lively picture playing fast.' – *Variety*

Mam'selle Striptease: see *Plucking the Daisy*

A Man, a Woman and a Bank
Canada 1979 101m CFI color
Bennett/McNichol

A civil engineer and a computer expert devise a foolproof way of robbing a bank.
We have been here before, except that these days the criminals are allowed to get away with it. Ho-hum.
w Raynold Gideon, Bruce A. Evans and Stuart Margolin *d* Noel Black *ph* Jack Cardiff *m* Bill Conti
☆ Donald Sutherland, Brooke Adams, Paul Mazursky

A Man about the House
GB 1947 95m bw
British Lion (Edward Black)

Two English ladies inherit an Italian villa and fall under the spell of the handsome handyman, who marries one of them and proceeds slowly to poison her.
Now clearly dull, at the time this seemed a fairly enterprising rehash of Gaslight, Kind Lady *and* Rebecca.
w J. B. Williams, Leslie Arliss *play* John Perry *novel Francis Brett Young d* Leslie Arliss *ph* Georges Perinal *m* Nicholas Brodszky *md* Philip Green *ad* Andre Andrejew *ed* Russell Lloyd
☆ Margaret Johnston (Agnes Isit), Dulcie Gray (Ellen Isit), Kieron Moore (Salvatore), Felix Aylmer (Ronnie Sanctuary), Lilian Braithwaite (Mrs Armitage), Guy Middleton (Sir Ben Dench), Victor Rietti (Peasant)

Man about the House
GB 1974 90m colour
EMI/Hammer (Roy Skeggs)

Two young women, their male flatmate and their landlords combine forces to prevent the terrace from being razed for redevelopment.
Mild and rather exhausting sex comedy from the TV series, as relentlessly single-minded as a 'Carry On'.
w Johnnie Mortimer, Brian Cooke *d* John Robins *ph* Jimmy Allen *m* Christopher Gunning
☆ Richard O'Sullivan, Paula Wilcox, Sally Thomsett, Yootha Joyce, Brian Murphy, Peter Cellier, Patrick Newell, Spike Milligan, Arthur Lowe

Man about Town *
US 1939 85m bw
Paramount (Arthur Hornblow Jnr)
A Broadway producer in London makes his girlfriend jealous.
Fairly amusing comedy-musical programmer.
w Morrie Ryskind *d* Mark Sandrich *ph* Ted Tetzlaff *md* Victor Young
☆ Jack Benny, Dorothy Lamour, Edward Arnold, Binnie Barnes, Phil Harris, Eddie Anderson, Monty Woolley, Isabel Jeans, Betty Grable, E. E. Clive
'Good comedy, rates okay biz.' – *Variety*

A Man Alone: see *The Killers (1946)*

A Man Alone *
US 1955 96m Trucolor
Republic
A wandering gunman is framed by other badmen.
Solemn, slow-moving but generally interesting Western, the star's first attempt at direction.
w John Tucker Battle *d* Ray Milland *ph* Lionel Lindon *m* Victor Young
☆ Ray Milland, Mary Murphy, Ward Bond, Raymond Burr, Arthur Space, Lee Van Cleef, Alan Hale Jnr

A Man and a Woman **
France 1966 102m Eastmancolor
Les Films 13

original title: *Un Homme et une Femme*
A racing driver and a script girl, both of whose spouses are dead, meet while visiting their children, and an affair leads to marriage.
Slight romantic drama so tricked out with smart images that it looks like a series of expensive commercials. A

great box-office success, but its director never again succeeded in this vein which he made his own.
w Claude Lelouch, Pierre Uytterhoeven *d* Claude Lelouch *ph* Jean Columb, Patrice Pouget
m Francis Lai
☆ *Anouk Aimée, Jean-Louis Trintignant*
'When in doubt, Lelouch's motto seems to be, use a colour filter or insert lyrical shots of dogs and horses; when in real doubt, use both.' – *Tom Milne, MFB*
'A slick item with all the Hollywood ingredients.' – *John Simon*
best foreign film; Claude Lelouch, Pierre Uytterhoeven
Claude Lelouch (as director); Anouk Aimée
Anouk Aimée

A Man and a Woman: Twenty Years Later
France 1986 120m Eastmancolor
Films 13/Warner
original title: *Un Homme Et Une Femme: Vingt Ans Déjà*
Slightly macabre attempt to extend the appeal with the same actors, the same technique, and even shots from Lelouch's other movies.
A bit of a wallow.
w Claude Lelouch, Pierre Uytterhoeven, Monique Lange, Jérôme Tonnerre *d* Claude Lelouch *ph* Jean-Yves Le Mener *m* Francis Lai
☆ Anouk Aimée, Jean-Louis Trintignant, Evelyne Bouix, Marie-Sophie Pochat

Man and His Mate: see *One Million BC*

Man at the Top *
GB 1973 87m Technicolor
Hammer/Dufton (Peter Charlesworth)
A pharmaceutical executive finds that his firm is marketing an unsafe drug.
Further adventures of the belligerent hero of Room at the Top *(qv), this time following a popular television series. All very fashionable and predictable.*
w Hugh Whitemore *d* Mike Vardy *ph* Bryan Probyn *m* Roy Budd
☆ Kenneth Haigh, Nanette Newman, Harry Andrews, John Quentin, Charlie Williams

The Man Behind the Gun
US 1952 82m Technicolor
Warner
A cavalry officer is sent to quell a rebellion and helps to found Los Angeles.
Cheerful Western programmer.
w John Twist *d* Felix Feist *ph* Bert Glennon
m David Buttolph
☆ Randolph Scott, Patrice Wymore, Dick Wesson, Phil Carey

The Man Behind the Mask
GB 1936 79m bw
Joe Rock
A mad scientist kidnaps a nobleman's daughter.
Serial-like hokum with interesting credits.
w Ian Hay, Syd Courtenay, Jack Byrd and Stanley Haynes *d* Michael Powell
☆ Hugh Williams, Maurice Schwartz, Jane Baxter, Donald Calthrop, Henry Oscar

A Man Betrayed
US 1941 82m bw
Armand Schaefer/Republic
GB title: *Citadel of Crime*
A hick lawyer in the big city smashes corruption.
Somewhat inconsequential melodrama which fails to come through with the powerful entertainment it promises.
w Isabel Dawn *d* John H. Auer
☆ John Wayne, Frances Dee, Edward Ellis, Wallace Ford, Ward Bond, Harold Huber, Alexander Granach, Barnett Parker

The Man Between *
GB 1953 101m bw
British Lion/London Films (Carol Reed)
Ivo Kern operates successfully as a West Berlin racketeer; love causes a softening of his attitudes and leads to his death.
Imitation Third Man *with an uninteresting mystery and a solemn ending. Good acting and production can't save it.*
w Harry Kurnitz *d* Carol Reed *ph* Desmond Dickinson *m* John Addison *ad* Andrei Andreiev
☆ James Mason, Hildegarde Neff, Claire Bloom, Geoffrey Toone, Ernst Schroeder
'Reed's love of photogenic corruption, his technical finesse, and his feeling for atmospheric intrigue almost make something really good out of a synthetic script.' – *Variety*
'A cold-hearted film about people with cold feet.' – *Daily Express*

Man Bites Dog **
Belgium 1992 96m bw
Metro/Les Artistes Anonymes (Rémy Belvaux, André Bonzel, Benoît Poelvoorde)
original title: *C'est arrivé près de chez vous*
A documentary film crew begins by recording the activities of a motiveless serial killer and ends by helping him with his murders.
A black comedy that makes some effective points about the relationship between cinema (or TV) and exploitation and voyeurism but which becomes ever harder to watch or enjoy, with its scenes of gang rape and murder. A remarkable, if sometimes repellent, first feature, nevertheless.
w Rémy Belvaux, André Bonzel, Benoît Poelvoorde, Vincent Tavier *d* Rémy Belvaux, André Bonzel, Benoît Poelvoorde *ph* André Bonzel *m* Jean-Marc Chenut *ed* Rémy Belvaux, Eric Dardill
☆ Benoît Poelvoorde, Jacqueline Poelvoorde-Pappaert, Nelly Pappaert, Jenny Drye, Malou Madou, Willy Vandenbroeck
'To encounter Man Bites Dog is to submit to a torrent of hilariously cruel humour, enacted without fuss or rancour, and inconceivably authentic.' – *Philip Strick, Sight and Sound*
'Offbeat, darkly hilarious ... Violent yet trenchant, potential sleeper should attract a cult following and will look just right on video.' – *Variety*
'Carefully shaped to draw us in and repel us, to make us laugh and wipe the smiles off our faces. The most horrendous scenes are calculated to force us into asking how we can bear to watch such things.' – *Philip French, Observer*

A Man Called Gannon
US 1969 105m Technicolor Techniscope
Universal
A wandering cowboy helps a widow rancher in her fight against encroaching cattlemen.
Adequate remake of Man Without a Star, *which somehow had much more stature.*
w Gene Kearney, D. D. Beauchamp and Borden Chase *d* James Goldstone
☆ Tony Franciosa, Michael Sarrazin, Judi West, Susan Oliver, John Anderson

A Man Called Horse *
US 1970 114m Technicolor Panavision
Cinema Center/Sanford Howard
In 1825 an English aristocrat is captured by Indians, lives with them and eventually becomes their leader.
Harrowing account of tribal life and customs, with much bloodshed and torture and most of the dialogue in Indian. Occasionally impressive but not exactly entertaining.
w Jack de Witt *story* Dorothy M. Johnson *d* Elliot Silverstein *ph* Robert Hauser *m* Leonard Rosenman
☆ Richard Harris, Judith Anderson, Jean Gascon, Manu Tupou
† Sequels 1976: *The Return of a Man Called Horse.* 1984: *Triumphs of a Man Called Horse.*

The Man Called Noon
GB/Spain/Italy 1973 95m Technicolor
Frontier/Montana/Finarco (Euan Lloyd)
A Western gunslinger loses his memory.
Childish Western melodrama in the violent manner.
w Scot Finch *novel* Louis L'Amour *d* Peter Collinson *ph* John Cabrera *m* Luis Bacalov
☆ Richard Crenna, Stephen Boyd, Rosanna Schiaffino, Farley Granger

A Man Called Peter *
US 1955 119m DeLuxe Cinemascope
TCF (Samuel G. Engel)
The life of Peter Marshall, a Scottish clergyman who became chaplain to the US Senate.
Careful but rather dreary biopic.
w Eleanore Griffin *book* Catherine Marshall *d* Henry Koster *ph* Harold Lipstein *m* Alfred Newman
☆ *Richard Todd*, Jean Peters, Marjorie Rambeau, Jill Esmond, Les Tremayne, Robert Burton
Harold Lipstein

A Man Called Sledge
Italy 1970 92m Techniscope
Dino de Laurentiis (Carl Olsen)
A bandit tries in vain to mastermind a bank robbery.
Curious change of pace for a genial star. A spaghetti Western without style but with plenty of violence, the result doesn't linger in the memory.
w Vic Morrow, Frank Kowalski *d* Vic Morrow *ph* Luigi Kuveiller
☆ James Garner, Dennis Weaver, Claude Akins, John Marley

A Man Called Sullivan: see *The Great John L.*

A Man Could Get Killed *
US 1966 98m Technicolor Panavision
Universal/Cherokee (Ernest Wehmeyer)
An American businessman in Lisbon is mistaken for a secret agent.
Minor thrill comedy with a confused plot and a willing cast.
w T. E. B. Clarke, Richard Breen *novel* Diamonds Are Danger by David Walker *d* Ronald Neame, Cliff Owen *ph* Gabor Pogany *m* Bert Kaemfert
☆ James Garner, Melina Mercouri, Sandra Dee, Tony Franciosa, Robert Coote, Roland Culver, Cecil Parker, Grégoire Aslan, Dulcie Gray, Martin Benson, Niall MacGinnis

A Man for All Seasons ****
GB 1966 120m Technicolor
Columbia/Highland (Fred Zinnemann)
Sir Thomas More opposes Henry VIII's divorce, and events lead inexorably to his execution.
Irreproachable film version of a play which has had its narrative tricks removed but stands up remarkably well. Acting, direction, sets, locations and costumes all have precisely the right touch.
w Robert Bolt play Robert Bolt d Fred Zinnemann ph Ted Moore m Georges Delerue pd John Box
☆ *Paul Scofield, Wendy Hiller,* Susannah York, *Robert Shaw,* Orson Welles, Leo McKern, Nigel Davenport, John Hurt, Corin Redgrave, Cyril Luckham, Jack Gwillim
'Mr Zinnemann has crystallized the essence of this drama in such pictorial terms as to render even its abstractions vibrant.' – *New York Times*
'A beautiful and satisfying film, the ultimate demonstration, perhaps, of how a fine stage play can be transcended and, with integrity and inspiration, turned into a great motion picture.' – *Judith Crist*
† Reports indicate that Charlton Heston badly wanted the role of Sir Thomas More.
best picture; Robert Bolt; Fred Zinnemann; Ted Moore; Paul Scofield
Wendy Hiller; Robert Shaw
best picture; best British film; Ted Moore; John Box; Paul Scofield

'If you've read the book, forget it!'
Man Friday
GB 1975 115m Eastmancolor Panavision
Avco-Embassy/ITC/ABC/Keep Films (Jules Buck)
The story of Robinson Crusoe told so that Friday appears the more intelligent.
A pointless and not very entertaining exercise which wears out its welcome very early.
w Adrian Mitchell *d* Jack Gold *ph* Alex Phillips *m* Carl Davis
☆ Peter O'Toole, Richard Roundtree
'Liberal intentions trail sadly through every sequence and cause absurd fluctuations of tone, since no one seems to have decided whether laborious slapstick, heavy portentousness or method acting is the best vehicle for the message.' – *Jill Forbes*

The Man from Blankley's
US 1930 67m bw
Warner
A drunken aristocrat goes to the wrong party and teaches those present, and himself, a thing or two.
Amusing star trifle, previously filmed as a silent.
w Harvey Thew, Joseph Jackson *story* F. Anstey *d* Alfred E. Green *ph* James Van Trees
☆ John Barrymore, Loretta Young, William Austin, Albert Gran, Emily Fitzroy
'Dickens comedy, in the Sennett vein, with the Barrymore finesse.' – *Variety*

The Man from Colorado
US 1948 99m Technicolor
Columbia (Jules Schermer)
A maladjusted Civil War veteran becomes a Western judge and rules by the gun.
Slightly unusual, watchable star Western.
w Robert D. Andrews, Ben Maddow *story* Borden Chase *d* Henry Levin *ph* William Snyder
m George Duning
☆ Glenn Ford, William Holden, Ellen Drew, Ray Collins, Edgar Buchanan, Jerome Courtland, James Millican, Jim Bannon
'No more humour than a lawyer's shingle, but it has suspense and some exciting shots of fist fights and burning houses.' – *Time*

The Man from Dakota *
US 1940 75m bw
MGM
GB title: *Arouse and Beware*
A Yankee soldier is taken prisoner by the South and becomes a spy.
Good period action piece.
w Laurence Stallings *novel* Mackinlay Kantor *d* Leslie Fenton
☆ Wallace Beery, Dolores Del Rio, John Howard, Donald Meek, H. B. Warner, Victor Varconi

Man from Del Rio
US 1956 82m bw
UA/Robert L. Jacks
A Mexican hobo becomes sheriff and forces the local badman to leave town.
Modest, efficient, rather brutal little Western.
w Richard Carr *d* Harry Horner *ph* Stanley Cortez *m* Fred Steiner
☆ Anthony Quinn, Katy Jurado, Peter Whitney, Douglas Fowley

The Man from Down Under
US 1943 103m bw
MGM
A veteran of World War I smuggles two orphans back into Australia.
Appallingly indulgent sentimental star vehicle, a mistake for all concerned.
w Wells Root, Thomas Seller *d* Robert Z. Leonard
☆ Charles Laughton, Binnie Barnes, Donna Reed, Richard Carlson, Horace McNally, Arthur Shields

'He came a thousand miles to kill someone he'd never seen!'
The Man from Laramie **
US 1955 104m Technicolor Cinemascope
Columbia (William Goetz)
A wandering cowman seeks revenge on those who killed his brother.
Grade-A Western with new-fangled touches of brutality touching off the wide screen spectacle.
w Philip Yordan, Frank Burt *d Anthony Mann ph* Charles Lang Jnr *m* George Duning *md* Morris Stoloff *ad* Cary Odell *ed* William Lyon
☆ *James Stewart* (Will Lockhart), Arthur Kennedy (Vic Hansbro), Donald Crisp (Alec Waggoman), Cathy O'Donnell (Barbara Waggoman), Alex Nicol (Dave Waggoman), Aline MacMahon (Kate Canaday), Wallace Ford, Jack Elam

The Man from Majorca *
Sweden 1984 105m colour
Cannon/Drakfilm (Göran Lindström)
original title: *Mannen Fròn Mallorca*
Two policemen are thwarted in their attempt to uncover a political and sexual scandal.
A taut thriller that maintains its suspense until the end.

wd Bo Widerberg *novel* Grisfesten by Leif G. W. Persson *ph* Thomas Wahlberg *m* Björn Jason Lindh *ad* Jan öquist *ed* Bo Widerberg
☆ Sven Wollter, Tomas von Brömssen, Hakan Serner, Ernst Günther, Thomas Hellberg, Ingvar Hirdvall, Niels Jensen

The Man from Monterey
US 1933 57m bw
Warner (Leon Schlesinger)
A US Army captain helps Mexican landowners prevent their lands from being taken over by unscrupulous speculators and saves the girl from marrying a villain.
A standard quickie that was Wayne's last Western for Warner, as he went on to better movies and paydays.
w Lesley Mason *d* Mack V. Wright
☆ John Wayne, Ruth Hall, Nina Quartero, Lillian Leighton, Luis Alberni, Francis Ford, Donald Reed

The Man from Morocco
GB 1944 116m bw
ABP (Warwick Ward)
Members of the international brigade are captured and later sent by Vichy to build a Sahara railway for the Germans; one escapes to London with vital information.
Stilted, meandering and extremely unconvincing melodrama with a star ill at ease.
w Warwick Ward, Edward Dryhurst, Marguerite Steen *story* Rudolph Cartier *d* Max Greene *ph* Basil Emmott
☆ Anton Walbrook, Margaretta Scott, Mary Morris, Reginald Tate, Peter Sinclair, David Horne

The Man from Nevada: see *The Nevadan*

The Man from Planet X
US 1951 70m bw
Sherrill Corwin/United Artists (Aubrey Wisberg and Jack Pollexfen)
On a remote Scottish island a spacecraft deposits a strange creature with a large head and mesmeric powers.
Early, minor, moderately pleasing fragment in the Close Encounters *cycle.*
w Aubrey Wisberg, Jack Pollexfen *d* Edgar G. Ulmer *ph* John Russell *m* Charles Koff
☆ Margaret Field, Raymond Bond, William Schallert

The Man from Snowy River
Australia 1982 104m Eastmancolor Panavision
Cambridge Films/Michael Edgley International (Geoff Burrowes)
In 1888, an orphan boy grows up with an obsession about wild horses.
Essentially no more than an Audie-Murphy-style Western given full down-under treatment. An Australian smash, a programmer elsewhere.
w John Dixon, Fred Cullen *poem* A. B. Paterson *d* George Miller *ph* Keith Wagstaff *m* Bruce Rowland
☆ Kirk Douglas, Jack Thompson, Sigrid Thornton, Tom Burlinson, Terence Donovan, Lorraine Bayly

The Man from Snowy River Part II: see *Return to Snowy River*

Man from Tangier
GB 1957 66m bw
Butcher's (W. G. Chalmers)
A pilot becomes mixed up with rival gangs trying to get their hands on a forger's valuable plates.
Dull, cramped thriller with little action and much talk in small rooms.
w P. Manning O'Brine *d* Lance Comfort *ph* Geoffrey Faithfull *md* Wilfred Burns *ad* John Stoll *ed* Peter Mayhew
☆ Robert Hutton, Lisa Gastoni, Martin Benson, Leonard Sachs, Derek Sydney, Robert Raglan, Harold Berens, Michael Balfour

The Man from the Alamo *
US 1953 79m Technicolor
U-I (Aaron Rosenberg)
A survivor of the Alamo is thought to be a deserter but proves his story and exposes a villain.
Satisfying Western programmer.
w Steve Fisher, D. D. Beauchamp *d* Budd Boetticher *ph* Russell Metty *m* Frank Skinner
☆ Glenn Ford, Victor Jory, Julia Adams, Hugh O'Brian

The Man from the Diners' Club *
US 1963 96m bw
Columbia/Dena/Ampersand (Bill Bloom)
A clerk accidentally lets a credit card go to a notorious gangster, and makes desperate efforts to retrieve it.
Minor star comedy with funny moments surviving a slapdash script.
w Bill Blatty *d* Frank Tashlin *ph* Hal Mohr *m* Stu Philips
☆ Danny Kaye, Telly Savalas, Martha Hyer, Cara Williams, Everett Sloane, George Kennedy

The Man from the Folies Bergère: see *Folies Bergère*

The Man from Tokyo: see *Tokyo Drifter*

The Man from U.N.C.L.E
This long-running one-hour TV series (1964–68) began as a spoof of James Bond, which was itself a spoof.
Not much more serious or convincing than Batman, *they caused a lot of people to suspend their disbelief.*
☆ Robert Vaughn (Napoleon Solo), David McCallum (Ilya Kuryakin), Leo G. Carroll (Mr Waverly)
† Several feature films were made up from various episodes, and did well in cinemas in some countries. They were: To Trap a Spy, The Spy with My Face, The Karate Killers, The Spy in the Green Hat, One of Our Spies Is Missing, The Helicopter Spies, How to Steal the World, and One Spy Too Many.

The Man from Utah
US 1934 55m bw
Lone Star (Paul Malvern)
At the urging of a US Marshal, a cowboy goes undercover to expose a gang organizing a crooked rodeo.
Dull Western, with some moderately interesting rodeo footage. It opens, uncharacteristically, with Wayne as a guitar-toting cowboy on a white horse, singing a love song in an unpleasing baritone.
w Lindsley Parsons *d* Robert Bradbury *ph* Archie Stout *m* William Barber *ed* Carl Pierson
☆ John Wayne, Polly Ann Young, Anita Compillo, Edward Peil, George Hayes, Yakima Canutt, George Cleveland

A Man from Wyoming
US 1930 70m bw
Paramount
A slow-speaking engineer joins the army, serves overseas and marries an ambulance driver.
Uncertain star vehicle which helped to mould his screen character.
w John Weaver and Albert Shelby Le Vino *d* Rowland V. Lee
☆ Gary Cooper, June Collyer, Regis Toomey, E. H. Calvert, Morgan Farley
'Bad enough to be good entertainment if taken as farce.' – *New York Evening Post.*

'Her body ached for the man she loved!'
The Man from Yesterday
US 1932 71m bw
Paramount
A man is reported missing in World War I, but years later his wife and her new fiancé find him in Switzerland, dying of gas poisoning.
Enoch Arden rides again, and very boringly.
w Oliver H. P. Garrett *d* Berthold Viertel *ph* Karl Struss
☆ Claudette Colbert, Clive Brook, Charles Boyer, Andy Devine, Alan Mowbray, Christian Rub
'Rather too late in the day to expect war scenes, and when the war peters out, there is only scenery and conversation.' – *Variety*

Man Hunt
US 1936 65m bw
Warner
A cub reporter hunts a bank robber.
Standard support action fare of its time.
w Roy Chanslor, Earl Felton *d* William Clemens *ph* Joseph Ruttenberg *ad* Esdras Hartley *ed* Louis Hesse
☆ William Gargan (Hank Dawson), Ricardo Cortez (Frank Kingman), Marguerite Churchill (Jane Carpenter), Chic Sale (Ed Hoggins), Maude Eburne (Mrs Hoggins), Don Barclay (Waffles)
'Script never lives up to the title's promise.' – *Variety*

Man Hunt **
US 1941 98m bw
TCF (Kenneth MacGowan)
A big game hunter misses a shot at Hitler and is chased back to England by the Gestapo.
Despite hilariously inaccurate English backgrounds, this is perhaps its director's most vivid Hollywood thriller, though watered down in tone from the original novel.
w Dudley Nichols *novel* Rogue Male by Geoffrey Household *d* Fritz Lang *ph* Arthur Miller *m* Alfred Newman
☆ Walter Pidgeon, Joan Bennett, George Sanders, John Carradine, Roddy McDowall, Ludwig Stossel, Heather Thatcher, Frederick Worlock
'A tense and intriguing thriller that is both propaganda and exciting entertainment.' – *Paul M. Jensen, 1969*
'In its manipulation of these dark and intent forces on a checkerboard, it manages to take your breath away.' – *Otis Ferguson*
† Remade for TV in 1976 as *Rogue Male*.

The Man I Killed: see *Broken Lullaby*

The Man I Married *
US 1940 79m bw
TCF (Raymond Griffith)
aka: *I Married a Nazi*
When an American couple take a European vacation, the wife is horrified to find her husband, who is of German parentage, agreeing with the Nazis.
Naïve but striking melodrama exploring attitudes of its time.
w Oliver H. P. Garrett *novel* Swastika by Oscar Shisgall *d* Irving Pichel *ph* Peverell Marley *m* David Buttolph
☆ Joan Bennett, Francis Lederer, Lloyd Nolan, Anna Sten, Otto Kruger, Maria Ouspenskaya, Ludwig Stossel, Johnny Russell

Man in a Cocked Hat: see *Carlton-Browne of the FO*

The Man in Grey **
GB 1943 116m bw
GFD/Gainsborough (Edward Black)
In Regency times, an aristocratic girl's love for her less fortunate friend is repaid by jealousy, treachery and murder.
Rather dully performed flashback costume melodrama which caught the public imagination in the middle of a dreary world war, especially as its evil leading characters were played by stars who rapidly went right to the top. The several imitations which followed, including The Wicked Lady, Jassy *and* Hungry Hill, *became known as the Gainsborough school.*
w Margaret Kennedy, Leslie Arliss, Doreen Montgomery *novel* Lady Eleanor Smith *d* Leslie Arliss *ph* Arthur Crabtree *m* Cedric Mallabey *ad* Walter Murton
☆ James Mason, Margaret Lockwood, Phyllis Calvert, Stewart Granger, Helen Haye, Nora Swinburne, Raymond Lovell, Martita Hunt
'There was not a moment when I would not gladly have dived for my hat.' – *James Agate*
'All the time-tested materials: gypsy fortune-teller; scowling, black-browed villain; gushy diary kept by a doe-eyed girl who munches candied violets; fire-breathing adventuress who dotes on discord and low-cut gowns…' – *Time*

'Even the one girl who loved enough to ask no questions – had to face the fearful truth!'
The Man in Half Moon Street
US 1944 91m bw
Paramount (Walter MacEwen)
A mysteriously handsome young scientist is actually a 90-year-old who has discovered a surgical method of preserving youth.
Boring screen version of a play which was conceived in an almost romantic vein; Hollywood has taken it too literally.
w Charles Kenyon *play* Barre Lyndon *d* Ralph Murphy *ph* Henry Sharp *m* Miklos Rozsa
☆ Nils Asther, Helen Walker, Brandon Hurst, Reinhold Schunzel
† Remade in straight horror vein as *The Man Who Could Cheat Death* (qv).

The Man in Her Life
Philippines 1998 103m colour
Star Pacific/Reyna (Armida Siguion-Reyna)
original title: *Ang Lalaki Sa Buhay Ni Selya*
A homosexual headmaster, scandalising the locals over his relationship with a married man, decides to marry the school's new teacher, who has left home to find her lover, a travelling salesman.
Amiable, but long-winded domestic drama that never fully engages with its subject matter.
w Bibeth Orteza *d* Carlos Siguion-Reyna *ph* Yam Laranas *m* Ryan Cayabyab *pd* Joey Luna *ed* Manet A. Dayrit
☆ Ricky Davao, Gardo Versoza, Rosanna Roces, Alan Paule, Eva Darren, Renato del Prado, Crispin Pineda

Man in Love *
France/Italy 1987 110m colour
Virgin/Fox/Camera One/Alexandra Films/JMS (Michel Seydoux, Diane Kurys)
original title: *Un Homme Amoureux*
A married American film star falls in love with an actress while making a movie in Italy.
Overlong romantic melodrama that generates little heat.
w Diane Kurys, Olivier Schatzky *d* Diane Kurys *ph* Bernard Zitzermann *m* Georges Delerue *ad* Dean Tavoularis *ed* Joelle Van Effenterre
☆ Peter Coyote, Greta Scacchi, Peter Riegert, Claudia Cardinale, John Berry, Vincent Lindon, Jamie Lee Curtis

The Man in Possession
US 1931 81m bw
MGM
A lady falls in love with the bailiff's man in temporary charge of her establishment.
Light comedy subsequently remade as Personal Property; *quite tolerable.*
w Sarah Y. Mason *play* H. M. Harwood *d* Sam Wood
☆ Robert Montgomery, Irene Purcell, Charlotte Greenwood, C. Aubrey Smith, Beryl Mercer, Reginald Owen, Alan Mowbray
'Should have no trouble where the censors don't interfere … where it gets by with the dirt, the dirt should get it over.' – *Variety*

The Man in Possession: see *Personal Property (1937)*

The Man in the Attic
US 1953 82m bw
TCF (Robert L. Jacks)
Remake of the much-remade *The Lodger*, this time with parsimonious production values and no style.
w Robert Presnell Jnr, Barre Lyndon *d* Hugo Fregonese *ph* Leo Tover *md* Lionel Newman
☆ Jack Palance, Constance Smith, Byron Palmer, Frances Bavier, Rhys Williams

The Man in the Back Seat *
GB 1961 57m bw
Independent Artists (Julian Wintle, Leslie Parkyn)
Two robbers fail to separate a bookie from the locked bag chained to his wrist, at first taking him with them they finally kill him and are apparently haunted by him.
Taut, downbeat little crime thriller which won a few critical plaudits.
w Malcolm Hulke, Eric Paice *d* Vernon Sewell *ph* Reg Wyer *m* Stanley Black
☆ Derren Nesbitt, Keith Faulkner, Carol White, Harry Locke

'Death at the carnival – as a killer takes over the switchback!'
Man in the Dark *
US 1953 70m bw 3-D
Columbia (Wallace MacDonald)
A convict submits to a brain operation which will remove his criminal tendencies. Unfortunately it also removes his memory, and on his release he is bewildered when gangsters expect him to know where the loot is hidden.
Silly low-budgeter which is only notable as the 3-D film which most exploited the short-lived medium. Apart

from a roller coaster ride, objects hurled at the audience include scissors, spiders, knives, forceps, fists and falling bodies.
w George Bricker, Jack Leonard *screenplay* The Man Who Lived Twice by William Sackheim *story Tom van Dyke, Henry Altimus d* Lew Landers *ph* Floyd Crosby *md* Ross Di Maggio *ad* John Meehan *ed* Viola Lawrence
☆ Edmond O'Brien (Steve Rawley), Audrey Totter (Peg Benedict), Ted de Corsia (Lefty), Horace MacMahon (Arnie), Nick Dennis (Cookie), Dayton Lummis (Dr Marston), Dan Riso (Jawald)

The Man in the Gray Flannel Suit *
US 1956 152m Eastmancolor Cinemascope
TCF (Darryl F. Zanuck)
A young New York executive is offered a demanding job but decides that his first loyalty is to his wife and children.
An amusingly accurate novel of Madison Avenue mores becomes a marathon emotional melodrama in which the mordant bits quickly give way to domestic problems and a guilt complex about a wartime affair, shown in lengthy flashback. It's all too much.
wd Nunnally Johnson *novel* Sloan Wilson *ph* Charles G. Clarke *m* Bernard Herrmann
☆ *Gregory Peck, Fredric March,* Jennifer Jones, Ann Harding, *Arthur O'Connell, Henry Daniell,* Marisa Pavan, Lee J. Cobb, Keenan Wynn, Gene Lockhart, Gigi Perreau, Connie Gilchrist, Joseph Sweeney

'Free Him!'
'Is he my wooer, my loved one? Or is he the tyrant who bleeds my people? Is he ardent lover – or cold-blooded killer? Let me look upon his face! Let me touch him!'

The Man in the Iron Mask **
US 1939 110m bw
Edward Small
King Louis XIV keeps his twin brother prisoner.
Exhilarating swashbuckler based on a classic novel, with a complex plot, good acting and the three musketeers in full cry.
w George Bruce novel Alexandre Dumas *d James Whale ph* Robert Planck *m* Lucien Moraweck, Lud Gluskin *ad* John DuCasse Schulze *ed* Grant Whytock
☆ *Louis Hayward* (Louis XIV/Philippe), *Warren William* (D'Artagnan), Alan Hale (Porthos), Bert Roach (Athos), Miles Mander (Aramis), Joan Bennett (Maria Theresa), *Joseph Schildkraut* (Fouquet), Walter Kingsford (Colbert), Marion Martin, Montagu Love, Albert Dekker
'Substantial entertainment for general appeal and satisfaction.' – *Variety*
'A sort of combination of *The Prisoner of Zenda* and *The Three Musketeers*, with a few wild west chases thrown in … not unentertaining.' – *Richard Mallett, Punch*
† Remade 1976 as a TV movie with Richard Chamberlain, and 1978 as *The Fifth Musketeer* (qv).
Lucien Moraweck, Lud Gluskin

The Man in the Iron Mask *
US 1998 132m DeLuxe
MGM/UA (Randall Wallace, Russell Smith)
When King Louis XIV rules badly and connives in the death of Athos's son, the former musketeers decide to replace him with his imprisoned twin brother.
A stolid version that limits the swashbuckling, and provides little else to excite, with its motley international quartet of musketeers and a twin performance from DiCaprio that fails to convince.
wd Randall Wallace *novel* Alexandre Dumas *ph* Peter Suschitzky *m* Nick Glennie-Smith *pd* Anthony Pratt *ed* William Hoy
☆ Leonardo DiCaprio, Jeremy Irons (Aramis), John Malkovich (Athos), Gérard Depardieu (Porthos), Gabriel Byrne (D'Artagnan), Anne Parillaud, Judith Godrèche, Edward Atterton, Peter Sarsgaard
'An unusually sober and serious-minded telling of Alexandre Dumas' classic tale, this handsome costumer is routinely made and comes up rather short in boisterous excitement.' – *Todd McCarthy, Variety*
† MGM discovered that the audience the movie attracted was 'directly related to the appeal of Leonardo DiCaprio', being 55 per cent female, and 46 per cent under-25.

The Man in the Middle *
GB 1964 94m bw Cinemascope
TCF/Pennebaker/Belmont (Walter Seltzer)
In India during World War II, an American lieutenant is indicted for murder and the defence counsel is instructed to lose the case.
Courtroom melodrama with unusual angles; quite intriguing, though the wide screen doesn't help.
w Keith Waterhouse, Willis Hall *novel The Winston Affair* by Howard Fast *d* Guy Hamilton *ph* Wilkie Cooper *m* John Barry
☆ Robert Mitchum, Trevor Howard, Keenan Wynn, Barry Sullivan, France Nuyen, Alexander Knox
'For once Mitchum seems to have an excuse for keeping his eyes at half mast.' – *Judith Crist*

The Man in the Mirror
GB 1936 82m bw
JH Productions (Julius Hagen)
A timid man's reflection steps out of the mirror and organizes him.
Modest comedy with a pleasing star.
w F. McGrew Willis, Hugh Mills *novel* William Garrett *d* Maurice Elvey *ph* Curt Courant
☆ *Edward Everett Horton,* Geneviève Tobin, Garry Marsh, Ursula Jeans, Alastair Sim, Aubrey Mather, Felix Aylmer
'High speed sequences of comic incident put over in fine style.' – *Cinema*

Man in the Moon
GB 1960 99m bw
Allied Film Makers/Excalibur (Michael Relph)
A man who earns his living as Mr Normal, a human guinea pig for scientific research, is chosen as the first astronaut.
Dated comedy which rather dismayingly turns from mild satire to outright farce and fantasy.
w Michael Relph, Bryan Forbes *d* Basil Dearden *ph* Harry Waxman *m* Philip Green
☆ Kenneth More, Shirley Anne Field, Michael Hordern, John Phillips, John Glyn-Jones, Charles Gray, Norman Bird

The Man in the Moon *
US 1991 99m Eastmancolor
UIP/MGM/Pathé (Mark Rydell)
In the 1950s, a 14-year-old girl falls in love with a 17-year-old boy, but he prefers her sister.
Weepy period account of growing-up, handled with skill.
w Jenny Wingfield *d* Robert Mulligan *ph* Freddie Francis *m* James Newton Howard *pd* Gene Callahan *ed* Trudy Ship
☆ Sam Waterston, Tess Harper, Gail Strickland, Reese Witherspoon, Jason London, Emily Warfield
'A disappointing return by Mulligan to the well-ploughed cliché.' – *Philip Strick, Sight and Sound*
'One of the most delicate and heart-warming movies of the year.' – *Roger Ebert*

The Man in the Net
US 1958 96m bw
UA/Mirisch-Jaguar (Walter Mirisch)
When a painter is accused of murdering his wife, he goes into hiding and is helped by children.
Extremely tedious and inept mystery, doubly disappointing in view of the credits.
w Reginald Rose *novel* Patrick Quentin *d* Michael Curtiz *ph* John Seitz *m* Hans Salter
☆ Alan Ladd, Carolyn Jones, Diane Brewster, John Lupton, Charles McGraw, Tom Helmore, John Alexander

Man in the Saddle
US 1951 87m Technicolor
Columbia/Scott-Brown (Harry Joe Brown)
GB title: *The Outcast*
A small rancher is victimized by his wealthy neighbour.
Fairly lively Western which develops into a series of gunfights.
w Kenneth Gamet *novel* Ernest Haycox *d* André de Toth *ph* Charles Lawton Jnr *m* George Duning *md* Maurice Stoloff *ad* George Brooks *ed* Charles Nelson
☆ Randolph Scott, Alexander Knox, Joan Leslie, Ellen Drew, Richard Rober, Alfonso Bedoya, Guinn 'Big Boy' Williams, Cameron Mitchell

Man in the Shadow *
US 1957 80m bw Cinemascope
U-I (Albert Zugsmith)
GB title: *Pay the Devil*
The sheriff of a small western town investigates a murder against the wishes of a powerful local rancher.
Mini-social drama in which the honest man wins out at last … and who would expect anything different. A brooding melodrama which delivers less than it promises.
w Gene L. Coon *d* Jack Arnold *ph* Arthur E. Arling *m* Hans Salter
☆ Jeff Chandler, Orson Welles, Colleen Miller, John Larch, Joe Schneider, Leo Gordon

The Man in the Sky *
GB 1956 87m bw
Ealing (Seth Holt)
US title: *Decision against Time*
A test pilot refuses to bale out when an engine catches fire; his plight is interwoven with scenes of his family, friends and associates.
Thin suspense drama with some effective moments but too many irrelevant asides.
w William Rose, John Eldridge *d* Charles Crichton *ph* Douglas Slocombe *m* Gerbrand Schurmann
☆ Jack Hawkins, Elizabeth Sellars, Walter Fitzgerald, Eddie Byrne, John Stratton, Victor Maddern, Lionel Jeffries, Donald Pleasence

The Man in the Trunk
US 1942 70m bw
TCF
The ghost of a murder victim helps a young attorney to nail the culprit.
Slightly uneasy spook comedy with a good star performance.
w John Larkin *d* Malcolm St Clair
☆ *Raymond Walburn,* Lynne Roberts, George Holmes, J. Carrol Naish, Dorothy Peterson

The Man in the White Suit ****
GB 1951 81m bw
Ealing (Sidney Cole)
A scientist produces a fabric that never gets dirty and never wears out. Unions and management are equally aghast.
Brilliant satirical comedy played as farce and put together with meticulous cinematic counterpoint, so that every moment counts and all concerned give of their very best.
w Roger MacDougall, John Dighton, Alexander Mackendrick d Alexander Mackendrick ph Douglas Slocombe m Benjamin Frankel
☆ *Alec Guinness, Joan Greenwood, Cecil Parker,* Vida Hope, *Ernest Thesiger,* Michael Gough, Howard Marion Crawford, Miles Malleson, *George Benson, Edie Martin*
'The combination of an ingenious idea, a bright, funny and imaginative script, skilful playing and perceptive brisk direction has resulted once more in a really satisfying Ealing comedy.' – *Richard Mallett, Punch*
script

Man in the Wilderness *
US 1971 105m Technicolor Panavision
Warner/Wilderness (Sanford Howard)
In 1820 in the Canadian northwest, a fur trapper is mauled by a grizzly and left for dead, but he learns to survive and sets out for revenge.
Endurance melodrama modelled after A Man Called Horse; *a bit stretched and only for the hardened, but taking an agreeably unromantic view of nature.*
w Jack de Witt *d* Richard Sarafian *ph* Gerry Fisher *m* Johnny Harris
☆ Richard Harris, John Huston, John Bindon, Prunella Ransome, Henry Wilcoxon, Ben Carruthers

The Man Inside
GB 1958 97m bw Cinemascope
Columbia/Warwick (Harold Huth)
A jeweller's book-keeper steals a priceless diamond and is trailed by various factions half across Europe.
Fairly modest and unenterprising British thriller which hadn't much hope of the world market it was aiming at.
w John Gilling, David Shaw *novel* M. E. Chaber *d* John Gilling *ph* Ted Moore *m* Richard Bennett
☆ Nigel Patrick, Jack Palance, Anita Ekberg, Anthony Newley, Bonar Colleano, Sid James, Donald Pleasence

A Man is Ten Feet Tall: see *Edge of the City*

A Man Like Eva *
West Germany 1983 89m colour
Blue Dolphin/Cinevista/Schier-Straub/Trio/Impuls/Maran (Horst Schier, Laurens Straub)
original title: *Ein Mann Wie Eva*
While making a film, its director marries the female star and seduces the male star.
Based on the messy, manipulative life of bisexual film director Rainer Werner Fassbinder, it has one of his leading ladies, Eva Mattes, in the role of the male director, surprising casting that works well and adds an extra spice to an already over-heated narrative.
w Radu Gabrea, Laurens Straub *d* Radu Gabrea *ph* Horst Schier *m* Verdi *ad* Herbert Buchenberger *ed* Dragos-Emmanuel Witowski
☆ Eva Mattes, Lisa Kreuzer, Werner Stocker, Charles Regnier, Carola Regnier, Charly Muhamed Huber, Albert Kitzl

Man Made Monster *
US 1940 57m bw
Universal (Jack Bernard)
GB title: *The Electric Man*
A scientist experiments with a man who is impervious to electric shock, and turns him into a walking robot.
A smart little semi-horror originally planned for Karloff and Lugosi.
w Joseph West *d* George Waggner *ph* Elwood Bredell *m* Hans Salter *md* Charles Previn *sp John P. Fulton*
☆ *Lon Chaney Jnr, Lionel Atwill,* Anne Nagel, Frank Albertson, Samuel S. Hinds

'Who were the women who twisted his life and love – gutting the flame of his incredible genius?'

Man of a Thousand Faces **
US 1957 122m bw Cinemascope
U-I (Robert Arthur)
The rise to fame of silent screen character actor Lon Chaney.
Moderately commendable biopic with a strong sense of period Hollywood, an excellent star performance, but too much sudsy emoting about deaf mute parents and an ungrateful wife.
w R. Wright Campbell, Ivan Goff, Ben Roberts *d* Joseph Pevney *ph* Russell Metty *m* Frank Skinner *ad Alexander Golitzen ed* Ted J. Kent *sp* Clifford Stine
☆ *James Cagney* (Lon Chaney), Dorothy Malone (Cleva Creighton Chaney), Robert Evans (Irving Thalberg), Roger Smith (Creighton Chaney at 21), *Marjorie Rambeau* (Gert), Jane Greer (Hazel Bennett), Jim Backus (Clarence Logan)
'The script and conception are so maudlin and degrading that Cagney's high dedication becomes somewhat oppressive.' – *Pauline Kael, 70s*
script

Man of Affairs: see *His Lordship (1936)*

Man of Affairs
GB 1937 70m bw
Gaumont British
When the foreign secretary is kidnapped, his twin brother impersonates him.
Lighthearted star vehicle which satisfied.
w Maude Howell and L. Du Garde Peach *play The Nelson Touch* by Neil Grant *d* Herbert Mason
☆ George Arliss, Romilly Lunge, Rene Ray, Jessie Winter, Allan Jeayes
'Business possibilities only moderate.' – *Variety*

Man of Aran **
GB 1934 75m bw
Gainsborough (Michael Balcon)

The primitive life of crofting and fishing folk in the west of Ireland.
A lowering documentary very typical of its maker: highly impressive scene for scene, but tedious as a whole; still, highly remarkable that it was made at all for the commercial cinema.
w Robert and Frances Flaherty *d* Robert Flaherty *m* John Greenwood
☆ Colman King, Maggie Dirane
'In so far as it is a rendering of the efforts of the Atlantic to overwhelm and demolish a wall of rock, it is magnificent; but the human note is inadequate and unnecessary.' – *E. V. Lucas, Punch*
'However real, it would have made better truth if it had been handled with more of the art of fiction.' – *Otis Ferguson*
'Six thousand feet of such fine and purposeful pictorial composition have seldom been seen on the screen.' – *Observer*

Man of Bronze: see *Jimmy Thorpe, All American*

Man of Conquest
US 1939 99m bw
Republic (Sol C. Siegel)
The life of Western hero Sam Houston, who became president of Texas.
Competent action/domestic biopic.
w Wells Root, E. E. Paramore Jnr *d* George Nicholls Jnr *ph* Joseph H. August *m* Victor Young *ad* John Victor Mackay
☆ Richard Dix, Joan Fontaine, Gail Patrick, Edward Ellis, Victor Jory, Robert Barrat, George Hayes, Ralph Morgan, Robert Armstrong, C. Henry Gordon, Janet Beecher
'A grown-up hoss opera, based on authentic and colorful history, with fairly believable characters, ample action and reasonable suspense.' – *Variety*
Ꞩ Victor Young; art direction

Man of Evil: see *Fanny by Gaslight*

Man of Flowers *
Australia 1983 91m Fujicolour
Flowers International (Jane Ballantyne, Paul Cox)

A model's relationship with her lover, a blackmailing, cocaine-snorting artist, and her admirer, a wealthy, repressed, middle-aged aesthete, leads to violence.
A study of sexual hang-ups that teeters on the edge of black farce.
w Paul Cox, Bob Ellis *d* Paul Cox *ph* Yuro Sokol *ad* Asher Bilu *ed* Tim Lewis
☆ Norman Kaye, Alyson Best, Chris Haywood, Sarah Walker, Werner Herzog

Man of Iron
US 1935 62m bw
Warner
A steel works foreman rises to the boardroom, but doesn't like it.
Rather obvious moral tale without much excitement.
w William Wister Haines, Dawn Powell *d* William McGann
☆ Barton MacLane, Mary Astor, John Eldredge, Dorothy Peterson, Joseph Crehan
'Unimportant programme material.' – *Variety*

Man of Iron *
Poland 1981 152m colour/bw
PRF/Filmowy X
original title: *Czowiek Z Zelaza*
The events of 1980 in Poland are seen through the eyes of a strike leader.
A stirring companion piece to Man of Marble*; hard tack for the entertainment seeker but as honest a piece of history as one is likely to get from a so-called fiction film.*
w Aleksander Scibor-Rylski d Andrzej Wajda
ph Edward Klosinski *m* Andrzej Korzynski
☆ Jerzy Radziwilowicz, Krystyna Janda, Marian Opania
Ꞩ best foreign film

Man of La Mancha *
† US 1972 132m DeLuxe
UA/PEA (Arthur Hiller)

Arrested by the Inquisition and thrown into prison, Miguel de Cervantes relates the story of Don Quixote.
Unimaginative but generally good-looking attempt to recreate on the screen an essentially theatrical experience.
w Dale Wasserman *play* Dale Wasserman *d* Arthur Hiller *ph Goffredo Rotunno m* Mitch Leigh *md* Laurence Rosenthal *ad* Luciano Damiani *ly* Joe Darion
☆ Peter O'Toole, Sophia Loren, James Coco, Harry Andrews, John Castle, Brian Blessed
'Needful of all the imagination the spectator can muster.' – *Variety*
Ꞩ Laurence Rosenthal

Man of Marble *
Poland 1978 165m colour
PRF/Zespol X (Andrzej Wajda)

original title: *Czlowiek Z Marmur*
Young film makers gather material on a political hero of the fifties.
An extended drama on the style of Citizen Kane *but with much more relevance to contemporary history. A key film to students of Poland, but too specialized for general entertainment.*
w Aleksander Scibor-Rylski *d* Andrzej Wajda *ph* Edward Klosinski *m* Andrzej Korzinski
☆ Jerzy Radziwilowicz, Krystyna Janda, Michael Tarkowski, Tadeusz Lomnicki

The Man of My Life: see *L'Homme de Ma Vie*

A Man of No Importance
GB/Ireland 1994 99m Eastmancolor
Clarence/Majestic/BBC/Little Bird (Jonathan Cavendish)

In Dublin in the early 60s, a middle-aged bus conductor, who is staging an amateur performance of Oscar Wilde's *Salome*, realizes that it is time to come out of the closet and admit that he is homosexual and in love with his driver.
A pointless and virtually witless exercise that resembles a timidly gay reworking of a third-rate Ealing comedy; it is heavy-handed whimsy weighed down by some broad acting.
w Barry Devlin *d* Suri Krishnamma *ph* Ashley Rowe *m* Julian Nott *pd* Jamie Leonard *ed* David Freeman
☆ Albert Finney, Brenda Fricker, Michael Gambon, Tara Fitzgerald, Rufus Sewell, Patrick Malahide, Anna Manahan
'Faced with a film as quietly bad, as lazy in its pathos (even the title is sentimental), it's hard to know whether to crush it with rock or to run circles round it sniggering.' – *Adam Mars-Jones, Independent*

Man of the East (dubbed)
Italy/France 1972 125m Technicolor Techniscope
UA/PEA/Artistes Associés (Alberto Grimaldi)
original title: *...E Poi Lo Chiamarono Il Magnifico*
An English fop is taught how to fight and shoot by three outlaws.
Over-long comedy Western, in which the jokes are few and far between.
w Enzo Barboni *d* E. B. Clutcher (Enzo Barboni) *ph* Aldo Giordani *m* Guido de Angelis, Maurizio de Angelis *ad* Enzo Bulgarelli *ed* Eugenio Alabiso
☆ Terence Hill (aka Mario Girotti) (Sir Thomas More), Yanti Somer (Candida), Gregory Walcott (Bull), Harry Carey (Holy Joe), Dominici Barto (Monkey), Riccardo Pizzuti (Morten Clayton)
'A predictable plot … is strung out to almost interminable length by the director's own script which never misses an opportunity to employ five sequences where one would do.' – *David Pirie, MFB*

Man of the Hour: see *Colonel Effingham's Raid*

The Man of the House
US 1995 96m Technicolor
Buena Vista/Walt Disney/Forever Girls (Bonnie Bruckheimer, Marty Katz)

A young boy attempts to sabotage his mother's romance with the lawyer who comes to live with them.
A dim and uninteresting account of male bonding in the woods; it is impossible to imagine at what audience it is aimed.
w James Orr, Jim Cruickshank *story* David Peckinpah, Richard Jefferies *d* James Orr *ph* Jamie Anderson *m* Mark Mancina *pd* Lawrence G. Paull *ed* Harry Keramidas
☆ Chevy Chase, Farrah Fawcett, Jonathan Taylor Thomas, George Wendt, David Shiner, Art LaFleur, Richard Portnow
'A dreadful film, with absolutely no redeeming features whatsoever – except that it does eventually end.' – *Derek Malcolm, Guardian*
'Jaw-droppingly awful.' – *Independent*

Man of the Moment
GB 1935 82m bw
Warner
An engaged young man saves a girl from suicide and falls in love with her.
Minor romantic comedy of predictable development.
w Roland Pertwee, Guy Bolton, A. R. Rawlinson *play* Yves Mirande *d* Monty Banks *ph* Basil Emmott *ad* Peter Proud
☆ Douglas Fairbanks Jnr, Laura La Plante, Claude Hulbert, Margaret Lockwood, Donald Calthrop, Monty Banks

Man of the Moment
GB 1955 88m bw
Rank (Hugh Stewart)
A Whitehall filing clerk has to pretend to be a high-level diplomat at an international conference in Geneva.
Slapstick comedy of the obvious kind, but one of the better showcases for Norman Wisdom's sentimental 'little man' act.
w Vernon Sylvaine, John Paddy Carstairs *story* Maurice Cowan *d* John Paddy Carstairs *ph* Jack Cox *m* Philip Green *ad* Cedric Dawe *ed* John Shirley
☆ Norman Wisdom, Lana Morris, Belinda Lee, Jerry Desmonde, Karel Stephanek, Garry Marsh, Inia te Wiata

Man of the People
US 1937 80m bw
Lucien Hubbard/MGM
An Italian immigrant works for a law degree but is forced in with crooks.
Political power play without much zest despite good acting.
w Frank Dolan *d* Edwin L. Marin
☆ Joseph Calleia, Thomas Mitchell, Florence Rice, Ted Healy, Catherine Doucet
'Patently primed for duals, where it can hold its own.' – *Variety*

Man of the West
US 1958 100m DeLuxe Cinemascope
UA/Ashton (Walter M. Mirisch)

In 1874 Arizona, a reformed gunman is cajoled by his old buddies to help them rob a bank.
Talkative, set-bound, cliché-ridden star Western with minor compensations.
w Reginald Rose *novel* Will C. Brown *d* Anthony Mann *ph* Ernest Haller *m* Leigh Harline
☆ Gary Cooper, Lee J. Cobb, Julie London, Arthur O'Connell, Jack Lord, John Dehner, Royal Dano, Robert Wilke

Man of the World
US 1931 71m bw
Paramount
A gentleman racketeer operates on American playboys in Paris.
Predictable but smooth star vehicle.
w Herman J. Mankiewicz *d* Richard Wallace
☆ William Powell, Carole Lombard, Wynne Gibson, Guy Kibbee, Lawrence Gray
'Anything better than moderate for gross must come through the star's personal pull.' – *Variety*

'He was the centrefold that revealed everything … but the truth.'
Man of the Year
US 1995 87m bw/colour
Artisan (Matt Keener)

Dirk Shafer, voted *Playgirl* magazine's Man of the Year in 1992, strives to conceal the fact that he is gay.
A light-hearted documentary that plays around with the form, also parodying straighter factual films.
wd Dirk Shafer *ph* Stephen Timberlake *m* Peitor Angell *pd* Michael Mueller *ed* Barry Silver, Ken Solomon
☆ Dirk Shafer, Vivian Paxton, Deidra Shafer, Michael Ornstein, Claudette Sutherland, Cal Bartlett, Beth Broderick

Man on a String
US 1960 92m bw
Columbia/Louis de Rochemont
GB title: *Confessions of a Counterspy*
A Russian-born Hollywood producer is asked by the Russians to work as a spy but becomes a double agent.
Slightly unbelievable biopic about Boris Morros, rather childlike in its simplicity and not too entertaining either.
w John Kafka, Virginia Shaler *book Ten Years a Counterspy* by Boris Morros *d* André de Toth *ph* Charles Lawton Jnr and others *m* George Duning
☆ Ernest Borgnine, Kerwin Mathews, Colleen Dewhurst, Alexander Scourby, Glenn Corbett, Vladimir Sokoloff

Man on a Swing
US 1975 108m Technicolor
Paramount (Howard B. Jaffe)
Investigations into a murder are helped by a would-be medium.
Overlong and confused psycho-mystery with one stand-out performance.
w David Zelag Goodman *d* Frank Perry *ph* Adam Holender *m* Lalo Schifrin
☆ Cliff Robertson, *Joel Grey*, Dorothy Tristan, Peter Masterson
'Runs out of interest long before it runs out of film.' – *Variety*

Man on a Tightrope *
US 1953 105m bw
TCF (Robert L. Jacks)
A Czech circus owner has trouble with the communist authorities and tries to escape.
Adventure story with cold war pretensions which virtually kill it.
w Robert Sherwood *d* Elia Kazan *ph* Georg Krause *m* Franz Waxman
☆ Fredric March, Cameron Mitchell, Adolphe Menjou, Gloria Grahame, Terry Moore, Richard Boone, John Dehner, Dorothea Wieck

The Man on America's Conscience: see *Tennessee Johnson*

Man on Fire
US 1957 95m bw
MGM (Sol C. Siegel)
When his wife divorces him, a middle-aged man refuses to hand over their son.
Low-key personal drama of very moderate interest and modest budget.
wd Ronald MacDougall *ph* Joseph Ruttenberg *m* David Raksin
☆ Bing Crosby, Inger Stevens, Mary Fickett, E. G. Marshall

Man on Fire
France/Italy 1987 92m Eastmancolor
Rank/Sept/FR3/Cima (Arnon Milchan)

An ex-CIA agent, working as a bodyguard in Italy, takes revenge on the gang who kidnapped a young girl he was protecting.
Uninteresting action movie, with a great deal of dull talk and hysterical acting interspersed by moments of violence that become ever more ludicrous. One of the many low points comes when Joe Pesci sings Johnny B. Goode.
w Eli Chouraqui, Sergio Donati *novel* A. J. Quinnell *d* Eli Chouraqui *ph* Gerry Fisher *m* John Scott *ad* Giantito Burchiellaro *ed* Noelle Boisson
☆ Scott Glenn, Brooke Adams, Danny Aiello, Joe Pesci, Jonathan Pryce, Paul Shenar, Laura

Morante, Alessandro Haber, Franco Trevisi, Jade Malle

† The film was cut by 30 seconds for its British video release.

The Man on the Eiffel Tower *

US 1949 82m Anscocolor

A & T (Irving Allen)

A crazy killer defies Inspector Maigret to discover his identity.

Early independent production, an unsatisfactory crime melodrama with international talent and Paris locations. Some quirky acting carries it through.

w Harry Brown *novel A Battle of Nerves* by Georges Simenon *d* Burgess Meredith *ph* Stanley Cortez *m* Michel Michelet

☆ Charles Laughton, Burgess Meredith, Franchot Tone, Robert Hutton, Jean Wallace, Patricia Roc, Wilfrid Hyde-White, Belita

† Some scenes were directed by Charles Laughton and some by Franchot Tone.

The Man on the Flying Trapeze *

US 1935 65m bw

Paramount (William Le Baron)

GB title: *The Memory Expert*

Adventures of an oppressed family man who is useful to his boss because of his prodigious memory.

Plotless rigmarole of shapeless comedy sketches, for star fans.

w Ray Harris, Sam Hardy, Jack Cunningham, Bobby Vernon *story* Charles Bogle (W. C. Fields) *d* Clyde Bruckman *ph* Al Gilks

☆ *W. C. Fields*, Kathleen Howard, Mary Brian, Grady Sutton, Vera Lewis, Lucien Littlefield, Oscar Apfel

'A series of gags unrelated to the title. Under average.' – *Variety*

"Hello, my name is Andy and people are talking about me!"

Man on the Moon *

US 1999 119m DeLuxe Panavision

Universal/Mutual/Jersey/Cinehaus (Danny DeVito, Michael Shamberg, Stacey Sher)

Biopic of stand-up, self-destructive comic Andy Kaufman, who enjoyed success on the TV sitcom *Taxi*, but then pushed at the bounds of comedy until his early death from cancer.

An intriguing story of an unusual and uncomfortable talent, with a good performance from Carrey; those who were never exposed to Kaufman's comedy are likely to need more convincing that he is worth this elaborate treatment.

w Scott Alexander, Larry Karaszewski *d* Milos Forman *ph* Anastas Michos *m* R.E.M. *pd* Patrizia von Brandenstein *ed* Christopher Tellefsen, Lynzee Klingman *cos* Jeffrey Kurland

☆ *Jim Carrey* (Andy Kaufman), Danny DeVito (George Shapiro), Courtney Love (Lynne Margulies), Paul Giamatti (Bob Zmuda), Vincent Schiavelli (Maynard Smith), Peter Bonerz (Ed Weinberger), Jerry Lawler (Himself), Gerry Becker (Stanley Kaufman), Leslie Lyles (Janice Kaufman)

'All the audience is left with is the impression of a thoroughly obnoxious man you'd never want to meet in real life, a hopeless neurotic of little discernible talent other than for making the lives of those around him miserable.' – *Todd McCarthy, Variety*

The Man on the Roof *

Sweden 1976 109m Eastmancolor

Svensk Filmindustri (Per Berglund)

original title: *Mannen pòa Taket*

A brutal policeman is murdered, and a rooftop sniper turns out to be the culprit.

Alternately vivid and lumbering police thriller with a regrettable tendency to moralize.

wd Bo Widerberg *novel The Abominable Man* by Max Sjöwall, Max Wahlöös *ph* Odd Geir Saether, Per Kallberg, others *m* Björn Lindh

☆ Carl-Gustaf Lindstedt, Gunnel Wadner, Hakan Serner, Sven Wollter

'A poet. A thief. Two strangers with nothing in common are about to trade their lives for a chance to cheat their destinies.'

The Man on the Train **

France 2002 90m colour Panavision

Pathé/Cine B/Zoulou Films/Rhone-Alpes/FCC/ Tubedale/Pandora/Cinema Parisien/Media Suits (Philippe Carcassonne)

original title: *L'Homme du Train*

In a small French town, an ageing bank robber and a retired teacher envy each other's way of life.

Delightful, intimate comedy of character that does not outstay its welcome; its two protagonists, a weary, itinerant tough guy and a prissily pedantic teacher, both contemplating the possibility of death, are given exemplary performances by Hallyday and Rochefort.

w Claude Klotz *d Patrice Leconte ph* Jean-Marie Drejou *m* Pascal Esteve *ad* Ivan Maussion *ed* Joëlle Hache

☆ *Jean Rochefort* (Manesquier), *Johnny Hallyday* (Milan), Jean-François Stévenin (Luigi), Charlie Nelson (Max), Pascal Parmentier (Sadko), Isabelle Petit-Jacques (Viviane), Édith Scob (Manesquier's sister)

'Has a wintry wit about it, and the modest incidents that define the two figures toying with transformation have a believable, saving naturalism.' – *Richard Schickel, Time*

'Delectable: Leconte has a taste for minor, chewed-up lives, and you can't help sighing with regret as he gathers his wits and hurries the plot toward an unnecessary climax.' – *Anthony Lane, New Yorker*

Man Proof

US 1937 74m bw

MGM (Louis D. Lighton)

In trying to win back her man a woman discovers she really loves someone else.

Modest romantic comedy which leaves its stars at sea.

w Vincent Lawrence, Waldemar Young, George Oppenheimer *novel The Four Marys* by Fanny Heaslip Lea *d* Richard Thorpe *ph* Karl Freund *m* Franz Waxman

☆ Myrna Loy, Franchot Tone, Walter Pidgeon, Rosalind Russell, Nana Bryant, Ruth Hussey

'A smartly produced, well-directed and excellently acted society comedy drama.' – *Variety*

The Man They Could Not Hang

US 1939 65m bw

Columbia

A scientist working on a mechanical heart causes the death of a volunteer student. He is executed, but his assistant restores him to life and he determines to murder those who convicted him.

Predictable horror hokum which set Karloff on his mad doctor cycle.

w Karl Brown *story* Leslie T. White, George W. Sayre *d* Nick Grinde *ph* Benjamin Kline *md* Morris Stoloff

☆ Boris Karloff, Lorna Gray, Robert Wilcox, Roger Pryor, Don Beddoe, Byron Foulger

A Man to Remember *

US 1938 80m bw

RKO (Robert Sisk)

At a small-town doctor's funeral, his life is remembered by mourners.

Modestly effective family film.

w Dalton Trumbo *novel Failure* by Katharine Haviland-Taylor *d Garson Kanin ph* J. Roy Hunt *m* Roy Webb

☆ Edward Ellis, Anne Shirley, Lee Bowman, William Henry, Granville Bates

'No sock for the marquee but a fine, well-made little picture.' – *Variety*

A Man to Respect

Italy/West Germany 1972 108m Technicolor Techniscope

Eagle/Verona Cinematografica/Paramount-Orion (Marina Cicogna)

aka: *Un Uomo da Rispettare*

On his release from jail, a safebreaker trains a young acrobat in his skills so that they can commit a double robbery.

An ingeniously plotted thriller that indulges in over-statement.

w Mino Roli *story* Franco Bucceri, Roberto Leoni *d* Michele Lupo *ph* Tonino Delli Colli *m* Ennio Morricone *ad* Francesco Bronzi *ed* Tony Zila

☆ Kirk Douglas, Giuliano Gemma, Florinda Bolkan

'A small triumph of dehumanised style.' – *Richard Combs, MFB*

'She Put Her Life In His Hands. Unfortunately, His Hands Have A Life Of Their Own.'

Man Trouble

US 1992 100m DeLuxe

First Independent/Penta/American Filmworks/ Budding Grove (Bruce Gilbert, Carole Eastman)

A dog-trainer becomes involved with an opera singer when she decides she needs a guard dog to protect her home.

An unlikely romance is at the centre of an even unlikelier narrative – and even if you swallow the implausibilities, the result is still sickly.

w Carole Eastman *d* Bob Rafelson *ph* Stephen H. Burum *m* Georges Delerue *pd* Mel Bourne *ed* William Steinkamp

☆ Jack Nicholson, Ellen Barkin, Harry Dean Stanton, Beverly D'Angelo, Michael McKean, Saul Rubinek, Viveka Davis

'An insultingly trivial star vehicle.' – *Variety*

'Unredeemedly awful.' – *Philip French, Observer*

The Man Upstairs *

GB 1958 88m bw

British Lion/ACT (Robert Dunbar)

A mild-mannered lodger becomes violent, injures a policeman, and barricades himself in his room.

Character melodrama reminiscent of both Fourteen Hours *and* Le Jour se Lève, *but not so interesting as either.*

w Alun Falconer *d* Don Chaffey *ph* Gerald Gibbs

☆ Richard Attenborough, Bernard Lee, Donald Houston, Dorothy Alison, Maureen Connell, Kenneth Griffith, Virginia Maskell, Patricia Jessel

The Man Who Broke the Bank at Monte Carlo *

US 1935 67m bw

Twentieth Century (Nunnally Johnson)

A Russian émigré becomes a taxi driver, wins a fortune at roulette, loses it all again, and returns happily to his cab.

Very mild, unconvincing and not very entertaining malarkey which rested squarely on its star, who carried it with aplomb.

w Nunnally Johnson *d* Stephen Roberts *ph* Ernest Palmer *md* Oliver Bradley

☆ Ronald Colman, Joan Bennett, Colin Clive, Nigel Bruce, Montagu Love, Frank Reicher, Ferdinand Gottschalk

'Nice production though lacks dash ... Colman at times seems to be playing under wraps. Should do fairly well.' – *Variety*

'The richest roles of romance and redemption they ever played!'

The Man Who Came Back

US 1930 74m bw

Fox

A reckless young man is reformed when he finds his erstwhile sweetheart now a drug addict in Hong Kong.

Earnest melodrama which not surprisingly damaged the talkie success of a celebrated screen team, and must now seem risible in the extreme.

w Edwin J. Burke *play* Jules Eckert Goodman *story and novel* John Fleming Wilson *d* Raoul Walsh *ph* Arthur Edeson *pd* Joseph Urban

☆ Janet Gaynor, Charles Farrell, Kenneth MacKenna, William Holden, Mary Forbes, Peter Gawthorne

'Gripping old melodrama of drugs and degradation tamed down and made into a cheerful sentimental piece. Co-star names make it a strong bid.' – *Variety*

'Sophisticates will give it one big horse laugh.' – *Photoplay*

The Man Who Came Back: see *Swamp Water* (1941)

The Man Who Came to Dinner ***

US 1941 112m bw

Warner (Jack Saper, Jerry Wald)

An acid-tongued radio celebrity breaks his hip while on a lecture tour, and terrorizes the inhabitants of the suburban home where he must stay for several weeks.

Delightfully malicious caricature of Alexander Woollcott which, though virtually confined to one set, moves so fast that one barely notices the lack of cinematic variety, and certainly provides more than a laugh a minute, especially for those old enough to understand all the references.

w Julius J. and Philip G. Epstein *play George S. Kaufman, Moss Hart d* William Keighley *ph* Tony Gaudio *m* Frederick Hollander

☆ *Monty Woolley* (Sheridan Whiteside), *Bette Davis* (Maggie Cutler), Ann Sheridan (Lorraine Sheldon), *Jimmy Durante* (Banjo (spoofing Harpo Marx)), *Reginald Gardiner* (Beverly Carlton (spoofing Noël Coward)), Richard Travis (Bert Jefferson), *Billie Burke* (Mrs Stanley), *Grant Mitchell* (Ernest Stanley), *Ruth Vivian*, *Mary Wickes*, George Barbier, Elisabeth Fraser

WHITESIDE (MONTY WOOLLEY) TO HIS NURSE, WHO WON'T LET HIM EAT CHOCOLATES: 'I had an aunt who ate a box of chocolates every day of her life. She lived to be a hundred and two, and when she had been dead three days, she looked healthier than you do now!'

NURSE (MARY WICKES): 'I am not only walking out on this case, Mr Whiteside, I am leaving the nursing profession. I became a nurse because all my life, ever since I was a little girl, I was filled with the idea of serving a suffering humanity. After one month with you, Mr Whiteside, I am going to work in a munitions factory. From now on, anything I can do to help exterminate the human race will fill me with the greatest of pleasure. If Florence Nightingale had ever nursed YOU, Mr Whiteside, she would have married Jack the Ripper instead of founding the Red Cross!'

WHITESIDE (INTRODUCING HIS SECRETARY): 'This ageing debutante, Mr Jefferson, I retain in my employ only because she is the sole support of her two-headed brother.'

BANJO (JIMMY DURANTE): 'Did you ever get the feeling that you wanted to stay, and still get the feeling that you wanted to go?'

BEVERLY CARLTON (REGINALD GARDINER IMPERSONATING NOËL COWARD): 'Don't tell me how you are, Sherry, I want none of the tiresome details. I've very little time, and so the conversation will be entirely about me, and I shall love it. Shall I tell you how I glittered through the South Seas like a silver scimitar, or would you rather hear how I finished a three-act play with one hand and made love to a maharaja's daughter with the other?'

† The inspiration for the play came after Alexander Woollcott had stayed with Moss Hart and, on leaving, had written in Hart's guest book, 'This is to certify that I had one of the most unpleasant times I ever spent.'

The Man Who Changed His Mind

GB 1936 66m bw

Gainsborough

US title: *The Man Who Lived Again*

A scientist dabbles in brain transplants.

Mild British-style horror piece; not a success.

w John L. Balderston, L. DuGarde Peach and Sidney Gilliat *d* Robert Stevenson

☆ Boris Karloff, Anna Lee, Donald Calthrop, John Loder, Frank Cellier, Cecil Parker

'A spine-freezer of routine construction. The accents are very limey and the way laboratory is pronounced may have American schoolchildren wondering.' – *Variety*

The Man Who Changed His Name

GB 1934 80m bw

Universal/Twickenham (Julius Hagen)

A wife begins to suspect that her husband is trying to murder her and her former lover.

Tepid comedy thriller that betrays its stage origins and is not helped by being somnambulistically acted and directed.

w H. Fowler Mear, Edgar Wallace *play* Edgar Wallace *d* Henry Edwards *ph* Sydney Blythe *md* W. L. Trytel *ad* James A. Carter *ed* Jack Harris, Michael C. Chorlton

☆ Lyn Harding, Betty Stockfeld, Leslie Perrins, Ben Welden, Aubrey Mather, Stanley Vine

The Man Who Cheated Himself

US 1950 81m bw

TCF (Jack M. Warner)

A woman shoots her husband and her homicide detective lover covers up for her.

Efficient crime melodrama.
w Seton I. Miller, Philip MacDonald *d* Felix Feist *ph* Russell Harlan *m* Louis Forbes
☆ Lee J. Cobb, Jane Wyatt, John Dall, Terry Frost

The Man Who Could Cheat Death
GB 1959 83m Technicolor
Paramount/Hammer (Anthony Nelson-Keys)
A surgeon looks 35 but is really 104, having had a series of gland operations performed on himself.
Vulgar, gory, gruesomely coloured Hammer version of a rather attractive play, previously filmed under its original title The Man in Half Moon Street *(qv). The shocks are routine, and entertainment value is minimal.*
w Jimmy Sangster *play* Barrie Lyndon *d* Terence Fisher *ph* Jack Asher *m* Richard Rodney Bennett
☆ Anton Diffring, Hazel Court, Christopher Lee, Arnold Marle, Delphi Lawrence, Francis de Wolff

The Man Who Could Work Miracles ***
GB 1936 82m bw
London (Alexander Korda)
A city clerk discovers he has the power to work miracles (given him by sportive gods) and nearly causes the end of the Earth.
Slow-moving but rather pleasing variation on a simple theme.
w Lajos Biro *story* H. G. Wells *d* Lothar Mendes *ph* Harold Rosson *m* Mischa Spoliansky
☆ *Roland Young*, Ralph Richardson, Ernest Thesiger, Edward Chapman, Joan Gardner, Sophie Stewart, Robert Cochran, George Zucco, Lawrence Hanray, George Sanders
'Supposedly a comedy. A weakling: little draw power on this side.' – *Variety*
'Sometimes fake poetry, sometimes unsuccessful comedy, sometimes farce, sometimes sociological discussion, without a spark of creative talent or a trace of film ability.' – *Graham Greene*

The Man Who Couldn't Get Enough: see *Confessions of a Sex Maniac*

The Man Who Cried *
GB/France/US 2000 100m colour
Universal/StudioCanal/Working Title/Adventure (Christopher Sheppard)
A Jewish woman, brought up in England, goes to Europe and America in search of her lost father and her religious identity.
A romantic melodrama with exuberant musical accompaniment, ravishingly photographed.
wd Sally Potter *ph* Sacha Vierny *m* Osvaldo Golijov *pd* Carlos Conti *ed* Hervé Schneid *cos* Lindy Hemming
☆ Christina Ricci (Suzie), Cate Blanchett (Lola), John Turturro (Dante Dominio), Johnny Depp (Cesar), Harry Dean Stanton (Felix Perlman), Claudia Lander-Duke (Young Suzie), Oleg Yankovsky (Father)
'A trite sob story.' – *Sunday Times*
'An aloof and uninvolving bore.' – *Damon Wise, Total Film*

The Man Who Cried Wolf
US 1937 67m bw
Universal
An actor continually confesses to crimes he didn't commit in the hope that when he does commit one he won't be believed.
An attractive idea rather poorly handled.
w Charles Grayson, Sy Bartlett *d* Lewis R. Foster
☆ Lewis Stone, Tom Brown, Barbara Read, Marjorie Main, Forrester Harvey
'Will get by as the number two feature on dual bills.' – *Variety*

The Man Who Dared
US 1933 72m bw
Fox
The life of a local politician, based on Mayor Cermak of Chicago.
Episodic but not unpleasant biopic; it adds up to very little, though.
w Dudley Nichols, Lamar Trotti *d* Hamilton McFadden
☆ Preston Foster, Zita Johann, Joan Marsh, Irene Biller, Leon Waycoff
'The most flattering account ever written of any man's life ... but as a commercial talker it's not likely to get very far. Even in Chicago they didn't care for it.' – *Variety*

The Man Who Fell to Earth *
GB 1976 138m colour Panavision
British Lion (Michael Deeley, Barry Spikings)
A visitor from another planet tries to colonize Earth, but his powers are destroyed and he ends an alcoholic cripple.
A weird piece of intellectual science fiction made weirder by longueurs of all varieties: obscure narrative, voyeuristic sex, pop music and metaphysics. Not an easy film or a likeable one, despite its great technical skill.
w Paul Mayersberg *novel* Walter Tevis *d* Nicolas Roeg *ph* Anthony Richmond *md* John Phillips
☆ David Bowie, Rip Torn, Candy Clark, Buck Henry
'Once you have pierced through its glittering veneer, you find only another glittering veneer underneath.' – *Michael Billington, Illustrated London News*
'There is a punch line, but it takes forever, and great expectations slump away.' – *Charles Champlin, L.A. News*
'You feel finally that all that has been achieved has been to impose an aura of mystery and enigma where essentially there is none; to turn a simple tale into the sort of accumulation of sensations that has become fashionable.' – *David Robinson, The Times*

The Man Who Finally Died
GB 1962 100m bw Cinemascope
British Lion/Magna/White Cross (Norman Williams)
A German-born Englishman returns to Bavaria for news of his father, and becomes involved in a spy plot.
Busy adaptation of a TV serial with a convoluted plot which might have been more pacily developed and better explained.
w Lewis Greifer, Louis Marks *d* Quentin Lawrence *ph* Stephen Dade *m* Philip Green
☆ Stanley Baker, Peter Cushing, Mai Zetterling, Eric Portman, Niall MacGinnis, Nigel Green, Barbara Everest, Harold Scott

The Man Who Found Himself
US 1937 67m bw
RKO (Cliff Reid)
A nurse helps a downcast doctor face his problems and renew his enthusiasm for life.
Simple-minded programmer.
w J. Robert Bren, Edmund Hartmann, G. V. Atwater *d* Lew Landers *ph* Roy Hunt
☆ John Beal, Joan Fontaine, Philip Huston, Jane Walsh, George Irving
'No names in this hokey B session ... flapdoodle with a capital F.' – *Variety*

The Man Who Had His Hair Cut Short *
Belgium 1966 94m bw
Belgian Cultural Ministry
A frustrated law clerk has an aberration after attending an autopsy and meeting again an old love.
Pessimistic case history with unpleasant details often brilliantly recorded.
w Anna de Pagter, André Delvaux *d* André Delvaux *ph* Ghislain Cloquet *m* Freddy Devreese
☆ Seene Rouffaer, Beata Tyszkiewicz, Hector Camerlynck

The Man Who Had Power over Women
GB 1970 89m Eastmancolor
Avco/Kettledrum
A successful public relations man comes to hate himself, his job and what it has done to his marriage.
Fashionable wallow in guilt and luxury, not very convincingly done.
w Allan Scott, Chris Bryant *novel* Gordon Williams *d* John Krish *ph* Gerry Turpin *m* Johnny Mandel
☆ Rod Taylor, Carol White, James Booth, Penelope Horner, Charles Korvin, Alexandra Stewart, Keith Barron

The Man Who Haunted Himself
GB 1970 94m Technicolor
ABP/Excalibur (Michael Relph)
After recovering from a road accident, a staid businessman finds that he has an evil doppelganger who steals his wife and his job.
Mildly effective if inexplicable story idea which served more suitably as a Hitchcock TV half hour and here, despite adequate production, outstays its welcome.
w Basil Dearden, Michael Relph *story* The Case of Mr Pelham by Anthony Armstrong *d* Basil Dearden *ph* Tony Spratling *m* Michael Lewis
☆ Roger Moore, Hildegarde Neil, Olga-Georges Picot, Anton Rodgers, Freddie Jones, Thorley Walters, John Carson, John Welsh

The Man Who Knew Too Little *
US 1997 94m Technicolor
Warner/Regency/Taurus (Arnon Milchan, Michael Nathanson, Mark Tarlov)
A holidaying American is mistaken for a hired killer.
Pleasant, undistinguished comedy that pokes fun at the sort of identity mix-up that Hitchcock used to better effect.
w Robert Farrar, Howard Franklin *novel* Watch That Man by Robert Farrar *d* Jon Amiel *ph* Robert Stevens *m* Chris Young *pd* Jim Clay *ed* Pamela Power, Paul Karasick
☆ Bill Murray, Peter Gallagher, Joanne Whalley, Alfred Molina, Richard Wilson, Geraldine James, John Standing, Anna Chancellor, Nicholas Woodeson
'Scores a reasonable number of laughs, but its ultimate impact is pretty mild.' – *Variety*

The Man Who Knew Too Much ***
GB 1934 84m bw
GFD/Gaumont British (Ivor Montagu)
A child is kidnapped by spies to ensure her father's silence, but he springs into action.
Splendid early Hitchcock which after a faded start moves into memorable sequences involving a dentist, an East End mission and the Albert Hall. All very stagey by today's standards, but much more fun than the expensive remake.
w A. R. Rawlinson, Charles Bennett, D. B. Wyndham Lewis, Edwin Greenwood, Emlyn Williams *d Alfred Hitchcock ph* Curt Courant *m* Arthur Benjamin
☆ *Leslie Banks*, Edna Best, *Peter Lorre*, Nova Pilbeam, Frank Vosper, Hugh Wakefield, Pierre Fresnay
'A natural and easy production that runs smoothly and has the hallmark of sincerity.' – *Variety*
'The film's mainstay is its refined sense of the incongruous.' – *Peter John Dyer, 1964*

'A single clash of cymbals that will rock the lives of an American family!'
The Man Who Knew Too Much *
US 1956 120m Technicolor Vistavision
(Paramount)
Flaccid remake of the above, twice as long and half as entertaining, though it does improve after a very slow start.
w John Michael Hayes, Angus MacPhail *d* Alfred Hitchcock *ph* Robert Burks *m* Bernard Herrmann
☆ James Stewart, Doris Day, Bernard Miles, Brenda de Banzie, Daniel Gelin, Ralph Truman, Mogens Wieth, Alan Mowbray, Hillary Brooke
'The balance between character and incident in the earlier film makes a far better thriller.' – *Observer*
'The remake is heavy and oppressive, the suspense often risible, and the moments of comic relief fall flat.' – *Sunday Times*
'Let's say the first version is the work of a talented amateur and the second was made by a professional.' – *Alfred Hitchcock*
song 'Que Sera Sera' (m/ly Jay Livingston, Ray Evans)

The Man Who Lived Again: see *The Man Who Changed His Mind*

The Man Who Lived Twice
US 1936 73m bw
Columbia (Ben Pivar)
An eminent doctor is unaware that he was formerly a criminal who was cured by a brain operation that also removed his memory; but his past begins to catch up with him.
Daft melodrama, acted with far more intensity than it deserves; there's a little pleasure to be gained from watching Bellamy play a disfigured murderer on the run before reverting to his more familiar blandness.
w Tom Van Dycke, Arthur Strawn, Fred Niblo Jnr *d* Harry Lachman *ph* James Van Trees *ed* Byron Robinson
☆ Ralph Bellamy, Marian Marsh, Thurston Hall, Isabel Jewell, Nana Bryant, Ward Bond, Henry Kolker, Willard Robertson
† It was remade in 1953 as *Man in the Dark* (qv).

The Man Who Lost Himself
US 1941 71m bw
Universal
A man back from the tropics finds himself playing the part of a lookalike millionaire.
Pleasantly nimble farce; not original but agreeable to watch.
w Eddie Moran *novel* H. DeVere Stacpoole *d* Edward Ludwig *ph* Victor Milner *ed* Milton Carruth
☆ Brian Aherne, Kay Francis, S. Z. Sakall, Henry Stephenson, Nils Asther, Sig Rumann

The Man Who Loved Cat Dancing
US 1973 114m Metrocolor Panavision
MGM (Martin Poll, Eleanor Perry)
A runaway wife is kidnapped by train thieves and comes to love one of them.
Outdoor variation on No Orchids for Miss Blandish, *remarkably lacking in any kind of entertainment value.*
w Eleanor Perry *novel* Marilyn Dunham *d* Richard Sarafian *ph* Harry Stradling Jnr *m* John Williams
☆ Sarah Miles, Burt Reynolds, Lee J. Cobb, Jack Warden, George Hamilton, Bo Hopkins, Robert Donner, Jay Silverheels
'Any number of things have gone wrong with this peculiarly dreary western.' – *Tom Milne*
'Sarah Miles undergoes more perils than Pauline.' – *Variety*

The Man Who Loved Redheads
GB 1954 90m Eastmancolor
British Lion/London Films (Josef Somlo)
Throughout his career, a diplomat seeks women who resemble the redhead with whom in youth he had had an idyllic affair.
West End theatrical moonshine, poorly filmed in ugly colour but saved by the cast.
w Terence Rattigan *play* Who Is Sylvia? by Terence Rattigan *d* Harold French *ph* Georges Périnal *m* Benjamin Frankel
☆ John Justin, Moira Shearer, *Roland Culver*, Gladys Cooper, Denholm Elliott, Harry Andrews, Patricia Cutts, Moyra Fraser, *Joan Benham*, Jeremy Spenser

'Deciding which woman in the world he loved most is driving him out of his mind!'
The Man Who Loved Women
France 1977 119m Eastmancolor
Les Films du Carrosse/PAA (Marcel Bebert)
A man spends his life in pursuit of women and dies in the chase.
Sour comedy which doesn't quite come off.
w François Truffaut, Michel Fermaud, Suzanne Schiffman *d* François Truffaut *ph* Nestor Almendros *m* Maurice Jaubert
☆ Charles Denner, Brigitte Fossey, Leslie Caron, Nelly Borgeaud, Nathalie Baye
'Doesn't just miss: it has virtually nothing.' – *Stanley Kauffmann*

The Man Who Loved Women
US 1983 110m Metrocolor
Columbia/Delphi/Blake Edwards (Blake Edwards, Tony Adams)
An American remake of the above, with even less success.
w Blake Edwards, Milton Wexler, Geoffrey Edwards *d* Blake Edwards *ph* Haskell Wexler *m* Henry Mancini
☆ Burt Reynolds, Julie Andrews, Kim Basinger, Marilu Henner, Cynthia Sikes, Jennifer Edwards

'The strangest story in the annals of naval espionage!'

The Man Who Never Was **

GB 1955 102m DeLuxe Cinemascope

Sumar/André Hakim

In 1943, the British secret service confuses the Germans by dropping a dead man into the sea with false documents.

Mainly enjoyable true life war story marred by an emotional romantic sub-plot with a double twist but helped by an equally fictitious spy hunt which cheers up the last half hour.

w Nigel Balchin *book* Ewen Montagu *d* Ronald Neame *ph* Oswald Morris *m* Alan Rawsthorne

☆ *Clifton Webb, Robert Flemyng*, Gloria Grahame, *Stephen Boyd*, Laurence Naismith, Josephine Griffin

Nigel Balchin

The Man Who Played God *

US 1932 81m bw

Warner

GB title: *The Silent Voice*

A musician goes deaf but finds satisfaction in helping a young student.

Stagey but effective star vehicle which Arliss also played as a silent film. Remade as Sincerely Yours *(qv).*

w Julien Josephson, Maude Howell *play The Silent Voice* by Jules Eckert Goodman *d* John G. Adolfi *ph* James Van Trees

☆ *George Arliss*, Violet Heming, Ivan Simpson, *Bette Davis*, Louise Closser Hale, Donald Cook, Ray Milland

'Will need all the Arliss name strength to pull average returns.' – *Variety*

The Man Who Reclaimed His Head *

US 1934 81m bw

Universal (Henry Henigson)

A writer who feels he has been betrayed and his brain sapped by his publisher takes a gruesome revenge.

Oddball period melodrama tailored rather unsuccessfully for a new star. Remade as Strange Confession *(see* Inner Sanctum*).*

w Jean Bart, Samuel Ornitz *play* Jean Bart *d* Edward Ludwig *ph* Merritt Gerstad *m* Heinz Roemheld

☆ *Claude Rains*, Joan Bennett, Lionel Atwill, Juanita Quigley, Henry O'Neill, Lawrence Grant

'Interesting screen diversion ... Far from a smash, but good enough to keep to the average level or above.' – *Variety*

The Man Who Shot Liberty Valance ***

US 1962 122m bw

Paramount/John Ford (Willis Goldbeck)

A tenderfoot becomes a hero for shooting a bad man, but the shot was really fired by his friend and protector.

Clumsy, obvious Western with the director over-indulging himself but providing some good scenes in comedy vein.

w James Warner Bellah, Willis Goldbeck *d* John Ford *ph* William H. Clothier *m* Cyril Mockridge

☆ James Stewart, John Wayne, Vera Miles, Lee Marvin, Edmond O'Brien, Andy Devine, Jeanette Nolan, John Qualen, Ken Murray, Woody Strode, Lee Van Cleef, Strother Martin, John Carradine

FAMOUS LINE: 'When truth becomes legend, print the legend.'

'Like Queen Victoria, John Wayne has become lovable because he stayed in the saddle into a new era.' – *Judith Crist*

'A heavy-spirited piece of nostalgia.' – *Pauline Kael, 1975*

'A film whose fascination lies less in what it is itself than in what it reveals about the art of its maker.' – *William S. Pechter*

The Man Who Talked Too Much

US 1940 75m bw

Warner (Edmund Grainger)

A smart defence attorney gets the goods on a gangster and decides to turn him in.

Below-par remake of The Mouthpiece *(qv), later filmed again as* Illegal *(qv).*

w Walter de Leon, Tom Reed *play The Mouthpiece* by Frank J. Collins *d* Vincent Sherman *ph* Sid Hickox

☆ George Brent, Brenda Marshall, Richard Barthelmess, Virginia Bruce, William Lundigan, John Litel, George Tobias, Henry Armetta, Alan Baxter

'Human or inhuman, no woman is safe!'

The Man Who Turned to Stone

US 1957 71m bw

Clover/Columbia

A girls' reformatory is taken over by a group of zombie scientists born in the 18th century.

Cheap horror item with a few choice moments for connoisseurs of the absurd.

w Raymond T. Marcus (Bernard Gordon) *d* Leslie Kardos *ph* Benjamin Kline

☆ Victor Jory, Ann Doran, Charlotte Austin, William Hudson, Paul Cavanagh

† Screenwriter Gordon wrote under a pseudonym because he was blacklisted at the time.

The Man Who Understood Women

US 1959 105m Eastmancolor

Cinemascope

TCF (Nunnally Johnson)

An arrogant, exhibitionist film producer finally alienates his long-suffering wife.

Something of an aberration, with good scenes submerged in an unholy mixture of sharp comedy and sentimental melodrama.

wd Nunnally Johnson *novel Colours of the Day* by Romain Gary *ph* Milton Krasner *m* Robert Emmett Dolan

☆ Henry Fonda, Leslie Caron, Myron McCormick, Cesare Danova, Marcel Dalio, Conrad Nagel, Harry Ellerbe

'A pretentious extravaganza on a romantic theme.' – *MFB*

'The Last Thing On His Mind Is Murder.'

The Man Who Wasn't There ***

US 2001 116m DeLuxe/bw

Entertainment/USA/Working Title/Gramercy (Ethan Coen)

In the late 1940s, an insignificant, small-town barber turned blackmailer finds himself in a situation he cannot control.

Stylish, stylized, highly polished, and leisurely thriller in the tradition of film noir, in which the guilty are undone by their own failures of character; it is impeccably written, photographed and acted.

w *Joel Coen, Ethan Coen d Joel Coen ph Roger Deakins m* Carter Burwell *pd* Dennis Gassner *ed* Roderick Jaynes, Tricia Cooke *cos* Mary Zophres

☆ *Billy Bob Thornton* (Ed Crane), Frances McDormand (Doris Crane), Michael Badalucco (Frank), James Gandolfini (Big Dave), Katherine Borowitz (Ann Nirdlinger), Jon Polito (Creighton Tolliver), Scarlett Johansson (Birdy Abundas), Richard Jenkins (Walter Abundas), Tony Shalhoub (Freddy Riedenschneider), Adam Alexi-Malle (Carcanogues)

'Steadily engrossing and devilishly funny, and, oh brother, does it look sharp.' – *Peter Travers, Rolling Stone*

'A work of finely fabricated art. For much of its length it gives enormous pleasure of a kind that comes from observing events interlocking inexorably.' – *Alexander Walker, London Evening Standard*

Roger Deakins

Roger Deakins

The Man Who Watched Trains Go By

GB 1952 80m Technicolor

Raymond Stross

aka: *Paris Express*

A clerk steals money in order to fulfil his wish of world travel, and this leads to murder.

Miscast minor Simenon, not exactly badly made but with no spark of excitement or suspense.

wd Harold French *novel* Georges Simenon *ph* Otto Heller *m* Benjamin Frankel

☆ Claude Rains, Marius Goring, Marta Toren, Anouk Aimée, Herbert Lom, Ferdy Mayne

The Man Who Would Be King *

US 1975 129m colour Panavision

Columbia/Allied Artists/Persky-Bright/Devon (John Foreman)

In India in the 1880s, two adventurers find themselves accepted as kings by a remote tribe, but greed betrays them.

After an ingratiating start this ambitious fable becomes more predictable, and comedy gives way to unpleasantness. Despite its sporadic high quality, one does not remember it with enthusiasm.

w John Huston, Gladys Hill *story* Rudyard Kipling *d* John Huston *ph* Oswald Morris *m* Maurice Jarre *pd* Alexander Trauner *ed* Russell Lloyd

☆ Sean Connery (Daniel Dravot), Michael Caine (Peachy Carnehan), Christopher Plummer (Rudyard Kipling), Saeed Jaffrey (Billy Fish), Jack May (District Commissioner), Shakira Caine

'Huston has now made a good picture – not up to the standard of his early best but with sweep and guts and with nicely overblown cinematic eloquence.' – *Stanley Kauffmann*

John Huston, Gladys Hill (script); Alexander Trauner

The Man Who Wouldn't Talk

US 1940 72m bw

Sol M. Wurtzel/TCF

A man on trial for murder has such a mysterious background that he may even be the victim.

Efficient remake of Paul Muni's The Valiant.

w Robert Ellis, Helen Logan, Lester Ziffren and Edward Ettinger *d* David Burton

☆ Lloyd Nolan, Jean Rogers, Richard Clarke, Eric Blore, Mae Marsh

The Man Who Wouldn't Talk

GB 1957 97m bw

British Lion/Everest (Herbert Wilcox)

A lady QC gets an acquittal for a man who can't defend himself on a murder charge because of loyalty to a scientist on the run.

Efficient courtroom melodrama based on a somewhat incredible and even uninteresting situation.

w Edgar Lustgarten *story* Stanley Jackson *d Herbert Wilcox ph Gordon Dines m* Stanley Black

☆ Anna Neagle, Anthony Quayle, Zsa Zsa Gabor, Katherine Kath, Dora Bryan, Patrick Allen

The Man with a Cloak *

US 1951 81m bw

MGM (Stephen Ames)

In 1848 New York, a mysterious stranger (who turns out to be Edgar Allan Poe) helps a young French girl to keep her inheritance.

Curious domestic melodrama set on MGM's choicest sets; its playful literary allusion causes it to fall between suspense thriller and character drama, but the acting keeps one watching.

w Frank Fenton *story* John Dickson Carr *d Fletcher Markle ph George Folsey m* David Raksin

☆ Joseph Cotten, Barbara Stanwyck, Leslie Caron, Louis Calhern, Joe de Santis, Jim Backus, Margaret Wycherly

The Man with a Hundred Faces: see *Crackerjack*

Man with a Million: see *The Million Pound Note*

The Man with an Umbrella: see *It Rains on Our Love*

The Man with Bogart's Face

US 1980 106m CFI color

TCF/Melvin Simon (Andrew J. Fenady)

An unremarkable private eye gets lots of assignments because he looks like Humphrey Bogart.

Amiably nostalgic romp, not too spoofy to be enjoyable for its own sake, but notably underproduced.

w Andrew J. Fenady *novel* Andrew J. Fenady *d* Robert Day *ph* Richard C. Glouner *m* George Duning

☆ Robert Sacchi, Misty Rowe, Michelle Phillips, Franco Nero, Olivia Hussey, Victor Buono, Herbert Lom, George Raft, Yvonne de Carlo, Jay Robinson, Mike Mazurki, Henry Wilcoxon, Victor Sen Yung

The Man with My Face

US 1951 77m bw

UA/Edward F. Gardner

A successful young man finds a double in his place at both home and office, and himself branded as an impostor.

Intriguing yarn which deserved a better production.

w Samuel W. Taylor, Edward J. Montagne, T. J. McGowan and Vincent Bogart *novel* Samuel W. Taylor *d* Edward J. Montagne

☆ Barry Nelson, Lynn Ainley, John Harvey, Carole Mathews, Jack Warden

The Man with Nine Lives *

US 1940 73m bw

Columbia

GB title: *Behind the Door*

A scientist believes he can cure cancer by freezing, but accidentally locks himself and his patients in an underground ice chamber for seven years, and goes berserk when thawed out.

Interesting, rather prophetic science fiction thriller which rather lacks the style required to put it over.

w *Karl Brown story* Harold Shumate *d* Nick Grinde *ph* Benjamin Kline

☆ *Boris Karloff*, Byron Foulger, Roger Pryor, Jo Ann Sayers

The Man with One Red Shoe

US 1985 93m colour

TCF (Victor Drai)

A violinist wearing odd shoes is mistaken for a spy and becomes a pawn in a battle being waged by rival factions for control of the CIA.

Farcical comedy that rarely achieves the right tempo or timing for its occasional jokes.

w Robert Klane *d* Stan Dragoti *ph* Richard H. Kline *m* Thomas Newman *pd* Dean E. Mitzner *ed* Bud Molin, O. Nicholas Brown

☆ Tom Hanks, Dabney Coleman, Lori Singer, Charles Durning, Jim Belushi, Carrie Fisher, Ed Herrmann, Irving Metzman, Tom Noonan, David Ogden Stiers

† It was a remake of the French film *Le Grand Blond avec une Chaussure Noire* (qv), written by Francis Veber and Yves Robert.

The Man with the Deadly Lens: see *Wrong Is Right*

The Man with the Golden Arm *

US 1956 119m bw

Otto Preminger

A Chicago poker dealer finally kicks the drug habit.

Sensational on its first release, with its cold turkey scenes, this now seems a muddled impressionist melodrama with echoes of the silent German cinema and much over-acting and miscasting all round. But Sinatra is good; and it is different...

w Walter Newman, Lewis Meltzer *novel* Nelson Algren *d* Otto Preminger *ph Sam Leavitt m Elmer Bernstein pd* Joe Wright *titles Saul Bass*

☆ *Frank Sinatra*, Kim Novak, Eleanor Parker, Darren McGavin, Arnold Stang, Robert Strauss, John Conte, Doro Merande, George E. Stone

'Nothing very surprising or exciting ... a pretty plain and unimaginative look-see at a lower depths character.' – *Bosley Crowther*

'A very inferior film ... the script is inexcusably clumsy, the sets are unbelievable and the casting is ridiculous.' – *Diana Willing, Films in Review*

'It has the same running time as Citizen Kane but it seems a whole lot longer.' – *Robert James*

Elmer Bernstein; Frank Sinatra; art direction

The Man with the Golden Gun *

GB 1974 125m Eastmancolor

UA/Eon (Harry Saltzman, Albert R. Broccoli)

James Bond goes to the Far East to liquidate a professional assassin named Scaramanga.

Thin and obvious Bond extravaganza with conventional expensive excitements.

w Richard Maibaum, Tom Mankiewicz *novel* Ian Fleming *d* Guy Hamilton *ph* Ted Moore, Oswald Morris *m* John Barry *pd* Peter Murton

☆ Roger Moore, Christopher Lee, Britt Ekland, Maud Adams, Hervé Villechaize, Clifton James, Richard Loo, Marc Lawrence

'The script lacks satiric insolence and the picture grinds on humourlessly.' – *New Yorker*

The Man with the Green Carnation: see *The Trials of Oscar Wilde*

Man with the Gun *
US 1955 83m bw
UA/Samuel Goldwyn Jnr
aka: *Deadly Peacemaker*
A gunfighter is hired to clean up a town overrun by hired guns.
A well-made Western, tough, grim and suspenseful.
w N. B. Stone Jnr, Richard Wilson *d* Richard Wilson *ph* Lee Garmes *m* Alex North *ad* Hilyard Brown *ed* Gene Milford
☆ Robert Mitchum, Jan Sterling, Karen Sharpe, Henry Hull, Emile Meyer, John Lupton, Barbara Lawrence, Ted DeCorsia, Leo Gordon, James Westerfield

The Man with the Movie Camera **
USSR 1928 60m approx bw silent
VUFKU
original title: *Chelovek sKinoapparatom*
A 'camera eye' documentary without any plot, showing, through a succession of street and interior scenes, all the tricks of which the instrument is capable; it takes a bow at the end.
Unique documentary which was understandably a sensation when it first appeared but now often seems merely quaint.
ph Mikhail Kaufman wd/ed Dziga Vertov
† A special edition DVD was released in 2002 with a new score composed by Michael Nyman.

The Man with Thirty Sons: see *The Magnificent Yankee*

The Man with Two Brains
US 1983 93m colour
Warner/Aspen (David V. Picker, William E. McEuen)
A surgeon, trapped in a frustrating marriage, falls in love with a brain in a jar.
Offbeat, broad comedy that is never as funny as it promises to be.
w Carl Reiner, Steve Martin, George Gipe *d* Carl Reiner *ph* Michael Chapman *m* Joel Goldsmith *ad* Polly Platt *ed* Bud Molin
☆ Steve Martin (Dr Michael Hfuhruhurr), Kathleen Turner (Dolores Benedict), David Warner (Dr Necessiter), Paul Benedict (Butler), Richard Brestoff (Dr Pasteur), James Cromwell (Realtor), Sissy Spacek (Brain's voice)
'Indefensible by any known standard of comedy form – or formlessness. It's not much of anything, but it moves along enjoyably.' – *Pauline Kael, New Yorker*

The Man with Two Faces *
US 1934 72m bw
Warner
An actor takes revenge on a scoundrel who had preyed on his sister.
Pleasing melodrama hinging on disguise; the Hays Office surprisingly allowed the hero to get away with it.
w Tom Reed, Niven Busch *play* The Dark Tower by George S. Kaufman, Alexander Woollcott *d* Archie Mayo *ph* Tony Gaudio
☆ *Edward G. Robinson*, Mary Astor, Ricardo Cortez, Louis Calhern, Mae Clarke, John Eldredge
'Fair fodder, but undistinguished in the main, and in spots very confusing.' – *Variety*

The Man with X-Ray Eyes: see *X–The Man with X-Ray Eyes*

The Man Within *
GB 1947 88m Technicolor
GFD/Production Film Service (Muriel and Sydney Box)
US title: *The Smugglers*
An orphan boy discovers that his mysterious new guardian is a smuggler.
Unconvincing period yarn which has managed to drain every vestige of subtlety from the novel, but at least looks good.
w Muriel and Sydney Box *novel* Graham Greene *d* Bernard Knowles *ph* Geoffrey Unsworth *m* Clifton Parker *md* Muir Mathieson *ad* Andrew Mazzei *ed* Alfred Roome *cos* Elizabeth Haffenden
☆ Michael Redgrave (Carlyon), Richard Attenborough (Andrews), Jean Kent (Lucy), Joan Greenwood (Elizabeth), Francis L. Sullivan (Mr Braddock), Felix Aylmer (Priest), Ronald Shiner (Cockney Harry), Basil Sydney (Sir Henry Merriman), Ernest Thesiger (Farne)
'With more style this might have been rather good. Outside of life more private than I am normally party to I can't recall hearing so many men so often say, to other men, I hate him! or I hate you!' – *James Agee*

The Man without a Body
GB 1957 80m bw
Eros/Filmplays (Guido Coen)
A tycoon with a brain tumour steals the head of Nostradamus and has it kept alive to replace his own.
Hilarious horror comic, inept in every department.
w William Grote *d* W. Lee Wilder, Charles Saunders *ph* Brendan J. Stafford *m* Albert Elms
☆ George Coulouris, Robert Hutton, Nadja Regin, Julia Arnall

The Man without a Face
US 1993 115m Technicolor
Entertainment/Icon (Bruce Davey)
A boy remembers how he was helped to enter a military academy by a disfigured former teacher who had become an outcast in the community.
A well-meaning but rather dull movie that makes heavy weather of a not very affecting drama.
w Malcolm MacRury *novel* Isabelle Holland *d* Mel Gibson *ph* Donald M. McAlpine *m* James Horner *pd* Barbara Dunphy *ed* Tony Gibbs
☆ Mel Gibson, Margaret Whitton, Fay Masterson, Gaby Hoffman, Geoffrey Lewis, Richard Masur, Nick Stahl, Viva
'The overall effect is sincere, sentimental and slightly uneasy.' – *Philip French, Observer*
'A contrived story, overloaded with pop psychology, that would never reach the big screen unless a major star insisted. As director, Mel Gibson proves no visual stylist.' – *Geoff Brown, The Times*

The Man Without a Past **
Finland/Germany/France 2002 97m colour
ICA/Sputnik Oy/Pandora/Pyramide (Aki Kaurismaki)
original title: *Mies Vailla Menneisyytta*
A man wakes up in a Helsinki hospital with amnesia and goes to live with the poor in a shanty town while he tries to rebuild his life.
Gentle humane comedy, full of keen observation and enjoyment of human foibles.
wd Aki Kaurismaki *ph* Timo Salminen *pd* Markku Patila, Jukka Salmi *ed* Timo Linnasalo
☆ Markku Peltola (M), Kati Outinen (Irma), Juhani Niemela (Nieminen), Kaija Pakarinen (Kaisa Nieminen), Sakari Kuosmanen (Anttila)
'Droll, reticent, flawlessly filmed fable of generosity.' – *Richard Corliss, Time*

Man without a Star *
US 1955 89m Technicolor
U-I (Aaron Rosenberg)
A wandering cowboy helps settlers to put up barbed wire against an owner of vast cattle herds.
Conventional but entertaining star Western.
w Borden Chase, D. D. Beauchamp *novel* Dee Linford *d* King Vidor *ph* Russell Metty *m* Hans Salter
☆ Kirk Douglas, Jeanne Crain, Claire Trevor, William Campbell, Jay C. Flippen, Mara Corday, Richard Boone
† Remade for TV as A Man Called Gannon.

Man, Woman and Child
US 1982 100m DeLuxe
Gaylord
A married professor discovers that he has a son by his only infidelity.
Angst among the well-to-do, from the author of Love Story.
w Erich Segal, David Zelag Goodman *novel* Erich Segal *d* Dick Richards *ph* Richard H. Kline *m* Georges Delerue
☆ Martin Sheen, Blythe Danner, Craig T. Nelson, David Hemmings, Nathalie Nell

Man, Woman and Sin
US 1927 85m approx (24 fps) bw silent
MGM
A reporter has an affair with his boss's mistress.
Glossy romantic drama marking the first screen appearance of a sensational stage star; her effect on screen was more muted.
w Alice Duer Miller *d* Monta Bell
☆ Jeanne Eagels, John Gilbert, Marc McDermott

Manbait: see *The Last Page*

The Manchurian Candidate ****
US 1962 126m bw
UA/MC (Howard W. Koch)
A Korean war 'hero' comes back a brainwashed zombie triggered to kill a liberal politician, his control being his own monstrously ambitious mother.
Insanely plotted but brilliantly handled spy thriller, a mixture of Hitchcock, Welles and All the King's Men.
w George Axelrod novel Richard Condon *d John Frankenheimer ph Lionel Lindon m* David Amram *pd Richard Sylbert*
☆ Frank Sinatra, Laurence Harvey, Janet Leigh, James Gregory, Angela Lansbury, Henry Silva, John McGiver
'The unAmerican film of the year.' – *Penelope Houston*
'An intelligent, funny, superbly written, beautifully played, and brilliantly directed study of the all-embracing fantasy in everyday social, emotional and political existence.' – *Philip Strick, 1973*
'Although it's a thriller, it may be the most sophisticated political satire ever to come out of Hollywood.' – *Pauline Kael, 70s*
Angela Lansbury

Mandalay
US 1934 65m bw
Warner
A lady of the tropics murders her lover and pushes his body through a porthole.
Steamy melodrama which the masses found absorbing.
w Austin Parker, Charles Kenyon *d* Michael Curtiz
☆ Kay Francis, Ricardo Cortez, Lyle Talbot, Ruth Donnelly, Shirley Temple, Warner Oland, Lucien Littlefield, Reginald Owen

Mandela *
US 1996 123m colour
Nubian Tales/Island/Clinica Estetico (Jonathan Demme, Edward Saxon, Jo Menell)
Documentary on the life of Nelson Mandela, from childhood through his involvement with the ANC, imprisonment for more than two decades and final triumph as president of a democratic South Africa.
Great subject, but a dull documentary, perhaps circumscribed by including a long interview with Mandela himself, which is often used as a commentary on the images; his need not to inflame those who opposed him for so long leads to blandness.
d Jo Menell, Angus Gibson *ph* Dewald Aukema, Peter Tischhauser *m* Cedric Gradus Samson, Hugh Masekela *ed* Andy Keir
'Very much the authorised biography ... The film-makers should still have tried harder to humanise him and the great struggle he led by opening up the complexities rather than closing down into pat clichés.' – *Kevin Macdonald, Sight and Sound*
documentary

Manden I Manen: see *The Dark Side of the Moon*

Mandingo
US 1975 126m Technicolor
Dino de Laurentiis (Peter Herald)
On a slave-breeding plantation in 1840 Louisiana, passions ride high.
Like Gone with the Wind *with all the characters on heat, this exuberant and unpleasant melodrama goes several points over the top from start to finish but proved to have wide appeal for the groundlings, in the* Tobacco Road *tradition of a wallow in other people's depravities.*
w Norman Wexler *play* Jack Kirkland *novel* Kyle Onstott *d* Richard Fleischer *ph* Richard H. Kline *m* Maurice Jarre *pd* Boris Leven
☆ James Mason, Susan George, Perry King, Richard Ward, Brenda Sykes, Ken Norton

Mandrake the Magician
US 1939 bw
Columbia
A world-famous magician trails an underworld leader called The Wasp.
Rather stylish serial exploits with the added effect of illusions.
d Sam Nelson, Norman Denning
☆ Warren Hull, Doris Weston, Al Kikume, Rex Downing, Don Beddoe
† Serial in 12 episodes.

'She'll find a home in every heart! She'll reach the heart of every home!'
Mandy ***
GB 1952 93m bw
Ealing (Leslie Norman)
US title: *The Crash of Silence*
A little girl, born deaf, is sent to a special school.
Carefully wrought and very sympathetic little semi-documentary film in which all the adults underplay in concession to a new child star who alas did not last long at the top.
w Nigel Balchin, Jack Whittingham *novel* This Day Is Ours by Hilda Lewis *d Alexander Mackendrick ph* Douglas Slocombe *m* William Alwyn
☆ *Jack Hawkins*, Terence Morgan, Phyllis Calvert, Mandy Miller, Godfrey Tearle, Dorothy Alison
'An extremely touching film, in spite of occasional obviousness in a plot never dull, and in spite of its subject never saccharine.' – *Dilys Powell*

Maneater of Kumaon
US 1948 78m bw
Monty Shaff-Frank Rosenberg/Universal
A doctor in the Himalayas helps track down a man-eating tiger.
Slightly unusual adventure story based on a currently popular book.
w Jeanne Bartlett and Lewis Meltzer *book* Jim Corbett *d* Byron Haskin
☆ Sabu, Wendell Corey, Joanne Page, Morris Carnovsky

Manèges *
France 1950 90m bw
Films Modernes-Discina (Emil Natan)
GB title: *The Wanton*
A scheming girl marries the middle-aged owner of a riding school and, with her greedy mother, milks him of his money.
A neat little melodrama with flashbacks so arranged that the girl, paralysed in an accident, seems for the first half to have an angelic character.
w Jacques Sigurd *d* Yves Allégret *ph* Jean Bourgoin
☆ *Simone Signoret*, Bernard Blier, *Frank Villard*, Jane Marken

The Mangler
US 1995 106m Technicolor
Guild/Distant Horizon/Allied/Anant Singh
After human blood falls on an industrial steam-iron at a laundry, it turns into a killer machine.
Ludicrous and stupid horror movie, full of gore but sadly lacking in any sense or the ability to scare.
w Tobe Hooper, Stephen Brooks, Peter Welbeck (Harry Alan Towers) *story* Stephen King *d* Tobe Hooper *ph* Amnon Salomon *m* Barrington Pheloung *pd* David Barkham *ed* David Heitner
☆ Robert Englund, Ted Levine, Daniel Matmor, Jeremy Crutchley, Vanessa Pike, Demetre Phillips, Lisa Morris
'Lackluster story and thesping should guarantee the would-be frightfest a short spin and quick fade at the box office.' – *Variety*

Manhandled
US 1949 97m bw
Paramount/Pine-Thomas
The secretary of a bogus psychiatrist becomes involved in a murder and finds herself in danger from all comers.
Modest, overlong suspenser with adequate production values.
w Lewis R. Foster, Whitman Chambers *novel The Man Who Stole a Dream* by L. S. Goldsmith *d* Lewis R. Foster *ph* Ernest Laszlo *m* David Chudnow
☆ Dorothy Lamour, Dan Duryea, Sterling Hayden, Irene Hervey, Harold Vermilyea, Philip Reed, Alan Napier, Art Smith, Irving Bacon

Manhattan ****
US 1979 96m bw Panavision
UA/Jack Rollins/Charles H. Joffe
Episodes in the sex life of a TV comedy writer with an obsession about New York.
As close to a summation of Woody Allen's views and oeuvre as anybody needs; some smart jabs about the lives we lead are sometimes bogged down in earnestness and half-comic despair.
w Woody Allen, Marshall Brickman *d* Woody Allen *ph* Gordon Willis *md* Tom Pierson
☆ Woody Allen, Diane Keaton, Meryl Streep, Mariel Hemingway, Michael Murphy
'Given that the identity of his films has increasingly been determined by his compulsion to talk about the things he finds important, but also by his fear of having them come out as anything but a joke, it is not surprising that he has scarcely been able to decide on a form for his "art": from the anything-for-a-laugh skittering of his early films, to the broad parodies and pastiches of his middle period, to the recent confessional/psychoanalytical mode.' – *Richard Combs, MFB*
'A masterpiece that has become a film for the ages by not seeking to be a film of the moment.' – *Andrew Sarris*
script; Mariel Hemingway
best picture

Manhattan Madness: see *Adventure in Manhattan*

Manhattan Melodrama **
US 1934 93m bw
MGM (David O. Selznick)
Two slum boys grow up friends, one as district attorney and the other as a gangster.
Archetypal American situation drama (cf Angels with Dirty Faces, Cry of the City, *etc), with the bad guy inevitably indulging in self-sacrifice at the end. An all-star cast makes it palatable in this case, though the film is inevitably dated.*
w Oliver H. P. Garrett, Joseph L. Mankiewicz *story* Arthur Caesar *d* W. S. Van Dyke *ph* James Wong Howe *m* William Axt
☆ William Powell, Clark Gable, Myrna Loy, Leo Carrillo, Nat Pendleton, George Sidney, Isabel Jewell, Thomas E. Jackson
'Action meller of the big town … replete with punchy, popularly-appealing ingredients.' – *Variety*
† *Manhattan Melodrama* gained some irrelevant fame as the movie John Dillinger was watching before he was cornered and shot.
Arthur Caesar

Manhattan Merry-go-round *
US 1937 82m bw
Republic
A sound recording studio is taken over by a band of racketeers.
Sufficient comedy plot to sustain a revue of historical interest.
w Harry Sauber, Frank Hummert *d* Charles F. Reisner *ad* Victor MacKay
☆ Phil Regan, Leo Carrillo, Ann Dvorak, Tamara Geva, James Gleason, Ted Lewis and his Orchestra, Cab Calloway and his Orchestra, the Kay Thompson Ensemble, Louis Prima and his Band, Gene Autry, Joe Di Maggio
'So much talent and novelty has been compressed within the limits of the film that customers dare not sneeze for fear of missing something … for the territorial distributors and independent theatres it is something to get excited about.' – *Variety*
Victor MacKay

Manhattan Murder Mystery *
US 1993 105m Technicolor
TriStar (Robert Greenhut)
A husband becomes concerned when his wife decides that the woman who lives next door has been murdered.
Amiable comedy whodunnit that jogs along nicely without arriving anywhere that is particularly interesting.
w Woody Allen, Marshall Brickman *d* Woody Allen *ph* Carlo Di Palma *pd* Santo Loquasto *ed* Susan E. Morse
☆ Woody Allen, Alan Alda, Anjelica Huston, Diane Keaton, Jerry Adler, Joy Behar, Ron Rifkin, Lynn Cohen, Melanie Norris
'Light, insubstantial and utterly devoid of the heavier themes Allen has grappled with in most of his recent outings, this confection keeps the chuckles coming and is mainstream enough in sensibility to be a modest success.' – *Variety*
'God, it's good to get a film which gives you only fun to worry about.' – *Alexander Walker*

Manhattan Parade
US 1931 77m Technicolor
Warner
Behind the scenes as a theatrical costumier tries to get into the revue business.
Aimless backstage comedy with turns.
w Robert Lord and Houston Branch *play* Sam Shipman *d* Lloyd Bacon
☆ Smith and Dale, Winnie Lightner, Charles Butterworth, Walter Miller, Luis Alberni
'A few laughs dot the scenery, and they're all this musical possesses in value.' – *Variety*

The Manhattan Project
US 1986 117m Technicolor
Cannon/Gladden (Jennifer Ogden, Marshall Brickman)
aka: *Deadly Game*
A clever student steals plutonium from a weapons laboratory and builds his own nuclear bomb; when the authorities track him down, he threatens to explode it.
Efficiently made but very silly thriller, a piece of teenage wish fulfilment.
w Marshall Brickman, Thomas Baum *d* Marshall Brickman *ph* Billy Williams *m* Philippe Sarde *pd* Philip Rosenberg *ed* Nina Feinberg
☆ John Lithgow, Christopher Collet, Cynthia Nixon, Jill Eikenberry, John Mahoney, Robert Sean Leonard

Manhunt: see *From Hell to Texas*

'Enter the mind of a serial killer… you may never come back.'
Manhunter **
US 1986 120m Technicolor Panavision
Recorded Releasing/Red Dragon/De Laurentiis Entertainment (Richard Roth)
An FBI agent with an ability to think like a killer tracks down a serial murderer.
Slick and glossy thriller, enjoyable enough if you can accept its premise.
novel Red Dragon by Thomas Harris *ph* Dante Spinotti *m* Michael Rubini, The Reds *pd* Mel Bourne *ed* Dov Hoenig *wd/p* Michael Mann
☆ William L. Petersen, Kim Greist, Joan Allen, Brian Cox, Dennis Farina, Stephen Lang, Tom Noonan, David Seaman, Benjamin Hendrickson
† It was remade in 2002 as *Red Dragon*, directed by Brett Ratner.

Le Mani sulla Città: see *Hands over the City*

Maniac
GB 1963 86m bw Hammerscope
Columbia/Hammer (Jimmy Sangster)
Murders by oxyacetylene torch in the Camargue, with the wrong lunatic going to the asylum.
Hammer's mark two plot, the shuddery murder mystery in which someone is not quite what he seems; feebly done in this case, with a fatally slow start.
w Jimmy Sangster *d* Michael Carreras *ph* Wilkie Cooper
☆ Kerwin Mathews, Donald Houston, Nadia Gray, Justine Lord

Maniac Cop
US 1988 85m colour
Medusa/Shapiro Glickenhaus Entertainment (Larry Cohen)
A former cop turns killer in New York.
Excessively violent thriller that is too implausible to be enjoyable.
w Larry Cohen *d* William Lustig *ph* Vincent J. Rabe *m* Jay Chataway *ad* Jonathan Hodges, Ann Cudworth *ed* David Kern
☆ Tom Atkins, Bruce Campbell, Laurene Landon, Richard Roundtree, William Smith, Robert Z'Dar, Sheree North

Maniac Cop 2
US 1990 88m Foto-Kem Panavision
Medusa/Movie House Sale/Fadd Enterprises (David Hodgins, Frank D'Alessio)
A murderous and deranged former policeman teams up with a mass murderer to terrorize New York.
Limply directed sequel that offers nothing new, but just increases the body count.
w Larry Cohen *d* William Lustig *ph* James Lemmo *m* Jay Chattaway *pd* Gene Abel, Charles Logola *ed* David Kern
☆ Robert Davi, Claudia Christian, Michael Lerner, Bruce Campbell, Laurene Landon, Robert Z'Dar, Clarence Williams III, Leo Rossi

'The Wrong Arm Of The Law Is Back.'
Maniac Cop 3: Badge of Silence
US 1992 81m Foto-Kem
Neo/First Look (Larry Cohen)
Resurrected by occult methods, a dead cop acts as a vigilante to protect the reputation of a policewoman, shot during a hold-up and accused of killing an innocent hostage.
An action adventure rather than a horror movie, with the maniac cop remaining a shadowy figure; it avoids predictability, has an inventive car chase and manages a moderate amount of suspense.
w Larry Cohen *d* William Lustig *ph* Jacques Haitkin *m* Joel Goldsmith *pd* Clark Hunter *ed* David Kern, Michael Eliot
☆ Robert Davi, Caitlin Dulany, Gretchen Becker, Paul Gleason, Jackie Earle Haley, Julius Harris, Grand Bush, Doug Savant, Robert Z'Dar
'A promising exploitation sequel, laced with Cohen's dark humour, which collapses in its final act into a series of dull stunts.' – *Sight and Sound*

Maniacs on Wheels: see *Once a Jolly Swagman*

Manifesto
US 1988 94m colour
Cannon/Menahem Golan, Yoram Globus
video title: *A Night of Love*
In an Eastern European village in the 1920s, a lecherous secret policeman waylays revolutionaries before a visit by a king.
Sex-obsessed black comedy that muffs its climaxes.
wd Dusan Makavejev *story* For a Night of Love by Emile Zola *ph* Tomislav Pinter *m* Nicola Piovani *pd* Velijo Despotovic *ed* Tony Lawson
☆ Alfred Molina, Camilla Soeberg, Simon Callow, Lindsay Duncan, Eric Stoltz, Rade Serbedzija, Chris Haywood, Linda Marlowe, Ronald Lacey

Manila Calling
US 1942 82m bw
TCF/Sol M. Wurtzel
Americans in the Philippines try to install a short-wave radio transmitter before the Japs take over.
Acceptable thick ear with professional trimmings.
w John Larkin *d* Herbert I. Leeds
☆ Lloyd Nolan, Carole Landis, Cornel Wilde, James Gleason, Martin Kosleck, Ralph Byrd

Manipulation *
GB 1991 5m colour
Tandem
A cartoon character tries to assert his independence from the artist who drew him.
A clever, if somewhat sterile, exercise in animation.
d Daniel Greaves *ed* Rod Howick
animated short

The Manitou
US 1978 104m CFI color Panavision
Herman Weist/Melvin Simon (William Girdler)
A fake spiritualist finds his girlfriend is possessed by the demon of a 400-year-old Indian.
Boring retread of The Exorcist.
w William Girdler, Jon Cedar, Tom Pope *novel* Graham Masterton *d* William Girdler *ph* Michel Hugo *m* Lalo Schifrin
☆ Tony Curtis, Susan Strasberg, Michael Ansara, Stella Stevens, Jon Cedar, Ann Sothern, Burgess Meredith, Paul Mantee

Mannen pò Taket: see *The Man on the Roof*

Mannequin
US 1937 95m bw
MGM (Joseph L. Mankiewicz)
The wife of a small-time crook gets a modelling job and falls for a shipping magnate.
Competent star melodrama about a working girl's harassments.
w Lawrence Hazard *d* Frank Borzage *ph* George Folsey *m* Edward Ward
☆ Joan Crawford, Spencer Tracy, Alan Curtis, Ralph Morgan, Mary Philips, Elizabeth Risdon, Leo Gorcey
'A star vehicle in which the star is so solemnly noble that you want to strangle her.' – *New Yorker*
song 'Always and Always' (*m* Edward Ward, *ly* Chet Forrest, Bob Wright)

Mannequin
US 1987 89m DuArt
TCF/Gladden (Art Levinson)
A window dresser falls in love with a mannequin who changes into a real live girl.
Feeble and never less than idiotic fantasy.
w Edward Rugoff, Michael Gottlieb *d* Michael Gottlieb *ph* Tim Suhrstedt *m* Sylvester Levay *pd* Josan Russo *ed* Richard Halsey, Frank Jiminez
☆ Andrew McCarthy (Joanthan Switcher), Kim Cattrall (Emmy), Estelle Getty (Claire Timkin), James Spader (Richards), G. W. Bailey (Felix), Carole Davis (Roxie), Stephen Vinovich (B. J. West), Christopher Maher (Armand), Meshach Taylor (Hollywood)
song 'Nothing's Gonna Stop Us Now' (*Albert Hammond, Diane Warren*)

Mannequin Two: On the Move
US 1991 95m colour
Rank/Gladden (Edward Rugoff)
A window dresser discovers that a mannequin holds the imprisoned spirit of a bewitched peasant girl.
Even less enjoyable than the original, if that's possible.
w Edward Rugoff, David Isaacs, Ken Levine, Betty Israel *d* Stewart Raffill *ph* Larry Pizer *m* David McHugh *ad* Norman B. Dodge Jnr *ed* Joan Chapman
☆ Kristy Swanson, William Ragsdale, Meshach Taylor, Terry Kizer, Stuart Pankin, Cynthia Harris, Andrew Hill Newman
'If this stiff ever shows any life, it will be a wonder indeed.' – *Variety*
'A messy rehash of clichés and tired jokes.' – *Empire*

Männer…: see *Men…*

Mano dello Straniero: see *The Stranger's Hand*

Manon *
France 1949 96m bw
Alcina (P. E. Decharme)
After the liberation, a girl who has been a collaborator becomes involved in the black market, passes from man to man, and ends up being shot by Arabs in the Sahara desert.
Oddball modernized version of Manon Lescaut, *with post-war pessimism and the glamour of sin going hand in hand. Worth comparing with* Gilda.
w Henri-Georges Clouzot, J. Ferry *novel* L'Abbé Prévost *d* Henri-Georges Clouzot *ph* Armand Thirard *m* Paul Misraki
☆ Michel Auclair, Cécile Aubry, Serge Reggiani, Gabrielle Dorziat
'A clever idea, handled cleverly, but without depth of feeling.' – *Penelope Houston*
'Though I have been going to the pictures since I wore rompers, I do not recall a more horrible film.' – *Leonard Mosley*

Manon des Sources
France 1952 190m bw
Films Marcel Pagnol
A Provençal girl who lives in the hills with her goats is thought to be a witch, and takes her revenge on the populace by stopping the water supply.
Insanely long idyll of the countryside with the writer-director unintentionally caricaturing himself.
wd Marcel Pagnol *ph* Willy *m* Raymond Legrand
☆ Jacqueline Pagnol, Raymond Péllégrin, Henri Vibert
'Something of an endurance test for all but the most enthusiastic Pagnol admirers.' – *John Gillett, MFB*
† Pagnol later expanded the story into two novels which were the basis for a two-part film, *Jean de Florette* (qv) and *Manon des Sources* (1986) (qv).

Manon des Sources ***
France 1986 114m colour Technovision
Renn Productions/A2/RAI 2/DD Productions (Roland Thenot)
A young girl avenges the wrong done to her father by a farmer and his nephew.
Absorbing drama of rural life, impeccably performed and directed.
w Claude Berri, Gérard Brach *novel* Marcel Pagnol *d* *Claude Berri* *ph* *Bruno Nuytten* *m* Jean-Claude Petit *pd* Bernard Vizat *ed* Geneviève Louveau, Hervé de Luze
☆ *Yves Montand, Daniel Auteuil, Emmanuelle Béart,* Hippolyte Girardot, Margarita Lozano, Gabriel Bacquier

Manpower *
US 1941 103m bw
Warner (Mark Hellinger)
Power linesmen fall out over a night-club hostess.
Yet another variation on Tiger Shark, *with vivid fisticuff and storm sequences supporting the star performers.*
w Richard Macaulay, Jerry Wald *d* Raoul Walsh *ph* Ernest Haller *m* Adolph Deutsch
☆ Edward G. Robinson, George Raft, Marlene Dietrich, Alan Hale, Frank McHugh, Eve Arden, Barton MacLane, Walter Catlett, Joyce Compton, Ward Bond
'The pace and cutting are those of the best gangster films ... the climax outdoes anything the Lyceum may have known.' – *William Whitebait*

Man's Best Friend
US 1993 87m DeLuxe
Guild/New Line/Roven-Cavello (Bob Engelman)
A reporter releases from an experimental laboratory a genetically altered dog that combines size and intelligence with the ability of a chameleon and the instincts of a killer.
A moderately entertaining, but gory, thriller that at least provides a welcome antidote to the Beethoven *series.*
wd John Lafia *ph* Mark Irwin *m* Joel Goldsmith *pd* Jaymes Hinkle *ed* Michael N. Knue *sp* Kevin Yagher
☆ Ally Sheedy, Lance Henriksen, Robert Constanzo, Frederic Lehne, John Cassini, J. D. Daniels, William Sanderson
'Combines increasingly gory black-comic bits ... with a plethora of gimmicks. The mixture is far from boring, but it coarsens the comedy about the hidden life of dogs.' – *Michael Sragow, New Yorker*
'How we all laughed at this movie's awful lines and clichéd plot contrivances, down to the closing, sequel-bound litter of pyscho puppies.' – *Sheila Johnston, Independent*

Man's Castle *
US 1933 70m bw
Columbia (Frank Borzage)
Romance blooms among the unemployed who live in a shanty town on the banks of the East River.
Depression moonshine which at the time was taken for realism; sociologically very interesting but very faded as entertainment.
w Jo Swerling *play* Lawrence Hazard *d* Frank Borzage *ph* Joseph August *m* W. Franke Harling
☆ Spencer Tracy, Loretta Young, Glenda Farrell, Walter Connolly, Arthur Hohl, Marjorie Rambeau, Dickie Moore
'A picture that goes contrary to normal entertainment appetites and tastes, its possibilities of going places look slender at best.' – *Variety*
'Heavily sentimental yet magically romantic.' – *New Yorker, 1977*

Man's Favorite Sport? *
US 1963 120m Technicolor
Universal/Gibraltar/Laurel (Howard Hawks)
A star salesman of fishing tackle finds his bluff called when he has to enter a fishing competition.
Over-extended romantic farce drawn by the director from memories of older and better films, such as Libeled Lady *and his own* Bringing Up Baby.
w John Fenton Murray, Steve McNeil *story* The Girl Who Almost Got Away by Pat Frank
d Howard Hawks *ph* Russell Harlan *m* Henry Mancini *ad* Alexander Golitzen, Tambi Larsen *ed* Stuart Gilmore *cos* Edith Head
☆ Rock Hudson (Roger Willoughby), Paula Prentiss (Abigail Page), Maria Perschy (Isolde Mueller), Charlene Holt (Tex Connors), John McGiver (William Cadwalader), Roscoe Karns (Major Phipps)
'Hawks' deadpan documentation of a physical gag is as effective as ever, but the overall pace of his direction is curiously contemplative, as though he were savoring all his past jokes for the last time.' – *Andrew Sarris*
† Leigh Brackett worked uncredited on the script, and also did rewrites during production.

Man's Hope: see *Espoir*

'Discover The Year's Most Passionate Film!'
'Jane Austen's Wicked Comedy.'
Mansfield Park *
GB/US 1999 112m DeLuxe
Buena Vista/Miramax HAL/BBC (Sarah Curtis)
A poor young girl goes to live with her wealthy relations and falls in love with her cousin.
Fanny Price, Austin's timid, neurasthenic heroine is here transformed into a forceful writer (based on Rozema's view of Jane Austen herself); other alterations include shifting the action back in time to make points about the slave trade. More seriously, other changes mean that Fanny is no longer the moral centre of the action, so that the point of the novel is lost.
wd Patricia Rozema *novel, letters and early journals* Jane Austen *ph* Michael Coulter *m* Lesley Barber *pd* Christopher Hobbs *ed* Martin Walsh *cos* Andrea Galer
☆ Embeth Davidtz (Mary Crawford), Jonny Lee Miller (Edmund Bertram), Alessandro Nivola (Henry Crawford), Frances O'Connor (Fanny Price), Harold Pinter (Sir Thomas Bertram), Lindsay Duncan (Lady Bertram/ Mrs Price), Sheila Gish (Mrs Norris), James Purefoy (Tom Bertram), Hugh Bonneville (Mr Rushworth), Justine Waddell (Julia Bertram), Victoria Hamilton (Maria Bertram), Sophia Myles (Susan), Hilton McRae (Mr Price), Hannah Taylor Gordon (Young Fanny), Charles Edwards (Yates)
'Rozema can't seem to hold a single tone for more than a few minutes, and she has too many other axes to grind besides just getting the story up on the screen.' – *Derek Elley, Variety*
'Seldom has a film played quite so fast and loose with an enduring literary work in the dubious cause of seeming "accessible" and "relevant".' – *Angie Errigo, Empire*

Manslaughter *
US 1922 80m approx (24 fps) bw silent
Paramount/Famous Players (Cecil B. de Mille)
An idle rich girl accidentally kills a man while driving, and is sent to prison, but falls for the district attorney who convicted her.
De Mille was here testing out his Ten Commandments *format, with a long flashback during the DA's speech to the idle rich of ancient Rome. It worked like a charm at the box-office.*
w Jeanie Macpherson *novel* Alice Duer Miller *d* Cecil B. de Mille *ph* Alvin Wyckoff
☆ Leatrice Joy, Thomas Meighan, Lois Wilson, John Miltern
† A 1930 sound remake for Paramount was directed by George Abbott, who also tried in vain to modernize the screenplay (by omitting the flashback). Claudette Colbert and Fredric March starred.

The Mantrap
US 1943 57m bw
Republic (George Sherman)
A retired Scotland Yard man helps the DA's office in a murder case.
Entertaining second feature with a geriatric hero; alas, the clues don't play quite fair.
w Curt Siodmak *d* George Sherman
☆ Henry Stephenson, Lloyd Corrigan, Joseph Allen Jnr, Dorothy Lovett

Mantrap
US 1961 93m bw Panavision
Paramount/Tiger (Edmond O'Brien, Stanley Frazen)
An honest man is lured by an old Marine friend into a hi-jack attempt which leads to the death of his wife.
Rather uninteresting melodrama, played and directed for more than it's worth.
w Ed Waters *novel* *Taint of the Tiger* by John D. Macdonald *d* Edmond O'Brien *ph* Loyal Griggs *m* Leith Stevens
☆ Jeffrey Hunter, David Janssen, Stella Stevens, Hugh Sanders

Manuela *
GB 1957 95m bw
British Lion/Ivan Foxwell
US title: *Stowaway Girl*
In a South American port, the engineer of a tramp steamer smuggles aboard a half caste girl, but it is the disillusioned captain who falls in love with her.
Downbeat seafaring melodrama, fine for those seeking a mood piece.
w William Woods *novel* William Woods *d* Guy Hamilton *ph* Otto Heller *m* William Alwyn
☆ Trevor Howard, Elsa Martinelli, Pedro Armendariz, Donald Pleasence

The Manxman
GB 1929 90m (24 fps) bw silent
British International (John Maxwell)
A fisherman thought drowned comes back to find that his girl is expecting his best friend's baby.
Stern romantic melodrama of virtually no interest despite its director.
w Eliot Stannard *novel* Hall Caine *d* Alfred Hitchcock *ph* Jack Cox
☆ Carl Brisson, Malcolm Keen, Anny Ondra, Randle Ayrton, Clare Greet
† Previously filmed in 1916 with Henry Ainley and Elizabeth Risdon.

Many Happy Returns
US 1934 62m bw
Paramount
A scatty girl jinxes her father's department store and a Hollywood studio.
Silly comedy with stops for vaudeville.
w J. P. McEvoy, Claude Binyon, Keene Thompson, Ray Harris *story* Lady Mary Cameron(!) *d* Norman Z. McLeod
☆ George Burns, Gracie Allen, Guy Lombardo and his Band, Veloz and Yolanda, Ray Milland, George Barbier, Joan Marsh, Franklin Pangborn, William Demarest, Larry Adler
'Often very funny, at other moments it lags.' – *Variety*

Many Rivers to Cross *
US 1955 94m Eastmancolor Cinemascope
MGM (Jack Cummings)
A trapper bound for Canada is helped by a sharp-shooting girl, and in return he saves her from marauding Indians.
Simple-minded, cheerful, quite refreshing Western compounded of equal parts comedy and action.
w Harry Brown, Guy Trosper *d* Roy Rowland *ph* John Seitz *m* Cyril Mockridge
☆ Robert Taylor, Eleanor Parker, Victor McLaglen, Josephine Hutchinson, Jeff Richards, Russ Tamblyn, James Arness, Alan Hale Jnr

'From a Kingdom of Ice to a Land of Fire ... A Love That Knows No Boundaries.'
Map of the Human Heart *
GB/Australia 1992 109m colour Panavision
Rank/Working Title/Map/Sunrise/Polygram/AFFC/Vincent Ward
An elderly Eskimo recalls to a surveyor the events of his life: how he helped map his remote part of the Arctic as a boy, was sent to Canada to cure his tuberculosis, served in the RAF and loved and lost a girl he met in hospital and later in England.
An ambitious, sprawling and flawed film that attempts to take in too much, in time and emotion – with a 'feel-good' ending that seems out of place with the tragic story that has gone before.
w Louis Nowra *story* Vincent Ward *d* Vincent Ward *ph* Eduardo Serra *m* Gabriel Yared *pd* John Beard *ed* John Scott, Frans Vandenburg
☆ Patrick Bergin, Anne Parillaud, Jason Scott Lee, John Cusack, Jeanne Moreau
'What we learn about the human heart remains a matter of guesswork, but as a map the film certainly offers some eye-catching perspectives.' – *Philip Strick, Sight and Sound*
'A true one-off, this is a poignant, thoughtfully drawn map of love, death and life.' – *Angie Errigo, Empire*
† The film was cut from 126m after it was shown at the Cannes Film Festival, and had an extra day's shooting in London to add scenes with Lee and Parillaud. The ending was also recut to give it a more upbeat feeling.

'A story about the amazing places life can take you.'
A Map of the World
US 1999 125m DeLuxe
Overseas (Kathleen Kennedy, Frank Marshall)
A farmer's wife discovers that speaking her mind causes her trouble and the possibility of a prison sentence.
Moderately intriguing drama of a woman in the wrong place and time, though it is too manipulative for its own good.
w Peter Hedges, Polly Platt *novel* Jane Hamilton *d* Scott Elliott *ph* Seamus McGarvey *m* Pat Metheny *pd* Richard Toyon *ed* Craig McKay, Naomi Geraghty *cos* Suzette Daigle
☆ Sigourney Weaver (Alice Goodwin), Julianne Moore (Theresa Collins), David Strathairn (Howard Goodwin), Ron Lea (Dan Collins), Arliss Howard (Paul Reverdy), Chloe Sevigny (Carole Mackessy), Louise Fletcher (Nellie), Dara Perlmutter (Emma), Kayla Perlmutter (Claire), Marc Donato (Robbie)
'An accomplished film that continually takes us beyond our first impressions of people and situations.' – *Kevin Thomas, Los Angeles Times*
'A soggy number, largely about child-rearing and its travails. It never really focuses.' – *Stanley Kaufmann, New Republic*

Mapantsula *
South Africa 1988 104m Agfacolor
Electric/One Look Productions/David Hannay Productions/Haverbeam (Max Montocchio)
A petty criminal in Soweto stands firm against police oppression.
Lively look at the underside of life in a black township, but lacking in depth.
w Oliver Schmitz, Thomas Mogotlane *d* Oliver Schmitz *ph* Rod Stewart *m* The Ouens *ad* Robin Hofmeyr *ed* Mike Baard
☆ Thomas Mogotlane, Thembi Mtshali, Peter Sephuma, Marcel Van Heerden, Eugene Majola, Dolly Rathebe, Darlington Michaels

El Mar *
Spain 1999 113m colour
Peccadillo/Massa d'Or/Paulo Branco/Isona Passola (Paulo Branco, Lluis Ferrando, Isona Passola)
aka: *The Sea*
In 1946, two men and a nurse, who witnessed two traumatic deaths during the Spanish Civil War, meet again in a tuberculosis sanitorium.
Overheated, claustrophic melodrama of repressed and violent love.
w Antonio Aloy, Biel Mesquida, Agustín Villaronga *d* Agustín Villaronga *ph* Jaime Peracaula *m* Javier Navarrete *ad* Francesc Candini *ed* Raul Roman
☆ Roger Casamajor (Ramallo), Bruno Bergonzini (Manuel Tur), Antonia Torrens (Francisca), Hernan Gonzalez (Galindo), Juli Mira (Eugeni Morell), Simon Andreu (Alcantara), Angela Molina (Carmen)
'Mixing religion, death and sex in just about equal proportions, this brooding item is probably too dark and bleak for most tastes.' – *David Stratton, Variety*

Mara Maru
US 1952 98m bw
Warner (David Weisbart)
A Manila salvage expert locates a sunken treasure and defeats crooks who are also in pursuit of it.
Lethargic but pleasant-looking star vehicle with a plot borrowed from The Maltese Falcon.
w N. Richard Nash, Philip Yordan, Sidney Harmon, Hollister Noble *d* Gordon Douglas *ph* *Robert Burks* *m* Max Steiner
☆ Errol Flynn, Ruth Roman, Raymond Burr, Paul Picerni, Richard Webb

Maracaibo
US 1958 88m Technicolor Vistavision
Paramount/Theodora (Cornel Wilde)
A Texan oil fire expert finds himself unexpectedly busy when on holiday in Venezuela.
Meandering action melodrama with too much local colour.
w Ted Sherdeman *novel* Stirling Silliphant *d* Cornel Wilde *ph* Ellsworth Fredericks *m* Laurindo Almeida
☆ Cornel Wilde, Jean Wallace, Abbe Lane, Francis Lederer, Joe E. Ross, Michael Landon

The Marat/Sade *
GB 1966 116m DeLuxe
UA/Marat Sade (Michael Birkett)
aka: *The Persecution and Assassination of Jean-Paul Marat as performed by the inmates of the Asylum of Charenton under the direction of the Marquis de Sade*
The title tells all, except that at the end the inmates go berserk.
Fairly plain filming of an Old Vic succès d'estime which it became fashionable to announce that one had seen and understood. The film makes no effort to attract the unbeliever.
w Adrian Mitchell *play* Peter Weiss *d* Peter Brook *ph* David Watkin *m* Richard Peaslee
☆ Glenda Jackson, Patrick Magee, Ian Richardson, Michael Williams, Robert Lloyd, Clifford Rose, Freddie Jones
'I loathed and detested doing the play. I couldn't wait for it to end. Then we all did the film and it was a shattering experience. People twitching, slobber running down their chins, everyone screaming from nerves and exhaustion.' – *Glenda Jackson*

Marathon Man ***
US 1976 126m Metrocolor
Paramount (Robert Evans, Sidney Beckerman)
A vicious Nazi returns from Uruguay to New York in search of diamonds which had been kept for him by his now-dead brother, and is outwitted by the young brother of an American agent he has killed.
Complex mystery thriller which seems to have things to mutter about freedom and McCarthyism and Nazism, but finally settles down to being a simple shocker with a nick-of-time climax. The presentation is dazzling.
w William Goldman *novel* William Goldman *d* *John Schlesinger* *ph* *Conrad Hall* *m* Michael Small *pd* Richard MacDonald
☆ Dustin Hoffman, *Laurence Olivier*, Roy Scheider, William Devane, Marthe Keller, Fritz Weaver, Marc Lawrence
'A film of such rich texture and density in its construction, so fascinatingly complex in its unfolding, so engrossing in its personalities, and so powerful in its performance and pace that the seduction of the senses has physical force.' – *Judith Crist, Saturday Review*
'Fashionably violent ... distinctly self-conscious ... conventionally moralistic ... and absolutely devoid of resonance.' – *Tom Milne, MFB*
'If at the film's end, you have followed the series of double and triple crosses, braved the torture scenes, and still don't know what it was about, you're bound to have company.' – *Paul Coleman, Film Information*
'A Jewish revenge fantasy.' – *Pauline Kael*
'He has made a most elegant, bizarre, rococo melodrama out of material which, when you think about it, makes hardly any sense at all.' – *Vincent Canby, New York Times*
Laurence Olivier

The Marauders
US 1955 81m Eastmancolor
MGM (Arthur M. Loew Jnr)
A rancher hires gunmen to drive away squatters, but the gunmen kill him and take over.
Slightly sinister Western with a plot probably worth trying again.
w Jack Leonard, Earl Fenton *novel* Alan Marcus *d* Gerald Mayer *ph* Harold Marzorati *m* Paul Sawtell
☆ Dan Duryea, Jeff Richards, Keenan Wynn, Jarma Lewis, Harry Shannon

March of the Wooden Soldiers: see *Babes in Toyland*

March or Die
GB 1977 107m Technicolor
ITC/Associated General (Dick Richards, Jerry Bruckheimer)
In 1918, tensions rise at a Foreign Legion outpost threatened by Arabs.
Incredibly old-hat romantic melodrama of the kind that was being spoofed forty years ago. The considerable talent involved seems unfortunately under instruction to take it seriously.
w David Zelag Goodman *d* Dick Richards *ph* John Alcott *m* Maurice Jarre
☆ Gene Hackman, Terence Hill (Mario Girotti), Catherine Deneuve, Max von Sydow, Ian Holm, Marcel Bozzuffi
† The writer and director more successfully revived a different set of clichés in *Farewell My Lovely*.

Marching Along: see *Stars and Stripes Forever*

Marco the Magnificent: see *The Fabulous Adventures of Marco Polo*

Mardi Gras
US 1958 107m DeLuxe Cinemascope
TCF (Jerry Wald)
In New Orleans at holiday time, a film star falls for a cadet.
Mindless musical using up available talent.
w Winston Miller, Hal Kanter *d* Edmund Goulding *ph* Wilfrid M. Cline *md* Lionel Newman
☆ Pat Boone, Christine Carere, Sheree North, Tommy Sands, Gary Crosby, Fred Clark, Richard Sargent, Barrie Chase
Lionel Newman

Mare Nostrum *
US 1925 110m approx bw silent
MGM
A Spanish captain loves a German spy.
Tragic romantic melodrama, a major attraction of its time.
w Willis Goldbeck *novel* Vicente Blasco Ibanez *d* Rex Ingram *ph* John Seitz
☆ Antonio Moreno, Alice Terry

Margaret's Museum **
Canada/GB 1995 100m colour
Ranfilm/Imagex/Télé-Action/Skyline (Mort Ransen, Christopher Zimmer, Claudio Luca, Steve Clark-Hall)
In the late 40s, in a small Novia Scotia town, a woman is driven to madness by the deaths of the men in her life, who had no option but to work as miners.
Compelling drama of female suffering that comes to an unexpected climax, and owes much to the equally unexpected performance of Bonham Carter as a working-class wife.
w Gerald Wexler, Mort Ransen *novel* *The Glace Bay Miner's Museum* by Sheldon Currie *d* Mort Ransen *ph* Vic Sarin *m* Milan Kymlicka *pd* William Fleming, David McHenry *ed* Rita Roy
☆ *Helena Bonham Carter*, Kate Nelligan, Clive Russell, Craig Olejnik, Andrea Morris, Peter Boretski, Kenneth Welsh
'A moving, funny pic that's actually quite uplifting for most of the time.' – *Brendan Kelly, Variety*
† Ransen spent most of the 90s trying to get backing for the film. In Canada's 1995 Genie awards it won plaudits for best writing, score, actress (Bonham Carter), supporting actress (Nelligan) and supporting actor (Welsh).

La Marge
France 1976 90m Eastmancolor
Paris Film/Robert and Raymond Hakim
aka: *The Margin*
aka: *The Streetwalker*
After receiving a letter telling him that his wife has committed suicide after his son was drowned, a husband working in Paris spends several days with a prostitute.
Trite tale of the wages of sin, filmed without much enthusiasm from the participants, despite a great deal of nudity and sexual activity.
wd Walerian Borowczyk *novel* André Pieyre de Mandiargues *ph* Bernard Daillencourt *ed* Louisette Hautecoeur
☆ Sylvia Kristel, Joe Dallesandro, André Falcon, Mireille Audibert, Denis Manuel
'Borowczyk is at his least impressive with this story.' – *Sight and Sound*
'His masterpiece.' – *Movie Collector*
† A dubbed version running for 80m has also been released on video.

'The girl of the moment in the picture of America's hey! hey! day!'
Margie ***
US 1946 94m Technicolor
TCF (Walter Morosco)
A married woman reminisces about her college days, when she married the French teacher despite her tendency to lose her bloomers at the most embarrassing moments.
Wholly pleasing nostalgia, very smartly and brightly handled.
w F. Hugh Herbert *stories* Ruth McKinney, Richard Bransten *d* Henry King *ph* Charles Clarke *md* Alfred Newman
☆ *Jeanne Crain*, Glenn Langan, *Alan Young*, Lynn Bari, Barbara Lawrence, Conrad Janis, Esther Dale
'Direction, script and settings skilfully interpret the fashions and crazes of the twenties.' – *MFB*

The Margin: see *La Marge*

Margin for Error *
US 1943 74m bw
TCF (Ralph Dietrich)
Just before World War II, the Nazi consul in New York is murdered in his own office.
Mildly intriguing whodunnit with the case solved by a Jewish cop.
w Lillie Hayward *play* Clare Boothe Luce *d* Otto Preminger *ph* Edward Cronjager *m* Leigh Harline
☆ Milton Berle, Joan Bennett, Otto Preminger, Carl Esmond, Howard Freeman, Poldy Dur, Hans von Twardowski

Le Marginal: see *The Outsider (1983)*

Marguerite de la Nuit *
France/Italy 1955 126m Technicolor
SNEG/Gaumont Actualités/Cino del Duca (Léon Carré)
An octogenarian signs a pact with the devil in return for his lost youth; but when he has it he causes the death of the woman he loves.
Expensive, sporadically interesting, but unpersuasive updating of Faust.
w Ghislaine Autant-Lara, Gabriel Arout *d* Claude Autant-Lara *ph* Jacques Natteau *m* René Cloërc
☆ Michèle Morgan, Yves Montand, Jean-François Calvé, Massimo Girotti

Le Mari de la coiffeuse: see *The Hairdresser's Husband*

Maria Chapdelaine *
France 1934 73m bw
Société Nouvelle
In a hard Quebec winter Maria loses her mother and her lover, but resists temptation by a man from the city.
Artistically telling drama, later flatly remade as The Naked Heart.
novel Louis Hémon *d* Julien Duvivier
☆ Madeleine Renaud, Jean Gabin, Suzanne Despres, Jean-Pierre Aumont
'A fine achievement, it gives the feeling of a sort of epic poem.' – *Variety*

Maria Marten, or The Murder in the Red Barn
GB 1935 67m bw
George King
A wicked Victorian squire kills his pregnant mistress and is haunted.
Stilted melodrama, ripely played, from a real-life case. (The villain's scalp is still exhibited in a museum at Bury St Edmunds.)
w Randall Faye *d* Milton Rosmer *ph* George Stretton *md* Lionel Claff *ad* D. W. Daniels *ed* Charles Saunders
☆ Tod Slaughter, Sophie Stewart, Eric Portman, Clare Greet, D. J. Williams
† Several versions had been made in silent days.

El Mariachi: see *under E*

Maria's Lovers
US 1984 103m colour
Cannon/Golan-Globus (Bosko Djordjevic, Lawrence Taylor-Mortorff)
A soldier returns from a Japanese prisoner-of-war camp to marry the girl of his dreams and discovers that he is impotent with her.
Turgid domestic drama, taken at a funereal pace and with acting that is unable to make the lugubrious script convincing; it is rather as if Tennessee Williams had been rewritten by William Faulkner.
w Gerard Brach, Andrei Konchalovsky, Paul Zindel, Marjorie David *d* Andrei Konchalovsky *ph* Juan Ruiz-Anchia *m* Gary S. Remal *pd* Jeannine Oppewall *ed* Humphrey Dixon
☆ Nastassja Kinski, John Savage, Robert Mitchum, Keith Carradine, Anita Morris, Bud Cort, Karen Young, Tracy (credited as Tracey) Nelson, John Goodman, Vincent Spano

Marie
US 1985 112m Technicolor Dunton vision
Dino de Laurentiis (Frank Capra Jnr)
A battered wife leaves her husband and becomes chairman of the Tennessee parole board.
An edifying biopic to which the only answer is, so what?
w John Briley *book* Peter Maas *d* Roger Donaldson *ph* Chris Menges *m* Francis Lai
☆ Sissy Spacek, Jeff Daniels, Morgan Freeman, Fred Thompson
'Blessed are the pure in heart but also deadly dull.' – *Time Out*
'A highly accomplished piece of work. It moves, it looks professional, and it's well acted.' – *Pauline Kael, New Yorker*
† Fred Thompson, who was the real-life Marie Ragghianti's lawyer, plays himself in the film. He then became a movie actor under the name Fred Dalton Thompson, appearing in *The Hunt for Red October* and *Die Hard 2* among other films.

Marie Antoinette *
US 1938 160m bw
MGM (Hunt Stromberg)
The last days of the French court before the revolution.
Too slow by half, and so glamorized and fictionalized as to lack all interest, this long delayed production stands only as an example of MGM's expensive prestige movies of the thirties.
w Claudine West, Donald Ogden Stewart, Ernest Vajda *d* W. S. Van Dyke *ph* William Daniels *m* Herbert Stothart *ad* Cedric Gibbons *montage* Slavko Vorkapich
☆ Norma Shearer, Tyrone Power, John Barrymore, Robert Morley, Gladys George, Anita Louise, Joseph Schildkraut, Henry Stephenson, Reginald Gardiner, Peter Bull, Albert Dekker, Cora Witherspoon, Barnett Parker, Joseph Calleia, Henry Kolker and also George Zucco, Henry Daniell, Harry Davenport, Barry Fitzgerald, Mae Busch, Robert Barrat
'Produced on a scale of incomparable splendour and extravagance, it approaches real greatness as cinematic historical literature.' – *Variety*
'A resplendent bore.' – *New Yorker, 1977*
Herbert Stothart; Norma Shearer; Robert Morley

Marie Baie des Anges: see *Angel Sharks*

La Marie du Port
France 1949 95m bw
Sacha Gordine
A Cherbourg restaurateur takes his mistress home for her father's funeral, and falls in love with her younger sister.
Slight romantic drama, well enough put over but not very memorable except for its slightly cynical mood.
w Louis Chavance, Marcel Carné *novel* Georges Simenon *d* Marcel Carné *ph* Henri Alekan *m* Joseph Kosma
☆ Jean Gabin, Blanchette Brunoy, Nicole Courcel, Claude Romain, Louis Seigner, Jeanne Marken, Carette

Marie Galante
US 1934 90m bw
Fox
A French girl stranded in the Canal Zone becomes involved in international intrigue.
Slightly unusual spy romance.
w Reginald Berkeley *novel* Jacques Deval *d* Henry King
☆ Spencer Tracy, Ketti Gallian, Ned Sparks, Helen Morgan, Sig Rumann, Leslie Fenton, Stepin Fetchit
'Production and handling should carry it to moderate grosses.' – *Variety*

Marie Octobre
France 1958 102m bw
Orex/SF/Abbey/Doxa (Lucien Viard)
US title: *Secret Meeting*
At a reunion dinner of a wartime resistance group, a traitor is exposed and killed.
Stultifying one-set talkfest employing Hitchcock's long-discarded ten-minute take.
w Julien Duvivier, Jacques Robert *novel* Jacques Robert *d* Julien Duvivier *ph* Robert Le Fèbvre *m* Jean Yatove *ad* Georges Wakhevitch
☆ Danielle Darrieux, Serge Reggiani, Bernard Blier, Paul Meurisse, Noel Roquevert, Lino Ventura, Paul Guers, Paul Frankeur

Marie Walewska: see *Conquest*

La Mariée Est Trop Belle: see *The Bride Is Much Too Beautiful*

La Mariée Etait en Noir: see *The Bride Wore Black*

Mariés de L'An Deux: see *The Scoundrel (1971)*

Marine Raiders
US 1944 90m bw
RKO (Robert Fellows)
The marines do battle in Guadalcanal.
Standard romantic flagwaver.
w Warren Duff *d* Harold Schuster *ph* Nick Musuraca *m* Roy Webb
☆ Pat O'Brien, Robert Ryan, Ruth Hussey, Frank McHugh, Barton MacLane

The Marines Fly High
US 1940 68m bw
RKO
Two leathernecks combat a mysterious South American villain.
Formula action fare, intended as a Flagg and Quirt adventure but made with a second team.
w Jerry Cady, A. J. Bolton *d* George Nicholls Jnr, Ben Stoloff
☆ Richard Dix, Chester Morris, Lucille Ball, John Eldredge, Steffi Duna

'Up to their necks in fights and loving!'
Marines Let's Go
US 1961 103m DeLuxe Cinemascope
TCF (Raoul Walsh)
Marines fighting in Korea are granted leave in Japan.
Brawling tragi-farce with predictable characters, a long way after What Price Glory.
w John Twist *story* Raoul Walsh *d* Raoul Walsh *ph* Lucien Ballard *m* Irving Gertz
☆ Tom Tryon, David Hedison, Tom Reese, Linda Hutchins, William Tyler
'A typically noisy, insensitive and maudlin tribute to the American Marines.' – *MFB*

Marius **
France 1931 125m bw
Marcel Pagnol/Paramount
The son of a Marseilles waterfront café owner gives up his sweetheart to go to sea.
Celebrated character drama which succeeds through the realism and vitality of its people and their dialogue.
w Marcel Pagnol *play* Marcel Pagnol *d* Alexander Korda *ph* Ted Pahle *m* Francis Grammon
☆ *Raimu, Pierre Fresnay*, Charpin, Orane Demazis
† Two sequels with the same players and from the same pen made this a famous trilogy: *Fanny* (qv) and *César* (qv).
†† *Port of Seven Seas* (MGM 1938) was a hammy and stagey Hollywood compression of the trilogy. See also *Fanny* (1960), a dull version of the stage musical, with the songs removed.

Marius et Jeanette *
France 1997 102m colour
Porter Frith/La Sept/Agat (Gilles Sandoz, Robert Guédiguian)
A security guard finds it difficult to cope with his new relationship with a single mother who has two young children.
A soft-centred romance about a couple experiencing hard times; the craft of its director and the performances of the cast compensate for its old-fashioned tone.
w Jean-Louis Milesi, Robert Guédiguian *d* Robert Guédiguian *ph* Bernard Cavalié *ed* Bernard Sasia
☆ Ariane Ascaride, Gérard Meylan, Pascale Roberts, Jacques Boudet, Frédérique Bonnal, Jean-Pierre Darroussin
'A rough-cut gem.' – *Empire*

Marjorie Morningstar
US 1958 123m Warnercolor
(Warner) United States Pictures (Milton Sperling)
A New York Jewish girl has great ambitions for herself but ends up a suburban housewife.
Stodgy 'woman's picture' with all talents somewhat uneasy in their assignments, mainly because the Jewish quality is imperfectly conveyed.
w Everett Freeman *novel* Herman Wouk *d* Irving Rapper *ph* Harry Stradling *m* Max Steiner
☆ Natalie Wood, Gene Kelly, Claire Trevor, Everett Sloane, Ed Wynn, Martin Milner, Carolyn Jones, George Tobias, Jesse White, Martin Balsam
† The first film in which perfume was credited.
song 'A Very Precious Love' (*m*Sammy Fain, *ly*Francis Webster)

'Lock me up! Please lock me up!'
The Mark *
GB 1961 127m bw Cinemascope
TCF/Raymond Stross/Sidney Buchman
A sexual psychopath finds on emerging from prison that his past still haunts him despite the help of his psychiatrist.
Worthy but evasive social drama which outstays its welcome but provides good performances.
w Sidney Buchman, Stanley Mann *d* Guy Green *ph* Douglas Slocombe *m* Richard Rodney Bennett
☆ Stuart Whitman, Maria Schell, *Rod Steiger*, Brenda de Banzie, Maurice Denham, Donald Wolfit, Paul Rogers, Donald Houston
'There is seriousness and care, but neither boldness nor passion … no hint of the truly sordid is allowed to seep through.' – *MFB*
Stuart Whitman

The Mark of Cain
GB 1947 88m bw
GFD/Two Cities (W. P. Lipscomb)
The attractive housekeeper of a Manchester businessman is blamed when his brother accidentally poisons him.
Turgid period melodrama in which few opportunities are offered and none taken.
w Francis Crowdy, Christianna Brand, W. P. Lipscomb *novel* *Airing in a Closed Carriage* by Joseph Shearing *d* Brian Desmond Hurst *ph* Erwin Hillier *m* Bernard Stevens *ad* Alexander Vetchinsky *ed* Sidney Stone
☆ Sally Gray, Eric Portman, Patrick Holt, Dermot Walsh, Denis O'Dea, Edward Lexy, Miles Malleson

'Positively The Most Horrifying Film Ever Made.'
'Likely to upset your stomach.'
Mark of the Devil (dubbed)
West Germany 1969 97m colour
Atlas/Hi-Fi Stereo 70 (Adrian Hoven)
original title: *Hexen geschändet und zu Tode gequält*
aka: *Austria 1700*
A bloodthirsty and lecherous witch-finder's activities are usurped by an even more sadistic aristocrat, acting in the name of the Church.
A nasty, garish horror that lingers over scenes of torture and brutality. The movie claims to be based on cases 'taken from authentic documents', but the result is the same old exploitative rubbish as usual.
w Sergio Casstner (Michael Armstrong), Percy Parker (Adrian Hoven) *d* Michael Armstrong *ph* Ernst W. Kulinke *m* Michael Holm *ad* Max Mellin *ed* Siegrun Jager
☆ Herbert Lom, Olivera Vuco, Udo Kier, Reggie Nalder, Herbert Fux, Michael Maien, Ingeborg Schoener, Johannes Buzalski, Gaby Fuchs
† The film was refused a certificate and never shown in British cinemas. It was released on video in the 1980s and quickly withdrawn before being given a British video release in 1993 with an 18 certificate. When it first opened in America, audiences were supplied with sick-bags as they went in.

The Mark of the Hawk
US 1958 84m Technicolor Superscope
Universal-International
An educated African fights for the emergence of his people by peaceful means.
Well-intentioned but muddled topical drama.
w H. Kenn Carmichael *d* Michael Audley
☆ Sidney Poitier, Juano Hernandez, Eartha Kitt, John McIntire, Marne Maitland, Patrick Allen

Mark of the Phoenix
GB 1959 65m bw
Butchers (W. G. Chalmers)
An American jewel thief becomes accidentally involved in a plan to smuggle into Russia a cigarette case made of a secret alloy.
Dull second feature; it is typical that its brief moments of action should take place in the dark.
w Norman Hudis *story* Desmond Cory *d* Maclean Rogers *ph* Geoffrey Faithfull *md* Wilfred Burns *ad* John Stoll *ed* Harry Booth
☆ Julia Arnall, Sheldon Lawrence, Anton Diffring, Eric Pohlmann, George Margo, Michael Peake, Martin Miller, Bernard Rebel, Roger Delgado

Mark of the Renegade
US 1951 81m Technicolor
Jack Gross/Universal-International
In 1824, a Mexican agent in California pretends to be a rotter in order to unmask villains.
Shakily constructed action piece which quickly wears out its welcome.
w Louis Solomon and Robert Hardy Andrews *story* Johnston McCulley *d* Hugo Fregonese
☆ Ricardo Montalban, Gilbert Roland, Cyd Charisse, J. Carrol Naish, Andrea King, George Tobias, Antonio Moreno

Mark of the Vampire *
US 1935 61m bw
MGM (E. J. Mannix)
A policeman tries to solve an old murder in an eerie house by hiring vaudeville performers to pose as vampires.
Semi-spoof horror which is flawed by lack of pace and a patchy script, but contains splendid visual moments. A remake of the Lon Chaney silent, London After Midnight.
w Guy Endore, Bernard Schubert *d* *Tod Browning* *ph* *James Wong Howe*
☆ Lionel Barrymore, Jean Hersholt, Elizabeth Allan, Bela Lugosi, Carol Borland, Lionel Atwill, Henry Wadsworth, Donald Meek, Jessie Ralph, Ivan Simpson, Holmes Herbert
'Deftly combines murder mystery, chiller and novelty elements for pretty good entertainment results.' – *Variety.*
'Even the adults in the audience may feel a bit skittery at the sight of two or three vampires, a bevy of bats, a drove of rodents, a herd of spiders and a cluster of cobwebs, not forgetting the swarm of fog.' – *New York Times*

The Mark of Zorro *
US 1920 90m (24 fps) bw silent
Douglas Fairbanks
A Mexican Robin Hood carves his initial wherever he turns up to harass the Spanish invaders.
A little faded now, but this swashbuckler opened up a whole new career for its star; the 1940 version clearly has more style.
novel *The Curse of Capistrano* by Johnston McCulley *d* Fred Niblo *ph* William McGann *m* William Perry
☆ *Douglas Fairbanks*, Marguerite de la Motte, Noah Beery

The Mark of Zorro ***
US 1940 94m bw
TCF (Raymond Griffith)
After being educated in Spain, Diego de Vega returns to California and finds the country enslaved and his father half-corrupted by tyrants. Disguising himself as a masked bandit, he leads the country to expel the usurpers.
Splendid adventure stuff for boys of all ages, an amalgam of The Scarlet Pimpernel *and* Robin Hood *to which in this version the director adds an overwhelming pictorial sense which makes it stand out as the finest of all.*
w John Taintor Foote, Garrett Fort, Bess Meredyth *d* *Rouben Mamoulian* *ph* *Arthur Miller* *m* *Alfred Newman* *ad* Richard Day, Joseph C. Wright
☆ *Tyrone Power, Basil Rathbone, J. Edward Bromberg*, Linda Darnell, Eugene Pallette, Montagu Love, Janet Beecher, Robert Lowery
Alfred Newman

The Mark of Zorro (dubbed)
Italy/France/Spain 1963 90m Eastmancolor Dyaliscope
CCM/Fidès/Benito Perojo (Harry Joe Brown)
original title: *Il Segno di Zorro*
US title: *Duel at the Rio Grande*
Returning from Spain to his Mexican home, an aristocrat discovers that his father has been killed and his lands confiscated by the governor on a false charge of treason.
Cut-rate swashbuckler with little of the necessary panache about it.
w Guido Malatesta, Casey Robinson *d* Nathan Juran *ph* Adalberto Albertini *m* Gregorio Garcia Segura *ad* Enrique Alarçon *ed* Alberto Gallitti, Antonio Boccianti
☆ Sean Flynn, Danielle de Metz, Armando Calvo, Mario Petri, Gaby André, Mino Doro, Folco Lulli, Alfredo Rizzo
† Nathan Juran directed the US dubbed version; the Italian version was directed by Mario Caiano

Marked for Death
US 1990 93m DeLuxe Super 35
TCF/Steamroller (Michael Grais, Mark Victor, Steven Seagal)
A former agent takes action against a Jamaican drug dealer and his gang.
Familiar scenario offering the usual mix of grunts and orchestrated violence.
w Michael Grais, Mark Victor *d* Dwight H. Little *ph* Ric Waite *m* James Newton Howard *pd* Robb Wilson King *ed* O. Nicholas Brown
☆ Steven Seagal, Basil Wallace, Keith David, Tom Wright, Joanna Pacula, Elizabeth Gracen, Bette Ford, Danielle Harris

Marked Woman *
US 1937 96m bw
Warner (Lou Edelman)
A night-club girl is persuaded to testify against an underworld boss.
A twist on the usual run of gangster melodramas, performed with the star's accustomed intensity and presented with the studio's usual panache.
w Robert Rossen, Abem Finkel *d* Lloyd Bacon *ph* George Barnes *m* Heinz Roemheld *md* Leo F. Forbstein
☆ Bette Davis, Humphrey Bogart, Jane Bryan, Eduardo Ciannelli, Isabel Jewell, Allen Jenkins, Mayo Methot, Lola Lane, Henry O'Neill
'Spotty draw depending on feminine reaction … there is nothing that is light, and very little that is funny.' – *Variety*
† Remade as *Lady Gangster*.

†† Humphrey Bogart's character was based on Thomas E. Dewey, and Eduardo Ciannelli's on Lucky Luciano.

Marlowe *
US 1969 95m Metrocolor
MGM (Gabriel Katzka, Sidney Beckerman)

Private eye Philip Marlowe is hired by a nervous girl to find her missing brother.
The authentic Chandler atmosphere is caught by this busy thriller, but there seems to be a deliberate attempt to make a confusing plot even more obscure, so that the end result is more tiresome than amusing.
w Stirling Silliphant *novel* *The Little Sister* by Raymond Chandler *d* Paul Bogart *ph* William H. Daniels *m* Peter Matz *ad* George W. Davis, Addison Hehr *ed* Gene Ruggiero
☆ *James Garner* (Philip Marlowe), *Rita Moreno* (Dolores Gonzales), *Sharon Farrell* (Orfamay Guest), *Bruce Lee* (Winslow Wong), Gayle Hunnicutt (Mavis Wald), Carroll O'Connor (Lt Christy French), William Daniels (Mr Crowell), Jackie Coogan (Grant W. Hicks), H. M. Wynant (Sonny Steelgrave), Kenneth Tobey (Sgt Fred Beifus)
'One does wonder whether the simple human squalor of the Bogart-Chandler era can ever be recaptured by an increasingly meretricious Hollywood.' – *MFB*

Marnie *
US 1964 130m Technicolor
Universal/Geoffrey Stanley Inc (Alfred Hitchcock)

A rich man marries a kleptomaniac and cures her, but a nightmare in her past makes her still sexually frigid.
Psychodrama with background crime and suspense, lethargically handled by the old master, who alone knows what he saw in it in the first place, as this heroine does not even have fire under her ice. The production is curiously artificial in many ways, from dummy horses to backcloths to back projection.
w Jay Presson Allen *novel* Winston Graham *d* Alfred Hitchcock *ph* Robert Burks *m* Bernard Herrmann *pd* Robert Boyle *ed* George Tomasini *cos* Edith Head
☆ Tippi Hedren (Marnie Edgar), Sean Connery (Mark Rutland), Martin Gabel (Sidney Strutt), Diane Baker (Lil Mainwaring), Louise Latham (Bernice Edgar), Bob Sweeney (Cousin Bob)

Maroc 7
GB 1967 91m Eastmancolor Panavision
Rank/Cyclone
The lady editor of a top fashion magazine doubles as a jewel thief and becomes involved in Moroccan intrigue.
Complex sub-Bond tale of cross and double cross; hardly worth following, really.
w David Osborn *d* Gerry O'Hara *ph* Ken Talbot *m* Kenneth Jones
☆ Gene Barry, Elsa Martinelli, Cyd Charisse, Leslie Phillips, Denholm Elliott, Alexandra Stewart, Eric Barker, Angela Douglas

Marooned *
US 1969 134m Technicolor Panavision 70
Columbia/Frankovich-Sturges (Frank Capra Jnr)

Three astronauts are stranded in space, and a rescue mission gets under way.
Very heavy-going space suspenser with all possible technical accomplishment but little life of its own.
w Mayo Simon *novel* Martin Caidin *d* John Sturges *ph* Daniel Fapp *pd* Lyle R. Wheeler
☆ Gregory Peck, Richard Crenna, David Janssen, James Franciscus, Gene Hackman, Lee Grant, Nancy Kovack, Mariette Hartley, Scott Brady
'In something like the plight of Ironman One, Sturges' work seems on the point of slowing to a standstill as it drifts further into projects of ever-increasing, self-effacing size and anonymous technical dexterity.' – *Richard Combs*
'It has all the zip, zest and zing of a moon walk, and I suspect a computer fed a dictionary could come up with better dialogue.' – *Judith Crist, 1973*
'A space epic with a horse-and-buggy script.' – *Pauline Kael*
special visual effects (Robbie Robertson)
Daniel Fapp

'The Marquis de Sade at his most bestial.'
Marquis
Belgium/France 1989 83m colour
ICA/Y. C. Aligator/Constellation/Tchin Tchin

Imprisoned in the Bastille in the 1780s, Marquis, an aristocratic spaniel, who passes the time by writing pornography and talking to his chatty penis, Colin, is accused of raping another prisoner, a cow impregnated by the king.
Bizarre, erotic fantasy about the Marquis de Sade by an iconoclastic French cartoonist in which all the characters are played by actors wearing animal masks. Its point remains obscure, though there are a few good jokes, as well as some unpleasant moments, along the way.
w Roland Topor, Henri Xhonneux *d* Henri Xhonneux *ph* Etienne Fauduet *m* Reinhardt Wagner *ad* Roland Topor *ed* Chantal Hymans
☆ Philippe Bizot, Bien de Moor, Gabrielle Van Damme, Olivier Duchaveau, Bernard Cogneux, Pierre Decuypere

'An erotic fantasy horror from the tortured pen of The Marquis de Sade.'
Marquis de Sade: Justine
W. Germany/Italy 1968 104m Eastmancolor
Antony Balch/Corona/Aica (Harry Alan Towers)

aka: *Justine and Julia*
A young woman flees from many attempts on her virtue, while her sister rises to a position of power through prostitution.
A sort of Carry On De Sade, a broad tale of the dangers of innocence, in which the director is unable to get convincing performances from a cast that is superior to most that have suffered at his hands.
w Peter Welbeck (Harry Alan Towers) *novel* Marquis de Sade *ph* Manuel Merino *m* Bruno Nicolai *ed* Nicholas Wentworth
☆ Romina Power (Justine), Maria Rohm (Juliette), Akim Tamiroff (Du Harpin), Jack Palance (Brother Antonin), Sylva Koscina (Jasmin), Klaus Kinski (De Sade), Horst Frank (Marquis de Bressac), Mercedes McCambridge (Madame Dusbois)

Marquise
France/Italy/Switzerland/Spain 1997 117m colour
Downtown/Stephan/France 3/AMLF/3 Emme/Multivideo (Nicola Venditti)
In 17th-century France, a dancer beds the playwright Molière to become an actress, and then begins an affair with his rival, Jean Racine.
Lurid melodrama of theatrical life and tragedy that never comes to life.
w Jean-François Josselin, Vera Belmont, Marcel Beaulieu, Gérard Mordillat *d* Vera Belmont *ph* Jean-Marie Dreujou *m* Jordi Savall, Marin Marais, Jean-Baptiste Lully *ad* Gianni Quaranta *ed* Martine Giordano, Babak Karimi
☆ Sophie Marceau, Bernard Giraudeau, Lambert Wilson, Patrick Timsit, Thierry Lhermitte, Anémone, Remo Girone, Romina Mondello, Estelle Skornik
'A muddled, decidedly soapified, not unintelligent yarn.' – *Empire*
'My worst movie.' – *Sophie Marceau*

The Marquise of O *
West Germany/France 1976 107m Eastmancolor
Janus/Films du Losange

At the end of the 18th century, during the Russian invasion of an Italian town, a noblewoman finds herself pregnant...
Careful novella with many ambiguities, more concerned with what might have happened than with what did. Interesting but exasperating.
wd Eric Rohmer story Heinrich von Kleist *ph* Nestor Almendros *m* Roger Delmotte
☆ Edith Clever, Bruno Ganz, Peter Luhr, Edda Seippel
'Some may find it slow, sentimental, naïve and old-fashioned; others leisurely, beautiful, controlled and illuminating. I found it both, often at the same time.' – *Alan Brien, Sunday Times*
'A bold, funny story becomes a formal, tame film, like a historical work recreated for educational TV.' – *New Yorker, 1980*

The Marriage Circle **
US 1924 78m (24 fps) bw silent
Warner

A bachelor on the loose becomes amorously involved in two marriages.
Feather-light comedy of manners which began a whole new American school, heavily influenced by various European masters.
w Paul Bern *play* *Only a Dream* by Lothar Schmidt *d Ernst Lubitsch ph* Charles Van Enger
☆ Monte Blue, Florence Vidor, Marie Prevost, Adolphe Menjou, Creighton Hale
'A vanished world of roses, kisses and embraces, of whispers and sighs, of a woman's shadowed arm encased in georgette beckoning across a moonlit garden ... and hand-kissing all over the place.' – *Herman G. Weinberg*
'At once perfect cinematography and perfect conventional drama.' – *Iris Barry, The Spectator*
'So slim a plot, so hackneyed if you will, is told with gaiety and a wit that lift it into the very first rank of screen comedy.' – *National Board of Review*
† Remade as *One Hour with You*, also by Lubitsch.

'It's the most hilarious proposition a wife ever had!'
The Marriage Go Round
US 1961 98m DeLuxe Cinemascope
TCF (Leslie Stevens)
A Swedish girl suggests to a married American professor that she borrow his body for mating purposes, believing they would produce the perfect child.
Silly, unfunny sex comedy.
w Leslie Stevens *play* Leslie Stevens *d* Walter Lang *ph* Leo Tover *m* Dominic Frontière
☆ James Mason, Susan Hayward, Julie Newmar, Robert Paige, June Clayworth
'As tedious as it is tasteless.' – *Evening Standard*
'It offers James Mason, an actor who couldn't crack a joke if it was a lichee nut, and Susan Hayward, a bargain basement Bette Davis whose lightest touch as a comedienne would stun a horse.' – *Time*

Marriage Is a Private Affair
US 1944 116m bw
MGM (Pandro S. Berman)
A spoilt rich girl becomes a petulant wife.
Abysmally slow, uninvolving and poorly acted star fodder.
w David Hertz, Lenore Coffee *novel* Judith Kelly *d* Robert Z. Leonard *ph* Ray June *m* Bronislau Kaper
☆ Lana Turner, James Craig, John Hodiak, Frances Gifford, Keenan Wynn, Natalie Schafer, Hugh Marlowe, Paul Cavanagh

The Marriage of a Young Stockbroker **
US 1971 95m DeLuxe
TCF/Lawrence Turman

A stockbroker who finds his life and his marriage dull tries voyeurism and extramarital sex.
Sardonic adult comedy of the battle between the sexes, pretty lively from start to finish.
w Lorenzo Semple Jnr novel Charles Webb *d* Lawrence Turman *ph* Laszlo Kovacs *m* Fred Karlin
☆ Richard Benjamin, Joanna Shimkus, Elizabeth Ashley, Adam West, Patricia Barry

The Marriage of Maria Braun *
West Germany 1978 119m Fujicolour
Albatros/Trio/WDR/FdA (Michael Fengler)

original title: *Die Ehe der Maria Braun*
Vicissitudes of a post-war bride who is eventually blown up in a gas explosion.
A mixture of solemnity and irony which keeps its basic points well concealed but, despite a sometimes flagging pace, more or less consistently entertains the eye.
w Peter Märthesheimer, Pea Fröhlich *d* Rainer Werner Fassbinder *ph* Michael Ballhaus *m* Peer Raben
☆ Hanna Schygulla, Klaus Löwitsch, Ivan Desny, Gottfried John

Marriage on the Rocks
US 1965 109m Technicolor Panavision
Warner/A-C/Sinatra (William H. Daniels)
An ad man and his wife decide to go to Mexico for a divorce but once there change their minds; she ends up accidentally married to his best friend.
All this talent retreats fearfully from a witless, tasteless script and slow handling. A dismal comedy.
w Cy Howard *d* Jack Donohue *ph* William H. Daniels *m* Nelson Riddle
☆ Frank Sinatra, Dean Martin, Deborah Kerr, Cesar Romero, Hermione Baddeley, Tony Bill, Nancy Sinatra, John McGiver
'A long, coarse, and nearly always unfunny comedy, hammered together for no apparent reason except to make money.' – *New Yorker*

The Marriage Playground
US 1929 70m bw
Paramount
Children of divorced rich parents wander round Europe in a group.
Slightly unusual drama of its day; sound technique very thin.
w J. Walter Ruben, Doris Anderson *novel* *The Children* by Edith Wharton *d* Lothar Mendes *ph* Victor Milner
☆ Fredric March, Kay Francis, Mary Brian, Lilyan Tashman, Huntley Gordon, Anita Louise

Married Before Breakfast
US 1937 70m bw
MGM
An impecunious inventor has a razorless shaving cream.
Scatty comedy which seldom amuses.
w George Oppenheimer, Everett Freeman, Harry Ruskin *d* Edwin L. Marin
☆ Robert Young, Florence Rice, June Clayworth, Barnett Parker, Warren Hymer
'It has practically nothing in its favour.' – *Variety*

Married but Single: see *This Thing Called Love*

Married to It
US 1993 112m DeLuxe
Orion (Thomas Baer)

Three ill-assorted couples, who meet through a school function, become friends while suffering marital problems.
A somewhat lifeless domestic comedy that never escapes the restraints of its over-schematic screenplay; it fails to animate its stock characters.
w Janet Kovalcik *d* Arthur Hiller *ph* Victor Kemper *m* Henry Mancini *pd* Robert Gundlach *ed* Robert C. Jones
☆ Beau Bridges, Stockard Channing, Robert Sean Leonard, Mary Stuart Masterson, Cybill Shepherd, Ron Silver
† The film was made in 1991 and not released for two years.

Married to the Mob **
US 1988 103m DuArt
Rank/Orion/Mysterious Arts (Kenneth Utt, Edward Saxon)

The wife of a murdered gangster tries to live an honest life after her husband's death.
Effervescent comedy-thriller that bubbles merrily along.
w Barry Strugatz, Mark R. Burns *d* Jonathan Demme *ph* Tak Fujimoto *m* David Byrne *pd* Kristi Zea *ed* Craig McKay
☆ Michelle Pfeiffer, Matthew Modine, Dean Stockwell, Mercedes Ruehl, Alec Baldwin, Trey Wilson, Joan Cusack
'A smart, genial entertainment that gives us plenty to look at and listen to.' – *Terrence Rafferty, New Yorker*
Dean Stockwell

A Married Woman *
France 1964 98m bw
Anouchka/Orsay (Philippe Dusart)

original title: *Une Femme Mariée*
A pilot's wife has an actor lover.
Fragments of character observation, in various cinematic techniques, build up into an intense personal study if not a plot.
wd Jean-Luc Godard ph Raoul Coutard *m* Claude Nougaro
☆ Macha Meril, Bernard Noel, Roger Leenhardt

'A minefield of paradoxes ... the essence of cinema 1965.' – *Peter John Dyer, MFB*

Marry Me
GB 1949 97m bw
GFD/Gainsborough (Betty Box)
Four stories of a marriage bureau.
A styleless portmanteau of anecdotes put over by a clear second team.
w Lewis Gilbert, Denis Waldock *d* Terence Fisher *ph* Ray Elton *m* Clifton Parker
☆ Derek Bond, Susan Shaw, Patrick Holt, Carol Marsh, David Tomlinson, Zena Marshall, Guy Middleton, Nora Swinburne, Jean Cadell, Mary Jerrold

Marry Me Again
US 1953 73m bw
RKO (Alex Gottlieb)
A man returns from war to find that his fiancée has inherited a million dollars.
Zany comedy with tilts at psychiatry: not too bad.
wd Frank Tashlin *ph* Robert de Grasse *m* Raoul Kraushaar
☆ Robert Cummings, Marie Wilson, Ray Walker, Mary Costa, Jess Barker

Marry the Girl
US 1937 66m bw
Warner
A crazy family owns a newspaper syndicate.
Fashionable comedy which goes far too far.
w Sig Herzig, Pat C. Flick, Tom Reed
novel Edward Hope *d* William McGann
☆ Mary Boland, Frank McHugh, Hugh Herbert, Mischa Auer, Carol Hughes, Allen Jenkins, Alan Mowbray, Hugh O'Connell
'Pic will probably get by on duals in the nabes and should be a panic with juve audiences. But it will probably lay an egg in first runs.' – *Variety*

The Marrying Kind *
US 1952 93m bw
Columbia (Bert Granet)
A couple seeking divorce tell their troubles to a judge, and change their minds.
Smart, New Yorkish, tragi-comic star vehicle which works pretty well.
w Ruth Gordon, Garson Kanin *d* George Cukor *ph* Joseph Walker *m* Hugo Friedhofer
☆ *Judy Holliday, Aldo Ray, Madge Kennedy,* Mickey Shaughnessy

The Marrying Man
US 1991 116m Technicolor
Warner/Hollywood Pictures/Silver Screen Partners IV/Odyssey (David Permut)
GB title: *Too Hot To Handle*
A playboy, forced to marry a gangster's girlfriend, finds himself repeating the experience several times.
A misfiring romantic comedy, both involved and uninvolving.
w Neil Simon *d* Jerry Rees *ph* Donald E. Thorin *m* David Newman *pd* William F. Matthews *ed* Michael Jablow
☆ Kim Basinger, Alec Baldwin, Elisabeth Shue, Armand Assante, Paul Reiser, Fisher Stevens, Peter Dobson, Steve Hytner
'A still-born romantic comedy of staggering ineptitude. Industry bad-mouthing of the stars during production was just a preview of the terrible picture.' – *Variety*
'A comedy that bounces skittishly down a lane that memory has not travelled in a while. Maybe it's silly. But it does awaken a nostalgic fondness for an era when celebrity dreaming was goofier, giddier and less consequential than it is now.' – *Richard Schickel, Time*

'Nice Planet. We'll Take It!'
Mars Attacks! *
US 1996 103m Technicolor Panavision
Warner (Tim Burton, Larry Franco)
Martians conquer the world, until they are defeated by being subjected to the singing of Slim Whitman.
The film begins brilliantly, with a stampede of flaming cows, but is then content to recycle, at great expense, the style of 50s sci-fi films while its cast parody their more serious roles; despite its occasional antic charm, it is not as enjoyable as it ought to be.
w Jonathan Gems *d* Tim Burton *ph* Peter Suschitzky *m* Danny Elfman *pd* Wynn Thomas *ed* Chris Lebenzon
☆ Jack Nicholson, Glenn Close, Annette Bening, Michael J. Fox, Pierce Brosnan, Sarah Jessica Parker, Martin Short, Lisa Marie, Rod Steiger, Danny DeVito, Lukas Haas, Natalie Portman, Jim Brown, Pam Grier, Joe Don Baker and also Tom Jones, Jerzy Skolimowsky, Barbet Schroeder
'A cult sci-fi comedy miscast as an elaborate all-star studio extravaganza. Continually inventive, parodistic sendup of alien invasion movies that owes its style to genre classics of the '50s, the technically brilliant picture possesses a quirky, somewhat facetious insider tone.' – *Todd McCarthy, Variety*

La Marseillaise *
France 1938 145m bw
Films La Marseillaise (André Zwoboda)
The story of the French revolution of 1789.
A rather disconnected epic which, despite a few splendid scenes, never moved its audiences to enthusiasm.
wd Jean Renoir *ph* Jean Bourgoin and others *md* Joseph Kosma
☆ Pierre Renoir, Lise Delemare, Louis Jouvet, Léon Larive, Georges Spanelly, Elisa Ruis, William Aguet
'France's super-super film production is a near flopperoo.' – *Variety*

The Marseille Contract
GB/France 1974 89m Eastmancolor
Warner/AIP/Kettledrum/PECF (Judd Bernard)
US title: *The Destructors*
An American narcotics agent in Paris hires an assassin to dispose of a drug smuggler.
Routine action melodrama with a jokey atmosphere not sustained by a downbeat script.
w Judd Bernard *d* Robert Parrish *ph* Douglas Slocombe *m* Roy Budd
☆ Michael Caine, Anthony Quinn, James Mason, Alexandra Stewart, Marcel Bozzuffi, Maurice Ronet

Marseilles trilogy: see *Marius; Fanny; César*

Marshmallow Moon: see *Aaron Slick from Punkin Crick*

Martha & Ethel **
US 1993 78m colour/bw
Columbia TriStar/Canobie (Jyll Johnstone)
A documentary on the lives of two nannies and the families they influence: Martha, 87, German-born and a disciplinarian, who worked for the same family for 30 years, bringing up five children; and Ethel, 88, from southern Carolina and easy-going, who was nanny to six children and still lives with her employer.
A fascinating glimpse into the lives of two ordinary but exceptional working women, including interviews with them and the children they raised through changing times.
d Jyll Johnstone *ph* Joseph Friedman *ed* Toby Shimin
'As light as a breeze, and there's a lot of bright, natural humour emanating from her subjects, but she raises dark questions.' – *Independent*

'Two's Company. Three's A Crowd. Four's A Catastrophe.'
Martha Meet Frank, Daniel & Laurence
GB 1998 90m colour
Film Four/Channel 4/Banshee (Grainne Marmion)
Three friends in London fall in love with the same young American woman.
A romantic comedy heavy with charm, but lacking in substance.
w Peter Morgan *d* Nick Hamm *ph* David Johnson *m* Edward Shearmur *pd* Max Gottlieb *ed* Michael Bradsell
☆ Monica Potter, Rufus Sewell, Tom Hollander, Joseph Fiennes, Ray Winstone
'Minuscule romantic comedy ... looks skimpy and feels plodding.' – *Alexander Walker*

Martha, Ruth & Edie
Canada 1988 90m Film House colour
Sunrise (Deepa Mehta Saltzman)
Three women tell each other of the most significant event in their lives.
Portmanteau movie of female bonding, which is no more rewarding than the more usual tales of the male variety.
w Anna Sandor, Janet Maclean, Barbara O'Kelly *story How I Met My Husband* by Alice Munro, *The California Aunts* by Cynthia Flood, *Guilt* by Betty Lambert *d* Norma Bailey, Daniele J. Suissa, Deepa Mehta Saltzman *ph* Doug Koch *m* Alexina Louie, Alex Pauk *ad* Tom Doherty *ed* Lara Mazur
☆ Jennifer Dale, Margaret Langrick, Andrea Martin, Tom Butler, Jeff Christensen, Page Fletcher, Lois Maxwell

Martin *
US 1978 95m colour
Laurel (Richard Rubinstein)
A disturbed youth may be a vampire or just a boy with sexual hangups and an appetite for blood.
Gory thriller with a sense of irony, making fun of the superstitions surrounding vampires yet utilizing them for its shocking climax.
wd George A. Romero *ph* Michael Gornick *m* Donald Rubinstein
☆ John Amplas, Lincoln Maazel, Christine Forrest, Elyane Nadeau, Tom Savini, Sarah Venable, Fran Middleton, Al Lavistsky

Martin Luther *
US/Germany 1953 114m bw
Louis de Rochemont/Lutheran Church Productions (Lothar Wolff)
The career and doubts of Martin Luther.
Frequently vivid, occasionally boring, small-scale account of the first Protestant.
w Allan Sloane, Lothar Wolff, others *d* Irving Pichel *ph* Joseph C. Brun *m* Mark Lothar *ad* Fritz Maurischat, Paul Markwitz
☆ *Niall MacGinnis,* John Ruddock, Pierre Lefèvre, Guy Verney, David Horne, Philip Leaver, Irving Pichel, Alexander Gauge
Joseph C. Brun; art direction

Martin Roumagnac
France 1946 99m bw
Alcina (Marc Le Pelletier)
The trial, with flashbacks, of a small-town businessman who has murdered his mistress.
Wholly unabsorbing and ordinary story of a crime passionnel, totally wasting its stars.
wd Georges Lacombe *ph* Roger Hubert *m* Marcel Mirouze
☆ Jean Gabin, Marlene Dietrich, Margo Lion, Marcel Hérrand

'Contaminating A Cinema Near You.'
The Martins
GB 2001 87m Technicolor Panavision
Icon/Tiger Aspect/Icon (Greg Brenman, Dixie Linder, Bruce Davey)
Anxious to give his family a better life, an unemployed man takes them on a holiday he has stolen.
A star vehicle for a comedian who has yet to prove himself a star on screen, and this witless hotchpotch won't help.
wd Tony Grounds *ph* David Johnson *m* Richard Hartley *pd* Michael Carlin *ed* Robin Sales
☆ Lee Evans (Robert Martin), Kathy Burke (Angie), Linda Bassett (Anthea), Eric Byrne (Little Bob), Terri Dumont (Katie), Frank Finlay (Mr Heath), Lennie James (PC Alex), Jack Shepherd (DI Branch)
'A confused mess that has nothing to say and yet still says it loudly.' – *Andrew Anthony, Observer*

Martin's Day
Canada 1985 98m Medallion
World Film Services/MGM-UA (Richard F. Dalton, Roy Krost)
An escaped convict and the young boy he kidnaps become friends.
Predictable melodrama which gets nowhere.
w Allan Scott, Chris Bryant *d* Alan Gibson *ph* Frank Watts *m* Wilfred Josephs *pd* Trevor Williams *ed* David de Wilde
☆ Richard Harris, Lindsay Wagner, James Coburn, Justin Henry, Karen Black, John Ireland

Marty ****
US 1955 91m bw
UA/Hecht-Hill-Lancaster (Harold Hecht)
A 34-year-old Bronx butcher fears he will never get a girl because he is unattractive, but at a Saturday night dance he meets a girl with similar fears. Unfortunately she is not Italian...
The first of the filmed teleplays which in the mid-fifties seemed like a breath of spring to Hollywood (they were cheap) and also brought in a new wave of talent. This is one of the best, its new naturalistic dialogue falling happily on the ear; but it has been so frequently imitated since that its revolutionary appearance is hard to imagine.
w Paddy Chayefsky play Paddy Chayefsky *d Delbert Mann ph Joseph LaShelle m* Roy Webb *ad* Edward S. Howarth, Walter Simonds
☆ *Ernest Borgnine, Betsy Blair, Esther Minciotti, Joe Mantell,* Karen Steele, Jerry Paris
'Something rare in the American cinema today: a subtle, ironic and compassionate study of ordinary human relationships.' – *Gavin Lambert*
† The original 1953 television version was also directed by Delbert Mann and starred Rod Steiger.
picture; Paddy Chayefsky; Delbert Mann; Ernest Borgnine
Joseph LaShelle; Betsy Blair; Joe Mantell; art direction
Ernest Borgnine; Betsy Blair

Marusa no onna: see *A Taxing Woman*

'A story about the years that keep us apart ... And the moments that bring us together.'
Marvin's Room *
US 1996 98m DeLuxe
Buena Vista/Miramax (Scott Rudin, Jane Rosenthal, Robert de Niro)
A woman who cares for her dying father and eccentric aunt discovers that she is terminally ill, and turns for help to her estranged sister, who has family troubles of her own.
A movie that betrays its theatrical origins, and which gives its cast the opportunity for acting with the stops full out, of which they take full advantage.
w Scott McPherson *play* Scott McPherson *d* Jerry Zaks *ph* Piotr Sobocinski *m* Rachel Portman *pd* David Gropman *ed* Jim Clark
☆ Meryl Streep, Leonardo DiCaprio, Diane Keaton, Robert de Niro, Hume Cronyn, Gwen Verdon, Hal Scardino, Dan Hedaya
'A film of many small but glorious moments.' – *Emanuel Levy, Variety*
'This seems a particularly nasty view of old age by a man who knew he'd never be around to experience it.' – *Mark Steyn, Spectator*
† Scott McPherson died of AIDS in 1992, aged 33.
Diane Keaton

The Marx Brothers at the Circus: see *At the Circus*

Mary Burns Fugitive *
US 1935 84m bw
Paramount (Walter Wanger)
The innocent girlfriend of a gangster is convicted through circumstantial evidence, escapes from prison and finds true love.
Competent meshing of well-tried thirties elements, a good typical wish-fulfilment melodrama of its time.
w Gene Towne, Graham Baker, Louis Stevens *d* William K. Howard *ph* Leon Shamroy
☆ Sylvia Sidney, Melvyn Douglas, Alan Baxter, Pert Kelton, Wallace Ford, Brian Donlevy, Esther Dale
'As a piece of synthetic studio slickness it has enough on the ball to qualify.' – *Variety*

Mary Forever: see *Mery per sempre*

Mary Jane's Pa
US 1935 70m bw
Warner
GB title: *Wanderlust*
A husband goes wandering for ten years. On his return, his wife has magnified what he left into a newspaper empire.
Adequate stagey comedy, well acted.
w Tom Reed, Peter Milne *play* Edith Ellis Furness *novel Norman Way d* William Keighley *ph* Ernest Haller *ad* Esdras Hartley *ed* Clarence Kolster

☆ Aline MacMahon, Guy Kibbee, Tom Brown, Robert McWade, Minor Watson, Nan Grey
'Okay for secondary bills.' – *Variety*

Mary Magdalene: see *The Sword and the Cross*

Mary Mary
US 1963 126m Technicolor
Warner (Mervyn Le Roy)
A publisher falls in love again with his ex-wife but finds she is being pursued by a film star.
Feeble film version of a lighter-than-air Broadway success, with the actors paralysed behind the footlights and the camera asleep in the stalls.
w Richard L. Breen *play* Jean Kerr *d* Mervyn Le Roy *ph* Harry Stradling *m* Frank Perkins
☆ Debbie Reynolds, Barry Nelson, Michael Rennie, Diane McBain

Mary of Scotland *
US 1936 123m bw
RKO (Pandro S. Berman)
Mary Stuart refuses to give up her claim to the English throne, and is eventually executed.
Sombre historical charade with splendid sets and atmosphere but suffering from script and performances that don't quite make it despite effort all round.
w Dudley Nichols *play* Maxwell Anderson *d* John Ford *ph* *Joseph H. August* *m* Nathaniel Shilkret *ad* *Van Nest Polglase, Carroll Clark*
☆ Katharine Hepburn, Fredric March, Donald Crisp, Florence Eldridge, Douglas Walton, John Carradine, Robert Barrat, Monte Blue, Moroni Olsen, Frieda Inescort, Alan Mowbray
'An unpromising and stagey play is fleshed out into a rich and confident exercise in filmcraft.' – *John Baxter, 1968*
'Events are walked through as though they were rooms in a museum, and closing time at three.' – *Otis Ferguson*

Mary Poppins ***
US 1964 139m Technicolor
Walt Disney (Bill Walsh)
In Edwardian London a magical nanny teaches two slightly naughty children to make life enjoyable for themselves and others.
Sporadically a very pleasant and effective entertainment for children of all ages, with plenty of brightness and charm including magic tricks, the mixing of live with cartoon adventures, and just plain fun. It suffers, however, from a wandering narrative in the second half (when Miss Poppins scarcely appears) and from Mr Van Dyke's really lamentable attempt at Cockney.
w Bill Walsh, Don da Gradi *novel* P. L. Travers *d* Robert Stevenson *ph* Edward Colman *m/ly* *Richard M. and Robert B. Sherman* *md* Irwin Kostal *pd* Tony Walton *ad* Carroll Clark, William H. Tuntke *ed* Cotton Warburton *sp* *Eustace Lycett, Peter Ellenshaw, Robert A. Mattey*
☆ *Julie Andrews*, David Tomlinson, Glynis Johns, Dick Van Dyke, Reginald Owen, Ed Wynn, Matthew Garber, Karen Dotrice, Hermione Baddeley, Elsa Lanchester, Arthur Treacher, Jane Darwell
'A charming, imaginative and technically superb movie musical, sparkling with originality, melody and magical performances.' – *Judith Crist*
Richard M. and Robert B. Sherman; Julie Andrews; song 'Chim Chim Cheree'; special visual effects; editing
best picture; script; Robert Stevenson; Edward Colman; Irwin Kostal; art direction
Julie Andrews

'They used every passion in their incredible duel, and every man in their savage games of intrigue!'
Mary Queen of Scots
GB 1971 128m Technicolor
Panavision
Universal/Hal B. Wallis
The story of Mary Stuart's opposition to Elizabeth I, her imprisonment and execution.
Schoolbook history in which none of the characters comes to life; dramatic movement is almost entirely lacking despite the liberties taken with fact.
w John Hale *d* Charles Jarrott *ph* Christopher Challis *m* John Barry *pd* Terry Marsh *ed* Richard Marden
☆ Vanessa Redgrave (Mary, Queen of Scots), Glenda Jackson (Elizabeth I), Trevor Howard (William Cecil), Patrick McGoohan (James Stuart), Nigel Davenport (James Hepburn), Timothy Dalton (Lord Henry Darnley), Ian Holm (David Riccio), Daniel Massey (Robert Dudley), Tom Fleming (Ballard)
'Without a better script, Hercules couldn't lift this story off the ground.' – *Pauline Kael, New Yorker*
John Barry; Vanessa Redgrave

'Evil is irresistible.'
Mary Reilly
US 1996 109m Technicolor
TriStar (Ned Tanen, Nancy Graham Tanen, Norma Heyman)
The new chambermaid in the household of Dr Jekyll is attracted by the doctor's lecherous assistant, Mr Hyde.
A handsome but dull attempt to turn Stevenson's tale of a split personality into a Jane Eyre-like romantic drama, but neither of the two leads is convincing and there is little sign of any attraction between them.
w Christopher Hampton *novel* Valerie Martin *d* Stephen Frears *ph* Philippe Rousselot *m* George Fenton *pd* Stuart Craig *ed* Lesley Walker
☆ Julia Roberts, John Malkovich, George Cole, Michael Gambon, Glenn Close, Kathy Staff, Michael Sheen, Ciaran Hinds
'Has plenty of production polish but little of the dramatic force and erotic spark needed.' – *Variety*
'I should never have done Mary Reilly. I knew that before I started. It was full of great design and photography, but it should have been a little BBC film.' – *Stephen Frears*
† The film, which cost $47m to make, flopped at the box-office.

Mary Shelley's Frankenstein *
US 1994 123m Technicolor
Columbia TriStar/American Zoetrope/Japan Satellite/IndieProd (Francis Ford Coppola, James V. Hart, John Veitch)
A scientist tells a sea captain how he gave life to a creature, which, when he refused to create a mate for it, took revenge on his family.
A bold and brash attempt to be true to the original novel, but which, like its monster, gets lost in the Arctic wastes and then confuses the narrative by focusing the attention on its over-production; it fails to dislodge the original film from folk memory.
w Steph Lady, Frank Darabont *novel* Mary Shelley *d* Kenneth Branagh *ph* Roger Pratt *m* Patrick Doyle *pd* Tim Harvey *ed* Andrew Marcus
☆ Robert DeNiro, Kenneth Branagh, Tom Hulce, Helena Bonham Carter, Aidan Quinn, Ian Holm, Richard Briers, John Cleese, Robert Hardy, Cherie Lunghi, Celia Imrie
'A highly paced costume drama that propels us along the trajectory of Frankenstein's ambition with a speed reminiscent of *Indiana Jones*.' – *Oscar Moore, Screen International*
'Much of *Frankenstein* is spectacular and hyperbolic, but in a good way. Kenneth Branagh has made a very fleshy and visceral movie, though not a horror movie in the normal sense.' – *David Denby, New York*
'A gargoyle short of the Gothic horror that made the original unforgettable.' – *Ingrid Pitt*
'More a case of Mary Shelley's Frankie Goes to Hollywood.' – *Adam Mars-Jones, Independent*
make-up

Mary Stevens M.D.
US 1933 71m bw
Warner
A lady doctor decides to have a baby before getting married.
Saucy drama which engrossed audiences in its day.
w Rian James *novel* Virginia Kellogg *d* Lloyd Bacon
☆ Kay Francis, Lyle Talbot, Glenda Farrell, Thelma Todd, Una O'Connor, Hobart Cavanaugh, Harold Huber
'Exceptionally good adult entertainment, with a pronounced feminine appeal.' – *Variety*

Maryland
US 1940 92m Technicolor
TCF (Gene Markey)
After her husband is killed in a fox-hunting accident, his wife tries to keep their son away from horses.
Over-lavish treatment of a trite story; money has been spent on everything except the script.
w Ethel Hill, Jack Andrews *d* Henry King *md* Alfred Newman
☆ Walter Brennan, Fay Bainter, Brenda Joyce, John Payne, Charles Ruggles, Hattie McDaniel, Marjorie Weaver, Sidney Blackmer, Ben Carter

Masala *
Canada 1991 106m colour
Metro/Divani/Telefilm Canada/Ontario Film Development/Ontario Arts Council (Srinivas Krishna, Camelia Freiberg)
The Hindu god Krishna grants a miracle to a Sikh family living in Toronto.
An irreverent small-scale movie that provides pleasure.
wd Srinivas Krishna *ph* Paul Sarossy *m* The West India Company, Leslie Winston *pd* Tamara Deverell *ed* Michael Munn
☆ Srinivas Krishna, Sakina Jaffrey, Zohra Segal, Saeed Jaffrey, Heri Johal, Madhuri Bhatia, Ronica Sajnani, Les Porter
'A highly entertaining work.' – *Sight and Sound*

La Maschera
Italy 1988 90m Eastmancolor
RAIDVE/Istituto Luce/Best International (Lilia Smecchia, Ettore Rosboch)
aka: *The Mask*
In the 18th century a young actress rejects the advances of a dissolute aristocrat and then falls in love with a mysterious masked stranger.
Lugubrious romance, concentrating on glossy surfaces.
w Adriano Apra, Fiorella Infascelli, Enzo Ungari, Ennio de Concini *d* Fiorella Infascelli *ph* Acacio de Almeida *m* Luis Bacalov *ad* Antonello Geleng *ed* Francisco Malvestito
☆ Helena Bonham Carter, Michael Maloney, Feodor Chaliapin Jnr, Roberto Herlitzka, Michele de Marchi, Alberto Cracco

La Maschera del Demonio: see *Mask of Satan*

The Mascot **
France 1916 20m bw
H. Rose/Gelma
The adventures of a toy dog, who goes to hell and back.
A mix of live action and stop-motion animation, amusing and macabre, by an early master of the craft.
wd Ladislaw Starewicz
† The film has been released on video with the feature-length *The Tale of the Fox* (qv) and four other shorts under the title *Ladislaw Starewicz: Selected Films*.

Masculin Féminin **
France/Sweden 1966 110m bw
Gala/Anouchka/Argos/Svensk/Sandrews (Philippe Dussart)
A young, romantic revolutionary imagines that he is in love with a would-be singer.
An exploration of pop culture and politics, in a sequence of episodes intercut with arbitrary happenings, and as much concerned with form as content, moving cinema away from straightforward narrative to something more abstract and less interesting.
wd Jean-Luc Godard *story* *La Femme de Paul* by Guy de Maupassant *ph* Willy Kurant *m* Francis Lai *ed* Agnès Guillemot
☆ Jean-Pierre Léaud, Chantal Goya, Catherine-Isabelle Duport, Marlène Jobert, Michel Debord, Birger-Malmsten, Eva Britt Strandberg, Brigitte Bardot, Françoise Hardy
'Godard's exercise in self-indulgence.' – *John Simon*
'That rare movie achievement: a work of grace and beauty in a contemporary setting.' – *Pauline Kael*
'By this defiantly unrealistic system of narrative, Godard manages to present us with all the problems facing his hero and facing boys of his generation.' – *Richard Roud*
'Mainly it seems to be a movie happening, in which Mr Godard can play whimsical and sometimes comical stunts, not leading to any clear conclusion as to the stability of youth. He himself, as a motion-picture maker, seems to have little more concentration-span than his saucy, good-looking youngsters, who evidently have none at all.' – *Bosley Crowther*
† For its American release, it was cut to 103m.

M*A*S*H ****
US 1970 116m DeLuxe Panavision
TCF/Aspen (Ingo Preminger, Leon Ericksen)
Surgeons at a mobile hospital in Korea spend what spare time they have chasing women and bucking authority.
Savage comedy of man's rebellion in the face of death, alternating sex farce with gory operation scenes; hailed as the great anti-everything film, and certainly very funny for those who can take it. It led to a television series which for once did not disgrace its original.
w *Ring Lardner Jnr* *novel* Richard Hooker *d* *Robert Altman* *ph* Harold E. Stine *m* Johnny Mandel
☆ Donald Sutherland, Elliott Gould, Tom Skerritt, Sally Kellerman, Robert Duvall, Jo Ann Pflug, René Auberjonois, Gary Burghoff
'Bloody funny. A hyper-acute wiretap on mankind's death wish.' – *Joseph Morgenstern*
'The laughter is blood-soaked and the comedy cloaks a bitter and terrible truth.' – *Judith Crist*
'A foul-mouthed, raucous, anti-establishment comedy, combining gallows humour, sexual slapstick and outrageous satire.' – *Les Keyser, Hollywood in the Seventies*
Ring Lardner Jnr
best picture; Robert Altman; Sally Kellerman

Mask **
US 1985 120m Technicolor
Universal/Martin Starger
A boy of 16 has a rare and disfiguring bone disease, but his mother fights for his rights.
More of a character study than a movie, this also has the problem of being emotionally hard to take; but one ends up respecting it.
w Anna Hamilton Phelan, from her true story of Rocky Dennis *d* *Peter Bogdanovich* *ph* Laszlo Kovacs *m* Dennis Ricotta *ed* Barbara Ford
☆ Cher, Sam Elliott, Eric Stoltz, Estelle Getty
'Anyone looking for a good uplifting cry should be well satisfied.' – *Variety*

The Mask: see *La Maschera (1988)*

'From Zero To Hero.'
The Mask **
US 1994 101m Foto-Kem
Entertainment/New Line/Dark Horse (Bob Engelman)
A wimpish bank clerk in a constant state of humiliation finds a mask that transforms him into a green-faced comic-book hero capable of humiliating everyone.
Antic, amusing comedy that finds a perfect setting for the exaggerated style of Jim Carrey: cartoon-style humour, borrowing heavily from Chuck Jones and Tex Avery. The jokes are often familiar, but never seen before in a real-life setting thanks to the spectacular digital special effects.
w Mike Werb *story* Michael Fallon, Mark Verheiden based on characters appearing in Dark Horse Comics *d* Chuck Russell *ph* John R. Leonetti *m* Randy Edelman *pd* Craig Stearns *ed* Arthur Coburn *sp* make-up: Greg Cannom; visual effects: Ken Ralston, Scott Squires, Steve 'Spaz' Williams, Industrial Light and Magic
☆ Jim Carrey, Peter Riegert, Cameron Diaz, Peter Greene, Amy Yasbeck, Richard Jeni, Orestes Matacena, Tim Bagley, Nancy Fish, Johnny Williams
'The story is predictable and has little imagination outside its technical prowess – some extraordinary special effects.' – *Derek Malcolm, Guardian*
'As dull-witted and straitjacketed by cliché as it is visually hellzapoppin, the film may be a watershed moment in the cultural current that looks to loot the baby-boomer memory banks for recyclable cinematic ideas.' – *Michael Atkinson, Sight and Sound*
visual effects

The Mask of Dimitrios **
US 1944 99m bw
Warner (Henry Blanke)
A timid Dutch novelist is drawn into a Middle-Eastern intrigue with money at the centre of it.
Generally successful international intriguer, moodily shot in evocative sets, and remarkable for its time in that the story is not distorted to fit romantic stars: character actors bear the entire burden.
w *Frank Gruber* novel Eric Ambler d *Jean Negulesco* ph *Arthur Edeson* m Adolph Deutsch
☆ *Peter Lorre, Sydney Greenstreet, Zachary Scott,* Faye Emerson, *Victor Francen, Steven Geray, Florence Bates, Eduardo Ciannelli, Kurt Katch,* John Abbott, Monte Blue
'The picture has more mood than excitement.' – *Pauline Kael, 70s*

The Mask of Fu Manchu **
US 1932 70m bw
MGM
Nayland Smith and his party are caught and threatened with torture by the yellow terror.
Highly satisfactory episode in the nefarious adventures of the master criminal, fast moving, humorous and very good to look at.
w John Willard, Edgar Woolf, Irene Kuhn stories Sax Rohmer d *Charles Brabin, Charles Vidor* ph *Tony Gaudio*
☆ *Boris Karloff, Myrna Loy, Lewis Stone,* Karen Morley, Charles Starrett, Jean Hersholt, Lawrence Grant
'The diabolical stuff is piled on so thick at the finish, audiences are liable to laugh where they oughtn't.' – *Variety*
'A tolerable, campy entertainment.' – *Pauline Kael, 70s*

Mask of Satan *
Italy 1960 84m bw
Galatea/Jolly (Massimo de Rita)
original title: *La Maschera del Demonio*
aka: *Black Sunday; Revenge of the Vampire*
A princess who was executed for witchcraft by her brother returns 200 years later to wreak vengeance on his descendants.
A stylish, though gruesome, horror movie.
w Mario Bava, Ennio de Concini, Marcello Coscia, Mario Serandrei d *Mario Bava* ph Mario Bava, Ubaldo Terzano sp Mario Bava
☆ Barbara Steele, John Richardson, Ivo Garrani, Andrea Cecchi, Arturo Dominici, Enrico Olivieri, Clara Bindi
'The greatest gothic horror movie ever made in Italy.' – *Empire*

Mask of the Avenger
US 1951 83m Technicolor
Columbia (Hunt Stromberg)
During the Austro-Italian War, a count's son avenges his father's death and exposes a traitor.
Very moderate swashbuckler on the lines of The Mark of Zorro.
w Jesse Lasky Jnr d Phil Karlson ph Charles Lawton Jnr m George Duning
☆ John Derek, Anthony Quinn, Jody Lawrance, Arnold Moss, Eugene Iglesias

The Mask of Zorro **
US 1998 136m CFI color Panavision
Columbia TriStar/Amblin/Zorro (Doug Claybourne, David Foster)
An ageing Zorro trains a young man to take his place and prevent the man who killed his wife and kidnapped his daughter from ruling over California.
An enjoyable, high-spirited return to the style of an old-fashioned swashbuckler, with added sex appeal.
w John Eskow, Ted Elliott, Terry Rossio d Martin Campbell ph Phil Meheux m James Horner pd Cecilia Montiel ed Thom Noble
☆ Antonio Banderas, Anthony Hopkins, Catherine Zeta-Jones, Stuart Wilson, Matt Letscher, Maury Chaykin, Tony Amendola, Pedro Armendariz, L. Q. Jones
'You haven't seen anything like this since the good old Indiana Jones days.' – *Alan Jones, Film Review*
sound; sound effects editing

Maskerade *
Austria 1935 87m bw
Tobis/Sascha
An inveterate ladies' man finds himself trapped.
Charming romantic comedy.
w Walter Reisch d Willi Forst ph Franz Planer
☆ Anton Walbrook, Paula Wessely, Olga Tscheshowa
'Not a real masterpiece like *Liebelei*, but it has the same b.o. elements.' – *Variety*

The Masque of the Red Death **
GB 1964 89m Pathécolor 'Scope
AIP/Alta Vista (George Willoughby)
A medieval Italian prince practises devil worship while the plague rages outside, but when he holds a ball, death is an uninvited guest.
Languorous, overstretched, often visually striking horror piece with some extremely effective touches among its longueurs.
w Charles Beaumont, R. Wright Campbell story Edgar Allan Poe d *Roger Corman* ph *Nicolas Roeg* m David Lee ad *Robert Jones* cos *Laura Nightingale*
☆ Vincent Price, Hazel Court, Jane Asher, Patrick Magee, John Westbrook

Masquerade *
GB 1965 101m Eastmancolor
UA/Novus (Michael Relph)
To avert friction between Arab states the young heir to one of them is abducted by a British secret service agent; but one of the plotters has other fish to fry.
Quite a lively spy romp with a spectacular action climax, but the plot is simply too complicated.
w Michael Relph, William Goldman novel *Castle Minerva* by Victor Canning d Basil Dearden ph Otto Heller m Philip Green pd Don Ashton
☆ Cliff Robertson, Jack Hawkins, Charles Gray, Bill Fraser, Marisa Mell, Michel Piccoli, John Le Mesurier

Masquerade
US 1988 91m colour
UIP/MGM (Michael I. Levy)
A gigolo marries a wealthy woman with the intention of murdering her for her money.
Dull thriller that fails to maintain interest.
w Dick Wolf d Bob Swaim ph David Watkin m John Barry pd John Kasarda ed Scott Conrad
☆ Rob Lowe, Meg Tilly, Kim Cattrall, Doug Savant, John Glover, Dana Delany, Erik Holland, Brian Davies, Barton Heyman
'A tranquil, sophisticated thriller.' – *Pauline Kael, New Yorker*

'A gay and gorgeous whirl of romance, adventure and rhythm ... in the billion-dollar pan-American postwar playground!'
Masquerade in Mexico
US 1945 96m bw
Paramount (Karl Tunberg)
A stranded showgirl is hired by a Mexican banker to entice a gigolo away from his wife.
Talent-starved remake of Midnight (qv), which seems second-hand even if you don't know why.
w Karl Tunberg d Mitchell Leisen ph Lionel Lindon m Victor Young
☆ Dorothy Lamour, Arturo de Cordova, Patric Knowles, Ann Dvorak, George Rigaud, Natalie Schafer, Mikhail Rasumny, Billy Daniels

The Masquerader *
US 1933 75m bw
Samuel Goldwyn
A drug-addicted politician is replaced by his lookalike cousin.
Pleasing dual role star vehicle with good production and support. Very much of its period.
w Howard Estabrook, Moss Hart play John Hunter Booth novel *Katherine Cecil Thurston* d Richard Wallace ph Gregg Toland m Alfred Newman
☆ *Ronald Colman,* Elissa Landi, *Halliwell Hobbes,* Juliette Compton, David Torrence
'A fine production with too much story handicap ... Colman's best is not enough.' – *Variety*
'The first amusing and believable tale of English politics and society ... made of all places in Hollywood.' – *Newsweek*

Masques *
France 1987 100m colour
Cannon/MK2 Productions/A2 (Marin Karmitz)
A thriller writer inveigles his way into the home of a TV game-show host to solve the mysterious disappearance of his sister.
Glossy, well-made thriller that promises more than it delivers, but is enjoyable for Noiret's performance as a hypocritically hearty television celebrity.
w Odile Barski, Claude Chabrol d Claude Chabrol ph Jean Rabier m Matthieu Chabrol ad Françoise Benoit-Fresco ed Monique Fardoulis
☆ Philippe Noiret, Robin Renucci, Bernadette Lafont, Monique Chaumette, Anne Brochet, Roger Dumas, Pierre-François Dumeniaud

Mass Appeal *
US 1984 100m Technicolor
Universal/Turman-Foster
An idealistic student matches wits with a compromising priest.
Amusing, opened-out version of a two-character play: good for minority audiences.
w Bill C. David play Bill C. David d Glenn Jordan ph Don Peterman m Bill Conti pd Philip Jefferies
☆ Jack Lemmon, Zeljko Ivanek, Charles Durning, Louise Latham
'Saved from damnation by the originality of its central theme and by the excellence of its acting.' – *Quentin Crisp*

Massacre Hill: see *Eureka Stockade*

Massacre in Rome
Italy 1973 103m Technicolor
Compagnia Cinematografica Champion (Carlo Ponti)
In 1944, after partisans blow up a detachment of SS troops in a Rome street, a German colonel makes an ineffectual attempt to resist an order to shoot 330 Italians in retaliation.
Moderately effective drama, based on a true story.
w Robert Katz, George Pan Cosmatos book *Death in Rome* by Robert Katz d George Pan Cosmatos ph Marcello Gatti m Ennio Morricone pd Morton Haack ed Françoise Bonnot, Roberto Silvi
☆ Richard Burton, Marcello Mastroianni, Leo McKern, John Steiner, Anthony Steel, Robert Harris, Peter Vaughan, Delia Boccardo

The Master Gunfighter
US 1975 120m Metrocolor Panavision
Avondale/Warner
In gold rush California, a mysterious avenger rights a variety of wrongs.
Pretentious Western which failed to advance the career of its somewhat over-confident creator.
w Harold Lapland d Tom Laughlin ph Jack Marta m Lalo Schifrin pd Albert Brenner
☆ Tom Laughlin, Ron O'Neal, Lincoln Kilpatrick, Barbara Carrera
† From a Japanese film *Goyokin* written by Kei Tasaka and Hideo Gosha

The Master of Ballantrae
GB 1953 89m Technicolor
Warner
Two brothers toss to decide which shall join Bonnie Prince Charlie's 1745 rebellion.
Half-hearted version of a classic adventure novel.
w Herb Meadow novel R. L. Stevenson d William Keighley ph Jack Cardiff m William Alwyn
☆ Errol Flynn, Anthony Steel, Roger Livesey, Beatrice Campbell, Felix Aylmer, Mervyn Johns, Jacques Berthier, Yvonne Furneaux, Ralph Truman
'All that can be salvaged from this rather unforgivable Anglo-American junket are some pleasant exteriors.' – *Gavin Lambert*

Master of Bankdam *
GB 1947 105m bw
GFD/Holbein (Nat Bronsten, Walter Forde, Edward Dryhurst)
19th-century chronicles of a mill-owning Yorkshire family.
Archetypal 'trouble at t'mill' saga with moderate production, good acting and undeniably compulsive story.
w Edward Dryhurst, Moie Charles novel *The Crowthers of Bankdam* by Thomas Armstrong d Walter Forde ph *Basil Emmott* m Arthur Benjamin md Muir Mathieson ad G. Patterson ed Terry Fisher cos Doris Lee
☆ *Tom Walls* (Simeon Crowther), Anne Crawford (Annie Pickersgill), Dennis Price (Joshua Crowther), Stephen Murray (Zebediah Crowther), Linden Travers (Clara Baker), Jimmy Hanley (Simeon Crowther Jnr), Nancy Price (Lydia Crowther), David Tomlinson (Lancelot Handel Crowther), Herbert Lomas (Tom France), Patrick Holt (Lemuel Pickersgill), Nicholas Parsons (Edgar Hoylehouse)

'He can get into any disguise... getting out is another story.'
Master of Disguise
US 2002 80m DeLuxe
Revolution/Happy Madison/Out of the Blue (Sid Ganis, Alex Siskin, Barry Bernardi, Todd Garner)
When his crime-fighting father is kidnapped, a restaurateur learns the family skills of disguise to rescue him.
Carvey shows himself to be a man of a thousand faces; what he cannot disguise, though, is that this is a tedious, woeful, witless movie.
w Dana Carvey, Harris Goldberg d Perry Andelin Blake ph Peter Lyons Collister m Marc Ellis pd Alan Au ed Peck Prior, Sandy Solowitz sp make-up fx: Kevin Yagher
☆ Dana Carvey (Pistachio), Jennifer Esposito (Jennifer), Harold Gould (Grandfather), James Brolin (Frabbrizio), Brent Spiner (Bowman), Edie McClurg (Mother), Maria Canals (Sophia)
'Everything in the film has been fine-tuned to produce the least possible mirth. I suppose we should be grateful that it doesn't last much longer than an hour.' – *Nicholas Barber, Independent*

Master of Lassie: see *The Hills of Home*

Master of the House *
Denmark 1925 107m bw
Palladium
original title: *Du Skal Aere Din Hustru*
A husband is cured of his domestic tyranny.
Enjoyable account of a man's comeuppance at the hands of his old nanny, one that is also perceptive about relationships.
w Carl Theodor Dreyer, Sven Rindom play *Tyraennens Fald* by Sven Rindom d Carl Theodor Dreyer ph George Schnéevoigt ad Carl Theodor Dreyer
☆ Johannes Meyer, Astrid Holm, Karin Nellemose, Clara Schonfeld, Mathilde Nielsen, Johannes Nielsen, Petrine Sonne

Master of the Islands: see *The Hawaiians*

Master of the World
US 1961 104m Magnacolor
AIP/Alta Vista (James H. Nicholson, Anthony Carras)
In 1848 a mad inventor takes to the air in his magnificent flying machine in the hope of persuading men to stop war.
Aerial version of Twenty Thousand Leagues under the Sea, *with cheap sets and much use of stock footage; some scenes however have a certain vigour.*
w Richard Matheson novel Jules Verne d William Witney ph Gil Warrenton m Les Baxter
☆ Vincent Price, Charles Bronson, Henry Hull, Mary Webster, David Frankham

The Master Plan
GB 1954 78m bw
Gibraltar
An American agent, concealing the fact that he suffers from blackouts, is sent to investigate information leakages in England.
Quite lively second feature spylarks.
wd Cy Endfield ph Jonah Jones
☆ Wayne Morris, Tilda Thamar, Norman Wooland, Mary Mackenzie, Arnold Bell

The Master Race
US 1944 96m bw
Edward Golden

German generals realize that the war is lost, and plan counter-measures.
Timely propaganda melodrama warning against premature rejoicing, from the producer of Hitler's Children.
wd Herbert J. Biberman.
☆ George Coulouris, Osa Massen, Stanley Ridges, Nancy Gates, Carl Esmond, Morris Carnovsky, Lloyd Bridges

The Masters
Italy 1975 100m Technospes
Campagnia Cinematografica Champion (Carlo Ponti)
original title: *Gente di rispetto*
A new and naïve schoolteacher in a small Sicilian town becomes involved in corrupt local politics after a man who insulted her is murdered by the Mafia.
Glossy thriller that fails to carry any conviction.
w Leo Benevenuti, Piero de Bernardi, Luigi Zampa *story* Giuseppe Fava *d* Luigi Zampa *ph* Ennio Guarnieri *m* Ennio Morricone *ad* Luigi Scaccianoce *ed* Franco Fraticelli
☆ James Mason, Jennifer O'Neill, Franco Nero, Orazio Orlando, Claudio Gora, Franco Fabrizi, Aldo Giuffré

Masters of Menace
US 1990 97m colour
Cinetel/Hertzberg-Hanson-Insana

A motorcycle gang violates its three-year probation in order to bury one of its members in Las Vegas.
Coarse and aimless send-up of biker movies, which at least ends appropriately, with a vat of manure.
w Tino Insana *d* Daniel Raskov *ph* Edward J. Pei *m* Hawk Wolinski *ed* Stephen Myers
☆ David Rasche, Catherine Bach, Lance Kinsey, Teri Copley, Ray Baker, David L. Lander
'Original humor was obviously not required.' – *Variety*
† Dan Aykroyd, Jim Belushi, John Candy and George Wendt appear in cameo roles.

Masters of the Universe
US 1987 106m Metrocolor
Edward R. Pressman/Cannon

He-Man defends the planet Eternia from the evil Skeletor.
Live action version of the TV cartoons of the toys of the comic strip. Pretty weak stuff, even for five-year-olds.
w David Odell *d* Gary Goddard *ph* Hanania Baer *m* Bill Conti *pd* William Stout *ed* Anne V. Coates
☆ Dolph Lundgren, Frank Langella, Meg Foster, Billy Barty

Masterson of Kansas
US 1955 73m Technicolor
Columbia (Sam Katzman)
The sheriff of Dodge City prevents an Indian uprising by saving an innocent man from the gallows.
Unhistorical two-bit Western.
w Douglas Heyes *d* William Castle *ph* Henry Freulich *md* Mischa Bakaleinikoff
☆ George Montgomery, Nancy Gates, James Griffith, Jean Willes

Mat: see *Mother*

Mat i syn: see *Mother and Son*

'Men worshipped her like a goddess, only to be betrayed by a kiss!'
Mata Hari **
US 1931 92m bw
MGM

The career of the famous lady spy of World War I.
Elaborate melodrama, pictorially satisfying and generally more entertaining than might be supposed, with both star and supporting cast in rich thespian form.
w Benjamin Glazer, Leo Birinsky, Doris Anderson, Gilbert Emery *d* George Fitzmaurice *ph* William Daniels
☆ *Greta Garbo*, Ramon Novarro, Lionel Barrymore, Lewis Stone, C. Henry Gordon, Karen Morley, Blanche Frederici
'Picture's strength is all in the players; an important grosser on that account.' – *Variety*

Mata Hari
US 1985 108m Eastmancolor
Rony Yacov/Cannon

The career of the famous lady spy of World War I.
Absurd melodrama which in places seems to be spoofing itself.
w Joel Ziskin *d* Curtis Harrington
☆ Sylvia Kristel, Christopher Cazenove, Oliver Tobias, Gaye Brown, William Fox

Mata Hari, Agent H21 *
France/Italy 1964 99m bw
Filmel/Les Films du Carrosse/Simar/Fida Cinematografica (Eugene Lepicier)
A rather unnecessary revamp of the same story, with interesting details but not much resonance.
w Jean-Louis Richard, François Truffaut *d* Jean-Louis Richard *ph* Michel Kelber *m* Georges Delerue *ad* Claude Pignot
☆ *Jeanne Moreau*, Jean-Louis Trintignant, Claude Rich, Frank Villard
'All that we are left with is a generous dollop of period charm, and the fascinating spontaneity of an actress.' – *Peter John Dyer, MFB*

Matador *
Spain 1988 106m colour
Iberoamericana de TV/Televisión Española (Andrés Vicente Gómez)

A lame, death-obsessed matador is smitten by a sex- and death-obsessed woman, the defending lawyer of a psychic, guilt-obsessed, would-be bullfighter who has confessed to a series of murders he did not commit.
An intense though unerotic treatment of decadent passions; it is comparatively restrained by its director's usual standards, avoiding camp, though it manages to encompass scenes of attempted rape, violent death, and masturbation to images of mutilation.
w Jesus Ferrero, Pedro Almodóvar *d* Pedro Almodóvar *ph* Angel Luis Fernández *m* Bernardo Bonezzi *ad* Roman Arango, José Morales, José Rosell *ed* Pepe Salcedo
☆ Assumpta Serna, Antonio Banderas, Bibi Andersen, Nacho Martinez, Eva Cobo, Julieta Serrano, Chus Lampreave, Carmen Maura, Eusebio Poncela
'Chips away at the surface elegance of the bourgeoisie to expose its private vices.' – *Sight and Sound*
'A piece of voluptuous tom-foolery.' – *Pauline Kael, New Yorker*

The Match
GB/US/Ireland 1999 96m Technicolor
Polygram/Propaganda/Irish Dreamtime (Allan Scott, Guymon Casady)

A pub football team, which has lost its annual match against a neighbouring inn for 99 years, gets ready to compete in the 100th game, with the loser agreeing to shut down his business.
Thoroughly predictable Scottish comedy about a group of losers discovering a winning community spirit; it might have worked had it been funny, or even amusing.
wd Mick Davis *ph* Witold Stok *m* Harry Gregson-Williams *pd* John Frankish *ed* Kate Williams
☆ Max Beesley (Wullie Smith), Isla Blair (Sheila Bailey), James Cosmo (Billy Bailey), Laura Fraser (Rosemary Bailey), Richard E. Grant (Gorgeous Gus), David Hayman (Scrapper), Ian Holm (Big Tam), Neil Morrissey (Mr Doris), Bill Paterson (Tommy), Iain Robertson (Danny Van Boy), Tom Sizemore (Buffalo), Pierce Brosnan (John McGee), Alan Shearer (Himself)
'Truly dire.' – *Guardian*

The Match Factory Girl **
Finland/Sweden 1990 70m Eastmancolor
Electric Pictures/Swedish Film Institute/ Viillealfa/Aki Kaurismäki

original title: *Tulitikkutehtaan Tytto*
A downtrodden factory girl takes her revenge on those who have taken her for granted.
Quietly savage comedy, filmed in a minimalist style.
wd Aki Kaurismäki *ph* Timo Salminen *pd* Risto Karhula *ed* Aki Kaurismäki
☆ Kati Outinen, Elina Salo, Esko Nikkari, Vesa Vierikko, Reijo Taipale, Silu Seppälä

The Match King
US 1932 80m bw
Warner
A world-famous match manufacturer gets into spectacular money difficulties.
Thinly veiled biopic of Ivar Kreuger; not at all bad.
w Houston Branch and Sidney Sutherland
d Howard Bretherton
☆ *Warren William*, Lili Damita, Glenda Farrell, Harold Huber
'Good entertainment, uncommonly well acted … in Swedish-populated sections should be top moneymaker.' – *Variety*

The Matchmaker *
US 1958 101m bw Vistavision
Paramount (Don Hartman)

In New York at the turn of the century, a rich merchant decides to marry again but the matchmaker he consults has her own eye on him.
Cold and lifeless version of an amusing play which also served as the basis for the musical Hello Dolly *(qv).*
w John Michael Hayes *play* Thornton Wilder
d Joseph Anthony *ph* Charles Lang *m* Adolph Deutsch
☆ Shirley Booth, Paul Ford, Anthony Perkins, Shirley MacLaine, Wallace Ford, Robert Morse, Perry Wilson
DOLLY LEVI (SHIRLEY BOOTH) TO THE AUDIENCE: 'Life's never quite interesting enough, somehow. You people who come to the movies know that.'
'Long static dialogue exchanges are further extended by frequent confidences expressed directly to the audience … but in spite of the general lack of pace, lightness and dimension there is still a great deal to enjoy.' – *Peter John Dyer*

La Maternelle *
France 1932 89m bw
Photosonor
A maid in a nursery school becomes devoted to the children and in particular to one who causes trouble when her friend decides to marry.
A touching drama of its day which now seems rather primitive.
w Jean Benoit-Lévy *d* Jean Benoit-Lévy, Marie Epstein *ph* Georges Asselin *m* Edouard Flament
☆ Madeleine Renaud, Paulette Elambert, Alice Tissot, Mady Berry
'By any standard the finest foreign-language talker shown in the US in a couple of years.' – *Variety*

Matewan **
US 1987 133m DuArt
Enterprise/Cinecom Entertainment/Film Gallery/Red Dog (Peggy Rajski, Maggie Renzi)

Striking miners battle against brutal owners determined to break the strike.
Engaging hard-edged political drama.
wd John Sayles *ph* Haskell Wexler *pd* Nora Chavooshian *ed* Sonya Polonsky
☆ Chris Cooper, Mary McDonnell, Will Oldham, David Strathairn, Ken Jenkins, Kevin Tighe, Gordon Clapp, James Earl Jones, Bob Gunton, Jace Alexander
Haskell Wexler

Matilda: see *Roald Dahl's Matilda*

Matilda
US 1978 105m Movielab
AIP/Albert S. Ruddy
A down-at-heel theatrical agent finds success with a boxing kangaroo.
Damon Runyon meets Walt Disney in an old-fashioned family audience picture for which there may no longer be an audience.
w Albert S. Ruddy, Timothy Galfas *novel* Paul Gallico *d* Daniel Mann *ph* Jack Woolf *m* Jerrold Immel *pd* Boris Leven
☆ Elliott Gould, Robert Mitchum, Harry Guardino, Clive Revill, Karen Carlson, Lionel Stander, Art Metrano, Roy Clark

'Lawrence Woolsey presents the end of civilisation as we know it. Make that … Proudly Presents'
Matinee *
US 1993 99m DeLuxe
Guild/Universal

At the time of the Cuban missile crisis, a B-movie-maker arrives at a US naval base to stage the premiere of his new horror film about a half-man, half-ant, incorporating the cinema-seat-shaking Rumblerama.
An enjoyable celebration of the nuclear-inspired, gimmicky horror movies of the 50s, brilliantly parodied; but it is hampered by a teen romance, presented without apparent irony, which might have been lifted from any drive-in movie of the period.
w Charlie Haas *story* Jerico *d* Joe Dante *ph* John Hora *m* Jerry Goldsmith *pd* Steven Legler *ed* Marshall Harvey
☆ *John Goodman*, Cathy Moriarty, Simon Fenton, Omri Katz, Lisa Jakub, Kellie Martin, Jesse Lee, Dick Miller, John Sayles
'Even when the film gets bogged down in romantic drivel, there are enough clever in-jokes and well-remembered period details to keep buffs happy.' – *Variety*
† The character played by Goodman is based on the showman-producer-director William Castle.

The Mating Game
US 1958 96m Metrocolor Cinemascope
MGM (Philip Barry Jnr)
An income-tax inspector becomes involved in the affairs of an unorthodox farming family.
Dismally unfunny adaptation for Americans of a very English novel; everyone works hard to no avail.
w William Roberts *novel The Darling Buds of May* by H. E. Bates *d* George Marshall *ph* Robert Bronner *m* Jeff Alexander
☆ Debbie Reynolds, Tony Randall, Paul Douglas, Fred Clark, Una Merkel, Philip Ober, Charles Lane, Philip Coolidge
'Every joke is driven past the point of exhaustion.' – *MFB*
† H. E. Bates's novel was the basis for a successful television series, *The Darling Buds of May* (1991–93), starring David Jason and Pam Ferris.

The Mating of Millie
US 1948 87m bw
Columbia
A self-confident young woman wants to adopt a small boy and tries to propel a bus driver into a marriage of convenience.
Amiable if protracted romantic comedy with dashes of sentiment and an obvious outcome.
w Louella MacFarlane, St Clair McKelway
d Henry Levin
☆ Glenn Ford, Evelyn Keyes, Willard Parker, Jimmy Hunt, Ron Randell

The Mating Season
US 1950 101m bw
Paramount (Charles Brackett)
A factory draughtsman marries an ambassador's daughter; his mother loses her job and comes incognito to work for them as a cook.
Uninteresting mechanical domestic comedy in which the young folk are dull and the older ones overplay.
w Walter Reisch, Charles Brackett, Richard Breen *d* Mitchell Leisen *ph* Charles Lang *m* Joseph J. Lilley
☆ Gene Tierney, John Lund, Miriam Hopkins, Thelma Ritter, Jan Sterling
Thelma Ritter

Matka Joanna od Aniolow: see *The Devil and the Nun*

'Believe the unbelievable.'
The Matrix ***
US/Australia 1999 136m Technicolor
Panavision
Warner/Village Roadshow/Groucho II (Joel Silver)

An insignificant worker turns out to be the promised leader who fights against the Matrix, an artificial intelligence that controls the world and consumes its inhabitants.
Spectacular special effects, slick design and the speed and vitality of the narrative overcome its deficiencies, particularly its derivative plot that draws on so many science-fiction clichés and conventions.
wd Andy Wachowski, *Larry Wachowski* *ph* Bill Pope *m* Don Davis *pd* Owen Paterson *ed* Zach

Staenberg sp Geoffrey Darrow; Bob McCarron; Makeup Effects Group Studio
☆ Keanu Reeves (Neo), Laurence Fishburne (Morpheus), Carrie-Anne Moss (Trinity), Hugo Weaving (Agent Smith), Gloria Foster (Oracle), Joe Pantoliano (Cypher), Marcus Chong (Tank), Paul Goddard (Agent Brown), Robert Taylor (Agent Jones), Julian Arahanga (Apoc), Matt Doran (Mouse), Belinda McClory (Switch), Anthony Ray Parker (Dozer)

'Eye-popping but incoherent extravaganza of morphing and superhuman martial arts. Ultra-cool visuals that truly deliver something new to the sci-fi action lexicon will make this time-jumping thriller a must-see among genre fans, especially guys in their teens and 20s.' – *Todd McCarthy, Variety*

'A dazzlingly nifty slice of sci-fi cool.' – *Empire*

† Yuen Wo-Ping was responsible for the kung fu choreography.

†† The film cost $60m to make and grossed $475m at cinemas around the world.

Zach Staenberg; sound (John Reitz, Gregg Rudloff, David Campbell, David Lee); sound effects editing (Dane A. Davis); visual effects (John Gaeta, Janek Sirrs, Steve Courtley, Jon Thum)

special visual effects; sound

'Free your mind.'
The Matrix Reloaded **
US 2003 138m Eastmancolor Panavision
Warner/Village Roadshow/NPV (Joel Silver)

As the last human outpost is threatened by machines, rebels against the system pin their hopes of survival on one man.

Now that our hero Neo can fly like Superman, this second instalment comes closer to other comic-book blockbusters: its set pieces may be bigger and better than anything done before, but they still remain action movie staples – car chases and fights on moving vehicles; the one brilliantly notable novelty is a fight between Neo and a hundred clones of Agent Smith.

wd Andy Wachowski, Larry Wachowski *ph* Bill Pope *m* Don Davis *pd* Owen Paterson *ed* Zach Staenberg *sp* John Gaeta; Animal Logic Films; Buf Compagnie; ESC; Giant Killer Robots; Sony Pictures Imageworks *cos* Kym Barrett *fight choreographer* Yuen Wo Ping

☆ Keanu Reeves (Neo), Laurence Fishburne (Morpheus), Carrie-Anne Moss (Trinity), Hugo Weaving (Agent Smith), Jada Pinkett Smith (Niobe), Gloria Foster (The Oracle), Harold Perrineau (Link), Monica Bellucci (Persephone), Harry Lennix (Commander Lock), Lambert Wilson (Merovingian), Randall Duk Kim (Keymaker), Neil Rayment (Twin #1), Adrian Rayment (Twin #2)

'More of a straight-ahead action movie than the original, and it's filled with spectacular mayhem.' – *David Ansen, Newsweek*

'Full of braindead cod philosophy and devoid of anything like a cogent plot, this nevertheless super sequel is a thrill ride that no film fan should miss.' – *Kevin O'Sullivan, Daily Mirror*

'Heavy-spirited and pompous, even faintly embarrassing.' – *David Denby, New Yorker*

'Utilization of serious thought does not in itself make the Matrix films more than the adolescent fodder that they are.' – *Stanley Kaufmann, New Republic*

A Matter of Dignity *
Greece 1957 104m bw
Finos (Anis Nohra)
original title: *To Telefteo Psemma*

The daughter of a bankrupt family reluctantly agrees to marry a millionaire, and the family's false values lead to tragedy.

Rather offbeat melodrama with the director in good form.

wd Michael Cacoyannis *ph* Walter Lassally *m* Manos Hadjidakis

☆ Ellie Lambetti, Georges Pappas, Athena Michaelidou

A Matter of Innocence: see *Pretty Polly*

A Matter of Life and Death ****
GB 1946 104m Technicolor
GFD/Archers (Michael Powell, Emeric Pressburger)
US title: *Stairway to Heaven*

A pilot with brain damage after bailing out is torn between this world and the next, but an operation puts things to rights.

Outrageous fantasy which seemed more in keeping after the huge death toll of a world war, and in any case learned the Hollywood lesson of eating its cake and still having it, the supernatural elements being capable of explanation. A mammoth technical job in the heavenly sequences, it deserves full marks for its sheer arrogance, wit, style and film flair.

wd Michael Powell, Emeric Pressburger ph Jack Cardiff m Allan Gray pd Hein Heckroth

☆ *David Niven, Roger Livesey, Kim Hunter, Marius Goring, Raymond Massey, Abraham Sofaer*

'Powell and Pressburger seem to have reached their heaven at last ... an illimitable Wembley stadium, surrounded by tinkly music and mists, from which all men of insight, if they were ever careless enough to get there, would quickly blaspheme their way out.' – *Richard Winnington*

'A dazzling mesh of visionary satire, postwar politics and the mystical side of English romanticism.' – *Tony Rayns, Time Out, 1979*

'Beautifully written, beautifully acted, beautifully executed ... you would think such formidable merits would add up to quite a film – and darned if they don't.' – *Time Out*

'This film, whether or not you find its philosophy half-baked, is downright good cinema, doing things that couldn't be done in any other medium' – *Tribune*

'It compelled attention and created emotion.' – *Basil Wright, 1972*

A Matter of Resistance: see *La Vie de Château*

'Some women are born to have a glorious affair with life ... !'
A Matter of Time
US/Italy 1976 97m Technicolor
(AIP)

An Italian country chambermaid is taught about life by a faded countess.

Interminable even in its abbreviated form, this woebegone fantasy is a tribute to his miscast daughter by a director who never had much sense of plot to begin with. It has to be seen to be believed.

w John Gay *novel The Film of Memory* by Maurice Druon *d* Vincente Minnelli *ph* Geoffrey Unsworth *m* Nino Oliviero

☆ Liza Minnelli, Ingrid Bergman, Charles Boyer, Tina Aumont, Gabriele Ferzetti, Spiros Andros

'So hackneyed, inept and stupid as to be almost amusing.' – *John Simon, New York*

'So spectacularly crazy that if Minnelli could only persuade Mel Brooks to put his name on it, *A Matter of Time* might yet be the comedy sleeper of the year.' – *Frank Rich, New York Post*

A Matter of Who
GB 1961 92m bw
MGM/Foray (Walter Shenson, Milton Holmes)

The World Health Organization tracks down a smallpox outbreak.

Curious blend of semi-documentary with suspense and comedy; not really a starter.

w Milton Holmes, Harold Buchman *magazine article* Patricia Lee, Paul Dickinson *d* Don Chaffey *ph* Erwin Hillier *m* Edwin Astley

☆ Terry-Thomas, Sonja Ziemann, Alex Nicol, Guy Deghy, Richard Briers, Clive Morton, Geoffrey Keen, Martin Benson, Honor Blackman, Carol White

† Harold Buchman's name was omitted from the original credits at the time because he was blacklisted.

Maurice *
GB 1987 140m Technicolor
Cinecom/Merchant Ivory (Ismail Merchant)

The life of a Cambridge homosexual.

Hothouse study of E. M. Forster's posthumously published and semi-autobiographical novel. An acquired taste, but many scenes have general appeal.

w Kit Hesketh-Harvey, James Ivory *d James Ivory ph* Pierre Lhomme *m* Richard Robbins *pd* Brian Ackland-Snow *ed* Katherine Wenning

☆ James Wilby, Hugh Grant, Rupert Graves, Denholm Elliott, Simon Callow, Billie Whitelaw, Ben Kingsley, Judy Parfitt

costume design (Jenny Beavan, John Bright)

Mauvais Sang: see *The Night Is Young*

Mauvaise Passe: see *The Escort (1999)*

'In Their Hands, A Deck Of Cards Was The Only Thing More Dangerous Than A Gun.'
Maverick *
US 1994 127m Technicolor Panavision
Warner/Icon (Bruce Davey, Richard Donner)

A gambler raises the money to take part in a poker championship, where his opponents include a woman who tried to rob him.

Based on the TV series that starred James Garner, this is a relaxed and rambling romp, a jokey tale of double-cross in a Western setting which would have been far better with its last half-hour excised.

w William Goldman *d* Richard Donner *ph Vilmos Zsigmond m* Randy Newman *pd* Tom Sanders

☆ Mel Gibson, Jodie Foster, James Garner, Graham Greene, James Coburn, Alfred Molina

'Good solid fun.' – *Empire*

† Danny Glover appears uncredited in a *Lethal Weapon* in-joke.

costume design

The Maverick Queen
US 1955 90m Trucolor Naturama
Republic

A lady rustler falls for a Pinkerton detective sent to arrest her.

Tedious Western in bilious colour.

w Kenneth Gamet, De Vallon Scott *novel* Zane Grey *d* Joseph Kane *ph* Jack Marta *m* Victor Young

☆ Barbara Stanwyck, Barry Sullivan, Scott Brady, Mary Murphy, Wallace Ford, Jim Davis

Max Dugan Returns **
US 1983 98m colour
TCF (Herbert Ross, Neil Simon)

A hard-up widow with a 15-year-old son is visited by her dying father who abandoned her when she was a child.

Slight, sentimental but gently amusing comedy.

w Neil Simon *d* Herbert Ross *ph* David M. Walsh *m* David Shire *ad* Albert Brenner *ed* Richard Marks

☆ Marsha Mason, Jason Robards, Donald Sutherland, Matthew Broderick

'A consistently happy comedic fable.' – *Variety*

Max Mon Amour
France/US 1986 97m colour
Electric/Greenwich Film/A2 (Serge Silberman)

The wife of a British diplomat in Paris falls in love with a chimpanzee.

Odd tale that strives for, but fails to achieve, an air of unease.

w Nagisa Oshima, Jean-Claude Carrière *d* Nagisa Oshima *ph* Raoul Coutard *m* Michel Portal *pd* Pierre Guffroy *ed* Hélène Plemiannikov

☆ Charlotte Rampling, Anthony Higgins, Bernard-Pierre Donnadieu, Victoria Abril, Anne-Marie Besse, Nicole Clafan, Pierre Etaix, Bernard Haller, Sabine Haudepin

Maxie
US 1985 98m DeLuxe
Orion/Aurora/Elsboy/Carter De Haven

The ghost of a twenties starlet revisits her old apartment and takes over the body of the wife of the tenant.

Heavenly comedy which would have been funnier in the forties.

w Patricia Resnick *novel Marion's Wall* by Jack Finney *d* Paul Aaron *ph* Fred Schuler *m* Georges Delerue *pd* John Lloyd *ed* Lynzee Klingman

☆ Glenn Close, Mandy Patinkin, Ruth Gordon, Barnard Hughes, Valerie Curtin

Maximum Overdrive
US 1986 97m Technicolor J-D-C Scope
Dino de Laurentiis (Martha Schumacher)

In a corner of North Carolina, all mechanical devices go haywire, and trucks menace a group of humans caught in a filling station.

Idiotic premise for sensational action sequences, which are well staged but go on too long.

wd Stephen King *ph* Armando Nannuzzi *m* AC/DC *pd* Giorgio Postiglione *ed* Evan Lottman

☆ Emilio Estevez, Pat Hingle, Laura Harrington, Yeardley Smith, John Short, Ellen McElduff, J. C. Quinn

† The plot was used again for a less effective TV movie *Trucks* in 1997.

Maximum Risk
US 1996 100m DeLuxe Panavision
Columbia (Moshe Diamant)

A French cop takes revenge on the gangsters who killed his twin brother by assuming his identity.

Standard action-film clichés are well orchestrated in this predictable fast-paced nonsense.

w Larry Ferguson *d* Ringo Lam *ph* Alexander Gruszynski *m* Robert Folk *pd* Steven Spence *ed* Bill Pankow

☆ Jean-Claude Van Damme, Natasha Henstridge, Zach Grenier, Jean-Hugues Anglade, Paul Ben-Victor, Stéphane Audran

'A visceral delight that refuses to be deterred by niceties of plot or character consistency and prefers sweat to emotion.' – *Leonard Klady, Variety*

Maya
US 1966 91m Technicolor
Panavision
MGM/King Brothers (Mary P. Murray, Herman King)

A teenage American boy arrives in India to visit his disillusioned father, who finally comes to understand him only after he has run away.

Good-looking but otherwise uninteresting animal drama which served as the pilot for a TV series.

w John Fante *d* John Berry *ph* Gunter Senftleben *m* Riz Ortolani

☆ Clint Walker, Jay North, I. S. Johar, Sajid Khan

Maybe Baby
US 1988 98m colour
Columbia/Tri-Star (Jerry Belson, Walter Coblenz)
US title: *For Keeps*

Two teenagers, who marry when pregnancy looms, face up to adult responsibilities.

Tiresome and sentimental account of young motherhood.

w Tim Kazurinsky, Denise DeClue *d* John G. Avildsen *ph* James Crabe *m* Bill Conti *pd* William J. Cassidy *ed* John G. Avildsen

☆ Molly Ringwald, Randall Batinkoff, Kenneth Mars, Miriam Flynn, Conchata Ferrell, Sharon Brown

'Unfunny, clichéd and dumbed down.' – *Steve Grant, Sunday Times*

Maybe Baby
GB/France 2000 104m DeLuxe
Redbus/Pandora/BBC (Phil McIntyre)

A BBC executive and his wife have difficulties with conceiving a child, which causes problems with their marriage.

A self-regarding comedy, since our hero is writing the script of the film we are watching and it is, we are told, brilliant; it doesn't live up to this word-of-mouth, but it may amuse in an idle moment.

wd Ben Elton *novel Inconceivable* by Ben Elton *ph* Roger Lanser *m* Colin Towns *pd* Jim Clay *ed* Peter Hollywood *cos* Anne Sheppard

☆ Hugh Laurie (Sam Bell), Joely Richardson (Lucy Bell), Adrian Lester (George), James Purefoy (Carl Phipps), Tom Hollander (Ewan Proclaimer), Joanna Lumley (Sheila), Rowan Atkinson (Mr James), Dawn French (Charlene), Emma Thompson (Druscilla), Rachael Stirling (Joanna), Matthew Macfadyen (Nigel)

'An innocuous and very English middle-class comedy.' – *Philip Kemp, Sight and Sound*

Maybe, Maybe Not: see *The Most Desired Man*

Mayerling **
France 1935 90m bw
Seymour Nebenzal/Nero Film
In 1889, imperial lovers are found dead in a country house.
Classic French version of a somewhat chilly subject.
w Joseph Kessel, V. Cube *novel* Claude Anet
d Anatole Litvak
☆ Charles Boyer, Danielle Darrieux, Marthe Regnier, Yolande Laffon, Suzy Prim
'As good a picture as Hollywood could produce, plus some local touches that are inaccessible to Hollywood.' – *Variety*

Mayerling
France/GB 1968 141m Eastmancolor Panavision
Corona/Winchester (Robert Dorfmann)
In 1889 the heir to the Habsburg Empire is forced into a suicide pact with his mistress.
Tedious dramatization of historical events which in 1935 had made a delicate French film but in these hands seems an endless and boring manipulation of doubtful events into turgid romance.
wd Terence Young *novel* Claude Anet *ph* Henri Alekan *m* Francis Lai *pd* Georges Wakhevitch
☆ Omar Sharif, Catherine Deneuve, James Mason, Ava Gardner, James Robertson Justice, Genevieve Page, Ivan Desny, Maurice Teynac

The Mayor of 44th Street
US 1942 86m bw
RKO (Cliff Reid)
Dance bands are threatened by hooligans demanding protection money.
Boring melodrama with music.
w Lewis R. Foster *d* Alfred E. Green *ph* Robert de Grasse *songs* Mort Greene, Harry Revel
☆ George Murphy, Anne Shirley, Richard Barthelmess, William Gargan, Joan Merrill, Millard Mitchell, Mary Wickes, Freddy Martin and band
song 'There's a Breeze on Lake Louise'

The Mayor of Hell *
US 1933 90m bw
Warner
A racketeer becomes superintendent of a reform school, and it changes his life.
Moderate star vehicle with a plot that did yeoman service thereafter in Dead End Kids films.
w Edward Chodorov *d* Archie Mayo *ph* Barney McGill *m* Leo F. Forbstein
☆ James Cagney, Madge Evans, Allen Jenkins, Dudley Digges, Frankie Darro
'Has the outline of a junior Big House. Offers exploitation easily.' – *Variety*
'Propaganda for nothing: like most of what comes out of Hollywood, it is entertaining trash.' – *Time*
† Remade in 1938 as *Crime School* with Humphrey Bogart, 1939 as *Hell's Kitchen* with Ronald Reagan.

Maytime **
US 1937 132m bw (sepia sequence)
MGM (Hunt Stromberg)
An opera star falls in love with a penniless singer but her jealous impresario shoots him.
Lush romantic musical which turns gradually into melodrama and ends in a ghostly reunion for the lovers. If that's what you like, it could scarcely be better done.
w Noel Langley *operetta* Rida Johnson Young
d Robert Z. Leonard *ph* Oliver T. Marsh
m Sigmund Romberg *md* Herbert Stothart
☆ Jeanette MacDonald, Nelson Eddy, John Barrymore, Herman Bing, Lynne Carver, Rafaela Ottiano, Paul Porcasi, Sig Rumann
'Click operetta ... cinch for the foreign market also.' – *Variety*
'Enjoyable for more than camp reasons ... the atmosphere of thwarted passion is compelling.' – *Pauline Kael, 70s*
† Shooting had begun in colour with Frank Morgan in Bing's part and Paul Lukas in Barrymore's; this footage, directed by Edmund Goulding, was abandoned on Irving Thalberg's death.
Herbert Stothart

Maytime in Mayfair
GB 1949 95m Technicolor
British Lion/Imperadio (Herbert Wilcox)
A playboy inherits a dress salon and falls for the lady manager.
Witless comedy fit to set one's teeth on edge, with over-acting and poor musical numbers. Not in the same street as its predecessor Spring in Park Lane.
w Nicholas Phipps *d* Herbert Wilcox *ph* Max Greene *md* Robert Farnon
☆ Anna Neagle, Michael Wilding, Nicholas Phipps, Peter Graves, Tom Walls
'Painstakingly refined.' – *MFB*

'The Suspense Novel That Startled the World.'
'The Deadliest Trap On Earth!'
The Maze
US 1953 81m bw 3-D
Allied Artists (Richard Heermance)
The heir to a title also inherits a family curse and turns into a giant frog.
Rather splendidly idiotic horror film which raises plenty of laughs but no frissons.
w Dan Ullman *story* Maurice Sandoz *d* William Cameron Menzies *ph* Harry Neumann *m* Marlin Skiles *pd* William Cameron Menzies *ad* David Milton *ed* John C. Fuller
☆ Richard Carlson (Gerald McTeam), Veronica Hurst (Kitty Murray), Katherine Emery (Edith Murray), Michael Pate (William), Lillian Bond (Margaret Dilling), Hillary Brooke (Peggy Lord), Owen McGiveney (Simon), John Dodsworth (Dr Bert Dilling), Stanley Fraser (Robert), Robin Hughes (Robert Robler)

Me and Him
US 1988 90m colour
Columbia/Egmont/Neue Constantin (Bernd Eichinger)
A New Yorker's penis begins to talk back to him.
A comedy about male chauvinism that fails to raise a smile.
w Warren D. Leight, Michael Junker, Doris Dörrie *novel* *Io e Lui* by Alberto Moravia *d* Doris Dörrie *ph* Helge Weindler *ed* Raimund Barthelmes
☆ Griffin Dunne, Ellen Greene, Steven Marcus, Craig T. Nelson, Kelly Bishop, Carey Lowell, Kara Glover, Kim Flowers

Me and Marlborough *
GB 1935 84m bw
GFD/Gainsborough (Michael Balcon)
In Marlborough's army, a woman takes the place of her soldier husband to prove his innocence of spying.
Curious period service farce, not quite a success but an interesting attempt at something different.
w Ian Hay, Marjorie Gaffney *story* W. P. Lipscomb, Reginald Pound *d* Victor Saville *ph* Charles Van Enger
☆ Cicely Courtneidge, Tom Walls, Barry McKay, Alfred Drayton
'In most cases the comedy is totally uncalled for and destroys the period atmosphere.' – *Variety*

Me and My Gal *
US 1932 79m bw
Fox
GB title: *Pier 13*
A cop on the beat romances a hashslinger and catches a crook.
Pleasant little programmer, very evocative of its period.
w Arthur Kober *d* Raoul Walsh *ph* Arthur Miller
☆ Spencer Tracy, Joan Bennett, George Walsh, Marion Burns, J. Farrell MacDonald, Noel Madison, Henry B. Walthall
'Lacking in nearly everything that makes box office.' – *Variety*
† Remade in 1949 as *Pier 13.*

Me and My Pal *
US 1933 20m bw
Hal Roach
Ollie becomes engrossed in a jigsaw puzzle and forgets to get married.
Oddball star comedy which nearly comes off but simply doesn't provide enough jokes.
w Stan Laurel *d* Charles Rogers, Lloyd French *ph* Art Lloyd *ed* Bert Jordan
☆ Stan Laurel, Oliver Hardy, James Finlayson, Eddie Dunn

Me and the Colonel
US 1958 110m bw
Columbia/Court-Goetz (William Goetz)
In 1940 an anti-semitic Polish colonel is obliged to flee from France in the company of a Jewish refugee.
Rather obvious war comedy with predictable but not very entertaining situations, sentiment, action and pathos. The stars cope well enough but the picture never picks up steam.
w S. N. Behrman, George Froeschel *play* Franz Werfel *d* Peter Glenville *ph* Burnett Guffey *m* George Duning
☆ Danny Kaye, Curt Jurgens, Nicole Maurey, Françoise Rosay, Akim Tamiroff, Martita Hunt, Alexander Scourby, Liliane Montevecchi, Ludwig Stossel

'From gentle to mental'
Me, Myself and Irene
US 2000 117m DuArt
TCF/Conundrum (Bradley Thomas, Bobby Farrelly, Peter Farrelly)
A Rhode Island state trooper with split personalities –one nice, the other nasty– falls in love with the woman he is escorting to New York.
Fans of Jim Carrey at his most manic will enjoy his mugging in this tasteless, episodic comedy; others will do well to stay as far away as possible.
w Peter Farrelly, Mike Cerrone, Bobby Farrelly *d* Bobby Farrelly, Peter Farrelly *ph* Mark Irwin *m* Peter Yorn, Lee Scott *pd* Sidney J. Bartholomew Jnr *ed* Christopher Greenbury *sp* makeup fx, animatronics: Alterian Studios *cos* Pamela Withers
☆ Jim Carrey (Charlie/Hank), Renee Zellweger (Irene), Chris Cooper (Lt Gerke), Robert Forster (Col Partington), Richard Jenkins (Agent Boshane), Rob Moran (Trooper Finneran), Traylor Howard (Layla), Daniel Greene (Dickie Thurman), Zen Gesner (Agent Peterson), Tony Cox (Limo Driver), Anthony Anderson (Jamaal), Rex Allen Jnr (Narrator), Mongo Brownlee (Lee Harvey), Jerod Mixon (Shonte Jnr)
'Goes out of its way to shock its audience with the bizarre and socially unacceptable antics of its protagonist.' – *Leslie Felperin, Sight and Sound*
'Jim Carrey's weakest effort to date, his talents wasted on a film which manages to be both unamusing and unpleasant by turns.' – *Empire*
† It took $90.6m at the US box office.

'Find out what happens when first love gets a second chance.'
Me Myself I *
Australia/France 1999 104m colour
Buena Vista/Gaumont/Films du Loup/Sedell (Fabien Liron)
A successful, single, thirtysomething female journalist finds herself transformed into the suburban wife of the man whose proposal of marriage she turned down 13 years earlier, and the mother of three children.
Enjoyable identity-switching comedy in which a woman gets to discover that the grass on the other side of the fence is no greener.
wd Pip Karmel *ph* Graeme Lind *m* Charlie Chan *pd* Murray Picknett *ed* Denise Haratzis *cos* Paul Warren, Ariane Weiss
☆ *Rachel Griffiths* (Pamela Drury), David Roberts (Robert Dickson), Sandy Winton (Ben), Yael Stone (Stacey), Shaun Loseby (Douglas), Trent Sullivan (Rupert)
'An exceedingly broad and obvious situation comedy that is nonetheless rooted in a great deal of recognizable truth.' – *Todd McCarthy, Variety*

Me, Natalie *
US 1969 111m DeLuxe
Cinema Center (Stanley Shapiro)
An unattractive 18-year-old girl moves into Greenwich Village and learns to accept herself as she is.
Basically very predictable but rather well done character study with excellent detail.
w A. Martin Zweiback *d* Fred Coe *ph* Arthur J. Ornitz *m* Henry Mancini
☆ Patty Duke, James Farentino, Martin Balsam, Elsa Lanchester, Salome Jens, Nancy Marchand, Al Pacino

Me Without You
GB/Germany 2001 108m Technicolor Panavision
Momentum/Road Movies/IoMFC/Dakota/Wave (Finola Dwyer)
The friendship and rivalry of two women, from their early years in London of the 1970s to university and beyond.
A sometimes engaging study of a relationship between opposites that is both supportive and destructive, and most perceptive on the pair's student years.
w Sandra Goldbacher, Laurence Coriat *d* Sandra Goldbacher *ph* Denis Crossan *m* Adrian Johnston *pd* Michael Carlin *ed* Michael Ellis
☆ Anna Friel (Marina), Michelle Williams (Holly), Kyle MacLachlan (Daniel), Oliver Milburn (Nat), Trudie Styler (Linda), Marianne Denicourt (Isabel), Nicky Henson (Ray), Allan Corduner (Max)
'Explores dysfunctional female relationships to the point where you drop with exhaustion. At least if you're a bloke you do.' – *Alexander Walker*

Me You Them: see *Eu Tu Eles*

Mean Guns
US 1996 96m Foto-Kem
Polygram/Filmwerks (Gary Schmoeller, Tom Karnowski)
A group of hitmen are gathered together in an unopened prison and told that the last three alive at the end of six hours can claim $10 million hidden in the building.
Explosive action movie, essentially men with guns running around shooting at one another.
w Andrew Witham *d* Albert Pyun *ph* George Mooradian *m* Tony Riparetti *ed* Ken Morrisey
☆ Christopher Lambert (Lou), Ice-T (Vincent Moon), Michael Halsey (Marcus), Deborah Van Valkenburgh (Cam), Tina Coté (Barb), Yuji Okomoto (Hoss), Thom Matthews (Crow), Hunter Doughty (Lucy), Kimberly Warren (Dee)
'Make no mistake, this is one of the worst films you will ever see.' – *Ben Mitchell, Guardian*

'Not Your Usual Suspects.'
Mean Machine
GB/US 2001 98m DeLuxe
Paramount/Ska/Ruddy/Morgan/Brad Grey (Matthew Vaughn)
A disgraced former England soccer captain, jailed for assault, coaches a prisoners' team in a game against the guards.
Unsuccessful attempt to make a star of a former footballer of limited acting ability, who was notorious for his tough-guy attitude on the field; the threadbare, hand-me-down script doesn't help.
w Charlie Fletcher, Chris Baker, Andrew Day *screenplay* Tracy Keenan Wynn *story* Albert S. Ruddy *d* Barry Skolnick *ph* Alex Barber *m* John Murphy *pd* Russell De Rozario *ed* Eddie Hamilton, Dayn Williams
☆ Vinnie Jones (Danny Meehan), Jason Statham (Monk), David Kelly (Doc), David Hemmings (Prison Governor), Vas Blackwood (Massive), Jason Flemyng (Bob), Danny Dyer (Billy the Limpet), Robbie Gee (Trojan)
'Another useless recycling of a brutal mid-'70s American sports movie.' – *Joe Leydon, San Francisco Examiner*
'It all seems like an unvarnished report on the state of English soccer today – or indeed the state of British cinema, reduced to the lowest common (and very common it is) denominator of laddish, loutish thuggery.' – *Alexander Walker, London Evening Standard*
† It is an Anglicised remake of Robert Aldrich's 1974 movie *The Longest Yard (qv).*

The Mean Machine (1974): see *The Longest Yard*

The Mean Season
US 1985 103m DeLuxe Panavision
Orion/Turman-Foster
A Miami police reporter becomes the personal spokesman for a murderous psychopath.
Tolerable murder thriller with asides on politics and the media.

w Leon Piedmont *novel In the Heat of the Summer* by John Katzenbach *d* Phillip Borsos *ph* Frank Tidy *m* Lalo Schifrin *pd* Philip Jefferies
☆ Kurt Russell, Mariel Hemingway, Richard Jordan, Richard Masur, Richard Bradford, Joe Pantoliano

Mean Streets ****
US 1973 110m Technicolor
Taplin-Perry-Scorsese (Jonathan T. Taplin)
Four young Italian-Americans use Tony's Bar as a base for drinking, brawling and hustling.
Relentlessly sordid melodrama with a good eye for realistic detail. The first film in which Scorsese announced himself as a major talent and discovered the subject matter that has served him so well.
w Martin Scorsese, Mardik Martin *d* Martin Scorsese *ph* Kent Wakeford *ed* Sid Levin
☆ *Harvey Keitel, Robert DeNiro*, David Proval, Amy Robinson, Richard Romanus
'Lacks a sense of story and structure ... unless a film-maker respects the needs of his audience, he can't complain if that audience fails to show up.' – *Variety*
'A thicker-textured rot than we have ever had in an American movie, and a deeper sense of evil.' – *New Yorker*
'Extraordinarily rich and distinguished on many levels.' – *Joseph Gelmis*

The Meanest Man in the World
US 1943 57m bw
TCF (William Perlberg)
An easy-going small-town lawyer finds that business picks up when he becomes tough and mean.
Very minor star comedy with a muddled opening followed by strictly rationed laughs.
w George Seaton, Allan House *play* George M. Cohan *d* Sidney Lanfield *ph* Peverell Marley *m* Cyril J. Mockridge *ad* Richard Day, Albert Hogsett *ed* Robert Bischoff
☆ Jack Benny, Priscilla Lane, Rochester, Edmund Gwenn, Anne Revere

The Meaning of Life: see *Monty Python's The Meaning of Life*

Meatballs
Canada 1979 92m Sonolab Color
Paramount (Dan Goldberg)
Adventures at an ineptly run summer camp.
Adolescent fun and games for easily pleased teens.
w Len Blum, Dan Goldberg, Harold Ramis, Janis Allen *d* Ivan Reitman *ph* Don Wilder *m* Elmer Bernstein *ad* David Charles *ed* Debra Karen
☆ Bill Murray (Tripper), Harvey Atkin (Morty), Russ Banham (Crockett), Ron Barry (Lance), Jack Blum (Spaz), Kate Lynch (Roxanne), Matt Craven (Hardware), Kristine DeBell (A.L.), Cindy Girling (Brenda)
'A smooth–running narrative that makes the camp hijinks part of an overall human mosaic... without the usual grossness and cynicism of many contempo comedy pix.' – *Variety*

Meatballs 4
US 1992 87m colour
Moviestore (Donald P. Borchers)
A water skier tries to prevent a lakeside summer camp being taken over by a ruthless developer.
Tired comedy with a predictable plot, occasionally enlivened by the action on water skis.
wd Bob Logan *ph* Vance Burberry *m* Steve Hunter *pd* Deborah Raymond *ed* Peter H. Verity
☆ Corey Feldman (Ricky Wade), Jack Nance (Neil Peterson), Sarah Douglas (Monica), Bojesse Christopher (Wes), Johnny Cocktails (Victor), J. Trevor Edmond (Howie), Paige French (Jennifer), John Mendoza (Dick)

'Rudy struck out two summers in a row... this will be his year to score!'
Meatballs III: Summer Job
Canada 1987 94m Sonolab color
(John Dunning, Don Carmody)
A wimp loses his virginity at summer camp with the aid of the ghost of a pornographic filmstar.
Tedious, frequently distasteful, no-brow, slapstick comedy; underlying all the antics is an adolescent fear of sex, or possibly its makers' fear of adolescent sex.
w Michael Paseorner, Radley Kesden *story* Carl Workman *d* George Mendeluk *ph* Peter Benison *m* Paul Zaza *pd* Charles Dunlop *ed* Debra Karen
☆ Sally Kellerman, Al Waxman, Patrick Dempsey, Shannon Tweed, Maury Chaykin, Isabelle Mejias, Ronnie Hawkins, George Suza

Meatballs Part II
Canada 1984 87m Movielab color
TriStar (Stephen Poe, Tony Bishop)
The future of a summer camp depends upon the outcome of a boxing match.
Raucous lowbrow comedy, a series of slapstick jokes and parodies.
w Bruce Singer *story* Martin Kitrosser, Carol Watson *d* Ken Wiederhorn *ph* Donald M. Morgan *m* Ken Harrison *pd* James William Newport *ed* George Berndt
☆ Archie Hahn (Jamie), John Mengatti (Flash), Tammy Taylor (Nancy), Kim Richards (Cheryl), Ralph Seymour (Eddie), Richard Mulligan (Giddy), Hamilton Camp (Hershey), John Larroquette (Meathead), Paul Reubens (Albert)

'The Mechanic must be dead sure ... or dead!'
The Mechanic
US 1972 100m Technicolor
UA/Chartoff/Winkler/Carlino
reissue title: *Killer of Killers*
A professional assassin under contract to the Mafia makes his missions look like accidents.
Violent thriller with a few pretensions, but too flashily made to be taken seriously.
w Lewis John Carlino *d* Michael Winner *ph* Richard Kline, Robert Paynter *m* Jerry Fielding
☆ Charles Bronson, Jan-Michael Vincent, Keenan Wynn, Jill Ireland
'A hymn to technological violence, efficiently and convincingly made.' – *George Melly, Observer*

Med Kaerlig Hilsen: see *Love Me Darling*

A Medal for Benny *
US 1945 77m bw
Paramount (Paul Jones)
An old rustic is the centre of small town celebrations in honour of his dead war hero son.
Satirical-sentimental location drama, effective but not memorable.
w Frank Butler *original story* John Steinbeck, Jack Wagner *d* Irving Pichel *ph* Lionel Lindon *m* Victor Young
☆ Dorothy Lamour, Arturo de Cordova, *J. Carrol Naish*, Mikhail Rasumny, Charles Dingle, Frank McHugh, Grant Mitchell
Academy Award nomination: original story; J. Carrol Naish

Medal for the General
GB 1944 99m bw
British National
An old general takes in evacuees and finds a new interest in life.
Uneventful character drama which seemed mildly pleasing at the time.
w Elizabeth Baron *novel* James Ronald *d* Maurice Elvey *ph* James Wilson
☆ Godfrey Tearle, Jeanne de Casalis, Morland Graham, Mabel Constanduros, John Laurie, Petula Clark

Medals: see *Seven Days Leave (1929)*

Medea *
Italy/France/West Germany 1970 118m Eastmancolor
San Marco/Number One/Janus (Franco Rossellini, Marina Cicogna)
Jason brings back as his wife the high priestess of the Golden Fleece, but her adjustment is to say the least uncomfortable.
In modern terms the case history of a psychopath, this weird production plays like an opera without music, and seems to have been designed as a vehicle for its charismatic star.
wd Pier Paolo Pasolini *play* Euripides *ph* Ennio Guarnieri
☆ *Maria Callas*, Giuseppe Gentile, Laurent Terzieff, Massimo Girotti

'He turned his back on civilization. Only to discover he had the power to save it.'
Medicine Man
US 1992 105m Technicolor Panavision
Guild/Cinergi (Andrew G. Vajna, Donna Dubrow)
A scientist, who has discovered a cure for cancer while working in the South American rain forest, is upset to find that his new research assistant is a woman.
Unpalatable mix of ecology and romance, with a long-delayed outcome that is predictable from the opening minutes.
w Tom Schulman, Sally Robinson *d* John McTiernan *ph* Donald McAlpine *m* Jerry Goldsmith
☆ Sean Connery, Lorraine Bracco, José Wilker, Rodolfo de Alexandre, Angelo Barra Moreira
'This jumbo-budget two-character piece suffers from a very weak script and a lethal job of miscasting.' – *Variety*
† Tom Schulman was reportedly paid $3 million for his script, with another $1 million being spent on rewrites. And still they got it wrong.

'A film dedicated to all those who are running away.'
Mediterraneo *
Italy 1991 90m Technicolor
Mayfair/Penta/AMA/Berlusconi (Gianni Minervini)
During the Second World War, eight Italian soldiers find themselves forgotten and stranded on an idyllic Aegean island.
Based on a true story, this is a pleasant, bitter-sweet, nostalgic comedy that prefers the past to the present.
w Vincenzo Monteleone *d* Gabriele Salvatores *ph* Italo Pettriccione *m* Giancarlo Bigazzi, Marco Falagiani *ad* Thalia Istikopoulos *ed* Nino Baragali
☆ Diego Abatantuono, Claudio Bigagli, Giuseppe Cederna, Claudio Bisio, Gigio Alberti, Ugo Conti, Memo Dini, Vasco Mirondola, Vanna Barba
'An ironic, gently amusing charmer, even though its anti-war elements jostle clumsily with its not entirely persuasive case for running away from real life's disappointments.' – *Angie Errigo, Empire*
Academy Award: best foreign film

The Medium *
Italy 1951 80m bw
Transfilm (Walter Lowendahl)
A fake medium feels a genuine manifestation, shoots at it and kills her assistant, but is still not sure whether he was responsible.
A filmic but not entirely satisfactory treatment of a modest but popular modern opera.
ph Enzo Serafin *wd/m Gian-Carlo Menotti, his opera co-d* Alexander Hammid
☆ Marie Powers, Anna Maria Alberghetti, Leo Coleman
Academy Award nomination: Gian-Carlo Menotti (for music)

Medium Cool **
US 1969 111m Technicolor
Paramount/H & J Pictures (Tully Friedman)
A TV news cameraman is made apathetic by the events around him.
Stimulating if overlong comment on the quality of life in the sixties, immaculately made and with a rather effective though obvious twist ending.
wd Haskell Wexler *ph* Haskell Wexler *m* Mike Bloomfield *ad* Leon Ericksen
☆ Robert Forster, Verna Bloom, Peter Bonerz, Marianna Hill, Sid McCoy
'A deeply moving questioning of America's violence and voyeurism.' – *Jan Dawson*
'I can't think of any film that tells one more about the texture of American life today.' – *Michael Billington, Illustrated London News*

'By the time he was eleven he had killed nine people!'
The Medusa Touch *
GB/France 1978 109m Technicolor
ITC/Bulldog/Citeca (Arnon Milchan, Elliott Kastner)
A novelist is haunted by the belief that he can cause disaster.
And he does, very predictably, while any intellectual excitement in the script is rapidly replaced by mere mayhem. Different, but not exciting.
w John Briley *novel* Peter Van Greenway *d* Jack Gold *ph* Arthur Ibbetson *m* Michael J. Lewis *sp* Doug Ferris
☆ Richard Burton, Lee Remick, Lino Ventura, Harry Andrews, Alan Badel, Jeremy Brett, Michael Hordern, Gordon Jackson

Meet Danny Wilson
US 1951 83m bw
U-I (Leonard Goldstein)
An overbearing crooner gets to the top with the help of gangsters.
Fairly abrasive star vehicle, almost amounting to self-parody.
w Don McGuire *d* Joseph Pevney *ph* Maury Gertsman *md* Joseph Gershenson
☆ *Frank Sinatra*, Shelley Winters, Alex Nicol, Raymond Burr

Meet Dr Christian
US 1939 68m bw
William Stephens/RKO
A dedicated small-town doctor has no concern for financial reward.
Adequate pot-boiler based on a radio character, and following Hersholt's popularity as Dr Dafoe.
w Ian McLellan Hunter, Harvey Gates, Ring Lardner Jnr *d* Bernard Vorhaus *ph* Robert Pittack
☆ Jean Hersholt, Dorothy Lovett, Robert Baldwin, Enid Bennett, Paul Harvey, Marcia Mae Jones
'First of a series ... profitable programme material for the family trade.' – *Variety*

'Sooner or later everyone does.'
Meet Joe Black
US 1998 180m DeLuxe
Universal/City Light (Martin Brest)
Death, in the form of a handsome young man, comes calling for a media tycoon and is attracted to the man's daughter.
A movie more than half in love with Brad Pitt; the camera swoons around him endlessly, while little of interest goes on elsewhere.
w Ron Osborn, Jeff Reno, Kevin Wade, Bo Goldman *play Death Takes a Holiday* by Alberto Casella, adapted by Walter Ferris *screenplay* Maxwell Anderson, Gladys Lehman *d* Martin Brest *ph* Emmanuel Lubezki *m* Thomas Newman *pd* Dante Ferretti *ed* Joe Hutshing, Michael Tronick *sp* Industrial Light & Magic
☆ Brad Pitt, Anthony Hopkins, Claire Forlani, Jake Weber, Marcia Gay Harden, Jeffrey Tambor, David S. Howard, Lois Kelly-Miller
† The film was a box-office flop, costing around $100m to make and market, and grossing around $43.25m at the US box-office.

Meet John Doe ***
US 1941 123m bw
Liberty Films (Frank Capra)
A tramp is hired to embody the common man in a phony political drive, and almost commits suicide.
Vividly staged but over-sentimental Capra extravaganza with high spots outnumbering low.
w Robert Riskin *d* Frank Capra *ph* George Barnes *m* Dimitri Tiomkin
☆ Gary Cooper, *Barbara Stanwyck*, Edward Arnold, Walter Brennan, James Gleason, Spring Byington, Gene Lockhart, Rod la Rocque, Irving Bacon, Regis Toomey, Ann Doran, Warren Hymer, Andrew Tombes
'Capra is as skilled as ever in keeping things moving along briskly and dramatically.' – *National Board of Review*
'The meanings were so distorted that the original authors sued ... It starts out in the confident Capra manner, but with a darker tone; by the end, you feel puzzled and cheated.' – *Pauline Kael, 70s*
Academy Award nomination: original story (Richard Connell, Robert Presnell)

Meet Me after the Show *
US 1951 88m Technicolor
TCF (George Jessel)
A musical star thinks she has discovered an affair between her husband and his glamorous backer.
Surprisingly bright routine musical.

w Mary Loos, Richard Sale *d* *Richard Sale*
ph *Arthur E. Arling* *md* Lionel Newman
songs Jule Styne, Leo Robin
☆ Betty Grable, Macdonald Carey, Rory Calhoun, Eddie Albert, Irene Ryan

Meet Me at Dawn
GB 1946 99m bw
Excelsior/Marcel Hellman
US title: *The Gay Duellist*
A professional duellist is commissioned to provoke a duel with a senator, but unwittingly hires the senator's daughter to play the injured party.
A totally laborious and artificial period comedy which never seems even to aspire to the style required.
w Lesley Storm, James Seymour, Maurice Cowan *story* *Le Tueur* by Anatole Litvak, Marcel Achard *d* Thornton Freeland *ph* Gunther Krampf *m* Mischa Spoliansky *ad* Norman Arnold *ed* E. B. Jarvis
☆ Hazel Court (Gabrielle Vermorel), William Eythe (Charles Morton), Stanley Holloway (Emile), Margaret Rutherford (Mme Vermorel), Basil Sydney (Georges Vermorel), Irene Browne (Madame Renault), George Thorpe (Senator Philipe Renault), Ada Reeve (Concierge), Graeme Muir (Count de Brissac), James Harcourt (Butler), Wilfrid Hyde-White (News Editor), Charles Victor (First Client)

Meet Me at the Fair
US 1952 87m Technicolor
U-I (Albert J. Cohen)
In 1900, an orphan joins a travelling medicine show.
Mildly pleasing open-air comedy drama.
w Irving Wallace *novel* *The Great Companions* by Gene Markey *d* Douglas Sirk *ph* Maury Gertsman *md* Joseph Gershenson
☆ Diana Lynn, Dan Dailey, Hugh O'Brian, Chet Allen, Rhys Williams

Meet Me in Las Vegas
US 1956 112m Eastmancolor
Cinemascope
MGM (Joe Pasternak)
▬
GB title: *Viva Las Vegas!*
A gambler's luck changes when he grabs the hand of a passing ballerina.
Listless song-and-dance extravaganza which wastes a great deal of talent.
w Isobel Lennart *d* Roy Rowland *ph* Robert Bronner *m* Georgie Stoll, Johnny Green *ch* Eugène Loring, Hermes Pan *ly* Sammy Cahn
☆ Dan Dailey, Cyd Charisse, Agnes Moorehead, Lili Darvas, Paul Henreid, Oscar Karlweis, Lena Horne, Jerry Colonna, Frankie Laine
'A large-scale musical of almost stupefying banality.' – *MFB*
🏆 Georgie Stoll, Johnny Green

Meet Me in St Louis ***
US 1944 113m Technicolor
MGM (Arthur Freed)
Scenes in the life of an affectionate family at the turn of the century.
Patchy but generally highly agreeable musical nostalgia with an effective sense of the passing years and seasons.
w Irving Brecher, Fred Finklehoffe *novel* Sally Benson *d* *Vincente Minnelli* *ph* George Folsey *md* Georgie Stoll
☆ *Judy Garland* (Esther Smith), *Margaret O'Brien* ('Tootie' Smith), Tom Drake (John Truett), Leon Ames (Mr Alonzo Smith), Mary Astor (Mrs Anne Smith), Lucille Bremer (Rose Smith), June Lockhart (Lucille Ballard), *Harry Davenport* (Grandpa), Marjorie Main, Joan Carroll, Hugh Marlowe, Robert Sully, Chill Wills
'A family group framed in velvet and tinsel ... it has everything a romantic musical should have.' – *Dilys Powell, 1955*
'A charming picture. There is much more in it than meets the ear.' – C. A. *Lejeune*
♫ 'Meet Me in St Louis'; 'The Boy Next Door'; 'Under the Bamboo Tree'; 'The Trolley Song'; 'You and I'; 'Have Yourself a Merry Little Christmas'
🏆 script; George Folsey; Georgie Stoll; song 'The Trolley Song' (*m/ly* Ralph Blane, Hugh Martin)

Meet Me on Broadway
US 1946 77m bw
Columbia (Burt Kelly)
A young musical director determines to hit Broadway.
Mild revue with a skimpy plot.
w George Bricker, Jack Henley *d* Leigh Jason *m/ly* Allen Roberts, Doris Fisher
☆ Marjorie Reynolds, Fred Brady, Jinx Falkenburg, Spring Byington, Gene Lockhart, Allen Jenkins

Meet Me Tonight
GB 1952 85m Technicolor
British Film Makers/Anthony Havelock Allan
Three short Noël Coward plays: *Red Peppers, Fumed Oak, Ways and Means.*
Regrettably bald treatment of three playlets which have not lasted well. A thoroughly artificial evening.
w Noël Coward *d* Anthony Pelissier *ph* Desmond Dickinson *m/ly* Noël Coward
☆ Ted Ray, Kay Walsh, Stanley Holloway, Betty Ann Davies, Nigel Patrick, Valerie Hobson

Meet Mr Callaghan
GB 1954 88m bw
Pinnacle
A private detective unmasks a rich man's killer.
Routine thick ear on American lines; moderately popular at the time, it spawned no sequels.
w Brock Williams *play* Gerald Verner (based on *novel* *The Urgent Hangman* by *Peter Cheyney*) *d* Charles Saunders *ph* Harry Waxman *m* Eric Spear
☆ Derrick de Marney, Harriet Johns, Peter Neil, Adrienne Corri, Delphi Lawrence, Belinda Lee

Meet Mr Lucifer *
GB 1953 81m bw
Ealing (Monja Danischewsky)
The Demon King in a tatty provincial pantomime dreams he is the devil preventing people from wasting time watching television.
Clean and occasionally amusing piece of topical satire on tellymania; but the prologue is funnier than the sketches.
w Monja Danischewsky *play* *Beggar My Neighbour* by Arnold Ridley *d* Anthony Pelissier *ph* Desmond Dickinson *m* Eric Rogers
☆ *Stanley Holloway*, Peggy Cummins, Jack Watling, Barbara Murray, Joseph Tomelty, Gordon Jackson, Jean Cadell, Kay Kendall, Ian Carmichael, Gilbert Harding, Charles Victor, Humphrey Lestocq

Meet Mr Penny
GB 1938 70m bw
British National
A meek clerk leads a revolt against a speculator who wants to build on allotments.
Early Ealing-style social comedy based on a radio character; of no abiding interest.
w Victor Kendall, Doreen Montgomery, from the character created by Maurice Moisiewicz *d* David MacDonald
☆ Richard Goolden, Vic Oliver, Fabia Drake, Kay Walsh, Patrick Barr, Hermione Gingold, Wilfrid Hyde-White

Meet Nero Wolfe *
US 1936 73m bw
Columbia
A corpulent stay-at-home sleuth solves a disappearance and a murder.
The film début of an engaging crime character, who oddly never made it to a series.
w Howard J. Green, Bruce Manning, Joseph Anthony *play* *Fer de Lance* by Rex Stout *d* Herbert Biberman *ph* Henry Freulich
☆ *Edward Arnold*, Lionel Stander, Joan Perry, Rita Hayworth, Victor Jory, Nana Bryant, Walter Kingsford, John Qualen

'The human race is about to be destroyed by people who wouldn't hurt a fly'
Meet the Applegates
US 1990 82m DuArt
Castle Premier/New World (Denise Di Novi)
US title: *The Applegates*
Giant insects, whose habitat in the Brazilian rain forests has been destroyed, disguise themselves as humans and go to America to wreck a nuclear power plant.
Ineffectual slapstick satire aimed at suburban life-styles.
w Redbeard Simmons, Michael Lehmann *d* Michael Lehmann *ph* Mitchell Dubin *m* David Newman *pd* John Hutman *ad* Kara Lindstrom, Adam Lustig *ed* Norman Hollyn
☆ Ed Begley Jnr, Stockard Channing, Dabney Coleman, Bobby Jacoby, Cami Cooper, Glenn Shadix, Susan Barnes, Adam Biesk
'This wayward movie has a great deal of charm.' – *MFB*

Meet the Baron
US 1933 79m bw
MGM
A nincompoop is fêted as the real Baron Münchhausen.
An incoherent script provides an opportunity for several comics to do their stuff.
w Herman J. Mankiewicz, Norman Krasna, Allen Rivkin, P. J. Wolfson, Arthur Kober, William K. Wells *d* Walter Lang
☆ Jack Pearl, Jimmy Durante, ZaSu Pitts, Ted Healy and his Stooges, Edna May Oliver, Henry Kolker
'Not so forte in the material division, but saved by its capable crew of comics.' – *Variety*

'Fish out of water...Surfers in Yellowstone'
Meet the Deedles
US 1998 92m Technicolor Panavision
Buena Vista/Walt Disney/DIC/Peak (Dale Pollock, Aaron Meyerson)
Two rich young slackers find themselves inadvertently working as trainee rangers in Yellowstone Park.
Vapid, dim-witted comedy, in which screaming and shouting too often substitute for meaningful dialogue.
w Jim Herzfeld, Dale Pollock *d* Steve Boyum *ph* David Hennings *m* Steve Bartek *pd* Stephen Storer *ed* Alan Cody
☆ Steve Van Wormer (Stew Deedle), Paul Walker (Phil Deedle), A. J. Langer (Lt Jesse Ryan), John Ashton (Capt Douglas Pine), Dennis Hopper (Frank Slater), Eric Braeden (Elton Deedle), Richard Lineback (Crabbe), Robert Englund (Nemo)
'Story's central absurdity is compounded by cheap jokes and scatological humor.' – *Variety*

Meet the Feebles
New Zealand 1989 97m colour
Arrow/Wingnut (Jim Booth, Peter Jackson)
A troupe of puppets indulge in sex, drugs, violence and general vulgarity.
A semi-pornographic horror with Muppet-like creatures that is determined to offend.
w Danny Mulheron, Frances Walsh, Stephen Sinclair, Peter Jackson *d* Peter Jackson *ph* Murray Milne *m* Peter Dasent *pd* Mike Kane *ed* Jamie Selkirk *sp* Steve Ingram
☆ Danny Mulheron and also the voices of: Donna Akersten, Stuart Devenie, Mark Hadlow, Ross Jolly, Brian Sergent, Peter Vere Jones, Mark Wright
'No excuse for spurting bodily secretions – blood, pus, vomit, or whatever – is passed up.' – *Sight and Sound*

Meet the Mayor
US 1938 63m bw
Frank Fay/Times
A veteran small-town elevator operator becomes involved in politics.
Curious semi-comedy in which the star uses up most of his old vaudeville routines.
w Walter DeLeon, Charles Belden, Frank Fay *d* Ralph Ceder
☆ Frank Fay, Ruth Hall, Hale Hamilton, George Meeker, Berton Churchill, Franklin Pangborn
'Flimsy meller for secondary duallers.' – *Variety*

Meet the Missus
US 1937 65m bw
Albert Lewis/RKO
A worm turns when his wife constantly involves him in newspaper contests.
Very slight farce for the rurals.
w Jack Townley, Bert Granet, Joel Sayre *story* *Lady Average* by Jack Goodman, Albert Rice *d* Joseph Santley
☆ Victor Moore, Helen Broderick, Anne Shirley, Alan Bruce, Willie Best
'Destined for the lower half of duals.' – *Variety*

Meet the Navy
GB 1946 85m bw (Technicolor sequence)
British National
The story of a revue featuring amateurs from the allied navies.
Patchy but generally good-natured wartime entertainment.
w Lester Cooper, James Seymour *d* Alfred Travers
☆ Lionel Murton, John Pratt, Oscar Naske, Alan Lund

'First comes love. Then comes the interrogation.'
Meet the Parents **
US 2000 108m DeLuxe
DreamWorks/Nancy Tenenbaum, Jane Rosenthal, Robert De Niro, Jay Roach
A teacher takes her accident-prone boyfriend, a male nurse, home to meet her mother and father, a humourless ex-CIA officer.
Polished, funny, old-fashioned farcical comedy with some impeccably-timed gags.
w Jim Herzfeld, John Hamburg *story* Greg Glienna, Mary Ruth Clarke *d* Jay Roach *ph* Peter James *m* Randy Newman *pd* Rusty Smith *ed* Jon Poll *cos* Daniel Orlandi
☆ Robert De Niro (Jack Byrnes), Ben Stiller (Greg Focker), Blythe Danner (Dina Byrnes), Teri Polo (Pam Byrnes), James Rebhorn (Larry Banks), Jon Abrahams (Denny Byrnes), Phyllis George (Linda Banks), Kali Rocha (Flight Attendant), Owen Wilson (Kevin Rawley), Tom McCarthy (Bob Banks), Nicole DeHuff (Debbie Byrnes)
'A film with lots of funny lines and actors doing an impeccable technical job, but it is somehow less than the sum of its parts.' – *Peter Bradshaw, Guardian*
'A flat-out hilarious mainstream comedy.' – *Todd McCarthy, Variety*
🏆 Randy Newman (song 'A Fool in Love')

Meet the People
US 1944 100m bw
MGM (E. Y. Harburg)
A Broadway musical star proves she isn't snooty by taking a job in a shipyard.
Thin propaganda musical which wastes a fair amount of talent.
w S. M. Herzig, Fred Saidy *play* Louis Lantz, Sol and Ben Barzman *d* Charles Reisner *ph* Robert Surtees *songs* various
☆ Lucille Ball, Dick Powell, Virginia O'Brien, Bert Lahr, Rags Ragland, June Allyson, Steve Geray, Phil Regan, Spike Jones and his City Slickers, Vaughn Monroe and his Orchestra

Meet the Stewarts
US 1942 74m bw
Columbia
Newlyweds have trouble when he's poor and she's used to rich living.
Modest marital comedy with young talent.
w Elizabeth Dunn, Karen de Wolf *d* Alfred E. Green
☆ William Holden, Frances Dee, Grant Mitchell

Meet Wally Sparks
US 1997 104m CFI color
Trimark/Largo (Leslie Greif)
Injured in an accident, the failing host of a scurrilous TV chat show takes over the governor's residence as a broadcasting studio.
A dim-witted variation on The Man Who Came to Dinner *that long overstays its welcome.*
w Rodney Dangerfield, Harry Basil *d* Peter Baldwin *ph* Richard Kline *m* Michel Colombier *pd* Bryan Jones *ed* Raul Davalos
☆ Rodney Dangerfield, Debi Mazar, Cindy Williams, Burt Reynolds, David Ogden Stiers, Alan Rachins
'A broad comedy of the kitchen sink school.' – *Variety*
† There are uncredited cameos by Tim Allen, Tony Danza, Jay Leno and Roseanne.

Meet Whiplash Willie: see *The Fortune Cookie*

'Love. Lust. Betrayal. Chaos. And the overture hasn't even begun.'

Meeting Venus *
GB 1990 120m colour
Warner/Enigma/BSB/County NatWest (David Puttnam)

A married Hungarian conductor, having problems over a performance of *Tannhäuser* to an international audience, has an affair with the principal singer.
Bold attempt at a European film, but one that works only fitfully.
w István Szabó, Michael Hirst *d* István Szabó *ph* Lajos Koltai *m* Richard Wagner *md* Marek Janowski *pd* Attila Kovacs *ed* Jim Clark
☆ Glenn Close, Niels Arestrup, Moscu Alcallay, Macha Meril, Johanna Ter Steege, Maite Nahyr, Victor Poletti, Marian Labuda
'A comedy with something to say, and the audacity to mix its laughs with a decent seriousness of purpose.' – *Derek Malcolm, Guardian*

Mein Kampf *
Sweden 1961 118m bw
Tõre Sjöberg/Minerva International

original title: *Den Blodiga Tiden*
A newsreel compilation tracing the rise and fall of Nazi Germany.
A simple but highly effective and reliable selection of actualities leaves conclusions to the viewer, letting the events speak for themselves. A powerful documentary.
wd Erwin Leiser *ed* Erwin Leiser

Het Meisje Met Het Rode Haar: see *The Girl with the Red Hair*

Melancholia
GB 1989 87m colour
BFI/Lichtblik Filmproduktion/Channel 4/ Norddeutscher Rundfunk/Film Fons Hamburg/ Hamburger Filmbüro (Colin MacCabe, Helga Bahr)

A German art critic, a former radical, is asked to take part in a political assassination in London.
Downbeat thriller built around an enigmatic protagonist.
w Andi Engel, Lewis Rodia *d* Andi Engel *ph* Denis Crossan *m* Simon Fisher Turner *pd* Jock Scott *ed* Christopher Roth
☆ Jeroen Krabbé, Susannah York, Ulrich Wildgruber, Jane Gurnett, Kate Hardie, Saul Reichlin, John Sparkes

Melba
GB 1953 113m Technicolor
Horizon (Sam Spiegel)

The life of the internationally famous Australian opera singer of Victorian days.
Moderately interesting recreation of a woman and an era, though dramatically rather stodgy.
w Harry Kurnitz *d* Lewis Milestone *ph* Ted Scaife *md* Muir Mathieson *ad* Andrei Andreiev
☆ Patrice Munsel, Robert Morley, Alec Clunes, Martita Hunt, Sybil Thorndike, John McCallum

O Melissokomos: see *The Beekeeper*

Mélo **
France 1986 112m colour
Artificial Eye/MK2/Films A2/CNC (Marin Karmitz)
A wife, tormented by her affair with another man, kills herself.
Deliberately theatrical treatment of a once-potent play of the 1920s that gives its principals a chance to revel in their roles.
wd Alain Resnais *play* Henry Bernstein *ph* Charlie Van Damme *m* Philippe Gérard *pd* Jacques Saulnier *ed* Albert Jurgenson, Jean-Pierre Besnard
☆ Sabine Azéma, Fanny Ardant, Pierre Aditi, André Dussollier, Jacques Dacqmine
† The same play was filmed as *Dreaming Lips* in 1936.

Melody
GB 1971 106m Eastmancolor
Hemdale/Sagittarius/Goodtimes (David Puttnam)

aka: *S.W.A.L.K.*
Calf love at school causes jealousy between two boys.
Tough-sentimental teenage comedy-drama of little interest to adults.
w Alan Parker *d* Waris Hussein *ph* Peter Suschitzky *m* Richard Hewson
☆ Jack Wild, Mark Lester, Tracy Hyde

Melody Cruise
US 1933 74m bw
Merian C. Cooper/RKO
A lady killer gets his come-uppance on board ship, but wins the girl he really wants.
Very messy mixture of comedy, romance and music.
w Mark Sandrich, Ben Holmes *d* Mark Sandrich
☆ Phil Harris, Charles Ruggles, Greta Nissen, Helen Mack, Chick Chandler
'Ought to be a moderate grosser ... the meat just isn't there for the principals, and they seem to feel it in their work.' – *Variety*

Melody for Two
US 1937 60m bw
Warner
A singing bandleader argues with his team and picks up with an all-girl crew.
Simple-minded peg for a few songs; rather a yawn.
w George Bricker, Luci Ward, Joseph K. Watson *d* Louis King
☆ James Melton, Patricia Ellis, Wini Shaw, Marie Wilson, Fred Keating, Dick Purcell
'Okay twin-bill fodder.' – *Variety*

Melody Inn: see *Riding High*

The Melody Lingers On
US 1935 65m bw
Edward Small
During World War I, an Italian soldier is killed after fathering an illegitimate baby, which grows up with no knowledge of mother, who watches from afar.
Old-fashioned tearjerker with musical background.
w Ralph Spence, Philip Dunne *novel* Lowell Brentano *d* David Burton
☆ Josephine Hutchinson, George Houston, John Halliday, Mona Barrie, Helen Westley, Laura Hope Crews
'Will probably wind up topping the duals.' – *Variety*

Melody of Life: see *Symphony of Six Million*

Melody of Youth: see *They Shall Have Music*

Melody Time *
US 1948 75m Technicolor
Walt Disney (Ben Sharpsteen)
An unlinked variety show of cartoon segments.
A mainly mediocre selection with the usual moments of high style: Once upon a Wintertime, Bumble Boogie, Johnny Appleseed, Little Toot, Trees, Blame it on the Samba, Pecos Bill.
wd various.
'There seems to be an obvious connection between the Disney artists' increasing insipidity and their increasing talent for fright, but I will leave it to accredited sado-masochists to make the discovery.' – *James Agee*

Melvin and Howard ***
US 1980 95m Technicolor
Universal (Terry Nelson)

The life of a factory worker is changed when a man he picks up in the Nevada desert claims to be Howard Hughes.
Eccentric comedy which has been compared to the work of Preston Sturges, but has an agreeable style of its own.
w Bo Goldman *d* Jonathan Demme *ph* Tak Fujimoto *m* Bruce Langhorne
☆ Paul Le Mat, Jason Robards Jnr, Mary Steenburgen, Elizabeth Cheshire, Michael J. Pollard, Gloria Grahame
'An almost flawless act of sympathetic imagination ... it's what might have happened if Jean Renoir had directed a comedy script by Preston Sturges.' – *New Yorker*
Bo Goldman; Mary Steenburgen
Jason Robards Jnr (supporting actor)

The Member of the Wedding *
US 1952 91m bw
Columbia/Stanley Kramer

A 12-year-old girl learns something about life when her sister gets married and a young boy dies.
Boringly contained in a kitchen set, this filmed play has interesting characters but is really not good enough for the talent involved.
w Edna and Edward Anhalt *play and novel* Carson McCullers *d* Fred Zinnemann *ph* Hal Mohr *m* Alex North
☆ Julie Harris, *Ethel Waters*, Brandon de Wilde, Arthur Franz, Nancy Gates, James Edwards
Julie Harris

Memed My Hawk
GB 1984 110m colour
Fuad Kavur/Peter Ustinov Productions
In 1923 Turkey, an inept tyrant chases one of his young villagers, who flees to the rebels.
Weird but not wonderful mix of comedy and melodrama in an unfamiliar and unattractive setting.
wd Peter Ustinov *novel* Yashar Kemal *ph* Freddie Francis *m* Manos Hadjidakis *ad* Veljko Despotovic *ed* Peter Honess
☆ Peter Ustinov, Herbert Lom, Denis Quilley, Michael Elphick, Simon Dutton

'Some Memories Are Best Forgotten.'

Memento ***
US 2000 116m FotoKem
Pathé/Newmarket/Summit/Team Todd (Suzanne Todd, Jennifer Todd)

In Los Angeles, an insurance investigator who has lost his short-term memory searches for the man who raped and murdered his wife.
Exceedingly clever, complex drama about identity and its meaning, and the search for a purpose in life, constructed so that the audience, too, experiences events without at first understanding their implications.
wd Christopher Nolan *story* Jonathan Nolan *ph* Wally Pfister *m* David Julyan *pd* Patti Podesta *ed* Dody Dorn *cos* Cindy Evans
☆ Guy Pearce (Leonard), Carrie-Anne Moss (Natalie), Joe Pantoliano (Teddy), Mark Boone Jnr (Burt), Stephen Tobolowsky (Sammy), Harriet Sansom Harris (Mrs Jankis), Callum Keith Rennie (Dodd)
'A remarkable psychological puzzle film.' – *Sight and Sound*
'Exciting, intriguing and exhausting.' – *Empire*
Christopher Nolan (Screenplay); Dody Dorn

Mémoire Traquée: see *Lapse of Memory*

Memoirs of a Survivor
GB 1981 115m Technicolor
EMI/Memorial (Michael Medwin, Penny Clark)
In the future, a single woman finds that urban civilization has decayed, and after many horrors finds refuge in an old Victorian house.
Unappetizing mixture of 1984 *and* Alice in Wonderland, *too despairing and plotless to find many takers.*
w Kerry Crabbe, David Gladwell *novel* Doris Lessing *d* David Gladwell *ph* Walter Lassally *m* Mike Thorn *pd* Keith Wilson *ed* William Shapter
☆ Julie Christie, Christopher Guard, Debbie Hutchings, Leonie Mellinger, Nigel Hawthorne, Pat Keen
'A film of wild ambition, sadly and hopelessly bungled.' – *Geoff Brown, MFB*

'Women want him for his wit. The C.I.A. wants him for his body. All Nick wants is his molecules back.'
'An adventure like you've never seen.'

Memoirs of an Invisible Man *
US 1992 99m Technicolor Panavision
Warner/Le Studio Canal Plus/Regency Enterprises/ Alcor (Bruce Bodner, Dan Kolsrud)

A CIA agent pursues a stock analyst who has turned invisible after an accident.
Clever special effects fail to compensate for the lacklustre script and uninspired performances.
w Robert Collector, Dana Olsen, William Goldman *novel* H. F. Saint *d* John Carpenter *ph* William A. Fraker *m* Shirley Walker *pd* Lawrence G. Paull *ed* Marion Rothman *sp* Industrial Light and Magic
☆ Chevy Chase, Daryl Hannah, Sam Neill, Michael McKean, Stephen Tobolowsky, Jim Norton
'Where's the wit? It fades into invisibility while you're watching it.' – *Los Angeles Times*

Memories of Me
US 1988 105m colour
MGM/Odyssey (Alan King, Billy Crystal, Michael Hertzberg)

After he suffers a heart attack, a surgeon attempts a reconciliation with his father, an unsuccessful actor working as a Hollywood extra.
Slick, wisecracking mix of comedy and drama in which everyone communicates in one-liners. It is sometimes funny, but more often creakingly sentimental in the manner of soap opera and sitcoms, with nothing to offer in the way of insight except another joke.
w Eric Roth, Billy Crystal *d* Henry Winkler *ph* Andrew Dintenfass *m* Georges Delerue *pd* William J. Cassidy *ed* Peter E. Berger
☆ Billy Crystal, Alan King, JoBeth Williams, Janet Carroll, David Ackroyd, Phil Fondacaro

The Memory Expert: see *The Man on the Flying Trapeze*

The Memphis Belle *
US/GB 1944 43m Technicolor
War Activities Commission
The last mission over Germany of a Flying Fortress.
Impressive on-the-spot documentary which provided a lot of library footage for later movies.
d William Wyler

Memphis Belle **
GB 1990 106m colour
Warner/Enigma (David Puttnam, Catherine Wyler)

In the Second World War, the crew of an American B-17 bomber fly their final mission over Germany.
Sentimental drama that is a throwback to war films of an earlier era.
w Monte Merrick *d* Michael Caton-Jones *ph* David Watkin *m* George Fenton *pd* Stuart Craig *ed* Jim Clark
☆ Matthew Modine, Eric Stoltz, Tate Donovan, D. B. Sweeney, Billy Zane, Sean Astin, Harry Connick Jnr, Reed Edward Diamond, Courtney Gains, Neil Giuntoli
'Another chapter in David Puttnam's peculiar cinema of history lessons without cinematic depth or sound dramatic portfolio.' – *Richard Combs, MFB*

'A completely new experience between men and women!'
'I was afraid I was gonna die ... now I'm afraid I'm gonna live!'

The Men ***
US 1950 85m bw
Stanley Kramer

reissue title: *Battle Stripe*
Paraplegic war veterans are prepared for civilian life; the fiancée of one of them helps overcome his problems.
Vivid semi-documentary melodrama, at the time rather shocking in its no-holds-barred treatment of sexual problems.
w Carl Foreman *d* Fred Zinnemann *ph* Robert de Grasse *m* Dimitri Tiomkin
☆ *Marlon Brando, Teresa Wright, Everett Sloane,* Jack Webb, Howard St John
'Don't be misled into feeling that to see this film is merely a duty; it is, simply, an experience worth having.' – *Richard Mallett, Punch*
'As a bold, brave motion picture, *The Men* is to be applauded; but it would be a mistake to imagine that noble intentions and the courage to speak in hitherto unmentionable medical jargon necessarily make great films.' – *Margaret Hinxman*
Carl Foreman

Men... **
West Germany 1985 99m colour
Artificial Eye/Olga Film/ZDF (Harald Kugler)

original title: *Männer...*
A bourgeois husband turns his wife's lover, a hippy artist, into a carbon copy of himself

Light-hearted indictment of men as overgrown children
wd Doris Dörrie *ph* Helge Weindler *m* Claus Bantzer *ed* Raimund Barthelmes, Jeanette Magerl
☆ Heiner Lauterbach, Uwe Ochsenknecht, Ulrike Kriener, Janna Marangosoff
'Dörrie's deadpan giddiness is likeable enough. The picture is insignificant, though – a piece of fluff without the wit that you might hope for.' – *Pauline Kael, New Yorker*

Men Are Not Gods
GB 1936 92m bw
UA/London (Alexander Korda)
An actor playing Othello nearly strangles his wife.
Tepid melodramatic attempt at a theme later used in A Double Life.
w Walter Reisch, G. B. Stern, Iris Wright
d Walter Reisch *ph* Charles Rosher *m* Geoffrey Toye *ad* Vincent Korda *ed* Henry Cornelius
☆ Miriam Hopkins, Sebastian Shaw, Rex Harrison, Gertrude Lawrence, A. E. Matthews, Val Gielgud, Laura Smithson
'A nearer approximation to box office quality than some recent London productions.' – *Variety*

Men Are Such Fools
US 1938 69m bw
Warner
The worm turns when his wife threatens to leave him for a singing career.
Mediocre is the word for this threadbare drama.
w Norman Reilly Raine, Horace Jackson *d* Busby Berkeley
☆ Wayne Morris, Humphrey Bogart, Priscilla Lane, Hugh Herbert, Penny Singleton

Men at Work
US 1990 98m DeLuxe
Entertainment/Epic Productions/Euphoria Films/ Sarlui/Diamant (Cassian Elwes)
Two garbage men find a corpse and set out to discover its killer.
Clumsily directed, witless rubbish.
wd Emilio Estevez *ph* Tim Suhrstedt *m* Stewart Copeland, Greg DeBelles *pd* Dins Danielsen *ed* Craig Bassett
☆ Charlie Sheen, Emilio Estevez, Leslie Hope, Keith David, Dean Cameron, John Getz, Hawk Wolinski, John Lavachielli, Geoffrey Blake
'This still manages to be an ordeal thanks to its endless procession of excrement jokes, kindergarten-level sex-jokes, contrived and pointless wandering around, and collection of arbitrary and oft-forgotten MacGuffins.' – *Kim Newman, MFB*

Men Behind Bars: see *Duffy of San Quentin*

Men Don't Leave
US 1990 115m CFI color
Warner (Jon Avnet)
Following the death of her husband in an accident, a widow with two sons strives to keep the family together.
Just about rises above the level of an average soap opera.
w Barbara Benedek, Paul Brickman *d* Paul Brickman *ph* Bruce Surtees *m* Thomas Newman *pd* Barbara Ling *ed* Richard Chew
☆ Jessica Lange, Arliss Howard, Joan Cusack, Kathy Bates, Tom Mason, Chris O'Donnell, Charlie Korsmo, Belita Moreno, Jim Haynie, Cory Carrier, Shannon Moffett

'Protecting The Earth From The Scum Of The Universe.'
Men in Black **
US 1997 90m Technicolor
Columbia/Amblin (Walter F. Parkes, Laurie MacDonald)
A cop is recruited to be the partner of a government agent whose task it is to track down illegal aliens.
Quick-witted science fiction with a couple of engaging, contrasting performances from its leads, and some excellent special effects, though a little more originality in its Earth-in-peril screenplay would have been welcome.
w Ed Solomon *comic* Lowell Cunningham *d* Barry Sonnenfeld *ph* Don Peterman *m* Danny Elfman *pd* Bo Welch *ed* Jim Miller *sp* Industrial Light and Magic; make-up: Rick Baker, David LeRoy Anderson
☆ Tommy Lee Jones (K), Will Smith (J), Linda Fiorentino (Laurel), Vincent D'Onofrio (Edgar), Rip Torn (Zed), Tony Shalhoub (Jeebs), Siobhan Fallon
'Undemanding popular entertainment with a modicum of irony to back it up. It never becomes camp. But it never becomes truly sophisticated either.' – *Derek Malcolm, Guardian*
† The film cost $90m and grossed $250m in the US and another $313m around the world.
make-up
Bo Welch; Danny Elfman

'Same Planet. New Scum.'
Men in Black II
US 2002 88m DeLuxe
Columbia/Amblin (Walter F. Parkes, Laurie MacDonald)
Two agents foil an alien plot to destroy the world and other parts of the universe.
A sequel that plods along the same track as the original, but with a little sense of fun or invention; a less derivative plot this time around would have been welcome.
w Robert Gordon, Barry Fanaro *Malibu comic* Lowell Cunningham *d* Barry Sonnenfeld *ph* Greg Gardiner *m* Danny Elfman *pd* Bo Welch *ed* Steven Weisberg, Richard Pearson *sp* ILM
☆ Tommy Lee Jones (Kay), Will Smith (Jay), Rip Torn (Zed), Lara Flynn Boyle (Serleena), Rosario Dawson (Laura Vasquez), Tony Shalhoub (Jeebs), Patrick Warburton (Agent Tee), Johnny Knoxville (Scrad/Charlie)
'Formulaic, flat and unfunny.' – *Sunday Times*
'Pretty much a disaster – repetitive beyond belief, and so busily inconsequential that it neutralizes your brain and leaves you with nothing to respond to.' – *David Denby, New Yorker*
'Strange, zany, generally amusing and very likeable without actually being all that hilarious or surprising.' – *Angie Errigo, Empire*

Men in Her Diary
US 1945 73m bw
Universal
A jealous woman tries to hire an unattractive girl as her husband's secretary.
Very mild lower-berth comedy.
w F. Hugh Herbert and Elwood Ullman *story* Kerry Shaw *d* Charles Barton
☆ Peggy Ryan, Jon Hall, Louise Allbritton, William Terry, Virginia Grey, Ernest Truex, Alan Mowbray, Eric Blore, Sig Rumann

Men in War
US 1957 104m bw
Security (Sidney Harmon)
Korea 1950: an infantry platoon is cut off from HQ and tries to take an enemy-occupied hill.
Stereotyped small-scale war heroics; the film makes its points but fails to entertain.
w Philip Yordan *novel* Day without End by Van van Praag *d* Anthony Mann *ph* Ernest Haller *m* Elmer Bernstein
☆ Robert Ryan, Robert Keith, Aldo Ray, Vic Morrow, James Edwards, Sen Yung

Men in White *
US 1934 80m bw
MGM (Monta Bell)
An ambitious intern is in love with an attractive socialite who resents his devotion to duty.
Popular but obvious star drama.
w Waldemar Young *play* Sidney Kingsley *d* Richard Boleslawski *ph* George Folsey
☆ Clark Gable, Myrna Loy, Jean Hersholt, Elizabeth Allan, Otto Kruger, C. Henry Gordon, Wallace Ford
'Belongs in the strictly adult class of pictures ... show spells money from plenty of angles.' – *Variety*

Men Must Fight
US 1933 73m bw
MGM
War comes to New York in 1940.
A forgotten pacifist tract which trod the same paths as did H. G. Wells; of historical interest only apart from a spectacular air raid climax.
w S. K. Lauren, Reginald Lawrence, C. Gardner Sullivan *d* Edgar Selwyn
☆ Robert Young, Diana Wynyard, May Robson, Phillips Holmes, Lewis Stone

Men o' War *
US 1929 20m bw
Hal Roach
Two sailors and two girls have adventures in a park.
Simple-minded early talkie star comedy featuring their famous soda fountain routine.
w H. M. Walker *d* Lewis R. Foster *ph* George Stevens, Jack Roach *ed* Richard Currier
☆ Stan Laurel, Oliver Hardy, James Finlayson, Anne Cornwall, Gloria Greer

Men of Boys' Town
US 1941 106m bw
MGM (John W. Considine Jnr)
Further adventures of Father Flanagan.
Mushy sequel to Boys' Town *(qv).*
w James Kevin McGuinness *d* Norman Taurog *ph* Harold Rosson *m* Herbert Stothart
☆ Spencer Tracy, Mickey Rooney, Bobs Watson, Larry Nunn, Lee J. Cobb, Mary Nash, Henry O'Neill, Darryl Hickman, Anne Revere

'History is made by those who break the rules.'
Men of Honor
US 2000 DeLuxe Super 35
TCF/Fox 2000/State Street (Robert Teitel, Bill Badalato)
GB title: *Men of Honour*
In the 1950s, Carl Brashear overcomes racial prejudice to be the US navy's first black deep-sea diver.
The sort of patriotic flagwaver that inspired the troops in time of war, this is a surprising movie to find being made at the end of the twentieth century; its simple-minded approach does scant justice to a remarkable life.
w Scott Marshall Smith *d* George Tillman Jnr *ph* Anthony B. Richmond *m* Mark Isham *pd* Leslie Dilley *ed* John Carter *cos* Salvador Perez
☆ Robert De Niro (Billy Sunday), Cuba Gooding Jnr (Carl Brashear), Charlize Theron (Gwen), Aunjanue Ellis (Jo), Hal Holbrook (Mr Pappy), David Keith (Capt Hartigan), Michael Rapaport (Snowhill), Powers Boothe (Capt Pullman), Joshua Leonard (Isert), David Conrad (Hanks)
'Full of easy-to-say, harder-to-do messages about never quitting and surmounting daunting obstacles, pic needs only a chorus of "Climb Every Mountain" to be complete.' – *Todd McCarthy, Variety*

Men of Means
Canada 1999 80m colour
Libra/Producers Network (Daniel D'Or, G. Philip Jackson)
In New York, a loan shark for the mob begins to develop a conscience and decides it is time to find another line of work.
Thuggish chase-thriller, of unpleasant people being nasty to one another; there are many better ways of passing the time.
w Shane Perez *d* George Mendeluk *ph* Ludek Bogner *m* Donald Quan *pd* Thomas Carnegie *ed* John Whitcher
☆ Michael Paré (Rico 'Bullet' Burke), Kaela Dobkin (Cleo), Raymond Serra (Tommy C.), Austin Pendleton (Jerry Trask), Mark Hutchinson (Joey), Tony Cucci (Angelo), Ron Holgate (Max), Tie Domi (Pete)

Men of Respect
US 1990 113m colour
Central City/Arthur Goldblatt (Ephraim Horowitz)
Told by a fortune-teller that he will become the next Mafia Godfather, a gangster is urged by his wife to make sure the prediction comes true.
Shakespeare's Macbeth *is the inspiration for this odd little thriller, with the plot sticking close to the original and some of the dialogue being repeated virtually word for word. But guilt over a murder seems an unlikely emotion for a hitman to feel.*
wd William Reilly *ph* Bobby Bukowski *m* Misha Segal *ad* William Barclay *ed* Elizabeth Kling
☆ John Turturro, Katherine Borowitz, Dennis Farina, Peter Boyle, Rod Steiger
'One has the feeling of watching an end-of-the-term show at Yale Drama School.' – *Philip French, Observer*
† An earlier thriller, *Joe Macbeth* (qv), also borrowed its plot from Shakespeare's play.

Men of Sherwood Forest
GB 1954 77m Eastmancolor
Hammer (Michael Carreras)
Robin Hood frees King Richard from bondage.
Fairly lively adventure romp on a low level.
w Allan MacKinnon *d* Val Guest *ph* Jimmy Harvey *m* Doreen Corwithen
☆ Don Taylor, Reginald Beckwith, Eileen Moore, David King-Wood, Patrick Holt, John Van Eyssen

Men of Texas
US 1942 81m bw
Universal (George Waggner)
At the end of the American Civil War, a Chicago journalist and a photographer are sent to Texas to find Sam Houston and discover an outlaw gang pretending to be patriots.
Flag-waving minor Western, quite lively when not overearnest.
w Harold Shumate, Richard Brooks *d* Ray Enright *ph* Milton Krasner *md* Edward Ward *ad* Jack Otterson *ed* Clarence Kolster
☆ Robert Stack, Broderick Crawford, Jackie Cooper, Anne Gwynne, Ralph Bellamy, Jane Darwell, Leo Carillo, John Litel

Men of the Sea: see *Midshipman Easy*

Men of Tomorrow
GB 1932 88m bw
Paramount/London Films (Alexander Korda)
Oxford students have more than academic work on their minds.
Dim comedy-drama with an interesting cast.
w Arthur Wimperis, Anthony Gibbs *play* Young Apollo by Anthony Gibbs *d* Leontine Sagan, Zoltan Korda *ph* Bernard Browne *ad* Vincent Korda *ed* Leontine Sagan
☆ Maurice Braddell, Joan Gardner, Emlyn Williams, Merle Oberon, Robert Donat

Men of Two Worlds
GB 1946 109m Technicolor
GFD/Two Cities (John Sutro)
US title: *Witch Doctor*
aka: *Kisenga, Man of Africa*
In Tanganyika, an educated native helps white men to counter the force of witch doctors and persuade tribes to leave an infected area.
Earnest but totally unpersuasive semi-documentary shot in unconvincing sets and garish colour.
w Thorold Dickinson, Joyce Cary, E. Arnot Robertson, Herbert Victor *d* Thorold Dickinson *ph* Geoffrey Unsworth, Desmond Dickinson *m* Arthur Bliss
☆ Eric Portman, Phyllis Calvert, Robert Adams, Orlando Martins, Arnold Marle, Cathleen Nesbitt, David Horne, Cyril Raymond

Men of War
US 1994 99m DeLuxe Super 35
MDP/Pomerance/Grandview Avenue (Arthur Goldblatt, Andrew Pfeffer)
A Swedish mercenary has a change of heart after hiring a gang of thugs to persuade some islanders in the South China Sea to part with their mining rights.
An action film that tries for a little originality and even wit in dealing with matters of morality versus expediency, but settles in the end for the usual over-the-top psychopathic villain and a gloating emphasis on violence.
w John Sayles, Ethan Reiff, Cyrus Voris *story* Stan Rogow *d* Perry Lang *ph* Ronn Schmidt *m* Gerald Gouriet *pd* Steve Spence, Jim Newport *ed* Jeffrey Reiner
☆ Dolph Lundgren, Charlotte Lewis, B. D. Wong, Anthony John Denison, Tim Guinee, Don Harvey, Trevor Goddard, Kevin Tighe
'Shot from an intelligent, witty, cliché-overturning script and featuring lashings of gritty violence, this is an action gem.' – *Film Review*

Men of Yesterday
GB 1936 82m bw
UK Films
Old army rivalries die down at a reunion.

Dated but interesting drama with interpolated variety talent.
w Gerald Elliott, Jack Francis *d* John Baxter
☆ Stewart Rome, Sam Livesey, Hay Petrie, Cecil Parker, George Robey, Ella Shields, Will Fyffe, Dick Henderson

Men on Her Mind: see *The Girl from Tenth Avenue*

Men with Guns *
US 1997 126m Technicolor
Lexington Road/Clear Blue Sky/IFC/Anarchists' Convention (R. Paul Miller, Maggie Renzi)
An ageing doctor goes to visit some former students, now working in poor villages, and discovers that they have been killed by those in authority.
A Spanish-language film from an American director, though not obviously set in any particular country; its narrative, about a man whose eyes are opened to the atrocities he has deliberately ignored, is a simple one, but told with feeling.
wd John Sayles *ph* Slawomir Idziak *m* Mason Daring *pd* Felipe Fernandez Del Paso *ed* John Sayles
☆ Federico Luppi, Damian Delgado, Dan Rivera, Tania Cruz, Damian Alcazar, Mandy Patinkin, Kathryn Grody, Iguandili Lopez, Nandi Luna Ramirez, Rafael de Quevedo, Roberto Sosa
'An absorbing, thoughtful and thoroughly rewarding watch.' – *Ian Freer, Empire*

'Dreamers Who Dare To Make Their Dreams Come True...'
Men with Wings
US 1938 106m Technicolor
Paramount (William Wellman)
Civil aviation pioneers fall out over a girl.
Disappointing epic from the maker of Wings, *with highly predictable story line, modest acting and ho-hum spectacle.*
w Robert Carson *d* William Wellman *ph* W. Howard Greene *m* W. Franke Harling, Gerard Carbonara
☆ Fred MacMurray, Ray Milland, Louise Campbell, Andy Devine, Lynne Overman, Porter Hall, Walter Abel, Virginia Weidler, Donald O'Connor
'To all women who love and admire the fearless heroes of the air, and who, with brave hearts, encourage them, hope, and pray for them.' – *director's dedication*
'Lavish air spectacle in Technicolor that means big business ... it will triumph through rain, sleet or snow.' – *Variety*

'Give the rats a taste of their own medicine!'
Men without Names
US 1935 67m bw
Paramount
Bank robbers are cornered in a small town and picked off by the FBI.
Routine crime feature, less exciting than it sounds.
w Marguerite Roberts, Kubec Glasmon, Dale Van Every *d* Ralph Murphy
☆ Fred MacMurray, Madge Evans, Lynne Overman, David Holt, John Wray, Dean Jagger
'Another of the new gangster films, and too flimsy. Grooved for the pops.' – *Variety*

Men without Women
US 1930 77m bw
Fox
Men in a submarine are trapped on the ocean bed.
Early talkie action drama noted more for its credits than its accomplishment.
w Dudley Nichols *d* John Ford *ph* Joseph H. August
☆ Kenneth MacKenna, Frank Albertson, Paul Page, Pat Somerset, Stuart Erwin, Warren Hymer, John Wayne
'Stunning, realistic picture that will make talk.' – *Variety*

Men Women: A User's Manual **
France 1996 122m colour 'Scope
Gala/UFD/Films 13/TF1/Canal+ (Claude Lelouch)
original title: *Hommes Femmes: Mode d'emploi*
An actor-turned-cop and an adulterous and successful businessman are among those who experience the trials of love, chance and betrayal.
Subtitled 'an inhuman comedy', this is an engrossing account about the loss of love and the search for it; despite the title, its perspective is a masculine one.
w Claude Lelouch, Rene Bonnell, Jean-Philippe Chatrier *d* Claude Lelouch *ph* Claude Lelouch, Philippe Pavans de Ceccatty *m* Francis Lai *pd* Jacques Bufnoir
☆ Fabrice Luchini, Bernard Tapie, Alessandra Martines, Pierre Arditi, Carlone Cellier, Ticky Holgado, Ophélie Winter, Anouk Aimée, Patrick Husson, Salome
'The intricate and suspense-laced narrative is a satisfying puzzle full of funny touches, just-missed opportunities and a few short cuts in social Darwinism.' – *Lisa Nesselson, Variety*
† Bernard Tapie, a controversial French businessman, had not acted before being cast in one of the leading roles, as a controversial businessman.

The Menace
US 1932 64m bw
Columbia
A convict escapes, gets a new face through plastic surgery, and plans his revenge.
Muddled melodrama.
w Dorothy Howell, Charles Logue, Roy Chanslor *novel* Feathered Serpent by Edgar Wallace *d* Roy William Neill
☆ Walter Byron, H. B. Warner, Bette Davis, Natalie Moorhead, William Davidson, Halliwell Hobbes
'A halting and frequently clumsy development leads to a weak climax.' – *Variety*

Menace
US 1934 58m bw
Paramount
Murders follow the suicide of a mining engineer.
Compact little dark house thriller with good stagey performances.
w Chandler Sprague, Anthony Veiller *story* Philip MacDonald *d* Ralph Murphy
☆ Gertrude Michael, Paul Cavanagh, Henrietta Crosman, John Lodge, Ray Milland, Berton Churchill, Halliwell Hobbes
'A pat specimen of the mystery film, expertly manipulated.' – *Variety*

'This is the truth. This is what's real.'
Menace II Society *
US 1993 97m Foto-Kem
First Independent/New Line (Darin Scott)
In the Watts district of Los Angeles, young blacks become involved in robbery and murder.
A harsh and violent movie that sticks close to the expectations of gangster films while claiming to be dealing with reality; its young directors show promise.
w Tyger Williams, Allen Hughes, Albert Hughes *d* Allen Hughes, Albert Hughes *ph* Lisa Rinzler *m* QD III *pd* Penny Barrett *ed* Christopher Koefoed
☆ Tyrin Turner, Jada Pinkett, Larenz Tate, Arnold Johnson, MC Eiht, Marilyn Coleman, Vonte Sweet, Clifton Powell, Samuel L. Jackson
'The clichés of racial stereotyping lie piled as high as the bodies ... It's a dreadfully inflammatory film to bring to our society. Hollywood is exporting too many of America's menaces.' – *Alexander Walker, London Evening Standard*
'A grim, nihilistic trip to the inner city ... Fierce, violent and searing in its observation, the film makes all previous excursions seem like a walk in the park.' – *Variety*

Menilmontant *
France 1924 50m (24 fps) bw silent
Dimitri Kirsanov (for his own company)
Respected but fairly impenetrable piece of avant-garde which appears to be about two sisters haunted by memories of the murder of their parents, for which they may or may not have been responsible.
wd Dimitri Kirsanov *ed* Dimitri Kirsanov
'A flurry of hand-held camera shots, incisive montages and elliptical progressions.' – *Geoff Brown, MFB, 1981*

The Men's Club
US 1986 100m colour
Atlantic Releasing/Howard Gottfried
Friends nearing forty get together and bemoan their lot.
Curious, talky, rather dreary piece which gets almost nowhere.
w Leonard Michaels *novel* Leonard Michaels *d* Peter Medak *ph* John Fleckenstein *m* Lee Holdridge *pd* Ken Davis *ed* Cynthia Scheider, David Dresser, Bill Butler
☆ Roy Scheider, Frank Langella, Harvey Keitel, Treat Williams, Richard Jordan, David Dukes, Craig Wasson, Stockard Channing, Jennifer Jason Leigh
'A club few will want to join ... a distasteful piece of work that displays the worst in men.' – *Variety*

Menschen am Sonntag: see *People on Sunday*

Mensonge *
France 1993 89m colour
Gala/Cuel Lavalette/France-3/Alain Sarde
aka: *The Lie*
A faithful wife discovers that she is both pregnant and HIV positive.
Interesting, though too easily resolved, exploration of relationships and the effect of AIDS on those innocently involved.
w Denis Saada, François Margolin *d* François Margolin *ph* Caroline Champetier *pd* Julie Sfez, Arnaud de Moleron *ed* Martine Giordano
☆ Nathalie Baye, Didier Sandre, Hélène Lapiower, Marc Citti, Dominique Besnehard, Christophe Bourseiller, Louis Ducreux, Adrien Beau
'Rather than flagging the disease as a metaphor of sanctification-through-degradation, it rolls it into a disease-of-the-week movie and uses it as a trigger for tears, lots of talk, pat ironies and soapy symbolism. And on that level, it's actually quite accomplished.' – *Steve Beard, Empire*

Mephisto ****
Hungary 1981 144m Eastmancolor
Mafilm/Manfred Durniok
In Germany in the twenties, an actor committed to the idea of a workers' theatre becomes a puppet of the Nazis.
Chilling and fiercely compelling melodrama of moral corruption, with a bravura performance from Brandauer as a man who willingly sells his soul.
w Peter Dobai, István Szabó *novel* Klaus Mann *d István Szabó* *ph* Lajos Koltai *m* Zdenko Tamassy
☆ *Klaus Maria Brandauer*, Ildikó Bánsági, Krystyna Janda
best foreign film

The Mephisto Waltz *
US 1971 109m DeLuxe
TCF/QM Productions
A satanic concert pianist on the point of death wills his soul into the body of a journalist.
Complex diabolical mumbo-jumbo with plenty of style.
w Ben Maddow *novel* Fred Mustard Stewart *d Paul Wendkos* *ph* William W. Spencer *m* Jerry Goldsmith
☆ Alan Alda, Jacqueline Bisset, Curt Jurgens, Barbara Parkins

Le Mépris: see *Contempt*

La Mer Cruelle
Kuwait 1983 107m bw
Sakr Films (Abbas Redha, Hassan Redha)
original title: *Bas Ya Bahar*
aka: *Sea of Silence*
In Kuwait before the discovery of oil, a youth becomes a pearl diver against his father's wishes.
Competent, but slow-moving and of interest mainly for its documentary content.
w Rahman Saleh *d* Khalid Al Siddiq *ph* Tanfig Al Amir *m* Abu Tariq *ed* Hassanof
☆ Saad Al Faraj, Mohammed Al Mansour, Hayat Al Fahd

The Mercenaries
GB 1968 100m Metrocolor Panavision
MGM/George Englund
US title: *Dark of the Sun*
In the Belgian Congo in 1960 a mercenary officer is ordered to bring back a fortune in diamonds by armoured train.
Basically an old-fashioned thriller about the hazards of a journey beset by brutish villains and damsels in distress, this unpleasant film is notable for the amount of sadistic action it crams into its running time.
w Quentin Werty, Adrian Spies *novel* Dark of the Sun by Wilbur Smith *d* Jack Cardiff *ph* Edward Scaife *m* Jacques Loussier *ed* Ernest Walter
☆ Rod Taylor, Yvette Mimieux, Kenneth More, Jim Brown, Peter Carsten, André Morell, Guy Deghy, Calvin Lockhart, Alan Gifford
'The violence done to the human body is matched by violence done to the intelligence by a stock adventure story given a gloss of topicality and social insult.' – *Judith Crist*

The Mercenary
Italy/Spain 1968 105m Technicolor Techniscope
United Artists/PEA/Delphos/Profilms 21 (Alberto Grimaldi)
aka: *A Professional Gun*
In revolutionary Mexico, a European gunfighter hires himself out to a group of rebellious peasants and turns them into a rampaging army.
Violent, action-packed spaghetti Western in which all the protagonists are motivated by greed and a pleasure in killing.
w Luciano Vincenzoni, Sergio Spina, Adriano Bolzoni, Sergio Corbucci *story* Franco Solinas, Giorgio Arlorio *d* Sergio Corbucci *ph* Alejandro Ulloa *m* Ennio Morricone, Bruno Nicolai *ad* Luis Vazquez *ed* Eugenio Alabiso
☆ Franco Nero, Tony Musante, Jack Palance, Giovanna Ralli, Franco Giacobini, Eduardo Fajardo, Franco Bessel, Alvaro de Luna
† A sequel, *Companeros* (qv), followed in 1970.

Merci La Vie **
France 1991 119m Eastmancolor/bw
Cine Valse/Film par Film/Orly/DD/SEDIF/A2 (Barnard Marescot)
A bored teenager befriends a girl with a venereal disease, who has been persuaded by a doctor to infect as many men as she can in order to provide him with patients.
Inventive, playful film which mixes the present day and the Nazi occupation of France, switching between reality, day-dreams and movies in which the girls appear – though the final effect may be more exhausting than invigorating.
wd Bertrand Blier *ph* Philippe Rousselot *pd* Theobald Meurisse *ed* Claudine Merlin
☆ Charlotte Gainsbourg, Anouk Grinberg, Gérard Depardieu, Michael Blanc, Jean Carmet, Catherine Jacob, Annie Girardot, Jean-Louis Trintignant, Thierry Frémont
'A bold, often exciting, sometimes frustrating but always challenging pic.' – *Variety*
'The art-house equivalent of a Hollywood rollercoaster where sensation is all and decorous values – logic, good taste, some ultimate meaning – get trampled in the rush to amaze.' – *Geoff Brown, The Times*

Merci Pour Le Chocolat *
France/Switzerland 2000 101m colour
Artificial Eye/MK2/CAB (Marin Karmitz)
US title: *Nightcap*
A piano student becomes involved with the family of a concert pianist who may have been her father.
Icy, ambiguous thriller that exposes the passionate secrets that underlie an apparently conventional bourgeois family.
w Caroline Eliacheff, Claude Chabrol *novel* The Chocolate Cobweb by Charlotte Armstrong *d* Claude Chabrol *ph* Renato Berta *m* Matthieu Chabrol *ad* Yvan Niclass *ed* Monique Fardoulis *cos* Elisabeth Tavernier
☆ Isabelle Huppert (Marie-Claire 'Mika' Muller), Jacques Dutronc (André Polonski), Anna Mouglalis (Jeanne Pollet), Rodolphe Pauly (Guillaume Polonski), Michel Robin (Dufreigne), Brigitte Catillon (Louise Pollet), Mathieu Simonet (Axel)
'A treat, a delicious blend of perversity, playfulness and deadly passion concealed

beneath the tranquil, moneyed surface.' – *Derek Elley, Variety*

Mercury Rising
US 1998 112m DeLuxe Panavision
Universal/Imagine (Brian Grazer, Karen Kehela)
A maverick agent protects an autistic child whose gift for mathematics makes him a security risk.
A by-the-numbers action flick, through which Willis glowers ferociously.
w Lawrence Konner, Mark Rosenthal *novel* Simple Simon by Ryne Douglas Peardon *d* Harold Becker *ph* Michael Seresin *m* John Barry *pd* Patrizia von Brandenstein *ed* Peter Honess *sp* Industrial Light & Magic
☆ Bruce Willis, Alec Baldwin, Miko Hughes, Chi McBride, Kim Dickens, Robert Stanton, Bodhi Pine Elfman, Carrie Preston, L. L. Ginter, John Carroll Lynch, Peter Stormare
'A real pot-boiler.' – *Guardian*

Merely Mary Ann
US 1931 74m bw
Fox
The maid of all work falls for the gentleman lodger.
Cinderella stuff redesigned for two popular stars, but of no lasting appeal.
w Jules Furthman *story* Israel Zangwill *d* Henry King
☆ Janet Gaynor, Charles Farrell, Beryl Mercer, J. M. Kerrigan, G. P. Huntley Jnr
'Bound to pull after a summer of gang violence, mystery shockers, and much sex urge study.' – *Variety*

'A Tale Of Wizards, Warriors, Myth And Magic.'
Merlin: The Return
GB 2000 88m colour
Peakviewing (Elizabeth Matthews, Paul Matthews)
A mad scientist reawakens King Arthur and his knights, who once again do battle with Mordred with the aid of a American boy.
Dire fantasy with a grating mix of modernity and medievalism; most of the cast wander around as if in a daze.
wd Paul Matthews *ph* Vincent G. Cox *m* Mark Thomas *pd* Edward Thomas *ed* Peter Davies
☆ Rik Mayall (Merlin), Tia Carrere (Joan Maxwell), Patrick Bergin (King Arthur), Adrian Paul (Lancelot), Craig Sheffer (Mordred), Julie Hartley (Guinevere), Leigh Greyvenstein (Kate), Byron Taylor (Richie), Grethe Fox (Morgana)
'Any parent caught taking their unfortunate child to see this film should be reported to the social services immediately.' – *Peter Bradshaw, Guardian*

Mermaids
US 1990 110m colour
Rank/Orion (Lauren Lloyd, Wallis Nichita, Patrick Palmer)
A daughter, torn between becoming a nun and her feelings for a handsome boy, resolves her difficulties with her flirtatious mother.
A romantic comedy uncertain whether it is trying for laughs or tears; it attempts, unsuccessfully, to settle for both.
w June Roberts *novel* Patty Dann *d* Richard Benjamin *ph* Howard Atherton *m* Jack Nitzsche *pd* Stuart Wurtzel *ed* Jacqueline Cambas
☆ Cher, Bob Hoskins, Winona Ryder, Michael Schoeffling, Christina Ricci, Caroline McWilliams, Jan Miner, Betsey Townsend
'It wavers between arch comedy and hollow melodrama, each desperately over-pitched.' – *Sight and Sound*
† Lasse Halstrom was replaced by Frank Oz as director before filming began. Two weeks after filming started, Richard Benjamin replaced Frank Oz. Winona Ryder's role as Cher's daughter was to have been played by Emily Lloyd until Cher objected that Lloyd did not look like her.

Merrill's Marauders *
US 1962 98m Technicolor Cinemascope
Warner/US Pictures (Milton Sperling)
Adventures of a crack US army unit in 1942 Burma.
Physically exhausting war adventure with emphasis on hand-to-hand fighting and much bloodshed.
w Samuel Fuller, Milton Sperling *novel* Charlton Ogburn Jnr *d* Samuel Fuller *ph* William Clothier *m* Howard Jackson *ed* Folmar Blangsted
☆ Jeff Chandler, Ty Hardin, Andrew Duggan, Peter Brown, Will Hutchins, Claude Akins

Merrily We Go to Hell
US 1932 78m bw
Paramount
GB title: *Merrily We Go to –*
A socialite marries a dipsomaniac journalist.
Glum problem drama.
w Edwin Justus Mayer *novel* I Jerry Take Thee Joan by Cleo Lucas *d* Dorothy Arzner *ph* David Abel
☆ Sylvia Sidney, Fredric March, Adrienne Allen, Richard Gallagher, Florence Burton, Esther Howard, Kent Taylor

Merrily We Live *
US 1938 90m bw
Hal Roach
A zany family hires a chauffeur who is actually a famous writer posing as a tramp.
Quite likeable compound of My Man Godfrey *and* You Can't Take It with You.
w Eddie Moran, Jack Jevne *d* Norman Z. McLeod *ph* Norbert Brodine *md* Marvin Hatley *ad* Charles D. Hall
☆ Constance Bennett, Brian Aherne, Billie Burke, Alan Mowbray, Patsy Kelly, Ann Dvorak, Tom Brown, Bonita Granville, Marjorie Rambeau, Clarence Kolb
'In the high cost bracket and rates top billing when dualled, with a chance it is strong enough to carry first runs as a single.' – *Variety*
Norbert Brodine; Billie Burke; title song (*m*Phil Craig, *ly*Arthur Quenzer); Charles D. Hall

Merry Andrew
US 1958 103m Metrocolor Cinemascope
MGM/Sol C. Siegel
A stuffy teacher in search of an ancient statue joins a travelling circus.
Deliberately charming star comedy which plumps too firmly for whimsy and, despite its professionalism, provokes barely a smile, let alone a laugh.
w Isobel Lennart, I. A. L. Diamond *story* Paul Gallico *ph* Robert Surtees *m* Saul Chaplin *d/ch* Michael Kidd *ly* Johnny Mercer
☆ Danny Kaye, Pier Angeli, Baccaloni, Noel Purcell, Robert Coote, Patricia Cutts, Rex Evans, Walter Kingsford, Tommy Rall, Rhys Williams

Merry Christmas, Mr Lawrence *
GB 1982 124m Eastmancolor
Recorded Picture/Cineventure/Oshima (Jeremy Thomas)
In a Japanese prisoner-of-war camp in Java in 1942, an English captive strikes up a strange relationship with the commandant.
Uncomfortably titled and unavoidably downbeat character drama with some unpleasant moments; despite good work all round it seems to head straight for every cliché perpetuated by The Bridge on the River Kwai.
w Nagisa Oshima, Paul Mayersberg *novel* The Seed and the Sower by Laurens van der Post *d* Nagisa Oshima *ph* Toichiro Narushima *m* Ryuichi Sakamoto
☆ David Bowie, Tom Conti, Ryuichi Sakamoto, Takeshi, Jack Thompson, Johnny Okura, Alistair Browning
'It always seems like a cocktail of saleable ingredients rather than genuine cinema.' – *Sunday Times*
Ryuichi Sakamoto

Merry Comes to Town
GB 1937 79m bw
Embassy/Sound City
US title: *Merry Comes to Stay*
A professor's family is disappointed when a relative visiting from America turns out to be as poor as they are.
Thin, predictable comedy with the visitor finally hailed as a saviour.
w Evadne Price *d* George King
☆ ZaSu Pitts, Guy Newall, Betty Ann Davies, Muriel George, Basil Langton
'A pleasant comedy which will improve with cutting.' – *Variety*

The Merry Frinks
US 1934 68m bw
First National
GB title: *Happy Family*
A sportswriter down on his luck has a crazy family.
And didn't everybody in the mid-thirties? But this one is crazy without being very funny.
w Gene Markey, Kathryn Scola *d* Alfred E. Green
☆ Aline MacMahon, Guy Kibbee, Allen Jenkins, Hugh Herbert, Frankie Darro
'The most disagreeable family group since Three Cornered Moon. Poor comedy and lacks names.' – *Variety.*

'A King's Ransom To Make America Laugh!'
Merry Go Round of 1938
US 1937 87m bw
Universal
Four vaudevillians adopt a small girl, and later head for Hollywood.
Sentimental farce with zany moments and an encouraging cast.
w Monte Brice, A. Dorian Otvos *d* Irving Cummings *ph* Joseph Valentine *ed* Ted J. Kent, Charles Maynard
☆ Jimmy Savo, Bert Lahr, Mischa Auer, Billy House, Alice Brady, Louise Fazenda
'First rate filmusical packed with laughs.' – *Variety*

The Merry Monahans
US 1944 90m bw
Universal (Michael Fessier, Ernest Pagano)
Adventures of a family of vaudeville performers.
Acceptable backstage comedy drama with good atmosphere.
w Michael Fessier, Ernest Pagano *d* Charles Lamont *ph* Charles Van Enger *m* Hans Salter
☆ Donald O'Connor, Jack Oakie, Rosemary de Camp, Peggy Ryan, Ann Blyth, Isabel Jewell, John Miljan
Hans Salter

A Merry War: see *Keep the Aspidistra Flying*

The Merry Widow *
US 1925 111m (24 fps) bw silent
MGM (Irving Thalberg)
A bankrupt king orders a nobleman to woo a wealthy American widow.
An operetta without music (or dialogue) is usually a poor thing, but the director added a few unpredictable touches.
w Erich von Stroheim, Benjamin Glazer *operetta* Victor Leon, Leo Stein *d* Erich von Stroheim *ph* Oliver Marsh, Ben Reynolds, William Daniels *m* William Axt, D. Mendoza
☆ Mae Murray, John Gilbert, Roy D'Arcy, Tully Marshall
† The story goes that when reproved by Thalberg for wasting film stock on, for instance, endless shots of a wardrobe full of shoes, von Stroheim remarked: 'The character has a foot fetish.' 'And you,' said Thalberg, 'have a footage fetish!'

'Surrender to the happy seduction of Ernst Lubitsch's most glorious picture holiday!'
The Merry Widow **
US 1934 99m bw
MGM
Patchy, but sometimes sparkling version.
w Samson Raphaelson, Ernest Vajda *d* Ernst Lubitsch *ph* Oliver T. Marsh *m* Franz Lehar *ad* Cedric Gibbons, Frederic Hope
☆ Maurice Chevalier, Jeanette MacDonald, Edward Everett Horton, Una Merkel, George Barbier, Donald Meek, Sterling Holloway, Shirley Ross
'Fine all-around job and an entertainment natural.' – *Variety*
'It is Lubitsch; it is also Hollywood; it is the cream of the American bourgeois film. It is a charlotte russe.' – *Peter Ellis, New Masses*
art direction

The Merry Widow
US 1952 105m Technicolor
MGM (Joe Pasternak)
Chill, empty remake.
w Sonya Levien, William Ludwig *d* Curtis Bernhardt *ph* Robert Surtees
☆ Fernando Lamas, Lana Turner, Richard Haydn, Una Merkel, Thomas Gomez, John Abbott
'Nothing has been omitted (except the spirit of the original).' – *MFB*
† Lana Turner's singing was dubbed by Trudy Erwin.

The Merry Wives of Reno *
US 1934 61m bw
Warner
Three couples go to a Reno hotel to get a divorce.
Amusing but scrappy comedy in the vein of the successful Convention City.
w Robert Lord *d* H. Bruce Humberstone
☆ Margaret Lindsay, Donald Woods, Guy Kibbee, Glenda Farrell, Ruth Donnelly, Hugh Herbert, Frank McHugh, Roscoe Ates, Hobart Cavanaugh
'Stylized farce with excellent cast and considerable humour.' – *Variety*

Merton of the Movies *
US 1947 82m bw
MGM
An innocent young man in Hollywood becomes a star.
The plot and characterizations of this old chestnut are resistible, but the Hollywood background is well managed and convincing.
w George Wells, Lou Breslow *novel* Harry Leon Wilson *d* Robert Alton *ph* Paul C. Vogel *m* David Snell
☆ Red Skelton, Virginia O'Brien, Alan Mowbray, Gloria Grahame, Leon Ames
† There were previous versions in 1924 and (as *Make Me a Star*) in 1932.

Mery per sempre
Italy 1988 106m Telecolor
BFI/Numero Uno (Claudio Bonivento)
aka: *Forever Mary*
aka: *Mary Forever*
In Sicily, a new liberal teacher at a reform school tries to win over the tough and suspicious pupils.
Downbeat documentary-style movie that substitutes earnestness for art.
w Sandro Petraglia, Stefano Rulli *novel* Aurello Grimaldi *d* Marco Risi *ph* Mauro Marchetti *m* Giancarlo Bigazzi *ad* Massimo Spano *ed* Claudio Di Mauro
☆ Michele Placido, Claudio Amendola, Francesco Benigno, Alessandro Di Sanzo

Mes Petites Amoureuses
France 1975 123m Eastmancolor
Gala/Elite (Pierre Cottrell)
A sex-obsessed schoolboy finds life full of frustrations when he goes to live with his mother and her Spanish lover.
A long-winded exploration of adolescence, which offers no fresh insights.
wd Jean Eustache *ph* Nestor Almendros *ed* Françoise Belleville, Alberto Yacelini, Vincent Cottrell
☆ Martin Loeb, Ingrid Caven, Jacqueline Dufranne, Dionys Mascolo, Henri Martinez, Pierre Edelman, Maurice Pialat

Mesa of Lost Women
US 1952 70m bw
Wade Williams Productions/Howco (G. William Perkins, Melvin Gordon)
A scientist experiments in the Mexican desert to combine the qualities of beautiful women and spiders.
Bizarre B-movie, ineptly directed, with portentous voice-over, a score played by piano and guitar, and two mad scientists, one of them one-eyed, as well as scantily clad female assistants and dwarfs, operating from a laboratory carved into a mountainside. It also has what may be the least erotic would-be seductive dance on film.
w Herbert Tevos *d* Herbert Tevos, Ron Ormond *ph* Karl Struss, Gil Warrenton *m* Hoyt S. Curtin *ed* W. Donn Hayes, Hugh Winn, Ray H. Lockert
☆ Jackie Coogan, Allan Nixon, Richard Travis, Mary Hill, Robert Knapp, Tandra Quinn
'A really barmy B-movie that has to be seen to be disbelieved.' – *The Dark Side*

The Message: see *Mohammed, Messenger of God*

Message in a Bottle
US 1999 132m Technicolor Panavision
Warner/Bel-Air/Tig (Denise Di Novi, Jim Wilson, Kevin Costner)

A female reporter finds a love letter in a bottle on a beach and traces the man who sent it.
Soporific and soft-centred romantic drama that is yet another nail in the coffin of Costner's career.
w Gerald DiPego *novel* Nicholas Sparks *d* Luis Mandoki *ph* Caleb Deschanel *m* Gabriel Yared *pd* Jeffrey Beecroft *ed* Steven Weisberg
☆ Kevin Costner, Robin Wright Penn, John Savage, Illeana Douglas, Robbie Coltrane, Paul Newman, Jesse James, Bethel Leslie, Tom Aldredge, Viveka Davis
'A prettily torpid film with the warm glow of a hazelnut coffee commercial.' – *Janet Maslin, New York Times*
'Dreary, lachrymose and incredibly poky tear-jerker.' – *Todd McCarthy, Variety*

A Message to Garcia *
US 1936 86m bw
TCF (Raymond Griffith)
During the Spanish-American war a Cuban girl helps an American agent get through to the rebel leader with a diplomatic message.
Agreeable embroidery of a historical incident: good production values and entertaining star performances.
w W. P. Lipscomb, Gene Fowler *book* Andrew S. Rowan *d* George Marshall *ph* Rudolph Maté *md* Louis Silvers *ad* William Darling
☆ Wallace Beery, Barbara Stanwyck, John Boles, Alan Hale, Herbert Mundin, Mona Barrie

The Messenger: The Story Of Joan Of Arc *
France 1999 158m colour Technovision
Columbia/Gaumont (Patrice Ledoux)

GB title: *Joan of Arc*
In the 15th century, a young girl, traumatised by the rape and murder of her sister by English soldiers, hears voices telling her to rid France of invaders and put the Dauphin on the throne.
Besson's action-film approach really needed Arnold Schwarzenegger in the title role to make it credible; here he concentrates on the spectacle and lets his cast do what they will, which is overact.
w Andrew Birkin, Luc Besson *d* Luc Besson *ph* Thierry Arbogast *m* Eric Serra *pd* Hugues Tissandier *ed* Sylvie Landra
☆ Milla Jovovich (Joan of Arc), John Malkovich (Charles VII), Dustin Hoffman (The Conscience), Faye Dunaway (Yolande D'Aragon), Pascal Greggory (Duke of Alencon), Vincent Cassel (Gilles de Rais), Tcheky Karyo (Dunois), Richard Ridings (La Hire), Desmond Harrington (Aulon)
'Both visually spectacular and staggeringly awful: a sense-pummeling, mind-numbing feast of bad ideas and laughable performances.' – *Michael Wilmington, Chicago Tribune*
'The lack of a plausible leading lady is enough to sink what is otherwise an eye-catching, although heavily '90s-style, telling of one of history's most frequently filmed stories.' – *Todd McCarthy, Variety*

'It's five miles wide ... It's coming at 30,000 mph ... and there's no place on Earth to hide!'
Meteor
US 1979 107m Movielab Panavision
Palladium (Sandy Howard, Gabriel Katzka)

A huge meteor, preceded by dangerous fragments, heads relentlessly towards Earth…
Talkative disaster movie with occasional moments of interest.
w Stanley Mann, Edmund H. North *d* Ronald Neame *ph* Paul Lohmann *m* Laurence Rosenthal *visual effects* Margo Anderson, William Cruse
☆ Sean Connery, Natalie Wood, Karl Malden, Brian Keith, Martin Landau, Trevor Howard, Henry Fonda, Joseph Campanella
'There are moments that make Godzilla look like a masterpiece.' – *Boxoffice*

The Meteor Man
US 1993 99m DeLuxe
MGM/Tinsel Townsend (Loretha C. Jones)

A schoolteacher hit by a meteor acquires super-human powers and begins to clean up his gang-ridden neighbourhood.
Mild morality tale for our times, pleasant enough, but it lacks impact.
wd Robert Townsend *ph* John A. Alonzo *m* Cliff Eidelman *pd* Toby Corbett *ed* Adam Bernardi *sp* Industrial Light and Magic
☆ Robert Townsend, Marla Gibbs, Eddie Griffin, Robert Guillaume, James Earl Jones, Bill Cosby, Frank Gorshin
'A cute skit expanded out of all proportion for the big screen.' – *Variety*
'Townsend's good nature will win most audiences over.' – *Adam Mars-Jones*

'Life Is A Negotiation.'
Metro
US 1997 117m Technicolor Panavision
Buena Vista/Touchstone/Caravan (Roger Birnbaum)

In San Francisco, a police hostage negotiator becomes involved in a battle of wits with a murderous jewel thief.
Murphy returns to familiar ground, as a smart, wise-cracking cop, but the style has worn thin through overuse; cast and director go through their predictable motions in an efficient but uninspired manner.
w Randy Feldman *d* Thomas Carter *ph* Fred Murphy *m* Steve Porcaro *pd* William Elliott *ed* Peter E. Berger
☆ Eddie Murphy (Scott Roper), Michael Rapaport (Kevin McCall), Michael Wincott (Michael Korda), Carmen Ejogo (Ronnie Tate), Denis Arndt (Capt. Frank Solis), Art Evans (Lt Sam Baffert), Donal Logue (Earl), Paul Ben-Victor (Clarence Teal), Kim Miyori (Detective Kimura)
'This formulaic ordeal – a notably sadistic exercise involving lots of beating, shooting, and stabbing.' – *Lisa Schwarzbaum, Entertainment Weekly*

Metroland
GB/Germany 1997 105m colour
Pandora/Blue Horizon/Mact/Filmania/BBC/Sogepaq (Andrew Bendel)

When an old friend from his bachelor days in Paris comes calling, a young advertising executive begins to have doubts about his settled life with a wife and young daughter.
Slight drama about the pull between a bourgeois and a bohemian existence; but there's something wrong when the only felt emotion comes in a vignette from John Wood as a teetotal commuter retiring after 42 years in the same firm with a farewell gift of a whisky decanter.
w Adrian Hodges *novel* Julian Barnes *d* Philip Saville *ph* Jean-François Robin *m* Mark Knopfler *pd* Don Taylor *ed* Greg Miller
☆ Christian Bale, Lee Ross, Emily Watson, Elsa Zylberstein, Rufus, Jonathan Aris, Ifan Meredith, Amanda Ryan, John Wood
'The film alternately whines and whimpers its way to a soporific end.' – *Demetrios Matheou, Sight and Sound*

Metropolis ***
Germany 1926 120m approx (24 fps) bw silent
UFA (Erich Pommer)

In the year 2000, the workers in a modernistic city live underground and unrest is quelled by the persuasion of a saintly girl, Maria; but a mad inventor creates an evil Maria to incite them to revolt.
Always somewhat overlong, and certainly heavy-going in places, this futuristic fantasy not only has many brilliant sequences which created genuine excitement and terror, but it inspired a great many Hollywood clichés to come, notably the Frankenstein theme. The BBC's version of the seventies, with an electronic music sound track, is the most satisfactory.
w Thea von Harbou d Fritz Lang ph Karl Freund, Günther Rittau ad Otto Hunte, Erich Kettelhut, Karl Volbrecht sp Eugene Schufftan
☆ *Brigitte Helm,* Alfred Abel, Gustav Fröhlich, Rudolf Klein-Rogge, Fritz Rasp
'It goes too far and always gets away with it.' – *New Yorker, 1978*
'A wonderful, stupefying folly.' – *New Yorker, 1982*
† In 1984 Giorgio Moroder put out his own new version, with tinted sequences and a re-edited running time of 83 minutes. It was received with a mixture of distaste, respect and caution. The latest version on video is 139m long.

Metropolis **
Japan 2001 108m colour
Columbia TriStar/Bandai Visual/Metropolis committee

In the future, a ruler's plans to create an all-powerful robot resembling his dead daughter are opposed by his adopted son.
Visually amazing animated feature, creating a monstrous world of inhumanely-scaled skyscrapers through which robots and people scurry; it is let down, though, by its often confusing narrative.
w Katsuhiro Otomo *comic book* Osamu Tezuka *d* Rintaro *m* Toshiyuki Honda *ad* Shuichi Hirata
☆ voices of: Yuka Imoto (Tima), Kei Kobayashi (Kenichi), Kohki Okada (Rock), Jamieson Price (Duke Red), Toshio Furukawa (General), Dave Mallow (Pero), Scott Weinger (Atlas)
'Inexplicable for much of its running time, *Metropolis* ends with a grand crescendo of escalating craziness.' – *J. Hoberman, Village Voice*
'Not a simple-minded animated cartoon, but a surprisingly thoughtful and challenging adventure that looks into the nature of life and love.' – *Roger Ebert, Chicago Sun-Times*

Metropolitan *
US 1935 79m bw
TCF (Darryl F. Zanuck)
A capricious prima donna walks out of the Metropolitan Opera and forms her own company.
Earnest and well-made melodrama with song; it earned critical plaudits but was a disappointment at the box-office.
w Bess Meredyth, George Marion Jnr *d* Richard Boleslawski *ph* Rudolph Maté *md* Alfred Newman
☆ Lawrence Tibbett, Alice Brady, Virginia Bruce, Cesar Romero, Thurston Hall, Luis Alberni
'Tibbett and exploitation should carry so-so operatic story into fair money.' – *Variety*

Metropolitan ***
US 1989 98m DuArt
Mainline/Westerly Film-Video/Allagash Films (Whit Stillman)

A left-wing student becomes a member of a group of rich young people intent on having a good time.
A conversation piece with wit and style to recommend it.
wd Whit Stillman ph John Thomas *m* Mark Suozzo, Tom Judson *ed* Christopher Tellefsen
☆ Carolyn Farina, Edward Clements, Christopher Eigeman, Taylor Nichols, Allison Rutledge-Parisi, Dylan Hundley, Isabel Gillies, Bryan Leder, Will Kempe
'A cast of attractive young newcomers plays out this ironic, arch, gently mocking and refreshingly original comedy with confident style.' – *David Robinson, The Times*
best original screenplay

Meurtres *
France 1950 91m bw
Cité Film/Fides
A doctor's wife suffering from an incurable illness begs him to give her an overdose of morphia; he does so and proposes to give himself up for murder; his family, afraid of scandal, try to have him certified.
A distinct change of pace for a star comedian, and not an unsuccessful one, though the satire is rather crudely handled.
w Charles Plisnier, Maurice Barry *d* Richard Pottier *ph* André Germain *m* Raymond Legrand
☆ *Fernandel,* Raymond Souplex, Jacques Varennes, Jeanne Moreau

'Love with the safety off.'
The Mexican
US 2001 123m Technicolor Panavision
DreamWorks/Newmarket (Lawrence Bender, John Baldecchi)

An incompetent crook is sent to Mexico to bring back a priceless pistol for his boss, while his girlfriend is taken hostage by a hitman to ensure he carries out the mission.
Interminable and dreary thriller, a mishmash of violence, romance and comedy; there is no spark between the two leads, which may be why they're kept apart for much of the movie.
w J. H. Wyman *d* Gore Verbinski *ph* Dariusz Wolski *m* Alan Silvestri *pd* Cecilia Montiel *ed* Craig Wood *cos* Colleen Atwood
☆ Brad Pitt (Jerry Welbach), Julia Roberts (Samantha), James Gandolfini (Leroy), Bob Balaban (Bernie Nayman), J. K. Simmons (Ted), David Krumholtz (Beck), Richard Coca (Car Thief), Michael Cerveris (Frank), Sherman Augustus (Well Dressed Black Man), Castulo Guerra (Joe the Pawnshop Owner), Gene Hackman (uncredited) (Arnold Margolese)
'An intensely whimsical shaggy-dog crime story that ricochets between goofy violence and some endearing personal moments.' – *Todd McCarthy, Variety*
'For this inconsequential yarn to work, the script needed to be short and sharp, and no amount of energy from the cast can disguise the fact that it is neither.' – *Tim Robey, Daily Telegraph*

Mexican Hayride
US 1948 77m bw
Universal (Robert Arthur)

Various swindlers come together at a Mexican bullfight.
A Cole Porter Broadway musical without the music makes an odd sort of vehicle for Abbott and Costello, but they inject a few good vaudeville gags.
w Oscar Brodney, John Grant *play* Herbert and Dorothy Fields *d* Charles Barton *ph* Charles Van Enger
☆ Bud Abbott, Lou Costello, Virginia Grey, John Hubbard, Pedro de Cordoba, Fritz Feld, Luba Malina

Mexican Spitfire
A series of second feature comedies nominally about a young businessman and his temperamental Mexican wife (Donald Woods and Lupe Velez), whose interest shifted firmly to the young man's accident-prone uncle Matt and his aristocratic boss Lord Epping, both of whom were played by the rubber-legged Ziegfeld comic Leon Errol at something near the top of his form. The plots made little sense, but the hectic situations provoked hearty roars of laughter. The films were all made by RKO, and all directed by Leslie Goodwins.
1939 The Girl from Mexico, Mexican Spitfire
1940 Mexican Spitfire Out West
1941 Mexican Spitfire's Baby, Mexican Spitfire at Sea
1942 Mexican Spitfire Sees a Ghost, Mexican Spitfire's Elephant
1943 Mexican Spitfire's Blessed Event

Mexicana
US 1945 83m bw
Republic (Alfred Santell)
The Frank Sinatra of Mexico is beset by bobbysoxers.
Thin excuse for a moderate musical.
w Frank Gill Jnr *d* Alfred Santell
☆ Tito Guizar, Constance Moore, Leo Carrillo, Howard Freeman, Steve Geray, Estelita Rodriguez

MGM's Big Parade of Comedy: see *The Big Parade of Comedy*

Mi Familia: see *My Family*

Mi Vida Loca: see *My Crazy Life*

Mia Eoniotita Ke Mia Mera: see *Eternity and a Day*

Miami Blues **
US 1990 97m
Rank/Orion/Tristes Tropiques (Jonathan Demme, Gary Goetzman)

A dogged policeman follows the trail of a murderous criminal who pretends to be an undercover cop.
Slick thriller with an undercurrent of lugubrious black humour.
wd George Armitage *novel* Charles Willeford *ph* Tak Fujimoto *m* Gary Chang *pd* Maher Ahmad *ed* Craig McKay, Bill Johnson
☆ Fred Ward, Jennifer Jason Leigh, Alec Baldwin, Cecilia Perez-Cervera, Georgie Cranford, Edward Saxon, Jose Perez, Obba Babatunde

'Love is great. Marriage is a completely different affair.'

Miami Rhapsody **
US 1995 95m Technicolor
Buena Vista/Hollywood/Cantaloupe (Barry Jossen, David Frankel)

A woman contemplating marriage observes the marital errors being committed by her siblings and friends.
Deft and observant comedy of relationships, smartly done and neatly worked out; the style is close to Woody Allen's, but lusher.
wd David Frankel *ph* Jack Wallner *m* Mark Isham *pd* J. Mark Harrington *ed* Steven Weisberg
☆ Sarah Jessica Parker, Gil Bellows, Antonio Banderas, Mia Farrow, Paul Mazursky, Kevin Pollak, Barbara Garrick, Naomi Campbell
'No more than superior American sitcom, and the film's wit goes no further than its immaculately tasteful interiors. But it was fun while it lasted, and, anyway, maybe it was never meant to be a long-term-commitment kind of thing.' – *Tom Shone, Sunday Times*
'An upscale Saturday date movie: not great but polished, amusing and above all competent – a quality which, these days, gives it a head start on most other comers.' – *Sheila Johnston, Independent*

The Miami Story
US 1954 75m bw
Columbia (Sam Katzman)
The syndicate is cracked by a reformed gangster.
Routine gangster alarms and excursions, like an extended Crime Does Not Pay.
w Robert E. Kent *d* Fred F. Sears *ph* Henry Freulich *m* Mischa Bakaleinikoff
☆ Barry Sullivan, Luther Adler, John Baer, Adele Jergens, Beverly Garland

'He's an angel ... Not a saint.'

Michael
US 1996 105m Technicolor
Rank/Castle Rock/Turner/Alphaville (Sean Daniel, Nora Ephron, James Jacks)

Tabloid reporters discover an angel, who turns out to be a charming, beer-swilling, womanizing slob.
Hellish attempt at a romantic comedy, in which unpleasant characters behave badly and fall in love.
w Nora Ephron, Delia Ephron, Peter Dexter, Jim Quinlan *d* Nora Ephron *ph* John Lindley *m* Randy Newman *pd* Dan Davis *ed* Geraldine Peroni
☆ John Travolta, Andie MacDowell, William Hurt, Bob Hoskins, Robert Pastorelli, Jean Stapleton, Teri Garr
'At once underwritten and overwritten. Rowdy, slapdash and unevenly directed, the movie is basically a collection of episodes tied together with a flimsy string.' – *Emanuel Levy, Variety*

Michael and Mary
GB 1931 85m bw
Gaumont
A husband thought dead for many years returns to disturb his wife's second marriage.
Acceptable comedy from a popular stage play; it headed its stars towards Hollywood.
w Angus MacPhail, Robert Stevenson, Lajos Biro *play* A. A. Milne *d* Victor Saville
☆ Herbert Marshall, Edna Best, Elizabeth Allan, Frank Lawton, D. A. Clarke-Smith

'An Epic Tale Of Passion And Destiny.'

Michael Collins *
US 1996 132m Technicolor
Warner/Geffen (Stephen Woolley)

Following the failure of the 1916 rising against the British, Michael Collins becomes a leading figure in the Irish Republican Army and, after negotiating the Anglo-Irish treaty, is repudiated by his former colleagues and assassinated.
Effective and dramatic political drama that simplifies the facts and has at its centre a glaring gap – Collins's negotiations with the British – into which the narrative unfortunately collapses.
wd Neil Jordan *ph* Chris Menges *m* Elliot Goldenthal *pd* Antony Pratt *ed* J. Patrick Duffner, Tony Lawson
☆ Liam Neeson, Aidan Quinn, Stephen Rea, Alan Rickman, Julia Roberts, Ian Hart, Richard Ingram, John Kenny
'Large-scale and comfortably epic in proportion, but, given that any film-maker has to make the best of his fictional way home without regarding facts as absolutely sacred, has a clear sense of history, or at least interprets it with intelligence.' – *Derek Malcolm, Guardian*
'A serious historical drama drained of serious history.' – *Ken Tucker, Entertainment Weekly*
† It won the Golden Lion for best film and Liam Neeson won the award for best actor at the 1996 Venice Film Festival.
Chris Menges; Elliot Goldenthal

Michael Shayne
The private eye created by Brett Halliday was featured in several second features starring Lloyd Nolan, mostly Eugene Forde for Fox. They were adequate time-passers without too much sparkle.
1940 Michael Shayne Private Detective
1941 Dressed to Kill, Just Off Broadway, The Man Who Wouldn't Die
1942 Time to Kill (a version of Chandler's The High Window), Blue White and Perfect

Michael Strogoff: see *The Soldier and the Lady*

The Michigan Kid
US 1947 70m Cinecolor
Universal

Several people hunt for treasure stolen from a stagecoach.
Lower-berth Western.
w Roy Chanslor *novel* Rex Beach *d* Ray Taylor
☆ Jon Hall, Victor McLaglen, Rita Johnson, Andy Devine, Byron Foulger, Milburn Stone

'A Romantic Comedy You Can't Refuse.'

Mickey Blue Eyes *
US 1999 103m Technicolor
Universal/Castle Rock/Simian (Elizabeth Hurley, Charles Mulvehill)

A very English auctioneer in New York becomes involved with the Mafia when he falls in love with a teacher, whose father is a mobster.
Intermittently amusing comedy of a clash between two cultures, though the mechanical contrivances of farce take over from the intended romantic comedy, and Grant's act as a floppy-haired bumbler is wearing a little thin.
w Adam Scheinman, Robert Kuhn *d* Kelly Makin *ph* Donald E. Thorin *m* Basil Poledouris *pd* Gregory Keen *ed* David Freeman *cos* Ellen Mirojnick
☆ Hugh Grant (Michael Felgate), James Caan (Frank Vitale), Jeanne Tripplehorn (Gina Vitale), Burt Young (Vito Graziosi), James Fox (Philip Cromwell), Joe Viterelli (Vinnie), Gerry Becker (Agent Connell), Maddie Corman (Carol), Tony Darrow (Angelo), Paul Lazar (Ritchie Vitale)
'An engaging, often very funny fish-out-of-water story.' – *Lael Loewenstein, Variety*
'A promising set-up; but all it develops into are knots of insane plot no one would waste time unpicking.' – *Alexander Walker, London Evening Standard*

Mickey One *
US 1965 93m bw
Columbia/Florin/Tatira (Arthur Penn, Harrison Starr)

A night-club entertainer runs away after an orgy to find some meaning in his life.
Obscure symbolic melodrama whose flashes of talent and interest needed firmer control.
w Alan Surgal *d* Arthur Penn *ph* Ghislain Cloquet *m* Eddie Sauter *pd* George Jenkins *ed* Aram Avakian
☆ Warren Beatty, Hurd Hatfield, Alexandra Stewart, Franchot Tone, Teddy Hart, Jeff Corey
'Arresting at first, it becomes more and more bogged down by its own pretensions, until one's main interest is simply in seeing it through.' – *MFB*

Mickey's Christmas Carol ***
US 1983 26m Technicolor
Disney

A cartoon version of Dickens with the parts played by familiar Disney characters; and a supreme re-establishment of the old Disney production values.
d Burney Mattinson
'For anyone over 35, this little jewel of a film is truly the Ghost of Christmas Past.' – *Gilbert Adair, MFB*
animated film

Micki and Maude *
US 1984 118m Metrocolor Panavision
Columbia/Delphi III/B.E.E. (Tony Adams)

A TV show host accidentally gets his wife and his mistress pregnant at the same time.
Wild and overlong farce with some undeniably funnier scenes than have been noted in the participants' work for some years.
w Jonathan Reynolds *d* Blake Edwards *ph* Harry Stradling Jnr *m* Lee Holdridge *pd* Rodger Maus *ed* Ralph E. Winters
☆ Dudley Moore, Amy Irving, Ann Reinking, Richard Mulligan, George Gaynes, Wallace Shawn, John Pleshette

Microcosmos **
France/Switzerland/Italy 1996 75m colour
Guild/Galatée/France 2/Bac/Delta/JMH/Urania (Jacques Perrin, Christophe Barratier, Yvette Mallet)

A day in the (mainly) insect life of a French meadow.
Intriguing, marvellously photographed documentary evocation of the often-ignored world beneath our feet; there is no commentary, so there is no explanation for the strange behaviour we witness, which detracts from the impact, as does the knowledge that some of the film was shot under studio conditions.
d Claude Nuridsany, Marie Pérennou *ph* Claude Nuridsany, Marie Pérennou, Hugues Ryffel, Thierry Machado *m* Bruno Coulais *ed* Marie-Josèphe Yoyotte, Florence Ricard *sp* Ex Machina; Jean-Pierre Maricourt
'What's on screen is no longer primary material but something staged to illustrate observations made elsewhere ... Alarm bells should ring when we're told that in some cases the real sounds "ring false in relation to the images", and have been faked. What sort of nature film is so willing to improve upon nature?' – *Adam Mars-Jones, Independent*

Midas Run
US 1969 104m Technicolor
Raymond Stross/MPI (Leon Chooluck)
GB title: *A Run on Gold*
An ageing secret service chief plans to hi-jack a bullion shipment.
Incompetently handled caper story with interest unwisely shifted for romantic purposes to the plotter's recruits.
w James D. Buchanan, Ronald Austin, Berne Giler *d* Alf Kjellin *ph* Ken Higgins *m* Elmer Bernstein
☆ Fred Astaire, Richard Crenna, Anne Heywood, Ralph Richardson, Roddy McDowall, Adolfo Celi, Maurice Denham, Cesar Romero

Middle Age Crazy
Canada 1980 91m DeLuxe
Barber International/Sid & Marty Krofft/Robert Cooper & Ronald Cohen

A 40-year-old husband begins to feel his age.
Mildly satirical sex comedy, all too easily forgotten among the rest.
w Carl Kleinschmitt *d* John Trent *ph* Reginald Morris *m* Matthew McCauley *ad* Jill Scott *ed* John Kelly
☆ Bruce Dern, Ann-Margret, Graham Jarvis, Eric Christmas

The Middle Man **
India 1975 131m bw
Connoisseur/Indus (Subir Guha)
original title: *Jana-Aranya*
Unable to find a job in overcrowded Calcutta, a young graduate has no option but to set up as a small 'middle man', buying goods cheaply and selling them at a profit, and slips into acting as a pimp for his customers.
Satirical, cutting portrait of the moral corruption of an innocent, which produces some fine ensemble acting from its cast.
wd Satyajit Ray *novel* Shankar *ph* Soumendu Roy *m* Satyajit Ray *ad* Ashoke Bose *ed* Dulal Dutt
☆ Pradip Mukherji, Satya Bannerji, Dipankar Dey, Lily Chakravarti, Aparna Sen, Goutam Chakravarti, Sudeshna Das, Utpal Dutt
'Nothing can detract from the film's overall success and its penetrating charm.' – *MFB*

Middle of Nowhere: see *The Webster Boy*

Middle of the Night **
US 1959 118m bw
Columbia (George Justin)
An elderly garment manufacturer falls in love with a young girl.
Serious and moving examination of a human predicament, shot against beautifully observed New York backgrounds.
w Paddy Chayefsky, *from his TV play* *d* Delbert Mann *ph* Joseph Brun *m* George Bassman
☆ Fredric March, Kim Novak, Glenda Farrell, Jan Norris, Lee Grant
'A work of greater cogency than his New York play script and of deeper maturity than his Marty.' – *Time*
'The best of the TV transformations into film.' – *Stanley Kauffmann*

The Middle Watch
GB 1930 112m bw
BIP
Female guests on board ship have to be hidden from the captain.
Naval froth in primitive talkie form; absurdly long but popular.
w Norman Walker, Frank Launder *play* Ian Hay, Stephen King-Hall *d* Norman Walker
☆ Owen Nares, Jacqueline Logan, Jack Raine, Dodo Watts, Reginald Purdell
† In 1939 ABPC made a smoother version with Jack Buchanan, Greta Gynt, David Hutcheson, Kay Walsh, Fred Emney and Reginald Purdell (in the same role); directed by Thomas Bentley. Another version followed in 1958, titled *Girls at Sea* (qv).

Middleton's Changeling *
GB 1997 96m Rank Colour Cinemascope
UIP/High Time (Marcus Thompson)
An aristocrat's daughter hires a hitman to murder the man her father wants her to marry, and finds herself drawn into sexual intrigue and further killings.
One of those Jacobean plays that still furnishes the basic plots for many films noir and revenge movies is here updated and cut about to provide some rough-and-ready entertainment.
wd Marcus Thompson *play* Thomas Middleton, William Rowley *ph* Richard K. J. Butland *pd* Rob Swinburn *ed* Marcus Thompson
☆ Ian Dury, Amanda Ray-King, Colm O Maonlai, Billy Connolly, Campbell Morrison, Moya Brady, Richard Mayes, Leo Wringer, Julia Tarnoky, James Maker, Vivian Stanshall
'In modern-day Alicante, characters wander around in Jacobean finery and baseball boots, alighting from horses to get into limousines. These Jarmanesque anachronisms misfire, not helped by the worst mismatch possible – blank verse does not sit well in the mouths of an inexperienced cast.' – *Edward Porter, Sunday Times*
† The original play was performed in the early 1620s and borrowed its plot from another work of the period, John Reynold's *God's Revenge against Murther*, adding a comic subplot that was probably the work of William Rowley, an actor noted for his roles as a fat clown.
†† The film took seven years to make, during which time Fernando Rey died before his scenes were filmed, and Vivian Stanshall before he could be voiced.

Midnight
US 1934 80m bw
Universal/All Star (Chester Erskine)

aka: *Call It Murder*
A jury foreman in a murder trial tips the scales in favour of guilty, but is haunted when his own daughter kills her lover.
Tepid family melodrama, very stagebound.
wd Chester Erskine *play* Paul and Claire Sifton *ph* William Steiner

☆ Sidney Fox, O. P. Heggie, Henry Hull, Humphrey Bogart, Margaret Wycherly, Lynne Overman, Richard Whorf, Cora Witherspoon

'It's pretty strong stuff and will hold audiences once they're in ... but it's not a good adaptation and is badly dialogued.' – *Variety*

Midnight ★★★
US 1939 95m bw
Paramount (Arthur Hornblow Jnr)
A girl stranded in Paris is hired by an aristocrat to seduce the gigolo paying unwelcome attention to his wife.
Sparkling sophisticated comedy which barely flags until a slightly disappointing ending; all the talents involved are in excellent form.
w *Billy Wilder, Charles Brackett* *story* Edwin Justus Mayer, Franz Schultz *d* *Mitchell Leisen* *ph* Charles Lang *m* Frederick Hollander
☆ *Claudette Colbert*, Don Ameche, *John Barrymore*, Francis Lederer, Mary Astor, Elaine Barrie, Hedda Hopper, Rex O'Malley

'Leisen's masterpiece, one of the best comedies of the thirties.' – *John Baxter, 1968*

'One of the authentic delights of the thirties.' – *New Yorker, 1976*

'It has the elements of an American *La Règle du Jeu*.' – *John Gillett*

'Just about the best light comedy ever caught by the camera.' – *Motion Picture Daily*

Midnight
US 1989 86m colour
SVS/Kuys Entertainment/Gomillion (Norman Thaddeus Vane, Gloria J. Morrison)
The hostess of a horror movie show on TV is targeted by a murderer.
Occasionally amusing spoof of horror films, though too stately to create any tension on its own account.
wd Norman Thaddeus Vane *ph* David Golia *m* Michael Weatherwax *ad* Mark Simon *ed* Sam Adelman
☆ Lynn Redgrave, Tony Curtis, Steve Parrish, Rita Gam, Gustav Vintas, Karen Witter, Frank Gorshin

'At the frontlines of life, near the end of innocence, came the beginning of manhood.'
A Midnight Clear ★★
US 1992 107m CFI color
Sovereign/Beacon/A&M (Dale Pollock, Bill Borden)
In the Ardennes Forest in 1944, a reconnaissance patrol composed of young and reluctant American soldiers goes disastrously wrong.
Effectively low-key, quietly ironic tale of the idiocies of war.
wd Keith Gordon *novel* William Wharton *ph* Tom Richmond *m* Mark Isham *pd* David Nichols *ed* Don Brochu
☆ Peter Berg, Kevin Dillon, Arye Gross, Ethan Hawke, Gary Sinise, Frank Whaley, John C. McGinley

'An extremely well-crafted and entirely absorbing movie.' – *Philip Thomas, Empire*

Midnight Club
US 1933 65m bw
Paramount
An American detective in London nabs a jewel gang.
Very tolerable smart-set crime melodrama.
w Seton I. Miller, Leslie Charteris *story* E. Phillips Oppenheim *d* Alexander Hall
☆ Clive Brook, George Raft, Helen Vinson, Alison Skipworth, Sir Guy Standing, Alan Mowbray

'Its London manners and locale lend it a polish which should renew interest in this school of celluloid melodramatics.' – *Variety*

'To tell you the truth, I ain't a real cowboy. But I'm one helluva stud!'
Midnight Cowboy ★★★★
US 1969 113m DeLuxe
UA/Jerome Hellman
A slightly dim-witted Texan comes to New York to offer his services as a stud for rich ladies, but spends a hard winter helping a tubercular con man.
Life in the New York gutter, brilliantly if not too accurately observed by a master showman with no heart.
w Waldo Salt *novel* James Leo Herlihy *d* *John Schlesinger* *ph* *Adam Holender* *md* John Barry *pd* John Robert Lloyd
☆ *Jon Voight, Dustin Hoffman*, Brenda Vaccaro, Sylvia Miles, John McGiver

'If only Schlesinger's directorial self-discipline had matched his luminous sense of scene and his extraordinary skill in handling actors, this would have been a far more considerable film.' – *Arthur Schlesinger Jnr (no relation)*

'A great deal besides cleverness, a great deal of good feeling and perception and purposeful dexterity.' – *Stanley Kauffmann*

Academy Award: best picture; Waldo Salt; John Schlesinger
Academy Award nomination: Dustin Hoffman; Jon Voight; Sylvia Miles
BAFTA: best picture; Waldo Salt; John Schlesinger; Dustin Hoffman; Jon Voight

Midnight Crossing
US 1987 104m Technicolor
Vestron/Team Effort/Limelite Studios (Mathew Hayden)
An insurance agent returns to a small Caribbean island to retrieve stolen treasure.
Glossily empty, often hysterical thriller that never rises above the ordinary.
w Roger Holzberg, Doug Weiser *d* Roger Holzberg *ph* Henry Vargas *m* Paul Buckmaster, Al Gorgoni *pd* José Duarte *ed* Earl Watson
☆ Faye Dunaway, Daniel J. Travanti, Kim Cattrall, Ned Beatty, John Laughlin

Midnight Dancers ★
Philippines 1994 100m colour
Tangent
original title: *Sibak*
Returning home to Manila, a poor youth joins his two brothers who work as 'macho dancers' in a homosexual night-club.
A gaudy exposé of Manila's gay sub-culture and the moral and social deprivations behind the thriving business of male prostitution; but one that is also concerned with the affirmations of love and desire.
w Ricardo Lee *d* Mel Chionglo *ph* George Tutanes *m* Nonong Buencamino *pd* Edgar Martin Littaua *ed* Jess Navarro
☆ Alex del Rosario, Lawrence David, Gandong Cervantes, Richard Cassity, Luis Cortes, John Mendoza, Danny Ramos, Leonard Manalansan, Perla Bautista
† The film was banned in the Philippines.

Midnight Episode
GB 1950 78m bw
Columbia/Triangle (Thomas Lageard)
An old busker stumbles over a dead body and a lot of money.
Tame British version of Raimu's French success Monsieur La Souris, *saved only by its star performance.*
w Rita Barisse, Reeve Taylor, Paul Vincent Carroll, David Evans, William Templeton *d* Gordon Parry *ph* Hone Glendinning
☆ Stanley Holloway, Natasha Parry, Leslie Dwyer, Reginald Tate, Meredith Edwards, Wilfrid Hyde-White, Joy Shelton

Midnight Express ★★
GB 1978 121m Eastmancolor
Columbia/Casablanca (Alan Marshall, David Puttnam)
Tribulations of an American student arrested in Turkey for carrying hashish.
Misleadingly-titled wallow in prison atrocities, extremely well made but certainly not entertaining and with little discernible point.
w Oliver Stone *memoirs* Billy Hayes *d* Alan Parker *ph* Michael Seresin *m* Giorgio Moroder
☆ Brad Davis, Randy Quaid, John Hurt, Irene Miracle, Bo Hopkins

'One of the ugliest sado-masochistic trips, with heavy homosexual overtones, that our thoroughly nasty movie age has yet produced.' – *Richard Schickel, Time*

'The film details all [the horrors] so relentlessly on one screaming note that it is rather like being hit in the gut until you no longer feel a thing.' – *Derek Malcolm, Guardian*

'Muted squalor with a disco beat in the background, all packaged as social protest.' – *New Yorker, 1982*

Academy Award: script; music
Academy Award nomination: best picture; Alan Parker; John Hurt
BAFTA: Alan Parker; John Hurt

Midnight Fear
US 1990 90m colour
Danyves/Crain
An alcoholic sheriff, investigating the murder of a woman skinned alive, suspects a deaf-mute who has escaped from an institution for the criminally insane.
Dreary psychological thriller, peopled by familiar and dull stereotypes.
w Chuck Hughes, Bill Crain, Craig Wasson *d* Bill Crain *ph* Michael Crain *m* Steve Edwards *pd* Pat Tagliaferro *ed* Brian Crain
☆ Craig Wasson, David Carradine, Page Fletcher, Mark Carlton, August West, Evan Richards

Midnight in Saint Petersburg
GB/Canada/Russia 1995 86m colour
Quebec 3099-3081/Lenfilm/Harry Palmer (Edward Simons, Kent Walwin, Alexander Goloutva, John Dunning, André Link)
In Russia, a British private investigator goes in search of some missing plutonium and a kidnapped ballet dancer.
Slack and uninteresting thriller, a sequel of sorts to Bullet to Beijing *(qv), and even worse than that flat film.*
w Peter Welbeck (Harry Alan Towers) *novel* Len Deighton *d* Douglas Jackson *ph* Peter Benison *m* Rick Wakeman *pd* Chris Tulloch *ed* Vidal Beique
☆ Michael Caine, Jason Connery, Michael Gambon, Michael Sarrazin, Tanya Jackson, Serge Houde, Anatoly Davidov

'Welcome To Savannah, Georgia. A City Of Hot Nights And Cold Blooded Murder.'
Midnight in the Garden of Good and Evil ★
US 1997 155m Technicolor
Warner/Malpaso/Silver (Clint Eastwood, Arnold Stiefel)
In Savannah, Georgia, a journalist investigates the shooting by a rich bachelor of his young male lover and his subsequent trial for murder.
Overlong retelling of a true story in an exotic setting; the leisurely style allows room for the characters to flower, but at the expense of the narrative tension.
w John Lee Hancock *book* John Berendt *d* Clint Eastwood *ph* Jack N. Green *m* Lennie Niehaus *pd* Henry Bumstead *ed* Joel Cox
☆ Kevin Spacey, John Cusack, Jack Thompson, The Lady Chablis (as herself), Alison Eastwood, Irma P. Hall, Paul Hipp, Jude Law, Dorothy Loudon, Anne Haney, Kim Hunter, Geoffrey Lewis

Midnight Lace ★
US 1960 108m Eastmancolor
Universal (Ross Hunter, Martin Melcher)
The wife of a rich Londoner is terrorized by threatening phone calls and voices in the fog.
Thoroughly silly rehash of Gaslight *and* The Boy Who Cried Wolf; *its glamorous accoutrements can't fight a lack of humour or predictable plot development.*
w Ivan Goff, Ben Roberts *play* *Matilda Shouted Fire* by Janet Green *d* David Miller *ph* Russell Metty *m* Frank Skinner
☆ Doris Day, Rex Harrison, John Gavin, Myrna Loy, Roddy McDowall, Herbert Marshall, Natasha Parry, John Williams, Anthony Dawson, Hermione Baddeley, Richard Ney, Rhys Williams, Doris Lloyd

Midnight Madonna
US 1937 56m bw
Paramount
There is a legal fight for custody of a child who has inherited a fortune.
Efficient programmer built around a new child actress, Kitty Clancy, who didn't take.
w Doris Malloy, Gladys Lehman *d* James Flood
☆ Warren William, Mady Correll, Edward Ellis, Robert Baldwin, Jonathan Hale

'It will be found fairly entertaining by the family trade.' – *Variety*

The Midnight Man
US 1974 117m Technicolor
Universal/Norlan (Roland Kibbee, Burt Lancaster)
An ex-cop, paroled after killing his wife's lover, takes a job as security guard and runs into a murder case.
Muddled mystery with pretentious characterization and bouts of violence.
wd Roland Kibbee, Burt Lancaster *novel* *The Midnight Lady and the Mourning Man* by David Anthony *ph* Jack Priestley *m* Dave Grusin
☆ Burt Lancaster, Susan Clark, Cameron Mitchell, Morgan Woodward, Harris Yulin, Robert Quarry, Joan Lorring, Lawrence Dobkin, Ed Lauter

'A thriller that has the impenetrability of Chandler but none of the flavour.' – *Tom Milne*

'Efficient enough but lifeless, and burdened with portentous sentiments about solitude, violence and the nature of the beast.' – *Sight and Sound*

Midnight Mary
US 1933 76m bw
MGM
A gangster's moll on trial for her life thinks back to her past.
Intolerable now, but a hit of its year despite star miscasting.
w Gene Markey and Anita Loos *d* William Wellman
☆ Loretta Young, Ricardo Cortez, Franchot Tone, Una Merkel, Andy Devine, Harold Huber

Midnight Melody: see *Murder in the Music Hall*

Midnight Patrol ★
US 1933 20m bw
Hal Roach
Incompetent policemen arrest their own chief as a burglar.
Good standard star slapstick.
w uncredited *d* Lloyd French
☆ Laurel and Hardy, Charlie Hall, Walter Plinge

Midnight Run ★★
US 1988 126m colour
UIP/Universal (Martin Brest)
A bounty hunter tries to bring in an embezzler, despite attempts by rivals, gangsters and the FBI to stop him.
Fast-paced action comedy, full of quick-fire wit and graced by some excellent performances.
w George Gallo *d* Martin Brest *ph* Donald Thorin *m* Danny Elfman *pd* Angelo Graham *ed* Billy Weber, Chris Lebenzon, Michael Tronick
☆ Robert DeNiro, Charles Grodin, Yaphet Kotto, John Ashton, Dennis Farina, Joe Pantoliano

Midnight Sting: see *Diggstown*

Midnight Taxi
US 1936 73m bw
TCF
A G-man becomes a taxi driver to rout a gang of counterfeiters.
Competent, predictable crime programmer.
w Lou Breslow, John Patrick *d* Eugene Forde
☆ Brian Donlevy, Frances Drake, Alan Dinehart, Sig Rumann, Gilbert Roland, Harold Huber, Lon Chaney Jnr

The Midshipmaid
GB 1932 84m bw
Gaumont
US title: *Midshipmaid Gob*
A naval commander loves the daughter of a politician out to effect navy cuts.
Very modest comedy with music, a key step in the star's success story.
w Ian Hay, Stephen King-Hall *play* Ian Hay, Stephen King-Hall *d* Albert de Courville *m* Noel Gay
☆ Jessie Matthews, Frederick Kerr, Basil Sydney, Nigel Bruce, Claud Allister, John Mills, George Zucco

Midshipman Easy
GB 1935 77m bw
ATP (Basil Dean, Thorold Dickinson)
US title: *Men of the Sea*
In 1790, young naval officers rescue a girl from Spanish bandits.
Stilted adventure story with interesting credits.

w Anthony Kimmins *novel* Frederick Marryat *d* Carol Reed *ph* John W. Boyle
☆ Hughie Green, Margaret Lockwood, Harry Tate, Robert Adams, Roger Livesey, Lewis Casson
'It is simply and dramatically cut, it contains the best fight I can remember on the screen, and I can imagine no child too sophisticated to be excited and amused.' – *Graham Greene*

A Midsummer Night's Dream: see *William Shakespeare's A Midsummer Night's Dream*

'Three centuries in the making!'
A Midsummer Night's Dream ***
US 1935 133m bw
Warner (Max Reinhardt)
Two pairs of lovers sort out their problems with fairy help at midnight in the woods of Athens.
Shakespeare's play is treated with remarkable respect in this super-glamorous Hollywood adaptation based on the Broadway production by Max Reinhardt. Much of it comes off, and visually it's a treat.
w Charles Kenyon, Mary McCall Jnr *play* William Shakespeare *d* *Max Reinhardt, William Dieterle* *ph* *Hal Mohr, Fred Jackman, Byron Haskin, H. F. Koenekamp* *m* Mendelssohn *md* *Erich Wolfgang Korngold* *ch* *Bronislawa Nijinska* *ad* *Anton Grot* *ed* *Ralph Dawson*
☆ *James Cagney*, Dick Powell, Jean Muir, Ross Alexander, Olivia de Havilland, Joe E. Brown, Hugh Herbert, Arthur Treacher, Frank McHugh, Otis Harlan, Dewey Robinson, *Victor Jory*, Verree Teasdale, *Mickey Rooney*, Anita Louise and also Grant Mitchell, Ian Hunter, Hobart Cavanaugh
'General b.o. chances could be improved by judicious pruning and appreciative selling ... a fine prestige picture not only for Warners but for the industry as a whole.' – *Variety*
'You must see it if you want to be in a position to argue about the future of the film!' – *Picturegoer*
'The publicity push behind the film is tremendous – it is going to be a success or everyone at Warner Brothers is going to get fired.' – *Robert Forsythe*
'Its assurance as a work of film technique is undoubted.' – *John Baxter, 1968*
'Its worst contradiction lies in the way Warners first ordered up a whole batch of foreign and high-sounding names to handle music, dances, general production – and then turned around and handed them empty vessels for actors.' – *Otis Ferguson*
photography; editing
best picture

A Midsummer Night's Dream
GB 1996 105m colour
Film Four/Edenwood/Arts Council/Capitol (Paul Arnott)
In Athens, a boy dreams a dream of lovers whose romances go wrong before they come right.
Originally staged by the Royal Shakespeare Company, this transfers unhappily to the screen as something of a nightmare, messy rather than magical, and too often ill-spoken.
wd Adrian Noble *play* William Shakespeare *ph* Ian Wilson *m* Howard Blake *pd* Anthony Ward *ed* Paul Hodgson, Peter Hollywood
☆ Lindsay Duncan, Alex Jennings, Desmond Barrit, Barry Lynch, Monica Dolan, Daniel Evans, Kevin Doyle, Emily Raymond, Alfred Burke, Osheen Jones
'It's so busy whipping up a stylistic storm that it lays low Shakespeare's true topic – love.' – *Matt Wolf, Variety*

A Midsummer Night's Sex Comedy *
US 1982 88m Technicolor
Warner/Orion/Rollins-Joffe (Robert Greenhut)
Around the turn of the century, a Wall Street broker expects various weekend guests at his country retreat.
Subdued, melancholy and rather uninventive Woody Allen variation on Smiles of a Summer Night.
wd Woody Allen *ph* Gordon Willis *m* from Mendelssohn *pd* Mel Bourne *ed* Susan E. Morse
☆ Woody Allen, Mia Farrow, José Ferrer, Julie Hagerty, Tony Roberts, Mary Steenburgen

Midway *
US 1976 131m Technicolor Panavision Sensurround
Universal/Mirisch Corporation (Walter Mirisch)
GB title: *The Battle of Midway*
The tide turns for the Americans when the Japanese attack the Pacific island of Midway in 1942.
Noisy flagwaver with confused strategy and too many stars in small parts.
w Donald S. Sanford *d* Jack Smight *ph* Harry Stradling Jnr *m* John Williams
☆ Charlton Heston, Henry Fonda, Robert Mitchum, Glenn Ford, Edward Albert, James Coburn, Hal Holbrook, Toshiro Mifune, Robert Wagner, Robert Webber, Ed Nelson, James Shigeta, Monte Markham, Christopher George, Glenn Corbett
'We are over-informed about the movements of every ship and plane, under-informed about how the battle was finally won, and positively swamped with tedious human interest.' – *Sight and Sound*

Mies Vailla Menneisyytta: see *The Man without a Past*

Mifune **
Denmark/Sweden 1999 101m colour
Alliance/Nimbus/Zentropa/DRTV/STV (Brigitte Hald, Morten Kaufmann)
original title: *Mifunes Sidste Sang*
After marrying his boss's daughter, a thrusting young businessman is forced by his father's death to return to the family farm and find a housekeeper to look after his mentally handicapped brother.
Enjoyable, though too often predictable, drama of a tart with a heart of gold redeeming a selfish yuppie.
w Soren Kragh-Jacobsen, Anders Thomas Jensen *d* Soren Kragh-Jacobsen *ph* Anthony Dod Mantle *m* Thor Backhausen, Karl Bille, Christian Sievert *ed* Valdis Oskarasdottir
☆ Anders W. Berthelsen (Kersten), Iben Hjejle (Liva), Jesper Asholt (Rud), Emil Tarding (Bjarke), Anders Hove (Gerner), Sofie Grabol (Claire), Paprika Steen (Pernille), Mette Bratlann (Nina)
'Well-constructed mixture of romance, sex and humor should be a crowd-pleaser in most territories.' – *David Stratton, Variety*

Mifunes Sidste Sang: see *Mifune*

'The quest for friendship is the noblest cause of all.'
'Courage comes in all sizes.'
The Mighty *
US 1998 100m DeLuxe
Miramax/Scholastic (Jane Startz, Simon Fields)
A small, physically handicapped but bright and brave boy forms a symbiotic friendship with a hulking near-illiterate youth.
Quirky movie about the attraction of opposites that thankfully avoids sentimentality.
w Charles Leavitt *novel* *Freak the Mighty* by Rodman Philbrick *d* Peter Chelsom *ph* John de Borman *m* Trevor Jones *pd* Caroline Hanania *ed* Martin Walsh
☆ Sharon Stone, Gena Rowlands, Harry Dean Stanton, Kieran Culkin, Elden Hanson, Gillian Anderson, James Gandolfini, Joe Perrino, Meat Loaf, Jenifer Lewis
'While the pic's core appeal is decidedly to young viewers, the material hits an emotional chord for all ages.' – *Leonard Klady, Variety*

Mighty Aphrodite **
US 1995 95m Technicolor
Miramax/Seetland/Jean Doumanian (Robert Greenhut)
A sports writer tries to rescue the mother of his adopted son from a life as a prostitute.
Witty comedy of love and marriage, not up to Allen's best, but highly enjoyable for all that.
wd Woody Allen *ph* Carlo DiPalma *pd* Santo Loquasto *ed* Susan E. Morse
☆ Woody Allen, Helena Bonham Carter, *Mira Sorvino*, Michael Rapaport, F. Murray Abraham, Claire Bloom, Olympia Dukakis, David Ogden Stiers, Jack Warden, Peter Weller, Dan Moran
'The suspicion lingers that Woody Allen deserves a good spanking, and not from a prostitute with a heart of gold. But, listen: humor and sentiment can triumph over stern morality any day. Once the picture gets going, it reminds us that Allen is also an artist with an acute feel for movie romance. So scruples be damned. This time, Mighty makes all righty.' – *Richard Corliss, Time*
Mia Sorvino
Woody Allen (as writer)

The Mighty Barnum *
US 1934 87m bw
Twentieth Century (Darryl F. Zanuck)
A fictionalized biopic of the great showman of the 1890s.
Lively without being very memorable.
w Gene Fowler, Bess Meredyth *play* Gene Fowler, Bess Meredyth *d* Walter Lang *ph* Peverell Marley *m* Alfred Newman
☆ Wallace Beery, Virginia Bruce, Adolphe Menjou, Janet Beecher, Rochelle Hudson

The Mighty Ducks
US 1992 101m Technicolor Panavision
Buena Vista/Walt Disney (Jordan Kerner, Jon Avnet)
GB title: *Champions*
video title: *The Mighty Ducks Are Champions*
A lawyer doing community service for drunk driving turns a group of drop-out kids into a winning hockey team.
Simple-minded and sentimental movie hymning the joys of team spirit.
w Steven Brill *d* Stephen Herek *ph* Thomas Del Ruth *m* David Newman *pd* Randy Ser *ed* Larry Bock, John F. Link
☆ Emilio Estevez, Joss Ackland, Lane Smith, Heidi King, Josef Sommer, Joshua Jackson
'A formulaic pic meant for children but actually focusing on a yuppie's struggle for redemption. Mildly entertaining but unexciting.' – *Variety*
† A sequel, *D2: The Mighty Ducks* (qv), followed in 1994.

'The ten most terrific thrills ever pictured!'
Mighty Joe Young *
US 1949 94m bw
RKO (Merian C. Cooper)
A little girl brings back from Africa a pet gorilla which grows to enormous size and causes a city to panic.
Rather tired comic-sentimental follow-up to King Kong, *with a tedious plot and variable animation but a few endearing highlights.*
w Ruth Rose *d* Ernest Schoedsack *ph* J. Roy Hunt *m* Roy Webb *sp* Willis O'Brien, Ray Harryhausen
☆ Terry Moore, Ben Johnson, Robert Armstrong, Frank McHugh, Douglas Fowley

Mighty Joe Young *
US 1998 114m colour Panavision
Buena Vista/Walt Disney/RKO (Ted Hartley, Tom Jacobson)
GB title: *Mighty Joe*
Fearing for the safety of a giant gorilla she has known since both were young, a woman takes him from Africa to live in LA.
An ecologically sound remake with splendid special effects, though it is no more successful than the original version as a successor to King Kong.
w Mark Rosenthal, Lawrence Konner *screenplay* Ruth Rose *story* Merian C. Cooper *d* Ron Underwood *ph* Don Peterman, Oliver Wood *m* James Horner *pd* Michael Corenblith *ed* Paul Hirsch *sp* creature designer: Rick Baker; Dreamquest Images; Industrial Light & Magic
☆ Charlize Theron, Bill Paxton, Rade Sherbedgia, Peter Firth, David Paymer, Regina King, Robert Wisdom, Naveen Andrews, Lawrence Pressman, Linda Purl, Mika Boorem, John Alexander
'Makes the most of modern technology, adding color, computer graphics and impressive animatronics to a rather predictable storyline.' – *Lael Loewenstein, Variety*
visual effects

The Mighty McGurk
US 1946 83m bw
Nat Perrin/MGM
In the Bowery in the 1890s, a bragging ex-fighter takes in a small boy.
Sentimental melodrama which unspools like a joint remake of The Champ *and* The Bowery.
w William R. Lipman, Grant Garrett, Harry Clork *d* John Waters
☆ Wallace Beery, Dean Stockwell, Edward Arnold, Aline MacMahon, Cameron Mitchell, Aubrey Mather

Mighty Morphin Power Rangers: The Movie
US 1995 95m DeLuxe
TCF/Saban/Toei (Haim Saban, Shuki Levy, Suzanne Todd)
Six teenagers who can transform themselves into Power Rangers, martial arts experts on the side of good, combat the evil Ivan Ooze.
Criticism is redundant faced with the movie version of a vapid though aggressive fantasy that was briefly many children's favourite television viewing. The TV original showed the joins between its tacky fights and special effects, filmed in Japan, and the remainder, made in America. The movie is considerably slicker, but as depressing in the low quality of its imagination.
w Arne Olsen, John Kamps *d* Bryan Spicer *ph* Paul Murphy *m* Graeme Revell *pd* Craig Stearns *ed* Wayne Wahrman
☆ Karan Ashley, Johnny Yong Bosch, Steve Cardenas, Jason David Frank, Amy Jo Johnson, David Yost, Paul Schrier, Jason Narvy, Paul Freeman
'A curious hybrid of tepid California teen drama and "chop socky" karate serial. Watching it provides the strange sensation of channel-surfing without having to touch the remote.' – *Stephen Amidon, Sunday Times*

The Mighty Quinn
US 1989 98m colour
UIP/MGM/Star partners II/A & M Films (Sandy Lieberson, Marion Hunt, Ed Elbert)
On a Caribbean island, the police chief investigates the murder of an American.
Routine thriller offering little in the way of suspense or excitement.
w Hampton Fancher *novel* *Finding Maubee* by A. H. Z. Carr *d* Carl Shenkel *ph* Jacques Steyn *m* Anne Dudley *pd* Roger Murray-Leach *ed* John Jympson
☆ Denzel Washington, James Fox, Mimi Rogers, M. Emmet Walsh, Sheryl Lee Ralph, Art Evans, Esther Rolle, Norman Beaton, Alex Colon
'A spy thriller, a buddy movie, a musical, a comedy, and a picture that is wise about human nature. And yet with all of those qualities, it never seems to strain. This is a graceful, almost charmed, entertainment.' – *Roger Ebert*

Mighty Ursus: see *Ursus*

The Mighty Warrior: see *The Vengeance of Ursus*

Mignon Has Left **
Italy/France 1988 90m Eastmancolor
Metro/Ellepi Film/Chrysalide Film/RAI/RAITRE (Leo Pescarolo, Guido de Laurentiis)
original title: *Mignon è Partita*
Adolescent traumas come to a head in a Rome household when their French cousin comes to stay.
A slight but charming study of children in the transition to adulthood, much admired by Continental audiences.
w Francesca Archibugi, Gloria Malatesta, Claudia Sbarigia *d* Francesca Archibugi *ph* Luigi Verga *m* Roberto Gatto, Battista Lena *ad* Massimo Spano *ed* Alfredo Muschietti
☆ Stefania Sandrelli, Jean-Pierre Duriez, Leonardo Ruta, Celine Beauvallet, Francesca Antonelli, Lorenzo de Pasqua, Eleonora Sambiagio, Daniele Zaccaria

The Mikado *
GB 1939 91m Technicolor
GFD/G and S (Geoffrey Toye, Joseph Somlo)
In Japan, a timid official is appointed Lord High Executioner and finds that his first intended victim is the Emperor's son, travelling incognito.

Agreeable film version of the classic Gilbert and Sullivan comic opera, with some of the D'Oyly Carte Company's most celebrated members in excellent form.
w Geoffrey Toye *opera* W. S. Gilbert *d* Victor Schertzinger *ph* Bernard Knowles *m* Arthur Sullivan
☆ Martyn Green, John Barclay, Sydney Granville, Kenny Baker, Jean Colin, Constance Willis
'An odd film that pulls this way and that way and never quite gets anywhere. On the credit side must be put down the colour and the music.' – *C. A. Lejeune*
† The 1966 version by British Home Entertainment featured a later D'Oyly Carte company including John Reed but suffered from a frozen camera and flat lighting, so that little of the original vivacity and charm came over

'He Knows F.A. About Football.'
Mike Bassett: England Manager
GB 2001 89m Technicolor
Entertainment/Film Council/Hallmark/AIN (Neil Peplow, Steve Barron)
A old-fashioned First Division manager is the only person who can be found to take charge of England in the World Cup.
Documentary-styled comedy with feeble and obvious jokes.
w Rob Sprackling, J. R. N. Smith *d* Steve Barron *ph* Mike Eley *m* Antony Genn, Duncan Mackay, Mark Neary *pd* John Reid *ed* Colin Green
☆ Ricky Tomlinson (Mike Bassett), Amanda Redman (Karine Bassett), Philip Jackson (Lonnie Urquart), Bradley Walsh (Dave Dodds), Phill Jupitus (Tommo Thompson), Ulrich Thomsen (Dr Hans Shoegaarten), Robert Putt (Jack Marshall), Martin Bashir (Interviewer), Geoffrey Hutchings (Gordon Lightfoot), Pelé (Himself)
'There's certainly room for a comedy of mismanagement, but not one in which every scene hammers individual stupidity and national inferiority into the mud.' – *Alexander Walker, London Evening Standard*

Mike's Murder
US 1984 97m Technicolor
Warner/Ladd Company/Skyeway
A bank teller decides to investigate the killing of the man she loved, an unstable, bisexual drug-dealer and tennis coach.
A turn-off: a combination of an unlikely narrative, a mediocre script, sleazy characters and indifferent performances.
wd James Bridges *ph* Reynaldo Villalobos *m* John Barry, Joe Jackson *pd* Peter Jamison *ed* Jeff Gourson, Dede Allen
☆ Debra Winger, Mark Keyloun, Darrell Larson, Brooke Alderson, Paul Winfield, Daniel Shor

Mikey and Nicky
US 1976 118m colour
Paramount (Michael Hausman)
Two crooks are old friends, but one has been hired to kill the other...
Intolerable improvisatory sentimental melodrama. Who on earth shells out the money for pictures like this?
wd Elaine May *ph* Victor Kemper *m* John Strauss *pd* Paul Sylbert *ed* John Carter
☆ Peter Falk (Mikey), John Cassavetes (Nicky), Ned Beatty (Kinney), Sanford Meisner (Dave Resnick), Rose Arrick (Annie), Joyce Van Patten (Jan), M. Emmet Walsh (Bus driver)
'An impenetrable, ugly and almost unendurable mess.' – *Frank Rich, New York Post*
'A pretext for Falk and Cassavetes to indulge in one of those long, lugubrious Actors' Studio exercises that wore out its welcome with the last frame of *Husbands* and the first frame of *The Killing of a Chinese Bookie*.' – *Molly Haskell, Village Voice*

The Milagro Beanfield War
US 1988 118m MGM Color
Universal (Robert Redford)
Impoverished farmers in New Mexico defy developers who try to take over their land.
Serious issues treated with quirky humour and visual lyricism.
w David Ward, John Nichols *book* John Nichols *d* Robert Redford *ph* Robbie Greenberg *m* Dave Grusin *ad* Joe Aubel
☆ Ruben Blades, Richard Bradford, Sonia Braga, Julie Carmen, James Gammon, John Heard, M. Emmet Walsh
'A very peculiar mixture of warmed-over movie conventions.' – *MFB*
Academy Award: Dave Grusin

'The kind of woman most men want ... and shouldn't have!'
Mildred Pierce **
US 1945 113m bw
Warner (Jerry Wald)
A dowdy housewife breaks with her husband, becomes the owner (through hard work) of a restaurant chain, and survives a murder case before true love comes her way.
A woman's picture par excellence, glossily and moodily photographed, with a star suffering in luxury on behalf of the most ungrateful daughter of all time.
w Ranald MacDougall, Catherine Turney *novel* James M. Cain *d Michael Curtiz ph Ernest Haller m Max Steiner ad Anton Grot*
☆ *Joan Crawford*, Jack Carson, Zachary Scott, *Eve Arden, Ann Blyth*, Bruce Bennett, George Tobias, Lee Patrick, Moroni Olsen
'Constant, lambent, virulent attention to money and its effects, and more authentic suggestions of sex than one hopes to see in American films.' – *James Agee*
Academy Award: Joan Crawford
Academy Award nomination: best picture; script; Ernest Haller; Eve Arden; Ann Blyth

Miles from Home *
US 1988 108m DeLuxe
Fox/Braveworld/Cinemcom/J & M Entertainment (Frederick Zollo, Paul Kurta)
Facing hard times, two brothers burn down their farm and take to the road.
Unconventional road movie with some interesting moments.
w Chris Gerolmo *d* Gary Sinise *ph* Elliot Davis *m* Robert Folk *pd* David Gropman *ed* Jane Schwartz Jaffe
☆ Richard Gere, Kevin Anderson, Brian Dennehy, Jason Campbell, Austin Bamgarner, Larry Poling, Terry Kinney, Penelope Ann Miller, Helen Hunt, John Malkovich

Military Policeman: see *Off Limits*

Militia
US 2000 90m Foto-Kem
Cinetel
An agent infiltrates a militia group that plans to kill the US President with missiles containing anthrax.
Dismal action flick with an opening borrowed from Terminator 2; the cast overact in an attempt to compensate for its poor quality.
w Steve Latshaw, William Carson *d* Jay Andrews (Jim Wynorski) *ph* Mario D'Ayala *m* Neal Acree *pd* Gilbert Alan *ed* William Daniels
☆ Dean Cain (Ethan Carter), Jennifer Beals (Julie Sanders), Frederic Forrest (William Fain), Stacy Keach (Montgomery), John Beck (Anderson), Brett Butler (Bobbi), Christopher Maleki (Staley)

Milk and Honey
Canada 1988 95m colour
Zenith/JA Film (Peter O'Brian)
In an attempt to improve her life, a Jamaican woman leaves her home and young son to work in Canada as a nanny.
Moderate domestic drama, given a little fillip by the novelty of its subject matter.
w Glen Salzman, Trevor Rhone *d* Rebecca Yates, Glen Salzman *ph* Guy Dufaux *m* Mickey Erbe, Maribeth Solomon *ad* François Seguin *ed* Bruce Nyznik
☆ Josette Simon, Lyman Ward, Djanet Sears, Fiona Reid, Leonie Forbes, Richard Mills

Milk Money
US 1994 109m DeLuxe
UIP (Kathleen Kennedy, Frank Marshall)
A big-city tart with a heart of gold returns to their homes three 12-year-old boys who paid to see her strip and falls for the father of one of them.
Uninteresting would-be romantic comedy, which fails on both counts.
w John Mattson *d* Richard Benjamin *ph* David Watkin *m* Michael Convertino *pd* Paul Sylbert *ed* Jacqueline Cambas
☆ Melanie Griffith, Ed Harris, Michael Patrick Carter, Malcolm McDowell, Anne Heche, Casey Siemaszko, Philip Bosco, Brian Casey
'Could curdle your stomach and the execution of the idea is just plain rancid ... obvious, loud, mean-spirited and has its mind in the gutter.' – *Variety*

The Milkman
US 1950 87m bw
Universal-International (Ted Richmond)
Two milkmen tangle with gangsters.
Odd little comedy which gets the benefit of the doubt more by bringing its stars together than by giving them anything to do.
w Albert Beich, James O'Hanlon, Martin Ragaway, Leonard Stern *d* Charles Barton *ph* Clifford Stine *m* Milton Rosen
☆ Donald O'Connor, Jimmy Durante, Joyce Holden, Piper Laurie, William Conrad, Paul Harvey, Henry O'Neill

The Milky Way *
US 1936 88m bw
Paramount/Harold Lloyd (Edward Sheldon)
A milkman becomes a prizefighter and overcomes a gang of crooks.
Modest Harold Lloyd comedy towards the end of his career; remade as The Kid from Brooklyn *(qv).*
w Grover Jones, Frank Butler, Richard Connell *play* Lynn Root, Harry Clork *d* Leo McCarey *ph* Alfred Gilks
☆ Harold Lloyd, Adolphe Menjou, Verree Teasdale, Helen Mack, William Gargan, George Barbier, Lionel Stander
'The work of many hands, all laid on expertly.' – *Otis Ferguson*
'One is more amazed than ever at the good fortune of this youngish man whose chief talent is not to act at all, to do nothing, to serve as a blank wall for other people to scrawl their ideas on.' – *Graham Greene*

The Milky Way *
France/Italy 1968 102m Eastmancolor
Greenwich/Medusa (Serge Silberman)
original title: *La Voie Lactée*
Two tramps set off on pilgrimage from Paris to a Spanish shrine, and have various surprising encounters.
A picaresque examination of Catholic doctrine, full of surface interest but requiring special knowledge for full appreciation.
w Luis Buñuel, Jean-Claude Carrière *d Luis Buñuel ph* Christian Matras *m* Luis Buñuel
☆ Laurent Terzieff, Paul Frankeur, Delphine Seyrig, Edith Scon
'A mere trifle wrapped in a triple cloak of befuddling obscurantism.' – *John Simon*

The Mill on the Floss
GB 1937 94m bw
Morgan/National Provincial
A Victorian mill owner and the lord of the manor start a family feud which ends in tragedy.
Romeo and Juliet in crinolines; a stilted and unpersuasive film of the book.
w John Drinkwater, Garnett Weston, Austin Melford, Tim Whelan *novel* George Eliot *d* Tim Whelan
☆ Geraldine Fitzgerald, Frank Lawton, James Mason, Victoria Hopper, Fay Compton, Griffith Jones, Mary Clare, Athene Seyler, Felix Aylmer
'A series of stiff little sequences, decorously posed.' – *New York Times.*

Millennium
US 1989 105m DeLuxe
Rank/First Millennium Partnership/Gladden Entertainment (Douglas Leiterman, Robert Vince)
The investigator of a mid-air collision of two planes discovers that people from the future are involved.
Implausible time travel story that never holds together or keeps an audience's interest.
w John Varley *story* Air Raid by John Varley *d* Michael Anderson *ph* Rene Ohashi *pd* Gene Rudolf *ed* Ron Wisman
☆ Kris Kristofferson, Cheryl Ladd, Daniel J. Travanti, Robert Joy, Lloyd Bochner, Brent Carver, David McIlwraith, Maury Chaykin, Al Waxman

Miller's Crossing **
US 1990 115m DuArt
Fox/Circle Films/Ted and Jim Pedas/Ben Barenholtz/Bill Durkin (Ethan Coen)
The duplicitous aide to a corrupt and powerful politician is caught in the crossfire between two rival gangsters.
Sombre, solidly made thriller, directed with a macabre skill.
w Joel Coen, Ethan Coen *d Joel Coen ph* Barry Sonnenfeld *m* Carter Burwell *pd* Dennis Gassner *ed* Michael Miller
☆ Gabriel Byrne, Marcia Gay Harden, John Turturro, Jon Polito, J. E. Freeman, Albert Finney, Mike Starr, Al Mancini, Richard Woods

Le Million ****
France 1931 89m bw
Tobis (Frank Clifford)
An artist and an ingratiating crook search Paris for a lost lottery ticket.
With its delicate touch, perfect sense of comedy timing and infectious use of recitative and song, this is superb screen entertainment using most of the medium's resources.
wd René Clair musical comedy Georges Berr, M. Guillemaud *ph* Georges Périnal *m Georges Van Parys, Armand Bernard, Philippe Parès ad* Lazare Meerson
☆ Annabella, René Lefèvre, *Paul Olivier*, Louis Allibert, Vanda Gréville, Raymond Cordy
'A good musical farce that ought to do well everywhere ... it has speed, laughs, splendid photography and a good cast.' – *Variety*
'René Clair at his exquisite best; no one else has ever been able to make a comedy move with such delicate inevitability.' – *New Yorker, 1978*
'I wanted an atmosphere of foolishness ... we put gauze between the actors and the sets, which created an illusion of unreality.' – *René Clair*
† The style of this film was developed and expanded in Hollywood by Lubitsch in *One Hour with You* and by Mamoulian in *Love Me Tonight*.

Million Dollar Baby
US 1941 100m bw
Warner (Hal B. Wallis, David Lewis)
A girl inherits a fortune and a lot of problems.
Very predictable but sometimes sprightly comedy with a hard-working cast.
w Richard Macaulay, Jerry Wald, Casey Robinson *story Miss Wheelwright Discovers America* by Leonard Spigelgass *d* Curtis Bernhardt *ph* Charles Rosher *m* Max Steiner
☆ Priscilla Lane, Jeffrey Lynn, Ronald Reagan, May Robson, Lee Patrick, Helen Westley, George Barbier, John Qualen, Walter Catlett, Nan Wynn

Million Dollar Duck
US 1971 92m Technicolor
Walt Disney (Bill Anderson)
A duck lays eggs with solid gold yolks, which provoke interest from gangsters as well as the government.
Minor Disney fantasy borrowed without permission from Mr Drake's Duck (qv).
w Roswell Rogers *d* Vincent McEveety *ph* William Snyder *m* Buddy Baker
☆ Dean Jones, Sandy Duncan, Joe Flynn, Tony Roberts

The Million Dollar Hotel *
Germany/US 1999 122m colour
Panavision
Icon/Road MoviesKintop (Deepak Nayar, Bono, Nicholas Klein, Bruce Davey, Wim Wenders)
An FBI agent investigates the death of the son of a media tycoon, who fell off the roof of a seedy Los Angeles hotel inhabited by social misfits.
An intermittently engaging look at the trashier side of American culture, though you need more than a collection of freaks and eccentrics to make an interesting movie.
w Nicholas Klein *idea* Bono *d* Wim Wenders *ph* Phedon Papamichael *m* Jon Hassell, Bono,

Daniel Lanois, Brian Eno *pd* Robbie Freed *ed* Tatiana S. Riegel
☆ Jeremy Davies (Tom Tom), Milla Jovovich (Eloise), Mel Gibson (Skinner), Jimmy Smits (Geronimo), Peter Stormare (Dixie), Amanda Plummer (Vivien), Gloria Stuart (Jessica), Tom Bower (Hector), Donal Logue (Charley Best), Bud Cort (Shorty), Julian Sands (Terence Scopey), Harris Yulin (Stanley Goldkiss), Richard Edson (Joe), Charlayne Woodard (Jean Swift), Tim Roth (Izzy Goldkiss)

'Profoundly irritating.' – *Times*

'Ultimately, the superb craftsmanship and cultish aura can't compensate for an underdeveloped and not very interesting story, especially when none of the characters is the least bit sympathetic or engaging.' – *David Stratton, Variety*

'Roaring laughs in a story built of goofer dust and frog fur!'

Million Dollar Legs *

US 1932 64m bw
Paramount

A mythical sport-ridden country decides to enter the Olympic Games.
The good gags in this film are weighted down by plodding treatment, and the general effect is more doleful than funny.
w Harry Myers, Nick Barrows, Joseph L. Mankiewicz *d* Edward F. Cline *ph* Arthur Todd
☆ W. C. Fields, Jack Oakie, Andy Clyde, Lyda Roberti, Ben Turpin, Hugh Herbert, Billy Gilbert, George Barbier, Susan Fleming

'One of the silliest and funniest pictures ever made.' – *New Yorker, 1977*

Million Dollar Legs

US 1939 59m bw
Paramount

College students back a favourite horse.
Very modest collegiate comedy.
w Lewis Foster, Richard English *d* Nick Grinde *ph* Harry Fischbeck
☆ Betty Grable, John Hartley, Donald O'Connor, Jackie Coogan, Buster Crabbe, Thurston Hall

Million Dollar Mermaid *

US 1952 115m Technicolor
MGM (Arthur Hornblow Jnr)

GB title: *The One Piece Bathing Suit*

The story of Australian swimmer Annette Kellerman.
Inaccurate biopic with a raison d'être *in its spectacular aquashow scenes, but nothing at all new in its script.*
w Everett Freeman *d* Mervyn Le Roy *ph* George J. Folsey *md* Adolph Deutsch *ch* *Busby Berkeley*
☆ *Esther Williams*, Victor Mature, Walter Pidgeon, David Brian, Jesse White, Maria Tallchief, Howard Freeman
George J. Folsey

Million Dollar Mystery: see *Money Mania*

Million Dollar Ransom

US 1934 67m bw
Universal

A racketeer consolidates his family affairs before being bumped off by his gang.
Slightly odd underworld melodrama, interesting but not very satisfying.
w William R. Lipman, Ben Ryan *story* Damon Runyon *d* Murray Roth
☆ Edward Arnold, Phillips Holmes, Mary Carlisle, Wini Shaw, Andy Devine

'Lacks names but offers fair possibilities.' – *Variety*

The Million Pound Note *

GB 1953 91m Technicolor
GFD/Group Films (John Bryan)
US title: *Man with a Million*

A man is given a million pounds in the form of a single banknote and finds it difficult to spend.
Fairly pleasing period comedy which wears its one joke pretty thin but is nicely decorated and acted.
w Jill Craigie *story* Mark Twain *d* Ronald Neame *ph* Geoffrey Unsworth *m* William Alwyn *ed* Clive Donner
☆ Gregory Peck, Jane Griffiths, Ronald Squire, Joyce Grenfell, A. E. Matthews, Reginald Beckwith, Hartley Power, Wilfrid Hyde-White

The Millionaire *

US 1931 80m bw
Warner

A bored millionaire retires and secretly buys a garage.
Fairly deft star comedy which well satisfied Depression audiences.
w Julien Josephson and Booth Tarkington *story* Earl Derr Biggers *d* John Adolfi
☆ *George Arliss*, Florence Arliss, Evalyn Knapp, David Manners, Noah Beery, J. Farrell MacDonald, James Cagney

'Should bring Arliss within mental reach of all theatres ... Should enjoy a substantial career.' – *Variety*

† Remade in 1947 as *That Way with Women* (qv)

A Millionaire for Christy

US 1951 91m bw
TCF (Bert Friedlob)

A lawyer's secretary is sent to Los Angeles to inform an heir of his good fortune, and decides to marry him.
Modest romantic comedy with plenty to be modest about.
w Ken Englund *d* George Marshall *ph* Harry Stradling *m* Victor Young
☆ Eleanor Parker, Fred MacMurray, Richard Carlson, Douglass Dumbrille

Millionaire Merry Go Round: see *Kicking the Moon Around*

'From naughty, notorious George Bernard Shaw, the sultry story of the beautiful babe in the Balmain gowns who pants for romance ... !'

The Millionairess *

GB 1960 90m DeLuxe Cinemascope
TCF/Dimitri de Grunwald (Pierre Rouve)

The richest woman in the world falls for a poor Indian doctor.
Messy travesty of a Shavian comedy that was never more than a star vehicle to begin with. Hardly any of it works despite the star cast, who are mostly miscast.
w Wolf Mankowitz *play* Bernard Shaw *d* Anthony Asquith *ph* Jack Hildyard *m* Georges Van Parys
☆ Sophia Loren, Peter Sellers, Alastair Sim, Vittorio de Sica, Dennis Price, Gary Raymond, Alfie Bass, Miriam Karlin, Noel Purcell

'The result, lacking any sort of dramatic cohesion or continuity and seemingly planned less as a film than as a series of haphazard effects, is merely tiring.' – *Peter John Dyer*

Millions

GB 1936 70m bw
Herbert Wilcox

A struggling composer is really the son of a millionaire.
Fairly lively comedy of rival self-made men.
w Michael Barringer *d* Leslie Hiscott *ph* Freddie Young
☆ Gordon Harker, Frank Pettingell, Richard Hearne, Jane Carr

Millions in the Air

US 1935 72m bw
Harold Hurley/Paramount

Complications of a radio amateur contest.
Scrappy comedy with more historical interest than entertainment value.
w Sig Herzig, Jane Storm *d* Ray McCarey
☆ Willie Howard, John Howard, Robert Cummings, Inez Courtney, Benny Baker, Dave Chasen, Wendy Barrie, Samuel S. Hinds

'Without a substantial monicker in the cast, it hasn't much to offer at the box office.' – *Variety*

Millions like Us **

GB 1943 103m bw
GFD/Gainsborough (Edward Black)

The tribulations of a family in wartime, especially of the meek daughter who goes into war work and marries an airman, who is killed.
Fragmentary but reasonably accurate picture of the Home Front during World War II; a little more humour would not have been out of place, but as propaganda it proved an effective weapon.
wd *Frank Launder, Sidney Gilliat* *ph* Jack Cox *md* Louis Levy *ad* John Bryan *ed* Alfred Roome
☆ Patricia Roc, Gordon Jackson, Moore Marriott, Eric Portman, Anne Crawford, Basil Radford, Naunton Wayne, Joy Shelton, Megs Jenkins

'There is an unsentimental warmheartedness which I hope we shall cling to and extend in filmed representations of the British scene.' – *Richard Winnington*

† The only picture Launder and Gilliat directed side by side on the floor.

Milou in May ***

France/Italy 1989 108m colour
Gala/Nouvelles Editions de Films/TFI/Ellepi Film (Jean-Yves Asselin)

Following the death of his mother, a 60-year-old man invites her relatives to the funeral.
Gentle, well-observed study of family relationships.
w Louis Malle, Jean-Claude Carrière *d* *Louis Malle* *ph* Renato Berta *m* Stéphane Grappelli *ed* Emmanuelle Castro
☆ *Michel Piccoli*, Miou-Miou, Michel Duchaussoy, Dominique Blanc, Harriet Walter, Bruno Carette, François Berléand, Martine Gautier, Paulette Dubost

'A film of Chekhovian generosity that never strays into sentimentality or cynicism.' – *Philip French, Observer*

Mimi

GB 1935 94m bw
BIP

In a Paris garret, a poor girl dies after encouraging a playwright.
La Bohème *without the music; not a good idea.*
w Clifford Grey, Paul Merzbach, Jack Davies, Denis Waldock *novel* *La Vie Bohème* by Henri Murger *d* Paul Stein
☆ Douglas Fairbanks Jnr, Gertrude Lawrence, Diana Napier, Harold Warrender, Carol Goodner, Richard Bird

Mimic *

US 1997 105m DeLuxe
Buena Vista/Dimension (Bob Weinstein, B. J. Rack, Ole Bornedal)

Mutant killer bugs, created to rid New York of a plague, evolve into creatures that resemble human beings.
Effective and atmospheric horror movie, with much of the action taking place in subway tunnels; its visual style creates unease without resorting to shock effects.
w Matthew Robbins, Guillermo Del Toro, Matthew Greenberg, John Sayles *story* Donald A. Wolheim *d* Guillermo Del Toro *ph* Dan Laustsen *m* Marco Beltrami *pd* Carol Spier *ed* Patrick Lussier *sp* creature design: Rob Bottin, Tyruben Ellingson
☆ Mira Sorvino, Jeremy Northam, Josh Brolin, Giancarlo Giannini, Charles S. Dutton, Alexander Goodwin, Alix Koromzay, F. Murray Abraham

'A murkily good job in scary subterranean suspense of the *Alien* kind, with sound effects prompting worse apocalyptic imaginings than the actual sight of the VW-sized bugs.' – *Alexander Walker, London Evening Standard*

'A cyclone of human emotion roars across the screen!'

Min and Bill **

US 1930 69m bw
MGM

A boozy old waterfront character and his wife try to keep her daughter from being placed in care.
Well-remembered and much-loved character comedy which led to the even more successful Tugboat Annie *with the same team.*
w Frances Marion, Marion Jackson *play* *Dark Star* by Lorna Moon *d* George Hill *ph* Harold Wenstrom
☆ *Marie Dressler*, *Wallace Beery*, Dorothy Jordan, Marjorie Rambeau, Donald Dillaway, Russell Hopton

'Comedy-drama of distinction. All ingredients for all theatres, from keys down.' – *Variety*

Marie Dressler

Mina Tannenbaum **

France 1993 128m colour
Mayfair/IMA/UGC/Christian Bourgois/La Sept/SFPC/L'Etang/Belbo/RTBF (Georges Benayoun)

Friends and relatives remember the life of a gifted Jewish artist, a misfit as a young girl, who kills herself after the relationships in her life go awry.
Assured exploration of the lives of two women growing up over 25 years, with men relegated to walk-on parts although the women also become marginalized; it starts light-heartedly and becomes much darker, while some of the narrative devices distance the audience, with the dead commenting on the action, and the women seen with 'ghosts' of how they might have been.
wd Martine Dugowson *ph* Dominique Chapuis *m* Peter Chase *ad* Philippe Chiffre *ed* Martine Barraqué, Dominique Gallieni
☆ Romane Bohringer, Elsa Zylberstein, Hugues Quester, Nils Tavernier, Stéphane Slima, Chantal Krief, Florence Thomassin, Eric Defosse, Jean-Philippe Ecoffey

'An unusual, sometimes uneven mix of comedy and melodrama. Yet it is a film of immense charm and humour which works surprisingly well.' – *Ginette Vincendeau, Sight and Sound*

Minbo No Onna **

Japan 1992 126m colour
Itami Films (Yasushi Tamaoki)
aka: *Anti-Extortion Woman*
aka: *The Gangster's Moll*

A female lawyer is hired to prevent yakuza from ruining a high-class hotel and blackmailing its manager.
Engaging, though sometimes broad, satire that changes tone into a more straightforward drama halfway through, mocking Japanese gangsters and exposing their methods of extortion and intimidation.
wd Juzo Itami *ph* Yonezo Maeda *m* Toshiyuki Honda *pd* Shuji Nakamura *ed* Akira Suzuki
☆ Nobuko Miyamoto, Yasuo Daichi, Takehiro Murata, Shiro Ito, Akira Nakao, Akira Takarada, Hideji Otaki, Norburo Mitani, Hosei Komatsu

† Japan's yakuza were not amused by the film: six days after its release Itami was hospitalized after being cut around the face and neck by gangsters. In a related incident in Tokyo, a man slashed a cinema screen during the showing of another of Itami's films.

The Mind Benders *

GB 1963 113m bw
Anglo-Amalgamated/Novus (Michael Relph)

A scientist undergoes an experiment aimed at depriving him of all sensation. It works too well; he becomes a sadist; and his colleagues can't reverse the process.
Matter-of-factly played hocus-pocus with spy asides; quite gripping while it's on, but in no way memorable.
w James Kennaway *d* Basil Dearden *ph* Denys Coop *m* Georges Auric
☆ Dirk Bogarde, John Clements, Mary Ure, Michael Bryant

The Mind of Mr Reeder *

GB 1939 75m bw
Jack Raymond

An elderly government employee unmasks a forger and murderer.
Entertaining crime comedy-drama which never quite realizes its potential.
w Bryan Edgar Wallace, Marjorie Gaffney, Michael Hogan *novel* Edgar Wallace *d* Jack Raymond
☆ Will Fyffe, Kay Walsh, George Curzon, Chili Bouchier, John Warwick

The Mind of Mr Soames

GB 1970 98m Technicolor
Columbia/Amicus (Teresa Bolland)

A man who has lived in a coma for thirty years is cured but faces the world as a new-born infant.
Ill-advised attempt at science fiction with meaning; its earnestness becomes a bore.
w John Hale, Edward Simpson *novel* Charles Eric Maine *d* Alan Cooke *ph* Billy Williams *m* Michael Dress
☆ Terence Stamp, Robert Vaughn, Nigel Davenport, Donal Donnelly, Christian Roberts, Vickery Turner, Scott Forbes

The Mind Reader *
US 1933 69m bw
Warner
A phoney mind reader tries to go straight for his wife's sake, and ends up in jail.
Reasonably mordant satirical drama with good performances.
w Wilson Mizner, Robert Lord *play* Vivian Cosby *d* Roy del Ruth
☆ *Warren William*, Constance Cummings, Allen Jenkins, Donald Dillaway, Mayo Methot, Clarence Muse
'Star performance plus laugh dialogue enough to send this into okay programmer class.' – *Variety*

Mind Your Own Business
US 1937 75m bw
Paramount/Emmanuel Cohen
Boy scouts help to capture gangsters.
Slightly rocky comedy which finally comes across as unsatisfactory.
w Dore Schary *story* John Francis Larkin *d* Norman Z. McLeod
☆ Charles Ruggles, Alice Brady, Lyle Talbot, Benny Baker, Jack La Rue, William Demarest, Frankie Darro
'It will have a tough time standing alone.' – *Variety*

Mine Own Executioner ***
GB 1947 108m bw
London Films (Anthony Kimmins, Jack Kitchin)
A lay psychiatrist undertakes the care of a mentally disturbed war veteran, but fails to prevent him from murdering his wife.
When this film first appeared it seemed like the first adult drama featuring sophisticated people to emerge from a British studio. Time and television have blunted its impact, but it remains a well told suspense melodrama with memorable characters.
w Nigel Balchin novel Nigel Balchin *d Anthony Kimmins ph* Wilkie Cooper *m* Benjamin Frankel *ad* William C. Andrews *ed* Richard Best
☆ *Burgess Meredith*, Kieron Moore, Dulcie Gray, Barbara White, Christine Norden, Michael Shepley, Walter Fitzgerald, John Laurie, Clive Morton
'The first psychoanalytical film that a grown-up can sit through without squirming.' – *Richard Winnington*
'One feels invigorated by having seen and understood other people's lives.' – *Daily Worker*

'His secret meant death to one man if he didn't talk ... to countless thousands if he did!'
Ministry of Fear **
US 1944 85m bw
Paramount (Seton I. Miller)
During World War II in England, a man just out of a mental hospital wins a cake at a village fair and finds himself caught up in bewildering intrigues.
Little to do with the novel, but a watchable, well-detailed little thriller on Hitchcock lines, once you forgive the usual phoney Hollywood England.
w Seton I. Miller *novel* Graham Greene *d Fritz Lang ph Henry Sharp m* Victor Young *ad* Hans Dreier, Hal Pereira *ed* Archie Marshek
☆ *Ray Milland* (Stephen Neale), Marjorie Reynolds (Carla Hilfe), Carl Esmond (Willi Hilfe), Hillary Brooke (Mrs Bellane), Dan Duryea (Cost/Travers), Percy Waram (Inspector Prentice), Alan Napier (Dr Forrester), Erskine Sanford (Mr Rennit)
'A crisp and efficiently made thriller with no pretension to intellectual content.' – *Paul Jensen*

The Miniver Story
GB 1950 104m bw
MGM (Sidney Franklin)
Mrs Miniver faces the tribulations of post-war Britain.
Glum sequel to Mrs Miniver, *with the dauntless heroine finally succumbing to a glossy but fatal disease. Well enough made, but very hard to take.*
w Ronald Millar, George Froeschel *d* H. C. Potter *ph* Joseph Ruttenberg *m* Miklos Rozsa
☆ Greer Garson, Walter Pidgeon, Cathy O'Donnell, John Hodiak, Leo Genn, Reginald Owen, Henry Wilcoxon, William Fox, Anthony Bushell

Minnie and Moskowitz *
US 1971 115m Technicolor
Universal (Al Rubin)
Two lonely Los Angeles misfits have a bumpy courtship.
Enjoyably aimless character comedy.
wd John Cassavetes *ph* Arthur J. Ornitz *m* Bob Harwood *ed* Robert Heffernan, Frederic Knudtson
☆ Gena Rowlands (Minnie Moore), Seymour Cassel (Seymour Moskowitz), Val Avery (Zelmo Swift), Tom Carey (Morgan Morgan)

Minor Mishaps **
Denmark 2002 109m colour
Artificial Eye/Zentropa (Ib Tardini)
original title: *Sma Ulykker*
After their mother dies unexpectedly, the children rally round to support their father.
With characters fleshed out rather than the usual ciphers, this is an engaging account of an often troubled group of siblings and their morose father that nevertheless functions well as a family unit.
w Kim Fupz Aakeson *d* Annette K. Olesen *ph* Morten Soborg *m* Jeppe Kaas *ed* Nicolaj Monberg
☆ Jorgen Kiil (John), Maria Wurgler Rich (Marianne), Jannie Faurschou (Eva), Henrik Prip (Tom), Jesper Christensen (Soren), Karen-Lise Mynster (Hanne), Tina Gylling (Ellen)
'By the end of this film we know and care as little about this family as we did at the beginning.' – *Geoffrey Mcnab, Sight and Sound*

'What would you do if you were accused of a murder you had not committed... yet?'
Minority Report *
US 2002 144m Technicolor Panavision
TCF
In a future where product placement is ubiquitous and pyschics identify murderers in advance of the crime, a cop goes on the run when he is accused of planning to kill a man he doesn't know.
Tense paranoid thriller that gives every indication of being brilliant until the halfway mark, when it becomes just another glossy action pic with the corniest of endings.
w Scott Frank, Jon Cohen *story* Philip K. Dick *d* Steven Spielberg *ph* Janusz Kaminski *m* John Williams *pd* Alex McDowell *ed* Michael Kahn *sp* ILM
☆ Tom Cruise (Chief John Anderton), Colin Farrell (Danny Witwer), Samantha Morton (Agatha), Max von Sydow (Director Lamar Burgess), Lois Smith (Dr Iris Hineman), Peter Stormare (Dr Solomon Eddie), Tim Blake Nelson (Gideon), Steve Harris (Jad)
'May be a shade too serious and contemplative to completely enchant the thrill-seeking masses, while simultaneously seeming too mainstream-minded and genre-bound to be entirely embraced by highbrows.' – *Todd McCarthy, Variety*
'My own minority report is that it stinks... sinks to the level of pornographically violent video games.' – *Andrew Sarris, New York Observer*
sound editing (Richard Hymns, Gary Rydstrom)

Minstrel Man *
US 1944 70m bw
PRC
A minstrel star seeks his long-lost daughter.
Interesting sidelights on old-time minstrel shows in a production somewhat less tatty than is usual from this company.
w Irwin Franklin, Pierre Gendron *d* Joseph H. Lewis *m* Leo Erdody, Ferde Grofe
☆ Benny Fields, Gladys George, Roscoe Karns
song, 'Remember Me to Carolina' (*m*Harry Revel, *ly*Paul Webster); music

A Minute to Pray, a Second to Die: see *Dead or Alive*

The Miracle
Italy 1948 40m bw
Tania Film (Roberto Rossellini)
A simple-minded peasant woman is seduced by a shepherd but believes her baby has been immaculately conceived.
Curious, rather unsatisfactory parable originally intended as part of a two-item tribute to the power of a star actress. (The other section, Cocteau's The Human Voice, *was withdrawn for copyright reasons.)*
w Tullio Pinelli, Roberto Rossellini, Federico Fellini *d* Roberto Rossellini *ph* Aldo Tonti *m* Renzo Rossellini
☆ Anna Magnani, Federico Fellini
'Acting on a plane scarcely known to the cinema.' – *Sunday Times*

'The mightiest story of fame and the flesh known to our time!'
The Miracle
US 1959 121m Technirama
Warner (Henry Blanke)
In Spain during the Peninsular War, a nun breaks her vows in order to follow a British soldier, and a statue of the Virgin Mary steps down to take her place.
And that's only the beginning in this very tall tale, full of heavy breathing, violent action and religiosity, from the old Max Reinhardt pageant. Quite incredible, and sloppily done.
w Frank Butler, Jean Rouverol *play* Karl Vollmoeller *d* Irving Rapper *ph* Ernest Haller *m* Elmer Bernstein
☆ Carroll Baker, Roger Moore, Walter Slezak, Vittorio Gassman, Katina Paxinou, Dennis King, Isobel Elsom, Torin Thatcher
† Jean Rouverol was blacklisted at the time of the film's original release and omitted from the credits.

The Miracle
GB 1990 97m colour
Palace/Promenade/British Screen/Film Four (Stephen Woolley, Redmond Morris)
An actress becomes the focus of the romantic attentions of an adolescent saxophonist.
Desultory tale of incipient incest with a few striking moments.
wd Neil Jordan *ph* Philippe Rousselot *m* Anne Dudley *pd* Gemma Jackson *ed* Joke Van Wijk
☆ Beverly D'Angelo, Donal McCann, Niall Byrne, Lorraine Pilkington, J. G. Devlin, Cathleen Delany, Tom Hickey, Shane Connaughton
'Insubstantial fare, with predictable situations and plotting.' – *Variety*

A Miracle Can Happen: see *On Our Merry Way*

Miracle in Milan **
Italy 1951 101m bw
PDS/ENIC (Vittorio de Sica)
A foundling goes to live with the poor on the outskirts of Milan, and his erstwhile guardian returns from heaven to help them repel capitalists and fly away on broomsticks to a better land.
An unlikely fable which manages to avoid all the obvious pitfalls and sends one out of the cinema in a warm glow.
w Cesare Zavattini, Vittorio de Sica *novel Toto il Buono* by Cesare Zavattini *d* Vittorio de Sica *ph* G. R. Aldo *m* Alessandro Cicognini
☆ Francesco Golisano, Brunella Bovo, Emma Gramatica, Paolo Stoppa

Miracle in Soho
GB 1957 93m Eastmancolor
Rank (Emeric Pressburger)
A Soho roadworker falls for a barmaid.
Rudimentary romantic whimsy in an unconvincing street set, with characters either too voluble or just plain dull.
w Emeric Pressburger *d* Julian Amyes *ph* Christopher Challis *m* Brian Easdale
☆ John Gregson, Belinda Lee, Cyril Cusack

'A street corner pick-up that worked a miracle of love! A picture of very special greatness!'
Miracle in the Rain **
US 1955 107m bw
Warner (Frank P. Rosenberg)
A plain New York girl falls for a soldier; when he is killed in action, he keeps their appointment on the church steps as a ghost.
Archetypal Hollywood schmaltz, half acute observation of amusing types, half sentimental whimsy, with a final supernatural touch of eating your cake and having it.
w Ben Hecht novel Ben Hecht *d Rudolph Maté ph Russell Metty m Franz Waxman*
☆ Jane Wyman, Van Johnson, Fred Clark, Eileen Heckart, William Gargan

The Miracle Maker
GB/Russia 1999 91m Technicolor
Icon/S4C/British Screen/Christmas (Naomi Jones, Renat Zinnurov)
Jesus leaves home to do God's work, performs miracles, is crucified and rises from the dead.
Reverential treatment of the Gospel story, told using animated clay figures.
w Murray Watts *d* Stanislav Sokolov, Derek Hayes *ph* Alexander Vikhanski *m* Anne Dudley *ad* Helena Livanova *ed* William Oswald, John Richards
☆ Featuring voices of: Ralph Fiennes, Michael Bryant, Julie Christie, Rebecca Callard, James Frain, Richard E. Grant, Ian Holm, William Hurt, Anton Lesser, Daniel Massey, Tim McInnerny, Alfred Molina, Bob Peck, Miranda Richardson, Anthony Sher, David Thewlis, Ken Stott
'Even as one admires the aesthetics and good intentions of this piece, the film falls flat since it's hard to feel in any way emotionally connected.' – *James Cameron-Wilson, Film Review*

The Miracle Man
US 1932 85m bw
Paramount
A gang of crooks is reformed by a faith healer they have exploited.
Adequate remake of the silent Lon Chaney vehicle; no sparks this time.
w Waldemar Young, Samuel Hoffenstein *play* Frank L. Packard, George M. Cohan *d* Norman Z. McLeod *ph* David Abel *m* W. Franke Harling
☆ Sylvia Sidney, Chester Morris, Irving Pichel, John Wray, Robert Coogan, Hobart Bosworth, Boris Karloff, Ned Sparks, Virginia Bruce

'50 minutes and counting...'
Miracle Mile *
US 1989 88m CFI color
Hemdale (John Daly, Derek Gibson)
A town panics as it learns that a nuclear strike is on the way.
Suspense and black humour are maintained to the final moments in an engagingly odd little movie.
wd Steve DeJarnatt *ph* Theo Van de Sande *m* Tangerine Dream *pd* Christopher Horner *ed* Stephen Semel, Kathie Weaver
☆ Anthony Edwards, Mare Winningham, John Agar, Lou Hancock, Mykel T. Williamson, Kelly Jo Minter, Kurt Fuller, Denise Crosby

The Miracle of Fatima: see *The Miracle of Our Lady of Fatima*

The Miracle of Morgan's Creek ***
US 1943 99m bw
Paramount (Preston Sturges)
Chaos results when a stuttering hayseed tries to help a girl accidentally pregnant by a soldier she met hazily at a dance.
Weird and wonderful one-man assault on the Hays Office and sundry other American institutions such as motherhood and politics; an indescribable, tasteless, roaringly funny mêlée, as unexpected at the time as it was effective, like a kick in the pants to all other film comedies.
wd Preston Sturges ph John Seitz *m* Leo Shuken, Charles Bradshaw
☆ Betty Hutton, Eddie Bracken, William Demarest, Diana Lynn, Porter Hall, Akim Tamiroff, Brian Donlevy, Alan Bridge
OFFICER KOCKENLOCKER (WILLIAM DEMAREST): 'Daughters. They're a mess no matter how you look at 'em. A headache till they get married – if they get married – and after that they get worse ... Either they leave their husbands and come back with four kids and move into your guest room or the husband loses his job and the whole caboodle comes back. Or else they're so homely that you can't get rid of them at all and they sit around like Spanish moss and shame you into an early grave.'
EMILY KOCKENLOCKER (DIANA LYNN): 'If you don't mind my mentioning it, father, I think you have a mind like a swamp.'
'Like taking a nun on a roller coaster.' – *James Agee*
'This film moves in a fantastic and irreverent whirl of slapstick, nonsense, farce, sentiment, satire, romance, melodrama – is there any

ingredient of dramatic entertainment except maybe tragedy and grand opera that hasn't been tossed into it?' – *National Board of Review*

'Bad taste, or no bad taste, I thoroughly enjoyed it.' – *Richard Mallett, Punch*

Preston Sturges (as writer)

The Miracle of Our Lady of Fatima
US 1952 102m Warnercolor
Warner (Bryan Foy)

GB title: *The Miracle of Fatima*

An account of the 1917 appearance of the Virgin Mary to three Portuguese peasant children.
Poorly staged religious film which manages to be less pro-Catholic than anti-communist, and was clearly seen by Jack L. Warner as a means of atoning for Mission to Moscow. *A real cold war piece.*
w Crane Wilbur, James O'Hanlon *d* John Brahm *ph* Edwin DuPar *m* Max Steiner *ad* Edward Carrere
☆ Gilbert Roland, Frank Silvera, Angela Clarke, Jay Novello
Max Steiner

The Miracle of the Bells
US 1948 120m bw
Jesse L. Lasky

The death of a glamorous film star causes a small-town miracle and a nationwide publicity stunt.
One hopes that this oddity was intended as a satire; as a straight entertainment it's more than a little icky, and good production values scarcely help.
w Ben Hecht *novel* Russell Janney *d* Irving Pichel *ph* Robert de Grasse *m* Leigh Harline
☆ Fred MacMurray, Alida Valli, Frank Sinatra, Lee J. Cobb

'An offensive exhibition of vulgar insensitivity.' – *MFB*

'I hereby declare myself the founding father of the Society for the Prevention of Cruelty to God.' – *James Agee*

The Miracle of the White Stallions *
US 1963 118m Technicolor
Walt Disney (Peter V. Herald)

GB title: *The Flight of the White Stallions*

During World War II the Nazis occupy Vienna and the owner of the Spanish Riding School guides his stallions to safety.
Adequate family adventure fare with a dull hero but interesting backgrounds.
w A. J. Carothers *d* Arthur Hiller *ph* Gunther Anders *m* Paul Smith
☆ Robert Taylor, Lilli Palmer, Eddie Albert, Curt Jurgens

Miracle on 34th Street ***
US 1947 94m bw
TCF (William Perlberg)

GB title: *The Big Heart*

A department store Santa Claus claims to be the real thing.
Mainly charming comedy fantasy which quickly became an American classic but does suffer from a few dull romantic stretches.
wd George Seaton *story* Valentine Davies *ph* Charles Clarke, Lloyd Ahern *m* Cyril Mockridge
☆ *Edmund Gwenn*, Maureen O'Hara, John Payne, Natalie Wood, Gene Lockhart, Porter Hall, William Frawley, Jerome Cowan, Thelma Ritter

'Altogether wholesome, stimulating and enjoyable.' – *Motion Picture Herald*

George Seaton (as writer); Valentine Davies; Edmund Gwenn
best picture

'Discover the Miracle.'
Miracle on 34th Street *
US 1994 114m DeLuxe
TCF (John Hughes)

A department store Santa Claus promises a child that he will bring her with a house, a father and a brother for Christmas.
A rather tired remake of the original which makes little attempt to engage with present-day realities, but gains from Attenborough's cuddly performance as Kriss Kringle.
w George Seaton, John Hughes *d* Les Mayfield *ph* Julio Macat *m* Bruce Broughton *pd* Doug Kraner *ed* Raja Gosnell
☆ *Richard Attenborough*, Elizabeth Perkins, Dylan McDermott, Mara Wilson, Robert Prosky, J. T. Walsh, James Remar, William Windom

'Glaringly predictable, and although some may succumb to its old-fashioned charm and naïvely simple message, others will find its look and feel too cloying.' – *Patricia Dobson, Screen International*

Miracle on Main Street *
US 1940 76m bw
RKO/Jack Skirball

A cabaret dancer finds an abandoned baby but her plans are thwarted by the return of her husband.
Odd, interesting but flatly handled melodrama.
w Sam Ornitz, Boris Ingster *story* Felix Jackson *d* Steve Sekely *ph* Charles Van Enger *m* Walter Jurmann, Hans Salter
☆ Walter Abel, Margo, William Collier, Jane Darwell, Lyle Talbot, Wynne Gibson

'Never give away what you can sell!'
The Miracle Woman *
US 1931 90m bw
Columbia (Harry Cohn)

A lady evangelist turns confidence trickster.
Mild satirical drama inspired by the career of Aimée Semple Macpherson.
w Jo Swerling *play* Bless You Sister by Robert Riskin, John Meehan *d* *Frank Capra* *ph* Joseph Walker
☆ Barbara Stanwyck, Sam Hardy, David Manners, Beryl Mercer, Russell Hopton

'Splendid programme leader, a big and strong film opening up numerous channels of publicity.' – *Variety*

'Such a beauty, well staged and handsomely lighted.' – *New Yorker, 1977*

The Miracle Worker *
US 1962 106m bw
UA/Playfilms (Fred Coe)

The childhood of Helen Keller, taught by Annie Sullivan after being left blind, deaf and dumb in an illness.
A moving real-life story is given hysterical treatment and the good scenes have a hard task winning through; in any case a documentary might have been more persuasive.
w William Gibson *play* William Gibson *d* Arthur Penn *ph* Ernest Caparros *m* Laurence Rosenthal *ad* George Jenkins
☆ *Anne Bancroft, Patty Duke*, Victor Jory, Inga Swenson, Andrew Prine, Beah Richards
Anne Bancroft; Patty Duke
William Gibson; Arthur Penn
Anne Bancroft

Miracles
US 1985 87m Technicolor Super Techniscope
Orion/Steve Roth, Bernard Williams

A chase begins when bank robbers kidnap an innocent couple.
Exhausting action comedy with no real finesse.
wd Jim Kouf *ph* John Alcott *m* Peter Bernstein *pd* Terence Marsh
☆ Tom Conti, Teri Garr, Paul Rodriguez, Christopher Lloyd

Miracles for Sale
US 1939 71m bw
MGM

An illusionist catches a murderer.
What could have been a smart mystery piece is sabotaged by stilted writing and direction, a muddled narrative style, and illusions which are patently faked by the camera.
w James Edward Grant, Marion Parsonnet, Harry Ruskin *novel* Death in a Top Hat by Clayton Rawson *d* Tod Browning *ph* Charles Lawton
☆ Robert Young, Florence Rice, Henry Hull, Frank Craven, Lee Bowman, William Demarest

'Unexciting whodunit … the plot stumbles over itself most of the time.' – *Variety*

Mirage **
US 1965 109m bw
U-I (Harry Keller)

During a New York power blackout, an executive falls to his death from a skyscraper and a cost accountant loses his memory.
Striking puzzler, rather slowly developed but generally effective and with a strong sense of place and timing.
w Peter Stone *novel* Walter Ericson *d* *Edward Dmytryk* *ph* Joe MacDonald *m* Quincy Jones *ad* Frank Arrigo, Alexander Golitzen *ed* Ted J. Kent
☆ *Gregory Peck, Diane Baker*, Walter Abel, *Walter Matthau*, Leif Erickson, Kevin McCarthy, Jack Weston, George Kennedy

'Worthy of Hitchcock at his vintage best.' – *Daily Express*

Miranda *
GB 1947 80m bw
GFD/Gainsborough/Sydney Box (Betty Box)

A doctor on holiday in Cornwall catches a mermaid and takes her to London disguised as an invalid.
Simple-minded comedy which scores a few easy laughs on obvious targets.
w Peter Blackmore *play* Peter Blackmore *d* Ken Annakin *ph* Ray Elton *m* Temple Abady *ed* Gordon Hales
☆ *Glynis Johns*, Griffith Jones, Googie Withers, *Margaret Rutherford*, David Tomlinson, Sonia Holm, John McCallum
† Sequel 1949, *Mad about Men*.

Miranda (dubbed)
Italy 1985 90m colour
San Francisco (Giovanni Bertolucci)

A woman keeps an inn and also manages to service a string of lovers.
From the opening shot of a woman's pubic hair and a man's bare bottom, we are in the tiresome world of Tinto Brass, a director who concentrates on voyeuristic, soft-focus scenes of sexual activity and displays no interest in style or narrative.
w Carla Cipriani, Tinto Brass *d* Tinto Brass *ph* Silvano Ippoliti *m* Riz Ortolani *ad* Paolo Biagetti *ed* Tinto Brass
☆ Serena Grandi, Andrea Occhipinti, Franco Interlenghi, Andy J. Forest, Franco Branciaroli

Mirror **
USSR 1974 106m bw/colour
Artificial Eye/Mosfilm Unit 4 (E. Waisberg)

original title: *Zerkalo*

An artist considers his relationships with his parents and with his wife and young son.
Intensely personal meditation, with the director's father reading his own poems and his mother playing the narrator's mother, which may baffle audiences, despite its assurance and visual beauty.
w Andrei Tarkovsky, Aleksandr Misharin *d* Andrei Tarkovsky *ph* Georgy Rerberg *m* Eduard Artemyev *ad* Nikolai Dvigubsky *ed* L. Feiginova
☆ Innokenti Smoktunovsky, Margarita Terekhova, L. Tarkovskaya, Philip Yankovsky, Ignat Daniltsev, Anatoli Solonitsin

'Tarkovsky's autobiographical essay in the interaction of private and collective memories, via a multi-layered structure of flashbacks, dream sequences and newsreel footage, is chillingly impressive even at its most hermetic.' – *Sight and Sound*

† Tarkovsky said of the film, 'We wanted to make a simple film which would signify only what was shown'. It was given a very restricted release in the USSR.

The Mirror
West Germany/Turkey 1984 94m colour
Von Vietinghoff Filmproduction/ZDF/Channel 4 (Joachim von Vietinghoff)
original title: *Der Spiegel Ayna*

A Turkish peasant reacts violently on discovering that the son of the local landowner is in love with his wife.
Ponderously told folk tale, full of stolid symbolism.
wd Erden Kiral *novel* The White Ox by Osman Sahin *ph* Kenan Ormanler *m* Brymor Jones
☆ Nur Surer, Suavi Eren, Hikmet Celik

'Mirror, mirror, on the wall, who's the killer among them all?'
The Mirror Crack'd
GB 1980 105m Technicolor
EMI/John Brabourne, Richard Goodwin

Murders result from the making of an all-star film in an English village.
After adventures on the Orient Express and the Nile, this follow-up in the Agatha Christie stakes seems woefully restricted with stilted dialogue and playing.
w Jonathan Hales, Barry Sandler *novel* Agatha Christie *d* Guy Hamilton *ph* Christopher Challis *m* John Cameron *pd* Michael Stringer
☆ Angela Lansbury, Geraldine Chaplin, Elizabeth Taylor, Rock Hudson, Tony Curtis, Edward Fox, Kim Novak, Marella Oppenheim, Charles Gray

'A story about just how wrong two people can be before they can be right…'
The Mirror Has Two Faces
US 1996 126m Technicolor
Columbia TriStar/Phoenix/Arnon Milchan/Barwood (Barbra Streisand, Arnon Milchan)

A dowdy academic marries a professor more interested in companionship than sex, until she reinvents herself as a desirable woman.
Creaky, frequently risible romantic hokum about the need to be adored, somewhat undermined by the fact that Streisand looks better before, rather than after, her transformation into a sex goddess.
w Richard LaGravenese *d* Barbra Streisand *ph* Dante Spinotti, Andrzej Bartkowiak *m* Marvin Hamlisch, Barbra Streisand *pd* Tom John *ed* Jeff Werner
☆ Barbra Streisand, Jeff Bridges, Pierce Brosnan, George Segal, Mimi Rogers, Brenda Vaccaro, Lauren Bacall, Austin Pendleton, Elle Macpherson

'A vanity production of the first order. A staggeringly obsessive expression of the importance of appearances, good looks and being adored, Barbra Streisand's third directorial outing is also, incidentally, a very old-fashioned wish-fulfillment romantic comedy that has been directed and performed in the broadest possible manner.' – *Todd McCarthy, Variety*

'I have never seen so many shots of a star staring into a mirror. Streisand seems to be in the unique position of being her own co-star for most of the movie. This has to be a cinema first: a romantic comedy for one.' – *Tom Shone, Sunday Times*

† It is based on the French film *Le Miroir à Deux Faces*, written by André Cayatte and Gerard Oury, directed by Cayatte in 1958 and starring Michele Morgan.

Lauren Bacall; song 'I Finally Found Someone' (*m/ly* Barbra Steisand, Marvin Hamlisch, Bryan Adams, Robert 'Mutt' Lange)

'In her book, there's a fine line between fantasy and reality – and she's walking it!'
The Misadventures of Margaret
GB/France 1998 93m DeLuxe
Feature/Mandarin/TF1/Lunatics and Lovers (Ian Benson)

A married American writer becomes excessively flirtatious as the result of researching a novel set in 18th-century France.
An odd comedy of sexual exploration that never quite manages the sophistication it needs.
wd Brian Skeet *novel* Rameau's Niece by Cathleen Schine *ph* Romain Winding *m* James Shearman *pd* Martin Childs *ed* Clare Douglas
☆ Parker Posey, Jeremy Northam, Craig Chester, Elizabeth McGovern, Brooke Shields, Corbin Bernsen, Justine Waddell, Patrick Bruel

'Coarse in the current female-laddish fashion, but not badly performed. And it's often verbally funny.' – *Philip French, Observer*

Mischief *
US 1985 93m DeLuxe
Jere Henshaw-Michael Nolin/TCF

Teenage anxieties in smalltown America in 1956
Clearly not for export, but a smooth piece of its kind.
w Noel Black *d* Mel Damski *ph* Donald E. Thorin *pd* Paul Peters *ed* Nick Brown
☆ Doug McKeon, Catherine Mary Stewart, Kelly Preston, Chris Nash

Les Misérables ****
US 1935 109m bw
Twentieth Century (Darryl F. Zanuck)
Unjustly convicted and sentenced to years in the galleys, Jean Valjean emerges to build up his life again but is hounded by a cruel and relentless police officer.
Solid, telling, intelligent version of a much-filmed classic novel; in adaptation and performance it is hard to see how this film could be bettered.
w W. P. Lipscomb *novel* Victor Hugo *d* Richard Boleslawski *ph* Gregg Toland *m* Alfred Newman *ed* Barbara McLean
☆ *Fredric March, Charles Laughton*, Cedric Hardwicke, Rochelle Hudson, Frances Drake, John Beal, Jessie Ralph, Florence Eldridge
'Brilliant filmization, sure fire for heavy money.' – *Variety*
'Unbelievably thrilling in all the departments of its manufacture ... a memorable experience in the cinema.' – *New York Times*
'A superlative effort, a thrilling, powerful, poignant picture.' – *New York Evening Post*
'Deserving of rank among the cinema's finest achievements.' – *New York World Telegram*
† Other versions of the story: 1909, 1913 (French); 1917 (William Farnum); 1923 (French: Gabriel Gabrio); 1929 as *The Bishop's Candlesticks* (Walter Huston); 1934 (French: Harry Baur); 1946 (Italian: Gino Cervi); 1952 (see below); 1956 (French: Jean Gabin; see below); 1978 (British: Richard Jordan)
best picture; Gregg Toland; editing

Les Misérables **
US 1952 106m bw
TCF (Fred Kohlmar)
Solemn remake, well done but lacking the spark of inspiration.
w Richard Murphy *d* Lewis Milestone *ph* Joseph LaShelle *m* Alex North
☆ Michael Rennie, Robert Newton, Edmund Gwenn, Debra Paget, Cameron Mitchell, Sylvia Sidney, Elsa Lanchester, James Robertson Justice, Joseph Wiseman, Rhys Williams

Les Misérables ***
France 1995 177m colour Super 35
Warner/Films 13/TF1/Canal (Claude Lelouch)
A former boxing champion who helps a Jewish couple during the Nazi occupation of France finds that his life begins to resemble that of Jean Valjean, the hero of Victor Hugo's novel.
An engrossing, intriguing, emotionally satisfying drama that both echoes and dramatizes Hugo's epic, revealing the timelessness of the story and the changes that time and circumstance might have made to its characters.
wd Claude Lelouch *novel* Victor Hugo *ph* Claude Lelouch, Philippe Pavans de Ceccatty *m* Francis Lai, Didier Barbelivien, Philippe Servain, Erik Berchot, Michel Legrand *ad* Jacques Bufnoir *ed* Hélène de Luze
☆ *Jean-Paul Belmondo*, Michel Boujenah, Alessandra Martines, Annie Girardot, Philippe Leotard, Clementine Celarie, Rufus, Ticky Holgado
'Hugely ambitious in both theme and scope and brimming with sheer delight in the medium.' – *Derek Elley, Variety*
'A righteous, passionate and witty soap opera.' – *Sarah Kerr, New Yorker*

Les Misérables *
US 1998 134m Technicolor Panavision
Entertainment/Mandalay (Sarah Radclyffe, James Gorman)
A former convict who makes good is hounded by a ruthless policeman.
Dour version of the classic novel, one that takes itself too seriously, repressing the romantic sweep of its narrative.
w Rafael Yglesias *novel* Victor Hugo *d* Bille August *ph* Jörgen Persson *m* Basil Poledouris *pd* Anna Asp *ed* Janus Billeskov-Jansen
☆ Liam Neeson, Geoffrey Rush, Uma Thurman, Claire Danes, Hans Matheson, Reine Brynolfsson, Peter Vaughan
'An impressive, brooding monolith of a film ... Unfortunately, it really isn't much fun, a cardinal sin in this sort of epic spectacle.' – *Andrew O'Hehir, Sight and Sound*

Les Misérables de Victor Hugo *
France/Italy 1958 210m Technicolor Technirama
Pathé/P.A.C./Serena (Paul Cadeac)
Jean Valjean escapes from prison and makes a new life for himself, but his old one catches up with him.
Stolid version of Hugo's classic, gaining what distinction it has from Gabin's performance.
w René Barjavel, Jean-Paul Le Chanois *d* Jean-Paul Le Chanois *ph* Jacques Natteau *m* Georges Van Parys *ad* Serge Pimenoff, Karl Schneider *ed* Emma Le Chanois
☆ *Jean Gabin* (Jean Valjean), Bernard Blier (Javert), Danièle Delorme, Serge Reggiani, Bourvil, Gianni Esposito, Martine Havet, Béatrice Altariba, Elfriede Florin, Jimmy Urbain, Jean Murat, Lucien Baroux, Silvia Monfort
† The film is sometimes shown in two parts. The best French version is that of Raymond Bernard, who made a three-part adaptation of the novel in 1933 starring Harry Baur under the titles *Tempête sous un Crane* (120m), *Les Thénardiers* (90m), and *Liberté, Liberté Chérie* (95m). He later cut it to a two-part film: *Jean Valjean* (109m) and *Cosette* (100m).

'Paul Sheldon used to write for a living. Now he's writing to stay alive.'
Misery **
US 1990 107m CFI color
Medusa/Castle Rock/Nelson (Andrew Scheinman, Rob Reiner)
A disturbed fan kidnaps an injured novelist and forces him to write a novel featuring her favourite heroine.
Impeccably directed, tense thriller.
w William Goldman *novel* Stephen King *d* Rob Reiner *ph* Barry Sonnenfeld *m* Marc Shaiman *pd* Norman Garwood *ed* Robert Leighton
☆ James Caan, Kathy Bates, Richard Farnsworth, Frances Sternhagen, Lauren Bacall, Graham Jarvis, Jerry Potter
'This astonishing film is a taut, darkly comic thriller and a post-modernist examination of the relationship between writer and reader, detached producer and vulnerable consumer, artist and critic.' – *Philip French, Observer*
Kathy Bates

'It shouts and sings with life ... explodes with love!'
The Misfits *
US 1961 124m bw
United Artists/Seven Arts (Frank E. Taylor)
Cowboys gather in the Nevada desert to rope wild mustangs, and a divorcee becomes involved with one of them.
Ill-fated melodrama whose stars both died shortly afterwards; a solemn, unattractive, pretentious film which seldom stops wallowing in self-pity.
w Arthur Miller *d* John Huston *ph* Russell Metty *m* Alex North *ad* Stephen Grimes, William Newberry *ed* George Tomasini
☆ Clark Gable (Gay Langland), Marilyn Monroe (Roslyn Taber), Montgomery Clift (Perce Howland), Eli Wallach (Guido), Thelma Ritter (Isabelle Steers), James Barton (Old man), Estelle Winwood (Church lady), Kevin McCarthy (Raymond Taber)
'The theme with its implications of an essentially male savagery suits Mr Huston, and he has drawn extraordinary qualities from all his chief players.' – *Dilys Powell*

Mishima *
US 1985 120m Technicolor Panavision
Coppola-Lucas/Warner
Fragments of autobiography by the self-destructing Japanese writer.
A complete switch-off for all but the initiated, this indulgent, delicate, violent kaleidoscope is half a work of art and half an utter waste of other people's money.
w Paul and Leonard Schrader *d* Paul Schrader *ph* John Bailey *m* Philip Glass
☆ Ken Ogata, Kanji Sawada, Yasosuke Bando

Misplaced
US 1989 95m colour
Subway (Lisa Zwerling)
In the early 80s, a Polish woman and her teenage son leave the political unrest of Poland to settle in Washington with family that she has not seen for more than 30 years.
Earnestly effective low-key drama of the problems of assimilation into a different culture, on a personal and a public level.
w Louis Yansen, Thomas DeWolfe *d* Louis Yansen *ph* Igor Sunara *m* Michael Urbaniak *pd* Beth Kuhn *ed* Michael Berenbaum
☆ John Cameron Mitchell, Viveca Lindfors, Elzbieta Czyzewska, Drew Snyder, Deirdre O'Connell, John Christopher Jones, Debralee Scott

Miss Amerigua
Paraguay/Sweden 1994 93m colour
FilmTeknik/Latino (Luis R. Vera)
A man returns home from Nicaragua to revenge the death of his father, which he witnessed as a boy, only to discover that the city is in the grip of a beauty competition.
Ham-fisted, if amiable and meandering, political farce.
w Luis R. Vera, Andrés Colmán *d* Luis R. Vera *ph* Mårten Nilsson *m* Jan Tolf *ad* Carlos dos Santos *ed* Lisskulla Moltke-Hoff
☆ Sonia Marchewka, Raquel Baeza, Ayesa Frutos, Jesús Perez, Hector Silva, Jorge Baez, Jorge Ramos
'Mild political satire with touches of magical realism that paints an agreeably sketchy portrait of a fictional South American town.' – *Ken Eisner, Variety*
† It was the first feature to be made in Paraguay for 30 years.

Miss Annie Rooney
US 1942 86m bw
Edward Small
Poor Irish girl loves rich boy.
A totally routine offering for a teenage star; no wonder she didn't make it.
w George Bruce *d* Edwin L. Marin *ph* Lester White *md* Edward Paul
☆ Shirley Temple, William Gargan, Guy Kibbee, Dickie Moore, Peggy Ryan, Gloria Holden, Jonathan Hale, Mary Field

'She's Got A Killer to Catch...Right After The Swimsuit Competition.'
Miss Congeniality *
US 2000 111m Technicolor
Warner/Castle Rock/Village Roadshow/NPV/Fortis (Sandra Bullock)
An uncouth, graceless FBI agent has to be transformed from an ugly duckling into a swan so that she can go undercover as a contestant in the Miss United States contest, which is being threatened by a terrorist.
A broad comedy of a familiar kind with a few good laughs among the pratfalls.
w Marc Lawrence *d* Donald Petrie *ph* Laszlo Kovacs *m* Edward Shearmur *ch* Scott Grossman *pd* Peter Larkin *ed* Billy Weber *cos* Susie De Santo
☆ Sandra Bullock (Gracie Hart), Michael Caine (Victor Melling), Benjamin Bratt (Eric Matthews), William Shatner (Stan Fields), Ernie Hudson (McDonald), John DiResta (Agent Clonsky), Candice Bergen (Kathy Morningside), Heather Burns (Cheryl 'Rhode Island'), Melissa De Sousa (Karen 'New York'), Steve Monroe (Frank Tobin)
'Happily, deliberately second-rate, as if its ideal audience consisted of weary airline passengers.' – *A.O. Scott, New York Times*

Miss Fane's Baby Is Stolen
US 1933 67m bw
Paramount
GB title: *Kidnapped*
A film star's baby is kidnapped.
Fairly straightforward crime yarn with comic asides.
w Adela Rogers St Johns, Rupert Hughes *d* Alexander Hall
☆ Dorothea Wieck, Alice Brady, Baby LeRoy, William Frawley, George Barbier, Alan Hale, Jack La Rue
'Box office as well as entertainment ... the first picture of its kind since the Lindbergh kidnapping.' – *Variety*

Miss Firecracker
US 1989 103m DuArt
Rank/Firecracker Company/Corsair (Fred Berner)
An orphaned girl enters her home-town beauty contest.
Unconvincing in its portrayal of a young woman discovering her individuality.
w Beth Hanley *play The Miss Firecracker Contest* by Beth Hanley *d* Thomas Schlamme *ph* Arthur Albert *m* David Mansfield, Homer Denison *pd* Maher Ahmad *ed* Peter C. Frank
☆ Holly Hunter, Mary Steenburgen, Tim Robbins, Alfre Woodard, Scott Glenn, Veanne Cox, Ann Wedgeworth, Trey Wilson, Amy Wright, Kathleen Chalfant

Miss Grant Takes Richmond *
US 1949 87m bw
Columbia (S. Sylvan Simon)
GB title: *Innocence Is Bliss*
A dumb secretary helps defeat crooks and improve the local housing situation.
Mildly amusing star comedy.
w Nat Perrin, Devery Freeman, Frank Tashlin *d* Lloyd Bacon *ph* Charles Lawton Jnr *m* Heinz Roemheld *md* Morris Stoloff
☆ Lucille Ball, William Holden, Janis Carter, James Gleason, Gloria Henry, Frank McHugh, George Cleveland
'One of the more delightful comedies of the season.' – *Lawrence J. Quirk*

Miss Julie *
Sweden 1950 87m bw
Sandrew (Rune Waldekranz)
In a lonely house, the count's daughter kills herself after being seduced by a valet.
Intense melodramatic fragment, just a little long for comfort.
wd Alf Sjöberg *play* August Strindberg *ph* Göran Strindberg *m* Dag Wirén
☆ *Anita Björk*, Ulf Palme, Anders Henrikson
'The outstanding achievement of the Swedish cinema in recent years.' – *Gavin Lambert, Sight and Sound*

'Worlds apart...bound by desire.'
Miss Julie *
GB/US 1999 101m colour
Optimum/Moonstone/Red Mullet (Mike Figgis, Harriet Cruikshank)
A footman begins a doomed love affair with his employer's flirtatious daughter.
A low budget version of Strindberg's study of sexual desire, power and ambition, shot on video with handheld cameras, which provide immediacy but also distract from the drama.
w Helen Cooper *play* August Strindberg *d* Mike Figgis *ph* Benoit Delhomme *m* Mike Figgis *pd* Michael Howells *ed* Matthew Wood
☆ Saffron Burrows (Miss Julie), Peter Mullan (Jean), Maria Doyle Kennedy (Christine)
'Worth seeing because films rarely contain characters of such quality and intricacy.' – *Film Review*

Miss London Ltd
GB 1943 99m bw
GFD/Gainsborough (Edward Black)
An escort agency is formed to assist soldiers on leave.
Flagwaving light entertainment with popular performers of the time.
w Val Guest, Marriott Edgar *d* Val Guest *ph* Basil Emmott *md* Louis Levy *songs* Manning Sherwin (m), Val Guest (ly)
☆ Arthur Askey, Anne Shelton, Evelyn Dall, Richard Hearne, Max Bacon, Jack Train, Peter Graves, Jean Kent

Miss Marple
Agatha Christie's inquisitive spinster detective was brought to the screen by director George Pollock and star Margaret Rutherford in four increasingly disappointing films for MGM.
1962 Murder She Said (qv)
1963 Murder at the Gallop
1964 Murder Most Foul, Murder Ahoy
See also *The Mirror Crack'd*.

Miss Mary
Argentina 1986 110m Eastmancolor
New World/GEA (Lita Stantic)
During the period between the two world wars, an English governess of a wealthy Argentinian family forms too close an attachment to the young son of the household.
An attempt to chart the social changes in Argentina, culminating in Perón's takeover, through the upheavals in one dysfunctional family; but the focus is too diffused, and there is little cohesion between its succession of effective individual episodes.
w Maria Luisa Bemberg, Jorge Goldenberg *d* Maria Luisa Bemberg *ph* Miguel Rodriguez *ed* Luisa Cesar d'Angiolillo
☆ Julie Christie, Nacha Guevara, Eduardo Pavlovsky, Luisina Brando, Gerardo Romano, Iris Marga, Guillermo Battaglia

Miss Pacific Fleet
US 1935 76m bw
Warner
Two stranded show girls enter a popularity contest to win the fare back home.
A comedy with little to laugh at.
w Lucille Newmark, Peter Milne, Patsy Flick *d* Ray Enright *ph* Arthur Todd *md* Leo F. Forbstein *ad* Esdras Hartley *ed* Clarence Kolster
☆ Glenda Farrell, Joan Blondell, Hugh Herbert, Allen Jenkins, Warren Hull, Guinn Williams
'Maybe OK for double feature bills, but that's the best it can hope for.' – *Variety*

Miss Pilgrim's Progress
GB 1949 82m bw
Daniel M. Angel
An American working girl in Britain helps to save a village from development.
Wholly artificial and unendearing comedy.
wd Val Guest *ph* Bert Mason *m* Phillip Martell
☆ Yolande Donlan, Michael Rennie, Garry Marsh, Emrys Jones, Reginald Beckwith, Helena Pickard, Jon Pertwee

Miss Pinkerton *
US 1932 66m bw
Warner
A private nurse helps a police detective to solve a murder case.
Pleasing little mystery comedy.
w Lillian Hayward, Niven Busch *story* Mary Roberts Rinehart *d* Lloyd Bacon *ph* Barney McGill
☆ Joan Blondell, George Brent, Mae Madison, John Wray, Ruth Hall, C. Henry Gordon, Elizabeth Patterson
'Formula mystery story ... picture is outdated and has nothing to draw.' – *Variety*
† Remade as *The Nurse's Secret* (1946).

Miss Robin Hood
GB 1952 78m bw
Group 3
A lady author pits her wits against crooks and saves an old lady's fortune.
Disappointing star comedy with no build-up.
w Val Valentine, Patrick Campbell, Geoffrey Orme *d* John Guillermin *ph* Arthur Grant *m* Temple Abady
☆ Margaret Rutherford, Richard Hearne, Michael Medwin, Peter Jones, James Robertson Justice, Sidney James, Dora Bryan

'She's The Only Dame With A Kiss Of Flame!'
Miss Sadie Thompson *
US 1953 91m Technicolor 3-D
Columbia (Lewis J. Rachmil)
On a Pacific island, a singer becomes involved with a marine, to the consternation of a local preacher.
Vigorous semi-musical remake of Rain *(qv); a good star vehicle, but not otherwise notable.*
w Harry Kleiner *d* Curtis Bernhardt *ph* Charles Lawton *m* George Duning *md* Morris W. Stoloff *ch* Lee Scott *ad* Carl anderson *ed* Viola Lawrence
☆ Rita Hayworth (Sadie Thompson), José Ferrer (Rev Alfred Davidson), Aldo Ray (Sgt Phil O'Hara), Russell Collins (Dr Robert MacPhail), Harry Bellaver (Joe Horn), Wilton Graf (Governor), Peggy Converse (Margaret Davidson), Charles Buchinsky (Bronson) (Edwards)
song 'Blue Pacific Blues' (*m* Lester Lee, *ly* Ned Washington)

'A story for lovers ... past, present and perfect!'
Miss Susie Slagle's
US 1946 88m bw
Paramount (John Houseman)
Romances of nursing students in 1910 Baltimore.
Modest melodramatic potboiler.
w Anne Froelick, Hugo Butler *novel* Augusta Tucker *d* John Berry *ph* Charles Lang Jnr *m* Daniele Amfitheatrof
☆ Veronica Lake, Joan Caulfield, Sonny Tufts, Lillian Gish, Ray Collins, Billy de Wolfe, Bill Edwards, Roman Bohnen, Morris Carnovsky, Lloyd Bridges

Miss Tatlock's Millions *
US 1948 101m bw
Paramount (Charles Brackett)
A stunt man impersonates the idiot heir to a fortune.
Tasteless but quite funny comedy with a cast of eccentrics indulging in enjoyable fooling.
w Charles Brackett, Richard L. Breen *d* Richard Haydn *ph* Charles Lang Jnr *m* Victor Young
☆ John Lund, Wanda Hendrix, Monty Woolley, Barry Fitzgerald, Robert Stack, Ilka Chase, Dorothy Stickney

Miss V from Moscow
US 1942 70m bw
PRC
A Russian spy impersonates a German spy in Paris.
Hilariously inept propaganda piece; since the Cold War it has been retitled Intrigue in Paris.
w Arthur St Claire and Sherman Lowe *d* Albert Herman
☆ Lola Lane, Noel Madison, Howard Banks

'Loyalty Without Question. Friendship Without Equal.'
Mrs Brown ***
GB 1997 103m colour
Miramax/Ecosse (Sarah Curtis)
Faithful Scottish servant John Brown lifts Queen Victoria out of her funereal gloom, arousing the jealousy of her other household staff.
Absorbing, deftly directed, excellently acted drama that, while concentrating on personal relationships, raises still-vital questions about the point and purpose of the monarchy.
w Jeremy Brock d John Madden ph Richard Greatrex m Stephen Warbeck *pd Martin Childs ed* Robin Sales
☆ *Judi Dench, Billy Connolly, Geoffrey Palmer, Anthony Sher*, Gerald Butler, Richard Pasco, David Westhead
'Possesses resonances that are rich, complex and instructive.' – *Richard Williams, Guardian*
† Executive producer Douglas Rae conceived the film in the 60s and originally planned to cast Sean Connery in the role of John Brown, but the film was then abandoned when he learned that the Royal Family was not happy with the project.
Judi Dench; make-up
Judi Dench; Deidre Clancy (costumes)

Mrs Brown, You've Got a Lovely Daughter
GB 1968 95m Metrocolor Panavision
MGM/Allen Klein
A young singer inherits a prize greyhound.
Inoffensive comedy musical with a swinging London background.
w Thaddeus Vane *d* Saul Swimmer *ph* Jack Hildyard *m/ly* Graham Couldman, Geoff Stephens, Kenny Young
☆ Peter Noone and Herman's Hermits, Stanley Holloway, Mona Washbourne, Lance Percival, Marjorie Rhodes

Mrs Caldicot's Cabbage War
GB 2001 110m colour
Arrow/Evolution/Cabbage (Andy Birmingham)
A widow leads residents of an old people's home in a revolt against the unfeeling way it is run.
Amiable but limp comedy that begins well but quickly runs of of steam; it might have made an amusing half-hour TV sitcom.
w Malcolm Stone *novel* Vernon Coleman *d* Ian Sharp *ph* Sue Gibson *m* Alan Lisk *pd* Malcolm Stone *ed* Gerry Hambling
☆ Pauline Collins (Mrs Caldicot), Peter Capaldi (Derek Caldicot), Anna Wilson-Jones (Veronica Caldicot), Gwenlian Davies (Audrey), Sheila Reid (Joyce), Frank Mills (Leslie), Frank Middlemass (Bernard), John Alderton (Hawksmoor), Isla Blair (Matron), Paul Freeman (Peter Jenkins), Martin Jarvis (JB)
'About 10 minutes in, I all but lost the will to live.' – *Peter Bradshaw, Guardian*

Mrs Dalloway **
GB/US/Netherlands 1997 97m Rank Colour
Artificial Eye/First Look (Stephen Bayly, Lisa Katselas Paré)
In the 20s, a society hostess looks back on her life and thinks of what might have been.
Gripping, pensive examination of the possibilities and missed opportunities of life.
w Eileen Atkins *novel* Virginia Woolf *d* Marleen Gorris *ph* Sue Gibson *m* Ilona Sekacz *pd* David Richens *ed* Michiel Reichwein
☆ Vanessa Redgrave, Natascha McElhone, Rupert Graves, Michael Kitchen, John Standing, Alan Cox, Lena Headey, Margaret Tyzack, Sarah Badel, Phyllis Calvert
'A highly romantic, deeply melancholy drama, the film offers psychological and existential insights about the inevitable effects – and price – of life choices.' – *Emanuel Levy, Variety*

'She makes dinner. She does windows. She reads bedtime stories. She's a blessing ... in disguise.'
Mrs Doubtfire *
US 1993 125m DeLuxe Panavision
TCF/Blue Wolf (Marcia Garces Williams, Robin Williams, Mark Radcliffe)
An unemployed actor, allowed only weekly visits to his two children, disguises himself as a nanny so that he can spend more time with them.
If you can accept Williams as a Scotswoman – he looks like a truck driver in drag and sounds like Miss Jean Brodie long past her prime – there is occasional slapstick amusement to be found in this over-long and sickly sweet comedy.
w Randi Mayem Singer, Leslie Dixon *novel Alias Madam Doubtfire* by Anne Fine *d* Chris Columbus *ph* Donald McAlpine *m* Howard Shore *pd* Angelo Graham *ed* Raja Gosnell *sp* Greg Cannom
☆ Robin Williams, Sally Field, Pierce Brosnan, Harvey Fierstein, Polly Holiday, Lisa Jakub, Matthew Lawrence, Mara Wilson, Robert Prosky
'Lessons are learned, loved ones are hugged, and personal growth is achieved – as usual, at the expense of the comedy. Some, apparently, including Williams, like it warm and cuddly, too. Nobody's perfect.' – *Terrence Rafferty, New Yorker*
'A really wholesome movie about a man in a bra; it's like watching a John Waters movie rewritten by John Hughes.' – *Libby Gelman-Waxner, Premiere*
'This Robin Williams-in-drag vehicle provides the comic with a slick surface for doing his shtick, within a story possessing broad family appeal.' – *Variety*
† The film was a success in America, taking more than $200m at the box-office.
make-up

Mrs Fitzherbert
GB 1947 99m bw
British National (Louis H. Jackson)
The Prince Regent secretly marries a Catholic widow.
Stilted, ill-cast historical charade.
wd Montgomery Tully *novel* Winifred Carter *ph* James Wilson *m* Hans May *ad* R. Holmes Paul *ed* Charles Hasse
☆ Peter Graves, Joyce Howard, Leslie Banks, Margaretta Scott, Mary Clare, Frederick Valk, Ralph Truman, John Stuart, Chili Bouchier

Mrs Loring's Secret: see *The Imperfect Lady*

Mrs Mike
US 1949 99m bw
Nassour/Huntingdon Hartford (Edward Gross)
A Mountie takes his new wife to live in the frozen northwest.
Predictable sentimental drama, well enough done to keep interest, but only just.
w Lewis Levitt, De Witt Bodeen *d* Louis King *ph* Joseph Biroc *m* Max Steiner
☆ Dick Powell, Evelyn Keyes, J. M. Kerrigan, Angela Clarke

Mrs Miniver **
US 1942 134m bw
MGM (Sidney Franklin)
An English housewife survives World War II.
This is the rose-strewn English village, Hollywood variety, but when released it proved a beacon of morale despite its false sentiment, absurd rural types and melodramatic situations. It is therefore beyond criticism, except that some of the people involved should have known better.
w Arthur Wimperis, George Froeschel, James Hilton, Claudine West *novel* Jan Struther *d* William Wyler *ph* Joseph Ruttenberg *m* Herbert Stothart *ed* Harold F. Kress
☆ *Greer Garson, Walter Pidgeon*, Teresa Wright, Richard Ney, Dame May Whitty, Henry Travers, Reginald Owen, Henry Wilcoxon, Helmut Dantine, Rhys Williams, Aubrey Mather
VICAR (HENRY WILCOXON) PREACHING FINAL SERMON IN BOMBED CHURCH: 'This is not only a war of soldiers in uniforms. It is a war of the people – of all the people – and it must be fought not only on the battlefield but in the cities and in the villages, in the factories and on the farms, in the home and in the heart of every man, woman and child who loves freedom. Well, we have buried our dead, but we shall not forget them. Instead, they will inspire us with an unbreakable determination to free ourselves and those who come after us from the tyranny and terror that threaten to strike us down. This is the people's war. It is our war. We are the fighters. Fight it, then. Fight it with all that is in us. And may God defend the right.'
'That almost impossible feat, a war picture that photographs the inner meaning, instead of the outward realism of World War II.' – *Time*
best picture; script; William Wyler; Joseph Ruttenberg; Greer Garson; Teresa Wright
Walter Pidgeon; Dame May Whitty; Henry Travers; Harold F. Kress

Mrs O'Malley and Mr Malone *
US 1950 69m bw
MGM (William H. Wright)
On a train to New York, a radio contest winner and a lawyer help solve a murder.
Lively second feature farce.
w William Bowers *d* Norman Taurog *ph* Ray June *m* Adolph Deutsch
☆ Marjorie Main, James Whitmore, Ann Dvorak, Fred Clark, Dorothy Malone, Phyllis Kirk

'A Woman Ahead Of Her Time. A Movie That Can't Be Missed.'
'New York in the 1920's. The only place to be was the Algonquin, and the only person to know was Dorothy Parker.'
Mrs Parker and the Vicious Circle
US 1994 124m colour Super 35
Artificial Eye/Miramax/Fine Line (Robert Altman)
Dorothy Parker, a successful Hollywood screenwriter, recalls her earlier days and love affairs with wits and writers in New York and her regard for Robert Benchley.
A disappointing biopic of a complex, unhappy and talented writer. Jennifer Jason Leigh's mannered performance and drawled monotone may be true to the externals of Dorothy Parker but render her witticisms in such an unintelligible way that it is surprising that anyone was able to record them.
w Alan Rudolph, Randy Sue Coburn *d* Alan Rudolph *ph* Jan Kiesser *m* Mark Isham *pd* François Séguin *ed* Suzy Elmiger
☆ Jennifer Jason Leigh, Matthew Broderick, Campbell Scott, Peter Gallagher, Jennifer Beals, Andrew McCarthy, Wallace Shawn, Martha Plimpton, Sam Robards, Lili Taylor, James LeGros
'Buys into the self-pity, morbidity and pathos of Dorothy Parker's writing and life, rather than her robustness, comic verve and bracing good sense; it also seems to buy into the modern therapised view that wounding wit is the first resort of the wounded.' – *Kevin Jackson, Independent*

Mrs Parkington
US 1944 124m bw
MGM (Leon Gordon)

A lady's maid marries a miner who becomes wealthy, and pushes her way into society.
Thoroughly unconvincing three-generation drama, with a bewigged and powdered star giving the boot to her conniving relations. It has production values and nothing else.
w Robert Thoeren, Polly James *novel* Louis Bromfield *d* Tay Garnett *ph* Joseph Ruttenberg *m* Bronislau Kaper
☆ Greer Garson, Walter Pidgeon, Edward Arnold, Agnes Moorehead, Cecil Kellaway, Gladys Cooper, Frances Rafferty, Tom Drake, Peter Lawford, Dan Duryea, Hugh Marlowe, Selena Royle
† The heroine is shown having a romance with Edward VII when Prince of Wales; special scenes were shot for the European version substituting Cecil Kellaway, who played Edward, by Hugo Haas who played a European king of indeterminate origin.
Academy Award nomination: Greer Garson; Agnes Moorehead

Mrs Pollifax – Spy
US 1970 110m DeLuxe
UA/Mellor (Frederick Brisson)
A respectable American matron offers her services to the CIA and sees active service in Albania.
Incredible comedy-dramatic vehicle for a star who won't give up. An obvious failure from the word go.
w C. A. McKnight *novel* Dorothy Gilman *d* Leslie Martinson *ph* Joseph Biroc *m* Lalo Schifrin
☆ Rosalind Russell, Darren McGavin
† C. A. McKnight was Rosalind Russell.

Mrs Pym of Scotland Yard
GB 1939 65m bw
Hurley/Grand National
A lady detective exposes a fake spiritualist.
A would-be series character bites the dust through plot malnutrition.
w Fred Elles, Peggy Barwell, Nigel Morland *novel* Nigel Morland *d* Fred Elles
☆ Mary Clare, Edward Lexy, Nigel Patrick, Anthony Ireland, Irene Handl

Mrs Soffel
US 1984 110m Metrocolor
MGM-UA/Edgar Scherick/Scott Rudin

In 1901 Pittsburgh, a warder's wife falls for a prisoner and helps him escape.
A basis in truth does not prevent this from being both glum and dull from beginning to end, and pretentious treatment doesn't help.
w Ron Nyswaner *d* Gillian Armstrong *ph* Russell Boyd *m* Mark Isham *pd* Luciana Arrighi *ed* Nicholas Beauman
☆ Diane Keaton, Mel Gibson, Matthew Modine, Edward Herrmann

Mrs Wiggs of the Cabbage Patch *
US 1934 80m bw
Paramount (Douglas MacLean)
Adventures of a poor family who live on the wrong side of the tracks in a broken down old shack.
A Depression fantasy of respectability and optimism, almost incredible to see now, although it plumbed the same never-never milieu as did Chaplin. Moments of comedy still please, but one does long for Mr Fields's delayed entry.
w William Slavens McNutt, Jane Storm *novel* Alice Hegan Rice *d* Norman Taurog *ph* Charles Lang
☆ Pauline Lord, *ZaSu Pitts*, *W. C. Fields*, Evelyn Venable, Kent Taylor, Charles Middleton, Donald Meek, Edith Fellows, Virginia Weidler, George Breakston
'A nasty all's-right-with-the-world burlesque of poverty, with emotions to tug at such heartstrings as are worn dangling from the mouth.' – *Otis Ferguson*

Mrs Wiggs of the Cabbage Patch
US 1942 80m bw
Paramount
Curiously quick remake, almost word for word, but without the moments of inspiration.
w Doris Anderson, Jane Storm, William Slavens McNutt *d* Ralph Murphy *ph* Leo Tover
☆ Fay Bainter, Hugh Herbert, Vera Vague, Barbara Britton, Carl Switzer, Moroni Olsen, Billy Lee

Mrs Winterbourne
US 1996 104m Technicolor
TriStar/A&M (Dale Pollock, Ross Canter, Oren Koules)

A poor, pregnant woman is mistaken for the widow of a millionaire and taken in by his family.
A thriller is here turned into a family comedy for no good reason.
w Phoef Sutton, Lisa-Maria Radano *story* *I Married a Dead Man* by Cornell Woolrich *d* Richard Benjamin *ph* Alex Nepomniaschy *m* Patrick Doyle *pd* Evelyn Sakash *ed* Jacqueline Cambas, William Fletcher
☆ Shirley MacLaine, Ricki Lake, Brendan Fraser, Miguel Sandoval, Loren Dean, Paula Prentiss
'A sappy, old-fashioned and predictable vehicle … that delivers requisite warmth but few laughs.' – *Brian Lowry, Variety*
† It is a remake of *No Man of Her Own* (qv), directed in 1950 by Mitchell Leisen and starring Barbara Stanwyck.

Missiles from Hell: see *The Battle of the V1*

Missing *
US 1982 122m Technicolor
Universal/Polygram/Peter Guber, Jon Peters (Edward and Mildred Lewis)

An American seeks his young son who has disappeared in Chile.
A further link in the chain of political thrillers from this director; well-wrought and compulsive but finally disappointing in its mixture of fact and fiction.
w Costa-Gavras, Donald Stewart *book* Thomas Hauser *d* *Costa-Gavras* *ph* Ricardo Aronovich *m* Vangelis *pd* Peter Jamison *ed* Françoise Bonnot
☆ *Jack Lemmon*, Sissy Spacek, Melanie Mayron, John Shea, Charles Cioffi, Richard Bradford
'Provocation and entertainment prove to be uneasy allies.' – *Tom Milne, MFB*
Academy Award: screenplay (adaptation)
Academy Award nomination: Jack Lemmon; best picture; Sissy Spacek
BAFTA: screenplay

Missing in Action
US 1984 101m Metrocolor
Cannon (Menahem Golan, Yoram Globus)

An American colonel, having been taken prisoner and escaped, returns to Vietnam to find other 'missing' men.
Naïve, violent, jingoistic romp which caused quite a lot of box-office business around the world.
w James Bruner *d* Joseph Zito *ph* Joao Fernandes *m* Jay Chattaway *ad* Ladi Wilheim, Toto Castillo *ed* Joel Goodman
☆ Chuck Norris, M. Emmet Walsh, Lenore Kasdorf, James Hong

Missing in Action 2 – The Beginning
US 1985 95m TVC Color
Cannon (Menahem Golan, Yoram Globus)

A prequel to the above, showing the colonel's first escape.
More cheaply made, it runs like a series of offcuts, with emphasis on unpleasant violence.
w Arthur Silver, Larry Levinson, Steve Bing *d* Lance Hool *ph* Jorge Stahl Jnr *m* Brian May *pd* Michael Baugh *ed* Mark Conte, Marcus Nanton
☆ Chuck Norris, Soon Teck-Oh, Cosie Costa, Steven Williams

The Missing Juror
US 1944 71m bw
Columbia
Members of a murder jury are killed off one by one.
Minor puzzle piece from the I Love a Mystery series.
w Charles O'Neal *d* Budd Boetticher
☆ Jim Bannon, Janis Carter, George Macready

Missing Link
US 1988 92m colour
Universal

A million years in the past, a solitary man-ape, the rest of his kind having been killed by humans, wanders across the African continent.
Quirky film with no dialogue, notable for some arresting wildlife photography – of nature red in tooth and claw – though it does not convince with its creation of a missing link between ape and humans, a hairy, harmless dimwit who walks into trees.
wd David and Carolyn Hughes *sp* make-up: Rick Baker
☆ Peter Elliott, Michael Gambon (narrator)

Missing Pieces
US 1991 92m colour
Rank/Aaron Russo Entertainment

An out-of-work writer and an unemployed musician are pursued by crooks as they try to solve a riddle that will net them a fortune.
A chase comedy that rounds up the usual clichés and then recycles them.
wd Leonard Stern *ph* Peter Stein *m* Marvin Hamlisch *pd* Michael Z. Hanan *ed* Evan Lottman
☆ Eric Idle, Robert Wuhl, Lauren Hutton, Bob Gunton, Richard Belzer, Bernie Kopell, Kim Lankford, Don Gibb

The Missing Rembrandt
GB 1932 82m bw
Twickenham
Sherlock Holmes saves a lady's honour and nails a blackmailer.
Not the best of this particular series, but Wontner is a Holmes to relish.
w Cyril Twyford, H. Fowler Mear *story* *Charles Augustus Milverton* by Arthur Conan Doyle *d* Leslie Hiscott *ph* Basil Emmott
☆ Arthur Wontner, Ian Fleming, Jane Welsh, Miles Mander, Francis L. Sullivan

Missing Ten Days: see *Ten Days in Paris*

The Mission **
GB 1986 128m Rank Colour JDC wide screen
Goldcrest/Kingsmere/Enigma/Fernando Ghia (David Puttnam)

In mid-18th-century South America, Jesuit priests fall foul of avaricious colonialists.
Sincere to the point of boredom, this 22-million-dollar would-be epic is short on plot development, long on superb photography of remote actualities.
w Robert Bolt *d* *Roland Joffé* *ph* *Chris Menges* *m* Ennio Morricone *pd* Stuart Craig, Norman Dorme *ed* Jim Clark
☆ Robert DeNiro, Jeremy Irons, Ray McAnally, Liam Neeson, Aidan Quinn, Ronald Pickup, Cherie Lunghi
Academy Award: Chris Menges
Academy Award nomination: best picture; Roland Joffe; Ennio Morricone; Jim Clark; art direction (Stuart Craig); sound (Jack Stephens); costumes (Enrico Sabbatini)
BAFTA: Ray McAnally; Ennio Morricone

'Expect the impossible.'
Mission: Impossible *
US 1996 110m DeLuxe Panavision
Paramount (Tom Cruise, Paula Wagner)

A secret agent sets out to discover who double-crossed him and killed his colleagues.
A movie very much in the James Bond style, with added paranoia; the gimmick-laden narrative makes little sense, but the set-piece stunts are spectacularly over-the-top.
w David Koepp, Robert Towne, Steven Zaillian *d* Brian de Palma *ph* Stephen H. Burum *m* Danny Elfman *pd* Norman Reynolds *ed* Paul Hirsch *sp* visual: John Knoll; make-up: Rob Bottin
☆ Tom Cruise, Jon Voight, Emmanuelle Beart, Henry Czerny, Jean Reno, Ving Rhames, Kristin Scott-Thomas, Vanessa Redgrave
'A headache with a great soundtrack and some lustrous set pieces.' – *Tom Shone, Sunday Times*
† The film is based on the TV series created by Bruce Geller, which ran from 1967 to 1973 and from 1988 to 1990. The theme music, which was written by Lalo Schifrin and also features in the movie, was a hit in 1968.
†† It was among the box-office successes of 1996, grossing more than $452m around the world.

'Expect the impossible again.'
Mission: Impossible 2
US 2000 123m Technicolor Panavision
Paramount (Tom Cruise, Paula Wagner)

A special agent is ordered to find a deadly virus stolen by a criminal mastermind.
Empty-headed action flick, even more like a James Bond adventure than its predecessor, with a risible narrative gimmick of face-mask disguises; the stunts are often spectacular, but as they are staged like circus turns, they rapidly become uninvolving.
w Robert Towne *story* Ronald D. Moore, Brannon Braga *d* John Woo *ph* Jeffrey L. Kimball *m* Hans Zimmer *pd* Tom Sanders *ed* Christian Wagner, Steven Kemper *cos* Lizzy Gardiner
☆ Tom Cruise (Ethan Hunt), Dougray Scott (Sean Ambrose), Thandie Newton (Nyah Hall), Ving Rhames (Luther Stickell), Richard Roxburgh (Hugh Stamp), John Polson (Billy Baird), Brendan Gleeson (McCloy), Rade Sherbedgia (Dr Nekhorvich), Anthony Hopkins (Boss)
'This self-destructs in 124 minutes.' – *Times*
'A pretty good ride, but so flashy, so empty, so utterly devoid of real risk, real sweat or real danger that in the end it's just *Mission: Improbable* or *Mission: Untenable*.' – *Peter Bradshaw, Guardian*
'Even more empty a luxury vehicle than its predecessor, "M:I 2" pushes the envelope in terms of just how much flashy packaging an audience will buy when there's absolutely nada inside.' – *Dennis Harvey, Variety*
† The film was the biggest international success of 2000, taking $545.4m at the box office worldwide.

Mission in Morocco
US/Spain 1959 79m bw
Republic/John Mather/Hispamer (Sergio Newman)

An oil-man goes to Morocco to investigate the murder of his partner and the whereabouts of a missing microfilm.
Sub-standard action adventure, with acting to match.
w Brian Clemens *story* Guy Elmes, Ken Annakin *d* Anthony Squire *ph* Cecilio Paniagua *m* Guenther Kauer *ad* Tadeo Villalba *ed* Max Benedict
☆ Lex Barker, Juli Reding, Fernando Rey, Silvia Morgan, Alfredo Mayo

'For centuries we've been looking for the origin of life on earth. We've been looking on the wrong planet.'
Mission to Mars
US 2000 112m Technicolor Panavision
Buena Vista/Touchstone (Tom Jacobson)

A rescue party goes to Mars to find the sole survivor of the first manned expedition to the planet, who has discovered evidence that it was once inhabited.
Grandiose attempt at science-fiction with a spiritual message; it never achieves lift-off.
w Jim Thomas, John Thomas, Graham Yost *d* Brian De Palma *ph* Stephen H. Burum *m* Ennio Morricone *pd* Ed Verreaux *ed* Paul Hirsch *sp* Industrial Light & Magic; Dream Quest Images; CIS Hollywood
☆ Gary Sinise (Jim McConnell), Tim Robbins (Woody Blake), Don Cheadle (Luke Graham), Connie Nielsen (Terri Fisher), Jerry O'Connell (Phil Ohlmyer), Kim Delaney (Maggie McConnell), Elise Neal (Debra Graham), Peter Outerbridge (Sergei Kirov), Jill Teed (Renee Cote), Kavan Smith (Nicholas Willis)
'Dull and eventually ludicrous while trying to be moving and profound.' – *Todd McCarthy, Variety*
'It's been a long time since such a grandiloquent souffle of majesty and silliness refused to rise on the big screen.' – *Elvis Mitchell, New York Times*

Mission to Moscow **
US 1943 112m bw
Warner (Robert Buckner)
The Russian career of US Ambassador Joseph E. Davies.
Stodgy but fascinating wartime propaganda piece viewing the Russians as warm-hearted allies; in the

later days of the McCarthy witch hunt, Jack L. Warner regretted he had ever allowed it to be made.
w Howard Koch *book* Joseph E. Davies
d Michael Curtiz *ph* Bert Glennon *m* Max Steiner *ad* Carl Weyl
☆ *Walter Huston*, Ann Harding, Oscar Homolka, George Tobias, Gene Lockhart, Eleanor Parker, Richard Travis, Helmut Dantine, Victor Francen, Henry Daniell, Barbara Everest, Dudley Field Malone, Roman Bohnen, Maria Palmer, Moroni Olsen and also Minor Watson

'A mishmash: of Stalinism with New Dealism with Hollywoodism with opportunism with shaky experimentalism with mesmerism with onanism, all mosaicked into a remarkable portrait of what the makers of the film think the Soviet Union is like – a great glad two-million-dollar bowl of canned borscht, eminently approvable by the Institute of Good Housekeeping.' – *James Agee*

Carl Weyl

The Missionary *
GB 1983 86m colour Panavision
HandMade Films (Michael Palin)

In 1906, a clergyman returns from darkest Africa and sets up a Mission to Fallen Women in the East End of London.
Sporadically amusing comedy of a reformer being tempted; the decoration is funnier than the central theme.
w Michael Palin *d* Richard Loncraine *ph* Peter Hannan *m* Mike Moran *ad* Norman Garwood
☆ Michael Palin, Maggie Smith, Michael Hordern, Trevor Howard, Denholm Elliott, Graham Crowden, Phoebe Nicholls, Roland Culver

'It leaves one with a half-frozen smile, in anticipation of a comic fulfilment which never quite happens.' – *Nick Roddick, MFB*

'A deliciously straight-faced acceptance of the palpably absurd.' – *Daily Mail*

Mississippi *
US 1935 75m bw
Paramount (Arthur Hornblow Jnr)
A showboat singer has a cloud on his reputation.
Mild period musical with occasional stops for comedy.
w Herbert Fields, Claude Binyon *story* Booth Tarkington *d* A. Edward Sutherland *ph* Charles Lang *m/ly* Rodgers and Hart
☆ Bing Crosby, W. C. Fields, Joan Bennett, Gail Patrick, Claude Gillingwater, John Miljan, Queenie Smith

'A dull film, rambling and hokey.' – *Variety*

Mississippi Burning **
US 1988 127m DeLuxe
Rank/Orion (Frederick Zollo, Robert F. Colesberry)

In Mississippi in the mid-1960s, FBI agents investigate the murder of three civil rights workers.
Melodramatic and sensational account of racism in action that caused controversy on its release because of its concentration on white activists; but it has a power that sweeps its audience along with it.
w Chris Gerolmo *d* Alan Parker *ph* *Peter Biziou*
m Trevor Jones *pd* Philip Harrison, Geoffrey Kirkland *ed* Gerry Hambling
☆ Gene Hackman, Willem Dafoe, Frances McDormand, Brad Dourif, R. Lee Ermey, Gailard Sartain, Stephen Tobolowsky, Michael Rooker, Pruitt Taylor Vince

Peter Biziou

best picture; Alan Parker; Gene Hackman; Frances McDormand; Gerry Hambling; best sound

Peter Biziou

Mississippi Gambler
US 1953 98m Technicolor
U-I (Ted Richmond)
A showboat gambler has trouble with a bad loser, but finally marries his sister.
Picturesque star melodrama with period settings and not much meat in the story.
w Seton I. Miller *d* Rudolph Maté *ph* Irving Glassberg *m* Frank Skinner
☆ Tyrone Power, Piper Laurie, John McIntire, Julia Adams, Dennis Weaver

'Romeo And Juliet Had It Easy.'
Mississippi Masala *
US 1991 113m colour
SCS/Odyssey/Cinecom/Film Four/Mirabai/Movieworks/Black River (Michael Nozick, Mira Nair)

A young Asian woman living in Mississippi falls in love with a black American, to the distress of both their families.
Uninvolving treatment of romance and racism.
w Sooni Taraporevala *d* Mira Nair *ph* Ed Lachman *m* L. Subramaniam *pd* Mitch Epstein *ed* Roberto Silvi
☆ Denzel Washington, Roshan Seth, Sarita Choudhury, Charles S. Dutton, Joe Seneca, Sharmila Tagore, Ranjit Chowdhry

'A film about racial issues which manages to avoid hatred and this leaves a joyously hopeful, if occasionally naive, aftertaste.' – *Empire*

The Mississippi Mermaid *
France/Italy 1969 123m Eastmancolor Dyaliscope
Films du Carrosse/PAA/Delphos (Marcel Berbert)

original title: *La Sirène du Mississippi*
After a courtship by mail, a factory owner on a remote African island finds that the girl who arrives by steamer does not fit his preconceptions...
Oddly obsessive romantic murder mystery: the hero continues to love the girl who tries to kill him, and at the end they are still together. Interesting when it is not uncomfortable.
wd François Truffaut *novel* *Waltz into Darkness* by William Irish *ph* Denys Clerval *m* Antoine Duhamel *ad* Claude Pignot *ed* Agnès Guillemot
☆ Jean-Paul Belmondo, Catherine Deneuve, Michel Bouquet, Nelly Borgeaud, Marcel Berbert

'One Steals. One Kills. One Dies.'
The Missouri Breaks
US 1976 126m DeLuxe
UA/Elliott Kastner/Robert B. Sherman

Montana ranchers and rustlers fight over land and livestock, and a hired killer shoots it out with a horse thief.
Savage, dislikeable Western with both stars over the top.
w Thomas McGuane *d* Arthur Penn *ph* Michael Butler *m* John Williams
☆ Marlon Brando, Jack Nicholson, Randy Quaid, Kathleen Lloyd, Frederic Forrest, Harry Dean Stanton

'It is typical of the film's richness and ambiguity that the title has about five possible punning meanings.' – *Michael Billington, Illustrated London News*

'Although listed as the director, Mr Penn finds himself perched on Brando's knee and manipulated as shamelessly as Edgar Bergen used to waggle Charlie McCarthy.' – *Benny Green, Punch*

'Nothing more than the self-conscious cleverness of some merry prankster with a blanket of scorn for all who don't share his flippancy.' – *William S. Pechter*

'A pair of million dollar babies in a five and ten cent flick.' – *Charles Champlin, Los Angeles Times*

'A picture of which it might be said they shouldn't make 'em like that any more ... a picture that explains very little, including why anyone thought it a work that demanded to be made.' – *Robert Hatch, Nation*

Mister 880 **
US 1950 90m bw
TCF (Julian Blaustein)
An elderly counterfeiter perplexes the US Secret Service.
Whimsical star comedy which moves along cheerfully enough to be a good example of the Hollywood programmer at its prime.
w Robert Riskin *d* Edmund Goulding *ph* Joseph LaShelle *m* Sol Kaplan
☆ *Edmund Gwenn*, Burt Lancaster, Dorothy McGuire, Millard Mitchell

Edmund Gwenn

Mr Ace
US 1946 84m bw
Benedict Bogeaus

A rich, spoiled congresswoman is backed by a gangster but gets religion.
Odd star drama, perfunctorily made.
w Fred Finklehoffe *d* Edwin L. Marin *ph* Karl Struss *m* Heinz Roemheld
☆ Sylvia Sidney, George Raft, Stanley Ridges, Sara Haden, Jerome Cowan

Mr and Mrs North
US 1941 68m bw
Irving Asher/MGM
Mr and Mrs find a corpse in their closet.
Reasonably lively transcription of a Broadway success.
w S. K. Lauren *play* Owen Davis *d* Robert B. Sinclair
☆ Gracie Allen, William Post Jnr, Paul Kelly, Rose Hobart, Virginia Grey, Tom Conway, Felix Bressart, Porter Hall, Millard Mitchell, Keye Luke, Jerome Cowan

Mr and Mrs Smith *
US 1941 95m bw
RKO (Harry E. Edington)

A much-married couple discover that their marriage wasn't legal.
Smartish matrimonial comedy, surprisingly but not obviously by the master of suspense.
w Norman Krasna *d* Alfred Hitchcock *ph* Harry Stradling *m* Edward Ward
☆ Carole Lombard, Robert Montgomery, Gene Raymond, Jack Carson, Philip Merivale, Lucile Watson, William Tracy

'I doubt that your interest or amusement will last as long as the picture.' – *Otis Ferguson*

Mr Arkadin: see *Confidential Report*

Mr Ashton Was Indiscreet: see *The Senator Was Indiscreet*

Mr Baseball
US/Japan 1992 109m DeLuxe Panavision
Buena Vista/Walt Disney/Universal/Outlaw/Pacific Artists/Dentsu (Fred Schepisi, Doug Claybourne, Robert Newmyer)

A failing American baseball player is traded to a Japanese team.
Unhappy comedy of a culture clash, unlikely to be of interest to anyone except the keenest and most undemanding fan of the sport.
w Gary Ross, Kevin Wade, Monte Merrick *story* Theo Pelletier, John Junkerman *d* Fred Schepisi *ph* Ian Baker *m* Jerry Goldsmith *pd* Ted Haworth *ed* Peter Honess
☆ Tom Selleck, Ken Takakura, Aya Takanashi, Dennis Haysbert, Toshi Shioya, Kohsuke Toyohara

'A strikeout is a strikeout. Universal's $40 million-plus exercise in cross-cultural comedy will land in a b.o. league of its own – in the cellar.' – *Variety*

Mr Belvedere Goes to College *
US 1949 88m bw
TCF (Samuel G. Engel)
A self-styled genius goes back to school and helps a college widow.
Flat follow up to Sitting Pretty *(qv), with only a few laughs.*
w Richard Sale, Mary Loos, Mary McCall Jnr
d Elliott Nugent *ph* Lloyd Ahern *m* Alfred Newman
☆ *Clifton Webb*, Shirley Temple, Alan Young, Tom Drake, Jessie Royce Landis, Kathleen Hughes, Taylor Holmes

Mr Belvedere Rings the Bell *
US 1951 87m bw
TCF (André Hakim)
Imperturbable Mr Belvedere enters an old folk's home under false pretences to test his theories of ageing.
A not unagreeable star vehicle for those who can stand the sentiment.
w Ranald MacDougall *play* *The Silver Whistle* by Robert E. McEnroe *d* Henry Koster *ph* Joseph LaShelle *m* Cyril Mockridge
☆ Clifton Webb, Joanne Dru, Hugh Marlowe, Zero Mostel, Doro Merande

Mr Big
US 1943 73m bw
Ken Goldsmith/Universal
Drama school students concoct a musical show.
Tolerable minor showcase for a new young star.
w Jack Pollexfen, Dorothy Bennett *d* Charles Lamont
☆ *Donald O'Connor*, Gloria Jean, Peggy Ryan, Robert Paige, Elyse Knox, Samuel S. Hinds, Florence Bates

Mr Billion *
US 1977 93m DeLuxe
TCF/Pantheon (Gabriel Katzka, Steve Bach, Ken Friedman)

An Italian garage mechanic becomes heir to a vast estate, providing he can get to San Francisco in time for the signing ceremony and outwit the villains trying to stop him.
Moderately engaging old-fashioned comedy-adventure.
w Ken Friedman, Jonathan Kaplan *d* Jonathan Kaplan *ph* Matthew F. Leonetti *m* Dave Grusin
☆ Terence Hill (Mario Girotti), Valerie Perrine, Jackie Gleason, Slim Pickens, William Redfield, Chill Wills

Mr Blandings Builds His Dream House ***
US 1948 84m bw
RKO (Norman Panama, Melvin Frank)

A New York advertising man longs to live in the Connecticut countryside, but finds the way to rural satisfaction is hard.
It hasn't the lightness and brightness of the book, but this is a fun film for the middle-aged who like to watch three agreeable stars doing their thing.
w *Norman Panama, Melvin Frank* *novel* *Eric Hodgins* *d* H. C. Potter *ph* James Wong Howe *m* Leigh Harline *md* Constantin Bakaleinikoff *ad* Albert S. D'Agostino, Carroll Clark *ed* Harry Marker
☆ *Cary Grant* (Jim Blandings), *Myrna Loy* (Muriel Blandings), *Melvyn Douglas* (Bill Cole), *Reginald Denny* (Simms), Louise Beavers (Gussie), Ian Wolfe (Smith), Harry Shannon (Tesander), Nestor Paiva (Joe Apollonio), Jason Robards (John Retch), Lex Barker (Carpenter Foreman)

'A bulls-eye for middle-class middlebrows.' – *James Agee*

'I loved it. That was really a pleasure to make.' – *H. C. Potter, 1973*

Mister Buddwing
US 1966 99m bw
MGM/DDD/Cherokee (Douglas Laurence, Delbert Mann)
GB title: *Woman without a Face*
An amnesiac wakes up in Central Park and goes in search of his identity.
Rather muddled melodrama in which the characters are so dull that by the time the flashbacks fall into place we scarcely care.
w Dale Wasserman *novel* *Buddwing* by Evan Hunter *d* Delbert Mann *ph* Ellsworth Fredericks *m* Kenyon Hopkins
☆ James Garner, Jean Simmons, Angela Lansbury, Suzanne Pleshette, Katharine Ross, George Voskovec, Jack Gilford, Joe Mantell, Raymond St Jacques

'Its distinction is its pretension, its banality and its complete success in making all the authentic New York backgrounds look like the studio's cheaper backdrops.' – *Judith Crist*

Mr Bug Goes to Town *
US 1941 78m Technicolor
Max Fleischer

aka: *Hoppity Goes to Town*
An urban community of insects is in danger from developers.
A cartoon feature which failed to make its mark despite clever detail; perhaps because insects make poor heroes, or because there simply wasn't enough plot.
d Dave Fleischer *m* Leigh Harline

Mr Chedworth Steps Out
Australia 1939 92m bw
Cinesound
In a period of redundancy a clerk has to take a job as a caretaker, but discovers a cache of counterfeit money.
Mild comedy-drama.

w Frank Harvey *d* Ken G. Hall
☆ Cecil Kellaway, Jean Hatton, James Raglan, Rita Pauncefort, Peter Finch

Mister Cinderella
US 1936 75m bw
Hal Roach/MGM
A meek-and-mild youth aspires to crash high society.
Milk-and-water comedy with insufficient get-up-and-go.
w Arthur Vernon Jones, Richard Flournoy, Jack Jevne *d* Edward Sedgwick
☆ Jack Haley, Betty Furness, Arthur Treacher, Raymond Walburn, Rosina Lawrence, Monroe Owsley

'Too crammed with slaptrap hokum to stand alone.' – *Variety*

Mister Cory
US 1957 92m Eastmancolor Cinemascope
U-I (Robert Arthur)
A small-time gangster leaves the Chicago slums to seek fame and fortune among the country-club set.
Modest star comedy drama.
wd Blake Edwards *ph* Russell Metty *m* Joseph Gershenson
☆ Tony Curtis, Martha Hyer, Charles Bickford, Kathryn Grant

'Don't let the fancy clothes fool you.'
Mr Deeds
US 2002 96m colour
Columbia/New Line/Happy Madison/Out of the Blue (Sid Ganis, Jack Giarraputo)
A small town pizzeria owner inherits a $40m media empire and outfoxes big city swindlers.
Witless and banal movie with moments of crude slapstick and cruder jokes.
w Tim Herlihy *story* Clarence Budington Kelland *film* Mr. Deeds Goes to Town by Robert Riskin, *d* Frank Capra *d* Steven Brill
☆ Adam Sandler (Longfellow Deeds), Winona Ryder (Babe Bennett), Peter Gallagher (Chuck Cedar), Jared Harris (Mac McGrath), Allen Covert (Marty), Erick Avari (Cecil Anderson), John Turturro (Emilio Lopez), Peter Dante (Murph), Conchata Ferrell (Jan), Harve Presnell (Preston Blake), Steve Buscemi (Crazy Eyes), John McEnroe (Himself), Rev. Al Sharpton (Himself)

'Might have been thrown together in even less time than it takes Sandler to get dressed in the morning; it feels sort of like the dumbest corporate comedy of 1987.' – *Owen Gleiberman, Entertainment Weekly*

'There is hardly anything more dismaying about American movie-goers than their affection for Sandler: can they not see him for the smug, charmless, oafish berk that he is?' – *Anthony Quinn, Independent*

† The film took more than $126m at the US box-office.

Mr Deeds Goes to Town ***
US 1936 118m bw
Columbia (Frank Capra)
A small-town poet inherits a vast fortune and sets New York on its heels by his honesty.
What once was fresh and charming now seems rather laboured in spots, and the production is parsimonious indeed, but the courtroom scene still works, and the good intentions conquer all.
w Robert Riskin story Opera Hat by Clarence Budington Kelland *d Frank Capra ph* Joseph Walker *m* Adolph Deutsch *md* Howard Jackson
☆ *Gary Cooper*, Jean Arthur, Raymond Walburn, Lionel Stander, Walter Catlett, George Bancroft, Douglass Dumbrille, H. B. Warner, Ruth Donnelly, *Margaret Seddon, Margaret McWade*

'I have an uneasy feeling he's on his way out. He's started to make pictures about themes instead of people.' – *Alistair Cooke*

'Everywhere the picture goes, from the endearing to the absurd, the accompanying business is carried through with perfect zip and relish.' – *Otis Ferguson*

'A comedy quite unmatched on the screen.' – *Graham Greene*

'The film culminates in a courtroom sequence that introduced the word "pixilated" to just about every American home, and set people to examining each other's casual scribbles or sketches – their "doodles".' – *Pauline Kael, 70s*

Frank Capra
best picture; Robert Riskin; Gary Cooper

Mr Denning Drives North
GB 1951 93m bw
London Films (Anthony Kimmins, Stephen Mitchell)
A wealthy man accidentally kills a criminal in love with his daughter; he hides the body, which then disappears.
Initially suspenseful but finally disappointing melodrama which seems to lack a twist or two.
w Alec Coppel *d* Anthony Kimmins *ph* John Wilcox *m* Benjamin Frankel
☆ John Mills, Phyllis Calvert, Sam Wanamaker, Freda Jackson

Mr Destiny
US 1990 105m colour
Buena Vista/Touchstone/Silver Screen Partners IV (James Orr, Jim Cruikshank)
A 35-year-old failure is given the chance to re-live his life as a success.
Dim comedy with the dimmer moral that everyone gets the life they deserve.
w James Orr, Jim Cruickshank *d* James Orr *ph* Alex Thomson *m* David Newman *pd* Michael Seymour *ed* Michael R. Miller
☆ James Belushi, Linda Hamilton, Michael Caine, Jon Lovitz, Hart Bochner, Bill McCutcheon, René Russo

'A heavy-handed by-the-numbers fantasy.' – *Variety*

Mr Dodd Takes the Air
US 1937 78m bw
Warner (Mervyn Le Roy)
A country cousin becomes a hit as a crooner.
Modest comedy for small towns.
w William Wister Haines, Elaine Ryan *story* Clarence Budington Kelland *d* Alfred E. Green *ph* Arthur Edeson *md* Adolph Deutsch *songs* Al Dubin, Harry Warren
☆ Kenny Baker, Jane Wyman, Alice Brady, Gertrude Michael, Frank McHugh, Luis Alberni, Henry O'Neill, Harry Davenport
Al Dubin and Harry Warren for 'Remember Me'

Mr Drake's Duck **
GB 1950 85m bw
Daniel M. Angel/Douglas Fairbanks
A duck lays a uranium egg, and a gentleman farmer finds himself at the centre of international military disagreement.
Brisk and amusing minor comedy deploying British comic types to good purpose.
wd Val Guest radio play Ian Messiter ph Jack Cox *m* Philip Martell
☆ Douglas Fairbanks Jnr, Yolande Donlan, Wilfrid Hyde-White, A. E. Matthews, Jon Pertwee, Reginald Beckwith, Howard Marion-Crawford, Peter Butterworth, Tom Gill

'One of the funniest films I have ever seen.' – *News of the World*

Mr Dynamite
US 1935 75m bw
Universal
An unconventional private detective outsmarts the police.
Amusing, wisecracking crime caper.
w Doris Malloy, Harry Clork *story* Dashiell Hammett *d* Alan Crosland
☆ Edmund Lowe, Jean Dixon, Esther Ralston, Victor Varconi, Minor Watson, Robert Gleckler

'Nice entertainment.' – *Variety*

Mr Emmanuel *
GB 1944 97m bw
Two Cities (William Sistrom)
In 1936 an elderly Jew visits Germany in search of the mother of an orphan boy.
Simply made but quite effective and unusual story giving Aylmer his only star part.
w Gordon Wellesley, Norman Ginsburg *novel* Louis Golding *d* Harold French *ph* Otto Heller
☆ *Felix Aylmer*, Greta Gynt, Walter Rilla, Peter Mullins, Ursula Jeans, Elspeth March, Meier Tzelniker

Mr Forbush and the Penguins *
GB 1971 101m Technicolor
EMI/PGI/Henry Trettin
A biologist is sent to the Antarctic to study penguins, and gets a new understanding of life.
Rather broken-backed animal film with a moral; pleasant enough, its two halves don't fit together.
w Anthony Shaffer *novel* Graham Billey *d Roy Boulting, Arne Sucksdorff ph* Harry Waxman, Ted Scaife *m* John Addison
☆ John Hurt, Hayley Mills, Tony Britton, Thorley Walters, Judy Campbell, Joss Ackland, Sally Geeson, Cyril Luckham

Mister Frost
France/GB 1990 104m colour
Blue Dolphin/AAA/Hugo Films/Overseas Multi Media (Xavier Gelin)
The devil incarnate tempts a hospital doctor.
Nonsensical and incomprehensible, a lurid mess from start to finish.
w Philippe Setbon, Brad Lynch *d* Philippe Setbon *ph* Dominique Brenguier *m* Steve Levine *ad* Max Berto *ed* Ray Lovejoy
☆ Jeff Goldblum, Alan Bates, Kathy Baker, Roland Giraud, Jean-Pierre Cassel, Daniel Gelin, François Negret, Maxime Leroux, Boris Bergman

'Staggeringly bad.' – *Philip French, Observer*

Mr Griggs Returns: see *The Cockeyed Miracle*

Mr Hobbs Takes a Vacation *
US 1962 116m DeLuxe Cinemascope
TCF (Jerry Wald)
A city dweller takes a seaside house for a family holiday, but it turns out to be a crumbling ruin.
Overlong, sloppy comedy which devotes too much time to teenage romance but manages occasional smiles.
w Nunnally Johnson *novel* Edward Streeter *d* Henry Koster *ph* W. C. Mellor *m* Henry Mancini
☆ James Stewart, Maureen O'Hara, Fabian, John Saxon, Marie Wilson, Reginald Gardiner, *John McGiver*

Mr Hobo: see *The Guvnor*

Mr Holland's Opus *
US 1995 143m Technicolor Panavision
Polygram/Interscope/Charlie Mopic (Ted Field, Michael Nolin, Robert W. Cort)
An ambitious composer takes a temporary job as a teacher and discovers that his true vocation is to inspire others with a love of music.
A relentlessly corny and sentimental drama that pulls out all the emotional stops as it plays slight variations on the themes of It's a Wonderful Life *and* Goodbye Mr Chips. *Its tone is populist: classical music is regarded as much less fun than jazz or rock.*
w Patrick Sheane Duncan *d* Stephen Herek *ph* Oliver Wood *m* Michael Kamen *pd* David Nichols *ed* Trudy Ship
☆ Richard Dreyfuss, Glenne Headly, Jay Thomas, Olympia Dukakis, W. H. Macy, Alicia Witt, Jean Louisa Kelly, Anthony Natale

'Older audiences will be moved by the story, but the crucial variable is to what extent younger viewers will embrace this schmaltzy, Capraesque saga that's not only set mainly in the past but also feels as if it were made back when.' – *Emanuel Levy, Variety*

Richard Dreyfuss

Mr Imperium
US 1951 87m Technicolor
MGM (Edwin H. Knopf)
GB title: *You Belong to My Heart*
An exiled king in Hollywood meets a famous film star with whom he once had a romance.
Minor romantic drama with songs.
w Edwin Knopf, Don Hartman *d* Don Hartman *ph* George J. Folsey *m* Bronislau Kaper *songs Harold Arlen (m), Dorothy Fields (ly)*
☆ Lana Turner, Ezio Pinza, Marjorie Main, Barry Sullivan, Cedric Hardwicke, Debbie Reynolds

'He's a proper Englishman in his heart. But Africa is in his soul'
Mr Johnson **
US 1990 101m Eastmancolor Panavision
TCF/Avenue Pictures (Michael Fitzgerald)
In West Africa in the 1920s a naïve and feckless clerk, who attempts to be more English than the English, destroys himself by seeking the easy way out of his problems.
Deftly acted and directed tragi-comedy of human fallibility and colonial attitudes.
w William Boyd *novel* Joyce Cary *d* Bruce Beresford *m* Georges Delerue *pd* Herbert Pinter *ed* Humphrey Dixon
☆ Pierce Brosnan, Edward Woodward, *Maynard Eziashi*, Beatie Edney, Denis Quilley, Bella Enahoro, Kwabena Manso, Nick Reding, Femi Fatoba

'Suffers the same fate as its title character, never coming close to being as important as it desperately wants to be.' – *Variety*

'A very generous, thoughtful and affecting movie.' – *Philip French, Observer*

Mr Jones
US 1993 114m Technicolor
Columbia TriStar/Rastar (Alan Greisman, Debra Greenfield)
A manic depressive begins an affair with the psychiatrist who treats him for his condition.
An unsatisfactory movie that was cut by the studio over the director's objections; the result is less a psychological drama than a standard Hollywood romance with a slightly different twist that gives Richard Gere the chance to display energy and charm.
w Eric Roth, Michael Cristofer *d* Mike Figgis *ph* Juan Ruiz Anchia *m* Maurice Jarre *pd* Waldemar Kalinowski *ed* Tom Rolf
☆ Richard Gere, Lena Olin, Anne Bancroft, Bruce Altman, Delroy Lindo, Tom Irwin, Lauren Tom

'Inoffensive rainy afternoon fodder, this is one Jones most cinemagoers would be wise not to keep up with.' – *Film Review*

Mister Kingstreet's War
US 1970 92m colour
H.R.S. Films (Thys Heyns)
aka: *Heroes Die Hard*
In Central Africa in 1939, an American game warden and his wife try to prevent the Italian and British armies from ruining his reserve, which contains the only water-holes in the area.
Clichéd drama – the baddie wears a black eye-patch – that makes no perceptible point and takes little advantage of the local flora and fauna.
w Percival Rubens, George Harding *d* Percival Rubens *ph* Grenville Middleton *m* Harry Sukman *ad* Roy Taylor *ed* John Bushelman
☆ John Saxon, Tippi Hedren, Rossano Brazzi, Brian O'Shaughnessy, Kerry Jordan, Joseph Sekatski

Mr Klein *
France/Italy 1976 123m Eastmancolor
Lira/Adel/Nova/Mondial Te-Fi (Raymond Danon, Alain Delon)
In 1942 Paris, a prosperous antique dealer is mistaken for a mysterious Jew of the same name, and despite the danger gradually assumes his identity.
Complex Kafkaesque character study: occasionally arresting but generally rather glum.
w Franco Solinas *d* Joseph Losey *ph* Gerry Fisher *m* Egisto Macchi, Pierre Porte
☆ Alain Delon, Jeanne Moreau, Suzanne Flon, Michael Lonsdale, Louis Seigner, Juliet Berto

Mr Love
GB 1986 91m colour
Warner/Goldcrest/Enigma (Susan Richards, Robin Douet)
A mild-mannered cinema projectionist develops an erroneous reputation as a Don Juan.
Ineffective character comedy with too few laughs and a minimum of accurate observation.
w Kenneth Eastaugh *d* Roy Battersby *ph* Clive Tickner *m* Willy Russell
☆ Barry Jackson, Maurice Denham, Margaret Tyzack, Linda Marlowe, Cristina Collier

'It renders would-be regional fantasy into something merely parochial.' – *Tim Pulleine, MFB*

Mr Lucky *
US 1943 98m bw
RKO (David Hempstead)

During World War II a gambling ship owner goes straight and instigates Bundles for Britain.
Unconvincing mixture of comedy and drama with the actors looking somewhat bewildered.
w Milton Holmes, Adrian Scott *d* H. C. Potter *ph* George Barnes *m* Roy Webb
☆ Cary Grant, Laraine Day, Charles Bickford, Gladys Cooper, Alan Carney, Henry Stephenson, Paul Stewart, Walter Kingsford
'If it weren't for Cary Grant's persuasive personality the whole thing would melt away to nothing at all.' – *Philip G. Hartung*
† Remade 1950 as *Gambling House*.

Mr Magoo
US 1997 87m colour
Buena Vista/Walt Disney (Ben Myron)

A myopic millionaire stumbles into trouble.
Tedious live-action version of the briefly witty UPA cartoons of the early 50s, with some misfiring slapstick and ponderous jokes.
w Pat Proft, Tom Sherohman *d* Stanley Tong *ph* Jingle Ma *m* Michael Tavera *pd* John Willett *ed* Stuart Pappe, David Rawlins, Michael R. Miller
☆ Leslie Nielsen, Kelly Lynch, Matt Keeslar, Nick Chinlund, Stephen Tobolowsky, Ernie Hudson, Jennifer Garner, Malcolm McDowell, Miguel Ferrer
'Unlikely to engage the younger audience for whom it is so obviously intended. When even the outtakes you see over the end titles don't raise a single titter, you know you're in trouble.' – *Bob McCabe, Empire*
† The National Federation of the Blind asked Disney to halt production because the character was insulting to the visually impaired. The credits include the announcement: 'Nothing in Mr Magoo should be interpreted as an accurate portrayal of blindness or poor eyesight.'

Mr Majestyk *
US 1974 103m DeLuxe
UA/Mirisch (Walter Mirisch)
A Colorado melon grower crosses swords with the local Mafia.
Violent but unexpectedly enjoyable action melodrama.
w Elmore Leonard *d* Richard Fleischer *ph* Richard Kline *m* Charles Bernstein
☆ Charles Bronson, Al Lettieri, Linda Cristal, Lee Purcell, Paul Keslo
'What I liked best about this trash is that Bronson begins each action sequence like Nureyev beginning a difficult solo.' – *Stanley Kauffmann*

Mr Mom
US 1983 91m Metrocolor
Fox/Sherwood (Lynn Loring)

GB title: *Mr Mum*
Dad loses his executive job and stays home to mind the kids while his wife works.
Obvious farce with too much messy slapstick and no real development.
w John Hughes *d* Stan Dragoti *ph* Victor J. Kemper *m* Lee Holdridge *pd* Alfred Sweeney *ed* Patrick Kennedy
☆ Michael Keaton, Teri Garr, Frederick Koehler, Martin Mull, Ann Jillian
'The jokes almost sink without trace in a hazy domestic setting straight from the hoariest sitcom.' – *Geoff Brown, MFB*

Mister Moses *
GB 1965 103m Technicolor Panavision
UA/Frank Ross/Talbot
A quack doctor is the only person who can persuade an African tribe to move before their land is flooded, and he leads them to their promised land.
Adventure spectacle with naïve biblical parallels; quite agreeable.
w Charles Beaumont, Monja Danischewsky *novel* Max Catto *d* Ronald Neame *ph* Oswald Morris *m* John Barry
☆ Robert Mitchum, Carroll Baker, Ian Bannen, Alexander Knox, Reginald Beckwith, Raymond St Jacques

Mr Moto
The Japanese detective created by John P. Marquand and played by Peter Lorre figured in several above-average second features of the late thirties, but the outbreak of war caused him to vanish.
The casts were interesting, the TCF production excellent, and the director usually Norman Foster. The 1965 attempt to revive the character with Henry Silva was painfully boring.
1937 Think Fast Mr Moto (with Virginia Field, Sig Rumann), Thank You Mr Moto (with Pauline Frederick, Sidney Blackmer)
1938 Mr Moto's Gamble (qv) (with Keye Luke, Lynn Bari), Mr Moto Takes a Chance (qv) (with Rochelle Hudson, J. Edward Bromberg), Mysterious Mr Moto (qv) (with Henry Wilcoxon, Erik Rhodes)
1939 Mr Moto's Last Warning (qv) (with Ricardo Cortez, George Sanders, Robert Coote, John Carradine), Mr Moto in Danger Island (qv) (with Jean Hersholt, Warren Hymer), Mr Moto Takes a Vacation (with Joseph Schildkraut, Lionel Atwill)
1965 The Return of Mr Moto

Mr Moto in Danger Island
US 1939 64m bw
TCF
Mr Moto investigates diamond smuggling in Puerto Rico with the aid of a dim-witted wrestler.
Moderately entertaining fast-paced programmer.
w Peter Milne *novel* John W. Vandercook *story* John Reinhardt, George Bricker *d* Herbert I. Leeds *ph* Lucien Andriot *md* Samuel Kaylin *ad* Richard Day, Chester Gore *ed* Harry Reynolds
☆ Peter Lorre, Jean Hersholt, Amanda Duff, Warren Hymer, Richard Lane, Leon Ames, Douglas Dumbrille
† Rewritten to feature Moto, the film was a remake of *Murder in Trinidad* (qv), which was made in 1934 by Seton I. Miller, starring Nigel Bruce. It was the last of the Moto series to be made, though it was released before *Mr Moto Takes a Vacation*.

Mr Moto Takes a Chance
US 1938 63m bw
TCF
Mr Moto thwarts two rebellions and helps save the life of a spy and two naïve American film-makers.
Enjoyable, though silly, jungle adventure set in Indonesia.
w Lou Breslow, John Patrick *story* Willis Cooper, Norman Foster *d* Norman Foster *ph* Virgil Miller *md* Samuel Kaylin *ad* Albert Hogsett *ed* Nick DeMaggio
☆ Peter Lorre, Rochelle Hudson, Robert Kent, Edward Bromberg, Chick Chandler, George Regis, Fredrik Vogeding

Mr Moto's Gamble
US 1938 71m bw
TCF
Mr Moto investigates the murder of a boxer in the ring.
An enjoyable, if silly, B feature; it is a more conventional mystery than most of the Moto series, owing to its origins as a movie intended to feature Charlie Chan.
w Charles Belden, Jerry Cady *d* James Tinling *ph* Lucien Andriot *ad* Bernard Herzbrun, Haldane Douglas *ed* Nick DeMaggio
☆ Peter Lorre, Keye Luke, Dick Baldwin, Lynn Bari, Douglas Fowley, Jayne Regan, Harold Huber, Maxie Rosenbloom, Ward Bond, Lon Chaney Jnr
† The script was originally intended as a Charlie Chan mystery, but was changed following the death of the star of that series, Warner Oland. It explains the appearance here of Key Luke as Chan's Number One son.

Mr Moto's Last Warning
US 1939 71m bw
TCF

Mr Moto outwits agents and double agents who gather in Port Said to scupper the French fleet in the Suez Canal.
Pleasant thriller with some heavy-handed comedy but displaying a notable collection of suave villains.
w Philip MacDonald, Norman Foster *d* Norman Foster *ph* Virgil Miller *md* Samuel Kaylin *pd* Bernard Herzbrun, Lewis Creber *ed* Norman Colbert
☆ Peter Lorre, Ricardo Cortez, Virginia Field, John Carradine, George Sanders, Joan Carol, Robert Coote, Leyland Hodgson

Mr & Mrs Bridge **
US 1990 124m Technicolor
Palace/Cineplex Odeon/Merchant Ivory/Robert Halmi (Ismail Merchant)

An inhibited lawyer snuffs out his wife's individuality during a long and apparently happy marriage.
Intriguing portrait of two self-limiting lives, made more effective by being played by a real-life husband and wife.
w Ruth Prawer Jhabvala *novels* Evan S. Connell *d* James Ivory *ph* Tony Pierce-Roberts *m* Richard Robbins *pd* David Gropman *ed* Humphrey Dixon
☆ *Paul Newman, Joanne Woodward*, Robert Sean Leonard, Margaret Walsh, Kyra Sedgwick, Blythe Danner, Simon Callow, Saundra McClain
'Brilliantly written and acted, and immensely watchable.' – *MFB*
Joanne Woodward

Mr Muggs Rides Again
US 1945 63m bw
Monogram/Pathé/Banner (Sam Katzman, Jack Dietz)
Framed by his crooked employer and suspended, a jockey rights wrongs and rides a winner.
Familiar East Side Kids material, mixing gangsters and guns, romance and gags in which the cast go through their usual routines with a notable lack of interest and enthusiasm.
w Harvey H. Gates *d* Wallace Fox *ph* Ira Morgan *md* Edward Kay *ad* David Milton *ed* William Austin
☆ Leo Gorcey, Huntz Hall, Billy Benedict, Nancy Brinkman, Bernard Thomas, George Meeker, Minerva Urecal, Johnny Duncan, Milton Kibbee

Mr Mum: see *Mr Mom*

Mr Music *
US 1950 113m bw
Paramount (Robert L. Welch)

A college girl is employed to keep an idle middle-aged songwriter's nose to the grindstone.
Bland musical remake of Accent on Youth *(qv); pleasant performances, moments of comedy, guest stars.*
w Arthur Sheekman *play* Samson Raphaelson *d* Richard Haydn *ph* George Barnes *ad* Hans Dreier, Earl Hedrick *songs* Johnny Burke, James Van Heusen
☆ Bing Crosby, Nancy Olson, Charles Coburn, Ruth Hussey, Marge and Gower Champion, Peggy Lee, Groucho Marx

Mr Nanny
US 1992 84m colour
Entertainment (Bob Engelman)

A child-hating wrestler acts as a bodyguard to the two small and mischievous children of an inventor.
Wearying comedy that might amuse the very young, in which Hulk Hogan can be seen trying, and failing, to find a suitable role for himself in the movies.
w Edward Rugoff, Michael Gottlieb *d* Michael Gottlieb *ph* Peter Stein *m* David Johansen, Brian Koonin *pd* Don de Fina *ed* Earl Ghaffari, Michael Ripps
☆ Terry 'Hulk' Hogan, Sherman Hemsley, Austin Pendleton, Robert Gorman, Madeline Zima, Raymond O'Connor, David Johansen
'A banal exercise in low-budget comedy.' – *Sight and Sound*

'Fight First ... Apologise Later.'
Mr Nice Guy *
Hong Kong 1997 113m Cineart Panavision
New Line/Raymond Chow/Golden Harvest (Chua Lam)

A television chef goes to the aid of an investigative reporter threatened by a gangster.
An entertaining mix of comedy and martial arts, undemanding to watch and with some enjoyable stunts.
w Edward Tang, Fibe Ma *d* Samo Hung *ph* Raymond Lam *m* J. Peter Robinson *pd* Horace Ma *ed* Peter Cheung
☆ Jackie Chan, Richard Norton, Gabrielle Fitzpatrick, Miki Lee, Karen McLymont, Vince Poletto, Barry Otto, Samo Hung
'Chock-a-block with stunts and gags ... definitely ranks as one of his most entertaining outings. Properly promoted and positioned, the film could prove to be his most popular outside Asia.' – *Leonard Klady, Variety*

Mr North *
US 1988 93m Metrocolor
Columbia TriStar/Heritage Entertainment/Showcase Productions (Steven Haft, Skip Steloff)

In the wealthy society of Newport in the 1920s, a young man angers the local doctor by gaining a reputation as a miracle healer.
Gentle, amusing fable, peopled by some engaging eccentrics.
w Janet Roach, John Huston, James Costigan *novel* Theophilus North by Thornton Wilder *d* Danny Huston *ph* Robin Vidgeon *m* David McHugh *pd* Eugene Lee *ed* Roberto Silvi
☆ Anthony Edwards, Robert Mitchum, Lauren Bacall, Harry Dean Stanton, Anjelica Huston, Mary Stuart Masterson, Virginia Madsen, Tammy Grimes, David Warner

Mr Peabody and the Mermaid
US 1948 89m bw
U-I (Nunnally Johnson)

A middle-aged husband imagines an affair with a mermaid.
Bone-headed quick-cash-in on Miranda *(qv); it never begins to work.*
w Nunnally Johnson *novel* Guy and Constance Jones *d* Irving Pichel *ph* Russell Metty *m* Robert Emmett Dolan
☆ William Powell, Ann Blyth, Irene Hervey, Andrea King, Clinton Sundberg

Mr Perrin and Mr Traill *
GB 1948 92m bw
GFD/Two Cities (Alexander Galperson)
A handsome young master at a boys' school incurs the jealousy of an embittered colleague.
Flat, over-acted but mildly watchable picturization of a well-known story.
w L. A. G. Strong *novel* Hugh Walpole *d* Lawrence Huntington *ph* Erwin Hillier *m* Alan Gray *ad* Tom Orahan
☆ Marius Goring, David Farrar, Greta Gynt, Edward Chapman, Raymond Huntley, Mary Jerrold, Finlay Currie, Ralph Truman

Mr Potts Goes to Moscow: see *Top Secret*

Mister Quilp
GB 1975 119m Technicolor Panavision
Reader's Digest (Helen M. Straus)
aka: *The Old Curiosity Shop*
In 1840 London, an antique-shop owner is in debt to a hunchback moneylender who has designs on his business.
The novel, with its villainous lead, is a curious choice for musicalizing, and in this treatment falls desperately flat, with no sparkle of imagination visible anywhere.
w Louis Kamp, Irene Kamp *novel* The Old Curiosity Shop by Charles Dickens *d* Michael Tuchner *ph* Christopher Challis *m* Anthony Newley *md* Elmer Bernstein *ch* Gillian Lynne *pd* Elliot Gould
☆ Anthony Newley, Michael Hordern, David Hemmings, Sarah-Jane Varley, David Warner, Paul Rogers, Jill Bennett
'Another soggy piece of family entertainment from Reader's Digest, who produced the toothless screen musicals of Tom Sawyer and Huckleberry Finn.' – *Philip French*
'Dickens shorn of sentiment, melodrama or love ... Mr Newley's Quilp, a galvanized Quasimodo on a permanent high, is something of a strain to watch.' – *Michael Billington, Illustrated London News*

'A wickedly comic tale of cold drinks, Barbies, a seige [sic], & a shot dog!'
'An unbelievable true story.'

Mr Reliable (A True Story)

Australia 1996 113m Cinevex
Polygram/AFFC/Hayes McElroy/Specific (Jim McElroy, Terry Hayes, Michael Hamlyn)

Police mistakenly believe that a convict is holding his girlfriend and her child hostage and besiege his house.
A ramshackle, misfiring comedy, apparently based on an actual incident in 1968, but with little sense of reality in evidence.
w Don Catchlove, Terry Hayes *d* Nadia Tass *ph* David Parker *m* Philip Judd *pd* Jon Dowding *ed* Peter Carrodus
☆ Colin Friels, Jacqueline McKenzie, Paul Sonkkila, Frank Gallacher, Lisa Hensley, Aaron Blabey, Geoff Morrell, Neil Fitzpatrick
'You should enjoy this charming, riotous comedy as a satire on the Australian condition.' – *Film Review*

Mr Ricco

US 1975 98m colour Panavision
MGM (Douglas Netter)
A defence counsel risks his life to prove his black client innocent.
Complex urban action thriller with a tired, ageing hero and impenetrable plot.
w Robert Hoban *d* Paul Bogart *ph* Frank Stanley *m* Chico Hamilton
☆ Dean Martin, Eugene Roche, Thalmus Rasulala, Denise Nicholas, Cindy Williams, Geraldine Brooks, Frank Puglia

Mister Roberts **

US 1955 123m Warnercolor Cinemascope
Warner/Leland Hayward

Life aboard a World War II cargo ship yearning for action.
A mixture of comedy and sentimentality which has become an American minor classic as a play; this film version is a shambling affair but gets most of the effects over.
w Frank Nugent, Joshua Logan *play* Thomas Heggen and Joshua Logan *novel* Thomas Heggen *d* John Ford, Mervyn Le Roy *ph* Winton Hoch *m* Franz Waxman
☆ *Henry Fonda, James Cagney, William Powell, Jack Lemmon*, Betsy Palmer, Ward Bond, Phil Carey, Ken Curtis, Harry Carey Jnr
'Probably the most eagerly awaited movie of the year. It is also one of the best.' – *Newsweek*
Jack Lemmon
best picture

Mr Robinson Crusoe

US 1932 76m bw
Douglas Fairbanks

A playboy takes a bet that he could live alone on a desert island ... but a girl turns up.
Mild adventure comedy with the star in subdued form.
w Douglas Fairbanks *d* A. Edward Sutherland *ph* Max Dupont *m* Alfred Newman
☆ Douglas Fairbanks, William Farnum, Earle Browne, Maria Alba

'A man so evil – his face could stop a heart!'

Mr Sardonicus

US 1961 90m bw
Columbia/William Castle
A surgeon is lured to an ex-girlfriend's remote home to cure her sadistic husband's crippled face.
Flatly handled, boring semi-horror.
w Robb White *d* William Castle *ph* Burnett Guffey *m* Von Dexter
☆ Ronald Lewis, Guy Rolfe, Audrey Dalton, Oscar Homolka

'It's lonely at the middle.'

Mr Saturday Night *

US 1992 119m colour
Columbia/Castle Rock/New Line (Billy Crystal)

In his dotage, a successful comedian looks back over his long career.
Intermittently amusing comedy, not helped by over-generous dollops of sentimentality.
w Billy Crystal, Lowell Ganz, Babaloo Mandel *d* Billy Crystal *ph* Don Peterman *m* Marc Shaiman *pd* Albert Brenner *ed* Kent Beyda
☆ Billy Crystal, David Paymer, Julie Warner, Helen Hunt, Ron Silver
'What's so special about this movie is that the funny parts are so funny, with gags coming too fast and too good to be assimilated on first hearing. At such moments, the main reaction is exhausted gratitude. It's as if you hired a painter to do your bathroom and he gave you the Sistine Chapel at no extra cost.' – *Richard Corliss, Time*
David Paymer

Mr Scoutmaster

US 1953 87m bw
TCF
A TV personality wants to understand children and is persuaded to take over a scout troop.
A star vehicle which starts promisingly enough in the Sitting Pretty *vein but quickly falls headlong into an abyss of sentimentality.*
w Leonard Praskins, Barney Slater *d* Henry Levin *ph* Joseph LaShelle *m* Cyril Mockridge *md* Lionel Newman
☆ Clifton Webb, Edmund Gwenn, George Winslow, Frances Dee, Veda Ann Borg

Mr Skeffington ***

US 1944 127m bw
Warner (Julius J. and Philip G. Epstein)

A selfish beauty finally turns to her discarded dull husband; when he is blind, he doesn't mind her faded looks.
Long, patchily made, but thoroughly enjoyable star melodrama.
w Julius J. and Philip G. Epstein *novel Elizabeth von Arnim* *d* Vincent Sherman *ph* Ernest Haller *m* Franz Waxman
☆ *Bette Davis, Claude Rains*, Walter Abel, Richard Waring, George Coulouris, John Alexander, Jerome Cowan
'An endless woman's page dissertation on What To Do When Beauty Fades.' – *James Agee*
'To call the film a good one would be to exaggerate; but entertaining and interesting, I insist, it is.' – *Richard Mallett, Punch*
Bette Davis; Claude Rains

Mr Skitch

US 1933 70m bw
Fox
A Missouri family heads for California.
Very passable star family entertainment.
w Anne Cameron *novel Green Dice* by Anne Cameron *d* James Cruze
☆ Will Rogers, ZaSu Pitts, Florence Desmond, Rochelle Hudson
'Enough laughs to please in general.' – *Variety*

'Stirring – in the seeing! Precious – in the remembering'

Mr Smith Goes to Washington ****

US 1939 130m bw
Columbia (Frank Capra)

Washington's youngest senator exposes corruption in high places, almost at the cost of his own career.
Archetypal high-flying Capra vehicle, with the little man coming out top as he seldom does in life. Supreme gloss hides the corn, helter-skelter direction keeps one watching, and all concerned give memorable performances. A cinema classic.
w Sidney Buchman *story* Lewis R. Foster *d* Frank Capra *ph* Joseph Walker *m* Dimitri Tiomkin *ad* Lionel Banks *montage* Slavko Vorkapich
☆ *James Stewart, Claude Rains, Jean Arthur, Thomas Mitchell, Edward Arnold*, Guy Kibbee, Eugene Pallette, Beulah Bondi, *Harry Carey*, H. B. Warner, Astrid Allwyn, Ruth Donnelly, Charles Lane, Porter Hall
SMITH (JAMES STEWART): 'I wouldn't give you two cents for all your fancy rules if, behind them, they didn't have a little bit of plain, ordinary kindness – and a little looking out for the other fella, too.'
'Timely and absorbing drama presented in best Capra craftsmanship.' – *Variety*
'More fun, even, than the Senate itself ... not merely a brilliant jest, but a stirring and even inspiring testament to liberty and freedom.' – *Frank S. Nugent, New York Times*
'It says all the things about America that have been crying out to be said again – and says them beautifully.' – *Los Angeles Times*
'The great American picture.' – *Billboard*
'I feel that to show this film in foreign countries will do inestimable harm to American prestige all over the world.' – *Joseph P. Kennedy, then American ambassador to Great Britain*
'A totally compelling piece of movie-making, upholding the virtues of traditional American ideals.' – *NFT, 1973*
'Very good, beautifully done and extremely entertaining; long, but worth the time it takes.' – *Richard Mallett, Punch*
'More of the heartfelt than is good for the stomach.' – *New Yorker, 1977*
Lewis R. Foster
best picture; Sidney Buchman; Frank Capra; Dimitri Tiomkin; James Stewart; Claude Rains; Harry Carey; Lionel Banks

Mr Soft Touch

US 1949 93m bw
Columbia
GB title: *House of Settlement*
A gangster is reformed at Christmas by a social worker.
Dewy-eyed romance with Damon Runyonish asides; only for soft touches.
w Orin Jannings *d* Henry Levin, Gordon Douglas *ph* Joseph Walker *m* Heinz Roemheld
☆ Glenn Ford, Evelyn Keyes, John Ireland, Beulah Bondi, Percy Kilbride, Roman Bohnen

Mister Ten Per Cent

GB 1967 84m Technicolor
ABPC (W. A. Whittaker)

An impresario stages a play, expecting it to flop in order to provide a tax loss, and finds himself with a hit on his hands.
A comedy vehicle for its diminutive, slapstick star, but too ramshackle to carry him very far.
w Norman Hudis, Charlie Drake *story* Mira Avrech *d* Peter Graham Scott *ph* Gerald Gibbs *m* Ron Goodwin *ch* Gillian Lynne *ad* Terence Knight *ed* Jack Harris
☆ Charlie Drake, Derek Nimmo, John Le Mesurier, Wanda Ventham, Anthony Nicholls, Noel Dyson, Ronald Radd, John Laurie, George Baker, Una Stubbs

Mr Topaze

GB 1961 84m Eastmancolor Cinemascope
TCF/Dimitri de Grunwald (Pierre Rouve)
US title: *I Like Money*
An honest ex-schoolmaster becomes prosperous when he joins some shady businessmen.
Predictable, sluggish character comedy, with a good actor unable to make it as a star. Or as a director.
w Pierre Rouve *play Topaze* by Marcel Pagnol *d* Peter Sellers *ph* John Wilcox *m* Georges Van Parys
☆ Peter Sellers, Herbert Lom, Leo McKern, Nadia Gray, Martita Hunt, John Neville, Billie Whitelaw, Michael Gough, Joan Sims, John Le Mesurier, Michael Sellers
'A film of minor pleasures and major inadequacies.' – *Penelope Houston, MFB*
† See also *Topaze* (1933).

Mr Universe

US 1951 79m bw
Laurel/Eagle Lion
Con men promote a new wrestler.
Fair low-class comedy with some laughs.
w Earle Kramer *d* Joseph Lerner *ph* Gerald Hirschfeld *m* Dimitri Tiomkin
☆ Bert Lahr, Jack Carson, Vincent Edwards, Janis Paige, Robert Alda

Mister V: see *Pimpernel Smith*

'Sometimes the wrong person is the only right person for you.'

Mr Wonderful

US 1992 97m Technicolor
Buena Vista/Samuel Goldwyn (Marianne Moloney)

A divorced couple decide to get together again.
A romantic comedy about star-crossed lovers becoming uncrossed that lacks force or passion.
wd Anthony Minghella from original screenplay by Amy Schor, Vicki Polon *ph* Geoffrey Simpson *m* Michael Gore *pd* Doug Kraner *ed* John Tintori
☆ Matt Dillon, Annabella Sciorra, Mary-Louise Parker, William Hurt, Vincent D'Onofrio, David Barry Gray, Dan Hedaya
'Makes a good shot at the difficult assignment of making romantic comedy for a modern audience.' – *Adam Mars-Jones, Independent*

Mr Wong

A cheeseparing set of second features from Monogram, based on stories by Hugh Wiley. *Boris Karloff was unsuitably cast as a Chinese detective, and in the last film he was replaced by Keye Luke. The films were directed by William Nigh.*
1938 Mr Wong Detective
1939 The Mystery of Mr Wong, Mr Wong in Chinatown
1940 The Fatal Hour, Doomed to Die (GB title: The Mystery of the Wentworth Castle)
1941 Phantom of Chinatown

Mr Wrong *

New Zealand 1985 89m colour
NZFC/Barclays (Robin Laing, Gaylene Preston)

aka: *Dark of the Night*
A young woman moves to the big city and discovers that the car she buys to make weekend visits to her parents appears to be haunted by a woman who was murdered by a hitch-hiker.
An intriguing psychological thriller, though occasionally it makes heavy weather of marrying its ghost story with a feminist account of a woman trying to survive among predatory men.
w Gaylene Preston, Geoff Murphy, Graeme Tetley *story* Elizabeth Jane Howard *d* Gaylene Preston *ph* Thom Burstyn *m* Jonathan Crayford *ad* Mike Becroft *ed* Simon Reece
☆ Heather Bolton, David Letch, Perry Piercy, Suzanne Lee, Margaret Umbers, Danny Mulheron, Gary Stalker, Kate Harcourt

'He loved her from afar. It wasn't far enough.'

Mr Wrong

US 1995 97m Technicolor
Buena Vista/Touchstone/Mandeville (Marty Katz)

A single 31-year-old woman discovers that her new romance is not the sensitive caring person he appears to be.
Weak one-joke comedy, so ill-constructed that all its jokes fall flat.
w Chris Matheson, Kerry Ehrin, Craig Munson *d* Nick Castle *ph* John Schwartzman *m* Craig Safan *pd* Doug Kraner *ed* Patrick Kennedy *cos* Ingrid Ferrin
☆ Ellen DeGeneres (Martha Alston), Bill Pullman (Whitman Crawford), Joan Cusack (Inga), Dean Stockwell (Jack Tramonte), John Livingston (Walter), Robert Goulet (Dick Braxton), Ellen Cleghorne (Jane), Polly Holiday (Mrs Alston), Camille Saviola (Consuela), Joan Plowright (Mrs Crawford), Hope Davis (Annie), Brad Henke (Bob)
'Takes an overworked genre – modern, angst-ridden romance – and drives it right around the bend.' – *John Anderson, LA Times*

Mr Wu *

US 1927 80m approx (24 fps) bw silent
MGM
A Chinese villain kills his daughter when she wants to marry an Englishman.
Turgid outmoded melodrama from a stage success: purely a star vehicle.
w Lorna Moon *play* Maurice Vernon, Harold Owen *d* William Nigh *ph* John Arnold
☆ Lon Chaney, Louise Dresser, Anna May Wong, Ralph Forbes, Renee Adoree, Holmes Herbert

Il Mistero di Oberwald: see *The Oberwald Mystery*

'Everybody's trying to get their girlfriend into the movies...'

Mistress *

US 1992 110m CFI color
Tribeca (Meir Teper, Robert DeNiro)

A writer-director discovers that all those approached to finance his movie have girlfriends who want a leading part in it, providing he changes the script to suit them.
Enjoyable satire on the dangers of integrity among minor players in a movie-making industry.
w Barry Primus, Jonathan L. Lawton *d* Barry Primus *ph* Sven Kirsten *m* Galt MacDermot *pd* Phil Peters *ed* Steve Weisberg

☆ Robert Wuhl, Martin Landau, Robert DeNiro, Jace Alexander, Laurie Metcalf, Danny Aiello, Christopher Walken, Eli Wallach, Tuesday Weld, Sheryl Lee Ralph, Ernest Borgnine

'Can't seem to decide if it's supposed to be a comedy about Hollywood small-timers trying to get an indie pic off the ground, or a somber drama in which greed and lust overwhelm art.' – *Variety*

Mix Me a Person

GB 1961 116m bw
Wessex (Sergei Nolbandov)

A barrister's psychiatrist wife takes on one of his failures, a client condemned to death for murder.
Once it gets started, a routine suspense thriller with the wrong man convicted and an espresso bar background. Not a very good one, though.
w Ian Dalrymple *novel* Jack Trevor Story *d* Leslie Norman *ph* Ted Moore *md* Muir Mathieson *songs* Johnny Worth
☆ Anne Baxter, Donald Sinden, Adam Faith, Walter Brown, Glyn Houston

Mixed Company

US 1974 109m DeLuxe
UA/Cornell (Melville Shavelson)

A basketball coach and his wife adopt several children of different races.
Room for One More *and then some, but not very interesting.*
w Melville Shavelson, Mort Lachman *d* Melville Shavelson *ph* Stan Lazan *m* Fred Karlin *pd* Stan Jolley
☆ Barbara Harris, Joseph Bologna, Lisa Gerritsen, Ariane Heller

Mixed Nuts

US 1995 97m Technicolor
TriStar (Paul Junger Witt, Tony Thomas, Joseph Hartwick)

The staff of a telephone help-line face eviction from their office as they are overwhelmed by eccentrics needing aid.
Absolutely absymal comedy, in which all hands sink without trace, leaving not a joke behind.
w Nora Ephron, Delia Ephron *Film* Le Père Noël est une ordure *d* Nora Ephron *ph* Sven Nykvist *m* George Fenton *pd* Bill Groom *ed* Robert Reitano
☆ Steve Martin, Madeline Kahn, Robert Klein, Anthony LaPaglia, Juliette Lewis, Rob Reiner, Adam Sandler, Rita Wilson, Garry Shandling

'It's a total misfire with no commercial vital signs registering on-screen.' – *Variety*

M'liss

US 1936 66m bw
RKO

A drunkard's daughter washes dishes in a Western saloon.
Laundered and fairly inept family version of a roistering tale.
w Dorothy Yost *story* Bret Harte *d* George Nicholls Jnr
☆ Anne Shirley, Guy Kibbee, John Beal, Douglass Dumbrille, Moroni Olsen, Arthur Hoyt

Mo' Better Blues *

US 1990 127m DeLuxe
UIP/40 Acres and a Mule Filmworks/Spike Lee

A jazz trumpeter redeems himself as a person, but loses out as a musician.
An unfocused narrative, caused by trying to say too much about too many things, results in an unsatisfactory film, though it has its moments.
wd Spike Lee *ph* Ernest Dickerson *m* Bill Lee *pd* Wynn Thomas *ed* Sam Pollard
☆ Denzel Washington, Spike Lee, Wesley Snipes, Joie Lee, Cynda Williams, Giancarlo Esposito, Robin Harris, Bill Nunn

'The film's movement is fitful and arbitrary – all mood swings and unpersuasive melodrama.' – *Richard Schickel, Time*

Mo' Money

US 1992 90m colour
Columbia TriStar/Columbia/A Wife N'Kids (Michael Rachmil)

After trying and failing to go straight, a hustler and his brother make money with a stolen credit card but also expose a big-time crook.
A vehicle of dubious morality, with some street-wise comedy, expertly delivered, from its star.
w Damon Wayans *d* Peter Macdonald *ph* Don Burgess *m* Jay Gruska *pd* William Arnold *ed* Hubert C. de La Bouillerie
☆ Damon Wayans, Stacey Dash, Joe Santos, John Diehl, Harry J. Lennix, Marlon Wayans, Mark Beltzman

'The comedy is, in truth, pretty feeble – rancid without the redeeming virtue of wit.' – *Sheila Johnston, Independent*
'If this is grown-up cinema, give me Peter Rabbit.' – *Geoff Brown, The Times*

The Mob *

US 1951 87m bw
Columbia (Jerry Bresler)
GB title: *Remember That Face*

A policeman works undercover to catch a dockside racketeer.
Tough, lively thriller with effectively sustained mystery and a serial-like finale.
w William Bowers d Robert Parrish ph Joseph Walker *m* George Duning
☆ Broderick Crawford, Richard Kiley, Ernest Borgnine, Neville Brand, Charles Bronson

Mob Town

US 1941 61m bw
Universal

A policeman tries to rehabilitate the young brother of an executed gangster.
Another spin-off from the Dead End Kids, quite unremarkable.
w Brenda Weisberg *d* William Nigh
☆ Dick Foran, Anne Gwynne, Billy Halop, Huntz Hall, Bernard Punsley, Gabriel Dell, Samuel S. Hinds

Mobsters

US 1991 104m DeLuxe
Universal (Steve Roth)
GB title: *Mobsters – The Evil Empire*

Four youths grow up to become gangsters Lucky Luciano, Meyer Lansky, Bugsy Siegel and Frank Costello.
Bungled attempt, full of gratuitous violence, to create an adolescent Godfather.
w Michael Mahern, Nicholas Kazan *d* Michael Karbelnikoff *ph* Lajos Koltai *m* Michael Small *pd* Richard Sylbert *ed* Scott Smith, Joe D'Augustine
☆ Christian Slater, Patrick Dempsey, Richard Grieco, Costas Mandylor, F. Murray Abraham, Lara Flynn Boyle, Michael Gambon, Christopher Penn, Anthony Quinn

'Armed with teen appeal thanks to its leads, this hollow pic may mow down strong boxoffice early but will start hemorrhaging quickly as mixed-to-poor word-of-mouth cuts off its legs.' – *Variety*

'America's greatest actor – as you like him!'

Moby Dick *

US 1930 75m bw
Warner

Captain Ahab returns minus a leg from fighting the white whale, and finds that his fiancée is too shocked to love him.
Mangled remake of a fine novel filmed in silent form as The Sea Beast.
w J. Grubb Alexander *novel* Herman Melville *d* Lloyd Bacon *ph* Robert Kurrie
☆ John Barrymore, Joan Bennett, Lloyd Hughes, May Boley, Walter Long

'Money picture, guaranteed by its action and by Barrymore.' – *Variety*

'In All The World – In All The Seas – In All Adventure There Is No Might Like The Might of Moby Dick.'

Moby Dick **

GB 1956 116m Technicolor
Warner/Moulin (John Huston)

A whaling skipper is determined to harpoon the white whale which robbed him of a leg.
Pretentious period adventure, rather too slowly developed, but full of interesting detail which almost outweighs the central miscasting.
w Ray Bradbury, John Huston *novel* Herman Melville *d* John Huston *ph* Oswald Morris *m* Philip Sainton
☆ Gregory Peck, Richard Basehart, Friedrich Ledebur, Leo Genn, Orson Welles, James Robertson Justice, Harry Andrews, Bernard Miles, Noel Purcell, Edric Connor, Joseph Tomelty, Mervyn Johns

'Interesting more often than exciting.' – *Variety*

Mockery

US 1927 75m approx (24 fps) bw silent
MGM

A noble peasant saves a countess from the Russian revolution.
Overly serious vehicle for a star more at ease in melodrama.
wd Benjamin Christensen *ph* Merritt B. Gerstad
☆ Lon Chaney, Barbara Bedford, Ricardo Cortez, Emily Fitzroy, Mack Swain

'Sexy. Cool. Mod.'

The Mod Squad

US 1999 94m DeLuxe
MGM (Ben Myron, Alan Riche, Tony Ludwig)

After infiltrating the counter-culture, three young hippie undercover agents discover that LA cops are involved with drug pushers.
Trivial movie version of an uninteresting TV series that recalls some of the worst of the 'swinging' films of the 60s.
w Stephen Kay, Scott Silver, Kate Lanier *characters created by* Buddy Ruskin *d* Scott Silver *ph* Ellen Kuras *m* B. C. Smith *pd* Patrick Sherman *ed* Dorian Harris
☆ Claire Danes, Giovanni Ribisi, Omar Epps, Dennis Farina, Josh Brolin, Steve Harris, Richard Jenkins, Larry Brandenburg, Lionel Mark Smith, Sam McMurray, Michael Lerner

'Foul word of mouth will spread quickly to send this exercise in pipsqueak crime-fighting back to its vid roots in short order.' – *Todd McCarthy, Variety*

† The TV series ran from 1968 to 1973 and starred Michael Cole, Clarence Williams III and Peggy Lipton as the three agents. It was based on the experiences of its creator, Bud Ruskin, a former cop who had been a member of an undercover narcotics squad.

The Model and the Marriage Broker

US 1951 103m bw
TCF (Charles Brackett)

A broker conceals her profession from a friend but gets the friend fixed up.
Moderate, unsurprising comedy somewhat overweighted by talent which can't express itself.
w Charles Brackett, Walter Reisch, Richard Breen *d* George Cukor *ph* Milton Krasner *m* Cyril Mockridge
☆ Thelma Ritter, Jeanne Crain, Scott Brady, Zero Mostel, Michael O'Shea, Nancy Kulp

The Model Murder Case: see *The Girl in the Headlines*

A Modern Hero *

US 1934 70m bw
Warner

A young circus rider becomes an automobile tycoon but overreaches himself.
Unconvincing moral tale, performed and presented with nice touches.
w Gene Markey, Kathryn Scola *novel* Louis Bromfield *d* G. W. Pabst
☆ Richard Barthelmess, Jean Muir, Marjorie Rambeau, Verree Teasdale, Florence Eldridge

'Essentially weak on plot and characterization.' – *Variety*

A Modern Hero: see *Knute Rockne, All American (1940)*

Modern Love

US 1990 109m CFI color Panavision
Skouras/SVS/Lyric (Robby Benson)

A man and a woman meet, marry, have a child and keep on smiling most of the time.
A story that is about as modern as Adam and Eve; it is given a resolutely old-fashioned comic treatment that quickly becomes tedious.
wd Robby Benson *ph* Christopher G. Tufty *m* Don Peake *pd* Carl E. Copeland *ed* Gib Jaffe
☆ Robby Benson, Karla DeVito, Rue McClanahan, Burt Reynolds, Frankie Valli, Kaye Ballard, Cliff Bemis, Louise Lasser, Lyric Benson

The Modern Miracle: see *The Story of Alexander Graham Bell*

Modern Romance *

US 1981 93m Metrocolor
Columbia (Andrew Scheinman, Martin Shafer)

A film editor leaves his girlfriend, then tries to get her back and becomes jealous of her every move.
Clever study of a neurotic in love, with some good jokes about the film business along the way.
w Albert Brooks, Monica Johnson *d* Albert Brooks *ph* Eric Saarinen *m* Lance Rubin *pd* Edward Richardson *ed* David Finfer
☆ Albert Brooks, Kathryn Harrold, Bruno Kirby, James L. Brooks, Meadowlark Lemon, George Kennedy, Jane Hallaren, Bob Einstein, Albert Henderson

'You'll never laugh as long and as loud again as long as you live! The laughs come so fast and so furious you'll wish it would end before you collapse!'

Modern Times ***

US 1936 87m bw
Charles Chaplin

An assembly-line worker goes berserk but can't get another job.
Silent star comedy produced in the middle of the sound period; flashes of genius alternate with sentimental sequences and jokes without punch.
wd Charles Chaplin *ph* Rollie Totheroh, Ira Morgan *m* Charles Chaplin
☆ *Charles Chaplin, Paulette Goddard*, Henry Bergman, Chester Conklin, Tiny Sandford

'A natural for the world market ... box office with a capital B.' – *Variety*
'A feature picture made out of several one- and two-reel shorts, proposed titles being *The Shop, The Jailbird, The Singing Waiter*.' – *Otis Ferguson*

Modern Vampires

US 1998 95m FotoKem
Storm/Muse (Brad Wyman, Chris Hanley)
GB title: *Revenant*

Vampire fighter Van Helsing co-opts an LA street gang to deal with an infestation of vampires in Hollywood.
A jokey, revisionist take on the vampire myths, with Van Helsing as a crypto-Nazi and Dracula as a ruler under threat from rebel vampires in a society that outdoes them in decadence; a great deal of blood is mixed in with the humour.
w Matthew Bright *d* Richard Elfman *ph* Robin Brown *m* Danny Elfman, Michael Wandmacher *pd* Robyn Costa *ed* Larry Bock
☆ Casper Van Dien (Dallas), Natasha Gregson Wagner (Nico), Gabriel Casseus (Time Bomb), Kim Cattrall (Ulrike), Craig Ferguson (Richard), Natasha Lyonne (Rachel), Natasha Andreichenko (Panthea), Robert Pastorelli (The Count), Udo Kier (Vincent), Rod Steiger (Dr Frederick Van Helsing), Flex (Trigger), Marco Hofschneider (Hans), Conchata Ferrell (Nico's Mom)

'A bloody, ugly, prurient affair that makes everyone connected with it look foolish.' – *Mick LaSalle, San Francisco Chronicle*

El Moderno Barba Azul: see *Boom in the Moon*

The Moderns **

US 1988 126m colour
Rank/Alive Films/Nelson (Carolyn Pfeiffer, David Blocker)

In Paris in the 1920s a struggling American expatriate artist agrees to fake some modern masterpieces.
Witty recreation of the past and an enjoyable dissection of the aspirations of the second-rate.
w Alan Rudolph, Jon Bradshaw *d Alan Rudolph ph* Toyomichoi Kurita *m* Mark Isham *pd* Steven Legler *ed* Debra T. Smith, Scott Brock

☆ Keith Carradine, Linda Fiorentino, Geneviève Bujold, Geraldine Chaplin, Wallace Shawn, John Lone, Kevin O'Connor, Elsa Raven, Ali Giron

'Beautifully shot and impeccably acted all the way down the cast list, weaving an astonishingly complex path through the "seems" and "is" of countless varieties of relationship, *The Moderns* is undoubtedly Rudolph's best film to date.' – *Tom Milne, MFB*

Modesty Blaise
GB 1966 119m Technicolor
TCF/Modesty Blaise Ltd (Joseph Janni)
Female arch-agent Modesty Blaise defends a shipload of diamonds against a sadistic master criminal.
Comic-strip adventures made by people with no sense of humour; Fu Manchu was much more fun.
w Evan Jones *comic strip* Peter O'Donnell, Jim Holdaway *d* Joseph Losey *ph* Jack Hildyard *m* Johnny Dankworth
☆ Monica Vitti, Dirk Bogarde, Terence Stamp, Harry Andrews, Michael Craig, Scilla Gabel, Clive Revill, Rossella Falk, Joe Melia

'Demonstrated that Joseph Losey is completely without a sense of humour when dealing with comedy.' – *Judith Crist*

Modigliani of Montparnasse: see *The Lovers of Montparnasse*

'Flaming love found in the savage heart of the jungle!'
Mogambo *
GB 1953 116m Technicolor
MGM (Sam Zimbalist)
The headquarters of a Kenyan white hunter is invaded by an American showgirl and a British archaeologist and his wife, and they all go off on a gorilla hunt.
Amiable, flabby remake of Red Dust, *with direction scarcely in evidence and the gorillas out-acting a genial cast.*
w John Lee Mahin *d* John Ford *ph* Robert Surtees, F. A. Young *m* A. N. Watkins
☆ Clark Gable, Ava Gardner, Grace Kelly, Donald Sinden, Laurence Naismith, Philip Stainton
† The story was also made as *Congo Maisie* in 1940.
Ava Gardner; Grace Kelly

La Moglie del Prete: see *The Priest's Wife*

Mohammed, Messenger of God
Lebanon 1976 182m Eastmancolor Panavision
Filmco International (Moustapha Akkad)
aka: *The Message*
The life of the seventh-century religious leader.
Predictably reverential and exceedingly tedious religious epic, rather like a lesser de Mille item and fatally handicapped by the decision never to show Mohammed at all.
w H. A. L. Craig (with Arab advice)
d Moustapha Akkad *ph* Jack Hildyard
m Maurice Jarre *pd* Tambi Larsen, Maurice Fowler
☆ Anthony Quinn, Irene Papas, Michael Ansara, Johnny Sekka, Michael Forest, André Morell

'For well over three hours this film stumbles, staggers, lurches and bumbles ahead, without any true rhythm, construction, vision, or even bare minimum of craft.' – *John Simon, New York*

Maurice Jarre

Mohawk
US 1956 79m Pathécolor
National Pictures (Edward L. Alperson)
An artist falls in love with the daughter of an Iriquois chief who is provoked into waging war on the settlers.
Amiable Western, with a modicum of originality in its narrative, though the implausibility of its romance is increased by the unconvincing performances of the actors playing the Indians.
w Maurice Geraghty, Milton Krims *d* Kurt Neumann *ph* Karl Struss *m* Edward L. Alperson Jnr *md* Raoul Kraushaar *pd* Ernst Fegté *ed* William B. Murphy
☆ Scott Brady, Rita Gam, Neville Brand, Allison Hayes, Lori Nelson, John Hoyt, Rhys Williams, Mae Clarke, Tommy Cook, Vera Vague, Ted de Corsia, John Hudson

Moi Drug Ivan Lapshin: see *My Friend Ivan Lapshin*

Le Moine: see *The Monk (1972)*

Mojo
GB 1997 93m Technicolor
Portobello/BBC/British Screen/Mojo (Paul Cowan)
In Soho of the 50s, a club-owner and a gangster battle over who controls a new rock singer.
Lurid melodrama which was a stage success, but transfers uneasily to the screen; it has its moments, particularly in a confrontation between Hart and Pinter, but they are few and far between.
wd Jez Butterworth *play* Jez Butterworth *ph* Bruno de Keyzer *m* Murray Gold *pd* Hugo Luczyc-Wyhowski *ed* Richard Milward
☆ Ian Hart, Ewen Bremner, Aiden Gillen, Martin Gwynn Jones, Hans Matheson, Andy Serkis, Ricky Tomlinson, Harold Pinter

'There's talent and substance to distract in a picture that never quite gels into an effective whole.' – *Darren Bignell, Empire*

'Horror crawls from the depths of the earth!'
The Mole People
US 1956 78m bw
Universal-International
Archaeologists fall down a shaft and find themselves in a subterranean civilization where mole people are ruled by albinos.
Thoroughly boring nonsense which would insult a Saturday matinée.
w Laszlo Gorog *d* Virgil Vogel *ph* Ellis Carter
☆ John Agar, Cynthia Patrick, Hugh Beaumont, Alan Napier

'The remarkable story of one woman's unbreakable spirit.'
Moll Flanders
US 1996 123m DeLuxe 'Scope
TCF/Spelling (John Watson, Richard B. Lewis, Pen Densham)
In 18th-century London, a poor woman becomes a prostitute and wife before escaping to a better life in the New World.
A very free adaptation of Defoe's novel, substituting a less interesting narrative, in which the bawdiness of the original is replaced by a tedious gentility.
wd Pen Densham *based on the character from the novel by* Daniel Defoe *ph* David Tattersall *m* Mark Mancina *pd* Caroline Hanania *ed* Neil Travis, James R. Symons
☆ Robin Wright, Morgan Freeman, Stockard Channing, John Lynch, Brenda Fricker, Geraldine James, Aisling Corcoran, Jim Sheridan, Jeremy Brett, Harry Towb

'Comprehensively dire.' – *Independent*

Molly
Australia 1983 82m colour
NSW Film Corp./Greater Union/M&L (Hilary Linstead)
A little girl, with the help of some circus children, looks after a singing dog when its owner is taken ill.
Amusing, although slow-moving, family film that will appeal most to soft-hearted sub-teens.
w Phillip Roope, Mark Thomas, Hilary Linstead, Ned Lander *d* Ned Lander *ph* Vincent Monton *md* Graeme Isaac *ad* Robert Dein *ed* Stewart Young
☆ Claudia Karvan, Garry McDonald, Reg Lye, Melissa Jaffer, Ruth Cracknell

Molly and Me
US 1945 76m bw
TCF
A cantankerous old man is tamed by his new housekeeper.
Sentimental little star vehicle.
w Leonard Praskins *d* Lewis Seiler *ph* Charles G. Clarke *m* Cyril Mockridge
☆ Gracie Fields, Monty Woolley, Reginald Gardiner, Roddy McDowall, Natalie Schafer, Edith Barrett
† This followed the more successful teaming of the stars in *Holy Matrimony*.

The Molly Maguires
US 1970 123m Technicolor Panavision
Paramount/Tamm (Martin Ritt, Walter Bernstein)
In the Pennsylvania coalmining district in the 1870s, an undercover detective exposes the leaders of a secret society.
Sober-sided and slow-moving account of actual events which also formed the basis for Conan Doyle's rather more entertaining The Valley of Fear. *Expensive, nicely photographed, but unpersuasive and empty.*
w Walter Bernstein *d* Martin Ritt *ph* James Wong Howe *m* Henry Mancini *ad* Tambi Larsen
☆ Richard Harris, Sean Connery, Samantha Eggar, Frank Finlay, Anthony Zerbe, Bethel Leslie, Art Lund

'The film's vague sense of grievance and harrowing circumstances hangs in the air like the smoky pall cast up by the anthracite workings.' – *Richard Combs*

'A cold, dry and rather perfunctory film.' – *Arthur Schlesinger Jnr*

Tambi Larsen

Mom and Dad Save the World
US 1992 88m Foto-Kem
Warner/HBO/Cinema Plus/Douglas (Michael Phillips)
A Californian couple are transported to an alien planet ruled by a mad dictator who has imprisoned the king.
A dim comedy for easily pleased children.
w Chris Matheson, Ed Solomon *d* Greg Beeman *ph* Jacques Haitkin *m* Jerry Goldsmith *pd* Craig Stearns *ed* W. O. Garret *sp* Alterian Studios; Perpetual Motion Pictures
☆ Teri Garr, Jeffrey Jones, Jon Lovitz, Thalmus Rasulala, Wallace Shawn, Eric Idle, Dwier Brown, Kathy Ireland

'With garish color, goofy-looking creatures in rubbery costumes and sets parodying old Flash Gordon serials, pic flaunts its modest budget with engaging candor.' – *Variety*

Moment by Moment
US 1979 105m Technicolor Panavision
Universal (Robert Stigwood)
A bored Beverly Hills wife has an affair with a young drifter.
Tedious proof that even the biggest new stars of the seventies can't carry a no-good picture.
wd Jane Wagner *ph* Philip Lathrop *m* Lee Holdridge *pd* Harry Horner
☆ John Travolta, Lily Tomlin, Andra Akers, Bert Kramer, Debra Feuer

'Little more than an animated snapshot of its leading man, baring body and soul to various effect ... truly terrible.' – *Gilbert Adair, MFB*

Un Moment d'Egarement: see *A Summer Affair*

Moment of Danger
GB 1960 87m bw
ABPC/Douglas Fairbanks Jnr
US title: *Malaga*
Thieves fall out and pursue each other to Malaga.
Falling between the stools of thriller and character drama, this is a poor effort in either category.
w David Osborn, Donald Ogden Stewart *novel* *The Scent of Danger* by Donald MacKenzie *d* Laslo Benedek *ph* Desmond Dickinson *m* Matyas Seiber
☆ Trevor Howard, Dorothy Dandridge, Edmund Purdom, Michael Hordern, Paul Stassino
† Donald Ogden Stewart's name was omitted from the film's original credits at the time because he was blacklisted.

Moment to Moment
US 1966 108m Technicolor
Universal (Mervyn Le Roy)
A housewife finds herself with a body on her hands.
Incredibly old-fashioned romantic/melodramatic malarkey set on the French Riviera but scarcely moving a step out of Hollywood. Lush settings made it marketable to women.
w John Lee Mahin, Alec Coppel *d* Mervyn Le Roy *ph* Harry Stradling *m* Henry Mancini
☆ Jean Seberg, *Honor Blackman*, Sean Garrison, Arthur Hill, Grégoire Aslan

Mommie Dearest
US 1981 129m Metrocolor
Paramount/Frank Yablans
An account of the private life of Joan Crawford, from the biography by her adopted daughter Christina, who claimed spectacular ill-treatment.
On the screen it all seemed too silly for words, and nobody cared anyway.
w Frank Yablans, Frank Perry, Tracy Hotchner, Robert Getchell *d* Frank Perry *ph* Paul Lohmann *m* Henry Mancini *pd* Bill Malley
☆ Faye Dunaway, Diana Scarwid, Steve Forrest, Howard da Silva (Louis B. Mayer)

'The only thing that is not transparent about this film is why it was ever made.' – *Jo Imeson, MFB*

The Mommy Market: see *Trading Mom*

Mon Homme
France 1996 99m colour Panavision
Artificial Eye/BAC/Alain Sarde
A contented prostitute takes in a tramp, who becomes her pimp; when he is imprisoned and she discovers he has been unfaithful, she becomes a housewife.
An oddly broken-backed and unsatisfactory movie, though it begins well as a brisk comedy of sexual needs before shifting into sentimentality and pointlessness.
wd Bertrand Blier *ph* Pierre Lhomme *m* *Barry White et al* *pd* Willy Holt, Georges Glon *ed* Claudine Merlin
☆ Anouk Grinberg, Gérard Lanvin, Valéria Bruni-Tedeschi, Olivier Martinez, Dominique Valadié, Jacques François, Michel Galabru, Robert Hirsch, Bernard Fresson, Aurore Clément, Jean-Pierre Léaud, Sabine Azéma

'Since pic isn't sure what it's about (except flying in the face of conventional morality), this stylish, keenly acted item runs out of both steam and substance before its less than satisying conclusion.' – *Lisa Nesselson, Variety*

Mon Oncle *
France 1956 116m Eastmancolor
Specta/Gray/Alterdel-Centaure (Louis Dolivet)
A small boy has less affection for his parents than for his vague, clumsy uncle.
Tiresomely long star vehicle, with Tati harping on his theory of detachment, i.e. keeping his comic character on the fringes of the action. It really doesn't work in a film of this length, and the jokes are thin.
w *Jacques Tati, Jacques Lagrange* *d* Jacques Tati *ph* Jean Bourgoin *m* Alain Romains, Franck Barcellini
☆ *Jacques Tati*, Jean-Pierre Zola, Adrienne Servatie, Alain Becourt, Yvonne Arnaud

'Deft, elusive, full of heart.' – *Brenda Davies, MFB*

'Cinema humour at its brilliant best.' – *Daily Worker*

best foreign film

Mon Oncle Américain: see *My American Uncle*

Mon Oncle Benjamin: see *Uncle Benjamin*

Mon Père, Ce Héros
France 1991 104m colour
Gala/Film Par Film/DD/Orly/TF1/Paravision/Canal (Jean-Louis Livi)
A teenage girl on holiday tells a boy she fancies that her father is a spy and her lover.
A dull and sentimental comedy that sanitizes incest.
wd Gérard Lauzier *ph* Patrick Blossier *m* François Bernheim *ad* Christian Marti *ed* Georges Klotz
☆ Gérard Depardieu, Marie Gillain, Patrick Mille, Catherine Jacob, Charlotte de Turckheim, Jean-François Rangasamy, Koomaren Chetty

'This syrupy teen romance would be all but unwatchable were it not for the presence of Depardieu.' – *Empire*

† The film was remade in America in 1994 as My *Father, the Hero*, again starring Gèrard Depardieu.

Mona Lisa **
GB 1986 104m Technicolor
HandMade/Palace (Stephen Woolley, Patrick Cassavetti)
An ex-con becomes chauffeur for a prostitute and becomes involved in the kinkier areas of the vice trade.
Only this actor could make a hit of this unsavoury yarn, with its highlights of sex and violence. But he did.
w Neil Jordan, David Leland d Neil Jordan ph Roger Pratt m Michael Kamen pd Jamie Leonard ed Lesley Walker
☆ *Bob Hoskins*, Cathy Tyson, Michael Caine, Robbie Coltrane, Clarke Peters, Sammi Davis
'A film to see again, with the certainty that each viewing will add something new.' – *MFB*
Bob Hoskins

Monache di Sant'Arcangelo: see *The Nun and the Devil*

Monday Morning *
France/Italy 2002 128m colour
Artificial Eye/Pierre Grise/Rhone-Alpes/Mikado (Martine Marignac, Maurice Tinchant, Roberto Cicutto, Luigi Musini)
original title: *Lundi Matin*
Tiring of his repetitive job and rural life with his family, a welder goes to Venice on an impulse.
Gentle, understated comedy of mundane life and incidents that meanders back to where it began.
wd Otar Iosseliani ph William Lubtchansky m Nicolas Zourabichvili pd Manu de Chauvigny ed Otar Iosseliani
☆ Jacques Bidou (Vincent), Arrigo Mozzo (Carlo), Anne Kravz-Tamavsky (Josephine), Narda Blanchet (Vincent's mother), Dato Tarielashvili (Nicolas), Anna Lamour-Flori (Berthe), Adrien Pachod (Gaston), Otar Iosseliani (Enzo de Martini)
'An impeccably made production which beautifully encapsulates a world of serenity and timelessness.' – *David Stratton, Variety*

Un Monde sans Pitié: see *A World without Pity*

Mondo Cane *
Italy 1961 105m Technicolor
Cineriz
aka: *A Dog's Life*
A documentary of thirty sequences of violently eccentric human behaviour, including cannibalism, pig killing, a dog meal restaurant, etc.
Emetic exploitation piece, quite glibly assembled. Its huge commercial success made one worry for the world.
wd Gualtiero Jacopetti ph Antonio Climati, Benito Frattari
song 'More' (m Riz Ortolani, Nino Oliviero, ly Norman Newell)

Money for Jam: see *It Ain't Hay*

Money from Home
US 1954 100m Technicolor 3-D
Paramount/Hal Wallis
A racing tipster and an assistant veterinary surgeon find themselves in charge of a horse.
A comedy with two strokes against it: the stars, and that never-never gangster land which was already a terrible cliché in the early fifties.
w Hal Kanter story Damon Runyon d George Marshall ph Daniel L. Fapp m Leigh Harline
☆ Dean Martin, Jerry Lewis, Marjie Millar, Pat Crowley, Richard Haydn, Robert Strauss, Gerald Mohr, Sheldon Leonard

Money Mania
US 1987 95m Technicolor J-D-C Scope
De Laurentiis (Stephen F. Kesten)
aka: *Million Dollar Mystery*
A dying man tells a group of people at a wayside diner that he has hidden four million dollars in four hiding places.
A vigorous reworking of It's a Mad Mad Mad Mad World, *even broader and cruder than the original.*
w Tim Metcalfe, Miguel Tejada-Flores, Rudy de Luca d Richard Fleischer ph Jack Cardiff m Al Gorgoni pd Jack G. Taylor Jnr ed John W. Wheeler
☆ Jamie Alcroft, Royce D. Applegate, Penny Baker, Eddie Deezen, Mack Dryden, Douglas Emerson, Tawny Ferée, H. B. Haggerty, Rich Hall, Tom Bosley

Money Movers
Australia 1978 90m colour
South Australian Film Corp (Matt Carroll)
A supervisor of a security firm plans a $20-million robbery.
An engaging, though occasionally violent, tale of crooked cops and double-crossing robbers.
wd Bruce Beresford novel The Money Movers by Devon Minchin ph Don McAlpine ed William Anderson, Jeanine Chialvo
☆ Terence Donovan, Tonny Bonner, Ed Devereaux, Charles 'Bud' Tingwell, Candy Raymond, Jeanie Drynan, Bryan Brown, Lucky Grills

The Money Pit
US 1986 91m DuArt
Universal/Steven Spielberg (Frank Marshall, Kathleen Kennedy, Art Levinson)
New Yorkers take on an old suburban house, and find it was no bargain.
Witless semi-remake of Mr Blandings Builds His Dream House, *with screams instead of subtlety and no real humour at all.*
w David Giler d Richard Benjamin ph Gordon Willis m Michel Colombier pd Patrizia von Brandenstein ed Jacqueline Cambas
☆ Tom Hanks, Shelley Long, Alexander Godunov, Maureen Stapleton, Joe Mantegna, Philip Bosco, Josh Mostel
'It begins unpromisingly and slides irrevocably downward from there.' – *Variety*

Money Talks
US 1997 96m DeLuxe Super 35
Entertainment/New Line (Walter Coblenz, Tracy Kramer)
A campaigning journalist shields an escaped convict in return for an exclusive story.
Indifferent thriller that seems a pale imitation of the Eddie Murphy–Nick Nolte pairing in 48 Hrs.
w Joel Cohen, Alec Sokolow d Brett Ratner ph Russell Carpenter, Robert Primes m Lalo Schifrin pd Robb Wilson King ed Mark Helfrich
☆ Chris Tucker, Charles Sheen, Heather Locklear, Gerard Ismaël, Damian Chapa, Elise Neal, Michael Wright, Veronica Cartwright, David Warner
'Chemistry between the mismatched stars is imperceptible. A new low point in Sheen's career slide.' – *Sight and Sound*

Money Train
US 1995 110m Technicolor Super 35
Columbia/Peters Entertainment (Jon Peters, Neil Canton)
Two New York cops who are foster brothers decide to rob a train carrying the money collected from the subway system each day.
A tired action movie, loud and unsubtle with performances to match.
w Doug Richardson, David Loughery d Joseph Ruben ph John W. Lindley m Mark Mancina pd Bill Groom ed George Bowers, Bill Pankow
☆ Wesley Snipes, Woody Harrelson, Jennifer Lopez, Robert Blake, Chris Cooper, Joe Grifasi
'Bounces along with a lame script and inconsistent pace.' – *Variety*
'A big, noisy headache of a movie.' – *Entertainment Weekly*

The Money Trap
US 1966 92m bw Panavision
MGM (Max E. Youngstein, David Karr)
A hard-up policeman turns to crime.
A cheap thriller decorated with waning stars; competent at the lowest level.
w Walter Bernstein novel Lionel White d Burt Kennedy ph Paul C. Vogel m Hal Schaefer
☆ Glenn Ford, Rita Hayworth, Elke Sommer, Ricardo Montalban, Joseph Cotten, Tom Reese, James Mitchum

Money, Women and Guns
US 1959 80m Eastmancolor Cinemascope
Universal-International
A murdered prospector scrawls a will before dying; a detective investigates the beneficiaries.
What could have been an effective Western whodunnit is jinxed by erratic writing and direction.
w Montgomery Pittman d Richard H. Bartlett ph Philip Lathrop ad Alexander Golitzen
☆ Jock Mahoney, Kim Hunter, Tim Hovey, Gene Evans, William Campbell, Lon Chaney Jnr, Tom Drake, James Gleason

Mongkok Kamun: see *As Tears Go By*

The Monk (dubbed)
France/Italy/West Germany 1972 90m Eastmancolor
Rank/Maya/Comacico/Peri/Tritone/Studio Films (Henry Lange)
original title: *Le Moine*
An abbot, seduced by a woman disguised as a monk, sinks into a life of debauchery and escapes punishment by selling his soul to the devil.
Ineptly directed, poorly dubbed version of the classic Gothic novel which makes one regret that Buñuel did not direct as well as writing the script.
w Luis Buñuel, Jean-Claude Carrière novel M. G. Lewis d Ado Kyrou ph Sacha Vierny m Piero Piccione ad Max Douy ed Eric Pluet
☆ Franco Nero, Nathalie Delon, Nicol Williamson, Nadja Tiller, Elizabeth Wiener, Denis Manuel
'A near disaster ... Kyrou's treatment, in fact, reduces the whole thing to the level of a kinky charade.' – *MFB*

The Monk
GB/Spain 1990 106m colour
Arrow/Celtic/Mediterraneo Cine-TV (Muir Sutherland, Paco Lara)
A priest is corrupted by a woman who enters his monastery disguised as a boy.
Highly coloured version of a Gothic classic, although it adds a touch of morality and repentance missing from the original.
wd Paco Lara novel M. G. Lewis ph Angel Luis Fernandez m Anton Garcia Abril pd Gumersindo Andres ed José Luis Matesanz sp Alberto Nombela
☆ Paul McGann, Sophie Ward, Isla Blair, Freda Dowie, Aitana Sanchez-Gijon, Laura Davenport, Suzanne Bertish, Mark Elstob

Monk Dawson
GB 1997 107m colour
De Warrenne (Tom Waller)
An outspoken monk leaves the priesthood to become a tabloid journalist, and then has second thoughts.
Glossy melodrama of the tug between spiritual and fleshy needs, but one that carries no great conviction.
w James Magrane novel Piers Paul Read d Tom Waller ph Teoh Gay Hian m Mark Jensen pd Harold Chapman ed Tom Waller
☆ John Michie, Ben Taylor, Paula Hamilton, Martin Kemp, Rupert Vansittart, Frances Tomelty, Rhona Mitra
'A rewarding low-budget British independent that really deserves to find an audience.' – *Mark Wyman, Sight and Sound*

'The 1931 nut crop is ready!'
Monkey Business ***
US 1931 81m bw
Paramount (Herman J. Mankiewicz)
Four ship's stowaways crash a society party and catch a few crooks.
The shipboard part of this extravaganza is one of the best stretches of Marxian lunacy, but after the Chevalier impersonations it runs out of steam. Who's grumbling?
w *S. J. Perelman, Will B. Johnstone, Arthur Sheekman* d Norman Z. McLeod ph Arthur L. Todd
☆ *Groucho Marx, Chico Marx, Harpo Marx, Zeppo Marx*, Thelma Todd, Rockcliffe Fellowes, Ruth Hall, Harry Woods
'Surefire for laughs despite working along familiar lines ... picture has started off by doing sweeping business all over, and no reason why it shouldn't continue to tickle wherever it plays.' – *Variety*

Monkey Business *
US 1952 97m bw
TCF (Sol C. Siegel)
original title: *Darling I Am Growing Younger*
A chimpanzee in a research lab accidentally concocts an elixir of youth.
Remarkably laboured comedy by and with top people; it can't fail to have funny moments, but they are few and far between.
w Ben Hecht, Charles Lederer, I.A.L. Diamond d Howard Hawks ph Milton Krasner m Leigh Harline
☆ Cary Grant, Ginger Rogers, *Charles Coburn*, Marilyn Monroe, Hugh Marlowe
CHARLES COBURN TO MARILYN MONROE (PLAYING HIS SECRETARY): 'Find someone to type this.'

Monkey Grip
Australia 1983 102m Eastmancolor
Mainline/Pavilion/Cinecom (Patricia Lovell)
A single mother begins an affair with a drug-addict.
Sprawling, downbeat story of suburban desolation and shiftless lives in Melbourne.
w Ken Cameron, Helen Graham novel Helen Graham d Ken Cameron ph David Gribble m Bruce Smeaton pd Clark Munro ed David Huggett
☆ Noni Hazlehurst, Colin Friels, Alice Garner, Harold Hopkins, Candy Raymond, Michael Caton, Tim Burns, Christina Amphlett

A Monkey in Winter *
France 1962 103m bw Totalvision
CIPRA/Cité (Jacques Bar)
aka: *Une Singe en Hiver*
aka: *It's Hot in Hell*
In a small Normandy resort, a hotel owner and a literary guest get drunk together and plan great fantasies, but finally return to their responsibilities.
Amiable, meandering star character comedy.
w François Boyer novel Antoine Blondin d Henri Verneuil ph Louis Page m Michel Magne
☆ *Jean Gabin, Jean-Paul Belmondo*, Suzanne Flon, Noël Roquevert, Paul Frankeur, Gabrielle Dorziat

Monkey on My Back
US 1957 93m bw
UA/Imperial/Edward Small
A Guadalcanal hero is given morphine to relieve malaria and becomes addicted.
Dreary case history sold as exploitation.
w Crane Wilbur, Anthony Veiller, Peter Dudley, from the experiences of Barney Ross d André de Toth ph Maury Gertsman m Paul Sawtell, Bert Shefter
☆ Cameron Mitchell, Dianne Foster, Jack Albertson, Paul Richards

Monkey Shines *
US 1988 109m DeLuxe
Rank/Orion (Charles Evans)
A student, paralysed in an accident, forms a deadly symbiotic relationship with a monkey trained to help him.
Deft psychological thriller, spoilt by its ending, which was forced on its director.
wd George A. Romero novel Michael Stewart ph James A. Contner m David Shire pd Cletus Anderson ed Pasquale Buba
☆ Jason Beghe, John Pankow, Kate McNeil, Joyce Van Patten, Christine Forrest

'He's Cute. He's Cuddly. He's A Klepto.'
Monkey Trouble
US 1994 95m Technicolor
Entertainment/New Line/Percy Main/Effe/Victor (Mimi Polk, Heidi Rufus Isaacs)
A small girl adopts a light-fingered monkey and cures him of his thieving ways, to the annoyance of his owner, an organ grinder in league with gangsters.
Amiable comedy for children, provided you don't mind its reliance for laughs on a domesticated performing monkey in waistcoat and fez.
w Franco Amurri, Stu Krieger d Franco Amurri ph Luciano Tovoli m Mark Mancina pd Les Dilley ed Ray Lovejoy, Chris Peppe

☆ Harvey Keitel, Thora Birch, Mimi Rogers, Christopher McDonald, Kevin Scannell, Finster
'A touching children's adventure that belongs among the great animal movies.' – *Variety*

'If It Yells, If It Swings, It's Got To Be Monkeybone!'
Monkeybone
US 2001 93m DeLuxe
TCF/1492 (Michael Barnathan, Mark Radcliffe)
A cartoonist in a coma goes into a surreal world of dreams, and his creation, a ribald monkey, takes over his body in real life.
Gross, unfunny comedy that seems uncertain of its purpose.
w Sam Hamm *graphic novel* Dark Town by Kaja Blackley, Vanessa Chong *d* Henry Selick *ph* Andrew Dunn *m* Anne Dudley *pd* Bill Boes *ed* Mark Warner, Jon Poll, Nicholas C. Smith *sp* Greg Cannom; Keith VanderLaan
☆ Brendan Fraser (Stu Miley), Bridget Fonda (Julie McElroy), Whoopi Goldberg (Death), Chris Kattan (Organ Donor Stu), Dave Foley (Herb), Giancarlo Esposito (Hypnos), Rose McGowan (Kitty), Megan Mullally (Kimmy), Lisa Zane (Medusa), voice of Monkeybone (John Turturro)
'The movie is booby-trapped with so many loud gags that some of its sneakier humor is nearly lost in the din...Imagine if Luis Buñuel had returned from the grave and hooked up with the Farrelly brothers.' – *A. O. Scott, New York Times*
'Too grotesque for children and just too silly for their parents.' – *Mick LaSalle, San Francisco Chronicle*

Monkeys Go Home
US 1966 101m Technicolor
Walt Disney (Ron Miller)
An American inherits a French olive farm and trains chimpanzees to harvest the crop.
Footling comedy with not much of an idea, let alone a plot.
w Maurice Tombragel *novel* The Monkeys by G. K. Wilkinson *d* Andrew V. McLaglen *ph* William Snyder *m* Robert F. Brunner
☆ Maurice Chevalier, Dean Jones, Yvette Mimieux, Bernard Woringer, Jules Munshin, Alan Carney
'Innocuous, extrovertly cheerful and good-humoured – and very dull.' – *MFB*

El Mono Loco: *see The Mad Monkey*

The Monolith Monsters
US 1957 77m bw
U-I (Howard Christie)
A meteorite lands in the desert and causes rocks to rise and expand, becoming toppling pillars which threaten a local community.
Dully-written science fiction with moderate special effects.
w Norman Jolley, Robert M. Fresco *d* John Sherwood *ph* Ellis Carter *md* Joseph Gershenson
☆ Lola Albright, Grant Williams, Les Tremayne, Phil Harvey

Monsieur Beaucaire *
US 1946 93m bw
Paramount (Paul Jones)
King Louis XV's bumbling barber impersonates a court dandy.
What seemed a lively period burlesque has faded somewhat with age, but it still has its moments. Any relation between this and the silent Valentino film is quite accidental.
w Melvin Frank, Norman Panama *d* George Marshall *ph* Lionel Lindon *md* Robert Emmett Dolan
☆ *Bob Hope*, Joan Caulfield, Patric Knowles, Marjorie Reynolds, Cecil Kellaway, Joseph Schildkraut, Reginald Owen, Constance Collier, Hillary Brooke, Douglass Dumbrille, Mary Nash
'Whether you yawn or rather wearily laugh depends chiefly on your chance state of mind.' – *James Agee*

Monsieur Hire **
France 1989 82m colour Panavision
Palace/Cinea/Hachette Premiere/FR3
A middle-aged voyeur, disliked by his neighbours and suspected by the police of murder, becomes involved with a young girl on whom he spies.
Meticulously stylish study of sexual obsession.
w Patrice Leconte, Patrick Dewolf *novel* Les Fiançailles de M. Hire by Georges Simenon *d Patrice Leconte* *ph* Denis Lenoir *m* Michael Nyman *pd* Ivan Mausson *ed* Joelle Hache
☆ *Michel Blanc*, Sandrine Bonnaire, André Wilms, Luc Thuillier
'Brilliantly conceived, admirably acted, and staged with stunning confidence.' – *Tom Milne, MFB*
'A classic pyschological thriller made with all the subtlety, elegance and skill which have placed the French at the head of the field in this genre.' – *Daily Telegraph*

Monsieur Hulot's Holiday ****
France 1953 91m bw
Cady/Discina (Fred Orain)
original title: *Les Vacances de Monsieur Hulot*
An accident-prone bachelor arrives at a seaside resort and unwittingly causes havoc for himself and everyone else.
Despite lame endings to some of the jokes, this is a film to set the whole world laughing, Hulot himself being an unforgettable character and some of the timing magnificent. One feels that it could very nearly happen.
w Jacques Tati, Henri Marquet *d* Jacques Tati *ph* Jacques Mercanton, Jean Mouselle *m* Alain Romans
☆ *Jacques Tati*, Nathalie Pascaud, Michèle Rolla, Valentine Camax
'The casual, amateurish air of his films clearly adds to their appeal: it also appears to explain their defects.' – *Penelope Houston, MFB*
'It had me laughing out loud with more enjoyment than any other comedy film this year.' – *Daily Express*
script

Monsieur Ripois et Son Némésis: *see Knave of Hearts*

Monsieur Verdoux **
US 1947 125m bw
Charles Chaplin
A bank cashier marries and murders rich women to support his real wife.
Interesting but unsatisfactory redrafting of the Landru case; the star is more dapper than funny, the moral is unconvincing, and the slapstick sequences too often raise yawns.
wd Charles Chaplin *ph* Rollie Totheroh *m* Charles Chaplin
☆ Charles Chaplin, Martha Raye, Isobel Elsom
'The cleverest and most brilliant film I have yet made.' – *Charles Chaplin*
'The result is pure Chaplin; and his genius alone has perfected the astonishing central portrait, among the few which, owing nothing to stage or fiction, belong entirely to the cinema.' – *Dilys Powell*
'Even today it will seem a failure to anyone who has taken half a dozen lessons in film technique.' – *Andrew Sarris, 1970*
Charles Chaplin (as writer)

Monsieur Vincent *
France 1947 113m bw
EDIC/UGC
The life of 17th-century St Vincent de Paul, who gave up all worldly goods to devote his life to the poor.
Earnest, realistic Catholic biopic.
w Jean-Bernard Luc, Jean Anouilh *d* Maurice Cloche *ph* Claude Renoir *m* J. J. Grunenwald
☆ *Pierre Fresnay*, Aimé Clairiond, Jean Debucourt, Lise Delemare
'In the sum of things writers and director, players, composer and technicians, have laboured together to make a film with a humanity which makes one forget the narrow criteria of cinema.' – *Dilys Powell*
best foreign film

Monsignor
US 1982 121m DeLuxe
TCF/Frank Yablans (Kurt Neumann)
An Irish cardinal supports the Vatican by doubtful financial means.
A largely boring roman à clef, with a sluggish story and uninspired performances.
w Abraham Polonsky, Wendell Mayes *novel* Jack Alain Leger *d* Frank Perry *ph* Billy Williams *m* John Williams *pd* John DeCuir
☆ Christopher Reeve, Geneviève Bujold, Fernando Rey, Jason Miller, Joe Cortese, Adolfo Celi, Leonardo Cimino
'Irrevocably grounded in a hash of breast-beating and pious platitudes.' – *Sight and Sound*

'The Rain Is Coming. And So Is The Family.'
Monsoon Wedding **
US/Italy/Germany/France 2001 113m Swiss Effects
Film4/IFC/Mirabai/Keyfilms/Pandora/Paradis (Caroline Baron, Mira Nair)
Relatives gather in Delhi for the marriage of a reluctant couple.
Colourful, enjoyably sprawling comedy on cross-cultural confusions among sophisticated middle-class Indian households.
w Sabrina Dhawan *d* Mira Nair *ph* Declan Quinn *m* Mychael Danna *pd* Stephanie Carroll *ed* Allyson C. Johnson *cos* Arjun Bhasin
☆ Naseeruddin Shah (Lalit Verma), Lillete Dubey (Pimmi Verma), Shefali Shetty (Ria Verma), Vasundhara Das (Aditi Verma), Parvin Dabas (Hemant Rai), Vijay Raaz (P. K. Dubei), Tilotama Shome (Alice), Rajat Kapoor (Tej Puri)
'Splashy, noisy and downright fun.' – *Variety*
'One of those joyous films that leaps over national boundaries and celebrates universal human nature.' – *Roger Ebert, Chicago Sun-Times*
† The film won the Golden Lion award at the Venice Film Festival in 2001.

The Monster
US 1925 70m approx (24 fps) bw silent
MGM
A scientist abducts passing motorists and uses them in his experiments at bringing the dead back to life.
Typical star grotesquerie without much flair.
w Willard Mack, Albert Kenyon *play* Crane Wilbur *d* Roland West
☆ Lon Chaney, Gertrude Olmstead, Hallam Cooley, Walter James

The Monster: *see I Don't Want to Be Born (1975)*

Monster: *see Humanoids of the Deep (1980)*

The Monster and the Girl
US 1940 64m bw
Paramount (Jack Moss)
A man is wrongfully executed and his brain is implanted in a gorilla, which goes on the rampage.
Curiously ineffectual considering its plot and cast, this little horror thriller seems to have been the first to use this particular situation, which became very well worn later.
w Stuart Anthony *d* Stuart Heisler *ph* Victor Milner *m* Sigmund Krumgold
☆ Paul Lukas, Ellen Drew, Joseph Calleia, George Zucco, Robert Paige, Rod Cameron, Phillip Terry, Onslow Stevens, Gerald Mohr
'The ape steals the picture.' – *Variety*

Monster City
Japan 1991 78m colour
Asahi Sonorama/Video Art/Japan Home Video/Hideyuki Kikuchi (Kenji Kurada, Makoto Sedani)
A boy and a girl set out to save the world from being taken over by demons.
Dull sequel to Wicked City, *with little to recommend it even to fans of anime.*
w Kaoru Okamura *d* Yoshiaki Kawajiri *ph* Kinichi Ishikawa *md* Motoichi Umeda *ad* Yuji Ikeda *ed* Nobuyuki Ogata
☆ Featuring the voices of Teresa Gallagher, Brad Lovelle, Alan Sherman, George Little, Bob Sessions, Gareth Armstrong
'Style, wit and an eerie twisted beauty are a refreshing change from the usual "rape 'n' pillage" supernatural fare.' – *Manga Mania*

The Monster Club
GB 1980 97m colour
ITC/Chips (Milton Subotsky)
A vampire introduces his victim to a club for ghouls and witches, who tell their stories.
A spoofy but not very entertaining variation on a too-familiar formula.
w Edward and Valerie Abraham *stories* R. Chetwynd-Hayes *d* Roy Ward Baker *ph* Peter Jessop *md* Graham Walker
☆ Vincent Price, John Carradine, Anthony Steel, Simon Ward, James Laurenson, Geoffrey Bayldon, Donald Pleasence, Richard Johnson, Britt Ekland, Anthony Valentine, Stuart Whitman, Patrick Magee

Monster from Green Hell
US 1956 71m bw/colour
Grosse-Krasne (Al Zimbalist)
Wasps sent into space and exposed to cosmic radiation in an experiment return to Earth as huge killer mutants with tiny wings.
Silly low-budget science fiction, with risible monsters, which has an underlying theme of the fear of a nuclear holocaust.
w Louis Vittes, Endre Bohem *d* Kenneth G. Crane *ph* Ray Flin *m* Albert Glasser *pd* Ernst Fegte *ed* Kenneth G. Crane *sp* Jack Rabin, Louis DeWitt
☆ Jim Davis, Robert E. Griffin, Barbara Turner, Joel Fluellen, Eduardo Ciannelli, Vladimir Sokoloff

Monster in a Box *
GB 1991 88m Eastmancolor
ICA/Jon Blair Film Co.
A monologue by actor Spalding Gray about his 'monster' of an autobiographical novel.
Engaging encounter with a master of the casual anecdote.
w Spalding Gray *play* Spalding Gray *d* Nick Broomfield *ph* Michael Coulter *m* Laurie Anderson *ed* Graham Hutchings
☆ Spalding Gray

The Monster Maker
US 1944 64m bw
Sigmund Neufeld/PRC
A doctor frustrated in love turns his girlfriend's father into a monster by injecting him with acromegaly, a distorting disease.
Ludicrous tinpot shocker.
w Pierre Gendron, Martin Mooney, Lawrence Williams *d* Sam Newfield
☆ Ralph Morgan, J. Carrol Naish, Tala Birell, Wanda McKay, Glenn Strange

'Horror that waited 100 million years becomes a terrifying reality!'
Monster on the Campus
US 1958 76m bw
Joseph Gershenson/Universal
A college professor studies a prehistoric fossilized fish, which turns everything that touches it into monsters.
Silly horror stuff with little to take the attention.
w David Duncan *d* Jack Arnold *ph* Russell Metty *md* Joseph Gershenson *ed* Ted J. Kent
☆ Arthur Franz, Whit Bissell, Joanna Moore, Judson Pratt, Nancy Walters, Troy Donahue, Phil Harvey, Helen Westcott

The Monster Squad *
Canada 1987 81m Metrocolor Panavision
Keith Barish/Taft/Tri-Star
Dracula, Frankenstein's monster, the Wolf Man, the Gill Man and the Mummy take refuge in a small American town.
Mildly amusing spoof for the teenage audience.
w Shane Black, Fred Dekker *d* Fred Dekker
☆ Stephen Macht, Duncan Regehr, Andre Gower, Robby Kiger, Tom Noonan

'Crawling Up From The Depths ... To Terrify And Torture!'
'A New Kind Of Terror To Numb The Nerves!'
The Monster that Challenged the World
US 1957 83m bw
Levy-Gardner-Laven/United Artists
A giant caterpillar lays eggs in California's Salton Sea: one hatches...
Overlong shocker for kids.
w Pat Fielder *d* Arnold Laven *ph* Lester White *m* Heinz Roemheld

☆ Tim Holt, Audrey Dalton, Hans Conried, Harlan Warde

The Monster Walks
US 1932 57m bw
Like/Action

A supposed paralytic plans the death of his rich niece.
Spooky house murder mystery, too hammy by half.
w Robert Ellis *d* Frank Strayer
☆ Sheldon Lewis, Mischa Auer, Martha Mattox, Vera Reynolds, Willie Best
'Not badly done, but lacking utterly in novelty.' – *Variety*

Monster Zero: see *Invasion of the Astro-Monsters*

'A lifetime of change can happen in a single moment.'
Monster's Ball **
US 2001 111m DeLuxe Panavision
Entertainment/Lions Gate (Lee Daniels)

In a small Georgia town, a black waitress unknowingly begins a relationship with a white former deathrow guard, who escorted her husband to the electric chair.
Violent deaths, beatings and racism form the background to this downbeat domestic drama, filmed in an understated manner that gives space for its unhappy characters to display their humanity.
w Milo Addica, Will Rokos *d* Marc Forster *ph* Roberto Schaefer *m* Asche and Spencer *pd* Monroe Kelly *ed* Matt Chesse
☆ Billy Bob Thornton (Hank Grotowski), Heath Ledger (Sonny Grotowski), Halle Berry (Leticia Musgrove), Peter Boyle (Buck Grotowski), Sean Combs (Lawrence Musgrove), Mos Def (Ryrus Cooper), Will Rokos (Warden Velasco), Milo Addica (Tommy Roulaine)
'The raw intimacy of some of the scenes – whether they take place at a diner, in the death house or in the bedroom – is breathtaking.' – *A. O. Scott, New York Times*
'It's a sour little soaper that ends 2001 on a downbeat note of suicidal despair.' – *Rex Reed, New York Observer*
Halle Berry
Milo Addica, Will Rokos

Monsters from an Unknown Planet (dubbed)
Japan 1975 80m colour Tohoscope
Miracle/Toho (Tomoyuki Tanaka)

original title: *Mekagojira No Gyakushu*
aka: *The Escape of Mechagodzilla; Terror of Mechagodzilla*
Godzilla is outclassed when aliens reanimate Mechagodzilla and loose Titanosaurus on Tokyo with the help of a renegade scientist and his cyborg daughter.
The usual nonsense from one of the later Godzilla movies, with the monsters inactive for much of the time.
w Yukiko Takayama *d* Inoshiro Honda
☆ Katsuhiko Sasaki, Tomoko Ai, Akihiko Mirata, Tadao Nakamaru, Katsumasu Uchida

'We Scare Because We Care.'
Monsters, Inc. **
US 2001 92m Technicolor
Buena Vista/Walt Disney/Pixar (Darla K. Anderson)

A little girl is stranded in Monstropolis, a town which is powered by children's screams and inhabited by nightmare creatures, who are frightened of her.
Marvellously animated movie that reveals another leap forward in computer animation; but there's a step back in content here, which is too cute and sentimental by half.
w Andrew Stanton, Daniel Gerson *story* Pete Docter, Jill Culton, Jeff Pidgeon, Ralph Eggleston *d* Pete Docter *m* Randy Newman *pd* Harley Jessup, Bob Pauley *ed* Jim Stewart
☆ voices of: John Goodman (Sulley), Billy Crystal (Mike Wazowski), Steve Buscemi (Randall Boggs), Mary Gibbs (Boo), James Coburn (Henry J. Waternoose), Jennifer Tilly (Celia), John Ratzenberger (Yeti), Frank Oz (Fungus)
'Pic is clever and jokey in a vaudeville sort of way, but lacks the heart and sheer imagination of the company's best work for Disney.' – *Todd McCarthy, Variety*
'Stingy on context, commentary, and the prism-ing view of pop culture that made the earlier films mint.' – *Michael Atkinson, Village Voice*
song 'If I Didn't Have You' (m/l Randy Newman)
animated feature film; Randy Newman; sound editing (Gary Rydstrom, Michael Silvers)

La Montagna del Dio Cannibale (dubbed)
Italy 1978 92m colour
Medusa/Dania (Luciano Martino)

aka: *The Mountain of the Cannibal God*
GB title: *Prisoner of the Cannibal God*
A woman goes in search of her husband, an anthropologist who has gone missing in the jungles of New Guinea.
Risible jungle adventure of a forgotten cannibal tribe, with some nasty moments of actual violence to animals, including a lizard eviscerated and skinned, a monkey swallowed by a snake.
w Cesare Frugoni, Sergio Martino *d* Sergio Martino *ph* Giancarlo Ferrando *m* Guido De Angelis, Maurizio De Angelis *pd* Massimo Antonello Geleng *ed* Eugenio Alabiso
☆ Ursula Andress (Susan Stevenson), Stacy Keach (Dr Edward Foster), Claudio Cassinelli (Manolo), Antonio Marsina (Arthur Stevenson), Franco Fantasia (Father Moses), Lanfranco Spinola, Carlo Longhi, Luigina Rocchi, Akushia Sellajaah, Dudley Wanaguru
'Very much a spiced-up dish of left-overs.' – *MFB*

Montana
US 1950 76m Technicolor
Warner (William Jacobs)

An Australian sheepman fights the cattle barons of Montana.
Modest Western from the star's declining years at Warner.
w James R. Webb, Borden Chase, Charles O'Neal *story* Ernest Haycox *d* Ray Enright *ph* Karl Freund *m* David Buttolph
☆ Errol Flynn, Alexis Smith, S. Z. Sakall, Douglas Kennedy, James Brown, Ian MacDonald

Montana Belle
US 1952 82m Trucolor
RKO (Howard Welsch)

The Daltons rescue Belle Starr and insist that she works with them on a dangerous raid.
Warmed-over Western melodramatics, quite unmemorable.
w Horace McCoy, Norman S. Hall *d* Allan Dwan *ph* Jack Marta *m* Nathan Scott
☆ Jane Russell, George Brent, Scott Brady, Forrest Tucker, Andy Devine, Jack Lambert, John Litel, Ray Teal
† The film was completed in 1948, but held over.

Montana Moon
US 1930 88m bw
MGM
A wealthy rancher's spoiled daughter is about to leave for New York when she falls for a handsome cowboy.
A long string of nothings with bursts of song; incompetent early talkie.
w Sylvia Thalberg, Frank Butler *d* Malcolm St Clair
☆ Joan Crawford, Johnny Mack Brown, Ricardo Cortez, Lloyd Ingraham, Cliff Edwards

Monte Carlo *
US 1930 94m bw
Paramount (Ernst Lubitsch)
A count passes himself off as a hairdresser to win a gambling lady.
Faded but charming romantic comedy with music, the first to show its director's sound style in full throttle, notably in the final 'Beyond the Blue Horizon' sequence.
w Ernest Vajda *play* The Blue Coast by Hans Muller *novel* Monsieur Beaucaire by Booth Tarkington *d* Ernst Lubitsch *ph* Victor Milner *m* W. Franke Harling *ad* Hans Dreier *songs* Leo Robin, Richard Whiting
☆ *Jack Buchanan, Jeanette MacDonald,* ZaSu Pitts, Tyler Brooke, Claud Allister, Lionel Belmore
'Nothing extra beyond usual par programmer.' – *Variety*
'Very stylish and sly, not to be missed.' – *New Yorker, 1978*

Monte Carlo or Bust: see *Those Daring Young Men in Their Jaunty Jalopies*

The Monte Carlo Story
Italy/US 1956 101m Technirama
Tatanus (Marcello Girosi)
A gambler looks for a rich wife, and finds instead a glamorous woman as penniless as himself: they become confidence tricksters but suffer a change of heart.
Lubitsch might have made something of it, but this is a flavourless pudding of a film and the stars can do nothing with it.
wd Sam Taylor *story* Marcello Girosi, Dino Risi *ph* Giuseppe Rotunno *m* Renzo Rossellini
☆ Marlene Dietrich, Vittorio de Sica, Arthur O'Connell, Mischa Auer, Natalie Trundy, Jane Rose, Renato Rascel

'He's a cowboy. She's a woman. He's the best at what he does. And so is she.'
Monte Walsh *
US 1970 108m Technicolor
Cinema Center (Hal Landers, Bobby Roberts)

Two ageing cowboys find life increasingly hard and hopeless; an old acquaintance kills one and is shot by the other.
'Realistic' Western developed in leisurely style with the emphasis on character and on the real drudgery of frontier life.
w David Z. Goodman, Lukas Heller *novel* Jack Schaefer *d* William A. Fraker *ph* David M. Walsh *m* John Barry
☆ Lee Marvin, Jack Palance, Jeanne Moreau, Mitch Ryan, Jim Davis
'As boring a western as ever involved a bronco-busting scene that alone cost almost half a million dollars.' – *Judith Crist*

Montenegro *
Sweden/GB 1981 96m Eastmancolor
Viking/Europa/Smart Egg (Bo Jonsson)

A housewife driven mad by boredom takes a lover and murders him.
Another case history in which the creator finds more symbolic meaning than the audience is likely to see. On the surface, a mildly entertaining piece of near-pornography.
wd Dusan Makavejev *ph* Tomislav Pinter *m* Kornell Kovach
☆ Susan Anspach, Erland Josephson, Bora Todorovic, Per Oscarsson

'A charming, wealthy English gentleman. Two beautiful women. If it only takes a moment to fall in love, imagine what can happen in...'
A Month by the Lake
US/GB 1994 91m Telecolor
Buena Vista/Miramax/Anuline (Robert Fox)

Holidaying in a villa on Lake Como in the mid-30s, a middle-aged English spinster tries to attract the attentions of an English major.
Moody, languid, reticent romance, pretty to look at but without much substance.
w Trevor Bentham *novella* H. E. Bates *d* John Irvin *ph* Pasqualino de Santis *m* Nicola Piovani *pd* Gianni Giovagnoni *ed* Peter Tanner
☆ Vanessa Redgrave, James Fox, Uma Thurman, Alida Valli, Alessandro Gassman, Carlo Cartier, Natalia Bizzi, Paolo Lombardi
'This isn't exactly a vacation to remember.' – *Sight and Sound*

A Month in the Country *
GB 1987 96m colour
Euston Films (Kenith Trodd)

In the English countryside, two men recover from the horrors of World War I.
Traditional British teledrama with much going for it despite a final lack of direction.
w Simon Gray *novel* J. L. Carr *d* Pat O'Connor *ph* Kenneth MacMillan *m* Howard Blake *pd* Leo Austin *ed* John Victor
☆ Colin Firth, Kenneth Branagh, Natasha Richardson, Patrick Malahide, Tony Haygarth, Richard Vernon

'Makes *Ben-Hur* look like an epic!'
Monty Python and the Holy Grail ***
GB 1975 90m Technicolor
EMI/Python (Monty) Pictures/Michael White (Mark Forstater)

King Arthur and his knights seek the Holy Grail.
Hellzapoppin-like series of linked sketches on a medieval theme; some slow bits, but often uproariously funny and with a remarkable visual sense of the Middle Ages.
w Graham Chapman, John Cleese, Terry Gilliam, Eric Idle, Michael Palin *d* Terry Gilliam, Terry Jones *ph* Terry Bedford *m* Neil Innes *pd* Roy Smith *ed* John Hackney
☆ Graham Chapman (King Arthur etc), John Cleese, Terry Gilliam, Eric Idle, Michael Palin
'The team's visual buffooneries and verbal rigmaroles are piled on top of each other with no attention to judicious timing or structure, and a form which began as a jaunty assault on the well-made revue sketch and an ingenious misuse of television's fragmented style of presentation, threatens to become as unyielding and unfruitful as the conventions it originally attacked.' – *Geoff Brown*

Monty Python's Life of Brian **
GB 1979 93m Eastmancolor
Hand Made Films (John Goldstone)

A contemporary of Jesus is mistaken for him and crucified.
Controversial middle-eastern romp which left its creators battered but extremely wealthy. In the face of such an onslaught of bad taste, criticism seems irrelevant.
w John Cleese, Graham Chapman, Eric Idle, Michael Palin, Terry Gilliam, Terry Jones *d* Terry Jones *ph* Peter Biziou *m* Geoffrey Burgon *ad* Roger Christian *ed* Julian Doyle
☆ Graham Chapman (Brian etc), John Cleese (Reg etc), Terry Gilliam, Eric Idle, Michael Palin (Pontius Pilate etc), Terry Jones (The Virgin Mandy etc), Kenneth Colley (Jesus the Christ), Gwen Taylor, Carol Cleveland (Mrs Gregory)

Monty Python's The Meaning of Life
GB 1983 90m Technicolor
Universal/Celandine/The Monty Python Partnership (John Goldstone)

A series of sketches in questionable taste.
Subjects include organ transplants, sex, death and the results of overeating.
w Graham Chapman, John Cleese, Terry Gilliam, Eric Idle, Michael Palin, Terry Jones *d* Terry Jones *ph* Peter Hannan *m* various *pd* Harry Lange *ed* Julian Doyle *animation* Terry Gilliam
☆ Graham Chapman, John Cleese, Eric Idle, Terry Jones, Michael Palin, Terry Gilliam, Carol Cleveland

Moon 44
West Germany 1989 99m colour Panavision
Medusa/Centropolis Filmproduktion (Dean Heyde, Roland Emmerich)

In the future, an undercover agent is sent to a far-away planet to unearth a saboteur.
Science fiction melodrama that borrows from most other recent films in the genre to little effect.
w Dean Heyde, Oliver Eberle *story* Roland Emmerich, Dean Heyde, Oliver Eberle, P. J. Mitchell *d* Roland Emmerich *ph* Karl Walter Undenlaub *m* Joel Goldsmith *pd* Oliver Scholl *ed* Tony Wigand
☆ Michael Pare, Lisa Eichhorn, Malcolm McDowell, Dean Devlin, Brian Thompson, Stephen Geoffreys, Leon Rippy, Jochen Nickel, Mechmed Yilmez

The Moon and Sixpence ***
US 1943 85m bw (colour sequence)
Albert Lewin/David L. Loew (Stanley Kramer)

A stockbroker leaves his wife and family, spends some selfish years painting in Paris and finally dies of leprosy on a South Sea island.

Pleasantly literary adaptation of an elegant novel based on the life of Gauguin; a little stodgy in presentation now, but much of it still pleases.
w Albert Lewin *novel* W. Somerset Maugham
d Albert Lewin *ph* John Seitz *m* Dimitri Tiomkin *ad* Gordon Willis *ed* Richard L. Van Enger
☆ *George Sanders* (Charles Strickland), *Herbert Marshall* (Geoffrey Wolfe), *Steve Geray* (Dirk Stroeve), Doris Dudley (Blanche Stroeve), Elena Verdugo (Ata), Florence Bates (Tiara Johnson), Heather Thatcher (Rose Waterford), Eric Blore (Captain Nichols), Albert Basserman (Dr Coutras)

'An admirable film until the end, when it lapses into Technicolor and techni-pathos.' – *James Agate*

🎗 Dimitri Tiomkin

The Moon in the Gutter

France/Italy 1983 130m Eastmancolor Panavision
Palace/Gaumont/TFI Films/SFPC/Opera Film Produzione (Lise Fayolle)
original title: *La Lune dans le Caniveau*

A stevedore, haunting the docks to find the man who raped his sister, becomes involved with a rich woman.
Relentlessly fashionable, now dated, low-life mystery that gets nowhere slowly.
w Jean-Jacques Beineix, Olivier Mergault *novel* David Goodis *d* Jean-Jacques Beineix *ph* Philippe Rousselot *m* Gabriel Yared *ad* Hilton McConnico *ed* Monique Prim, Yves Deschamps
☆ Gérard Depardieu, Nastassia Kinski, Victoria Abril, Beatrice Reading, Gabriel Monnet, Dominique Pinon, Milena Vukotic, Vittorio Mezzogiorno

The Moon Is Blue *

US 1953 99m bw
Otto Preminger

A spry young girl balances the attractions of a middle-aged lover against her young one.
Paper-thin comedy partly set on top of the Empire State Building (and thereafter in a dowdy set); mildly amusing in spots, it gained notoriety, and a Production Code ban, by its use of such naughty words as 'virgin' and 'mistress'.
w F. Hugh Herbert *play* F. Hugh Herbert *d* Otto Preminger *ph* Ernest Laszlo *m* Herschel Burke Gilbert *ed* Otto Ludwig
☆ Maggie McNamara, David Niven, William Holden, Tom Tully, Dawn Addams

PATTY (MAGGIE MCNAMARA): 'Men are usually bored with virgins. I'm so glad you're not ... Have you a mistress?'
DONALD: 'Don't you think it's better for a girl to be preoccupied with sex than occupied with it?'

'It adds nothing to the art of cinema and certainly does not deserve the attention it will get for flouting the Production Code.' – *Philip T. Hartung*

† The film was made simultaneously in German, as *Die Jungfrau auf dem Dach*, with Hardy Kruger, Johanna Matz and Johannes Heesters.

🎗 Maggie McNamara; title song (*m* Herschel Burke Gilbert, *ly* Sylvia Fine); editing

The Moon Is Down **

US 1943 90m bw
TCF (Nunnally Johnson)

A Norwegian village resists the Nazis.
Sombre, talkative, intelligent little drama, the best of the resistance films, shot on the set of How Green Was My Valley *(with snow covering).*
w Nunnally Johnson *novel* John Steinbeck *d* Irving Pichel *ph* Arthur Miller *m* Alfred Newman *ad* James Basevi, Maurice Ransford *ed* Louis Loeffler
☆ *Henry Travers*, Cedric Hardwicke, Lee J. Cobb, Dorris Bowdon, Margaret Wycherly, Peter Van Eyck, John Banner

'This may well be a true picture of Norway and its people. But it fails to strike fire, to generate passion. It leaves one feeling rather proud but also sad.' – *Bosley Crowther*

Moon over Miami *

US 1941 92m Technicolor
TCF (Harry Joe Brown)

Two sisters seek rich husbands in Florida.
Musical remake of Three Blind Mice, *which was suspiciously similar to* Golddiggers of Broadway, The Greeks Had a Word for Them, *etc., and the later* How to Marry a Millionaire *and* Three Little Girls in Blue. *In short, a Hollywood standard, not too badly done.*
w Vincent Lawrence, Brown Holmes *d* Walter Lang *ph* Peverell Marley, Leon Shamroy *md* Alfred Newman *songs* Leo Robin, Ralph Rainger
☆ Don Ameche, Betty Grable, Carole Landis, Robert Cummings, Charlotte Greenwood, Jack Haley, Cobina Wright Jnr, Robert Greig

Moon over Parador

US 1988 104m DeLuxe
UIP/Universal (Paul Mazursky)

An actor is kidnapped and forced to impersonate the president of a Caribbean country.
Occasionally amusing, but the joke is too thin to bear much watching.
w Leon Capetanos, Paul Mazursky *story* Charles G. Booth *d* Paul Mazursky *ph* Donald McAlpine *m* Maurice Jarre *pd* Pato Guzman *ed* Stuart Pappe
☆ Richard Dreyfuss, Raul Julia, Sonia Braga, Jonathan Winters, Fernando Rey, Sammy Davis Jnr, Michael Greene, Polly Holliday, Milton Goncalves, Charo, Marianne Sagebrecht

Moon Pilot **

US 1961 98m Technicolor
Walt Disney (Ron Miller)

A reluctant astronaut falls in love with a girl from outer space, who finally accompanies him on his mission.
Engaging science-fiction spoof with good performances.
w Maurice Tombragel *serial* Robert Buckner *d* James Neilson *ph* William Snyder *m* Peter Smith *sp* Eustace Lycett
☆ Edmond O'Brien, Tom Tryon, Brian Keith

The Moon Spinners *

GB 1964 119m Technicolor
Walt Disney (Bill Anderson)

A young girl holidaying in Crete becomes involved with jewel robbers.
Teenage adventure against attractive locations; quite agreeable but overlong.
w Michael Dyne *novel* Mary Stewart *d* James Neilson *ph* Paul Beeson *m* Ron Grainer
☆ Hayley Mills, Peter McEnery, Eli Wallach, Joan Greenwood, John Le Mesurier, *Pola Negri*

Moon Warriors

Hong Kong 1992 83m colour
Team Work (Andy Lau)

An exiled prince, escaping from his usurping brother's army, finds refuge with a fisherman and his friendly killer whale.
Epic romance with spectacular, acrobatic sword fights, and good to look at despite its often trite narrative.
w Ching Siu Tung *d* Samo Hung
☆ Andy Lau, Maggie Cheung, Anita Mui, Kenny Bee

'Delirious feudal martial arts adventure which boasts expensive production values, well-composed widescreen images and flawless choreography ... highly enjoyable.' – *Sight and Sound*

'The number one space western!'
Moon Zero Two

GB 1969 100m Technicolor
Hammer (Michael Carreras)

In 2021, the moon is being colonized and crooks are trying to get control of an asteroid.
A self-acknowledged 'space western' which has a few bright ideas but suffers from a childish script.
w Michael Carreras *story* Gavin Lyall, Frank Hardman, Martin Davidson *d* Roy Ward Baker *ph* Paul Beeson *m* Don Ellis
☆ James Olson, Catherina von Schell, Warren Mitchell, Ori Levy, Adrienne Corri, Dudley Foster, Bernard Bresslaw, Neil McCallum

'It's all just about bad enough to fill older audiences with nostalgia for the inspired innocence of Flash Gordon, or even the good old days of Abbott and Costello in outer space.' – *MFB*

Moonfleet *

US 1955 87m Eastmancolor Cinemascope
MGM (John Houseman)

In Dorset in 1770 an orphan boy finds that his elegant guardian leads a gang of smugglers.
Period gothic melodrama which nearly, but not quite, comes off; the script simply doesn't build to the right climax, and too many characters come to nothing. But there are splendid moments.
w Margaret Fitts, Jan Lustig *novel* J. Meade Falkner *d* Fritz Lang *ph* Robert Planck *m* Miklos Rozsa
☆ Stewart Granger, Jon Whiteley, George Sanders, Joan Greenwood, Viveca Lindfors, Liliane Montevecchi, Melville Cooper, Sean McClory, John Hoyt, Alan Napier

'A film as funny, complicated and real ... as life itself.'
Moonlight and Valentino

US 1995 104m Technicolor Panavision
Polygram/Working Title (Alison Owen, Eric Fellner, Tim Bevan)

Her friend, a sister and her divorced stepmother help a young academic cope with the unexpected death of her husband.
Talky drama of female bonding and dealing with grief that has some, but not enough, effective moments.
w Ellen Simon *play* Ellen Simon *d* David Anspaugh *ph* Julio Macat *m* Howard Shore *pd* Robb Wilson King *ed* David Rosenbloom
☆ Elizabeth Perkins, Gwyneth Paltrow, Jon Bon Jovi, Kathleen Turner, Whoopi Goldberg, Jeremy Sisto, Josef Sommer

'"Gently dreary" would be the best chosen words for this film which is so slow at times it is almost stationary.' – *Marianne Gray, Film Review*

Moonlight in Havana

US 1942 63m bw
Bernard W. Burton/Universal

A baseball catcher goes to Havana for spring training.
Another in the long line of lightweight musical supports from this studio.
w Oscar Brodney *d* Anthony Mann
☆ Allan Jones, Jane Frazee, Marjorie Lord, William Frawley, the Jiving Jacks and Jills

'In life and love, expect the unexpected.'
Moonlight Mile *

US 2002 117m Technicolor Panavision
Buena Vista/Touchstone/Hyde Park/Reveal/Gran Via/Punch (Mark Johnson, Brad Silberling)

A businessman and his wife, mourning over the accidental death of their daughter, invite her fiancé to live with them, not knowing that their romance was over.
Over-sweet account of how various individuals cope with loss; it has its moments, though they are not as many as one would hope.
wd Brad Silberling *ph* Phedon Papamichael *m* Mark Isham *pd* Missy Stewart *ed* Lisa Zeno Churgin
☆ Jake Gyllenhaal (Joe Nast), Dustin Hoffman (Ben Floss), Susan Sarandon (JoJo Floss), Holly Hunter (Mona Camp), Ellen Pompeo (Bertie Knox), Richard T. Jones (Ty), Allan Corduner (Stan Michaels), Dabney Coleman (Mike Mulcahey)

'Full of sharp acting and home truths, but its ambition to be different finally surrenders to its need to be loved.' – *Richard Corliss, Time*
'Awkward tragicomedy about bereavement that features a strong cast but a feeble script.' – *Anthony Quinn, Independent*

Moonlight Sonata *

GB 1937 90m bw
Pall Mall (Lothar Mendes)

Stranded victims of a plane crash are affected by the art of a famous pianist.
Curious, slight, unexpected play-on-film designed to showcase the talent of Paderewski.
w Edward Knoblock, E. M. Delafield *d* Lothar Mendes *ph* Jan Stallich
☆ *Ignace Paderewski*, Eric Portman, *Marie Tempest*, Charles Farrell, Barbara Greene, Binkie Stuart

'Should make good with class audiences.' – *Variety*
'Dame Marie is a sparking line-tosser who keeps the script alive when Paderewski (then 77) is not putting it to music.' – *New York Times*

The Moonlighter

US 1953 77m bw 3-D
Warner (Joseph Bernhard)

A cattle rustler moves towards reforming.
Ho-hum Western which offers its stars little to work with and was not even very exciting in 3-D.
w Niven Busch *d* Roy Rowland *ph* Bert Glennon *m* Heinz Roemheld
☆ Fred MacMurray, Barbara Stanwyck, Ward Bond, William Ching, John Dierkes, Morris Ankrum

Moonlighting ***

GB 1982 97m colour
Michael White/Channel 4 (Mark Shivas, Jerzy Skolimowski)

In 1981 four Polish building workers arrive in London to renovate a house for their boss and make a quick profit. The scheme is somewhat upset by the news of martial law at home...
Very interesting and well-acted anecdote, virtually constructed out of the headlines.
wd Jerzy Skolimowski *ph* Tony Pierce Roberts *m* Stanley Myers *pd* Tony Woollard *ed* Barrie Vince
☆ Jeremy Irons, Eugene Lipinski, Jiri Stanislaw, Eugeniusz Haczkiewicz

The Moonraker *

GB 1957 82m Technicolor
ABPC (Hamilton Inglis)

During the English Civil War, a noble highwayman smuggles the king's son into France.
Likeable swashbuckler which confines its second half to suspense at an inn, a who-is-it rather than a whodunnit. Good fun.
w Robert Hall, Wilfred Eades, Alistair Bell *play* Arthur Watkyn *d* David MacDonald *ph* Max Greene *m* Laurie Johnson
☆ George Baker, Sylvia Syms, Marius Goring, Peter Arne, Richard Leech, Clive Morton, Paul Whitsun-Jones, Gary Raymond, John Le Mesurier (Oliver Cromwell), Patrick Troughton, Michael Anderson Jnr

Moonraker

GB 1979 126m Technicolor Panavision
UA/Eon (Albert R. Broccoli)

James Bond investigates the disappearance of a space shuttle during a test flight.
Adventures in Venice, Rio and the upper Amazon; all very repetitive and no longer more than faintly amusing.
w Christopher Wood *novel* Ian Fleming *d* Lewis Gilbert *ph* Jean Tournier *m* John Barry *pd* Ken Adam
☆ Roger Moore, Lois Chiles, Michael Lonsdale, Richard Kiel, Geoffrey Keen, Lois Maxwell, Bernard Lee

'Conspicuously expensive production values but an unmistakably cut price plot.' – *Sight and Sound*

Moonrise *

US 1948 90m bw
Republic/Frank Borzage Productions (Charles F. Haas)

A murderer's son is driven into violence by memories and fears of his childhood.
Broody melodrama set against a remote village and swamp background; not a very interesting story, but memorable detail.
w Charles Haas *d Frank Borzage* *ph* John L. Russell *m* William Lava *ed* Harry Keller
☆ Gail Russell, Dane Clark, Ethel Barrymore, Allyn Joslyn, Rex Ingram

'The story is told with a unity of mood, sombre and poignant, set by some impressionistic opening passages and sustained by the slow yet firmly compressed style and the strong, low-toned images.' – *Gavin Lambert*

'If the world is sane – then they're completely mad!'

The Moon's Our Home *

US 1936 80m bw

Paramount (Walter Wanger)

A headstrong actress marries an adventurer on impulse, and they both try to work it out.

Light, bright romantic comedy with the zany tinge then in fashion.

w Isabel Dawn, Boyce DeGaw *novel* Faith Baldwin *d* William A. Seiter *ph* Joseph Valentine *m* Gerard Carbonara

☆ Margaret Sullavan, Henry Fonda, Beulah Bondi, Charles Butterworth, Margaret Hamilton, Dorothy Stickney, Lucien Littlefield

'It isn't, of course, as good as all that; nothing is as good as all that in the cinema, but the great commercial wheels don't grind here quite so effortlessly; a little satire, a little imagination, a little feeling for human inconsistency, has got into the works.' – *Graham Greene, The Spectator*

The Moonshine War

US 1970 100m Metrocolor Panavision

MGM/Filmways (James C. Pratt, Leonard Blair)

In Kentucky just before the repeal of prohibition, a corruptible revenue agent regrets bringing in a sadistic crook to help confiscate illegal whisky.

Downright peculiar hillbilly melodrama, neither straight nor satirical; interesting only in fits and starts.

w Elmore Leonard *novel* Elmore Leonard *d* Richard Quine *ph* Richard H. Kline *m* Fred Karger

☆ Patrick McGoohan, Richard Widmark, Alan Alda, Melodie Johnson, Will Geer

'Patrick McGoohan walked over to me the only day I was on the set and said, "What's it like to hear your lines all fucked up?"{?is0p1.5°' – *Elmore Leonard*

The Moonspinners: see *The Moon Spinners*

Moonstruck *

US 1987 102m Technicolor

Patrick Palmer/Norman Jewison

Young widow falls for the estranged brother of her husband-to-be.

Noisy, sometimes heavy-handed romantic comedy of Italian-American manners.

w John Patrick Shanley *d* Norman Jewison *ph* David Watkin *m* Dick Hyman *pd* Philip Rosenberg

☆ Cher, Nicolas Cage, Vincent Gardenia, Olympia Dukakis, Danny Aiello

Cher; John Patrick Shanley; Olympia Dukakis

best picture; Norman Jewison; Vincent Gardenia

Moontide *

US 1942 94m bw

TCF (Mark Hellinger)

A seaman cares for an unhappy waif.

A Hollywood attempt at romantic melodrama in the French manner. It looks good, and the cast is fine, but everything is just a bit too glum.

w John O'Hara *novel* Willard Robertson *d* Archie Mayo *ph* Charles G. Clarke *m* Cyril Mockridge, David Buttolph

☆ Jean Gabin, Ida Lupino, Claude Rains, Thomas Mitchell, Jerome Cowan, Sen Yung, Tully Marshall, Helene Reynolds

Charles G. Clarke

Moonwalker

US 1988 93m

Warner/Ultimate Productions

Episodic look at the life and performances of Michael Jackson, culminating in a fantasy in which he stops a gangster turning children into junkies.

Strictly for fans.

w David Newman *story* Michael Jackson *d* Colin Chilvers, Jerry Kramer *ph* John Hora, Tom Ackerman, Bob Collins, Fred Elmes, Crescenzo Notarile *m* Bruce Broughton *pd* Michael Ploog *ed* David E. Blewitt, Mitchell Sinoway, Dale Beldin

☆ Michael Jackson, Joe Pesci, Sean Lennon, Kellie Parker, Brandon Adams

The Morals of Marcus

GB 1936 75m bw

Real Art (W. J. Locke)

A girl escapes from a Middle Eastern harem by stowing away with a British aristocrat.

Feeble 'naughty' comedy, killed by lack of wit and pace.

w Guy Bolton, Miles Mander *play* W. J. Locke *d* Miles Mander *ph* John W. Boyle

☆ Lupe Velez, Ian Hunter, Adrianne Allen, Noel Madison, J. H. Roberts, H. F. Maltby

'Acceptable feature for general consumption.' – *Variety*

Die Mörder Sind Unter Uns: see *The Murderers Are Among Us*

More American Graffiti

US 1979 111m Technicolor

Universal/Lucasfilm (Howard Kazanjian)

In 1964, American small-town teenagers quarrel over drugs and drag racing.

Tedious sequel to a movie which was more than enough.

wd Bill L. Norton *ph* Caleb Deschanel *m* various

☆ Candy Clark, Bo Hopkins, Ron Howard, Paul Le Mat, Mackenzie Phillips, Richard Bradford

'What once was a crate of dynamite has been cosmetically giftwrapped à la Happy Days.' – *Cynthia Rose, MFB*

More Dead Than Alive

US 1968 99m DeLuxe

United Artists/Aubrey Schenck

Revenge erupts some years after a violent jail break.

Eccentric and pretentious Western with a complex story which might have intrigued if handled better.

w George Schenck *d* Robert Sparr *ph* Jack Marquette *m* Philip Springer

☆ Clint Walker, Vincent Price, Anne Francis, Paul Hampton, Mike Henry, Craig Littler

More than a Secretary

US 1936 80m bw

Columbia

A dowdy secretary loses her glasses and wins her boss.

That old story, and the treatment isn't anything to get excited about either.

w Dale Van Every, Lynn Starling *d* Alfred E. Green

☆ Jean Arthur, George Brent, Lionel Stander, Ruth Donnelly, Reginald Denny, Dorothea Kent, Charles Halton

'Fair b.o. possibilities, but the story doesn't belong on the same block as the production afforded to it.' – *Variety*

The More the Merrier ***

US 1943 104m bw

Columbia (George Stevens)

In crowded Washington during World War II, a girl allows two men to share her apartment and falls in love with the younger one.

Thoroughly amusing romantic comedy with bright lines and situations; remade less effectively as Walk Don't Run *(qv).*

w Robert Russell, Frank Ross, Richard Flournoy, Lewis R. Foster *d* George Stevens *ph* Ted Tetzlaff *m* Leigh Harline *md* Morris Stoloff

☆ *Jean Arthur, Joel McCrea, Charles Coburn*, Richard Gaines, Bruce Bennett

'The gayest comedy that has come from Hollywood in a long time. It has no more substance than a watermelon, but is equally delectable.' – *Howard Barnes*

'Farce, like melodrama, offers very special chances for accurate observation, but here accuracy is avoided ten times to one in favour of the easy burlesque or the easier idealization which drops the bottom out of farce. Every good moment frazzles or drowns.' – *James Agee*

† Garson Kanin has claimed to have written virtually all the script.

Charles Coburn

best picture; script; original story (Frank Ross, Robert Russell); George Stevens; Jean Arthur

The More Things Change...

Australia 1985 95m Eastmancolor

Panvision

Syme International/NSWFC (Jill Robb)

A successful journalist tries to cope with the strains of a demanding job and marriage when her husband decides to move to the country to become self-sufficient.

Small-scale, routine drama of a marriage in trouble; nothing out of the ordinary.

w Moya Wood *d* Robyn Nevin *ph* Dan Burstall *m* Peter Best *pd* Josephine Ford *ed* Jill Bilcock

☆ Judy Morris, Barry Otto, Victoria Longley, Peter Carroll, Louise Le Nay, Lewis Fitz-Gerald, Owen Johnson

Morgan – A Suitable Case for Treatment ***

GB 1966 97m bw

British Lion/Quintra (Leon Clore)

US title: *Morgan!*

A young woman determines to leave her talented but half-mad artist husband, who has a fixation on gorillas and behaves in a generally uncivilized manner.

Archetypal sixties marital fantasy, an extension of Look Back in Anger *in the mood of swinging London. As tiresome as it is funny – but it is funny.*

w David Mercer play David Mercer *d Karel Reisz ph Larry Pizer, Gerry Turpin m* Johnny Dankworth

☆ Vanessa Redgrave, *David Warner*, Robert Stephens, Irene Handl, Newton Blick, Nan Munro

'Poor Morgan: victim of a satire that doesn't bite, lost in a technical confusion of means and ends, and emerging like an identikit photograph, all bits and pieces and no recognizable face.' – *Penelope Houston*

'The first underground movie made above ground.' – *John Simon*

'I think Morgan is so appealing to college students because it shares their self-view: they accept this mess of cute infantilism and obsessions and aberrations without expecting the writer and director to resolve it and without themselves feeling a necessity to sort it out.' – *Pauline Kael*

Vanessa Redgrave

David Mercer

Morituri: The Saboteur: see *The Saboteur, Code Name Morituri*

The Morning After

US 1986 103m DeLuxe

TCF/Lorimar/American Filmworks (Bruce Gilbert)

A drunken actress wakes up one morning next to a man with a dagger in his heart.

A mystery which starts as intriguing but is insufficiently developed and peters out into a series of casual encounters between unattractive people.

w James Hicks *d* Sidney Lumet *ph* Andrzej Bartkowiak *m* Paul Chihara *pd* Albert Brenner *ed* Joel Goodman

☆ Jane Fonda, Jeff Bridges, Raul Julia, Diane Salinger

Jane Fonda

Morning Departure *

GB 1950 102m bw

Rank/Jay Lewis (Leslie Parkyn)

US title: *Operation Disaster*

Twelve men are caught in a trapped submarine, and only eight can escape.

Archetypal stiff-upper-lip service tragedy, which moves from briskness to a slow funereal ending.

w William Fairchild *play* Kenneth Woollard *d* Roy Baker *ph* Desmond Dickinson

☆ John Mills, Richard Attenborough, Nigel Patrick, Lana Morris, Peter Hammond, Helen Cherry, James Hayter, Andrew Crawford, George Cole, Michael Brennan, Wylie Watson, Bernard Lee, Kenneth More

Morning Glory **

US 1933 74m bw

RKO (Pandro S. Berman)

A young actress comes to New York determined to succeed.

Marvellously evocative theatrical drama which provided a strong star part for a fresh young actress and surrounded her with accomplished thespians. Remade to much less effect as Stage Struck *(qv).*

w Howard J. Green *play* Zoe Akins *d* Lowell Sherman *ph* Bert Glennon *m* Max Steiner

☆ *Katharine Hepburn, Douglas Fairbanks Jnr, Adolphe Menjou*, Mary Duncan, C. Aubrey Smith, Don Alvarado

'Star vastly superior to this sometimes misdirected arty story.' – *Variety*

Katharine Hepburn

Morning Glory

US 1993 95m Foto-Kem

Overseas/Dove Audio (Michael Viner)

In 1941, a former convict, who answers an advert for a husband by a pregnant widow with three children, is accused of murder when the town's good-time girl is killed.

Dull and predictable small-town soap opera, given a plodding treatment.

w Charles Jarrott, Deborah Raffin *novel* Lavyrle Spencer *d* Steven Hilliard Stern *ph* Laszlo George *m* Jonathan Elias *ad* David Hiscox *ed* Richard Benwick

☆ Christopher Reeve, Deborah Raffin, Lloyd Bochner, Nina Foch, Helen Shaver, J. T. Walsh

Morning of the Earth

Australia 1972 80m colour

Woolloomooloo/AFD (David Elfick)

Documentary film that tries to communicate the pleasure and adrenalin rush of surfing big waves in Australia and Hawaii.

Surfers are likely to enjoy this the most; the images of sand, sea and surfers have a charm, though after a while one wave begins to look much like another.

d Albert Falzon *ph* Albert Falzon *m* G. *Wayne Thomas, Brian Cadd, Taman Shud et al ed* Grant Shanks

☆ Nat Young, Chris Brock, Stephen Cooney, David Treloar, Mark Warren, Rusty Miller, Michael Peterson, Terry Fitzgerald, Ted Spencer, Reno Abelliro, Jerry Lopez

'Revealing the amazing things a woman will do for love!'

Morocco ***

US 1930 97m bw

Paramount (Louis D. Lighton)

A cabaret singer arrives in Morocco and continues her wicked career by enslaving all the men in sight; but true love reaches her at last.

The star's first American film reveals her quintessence, and although wildly dated in subject matter remains a perversely enjoyable entertainment.

w Jules Furthman *novel Amy Jolly* by Benno Vigny *d Josef von Sternberg ph* Lee Garmes *m* Karl Hajos *ad* Hans Dreier

☆ *Marlene Dietrich*, Gary Cooper, Adolphe Menjou, Ullrich Haupt, Juliette Compton, Francis McDonald

'Lightweight story with good direction ... needs plenty of exploitation to do over average.' – *Variety*

'A definite step forward in the art of motion pictures.' – *National Board of Review*

'A cinematic pattern, brilliant, profuse, subtle, and at almost every turn inventive.' – *Wilton A. Barrett*

'Enchantingly silly, full of soulful grand passions, drifting cigarette smoke, and perhaps a few too many pictorial shots of the Foreign Legion marching this way and that.' – *New Yorker, 1979*

Josef von Sternberg; Lee Garmes; Marlene Dietrich; Hans Dreier

Morons from Outer Space

GB 1985 91m colour

Thorn EMI (Barry Hanson)

Dopey space travellers arrive on Earth.

Spoofy comedy which, apart from staging a spectacular motorway landing and mocking various popular film genres, never decides where to go.

w Griff Rhys Jones, Mel Smith *d* Michael Hodges *ph* Phil Meheux *m* Peter Brewis

☆ Mel Smith, Griff Rhys Jones, Paul Bown, Joanne Pearce, Jimmy Nail, Dinsdale Landen, James B. Sikking

'It remains stuck on the launch pad.' – *Variety*

Morris West's The Naked Country: see *The Naked Country*

Mortal Kombat
US 1995 101m colour
First Independent/New Line/Threshold (Lawrence Kasanoff)

Good guys with muscles battle evil in an attempt to save the world from the denizens of another universe.
On its level, of mindless, violent entertainment, this can be counted something of a success: it is the first film based on a video game to reproduce some of the visceral excitement of the original.
w Kevin Droney *d* Paul Anderson *ph* John R. Leonetti *m* George S. Clinton *pd* Jonathan Carlson *ed* Martin Hunter
☆ Christopher Lambert, Robin Shou, Cary-Hiroyuki Tagawa, Bridgette Wilson, Talisa Soto, Chris Casamassa, Linden Ashby
'It is well-served by a cast clearly well-versed in dopey grinning. All the actors have to do is talk, fight a bit, and vaguely resemble their digitised counterparts. Tough gig.' – *Guardian*

Mortal Kombat 2: Annihilation
US 1997 94m Foto-Kem
Entertainment/New Line/Threshold/Lawrence Kasanoff

Martial artists who triumphed over evil are attacked by a wicked emperor who wants to create hell on Earth.
There is a problem in converting the mindless mayhem of video games to the mindless mayhem of action films: the latter require an engaging narrative to replace the interactive charms of the former, something this mess fails to achieve.
w Brent V. Friedman, Bryce Zabel *d* John R. Leonetti *ph* Matthew F. Leonetti *m* George S. Clinton *pd* Charles Wood *ed* Peck Prior *sp* Chuck Comisky, Alison Savitch
☆ Robin Shou, Talisa Soto, James Remar, Sandra Hess, Lynn Red Williams, Brian Thompson, Reiner Schoene
'Consists largely of choppily edited fight scenes (usually involving somersaults and back flips) combined with various computer graphic effects.' – *Variety*

Mortal Passions
US 1990 98m Foto-Kem
Gibraltar (Gwen Field)

A lying wife, attempting to manipulate her lover into killing her weak husband, finds herself unexpectedly involved in murder.
A feeble, vacuous attempt at a thriller in the tradition of film noir, with dull characters, uninteresting dialogue and no suspense.
w Alan Moscowitz *d* Andrew Lane *ph* Christian Sebaldt *m* Parmer Fuller *pd* Robert Sissman *ed* Kimberly Ray
☆ Zach Galligan, Krista Errickson, Michael Bowen, Luca Bercovici, Sheila Kelley, Cassandra Gava, David Warner

'The love story of today with the popular stars of The Shop Around the Corner!'
The Mortal Storm **
US 1940 100m bw
MGM (Sidney Franklin)
A German family in the thirties is split by Nazism.
Solid anti-Nazi melodrama typical of the period before America entered the war; good performances outweigh unconvincing studio sets.
w Claudine West, George Froeschel, Anderson Ellis *novel* Phyllis Bottome *d Frank Borzage* *ph* William Daniels *m* Edward Kane
☆ Margaret Sullavan, Robert Young, James Stewart, Frank Morgan, Robert Stack, Bonita Granville, Irene Rich, Maria Ouspenskaya
† The film caused Goebbels to ban the showing of MGM pictures in all German territories.

'Murder is a secret that should never be shared.'
Mortal Thoughts *
US 1991 103m DeLuxe
Columbia TriStar/New Visions/Polar/Rufglen (John Fiedler, Mark Tarlov)

Two women, who are best friends, are questioned about the murder of the husband of one of them.
Entertaining thriller which sustains its mystery to the end.
w William Reilly, Claude Kerven *d* Alan Rudolph *ph* Elliot Davis *m* Mark Isham *pd* Howard Cummings *ed* Tom Walls
☆ Demi Moore, Glenne Headly, Bruce Willis, John Pankow, Harvey Keitel, Billie Neal, Frank Vincent
'A bravely downbeat movie.' – *Empire*

Morte a Venezia: see *Death in Venice*

La Morte Vivante: see *The Living Dead Girl*

Mortifero: see *The Stranger (1987)*

Morvern Callar *
GB/Canada 2001 98m colour
Momentum/Alliance Atlantis/BBC/Company (Robyn Slovo, Charles Pattinson, George Faber)

A Scottish supermarket worker strikes lucky when she passes off her dead boyfriend's novel as her own work.
A grim fairy-tale, a psychological fantasy of feckless escape from the world, that occasionally charms.
w Lynne Ramsay, Liana Dognini *novel* Alan Warner *d* Lynne Ramsay *ph* Alwin Kuchler *pd* Jane Morton *ed* Lucia Zucchetti
☆ Samantha Morton (Morvern Callar), Kathleen McDermott (Lanna), Raife Patrick Burchell (Boy in Room 1022), Dan Cadan (Dazzer), Carolyn Calder (Sheila Tequila), Jim Wilson (Tom Boddington), Dolly Wells (Susan), Ruby Milton (Couris Jean)
'This minimalist film is slightly hobbled by its minimal plot; it's the crucial difference between a movie with moments of greatness and a great movie.' – *Elvis Mitchell, New York Times*
'A mesmeric, startling and sometimes baffling movie from Lynne Ramsay and it announces her as one of the most distinctive talents in British cinema.' – *Peter Bradshaw, Guardian*

Moscow Distrusts Tears *
USSR 1979 148m Sovcolor
Mosfilm (V. Kuchinsky)
original title: *Moskva Slezam Ne Verit*
US title: *Moscow Does Not Believe In Tears*
In Moscow in 1958, three working girls have love affairs. Twenty years later they compare notes.
Odd portmanteau drama, most interesting for its picture of life in Russia.
w Valentin Chernykh *d* Vladimir Menshov *ph* Igor Slabnevich *m* Sergei Nikitin
☆ Vera Alentova, Alexei Batalov, Irina Muravera, Alexander Fatiushin, Raisa Ryazanova, Boris Smorchkov
best foreign film

Moscow Nights
GB 1936 75m bw
London Films/Capitol Films (Alexis Granowsky, Max Schach)

US title: *I Stand Condemned*
A Russian girl sacrifices her virtue to save her lover from execution.
Cardboard melodrama of pre-revolutionary Moscow; not by any means a classic.
w Erich Seipmann *novel* Pierre Benoît *d* Anthony Asquith *ph* Phil Tannura *md* Muir Mathieson *ad* Vincent Korda *ed* Francis Lyon
☆ Laurence Olivier, Penelope Dudley Ward, Harry Baur, Robert Cochran, Morton Selten, Athene Seyler
'Completely bogus … The direction is puerile.' – *Graham Greene, The Spectator*
† This was based directly on a 1934 French film, *Nuits Moscovites*, with Annabella, Pierre-Richard Willm, and Harry Baur.

Moscow on the Hudson *
US 1984 117m Metrocolor
Columbia/Delphi (Paul Mazursky)

A Soviet circus artiste defects in New York but has second thoughts.
Not so much a political comedy as an immigrant one, with the Big Apple shown at its worst. As such, occasionally funny in a desperate way, but overlong.
w Paul Mazursky, Leon Capetanos *d* Paul Mazursky *ph* Donald McAlpine *m* David McHugh *pd* Pato Guzman
☆ Robin Williams, Maria Conchita Alonso, Cleavant Derricks, Alejandro Rey, Savely Kramarov

The Mosquito Coast *
US 1986 117m Technicolor
Saul Zaentz/Jerome Hellman

A frustrated visionary packs up and moves his family to a remote Caribbean island, where he fails to notice the seeds of downfall.
An antidote to Robinson Crusoe *which is often wryly amusing, but the leading character is too hysterical and his fall too complete to make good drama.*
w Paul Schrader *novel* Paul Theroux *d* Peter Weir *ph* John Seale *m* Maurice Jarre *pd* John Stoddart *ed* Thom Noble
☆ *Harrison Ford*, Helen Mirren, River Phoenix, Jadrien Steele, André Gregory
'In the end there is barely a thread of hope to take home, other than some strikingly beautiful and sad images of a man grasping for something just beyond his reach.' – *Variety*

Mosquito Squadron
GB 1968 90m DeLuxe
Lewis J. Rachmil/UA
In 1944, the RAF tries out bouncing bombs in a French offensive.
Very minor and belated war heroics for double-billing.
w Donald Sanford, Joyce Perry *d* Boris Sagal *ph* Paul Beeson *m* Frank Cordell
☆ David McCallum, Suzanne Neve, David Buck, Dinsdale Landen, Charles Gray

Moss Rose
US 1947 82m bw
TCF (Gene Markey)
A Victorian chorus girl suspects her aristocratic admirer of being a murderer.
Absurd, stilted mystery melodrama with a better-looking production than it deserves.
w Jules Furthman, Tom Reed *d* Gregory Ratoff *ph* Joe MacDonald *m* David Buttolph
☆ Peggy Cummins, Victor Mature, Ethel Barrymore, Vincent Price

The Most Dangerous Game ***
US 1932 63m bw
(RKO)

GB title: *The Hounds of Zaroff*
A mad hunter lures guests on to his island so that he can hunt them down like animals.
Dated but splendidly shivery melodrama with moments of horror and mystery and a splendidly photographed chase sequence. Much imitated in curious ways, and not only by direct remakes such as A Game of Death *and* Run for the Sun *(qv).*
w James Creelman story Richard Connell d Ernest B. Schoedsack, Irving Pichel ph Henry Gerrard m Max Steiner
☆ *Leslie Banks*, Joel McCrea, Fay Wray, Robert Armstrong, Noble Johnson
'Futile stab at horror film classification, ineffective as entertainment and minus cast names to compensate.' – *Variety*

The Most Dangerous Man in the World
GB 1969 99m DeLuxe Panavision
TCF/APJAC (Mort Abrahams)
US title: *The Chairman*
A top scientist is sent by western intelligence on a mission into Red China, with a transmitter and a detonator implanted in his skull.
Wild Boys' Own Paper adventure which regrettably slows down in the middle for political philosophizing.
w Ben Maddow *novel* The Chairman by Jay Richard Kennedy *d* J. Lee-Thompson *ph* Ted Moore *m* Jerry Goldsmith
☆ Gregory Peck, Anne Heywood, Arthur Hill, Conrad Yama, Francisca Tu, Keye Luke, Alan Dobie, Ori Levy

The Most Desired Man
Germany 1994 94m colour
Gala/Neue Constantin/Olga (Bernd Eichinger)
original title: *Der Bewegte Mann*
After he is thrown out of their flat by his girlfriend, a handsome philanderer moves in with two homosexual men, who both fall for him.
Perhaps something has been lost in the translation, but this highly regarded (in Germany) comedy has little wit and not much humour.
wd Sönke Wortmann *comics* Der Bewegte Mann, Pretty Baby *by* Ralf König *ph* Gernot Roll *m* Torsten Breuer *pd* Monika Bauert *ed* Ueli Christen
☆ Til Schweiger, Katja Reimann, Joachim Krol, Rufus Beck, Armin Rohde, Nico van der Knapp, Antonia Lang
'Capped by endearing performances all round, this is a very funny movie which should ring recognition bells with under-35s of every romantic persuasion.' – *Empire*
'Ends up being a drab miscalculation.' – *Sight and Sound*
† It is the highest-grossing German film so far released in Germany.

The Most Terrible Time of My Life: see *Waga Jinsei Saiaku No Toki*

Most Wanted
US 1997 99m DeLuxe Super 35
New Line/Ivory Way (Eric L. Gold)

A former marine, working as an undercover agent, becomes the chief suspect when the President's wife is murdered.
Formulaic conspiracy-and-chase thriller; its only interest lies in another over-the-top performance from Voight as a crazed general.
w Keenen Ivory Wayans *d* David Glenn Hogan *ph* Marc Reshovsky *m* Paul Buckmaster *pd* Jean-Philippe Carp *ed* Michael J. Duthie
☆ Keenen Ivory Wayans, Jon Voight, Jill Hennessy, Paul Sorvino, Eric Roberts, Robert Culp, Wolfgang Bodison, Simon Baker Denny
'Plays like a made-for-video B movie that somehow won the lottery and got a theatrical release.' – *Joe Leydon, Variety*

'It takes all kinds of critters to make Farmer Vincent's fritters!'
Motel Hell
US 1980 106m Technicolor
United Artists/Camp Hill (Herb Jaffe)

Benign motel owners are famous for their spiced meat, which is in fact made from their human guests.
Horror comic intended to amuse, but too repulsive to do so.
w Robert Jaffe, Steven-Charles Jaffe *d* Kevin Connor *ph* Thomas Del Ruth *m* Lance Rubin
☆ Rory Calhoun, Paul Linke, Nancy Parsons, Nina Axelrod, Wolfman Jack

Mother ***
USSR 1926 90m approx (24 fps) bw silent
Mezhrabpom-Russ

original title: *Mat*
A mother incriminates her strike-breaking son, but realizes her error.
Propagandist social melodrama which is also brilliantly conceived and edited, with sequences matching those of Eisenstein.
w N. Zarkhi, V. I. Pudovkin *novel* Maxim Gorky *d V. I. Pudovkin* *ph* A. Golovnia
☆ Vera Baranovskaya, Nikolai Batalov
† Other versions appeared in 1920 and ({KW}d{/KW}Mark Donskoi) 1955

Mother and Son ***
Russia/Germany 1997 71m colour
Zero/O-Film/Severnij Fond/Lenfilm

original title: *Mat i syn*
In a large house near the sea, a son tends his dying mother.
A gently lyrical film about love and the immanence of death, and the beauty of the natural world. It has little dialogue, the actors are not professional, and it has no action in the conventional sense; yet it maintains a hushed, hypnotic hold.
w Yuri Arabov *d* Alexandr Sokurov *ph* Alexei Yodorov *m* Mikhail Ivanovich Glinka, Otmar Nussio *ad* Vera Zelinskaya *ed* Leda Semyonova
☆ Gudrun Geyer, Alexei Ananishov
'Its majestic, affective power makes most of cinema seem trivial, raucous, faked.' – *Julian Graffy, Sight and Sound*

The Mother and the Whore **

France 1973 219m bw

Gala/Films du Losange/Elite/Cine Qua Non/Simar/V.M. (Pierre Cottrell)

original title: *La Maman et la Putain*

A charming but idle man, who lives with his older mistress, dates a young nurse who moves in with them.

A long, sometimes desultory, but often engrossing debate on love, fidelity, sex, marriage and the comedy of human affairs.

wd Jean Eustache *ph* Pierre Lhomme, Jacques Renard, Michel Cenet *m* Mozart, Offenbach and others *ed* Jean Eustache, Denise de Casabianca

☆ Jean-Pierre Léaud, Françoise Lebrun, Bernadette Lafont, Isabelle Weingarten, Jacques Renard, Jean Eustache

'What is extraordinary is that Eustache mesmerises us into caring about each emotional quaver, creating suspense from seemingly inert surfaces, a tension between elusive sensibility and indisputable presence.' – *Jan Dawson, MFB*

Mother Carey's Chickens

US 1938 82m bw

RKO (Pandro S. Berman)

The tribulations of a small-town family in the 1890s.

Modest domestic drama, not totally unpleasing.

w S. K. Lauren, Gertrude Purcell *novel* Kate Douglas Wiggin *d* Rowland V. Lee *ph* Roy Hunt *m* Frank Tours

☆ Anne Shirley, Ruby Keeler, Fay Bainter, James Ellison, Walter Brennan, Donnie Dunagan, Frank Albertson, Alma Kruger, Jackie Moran, Virginia Weidler, Margaret Hamilton

† Remade 1963 as *Summer Magic*.

Mother Didn't Tell Me

US 1950 88m bw

TCF (Fred Kohlmar)

A working girl marries a doctor and their off duty hours don't coincide.

Thin comedy.

wd Claude Binyon *novel The Doctor Wears Three Faces* by Mary Baird *ph* Joseph LaShelle *m* Cyril Mockridge

☆ Dorothy McGuire, William Lundigan, June Havoc, Gary Merrill, Jessie Royce Landis

Mother Is a Freshman

US 1948 80m Technicolor

TCF

GB title: *Mother Knows Best*

A mother goes to college and falls for the teacher with whom her daughter is infatuated.

Thin romantic comedy lacking the piquancy at which it aims.

w Mary Loos, Richard Sale *d* Lloyd Bacon *ph* Arthur Arling *m* Alfred Newman

☆ Loretta Young, Van Johnson, Rudy Vallee, Barbara Lawrence, Betty Lynn, Robert Arthur

Mother Joan of the Angels: see *The Devil and the Nun*

Mother, Jugs and Speed

US 1976 98m DeLuxe Panavision

TCF (Joseph R. Barbera)

Comic and tragic events in the lives of Los Angeles drivers of private commercial ambulances.

Black comedy of incidents ranging from farcical to sentimental, sometimes funny but basically unacceptable in either vein.

w Tom Mankiewicz *d* Peter Yates *ph* Ralph Woolsey *m* various *md* Joel Sill

☆ Bill Cosby, Raquel Welch, Harvey Keitel, *Allen Garfield*, Bruce Davison, Larry Hagman

'The writer has found a way to get into the underbelly of a city, to survey the twilight territory where tragedy and comedy trip over each other and make an unsightly mess.' – *Time*

Mother Knows Best: see *Mother Is A Freshman*

'The lure of gold can make a man do anything!'

Mother Lode

US 1982 101m colour

Agamemnon/Martin Shafter, Andrew Scheinman (Fraser Clarke Heston, Andrew Snell)

A villainous miner stops at nothing to protect his goldfield.

More-or-less old-fashioned Western with a change of pace for the star. No world beater, but not bad.

w Fraser Clarke Heston, Peter Snell *d* Charlton Heston *ph* Richard Leiterman *m* Ken Wannberg *pd* Douglas Higgins

☆ Charlton Heston, Nick Mancuso, Kim Basinger, John Marley

'Howard W. Campbell, Jr. Is The Most Patriotic American In The Third Reich.'

Mother Night **

US 1996 110m bw/Foto-Kem

Fine Line/Whyaduck (Keith Gordon, Robert B. Weide)

While awaiting trial for war crimes, a German-born American recalls his career as an Allied agent and a Nazi sympathizer.

An engrossing attempt to film a complex novel concerned with moral relativities, although, despite its intelligence, it doesn't quite capture the original's ironic humour.

w Robert B. Weide *novel* Kurt Vonnegut *d* Keith Gordon *ph* Tom Richmond *m* Michael Convertino *pd* François Seguin *ed* Jay Rabinowitz

☆ *Nick Nolte*, Sheryl Lee, Alan Arkin, John Goodman, Kirsten Dunst, Arye Gross, Frankie Faison, David Straithairn, Bernard Behrens, Henry Gibson

'A movie that offers no easy rewards, this is still a deeply satisfying experience.' – *Bob McCabe, Empire*

Mother Riley Meets the Vampire

GB 1952 74m bw

Renown (John Gilling)

US title: *My Son the Vampire*

An old washerwoman accidentally catches a robot-wielding crook called The Vampire.

Childish farce notable for Lucan's last appearance in his dame role, and Lugosi's last substantial appearance of any kind – two pros at the end of their tether.

w Val Valentine *d* John Gilling *ph* Stan Pavey *m* Linda Southworth

☆ Arthur Lucan, Bela Lugosi, Dora Bryan, Richard Wattis

'Stupid, humourless and repulsive.' – *MFB*

Mother, Sir!: see *Navy Wife*

Mother Wore Tights *

US 1947 109m Technicolor

TCF (Lamar Trotti)

Recollections of a vaudeville team and their growing family.

Well-mounted, reasonably charming family musical, one of the best of the many TCF examples of this genre.

w Lamar Trotti *book* Miriam Young *d* Walter Lang *ph* Harry Jackson *md* Alfred Newman, Charles Henderson

☆ *Betty Grable, Dan Dailey*, Mona Freeman, Connie Marshall, Vanessa Brown, Robert Arthur, Sara Allgood, William Frawley, Ruth Nelson

Alfred Newman, Charles Henderson

Harry Jackson; song 'You Do' (*m*Josef Myrow, *ly*Mack Gordon)

Mother's Boys

US 1994 95m colour

Miramax/CBS (Jack E. Freedman, Wayne S. Williams, Patricia Herskovic)

A mother who left her husband and three sons decides she wants to return, despite the fact that no one wants her back.

Uninteresting attempt at a psychological thriller-cum-chiller, with an unconvincing script that steers clear of any suspense or emotional involvement.

w Barry Schneider, Richard Hawley *novel* Bernard Taylor *d* Yves Simoneau *ph* Elliot Davis *m* George S. Clinton *ad* David Bomba *ed* Michael Ornstein

☆ Jamie Lee Curtis, Peter Gallagher, Joanne Whalley-Kilmer, Vanessa Redgrave, Luke Edwards, Joss Ackland, Colin Ward, Joey Zimmerman

'A film that has an uninteresting beginning, an exploitative middle that actually cheats by genre standards, and a ludicrous climax that is borderline laughable.' – *Emanuel Levy, Variety*

'What do you see?'

The Mothman Prophecies

US 2001 119m colour Super 35

Helkon SK/Screen Gems/Lakeshore (Tom Rosenberg, Gary Lucchesi, Gary Goldstein)

A journalist investigates paranormal happenings that seem to be connected to the death of his wife and presage some disaster.

A gloomy trip into the twilight zone with a movie that follows the usual ominous conventions of the horror genre, but dispenses with the monster.

w Richard Hatem *book* John A. Keel *d* Mark Pellington *ph* Fred Murphy *m* Tomandandy *pd* Richard Hoover *ed* Brian Berdan *sp* Cinesite

☆ Richard Gere (John Klein), Laura Linney (Connie), Will Patton (Gordon Smallwood), Debra Messing (Mary Klein), Lucinda Jenney (Denise Smallwood), Alan Bates (Alexander Leek), David Eigenberg (Ed Fleischman), Ann McDonough (Lucy Griffin)

'A portentous journey into cinematic doom which fails to fully evoke its chilling and tragic dimensions.' – *Robert Koehler, Variety*

'Solemn, credulous junk.' – *Observer*

La Motocyclette: see *Girl on a Motorcycle*

Motorcycle Gang

US 1957 78m bw

AIP/Golden State (Alex Gordon)

A bad boy returns from prison to antagonize the local law-abiding motorcycle club.

Low-budget, low-grade drive-in movie, though its dialogue, written in what purports to be the latest teenage slang ('You're not hip to this new lingo. Miger? Mad tiger') has acquired a period curiosity.

w Lou Rusoff *d* Edward L. Cahn *ph* Frederick E. West *m* Albert Glasser *ad* Don Ament *ed* Richard C. Meyer

☆ Anne Neyland, Steve Terrell, John Ashley, Carl Switzer, Raymond Hatton, Wayne Taylor, Hal Bogart, Edmund Cobb

Mouchette *

France 1966 90m bw

Argos/Parc (Anatole Dauman)

An unloved 14-year-old schoolgirl contemplates her unhappy life with her alcoholic father and dying mother.

Grim, austere, unsparing examination of the misery of an outsider.

wd Robert Bresson *novel Nouvelle Histoire de Mouchette* by Georges Bernanos *ph* Ghislain Cloquet *m* Jean Wiener, Monteverdi *ad* Pierre Guffroy *ed* Raymond Lamy

☆ Nadine Nortier, Jean-Claude Guilbert, Marie Cardinal, Paul Hébert, Jean Vimenet, Marie Susini

Moulin Rouge

US 1934 69m bw

Twentieth Century (Darryl F. Zanuck)

The wife of a songwriter impersonates her own sister in order to revitalize her marriage and her stage career.

Predictable minor star vehicle, quite competently done.

w Nunnally Johnson, Henry Lehrman *play* Lyon de Bri *d* Sidney Lanfield *ph* Charles Rosher *md* Alfred Newman *songs* Harry Warren, Al Dubin

☆ Constance Bennett, Franchot Tone, Tullio Carminati, Helen Westley, Andrew Tombes, Hobart Cavanaugh

Moulin Rouge **

GB 1952 119m Technicolor

Romulus (Jack Clayton)

Fictional biopic of Toulouse Lautrec.

The dramatic emphasis is on the love affairs of the dwarfish artist, but the film's real interest is in its evocation of 19th-century Montmartre, and especially in the first twenty-minute can-can sequence. Nothing later can stand up to the exhilaration of this, and the film slowly slides into boredom.

w John Huston, Anthony Veiller *novel* Pierre La Mure *d* John Huston *ph* Oswald Morris *m* Georges Auric *ad Paul Sheriff ed* Ralph Kemplen *cos Marcel Vertes*

☆ José Ferrer (Henri de Toulouse-Lautrec), Zsa Zsa Gabor (Jane Avril), Katherine Kath (La Goulue), Colette Marchand (Marie Charlet), Suzanne Flon (Myriamme Hayem), Muriel Smith (Aicha), Lee Montague (Maurice Joyant), Harold Kasket (Zidler), Jill Bennett (Sarah), Christopher Lee (Seurat), Peter Cushing (Marcel de la Voisier)

Paul Sheriff; Marcel Vertes

picture; John Huston (as director); José Ferrer; Colette Marchand; Ralph Kemplen

'Some Things Are Worth The Risk.'

Moulin Rouge *

Australia/US 2001 128m DeLuxe Panavision

TCF/Bazmark (Martin Brown, Baz Luhrmann, Fred Baron)

In 19th-century Paris, a penniless poet vies with a rich aristocrat for the love of a courtesan.

Hyperkinetic, attention-seeking pop variation on La Bohème and La Traviata that is so over the top it parodies itself; its modern songs cannot carry the weight of emotion piled upon them, though it might have helped to have had a few singers in the cast.

w Baz Luhrmann, Craig Pearce *d* Baz Luhrmann *ph* Donald M. McAlpine *m* Craig Armstrong *md* Marius DeVries *pd* Catherine Martin *ed* Jill Bilcock *cos* Catherine Martin, Angus Strathie

☆ Nicole Kidman (Satine), Ewan McGregor (Christian), John Leguizamo (Toulouse-Lautrec), Jim Broadbent (Zidler), Richard Roxburgh (Duke of Worcester), Garry McDonald (The Doctor), Matthew Whittet (Satie), Kerry Walker (Marie), Kylie Minogue (Green Fairy)

'A tour de force of artifice, a dazzling pastiche of musical and visual elements at the service of a blatantly artificial story.' – *Todd McCarthy, Variety*

'Like being thrust into the middle of a loud and frantic party whether you want to be there or not. You can go with it or resist it, be exhilarated or worn out. But forgetting the experience is not one of your options.' – *Kenneth Turan, Los Angeles Times*

'Overwrought and underwhelming…This tawdry bauble has less drama and lousier karaoke than any given episode of *Ally McBeal*.' – *J. Hoberman, Village Voice*

♫ 'Nature Boy'; 'Lady Marmalade'; 'Children of the Revolution'; 'Diamonds Are a Girl's Best Friend'; 'Material Girl'; 'Your Song'; 'Sound of Music'; 'One Day I'll Fly Away'; 'All You Need is Love'; 'Like a Virgin'; 'Come What May'; 'Fool To Believe'; 'The Show Must Go On'

Catherine Martin (art direction); Catherine Martin, Angus Strathie (costumes)

picture; Nicole Kidman; Donald M. McAlpine; Jill Bilcock; Maurizio Silvi, Aldo Signoretti; sound (Andy Nelson, Anna Behlmer, Roger Savage, Guntis Sics)

Jim Broadbent; sound; music

The Mountain *

US 1956 105m Technicolor Vistavision

Paramount (Edward Dmytryk)

After an airplane crash the wreck is difficult to reach. A young man sets off alone to loot it, and his elder brother follows to stop him.

An indeterminate production in which one believes neither the setting, the plot nor the characters, especially not with Vistavision making everything sharply unreal and the brothers seeming two generations apart.

w Ranald MacDougall *novel* Henri Troyat *d* Edward Dmytryk *ph* Franz Planer *m* Daniele Amfitheatrof

☆ Spencer Tracy, Robert Wagner, Claire Trevor, William Demarest, E. G. Marshall

'A terrible picture. It goes on forever and it's bad.' – *Claire Trevor*

The Mountain Eagle

GB 1926 72m approx (24 fps) bw silent

Gainsborough/Emelka (Michael Balcon)

US title: *Fear o' God*

A young schoolmistress resists the attentions of a businessman, escapes to the mountains, and marries a recluse.

Unremarkable romantic drama; one of the lost Hitchcock films.

w Eliot Stannard *d* Alfred Hitchcock *ph* Baron Ventimiglia
☆ Nita Naldi, Bernard Goetzke, Malcolm Keen

Mountain Justice
US 1937 82m bw
Warner
A frightened hillbilly girl kills her brutal father and is protected by a lawyer.
Involved backwoods melodrama, not really worth the trouble.
w Norman Reilly Raine, Luci Ward *d* Michael Curtiz
☆ Josephine Hutchinson, George Brent, Robert Barrat, Guy Kibbee, Mona Barrie, Margaret Hamilton, Robert McWade
'Too much plot, but okay for duals.' – *Variety*

The Mountain Men
US 1980 102m Metrocolor Panavision
Columbia (Martin Ransohoff)
Two 19th-century trappers have adventures with Indians.
Rumbustious, foul-mouthed and lethargic Western of the primitive kind; no possible interest.
w Fraser Clarke Heston *d* Richard Lang *ph* Michel Hugo *m* Michel Legrand
☆ Charlton Heston, Brian Keith, Victoria Racimo, Stephen Macht, John Glover
'It plays like a Sunn Classic four-waller uncomfortably spiced up with violence and profanity.' – *Variety*.

'It's The Snappiest Ole Swing Music, An' It's Echoin' Thru The Land.'
Mountain Music
US 1937 76m bw
Paramount
A hillbilly runs from a marriage and loses his memory.
Tiresome comedy with music.
w J. C. Moffitt, Duke Atterbury, Russel Crouse, Charles Lederer *story* Mackinlay Kantor *d* Robert Florey
☆ Martha Raye, Bob Burns, John Howard, George Hayes, Rufe Davis, Fuzzy Knight
'Burns and Raye have trouble topping a cast. Mild and minor.' – *Variety*

The Mountain of the Cannibal God: see *La Montagna del Dio Cannibale*

The Mountain Road
US 1960 102m bw
Columbia/William Goetz
In 1944 China, an American officer helps peasants against the Japanese.
Confused and rather dreary war adventure with pretensions.
w Alfred Hayes *novel* Theodore White *d* Daniel Mann *ph* Burnett Guffey *m* Jerome Moross *md* Morris Stoloff
☆ James Stewart (Major Baldwin), Lisa Lu (Mme Sue-Mei Hung), Glenn Corbett (Collins), Henry Morgan (Michaelson), Frank Silvera (General Kwan), James Best (Niergaard), Mike Kellin, Frank Maxwell, Alan Baxter

Mountains of the Moon **
US 1989 136m Technicolor
Guild/Carolco/IndieProd (Daniel Melnick)
Explorers Richard Burton and John Hanning Speke go in search of the source of the Nile.
Exuberant and engrossing epic that catches the mood of the times.
w William Harrison, Bob Rafelson *story* *Burton and Speke* by William Harrison *d* Bob Rafelson *ph* Dick Pope *m* Michael Small *pd* Norman Reynolds *ed* Thom Noble
☆ Patrick Bergin, Iain Glen, Richard E. Grant, Fiona Shaw, John Savident, James Villiers, Adrian Rawlins, Peter Vaughan, Delroy Lindo, Bernard Hill
'Somehow it conveys, as few movies ever have, the miserable realities that underlay the 19th century's heroic age of exploration.' – *Richard Schickel, Time*
'Worth seeing principally because it is a real film, by a director who understands the true nature of cinema as a visual medium.' – *Derek Malcolm, Guardian*

'Mother and daughter! Rivals in love!'
Mourning Becomes Electra *
US 1947 170m bw
RKO/Theatre Guild (Dudley Nichols)
Murder, doom and guilt affect a New England family at the end of the Civil War.
A mark for trying is all. This is a clearly fated attempt to film the unfilmable, a long and lugubrious updating of Sophocles with more than its share of risible moments.
wd Dudley Nichols *play* Eugene O'Neill *ph* George Barnes *m* Richard Hagemann *ad* Albert D'Agostino
☆ Michael Redgrave, Rosalind Russell, Katina Paxinou, Kirk Douglas, Raymond Massey, Nancy Coleman, Leo Genn
'A star cast fumbles with helpless and sometimes touching ineptitude.' – *Gavin Lambert*
'Within its own terms of mistaken reverence, a good, straight, deliberately unimaginative production.' – *James Agee*
'It is apparent from their accents that they have only recently become a family.' – *Pauline Kael, 70s*
Michael Redgrave; Rosalind Russell

'The squeak shall inherit the earth'
Mouse Hunt **
US 1997 97m Technicolor
DreamWorks (Alan Riche, Tony Ludwig, Bruce Cohen)
Two antagonistic brothers attempt to get rid of a mouse that inhabits the derelict mansion they inherit.
Slick slapstick comedy with a dark, Gothic tone that only lightens at the very end. There's an occasional nod to Laurel and Hardy, but the edgy humour owes much more to Tom and Jerry.
w Adam Rifkin *d* Gore Verbinski *ph* Phedon Papamichael *m* Alan Silvestri *pd* Linda DeScenna *ed* Craig Wood *sp* Stan Winston
☆ Nathan Lane (Ernie Smuntz), Lee Evans (Lars Smuntz), Vicki Lewis (April Smuntz), Maury Chaykin (Alexander Falko), Eric Christmas (Lawyer), Michael Jeter (Quincy Thorpe), Christopher Walken (Caesar), Debra Christofferson (Ingrid), Camilla Soeberg (Hilde), William Hickey (Rudolf Smuntz)
'This often screamingly funny comedy about a resilient rodent has enough across-the-board appeal to click with audiences of all ages.' – *Joe Leydon, Variety*
† The picture is dedicated to William Hickey, who died soon after his filming was completed.

The Mouse on the Moon
GB 1963 85m Eastmancolor
UA/Walter Shenson
The tiny duchy of Grand Fenwick discovers that its home-made wine makes excellent rocket fuel.
Piddling sequel to The Mouse that Roared, *suffering from a hesitant script, too few jokes, and overacting.*
w Michael Pertwee *novel* Leonard Wibberley *d* Richard Lester *ph* Wilkie Cooper *m* Ron Grainer
☆ Margaret Rutherford, Ron Moody, Bernard Cribbins, David Kossoff, Terry-Thomas, Michael Crawford

The Mouse that Roared **
GB 1959 85m Technicolor
Columbia/Open Road (Carl Foreman)
The tiny duchy of Grand Fenwick is bankrupt, and its minister decides to declare war on the United States, be defeated, and receive Marshall Aid.
Lively comedy which sounds rather better than it plays, but has bright moments.
w Roger Macdougall, Stanley Mann *novel* Leonard Wibberley *d* Jack Arnold *ph* John Wilcox *m* Edwin Astley *ad* Geoffrey Drake *ed* Raymond Poulton
☆ Peter Sellers (Tully Bascombe/Grand Duchess/Prime Minister), Jean Seberg (Helen), David Kossoff (Professor Kokintz), William Hartnell (Will), Leo McKern (Benter), Macdonald Parke (Snippe5), Harold Kasket (Pedro), Timothy Bateson (Roger)
'The kind of irrepressible topical satire whose artistic flaws become increasingly apparent but whose merits outlast them.' – *Peter John Dyer*

Mouth to Mouth
Australia 1978 94m colour
Vega (Jon Sainken)
Two sisters, who squat in a deserted warehouse and live by petty theft and occasional prostitution, form a casual relationship with two young men looking for work.
A dull slice of Melbourne low-life, peopled by no-hopers looking for something to rebel against.
wd John Duigan *ph* Tom Cowan *m* Roy Ritchie *ad* Tracy Watt *ed* Tony Paterson
☆ Kim Krejus, Sonia Peat, Ian Gilmour, Sergio Frazzetto, Walter Pym, Michael Carman

The Mouthpiece **
US 1932 90m bw
Warner (Lucien Hubbard)
A prosecuting counsel successfully turns to defence but becomes corrupt.
A hard-hitting and entertaining melodrama allegedly based on the career of William Fallon, a New York lawyer.
w Joseph Jackson, Earl Baldwin *d* James Flood, Elliott Nugent *ph* Barney McGill
☆ *Warren William*, Sidney Fox, Aline MacMahon, John Wray, Ralph Ince, Guy Kibbee
'First-grade melodrama, a bet for all grades of houses.' – *Variety*

Le Mouton a Cinq Pattes: see *The Sheep Has Five Legs*

Move
US 1970 88m DeLuxe Panavision
TCF
A frustrated playwright writes pornography to make money; he moves to a larger apartment but his mind is full of fantasies.
None of which are of much interest to the paying customers, the movie being drenched with self-pity.
w Joel Lieber, Stanley Hart *novel* Joel Lieber *d* Stuart Rosenberg
☆ Elliott Gould, Paula Prentiss, Genevieve Waite, John Larch, Joe Silver

Move Over Darling **
US 1963 103m DeLuxe Cinemascope
TCF/Arcola/Arwin (Aaron Rosenberg, Marty Melcher)
A wife who has spent five years shipwrecked on a desert island returns to find that her husband has just remarried.
Thin but fitfully amusing remake of My Favorite Wife; *sheer professionalism gets it by.*
w Hal Kanter, Jack Sher *d* Michael Gordon *ph* Daniel L. Fapp *m* Lionel Newman
☆ Doris Day, James Garner, Polly Bergen, Thelma Ritter, Chuck Connors, Fred Clark

Movers and Shakers
US 1985 79m Metrocolor
MGM-UA/BHC (Charles Grodin, William Asher)
A Hollywood writer tries to cope with a difficult project while having personal problems with his wife.
Mishmash of unrealized anecdotes with pauses for studio in-jokes. Despite the talent, it could never have worked, not even under the previously announced title Dreamers.
w Charles Grodin *d* William Asher *ph* Robbie Greenberg *m* Ken and Mitzie Welch
☆ Walter Matthau, Charles Grodin, Vincent Gardenia, Tyne Daly, Bill Macy, Gilda Radner, Steve Martin, Nita Talbot
'Only occasionally amusing: faces a bleak box-office future.' – *Variety*

Movie Crazy **
US 1932 82m bw
Harold Lloyd
A filmstruck young man is mistakenly invited to Hollywood for a film test.
The silent comedian is not quite at his best in this early sound comedy, but it contains his last really superb sequences and its picture of Hollywood is both amusing and nostalgic.
w Harold Lloyd and others *d* Clyde Bruckman *ph* Walter Lundin
☆ Harold Lloyd, Constance Cummings
'A corking comedy, replete with wow belly laughs. Sure-fire.' – *Variety*

Movie Movie **
US 1978 106m bw/colour
ITC (Stanley Donen)
A pastiche of a thirties double bill, including a boxing yarn (*Dynamite Hands*) and a Busby-Berkeley style girlie show (*Baxter's Beauties of 1933*).
Unfortunately there weren't enough paying customers to appreciate the spoofs, which are pretty patchy anyway; but golden moments stay in the mind.
w Larry Gelbart, Sheldon Keller *d* Stanley Donen *ph* Chuck Rosher Jnr, Bruce Surtees *m* Ralph Burns *ch* Michael Kidd
☆ George C. Scott, Trish Van Devere, Red Buttons, Eli Wallach, Michael Kidd, Barbara Harris, Barry Bostwick, Art Carney, Jocelyn Brando
'Camp, which has to do with a switch of vision from one era to another, cannot be created, and where it is, as this and previous attempts testify, it is immediately swallowed in its own idiocy.' – *Richard Combs, MFB*

Movietone Follies of 1930
US 1930 70m bw
Fox
A rich boy courts a chorus girl, and her friends give a show on his estate.
Thin, fumbling drama which doesn't remember to become a musical till it's halfway through, and even then has little spark.
w William K. Wells *d* Ben Stoloff *ph* William O'Connell *md* Arthur Kay
☆ El Brendel, Marjorie White, William Collier Jnr, Miriam Seegar, Frank Richardson

Moving
US 1988 89m Technicolor
Warner (Stuart Cornfeld)
A traffic engineer runs into all kinds of trouble when he decides to move his family from New Jersey to Idaho.
Disappointingly predictable comedy, making all the obvious jokes in a leaden way.
w Andy Breckman *d* Alan Metter *ph* Donald McAlpine *m* Howard Shore *pd* David L. Snyder *ed* Alan Balsam
☆ Richard Pryor, Beverly Todd, Randy Quaid, Dave Thomas, Dana Carvey, Stacey Dash, Gordon Jump, Morris Day

The Moving Target: see *Harper*

Moving Violation *
US 1976 91m DeLuxe
TCF/Roger Corman
Small-town teenagers are pursued by the sheriff because they saw him commit a murder.
Old hat suspenser with a smart new line in thrills.
w David R. Osterhout, William Norton d Charles S. Dubin *ph* Charles Correll *m* Don Leake
☆ Stephen McHattie, Kay Lenz, Eddie Albert, Lonny Chapman, Will Geer
'Probably the most hair-raising pursuit sequences in the history of film.' – *Cleveland Amory*

Moving Violations
US 1985 90m DeLuxe
Ufland-Roth-IPI-James G. Robinson/TCF
Misadventures of trainee traffic school cops.
Wasn't Police Academy *bad enough?*
w Neal Israel, Pat Proft *d* Neal Israel
☆ John Murray, Jennifer Tilly, James Keach, Brian Backer

Mua He Chieu Thang Dung
France/Germany/Vietnam 2000 112m colour
Artificial Eye/Lazennec/Canal+/Arte France/Hang Phim Truyen (Christophe Rossignon)
aka: *At the Height of Summer*
US title: *The Vertical Ray of the Sun*
In Hanoi, three sisters, two of them married, come to terms with the men in their life.
Ravisingly photographed domestic drama, set between memorial celebrations of the death of parents, that deals with the pains and pleasures of love and the familiar.
wd Tran Anh Hung *ph* Mark Lee *m* Ton That Tiet *pd* Benoit Barouh *ed* Mario Battistel

☆ Tran Nu Yen Khe (Lien), Nguyen Nhu Quynh (Suong), Le Khanh (Khanh), Ngo Quang Hai (Hai), Chu Hung (Quoc), Tran Manh Cuong (Kien), Le Tuan Anh (Tuan), Le Ngoc Dung (Huong)

'Beautiful, languorous, passive – it plays like background music for itself.' – *Roger Ebert, Chicago Sun-Times*

'A Romantic Comedy For Anyone Who's Ever Been In Love.'

Much Ado about Nothing **

GB 1993 111m Technicolor

Samuel Goldwyn/Renaissance (Steven Evans, David Parfitt, Kenneth Branagh)

A man and a woman who have sworn never to marry are tricked into falling in love with each other.

A lively version of Shakespeare's witty romantic comedy, but suffering from some miscasting, plodding direction and rather too much forced jollity to be entirely successful.

wd Kenneth Branagh *play* William Shakespeare *ph* Roger Lanser *m* Patrick Doyle *pd* Tim Harvey *ed* Andrew Marcus

☆ Kenneth Branagh, *Richard Briers*, Michael Keaton, Denzel Washington, Robert Sean Leonard, Keanu Reeves, Emma Thompson, Kate Beckinsale, Brian Blessed, Patrick Doyle, Imelda Staunton, Phyllida Law, Ben Elton

'This isn't the best Shakespeare on film ... but it may be the best movie Shakespeare.' – *Richard Corliss, Time*

'Triumphantly romantic, comic and emotionally alive.' – *Vincent Canby, New York Times*

'One of the few movies of recent years that could leave audiences weeping for joy.' – *David Denby, New York*

Much Too Shy

GB 1942 92m bw

Columbia (Ben Henry)

A gormless handyman gets into trouble when the portraits of his lady clients are sold to an advertising agency with nude bodies added to them.

A slightly vulgar and talkative farce which restricts the star.

w Ronald Frankau *d* Marcel Varnel *ph* Arthur Crabtree

☆ George Formby, Kathleen Harrison, Hylda Bayley, Eileen Bennett, Joss Ambler, Jimmy Clitheroe

Muddy River *

Japan 1981 105m bw

Unifilm/Contemporary/Kimura Productions (Motoyasu Kimura)

original title: *Doro No Kawa*

Two nine-year-old boys become friends and try to make sense of the adult world around them.

A small and charming story, sharply observed and photographed.

w Takaki Shigemori *novel* Teru Miyamoto *d* Kohei Oguri *ph* Shohei Ando *m* Kuroudo Mori *ad* Akira Naito *ed* Nobuo Ogawa

☆ Nobutaka Asahara, Takahiro Tamura, Yumiko Fujita, Masako Yagi, Minoru Sakurai, Makiko Shibata, Mariko Kaga

♀ best foreign film

Der Müde Tod: see *Destiny*

The Mudlark **

GB 1950 98m bw

TCF (Nunnally Johnson)

A scruffy boy from the docks breaks into Windsor Castle to see Queen Victoria and ends her fifteen years of seclusion.

A pleasant whimsical legend which could have done without the romantic interest, but which despite an air of unreality provides warm-hearted, well upholstered entertainment for family audiences.

w Nunnally Johnson novel Theodore Bonnet *d Jean Negulesco ph Georges Périnal m* William Alwyn *ad* C. P. Norman

☆ *Alec Guinness*, Irene Dunne, *Andrew Ray*, Anthony Steel, Constance Smith, *Finlay Currie, Edward Rigby*

La Muerte de un Burocrata: see *Death of a Bureaucrat*

Muerte de un Ciclista: see *Death of a Cyclist*

Mug Town

US 1942 60m bw

Universal

The Little Tough Guys get mixed up with hi-jackers.

A failing entry in this series: the ageing teenagers shortly decided to play for laughs.

w Brenda Weisberg, Harold Tarshis, Harry Sucher and Lewis Amster *d* Ray Taylor

☆ Billy Halop, Huntz Hall, Bernard Punsley, Gabriel Dell, Grace McDonald, Edward Norris, Jed Prouty

Mùi Du Du Xanh: see *The Scent of the Green Papaya*

Mujeres al Borde de un Ataque de Nervios: see *Women on the Verge of a Nervous Breakdown*

Mulan *

US 1998 88m Technicolor

Buena Vista/Walt Disney (Pam Coats)

A Chinese girl disguises herself as a warrior and rescues the Emperor from the barbarian hordes threatening the country.

An animated film that will no doubt be enjoyed by its target audience; for adults it offers less, despite its attractive style, incorporating something of a Chinese approach to art within the familiar Disney manner.

w Rita Hsiao, Christopher Sanders, Philip Lazebnik, Raymond Singer, Eugenia Bostwick-Singer *story* Robert D. San Souci *d* Barry Cook, Tony Bancroft *m* Jerry Goldsmith *m/ly* Matthew Wilder, David Zippel *pd* Hans Bacher *ed* Michael Kelly

☆ Featuring the voices of: Ming-Na Wen (singing: Lea Salonga), Eddie Murphy, B. D. Wong (singing: Donny Osmond), Harvey Fierstein, Jerry S. Tondo, Gedde Watanabe (singing: Matthew Wilder), James Hong, Miguel Ferrer, Soon-Tek Oh, Freda Foh Shen, Pat Morita, June Foray (singing: Marni Nixon), George Takei, Miriam Margolyes, James Shigeta, Frank Welker

'Quite likely the first animated cross-dressing action musical.' – *Todd McCarthy, Variety*

'Kids are going to love this movie.' – *Observer*

♀ Jerry Goldsmith, Matthew Wilder, David Zippel

'A Love Story In The City Of Dreams.'

Mulholland Dr. **

US/France 2001 146m FotoKem

Pathé/Alain Sarde/Studio-Canal/Asymmetrical (Mary Sweeney, Alain Sarde, Neal Edelstein, Michael Polaire, Tony Krantz)

aka: *Mulholland Drive*

A would-be actress goes to Hollywood in search of stardom and finds disappointment, heartbreak and, possibly, death instead.

Based in part on an abortive pilot for a TV series, this recycles too many motifs from Lynch's previous work, from a mysterious dwarf to slipping and shared identities and contrived coincidences. But, showing life as a succession of power struggles, it holds the attention, even if, under the deliberate obfuscation, it seems no more than a trite stripping away of the false tinsel of Hollywood to reveal the real tinsel beneath.

wd David Lynch *ph* Peter Deming *m* Angelo Badalamenti *pd* Jack Fisk *ed* Mary Sweeney *cos* Amy Stofsky

☆ Justin Theroux (Adam Kesher), Naomi Watts (Betty Elms), Laura Elena Harring (Rita), Ann Miller (Coco Lenoix), Dan Hedaya (Vincenzo Castigliane), Mark Pellegrino (Joe), Brian Beacock (Studio Singer), Robert Forster (Det Harry McKnight)

'Endless tedious mind-rot.' – *Barbara Ellen, Times*

'Compelling but intentionally inscrutable return of the "weird" David Lynch that will please his hardcore fans even if it has them scratching their heads as well.' – *Todd McCarthy, Variety*

♀ David Lynch (as director)

Mary Sweeney

'A New Kind Of Law Enforcement.'

Mulholland Falls *

US 1996 107m DeLuxe

Polygram/MGM/Largo/Zanuck (Richard D. Zanuck, Lili Fini Zanuck)

In Los Angeles in the 50s, four detectives investigate the death of a woman who is linked with work at an atomic test site.

Period thriller that looks better than it plays; it never fully engages an audience's attention, and the ending is unsatisfactory.

w Pete Dexter, Floyd Mutrux *d* Lee Tamahori *ph* Haskell Wexler *m* Dave Grusin *pd* Richard Sylbert *ed* Sally Menke

☆ Nick Nolte, Melanie Griffith, Chazz Palminteri, Michael Madsen, Chris Penn, Treat Williams, Jennifer Connelly, Daniel Baldwin, Andrew McCarthy, John Malkovich, Bruce Dern, Ed Lauter

'It will pleasure everyone in love with the old Forties landscape of no-nonsense cynicism that Bogart and Stanwyck sculpted.' – *Alexander Walker*

'She's always known he's the one. She didn't know he was also the two, the three and the four...'

Multiplicity

US 1996 117m Technicolor Panavision

Columbia (Trevor Albert, Harold Ramis)

A workaholic runs into problems when he clones himself in order to spend more time with his wife and children.

A clever concept, which ought to have resulted in a much funnier comedy instead of this conventional farce, though Keaton does well in differentiating his various roles.

w Chris Miller, Mary Hale, Lowell Ganz, Babaloo Mandel *d* Harold Ramis *ph* Laszlo Kovacs *m* George Fenton *pd* Jackson DeGovia *ed* Pem Herring, Craig Herring

☆ Michael Keaton, Andie MacDowell, Harris Yulin, Richard Masur, Eugene Levy, Ann Cusack, John de Lancie, Brian Doyle-Murray

'Afterwards you can't help wishing you'd got someone else to watch it for you.' – *Tom Shone, Sunday Times*

'Some towns have all the fun.'

Mumford

US 1999 112m colour

Buena Vista/Touchstone (Charles Okun, Lawrence Kasdan)

A new psychiatrist in town, who attracts many new patients, is not all he seems to be.

Mild and underdeveloped small-town comedy.

wd Lawrence Kasdan *ph* Ericson Core *m* James Newton Howard *pd* Jon Hutman *ed* Carol Littleton, William Steinkamp

☆ Loren Dean (Mumford), Hope Davis (Sofie Crisp), Jason Lee (Skip Skipperton), Alfre Woodard (Lily), Mary McDonnell (Althea Brockett), Pruitt Taylor Vince (Henry Follett), Zooey Deschanel (Nessa Watkins), Martin Short (Lionel Dillard), David Paymer (Dr Ernest Delbanco), Jane Adams (Dr Phyllis Sheeler), Dana Ivey (Mrs Crisp), Kevin Tighe (Mr Crisp)

'It's neither funny, heart-warming nor star-powered enough to motivate the public to turn out in very large numbers.' – *Todd McCarthy, Variety*

'It comes to life!'

'A love story that lived for three thousand years!'

The Mummy **

US 1932 72m bw

Universal (Stanley Bergerman)

An Egyptian mummy comes back to life and covets a young girl.

Strange dreamlike horror film with only fleeting frissons but plenty of narrative interest despite the silliest of stories and some fairly stilted acting.

w John L. Balderston d Karl Freund ph Charles Stumar m Tchaikovsky *ad Willy Pogany ed* Milton Carruth *sp* make-up: Jack Pierce

☆ *Boris Karloff*, Zita Johann, David Manners, Arthur Byron, Edward Van Sloan

'Should show profit despite fairy tale theme.' – *Variety*

'It beggars description ... one of the most unusual talkies ever produced.' – *New York Times*

'Editing very much in the Germanic style, magnificent lighting and a superb performance from Karloff make this a fantasy almost without equal.' – *John Baxter, 1968*

† The star was billed simply as 'Karloff the uncanny'.

The Mummy *

GB 1959 88m Technicolor

Hammer (Michael Carreras)

A mummy brought back to England by archaeologists wakes up and goes on the rampage.

Typical Hammer vulgarization of a Hollywood legend; starts slowly and unpleasantly, but picks up speed and resource in the last half hour.

w Jimmy Sangster *d* Terence Fisher *ph* Jack Asher *m* Frank Reizenstein

☆ Peter Cushing, Christopher Lee, Yvonne Furneaux, Eddie Byrne, Felix Aylmer, Raymond Huntley, John Stuart

† Hammer sequels, of little interest, were *Curse of the Mummy's Tomb* (1964), *The Mummy's Shroud* (1966) and *Blood from the Mummy's Tomb* (1971).

'The Legend Rises Again.'

The Mummy *

US 1999 124m DeLuxe Panavision

Universal/Alphaville (James Jacks, Sean Daniel)

An Egyptian priest, who was mummified alive more than two thousand years previously, is revived when his burial place is discovered by an American explorer.

A tongue-in-the-cheek Boy's Own adventure, which is played mostly for laughs and the occasional shock, and is notable only for its computer-generated special effects.

wd Stephen Sommers *ph* Adrian Biddle *m* Jerry Goldsmith *pd* Allan Cameron *ed* Bob Ducsay *sp* John Andrew Berton Jnr; Chris Corbould; Nick Dudman

☆ Brendan Fraser, Rachel Weisz, John Hannah, Arnold Vosloo, Kevin J. O'Connor, Jonathan Hyde, Oded Fehr, Erick Avari, Stephen Dunham, Corey Johnson, Tuc Watkins

'Universal's attempt to find gold by bringing to new life one of the mustier items in its vaults is pure hokum and scarcely of the first order.' – *Todd McCarthy, Variety*

† The film was a box-office success, taking $43.3m in its first three days at the US box-office, the ninth-best opening gross so far. It went on to gross more than $155m at the US box-office.

♀ sound (Leslie Shatz, Chris Carpenter, Rick Kline, Chris Munro)

'Adventure Is Reborn.'

The Mummy Returns

US 2001 129m DeLuxe Panavision

Universal/Alphaville (James Jacks, Sean Daniel)

A young boy discovers in an Egyptian tomb a bracelet that results in the resurrection of the mummy of Imhotep and of his ancient adversary, the Scorpion King, threatening the future of the world.

Woefully unimaginative adventure that is no more than an overblown Saturday morning serial; it shuffles musty narrative artifices, mainly derived from pulp fiction of eighty years ago, and downplays the Mummy in favour of unexciting computer-generated effects.

wd Stephen Sommers *ph* Adrian Biddle *m* Alan Silvestri *pd* Allan Cameron *ed* Bob Ducsay, Kelly Matsumoto *sp* Industrial Light & Magic

☆ Brendan Fraser (Rick O'Connell), Rachel Weisz (Evelyn/Nefertiti), John Hannah (Jonathan), Arnold Vosloo (Imhotep), Oded Fehr (Ardeth Bay), Patricia Velasquez (Meela/Anck-Su-Namun), Alex (Freddie Boath), Alun Armstrong (Curator), The Rock (The Scorpion King), Adewale Akinnuoye-Agbaje (Lock-Nah), Shaun Parkes (Izzy)

'May be the least original motion picture ever, and there's a lot of competition for that title these days...This enterprise is to the movies what an average boy band is to pop; just because there's an audience for it doesn't mean it's any good.' – *Elvis Mitchell, New York Times*

'This follow-up still lacks the wit and elan that would have made this burgeoning series more than a popcorn-picture franchise. But the widescreen here virtually bursts with visual goodies.' – *Todd McCarthy, Variety*

† The film cost $100m to make. It had the second biggest opening in cinema history, taking $68.1m at the US box-office.

Mummy's Boys
US 1936 68m bw
RKO (Lee Marcus)
Two ditch diggers in Egypt encounter some dirty work by a mad archaeologist.
Ho-hum comedy with tired old gags.
w Jack Townley, Philip G. Epstein, Charles Roberts *d* Fred Guiol *ph* Jack MacKenzie *md* Roy Webb
☆ Bert Wheeler, Robert Woolsey, Barbara Pepper, Moroni Olsen, Willie Best
'Poorly acted, raggedly written ... net result of the dialogue is about four snickers.' – *Variety*

'Egypt's ancient loves live again in evil!'
The Mummy's Curse
US 1945 62m bw
Universal (Oliver Drake)
Sequel to *The Mummy's Ghost* (qv), notable for many loose ends of narrative.
Last of the Universal mummy films (until Abbott and Costello met him).
w Bernard Schubert *d* Leslie Goodwins
☆ Peter Coe, Martin Kosleck, Kay Harding, Kurt Katch, Virginia Christine, Lon Chaney Jnr
'This film contains the most nauseous horror imaginable and is not for the squeamish.' – *MFB*
† See also *Abbott and Costello Meet the Mummy.*

'Nameless! Fleshless! Deathless!'
The Mummy's Ghost
US 1944 60m bw
Universal (Ben Pivar)
The slow but unstoppable Kharis is now on the trail of his long-lost princess.
A slight improvement on its predecessor, The Mummy's Tomb.
w Griffin Jay, Henry Sucher, Brenda Weisberg *d* Reginald LeBorg *ph* Virgil Miller *md* Paul Sawtell
☆ John Carradine, George Zucco, Ramsay Ames, Robert Lowery, Barton MacLane, Lon Chaney Jnr

'Tomb of a thousand terrors!'
The Mummy's Hand **
US 1940 67m bw
Universal (Ben Pivar)
The high priest of an evil sect revivifies an Egyptian mummy and uses it to kill off members of an archaeological expedition.
Semi-sequel to 1932's The Mummy, *economically using the same flashback. It starts off in comedy vein, but the last half hour is among the most scary in horror film history.*
w Griffin Jay, Maxwell Shane *d* Christy Cabanne *ph* Elwood Bredell
☆ Dick Foran, Wallace Ford, *George Zucco,* Cecil Kellaway, Peggy Moran, *Tom Tyler, Eduardo Ciannelli*
† Sequels, of decreasing merit, were *The Mummy's Tomb* (1942) (in which the heroes of *The Mummy's Hand* are killed off), *The Mummy's Ghost* (1944) and *The Mummy's Curse* (1944). See also *Abbott and Costello Meet the Mummy.*

'Buried alive for 3700 years! Brought back to live, love and kill!'
'Beware the beat of the cloth-wrapped feet!'
The Mummy's Shroud
GB 1966 84m Technicolor
Hammer (Anthony Nelson-Keys)
In the twenties, an exhumed mummy brought to the city museum is restored to life and slaughters those who disturbed his rest.
Uninventive rehash of every other mummy movie; too hackneyed to be saved even by a good cast and production values.
wd John Gilling *ph* Arthur Grant *m* Don Banks
☆ John Phillips, André Morell, David Buck, Elizabeth Sellars, Catherine Lacey, Maggie Kimberley, Michael Ripper, Tim Barrett, Roger Delgado, Dickie Owen

'Eyes That Crawl With Madness! Hands That Creep Like Cobras!'
The Mummy's Tomb
US 1942 61m bw
Ben Pivar/Universal
The aged high priest sends a young disciple to America, where Kharis dutifully kills off those who violated his tomb.
Shoddily made sequel to The Mummy's Hand, *with much re-used footage; astonishingly, it broke box-office records for its year, and provoked two more episodes.*
w Griffin Jay, Henry Sucher *d* Harold Young *ph* George Robinson *ad* Jack Otterson *ed* Milton Carruth
☆ Turhan Bey, George Zucco, Dick Foran, Wallace Ford, Elyse Knox, Lon Chaney Jnr

Mumsy, Nanny, Sonny and Girly
GB 1969 102m Eastmancolor
CIRO/Brigitte (Ronald J. Kahn)
aka: *Girly*
Two adolescents bring home lonely people as playthings for a homicidal family.
Revolting black comedy for masochists, representing the British cinema at its lowest ebb.
w Brian Comport *play* Maisie Mosco *d* Freddie Francis *ph* David Muir *m* Bernard Ebbinghouse
☆ Michael Bryant, Ursula Howells, Pat Heywood, Howard Trevor, Vanessa Howard

Münchausen **
Germany 1943 134m Agfacolor
UFA (Eberhard Schmidt)
aka: *The Adventures of Baron Münchausen*
In the 1940s Baron Münchausen tells stories of his fabulous ancestor who, it is soon clear, is himself, having been given immortality by a magician.
Lavish but somewhat stilted spectacle, produced on the orders of Nazi propagandist Joseph Goebbels to mark the studio's twenty-fifth anniversary. His influence is evident in the way that all other nationalities are shown as comic.
w Berthold Bürger (Erich Kästner) *d* Josef von Baky *ph* Werner Krien *m* Georg Haentzschel *ad* Emil Hasler, Otto Gulstorff
☆ Hans Albers, Wilhelm Bendow, Michael Bohnen, Marina von Ditmar, Hans Brausewetter, Brigitte Horney, Käthe Haack
† Kästner used a pseudonym because his writings had been banned since 1933. After the film was released, Hitler ordered that he should receive no further commissions.

Munkbrogreven: see *The Count of the Old Town*

The Muppet Christmas Carol *
US 1992 86m colour
Buena Vista/Walt Disney/Jim Henson (Brian Henson, Martin G. Baker)
A Christmas-hating miser is reformed by the visitations of five ghosts.
Cheerful adaptation of the perennial story, in a version that should appeal to the young.
w Jerry Juhl *story* A Christmas Carol by Charles Dickens *d* Brian Henson *ph* John Fenner *m* Miles Goodman *m/ly* Paul Williams *pd* Val Strazovec *ed* Michael Jablow *sp* The Computer Film Company
☆ Michael Caine, Steven MacKintosh, Meredith Brown, Robin Weaver, Kermit the Frog, Miss Piggy, The Great Gonzo, Fozzie Bear
'The film sinks into a quagmire of sentimentality; the Muppets withdraw discreetly during Scrooge's ghostly visitations and the dominant flavour is more saccharine than humbug. Nice try, though.' – *Sheila Johnston, Independent*

'More entertainment than humanly possible!'
The Muppet Movie **
GB 1979 97m Eastmancolor
ITC (Jim Henson)
Kermit the Frog and friends travel across America to Hollywood and are offered a film contract by Lew Lord, the famous impresario.
Technically an adroit transfer of the celebrated puppets from their TV backstage milieu to a wider canvas; but the latter tends to dwarf them, the material is very variable, the guest stars look embarrassed and the show goes on too long.
w Jerry Juhl, Jack Burns *d* James Frawley *ph* Isidore Mankofsky *m* Paul Williams, Kenny Ascher *pd* Joel Schiller
☆ Charles Durning, Edgar Bergen, Bob Hope, Milton Berle, Mel Brooks, James Coburn, Dom DeLuise, Elliott Gould, Cloris Leachman, Telly Savalas, Orson Welles
Paul Williams, Kenny Ascher; song 'The Rainbow Connection'

Muppet Treasure Island
US 1996 99m Technicolor
Buena Vista/Walt Disney/Jim Henson (Martin G. Baker, Brian Henson)
The adventures of an orphan who is given a map to buried pirate treasure and sets sail to find it.
A rollicking, unmemorable musical treatment of an oft-told tale which has some difficulty accommodating the story to its Muppet characters: Miss Piggy appears as Benjamina Gunn, Fozzie Bear is Squire Trelawney and Kermit becomes Captain Smollett.
w Jerry Juhl, Kirk R. Thatcher, James V. Hart *novel* Robert Louis Stevenson *d* Brian Henson *ph* John Fenner *m* Hans Zimmer *m/ly* Barry Mann, Cynthia Weil *pd* Val Strazovec *ed* Michael Jablow
☆ Tim Curry, Kevin Bishop, Steve Whitmire, Frank Oz, Billy Connolly, David Goelz, Jennifer Saunders
'A breezily entertaining yet old-fashioned brew.' – *Empire*

'The Ultimate Muppet Trip.'
Muppets from Space
GB/US 1999 88m DeLuxe
Columbia/Jim Henson Pictures (Brian Henson, Martin G. Baker)
Gonzo discovers he is an alien and that his relatives are coming to take him home.
Lacklustre movie with few jokes and unexciting action that concentrates on one of the least charismatic of Henson's creations.
w Jerry Juhl, Joseph Mazzarino, Ken Kaufman *d* Tim Hill *ph* Alan Caso *m* Jamshied Sharifi *ch* Toni Basil *pd* Stephen Marsh *ed* Michael A. Stevenson, Richard Pearson
☆ Jeffrey Tambor (K. Edgar Singer), F. Murray Abraham (Noah), Rob Schneider (TV Producer), Josh Charles (Agent Barker), Ray Liotta (Gate Guard), David Arquette (Dr Tucker), Andie MacDowell (Shelley Snipes), Kathy Griffin (Armed Guard), Pat Hingle (General Luft), Hollywood Hogan (Man in Black) and also voices of: Dave Goelz, Steve Whitmire, Bill Barretta, Jerry Nelson, Brian Henson, Kevin Clash, Frank Oz
'Ploddingly whimsical caper.' – *Entertainment Weekly*
'The movie peaks very early, and never quite regains its early momentum until the end. But even in its slackest moments you've been put in such a good mood you can let them get away with the occasional lapse.' – *Lee Binding, Film Review*

The Muppets Take Manhattan *
US 1984 94m Technicolor
Tri-Star (David Lazer)
The Muppets' varsity show is promised a New York opening.
Probably the best of the Muppet features, but by the time of its arrival the early brilliance had been forgotten and even Miss Piggy had worn out her welcome.
w Frank Oz, Tom Patchett, Jay Tarses *d* Frank Oz *ph* Bob Paynter *m* Ralph Burns
☆ Dabney Coleman, Art Carney, James Coco, Joan Rivers, Gregory Hines, Linda Lavin
Jeffrey Moss (music)

Le Mur: see *The Wall*

La Mura de Malapaga: see *Au delà des Grilles*

Murder **
GB 1930 92m bw
British International (John Maxwell)
A girl is convicted of murder, but one of the jurors sets out to prove her innocent.
Interesting early Hitchcock, a rare whodunnit for him.
w Alma Reville *novel* Enter Sir John by Clemence Dane, Helen Simpson *d* Alfred Hitchcock *ph* Jack Cox
☆ *Herbert Marshall,* Norah Baring, Phyllis Konstam, Edward Chapman, Miles Mander, Esmé Percy, Donald Calthrop
'If Hitchcock produced in Hollywood and was wise enough to keep his films to six or seven reels, he might be a rave anywhere.' – *Variety*

Murder Ahoy
GB 1964 74m bw
MGM (Lawrence P. Bachmann)
Miss Marple investigates murders on a naval cadet training ship.
Weakest of the Marple mysteries: all chat and no interest.
w David Pursall, Jack Seddon *d* George Pollock *ph* Desmond Dickinson *m* Ron Goodwin *ad* Bill Andrews *ed* Ernest Walter
☆ Margaret Rutherford (Miss Marple), Lionel Jeffries (Capt. Rhumstone), Stringer Davis (Mr Stringer), Charles Tingwell (Det. Insp. Craddock), William Mervyn (Breeze-Connington), Joan Benham (Matron Alice Fanbraid), Nicholas Parsons (Dr Crump), Miles Malleson (Bishop), Henry Oscar (Lord Rudkin), Derek Nimmo (Humbert), Francis Matthews (Compton), Gerald Cross (Brewer)

Murder among Friends
US 1941 61m bw
Ralph Dietrich-Walter Morosco/TCF
Subscribers to a 200,000-dollar insurance policy die one by one.
Pleasingly efficient supporting mystery.
w John Larkin *d* Ray McCarey
☆ John Hubbard, Marjorie Weaver, Cobina Wright Jnr, Mona Barrie, Douglass Dumbrille, Sidney Blackmer, Lucien Littlefield, Milton Parsons

'This address changes all the rules'
Murder at 1600
US 1997 107m Technicolor Panavision
Warner/Monarchy/Regency (Arnold Kopelson, Arnon Milchan)
A detective who investigates the murder of the mistress of the President's son in the White House discovers a conspiracy that threatens the nation.
Dull and unconvincing thriller, lacking both mystery and suspense.
w Wayne Beach, David Hodgin *d* Dwight Little *ph* Steven Bernstein *m* Christopher Young *pd* Nelson Coates *ed* Billy Weber, Leslie Jones
☆ Wesley Snipes (Detective Harlan Regis), Diane Lane (Nina Chance), Daniel Benzali (Nick Spikings), Dennis Miller (Detective Stengel), Alan Alda (Alvin Jordan), Ronny Cox (President Jack Neil), Diane Baker (Kitty Neil), Tate Donovan (Kyle Neil), Mary Moore (Carla Town), Harris Yulin
'A trashy movie that's intermittently intriguing and enjoyable on its own terms.' – *Emanuel Levy, Variety*

Murder at Monte Carlo
GB 1934 70m bw
Warner (Irving Asher)
A professor is murdered for his roulette system.
Modest second feature notable only as a springboard for the career of its star.
w John Hastings Turner, Michael Barringer *novel* Tom Van Dyke *d* Ralph Ince *ph* Basil Emmott
☆ Errol Flynn, Eve Gray, Paul Graetz, Molly Lamont, Ellis Irving

Murder at the Baskervilles: see *Silver Blaze*

'By the first lady of mystery – with the last word in detectives!'
Murder at the Gallop *
GB 1963 81m bw
MGM (George H. Brown)
Miss Marple investigates when an old man is apparently frightened to death by a cat.
Probably the best of the Marples, with a good sense of place and lively performances.
w James P. Cavanagh *novel* After the Funeral by Agatha Christie *d* George Pollock *ph* Arthur Ibbetson *m* Ron Goodwin *ad* Frank White

☆ Margaret Rutherford, Flora Robson, Robert Morley, Stringer Davis, Charles Tingwell, Duncan Lamont, James Villiers, Robert Urquhart, Katya Douglas

Murder at the Vanities *
US 1934 95m bw
Paramount (E. Lloyd Sheldon)
Murder backstage at the first night of Earl Carroll's Vanities.
Curious, stylish mixture of musical numbers, broad comedy and mystery. Dated, but fun.
w Carey Wilson, Joseph Gollomb, Sam Hellman *d* Mitchell Leisen *ph* Leo Tover *md* Rudolph Kopp *songs* Arthur Johnston, Sam Coslow
☆ Jack Oakie, Victor McLaglen, Carl Brisson, Kitty Carlisle, Dorothy Stickney, Gertrude Michael, Jessie Ralph, Gail Patrick
'Above average and for the masses ... long but does not drag.' – *Variety*
'It can boast lavish staging, tuneful melodies, and a host of attractive girls.' – *New York Times*

Murder at the Windmill
GB 1949 70m bw
Daniel Angel and Nat Cohen
US title: *Murder at the Burlesque*
At London's famous girlie show, a front row patron is murdered.
Rather rushed-looking whodunnit with interesting detail.
wd Val Guest *ph* Bert Mason *md* Phillip Martell
☆ Garry Marsh, Jack Livesey, Jon Pertwee, Diana Decker, Jimmy Edwards, Eliot Makeham

Murder by Contract *
US 1958 81m bw
Columbia/Orbin (Leon Chooluck)
A professional killer makes a fatal mistake and is shot down by police.
Low-budgeter which seemed stark and original at the time, but television has familiarized its contents. Moody, contrasty photography and restrained style give it a minor distinction.
w Ben Simcoe *d* Irving Lerner *ph* Lucien Ballard *m* Perry Botkin
☆ Vince Edwards, Philip Pine, Herschel Bernardi, Caprice Toriel
'Ice cold and completely unsentimental.' – *John Gillett*

'A bloody funny movie!'
Murder by Death *
US 1976 94m Metrocolor
Columbia/Ray Stark
Several (fictional) detectives are invited to stay at the home of a wealthy recluse, and mystery and murder follow.
Sometimes thin but generally likeable spoof of a longstanding genre; the stars seize their opportunities avidly, and the film does not outstay its welcome.
w Neil Simon *d* Robert Moore *ph* David M. Walsh *m* Dave Grusin *pd* Stephen Grimes
☆ Peter Falk, Alec Guinness, Peter Sellers, Truman Capote, Estelle Winwood, Elsa Lanchester, Eileen Brennan, James Coco, David Niven, Maggie Smith, Nancy Walker
'Plenty of scene-stealing actors but not many scenes worth stealing.' – *Michael Billington, Illustrated London News*
'Polished performances fail to compensate for a vacuous and frustratingly tortuous plot.' – *Sight and Sound*
'It seems to me that if you haven't watched the real Thin Man and the real Bogie in the real *Maltese Falcon* you won't see the joke; and if you have watched them, the joke is not good enough.' – *Dilys Powell, Sunday Times*

Murder by Decree
GB/Canada 1978 112m Metrocolor
Avco/Decree Productions/Saucy Jack (René Dupont, Bob Clark)
Sherlock Holmes investigates the matter of Jack the Ripper and comes upon a Masonic conspiracy.
Interminably long and unpardonably muddled variation on this over-familiar theme, with halts for the performances of guest artists and no clear grip on narrative or character.
w John Hopkins *d* Bob Clark *ph* Reginald H. Morris *m* Carl Zittrer, Paul Zaza *pd* Harry Pottle
☆ Christopher Plummer, James Mason, Anthony Quayle, David Hemmings, Susan Clark, John Gielgud, Donald Sutherland, Frank Finlay, Geneviève Bujold

Murder by Illusion: see *FIX*

'Let The Mind Games Begin.'
Murder by Numbers
US 2002 120m Technicolor
Warner/Castle Rock (Barbet Schroeder, Susan Hoffman, Richard Crystal)
A tough cop suspects two high-school students of committing a random murder.
An unconvincing star vehicle of startling unoriginality.
w Tony Gayton *d* Barbet Schroeder *ph* Luciano Tovoli *m* Clint Mansell *pd* Stuart Wurtzel *ed* Lee Percy
☆ Sandra Bullock (Cassie Mayweather), Ryan Gosling (Richard Haywood), Michael Pitt (Justin Pendleton), Agnes Bruckner (Lisa Mills), Chris Penn (Ray), R. D. Call (Captain Rod Cody), Ben Chaplin (Sam Kennedy)
'Endeavors to turn the standard murder-mystery formula inside out but ends up making it even more boring and predictable than usual.' – *Andrew O'Hehir, Salon.com*

Murder by Television
US 1935 60m bw
Edward M. Spitz/Imperial
The inventor of a television process is murdered.
Static whodunnit with the star as twin brothers. Only a curio.
w Joseph O'Donnell *d* Clifford Sanforth *ph* Arthur Reed *m* Oliver Wallace
☆ Bela Lugosi, June Collyer, Huntley Gordon, George Meeker

Murder by the Clock
US 1931 76m bw
Paramount
Creepy goings on in an old house after the death of a dowager who has built herself a tomb from which she can escape if buried alive.
Tasteless chiller which had the distinction of being withdrawn from British circulation after public protests.
w Henry Myers, Rufus King, Charles Beahan *play* Charles Beahan *novel* Rufus King *d* Edward Sloman *ph* Karl Struss
☆ Lilyan Tashman, William 'Stage' Boyd, Regis Toomey, Irving Pichel, Blanche Frederici, Walter McGrail
'Lacking in punch as a strongie for first runs. Below that should do oke.' – *Variety*

Murder Can Be Deadly: see *The Painted Smile*

Murder Goes to College
US 1937 77m bw
Paramount
A reporter on vacation helps solve a campus killing.
Reasonably lively comedy mystery which might have started a series, but didn't.
w Brian Marlow, Eddie Welch, Robert Wyler *novel* Kurt Steele *d* Charles Reisner
☆ Roscoe Karns, Lynne Overman, Marsha Hunt, Astrid Allwyn, Harvey Stephens, Larry Crabbe
'Dialogue crackles with humour ... this whodunit will be welcome material on many programmes.' – *Variety*

'You'll die laughing!'
Murder He Says **
US 1945 91m bw
Paramount (E. D. Leshin)
An insurance salesman stays with a homicidal family of hillbillies.
A curious black farce which seems to be compounded of Cold Comfort Farm and The Red Inn. Very funny, and ahead of its time.
w Lou Breslow *d* George Marshall *ph* Theodor Sparkuhl
☆ Fred MacMurray, Marjorie Main, Helen Walker, Peter Whitney, Jean Heather, Porter Hall, Mabel Paige

Murder in a Blue World: see *Una Gota De Sangre Para Morir Amando*

'What If The Perfect Crime Was All In Your Mind?'
Murder in Mind
US/GB 1996 85m CFI color
Lakeshore/Evergreen/BBC/Alva/Storyteller (Vicki Slotnick, Jeremy Paige)
A psychiatrist who uses hypnotic techniques is called in by the police to examine a woman accused of murdering her wealthy husband.
Tricksy thriller that betrays its stage origins, relying entirely on narrative twists to maintain interest and distract attention from its implausibilities.
w Michael Cooney *play* Michael Cooney *d* Andrew Morahan *ph* John Aranson *m* Paul Buckmaster *pd* Ben Morahan *ed* Andrea MacArthur
☆ Nigel Hawthorne, Mary Louise Parker, Jimmy Smits, Gailard Sartain, Jason Scott Lee

Murder in Reverse
GB 1945 88m bw
British National
After long imprisonment for a supposed murder, a convict comes out and hunts down the victim, who isn't really dead.
A reasonable crime entertainment of its day which seemed to introduce a new star; but it hasn't worn well.
wd Montgomery Tully *novel* Austin Small *ph* Ernest Palmer *m* Hans May
☆ William Hartnell, Jimmy Hanley, Chili Bouchier, John Slater, Dinah Sheridan, Wylie Watson

Murder in the Big House
US 1942 67m bw
Warner
Two reporters uncover a murder ring in a prison.
Acceptable second feature which catapulted its star to fame – at another studio.
w Raymond Schrock *d* B. Reeves Eason
☆ Van Johnson, George Meeker, Faye Emerson, Frank Wilcox
† A previous 1936 version was called *Jailbreak* and starred Craig Reynolds. *Murder in the Big House* was reissued in 1945 as *Born for Trouble*.

Murder in the Blue Room
US 1944 61m bw
Frank Gross/Universal
Volunteering to sleep in a room where a murder was committed, a guest is found dead.
Tepid remake of The Secret of the Blue Room.
w I. A. L. Diamond, Stanley Davis *d* Leslie Goodwins
☆ Anne Gwynne, Donald Cook, John Litel, Grace McDonald, June Preisser, Regis Toomey

Murder in the Cathedral
GB 1951 136m bw
Film Traders/George Hoellering
The 12th-century struggle between Henry II and his archbishop culminates in the assassination of Becket in Canterbury Cathedral.
Plainly filmed, slightly amateur version of the celebrated verse play; scarcely a rewarding cinematic experience.
wd George Hoellering *play* T. S. Eliot *ph* David Kosky *m* Laszlo Lajtha *ad* Peter Pendrey
☆ Father John Grosner, Alexander Gauge, David Ward, George Woodbridge, Basil Burton, Paul Rogers, Niall MacGinnis, Mark Dignam, Leo McKern
'A curious ordeal for the audience ... a no-man's-land between cinema and drama has been discovered, rather than any extension of either.' – *Gavin Lambert*

Murder in the Family
GB 1938 75m bw
TCF
Who killed rich Aunt Octavia?
Mild whodunnit with interesting cast.
w David Evans *novel* James Ronald *d* Al Parker
☆ Barry Jones, Jessica Tandy, Evelyn Ankers, Donald Gray, David Markham, Glynis Johns, Roddy McDowall

'One Broke His Silence. The Other Broke The System'
Murder in the First *
US 1995 122m Foto-Kem
Guild/Canal/Wolper (Marc Frydman, Mark Wolper)
In the early 40s, a young lawyer defends on a murder charge a prisoner who spent three years in solitary confinement in Alcatraz and exposes the brutalities of the system.
Effective and powerful courtroom drama, with some good performances; yet right and wrong are so clearly delineated from the opening scenes that there is no tension, apart from that supplied by the nervy camerawork.
w Dan Gordon *d* Marc Rocco *ph* Fred Murphy *m* Christopher Young *pd* Kirk M. Petruccelli *ed* Russell Livingstone
☆ Christian Slater, *Kevin Bacon*, Gary Oldman, Embeth Davidtz, Bill Macy, Stephen Tobolowsky, Brad Dourif, Mia Kirshner, Kyra Sedgwick
'From among the flotsam of prison movie clichés emerges a flawed but stirring piece of entertainment.' – *Empire*

Murder in the Fleet
US 1935 70m bw
MGM (Lucien Hubbard)
Sabotage on a navy cruiser turns out to be the work of a mad inventor.
Weak and confused mixture of melodrama and comedy.
wd Edward Sedgwick *ph* Milton Krasner
☆ Robert Taylor, Jean Parker, Jean Hersholt, Ted Healy, Una Merkel, Nat Pendleton, Raymond Hatton, Donald Cook, Mischa Auer

Murder in the Music Hall
US 1946 84m bw
Republic (Herman Millakowsky)
reissue title: *Midnight Melody*
A former criminal, now Broadway producer, is murdered on opening night.
Humdrum extravaganza built round its star, whose last skating appearance this was.
w Frances Hyland, Laszlo Gorog *d* John English *ph* John Alton *md* Walter Scharf
☆ Vera Hruba Ralston, William Marshall, Helen Walker, Nancy Kelly, William Gargan, Ann Rutherford, Julie Bishop, Jerome Cowan, Edward Norris, Paul Hurst, Jack La Rue

Murder in the Private Car *
US 1934 60m bw
Lucien Hubbard/MGM
GB title: *Murder on the Runaway Train*
Mysteries proliferate aboard a fast-moving train.
Adequate second feature which builds up to a remarkably well-staged climax in a runaway carriage.
w Ralph Spence, Edgar Allan Woolf, Al Boasberg, Harvey Thew *d* Harry Beaumont
☆ Russell Hardie, Charles Ruggles, Mary Carlisle, Una Merkel, Porter Hall
'About the swiftest 61 minutes of entertainment you are ever likely to see.' – *Picturegoer*

The Murder in Thornton Square: see *Gaslight (1944)*

Murder in Times Square
US 1943 72m bw
Columbia
An actor-playwright is suspected of four theatrical murders.
Standard detection work with some slight claim to sophistication.
w Stuart Palmer, Paul Gangelin *d* Lew Landers
☆ Edmund Lowe, Sidney Blackmer, Marguerite Chapman, John Litel

Murder in Trinidad
US 1934 74m bw
Fox
A quiet detective solves a murder in the tropics.
Modest whodunnit with Nigel Bruce for once playing the sleuth instead of Watson.
w Seton I. Miller *novel* John W. Vandercook *d* Louis King
☆ Nigel Bruce, Heather Angel, Victor Jory, Murray Kinnell, Douglas Walton, J. Carrol Naish
'Amusing, but not particularly intriguing.' – *Variety*

Murder Inc: see *The Enforcer*

Murder, Incorporated
US 1960 103m bw Cinemascope
TCF (Burt Balaban)
In the thirties, Anastasia and Lepke build up their crime syndicate which spreads terror through New York.

Tedious and poorly made gangster thriller, unforgivable faults considering the many admirable models it has to follow.
w Irv Tunick, Mel Barr *d* Burt Balaban, Stuart Rosenberg *ph* Gayne Rescher *m* Frank de Vol
☆ Stuart Whitman, May Britt, Henry Morgan, Peter Falk, David J. Stewart, Simon Oakland, Morey Amsterdam
Peter Falk

Murder Is News: see *The Delavine Affair*

The Murder Man *
US 1935 84m bw
MGM (Harry Rapf)
A reporter investigating a murder becomes one of the suspects.
Good low-key melodrama with an interesting cast.
w Tim Whelan, John C. Higgins *d* Tim Whelan *ph* Lester White *m* William Axt
☆ Spencer Tracy, Virginia Bruce, Lionel Atwill, James Stewart, Harvey Stephens, William Collier Snr
'It will please in the lesser houses.' – *Variety*

Murder Most Foul
GB 1964 91m bw
MGM/Lawrence P. Bachmann (Ben Arbeid)
Refusing to return a guilty verdict, juror Miss Marple makes her own murder investigation backstage at a third-rate repertory company.
Moderate Marple mystery which hasn't quite found the light touch it seeks.
w David Pursall, Jack Seddon *novel Mrs McGinty's Dead* by Agatha Christie *d* George Pollock *ph* Desmond Dickinson *m* Ron Goodwin *ed* Ernest Walter
☆ Margaret Rutherford, Ron Moody, Charles Tingwell, Andrew Cruickshank, Megs Jenkins, Ralph Michael, James Bolam, Stringer Davis, Francesca Annis, Dennis Price, Terry Scott

Murder My Sweet: see *Farewell My Lovely (1944)*

The Murder of Dr Harrigan
US 1935 67m bw
Warner
A hospital founder disappears while on his way to the operating room.
Formula murder mystery without much special interest.
w Peter Milne, Sy Bartlett *novel* Mignon G. Eberhart *d* Frank McDonald
☆ Kay Linaker, Ricardo Cortez, Mary Astor, John Eldredge, Joseph Crehan, Frank Reicher
'Will probably do no better than mildly.' – *Variety*

Murder on a Honeymoon
US 1935 74m bw
RKO (Kenneth Macgowan)
When a passenger dies on a holiday flight, a schoolmistress is convinced that it is murder.
Deft little comedy thriller that has acquired a period charm.
w Seton I. Miller, Robert Benchley *story Puzzle of the Pepper Tree* by Stuart Palmer *d* Lloyd Corrigan *ph* Nick Musuraca *md* Alberto Colombo *ad* Van Nest Polglase, Perry Ferguson *ed* William Morgan
☆ Edna May Oliver, James Gleason, Lola Lane, Chick Chandler, George Meeker, Dorothy Libaire, Morgan Wallace, Leo G. Carroll
† It was the third, and last, film in the Hildegarde Withers series starring Edna May Oliver, following on from *Penguin Pool Murder* and *Murder on the Blackboard* (qqv).

Murder on Diamond Row: see *The Squeaker*

Murder on Monday: see *Home at Seven*

Murder on the Blackboard
US 1934 72m bw
RKO (Kenneth Macgowan)
When the music teacher is murdered at her school, Hildegarde Withers helps the police with their enquiries.
Pleasant little mystery, with some enjoyable exchanges between Gleason's inspector and Oliver's tart-tongued teacher.
w Willis Goldbeck *story* Stuart Palmer *d* George Archainbaud *ph* Nick Musuraca *md* Max Steiner *ad* Van Nest Polglase, Albert D'Agostino *ed* Archie F. Marsheck
☆ Edna Mae Oliver, James Gleason, Bruce Cabot, Gertrude Michael, Regis Toomey, Tully Marshall, Fredrik Vogeding, Edgar Kennedy
† It was the second film in the Hildegarde Withers series. See also: *Penguin Pool Murder, Murder on a Honeymoon.*

Murder on the Orient Express **
GB 1974 131m Technicolor
EMI/GW Films (John Brabourne, Richard Goodwin)
In the early thirties, Hercule Poirot solves a murder on a snowbound train.
Reasonably elegant but disappointingly slackly-handled version of a classic mystery novel. Finney overacts and his all-star support is distracting, while as soon as the train chugs into its snowdrift the film stops moving too, without even a dramatic 'curtain'.
w Paul Dehn *novel* Agatha Christie *d* Sidney Lumet *ph* Geoffrey Unsworth *m* Richard Rodney Bennett *pd* Tony Walton
☆ Albert Finney, *Ingrid Bergman*, Lauren Bacall, Wendy Hiller, Sean Connery, Vanessa Redgrave, Michael York, Martin Balsam, Richard Widmark, Jacqueline Bisset, Jean-Pierre Cassel, Rachel Roberts, George Coulouris, *John Gielgud*, Anthony Perkins and also Colin Blakely, Jeremy Lloyd, Denis Quilley
'Audiences appear to be so hungry for this type of entertainment that maybe it hardly matters that it isn't very good.' – *Judith Crist*
Ingrid Bergman
Paul Dehn; Geoffrey Unsworth; Richard Rodney Bennett; Albert Finney
Richard Rodney Bennett; John Gielgud; Ingrid Bergman

Murder She Said *
GB 1961 87m bw
MGM (George H. Brown)
An elderly spinster investigates after seeing a woman strangled in a passing train.
Frightfully British and disappointingly tame adaptation of an Agatha Christie character, with only the star (who is somewhat miscast) holding one's attention.
w David Pursall, Jack Seddon *novel 4.50 from Paddington* by Agatha Christie *d* George Pollock *ph* Geoffrey Faithfull *m* Ron Goodwin *ed* Ernest Walter
☆ *Margaret Rutherford*, Charles Tingwell, Muriel Pavlow, Arthur Kennedy, James Robertson Justice, Thorley Walters, Gerald Cross, Conrad Phillips
† Thanks to Miss Rutherford's popularity, three increasingly poor sequels were made: *Murder at the Gallop* (qv) (1963), *Murder Most Foul* (qv) (1964), *Murder Ahoy* (qv) (1964).

Murder Will Out: see *The Voice of Merrill*

Murder without Crime
GB 1950 76m bw
ABPC
A blackmailer extracts money for a crime not yet committed.
Thin four-hander from a rather mysterious West End success.
wd J. Lee-Thompson *play Double Error* by J. Lee-Thompson *ph* William McLeod *m* Philip Green
☆ Dennis Price, Derek Farr, Joan Dowling, Patricia Plunkett

The Murderer Lives at 21: see *L'Assassin habite au 21*

The Murderers Are Among Us *
Germany 1947 87m bw
Defa
original title: *Die Mörder Sind Unter Uns*
In the ruins of Berlin several post-war characters indulge in gloomy self-examination.
Almost a caricature of what one would expect from a defeated people, this now-curious item has a certain power of its own.
wd Wolfgang Staudte *ph* Friedl Behn-Grund, Eugen Klagemann *m* Ernst Roters
☆ Hildegard Knef, Ernst Fischer, Arno Paulsen
'It is sombre, slow, intense, tragically moving and in common with the post-war Italian films as true as it can be to the surrounding reality. It would seem that only the impoverished and defeated can focus the camera lens on life.' – *Richard Winnington*

Murderer's Row
US 1966 108m Technicolor
Columbia/Meadway-Claude/Euan Lloyd
Matt Helm tracks down an international villain who has kidnapped an inventor.
Witless and uninventive spy spoof which drags itself wearily along but never attempts an explanation of its own title.
w Herbert Baker *novel* Donald Hamilton *d* Henry Levin *ph* Sam Leavitt *m* Lalo Schifrin
☆ Dean Martin, Ann-Margret, Karl Malden, Camilla Sparv, James Gregory, Beverly Adams, Tom Reese

'The blood will run cold in your veins!'
Murders in the Rue Morgue *
US 1932 62m bw
Universal (Carl Laemmle Jnr)
A series of grisly murders prove to be the work of a trained ape.
A distant relation of the original story, mildly interesting for its obvious Caligari influences, but not very good in any way.
w Tom Reed, Dale Van Every, John Huston *story* Edgar Allan Poe *d* Robert Florey *ph* Karl Freund *ed* Milton Carruth
☆ Bela Lugosi, Sidney Fox, Leon Ames, Bert Roach, Brandon Hurst
'Synthetic studio rewrite ... Poe wouldn't recognize his story.' – *Variety*

'Where sights of passion end in screams of terror!'
Murders in the Rue Morgue *
US 1971 86m Foto Film Color
AIP (Louis M. Heyward)
Poe's story is being presented at a Grand Guignol theatre in Paris, and when murders happen within the company Inspector Vidocq comes to investigate.
Playfully plotted chiller which has more to do with The Phantom of the Opera *than with Poe. A good time-waster for addicts.*
w Charles Wicking, Henry Slesar *d Gordon Hessler ph* Manuel Berengier *m* Waldo de Los Rios
☆ Jason Robards Jnr, Herbert Lom, Lilli Palmer, Adolfo Celi, Michael Dunn, Christine Kaufmann

Murders in the Zoo
US 1933 64m bw
Paramount
A jealous zoologist finds interesting ways to murder any man who shows interest in his wife.
Modest time-passer with a rampant star.
w Philip Wylie, Seton I. Miller *d* A. Edward Sutherland *ph* Ernest Haller
☆ Lionel Atwill, Charles Ruggles, Kathleen Burke, John Lodge, Randolph Scott, Gail Patrick
'Has what it takes to chill and entertain.' – *Variety*

Muriel *
France/Italy 1963 116m Eastmancolor
Argos/Alpha/Eclair/Films de la Pléiade/Dear Films (Anatole Dauman)
aka: *Muriel, ou le Temps d'un Retour*
A widow and her stepson are both misled by memories of past loves.
Elusive character drama which, though over-generous in length, fails to satisfy.
w Jean Cayrol *d* Alain Resnais *ph* Sacha Vierny *m* Hans Werner Henze
☆ Delphine Seyrig, Jean-Pierre Kérien, Nita Klein, Jean-Baptiste Thierrée
'One has to watch and listen with every nerve alert.' – *Tom Milne, MFB*

Muriel, ou le Temps d'un Retour: see *Muriel*

'A Story of Love, Laughter and the Pursuit of Matrimony.'
Muriel's Wedding *
Australia 1994 105m colour
Buena Vista/CIBY 2000/AFFC (Lynda House, Jocelyn Moorhouse)
A fat, unhappy 22-year-old, the butt of her companions, robs her father and sets out to enjoy herself and find a husband.
Enjoyable, rumbustious soap opera, poking fun at small-time political corruption and the small-town desire for marriage at any cost, though it offers little that is positive and the constant presence of Abba on the soundtrack does little for its feel-good qualities.
wd P. J. Hogan *ph* Martin McGrath *m* Peter Best *pd* Patrick Reardon *ed* Jill Bilcock
☆ *Toni Collette*, Bill Hunter, Rachel Griffiths, Jeanie Drynan, Gennie Nevinson, Matt Day, Daniel Lapaine, Sophie Lee, Chris Haywood
'The film would be more convincing in poking fun at the world of soap opera if it didn't reach for the instant dramas of illness and breakdown, cancer and kleptomania in such a soapy way.' – *Adam Mars-Jones, Independent*
'Provides a nicely vicious portrait of Australian suburban life, with its young people aiming to be as much like their peers as possible and the older generation piously performing moral somersaults to justify their tepid respectability.' – *Derek Malcolm, Guardian*
† The film won the 1994 Australian Film Institute awards for best film, best actress (Toni Colette), best supporting actress (Rachel Griffiths), and sound.

Murmur of the Heart: see *Le Souffle au Coeur*

Un Muro de Silencio: see *Black Flowers*

Murph the Surf: see *Live a Little, Steal a Lot*

Murphy's Law
US 1986 100m TVC Color
Cannon (Pancho Kohner)
A tough LA cop with a drink problem is arrested for his ex-wife's murder.
Unattractively violent and foul-mouthed urban thriller in the wake of Dirty Harry.
w Gail Morgan Hickman *d* J. Lee Thompson *ph* Alex Phillips *m* Marc Donahue, Valentine McCallum
☆ Charles Bronson, Carrie Snodgress, Kathleen Wilhoite, Robert F. Lyons, Richard Romanus

Murphy's Romance
US 1985 107m Metrocolor Panavision
Columbia/Martin Ritt-Fogwood (Laura Ziskin)
A divorcée determined to make a living as a horse trainer in rural Arizona falls for the ageing local chemist.
Well-meaning but somewhat yawnworthy romantic comedy-drama which might almost have strayed from the days of the Hardy family.
w Harriet Frank Jnr, Irving Ravetch *d* Martin Ritt *ph* William A. Fraker *m* Carole King *pd* Joel Schiller
☆ Sally Field, James Garner, Brian Kerwin, Corey Haim
'Sweet and homey, but falls far short of compelling film-making.' – *Variety*
James Garner; photography

Murphy's War *
GB 1971 108m Eastmancolor Panavision
Hemdale/Yates-Deeley (Michael Deeley)
A torpedoed British merchantman in Venezuela devotes himself to bombing a U-boat from a home-made plane.
Modest adventure story with the star in better form than the script.
w Stirling Silliphant *novel* Max Catto *d* Peter Yates *ph* Douglas Slocombe *m* John Barry
☆ *Peter O'Toole*, Sian Phillips, Philippe Noiret, Horst Janson

Muscle Beach Party
US 1964 94m Pathécolor Panavision
AIP (James H. Nicholson, Robert Dillon)
A fickle, rich Italian widow falls for a teenage surfer and plans to make him a star, to the annoyance of his friends, whose beach has been invaded by body-builders.
Tiresome comedy of teenage bonding, one of the many pumped out in the mid-60s and marked by banal plot, dialogue and songs, though providing brief employment for some ageing actors and comedians.
w Robert Dillon *d* William Asher *ph* Harold Wellman *m* Les Baxter *m/ly* Roger Christian, Gary Usher, Brian Wilson, Guy Hemric, Jerry

Styner *ad* Lucius Croxton *ed* Eve Newman, Fred Feitshans
☆ Frankie Avalon, Annette Funicello, Luciana Paluzzi, John Ashley, Don Rickles, Peter Turgeon, Jody McCrea, Dick Dale and the Del Tones, Candy Johnson, Morey Amsterdam, Buddy Hackett, Little Stevie Wonder, Peter Lorre
† It was a sequel to *Beach Party* and was followed by *Bikini Beach* and *Pajama Party* (qqv).

'If You Want A Leg Up In Hollywood, It's Time You Met...'
The Muse **
US 1999 96m DeLuxe
Entertainment/October (Herb Nanas)
A Hollywood screenwriter in trouble meets a woman claiming to be a daughter of Zeus, who offers to inspire him providing that he indulges her every whim.
Sourly amusing take on what constitutes success and failure in Hollywood, though slackly directed.
w Albert Brooks, Monica Johnson *d* Albert Brooks *ph* Thomas Ackerman *m* Elton John *pd* Dina Lipton *ed* Peter Teschner
☆ Albert Brooks (Steven Philips), Sharon Stone (Sarah), Andie MacDowell (Laura Phillips), Jeff Bridges (Jack Warrick), Mark Feuerstein (Josh Martin), Steven Wright (Stan Spielberg), Bradley Whitford (Hal), Mario Opinato (European Man), Dakin Matthews (Dr Jacobson), Concetta Tomei (Nurse Rennert)
'Brooks will always be funny; but, if anything, his own muse deserts him here, revealing a man with a cynical view of the town he works in.' – *Bob McCabe, Empire*
† Cybill Shepherd, Lorenzo Lamas, Jennifer Tilly, Rob Reiner, James Cameron and Martin Scorsese appear as themselves.

Mushrooms
Australia 1994 93m colour
J.A.M./AFFC/Rosen-Harper
The ageing widows of two fences have problems when a police sergeant becomes a lodger at the same time as a violent criminal seeks refuge in their house.
Gruesome black comedy, done with a certain style, but likely to be best enjoyed by cannibals.
wd Alan Madden *ph* Louis Irving *m* Paul Grabowsky *pd* George Liddle *ed* Henry Dangar
☆ Julia Blake, Simon Chilvers, Lynette Curran, Brandon Burke, George Shevtsov, Boris Brkic

The Music Box ****
US 1932 30m bw
Hal Roach
Two delivery men take a piano to a house at the top of a flight of steps.
Quintessential Laurel and Hardy, involving almost all their aspects including a slight song and dance. With Billy Gilbert.
w H. M. Walker *d* James Parrott
best short

'As a lawyer all she wanted was the truth. As a daughter all she wanted was his innocence. How well do you really know your father?'
Music Box *
US 1989 126m colour Cinemascope
Guild/Carolco (Irwin Winkler)
A lawyer defends her father against charges that he was a war criminal.
An effectively melodramatic courtroom drama, but no more than that, despite winning the Golden Bear at the Berlin Film Festival in 1990.
w Joe Eszterhas *d* Costa-Gavras *ph* Patrick Blossier *m* Philippe Sarde *pd* Jeannine Claudia Oppewall *ed* Joelle Van Effenterre
☆ Jessica Lange, Armin Mueller-Stahl, Frederic Forrest, Donald Moffat, Lukas Haas, Cheryl Lynn Bruce, Mari Torocsik, J. S. Block, Sol Frieder
Jessica Lange

Music for Madame
US 1937 81m bw
RKO (Jesse L. Lasky)
An opera singer goes to Hollywood and becomes the dupe of jewel thieves.
Tolerable star musical with rather stale comedy elements.
w Gertrude Purcell, Robert Harari *d* John G. Blystone
☆ Nino Martini, Joan Fontaine, Alan Mowbray, Erik Rhodes, Alan Hale, Billy Gilbert, Grant Mitchell, Lee Patrick
'Seems that Nino just can't make the grade as a film star.' – *Variety*

Music for Millions *
US 1944 117m bw
MGM (Joe Pasternak)
A small girl helps her pregnant sister who is a member of José Iturbi's orchestra.
Dewy-eyed wartime musical, full of popular classics, sentimentality and child interest, all smoothly packaged. As an example of what the public wanted in 1944, quite an eye-opener.
w Myles Connolly *d* Henry Koster *ph* Robert Surtees *md* George Stoll
☆ *Margaret O'Brien*, June Allyson, José Iturbi, Jimmy Durante, Marsha Hunt, Hugh Herbert, Harry Davenport, Connie Gilchrist
Myles Connelly

Music Hath Charms *
GB 1935 70m bw
BIP (Walter C. Mycroft)
A dance band's broadcast has various effects on listeners.
Pleasing, modest portmanteau of sketches with music.
w L. du Garde Peach, Jack Davies Jnr *d* Thomas Bentley, Alexander Esway, Walter Summers, Arthur Woods *ph* Horace Wheddon, Jack Cox, Bryan Langley, Otto Kanturek *ad* Clarence Elder *ed* J. Corbett
☆ Henry Hall and his Orchestra, Carol Goodner, W. H. Berry, Arthur Margetson, Antoinette Cellier, Billy Milton

Music in Darkness: see *Music Is My Future*

Music in Manhattan
US 1944 81m bw
RKO
A Broadway actress is rumoured to be secretly married to a war hero, much to the annoyance of her fiancé.
A minor musical that gets up a little comic steam until the unmemorable songs cool it down.
w Lawrence Kimble *story* Maurice Tombragel, Hal Smith, Jack Scholl *d* John H. Auer *ph* Russell Metty *m* Leigh Harline *m/ly* Herb Magidson, Lew Pollack
☆ Anne Shirley, Dennis Day, Phillip Terry, Raymond Walburn, Jane Darwell, Patti Brill, Nino Menendez, Charlie Barnet, Jason Robards

Music in My Heart
US 1940 70m bw
Columbia
An alien singer wins the lead in a Broadway musical, which prevents him from being deported.
Forgettable second feature which was its leading lady's last stepping stone before stardom.
w James Edward Grant *d* Joseph Santley
☆ Rita Hayworth, Tony Martin, Edith Fellows, Alan Mowbray, George Tobias, Eric Blore, André Kostelanetz and his orchestra
song 'It's a Blue World' (*m/ly* Chet Forrest, Bob Wright)

Music in the Air
US 1934 85m bw
Fox (Erich Pommer)
An opera singer is torn between two men.
Heavy-going light entertainment.
w Howard Young, Billy Wilder *play* Oscar Hammerstein II, Jerome Kern *d* Joe May *ph* Ernest Palmer
☆ Gloria Swanson, John Boles, Douglass Montgomery, June Lang, Al Shean, Reginald Owen, Joseph Cawthorn, Hobart Bosworth
'Mild operetta of class appeal, which limits its b.o. sturdiness.' – *Variety*

Music Is Magic
US 1935 67m bw
TCF
By a series of unexpected events, a young girl becomes a Hollywood star.
Unpretentious and fairly snappy musical which still provides moments to enjoy.
w Edward Eliscu, Lou Breslow *d* George Marshall
☆ Alice Faye, Bebe Daniels, Ray Walker, Frank Mitchell, Jack Durant, Hattie McDaniel
'One of those flighty affairs that will have trouble getting past the dual barricade.' – *Variety*

Music Is My Future *
Sweden 1948 85m bw
Terrafilm (Lorens Marmstedt)
original title: *Musik i Mörker*
aka: *Music In Darkness, Night is My Future*
Blinded in an accident, a young pianist forms a relationship with a poor girl.
Saved from its persistent sentimentality by occasional stringency, it survives as an early example of a developing talent.
w Dagmar Edquist *novel* Dagmar Edquist *d* Ingmar Bergman *ph* Göran Strindberg *m* Erland von Koch *ad* P. A. Lundgren *ed* Lennart Wallén
☆ Mai Zetterling, Birger Malmsten, Olaf Winnerstrand, Naima Wifstrand, Bibi Skoglund, Hilda Borgström, Douglas Hage, Gunnar Björnstrand, Bengt Eklund
'My fourth film became a modest success, thanks to Lorens Marmstedt's wisdom, thoughtfulness and patience … It was he who taught me how to make films.' – *Ingmar Bergman, The Magic Lantern*

'The story of a homosexual who married a nymphomaniac!'
The Music Lovers *
GB 1970 123m Eastmancolor Panavision
UA/Rossfilms (Roy Baird)
Homosexual composer Tchaikovsky is impelled to marry, loses his sponsor, drives his wife into an asylum and dies of cholera.
Absurd fantasia on the life of a great composer, produced in a manner reminiscent of MGM's sillier musicals; up to a point hysterically (and unintentionally) funny, then rather sickening.
w Melvyn Bragg *book Beloved Friend* by C. D. Bowen, Barbara von Meck *d Ken Russell* *ph* Douglas Slocombe *md* André Previn
☆ Richard Chamberlain, *Glenda Jackson*, Christopher Gable, Max Adrian, Isabella Telezynska, Maureen Pryor, Andrew Faulds
'Tchaikovsky has been made the excuse for a crude melodrama about sex.' – *Konstantin Bazarov*
'Libellous not only to the composer but to his music.' – *Roger Ebert*

The Music Man ***
US 1962 151m Technirama
Warner (Morton da Costa)
A confidence trickster persuades a small-town council to start a boys' band, with himself as the agent for all the expenses.
Reasonably cinematic, thoroughly invigorating transference to the screen of a hit Broadway musical. Splendid period 'feel', standout performances, slight sag in second half.
w Marion Hargrove *book* Meredith Willson *d Morton da Costa* *ph* Robert Burks *md* Ray Heindorf *ch* Onna White *songs Meredith Willson*
☆ *Robert Preston*, Shirley Jones, Buddy Hackett, *Hermione Gingold*, Pert Kelton, Paul Ford
'This is one of those triumphs that only a veteran performer can have; Preston's years of experience and his love of performing come together joyously.' – *Pauline Kael*
† Robert Preston, who originated the part on Broadway, was only offered the film role after Cary Grant had turned it down.
Ray Heindorf
best picture

The Music of Chance *
US 1993 97m Foto-Kem
Feature film/I.R.S. Media/American Playhouse (Frederick Zollo, Dylan Sellers)
Two millionaires force two poker players, who lose all their money in a game, to work off the debt by remaining on their estate and building a wall.
A good-looking, well-acted, minimalist, lightweight drama of men trapped by their own greed.
w Philip Haas, Belinda Haas *novel* Paul Auster *d* Philip Haas *m* Philip Johnston *pd* Hugo Luczyc-Wyhowski *ed* Belinda Haas
☆ James Spader, Mandy Patinkin, M. Emmet Walsh, Charles Durning, Joel Grey, Samantha Mathis, Christopher Penn
'A lean, convincing fable in the tradition of Kafka, Borges and Pinter.' – *Philip French, Observer*

'She gave them a gift they could never imagine. They gave the system a fight it would never forget.'
Music of the Heart *
US 1999 124m DeLuxe
Miramax (Marianne Maddalena, Susan Kaplan, Allan Miller, Walter Scheuer)
Abandoned by her husband, a mother of two small children becomes a noted children's violin teacher; when her work is threatened by cuts in funding, she organises a charity concert at Carnegie Hall.
A heartening true life story re-told without much subtlety or finesse; Craven goes unashamedly for tears as he more usually does for shocks.
w Pamela Gray *documentary Small Wonders* by Allan and Lana Miller *d* Wes Craven *ph* Peter Deming *m* Mason Daring *pd* Bruce Miller *ed* Patrick Lussier
☆ Meryl Streep (Roberta Guaspari), Aidan Quinn (Brian Sinclair), Angela Bassett (Janet Williams), Cloris Leachman (Isabel Vasquez), Josh Pais (Dennis), Jay O. Sanders (Dan), Charlie Hofheimer (Nick), Kieran Culkin (Lexi), Michael Angarano (Nick (7)), Henry Dinhofer (Lexi (5))
'A gloriously sentimental true-life drama in which Meryl Streep offers another indelible portrayal.' – *David Stratton, Variety*
† Isaac Stern, Itzhak Perlman, and Arnold Steinhardt appear as themselves.
Meryl Streep; song 'Music of My Heart' (*m/l* Diane Warren)

The Music Room **
India 1958 100m bw
Satyajit Ray Productions
original title: *Jalsaghar*
An elderly and reclusive aristocratic connoisseur of music stages a magnificent musical evening in his crumbling palace as a gesture of defiance at the modern world.
Elegant, small-scale work of a man destroying himself through his obsessive pride.
wd Satyajit Ray *story* Tarasankar Banerjee *ph* Subrata Mitra *m* Vilayat Khan *ad* Bansi Chandragupta *ed* Dulal Dutta
☆ Chhabi Biswas, Padman Devi, Pinaki Sen Gupta, Gangapada Bose
'A deeply felt, extremely tedious film. On the one hand its western derivations are patent (the Greek-revival mansion no more than the Chekhovian theme). On the other hand its chief indigenous element, the Indian music, is simply uncongenial and tiresome to our ears. No doubt these are excellent musical performances for those who understand them, but they make us start counting the bulbs in the theater chandelier.' – *Stanley Kauffman*
'A great, flawed, maddening film – hard to take but probably impossible to forget. It's often crude and it's poorly constructed, but it's a great experience.' – *Pauline Kael*
† The film was hampered by casting an unmusical actor in the leading role.

The Music Teacher *
Belgium 1988 98m Fujicolour
Mainline/RTBF/K2-One (Alexandre Pletser)
original title: *Le Maître de Musique*
Protégées of two rival singing teachers engage in a contest.
Resolutely old-fashioned drama, done with a certain style.
w Gérard Corbiau, André Corbiau *story* Luc Jabon, Gérard Corbiau *d* Gérard Corbiau *ph* Walther Van Den Ende *m* Ronald Zollman *ad* Zouc Lanc *ed* Denise Vindevogel
☆ José Van Dam, Anne Roussel, Philippe Volter, Sylvie Fennec, Patrick Bauchau, Johan Leysen, Marc Schreiber
'Verbal and visual clichés provide the setting for a selection of popular operatic gems. Culture of this kind makes gun-reaching Goerings of us all.' – *Philip French, Observer*
best foreign film

Musik I Mörker: see *Music Is My Future*

Musíme Si Pomàhat: see *Divided We Fall*

'As You've Never Seen It Before'
The Musketeer
US 2001 105m Technicolor
Universal/Miramax/D'Artagnan/Apollomedia/Q&Q/Carousel (Moshe Diamant)

D'Artagnan becomes involved in a political struggle for France when he sets out to avenge his parents' death.
Dire version of the familiar story, with a dull hero, unspeakable dialogue, overblown supporting performances and Hong Kong-styled martial arts to sabotage any sense of period.
w Gene Quintano *novel* The Three Musketeers by Alexandre Dumas *d* Peter Hyams *ph* Peter Hyams *m* David Arnold *pd* Philip Harrison *ed* Terry Rawlings *fight choreography* Xin-Xin Xiong
☆ Justin Chambers (D'Artagnan), Catherine Deneuve (The Queen), Mena Suvari (Francesca), Stephen Rea (Cardinal Richelieu), Tim Roth (Febre), Bill Treacher (Bonacieux), Daniel Mesguich (Louis XIII), David Schofield (Rochefort)
'If this is Dumas, there's a "b" in the middle and an extra "s" at the end.' – *Mike Clark, USA Today*
'Belongs to the school of new-style adventure movies that confuse visual energy with visual coleslaw.' – *Stephen Holden, New York Times*

Muss 'em Up
US 1936 70m bw
RKO/Pandro S. Berman
A cop with a Philo Vance complex routs out gangsters.
Competent crime programmer.
w Erwin Gelsey, James Edward Grant *d* Charles Vidor
☆ Preston Foster, Margaret Callahan, Alan Mowbray, Ralph Morgan, Guinn Williams, Maxie Rosenbloom
'Enough comedy and other values to make it fairly passable fare.' – *Variety*

Mustang Country
US 1976 79m Technicolor
Universal (John Champion)
In 1925 Montana, a rancher comes out of retirement to help to round up a wild stallion.
Mild outdoor yarn for family audiences.
wd John Champion *ph* J. Barry Herron *m* Lee Holdridge
☆ Joel McCrea, Nika Mina, Robert Fuller, Patrick Wayne

The Mutations
GB 1974 92m Eastmancolor
Columbia/Getty (Robert D. Weinbach)

A bio-chemist uses circus freaks in his experiments to find the perfect synthesis of plant and animal.
Tasteless horror film with little style of any kind.
w Robert D. Weinbach, Edward Mann *d* Jack Cardiff *ph* Paul Beeson *m* Basil Kirchin
☆ Donald Pleasence, Tom Baker, Brad Harris, Julie Ege, Michael Dunn, Scott Antony, Jill Haworth, Lisa Collings
'Bloody awful!' – *Julie Ege*

Mute Witness **
GB 1995 90m colour
Columbia TriStar/Cobblestone (Alexander Buchman, Norbert Soentgen, Anthony Waller)

In a Moscow film studio, a mute make-up artist is locked in at night and witnesses the filming of a real-life murder.
Tense, darkly comic chase thriller that maintains an exciting level of suspense and plays some clever tricks along the way.
wd Anthony Waller *ph* Egon Werdin *m* Wilbert Hirsch *pd* Matthias Kammermeir *ed* Peter Adam
☆ Mary Sudina, Fay Ripley, Evan Richards, Oleg Jankowskij, Igor Volkow, Sergei Karlenkov, Alec Guinness
'A seductive piece of real filmmaking that should keep audiences hyperventilating to the last reel.' – *Variety*

Mutiny
US 1952 77m Technicolor
King Brothers/United Artists

During the war of 1812, an American ship runs the English blockade to collect gold bullion from France.
Fairly lively swashbuckler.
w Philip Yordan, Sidney Harmon *d* Edward Dmytryk *ph* Ernest Laszlo *m* Dimitri Tiomkin
☆ Mark Stevens, Angela Lansbury, Patric Knowles, Gene Evans, Rhys Williams

Mutiny in the Big House
US 1939 83m bw
Monogram
A chaplain is at the centre of a prison break, and tries to calm the mob.
Archetypal cellblock movie, and not the worst of them.
w Robert D. Andrews, Martin Mooney *d* William Nigh
☆ Charles Bickford, Barton MacLane
'Will edge toward the profit side of the ledger for the pop-pricers.' – *Variety*

The Mutiny of the Elsinore
GB 1937 79m bw
Argyle British
A reporter on a sailing ship for a story finds himself in the middle of a mutiny.
Very studio-bound seafaring adventure.
w Walter Summers and Beaufoy Milton *novel* Jack London *d* Roy Lockwood *ph* Bryan Langley *m* Guy Jones
☆ Paul Lukas, Lyn Harding, Kathleen Kelly, Clifford Evans

'They'll take this town by storm ... fighting, laughing, loving, breaking every law of the seven seas!'
Mutiny on the Bounty ***
US 1935 135m bw
MGM (Irving Thalberg, Albert Lewin)

An 18th-century British naval vessel sets off for South America but during a mutiny the captain is cast adrift and the mutineers settle in the Pitcairn Islands.
A still-entertaining adventure film which seemed at the time like the pinnacle of Hollywood's achievement but can now be seen to be slackly told, with wholesale pre-release editing very evident. Individual scenes and performances are however refreshingly well-handled.
w Talbot Jennings, Jules Furthman, Carey Wilson *book* Charles Nordhoff, James Hall *d Frank Lloyd* *ph* Arthur Edeson *m* Herbert Stothart *ed* Margaret Booth
☆ *Charles Laughton, Clark Gable,* Franchot Tone, Movita, Dudley Digges, Henry Stephenson, Donald Crisp, Eddie Quillan, Francis Lister, Spring Byington, Ian Wolfe
BLIGH (CHARLES LAUGHTON): 'Casting me adrift 3,500 miles from a port of call! You're sending me to my doom, eh? Well, you're wrong, Christian. I'll take this boat, as she floats, to England if I must. I'll live to see you – all of you – hanging from the highest yardarm in the British fleet...'
'Nothing to stand in the way of a box office dynamite rating.' – *Variety*
'Incidents are made vivid in terms of the medium – the swish and pistol crack of the lash, the sweating lean bodies, the terrible labour, and the ominous judgment from the quarterdeck.' – *Otis Ferguson*
best picture
script; Frank Lloyd; Herbert Stothart; Charles Laughton; Clark Gable; Franchot Tone (whose role was originally to have been played by Robert Montgomery); Margaret Booth

Mutiny on the Bounty
US 1962 185m Technicolor Ultra Panavision 70
MGM/Arcola (Aaron Rosenberg)

Overlong and unattractive remake marred principally by Brando's English accent and various production follies, not to mention his overlong and bloody death scene.
The shipboard sadism still works pretty well, but after the landing in Tahiti boredom takes over.
w Charles Lederer *d* Lewis Milestone *ph* Robert Surtees *m* Bronislau Kaper
☆ Trevor Howard, Marlon Brando, Richard Harris, Hugh Griffith, Tarita, Richard Haydn, Percy Herbert, Duncan Lamont, Gordon Jackson, Chips Rafferty, Noel Purcell
best picture; Robert Surtees; Bronislau Kaper; Song 'Follow Me' (*m* Bronislau Kaper, *ly* Paul Francis Webster)

Mutiny on the Buses
GB 1972 89m Technicolor
MGM-EMI/Hammer (Ronald Wolfe, Ronald Chesney)
A bus driver, who is trying to raise the money to get married, finds his life complicated by his incompetent out-of-work brother-in-law and a fierce new depot manager.
Dreadful, broad slapstick comedy, based on a TV sitcom, with jokes that are both feeble and heavy-handed.
w Ronald Wolfe, Ronald Chesney *d* Harry Booth *ph* Mark McDonald *m* Ron Grainer *md* Philip Martell *ad* Scott MacGregor *ed* Archie Ludski
☆ Reg Varney (Stan Butler), Doris Hare (Mrs Butler), Anna Karen (Olive), Michael Robbins (Arthur), Bob Grant (Jack), Stephen Lewis (Inspector Blake), Pat Ashton (Nora), Janet Mahoney (Susy), Caroline Dowdeswell (Sandra), Kevin Brennan (Mr Jenkins), Bob Todd (New Inspector), David Lodge (Safari Guide)
'Shot in the same flat, one-dimensional style as its predecessor and appears even more hard up for humour.' – *Paul Madden, MFB*
† It was a sequel to *On the Buses* (qv).

My Ain Folk ***
GB 1973 55m bw
Connoisseur/BFI (Nick Nascht)

Following the death of his maternal grandmother, a boy is reluctantly taken in by his father's mother until he goes away to an orphanage.
Stark account of narrow and damaged lives, told with an intense sympathy.
wd Bill Douglas *ph* Gale Tattersall *ed* Peter West
☆ Stephen Archibald, Hughie Restorick, Jean Taylor Smith, Bernard McKenna, Mr Munro, Paul Kermack, Helena Gloag, Jessie Combe
'A very considerable work of art, more profound, more terrible and ultimately more inspiring than My Childhood, all of whose virtues it shares.' – *Elizabeth Sussex, MFB*
† The second part of an autobiographical trilogy that began with *My Childhood* and was completed by *My Way Home* (qqv).

My American Cousin *
Canada 1985 95m Alpha Cine
Borderline/Okanagan/Peter O'Brian

In the summer of 1959, a 12-year-old girl falls for her blond Californian cousin when he arrives in his red Cadillac on a visit to her home in British Columbia.
Gently nostalgic film of family life and mild teenage rebellion, with a rock soundtrack.
wd Sandy Wilson *ph* Richard Leiterman *ad* Phil Schmidt *ed* Haida Paul
☆ Margaret Langrick, John Wildman, Richard Donat, Jane Mortifee, T. J. Scott, Camille Henderson, Darsi Bailey, Allison Hale, Samantha Jocelyn
† The film won Canadian Genie awards for best film, director, screenplay, editing, actress (Margaret Langrick), and actor (John Wildman).

My American Uncle ***
France 1980 126m Eastmancolor
Andrea Films/TFI (Philippe Dussart)
original title: *Mon Oncle Américain*
Professor Henri Laborit explains the lives of two men and a woman in terms of animal behaviour.
Fascinatingly assembled but basically pessimistic dissection of human life, in the director's most meticulous style. The American uncle is the piece of good luck which may be just around the corner (but probably isn't).
w Jean Gruault *books* Henri Laborit *d* Alain Resnais *ph* Sacha Vierny *m* Arié Dzierlatka
☆ Gérard Depardieu, Nicole Garcia, Roger Pierre, Henri Laborit
screenplay

My Beautiful Laundrette *
GB 1985 97m colour
Working Title/SAF/Channel 4 (Sarah Radclyffe, Tim Bevan)

A young south London Asian manages his uncle's launderette and falls for a white racist boy.
Made for TV, but fashionable enough to get critical acclaim and cinema distribution, this soft-centred anecdote was a bit of a puzzle to those neither Asian nor homosexual.
w Hanif Kureishi *d* Stephen Frears *ph* Oliver Stapleton *m* Ludus Tonalis
☆ Saeed Jaffrey, Roshan Seth, Daniel Day-Lewis, Gordon Warnecke, Shirley Anne Field, Rita Wolf
best original screenplay

My Best Friend's Girl
France 1983 100m Eastmancolor
Cannon/Renn Productions/Sara Films (Alain Sarde)

original title: *La Femme de Mon Pote*
A day worker asks his friend, a night worker, to look after his girlfriend.
Mildly amusing comedy.
w Bertrand Blier, Gérard Brach *d* Bertrand Blier *ph* Jean Penzer, Yves Agostini, Michel Coteret, Eric Vallée *m* J. J. Cale *ed* Claudine Merline, Sylvie Quester, Annick Menier, Jeanne Kef
☆ Coluche, Isabelle Huppert, Thierry Lhermitte, Farid Chopel, François Perrot, Daniel Colas, Frédérique Michot

'Julianne fell in love with her best friend the day he decided to marry someone else.'
My Best Friend's Wedding **
US 1997 105m Technicolor Panavision
Columbia TriStar/Predawn (Jerry Zucker, Ronald Bass)

When she discovers that her former lover is about to marry, a woman decides to break up the romance and win him back for herself.
Enjoyable, slightly tart comedy, with a star turn from Everett to compensate for the occasional predictability of the plot.
w Ronald Bass *d* P. J. Hogan *ph* Laszlo Kovacs *m* James Newton Howard *pd* Richard Sylbert *ed* Garth Craven
☆ Julia Roberts (Julianne Potter), Dermot Mulroney (Michael O'Neal), Cameron Diaz (Kimmy Wallace), *Rupert Everett* (George Downes), Philip Bosco (Walter Wallace), M. Emmet Walsh (Joe O'Neal), Rachel Griffiths (Samantha Newhouse)
'Straddling several genres, the film has an underlying veracity that should strike an emotional chord with audiences.' – *Leonard Klady, Variety*
† After preview audiences liked the character played by Rupert Everett, extra scenes involving him were shot, and a new ending added.
†† It was one of the most successful movies of the year, grossing more than $126m in the US, and another $129m elsewhere in the world.
James Newton Howard

My Best Girl *
US 1927 84m (24 fps) bw silent
Mary Pickford Corporation
A shopgirl falls for a co-worker, unaware that he is the son of the owner.
The star's last silent film is a charming comedy which tends to fade in the memory.
w Allen McNeil, Tim Whelan *d* Sam Taylor *ph Charles Rosher* *m* Gaylord Carter
☆ *Mary Pickford,* Charles 'Buddy' Rogers, Sunshine Hart, Lucien Littlefield, Hobart Bosworth
Charles Rosher

'Love is here to stay...So is her family'
My Big Fat Greek Wedding **
US/Canada 2002 95m DeLuxe
Entertainment/Gold Circle/HBO/MPH/Playtone (Rita Wilson, Tom Hanks, Gary Goetzman)

A Greek-American woman horrifies her large family by deciding to marry a non-Greek.
Warm and lively comedy that is just saved from its reliance on stereotyped characters and situations by its generous humanity.
w Nia Vardalos *play* Nia Vardalos *d* Joel Zwick *ph* Jeffrey Jur *m* Chris Wilson, Alexander Janko *pd* Gregory Keen *ed* Mia Goldman

☆ Nia Vardalos (Toula), John Corbett (Ian), Michael Constantine (Gus), Lainie Kazan (Maria), Andrea Martin (Aunt Voula), Joey Fatone (Angelo), Gia Carides (Nikki), Louis Mandylor (Nick)

'Just a routinely sentimental/slapstick march toward the altar, sans any real comic invention.' – *Dennis Harvey, Variety*

'Insufferably cute pile of tripe.' – *Joe Queenan*

† The film was the unexpected hit of the year, taking $241.4m at the US box-office and another $115m elsewhere in the world. It also spawned a TV sitcom *My Big Fat Greek Life.*

Ꭾ Nia Vardalos (as writer)

'Perhaps it is not for the living to know the truth about reincarnation!'

'If you give away the ending, may your blood run cold forever!'

My Blood Runs Cold
US 1965 108m bw Panavision
Warner (William Conrad)

A spoilt heiress meets a strange young man who claims she is the reincarnation of a long dead charmer; he turns out to be a madman who has come across an old diary.

Initially intriguing but eventually exhausting melodrama with a weak solution.

w John Mantley *d* William Conrad *ph* Sam Leavitt *m* George Duning

☆ Troy Donahue, Joey Heatherton, Barry Sullivan, Jeanette Nolan

'Not all that bad, but not worth missing *I Love Lucy* for either.' – *Leonard Maltin*

My Blue Heaven
US 1950 96m Technicolor
TCF (Sol C. Siegel)

A pair of troupers want a family, by adoption if not otherwise.

Routine musical drenched in sentimentality.

w Lamar Trotti, Claude Binyon *d* Henry Koster *ph* Arthur E. Arling *m* Alfred Newman *songs Harold Arlen (m), Ralph Blane (ly)*

☆ Betty Grable, Dan Dailey, Mitzi Gaynor, David Wayne, Jane Wyatt, Una Merkel

My Blue Heaven
US 1990 95m Technicolor
Warner (Herbert Ross, Anthea Sylbert)

Relocated in a small town, a gangster who has turned state's evidence decides not to go straight.

Dull comedy, broadly acted and directed.

w Nora Ephron *d* Herbert Ross *ph* John Bailey *m* Ira Newborn *pd* Charles Rosen *ed* Stephen A. Rotter, Robert Reitano

☆ Steve Martin, Rick Moranis, Joan Cusack, Melanie Mayron, William Irwin, Carol Kane, William Hickey, Deborah Rush, Daniel Stern, Jesse Bradford

My Bodyguard
US 1980 96m CFI color
Market Street/Melvin Simon

A 15-year-old Chicago boy has trouble at school.

Oddly titled, uncommercial but quite watchable drama of adolescence. Not surprisingly, it failed to find an audience.

w Alan Ormsby *d* Tony Bill *ph* Michael D. Margulies *m* Dave Grusin *pd* Jackson de Govia

☆ Chris Makepeace, Adam Baldwin, Ruth Gordon, Matt Dillon, Martin Mull, John Houseman

My Boyfriend's Back
US 1993 84m DeLuxe
Buena Vista/Touchstone (Sean S. Cunningham)

A high-school student, killed in a bungled robbery planned to impress a girl, returns as a zombie to demonstrate his undying love.

Ghoulish and unedifying horror.

w Dean Lorey *d* Bob Balaban *ph* Mac Ahlberg *m* Harry Manfredini *pd* Michael Hanan *ed* Michael Jablow

☆ Andrew Lowery, Traci Lind, Danny Zorn, Edward Herrmann, Mary Beth Hurt, Austin Pendleton, Cloris Leachman, Paxton Whitehead

'Lacking any redeeming quality, it's a matter of days before this tasteless pic is buried without trace in the sands of Hollywood.' – *Variety*

My Brilliant Career ***
Australia 1979 100m Eastmancolor
NSW Film Corporation/Margaret Fink

The daughter of an Australian bush farmer at the turn of the century dreams of the world beyond and writes a memoir.

Pleasing but very slow picture of a world gone by.

w Eleanor Witcombe *novel* Miles Franklin *d* Gillian Armstrong *ph* Don McAlpine *m* Nathan Waks

☆ *Judy Davis*, Sam Neill, Wendy Hughes, Robert Grubb, Max Cullen

Judy Davis

My Brother Jonathan
GB 1947 108m bw
ABP (Warwick Ward)

The life of a small-town doctor who wanted to be a great surgeon.

Unobjectionable, unexciting novel-on-film with the typically British artificial studio look of the time.

w Leslie Landau, Adrian Arlington *novel* Francis Brett Young *d* Harold French *ph* Derick Williams *m* Hans May *ad* Douglas Daniels *ed* Chalres Hasse

☆ Michael Denison, Dulcie Gray, Ronald Howard, Stephen Murray, Mary Clare, Finlay Currie, Beatrice Campbell

My Brother Talks to Horses
US 1946 93m bw
MGM (Samuel Marx)

A boy who can talk to horses finds himself in demand by racetrack gamblers.

Well-mounted but uninspired whimsy with a fatal lack of pace.

w Morton Thompson *novel Joe the Wounded Tennis Player* by Morton Thompson *d* Fred Zinnemann *ph* Joseph Ruttenberg *m* Rudolph Kopp

☆ Butch Jenkins, Peter Lawford, Charlie Ruggles, Edward Arnold, Beverly Tyler, Spring Byington

My Brother Tom
GB/Germany 2001 111m DeLuxe
Film4/Film Council/British Screen/W.O.W./Trijbits (Carl Schonfeld)

An unhappy teenage girl forms a close relationship with an abused boy who spends most of his time in a wood.

Shot on digital video, the film has an intense sense of reality about it, in its portrait of misunderstood adolescents, but that does not survive the increasingly melodramatic nature of the narrative.

w Dom Rotheroe, Alison Beeton-Hilder *d* Dom Rotheroe *ph* Robby Muller *pd* Isolde Sommerfeldt *ed* David Charap

☆ Jenna Harrison (Jessica), Ben Whishaw (Tom), Adrian Rawlins (Jack), Jonathan Hackett (Tom's Dad), Richard Hope (Jessica's Dad), Judith Scott (Jessica's Mum), Honeysuckle Weeks (Sarah)

'Notable for its atmospheric fairy-tale setting, its dark intensity and aching depiction of adolescent vulnerability, the overwrought drama nonetheless fails to summon the edge and emotional truth that it aims for.' – *David Rooney, Variety*

'A more amateurish, misbegotten and badly made film it would be hard to find this year.' – *Alexander Walker, London Evening Standard*

My Brother's Keeper
GB 1948 91m bw
GFD/Gainsborough (Anthony Darnborough)

Two convicts escape, handcuffed together; one is violent, the other innocent.

Pre-Defiant Ones social melodrama, quite well made but suffering from miscasting.

w Frank Harvey *story* Maurice Wiltshire *d* Alfred Roome, Roy Rich *ph* Gordon Lang *m* Clifton Parker

☆ Jack Warner, George Cole, Jane Hylton, David Tomlinson, Bill Owen, Raymond Lovell, Yvonne Owen, Beatrice Varley

My Buddy *
US 1944 67m bw
Eddy White/Republic

A World War I veteran is forced into crime.

Not a new message, but a second feature with sincerity and conviction. A better title would have helped.

w Arnold Manoff, Prescott Chaplin *d* Steve Sekely

☆ Don Barry, Alexander Granach, Ruth Terry, Lynne Roberts, Emma Dunn, John Litel, George E. Stone

My Childhood ***
GB 1972 48m bw
Connoisseur/BFI (Geoffrey Evans)

An eight-year-old boy lives with his half-brother and ailing grandmother in dire poverty in a Scottish mining village.

Passionate, autobiographical account of a life of almost total bleakness observed with scrupulous honesty.

wd Bill Douglas *ph* Mick Campbell *ed* Brand Thumim

☆ Stephen Archibald, Hughie Restorick, Jean Taylor Smith, Karl Fieseler, Paul Kermack, Helena Gloag

'The story unfolds with pathos, tension and considerable humour.' – *MFB*

† The first part of an autobiographical trilogy that was followed by *My Ain Folk* and *My Way Home* (qqv).

My Cousin Rachel *
US 1952 98m bw
TCF (Nunnally Johnson)

A Cornish gentleman dies in Italy after marrying a mysterious lady; when she comes to England she arouses the hostility, and love, of her husband's foster son.

Well-wrought but dramatically unsatisfactory Victorian melodrama from a bestseller; plenty of suspicion but no solution makes Rachel a dull girl.

w Nunnally Johnson *novel* Daphne du Maurier *d* Henry Koster *ph* Joseph LaShelle *m* Franz Waxman *ad* Lyle Wheeler, John DeCuir

☆ Olivia de Havilland, Richard Burton, John Sutton, Audrey Dalton, Ronald Squire

Ꭾ Joseph LaShelle; Richard Burton; art direction

My Cousin Vinny *
U.S. 1992 119m DeLuxe
TCF/Peter V. Miller Investment Corp. (Dale Launer, Paul Schiff)

An inexperienced New York lawyer goes to Alabama to defend his cousin who is charged with murder.

Ramshackle comedy that raises an occasional smile and one or two laughs.

w Dale Launer *d* Jonathan Lynn *ph* Peter Deming *m* Randy Edelman *pd* Victoria Paul *ed* Tony Lombardo

☆ Joe Pesci, Ralph Macchio, Marisa Tomei, Mitchell Whitfield, Fred Gwynne, Lane Smith, Austin Pendleton, Bruce McGill, Maury Chaykin

'The bits and pieces never quite add up. Somewhere during this film's making I suspect that half the script was mysteriously lost down a street grating.' – *Nigel Andrews, Financial Times*

Marisa Tomei

My Crasy Life
US 1992 98m colour
BBC/FR3 (Daniel Marks, Cameron Allan)

American-Samoan members of a Californian street-gang talk about their violent lives.

Unilluminating mix of documentary and fiction about the inarticulate young being assimilated into a ghetto culture.

w Jean-Pierre Gorin, Howard Rodman *d* Jean-Pierre Gorin *ph* Babette Mangolte *m* Joyi Yuasa *ed* Brad Thumin

'An aggravatingly tedious docu-drama.' – *Variety*

'Lipstick and attitude – the girls from Echo Park are hard!'

My Crazy Life
US 1993 95m DeLuxe
aka: *Mi Vida Loca*

In Los Angeles, Hispanic teenagers, members of a street gang, hang out, talk tough and try to make sense of their lives and the men they become involved with.

Voice-overs rob this account of young street-wise women of much of its dramatic impact; the narrative interest is slight and the performances often amateurish despite their authenticity.

wd Allison Anders *ph* Rodrigo Garcia *m* John Taylor *pd* Jane Stewart *ed* Kathryn Himoff, Tracy Granger

☆ Angel Aviles, Seidy Lopez, Jacob Vargas, Mario Marron, Nelida Lopez, Jessie Borrego, Magali Alvarado

'Dramatically fuzzy and very flat visually and in performance.' – *Variety*

'She was everything the west was – young, fiery, exciting!'

My Darling Clementine ***
US 1946 98m bw
TCF (Samuel G. Engel)

Wyatt Earp cleans up Tombstone and wipes out the Clanton gang at the OK corral.

Archetypal Western mood piece, full of nostalgia for times gone by and crackling with memorable scenes and characterizations.

w Samuel G. Engel, Winston Miller *book Wyatt Earp, Frontier Marshal* by Stuart N. Lake *d John Ford ph Joe MacDonald m Cyril Mockridge*

☆ *Henry Fonda, Victor Mature, Walter Brennan,* Linda Darnell, Cathy Downs, Tim Holt, Ward Bond, *Alan Mowbray*, John Ireland, Jane Darwell

'Every scene, every shot is the product of a keen and sensitive eye.' – *Bosley Crowther*

'Considerable care has gone to its period reconstruction, but the view is a poetic one.' – *Lindsay Anderson*

My Daughter Joy
GB 1950 81m bw
London Films/Gregory Ratoff
US title: *Operation X*

In order to cement a new trade pact, an international financier plans to marry his daughter to the son of an African sultan.

Turgid melodrama swamping some good actors.

w Robert Thoeren, William Rose *novel* David Golder by Irene Neirowsky *d* Gregory Ratoff *ph* Georges Périnal *m* Raymond Gallois-Montbrun

☆ Edward G. Robinson, Peggy Cummins, Nora Swinburne, Richard Greene, Finlay Currie, Gregory Ratoff, Ronald Adam, Walter Rilla, James Robertson Justice, David Hutcheson

My Dear Miss Aldrich
US 1937 73m bw
MGM

The glamorous new owner of a newspaper never agrees with its editor.

Skilful light comedy with good work all round.

w Herman Mankiewicz *d* George B. Seitz

☆ Maureen O'Sullivan, Walter Pidgeon, Edna May Oliver, Rita Johnson, Janet Beecher

My Dear Secretary
US 1948 96m bw
Cardinal/UA

A secretary marries her boss and becomes jealous of his new secretary.

Slow-paced, frivolous romantic comedy.

wd Charles Martin

☆ Kirk Douglas, Laraine Day, Keenan Wynn, Rudy Vallee, Helen Walker, Florence Bates, Alan Mowbray

My Dinner with André *
US 1981 111m Movielab
André Company/George W. George/Michael White

Two men start a dinner table conversation which becomes a philosophical argument.

Curious two-hander which can please the right audience when it's in the mood; for selling tickets, forget it.

w Wallace Shawn, André Gregory *d* Louis Malle *ph* Jeri Sopanen *m* Allen Shawn *pd* David Mitchell *ed* Suzanne Baron

☆ *Wallace Shawn, André Gregory,* Jean Lenauer, Roy Butler

'A magical mystery tour of thoughts, dreams, fantasies and emotions.' – *Time Out*

'An adventure through a magically cracked looking glass.' – *San Francisco Chronicle*

'A dazzling cerebral comedy of ideas.' – *Los Angeles Times*

'Every Family Needs An Optimist.'

My Dog Skip *

US 2000 95m DeLuxe

Warner/Alcon (Broderick Johnson, Andrew A. Kosove, Mark Johnson, John Lee Hancock)

In Mississippi in the 1940s, a shy nine-year-old boy learns to cope with life with the help of his dog.

Nostalgic account of growing up that has plenty of charm, though it is tinged with too much sentimentality.

w Gail Gilchriest *book* Willie Morris *d* Jay Russell *ph* James L. Carter *m* William Ross *pd* David J. Bomba *ed* Harvey Rosenstock, Gary Winter *cos* Edi Giguere

☆ Frankie Muniz (Willie Morris), Diane Lane (Ellen Morris), Luke Wilson (Dink Jenkins), Kevin Bacon (Jack Morris), Caitlin Wachs (Rivers Applewhite), Bradley Coryell (Big Boy Wilkinson), Daylan Honeycutt (Henjie Henick), Cody Linley (Spit McGee), Peter Crombie (Junior Smalls), Clint Howard (Millard), Harry Connick Jnr (Narrator)

'Family entertainment that has no ambition beyond continuing America's love affair with the pet pooch.' – *Anthony Quinn, Independent*

My Dream Is Yours

US 1949 101m Technicolor

Warner (Michael Curtiz)

A Hollywood talent scout discovers a new singer.

Competent, forgettable musical.

w Harry Kurnitz, Dane Lussier *d* Michael Curtiz *ph* Ernest Haller *m* Harry Warren *ch* Le Roy Prinz *ly* Ralph Blane

☆ Doris Day, Jack Carson, Lee Bowman, Adolphe Menjou, Eve Arden, S. Z. Sakall

† A remake of *Twenty Million Sweethearts*.

My English Grandfather **

USSR 1986 75m colour/bw

Georgia Film Studios

aka: *Robinson Crusoe in Georgia*

A Russian composer dedicates his new symphony to his English grandfather, sent to Georgia to maintain the London–Delphi telephone line, who takes up residence in the three metres around a telephone post which remain British territory when the revolution comes.

Enjoyable and quirky drama, with ironic and comic overtones, which shuttles between the present, in colour, and the past, mainly in monochrome.

w Irakli Kvirikadze *d* Nana Djordjadze *ph* Levan Paatashvili *m* Enri Lolashvili *ad* Vakhtang Rurua

☆ Zhanri Lolashvili, Nineli Chankvetadze, Guram Pirtskhalava, Gudja Burduli, Rusudan Bolkvadze, Tiko Eliosidze

My Fair Lady ***

US 1964 175m Technicolor Super Panavision 70

CBS/Warner (Jack L. Warner)

Musical version of *Pygmalion*, about a flower girl trained by an arrogant elocutionist to pass as a lady.

Careful, cold transcription of a stage success; cinematically quite uninventive when compared with Pygmalion *itself, but a pretty good entertainment.*

w Alan Jay Lerner *play* *Pygmalion* by Bernard Shaw *d* George Cukor *ph* *Harry Stradling* *m* Frederick Loewe *md* André Previn *ch* Hermes Pan *ad* Gene Allen *ed* William Ziegler *cos* Cecil Beaton

☆ *Rex Harrison*, Audrey Hepburn, Stanley Holloway, Wilfrid Hyde-White, Gladys Cooper, Jeremy Brett, Theodore Bikel, Isobel Elsom, Mona Washbourne, Walter Burke

'The property has been not so much adapted as elegantly embalmed.' – *Andrew Sarris*

† Audrey Hepburn's singing was dubbed by Marni Nixon. In the restored 30th-anniversary laser disc edition, Hepburn can be heard singing two songs – 'Wouldn't It Be Luvverly' and 'Show Me' – on alternate tracks on the disc.

best picture; George Cukor; Harry Stradling; Rex Harrison; André Previn (scoring of music); costumes; sound

Alan Jay Lerner; Stanley Holloway; Gladys Cooper; editing

best picture

My Family

US 1995 125m colour

Entertainment/New Line/Majestic/American Playhouse/American Zoetrope/Newcomm/Anna Thomas

aka: *Mi Familia*

UK video title: *East L.A.*

The life of a Mexican family in California over three generations, from the 20s to the 80s.

A soft-centred domestic saga that never quite engages the heart or the mind.

w Gregory Nava, Anna Thomas *d* Gregory Nava *ph* Edward Lachman *m* Pepe Avila, Mark McKenzie *pd* Barry Robison *ed* Nancy Richardson

☆ Jimmy Smits, Esai Morales, Eduardo Lopez Rojas, Jenny Gago, Elpidia Carrillo, Lupe Ontiveros, Edward James Olmos, Scott Bakula

'More a superior television soap than a proper film.' – *Derek Malcolm, Guardian*

make-up

My Father Is Coming

Germany/US 1991 81m TVC Color

Out on a Limb/Hyane/Hyena (Monika Treut)

A German would-be actress in New York auditions for a sex movie, makes friends with a transsexual and goes to bed with a Puerto Rican woman.

A movie without a redeeming feature, other than its short running time.

w Monika Treut, Bruce Benderson, Sarah Schulman *d* Monika Treut *ph* Elfi Mikesch *m* David Van Tieghem *pd* Robin Ford *ed* Steve Brown

☆ Alfred Edel, Shelley Kästner, Annie Sprinkle, Mery Lou Graulau, David Bronstein, Michael Massee

'A scrappy little film, ill-scripted, photographed and, in particular, directed, and the weird, but very likeable cast is the only reason to see it.' – *Sheila Johnston, Independent*

'Treut's film seems to condemn rather than celebrate the effects of implementing consumerist notions of choice within the field of sexuality.' – *Verina Glaessner, Sight and Sound*

My Father, the Hero

US 1994 90m Technicolor

Buena Vista/Touchstone/Cité (Jacques Bar, Jean-Louis Livi)

A young girl on holiday in the Caribbean pretends that her father is actually her lover.

Dull and corny comedy, with little appeal to any age group.

w Francis Veber, Charlie Peters *d* Steve Miner *ph* Daryn Okada *m* David Newman *pd* Christopher Nowak *ed* Marshall Harvey

☆ Gérard Depardieu, Katherine Heigl, Emma Thompson, Dalton James, Lauren Hutton, Faith Prince, Stephen Tobolowsky, Ann Hearn

'You don't have to be a black-polo-neck-wearing francophile to see that hardly a single remake of a French movie has been any good. Let us hope the flopping of this latest atrocity augurs the cessation of this insidious Hollywood habit.' – *Leslie Felperin Sharman, Sight and Sound*

† The film is a remake of *Mon Père, Ce Héros*, which also starred Gérard Depardieu.

My Father's Glory: see *La Gloire de mon père*

My Favorite Blonde ***

US 1942 78m bw

Paramount (Paul Jones)

A burlesque comic travelling by train helps a lady in distress and lives to regret it.

Smartly paced spy comedy thriller, one of its star's best vehicles.

w Don Hartman, Frank Butler, Melvin Frank, Norman Panama d Sidney Lanfield ph William Mellor *m* David Buttolph

☆ *Bob Hope, Madeleine Carroll, Gale Sondergaard,* George Zucco, Lionel Royce, Walter Kingsford, Victor Varconi

My Favorite Brunette *

US 1947 87m bw

Paramount/Hope Enterprises (Daniel Dare)

A photographer gets mixed up with mobsters.

Pretty fair star vehicle which half-heartedly spoofs Farewell My Lovely.

w Edmund Beloin, Jack Rose *d* Elliott Nugent *ph* Lionel Lindon *m* Robert Emmett Dolan

☆ Bob Hope, Dorothy Lamour, Peter Lorre, Lon Chaney Jnr, John Hoyt, Charles Dingle, Reginald Denny

My Favorite Martian

US 1999 93m Technicolor

Buena Vista/Walt Disney (Robert Shapiro, Jerry Leider, Mark Toberoff)

A TV producer rescues a stranded Martian, who has the ability to assume human form.

Yet another lumbering attempt to turn a forgotten sitcom into a movie, and yet more evidence that dead television comedy isn't worth reviving.

w Sherri Stoner, Deanna Oliver *TV serial* John L. Greene *d* Donald Petrie *ph* Thomas Ackerman *m* John Debney *pd* Sandy Veneziano *ed* Malcolm Campbell *sp* Phil Tippett, John T. Van Vliet; Alec Gillis, Tom Woodruff Jnr

☆ Christopher Lloyd, Jeff Daniels, Elizabeth Hurley, Daryl Hannah, Wallace Shawn, Christine Ebersole, Michael Lerner, Ray Walston

'The kind of leering, obnoxious picture that seizes you by the neck and gnaws at your skull like a giant, snot-nosed child.' – *New York Post*

† The TV series, starring Ray Walston and Bill Bixby, ran from 1963 to 1966.

My Favorite Spy

US 1942 86m bw

RKO

The bandleader Kay Kyser has to postpone his honeymoon when he is called up and set to spy-catching.

Fairly slick nonsense featuring a band popular at the time.

w Sig Herzig, William Bowers *d* Tay Garnett *ph* Robert de Grasse

☆ Kay Kyser, Ginny Simms, Ish Kabibble, Ellen Drew, Jane Wyman

My Favorite Spy *

US 1951 93m bw

Paramount (Paul Jones)

A burlesque comic is asked by the US government to pose as an international spy who happens to be his double.

Moderately funny star vehicle with more willing hands than good ideas. The chase finale however is worth waiting for.

w Edmund Hartmann, Jack Sher *d* Norman Z. McLeod *ph* Victor Milner *m* Victor Young

☆ Bob Hope, Hedy Lamarr, Francis L. Sullivan, Arnold Moss, Mike Mazurki, Luis Van Rooten

'The funniest, fastest honeymoon ever screened!'

My Favorite Wife ***

US 1940 88m bw

RKO (Leo McCarey)

A lady explorer returns after several shipwrecked years to find that her husband has married again.

A well-worn situation gets its brightest treatment in this light star vehicle.

w Sam and Bella Spewack, Leo McCarey d Garson Kanin ph Rudolph Maté *m* Roy Webb *ad* Van Nest Polglase *ed* Robert Wise

☆ *Cary Grant, Irene Dunne,* Randolph Scott, Gail Patrick, Ann Shoemaker, Donald MacBride

'One of those comedies with a glow on it.' – *Otis Ferguson*

† Other variations (qv): *Too Many Husbands, Our Wife, Three for the Show, Move Over Darling.*

story; Roy Webb; art direction

'I can't go on *live*! I'm a movie star, not an actor!'

My Favorite Year ***

US 1982 92m Metrocolor

MGM-UA/Brooksfilms/Michael Gruskoff

In 1954, a legendary Hollywood star noted for wine and women is unwisely invited to star in a television series.

A good-humoured and well-researched romp with a central character not too far removed from Errol Flynn.

w Norman Steinberg, Dennis Palumbo *d* Richard Benjamin *ph* Gerald Hirschfeld *m* Ralph Burns *pd* Charles Rosen *ed* Richard Chew

☆ *Peter O'Toole,* Mark Linn-Baker, Jessica Harper, Joseph Bologna, Bill Macy, Lainie Kazan, Lou Jacobi, Cameron Mitchell

'A field day for a wonderful bunch of actors.' – *Variety*

Peter O'Toole

My Fellow Americans

US 1996 101m colour

Warner/Peters/Storyline (Jon Peters)

Two ageing and antagonistic former presidents of the USA are forced to co-operate with one another when they find themselves targeted for assassination.

An uneasy mix of weak political satire and thriller, with the Odd Couple pairing of Lemmon as an uptight conservative and Garner as a libidinous liberal, swopping insults as they dodge bullets.

w E. Jack Kaplan, Richard Chapman, Peter Tolan *d* Peter Segal *ph* Julio Macat *m* William Ross *pd* James Bissell *ed* William Kerr

☆ Jack Lemmon (Russell P. Kramer), James Garner (Matt Douglas), Dan Aykroyd (William Haney), John Heard (Ted Matthews), Sela Ward (Kaye Griffin), Wilford Brimley (Joe Hollis), Everett McGill (Col Paul Tanner), Bradley Whitford (Carl Witnaur), Lauren Bacall (Margaret Kramer), James Rebhorn (Charlie Reynolds)

My First 40 Years

Italy 1989 107m Technicolor

Columbia TriStar/CG Silver Film/Reteitalia (Mario Cecchi Gori, Vittorio Cecchi Gori)

A fashion designer recalls her numerous affairs on her fortieth birthday.

Charmless romantic drama, not helped by some inept dubbing.

w Enrico Vanzina, Carlo Vanzina *novel I Miei Primi 40 Anni* by Marina Ripa Di Meana *d* Carlo Vanzina *ph* Luigi Kuveiller *m* Umberto Smaila *ad* Mario Chiari *ed* Ruggero Mastroianni

☆ Carol Alt, Elliott Gould, Jean Rochefort, Pierre Cosso, Massimo Venturiello, Isabel Russinova, Paolo Quattrini, Riccardo Garrone, Capucine

'Mismatched. Misguided. Unmistakably friends.'
'Meet the new odd couple.'

My First Mister

US 2001 109m DeLuxe 'Scope

Paramount/Total/Film Roman/Firelight/Apollo Media (Mitchell Solomon, Sukee Chew, Anne Kurtzman, Carol Baum, Jane Goldenring)

An unhappy teenager goes to work for a fussy shopkeeper, and the experience changes them both.

A sitcom masquerading as a movie, and abandoning a character study of two misfits for mawkish sentimentality.

w Jill Franklyn *d* Christine Lahti *ph* Jeffrey Jur *m* Steve Porcaro *pd* Dan Bishop *ed* Wendy Greene Bricmont

☆ Albert Brooks (Randall), Leelee Sobieski (Jennifer), Desmond Harrington (Randy), Carol Kane (Mrs Benson), Mary Kay Place (Patty), Michael McKean (Bob), John Goodman (Benjamin)

'Mild, obvious but not entirely unappealing.' – *Todd Mccarthy, Variety*

My First Wife *

Australia 1984 98m colour

Artificial Eye/Dofine Productions/Film Victoria/Spectrafilm (Jane Ballantyne, Paul Cox)

A composer is heart-stricken when his wife decides to leave him.

Passionate, emotionally painful study of relationships over two generations that comes to the somewhat pat conclusion that the family is everything.

w Paul Cox, Bob Ellis *d* Paul Cox *ph* Yuri Sokol *m* Gluck, Orff, Haydn and others *pd* Asher Bilu *ed* Tim Lewis

☆ John Hargreaves, Wendy Hughes, Lucy Angwin, David Cameron, Anna Jemison, Charles Tingwell, Betty Lucas, Robin Lovejoy

'I was a good girl – wasn't I?'

My Foolish Heart *

US 1949 98m bw

Samuel Goldwyn

A woman deceives her husband into thinking her forthcoming child is his.

A 'woman's picture' par excellence, and among the first to benefit from commercial plugging of a schmaltzy theme tune.

w Julius J. and Philip G. Epstein *story* J. D. Salinger *d* Mark Robson *ph* Lee Garmes *m* Victor Young
☆ Susan Hayward, Dana Andrews, Kent Smith, Robert Keith, Gigi Perreau, Lois Wheeler, Jessie Royce Landis

'Obviously designed to pull the plugs out of the tear glands and cause the ducts to overflow.' – *Bosley Crowther, New York Times*

'In its dry-eyed moments, this damp fable is brightened by some well-written patches of wryly amusing dialogue.' – *Time*

Susan Hayward; title song (*m*Victor Young, *ly*Ned Washington)

My Forbidden Past
US 1951 81m bw
RKO (Polan Banks)

A New Orleans beauty seeks vengeance when her cousin prevents her marriage.
Stuffy period melodrama with vigorous performances.
w Marion Parsonnet *novel* Polan Banks *d* Robert Stevenson *ph* Harry J. Wild *m* Frederick Hollander *ad* Albert S. D'Agostino
☆ Ava Gardner, Melvyn Douglas, Robert Mitchum, Janis Carter, Lucile Watson

My Friend Flicka *
US 1943 89m Technicolor
TCF (Ralph Dietrich)

Adventures of a young boy and his pet colt.
Winsome boy-and-horse story, one of the most popular family films of the forties. Sequel 1945 with virtually the same cast: Thunderhead Son of Flicka.
w Lillie Hayward *novel* Mary O'Hara *d* Harold Schuster *ph* Dewey Wrigley *m* Alfred Newman
☆ Roddy McDowall, Preston Foster, Rita Johnson, James Bell, Jeff Corey

My Friend Irma *
US 1949 103m bw
Paramount/Hal B. Wallis

Dumb blonde Irma's con man boyfriend lends her apartment to two soda jerks.
Comic strip humour responsible for the screen début of Martin and Lewis. Sequel 1950: My Friend Irma Goes West.
w Cy Howard, Parke Levy *radio show* Cy Howard *d* George Marshall *ph* Leo Tover *m* Roy Webb
☆ *Marie Wilson*, John Lund, Diana Lynn, *Dean Martin, Jerry Lewis*, Don Defore, Hans Conried, Kathryn Givney

My Friend Irma Goes West
US 1950 90m bw
Paramount/Hal Wallis
Irma's friends Steve and Seymour are offered a Hollywood contract and have adventures on the train.
Witless farce of mild historical interest.
w Cy Howard, Parke Levy *d* Hal Walker *ph* Lee Garmes *m* Leigh Harline
☆ John Lund, Marie Wilson, Dean Martin, Jerry Lewis, Diana Lynn, Corinne Calvet, Lloyd Corrigan

'The general mental level can be judged from the fact that the performance of the chimpanzee seems the most natural thing in the film.' – *MFB*

My Friend Ivan Lapshin **
USSR 1986 99m bw/colour
Metro/Lenfilm
Memories of life in a provincial Russian town in the 1930s, where a harassed policeman pursues a criminal gang.
Made in 1982, but not shown for four years, this is a well-observed, well-directed and acted slice-of-Soviet-life.
w Eduard Volodarski *d* Alexei Gherman *ph* Valeri Fedosov *m* Arkadi Gagulachvili *ad* Yuri Pougatch *ed* L. Semionovi
☆ Andrei Boltnev, Nina Rousianova, Andrei Mironov, Alexei Zharkov, Z. Adamovich, A. Filippenko

'It takes a girl like Rita to play a gal like Sal!'
My Gal Sal *
US 1942 103m Technicolor
TCF (Robert Bassler)
The career and romances of songwriter Paul Dresser.
Conventional 1890s musical biopic, more vigorous and likeable than most.
w Seton I. Miller, Darrell Ware, Karl Tunberg *book* *My Brother Paul* by Theodore Dreiser *d* Irving Cummings *ph* Ernest Palmer *md* Alfred Newman *ad* Richard Day, Joseph Wright
☆ *Rita Hayworth, Victor Mature*, John Sutton, Carole Landis, James Gleason, Phil Silvers, Walter Catlett, Mona Maris, Frank Orth
† The title role was intended for Alice Faye, but she was pregnant. Irene Dunne was too busy, Mae West refused, and Betty Grable didn't test well.
†† Rita Hayworth's singing was dubbed by Nan Wynn.
Richard Day, Joseph Wright
Alfred Newman

My Geisha
US 1962 120m Technirama
Paramount/Steve Parker

A director makes a film in Japan; his wife disguises herself as a geisha and gets the leading role.
Silly, overstretched comedy with pretty locations.
w Norman Krasna *d* Jack Cardiff *ph* Shunichuro Nakao *m* Franz Waxman
☆ Shirley Maclaine, Yves Montand, Robert Cummings, Edward G. Robinson, Yoko Tani

My Giant
US 1998 103m Technicolor
Columbia/Castle Rock/Face (Billy Crystal)

An unsuccessful agent discovers a giant-sized Romanian and takes him to America to make him into a movie star.
Strangely unappealing drama that veers between mawkishness and acerbity and seems uncertain about the point of its odd central relationship.
w David Seltzer, Billy Crystal *d* Michael Lehman *ph* Michael Coulter *m* Marc Shaiman *pd* Jackson DeGovia *ed* Stephen Semel
☆ Billy Crystal, Kathleen Quinlan, Gheorghe Muresan, Joanna Pacula, Zane Carney, Rider Strong, Steven Seagal (as himself), Harold Gould, Doris Roberts, Philip Sterling, Heather Thomas

'An uneven film with limited commercial appeal.' – *Variety*

'Mac's back and he's not alone...'
My Girl
US 1991 102m Technicolor
Columbia TriStar/Imagine (Brian Grazer)

In the 1970s, the 11-year-old daughter of an undertaker comes to terms with her widowed father's romance and the death of a friend.
Slick, over-sentimental account of growing up, part of Hollywood's early 90s cycle of films centred on children. It provided the first screen kiss for Culkin.
w Laurice Elehwany *d* Howard Zieff *ph* Paul Elliott *m* James Newton Howard *pd* Joseph T. Garrity *ed* Wendy Greene Bricmont
☆ Dan Aykroyd, Jamie Lee Curtis, Macaulay Culkin, Anna Chlumsky, Richard Masur, Griffin Dunne, Ann Nelson

'As pleasant as a warm summer day and as ephemeral.' – *Variety*

'A hilarious mix of schmaltz, angst and shlock. In other words a joy to watch. One asks hopefully, it can't get worse, surely, can it? But it does.' – *Alexander Walker, London Evening Standard*

My Girl II
US 1994 99m colour
Columbia TriStar/Imagine (Brian Grazer)

In the mid-70s, a young teenage girl travels to Los Angeles to find out more about her mother, who died giving birth to her.
Enjoyable enough sentimental domestic drama, although its appeal is likely to be limited to those of the same gender and age group as its heroine.
w Janet Kovalcik *d* Howard Zieff *ph* Paul Elliott *m* Cliff Eidelman *pd* Charles Rosen *ed* Wendy Greene Bricmont
☆ Dan Aykroyd, Jamie Lee Curtis, Anna Chlumsky, Richard Masur, Austin O'Brien, Christine Ebersole, Aubrey Morris, Gerrit Graham, Keone Young

'Pleasant, painless and, as sequels go, genuinely ambitious in its efforts to be a continuation rather than just a retread.' – *Joe Leydon, Variety*

My Girl Tisa ***
US 1948 95m bw
United States Pictures (Milton Sperling)
An immigrant girl in New York in the 1890s falls for an aspiring politician, is threatened with deportation but saved by the intervention of Theodore Roosevelt.
Charming period fairy tale with excellent background detail and attractive performances.
w Allen Boretz *play* Lucille S. Prumbs, Sara B. Smith *d* *Elliott Nugent* *ph* Ernest Haller *m* Max Steiner
☆ *Lilli Palmer, Sam Wanamaker, Alan Hale, Stella Adler*, Akim Tamiroff

My Girlfriend's Boyfriend *
France 1987 102m colour
Artificial Eye/AAA/Les Films Du Losange (Margaret Menegoz)

original title: *L'Ami de Mon Amie*
Two young couples find themselves attracted to each other's partner.
Charming conversation piece, the sixth in Rohmer's series of Comedies and Proverbs.
wd Eric Rohmer *ph* Bernard Lutic, Sabine Lanceline *m* Jean-Louis Valero *ed* Luisa Garcia
☆ Emmanuelle Chaulet, Sophie Renoir, Anne-Laure Meury, Eric Vieillard, François-Eric Gendron

'Fluff of a rarefied order. The movie is so rigorous and elegant and extreme that it seems, finally, to be about its own weightlessness – not so much a thin romantic comedy as a comic meditation on the thinness of romance.' – *Terrence Rafferty, New Yorker*

My Gun Is Quick
US 1957 90m bw
United Artists/Victor Saville
Mike Hammer investigates the murder of a bar girl and is led to rival gangs of jewel thieves.
Impenetrably plotted but quite violent brew of typical Spillane ingredients.
w Richard Collins, Richard Powell *novel* Mickey Spillane *d* George A. White, Phil Victor *ph* Harry Neumann *m* Marlin Skiles
☆ Robert Bray, Whitney Blake, Pat Donahue, Pamela Duncan, Booth Colman

My Heart Goes Crazy: see *London Town*

My Heart Is Calling
GB 1935 91m bw
Cine-Allianz (Ivor Montagu, Arnold Pressburger)
An opera singer falls for a stowaway to Monte Carlo.
Musical trifle with little to be said for or against it.
w Sidney Gilliat *story* Ernst Marischka *d* Carmine Gallone *ph* Glen MacWilliams *m* Robert Stolz
☆ Jan Kiepura, Marta Eggerth, Sonnie Hale, Hugh Wakefield, Ernest Thesiger, Marie Lohr

My Hero: see *A Southern Yankee*

My Heroes Have Always Been Cowboys
US 1991 106m DeLuxe
Samuel Goldwyn (Martin Poll, E. K. Gaylord II)

A rodeo rider, returning home to look after his ageing father, resumes his relationship with an old girlfriend and decides to try for the big time once more.
Moderate but unoriginal drama of domestic wranglings, with some spectacular bull-riding footage at the climax.
w Joel Don Humphreys *d* Stuart Rosenberg *ph* Bernd Heinl *m* James Horner *ed* Dennis M. Hill
☆ Scott Glenn, Kate Capshaw, Ben Johnson, Tess Harper, Balthazar Getty, Gary Busey, Mickey Rooney, Clarence Williams III, Dub Taylor, Clu Gulager

'Pic casts its lot with the underdog in true American fashion, but is bland and unexciting.' – *Variety*

My Hustler *
US 1965 70m bw
Vaughan/Factory Films (Andy Warhol)
Two men and two women compete for the sexual attentions of a blond hustler.
An apparently unedited two reels of film that, for all its apparent casualness and spontaneity, maintains its interest.
w Chuck Wein *d* Andy Warhol *ph* Andy Warhol
☆ Paul America, Ed Hood, Joseph Campbell, John McDermott, Genevieve Charbon, Dorothy Dean

'A complex and unified whole, in which the form and the content relate in new and surprising ways. The film is the clearest guide we have to the innovations which are uniquely Warhol's.' – *Tony Rayns, MFB*

'The downer, and it is a major one, is that these shallow, one-dimensional people are worth examining at all. They, and their situation, like their existence, are not really worth a second look, let alone seventy minutes of film.' – *Peter Buckley, Films and Filming*

My Kingdom
GB 2001 116m DeLuxe
Metro Tartan/Sky/Close Grip/Primary (Neal Weisman, Gabriela Bacher)

An ageing gangster lives to regret handing over his organisation to his daughters.
A trite thriller based on King Lear, and as sadistic without being in the least tragic.
w Nick Davies, Don Boyd *inspired by* *King Lear* by William Shakespeare *d* Don Boyd *ph* Dewald Aukema *m* Deirdre Gribbin, Simon Fisher Turner *pd* Luana Hanson *ed* Adam Ross
☆ Richard Harris (Sandeman), Lynn Redgrave (Mandy), Tom Bell (Quick), Emma Catherwood (Jo), Aidan Gillen (Barry Puttnam), Louise Lombard (Kath), Paul McGann (Dean), Jimi Mistry (Jug)

'Bleakly satisfying drama.' – *Film Review*

My Kingdom for a Cook
US 1943 81m bw
P. J. Wolfson/Columbia
An English author on a US lecture tour steals his hostess's cook.
Curious comedy with the star seeming to play an unsympathetic Alexander Woollcott type.
w Harold Goldman, Andrew Solt, Joseph Hoffman, Jack Henley *d* Richard Wallace
☆ Charles Coburn, Marguerite Chapman, Bill Carter, Isobel Elsom, Ed Gargan

My Learned Friend ***
GB 1943 76m bw
Ealing (Michael Balcon)
A shady lawyer is last on a mad ex-convict's murder list of those who helped get him convicted.
Madcap black farce, plot-packed and generally hilarious; the star's last vehicle, but one of his best, with superbly timed sequences during a pantomime and on the face of Big Ben.
w *John Dighton, Angus MacPhail* *d* *Basil Dearden, Will Hay* *ph* Wilkie Cooper *m* Ernest Irving *ad* Michael Relph
☆ *Will Hay, Claude Hulbert, Mervyn Johns*, Ernest Thesiger, Charles Victor, Lloyd Pearson, Maudie Edwards, G. H. Mulcaster, Gibb McLaughlin

My Left Foot **
GB 1989 103m Technicolor
Palace/Fernadale Films/Granada TV International/Radio Telefis Eireann (Noel Pearson)

Biopic of the Irish writer and painter Christy Brown, crippled from birth by cerebral palsy.
Pedestrian narrative, relying on cinematic clichés, but enlivened by the intensity of Day-Lewis's performance and some good ensemble acting.
w Shane Connaughton, Jim Sheridan *book* Christy Brown *d* Jim Sheridan *ph* Jack Conroy *m* Elmer Bernstein *pd* Austen Spriggs *ed* J. Patrick Duffner
☆ *Daniel Day-Lewis, Ray McAnally*, Brenda Fricker, Ruth McCabe, Fiona Shaw, Eanna MacLiam, Alison Whelan, Declan Croghan, Hugh O'Conor, Cyril Cusack
Daniel Day-Lewis; Brenda Fricker
best picture; best director; best adapted screenplay
Daniel Day-Lewis; Ray McAnally (as supporting actor)

My Life
US 1993 116m Technicolor
Guild/Zucker Brothers (Jerry Zucker, Bruce Joel Rubin, Hunt Lowry)
A man dying of cancer decides to make a videotape explaining himself to his unborn son.
A film that is interesting as a social document, in articulating American attitudes to life and its championing of childish attitudes, but which is much less successful as a movie, content to evoke easy tears.
wd Bruce Joel Rubin *ph* Peter James *m* John Barry *pd* Neil Spisak *ed* Richard Chew
☆ Michael Keaton, Nicole Kidman, Bradley Whitford, Queen Latifah, Michael Constantine, Rebecca Schull, Mark Lowenthal, Haing S. Ngor
'The sincere, often touching story tugs shamelessly at the heart strings.' – *Variety*
'This bravely sentimental Hollywood film misses the mark.' – *Derek Malcolm, Guardian*
'The sort of New Age film that believes in everything and nothing at the same time, and turns every emotion into a therapy-wallow.' – *Adam Mars-Jones, Independent*

My Life and Times with Antonin Artaud *
France 1993 90m bw
Metro Tartan/Archipel 33/Laura/La Sept/France 2 (Denis Freyd)
original title: *En compagnie d'Antonin Artaud*
In 1946, an unsuccessful poet becomes a friend of Artaud, the writer and actor, on his release from the asylum where he has been held for nine years.
An understated biopic of the last two years of Artaud's life, as witnessed by a young admirer; despite its portrait of a driven, self-obsessed man only slightly sane, it has both charm and wit.
w Gérard Mordillat, Jérôme Prieur *book* Jacques Prevel *d* Gérard Mordillat *ph* François Catonné *m* Jean-Claude Petit *ad* Jean-Pierre Clech *ed* Sophie Rouffio
☆ Sami Frey, Marc Barbé, Julie Jézéquel, Valérie Jeannet, Clotilde de Bayser, Charlotte Valandrey
'Compulsively told, its (sometimes heavyweight) intellectualizing never fails to engage both the mind and the eye.' – *Nigel Robinson, Film Review*

My Life as a Dog **
Sweden 1985 101m Fujicolour
Svensk Filmindustri/Film-Teknik
original title: *Mitt Liv Som Hund*
12-year-old Ingemar learns to cope with his mother's illness and death, and his own propensity for getting into trouble, while staying with his aunt and uncle in the country.
By turns painful and funny, the film manages to achieve genuine charm while steering clear of sentimentality.
w Lasse Hallström, Reidar Jonsson, Brasse Brännström, Per Berglund *novel* Reidar Jonsson *d* Lasse Hallström *ph* Jörgen Persson, Rolf Lindström *m* Björn Isfält
☆ Anton Glanzelius, Manfred Serner, Anki Lidén, Tomas von Bromssen, Melinda Kinnaman, Ing-Marie Carlsson
best director; best adapted screenplay

My Life with Caroline *
US 1941 81m bw
RKO (Lewis Milestone)
An understanding husband thinks his high-spirited wife may be having an affair.
Very minor romantic comedy with an agreeable air but no substance whatever.
w John Van Druten, Arnold Belgard *d* Lewis Milestone *ph* Victor Milner *m* Werner Heymann
☆ Ronald Colman, Anna Lee, Reginald Gardiner, Charles Winninger, Gilbert Roland

My Little Chickadee *
US 1939 83m bw
Universal (Lester Cowan)
A shady lady and an incompetent cardsharp unmask a villain in the old West.
A clash of comedy personalities which is affectionately remembered but in truth does not play very well apart from the odd line.
w Mae West, W. C. Fields *d* Edward F. Cline *ph* Joseph Valentine *m* Frank Skinner *md* Charles Previn
☆ *Mae West, W. C. Fields*, Joseph Calleia, Dick Foran, Margaret Hamilton
'It obstinately refuses to gather momentum.' – *The Times*
'A classic among bad movies ... the satire never really gets off the ground. But the ground is such an honest mixture of dirt, manure and corn that at times it is fairly aromatic.' – *Pauline Kael, 1968*

'Fear Is Not Knowing. Terror Is Finding Out.'
My Little Eye *
GB/France/US 2002 95m Technicolor
Momentum/Universal/StudioCanal/Working Title/WT (Jonathan Finn, Jane Villiers, David Hilton, Alan Greenspan)
Five contestants, who join a TV project to stay in a remote and isolated house for six months, begin to panic when one of them is murdered.
Deft thriller that makes confident use of the tricks of reality television and webcasts, though in the end it's just another slasher movie.
w David Hilton, James Watkins *d* Marc Evans *ph* Hubert Taczanowski *m* Bias *pd* Crispian Sallis *ed* Marguerite Arnold
☆ Sean CW Johnson (Matt), Kris Lemche (Rex), Stephen O'Reilly (Danny), Laura Regan (Emma), Jennifer Sky (Charlie), Bradley Cooper (Travis Patterson), Nick Mennell (Cop)
'Effective enough, though it doesn't bear thinking about too much' – *Philip French, Observer*

My Little Girl *
US 1986 117m colour
Hemdale (Ismail Merchant)
A privileged teenager encounters problems when she goes to work at a centre for children in care.
Well-acted, moderately engaging drama of innocence and experience.
w Connie Kaiserman, Nan Mason *d* Connie Kaiserman *ph* Pierre Lhomme *m* Richard Robbins *pd* Dan Leigh *ed* Katherine Wenning
☆ James Earl Jones, Geraldine Page, Mary Stuart Masterson, Anne Meara, Pamela Payton Wright, Peter Michael Goetz, Peter Gallagher, Erika Alexander, Traci Lin

My Little Pony
US 1986 100m Technicolor
Sunbow/Hasbro
The inhabitants of Ponyland fear the wicked witch Hydia.
Immensely distended cartoon meant to plug a fashionable line of children's dolls.
w George Arthur Bloom *d* Michael Jones
† Animated in Japan.

'A Modern Girl Having A Modern Good Time.'
My Lucky Star *
US 1938 84m bw
TCF (Harry Joe Brown)
A shopgirl is innocently caught in a compromising situation with the owner's son.
Fluffy comedy, acceptable as a background for skating sequences.
w Harry Tugend, Jack Yellen *story* Karl Tunberg, Don Ettlinger *d* Roy del Ruth *ph* John Mescall *md* Louis Silvers *songs* Mack Gordon, Harry Revel
☆ *Sonja Henie*, Richard Greene, Joan Davis, Buddy Ebsen, Cesar Romero, Arthur Treacher, George Barbier, Louise Hovick, Billy Gilbert

My Man Godfrey ***
US 1936 90m bw
Universal (Gregory La Cava)
A zany millionaire family invite a tramp to be their butler and find he is richer than they are.
Archetypal Depression concept which is also one of the best of the thirties crazy sophisticated comedies, though its pacing today seems somewhat unsure.
w Morrie Ryskind, Eric Hatch, Gregory La Cava *d Gregory La Cava* *ph* Ted Tetzlaff *m* Charles Previn *ad* Charles D. Hall *ed* Ted J. Kent
☆ *Carole Lombard, William Powell, Alice Brady, Mischa Auer*, Eugene Pallette, Gail Patrick, Alan Mowbray, Jean Dixon
script; Gregory La Cava (as director); Carole Lombard; William Powell; Alice Brady; Mischa Auer

'The butler did it! He made every lady in the house oh so very happy!'
My Man Godfrey
US 1957 92m Technicolor Cinemascope
U-I (Ross Hunter)
The daughter of a rich and eccentric family hires an illegal immigrant as her butler.
Tepid remake which without the period background, and in unsuitable wide screen, raises very few laughs.
w Everett Freeman, Peter Berneis, William Bowers *d* Henry Koster *ph* William Daniels *m* Frank Skinner *ad* Alexander Golitzen, Richard H. Riedel *ed* Milton Carruth
☆ June Allyson, David Niven, Jessie Royce Landis, Jay Robinson, Robert Keith, Martha Hyer, Eva Gabor

My Mother's Castle: see *Le Château de ma Mère*

My Mother's Courage *
Germany/Austria/GB 1995 90m colour
Clarence/Sentana/Little Bird/Vega (Michael Verhoeven)
An author, celebrating his 80th birthday, explains that we are to see a film based on his novel about his mother's escape from a Nazi train taking her from Budapest to Auschwitz.
A small-scale sidelight on the horror of the concentration camps, effective and moving in its focus on a fortunate individual.
wd Michael Verhoeven *novel* George Tabori *ph* Michael Epp, Theo Bierkens *m* Julian Nott, Simon Verhoeven *ed* David Freeman
☆ Pauline Collins, Ulrich Tukur, Heirbert Sasse, Natalie Morse, Robert Giggenbach, Günther Bothur, Simon Verhoeven, George Tabori (as himself)
'Achieves its aims with something of a twinkle in its eye. For that, it's rather remarkable, in its understated way.' – *Nick Kimberley, Sight and Sound*

My Name Is Joe ***
GB/Germany 1998 105m colour
Parallax/Road Movies (Rebecca O'Brien)
In Glasgow, a reformed alcoholic ruins his developing relationship with a nurse when he agrees to carry drugs for a local gangster in order to help a friend stay out of trouble.
Grim, compassionate account of deprivation, and the desperation of poverty, in which only the energy of Mullan's performance offers any optimism for the future.
w Paul Laverty *d* Ken Loach *ph* Barry Ackroyd *m* George Fenton *pd* Martin Johnson *ed* Jonathan Morris
☆ Peter Mullan, Louise Goodall, David McKay, Annemarie Kennedy, David Hayman, Gary Lewis, Lorraine McIntosh
'Ken Loach works very near the top of his form, his angrily unblinkered vision of life at the rough end of modern Britain tempered with humanity, humour and a storyline that could almost come from a classic screwball romantic comedy.' – *Kim Newman, Empire*
† Peter Mullan won the best actor award at the Cannes Film Festival of 1998.
†† The film was subtitled for American audiences.

My Name Is Julia Ross **
US 1945 65m bw
Columbia
A girl is kidnapped and forced to impersonate an heiress.
A very good second feature which has been culted into a reputation beyond its worth, though it is undeniably slick and entertaining.
w Muriel Roy Bolton *novel The Woman in Red* by Anthony Gilbert *d Joseph H. Lewis* *ph* Burnett Guffey *md* Mischa Bakaleinikoff
☆ Nina Foch, Dame May Whitty, George Macready, Roland Varno, Doris Lloyd
'A superior, well-knit thriller.' – *Don Miller*
'A likeable, unpretentious, generally successful attempt to turn good trash into decently artful entertainment.' – *James Agee*

My Name Is Nobody *
Italy/France/West Germany 1973 116m Technicolor Panavision
Gala/Rafran/Jacques Leitienne/Alcinter/Société Imp. Ex. Ci./Rialto (Claudio Mancini)
original title: *Il mio nome è Nessuno*
A young admirer persuades an ageing gunfighter to end his career in an explosive fashion.
This is less a conventional Western and more a comic horse opera, complete with a tombstone bearing the name of Sam Peckinpah and with Wagner's Ride of the Valkyrie*, scored country and western style, accompanying the 150-strong Wild Bunch as they thunder by. Along the way it makes the occasional interesting comment about the reality and the mythology of the West.*
w Ernesto Gastaldi *story* Fulvio Morsella, Ernesto Gastaldi, from an idea by Sergio Leone *d* Tonino Valerii *ph* Giuseppe Ruzzolini, Armando Nannuzzi *m* Ennio Morricone *ad* Gianni Polidori *ed* Nino Baragli
☆ Henry Fonda, Terence Hill (Mario Girotti), Jean Martin, Piero Lulli, Leo Gordon, Neil Summers, R. G. Armstrong, Steve Kanaly, Geoffrey Lewis
'Constitutes an explicit, thoroughgoing critique of Sam Peckinpah's work up to 1970, and if its own whimsical/elegiac tone is closer to the romantic comedy of Cable Hogue than to the romantic tragedies of *Major Dundee* and *The Wild Bunch*, then that signifies the warmth of its engagement with its subject rather than any reluctance to face up to Peckinpah's capacity for nihilism.' – *Tony Rayns, MFB*

My New Gun
US 1992 99m Foto-Kem
Feature/IRS (Michael Flynn)
A housewife finds that her life becomes full of danger after her husband buys her a gun and she lends it to her neighbour.
A one-joke suburban sitcom that misses most of its targets.
wd Stacy Cochran *ph* Ed Lachman *m* Pat Irwin *pd* Tony Corbett *ed* Camilla Toniolo
☆ James LeGros, Diane Lane, Stephen Collins, Tess Harper, Bruce Altman, Maddie Corman, Phillip Seymour, Bill Raymond
'Feeble farrago ... flimsily inept.' – *Tom Hutchinson, Film Review*
'In a word? Dull.' – *Independent*

My Night with Maud: see *Ma Nuit chez Maud*

My Old Man's a Fireman: see *The Chief*

My Outlaw Brother
US 1951 78m bw
Eagle Lion
A young man is shocked to find that his elder brother is a notorious bandit.
Glum little semi-Western, unpersuasively cast.
w Gene Fowler Jnr *d* Elliott Nugent
☆ Mickey Rooney, Robert Preston, Robert Stack, Wanda Hendrix

'Wherever, Whatever, Have a nice day.'
My Own Private Idaho *
US 1991 102m Alpha Cine
New Line (Laurie Parker)
A narcoleptic male prostitute makes friends with a slumming rich youth.
A variation on Shakespeare's Henry IV*, complete with a seductive but dangerous Falstaffian figure, which becomes a distracting device, lessening the film's impact.*
wd Gus Van Sant *ph* Eric Alan Edwards, John Campbell *pd* David Brisbin *ed* Curtiss Clayton
☆ River Phoenix, Keanu Reeves, James Russo, William Richert, Rodney Harvey, Michael Parker, Udo Kier
'One of those ambitious, over-reaching disappointments that is more interesting than some conservative successes.' – *Variety*
'It's a beautiful disaster, like a bomb test in the middle of nowhere.' – *New Yorker*

My Pal Gus
US 1952 84m bw
TCF (Stanley Rubin)
A business man has a five-year-old problem son and in sorting him out falls in love with his schoolteacher.
Unrewarding domestic drama with actors who look as though they would rather be somewhere else.
w Fay and Michael Kanin *d* Robert Parrish *ph* Leo Tover *m* Leigh Harline
☆ Richard Widmark, Joanne Dru, Audrey Totter, George Winslow, Joan Banks, Regis Toomey, Ludwig Donath

My Pal Trigger
US 1946 79m bw
Armand Schaefer/Republic
A cowboy tracks down the man who killed his horse's sire.
Folksy Western drama, a cut above the usual Rogers episode.
w Jack Townley, John K. Butler *d* Frank McDonald
☆ Roy Rogers, Dale Evans, Jack Holt, George 'Gabby' Hayes, Roy Barcroft

My Reputation
US 1946 96m bw
Warner (Henry Blanke)
A widow is talked about for dispensing too soon with her weeds.
Dim drama, hastily shot on familiar sets with a reach-me-down script.
w Catherine Turney *novel* *Instruct My Sorrows* by Clare Jaynes *d* Curtis Bernhardt *ph* James Wong Howe *m* Max Steiner
☆ Barbara Stanwyck, George Brent, Warner Anderson, Lucile Watson, John Ridgely, Eve Arden, Jerome Cowan, Esther Dale, Scotty Beckett

My Science Project
US 1985 91m Technicolor Panavision
Touchstone/Silver Screen Partners
A high school student investigates an old UFO and finds an energy-absorbing machine which can materialize objects from the past and future.
Disney-style fare with teenage sex: the mixture may not be for many.
wd Jonathan R. Betuel *ph* David M. Walsh *m* Peter Bernstein
☆ John Stockwell, Danielle von Zerneck, Fisher Stevens, Raphael Sbarge, Richard Masur, Dennis Hopper

My Sister Eileen *
US 1942 96m bw
Columbia (Max Gordon)
Two Ohio girls come to New York and live with some zany friends in a Greenwich Village basement apartment.
Rather strained high jinks which were, not surprisingly, later musicalized.
w Ruth McKinney, Joseph Fields, Jerome Chodorov *book* Ruth McKinney *d* Alexander Hall *ph* Joseph Walker *md* Morris Stoloff
☆ Rosalind Russell, Janet Blair, Brian Aherne, Allyn Joslyn, George Tobias, Elizabeth Patterson, June Havoc
Rosalind Russell

'Gayest Show Ever To Go Singing Across The CinemaScope Screen!'
My Sister Eileen *
US 1955 108m Technicolor Cinemascope
Columbia (Fred Kohlmar)
Two Ohio girls move to an eccentric rooming house in Greenwich Village.
A musical version of a collection of stories that became a book, a film and a play: watchable but hardly stimulating.
w Blake Edwards, Richard Quine *play* Joseph Fields, Jerome Chodorov *d* Richard Quine *ph* Charles Lawton Jnr *m* George Duning *md* Morris Stoloff *ch* Bob Fosse *songs* Jule Styne, Leo Robin
☆ *Betty Garrett*, Janet Leigh, Jack Lemmon, Bob Fosse, Kurt Kasznar, Horace MacMahon, Dick York
'Even those well-acquainted with all of the material will find a freshness here that assures acceptance.' – *Variety*
† The play was also the basis of a later Broadway musical, *Wonderful Town*.

My Six Convicts *
US 1952 104m bw
Columbia/Stanley Kramer
A psychologist joins the staff of an American prison and gains the trust of six inmates.
Moderately interesting semi-documentary melodrama marred by a conventional prison break climax.
w Michael Blankfort *book* Donald Powell Wilson *d* Hugo Fregonese *ph* Guy Roe *m* Dmitri Tiomkin
☆ John Beal, *Millard Mitchell*, *Gilbert Roland*, Marshall Thompson, Regis Toomey

My Six Loves
US 1963 101m Technicolor
Paramount/Gant Gaither
A musical comedy star goes to the country for a rest and with the help of the local minister adopts six scruffy children.
Icky sentimental comedy for the easily pleased.
w John Fante, Joseph Calvelli, William Wood *d* Gower Champion *ph* Arthur E. Arling *m* Walter Scharf *songs* Jimmy Van Heusen, Sammy Cahn
☆ Debbie Reynolds, David Janssen, Cliff Robertson, Eileen Heckart
'Enough to make you settle for cyclamates – or cyanide.' – *Judith Crist, 1973*

My Son Alone: see *American Empire*

My Son John
US 1952 122m bw
Paramount/Rainbow (Leo McCarey)
An American Catholic family is horrified when its eldest son is revealed as a communist.
The lower depths of Hollywood's witch hunt cycle are marked by this Goldwynesque family saga, all sweetness and light, in which the commie son is treated as though he had rabies. Purely as entertainment the plot is pretty choppy and defeats all attempts at acting.
w Myles Connolly, Leo McCarey *d* Leo McCarey *ph* Harry Stradling *m* Robert Emmett Dolan
☆ Helen Hayes, Robert Walker, Dean Jagger, Van Heflin, Minor Watson, Frank McHugh, Richard Jaeckel
Leo McCarey (original story)

'Their tangled loves wove a web of hate!'
My Son, My Son *
US 1940 117m bw
Edward Small
A man who becomes rich spoils his son and lives to regret it.
Solid narrative from a bestseller.
w Lenore Coffee *novel* Howard Spring *d* Charles Vidor *ph* Harry Stradling *m* Edward Ward *ad* John DuCasse Schulze
☆ Brian Aherne, Madeleine Carroll, Louis Hayward, Laraine Day, Henry Hull
art direction

My Son the Fanatic **
GB 1997 86m Metrocolor
BBC/UGC/Arts Council/Zephyr (Chris Curling)
A Pakistani taxi driver, who has embraced British ways, is horrified by his son's reversion to a fundamentalist religious outlook.
Engrossing domestic drama with a twist, as the young uphold traditional values; it makes some effective points about tolerance and bigotry and the clash between cultures and generations.
w Hanif Kureishi *story* Hanif Kureishi *d* Udayan Prasad *ph* Alan Almond *m* Stephen Warbeck *pd* Grenville Horner *ed* David Gamble
☆ Om Puri, Rachel Griffiths, Stellan Skarsgard, Akbar Kurtha, Gopi Desai, Harish Patel, Sarah Jane Potts
'An engagingly offbeat love story.' – *Variety*

My Son the Vampire: see *Mother Riley Meets the Vampire*

My Stepmother Is an Alien
US 1988 108m Film House colour
Columbia TriStar/Weintraub Entertainment (Ronald Parker, Franklin R. Levy)
A scientist marries a beautiful woman from another planet.
Feeble comedy with little point and no taste.
w Jerico, Herschel Weingrod, Timothy Harris, Jonathan Reynolds *d* Richard Benjamin *ph* Richard H. Kline *m* Alan Silvestri *pd* Charles Rosen *ed* Jacqueline Cambas, Brian Chambers
☆ Dan Aykroyd, Kim Basinger, Jon Lovitz, Alyson Hannigan, Joseph Maher, Seth Green, Ann Prentiss, Wesley Mann, Tony Jay, Peter Bromilow

My Sweet Little Village **
Czechoslovakia 1985 100m colour
Cannon/Barrandov Film Studio '85 (Jan Suster)
Life in a small village, where a mentally-retarded worker is forced to move to Prague.
Charming, good-hearted film of a small community where individuality flourishes.
w Zdenek Sverak *d* Jiri Menzel *ph* Jaromir Sofr *m* Jiri Sust *pd* Zbyner Hoch *ed* Jiri Brozeck
☆ Janos Ban, Marian Labuda, Rudolf Hrusinsky, Milena Dvorska, Ladislav Zupanic, Petr Cepek
best foreign film

My Teenage Daughter
GB 1956 100m bw
British Lion/Everest (Herbert Wilcox)
US title: *Teenage Bad Girl*
A widow's seventeen-year-old daughter meets an aggressive young man and ends up in court.
Predictable domestic drama, a tame British version of Rebel without a Cause.
w Felicity Douglas *d* Herbert Wilcox *ph* Max Greene
☆ Anna Neagle, Sylvia Syms, Kenneth Haigh, Norman Wooland, Wilfrid Hyde-White, Julia Lockwood, Helen Haye

'School's out...but Bobby's education has just begun!'
My Tutor
US 1982 97m DeLuxe
Crown
Two teenage boys try to lose their virginity.
As woeful as it sounds.
w Joe Roberts *d* George Bowers *ph* Mac Ahlberg *m* Webster Lewis
☆ Matt Lattanzi, Caren Kaye, Kevin McCarthy, Arlene Golonka, Crispin Slater

My Two Husbands: see *Too Many Husbands*

My Uncle Antoine
Canada 1971 110m Eastmancolor
National Film Board of Canada
In a Quebec village a young boy reluctantly helps his undertaker uncle to deliver a coffin.
French-speaking comedy drama with a sour edge, as thoughts of death mar a family Christmas.
w Clément Perron *d* Claude Jutra *ph* Michel Brault *m* Jean Cousineau
☆ Jacques Gagnon, Lyne Champagne, Jean Duceppe, Olivette Thibault

My Way Home **
GB 1979 72m bw
BFI (Judy Cottam, Richard Craven)
Leaving a children's home to become a miner and then a tramp, a young man's miserable life changes for the better when he is called up for National Service and goes to Egypt.
The poverty of the lives depicted is mirrored by the directorial style – austere, spare, non-committal – to create a Calvinist masterpiece illumined by a little hope.
wd Bill Douglas *ph* Ray Orton *ad* Oliver Bouchier, Elsie Restorick *ed* Mick Audsley
☆ Stephen Archibald, Paul Kermack, Jessie Combe, William Carrol, Morag McNee, Lennox Milne, Gerald James
† The third of a trilogy of autobiographical films that began with *My Childhood* and *My Ain Folk* (qqv).

My Wife's Best Friend
US 1952 87m bw
TCF
A wife learns of her husband's infidelity, and imagines how Cleopatra, Joan of Arc and other historical figures might handle the situation.
A sharp little comedy rather similar to Unfaithfully Yours.
w Isobel Lennart *d* Richard Sale
☆ Anne Baxter, Macdonald Carey, Cecil Kellaway, Casey Adams, Catherine McLeod

My Wife's Family
GB 1931 80m bw
BIP
A wife thinks her husband has an illegitimate child.
Archetypal British farce. This may be the best version; it was also made with Charlie Clapham in 1941 and with Ronald Shiner in 1956.
w Fred Duprez and Val Valentine *play* Fred Duprez, Hal Stephens and Harry B. Linton *d* Monty Banks
☆ Gene Gerrard, Muriel Angelus, Jimmy Godden, Amy Veness

My Wild Irish Rose
US 1947 101m Technicolor
Warner (William Jacobs)
The ups and downs of Irish tenor Chauncey Olcott and his encounters with Lillian Russell.
Inoffensive but not very exciting period musical, rather lacking in humour.
w Peter Milne *book* Rita Ilcott *d* David Butler *ph* Arthur Edeson *m* Ray Heindorf, Max Steiner *ch* Le Roy Prinz
☆ Dennis Morgan, Arlene Dahl, Andrea King, Alan Hale, George Tobias
Ray Heindorf, Max Steiner

My World Dies Screaming: see *Terror in the Haunted House*

'At last, the book that couldn't be written is now the motion picture that couldn't be made!'
Myra Breckinridge
US 1970 94m DeLuxe Panavision
TCF (Robert Fryer)
After a sex-change operation a film critic goes to Hollywood to accomplish the deflation of the American male.
A sharply satirical novel has been turned into a sleazy and aimless picture which became a watershed of permissiveness; after international outcry it was shunned even by its own studio. A few good laughs do emerge from the morass, but even the old clips are misused.
w Mike Sarne, David Giler *novel* Gore Vidal *d* Mike Sarne *ph* Richard Moore *m* John Philips *md* Lionel Newman
☆ *Mae West*, Raquel Welch, John Huston, Rex Reed, Jim Backus, John Carradine, Andy Devine
'Whatever the novel may be like, it surely cannot be this sort of witless, lip-smacking, continuously inept cop-out.' – *John Simon*
'About as funny as a child molester.' – *Time*
'A disjointed patchwork of leers, vulgarity and general ineptness.' – *Cue*
'An incompetent attempt at exploitation by an industry that knew once, at the very least, how to make a dishonest buck.' – *Newsweek*
'I don't want subtlety. I want vulgarity.' – *Michael Sarne*

The Mysterious Dr Fu Manchu
US 1929 80m bw
Paramount
After the Boxer rebellion an evil Chinese seeks the death of British officers.
First but not the worst of the yellow peril's sinister adventures; to be taken for what it is, however.
w Florence Ryerson, Lloyd Corrigan *d* Rowland V. Lee
☆ Warner Oland, Jean Arthur, Neil Hamilton, O. P. Heggie, William Austin

Mysterious Intruder
US 1946 62m bw
Columbia
A private detective seeks a missing heiress.
Intriguing minor thriller, part of the Whistler *series.*
w Eric Taylor *d* William Castle
☆ Richard Dix, Barton MacLane, Nina Vale, Regis Toomey

Mysterious Invader: see *The Astounding She-Monster*

Mysterious Island *
GB 1961 101m Technicolor
Columbia/Ameran (Charles Schneer)
Union officers escape by balloon and join shipwrecked English ladies on a strange island where they are menaced by prehistoric monsters and helped by Captain Nemo.

Rambling, lively juvenile adventure with good moments and excellent monsters.
w John Prebble, Dan Ullman, Crane Wilbur *novel* Jules Verne *d* Cy Endfield *ph* Wilkie Cooper *m* Bernard Herrmann *sp* Ray Harryhausen
☆ Joan Greenwood, Michael Craig, Herbert Lom, Michael Callan, Gary Merrill
† An early sound version was made by MGM in 1929, directed by Lucien Hubbard. Despite Technicolor and a cast which included Lionel Barrymore it was judged unsatisfactory, and concentrated less on stop-frame monsters than on the submarine elements ignored in the above but remade in *Captain Nemo and the Underwater City* (qv).

The Mysterious Lady
US 1928 84m (24 fps) bw silent
MGM
A glamorous Russian spy has to save her lover from execution as a traitor.
Threadbare star melodrama.
w Bess Meredyth *d* Fred Niblo *ph* William Daniels
☆ Greta Garbo, Conrad Nagel, Gustav von Seyffertitz

Mysterious Mr Moto
US 1938 62m bw
TCF
Mr Moto goes to London to expose the leader of The League of Assassins, Continental criminals who work as contract killers.
One of the lesser episodes in the series; the problem is what one character calls 'local character': London has rarely looked so unconvincing.
w Philip MacDonald, Norman Foster *d* Norman Foster *ph* Virgil Miller *md* Samuel Kaylin *ad* Bernard Herzbrun, Lewis Creber *ed* Norman Colbert
☆ Peter Lorre, Mary Maguire, Henry Wilcoxon, Erik Rhodes, Harold Huber, Leon Ames, Forrester Harvey, Karen Sorrell

Mysterious Mr Wong
US 1935 60m bw
Monogram
A mandarin in New York's Chinatown will stop at nothing to collect the twelve coins of Confucius.
Tolerable programme filler with old-fashioned thrills.
w Nina Howatt *story* Stephen Keeler *d* William Nigh
☆ Bela Lugosi, Wallace Ford, Arline Judge, Fred Warren
'Passably exciting.' – *Variety*

Mystery, Alaska
US 1999 118m Technicolor Panavision
Buena Vista/Hollywood/Baldwin/Cohen–Rocking Chair (David E. Kelley, Howard Baldwin)
Life in an ice-hockey crazy, small Alasakan town is turned upside down when a match is arranged between its amateur players and New York professionals.
Genial but unremarkable tale of a small town entirely inhabited by stereotypical characters; the narrative strays into too many dull subplots to maintain any momentum.
w David E. Kelley, Sean O'Byrne *d* Jay Roach *ph* Peter Deming *m* Carter Burwell *pd* Rusty Smith *ed* Jon Poll *cos* Deena Appel
☆ Russell Crowe (John Biebe), Hank Azaria (Charles Danner), Mary McCormack (Donna Biebe), Burt Reynolds (Judge Walter Burns), Lolita Davidovich (Mary Jane Pitcher), Ron Eldard ('Skank' Marden), Colm Meaney (Mayor Scott Pitcher), Maury Chaykin (Bailey Pruitt), Michael McKean, Judith Ivey (Joanne Burns), Rachel Wilson (Marla Burns), Michael Buie (Connor Banks), Ryan Northcott (Stevie Weeks), Scott Grimes ('Birdie' Burns), Mike Myers (Donnie Shulzhoffer) and also Little Richard
'Curiously mild and underwhelming.' – *Variety*

Mystery Date
US 1991 99m DeLuxe
Orion (Cathleen Summers)
Out on a date with a new girlfriend, a shy youth is mistaken for a thief and a killer.
Dim, blackish 'teen comedy that tries hard to amuse and fails miserably.
w Parker Bennett, Terry Runté *d* Jonathan Wacks *ph* Oliver Wood *m* John DuPrez *pd* John Willett *ed* Tina Hirsch
☆ Ethan Hawke, Teri Polo, Brian McNamara, Fisher Stevens, Tony Rosato, Don Davis, James Hong, Victor Wong, B. D. Wong
'A reasonably entertaining pic but too lame to generate word-of-mouth.' – *Variety*

Mystery Liner
US 1934 62m bw
Monogram
Several murders take place at sea on a passenger liner.
Reputedly above-average whodunnit.
w Wellyn Totman *novel The Ghost of John Holling* by Edgar Wallace *d* William Nigh
☆ Noah Beery, Astrid Allwyn, Cornelius Keefe, Gustav von Seyffertitz, Edwin Maxwell
'Too good for the lesser grinds: exceptional indie entertainment.' – *Variety*

'They're Not Your Classic Superheroes... They're The Other Guys.'
Mystery Men *
US 1999 120m DeLuxe
Universal/Dark House (Lawrence Gordon, Mike Richardson, Lloyd Levin)
An odd group of incompetent would-be superheroes attempt to fight crime.
An often amusing send-up of superheroes, slickly made and with an excellent cast, though it would have been a much funnier film had it been half-an-hour shorter.
w Neil Cuthbert *comic book* Bob Burden *d* Kinka Usher *ph* Stephen H. Burum *m* Stephen Warbeck *pd* Kirk M. Petruccelli *ed* Conrad Buff
☆ Hank Azaria (Blue Raja), Janeane Garofalo (Bowler), William H. Macy (Shoveler), Kel Mitchell (Invisible Boy), Paul Reubens (Spleen), Ben Stiller (Mr Furious), Wes Studi (Sphinx), Greg Kinnear (Captain Amazing), Lena Olin (Dr Anabel Lee), Geoffrey Rush (Casanova Frankenstein), Tom Waits (Doc Heller), Eddie Izzard (Tony P), Claire Forlani (Monica), Ricky Jay (Vic Weems), Louise Lasser (Violet)
'A better action movie than the last *Batman* and funnier than most recent comedies.' – *Hot Dog*

The Mystery of Alexina
France 1985 90m colour
Electric Pictures/Les Cinéastes Associés/TF1
original title: *Mystère Alexina*
A convent-educated girl discovers that in reality she is masculine.
Although based on the diary of a 19th-century hermaphrodite, it fails to explore the subject in any depth, preferring a glossy romanticism instead.
w Jean Gruault, René Feret *d* René Feret *ph* Bernard Zitzermann *m* Anne-Marie Deschamps *ed* Ariane Boeglin
☆ Philippe Vuillemin, Valerie Stroh, Véronique Silver, Bernard Freyd, Marianne Basler, Pierre Vial

'A thing to bewitch your senses for days and days! Charming in the thrills! Gripping in the suspense!'
The Mystery of Edwin Drood *
US 1935 85m bw
Universal
In a cathedral town, a drug-addicted choirmaster is his nephew's rival for the hand of Rosa Bud.
Fairly creditable attempt to deal with a famous unfinished novel. Slightly stilted, but good visuals and performances.
w John L. Balderston, Gladys Unger, Bradley King, Leopold Atlas *novel* Charles Dickens *d Stuart Walker ph* George Robinson *m* Edward Ward
☆ Claude Rains, Douglass Montgomery, Heather Angel, David Manners, E. E. Clive, Valerie Hobson

The Mystery of Edwin Drood
GB 1993 112m Metrocolor
Mayfair/First Standard Media (Keith Hayley)
An opium-addicted choirmaster becomes obsessed with the fiancée of his nephew and plots to marry her.
A low-budget thriller that fails to match Dickens's lurid imaginings and makes a poor job of completing the novel satisfactorily.
wd Timothy Forder *novel* Charles Dickens *ph* Martin McGrath *m* Kick Production *pd* Edward Thomas *ed* Sue Alhadeff
☆ Robert Powell, Nanette Newman, Gemma Craven, Jonathan Phillips, Rupert Rainsford, Michelle Evans, Rosemary Leach, Finty Williams, Ronald Fraser, Glyn Houston, Andrew Sachs, Freddie Jones, Barry Evans
'The only mystery about this Edwin Drood is why anyone bothered to make it.' – *Philip Kemp, Sight and Sound*

The Mystery of Kaspar Hauser: see *The Enigma of Kaspar Hauser*

The Mystery of Mr X *
US 1934 84m bw
MGM (Lawrence Weingarten)
In foggy London, a jewel thief protects himself by finding the murderer of several policemen.
Passable mystery, later remade as The Hour of Thirteen.
w Howard Emmett Rogers, Philip MacDonald, Monckton Hoffe *novel X vs Rex* by Philip MacDonald *d* Edgar Selwyn *ph* Oliver T. Marsh
☆ Robert Montgomery, Elizabeth Allan, Lewis Stone, Ralph Forbes, Henry Stephenson, Forrester Harvey
'One of the best-made mystery mellers yet.' – *Variety*

The Mystery of the 13th Guest
US 1943 60m bw
Lindsley Parsons/Monogram
A girl beneficiary under her uncle's will is menaced when she goes to visit.
Ham-fisted remake of The Thirteenth Guest, *which was a mite too complex in the first place. This version makes no sense at all and is cheaply produced.*
w Charles Marion, Tim Ryan *play* Armitage Trail *d* William Beaudine
☆ Helen Parrish, Dick Purcell, Tim Ryan, Frank Faylen

The Mystery of the Mary Celeste
GB 1935 80m bw
Hammer
US title: *Phantom Ship*
A mad sailor kills his fellow crew members and jumps overboard.
Unpersuasive solution to an unsolved mystery in a production which sounds more interesting than it is.
wd Denison Clift
☆ Bela Lugosi, Shirley Grey, Arthur Margetson, Edmund Willard, Dennis Hoey
'Very strong stuff for those who like tragic entertainment.' – *Variety*

'Images of wax that throbbed with human passion. Almost woman! What did they lack?'
Mystery of the Wax Museum ***
US 1933 77m Technicolor
Warner (Henry Blanke)
A sculptor disfigured in a fire builds a wax museum by covering live victims in wax.
Archetypal horror material is augmented by a sub-plot about drug-running and an authoritative example of the wisecracking reporter school of the early thirties. The film is also notable for its highly satisfactory use of two-colour Technicolor and for its splendid art direction. Remade 1953 as House of Wax *(qv).*
w Don Mullally, Carl Erickson play Charles S. Belden *d Michael Curtiz ph Ray Rennahan ad Anton Grot*
☆ *Lionel Atwill,* Fay Wray, *Glenda Farrell, Frank* McHugh, Gavin Gordon, Allen Vincent, Edwin Maxwell
ATWILL: 'I offer you immortality, my child. Think of it: in a thousand years you shall be as lovely as you are now!'
'Would have been certain of better gate support a year ago. Recognizing this, the Technicolor and hyper-weirdness were apparently mandatory studio precautions to offset the element of belated arrival.' – *Variety*
'Marvellously grisly chiller.' – *Judith Crist, 1977*
'Its most telling details are its horrific ones. The fire at the beginning, with lifelike figures melting into grisly ooze; night time in the city morgue, with a dead body suddenly popping up as a side effect of embalming fluid; chases through shadows as the ghoulish sculptor collects bodies for his exhibit; and the shock when Atwill's homemade wax face crumbles to the floor and exposes the hidden demon.' – *Tom Shales, The American Film Heritage, 1972*

The Mystery of the Wentworth Castle: see *Mr Wong*

The Mystery of the Yellow Room *
France 1931 96m bw
Osso
An attempt is made on the life of a scientist's daughter.
Complex mystery which has maintained some reputation.
wd Marcel L'Herbier *novel* Gaston Leroux *ph* L. H. Burel *m* Edouard Flament
☆ Hugette Ex-Duclos, Roland Toutain, Maxime Desjardins

Mystery Science Theater 3000: The Movie
US 1996 73m DeLuxe
Gramercy/Best Brains (Jim Mallon)
A mad scientist forces an astronaut and his robots to watch an edited version of the 50s sci-fi movie *This Island Earth*.
A joke that anyone can play at home, since it consists of three characters, seen in silhouette at the bottom of the screen, making fun of an old movie; occasionally the remarks are amusing, but more often they are irritating.
w Michael J. Nelson, Trace Beaulieu, Jim Mallon, Kevin Murphy, Mary Jo Pehl, Paul Chaplin, Bridget Jones *d* Jim Mallon *ph* Jeff Stonehouse *m* Billy Barber *pd* Jef Maynard *ed* Bill Johnson
☆ Michael J. Nelson, Trace Beaulieu, Kevin Murphy, Jim Mallon, John Brady
'Infectiously funny while it's unspooling but instantly forgettable, goofy item will play best to teenagers in an altered state and looks unlikely to go beyond cult status.' – *Todd McCarthy, Variety*

Mystery Street *
US 1950 93m bw
MGM (Frank E. Taylor)
Harvard medical scientists help solve a murder by examining the victim's bones.
Standard semi-documentary police thriller; well paced and quite entertaining.
w Sydney Boehm, Richard Brooks d John Sturges *ph* John Alton *m* Rudolph Kopp
☆ Ricardo Montalban, Sally Forrest, Elsa Lanchester, Bruce Bennett, Marshall Thompson, Jan Sterling
Leonard Spigelgass (original story)

Mystery Train **
US 1989 110m DuArt
Palace/JVC (Jim Stark)
Episodic film involving two Elvis Presley fans in Memphis, an Italian woman who sees Elvis's ghost and a Presley look-alike, all of whom converge on a seedy hotel for the night.
Rambling, leisurely film that contains a multitude of small pleasures.
wd Jim Jarmusch *ph* Robby Müller *m* John Lurie *pd* Dan Bishop *ed* Melody London
☆ Masatoshi Nagase, Youki Kudoh, Screamin' Jay Hawkins, Cinque Lee, Rufus Thomas, Nicoletta Braschi, Elizabeth Bracco, Joe Strummer, Rick Aviles, Steve Buscemi

The Mystic Masseur
GB/India 2001 118m colour
Miracle/Merchant Ivory/Pritish Nandy Communications (Nayeem Hafizka, Richard Hawley)
An unsuccessful school teacher returns home and, after making his name as a healer and masseur, becomes a politician.
Uninvolving, episodic plod through a not very engaging life, told with little feel for character or setting.
w Caryl Phillips *novel* V. S. Naipaul *d* Ismail Merchant *ph* Ernie Vincze *m* Richard Robbins, Zakir Hussain *pd* Lucy Richardson *ed* Roberto Silvi *cos* Michael O'Connor
☆ Om Puri (Ramlogan), James Fox (Mr Stewart), Aasif Mandvi (Ganesh), Sanjeev Bhaska (Beharry), Ayesha Dharker (Leela), Jimi Mistry (Partap), Zohra Segal (Auntie), Sakina Jaffrey (Suruj Mooma)
'The combination of ... lack of substance and Merchant's lack of flair doesn't make for

scintillating cinema.' – *Edward Porter, Sunday Times*

'A limp though not dislikeable affair.' – *Observer*

Mystic Pizza

US 1988 104m colour

Virgin/Samuel Goldwyn Company (Mark Levinson, Scott Rosenfelt)

Three young women experience love and affairs for the first time.

Likely to appeal to a young female audience and offering little of interest to anyone else.

w Amy Jones, Perry Howze, Randy Howze, Alfred Uhry *story* Amy Jones *d* Donald Petrie *ph* Tim Suhrstedt *m* David McHugh *pd* David Chapman *ed* Marion Rothman, Don Brochu

☆ Vincent Phillip D'Onofrio, Annabeth Gish, William R. Moses, Julia Roberts, Adam Storke, Lili Taylor, Conchata Ferrell, Porscha Radcliffe

The Myth of Fingerprints

US 1997 90m DuArt

Feature Film/Good Machine/Eureka (Mary Jane Skalski, Tim Perell, Bart Freundlich)

Four children return home to their ageing parents for the Thanksgiving weekend.

A predictable slice of dysfunctional family life, with a distant, overbearing father and a forgiving mother.

wd Bart Freundlich *ph* Stephen Kazmierski *m* David Bridie, John Phillips *pd* Susan Bolles *ed* Kate Williams, Ken J. Sackheim

☆ Arija Bareikis, Blythe Danner, Hope Davis, Laurel Holloman, Brian Kerwin, James LeGros, Julianne Moore, Roy Scheider, Michael Vartan, Noah Wyle

'This is one angst-ridden family saga that needn't be a totally repellent experience.' – *Empire*

Nada ***
France/Italy 1974 134m Eastmancolor
Academy/Connoisseur/Verona/Films La Boétie (André Génovès)

A tough policeman tracks down a group of anarchists who kidnap the American Ambassador in Paris.
Bleak and violent film, expertly made, in which it is difficult to tell the good guys from the bad.
w Jean-Patrick Manchette *novel* Jean-Patrick Manchette *d* *Claude Chabrol* *ph* Jean Rabier *m* Pierre Jansen *ad* Guy Littaye *ed* Jacques Gaillard
☆ Fabio Testi, Michel Duchaussoy, Maurice Garrel, Michel Aumont, Lou Castel, Didier Kaminka, Lyle Joyce, Viviane Romance
'Chabrol's most profoundly cynical film to date ... he lays bare the cause-and-effect mechanism of terrorism.' – *Jan Dawson, MFB*

Nadine
US 1987 88m Metrocolor
Columbia TriStar/ML Delphi (Arlene Donovan)

Husband and wife on the brink of divorce are drawn together by a suspicious killing.
Unresolvedly old-fashioned comedy which seems to need the Cary Grant touch.
wd Robert Benton *ph* Nestor Almendros *m* Howard Shore *pd* Paul Sylbert *ed* Sam O'Steen
☆ Jeff Bridges, Kim Basinger, Rip Torn, Gwen Verdon, Glenne Headly, Jerry Stiller

'Hurry, The Dead Travel Fast!'
Nadja
US 1995 100m bw
ICA/Kino Link (Mary Sweeney, Amy Hobby)

Dracula's daughter attempts to revive her father while beginning an affair with the wife of the nephew of vampire hunter Van Helsing.
Despite being executive-produced by David Lynch, this is more an exhumation than a revival of an increasingly tired genre: the narrative owes much to Dracula's Daughter, *merely adding a lesbian twist, and its use of the toy camera Pixelvision to suggest a vampire's-eye view emphasizes that the project lacks any sharpness of style.*
wd Michael Almereyda *ph* Jim Denault *m* Simon Fisher Turner *pd* Kurt Ossenfort *ed* David Leonard
☆ Suzy Amis, Elina Löwensohn, Galaxy Craze, Martin Donovan, Peter Fonda, Karl Geary, Jared Harris
'Almost completely devoid of urgency or warmth. A calculated attempt to evoke the zero degree existential dreadfulness of its immortal predators' lifestyles, the film is a pretty slow one to watch.' – *Kim Newman*

Nagisa no Sindbad: see *Like Grains of Sand*

Naked *
GB 1993 131m Metrocolor
First Independent/Thin Man/Film Four (Simon Channing-Williams)

Running away from Manchester, where he rapes a woman, an unemployed, compulsively talkative misogynist comes to London and moves in with a former girlfriend.
A saga of an unlovely man out to destroy himself and others, which is bleak and despairing at its best, but more often is embittered overstatement and caricature.
wd Mike Leigh *ph* Dick Pope *m* Andrew Dickson *pd* Alison Chitty *ed* Jon Gregory
☆ *David Thewlis*, Lesley Sharp, Katrin Cartlidge, Greg Cruttwell, Claire Skinner, Peter Wight, Ewen Bremner, Susan Vidler
'It would be hard to imagine a film much sourer than *Naked*, but sourness is not a fault, merely a characteristic. Hollowness, now, self-indulgence, a sort of gloating emotional ugliness – those are faults.' – *Adam Mars-Jones, Independent*
'This is a neorealist monster movie, and the monster won't lie down and die – he just keeps coming.' – *Gavin Smith, Film Comment*
'A startling leap from the petty comic viciousness of Mike Leigh's domestic satires into darker, more complex philosophical territory.' – *Claire Monk, Sight and Sound*
† David Thewlis won the award for best actor, and Mike Leigh for best director, at the Cannes Film Festival in 1993.

Naked Alibi
US 1954 85m bw
U-I (Ross Hunter)
The police track a homicidal baker to a Mexican border town.
Modest police thriller which sags after it crosses the border.
w Lawrence Roman *d* Jerry Hopper *ph* Russell Metty *m* Hans Salter
☆ Sterling Hayden, Gene Barry, Gloria Grahame, Marcia Henderson, Casey Adams, Chuck Connors

The Naked and the Dead
US 1958 131m Technicolor RKOscope
RKO Teleradio/Gregjac (Paul Gregory)

Adventures of an army platoon in the Pacific war.
Shorn of the four letter words which made the novel notorious, this is a routine war film, neither very good nor very bad.
w Denis and Terry Sanders *novel* Norman Mailer *d* Raoul Walsh *ph* Joseph LaShelle *m* Bernard Herrmann
☆ Aldo Ray, Cliff Robertson, Raymond Massey, William Campbell, Richard Jaeckel, James Best, Joey Bishop, Robert Gist, Jerry Paris, L. Q. Jones
'One of the worst movies ever made.' – *Norman Mailer*

Naked as Nature Intended
GB 1961 65m Eastmancolor
Compass/Markten (Harrison Marks)

Five women visit British tourist attractions before going to a Cornish naturist resort, where they briefly take off their clothes and romp in the sun.
Innocuous film that helped start the British sexploitation cycle of the 60s and 70s and made Pamela Green the best-known unclothed actress of her time.
wd Harrison Marks *ph* Roy Poynter
☆ Pamela Green, Jackie Salt, Petrina Forsyth, Stuart Samuels, Bridget Leonard, Angela Jones
† The film was originally going to be titled *Cornish Holiday*. It was at first banned by the British Board of Film Censors, but the makers submitted it to the London County Council and other local authorities who passed it for exhibition, forcing the BBFC to change its policy and certify such films.

'The Most Exciting Story Of The World's Most Exciting City!'
The Naked City ****
US 1948 96m bw
Universal (Mark Hellinger)

New York police track down a killer.
Highly influential documentary thriller which, shot on location in New York's teeming streets, claimed to be giving an impression of city life; actually its real mission was to tell an ordinary murder tale with an impressive accumulation of detail and humour. The narrator's last words became a cliché: 'There are eight million stories in the naked city. This has been one of them.'
w Malvin Wald, Albert Maltz d Jules Dassin ph William Daniels *m* Frank Skinner, Miklos Rozsa *md* Milton Schwarzwald *ed Paul Weatherwax*
☆ *Barry Fitzgerald, Don Taylor*, Howard Duff, Dorothy Hart, Ted de Corsia, Adelaide Klein
William Daniels; Paul Weatherwax
original story (Malvin Wald)

The Naked Country
Australia 1985 90m colour
Naked Country Productions (Ross Dimsey)

aka: *Morris West's The Naked Country*
In the outback, a rancher engaged in a bloody conflict with the aborigines over land they regard as sacred comes to understand their attitudes through his suffering.
An Australian variation on cowboys and Indians, average for the most part though managing a rousing climax reminiscent of Sam Peckinpah in its theme of redemption through violence.
w Tim Burstall, Ross Dimsey *novel* Morris West *d* Tim Burstall *ph* David Eggby *m* Bruce Smeaton *ad* Philip Warner *ed* Tony Paterson
☆ John Stanton, Rebecca Gilling, Ivar Kants, Tommy Lewis, Donald Blitner, Simon Chilvers, Malcolm Cork, John Jarratt

The Naked Dawn
US 1956 82m Technicolor
Universal-International
A hired robber finds that his boss is not to be trusted.
Heavy-going Mexican Western.
w Nina and Herman Schneider (Julian Zimet) *d* Edgar G. Ulmer *ph* Frederick Gately *m* Herschel Burke Gilbert
☆ Arthur Kennedy, Eugene Iglesias, Betta St John
† Screenwriter Julian Zimet was blacklisted, so at the time of the film's release the screenplay was credited to Zimet's brother-in-law and his wife.

Naked Earth
GB 1958 96m bw Cinemascope
TCF/Foray Films (Adrian Worker)
In 1895 a young Irish farmer goes to Africa to grow tobacco, but moves on to crocodile hunting.
Predictable and uninteresting epic of endurance; not very convincing either.
w Milton Holmes *d* Vincent Sherman *ph* Erwin Hillier
☆ Richard Todd, Juliette Greco, John Kitzmiller, Finlay Currie, Laurence Naismith, Christopher Rhodes, Orlando Martins
† Screenwriter Harold Buchman was forced to take his name off the credits of the film because he was blacklisted.

The Naked Edge
GB 1961 100m bw
UA/Pennebaker/Baroda (Walter Seltzer, George Glass)

A successful executive is suspected by his wife of an old murder in which he testified against the man who was convicted.
Dreary thriller which piles up red herrings in shoals, then abandons them all for a razor-and-bathroom finale.
w Joseph Stefano *novel First Train to Babylon* by Max Ehrlich *d* Michael Anderson *ph* Erwin Hillier *m* William Alwyn
☆ Gary Cooper, Deborah Kerr, Peter Cushing, Eric Portman, Diane Cilento, Hermione Gingold, Michael Wilding, Ronald Howard

The Naked Face
US 1984 106m Metrocolor
Cannon (Rony Yacov)

A Chicago psychiatrist finds himself a potential victim of the Mafia.
Muddled and violent mystery with a rather boring solution.
wd Bryan Forbes *novel* Sidney Sheldon *ph* David Gurfinkel *m* Michael J. Lewis *pd* William Fosser
☆ Roger Moore, Rod Steiger, Elliott Gould, Anne Archer, David Hedison, Art Carney, Ron Parady

Naked Fury
GB 1959 60m bw
Butcher's/Coenda (Guido Coen)
A robbery goes wrong when a gang is forced to take the night watchman's daughter as well as their loot.
Unconvincing thriller in which most of the crooks act like gentlemen, which robs the drama of any suspense as well as credibility.
w Brock Williams *story* Guido Coen *d* Charles Saunders *ph* Jimmy W. Harvey *m* Edwin Astley *ad* Duncan Sutherland *ed* Peter Pitt
☆ Reed de Rouen, Kenneth Cope, Leigh Madison, Arthur Lovegrove, Alexander Field, Tommy Eytle, Ann Lynn, Marianne Brauns, Arthur Gross

Naked Gun 2½: The Smell of Fear
US 1991 85m Technicolor
UIP/Paramount/Zucker/Abrahams/Zucker (Robert K. Weiss)

A clumsy police lieutenant investigates an attempt to kill a solar energy expert.
The mixture as before, although this time around the slapstick comedy is enlivened with fewer good jokes.
w David Zucker, Pat Proft *d* David Zucker *ph* Robert Stevens *m* Ira Newborn *pd* John J. Lloyd *ed* James Symons, Chris Greenbury
☆ Leslie Nielsen, Priscilla Presley, George Kennedy, O.J. Simpson, Robert Goulet, Richard Griffiths, Jacqueline Brookes, Anthony James, Lloyd Bochner
'At least two-and-a-half times less funny than its hilarious progenitor.' – *Variety*
'An appealing rag-bag of the ribald and the ridiculous, showing only the slightest signs of running out of steam.' – *Philip Strick, Sight and Sound*

Naked Gun 33⅓: The Final Insult *
US 1994 82m DeLuxe
Paramount (Robert K. Weiss, David Zucker)

Detective Frank Drebin retires from the force and is persuaded to return as an undercover cop.
With some new jokes this time around, and deft parodies, this is the funniest of the series so far.
w Pat Proft, David Zucker, Robert LoCash *d* Peter Segal *ph* Robert Stevens *m* Ira Newborn *pd* Lawrence G. Paull *ed* Jim Symons
☆ Leslie Nielsen, Priscilla Presley, George Kennedy, O. J. Simpson, Fred Ward, Kathleen Freeman, Anna Nicole Smith, Ellen Greene, Ed Williams
'Loaded with the usual barrage of irreverent, politically incorrect and virtually non-stop gags.' – *Variety*

The Naked Gun: From the Files of Police Squad *
US 1988 85m Technicolor
UIP/Paramount (Robert K. Weiss)

A bungling detective foils attempts to assassinate the Queen in Los Angeles.
A barrage of gags, some good, some dreadful, is harnessed to a limp narrative. Not as funny as it should be.
w Jerry Zucker, Jim Abrahams, David Zucker, Pat Proft *d* David Zucker *ph* Robert Stevens *m* Ira Newborn *pd* John J. Lloyd *ed* Michael Jablow
☆ Leslie Nielsen, Priscilla Presley, Ricardo Montalban, George Kennedy, O. J. Simpson, Susan

Digital Video Disc Region 2 · Digital Video Disc Region 1 · Soundtrack released on compact disc · ☆ Cast in approximate order of importance · † Points of interest · Notable songs · Academy Award · Academy Award nomination · BAFTA

Beaubian, Nancy Marchand, Raye Birk, Jeannette Charles

'Quickly and efficiently establishes its pattern of wildly escalating absurdity within each scene, combined with a series of gags related to each character throughout the film.' – *Philip Strick, MFB*

The Naked Hills

US 1955 73m Pathécolor
Allied Artists/La Salle (Josef Shaftel)

Starting in 1849, a young prospector spends his life looking for gold.
Curious, mildly interesting saga with an obsession instead of a plot.
wd Josef Shaftel *ph* Frederick Gately *m* Herschel Burke Gilbert
☆ David Wayne, Marcia Henderson, Keenan Wynn, James Barton, Jim Backus, Denver Pyle

Naked in New York *

US 1993 86m colour
Fine Line/Pandora (Frederick Zollo)

A young hopeful playwright reflects on his upbringing in a fatherless home, his on-and-off relationship with his girlfriend and the way his life is taken over by others.
Pleasant low-key drama of the young attempting to come to terms with the compromises of life.
w Dan Algrant, John Warren *d* Dan Algrant *ph* Joey Forsyte *m* Angelo Badalamenti *pd* Kalina Ivanov *ed* Bill Pankow
☆ Eric Stoltz, Mary-Louise Parker, Ralph Macchio, Jill Clayburgh, Tony Curtis, Kathleen Turner, Timothy Dalton, Roscoe Lee Browne, Whoopi Goldberg, Eric Bogosian, Quentin Crisp

'A charming, creative, but slightly inconsistent look at the dreams and loves of the artsy twentysomethings.' – *Variety*

† Martin Scorsese became the film's executive producer after reading Algrant's semi-autobiographical script.

The Naked Jungle *

US 1954 95m Technicolor
Paramount/George Pal (Frank Freeman Jnr)

In 1901 a young woman is married by proxy to a South American cocoa planter, and when she arrives at his jungle home she has to conquer not only him but an army of soldier ants.
Mixture of Rebecca *elements with a more unusual kind of thrill; all quite watchable, and the ant scenes very effective.*
w Philip Yordan, Ranald MacDougall *story Leiningen Versus the Ants* by Carl Stephenson *d* Byron Haskin *ph* Ernest Laszlo *m* Daniele Amfitheatrof
☆ Charlton Heston, Eleanor Parker, William Conrad, Abraham Sofaer, John Dierkes, Douglas Fowley

The Naked Kiss *

US 1964 92m bw
Allied Artists/F and F/AA (Samuel Fuller)

A prostitute tries to enter mainstream society.
Tough early work by a director who never compromised but seldom hit the public fancy.
wd Samuel Fuller *ph* Stanley Cortez *m* Paul Dunlap *ad* Eugene Lourie *ed* Jerome Thoms
☆ Constance Towers, Anthony Eisley, Michael Dante, Virginia Grey, Patsy Kelly, Betty Bronson

'Exterminate all rational thought.'

Naked Lunch *

Canada/GB 1991 115m Film House colour
First Independent (Jeremy Thomas)

In the 1950s, a drug-addicted writer kills his wife while trying to emulate William Tell and flees to Interzone, an exotic place of paranoid fantasy.
Instead of the savagery and rampant homosexuality of the original, the film concerns the act of the book's creation, through the hallucinatory experiences of a writer, based on Burroughs, among the expatriate artistic community of Tangier. All that is carried over from the novel is the title and lack of narrative coherence.
wd David Cronenberg *novel* William S. Burroughs *ph* Peter Suschitzky *m* Howard Shore, Ornette Coleman (alto sax solos) *pd* Carol Spier *ed* Ronald Sanders *sp* creature effects: Chris Walas Inc.
☆ Peter Weller, Judy Davis, Ian Holm, Julian Sands, Roy Scheider, Monique Mercure, Nicholas Campbell, Michael Zelniker, Robert A. Silverman, Joseph Scorsiani

'A fascinating, demanding, mordantly funny picture that echoes many of the book's chief concerns, but also stands as a distinctively personal creation in its own right.' – *Variety*

'It's impossible to make a movie out of *Naked Lunch*. A literal translation just wouldn't work. It would cost $400 million to make and would be banned in every country of the world.' – *David Cronenberg*

The Naked Maja

Italy/US 1959 112m Technirama
MGM/Titanus (Goffredo Lombardo)

Peasant Francisco Goya becomes a famous painter through the influence of the Duchess of Alba.
Boring and unconvincing biopic.
w Giorgio Prosperi, Norman Corwin, Albert Lewin, Oscar Saul *d* Henry Koster *ph* Giuseppe Rotunno *m* Francesco Lavagnino
☆ Anthony Franciosa, Ava Gardner, Amedeo Nazzari, Gino Cervi, Lea Padovani, Massimo Serrato

'This travesty of Goya's life, country and period adds up to nothing more entertaining than a perfunctory, heavy-handed pageant.' – *MFB*

'Chiropractor by day. Wrestler by night.'

The Naked Man *

US 1998 93m FotoKem
October (Ben Barenholtz)

A chiropractor-cum-wrestler becomes an all-action crusader for spinal integrity after his family is murdered.
Quirky comedy with some funny moments, including a shabby detective who makes Colombo look like Lord Peter Wimsey; but its stylised approach and broad tone cannot encompass the gruseome deaths which punctuate the action.
w J. Todd Anderson, Ethan Coen *d* J. Todd Anderson *ph* Jeff Barklage *m* Edward Bilous *pd* Kathleen M. McKernin *ed* Tricia Cooke, Mark Cretcher
☆ Michael Rapaport (Ed Bliss Jnr), Arija Bareikis (Kim), Rachael Leigh Cook (Delores), Martin Ferrero (Sammy), Joe Grifasi (Kaski), John Carroll Lynch (Driver), Michael Jeter (Sticks), John Slattery (Burns)

The Naked Night: see *Sawdust and Tinsel*

The Naked Prey *

US 1966 94m Technicolor Panavision
Paramount/Theodora/Sven Persson (Cornel Wilde)

In 1840, a white hunter becomes brutalized when a tribe hunts him down as though he were a lion.
Savage adventure story with bloodthirsty detail; unusual and certainly effective.
w Clint Johnston, Don Peters *d* Cornel Wilde *ph* H. A. R. Thomson *md* Andrew Tracy, from African folk music
☆ Cornel Wilde, Gert Van Den Berg, Ken Gampu

'Overtones pretentious, but it tries.' – *Sight and Sound*

script

The Naked Runner

GB 1967 104m Techniscope
Warner/Artanis (Brad Dexter)

British intelligence conceive a plan to turn an innocent businessman into a spy killer.
Silly espionage thriller further marred by its director's penchant for making a zany composition of every frame.
w Stanley Mann *novel* Francis Clifford *d* Sidney J. Furie *ph* Otto Heller *m* Harry Sukman
☆ Frank Sinatra, Peter Vaughan, Derren Nesbitt, Nadia Gray, Toby Robins, Cyril Luckham, Edward Fox, Inger Stratton

'It might be a good movie to read by if there were light in the theatre.' – *Pauline Kael*

The Naked Spur *

US 1952 91m Technicolor
MGM (William H. Wright)

A bounty hunter has trouble getting his quarry back to base.
Standard big-studio Western shot in Colorado, with all characters motivated by greed.
w Sam Rolfe, Harold Jack Bloom *d* Anthony Mann *ph* William Mellor *m* Bronislau Kaper
☆ James Stewart, Robert Ryan, Janet Leigh, Millard Mitchell

script

The Naked Street

US 1955 83m bw
Edward Small

A racketeer's daughter marries a worthless crook: her father saves him from the electric chair but he murders again.
Semi-documentary exposé melodrama about unpleasant people; reasonably proficient on its level.
w Maxwell Shane, Leo Katcher *d* Maxwell Shane *ph* Floyd Crosby *m* Ernest Gold *md* Emil Newman
☆ Anthony Quinn, Anne Bancroft, Farley Granger, Peter Graves

Naked Tango

US 1990 92m DeLuxe
Blue Dolphin/Sugarloaf/Gotan/Towa/Praesens/Grupo Baires (David Weisman)

In the 1920s a bored wife assumes the identity of a suicide, marries a dubious night-club owner in Buenos Aires, and falls in love with a tango-dancing gangster.
Luridly directed and acted, over-the-top romance that fails to convince, particularly in its attempt at a period setting.
wd Leonard Schrader *story* inspired by the work of Manuel Puig *ph* Juan Ruiz-Anchia *m* Thomas Newman *pd* Anthony Pratt *ed* Lee Percy, Debra McDermott
☆ Vincent D'Onofrio, Mathilda May, Esai Morales, Fernando Rey, Cipe Lincovsky, Josh Mostel, Patricio Bisso, Constance McCashin

'Too morbid and narrowly conceived to interest mainstream audiences.' – *Variety*

The Naked Truth *

GB 1957 92m bw
Rank/Mario Zampi

US title: *Your Past is Showing*

Celebrities band together to kill a blackmailer who threatens to expose unsavoury aspects of their lives.
Frenzied black farce, quite a lot of which comes off.
w Michael Pertwee *d* Mario Zampi *ph* Stan Pavey *m* Stanley Black
☆ Peter Sellers, Terry-Thomas, Peggy Mount, Dennis Price, Shirley Eaton, Georgina Cookson

Naked under Leather: see *Girl on a Motorcycle*

The Naked Vampire: see *La Vampire Nue*

Naked Warriors: see *The Arena*

Namayeh Nazdik: see *Close-Up*

'Even men of God can trade with the Devil'

The Name of the Rose *

US 1986 130m colour
TCF/Bernd Eichinger/Bernd-Schaefers/Cristaldi/Ariane/ZDF

In the 14th century, an English monk's visit to an Italian abbey is soured by a series of murders.
Curious, remote, randomly developed and edited, this can never have been an obvious candidate for box-office success: yet it did pretty well.
w Andrew Birkin, Gerard Brach, Howard Franklin, Alain Godard *novel* Umberto Eco *d* Jean-Jacques Annaud *ph* Tonino Delli Colli *m* James Horner *pd* Dante Ferretti *ed* Jane Seitz
☆ Sean Connery, F. Murray Abraham, Christian Slater, Michael Lonsdale, Elya Baskin

'A plodding misfire ... sorrowfully mediocre.' – *Variety*

Sean Connery

Namu the Killer Whale *

US 1966 88m DeLuxe
United Artists (Lazlo Benedek)

A marine biologist traps a killer whale in a small cove so that he can study it, causing fear and suspicion among the local fishermen and villagers.
Pleasant movie of prejudice overcome by reason and example, aimed at a family audience and treating its animals with respect.
w Arthur Weiss *d* Laslo Benedek *ph* Lamar Boren *m* Samuel Matlovsky *ad* Eddie Imazu *ed* Erwin Dumbrille
☆ Robert Lansing, John Anderson, Richard Erdman, Lee Meriwether, Robin Mattson, Joe Higgins, Michael Shea

Nana *

US 1934 89m bw
Samuel Goldwyn

GB title: *Lady of the Boulevards*

The high life and subsequent degradation of a Parisian demi-mondaine in the 1890s.
Stylish yet stolid slice of le beau monde, *intended to create a new star.*
w Willard Mack, Harry Wagstaff Gribble *novel* Emile Zola *d Dorothy Arzner ph* Gregg Toland *m* Alfred Newman
☆ Anna Sten, Lionel Atwill, Phillips Holmes, Richard Bennett, Mae Clarke, Muriel Kirkland, Reginald Owen, Jessie Ralph

'The star's resources should be sufficient to offset some of the lesser script deficiencies.' – *Variety*

Nana

France/Italy 1955 100m
Cygno Films/FLF (Jacques Roitfeld)

A courtesan and actress comes to grief.
Glossily unconvincing version, with a performance in the title role in the style of Lucille Ball.
w Henri Jeanson, Albert Valentin *d* Christian-Jaque *ph* Christian Matras *m* Georges Van Parys *ad* Robert Gys *ed* Jacques Desagneaux
☆ Charles Boyer, Martine Carol, Walter Chiari, Marguerite Pierry, Paul Frankeur, Elisa Cegani, Dora Doll, Jacques Castlelot, Noel Roquevert

Nancy Drew

This series of second features starring Bonita Granville as a teenage small-town detective was moderately well received but quickly forgotten. The character was created in novels by Edward Stratemeyer and his daughter Harriet Evans; the films were all directed by William Clemens for Warner.
1938 Nancy Drew, Detective
1939 Nancy Drew, Reporter, Nancy Drew, Trouble Shooter, Nancy Drew and the Hidden Staircase

Nancy Goes to Rio

US 1950 99m Technicolor
MGM (Joe Pasternak)

Two actresses, mother and daughter, are both after the same part.
Mild shipboard musical.
w Sidney Sheldon *d* Robert Z. Leonard *ph* Ray June *m* George Stoll
☆ Jane Powell, Ann Sothern, Carmen Miranda, Barry Sullivan, Louis Calhern, Fortunio Bonanova, Hans Conried

Nancy Steele is Missing *

US 1937 85m bw
TCF (Nunnally Johnson)

Crooks try to pass off a girl as the long lost heir to a fortune.
Slightly unusual, well cast melodrama.
w Gene Fowler, Hal Long *novel* C. F. Coe *d* George Marshall *ph* Barney McGill *m* David Buttolph
☆ Victor McLaglen, Peter Lorre, June Lang, Jane Darwell, John Carradine, Walter Connolly

The Nanny *

GB 1965 93m bw
ABP/Hammer (Jimmy Sangster)

A 10-year-old boy hates his nanny, and with good reason, for she is a neurotic murderess.
Muted Hammer experiment in psycho- pathology, with too much equivocation before the dénouement; the star's role allows few fireworks, and the plot is rather unpleasant.

w Jimmy Sangster *novel* Evelyn Piper *d* *Seth Holt* *ph* Harry Waxman *m* Richard Rodney Bennett
☆ Bette Davis, Jill Bennett, William Dix, James Villiers, Wendy Craig, Pamela Franklin, Maurice Denham

Nanook of the North *
US 1921 57m bw silent
Revillon Frères
The life of an Eskimo and his family.
Primitive but trail-blazing documentary, hard to sit through for modern audiences.
wd/ph/ed *Robert Flaherty*
'In a day of emotional and artistic deliquescence on the screen. a picture with the fresh strength and pictorial promise of Nanook of the North is in the nature of a revolution.' – *Frances Taylor Patterson*
† Nanook himself died of hunger on the ice shortly after the film was released.

Nanou
GB/France 1986 110m Eastmancolor
Umbrella-Caulfield/Arion
A young English girl, travelling through France, has an affair with a political activist.
Unsatisfactory film of an unsatisfactory romance.
wd Conny Templeman *ph* Martin Fuhrer *m* John Keane *pd* Andrew Mollo *ed* Tom Priestley
☆ Imogen Stubbs, Jean-Philippe Ecoffey, Daniel Day-Lewis, Lou Castel, Valentine Pelka, Anne-Marie Jabraud, Dominique Rousseau, Michel Robin, Roger Ibanez

Napló Gyermekeimnek: see *Diary for My Children*

Napoleon ****
France 1927 378m approx (24 fps) bw (some colour) silent
WESTI/Société Générale de Films
The early life of Napoleon.
A cinematic epic which, although brilliant in most particulars, owes its greatest interest to its narrative sweep, its flair for composition and its use of triptych screens which at the end combine to show one giant picture, the clear precursor of Cinerama. In 1934 Gance revised his film and added stereophonic sound.
ph various *m* Arthur Honegger *wd/ed* *Abel Gance*
☆ Albert Dieudonné, Antonin Artaud, Pierre Batcheff
† The 1934 version ran 140m and included three-dimensional sound.

Napoleon and Samantha
US 1972 91m Technicolor
Walt Disney (Winston Hibler)
When his old guardian dies, a small boy and his girl friend run away with their pet lion.
Patchy, episodic action drama for older children, with a very sleepy lion.
w Stewart Raffill *d* Bernard McEveety
ph Monroe Askins *m* Buddy Baker
☆ Michael Douglas, Will Geer
Buddy Baker

Nära Livet: see *So Close to Life*

Narayama Bushi-Ko: see *The Ballad of Narayama*

Narc *
US 2002 105m DeLuxe
UIP/Lions Gate/Tiara Blu/Cutting Edge (Diane Nabatoff, Ray Liotta, Michelle Grace)
In Detroit, a disgraced undercover cop is forced to find the drug dealers who killed a colleague, in order to be rehabilitated.
Tough, rough-edged thriller about policemen on the edge of compromise and criminality.
wd Joe Carnahan *ph* Alex Nepomnischy *m* Cliff Martinez *pd* Taava Sooder *ed* John Gilroy
☆ Ray Liotta (Lt Henry Oak), Jason Patric (Nick Tellis), Chi McBride (Capt. Cheevers), Busta Rhymes (Beery), Anne Openshaw (Katherine Calvess), Richard Chevolleau (Steeds), John Ortiz (Ruiz)
'A movie that bristles with energy, from its stand-out, hand-held opening chase to its brutal, bloody denouement.' – *Alan Morrison, Empire*

The Narrow Corner
US 1933 71m bw
Warner
On an eastern island, a man on the run for murder finds he can't escape his fate.
Mediocre adaptation of a Somerset Maugham novel in which very little happens; the added love interest doesn't help.
w Robert Presnell *d* Alfred E. Green
☆ Douglas Fairbanks Jnr, Ralph Bellamy, Dudley Digges, Arthur Hohl, Patricia Ellis
'Considerably better than fair.' – *Variety*
† Remade three years later as *Isle of Fury* (qv).

The Narrow Margin ***
US 1952 70m bw
RKO (Stanley Rubin)
Police try to guard a prosecution witness on a train from Chicago to Los Angeles.
Tight little thriller which takes every advantage of its train setting. What the trade used to call a sleeper, it gave more satisfaction than many a top feature.
w Earl Fenton *d* *Richard Fleischer* *ph* *George E. Diskant*
☆ *Charles McGraw, Marie Windsor*, Jacqueline White, Queenie Leonard
'A taut, breathlessly fast and highly suspenseful "sleeper" par excellence.' – *Time Out, 1986*
original story (Martin Goldsmith, Jack Leonard)

'They Want Her Dead. He Needs Her Alive.'
Narrow Margin
US 1990 97m Technicolor Panavision
Guild/Carolco (Jonathan A. Zimbert)
A district attorney and a key witness in a trial take refuge on a train from pursuing gangsters.
Inferior remake of the 1952 film, with little sense of suspense.
w Earl Fenton Jnr *story* Martin Goldsmith, Jack Leonard *m* Bruce Broughton *pd* Joel Schiller *ad* Kim Mooney *ed* James Mitchell *d/ph* Peter Hyams
☆ Gene Hackman, Anne Archer, James B. Sikking, J. T. Walsh, M. Emmet Walsh, Susan Hogan, Nigel Bennett, J. A. Preston
† *Variety* reported that while the original film cost $230,000 to make, the remake was nearly a hundred times more expensive, at $21 million.

The Narrowing Circle
GB 1955 66m bw
Fortress Films/Eros
Murder on the staff of a magazine.
Very tolerable mystery which wastes no time and plays fair.
w Doreen Montgomery *novel* Julian Symons
d Charles Saunders *ph* Jonah Jones *m* Reg Owen
☆ Paul Carpenter, Hazel Court, Ferdy Mayne, Russell Napier, Trevor Reid

'The damnedest thing you ever saw!'
Nashville ***
US 1975 161m Metrocolor Panavision
Paramount/ABC (Robert Altman)
A political campaign in Nashville organizes a mammoth pop concert to gain support.
Kaleidoscopic, fragmented, multi-storied musical melodrama, a mammoth movie which can be a bore or an inspiration according to taste. Certainly many exciting moments pass by, but the length is self-defeating.
w Joan Tewkesbury *d* *Robert Altman* *ph* Paul Lohmann *md* Richard Baskin
☆ Geraldine Chaplin, David Arkin, Barbara Baxley, Ned Beatty, Karen Black, Keith Carradine, Henry Gibson, Keenan Wynn, Lily Tomlin, Ronee Blakley
'A gigantic parody … crammed with samples taken from every level of Nashville society, revealed in affectionate detail bordering on caricature in a manner that would surely delight Norman Rockwell.' – *Philip Strick*
'Wildly over-praised Altman, with all the defects we once looked on as marks of healthy ambitiousness: terrible construction, messy editing, leering jokes at its own characters, unending pomposity.' – *Time Out, 1980*
song 'I'm Easy' (m/ly Keith Carradine)
best picture; Robert Altman; Lily Tomlin; Ronee Blakley

The Nasty Girl ***
West Germany 1990 92m Eastmancolor
Mainline/Sentana/ZDF
original title: *Das Schreckliche Mädchen*
Despite local hostility, a girl researches into events in her home town during the Nazi regime.
A witty and exuberant social satire, using very effectively a documentary approach to the subject.
wd *Michael Verhoeven* *ph* Axel de Roche *m* Mike Hertung, Elmar Schloter, Billy Gorlt, Lydie Auvray *ad* Hubert Popp *ed* Barbara Hennings
☆ Lena Stolze, Monika Baumgartner, Michael Gahr, Fred Stillkrauth, Elisabeth Bertram, Robert Giggenbach, Karin Thaler, Hans-Reinhard Muller
best foreign film
best foreign film

Nasty Habits *
GB 1976 92m Technicolor
Brut/Bowden (Robert Enders)
An abbess dies and the nuns vie for succession.
Satirical comedy rather obviously based on the Watergate scandals; initially amusing, but very tiresome by the end.
w Robert Enders *novel* *The Abbess of Crewe* by Muriel Spark *d* Michael Lindsay-Hogg
ph Douglas Slocombe *m* John Cameron
☆ Glenda Jackson, Melina Mercouri, Geraldine Page, Sandy Dennis, Anne Jackson, Anne Meara, Edith Evans, Susan Penhaligon, Rip Torn, Eli Wallach, Jerry Stiller
'The sort of material just about fit for a half-hour TV sketch.' – *Richard Combs, MFB*

Nasty Neighbours
GB 2000 88m colour
Redbus
Family rivalries erupt when a brash young couple move in next door to a middle-aged suburban couple.
Tiny comedy that looks lost on the big screen: the most exciting moment comes when one neighbour damages the other's prize pansies.
wd Debbie Isitt *play* Debbie Isitt *ph* Simon Reeves, Sam McCurdy *m* Jocelyn Pook *pd* Tim Streater *ed* Nicky Ager *cos* Sally Plum
☆ Ricky Tomlinson (Harold Peach), Marion Bailey (Jean Peach), Phil Daniels (Chapman), Rachel Fielding (Mrs Chapman), Hywel Bennett (The Boss), Dawn Butler (Travel agent), Nick Whitfield (Estate agent), Gordon Coulson (Stan)
'Characters and incidents are strictly from stock, and pretty dated stock at that.' – *Philip Kemp, Sight and Sound*

The National Health *
GB 1973 97m Eastmancolor
Columbia (Ned Sherrin, Terry Glinwood)
Life in the general men's ward of a large antiquated hospital.
Acerbic comedy from a National Theatre play which mixes tragedy and farce into a kind of Carry on Dying.
w *Peter Nichols* *play* Peter Nichols *d* *Jack Gold*
ph John Coquillon *m* Carl Davis *pd* Ray Simm
☆ *Jim Dale*, Lynn Redgrave, Eleanor Bron, Sheila Scott-Wilkinson, Donald Sinden, Colin Blakely, Clive Swift

National Lampoon Goes to the Movies: see *National Lampoon's Movie Madness*

'It was the Deltas against the rules... the rules lost!'
National Lampoon's Animal House *
US 1978 109m Technicolor
Universal (Matty Simmons, Ivan Reitman)
On an American campus around 1962, scruffy newcomers challenge the elegant élite.
A ragbag of college gags, of interest only to those who have had the experience; but its success caused much imitation, especially in American television.
w Harold Ramis, Douglas Kenney, Chris Miller
d John Landis *ph* Charles Correll *m* Elmer Bernstein
☆ John Belushi, Tim Matheson, John Vernon, Donald Sutherland, Verna Bloom, Cesare Danova, Mary Louise Weller

National Lampoon's Christmas Vacation
US 1989 97m colour
Warner/Hughes Entertainment (John Hughes, Tom Jacobson)
A father decides to give the family an old-fashioned Christmas at home.
Unsubtle comedy that always goes for the easy laugh.
w John Hughes *d* Jeremiah S. Chechik
ph Thomas Ackerman *m* Angelo Badalmenti
pd Stephen Marsh *ed* Jerry Greenberg
☆ Chevy Chase, Beverly D'Angelo, Randy Quaid, Diane Ladd, E. G. Marshall, Doris Roberts, Julia Louis-Dreyfus, Mae Questel, William Hickey

National Lampoon's Class Reunion
US 1982 85m Metrocolor
Fox/ABC Productions (Matty Simmons)
The class of '72 foregathers at Lizzie Borden High, where a murderer is lurking.
An entertainment in which the presentation is better than the material, which is a vague spoof of high school and horror films.
w John Hughes *d* Michael Miller *ph* Phil Lathrop *m* Peter Bernstein, Mark Goldenberg *pd* Dean Edward Mitzner *ed* Richard C. Meyer, Ann Mills
☆ Gerrit Graham, Michael Lerner, Fred McCarren, Miriam Flynn, Stephen Furst

National Lampoon's European Vacation
US 1985 94m Technicolor
Warner (Matty Simmons)
An American family determines to see Europe.
Hopelessly unfunny and simple-minded comedy, lacking even the usual schoolboy smut.
w John Hughes, Robert Klane *d* Amy Heckerling
ph Bob Paynter *m* Charles Fox *pd* Bob Cartwright *ed* Paul Herring
☆ Chevy Chase, Beverly D'Angelo, Jason Lively, Dana Hill, Eric Idle

'See it before they make the sequel!'
National Lampoon's Loaded Weapon 1
US 1993 83m DeLuxe
Guild/New Line (Suzanne Todd, David Willis)
Two cops investigate a cocaine-cookie smuggling ring.
A lacklustre parody of the Lethal Weapon *movies; it not only has no style, it does not even have any jokes.*
w Don Holley, Gene Quintano *d* Gene Quintano
ph Peter Dening *m* Robert Folk *pd* Jaymes Hinkle *ed* Christopher Greenbury
☆ Emilio Estevez, Samuel L. Jackson, Jon Lovitz, Tim Curry, Kathy Ireland, Frank McRae, William Shatner, James Doohan, F. Murray Abraham
'This would-be comedy is very short on laughs and virtually all are given away in its trailer.' – *Variety*

National Lampoon's Movie Madness
US 1981 89m Technicolor Panavision
UA (Matty Simmons)
aka: *National Lampoon Goes to the Movies*
Three parodies of movie genres: an insurance salesman seeks personal growth; a stripper becomes First Lady in three days; a young cop learns how to be tough.
Cinema audiences were spared this inept and witless display, though it turns up on late-night TV to bore the unwary.
w Tod Carroll, Shary Flenniken, Pat Mephitis, Gerald Sussman, Ellis Weiner *d* Bob Giraldi, Henry Jaglom *ph* Charles Correll, Tak Fujimoto *m* Andy Stein *ad* Alexander A. Mayer *ed* James Coblentz, Bud S. Isaacs
☆ Robby Benson, Richard Widmark, Diane Lane, Candy Clark, Christopher Lloyd, Peter Riegert, Ann Dusenberry, Elisha Cook, Robert Culp

National Lampoon's Senior Trip
US 1995 91m colour
New Line/Alliance (Wendy Grean)
High-school seniors cause political mayhem when the US President invites them to Washington.
Dim and dumb comedy with jokes that rarely rise above the subjects of flatulence and vomit; sick-making it is.
w Roger Kumble, I. Marlene King *d* Kelly Makin
ph François Protat *m* Steve Bartek *pd* Gregory Keen *ed* Stephen Lawrence

☆ Matt Frewer, Valerie Mahaffey, Lawrence Dane, Thomas Chong, Jeremy Renner, Rob Moore
'A witless item.' – *Variety*

National Lampoon's Vacation
US 1983 98m Technicolor
Warner (Matty Simmons)
An inventor drives his family on a holiday starting in Chicago and ending in California, but the journey is fraught with disaster.
Episodic, more or less straight black comedy, with detail more often boring or repellent than funny.
w John Hughes *d* Harold Ramis *ph* Victor J. Kemper *m* Ralph Burns *pd* Jack Collis *ed* Paul Herring
☆ Chevy Chase, Imogene Coca, Beverly D'Angelo, Randy Quaid, Eddie Bracken

'Don't Graduate. Celebrate.'
National Lampoon's Van Wilder
US/Germany 2001 92m Fotokem
Momentum/Artisan/MyriadIn/Motion AG/WMF V/ Tapestry (Robert L. Levy, Peter J. Abrams, Andrew Panay, Jonathon Komack-Martin)
GB title: *Van Wilder Party Liaison*
An eternal student has no desire to graduate as long as he can continue to party.
Gruesome concoction of coarse and feeble jokes, mainly concerning masturbation and vomit; it is like Animal House without the animals.
w Brent Goldberg, David T. Wagner *d* Walt Becker *ph* James Bagdonas *m* David Lawrence *pd* Rachel Kamerman *ed* Dennis M. Hill
☆ Ryan Reynolds (Van Wilder), Tara Reid (Gwen Pearson), Tim Matheson (Vance Wilder Snr), Kal Penn (Taj Mahal Badalandabad), Teck Holmes (Hutch), Daniel Cosgrove (Richard Bagg), Deon Richmond (Mini Cochran)
'Dreadful.' – *Observer*
'Painfully flat gross-out comedy.' – *Rolling Stone*

'They only look like cops.'
National Security
US/GB 2003 88m colour
Columbia/Outlaw/Intermedia/Firm Films (Bobby Newmyer, Jeff Silver, Michael Green)
Two antagonistic security guards team up to foil a ruthless robber.
Dim comedy that cannot even raise a smile; Lawrence's performance is notably charmless.
w Jay Scherick, David Ronn *d* Dennis Dugan *ph* Oliver Wood *m* Randy Edelman *pd* Larry Fulton *ed* Debra Neil-Fisher
☆ Martin Lawrence (Earl Montgomery), Steve Zahn (Hank Rafferty), Colm Feore (Det. Frank McDuff), Bill Duke (Lt Washington), Eric Roberts (Nash), Timothy Busfield (Charlie Reed), Robinne Lee (Denise), Matt McCoy (Robert Barton)
'A film that's both laugh out loud funny and surprisingly subtle.' – *Kevin Thomas, Los Angeles Times*
'Can you believe there are movie producers who still think it worthwhile ripping off *Beverly Hills Cop?*' – *Anthony Quinn, Independent*

National Velvet *
US 1945 125m Technicolor
MGM (Pandro S. Berman)
Children train a horse to win the Grand National.
A big bestseller from another era; its flaws of conception and production quickly became evident.
w Theodore Reeves, Helen Deutsch *novel* Enid Bagnold *d* Clarence Brown *ph* Leonard Smith *m* Herbert Stothart *ed* *Robert J. Kern*
☆ Mickey Rooney, Elizabeth Taylor, *Anne Revere*, Donald Crisp, Angela Lansbury, Jackie Jenkins, Reginald Owen, Terry Kilburn, Norma Varden, Alec Craig, Arthur Shields, Dennis Hoey
† Sequel 1978: *International Velvet*.
Anne Revere; Robert J. Kern
Clarence Brown; Leonard Smith

Nationale 7: see *Uneasy Riders*

Native Son
US 1986 112m colour
Cinecom/Diane Silver/American Playhouse/Cinetudes
A poor black teenager commits murder.
Heavy-going adaptation of a novel seen in some American quarters as a symbol of classic guilt.
w Richard Wesley *novel* Richard Wright *d* Jerrold Freedman *ph* Thomas Burstyn *m* James Mtume
☆ Carroll Baker, Akousuwa Busia, Matt Dillon, Art Evans, Elizabeth McGovern, John McMartin, Geraldine Page
† A low-budget Argentine version had been filmed in 1950 by Pierre Chenal, with the author in the leading role

Nattevagten: see *Nightwatch*

Nattlek: see *Night Games*

Nattvardsgästerna: see *Winter Light*

'He lived for a dream that wouldn't die.'
The Natural *
US 1984 137m Technicolor
Tri-Star/Delphi II (Mark Johnson)
The life of a baseball star who reaches the heights and can only fall.
Curious attempt to modernize the King Arthur legend, with a baseball bat substituting for Excalibur and hints of magic everywhere. A generally mystifying if occasionally an attractive experience.
w Roger Towne, Phil Dusenberry *novel* Bernard Malamud *d* Barry Levinson *ph* Caleb Deschanel *m* Randy Newman
☆ Robert Redford, Robert Duvall, Glenn Close, Kim Basinger, Wilford Brimley, Barbara Hershey, Robert Prosky, Joe Don Baker, Richard Farnsworth
Glenn Close (supporting actress); photography; music; art direction

'In The Media Circus Of Life, They Were The Main Attraction.'
Natural Born Killers *
US 1994 119m Technicolor
Warner/Regency/Alcor/JD/Ixtlan/New Regency (Jame Hamsher, Don Murphy, Clayton Townsend)
A young couple become mass murderers and media favourites.
An over-the-top assault on an audience's sensibilities, making its points with a heavy hand and a brutally jokey style, utilizing every movie- and video-making style in its deadly assault through a dislocating barrage of images. The message of all this manipulation is that the media manipulate violence for their own sensationalist aims. As a technical exercise, it is dazzling; as a contribution to a moral debate, it is deadening.
w David Veloz, Richard Rutowski, Oliver Stone *story* Quentin Tarantino *ph* Robert Richardson *pd* Victor Kempster *ed* Hank Corwin, Brian Berdan
☆ Woody Harrelson (Mickey), Juliette Lewis (Mallory), Robert Downey Jnr (Wayne Gale), Tommy Lee Jones (Dwight McClusky), Rodney Dangerfield (Mallory's Dad), Edie McClurg (Mallory's Mom)
'Plunders every visual trick of avant-garde and mainstream cinema – morphing, back projection, slow motion, animation and pixilation on five kinds of film stock – and, for two delirious hours, pushes them in your face like a Cagney grapefruit. The actors go hyper-hyper, the camera is ever on the bias, the garish colors converge and collide into a vision of America in heat. The ride is fun, too, daredevil fun of the sort only Stone seems willing to provide in this timid-film era.' – *Richard Corliss, Time*
'The oddest thing about this would-be satire is that, for all the gore and hysteria, the film doesn't feel particularly impassioned; it's a frivolous barrage.' – *Terrence Rafferty, New Yorker*
'Oliver Stone would have a lot more chance of proving the proposition that violence is only exciting at second hand if he himself were able to show a prison riot without adding a pounding rock soundtrack. What makes him think he's a critic of an over-stimulated society when synthetic adrenalin is his stock-in-trade?' – *Adam Mars-Jones, Independent*
'How is it possible that Stone has made a picture of such staggering awfulness and jaw-dropping amateurishness?' – *Henry Joyce, Movie Collector*
'Isn't so much a cry against the dying of the light as the kind of movie that dims the light in the first place. We all make mistakes. But this time Stone has made a colossal blunder.' – *Derek Malcolm, Guardian*
'It's like watching two weeks of television in two hours.' – *Oliver Stone*
† Quentin Tarantino objected when his original script was rewritten by Stone.
†† Although the video was given an '18' certificate in Britain, Warner Home Video withdrew its UK release indefinitely following mass killings in Scotland and Tasmania in 1996.

A Natural Born Salesman: see *Earthworm Tractors*

The Nature of the Beast *
GB 1988 95m colour
Cannon/Film Four International/British Screen (Joanna Smith)
In a small industrial town, where unemployment is rife, a young boy and his friend stalk a mysterious beast that is killing animals.
An unsuccessful allegory of social disintegration that stays in the shadow of Kes.
w Janni Howker *novel* Janni Howker *d* Franco Rosso *ph* Nat Crosby *m* Stanley Myers, Hans Zimmer *pd* Jamie Leonard *ed* George Akers
☆ Lynton Dearden, Paul Simpson, Tony Melody, Freddie Fletcher, Dave Hill, Roberta Kerr, David Fleeshman

The Nature of the Beast: see *Hatchet Man (1994)*

Naughty Arlette: see *The Romantic Age*

Naughty Blue Knickers: see *The Folies of Elodie*

Naughty but Nice
US 1939 90m bw
Warner (Sam Bischoff)
A professor of classical music accidentally writes a popular song.
Mildly amusing comedy musical with all the tunes adapted from the classics (cf That Night with You*).*
w Jerry Wald, Richard Macaulay *d* Ray Enright *ph* Arthur L. Todd *songs* Harry Warren, Johnny Mercer
☆ Dick Powell, Ann Sheridan, Ronald Reagan, Gale Page, ZaSu Pitts, Jerry Colonna

Naughty Marietta **
US 1935 106m bw
MGM (Hunt Stromberg)
A French princess goes to America and falls in love with an Indian scout.
Period operetta which set the seal of success on the MacDonald-Eddy team. In itself, dated but quite pleasing for those who like the genre.
w John Lee Mahin, Frances Goodrich, Albert Hackett *operetta* Rida Johnson Young *d* W. S. Van Dyke *ph* William Daniels *m* Victor Herbert *ad* Cedric Gibbons
☆ *Jeanette MacDonald, Nelson Eddy*, Frank Morgan, Elsa Lanchester, Douglass Dumbrille, Joseph Cawthorn, Cecilia Parker, Walter Kingsford
'Slow-moving operetta which singing must sustain.' – *Variety*
'When these two profiles come together to sing Ah Sweet Mystery of Life, it's beyond camp, it's in a realm of its own.' – *Judith Crist, 1977*
best picture

The Naughty Nineties
US 1945 72m bw
Universal (Edward L. Hartmann, John Grant)
Two incompetents help an old showboat owner.
Dim star comedy apart from the team's rendition of their most famous routine, 'Who's On First'.
w Edmund L. Hartmann, John Grant, Edmund Joseph, Hal Fimberg *d* Jean Yarbrough *ph* George Robinson
☆ Bud Abbott, Lou Costello, Henry Travers, Alan Curtis, Rita Johnson, Joe Sawyer

The Navigator ***
US 1924 63m approx (24 fps) bw silent
Metro-Goldwyn/Buster Keaton (Joseph M. Schenck)
A millionaire and his girl are the only people on a transatlantic liner marooned in mid-ocean.
A succession of hilarious sight gags: the star in top form.
w Jean Havez, Clyde Bruckman, J. A. Mitchell *d* Buster Keaton, Donald Crisp *ph* Elgin Lessley, Byron Houck
☆ *Buster Keaton*, Kathryn McGuire
'Studded with hilarious moments and a hundred and one adroit gags.' – *Photoplay*

The Navigator: A Medieval Odyssey **
Australia 1988 91m colour/bw
Recorded Releasing/Arenafilm (John Maynard, Gary Hannam)
Medieval villagers, fearful of the Black Death, go on a pilgrimage through a mine and emerge in the modern world.
Oddly disturbing fable, imaginatively presented.
w Vincent Ward, Kely Lyons, Geoff Chapple *d* Vincent Ward *ph* Geoffrey Simpson *m* Davood A. Tabrizi *pd* Sally Campbell *ed* John Scott
☆ Bruce Lyons, Chris Haywood, Hamish McFarlane, Marshall Napier, Noel Appleby, Paul Livingstone, Sarah Pierse, Mark Wheatley, Tony Herbert

The Navigators **
GB/Spain/Germany 2001 96m colour
BFI/Parallax/Road Movies/Tornasol/Alta (Rebecca O'Brien)
When British Rail is privatised, a group of workers responsible for track maintenance discover that their skills are no longer valued.
Topical drama, full of righteous anger at the dismantling of Britain's rail service to the detriment of efficiency and safety, but the script is sometimes too polemical for its own good.
w Rob Dawber *d* Ken Loach *ph* Mike Eley, Barry Ackroyd *m* George Fenton *pd* Martin Johnson *ed* Jonathan Morris
☆ Dean Andrews (John), Tom Craig (Mick), Joe Duttine (Paul), Steve Huison (Jim), Venn Tracey (Gerry), Andy Swallow (Len), Sean Glenn (Harpic), Charlie Brown (Jack), Juliet Bates (Fiona), Angela Saville (Tracy)
'A very low-key, modest film, but an important one, and one to which audiences, given the chance, should certainly respond.' – *David Stratton, Variety*

'It is not the victory that is important, it is how the game is played!'
Navy Blue and Gold
US 1937 93m bw
Sam Zimbalist/MGM
An unpopular naval cadet makes good.
Ingenuous flagwaver, like a wrap-up of umpteen others but with better production.
w George Bruce *d* Sam Wood
☆ Robert Young, James Stewart, Florence Rice, Billie Burke, Lionel Barrymore, Tom Brown, Samuel S. Hinds, Paul Kelly
'Expertly made and sure box office.' – *Variety*

Navy Blues
US 1941 109m bw
Warner (Jerry Wald)
Naval ratings get into trouble in Honolulu.
Undernourished musical comedy with not too much of either commodity.
w Jerry Wald, Richard Macaulay, Arthur T. Horman *d* Lloyd Bacon *ph* Tony Gaudio *ch* Seymour Felix *songs* Arthur Schwartz, Johnny Mercer
☆ Ann Sheridan, Jack Oakie, Martha Raye, Jack Haley, Herbert Anderson, Jack Carson, Richard Lane, Jackie Gleason, Howard da Silva

The Navy Comes Through
US 1942 81m bw
RKO
The story of a merchant marine ship.
Propaganda potboiler with a reasonably efficient cast and production.
w Roy Chanslor, Aeneas Mackenzie *story* Borden Chase *d* A. Edward Sutherland *ph* Nick Musuraca *m* Roy Webb
☆ Pat O'Brien, George Murphy, Jane Wyatt, Jackie Cooper, Carl Esmond, Max Baer, Desi Arnaz, Ray Collins

Navy SEALS
US 1990 114m Technicolor
Rank/Orion (Brenda Feigen, Bernard Williams)
Naval commandos attempt to kidnap an Arab terrorist and destroy a missile store in Lebanon.
Flaccid action picture, peopled by comic-strip stereotypes and full of nothing but sound and fury.
w Chuck Pfarrer, Gary Goldman *d* Lewis Teague *ph* John A. Alonzo *m* Sylvester Levay *pd* Guy J. Comtois, Veronica Hadfield *ed* Don Zimmerman
☆ Charlie Sheen, Michael Biehn, Joanne Whalley-Kilmer, Rick Rossovich, Cyril O'Reilly, Bill Paxton, Dennis Haysbert, Paul Sanchez
'Quite what this balefully predictable action-adventure is trying to prove totally escapes me. Unless it is that there is nothing much these days that the American public won't take in the way of flag-waving juvenilia.' – *Derek Malcolm, Guardian*

The Navy Steps Out: see *A Girl, a Guy and a Gob*

The Navy versus The Night Monsters
US 1965 90m DeLuxe
Standard Club (George Edwards)
aka: *Monsters of the Night*
aka: *Night Crawlers*
Botanical specimens taken from the Antarctic to a remote naval base include man-eating plants.
There is a certain silly pleasure to be derived from watching Mamie Van Doren being threatened by carnivorous vegetables, which hardly look a match for her, but The Day of the Triffids *it isn't, despite some atmospheric photography.*
wd Michael A. Hoey *novel Monsters from the Earth's End* by Murray Leinster *ph* Stanley Cortez *m* Gordon Zahler *ad* Paul Sylos *ed* George White
☆ Anthony Eisley, Mamie Van Doren, Walter Sande, Bobby Van, Billy Gray, Phillip Terry, Pamela Kellino

Navy Wife
US 1935 72m bw
Fox
A girl who marries a navy doctor is unhappy with the life.
Routine domestic drama with a propaganda angle.
w Sonya Levien *novel Beauty's Daughter* by Kathleen Norris *d* Allan Dwan
☆ Claire Trevor, Ralph Bellamy, Jane Darwell, Ben Lyon, Warren Hymer, Kathleen Burke
'Problem play for the duals.' – *Variety*

Navy Wife
US 1956 83m bw
Allied Artists
GB title: *Mother, Sir!*
A commander's wife visits her husband in Japan and learns about Japanese attitudes.
Silly hands-across-the-sea comedy which takes a long time to get nowhere.
w Kay Lenard *d* Edward Bernds *ph* Wilfred Cline *m* Hans Salter
☆ Joan Bennett, Gary Merrill, Shirley Yagamuchi, Judy Nugent

Nazarin *
Mexico 1958 94m bw
Barbachano Ponce
A Catholic priest tries to take the teachings of Christ literally, but is drastically misunderstood.
A black atheistic satire pretty typical of its director, but not among his most enjoyable works.
w Julio Alejandro, Luis Buñuel *novel* Benito Perez Galdos *d Luis Buñuel* *ph* Gabriel Figueroa
☆ Francisco Rabal, Marga Lopez, Rita Macedo, Ignacio Lopez Tarso

Nazi Agent *
US 1942 84m bw
MGM (Irving Asher)
A German-American is forced by his Nazi twin to help a group of German spies.
Modest suspenser with a plot twist similar to The Great Impersonation *and* Dead Ringer.
w Paul Gangelin, John Meehan Jnr *d* Jules Dassin *ph* Harry Stradling *m* Lennie Hayton
☆ Conrad Veidt, Ann Ayars, Frank Reicher, Dorothy Tree, Martin Kosleck

Neak Sre: see *Rice People*

The Neanderthal Man
US 1953 75m bw
United Artists/Global
A scientist transforms a cat into a sabre-toothed tiger and himself into a neanderthal man; he is then eaten by the tiger.
By no means as amusing as it sounds.
w Aubrey Wisberg, Jack Pollexfen *d* E. A. Dupont *ph* Stanley Cortez
☆ Robert Shayne, Richard Crane, Doris Merrick, Joyce Terry

Near Dark
US 1987 94m colour
Entertainment/Scotti Brothers/International Video Entertainment (Steven-Charles Jaffe)
A cowboy is seduced into joining a roving gang of vampires.
Fast moving, moderately successful attempt to bring the vampire movie screaming into the 20th century.
w Eric Red, Kathryn Bigelow *d* Kathryn Bigelow *ph* Adam Greenberg *m* Tangerine Dream *pd* Stephen Altman *ed* Howard Smith
☆ Adrian Pasdar, Jenny Wright, Lance Henriksen, Bill Paxton, Jenette Goldstein, Tim Thomerson, Joshua Miller
'Projects a truly upsetting image of revulsion and horror, and its scenes of blood-letting – especially a long spectacular set piece featuring the killing of the clientele of a lowlife tavern – are not merely gross, but genuinely disturbing.' – *Henry Sheehan, L.A. Reader*

Near Misses: see *Near Mrs*

Near Mrs
US/France 1991 89m colour
Chrysalide/Canal+/Movie Group (Monique Annaud)
aka: *Near Misses*
A bigamist runs into difficulties when he assumes the identity of a marine in order to have a dirty weekend with his mistress.
Frenetic but rarely amusing farce; its opening sequence of multiple murder kills the fun before the film has begun.
w Peter Baloff, David Wollert *d* Baz Taylor *ph* Yves Dahan *m* Didier Vasseur *ad* Nicolas Prier *ed* Michele Robert-Lauliac
☆ Judge Reinhold, Casey Siemaszko, Rebecca Pauly, Cecile Paoli, Kashia Figura, Muriel Combeau, Andrzej Jagora

The Near Room
GB 1995 90m colour
Metrodome/Inverclyde/Glasgow Film Fund/British Screen (Len Crooks)
An investigative journalist, who is hired by his former wife to track down a missing teenager involved in prostitution and drugs, realizes that she is the illegimate daughter he abandoned at birth.
A low-budget film noir, stylishly made but lacking conviction and often bordering on the incomprehensible.
w Robert Murphy *d* David Hayman *ph* Kevin Rowley *m* James Grant, Paul McGeechan *pd* Andy Harris *ed* Martin Sharpe
☆ Adrian Dunbar, David O'Hara, Julie Graham, David Hayman, Tom Watson, James Ellis, Robert Pugh, Emma Faulkner, Andy Serkis, Peter McDougall
'Aspires to delve into the dark side: to show madness, violence and exploitation. Instead, it is as ludicrous and as luridly enjoyable as an old B-movie.' – *Geoffrey Macnab, Sight and Sound*

Nearly a Nasty Accident
GB 1961 91m bw
British Lion/Britannia/Marlow (Bertram Ostrer)
A mild-mannered aircraftman causes disaster wherever he goes.
Familiar faces just about save from disaster this underscripted comedy for indulgent audiences.
w Jack Davies, Hugh Woodruff *play Touch Wood* by David Stringer, David Carr *d* Don Chaffey *ph* Paul Beeson *m* Ken Jones
☆ Kenneth Connor, Jimmy Edwards, Shirley Eaton, Richard Wattis, Ronnie Stevens, Jon Pertwee, Eric Barker, Peter Jones, Jack Watling, Joyce Carey, Terry Scott

'Neath the Arizona Skies
US 1934 54m bw
Monogram/Lone Star (Paul Malvern)
A cowboy searches for the father of a young Indian girl, who is heiress to oil riches, and threatened by bandits.
One of the nine films that Wayne rolled out in the same year, and a standard production-line effort, with the usual fist- and gunfights, chases, and good triumphing over evil.
w Burl Tuttle *d* Harry Fraser *ph* Archie Stout *ad* E. R. Hickson *ed* Charles Hunt
☆ John Wayne, Sheila Terry, Shirley Jane Rickert, Jack Rockwell, Yakima Canutt, Weston Edwards, Buffalo Bill Jnr, George Hayes

'Three men and a woman face death beside a man they want to kill!'
The Nebraskan
US 1953 66m Technicolor 3D
Columbia
An army scout proves the innocence of an Indian supposed to have murdered a Sioux chief.
Two-bit Western which looked even worse in three dimensions.
w David Lang, Martin Berkeley *d* Fred F. Sears
☆ Phil Carey, Roberta Haynes, Wallace Ford, Richard Webb, Lee Van Cleef

Necessary Roughness
US 1991 104m Technicolor
UIP/Paramount (Mace Neufeld, Robert Rehme)
After a college football team has been dismissed for corruption, a coach attempts to create a new squad from unathletic students.
Drear movie that is never less than predictable and never more than tedious.
w Rick Natkin, David Fuller *d* Stan Dragoti *ph* Peter Stein *m* Bill Conti *pd* Paul Peters *ed* John Wright, Steve Mirkovich, Wayne Wahrman
☆ Scott Bakula, Robert Loggia, Hector Elizondo, Harley Jane Kozak, Larry Miller, Sinbad, Fred Dalton Thompson
'All the expected clichés of the losers-make-a-comeback plot.' – *Variety*
'As phoney as the Astroturf on which most of it takes place.' – *Philip French, Observer*

Necromancy
US 1973 83m colour
Cinerama (Bert I. Gordon)
Two young people become involved in small-town witchcraft.
Low-key, low-talent thriller overbalanced by its star.
wd Bert I. Gordon *ph* Winton C. Hoch *m* Fred Karger
☆ Orson Welles, Pamela Franklin, Michael Ontkean, Lee Purcell

'It'll Take You To Hell and Back...'
Necronomicon
US 1993 Foto-Kem
August/Davis Film/Brian Yuzna (Samuel Hadida, Brian Yuzna)
Horror writer H. P. Lovecraft discovers that a copy of the *Necronomicon*, containing the secrets of the universe, is in America and seeks it out to inspire his work.
Dull compendium of three stories of demonic possession, with cheesey special effects and little that will either thrill or terrify.
w Brent V. Friedman, Christophe Gans, Kazunori Ito, Brian Yuzna *d* Brian Yuzna, Christophe Gans, Shusuke Kaneko *ph* Gerry Lively, Russ Brandt *m* Joseph Lo Duca, Daniel Licht *pd* Antony Tremblay *ed* Christopher Roth *sp* Thomas C. Rainone, John Vulich, Magic Media, Screaming Mad George, Todd Masters, Bart Mixon's Monster Fixin's and others
☆ Jeffrey Combs, Bruce Payne, Belinda Bauer, David Warner, Signy Coleman, Don Calfa, Bess Meyer, Millie Perkins, Dennis Christopher, Maria Ford, Richard Lynch
'B horror movies are often fun but this is Pillocksville.' – *Derek Malcolm, Guardian*

Necronomicon – Geträumte Sünden: see *Succubus*

Ned Kelly
GB 1970 103m Technicolor
UA/Woodfall (Neil Hartley)
The career of a 19th-century Australian outlaw.
Obstinately unlikeable action picture with some kind of message which never becomes clear amid all the cleverness.
w Tony Richardson, Ian Jones *d* Tony Richardson *ph* Gerry Fisher *m* Shel Silverstein *pd* Jocelyn Herbert
☆ Mick Jagger, Allen Bickford, Geoff Gilmour, Mark McManus

'The town of Castle Rock just made a deal with the Devil ... Now it's time to pay!'
Needful Things
US 1993 120m Technicolor
Rank/Castle Rock/New Line (Jack Cummins)
The owner of an antique shop creates havoc and murder by offering customers what they want in return for carrying out practical jokes on their neighbours.
A down-market version of Faust that provides some moments of black comedy in its depiction of small-town rivalries, but outstays its welcome.
w W. D. Richter *novel* Stephen King *d* Fraser C. Heston *ph* Tony Westman *m* Patrick Doyle *pd* Douglas Higgins *ed* Rob Kobrin *sp* make-up: Tibor Furkas
☆ Max von Sydow, Ed Harris, Bonnie Bedelia, Amanda Plummer, J. T. Walsh, Ray McKinnon, Duncan Fraser, Shane Meier, Valri Bromfield
'This darkly comic picture proves a sadistic, mean-spirited, overlong exercise that should have a devilish time sustaining any box-office fire.' – *Brian Lowry, Variety*

Negatives *
GB 1968 98m Eastmancolor
Crispin/Kettledrum (Judd Bernard)
Three people indulge in sexual fantasies involving Dr Crippen and Baron von Richthofen.
Smoothly done but impenetrable psychological poppycock: what is fact and what is fancy, only the author knows.
w Peter Everett, Roger Lowry *novel* Peter Everett *d* Peter Medak *ph* Ken Hodges *m* Basil Kirchin
☆ Glenda Jackson, Peter McEnery, Diane Cilento, Maurice Denham, Stephen Lewis, Norman Rossington

'Justice At Any Price.'
The Negotiator
US 1998 138m Technicolor Panavision
Warner/Regency/Mandeville/Taurus (David Hoberman, Arnon Milchan)
Realizing that he is being set up by his colleagues, a police hostage negotiator takes hostages of his own, and is besieged by corrupt cops who want him dead.
A noisy thriller that delivers big bangs and obtrusive acting.
w James DeMonaco, Kevin Fox *d* F. Gary Gray *ph* Russell Carpenter *m* Graeme Revell *pd* Holger Gross *ed* Christian Wagner
☆ Samuel L. Jackson, Kevin Spacey, David Morse, Ron Rifkin, John Spencer, J. T. Walsh, Regina Taylor, Siobahn Fallon, Paul Giamatti
'Doesn't stretch the Hollywood thriller much beyond its big, loud self-important traditions.' – *Anthony Quinn, Independent*

Neighbors *
US 1981 94m Technicolor
Columbia/Zanuck-Brown
A staid suburbanite is first irritated, then taken over by his splashy neighbours.
Hit-or-miss but generally quite funny comedy in a style familiar to viewers of American late night television.
w Larry Gelbart *novel* Thomas Berger *d* John G. Avildsen *ph* Gerald Hirschfeld *m* Bill Conti *pd* Peter Larkin *ed* Jan Kurson
☆ John Belushi, Dan Aykroyd, Kathryn Walker, Cathy Moriarty, Igors Gavon, Dru-Ann Chukron

Neither the Sea nor the Sand
GB 1972 94m Eastmancolor
LMG/Portland (Jack Smith, Peter Fetterman)
Holidaying in Jersey, a married woman begins a love-affair with a local man which survives his sudden death.
An attempt at a Gothic romance ruined by half-hearted acting and direction; all that remains is a dull zombie movie and an unpleasant exercise in necrophilia.
w Gordon Honeycombe, Rosemary Davies *novel* Gordon Honeycombe *d* Fred Burnley *ph* David Muir *m* Nachum Heiman *ad* Michael Bastow *ed* Norman Wanstall
☆ Susan Hampshire, Frank Finlay, Michael Petrovitch, Michael Craze, Jack Lambert, Betty Duncan, David Garth, Tony Booth
'To depict the macabre in the midst of the everyday requires a greater degree of artifice than is displayed here.' – *MFB*
'Hampshire and Petrovitch are no Heathcliff and Cathy, and the director's "realistic" style which stops short at the genuinely macabre makes a mockery of the story's metaphysical overtones.' – *Films and Filming*

Nel Segno di Roma: see *Sign of the Gladiator*

'An Extraordinary Motion Picture About the Power of Innocence.'
'Her heart. Her soul. Her language are a mystery ... A mystery called...'
Nell
US 1994 113m colour Panavision
Polygram/Egg Pictures/Lost Pond (Jodie Foster, Renée Missel)
Two doctors study, and try to communicate with, a young woman, brought up in the wilderness and speaking a language only she and her speech-impaired mother, now dead, can understand.
This is little more than an ordinary romance between two opposites, spiced with a bizarre turn from Jodie Foster; it confuses innocence and ignorance.
w William Nicholson, Mark Handley *play* *Idioglossia* by Mark Handley *d* Michael Apted *m* Mark Isham *pd* Dante Spinotti *ed* Jim Clark
☆ Jodie Foster, Liam Neeson, Natasha Richardson, Richard Libertini, Nick Searcy, Robin Mullins, Jeremy Davies
'One of those films about the mentally challenged that is so anxious to be politically correct that it over-compensates every which way it can.' – *Derek Malcolm, Guardian*
Jodie Foster

Nell Gwyn **
GB 1934 85m bw
B and D (Herbert Wilcox)
The affair of Charles II and an orange seller.
Naïve, vivid account of a famous couple; physically cheap and rather faded, but the best film on the subject and one of the best covering this period.
w Miles Malleson *d* Herbert Wilcox *ph* F. A. Young
☆ Anna Neagle, Cedric Hardwicke, Jeanne de Casalis, Muriel George, Miles Malleson, Esmé Percy, Moore Marriott
'Slow costumer, also lacking marquee value.' – *Variety*

Nelly and M Arnaud **
France/Germany/Italy 1995 106m colour
Guild/TFI/Cecchi Gori/Prokino/Canal/Alain Sarde
A young wife leaves her husband to form an uneasy relationship with a wealthy elderly businessman for whom she works as a secretary.
A cool, immacutely acted, restrained drama of two people unable or unwilling to resolve their feelings for one another.
w Claude Sautet, Jacques Fieschi, Yves Ulmann *d* Claude Sautet *ph* Jean-François Robin *m* Philippe Sarde *pd* Carlos Conti *ed* Jacqueline Thiedot
☆ *Emmanuelle Béart, Michel Serrault*, Jean-Hugues Anglade, Claire Nadeau, Françoise Brion, Michèle Laroque, Michel Lonsdale
'Orchestrates the progress of the obsessional relationship with the precision that only a director fully in command of both his style and material can muster. As a quiet, intimate dissection of the emotions, it is hard to beat.' – *Derek Malcolm, Guardian*

The Nelson Affair: see *Bequest to the Nation*

The Nelson Touch: see *Corvette K 225*

'In The Future ... It Pays To Be More Than Human.'
Nemesis
US 1993 95m colour
Imperial (Ash R. Shah, Eric Karson, Tom Karnowski)
In Los Angeles in 2027, where most people speak with thick foreign accents, a cop shot to pieces is reassembled as an android for a special assignment and uncovers a plot to take over the world.
Derivative and violent action film, strictly for those whose idea of a good time is bimbos with big guns.
w Rebecca Charles *d* Albert Pyun *ph* George Mooradian *m* Michel Rubini *pd* E. Colleen Saro *ed* David Kern, Mark Conte *sp* Gene Warren Jnr, Fantasy II Film Effects
☆ Olivier Gruner, Tim Thomerson, Cary-Hiroyuki Tagawa, Merle Kennedy, Yuji Okumoto, Marjorie Monaghan, Brion James, Deborah Shelton
'Fails in almost every respect.' – *Variety*

The Neon Bible *
GB/US 1995 92m Metrocolor Cinemascope
Artificial Eye/Mayfair/Scala/Channel 4 (Elizabeth Karlsen, Olivia Stewart)
A boy grows up in Georgia in the 1940s, living with a harsh and unsuccessful father and his increasingly demented mother, with only his aunt, a singer, adding any colour to his narrow life.
A carefully composed account of a very limited and repressed existence, much in the style of Davies's earlier The Long Day Closes, *but lacking its wider resonance.*
wd Terence Davies *novel* John Kennedy Toole *ph* Mick Coulter *pd* Christopher Hobbs *ed* Charles Rees
☆ Gena Rowlands, Jacob Tierney, Diana Scarwid, Denis Leary, Leo Burmester, Frances Conroy, Peter McRobbie, Drake Bell
'Kitchen-sink drama that pulls its own plug.' – *Tom Shone, Sunday Times*

The Neptune Disaster: see *The Neptune Factor*

'Wherever you've been – this is where you've never been before!'
The Neptune Factor
Canada 1972 98m DeLuxe Panavision
TCF/Quadrant/Bellevue-Pathé (Sanford Howard)
later retitled: *The Neptune Disaster*
American oceanologists conduct an experiment in underwater living.
Wet 'actioner' in which very little happens except a few porthole views of magnified fish.
w Jack de Witt *d* Daniel Petrie *ph* Harry Makin *m* Lalo Schifrin
☆ Ben Gazzara, Walter Pidgeon, Yvette Mimieux, Ernest Borgnine, Chris Wiggins

Neptune's Daughter *
US 1949 93m Technicolor
MGM (Jack Cummings)
A lady bathing suit designer has a South American romance.
Generally thought one of the better aquatic musicals, and certainly very typical of them and its studio at this time.
w Dorothy Kingsley *d* Edward Buzzell *ph* Charles Rosher *m* George Stoll *songs* Frank Loesser
☆ Esther Williams, Red Skelton, Ricardo Montalban, Betty Garrett, Keenan Wynn, Xavier Cugat and his Orchestra, Mike Mazurki, Ted de Corsia, Mel Blanc
song 'Baby, It's Cold Outside'

Neskolko Intervyu Po Lichnyam Voprosam: see *Several Interviews On Personal Problems*

The Net
GB 1953 86m bw
Rank/Two Cities (Anthony Darnborough)
US title: *Project M7*
Tension among boffins in an aviation research station leads to murder and the discovery of a spy.
Low-key suspenser, quite adequately presented.
w William Fairchild *novel* John Pudney *d* Anthony Asquith *ph* Desmond Dickinson *m* Benjamin Frankel
☆ Phyllis Calvert, Noel Willman, Herbert Lom, James Donald, Robert Beatty, Muriel Pavlow, Walter Fitzgerald, Maurice Denham

The Net
US 1995 112m Technicolor
Columbia (Irwin Winkler, Rob Cowan)
A reclusive software tester's life is threatened after she discovers a conspiracy that allows crooks to gain access to, and manipulate, top-secret data held on government computers.
A dully paranoid thriller that is a bad imitation of Hitchcock. Its plot is full of implausibilities and it is also computer illiterate, which doesn't help, though Sandra Bullock's performance does, even if it is not enough to save the film.
w John Brancato, Michael Ferris *d* Irwin Winkler *ph* Jack N. Green *m* Mark Isham *pd* Dennis Washington *ed* Richard Halsey
☆ Sandra Bullock, Jeremy Northam, Dennis Miller, Diane Baker, Wendy Gazelle, Ken Howard, Ray McKinnon
'This high-tech but modestly scaled meller adroitly alternates between anxiety provoked by powerful computers and old-fashioned peril posed by duplicitous men, dark alleys, speeding cars and deserted warehouses.' – *Todd McCarthy, Variety*
† The film was the basis of a US TV series, *The Net*, starring Brooke Langton.

'Television will never be the same!'
'Prepare yourself for a perfectly outrageous motion picture!'
Network ****
US 1976 121m Metrocolor Panavision
MGM/UA (Howard Gottfried, Fred Caruso)
A network news commentator begins to say what he thinks about the world and becomes a new messiah to the people and an embarrassment to his sponsors.
A deliberately melodramatic satire on media corruption, it is passionate and compulsively watchable in its attack on demagoguery and in its depiction of the dangerous madness exploited by the mass media. What once seemed overheated satire has come, with time, to resemble accurate reporting. Its very existence in a commercial system is as remarkable as its box-office success.
w *Paddy Chayefsky* *d* Sidney Lumet *ph* Owen Roizman *m* Elliot Lawrence
☆ *Peter Finch, William Holden*, Faye Dunaway, Robert Duvall, Wesley Addy, Ned Beatty, Beatrice Straight, John Carpenter
HOWARD BEALE (PETER FINCH) ON LIVE TELEVISION: 'I don't know what to do about the depression and the inflation and the Russians and the crime in the streets. All I know is that first you've got to get mad. You've got to say: "I'm a human being, god damn it, my life has some value!" So I want you to get up now. I want all of you to get up out of your chairs. I want you to get up right now and go to the window, open it and stick your head out and yell "I'm mad as hell, and I'm not going to take this any more!"'
DITTO: 'Ladies and gentlemen, I would like at this moment to announce that I will be retiring from this programme in two weeks' time because of poor ratings. Since this show was the only thing I had going for me in my life, I have decided to kill myself. I'm going to blow my brains out right on this programme a week from today.'
MAX SCHUMACHER (WILLIAM HOLDEN): 'You're television incarnate, Diana, indifferent to suffering, insensitive to joy. All of life is reduced to the common rubble of banality. War, murder, death – all the same to you as bottles of beer, and the daily business of life is a corrupt comedy. You even shatter the sensations of time and space into split seconds and instant replays. You're madness, Diana.'
'The cast of this messianic farce take turns yelling at us soulless masses.' – *New Yorker*
'Too much of this film has the hectoring stridency of tabloid headlines.' – *Michael Billington, Illustrated London News*
† The theme was taken up a year later in the shortlived TV series *W.E.B.*
Paddy Chayefsky; Peter Finch; Faye Dunaway; Beatrice Straight
best picture; Sidney Lumet; Owen Roizman; William Holden; Ned Beatty
Peter Finch

Nevada Smith *
US 1966 131m Eastmancolor Panavision
Avco/Solar (Joe Levine, Henry Hathaway)
A cowboy takes a long revenge on the outlaws who murdered his parents.
Violent, sour, occasionally lively but frequently boring Western melodrama on a well worn theme.
w John Michael Hayes, from the 'early life' of a character in The Carpetbaggers by Harold Robbins
d Henry Hathaway *ph* Lucien Ballard *m* Alfred Newman
☆ Steve McQueen, Karl Malden, Brian Keith, Suzanne Pleshette, Arthur Kennedy, Janet Margolin, Howard da Silva, Raf Vallone, Pat Hingle

The Nevadan
US 1950 81m Cinecolor
Harry Joe Brown/Columbia
GB title: *The Man from Nevada*
A marshal recovers stolen gold.
Solid Western programmer, compromised by poor colour.
w George W. George, George F. Slavin *d* Gordon Douglas *ph* Charles Lawton Jnr *m* Arthur Morton
☆ Randolph Scott, Dorothy Malone, Forrest Tucker, Frank Faylen, George Macready

Never a Dull Moment
US 1943 60m bw
Universal
Three comedians prevent a night-club owner from carrying out a robbery.
The last thin vehicle for a famous comedy trio; even here they have their moments.
w Mel Ronson, Stanley Roberts *d* Edward Lilley
☆ The Ritz Brothers, Frances Langford, Mary Beth Hughes, George Zucco, Franklin Pangborn

Never a Dull Moment
US 1950 89m bw
RKO (Harriet Parsons)
A lady music critic marries a rodeo cowboy and finds life hard down on the ranch.
Very mild star programmer.
w Lou Breslow, Doris Anderson *novel* *Who Could Ask for Anything More?* by Kay Swift *d* George Marshall *ph* Joseph Walker *m* Frederick Hollander *md* Constantin Bakaleinikoff
☆ Irene Dunne, Fred MacMurray, William Demarest, Andy Devine, Gigi Perreau, Natalie Wood, Philip Ober, Jack Kirkwood

Never a Dull Moment
US 1967 100m Technicolor
Walt Disney (Ron Miller)
An unsuccessful actor is mistaken for a notorious gangster.
Slapstick romp with vigour but not much flair.
w A. J. Carothers *novel* John Godey *d* Jerry Paris *ph* William Snyder *m* Robert F. Brunner
☆ Dick Van Dyke, Edward G. Robinson, Dorothy Provine, Henry Silva, Joanna Moore, Tony Bill, Slim Pickens, Jack Elam

'Some Things Are Worth Waiting For.'
'The Class Geek Just Turned Chic.'
Never Been Kissed
US 1998 107m DeLuxe Panavision
TCF/Fox 2000/Flower/Bushwood (Sandy Isaac, Nancy Juvonen)
A journalist in her mid-20s pretends to be a high-school girl so that she can write a feature on modern teenagers.
Mildly amusing comedy of a clash between generations, in which the teens are cool and the adults are silly; teenagers are most likely to enjoy it.
w Abby Kohn, Marc Silverstein *d* Raja Gosnell *ph* Alex Nepomniaschy *m* David Newman *pd* Steven Jordan *ed* Debra Chiate, Marcelo Sansevieri
☆ Drew Barrymore (Josie Geller), David Arquette (Rob Geller), Michael Vartan (Sam Coulson), Leelee Sobieski (Aldys), Jeremy Jordan (Guy Perkins), Molly Shannon (Anita), Garry Marshall

(Rigfort), John C. Reilly (Gus), Sean Whalen (Merkin)

'If you like your cinema entertainment broad and drippy, then this is for you.' – *James Cameron-Wilson, Film Review*

'They thought he couldn't do the job: that's why they chose him!'

Never Cry Wolf

US 1983 105m Technicolor

Walt Disney

A scientist is dumped alone in the Arctic to collect evidence against wolves.

Weird fable whose comic asides diminish its serious intent, and whose leading characterization is so eccentric as to bewilder any audience.

w Curtis Hanson, Sam Hamm, Richard Kletter *book* Farley Mowat *d* Carroll Ballard

☆ Charles Martin Smith, Brian Dennehy, Samson Jorah

'There are sequences in this movie that make your jaw drop open out of genuine amazement. To put it simply, he shows you sights you've never seen before ... It's no mere environmentalist film, but a meditation on survival and the story of its hero's inner rebirth.' – *David Ansen, Newsweek*

Never Give a Sucker an Even Break *

US 1941 70m bw

Universal

GB title: *What a Man*

W. C. Fields dives off an aeroplane into the lap of a young woman who has never seen a man; she falls in love with him.

Stupefyingly inept in its scripting and pacing, this comedy is often irresistibly funny because of the anti-everything personality of its writer-star. No one else could have got away with it, or would have been likely to try.

w John T. Neville, Prescott Chaplin *story* Otis Criblecoblis (W. C. Fields) *d* Edward F. Cline *ph* Charles Van Enger *m* Frank Skinner

☆ *W. C. Fields*, Gloria Jean, Leon Errol, Butch and Buddy, Franklin Pangborn, Anne Nagel, Mona Barrie, Susan Miller, Margaret Dumont

'A beautifully timed exhibition of mock pomposity, puzzled ineffectualness, subtle understatement and true-blue nonchalance.' – *James Agee*

Never Give an Inch: see *Sometimes a Great Notion*

Never Let Go

GB 1960 91m bw

Rank/Julian Wintle-Leslie Parkin (Peter de Sarigny)

A travelling salesman has his car stolen and stands up to the sadistic gang boss responsible.

Brutishly unattractive thriller, apparently designed for the sole purpose of giving Peter Sellers a villainous part.

w Alun Falconer *d* John Guillermin *ph* Christopher Challis *m* John Barry

☆ Richard Todd, Peter Sellers, Elizabeth Sellars, Adam Faith, Carol White, Mervyn Johns, Noel Willman

Never Let Me Go

GB 1953 94m bw

MGM (Clarence Brown)

After World War II an American correspondent marries a Russian ballerina but is later deported by the authorities.

Ho-hum romantic melodrama, quite interestingly cast.

w Ronald Millar, George Froeschel *novel Came the Dawn* by Roger Bax *d* Delmer Daves *ph* Robert Krasker *m* Hans May

☆ Clark Gable, Gene Tierney, Richard Haydn, Belita, Bernard Miles, Kenneth More, Karel Stepanek, Theodore Bikel, Frederick Valk

Never Look Back

GB 1952 73m bw

Exclusive/Hammer (Michael Carreras)

A lady barrister finds she must defend an old boyfriend on a murder charge.

Plausible drama which never quite comes to the boil.

w John Hunter, Guy Morgan, Francis Searle *d* Francis Searle *ph* Reginald Wyer *m* Temple Abady

☆ Rosamund John, Hugh Sinclair, Guy Middleton, Henry Edwards, Terence Longdon

Never Love a Stranger

US 1958 93m bw

Harold Robbins/Allied Artists (Peter Gettlinger)

A Catholic boy who has become a gangster helps his Jewish friend who has become assistant district attorney to trap a vicious hoodlum.

The old Manhattan Melodrama theme is dusted off once again, this time to very little effect.

w Harold Robbins, Richard Day *novel* Harold Robbins *d* Robert Stevens *ph* Lee Garmes *m* Raymond Scott

☆ John Drew Barrymore, Steve McQueen, Robert Bray, Lita Milan, R. G. Armstrong, Salem Ludwig

Never on Sunday *

Greece 1959 97m bw

Lopert/Melinafilm (Jules Dassin)

original title: *Pote tin Kyriaki*

An American scholar in Greece is infatuated by a prostitute and sets about improving her.

Amiable if rather shoddy variation on Pygmalion*: the star performance and the music carried it, along with its own naughtiness, to success.*

wd Jules Dassin *ph* Jacques Natteau *m* Manos Hadjidakis

☆ *Melina Mercouri*, Jules Dassin, Georges Foundas, Titos Vandis, Despo Diamantidou

'It barely stands scrutiny, but it communicates cheerfulness, and this in itself is no mean achievement.' – *Penelope Houston, MFB*

title song (Manos Hadjidakis)

direction; script; Melina Mercouri

Never Put It in Writing *

GB 1963 93m bw

MGM/Andrew Stone

A young executive tries to recover from the mail an indiscreet letter he has written to his boss.

Frantic hit-or-miss farcical comedy distinguished by Dublin locations and cast.

wd Andrew Stone *ph* Martin Curtis *m* Frank Cordell

☆ Pat Boone, Fidelma Murphy, Reginald Beckwith, John Le Mesurier, Colin Blakely, Milo O'Shea

Never Say Die *

US 1939 80m bw

Paramount (Paul Jones)

A millionaire hypochondriac is convinced he is dying.

Thin farce with Hope on the very brink of stardom; some bright moments.

w Don Hartman, Frank Butler, Preston Sturges *d* Elliott Nugent *ph* Leo Tover *md* Boris Morros

☆ Martha Raye, Bob Hope, Andy Devine, Alan Mowbray, Gale Sondergaard, Sig Rumann, Ernest Cossart, Monty Woolley, Christian Rub

'Needs strong support for top dual spots.' – *Variety*

'The most enjoyable film for weeks ... consistently absurd ... no dignity, no passion, and a magnificent cast.' – *Graham Greene*

Never Say Goodbye

US 1946 97m bw

Warner (William Jacobs)

A seven-year-old girl draws her divorced parents back together.

Highly derivative romantic comedy mishmash which did its star's career no good at all.

w James V. Kern, I. A. L. Diamond, Lewis R. Foster, Ben and Norma Barzman *d* James V. Kern *ph* Arthur Edeson *m* Frederick Hollander

☆ Errol Flynn, Eleanor Parker, Lucile Watson, S. Z. Sakall, Donald Woods, Patti Brady, Forrest Tucker, Hattie McDaniel

Never Say Goodbye

US 1955 96m Technicolor

U-I (Albert J. Cohen)

In 1945 Berlin an American army doctor marries a pianist who is later trapped in the Russian zone; they meet years later in America.

Romantic drama aimed at a female audience, remade from This Love of Ours *(qv).*

w Charles Hoffman *d* Jerry Hopper *ph* Maury Gertsman *m* Frank Skinner

☆ Rock Hudson, George Sanders, Cornell Borchers, Ray Collins, David Janssen

Never Say Never Again *

GB 1983 134m Technicolor Panavision

Warner/Woodcote/Taliafilm (Jack Schwartzman)

James Bond foils a world domination attempt by Blofeld.

Reasonably enjoyable mishmash of Bondery; the plot is technically a remake of Thunderball*, not that it matters much until the end, when the underwater stuff becomes tiresome because one hardly knows who is under the masks.*

w Lorenzo Semple Jnr *d* Irvin Kershner *ph* Douglas Slocombe *m* Michel Legrand *pd* Philip Harrison, Stephen Grimes

☆ Sean Connery, Klaus Maria Brandauer, Max von Sydow, Barbara Carrera, Kim Basinger, Bernie Casey, Alec McCowen, Edward Fox, Rowan Atkinson

'Q' (Alec McCowen): 'Good to see you again, Mr Bond. Let's get back to some gratuitous sex and violence, I say.'

Never So Few

US 1959 124m Metrocolor Cinemascope

MGM/Canterbury (Edmund Grainger)

Adventures of World War II Americans commanding Burmese guerrillas.

Jungle actioner with pauses for philosophizing; well enough made but not very interesting.

w Millard Kaufman *novel* Tom Chamales *d* John Sturges *ph* William H. Daniels *m* Hugo Friedhofer

☆ Frank Sinatra, Gina Lollobrigida, Peter Lawford, Steve McQueen, Paul Henreid, Richard Johnson, Brian Donlevy, Charles Bronson, Dean Jones

Never Steal Anything Small

US 1958 94m Eastmancolor Cinemascope

U-I (Aaron Rosenberg)

The reformation of a corrupt but sympathetic dockers' union boss.

Curious semi-musical which doesn't come off at all despite excellent credentials.

wd Charles Lederer *play The Devil's Hornpipe* by Rouben Mamoulian, Maxwell Anderson *ph* Harold Lipstein *m* Allie Wrubel *ch* Hermes Pan *ly* Maxwell Anderson

☆ James Cagney, Shirley Jones, Roger Smith, Cara Williams, Nehemiah Persoff, Royal Dano, Anthony Caruso

'The closest thing to it, I'd say, is *The Threepenny Opera*. It's witty, and it has some good radical lyrics. Films must have some comment to make.' – *James Cagney*

Never Take No for an Answer *

GB 1951 82m bw

Constellation (Anthony Havelock-Allan)

A small boy goes to Rome to get permission from the Pope to take his sick donkey to be blessed in the church.

Slight, easy-going whimsy with attractive sunlit locations.

w Paul and Pauline Gallico *novel The Small Miracle* by Paul Gallico *d* Maurice Cloche, Ralph Smart *ph* Otto Heller *m* Nino Rota

☆ Vittorio Manunta, Denis O'Dea, Guido Cellano, Nerio Bernardi

'The main pleasures of this slender film are visual ones.' – *MFB*

† Remade as a TV movie *The Small Miracle*.

Never Take Sweets from a Stranger

GB 1960 81m bw Megascope

Hammer/Columbia

In a Canadian town, a respected elderly man is accused of improper sexual advances to a child.

In the awful warning category, and rather predictable.

w John Hunter *play The Pony Cart* by Roger Garis *d* Cyril Frankel *ph* Freddie Francis *m* Elisabeth Lutyens

☆ Gwen Watford, Patrick Allen, Felix Aylmer, Niall MacGinnis, Bill Nagy, Janina Faye, Michael Gwynn

Never Talk to Strangers

Canada/US 1995 86m DeLuxe

Columbia TriStar/Never Talk to Strangers/Alliance (Andras Hamori, Jeffrey R. Neuman, Martin J. Wiley)

A criminal psychologist, who is examining a serial killer, begins to receive death threats.

Risible thriller, stuffed with clichés and given a fashionable gloss with talk of multiple personality disorders and repressed memory syndrome; it is one memory that most audiences will be anxious to suppress.

w Lewis Green, Jordan Rush *d* Peter Hall *ph* Elemér Ragályi *m* Pino Donaggio *pd* Linda del Rosario, Richard Paris *ed* Roberto Silvi

☆ Rebecca De Mornay, Antonio Banderas, Dennis Miller, Len Cariou, Harry Dean Stanton, Beau Starr, Tim Kelleher, Eugene Lipinski

'The plot is so silly and the screenplay so unconvincing that nothing could be done to save it.' – *Derek Malcolm, Guardian*

Never the Twain Shall Meet

US 1931 89m bw

MGM

A young lawyer goes native when he falls for a South Sea island girl.

Stilted misalliance melodrama, previously made in 1925 as a silent with Bert Lytell and Anita Stewart; its faded notions simply didn't survive sound.

w Ruth Cummings and Edwin Justus Mayer *novel* Peter B. Kyne *d* W. S. Van Dyke

☆ Leslie Howard, Conchita Montenegro, Karen Morley, C. Aubrey Smith

Never to Love: see *A Bill of Divorcement (1940)*

Never Too Late

US 1965 104m Technicolor Panavision

Warner/Lear-Yorkin (Norman Lear)

A well-to-do middle-aged housewife discovers she is pregnant.

Predictable, rather hysterical domestic comedy, flatly developed from a successful play which offered two star parts for old stagers.

w Sumner Arthur Long *play* Sumner Arthur Long *d* Bud Yorkin *ph* Philip Lathrop *m* David Rose

☆ *Paul Ford, Maureen O'Sullivan*, Connie Stevens, Jim Hutton, Lloyd Nolan, Henry Jones, Jane Wyatt

Never Too Young to Rock

GB 1975 99m Fujicolour

GTO (Greg Smith, Ron Inkpen)

After rock'n'roll is no longer shown on TV in the near future, one man gathers together leading groups to perform at a concert to get the ban overturned, hampered by his elderly driver.

An inept comedy by a director who believes punch-ups and chickens are automatically funny. It is an excuse for a succession of performances by various bubblegum and glam-rock groups, including Mud performing Tiger Feet*, a No. 1 hit at the time, and the Glitter Band.*

w Ron Inkpen, Dennis Abey *d* Dennis Abey *ph* Harvey Harrison *ad* Denis Gordon-Orr *ed* Ray Lovejoy

☆ Peter Denyer, Freddie Jones, Sheila Steafel, Joe Lynch, John Clive, Peter Noone, Sally James, Scott Fitzgerald, Mud, Bob Kerr's Whoopee Band, The Glitter Band, The Rubettes, Slick

Never Wave at a WAC

US 1952 87m bw

Independent Artists (Frederick Brisson)

GB title: *The Private Wore Skirts*

A Washington hostess joins the WACs and finds she can't get beyond the rank of private.

Pattern comedy, unconvincing in all respects but with a smattering of funny moments. Flagwaving takes over towards the end.

w Ken Englund *d* Norman Z. McLeod *ph* William Daniels *m* Elmer Bernstein

☆ Rosalind Russell, Paul Douglas, Marie Wilson, William Ching, Leif Erickson, Arleen Whelan, Charles Dingle

'A boy who needs a friend finds a world that needs a hero in a land beyond imagination!'

The Neverending Story *

West Germany 1984 94m Technicolor Technovision

Warner/Bavaria Studios/WDR/Neue Constantin Filmproduktion (Bernd Eichinger, Dieter Geissler)

A reluctant student reads a book instead: dealing with mystical monsters and make-believe, it takes him back into their world.

Slow-starting fantasy with agreeable enough creations but not a lot of humour despite its intended stimulus to the imagination.

wd Wolfgang Petersen *novel* Michael Ende *ph* Jost Vacano *m* Klaus Doldinger, Giorgio Moroder *pd* Rolf Zehetbauer *ed* Jane Seitz

☆ Barret Oliver, Gerald McRaney, Moses Gunn, Patricia Hayes

The Neverending Story II: The Next Chapter

Germany 1990 89m Eastmancolor Panavision

Warner/Soriba & Dehle (Dieter Geissler)

A boy and his fantasy alter-ego search for an imprisoned empress in a fairy-tale land of dreams.

Sequel that does little to expand the imagination.

w Karin Howard *novel* Michael Ende *d* George Miller *ph* Dave Connell *m* Robert Folk *pd* Bob Laing, Götz Weidner *ed* Peter Hollywood, Chris Blunden *sp* creature effects Colin Arthur

☆ Jonathan Brandis, Kenny Morrison, Clarissa Burt, Alexandra Johnes, Martin Umbach, John Wesley Shiff, Helena Michell, Chris Burton, Thomas Hill

The Neverending Story III

Germany 1994 95m Agfacolor

Warner/Cinevox/Babelsberg/Dieter Geissler

School bullies corrupt the book of the Neverending Story, so that the kingdom of Fantasia begins to decay and some of its inhabitants escape into the real world.

Limp sequel that cuts down on the magic and sets most of the action in a dull, real world of shopping malls and school.

w Jeff Lieberman *story* Karin Howard *d* Peter Macdonald *ph* Robin Vidgeon *m* Peter Wolf *pd* Rolf Zehetbauer *ed* Michael Bradsell

☆ Jason James Richter, Melody Kay, Freddie Jones, Ryan Bollman, Jack Black, Tracey Ellis, Kevin McNulty, Carole Finn, Julie Cox

'A charmless, desperate reworking ... aimed at a generation of moppets with one finger on the fast forward button.' – *Derek Elley, Variety*

The New Adventures of Don Juan: see *The Adventures of Don Juan*

The New Adventures of Get-Rich-Quick Wallingford

US 1931 76m bw

MGM

Exploits of an attractive go-getter.

Reliable comedy of its day.

w Charles MacArthur *novel* G. R. Chester *d* Sam Wood

☆ William Haines, Jimmy Durante, Leila Hyams, Guy Kibbee

The New Adventures of Pippi Longstocking

US/Sweden 1988 100m DeLuxe

Columbia/Svensk Filmindustri (Gary Mehlman, Walter Moshay)

Pippi Longstocking causes havoc when she returns home alone from a sea voyage.

The classic children's stories were turned into some dreary Swedish movies; this American effort is no better, being tiresome, dull and witless, unsuited to any age of audience.

wd Ken Annakin *novel* Astrid Lindgren *ph* Roland 'Ozzie' Smith *m* Misha Segal *pd* Jack Senter *ed* Ken Zemke

☆ Tami Erin, Eileen Brennan, Dennis Dugan, Dianne Hull, George di Cenzo, John Schuck, Dick Van Patten

The New Age

US 1994 110m Technicolor

Warner/Regency/Alcor (Nick Wechsler, Keith Addis)

A couple's upwardly mobile progress, founded on the belief that shopping is good, comes to an abrupt stop.

A bleak look at a vapid society, so distanced from the characters it dispassionately observes that they dwindle to the level of uninteresting insects.

wd Michael Tolkin *ph* John H. Campbell *m* Mark Mothersbaugh *pd* Robin Standefer *ed* Suzanne Fenn

☆ Peter Weller, Judy Davis, Patrick Bauchau, Corbin Bernsen, Jonathan Hadary, Patricia Heaton, Samuel L. Jackson, Adam West

'Suffers from the pretentiousness it is surely designed to expose.' – *Derek Malcolm, Guardian*

The New Babylon *

USSR 1929 80m approx (24 fps) bw silent

Sovkino

original title: *Novyi Vavilon*

The rise and fall of the 1871 French commune, seen through the eyes of a girl department store worker.

Propagandist socio-historical melodrama, most interesting now for its sub-Eisenstein technique.

wd Leonid Trauberg, Grigori Kozintsev *ph* Andrei Moskvin, Yevgeni Mikhailov *m* Dmitri Shostakovich *ad* Yevgeni Enei

☆ Yelena Kuzmina, Pyotr Sobelevsky, Sophie Magarill

'A slow decorative romantic picture.' – *Graham Greene*

The New Barbarians

Italy 1983 91m Telecolor

Entertainment/Deaf International (Fabrizi de Angelis)

original title: *I Nuovi Barbari*

In a post-holocaust future, two wandering warriors destroy a vicious gang of murdering homosexuals.

Mad Max, *Italian-style, in an untalented low-budget rip-off.*

w Tito Carpi, Enzo Girolami *d* Enzo G. Castellari *ph* Fausto Amicucci *m* Claudio Simonetti *pd* Antonio Visune *ed* Gianfranco Amicucci

☆ Fred Williamson, Timothy Brent, George Eastman, Anna Kanakis, Thomas Moore

The New Centurions *

US 1972 103m Eastmancolor Panavision

Columbia/Chartoff-Winkler

GB title: *Precinct 45: Los Angeles Police*

An old cop teaches a new one.

'Realistic' crime prevention saga which spawned the TV series Police Story *and* Police Woman. *Well done within its limits.*

w Stirling Silliphant *novel* Joseph Wambaugh *d* Richard Fleischer *ph* Ralph Woolsey *m* Quincy Jones

☆ George C. Scott, Stacy Keach, Jane Alexander, Rosalind Cash, Scott Wilson

The New Eve *

France/Portugal 1999 94m colour

Gala/Gemini/Arte France/Mandragoa (Paulo Branco)

original title: *La Nouvelle Eve*

A party- and sex-loving woman, who is dissatisfied with life and loathes domesticity, finds herself obsessed by a middle-aged married man.

Intermittently amusing study of an emotional woman who wants the impossible; it has its longeurs, though many individual scenes are arresting.

w Catherine Corsini, Marc Syrigas *d* Catherine Corsini *ph* Agnès Godard *ad* Solange Zeitoun *ed* Sabine Mamou *cos* Anne Schotte

☆ Karin Viard (Camille), Pierre-Loup Rajot (Alexis), Catherine Frot (Isabelle), Sergi Lopez (Ben), Laurent Lucas (Emile), Mireille Roussel (Louise), Nozha Khouadra (Solveig), Valentine Vidal (Sophie)

'Pithy portrait of an irresponsible and free-spirited scatterbrain who's alternately endearing and exasperating, pic pokes fun at both bourgeois coupledom and the swinging singles scene.' – *Lisa Nesselson, Variety*

New Face in Hell: see *P.J.*

New Faces *

US 1954 99m Eastmancolor Cinemascope

Edward L. Alperson (Leonard Sillman)

A revue goes on despite money problems.

Five minutes of plot, ninety-five minutes of revue from the Broadway stage; mostly quite amusing, and chiefly notable for introducing Eartha Kitt with all her standards.

w various *d* Harry Horner *ph* Lucien Ballard *m* Raoul Kraushaar *revue deviser* John Murray Anderson

☆ *Eartha Kitt*, Ronny Graham, Alice Ghostley, Robert Clary, Paul Lynde

New Faces of 1937

US 1937 105m bw

RKO

Talent auditions for a Broadway show.

Shapeless agglomeration of variety acts with a wisp of story; the level of talent is not outstandingly high.

w Nat Perrin, P. G. Epstein, Irving Brecher, Harold Russell, Harry Clork, Howard J. Green *story* Shoestring by George Bradshaw *d* Leigh Jason

☆ Joe Penner, Milton Berle, Parkyakarkus, Harriet Hilliard, Jerome Cowan, Bert Gordon, Ann Miller, Richard Lane

'A hodgepodge of vaudeville, night club and radio talent, unskilfully blended and rather inanely promulgated.' – *Variety*

New Frontier

US 1939 57m bw

Republic (William Berke)

aka: *Frontier Horizon*

aka: *Raiders of the Wasteland*

Cowboys come to the rescue of settlers who are losing their land to crooked dam builders.

A typical action-packed adventure for the Three Mesquiteers, which was also Wayne's last film in the series before he went on to better movies.

w Betty Burbridge, Luci Ward *d* George Sherman *ph* Reggie Lanning *m* William Lava

☆ John Wayne, Ray Corrigan, Raymond Hatton, Phylis Isley (Jennifer Jones), Eddy Waller, LeRoy Mason, Sammy McKim

The New Gulliver *

USSR 1933 85m approx bw

Gulliver's Travels is retold in puppet form, but the plot has become a satire against capitalism.

Interesting both as animation and as propaganda.

w A. Ptoushko, B. Roshal *d* Alexander Ptoushko, A. Vanitchkin

'The invention is often delightful (one wonders how such humour in detail can exist with so humourless a philosophy), and the marvellous ingenuity of the puppets is beyond praise.' – *Graham Greene, The Spectator*

'Popularity isn't a contest... It's a war!'

The New Guy

US 2002 88m DeLuxe

Columbia/Revolution (Todd Garner, Gordon Gray, Mark Ciardi)

An unpopular teenager changes schools so that he can re-invent himself as a cool guy.

An all-American theme given a trite treatment; it makes a new low in the current stream of dreary high-school comedies;

w David Kendall *d* Ed Decter *ph* Michael D. O'Shea *m* Ralph Sall *pd* Dina Lipton *ed* David Rennie

☆ DJ Qualls (Dizzy), Eliza Dushku (Danielle), Zooey Deschanel (Nora), Lyle Lovett (Bear), Jerod Mixon (Kirk), Illeana Douglas (Kiki Pierce), Parry Shen (Glen), Kurt Fuller (Mr Undine)

'Bad beyond belief and ridiculous beyond description.' – *Michael Wilmington, Chicago Tribune*

'A trashy, crass piece of work that panders to the anxieties and desires of adolescents without a scintilla of sympathy or coherence.' – *Ann Hornaday, Washington Post*

The New Interns

US 1964 123m bw

Columbia (Robert Cohn)

Young doctors at a city hospital have trouble saving a rapist and his victim.

Unnecessary sequel to The Interns, *its 'realism' requiring large pinches of salt.*

w Wilton Schiller *d* John Rich *ph* Lucien Ballard *m* Earle Hagen

☆ George Segal, Telly Savalas, Michael Callan, Dean Jones, Inger Stevens, Stefanie Powers, Lee Patrick

New Jack City **

US 1991 100m Technicolor

Warner (Doug McHenry, George Jackson)

Undercover cops go after a successful gangster dealing drugs in Harlem.

Fast-moving, street-wise thriller with an anti-drugs stance.

w Thomas Lee Wright, Barry Michael Cooper *d* Mario Van Peebles *ph* Francis Kenny *m* Michel Colombier *pd* Charles C. Bennett *ed* Steven Kemper, Kevin Stitt

☆ Wesley Snipes, Ice T, Allen Payne, Chris Rock, Mario Van Peebles, Michael Michele, Bill Nunn, Russell Wong, Bill Cobbs

'A provocative, pulsating update on gangster pics.' – *Variety*

New Jersey Drive

US 1995 95m Technicolor

Universal/Gramercy/40 Acres and a Mule Filmworks/Shooting Gallery (Larry Meistrich, Bob Gosse)

Police engage in a war with young black joyriders and car thieves.

Gritty but unconvincing urban melodrama; its feeling for street life doesn't compensate for its reliance on stereotypical characters and situations.

wd Nick Gomez *ph* Adam Kimmel *m* Wendy Blackstone *pd* Lester Cohen *ed* Tracy Granger

☆ Sharron Corley, Gabriel Casseus, Saul Stein, Gwen McGee, Andre Moore, Donald Adeosun Faison, Conrad Meertin, Christine Baranski

'Lack of a discernible point of view on this out-of-control lawlessness and mayhem until the final minutes is a nagging problem throughout, leaving the viewer nowhere to put one's concerns or sympathies.' – *Todd McCarthy, Variety*

A New Kind of Love

US 1963 110m Technicolor

Paramount/Llenroc (Melville Shavelson)

An American dress designer in Paris is softened by a boorish newspaper columnist.

Very thin sex comedy, dressed to kill but with nowhere to go.

wd Melville Shavelson *ph* Daniel Fapp *m* Leith Stevens

☆ Paul Newman, Joanne Woodward, Maurice Chevalier, Thelma Ritter, George Tobias

Leith Stevens

The New Land: see *The Emigrants*

A New Leaf *

US 1970 102m Movielab

Paramount/Aries/Elkins (Joe Manduke)

A middle-aged playboy, close to bankruptcy, thinks of acquiring a wealthy wife.

Agreeably mordant comedy which sparkles in patches rather than as a whole.

wd Elaine May *story* *The Green Heart* by Jack Ritchie *ph* Gayne Rescher *m* John Mandel, Neal Hefti *pd* Richard Fried

☆ *Walter Matthau, Elaine May*, Jack Weston, George Rose, William Redfield, James Coco

'Unashamedly a thirties fairy tale in modern, but not fashionable, dress.' – *Jan Dawson*

A New Life

US 1988 104m Technicolor Panavision

Paramount (Martin Bregman)

A middle-aged couple divorce and find new partners and problems.

Occasionally wry, but more often sentimental, romantic comedy.

wd Alan Alda *ph* Kelvin Pike *m* Joseph Turrin *pd* Barbara Dunphy *ed* William Reynolds

☆ Alan Alda, Ann-Margret, Hal Linden, Veronica Hamel, John Shea, Mary Kay Place

New Mexico
US 1952 78m Anscocolor
United Artists (Irving Allen)
A cavalry officer tries to make peace with the Indians, but when an Indian child is accidentally killed a savage war breaks out.
Standard Western, not badly made.
w Max Trell *d* Irving Reis *ph* William Snyder *m* Lucien Moraweck, Rene Garriguenc
☆ Lew Ayres, Marilyn Maxwell, Robert Hutton, Andy Devine, Raymond Burr, Jeff Corey

New Moon *
US 1940 105m bw
MGM (Robert Z. Leonard)
Romance in old French Louisiana.
Stalwart adaptation of an operetta previously filmed in 1930 with Lawrence Tibbett and Grace Moore.
w Jacques Deval, Robert Arthur *d* Robert Z. Leonard *ph* William Daniels *m/ly* Sigmund Romberg, Oscar Hammerstein
☆ *Jeanette MacDonald, Nelson Eddy*, Mary Boland, George Zucco, H. B. Warner, Stanley Fields, Grant Mitchell

New Morals for Old
US 1932 77m bw
MGM
John Van Druten's play *After All*, about the generation gap in the London aristocracy, was here rather unwisely translated to the American middle class and emerged as a decided curiosity.
w Zelda Sears, Wanda Tuchock *d* Charles Brabin
☆ Robert Young, Myrna Loy, Jean Hersholt, Lewis Stone, Laura Hope Crews, Elizabeth Patterson
'A weak sister, swathed in gloom, muddled, and without names that will draw.' – *Variety*

New Orleans *
US 1947 89m bw
Jules Levey
How jazz was born, according to the movies.
Routine low-budgeter enlivened by a splendid array of guest musicians.
w Elliot Paul, Dick Irving Hyland *d* Arthur Lubin *ph* Lucien Andriot *md* Nathaniel Finston
☆ *Louis Armstrong and his All Stars*, Arturo de Cordova, Dorothy Patrick, Richard Hageman, *Billie Holiday, Meade Lux Lewis, Woody Herman and his Orchestra*
† Richard Hageman's piano-playing was dubbed by Arthur Schutt.

New World Disorder
GB 1999 94m Technicolor
Promark/Videal/Carousel (Silvio Muraglia, Tom Reeve)
An old-fashioned cop and a young female FBI agent clash during an investigation of a murder in a high-tech computer firm in Silicon Valley.
Ludicrously overheated thriller, notable for its low-resolution acting, direction and script.
w Jeffrey Smith, Ehren Kruger *d* R. C. Spence *ph* Ivan Strasburg *m* Gast Waltzing *pd* Humphrey Bangham *ed* Graham Walker
☆ Rutger Hauer (David Marx), Andrew McCarthy (Kurt Bishop), Tara Fitzgerald (Kris Paddock), Hari Dhillon (Mark Ohal), Branwell Donaghey (Leo), Lawrence Elman (Maximilian Biggs)
† Despite its ostensible setting in Silicon Valley, the movie was shot in Luxembourg

New Year's Day *
US 1989 92m Technicolor
Contemporary/International Rainbow/Jagfilm (Judith Wolinsky)
A writer moves back from Los Angeles to his New York apartment and becomes involved in the lives of three young women, his previous tenants, and their friends.
A conversation piece, in which a varied group sound off about their lives and loves in a manner ranging from the engaging to the uninteresting; worth a listen for the most part.
wd Henry Jaglom *ph* Joey Forsyte *ad* Barbara Flood *ed* Ruth Zucker Ward
☆ Maggie Jakobson, Gwen Welles, Henry Jaglom, David Duchovny, Milos Forman, Michael Emil, Donna Germain, Tracy Reiner, Harvey Miller, Irene Moore
'Warm, perceptive, wryly comic.' – *Philip French, Observer*

'12 reasons to live. 12 reasons to die.'
New Year's Day
GB/France 1999 101m DeLuxe 'Scope
Optimum/Flashpoint/Alchymie/ECF/Liberator/Canal+ (Stephen Cleary, Simon Channing-Williams)
Two teenagers, who are the only survivors of an avalanche that killed their friends, agree to carry out twelve anti-social tasks in a year before they kill themselves.
Tame and shallow drama of adolescent angst, lacking the necessary sense of danger.
w Ralph Brown *d* Suri Krishnamma *ph* John de Borman *m* Julian Nott *pd* Eve Stewart *ed* Adam Ross
☆ Andrew Lee Potts (Jake), Robby Barry (Steven), Marianne Jean-Baptiste (Veronica), Jacqueline Bisset (Geraldine), Anastasia Hille (Shelley), Michael Kitchen (Robin), Ralph Brown (Mr Diamond), Sue Johnston (Mrs Fisher)
'There are false notes everywhere: all the rebellion is a fantasy, miles away from real grief or real adolescent pain.' – *Peter Bradshaw, Guardian*

New York Confidential
US 1955 87m bw
Warner/Russel Rouse, Clarence Greene
The head of a crime syndicate is assassinated by his own hired killer.
Unexciting 'realistic' thriller with the gangsters presented as family and businessmen; seventeen years later The Godfather *did it rather better.*
w Clarence Greene, Russel Rouse *d* Russel Rouse *ph* Edward Fitzgerald *m* Joseph Mullendore *pd* Fernando Carrere
☆ Broderick Crawford, Richard Conte, Anne Bancroft, Marilyn Maxwell, Onslow Stevens, J. Carrol Naish, Barry Kelley, Mike Mazurki, Celia Lovsky

The New York Hat *
US 1912 10m approx (24 fps) bw silent
D. W. Griffith
A small-town minister is gossiped about when he buys a hat for a young girl.
Influential early short story film with good local backgrounds.
w Anita Loos *d D. W. Griffith ph* Billy Bitzer
☆ *Mary Pickford*, Lionel Barrymore, Lillian Gish, Dorothy Gish, Robert Harron, Mack Sennett, Mae Marsh

New York, New York *
US 1977 153m Technicolor Panavision
UA/Chartoff-Winkler (Gene Kirkwood)
In the late forties in New York, a single-minded saxophonist fails to do right by his girlfriend, who becomes a Hollywood star.
A clever recreation of the big band era, hampered by gross overlength, unattractive characters and a pessimistic plot.
w Earl Mac Rauch, Mardik Martin *d* Martin Scorsese *ph* Laszlo Kovacs *md* Ralph Burns *pd* Boris Leven
☆ Liza Minnelli, Robert DeNiro, Lionel Stander, Barry Primus
'A dazzling modern musical, this is one of the rare films which is actually constructed with as much passion as it depicts.' – *Judith Williamson*

New York Nights
US 1929 81m bw
UA/Talmadge
A musical comedy star has a husband who drinks, and she accepts help from a gangster.
The star's sound début was a hit-and-miss affair composed of familiar elements.
w Jules Furthman *play Tin Pan Alley* by Hugh Stanislaus Stange *d* Lewis Milestone
☆ Norma Talmadge, Gilbert Roland, John Wray, Lilyan Tashman, Roscoe Karns
'Good performance, fair picture.' – *Variety*

New York Stories **
US 1989 124m Technicolor
Warner/Touchstone (Robert Greenhut)
Anthology of three stories: 'Life Lessons', dealing with a painter's attitude to life and art; 'Life Without Zoë', in which a 12-year-old girl brings her parents back together; and 'Oedipus Wrecks', in which a son is tyrannized by his mother materializing in the sky over New York.
Worth watching for Scorsese's sharp look at the art world and Allen's ultimate Jewish mother joke. Sandwiched between them is Coppola at his most disastrously winsome.
w Richard Price, Francis Coppola, Sofia Coppola, Woody Allen *d* Martin Scorsese, Francis Coppola, Woody Allen *ph* Nestor Almendros, Vittorio Storaro, Sven Nykvist *m* Carmine Coppola, Kid Creole and the Coconuts *pd* Kristi Zea, Dean Tavoularis, Santo Loquasto *ed* Thelma Schoonmaker, Barry Malkin, Susan E. Morse
☆ Nick Nolte, Patrick O'Neal, Rosanna Arquette, Heather McComb, Talia Shire, Gia Coppola, Giancarlo Giannini, Woody Allen, Marvin Chatinover, Mae Questel, Mia Farrow

New York Town
US 1941 94m bw
Paramount (Anthony Veiller)
A girl new to the Big Apple befriends a sidewalk photographer.
Flat romantic comedy, a soufflé which doesn't rise despite the talents involved.
w Lewis Seltzer (and, uncredited, Preston Sturges) *d* Charles Vidor (and Sturges) *ph* Charles Schoenbaum *m* Leo Shuken
☆ Fred MacMurray, Mary Martin, Robert Preston, Akim Tamiroff, Lynne Overman, Eric Blore, Cecil Kellaway, Fuzzy Knight

Newman's Law
US 1974 99m Technicolor
Universal (Richard Irving)
A cop uses unconventional methods to trap drug smugglers.
Very routine police actioner, just above TV movie level.
w Anthony Wilson *d* Richard Heffron *ph* Vilis Lapenieks *m* Robert Prince
☆ George Peppard, Roger Robinson, Eugene Roche, Gordon Pinsent, Abe Vigoda

The News Boys: see *Newsies*

News Is Made at Night
US 1939 72m bw
TCF
To boost circulation, a news editor pins a string of murders on a well-known gangster, and soon regrets it.
Pacy crime comedy-drama, very acceptable as the lower half of a double bill.
w John Larkin *d* Alfred Werker
☆ Preston Foster, Lynn Bari, Eddie Collins, Russell Gleason, George Barbier, Charles Halton
'Above average B; should do all right where properly placed.' – *Variety*

Newsboys' Home
US 1939 73m bw
Universal
A girl inherits a newspaper which sponsors a home for boys.
Modest debut for the East Side Kids, a spin-off group from the Dead End Kids.
w Gordon Kahn *d* Harold Young
☆ Jackie Cooper, Edmund Lowe, Wendy Barrie, Edward Norris, Samuel S. Hinds; and Elisha Cook Jnr, Hally Chester, Harris Berger, David Gorcey, Billy Benedict, Charles Duncan
'Another in the tough kid cycle. Will easily handle its end of dual depots.' – *Variety*

Newsfront ***
Australia 1978 110m colour/bw
Palm Beach Productions (David Elfick)
In the fifties, rival news teams battle to get the best shots for cinema newsreels.
Lively nostalgic feature with slick modern technique.
wd Phillip Noyce, from a concept by David Elfick ph Vincent Monton *pd* Lissa Coote *ed* John Scott
☆ Bill Hunter, Wendy Hughes, Gerard Kennedy, Chris Haywood

Newsies
US 1992 121m Technicolor Panavision
Warner/Walt Disney/Touchwood Pacific Partners I (Michael Finnell)
In the 1890s news boys in New York call a strike when a newspaper publisher charges them more for his papers.
Unsuccessful attempt to create a youthful musical – the model seems to be Oliver! *but it lacks any Dickensian dimension despite its subplot of the exploitation of child labour.*
w Bob Tzudiker, Noni White *d* Kenny Ortega *ph* Andrew Laszlo *m* Alan Menken *ch* Kenny Ortega, Peggy Holmes *pd* William Sandell *ed* William Reynolds
☆ Christian Bale, Bill Pullman, Ann-Margret, Robert Duvall, David Moscow, Ele Keats, Kevin Tighe, Luke Edwards
'With many catchy if forgettable ditties littered throughout, one is led to the inevitable conclusion that nine-year-old girls will just love it.' – *Angie Errigo, Empire*

The Newton Boys
US 1998 122m colour Panavision
TCF/Detour (Anne Walker-McBay)
In the 20s, four rural brothers become bank robbers.
Atmospheric but somewhat lethargic drama, set in a period of change.
w Richard Linklater, Claude Stanush, Clark Lee Walker *book* Claude Stanush *d* Richard Linklater *ph* Peter James *m* Edward D. Barnes *pd* Catherine Hardwicke *ed* Sandra Adair
☆ Matthew McConaughey, Skeet Ulrich, Ethan Hawke, Vincent D'Onofrio, Julianna Margulies, Dwight Yoakam, Chloe Webb
'A story that's too diffuse and lacks a discernible point of view that would make it dramatically engaging.' – *Variety*
† The film was released direct to video in Britain.

'Best friends make the best mistakes.'
The Next Best Thing
US 2000 108m DeLuxe
Paramount/Lakeshore (Tom Rosenberg, Leslie Dixon, Linne Radmin)
A yoga instructor and her gay friend, parents of a six-year-old son, fall out when she finds the man she wants to marry.
A movie that may appeal to fans of Madonna, but otherwise does little to add to the gaiety of nations, with its awkaward drama that resorts to court scenes in the hope of adding a little excitement to a bland, romantic serio-comedy.
w Thomas Ropelewski *d* John Schlesinger *ph* Elliot Davis *m* Gabriel Yared *pd* Howard Cummings *ed* Peter Honess *cos* Ruth Myers
☆ Rupert Everett (Robert), Madonna (Abbie), Benjamin Bratt (Ben), Michael Vartan (Kevin), Josef Sommer (Richard Whittaker), Lynn Redgrave (Helen Whittaker), Malcolm Stumpf (Sam), Neil Patrick Harris (David), Illeana Douglas (Elizabeth Ryder), Mark Valley (Cardiologist), Suzanne Krull (Annabel), Stacy Edwards (Finn)
'Resoundingly adequate Advanced Family Values comedy-drama.' – *Variety*

'The suburbs make the hood look good.'
Next Friday
US 2000 98m DeLuxe
Entertainment/New Line/Cubevision (Ice Cube)
Hiding from a thug, a unemployed man leaves his neighbourhood to stay with his lottery-rich uncle in the suburbs.
Amiable enough romp, a sequel of sorts to Friday (qv), which ambles along without getting anywhere very interesting.
w Ice Cube *d* Steve Carr *ph* Christopher J. Baffa *m* Terence Blanchard *pd* Dina Lipton *ed* Elena Maganini
☆ Ice Cube (Craig Jones), Mike Epps (Day-Day), Justin Pierce (Roach), John Witherspoon (Mr Jones), Don "DC" Curry (Uncle Elroy), Jacob Vargas (Joker), Lobo Sebastian (Lil Joker), Rolando Molina (Baby Joker), Lisa Rodriguez (Karla)
'There are a good few laughs but few surprises.' – *Joe Leydon, Variety*

The Next Karate Kid
US 1994 104m Technicolor
Columbia (Jerry Weintraub)

An unhappy teenage girl, whose parents died in a car crash, discovers that karate is a means of gaining self-respect.
This is another series running out of steam; the attempt to revive it by changing the gender of its protagonist yields small returns, since otherwise the story is as before.
w Mark Lee *d* Christopher Cain *ph* Laszlo Kovacs *m* Bill Conti *pd* Walter P. Martishius *ed* Ronald Roose
☆ Pat Morita, Hilary Swank, Michael Ironside, Constance Towers, Christian Conrad, Arsenio Trinidad, Michael Cavalieri
'Wholesome apprenticeship tale has its scattered moments of humor and insight but lacks sustained verve.' – *Variety*

The Next Man
US 1976 107m Technicolor
Artists Entertainment Complex (Martin Bregman)
A female assassin is hired to kill the Saudi Arabian Minister of State at the United Nations.
Fractured and uninteresting thriller in which all manner of cinematic styles obscure the storyline but point up the lack of narrative skill.
w Mort Fine, Alan R. Trustman, David M. Wolf, Michael Chapman *d* Richard C. Sarafian *ph* Michael Chapman *m* Michael Kamen *pd* Gene Callahan
☆ Sean Connery, Cornelia Sharpe, Albert Paulsen, Adolfo Celi, Charles Cioffi
'The director takes forever to set up the film's premise, and then he lingers over interminable street festivals and lush scenery.' – *Dave Pomeroy, Film Information*

The Next of Kin ***
GB 1942 102m bw
Ealing (S. C. Balcon)

Careless talk causes loss of life in a commando raid.
A propaganda instructional film which was made so entertainingly that it achieved commercial success and remains an excellent example of how to make a bitter pill palatable.
w Thorold Dickinson, Basil Bartlett, Angus Macphail, John Dighton *d* Thorold Dickinson *ph* Ernest Palmer *m* William Walton
☆ Mervyn Johns, Nova Pilbeam, Stephen Murray, Reginald Tate, Basil Radford, Naunton Wayne, Geoffrey Hibbert, Philip Friend, Mary Clare, Basil Sydney
'The detail everywhere is curious and surprising, with something of the fascination of a Simenon crime being unravelled.' – *William Whitebait*

Next of Kin
Australia 1982 86m Eastmancolor
Miracle/SIS Productions/Filmco (Robert Le Tet)
A young girl teacher inherits an old people's home, and finds murder lurking.
Slow-starting but finally over-the-top melodrama, with elements borrowed from Psycho, Taste of Fear *and a score of other creepies.*
w Michael Heath, Tony Williams *d* Tony Williams *ph* Gary Hansen *m* Klaus Schulze *ad* Richard Francis, Nick Hepworth *ed* Max Lemon
☆ Jackie Kerin, John Jarratt, Alex Scott, Gerda Nicolson
'Genre awareness is one thing; a dreary sense of déjà vu is another matter entirely.' – *Paul Taylor, MFB*

Next of Kin
US 1989 108m Metrocolor
Warner/Lorimar (Les Alexander, Don Enright)

Two brothers, one a cop, the other a hillbilly, take their revenge when another brother is killed by gangsters.
Dreary action movie of no originality.
w Michael Jenning, Jeb Stuart *d* John Irvin *ph* Steven Poster *m* Jack Nitzsche, Gary Chang, Todd Hayen *pd* Jack T. Collis *ed* Peter Honess
☆ Patrick Swayze, Liam Neeson, Adam Baldwin, Helen Hunt, Andreas Katsulas, Bill Paxton, Ben Stiller, Michael J. Pollard, Ted Levine

The Next One
US 1984 105m colour
Allstar Productions (Constantine Vlachakis)

An American widow, living on a Greek island, becomes involved with a mysterious stranger she finds washed up on the beach.
Glossy, dull fantasy about a man from the future with a Christ complex, made in 1981.
wd Nico Mastorakis *ph* Ari Stavrou *m* Stanley Myers *pd* Paul Acciari *ed* George Rosenberg
☆ Keir Dullea, Adrienne Barbeau, Peter Hobbs, Phaedon Georgitsis, Betty Arvanitis, Jeremy Licht

Next Stop Greenwich Village *
US 1975 111m Movielab
TCF (Paul Mazursky, Tony Ray)

In 1953 in a poor quarter of New York, a young Jew tries to stretch his wings.
A bumper bundle of Jewish clichés dressed up as autobiography, and switching abruptly from comedy to tragedy and back. Vivid, but not exactly entertaining.
wd Paul Mazursky *ph* Arthur Ornitz *m* Bill Conti
☆ Lenny Baker, Shelley Winters, Ellen Greene, Lois Smith, Dori Brenner
'Some tartly comic observation, but the fragmented structure keeps the mixture inert.' – *Sight and Sound*

The Next Time I Marry
US 1938 64m bw
RKO
In order to become the richest girl in America, an heiress must marry in haste.
Tedious comedy which falls apart halfway.
w John Twist, Helen Meinardi *d* Garson Kanin *ph* Russell Metty *md* Roy Webb
☆ Lucille Ball, James Ellison, Lee Bowman, Granville Bates, Mantan Moreland
'A very poor entry. The story is banal, production values poor, direction sloppy and most of the performances bad.' – *Variety*

Next Time We Live: see *Next Time We Love*

Next Time We Love
US 1936 87m bw
Universal (Paul Kohner)
GB title: *Next Time We Live*
The wife of a war correspondent has plenty of time for romance.
Romantic drama which badly needs an injection of comedy.
w Melville Baker *stories* Ursula Parrott *d* Edward H. Griffith *ph* Joseph Valentine *m* Franz Waxman *ad* Charles D. Hall *ed* Ted J. Kent
☆ Margaret Sullavan, Ray Milland, James Stewart, Grant Mitchell, Robert McWade
'Draggy, complex tale ... will have to be sold on the star's past performances.' – *Variety*

Next to No Time
GB 1958 93m Eastmancolor
British Lion/Montpelier (Albert Fennell)
A meek-and-mild engineer crossing the Atlantic gains confidence when told that anything is possible during the hour 'lost' every day.
Whimsical comedy which never gains momentum.
wd Henry Cornelius *story* The Enchanted Hour by Paul Gallico *ph* Freddie Francis *m* Georges Auric
☆ Kenneth More, Betsy Drake, Bessie Love, Harry Green, Roland Culver, Reginald Beckwith, John Welsh, John Laurie, Howard Marion-Crawford

The Next Voice You Hear *
US 1950 83m bw
MGM (Dore Schary)

God speaks to mankind on the radio, and the life of Joe Smith American is changed.
Soppy parable, the archetypal instance of Schary's reign of do-goodery at MGM. (He wrote a book about it, Case History of a Movie.*) The idea is handled with deadly reverence, and falls quite flat, while the depiction of the inhabitants of American suburbia is depressing.*
w Charles Schnee *d* William Wellman *ph* William Mellor *m* David Raksin
☆ James Whitmore, Nancy Davis, Lillian Bronson, Jeff Corey
'The sins of the American working man are singularly uninteresting and their obliteration seems scarcely to require the very voice of God.' – *Henry Hart*

Ngati *
New Zealand 1987 90m colour
Pacific/NZFC (John O'Shea)
In the late 40s, a young Australian-born doctor returns to the small New Zealand community where his father lived and his mother, a Maori, died.
Austere and affecting study of the sometimes uneasy relations between two cultures, and between modern and traditional attitudes to life, filmed in a deliberately spare manner.
w Tama Poata *d* Barry Barclay *ph* Rory O'Shea *m* Dalvanius *ad* Matthew Murphy *ed* Dell King
☆ Tuta Ngarimu Tamati, Iranui Haig, Tawai Moana, Michael Tibble, Oliver Jones, Wi Kuki Kaa, Ross Girven

Ni ju-seiki Shonen Dokuhon: see *Circus Boys*

Ni Neibian Jidian: see *What Time Is It There?*

'A raging torrent of emotion that even nature can't control!'
Niagara ***
US 1952 89m Technicolor
TCF (Charles Brackett)

While visiting Niagara Falls, a faithless wife is plotting to murder her husband, but he turns the tables.
Excellent suspenser with breathtaking locations; in the best Hitchcock class though slightly marred by the emphasis on Monroe's wiggly walk (it was her first big part).
w Charles Brackett, Walter Reisch, Richard Breen *d* Henry Hathaway *ph* Joe MacDonald *m* Sol Kaplan
☆ Joseph Cotten, Jean Peters, Marilyn Monroe, Don Wilson, Casey Adams
'The story is most imaginatively treated, the production values are excellent.' – *CEA Film Report*
'Seen from any angle, the Falls and Miss Monroe leave little to be desired.' – *New York Times*
'A masterly example of fluid screen narrative.' – *Charles Higham*
'It would have turned out a much better picture if James Mason had played the husband as I wanted. He has that intensity, that neurotic edge. He was all set to do it, but his daughter Portland said she was sick of seeing him die in his pictures.' – *Henry Hathaway*
'This isn't a good movie but it's compellingly tawdry and nasty ... the only movie that explored the mean, unsavoury potential of Marilyn Monroe's cuddly, infantile perversity.' – *Pauline Kael, 70s*

Niagara Falls
US 1941 43m bw
Hal Roach
Confusion reigns in a hotel overlooking the falls.
Potted farce in the producer's season of 'shorties'; not the worst, but far from brilliant.
w Paul Gerard Smith, Hal Yates, Eugene Conrad *d* Gordon Douglas
☆ ZaSu Pitts, Slim Summerville, Tom Brown, Marjorie Woodworth, Chester Clute

Nice Girl? *
US 1941 95m bw
Universal (Joe Pasternak)
A teenager finds herself in demand by two older men.
Amusing romantic trifle supposed to mark the growing up of Universal's great teenage star.
w Richard Connell, Gladys Lehman *d* William A. Seiter *ph* Joseph Valentine *md* Charles Previn
☆ Deanna Durbin, Franchot Tone, Robert Stack, Walter Brennan, Robert Benchley, Helen Broderick, Ann Gillis

A Nice Girl Like Me
GB 1969 91m Eastmancolor
Anglo Embassy/Partisan (Roy Millichip)
A sheltered young lady sets out to see life but keeps getting pregnant.
Insufferable romantic whimsy, made to look like a marathon TV commercial but never so interesting.
w Anne Piper, Desmond Davis *d* Desmond Davis *ph* Gil Taylor, Manny Wynn *m* Pat Williams
☆ Barbara Ferris, Harry Andrews, Gladys Cooper, Joyce Carey, Bill Hinnant, James Villiers, Christopher Guinee, Fabia Drake
'High-toned woman's magazine nostalgia.' – *MFB*

Nice Girls Don't Explode
US 1987 92m colour
New World/Nice Girls (Douglas Curtis, John Wells)

An over-protective mother persuades her teenage daughter that she will cause fires whenever she becomes sexually excited.
Dim and exceedingly unfunny comedy, taken at a painfully slow pace.
w Paul Harris *d* Chuck Martinez *ph* Stephen Katz *m* Anthony Marinelli, Brian Banks *pd* Sarina Rotstein *ed* Wende Phifer Mate
☆ Barbara Harris, Michelle Meyrink, William O'Leary, Wallace Shawn, James Nardini, Irwin Keyes, Belinda Wills

A Nice Little Bank That Should Be Robbed
US 1958 87m bw Cinemascope
TCF (Anthony Muto)
GB title: *How to Rob a Bank*
Two incompetent crooks rob a bank and buy a racehorse.
Feeble comedy, a sad waste of its stars.
w Sydney Boehm *d* Henry Levin *ph* Leo Tover *m* Lionel Newman
☆ Mickey Rooney, Tom Ewell, Mickey Shaughnessy, Dina Merrill

Nicholas and Alexandra *
GB 1971 189m Eastmancolor Panavision
Columbia/Horizon (Sam Spiegel)

The life of Tsar Nicholas II from 1904 to the execution of the family in 1918.
Inflated epic of occasional interest, mainly for its sets; generally heavy going.
w James Goldman *book* Robert K. Massie *d* Franklin Schaffner *ph* Frederick A. Young *m* Richard Rodney Bennett *pd* John Box *ed* Ernest Walter
☆ Michael Jayston, Janet Suzman, Laurence Olivier, Jack Hawkins, Tom Baker, Harry Andrews, Michael Redgrave, Alexander Knox
† Original preferred casting: Rex Harrison, Vanessa Redgrave
art direction; costumes (Yvonne Blake, Antonio Castillo)
best picture; Frederick A. Young; Richard Rodney Bennett; Janet Suzman

Nicholas Nickleby **
GB 1947 108m bw
Ealing (John Croydon)

The adventures of a Victorian schoolmaster, deprived of his rightful fortune, who joins a band of travelling entertainers.
Quite tasteful and expert but too light-handed potted version of Dickens, which suffered by comparison with the David Lean versions.
w John Dighton *novel* Charles Dickens *d* Alberto Cavalcanti *ph* Gordon Dines *m* Lord Berners *md* Ernest Irving *ad* Michael Relph *ed* Leslie Norman
☆ Derek Bond (Nicholas Nickleby), *Cedric Hardwicke* (Ralph Nickleby), *Alfred Drayton* (Wackford Squeers), *Sybil Thorndike* (Mrs Squeers), Stanley Holloway (Vincent Crummles), James Hayter (Cheeryble Brothers), Sally Ann Howes (Kate Nickleby), Jill Balcon (Madeline Bray), Cyril Fletcher (Alfred Mantalini), Fay Compton (Madame Mantalini), Bernard Miles (Newman Noggs), Athene Seyler (Miss LaCreevy), Vida Hope (Fanny Squeers), Aubrey Woods (Smike), Patricia Hayes (Phoebe) and also Cathleen Nesbit (Miss Knag), Vera Pearce (Mrs Crummles), Una Bart (Infant Phenomenon), George Relph, Michael Shepley, Cecil Ramage
'Here's richness! Not all the novel, perhaps, but enough to make a film full of the Dickens spirit.' – *Star*

Nick Carter, Master Detective
US 1939 57m bw
MGM (Lucien Hubbard)
Carter uncovers a spy ring in a plane factory.

Dull, devitalized version of the old dime novel adventures; generally characterless and unmemorable.
w Bertram Millhauser *d* Jacques Tourneur *ph* Charles Lawton Jnr *m* Edward Ward
☆ Walter Pidgeon, Rita Johnson, Henry Hull, Stanley Ridges, Donald Meek, Addison Richards, Milburn Stone, Martin Kosleck
'Just another screen sleuth.' – *Variety*

Nick of Time
US 1995 89m DeLuxe
Paramount (John Badham)
A man is given 90 minutes to kill the Governor of California or his young daughter will die.
A thriller in which real time and the film's time are the same, but it still drags at times, failing to create the necessary suspense, owing mainly to the spiralling absurdity of its narrative.
w Patrick Sheane Duncan *d* John Badham *ph* Roy H. Wagner *m* Arthur B. Rubinstein *pd* Philip Harrison *ed* Frank Morriss, Kevin Stitt
☆ Johnny Depp, Christopher Walken, Courtney Chase, Charles S. Dutton, Roma Maffia, Marsha Mason, Peter Strauss, Gloria Reuben
'This OK but undistinguished thriller takes a simple Hitchcockian premise and milks things about as well as it can, given its confines, before a rather silly and abrupt conclusion.' – *Brian Lowry, Variety*

The Nickel Queen
Australia 1971 89m colour
Fox/Rank/Woomera (Bob Austin, Lee Robinson)
A back country barmaid becomes a rich woman with a nickel share in the mineral boom; but she is swindled by con men.
Mild comedy-drama.
w Henry C. James, John McCallum, Joy Cavill *d* John McCallum *ph* John Williams *m* Sven Libaek
☆ Googie Withers, John McCallum, John Laws, Ed Devereaux

The Nickel Ride
US 1975 110m DeLuxe
TCF
A wheeler dealer in downtown Los Angeles learns that he is marked for elimination.
Unpleasant and entirely uninteresting low-life crime melodrama.
w Eric Roth *d* Robert Mulligan
☆ Jason Miller, Linda Haynes, Victor French, John Hillerman, Bo Hopkins

Nickelodeon *
US/GB 1976 122m Metrocolor
Columbia/EMI/Chartoff-Winkler (Frank Marshall)
In 1910, various characters come together to make movies, finally attending the 1915 opening in Hollywood of *The Birth of a Nation*.
What should have been a hugely entertaining chunk of comic nostalgia is killed stone dead by embarrassed acting, poor timing, and a general lack of funny ideas, despite having so much to borrow from.
w W. D. Richter, Peter Bogdanovich *d* Peter Bogdanovich *ph* Laszlo Kovacs *md* Richard Hazard
☆ Ryan O'Neal, Burt Reynolds, Tatum O'Neal, Brian Keith, Stella Stevens, John Ritter, Jane Hitchcock
'Ponderous slapstick and a pathetic parody of Harold Lloyd.' – *Sight and Sound*
'Another collection of scenes from other people's films.' – *Howard Kissel, Women's Wear Daily*
'The slightest familiarity with the early works of Hal Roach – not to mention D. W. Griffith, here pretentiously quoted – reveals how little Bogdanovich understands his vastly superior predecessors.' – *Robert Asahina, New Leader*
'The crudest, stupidest, unfunniest farce of this or any other year.' – *John Simon, New York*

Nick's Movie: see *Lightning Over Water*

Nicky and Gino
US 1988 109m DeLuxe
Rank/Orion (Marvin Minoff, Mike Farrell)
aka: *Dominick and Eugene*
A hospital doctor tries to keep his brain-damaged twin brother out of trouble.
Sentimental drama of no particular distinction.
w Alvin Sargent, Corey Blechman *story* Danny Porfirio *d* Robert M. Young *ph* Curtis Clark *m* Trevor Jones *pd* Doug Kraner *ed* Arthur Coburn
☆ Tom Hulce, Ray Liotta, Jamie Lee Curtis, Todd Graff, Bill Cobbs, David Strathairn, Mimi Cecchini, Robert Levine

Nico: see *Above the Law*

The Niebelungen ***
Germany 1924 bw silent
Decla-Bioscop (Erich Pommer)
Part 1: *Siegfried*, 115m approx (24 fps)
Part 2: *Kriemheld's Revenge*, 125m approx (24 fps)
Siegfried kills a dragon and marries a princess of Burgundy but the fierce queen Brunhilde arranges his death. His widow marries Attila the Hun and they massacre the Burgundians.
Stately, warlike legends are transformed into a slow, chilling, awe-inspiring sequence of films, the décor being of special interest. The films were conceived as a tribute to the German nation, and were among Hitler's favourites.
w Thea von Harbou *d* Fritz Lang *ph* Carl Hoffman, Günther Rittau *ad* Otto Hunte, Karl Vollbrecht, Erich Kettelhut
☆ Paul Richter, Marguerite Schön, Theodor Loos, Hannah Ralph, Rudolf Klein-Rogge

'They all loved him – a schoolteacher, a night club hostess, and a luscious society bud!'
Night after Night *
US 1932 76m bw
Paramount
An ex-boxer seeking refinement buys a night-club and falls for a socialite.
Dim little drama which is remembered for introducing Mae West to the screen with her famous line, 'Goodness had nothing to do with it'.
w Vincent Laurence *novel* Single Night by Louis Bromfield *d* Archie Mayo *ph* Ernest Haller
☆ George Raft, Constance Cummings, Wynne Gibson, *Mae West*, Alison Skipworth, Roscoe Karns, Louis Calhern
'Mae West stole everything but the cameras. I never made another picture with her. I knew she had me licked.' – *George Raft*

Night Ambush: see *Ill Met by Moonlight*

Night and Day *
US 1946 132m Technicolor
Warner (Arthur Schwarz)
The life of Cole Porter.
Or rather, a fictitious story about a composer who happens to be called Cole Porter. A careful but undistinguished musical with pleasant moments.
w Charles Hoffman, Leo Townsend, William Bowers *d* Michael Curtiz *ph* Peverell Marley, William V. Skall *m/ly* Cole Porter *md* Max Steiner, Ray Heindorf *ch* Le Roy Prinz
☆ Cary Grant, Alexis Smith, Monty Woolley, Mary Martin, Ginny Simms, Jane Wyman, Eve Arden, Victor Francen, Alan Hale, Dorothy Malone
Max Steiner, Ray Heindorf

Night and Day *
France 1991 100m colour
Artificial Eye/Pierre Grise Productions (Martine Marignac, Maurice Tinchant)
original title: *Nuit et Jour*
A woman has simultaneous and passionate affairs with two men.
A celebration of guilt-free sex, rather than love, with men depicted as adjuncts to a strong woman.
wd Chantal Akerman *ph* Jean-Claude Neckelbrouck *m* Marc Herouet *ad* Michel Vandestein, Dominique Douret *ed* Francine Sandberg, Camille Bordes-Resnais
☆ Guillaine Londez, Thomas Langmann, François Negret, Nicole Colchat, Pierre Laroche

Night and Fog *
France 1955 31m Eastmancolor
Argos/Como
original title: *Nuit et Brouillard*
An account of the concentration camp at Auschwitz, contrasted with the peaceful surroundings ten years after its disbandment.
An official film of great dignity.
ph Ghislain Cloquet, Sacha Vierny *d/ed* Alain Resnais

Night and the City
GB 1950 101m bw
TCF (Samuel G. Engel)
A crooked wrestling promoter is tracked down by an underworld gang.
A fated attempt to extend the success of Naked City *in a London setting; the surface is accomplished enough, but the plot and characters are just plain dull, especially as little is seen of the police.*
w Jo Eisinger *novel* Gerald Kersh *d* Jules Dassin *ph* Max Greene *m* Benjamin Frankel
☆ Richard Widmark, Gene Tierney, Googie Withers, Hugh Marlowe, Herbert Lom
'Brilliantly photographed, it is an example of neo-expressionist techniques at their most potent.' – *Richard Roud, 1964*

'When you're down to your last dream, you either live it or lose it.'
Night and the City
US 1992 104m colour
First Independent/Penta/Tribeca (Jane Rosenthal, Irwin Winkler)
A small-time lawyer talks himself into trouble when he sets up as a boxing promoter and has an affair with the wife of one of his backers.
Dully directed, the movie comes to life only spasmodically; for the most part, it just lies there, completely inert.
w Richard Price *novel* Gerald Kersh *d* Irwin Winkler *ph* Tak Fujimoto *m* James Newton Howard *pd* Peter Larkin *ed* David Brenner
☆ Robert DeNiro, Jessica Lange, Cliff Gorman, Jack Warden, Alan King, Eli Wallach, Barry Primus
'It resembles a cigarette lighter with a worn flint and a dry wick that never ignites, leaving everyone with bruised thumbs from vainly flicking the spiked wheel.' – *Philip French, Observer*
'A useless film.' – *Rupert Murdoch*
† A remake of Jules Dassin's 1950 film.

The Night Angel
US 1931 75m bw
Paramount
A Prague lawyer falls for the daughter of the brothel keeper he has sent to prison, and after killing a jealous suitor is himself accused of murder.
Would-be Dietrichean high-style melodrama which did its stars no good at all and virtually ended Miss Carroll's career.
wd Edmund Goulding
☆ Fredric March, Nancy Carroll, Alan Hale, Alison Skipworth, Katherine Emmett
'Mild and frequently boring entertainment of the kind that can just about last a week in most of the de luxers.' – *Variety*

A Night at the Opera ****
US 1935 96m bw
MGM (Irving Thalberg)
Three zanies first wreck, then help an opera company.
Certainly among the best of the Marxian extravaganzas, and the first to give them a big production to play with as well as musical interludes by other than themselves for a change of pace. The mix plays beautifully.
w George S. Kaufman, Morrie Ryskind d Sam Wood *ph* Merritt Gerstad *md* Herbert Stothart *ad* Cedric Gibbons, Ben Carre *ed* William LeVanway
☆ *Groucho Marx* (Otis B. Driftwood), *Chico Marx* (Fiorello), *Harpo Marx* (Tomasso), *Margaret Dumont* (Mrs Claypool), Kitty Carlisle (Rosa Castaldi), Allan Jones (Riccardo Baroni), Walter Woolf King (Rodolfo Lassparri), *Sig Rumann* (Herman Gottlieb)
'Corking comedy with the brothers at par and biz chances excellent … songs in a Marx picture are generally at a disadvantage because they're more or less interruptions, the customers awaiting the next laugh.' – *Variety*
† Zeppo Marx absented himself from here on.

'Score!'
A Night at the Roxbury
US 1998 81m DeLuxe
Paramount/SNL (Lorne Michaels, Amy Heckerling)
Two brothers, desperate to be cool, manage against the odds to be allowed into an exclusive LA night-club.
Yet another comic spin-off from the US TV series Saturday Night Live; *on the big screen, it is dumb, stupid and not at all funny.*
w Steve Koren, Will Ferrell, Chris Kattan *d* John Fortenberry *ph* Francis Kenny *m* David Kitay *pd* Steven Jordan *ed* Jay Kamen
☆ Will Ferrell, Chris Kattan, Molly Shannon, Dan Hedaya, Richard Grieco (as himself), Loni Anderson, Elisa Donovan, Gigi Rice, Lochlyn Munro
'We have to survive on a diet of low calorie slapstick and quick-fix buffoonery. Even at just 82 minutes it can still seem like an hour-and-a-half too long.' – *Trevor Lewis, Empire*

Night Beat
GB 1948 91m bw
BLPA (Harold Huth)
Demobbed, a commando becomes a policeman and his friend becomes a crook.
Manhattan Melodrama, *British style; no more than an adequate offering of its type.*
w T. J. Morrison, Roland Pertwee, Guy Morgan *d* Harold Huth *ph* Vaclav Vich *m* Benjamin Frankel *ad* F. Bellan *ed* Grace Garland
☆ Anne Crawford, Maxwell Reed, Ronald Howard, Christine Norden, Hector Ross, Sidney James

Night Boat to Dublin
GB 1945 99m bw
ABP (Hamilton Inglis)
An MI5 man saves an atom scientist from kidnapping.
Generally watchable low key thriller with familiar British ingredients.
w Lawrence Huntington, Robert Hall *d* Lawrence Huntington *ph* Otto Heller
☆ Robert Newton, Raymond Lovell, Muriel Pavlow, Guy Middleton, Herbert Lom, Martin Miller, Marius Goring

The Night Caller *
GB 1965 84m bw
New Art/Armitage
US title: *Blood Beast from Outer Space*
An alien being arrives on Earth to abduct girls for genetic purposes.
Reasonably well made science fiction thriller.
w Jim O'Connolly *novel* Frank Crisp *d* John Gilling *ph* Stephen Dade *m* Johnny Gregory
☆ John Saxon, Maurice Denham, Patricia Haines, Alfred Burke, John Carson, Jack Watson, Warren Mitchell

Night Caller (dubbed)
France/Italy 1975 125m Eastmancolor
Columbia-Warner/Cerito/Mondial (Henri Verneuil)
original title: *Peur sur la Ville*
A moody inspector, obsessed with his personal vendetta against a crook, pays little attention to tracking down a serial killer who is murdering women.
Slight but enjoyable thriller, with some fancy stunts to enliven a familiar story.
w Henri Verneuil, Francis Veber *d* Henri Verneuil *ph* Jean Penzer *m* Ennio Morricone *ad* Jean André *ed* Pierre Gillette, Henri Lanoë
☆ Jean-Paul Belmondo, Charles Denner, Catherine Morin, Adalberto-Maria Merli, Lea Massari, Giovanni Cianfriglia, Rosy Varte, Henri-Jacques Huet
'A routine policier, which seems to have one eye on the American tough cop series.' – *John Gillett, MFB*

Night Club Hostess: see *Unmarried*

Night Club Lady
US 1932 66m bw
Columbia
A police commissioner solves the murder of a night-club hostess.
Straightforward cops and killers melodrama with the star in his first non-romantic role.

w Robert Riskin *novel* Anthony Abbott *d* Irving Cummings
☆ Adolphe Menjou, Mayo Methot, Skeets Gallagher, Blanche Friderici, Nat Pendleton

Night Club Scandal
US 1937 74m bw
Paramount
A society doctor murders his wife and incriminates her lover.
Smooth second feature remake of Guilty as Hell, *chiefly notable for its star's last controlled performance.*
w Lillie Hayward *play Riddle Me This* by Daniel Rubin *d* Ralph Murphy *ph* Leo Tover
☆ *John Barrymore*, Lynne Overman, Charles Bickford, Elizabeth Patterson, Evelyn Brent, Louise Campbell, J. Carrol Naish

Night Court
US 1932 90m bw
MGM
GB title: *Justice for Sale*
A corrupt judge frames a girl on a prostitution charge.
Tough star melodrama.
w Mark Hellinger, Bayard Veiller, Charles Beehan, Lenore Coffee *d* W. S. Van Dyke
☆ Walter Huston, Lewis Stone, Anita Page, Phillips Holmes, Jean Hersholt
'Political frame-up of women is made the subject of a vigorous melodrama, though it comes after the New York scandal on the subject is largely forgotten.' – *Variety*

Night Crawlers: see *The Navy versus The Night Monsters*

Night Creatures: see *Captain Clegg*

Night Crossing
(family) US 1982 106m Technicolor
Walt Disney (Tom Leetch)
(NTSC) (colourised)
East Germans escape to the west via air balloon.
Well-meaning melodrama which sadly lacks plot development and suspense, and is also rather miserable to look at.
w John McGreevey *d* Delbert Mann *ph* Tony Imi *m* Jerry Goldsmith
☆ John Hurt, Jane Alexander, Doug McKeon, Frank McKeon, Beau Bridges, Glynnis O'Connor, Ian Bannen

The Night Digger
GB 1971 100m colour
MGM
A frustrated spinster protects a handyman clearly guilty of murder, and runs away with him.
How this came to be made at all when the Finney version of Night Must Fall *had recently flopped is a mystery; it had so little box-office appeal that it was barely released.*
w Roald Dahl *story* Joy Cowley *d* Alastair Reid
☆ Patricia Neal, Nicholas Clay, Pamela Browne, Jean Anderson, Yootha Joyce, Peter Sallis, Graham Crowden

Night Eyes
US/India 1990 98m colour
Amritraj-Baldwin (Ashok Amritraj)
(NTSC)
A rock star hires a security guard to look after his estranged wife, hoping to catch her in an affair.
Cheap, unsubtle thriller of the sort that gives direct-to-video movies a bad name: the dialogue sounds as if it was bought by the yard, and the acting and direction are uninteresting.
w Tom Citrano, Andrew Stevens *d* Jag Mundhra *ph* James Mathers *m* Richard Glasser *pd* Brian McCabe *ed* David H. Lloyd
☆ Andrew Stevens, Tanya Roberts, Warwick Sims, Karen Elise Baldwin, Cooper Huckabee, Stephen Meadows, Chick Vennera
† It was followed by three sequels, none of which managed to be any more watchable.

'In a city of nine million people is there room for one honest man?'
Night Falls on Manhattan *
US 1997 114m DuArt
Paramount/Spelling (Thom Mount, Josh Kramer)
(PAL) (NTSC) (laser) (laser)
Investigating the shooting of his father, a policeman, by a drug dealer, an honest cop-turned-lawyer uncovers high-level corruption.
Effective investigative drama on a somewhat familiar theme, but given urgency by the lead performances.
wd Sidney Lumet *novel Tainted Evidence* by Robert Daley *ph* David Watkin *m* Mark Isham *pd* Philip Rosenberg *ed* Sam O'Steen
☆ Andy Garcia, Richard Dreyfuss, Lena Olin, Ian Holm, James Gandolfini, Colm Feore, Ron Liebman
'Intelligent and reasonably compelling, this is solid fare.' – *Empire*

Night Fighters: see *A Terrible Beauty*

Night Flight *
US 1933 84m bw
MGM (David O. Selznick)
The president of a civil airline insists that dangerous night flights must continue as a mark of progress.
Spurious, unsatisfactory, multi-star air melodrama lacking both narrative flow and the common touch.
w Oliver H. P. Garrett *stories* Antoine de St Exupéry *d* Clarence Brown *ph* Oliver T. Marsh, Elmer Dyer, Charles Marshall
☆ John Barrymore, Helen Hayes, Lionel Barrymore, Clark Gable, Robert Montgomery, Myrna Loy, William Gargan, C. Henry Gordon
'Punch aviation film with a flock of potent marquee names.' – *Variety*
'It is in the sense it conveys of human beings caught in the swift machinery of modern living that *Night Flight* soars above other pictures of its kind.' – *James Shelley Hamilton*

Night Full of Rain: see *The End of the World (in our usual bed in a night full of rain)*

Night Games *
Sweden 1966 105m bw
Sandrews (Lena Malmsjö)
original title: *Nattlek*
A 35-year-old man is sexually inhibited by memories of his dead mother's passions and perversions.
Curious Freudian parable apparently intended as a comment on the state of Europe. Audiences found it merely peculiar.
wd Mai Zetterling novel Mai Zetterling *ph* Rune Ericson *m* Jan Johansson, George Riedel
☆ Ingrid Thulin, Keve Hjelm, Lena Brundin, Naima Wifstrand
'The best one can say is that it never lets up for a moment.' – *David Wilson, MFB*

Night Games
US 1980 100m Technicolor
Golden Harvest/Avco
(NTSC) (colourised)
A neurotic Beverly Hills housewife is terrified of men.
Crazy mix of case history, eroticism and suspense with insufficient of any to satisfy fans.
w Anton Diether, Clarke Reynolds *d* Roger Vadim *ph* Denis Lewiston *m* John Barry
☆ Cindy Pickett, Joanna Cassidy, Barry Primus

Night Hair Child
GB 1971 89m Movielab
Leander/Harry Alan Towers (Graham Harris)
A 12-year-old boy makes sexual advances to his stepmother.
Corrupt voyeuristic weirdie which has to be seen to be believed.
w Trevor Preston *d* James Kelly *ph* Harry Waxman *m* Stelvio Cipriani
☆ Mark Lester, Britt Ekland, Hardy Kruger, Harry Andrews, Lilli Palmer

'Was his strange power a blessing or a curse? He was a refugee from love – because he could foretell that their marriage and their kisses would dissolve in a tragedy of tears!'
Night Has a Thousand Eyes
US 1948 80m bw
Paramount (André Boehm)
A vaudeville mentalist finds that he really does have the power to predict the future.
Predictable supernatural melodrama closely modelled on The Clairvoyant *(qv); quite nicely made but simply not exciting.*
w Barre Lyndon, Jonathan Latimer *novel* Cornell Woolrich *d* John Farrow *ph* John F. Seitz *m* Victor Young
☆ *Edward G. Robinson*, Gail Russell, John Lund, Virginia Bruce, William Demarest, Richard Webb, Jerome Cowan
'For those who like sweet hocus-pocus and Edward G. Robinson.' – *Sunday Express*

The Night Has Eyes *
GB 1942 79m bw
ABP (John Argyle)
(NTSC)
US title: *Terror House*
A young teacher disappears on the Yorkshire moors; her friend goes in search, and comes under the influence of a strange young man and his sinister housekeeper.
Stagey but effective little thriller, with oodles of fog and bog to help the suspense.
w Alan Kennington *d* Leslie Arliss *ph* Günther Krampf *m* Charles Williams
☆ *James Mason*, Joyce Howard, *Wilfrid Lawson*, Mary Clare, Tucker McGuire, John Fernald
'Some ingenuity and not a little style.' – *The Times*

The Night Holds Terror *
US 1955 86m bw
Columbia (Andrew Stone)
Three gunmen on the run kidnap a factory worker and hold him to ransom.
Effective, detailed, low-budget police melodrama; its plot may be over familiar now, but at the time it was refreshing and the whole film an intelligent exercise in suspense.
wd Andrew Stone ph Fred Jackman Jnr *m* Lucien Cailliet
☆ Jack Kelly, Hildy Parks, John Cassavetes, David Cross, Edward Marr, Jack Kruschen

A Night in Cairo: see *The Barbarian*

A Night in Casablanca **
(family) US 1946 85m bw
David L. Loew
(PAL)
Three zanies rout Nazi refugees in a North African hotel.
The last authentic Marxian extravaganza; it starts uncertainly, builds to a fine sustained frenzy, then peters out in some overstretched airplane acrobatics.
w Joseph Fields, Roland Kibbee, Frank Tashlin *d* Archie Mayo *ph* James Van Trees *m* Werner Janssen *pd* Duncan Cramer
☆ *Groucho Marx, Chico Marx, Harpo Marx, Sig Rumann, Lisette Verea*, Charles Drake, Lois Collier, Dan Seymour
KORNBLOW (GROUCHO MARX): 'I don't mind being killed, but I resent hearing it from a character whose head comes to a point.'
KORNBLOW: 'From now on the essence of this hotel will be speed. If a customer asks you for a three-minute egg, give it to him in two minutes. If he asks you for a two-minute egg, give it to him in one minute. If he asks you for a one-minute egg, give him the chicken and let him work it out for himself.'
BEATRICE (LISETTE VEREA): 'My name's Beatrice Ryner. I stop at the hotel.'
KORNBLOW: 'My name's Ronald Kornblow. I stop at nothing.'
'It is beside the main point to add that it isn't one of their best movies; for the worst they might ever make would be better worth seeing than most other things I can think of.' – *James Agee*

A Night in Havana: see *The Big Boodle*

A Night in Paradise
US 1946 84m Technicolor
(Universal)
Aesop falls in love at the court of King Croesus.
Deadly boring, unintentionally funny Arabian Nights farrago without the saving grace of action.
w Ernest Pascal, Emmet Lavery *novel Peacock's Feather* by George S. Hellman *d* Arthur Lubin *ph* Hal Mohr *m* Frank Skinner *ad* Alexander Golitzen, John B. Goodman *ed* Milton Carruth
☆ Merle Oberon, Turhan Bey, Thomas Gomez, Gale Sondergaard, Ray Collins, George Dolenz, John Litel, Ernest Truex, Jerome Cowan, Douglass Dumbrille

A Night in the Life of Jimmy Reardon: see *Jimmy Reardon*

Night into Morning
US 1951 86m bw
MGM (Edwin H. Knopf)
A college professor loses his wife and son in an accident; despair drives him to drink and attempted suicide.
Well-made and well-meaning melodrama whose virtual absence of plot makes it seem by the end merely maudlin.
w Karl Tunberg, Leonard Spigelgass *d* Fletcher Markle *ph* George Folsey *m* Carmen Dragon
☆ Ray Milland, Nancy Davis, John Hodiak, Lewis Stone, Jean Hagen, Rosemary de Camp
'Tediously uneventful, as sincere and futile as a note of condolence.' – *Time*

The Night Is Ending: see *Paris After Dark*

Night Is My Future: see *Music Is My Future*

The Night Is Young
US 1934 82m bw
MGM
A European archduke loves a ballerina.
High-class musical which failed despite an intriguing cast and a Romberg and Hammerstein score.
w Vicki Baum *d* Dudley Murphy
☆ Evelyn Laye, Ramon Novarro, Una Merkel, Edward Everett Horton, Rosalind Russell, Charles Butterworth, Herman Bing, Henry Stephenson, Donald Cook
'Disappointing entertainment ... feeble in plot, with a cast struggling to carry assignments and failing to ignite any real romantic fire, film also seems to lack a single strong musical number.' – *Variety*

The Night Is Young
France 1986 119m colour
Artificial Eye/Les Films Plain Chant/Soporfilms/FR3 (Philippe Diaz)
(PAL)
original title: *Mauvais Sang*
In the future, a gang of criminals sets out to steal an antidote to a disease which kills those who indulge in sex without love.
Chic, slight tale, influenced for the bad by Godard.
wd Leos Carax *ph* Jean-Yves Escoffier *pd* Michel Vandestien *ed* Nelly Quettier
☆ Michel Piccoli, Juliette Binoche, Denis Lavant, Hans Meyer, Julie Delpy, Carroll Brooks, Hugo Pratty

Night Key
US 1937 67m bw
Universal (Robert Presnell)
An inventor's idea is stolen by his former partner, and he takes an appropriate revenge.
Low-key star melodrama: competent, but no great shakes.
w Tristram Tupper, John C. Moffitt *d* Lloyd Corrigan *ph* George Robinson *m* Louis Forbes *make-up* Jack Pierce
☆ Boris Karloff, Jean Rogers, Warren Hull, Samuel S. Hinds, Alan Baxter, Ward Bond, Edwin Maxwell
'Mildly entertaining dualler ... one of those impossible gadget yarns with liberal injections of cops and robbers stuff.' – *Variety*

The Night Life of the Gods
US 1935 75m bw
Universal
An inventor turns statues into people, and vice versa.
Fantasy comedy from a well-known comic novel; interesting despite low level of invention.
w Barry Trivers *novel* Thorne Smith *d* Lowell Sherman *ph* John Mescall *ed* Ted J. Kent
☆ Alan Mowbray, Florine McKinney, Richard Carle, Peggy Shannon
'Universal has managed to keep in the fun and restrain it from getting too rough.' – *Variety*

Night Mail ***
GB 1936 24m bw
GPO Film Unit (John Grierson)
A 'film poem' showing the journey of the mail train from London to Glasgow.
One of the best and most influential of British documentaries: despite a few absurdities, it remains a pleasure to watch.
wd Basil Wright, Harry Watt poem W. H. Auden *ph J. Jones, H. E. Fowle m Benjamin Britten sound arrangements* Alberto Cavalcanti

'The final sequences as the train drives at dawn through the northern moors, the sheep-dog racing the train and the rabbits scurrying to cover, set to the simple visual verses of Mr Auden, are extraordinarily exciting.' – *Graham Greene, The Spectator*

Night Mayor
US 1932 65m bw
Columbia
The Mayor of New York pays too much attention to night life and not enough to his desk.
Thinly veiled account of the Jimmy Walker affair, released after Walker had been discredited. As entertainment, punchy, but in the end only fair.
w Gertrude Purcell, Sam Marx *d* Ben Stoloff
☆ Lee Tracy, Evalyn Knapp, Eugene Pallette, Warren Hymer, Donald Dillaway, Astrid Allwyn
'It is a safe general statement that the screen ought never to exploit a public character who is the center of debate.' – *Variety*

Night Monster
US 1942 73m bw
Universal (Ford Beebe)
GB title: *House of Mystery*
Murders are committed in a spooky house by a cripple who produces synthetic legs by self-hypnotism.
Stilted, creaky would-be thriller with a good cast and an impertinent plot.
w Clarence Upson Young *d* Ford Beebe *ph* Charles Van Enger *m* H. J. Salter *ad* Jack Otterson, Richard H. Riedel *ed* Milton Carruth
☆ Ralph Morgan, Don Porter, Irene Hervey, Bela Lugosi, Lionel Atwill, Nils Asther, Leif Erickson, Frank Reicher

'Night, Mother
US 1986 96m DeLuxe
Universal/Aaron Spelling, Alan Greisman
A mother gets to grips with the problems of her suicidal daughter.
Rueful drama which pares down the nerve ends but was clearly not designed for box-office, and remains a play rather than a film.
w Marsha Norman *play* Marsha Norman *d* Tom Moore *ph* Stephen M. Katz *m* David Shire
☆ Anne Bancroft, Sissy Spacek, Ed Berke, Carol Robbins

'Maybe he would find the girl – maybe he would find himself!'
Night Moves *
US 1975 99m Technicolor
Warner/Hiller/Layton (Robert M. Sherman)
A private eye is engaged to find a runaway teenager.
Apparently a Chandlerish mystery, this is really a Pinterish audience-teaser with obsessions about communication and the meaning of life. A smart-ass entertainment for eager trendies.
w Alan Sharp *d* Arthur Penn *ph* Bruce Surtees *m* Michael Small *pd* George Jenkins
☆ Gene Hackman, Jennifer Warren, Edward Binns, Harris Yulin, Kenneth Mars
'Beneath the complicated unravelling of a mystery, an anti-mystery, with the hero's detection registering as an evasion of his own problems; beneath a densely charted intrigue of betrayals and cross purposes, a cryptic void...' – *Jonathan Rosenbaum*
'A suspenseless suspenser ... there's very little rhyme or reason for the plot's progression.' – *Variety*
'Rich and dense enough to set up reverberations long after one has left the cinema.' – *Michael Billington, Illustrated London News*

Night Must Fall **
US 1937 117m bw
MGM (Hunt Stromberg)
A bland young bellboy who is really a psychopathic murderer attaches himself to the household of a rich old lady.
Unconvincing but memorable Hollywood expansion of an effective British chiller.
w John Van Druten *play* Emlyn Williams *d* Richard Thorpe *ph* Ray June *m* Edward Ward
☆ *Robert Montgomery*, Rosalind Russell, *May Whitty*, Alan Marshal, Merle Tottenham, Kathleen Harrison, Matthew Boulton, E. E. Clive
'Too long and not box office ... tedious, slow, and even dull in spots.' – *Variety*
'A pretty little murder play has made a long dim film.' – *Graham Greene*
'The most exhilarating shrouds of horror hang over it. It represents a provocative imagination, a skilled adapter, a sensitive director, a splendid acting job.' – *Bland Johaneson, New York Daily Mirror*
† Louis B. Mayer so disliked this film that at the New York première he ordered the distribution of leaflets disowning it on behalf of MGM.
Academy Award nomination: Robert Montgomery; May Whitty

Night Must Fall
GB 1964 105m bw
MGM (Albert Finney, Karel Reisz)
Dreary remake with a mannered star performance and the emphasis on axe murders. A mistake from beginning to end.
w Clive Exton *d* Karel Reisz *ph* Freddie Francis *m* Ron Grainer
☆ Albert Finney, Susan Hampshire, Mona Washbourne, Sheila Hancock, Michael Medwin, Joe Gladwin, Martin Wyldeck
'Not so much a thriller as a typically humourless example of that overworked genre known as psychological drama ... [Finney] constantly recalls a ventriloquist's dummy.' – *MFB*

The Night My Number Came Up *
GB 1954 94m bw
Ealing (Tom Morahan)
A man dreams that his plane will crash, and the dream begins to come true.
Intriguing little melodrama which badly lacks a twist ending and foxes itself by a flashback construction which leaves very little open to doubt. Production generally good.
w R. C. Sherriff *d* Leslie Norman *ph* Lionel Banes *m* Malcolm Arnold
☆ Michael Redgrave, Alexander Knox, Sheila Sim, Denholm Elliott, Ursula Jeans, George Rose, Nigel Stock, Michael Hordern, Ralph Truman, Victor Maddern, Bill Kerr, Alfie Bass
'A story which, in its delicately measured suspenses and reliefs, has been beautifully built.' – *Times Educational Supplement*
'The idea of destiny as predestiny is an old psychological trump, but it still takes tricks.' – *Time*
† The story was taken from a personal account by Sir Victor Goddard.

Night Nurse *
US 1931 72m bw
Warner
A nurse uncovers a plot by other members of the household against her patient's children.
Fast-moving melodrama with solid star performances; just what the public wanted in 1931.
w Oliver H. P. Garrett, Charles Kenyon *novel* Dora Macy *d* William Wellman *ph* Chick McGill *md* Leo Forbstein *ad* Max Parker *ed* Edward M. McDermott
☆ Barbara Stanwyck, Ben Lyon, Joan Blondell, Clark Gable, Charles Winninger, Vera Lewis, Blanche Frederici, Charlotte Merriam
'A conglomeration of exaggerations, often bordering on serial dramatics.' – *Hollywood Reporter*

Night of Counting the Years **
Egypt 1969 102m colour
Egyptian Cinema General Organization
original title: *El Mumia*
Horrified to discover that his tribe has grown rich by robbing the tombs of the Pharaohs, a young leader faces the dilemma of what to do about it.
Engrossing, if rather stately, account of a moral choice against the magnificent background of Egypt's past. The film was sponsored by Italian director Roberto Rossellini.
wd Shadi Abdelsalam *ph* Abdel Aziz Fahmy *m* Mario Nascimbene *ad* Salah Marei *ed* Kamal Abou
☆ Ahmed Marel (Wanniss), Zouzou El Hakim (Mother), Ahmad Hegazi (Brother), Nadia Loutfy (Zeena), Gaby Karraz (Maspero)
'Film-making of the highest order.' – *MFB*

Night of Dark Shadows
US 1971 97m Metrocolor Panavision
MGM (Dan Curtis)
aka: *Curse of Dark Shadows*
After moving to his ancestral home, an artist begins to experience strange and violent visions of the past.
Tame tale of the supernatural that fails to hold one's interest.
w Sam Hall *story* Sam Hall, Dan Curtis *d* Dan Curtis *ph* Richard Shore *m* Robert Cobert *pd* Trevor Williams *ed* Charles Goldsmith
☆ David Selby, Grayson Hall, Lara Parker, John Karlen, Nancy Barrett, James Storm, Thayer David, Christopher Pennock, Diana Millay, Kate Jackson
† The film was an unsuccessful follow-up to Curtis's 1970 film *House of Dark Shadows* (qv).

The Night of January 16th
US 1941 79m bw
Paramount
A secretary is arrested for her boss's murder; but is he really dead?
A stage thriller full of theatrical trickery becomes a very mundane film.
w Delmer Daves, Robert Pirosh, Eve Greene *play* Ayn Rand *d* William Clemens
☆ Robert Preston, Ellen Drew, Nils Asther, Margaret Hayes

The Night of June 13th
US 1932 76m bw
Paramount
A suburban street is transformed when one of its residents goes on trial for murder.
Combination courtroom and slice-of-life drama which satisfied most audiences.
w Agnes Brand Leahy, Brian Marlow, William Slavens McNutt *story* Vera Caspary *d* Stephen Roberts
☆ Clive Brook, Lila Lee, Mary Boland, Adrianne Allen, Gene Raymond, Frances Dee, Charley Grapewin
'Absorbingly worked out with fascinating character study and a touch of satire.' – *Variety*

A Night of Love: see *Manifesto*

'What happens after they turn the lights out on Broadway?'
The Night of Nights
US 1939 86m bw
Paramount
A once-famous Broadway writer, now a drunk, tries to ensure his daughter's fame.
Curious downbeat melodrama without the courage of its convictions, or the actors to give the right bravura performances.
w Donald Ogden Stewart *d* Lewis Milestone
☆ Pat O'Brien, Olympe Bradna, Reginald Gardiner, Roland Young
'Backstage drama lightened by direction and cast performances. Nominal supporter for key duals.' – *Variety*

The Night of San Lorenzo **
Italy 1981 107m Agfacolor
UA/Premier/RAI/Ager Cinematografica (Giuliani G. de Negri)
original title: *La Notte Di San Lorenzo*
aka: *Night of the Shooting Stars*
In the Second World War a six-year-old girl watches events in her town as American forces advance to liberate it.
Touching, powerfully nostalgic study of a community in ferment.
wd Paolo Taviani, Vittorio Taviani *ph* Franco Di Giacomo *m* Nicola Piovani *ad* Gianni Sbarra *ed* Roberto Perpignani
☆ Omero Antonutti, Margarita Lozano, Claudio Bigagli, Massimo Bonetti, Norma Martelli, Enrica Maria Modugno, Sabina Vannucchi

Night of the Big Heat
GB 1967 94m Eastmancolor
Tom Blakeley/Planet
US title: *Island of the Burning Damned*
Invaders from outer space take over a remote Scottish island and make it unbearably hot so that they can survive.
Sloppily made and over-prolonged science fiction with far too much irrelevant talk.
w Ronald Liles *novel* John Lymington *d* Terence Fisher *ph* Reginald Wyer *m* Malcolm Lockyer
☆ Christopher Lee, Peter Cushing, Patrick Allen, Sarah Lawson, Jane Merrow, William Lucas, Kenneth Cope

Night of the Bloody Apes (dubbed)
Mexico 1970 82m Eastmancolor
Grand National/Unistar (Alfredo Salazar)
original title: *Horriplante Bestia Humana*
aka: *Gomar the Human Gorilla*
In an attempt to save his son's life, a doctor gives him the heart of a gorilla, causing him to change into a murderous ape.
Bizarre horror that may appeal to lovers of terrible movies; it borrows from every major film of the genre, from Jekyll and Hyde *and* Frankenstein *to* King Kong *and* The Murders of the Rue Morgue.
w René Cardona, René Cardona Jnr *d* René Cardona *ph* Raúl Martinez Solares *m* Antonio Diaz Conde *ad* Carlos Arjona *ed* Jorge Bustos *sp* Javier Torres Torija
☆ José Elias Moreno, Carlos López Moctezuma, Armando Silvestre, Norma Lazareno, Agustin Martinez Solares, Noelia Noel
'Patience is severely tried by the stately pace, the endless expressions of paternal devotion, and the script's risible attempts to offer medical explanations and justifications.' – *Tom Milne, MFB*

Night of the Comet
US 1984 98m colour
Atlantic/Thomas Coleman-Michael Rosenblatt (Andrew Lane, Wayne Crawford)
In Los Angeles two sisters are the only survivors of a cosmic storm that kills the population or turns them into zombies.
Low-budget science-fiction thriller, done with humour and some imagination.
wd Thom Eberhardt *ph* Arthur Albert *m* David Richard Campbell *pd* John Muto *ed* Fred Stafford
☆ Robert Beltran, Catherine Mary Stewart, Kelli Maroney, Sharon Farrell, Mary Woronov, Geoffrey Lewis

Night of the Cyclone
US 1990 90m colour
Maroon (Edgar Bold)
aka: *Perfume of the Cyclone*
A maverick Chicago cop goes to a tropical island to find his spoilt 16-year-old daughter, who has not returned from a modelling assignment.
Glossy thriller that is both exotic and uninteresting, affected and very ordinary.
w Rick Brotherhood *d* David Irving *ph* James Robb *m* David Pollecutt *pd* Graeme Orwin *ed* Ettie Feldman
☆ Kris Kristofferson, Jeff Meek, Marisa Berenson, Winston Ntshona, Dick Reineke, Marcel van Heerden, Alla Korot

Night of the Demon ***
GB 1957 87m bw
Columbia/Sabre (Frank Bevis)
US title: *Curse of the Demon*
An occultist despatches his enemies by raising a giant medieval devil.
Despite dim work from the leads, this supernatural thriller is intelligently scripted and achieves several frightening and memorable sequences in the best Hitchcock manner.
w Charles Bennett, Hal E. Chester story Casting the Runes by *M. R. James d Jacques Tourneur ph* Ted Scaife *m* Clifton Parker *ad* Ken Adam
☆ Dana Andrews, Peggy Cummins, *Niall MacGinnis, Athene Seyler*, Brian Wilde, Maurice Denham, Ewan Roberts, Liam Redmond, Reginald Beckwith

Night of the Demons
US 1988 92m colour
Meridian/Paragon (Joe Augustyn, Jeff Geoffray, Walter S. Josten)
Teenagers release demonic spirits when they hold a Halloween party in a mortuary.
Direly predictable, cheaply produced horror flick with some gruesome make-up effects.

w Joe Augustyn *d* Kevin S. Tenney *ph* David Lewis *m* Dennis Michael Tenney *ad* Ken Aichele *ed* Daniel Duncan *sp* make-up: Steve Johnson
☆ Alvin Alexis, Alison Barron, Lance Fenton, William Gallo, Hal Havins, Mimi Kinkade, Linnea Quigley; Lance Fenton

'Angela's Back ... And She's Throwing Another Party ... Trick Or Treat, Sucker!'

Night of the Demons 2
US 1994 98m colour
Republic/Blue Rider (Walter Josten, Jeff Geoffray)
aka: *Night of the Demons: Angela's Revenge*
A girl invites fellow students to a creepy old house for Halloween night, causing the malevolent spirit of its former owner to wreak havoc and create zombie killers.
A more polished retread of the original, with the welcome addition of graveyard humour.
w Joe Augustyn, James Penzi *d* Brian Trenchard-Smith *ph* David Lewis *m* Jim Manzie *pd* Wendy Guidery *ed* Daniel Duncan *sp* prosthetic make-up: Steve Johnson
☆ Cristi Harris, Bobby Jacoby, Merle Kennedy, Amelia Kinkade, Rod McCary, Zoe Trilling, Jennifer Rhodes
'Rises above most slice-and-dice fare and may tantalize some more discriminating palettes in addition to the usual teen suspects.' – *Variety*

Night of the Doomed
Italy 1965 97m bw
Emmeci (Carlo Caiano)
original title: *Amanti d'Oltretomba*
GB title: *The Faceless Monster; US title: Nightmare Castle*
A sadistic scientist tries to drive his dead wife's stepsister, who has inherited her money, insane.
Lurid thriller that circles endlessly around Barbara Steele, running the gamut of emotions in two roles.
w Carlo Caiano, Fabio de Agostini *d* Allan Grunewald (Mario Caiano) *ph* Enzo Barboni *m* Ennio Morricone *ad* Massimo Tavazzi *ed* Renato Cinquini
☆ Barbara Steele, Paul Muller, Helga Liné, Laurence Clift, Rik Battaglia, Giuseppe Addobbati

Night of the Eagle **
GB 1961 87m bw
Independent Artists (Albert Fennell)
US title: *Burn, Witch, Burn*
At a medical school, a jealous witch sets an evil force on her rival.
Pretty good supernatural thriller, let down by leading performances and sustained by character roles and solid production values in creepy sequences.
w Charles Beaumont, Richard Matheson, George Baxt *novel* Conjure Wife by Fritz Leiber Jnr *d* Sidney Hayers *ph* Reg Wyer *m* William Alwyn
☆ *Margaret Johnston*, Janet Blair, Peter Wyngarde, Anthony Nicholls, Reginald Beckwith, Kathleen Byron

The Night of the Following Day *
US 1969 100m Technicolor
Universal/Gina (Hubert Cornfield)
A young girl arriving in Paris to stay with her father is kidnapped and held to ransom by an eccentric gang.
Straightforward suspense thriller with delusions of grandeur; the second half bogs down in pretentious talk and the end suggests that the whole thing was a dream.
w Hubert Cornfield, Robert Phippeny *novel* The Snatchers by Lionel White *d* Hubert Cornfield *ph* Willy Kurant *m* Stanley Myers
☆ Marlon Brando, Richard Boone, Rita Moreno, Pamela Franklin, Jess Hahn

Night of the Garter
GB 1933 86m bw
British and Dominions (Herbert Wilcox)
A newly married man tries to retrieve an intimate gift from an old flame.
One of the best-remembered comedies of Sydney Howard.
w Austin Melford, Marjorie Gaffney *play* Getting Gertie's Garter by Avery Hopwood, Wilson Collison *d* Jack Raymond
☆ Sydney Howard, Winifred Shotter, Elsie Randolph, Austin Melford

The Night of the Generals **
GB 1967 148m Technicolor Panavision
Columbia/Horizon/Filmsonor (Sam Spiegel)
A German intelligence agent tracks down a psychopathic Nazi general who started killing prostitutes in Warsaw during World War II.
A curiously bumpy narrative which is neither mystery nor character study but does provide a few effective sequences and impressive performances. The big budget seems well spent.
w Joseph Kessel, Paul Dehn *novel* Hans Helmut Kirst *d* Anatole Litvak *ph* Henri Decaë *m* Maurice Jarre *pd* Alexander Trauner
☆ Peter O'Toole, *Omar Sharif, Tom Courtenay*, Donald Pleasence, Joanna Pettet, *Philippe Noiret*, Charles Gray, Coral Browne, John Gregson, Harry Andrews, Nigel Stock, Christopher Plummer, Juliette Greco
'The "who" is obvious from the first and the "dunnit" interminable.' – *Judith Crist, 1973*
'Lurid and vivid, if nothing else.' – *Robert Windeler*

Night of the Ghouls
US 1958 75m bw
Wade Williams (Edward D. Wood Jnr)
aka: *Revenge of the Dead*
Dr Acula, a fake medium, takes up residence in a haunted house where he manages to raise the dead.
Aficianados of the work of the totally inept Wood may enjoy this, since it has all the hallmarks of his movies: bad acting, irrelevant voice-over and hopeless direction, although it lacks the delirium of Plan 9 from Outer Space.
wd Edward D. Wood Jnr *ph* William C. Thompson *md* Gordon Zahler *ad* Kathleen O'Hara Everett
☆ Criswell, Kenne Duncan, 'Duke' Moore, Valda Hansen, Tor Johnson, John Carpenter, Paul Marco

The Night of the Grizzly
US 1966 102m Techniscope
Paramount (Burt Dunne)
A Wyoming ex-sheriff kills a marauding bear and earns the respect of his son.
Stout-hearted family film, rather sluggishly made.
w Warren Douglas *d* Joseph Pevney *ph* Harold Lipstein, Loyal Griggs *m* Leith Stevens
☆ Clint Walker, Martha Hyer, Keenan Wynn, Leo Gordon, Kevin Brodie, Nancy Kulp, Ellen Corby, Jack Elam, Ron Ely

'The scenes! The story! The stars! But above all – the suspense!'

The Night of the Hunter ***
US 1955 93m bw
UA/Paul Gregory
A psychopathic preacher goes on the trail of hidden money, the secret of which is held by two children.
Weird, manic fantasy in which evil finally comes to grief against the forces of sweetness and light (the children, an old lady, water, animals). Although the narrative does not flow smoothly there are splendidly imaginative moments, and no other film has ever quite achieved its texture.
w James Agee *novel* Davis Grubb *d* Charles Laughton *ph* Stanley Cortez *m* Walter Schumann
☆ Robert Mitchum, Shelley Winters, Lillian Gish, Don Beddoe, Evelyn Varden, Peter Graves, James Gleason
PREACHER (ROBERT MITCHUM): 'Lord, you sure knew what you was doing when you brung me to this very cell at this very time. A man with ten thousand dollars hid somewhere, and a widder in the makin'.'
'One of the most frightening movies ever made.' – *Pauline Kael, 1968*
'A genuinely sinister work, full of shocks and over-emphatic sound effects, camera angles and shadowy lighting.' – *NFT, 1973*
'One of the most daring, eloquent and personal films to have come from America in a long time.' – *Derek Prouse*

'One man ... three women ... one night!'

The Night of the Iguana ***
US 1964 125m bw
MGM/Seven Arts (Ray Stark)
A disbarred clergyman becomes a travel courier in Mexico and is sexually desired by a teenage nymphomaniac, a middle-aged hotel owner and a frustrated itinerant artist.
The author is most tolerable when poking fun at his own types, and this is a sharp, funny picture with a touch of poetry.
w Anthony Veiller *play* Tennessee Williams *d* John Huston *ph* Gabriel Figueroa *m* Benjamin Frankel *ad* Stephen Grimes
☆ *Richard Burton*, Deborah Kerr, Ava Gardner, Sue Lyon, *Grayson Hall, Cyril Delevanti*
'Whatever poetry it had seems to have leaked out.' – *New Yorker, 1982*
Gabriel Figueroa; Grayson Hall

Night of the Juggler
US 1980 100m Technicolor
Columbia
A New Yorker relentlessly pursues the kidnapper of his daughter.
Average chase thriller with good location staging of car crashes.
w Bill Norton Snr, Rick Natkin *novel* William P. McGivern *d* Robert Butler *ph* Victor J. Kemper *m* Art Kane
☆ James Brolin, Cliff Gorman, Richard Castellano, Abby Bluestone

Night of the Laughing Dead: see *The House in Nightmare Park*

'There's a herd of killer rabbits heading this way!'

Night of the Lepus
US 1972 88m Metrocolor
MGM (A. C. Lyles)
A serum meant to control a surplus of rabbits instead produces monster varieties four feet tall.
Tolerable sci-fi tailored to a very tired formula.
w Don Holiday, Gene R. Kearney *novel* The Year of the Angry Rabbit by Russell Braddon *d* William F. Claxton *ph* Ted Voigtlander *m* Jimmie Haskell
☆ Stuart Whitman, Rory Calhoun, Janet Leigh, Paul Fix, DeForest Kelley
'For insomniacs with lax standards.' – *Judith Crist*

The Night of The Living Dead ***
US 1968 98m bw
Image Ten
Flesh-eating zombies, activated by radiation from a space rocket, ravage the countryside.
Gruesome horror comic with effective moments; the director was still doing the same schtick ten years later. One of the most influential, and most imitated, of modern horror movies.
w John A. Russo *d/ph* George A. Romero
☆ Judith O'Dea, Duane Jones, Karl Hardman, Keith Wayne
'The best film ever made in Pittsburgh.' – *Anon.*
'Casts serious aspersions on the integrity of its makers ... the film industry as a whole and exhibs who book the pic, as well as raising doubts about the future of the regional cinema movement and the moral health of filmgoers who cheerfully opt for unrelieved sadism.' – *Variety*

Night of The Living Dead
US 1990 89m TVC Color
Columbia/21st Century/George A. Romero/Menahem Golan (John A. Russo, Russ Steiner)
Cannibalistic corpses rise from their graves to terrorize people trapped in a farmhouse.
Remake lacking the relentless intensity of the original.
w George A. Romero *d* Tom Savini *ph* Frank Prinzi *m* Paul McCollough *ad* James Feng *ed* Tom Dubensky
☆ Tony Wood, Patricia Tallman, Tom Towles, McKee Anderson, William Butler, Katie Finnerman, Bill Mosley, Heather Mazur
'A crass bit of cinematic grave-robbing.' – *Variety*

The Night of the Party
GB 1934 60m bw
Gaumont-British (Jerome Jackson)
A game of murder at a dinner party leads to a real one.

Solid supporting thriller with interesting credits.
w Ralph Smart *play* Roland Pertwee, John Hastings Turner *d* Michael Powell *ph* Glen MacWilliams *ad* Alfred Junge
☆ Leslie Banks, Jane Baxter, Viola Keats, Ian Hunter, Ernest Thesiger, Malcolm Keen
'Nothing original, but good entertainment.' – *Variety*

'Assigned to kill ... There can be no escape.'

Night of the Running Man
US 1994 89m CFI color
Trimark/American World (Mark L. Lester, Dana Dubovsky, George W. Perkins)
A Las Vegas taxi driver finds a suitcase containing a million stolen dollars in his cab and goes on the run with it, hunted by a ruthless hitman from the Mob.
Unpleasantly violent and sleazy chase thriller with a narrative that favours repetition over invention.
w Lee Wells *novel* Lee Wells *d* Mark L. Lester *ph* Mark Irwin *m* Christopher Franke *pd* Alfred Sole *ed* David Berlatsky
☆ Scott Glenn, Andrew McCarthy, Janet Gunn, Wayne Newton, John Glover, Peter Lacangelo, Matthew Laurance
'A run-of-the-mill thriller plucked from obscurity by its prolonged torture sequence which will have even hardened viewers squirming.' – *Sight and Sound*

Night of the Shooting Stars: see *The Night of San Lorenzo*

Night on Earth **
US 1992 129m colour
Electric/Locus Solus/Victor/Victor Musical Industries/Pyramide/Canal/Pandora/Channel 4 (Jim Jarmusch)
Five individuals take simultaneous taxi rides in five cities: Los Angeles, New York, Paris, Rome and Helsinki.
Engaging series of shaggy dog stories, expertly told.
wd Jim Jarmusch *ph* Frederick Elmes *m* Tom Waits *ed* Jay Ribinowitz
☆ Winona Ryder, Gena Rowlands, Giancarlo Esposito, Armin Mueller-Stahl, Rosie Perez, Isaach de Bankolé, Béatrice Dalle, Roberto Benigni, Paolo Bonacelli, Matti Pellonpää
'For the most part, the movie induces in the viewer an eerie, suspended feeling that mimics the time-stands-still monotony of a long airplane journey. It tries for a chipper, lighthearted tone, but it gives the audience a gruelling flight – a red-eye to nowhere.' – *Terrence Rafferty, New Yorker*

Night on the Town
US 1987 99m DeLuxe
Touchstone/Silver Screen Partners III/Debra Hill/Linda Obst
US title: *Adventures in Babysitting*
Babysitting young children, a girl takes them for a ride in her car and unwittingly becomes a target for gangsters.
A sequence of tepid chases aimed at an undemanding audience.
w David Simkins *d* Chris Columbus *ph* Ric Waite *m* Michael Kamen *pd* Todd Hallowell *ad* Gregory Keen *ed* Fredric Steinkamp
☆ Elisabeth Shue, Maia Brewton, Keith Coogan, Anthony Rapp, Calvin Levels

Night Owls *
US 1930 20m bw
Hal Roach
A policeman wanting to record an arrest bribes two tramps to burgle a house.
The stars at their most hilariously incompetent, unable even to get through a doorway efficiently.
w Leo McCarey, H. M. Walker *d* James Parrott *ph* George Stevens *ed* Richard Currier
☆ Stan Laurel, Oliver Hardy, Edgar Kennedy, James Finlayson

Night Passage *
US 1957 90m Technirama
U-I (Aaron Rosenberg)
A railroad worker entrusted with a payroll finds that the bandits trying to rob it are led by his own brother.

Obscurely titled and rather empty Western providing standard excitements.
w Borden Chase *d* James Neilson *ph* William Daniels *m* Dimitri Tiomkin
☆ James Stewart, Audie Murphy, Dan Duryea, Brandon de Wilde, Dianne Foster, Elaine Stewart

'You have never really seen Gregory Peck until you see him in CinemaScope!'
'We didn't say nice people, we said *night people*!'
Night People *
US 1954 93m Technicolor Cinemascope
TCF (Nunnally Johnson)
When a US corporal stationed in Berlin is kidnapped by the Russians, his influential father flies into action.
Curiously titled cold war suspenser which would have been more memorable if not in Cinemascope; the pace and talent are visible, but the wide screen and poor colour dissipate them.
wd Nunnally Johnson ph Charles G. Clarke
m Cyril Mockridge
☆ Gregory Peck, Broderick Crawford, Anita Bjork, Walter Abel, Rita Gam, Buddy Ebsen, Jill Esmond, Peter Van Eyck
original story (Jed Harris, Tom Reed)

'Seven in the skies over China – and one of them a dangerous Axis spy!'
Night Plane from Chungking
US 1942 69m bw
Paramount
Assorted international passengers are flown from Chungking to India, but one of their number is a German spy who will kill to get his hands on vital information.
A lower-case 'who is it' based on Shanghai Express. *Not bad according to its lights.*
w Earl Felton, Theodore Reeves, Lester Cole
d Ralph Murphy *ph* Theodor Sparkuhl *m* Gerard Carbonara
☆ Ellen Drew, Robert Preston, Otto Kruger, Steve Geray, Ernest Dorian, Tamara Geva, Sen Yung

'The most controversial film of our time!'
The Night Porter
Italy 1973 118m Technicolor
Lotar Films (Robert Gordon Edwards, Esa de Simone)
The wife of an opera conductor recognizes a hotel porter as the sadistic SS commandant of a concentration camp in which she spent the war years; they now resume a sado-masochistic love affair.
A downright deplorable film, with no cinematic skill or grace to excuse it; the visuals are as loathsome as the sound is indecipherable, and the sheer pointlessness of it is insulting.
w Liliana Cavani, Italo Moscati *d* Liliana Cavani
ph Alfio Contini *m* Daniele Paris
☆ Dirk Bogarde, Charlotte Rampling, Philippe Leroy, Gabriele Ferzetti, Isa Miranda
'Its claim to be saying something important is offensive, but the picture is too crudely trumped up to be a serious insult.' – *New Yorker*

Night Ride
GB 1937 70m bw
Paramount
Unemployed lorry drivers start an independent co-operative.
Brisk action programmer.
w Ralph Bettinson *d* John Paddy Carstairs
☆ Julian Vedey, Wally Patch, Jimmy Hanley, Joan Ponsford

Night Shift
US 1982 106m Technicolor
Warner/Ladd (Brian Grazer)
A weary financial analyst becomes a morgue attendant and finds himself involved with gangsters and pimps.
Unattractive comedy that outstays its welcome, which wasn't very enthusiastic in the first place.
w Lowell Ganz, Babaloo Mandel *d* Ron Howard
ph James Crabe *m* Burt Bacharach *pd* Jack Collis
☆ Henry Winkler, Michael Keaton, Shelley Long, Gina Hecht

Night Song
US 1947 101m bw
RKO (Harriet Parsons)
A wealthy socialite falls for a blind pianist and pretends to be blind also, and poor to boot.
Silly, pretentious soaper, moodily photographed.
w Frank Fenton, Irving Hyland, De Witt Bodeen
d John Cromwell *ph Lucien Ballard m* Leith Stevens
☆ Dana Andrews, Merle Oberon, Hoagy Carmichael, Ethel Barrymore, Artur Rubinstein, Eugene Ormandy

Night Sun *
Italy/France/Germany 1990 113m
Eastmancolor
Artificial Eye/Filmtre/Raiuno/Capoul/Interpool/Sara/Direkt (Giuliani G. de Negri)
original title: *Il sole anche di notte*
In 18th-century Italy, a nobleman, upset to discover that he is expected to marry the king's mistress, becomes a hermit credited with miraculous powers.
Austere fable of a search for salvation that is likely to tire most audiences before the end.
w Paolo and Vittorio Taviani, Tonino Guerra
story Father Sergius by Leo Tolstoy *d* Paolo and Vittorio Taviani *ph* Giuseppe Lanci *m* Nicola Piovani *ad* Gianni Sbarra *ed* Roberto Perpignani
☆ Julian Sands, Charlotte Gainsbourg, Nastassja Kinski, Massimo Bonetti, Margarita Lozano, Patricia Millardet, Rudiger Vogler, Pamela Villoresi
'A hauntingly spiritual film which is never afraid to explore the unfashionable themes of longing, solitude and meditation.' – *Sight and Sound*

The Night the Lights Went Out in Georgia
US 1981 120m Technicolor
Avco Embassy/Viacom (Elliot Geisinger, Howard Kuperman, Ronald Saland, Howard Smith)
A young girl tries to guide her rambunctious brother to success as a country and western singer.
A poorly constructed narrative ensures that the level of interest remains low.
w Bob Bonney *d* Ronald F. Maxwell *ph* Bill Butler *m* David Shire *pd* Gene Rudolf *ed* Anne Goursaud *song* Bobby Russell
☆ Kristy McNichol, Dennis Quaid, Don Stroud, Mark Hamill, Arlen Dean Snyder

The Night They Invented Striptease: see *The Night They Raided Minsky's*

The Night They Killed Rasputin
France/Italy 1960 95m Eastmancolor
Faro/Explorer/Rialto
original title: *Les Nuits de Raspoutine*
In 1916, a prince leads a gang of aristocrats to kill Rasputin, a monk who exercises an evil power over the Russian court and the Tsarina.
This is bad history and not a very good film, with a great deal of posturing from its cast.
w Ugo Liberatore, André Tabet *d* Pierre Chenal
ph Adalberto Albertini *m* Angelo Francesco Lavagnino *ad* Arrigo Equini *ed* Antonietta Zita
☆ Edmund Purdom, Gianna Maria Canale, Jany Clair, John Drew Barrymore, Ugo Sasso, Giulia Rubini

The Night They Raided Minsky's **
US 1968 99m DeLuxe
UA/Tandem (Norman Lear)
GB title: *The Night They Invented Striptease*
Various human problems are posed and solved during a night at a burlesque theatre.
Marvellous kaleidoscopic ragbag of brilliant fragments which unfortunately don't cohere in the mind into a really memorable film, though it gives detailed pleasure on every viewing.
w Arnold Schulman, Sidney Michaels, Norman Lear *book* Rowland Barber *d William Friedkin ph Andrew Laszlo m Charles Strouse ch* Danny Daniels *pd William Eckart, Jean Eckart*
narrator Rudy Vallee
☆ Jason Robards, Britt Ekland, *Norman Wisdom*, Forrest Tucker, Joseph Wiseman, Bert Lahr, Harry Andrews, Denholm Elliott, Elliott Gould, Jack Burns
'The Fanny Brice country stunningly brought to life – every face a snapshot of yesterday.' – *Alexander Walker*
'It's lightweight and disorganized; it's a shambles; yet a lot of it is charming, and it has a wonderful seedy chorus line – a row of pudgy girls with faces like slipped discs.' – *Pauline Kael, New Yorker*
'A brilliant pastiche of classic American burlesque on the lower east side in the twenties.' – *Time*
'An entire way of life is encapsulated' – *Morning Star*

'Was she human?'
Night Tide
US 1961 84m bw
Virgo Films
A sailor falls in love with a fairground freak show girl who may be a real mermaid.
Cheaply made and very derivative romantic fantasy which seemed to hold a promise never fulfilled.
wd Curtis Harrington *ph* Vilis Lapenieks
m David Raksin
☆ Dennis Hopper, Linda Lawson, Gavin Muir, Luana Anders

A Night to Remember *
US 1943 91m bw
Columbia (Samuel Bischoff)
A Greenwich Village mystery-writing couple try to solve a murder.
Reasonably sparkling comedy whodunnit with a zany tinge.
w Richard Flournoy, Jack Henley *d* Richard Wallace *ph* Joseph Walker *m* Werner Heymann
md Morris Stoloff
☆ *Loretta Young, Brian Aherne*, Jeff Donnell, William Wright, Sidney Toler, Gale Sondergaard, Donald MacBride, Lee Patrick, Blanche Yurka
'A first-rate gloom chaser.' – *Picture Show*

A Night to Remember ***
GB 1958 123m bw
Rank (William Macquitty)
The story of the 1912 sea disaster when the *Titanic* struck an iceberg.
A major film enterprise featuring hundreds of cameos, none discernibly more important than the other. On this account the film seems alternately stiff and flabby as narrative, but there is much to enjoy and admire along the way, though the sense of awe is dissipated by the final model shots.
w Eric Ambler *book* Walter Lord *d Roy Baker*
ph Geoffrey Unsworth m William Alwyn
☆ Kenneth More, Honor Blackman, Michael Goodliffe, David McCallum, George Rose, Anthony Bushell, Ralph Michael, John Cairney, Kenneth Griffith, Frank Lawton, Michael Bryant
'A worthy, long-drawn-out documentary, with noticeably more honesty about human nature than most films, but little shape or style.' – *Kenneth Cavender*

Night Train: see *Night Train to Munich*

Night Train
GB 1999 92m colour
Alternative/Subotica (Tristan Lynch)
An ex-convict, still being hunted by a gangster, hides out in a Dublin boarding house, where he plays with a giant train set and forms a relationship with his landlady's daughter.
Tepid romance of two misfits who find that they fit together, which suddenly becomes a violent escapist drama for no good reason.
w Aodhan Madden *d* John Lynch *ph* Seamus Deasy *m* Adam Lynch *pd* Alan Farquaharson
ed J. Patrick Duffner
☆ John Hurt (Michael Poole), Brenda Blethyn (Alice Mooney), Pauline Flanagan (Mrs Mooney), Rynagh O'Grady (Winnie), Peter Caffrey (Walter), Paul Roe (Blake), Lorcan Cranitch (Billy), Cathy White (Liz)
'Grey, parochial and unambitious.' – *Edward Porter, Sunday Times*

Night Train to Munich ***
GB 1940 93m bw
TCF (Edward Black)
aka: *Gestapo*
aka: *Night Train*
A British agent poses as a Nazi in order to rescue a Czech inventor.
First-rate comedy suspenser obviously inspired by the success of The Lady Vanishes *and providing much the same measure of thrills and laughs.*
w Frank Launder, Sidney Gilliat novel Report on a Fugitive by Gordon Wellesley *d Carol Reed*
ph Otto Kanturek *m* Charles Williams *md* Louis Levy
☆ Margaret Lockwood, *Rex Harrison, Basil Radford, Naunton Wayne*, Paul Henreid, Keneth Kent, Felix Aylmer, Roland Culver, *Eliot Makeham, Raymond Huntley*, Wyndham Goldie
'A very nice triumph of skill and maturity in films, and thus a pleasure to have.' – *Otis Ferguson*
Gordon Wellesley

Night Train to Venice
Germany 1993 97m colour
Take Munich (Toni Hirtreiter)
A journalist travelling to Venice to deliver an exposé of fascist groups falls in love with an actress he meets on the Orient Express; also on board is a gang of neo-Nazi thugs.
A senseless and incomprehensible thriller with occult overtones, one in which everyone behaves oddly, never making a normal response to any situation. Irrelevant dream sequences interrupt what action there is; it ends with the lines: 'Imagine you woke up one day and realized it was all a dream.' This is a nightmare.
w Leo Tichat, Toni Hirtreiter *d* Carlo U. Quinterio *ph* Armando Nannuzzi *m* Wolfgang Hammerschmid *pd* Heinz Eickmeyer *ed* Wicktor Grodecki
☆ Hugh Grant, Tahnee Welch, Malcolm McDowell, Evelyn Opela, Samy Langs, Rachel Rice, Kristina Soederbaum
'A work of such thoroughgoing ineptitude it makes even Ed Wood's movies look like they're touched by genius.' – *Film Review*
'Too deadingly awful to be enjoyably bad.' – *Variety*

Night unto Night *
US 1949 85m bw
Warner (Owen Crump)
An epileptic scientist falls for a girl hallucinated by the ghost of her dead husband.
Cheerless nuthouse melodrama, one of the well-meant aberrations which Hollywood studios used to produce as a sop to conscience.
w Kathryn Scola *novel* Philip Wylie *d Don Siegel*
ph Peverell Marley *m* Franz Waxman
☆ Ronald Reagan, Viveca Lindfors, Rosemary de Camp, Broderick Crawford, Osa Massen, Craig Stevens, Erskine Sanford

'Locked in the cold asylum of the mind – a sane man stalks his prey!'
The Night Visitor
Sweden/US 1971 102m Eastmancolor
UMC/Hemisphere
Imprisoned for an axe murder he didn't commit, a man escapes and takes revenge.
Overdone Grand Guignol which simply doesn't come off.
w Guy Elmes *story Salem Came to Supper* by Samuel Roecca *d* Laslo Benedek
☆ Max von Sydow, Trevor Howard, Liv Ullmann, Rupert Davies, Per Oscarsson, Andrew Keir

'Do you know that a dream can kill you?'
The Night Walker *
US 1965 86m bw
U-I/William Castle
The widow of a tough executive, killed and disfigured in an explosion, is haunted in her dreams not only by him but by a mysterious lover who turns up in reality.
Stiff and unconvincing but still fairly frightening low-budget shocker with a plot twist or two.
w Robert Bloch d William Castle *ph* Harold Stine
m Vic Mizzy
☆ Robert Taylor, *Barbara Stanwyck*, Lloyd Bochner, Rochelle Hudson, Judi Meredith, Hayden Rorke

Night Was Our Friend
GB 1951 61m bw
Monarch (Gordon Parry)
Returning home after being thought dead for two years, an unhinged explorer discovers that his wife is in love with another man.
Gloomy psychological drama that never quite comes to life.
w Michael Pertwee *play* Michael Pertwee
d Michael Anderson *ph* Moray Grant

☆ Elizabeth Sellars, Michael Gough, Ronald Howard, Marie Ney, Edward Lexy, Nora Gordon, John Salew

Night Watch
GB 1973 98m Technicolor
Avco/Brut (David White)

A widow recovering from a nervous breakdown keeps seeing bodies in the night. Her friends try to help, but things are not quite what they seem.
Predictable coiled-spring shocker which goes curiously flat despite a star cast and lashings of blood. Perhaps we have all been here once too often.
w Tony Williamson *play* Lucille Fletcher *d* Brian G. Hutton *ph* Billy Williams *m* John Cameron
☆ Elizabeth Taylor, Laurence Harvey, Billie Whitelaw, Robert Lang, Tony Britton, Bill Dean
'It has all the trappings of a Joan Crawford vehicle of the forties, with numerous elegant dresses for Miss Taylor, an appropriately unbecoming wardrobe for Miss Whitelaw, and a set which is an art director's dream.' – *Brenda Davies*
'Elizabeth Taylor's gowns are by Valentino, her jewellery is by Van Cleef and Arpels, even her kitchen is by Westinghouse. And she is still going out of her mind.' – *Alexander Walker*

The Night We Dropped a Clanger
GB 1959 86m bw
Rank/Sydney Box/Four Star
US title: *Make Mine a Double*
During World War II, a wing commander's double is accidentally sent to the front line in his place.
Feeble take-off on I Was Monty's Double; *a few bright gags survive.*
w John Chapman *d* Darcy Conyers *ph* Ernest Steward *m* Edwin Braden
☆ Brian Rix, Cecil Parker, William Hartnell, Leslie Phillips, Leo Franklyn, John Welsh, Liz Fraser

The Night We Got the Bird
GB 1960 82m bw
British Lion/Rix-Conyers
A husband is driven bonkers by a talking parrot which he believes to be the reincarnation of his predecessor.
Pretty awful farce with the sole virtue of a frantic pace.
w Ray Cooney, Tony Hilton, Darcy Conyers *d* Darcy Conyers *ph* S. D. Onions *m* Tommy Watt
☆ Brian Rix, Dora Bryan, Ronald Shiner, Leo Franklyn, Irene Handl, John Slater, Liz Fraser, Reginald Beckwith, Robertson Hare, John Le Mesurier, Terry Scott

The Night We Never Met
US 1993 99m DuArt
Guild/Miramax (Michael Peyser)

Three young New Yorkers organize a time-share on a Greenwich Village apartment, but the days on which each uses the place become confused.
Brash and not very likeable farce that will mean little outside the city in which it is set.
wd Warren Leight *ph* John A. Thomas *m* Evan Lurie *pd* Lester Cohen *ed* Camilla Toniolo
☆ Matthew Broderick, Annabella Sciorra, Kevin Anderson, Jeanne Tripplehorn, Justine Bateman, Michael Mantell, Christine Baranski
'If you're in the mood to indulge in some light cultural snobbery, you'll enjoy this film ... a rickety structure with trendy interior design, an old-fashioned sex comedy for the nouveau hip.' – *Leslie Felperin Sharman, Sight and Sound*

Night without Stars
GB 1951 86m bw
Hugh Stewart/GFD
A blind lawyer solves the death of a traitor.
Enervated romantic melodrama.
w Winston Graham *novel* Winston Graham *d* Anthony Pelissier *ph* Guy Green *m* William Alwyn
☆ David Farrar, Nadia Gray, Maurice Teynac, Gilles Queyant

Night World
US 1932 58m bw
Universal
Characters with an assortment of problems congregate in a night-club.
Tolerable slice-of-life drama with interesting cast.
w Richard Schayer *story* P.J. Wolfson and Allen Rivkin *d* Hobart Henley
☆ Lew Ayres, Boris Karloff, Mae Clarke, Russell Hopton, George Raft, Dorothy Revier, Bert Roach, Hedda Hopper
'Sum total is an impression that this was a two-reeler blown up into five.' – *Variety*

Night Zoo
Canada 1987 115m colour
Hendring/Oz Productions/National Film Board Of Canada (Roger Frappier, Pierre Gendron)

original title: *Un Zoo la Nuit*
A drug dealer, out of prison on parole, is reconciled with his father and outwits his former bosses, who include a sadistic homosexual cop.
Lurid thriller which, inexplicably, was much honoured in its home country.
wd Jean-Claude Lauzon *ph* Guy Dufaux *m* Jean Corriveau *ad* Jean-Baptiste Tard *ed* Michel Arcand
☆ Roger Le Bel, Gilles Maheu, Lorne Brass, Germain Houde, Jerry Snell, Corrado Mastropasqua, Lynne Adams, Amulette Garneau, Anna-Maria Giannotti

Nightbreed
US 1990 102m Technicolor
Fox/Morgan Creek (Gariella Martinelli)

A teenager discovers Midian, a world of shape-shifting monsters.
Novel horror movie, in which the monsters are nicer than the humans, but without much narrative drive.
wd Clive Barker *novel* *Cabal* by Clive Barker *ph* Robin Vidgeon *pd* Steve Hardie, Mark Haskins *ed* Richard Marden, Mark Goldblatt *sp* Image Animation
☆ Craig Sheffer, Anne Bobby, David Cronenberg, Charles Haid, Hugh Quarshie, Hugh Ross, Doug Bradley, Catherine Chevalier, Malcolm Sith, Bob Sessions, Oliver Parker

Nightcap: see *Merci Pour Le Chocolat*

The Nightcomers *
GB 1971 96m Technicolor
Scimitar/Kastner-Kanter-Ladd (Michael Winner)

How the ghost-ridden children in *The Turn of the Screw* became evil; they became involved in aberrant sexual activities between the gardener and the housekeeper, and finally murdered the former.
Despite its unexpected literariness this is unpleasant and unconvincing nonsense with a boring script punctuated by shock cuts and very little period feel.
w Michael Hastings *d* Michael Winner *ph* Robert Paynter *m* Jerry Fielding *ad* Herbert Westbrook *ed* Frederick Wilson
☆ Stephanie Beacham (Miss Jessel), Marlon Brando (Peter Quint), Thora Hird (Mrs Grose), Harry Andrews (Master of the House), Verna Harvey (Flora), Christopher Ellis (Miles), Anna Palk (New governess)
'It leaves the viewer cold – perhaps even repelled. How could anybody think this movie would be entertaining?' – *Pauline Kael, New Yorker*

Nightfall: see *Abendland*

Nightfall *
US 1956 78m bw
Columbia (Ted Richmond)
The police and two bank robbers chase an innocent artist who happens to know that the loot is hidden in a Wisconsin snowdrift.
Occasionally stylish but obscurely narrated suspenser.
w Stirling Silliphant *novel* David Goodis *d* *Jacques Tourneur* *ph* Burnett Guffey *m* George Duning
☆ Anne Bancroft, Aldo Ray, Brian Keith, James Gregory, Jocelyn Brando, Frank Albertson

Nighthawks
GB 1978 113m Eastmancolor
Cinegate/Nashburgh/Four Corner Films (Ron Peck, Paul Hallam)

The life of an actively homosexual schoolteacher.
Painful low-life drama with many signs of its amateur status.
wd Ron Peck, Paul Hallam *ph* Joanna Davis, Patrick Duval, Sebastian Dewsbery, Ian Owles, Steve Shaw *m* David Graham Ellis *ad* Jan Sender *ed* Richard Taylor, Mary Pat Leece, Debra Daley, Tim Horrocks
☆ Ken Robertson and non-professionals

Nighthawks
US 1981 99m Technicolor
Universal/Herb Nanas (Martin Poll)

New York cops track an international terrorist.
Kojak-style thriller with a rather glum attitude to its subject.
w David Shaber *d* Bruce Malmuth *ph* James A. Contner *m* Keith Emerson
☆ Sylvester Stallone, Billy Dee Williams, Rutger Hauer, Lindsay Wagner, Persis Khambatta, Nigel Davenport

Nighthawks 2: Strip Jack Naked
GB 1991 94m bw/colour
BFI/Channel 4 (Ron Peck)

An autobiographical documentary on the background to the making of *Nighthawks*, including material cut from the original film.
An amateurish and boring film, on the level of a home movie, and a demonstration that earnestness can be trying.
w Ron Peck, Paul Hallam *d* Ron Peck *ph* Ron Peck, Christopher Hughes *m* Adrian James Carbutt *ed* Ron Peck, Adrian James Carbutt
☆ John Brown, John Daimon, Nick Bolton

Nightmare: see *Nightmares in a Damaged Brain*

Nightmare
US 1942 81m bw
Universal (Dwight Taylor)
A gambler in wartime London helps a beautiful girl escape from Nazi spies.
Thin espionage thriller with a good sequence or two and a smooth villain.
w Dwight Taylor *novel* *Escape* by Philip MacDonald *d* Tim Whelan *ph* George Barnes *m* Frank Skinner
☆ Brian Donlevy, Diana Barrymore, *Gavin Muir*, Henry Daniell, Hans Conried, Arthur Shields

Nightmare *
US 1956 89m bw
UA/Pine-Thomas/Shane (Maxwell Shane)
A young musician is hypnotized into committing a murder, and reconstructs his actions with the help of his policeman brother-in-law.
Lethargic remake of the ingenious Fear in the Night *(qv). Watchable.*
wd Maxwell Shane *novel* Cornell Woolrich *ph* Joseph Biroc *m* Herschel Burke Gilbert
☆ *Edward G. Robinson*, Kevin McCarthy, Virginia Christine, Connie Russell
'A chilling, highly suspenseful little item.' – *Motion Picture Herald*

'Three shocking murders ... did she dream them? ... or do them?'
Nightmare *
GB 1964 82m bw Hammerscope
U-I/Hammer (Jimmy Sangster)
18-year-old Janet still has nightmares after seeing her mad mother kill her father six years ago; brought home, even more frightening visions afflict her.
Genuinely scary Diabolique*-type mystery with the usual Hammer borrowings put to good use.*
w *Jimmy Sangster* *d* Freddie Francis *ph* John Wilcox *m* Don Banks
☆ *Moira Redmond*, David Knight, Brenda Bruce, John Welsh, *Jennie Linden*

Nightmare Alley **
US 1947 112m bw
TCF (George Jessel)
A fairground barker becomes a successful confidence trickster dealing with the supernatural, but finally sinks to the depths.
Unusual road to ruin melodrama, a striking oddity from Hollywood at the time, and still quite interesting and well done.
w *Jules Furthman* *novel* William Lindsay Gresham *d* Edmund Goulding *ph* *Lee Garmes* *m* Cyril Mockridge
☆ *Tyrone Power*, Coleen Gray, Joan Blondell, *Taylor Holmes*, Helen Walker, Mike Mazurki, Ian Keith
'The picture goes just short of all that might have made it very interesting ... even so, two or three sharply comic and cynical scenes make it worth seeing.' – *James Agee*

The Nightmare before Christmas ***
US 1993 75m Technicolor
Buena Vista/Touchstone (Tim Burton, Denise Di Novi)

aka: *Tim Burton's The Nightmare before Christmas*
Jack Skellington, Pumpkin King of Halloween Town, tries to take over Christmas as well.
Imaginative, superbly animated (using stop-motion techniques with figures) musical, although children may not warm to its quirky humour.
w Caroline Thompson, Michael McDowell *story* Tim Burton *d* Henry Selick *m/ly* *Danny Elfman* *ed* Stan Webb *sp* Pete Kozachik, Eric Leighton, Ariel Velasco Shaw, Gordon Baker
☆ Featuring the voices of Danny Elfman, Chris Sarandon, Catherine O'Hara, William Hickey, Glenn Shadix, Paul Reubens
'The dazzling techniques employed here create a striking look that has never been seen in such a sustained form before, making this a unique curio that will appeal to kids and film enthusiasts alike.' – *Variety*
'An animated fun-house for eeek freaks of all ages.' – *Peter Travers, Rolling Stone*
'It displays more inventiveness than some studios can manage in an entire year.' – *Kenneth Turan, Los Angeles Times*
visual effects

Nightmare Castle: see *Night of the Doomed*

'Now They Are Everywhere! There Is No Escape!'
Nightmare City
Italy/Spain 1980 88m colour
Lotus/Dialchi (Luis Méndez, Diego Alchimede)

original title: *Incubo Sulla Città Contaminata*
aka: *City of the Walking Dead*
A TV reporter discovers that a nuclear accident has turned a planeload of people into blood-drinking zombies.
Gory horror movie with a script that even the director thought was bad.
w Antonio Cesare Corti, Luis María Delgado, Piero Regnoli *d* Umberto Lenzi *ph* Hans Burman *m* Stelvio Cipriani *ad* Mario Molli *ed* Daniele Alabiso
☆ Hugi Stiglitz (Dean Miller), Mel Ferrer (General Murchison), Laura Trotter (Dr Anna Miller), Maria Rosaria Omaggio (Sheila Holmes), Francisco Rabal (Major Warren Holmes), Sonia Viviani (Cindy)

Nightmare in the Sun *
US 1963 81m DeLuxe
Afilmco (Marc Lawrence, John Derek)

A rich man kills his wife and blames a hitch-hiker who has had a brief affair with her.
Modest independent melodrama, quite interestingly made though not entirely effective.
w Ted Thomas *d* Marc Lawrence *ph* Stanley Cortez *m* Paul Glass
☆ John Derek, Ursula Andress, Arthur O'Connell, Aldo Ray

'See Freddy – before he sees you!'
A Nightmare on Elm Street
US 1984 91m DeLuxe
New Line/Media/Smart Egg/Elm Street Venture/Robert Shaye

Suburban teenagers find their communal dreams becoming reality when they are menaced by a creepy figure with knives for fingernails.
Unpleasant semi-splatter movie which was well enough made to take a lot of money.
wd Wes Craven *ph* Jacques Haitkin *m* Charles Bernstein *pd* Greg Fonseca *ed* Rick Shaine *sp* Jim Doyle
☆ John Saxon (Lt Thompson), Ronee Blakley (Marge Thompson), Heather Langenkamp (Nancy Thompson), Amanda Wyss (Tina Gray), Nick Corri (Rod Lane), Robert Englund (Freddy Krueger), Johnny Depp (Glen Lantz), Charles Fleischer (Dr King)

A Nightmare on Elm Street Part Four: The Dream Master
US 1988 93m Metrocolor
Palace/New Line Cinema/Heron Communications/Smart Egg Pictures (Robert Shaye, Rachel Talalay)

As Freddy goes on his usual killing spree, a teenager discovers that she can destroy him.
A mixture, as before, of spectacularly unpleasant special effects and grotesque humour, except that Freddy is now firmly established as the star.
w Brian Helgeland, Scott Pierce *story* Brian Helgeland, William Kotzwinkle *d* Renny Harlin *ph* Steven Fierberg *m* Craig Safan *pd* Mick Strawn, C. J. Strawn *ed* Michael N. Knue, Chuck Weiss, Jack Tucker, Charley Coleman
☆ Robert Englund, Rodney Eastman, Danny Hassel, Andras Jones, Tuesday Knight, Toy Newkirk, Ken Sagoes
'The fact remains that the child-killer of Elm Street has simply run out of things to do and say.' – *MFB*

A Nightmare on Elm Street Part Three: Dream Warriors
US 1987 96m DeLuxe
Heron/Smart Egg/New Line/Robert Shaye

Freddy now invades the minds of teenagers under group hypnosis for nightmares.
Diminishing returns set in as this tedious bloodbath (all in the mind) gets under way.
w Wes Craven, Bruce Wagner *d* Chuck Russell *ph* Roy H. Wagner *m* Angelo Badalamenti, Don Dokken *ad* Mick Strawn, C. J. Strawn *ed* Terry Stokes
☆ Heather Langenkamp, Patricia Arquette, Larry Fishburne, Robert Englund, Priscilla Pointer, Craig Wasson

A Nightmare on Elm Street Part Two: Freddy's Revenge
US 1985 84m DeLuxe
Heron/Smart Egg/New Line/Robert Shaye

Freddy comes back and tries to take over the mind and body of a young boy.
More horror nonsense in the same mould as the above.
w David Chaskin *d* Jack Sholder *ph* Jacques Haitkin *m* Christopher Young *ed* Bob Brady
☆ Mark Patton, Kim Myers, Hope Lange, Clu Gulager, Robert Englund
'Much as one loves watching unpleasant American teenagers ripped to death, the slasher formula has worn thin of late.' – *Time Out*

A Nightmare on Elm Street: The Dream Child
US 1989 89m Metrocolor
Enterprise/New Line Cinema/Heron Communications/Smart Egg Pictures (Robert Shaye, Rupert Harvey)

Freddy attempts to possess a girl's unborn child.
The murderer of the young continues in an incoherent sequel with some clever special effects. It is time that Freddy was laid to rest.
w Leslie Bohem *story* John Skipp, Craig Spector, Leslie Bohem *d* Stephen Hopkins *ph* Peter Levy *m* Jay Ferguson *pd* C. J. Strawn *ed* Chuck Weiss, Brent Schoenfeld
☆ Robert Englund, Lisa Wilcox, Kelly Jo Minter, Danny Hassel, Erika Anderson, Nick Mele, Whitby Hertford, Joe Seely
'The scariest idea in the film, underlined by yet another open ending, is the possibility that this nightmare will never end, the non-existent story spinning out forever.' – *Kim Newman, MFB*
† The sequel was *Freddy's Dead: The Final Nightmare* (qv)

'The Dream You Can't Escape Alive!'
Nightmares in a Damaged Brain
US 1981 97m Technicolor
Watchgrove/Goldmine (John L. Watkins, William Milling)

aka: *Nightmare*
A murderous psychopath, tormented by nightmares, terrorises a single mother and her children.
Ineptly made, badly acted, derivative horror that gained a little notoriety in the mid-80s when it was withdrawn during the "video nasties" controversy.
wd Romano Scavolini *ph* Gianni Fiore *m* Jack Eric Williams *ad* Jan Foster, Gary Olson *ed* Robert T. Megginson *sp* Tom Savini
☆ Baird Stafford (George Tatum), Sharon Smith (Susan Temper), C. J. Cook (C. J. Temper), Mik Cribben (Bob Rosen), Danny Ronen (Kathy the Babysitter)
'Dismayingly routine.' – *MFB*
'Severed heads and axings galore, but the end result is not that memorable.' – *Allan Bryce, Dark Side*
† The 1981 GB release was cut, running for 93m. The DVD version, released in 2002, runs for 96m

Nights of Cabiria: see *Cabiria*

The Nights of Lucretia Borgia
Italy/France 1959 92m Eastmancolor Totalscope
Fidès/Musa Cinematografica (Carlo Caiano)
original title: *Le Notti di Lucrezia Borgia*
aka: *Nights of Temptation*
Lucretia Borgia falls in love with one of her brother's soldiers, who loves another.
Silly historical romp, occasionally enjoyable in the way that bad films can be.
w Sergio Grieco, Mario Caiano, Aldo Segri, Duncan Elliot, Barbara Sohmers *play Lucrece Borgia* by Victor Hugo *d* Sergio Grieco *ph* Massimo Dallamano *m* Alexandre Derevitsky *ad* Saverio D'Eugenio *ed* Enzo Alfonsi
☆ Belinda Lee, Michèle Mercier, Jacques Sernas, Arnoldo Foa, Franco Fabrizio, Marco Tulli

Nightshift: see *Trois Huit*

Nightwatch *
Denmark 1994 105m colour
Metro Tartan/Thura/DR TV/Danske Filminstitut (Michael Obel)

original title: *Nattevagten*
A law student who also works as a night watchman in a morgue is suspected of killing and scalping prostitutes.
Slow but suspenseful thriller that comes near to equating sex and death; it manages some jokes to lighten its pervading and chilling claustrophobia.
wd Ole Bornedal *ph* Dan Laustsen *m* Joachim Holbek *ad* Soren Krag Sorensen *ed* Camilla Skousen
☆ Nicolai Coster Waldau, Sofie Grabol, Kim Bodnia, Ulf Pilgaard, Lotte Andersen, Rikke Louise Andersson, Stig Hoffmeyer
'The movie took Scandinavia by storm, which says something rather quaint about Scandinavia's desire to import the blueprint for the serial killer movie and make their own version with local ingredients. Like a Big Mac, it's a bit stale by the time it's re-exported.' – *Tom Shone, Sunday Times*

Nightwatch
US 1998 101m colour
Miramax/Dimension (Michael Obel)

A student takes a job in a city morgue, and is suspected of being a serial killer.
Although it retains its original director, this American remake of a Danish thriller has lost the creepiness that made it memorable.
w Steven Soderbergh, Ole Bornedal *d* Ole Bornedal *ph* Dan Lausten *m* Joachim Holbeck *pd* Richard Hoover *ed* Sally Menke
☆ Ewan McGregor, Nick Nolte, Josh Brolin, Patricia Arquette, Alix Koromzay, John C. Reilly, Brad Dourif
'A laboured black comedy which is overacted, overwritten and far too conceited for its own good.' – *Sight and Sound*

Nightwing
Netherlands 1979 105m Metrocolor
Columbia/Polyc/Martin Ransohoff

In Arizona, mysterious deaths turn out to be caused by plague-bearing vampire bats.
Tedious shocker in the vein of Them *but with 'modern' unpleasantness of detail.*
w Steve Shagan, Bud Shrake *novel* Martin Cruz Smith *d* Arthur Hiller *ph* Charles Rosher *m* Henry Mancini
☆ David Warner, Kathryn Harrold, Stephen Macht, Strother Martin, Nick Mancuso, Ben Piazza

'Genius. Madman. Animal. God.'
Nijinsky *
US 1980 125m Metrocolor
Paramount/Hera (Harry Saltzman)

The rise and fall of a great dancer groomed for stardom in the Ballets Russes by the impresario Diaghilev.
Rather boringly scripted with the emphasis on homosexual love, this film finally survives through its electrifying personalities and its strong sense of period.
w Hugh Wheeler *d* Herbert Ross *ph* Douglas Slocombe *md* John Lanchbery *pd John Blezard*
☆ *Alan Bates, George de la Pena*, Leslie Browne, *Alan Badel*, Colin Blakely, Ronald Pickup, Ronald Lacey, Jeremy Irons, Anton Dolin, Janet Suzman, Sian Phillips, members of the London Festival Ballet
'The impression is left of a fascinating subject which proved too challenging for its makers, who settle eventually for what is uncomfortably near *All About Eve* with Bette Davis in a dinner jacket and Anne Baxter in a jock strap.' – *Alan Brien, Sunday Times*

Nikita *
France/Italy 1990 117m Eastmancolor Technovision
Palace/Gaumont/Cecci/Tiger (Jérôme Chalou)

aka: *La Femme Nikita*
A young criminal turns assassin for the intelligence services.
Implausible, though stylish and very watchable, thriller.
wd Luc Besson *ph* Thierry Arbogast *m* Eric Serra *pd* Dan Weil *ed* Olivier Mauffroy
☆ Anne Parillaud, Jean-Hugues Anglade, Tcheky Karyo, Jeanne Moreau, Jean Reno, Roland Blanche, Marc Duret
'An absurd, shrill, ultraviolent but soft-centered urban thriller.' – *Variety*
† In 1997 the film was turned into a successful US TV series, *La Femme Nikita*, starring Peta Wilson.

Nikki, Wild Dog of the North *
US 1961 74m Technicolor
Walt Disney (Winston Hibler)

The life of a Canadian trapper's wolf dog.
Pleasing 'true life fiction' which didn't quite reach top feature status.
w Ralph Wright, Winston Hibler *novel* James Oliver Curwood *d* Jack Couffer *m* Oliver Wallace
☆ Emile Genest, Jean Coutu

Nikogarsnja Zemlja **
France/Italy/Belgium/U.K/Slovenia 2001 98m colour CinemaScope
Momentum/Noe/Fabrica/Man's Films/Counihan-Villiers/Maj-Casablanca (Frederique Dumas-Zajdela, Marc Baschet, Cedomir Kolar)

aka: *No Man's Land*
In 1993, a Bosnian and a Serb find themselves isolated in a trench with a booby-trapped soldier.
Witty, angry satire on the large and small idiocies of war, from the inadequacies of international peace-keepers to the compliance of reporters and the determination of two men to kill another one when, in other circumstances, they might have been friends.
wd Danis Tanovic *ph* Walther Vanden Ende *m* Danis Tanovic *pd* Dusko Milavec *ed* Francesca Calvelli
☆ Brancko Djuric (Chiki), Rene Bitoraja (Nino), Filip Sovagovic (Chera), Georges Siatidis (Marchand), Katrin Cartlidge (Jane Livingstone), Simon Callow (Col Soft), Serge-Henri Valcke (Capt Dubois)
'A smart, entertainingly acrid thumbnail sketch of the ironies and absurdities of the Bosnian war.' – *Peter Bradshaw, Guardian*
† In 2001, Danis Tanovic won the European Film Award, and the Cannes Film Festival Award, for best screenplay.
foreign film

Nil by Mouth **
GB 1997 128m DuArt
TCF/SE8 (Luc Besson, Douglas Urbanski, Gary Oldman)

In South London, a violent alcoholic terrorizes his family.
A bleak and unsparing account of devastated life in the slums, where drinks and drugs provide a momentary escape and masculinity is measured by the size of the fist; this semi-autobiographical drama is given vitality by the conviction of its performances.
wd Gary Oldman ph Ron Fortunato *m* Eric Clapton *pd* Hugo Luczyc-Wyhowski *ed* Brad Fuller
☆ *Ray Winstone, Kathy Burke*, Charlie Creed-Miles, Laila Morse, Edna Doré, Chrissie Cotterill, Jon Morrison, Jamie Forman
'A film of hard, unyielding brilliance that, given the choice, I would quite happily unwatch.' – *Tom Shone, Sunday Times*
† Kathy Burke won the best actress award at the Cannes Film Festival in 1997, and Gary Oldman the best director award at the 1997 Edinburgh Film Festival.
best British film; Gary Oldman (as writer)

Nilouhe, Nuer: see *Daughter of the Nile*

9/30/55 *
US 1977 101m colour
Columbia (Jerry Weintraub)
The death of James Dean on 30 September 1955 has a devastating effect on a teenager at an Arkansas college who identifies with him.
Effective story of adolescent feelings and frustrations.
wd James Bridges *ph* Gordon Willis *m* Leonard Rosenman *ad* Robert Luthardt *ed* Jeff Gourson
☆ Richard Thomas, Susan Tyrrell, Deborah Benson, Lisa Blount, Thomas Hulce, Dennis Quaid, Dennis Christopher
'This is the sort of low-budget, personal moviemaking that Hollywood is presumed to shy away from, and it would be a shame if it got overlooked.' – *David Ansen, Newsweek*
† Leonard Rosenman wrote the music for two films starring James Dean, *East of Eden* and *Rebel without a Cause*.

Nine and a Half Weeks
US 1986 113m colour
MGM/UA/PSO/Sidney Kimmel/Keith Barish/Jonesfilm/Galactic Films/Triple Ajaxx (Anthony Rufus Isaacs, Zalman King)

A Wall Street executive and an art gallery employee embark upon a passionate affair.
Crash course in hot sex for those who wish to major in such studies; of no other interest despite its aspirations to being some sort of art.
w Patricia Knop, Zalman King, Sarah Kernochan *novel* Elizabeth McNeill *d* Adrian Lyne *ph* Peter Biziou *m* Jack Nitzsche *pd* Ken Davis
☆ Mickey Rourke, Kim Basinger, Margaret Whitton, David Margulies, Christine Baranski
'The virtual absence of anything happening between them – like plausible attraction, amazing sex or, God forbid, good dialogue – leaves one great hole on the screen for two hours.' – *Variety*

Nine Days a Queen: see *Tudor Rose*

9 Deaths of the Ninja
US 1985 94m colour
Crown International (Ashok Amritraj)
An anti-terrorist outfit rescues hostages captured by a mad German drug dealer.
Bungled attempt at a comic martial arts movie.
wd Emmett Alston *ph* Roy H. Wagner *m* Cecile Colayco *pd* Rodell Cruz *ed* Emmett Alston, Robert E. Waters
☆ Sho Kosugi, Brent Huff, Emilia Lesniak, Regina Richardson, Vijay Amritraj, Blackie Dammett

Nine Hours to Rama
GB 1962 125m DeLuxe Cinemascope
TCF/Red Lion (Mark Robson)
Events leading to the assassination of Mahatma Gandhi.
Fictionalized, sensationalized and very dull, this multi-character drama holds interest only for snatches of acting and location backgrounds.
w Nelson Gidding *novel* Stanley Wolpert *d* Mark Robson *ph* Arthur Ibbetson *m* Malcolm Arnold *ad* Elliot Scott, Ram Yedekar *ed* Ernest Walter
☆ José Ferrer (Supt Gopal Das), Diane Baker (Sheila), Robert Morley (P.K. Mussadi), J. S. Casshyap (Mahatma Gandhi), Horst Buchholz (Naturam Godse), Harry Andrews (Gen Singh), Valerie Gearon (Rani Mehta), Don Borisenko (Naryan Apte)

'The only interesting line in the movie is the thick brown one visible on the inside of every white collar.' – *John Simon*

976-Evil
US 1988 100m colour
Medusa/Cinetel/Horrorscope (Lisa M. Hansen)

A teenager gains evil powers after summoning a demon by telephone.
Directed by the star of A Nightmare on Elm Street *and its sequels, it resembles those films in its mixture of grotesque humour and gruesome special effects.*
w Rhet Topham, Brian Helgeland *d* Robert Englund *ph* Paul Elliott *m* Thomas Chase, Steve Rucker *ad* David Brian Miller *ed* Stephen Myers
☆ Stephen Geoffreys, Patrick O'Bryan, Sandy Dennis, Jim Metzler, Maria Rubell, Robert Picardo, Lezlie Deane, J. J. Cohen, Paul Wilson

Nine Lives Are Not Enough
US 1941 63m bw
Warner
A reporter solves a multi-murder in a boarding house.
Lively second feature which moves at a commendable pace.
w Fred Niblo Jnr *d* A. Edward Sutherland
☆ Ronald Reagan, Howard da Silva, James Gleason, Ed Brophy, Faye Emerson, Peter Whitney, Charles Drake

The Nine Lives of Fritz the Cat
US 1974 76m DeLuxe
AIP/Two Gees (Steve Krantz)

Stoned on pot, a cat dreams of the lives he might have led.
An animated sequel of sorts to Fritz the Cat *(qv), but done by other, cruder hands and lacking imagination and wit; it is far removed from Robert Crumb's original.*
w Fred Halliday, Eric Monte, Robert Taylor *d* Robert Taylor *m* Tom Scott and the LA Express *ed* Marshall M. Borden
☆ Featuring the voices of Skip Hinnant, Reva Rose, Bob Holt, Fred Smoot, Robert Ridgely
'Boringly diffuse, completely negating any possible shock effect through the overwhelming quantity of obscenity and gutter language.' – *David Rider, MFB*

The Nine Lives of Tomas Katz
Germany/GB 1999 87m bw
NFT/Geissendorfer/G2/Strawberry Vale (Caroline Hewitt)
In London, a stranger emerges from a sewer and takes over the identities of the people he meets so that he can cause chaos and bring about the apocalypse.
Weird, low-budget surrealism that is defiantly original and obscure; crossword-puzzlers may be able to tease some meaning from it.
w Ben Hopkins, Thomas Browne *d* Ben Hopkins *ph* Julian Court *m* Dominik Scherrer *pd* Gideon Davey *ed* Alan Levy
☆ Thomas Fisher (No/Tomas Katz), Ian McNeice (Inspector), Tim Barlow (Mr Browne), Janet Henfrey (Janice Waily), Will Keen (Cuthbert), Tony Maudsley (Taxi driver), David De Keyser (Exhumed Rabbi)
'Beyond art school outings, pic's only audience will be the director's friends and family.' – *Derek Elley, Variety*
'Nothing so obvious as a plot is allowed to cramp this movie's style as it swoops weirdly across the dream landscape of London like a demented, dishevelled bird.' – *Peter Bradshaw, Guardian*

Nine Men *
GB 1943 68m bw
Ealing
A sergeant and a handful of men in an old fort hold off the Italians in the Libyan desert.
Sharp semi-documentary of the war which paled against the mightier epics to follow.
wd Harry Watt *ph* Roy Kellino *m* John Greenwood
☆ Jack Lambert, Gordon Jackson, Frederick Piper, Grant Sutherland, Bill Blewett

'Ready or Not.'
Nine Months
US 1995 103m DeLuxe Panavision
TCF/1492 (Ann François, Chris Columbus, Mark Radcliffe, Michael Barnathan)

An English child psychologist working in San Francisco is horrified to discover that his girlfriend is pregnant.
A still-born comedy, bereft of wit or style, in which Hugh Grant acts embarrassed for most of the time, as well he might.
wd Chris Columbus *ph* Donald McAlpine *m* Hans Zimmer *pd* Angelo P. Graham *ed* Raja Gosnell
☆ Hugh Grant, Julianne Moore, Tom Arnold, Joan Cusack, Jeff Goldblum, Robin Williams
'A dim-witted romp that makes little use of its leading man – if Tinseltown is looking for the next Cary Grant, this isn't the vehicle.' – *Denis Seguin, Screen International*
'Truly dreadful.' – *Guardian*
† It is based on a French film, *Neuf Mois*, written and directed by Patrick Brauodé.

Nine Queens: see *Nueve Reinas*

Nine to Five *
US 1980 110m DeLuxe
TCF/IPC (Bruce Gilbert)

Three office women plot to get rid of their boss, and nearly make it.
Sporadically agreeable comedy somewhat reminiscent of Sturges's Unfaithfully Yours.
w Colin Higgins, Patricia Resnick *d* Colin Higgins *ph* Reynaldo Villalobos *m* Charles Fox *pd* Dean Mitzner
☆ Jane Fonda, Dolly Parton, Lily Tomlin, Dabney Coleman, Sterling Hayden, Elizabeth Wilson, Henry Jones
'An effective escapist feast with lotsa funny physical schtick.' – *Variety*
title song (Dolly Parton)

1900 *
Italy/France/West Germany 1976 320m Technicolor
TCF/PEA/Artistes Associés/Artemis (Alberto Grimaldi)

original title: *Novecento*
The political and personal vicissitudes of a noble Italian family between 1900 and 1945
Immensely long and heavy-going study of the rise of fascism in the form of a family saga. For specialists only.
w Bernardo Bertolucci, Franco Arcalli, Giuseppe Bertolucci *d* Bernardo Bertolucci *ph* Vittorio Storaro *m* Ennio Morricone *ad* Enzo Frigiero
☆ Burt Lancaster, Robert de Niro, Gérard Depardieu, Dominique Sanda, Donald Sutherland, Sterling Hayden
'Exasperatingly uneven, but its most powerful moments can't be matched by any movie since Godfather Two.' – *Time*
'Bertolucci tried to write a 19th-century novel on film: the result is appalling, yet it has the grandeur of a classic visionary folly.' – *New Yorker*
† The film was normally shown in two separate parts.

19/19
GB 1984 99m colour/bw
BFI/Channel 4 (Nita Amy)
Two former patients of Sigmund Freud meet in old age to recall their past treatment.
Interminable and unilluminating conversation piece, intercut with documentary footage and flashbacks that illustrate what has just been said.
w Hugh Brody, Michael Ignatieff *d* Hugh Brody *ph* Ivan Strasburg *m* Brian Gascoigne *ad* Caroline Amies *ed* David Gladwell
☆ Paul Scofield, Maria Schell, Frank Finlay, Diana Quick, Clare Higgins, Colin Firth

1941 *
US 1979 118m Metrocolor Panavision
Columbia/Universal/A-Team (John Milius)

Just after Pearl Harbor, a stray Japanese submarine terrorizes Hollywood.
Absurdly over-budgeted manic farce which substitutes noise for wit and slapstick for comedy; it fails on every level.
w Robert Zemeckis, Bob Gale *d* Steven Spielberg *ph* William A. Fraker *m* John Williams *pd* Dean Edward Mitzner
☆ Dan Aykroyd, Ned Beatty, John Belushi, Lorraine Gary, Murray Hamilton, Christopher Lee, Tim Matheson, Toshiro Mifune, Warren Oates, Robert Stack, Elisha Cook Jnr
'So overloaded with visual humour of rather monstrous nature that the feeling emerges that once you've seen ten explosions, you've seen them all.' – *Variety*
'Aimed at young audiences, who deserve better fun.' – *New Yorker*
'Its sheer relentless physicality, its elaborately orchestrated pointlessness on every other level, make it probably the purest demonstration of what it means to have two of the all-time commercial blockbusters to one's record and one's hands firmly on the fantasy machine.' – *Richard Combs, MFB*
'Spielberg intended it as "a stupidly outrageous celebration of paranoia" ... audiences found it curiously unfunny and elephantine.' – *Les Keyser, Hollywood in the Seventies*
William A. Fraker

1969
US 1988 96m colour
Entertainment/Atlantic (Daniel Grodnick, Bill Badalato)

As the Vietnam War gets under way, two small-town youths protest for peace.
A nostalgic wallow that never rises above cliché.
wd Ernest Thompson *ph* Jules Brenner *m* Michael Small *pd* Marcia Hinds *ed* William Anderson
☆ Robert Downey Jnr, Kiefer Sutherland, Bruce Dern, Mariette Hartley, Winona Ryder, Joanna Cassidy, Christopher Wynne

1984 *
GB 1955 91m bw
Holiday (N. Peter Rathvon)
Europe has become the fascist state of Oceania, ruled by Big Brother; Winston Smith yearns for the old days, and is brainwashed.
The famous prophecy of a dehumanized future is followed with reasonable fidelity apart from the defiant ending, but the novel is too literary for cinematic success and the result is too often both downbeat and boring.
w William P. Templeton, Ralph Bettinson *novel George Orwell d Michael Anderson ph* C. Pennington Richards *m* Malcolm Arnold
☆ Michael Redgrave, Edmond O'Brien, Jan Sterling, David Kossoff, Mervyn Johns, Donald Pleasence

'Will ecstasy be a crime – in the terrifying world of the future?'
1984 *
GB 1984 110m Eastmancolor
Umbrella/Rosenblum/Virgin (Simon Perry)

Winston Smith comes to love Big Brother after being brainwashed and taught Doublethink.
Pointless, perhaps, to make a prophetic film in the year it was supposed to be prophesying, but this version adds a few twists to Orwell's nightmarish original and is well if sometimes confusingly made.
wd Michael Radford *novel* George Orwell *m* Dominic Muldowney *pd* Allan Cameron *ed* Tom Priestley *d/ph* Roger Deakins
☆ John Hurt, Richard Burton, Suzanna Hamilton, Cyril Cusack, Gregor Fisher, James Walker
'A tale of unrelieved bleakness is told with relentless accuracy to Mr Orwell's novel, to which it is a kind of homage.' – *Quentin Crisp*

99 and 44/100 Per Cent Dead
US 1974 98m DeLuxe Panavision
TCF/Joe Wizan/Vashon

aka: *Call Harry Crown*
A losing gang boss hires a trouble shooter.
Violent gangster melodrama apparently intended as a black comedy; if so, as clumsy as its title.
w Robert Dillon *d* John Frankenheimer *ph* Ralph Woolsey *m* Henry Mancini
☆ Richard Harris, Edmond O'Brien, Bradford Dillman, Ann Turkel, Chuck Connors, Constance Ford
'Esthetically, commercially and morally, a quintessential fiasco.' – *Variety*
† The title in fact spoofs an ad familiar to Americans for a soap which was said to be '99 and 44/100 per cent pure'.

99 River Street *
US 1953 83m bw
UA/Edward Small
A taxi driver becomes involved in a diamond robbery.
Adequate thick ear with quite good detection and action sequences.
w Robert Smith *d Phil Karlson ph* Franz Planer
☆ John Payne, Evelyn Keyes, Frank Faylen, Brad Dexter, Peggie Castle

92 in the Shade *
US 1975 88m colour
United Artists (George Pappas)

A drifter who becomes a fishing guide in Florida's Key West finds himself in competition with the captain of another fishing boat.
For the most part, an engaging and atmospheric study of coolly observed eccentricity, though lacking any narrative thrust.
wd Thomas McGuane *novel* Thomas McGuane *ph* Michael C. Butler *m* Michael J. Lewis *ed* Ed Rothkowitz
☆ Peter Fonda, Warren Oates, Margot Kidder, Elizabeth Ashley, Burgess Meredith, Harry Dean Stanton, Sylvia Miles, William Hickey, Louise Latham
† The film was recut and re-released in 1981.

'He has the Power. He can stop the killings. He is the...'
Ninja Dragon (dubbed)
Hong Kong 1986 87m colour
IFD Films and Arts (Joseph Lai, Betty Chan)

The daughter of a murdered gang-leader returns to take over his territory and precipitates a power struggle between rival gangsters on the streets of Shanghai.
Ludicrous thriller, with unconvincing martial arts interludes, notable for its high body-count and for having not one redeeming character in its large cast; with its hooded avenger, wearing a great deal of eye-liner, and cackling black-hatted hoodlums, its overwrought style can best be described as high camp.
wd Godfrey Ho *story* Frank Hor, AAV Creative Unit *d* Joseph Lai *ph* Raymond Chang *m* Stephen Tsang *pd* Hiram Lai *ed* Nicky Au *sp* Simon Chu
☆ Richard Harrison, Bruce Stallion, Melvin Pitcher, Konrad Chang, Lily Lan, Freya Patrick

Ninja in a Lion's Den: see *Long Zhi Ren Zhe*

'The picture that kids the commissars!'
'Garbo laughs!'
'Don't pronounce it – see it!'
Ninotchka ***
US 1939 110m bw
MGM (Ernst Lubitsch)

A Paris playboy falls for a communist emissary sent to sell some crown jewels.
Sparkling comedy on a theme which has been frequently explored; delicate pointing and hilarious character comedy sustain this version perfectly until the last half hour, when it certainly sags; but it remains a favourite Hollywood example of this genre.
w Charles Brackett, Billy Wilder, Walter Reisch story Melchior Lengyel *d Ernst Lubitsch ph William Daniels m* Werner Heymann
☆ *Greta Garbo, Melvyn Douglas, Sig Rumann, Alexander Granach, Felix Bressart*, Ina Claire, Bela Lugosi
PROLOGUE: THIS PICTURE TAKES PLACE IN PARIS IN THOSE WONDERFUL DAYS WHEN A SIREN WAS A BRUNETTE AND NOT AN ALARM – AND IF A FRENCHMAN TURNED OUT THE LIGHT IT WAS NOT ON ACCOUNT OF AN AIR RAID!
NINOTCHKA (GRETA GARBO): 'I must have a complete report of your negotiations and a detailed expense account.'
BULJANOFF (FELIX BRESSART): 'No, non, Ninotchka. Don't ask for it. There is an old

Turkish proverb that says, if something smells bad, why put your nose in it?'

NINOTCHKA: 'And there is an old Russian saying, the cat who has cream on his whiskers had better find good excuses.'

NINOTCHKA: 'The last mass trials were a great success. There are going to be fewer but better Russians.'

'High calibre entertainment for adult audiences, and a top attraction for the key de-luxers.' – *Variety*

'The Lubitsch style, in which much was made of subtleties – glances, finger movements, raised eyebrows – has disappeared. Instead we have a hard, brightly lit, cynical comedy with the wisecrack completely in control.' – *John Baxter, 1968*

† William Powell and Robert Montgomery were formerly considered for the Melvyn Douglas role.

best picture; script; story; Greta Garbo

The Ninth Configuration

US 1980 105m Metrocolor Panavision
ITC/Lorimar (William Peter Blatty)

A new psychiatrist in a compound of military misfits becomes the victim of a terror campaign.
Weirdly obscure would-be thriller which only mystifies and annoys.
wd William Peter Blatty *novel Twinkle, Twinkle 'Killer' Kane* by William Peter Blatty *ph* Gerry Fisher *m* Barry DeVorzon *pd* Bill Malley, J. Dennis Washington *ed* Peter Taylor
☆ Stacy Keach (Col Vincent Kane), Scott Wilson (Capt. Billy Cutshaw), Jason Miller (Lt Frankie Reno), Ed Flanders (Col Hudson Kane), Neville Brand (Maj. Marvin Groper), Moses Gunn (Maj. Nammack), Robert Loggia (Lt Bennish), Joe Spinell (Lt Spinell)

'Quite astonishingly garbled, trailing yards of portentous religious allegory.' – *Observer*

'The pretensions are enough to raise the *Titanic* – and sink it again.' – *Guardian*

† Blatty released a longer version, running for 118m, in 1985.

'Leave the unknown alone.'
The Ninth Gate *

France/Spain 1999 127m colour Super 35
Artisan/R.P./OrlyTF1/Kino Vision/Origen/Bac/Canal+/Via Digital (Roman Polanski)

A wealthy New York collector hires a rare-book dealer to check the authenticity of a 17th century book said to have been co-authored by the devil.
An uncertain tone bedevils this tale of decadence and satanism among the very rich, veering as it does between horror and satire; ultimately, it's nothing very much.
w Enrique Urbizu, John Brownjohn, Roman Polanski *novel El Club Dumas* by Arturo Perez-Reverte *d* Roman Polanski *ph* Darius Khondji *m* Wojciech Kilar *pd* Dean Tavoularis *ed* Herve de Luze *cos* Anthony Powell
☆ Johnny Depp (Dean Corso), Frank Langella (Boris Balkan), Lena Olin (Liana Telfer), Emmanuelle Seigner (The Girl), Barbara Jefford (Baroness Kessler), Jack Taylor (Victor Fargas), Jose Lopez Rodero (Pablo and Pedro Ceniza), James Russo (Bernie)

'About as scary as a sock-puppet re-enactment of *The Blair Witch Project* and not nearly as funny.' – *Elvis Mitchell, New York Times*

The Ninth Guest

US 1934 65m bw
Columbia

Eight people are trapped by a murderer in a penthouse suite.
Whodunnit which must have been seen by Agatha Christie before she wrote And Then There Were None. *This version however is flatly scripted and characterized, with no real interest in the (unlikely) outcome.*
w Garnett Weston *novel* Gwen Bristow *stage play* Owen Davis *d* Roy William Neill
☆ Donald Cook, Genevieve Tobin, Hardie Albright, Edward Ellis, Edwin Maxwell, Vince Barnett, Samuel S. Hinds

'It ought to get a neat return in most spots.' – *Variety*

Nirvana Street Murder

Australia 1990 75m colour
AFC (Fiona Cochrane)

An abattoir worker tries to keep control of his own life, and that of his simple-minded, violent brother, who has hazy notions of right and wrong.
A short, grimly realistic working-class drama that quickly degenerates into unconvincing melodrama.
wd Aleksi Vellis *ph* Mark Lane *pd* Lisa Thompson *ed* Aleksi Vellis
☆ Mark Little, Ben Mendelsohn, Mary Coustas, Sheila Florance, Roberto Micale, Tamara Saulwick, Yiorgo, Russell Gilbert

The Nitwits

US 1935 81m bw
RKO

Two cigar-stand assistants solve the murder of a music publisher.
Overlong crime comedy with a good finale.
w Fred Guiol, Al Boasberg, Stuart Palmer
d George Stevens
☆ Bert Wheeler, Robert Woolsey, Fred Keating, Betty Grable, Evelyn Brent

'Fair.' – *Variety*

Niu-Peng **

China/France 1989 100m colour
Titane/Flach Film/La Sept (Jean-Luc Ormieres)
aka: *China, My Sorrow*

A 13-year-old boy is sent to Niu-Peng, a detention centre for 'the re-education of enemies of the people', for listening to love songs on his record-player.
Moving and compassionate account of a community of independent spirits surviving in the face of intransigence.
w Dai Sijie, Shan Yuan Zhu *d* Dai Sijie *ph* Jean-Michael Humeau *m* Chen Qi Gang *ad* Christian Marti *ed* Chantal Delattre
☆ Guo Liang Yi, Tien Quan Nghieu, Vuong Han Lai, Sam Chi-Vy, Truong Loi

Nixon ***

US 1995 192m Technicolor Panavision
Entertainment/Illusion/Cinergi (Clayton Townsend, Oliver Stone, Andrew G. Vajna)

As the Watergate cover-up begins to unravel, Richard Nixon recalls his past, from his Quaker childhood to his marriage and the triumphs of his political career.
A boldly conceived film on the corruption of power. It attempts to cast Nixon as the protagonist of a tragedy in a Shakespearean mould – like Macbeth, he clambers over the dead bodies of others to seize power and to retain it. While the film fails to show that Nixon had sufficient stature to qualify as a tragic hero, it does provide a fascinating portrait of a flawed and envious man, seeking support from dubious allies and brought down by his own failings. Hopkins is utterly convincing in the title role.
w Stephen J. Rivele, Christopher Wilkinson, Oliver Stone *d* Oliver Stone *ph* Robert Richardson *m* John Williams *pd* Victor Kempster *ed* Brian Berdan, Hank Corwin
☆ *Anthony Hopkins* (Nixon), *Joan Allen* (Pat Nixon), Powers Boothe (Alexander Haig), Ed Harris (E. Howard Hunt), E. G. Marshall (John Mitchell), David Paymer (Ron Ziegler), David Hyde Pierce (John Dean), Paul Sorvino (Henry Kissinger), J. T. Walsh (John Erlichman), James Woods (H. R. Haldeman), Mary Steenburgen (Hannah Nixon)

'Inescapably interesting due to the parade of recent history on view, but it finally emerges as an honorable, and rather too strenuous, failure.' – *Todd McCarthy, Variety*

'Achieves the dubious distinction of being a film about Nixon that is actually more paranoid than Nixon was.' – *Tom Shone, Sunday Times*

Anthony Hopkins, Joan Allen; John Williams; screenplay

Nô *

Canada 1998 85m colour/bw
Alliance/In Extremis Images/Telefilm Canada/Sodec (Bruno Jobin)

In 1970, at a time of martial law in Quebec, a pregnant Canadian actress decides to return home to her lover, who has become involved with violent separatists.
An enjoyable, cleverly constructed movie that moves from stylized comedy to realistic drama, though its political concerns are too local to mean much in the wider world.
w Robert Lepage, Andre Morency *play The Seven Branches of the River Ota* by Robert Lepage
d Robert Lepage *ph* Pierre Mignot *m* Michel F. Cote, Bernard Falaise *pd* Fanfan Boudreau
ed Aube Foglia
☆ Anne-Marie Cadieux, Alexis Martin, Marie Brassard, Richard Fréchette, Marie Gignac, Eric Bernier

'Witty, always intriguing and amusing, and maintains the director's reputation as an inventive cinematic stylist.' – *Richard Falcon, Sight and Sound*

No Big Deal

US 1984 86m Movielab
Kandel/Film Gallery/Cinétudes (Gale Goldberg, Christine Jurzykowski)

A juvenile delinquent fails to make the grade.
Drear high-school drama of adolescent angst, indifferently acted and directed.
w Jeffrey Kindley *book Would You Settle for Improbable?* by P. J. Petersen *d* Robert Charlton
ph Jeff Lion Weinstock *m* Lynn Ahrens
ad Joshua Harrison *ed* Margot Francis
☆ Kevin Dillon, Christopher Gartin, Mary Joan Negro, Jane Krakowski, Stacy Lauren, Daniel Hess, Wayne Daniels, Tammy Grimes, Sylvia Miles

No Blade of Grass

GB 1970 97m Metrocolor Panavision
MGM (Cornel Wilde)

Industrial pollution sets a destructive virus ruining the crops of the world; anarchy spreads through Britain and one family takes refuge in the Lake District.
Apocalyptic sci-fi, moderately well done though so humourless as to be almost funny.
w Sean Forestal, Jefferson Pascal *novel The Death of Grass* by John Christopher *d* Cornel Wilde
ph H. A. R. Thomson *m* Burnell Whibley
☆ Nigel Davenport, Jean Wallace, Patrick Holt, John Hamill

'When Corruption Strikes the Police Force... Trust No One!'
No Code of Conduct

US 1998 93m FotoKem
Nu Image/Millennium/Sheen/Michaels (Avi Lerner, Elie Samaha, Danny Dimbort, Trevor Short)

A cop with family problems tracks down drug dealers attempting to shift a $50m consignment of heroin.
Banal, loud and ludicrous movie, recycling a familiar narrative without style or impact, and with an irritating method of cutting between one predictable scene and the next. Ironically, at the beginning Martin Sheen's retiring policeman tells young recruits that police-work bears no resemblance to TV cop shows; what follows includes all the worst moments of the genre.
w Brett Michaels, Charles Sheen, Shane Stanley, William Gucwa, Edward Masterson *d* Bret Michaels *ph* Adam Kane *m* Bret Michaels, Kyle Level *pd* Marc Fisichella *ed* Shane Stanley
☆ Charles Sheen (Jake Peterson), Martin Sheen (Bill Peterson), Mark Dasascos (Paul Delucca), Paul Gleason (Bagwell), Joe Lando (Willdog), Courtney Gains (Cameron), Meredith Salinger (Rebecca Peterson), Joe Estevez (Pappy), Tina Nguyen (Shi), Ron Masak (Julian Disanto)

No Deposit, No Return

US 1976 112m Technicolor
Walt Disney (Ron Miller)

Airport confusion causes crooks to abduct (unwittingly) a millionaire's grandchildren; the millionaire gives chase.
Overlong and tedious action comedy which makes little sense.
w Arthur Alsberg, Don Nelson *d* Norman Tokar
ph Frank Phillips *m* Buddy Baker
☆ David Niven, Darren McGavin, Don Knotts, Herschel Bernardi, Barbara Feldon, John Williams, Vic Tayback, Kim Richards

'Once again one is left wondering why there should be such an unbridgeable gulf between the brilliant professionalism and sometimes innovative genius of the Disney animated films, and the dull artlessness of the majority of their live-action pictures.' – *Philip French, The Times*

'You can't throw so many young couples together and not expect explosions!'
No Down Payment **

US 1957 105m bw Cinemascope
TCF (Jerry Wald)

Tension among smart suburban couples in a Los Angeles housing development.
Lively domestic melodrama, very useful to sociologists as a mirror of its times.
w Philip Yordan novel John McPartland *d Martin Ritt ph* Joseph LaShelle *m* Leigh Harline
☆ Joanne Woodward, Tony Randall, Sheree North, Jeffrey Hunter, Cameron Mitchell, Patricia Owens, Barbara Rush, Pat Hingle

No End *

Poland 1984 107m colour
Artificial Eye/Zespoly Filmowe (Ryszard Chutkowski)
original title: *Bez Konca*

The ghost of a radical lawyer watches over his wife and son and an elderly lawyer who has taken over his final case, defending the leader of a strike.
Intense domestic and political drama, set against a background of the imposition of martial law.
w Krzysztof Kieslowski, Krzysztof Piesiewicz
d Krzysztof Kieslowski *ph* Jacek Petrycki
m Zbigniew Preisner *ad* Allan Starski
ed Krystyna Rutowska
☆ Grazyna Szapolowska, Maria Pakulnis, Aleksander Bardini, Jerzy Radziwilowicz, Artur Barcis, Michel Bajor, Marek Kondrat

No Escape

GB 1936 85m bw
Pathé Welwyn

A man pretends to be dead as a hoax, and when he is found so, his accomplice is suspected.
Twisty thriller from a popular play.
w George Goodchild, Frank Witty *play No Exit* by George Goodchild, Frank Witty *d* Norman Lee
☆ Valerie Hobson, Leslie Perrins, Robert Cochran, Billy Milton, Henry Oscar

'Good programme picture for almost anywhere.' – *Variety*

'No Guards. No Walls.'
No Escape

US 1994 118m Eastmancolor Arriscope
Savoy/Allied Filmmakers/Pacific Western (Gale Anne Hurd)

In 2022, when prisons have been privatized, a vicious warden illegally dumps a convicted soldier on a remote island where gangs of criminals, some violent, one attempting to be civilized, strive for supremacy.
Slick action movie that follows conventional lines and, despite its future setting, most closely resembles ancient jungle escape stories; all it lacks is Tarzan.
w Michael Gaylin, Joel Gross *novel The Penal Colony* by Richard Herley *d* Martin Campbell
ph Phil Meheux *m* Graeme Revell *pd* Allan Cameron *ed* Terry Rawlings
☆ Ray Liotta, Lance Henriksen, Stuart Wilson, Kevin Dillon, Kevin J. O'Connor, Don Henderson, Ian McNeice, Jack Shepherd, Michael Lerner, Ernie Hudson

'This offers muscular widescreen thrills, but is sorely lacking in any cranial tissue.' – *Jack Yeovil, Empire*

No Funny Business

GB 1933 75m bw
John Stafford

Two professional co-respondents are sent to the Riviera; each mistakes the other as his client.
Stagey farce, notable for its unlikely star teaming and its hilariously dated style.
w Victor Hanbury, Frank Vosper, Dorothy Hope
d John Stafford, Victor Hanbury *ph* Bryan Langley *songs* Noel Gay, Clifford Grey
☆ Gertrude Lawrence, Laurence Olivier, Jill Esmond, Edmund Breon, Gibb McLaughlin, Muriel Aked

No Greater Glory

US 1934 78m bw
Columbia

Boys learn through their play that there is no greater glory than to die for one's country.
Glum parable which probably worked better in the original German.

w Jo Swerling *film script The Paul Street Boys* by Ferenc Molnar *d* Frank Borzage
☆ George Breakston, Jimmy Butler, Jackie Searl, Frankie Darro, Ralph Morgan, Christian Rub
'Not for the general trade, but a prospective hit in the arties.' – *Variety*

No Habra Mas Penas Ni Olvido: see *A Funny Dirty Little War*

'Turn back, I tell you! Any minute may be too late!'
No Highway **
GB 1951 98m bw
TCF (Louis D. Lighton)
US title: *No Highway in the Sky*
During a transatlantic flight, a boffin works out that the plane's tail is about to fall off from metal fatigue.
The central premise of this adaptation from a popular novel is fascinating, but the romantic asides are a distraction and the characters cardboard; the film still entertains through sheer professionalism.
w R. C. Sherriff, Oscar Millard, Alec Coppel *novel* Nevil Shute *d* Henry Koster *ph* Georges Périnal
☆ James Stewart, Marlene Dietrich, Glynis Johns, Jack Hawkins, Janette Scott, Elizabeth Allan, Kenneth More, Niall MacGinnis, Ronald Squire

No Highway in the Sky: see *No Highway*

No Leave, No Love
US 1946 118m bw
MGM (Joe Pasternak)
Sailors on leave meet an English girl.
Witless, overlong musical extravaganza.
w Charles Martin, Leslie Karkos *d* Charles Martin *ph* Harold Rosson, Robert Surtees *md* Georgie Stoll
☆ Van Johnson, Pat Kirkwood, Keenan Wynn, Guy Lombardo and his Orchestra, Edward Arnold, Marie Wilson, Leon Ames

No Limit *
GB 1935 79m bw
ATP (Basil Dean)
A motor mechanic enters for the TT Races.
Lively star comedy with Isle of Man locations.
w Tom Geraghty, Fred Thompson *story* Walter Greenwood *d* Monty Banks *ph* Bob Martin
☆ George Formby, Florence Desmond, Edward Rigby, Jack Hobbs, Peter Gawthorne, Alf Goddard

No Love for Johnnie *
GB 1960 111m bw Cinemascope
Rank/Five Star (Betty E. Box)
The personal and political problems of a Labour MP.
Predictable but quite lively study of ambition and frustration, with good cameos; Cinemascope all but ruins its impact.
w Nicholas Phipps, Mordecai Richler *novel* Wilfred Fienburgh *d* Ralph Thomas *ph* Ernest Steward *m* Malcolm Arnold
☆ *Peter Finch*, Mary Peach, *Stanley Holloway*, Donald Pleasence, Billie Whitelaw, Hugh Burden, Rosalie Crutchley, Michael Goodliffe, Mervyn Johns, Geoffrey Keen, Paul Rogers, Dennis Price, Peter Barkworth, Fenella Fielding, Gladys Henson
Peter Finch

No Man Is an Island
US 1962 114m Eastmancolor
U-I/Gold Coast (John Monks Jnr, Richard Goldstone)
GB title: *Island Escape*
After the Japanese attack on Guam, a radioman finds refuge in a leper colony and sets up his own resistance unit.
Unexceptionable war adventure in the jungle.
wd John Monks Jnr, Richard Goldstone *ph* Carl Kayser *m* Restie Umali
☆ Jeffrey Hunter, Marshall Thompson, Barbara Perez, Ronald Remy
'Good clean fun for right-minded teenagers.' – *MFB*

'He was a hit and run lover ... personally, he preferred a cigarette to any dame!'
No Man of Her Own *
US 1933 98m bw
Paramount
A big-time gambler marries a local girl on a bet and tries to keep her innocent of his activities.
Star romantic comedy drama, quite professionally assembled and played.
w Maurine Watkins, Milton H. Gropper *d* Wesley Ruggles *ph* Leo Tover
☆ Clark Gable, Carole Lombard, Dorothy Mackaill, Grant Mitchell, George Barbier, Elizabeth Patterson, J. Farrell MacDonald
'Entertaining film with national appeal.' – *Variety*
'Just about everything that the ordinary picture fan looks for: drama, romance, comedy, strong build-ups, exciting climaxes, a fine line of human interest.' – *Film Daily*

No Man of Her Own *
US 1950 98m bw
Paramount (Richard Maibaum)
A pregnant wanderer is involved in a train crash and assumes the identity of the wife of a dead passenger.
Glossy star melodrama, very watchable.
w Catherine Turney, Sally Benson, Mitchell Leisen *novel* William Irish (Cornell Woolrich) *d Mitchell Leisen ph* Daniel L. Fapp *m* Hugo Friedhofer
☆ *Barbara Stanwyck*, John Lund, Lyle Bettger, *Jane Cowl*, Phyllis Thaxter, Henry O'Neill, Richard Denning

No Man's Land: see *Nikogarsnja Zemlja*

No Man's Land *
France/Switzerland 1985 110m colour
Filmograph/MK2 (Alain Tanner, Marin Karmitz)
A group of smugglers, each wanting a better way of life, operate on the borders of France and Switzerland.
Coolly detached account of people on the point of breakdown.
wd Alain Tanner *ph* Bernard Zitzermann *m* Terry Riley *pd* Alain Nicolet *ed* Laurent Uhler
☆ Jean-Philippe Ecoffey, Betty Berr, Marie-Luce Felber, Hugues Quester, Myriam Mézières

No Man's Land
1987 105m colour
Rank/Orion (Joseph Stern, Dick Wolf)
A young undercover cop falls in love with the sister of the car thief he is trying to bring to justice.
Moderate low-key thriller with lacklustre performances.
w Dick Wolf *d* Peter Werner *ph* Hiro Narita *m* Basil Poledouris *pd* Paul Peters *ed* Steve Cohen
☆ D. B. Sweeney, Charlie Sheen, Lara Harris, Randy Quaid, Bill Duke, R. D. Call, Arlen Dean Snyder, M. Emmet Walsh, Al Shannon
foreign film

No Mercy
US 1986 105m Metrocolor
Tri-Star/Delphi IV (D. Constantine Conte)
Policemen pretend to be hit men in an attempt to infiltrate a murder-by-contract organization.
Fashionable violence, slick production, nothing new.
w Jim Carabatsos *d* Richard Pearce *ph* Michael Brault *m* Alan Silvestri *pd* Patrizia von Brandenstein *ed* Jerry Greenberg, Bill Yahraus
☆ Richard Gere, Kim Basinger, Jeroen Krabbe, George Dzundza, Gary Basaraba, William Atherton

No Mercy, No Future
West Germany 1981 100m colour
Mainline/Helma Sanders-Brahms
original title: *Die Berührte*
A suicidal schizophrenic wanders through Berlin looking for Christ and indulging in casual affairs.
Uncompromisingly downbeat study of madness that provides a succession of shocking images which become hard to bear.
wd Helma Sanders-Brahms *ph* Thomas Mauch *m* Manfred Opitz, Harald Grosskopf *ed* Ursula West, Hanni Lewerenz
☆ Elisabeth Stepanek, Hubertus von Weyrauch, Irmgard Mellinger, Nguyen Chi Canh

No Minor Vices
US 1948 96m bw
(MGM) Enterprise (Lewis Milestone)
A doctor brings home an artist friend who proceeds to wreck his household.
Interminable thin comedy which gives no clue as to what the talent involved thought it was doing.
w Arnold Manoff *d* Lewis Milestone *ph* George Barnes *m* Franz Waxman
☆ Dana Andrews, Lilli Palmer, Louis Jourdan, Jane Wyatt, Norman Lloyd

No More Ladies
US 1935 79m bw
MGM
A society girl thinks that by marrying a rake she can reform him.
Breezy sophisticated comedy which doesn't quite maintain its impetus.
w Donald Ogden Stewart, Horace Jackson *play* A. E. Thomas *d* Edward H. Griffith, George Cukor *ph* Oliver T. Marsh *m* Edward Ward
☆ Joan Crawford, Robert Montgomery, Franchot Tone, Charles Ruggles, Edna May Oliver, Gail Patrick, Reginald Denny, Arthur Treacher
'Sophistication plus in society setting and probably too much on the ultra side for sock appreciation. But okay.' – *Variety*

No More Women
US 1934 73m bw
Paramount
Deep-sea divers compete for jobs and a woman.
Flagg and Quirt in all but name, with action melodrama largely substituted for skirt-chasing.
w Delmer Daves, Lou Breslow *story* John M. Strong *d* Albert S. Rogell
☆ Edmund Lowe, Victor McLaglen, Sally Blane, Minna Gombell, Harold Huber
'Quirt and Flagg under the Hays morality code, and they can't take it.' – *Variety*

No, My Darling Daughter
GB 1961 96m bw
Rank/Five Star/Betty E. Box-Ralph Thomas
Chaos ensues when a tycoon's daughter is thought to be eloping with an American boyfriend.
Clumsy comedy with moments of brightness provided by the actors.
w Frank Harvey *play A Handful of Tansy* by Harold Brooke, Kay Bannerman *d* Ralph Thomas *ph* Ernest Steward *m* Norrie Paramor
☆ Michael Redgrave, Michael Craig, Roger Livesey, Rad Fulton, Juliet Mills, Renee Houston, Joan Sims, Peter Butterworth

No Name on the Bullet
US 1958 77m Eastmancolor Cinemascope
Universal (Howard Christie, Jack Arnold)
A hired gunman books into the hotel of a small Western town, and everybody wonders who he is after.
Tolerable Western programmer with more emphasis than usual on characterization.
w Gene L. Coon *d* Jack Arnold *ph* Harold Lipstein *m* Herman Stein
☆ Audie Murphy, Charles Drake, Joan Evans, R. G. Armstrong, Willis Bouchey, Karl Swenson

No, No, Nanette
US 1930 90m approx bw with Technicolor sequences
Warner
A married bible publisher secretly helps three girls, who all visit him on the same day.
Early talkie version of the rather naïve musical hit, with a priceless moment or two among the dross.
w Howard Emmett Rogers *play* Otto Harbach, Frank Mandel *d* Clarence Badger *ch* Larry Ceballos
☆ Bernice Claire, Lucien Littlefield, Lilyan Tashman, Bert Roach, ZaSu Pitts
♫ 'Dance of the Wooden Shoes'; 'As Long as I'm with You'; 'King of the Air'; No, No, Nanette'; 'Dancing to Heaven'; 'Tea for Two'; 'I Want to Be Happy'

No No Nanette
US 1940 90m bw
RKO/Suffolk (Herbert Wilcox)
Slightly altered remake with too little attention to the musical numbers.
w Ken Englund *d* Herbert Wilcox *md* Anthony Collins
☆ Anna Neagle, Richard Carlson, Victor Mature, Helen Broderick, Roland Young, ZaSu Pitts, Eve Arden, Billy Gilbert
'It's overboard on inaction, with most of the dead wood up front.' – *Variety*
♫ 'No, No Nanette'; 'I Want to Be Happy'; 'Tea for Two'

No Orchids for Miss Blandish
GB 1948 102m bw
Alliance/Tudor (A. R. Shipman, Oswald Mitchell)
An heiress is kidnapped by gangsters and falls for their psychopathic leader.
Hilariously awful gangster movie from a bestselling shocker. Everyone concerned is all at sea, and the result is one of the worst films ever made.
wd St John L. Clowes *novel* James Hadley Chase *ph* Gerald Gibbs *m* George Melachrino *ad* Harry Moore *ed* Manuel Del Campo
☆ Jack La Rue, Linden Travers, Hugh McDermott, Walter Crisham, Lily Molnar, Zoe Gail
'This must be the most sickening exhibition of brutality, perversion, sex and sadism ever to be shown on a cinema screen ... with pseudo-American accents the actors literally battle their way through a script laden with suggestive dialogue.' – *MFB*
'A most vicious display of sadism, brutality and suggestiveness.' – *Milton Shulman, Evening Standard*
'The morals are about level with those of a scavenger dog.' – *Daily Express*
'It has all the morals of an alley cat and all the sweetness of a sewer.' – *Observer*
'The worst film I have ever seen.' – *Sunday Express*
† Remade as *The Grissom Gang* (qv).

No Parking
GB 1938 72m bw
Herbert Wilcox
A car park attendant is mistaken for an American killer.
Modest, entertaining star comedy.
w Gerald Elliott *story* Carol Reed *d* Jack Raymond *ph* Francis Carver
☆ Gordon Harker, Leslie Perrins, Irene Ware, Cyril Smith

No Peace among the Olives
Italy 1950 99m bw
Lux (Domenico Davanzati)
A young shepherd goes home after the war and finds himself at war again – against a local racketeer.
A rather crude melodrama comparable with the American Thieves' Highway and other films noirs of the time.
w Giuseppe de Santis and others *d* Giuseppe de Santis *ph* Pietro Portalupi *m* Goffredo Petrassi
☆ Lucia Bose, Raf Vallone, Folco Lulli, Dante Maggio

No Place for Jennifer
GB 1949 90m bw
ABPC
Divorcing parents think again when their twelve-year-old daughter runs away.
Very predictable tearjerker which kept box offices busy in its day.
w J. Lee-Thompson *novel No Difference to Me* by Phyllis Hambledon *d* Henry Cass *ph* William McLeod *m* Allan Gray
☆ Leo Genn, Rosamund John, Janette Scott, Beatrice Campbell, Guy Middleton, Anthony Nicholls, Jean Cadell

No Problem! (dubbed) *
France 1975 100m Eastmancolor
Gaumont International 2000 (Alain Poiré)
original title: *Pas de Problème*
Enlisting the aid of a medical student in ridding her flat of a dead man, a young woman triggers a series of mishaps.
A hectic farce that, despite some unsympathetic dubbing, manages to raise a few smiles.
w Jean-Marie Poiré *d* Georges Lautner *ph* Maurice Fellous *m* Philippe Sarde *ed* Michelle David
☆ Miou-Miou, Bernard Menez, Jean Lefebvre, Anny Duperey, Henri Guybet, Renée Saint-Cyr, Patrick Dewaere (cameo)

No Questions Asked
US 1951 80m bw
MGM (Nicholas Nayfack)
A young lawyer undertakes shady business and finds himself framed for murder.
Well made second feature on conventional lines.
w Sidney Sheldon *d* Harold Kress *ph* Harold Lipstein *m* Leith Stevens
☆ Barry Sullivan, George Murphy, Arlene Dahl, Jean Hagen, William Reynolds, Mari Blanchard

No Regrets for Our Youth **
Japan 1946 110m bw
Toho (Keiji Matsuzaki)
original title: *Waga Seishun ni Kui Nashi*
The urbane widow of a left-wing journalist goes to live and work with his parents, who are peasants.
A moving account of the cost of individual survival, and of liberal ideals, at a time of repression and militarism in Japan.
w Eijiro Hisaita, Akira Kurosawa *d* Akira Kurosawa *ph* Asakazu Nakai *m* Tadashi Hattori
☆ Setsuko Hara, Susumu Fujita, Denjiro Okochi, Eiko Miyoshi, Kokuten Kodo, Haruko Sugimura

No Resting Place
GB 1951 77m bw
Colin Lesslie
A wandering Irish tinker accidentally kills a man and is hounded by a Civil Guard.
Interesting attempt at realistic location drama, suffering from a dejected plot and unsympathetic characters.
w Paul Rotha, Colin Lesslie, Michael Orrom *novel* Ian Niall *d* Paul Rotha *ph* Wolfgang Suschitzky *m* William Alwyn
☆ Michael Gough, Noel Purcell, Jack MacGowran

No Retreat, No Surrender
US 1986 90m Technicolor
Entertainment/New World/Seasonal/Balcor (Ng See Yuen)
An American kick-boxer, aided by the ghost of Bruce Lee, conquers a Russian champion who beat up his father.
Standard martial arts revenge movie, with Van Damme as the villain of the piece.
w Keith W. Strandberg *story* Ng See Yuen, Corey Yuen *d* Corey Yuen *ph* John Huneck, David Golia *m* Paul Gilreath *ed* Alan Poon, Mark Pierce, James Melkonian, Dane Davis
☆ Jean-Claude Van Damme, Kurt McKinney, J. W. Fails, Kathie Sileno, Kim Tai Chong, Kent Lipham

No Road Back
GB 1957 83m bw
Gibraltar/RKO (Steven Pallos)
A doctor discovers that his blind mother and fiancée are involved with a gang of violent thieves.
Agreeable time-waster, competently made but unexciting and notable mainly for one of Connery's early performances, as a Scottish crook with a speech impediment.
w Charles A. Leeds, Montgomery Tully *play* Falkland L. Cary, Philip Weathers *d* Montgomery Tully *ph* Lionel Banes *m* John Veale *md* Philip Martell *ad* John Stoll *ed* Jim Connock
☆ Skip Homeier, Paul Carpenter, Patricia Dainton, Norman Wooland, Margaret Rawlings, Eleanor Summerfield, Alfie Bass, Sean Connery

No Room at the Inn
GB 1948 82m bw
British National (Ivan Foxwell)
A monstrous woman half-starves evacuees and turns her house into a brothel.
Absurd melodrama from a play which was popular because it offered a full-blooded star performance. The film is less convincing but works pretty well on its level.
w Ivan Foxwell, Dylan Thomas *play* Joan Temple *d* Daniel Birt *ph* James Wilson
☆ *Freda Jackson*, Joy Shelton, Hermione Baddeley, Joan Dowling, Harcourt Williams, Sydney Tafler, Frank Pettingell, Niall MacGinnis

No Room for the Groom *
US 1952 82m bw
Universal-International (Ted Richmond)
An army veteran returns to his wife, who has moved in with her family without telling them of her marriage.
Amiable comedy which rises to a fair pitch of frenzy.
w Joseph Hoffman *story* Darwin H. Teilhet *d* Douglas Sirk *ph* Clifford Stine *m* Frank Skinner
☆ Tony Curtis, Piper Laurie, Don Defore, *Spring Byington*, Lee Aaker, Jack Kelly, Lillian Bronson

No Sad Songs for Me
US 1950 89m bw
Columbia (Buddy Adler)
A young wife discovers she has only eight months to live, and spends it planning her husband's future.
Well-meant but rather icky melodrama featuring one of those beautiful illnesses that appear to have no physical effect.
w Howard Koch *novel* Ruth Southard *d* Rudolph Maté *ph* Joseph Walker *m* George Duning
☆ Margaret Sullavan, Wendell Corey, Viveca Lindfors, Natalie Wood, John McIntire
Academy Award nomination: George Duning

No Secrets
GB 1982 90m colour
Fulsetcourt (Elizabeth Curran)
With the help of a female spy, an African emperor kidnaps two US astronauts and demands a huge ransom.
An unbelievably atrocious movie: a crude mix of dim-witted script, bad acting and heavy-handed, mistimed comedy.
w George Fowler, Peter Curran *d* Peter Curran *ph* David Mason *ed* Peter Curran
☆ Oliver Reed, Sylvaine Charlet, Peter Cushing, Keenan Wynn, Edwin Manda, Wilfrid Hyde-White, Hilary Pritchard, Melvyn Hayes

No Sex Please, We're British
GB 1973 91m Technicolor
Columbia/BHP (John R. Sloan)
Confusion ensues when a wrongly addressed parcel of dirty postcards arrives at a bank.
Fairly lively farce with everything from mistaken identity to falling trousers.
w Anthony Marriott, Johnnie Mortimer, Brian Cooke *play* Anthony Marriott, Alistair Foot *d* Cliff Owen *ph* Ken Hodges *m* Eric Rogers
☆ Ronnie Corbett, Arthur Lowe, Beryl Reid, Ian Ogilvy, Susan Penhaligon, David Swift, Michael Bates

No Sleep Till Dawn: see *Bombers B52*

No Smoking
GB 1955 72m bw
Tempean (Robert S. Baker, Monty Berman)
Tobacco companies take action when a simple-minded village chemist invents a no-smoking pill that works.
Dreary B-feature comedy with a ludicrous plot that failed to make an amiable radio comedian funny on the screen.
w Kenneth Hayles, Phil Park *play* George Moresby-White, Rex Rientis *d* Henry Cass *ph* Monty Berman *m* Ivor Slaney *md* Stanley Black *ad* Wilfred Arnold *ed* Jack Slade
☆ Reg Dixon, Belinda Lee, Lionel Jeffries, Ruth Trouncer, Alexander Gauge, Myrtle Rowe, Arthur Young, Hal Osmond, Tom Gill, Ronnie Stevens

No Surrender *
GB 1985 104m colour
Dumbarton/NFFC/Lauron/Film Four International (Mamoun Hassan)
Irish factions collide in a Liverpool club.
Black comedy typical of the author of Boys from the Black Stuff.
w Alan Bleasdale *d* Peter Smith *ph* Mick Coulter *m* Daryl Runswick
☆ Michael Angelis, Avis Bunnage, James Ellis, Ray McAnally, Tom Georgeson, Bernard Hill, J. G. Devlin

'Monstrous and marvellous, it combines the disturbing, the disorienting and the downright daft.' – *Paul Taylor, MFB*

No Time for Comedy *
US 1940 93m bw
Warner (Robert Lord)
A playwright is depressed by the times and has lost the knack of making people laugh.
Smooth film version of a thoughtful romantic comedy play.
w Julius J. and Philip G. Epstein *play S. N. Behrman* *d* William Keighley *ph* Ernest Haller *m* Heinz Roemheld
☆ James Stewart, Rosalind Russell, Charles Ruggles, Genevieve Tobin, Allyn Joslyn, Clarence Kolb, Louise Beavers

'Claudette loves the men with muscles!'
No Time for Love *
US 1943 83m bw
Paramount (Mitchell Leisen)
A lady photographer falls for the foreman of a crew digging a tunnel under the Hudson.
Agreeable romantic slapstick farce.
w Claude Binyon *d* Mitchell Leisen *ph* Charles Lang Jnr *m* Victor Young *ad* Hans Dreier, Robert Usher
☆ Claudette Colbert, Fred MacMurray, Ilka Chase, Richard Haydn, June Havoc, Marjorie Gateson, Bill Goodwin
Academy Award nomination: art direction

No Time for Sergeants
US 1958 111m bw
Warner (Mervyn Le Roy)
Adventures of a hillbilly army conscript.
Heavy-handed adaptation of the stage success, a real piece of filmed theatre with not much sparkle to it.
w John Lee Mahin *play* Ira Levin *novel* Mac Hyman *d* Mervyn Le Roy *ph* Harold Rosson *m* Ray Heindorf
☆ *Andy Griffith*, William Fawcett, Murray Hamilton, Nick Adams, Myron McCormick, Bartlett Robinson

No Time for Tears
GB 1957 86m Eastmancolor Cinemascope
ABPC (W. A. Whittaker)
Problems of a children's hospital.
Totally predictable British tearjerker with a happy ending.
w Anne Burnaby *d* Cyril Frankel *ph* Gilbert Taylor *m* Francis Chagrin
☆ Anna Neagle, Anthony Quayle, Sylvia Syms, Flora Robson, George Baker, Alan White, Daphne Anderson, Michael Hordern, Joan Hickson, Sophie Stewart, Rosalie Crutchley

No Trace
GB 1950 70m bw
Eros/Tempean (Robert S. Baker, Monty Berman)
An English crime novelist is invited by the police to help investigate a murder he has committed.
Ingenious minor thriller, not helped by being directed at a plodding pace.
wd John Gilling *story* Robert S. Baker, Carl Nystrom *ph* Monty Berman *m* John Lanchberry *md* Eric Robinson *ad* Walter Scott *ed* Gerald Landau
☆ Hugh Sinclair, Dinah Sheridan, John Laurie, Dora Bryan, Barry Morse, Beatrice Varley, Michael Brennan, Michael Ward

No Trees in the Street
GB 1958 96m bw
ABP/Allegro (Frank Godwin)
Problems of a London slum family in the thirties.
Artificial and unconvincing attempt at a London Love on the Dole, dragged up and redigested in a later era when 'realism' was thought to be fashionable.
w Ted Willis *play* Ted Willis *d* J. Lee-Thompson *ph* Gilbert Taylor *m* Laurie Johnson
☆ Sylvia Syms, Herbert Lom, Joan Miller, Melvyn Hayes, Stanley Holloway, Liam Redmond, Ronald Howard, Carole Lesley, Lana Morris, Lily Kann

'Nothing remains but crude sensationalism and several moments of unconscious humour.' – *MFB*

No Way Home *
US 1996 93m DuArt
Blue Dolphin/Back Alley/Orenda (Lisa Bruce, Robert Nickson)
A gentle, dim-witted man leaves jail after serving a six-year sentence for murder to live with his drug-dealing brother and new sister-in-law, who is a stripper.
Effective, low-key, foul-mouthed drama of sibling differences for the most part, until it resolves its narrative problems with a melodramatic climax.
wd Buddy Giovinazzo *ph* Claudia Raschke *m* Rick Giovinazzo *pd* Phyllis Cedar *ed* Stan Warnow
☆ Tim Roth, James Russo, Deborah Kara Unger, Joseph Ragno, Catherine Kellner, Saul Stein, Bernadette Penotti

'This feels like a down-market Martin Scorsese movie – which makes it engaging enough.' – *Amanda Lipman, Sight and Sound*

No Way Out *
US 1950 106m bw
TCF (Darryl F. Zanuck)
A crook stirs up racial feeling against a black doctor in whose hands his brother has died.
Vivid, hard-hitting melodrama with a hospital background and a strong sociological flavour.
w Joseph L. Mankiewicz, Lesser Samuels *d* Joseph L. Mankiewicz *ph Milton Krasner* *m* Alfred Newman
☆ Richard Widmark, Sidney Poitier, Linda Darnell, Stephen McNally, Harry Bellaver, Stanley Ridges, Ossie Davis, Ruby Dee

'A production designed solely for purposes of agitation and propaganda, unworthy of literary or cinematic consideration.' – *Henry Hart, Films in Review*

Academy Award nomination: script

No Way Out *
US 1987 116m Metrocolor
Orion/Neufeld/Ziskin/Garland (Laura Ziskin, Robert Garland)
A Pentagon officer is convinced his boss is guilty of murder, but the evidence points to himself.
Fast-paced remake of The Big Clock *(qv) which does not efface the memory of the original.*
w Robert Garland *novel* Kenneth Fearing *d* Roger Donaldson *ph* John Alcott *m* Maurice Jarre *pd* Dennis Washington
☆ Kevin Costner, Gene Hackman, Sean Young, Will Patton, Howard Duff, George Dzundza

No Way to Treat a Lady *
US 1968 108m Technicolor
Paramount/Sol C. Siegel
A mass murderer of women who is also a master of disguise has a running battle with a police detective.
Curious mixture of star show-off piece, murder mystery, black farce, suspense melodrama and Jewish comedy. Bits of it come off very well, but it's a bumpy ride.
w John Gay *novel* William Goldman *d* Jack Smight *ph* Jack Priestley *m* Stanley Myers
☆ *Rod Steiger, George Segal*, Lee Remick, Eileen Heckart, Murray Hamilton, Michael Dunn

'The sweetest love story ever told! The epic drama of the age! Drama with a world sweep, colossal and sublime!'
Noah's Ark **
US 1929 135m bw
Warner
The biblical story of Noah is paralleled, rather loosely, with a tragedy of World War I.
Naïve but fascinating Hollywood epic which in patches triumphantly overcomes the problems of the part-talkie period and is always fascinating to look at.
w Anthony Coldeway, Darryl F. Zanuck *d Michael Curtiz* *ph Hal Mohr, Barney McGill* *pd Anton Grot*
☆ Dolores Costello, Noah Beery, Louise Fazenda, Guinn Williams, Paul McAllister, Myrna Loy, George O'Brien

'The biggest and best edited picture of the industry ... mobs, Niagaras, train wrecks, war aplenty, crashes, deluges and everything that goes to give the picture fan a thrill.' – *Variety*

'Staggering ... the greatest thing the screen has done.' – *The Film Spectator*

† On première it was Warner's longest film, but the release version was cut by nearly half.

Nob Hill *
US 1945 95m Technicolor
TCF (André Daven)
In the gay 1890s, a San Francisco saloon owner tries to step into society and win one of its most eligible young ladies.
Engaging period musical drama with all talents working well.
w Wanda Tuchock, Norman Reilly Raine *d* Henry Hathaway *ph* Edward Cronjager *m* David Buttolph *md* Emil Newman, Charles Henderson

☆ George Raft, Joan Bennett, Peggy Ann Garner, Vivian Blaine, Alan Reed, B. S. Pully, Edgar Barrier

Nobi: see *Fires on the Plain*

Nobody Lives Forever
US 1946 100m bw
Warner (Robert Buckner)
A con man fleeces a rich widow, then falls in love with her.
Forgettable romantic melodrama.
w W. R. Burnett *d* Jean Negulesco *ph* Arthur Edeson *m* Adolph Deutsch
☆ John Garfield, Geraldine Fitzgerald, Walter Brennan, Faye Emerson, George Coulouris, George Tobias

Nobody Runs Forever *
GB 1968 101m Eastmancolor
Rank/Selmur (Betty E. Box)
US title: *The High Commissioner*
An Australian detective is sent to arrest the high commissioner in London on a charge of murdering his first wife.
Sub-Hitchcock thriller which comes to life in patches but has a plot and dialogue which obviously embarrass the actors.
w Wilfred Greatorex *novel The High Commissioner* by Jon Cleary *d* Ralph Thomas *ph* Ernest Steward *m* Georges Delerue
☆ Rod Taylor, Christopher Plummer, Lilli Palmer, Camilla Sparv, Daliah Lavi, Clive Revill, Lee Montague, Calvin Lockhart, Derren Nesbitt, Leo McKern, Franchot Tone

Nobody's Baby
US 1937 67m bw
MGM (Hal Roach)
Girls at a training school for nurses find themselves looking after a baby.
Lightweight comedy filler.
w Harold Law, Hal Yates, Pat C. Flick *d* Gus Meins
☆ Lyda Roberti, Patsy Kelly, Lynne Overman, Robert Armstrong, Rosina Lawrence, Don Alvarado, Tom Dugan
'Agreeable enough number two feature for duals.' – *Variety*

Nobody's Fool
US 1986 107m CFI color
Enterprise/Island (James C. Katz, Jon S. Denny)
A small-town girl with a mild past falls for a lighting technician with a visiting theatrical troupe.
Much ado about nothing; good observant touches don't stifle the yawns.
w Beth Henley *d* Evelyn Purcell *ph* Mikhail Suslov *m* James Newton Howard *pd* Jackson DeGovia *ed* Dennis Virkler
☆ Rosanna Arquette, Eric Roberts, Mare Winningham, Jim Youngs, Louise Fletcher, Gwen Welles

'In A Town Where Nothing Ever Happens ... Everything Is About To Happen To Sully.'
Nobody's Fool *
US 1994 110m colour
TCF/Paramount/Capella/Scott Rudin/Cinehaus (Scott Rudin, Arlene Donovan)
In a small town, a 60-year-old handyman, for whom life has rarely gone right, has one more chance to make good.
A story of understated charm that also observes sharp-edged and unsuccessful relationships with a beady eye.
wd Robert Benton *novel* Richard Russo *ph* John Bailey *m* Howard Shore *pd* David Gropman *ed* John Bloom
☆ Paul Newman, Jessica Tandy, Bruce Willis, Melanie Griffith, Dylan Walsh, Pruitt Taylor Vince, Gene Saks, Philip Bosco
'Shrewd, agreeable, ultimately dishonest.' – *Richard Schickel, Time*
'A nice film, funny and doleful at the same time, which says more than most about those small things which, taken together, make up most of our everyday lives.' – *Derek Malcolm, Guardian*
Paul Newman; Robert Benton (Screenplay)

Nobody's Perfect
US 1968 103m Techniscope
Universal (Howard Christie)
An ex-naval officer returns to Japan to make amends for stealing a buddha.
Flatfooted comedy adventure.
w John D. F. Black *novel The Crows of Edwina Hill* by Allan R. Bosworth *d* Alan Rafkin *ph* Robert H. Wyckoff *m* Irving Gertz
☆ Doug McClure, Nancy Kwan, Steve Carlson, James Whitmore, David Hartman, Gary Vinson, James Shigeta

Noce Blanche
France 1989 92m colour
Gala/Les films du Losange/La Sept/La Sorcière Rouge/Sofia/Investimage 2 (Margaret Menégoz)
A middle-aged teacher has a stormy affair with his seventeen-year-old pupil.
Cliché-ridden account of mid-life fantasies and adolescent problems, from drugs to prostitution, that offers little in the way of enlightenment.
wd Jean-Claude Brisseau *ph* Romain Winding *ad* Maria-Luisa Garcia *ed* Maria-Luisa Garcia
☆ Vanessa Paradis, Bruno Cremer, Ludmila Mikael, François Negret, Jean Daste, Véronique Silver, Philippe Tuin

La Noche del Terror Ciego: see *Tombs of the Blind Dead*

Nocturne *
US 1946 87m bw
RKO (Joan Harrison)
A police detective investigates the death of a composer.
Amusingly self-mocking crime thriller, quite smoothly done in all departments.
w Jonathan Latimer d Edwin L. Marin ph Harry J. Wild *m* Leigh Harline
☆ *George Raft*, Lynn Bari, Virginia Huston, Joseph Pevney, Myrna Dell, Edward Ashley, Walter Sande, Mabel Paige
'As for the plot, I confess I could not follow it, nor did I care.' – *Paul Holt, Daily Express*

Noi Tre
Italy 1984 96m colour
Instituto Luce/Duea Film/RAI (Paolo Bacchi, Francesco Guerrieri)
aka: *The Three of Us*
On a summer visit to the estate of an Italian count, the young Mozart falls in love.
Pleasant but inconsequential pastoral idyll which treats the composer as an exceptionally innocent adolescent.
w Pupi Avati, Antonio Avati, Cesare Bornazzini *d* Pupi Avati *ph* Pasquale Rachini *m* Riz Ortolani *pd* Giancarlo Basili, Leonardo Scarpa *ed* Amedeo Salfa
☆ Lino Capolicchio, Gianni Cavina, Carlo Delle Piane, Ida Di Benedetto, Giulio Pizzirani

La Noia: see *The Empty Canvas*

Noir et Blanc
France 1986 80m bw
Electric/Les Films Du Volcan
A timid accountant forms a sado-masochistic relationship with a black masseur.
Claustrophobic study of sexual obsession which eschews sensationalism.
wd Claire Devers *story Desire and the Black Masseur* by Tennessee Williams *ph* Daniel Desbois, Christopher Doyle, Alain Lasfargues, Jean-Paul de Costa *pd* Claire Devers *ed* Fabienne Alvarez, Yves Sarda
☆ Francis Frappat, Jacques Martial, Joséphine Fresson, Marc Berman, Claire Rigollier

Noises Off
US 1992 104m Technicolor
Warner/Touchstone/Touchstone Pacific Partners 1/Amblin (Frank Marshall)
The American cast of a British sex comedy suffers a series of disasters, on-stage and off, during a pre-Broadway tour.
Brave though misguided attempt to transfer to the screen an intensely theatrical work, depending on live performance for its effect. It begins well but soon ceases to amuse.
w Marty Kaplan *play* Michael Frayn *d* Peter Bogdanovich *ph* Tim Suhrstedt *m* Phil Marshall *pd* Norman Newberry *ed* Lisa Day
☆ Carol Burnett, Michael Caine, Denholm Elliott, Julie Hagerty, Marilu Henner, Mark Linn-Baker, Christopher Reeve, John Ritter, Nicollette Sheridan
'Serves up plenty of laughs, and in many ways it stands as a model transfer of a play to the screen.' – *Variety*
'If I say that I laughed till I cried, I have a dreadful fear the words will be ripped out and stuck on the poster. But I did.' – *Nigel Andrews, Financial Times*
'On screen, *Noises Off* fails in the only way that films can fail – bit by bit. But utterly.' – *Adam Mars-Jones, Independent*

Nomads
US 1985 100m Eastmancolor
PSO/Elliott Kastner/Cinema 7 (George Pappas, Cassian Elwes)
An anthropologist settling in Los Angeles is haunted by vengeful spirits of remote tribes he had investigated.
Stylish nonsense, but nonsense none the less: it would have seemed more striking if it hadn't been five-hundredth in line.
wd John McTiernan *ph* Stephen Ramsey *m* Bill Conti *pd* Marcia Hinds
☆ Pierce Brosnan, Lesley-Anne Down, Anna Maria Monticelli, Adam Ant, Hector Mercado

Non Stop New York
GB 1937 71m bw
GFD/Gaumont (Michael Balcon)
In 1940, gangsters on a transatlantic airliner try to kill a key witness.
Slightly futuristic thriller of its time, now hilariously dated but quite entertaining as well as giving a rare picture of air travel in the thirties.
w Curt Siodmak, Roland Pertwee, J. O. C. Orton, Derek Twist *novel Sky Steward* by Ken Attiwill *d* Robert Stevenson *ph* Max Greene *md* Louis Levy
☆ John Loder, Anna Lee, Francis L. Sullivan, Frank Cellier, Desmond Tester, Athene Seyler, Jerry Verno

None but the Brave: see *For the Love of Mike (1960)*

None but the Brave
US 1965 105m Technicolor Panavision
Warner/Eiga/Toho/Artanis (Frank Sinatra)
During World War II a plane carrying US Marines to the Pacific front crashlands on an island held by Japanese.
Anti-war melodrama in which the action scenes are more memorable than the admirable sentiments.
w John Twist, Katsuya Susaki *story* Kikumaru Okuda *d* Frank Sinatra *ph* Harold Lipstein *m* Johnny Williams
☆ Frank Sinatra, Clint Walker, Tommy Sands, Tony Bill, Brad Dexter

'When is the world coming out of its midnight? When is the human race going to get off its knees?'
None but the Lonely Heart *
US 1944 113m bw
RKO (David Hempstead)
In the thirties, a Cockney drifter finds himself when he learns that his mother is dying.
Wildly astonishing moodpiece to come from Hollywood during World War II; its picture of East End low life is as rocky as its star performance, but it started Miss Barrymore on the west coast career which sustained her old age.
wd Clifford Odets *novel* Richard Llewellyn *ph* George Barnes *m* Hanns Eisler *md* Constantin Bakaleinikoff *ed* Roland Gross
☆ Cary Grant, *Ethel Barrymore*, June Duprez, Barry Fitzgerald, Jane Wyatt, George Coulouris, Dan Duryea, Konstantin Shayne, Morton Lowry, Helene Thimig
'A perplexing mixture of good and bad, authentic and phony.' – *Hermione Rich Isaacs, Theatre Arts*
Ethel Barrymore
Hanns Eisler; Cary Grant; Roland Gross

None Shall Escape *
US 1944 85m bw
Columbia (Sam Bischoff)
The career of a Nazi officer shown as flashbacks from his trial as a war criminal.
Taut topical melodrama reflecting the mood of the time.
w Lester Cole *d* André de Toth *ph* Lee Garmes *m* Ernst Toch
☆ Alexander Knox, Marsha Hunt, Henry Travers, Dorothy Morris, Richard Crane
original story (Alfred Neumann, Joseph Thau)

De Noorderlingen: see *The Northerners*

Noose
GB 1948 98m bw
ABPC/Edward Dryhurst
A Soho black market gang is exposed.
Vivid though rather tatty film version of a West End play success.
w Richard Llewellyn *play* Richard Llewellyn *d* Edmond T. Gréville *ph* Hone Glendinning *m* Charles Williams
☆ Nigel Patrick, Carole Landis, Derek Farr, Joseph Calleia, Stanley Holloway, Hay Petrie, John Slater

Noose: see *Snitch (1998)*

The Noose Hangs High
US 1948 77m bw
Eagle-Lion
Two window washers are hired by a crooked bookie who finds their incompetence hard to tolerate when they lose his winnings.
Thin star comedy filled with the team's cornier routines, not too cleverly revived.
w John Grant and Howard Harris *d* Charles Barton
☆ Bud Abbott, Lou Costello, Leon Errol, Joseph Calleia, Murray Leonard, Cathy Downs, Mike Mazurki, Fritz Feld
† A previous film of the same story was made in 1939 under the title *For Love or Money*, with June Lang, Robert Kent and Ed Brophy.

Nor the Moon By Night
GB 1958 92m Eastmancolor
Rank (John Stafford)
US title: *Elephant Gun*
An African game warden marries a longtime penfriend who finds that Africa presents unexpected problems.
Paperback romance with pleasant backgrounds.
w Guy Elmes *novel* Joy Packer *d* Ken Annakin *ph* Harry Waxman *m* James Bernard
☆ Belinda Lee, Michael Craig, Patrick McGoohan, Anna Gaylor, Eric Pohlmann
'Neither character nor incident nor theme has any coherence or interest.' – *MFB*

Nora
GB/Ireland/Germany 2000 107m DeLuxe
Alliance/Natural Nylon/IAC/Volta/Road Movies//Gam/Metropolitan/IFB (Bradley Adams, Damon Bryant, Tracey Seaward)
In the early 1900s Nora Barnacle moves from Galway to Dublin and begins a stormy relationship with the writer James Joyce.
This portrait of the artist's wife and muse as a young, free-spirited woman is oddly uncompelling, reducing her to little more than an orgasmic 'yes', despite Lynch's efforts to give some body to an underwritten role; but it is handsomely photographed.
w Pat Murphy, Gerard Stembridge *book* Brenda Maddox *d* Pat Murphy *ph* Jean François Robin *m* Stanislas Syrewicz *pd* Alan Macdonald *ed* Pia Di Ciaula *cos* Consolata Boyle
☆ Ewan McGregor (James Joyce), Susan Lynch (Nora Barnacle), Peter McDonald (Stanislaus Joyce), Roberto Citran (Roberto Prezioso), Veronica Duffy (Annie Barnacle), Aedin Moloney (Eva Joyce), Pauline McLynn (Miss Kennedy), Andrew Scott (Michael Bodkin), Alan Devine (Gogarty), Vinnie McCabe (Uncle Tommy), Paul Hickey (Curran), Kate O'Toole (Miss Delahunty), Darragh Kelly (Cosgrave)
'It's as hard to watch as it is to read Joyce's *Ulysses* – but less rewarding.' – *Demetrious Matheou, Total Film*

'A mouth like hers is just for kissing ... not for telling!'

Nora Prentiss *
US 1946 117m bw
Warner (William Jacobs)
A doctor falls for a café singer who ruins his life.
Standard star melodrama aimed at women, and appreciated by them.
w N. Richard Nash *story* Paul Webster, Jack Sobell *d* Vincent Sherman *ph* James Wong Howe *m* Franz Waxman
☆ Ann Sheridan, Kent Smith, Bruce Bennett, Robert Alda, Rosemary de Camp, John Ridgely, Wanda Hendrix

Norma Rae *
US 1979 114m DeLuxe Panavision
TCF (Tamara Asseyev, Alex Rose)
A Southern girl becomes an angry union organizer.
Well-intentioned and well-acted pamphlet of political enlightenment with an inevitably ambivalent attitude.
w Irving Ravetch, Harriet Frank Jnr *d* Martin Ritt *ph* John A. Alonzo *m* David Shire *pd* Walter Scott Herndon
☆ *Sally Field*, Beau Bridges, Ron Leibman, Pat Hingle, Barbara Baxley
Sally Field; song 'It Goes Like It Goes' (*m* David Shire, *ly* Norman Gimbel)
best picture; best script

Normal Life
US 1996 103m colour
First Independent/Spelling/Fine Line (Richard Maynard)
A Chicago cop marries an alcoholic, drug-addicted blonde, loses his job and turns bank robber.
Bleak, documentary-style narrative of a downward spiral into despair and death, based on a true story.
w Peg Haller, Bob Schneider *d* John McNaughton *ph* Jean DeSegonzac *m* Robert McNaughton *pd* Rick Paul *ed* Elena Maganini
☆ Luke Perry, Ashley Judd, Bruce Young, Jim True, Edmund Wyson, Michael Skewes, Dawn Maxey
'Hasn't quite been able to translate its diverse raw elements into fully formed drama.' – *Variety*

Norman, Is That You?
US 1976 92m Metrocolor
MGM (George Schlatter)
Adulterous parents find that their son is a homosexual.
Unattractive comedy roughly filmed and given a black ambience. Not worth buying a ticket.
w Ron Clark, Sam Bobrick *play* Ron Clark, Sam Bobrick *d* George Schlatter *ph* Gayne Rescher *m* William Goldstein
☆ Redd Foxx, Pearl Bailey, Dennis Dugan, Michael Warren, Tamara Dobson

The Norseman
US 1978 90m Movielab Panavision
AIP/Charles B. Pierce/Fawcett Majors
A Viking heads across the sea to America in search of his long lost father.
Low grade hokum for the easily pleased.
wd Charles B. Pierce *ph* Robert Bethard *m* Jaime Mendoza-Nava
☆ Lee Majors, Cornel Wilde, Mel Ferrer, Jack Elam, Chris Connelly

El Norte **
GB/US 1983 139m
Independent Productions/American Playhouse Theatre/Channel 4 (Anna Thomas)
Fleeing from a murderous army in Guatemala, a brother and sister travel north to try to make a new life in the United States.
Conceived on a grand scale and often moving, it is nevertheless too long to bear its fragile narrative.
w Gregory Nava, Anna Thomas *d* Gregory Nava *ph* James Glennon *ed* Betsy Blankett
☆ Zaide Silvia Gutierrez, David Villalpando, Ernesto Gomez Cruz, Alicia del Lago, Eraclio Zepeda
screenplay

'North's hopping mad with his parents and now he's off on a world wide adventure!'

North
US 1994 88m Technicolor
Rank/Columbia/Castle Rock (Rob Reiner, Alan Zweibel)
An 11-year-old boy, who decides to divorce his parents, sets out to find the ideal mother and father.
A disaster, unless you can derive pleasure from Bruce Willis dressed as a fluffy, bright pink bunny rabbit; it is neither amusing nor adventurous and fails to be interesting or enlightening as it drags its child hero from one grotesque encounter to another.
w Alan Zweibel, Andrew Scheinman *novel* Alan Zweibel *d* Rob Reiner *ph* Adam Greenberg *m* Marc Shaiman *pd* J. Michael Riva *ed* Robert Leighton
☆ Elijah Wood, Bruce Willis, Jon Lovitz, Matthew McCurley, Alan Arkin, Abe Vigoda, Richard Belzer, Kathy Bates, Jason Alexander, Dan Aykroyd, Kelly McGillis, Alexander Godunov
'The director, Rob Reiner, slips on a banana peel and crushes an entire cast in this fantasy.' – *Michael Sragow, New Yorker*
'Embarrassingly bad.' – *Guardian*

The North Avenue Irregulars
US 1978 99m Technicolor
Disney
GB title: *Hill's Angels*
A Presbyterian minister becomes an undercover agent for the FBI, helping to expose a crooked gambling syndicate.
Very heavy comedy which seems to find itself much funnier than the audience does.
w Don Tait *novel* the Rev. Albert Fay Hill *d* Bruce Bilson *ph* Leonard South *m* Robert F. Brunner
☆ Edward Herrmann, Barbara Harris, Susan Clark, Karen Valentine, Michael Constantine, Cloris Leachman, Patsy Kelly, Douglas Fowley, Alan Hale Jnr

North by Northwest ****
US 1959 136m Technicolor Vistavision
MGM (Alfred Hitchcock)
A businessman is mistaken for a spy, and enemy agents then try to kill him because he knows too much.
Delightful chase comedy-thriller with a touch of sex, a kind of compendium of its director's best work, with memories of The 39 Steps, Saboteur *and* Foreign Correspondent *among others.*
w Ernest Lehman d Alfred Hitchcock ph Robert Burks m Bernard Herrmann ad William A. Horning, Robert Boyle, Merrill Pye ed George Tomasini
☆ *Cary Grant*, Eva Marie Saint, James Mason, Leo G. Carroll, Martin Landau, Jessie Royce Landis, Adam Williams
'It is only when you adopt the basic premise that Cary Grant could not possibly come to harm that the tongue in Hitchcock's cheek becomes plainly visible.' – *Hollis Alpert, Saturday Review*
'North by Northwest is never brutal. Mr Grant calls it a comedy; I would agree that it is consistently entertaining, its excitement pointed by but never interrupted by the jokes.' – *Dilys Powell*
'You get a lot of entertainment for your money. You get a couple of clever, sophisticated screen actors and an elegant actress with a fine-drawn, exciting face. You get one scene that will be talked about as long as people talk about films at all.' – *C. A. Lejeune*
Ernest Lehman; art direction; editing

North Dallas Forty
US 1979 118m Metrocolor
Paramount (Frank Yablans)
The gruelling life of a professional football player, laced with drugs, sex and alcohol.
Well made but generally unattractive, the kind of movie for which one wouldn't expect to find an audience.
w Frank Yablans, Ted Kotcheff, Peter Gent *novel* Peter Gent *d* Ted Kotcheff *ph* Paul Lohmann *m* John Scott *pd* Alfred Sweeney
☆ Nick Nolte, Mac Davis, Charles Durning, Dayle Haddon, Bo Svenson

North Sea Hijack
GB 1979 100m Technicolor
Universal/Cinema Seven (Mo Rothman)
US title: *ffoulkes*
A British oil rig in the North Sea is held for ransom.
Asinine Boys' Own Paper adventure story with the very minimum of thrills and a totally miscast hero.
w Jack Davis *novel Esther, Ruth and Jennifer* by Jack Davis *d* Andrew V. McLaglen *ph* Tony Imi *m* Michael J. Lewis *pd* Maurice Carter
☆ Roger Moore, Anthony Perkins, James Mason, Michael Parks, David Hedison, Jack Watson, George Baker, Faith Brook

North Star *
US 1943 105m bw Technovision
Samuel Goldwyn (William Cameron Menzies)
aka: *Armored Attack*
A Russian village defends itself against the Nazi onslaught.
Highly artificial propaganda piece later disowned by its makers and retitled. Good acting can't make its mark when the Russian steppes become a never-never land.
w Lillian Hellman *d* Lewis Milestone *ph* James Wong Howe *m* Aaron Copland *ad* Perry Ferguson
☆ Anne Baxter, Farley Granger, Jane Withers, Dana Andrews, Walter Brennan, Erich von Stroheim, Dean Jagger, Ann Harding, Carl Benton Reid, Walter Huston
'Putting American villagers into Russian costumes and calling them by Russian names is never going to deceive this old bird.' – *James Agate*
'Its failure is the case history of every Hollywood film that steps out of its scope.' – *Richard Winnington*
'Something to be seen more in sorrow than in anger and more in the attitude of the diagnostician in any emotion at all.' – *James Agee*
Lillian Hellman; James Wong Howe; Aaron Copland; Perry Ferguson

North Star
GB/France/Norway/Italy 1996 88m colour
Warner/Regency/AFCL/M6/Federal (Anne François)
In Alaska in the 1890s, a halfbreed trapper earns the enmity of a crooked businessman when he refuses to mine for gold on land that he considers sacred.
Broadly acted chase drama that lacks any impetus or dramatic interest.
w Sergio Donati, Lorenzo Donati, Paul Ohl *novel* Will Henry *story Gilles Behat, Philippe Schwartz, Marc Pecas d* Nils Gaup *ph* Bruno de Keyzer *m* Bruce Rowland *pd* Ben Morahan *ed* Kant Pan, Michael A. Hoey
☆ James Caan, Christopher Lambert, Catherine McCormack, Burt Young
'Drearily uninspired.' – *Variety*

North to Alaska *
US 1960 122m DeLuxe Cinemascope
TCF (Henry Hathaway)
In 1900, two successful gold prospectors have woman trouble.
Good-natured brawling adventure story which could do with cutting but is certainly the type of action movie they don't make 'em like any more.
w John Lee Mahin, Martin Rackin, Claude Binyon *play Birthday Gift* by Ladislas Fodor *d* Henry Hathaway *ph* Leon Shamroy *m* Lionel Newman
☆ John Wayne, Stewart Granger, Fabian, Capucine, Ernie Kovacs, Mickey Shaughnessy, Karl Swenson, Joe Sawyer, John Qualen

Northern Pursuit *
US 1943 94m bw
Warner (Jack Chertok)
A Mountie tracks a stranded Nazi pilot through the Canadian wastes.
Rather unusual star actioner, not badly done.
w Frank Gruber, Alvah Bessie *d* Raoul Walsh *ph* Sid Hickox *m* Adolph Deutsch
☆ Errol Flynn, Helmut Dantine, Julie Bishop, John Ridgely, Gene Lockhart, Tom Tully, Bernard Nedell

The Northerners *
Holland 1993 105m colour
Mayfair/First Floor (Laurens Geels, Dick Maas)
original title: *De Noorderlingen*
In the only occupied street on a half-built housing estate at the edge of nowhere, everyone is acting rather strangely.
A cool and bizarre comedy of frustrated lives and eccentric behaviour.
w Alex Van Warmerdam, Aat Ceelen *d* Alex Van Warmerdam *ph* Marc Felperlaan *m* Vincent Van Warmerdam *pd* Rikke Jelier *ed* René Wiegmans
☆ Leonard Lucieer, Jack Wouterse, Rudolf Lucieer, Alex Van Warmerdam, Annet Malherbe, Loes Wouterson, Veerle Dobbelaere
'Witty and original comedy ... Showcases a vision and style reminiscent of both Jacques Tati and Aki Kaurismäki.' – *Variety*
'Mean-spirited in its emphasis on the characters' physical indignity, this is a cold, unwelcoming movie whose studied weirdness soon becomes wearisome in the extreme.' – *Kim Newman*

Northwest Frontier ***
GB 1959 129m Eastmancolor Cinemascope
Rank/Marcel Hellman
US title: *Flame Over India*
In 1905 an English officer during a rebellion escorts a young Hindu prince on a dangerous train journey.
Thoroughly enjoyable Boys' Own Paper adventure story with excellent set-pieces and a spot-the-villain mystery.
w Robin Estridge d J. Lee-Thompson ph Geoffrey Unsworth m Mischa Spoliansky
☆ Kenneth More, Lauren Bacall, Herbert Lom, Ursula Jeans, Wilfrid Hyde-White, I. S. Johar, Eugene Deckers, Ian Hunter
'*Northwest Frontier* seems to have borrowed its eccentric engine from *The General*, its hazardous expedition from *Stagecoach* and its background of tribal violence from *The Drum*.' – *Penelope Houston*

'Ten stars! Two love stories! One thousand thrills!'

Northwest Mounted Police *
US 1940 125m Technicolor
Paramount (Cecil B. de Mille)
A Texas Ranger seeks a fugitive in Canada.
Typical big-scale action concoction by de Mille, but in this case none of it's very memorable and the detail is poor.
w Alan Le May, Jesse Lasky Jnr, C. Gardner Sullivan *d* Cecil B. de Mille *ph* Victor Milner, Howard Greene *m* Victor Young *ad* Hans Dreier, Roland Anderson *ed* Anne Bauchens
☆ Gary Cooper, Paulette Goddard, Madeleine Carroll, Preston Foster, Robert Preston, George Bancroft, Lynne Overman, Akim Tamiroff, Walter Hampden, Lon Chaney Jnr, Montagu Love, George E. Stone
'Two hours of colour, killing, kindness and magnificent country.' – *Otis Ferguson*
'A movie in the grand style. God's own biggest trees and mountains for prop and backdrop; staunch courage and lofty aims among the good people; cunning and treachery lurking within the sinister forces; the ominous note of doom finally stifled by the fortitude of noble men.' – *Time*
Anne Bauchens
Victor Milner, Howard Greene; Victor Young; art direction

Northwest Outpost
US 1947 91m bw
Republic (Allan Dwan)
GB title: *End of the Rainbow*
Adventures of California cavalrymen.
Milk-and-water adventures in a forgettable operetta.
w Elizabeth Meehan, Richard Sale *d* Allan Dwan *ph* Reggie Lanning *m* Rudolf Friml
☆ Nelson Eddy, Ilona Massey, Hugo Haas, Elsa Lanchester

'Half men, half demons, warriors such as the world has never known ... they lived with death and danger for the women who hungered for their love!'

Northwest Passage (Part One, Rogers' Rangers) ***
US 1940 126m Technicolor
MGM (Hunt Stromberg)

Colonial rangers fight it out with hostile Indians.
Part Two was never made, but no one seemed to mind that the characters in Part One never got round to seeking the titular sea route. The adventures depicted had the feel of historical actuality, and the star was well cast.
w Laurence Stallings, Talbot Jennings *novel* Kenneth Roberts *d* *King Vidor* *ph* Sidney Wagner, William V. Skall *m* Herbert Stothart
☆ *Spencer Tracy*, *Robert Young*, Ruth Hussey, Walter Brennan, Nat Pendleton, Robert Barrat, Lumsden Hare, Donald MacBride
Sidney Wagner, William V. Skall

Northwest Stampede
US 1948 79m Cinecolor
Eagle-Lion (Albert S. Rogell)
The female foreman of a horse ranch hires a new hand, not knowing that he is the son of its recently dead owner, come to claim his inheritance.
An easy-going outdoor drama, although it is a slightly uncomfortable mix of documentary-style footage of rodeo events and capturing and breaking wild horses, and a broadly comic battle of the sexes.
w Art Arthur, Lillie Hayward *Saturday Evening Post article* *Wild Horse Roundup* by Jean Muir *d* Albert S. Rogell *ph* John W. Boyle *m* Paul Sawtell *md* Irving Friedman *ad* Edward L. Ilou *ed* Philip Cahn
☆ Joan Leslie, James Craig, Jack Oakie, Chill Wills, Victor Kilian, Stanley Andrews, Ray Bennett, Lane Chandler

Norwood
US 1969 95m Technicolor
Paramount/Hal B. Wallis
A Vietnam veteran returns to his Texas home but feels restless and decides to become a radio singer.
A rather ordinary film about an innocent abroad, neither very funny nor very moving.
w Marguerite Roberts *d* Jack Haley Jnr *ph* Robert B. Hauser *m* Al de Lory
☆ Glen Campbell, Kim Darby, Joe Namath, Carol Lynley, Pat Hingle, Tisha Sterling, Dom DeLuise, Jack Haley, Cass Daley, Gil Lamb

Nosferatu ***
Germany 1921 72m approx (24 fps) bw
Prana

Count Dracula goes to Bremen and is destroyed by sunlight.
An unofficial treatment of the Bram Stoker novel, with a terrifying count and several splendid moments. It took its director to Hollywood.
w Henrik Galeen *d* *F. W. Murnau* *ph* Fritz Arno Wagner *ad* *Albin Grau*
☆ *Max Schreck*, Gustav von Wangenheim, Greta Schröder, Alexander Granach

Nosferatu a Venezia: see *Vampires in Venice*

Nosferatu, Phantom der Nacht: see *Nosferatu the Vampyre*

Nosferatu the Vampyre *
West Germany/France 1979 107m Eastmancolor
Gaumont/Werner Herzog Filmproduktion

original title: *Nosferatu, Phantom der Nacht*
Excruciatingly slow retread of the German silent film.
Despite the star's splendidly loathsome appearance, the overall is no improvement, and the colour in the English prints is quite dreadful.
wd Werner Herzog *ph* Jörg Schmidt-Reitwein *m* Popol Vuh
☆ *Klaus Kinski*, Isabelle Adjani, Bruno Ganz, Walter Ladengast
'Like a dream from which you keep waking with indigestion.' – *Guardian*

Nostalgia *
Italy 1983 126m Eastmancolor
Artificial Eye/Opera Film/Sovin Film/RAI (Francesco Casati)

A Russian writer in Italy meets a social outcast who is expecting the end of the world.
Indescribably doomladen, occasionally beautiful, stylistically interesting and for the most part very boring parable of a kind unique to this director.
w Andrei Tarkovsky, Tonino Guerra *d* Andrei Tarkovsky *ph* Giuseppe Lanci *ad* Andrea Crisanti *ed* Erminia Marani, Amedeo Salfa
☆ Oleg Jankovsky, Erland Josephson, Domiziana Giordano
'Tarkovsky... may well be a film poet but he's a film poet with a tiny vocabulary. The same, eventually- boring images keep recurring in film after film – shots of damp landscapes, marshes, hills in fog, and abandoned buildings with roofs that leak.' – *Vincent Canby, New York Times*

'There's Still Time To Understand His Words...'

Nostradamus
GB/Germany 1994 118m DeLuxe
First Independent/Allied/Vereinigte (Edward Simons, Harald Reichebner)

In the early 16th century, a French scientist is persecuted for his visions of future catastrophic events.
Rambling bio-pic, with its visionary hero watching modern newsreels in a bowl of water, which fails to tell its audience anything it didn't know about the present and reveals the past as a time of hysterical sexually influenced power struggles; not even Hauer, as 'The Mystic Monk' in an illuminated hat, can save it.
w Knut Boeser, Brian Clark *story* Piers Ashworth, Roger Christian *d* Roger Christian *ph* Denis Crossan *m* Barrington Pheloung *pd* Peter J. Hampton *ed* Alan Strachan
☆ Tcheky Karyo, Amanda Plummer, Julia Ormond, Assumpta Serna, Rutger Hauer, F. Murray Abraham, Anthony Higgins, Diana Quick, Michael Gough, Maja Morgenstern
'Crushingly dull.' – *Sheila Johnston, Independent*

'The Teen Mother Of All Movies!'

Not Another Teen Movie
US 2001 89m DeLuxe
Columbia/Original (Neal H. Moritz)

A high school football star accepts a bet that he can turn any girl into the prom queen.
A movie with more writers than jokes, and those few involve flatulence and other bodily functions, so that it is indistinguishable from any other teen movie.
w Michael G. Bender, Adam Jay Epstein, Andrew Jacobson, Phil Beauman, Buddy Johnson *d* Joel Gallen *ph* Reynaldo Villalobos *m* Theodore Shapiro *pd* Joseph T. Garrity *ed* Stephen Welch
☆ Chyler Leigh (Janey Briggs), Chris Evans (Jake Wyler), Jaime Pressly (Priscilla), Eric Christian Olsen (Austin), Mia Kirshner (Catherine), Deon Richmond (Malik)
'Give it a wide berth.' – *Observer*

Not as a Stranger **
US 1955 135m bw
UA/Stanley Kramer

A medical student has professional and personal struggles.
Earnest filming of a bestseller, with all the actors too old for their parts.
w Edna and Edward Anhalt *novel* Morton Thompson *d* Stanley Kramer *ph* Franz Planer *m* George Antheil *pd* Rudolph Sternad
☆ Robert Mitchum, Olivia de Havilland, Broderick Crawford, Frank Sinatra, Gloria Grahame, Charles Bickford, Myron McCormick, Lon Chaney Jnr, Jesse White, Henry Morgan, Lee Marvin, Virginia Christine

Not Now, Comrade
GB 1977 90m Technicolor
EMI/Not Now (Martin C. Chute)
A defecting Russian ballet dancer, and his girlfriend, a stripper, are offered refuge by the daughter of a top-ranking Ministry of Defence official, without the knowledge of her father.
Depressing, frenetic farce that worked on the stage but looks lost, cramped and merely silly on the screen.
w Ray Cooney *play* *Chase Me, Comrade* by Ray Cooney *d* Harold Snoad, Ray Cooney *ph* Jack Hildyard *m* Harry Robinson *ad* Edward Marshall *ed* Peter Thornton
☆ Leslie Phillips, Roy Kinnear, Windsor Davies, Don Estelle, Michele Dotrice, Ray Cooney, June Whitfield, Carol Hawkins, Lewis Fiander, Ian Lavender
'Settles into the familiar round of harmless double entendres buried in the ramifications of a mistaken-identity plot played by the familiar troupers of British farce ... mirthless.' – *John Pym, MFB*

Not Now, Darling
GB 1972 97m Eastmancolor
LMG/Sedgemoor/Not Now Films

A furrier gets into a complicated situation when he arranges for his mistress to have a cheap mink coat.
Interminable film version (in Multivista, a shoot-and-edit equivalent to TV taping which gives a dingy look and can only work in a single set) of a West End farce which wasn't marvellous to begin with.
w John Chapman *play* Ray Cooney *d* Ray Cooney, David Croft *ph* Alan Hume *m* Cyril Ornadel
☆ Leslie Phillips, Ray Cooney, Moira Lister, Julie Ege, Joan Sims, Derren Nesbitt, Barbara Windsor, Jack Hulbert, Cicely Courtneidge, Bill Fraser

Not of This Earth **
US 1957 72m bw
AA (Roger Corman)

An alien comes to Earth in human form in search of blood which may save his planet.
Modestly budgeted minor sci-fi; ruthless, original and competent.
w *Charles Griffith*, *Mark Hanna* *d* *Roger Corman* *ph* John Mescall *m* Ronald Stein
☆ *Paul Birch*, Beverly Garland, Morgan Jones

'In her village, she was the teacher... In the city, she discovered how much she had to learn.'

Not One Less *
China 1999 106m colour
Columbia/Guangxi/Bejing New Picture (Zhao Yu)

original title: *Yi Ge Dou Bu Neng Shao*
Promised a bonus if numbers at the village school do not fall any lower, a 13 year-old temporary teacher goes to the city in search of a missing pupil.
Zhang Yimou coaxes good performances from a cast of non-professionals in a small-scale movie that begins as a vivid portrait of modern China before succumbing to sentimentality, complete with a plug for Coca-Cola, and a contrived, feel-good ending.
w Shi Xiangsheng *d* Zhang Yimou *ph* Hou Yong *m* San Bao *pd* Cao Jiuping *ed* Zhai Ru *cos* Dong Huamiao
☆ Wei Minzhi (Wei Minzhi), Zhang Huike (Zhang Huike), Tian Zhenda (Village chief), Gao Enman (Teacher Gao), Sun Zhimei (Sun Zhimei), Feng Yuying (TV receptionist), Li Fanfan (TV host)
'The story is simple, moving and universal.' – *Variety*
† The film won the Golden Lion at the 1999 Venice Film Festival.

Not Quite Jerusalem
GB 1985 114m colour
Rank/Acorn/Lewis Gilbert

An Israeli girl and an American volunteer fall in love on the kibbutz.
A curious misfire. Interest in the subject is cancelled out by unattractive, slangy or caricatured people and by a muddled approach suggesting that a fairer title might have been Carry on Terrorist.
w Paul Kember *play* Paul Kember *d* Lewis Gilbert *ph* Tony Imi *m* Rondo Veneziano
☆ Joanna Pacula, Sam Robards, Kevin McNally, Todd Graff, Selina Cadell

Not So Dumb
US 1929 80m bw
MGM
A naïve girl throws a big party in the hope of advancing her boyfriend's career.
Popular comedy of its time.
w Wanda Tuchock, Edwin Justus Mayer *play* *Dulcy* by George S. Kaufman, Marc Connolly *d* King Vidor
☆ Marion Davies, Elliott Nugent, Raymond Hackett, Franklin Pangborn, Julia Faye
† Previously made as *Dulcy* by Warner in 1923, directed by Sidney Franklin, with Constance Talmadge.

Not Wanted on Voyage
GB 1957 82m bw
Renown
A necklace is stolen on an ocean liner.
Feeble fun from an old play.
w Michael and Roland Pertwee and others *play* Evadne Price, Ken Attiwill *d* Maclean Rogers *ph* Arthur Grant *m* Tony Lowry
☆ Ronald Shiner, Brian Rix, Griffith Jones, Katie Boyle, Fabia Drake, Michael Brennan

Not with My Wife, You Don't!
US 1966 119m Technicolor
Warner/Fernwood/Reynard (Norman Panama, Joel Freeman)
A Korean war veteran is furious when an old rival turns up in London and again makes eyes at his wife.
Extraordinarily flat star comedy of cross and double cross among friends.
w Norman Panama, Larry Gelbart, Peter Barnes *d* Norman Panama *ph* Charles Lang, Paul Beeson *m* Johnny Williams *pd* Edward Carrere *ed* Aaron Stell
☆ Tony Curtis (Tom Ferris), George C. Scott ('Tank' Martin), Virna Lisi (Julie Ferris), Carroll O'Connor (General Parker), Richard Eastham (General Walters), Eddie Ryder (Sgt Gilroy), George Tyne (Sgt Dogerty)
'About as frothy as a tin of dehydrated milk.' – *MFB*
'It has all the verve, subtlety and sophistication of its title.' – *Judith Crist*

Not without My Daughter
US 1991 114m colour
UIP/MGM/Pathé (Harry J. and Mary Jane Ufland)

Accompanying her Iranian husband to his homeland for a holiday, an American-born wife discovers that she and her young daughter will not be permitted by him to return to America.
A plodding account of a true story, told with little imagination or flair.
w David W. Rintels *book* Betty Mahmoody, William Hoffer *d* Brian Gilbert *ph* Peter Hannan *m* Jerry Goldsmith *pd* Anthony Pratt *ed* Terry Rawlings
☆ Sally Field, Alfred Molina, Sheila Rosenthal, Roshan Seth, Sarah Badel, Soudabeh Farrokhnia
'It is certainly as propaganda that the film is most successful, for its artlessness in all other respects will be noticeable even to those who may be convulsed by the central dilemma.' – *Variety*
'Fits with eerie precision into the cycle of paranoid and xenophobic Hollywood films familiar from the Cold War era.' – *Verina Glaessner, Sight and Sound*

Notebook on Cities and Clothes *
Germany 1989 80m colour
Road Movies

A documentary on the Japanese fashion designer Yohji Yamamoto and his relationship to, and with, Tokyo and Paris.
A quirky examination of the images we create of ourselves and the people we really are, or may be, in a world of quick change. Yamamoto is thoughtful but not particularly articulate about his work, other than when expressing his enjoyment of irresponsibility, which contrasts with Wenders's fussily pedantic style. The quality of the images is variable, owing to much of the material being shot with a video camera.
wd Wim Wenders *ph* Robby Müller, Muriel Edelstein, Uli Kidicke, Wim Wenders, Masatoshi Nakajima, Masashi Chikamori *m* Laurent Petitgand *ed* Dominique Auvray

Nothing but a Man *
US 1964 95m bw
Roemer-Young/DuArt (Robert Young, Michael Roemer, Robert Rubin)

In a small Southern town, a black railroad worker, who decides to marry and settle down, runs into trouble with the locals when he asserts his independence.
One of the first movies to treat the subject of racial discrimination without condescension, it is effective and engaging for the most part with its documentary-style approach, even though Abbey Lincoln's wife is too good to be true.
w Michael Roemer, Robert Young d Michael Roemer ph Robert Young ed Luke Bennett
☆ Ivan Dixon, Abbey Lincoln, Julius Harris, Gloria Foster, Martin Priest, Leonard Parker, Yaphet Kotto, Stanley Greene
'A fine film – a first one that sets a towering standard for its makers.' – *Judith Crist*

Nothing but the Best **
GB 1964 99m Eastmancolor
Anglo Amalgamated/Domino (David Deutsch)

An ambitious clerk learns to fight his way to the top by cheek and one-upmanship.
Hard, skilful, rather unattractive comedy with interesting social comments on its time.
w *Frederic Raphael* d *Clive Donner* ph Nicolas Roeg m Ron Grainer ad Reece Pemberton
☆ *Alan Bates, Denholm Elliott,* Harry Andrews, Millicent Martin, Pauline Delany
'It is a film with a smooth, smiling elegant fun, witty but never concentrating on wit to the detriment of tension; it makes a logical step-by-step progression towards a climax which is hilarious in a Stygian way without resort to the usual bangabout.' – *Dilys Powell*

'The nightmare has already killed five people. Now it's yours to live!'
Nothing but the Night *
GB 1972 90m Eastmancolor
Rank/Charlemagne (Anthony Nelson Keys)

The trustees of an orphanage die off mysteriously, and it seems that the orphans themselves are responsible.
Convoluted murder mystery with horror elements and a twist hardly worth waiting for; earnest performances help.
w Brian Hayles novel John Blackburn d Peter Sasdy ph Ken Talbot m Malcolm Williamson
☆ Christopher Lee, Peter Cushing, Diana Dors, Georgia Brown, Keith Barron, John Robinson

Nothing but the Truth
US 1941 90m bw
Paramount (Arthur Hornlow Jnr)
A stockbroker takes a bet that he can tell the absolute truth for twenty-four hours.
Rather unsurprising version of a stage comedy previously filmed as a silent. It lacks the style one might expect from the team which made The Cat and the Canary.
w Don Hartman, Ken Englund play James Montgomery novel *Frederic S. Isham* d Elliott Nugent ph Charles Lang
☆ Bob Hope, Paulette Goddard, Edward Arnold, Leif Erickson, Glenn Anders, Helen Vinson, Grant Mitchell, Willie Best

Nothing but Trouble
US 1944 70m bw
MGM (B. F. Ziedman)

A chef and butler accidentally prevent a poison plot against a young king.
Feebly-devised star comedy, their last for a big studio.
w Russel Rouse, Ray Golden d Sam Taylor ph Charles Salerno Jnr m Nathaniel Shilkret ad Cedric Gibbons, Henry McAfee ed Conrad Nervig
☆ Stan Laurel, Oliver Hardy, Mary Boland, Henry O'Neill, David Leland

Nothing but Trouble
US 1991 94m Technicolor
Warner/Applied Action (Robert K. Weiss)

A New York couple find themselves stranded in a village where a centenarian judge has absolute rule.
Exceedingly dismal comedy, in which a group of self-indulgent comedians, having been given a great deal of rope, proceed to hang themselves; it is not a pretty sight.
wd Dan Aykroyd story Peter Aykroyd ph Dean Cundey m Michael Kamen pd William Sandell ed Malcolm Campbell, James Symons
☆ Chevy Chase, Dan Aykroyd, John Candy, Demi Moore, Valri Bromfield, Taylor Negron, Bertila Damas, Raymond J. Barry, Brian Doyle-Murray, Peter Aykroyd
'Astonishingly poor effort ... one of the longest 94 minutes on record.' – *Variety*
'Combines absolute failure as a comedy with a surprisingly interesting and disgusting vision of grotesque America.' – *Kim Newman, Sight and Sound*

Nothing in Common
US 1986 118m Metrocolor Super 35
Tri-Star/Rastar (Alexandra Rose)

Problems of an eccentric family when mum decides to walk out after 36 years.
Edgy comedy which misfires in all directions.
w Rick Podell, Michael Preminger d Garry Marshall ph John A. Alonzo m Patrick Leonard
☆ Jackie Gleason, Eva Marie Saint, Tom Hanks, Hector Elizondo, Barry Corbin, Bess Armstrong

Nothing Lasts Forever *
US 1984 82m bw/Metrocolor
MGM/Broadway (Lorne Michaels)
The adventures of an innocent returning from abroad and seeking artistic fulfilment in a New York he hardly recognizes.
Engagingly bizarre comedy, part parody of 30s biopics, which eventually goes out of control as it takes our hero on a shopping trip to the Moon.
wd Tom Schiller ph Fred Schuler m Howard Shore pd Woods Mackintosh ed Kathleen Dougherty, Margot Francis
☆ Zach Galligan, Apollonia Van Ravenstein, Lauren Tom, Dan Aykroyd, Imogene Coca, Anita Ellis, Eddie Fisher, Sam Jaffe, Bill Murray, Paul Rogers, Mort Sahl

Nothing Personal
US 1980 97m Movielab
AIP (David M. Perlmutter)

A professor and a lady lawyer try to stop seal hunting.
The subject is an unsuitable starting point for a thin and zany comedy which gets nowhere and stays there.
w Robert Kaufman d George Bloomfield ph Arthur Ibbetson, Laszlo George m Peter Mann
☆ Donald Sutherland, Suzanne Somers, Lawrence Dane, Roscoe Lee Browne

Nothing Personal
GB/Ireland 1995 85m Metrocolor
Film Four/Irish Film Board/British Screen/Little Bird (Jonathan Cavendish, Tracey Seaward)
In Belfast in the mid-70s, armed conflict between republican and loyalist paramilitary groups claims innocent lives.
A well-made drama of the Irish troubles, showing faults on both sides, but one that is likely to leave a viewer little wiser, other than with the conclusion that violence causes more problems than it solves.
w Daniel Mornin novel *All Our Fault* by Daniel Mornin d Thaddeus O'Sullivan ph Dick Pope m Philip Appleby pd Mark Geraghty ed Michael Parker
☆ Ian Hart, John Lynch, James Frain, Michael Gambon, Gary Lydon, Ruaidhri Conroy, Maria Doyle Kennedy, Jeni Courtney, Gerard McSorley
'A film to laud for the courage and sincerity of its aspirations rather than its modest, perhaps muffled achievement.' – *Trevor Johnston, Sight and Sound*

'Boy Makes Girl Make Fool Of New York.'
Nothing Sacred ***
US 1937 77m Technicolor
David O. Selznick

A girl thought to be dying of a rare disease is built up by the press into a national heroine; but the diagnosis was wrong.
Hollywood's most bitter and hilarious satire, with crazy comedy elements and superb wisecracks; a historical monument of screen comedy, though its freshness at the time can't now be recaptured.
w *Ben Hecht* story *Letter to the Editor* by James H. Street d William Wellman ph W. Howard Greene m Oscar Levant
☆ *Carole Lombard, Fredric March, Walter Connolly,* Charles Winninger, Sig Rumann, Frank Fay, Maxie Rosenbloom, Margaret Hamilton, Hedda Hopper, Monty Woolley, Hattie McDaniel, Olin Howland, John Qualen
DOCTOR (CHARLES WINNINGER): 'I'll tell you briefly what I think of newspapermen. The hand of God, reaching down into the mire, couldn't elevate one of them to the depths of degradation.'
EDITOR (WALTER CONNOLLY): 'I am sitting here, Mr Cook, toying with the idea of cutting out your heart and stuffing it – like an olive!'
'Hit comedy ... will be one of the big grossers of the year.' – *Variety*
'Because it does hold up a mirror, even though a distorting mirror, to a very real world of ballyhoo and cheap sensationalism, the pleasure to be obtained from it is something more than the usual mulish guffaw.' – *Spectator*
† Refashioned in 1953 as a stage musical, *Hazel Flagg*, with Jule Styne; this in turn became a Martin and Lewis comedy *Living It Up* (Jerry Lewis in the Carole Lombard part).

'Slick advertising guy who's lost it. Small-time thief who can't find it. When life sucks this bad, you may as well blow it all...'
Nothing to Lose
US 1997 98m Technicolor Panavision
Buena Vista/Touchstone (Martin Bregman, Dan Jinks, Michael Bregman)

Believing that his wife is having an affair with his boss, an advertising executive goes on the rampage with the aid of a petty thief.
Tired and dim-witted action comedy in desperate search of an audience.
wd Steve Oedekerk ph Donald E. Thorin m Robert Folk pd Maria Caso ed Malcolm Campbell
☆ Tim Robbins, Martin Lawrence, John C. McGinley, Giancarlo Esposito, Michael McKean, Susan Barnes
'Sharper and funnier than you'd expect from a racist, formulaic comedy starring a high-minded director and an angry sitcom star.' – *Entertainment Weekly*

'Fateful Fascination! Electric Tension!'
'The screen's top romantic stars in a melodramatic masterpiece!'
Notorious ***
US 1946 101m bw
RKO (Alfred Hitchcock)

In Rio, a notorious lady marries a Nazi renegade to help the US government but finds herself falling in love with her contact.
Superb romantic suspenser containing some of Hitchcock's best work.
w *Ben Hecht* d *Alfred Hitchcock* ph Ted Tetzlaff m Roy Webb
☆ *Cary Grant, Ingrid Bergman, Claude Rains,* Louis Calhern, Leopoldine Konstantin, Reinhold Schünzel
'Velvet smooth in dramatic action, sharp and sure in its characters, and heavily charged with the intensity of warm emotional appeal.' – *Bosley Crowther*
'The suspense is terrific.' – *New Yorker, 1976*
'A film in the supercharged American idiom which made *Casablanca* popular.' – *Hermione Rich Isaacs, Theatre Arts*
Academy Award nomination: Ben Hecht; Claude Rains

A Notorious Gentleman
US 1935 73m bw
Universal
A man plans murder and incriminates the victim's fiancée.
Basically intriguing crime yarn spoiled by over-enthusiastic direction.
w Leopold Atlas, Robert Trasker d Edward Laemmle
☆ Charles Bickford, Helen Vinson, Sidney Blackmer, Onslow Stevens, Dudley Digges
'Too heavily handled for first consideration.' – *Variety*

Notorious Gentleman: see *The Rake's Progress (1945)*

The Notorious Landlady
US 1962 127m bw
Columbia/Kohlmar/Quine (Fred Kohlmar)
An American diplomat in London takes rooms with a murder suspect; after many mysterious happenings he helps to clear her.
Flatly whimsical goings on in comical old London, complete with fog and eccentrics. The actors all try hard but are deflated by the script.
w Larry Gelbart, Richard Quine d Richard Quine ph Arthur E. Arling m George Duning
☆ Kim Novak, Jack Lemmon, Fred Astaire, Lionel Jeffries, Estelle Winwood, Maxwell Reed
'A picture that is entertaining and exciting, often simultaneously, and that ends with a wildly funny chase.' – *Edith Oliver, New Yorker*

The Notorious Sophie Lang
US 1934 60m bw
Paramount
A lady jewel thief matches wits with a rival from abroad.
Frothy crime comedy which isn't quite smart enough to avoid boredom.
w Anthony Veiller d Ralph Murphy
☆ Gertrude Michael, Paul Cavanagh, Arthur Byron, Alison Skipworth, Leon Errol
'No marquee strength, but nice pace and some genuine amusement.' – *Variety*
† There was a sequel in 1937, *Sophie Goes West*, also starring Gertrude Michael, directed by Charles Reisner.

Notre Histoire: see *Our Story*

La Notte *
Italy/France 1960 121m bw
Nepi/Sofitedip/Silver

A moderately successful novelist and his wife begin to question their marriage and their life.
Slow but engaging character drama set during one night in Milan.
w Michelangelo Antonioni, Ennio Flaiano, Antonio Guerra d *Michelangelo Antonioni* ph Gianni di Venanzo m Giorgio Gaslini
☆ Marcello Mastroianni, Jeanne Moreau, Monica Vitti, Bernhard Wicki
'A film of supreme, of ferocious elegance: a film belonging in its rejection of the traditional forms of narrative to the new worlds of fiction.' – *Dilys Powell*

La Notte di San Lorenzo: see *The Night of San Lorenzo*

Le Notti di Cabiria: see *Cabiria*

Notting Hill **
US/GB 1999 123m DeLuxe Super 35
Polygram/Working Title (Duncan Kenworthy)

In a fashionable part of London, a diffident English bookseller becomes romantically involved with a famous American film star.
Slight but clever and often funny romantic comedy, making witty use of national stereotypes.
w Richard Curtis d Roger Michell ph Michael Coulter m Trevor Jones pd Stuart Craig ed Nick Moore
☆ Julia Roberts, Hugh Grant, Hugh Bonneville, Emma Chambers, James Dreyfus, Rhys Ifans, Tim McInnerny, Gina McKee, Richard McCabe, Alec Baldwin
'Solid, crowd-pleasing entertainment.' – *Empire*
BAFTA: audience award

Nous Sommes Tous les Assassins *
France 1952 108m bw
UGC
aka: *Are We All Murderers?*
An illiterate youth is taught to kill during the war; afterwards he kills again for money and is sent for execution.
A solemn sermon on capital punishment, and a powerful though rather glib one.
w André Cayatte, Charles Spaak d André Cayatte ph Jean Bourgoin
☆ Marcel Mouloudji, Raymond Pellégrin, Antoine Balpêtre, Claude Laydu

Les Nouveaux Messieurs *
France 1928 135m approx (24 fps) bw silent
Albatros/Séquance
A glamorous dancer forsakes a count for a rising trade union official.
Lengthy political satire which caused a few headlines when first released.
w Charles Spaak, Jacques Feyder *play* Robert de Flers, Francis de Grosset *d* Jacques Feyder *ph* Georges Périnal, Maurice Defassiaux *ad* Lazare Meerson
☆ Albert Préjean, Gaby Morlay, Henri Roussel

La Nouvelle Eve: see *The New Eve*

Novecento: see *1900*

A Novel Affair: see *The Passionate Stranger*

Novembermond
West Germany 1984 106m colour
ICA/Ottokar Runze Film/Sun 7
A Jewish refugee fleeing from Nazi Germany has a lesbian love affair in Germany.
Slight, anecdotal film with little insight into the period.
wd Alexandra von Grote *ph* Bernard Zitzermann *ad* Helger Gross, Jean-Pierre Balzerolla *ed* Susan Lahaye
☆ Gabrile Osburg, Christine Millet, Danièle Delorme, Bruno Pradal, Stéphane Garcin, Louise Martini

'Till *Death* They Do Part!'
La Novia Ensangrentada
Spain 1972 102m colour
Eagle/Morgana
aka: *The Blood Spattered Bride*
A newly married man discovers that his bride is haunted by a woman who killed her husband on their wedding night two hundred years before.
Coarse and unattractive vampire movie; the narrative leaves too much unexplained.
wd Vicente Aranda *novella Carmila* by Sheridan Le Fanu *ph* Fernando Arribas *m* Antonio Perez Olea *pd* Juan Alberto Soler *ed* Pablo Gonzalez del Amo *sp* Antonio Molina
☆ Simon Andreu (Husband), Maribel Martín (Susan), Alexandra Bastedo (Mircala/Carmila), Dean Selmier (Doctor), Rosa Ma Rodrígues (Carol), Montserrat Julio (Maid), Angel Lombarte (Servant)
'Unappealing combination of explicit brutality and sadistic sexism.' – *Scott Meek, MFB*

The Novices (dubbed)
France/Italy 1970 95m Eastmancolor
Scotia-Barber/Les Films La Boétie/Rizzoli (André Génovès)
original title: *Les Novices*
After trying to become a prostitute in Paris, a nun decides that convent life is best.
Occasionally amusing comedy, sabotaged by its unsympathetic and out-of-sync dubbing.
wd Guy Casaril *ph* Claude Lecomte *m* François de Roubaix *ed* Nicole Gauduchon
☆ Brigitte Bardot, Annie Girardot, Lucien Barjon, Angelo Bardi, Jean Carmet, Jess Hahn
† The film was cut to 90m on its British release.

'Crime Is Not Only Done By Criminals.'
Novocaine
US 2001 94m DeLuxe
Artisan (Paul Mones, Daniel M. Rosenberg)
A dentist falls for a woman who is only interested in his drugs.
A black farce without laughs; it rapidly spins out of control of its actors and director.
wd David Atkins *ph* Vilko Filac *m* Steve Bartek *pd* Sharon Seymour *ed* Melody London
☆ Steve Martin (Dr Frank Sangster), Helena Bonham Carter (Susan Ivey), Laura Dern (Jean Noble), Elias Koteas (Harlan Sangster), Scott Caan (Duane), Keith David (Detective Lunt), Lynne Thigpen (Pat)
'O.K., so it's different and peculiar. It's also confused, repulsive and unconvincing. I've had more fun at root canals.' – *Rex Reed, New York Observer*

Novyi Vavilon: see *The New Babylon*

Now About These Women ... *
Sweden 1964 80m Eastmancolor
Svensk Filmindustri
aka: *All These Women*
A critic comes to stay with a famous cellist whose biography he is writing, but his efforts are hampered by all the women in the house.
Virtually indescribable black farce comedy which doesn't really work, yet, as always with this director, is continually of interest.
w Erland Josephson, Ingmar Bergman *d* Ingmar Bergman *ph* Sven Nykvist *m* Erik Nordgren
☆ Jarl Kulle, Georg Funkquist, Eva Dahlbeck, Karen Kavli, Harriet Andersson, Bibi Andersson, Gertrud Fridh

Now and Forever *
US 1934 82m bw
Paramount (Louis D. Lighton)
A jewel thief and his mistress are taught a thing or two by his small daughter.
Odd mixture of comedy and drama which was box-office at the time but seems pretty dated after nearly fifty years, though technically very smooth.
w Vincent Lawrence, Sylvia Thalberg *d* Henry Hathaway *ph* Harry Fischbeck
☆ Gary Cooper, Carole Lombard, Shirley Temple, Guy Standing, Charlotte Granville, Gilbert Emery, Henry Kolker
'Cinch b.o. entertainment.' – *Variety*
'Expertly contrived to furnish first-rate entertainment.' – *Thornton Delehanty, New York Post*

Now and Forever
GB 1955 91m Technicolor
ABPC/Mario Zampi
A lonely schoolgirl plans an elopement and is chased across England by two sets of parents.
Teenage romance with elements of both farce and melodrama. It seemed to please at the time.
w R. F. Delderfield, Michael Pertwee *play The Orchard Walls* by R. F. Delderfield *d* Mario Zampi *ph* Erwin Hillier *m* Stanley Black
☆ Janette Scott, Vernon Gray, Kay Walsh, Jack Warner, Pamela Brown, Charles Victor, Wilfrid Lawson, Marjorie Rhodes, Sonia Dresdel, Ronald Squire, David Kossoff

'A summer when four friends made a promise to return anytime they needed each other. Twenty years later, that time has come.'
Now and Then
US 1995 96m DeLuxe
First Independent/New Line/Moving Pictures (Suzanne Todd, Demi Moore)
A novelist, an actress and a doctor meet at the home of a pregnant friend and recall their childhood friendship.
Routine coming-of-age drama, given an overtly sentimental and nostalgic treatment.
w I. Marlene King *d* Lesli Linka Glatter *ph* Ueli Steiger *m* Cliff Eidelman *pd* Gershon Ginsburg *ed* Jacqueline Cambas
☆ Rosie O'Donnell, Christina Ricci, Melanie Griffith, Thora Birch, Demi Moore, Gaby Hoffmann, Rita Wilson, Ashleigh Aston Moore, Janeane Garofalo, Lolita Davidovich
'Semi-autobiographical screenplay is so predictable, audiences may grow impatient while waiting for the inevitable to occur.' – *Variety*

Now Barabbas...
GB 1949 87m bw
Warner/Anatole de Grunwald
aka: *Now Barabbas Was a Robber*
Stories of men in prison.
Thinly intercut dramas; from a stage success.
w Anatole de Grunwald *play* William Douglas Home *d* Gordon Parry *ph* Otto Heller
☆ Richard Greene, Cedric Hardwicke, William Hartnell, Kathleen Harrison, Leslie Dwyer, Richard Burton, Kenneth More, Ronald Howard, Stephen Murray, Beatrice Campbell, Betty Ann Davies, Alec Clunes

Now Barabbas Was a Robber: see *Now Barabbas...*

Now I'll Tell
US 1934 72m bw
Fox (Winfield Sheehan)
GB title: *When New York Sleeps*
The story of Arnold Rothstein, gambler-racketeer of the twenties, as told by his widow.
Competent crime/domestic programmer.
wd Edwin Burke *ph* Ernest Palmer *m* Hugo Friedhofer
☆ Spencer Tracy, Helen Twelvetrees, Hobart Cavanaugh, Alice Faye, G. P. Huntley Jnr, Shirley Temple, Leon Ames
'In spite of the breezy sequences with which it starts, it quickly gets improbable and goes from bad to maudlin.' – *Otis Ferguson*

Now Voyager ***
US 1942 117m bw
Warner (Hal B. Wallis)
A dowdy frustrated spinster takes the psychiatric cure and embarks on a doomed love affair.
A basically soggy script still gets by, and how, through the romantic magic of its stars, who were all at their best; and suffering in mink went over very big in wartime.
w Casey Robinson *novel* Olive Higgins Prouty *d Irving Rapper ph* Sol Polito *m* Max Steiner *ad* Robert Haas *ed* Warren Low
☆ *Bette Davis, Claude Rains, Paul Henreid*, Gladys Cooper, John Loder, Bonita Granville, Ilka Chase, Lee Patrick, Charles Drake, Franklin Pangborn, Janis Wilson
CHARLOTTE (BETTE DAVIS): 'Oh, Jerry, don't let's ask for the moon. We have the stars!'
'If it were better, it might not work at all. This way, it's a crummy classic.' – *New Yorker, 1977*
Max Steiner
Bette Davis; Gladys Cooper

Now You See Him Now You Don't
US 1972 88m Technicolor
Walt Disney
Two students discover an elixir of invisibility and help prevent a gangster from taking over the college.
Flat Disney frolic with fair trick effects.
w Joseph L. McEveety *d* Robert Butler *ph* Frank Phillips *m* Robert F. Brunner *sp* Eustace Lycett, Danny Lee
☆ Kurt Russell, Cesar Romero, Joe Flynn, Jim Backus, William Windom, Edward Andrews, Richard Bakalyan

Nowhere *
US/France 1997 82m colour
Pathé/Kill/Desperate/Blurco/Why Not (Andrea Sperling, Gregg Araki)
A group of friends indulge in a variety of sexual experiences.
Delirious send-up of high-school movies – one character turns into a giant cockroach – with alienated teenagers indulging in polymorphous perversities.
wd Gregg Araki *ph* Arturo Smith *pd* Patti Podesta *ed* Gregg Araki
☆ James Duval (Dark), Rachel True (Mel), Nathan Bexton (Montgomery), Chiara Mastroianni (Kriss), Debi Mazar (Kozy), Kathleen Robertson (Lucifer), Joshua Gibran Mayweather (Zero), Christina Applegate (Dingbat), Jordan Ladd (Alyssa), Ryan Phillippe (Shad), Heather Graham (Lilith)
'Without a doubt his most accessible, sensual and superficially entertaining movie to date.' – *Emanuel Levy, Variety*
'Its storm of sex and violence celebrates American pop culture with punning, postmodern artifice.' – *Liese Spencer, Sight and Sound*

'1938. One family's story of a homeland lost and a new one found...'
Nowhere in Africa **
Germany 2001 141m colour
Optimum/MTM/Constantin/Bavaria Film/MC-One (Peter Herrmann)
The experiences of a Jewish lawyer, his wife and daughter, who leave Germany for a tougher, poorer life on a farm in Kenya.
Engaging account of an unlooked-for colonial adventure, as seen through the eyes of a young girl, and encompassiing marital problems and homesickness along the way.
wd Caroline Link *novel* Stefanie Zweig *ph* Gernot Roll *m* Niki Reiser *pd* Susann Bieling, Uwe Szielasko *ed* Patricia Rommel
☆ Juliane Koehler (Jettel Redlich), Merab Ninidze (Walter Redlich), Matthias Habich (Suesskind), Sidede Onyulo (Owuor), Lea Kurka (Regina Redlich (younger)), Karoline Eckertz (Regina Redlich (older)), Gerd Heinz (Max), Hildegard Schmahl (Ina)
'This is an intelligent epic told without special pleading, a film able to cut deep enough to reveal a keen specificity of experience.' – *Kenneth Turan, Los Angeles Times*
'Has the sturdiness of an old-fashioned Hollywood epic. What isn't Hollywood is Link's refusal to tell the audience how to feel at every moment.' – *David Ansen, Newsweek*
foreign film

Nowhere to Go
GB 1958 87m bw
Ealing (Eric Williams)
A thief escapes from prison but can get no help from the underworld and is accidentally shot after being sheltered by a socialite.
Glum character melodrama which fails to sustain interest despite the best intentions.
w Seth Holt, Ken Tynan *book* Donald MacKenzie *d* Seth Holt *ph* Paul Beeson *m* Dizzy Reece
☆ George Nader, Maggie Smith, Bernard Lee, Geoffrey Keen, Andree Melly, Bessie Love, Howard Marion Crawford

Nowhere to Hide: see *Injeong Sajeong Bolgeos Eobsda*

'When the law can't protect the innocent ... it takes an outlaw to deliver justice.'
Nowhere to Run
US 1992 94m Technicolor
Columbia (Craig Baumgarten, Gary Adelson)
An escaped prisoner helps a widow and her two young sons who are being threatened by an evil property developer.
Tedious action movie with a little added sentimentality, intended, but failing, to give its star a wider appeal.
w Joe Eszterhas, Leslie Bohem, Randy Feldman *d* Robert Harmon *ph* David Gribble *m* Mark Isham *pd* Dennis Washington *ed* Zach Staenberg, Mark Helfrich
☆ Jean-Claude Van Damme, Rosanna Arquette, Kieran Culkin, Ted Levine, Tiffany Taubman, Edward Blatchford, Anthony Starke, Joss Ackland
'A relentlessly corny and shamelessly derivative vehicle.' – *Variety*

Noz w Wodzie: see *Knife in the Water*

Nuclear Run: see *The Chain Reaction*

The Nude Bomb
US 1980 94m Technicolor
Universal/Time-Life Films (Jennings Lang)
aka: *The Return of Maxwell Smart*
An incompetent secret agent chases a missile launching villain.
Curious and unsatisfactory attempt to revive a twenty-year-old TV situation comedy minus half its personnel.
w Arne Sultan, Bill Dana, Leonard B. Stern *d* Clive Donner *ph* Harry L. Wolf *m* Lalo Schifrin *pd* William Tuntke *ed* Walter Hannemann
☆ Don Adams, Sylvia Kristel, Dana Elcar, Rhonda Fleming, Andrea Howard, Norman Lloyd
'Fans of the vidshow will derive much more enjoyment by crowding round their television sets with a bowl of popcorn watching *Get Smart* reruns.' – *Variety.*

Nueve Reinas *
Argentina 2001 114m colour
Optimum/Patagonik (Pablo Bossi)
aka: *Nine Queens*
A conman persuades a younger operator to become his new partner in a scam involving forged copies of rare stamps.
Much lauded in its home country, this moderately clever slow-paced movie of con-men in a collapsing economy does not always play fair with its audience, who may also feel cheated by the end.

wd Fabian Bielinsky *ph* Marcelo Camorino *m* Cesar Lerner *pd* Marcelo Salvioli *ed* Sergio Zottola
☆ Ricardo Darin (Marcos), Gaston Pauls (Juan), Leticia Bredice (Valeria), Tomas Fonzi (Federico), Ignasi Abadal (Vidal Gandolfo), Alejandro Awada (Washington), Antonio Ugo (D'Agostino), Oscar Nunez (Sandler)

'A clever, entertaining and amusing piece of film-making.' – *Derek Malcolm, Guardian*

La Nuit Américaine: see *Day for Night*

La Nuit de Varennes *
France/Italy 1982 165m Eastmancolor Technovision
Electric/Contemporary/Gaumont-FR3/Opera Film (Renzo Rossellini)

In the early days of the French Revolution, a mixed coachload of travellers, including Restif de la Bretonne, Tom Paine and Casanova, make their way to Varennes, where King Louis is held captive.
Moderately engaging historical tale that does not take itself, or the times, too seriously.
w Sergio Amidei, Ettore Scola *d* Ettore Scola *ph* Armando Nannuzzi *m* Armando Trovajoli *pd* Dante Ferretti *ed* Raimondo Crociani
☆ Jean-Louis Barrault, Marcello Mastroianni, Hanna Schygulla, Harvey Keitel, Jean-Claude Brialy, Daniel Gelin, Andrea Ferreol, Michael Vitold, Laura Betti

Nuit et Brouillard: see *Night and Fog*

Les Nuits de la Pleine Lune: see *Full Moon in Paris*

Les Nuits Fauves: see *Savage Nights*

Number One
US 1969 105m DeLuxe
Walter Seltzer
Age and injury overtake a quarterback, once regarded as the greatest.
Unconvincing sporting drama, which plods around its subject-matter without creating anything of even passing interest.
w David Moessinger *d* Tom Gries *ph* Michel Hugo *m* Dominic Frontiere *ad* Arthur Loel *ed* Richard Brockway
☆ Charlton Heston, Jessica Walter, Bruce Dern, John Randolph, Diana Muldaur, Al Hirt, Roy Jenson, Mike Henry, Bobby Troup, Richard Elkins, Ernie Barnes

Number One
GB 1984 106m Technicolor
Videoform (Mark Forstater, Raymond Day)
Adventures of a snooker hall hustler.
Unappetizingly foul-mouthed low-life saga.
w G. F. Newman *d* Les Blair *ph* Bahram Manocheri *m* David Mackay *pd* Martin Johnson *ed* Jon Gregory
☆ Bob Geldof, Mel Smith, Alison Steadman, P. H. Moriarty, Phil Daniels, Alfred Molina

Number One Fan
US 1994 93m CFI color
MCEG Sterling
A film star is seduced by an unbalanced female fan, who is determined to have him for herself.
Lurid and increasingly risible thriller, notable only for the number of children of successful stars that it features.
w Anthony Laurence Greene *d* Jane Simpson *ph* Sead Mutarevic *m* Robert J. Walsh *pd* Gary Randall *ed* Ivan Ladizinsky
☆ Chad McQueen, Catherine Mary Stewart, Rennee Ammann, Paul Bartel, Charles Matthau, Hoyt Axton, Dean Morris, Mary Woronow, Eric Da Re, Dick Miller

Number One with a Bullet
US 1987 101m colour
Cannon
An LA detective is obsessed with busting a big drug dealer who is also a pillar of the community.
Ho-hum policier with routine violence.
w Gail Morgan Hickman and others *d* Jack Smight
☆ Robert Carradine, Billy Dee Williams, Valerie Bertinelli, Peter Graves, Doris Roberts

Number Seventeen *
GB 1932 63m bw
BIP (John Maxwell)
A girl jewel thief reforms and helps the police track down her former gang.
Minor Hitchcock thriller largely confined to a single interior until the final train chase, which despite obvious models remains exhilarating.
w Alfred Hitchcock, Alma Reville, Rodney Ackland *play* J. Jefferson Farjeon *d Alfred Hitchcock ph* Jack Cox
☆ Leon M. Lion, Anne Grey, John Stuart, Donald Calthrop, Barry Jones, Garry Marsh

'Only spasmodically good photography and usual slow tempo British direction. Wonder why they can't speed up a picture? Maybe it's the tea.' – *Variety*

† The same play had been filmed as a silent in 1928 by Geza Bolvary, with Guy Newall; it was shot in Germany.

The Nun and the Devil
Italy/France 1973 102m Technicolor
PAC/Splendida/Jacques Leitienne (Tonino Cervi)
original title: *Monache di Sant'Arcangelo*
aka: *The Nuns of Saint Archangel*
At an Italian convent in the 1570s, one sister uses any means at her disposal to become Mother Superior.
Sex and death among the nuns turns out to be a dull affair.
wd Domenico Paolella *story* Stendhal *ph* Giuseppe Ruzzolini *m* Piero Piccioni *ed* Nino Baragli
☆ Anne Heywood, Ornella Muti, Duilio del Prete, Martine Brochard, Luc Merenda, Claudia Gravi

'Basically a sexploitation piece of exceeding dignity, it boasts a modestly attractive visual surface, with deft photography and neat compositions, and suffers from a debilitating lack of dramatic impetus.' – *Geoff Brown, MFB*

† The version released in Britain ran for 93m.

The Nuns of Saint Archangel: see *The Nun and the Devil*

'The Story of an Immaculate Deception.'
Nuns on the Run
GB 1990 92m Technicolor
Palace/Handmade Films (Michael White)
Two petty criminals disguise themselves as nuns to escape capture.
Broad, slapstick comedy that provides scant amusement, although it went down well in America.
wd Jonathan Lynn *ph* Michael Garfath *m* Hidden Faces *pd* Simon Holland *ed* David Martin
☆ Eric Idle, Robbie Coltrane, Camille Coduri, Janet Suzman, Doris Hare, Lila Kaye, Robert Patterson, Robert Morgan, Winston Dennis, Tom Hickey

'Filmed in Belgium, Italy, Africa ... and mostly in the conscience of a beautiful young girl!'
The Nun's Story ***
US 1959 151m Technicolor
Warner (Henry Blanke)
A Belgian girl joins a strict order, endures hardship in the Congo, and finally returns to ordinary life.
The fascinating early sequences of convent routine are more interesting than the African adventures, but this is a careful, composed and impressive film with little Hollywood exaggeration.
w Robert Anderson book Kathryn C. Hulme d Fred Zinnemann ph Franz Planer m Franz Waxman ed Walter Thompson
☆ *Audrey Hepburn, Peter Finch,* Edith Evans, Peggy Ashcroft, Dean Jagger, Mildred Dunnock, Patricia Collinge, Beatrice Straight

'A major directorial achievement ... the best study of the religious life ever made in the American cinema.' – *Albert Johnson, Film Quarterly*

Academy Award nomination: picture; Robert Anderson; Fred Zinnemann; Franz Planer; Franz Waxman; Audrey Hepburn; editing
BAFTA: Audrey Hepburn

I Nuovi Barbari: see *The New Barbarians*

Nuovo Cinema Paradiso: see *Cinema Paradiso*

'She's chasing a dream...they're chasing her.'
'She Needs To See A Doctor.'
Nurse Betty **
US 2000 108m Technicolor
Gramercy/Pacifica/Propaganda/ab'-strakt/IMF (Gail Mutrux, Steve Golin)
After seeing her drug-dealing husband murdered, a waitress in a small Kansas town believes she is in love with a doctor in her favourite soap opera and travels to California to meet him.
A comic thriller with a sour edge, balancing precariously on the point where television-fuelled fantasy spills over into real life.
w John C. Richards, James Flamberg *d* Neil LaBute *ph* Jean Yves Escoffier *m* Rolfe Kent *pd* Charles Breen *ed* Joel Plotch, Steven Weisberg *cos* Lynette Meyer
☆ Renée Zellweger (Betty Sizemore), Morgan Freeman (Charlie), Chris Rock (Wesley), Greg Kinnear (Dr David Ravell/George McCord), Aaron Eckhart (Del), Tia Texada (Rosa), Crispin Glover (Roy), Pruitt Taylor Vince (Ballard), Allison Janney (Lyla), Kathleen Wilhoite (Sue Ann), Harriet Sanson Harris (Ellen), Laird Macintosh (Dr Lonnie Walsh)

'A weirdly uneven, ultimately dissatisfying experience.' – *Empire*

'A clever, vastly entertaining film.' – *Variety*

Nurse Edith Cavell
US 1939 98m bw
Imperator/RKO
The story of a British nurse executed as a spy during World War I; previously filmed in 1930 as *Dawn* with Sybil Thorndike.
This is a moderately touching but uninspired treatment.
w Michael Hogan *novel Dawn* by Reginald Berkeley *d* Herbert Wilcox *m* Anthony Collins
☆ Anna Neagle, George Sanders, May Robson, Edna May Oliver, Alan Marshal

'Excellently produced documentary film, but not for general audience appeal ... no light moments to relieve the tragic aspects.' – *Variety*

'Miss Neagle looked nice as Queen Victoria, she looks just as nice as Nurse Cavell: she moves rigidly on to the set, as if wheels were concealed under the stately skirt: she says her piece with flat dignity and trolleys out again – rather like a mechanical marvel from the World's Fair.' – *Graham Greene, The Spectator*

Academy Award nomination: Anthony Collins

Nurse on Wheels
GB 1963 86m bw
Anglo Amalgamated/GHW (Peter Rogers)
Adventures of a young District Nurse.
Part sentimental, part Carry On; watchable of its curious kind.
w Norman Hudis *novel Nurse Is a Neighbour* by Joanna Jones *d* Gerald Thomas *ph* Alan Hume *m* Eric Rogers
☆ Juliet Mills, Ronald Lewis, Joan Sims, Raymond Huntley, Athene Seyler

The Nursemaid Who Disappeared
GB 1939 86m bw
Warner
A domestic agency hides a gang of kidnappers.
Fairly pleasing mystery of the old school.
w Paul Gangelin and Connery Chappell *novel* Philip MacDonald *d* Arthur Woods
☆ Arthur Margetson, Peter Coke, Lesley Brook, Edward Chapman, Coral Browne, Martita Hunt

The Nurse's Secret
US 1941 56m bw
First National/Warner
A hired nurse solves her patient's murder.
Potboiling remake of Miss Pinkerton, *rather better written than the original.*
w Anthony Coldeway *d* Noel M. Smith
☆ Lee Patrick, Regis Toomey, Julie Bishop, Charles D. Waldron, Charles Trowbridge, Leonard Mudie

Nutcracker
GB 1982 101m Eastmancolor
Rank/Ezshaw (Panos Nicolaou)
A Russian ballerina defects in London but finds that she is being used for business/political purposes.
Weird, dated and utterly mediocre melodrama with pauses for sexual revels. Not a goer.
w Raymond Christodoulou *d* Anwar Kawadri *ph* Peter Jessop *m* Simon Park
☆ Joan Collins, Carol White, Paul Nicholas, Finola Hughes, William Franklyn, Murray Melvin

Nutcracker – The Motion Picture *
US 1986 85m colour
Entertainment/Hyperion/Kushner/Locke
A movie based on the Pacific Northwest Ballet company's version of the classic ballet.
The restless and moody direction does not always do justice to the dancing, although it effectively conjures a slightly sinister atmosphere.
d Carroll Ballard *ph* Stephen M. Burum *m* Tchaikovsky *pd* Maurice Sendak *ed* John Nutt, Michael Silvers
☆ Hugh Bigney, Vanessa Sharp, Patricia Barker, Wade Walthall

Nuts
US 1987 116m Technicolor
Warner (Barbra Streisand)
Classy prostitute kills a client; at her trial she battles against attempts to find her mentally unstable.
Star vehicle, strictly for fans.
w Tom Topor and others *play* Tom Topor *d* Martin Ritt *ph* Andrzej Bartkowiak *m* Barbra Streisand *pd* Joel Schiller
☆ Barbra Streisand, Richard Dreyfuss, Maureen Stapleton, Karl Malden, Eli Wallach

The Nutty Professor
US 1963 107m Technicolor
Paramount/Jerry Lewis (Ernest D. Glucksman)
An eccentric chemistry professor discovers an elixir which turns him into a pop idol.
Long dreary comedy which contains patches of its star at somewhere near his best; but even Dr Jekyll and Mr Hyde *is funnier.*
w Jerry Lewis, Bill Richmond *d* Jerry Lewis *ph* W. Wallace Kelley *m* Walter Scharf *ad* Hal Pereira, Walter Tyler *ed* John Woodcock
☆ Jerry Lewis, Stella Stevens, Howard Morris, Kathleen Freeman, Del Moore, Les Brown and His Band of Renown

The Nutty Professor *
US 1996 95m DeLuxe
UIP/Universal/Imagine (Brian Grazer, Russell Simmons)
A shy, fat chemistry professor discovers a formula that turns him into a slim, brash man-about-town.
One of the few remakes that is an improvement on the original, with Murphy demonstrating his abilities by playing an entire family at dinner; the humour is broad, but occasionally beguiling.
w David Sheffield, Barry W. Blaustein, Tom Shadyac, Steve Oedekerk *film* Jerry Lewis, Bill Richmond *d* Tom Shadyac *ph* Julio Macat *m* David Newman *pd* William Elliott *ed* Don Zimmerman *sp* make
☆ Eddie Murphy, Jada Pinkett, James Coburn, Larry Miller, Dave Chappelle, John Ales

'Combining the riotously funny and the sweetly sentimental, the new outing is a welcome entry in a season suffering from a paucity of comedy.' – *Variety*

† It was among the box-office successes of 1996, grossing around $254m around the world.
†† A sequel is planned.
Academy Award: Rick Baker, David Leroy Anderson

'Eddie Murphy Is The Klumps!'

Nutty Professor II: The Klumps

US 2000 106m DeLuxe

Universal/Imagine (Brian Grazer)

A fat professor discovers that his slim but unpleasant alter ego has become a separate person.

A too often crude and tasteless sequel that is notable for Murphy's impersonation of the entire Klump family.

w Barry W. Blaustein, David Sheffield, Paul Weitz, Chris Weitz *d* Peter Segal *ph* Dean Semler *m* David Newman *pd* William Elliott *ed* William Kerr *sp* makeup fx: Rick Baker *cos* Sharen Davis

☆ Eddie Murphy (Sherman Klump/Buddy Love/Granny Klump/ Mama Klump/Papa Klump/Young Papa Klump/Ernie Klump/Lance Perkins), Janet Jackson (Denise Gaines), Larry Miller (Dean Richmond), John Ales (Jason), Richard Gant (Denise's Father), Anna Maria Horsford (Denise's Mother), Melinda McGraw (Leanne Guilford), Jamal Mixon (Ernie Klump Jnr)

'As silly and as marginally endearing as its high-earning predecessor.' – *Adam Mars-Jones, Times*

'A heavy handful of comic crudity with gross-out gags.' – *Cosmo Landesman, Sunday Times*

'Everything Comes Full Circle...'
O
US 2001 95m colour
Buena Vista/Chickie the Cop/Daniel Fried/Rhulen Entertainment

At an exclusive Southern school, the only black pupil, a baseball star, arouses the jealousy of the coach's son over his romance with a white girl.
What a noble play is here overthrown in this high school variation on Shakespeare's Othello, which does no more than trivialise the drama.
w Brad Kaaya *d* Tim Blake Nelson *ph* Russell Lee Fine *m* Jeff Danna *pd* Dina Goldman *ed* Kate Sanford
☆ Mekhi Phifer (Odin James), Josh Hartnett (Hugo Goulding), Julia Stiles (Desi Brable), Elden Henson (Roger Rodriguez), Michael Casio (Andrew Keegan), Rain Phoenix (Emily), John Heard (Dean Brable), Anthony 'A. J.' Johnson (Dell), Martin Sheen (Coach Duke Goulding)
'Something that never should have gone further than a class assignment to see if it could be made to work. It doesn't.' – *Todd McCarthy, Variety*
'All the conflicts have been laid out in fairly simple terms, as if the writer was in a hurry to get to the point before the butterlike topping on the audience's popcorn congealed.' – *Elvis Mitchell, New York Times*
† The movie was completed in 1999, but its release was delayed following a high school shooting in America.

O Brother, Where Art Thou? ***
US 2000 106m DeLuxe
Universal/Touchstone/StudioCanal/Working Title (Ethan Coen)

In Mississippi in the 1930s, three convicts escape a chain gang and go in search of buried treasure.
No one, least of all its makers, would take seriously the claim that this is based on Homer: rather it journeys through more modern American myths and legends with a lightly satirical touch and enormous charm; it comes closer than most modern movies to re-inventing the musical as a potent form of entertainment.
w Ethan and Joel Coen poem The Odyssey by Homer *d Joel Coen ph Roger Deakins m* T Bone Burnett *pd* Dennis Gassner *ed* Roderick Jaynes, Tricia Cooke *cos* Mary Zophres
☆ *George Clooney* (Everett Ulysses McGill), John Turturro (Pete), Tim Blake Nelson (Delmar), Charles Durning (Pappy O'Daniel), John Goodman (Big Dan Teague), Michael Badalucco (George Nelson), Holly Hunter (Penny), Stephen Root (Radio Station Man), Chris Thomas King (Tommy Johnson), Wayne Duvall (Homer Stokes), Daniel Von Bargen (Sheriff Cooley)
'The pace of the action, the brilliance of the dialogue, the spinning of a narrative out of scraps of Faulkner and *Moby Dick*, all consolidate the reputation that the brothers have earned.' – *Adam Mars-Jones, Times*
'It's such a charming, happy and beautiful film that the only possible response is one of admiration and gratitude.' – *Edward Porter, Sunday Times*
† The title is taken from the serious movie that the hero of Preston Sturges' *Sullivan's Travels* intended to make.
†† George Clooney's singing is dubbed by Dan Tyminski.
script (Ethan Coen, Joel Coen)

O. C. and Stiggs
US 1987 109m Metrocolor Panavision
MGM (Robert Altman, Peter Newman)
Two teenagers spend their summer playing practical jokes, particularly on their obnoxious neighbour.
Tedious comedy with an air of desperate improvisation about it.
w Donald Cantrell, Ted Mann *story* Tod Carroll, Ted Mann *d* Robert Altman *ph* Pierre Mignot *m* King Sunny Ade and his African Beats *pd* Scott Bushnell *ed* Elizabeth Kling
☆ Daniel H. Jenkins, Neill Barry, Paul Dooley, Jane Curtin, Jon Cryer, Ray Walston, Louis Nye, Tina Louise, Dennis Hopper, Melvin Van Peebles

O Despertar da Besta: see *Ritual Dos Sadicos*

O Dragao da Maldade contra o Santo Guerreiro: see *Antonio das Mortes*

O.H.M.S.
GB 1936 86m bw
Gaumont (Geoffrey Barkas)
US title: *You're in the Army Now*
British forces fighting in China are joined by an American gangster on the run, who dies a hero.
Stiff-upper-lip adventure of no particular interest.
w Bryan Edgar Wallace, Austin Melford, A. R. Rawlinson *story* Lesser Samuels, Ralph Bettinson *d* Raoul Walsh *ph* Roy Kellino
☆ John Mills, Wallace Ford, Anna Lee, Frank Cellier, Grace Bradley, Frederick Leister
'As near 100% entertainment value as can reasonably be hoped for without the employment of a superstar, super-cast, super-director and super-production.' – *Variety*

O. Henry's Full House **
US 1952 117m bw
TCF (André Hakim)
GB title: *Full House*
John Steinbeck introduces five stories by O. Henry.
Modelled on the success of Quartet (qv), this compendium was less successful because these turn-of-the-century tales of New York depend less on character than on the sting in the tail; but the cast and production were lavish.
The Cop and the Anthem:
w Lamar Trotti *d* Henry Koster *ph* Lloyd Ahern with Charles Laughton, David Wayne, Marilyn Monroe
The Clarion Call:
w Richard Breen *d* Henry Hathaway *ph* Lucien Ballard with Dale Robertson, Richard Widmark
The Last Leaf:
*w*Ivan Goff, Ben Roberts *d* Jean Negulesco *ph* Joe MacDonald with Anne Baxter, Jean Peters, Gregory Ratoff
The Ransom of Red Chief:
w Nunnally Johnson *d* Howard Hawks *ph* Milton Krasner with Fred Allen, Oscar Levant
The Gift of the Magi:
w Walter Bullock *d*Henry King *ph*Joe MacDonald with Jeanne Crain, Farley Granger
m Alfred Newman

'Smile while you're makin' it/Laugh while you're takin' it/Even though you're fakin' it/Nobody's gonna know...'
O Lucky Man! ***
GB 1973 174m Eastmancolor
Warner/Memorial/Sam (Michael Medwin, Lindsay Anderson)

The odyssey of a trainee salesman who after a while as an international financier settles down to be a do-gooder.
Modern revue-style version of Candide/Decline and Fall; *very hit or miss in style and effect, and hellishly overlong, but with good things along the way.*
w David Sherwin *d* Lindsay Anderson *ph* Miroslav Ondricek *m Alan Price pd* Jocelyn Herbert
☆ *Malcolm McDowell, Arthur Lowe, Ralph Richardson*, Rachel Roberts, Helen Mirren, Mona Washbourne, Dandy Nichols
'A sort of mod Pilgrim's Progress.' – *New Yorker*
Alan Price; Arthur Lowe

O Mary This London
GB 1994 90m colour
BBC (Helen Greaves)
Two Irish teenagers and their girlfriend come to London in search of adventure and an abortion.
A desultory, episodic road movie that manages to caricature the English and the Irish without creating any identity of its own.
w Shane Connaughton *d* Suri Krishnamma *ph* Sean Van Hales *m* Stephen Warbeck *ed* Sue Wyatt
☆ Jason Barry, Oba Seagrave, Dylan Tighe, Ram John Holder, Lesley Manville, John Otway
'The writer of this dismal, overlong farrago did his research in three London hostels; which suggests that the young Irish people he talked to must enjoy playing up all the most damaging stereotypes of their nation.' – *Hugh Hebert, Guardian*
'An implausible production, full of cultural clichés and based on a plot which threw in a dollop of mindless violence whenever things began to pall. The fact that much of the dialogue sounded like a preliminary read-through by an amateur dramatic society might be taken as a clever way of symbolising the inarticulateness of the characters, but somehow I don't think it was that smart.' – *John Naughton, Observer*
† Seen first in BBC-TV's *Screen Two* series, it was shown in cinemas in the United States.

'He's deep in danger, deeper in love!'
O.S.S. *
US 1946 107m bw
Paramount (Richard Maibaum)
American spies are parachuted into France in 1943.
Espionage heroics with an unhappy ending and a slight documentary flavour. Not bad of its kind.
w Richard Maibaum *d Irving Pichel ph* Lionel Lindon *m* Daniele Amfitheatrof, Heinz Roemheld
☆ Alan Ladd, Geraldine Fitzgerald, Patric Knowles, John Hoyt, Don Beddoe

O-Kay for Sound *
GB 1937 85m bw
GFD/Gainsborough (Edward Black)
The Crazy Gang runs amok in a film studio.
Patchy farce with music hall talents of the time.
w Marriott Edgar, Val Guest, R. P. Weston, Bert Lee *d* Marcel Varnel *ph* Jack Cox *m/ly* Michael Carr, Jimmy Kennedy *md* Louis Levy *pd* Vetchinsky *ed* R. E. Dearing
☆ Bud Flanagan, Chesney Allen, Jimmy Nervo, Teddy Knox, Charlie Naughton, Jimmy Gold, Fred Duprez, Enid Stamp-Taylor, Graham Moffatt, Meinhart Maur, H. F. Maltby, Peter Dawson, The Radio Three, The J. Sherman Fisher Girls

Oasis
France/Germany 1956 100m approx Eastmancolor Cinemascope
TCF/Roxy/Criterion (Gerd Oswald, Luggi Waldleitner)
An ex-pilot gets involved with two attractive women who are smuggling gold across the Sahara.
Glum romantic adventure.
w Joseph and Georges Kessel *d* Yves Allégret *ph* Roger Hubert *m* Paul Misraki
☆ Pierre Brasseur, Michèle Morgan, Cornell Borchers, Grégoire Aslan

Obchod na Korze: see *The Shop on Main Street*

Obecna Skola: see *Elementary School*

Oberst Redl: see *Colonel Redl*

The Oberwald Mystery
Italy 1980 129m colour
Artificial Eye/Polytel International/RAI (Sergio Benevenuti, Alessandro von Norman)
original title: *Il Mistero di Oberwald*
The queen of a Middle European country falls in love with an assassin who looks like her dead husband.
Shot on videotape and transferred to film, it is in unpleasing colour and takes an understated approach to a melodramatic work.
w Michelangelo Antonioni, Tonino Guerra *play L'Aigle A Deux Têtes* by Jean Cocteau *d* Michelangelo Antonioni *ph* Luciano Tovoli *m* Strauss, Schoenberg, Brahms *ad* Mischa Scandella *ed* Michelangelo Antonioni, Francesco Grandoni
☆ Monica Vitti, Franco Branciaroli, Luigi Diberti, Elisabetta Pozzi, Amad Saha Alan, Paolo Bonacelli

Object of Beauty
US/GB 1991 103m colour
Samuel Goldwyn/Winston/Avenue/BBC (Jon S. Denny, Alex Gohar)

In a luxurious London hotel, a deaf-mute maid steals a Henry Moore bronze from the bedroom of an adulterous American couple.
Dull and muted romantic comedy with obnoxious protagonists.
wd Michael Lindsay-Hogg *ph* David Watkin *m* Tom Bahler *pd* Derek Dodd *ed* Ruth Foster
☆ John Malkovich, Andie MacDowell, Lolita Davidovich, Rudi Davies, Joss Ackland, Bill Paterson, Ricci Harnett, Peter Riegert, Jack Shepherd
'A mildly diverting but empty picture.' – *Variety*

'Sometimes The Most Desirable Relationship Is The One You Can't Have.'
The Object of My Affection
US 1998 111m DuArt
TCF (Laurence Mark)

As they lose their existing boyfriends, a pregnant woman and a gay teacher develop a close relationship.
Another contemporary American take on relationships, which seems predicated on a dislike of sexual activities, insisting that a homosexual man is a woman's best friend.
w Wendy Wasserstein *novel* Stephen McCauley *d* Nicholas Hytner *ph* Oliver Stapleton *m* George Fenton *pd* Jane Musky *ed* Tariq Anwar
☆ Jennifer Aniston, Paul Rudd, Alan Alda, Nigel Hawthorne, John Pankow, Tim Daly, Allison Janney, Steve Zahn, Amo Gulinello, Bruce Altman, Kevin Carroll
'Tries to mix the messy realities of mismatched relationships with the structural neatness of a musical-comedy view of the world, with mild, occasionally diverting results.' – *Todd McCarthy, Variety*

Objective Burma! *
US 1945 142m bw
Warner (Jerry Wald)

Exploits of an American platoon in the Burma campaign.
Overlong but vivid war actioner which caused a diplomatic incident by failing to mention the British contribution.
w Ranald MacDougall, Lester Cole, Alvah Bessie *d Raoul Walsh ph* James Wong Howe *m* Franz Waxman *ed* George Amy
☆ Errol Flynn, James Brown, William Prince, George Tobias, Henry Hull, Warner Anderson, John Alvin

'At the rate Errol Flynn and co. knock off the Japanese, it may make you wonder why the war need outlast next weekend.' – *Time*

'I am amazed that Warner Brothers ever made it, or having made it failed to think again and smother it.' – *Reynolds News*

† The film was not released in Britain until 1952, and then with an apologetic prologue.

original story (Alvah Bessie); Franz Waxman; George Amy

The Obliging Young Lady
US 1941 80m bw
RKO

A secretary escorts a wealthy child out of town while her parents wrangle over custody.
Tedious comedy with interest occasionally provided by the supporting cast.
w Frank Ryan, Bert Granet *d* Richard Wallace
☆ Joan Carroll, Ruth Warrick, Edmond O'Brien, Eve Arden, Franklin Pangborn, Marjorie Gateson, John Miljan, George Cleveland, Luis Alberni, Charles Lane

The Oblong Box
GB 1969 95m Eastmancolor
AIP (Gordon Hessler)

One of two 19th-century brothers is mysteriously disfigured and buried alive; he recovers and runs amok.
Nastily effective horror film with a frail story but good background detail.
w Lawrence Huntington *d* *Gordon Hessler*
ph John Coquillon *m* Harry Robinson
☆ Vincent Price, Christopher Lee, Alastair Williamson, Hilary Dwyer, Peter Arne, Maxwell Shaw, Rupert Davies

'A pervasive aura of evil.' – *MFB*

Obsessed: see *The Late Edwina Black (1951)*

Obsessed
Canada 1989 100m colour
Telescene (Robin Spry, Jamie Brown)

A mother is determined to track down and bring to justice the hit-and-run driver who killed her skateboarding son.
A movie as relentlessly one-track as its title suggests; it is well enough done, but somewhat wearing, and less than believable, by the end.
w Douglas Bowie, Robin Spry *novel* *Hit and Run* by Tom Alderman *d* Robin Spry *ph* Ron Stannett *m* Jean-Alain Roussel *pd* Claude Paré *ed* Diann Ilnicki
☆ Kerrie Keane, Daniel Pilon, Saul Rubinek, Alan Thicke, Mireille Deyglun, Leif Anderson, Colleen Dewhurst

Obsession *
GB 1948 98m bw
GFD/Independent Sovereign (Nat Bronsten)
US title: *The Hidden Room*

A doctor decides to kill his wife's lover by imprisoning him in a lonely cellar while he accumulates enough acid to destroy all traces of his body.
Implausible, overstretched thriller, carefully enough done to be bearable.
w Alec Coppel *play* *A Man About a Dog* by Alec Coppel *d* Edward Dmytryk *ph* C. Pennington Richards *m* Nino Rota
☆ Robert Newton, Sally Gray, Phil Brown, Naunton Wayne

Obsession *
US 1976 98m Technicolor Panavision
Columbia (Robert S. Bremson)

A widower with guilt feelings meets the double of his dead wife and is drawn into a strange plot.
Hitchcockian adventure with a few unwise attempts at seriousness, à la Don't Look Now. *Generally entertaining, skilled and quite rewarding.*
w Paul Schrader *d* Brian de Palma *ph* Vilmos Zsigmond *m* Bernard Herrmann *ad* Jack Senter *ed* Paul Hirsch
☆ Cliff Robertson, Geneviève Bujold, John Lithgow, Sylvia Williams, Wanda Blackman, Patrick McNamara

'An unholy mess. Intended as an *hommage* to Hitchcock ... it attitudinizes [also] towards the old-fashioned tearjerker and towards the sophisticated European film, with cultural references strewn like breadcrumbs along the way of Hansel and Gretel...' – *John Simon, New York*

'Merely a mannered cerebral exercise without any emotional underpinning or unconscious feeling of its own.' – *Andrew Sarris, Village Voice*

Bernard Herrmann

Occupe-Toi d'Amélie ***
France 1949 95m bw
Lux (Louis Wipf)
aka: *Keep an Eye on Amelia*

A Parisian cocotte agrees to go through a mock marriage ceremony with her lover's best friend to fool his uncle: but the ceremony turns out to be real.
Hilarious and superbly stylized adaptation of a period boulevard farce: the play starts in a theatre, showing the audience, but gradually cinema technique takes over. Acting, timing and editing are all impeccable, and the production stands as a model of how such things should be done.
w *Jean Aurenche, Pierre Bost* *play* Georges Feydeau *d* *Claude Autant-Lara* *ph* André Bac *m* René Cloërc
☆ *Danielle Darrieux, Jean Desailly*, Bourvil, Carette, Grégoire Aslan

'Even those who do not respond to the artificialities of French vaudeville will admire the ingenuity and elegance of treatment.' – *Gavin Lambert, MFB*

'Most people, I think, could see it with considerable enjoyment even twice on the same evening.' – *Richard Mallett, Punch*

Ocean's Eleven *
US 1960 128m Technicolor Panavision
Warner/Dorchester (Lewis Milestone)

A gang of friends plan to rob a Las Vegas casino.
Self-indulgent and overlong caper comedy which marked Hollywood's entry into a subsequently much overworked field. In this case the plot stops all too frequently for guest spots and in-jokes.
w Harry Brown, Charles Lederer *d* Lewis Milestone *ph* William H. Daniels *m* Nelson Riddle
☆ Frank Sinatra, Peter Lawford, Sammy Davis Jnr, Richard Conte, Dean Martin, Angie Dickinson, Cesar Romero, Joey Bishop, Patrice Wymore, Akim Tamiroff, Henry Silva, Ilka Chase

'Are You In Or Out?'
Ocean's Eleven
US 2001 116m Technicolor Super 35
Warner/Village Roadshow/NPV/JW/Section Eight (Jerry Weintraub)

Released from prison, a conman recruits old friends to rob three Las Vegas casinos.
A remake as self-indulgent as the original, though slightly more fun; a little more wit, and less striving to seem cool, would have been welcome.
w Ted Griffin *screenplay* Harry Brown, Charles Lederer *story* George Clayton Johnson, Jack Golden Russell *d* Steven Soderbergh *ph* Peter Andrews *m* David Holmes *pd* Philip Messina *ed* Stephen Mirrione *cos* Jeffrey Kurland
☆ George Clooney (Danny Ocean), Matt Damon (Linus), Andy Garcia (Terry Benedict), Brad Pitt (Rusty Ryan), Julia Roberts (Tess Ocean), Casey Affleck (Virgil Malloy), Scott Caan (Turk Malloy), Don Cheadle (Basher Tarr), Elliott Gould (Reuben Tishkoff), Eddie Jemison (Livingston Dell), Bernie Mac (Frank Catton), Shaobo Qin (Yen), Carl Reiner (Saul Bloom)

'Made with so much wit and brains and dazzle and virtuosity that the sheer speed and cleverness of the caper hits you like a shot of pure oxygen.' – *Owen Gleiberman, Entertainment Weekly*

'High-style nonsense.' – *Sight and Sound*

'Slick and studiously cool—with plenty of visual flourishes but not too much soul.' – *J. Hoberman, Village Voice*

October ****
USSR 1927 95m approx bw silent
Sovkino

In 1917, the Kerensky regime is overthrown by the Bolsheviks.
A propaganda masterpiece whose images have all too often been mistaken and used for genuine newsreel. Cinematically, an undoubted masterpiece.
w Sergei M. Eisenstein, Grigory Alexandrov
d *Sergei* M. *Eisenstein* *ph* Edouard Tissé, V. Popov

The October Man **
GB 1947 98m bw
GFD/Two Cities (Eric Ambler)

After an accident which causes a head injury and subsequent depression, a lonely man staying at a small hotel is suspected of a local murder.
Nice blend of character study, mystery and suspense, with excellent attention to suburban detail.
w *Eric Ambler* *d* *Roy Baker* *ph* *Erwin Hillier*
m Kenneth Pakeman *md* Muir Mathieson
ad Alex Vetchinsky *ed* Alan L. Jaggs
☆ *John Mills* (Jim Ackland), Joan Greenwood (Jenny Carden), Edward Chapman (Mr Peachey), Kay Walsh (Molly), Catherine Lacey (Miss Selby), Joyce Carey (Mrs Vinton), Adrianne Allen (Joyce Carden), Felix Aylmer (Dr Martin), Frederick Piper (Godby), Patrick Holt (Harry), Juliet Mills (Little Girl)

'This film of psychological suspense tells its complicated story with complete clarity, but it is mainly to be noted for its settings.' – *Basil Wright, 1972*

'A new type of thriller in which tension is heightened by the vivid realism of its setting and the complete credibility of its characters.' – *Reynolds News*

October Moth
GB 1959 54m bw
Independent Artists

A mentally retarded farmhand goes berserk after causing a fatal car crash.
Unattractive and singularly pointless little melodrama which neither edifies nor entertains.
wd John Kruse *ph* Michael Reed *m* Humphrey Searle
☆ Lana Morris, Lee Patterson, Peter Dyneley, Robert Cawdron

'A boy who could see the future. A father stuck in the past. A dream that wouldn't die.'
October Sky
US 1999 107m DeLuxe Panavision
Universal Pictures (Charles Gordon, Larry Franco)

Inspired by the sight of Sputnik, a teenager in a coal-mining town decides to build his own rocket with a little help from his friends.
Based on the biography of a man who became a NASA engineer, this is a gently nostalgic flag-waver of small-town Americana in the 50s, amiable but forgettable.
w Lewis Colick *book* *Rocket Boys* by Homer H. Hickam Jnr *d* Joe Johnston *ph* Fred Murphy *m* Mark Isham *pd* Barry Robinson *ed* Robert Dalva
☆ Jake Gyllenhaal (Homer Hickam), Chris Cooper (John Hickam), Laura Dern (Miss Riley), Chris Owen (Quentin), William Lee Scott (Roy Lee), Chad Lindberg (O'Dell), Natalie Canerday (Elsie Hickam), Scott Miles (Jim Hickam), Randy Stripling (Leon Bolden), Chris Ellis (Principal Turner)

'A feelgood movie of some power.' – *Empire*

'A Cruise to Hell.'
Octopus
US 2000 100m colour
Nu Image (David Varod, Danny Lerner, Boaz Davidson)

An American nuclear submarine with a dangerous terrorist on board is attacked by a giant, mutant octopus.
Feeble attempt to combine a spy thriller with horror; the cast compensate for its cheapness by over-acting.
w Michael D. Weiss *story* Boaz Davidson *d* John Eyres *ph* Adolfo Bartoli *m* Marco Marinangeli *pd* Carlos DaSilva *ed* Amanda I. Kirpaul *sp* Willie Botha; Mark Harris
☆ Jay Harrington (Roy Turner), Ravil Isyanov (Casper), David Beecroft (Captain Shaw), Carolyn Lowery (Dr Lisa Finch), Ricco Ross (Brickman), Jeff Nuttall (Henry Campbell), George Stanchev (Salvanto), Martin McDougall (Taylor)

Octopussy
GB 1983 131m Technicolor Panavision
Eon/Danjaq (Albert R. Broccoli)

James Bond takes on an evil Afghan prince and a glamorous woman who plan between them to plunder Tsarist treasures.
Bond at the end of his tether: such far-stretched adventures have become merely a tedious way of passing the time.
w George MacDonald Fraser, Richard Maibaum, Michael G. Wilson *d* John Glen *ph* Alan Hume *m* John Barry *pd* Peter Lamont
☆ Roger Moore, Maud Adams, Louis Jourdan, Kristina Wayborn, Kabir Bedi, Desmond Llewelyn, Lois Maxwell

'As the films drift further and further into self-parody, no one seems to notice and no one (at any rate in box office terms) seems to mind.' – *Nick Roddick, MFB*

The Odd Couple **
US 1968 105m Technicolor Panavision
Paramount (Howard W. Koch)

A fussy divorce-shocked newswriter moves in with his sloppy sportscaster friend, and they get on each other's nerves.
Straight filming of a funny play which sometimes seems lost on the wide screen, but the performances are fine.
w *Neil Simon* *play* Neil Simon *d* Gene Saks *ph* Robert B. Hauser *m* Neal Hefti
☆ *Jack Lemmon, Walter Matthau*, John Fiedler, Herb Edelman, David Sheiner, Larry Haines, Monica Evans, Carole Sheely, Iris Adrian

OSCAR (WALTER MATTHAU): 'I can't take it anymore, Felix. I'm crackin' up. Everything you do irritates me. And when you're not here, the things I know you're gonna do when you come in irritate me. You leave me little notes on my pillow. I told you 158 times I cannot stand little notes on my pillow. "We are all out of cornflakes, F.U." It took me three hours to figure out that F.U. was Felix Ungar. It's not your fault, Felix. It's a rotten combination, that's all.'

Neil Simon

The Odd Couple II
US 1998 96m DeLuxe Panavision
UIP/Paramount (Neil Simon, Robert W. Cort, David Madden)

The adventures of two fathers, whose children are marrying one another, on the road to Los Angeles.
Not content with the derivative Grumpy Men *series, Lemmon and Matthau revive their earlier, grumpiest success; but it lacks any semblance of life.*
w Neil Simon *d* Howard Deutch *ph* Jamie Anderson *m* Alan Silvestri *pd* Dan Bishop *ed* Seth Flaum
☆ Jack Lemmon, Walter Matthau, Christine Baranski, Barnard Hughes, Jonathan Silverman, Jean Smart, Lisa Waltz

'The film feels like an extended television episode.' – *Sight and Sound*

The Odd Job
GB 1978 86m colour
Charisma/Steve O'Rourke (Mark Forstater, Graham Chapman)

A husband, upset because his wife has left him, hires an odd-job man to kill him; then his wife returns...
Listless comedy that lacks the necessary invention or style to be funny.
w Bernard McKenna, Graham Chapman *d* Peter Medak *ph* Ken Hodges *m* Howard Blake *ad* Tony Curtis *ed* Barrie Vince
☆ Graham Chapman, David Jason, Simon Williams, Diana Quick, Edward Hardwicke, Bill Paterson, Michael Elphick, Joe Melia, Carolyn Seymour, Richard O'Brien

Odd Man Out ***
GB 1946 115m bw
GFD/Two Cities (Carol Reed)
US title: *Gang War*

An IRA gunman, wounded and on the run in Belfast, is helped and hindered by a variety of people.
Superbly crafted but rather empty dramatic charade, visually and emotionally memorable but with nothing whatever to say.

w F. L. Green, R. C. Sherriff *novel* F. L. Green *d* *Carol Reed* *ph* *Robert Krasker* *m* William Alwyn *ad* Roger Furse *ed* Fergus McDonnell
☆ *James Mason* (Johnny), *Robert Newton* (Lukey), *Kathleen Ryan* (Kathleen), *F. J. McCormick* (Shell), Cyril Cusack (Pat), Robert Beatty (Dennis), Fay Compton (Rosie), Dan O'Herlihy (Nolan), Denis O'Dea (Head Constable), Maureen Delany (Theresa), Joseph Tomelty (Carby), William Hartnell (Barman), Beryl Measor (Maudie)

'The story seems to ramify too much, to go on too long, and at its unluckiest to go arty. Yet detail by detail *Odd Man Out* is made with great skill and imaginativeness and with a depth of ardour that is very rare.' – *James Agee*

'Quite simply the most imaginative film yet produced in England, comparable with *Quai des Brumes* and *Le Jour se Lève*.' – *William Whitebait, New Statesman*

Fergus McDonnell
British picture

Odds against Tomorrow *
US 1959 96m bw
UA/Harbel (Robert Wise)

Three crooks plan to rob a bank, but two of them cause the enterprise to fail because of their own racist hatreds.
Sour, glossy crime thriller with elementary social significance.
w John O. Killens (Abraham Polonsky), Nelson Gidding *novel* William P. McGivern *d* *Robert Wise* *ph* *Joseph Brun* *m* John Lewis
☆ Robert Ryan, Harry Belafonte, *Ed Begley*, Shelley Winters, Gloria Grahame, Will Kuluva, Kim Hamilton

'An efficient but unnecessarily portentous thriller.' – *Penelope Houston*

† Abraham Polonsky was excluded from the screenwriting credit because he was blacklisted at the time.

Ode to Billy Joe *
US 1976 106m CFI color
Columbia-Warner/Max Baer Productions (Max Baer, Roger Camras)

In Mississippi in the early 1950s a 17-year-old youth, who is in love with a 15-year-old girl, is driven to kill himself.
Based on the hit song of the 1960s by Bobbie Gentry, a melodramatic account of the frustrations of growing up in a small town.
w Herman Raucher *d* Max Baer *ph* Michel Hugo *m* Michel Legrand *ad* Philip Jefferies *ed* Frank E. Morriss
☆ Robby Benson, Glynnis O'Connor, Joan Hotchkis, Sandy McPeak, James Best, Terence Goodman, Becky Brown

'The ultimate tribute earned by the film is that it retrospectively makes Bobbie Gentry's song sound still better – the distillation of a complex experience charted by the film rather than just an isolated epigram and postscript framing it.' – *Jonathan Rosenbam, MFB*

'Unusually refreshing and moving' – *Films and Filming*

The Odessa File **
GB 1974 129m Eastmancolor Panavision
Columbia/Domino/Oceanic (John Woolf)

In 1963, a young German reporter tracks down a gang of neo-Nazis.
Elaborate but uninvolving suspenser with several excellent cliffhanging sequences and a let-down climax.
w Kenneth Ross, George Markstein *novel* Frederick Forsyth *d* Ronald Neame *ph* Oswald Morris *m* Andrew Lloyd Webber *pd* Rolf Zehetbauer
☆ *Jon Voight*, Maria Schell, Maximilian Schell, Mary Tamm, Derek Jacobi, Peter Jeffrey, *Noel Willman*

'As resistible a parcel of sedative entertainment as ever induced narcolepsy in a healthy man.' – *Benny Green, Punch*

Odette *
GB 1950 123m bw
Herbert Wilcox

A Frenchwoman with an English husband spies for the French resistance, is caught and tortured.
Deglamorized true life spy story with emotional moments let down by generally uninspired handling, also by the too well-known image of its star, who however gives a remarkable performance.
w Warren Chetham Strode *book* Jerrard Tickell *d* Herbert Wilcox *ph* Max Greene *m* Anthony Collins
☆ Anna Neagle, Trevor Howard, Peter Ustinov, Marius Goring

'As a work of art, pretty flat ... though innumerable people will find it moving and impressive, they will have done the work themselves.' – *Richard Mallett, Punch*

'She always gets a part.'
Odishon *
Japan 1999 115m colour
Metro Tartan/Omega (Akemi Suyama, Satoshi Hukushima)

aka: *Audition*
A middle-aged widower and TV producer auditions actresses as a means of finding a new wife, and gets more than he has bargained for.
Chilling and ultimately extremely violent and gruesome drama that opens in a leisurely fashion before overturning its audience's expectations, climaxing with a tortured, hallucinatory finale that many may find unwatchable.
w Daisuke Tengan *novel* Ryu Murakami *d* Takashi Miike *ph* Hideo Yamamoto *m* Koji Endo *pd* Tatsuo Ozeki *ed* Yasushi Shimamura
☆ Ryo Ishibashi (Shigeharu Aoyama), Eihi Shiina (Asami Yamasaki), Jun Kunimura (Yoshikawa), Miyuki Matsuda (Ryoko Aoyama), Ren Osugi (Shibata), Tetsu Sawaki (Shigehiko Aoyama), Renji Ishibashi (Old Man)

'The best-disguised psychotronic splatter flick in recent memory... a lethally poised Venus flytrap of a movie.' – *Dennis Lim, Village Voice*

'The grimmest exploitation of sadistic violence I have seen in months... pornographic.' – *Alexander Walker, London Evening Standard*

Odongo
GB 1956 85m Technicolor Cinemascope
Warwick/Columbia
A collector of animals for zoos runs into various kinds of trouble during an African safari.
Elementary jungle adventure centring on a small Sabu-like jungle boy. For the now extinct family audience.
wd John Gilling *ph* Ted Moore *m* George Melachrino
☆ Macdonald Carey, Rhonda Fleming, Juma, Eleanor Summerfield, Francis de Wolff, Earl Cameron

Oedipus Rex **
Italy/Morocco 1967 110m Technicolor Panoramica
Arco/Somafis

original title: *Edipo Re*
Oedipus, returning to his home of Thebes, suffers through unwittingly killing his father and marrying his mother.
Austerely involving adaptation of the Greek tragedy, sandwiched between scenes set in modern Italy.
wd Pier Paolo Pasolini *play* Sophocles *ph* Giuseppe Ruzzolini *ad* Luigi Scaccianoce *ed* Nino Baragli
☆ Franco Citti, Silvana Mangano, Carmelo Bene, Julian Beck, Pier Paolo Pasolini, Alida Valli, Ninetto Davoli

Of Freaks and Men **
Russia 1998 94m sepia/bw
Metro Tartan/STV/Soiuzkino (Sergei Selyanov, Oleg Botogov)

original title: *Po Urodov i Liudei*
In St. Petersburg in the early 1900s, a pornographer and his assistant destroy two families by exposing them to photographs of scenes of flagellation.
A genuinely original and very strange movie, tinted to look like old photographs and dealing with the corruption and liberation that photography and film brings in its wake.
d Alexei Balabanov *ph* Sergei Astakhov *pd* Vera Zelinskaya *ed* Marina Lipartia *cos* Nadya Vasilyeva
☆ Sergei Makovetskii (Johan), Dinara Drukarova (Lisa), Lika Nevolina (Ekaterina Kirillovna), Victor Sukhorukov (Victor Ivanovich), Alyesha De (Kolya), Chingiz Tsydendabayev (Tolya), Vadim Prokhorov (Pytilov), Alexandr Mezentsev (Dr Stasov), Darya Lesnikova (Grunya), Igor Shibanov (Radlov), Tatyana Polonskaya (Darya)

'A film of pungent and distinctive flavour, maybe not to all tastes; but, for its originality and style, it must be seen.' – *Peter Bradshaw, Guardian*

'Thought-provoking, funny, disturbing, utterly involving.' – *Steven Gaydos, Variety*

Of Human Bondage **
US 1934 83m bw
(RKO)

A well-to-do Englishman is brought down by his infatuation with a sluttish waitress.
This version of the famous novel brought Bette Davis to prominence but is not otherwise any better than the others.
w Lester Cohen *novel* W. Somerset Maugham *d* John Cromwell *ph* Henry W. Gerrard *m* Max Steiner *ad* Van Nest Polglase, Carroll Clark *ed* William Morgan
☆ *Leslie Howard*, *Bette Davis*, Frances Dee, Reginald Owen, Reginald Denny, Kay Johnson, Alan Hale

'Stars and the novel rep will have to carry a lethargic romance.' – *Variety*

'A totally obtuse concoction, serving only to demonstrate how untalented an actress Bette Davis was before she perfected those camp mannerisms.' – *John Simon, 1967*

Of Human Bondage *
US 1946 105m bw
Warner (Henry Blanke)
A doctor suffers through his infatuation with a common waitress.
Good-looking but thoroughly dull remake of Maugham's novel.
w Catherine Turney *novel* Somerset Maugham *d* Edmund Goulding *ph* Peverell Marley *m* Erich Wolfgang Korngold *ad* Henry Kelso, Hugh Reticker *ed* Clarence Kolster
☆ Paul Henreid, Eleanor Parker, Alexis Smith, Edmund Gwenn, Patric Knowles, Janis Paige, Henry Stephenson

Of Human Bondage
GB 1964 99m bw
MGM/Seven Arts (James Woolf)

An upper-class doctor is brought low by his relationship with a waitress.
Disastrous remake with both star roles miscast.
w Bryan Forbes *d* Henry Hathaway, Ken Hughes *ph* Oswald Morris *m* Ron Goodwin *pd* John Box
☆ Laurence Harvey, Kim Novak, Nanette Newman, Roger Livesey, Jack Hedley, Robert Morley, Siobhan McKenna, Ronald Lacey

Of Human Hearts *
US 1938 100m bw
MGM (John Considine Jnr)
A 19th-century idyll of middle America and especially of a preacher and his wayward son.
Curious all-American moral fable, splendidly made and acted.
w Bradbury Foote *novel* *Benefits Forgot* by Honoré Morrow *d* Clarence Brown *ph* Clyde de Vinna *m* Herbert Stothart
☆ Walter Huston, James Stewart, Beulah Bondi, Gene Reynolds, Charles Coburn, Guy Kibbee, John Carradine, Gene Lockhart, Ann Rutherford

'Long on narrative and short on romance ... the box office reaction is likely to dampen the enthusiasm of those who believe the film possesses any wide public appeal.' – *Variety*

† The title was chosen via a radio contest, the winner being a high-school student.

Beulah Bondi

Of Love and Desire
US 1963 97m DeLuxe
New World (Victor Stoloff)
An engineer in Mexico takes up with the boss's nymphomaniac sister.
Unwise sensationalist vehicle for an ageing leading lady who is past such carryings on.
w Laslo Gorag, Richard Rush *d* Richard Rush *ph* Alex Phillips *m* Ronald Stein
☆ Merle Oberon, Steve Cochran, John Agar, Curt Jurgens

'I'm decent, I tell ya! Nobody's got the right to call me names!'
'The picture Hollywood said could never be made!'
Of Mice and Men ***
US 1939 107m bw
Hal Roach (Lewis Milestone)

An itinerant worker looks after his mentally retarded cousin, a giant who doesn't know his own strength.
A strange and unexpected tragedy which has strength and is very persuasively made but seems somehow unnecessary.
w Eugene Solow *novel* John Steinbeck *d* *Lewis Milestone* *ph* *Norbert Brodine* *m* Aaron Copland
☆ *Burgess Meredith*, *Lon Chaney Jnr*, *Betty Field*, Charles Bickford, Roman Bohnen, Bob Steele, Noah Beery Jnr

'The film is excellently acted by everyone ... there are, mercifully, no stars to intrude their tedious flat personalities into this picture of life. It is a picture which, for all its grief, is not depressing; and if it should be said that this is no time for adding to one's own melancholy, let me reply that it is sometimes well not to lose from sight the individual pity of the lives of men.' – *Dilys Powell*

best picture; Aaron Copland

'We have a dream. Someday we'll have a little house and a couple of acres. A place to call home.'
Of Mice and Men *
US 1992 111m DeLuxe
UIP/MGM (Russ Smith, Gary Sinise)

While dreaming of better times, an itinerant farm worker tries to keep his companion, a dim but well-meaning giant, out of trouble.
Despite the good intentions of those involved, a strangely unemotional and inert remake.
w Horton Foote *novel* John Steinbeck *d* Gary Sinise *ph* Kenneth MacMillan *m* Mark Isham *pd* David Gropman *ed* Robert L. Sinise
☆ John Malkovich, Gary Sinise, Ray Walston, Casey Siemaszko, Sherilyn Fenn, John Terry

'Little more than a lacklustre ramble through an old favourite.' – *Geoffrey Macnab, Sight and Sound*

Ofelas: see *Pathfinder*

Off and Running
US 1991 90m colour
Rank/Aaron Russo Entertainment (Aaron Russo, William C. Carraro)
An actress flees from the killer of her fiancé while she tries to discover why he was murdered.
Misfiring romantic comedy with some violent action thrown in for bad measure.
w Mitch Glazer *d* Edward Bianchi *ph* Andrzej Bartkowiak *m* Mason Daring *ad* Norman E. Weber *ed* Rick Shaine
☆ Cyndi Lauper, David Keith, Johnny Pinto, David Thornton, Richard Belzer, José Perez, Anita Morris, Hazen Gifford

Off Beat
US 1986 92m DeLuxe
Buena Vista/Touchstone/Ufland/Roth/Ladd

An accident-prone librarian, persuaded by his policeman friend to take his place at a charity dance competition, falls in love with a female cop and continues with his impersonation.
A pleasant, though undistinguished romantic comedy, undermining macho posturings.
w Mark Medoff *story* Dezso Magyar *d* Michael Dinner *ph* Carlo DiPalma *m* James Horner *pd* Woods Mackintosh *ed* Dede Allen, Angelo Corrao
☆ Judge Reinhold, Meg Tilly, Cleavant Derricks, Harvey Keitel, Joe Mantegna, Jacques D'Amboise, Amy Wright, John Turturro, James Tolkan, Fred Gwynne

Off Limits: see *Saigon*

Off Limits
US 1953 89m bw
Paramount (Harry Tugend)
GB title: *Military Policemen*
A boxing manager trains a young fighter in the military police.
Flat star comedy.

w Hal Kanter, Jack Sher *d* George Marshall
ph *Peverell Marley* *m* Van Cleave
☆ Bob Hope, Mickey Rooney, Marilyn Maxwell, Marvin Miller

Off the Beaten Track: see *Behind the Eight Ball*

Off the Dole
GB 1935 89m bw
Mancunian
An amateur detective catches burglars.
Artless comedy shot on a minuscule budget; it helped to make George Formby a star.
wd *Arthur Mertz*
☆ George Formby, Beryl Formby, Constance Shotter, Dan Young

Off the Record
US 1939 71m bw
Warner
A star reporter exposes the mob's use of youngsters as spotters in the gambling racket.
Predictable crime support.
w Niven Busch, Lawrence Kimble, Earl Baldwin
d James Flood
☆ Pat O'Brien, Joan Blondell, Bobby Jordan, Alan Baxter, Morgan Conway
'Stereotype dualler.' – *Variety*

Offbeat *
GB 1960 72m bw
British Lion/Northiam (M. Smedley Aston)
An MI5 undercover man finds himself sympathizing with a gang of robbers and falling in love with one of them.
Sharply observed thriller which gets a bit glum in dealing with its rather contrived 'switch'.
w Peter Barnes *d* Cliff Owen *ph* Geoffrey Faithfull *m* Ken Jones
☆ William Sylvester, Mai Zetterling, Anthony Dawson, John Meillon, John Phillips, Victor Brooks, Joseph Furst, Neil McCarthy, Harry Baird

The Offence *
GB 1972 113m DeLuxe
United Artists/Tantallon (Denis O'Dell)
A tough police inspector bullies a suspected child molester.
Tortuous psychological study on the fringe of hysteria; good performances.
w John Hopkins *play* *This Story of Yours* by John Hopkins *d* Sidney Lumet *ph* Gerry Fisher
m Harrison Birtwistle
☆ Sean Connery, Trevor Howard, Ian Bannen, Vivien Merchant

Offending Angels
GB 2000 93m colour
Guerrilla Films/Pants (Andrew Rajan)
Guardian angels give hope for the future to two young men, addicts of drugs and pornography.
Muddled metaphysical fable of no discernible purpose.
w Andrew Rajan, Tim Moyler *d* Andrew Rajan
ph Alvin Leong *m* Martin Ward *ad* Annie Gosney *ed* Roger Burgess, Catherine Fletcher
☆ Susannah Harker (Paris), Andrew Lincoln (Sam), Shaun Parkes (Zeke), Andrew Rajan (Baggy), Paula O'Grady (Alison), Marion Bailey (Mentor), Michael Cochrane (Mentor), Sophie Dix (Mandy)
'An excruciating British fantasy romcom, where the direction's out to lunch and the script's three or four drafts away from anything usable.' – *Peter Bradshaw, Guardian*

Office Killer
US 1997 83m Technicolor
Strand/Good Machine/Kardana/Swinsky (Christine Vachon, Pamela Koffler)
Problems escalate on a magazine when a copy editor accidentally electrocutes a writer and discovers that she enjoys killing.
Dimly lit experimental movie, directed by a fashionable photographer, that has all the attraction of the most inept 'B' movie ever.
w Elise MacAdam, Tom Kalin, Todd Haynes
d Cindy Sherman *ph* Russell Fine *m* Evan Lurie
pd Kevin Thompson *ed* Merril Stern
☆ Carol Kane, Molly Ringwald, Jeanne Tripplehorn, Barbara Sukowa, Michael Imperioli, David Thornton, Mike Hodge, Alice Drummond
'Deep-sixed by klutzy direction, mostly sophomoric performances and a script so flat it isn't even laughably bad, *Office Killer* sinks like a stone.' – *Derek Elley, Variety*
† The film was a low-budget production, costing $300,000.

Office Space **
US 1999 89m DeLuxe
TCF (Michael Rotenberg, Daniel Rappaport)
After a visit to an occupational hypnotherapist goes wrong, a downhearted computer programmer ceases to care about his boring job.
Witty demolition of corporate culture, deftly skewering all the petty nuisances of office routine.
wd Mike Judge *animated shorts* *Milton* by Mike Judge *ph* Tim Suhrstedt *m* John Frizzell
pd Edward McAvoy *ed* David Rennie
☆ Ron Livingston (Peter Gibbons), Jennifer Aniston (Joanne), Stephen Root (Milton), Gary Cole (Bill Lumbergh), John C. McGinley (Bob Slydell), Diedrich Bader (Lawrence), David Herman (Michael Bolton), Ajay Naidu (Samir), Michael McShane (Dr Swanson), Richard Riehle (Tom Smykowski)
'This satirical comedy about white-collar wage-slavery is amusing and accessible enough to have wide-ranging appeal.' – *Joe Leydon, Variety*

An Officer and a Gentleman *
US 1982 126m Metrocolor
Paramount/Lorimar (Martin Elfand)
A potential officer suffers thirteen weeks of agony at the Naval Aviation Officer Candidate School.
Old-hat stuff given a fresh look and some smart acting.
w Douglas Day Stewart *d* Taylor Hackford
ph Donald Thorin *m* Jack Nitzsche *pd* Philip M. Jefferies
☆ Richard Gere, Debra Winger, *Louis Gossett Jnr*, David Keith, Lisa Blount, Lisa Eilbacher
'Shamelessly manipulative, but whether the manipulations are funny, dramatic or tear-jerking, it knows exactly what and how to deliver.' – *Sunday Telegraph*
† John Travolta turned down the lead because 'I was just more interested in pursuing my actual life as a jet pilot than my film life as a jet pilot'.
Louis Gossett Jnr (as supporting actor); song 'Up Where We Belong' by Jack Nitzsche, Buffy Sainte-Marie (*m*), Will Jennings (*ly*)
Debra Winger; original screenplay; editing (Peter Zinner); music

The Officers' Ward: see *La Chambre des Officiers*

The Official Version **
Argentina 1985 115m Eastmancolor
Virgin/Almi/HistoriasCinematograficas/Progress Communications (Marcelo Pineyro)
original title: *La Historia Official*
aka: *The Official Story*
A teacher begins to realize that her adopted daughter was probably the child of parents murdered by the regime under which she lives.
Strong and moving drama of the stirrings of a political conscience.
w Aida Bortnik, Luis Puenzo *d* Luis Puenzo
ph Felix Monti *m* Atilio Stampone *ad* Abel Facello *ed* Juan Carlos Macias
☆ Hector Alterio, Norma Aleandro, Chela Ruiz, Chunchuna Villafane, Hugo Arana, Patricio Contreras
best foreign film
screenplay

Offret: see *The Sacrifice*

Oggi a Me ... Domani a Te!: see *Today It's Me, Tomorrow You!*

Oh Dad, Poor Dad, Mamma's Hung You in the Closet and I'm Feelin' So Sad
US 1966 86m Technicolor
Paramount/Seven Arts (Ray Stark, Stanley Rubin)
A dead father helps his son to get married despite his mother's influence to the contrary.
Zany black comedy which never really worked on the stage, let alone the screen.
w Ian Bernard *play* Arthur Kopit *d* Richard Quine *ph* Geoffrey Unsworth *m* Neal Hefti
☆ Rosalind Russell, Jonathan Winters, Robert Morse, Hugh Griffith, Barbara Harris, Lionel Jeffries, Cyril Delevanti, Hiram Sherman

Oh, Daddy!
GB 1935 77m bw
Gaumont-British/Gainsborough (Michael Balcon)
Aristocratic and abstemious members of the League of Purity are converted to pleasure by a trip to London.
A not very successful transfer of a stage play to the screen, though the stars occasionally show why they were so admired by their theatre audiences.
w Michael Powell, Austin Melford *play* Franz Arnold, Ernst Bach *d* Graham Cutts, Austin Melford *ph* Mutz Greenbaum (Max Greene)
m/ly Sam Coslow *md* Louis Levy *ad* Ernö Metzner *ed* Charles Frend
☆ Leslie Henson, Frances Day, Robertson Hare, Barry Mackay, Marie Löhr, Alfred Drayton, Tony de Lungo, Daphne Courtney

Oh Doctor
US 1937 67m bw
Universal
A rich hypochondriac is the target of confidence tricksters.
Moderate star comedy.
d Edmund Grainger
☆ Edward Everett Horton, Donrue Leighton, Eve Arden, Thurston Hall, William Demarest
'Smooth dialogue keeps this hokey picture from going completely corkscrew.' – *Variety*

Oh! For a Man!: see *Will Success Spoil Rock Hunter?*

'It's an almighty laugh!'
Oh, God *
US 1977 104m Technicolor
Warner (Jerry Weintraub)
A bewildered supermarket manager is enlisted by God to prove to the world that it can only work if people try.
Overlong but generally amiable reversion to the supernatural farces of the forties: its success seems to show that people again need this kind of comfort.
w Larry Gelbart *novel* Avery Corman *d* Carl Reiner *ph* Victor Kemper *m* Jack Elliott
☆ *George Burns*, John Denver, Ralph Bellamy, Donald Pleasence, Teri Garr, William Daniels, Barnard Hughes, Paul Sorvino, Barry Sullivan, Dinah Shore, Jeff Corey, David Ogden Stiers
'Undeniably funny and almost impossible to dislike.' – *Tom Milne, MFB*
'Basically a single-joke movie: George Burns is God in a football cap.' – *Pauline Kael, New Yorker*
Larry Gelbart

Oh God Book Two
US 1980 94m Technicolor
Warner (Gilbert Cates)
God enlists a child to remind people that he is still around.
Crass sequel with sentiment replacing jokes.
w Josh Greenfeld, Hal Goldman, Fred S. Fox, Seaman Jacobs, Melissa Miller *d* Gilbert Cates
ph Ralph Woolsey *m* Charles Fox *pd* Preston Ames *ed* Peter E. Berger
☆ George Burns, Suzanne Pleshette, David Birney, Louanne, Howard Duff, Hans Conried, Wilfrid Hyde-White

Oh God, You Devil
US 1984 96m Technicolor
Warner (Robert M. Sherman)
A struggling musician sells his soul to the devil in exchange for success.
A comic version of Faust, appended to the two films in which George Burns played God; he now puts on the other hat to fairly, but not very, comic effect.
w Andrew Bergman *d* Paul Bogart *ph* King Baggot *m* David Shire *pd* Peter Wooley
ed Andy Zall
☆ George Burns, Ted Wass, Ron Silver, Roxanne Hart, Eugene Roche

Oh Heavenly Dog
US 1980 103m DeLuxe
Mulberry Square/TCF
A private eye is reincarnated as a dog and solves his own murder.
Witless fantasy comedy, an uncredited remake of You Never Can Tell *which also rates as a Benji movie with curious additions of sex and profanity. A total muddle.*
w Rod Browning, Joe Camp *d* Joe Camp
☆ Chevy Chase, Jane Seymour, Omar Sharif, Robert Morley, Alan Sues

Oh Men! Oh Women!
US 1957 90m Eastmancolor Cinemascope
TCF (Nunnally Johnson)
A psychoanalyst discovers that his wife is involved with two of his patients.
Scatty Broadway comedy which strains the patience.
wd Nunnally Johnson *play* Edward Chodorov
ph Charles G. Clarke *m* Cyril Mockridge
☆ David Niven, Ginger Rogers, Dan Dailey, Barbara Rush, Tony Randall
'The ugliest sort of fun.' – *Observer*
'Cinemascope discovers a solution to the problem of filling its wide screen; the characters spend most of their time full length on the psychoanalyst's couch.' – *Sunday Times*

Oh Mr Porter ****
GB 1937 84m bw
GFD/Gainsborough (Edward Black)
The stationmaster of an Irish halt catches gun-runners posing as ghosts.
Marvellous star comedy showing this trio of comedians at their best, and especially Hay as the seedy incompetent. The plot is borrowed from The Ghost Train, *but each line and gag brings its own inventiveness. A delight of character comedy and cinematic narrative.*
w *Marriott Edgar, Val Guest, J. O. C. Orton*
story Frank Launder *d* *Marcel Varnel* *ph* Arthur Crabtree *md* Louis Levy
☆ *Will Hay, Moore Marriott, Graham Moffatt*, Dave O'Toole, Dennis Wyndham
'That rare phenomenon: a film comedy without a dud scene.' – *Peter Barnes, 1964*
'Behind it lie the gusty uplands of the British music hall tradition, whose rich soil the British film industry is at last beginning to exploit.' – *Basil Wright*

Oh Rosalinda!
GB 1955 105m Technicolor Cinemascope
ABP/Powell and Pressburger
A playboy in four-power Vienna plays a practical joke on four officers and the flirtatious wife of one of them.
Lumbering attempt to modernize Die Fledermaus, *unsuitably wide-screened and totally lacking the desired Lubitsch touch. A monumental step in the decline of these producers, and a sad stranding of a brilliant cast.*
wd Michael Powell, Emeric Pressburger
ph Christopher Challis *m* Johann Strauss
ad Hein Heckroth
☆ *Anton Walbrook*, Michael Redgrave, Anthony Quayle, Mel Ferrer, Dennis Price, Ludmilla Tcherina

Oh What a Lovely War **
GB 1969 144m Technicolor Panavision
Paramount/Accord (Brian Duffy, Richard Attenborough)
A fantasia with music on World War I.
A brave all-star attempt which comes off only in patches; the pier apparatus from the stage show really doesn't translate, the piece only works well when it becomes cinematic, as in the recruiting song and the final track-back from the graves. But there are many pleasures, as well as yawns, along the way.
w Len Deighton *stage show* Joan Littlewood, Charles Chilton *d* Richard Attenborough
ph *Gerry Turpin* *m* various *md* Alfred Ralston
pd *Don Ashton*
☆ Ralph Richardson, Meriel Forbes, John Gielgud, Kenneth More, John Clements, Paul Daneman, Joe Melia, Jack Hawkins, John Mills, Maggie Smith, Michael Redgrave, Laurence Olivier, Susannah York, Dirk Bogarde, Phyllis Calvert and also Vanessa Redgrave
'This musical lampoon is meant to stir your sentiments, evoke nostalgia, and make you react to the obscenity of battles and bloodshed, and apparently it does all that for some people.' – *New Yorker, 1977*

'A naïve, sentimental, populist affair, using many (too many) clever devices yet making the same old simplistic statements.' – *John Simon*

'An overlong and rarely cinematic musical satire that ladles its anti-war message on by the bucketload.' – *Time Out, 1984*

cinematography; production design; Laurence Olivier

Oh, What a Night
Canada 1992 93m colour
Norstar (Peter Simpson)

In the 50s, a teenager moves with his father to live in Ontario and becomes infatuated with a married woman.
Routine drama of teenage fumblings to a soundtrack of gentler hits of the period.
w Richard Nielsen *d* Eric Till *ph* Brian R. R. Hebb *m* Ian Thomas *ad* David Moe *ed* Susan Shipton
☆ Corey Haim, Barbara Williams, Keir Dullea, Genevieve Bujold, Robbie Coltrane, Andrew Miller

Oh You Beautiful Doll *
US 1949 93m Technicolor
TCF (George Jessel)
Fred Fisher wants to write opera but is more successful with pop songs.
Standard turn-of-the-century biopic, very pleasantly handled and performed.
w Albert and George Lewis *d* John M. Stahl *ph* Harry Jackson *md* Alfred Newman
☆ S. Z. Sakall, Mark Stevens, June Haver, Charlotte Greenwood, Jay C. Flippen, Gale Robbins

O'Hara's Wife
US 1982 87m DeLuxe
David-Panzer

A widower is helped by his wife's ghost.
Rather icky sentimental comedy.
w James Nasella, William S. Bartman *d* William S. Bartman
☆ Ed Asner, Mariette Hartley, Jodie Foster, Perry Lang, Tom Bosley, Ray Walston

Oil for the Lamps of China *
US 1935 98m bw
Warner (Robert Lord)
The career in China of an American oil company representative.
Adequate general audience picture from a bestseller.
w Laird Doyle *novel* Alice Tisdale Hobart *d* Mervyn Le Roy *ph* Tony Gaudio *m* Heinz Roemheld *md* Leo F. Forbstein
☆ Pat O'Brien, Josephine Hutchinson, Jean Muir, Lyle Talbot, Arthur Byron, John Eldredge, Henry O'Neill, Donald Crisp

'Long and choppy version of a best-seller novel. Little marquee strength will probably mean light returns.' – *Variety*

'Far above average in performance, direction and content.' – *John Baxter, 1968*

† Remade 1941 as *Law of the Tropics*.

Okay America
US 1932 80m bw
Universal
GB title: *Penalty of Fame*
A brash reporter saves a politician's daughter from kidnapping.
Okay melodrama remade in 1939 as Risky Business.
w William Anthony McGuire *d* Tay Garnett
☆ Lew Ayres, Maureen O'Sullivan, Louis Calhern, Walter Catlett, Edward Arnold

OK Connery: see *Operation Kid Brother*

'A picture straight from the heart of America!'
Oklahoma! **
US 1955 143m Technicolor Todd-AO
Magna/Rodgers and Hammerstein (Arthur Hornblow Jnr)

A cowboy wins his girl despite the intervention of a sinister hired hand.
Much of the appeal of the musical was in its simple timeworn story and stylized sets; the film makes the first merely boring and the latter are replaced by standard scenery, not even of Oklahoma. The result is efficient rather than startling or memorable.
w Sonya Levien, William Ludwig *book* Oscar Hammerstein *play* *Green Grow the Rushes* by Lynn Riggs *d* Fred Zinnemann *ph* Robert Surtees *m* Robert Russell Bennett, Jay Blackton, Adolph Deutsch *pd* Oliver Smith *ed* Gene Ruggiero, George Boemler *songs* Richard Rodgers, Oscar Hammerstein II
☆ Gordon MacRae, Shirley Jones, Rod Steiger, Gloria Grahame, Charlotte Greenwood, Gene Nelson, Eddie Albert
♫ 'Oh, What a Beautiful Mornin''; 'The Surrey with the Fringe on Top'; 'Kansas City'; 'I Cain't Say More'; 'Many a New Day'; 'People Will Say We're in Love'; 'Pore Jud'; 'Out of My Dreams'; 'The Farmer and the Cowman'; 'All or Nothing'; 'Oklahoma!'
music score
Robert Surtees; editing

'A story of wooden derricks, iron men, and a defiant woman!'
Oklahoma Crude *
US 1973 111m Technicolor
Columbia/Stanley Kramer

In 1913, a drifting oil man stops to help a girl develop her rig.
Dour, downbeat melodrama with restricted action and much bad language; within its lights quite entertaining, but odd.
w Marc Norman *d* Stanley Kramer *ph* Robert Surtees *m* Henry Mancini *pd* Alfred Sweeney
☆ Faye Dunaway, George C. Scott, John Mills, Jack Palance, Woodrow Parfrey

The Oklahoma Kid **
US 1939 80m bw
Warner (Samuel Bischoff)

During the settlement of the Cherokee Strip a cowboy avenges the unjust lynching of his father.
Competent but slightly disappointing star Western memorable for the clash in this guise of its protagonists, more usually seen as gangsters.
w Warren Duff, Robert Buckner, Edward E. Paramore *d* Lloyd Bacon *ph* James Wong Howe *m* Max Steiner
☆ *James Cagney, Humphrey Bogart*, Rosemary Lane, Donald Crisp, Harvey Stephens, Charles Middleton, Edward Pawley, Ward Bond

'Its b.o. potency will depend on Cagney's name and draw, rather than story or production, neither of which is commendable.' – *Variety*

'There's something entirely disarming about the way he has tackled horse opera, not pretending for a minute to be anything but New York's Jimmy Cagney all dressed up as a Robin Hood of the old west.' – *Frank Nugent*

The Oklahoma Woman
US 1956 72m bw SuperScope
ARC/Sunset (Roger Corman)
After six years in jail, a gunfighter returns home in search of a quiet life to find that his former girlfriend is taking over the town.
Cliché-ridden Western that follows a familiar story with no sign of enthusiasm.
w Lou Rusoff *d* Roger Corman *ph* Fred West *m* Ronald Stein *ed* Ronald Sinclair
☆ Richard Denning, Peggie Castle, Cathy Downs, Touch Connors, Martin Kingsley, Tudor Owen, Jonathan Haze, Richard Miller, Edmund Cobb

The Oklahoman
US 1956 78m DeLuxe Cinemascope
Walter Mirisch/Allied Artists

A widowed doctor becomes the subject of gossip when he takes an Indian girl for his housekeeper.
Rather curious domestic Western which erupts into action sequences but devotes too much time to talk and romance.
w Daniel B. Ullman *d* Francis D. Lyon *ph* Carl Guthrie *m* Hans Salter
☆ Joel McCrea, Barbara Hale, Brad Dexter, Gloria Talbott, Michael Pate

Old Acquaintance **
US 1943 110m bw
Warner (Henry Blanke)
Two jealous lady novelists interfere in each other's love lives.
A dated but rather splendid battle of the wild cats, with two stars fighting their way through a plush production and a rather overlong script.
w John Van Druten, Lenore Coffee *play* John Van Druten *d* Vincent Sherman *ph* Sol Polito *m* Franz Waxman
☆ *Bette Davis, Miriam Hopkins*, Gig Young, John Loder, Dolores Moran, Philip Reed, Roscoe Karns, Anne Revere

'The odd thing is that the two ladies and the director can make the whole business look fairly intelligent, detailed and plausible; and that on the screen such trash can seem, even, mature and adventurous.' – *James Agee*

'Trashy fun, on an unusually literate level.' – *New Yorker, 1978*

Old and New: see *The General Line*

Old Bones of the River *
GB 1938 90m bw
GFD/Gainsborough (Edward Black)
A teacher in Africa accidentally quells a native rising.
Tediously funny star comedy; enough said.
w Marriott Edgar, Val Guest, J. O. C. Orton *character* Edgar Wallace *d* Marcel Varnel *ph* Arthur Crabtree *m* Louis Levy *ad* Vetchinsky
☆ *Will Hay, Moore Marriott, Graham Moffatt*, Robert Adams, Jack Livesey

Old Boyfriends *
US 1978 103m Technicolor
Edward R. Pressman Productions (Paul Schrader)

A divorcee survives a nervous breakdown and goes on a journey of her past life to find out where she went wrong.
Low-key and somehow rather flat romantic odyssey, with interesting sequences and characters muted by the director's jaundiced eye.
w Paul and Leonard Schrader *d* Joan Tewkesbury *ph* William A. Fraker *m* David Shire
☆ Talia Shire, Richard Jordan, John Belushi, Keith Carradine, John Houseman, Buck Henry, Bethel Leslie

The Old Curiosity Shop *
GB 1934 95m bw
BIP (Walter C. Mycroft)
The lives of a gambler and his granddaughter are affected by a miserly dwarf.
Heavy-going Dickens novel given reasonably rich production and well enough acted; sentimentality prevented a remake until the unsuccessful Mister Quilp (qv) *in 1975.*
w Margaret Kennedy, Ralph Neale *novel* Charles Dickens *d* Thomas Bentley *ph* Claude Friese-Greene
☆ *Hay Petrie*, Ben Webster, Elaine Benson, Beatrice Thompson, Gibb McLaughlin, Reginald Purdell, Polly Ward

The Old Curiosity Shop: see *Mister Quilp (1975)*

'Beware The Night!'
The Old Dark House ****
US 1932 71m bw
Universal (Carl Laemmle Jnr)

Stranded travellers take refuge in the house of a family of eccentrics.
Marvellous horror comedy filled with superb grotesques and memorable lines, closely based on a Priestley novel but omitting the more thoughtful moments. A stylist's and connoisseur's treat.
w Benn W. Levy, R. C. Sherriff novel Benighted *by J. B. Priestley d James Whale ph Arthur Edeson ad Charles D. Hall ed* Clarence Kolster
☆ *Melvyn Douglas, Charles Laughton, Raymond Massey, Boris Karloff, Ernest Thesiger, Eva Moore*, Gloria Stuart, Lillian Bond, Brember Wills, John Dudgeon (Elspeth Dudgeon)

'Somewhat inane, it's a cinch for trick ballyhooing. Better for the nabes than the big keys.' – *Variety*

'An unbridled camp fantasy directed with great wit.' – *Charles Higham*

'Each threat as it appears is revealed to be burlap and poster paint ... despite storm, attempted rape and a remarkable final chase, the film is basically a confidence trick worked with cynical humour by a brilliant technician.' – *John Baxter, 1968*

'Basically a *jeu d'esprit* in which comedy of manners is edged into tragedy of horrors, the film never puts a foot wrong.' – *Tom Milne, MFB, 1978*

'The ghost doesn't walk in this family – it runs riot!'
The Old Dark House
GB 1962 86m Eastmancolor
Columbia/Hammer/William Castle
An American accepts an invitation to visit Femm Manor and finds the inhabitants either mad or homicidal.
A travesty which has nothing to do with the 1932 film and possesses no merit of its own. The cast is left floundering.
w Robert Dillon *d* William Castle *ph* Arthur Grant *m* Benjamin Frankel
☆ Tom Poston, Janette Scott, Robert Morley, Joyce Grenfell, Mervyn Johns, Fenella Fielding, Peter Bull

Old Dracula: see *Vampira*

'Come and meet a grand old sinner!'
Old English
US 1930 87m bw
Warner
In order to provide for his grandchildren, a financier makes certain illegal arrangements which involve his prearranged death.
Satisfying pattern play arranged for its star.
w Walter Anthony, Maude Howell *play* John Galsworthy *d* Alfred E. Green
☆ *George Arliss*, Leon Janney, Doris Lloyd, Betty Lawford, Ivan Simpson

'Will call for most careful placement by chains and indies to draw the class trade it will only appeal to.' – *Variety*

Old Enough
US 1984 91m colour
Silverfilm (Dina Silver)

During one summer, a rich girl learns about life from a poor girl.
A dull movie about the first slow stirrings of adolescence.
wd Marisa Silver *ph* Michael Ballhaus *m* Julian Marshall *pd* Jeffrey Townsend *ed* Mark Burns
☆ Sarah Boyd, Rainbow Harvest, Neill Barry, Danny Aiello, Fran Brill

Old Gringo
US 1989 120m DeLuxe
Columbia TriStar (Lois Bonfiglio)

The writer Ambrose Bierce and an American schoolteacher become involved in the Mexican revolution of Pancho Villa.
Confused romantic drama that attempts large gestures and bungles even small ones.
w Aida Bortnik, Luis Puenzo *novel* *Gringo Viejo* by Carlos Fuentes *d* Luis Puenzo *ph* Felix Monti *m* Lee Holdridge *pd* Stuart Wurtzel, Bruno Rubeo *ed* Juan Carlos Macias, William Anderson, Glenn Farr
☆ Jane Fonda, Gregory Peck, Jimmy Smits, Patricio Contreras, Jenny Gago, Gabriela Roel, Sergio Calderon
† The film cost $25m and took around $2m at the US box-office.

Old Hutch
US 1936 80m bw
MGM
An idler finds a fortune but can't spend it because everybody knows he hasn't worked for years.
Satisfactory star comedy.
w George Kelly *d* J. Walter Ruben
☆ Wallace Beery, Elizabeth Patterson, Eric Linden, Cecilia Parker, Donald Meek, Virginia Grey

'Hasn't the backbone usually associated with Wallace Beery's vehicles. A nice light comedy which will doubtless garner fair box office.' – *Variety*

Old Iron
GB 1938 80m bw
TW Productions/British Lion
A shipping magnate disowns his son for marrying against his will, but a car accident reconciles them.
Very boring drama, an odd choice for this star, who can't cope with it.
w Ben Travers *d* Tom Walls
☆ Tom Walls, Eva Moore, Cecil Parker, Richard Ainley, David Tree, Enid Stamp-Taylor

'An embarrassing little stage comedy of parental affection, shot hurriedly from the front as you would shoot a charging lion.' – *Graham Greene*

The Old Lady Who Walked in the Sea
France 1991 94m colour
Gala/Blue Dahlia/SFC/A2/Little Bear/JM Productions (Gérard Jourd'hui)
original title: *La vieille qui marchait dans la mer*
Two aged confidence tricksters fall out after they take on a young apprentice in crime.
A defiantly tasteless and foul-mouthed comedy that somehow manages to charm as well, mainly due to Moreau's imperious performance.
w Dominique Roulet, Laurent Heynemann *novel* San Antonio *d* Laurent Heynemann *ph* Robert Alazraki *m* Philippe Sarde *pd* Valérie Grall *ed* Jacques Comets
☆ *Jeanne Moreau*, Michel Serrault, Luc Thuillier, Geraldine Danon, Jean Bouchaud, Marie-Dominique Aumont, Hester Wilcox
'A film to test the audience's patience.' – *Geoff Brown, The Times*
'Tasteless, vulgar and even badly shot.' – *Derek Malcolm, Guardian*

The Old Maid **
US 1939 95m bw
Warner (Henry Blanke)
When her suitor is killed in the Civil War, an unmarried mother lets her childless cousin bring up her daughter as her own.
A 'woman's picture' par excellence, given no-holds-barred treatment by all concerned but a little lacking in surprise.
w Casey Robinson *play* Zoe Akins *novel Edith Wharton d Edmund Goulding ph Tony Gaudio m* Max Steiner *md* Leo F. Forbstein
☆ Bette Davis, Miriam Hopkins, George Brent, Jane Bryan, Donald Crisp, Louise Fazenda, James Stephenson, Jerome Cowan, William Lundigan, Rand Brooks
'Stagey, sombre and generally confusing fare. Must aim for the femme trade chiefly.' – *Variety*
'It is better than average and sticks heroically to its problem, forsaking all delights and filling a whole laundry bag with wet and twisted handkerchiefs.' – *Otis Ferguson*
'The picture isn't bad, but it trudges along and never becomes exciting.' – *New Yorker, 1977*

The Old Man and the Sea *
US 1958 89m Technicolor
Warner/Leland Hayward
An old fisherman dreams of hooking a great fish.
Expensive but poor-looking and stultifyingly dull one-character drama with variable production effects, a low key Moby Dick. *Interesting but not effective.*
w Peter Viertel *novella Ernest Hemingway d* John Sturges *ph* James Wong Howe, Floyd Crosby, Tom Tutweiler, Lama Boren *m* Dimitri Tiomkin
☆ Spencer Tracy, Felipe Pazos, Harry Bellaver
'A literary property about as suited for the movie medium as *The Love Song of J. Alfred Prufrock*.' – *Time*
'A strange amalgam of practically unassisted acting, good camerawork and editing, and a lot of special effects.' – *Ernest Callenbach, Film Quarterly*
'Tracy struggles valiantly with the endless monologues ... misguided in the extreme.' – *Time Out, 1984*
'This is not a picture audiences are going to tear down the doors to see.' – *Motion Picture Herald*
† It was remade as a TV film in 1990, starring Anthony Quinn.
Dimitri Tiomkin
James Wong Howe; Spencer Tracy

Old Man Rhythm
US 1935 75m bw
Radio
A wealthy businessman becomes a college freshman to prevent his son marrying a gold-digger.
Amiable, relentlessly cheerful musical entertainment that passes the time pleasantly.
w Sig Herzig, Ernest Pagano, H. W. Hanemann *d* Edward Ludwig *ph* Nick Musuraca *m/ly* Lewis Gensler, Johnny Mercer *md* Roy Webb *ch* Hermes Pan *ad* Van Nest Polglase *ed* George Crone
☆ Charles Buddy Rogers, George Barbier, Barbara Kent, Grace Bradley, Betty Grable, Eric Blore, Erik Rhodes, John Arledge, Johnny Mercer, Donald Meek

Old Mother Riley
This Irish washerwoman with flailing arms and a nice line in invective was a music hall creation of Arthur Lucan, a variation of a pantomime dame. His wife Kitty McShane played Mother Riley's daughter, and despite personal difficulties they were top of the bill for nearly 30 years. Their first film was *Stars on Parade*, a collection of music-hall acts, in 1935.
The films were very cheaply made and the padding is difficult to sit through, but Lucan at his best is a superb comedian: they were made for small independent companies such as Butcher's and usually directed by Maclean Rogers.
1937 Old Mother Riley
1938 Old Mother Riley in Paris
1939 Old Mother Riley MP, Old Mother Riley Joins Up
1940 Old Mother Riley in Business, Old Mother Riley's Ghosts
1941 Old Mother Riley's Circus
1942 Old Mother Riley in Society
1943 Old Mother Riley Detective, Old Mother Riley Overseas
1944 Old Mother Riley at Home
1947 Old Mother Riley's New Venture
1949 Old Mother Riley's Jungle Treasure
1950 Old Mother Riley Headmistress (qv)
1952 Mother Riley Meets the Vampire

Old Mother Riley Headmistress
GB 1950 75m bw
Renown (Harry Reynolds)
Old Mother Riley, annoyed that her daughter has been unfairly sacked as a music teacher, buys the school.
A lacklustre comedy that fails to capitalize on Arthur Lucan's anarchic knockabout skills, insisting on a sympathetic mother–daughter relationship rather than the antagonistic one of his music-hall act.
w John Harlow, Ted Kavanagh *story* Jackie Marks, Con West *d* John Harlow *ph* James Wilson *md* George Melachrino *ad* C. Wilfred Arnold *ed* Douglas Myers
☆ Arthur Lucan, Kitty McShane, Willer Neal, Cyril Smith, C. Denier Warren, Enid Hewit, Paul Sheridan, Harry Herbert, The Luton Girls' Choir

The Old Woman Who Walked in the Sea:
see *The Old Lady Who Walked in the Sea*

Old Yeller *
US 1957 83m Technicolor
Walt Disney
The love of a boy for his dog.
Archetypal family movie set in a remote rural area.
w Fred Gipson, William Tunberg *novel* Fred Gipson *d* Robert Stevenson *ph* Charles P. Boyle *m* Oliver Wallace
☆ Dorothy McGuire, Fess Parker, Tommy Kirk, Kevin Corcoran, Jeff York, Chuck Connors

'You dastard! Get thee hence or I shall smite thee in the puss!'
The Old-Fashioned Way *
US 1934 74m bw
Paramount/ (William Le Baron)
Adventures of The Great McGonigle and his troupe of travelling players.
Period comedy tailored for its star and incorporating fragments of The Drunkard. *Not so funny as it might be, but essential for students.*
w Garnett Weston, Jack Cunningham, Charles Bogle (W. C. Fields) *d* William Beaudine *ph* Benjamin Reynolds *m* Harry Revel
☆ *W. C. Fields*, Joe Morrison, Judith Allen, Jan Duggan, Jack Mulhall, Baby Leroy

The Oldest Profession
France/West Germany/Italy 1967 115m Eastmancolor
Gibe/Francoriz/Rialto/Rizzoli
Six sketches about prostitution.
Very variable portmanteau, with moments of interest towards the end.
w Ennio Flaiano, Daniel Boulanger, Georges and André Tabet, Jean Aurenche, Jean-Luc Godard *d* Franco Indovina, Mauro Bolognini, Philippe de Broca, Michel Pfleghar, Claude Autant-Lara, Jean-Luc Godard
☆ Michele Mercier, Elsa Martinelli, Jeanne Moreau, Jean-Claude Brialy, Raquel Welch, Nadia Gray, Anna Karina

Oleanna
US 1994 89m DuArt
Samuel Goldwyn/Channel 4/Bay Kinescope (Patricia Wolff, Sarah Green)
An unhappy and pedantic professor is accused of sexually harassing a female student, who finds herself unable to understand the course he is teaching.
A controversial and successful two-character play transfers poorly to the screen, where the performances seem too aggressive to compel attention; it is less to do with sexual or male–female relationships than with an exploration of how we use language and what we mean by what we say.
wd David Mamet *play* David Mamet *ph* Andrzej Sekula *m* Rebecca Pidgeon *ed* Barbara Tulliver
☆ William H. Macy, Debra Eisenstadt
'This film never finds the magic balance between genre convention and sociopolitical currents. Its relevance to sexual harassment is on the same level as "The Hand That Rocks the Cradle's" analysis of contemporary babysitting.' – *Leonard Klady, Variety*

'Much much more than a musical!'
Oliver! ***
GB 1968 146m Technicolor
Panavision 70
Columbia/Warwick/Romulus (John Woolf)
A musical version of *Oliver Twist*.
The last, perhaps, of the splendid film musicals which have priced themselves out of existence; it drags a little in spots but on the whole it does credit both to the show and the original novel, though eclipsed in style by David Lean's straight version.
w Vernon Harris *play* Lionel Bart *novel Charles Dickens d Carol Reed ph Oswald Morris m* Lionel Bart *md* John Green *ch Onna White pd John Box ed* Ralph Kemplen
☆ *Ron Moody*, Oliver Reed, Harry Secombe, Mark Lester, Shani Wallis, *Jack Wild*, Hugh Griffith, Joseph O'Conor, Leonard Rossiter, Hylda Baker, Peggy Mount, Megs Jenkins
'Only time will tell if it is a great film but it is certainly a great experience.' – *Joseph Morgenstern*
'There is a heightened discrepancy between the romping jollity with which everyone goes about his business and the actual business being gone about ... such narrative elements as the exploitation of child labour, pimping, abduction, prostitution and murder combine to make Oliver! the most non-U subject ever to receive a U certificate.' – *Jan Dawson*
best picture; Carol Reed; John Green; Onna White; sound
Vernon Harris; Oswald Morris; Ron Moody; Jack Wild; costumes (Phyllis Dalton); editing

Oliver and Company *
US 1988 74m Metrocolor
Warner/Walt Disney/Silver Screen Partners III
A kitten becomes friends with a gang of criminal dogs and their human master.
Episodic film, short on charm, that only now and then provides glimpses of stylish animation.
w Jim Cox, Timothy J. Disney, James Mangold *novel Oliver Twist* by Charles Dickens *d* George Scribner *m* J. A. C. Redford *ad* Dan Hansen *ed* Jim Melton, Mark Hester
☆ Featuring the voices of Joey Lawrence, Bill Joel, Cheech Marin, Richard Mulligan, Roscoe Lee Browne, Sheryl Lee Ralph, Dom DeLuise, Taurean Blacque, Carl Weintraub, Robert Loggia, Natalie Gregory, William Glover, Bette Midler

Oliver the Eighth
US 1933 20m bw
Hal Roach
Ollie goes on a blind date, and the lady turns out to be homicidal.
Star farce which never quite rises to the occasion; pleasant fooling but no more.
w anon *d* Lloyd French *ph* Art Lloyd *ed* Bert Jordan
☆ Stan Laurel, Oliver Hardy, Mae Busch, Jack Barty

Oliver Twist ****
GB 1948 116m bw
GFD/Cineguild (Ronald Neame)
A foundling falls among thieves but is rescued by a benevolent old gentleman.
Simplified, brilliantly cinematic version of a voluminous Victorian novel, beautiful to look at and memorably played, with every scene achieving the perfect maximum impact.
w David Lean, Stanley Haynes novel Charles Dickens d David Lean ph Guy Green m Arnold Bax *md* Muir Mathieson *pd John Bryan ed* Jack Harris *cos* Margaret Furse
☆ *Alec Guinness* (Fagin), *Robert Newton* (Bill Sikes), *Francis L. Sullivan* (Mr Bumble), *John Howard Davies* (Oliver Twist), *Kay Walsh* (Nancy), *Anthony Newley* (The Artful Dodger), *Henry Stephenson* (Mr Brownlow), *Mary Clare* (Mrs Corney), *Gibb McLaughlin* (Mr Sowerberry), *Diana Dors* (Charlotte)
'A thoroughly expert piece of movie entertainment.' – *Richard Winnington*
'A brilliant, fascinating movie, no less a classic than the Dickens novel which it brings to life.' – *Time*

Oliver's Story
US 1978 92m Technicolor
Paramount (David V. Picker)
A sequel to *Love Story*, showing how Oliver succumbed to depression but finally found another girlfriend.
Love means never having to watch this trendy rubbish.
w Erich Segal, John Korty *d* John Korty *ph* Arthur Ornitz *m* Francis Lai, Lee Holdridge
☆ Ryan O'Neal, Candice Bergen, Nicola Pagett, Edward Binns, Ray Milland

Olivier, Olivier **
France 1992 109m Eastmancolor
Gala/Oliane/A2 (Marie-Laure Reyre)
A middle-class family is thrown into confusion when a 15-year-old male prostitute claims to be the son who vanished six years earlier.
Engrossing examination of identity, credulity and family harmony.
w Agnieszka Holland, Yves Lapointe, Régis Debray *d* Agnieszka Holland *ph* Bernard Zitzermann *m* Zbigniew Preisner *pd* Helene Bourgy *ed* Isabelle Lorente
☆ François Cluzet, Brigitte Roüan, Jean-François Stévenin, Grégoire Colin, Marina Golovine, Frédéric Quiring
'What could have been a deadly mysterious tale becomes modestly intriguing, almost prosaic.' – *Geoff Brown, The Times*
'A seemingly simple but intriguing and ultimately powerful film.' – *Variety*

Olly Olly Oxen Free
US 1978 93m Metrocolor
Rico Lion (Richard A. Colla)
aka: *The Great Balloon Adventure*
A junkyard proprietress helps two young children to launch a decrepit hot-air balloon.
Simpleminded children's adventure with a surprising star.
w Eugene Poinc *d* Richard A. Colla *ph* Gayne Rescher *m* Bob Alcivar *pd* Peter Wooley
☆ Katharine Hepburn, Kevin McKenzie, Dennis Dimster

Los Olvidados *
Mexico 1951 88m bw
Utramar/Oscar Dancigers
aka: *The Young and the Damned*
A good boy is contaminated by the young thugs in Mexico City's slums, and both he and his tormentor die violently.
Sober but penetrating analysis of social conditions leading to violence. The film was widely acclaimed, yet its very proficiency and excellent photography tend to glamorize its subject. Compare, however, the Hollywood resolutions of Dead End, *on a similar subject.*

w Luis Buñuel, Luis Alcoriza, Oscar Dancigers *d* Luis Buñuel *ph* Gabriel Figueroa *m* Gustavo Pitaluga
☆ Alfonso Mejia, Miguel Inclan, Estela Inda, Roberto Cobo

'I shall not put *Los Olvidados* among the films I have most enjoyed; but I am far from sure that it should not go among the monuments of the cinema.' – *Dilys Powell*

Olympische Spiele ***
Germany 1936 225m bw
Leni Riefenstahl

An account of the Berlin Olympic Games.
This magnificent film is in no sense a mere reporting of an event. Camera movement, photography and editing combine with music to make it an experience truly olympian, especially in the introductory symbolic sequence suggesting the birth of the games. It was also, dangerously, a hymn to Nazi strength.
ph Hans Ertl, Walter Franz and 42 others
m Herbert Windt *d/ed* Leni Riefenstahl
assistant Walter Ruttman

'Here is the camera doing superbly what only the camera can do: refashioning the rhythms of the visible; of the moment seen.' – *Dilys Powell*

† Part 1 runs to 118m, and Part 2 to 107m.

The Omaha Trail
US 1942 62m bw
MGM
The laying of train track across the west causes Indian wars.
Brisk second-feature Western with good production values.
w Jesse Lasky Jnr, Hugo Butler *d* Edward Buzzell
☆ James Craig, Dean Jagger, Edward Ellis, Chill Wills, Donald Meek, Pamela Blake, Howard da Silva

'One thousand years ago, Omar Khayyam was a poet, a scientist and military leader so great that an army of Assassins dedicated to world domination fell before his genius!'
Omar Khayyam
US 1956 101m Technicolor Vistavision
Paramount (Frank Freeman Jnr)
The Persian poet and philosopher defends his Shah against the Assassins.
Clean but dull Arabian Nights fantasy with pantomime sets and no humour.
w Barre Lyndon *d* William Dieterle *ph* Ernest Laszlo *m* Victor Young
☆ Cornel Wilde, Michael Rennie, Raymond Massey, John Derek, Yma Sumac, Sebastian Cabot, Debra Paget

L'Ombre du Doute: see *A Shadow of a Doubt*

'Robots rule the Earth. Only one man can stop them.'
Omega Doom
US 1995 86m colour
Largo/Toga/Filmwerks (Gary Schmoeller, Tom Karnowski)
In a future nuclear winter, an android programmed to know the difference between right and wrong fights against rival robot gangs determined to rid the world of humanity.
Tepid science-fiction, influenced by the styles of spaghetti westerns and kung-fu movies, and a narrative that owes something to A Fistful of Dollars*; but genre fans will be disappointed by the confusing and lacklustre action.*
w Ed Naha, Albert Pyun *d* Albert Pyun
ph George Mooradian *m* Tony Riparetti
pd Nenad Pecur *ed* Ken Morrisey, Joe Shugart
sp makeup: Maurine Schlenz, Dan Robert
cos Shelley Boies
☆ Rutger Hauer (Omega Doom), Shannon Whirr, Tina Coté, Anna Katarina, Jill Pierce, Jahi Zuri, Cynthia Ireland, Simon Poland, Earl White, Norbert Weisser (The Head)

The Omega Man *
US 1971 98m Technicolor Panavision
Warner/Walter Seltzer
In 1977 a plague resulting from germ warfare has decimated the world's population; in Los Angeles, one man wages war against loathsome carriers of the disease.
'Realistic' version of a novel which was about vampires taking over, and was previously filmed unsatisfactorily as The Last Man on Earth. *This nasty version rises to a few good action sequences but is bogged down by talk in between.*
w John William Corrington, Joyce H. Corrington *novel I am Legend* by Richard Matheson *d* Boris Sagal *ph* Russell Metty *m* Ron Grainer
☆ Charlton Heston, Rosalind Cash, Anthony Zerbe

'Good morning. You are one day closer to the end of the world!'
The Omen **
US 1976 111m DeLuxe Panavision
TCF (Harvey Bernhard)
The adopted child of an ambassador to Great Britain shows unnerving signs of being diabolically inspired.
Commercially successful variation on The Exorcist, *quite professionally assembled and more enjoyable as entertainment than its predecessor.*
w David Seltzer *d Richard Donner ph* Gil Taylor *m* Jerry Goldsmith
☆ Gregory Peck, Lee Remick, David Warner, Billie Whitelaw, Leo McKern, Harvey Stevens, Patrick Troughton, Anthony Nicholls, Martin Benson

'A cut above the rest in that it has an ingenious premise, a teasingly labyrinthine development, a neat sting in its tail, and enough confidence in its own absurdities to carry them off.' – *David Robinson, The Times*

'Dreadfully silly ... its horrors are not horrible, its terrors are not terrifying, its violence is ludicrous.' – *New York Times*

'More laughs than an average comedy.' – *Judith Crist*

'I did it strictly for the money.' – *David Seltzer*

† See *Damien: Omen II* and *The Final Conflict.*
†† Gregory Peck inherited his role from Charlton Heston, who turned it down.
Jerry Goldsmith
song 'Ave Satani'

Omen III: The Final Conflict: see *The Final Conflict*

Omen IV: The Awakening
US 1991 97m colour
TCF/FNM (Harvey Bernhard)
A wealthy couple adopt a young girl who turns out to be the daughter of the Anti-Christ.
An American TV movie, virtually rehashing The Omen, *that was given a cinema release elsewhere, it has all the sins of a film made for the small screen, looking cheap and clearly intended for audiences with brief attention spans.*
w Brian Taggert *d* Jorge Montesi, Dominique Othenin-Girard *ph* Martin Fuhrer *m* Jonathan Sheffer *pd* Richard Wilcox *ed* Frank Irvine
☆ Faye Grant, Michael Woods, Michael Lerner, Madison Mason, Asia Vieira

'This mainly serves to remind you that, silly though they were, the earlier films were at least quality entertainment. Further sequels would be as welcome as a plague of locusts.' – *Kim Newman, Empire*

'While pic offers a few creepy moments, its structure is so convoluted that it's sheer hell to follow.' – *Variety*

On a Clear Day You Can See Forever *
US 1970 129m Technicolor Panavision
Paramount (Howard Koch)
A psychiatric hypnotist helps a girl to stop smoking, and finds that in trances she remembers previous incarnations.
Romantic musical which tries, and fails, to substitute wispy charm for its original Broadway vitality. There are compensations.
w Alan Jay Lerner *play* Alan Jay Lerner
d Vincente Minnelli *ph* Harry Stradling
m Burton Lane
☆ Barbra Streisand, Yves Montand, Bob Newhart, Larry Blyden, Jack Nicholson, Simon Oakland

On an Island with You
US 1948 104m Technicolor
MGM (Joe Pasternak)
A film actress on location in the South Seas is chased by a naval officer.
Below par musical which far outstays its welcome.
w Dorothy Kingsley, Dorothy Cooper, Charles Martin, Hans Wilhelm *d* Richard Thorpe
ph Charles Rosher *md* George Stoll
☆ Esther Williams, Peter Lawford, Jimmy Durante, Ricardo Montalban, Cyd Charisse, Xavier Cugat and his Orchestra

On Approval ***
GB 1943 80m bw
(GFD)
An Edwardian duke and an American heiress plan a chaperoned trial marriage in a remote Scottish castle.
Sparkling comedy of manners made even more piquant by careful casting and mounting; a minor delight.
w Clive Brook, Terence Young play Frederick Lonsdale d Clive Brook ph C. Friese-Greene
m William Alwyn
☆ *Clive Brook, Beatrice Lillie, Googie Withers, Roland Culver,* O. B. Clarence, Lawrence Hanray, Hay Petrie

'Totally diverting, highly cinematic.' – *NFT, 1974*

'There has probably never been a richer, funnier anthology of late-Victorian mannerisms.' – *Time*

'I enjoyed it so thoroughly that I have to fight off superlatives.' – *James Agee*

† Also filmed in 1930 by Tom Walls for Herbert Wilcox, with Walls, Yvonne Arnaud, Winifred Shotter and Edmund Breon.

On Borrowed Time *
US 1939 98m bw
MGM (Sidney Franklin)
An old man refuses to die and chases Death up the apple tree.
Amiable, very American fantasy with much sentiment and several effective moments.
w Alice Duer Miller, Frank O'Neill, Claudine West *novel* Lawrence Edward Watkin *d* Harold S. Bucquet *ph* Joseph Ruttenberg *m* Franz Waxman
☆ *Lionel Barrymore,* Bobs Watson, Beulah Bondi, *Cedric Hardwicke* (Mr Brink), Una Merkel, Ian Wolfe, Philip Terry, Eily Malyon

'General audiences may cotton to the novelty ... artistically fine prestige production.' – *Variety*

'A weird, wild, totally unpredictable fantasy with dream sequences more like Buñuel than anything in the cinema.' – *John Russell Taylor, 1965*

On Connaît la Chanson: see *Same Old Song*

On Dangerous Ground
US 1951 82m bw
RKO (John Houseman)
A tough cop falls in love with the blind sister of a mentally defective murderer.
Pretentious Hollywood film noir *in the Gabin manner, partly redeemed by its glossy surface.*
w A. I. Bezzerides *novel* George Butler
d Nicholas Ray *ph George E. Diskant m* Bernard Herrmann
☆ Robert Ryan, Ida Lupino, Ward Bond, Ed Begley, Cleo Moore, Charles Kemper

'His battle to save the Alaskan wilderness and protect its people can only be won...'
On Deadly Ground
US 1994 101m Technicolor Clairmont Scope
Warner/Seagal/Nasso (Steven Seagal, Julius R. Nasso, A. Kitman Ho)
A former CIA agent protects the Alaskan environment against a wicked oil mogul.
Risible action movie in which the pollution-count is high, particularly since Seagal's notion of saving the environment is to destroy it and everyone who stands in his way.
w Ed Horowitz, Robin U. Russin *d* Steven Seagal *ph* Ric Waite *m* Basil Poledouris *pd* William Ladd Skinner *ed* Robert Ferreti, Don Brochu
☆ Steven Seagal, Michael Caine, Joan Chen, John C. McGinley, R. Lee Ermey, Shari Shattuck, Billy Bob Thornton, Richard Hamilton, Chief Irvin Brink

'A vanity production parading as a social statement. It nonetheless has enough sound, fury and flash to satisfy the action crowd who have propped up Seagal's career.' – *Variety*

'Seagal, of course, remains exactly himself – a human bullet winging its way towards the flabby guts of the baddies. But he seems to be getting a little older now, and the martial arts are not as spectacular.' – *Derek Malcolm*

On Dress Parade
US 1939 62m bw
Warner
The Dead End Kids go to military school.
Cleaned-up comedy-drama, the last for the Kids before they split up.
w Tom Reed, Charles Belden *d* William Clemens
☆ Billy Halop, Leo Gorcey, Huntz Hall, Bobby Jordan, Gabriel Dell, Bernard Punsley, John Litel, Frankie Thomas

'It just doesn't ring true. Dualler.' – *Variety*

On Friday at Eleven
West Germany/France/Italy 1960 93m bw
Corona/Criterion/Erredi (Alexander Gruter)
aka: *The World in My Pocket*
A cold-hearted gang plans to rob a heavily armoured American army truck.
Unsurprising but vaguely unpleasant thriller with nary a character left alive at the end.
w Frank Harvey *novel* James Hadley Chase
d Alvin Rakoff *ph* Vaclav Vich *m* Claude Bolling
☆ Rod Steiger, Nadja Tiller, Peter Van Eyck, Jean Servais, Ian Bannen

'Growing up isn't easy at any age'
On Golden Pond ***
US 1981 109m colour Panavision
ITC/IPC (Bruce Gilbert)
An 80-year-old, his wife and his daughter spend a holiday at their New England lakeside cottage.
A film remarkable not so much for what it is – a well-acted, decent screen presentation of a rather waffling and sentimental play – as for the fact that in the sophisticated eighties enough people paid to see it to make it a box-office record-breaker. This was mainly due to affection for its star, whose last film it was, but also to an American desire for a reversion to the old values of warmth and humanity after the sex and violence which the screen had lately been offering.
w Ernest Thompson *play* Ernest Thompson
d Mark Rydell *ph* Billy Williams *m* Dave Grusin
ed Robert L. Wolfe
☆ *Henry Fonda, Katharine Hepburn,* Jane Fonda, Doug McKeon, Dabney Coleman

'Moments of truth survive some cloying contrivance; Rydell directs on bended knees.' – *Sight and Sound*

'Two of Hollywood's best-loved veterans deserve a far better swansong than this sticky confection.' – *Time Out*

'The kind of uplifting twaddle that traffics heavily in rather basic symbols: the gold light on the pond stands for the sunset of life, and so on.' – *Pauline Kael, New Yorker*

Ernest Thompson; Henry Fonda; Katharine Hepburn
picture; Mark Rydell; Jane Fonda; Robert L. Wolfe; Dave Grusin; Billy Williams; sound (Richard Portman, David M. Ronne)
Katharine Hepburn

On Her Majesty's Secret Service **
GB 1969 140m Technicolor Panavision
UA/Eon/Danilaq (Harry Saltzman, Albert R. Broccoli)
James Bond tracks down master criminal Blofeld in Switzerland.
Perhaps to compensate for no Sean Connery and a tragic ending, the producers of this sixth Bond opus shower largesse upon us in the shape of no fewer than four protracted and spectacular climaxes. Splendid stuff, but too much of it, and the lack of a happy centre does show.
w Richard Maibaum *novel* Ian Fleming *d* Peter Hunt *ph* Michael Reed, Egil Woxholt, Roy Ford, John Jordan *m* John Barry *pd* Syd Cain
☆ George Lazenby, Diana Rigg, Telly Savalas, Ilse Steppat, Gabriele Ferzetti, Yuri Borienko, Bernard Lee, Lois Maxwell

'Put on your straw boater and *Cuddle Up A Little Closer!*'

On Moonlight Bay **

US 1951 95m Technicolor
Warner (William Jacobs)

Family crises, to do with growing up and young love, in a 1917 Indiana town.
Pleasant musical, competently made, from the Penrod stories, with the emphasis switched to big sister.
w Melville Shavelson, Jack Rose *stories* Booth Tarkington *d* Roy del Ruth *ph* Ernest Haller *md* Ray Heindorf
☆ Doris Day, Gordon MacRae, Leon Ames, Rosemary de Camp, Billy Gray
† See also *By the Light of the Silvery Moon*, a companion piece.

On My Way to the Crusades I Met a Girl Who...: see *The Chastity Belt*

On Our Merry Way *

US 1948 107m bw
Miracle Productions (Benedict Bogeaus, Burgess Meredith)
aka: *A Miracle Can Happen*

A reporter is urged by his wife to dig up some human interest stories.
Frail compendium of anecdotes which barely work.
w Laurence Stallings *story* Arch Oboler *d* King Vidor, Leslie Fenton (also John Huston, George Stevens, uncredited) *ph* Joseph August, Gordon Avil, John Seitz, Edward Cronjager *m* Heinz Roemheld *md* David Chudnow, Skitch Henderson
☆ Burgess Meredith, Paulette Goddard, Fred MacMurray, Hugh Herbert, James Stewart, Dorothy Lamour, Victor Moore, Henry Fonda, William Demarest

On Our Selection

Australia 1932 99m bw
Australasian Films

The life of the Rudd family in rural Queensland.
Predictable plot complications and loveable characters.
w Bert Bailey, Ken G. Hall *d* Ken G. Hall
☆ Bert Bailey, Fred McDonald, Alfreda Bevan, Jack McGowan
† Subsequent Rudd adventures included *Dad and Dave Come to Town* (1938) and *Dad Rudd M.P.* (1940).

On Stage Everybody

US 1945 65m bw
Universal

A vaudevillian helps youngsters put on a radio show.
Tired musical support.
w Warren Wilson, Oscar Brodney *d* Jean Yarbrough
☆ Jack Oakie, Peggy Ryan, Johnny Coy, Julie London, Otto Kruger

On Such a Night

US 1937 71m bw
Emmanuel Cohen/Paramount

Gangsters get caught in a Mississippi flood.
Confusing action yarn which fizzles out before it gets going.
w Doris Malloy, William Lipman, and various hands *d* E. A. Dupont
☆ Grant Richards, Roscoe Karns, Karen Morley, Eduardo Ciannelli, Alan Mowbray, Robert McWade
'So many baffling twists that the thread of the narrative is soon lost.' – *Variety*

On Such a Night *

GB 1955 37m Eastmancolor
Screen Audiences/Rank

An American is initiated into the splendours of Glyndebourne Opera.
Modestly pleasing documentary with fictionalized bookends.
w Paul Dehn *d* Anthony Asquith
☆ David Knight, Josephine Griffin, Marie Lohr

'The tops in swank! The smoothest in rhythm! The greatest in stars! The newest in love! The fastest in dancing! The last word in entertainment!'

On the Avenue **

US 1937 89m bw
TCF (Gene Markey)

An heiress rages because she is being satirized in a revue, but later falls in love with the star.
Bright musical which keeps moving and uses its talents wisely.
w Gene Markey, William Conselman *d* Roy del Ruth *ph* Lucien Andriot *m/ly* Irving Berlin *ch* Seymour Felix
☆ *Dick Powell, Madeleine Carroll, The Ritz Brothers*, George Barbier, Alice Faye, Walter Catlett, Joan Davis, E. E. Clive
'An amusing revue, with a pleasant score and a disarming informality in its production to lure us into liking it.' – *New York Times*
† Revamped as *Let's Make Love* (qv)
♫ 'He Ain't Got Rhythm'; 'The Girl on the Police Gazette'; 'This Year's Kisses'; 'I've Got My Love to Keep Me Warm'. The title song was dropped before release.

On the Beach **

US 1959 134m bw
United Artists/Stanley Kramer

When most of the world has been devastated by atomic waste, an American atomic submarine sets out to investigate.
Gloomy prophecy which works well in spasms but is generally too content to chat rather than imagine. A solid prestige job nevertheless.
w John Paxton, James Lee Barrett *novel* Nevil Shute *d* *Stanley Kramer* *ph* *Giuseppe Rotunno, Daniel Fapp* *m* Ernest Gold *pd* *Rudolph Sternad* *ed* Frederic Knudtson
☆ Gregory Peck, Ava Gardner, *Fred Astaire*, Anthony Perkins, Donna Anderson, John Tate, Lola Brooks
'Its humanism is clearly of the order that seeks the support of a clamorous music score. The characters remain little more than spokesmen for timid ideas and Salvation Army slogans, their emotions hired from a Hollywood prop room; which is all pretty disturbing in a film about nothing less than the end of the world.' – *Robert Vas*
Ernest Gold; editing

On the Beat

GB 1962 105m bw
Rank (Hugh Stewart)

A Scotland Yard car park attendant manages to capture some crooks and become a policeman.
Busy but flat comedy vehicle, never very likeable.
w Jack Davies *d* Robert Asher *ph* Geoffrey Faithfull *m* Philip Green
☆ Norman Wisdom, Jennifer Jayne, Raymond Huntley, David Lodge, Esma Cannon, Terence Alexander

On the Black Hill *

GB 1988 117m colour
BFI/Channel 4/British Screen

Twin brothers grow up on a Welsh hill farm.
Unsentimental and episodic narrative of limited lives, but not without its longueurs.
wd Andrew Grieve *novel* Bruce Chatwin *ph* Thaddeus O'Sullivan *m* Robert Lockhart *ad* Jocelyn James *ed* Scott Thomas
☆ Mike Gwilym, Robert Gwilym, Bob Peck, Gemma Jones, Jack Walters, Nesta Harris, Huw Toghill, Gareth Toghill

On the Buses

GB 1971 88m Technicolor
MGM-EMI/Hammer (Ronald Wolfe, Ronald Chesney)

Women drivers cause trouble at a bus depot.
Grotesque, ham-handed farce from a TV series which was sometimes funny; this is merely vulgar.
w Ronald Wolfe, Ronald Chesney *d* Harry Booth *ph* Mark MacDonald *m* Max Harris *pd* Scott MacGregor *ed* Archie Ludski
☆ Reg Varney (Stan Butler), Doris Hare (Stan's Mum), Anna Karen (Olive), Michael Robbins (Arthur), Stephen Lewis ('Blakey'), Bob Grant (Jack), Andrea Lawrence (Betty), Pat Ashton (Sally), Brian Oulton (Manager), Pamela Cundell (Ruby), Pat Coombs (Vera), Wendy Richards (Housewife), David Lodge (Busman)
'Reaches a new low in British production standards.' – *MFB*
† *Mutiny on the Buses* (qv) followed in 1972 and *Holiday on the Buses* (qv) in 1973. Both were deplorably witless.
†† It was the highest earning British film of 1971.

On the Carpet: see *Little Giant*

On the Double *

US 1961 92m Technicolor Panavision
Paramount/Dena-Capri (Jack Rose)

During World War II, an American private is asked to impersonate a British intelligence officer.
From the plot and the talents it seems one might start laughing at this while still in the queue, but in fact most of it goes sadly awry and it never quite comes to the boil.
w Jack Rose, Melville Shavelson *d* Melville Shavelson *ph* Harry Stradling, Geoffrey Unsworth *m* Leith Stevens
☆ Danny Kaye, Dana Wynter, Wilfrid Hyde-White, Diana Dors, Margaret Rutherford, Allan Cuthbertson, Jesse White

On the Fiddle *

GB 1961 97m bw
Anglo-Amalgamated/S. Benjamin Fisz
US title: *Operation Snafu*

A wide boy and a slow-witted gypsy have comic and other adventures in the RAF.
Curious mixture of farce and action, more on American lines than British, but quite entertainingly presented.
w Harold Buchman *novel* *Stop at a Winner* by R. F. Delderfield *d* Cyril Frankel *ph* Ted Scaife *m* Malcolm Arnold
☆ Alfred Lynch, Sean Connery, Cecil Parker, Wilfrid Hyde-White, Kathleen Harrison, Alan King, Eleanor Summerfield, Eric Barker, Terence Longdon, John Le Mesurier, Harry Locke

On the Night of the Fire *

GB 1939 94m bw
GFD/G & S (Josef Somlo)
US title: *The Fugitive*

A barber kills the blackmailer of his wife.
Dour little drama, rather unusual for pre-war British studios.
w Brian Desmond Hurst, Terence Young *novel* F. L. Green *d* Brian Desmond Hurst *ph* Gunther Krampf
☆ Ralph Richardson, Diana Wynyard, Romney Brent, Mary Clare, Henry Oscar, Frederick Leister
'The kind of film either liked very much or very little ... absorbingly entertaining, and b.o. should profit considerably by word of mouth.' – *Variety*

On the Riviera **

US 1951 90m Technicolor
TCF (Sol C. Siegel)

A cabaret artist is persuaded to pose as a philandering businessman.
Remake of Folies Bergère *and* That Night in Rio *(see also* On the Double*); disliked at the time and accused of tastelessness, it now seems smarter and funnier than comparable films of its era.*
w Valentine Davies, Phoebe and Henry Ephron *d* *Walter Lang* *ph* Leon Shamroy *m* Alfred Newman *ad* Lyle Wheeler, Leland Fuller
☆ *Danny Kaye*, Corinne Calvet, Gene Tierney, Marcel Dalio, Jean Murat
Alfred Newman; art direction

On the Run

Hong Kong 1988 96m colour
Bo Ho/Mobile (Raymond Chow)

A cop and the hit-woman who killed his wife go on the run from a gang of corrupt and violent policemen who are dealing in heroin.
Brutal, hard-boiled thriller with a great deal of slaughter and not much plausibility.
wd Alfred Cheung *m* Lam Man Yee *pd* Chen Yu *ad* Kih Chung Man, Loo Kah Hiu
☆ Yuen Biao, Patricia Ha, Kao Fei, Yuen Wah, Loh Lieh, Chan Yoke Lin
'More than just good Hong Kong noir, it is good film noir.' – *Jim Morton, Sex and Zen & A Bullet in the Head*

On the Threshold of Space

US 1956 96m Eastmancolor Cinemascope
TCF (William Bloom)

The USAF medical corps explores human reactions at high altitudes.
Semi-documentary flagwaver with dreary domestic asides; very dated now, and of no particular nostalgic interest.
w Simon Wincelberg, Francis Cockrell *d* Robert D. Webb *ph* Joe MacDonald *m* Lyn Murray
☆ Guy Madison, Virginia Leith, John Hodiak, Dean Jagger, Warren Stevens

On the Town ****

US 1949 98m Technicolor
MGM (Arthur Freed)

Three sailors enjoy 24 hours' leave in New York.
Most of this brash location musical counts as among the best things ever to come out of Hollywood; the serious ballet towards the end tends to kill it, but it contains much to be grateful for.
w Betty Comden, Adolph Green *ballet* Fancy Free by Leonard Bernstein *ph* *Harold Rosson* *md* Lennie Hayton, Roger Edens *d/ch* *Gene Kelly, Stanley Donen* *songs* various
☆ *Gene Kelly, Frank Sinatra, Jules Munshin, Vera-Ellen, Betty Garrett, Ann Miller*, Tom Dugan, Florence Bates, Alice Pearce
'A film that will be enjoyed more than twice.' – *Lindsay Anderson*
'So exuberant that it threatens at moments to bounce right off the screen.' – *Time*
'The speed, the vitality, the flashing colour and design, the tricks of timing by which motion is fitted to music, the wit and invention and superlative technical accomplishment make it a really exhilarating experience.' – *Richard Mallett, Punch*
♫ 'New York, New York'; 'Prehistoric Man'; 'I Can Cook Too'; 'Main Street'; 'You're Awful'; On the Town'; 'Count on Me'
Lennie Hayton, Roger Edens

On the Twelfth Day *

GB 1956 23m Eastmancolor
George K. Arthur/Bahamian

A balletic presentation of the song about the 12 days of Christmas, with plenty of maids a'milking and lords a'leaping.
A refreshing and extravagant novelty.
w James Matthews, Val Valentine *d* *Wendy Toye* *ph* Arthur Grant *pd* Ronald Searle
☆ Wendy Toye, Franklin Bennett, David O'Brien

On the Waterfront ****

US 1954 108m bw
Columbia/Sam Spiegel

After the death of his brother, a young stevedore breaks the hold of a waterfront gang boss.
Intense, broody dockside thriller with 'method' performances; very powerful of its kind, and much imitated.
w Budd Schulberg *novel* Budd Schulberg *d* *Elia Kazan* *ph* *Boris Kaufman* *m* Leonard Bernstein *ad* Richard Day *ed* Gene Milford
☆ *Marlon Brando*, Eva Marie Saint, *Lee J. Cobb*, Rod Steiger, Karl Malden, Pat Henning, Leif Erickson, James Westerfield, John Hamilton
TERRY (MARLON BRANDO): 'It was you, Charley. You and Mickey. Like the night the two of you's come in the dressing room and says, "Kid, this ain't your night. We're going for the price on Wilson." *It ain't my night.* I'd of taken Wilson apart that night! I was ready. Remember the early rounds throwing them combinations? So what happens? This bum Wilson he gets the title shot. Outdoors in the ball park! And what do I get? A couple of bucks and a one-way ticket to Palookaville.
'It was you, Charley. You was my brother. You should have looked out for me instead of making me take them dives for the short end money.'
CHARLEY (ROD STEIGER): 'I always had a bet down for you. You saw some money.'
TERRY: 'See! You don't understand! I could've been a contender. I could've had class and been somebody. Real class. Instead of a bum. It was you, Charley.'
'An uncommonly powerful, exciting and imaginative use of the screen by gifted professionals.' – *New York Times*
'A medley of items from the Warner gangland pictures of the thirties, brought up to date.' – *Steven Sondheim, Films in Review*
best picture; Budd Schulberg; Elia Kazan; Boris Kaufman; Richard Day; Marlon Brando; Eva Marie Saint; editing
Leonard Bernstein; Lee J. Cobb; Rod Steiger; Karl Malden
Marlon Brando

On the Yard
US 1979 102m Technicolor
Midwest (Joan Micklin Silver)
In a tough jail, the controlling convict finds his authority challenged by a wife-killer and a new guard captain.
Bleak drama of prison life, conveying the futility of existence inside, but not much else.
w Malcolm Braly *novel* Malcolm Braly *d* Raphael D. Silver *ph* Alan Metzger *m* Charles Gross *ad* Leon Harris *ed* Evan Lottman
☆ John Heard, Thomas Waites, Mike Kellin, Richard Bright, Joe Grifasi, Lane Smith, Richard Hayes

On Top of Old Smoky
US 1953 60m bw
Columbia/Gene Autry (Armand Schaefer)
Gene Autry is mistaken for a Texas Ranger when he intervenes in a row between freight operators and a young woman operating a toll road.
Amiable light Western that ambles along, arousing mild interest as it goes.
w Gerald Geraghty *d* George Archainbaud *ph* William Bradford *md* Mischa Bakaleinikoff *ad* George Brooks *ed* James Sweeney
☆ Gene Autry, Smiley Burnette, Gail Davis, Grandon Rhodes, Sheila Ryan, Kenne Duncan, Cass County Boys, Champion

On Trial
US 1939 60m bw
Warner
A man kills his wife's lover and is put on trial for murder.
Dozy film version of a once sensational play.
w Don Ryan *play* Elmer Rice *d* Terry Morse
☆ John Litel, Margaret Lindsay, Edward Norris, James Stephenson
'Strictly dual fodder, talking along for an hour without going anywhere.' – *Variety*

On Wings of Song: see *Love Me Forever*

On with the Show
US 1929 98m Technicolor (two-colour)
Warner
Crude early talkie musical revue with historical interest.
w Robert Lord *play Shoestring* by Humphrey Pearson *d* Alan Crosland *ph* Tony Gaudio *m/ly* Harry Akst, Grant Clarke *ch* Larry Ceballos
☆ Betty Compson, Louise Fazenda, Sally O'Neil, Joe E. Brown, Ethel Waters, Arthur Lake

On Your Toes *
US 1939 94m bw
Warner (Robert Lord)
Backstage jealousies at the ballet.
Smooth film version of a top Broadway show of its time.
w Jerry Wald, Richard Macaulay *play* George Abbott *d* Ray Enright *ph* James Wong Howe, Sol Polito *m/ly Richard Rodgers, Lorenz Hart*
☆ Vera Zorina, Eddie Albert, Alan Hale, Frank McHugh, James Gleason, Donald O'Connor, Gloria Dickson
'Box office prospects appear to be pretty good, but more than the average campaigning should be indulged.' – *Variety*

Once a Crook
GB 1941 81m bw
TCF
A publican with a shady past helps his son who is in trouble with the law.
Low-key character comedy for two stars who would benefit from a greater tendency to farce.
w Roger Burford *play* Evadne Price, Ken Attiwill *d* Herbert Mason
☆ Gordon Harker, Sydney Howard, Frank Pettingell, Carla Lehmann, Bernard Lee, Kathleen Harrison, Cyril Cusack

Once a Jolly Swagman *
GB 1948 100m bw
GFD/Wessex (Ian Dalrymple)
US title: *Maniacs on Wheels*
A factory worker becomes a speedway rider.
Competent sporting drama of no particular interest.
w William Rose, Jack Lee *d* Jack Lee *ph* H. E. Fowle *m* Bernard Stevens
☆ Dirk Bogarde, Renée Asherson, Bonar Colleano, Bill Owen

Once a Lady
US 1931 65m bw
Paramount
An illegitimate baby grows up to meet her mother without recognizing her.
A plot that was often tried out during the early thirties, seldom more boringly than on this occasion.
w Zoe Akins, Samuel Hoffenstein *play The Second Life* by Rudolf Bernauer, Rudolf Oesterreicher *d* Guthrie McClintic
☆ Ruth Chatterton, Ivor Novello, Jill Esmond, Geoffrey Kerr, Doris Lloyd
'Another crying towel special.' – *Variety*

Once a Sinner
US 1930 71m bw
Fox
A girl criminal reforms but almost loses the love of her new boyfriend when he finds out about her past.
Transparent melodrama, strictly for indulgent ladies.
w George Middleton *d* Guthrie McClintic *ph* Arthur L. Todd
☆ Dorothy Mackaill, Joel McCrea, John Halliday, C. Henry Gordon, Ilka Chase, Clara Blandick, George Brent
'Slow drama that needs plenty of support.' – *Variety*

Once a Thief
US 1965 107m bw Panavision
MGM/Cipra/RN/Fred Engel (Jacques Bar)
An ex-convict is hounded by a vengeful cop.
Glum crime melodrama gleamingly photographed but otherwise quite routine.
w Zekial Marko *d* Ralph Nelson *ph Robert Burks* *m* Lalo Schifrin
☆ Alain Delon, Ann-Margret, Van Heflin, Jack Palance, John Davis Chandler

Once a Thief
Hong Kong 1991 108m colour
Milestone (Linda Kuk, Terence Chang)
original title: *Zongheng Sihai*
A criminal gang of two men and a woman, stealing paintings in France, decide to take their revenge after they are double-crossed by their mentor.
A mix of crime caper and romantic comedy, of minimal appeal other than to aficionados of its cultish director's delight in unlikely violence.
w John Woo, Clifton Ko, Janet Chun *d* John Woo *ph* Poon Hang Seng *m* Violet Lam *ad* James Leung *ed* David Wu
☆ Chow Yun-Fat, Leslie Cheung, Cherie Chung
'Packed with so many hilarious, violent action sequences that it becomes silly sophomoric fun.' – *Variety*
† It was given a US makeover in 1995 to emerge as *John Woo's Once a Thief* (qv).

Once Around **
US 1991 114m colour
Universal/Cinecom (Amy Robinson, Griffin Dunne)
Urged by her loving family to marry, a thirtyish woman chooses as a husband a brash and vulgar salesman who does not win their approval.
Perceptive drama of the swings and roundabouts of marital and family life.
w Malia Scotch Marmo *d* Lasse Hallström *ph* Theo Van de Sande *m* James Horner *ad* David Gropman *ed* Andrew Monshein
☆ Richard Dreyfuss, Holly Hunter, Danny Aiello, Laura San Giacomo, Gena Rowlands, Roxanne Hart, Griffin Dunne
'An intelligently engaging domestic comedy-drama.' – *Variety*

Once Before I Die
US 1966 97m Eastmancolor
F.8 Productions (John Derek)
In the Philippines, after a Jap aerial attack, a cavalry major's girlfriend causes complications in her bids to escape.
Mildly hilarious action melodrama in which the star's superstructure is made the focus of the action.
w Vance Skarstedt *d* John Derek *ph* Arthur Arling *m* Emmanuel Vardi
☆ Ursula Andress, John Derek, Richard Jaeckel, Rod Lauren

'Mark Kendell just found out that his one-night stand has been around for centuries.'
Once Bitten
US 1985 93m Metrocolor
Villard-Wald-Hilderbrand
Teenage sex problems are complicated by a visiting vampiress who needs the blood of a virgin three times before Hallowe'en.
Dispiriting attempt to mix genres without even a tinge of talent or sophistication.
w David Hines, Jeffrey Hause, Jonathan Roberts *d* Howard Storm
☆ Lauren Hutton, Jim Carrey, Karen Kopins, Cleavon Little
'Mr Storm might have found his ideas for the tone of this movie written on high school locker walls.' – *People*

Once in a Blue Moon
US 1936 65m bw
Paramount
Adventures of an innocent abroad in contemporary Russia.
Would-be satire which was seen by very few people indeed.
wd Ben Hecht, Charles MacArthur
☆ Jimmy Savo, Nikita Balieff, Whitney Bourne, Cecilia Loftus
'A dud. The exhibitors who are kidded into playing it won't be very happy afterwards.' – *Variety*
† Produced in 1934.

Once in a Lifetime *
US 1933 80m approx bw
Universal (Carl Laemmle Jnr)
How a script was sold in old-time Hollywood.
Half good-humoured, half-scathing satire on Hollywood; technique dated, content still amusing.
w Seton I. Miller *play* Moss Hart, George S. Kaufman *d* Russell Mack *ph* George Robinson
☆ Jack Oakie, Sidney Fox, Aline MacMahon, Russell Hopton, ZaSu Pitts, Louise Fazenda, Gregory Ratoff, Onslow Stevens
'Idol-smashing satire, strictly for the initiated.' – *Variety*

Once in Paris
US 1978 100m TVC Color
Frank D. Gilroy
A naïve American writer is introduced to the delights of Paris by a worldly chauffeur and an amorous British noblewoman.
A movie that adds up to very little, but pleases along the way.
wd Frank D. Gilroy
☆ Wayne Rogers, Gayle Hunnicutt, Jack Lenoir, Philippe March, Tanya Lopert

'The darkest alleys of love among the international set!'
Once Is Not Enough
US 1975 122m Movielab Panavision
Paramount/Sujac/Aries (Howard W. Koch)
aka: *Jacqueline Susann's Once Is Not Enough*
The daughter of a movie producer is corrupted by his circle.
Old-fashioned jet-set melodrama with new-fashioned sexual novelties.
w Julius J. Epstein *novel* Jacqueline Susann *d* Guy Green *ph* John A. Alonzo *m* Henry Mancini *pd* John DeCuir
☆ Kirk Douglas, Alexis Smith, David Janssen, George Hamilton, Melina Mercouri, Gary Conway, Brenda Vaccaro, Deborah Raffin
Brenda Vaccaro

Once More My Darling
US 1949 92m bw
Universal (Joan Harrison)
A young girl is romantically pursued by an older man.
Tame comedy.
w Robert Carson *d* Robert Montgomery *ph* Franz Planer *m* Elizabeth Firestone
☆ Robert Montgomery, Ann Blyth, Jane Cowl, Taylor Holmes, Charles McGraw

Once More with Feeling
GB 1960 92m Technicolor
Columbia/Stanley Donen
The volatile private life of an orchestral conductor.
Thin comedy from a West End play, something between a shouting match and a fashion show.
w Harry Kurnitz *play* Harry Kurnitz *d* Stanley Donen *ph* Georges Périnal *md* Muir Mathieson *pd* Alexander Trauner
☆ Yul Brynner, Kay Kendall, Geoffrey Toone, Maxwell Shaw, Mervyn Johns, Martin Benson, Gregory Ratoff

Once Upon a Crime
US 1992 94m Technicolor
Entertainment/Troublemakers/Dino de Laurentiis
Two Americans in Europe, hoping to collect a reward for finding a valuable dog, are suspected of murdering the animal's owner.
Hysterically unamusing comedy, performed in a frantic style.
w Charles Shyer, Nancy Myers, Steve Kluger *story* Rodolfo Sonego *d* Eugene Levy *ph* Giuseppe Rotunno *m* Richard Gibbs *pd* Pier Luigi Basile *ed* Patrick Kennedy
☆ John Candy, James Belushi, Cybill Shepherd, Sean Young, Richard Lewis, Ornella Muti, Giancarlo Giannini, George Hamilton, Joss Ackland
'An overacted, unfunny, unexciting comedy-thriller.' – *Philip French, Observer*
'The film gives the impression of having been assembled, at great haste and in a state of panic, from bits and pieces left over from several other "international comedies".' – *Philip Kemp, Sight and Sound*
'Abysmal comedy.' – *Variety*
† A remake of *Crimen*, directed by Mario Camerini in 1960.

Once Upon a Dream
GB 1948 84m bw
Triton/Rank
An officer's wife has a romantic dream about her husband's batman, and comes to believe it true.
Very wispy comedy which does none of its principals any good.
w Patrick Kirwan, Victor Katona *d* Ralph Thomas
☆ Googie Withers, Griffith Jones, Guy Middleton, Raymond Lovell, Hubert Gregg

Once Upon a Forest
US 1992 71m CFI color
TCF/Hanna-Barbera/HTV (David Kirschner, Jerry Mills)
After toxic waste destroys their environment, a mouse, a mole and a hedgehog have two days to find herbs that will save the life of their friend, a badger.
Dull and unimaginative animated movie that is unlikely to engage anyone's attention.
w Mark Young, Kelly Ward *story* Rae Lambert *d* Charles Grosvenor *m* James Horner *pd* Carol Holman Grosvenor, Bill Proctor *ed* Pat A. Foley
☆ Featuring the voices of Michael Crawford, Ben Vereen, Ellen Blain, Ben Gregory, Paige Gosney, Elizabeth Moss, Paul Elding, Janet Waldo
'It might, just, be of mild interest to the very young. But most kids, you suspect, are unregenerate sadists who will run a mile from something so earnestly improving.' – *Sheila Johnston, Independent*
'One long yawn.' – *Geoff Brown, The Times*

Once Upon a Honeymoon *
US 1942 116m bw
RKO (Leo McCarey)
An American radio correspondent and an ex-burlesque queen cheat the Nazis – and her husband – in Europe during World War II.
Smooth but curious mixture of comedy and drama, a satisfactory but unmemorable star vehicle.
w Sheridan Gibney, Leo McCarey *d* Leo McCarey *ph* George Barnes *m* Robert Emmett Dolan
☆ Cary Grant, Ginger Rogers, Walter Slezak, Albert Dekker, Albert Bassermann, Ferike Boros, Harry Shannon
'The attempt to play for both laughs and significance against a terrifying background of Nazi aggression is on the whole a little disappointing.' – *Newsweek*

Once Upon a Horse
US 1958 85m bw Cinemascope
Universal (Hal Kanter)

Two cowboys steal a herd of cattle but can't afford to feed them.
Unprepossessing comedy vehicle for a team which found success only on television.
wd Hal Kanter *ph* Arthur Arling *m* Frank Skinner *ad* Robert Clatworthy *ed* Milton Carruth
☆ Dan Rowan, Dick Martin, Martha Hyer, Leif Erickson, Nita Talbot, James Gleason

Once Upon a Time *
US 1944 89m bw
Columbia (Louis Edelman)

A luckless producer makes a sensation out of a boy and his dancing caterpillar.
Thin whimsical comedy, too slight to come off given such standard treatment, but with nice touches along the way.
w Lewis Meltzer, Oscar Saul *radio play* My Client Curley by *Norman Corwin, Lucille F. Herrmann*
d Alexander Hall *ph* Franz Planer *m* Frederick Hollander
☆ Cary Grant, Janet Blair, James Gleason, Ted Donaldson, Howard Freeman, William Demarest, Art Baker, John Abbott

'There just isn't enough material here for a full-length feature.' – *Philip T. Hartung*

'It would be nice to see some screen fantasy if it were done by anyone with half a heart, mind and hand for it. But when the studios try to make it, duck and stay hid till the mood has passed.' – *James Agee*

'As boys they said they would die for each other. As men, they did.'
Once Upon a Time in America ****
US 1984 228m Technicolor
Warner/Embassy/Ladd/PSO (Arnon Milchan)

The lives of four gangsters between 1922 and 1968.
Vast, sprawling, violent crime saga that is both the epitome and summation of gangster movies, a powerful, almost operatic drama of waste and despair.
w Leonardo Benvenuti, Piero de Bernardi, Enrico Medioli, Franco Arcalli, Franco Ferrini, Sergio Leone *novel* The Hoods by David Aaronson ('Harry Grey') *d Sergio Leone ph* Tonino Delli Colli *m* Ennio Morricone *ed* Nino Baragli
☆ Robert DeNiro, James Woods, Elizabeth McGovern, Treat Williams, Tuesday Weld, Burt Young, Danny Aiello, William Forsythe

'It is, finally, a heart-breaking story of mutual need. By matching that need with his own need to come to terms with his own cultural memories, Leone has made his most oneiric and extraordinary film.' – *Tony Rayns, MFB*

music

'Never was a hero needed more...'
Once Upon a Time in China *
Hong Kong 1991 140m colour Panavision
Film Workshop 1 (Zhen Wen Huai, Tsui Hark)

original title: *Wong Fei Hung*
Concerned about the growing Western influences in China, a martial master finds himself arrayed against a combination of triads, English, Americans selling the locals into slavery and prostitution, and government officials.
Anti-West martial arts movie, notable for the vigour and speed of its many scenes of fighting action.
w Tsui Hark, Yuan Zao Zhi, Liang Yao Min, Deng Bi Yan *d* Tsui Hark *ph* Chong Zhi Wen, Bill Huang, Arthur Huang, Ardy Chan *m* James Wong, Dai Le Ming *pd* David Luo, Jin Yang Xiang *ed* Mak Zhi Shang
☆ Jet Li, Yuan Biao, Rosamund Kwan, Ken Chung, Jacky Cheung, Wu Ma, Liu Xun, Yuan Xian Ren

'A tinned spaghetti western.'
Once Upon a Time in the Midlands
GB/Germany 2002 103m colour 'Scope
Film4/Film Council/Senator/EMMI/Slate/Big Arty (Andrea Calderwood)

A tough Glaswegian goes to the Midlands to reclaim his girlfriend and daughter, who are now living with a garage owner who likes to avoid trouble.
A minor account of domestic trials couched in the terms of a Sergio Leone movie, but the method merely emphasises the secondhand nature of the narrative and adds nothing to the pawky tone.
w Paul Fraser, Shane Meadows *d* Shane Meadows *ph* Brian Tufano *m* John Lunn *pd* Crispian Sallis *ed* Peter Beston, Trevor Waite
☆ Robert Carlyle (Jimmy), Rhys Ifans (Dek), Kathy Burke (Carol), Shirley Henderson (Shirley), Ricky Tomlinson (Charlie), Finn Atkins (Marlene)

'Enjoyable enough, but the un-originality of the script, plot and characters, means it will probably play a lot more convincingly on TV.' – *Jonathan Ross, Daily Mirror*

'Comedy-wise, there are few laughs, and the emotional heart of the story fails to grip.' – *Cosmo Landesman, Sunday Times*

Once Upon a Time in the West ***
Italy/US 1969 165m Techniscope
Paramount/Rafran/San Marco (Fulvio Morsella)

A lonely woman in the old west is in danger from a band of gunmen.
Immensely long and convoluted epic Western marking its director's collaboration with an American studio and his desire to make serious statements about something or other. Beautifully made, empty, and very violent.
w Sergio Leone, Sergio Donati *d* Sergio Leone *ph* Tonino Delli Colli *m* Ennio Morricone
☆ Henry Fonda, Claudia Cardinale, Jason Robards, Charles Bronson, Gabriele Ferzetti, Keenan Wynn, Paolo Stoppa, Lionel Stander, Jack Elam, Woody Strode
† This film has the longest credits of all: they sprawl through the first twelve minutes.

Once Were Warriors ***
New Zealand 1994 103m Eastmancolor
Entertainment/Communicado/NZFC/Avalon/New Zealand On Air (Robin Scholes)

In Auckland, a Maori woman attempts to bring up her children, including a bookish daughter and a son attracted to street gangs, and to cope with her unemployed, heavy-drinking and violent husband.
A powerfully emotional and often disturbing drama of the dispossessed, making its points with sledgehammer force, but also giving a place to the tenderness and pride that exist within a family forced to the edges of society.
w Riwia Brown *novel* Alan Duff *d Lee Tamahori ph* Stuart Dryburgh *m* Murray Grindley, Murray McNabb *pd* Michael Kane *ed Michael Horton*
☆ *Rena Owen, Temuera Morrison,* Mamaengaroa Kerr-Bell, Julian Arahanga, Taungaroa Emile, Rachael Morris, Joseph Kairau, Clifford Curtis

'Unflinchingly scans the domestic tragedy which can be found in any culture where hope is a luxury no one can afford.' – *Time*

'It's certainly operatic in style and melodramatic in concept. It shouldn't work as well as it does. But by flinging caution to the winds, it winds up mightily effective.' – *Derek Malcolm, Guardian*

† It took more money at the New Zealand box-office than any other film so far.
†† A sequel *What Becomes of the Broken-Hearted?* (qv) followed in 1999.

'Stealing the power of the universes one by one.'
The One
US 2001 87m DeLuxe Clairmont widescreen
Columbia/Revolution/Hard Eight (Glen Morgan, Steven Chasman)

A man seeks ultimate power by finding and killing his other selves that exist in parallel universes.
An intriguing concept that is used only as a means of having Jet Li fight himself, which isn't as interesting as having him beat up other people.
w Glen Morgan, James Wong *d* James Wong *ph* Robert McLachlan *m* Trevor Rabin *pd* David L. Snyder *ed* James Coblentz *martial arts choreographer* Cory Yuen
☆ Jet Li (Gabe/Yulaw/Lawless), Carla Gugino (T.K./Massie Walsh), Delroy Lindo (Roedecker/Attendant), Jason Statham (Funsch), James Morrison (Aldrich/'A' World Inmate #1), Dylan Bruno (Yates), Richard Steinmetz (D'Antoni)

'It aims low and hits its audience squarely in the nuts.' – *James Christopher, Times*

One Against Seven: see *Counterattack*

A One and a Two... ***
Taiwan/Japan 2000 173m Eastmancolor
ICA/1+2 Seisaku Iinkai/Pony Canyon/Omega/Hakuhodo/Atom (Shinya Kawai, Naoko Tsukeda)

original title: *Yi Yi*
While his mother-in-law lapses into a coma, his wife goes to a spiritual retreat, his daughter begins troubled relationships with boys and his son is in trouble at school, a middle-aged man, whose computer firm is failing, meets an old flame and wonders whether his life might have been different.
A cool dissection of three generations of a family, at different but similar points in their trajectories, this wry, detailed narrative, circling at a distance around its protagonists, provides many pleasures, as well as insights into the human condition.
wd Edward Yang *ph* Yang Wei-han *m* Peng Kai-li *pd* Peng Kai-li *ed* Chen Bo-wen
☆ Wu Nien-jen (NJ Jian), Elaine Jin (Min-Min), Issey Ogata (Mr Ota), Kelly Lee (Ting-Ting), Jonathan Chang (Yang-Yang), Chen Hsi-sheng (A-Di), Ko Su-yun (Sherry), Michael Tao (Da-Da), Hsiao Shu-shen (Xiao Yan), Adrian Lin (Lili)

'No narrative outline can hope to convey anything of the novelistic density of character and incident in Edward Yang's wonderful film.' – *Tony Rayns, Sight and Sound*

'A movie of formidable intelligence and observation, marbled with moments of magical abstraction.' – *Derek Elley, Variety*

† It won the Palme D'Or as best film at the Cannes Film Festival in 2000.

The One and Only
US 1978 98m Movielab
Paramount/First Artists (Steve Gordon, David V. Picker)

A stage-struck egomaniac finds success at the expense of happiness with his wife.
Uneasy mixture of farce and sentiment intended as a star vehicle, but not a very successful one.
w Steve Gordon *d* Carl Reiner *ph* Victor J. Kemper *m* Patrick Williams
☆ Henry Winkler, Kim Darby, Gene Saks, William Daniels, Polly Holiday, Herve Villechaize, Harold Gould, Richard Lane

The One and Only
GB/France 2002 91m DeLuxe
Pathé/TF1/Film Council/Assassin (Leslee Udwin)
On Tyneside, a widower, who is recovering from an unhappy marriage, falls for the unhappy wife of a footballer.
Dull romance that is mired in cliché and corn.
w Peter Flannery *Danish film Den Eneste Ene* by Susanne Bier *d* Simon Cellan Jones *ph* Remi Adefarasin *m* Gabriel Yared; *pd* Zoe Macleod *ed* Pia Di Ciaula
☆ Richard Roxburgh (Neil), Justine Waddell (Stevie), Jonathan Cake (Sonny), Aisling O'Sullivan (Jenny), Patsy Kensit (Stella), Michael Hodgson (Stan), Kerry Rolfe (Sharon)

'Deeply and insultingly awful comedy.' – *Peter Bradshaw, Guardian*

'Get Ready To Hear! Get ReadyTo Cheer!'
The One and Only Genuine Original Family Band
US 1968 110m Technicolor
Disney

Adventures of a Republican family at the 1888 convention.
Long and rather muddled family comedy with politics and music; not a winner anywhere.
w Lowell S. Hawley *book* Laura Bower Van Nuys *d* Michael O'Herlihy
☆ Walter Brennan, Buddy Ebsen, John Davidson, Lesley Ann Warren, Janet Blair, Kurt Russell, Richard Deacon

One Armed Boxer
Hong Kong 1972 97m Eastmancolor 'Scope
Cathay/Champion (Raymond Chow)

original title: *Dop Bey Kuan Wan*
A young boxer seeks revenge after he loses an arm in a fight against a gang leader and his assorted thugs, each expert in a different martial art.
Little more than a series of fight sequences, which are well choreographed and will no doubt appeal to fans of the genre.
wd Wang Yu *ph* Mo Shen Ku *m* Wang Fu Ling, Wang Ping *ed* Cheng Hung Min
☆ Wang Yu, Tang Shin, Tien Yeh, Lung Fei, Wu Tung Choo, Pan Chun Lin, San Mao

'The photography and cutting of the fights is, as usual, highly expert, with a splendid sense of movement.' – *MFB*

† The film was cut to 92m for its British release.

One Body Too Many
US 1944 74m bw
Pine-Thomas/Paramount

An insurance salesman arrives at a spooky house to find his prospect murdered.
Comedy melodrama which could have been a lot funnier and more melodramatic; once more, the butler didn't do it.
w Winston Miller, Maxwell Shane *d* Frank McDonald
☆ Jack Haley, Bela Lugosi, Jean Parker, Bernard Nedell, Blanche Yurka, Douglas Fowley, Lyle Talbot

One Born Every Minute: see *The Flim Flam Man*

One Dangerous Night
US 1943 77m bw
Columbia (David Chatkin)
Reformed jewel thief The Lone Wolf is accused of the murder of a society blackmailer.
Entertaining, fast-paced little thriller, with the usual comedy of bumbling cops kept to the minimum.
w Donald Davis *story* Arnold Phillips, Max Nosseck *d* Michael Gordon *ph* L. W. O'Connell *md* M. W. Stoloff *ad* Lionel Banks *ed* Viola Lawrence
☆ Warren William, Eric Blore, Marguerite Chapman, Mona Barrie, Tala Birell, Margaret Hayes, Ann Savage, Thurston Hall, Warren Ashe

'September 5, 1972. The Munich Games. On This Day, There Would Be No Winners.'
One Day in September **
GB 1999 95m colour
Redbus/Passion Pictures (Arthur Cohn, John Battsek)

Documentary on the events at the 1972 Olympic Games in Munich, when Palestinians took Israeli atheletes hostage.
Fascinating documentary that includes interviews with the one surviving Palestinian, Jamal Al Gashey, and also demonstrates the incompetence of the rescue attempt, and the German government's complicity in letting the Palestinians go free.
d Kevin Macdonald *ph* Alwin Kuchler, Neve Cunningham *m* Alex Heffes, Craig Armstrong *ed* Justine Wright
☆ Michael Douglas (Narrator)

'As a dramatic replay of the past, it's terrific: too bad it didn't try harder to say something new.' – *Cosmo Landesman, Sunday Times*

documentary

One Day in the Life of Ivan Denisovich *
GB 1971 105m Eastmancolor
Group W/Leontes/Norsk (Caspar Wrede)

Life in a Siberian labour camp in 1950.
A fairly successful book adaptation, as far as mere pictures can cope with the harrowing detail.
w Ronald Harwood *novel* Alexander Solzhenitsyn *d* Caspar Wrede *ph Sven Nykvist m* Arne Nordheim
☆ *Tom Courtenay,* Espen Skjonberg, James Maxwell, Alfred Burke, Eric Thompson, Matthew Guinness

'The film's general air of earnestness deflects rather than stimulates involvement.' – *David Wilson*

One Deadly Summer *
France 1983 133m Eastmancolor
Premier/SNC/CAPAC/TFI (Christine Beytout)

original title: *L'été Meurtrier*
A nineteen-year-old girl seduces a villager into marrying her as the first step in a long-delayed act of revenge.
Moody psychological thriller, an award-winner in France, that grows more engrossing as it continues.

w Sebastien Japrisot *novel* Sebastien Japrisot *d* Jean Becker *ph* Etienne Becker *m* Georges Delerue *ad* Jean-Claude Gallouin *ed* Jacques Witta
☆ Isabelle Adjani, Alain Souchon, Suzanne Flon, Jenny Clève, Michel Galabru, François Cluzet

One Desire
US 1955 94m Technicolor
U-I (Ross Hunter)
The romantic career of the lady owner of a gambling saloon.
Tawdry 1890s drama which never really gets going.
w Lawrence Roman, Robert Blees *novel Tacey Cromwell* by Conrad Richter *d* Jerry Hopper *ph* Maury Gertsman *m* Frank Skinner *md* Joseph Gershenson *ad* Carroll Clark, Alexander Golitzen *ed* Milton Carruth
☆ Anne Baxter, Rock Hudson, Julia Adams, Natalie Wood, Barry Curtis, William Hopper, Carl Benton Reid
'The standards of writing and characterization belong to a Victorian servant girl's paper-covered romance.' – *MFB*

One Exciting Night
GB 1944 89m bw
Columbia British
A singing welfare worker averts a plan to steal a Rembrandt.
Very ho-hum stuff for a very popular but histrionically untried star.
w Howard Irving Young, Peter Fraser, Margaret Kennedy, Emery Bonnet *d* Walter Forde
☆ Vera Lynn, Donald Stewart, Mary Clare, Frederick Leister, Richard Murdoch

One Eyed Jacks
US 1961 141m Technicolor Vistavision
Paramount/Pennebaker (Frank P. Rosenberg)
An outlaw has a running battle with an old friend.
Grossly self-indulgent Western controlled (unwisely) by its star, full of solemn pauses and bouts of violence.
w Guy Trosper, Calder Willingham *novel The Authentic Death of Hendry Jones* by Charles Neider *d* Marlon Brando *ph* Charles Lang Jnr *m* Hugo Friedhofer
☆ Marlon Brando, Karl Malden, Pina Pellicer, Katy Jurado, Slim Pickens, Ben Johnson, Timothy Carey, Elisha Cook Jnr
'This is not the ordinary Western; not the ordinary good Western; not even the ordinary extraordinary Western … The figures and the background, the colour and the movement repeatedly unite in compositions of mesmerizing beauty.' – *Dilys Powell*
'The picture is of variable quality: it has some visual grandeur; it also has some bizarrely brutal scenes. It isn't clear why Brando made this peculiarly masochistic revenge fantasy, or whether he hoped for something quite different from what he finished with.' – *Pauline Kael*
Charles Lang Jnr

One False Move ***
US 1992 105m colour
Metro/I.R.S. Media (Jesse Beaton, Ben Myron)
Two killers on the run with their black girlfriend head for a small town in Alabama where the local police chief and two big city detectives are waiting for them.
A tough, complex, suspenseful thriller-cum-road movie that also finds room to concern itself with relationships and racism.
w Billy Bob Thornton, Tom Epperson *d Carl Franklin ph* James L. Carter *m* Peter Haycock, Derek Holt *pd* Gary T. New *ed* Carole Kravetz
☆ Bill Paxton, Cynda Williams, Billy Bob Thornton, Michael Beach, Jim Metzler, Earl Billings, Natalie Canerday
'Gives film buffs that special jolt they're always looking for.' – *Jami Bernard, New York Post*
'A crime film that lifts you up and carries you along in an ominously rising tide of tension, building to an emotional pay-off of amazing power.' – *Roger Ebert*

One Fine Day
US 1996 109m DeLuxe
TCF/Fox 2000/Via Rosa (Lynda Obst)
Two busy single parents fall in love with each other.
Bland and sentimental romantic comedy.
w Terrel Seltzer, Ellen Simon *d* Michael Hoffman *ph* Oliver Stapleton *m* James Newton Howard *pd* David Gropman *ed* Garth Craven
☆ Michelle Pfeiffer, George Clooney, Mae Whitman, Alex D. Linz, Charles Durning, Jon Robin Baitz, Ellen Greene, Joe Grifasi, Pete Hamill
'Made with the right breezy insouciance and performed with consummate flair and sexy star appeal.' – *Todd McCarthy, Variety*
'Was it a great film? Absolutely not.' – *George Clooney*
song 'For the First Time' (*m/ly* James Newton Howard, Jud J. Friedman, Allan Dennis Rich)

One Flew over the Cuckoo's Nest ****
US 1975 134m DeLuxe
UA/Fantasy Films (Saul Zaentz, Michael Douglas)
A cheerful immoralist imprisoned for rape is transferred for observation to a state mental hospital.
Wildly and unexpectedly commercial film of a project which had lain dormant for fourteen years, this amusing and horrifying film conveniently sums up anti-government attitudes as well as make love not war and all that. It's certainly impossible to ignore.
w Lawrence Hauben, Bo Goldman *novel Ken Kesey d Milos Forman ph* Haskell Wexler *m* Jack Nitzsche *pd* Paul Sylbert
☆ *Jack Nicholson, Louise Fletcher*, William Redfield, Will Sampson, Brad Dourif, Christopher Lloyd
'Lacks the excitement of movie art, but the story and the acting make the film emotionally powerful.' – *New Yorker*
† Kirk Douglas bought the rights to the book and starred in a Broadway adaptation of it, but he was unable to obtain backing for a film version. When Michael Douglas obtained finance from outside the movie industry, his father was too old to play the lead role. James Caan turned down the role. Louise Fletcher's role was turned down by Anne Bancroft, Angela Lansbury and Ellen Burstyn.
best picture; script; Milos Forman; Jack Nicholson; Louise Fletcher
Haskell Wexler; Jack Nitzsche; Brad Dourif
best picture; Milos Forman; Jack Nicholson; Louise Fletcher; Brad Dourif

One Foot in Heaven *
US 1941 108m bw
Warner (Robert Lord, Irving Rapper)
The small-town doings of a methodist minister.
Slow but pleasing chronicle, nicely assembled.
w Casey Robinson *biography* (of his father) Hartzell Spence *d* Irving Rapper *ph* Charles Rosher *m* Max Steiner
☆ *Fredric March*, Martha Scott, Beulah Bondi, Gene Lockhart, Elisabeth Fraser, Harry Davenport, Laura Hope Crews, Grant Mitchell, Moroni Olsen, Ernest Cossart, Jerome Cowan
'A clean, sweet, decent picture.' – *Cecilia Ager*
best picture

One Foot in Hell
US 1960 89m DeLuxe Cinemascope
TCF (Sydney Boehm)
The sheriff of a small Western town is secretly plotting revenge on the townfolk for their long-ago treatment of his wife.
Unusual Western suspenser with plenty of violent action and an extremely equivocal hero.
w Aaron Spelling, Sydney Boehm *d* James B. Clark *ph* William C. Mellor *m* Dominic Frontière
☆ Alan Ladd, Dan O'Herlihy, Don Murray, Dolores Michaels, Barry Coe, Larry Gates, John Alexander

One for the Book: see *The Voice of the Turtle*

One Frightened Night
US 1935 67m bw
Mascot
Relatives assemble in a spooky house in the hope of inheriting an old man's wealth.
Low-budget thriller that sometimes seems like a spoof of The Cat and the Canary.
w Wellyn Totman *d* Christy Cabanne *ph* Ernest Miller, William Nobles
☆ Charles Grapewin, Mary Carlisle, Arthur Hohl, Evalyn Knapp, Wallace Ford, Hedda Hopper, Lucien Littlefield, Regis Toomey, Rafaela Ottiano

One from the Heart *
US 1982 101m Metrocolor
Zoetrope Studios (Gray Frederickson, Fred Roos, Armyan Bernstein)
On Independence Day in Las Vegas, a pair of lovers quarrel and make up.
Extraordinarily slim (for its cost) romantic fantasy which makes one wonder why, of all stories in the world, its creator chose this one. It does however boast attractive visuals.
w Armyan Bernstein, Francis Coppola *d* Francis Coppola *ph* Vittorio Storaro *m* Tom Waits *pd* Dean Tavoularis
☆ Frederic Forrest, Teri Garr, Raul Julia, Nastassja Kinski, Lainie Kazan, Harry Dean Stanton
'Giddy heights of visual imagination and technical brilliance are lavished on a wafer-thin story.' – *Variety*
'If this is the essence of cinema, then Salvador Dali is the essence of painting.' – *Sunday Times*
'A very beautiful film, the background of which totally drowns a wafer-thin plot. A musical non-musical, a spectacular nonspectacular, a fantasy with realist aspirations.' – *Guardian*
'Escapism running away with itself.' – *Standard*
original song score

One Good Cop
US 1991 105m colour
Hollywood/Silver Screen Partners IV (Laurence Mark)
A policeman and his wife run into problems when they try to adopt the three young girls of his murdered partner.
Mundane and manipulative drama that is never arresting.
wd Heywood Gould *ph* Ralf Bode *m* David Foster, William Ross *ad* Sandy Veneziano *ed* Richard Marks
☆ Michael Keaton, René Russo, Anthony LaPaglia, Kevin Conway, Rachel Ticotin, Tony Plana, Benjamin Bratt
'Excruciating dialogue, stagnant ideas and acting more wooden than Sherwood Forest.' – *Sight and Sound*

One Good Turn
US 1931 20m bw
Hal Roach
Two odd-job men see their benefactress rehearsing a play, and think she is really being evicted.
Moderate star comedy with nice moments.
w H. M. Walker *d* James W. Horne *ph* Art Lloyd *ed* Richard Currier
☆ Stan Laurel, Oliver Hardy, Mary Carr, Billy Gilbert, James Finlayson, Snub Pollard

One Good Turn
GB 1954 90m bw
GFD/Two Cities (Maurice Cowan)
An orphan stays on to become an odd job man, and tries to raise money to buy an old car.
The star's second comedy is an almost unmitigated disaster, disjointed and depending too much on pathos.
w Maurice Cowan, John Paddy Carstairs, Ted Willis *d* John Paddy Carstairs *ph* Jack Cox *m* John Addison
☆ Norman Wisdom, Joan Rice, Shirley Abicair, Thora Hird, William Russell, Richard Caldicot

One Heavenly Night
US 1930 82m bw
Samuel Goldwyn
A flower girl in a Budapest music hall finds herself imitating the absent star.
Would-be-Lubitsch-like musical comedy which doesn't quite succeed in its pleasant aims.
w Sidney Howard *story* Louis Bromfield *d* George Fitzmaurice *ph* George Barnes, Gregg Toland
☆ Evelyn Laye, John Boles, Leon Errol, Lilyan Tashman, Hugh Cameron, Lionel Belmore
'It will satisfy the customers, but lacks the intrinsic quality that makes 'em talk and recommends it as an entertainment for big grosses.' – *Variety*

'There's nothing more dangerous than a familiar face.'
One Hour Photo **
US 2002 95m DeLuxe
TCF/Fox Searchlight/Catch 23/Killer/Madjak (Christine Vachon, Pamela Koffler, Stan Wlodkowski)
A lonely photo developer becomes obsessed with a suburban family whose snapshots he prints.
Creepy thriller of a voyeur that gets tightly contained performance from Williams as a man going over the edge of madness; the meticolous use of colour and space adds to its chilling quality.
d Mark Romanek *ph* Jeff Cronenweth *m* Reinhold Heil, Johnny Klimek *pd* Tom Foden *ed* Jeffrey Ford
☆ Robin Williams (Seymour "Sy" Parrish), Connie Nielsen (Nina Yorkin), Michael Vartan (Will Yorkin), Gary Cole (Bill Owens), Dylan Smith (Jake Yorkin), Eriq La Salle (Detective Van Der Zee), Erin Daniels (Maya Burson)
'What damps down the psychological power… is director Mark Romanek's reluctance to let the film become as idiosyncratically unnerving as its main character.' – *David Sterritt, Christian Science Monitor*

One Hour with You: see *The Marriage Circle (1924)*

'Gayest screen event of the year!'
One Hour with You ***
US 1932 84m bw
Paramount (Ernst Lubitsch)
The affairs of a philandering Parisian doctor.
Superbly handled comedy of manners in Lubitsch's most inventive form, handled by a most capable cast. Unique entertainment of a kind which is, alas, no more.
w Samson Raphaelson play Only a Dream by Lothar Schmidt *d George Cukor, Ernst Lubitsch ph* Victor Milner *m Oscar Straus, Richard Whiting ad Hans Dreier ly Leo Robin*
☆ *Maurice Chevalier, Jeanette MacDonald*, Genevieve Tobin, *Roland Young*, Charles Ruggles, George Barbier
'Sure fire if frothy screen fare, cinch b.o. at all times.' – *Variety*
'A brand new form of musical entertainment … he has mixed verse, spoken and sung, a smart and satiric musical background, asides to the audience, and sophisticated dialogue, as well as lilting and delightful songs … The result is something so delightful that it places the circle of golden leaves jauntily upon the knowing head of Hollywood's most original director.' – *Philadelphia Inquirer*
† A remake of Lubitsch's silent success *The Marriage Circle*.
best picture

One Hundred and One Dalmatians ***
US 1961 79m Technicolor
Walt Disney
The dogs of London help save puppies which are being stolen for their skins by a cruel villainess.
Disney's last really splendid feature cartoon, with the old flexible style cleverly modernized and plenty of invention and detail in the story line. The London backgrounds are especially nicely judged.
w Bill Peet *novel* Dodie Smith *d* Wolfgang Reitherman, Hamilton S. Luske, Clyde Geronimi *m* George Bruns
☆ Featuring the voices of Rod Taylor, Cate Bauer, Betty Lou Gerson, J. Pat O'Malley
'It has the freshness of the early short colour-cartoons without the savagery which has often disfigured the later feature-length stories.' – *Dilys Powell*

'When schools become war zones and both sides start taking casualties, what then?'
187
US 1997 119m DeLuxe
Warner/Anna K/Icon (Bruce Davey, Stephen McEveety)
A New York teacher recovers from being stabbed by a pupil sufficiently to move to a Los Angeles school, where he reacts violently when he is threatened by some of his students.
Risible and confused melodrama, from which an audience can learn nothing and enjoy even less.

w Scott Yagemann *d* Kevin Reynolds *ph* Ericson Core *pd* Stephen Storer *ed* Stephen Semel
☆ Samuel L. Jackson, John Heard, Kelly Rowan, Clifton Gonzalez Gonzalez, Tony Plana, Karina Arroyave, Lobo Sebastian

'"A teacher wrote this movie," the final credit reads. It might have made more sense to hire a screenwriter.' – *Richard Williams, Guardian*

One Hundred Men and a Girl ***
US 1937 84m bw
Universal (Joe Pasternak)

A young girl persuades a great conductor to form an orchestra of unemployed musicians.
Delightful and funny musical fable, an instance of the Pasternak formula of sweetness and light at its richest and best.
w Bruce Manning, Charles Kenyon, Hans Kraly d Henry Koster ph Joseph Valentine *m* Charles Previn *ed* Bernard W. Burton *songs* various
☆ *Deanna Durbin, Adolphe Menjou, Leopold Stokowski, Alice Brady, Mischa Auer, Eugene Pallette,* Billy Gilbert, Alma Kruger, Jed Prouty, Frank Jenks, Christian Rub

'Smash hit for all the family ... something new in entertainment.' – *Variety*

'Apart from its value as entertainment, which is considerable, it reveals the cinema at its sunny-sided best.' – *New York Times.*

'An original story put over with considerable skill.' – *MFB*

Charles Previn
best picture; original story (Hans Kraly); editing

'This Time The Magic Is Real.'
101 Dalmatians
US 1996 103m Technicolor
Panavision
Buena Vista/Walt Disney/Great Oaks (John Hughes, Ricardo Mestres)

After their owners marry, two dalmatians protect their numerous puppies from a fur-loving woman who wants to turn them into a fur coat.
Live-action remake of a successful animated feature which lacks the charm of the original.
w John Hughes *novel The One Hundred and One Dalmatians* by Dodie Smith *d* Stephen Herek *ph* Adrian Biddle *m* Michael Kamen *pd* Assheton Gorton *ed* Industrial Light and Magic; Jim Henson's Creature Shop
☆ Glenn Close, Jeff Daniels, Joan Plowright, Joely Richardson, Hugh Laurie, Mark Williams, John Shrapnel

'Relentlessly cuddlesome enough to make this, if not enchanting, then sufficiently chucklesome and likeable to send family audiences home with their tails wagging.' – *Angie Errigo, Empire*

'30 below zero, five hours of daylight, what else can you do but get wrecked?'
101 Reykjavik *
Iceland/France/Denmark/Norway 2000 89m colour
Metrodome/101/Zentropa/Liberator/Filmhuset (Ingvar Thordarson, Baltasar Kormakur)

An unemployed 30-year-old layabout falls for his mother's lesbian flamenco teacher; so does his mother.
Amiable comedy of indolence getting its come-uppance.
wd Baltasar Kormakur *novel* Hallgrimur Helgason *ph* Peter Steuger *m* Damon Albarn, Einar Orn Benediktsson *ed* Skule Eriksen, Sigvaldi Karason
☆ Hilmir Snaer Gudnason (Hlynur), Victoria Abril (Lola Milagros), Hanna Maria Karlsdottir (Berglind), Baltasar Kormakur (Thröstur), Olafur Darri Olafsson (Marri), Thrudur Vilhjalmdottir (Hofi)

'Funny, touching, off-the-wall relationer.' – *Variety*

'A lumpy dish of second-hand hippiness – undercooked and over-familiar.' – *Alexander Walker*

One Hundred Per Cent Pure: see *The Girl from Missouri*

100 Rifles *
US 1969 109m DeLuxe
TCF/Marvin Schwartz

In war-torn Mexico, a black American sheriff and his prisoner become involved in a girl's fight for vengeance after her father's death.
Blood-soaked adventure with plenty of tough action and tight pace. A little too purposeful in its unpleasantness to be very entertaining.
w Clair Huffaker, Tom Gries *novel* Robert MacLeod *d* Tom Gries *ph* Cecilio Paniagua *m* Jerry Goldsmith
☆ Jim Brown, Raquel Welch, Burt Reynolds, Fernando Lamas, Dan O'Herlihy, Hans Gudegast

120 Days of Sodom *
Italy/France 1975 117m Technicolor
PEA/PAA

aka: *Salo*
After the Italian campaign of 1944, four local dignitaries marry each other's daughters, withdraw with a bevy of nubile girls to a mountain retreat, and tell each other sado-masochistic sexual adventures.
Whether you regard this bleak film as obscene or as a relentless examination of the effects of capitalism on sexuality, its scenes of brutal consumption, rape and torture make it difficult to watch; its despair is palpable.
wd Pier Paolo Pasolini *novel* Marquis de Sade *ph* Tonino delli Colli *ad* Dante Ferretti
☆ Paolo Bonacelli, Giorgio Cataldi, Uberto P. Quintavalle, Aldo Valetti

'One of the most scandalous films ever made...comments on the exercise of power, and on a consumer culture where a limitless choice of gratifications disguises an absence of all choice and all resistance.' – *Gary Indiana*

102 Dalmatians
US 2000 100m Technicolor
Buena Vista/Walt Disney (Edward S. Feldman)

Despite being taught to like dogs, Cruella De Vil lapses into her old ways and longs once more for a Dalmatian coat.
This is not so much a sequel, but virtually a remake of Disney's first live-action version of the story, only much duller.
w Kristen Buckley, Brian Regan, Bob Tzudiker, Noni White *novel The One Hundred and One Dalmatians* by Dodie Smith *d* Kevin Lima *ph* Adrian Biddle *m* David Newman *pd* Assheton Gorton *ed* Gregory Perler *cos* Anthony Powell
☆ Glenn Close (Cruella De Vil), Ioan Gruffudd (Kevin Shepherd), Alice Evans (Chloe Simon), Tim McInnerny (Alonso), Ian Richardson (Mr Torte), Gerard Depardieu (Jean Pierre Le Pelt), Ben Crompton (Ewan), Carol Macready (Agnes), Jim Carter (Detective Armstrong), Ron Cook (Mr Button), David Horovitch (Doctor Pavlov), Timothy West (Judge), Eric Idle (Voice of Waddlesworth)

'Goes through the motions and big set pieces with the prosaic proficiency of a formulaic sequel.' – *Cosmo Landesman, Sunday Times*

Anthony Powell

One in a Million **
US 1936 94m bw
TCF (Raymond Griffith)
The daughter of a Swiss innkeeper becomes an Olympic ice-skating champion.
Sonja Henie's film debut shows Hollywood at its most professional, making entertainment out of the purest moonshine with considerable injections of novelty talent.
w Leonard Praskins, Mark Kelly *d* Sidney Lanfield *ph* Edward Cronjager *md* Louis Silvers *ch* Jack Haskell *songs* Sidney Mitchell, Lew Pollack
☆ *Sonja Henie*, Don Ameche, *The Ritz Brothers*, Jean Hersholt, Ned Sparks, Arline Judge, Dixie Dunbar, Borrah Minevitch and his Rascals, Montagu Love

'A very entertaining, adroitly mixed concoction of romance, music, comedy and skating ... Miss Henie is a screen find.' – *Variety*

Jack Haskell

One Is a Lonely Number *
US 1972 97m Metrocolor
MGM (Stan Margulies)
When her husband leaves her, a woman tries to develop new interests.
Satirical sentimental view of American divorce, with interesting moments.
w David Seltzer *novel* Rebecca Morris *d* Mel Stuart *ph* Michel Hugo *m* Michel Legrand
☆ Trish Van Devere, Monte Markham, Melvyn Douglas, Janet Leigh

One Little Indian
US 1973 91m Technicolor
Walt Disney (Winston Hibler)

A cavalry corporal escapes from jail and falls in with a ten-year-old Indian.
Sentimental semi-Western, a bit dull for Disney apart from a camel.
w Harry Spalding *d* Bernard McEveety *ph* Charles F. Wheeler *m* Jerry Goldsmith
☆ James Garner, Vera Miles, Pat Hingle, Morgan Woodward, John Doucette

One Magic Christmas
Canada 1985 88m DeLuxe
Silver Screen/Telefilm Canada/Walt Disney (Peter O'Brian, Fred Roos)

An angel interferes in the lives of a family with problems.
Decidedly downbeat Christmas fantasy: daddy gets drowned, mother is a nut, and the angel looks like a tramp. Santa Claus puts in an appearance for a happy finale, but It's a Wonderful Life *should sue for plagiarism.*
w Thomas Meecham *d* Phillip Borsos *ph* Frank Tidy *m* Michael Conway *pd* Bill Brodie *ed* Sidney Wolinsky
☆ Mary Steenburgen, Gary Basaraba, Harry Dean Stanton, Arthur Hill

One Man Mutiny: see *The Court Martial of Billy Mitchell*

One Man's Journey
US 1933 72m bw
RKO
The career of a rural doctor for whom fame arrives too late.
Pleasant, predictable, rather downbeat small-town drama.
w Lester Cohen, Sam Ornitz *story Failure* by Katharine Haviland Taylor *d* John Robertson
☆ Lionel Barrymore, May Robson, Dorothy Jordan, Joel McCrea, Frances Dee, David Landau, Samuel S. Hinds

'Carries sympathetic interest and appeal.' – *Variety*

One Man's Way
US 1964 105m bw
UA
A crime reporter becomes a priest.
Rather self-conscious biography of Norman Vincent Peale, adequately assembled but containing no surprises.
w Eleanore Griffin, John W. Bloch *book Minister to Millions* by Arthur Gordon *d* Denis Sanders
☆ Don Murray, Diana Hyland, William Windom, Virginia Christine, Carol Ohmart

One Mile from Heaven
US 1937 68m bw
TCF
A girl reporter makes hay with the story of a black woman who is raising a white child.
Curious mixture of melodrama and wisecracking farce, with tap dancing from Bill Robinson thrown in.
w Lou Breslow, John Patrick *d* Allan Dwan
☆ Claire Trevor, Sally Blane, Douglas Fowley, Fredi Washington, Ralf Harolde

'Whether the theme fits into the popular groove is something to think about.' – *Variety*

'The most exciting adventure in a million years!'
One Million BC *
US 1940 80m bw
Hal Roach

GB title: *Man and His Mate*
aka: *The Cave Dwellers*
Life between warring tribes of primitive man in the stone age.
Impressive-looking but slow-moving grunt-and-groan epic originally based on D. W. Griffith's Man's Genesis *and on which Griffith did some work. The totally unhistoric dinosaurs (which had disappeared long before man arrived) are impressively concocted by magnifying lizards.*
w Mickell Novak, George Baker, Joseph Frickert *d* Hal Roach, Hal Roach Jnr, D. W. Griffith *ph Norbert Brodine m* Werner R. Heymann
☆ Victor Mature, Carole Landis, Lon Chaney Jnr, John Hubbard, Nigel de Brulier, Conrad Nagel

Werner R. Heymann

'This is the way it was!'
One Million Years BC *
GB 1966 100m Technicolor
Hammer (Michael Carreras)

A vague remake of the above, with animated monsters.
Not badly done, with some lively action.
w Michael Carreras *d* Don Chaffey *ph* Wilkie Cooper *m* Mario Nascimbene
☆ John Richardson, Raquel Welch, Robert Brown, Percy Herbert, Martine Beswick

'Very easy to dismiss the film as a silly spectacle; but Hammer production finesse is much in evidence and Don Chaffey has done a competent job of direction. And it is all hugely enjoyable.' – *David Wilson*

One Minute to Zero
US 1952 105m bw
RKO (Edmund Grainger)

In Korea a US colonel is evacuating American civilians but is forced to bomb refugees.
Flat war film with Something To Say and the star at his most humourless.
w Milton Krims, William Haines *d* Tay Garnett *ph* William E. Snyder *m* Victor Young *md* Constantin Bakaleinikoff
☆ Robert Mitchum, Ann Blyth, William Talman, Charles McGraw, Richard Egan

One More Kiss
GB 1999 102m Technicolor Panavision
Metrodome/Mob/Jam/Freewheel (Vadim Jean, Paul Brooks)
A young woman returns home to Britain to die and to ask a former boyfriend, who is now married, to be with her during her last days.
Tear-jerking drama that, despite its terminal theme, tries to keep death at a distance.
w Suzie Halewood *d* Vadim Jean *ph* Mike Fox *m* David A. Hughes, John Murphy *pd* Simon Hicks *ed* Joe McNally
☆ Gerard Butler (Sam), James Cosmo (Frank), Valerie Edmond (Sarah), Valerie Gogan (Charlotte), Carl Proctor (Barry), Danny Nussbaum (Jude), Dilys Miller (Mary), Ron Guthrie (Robin)

'A glossy romance of the Mills and Boon kind...would have played better had some of the gloss been scraped off.' – *Alexander Walker*

One More River *
US 1934 88m bw
Universal (James Whale)
GB title: *Over the River*
A wife runs away from her husband, and he sets detectives on her and her lover.
Old-fashioned, well made picturization of a novel.
w R. C. Sherriff *novel* John Galsworthy *d* James Whale *ph* John Mescall *m* W. Franke Harling
☆ Colin Clive, Diana Wynyard, C. Aubrey Smith, Jane Wyatt, Lionel Atwill, Mrs Patrick Campbell, Frank Lawton, Reginald Denny, Henry Stephenson, Alan Mowbray, E. E. Clive

'Galsworthy beautifully transmuted to the screen ... Very British and ultra, but should prove nice enough b.o.' – *Variety*

'Taste, elegance, narrative drive and a deliberate nostalgia for the Galsworthy period.' – *Peter John Dyer, 1966*

'One of the finest courtroom episodes ever projected on a screen.' – *Motion Picture Herald*

One More Spring *
US 1935 87m bw
Fox (Winfield Sheehan)
Three strangers, in reduced circumstances due to the Depression, meet in Central Park and pool their resources.
Topical serio-comedy which looks pretty dated but still serves as a summation of American mid-thirties attitudes.
w Edwin Burke *novel* Robert Nathan *d* Henry King *ph* John Seitz *md* Arthur Lange

☆ Janet Gaynor, Warner Baxter, Walter Woolf King, Grant Mitchell, Jane Darwell, Roger Imhof, John Qualen, Dick Foran, Stepin Fetchit

'Whimsical comedy with plenty of laughs. Should do well.' – *Variety*

One More Time
GB 1969 93m DeLuxe
UA/Chrislaw-Tracemark (Milton Ebbins)
Two London club owners become involved with spies, gangsters and jewel-thieves.
The stars of the tedious Salt and Pepper *are reunited for an even less amusing film.*
w Michael Pertwee *d* Jerry Lewis *ph* Ernest Steward *m* Les Reed
☆ Peter Lawford, Sammy Davis Jnr, Esther Anderson, Maggie Wright

One More Tomorrow *
US 1946 89m bw
Warner (Henry Blanke)
A wealthy playboy marries a left-wing photographer and buys up her magazine.
An interesting but dated play fails to come to life because neither cast nor director seem to understand what it's about.
w Charles Hoffman, Catherine Turney, Julius J. and Philip G. Epstein *play The Animal Kingdom* by Philip Barry *d* Peter Godfrey *ph* Bert Glennon *m* Max Steiner
☆ Ann Sheridan, Dennis Morgan, Jack Carson, Alexis Smith, Jane Wyman, Reginald Gardiner, John Loder, Marjorie Gateson

One More Train to Rob
US 1971 108m Technicolor
Universal (Robert Arthur)
A train robber comes out of prison and warily takes up with his old partners.
Undistinguished Western which tries to be funny and serious at the same time.
w Don Tait, Dick Nelson *d* Andrew V. McLaglen *ph* Alric Edens *m* David Shire
☆ George Peppard, Diana Muldaur, John Vernon, France Nuyen, Steve Sandor

One New York Night *
US 1935 80m bw
MGM (Bernard Hyman)
GB title: *The Trunk Mystery*
A young farmer in Manhattan on a visit finds a body in the hotel room next to his.
Slick comedy thriller very typical of its date and studio.
w Frank Davis *play* Edward Childs Carpenter *d* Jack Conway
☆ Franchot Tone, Una Merkel, Steffi Duna, Conrad Nagel, Charles Starrett, Harold Huber

'Sprightly devised murder mystery accounting for plenty of laughs ... studded with multiple touches of production value.' – *Variety*

'A comedy of astonishing intelligence and finish ... it ought to take its place immediately with the classics.' – *Graham Greene*

'She's three men over the legal limit.'
One Night at McCool's
US 2001 93m DeLuxe
Entertainment/October/Furthur (Michael Douglas, Allison Lyon Segan)
🎧
A bartender, a lawyer and a detective all fall for the same ruthless woman.
Ramshackle comedy that suffers from the miscasting of Liv Tyler as a femme fatale, though there's enjoyment to be found elsewhere, notably in Douglas's toothy, bingo-playing hit-man.
w Stan Seidel *d* Harald Zwart *ph* Karl Walter Lindenlaub *m* Marc Shaiman *pd* Jon Gary Steele *ed* Bruce Cannon *cos* Ellen Mirojnick
☆ Liv Tyler (Jewel), Matt Dillon (Randy), John Goodman (Detective Dehling), Paul Reiser (Carl), Michael Douglas (Mr Burmeister), Richard Jenkins (Father Jimmy), Reba McEntire (Dr Green), Andrew Silverstein (Utah), Andrea Bendewald (Karen), Eric Schaeffer (Greg Spradling), Leo Rossi (Joey Dinardo)

'Packs a lot into one night, but it's wearying. It's like a kid determined to show you every toy in his room, and there's nowhere to escape.' – *Elvis Mitchell, New York Times*

One Night in Lisbon
US 1941 97m bw
Paramount (Edward H. Griffith)
During World War II an American flyer falls for a British socialite who is being used by the government as a decoy for spies.
Flabby romantic comedy-drama which mostly wastes a good cast.
w Virginia Van Upp *play There's Always Juliet* by John Van Druten *d* Edward H. Griffith *ph* Bert Glennon *m* Sigmund Krumgold
☆ Madeleine Carroll, Fred MacMurray, Edmund Gwenn, Patricia Morison, Billie Burke, John Loder, Dame May Whitty, Reginald Denny, Billy Gilbert

One Night in the Tropics
US 1940 69m bw
Universal (Leonard Spigelgass)
Holidays on a Caribbean island lead to a double wedding.
Very lightweight comedy-musical notable only for introducing Abbott and Costello.
w Gertrude Purcell, Charles Grayson *play Love Insurance* by Earl Derr Biggers *d* A. Edward Sutherland *ph* Joseph Valentine *m/ly* Oscar Hammerstein II, Jerome Kern, Otto Harbach, Dorothy Fields *md* Charles Previn *ch* Larry Ceballos *ad* Jack Otterson *ed* Milton Carruth
☆ Allan Jones, Nancy Kelly, Bud Abbott, Lou Costello, Robert Cummings, Leo Carrillo, Peggy Moran, Mary Boland

One Night of Love **
US 1934 95m bw
Columbia (Harry Cohn)
An opera star rebels against her demanding teacher.
Light classical musical which was a surprising box-office success and brought Hollywood careers for Lily Pons, Gladys Swarthout, Miliza Korjus, etc.
w Dorothy Speare, Charles Beahan, S. K. Lauren, James Gow, Edmund North *d Victor Schertzinger* *ph* Joseph Walker *m* Victor Schertzinger, Gus Kahn *md* Pietro Cimini *ed* Gene Milford
☆ *Grace Moore, Tullio Carminati*, Lyle Talbot, Mona Barrie, Nydia Westman, Jessie Ralph, Luis Alberni, Jane Darwell
score
best picture; direction; Grace Moore; editing

One Night Stand
US 1994 92m Foto-Kem
New World/New Horizons/Schwartzman (Alida Camp)
aka: *Before the Night*
An unhappy, restless career woman falls for a man who picks her up in a night-club and discovers that he is suspected of murdering his wife.
Unconvincing and extremely boring romantic drama, along the lines of a TV soap opera, with trite dialogue.
w Marty Casella *d* Talia Shire *ph* Arthur Albert *m* David Shire *pd* Rusty Smith *ed* Jim Prior
☆ Ally Sheedy, A. Martinez, Frederic Forrest, Diane Salinger, Gina Hecht, Don Novello, Jodi Thelen, Robin Frates, Elsa Raven

'It was just one night that changed everything.'
One Night Stand *
US 1997 102m DeLuxe
Entertainment/New Line/Red Mullet (Mike Figgis, Annie Stewart, Ben Myron)
Visiting New York, a director of commercials spends the night with a woman he meets at his hotel, and finds he misses her when he returns home to his wife.
Slick, well-acted account of a burgeoning romance, but very forgettable.
wd Mike Figgis *ph* Declan Quinn *m* Mike Figgis *pd* Waldemar Kalinowski *ed* John Smith
☆ Wesley Snipes, Nastassja Kinski, Robert Downey Jnr, Ming-Na Wen, Kyle MacLachlan, Glenn Plummer, Amanda Donohoe, Thomas Haden Church, Julian Sands

'It's beautiful to look at, but shallow and trivial ... flashy, phoney and as ephemeral as its title.' – *Alexander Walker, London Evening Standard*

† Joe Eszterhas was reportedly paid $3m for his original script, which was to have been directed by Adrian Lyne; Figgis rewrote it, keeping only the title and the plot device.
†† Wesley Snipes won the best actor award at the Venice Film Festival.

One Night with You
GB 1948 92m bw
Two Cities/Rank
An English girl and an Italian tenor, stranded by a train failure, are taken for forgers.
Rather frantic but occasionally amusing Italian-set comedy.
w Caryl Brahms, S. J. Simon *d* Terence Young *ph* André Thomas *m* Lambert Williamson *ad* Terence Verity
☆ Nino Martini, Patricia Roc, Hugh Wakefield, Bonar Colleano, Guy Middleton, Stanley Holloway, Irene Worth, Charles Goldner

One of Our Aircraft Is Missing *
GB 1941 102m bw
British National (Michael Powell, Emeric Pressburger)
A bomber is grounded after a raid and its crew is helped by the Dutch resistance.
Efficient propaganda piece which starts vigorously but gets bogged down in talk.
wd Michael Powell, Emeric Pressburger
ph Ronald Neame *ed* David Lean
☆ Godfrey Tearle, Eric Portman, Hugh Williams, Bernard Miles, Hugh Burden, Emrys Jones, Googie Withers, Pamela Brown, Peter Ustinov, Joyce Redman, Hay Petrie, Robert Helpmann, Alec Clunes
script

One of Our Dinosaurs Is Missing *
US 1975 94m Technicolor
Walt Disney (Bill Walsh)
In the 1920s a strip of secret microfilm is smuggled out of China and hidden in a dinosaur's skeleton in the Natural History Museum.
Unexceptionable family comedy with everyone trying hard; somehow it just misses, perhaps because it is told through talk rather than cinematic narrative.
w Bill Walsh *novel The Great Dinosaur Robbery* by David Forrest *d* Robert Stevenson *ph* Paul Beeson *m* Ron Goodwin
☆ Helen Hayes, Peter Ustinov, Derek Nimmo, Clive Revill, Joan Sims, Bernard Bresslaw, Roy Kinnear, Deryck Guyler, Richard Pearson

One on One
US 1977 98m colour
Warner (Martin Hornstein)
An idealistic young basketball star finds life hard after he wins a scholarship to university.
Dull teen drama of a misfit making good.
w Robby Benson, Jerry Segal *d* Lamont Johnson *ph* Donald M. Morgan *m* Charles Fox *ad* Sherman Laudermilk *ed* Robbe Roberts
☆ Robby Benson, Annette O'Toole, G. D. Spradlin, Gail Strickland, Melanie Griffith

The One Piece Bathing Suit: see *Million Dollar Mermaid*

One Plus One
GB 1968 104m Eastmancolor
Connoisseur/Cupid (Michael Pearson, Iain Quarrier)
aka: *Sympathy for the Devil*
As the Rolling Stones rehearse their song 'Sympathy for the Devil', the film cuts between black militants, a television interview about revolution and its relationship with culture, and a bookshop where someone recites excerpts from *Mein Kampf*.
A confused revolutionary statement, with Godard trying to annex rock 'n' roll for his own impenetrable purposes. The last words in the film are the director's, stating that he is fed up and wants to go home; his audience is likely to have left earlier.
wd Jean-Luc Godard *ph* Tony Richmond *m* The Rolling Stones *ed* Ken Rowles
☆ Jean-Luc Godard (voice), Sean Lynch (voice), Mick Jagger, Keith Richard, Brian Jones, Charlie Watts, Bill Wyman, Anne Wiazemsky, Iain Quarrier, Frankie Dymon Jnr, Nike Arrighi

'Regardless of the effectiveness of certain scenes and sequences, one is left with the feeling that the film as a whole doesn't add up. But this is falling into the trap Godard has set for us: it is not meant to add up, and it won't.' – *Richard Roud, MFB*

† The producers increased Godard's cut by five minutes to 109m to include a full version of the Stones' song 'Sympathy for the Devil' at the end of the film.

One Rainy Afternoon *
US 1935 79m bw
Pickford-Lasky
In a cinema one afternoon, a gigolo kisses the wrong girl.
Rather heavy-handed light comedy with interesting credentials.
w Stephen Morehouse Avery, Maurice Hanline *play* Emeric Pressburger and René Pujal *d* Rowland V. Lee
☆ Francis Lederer, Ida Lupino, Roland Young, Hugh Herbert, Erik Rhodes, Mischa Auer

'Mr Lee has given a useful demonstration of how not to direct this kind of story: he has been remorselessly logical when he should have been crazy; his only idea of humour is speed and noise, not speed of thought or situation, but just literal speed of walking and talking.' – *Graham Greene, The Spectator*

One Spy Too Many
US 1966 102m Metrocolor
MGM/Arena (David Victor)
A modern-day Alexander the Great is foiled in his attempt to conquer the world.
Trivial spy caper, edited from episodes of the television series The Man from U.N.C.L.E.
w Dean Hargrove *d* Joseph Sargent *ph* Fred Koenekamp *m* Gerald Fried *ad* George W. Davis, Merrill Pye *ed* Henry Berman
☆ Robert Vaughn, David McCallum, Rip Torn, Dorothy Provine, Leo G. Carroll, David Opatoshu, David Sheiner

One Summer Love
US 1976 97m colour Panavision
AIP
aka: *Dragonfly*
A young man leaves mental hospital for his Connecticut home, only to find everyone there nuttier than he is.
Over-the-top melodrama.
w N. Richard Nash *d* Gilbert Cates
☆ Beau Bridges, Susan Sarandon, Mildred Dunnock, Michael B. Miller

One Sunday Afternoon **
US 1933 93m bw
Paramount (Louis D. Lighton)
In 1910, a Brooklyn dentist feels he has married the wrong girl, but discovers that his choice was the right one.
Pleasant period comedy drama which was twice remade: as The Strawberry Blonde *(qv) and see below.*
w William Slavens McNutt, Grover Jones *play* James Hagan *d* Stephen Roberts *ph* Victor Milner
☆ *Gary Cooper*, Frances Fuller, Fay Wray, Neil Hamilton, Roscoe Karns

'Still pitched in stage tempo and unfolds haltingly.' – *Variety*

One Sunday Afternoon
US 1948 90m Technicolor
Warner (Jerry Wald)
Pleasant but undistinguished musical remake of the above.
w Robert L. Richards *d* Raoul Walsh *ph* Sid Hickox, Wilfrid M. Cline *md* Ray Heindorf *ad* Anton Grot
☆ Dennis Morgan, Dorothy Malone, Janis Paige, Don Defore, Ben Blue

'A lackadaisical and uninspired jaunt down memory lane.' – *New Yorker, 1978*

The One that Got Away **
GB 1957 111m bw
Rank (Julian Wintle)
A German flyer, Franz von Werra, is captured and sent to various British prisoner-of-war camps, from all of which he escapes.
True-life biopic, developed in a number of suspense and action sequences, all very well done.
w Howard Clewes book Kendal Burt, James Leasor *d* Roy Baker *ph* Eric Cross *m* Hubert Clifford
☆ *Hardy Kruger*, Michael Goodliffe, Colin Gordon, *Alec McCowen*

One Third of a Nation *
US 1939 79m bw
Federal Theatre (Dudley Murphy)

A shopgirl persuades a landlord to tear down his dangerous slums and put up good buildings.
Naïve do-goodery, not too persuasively managed.
w Dudley Murphy, Oliver H. P. Garrett *play* Arthur Arent *d* Dudley Murphy *ph* William Mellor *m* Nathaniel Shilkret
☆ Sylvia Sidney, Leif Erickson, Myron McCormick, Hiram Sherman, Sidney Lumet, Percy Waram
'No worse and rather better than a commensurate modest-budgeter essayed on the coast ... the cinematic transition however seems to have almost wholly ditched the Federal Housing "living newspaper" purpose of the stage version, emphasizing the boy-meets-girl premise against the shocking slum background.' – *Variety*

The One Thousand Plane Raid
US 1969 94m DeLuxe
Oakwood/UA
An American colonel persuades top brass of the need for daylight bombing of Germany.
Reasonable routine war action drama.
w Donald S. Sanford *d* Boris Sagal
☆ Christopher George, Laraine Stephens, J. D. Cannon, Gary Marshall, Michael Evans, Ben Murphy

'The Gal Who Invented Love!'
One Touch of Venus *
US 1948 82m bw
Universal/Lester Cowan

In a fashionable department store, a statue of Venus comes to life and falls for a window dresser.
Pleasant satirical comedy, watered down from the Broadway original.
w Harry Kurnitz, Frank Tashlin *play* S. J. Perelman, Ogden Nash *d* William A. Seiter *ph* Franz Planer *ad* Bernard Herzbrun, Emrich Nicholson *songs* Kurt Weill
☆ Ava Gardner, Robert Walker, Eve Arden, Dick Haymes, Olga San Juan, Tom Conway

One, Two, Three **
US 1961 115m bw Panavision
United Artists/Mirisch/Pyramid (Billy Wilder)

An executive in West Berlin is trying to sell Coca Cola to the Russians while preventing his boss's daughter from marrying a communist.
Back to Ninotchka *territory, but this time the tone is that of a wild farce which achieves fine momentum in stretches but also flags a lot in between, teetering the while on the edge of taste.*
w Billy Wilder, I. A. L. Diamond *play* Ferenc Molnar *d* *Billy Wilder* *ph* Daniel Fapp *m* André Previn
☆ *James Cagney*, Horst Buchholz, Arlene Francis, Pamela Tiffin, Lilo Pulver, Howard St John, Leon Askin
'A sometimes bewildered, often wonderfully funny exercise in nonstop nuttiness.' – *Time*
'This first-class featherweight farce is a serious achievement.' – *Stanley Kauffmann*
Daniel Fapp

One Way Passage *
US 1932 69m bw
Warner (Robert Lord)
On an ocean voyage, a dying girl falls in love with a crook going home to face a life sentence.
Pattern melodrama which stood Hollywood in good stead.
w Wilson Mizner, Joseph Jackson, Robert Lord *d* Tay Garnett *ph* Robert Kurrie *m* W. Franke Harling
☆ William Powell, Kay Francis, Frank McHugh, Aline MacMahon, Warren Hymer, Herbert Mundin, Roscoe Karns, Stanley Fields
'Will reach house averages for this time of year.' – *Variety*
† Remade as *'Til We Meet Again* (qv).
original story (Robert Lord)

One Way Pendulum
GB 1964 85m bw
UA/Woodfall (Michael Deeley)
A suburban clerk leads a dream existence; his son teaches speak-your-weight machines to sing, while he sets an imaginary murder trial in motion.
A nonsense play (which has many adherents) resists the literalness of the camera eye.
w N. F. Simpson *play* N. F. Simpson *d* Peter Yates *ph* Denys Coop *m* Richard Rodney Bennett
☆ Eric Sykes, George Cole, Julia Foster, Jonathan Miller, Peggy Mount, Alison Leggatt, Mona Washbourne

One Way to Love
US 1945 83m bw
Burt Kelly/Columbia
A Chicago radio writer gets a chance in Hollywood.
Hit-and-miss romantic comedy which takes place largely on a westbound train.
w Joseph Hoffman, Jack Henley, Lester Lee, Larry Marks *d* Ray Enright
☆ Willard Parker, Marguerite Chapman, Hugh Herbert, Chester Morris, Jerome Cowan, Janis Carter

One Wedding and Lots of Funerals: see *Leprechaun 2*

One Wild Moment: see *A Summer Affair*

One Wild Night
US 1938 63m bw
John Stone/TCF
Four small-town citizens anxious for vacations away from their wives plot their own kidnapping.
Tolerable second feature comedy, but the plot might have been better developed.
w Charles Belden, Jerry Cady *d* Eugene Forde
☆ June Lang, Dick Baldwin, Lyle Talbot, J. Edward Bromberg, Sidney Toler, William Demarest, Andrew Tombes, Spencer Charters

One Wild Oat
GB 1951 78m bw
Coronet/Eros
An old flame tries to blackmail a highly respectable solicitor.
Modest film version of a popular West End farce.
w Vernon Sylvaine, Lawrence Huntington *play* Vernon Sylvaine *d* Charles Saunders *ph* Robert Navarro *m* Stanley Black
☆ Robertson Hare, Stanley Holloway, Sam Costa, Andrew Crawford, Vera Pearce, Robert Moreton, Irene Handl

One Woman or Two: see *Une Femme ou Deux*

One Woman's Story: see *The Passionate Friends*

One-Trick Pony *
US 1980 98m Technicolor
Warner (Michael Tannen)

A veteran rock musician attempts to hold on to his integrity as his career and marriage disintegrate.
An episodic account, broken by songs that carry, not always successfully, the movie's emotional weight; but the scenes detailing the business side of popular music, dealing with a crass DJ and an unsympathetic producer and record boss, have an authentic bitterness about them.
w Paul Simon *d* Robert M. Young *ph* Dick Bush *m/ly* Paul Simon *pd* David Mitchell *ed* Edward Beyer, Barry Malkin, David Ray
☆ Paul Simon, Blair Brown, Rip Torn, Joan Hackett, Allen Goorwitz (Garfield), Mare Winningham, Michael Pearlman, Lou Reed, Daniel Stern
† The film also includes performances by the B-52s, Sam and Dave and the Lovin' Spoonful, and a brief appearance by Tiny Tim.

A One-Way Ticket: see *Un Pasaje de Ida*

One-Way Ticket
US 1935 66m bw
Columbia
A convicted bank robber falls in love with the warden's daughter.
Prison break drama which seems to be trying to make a point but is not sure what.
w Vincent Lawrence, Joseph Anthony, Oliver H. P. Garrett, Grover Jones *novel* Ethel Turner *d* Herbert Biberman
☆ Lloyd Nolan, Walter Connolly, Peggy Conklin, Edith Fellows, Nana Bryant, Thurston Hall
'It is "different" at the cost of credulity.' – *Variety*

'From Alexander Pushkin's timeless masterpiece of love and obsession.'
Onegin *
GB/US 1998 106m DeLuxe
Entertainment/Seven Arts/Baby/Protagonist (Ileen Maisel, Simon Bosanquet)

An aristocrat rejects the love of a young woman and lives to regret his action.
Sumptuous version of a classic tale of doomed love, but one that has an unwonted air of Anglo-Saxon repression about it; and Tyler is miscast.
w Peter Ettedgui, Michael Ignatieff *verse novel* Aleksandr Pushkin *d* Martha Fiennes *ph* Remi Adefarasin *m* Magnus Fiennes *pd* Jim Clay *ed* Jim Clark
☆ Ralph Fiennes (Evgeny Onegin), Liv Tyler (Tatyana Larin), Toby Stephens (Vladimir Lensky), Lena Headey (Olga Larin), Martin Donovan (Prince Nikitin), Alun Armstrong (Zaretsky), Harriet Walter (Mme Larina), Irene Worth (Princess Alina), Jason Watkins (Guillot), Francesca Annis (Katiusha)
'There's something frozen about her film, despite its immense decorative appeal.' – *Adam Mars-Jones, Times*
'Diminishes Alexander Pushkin's epic 19th-century novel ... into a cramped little soap opera whose two stars are painfully mismatched.' – *Janet Maslin, New York Times*

Onibaba *
Japan 1964 104m bw Tohoscope
Kindai Eiga Kyokai/Tokyo Eiga

aka: *The Hole*
In medieval times on a remote marshy plain, mother and daughter live by killing stray soldiers and selling their armour, until daughter takes one for a lover and mother becomes jealous.
A kind of original horror legend is told by this strange, compelling piece with its frequent moments of nastiness. It remains, perhaps mercifully, unique.
wd Kaneto Shindo *ph* Kiyomi Juroda *m* Hikaru Hayashi
☆ Nobuko Otowa, Jitsuko Yoshimura, Kei Sato
'The film is the most ardent and unflinching celebration of sex. It shows with equal faithfulness the ecstasies of its fulfilment and the agonies of its frustration.' – *John Simon*

'What happened is true ... but the real crime is what happened after!'
The Onion Field
US 1979 126m Eastmancolor
Black Marble (Walter Coblenz)

Two policemen are shot at by a manic killer, and the one who survives finds that he is suspected of cowardice and has to resign from the force.
Well meaning but lumbering case history. The author must carry the blame, as for once the picture was made exactly on his terms.
w Joseph Wambaugh *novel* Joseph Wambaugh *d* Harold Becker *ph* Charles Rosher *m* Eumir Deodato *pd* Brian Eatwell
☆ John Savage, James Woods, Franklyn Seales, Ted Danson, Ronny Cox, David Huffman

Onionhead
US 1958 110m bw
Warner (Jules Schermer)
Adventures of a ship's cook in the US Coastguard.
Service comedy that must have seemed funnier in the US than in Britain.
w Nelson Gidding *novel* Weldon Hill *d* Norman Taurog *ph* Harold Rosson *md* Ray Heindorf
☆ Andy Griffith, Felicia Farr, Walter Matthau, Erin O'Brien, Joe Mantell, Ray Danton, Roscoe Karns, James Gregory, Tige Andrews
† An attempt to cash in on the success of *No Time for Sergeants*.

'Romance as glorious as the towering Andes!'
Only Angels Have Wings **
US 1939 121m bw
Columbia (Howard Hawks)

Tension creeps into the relationships of the men who fly cargo planes over the Andes when a stranded showgirl sets her cap at the boss.
For an action film this is really too restricted by talk and cramped studio sets, and its theme was more entertainingly explored in Red Dust*. Still, it couldn't be more typical of the Howard Hawks film world, where men are men and women have to be as tough as they are.*
w Jules Furthman *story* Howard Hawks *d* Howard Hawks *ph* Joseph Walker, Elmer Dyer *m* Dimitri Tiomkin *md* Morris Stoloff
☆ Cary Grant, Jean Arthur, Rita Hayworth, Richard Barthelmess, Thomas Mitchell, Sig Rumann, Victor Kilian, John Carroll, Allyn Joslyn
'All these people did the best they could with what they were given – but look at it.' – *Otis Ferguson*

The Only Game in Town
US 1969 113m DeLuxe
TCF (Fred Kohlmar)

A Las Vegas chorus girl and a piano player have an unhappy life because of his gambling fever.
Uninteresting two-header from a play that didn't make it; no light relief, no action, and not even very good acting.
w Frank D. Gilroy *play* Frank D. Gilroy *d* George Stevens *ph* Henri Decaë *m* Maurice Jarre
☆ Elizabeth Taylor, Warren Beatty, Charles Braswell, Hank Henry
'It epitomizes the disaster the studio and star systems foist on films ... the only two-character tale around to cost $11 million.' – *Judith Crist*
† Frank Sinatra was originally cast but walked out after production started; Warren Beatty astonishingly chose to do this rather than *Butch Cassidy and the Sundance Kid*.

Only the Best: see *I Can Get It for You Wholesale*

'A comedy for anyone who's ever had a mother.'
Only the Lonely
US 1991 104m DeLuxe
TCF/Hughes Entertainment (John Hughes, Hunt Lowry)

A mother-dominated cop falls in love with a shy beautician at his neighbourhood undertakers.
Soft-centred, sentimental drama that lacks the courage to be convincing.
wd Chris Columbus *ph* Julio Macat *m* Maurice Jarre *ch* Monica Devereux *pd* John Muto *ed* Raja Gosnell
☆ John Candy, Maureen O'Hara, Ally Sheedy, Anthony Quinn, James Belushi, Kevin Dunn, Milo O'Shea, Bert Remsen, Macaulay Culkin
† It was Maureen O'Hara's first film for 20 years.

'On The Streets Survival Is The Only Law.'
Only the Strong
US 1993 96m Eastmancolor
Rank/Polygram/Freestone/Davis (Samuel Hadida, Stuart S. Shapiro, Steven G. Menkin)

An expert in the Brazilian martial art of capoeira teaches it to a school's 12 toughest kids to give them self-respect.
Apart from its use of Brazil's dance-based method of beating opponents to pulp, a standard, forgettable film of its type, surprisingly given a cinema release.
w Sheldon Lettich, Luis Esteban *d* Sheldon Lettich *ph* Edward Pei *m* Harvey J. Mason *pd* J. Mark Harrington *ed* Stephen Semel
☆ Mark Dacascos, Geoffrey Lewis, Paco Christian Prieto, Stacey Travis, Todd Susman, Richard Coca
'I strained my neck just watching it, largely because I kept nodding off. I imagine Sheldon Lettich, the director, might have done so too. At any rate, he must have written it in a doze.' – *Derek Malcolm, Guardian*

'They were six and they fought like six hundred!'

Only the Valiant
US 1950 105m bw
(Warner)

A tough cavalry officer in a lonely fort wins a battle against Indians.
Standard top-of-the-bill Western; competent but not very gripping.
w Edmund H. North, Harry Brown *d* Gordon Douglas *ph* Lionel Lindon *m* Franz Waxman
☆ Gregory Peck, Ward Bond, Gig Young, Lon Chaney Jnr, Barbara Payton, Neville Brand

Only Two Can Play ***
GB 1962 106m bw
British Lion/Vale (Launder and Gilliat)

A much married assistant librarian in a Welsh town has an abortive affair with a councillor's wife.
Well characterized and generally diverting 'realistic' comedy which slows up a bit towards the end but contains many memorable sequences and provides its star's last good character performance.
w Bryan Forbes novel That Uncertain Feeling by Kingsley Amis d Sidney Gilliat ph John Wilcox *m* Richard Rodney Bennett *ad* Albert Witherick
☆ *Peter Sellers, Mai Zetterling, Virginia Maskell,* Richard Attenborough, Raymond Huntley, John Le Mesurier, *Kenneth Griffith*
'It has a kind of near-truth which is at once hilarious and faintly macabre.' – *Dilys Powell*

Only When I Larf *
GB 1968 103m Eastmancolor
Paramount/Beecord (Len Deighton, Brian Duffy, Hugh Attwooll)
The adventures of three confidence tricksters.
Quite likeable but unmemorable 'with it' comedy of the sixties; the tricks are more amusing than the characterization.
w John Salmon *novel* Len Deighton *d* Basil Dearden *ph* Anthony Richmond *m* Ron Grainer
☆ *Richard Attenborough,* David Hemmings, Alexandra Stewart, Nicholas Pennell, Melissa Stribling, Terence Alexander, Edric Connor, Calvin Lockhart, Clifton Jones

Only When I Laugh
US 1981 120m Metrocolor
Columbia (Roger M. Rothstein, Neil Simon)

GB title: *It Hurts Only When I Laugh*
An alcoholic actress tries to rebuild her life.
Last desperate fling (one hopes) of the Neil Simon industry, dispensing in this case more bitter tears than laughs, and generally failing to stay the course.
w Neil Simon *play The Gingerbread Lady* by Neil Simon *d* Glenn Jordan *ph* David M. Walsh *m* David Shire
☆ Marsha Mason, Kristy McNichol, James Coco, Joan Hackett, David Dukes, John Bennett Perry
'One can almost hear the click of typewriter keys.' – *Geoff Brown, MFB*
Marsha Mason; James Coco (supporting actor); Joan Hackett (supporting actress)

Only Yesterday *
US 1933 105m bw
Universal
An unmarried mother is seduced twice by the same man.
One that Ross Hunter didn't get around to remaking … and a good job too.
w William Hurlbut, George O'Neill, Arthur Richman *d* John M. Stahl *ph* Merritt Gerstad *m* Constantine Bakaleinikoff *ad* Charles D. Hall *ed* Milton Carruth
☆ Margaret Sullavan, John Boles, Billie Burke, Reginald Denny, Edna May Oliver, Benita Hume
'The film needs little more praise than that it warrants its unusual length.' – *Variety*
† The original intention seems to have been to mirror recent history as in Frederick Lewis Allen's book of the same title.

Only You *
US 1994 108m Technicolor
Columbia TriStar/Fried/Woods Films/Yorktown (Norman Jewison, Cary Wood, Robert N. Fried, Charles Mulvehill)

In Italy, a woman pursues the man she believes, on the evidence of a fortune teller, she is destined to marry and finds the love of her life.
Sugary, glossy, nostalgic romantic comedy that deliberately harks back to the 50s Roman Holiday, *starring Audrey Hepburn and Gregory Peck, and which seems even more old-fashioned.*
w Diane Drake *d* Norman Jewison *ph* Sven Nykvist *m* Rachel Portman *pd* Luciana Arrighi *ed* Stephen Rivkin
☆ Marisa Tomei, Robert Downey Jnr, Bonnie Hunt, Billy Zane, Joaquim de Almeida, Fisher Stevens
'Populated by characters who believe in pursuing their amorous destinies as long as it involves staying in five-star hotels, handsomely turned-out trifle has a healthy dose of highly calculated commercial appeal, especially to those who are ready to swallow cornball romance without worrying about excess sweets.' – *Todd McCarthy, Variety*

Ooh, You Are Awful *
GB 1972 97m Eastmancolor
British Lion/Quintain (E. M. Smedley Aston)

US title: *Get Charlie Tully*
A London con man seeks a fortune, the clue to which is tattooed on the behind of one of several girls.
Amusing star vehicle with plenty of room for impersonations and outrageous jokes.
w John Warren, John Singer *d Cliff Owen ph* Ernest Steward *m* Christopher Gunning
☆ *Dick Emery,* Derren Nesbitt, Ronald Fraser, Pat Coombs, William Franklyn, Brian Oulton, Norman Bird

Open City **
Italy 1945 101m bw
Minerva

original title: *Roma, Città Aperta*
Italian underground workers defy the Nazis in Rome towards the end of the war.
A vivid newsreel quality is achieved by this nerve-stretching melodrama in which all the background detail is as real as care could make it.
w Sergio Amidei, Federico Fellini *d Roberto Rossellini ph* Ubaldo Arata *m* Renzo Rossellini
☆ Aldo Fabrizi, *Anna Magnani,* Marcello Pagliero, Maria Michi
script

Open Season
US/Spain/Switzerland 1974 104m
Eastmancolor Panavision
Impala/Arpa (George H. Brown, Jose S. Vicuna)
Three young criminals hunt human prey, but one of their victims takes his own revenge.
Rough, flashy, violent melodrama which pretends to have something to say but in fact is merely sensationalist.
w David Osborn, Liz Charles Williams *d* Peter Collinson *ph* Fernando Arribas *m* Ruggero Cini
☆ Peter Fonda, Cornelia Sharpe, John Phillip Law, Richard Lynch, Albert Mendoza, William Holden
'An offensive, gamy potboiler.' – *Variety*
'Both patience and the plot line are severely strained by the artiness Collinson frequently indulges, with frozen shots to mark the moments of truth and a meaningless punctuation throughout of long shots, angles and flashes.' – *Tom Milne*

Open Your Eyes: see *Abre Los Ojos*

Opening Night
US 1978 144m Metrocolor
Faces Distribution (Al Ruban)

A Broadway actress is on the point of a nervous breakdown.
Interminable addition to the director's list of unwatchable personal films.
wd John Cassavetes *ph* Al Ruban *m* Bo Horwood
☆ Gena Rowlands, Ben Gazzara, John Cassavetes, Joan Blondell, Paul Stewart, Zohra Lampert, Laura Johnson
'Shrill, puzzling, depressing and overlong.' – *Variety*

L'Opéra de Quat' Sous: see *Die Dreigroschenoper*

Opera do Malandro
Brazil 1986 105m colour
Goldwyn/MK2/Austra/TF1 (Marin Karmitz, Ruy Guerra)
A pro-American pimp in pro-Nazi Brazil becomes involved with the daughter of his enemy, a corrupt night-club owner.
A South American treatment of Brecht's Threepenny Opera *without Kurt Weill's music or much to recommend it.*
w Chico Buarque, Orlando Senna, Ruy Guerra *d* Ruy Guerra *ph* Antonio Luis Mendes *m* Chico Buarque *ed* Mair Tavares, Ide Lacreta, Kenout Peltier
☆ Edson Celulari, Claudia Ohana, Elba Ramalho, Ney Latorraca, Fabio Sabag, J. C. Violla, Wilson Grey

Operation Amsterdam *
GB 1958 104m bw
Rank/Maurice Cowan

In 1940 spies are sent into Holland to prevent the invading Germans from finding Amsterdam's stock of industrial diamonds.
Semi-documentary war adventure, well mounted and played.
w Michael McCarthy, John Eldridge *book Adventure in Diamonds* by David Walker *d Michael McCarthy ph* Reg Wyer *m* Philip Green
☆ Peter Finch, Tony Britton, Eva Bartok, Alexander Knox, Malcolm Keen, Tim Turner, John Horsley, Melvyn Hayes, Christopher Rhodes

Operation Bullshine
GB 1959 84m Technicolor
ABPC
In 1942, complications ensue when an ATS private suspects her husband of infidelity.
Flabby army comedy with a few laughs.
w Anne Burnaby, Rupert Lang, Gilbert Gunn *d* Gilbert Gunn *ph* Gilbert Taylor *m* Laurie Johnson
☆ Donald Sinden, Barbara Murray, Carole Lesley, Ronald Shiner, Naunton Wayne, Daniel Massey, Dora Bryan

Operation CIA
US 1965 90m bw
Allied Artists

An agent is rushed to Saigon to find a secret message which was never delivered.
Crude thick ear with a few suspenseful moments.
w Bill S. Ballinger, Peer J. Oppenheimer *d* Christian Nyby *ph* Richard Moore *m* Paul Dunlap
☆ Burt Reynolds, John Hoyt, Daniele Aubry, Kieu Chinh, Cyril Collick

Operation Condor
Hong Kong 1991 103m colour
Technovision
Golden Harvest/Golden Way (Raymond Chow)
original title: *Feiying Gaiwak*
aka: *The Armor of God II*
A Chinese explorer is hired by a Spanish aristocrat to find a hoard of Nazi gold buried in the Sahara Desert.
Genial and energetic martial arts movie, less effective than usual because the action is removed from its normal Hong Kong context, though no doubt its desert setting seemed exotic to its home audience.
w Jackie Chan, Edward Tang, Ma Mei-ping *d* Jackie Chan *ph* Arthur Wong *m* Peter Pau *ad* Oliver Wong, Eddie Ma, Lou Ka-yiu *ed* Peter Cheung
☆ Jackie Chan, Carol Cheng, Eva Cobo de Garcia, Shoko Ikeda
'A breezy actioneer that's always watchable.' – *Variety*
† The film was the most expensive so far made in Hong Kong, at a cost of $15 million ($HK115).

Operation Crossbow *
GB 1965 116m Metrocolor Panavision
MGM/Carlo Ponti

aka: *The Great Spy Mission*
In World War II, trained scientists are parachuted into Europe to destroy the Nazi rocket-making plant at Peenemunde.
Unlikely, star-packed war yarn with more passing tragedy than most, all obliterated by a shoot-em-up James Bond finale.
w Richard Imrie (Emeric Pressburger), Derry Quinn, Ray Rigby *d* Michael Anderson *ph* Erwin Hillier *m* Ron Goodwin *ed* Ernest Walter
☆ George Peppard, Tom Courtenay, John Mills, Sophia Loren, Lilli Palmer, Anthony Quayle, Patrick Wymark, Jeremy Kemp, Paul Henreid, Trevor Howard, Sylvia Syms, Richard Todd, Richard Johnson

Operation Daybreak
US 1975 119m Technicolor
Warner/Howard R. Schuster/American Allied (Carter de Haven)
In 1941, Czech patriots kill the hated Nazi Heydrich and are hunted down.
Curiously-timed evocation of wartime resistance adventures, too realistic for the squeamish and certainly not very entertaining despite a fair level of professionalism.
w Ronald Harwood *novel Seven Men at Daybreak* by Alan Burgess *d* Lewis Gilbert *ph* Henri Decaë *m* David Hentschel
☆ Timothy Bottoms, Martin Shaw, Joss Ackland, Nicola Pagett, Anthony Andrews, Anton Diffring, Carl Duering, Diana Coupland

Operation Delta Force
US 1997 93m colour
Nu Image/Monodfin (Danny Lerner, Boaz Davidson)

An elite military team deals with South African terrorists who threaten to unleash the Ebola virus upon the world.
Episodic action movie that consists of one long chase filled with gun battles and explosions; there are many better (and few worse) ways of passing the time than watching this.
w David Sparling *d* Sam Firstenberg *ph* Yossi Wein *m* Serge Colbert *pd* Richard Varod *ed* Omer Tal, Henry Richardson
☆ Jeff Fahey (Lang), Ernie Hudson (Tipton), Rob Stewart (Sparks), Frank Zagarino (McKinney), Joe Lara (Nash), Todd Jensen (Hutch), Natasha Sunderland (Marie), Hal Holbrook (Henshaw), Gideon Emery (Bowers), Tshepo Nzimande (DiBlase), Dan Robbertse (Pretorius)

Operation Delta Force II: Mayday
US 1998 98m colour
Nu Image/New World Services (Danny Lerner)

An elite US military team are called into action after a terrorist hijacks a Russian submarine and threatens nuclear destruction of American and Russian cities.
Dull and confusing action pic, with a sentimental subplot about father-son bonding; it is needlessly loud and violent, with much macho posturing.
w David Sparling *d* Yossi Wein *ph* Peter Belcher *m* Russell Stirling, Wessel van Rensburg *pd* David Varod *ed* Felix Meyburgh Jnr
☆ Michael McGrady (Capt Skip Lang), J. Kenneth Campbell (Lukash), Dale Dye (Admiral Halsey Lang), Greg Melvill-Smith (Sergei), Robert Whitehead (Mikhail), Simon Jones (Vickers), Robert Patteri (McKinney), Todd Jensen (Lombardi), Spencer Rochfort (Hutch), Gavin Hood (Sparks), James Whyle (Bagley), Brian O'Shaughnessy (Admiral Henshaw)

Operation Delta Force III: Clear Target
US 1998 96m colour
Nu Image/Nu World (Danny Lerner)

Delta Force deals with a Colombian drug baron who hijacks a US submarine so he can fire biological weapons at the UN headquarters in New York.
An action film reduced to its bare essentials: characterisation is minimal, dialogue is no more than shouted commands and the occasional grunt through clenched teeth, and the narrative is one long gun-battle, during which the enemy body count is high, and our heroes endure the odd scratch.
w David Sparling *story* Danny Lerner *d* Mark Roper *ph* Johan Scheepers *m* Serge Colbert *pd* David Varod *ed* Gerard Jakubowicz
☆ Jim Fitzpatrick (Skip Lang), Greg Collins (McKinney), Danny Keogh (Salvatore), Simon Jones (Vickers), Gavin Hood (Sparks), Darcy La Pier (Ariana Decker), Bryan Genesse (Hutch),

David Dukas (Lombardi), Brian O'Shaughnessy (Admiral Norman Henshaw)

Operation Delta Force IV: Deep Fault
US 1999 104m colour
Nu Image (Danny Lerner, David Varod)

US special forces deal with a double-crossing Serbian general and a Cuban-American who plans to use a nucelar weapon to cause a major earthquake along the San Andreas fault..
The threadbare franchise continues with a movie that is one long gun-battle in various locations; the topicality of the scenario adds nothing to the predictable gung-ho action.
w David Sparling *story* Danny Lerner *d* Mark Roper *ph* Adolfo Bartoli *m* Serge Colbert *pd* David Varod *ed* Omer Tal
☆ Joe Lara (McKinney), Greg Collins (Skip Lang), Justin Williams, Gary Hudson, Johnny Messner, Hayley Du Mond, John Laughlin

'They are back again with a vengeance.'
Operation Delta Force V: Random Fire
US 1999 94m colour
Nu Image/Do (Marlow De Mardt, Brigid Olen, Danny Lerner)
After African troops kill two American ambassadors and their families and send a suicide bomber to a Boston conference, Delta Force go into action to kill the rebel leader.
The stupefying mixture as before: tough guy dialogue ("Goodbyes are for women"), gung ho action, mindless heroics and endless explosions – to which is added some absurd brain-washing by a dastardly Russian psychiatrist.
w Bernard Stone *story* Danny Lerner *d* Yossi Wein *ph* Peter Belcher *m* Serge Colbert *pd* Zack Grobler *ed* Amanda I. Kirpaul
☆ Trae Thomas (Brad Kennedy), Pepper Sweeney (Charlie), Todd Jensen (Bob Johnson), Emily Whitfield (Karen Sommers), Ron Smerczak (General Thompson), Toni Caprari (Jafari Bin Kasim), Anthony Bishop (Skip Loomis)

Operation Disaster: see *Morning Departure*

Operation Dumbo Drop
US 1995 107m colour Panavision
Buena Vista/Walt Disney (Diane Nabatoff, David Madden)

US soldiers in Vietnam have five days to deliver an elephant to villagers whose beast was killed by the Vietcong.
Amiable movie that ignores the realities of war for the story of an appealing animal.
w Gene Quintano, Jim Kouf *story* Jim Morris *d* Simon Wincer *ph* Russell Boyd *m* David Newman *pd* Paul Peters *ed* O. Nicholas Brown
☆ Danny Glover, Ray Liotta, Denis Leary, Doug E. Doug, Corin Nemec, Dinh Thien Le, Tcheky Karyo
'A well-crafted and entertaining pic with broad, cross-generational appeal.' – *Variety*

Operation Eichmann
US 1961 94m bw
Allied Artists

After the war, the Nazi who exterminated six million Jews escapes from Europe but is eventually recaptured.
Crude exploitation item designed to cash in on Eichmann's trial, a documentary on which would have been much more interesting.
w Lewis Copley (Lester Cole) *d* R. G. Springsteen *ph* Joseph Biroc *m* Alex Alexander
☆ Werner Klemperer (Eichmann), Ruta Lee, Donald Buka, John Banner
† Lewis Copley was a pseudonym used by Lester Cole after he was blacklisted.

Operation Golden Phoenix
Canada 1994 95m colour
Le Monde/Film One (Jalal Merhi)

Double-crossed by a friend, a security agent is robbed of a pendant that reveals the whereabouts of the lost treasure of the Ottoman Empire.
Trivial, slow-moving thriller with a feeble script and badly acted performances.
w J. Stephen Maunder, Kevin Ward *story* Samir Ghouseine *d* Jalal Merhi *ph* Mark Willis, Curtis Petersen *m* Varouje *pd* Jasna Stefanovic *ed* Kevin Schjerning
☆ Jalal Merhi (Mark Assante), Loren Avedon (Ivan Jones), James Hong (Mr Chang), Karen Sheperd (Princess Tara), Al Waxman (Chief Gordon), Joseph Nano (Professor Amid), Ala'a Zalzali (Walter), Guylaine St Onge (Princess Angelica)

Operation Kid Brother
Italy 1967 105m Techniscope
Dario Sabatello

aka: *OK Connery*
007's brother defeats an international mastermind with the help of a Scottish archery team.
Very elementary James Bond spoof, with a confusing array of old and new elements but less than the required minimum of style.
w Paolo Levi, Vincenzo Mannino, Carlo Tritto *d* Alberto de Martino *ph* Alejandro Ulloa *m* Ennio Morricone
☆ Neil Connery, Daniela Bianchi, Adolfo Celi, Bernard Lee, Lois Maxwell, Agata Flori
'A grotesque parody of a parody … bad enough to be hysterically funny.' – *MFB*
† Neil Connery is Sean's kid brother.

Operation Mad Ball *
US 1957 105m bw
Columbia (Jed Harris)
American troops in Normandy are forbidden to fraternize with nurses, but a clandestine dance is arranged.
Madcap army farce which keeps promising to be funnier than it is.
w Arthur Carter, Jed Harris, Blake Edwards *play* Arthur Carter *d* *Richard Quine* *ph* Charles Lawton Jnr *m* George Duning
☆ Jack Lemmon, Ernie Kovacs, Kathryn Grant, Mickey Rooney, James Darren, Arthur O'Connell
'A routine regimental farce, but fast and snafurious.' – *Time*

Operation Pacific
US 1950 109m bw
Warner (Louis F. Edelman)

Adventures of a submarine commander in the Pacific war.
Routine war heroics, tolerably done but overstretched.
wd George Waggner *ph* Bert Glennon *m* Max Steiner
☆ John Wayne, Patricia Neal, Ward Bond, Scott Forbes, Phil Carey, Paul Picerni, William Campbell, Martin Milner

Operation Petticoat *
US 1959 124m Eastmancolor
Universal/Granart (Robert Arthur)

During World War II, a crippled submarine is refloated by fair means and foul, and a party of nurses is taken aboard.
Flabby comedy with good moments, but not many.
w Stanley Shapiro, Maurice Richlin *story* Paul King, Joseph Stone *d* Blake Edwards *ph* Russell Harlan *m* David Rose *ad* Alexander Golitzen, Robert E. Smith *ed* Ted J. Kent, Frank Gross
☆ Cary Grant, Tony Curtis, Joan O'Brien, Dina Merrill, Gene Evans, Arthur O'Connell, Richard Sargent, Virginia Gregg
'Grant is a living lesson in getting laughs without lines.' – *Variety*
🎗 story and screenplay

Operation St Peter's
Italy 1968 100m colour
Paramount/Turi Vasile
Three thieves steal Michelangelo's *Pietà* and sell it for forty dollars to an American gangster.
Rather surprisingly watchable comedy chase, with the star parodying his past roles.
w Ennio de Concini, Adriano Baracco, Roberto Gianviti, Lucio Fulci *d* Lucio Fulci
☆ Edward G. Robinson, Lando Buzzanca, Heinz Ruhmann, Jean-Claude Brialy

Operation Secret
US 1952 108m bw
Warner (Henry Blanke)
A traitor in the French resistance movement shoots a colleague, and the wrong man is accused.
Belated World War II adventure which gives the impression of having been discarded by Errol Flynn.
w James R. Webb, Harold Medford *d* Lewis Seiler *ph* Ted McCord *m* Roy Webb *ed* Clarence Kolster
☆ Cornel Wilde, Steve Cochran, Paul Picerni, Karl Malden

Operation Snafu: see *On the Fiddle*

Operation Thunderbolt *
Israel 1977 117m Eastmancolor Panavision
GS Films (Menahem Golan, Yoram Globus)

aka: *Entebbe: Operation Thunderbolt*
An account of the rescue of Israeli hostages from terrorists who have hijacked their plane to Entebbe.
Victory at Entebbe and Raid on Entebbe were made with all-star casts for American television. This home-grown account of a famous deed is more modest yet more authoritative.
w Clarke Reynolds *d* Menahem Golan *ph* Adam Greenberg *m* Dov Seltzer
☆ Klaus Kinski, Assaf Dayan, Ori Levy, Yehoram Geon, Mark Heath
🎗 best foreign film

Operation Undercover: see *Report to the Commissioner*

Operation X: see *My Daughter Joy*

Operator 13
US 1934 86m bw
MGM/Cosmopolitan (Lucien Hubbard)
GB title: *Spy 13*
During the Civil War an actress becomes a Union spy.
Elaborate period romance with action highlights.
w Harry Thew, Zelda Sears, Eve Greene *d* Richard Boleslawski *ph* *George Folsey* *m* William Axt
☆ Marion Davies, Gary Cooper, Jean Parker, Katherine Alexander, Ted Healy, Russell Hardie, Henry Wadsworth, Douglass Dumbrille
'Will please generally … one of Davies' best.' – *Variety*
🎗 George Folsey

Opposing Force
US 1986 97m DeLuxe
Orion (Tamar E. Glaser, Daniel A. Berk)

aka: *Hellcamp*
The brutal, power-crazed commandant of a simulated prison camp, run as part of a military escape-and-evasion exercise, loses control after he rapes the only woman on the course.
An unpleasant and unconvincing action movie, stupidly violent.
w Gil Cowan *d* Eric Karson *ph* Michael A. Jones *m* Marc Donahue *pd* Art Nicdao *ed* Mark Conte
☆ Tom Skerritt, Lisa Eichhorn, Anthony Zerbe, Richard Roundtree, Robert Wightman, John Considine

'You'll laugh, you'll cry, you'll be offended.'
The Opposite of Sex ***
US 1998 105m Foto-Kem
Sony/Rysher (David Kirkpatrick, Michael Besman)

A teenager runs away from home, seduces her gay brother's boyfriend, and runs off with him to LA.
Tough, tart, smart movie, which makes fun of the usual rites-of-passage stories and has enough twists in its plot to provide a continual surprise.
wd *Don Roos* *ph* Hubert Taczanowski *m* Mason Daring *pd* Michael Clausen *ed* David Codron
☆ *Christina Ricci*, Martin Donovan, *Lisa Kudrow*, Lyle Lovett, Johnny Galecki, Ivan Sergei
'A delight on every conceivable level.' – *Andy Medhurst, Sight and Sound*

The Opposite Sex
US 1956 116m Metrocolor Cinemascope
MGM (Joe Pasternak)

A New York socialite divorces her unfaithful husband but finally takes him back.
Softened, musicalized version of The Women *(qv); very patchy, shapeless, and not nearly sharp enough.*
w Fay and Michael Kanin *play* Clare Boothe *d* David Miller *ph* Robert Bronner *m* Nicholas Brodszky *songs* Nicholas Brodszky, Sammy Cahn
☆ June Allyson, Dolores Gray, Joan Collins, Ann Sheridan, Agnes Moorehead, Joan Blondell, Barbara Jo Allen, Charlotte Greenwood

The Opposite Sex and How to Live with Them
US 1993 86m CFI color
Spelling/Outlaw/Once Upon A Time (Stanley M. Brooks, Robert Newmyer)

Two Jewish men court WASP women and insist on discussing their attitudes at length with the audience.
An experience akin to being buttonholed by a bore in a bar.
w Noah Stern *d* Matthew Meshekoff *ph* Jacek Laskus *m* Ira Newborn *pd* Alex Tavoularis *ed* Adam Weiss
☆ Arye Gross, Courteney Cox, Kevin Pollak, Julie Brown, Mitchell Ryan, Phil Bruns

The Optimists of Nine Elms *
GB 1973 110m Eastmancolor
Cheetah/Sagittarius (Adrian Gaye, Victor Lyndon)

Children of a London slum make friends with an old busker.
Gentle, sentimental, quite well-observed piece of wistful melancholia, falsified by its star performance.
wd *Anthony Simmons* *novel* Anthony Simmons *ph* Larry Pizer *m* George Martin *co-w* Tudor Gates
☆ Peter Sellers, Donna Mullane, John Chaffey, David Daker, Marjorie Yates
'Told with economy and sensitivity, this underrated film establishes Tony Simmons as a first-rate director and justifies the risk Sellers took in tackling a difficult role in an offbeat subject.' – *Ken Russell, Fire over England*

The Oracle
GB 1952 83m bw
Group Three (Colin Lesslie)
US title: *The Horse's Mouth*
A reporter discovers that a village well in Ireland contains an oracle which can predict the future.
Weak sub-Ealing comedy which aims to please and gets a few laughs. All very British.
w Patrick Campbell *d* C. M. Pennington-Richards *ph* Wolfgang Suschitzky *m* Temple Abady
☆ Robert Beatty, Virginia McKenna, Mervyn Johns, Gilbert Harding

'It's not just a place. It's a state of mind.'
Orange County
US 2001 82m DeLuxe
Paramount/MTV (Scott Rudin, Van Toffler, David Gale, Scott Aversano)

A surfer refuses to accept his rejection by Stanford University, which will prevent him from realising his dream of becoming a writer.
Low key 'teen comedy, of interest only because it features some second generation Hollywood names behind and before the cameras (and let's hope their parents managed to enjoy it).
w Mike White *d* Jake Kasdan *ph* Greg Gardiner *m* Michael Andrews *pd* Gary Frutkoff *ed* Tara Timpone *cos* Debra McGuire
☆ Colin Hanks (Shaun Brumder), Jack Black (Lance), Catherine O'Hara (Cindy Beugler), Schuyler Fisk (Ashley), John Lithgow (Bud Brumder), Harold Ramis (Don Durkett), Jane Adams (Mona), Garry Marshall (Arthur Gantner), Dana Ivey (Vera Gantner), Chevy Chase (Principal Harbert), Lily Tomlin (Charlotte Cobb)
'A very slight amusement that faintly echoes every other suburban teen comedy that's been made over the past 30 years.' – *Todd McCarthy, Variety*

Orca – Killer Whale
US 1977 92m Technicolor Panavision
Famous Films/Dino de Laurentiis (Luciano Vincenzoni)

Off Newfoundland, a killer whale takes revenge for its mate's death.
A rather unpleasant attempt to mix horror and thrills with ecology: not very entertaining, and not for the squeamish.

w Luciano Vincenzoni, Sergio Donati *d* Michael Anderson *ph* Ted Moore, J. Barry Herron *m* Ennio Morricone
☆ Richard Harris, Charlotte Rampling, Will Sampson, Keenan Wynn
'The biggest load of cod imaginable.' – *Philip Bergson, Sunday Times*
'There are more thrills to be had in the average dolphinarium.' – *Sight and Sound*

Orchestra Wives **
US 1942 97m bw
TCF (William Le Baron)
A small town girl marries the trumpet player of a travelling swing band.
Fresh and lively musical of its period, full of first-class music and amusing backstage backbiting.
w Karl Tunberg, Darrell Ware *d* Archie Mayo *ph* Lucien Ballard *md* Alfred Newman
☆ Ann Rutherford, George Montgomery, Lynn Bari, *Glenn Miller and his Orchestra*, Carole Landis, Jackie Gleason, Cesar Romero
'A natural for any theatre that hasn't got an ironclad rule against jive.' – *Hollywood Reporter*
song 'I've Got a Girl in Kalamazoo' (*m* Harry Warren, *ly* Mack Gordon)

Orchids to You *
US 1935 74m bw
Robert T. Kane/Fox
A florist pulls several strokes to prevent an attorney from taking over her lease.
Amusing comedy drama which failed through lack of strong names.
w William Hurlbut, Bartlett Cormack, Glenn Tryon, Howard Estabrook *d* William A. Seiter
☆ John Boles, Jean Muir, Charles Butterworth, Ruthelma Stevens, Arthur Lake, Spring Byington
'One of those productions that just misses the top rung.' – *Variety*

Ordeal by Innocence
US 1985 88m Eastmancolor
Cannon (Jenny Craven)
An explorer returning from an Antarctic trip discovers that an acquaintance has been hanged for murder, and he might have saved him.
Rather dim Agatha Christie adaptation (though set in her favourite Devon from her favourite book), with workaday actors and a most unsuitable music score. By the time the end comes, nobody could possibly care who done it.
w Alexander Stuart *d* Desmond Davis *ph* Billy Williams *m* Dave Brubeck
☆ Donald Sutherland, Christopher Plummer, Faye Dunaway, Sarah Miles, Ian MacShane, Diana Quick, Annette Crosbie, Michael Elphick, Phoebe Nicholls

Order of Death
Italy 1983 101m colour
New Line/Virgin/RAI (Elda Ferri)
A corrupt cop and a cop-killer form a sado-masochistic relationship.
Confused personalities battle it out in an exaggerated, bombastic psychological thriller.
w Ennio de Concini, Hugh Fleetwood *novel* Hugh Fleetwood *d* Roberto Faenza *ph* Giuseppe Pinori *m* Ennio Morricone *ad* Giantito Burchiellaro *ed* Nini Baragli
☆ Harvey Keitel, John Lydon, Nicole Garcia, Leonard Mann, Sylvia Sidney, Carlo Romanelli, Bob Kelly, Tony Mayer

Orders Are Orders
GB 1954 78m bw
Group 3 (Donald Taylor)
Flabby update of *Orders Is Orders* with an interesting cast below par.
w Donald Taylor, Geoffrey Orme *d* David Paltenghi *ph* Arthur Grant *m* Stanley Black
☆ Peter Sellers, Brian Reece, Sid James, Tony Hancock, Margot Grahame, Raymond Huntley, Maureen Johnson, June Thorburn, Bill Fraser

Orders Is Orders *
GB 1933 88m bw
Gaumont British (Michael Balcon)
An army barracks is disrupted when an American film company gets permission to work there.
Breezy farce which pleased at the time.
w Leslie Arliss, Sidney Gilliat *play* Ian Hay, Anthony Armstrong *d* Walter Forde *ph* Glen MacWilliams
☆ Charlotte Greenwood, James Gleason, Cedric Hardwicke, Cyril Maude, Ian Hunter, Ray Milland, Jane Carr, Donald Calthrop, Eliot Makeham, Wally Patch, Finlay Currie
'A wow from start to finish.' – *Variety*

'They made this boy a cold-blooded killer!'
Orders to Kill *
GB 1958 111m bw
British Lion/Lynx (Anthony Asquith, Anthony Havelock-Allan)
During World War II a bomber pilot undertakes a mission to parachute into occupied France and kill a double agent, who turns out afterwards to have been innocent.
Strong, hard-to-take but well made war story about the effect of war on conscience.
w Paul Dehn d Anthony Asquith ph Desmond Dickinson *m* Benjamin Frankel
☆ *Paul Massie, Irene Worth*, James Robertson Justice, *Leslie French*, Eddie Albert, Lillian Gish, John Crawford, Jacques Brunius, Lionel Jeffries
Paul Dehn; Irene Worth; Paul Massie (newcomer)

Ordet *
Denmark 1957 126m bw
Palladium (Carl Theodor Dreyer)
In a God-fearing village, a father and his three sons have various religious experiences.
Hard-to-take intellectual drama of the faith, very slow and austere but strangely compelling.
wd Carl Theodor Dreyer *ph* Henning Bendtsen *m* Poul Schierbeck
☆ Henrik Malberg, Emil Hass Christensen, Preben Lerdorff-Rye, Caj Kristensen

'A smash and grab masterpiece.'
Ordinary Decent Criminal
Ireland/GB/Germany/US 2000 90m Technicolor Super 35
Icon/Little Bird/Tatfilm/Trigger Street/Miramax/IFB/Greenlight/Filmstiftung (Jonathan Cavendish)
In Dublin, a notorious criminal runs rings around the police in a series of audacious thefts.
Partly based on the true-life exploits of Martin Cahill, this is a run-of-the-mill thriller with some unconvincing casting.
w Gerard Stembridge *d* Thaddeus O'Sullivan *ph* Andrew Dunn *m* Damon Albarn *pd* Tony Burrough *ed* William Anderson
☆ Kevin Spacey (Michael Lynch), Linda Fiorentino (Christine), Peter Mullan (Stevie), Stephen Dillane (Det. Sgt Noel Quigley), Helen Baxendale (Lisa), David Hayman (Tony), Patrick Malahide (Commissioner Daly), Gerard McSorley (Harrison)
'You just feel like you've seen it all before.' – *Bob McCabe, Empire*
† A better film dealing with Martin Cahill is John Boorman's *The General* (qv).

'Everything is in its proper place – except the past!'
Ordinary People ***
US 1980 124m Technicolor
Paramount/Wildwood (Ronald L. Schwary)
The eldest son of a well-heeled American family is drowned, and the survivors take stock and indulge in recriminations.
An actor's piece which on that level succeeds very well, and accurately pins down a certain species of modern American family.
w Alvin Sargent novel Judith Guest *d Robert Redford ph* John Bailey *m* Marvin Hamlisch
☆ Donald Sutherland, *Mary Tyler Moore, Timothy Hutton*, Judd Hirsch, Elizabeth McGovern, M. Emmet Walsh
'This is an academic exercise in catharsis: it's earnest, it means to improve people, and it lasts a lifetime.' – *New Yorker*
best film; Alvin Sargent; Robert Redford; Timothy Hutton
Mary Tyler Moore; Judd Hirsch (supporting actor)

The Oregon Trail
US 1959 86m DeLuxe Cinemascope
TCF
A New York reporter in 1846 is sent to cover a westward trek.
Prototype settlers vs Indians Western with all the expected incident.
w Louis Vittes, Gene Fowler Jnr *d* Gene Fowler Jnr *ph* Kay Norton *m* Paul Dunlap
☆ Fred MacMurray, William Bishop, Nina Shipman, Gloria Talbott, Henry Hull, John Carradine, Elizabeth Patterson

Orfeu Negro: see *Black Orpheus*

The Organization
US 1971 108m DeLuxe
UA/Mirisch (Walter Mirisch)
San Francisco policemen combat an international drug smuggling organization.
The third and weakest adventure of Virgil Tibbs, black policeman of In the Heat of the Night. *Absolutely routine.*
w James R. Webb *d* Don Medford *ph* Joseph Biroc *m* Gil Melle
☆ Sidney Poitier, Barbara McNair, Sheree North, Gerald S. O'Loughlin

'Making sex safe again!'
Orgazmo
US 1997 90m colour
October/Kuzui Enterprises/MDP/Avenging Conscience (Fran Rubel Kuzui, Jason McHugh, Matt Stone)
A naïve Mormon actor is persuaded to take the leading role of Captain Orgazmo in a pornographic movie.
Drear and feeble send-up of porn and superheroes that is enough to give comedy a bad name.
wd Trey Parker *ph* Kenny Gioseffi *m* Paul Robb *pd* Tristan Paris Bourne *ed* Trey Parker, Michael R. Miller
☆ Trey Parker, Dian Bachar, Robyn Lynne, Michael Dean Jacobs, Ron Jeremy, Andrew W. Kemler
'Patchy, clumsy and almost unwatchable. The laughs are few, and feebly silly at best.' – *Mark Sinker, Sight and Sound*
'Massively inventive and spiked with perversely wicked humor.' – *Emanuel Levy, Variety*

Orient Express *
US 1934 71m bw
Fox
Various stories conflict on the Orient Express.
Moderately successful multi-drama in the wake of Grand Hotel.
w Paul Martin, Carl Hovey, Oscar Levant, William Conselman *novel* Graham Greene *d* Paul Martin
☆ Heather Angel, Ralph Morgan, Norman Foster, Herbert Mundin, Una O'Connor, Irene Ware, Dorothy Burgess
'Rather too much story all of a sudden; auditors may be lulled to quiet by the easy, non-exciting early action.' – *Variety*

Oriental Dream: see *Kismet (1944)*

'It's time for some respect.'
Original Gangstas *
US 1996 98m DeLuxe
Orion/Po' Boy (Fred Williamson)
A former gang leader, now a respected football coach, returns home to recruit some old friends to deal with the violent criminals who shot his father, a shopkeeper in Gary, Indiana, described as 'the city with the highest murder rate in the USA'.
Some of the originators of the blaxploitation movies of the 70s return in a brash, energetic action movie, fuelled by a righteous anger at urban degradation, mob rule, and the specious platitudes of politicians.
w Aubrey Rattan *d* Larry Cohen *ph* Carlos Gonzalez *m* Vladimir Horunzhy *pd* Elayne Barbara Ceder *ed* David Kern, Peter B. Ellis
☆ Fred Williamson, Jim Brown, Pam Grier, Richard Roundtree, Paul Winfield, Isabel Sanford, Ron O'Neal, Robert Forster, Charles Napier, Wings Hauser, Frank Pesce, Dru Down, Shyheim
'Everyone involved gets a job done without much fuss and with the cool savvy that makes the film a satisfying diversion.' – *Variety*

'Love's A Killer'
Original Sin
US/France 2001 116m DeLuxe Super 35
TCF/MGM/Hyde Park (Denise Di Novi, Kate Guinzburg, Carol Lees)
In the 1880s, a Cuban plantation owner advertises for a wife and gets a con-woman.
Over-the-top, over-indulgent melodramatic hokum.
wd Michael Cristofer *novel Waltz Into Darkness* by Cornell Woolrich *ph* Rodrigo Prieto *m* Terence Blanchard *pd* David J. Bomba *ed* Eric Sears
☆ Antonio Banderas (Luis Antonio Vargas), Angelina Jolie (Julia Russell/Bonny Castle), Thomas Jane (Walter Downs), Jack Thompson (Alan Jordan), Gregory Itzin (Colonel Worth)
'Lavish and florid, the corny venture falls into so-bad-it's-good territory' – *Lisa Nesselson, Variety*
'It's hard to keep a straight face just thinking of Mr Banderas and Ms. Jolie in the same shot, but "Original Sin" will bore the giggles right out of you.' – *Elvis Mitchell, New York Times*
† Cornell Woolrich's novel also formed the basis of François Truffaut's 1969 film *Mississippi Mermaid* (*qv*).

Orion's Belt
Norway 1985 103m Eastmancolor
Enterprise/Filmeffekt (Dag Alveberg, Petter Borgli)
original title: *Orions Belte*
Three sailors discover a Soviet spy station.
Plodding Cold War thriller.
w Richard Harris *novel* Jon Michelet *d* Ola Solum *ph* Harald Paalgard *m* Geir Bohren, Bent Aserud *ad* Harald Egede-Nissen *ed* Bjorn Breigutu, Yngve Refseth
☆ Helge Jordal, Sverre Anker Ousdal, Hans Ola Sorlie, Kjersti Holmen, Vidar Sandem, Nils Johnson

Orlando **
GB/Russia/France/Italy/Netherlands 1992 93m Eastmancolor
Electric/Adventure Pictures/Lenfilm/Mikado/Sigma/British Screen (Christopher Sheppard)
In a life that lasts for 400 years, a male favourite of Queen Elizabeth I undergoes a sex change and becomes a 20th-century woman.
A divertingly different romp, amusing and occasionally provocative in its examination of identity and gender.
wd Sally Potter *novel* Virginia Woolf *ph* Alexsei Rodionov *m* David Motion, Sally Potter *pd* Ben Van Os, Jan Roelfs *ed* Herve Schneid
☆ Tilda Swinton, Billy Zane, Lothaire Bluteau, John Wood, Charlotte Valandrey, Heathcote Williams, Quentin Crisp, Peter Eyre, Thom Hoffman, Jimmy Somerville, Dudley Sutton, Anna Healy
'Exciting, wonderfully witty entertainment for discriminating auds.' – *Variety*
Ben Van Os, Jan Roelfs; costume design (Sally Potter)

L'Oro di Napoli: see *Gold of Naples*

O'Rourke of the Royal Mounted: see *Saskatchewan*

Orphans
US 1987 120m colour
Lorimar
Two outcast brothers have their lives transformed by a gangster.
Photographed talk-piece which could hope for few takers among the general audience: one for actor-fanciers.
w Lyle Kessler *play* Lyle Kessler *d* Alan J. Pakula *ph* Donald McAlpine *m* Michael Small
☆ Albert Finney, Matthew Modine, Kevin Anderson, John Kellogg

'Are Your Parents A Burden?'
Orphans **
GB 1999 95m colour
Downtown/Channel 4 (Frances Higson)
Three brothers and their handicapped sister mourn the death of their mother in different ways.
A raw-edged, energetic, dark comedy of working-class life in Glasgow; it takes some imaginative risks as it veers between knockabout comedy and stark tragedy.

wd Peter Mullan *ph* Grant Scott Cameron *m* Craig Armstrong *pd* Campbell Gordon *ed* Colin Monie
☆ Gary Lewis, Douglas Henshall, Rosemarie Stevenson, Stephen McCole, Frank Gallagher, Malcolm Shields

'The milk of human kindness hasn't merely soured in Peter Mullan's transcendentally nasty comedy ... It has so poisoned the air of Glasgow that its clammy atmosphere seems charged with petty malice.' – *Stephen Holden, New York Times*

'Can a woman love more than one man?'
Orphans of the Storm ★
US 1921 124m (24 fps) bw silent
D. W. Griffith

Two sisters are caught up in the French revolution of 1789.
Half melodrama, half epic, this celebrated film survives chiefly by its careful attention to historical detail and by the excitement of its crowd scenes.
w D. W. Griffith *play* Adolph Ennery *d D. W. Griffith* *ph* Henrick Sartov
☆ Lillian Gish, Dorothy Gish, Joseph Schildkraut, Lucille La Verne, Morgan Wallace, Frank Puglia, Creighton Hale

'There is scarcely a scene or an effect in the entire production that is not beautiful to look upon, and there is scarcely a moment that is not charged with intense dramatic power.' – *Robert E. Sherwood, Life*

Orphée ★★★
France 1949 112m bw
André Paulvé 1/Films du Palais Royal

Death, represented by a princess, falls in love with Orpheus, a poet, and helps him when he goes into hell in pursuit of his dead love.
Fascinating poetic fantasy which may have been finally unintelligible but was filled to overflowing with memorable scenes and cinematic tricks, from the entry to the hereafter through a mirror to intercepted code messages such as 'L'oiseau compte avec ses doigts'. The closest the cinema has got to poetry.
wd Jean Cocteau *play* Jean Cocteau *ph Nicolas Hayer* *m Georges Auric* *ad Jean d'Eaubonne*
☆ *Jean Marais, François Périer, Maria Casarès,* Marie Déa, Edouard Dermithe, Juliette Greco

'It is a drama of the visible and the invisible ... I interwove many myths. Death condemns herself in order to help the man she is duty bound to destroy. The man is saved but Death dies: it is the myth of immortality.' – *Jean Cocteau*

† See the sequel *Le Testament d'Orphée*.
†† The film was dedicated to its designer Christian Bérard (1902–49).

The Oscar ★
US 1966 118m Pathécolor
Paramount/Greene-Rouse (Russel Rouse)

On the night of the Academy Awards his friend recalls a heel's rise to stardom.
Squalid, sensationalist account of Hollywood mores; one hopes it isn't quite true.
w Harlan Ellison, Russel Rouse, Clarence Greene *novel* Richard Sale *d* Russel Rouse *ph* Joseph Ruttenberg *m* Percy Faith
☆ Stephen Boyd, Elke Sommer, Tony Bennett, Eleanor Parker, Milton Berle, Joseph Cotten, Jill St John, Edie Adams, Ernest Borgnine, Ed Begley, Walter Brennan, Broderick Crawford, James Dunn, Peter Lawford, Edith Head and also Hedda Hopper, Merle Oberon, Bob Hope, Frank Sinatra

'This is the sort of film that only Hollywood could make, and on that level it is preposterously enjoyable.' – *David Wilson*

'That true movie rarity – a picture that attains a perfection of ineptitude quite beyond the power of words to describe.' – *Richard Schickel*

'When Chicago's Toughest Gangster Promises to Go Straight... Everybody Gets Into The Act!'
Oscar
US 1991 109m Technicolor
Warner/Touchstone/Silver Screen Partners IV (Leslie Belzberg)

A gangster who is trying to reform attempts to sort out the marital problems of his daughters.
Leaden attempt at a screwball comedy, and one that sinks under its own witlessness.
w Michael Barrie, Jim Mulholland *play* Claude Magnier *d* John Landis *ph* Mac Ahlberg *m* Elmer Bernstein *pd* Bill Kenney *ed* Dale Beldin, Michael R. Miller
☆ Sylvester Stallone, Ornella Muti, Kirk Douglas, Peter Riegert, Chazz Palminteri, Vincent Spano, Marisa Tomei, Tim Curry, Don Ameche, Yvonne DeCarlo, Linda Gray

'Zany farce generates a fair share of laughs but still probably remains too creaky a conceit for modern audiences to go for in a big way.' – *Variety*

† Magnier's play was first filmed in France in 1967, directed by Eduardo Molinaro and starring Louis de Funes.

Oscar and Lucinda ★★
Australia 1997 132m Atlab Panavision
Fox/AFFC/Meridian (Robin Dalton, Timothy White)

A gambling-mad English missionary makes one last bet with a wealthy Australian woman: that he can transport a glass chapel she has designed to a remote part of the country.
An imaginative, flawed attempt to encompass a strange and obsessive drama of the varieties of faith.
w Laura Jones *novel* Peter Carey *d* Gillian Armstrong *ph* Geoffrey Simpson *m* Thomas Newman *pd* Luciana Arrighi *ed* Nicholas Beauman
☆ Ralph Fiennes, Cate Blanchett, Ciaran Hinds, Tom Wilkinson, Richard Roxburgh, Clive Russell, Barry Otto, Geoffrey Rush

Oscar Wilde ★★
GB 1959 96m bw
Vantage (William Kirby)
Scandal strikes Oscar Wilde through his involvement with Lord Alfred Douglas.
Competent, well acted version of well-known events of the 1890s, with Morley in his original stage role; generally more satisfactory than The Trials of Oscar Wilde *which was shot simultaneously.*
w Jo Eisinger *d* Gregory Ratoff *ph* Georges Périnal *m* Kenneth V. Jones
☆ *Robert Morley,* John Neville, Phyllis Calvert, *Ralph Richardson,* Dennis Price, Alexander Knox, Edward Chapman, Martin Benson, Robert Harris, Henry Oscar, William Devlin

O'Shaughnessy's Boy
US 1935 88m bw
MGM
A circus performer is reunited with the son his wife took away in childhood.
Shameless sentiment which failed to repeat for its stars the success of The Champ.
w Leonard Praskins, Otis Garrett *d* Richard Boleslawski
☆ Wallace Beery, Jackie Cooper, Leona Maricle, Sara Haden, Henry Stephenson, Spanky MacFarland

'Far too much crying. Good production will help.' – *Variety*

'Every Body Needs A Hero.'
'He's one cell of a guy.'
Osmosis Jones ★
US 2001 96m Technicolor
Warner/Conundrum (Bradley Thomas, Peter Farrelly, Bobby Farrelly, Zak Penn, Dennis Edwards)

A maverick white blood cell cop and his buddy, a cold pill, track down a killer virus in the human they inhabit.
A comedy that mixes some dull live action with much more inventive animation, in which the body is seen as a vast metropolis of different districts, giving the opportunity for parodies of many movie genres.
w Marc Hyman *Animation Directors* Piet Kroon, Tom Sito *d* Peter Farrelly, Bobby Farrelly *ph* Mark Irwin *m* Randy Edelman *pd* Steve Pilchar, Sidney Jackson Bartholomew Jnr *ed* Lois Freeman-Fox, Stephen R. Schaffer, Sam Seig
☆ Bill Murray (Frank), Molly Shannon (Mrs Boyd), Chris Elliott (Bob), Elena Franklin (Shane), Danny Murphy (Zookeeper Superintendent), voices of: Chris Rock (Osmosis Jones), Laurence Fishburne (Thrax), David Hyde Pierce (Drix), Brandy Norwood (Leah), William Shatner (The Mayor), Ron Howard (Tom Colonic)

'Likely to entertain kids, who seem to like jokes about anatomical plumbing. For adults, there is the exuberance of the animation and the energy of the whole movie, which is just plain clever.' – *Roger Ebert, Chicago Sun-Times*

Ososhiki: see *Death Japanese Style*

Ossessione ★★
Italy 1942 135m bw
ICI

A wanderer falls for the wife of an innkeeper and they murder him, but fate takes a hand.
Unofficial remake of The Postman Always Rings Twice, *barely released outside Italy. A powerful melodrama credited with starting the neo-realist school.*
w Antonio Pietrangeli, Giuseppe de Santis, Gianni Puccini, Luchino Visconti, Mario Alicata *d Luchino Visconti* *ph* Aldo Tonti, Domenico Scala *m* Giuseppe Rosati
☆ Massimo Girotti, Clara Calamai, Elio Marcuzzo
† Other versions: *Le Dernier Tournant* (France 1939); *The Postman Always Rings Twice* (US 1945); *The Postman Always Rings Twice* (US 1981).

Ostatni Etap: see *The Last Stage*

The Osterman Weekend
US 1983 102m DeLuxe
Davis-Panzer/Fox

A CIA chief tries to convince a powerful TV journalist that several of his trusted informants are Soviet agents.
Convoluted bloodbath with absolutely nothing new in its locker.
w Alan Sharp, Ian Masters *novel* Robert Ludlum *d* Sam Peckinpah *ph* John Coquillon *m* Lalo Schifrin
☆ Rutger Hauer, John Hurt, Burt Lancaster, Craig T. Nelson, Dennis Hopper, Chris Sarandon, Meg Foster, Helen Shaver

'A competent, professional, but thoroughly impersonal meller.' – *Variety*

Otac Na Slu a benom Putu: see *When Father Was Away On Business*

Otello ★
US/Italy 1986 120m Eastmancolor
Cannon/RAI (John Thompson, Fulvio Lucisano)

An adaptation of Verdi's opera, based on Shakespeare's play.
A visually splendid transcription, which however did not hit the mark with audiences.
wd Franco Zeffirelli *ph* Ennio Guarnieri *m* Giuseppe Verdi *ed* Peter Taylor, Franca Silvi
☆ Placido Domingo, Katia Ricciarelli, Justino Diaz, Petra Malakova
costumes (Anna Anni, Maurizio Millenotti)

Otenki Onesan: see *A Weatherwoman*

Otesanek ★
Czech Republic/GB/Japan 2000 132m colour
Film4/Athanor/Illuminations/Barrandov Biografia (Jaromir Kallista, Jan Svankmajer, Keith Griffiths)
aka: *Little Otik*
A childless couple adopt a tree stump which comes to voracious life.
An overlong black comedy, with the insistent repetition of a grim fairy-tale.
wd Jan Svankmajer *ph* Juraj Galvanek *ad* Eva and Jan Svankmajer *ed* Marie Zemanova
☆ Veronika Zilkova (Bozena), Jan Hartl (Karel), Kristina Adamcova (Alzbetka), Jaroslava Kretschmerova (Her mother), Pavel Novy (Her father)

'Boldly bizarre, darkly funny but poignant.' – *Kevin Thomas, Los Angeles Times*

Othello ★
US/France 1951 91m bw
Mercury/Films Marceau (Orson Welles)

Shakespeare's play as rearranged by Orson Welles at the start of his European wanderings; modest budget, flashes of brilliance, poor technical quality, variable acting.
Not really the best way to film Shakespeare.
wd Orson Welles *play* William Shakespeare *ph* Anchise Brizzi, George Fanto, Obadan Troania, Roberto Fusi, G. Araldo *m* Francesco Lavagnino, Alberto Barberis *ad* Alexander Trauner
☆ Orson Welles, Michael MacLiammoir, Fay Compton, Robert Cook, Suzanne Cloutier, Michael Laurence, Hilton Edwards, Doris Dowling
† Michael MacLiammoir's book *Put Money in Thy Purse* is a witty account of the sporadic, poverty-stricken making of the film.

Othello ★
GB 1965 166m Technicolor Panavision
BHE (Richard Godwin)

A record of the National Theatre production, disappointing in terms of cinema but a valuable record of a famous performance.
d Stuart Burge *ph* Geoffrey Unsworth *md* Richard Hampton
☆ Laurence Olivier, Frank Finlay, Joyce Redman, Maggie Smith, Derek Jacobi, Robert Lang, Anthony Nicholls

'What the director does is keep the camera moving among the actors with the most intelligent precision.' – *Observer*

Laurence Olivier; Frank Finlay; Joyce Redman; Maggie Smith

'Envy greed jealousy and love.'
Othello ★
US 1995 124m Technicolor
Columbia/Castle Rock/Dakota/Imminent (Luc Roeg, David Barron)

A black soldier woos, wins and loses the love of his life.
A good-looking version of Shakespeare's play but hampered by some inadequate speaking of the verse. Othello is robbed of much of his charisma by having his speeches, the means by which he won Desdemona, cut short. Branagh survives the experience best.
wd Oliver Parker *ph* David Johnson *m* Charlie Mole *pd* Tim Harvey *ed* Tony Lawson
☆ Laurence Fishburne (Othello), Irene Jacob (Desdemona), Kenneth Branagh (Iago), Nathaniel Parker, Michael Maloney, Anna Patrick, Nicholas Farrell, Indra Ove

'Colorful and intimate production is relatively conventional and unremarkable as an interpretation, but is well performed by its two male leads and clearly staged and enunciated for ready comprehension by a mass audience.' – *Todd McCarthy, Variety*

'Pitched at audiences as a sort of psychological thriller about sexual jealousy: *Basic Instinct* with better dialogue and a handkerchief instead of an ice pick.' – *Tom Shone, Sunday Times*

† The film's trailer went: 'In the time of heroes there was but one great general. His bravery in battle was legendary, his devotion to his love unchallenged. His name was Othello. Under the cover of darkness and against her father's will, he took Desdemona into his heart. The great general and his true love were secretly wed. Some men die for glory, some men fight for love. One man lives for revenge. His was the soul of a traitor, and the opportunity he seized will change their lives forever...'
†† Only a third of Shakespeare's dialogue remains in this version. The director explained, 'I thought it would be interesting to make it more of a punchy, pacey number.'

The Other ★
US 1972 100m DeLuxe
TCF/Rex-Benchmark (Tom Tryon)

A boy insists that his dead twin is responsible for several unexplained deaths.
Subtle family ghost story for intellectuals; a bit pretentious and restrained for popular success.
w Tom Tryon *novel* Tom Tryon *d* Robert Mulligan *ph* Robert Surtees *m* Jerry Goldsmith *pd* Albert Brenner
☆ Uta Hagen, Diana Muldaur, Chris Connelly, Victor French

Other Halves
New Zealand 1984 95m Eastmancolor
Oringham/Galatea (Tom Finlayson, Dean Hill)
A middle-class woman, recovering from a breakdown and the end of her marriage, falls for a homeless and delinquent 16-year-old Maori youth.
Confused melodrama of racial intolerance and an unlikely love affair, unconvincing for the most part.

w Sue McCauley *novel* Sue McCauley *d* John Laing *ph* Leon Narbey *m* Don McGlashan *pd* Robert Gillies *ed* Harley Oliver
☆ Lisa Harrow, Mark Pilisi, Clare Clifford, Bruce Purchase, Emma Piper, Paul Gittins, John Bach

'Her every exciting moment was an unforgettable experience!'
The Other Love
US 1947 96m bw
Enterprise (David Lewis)

At a Swiss sanatorium, a lady concert pianist who is dying falls in love with her doctor.
Fairly icky 'woman's picture' with uncomfortable performances.
w Ladislas Fodor, Harry Brown *story* Erich Maria Remarque *d* André de Toth *ph* Victor Milner *m* Miklos Rozsa
☆ Barbara Stanwyck, David Niven, Richard Conte, Gilbert Roland, Joan Lorring, Lenore Aubert

Other Men's Women
US 1931 70m bw
Warner
A train driver falls for his partner's wife.
Stilted heavy-breathing melodrama.
w William K. Wells *d* William A. Wellman
☆ Grant Withers, James Cagney, Mary Astor, Joan Blondell, Regis Toomey
'Good railroad melo for the lesser run theatres.' – *Variety*

'Meet Larry the Liquidator. Arrogant. Greedy. Self-centered. Ruthless. You gotta love the guy.'
Other People's Money *
US 1991 101m Technicolor
Warner/Yorktown (Norman Jewison, Ric Kidney)

A selfish asset-stripper attempts to take over an old-established company and its attractive young lawyer.
Entertaining comedy of the conflict between big-city and small-town values in the modern manner: that is, greed wins.
w Alvin Sargent *play* Jerry Sterner *d* Norman Jewison *ph* Haskell Wexler *m* David Newman *pd* Philip Rosenberg *ed* Lou Lombardo, Michael Pacek, Hubert de la Bouillerie
☆ Danny DeVito, Gregory Peck, Penelope Ann Miller, Piper Laurie, Dean Jones, R. D. Call, Mo Gaffney, Bette Henritze

'The romance of passion and power!'
The Other Side of Midnight
US 1977 166m DeLuxe Panavision
TCF/Frank Yablans, Martin Ransohoff (Howard W. Koch Jnr)

Before and after World War II a young Parisienne courts an American flyer, but her tycoon husband eventually exacts a grim revenge on both of them.
Turgid and interminable adaptation of a best-seller, with no likeable characters and several unpleasant sequences.
w Herman Raucher, Daniel Taradash *novel* Sidney Sheldon *d* Charles Jarrott *ph* Fred J. Koenekamp *m* Michel Legrand *pd* John DeCuir
☆ Marie-France Pisier, John Beck, Susan Sarandon, Raf Vallone, Clu Gulager, Christian Marquand
'After 166 minutes the feeling that one has actually lived through it all is a little too real for comfort.' – *David Badder, MFB*
'A fatuous, money-spinning film from the fatuous, money-spinning book.' – *New Yorker*
'Right down to the nonsense title, this epic of schlock restores the era of *Now Voyager* ... the movie equivalent of a good bad read.' – *Time Out*

'Once in your life – may someone love you like this!'
The Other Side of the Mountain
US 1975 102m Technicolor
Universal/Filmways/Larry Peerce (Edward S. Feldman)

GB title: *A Window to the Sky*
A girl skiing champion is paralysed by polio.
Maudlin tearjerker based on a real case; altogether too much of a good thing.
w David Seltzer *book* *A Long Way Up* by E. G. Valens *d* Larry Peerce *ph* David M. Walsh *m* Charles Fox
☆ Marilyn Hassett, Beau Bridges, Belinda Montgomery, Nan Martin, William Bryant, Dabney Coleman
song 'Richard's Window' (*m*Charles Fox, *ly*Norman Gimbel)

'For everyone who believes in happy endings!'
The Other Side of the Mountain Part Two
US 1977 99m Technicolor
Universal/Filmways (Edward S. Feldman)

Crippled skier Jill Kinmont becomes a teacher and falls in love again.
More true-life weepie material spun out from the first successful film; the sequel is quickly forgettable.
w Douglas Day Stewart *d* Larry Peerce *ph* Ric Waite *m* Lee Holdridge
☆ Marilyn Hassett, Timothy Bottoms, Nan Martin, Belinda J. Montgomery

'A love story for the romantically challenged.'
The Other Sister
US 1999 129m Technicolor Panavision
Buena Vista/Touchstone (Mario Iscovich, Alexandra Rose)

In San Francisco, two mentally retarded young people fall in love.
Manipulative, sentimental romantic tale that resembles a couple of episodes from a TV soap opera.
w Garry Marshall, Bob Brunner, Alexandra Rose, Blair Richwood *d* Garry Marshall *ph* Dante Spinotti *m* Rachel Portman *pd* Stephen J. Lineweaver *ed* Bruce Green
☆ Juliette Lewis (Carla), Diane Keaton (Elizabeth), Tom Skerritt (Radley), Giovanni Ribisi (Danny), Poppy Montgomery (Caroline), Sarah Paulson (Heather), Linda Thorson (Drew), Joe Flanigan (Jeff), Juliet Mills (Winnie), Hector Elizondo (Ernie)
'The sentiments are so perniciously calculated to extract tears that it left me stone cold.' – *James Christopher, Times*

'The Heart Is Deceitful, Who Can Know It?'
Other Voices, Other Rooms *
US 1995 98m colour
Dowtown/Golden Eye (Peter Wentworth, David Rocksavage)

A teenage boy is summoned by his cousin to a Southern mansion where his father lies paralysed.
Muted gothic romance, a work of intense, somewhat precious imagination that does not translate well to the screen.
w Sara Flanigan, David Rocksavage *novel* Truman Capote *d* David Rocksavage *ph* Paul Ryan *m* Chris Hajian *pd* Amy McGary *ed* Cynthia Scheider
☆ Lothaire Bluteau (Randolph Skully), Anna Thomson (Amy Skully), David Speck (Joel Sansom), April Turner (Missouri Fever), Frank Taylor (Edward R. Sansom), Leonard Watkins (Jesus Fever), Audrey Dollar (Idabell Thompkins), Elizabeth Byler (Florabell Thompkins), Moses Gibson (Little Sunshine), Bob Kingdom (narrator)
'A torturous experience at best.' – *Film Review*

'Sooner Or Later They Will Find You.'
The Others *
Spain/US 2001 104m colour
Buena Vista/Miramax/Cruise-Wagner/Escorpion/Sogecine/Canal+ (Fernando Bovaira, Jose Luis Cuerda, Sunmin Park)

In the late 1940s, a worried mother experiences strange phenomena while trying to protect her two children, who are allergic to daylight.
Chilling little drama, set in the past when people had servant problems; sometimes predictable, it is held together by Kidman's performance as a neurotic woman on the edge of hysteria.
wd Alejandro Amenábar *ph* Javier Aguirresarobe *m* Alejandro Amenábar *pd* Benjamin Fernandez *ed* Nacho Ruiz Capillas *cos* Sonia Grande
☆ Nicole Kidman (Grace), Christopher Eccleston (Charles), Fionnula Flanagan (Mrs Mills), Elaine Cassidy (Lydia), Eric Sykes (Mr Tuttle), Alakina Mann (Anne), James Bentley (Nicholas), Renée Asherson (Old lady)
'This is one scary movie, not because we see ghosts or monsters, but because Kidman makes us feel her fear as our own.' – *Amy Taubin, Village Voice*
'An unconvincing, pretentiously artsy pastiche of just about every hoary old gothic thriller you can think of.' – *Lou Lumenick, New York Post*

Otley **
GB 1968 91m Technicolor
Columbia/Open Road (Bruce Cohn Curtis)
An inoffensive Londoner falls in with spies and murderers.
Semi-spoof comedy thriller taking in James Bondery and the swinging London set. Generally pretty funny, but not entirely certain of its own motives.
w Ian La Frenais, Dick Clement *novel* Martin Waddell *d* Dick Clement *ph* Austin Dempster *m* Stanley Myers
☆ *Tom Courtenay*, Romy Schneider, Alan Badel, James Villiers, Leonard Rossiter, Freddie Jones, James Bolam, Fiona Lewis

Otto e Mezzo: see *Eight and a Half*

Our Betters *
US 1933 83m bw
RKO (David O. Selznick)
An American woman in London finds her titled husband is unfaithful and sets about causing society scandals.
Dimly adapted West End success makes an interesting but unamusing film.
w Jane Murfin, Harry Wagstaff Gribble *play* W. Somerset Maugham *d* George Cukor *ph* Charles Rosher *md* Max Steiner
☆ Constance Bennett, Violet Kemble Cooper, Alan Mowbray, Gilbert Roland, Phoebe Foster, Charles Starrett, Grant Mitchell, Anita Louise, Minor Watson, Hugh Sinclair
'It's all very English and so sophisticated ... they will really have to go for Constance Bennett to go for this picture.' – *Variety*
'One of those familiar dreams of high life in which we are asked to admire even while we condemn the superb immorality of our almost godlike betters.' – *The Times*

Our Blushing Brides: see *Our Dancing Daughters*

Our Daily Bread *
US 1934 80m bw
(UA)

A young couple in the Depression inherit a broken-down farm and make it work.
A rather drab sequel to The Crowd, *with an irrigation ditch finale in clear imitation of Eisenstein.*
w Elizabeth Hill *story* King Vidor *d* King Vidor *ph* Robert Planck *m* Alfred Newman
☆ Karen Morley, Tom Keene, John Qualen, Barbara Pepper, Addison Richards
'Regardless of the scepticism on the matter of box office, and its chances seem thin, it ranks as a fine effort.' – *Variety*
'With the arrival of the ditchdigging sequence, all that has gone before seems but buildup for this compelling climax.' – *Eileen Bowser, Film Notes, 1969*
† Vidor so desperately wanted to make the film that, discovering its theme to be unpopular with sponsors, he pawned everything he owned to finance it.

Our Dancing Daughters *
US 1928 86m approx (24 fps) bw silent
MGM/Cosmopolitan (Hunt Stromberg)

A wild young socialite knows when to stop, and makes a good marriage; her friend doesn't and falls to her death while drunk.
Mild exploitation piece of its time which swept Joan Crawford to stardom after her dance in her underwear.
w Josephine Lovett *d* Harry Beaumont *ph* George Barnes
☆ Joan Crawford, John Mack Brown, Dorothy Sebastian, Anita Page, Nils Asther
† Sequels: *Our Modern Maidens* (silent, 1929) with JC, Rod La Rocque, Douglas Fairbanks Jnr, Anita Page, *w* Josephine Lovett; *Our Blushing Brides* (sound, 1930) with JC, Robert Montgomery, Anita Page, Dorothy Sebastian, Raymond Hackett, *w* Bess Meredyth and John Howard Lawson. Neither was remarkable.
Josephine Lovett; George Barnes

Our Fighting Navy
GB 1937 75m bw
Herbert Wilcox
US title: *Torpedoed*
In South America, a British naval captain saves the consul's daughter from a revolutionary.
Tuppenny blood heroics, unconvincingly staged.
w 'Bartimeus', Guy Pollock, H. T. Bishop, Gerald Elliott, Harrison Owens *d* Norman Walker
☆ Robert Douglas, H. B. Warner, Noah Beery, Richard Cromwell, Hazel Terry, Esme Percy

Our Girl Friday
GB 1953 87m Eastmancolor
Renown

US title: *The Adventures of Sadie*
Four shipwrecked survivors are washed up on a desert island.
Coy sex comedy for the family; pretty unbearable.
wd Noel Langley *ph* Wilkie Cooper *m* Ronald Binge
☆ Kenneth More, Joan Collins, George Cole, Robertson Hare, Hermione Gingold, Walter Fitzgerald

Our Hearts Were Growing Up
US 1946 83m bw
Daniel Dare/Paramount
Our two heroines experience their college days during the roaring twenties.
Rather stiffly made but fitfully amusing sequel to the above.
w Norman Panama, Melvin Frank *d* William D. Russell
☆ Gail Russell, Diana Lynn, Brian Donlevy, James Brown, William Demarest, Bill Edwards, Billy DeWolfe, Sara Haden

Our Hearts Were Young and Gay *
US 1944 81m bw
Paramount (Sheridan Gibney)
Two well-to-do flappers of the twenties find fun and romance in Paris.
A pleasant, undemanding piece of nostalgia based on a popular biography.
w Sheridan Gibney *book* Cornelia Otis Skinner, Emily Kimbrough *d* Lewis Allen *ph* Theodor Sparkuhl *m* Werner Heymann
☆ Gail Russell, Diana Lynn, Charles Ruggles, Dorothy Gish, Beulah Bondi, James Brown, Bill Edwards, Jean Heather

Our Hospitality ***
US 1923 70m approx (24 fps) bw silent
Metro/Buster Keaton (Joseph M. Schenck)

Around 1850, a Southerner returns home to claim his bride and finds himself in the middle of a blood feud.
Charming rather than hilarious star comedy with a splendid ancient train and at least one incredible stunt by the star.
w Jean Havez, Joseph Mitchell, Clyde Bruckman *d* Buster Keaton, Jack Blystone *ph* Elgin Lesley, Gordon Jennings
☆ *Buster Keaton*, Natalie Talmadge, Joe Keaton, Buster Keaton Jnr
'A novelty mélange of dramatics, low comedy, laughs and thrills ... one of the best comedies ever produced.' – *Variety*

Our Leading Citizen
US 1939 87m bw
George Arthur/Paramount
A philosophical lawman tries to deal with labour unrest in his community.
Another attempt to make a star out of a character who appealed only in rural districts.
w John C. Moffitt *stories* Irvin S. Cobb *d* Alfred Santell
☆ Bob Burns, Susan Hayward, Joseph Allen, Charles Bickford, Elizabeth Patterson, Clarence Kolb, Paul Guilfoyle
'Confusing and burdensome script ... programme supporter.' – *Variety*

Our Little Girl
US 1935 63m bw
Fox (Edward Butcher)
A doctor's daughter brings her parents together.
One of the child star's thinner and more sentimental vehicles.
w Stephen Morehouse Avery, Allen Rivkin, Jack Yellen *story* *Heaven's Gate* by Florence Leighton

Pfalzgraf *d* John Robertson *ph* John Seitz *md* Oscar Bradley
☆ Shirley Temple, Joel McCrea, Rosemary Ames, Lyle Talbot, Erin O'Brien-Moore
'She should easily satisfy her following and assure business.' – *Variety*

Our Man Flint *
US 1965 108m DeLuxe Cinemascope
TCF (Saul David)
An American secret agent and super stud fights an organization bent on controlling the world through its weather.
Comic strip imitation of James Bond; in its wild way the first instalment scored a good many laughs, but the sequel, In Like Flint *(qv), quickly ended the series.*
w Hal Fimberg, Ben Starr *d* Daniel Mann *ph* Daniel L. Fapp *m* Jerry Goldsmith
☆ *James Coburn*, Lee J. Cobb, Gila Golan, Edward Mulhare, Benson Fong, Sigrid Valdis
'Despite the fact that everyone from designers to actors seems to be having a ball, the film somehow goes over the edge of parody – ultimately it looks suspiciously like a case of wish-fulfilment.' – *John Gillett*

Our Man in Havana *
GB 1959 112m bw Cinemascope
Columbia/Kingsmead (Carol Reed)
A British vacuum cleaner salesman in Havana allows himself to be recruited as a spy, and wishes he hadn't.
The wry flavour of the novel does not really translate to the screen, and especially not to the wide screen, but a few lines and characters offer compensation.
w Graham Greene *novel* Graham Greene *d* Carol Reed *ph* Oswald Morris *m* Hermanos Deniz Cuban Rhythm Band
☆ Alec Guinness, *Noël Coward*, Burl Ives, Maureen O'Hara, Ernie Kovacs, *Ralph Richardson*, Jo Morrow, Paul Rogers, Grégoire Aslan, Duncan Macrae
'The main weakness is the absence of economic, expressive cutting and visual flow. As a result ... stretches of dialogue become tedious to watch; and the essential awareness of the writer's shifting tensions yields disappointingly to the easier mannerisms of any conventional comedy-thriller.' – *Peter John Dyer*

Our Man in Marrakesh
GB 1966 92m Technicolor
Harry Alan Towers
US title: *Bang Bang, You're Dead*
A tourist becomes involved with gangsters.
Thin comedy-thriller with exotic locations.
w Peter Yeldham *d* Don Sharp *ph* Michael Reed *m* Malcolm Lockyer
☆ Tony Randall, Senta Berger, Terry-Thomas, Herbert Lom, Wilfrid Hyde-White, Grégoire Aslan, Klaus Kinski

Our Miss Brooks
US 1955 85m bw
Warner
A lady teacher finds that the professor to whom she is engaged is tied to mother's apron strings.
Verbose comedy considerably less funny than the TV series from which it was spun off.
w Al Lewis, Joseph Quillan *d* Al Lewis
☆ Eve Arden, Gale Gordon, Robert Rockwell, Don Porter, Jane Morgan, Richard Crenna, Nick Adams

Our Miss Fred *
GB 1972 96m Technicolor
EMI/Willis World Wide (Josephine Douglas)
In World War II France, an actor escapes in women's clothes when his troupe is captured by the Nazis.
A carefully nurtured vehicle for Britain's top female impersonator somehow doesn't come off; celluloid both constrains his range and reveals his inadequacies.
w Hugh Leonard *d* Bob Kellett *ph* Dick Bush *m* Peter Greenwell
☆ *Danny La Rue*, Alfred Marks, Lance Percival, Lally Bowers, Frances de la Tour, Walter Gotell

Our Modern Maidens: see *Our Dancing Daughters*

Our Mother's House
GB 1967 105m Metrocolor
MGM/Filmways (Jack Clayton)
When mother dies, seven children, who don't want to go to an orphanage, bury her in the garden. Then their ne'er-do-well father turns up.
Unpleasant and rather boring melodrama, too silly to have much dramatic impact.
w Jeremy Brooks, Haya Harareet *novel* Julian Gloag *d* Jack Clayton *ph* Larry Pizer *m* Georges Delerue
☆ Dirk Bogarde, Margaret Brooks, Pamela Franklin, Mark Lester, Yootha Joyce, Anthony Nicholls
'The children begin to display an alarming variety of accents ... and when Dirk Bogarde enters, doing a rich Bill Sykes act as the long lost wicked father to a predominantly genteel family, the whole structure collapses.' – *Tom Milne*
'Clayton succeeds where upstarts have failed in capturing the essence of the horror-suspense film – and that is the realization that the monsters among us are human.' – *Judith Crist*

Our Neighbours the Carters
US 1939 85m bw
Paramount
A small-town pharmacist is so poor that he considers an offer from a wealthy friend to adopt one of his children.
A small-town saga of smiles and tears, much appreciated at the time.
w S. K. Lauren, Renaud Hoffman *d* Ralph Murphy
☆ Fay Bainter, Frank Craven, Genevieve Tobin, Edmund Lowe
'Neatly set up as a programmer for the family trade.' – *Variety*

Our Relations ***
US 1936 65m bw
Hal Roach/Stan Laurel Productions
Two sailors entrusted with a diamond ring get mixed up with their long lost and happily married twin brothers.
A fast-moving comedy which contains some of Laurel and Hardy's most polished work as well as being their most satisfying production.
w Richard Connell, Felix Adler, Charles Rogers, Jack Jevne *story* *The Money Box* by W. W. Jacobs *d Harry Lachman ph Rudolph Maté*
☆ *Stan Laurel, Oliver Hardy*, James Finlayson, Alan Hale, Sidney Toler, Daphne Pollard, Iris Adrian, Noel Madison, Ralf Harolde, *Arthur Housman*

Our Story
France 1984 111m Eastmancolor
Artificial Eye/Adel Productions/Sara Films-A2 (Alain Sarde)
original title: *Notre Histoire*
A boozy traveller falls for a beautiful woman he meets on a train.
Sub-Buñuel surrealism that is an irritant rather than a pleasure.
wd Bertrand Blier *ph* Jean Penzer *m* Martinu, Beethoven, Schubert and others *ad* Bernard Evien *ed* Claudine Merlin
☆ Alain Delon, Nathalie Baye, Michel Galabru, Geneviève Fontanel, Jean-Pierre Darroussin, Gérard Darmon

'The story of a love affair that lasted a lifetime!'
Our Town **
US 1940 90m bw
Principal Artists/Sol Lesser
Birth, life and death in a small New Hampshire community.
One of the main points of the play, the absence of scenery, is abandoned in this screen version, and the graveyard scene has to be presented as a dream, but the film retains the narrator and manages to make points of its own while absorbing the endearing qualities which made the play a classic.
w Thornton Wilder, Frank Craven, Harry Chantlee *play* Thornton Wilder *d Sam Wood* *ph* Bert Glennon *m* Aaron Copland *pd William Cameron Menzies*
☆ *Frank Craven*, William Holden, *Martha Scott, Thomas Mitchell, Fay Bainter, Guy Kibbee, Beulah Bondi*, Stuart Erwin
'You can nearly smell things cooking, and feel the night air.' – *Otis Ferguson*
best picture; Aaron Copland; Martha Scott; art direction

Our Very Own
US 1950 93m bw
Samuel Goldwyn
A girl is shocked to discover that she is adopted.
Another Goldwyn foray into chintzy, middle-class, small-town America, but not a winning example.
w F. Hugh Herbert *d* David Miller *ph* Lee Garmes *m* Victor Young *sp* Richard Day
☆ Ann Blyth, Farley Granger, Joan Evans, Jane Wyatt, Ann Dvorak, Donald Cook, Natalie Wood, Gus Schilling, Phyllis Kirk

Our Vines Have Tender Grapes *
US 1945 105m bw
MGM (Robert Sisk)
Life in a Norwegian farm community in southern Wisconsin.
Unexceptionable family picture produced in MGM's best manner.
w Dalton Trumbo *novel* George Victor Martin *d* Roy Rowland *ph* Robert Surtees *m* Bronislau Kaper
☆ Edward G. Robinson, Margaret O'Brien, James Craig, Agnes Moorehead, Jackie 'Butch' Jenkins, Morris Carnovsky, Frances Gifford, Sara Haden

Our Wife *
US 1931 20m bw
Hal Roach
Stan helps Ollie to elope.
Good standard star comedy with a rather disappointing third sequence as three people try to get into a car designed for one.
w H. M. Walker *d* James W. Horne *ph* Art Lloyd *ed* Richard Currier
☆ Stan Laurel, Oliver Hardy, James Finlayson, Jean London, Ben Turpin, Charley Rogers

Our Wife
US 1941 95m bw
Columbia (John M. Stahl)
A composer is romantically torn between a lady scientist and his own ex-wife.
Middling romantic comedy of a kind very familiar at the time.
w P. J. Wolfson *play* Lillian Day, Lyon Mearson *d* John M. Stahl *ph* Franz Planer *m* Leo Shuken
☆ Melvyn Douglas, Ruth Hussey, Ellen Drew, Charles Coburn, John Hubbard, Harvey Stephens

Ourselves Alone
GB 1936 87m bw
British International
An Irish colleen has a brother in the IRA and a lover in the British Army.
Rather tired hawking of a theme already treated in Beloved Enemy.
w Dudley Leslie, Marjorie Jeans, Dennis Johnstone *play* Dudley Sturrock, Noel Scott *d* Brian Desmond Hurst, Walter Summers
☆ Antoinette Cellier, Niall MacGinnis, John Lodge, John Loder, Clifford Evans
'Will find tough sledding because of the subject matter.' – *Variety*
'One of the silliest pictures which even an English studio has yet managed to turn out.' – *Graham Greene, The Spectator*

Out Cold
US 1989 92m CFI color
Hemdale (George G. Braunstein, Ron Hamady)
Believing that he has inadvertently killed his partner, a butcher covers up the crime with the help of the widow, who is the real murderer.
Limp comedy that quickly runs out of ideas.
w Leonard Glasser, George Malko *d* Malcolm Mowbray *ph* Tony Pierce-Roberts *m* Michel Colombier *pd* Linda Pearl *ed* Dennis M. Hill
☆ John Lithgow, Teri Garr, Randy Quaid, Bruce McGill, Lisa Blount, Alan Blumenfeld, Morgan Paull, Barbara Rhoades

Out for Justice
US 1991 91m Technicolor Panavision
Warner (Steven Seagal, Arnold Kopelson)
In Brooklyn, a cop hunts down the drug-crazed killer who murdered his best friend.
Despite the title, our hero is out for revenge, and the bloodier the better. The familiar theme is played out with the maximum amount of violence.
w David Lee Henry *d* John Flynn *ph* Ric Waite *m* David Michael Frank *pd* Gene Rudolf *ed* Robert A. Ferretti, Donald Brochu
☆ Steven Seagal, William Forsythe, Jerry Orbach, Jo Champa, Shareen Mitchell, Sal Richards, Gina Gershon, Jay Acovone
'Steven Seagal should snap off another hefty chunk of box-office with this latest lame-brained excuse to showcase his bone-breaking talents.' – *Variety*

Out in Fifty
US 1999 100m CFI
Amco/Urban (Ami Artzi, BoJesse Christopher, Scott Leet)
After he gets out of prison, an ex-convict is stalked by the vengeful LA cop whose wife he accidentally killed.
Another giant step in the disintegration of Rourke's career: you cannot go much lower, in cinematic terms, than starring in this crude, posturing, self-indulgent and badly-acted and -scripted thriller.
wd BoJesse Christopher, Scott Leet *ph* Sharon Meir *m* Steve Edwards *pd* Linda Keil *ed* Ross Guidici
☆ Mickey Rourke (Jack Bracken), BoJesse Christopher (Steven Fisher), Nina Ofenböck (Gloria Fisher), Nikki Bokal (Sarah Brawn), Scott Leet (Raymond Frye), Peter Greene (Tony Grayson), Christina Applegate (Lillah), Alexis Arquette (Kim), Balthazar Getty (Lefty), James Avery (Cappy), Abraham Benrubi (Spike)

Out of Africa **
US/GB 1985 150m Rank Colour
Technovision
Mirage/Sydney Pollack
In 1914 Karen Blixen arrives in Africa for a marriage of convenience with a German baron who ignores her; a white hunter remedies the situation.
Heavy going but critically lauded transcription of a semi-classic which ambles along for an extremely long time without really getting anywhere.
w Kurt Luedtke *writings* Isak Dinesen (Karen Blixen) *d* Sydney Pollack *ph David Watkin* *m* John Barry *pd* Stephen Grimes *ed* Frederic Steinkamp, William Steinkamp
☆ Meryl Streep, Robert Redford, Klaus Maria Brandauer, Michael Kitchen, Michael Gough
'It's a long way to go for a downbeat ending.' – *Variety*
'The film purrs pleasantly along like one of its own big cats.' – *Sight and Sound*
best picture; Sydney Pollack; David Watkin; John Barry; Kurt Luedtke; Stephen Grimes; sound
Meryl Streep; Klaus Maria Brandauer; Frederic Steinkamp, William Steinkamp
Kurt Luedtke; David Watkin

Out of Depth
GB 1999 99m colour
Steon/Redbus (Stephen Cranny)
In London, a graphic designer becomes reluctantly involved with gangsters and drug dealers.
An unappetising slice of low-life, as predictable as it is dull.
wd Simon Marshall *ph* Adam Suschitzky *m* Barry Adamson *pd* Philip Robinson *ed* St John O'Rorke
☆ Sean Maguire (Paul), Danny Midwinter (Steve), Nicholas Ball (Lenny), Phil Cornwell (Ed), Josephine Butler (Sarah), Leigh Lawson (Tate), Clive Russell (Tinker), Rita Tushingham (Maggie)
'Banal, often risible crime movie that works in black and white with various familiar shades of Kray.' – *Philip French, Observer*

Out of Order *
West Germany 1984 88m colour
Laura/Mutoskop (Thomas Schühly, Matthias Deyle)
original title: *Abwärts*
In an office block at night, four people are trapped in a lift with an alarm system that does not work.
Well-made, moderately gripping thriller, although it might have been better with a few more people trapped, to provide more variation on what threatens to stay close to cliché for most of its length.

w Carl Schenkel, Frank Göhre *d* Carl Schenkel *ph* Jacques Steyn *m* Jacques Zwart *ed* Norbert Herzner
☆ Götz George, Renee Soutendijk, Wolfgang Kieling, Hannes Jaenicke, Kurt Raab

Out of Rosenheim: see *Bagdad Café*

Out of Season *
GB 1975 90m Technicolor
EMI/Lorimar (Robert Enders, Merv Adelson)
One winter in an English seaside resort, an old love is rekindled.
Restrained sexual fireworks in the old French manner, well enough done with excellent atmosphere but a shade overlong and marred by the need to indulge in modern tricks such as a deliberately ambiguous ending.
w Reuben Bercovitch, Eric Bercovici *d* Alan Bridges *ph* Arthur Ibbetson *m* John Cameron
☆ Cliff Robertson, Vanessa Redgrave, Susan George, Edward Evans

Out of Sight ***
US 1998 123m DeLuxe
Universal/Jersey (Danny de Vito, Michael Shamberg, Stacey Sher)
A bank robber and a federal marshal fall for each other, despite being on opposite sides of the law.
A thriller disguised as a romantic comedy, acted and directed with the necessary light touch.
w Scott Frank *novel* Elmore Leonard *d* Steven Soderbergh *ph* Elliot Davis *m* Cliff Martinez *pd* Gary Frutkoff *ed* Anne V. Coates
☆ George Clooney, Jennifer Lopez, Vingh Rhames, Don Cheadle, Dennis Farina, Albert Brooks
'There's no getting away with the simplicity of its success – great script based on a good book, good actors working with great characters, a great director empowered to be great again.' – *Ian Nathan, Empire*
Scott Frank; Anne V. Coates

Out of the Blue
GB 1931 88m bw
BIP
An aristocrat's daughter loves the radio singer who is engaged to her sister.
Dated frou-frou with interesting talent.
w R. P. Weston, Frank Miller, Bert Lee *play Little Tommy Tucker* by Caswell Garth and Desmond Carter *d* Gene Gerrard, John Orton *ph* Ernest Palmer, Arthur Crabtree *m* Vivian Ellis
☆ Jessie Matthews, Gene Gerrard, Kay Hammond, Kenneth Kove, Binnie Barnes

Out of the Blue
US 1947 86m bw
Eagle Lion
A Greenwich village artist thinks a girl who has passed out in his apartment is dead, and tries to hide the body.
Tasteless and very unfunny farce.
w Vera Caspary, Walter Bullock, Edward Eliscu *d* Leigh Jason
☆ George Brent, Carole Landis, Ann Dvorak, Turhan Bey, Virginia Mayo, Elizabeth Patterson, Julia Dean, Richard Lane

'Her dad's in prison...Her mom's on drugs...The only adult she admires is Johnny Rotten.'
Out of the Blue
Canada 1980 94m colour
Sanctuary (Leonard Yakir, Gary Jules Jouvenat)
A wayward teenage punk, with a drug-addicted mother and a drunken, sexually abusive ex-convict for a father, finds her life unendurable.
At least she can count herself fortunate that she didn't have to sit through this film.
w Leonard Yakir, Brenda Nelson *d* Dennis Hopper *ph* Marc Champion *m* Tom Lavin, Neil Young *ad* David Hiscox *ed* Doris Dyck
☆ Linda Manz, Dennis Hopper, Sharon Farrell, Don Gordon, Raymond Burr
'"I've never endorsed anything before, but if a masterpiece comes along, people should see it," states Jack Nicholson…it's hard to disagree.' – *Sight and Sound, 2002*

Out of the Clouds
GB 1954 88m Eastmancolor
Ealing (Michael Balcon, Michael Relph)
Several personal stories mesh against a background of London airport during a fog.
A dull compendium of stories with a background of documentary detail which is now fascinating because it's so dated.
w John Eldridge, Michael Relph *novel* John Fores *d* Michael Relph, Basil Dearden *ph* Paul Beeson *m* Richard Addinsell
☆ Anthony Steel, Robert Beatty, David Knight, Margo Lorenz, James Robertson Justice, Eunice Gayson, Isabel Dean, Gordon Harker, Bernard Lee, Michael Howard, Marie Lohr, Esma Cannon, Abraham Sofaer
'The film relies considerably on small-time players and marginal incidents; the detail, however, never looks like adding up to a satisfactory whole.' – *Penelope Houston*

Out of the Dark
US 1988 89m colour
Medusa/Zel Films (Zane W. Levitt)
Cops investigate a series of sex-related murders by a man dressed as a clown.
Camp horror film, full of sniggers at its own nastiness.
w J. Gregory de Felice, Zane W. Levitt *d* Michael Schroeder *ph* Julio Macat *m* Paul F. Antonelli, David Wheatley *pd* Robert Schulenberg *ed* Mark Manos
☆ Cameron Dye, Karen Black, Lynn Danielson, Karen Witter, Tracey Walter, Silvana Gallardo, Bud Cort, Geoffrey Lewis, Divine, Paul Bartel, Tab Hunter

Out of the Fog *
US 1941 86m bw
Warner (Henry Blanke)
Gangsters move in to terrorize an innocent Brooklyn family.
Standard exploration of a situation which became routine.
w Robert Rossen, Jerry Wald, Richard Macaulay *play The Gentle People* by Irwin Shaw *d* Anatole Litvak *ph* James Wong Howe
☆ Ida Lupino, John Garfield, Thomas Mitchell, Eddie Albert, George Tobias, Aline MacMahon, Jerome Cowan, John Qualen, Leo Gorcey
'Has succeeded in converting a disappointing stage work into a vastly entertaining motion picture.' – *New York Herald Tribune*

'You're no good and neither am I. We deserve each other!'
Out of the Past **
US 1947 97m bw
RKO (Warren Duff)
GB title: *Build My Gallows High*
A private detective is hired by a hoodlum to find his homicidal girlfriend; he does, and falls in love with her.
Moody film noir *with Hollywood imitating French models; plenty of snarling and a death-strewn climax.*
w Geoffrey Homes *novel Build My Gallows High* by Geoffrey Homes *d* Jacques Tourneur *ph* Nicholas Musuraca *m* Roy Webb
☆ *Robert Mitchum, Jane Greer, Kirk Douglas,* Rhonda Fleming, Richard Webb, Steve Brodie, Virginia Houston, Dickie Moore
'Is this not an outcrop of the national masochism induced by a quite aimless, newly industrialized society proceeding rapidly on its way to nowhere?' – *Richard Winnington*
'Mitchum is so sleepily self-confident with the women that when he slopes into clinches you expect him to snore in their faces.' – *James Agee*

'The First Film Made In Outer Space.'
Out of the Present *
Germany/France/Belgium/Russia 1995 96m colour
Downtown/Bremer Institut/Fernsehen (Elke Peters)
A documentary about life on the Russian Mir space station in the early 90s.
Using film shot by Sergei Krikalev, who spent ten months aboard Mir, this is a fascinating glimpse of a confined life in space.
wd Andrei Ujica *ph* Vadim Yusov *m* Johann Strauss, Peter Lazonby *ed* Ralf Henninger, Heldi Leihbecher
☆ Anatoli Artesbarski, Sergei Krikalev, Helen Sharman, Viktor Afanasiev, Musa Monarov

'The laugh-a-minute lowdown on the birth of swoon!'
Out of this World
US 1945 96m bw
Paramount (Sam Coslow)
A Western Union messenger becomes a hit crooner and a national phenomenon.
Very mild comedy with the gimmick that Bing Crosby dubbed the singing.
w Walter de Leon, Arthur Phillips *d* Hal Walker *ph* Stuart Thompson *m* Victor Young
☆ Eddie Bracken, Veronica Lake, Diana Lynn, Cass Daley, Parkyakarkus, Donald MacBride, Florence Bates, Carmen Cavallero

'When they take you for an out-of-towner, they really take you.'
The Out of Towners *
US 1970 98m Movielab
Paramount/Jalem (Paul Nathan)
An executive and his wife fly into New York for an interview, but their encounter with the city is a mounting series of traumatic disasters.
A love-hate relationship with a city demonstrated by a resident is something of an in-joke and becomes increasingly hysterical and unsympathetic, but there are bright moments in this company.
w Neil Simon *d* Arthur Hiller *ph* Andrew Laszlo *m* Quincy Jones
☆ Jack Lemmon, Sandy Dennis
'Technically the sloppiest as well as the most witlessly uncomfortable movie for some time.' – *Roger Greenspun, New York Times*

Out on a Limb
US 1992 83m DeLuxe
Universal/Interscope (Michael Hertzberg)
Asked by her teacher to describe her summer vacation, a young girl tells a story involving mistaken indentity, kidnapping, murder and romance.
Witless black farce, neatly plotted but with a hapless, wimpish hero and a leaden pace.
w Daniel Goldin, Joshua Goldin *d* Francis Veber *ph* Donald E. Thorin *m* Van Dyke Parks *pd* Stephen Marsh *ed* Glenn Farr
☆ Matthew Broderick, Jeffrey Jones, Heidi Kling, John C. Reilly, Courtney Peldon, Nancy Lenehan, Marian Mercer, David Margulies, Michael Monks

Out to Sea
US 1997 109m DeLuxe
TCF (John Davis, David T. Friendly)
A gambler in search of a wealthy wife signs on as a dance host aboard a luxury liner and tricks his brother-in-law into accompanying him on the cruise.
Nostalgic, old-fashioned comedy that provides a modicum of amusement.
w Robert Nelson Jacobs *d* Martha Coolidge *ph* Lajos Koltai *m* David Newman *pd* James Spencer *ed* Anne V. Coates
☆ Jack Lemmon, Walter Matthau, Dyan Cannon, Gloria DeHaven, Brent Spiner, Elaine Stritch, Hal Linden, Donald O'Connor, Edward Mulhare, Rue McClanahan
'Mildly amusing and unabashedly retrograde trifle that, except for a few naughty words, resembles glossy studio product of a generation or so ago.' – *Joe Leydon, Variety*

'They fell in love 24 years ago … and in the next 24 hours they'll remember why.'
The Out-of-Towners
US 1999 91m colour
Paramount (Robert Cort, David Madden, Robert Evans, Teri Schwartz)
A long-time married couple visit New York, where everything goes wrong except their feelings for one another.
Lamentably dull remake of a comedy that left much to be desired the first time around.
w Marc Lawrence *play* Neil Simon *d* Sam Weisman *ph* John Bailey *m* Marc Shaiman *pd* Ken Adam *ed* Kent Beyda
☆ Steve Martin, Goldie Hawn, John Cleese, Mayor Rudolph Giuliani (as himself)
'So feeble and unfocused as to make the Farrelly brothers of *There's Something about Mary* appear to have been suckled at the bosom of Aristophanes.' – *Lawrence Van Gelder, New York Times*

Outback *
Australia 1970 109m Technicolor
NIT/Group W (George Willoughby)
A young teacher becomes involved in the rougher side of life in a remote Australian village.
A convincingly brutal picture of a community whose interests range from homosexuality to a bloody kangaroo hunt.
w Evan Jones *novel Wake in Fright* by Kenneth Cook *d* Ted Kotcheff *ph* Brian West *m* John Scott
☆ Gary Bond, Donald Pleasence, Chips Rafferty

Outback
Australia/US 1989 94m colour
Samuel Goldwyn/Burrowes (John Sexton)
In Australia at the turn of the century, a wealthy American entrepreneur and a drover both risk everything for the love of a young heiress threatened by an unscrupulous landowner.
Opulent period drama, enjoyable enough in its lush, romantic way but populated by stock characters.
w John Sexton *d* Ian Barry *ph* Ross Berryman *m* Mario Millo *pd* Owen Paterson *ed* Henry Dangar
☆ Jeff Fahey, Tushka Bergen, Steven Vidler, Richard Moir, Shane Briant, Drew Forsythe, Sandy Gore

'An animal carries a deadly virus ... And the greatest medical crisis in history begins.'
'Try to remain calm.'
Outbreak
US 1995 127m Technicolor
Warner/Punch (Arnold Kopelson, Wolfgang Petersen, Gail Katz)
A US Army expert saves the world from a deadly virus that spreads from Africa to the States and his own gung-ho generals.
An increasingly risible thriller that begins well and then becomes a fevered exercise in sub-James Bond heroics, with a military villain straight out of a comic book.
w Laurence Dworet, Robert Roy Pool *d* Wolfgang Petersen *ph* Michael Ballhaus *m* James Newton Howard *pd* William Sandell *ed* Neil Travis, Lynzee Klingman, William Hoy *sp* John Frazier; Boss Film Studios
☆ Dustin Hoffman, Rene Russo, Morgan Freeman, Kevin Spacey, Cuba Gooding Jnr, Donald Sutherland, Patrick Dempsey, Zakes Mokae, Malick Bowens
'The entire film has been put together with such skill and attention to viewer excitement that audiences will readily swallow the whole enchilada without a burp. A highly topical and alarming cautionary tale that's been socked over for maximum visceral impact.' – *Todd McCarthy, Variety*
'A pallid epic about an appalling epidemic.' – *Time*
† Five other screenwriters worked uncredited on the script: Neil Jiminez, Ted Tally, Jeb Stuart, Carrie Fisher and Dan Gilroy.

The Outcast: see *Man in the Saddle*

The Outcast
US 1954 87m Trucolor
Republic (Herbert J. Yates)
A cowboy returns home to claim the ranch his uncle stole from him.
Fast-paced Western that relies on non-stop action to distract attention from its clichéd narrative.
w John K. Butler, Richard Wormser *story* Todhunter Ballard *d* William Witney *ph* Reggie Lanning *m* R. Dale Butts *ad* Frank Arrigo *ed* Tony Martinelli
☆ John Derek, Joan Evans, Jim Davis, Slim Pickens, Harry Carey Jnr

Outcast Lady
US 1934 79m bw
MGM
GB title: *A Woman of the World*
A spoilt rich girl goes from man to man but helps her drunken brother.
Modest remake of the Garbo vehicle A Woman of Affairs.
w Zoe Akins *novel The Green Hat* by Michael Arlen *d* Robert Z. Leonard

☆ Constance Bennett, Hugh Williams, Mrs Patrick Campbell, Elizabeth Allan, Henry Stephenson, Leo G. Carroll

'Even her love was primitive!'

Outcast of the Islands **

GB 1951 102m bw

London Films (Carol Reed)

A shiftless trader finds a secret Far Eastern trading post where he can be happy – but even here he becomes an outcast.

An interesting but not wholly successful attempt to dramatize a complex character study. It looks great and is well acted.

w William Fairchild *novel* Joseph Conrad *d* Carol Reed *ph* *John Wilcox* *m* Brian Easdale

☆ *Trevor Howard*, Ralph Richardson, Kerima, Robert Morley, Wendy Hiller, George Coulouris, Frederick Valk, Wilfrid Hyde-White, Betty Ann Davies

'The script is so overwhelmed by the narrative itself that the characters and relationships fail to crystallize ... while the handling is often intelligent, ingenious, and has its effective moments, no real conception emerges.' – *Gavin Lambert*

'Its sordidness is not veneered by the usual lyricism of Hollywood.' – *London Evening News*

'The most powerful film ever made in this country.' – *Observer*

The Outcasts of Poker Flat

US 1937 68m bw

RKO (Robert Sisk)

Four undesirables are run out of town and stuck in a mountain cabin during a snowstorm.

Overstretched anecdote with a predictably downbeat finale and not much action.

w John Twist, Harry Segall *story* Bret Harte *d* Christy Cabanne *ph* Robert de Grasse

☆ Preston Foster, Jean Muir, Van Heflin

The Outcasts of Poker Flat

US 1952 80m bw

TCF (Julian Blaustein)

Good-looking but equally undramatic remake of the above.

w Edmund H. North *d* Joseph M. Newman *ph* Joseph LaShelle *m* Hugo Friedhofer

☆ Dale Robertson, Anne Baxter, Cameron Mitchell, Miriam Hopkins

'Fails badly either as dramatic or as western fare ... best where two features prevail.' – *Variety*

The Outfit *

US 1974 103m Metrocolor

MGM (Carter de Haven)

A bank robber comes out of prison to discover that gangsters have murdered his brother and intend to kill him.

Slick, tough thriller with slick, tough dialogue and performances to match; the taut direction maintains suspense even when the action becomes predictable.

wd John Flynn *novel* Richard Stark *ph* Bruce Surtees *m* Jerry Fielding *ad* Tambi Larsen *ed* Ralph E. Winters

☆ Robert Duvall, Karen Black, Joe Don Baker, Robert Ryan, Timothy Carey, Richard Jaeckel, Sheree North, Felice Orlandi, Joanna Cassidy, Elisha Cooke

'Even in space, the ultimate enemy is man!'

'On Jupiter's moon, something deadly is happening!'

Outland

GB 1981 109m Technicolor Panavision

Warner/Ladd (Richard A. Roth)

The marshal of a mining base on the third moon of Jupiter waits for hired killers to arrive from Earth and try to assassinate him.

Ludicrous, over-plotted outer-space version of High Noon, *in such thick colour that the action is hard to follow.*

wd Peter Hyams *ph* Stephen Goldblatt *m* Jerry Goldsmith *pd* Philip Harrison

☆ Sean Connery, Peter Boyle, Frances Sternhagen, James B. Sikking, Kika Markham, Clarke Peters

'Acres of footage are expended on the same old dreary electronic gadgetry and the same old hollowly echoing metalwork sets.' – *Tom Milne, MFB*

'Action! Thrills! Sensations! Primitive Love!'

The Outlaw *

US 1943 126m bw

Howard Hughes

Billy the Kid, Doc Holliday and Pat Garrett meet up at a way station and quarrel over a half-breed girl.

Half-baked Western with much pretentious chat and the main interest squarely focused on the bosom of the producer's new discovery. This aspect kept censorship ballyhoo going for six years before the film was finally released in truncated form, and audiences found it not worth the wait, though it does look good.

w Jules Furthman *d* Howard Hughes *ph* *Gregg Toland* *md* Victor Young

☆ Jack Beutel, Jane Russell, Thomas Mitchell, Walter Huston

'A Western employing every ingredient ever used in this brand of production, but in such a naive fashion that you will laugh – not with the picture but at it.' – *Ewart Hodgson, News of the World*

† Despite the controversy, the British Board of Film Censors gave the film a 'U' certificate, which meant that children could see it.

Outlaw Blues

US 1977 101m Technicolor

Warner/Fred Weintraub–Paul Heller (Steve Tisch)

An ex-con finds that a singing star has stolen his song.

Fashionable comedy-melodrama with no great entertainment value despite action scenes towards the end.

w B. W. L. Norton *d* Richard T. Heffron *ph* Jules Brenner *m* Charles Bernstein

☆ Peter Fonda, Susan Saint James, John Crawford, James Callahan, Michael Lerner

The Outlaw Josey Wales *

US 1976 135m DeLuxe Panavision

Warner/Malpaso (Robert Daley)

A Westerner gradually avenges the death of his wife at the hands of bandits.

Bloodthirsty actioner in the star's usual mould; likely to prove unintentionally funny for hardened addicts.

w Phil Kaufman, Sonia Chernus *novel* Gone to Texas by Forrest Carter *d* Clint Eastwood *ph* Bruce Surtees *m* Jerry Fielding

☆ Clint Eastwood, Chief Dan George, Sondra Locke, John Vernon, Bill McKinney

'If only the actors hadn't got in the way of the scenery, it would have been a very beautiful film indeed.' – *Benny Green, Punch*

Jerry Fielding

Outpost in Malaya: see *The Planter's Wife*

Outpost in Morocco

US 1949 92m bw

Joseph N. Ermolieff

A romantic Foreign Legion officer falls for the daughter of an enemy Arab.

Despite authentic locations and the cooperation of the Legion this is a stolid piece of work, too dull even for children's matinees.

w Charles Grayson, Paul de St Columbe *d* Robert Florey *ph* Lucien Andriot

☆ George Raft, Akim Tamiroff, Marie Windsor, John Litel, Eduard Franz

Outrage

US 1950 75m bw

Filmmakers (Collier Young)

A girl who has been raped is almost unhinged by the experience.

Well-meaning low-budgeter, thin in entertainment value.

w Ida Lupino, Collier Young, Malvin Wald *d* Ida Lupino *ph* Archie Stout *m* Paul Sawtell *md* Constantin Bakaleinikoff *pd* Harry Horner

☆ Mala Powers, Tod Andrews, Robert Clarke, Raymond Bond, Lilian Hamilton

'An unconvincing mixture of sensationalism, sentiment and half-baked sociology.' – *MFB*

The Outrage *

US 1964 97m bw Panavision

MGM/Harvest/February/Ritt/Kayos (A. Ronald Lubin)

Conflicting views of a Western murder.

Wildly ineffective remake of Rashomon, *with everyone strangely overacting and little sense of the West as it is normally depicted.*

w Michael Kanin *d* Martin Ritt *ph* James Wong Howe *m* Alex North

☆ Paul Newman, Edward G. Robinson, Laurence Harvey, Claire Bloom, William Shatner, Albert Salmi

Outrageous Fortune *

US 1987 100m DeLuxe

Touchstone/Interscope (Ted Field, Robert Cort)

Two disparate women are in love with the same man, who is wanted by the CIA and the KGB.

Chase comedy with sex elements and plenty going on: old-fashioned jokes wrapped up in a modern package.

w Leslie Dixon *d* Arthur Hiller *ph* David M. Walsh *m* Alan Silvestri *pd* James D. Vance

☆ Shelley Long, Bette Midler, Peter Coyote, Robert Prosky, John Schuck

'Really a risqué film for a conservative audience.' – *Daily Variety*

The Outriders

US 1950 93m Technicolor

MGM (Richard Goldstone)

Three Confederate soldiers escape from a Yankee prison camp.

Competent star Western with solid production values.

w Irving Ravetch *d* Roy Rowland *ph* Charles Schoenbaum *m* André Previn *ed* Robert J. Kern

☆ Joel McCrea (Will Owen), Arlene Dahl (Jen Gort), Barry Sullivan (Jesse Wallace), Claude Jarman Jnr (Roy Gort), Ramon Novarro (Don Antonio Chaves), James Whitmore (Clint Priest), Jeff Corey (Keeley), Ted de Corsia (Bye), Martin Garralaga (Father Damasco)

The Outside Man **

France/Italy 1972 104m DeLuxe

United Artists/Cité Films/Mondial TE.FI (Jacques Bar)

original title: *Un Homme est Mort*

After he has killed a Mafia boss in Los Angeles to pay off his debts, a Frenchman discovers that he is to be killed and goes on the run from his assassin.

Well-made thriller full of unexpected twists and turns, with some intriguing set-pieces, including a shoot-out at a funeral.

w Jean-Claude Carrière, Jacques Deray, Ian McLellan Hunter *d* Jacques Deray *ph* Terry K. Meade, Silvano Ippoliti *m* Michel Legrand *pd* Marvin March *ed* Henri Lanoe, William K. Chulack

☆ Jean-Louis Trintignant, Ann-Margret, Roy Scheider, Angie Dickinson, Georgia Engel, Felice Orlandi, Talia Shire

'A neat, intriguing thriller which never gets ambitions above its station.' – *Tom Milne, MFB*

Outside the Law

US 1930 76m bw

Universal

A girl becomes involved between two crooks planning a bank robbery.

Incompetent early talkie with some familiar talents all at sea.

w Tod Browning, Garrett Fort *d* Tod Browning

☆ Mary Nolan, Edward G. Robinson, Owen Moore, Edwin Sturgis

'One of the worst examples of claptrap since sound came in ... no continuity and the director lets the cast run wild.' – *Variety*

The Outsider

GB 1931 93m bw

Cinema House/MGM

A 'quack' osteopath is finally able to make a surgeon's crippled daughter walk.

Cast-iron theatre and a fairly successful quota quickie which was also released in America.

w Harry Lachman, Alma Reville *play* Dorothy Brandon *d* Harry Lachman *ph* Günther Krampf *ad* Wilfred Arnold

☆ Harold Huth, Joan Barry, Norman McKinnel, Frank Lawton, Mary Clare

The Outsider

GB 1939 90m bw

ABPC

Sturdy remake of the above.

w Dudley Leslie *d* Paul Stein

☆ George Sanders, Mary Maguire, Frederick Leister, Peter Murray Hill, Kathleen Harrison

'Up-to-date and should appeal to popular-priced audiences.' – *Variety*

The Outsider: see *The Guinea Pig (1948)*

The Outsider

US 1961 108m bw

U-I (Sy Bartlett)

Ira Hayes, a simple Red Indian, becomes a war hero but cannot reconcile himself to living in a white society.

Prolonged biopic which proves a shade too much for an eager star; it's all earnest and mildly interesting but not cinematically compulsive.

w Stewart Stern *d* Delbert Mann *ph* Joseph LaShelle *m* Leonard Rosenman

☆ Tony Curtis, James Franciscus, Bruce Bennett, Gregory Walcott, Vivian Nathan, Edmund Hashim, Stanley Adams

The Outsider *

France 1983 95m Eastmancolor

Cerito/Ariane (Dominique Rigaux)

original title: *Le Marginal*

A tough and reckless Parisian cop runs into trouble when he is sent to Marseille to sort out the local drug smugglers.

Fast-moving low-life thriller, with a maverick hero patterned after Dirty Harry, but much dirtier.

w Jacques Deray, Jean Herman *d* Jacques Deray *ph* Xaver Schwarzenberger *m* Ennio Morricone *ad* Eric Moulard *ed* Albert Jurgenson

☆ Jean-Paul Belmondo, Henry Silva, Carlos Sotto Mayor, Pierre Vernier, Maurice Barrier, Tcheky Karyo, Claude Brosset

The Outsiders: see *Bande à Part (1964)*

The Outsiders

US 1983 91m Technicolor Panavision

Zoetrope/Warner

A young punk leads a high school gang against another rather higher in the social scale.

Oddball youth melodrama, a curious choice for a director with big successes behind him.

w Katherine Knutsen Rowell *novel* S. E. Hinton *d* Francis Ford Coppola *ph* Stephen H. Burum *m* Carmine Coppola *pd* Dean Tavoularis

☆ Matt Dillon, Ralph Macchio, C. Thomas Howell, Patrick Swayze, Rob Lowe, Emilio Estevez, Tom Cruise

'No more than a well-acted teen film.' – *Motion Picture Guide*

Outward Bound *

US 1930 82m bw

Warner

Passengers on a strange liner discover that they are all dead and heading for purgatory.

Early sound version of a popular twenties play which does not translate too well to cinematic forms and now seems very dated apart from a couple of performances; remade as Between Two Worlds *(qv).*

w J. Grubb Alexander *play* Sutton Vane *d* Robert Milton *ph* Hal Mohr

☆ *Leslie Howard*, Douglas Fairbanks Jnr, Alec B. Francis, Helen Chandler, Beryl Mercer, Alison Skipworth, Montagu Love, Dudley Digges

'Intelligentsia subject that must be spotted carefully ... seems to lack the essentials of mass entertainment.' – *Variety*

Over Her Dead Body: see *Enid Is Sleeping*

Over My Dead Body

US 1942 67m bw

Walter Morosco/TCF

A writer plans commercial success by pleading guilty to an imaginary crime, but truth is stranger than fiction.

Over-talkative crime comedy.

w Edward James *novel* James O'Hanlon *d* Malcolm St Clair

☆ Milton Berle, Mary Beth Hughes, Reginald Denny, Frank Orth, J. Pat O'Malley

Over She Goes *

GB 1937 74m bw

ABPC

An old friend helps a nobleman to thwart a blackmailer.

Lively comedy vehicle for a forgotten star.

w Elizabeth Meehan, Hugh Brooke *play* Stanley Lupino *d* Graham Cutts *ph* Otto Kanturek *m* Billy Mayerl
☆ Stanley Lupino, Laddie Cliff, Gina Malo, Claire Luce, Max Baer, Sally Gray, Syd Walker

Over the Brooklyn Bridge
US 1983 106m Metrocolor
Golan-Globus
Misadventures of a family-ridden Jewish restaurant owner in New York.
Frantic ethnic comedy with an unsympathetic hero.
w Arnold Somkin *d* Menahem Golan *ph* Adam Greenberg *m* Pino Donaggio
☆ Elliott Gould, Margaux Hemingway, Sid Caesar, Shelley Winters, Burt Young, Carol Kane
'The film's lip service to liberalism is offset by a blatantly sexist storyline.' – *Ruth Baumgarten, MFB*

Over the Edge *
US 1979 95m colour
Orion (George Litto)
In a new Colorado development, bored, affluent teenagers go on the rampage.
Slick, violent movie about the disaffected young that for some reason never found a responsive audience.
w Charlie Hass, Tom Hunter *d* Jonathan Kaplan *ph* Andrew Davis *m* Sol Kaplan *pd* Jim Newport *ed* Robert Bargere
☆ Michael Kramer, Pamela Ludwig, Matt Dillon, Vincent Spano, Tom Fergus, Harry Northup, Ellen Geer
'Sensationally effective ... exploitation movie. In their opportunistic way, the fellows who made it get at the social truths and middle-class nightmares more effectively than most "responsible" filmmakers would.' – *David Denby, New York*

Over the Hill
US 1931 87m bw
Fox
An ageing mother is sent to the poorhouse by her hard-hearted older son, but rescued by her ne'er-do-well younger one.
Sound remake of a silent success which in 1920 made a star of Mary Carr, who thereafter specialized in playing dear old ladies.
w Tom Barry, Jules Furthman *poems* Will Carleton *d* Henry King
☆ James Dunn, Sally Eilers, Mae Marsh, Edward Crandall, James Kirkwood
'There isn't a single overacted scene and there isn't a sequence that doesn't reach straight to the heart.' – *Variety*

Over the Hill *
Australia 1993 102m colour Panavision
Rank/Village Roadshow/Glasshouse (Robert Caswell, Bernard Terry)
The adventures in the Australian outback of a 60-year-old American widow, who flees from a dull life in Maine to visit her estranged and ambitious daughter in Sydney.
A gentle road movie, enjoyably done, about a woman's refusal to give up on life.
w Robert Caswell *book* *Alone in the Australian Outback* by Gladys Taylor *d* George Miller *ph* David Connell *m* David McHugh *pd* Graham 'Grace' Walker *ed* Henry Dangar
☆ Olympia Dukakis, Sigrid Thornton, Derek Fowlds, Bill Kerr, Steve Bisley, Martin Jacobs, Gerry Connolly, Andrea Moore

Over the Moon
GB 1940 78m Technicolor London Films (Alexander Korda)
A poor girl comes into a fortune but this does not help her romance with a proud young doctor.
Insubstantial comedy which turns itself into a European travelogue before petering out.
w Anthony Pelissier, Arthur Wimperis, Alec Coppel *d* Thornton Freeland *ph* Harry Stradling *m* Mischa Spoliansky
☆ Merle Oberon, Rex Harrison, Ursula Jeans, Robert Douglas, Louis Borell, Zena Dare, Peter Haddon, David Tree
† Made in 1937–8, but not released.

Over the River: see *One More River*

Over the Top
US 1987 93m Metrocolor Panavision
Cannon (Menahem Golan, Yoram Globus)
An arm wrestler tries to win the love of his son.
Mundane melodrama which its star couldn't carry.
w Stirling Silliphant, Sylvester Stallone *d* Menahem Golan *ph* David Gurfinkel *m* Giorgio Moroder *pd* James Schoppe *ed* Don Zimmerman, James Symons
☆ Sylvester Stallone, Robert Loggia, Susan Blakely, Rick Zumwalt, David Mendenhall
'Routinely made in every respect.' – *Daily Variety*

Over the Wall
US 1938 72m bw
Warner
A man wrongly convicted of murder fights the prison system.
Predictable semi-documentary thriller from the prolific pen of Warden Lewis E. Lawes; just an efficient second feature.
w Crane Wilbur, George Bricker *d* Frank MacDonald
☆ Dick Foran, John Litel, June Travis, Dick Purcell, Veda Ann Borg, George E. Stone
'Authentic melodrama, headed for nice biz.' – *Variety*

Over Twenty-One
US 1945 102m bw
Columbia (Sidney Buchman)
A famous lady screenwriter copes with wartime domestic problems while her husband is off at the war.
Thin star comedy based on Ruth Gordon's play about her own predicament; not for the wider audience, and not very good anyway.
w Sidney Buchman *play* Ruth Gordon *d* Alexander Hall *ph* Rudolph Maté *m* Marlin Skiles
☆ Irene Dunne, Alexander Knox, Charles Coburn, Jeff Donnell, Lee Patrick, Phil Brown, Cora Witherspoon

Overboard
US 1987 112m colour
UIP/MGM (Alexandra Rose, Anthea Sylbert)
An heiress suffering from amnesia is claimed as a wife by a carpenter with three kids.
Mild amusement is provided by a predictable comedy.
w Leslie Dixon *d* Garry Marshall *ph* John A. Alonzo *m* Alan Silvestri *ad* James Shanahan, Jim Dultz *ed* Dov Hoenig, Sonny Baskin
☆ Goldie Hawn, Kurt Russell, Edward Herrmann, Katherine Helmond, Roddy McDowall, Michael Hagerty, Jeffrey Wiseman

Overdrive
US 1997 95m Foto-Kem
Pacific Trust/Libra (Cheryl Parnell, Darin Spillman)
An out-of-control racing driver becomes involved with a secret agent who is being stalked by the spy she is attempting to blackmail.
A truly terrible thriller that commits the crimes of being dull, amoral and cliché-ridden.
w Malcolm Stephens *d* Lev L. Spiro *ph* Christopher Baffa *ed* Dan Holland
☆ Steve Guttenberg, Robert Wagner, Kaela Dobkin, Stephen Meadows, Richard Arquette, Frantz Turner, Alex Hyde-White

The Overlanders **
Australia 1946 91m bw
Ealing (Ralph Smart)
In 1943 a drover saves a thousand head of cattle from the Japanese by taking them two thousand miles across country.
Attractive, easy-going semi-Western, the first and best of several films made by Ealing Studios in Australia.
wd Harry Watt *ph* Osmond Borradaile *m* John Ireland
☆ Chips Rafferty, John Nugent Hayward, Daphne Campbell
'Let us congratulate Harry Watt on the absence of kangaroos and camp-fire songs, items which few directors could have resisted.' – *Richard Winnington*

Overlord *
GB 1975 83m bw
EMI/Jowsend (James Quinn)
An eighteen-year-old is called up in early 1944 and killed in the D-Day landings.
Semi-documentary recreating a time in history (with much aid from newsreels) but making no discernible point. Interesting, though.
w Stuart Cooper, Christopher Hudson *d* Stuart Cooper *ph* John Alcott *m* Paul Glass
☆ Brian Stirner, Davyd Harries, Nicholas Ball, Julie Neesam

Owd Bob *
GB 1938 78m bw
GFD/Gainsborough (Edward Black)
US title: *To the Victor*
A Cumberland farmer's faithful dog is accused of killing sheep.
Sentimental yarn with good location backgrounds; the plot was later reused as Thunder in the Valley.
w Michael Hogan, J. B. Williams *novel* Alfred Olivant *d* Robert Stevenson *ph* Jack Cox *md* Louis Levy
☆ Will Fyffe, John Loder, Margaret Lockwood, Moore Marriott, Graham Moffatt, Wilfred Walter, Elliot Mason

'When she starts mixing business with pleasure, she goes out of business'
The Owl and the Pussycat *
US 1970 96m Eastmancolor Panavision
Columbia/Rastar (Ray Stark)
A bookstore assistant reports a fellow tenant for prostitution, and when she is evicted she moves in with him.
Wacky, bawdy double act which starts promisingly but outstays its welcome. A solid step forward in permissiveness, with kinky behaviour as well as four-letter words.
w Buck Henry *play* Bill Manhoff *d* Herbert Ross *ph* Harry Stradling, Andrew Laszlo *m* Richard Halligan
☆ *Barbra Streisand, George Segal*, Robert Klein, Allen Garfield
'If computers ever turn out romantic comedies, the results will look like this.' – *Stanley Kauffmann*

The Ox **
Sweden/Norway/Denmark 1992 92m Eastmancolor
Artificial Eye/Sweetland (Jean Doumanian)
original title: *Oxen*
In a time of famine, a man kills his employer's ox in order to feed his starving family and is condemned to hard labour in prison for life.
A harrowing and humane story of hardship and forgiveness, much in the Bergman manner and as visually striking as you'd expect from a great cinematographer in his directorial debut.
w Sven Nykvist, Lasse Summanen *d* Sven Nykvist *ph* Sven Nykvist *m* Greig and others *pd* Peter Høimark *ed* Lasse Summanen
☆ Max von Sydow, Stellan Skarsgård, Ewa Fröling, Erland Josephson, Liv Ullmann
'Much more than just another snowy Scandinavian tale, this infuses its bleakness with tenderness and compassion while remaining a million miles away from sentimentality.' – *Empire*
best foreign film

The Ox-Bow Incident **
US 1943 75m bw
TCF (Lamar Trotti)
GB title: *Strange Incident*
A cowboy is unable to prevent three wandering travellers being unjustly lynched for murder.
Stark lynch law parable, beautifully made but very depressing.
w Lamar Trotti *novel* Walter Van Tilburg Clark *d* *William Wellman* *ph* *Arthur Miller* *m* Cyril Mockridge
☆ *Henry Fonda*, Henry Morgan, Jane Darwell, Anthony Quinn, Dana Andrews, Mary Beth Hughes, William Eythe, Harry Davenport, *Frank Conroy*
'Realism that is as sharp and cold as a knife.' – *Frank S. Nugent, New York Times*
'Very firm, respectable, and sympathetic; but I still think it suffers from rigor artis.' – *James Agee*
best picture

Oxen: see *The Ox*

Oxford Blues
US 1984 97m colour
Winkast/Baltic Industrial (Peter Kohn, David Wimbury)
A Los Angeles casino worker wins enough to finance an Oxford education.
Sexed-up version of A Yank at Oxford; *only tolerable when the tone gets close to the original.*
wd Robert Boris *ph* John Stanier *m* John Du Prez
☆ Rob Lowe, Ally Sheedy, Alan Howard, Amanda Pays, Julian Sands, Julian Firth, Michael Gough, Aubrey Morris

Oxygen
US 1999 92m DeLuxe
Curb/Paddy Wagon/Abandon (Jonathan Stern, Richard Shepard, Carole Curb Nemoy, Mike Curb)
A female cop with a self-destructive, masochistic personality interrogates an arrogant young kidnapper who has buried alive the wife of a millionaire.
Slick. moderately engaging thriller that over-uses a familiar device, suggesting that a cop and criminal are somehow similar; in the process, the suspense leaks away.
wd Richard Shepard *ph* Sarah Cawley *m* Rolfe Kent *pd* Rowena Rowling *ed* Adam Lichtenstein
☆ Adrien Brody (Harry), Maura Tierney (Madeline Foster), James Naughton (Clark Hannon), Terry Kinney (Tim), Laila Robins (Frances Hannon), Paul Calderon (Jesse), Dylan Baker (Jackson Lantham), Olek Krupa (Madeline's Lover)
'The more the film focuses on the psychological cat-and-mouse game... the more it loses momentum and its claims to credibility.' – *Lawrence Van Gelder, New York Times*

P

PCU
US 1994 95m DeLuxe
TVF (Paul Schiff)
A freshman at Port Chester University becomes involved with a group of students fighting the pervading atmosphere of political correctness and sensitivity to others.
Crude and boisterous romp for the young and unstudious.
w Adam Leff, Zak Penn *d* Hart Bochner *ph* Reynaldo Villalobos *m* Steve Vai *pd* Steven Jordan *ed* Nicholas C. Smith
☆ Jeremy Piven, Chris Young, David Spade, Megan Ward, Sarah Trigger, Jon Favreau, Jake Busey, Jessica Walter

'Gun in one hand – woman in the other!'
P.J.
US 1967 109m Techniscope
Universal (Edward J. Montagne)
GB title: *New Face in Hell*
A down-at-heel private eye takes a job as bodyguard to a boorish businessman.
Routine thick ear with a predictable turnabout plot.
w Philip Reisman Jnr *story* Edward J. Montagne *d* John Guillermin *ph* Loyal Griggs *m* Neal Hefti
☆ George Peppard, Gayle Hunnicutt, Raymond Burr, Susan St James, Coleen Gray, Jason Evers, Wilfrid Hyde-White, Severn Darden
'Enough action to keep you from noticing that the plot doesn't make any sense.' – *Judith Crist*

P.K. and the Kid
US 1982 89m CFI color
Sunn Classic (Joe Roth)
A teenager, running away from her brutal stepfather, goes on the road with a contestant heading for the world arm-wrestling championships in Los Angeles.
Mundane teen pic with too much concentration on the world's least photogenic sport.
w Neal Barbera *d* Lou Lombardo *ph* Ed Koons *m* James Horner *pd* Chet Allen *ed* Tony Lombardo
☆ Paul Le Mat, Molly Ringwald, Alex Rocco, Charles Hallahan, John Di Santi, Fionnula Flanagan, Bert Remsen, Leigh Hamilton, Esther Rolle

PT 109
US 1963 140m Technicolor Panavision
Warner (Brian Foy)
Adventures of president-to-be John F. Kennedy when he was a naval lieutenant in the Pacific during World War II.
Extraordinarily protracted and very dull action story which seems to have been overawed by its subject.
w Richard L. Breen *d* Leslie H. Martinson *ph* Robert Surtees *m* William Lava, David Buttolph
☆ Cliff Robertson, Ty Hardin, James Gregory, Robert Blake

'A killer and a girl – trapped in America's first air raid!'
Pacific Blackout
US 1942 76m bw
Paramount (Sol C. Siegel)
An inventor escapes from jail and proves his innocence during a practice air raid blackout.
Minor melo which proved profitably topical, being released shortly after the Japanese attack on Pearl Harbor.
w Lester Cole, W. P. Lipscomb *d* Ralph Murphy *ph* Theodor Sparkuhl
☆ Robert Preston, Martha O'Driscoll, Philip Merivale, Eva Gabor, Louis Jean Heydt, Thurston Hall

Pacific Destiny
GB 1956 97m Eastmancolor Cinemascope
James Lawrie
Experiences of a British colonial servant in the South Seas.
Pleasant episodic drama which needed a firmer hand all round.
w Richard Mason *autobiography A Pattern of Islands* by Sir Arthur Grimble *d* Wolf Rilla *ph* Martin Curtis *m* James Bernard
☆ Denholm Elliott, Susan Stephen, Michael Hordern

Pacific Heights *
US 1990 104m DeLuxe
Fox/Morgan Creek (Scott Rudin, William Sackheim)
A young couple let part of their house to a dangerously unbalanced tenant.
A suburban horror that rapidly goes over the top into unconvincing melodrama.
w Daniel Pyne *d* John Schlesinger *ph* Amir Mokri *m* Hans Zimmer *pd* Neil Spisak *ed* Mark Warner, Steven Ramirez
☆ Melanie Griffith, Matthew Modine, Michael Keaton, Mako, Nobu McCarthy, Laurie Metcalf, Carl Lumbly, Dorian Harewood, Luca Bercovici, Tippi Hedren

Pacific Liner
US 1938 73m bw
RKO
Cholera breaks out on a ship bound from Shanghai to San Francisco.
Rather a depressing melodrama with all the action below decks, and very slow at that.
w John Twist, Anthony Coldeway, Henry Roberts Symonds *d* Lew Landers
☆ Victor McLaglen, Chester Morris, Wendy Barrie, Alan Hale, Barry Fitzgerald, Halliwell Hobbes, Cy Kendall
'Drab melodrama with little of interest to hold attention.' – *Variety*
music (Robert Russell Bennett)

Pacific Rendezvous
US 1942 76m bw
MGM
A coding expert breaks up an enemy spy ring.
Competent propaganda potboiler, rehashed from the rather smarter Rendezvous, *which was set one war earlier.*
w Harry Kurnitz, P. J. Wolfson, George Oppenheimer *d* George Sidney
☆ Lee Bowman, Jean Rogers, Mona Maris, Carl Esmond, Paul Cavanagh, Blanche Yurka

Paciorki Jednego Różańca: see *The Beads of One Rosary*

The Pack
US 1977 99m colour
Warner (Fred Weintraub, Paul Heller)
Abandoned dogs on a remote island turn on holidaymakers.
The Birds *becomes* The Dogs; *competently made but unsurprising thriller.*
wd Robert Clouse *novel* Dave Fisher *ph* Ralph Woolsey *m* Lee Holdridge *ed* Peter Berger *sp* Milton Rice
☆ Joe Don Baker, Hope Alexander Willis, Richard B. Shull, R. G. Armstrong

Pack Up Your Troubles *
US 1931 68m bw
Hal Roach
Two World War I veterans try to look after their late pal's orphan daughter.
Patchy comedy vehicle in which too many gags are not fully thought out or timed.
w H. M. Walker *d* George Marshall, Ray McCarey *ph* Art Lloyd *ed* Richard Currier
☆ Stan Laurel, Oliver Hardy, Donald Dillaway, Mary Carr, Charles Middleton, Dick Cramer, James Finlayson, Tom Kennedy, Billy Gilbert

Pack Up Your Troubles *
US 1939 75m bw
TCF
GB title: *We're in the Army Now*
Exploits in Flanders of three zany soldiers.
Good slapstick antics in an unfamiliar venue.
w Lou Breslow, Owen Francis *d* H. Bruce Humberstone
☆ The Ritz Brothers, Jane Withers, Joseph Schildkraut, Lynn Bari, Stanley Fields
'A pretty good programmer in the B division.' – *Variety*

The Package
US 1989 108m DeLuxe
Rank/Orion (Beverly J. Camhe, Tobie Haggerty)
An army sergeant discovers an assassination plot after the escape of a prisoner he is escorting.
Unconvincing and melodramatic thriller that rarely grips the attention.
w John Bishop *d* Andrew Davis *ph* Frank Tidy *m* James Newton Howard *pd* Michael Levesque *ed* Don Zimmerman, Billy Weber
☆ Gene Hackman, Joanna Cassidy, Tommy Lee Jones, Dennis Franz, Reni Santoni, Pam Grier, Chelcie Ross, Ron Dean, Kevin Crowley

Le Pacte des Loups **
France 2001 142m colour 'Scope
Pathé/StudioCanal/Davis/TF1 (Richard Grandpierre, Samuel Hadida)
aka: *Brotherhood of the Wolf*
In the 1760s, a scientist and his Iroquois martial arts expert investigate a series of killings by a wolf-like creature in rural France.
A delirious mix of kung fu fighting, aristocratic shenanigans, Hammer horror and religious and political conspiracies; it is a stylish, enjoyable diversion.
w Christophe Gans, Stéphane Cabel *d* Christophe Gans *ph* Dan Laustsen *m* Joseph Lo Duca *pd* Guy Claude François *ed* David Wu, Sébastien Prangère *sp* beast designer: Igor Chevalier; beast fx Jim Henson's Creature Shop *fight choreographer* Philip Kwok
☆ Samuel Le Bihan (Grégoire de Fronsac), Mark Dacascos (Mani), Émilie Dequenne (Marianne de Morangias), Vincent Cassel (Jean-François de Morangias), Monica Bellucci (Sylvia), Jérémie Rénier (Thomas d'Apcher), Jean Yanne (Le Comte de Morangias), Jean-François Stévenin (Henri Sardis)
'You have to admire a movie that endeavors to moosh together every successful cross-cultural action picture ever made.' – *David Edelstein, Slate*
'Such a smooth amalgamation of hilariously disparate varieties of ripe cheese that the effect is brutely cheering.' – *Michael Atkinson, Village Voice*

The Pad, and How to Use It *
US 1966 86m Technicolor
Universal (Ross Hunter)
A shy young man has his first date.
Pleasant, odd little comedy apparently made in emulation of The Knack.
w Thomas C. Ryan, Ben Starr *play The Private Ear* by Peter Shaffer *d* Brian G. Hutton *ph* Ellsworth Fredericks *m* Russ Garcia *ad* Alexander Golitzen, George Webb *ed* Milton Carruth
☆ Brian Bedford, James Farentino, Julie Sommars, Edy Williams, Nick Navarro

Paddy O'Day
US 1935 73m bw
TCF (Sol M. Wurtzel)
An Irish child emigrates to America to find that her mother has died.
One of the more satisfactory vehicles for a child star maintained by the studio as an antidote to the cuter antics of Shirley Temple.
w Lou Breslow, Edward Eliscu *story* Sonya Levien *d* Lewis Seiler *ph* Arthur Miller *m* Harry Akst, Troy Sanders
☆ *Jane Withers*, Pinky Tomlin, Rita Hayworth, Jane Darwell, Francis Ford

Paddy the Next Best Thing
US 1933 75m bw
Fox
Adventures of an Irish tomboy in New York.
Modest star comedy from a popular play.
w Edwin Burke *play* Gertrude Page *d* Harry Lachman *ph* John Seitz
☆ Janet Gaynor, Warner Baxter, Walter Connolly, Harvey Stephens, Margaret Lindsay
'Easy entertainment: excellent, wholesome and amusing.' – *Variety*

Padella Calibro 38: see *Panhandle Calibre 38*

Padre Padrone ***
Italy 1977 113m Eastmancolor
Radiotelevisione Italia (Tonino Paoletti)
aka: *Father and Master*
The author recounts how he grew up with a violent and tyrannical father.
A vivid chunk of autobiography with food for thought on several levels, and a clever piece of film-making to boot.
wd Paolo Taviani, Vittorio Taviani book Gavino Ledda *ph* Mario Masini *md* Egisto Macchi
☆ Omero Antonutti, Saverio Marconi, Marcella Michelangeli

The Pagan
US 1929 85m approx bw
MGM
A South Sea islander falls for the daughter of a white trader.
Highly commercial star vehicle apparently made as an afterthought to White Shadows in the South Seas.
w Dorothy Farnum *d* W. S. Van Dyke
☆ Ramon Novarro, Renee Adoree, Dorothy Janis, Donald Crisp

Pagan Lady
US 1931 70m bw
Columbia
A nice American boy in Havana falls for a girl who is no better than she should be.
Sultry melodrama reminiscent of Rain *but of no intrinsic merit.*
w Ben Glazer *play* William Dubois *d* John Francis Dillon
☆ Evelyn Brent, Conrad Nagel, Charles Bickford, Roland Young, William Farnum
'Something of a lightweight; the storm is quite the best thing in the picture.' – *Variety*

Pagan Love Song
US 1950 76m Technicolor
MGM (Arthur Freed)
An American schoolteacher marries a Tahitian girl.
Very mild musical potboiler using familiar talents.
w Robert Nathan, Jerry Davis *d* Robert Alton *ph* Charles Rosher *m* Harry Warren *ly* Arthur Freed
☆ Esther Williams, Howard Keel, Rita Moreno, Minna Gombell

Page Miss Glory *
US 1935 90m bw
Warner/Cosmopolitan
A con man wins a beauty contest with a composite photograph of a non-existent girl.
Amusing comedy-musical, unjustly forgotten.
w Delmer Daves, Robert Lord *play* Joseph Schrank, Philip Dunning *d* Mervyn Le Roy *ph* George Folsey *m/ly* Harry Warren, Al Dubin
☆ Dick Powell, Marion Davies, Frank McHugh, Pat O'Brien, Mary Astor, Lyle Talbot, Patsy Kelly, Allen Jenkins, Barton MacLane

'All The Adventure Your Imagination Can Hold.'
The Pagemaster
US 1994 75m colour
TCF/Turner (David Kirschner, Paul Gertz)
A timid child takes refuge in a library and, changed into a cartoon figure, has to undergo three tests of courage before he can go home.
Intended as an encouragement for children to read books, the movie's more likely effect is to discourage them from going to the cinema; the lack of imagination in the script is deadening to the spirit as Long John Silver, Dr Jekyll and Mr Hyde and others join in dull animated adventures.
w David Casci, David Kirschner, Ernie Contreras *d* Joe Johnston, Maurice Hunt (animation director) *ph* Alexandra Gruszynski *m* James Horner *pd* Gay Lawrence, Valeria Ventura *ed* Roy Forge Smith
☆ Macaulay Culkin, Christopher Lloyd, Ed Begley Jnr, Mel Harris and also the voices of Patrick Stewart, Whoopi Goldberg, Frank Welker, Leonard Nimoy
'Plays like a slickly produced afternoon special and should be limited in its appeal to the youngest of kids.' – *Brian Lowry, Variety*

Pagliacci *
GB 1936 92m colour
Trafalgar
US title: *A Clown Must Laugh*
A jealous clown kills his wife and her lover.
A surprising British enterprise of the time which did fairly well at the box-office, presumably because of the colour.
w Monckton Hoffe, Roger Burford, Ernest Betts *opera* Ruggiero Leoncavallo *d* Karl Grune *ph* Otto Kanturek *pd* Oscar Werndorff *ly* John Drinkwater
☆ Richard Tauber, Steffi Duna, Diana Napier, Arthur Margetson, Esmond Knight, Jerry Verno

Pagliacci *
Italy 1948 104m bw
Itala Film/Titanus (Mario Bisi)
The leader of a theatrical troupe kills his wife and her lover after he realizes that the performance they are staging resembles his own situation.
A slightly clumsy attempt to open up the opera by filming it in the open air and casting actors in the leading roles, with their singing dubbed. Worth seeing for the acting and singing of Tito Gobbi, who appears as the Prologue, as Nedda's would-be lover Tonio, and as her lover Silvio.
w Anton Giulio Majano, Mario Costa, Carlo Castelli *d* Mario Costa *ph* Mario Bava *md* Giuseppe Morelli *ad* Ottavio Scotti *ed* Otello Colangeli
☆ Tito Gobbi, Afro Poli (singing by Galliano Masini), Gina Lollobrigida (singing by Onella Fineschi), Filippo Morucci (singing by Gino Sinimberghi)

Paid *
US 1930 80m bw
MGM
GB title: *Within the Law*
A woman sent to prison unjustly plots revenge on those responsible.
Reliable melodrama with the heroine eventually forgiving and forgetting.
w Charles MacArthur, Lucien Hubbard *play Within the Law* by Bayard Veiller *d* Sam Wood *ph* Charles Rosher
☆ Joan Crawford, Kent Douglass, Robert Armstrong, Marie Prévost, John Miljan, Polly Moran

Paid in Full
US 1949 105m bw
Paramount/Hal B. Wallis
A woman is responsible for the death of her sister's child, and becomes pregnant herself in the knowledge that giving birth will be fatal to her.
Stolid, contrived tearjerker.
w Robert Blees, Charles Schnee *d* William Dieterle *ph* Leo Tover *m* Victor Young
☆ Lizabeth Scott, Diana Lynn, Robert Cummings, Eve Arden, Ray Collins, Frank McHugh, Stanley Ridges, Louis Jean Heydt
'Aimed straight at the lachrymal glands, if it can be said to be aimed at anything. The dialogue is appalling.' – *C. A. Lejeune*

A Pain in the A–: see *L'Emmerdeur*

'Ben and pardner shared everything – even their wife!'
Paint Your Wagon *
US 1969 164m Technicolor
Panavision 70
Paramount/Alan Jay Lerner (Tom Shaw)
During the California Gold Rush, two prospectors set up a Mormon menage with the same wife.
Good-looking but uncinematic and monumentally long version of an old musical with a new plot and not much dancing. There are minor pleasures, but it really shouldn't have been allowed.
w Paddy Chayefsky *musical play Alan Jay Lerner, Frederick Loewe* *d* Joshua Logan *ph* William A. Fraker *md* Nelson Riddle *pd* John Truscott
☆ Lee Marvin, Clint Eastwood, Jean Seberg, Harve Presnell, Ray Walston
'One of those big movies in which the themes are undersized and the elements are juggled around until nothing fits together right and even the good bits of the original show you started with are shot to hell.' – *Pauline Kael*
† Jean Seberg's singing was dubbed by Anita Gordon.
Nelson Riddle

Painted Angels
GB/Canada 1998 109m colour
Artificial Eye/Shaftesbury/Greenpoint/Heartland/British Screen (Ann Scott, Christine Jennings, Stephen Onda)
Five prostitutes lead tawdry lives in a frontier-town brothel in the American West of the 1870s.
Glum portrait of unhappy working women in desperate circumstances; its depiction may well be accurate, but it is not involving.
w Anna Mottram, Jon Sanders *d* Jon Sanders *ph* Gerald Packer *m* Douglas Finch *pd* Hayden Griffin *ed* Maysoon Pachachi
☆ Brenda Fricker, Kelly McGillis, Meret Becker, Bronagh Gallagher, Lisa Jakub, Anna Mottram, Josiah Wu, Kent Allan

Painted Boats
GB 1945 63m bw
Ealing
US title: *The Girl on the Canal*
Romance among the bargees.
Excessively thin location drama, which nevertheless has an early place in the Ealing tradition.
w Louis MacNeice, Michael McCarthy *d* Charles Crichton
☆ Jenny Laird, Bill Blewett, Robert Griffith, May Hallatt

Painted Desert
US 1938 59m bw
RKO (Bert Gilroy)
A rancher becomes a miner for romantic reasons but has to overcome a crooked banker and his followers.
A B-Western with B-picture acting and direction. A remake of a 1931 movie starring William Boyd, it contains footage from the earlier film.
w John Rathmell, Oliver Drake *story* Jack Cunningham *d* David Howard *ph* Harry Wild *md* Roy Webb *ad* Van Nest Polglase *ed* Frederic Knudtson
☆ George O'Brien, Laraine Day, Ray Whitley, Fred Kohler Snr, Stanley Fields, William V. Mong, Maude Allen

Painted Heart
US 1992 90m colour
Metro Tartan/Second Son (Mark Pollard, Randall Poster)
A house-painter suspects that his boss is the Lipstick Murderer, who kills old men and paints their faces.
Determinedly eccentric movie of small-town America, slow-moving whimsy in which even the sane residents behave in an odd manner.
wd Michael Taav *ph* Robert Yeoman *m* John Wesley Harding, Jeff Charbonneau *pd* Mark Friedberg *ed* Nancy Richardson
☆ Will Patton, Bebe Neuwirth, Casey Siemaszko, Robert Pastorelli, Mark Boone Jnr, Richard Hamilton, Jayne Haynes
'It's ultimately hopelessly self-indulgent, and a little bit like watching paint dry.' – *David Richardson, Film Review*

The Painted Smile
GB 1962 60m bw
Planet/Mancunian (Tom Blakeley)
US title: *Murder Can Be Deadly*
A student who goes out for a celebration in a night-club becomes involved in a murder.
Dreary thriller that makes little sense, and is sadly lacking in suspense or interest.
w Pip and Jane Baker *idea* Brock Williams *d* Lance Comfort *ph* Basil Emmot *m* Martin Slavin *ad* George Provis *ed* John Trumper
☆ Liz Fraser, Kenneth Griffith, Tony Wickert, Ray Smith, Nanette Newman, David Hemmings, Harold Berens, Peter Reynolds, Craig Douglas

The Painted Veil *
US 1934 84m bw
MGM (Hunt Stromberg)
In China, a doctor's wife gives up her lover to join her husband fighting an epidemic.
Soulful melodrama which seemed much more acceptable in this version than in the summer stock style remake The Seventh Sin.
w John Meehan, Salka Viertel, Edith Fitzgerald *novel* W. Somerset Maugham *d* Richard Boleslawski *ph* William Daniels *m* Herbert Stothart
☆ Greta Garbo, George Brent, Herbert Marshall, Warner Oland, Jean Hersholt
'Confused and slow, but extra heavy name cast should get it by.' – *Variety*

Painted Woman
US 1932 73m bw
Fox
A floozie stranded on a South Sea island resists offers of help from several men.
Another variation on Rain, *and not the best.*
w Guy Bolton, Leon Gordon *novel After the Rain* by A. C. Kennedy *d* John Blystone
☆ Spencer Tracy, Peggy Shannon, William 'Stage' Boyd, Irving Pichel, Raul Roulien
'It's hard to see how the studio figured a good picture would result from the material at hand.' – *Variety*

Painting the Clouds with Sunshine
US 1951 86m Technicolor
Warner (William Jacobs)
Three singing sisters go to Las Vegas in search of rich husbands.
Yet another revamp of the original Gold Diggers *(qv), and not a very lively one.*
w Harry Clork, Roland Kibbee, Peter Milne *d* David Butler *ph* Wilfred Cline
☆ Virginia Mayo, Gene Nelson, Dennis Morgan, S. Z. Sakall, Lucille Norman, Tom Conway

A Pair of Briefs
GB 1961 90m bw
Rank/Betty E. Box-Ralph Thomas
Barristers Tony and Frances fall in love while opposing each other in court.
Adam's Rib *need have no fears; this is the palest of imitations.*
w Nicholas Phipps *play How Say You* by Harold Brooke, Kay Bannerman *d* Ralph Thomas *ph* Ernest Steward *m* Norrie Paramor
☆ Michael Craig, Mary Peach, Brenda de Banzie, James Robertson Justice, Roland Culver, Liz Fraser, Ron Moody, Jameson Clark, Charles Heslop

Paisà *
Italy 1946 115m bw
Foreign Film Productions/OFI
Six episodes in the Battle of Italy between 1943 and 1945.
More important historically than dramatically, Paisà *was always a somewhat disappointing experience, especially as the earlier episodes are stronger than the later ones. Like* Open City, *it was partly improvised and had a gritty documentary quality.*
w Federico Fellini, Roberto Rossellini *d* Roberto Rossellini *ph* Otello Martelli *m* Renzo Rossellini
☆ William Tubbs, Gar Moore, Maria Michi and non-professionals
'It brings to the picture of war a pity at once savage and tender which is quite foreign to the studio-made film – or, come to that, the contemporary documentary film.' – *Dilys Powell*
script

The Pajama Game ***
US 1957 101m Warnercolor
Warner/George Abbott
Workers in a pajama factory demand a pay rise, but their lady negotiator falls for the new boss.
Brilliantly conceived musical on an unlikely subject, effectively concealing its Broadway origins and becoming an expert, fast-moving, hard-hitting piece of modern musical cinema.
w George Abbott, Richard Bissell book Seven and a Half Cents by Richard Bissell d Stanley Donen *ph* Harry Stradling *ch Bob Fosse songs Richard Adler, Jerry Ross*
☆ *Doris Day*, John Raitt, *Eddie Foy Jnr*, Reta Shaw, Carol Haney

The Pajama Girl Case (dubbed)
Italy/Spain 1978 105m colour
Capitol (Giorgio Salvioni)
original title: *La Ragazza dal Pigiama Giallo*
aka: *Pyjama Girl*
A retired police inspector goes back to work to solve the murder of an unknown woman found on a beach.
Dull thriller, with Milland looking as though he would rather be somewhere else.
wd Flavio Mogherini *ph* Carlo Carlini *m* Riz Ortolani *pd* Franco Velchi *ed* Adriani Tagliavia
☆ Ray Milland, Dalila Di Lazzaro, Michele Placido, Howard Ross, Ramiro Oliveros, Rod Mullinar, Mel Ferrer

Pajama Party
US 1964 85m Pathécolor Panavision
AIP (James Nicholson, Samuel Z. Arkoff)
A Martian, a scout for an invasion of Earth, changes his mind after meeting some partying teenagers.
The beach party formula almost as usual, except that the beach is abandoned in this bland teen mix of romance and forgettable songs.
w Louis M. Heyward *d* Don Weis *ph* Floyd Crosby *m* Les Baxter *m/ly* Guy Hemric, Jerry Styner *ch* David Winters *ad* Daniel Haller *ed* Fred R. Feitshans, Eve Newman
☆ Tommy Kirk, Annette Funicello, Elsa Lanchester, Buster Keaton, Harvey Lembeck, Jesse White, Jody McCrea, Dorothy Lamour, Candy Johnson
† It was a follow-up to *Bikini Beach* and was followed by *Beach Blanket Bingo* (qqv).

Pal Joey **
US 1957 109m Technicolor
Columbia/Essex-Sidney (Fred Kohlmar)
The rise of a night-club entertainer who is also a heel.
Smart musical which begins very brightly indeed but slides off alarmingly into conventional sentiment.
w Dorothy Kingsley *play* John O'Hara *stories John O'Hara* *d* George Sidney *ph* Harold Lipstein *ad* Walter Holscher *ed* Viola Lawrence, Jerome Thomas *songs Richard Rodgers, Lorenz Hart*
☆ *Frank Sinatra, Rita Hayworth,* Kim Novak, Bobby Sherwood, Hank Henry, Elizabeth Patterson, Barbara Nichols
† Rita Hayworth's singing was dubbed by Jo Ann Greer, and Kim Novak's by Trudy Erwin.
Walter Holscher; editing

Pale Rider
US 1985 115m Technicolor Panavision
Warner/Malpaso (Clint Eastwood)

Harassed gold prospecting families are helped by a mysterious avenger.
Unreeling like a supernatural Shane, *this is a violent and pretentious Western with nothing to be pretentious about.*
w Michael Butler, Dennis Shryack *d* Clint Eastwood *ph* Bruce Surtees *m* Lennie Niehaus *pd* Edward Carfagno *ed* Joel Cox
☆ Clint Eastwood, Michael Moriarty, Carrie Snodgress, Christopher Penn, Richard Dysart, Richard Kiel

The Paleface ***
US 1948 91m Technicolor
Paramount (Robert L. Welch)

Calamity Jane undertakes an undercover mission against desperadoes, and marries a timid dentist as a cover.
Splendid wagon train comedy Western with the stars in excellent form.
w Edmund Hartman, Frank Tashlin d Norman Z. McLeod *ph* Ray Rennahan *m* Victor Young
☆ *Bob Hope, Jane Russell,* Robert Armstrong, Iris Adrian, Robert Watson, Jackie Searl, Joe Vitale, Clem Bevans, Charles Trowbridge
† Sequel: *Son of Paleface* (qv); remake, *The Shakiest Gun in the West* (1968).
song 'Buttons and Bows' (*m* Jay Livingston, *ly* Ray Evans)

The Pallbearer
US 1996 97m DeLuxe
Miramax (Jeffrey Abrams, Paul Webster)

An unemployed graduate, asked to be the pallbearer at the funeral of a friend whom he cannot remember, is seduced by the dead youth's mother.
A limp comedy that owes much to The Graduate, *but remains no more than a very pale shadow of that film.*
w Jason Katims, Matt Reeves *d* Matt Reeves *ph* Robert Elswit *m* Stewart Copeland *pd* Robert Standefer *ed* Stan Salfas
☆ David Schwimmer, Gwyneth Paltrow, Michael Rapaport, Toni Collette, Barbara Hershey, Carol Kane, Michael Vartan, Bitty Schram
'A passably entertaining seriocomedy.' – *Variety*
† The film flopped, taking $5.7m at the US box-office.

The Palm Beach Story ***
US 1942 88m bw
Paramount (Paul Jones)

The wife of a penurious engineer takes off for Florida to set her sights on a millionaire.
Flighty comedy, inconsequential in itself, but decorated with scenes, characters and zany touches typical of its creator, here at his most brilliant if uncontrolled.
wd Preston Sturges *ph* Victor Milner *m* Victor Young
☆ *Claudette Colbert, Joel McCrea, Rudy Vallee,* Mary Astor, Sig Arno, Robert Warwick, Torben Meyer, Jimmy Conlin, William Demarest, Jack Norton, Robert Greig, Roscoe Ates, Chester Conklin, Franklin Pangborn, Alan Bridge and also *Robert Dudley*
HACKENSACKER (RUDY VALLEE): 'That's one of the tragedies of this life, that the men most in need of a beating up are always enormous.'
WEENIE KING (ROBERT DUDLEY): 'Anyway, I'd be too old for you. Cold are the hands of time that creep along relentlessly, destroying slowly but without pity that which yesterday was young. Alone, our memories resist this disintegration and grow more lovely with the passing years. That's hard to say with false teeth.'
'Surprises and delights as though nothing of the kind had been known before … farce and tenderness are combined without a fault.' – *William Whitebait*
'Minus even a hint of the war … packed with delightful absurdities.' – *Variety*

Palm Springs
US 1936 74m bw
Paramount
GB title: *Palm Springs Affair*
An elderly Englishman becomes a gambler in order to give his daughter the appropriate upbringing.
Slight romantic comedy which gave a young Englishman a foothold in Hollywood.
w Joseph Fields *d* Aubrey Scotto
☆ David Niven, Sir Guy Standing, Frances Langford, Ernest Cossart, Spring Byington

Palm Springs Affair: *see Palm Springs*

Palm Springs Weekend
US 1963 100m Technicolor
Warner (Michael Hoey)

Various holidaymakers at Palm Springs get romantically involved.
Youth-oriented farce, better produced than most but basically a depressing experience.
w Earl Hamner Jnr *d* Norman Taurog *ph* Harold Lipstein *m* Frank Perkins
☆ Troy Donahue, Ty Hardin, Connie Stevens, Stefanie Powers, Robert Conrad, Jack Weston, Andrew Duggan

'In A Town This Bad It's No Use Being Good.'
Palmetto
US/Germany 1998 114m Technicolor Panavision
Warner/Castle Rock/Rialto (Mathias Wendlandt)

An ex-journalist is hired by a seductive woman to stage the kidnapping of her daughter so that she can extort money from the girl's father, a dying millionaire.
A laboured attempt at a film noir, which is taken at too leisurely a pace to provide any thrills or suspense.
w E. Max Frye *novel Just Another Sucker* by *James Hadley Chase d* Volker Schlöndorff *ph* Thomas Kloss *m* Klaus Dolinger *pd* Clare Jenora Bowin *ed* Peter Przygodda
☆ Woody Harrelson, Elisabeth Shue, Gina Gershon, Rolf Hoppe, Michael Rapaport, Chloe Sevigny, Tom Wright, Marc Macauley
'May well have coined a new genre: the unthriller.' – *Gaby Wood, Guardian*
'The film deserves a new subgenre of its own, that of sitcom noir.' – *Edward Porter, Sunday Times*

Palmy Days
US 1932 77m bw
Samuel Goldwyn

Shady fortune tellers find a willing stooge.
Dated star comedy.
w Eddie Cantor, Morrie Ryskind, David Freedman, Keene Thompson *d* A. Edward Sutherland *ph* Gregg Toland *ch* Busby Berkeley
☆ Eddie Cantor, Charlotte Greenwood, Charles Middleton, George Raft, Walter Catlett
'Heavily hoked but funny throughout.' – *Variety*

Palooka
US 1934 80m bw
Reliance (Edward Small)

GB title: *The Great Schnozzle*
An eccentric manager makes a prizefighter of a country cousin.
Fairly amusing first-feature version of the strip cartoon hero Joe Palooka.
w Jack Jevne, Arthur Kober, Gertrude Purcell *strip* Ham Fisher *d* Ben Stoloff
☆ Jimmy Durante (Knobby Walsh), Stuart Erwin, Lupe Velez, Marjorie Rambeau, Robert Armstrong, Mary Carlisle, William Cagney, Thelma Todd
'A laugh riot, the nearest approach to a Marx picture that's been around.' – *Variety*

Palookaville *
US 1995 92m DuArt
Metrodome/Playhouse International/Samuel Goldwyn/Redwave (Uberto Pasolini)

In New Jersey, three unemployed young men turn to crime with unpredictable results.
Amiable comic drama of incompetents failing to cope with the cost and problems of living.
w David Epstein *d* Alan Taylor *ph* John Thomas *m* Rachel Portman *pd* Anne Stuhler *ed* David Leonard
☆ William Forsythe, Vincent Gallo, Adam Trese, Gareth Williams, Lisa Gay Hamilton, Bridgit Ryan, Kim Dickens
'A refreshing and hilarious alternative to the cool-guys-with-guns flick.' – *Empire*

Paltoquet
France 1986 92m colour
Artificial Eye/Elefilm/Erato/Soprofilm/TF1/Sofia/Sofima (Rosalinde Damamme)
A detective tries to discover which habitué of a seedy bar, with its shiftless waiter, is a killer.
Intellectual thriller in which film theory has precedence over practice, resulting in tedium.
wd Michel Déville *novel On A Tué Pendant L'Escale* by Franz-Rudolf Falk *ph* André Diot *m* Dvořák, Janáček *pd* Thierry Leproust *ed* Raymonde Guyot
☆ Jeanne Moreau, Michel Piccoli, Fanny Ardant, Daniel Auteuil, Richard Bohringer, Philippe Léotard, Claude Piéplu, Jean Yanne

Pan-Americana *
US 1945 85m bw
RKO (Sid Rogell)
A New York magazine sends editors around South America to choose the prettiest girl of each nation.
Slick, mindless musical with good numbers.
w Lawrence Kimble *d* John H. Auer *ph* Frank Redman *md* Constantin Bakaleinikoff *ch* Charles O'Curran
☆ Audrey Long, Phillip Terry, Robert Benchley, Eve Arden, Ernest Truex, Marc Cramer

Panama Hattie
US 1942 79m bw
MGM (Arthur Freed)

A showgirl in Panama helps to capture Nazis.
Dim film version of a Broadway musical, stripped of most of its music and more like a Maisie comedy.
w Jack McGowan, Wilkie Mahoney *musical play Herbert Fields, B. G. de Sylva, Cole Porter d* Norman Z. McLeod *ph* George Folsey *md* George Stoll
☆ Ann Sothern, Dan Dailey, Red Skelton, Marsha Hunt, Rags Ragland, Virginia O'Brien, Alan Mowbray, Ben Blue, Carl Esmond

Pancho Villa
Spain 1971 93m Technicolor
Granada Films (Bernard Gordon)

In 1916 Villa is rescued from execution and starts a reign of terror.
Mexican banditry played half for laughs and half for real; not a successful compromise.
w Julian Halevy (Julian Zimet) *story* Gene Martin *d* Eugenio Martin *ph* Alejandro Ulloa *m* Anton Garcia-Abril
☆ Telly Savalas, Clint Walker, Chuck Connors
† Screenwriter Zimet wrote under a pseudonym because of the blacklist.

'Their poems have crossed centuries, but now their secrets will be revealed.'
Pandaemonium
GB/US 2000 124m colour
Optimum/BBC/Mariner/Film Council/Moonstone (Jane Robertson)

In 1813, Samuel Taylor Coleridge recalls his long friendship with fellow poet William Wordsworth.
A bizarre attempt to suggest that romantic poets were the new rock'n'roll; a fervid, anachronistic romp, frequently risible, which casts Coleridge in the role of hero, and Wordsworth as the villain.
w Frank Cottrell Boyce *d* Julien Temple *ph* John Lynch *m* Dario Marianelli *pd* Laurence Dorman *ed* Niven Howie
☆ Linus Roache (Samuel Coleridge), John Hannah (William Wordsworth), Samantha Morton (Sara Coleridge), Emily Woof (Dorothy Wordsworth), Emma Fielding (Mary Wordsworth), Andy Serkis (John Thelwall), Samuel West (Robert Southey)
'Among the most vulgar travesties of English literature I've seen in years certainly since Ken Russell gave up the ghost.' – *Alexander Walker*
'Literate and handsome… As they have for centuries, writers like these make rewarding company.' – *Lawrence Van Gelder, New York Times*

Pandora and the Flying Dutchman *
GB 1950 122m Technicolor
Romulus (Albert Lewin)

A cold but beautiful American woman in Spain falls for a mystery man who turns out to be a ghostly sea captain; she dies so as to be with him.
Pretentious, humourless, totally unpersuasive fantasy of the kind much better done in Portrait of Jennie. *The writer-director wears Omar Khayyam's moving finger to the bone, and the actors look thoroughly unhappy; even the colour is a bit thick.*
wd Albert Lewin *ph* Jack Cardiff *m* Alan Rawsthorne *ad* John Bryan
☆ James Mason, Ava Gardner, Harold Warrender, Nigel Patrick, Sheila Sim, Mario Cabre, John Laurie, Pamela Kellino, Marius Goring
'Conspicuous in its confident assumption of scholarship and its utter poverty of imagination and taste.' – *C. A. Lejeune*
'It might have been enjoyably silly but for Lewin's striving to be classy and an air of third-rate decadence that hangs about it. This is an Anglo-American co-production and one of the occasions, I think, when we might be generous and let Hollywood have all the credit.' – *Richard Winnington*

Pandora's Box *
Germany 1929 97m approx (24 fps) bw silent
Nero Film

original title: *Die Büchse der Pandora*
aka: *Lulu*
A woman murders her lover, becomes a prostitute, and is murdered in London by Jack the Ripper.
Oddball fantasy on a few favourite German themes: very watchable, and benefiting from its star performance.
w G. W. Pabst, Laszlo Wajda *plays 'Erdgeist' and 'Pandora's Box' by Franz Wedekind d G. W. Pabst ph* Günther Krampf
☆ *Louise Brooks* (Lulu), Fritz Kortner (Dr Peter Schon), Franz Lederer (Alwa Schön), Gustav Diessl (Jack the Ripper)
'A disconnected melodramatic effusion.' – *Mordaunt Hall, New York Times*
† Remade in Austria in 1962 as *No Orchids for Lulu*, with Nadja Tiller.

Panhandle
US 1948 84m bw
Champion-Edwards/Allied Artists
A reformed gunman avenges the murder of his brother.
Solid co-feature Western.
w Blake Edwards, John C. Champion *d* Lesley Selander *ph* Harry Neumann
☆ Rod Cameron, Cathy Downs, Reed Hadley, Anne Gwynne, Blake Edwards

Panhandle Calibre 38 (dubbed)
Italy 1972 90m SPES colour
Cinegai (F. T. Gay)
original title: *Padella Calibro 38*
An ageing gunslinger and his convent-educated son are hired to take a million dollars of Confederate gold across bandit-filled country.
Coarse, slapstick spaghetti Western, taken at a very leisurely tempo.
w Mario Amendola, Massimo Franciosa, Luisa Montagnana, Toni Secchi *d* Toni Secchi *ph* Giorgio Regis *m* Franco Micalizzi *ad* Luciano Puccini *ed* Luciano Anconetani
☆ Scott Holden, Delia Boccardo, Keenan Wynn, Giorgio Trestini, Mimmo Palmara, Franco Fabrizi, Philippe Leroy

Panic Button
US 1963 98m bw
Gorton Associates
A has-been film star is hired by gangsters to star in a film which must lose money; but it wins the Venice Festival award.
Artless and padded comedy with good moments provided by an intriguing cast.
w Hal Biller *d* George Sherman *ph* Enzo Serafin *m* Georges Garvarentz
☆ Maurice Chevalier, Akim Tamiroff, Jayne Mansfield, Eleanor Parker, Michael Connors

The Panic in Needle Park
US 1971 110m DeLuxe
Gadd Productions (Dominick Dunne)

Drug addiction problems in a New York ghetto.
Vivid, intimate but overlong and unsympathetic account of a junkie and his mistress.
w Joan Didion, John Gregory Dunne *novel* James Mills *d* Jerry Schatzberg *ph* Adam Holender *m* none

☆ Al Pacino, Kitty Winn, Alan Vint, Richard Bright, Kiel Martin

Panic in the Parlor: see *Sailor Beware (1956)*

Panic in the Streets ***
US 1950 96m bw
TCF (Sol C. Siegel)
On the New Orleans waterfront, public health officials seek a carrier of bubonic plague.
Semi-documentary suspenser in the Naked City *manner; location Hollywood at its best.*
w Richard Murphy, Edward and Edna Anhalt *d* Elia Kazan *ph* Joe MacDonald *m* Alfred Newman
☆ *Richard Widmark, Jack Palance,* Paul Douglas, Barbara Bel Geddes, Zero Mostel
'Elia Kazan directs this tough and unique story with the speed, imagination and ruthlessness that it needs.' – *Milton Shulman*
'A model of what an action story should be ... every department is admirably handled.' – *Richard Mallett, Punch*
original story (Edward and Edna Anhalt)

Panic in Year Zero *
US 1962 93m bw Cinemascope
AIP (Lou Rusoff, Arnold Houghland)
Adventures of a family on a fishing trip in the mountains when Los Angeles is blasted by a nuclear attack.
Mildly interesting catalogue of predictable events – thugs, looting, fear of fall-out – in a simple-minded script finishing with a hopeful meeting of the UN.
w Jay Simms, John Morton *d* Ray Milland *ph* Gil Warrenton *m* Les Baxter
☆ Ray Milland, Jean Hagen, Frankie Avalon, Joan Freeman

Panic on the Trans-Siberian Express: see *Horror Express*

'It was supposed to be the safest room in the house.'
Panic Room
US 2002 112m DeLuxe Panavision
Columbia TriStar/Indelible (Gavin Polone, Judy Hofflund, David Koepp, Cean Chaffin)
Violent robbers break into a house to recover treasure hidden in an impregnable room where a mother and her young daughter have taken refuge.
The camera prowls, swoops, glides and slips through small spaces in an attempt to enliven this dingy, claustrophobic thriller that becomes increasingly clichéd, predictable and corny, so that all suspense quickly leaks away.
w David Koepp *d* David Fincher *ph* Conrad W. Hall, Darius Khondji *m* Howard Shore *pd* Arthur Max *ed* James Haygood, Angus Wall
☆ Jodie Foster (Meg Altman), Forest Whitaker (Burnham), Dwight Yoakam (Raoul), Jared Leto (Junior), Kristen Stewart (Sarah Altman), Ann Magnuson (Lydia Lynch), Ian Buchanan (Evan Kurlander), Patrick Bauchau (Stephen Altman)
'Smartly plotted, convincingly acted and brilliantly executed technically, this engrossing thriller adds some clever modern wrinkles to the time-tested formula of sinister intruders threatening innocents in their home.' – *Todd McCarthy, Variety*
'For all the script's self-referential pop-cultural popcorn, the skirmishes for power waged among victims and predators settle into an undistinguished rhythm of artificial suspense.' – *Lisa Schwarzbaum, Entertainment Weekly*
† Jodie Foster replaced Nicole Kidman, who had to quit filming because of a knee injury. Cinematographer Darius Khondji also left, after creative differences with the director.

Pánico en el Transiberiano: see *Horror Express*

Panique *
France 1946 98m bw
Filmsonor
A respectable man knows who committed a murder, and the murderer cunningly swings the blame onto him.
Careful suspenser with a twist ending.
w Charles Spaak, Julien Duvivier *novel* Georges Simenon *d* Julien Duvivier *ph* Nicolas Hayer
☆ *Michel Simon,* Viviane Romance, Paul Bernard
'Whether you like it or not, you may be forced to agree that it's a near-perfect movie.' – *Pauline Kael, 1972*

Panther
US 1995 124m DeLuxe/bw
Polygram/Working Title/Tribeca/MVP (Mario Van Peebles, Melvin Van Peebles, Preston L. Holmes)
A black Vietnam veteran recalls his role in the Black Panther Party, which was formed in the mid-60s and soon faced infiltration and attacks by the FBI, culminating in the Bureau's involvement in introducing cheap heroin to the ghettos.
A melodramatic account of the black rights struggle and the highly publicized activities of the Panthers which abandons fact to indulge in wild fiction, to the detriment of the film.
w Melvin Van Peebles *novel* Melvin Van Peebles *d* Mario Van Peebles *ph* Eddie Pei *m* Stanley Clarke *pd* Richard Hoover *ed* Earl Watson
☆ Kadeem Hardison, Bokeem Woodbine, Joe Don Baker, Courtney B. Vance, Tyrin Turner, Marcus Chong, James Russo, Chris Rock, Richard Dysart, M. Emmet Walsh, Jenifer Lewis, Wesley Johnson, Nefertiti
'A crudely schematic propaganda thriller.' – *Alexander Walker*

The Panther's Claw
US 1942 73m bw
PRC
Thatcher Colt solves a blackmail case which ends in murder.
Unassuming but efficient second-feature mystery.
w Martin Mooney, Anthony Abbott *d* William Beaudine
☆ Sidney Blackmer, Byron Foulger, Rick Vallin

Panther's Moon: see *Spy Hunt*

Paoda Shuang Deng: see *Red Firecracker, Green Firecracker*

Papa's Delicate Condition
US 1963 98m Technicolor
Paramount/Amro (Jack Rose)
At the turn of the century in a small Texas town an amiable family man gets into scrapes when he drinks too much.
Basically pleasing period comedy which suffers from slow, stiff treatment.
w Jack Rose *book* Corinne Griffith *d* George Marshall *ph* Loyal Griggs *m* Joseph J. Lilley
☆ Jackie Gleason, Glynis Johns, Charles Ruggles, Charles Lane, Laurel Goodwin, Juanita Moore, Elisha Cook Jnr, Murray Hamilton
song 'Call Me Irresponsible' (*m* James Van Heusen, *ly* Sammy Cahn)

'They put together New York's fastest moving newspaper. They search for truth, they strive for justice ... then print what they can get away with.'
'Never let the truth get in the way of a good story.'
The Paper **
US 1994 112m DeLuxe
Universal/Imagine (Brian Grazer, Frederick Zollo)
A day in the life of the metropolitan editor of a struggling New York tabloid, who has to sort out career and family problems, which include a job offer from a better paper, an emasculating managing editor and an anxious and pregnant wife.
Entertaining, though soft-centred, slice of journalism, but lacking that occupation's bracing cynicism, and somewhat remote from reality.
w David Koepp, Stephen Koepp *d* Ron Howard *ph* John Seale *m* Randy Newman *pd* Todd Hallowell *ed* Daniel Hanley, Michael Hill
☆ Michael Keaton, Glenn Close, Marisa Tomei, Robert Duvall, Randy Quaid, Jason Alexander, Spalding Gray, Catherine O'Hara, Lynne Thigpen
'Howard may take on large, semi-serious topics, but he always intends to make cotton candy of them in the end.' – *Michael Atkinson, Sight and Sound*
'It naturally lacks the edge of the *great* media farces, but there's a lot of sparkling fun to be had.' – *Angie Errigo, Empire*
song 'Make Up Your Mind'

Paper Bullets
US 1941 69m bw
King Brothers/PRC
Three orphanage pals grow up to be involved in crime.
Fast-moving second feature.
w Martin Mooney *d* Phil Rosen
☆ Joan Woodbury, Jack La Rue, Alan Ladd, Linda Ware, Vince Barnett, Gavin Gordon, John Archer

The Paper Chase **
US 1973 111m DeLuxe Panavision
TCF (Robert C. Thompson, Rodrick Paul)
A Harvard law graduate falls in love with the divorced daughter of his tetchiest professor.
A thoughtful analysis of attitudes to learning turns into just another youth movie.
wd James Bridges *novel* John Jay Osborn Jnr *ph* Gordon Willis *m* John Williams
☆ Timothy Bottoms, Lindsay Wagner, *John Houseman,* Graham Bickel
'A slightly unfocused account of conformism and milk-mild rebellion on the campus.' – *Sight and Sound*
'A worthy film which engages the eye and the brain.' – *Benny Green, Punch*
John Houseman
James Bridges (as writer)

Paper Lion
US 1968 105m colour
Stuart Millar/United Artist
The training of a professional football player.
Rather single-minded sporting biography from a book by George Plimpton.
w Lawrence Roman *d* Alex March
☆ Alan Alda, Lauren Hutton, David Doyle, Sugar Ray Robinson

'Trust me. I'm a doctor.'
Paper Mask **
GB 1990 105m colour
Enterprise/Film Four International (Christopher Morahan)
A hospital porter pretends to be a doctor.
Chilling and enjoyable small-scale thriller.
w John Collee *d* Christopher Morahan *ph* Nat Crosby *m* Richard Harvey *pd* Caroline Hanania *ed* Peter Coulson
☆ Paul McGann, Amanda Donohoe, Frederick Treves, Tom Wilkinson, Barbara Leigh-Hunt, Jimmy Yuill, Mark Lewis Jones, John Warnaby, Alexandra Mathie

'As P. T. Barnum put it, "There's a sucker born every minute".'
Paper Moon **
US 1973 103m bw
Paramount/Saticoy (Peter Bogdanovich)
In the American midwest in the thirties, a bible salesman and a plain little girl make a great con team.
Unusual but overrated comedy, imperfectly adapted from a very funny book, with careful but disappointing period sense and photography. A lot more style and gloss was required.
w Alvin Sargent *novel* *Addie Pray* by *Joe David Brown* *d* Peter Bogdanovich *ph* Laszlo Kovacs *m* popular songs and recordings
☆ *Ryan O'Neal, Tatum O'Neal,* Madeline Kahn, John Hillerman
'I've rarely seen a film that looked so unlike what it was about.' – *Stanley Kauffmann*
'At its best the film is only mildly amusing, and I'm not sure I could recall a few undeniable highlights if pressed on the point.' – *Gary Arnold*
'Bogdanovich once again deploys the armoury of nostalgia with relentless cunning to evoke the threadbare side of American life forty years ago ... one of those rare movies which engages at least two of the senses.' – *Benny Green, Punch*
'It is so enjoyable, so funny, so touching that I couldn't care less about its morals.' – *Daily Telegraph*
Tatum O'Neal
Alvin Sargent; Madeline Kahn

Paper Tiger
GB 1975 99m Technicolor
Maclean and Co (Euan Lloyd)
An ageing Englishman becomes tutor to the son of the Japanese ambassador in a Pacific state, and finds he has to live his heroic fantasies in reality.
Uneasy adventure comedy drama which might, given more skilled handling, have been much better than it is.
w Jack Davies *d* Ken Annakin *ph* John Cabrera *m* Roy Budd
☆ David Niven, Toshiro Mifune, Hardy Kruger, Ando, Ivan Desny, Irene Tsu, Miiko Taka, Ronald Fraser, Jeff Corey
'Makes no demands, except on 99 minutes of our time.' – *Michael Billington, Illustrated London News*

'He's hard, tough... and doesn't give a XXXX for anything... except romantic novels.'
Paperback Hero *
Australia 1998 97m colour
AFFC/Paperback (Lance W. Reynolds, John Winter)
A truck driver who lives in the outback persuades a waitress to pose as the author of a best-selling romantic novel that he has written.
Amiable, though predictable, romantic comedy, with a few sideswipes at macho attitudes on the way.
wd Antony J. Bowman *ph* David Burr *m* Burkhard Dallwitz *pd* Jon Dowding *ed* Veronika Jenet
☆ Claudia Karvan (Ruby), Hugh Jackman (Jack), Angie Milliken (Ziggy), Andrew S. Gilbert (Hamish), Jeanie Drynan (Suzie), Bruce Venables (Artie), Barry Rugless (Mad Pete), Tony Barry (Mack)
'The pace is slow, the plot is predictable and all the characters are cardboard cutouts.' – *Cosmo Landesman, Sunday Times*

Paperhouse
GB 1988 92m Technicolor
Vestron/Working Title (Tim Bevan, Sarah Radcliffe)
An 11-year-old girl has fainting fits which take her into a dangerous fantasy world that resembles her drawings.
Slow-moving, shallow fantasy.
w Matthew Jacobs *novel* *Marianne's Dream* by Catherine Storr *d* Bernard Rose *ph* Mike Southon *m* Hans Zimmer, Stanley Myers *pd* Gemma Jackson *ed* Dan Rae
☆ Charlotte Burke, Ben Cross, Glenne Headly, Elliott Spiers, Gemma Jones

Papillon *
US 1973 150m Technicolor Panavision
Papillon Partnership/Corona/General Production Co (Robert Dorfmann)
Filmed autobiography of life on Devil's Island.
Overlong and rather dreary film of a bestseller; it determinedly rubs the audience's nose in ordure from the start, and the final successful escape is one try too many.
w Dalton Trumbo, Lorenzo Semple Jnr *book* Henri Charrière *d* Franklin Schaffner *ph* Fred Koenekamp *m* Jerry Goldsmith
☆ Steve McQueen, Dustin Hoffman, Victor Jory, Don Gordon, Anthony Zerbe, George Coulouris, Woodrow Parfrey
'A $2\frac{1}{2}$-hour epic trampling the corn growing round the theme of man's inhumanity to man.' – *Sight and Sound*
'Papillon offers torture as entertainment but winds up making entertainment a form of torture ... a tournament of brutality unrelieved by imagination.' – *Paul D. Zimmermann*
'So overloaded with details that the stars are almost lost in exposition, repetition and unfocused drama.' – *Judith Crist, 1977*
'So solemn one would think it the story of a pope at the very least.' – *New Yorker, 1980*
Jerry Goldsmith

Parachute Jumper
US 1932 70m bw
Warner
Ex-flying Marines out of a job fall in with gangsters.
Easy-going adventure yarn with agreeable players.
w Rian James, John Francis Larkin *d* Alfred E. Green

☆ Douglas Fairbanks Jnr, Bette Davis, Leo Carrillo, Claire Dodd, Frank McHugh, Harold Huber

'Breezy treatment of a not very brilliant yarn.' – *Variety*

Parade *

France/Sweden 1974 85m Technicolor
Gray Film/Sveriges Radio

Jacques Tati introduces a series of acts in a small-scale circus.

Pleasant, sometimes boring variety show, to be included in the Tati canon for completeness; it does include some of his unique pieces of mime.

wd Jacques Tati *ph* Jean Badal, Gunnar Fischer *m* Charles Dumont

'A curious, unresolved envoi.' – *John Pym, MFB*

'Moments of great good humour and flashes of incomparable magic.' – *Sight and Sound*

The Paradine Case **

US 1947 115m bw
Selznick

A barrister falls in love with his client, who is suspected of murder.

A stodgy and old-fashioned script is given gleaming treatment; this and the acting make it seem better thirty years later than it did on release.

w David O. Selznick *novel* Robert Hichens *d Alfred Hitchcock ph Lee Garmes m* Franz Waxman

☆ Gregory Peck, *Alida Valli*, Ann Todd, Louis Jourdan, *Charles Laughton*, Charles Coburn, Ethel Barrymore, Leo G. Carroll

'This is the wordiest script since the death of Edmund Burke.' – *James Agee*

'The characters and their problems don't make much imprint on a viewer; if you can't remember whether you've seen the picture or not, chances are you did and forgot it.' – *New Yorker, 1976*

† Original choices were Olivier instead of Peck, Garbo instead of Valli, and Robert Newton instead of Jourdan.

Ethel Barrymore

Paradise *

US 1991 110m Technicolor
Buena Vista/Touchstone/Touchwood Pacific Partners I/ Interscope/Jean-François Lepetit (Scott Kroopf, Patrick Palmer)

A ten-year-old boy makes friends with a young girl when he goes to spend the summer with a childless couple.

Sentimentality is kept at bay for the most part and charm predominates in a gently effective narrative.

wd Mary Agnes Donoghue *ph* Jerzy Zielinski *m* David Newman *pd* Evelyn Sakash, Marcia Hinds *ed* Eva Gardos, Debra McDermott

☆ Melanie Griffith, Don Johnson, Elijah Wood, Thora Birch, Sheila McCarthy, Eve Gordon, Louise Latham, Greg Travis, Sarah Trigger, Richard K. Olsen

'Excellent ensemble acting and a feel-good payoff to this bittersweet tale could produce a sleeper hit.' – *Variety*

† A remake of *Le Grand Chemin* (qv), directed in 1987 by Jean-Loup Hubert.

Paradise Alley

US 1978 107m Technicolor
Universal/Force Ten (John F. Roach, Ronald A. Suppa)

The adventures of three wrestling brothers in New York's Hell's Kitchen during the forties.

Fashionable update of the City for Conquest *school, not in itself very interesting despite amusing bits.*

wd Sylvester Stallone *ph* Laszlo Kovacs *m* Bill Conti *pd* John W. Corso

☆ Sylvester Stallone, Kevin Conway, Anne Archer, Joe Spinell, Armand Assante, Lee Canalito

Paradise for Three

US 1937 78m bw
MGM
GB title: *Romance for Three*

A businessman goes to Germany to find out how the workers live.

An interesting premise leads inevitably into a flimsy romantic comedy.

w George Oppenheimer, Harry Ruskin *d* Edward Buzzell

☆ Robert Young, Frank Morgan, Mary Astor, Edna May Oliver, Florence Rice, Reginald Owen, Henry Hull, Sig Rumann, Herman Bing

Paradise for Two

GB 1937 77m bw
Günther Stapenhorst/Denham
US title: *Gaiety Girls*

A millionaire posing as a reporter is asked to pose as a millionaire.

Cheerful comedy-romance.

w Robert Stevenson, Arthur Macrae *d* Thornton Freeland *ph* Gunther Krampf *m* Mischa Spoliansky *ad* Vincent Korda, Shamoon Nadir *ed* E. B. Jarvis

☆ Jack Hulbert, Patricia Ellis, Arthur Riscoe, Googie Withers, Sydney Fairbrother, Wylie Watson, David Tree

Paradise Hawaiian Style

US 1965 91m Technicolor
Paramount/Hal Wallis/Joseph H. Hazen

An amorous airline pilot returns to Hawaii and sets up a helicopter service.

Mindless musical vehicle for an increasingly resistible star.

w Allan Weiss, Anthony Lawrence *d* Michael Moore *ph* W. Wallace Kelley *md* Joseph J. Lilley

☆ Elvis Presley, Suzanna Leigh, James Shigeta, Irene Tsu

Paradise Lagoon: see *The Admirable Crichton*

'Courage echoes forever.'

Paradise Road *

Australia/US 1997 115m colour
Panavision
TCF/YTC/Village Roadshow (Sue Milliken, Greg Coote)

During the Second World War, women survivors of a shipwreck are imprisoned by the Japanese; some keep their morale high by forming a vocal orchestra.

Based on a true story, this should be more affecting than it is; it is too often shallow and manipulative to be moving.

wd Bruce Beresford *story* David Giles, Martin Meader *diaries by Betty Jeffrey in* White Coolies *ph* Peter James *m* Ross Edwards *pd* Herbert Pinter *ed* Tim Wellburn

☆ Glenn Close, Pauline Collins, Cate Blanchett, Frances McDormand, Julianna Margulies, Jennifer Ehle, Wendy Hughes, Johanna Ter Steege, Elizabeth Spriggs, Clyde Kusatsu

'This powerful account of female friendship and bonding under the most cruel conditions lacks the narrative focus and dramatic shapeliness to generate emotional excitement.' – *Emanuel Levy, Variety*

The Parallax View ***

US 1974 102m Technicolor Panavision
Paramount/Gus/Harbour/Doubleday (Alan J. Pakula)

Witnesses to a political assassination are systematically killed, despite the efforts of a crusading journalist.

Stylish, persuasive political thriller with a downbeat ending; the villains win.

w David Giler, Lorenzo Semple Jnr *novel* Loren Singer *d* Alan J. Pakula *ph* Gordon Willis *m* Michael Small

☆ Warren Beatty, Paula Prentiss, William Daniels, Hume Cronyn, Walter McGinn

'Pakula at his best ... the test sequence is one of the most celebrated, manipulating the audience as it bombards Beatty's psyche.' – *Les Keyser, Hollywood in the Seventies*

'It is terribly important to give an audience a lot of things they may not get as well as those they will, so that finally the film does take on a texture and is not just simplistic communication.' – *Alan J. Pakula*

Paramount on Parade *

US 1930 102m bw (Technicolor sequence)
Paramount (Elsie Janis)

A revue featuring Paramount contract stars.

A ragged affair by any standard, but worth a look for a couple of Chevalier's numbers.

w various *d* Dorothy Arzner, Otto Brower, Edmund Goulding, Victor Heerman, Edwin H. Knopf, Rowland V. Lee, Ernst Lubitsch, Lothar Mendes, Victor Schertzinger, A. Edward Sutherland, Frank Tuttle *ph* Harry Fischbeck, Victor Milner *m* various

☆ Richard Arlen, Jean Arthur, George Bancroft, Clara Bow, Nancy Carroll, Ruth Chatterton, Maurice Chevalier, Gary Cooper, Leon Errol, Kay Francis, Harry Green, Mitzi Green, Dennis King, Fredric March, Nino Martini and also Jack Oakie, Charles 'Buddy' Rogers, Lillian Roth, Fay Wray, Clive Brook, Warner Oland, Eugene Pallette, William Powell

'Pip revue packed with laughs and talent.' – *Variety*

'It ran for less than two hours but I came out of the theater several years older.' – *Robert Benchley*

Paranoia

Italy/Spain 1969 88m Technicolor
Techniscope
Eagle/Tritone/Medusa/D.I.A.
aka: *A Quiet Place to Kill*

A jealous wife plots to murder her philandering husband with the help of his former wife.

Lacklustre thriller that seemingly failed to engage the interest of director or cast.

w Rafael Romero Marchent, Marcello Coscia, Bruno di Geronimo *d* Umberto Lenzi *ph* Guglie Imo Mancori *m* Gregorio Garcia Segura *ad* Wolfgang Burmann *ed* Antonio Ramirez, Enzo Alabiso

☆ Carroll Baker, Jean Sorel, Marina Coffa, Anna Proclemer, Alberto Dalbes

'A sun-struck little thriller so listlessly plotted – between Majorca beach and luxury poolside – that not even the occasional homicide can shake its mildly enervated holiday air.' – *Richard Combs, MFB*

† The film was cut to 77m on its British release.

'Suddenly, she knew the lips burning on hers did not belong to any normal man!'

Paranoiac *

GB 1963 80m bw Cinemascope
U-I/Hammer (Anthony Hinds)

An heiress is saved from a suicide attempt by a young man claiming to be her dead brother.

A complex maze of disguise, mistaken identity, family curses and revelations of something nasty in the woodshed, out of Psycho *by* Taste of Fear. *Not very good in itself, but interesting in its borrowings.*

w Jimmy Sangster *d* Freddie Francis *ph* Arthur Grant *m* Elisabeth Lutyens

☆ Oliver Reed, Janette Scott, Alexander Davion, Sheila Burrell, Liliane Brousse, Maurice Denham, John Bonney

Les Parapluies de Cherbourg **

France/West Germany 1964 92m
Eastmancolor
Parc/Madeleine/Beta
aka: *The Umbrellas of Cherbourg*

A shopgirl loves a gas station attendant. He goes on military service; she finds she is pregnant and marries for security. Years later they meet briefly by accident.

Unexpected, charming, pretty successful screen operetta with only sung dialogue. Careful acting and exquisite use of colour and camera movement paste over the thinner sections of the plot.

wd Jacques Demy ph Jean Rabier m Michel Legrand, Jacques Demy ad Bernard Evein

☆ Catherine Deneuve, *Anne Vernon*, Nino Castelnuovo

'Poetic neo-realism.' – *Georges Sadoul*

'We are told that in Paris the opening night audience wept and the critics were ecstatic. It would have made a little more sense the other way round.' – *John Simon*

best foreign film; script; Michel Legrand, Jacques Demy; song 'I Will Wait for You'; scoring

'The First Futristic Monster Movie In 3-D!'

Parasite

US 1982 85m Metrocolor StereoVision 3-D
Embassy/Charles Band

In a post-holocaust 1992, a scientist battles to control a virulent flesh-eating parasite he has developed.

Silly sci-fi horror, in which three-dimensional effects take precedence over sense and logic.

w Alan J. Adler, Michael Shoob, Frank Levering *d* Charles Band *ph* Mac Ahlberg *m* Richard Band *ad* Pamela B. Warner *ed* Brad Arensman *sp* parasite effects: Stan Winston, James Kagel, Lance Anderson

☆ Robert Glaudini, Demi Moore, Luca Bercovici, James Davidson, Vivian Blaine, Al Fann, Tom Villard, Scott Thomson

† The film was a hit, owing mainly to its excellent 3-D and scenes such as one in which, in close-up so that it was right in the viewer's face, blood oozes out of the end of a pipe on which a man is impaled. A sequel was announced but never, so far, made.

The Parasite Murders

Canada 1974 87m colour
Target/Cinepix/Canadian Film Development Corp. (Ivan Reitman)
aka: *Shivers*
US title: *They Came from Within*

Parasites that turn people into diseased sex maniacs infect the inhabitants of a luxury hotel.

Bloody and violent horror movie, the first to explore its director's obsession with the alteration of the human body from one form to another.

wd David Cronenberg *ph* Robert Saad *ad* Erla Gliserman *ed* Patrick Dodd *sp* Joe Blasco

☆ Paul Hampton, Joe Silver, Lynn Lowry, Allan Migicovsky, Susan Petrie, Barbara Steele, Ronald Mlodzik

'A fresh and diverting variation of a hoary entertainment formula.' – *Richard Combs, MFB*

'I was saying "I love sex, but I love sex as a venereal disease. I am syphilis. I am enthusiastic about it, but in a very different way from you".' – *David Cronenberg*

Paratrooper: see *The Red Beret*

Pardners

US 1956 88m Technicolor
Vistavision
Paramount (Paul Jones)

An incompetent idiot goes west and accidentally cleans up the town.

Stiff Western star burlesque, a remake of Rhythm on the Range.

w Sidney Sheldon *d* Norman Taurog *ph* Daniel Fapp *songs* Sammy Cahn, Jimmy Van Heusen

☆ Dean Martin, Jerry Lewis, Agnes Moorehead, Lori Nelson, John Baragrey, Jeff Morrow, Lon Chaney Jnr

Pardon Mon Affaire *

France 1977 108m Eastmancolor
Gaumont/La Guéville (Daniel Deschamps)
aka: *Un Eléphant ça Trompe Enormément*

A middle-aged married man discovers that he is a very unsuccessful adulterer.

Unsubtle comedy that was successful in France, though it does not travel well.

w Jean-Loup Dabadie, Yves Robert *d* Yves Robert *ph* René Mathelin *m* Vladimir Cosma *ad* Jean-Pierre Kohut-Svelko *ed* Gérard Pollicand

☆ Jean Rochefort, Claude Brasseur, Guy Bedos, Victor Lanoux, Daniele Delorme, Anny Duperey

† The film was remade by Hollywood as *The Woman In Red* (qv), directed by Gene Wilder.

Pardon My Past *

US 1945 88m bw
Columbia

A man unwittingly takes on the problems of his double, a shady playboy.

Amusing mistaken identity comedy.

w Earl Felton, Karl Kamb *d* Leslie Fenton *ph* Russell Metty *m* Dimitri Tiomkin

☆ Fred MacMurray, Marguerite Chapman, Akim Tamiroff, Rita Johnson, William Demarest, Harry Davenport

Pardon Us *

US 1931 55m bw
Hal Roach
aka: *Jailbirds*

Two zany bootleggers find themselves in and out of prison.

Patchy star comedy which finds the boys on the whole not in quite their best form.

w H. M. Walker *d* James Parrott *ph* George Stevens *ed* Richard Currier

☆ Stan Laurel, Oliver Hardy, Wilfred Lucas, Walter Long, James Finlayson

'Their first full-length, with not over two reels of value.' – *Variety*

† Boris Karloff replaced Walter Long in the French version of the film.

The Parent Trap *

US 1961 129m Technicolor
Walt Disney (George Golitzen)

Twin daughters of separated parents determine to bring the family together again.
Quite bright but awesomely extended juvenile romp.
wd David Swift *novel* *Das Doppelte Lottchen* by Erich Kästner *ph* Lucien Ballard *m* Paul Smith
☆ *Hayley Mills*, Maureen O'Hara, Brian Keith, Charles Ruggles, Leo G. Carroll, Una Merkel, Joanna Barnes, Cathleen Nesbitt, Ruth McDevitt, Nancy Kulp

The Parent Trap *

US 1998 127m
Buena Vista/Disney (Charles Shyer)

Twins separated when very young discover each other and decide to bring together again their divorced parents.
Overlong remake that is on the bland side, but also bright and cheerful.
w David Swift, Nancy Meyers, Charles Shyer *book* *Das Doppelte Lottchen* by Erich Kastner *d* Nancy Meyers *ph* Dean A. Cundey *m* Alan Silvestri *pd* Dean Tavoularis *ed* Stephen A. Rotter
☆ Lindsay Lohan, Dennis Quaid, Natasha Richardson, Elaine Hendrix, Lisa Ann Walter, Simon Kunz, Polly Holliday, Maggie Wheeler, Ronnie Stevens

'Slick, sentimental and exceptionally well cast.' – *Variety*

Parenthood **

US 1989 99m DeLuxe Panavision
UIP/Imagine Entertainment (Brian Grazer)

Three generations of fathers and sons try to come to terms with each other.
Expertly packaged, frequently funny, sometimes accurate, but more often sentimental, study of paternal relationships (maternal relationships are defined in terms of the absence of a father).
w Lowell Ganz, Babaloo Mandel *d* Ron Howard *ph* Donald McAlpine *m* Randy Newman *pd* Todd Hallowell *ed* Michael Hill, Daniel Hanley
☆ Steve Martin, Tom Hulce, Rick Moranis, Martha Plimpton, Keanu Reeves, Jason Robards, Mary Steenburgen, Dianne Wiest
Dianne Wiest; song 'I Love To See You Smile' (*m/l* Randy Newman)

'There's A New Name For Terror'
Parents

US 1988 82m colour
Vestron/Parents Productions (Bonnie Palef-Woolf)

A child in small-town America of the 1950s discovers that his parents are cannibals.
Black comedy all the more unsettling because of its resolutely suburban setting.
w Christopher Hawthorne *d* Bob Balaban *ph* Ernest Day, Robin Vidgeon *m* Angelo Badalamenti, Jonathan Elias *ad* Andris Hausmanis *ed* Bill Pankow
☆ Randy Quaid, Mary Beth Hurt, Sandy Dennis, Bryan Madorsky, Juno Mills-Cockell, Kathryn Grody, Deborah Rush, Graham Jarvis

'The most interesting and exciting directorial debut that I have encountered in some time – a "failure" that makes most recent successes seem like cold mush.' – *Jonathan Rosenbaum, Chicago Reader*

Les Parents Terribles **

France 1948 98m bw
Sirius

Life with a family in which the children are as neurotic as the parents.
Alternately hilarious and tragic, this is a fascinating two-set piece of filmed theatre, with every performance a pleasure.
wd *Jean Cocteau* *play* Jean Cocteau *ph* Michel Kelber *m* Georges Auric *ad* Christian Bérard, Guy de Gastyne
☆ *Jean Marais*, *Yvonne de Bray*, Gabrielle Dorziat, Marcel André, Josette Day

† In 1953 a curious and unsatisfactory British version was made by Charles Frank under the title *Intimate Relations*, with Marian Spencer, Russell Enoch, Ruth Dunning, Harold Warrender and Elsy Albiin.

Le Parfum d'Yvonne *

France 1994 89m colour
Artificial Eye/Lambart/Zoulou/CECR-A/M6 (Thierry de Ganay)

aka: *Yvonne's Perfume*

A man remembers a holiday by Lake Geneva, when he was avoiding service in the Algerian war, one that changed his life after he became involved with a beautiful actress and her reckless friend, an elderly homosexual doctor.
Slight, leisurely, bitter-sweet romance among the idle, set against the background of privilege.
wd Patrice Leconte *novel* *Villa Triste* by Patrick Modiano *ph* Eduardo Serra *m* Pascal Estève *ad* Ivan Maussion *ed* Joëlle Hache
☆ *Jean-Pierre Marielle*, Hippolyte Girardot, Sandra Majani, Richard Bohringer, Paul Guers, Corinne Marchand, Philippe Magnan

'Good playing, particularly from Marielle, some fine widescreen camerawork and a certain sense of melancholy, even as the gaiety is outlined, prevents the film falling into bathos. But it's a near thing.' – *Derek Malcolm, Guardian*

'Stunningly lensed widescreen memoir captured at the intersection of insouciance and longing.' – *Variety*

Paris

US 1929 88m bw/colour
Warner

An American stage star, her fiancé, her partner and her mother-in-law-to-be converge on the Champs Elysées.
Shaky musical with interesting talent, but bereft of its original Cole Porter score.
w Hope Loring *d* Clarence Badger
☆ Irene Bordoni, Jack Buchanan, Louise Closser Hale, Jason Robards

Paris after Dark

US 1943 85m bw
TCF

GB title: *The Night Is Ending*

In wartime Paris a doctor leads the resistance forces.
Propaganda potboiler, quite neatly made and cast.
w Howard Buchman *d* Leonide Moguy *ph* Lucien Andriot
☆ George Sanders, Philip Dorn, Brenda Marshall, Marcel Dalio, Madeleine LeBeau

Paris Belongs to Us

France 1961 140m bw
AJYM/Films du Carrosse (Roland Nonia)

original title: *Paris Nous Appartient*

A student becomes involved with a group unsuccessfully rehearsing a Shakespearean play who fear a conspiracy to take over the world.
Overlong, often pretentious and frequently amateurish, Rivette's first feature reflects an adolescent despair of the future.
w Jacques Rivette, Jean Gruault *d* Jacques Rivette *ph* Charles Bitsch *m* Philippe Arthuys *ed* Denise de Casablanca
☆ Betty Schneider, Gianni Esposito, Françoise Prévost, Daniel Crohem, François Maistre, Jean-Marie Robain, Hans Lucas, Jean-Claude Brialy

Paris Blues *

US 1961 98m Technicolor
UA/Pennebaker/Diane/Jason/Monica/Monmouth (Sam Shaw)

Two jazz musicians have romantic problems in Paris.
Semi-serious mini-drama with emphasis on the music; one is not quite sure what the actors thought they were up to.
w Jack Sher, Irene Kamp, Walter Bernstein *novel* Harold Flender *d* Martin Ritt *ph* Christian Matras *m* Duke Ellington
☆ Paul Newman, Joanne Woodward, Sidney Poitier, Louis Armstrong, Diahann Carroll, Serge Reggiani, Barbara Laage

'All wrong from beginning to end.' – *Sidney Poitier*

Duke Ellington

Paris by Night

GB 1988 103m Eastmancolor
Virgin/British Screen/Film Four International/Zenith

Harassed by personal problems, a Conservative MP in the European Parliament is driven to extreme actions.
Unsatisfactory political drama, intended to expose social and moral hypocrisies but rarely rising above melodrama.
wd David Hare *ph* Roger Pratt *m* Georges Delerue *pd* Anthony Pratt *ed* George Akers
☆ Charlotte Rampling, Michael Gambon, Robert Hardy, Iain Glen, Jane Asher, Andrew Ray, Niamh Cusack, Jonathan White, Linda Bassett, Robert Flemyng, Robert David MacDonald

Paris Express: see *The Man Who Watched Trains Go By*

'Sometimes the most erotic place to go is inside yourself.'
Paris France

Canada 1993 105m Eastmancolor/bw
Feature Film/Alliance/Lightshow (Eric Norlen, Allan Levine)

A writer comes between a publisher and his wife.
An absurd mishmash of sex and literary musings, resembling a pornographer's fantasy of the artistic life in which coupling and writing are seen as complementary activities.
w Tom Walmsley *novel* Tom Walmsley *d* Gerard Ciccoritti *ph* Barry Stone *m* John McCarthy *pd* Marian Wihak *ed* Roushell Goldstein
☆ Leslie Hope, Peter Outerbridge, Victor Ertmanis, Dan Lett, Raoul Trujillo

'A pretentiously steamy piece of Canadian erotica.' – *Derek Malcolm, Guardian*

'An unerotic bonkathon chock-full of unintentional laughs, hysterical performances and flaccid members.' – *Film Review*

Paris Holiday *

US 1957 101m Technirama
UA/Tolda (Bob Hope)

An American comedian meets a French one in Paris, and both have narrow escapes because their script contains the clue to a gang of counterfeiters.
Amiable location romp with the stars in pretty good form.
w Edmund Beloin, Dean Riesner *d* Gerd Oswald *ph* Roger Hubert *m* Joseph J. Lilley
☆ Bob Hope, Fernandel, Anita Ekberg, Martha Hyer, André Morell, Maurice Teynac, Jean Murat, Preston Sturges

Paris Honeymoon

US 1938 85m bw
Paramount

An American in Paris persuades his fiancée to forget a French nobleman.
Candy floss musical for star fans.
w Frank Butler, Don Hartman *d* Frank Tuttle *ph* Karl Struss *m/ly* Leo Robin *md* Boris Morros
☆ Bing Crosby, Franciska Gaal, Akim Tamiroff

'Entertaining offering that will click substantially at the box office.' – *Variety*

Paris in Spring

US 1935 81m bw
Paramount

GB title: *Paris Love Song*

Four visitors change partners in the romantic city.
Predictable romance with good ingredients.
w Samuel Hoffenstein, Franz Schulz, Keene Thompson *play* Dwight Taylor *d* Lewis Milestone
☆ Mary Ellis, Tullio Carminati, Lynne Overman, Ida Lupino

'In everything except the unhappy choice of narrative it comes close to being an ideal production.' – *Variety*

Paris Interlude

US 1934 72m bw
MGM

American newspapermen hang out in a Paris bar.
Aimless comedy-drama which fails to achieve the intended mood of world-weariness.
w Wells Root *play* *All Good Americans* by S. J. and Laura Perelman *d* Edwin L. Marin
☆ Madge Evans, Otto Kruger, Robert Young, Una Merkel, Ted Healy, Louise Henry, Edward Brophy

'60 minutes instead of 72 would still have left something to be desired – further cutting.' – *Variety*

Paris Is Burning **

US 1990 78m colour
ICA/OffWhite (Jennie Livingston)

Documentary about gay black men who compete for prizes at drag balls.
Fascinating glimpse of an enclosed world, reported with insight and sensitivity.
d *Jennie Livingston* *ph* Paul Gibson *ed* Jonathan Oppenheim
☆ Paris Dupree, Andre Christian, Dorian Corey, Pepper Labeija, Willi Ninja

'A masterpiece of underworld reportage.' – *Sight and Sound*

Paris Love Song: see *Paris in Spring*

Paris Model

US 1953 88m bw
Albert Zugsmith/Columbia

Stories involving four copies of the same Paris gown.
Depressing dramatic package with production values at a low ebb and some pleasant talents going awry.
w Robert Smith *d* Alfred E. Green *ph* William Bradford *m* Albert Glasser
☆ Paulette Goddard, Eva Gabor, Marilyn Maxwell, Barbara Lawrence, Tom Conway, Leif Erickson, Florence Bates, Cecil Kellaway, Robert Hutton

'Wasn't it dreadful?' – *Marilyn Maxwell*

Paris Nous Appartient: see *Paris Belongs to Us*

Paris Qui Dort *

France 1923 40m approx (24 fps) bw silent
Films Diamant (Maurice Diamant-Berger)

aka: *The Crazy Ray*

A mad scientist invents a ray which brings everyone but six people in Paris to a halt.
Mildly entertaining semi-professional comedy showing several of its director's most engaging traits.
ph Maurice Défassiaux, Paul Guichard *wd/ed* *René Clair*
☆ Henri Rollan, Albert Préjean, Marcel Vallée, Madeleine Rodrigue

Paris, Texas **

West Germany/France 1984 148m colour
Road Movies/Argos (Don Guest, Anatole Dauman)

After separating from his wife a man goes missing and is later found in the small town where he was born.
Long, enigmatic but generally fascinating puzzle-without-a-solution, about people who never find what they want.
w Sam Shepard *d* *Wim Wenders* *ph* Robby Müller *m* Ry Cooder
☆ Harry Dean Stanton, Dean Stockwell, Aurore Clement, Hunter Carson, Nastassja Kinski, Bernhard Wicki

† Filmed in English.

best director

Paris Trout **

US 1991 99m CFI color Panavision
Palace/Viacom (Frank Konigsberg, Larry Sanitsky)

In the 1940s, in a small town in Georgia, a bigoted white store-owner is amazed to be tried for shooting a black girl and wounding her mother in a dispute over a car.
Powerful if predictable drama of racial hatred and a disintegrating marriage, though not helped by a portentous voice-over narration.
w Pete Dexter *novel* Pete Dexter *d* Stephen Gyllenhaal *ph* Robert Elswit *m* David Shire *pd* Richard Sherman *ed* Harvey Rosenstock
☆ Dennis Hopper, Barbara Hershey, Ed Harris, Ray McKinnon, Tina Lifford, Darnita Henry, Eric Ware, Ronreaco Lee, Gary Bullock

Paris Underground
US 1945 97m bw
(UA)
GB title: *Madame Pimpernel*
Two women caught in Paris when the Nazis invade continue their resistance activities.
Artificial and not very exciting flagwaver.
w Boris Ingster, Gertrude Purcell *novel* Etta Shiber *d* Gregory Ratoff *ph* Lee Garmes *m* Alexander Tansman
☆ Constance Bennett, Gracie Fields, George Rigaud, Kurt Kreuger, Leslie Vincent
'Mainly trash, involving enough handsome young men, in various poses of gallant gratitude, to satisfy Mae West in her prime.' – *James Agee*
Alexander Tansman

Paris Vu Par... **
France 1965 98m colour
Films du Losange/Les Films du Cyprès/Barbet Schroeder
aka: *Six in Paris*
Six short stories set in different parts of Paris: in Douchet's 'Saint Germain-des-Prés', an American girl is seduced by appearances. In Rouch's 'Gard du Nord', a discontented wife is offered the freedom that she thinks she desires. In Pollet's 'Rue St Denis', a dull dishwasher takes a prostitute back to his dingy flat. In Rohmer's 'Place de l'étoile', a fastidious shirt-salesman thinks he has killed someone in a roadside brawl. In Godard's 'Montparnasse et Levallois', a girl believes she has mixed up telegrams sent to her two lovers. In Chabrol's 'La Muette Chabrol', a young boy buys ear-plugs to avoid listening to his parents' quarrel and so misses a vital cry for help.
Enjoyable, ironic anecdotes by six French 'New Wave' directors, originally shot in 16mm using hand-held cameras and natural lighting to achieve an appropriately offhand style.
wd Jean Douchet; Jean Rouch; Jean-Daniel Pollet; Eric Rohmer; Jean-Luc Godard; Claude Chabrol *ph* Nestor Almendros; Etienne Becker; Alain Levent; Albert Maysles; Jean Rabier *ed* Jacqueline Raynal
☆ Barbara Wilkind, Jean-François Chappey, Jean-Pierre Andréani; Nadine Ballot, Barbet Schroeder, Gilles Quéant; Micheline Dax, Claude Melki; Jean-Michel Rouzière, Marcel Gallon; Joanna Shimkus, Philippe Hiquily, Serge Davri; Stéphane Audran, Gilles Chusseau, Claude Chabrol

Paris When It Sizzles
US 1963 110m Technicolor
Paramount (Richard Quine, George Axelrod)
A film writer tries out several script ideas with his secretary as heroine and himself as hero or villain.
As a French film called La Fête à Henriette *this was a charming whimsy, but Hollywood made it heavy-handed and boring, especially as no one in it seems to be having much fun.*
w George Axelrod *screenplay* Julien Duvivier, Henri Jeanson *d* Richard Quine *ph* Charles Lang Jnr *m* Nelson Riddle *ad* Jean d'Eaubonne *ed* Archie Marshek *cos* Hubert de Givenchy, Christian Dior
☆ William Holden (Richard Benson), Audrey Hepburn (Gabrielle Simpson), Grégoire Aslan (Police Inspector), Noël Coward (Alexander Meyerheimer), Raymond Bussières (Gangster), Tony Curtis (Second policeman), Marlene Dietrich, Mel Ferrer
'The new script embalms the original instead of reviving it.' – *Stanley Kauffmann, New Republic*

Park Row *
US 1952 83m bw
UA/Samuel Fuller
Conflict breaks out between two newspapers in 1886 New York.
Earnest but flat low-budgeter of a rather unusual kind.
wd Samuel Fuller *ph* Jack Russell *m* Paul Dunlap *ad* Theobold Holsopple
☆ Gene Evans, Mary Welch, Bela Kovacs, Herbert Heyes, Forrest Taylor

Parker
GB 1984 97m colour
Moving Picture Company (Nigel Stafford-Clark)
A British businessman turns up after claiming to have been kidnapped in Munich, but the police don't necessarily believe him.
Suspense thriller hampered by overblown bits of ambivalence which prevent sympathy from lodging in any quarter.
w Trevor Preston *d* Jim Goddard *ph* Peter Jessop *m* Richard Hartley
☆ Bryan Brown, Cherie Lunghi, Kurt Raab, Bob Peck, Beate Finkh

Parlor, Bedroom and Bath
US 1931 72m bw
MGM
GB title: *Romeo in Pyjamas*
A mild-mannered husband has trouble when he becomes a landlord.
Rather flatfooted farce, on a par with the star's other talkies.
w Richard Schayer, Robert Hopkins *play* Charles W. Bell, Mark Swan *d* Edward Sedgwick
☆ Buster Keaton, Charlotte Greenwood, Reginald Denny, Cliff Edwards
'Funny, clean enough for kids, and generally well made.' – *Variety*
† The film was largely shot on location in Keaton's own house.

'As though torn from life's pages!'
Parnell *
US 1937 115m bw
MGM (John M. Stahl)
A 19th-century Irish politician comes to grief through his love for a married woman.
Well made but miscast biopic, a resounding thud at the box-office.
w John Van Druten, S. N. Behrman *play* Elsie T. Schauffler *d* John M. Stahl *ph* Karl Freund *m* William Axt
☆ Clark Gable, Myrna Loy, Edmund Gwenn, Edna May Oliver, Alan Marshal, Donald Crisp, Billie Burke, Berton Churchill, Donald Meek, Montagu Love, George Zucco
'Dull and overlong historical drama ... word of mouth is likely to be poor.' – *Variety*
'A singularly pallid, tedious and unconvincing drama.' – *Frank Nugent*
'Poor though the picture may be, it is pleasing to think how clean a film magnate's wish-fulfilments are, how virginal and high-minded the tawdry pathetic human past becomes when the Mayers and Goldwyns turn the magic ring.' – *Graham Greene*

'Fighting Crime The Only Way He Knows How Badly.'
The Parole Officer
GB 2001 93m Technicolor
UIP/DNA/Universal/Film Council/Figment/Toledo (Duncan Kenworthy, Andrew Macdonald, Callum McDougall)
A probation officer is forced to stage a bank robbery so that he can clear himself of being framed for murder.
Slapdash, bumbling comedy of low ambition.
w Steve Coogan, Henry Normal *d* John Duigan *ph* John Daly *m* Alex Heffes *pd* Tom Brown *ed* David Freeman
☆ Steve Coogan (Simon Garden), Lena Headey (Emma), Stephen Dillane (Det. Insp. Burton), Om Puri (George), Steven Waddington (Jeff), Ben Miller (Colin), Jenny Agutter (Sarah), Emma Williams (Kirsty), Omar Sharif (Victor Bonderenko)
'A bog-standard caper comedy with deviations into gross-out interludes to please the American teens and any dumbed-down Brits.' – *Alexander Walker, London Evening Standard*

Parrish
US 1961 137m Technicolor
Warner (Delmer Daves)
A young tobacco plantation worker has an ample sex life and the luck to become boss.
Predictable trudge through scenes from a bestselling novel, less offensive than most such adaptations.
wd Delmer Daves *novel* Mildred Savage *ph* Harry Stradling *m* Max Steiner
☆ Troy Donahue, Claudette Colbert, Karl Malden, Dean Jagger, Connie Stevens, Diane McBain, Sharon Hugueny

Parsifal **
West Germany 1982 255m colour
Artificial Eye/Gaumont/TMS
Cinematic version of Wagner's opera of the knights of the Holy Grail.
Imaginative treatment, set around the composer's death mask, with a youth and a girl playing Parsifal; its actors are dubbed by singers.
d Hans Jürgen Syberberg *ph* Igor Luther *m* Richard Wagner *md* Armin Jordan *ed* Jutta Brandstaedter, Marianne Fehrenberg
☆ Michael Kutter, Karin Krick, Edith Clever, Armin Jordan, Robert Lloyd, Aage Haugland, Martin Sperr and also the voices of Rainer Goldberg, Yvonne Minton and Wolfgang Schöne

Une Partie de Campagne ***
France 1936 40m bw
Pantheon/Pierre Braunberger
aka: *A Day in the Country*
Around 1880, a Parisian tradesman and his family picnic one Sunday in the country, and one of the daughters falls in love.
An unfinished film which was much admired for its local colour, like an impressionist picture come to life.
wd Jean Renoir *story* Guy de Maupassant *ph* Claude Renoir, Jean Bourgoin *m* Joseph Kosma
☆ Sylvia Bataille, Georges Darnoul, Jane Marken, Paul Temps
'Nothing can tarnish the intense lyrical simplicity underlaid with an aching irony and made almost unbearable by the yearning musical score of Kosma. This is everybody's lost love.' – *Richard Winnington*

Une Partie de Plaisir *
France 1975 100m colour
La Boétie/Sunchild/Gerico (André Génoves)
The analysis of a divorce.
Bitter comedy drama, with the director's usual scriptwriter playing out his own life story. A little too incestuous for its own good, but with striking moments.
w Paul Gegauff *d* Claude Chabrol *ph* Jean Rabier *m* Beethoven, Brahms, Schubert *ad* Guy Littaye *ed* Jacques Gaillard
☆ Paul Gegauff, Danielle Gegauff, Paula Moore, Michel Valette, Cecile Vassort, Pierre Santini

Parting Glances *
US 1986 90m DuArt
Rondo (Yoran Mandel, Arthur Silverman)
A gay couple, one of whom is going to work in Africa, spend their last day together with friends.
A low-key drama of love, death and companionship in a community haunted by the fear of death; it was one of the first movies to confront the trauma of AIDS.
wd Bill Sherwood *ph* Jacek Laskus *pd* John Loggia
☆ Richard Ganoung, John Bolger, Steve Buscemi, Kathy Kinney, Adam Nathan, Yolande Bavan, Patrick Tull
'Is skilfully constructed and artfully shot, and boasts impressive acting.' – *MFB*
† Bill Sherwood died of AIDS in 1990.

Parting Shots
GB 1998 98m colour
UIP/Scimitar/Michael Winner
Told that he has only six weeks to live, a photographer decides to kill all the people who have humiliated him.
An extravagant waste of talent; with a miscast lead and a leaden script, it reworks the director's Death Wish *as a comedy, but isn't as funny.*
w Michael Winner, Nick Mead *d* Michael Winner *ph* Ousama Rawi *m* Les Reed *pd* Crispian Sallis *ed* Chris Barnes, Arnold Crust (Michael Winner)
☆ Chris Rea, Felicity Kendall, Bob Hoskins, Ben Kingsley, Joanna Lumley, Oliver Reed, Diana Rigg, John Cleese, Gareth Hunt, Peter Davison, Patrick Ryecart, Nicky Henson, Edward Hardwicke
'Sucks on every conceivable level. Its technical ineptitude and dramatic impotence simply beggar belief.' – *Andrew Collins, Empire*
'A thoroughbred contender for the crown "Worst Film Ever Made".' – *Observer*

Partners
US 1982 98m Movielab
Titan (Aaron Russo)
Two Los Angeles police officers, one straight and one gay, investigate the murder of a homosexual.
Uneasy comedy-melodrama of somewhat mysterious purpose.
w Francis Veber *d* James Burrows *ph* Victor J. Kemper *m* Georges Delerue
☆ John Hurt, Ryan O'Neal, Kenneth McMillan, Robyn Douglass, Jay Robinson

Partners in Crime
US 1937 66m bw
Paramount
A private eye stumbles on a plot to victimize the reform candidate in a local election.
Reliable second feature with few surprises.
w Garnett Weston *novel* Kurt Steel *d* Ralph Murphy
☆ Lynne Overman, Roscoe Karns, Muriel Hutchinson, Anthony Quinn, Inez Courtney, Charles Halton, Lucien Littlefield
'A cockeyed affair, perforated with surprises.' – *Variety*

The Party *
US 1968 98m DeLuxe Panavision
UA/Mirisch/Geoffrey (Blake Edwards)
An accident-prone Indian actor is accidentally invited to a swank Hollywood party and wrecks it.
Would-be Tatiesque comedy of disaster, occasionally well-timed but far too long for all its gloss.
w Blake Edwards, Tom and Frank Waldman *d* Blake Edwards *ph* Lucien Ballard *m* Henry Mancini *pd* Fernando Carrere
☆ Peter Sellers, Claudine Longet, Marge Champion, Fay McKenzie, Steve Franken, Buddy Lester
'One thing the old movie makers did know is that two reels is more than enough of this stuff.' – *Wilfred Sheed*
'It is only rarely that one laughs or even smiles; mostly one just chalks up another point for ingenuity.' – *Tom Milne*

The Party and the Guests *
Czechoslovakia 1966 71m bw
Barrandov Studio
original title: *O Slavnosti A Hostech*
A reluctant guest at an outdoor birthday and wedding party refuses to join in the celebrations.
Biting political allegory on the nature of tyranny.
w Ester Krumbachová, Jan N&ecaronmec *d* Jan Němec *ph* Jaromir Sofr *m* Karel Mares
☆ Helena Pejsková, Jana Pracharova, Zdena Skvorecká, Pavel Bosek, Karel Mares, Evald Schorm, Jan Klusak, Jiři Němec, Wan Vyskocil

Party Girl
US 1958 98m Metrocolor Cinemascope
MGM/Euterpe (Joe Pasternak)
In twenties Chicago, a lawyer wins a girl from a gangster.
Heavy-handed Scarface*-style saga which at one time won a curious reputation for being a satire.*
w George Wells *d* Nicholas Ray *ph* Robert Bronner *m* Jeff Alexander
☆ Robert Taylor, Cyd Charisse, Lee J. Cobb, John Ireland, Kent Smith, Claire Kelly, Corey Allen

Party, Party
GB 1983 98m colour
A & M Records
A teenager throws a drunken party while his parents are out.
Ghastly British rubbish: no plot and nothing to laugh at at all, just young people making asses of themselves.
w Daniel Peacock, Terry Winsor *d* Terry Winsor *ph* Syd Macartney
☆ Daniel Peacock, Karl Howman, Perry Fenwick, Sean Chapman, Phoebe Nicholls, Caroline Quentin

Party Wire
US 1935 70m bw
Columbia
Small-town gossipers listen in on party wires and draw the wrong conclusions.
Multi-stranded comedy-drama; not important but quite pleasant.

w Ethel Hill, John Howard Lawson, Bruce Manning *d* Erle C. Kenton
☆ Jean Arthur, Victor Jory, Helen Lowell, Charley Grapewin, Clara Blandick, Maude Eburne
'Entertaining for the family trade.' – *Variety*

The Party's Over
GB 1963 94m bw
Tricastle (Anthony Perry)
An American girl joins a group of Chelsea beatniks and dies in a fall from a balcony; her father investigates.
Tasteless and boring swinging London trash which became notorious when its producers (Rank) disowned it because it features a party at which a man makes love to a dead girl. An unattractive display of moral squalor.
w Marc Behm *d* Guy Hamilton *ph* Larry Pizer *m* John Barry
☆ Oliver Reed, Eddie Albert, Ann Lynn, Louise Sorel

Pas de Problème: see *No Problem!*

Un Pasaje de Ida
Dominican Republic 1988 90m colour
Producciones Testimonio (Agliberto Melendez)
aka: *A One-Way Ticket*
A ship's captain, who is smuggling 40 men to America, panics when police come aboard to search the vessel.
A competent exposé of high-level corruption and low-level greed which gains some resonance from its harrowing climax, based as it is on a true story.
w Agliberto Melendez, Adelso Cass, Danilo Taveras *d* Agliberto Melendez *ph* Pedro Guzman Cordero *m* Rafael Solano *pd* Orlando Menicucci *ed* Pericles Mejia
☆ Horacio Veloz, Miguel Buccarelli, Victor Checo, Felix German, Pepito Guerra, Nini German, Giovanni Cruz, Delta Soto

Pasazerka: see *Passenger*

Pascali's Island *
GB 1988 104m Metrocolor
Virgin/Avenue Pictures/Initial/Film Four International
On an Aegean island, a Turkish spy and an English con man attempt to double-cross one another.
Elegant period drama full of an understated sexual tension.
wd James Dearden *novel* Barry Unsworth *ph* Roger Deakins *m* Loek Dikker *pd* Andrew Mollo *ed* Edward Marnier
☆ *Ben Kingsley, Charles Dance, Helen Mirren*, Stefan Gryff, George Murcell, Nadim Sawalha, T. P. McKenna, Sheila Allan

Pasqualino Settebellezze: see *Seven Beauties*

The Passage
GB 1978 98m Eastmancolor Technovision
Hemdale/Passage/Lester Goldsmith-Maurice Binder (John Quested)
A Basque shepherd guides a scientist and his family from occupied France over the mountains into Spain.
Routine war suspenser given an unnecessary taint of sadism. Only those addicted to unpleasant detail will enjoy it.
w Bruce Micolaysen *novel The Perilous Passage* by Bruce Micolaysen *d* J. Lee Thompson *ph* Michael Reed *m* Michael J. Lewis
☆ Anthony Quinn, James Mason, Malcolm McDowell, Patricia Neal, Kay Lenz, Paul Clemens, Christopher Lee
'Utter rubbish.' – *Malcolm McDowell*

Le Passage du Rhin: see *The Crossing of the Rhine*

Passage Home
GB 1955 102m bw
GFD/Group Films (Julian Wintle)
In 1931, tensions run high on a merchant ship when the captain accepts an attractive girl as passenger from South America.
Obvious melodrama complete with drunken captain and storm at sea; not badly done if it must be done at all.
w William Fairchild *novel* Richard Armstrong *d* Roy Baker *ph* Geoffrey Unsworth *m* Clifton Parker
☆ Peter Finch, Anthony Steel, Diane Cilento, Cyril Cusack, Geoffrey Keen, Hugh Griffith, Duncan Lamont, Bryan Forbes, Gordon Jackson, Michael Craig

A Passage to India **
GB 1984 163m Technicolor
EMI/John Brabourne-Richard Goodwin/HBO/John Heyman/Edward Sands
An English girl in India accuses an Indian doctor of rape.
Another film about India under the Raj seems somewhat redundant after The Jewel in the Crown, Gandhi *and* The Far Pavilions, *but at least under David Lean's direction this is intelligent and good to look at.*
novel E. M. Forster *play Santha Rama Rau* *ph* Ernest Day *m* Maurice Jarre *pd* John Box *wd/ed David Lean* *cos* Judith Moorcroft
☆ Judy Davis, Alec Guinness, Victor Banerjee, Peggy Ashcroft, James Fox, Nigel Havers, Richard Wilson, Antonia Pemberton, Michael Culver, Art Malik, Saeed Jaffrey, Ann Firbank, Clive Swift, Sandra Hotz
Peggy Ashcroft (supporting actress); music
best picture; direction; Judy Davis; adapted screenplay; photography; editing; art direction
Peggy Ashcroft

Passage to Marseilles *
US 1944 110m bw
Warner (Hal B. Wallis)
Convicts escape from Devil's Island and join the Free French.
A rare example of a film boasting flashbacks within flashbacks within flashbacks, this confusing if sometimes entertaining all-star saga is done to death by its unconvincing flagwaving endpapers which prevent it from being at all comparable with Casablanca, *as was clearly intended.*
w Casey Robinson, Jack Moffitt *story* Charles Nordhoff, James Hall *d* Michael Curtiz *ph* James Wong Howe *m* Max Steiner
☆ Humphrey Bogart, Michèle Morgan, Claude Rains, Philip Dorn, Sydney Greenstreet, Peter Lorre, Helmut Dantine, George Tobias, John Loder, Victor Francen, Eduardo Ciannelli
'Invincibly second rate.' – *Richard Mallet, Punch*

Passage West
US 1951 81m Technicolor
Pine-Thomas/Paramount
Religious pioneers headed west are menaced by escaped convicts.
Entertaining minor Western.
w Lewis R. Foster *story* Nedrick Young (Alvah Bessie) *d* Lewis R. Foster *ph* Loyal Griggs *m* Mahlon Merrick
☆ John Payne, Dennis O'Keefe, Arleen Whelan, Peter Hanson
† Because Bessie had been blacklisted, Nedrick Young fronted for him until he, too, was blacklisted.

Passager de la Pluie: see *Rider on the Rain*

Passe-Passe: see *Quicker than the Eye*

Passed Away
US 1992 96m Technicolor
Hollywood/Touchwood (Larry Brezner, Timothy Marx)
After his elderly father dies, and the family gathers for a wake, the eldest son decides it is time to take risks with his life.
Mundane domestic comedy, too predictable to be enjoyable; like its central character it settles for safety and familiarity.
wd Charlie Peters *ph* Arthur Albert *m* Richard Gibbs *pd* Catherine Hardwicke *ed* Harry Keramidas
☆ Bob Hoskins (Johnny Scanlan), Blair Brown (Amy Scanlan), Tim Curry (Boyd Pinter), Frances McDormand (Nora Scanlan), William Petersen (Frank Scanlan), Pamela Reed (Terry Scanlan), Peter Riegert (Peter Syracusa), Maureen Stapleton (Mary Scanlan), Nancy Travis (Cassie Slocombe), Jack Warden (Jack Scanlan)

Passenger *
Poland 1963 63m bw Dyaliscope
Kadr
original title: *Pasazerka*
A German woman on a liner sees a woman she thinks she recognizes, and realizes that it is one of her charges when she was an official in a concentration camp.
Minor but effective character drama, in essence an investigation of guilt. The director died during its making, so some scenes are replaced by still photographs.
wd Andrzej Munk *play* Zofia Posmysz-Piasecka *ph* Krzysztof Winiewicz
☆ Aleksandra Slaska, Anna Ciepielewska

'I used to be somebody else; but I traded myself in...'
The Passenger *
Italy/France/Spain 1975 119m Metrocolor
MGM/CCC/Concordia/CIPI (Carlo Ponti)
aka: *Profession: Reporter*
A TV reporter in a desert hotel changes identities with a dead man and finds he is now an African gun runner being drawn irresistibly towards his own death.
Pretty much in the style of Blow Up, *but this time with no frills of fashion or nudity to bring the public in. After this, Antonioni was given up by the commercial cinema.*
w Mark Peploe, Peter Wollen, Michelangelo Antonioni *d* Michelangelo Antonioni *ph* Luciano Tovoli *md* Ivan Vandor
☆ Jack Nicholson, Maria Schneider, Jenny Runacre, Ian Hendry
'A film of real romance, depth and power ... the very quintessence of cinema.' – *Michael Billington, Illustrated London News*

'He's an ex-cop with a bad mouth, a bad attitude, and a bad seat. For the terrorists on flight 163 ... he's very bad news.'
Passenger 57
US 1992 84m Technicolor
Warner (Lee Rich, Dan Paulson, Dylan Sellers)
An ex-cop goes into action when terrorists hijack his plane.
A Die Hard*-style thriller, entertaining enough although inevitably predictable.*
w David Loughery, Dan Gordon, Stewart Raffill *d* Kevin Hooks *ph* Mark Irwin *m* Stanley Clarke *pd* Jaymes Hinkle *ed* Richard Nord
☆ Wesley Snipes, Bruce Payne, Tom Sizemore, Alex Datcher, Bruce Greenwood, Robert Hooks, Elizabeth Hurley, Michael Horse
'About as fresh as an in-flight meal. Even so, it has a certain appetizing quality about it.' – *Guardian*

Passing Clouds: see *Spellbound*

The Passing of the Third Floor Back *
GB 1935 90m bw
Gaumont (Ivor Montagu)
A Christ-like visitor stays at a London boarding house and changes the lives of the inmates.
Competent film version of a famous, sentimental, dated play.
w Michael Hogan, Alma Reville *play* Jerome K. Jerome *d* Berthold Viertel *ph* Curt Courant *m* Hubert Bath
☆ *Conrad Veidt*, René Ray, Anna Lee, Frank Cellier, Mary Clare, Beatrix Lehmann, Cathleen Nesbitt, Sara Allgood
'Drawing power of the book, the play, the picturization and the star should, on form, be invincible.' – *Variety*
'The pious note has been toned down, the milk of human kindness has been agreeably watered, and the types in the small London private hotel are observed with malicious realism.' – *Graham Greene*

Passion: see *Madame Dubarry (1919)*

Passion
US 1954 84m Technicolor
Benedict Bogeaus/RKO
Jealousy erupts between ranchers in Spanish California.
Peculiarly titled Western of no merit whatsoever.
w Beatrice A. Dresher, Joseph Leytes *d* Allan Dwan *ph* John Alton *m* Louis Forbes
☆ Yvonne de Carlo, Cornel Wilde, Raymond Burr, Lon Chaney Jnr, Rodolfo Acosta, John Qualen

Passion *
France 1982 88m Eastmancolor
Artificial Eye/Sonimage/Sara Films/A2/Film et Video Productions (Alain Sarde)
A Polish film director has an affair with the wife of a factory owner who is trying to cope with a threatened strike.
Visually complex examination of film-making, work, love and betrayal.
wd Jean-Luc Godard *ph* Raoul Coutard *m* Ravel, Mozart and others *ad* Serge Marzolff
☆ Isabelle Huppert, Hanna Schygulla, Michel Piccoli, Jerzy Radziwilowicz, László Szabó, Jean-François Stevenin, Patrick Bonnel, Sophie Loucachevsky

Passion Fish
US 1992 134m DuArt
Atchafalaya (Sarah Green, Maggie Renzi)
A new nurse with problems of her own gives a crippled TV actress a reason to live.
A well-acted but constricting domestic drama.
wd John Sayles *ph* Roger Deakins *m* Mason Daring *pd* Dan Bishop, Dianna Freas *ed* John Sayles
☆ Mary McDonnell, Alfre Woodard, David Strathairn, Vondie Curtis-Hall, Nora Dunn, Sheila Kelley, Angela Bassett, Leo Burmester
'Pic has a measure of charm, plenty of validity and some fine scenes, but lacks the intensity that would have made it galvanizing or transcendent.' – *Variety*
Mary McDonnell; John Sayles

Passion Flower
US 1930 78m bw
MGM
Two rich girls marry beneath them.
Tedious romantic drama about class and true love.
w Martin Flavin, L. E. Johnson, Edith Fitzgerald *novel* Kathleen Norris *d* William de Mille
☆ Kay Francis, Kay Johnson, Charles Bickford, Lewis Stone, ZaSu Pitts, Dickie Moore, Winter Hall
'A flock of talent, but talent doesn't always count on a marquee.' – *Variety*

A Passion for Murder
Canada 1992 92m colour
The Fare/Actra (Robert Vince, Vonnie von Helmont)
aka: *Black Ice*
Following the death of the corrupt politician who was her lover, a female secret agent enlists the help of a friendly taxi driver when she is stalked by a killer from the CIA.
A chase thriller taken at a too-leisurely pace, and demonstrating too great an interest in the passing landscape, to maintain much suspense.
w Arne Olsen, John Alan Schwartz *d* Neill Fearnley *ph* David Geddes *m* Asmin Bahtia *pd* Deanna Rhode *ed* Alan Lee
☆ Joanna Pacula, Michael Nouri, Michael Ironside, Lee J. Campbell, Victor Cowie, Mickey Jones

'When nature divides, the spirit unites.'
Passion in the Desert *
US 1997 93m colour
Fine Line/Roland (Jamil Dehlavi, Lavinia Currier)
Lost in the Sahara, a Napoleonic officer forms a loving relationship with a female leopard.
An unusual and imaginative movie that manages without much dialogue to raise philosophical questions of man's place within the natural world.
w Lavinia Currier, Martin Edmunds *novella Honoré de Balzac* *d* Lavinia Currier *ph* Alexei Rodionov *m* Joseph Nieto *pd* Amanda McArthur *ed* Nicolas Gaster
☆ Ben Daniels, Michel Piccoli, Paul Meston, Kenneth Collard, Nadi Odeh

'If You Go Down To The Woods Tonight...'

The Passion of Darkly Noon
GB/Germany/Belgium 1995 101m colour
Entertainment/Fugitive/Die Hauskunst/Keytsman (Dominic Anciano, Frank Henschke, Alain Keytsman)

A 17-year-old runaway from a strict religious community is given shelter by a carpenter and the woman he lives with.
Portentous and overwrought fable, involving incest and murder, full of symbols that will no doubt mean something to someone.
wd Philip Ridley *ph* John de Borman *m* Nick Bicât *pd* Hubert Pouillé *ed* Leslie Healey
☆ Brendan Fraser, Ashley Judd, Viggo Mortensen, Loren Dean, Grace Zabriskie, Lou Myers, Kate Harper
'Looks and sounds like a B-movie with symbolic pretensions.' – *Derek Malcolm, Guardian*

The Passion of Joan of Arc **
France 1928 110m bw silent
Société Générale des Films
original title: *La Passion de Jeanne d'Arc*
On her last day on Earth, Joan of Arc is subjected to five increasingly threatening interrogations before being burned at the stake.
Austerely moving drama, using close-ups to give intense scrutiny to Joan and her accusers, drawing in the audience to become involved in the action.
w Carl Dreyer, Joseph Delteil *d* *Carl Dreyer* *ph* *Rudolph Maté* *ad* Hermann Warm, Jean Hugo *ed* Carl Dreyer
☆ *Renée Falconetti*, Eugène Silvain, Maurice Schutz, Michel Simon, Antonin Artaud, Louis Ravet, André Berley, Jean d'Yid
'One of the greatest of all movies ... Falconetti's Joan may be the finest performance ever recorded on film.' – *Pauline Kael*
'Isn't worth a dollar to any commercial regular picture theatre in the US.' – *Variety*
† Lilian Gish was first considered for the role of Joan. Falconetti never made another film. After its first showing the film was cut by the French authorities and was banned by the British until 1930.

Passion: The Story of Percy Grainger *
Australia/US 1999 98m Technicolor
AFFC/Hollywood Partners/Movie Network (Matt Carroll)
In 1914, the Australian pianist and composer Percy Grainger enjoys success in London while involved in a seemingly-incestuous relationship with his domineering, syphilitic mother, and a sado-masochistic one with a young musician who wants to marry him.
Good acting and some attractive locations enliven a drama that seems constrained by its period setting; the narrative requires a more flamboyant approach.
w Don Watson *screenplay* George and Peter Goldsworthy *play* *Percy & Rose* by Rob George *d* Peter Duncan *ph* *Martin McGrath* *md* Christine Woodruff *pd* *Murray Picknett* *ed* Simon Martin *cos* *Terry Ryan*
☆ Barbara Hershey (Rose), Richard Roxburgh (Percy), Emily Woof (Karen Holten), Claudia Karvan (Alfhild de Luce), Simon Burke (Herman Sandby), Linda Cropper (Mrs Lowery), Julia Blake (Queen Alexandra), Bille Brown (John Grainger)
'A seductive mix for broad-minded buffs of Grainger's oeuvre, but likely to prove of limited appeal to general auds.' – *Derek Elley, Variety*
† John Bird's biography *Percy Grainger* was also used for research.

A Passion to Kill
US 1994 93m colour
A-Pix/Rysher (Bruce Cohn Curtis)
aka: *Rules of Obsession*
A psychiatrist falls for his best friend's wife, who may be a killer.
Dull, totally predictable thriller that is most likely to turn up as a filler on late-night TV; even there, it is best avoided.
w William Delligan *d* Rick King *ph* Paul Ryan *m* Robert Sprayberry *pd* Ivo Cristante *ed* David H. Lloyd
☆ Scott Bakula (David), Chelsea Field (Diana), Sheila Kelley (Beth), John Getz (Jerry), Rex Smith (Ted), Eddie Vélez (Morales), Michael Warren (Martindale), Michael Cavanaugh (Robinson), France Nuyen (Lou Mazaud)
'An entirely formulaic soft-sex soap'n'slasher indistinguishable from the hundreds of cable-ready pix already clogging up the airwaves.' – *Steven Gaydos, Variety*

The Passionate Friends **
GB 1948 91m bw
GFD/Cineguild (Ronald Neame)
US title: *One Woman's Story*
A woman marries an older man, then meets again her young lover.
A simple and obvious dramatic situation is tricked out with flashbacks and the inimitable high style of its director to make a satisfying entertainment.
w Eric Ambler *novel* H. G. Wells *d* David Lean *ph* Guy Green *m* Richard Addinsell
☆ Ann Todd, Trevor Howard, Claude Rains, Betty Ann Davies, Isabel Dean, Arthur Howard, Wilfrid Hyde-White
'Mr Lean plants his clues with the certainty of a master of the detective story, and heightens their effect with a sure handling of camera and sound track.' – *The Times*
† Ronald Neame began as director, but was replaced by David Lean, his partner in Cineguild, and instead took over the role of producer from Eric Ambler. Lean replaced Marius Goring with Trevor Howard.

The Passionate Plumber
US 1932 73m bw
MGM
A woman hires a professional lover to fend off the man she really loves but thinks she shouldn't have.
Much revamped farce version of a comedy made straight in 1927 and 1942. All flopped, but this is the worst.
w Laurence E. Johnson *play* *Her Cardboard Lover* by Frederick Lonsdale *d* Edward Sedgwick
☆ Buster Keaton, Jimmy Durante, Irene Purcell, Polly Moran, Gilbert Roland, Mona Maris, Maude Eburne
'Another lay-me-down-to-sleeper for box offices.' – *Variety*

The Passionate Sentry: see *Who Goes There?*

The Passionate Stranger
GB 1956 97m bw/Eastmancolor
British Lion/Beaconsfield (Peter Rogers, Gerald Thomas)
US title: *A Novel Affair*
A lady novelist bases a character on her virile chauffeur; he reads the book and thinks she fancies him.
Feeble comedy, half of it consisting of a dramatization of the heroine's very dull novel.
w Muriel and Sydney Box *d* Muriel Box *ph* Otto Heller *m* Humphrey Searle
☆ Ralph Richardson, Margaret Leighton, Carlo Justini, Patricia Dainton, Marjorie Rhodes, Thorley Walters, Frederick Piper

Passionate Summer
GB 1958 104m Eastmancolor
Briar/Kenneth Harper
A divorced headmaster at a Jamaican school is loved by three women.
Silly melodrama with splendid backgrounds ruined by poor colour.
w Joan Henry *novel* *The Shadow and the Peak* by Richard Mason *d* Rudolph Cartier *ph* Ernest Steward *m* Angelo Lavagnino
☆ Virginia McKenna, Bill Travers, Yvonne Mitchell, Alexander Knox, Ellen Barrie, Carl Mohner
'The climactic hurricane does little to dispel the overall feeling of emotional suffocation.' – *MFB*

La Passione
GB 1996 109m colour
Warner/Fugitive (Chris Rea)
A working-class boy makes a fortune with a secret family formula and becomes a racing driver, but does not find happiness.
A movie of quite startling banality, little more than an elongated music video.
w Chris Rea *d* John B. Hobbs *ph* Roger Bonnici *m* Chris Rea *pd* Garry Freeman *ed* Paul Endacott
☆ Shirley Bassey, Sean Gallagher, Thomas Orange, Paul Shane, Jan Ravens, Carmen Silvera, Keith Barron
'The style is strained and vacuous.' – *George Perry, Sunday Times*

Passione d'Amore
Italy/France 1982 119m Eastmancolor
Connoisseur/Rizzoli Films/Massfilm/Marceau Cocinor (Franco Committou, Gino Santarelli)

A neurotic and unattractive woman becomes infatuated with a handsome young army captain.
Turgid 19th-century melodrama.
w Ruggero Maccari, Ettore Scola *novel* *Fosca* by Ignio Ugo Tarchetti *d* Ettore Scola *ph* Claudio Ragona *m* Armando Trovagoli *ad* Fiorenzo Senese *ed* Raimondo Crociani
☆ Valeria D'Obici, Bernard Giraudeau, Jean-Louis Trintignant, Massimo Girotti, Bernard Blier, Laura Antonelli

Passport to Destiny
US 1943 65m bw
RKO (Herman Schlom)
During the Second World War, a London charlady takes her scrubbing brush and bucket and makes her way to Berlin to assassinate Hitler, protected by her dead husband's lucky charm.
One of the silliest movies ever made, even by the standards of wartime propaganda: the risible narrative makes no sense at all, though Lanchester acts as if her life depended upon her performance.
w Val Burton, Muriel Roy Bolton *d* Ray McCarey *ph* Jack Mackenzie *m* Roy Webb *md* C. Bakaleinikoff *ad* Albert D'Agostino, Jack Okey *ed* Robert Swink
☆ Elsa Lanchester, Gordon Oliver, Lenore Aubert, Lionel Royce, Fritz Feld, Joseph Vitale, Gavin Muir, Lloyd Corrigan, Anita Bolster, Lumsden Hare
† Charles Laughton appears in a photograph as Elsa Lanchester's husband.

Passport to Fame: see *The Whole Town's Talking*

Passport to Hell
US 1932 72m bw
Fox
A woman tainted by scandal moves from country to country and marries a German commandant in the Cameroons to avoid internment.
Reasonably lively drama which ends less well than it began.
w Bradley King, Leon Gordon, Harry Hervey *d* Frank Lloyd
☆ Elissa Landi, Paul Lukas, Warner Oland, Alexander Kirkland, Donald Crisp
'Not a de luxer; Broadway spotted because of the product shortage.' – *Variety*

Passport to Pimlico **
GB 1949 84m bw
Ealing (E. V. H. Emmett)

Part of a London district is discovered to belong to Burgundy, and the inhabitants find themselves free of rationing restrictions.
A cleverly detailed little comedy which inaugurated the best period of Ealing, its preoccupation with suburban man and his foibles. Not exactly satire, but great fun, and kindly with it.
w T. E. B. Clarke *d* *Henry Cornelius* *ph* Lionel Banes *m* *Georges Auric*
☆ Stanley Holloway, *Margaret Rutherford*, Basil Radford, Naunton Wayne, Hermione Baddeley, John Slater, Paul Dupuis, Jane Hylton, Raymond Huntley, Betty Warren, Barbara Murray, Sydney Tafler
'One of the most felicitous and funny films since the age of the René Clair comedies.' – *C. A. Lejeune*
† The film was based on a genuine news item. The Canadian government presented to the Netherlands the room in which Princess Juliana was to bear a child.
T. E. B. Clarke

Passport to Shame
GB 1959 88m bw
United/Cory/Eros
US title: *Room 43*
A taxi driver rescues his girl from the white slave business.
Would-be seamy melodrama which just about serves its purpose.
w Patrick Alexander *d* Alvin Rakoff *ph* Jack Asher *m* Ken Jones
☆ Eddie Constantine, Diana Dors, Odile Versois, Herbert Lom, Brenda de Banzie, Robert Brown

Passport to Suez
US 1943 71m bw
Columbia (Wallace MacDonald)
In Alexandria, the Lone Wolf foils Nazi spies who steal British plans that will enable them to destroy the Suez canal.
An over-complicated minor thriller, more interested in propaganda than suspense.
w John Stone *story* Alden Nash *d* André de Toth *ph* L. W. O'Connell *md* M. W. Stoloff *ad* Lionel Banks *ed* Mel Thorsen
☆ Warren William, Eric Blore, Ann Savage, Robert Stanford, Sheldon Leonard, Lloyd Bridges, Gavin Muir
† It was André de Toth's first feature in the US. According to *Fragments*, his autobiography, he was told 'the script stinks, but do the best you can'. The film had a seven-day shooting schedule and he finished it seven days late.

Passport to Treason
GB 1956 80m bw
Mid Century/Eros
A detective traces the death of his colleague to fascists working within an alleged peace group.
Stock melodramatic situations straightforwardly presented make this a watchable support.
w Kenneth Hales, Norman Hudis *d* Robert S. Baker *ph* Monty Berman *m* Stanley Black
☆ Rod Cameron, Lois Maxwell, Clifford Evans, John Colicos, Ballard Berkeley

The Password Is Courage *
GB 1962 116m bw
MGM/Andrew and Virginia Stone
In Europe during World War II, Sgt-Major Charles Coward has a career of escapes and audacious anti-Nazi exploits.
Lively, slightly over-humorous account of one man's war, well mounted and shot entirely on location.
wd Andrew L. Stone *biography* John Castle *ph* David Boulton
☆ Dirk Bogarde, Maria Perschy, Alfred Lynch, Nigel Stock, Reginald Beckwith
'The experiences are, it seems, mainly true but they do not seem so.' – *Guardian*

Past Midnight
US 1991 96m Foto-Kem
Cinetel (Lisa M. Hansen)

A social worker begins an affair with a paroled prisoner, convicted of murdering his pregnant wife.
Utterly predictable thriller, taken at a slow pace that does nothing to disguise its deficiencies.
w Frank Norwood *d* Jan Eliasberg *ph* Robert Yeoman *m* Steve Barteck *pd* Sharon Seymour *ed* Christopher Rouse
☆ Rutger Hauer, Natasha Richardson, Clancy Brown, Guy Bond, Ernie Lively, Tom Wright

Pastor Hall *
GB 1940 97m bw
Charter (John Boulting)
The story of a German village pastor shot for denouncing the Nazis. Inspired by the life of Martin Niemöller (1892–1984), who survived eight years in concentration camps.
A courageous film of its time, not very interesting dramatically or cinematically.
w Leslie Arliss, Haworth Bromley, Anna Reiner *play* Ernst Toller *d* Roy Boulting *ph* Max Greene
☆ *Wilfrid Lawson*, Nova Pilbeam, Seymour Hicks, Marius Goring, Percy Walsh, Brian Worth, Peter Cotes, Hay Petrie

'Not much meat on her, but what there is is cherce!'

Pat and Mike **
US 1952 95m bw
MGM (Lawrence Weingarten)

A small-time sports promoter takes on a female intellectual multi-champion.
A comedy which amuses because of its star playing, but doesn't really develop. All very easy going, with guest appearances from sporting personalities.
w Ruth Gordon, Garson Kanin *d* George Cukor *ph* William Daniels *m* David Raksin
☆ *Spencer Tracy*, *Katharine Hepburn*, Aldo Ray, William Ching, Sammy White, Jim Backus, Phyllis Povah
'They do not, like the Lunts, give the impression of a rigid calculated effect; rather, they complement and stimulate each other.' – *MFB*
script

Pat Garrett and Billy the Kid

US 1973 106m Metrocolor Panavision
MGM (Gordon Carroll)

An outlaw-turned-sheriff tracks down his former partner.

Blood-spattered version of a Western legend, with violence always to the fore, accentuated by the impossibility of listening to the dialogue because of poor direction and recording.

w Rudolph Wurlitzer *d* Sam Peckinpah *ph* John Coquillon *m* Bob Dylan

☆ James Coburn, Kris Kristofferson, Bob Dylan, Richard Jaeckel, Katy Jurado, Slim Pickens, Chill Wills, Jason Robards Jnr

'A sombre, intense, downbeat essay on the truth behind the legend and the legend behind the truth.' – *Sight and Sound*

'Shows what Peckinpah can do when he doesn't put his mind to it.' – *Stanley Kauffmann*

'A rash adventure in inadvertent self-parody.' – *William S. Pechter*

'Ambitious, erotic, peculiarly unrealized...' – *Pauline Kael, New Yorker*

'Laughter is contagious.'

Patch Adams

US 1998 115m DeLuxe
Universal/Blue Wolf-Farrell/Minoff-Bungalow 78 (Barry Kemp, Mike Farrell, Marvin Minoff, Charles Newirth)

A doctor discovers that clowning promotes health, and sets up his own hospital to prove it.

Cloyingly sweet drama that is based on a true story but here bears no resemblance to any reality; it is merely an opportunity for Williams to be alternately manic and misty-eyed.

w Steve Oedekerk *book* *Gesundheit – Good Health Is a Laughing Matter* by Hunter Doherty Adams with Maureen Mylander *d* Tom Shadyac *ph* Phedon Papamichael *m* Marc Shaiman *pd* Linda DeScenna *ed* Don Zimmerman

☆ Robin Williams, Daniel London, Monica Potter, Philip Seymour Hoffman, Bob Gunton, Peter Coyote, Josef Sommer, Irma P. Hall, Frances Lee McCain, Harvey Presnell, Daniella Kuhn, Jake Bowen, Michael Jeter, Harold Gould, Richard Kiley

'A comedy that neglects the humble task of making an audience laugh in favour of the more vainglorious task of delivering a 90-minute lecture on the positive benefits laughter has for your kidneys.' – *Tom Shone, Sunday Times*

Ᾱ Marc Shaiman

A Patch of Blue *

US 1965 105m bw Panavision
MGM/Pandro S. Berman

A blind girl who lives in a slum is helped by a Negro with whom she falls in love without realizing his colour.

Polished tearjerker with racial overtones; nicely done for those who can take it.

wd Guy Green *novel* *Be Ready with Bells and Drums* by Elizabeth Kata *ph* Robert Burks *m* Jerry Goldsmith

☆ Sidney Poitier, Elizabeth Hartman, Shelley Winters, Wallace Ford, Ivan Dixon, Elisabeth Fraser, John Qualen

🏆 Shelley Winters

Ᾱ Robert Burks; Jerry Goldsmith; Elizabeth Hartman

'He wants YOU to have his baby!'

Paternity

US 1981 93m Movielab
Paramount (Jerry Tokofsky)

A middle-aged bachelor decides to father a son via a hired mother, who will then return the child to him.

Tastelessly up-dated Hollywood romance with predictable complications. Not worth sitting through.

w Charlie Peters *d* David Steinberg *ph* Bobby Byrne *m* David Shire

☆ Burt Reynolds, Beverly D'Angelo, Norman Fell, Paul Dooley, Elizabeth Ashley, Lauren Hutton, Juanita Moore

Pather Panchali ****

India 1955 115m bw
Government of West Bengal

In a small Bengal village, the son of a would-be writer grows up in poverty and tragedy before setting off with what remains of the family to seek a living in Benares.

A remarkable first film of a director now famous, showing that people are much the same though the details of their daily lives may be different. The pace may be slow but the content is mainly absorbing.

wd Satyajit Ray *novels* Bhibuti Bashan Bannerjee *ph* Subrata Mitra *m* Ravi Shankar

☆ Kanu Banerjee, Karuna Banerjee, Uma Das Gupta, Subir Bannerjee, Chunibala

'It has been left to the Indian cinema to give us a picture of a childhood which preserves under the shadow of experience not only its innocence but its gaiety.' – *Dilys Powell*

† The film was the first part of a trilogy and was followed by *Aparajito* (1956) and *The World of Apu* (1959).

Pathfinder **

Norway 1987 86m colour
Guild/Filmkameratene/Norsk Film (John M. Jacobson)

original title: *Ofelas*

A gang of ruthless raiders capture a 16-year-old boy and force him to lead them to his village so that they may plunder it.

Based on an ancient Lapp folk-tale, this is a simple, direct, marvellously exciting adventure shot in a snow- and ice-bound landscape.

wd Nils Gaup *ph* Erling Thurmann-Andersen *m* Nils-Aslak Valkeapaa *pd* Harald Egede-Nissen *ed* Niels Pagh Andersen

☆ Mikkel Gaup, Nils Utsi, Svein Scharffenberg, Helgi Skulason, Sverre Porsanger, Svein Birger Olsen

Ᾱ best foreign film

Paths of Glory ****

US 1957 86m bw
UA/Bryna (James B. Harris)

In 1916 in the French trenches, three soldiers are courtmartialled for cowardice.

Incisive melodrama chiefly depicting the corruption and incompetence of the high command; the plight of the soldiers is less interesting. The trench scenes are the most vivid ever made, and the rest is shot in genuine castles, with resultant difficulties of lighting and recording; the overall result is an overpowering piece of cinema.

w Stanley Kubrick, Calder Willingham, Jim Thompson *novel* Humphrey Cobb *d* *Stanley Kubrick* *ph* *Georg Krause* *m* Gerald Fried

☆ *Kirk Douglas*, *Adolphe Menjou*, *George Macready*, Wayne Morris, Richard Anderson, Ralph Meeker, Timothy Carey

'A bitter and biting tale, told with stunning point and nerve-racking intensity.' – *Judith Crist*

'Beautifully performed, staged, photographed, cut and scored.' – *Colin Young*

The Patient Vanishes: see *This Man Is Dangerous*

Patrick

Australia 1978 110m colour
AIFC (Anthony I. Ginnane, Richard Franklin)

A new nurse discovers that an apparently comatose young man, hospitalized after killing his mother and her lover, possesses psychic powers that can kill those he dislikes.

Slick but derivative thriller, well enough done in its low-budget way but lacking suspense as well as originality.

w Everett de Roche *d* Richard Franklin *ph* Don McAlpine *m* Brian May *ad* Leslie Binns *ed* Edward McQueen-Mason

☆ Susan Penhaligon, Robert Helpmann, Rod Mullinar, Bruce Barry, Julia Blake, Helen Hemingway, Robert Thompson

'The film's intrinsic interest is minimal.' – *MFB*

† The US release ran for 96m.

Patrick the Great *

US 1944 88m bw
Universal (Howard Benedict)

An actor whose career is waning is jealous of his young son.

Slick teenage family comedy, virtually a one-man show for O'Connor.

w Jane Hall, Bertram Millhauser, Dorothy Bennett, Frederick Kohner, Ralph Block *d* Frank Ryan *ph* Frank Redman *m* Hans Salter *ad* John B. Goodman, Abraham Grossman *ed* Ted J. Kent

☆ *Donald O'Connor*, Donald Cook, Peggy Ryan, Frances Dee, Eve Arden, Thomas Gomez, Gavin Muir, Andrew Tombes

The Patriot **

US 1928 110m approx (24 fps) bw silent
Paramount (Ernst Lubitsch)

Mad Czar Paul I is assassinated by his chief adviser for the good of the state.

Historical melodrama with a good many comedy touches: the director makes the most of both aspects, but they don't in the end hang together despite bravura acting.

w *Hans Kraly* *novel* Alfred Neumann *d* *Ernst Lubitsch* *ph* Bert Glennon *ad* Hans Dreier

☆ *Emil Jannings*, Lewis Stone, Florence Vidor, Neil Hamilton

'I believe this picture the most suggestive we ever ran. Just another reason why we need censorship. Small-town exhibitors need clean pictures.' – *Ohio exhibitor's report in Motion Picture Herald*

🏆 Hans Kraly

Ᾱ best picture; Ernst Lubitsch; Lewis Stone; Hans Dreier

The Patriot

West Germany 1979 120m bw/colour
The Other Cinema/Kairos Film/ZDF (Alexander Kluge)

original title: *Die Patriotin*

A schoolteacher looks for new ways of presenting the history of Germany.

Intellectually austere examination of Germany's past and future, using newsreels, commentary and documentary footage; as cinema it is inert and condescending.

wd Alexander Kluge *ph* Thomas Mauch, Jörg Schmidt-Reitwein, Werner Lring, Gunther Hörmann *ed* Beate Mainka-Jellinghaus

☆ Hannelore Hoger, Alfred Edel, Alexander von Eschwege, Hans Heckel, Beate Holle, Curt Jürgens, Dieter Mainka, Willi Münch

The Patriot

US 1986 88m Foto-Kem
Crown International/Patriot (Michael Bennett)

A former commando, now a diver on oil rigs, rejoins the navy to track down terrorists who have stolen some nuclear warheads.

Dull and jingoistic action movie which is always predictable, and also clumsy and contrived.

w Andy Ruben, Katt Shea Ruben *d* Frank Harris *ph* Frank Harris *m* Jay Ferguson *ad* Brad Einhorn *ed* Richard E. Westover

☆ Gregg Henry, Simone Griffeth, Michael J. Pollard, Jeff Conaway, Stack Pierce, Leslie Nielsen

The Patriot *

US/Germany 2000 165m DeLuxe Panavision
Columbia/Mutual/Centropolis (Dean Devlin, Mark Gordon, Gary Levinsohn)

In the 1770s, after one of his sons is killed and another wounded, a Southern plantation owner joins the war of independence against the British.

Simple-minded and inaccurate history, in which Gibson does his familiar Mad Max turn, as an out-of-control action hero; but the movie, though overlong, has a commendable energy and verve.

w Robert Rodat *d* Roland Emmerich *ph* Caleb Deschanel *m* John Williams *pd* Kirk M. Petruccelli *ed* David Brenner *cos* Deborah L. Scott

☆ Mel Gibson (Benjamin Martin), Heath Ledger (Gabriel Martin), Joely Richardson (Charlotte Selton), Jason Isaacs (Col William Tavington), Chris Cooper (Col Harry Burwell), Tcheky Karyo (Jean Villeneuve), Rene Auberjonois (Rev Oliver), Lisa Brenner (Anne Howard), Tom Wilkinson (Gen Cornwallis), Donal Logue (Dan Scott), Leon Rippy (John Billings), Adam Baldwin (Loyalist/Captain Wilkins), Gregory Smith (Thomas Martin), Mika Boorem (Margaret Martin)

'If Nazis had won the war in Europe, and their propaganda ministry had decided to make a film about the American Revolution, *The Patriot* is the sort of movie you could expect to see.' – *Jonathan Foreman, Salon.com*

'Begins brightly, concludes on a tiresome and formulaic note. A shame.' – *James Mottram, Film Review*

Ᾱ Caleb Deschanel; John Williams; sound (Kevin O'Connell, Greg P. Russell, Lee Orloff)

'Not for honour. Not for country. For his wife and child.'

Patriot Games

US 1992 117m Technicolor Panavision
UIP/Paramount (Mace Neufeld, Robert Rehme)

In London, a former CIA agent shoots an IRA terrorist in a street battle and becomes a target for the organization's revenge on his return to the States.

Muddled and melodramatic, it relies on nationalistic clichés and violent set-pieces rather than narrative coherence; it is certainly not for posterity.

w W. Peter Iliff, Donald Stewart, Steven Zaillian *novel* Tom Clancy *d* Phillip Noyce *ph* Donald McAlpine *m* James Horner *pd* Joseph Nemec III *ed* Neil Travis, William Hoy

☆ Harrison Ford, Anne Archer, Patrick Bergin, Sean Bean, Thora Birch, James Fox, Samuel L. Jackson, Polly Walker, J. E. Freeman, James Earl Jones, Richard Harris, Hugh Fraser, David Threlfall, Alun Armstrong

'A star turn and smart action sequences enliven an otherwise abstract film.' – *Time*

'It flounders from one absurdity to another, with results that are hilarious when they aren't insulting.' – *Adam Mars-Jones, Independent*

'Mindless, morally repugnant and ineptly directed to boot.' – *Variety*

El Patrullero: see *Highway Patrolman*

The Patsy *

US 1928 80m approx (24 fps) bw silent
MGM (Irving Thalberg)

GB title: *The Politic Flapper*

Tired of being taken for granted, a girl puts on a surprising show for her family.

Amusing comedy which, in sound, might have made Miss Davies a bigger star than she ever became.

w Agnes Christine Johnston *play* Barry Connors *d* King Vidor

☆ *Marion Davies*, Marie Dressler, Lawrence Gray, Del Henderson, Jane Winton

'Marion Davies is in my opinion Filmland's Funniest Female, the only one I would mention in the same breath as Charlie Chaplin.' – *A. P. Herbert, Punch*

The Patsy

US 1964 101m Technicolor
Paramount/Jerry Lewis (E. J. Glucksman)

Hollywood executives try to mould a bellboy to replace a deceased comedian.

A few mildly funny scenes scarcely atone for a long raucous comedy in which the star upstages his betters.

wd Jerry Lewis *ph* Wallace Kelley *m* David Raksin

☆ Jerry Lewis, Everett Sloane, Peter Lorre, John Carradine, Phil Harris, Hans Conried, Ina Balin

'Inside the skyscraper jungle! Ruthless men and ambitious women clawing for control of a billion-dollar empire!'

Patterns ***

US 1956 88m bw
UA/Jed Harris, Michael Myerberg

GB title: *Patterns of Power*

The tough boss of a New York corporation forces a showdown between a young executive and the older ineffectual man who he hopes will resign.

Tense little boardroom melodrama with domestic asides, one of the best of the filmed TV plays of the mid-fifties.

w *Rod Serling* *play* Rod Serling *d* *Fielder Cook* *ph* Boris Kaufman

☆ Van Heflin, Everett Sloane, Ed Begley, Beatrice Straight, Elizabeth Wilson

Patterns of Power: see *Patterns*

Patti Rocks *

US 1987 87m colour
Premier/FilmDallas (Gwen Field, Gregory M. Cummins)

A married man takes an old, but estranged, friend on a long car ride to the home of his pregnant girlfriend.
Low-budget movie concentrating on character development, though the likelihood of the slobbish male and the sensitive woman ever being attracted to one another seems remote.
w David Burton Morris, Chris Mulkey, John Jenkins, Karen Landry d David Burton Morris ph Gregory M. Cummins m Doug Maynard ad Charlotte Whitaker ed Gregory M. Cummins
☆ Chris Mulkey, John Jenkins, Karen Landry, David L. Turk, Stephen Yoakam

'Nobody ever won a war by dying for his country. He won it by making the other poor dumb bastard die for his country!'

Patton ***

US 1969 171m DeLuxe Dimension 150
TCF (Frank McCarthy)

GB title: *Patton – Lust for Glory*
World War II adventures of an aggressive American general.
Brilliantly handled wartime character study which is also a spectacle and tries too hard to have it both ways, but as a piece of film-making is hard to beat.
w Francis Ford Coppola, Edmund H. North d *Franklin Schaffner* ph *Fred Koenekamp* m *Jerry Goldsmith* ad Urie McCleary, Gil Parrondo ed Hugh S. Fowler
☆ *George C. Scott*, Karl Malden, Michael Bates, Stephen Young, Michael Strong, Frank Latimore
'Here is an actor so totally immersed in his part that he almost makes you believe he is the man himself.' – *John Gillett*
best picture; script; Franklin Schaffner; George C. Scott; art direction; editing; sound (Douglas Williams, Don Bassman)
Fred Koenekamp; Jerry Goldsmith; special visual effects

Patton – Lust for Glory: see *Patton*

Patty Hearst *

US/GB 1988 104m DeLuxe
Entertainment/Atlantic Entertainment/Zenith (Marvin Worth)

After being kidnapped and imprisoned by a revolutionary group, a wealthy, privileged teenager joins in their terrorist activities.
Based on fact, though impressionistic in approach, it concerns itself, not always successfully, with questions of identity and personal responsibility.
w Nicholas Kazan book *Every Secret Thing* by Patricia Campbell Hearst with Alvin Moscow d Paul Schrader ph Bojan Bazelli, Stuart Barbee m Scott Johnson pd Jane Musky ed Michael R. Miller
☆ Natasha Richardson, William Forsythe, Ving Rhames, Frances Fisher, Jodi Long, Olivia Barash, Dana Delany, Marek Johnson, Kitty Swink, Peter Kowanko

Paula: see *Framed (1947)*

Paula

US 1952 80m bw
Columbia (Buddy Adler)
GB title: *The Silent Voice*
A barren wife causes a boy's deafness in an accident; she cures and adopts him.
Adequate woman's picture, a vehicle for a star and a luxuriant wardrobe.
w James Poe, William Sackheim d Rudolph Maté ph Charles Lawton Jnr m George Duning
☆ Loretta Young, Kent Smith, Alexander Knox, Tommy Rettig

'The journey of a thousand miles begins with a single parrot'

Paulie

US 1998 91m Technicolor
DreamWorks/Mutual Film (Mark Gordon, Gary Levinsohn, Allison Lyon Segan)

A wisecracking parrot explains to a cleaner how he came to be shut in the basement of an LA animal-study institute.
Intermittently enjoyable movie, though its style may not suit the kids for whom it is presumably intended.
w Laurie Craig d John Roberts ph Tony Pierce-Roberts m John Debney pd Dennis Washington ed Bruce Cannon sp animatronics: Stan Winston
☆ Gena Rowlands, Tony Shalhoub, Cheech Marin, Bruce Davison, Jay Mohr (voice), Trini Alvarado, Buddy Hackett, Hallie Kate Eisenberg, Matt Craven
'The script, intent on fable status, cannot stop wading into territory and language unsuitable for toddlers.' – *Geoff Brown, The Times*

Pauline at the Beach **

France 1983 94m colour
Gala/Les Films Du Losange/Les Films Ariane (Margaret Menegoz)

original title: *Pauline à la Plage*
A young girl observes her older cousin's disastrous holiday romances.
Delicately witty, eminently civilized entertainment.
wd Eric Rohmer ph Nestor Almendros m Jean-Louis Valero ed Cécile Decugis
☆ Arielle Dombasle, Amanda Langlet, Pascal Greggory, Féodor Atkine, Simon de la Brosse, Rosette

Pauline et Paulette *

Belgium/Netherlands/France 2001 78m colour
Columbia TriStar/K2/RTBF/VRT/K-Star/TF1/NCRV (Dominique Janne)

aka: *Pauline and Paulette*
Two elderly sisters squabble over which of them should care for their mentally retarded sibling.
Cool and detached account of provincial Belgian life that eschews easy answers in favour of flawed humanity.
w Lieven Debrauwer, Jacques Boon d Lieven Debrauwer ph Michel van Laer m Frederic Devreese ad Hilde Duyck ed Philippe Ravoet
☆ Dora van der Groen (Pauline), Ann Petersen (Paulette), Rosemarie Bergmans (Cecile), Idwig Stephane (Albert), Julienne De Bruyn (Martha)
'Rather than assaulting you with self-congratulatory tears, it leaves you with a bittersweet glow of wisdom and an appreciation of the small triumphs and difficult labors of love.' – *A. O. Scott, New York Times*
'A charmless, thoughtless movie.' – *Sight and Sound*

Paura e Amore: see *Three Sisters*

Paura nella Città dei Morti Viventi: see *City of The Living Dead*

The Pawnbroker **

US 1965 114m bw
Landau-Unger (Worthington Miner)

A Jew in slummy New York is haunted by his experiences in Nazi prison camps.
Engrossing, somewhat over-melodramatic character study, generally well done.
w David Friedkin, Morton Fine novel Edward Lewis Wallant d Sidney Lumet ph Boris Kaufman m Quincy Jones
☆ *Rod Steiger*, Brock Peters, Geraldine Fitzgerald, Jaime Sanchez, Thelma Oliver, Juano Hernandez
'Might have been a great film had the director been able to restrain his dual tendency towards artiness and towards slickness.' – *Judith Crist*
'The film is trite, and you can see the big pushes for powerful effects, yet it isn't negligible.' – *Pauline Kael*
Rod Steiger
Rod Steiger

Paws *

GB/Australia 1997 84m Atlab
Polygram/AFFC/Latent Image/NSWFTO (Andrena Finlay, Vicki Watson)
A Jack Russell terrier with the power of speech leads his new-found family to hidden wealth.
Pleasant, tail-wagging family film that is eager to please.
w Harry Crips d Karl Zwicky ph Geoff Burton m Mario Millo pd Stephen Jones-Evans ed Nicholas Holmes sp D-Film Services
☆ Billy Connolly (voice), Nathan Cavaleri, Emile Francois, Jon Petruzzi, Caroline Gillmer, Rachel Blake, Sandy Gore, Norman Kaye
'It's really quite lovable, not to mention fully housebroken of anything that might disturb younger viewers.' – *Leslie Felperin, Sight and Sound*

'Sometimes The Simplest Idea Can Make The Biggest Difference.'

Pay It Forward

US 2000 122m Technicolor
Warner/Bel Air/Tapestry (Steven Reuther, Peter Abrams, Robert Levy)

Asked to think of an idea to change the world, a young schoolboy suggests that each person do a good turn for three other people, each of whom must do a kind act to three others.
Here is a concept looking for a dramatic context to give it life, and finding only a fatal sentimental contrivance.
w Leslie Dixon book Catherine Ryan Hyde d Mimi Leder ph Oliver Stapleton m Thomas Newman pd Leslie Dilley ed David Rosenbloom cos Renee Ehrlich Kalfus
☆ Kevin Spacey (Eugene Simonet), Helen Hunt (Arlene McKinney), Haley Joel Osment (Trevor McKinney), Chris Chandler (Jay Mohr), James Caviezel (Jerry), Jon Bon Jovi (Ricki), Angie Dickinson (Grace), David Ramsey (Sidney), Gary Werntz (Thorsen)
'An unusual film that intelligently avoids numerous potential pitfalls even if its central earnestness is ultimately inescapable.' – *Todd McCarthy, Variety*
'Some of us are bound to take umbrage at the film's vulgar manipulations. Set in terminally tacky Las Vegas, *Pay It Forward* is as rigged as a casino slot machine, preying on people's hopes but paying off only for the house.' – *Richard Schickel, Time*

Pay or Die! *

US 1960 109m bw
Allied Artists (Richard Wilson)

In 1906, a New York Italian police detective forms a special squad to combat the Black Hand.
Tough, convincing period melodrama.
w Richard Wilson, Bertram Millhauser d *Richard Wilson* ph Lucien Ballard m David Raksin ad Fernando Carrere
☆ Ernest Borgnine, Alan Austin, Zohra Lampert, Robert F. Simon, Renata Vanni

'Get Ready To Root For The Bad Guy.'

Payback

US 1999 101m DeLuxe
Paramount/Icon (Bruce Davey)

Betrayed by his fellow crooks, a robber decides to get his revenge and his share of the loot.
Ugly, brutish thriller with drawn-out scenes of gratuitous violence.
w Brian Helgeland, Terry Hayes novel *The Hunter* by Richard Stark d Brian Helgeland ph Ericson Core m Chris Boardman pd Richard Hoover ed Kevin Stitt
☆ Mel Gibson (Porter), Gregg Henry (Val), Maria Bello (Rosie), Deborah Kara Unger (Lynn), David Paymer (Stegman), Bill Duke (Detective Hicks), Jack Conley (Detective Leary), William Devane (Carter), Kris Kristofferson (Bronson), John Glover (Phil), Lucy Alexis Liu (Pearl)
'A passable, intermittently enjoyable entertainment.' – *Variety*
'What one word might best describe *Payback*. How about "loathsome"?' – *Stephen Holden, New York Times*
† John Boorman's 1967 *Point Blank* (qv) is based on the same novel.
†† Gibson, whose company produced the movie, had a quarter of it remade by an unnamed director because he thought Helgeland's version lacked impact. In order to achieve its dark look, an image of the film in black and white was overlaid on the colour print.

Payday

US 1972 103m colour
Cinerama/Pumice/Fantasy (Ralph J. Gleason)

An over-age pop singer has personal problems which erupt into violence.
Well made, dislikeable melodrama.
w Don Carpenter d Daryl Duke ph Richard C. Glouner md Ed Bogas
☆ Rip Torn, Ahna Capri, Elayne Heilveil, Michael C. Gwynne
'Explores the Nashville-centered world of country with an easy authenticity which makes this nothing like a repetition of what has been before.' – *Charles Champlin*

Paydirt: see *There Goes the Neighborhood*

Paying the Penalty: see *Underworld*

Payment Deferred *

US 1932 75m bw
MGM (Irving Thalberg)
A man desperate for money poisons his wealthy nephew.
Watchable photographed play.
w Ernest Vajda, Claudine West play Jeffrey Dell d Lothar Mendes ph Merritt Gerstad
☆ Charles Laughton, Maureen O'Sullivan, Ray Milland, Dorothy Peterson, Verree Teasdale, Billy Bevan, Halliwell Hobbes
'In spite of its excellence, it will probably prove indifferent box office.' – *Variety*

Payment on Demand *

US 1951 90m bw
RKO/Jack H. Skirball
A happy wife and mother is appalled when her husband asks for a divorce.
A star suffers her way through luxury to a happy ending; good enough stuff for its intended audience.
w Bruce Manning, Curtis Bernhardt d Curtis Bernhardt ph Leo Tover m Victor Young
☆ Bette Davis, Barry Sullivan, Jane Cowl, Kent Taylor, Betty Lynn, John Sutton, Frances Dee, Otto Kruger
'An absolutely typical Joan Crawford picture except that Bette Davis happens to be in the Joan Crawford part.' – *Richard Mallett, Punch*

The Payoff

US 1943 74m bw
PRC/Jack Schwarz
A star reporter nabs the killer of a prosecuting attorney.
A fading star in a role he had played several times before.
w Edward Dein d Arthur Dreifuss
☆ Lee Tracy, Tom Brown, Tina Thayer, Evelyn Brent, Jack La Rue

Payroll *

GB 1961 105m bw
Anglo Amalgamated/Lynx (Norman Priggen)

Small-time crooks snatch £100,000, but after the getaway things begin to go wrong.
Tense, vivid, thoroughly predictable Rififi*-style thriller, handled with solid professionalism.*
w George Baxt novel Derek Bickerton d *Sidney Hayers* ph *Ernest Steward* m Reg Owen
☆ Michael Craig, Billie Whitelaw, Françoise Prévost, Kenneth Griffith, William Lucas, Tom Bell, Barry Keegan, Joan Rice, Glyn Houston

'In the fall of 1997, every nuclear device in the world will be accounted for ... Except one.'

The Peacemaker

US 1997 123m Technicolor 'Scope
DreamWorks (Walter Parkes, Branko Lustig)

An American scientist and a military agent reluctantly team up to track down a stolen nuclear warhead in New York.
Frantic attempt at a topical thriller, set against the background of Russian gangsters and Bosnian unrest; it fails to deliver.
w Michael Schiffer article Leslie Cockburn, Andrew Cockburn d Mimi Leder ph Dietrich

Lohmann *m* Hans Zimmer *pd* Leslie Dilley *ed* David Rosenbloom
☆ George Clooney, Nicole Kidman, Marcel Iures, Alexander Baluev, Rene Medvesek, Gary Werntz, Randall Batinkoff, Jim Haynie, Armin Mueller-Stahl
'Another machine-tooled slab of Hollywood brutality.' – *Sunday Times*
'Standard action-film stuff.' – *Time*
† It was the first release from the new studio DreamWorks SKG (initials which stand for Steven Spielberg, Jeffrey Katzenberg and David Geffen).

Peach O'Reno
US 1931 66m bw
RKO-Pathé
Two incompetent lawyers work on a divorce case.
Burlesque-style comedy with cabaret asides. Thin stuff.
w Ralph Spence, Tim Whelan *d* William Seiter
☆ Bert Wheeler, Robert Woolsey, Dorothy Lee, Joseph Cawthorn, Cora Witherspoon, Zelma O'Neal
'Less than average; low comedy laughs for the minor spots.' – *Variety*

'Get Your Priorities Straight.'
Peaches
Ireland 2000 86m colour
Optimum/Stone Ridge/IFB (Ronan Glennane)
A failing student spends the summer living in London and trying to sleep with as many girls as possible before discovering true love.
A successful play about a callow youth makes an unsuccessful transition to the screen, where it seems as unfinished as its protagonist.
wd Nick Grosso *play* Nick Grosso *ph* Brendan Galvin *pd* Jessica Coyle *ed* Niamh Fagan
☆ Matthew Rhys (Frank), Kelly Reilly (Cherry), Justin Salinger (Johnny), Matthew Dunster (Pete), Sophie Okonedo (Pippa), Emily Hillier (Niki), Stephanie Bagshaw (Linda)
'Watching this film is like being whinged at for an hour and a half.' – *Peter Bradhsaw, Guardian*

The Pearl *
US/Mexico 1948 72m bw
RKO/Oscar Dancigers
In a remote Mexican village, a simple shell diver finds a pearl of great price, but finds his life complicated as a result.
A fable which at the time seemed to have considerable quality, being the first Mexican film to receive international distribution.
w John Steinbeck, Emilio Fernandez, Jack Wagner *d* Emilio Fernandez *ph* Gabriel Figueroa *m* Antonio Diaz Conde
☆ Pedro Armendariz, Maria Elena Marques, Alfonso Bedoya

'It was the end of innocence, and the dawn of a nation's greatest glory.'
'Not Since Titantic Have The Critics Been So Out Of Touch With Their Readers.'
Pearl Harbor
US 2001 182m Technicolor Panavision
Buena Vista/Touchstone (Jerry Bruckheimer, Michael Bay)
Two farmboys, childhood friends, grow up to become Army pilots, fall in love with the same woman, survive the Japanese attack on Pearl Harbor, and take part in a retaliatory bombing raid on Tokyo.
Mountainous labours have resulted in a simple-minded, flagwaving mouse of a movie, glib, glossy and frequently banal: the central romance is bad soap opera, and is acted that way, while the action has all the reality of a video game.
w Randall Wallace *d* Michael Bay *ph* John Schwartzman *m* Hans Zimmer *pd* Nigel Phelps *ed* Chris Lebenzon, Steven Rosenblum, Mark Goldblatt, Roger Barton *sp* Industrial Light & Magic *cos* Michael Kaplan
☆ Ben Affleck (Rafe McCawley), Josh Hartnett (Danny Walker), Kate Beckinsale (Evelyn Johnson), Cuba Gooding Jnr (Doris 'Dorie' Miller), Tom Sizemore (Earl), Jon Voight (President Roosevelt), Admiral Kimmel (Colm Feore), Mako (Admiral Yamamoto), Alec Baldwin (Doolittle), William Lee Scott (Billy), Michael Shannon (Gooz), Scott Wilson (General Marshall), Peter Firth (Captain of the West Virginia), Catherine Kellner (Barbara), Dan Aykroyd (Captain Thurman)
'Rarely, perhaps never, in the field of movies about human conflict has so much money, effort and technical expertise resulted in such a vapid piece of schmaltz.' – *Ian Buruma, Guardian*
'Has as little interest in character as it does, ultimately, in history. For all its epic pretensions (as if epic were a matter of running time, tumescent music and earnest voice-over pronouncements), the movie works best as a bang-and-boom action picture.' – *A.O. Scott, New York Times*
'The film has been directed without grace, vision, or originality, and although you may walk out quoting lines of dialog, it will not be because you admire them.' – *Roger Ebert, Chicago Sun-Times*
'Features a script that Jack Warner would have found wanting even for a propaganda meller at the time, along with a cast perfectly in tune with its shallowness.' – *Todd McCarthy, Variety*
'A blockbuster entertainment that has passion, valor and tremendous action.' – *Kevin Thomas, LA Times*
† The film cost $135m, with another $5m being spent on its premiere aboard an aircraft carrier.
†† It took $75.1m at the US box-office in its first four days, the second biggest four-day opening in cinema history.
sound editing (George Watters II, Christopher Boyes)
song 'There You'll Be' (m/l Diane Warren); sound (Kevin O'Connell, Greg P. Russell, Peter J. Devlin); visual effects (Eric Brevig, John Frazier, Ed Hirsh, Ben Snow)

'The Master Minds Tackle The Master Crimes!'
The Pearl of Death **
US 1944 67m bw
Universal (Howard S. Benedict)
When a valuable pearl is stolen, Sherlock Holmes has only his own cleverness to blame; but he redeems himself by trapping 'The Creeper'.
An amusing picturization of Doyle's The Six Napoleons, *with the addition of a horror figure; it plays very well and is certainly among the best of this series.*
w Bertram Millhauser *d* Roy William Neill *ph* Virgil Miller *m* Paul Sawtell
☆ *Basil Rathbone, Nigel Bruce,* Dennis Hoey, Miles Mander, Rondo Hatton, Evelyn Ankers

Peau d'Espion: see *To Commit A Murder*

La Peau Douce: see *Silken Skin*

The Pebble and the Penguin
US 1995 74m Technicolor
Warner/Don Bluth Ireland (Russell Boland)
A shy penguin searches for the perfect pebble to give to his intended.
Unadventurous animated film that lacks a captivating story, substituting a string of unconnected episodes of varying interest.
w Rachel Koretsky, Steve Whitestone *d* Don Bluth *m* Mark Watters *m/ly* Barry Manilow, Bruce Sussman
☆ Featuring the voices of: Martin Short, Annie Golden, Tim Curry, James Belushi, Shani Wallis, Scott Bullock
'A sweet, enjoyable romantic tale more likely to succeed as an afternoon diversion on home video than on the big screen.' – *Variety*

Pecker
US 1998 87m Technicolor
Fine Line/Polar Entertainment (John Fiedler, Mark Tarlov)
A Baltimore amateur photographer, who takes snapshots of his friends, is fêted by the New York art establishment, while the subjects of his work are humiliated.
Blandly camp satire on big-city tastes and people, though what it offers in its place is even less enticing.
wd John Waters *ph* Robert Stevens *m* Stewart Copeland *pd* Vincent Peranio *ed* Janice Hampton
☆ Edward Furlong (Pecker), Christina Ricci (Shelley), Lili Taylor (Rorey), Mary Kay Place (Joyce), Martha Plimpton (Tina), Brendan Sexton III (Matt), Mark Joy (Jimmy), Mink Stole (Precinct Captain)
'A pleasant but ephemeral spoof that may disappoint Waters' hardcore fans while not recruiting many new devotees.' – *Emanuel Levy, Variety*

Peck's Bad Boy
US 1934 70m bw
Fox/Sol Lesser
Adventures of a well-intentioned but accident-prone boy in a midwestern town.
Old-fashioned American juvenile classic, modestly well done.
w Bernard Schubert, Marguerite Roberts *story* G. W. Peck *d* Edward F. Cline
☆ Jackie Cooper, Jackie Searl, Dorothy Peterson, Thomas Meighan
† Previously made in 1921 with Jackie Coogan. Cline also directed a sequel, *Peck's Bad Boy with the Circus* starring Tommy Kelly, in 1938.

Pee-wee's Big Adventure *
US 1985 92m colour
Mainline/Aspen Film Society/Robert Shapiro
Pee-wee Herman loses his red bicycle and goes looking for it.
Starring an American TV comedian who acts like a small child, this offbeat, episodic comedy has some amusing moments.
w Phil Hartman, Paul Reubens, Michael Varhol *d* Tim Burton *ph* Victor J. Kemper *m* Danny Elfman *pd* David L. Snyder *ed* Billy Weber
☆ Paul Reubens, Elizabeth Daily, Mark Holton, Diane Salinger, Judd Omen, Jon Harris, Carmen Filpi, Tony Bill, James Brolin, Morgan Fairchild
'This slapstick fantasy has the bouncing-along inventiveness of a good cartoon.' – *Pauline Kael, New Yorker*

Peeper
US 1975 87m DeLuxe Panavision
TCF/Chartoff-Winkler (Ron Buck)
In 1947 Los Angeles, a poor British private eye gets into trouble when he seeks a man's lost daughter.
Semi-spoofing Chandleresque caper which is never quite funny or quite thrilling enough.
w W. D. Richter *novel* Deadfall by Keith Laumer *d* Peter Hyams *ph* Earl Rath *m* Richard Clements
☆ Michael Caine, Natalie Wood, Kitty Winn, Thayer David, Liam Dunn
'Flimsy whimsy.' – *Variety*

'More horrible than horror! More terrible than terror!'
Peeping Tom *
GB 1959 109m Eastmancolor
Anglo Amalgamated/Michael Powell
A film studio focus puller is obsessed by the lust to murder beautiful women and photograph the fear on their faces.
Thoroughly disagreeable suspenser, a kind of compendium of the bad taste the director showed in flashes during his career.
w Leo Marks *d* Michael Powell *ph* Otto Heller *m* Brian Easdale
☆ Carl Boehm, Moira Shearer, Anna Massey, Maxine Audley, Esmond Knight, Michael Goodliffe, Shirley Anne Field, Jack Watson
'Perhaps one would not be so disagreeably affected by this exercise in the lower regions of the psychopathic were it handled in a more bluntly debased fashion.' – *Dilys Powell*
'Of enormous and deserved reputation.' – *Time Out, 1982*

Peg o' My Heart
US 1933 86m bw
MGM
To the concern of his family, an English nobleman falls for an Irish colleen.
Half-hearted version of a famous lavender-tinted stage hit previously filmed in the twenties with its original star Laurette Taylor; but by 1933 its time was past.
w Frances Marion *play* J. Hartley Manners *d* Robert Z. Leonard
☆ Marion Davies, Onslow Stevens, Alan Mowbray, Robert Greig, Irene Browne, J. Farrell MacDonald, Juliette Compton
'Just an 86-minute Irish monologue … undeservedly flattered by an almost perfect production.' – *Variety*

Peg of Old Drury *
GB 1935 76m bw
British and Dominions/Herbert Wilcox
The romance of 18th-century actress Peg Woffington with David Garrick.
Primitive but vivacious historical romp with adequate star performances.
w Miles Malleson *play* Masks and Faces by Charles Reade, Tom Taylor *d* Herbert Wilcox *ph* F. A. Young
☆ *Anna Neagle,* Cedric Hardwicke, Jack Hawkins, Margaretta Scott, Hay Petrie
'I never tired of Miss Neagle's physical appearance, which was as pretty as a Chelsea figure. The whole film indeed is very pretty, with the sentiment neatly handled. But prettiness is a quality one wants, if at all, in small quantities.' – *Graham Greene, The Spectator*

Peggy Sue Got Married **
US 1986 104m DeLuxe
Tri-Star/Rastar (Paul R. Gurian)
A disillusioned woman goes to her 25th high school reunion and finds herself reliving her young life.
It plays like an extended Twilight Zone, *but with plenty of interesting details to back up an excellent leading performance.*
w Jerry Leichtling, Arlene Sarner *d* Francis Coppola *ph* Jordan Cronenweth *m* John Barry *pd* Dean Tavoularis *ed* Barry Malkin
☆ *Kathleen Turner,* Nicolas Cage, Barry Miller, Catherine Hicks, Maureen O'Sullivan, Leon Ames, Helen Hunt, Don Murray, Barbara Harris, Kevin J. O'Connor
'Provocative, well acted, stylish and uneven.' – *Variety*
Jordan Cronenweth; Theodora Van Runkle (costumes); Kathleen Turner

Peking Express
US 1951 90m bw
Paramount/Hal B. Wallis
In communist China, an assortment of people are aboard a train which is diverted by outlaws.
Pot-boiling remake of Shanghai Express *(qv); an adequate time-passer.*
w John Meredyth Lucas *d* William Dieterle *ph* Charles Lang *m* Dimitri Tiomkin
☆ Joseph Cotten, Corinne Calvet, Edmund Gwenn, Marvin Miller
'Lacks flavour or distinction.' – *Leonard Maltin*

The Peking Medallion
Italy/Germany/France 1966 87m Technicolor
CCC/Criterion/Senior (Artur Brauner)
original title: *Il Sigillo di Pechino*
US title: *The Corrupt Ones*
A freelance photographer searches for buried treasure while fighting off the attentions of two rival gangs.
Routine chase thriller with a cast that tries to get the most out of a pedestrian script.
w Brian Clemens *story* Ladislas Fodor *d* James Hill *ph* Heinz Pehlke *m* Georges Garvarentz *ad* Hans-Jürgen Kiebach *ed* Alfred Srp
☆ Robert Stack, Elke Sommer, Nancy Kwan, Christian Marquand, Werner Peters, Maurizio Arena, Dean Heyde, Marisa Merlini

'Two Supreme Court Justices have been assassinated. One lone law student has stumbled upon the truth. An investigative journalist wants her story. Everyone else wants her dead.'
The Pelican Brief
US 1993 141m Technicolor
Warner (Alan J. Pakula, Pieter Jan Brugge)
A law student is stalked by hitmen after she speculates on the reasons behind the killings of two leading judges.
Mundane chase movie, a paranoid thriller that rarely rings true and mainly consists of Julia Roberts being chased but not caught. Her fans may enjoy it.
wd Alan J. Pakula *novel* John Grisham *ph* Stephen Goldblatt *m* James Horner *pd* Philip Rosenberg *ed* Tom Rolf, Trudy Ship
☆ Julia Roberts, Denzel Washington, Sam Shepard, John Heard, Tony Goldwyn, James B. Sikking, William Atherton, Robert Culp, Stanley Tucci, Hume Cronyn, John Lithgow
'This crackling thriller will have a long, prosperous box-office flight.' – *Variety*

'Pakula allows everyone to be briefly implicated, with menace poured on by the gallon, but fails to raise a spark of interest.' – *Lizzie Francke, Sight and Sound*

Pelle Erobreren: see *Pelle the Conqueror*

Pelle the Conqueror **\
Denmark/Sweden 1987 150m colour\
Curzon/Danish Film Institute/Swedish Film Institute/Svensk Filmindustri/Per Holst\
original title: *Pelle Erobreren*\
In the early 1900s, the young son of a Swedish immigrant worker enduring hardship on a Danish farm learns to be self-sufficient.\
Winner of the Palme D'Or at the Cannes Film Festival in 1988, it matches an epic scope with domestic detail in a finely acted, beautifully photographed movie.\
wd Bille August *novel* Martin Andersen Nexö *ph* Jörgen Persson *m* Stefan Nilsson *pd* Anna Asp *ed* Janus Billeskov Jansen\
☆ Max von Sydow, Pelle Hvenegaard, Erik Paaske, Kristina Tornqvist, Morten Jørgensen, Alex Strøbye, Astrid Villaume, Björn Granath\
† It was released on video in two versions, one subtitled, one dubbed by American actors.\
best foreign film\
Max von Sydow

The Penalty\
US 1941 81m bw\
MGM (Jack Chertok)\
The son of a gangster is regenerated by farm life and turns against his father.\
Antediluvian sweetness and light which wastes a good cast.\
w Harry Ruskin, John C. Higgins *d* Harold S. Bucquet *ph* Harold Rosson *m* David Snell\
☆ Edward Arnold, Lionel Barrymore, Marsha Hunt, Robert Sterling, Gene Reynolds

Penalty of Fame: see *Okay America*

Pendulum *\
US 1969 102m Technicolor\
Columbia/Pendulum (Stanley Niss)\
A convicted murderer and rapist is freed on appeal and kills the wife of the detective who arrested him.\
Heavy-going police melodrama, efficient but not very interesting.\
w Stanley Niss *d* George Schaefer *ph* Lionel Lindon *m* Walter Scharf\
☆ George Peppard, Jean Seberg, Richard Kiley, Charles McGraw, Robert F. Lyons, Madeleine Sherwood

Penelope\
US 1966 98m Metrocolor Panavision\
MGM/Euterpe (Joe Pasternak, Arthur Loew Jnr)\
The wife of a bank vice-president is a bank robber and kleptomaniac.\
Would-be cute comedy which only sickens one for wasting its talent.\
w George Wells *novel* E. V. Cunningham *d* Arthur Hiller *ph* Harry Stradling *m* Johnny Williams\
☆ Natalie Wood, Ian Bannen, Dick Shawn, Peter Falk, Jonathan Winters, Lila Kedrova, Lou Jacobi, Norma Crane, Arthur Malet, Jerome Cowan

Penguin Pool Murder\
US 1932 70m bw\
RKO (Kenneth Macgowan)\
A spinster schoolteacher helps a police inspector solve the murder of a man found floating in the penguin pool.\
Enjoyable minor mystery with the emphasis on the tart relationship between teacher and cop.\
w Willis Goldbeck *novel* Stuart Palmer *story* Lowell Brentano *d* George Archainbaud *ph* Henry Gerrard *m* Max Steiner *ed* Jack Kitchin\
☆ Edna May Oliver, James Gleason, Robert Armstrong, Mae Clarke, Donald Cook, Edgar Kennedy, Clarence H. Wilson, James Donlan, Gustav von Seyffertitz\
† It was the first of three films featuring Edna Mae Oliver as Hildegarde Withers, and was followed by *Murder on the Blackboard* and *Murder on a Honeymoon* (qqv).

Penitentiary\
US 1938 78m bw\
Columbia\
A district attorney becomes prison warden, and his daughter falls for a convict.\
Scene-for-scene remake of The Criminal Code *(qv) but considerably less dynamic.*\
w Fred Niblo Jnr, Seton I. Miller *play* Martin Flavin *d* John Brahm\
☆ Walter Connolly, John Howard, Jean Parker, Robert Barrat, Marc Lawrence, Arthur Hohl, Paul Fix

Penn of Pennsylvania\
GB 1941 79m bw\
British National (Richard Vernon)\
US title: *The Courageous Mr Penn*\
Persecuted Quakers leave England for America.\
Stodgily fictionalized history.\
w Anatole de Grunwald *book William Penn* by C. E. Vulliamy *d* Lance Comfort *ph* Ernest Palmer\
☆ Clifford Evans, Deborah Kerr, Denis Arundell, Aubrey Mallalieu, Henry Oscar, Max Adrian

Pennies from Heaven\
US 1936 81m bw\
Columbia (Emanuel Cohen)\
A wanderer protects a homeless little girl from the truant officer.\
Mild star musical, lucky enough to have a hit title song.\
w Jo Swerling *novel The Peacock Feather* by Katharine Leslie Moore *story William Rankin* *d* Norman Z. McLeod *ph* Robert Pittack *m* Arthur Johnston\
☆ Bing Crosby, Edith Fellows, Madge Evans, Donald Meek, Louis Armstrong and his band\
song 'Pennies from Heaven' (*m*Arthur Johnson, *ly*Sidney Mitchell)

Pennies from Heaven *\
US 1981 108m Metrocolor\
MGM/Hera (Nora Kaye, Herbert Ross)\
In 1934 Chicago, a sheet music salesman consoles himself for his drab and tragic life by fantasies induced by his songs.\
The essence of Dennis Potter's British TV serial was hard enough to get at; transposed to America it becomes unattractive nonsense, and the song sequences are not even well staged despite the enormous expense.\
w Dennis Potter *d* Herbert Ross *ph* Gordon Willis *md* Marvin Hamlisch, Billy May *pd* Ken Adam\
☆ Steve Martin, Bernadette Peters, Christopher Walken, Jessica Harper, John McMartin\
'All flash and style and no heart.' – *Roger Ebert*\
Dennis Potter

Penny Gold\
GB 1973 90m colour\
Fanfare (George H. Brown)\
Police investigate the murder of a young woman involved in dealing in rare stamps.\
Direly unimaginative thriller, all dull talk and no action; any audience is likely to have anticipated its final twist within the first ten minutes.\
w David Osborn, Liz Charles-Williams *d* Jack Cardiff *ph* Ken Hodges *m* John Scott *ad* Bert Davey *ed* John Trumper\
☆ James Booth, Francesca Annis, Nicky Henson, Joss Ackland, Richard Heffer, Sue Lloyd, Joseph O'Conor, Una Stubbs, Penelope Keith

Penny Paradise\
GB 1938 72m bw\
ATP (Basil Dean)\
A tugboat captain thinks he has won the football pools; but the coupon wasn't posted.\
An old, old story, put over with modest effectiveness.\
w Tommy Thompson, W. L. Meade, Thomas Browne *d* Carol Reed *ph* Ronald Neame, Gordon Dines *m/ly* Harry Parr-Davies, Harry O'Donovan *ad* Wilfrid Shingleton *ed* Ernest Aldridge\
☆ Edmund Gwenn, Betty Driver, Jimmy O'Dea, Maire O'Neill, Jack Livesey

Penny Points to Paradise\
GB 1951 77m bw\
Advance/Adelphi\
A pools winner takes cash but nearly loses it to a forger.\
Abysmally made comedy, only interesting as an early teaming of the Goons.\
w John Ormonde *d* Tony Young *ph* Bert Mason *m* Spike Milligan\
☆ Harry Secombe, Peter Sellers, Spike Milligan, Alfred Marks, Bill Kerr, Freddie Frinton, Paddie O'Neil

The Penny Pool\
GB 1937 85m bw\
Mancunian (John Blakeley)\
A store foreman tries to cheat one of the workers out of her football pool winnings.\
Threadbare comedy, subtitled 'A Merry Musical Burlesque', with musical interludes that preserve the slapstick music-hall act of Duggie Wakefield, which does not wear well, and some of the lesser performers of the era, including a yodelling accordion band.\
w Arthur Mertz *d* George Black Jnr *ph* James Burger *m* Julian Niman *m/ly* Arthur Mertz, Albert Stanbury *ad* George Ward *ed* B. Bayley\
☆ Duggie Wakefield, Billy Nelson, Chuck O'Neil, Jack Butler, Tommy Fields, Luanne Shaw, Charles Sewell, Harry Terry, Howard Douglas

Penny Princess\
GB 1952 94m Technicolor\
Rank/Conquest (Frank Godwin)\
A New York shopgirl inherits a tiny European state and boosts its economy by marketing a mixture of cheese and schnapps.\
Thin, spoofy comedy with mild moments of fun.\
wd Val Guest *ph* Geoffrey Unsworth *m* Ronald Hammer\
☆ Dirk Bogarde, Yolande Donlan, A. E. Matthews, Anthony Oliver, Edwin Styles, Reginald Beckwith, Kynaston Reeves, Peter Butterworth, Laurence Naismith, Mary Clare, Desmond Walter-Ellis

Penny Serenade *\
US 1941 120m bw\
Columbia (Fred Guiol)\
Courtship, marriage and the death of two children are recollected by a woman contemplating divorce.\
Well-played but uneasy film which veers suddenly and disconcertingly from light comedy into tragedy.\
w Morrie Ryskind *d* George Stevens *ph* Joseph Walker *m* W. Franke Harling\
☆ Cary Grant, Irene Dunne, Beulah Bondi, Edgar Buchanan, Ann Doran\
'To make something out of very little, and that so near at hand, is one of the tests of artistry.' – *Otis Ferguson*\
'A tear compeller showing how Cary Grant and Irene Dunne lose first their own baby and then the one they adopt. Which, as Lady Bracknell would certainly have observed, looks like carelessness.' – *James Agate*\
Cary Grant

Penrod and Sam\
US 1937 68m bw\
Warner\
Exploits of a club for juvenile sleuths.\
Start of a second feature series which had little to do with the original period characters but was generally well received. Later the same year came Penrod and his Twin Brother, *and in 1938* Penrod's Double Trouble.\
w Lillie Hayward, Hugh Cummings from the characters created by Booth Tarkington *d* William McGann\
☆ Billy Mauch, Frank Craven, Spring Byington, Craig Reynolds, Charles Halton\
'Should serve as a nucleus for swell exploitation tie-ups.' – *Variety*\
† There had been an earlier version in 1931, starring Leon Janney; and the family turned up again in the Doris Day musicals *On Moonlight Bay* and *By the Light of the Silvery Moon*.

'The Most Challenging Sport Has Just Become The Deadliest Game.'\
Pentathlon\
Germany 1994 97m Foto-Kem\
First Independent/Live/PFG (Martin E. Caan, Dolph Lundgren)\
The East German Olympic pentathlon gold medallist defects to the US, where, following the fall of the Berlin Wall, he is followed by his former trainer and a gang of neo-Nazi assassins.\
Risible melodrama which swiftly runs out of ideas; you keep thinking it cannot get any worse, but it does, with David Soul cackling manfully as the villain of the piece.\
w William Stadiem, Gary McDonald, Gary DeVore, Bruce Malmuth *d* Bruce Malmuth *ph* Misha Suslov *m* David Spear *pd* Jaymes Hinkle *ed* Richard Nord, Joseph Gutowski\
☆ Dolph Lundgren, David Soul, Renee Coleman, Daniel Riordan, David Drummond, Philip Bruns, Roger E. Mosley

Penthouse *\
US 1933 90m bw\
MGM/Hunt Stromberg\
GB title: *Crooks in Clover*\
When he outlives his usefulness to the underworld, a lawyer is framed for murder.\
Sprightly murder comedy-drama which plays like a try-out for The Thin Man.\
w Frances Goodrich, Albert Hackett *d* W. S. Van Dyke\
☆ Warner Baxter, Myrna Loy, C. Henry Gordon, Nat Pendleton, Charles Butterworth, George E. Stone\
'Well-sustained crime solution with smashing climax and arresting title.' – *Variety*

The Penthouse\
GB 1967 96m Eastmancolor\
Paramount/Tahiti (Harry Fine)\
Illicit lovers in an unfinished block of flats are terrorized by intruders.\
Thoroughly objectionable and unpleasant melodrama with no attractive characters and no attempt to explain itself.\
wd Peter Collinson *play The Meter Man* by J. Scott Forbes *ph* Arthur Lavis *m* John Hawkesworth\
☆ Suzy Kendall, Terence Morgan, Tony Beckley, Norman Rodway, Martine Beswick\
'Pornography in Pinter's clothing.' – *MFB*

The People against O'Hara *\
US 1951 102m bw\
MGM (William H. Wright)\
An ex-alcoholic defence lawyer sacrifices himself to prove his client's innocence.\
Formula drama, well made and entertainingly performed, with snatches of bright dialogue.\
w John Monks Jnr *novel* Eleazar Lipsky *d* John Sturges *ph* John Alton *m* Carmen Dragon\
☆ Spencer Tracy, Diana Lynn, Pat O'Brien, John Hodiak, James Arness, Arthur Shields, Eduardo Ciannelli, Louise Lorimer

The People Next Door\
US 1970 93m DeLuxe\
Avco Embassy (Herb Brodkin)\
Suburban parents have trouble with their drug-addicted teenage daughter.\
Hysterical melodrama with good credentials.\
w J. P. Miller *TV play* J. P. Miller *d* David Greene *ph* Gordon Willis *m* Don Sebesky\
☆ Eli Wallach, Julie Harris, Hal Holbrook, Cloris Leachman, Stephen McHattie, Nehemiah Persoff\
'As unlovely a picture of suburban living as one is likely to see.' – *Judith Crist*

People on Sunday **\
Germany 1929 72m approx (24 fps) bw silent\
Filmstudio 1929\
original title: *Menschen am Sonntag*\
Two couples spend a flirtatious day in Berlin's countryside.\
Influential semi-documentary with fascinating credits, using amateur actors playing themselves.\
w Billy Wilder, Curt Siodmak *d* Robert Siodmak, Fred Zinnemann, Edgar G. Ulmer *ph* Eugen Schüfftan\
☆ Brigitte Borchert, Christl Ehlers, Annie Schreyer, Wolfgang von Waltershausen

The People that Time Forgot\
GB 1977 90m Technicolor\
AIP/Amicus (John Dark)\
Major McBride tries to rescue his old friend from a prehistoric island on which he disappeared in 1916.

Tepid sequel to The Land that Time Forgot: *even the dinosaurs don't rise to the occasion.*
w Patrick Tilley *d* Kevin Connor *ph* Alan Hume *m* John Scott *pd* Maurice Carter
☆ Patrick Wayne, Sarah Douglas, Dana Gillespie, Doug McClure, Thorley Walters, Shane Rimmer, Tony Britton

'They'll devour everything but your screams.'
The People under the Stairs *
US 1991 102m DeLuxe
UIP/Universal/Alive (Marianne Maddalena, Stuart M. Besser)
A 13-year-old boy discovers that the wealthy couple he attempts to rob have imprisoned in their cellar kidnapped youths who have become damaged mutants.
An effective horror film, or possibly a less effective allegory about the exploitation of the urban poor.
wd Wes Craven *ph* Sandi Sissel *m* Don Peake *pd* Bryan Jones *ed* James Coblentz, Tom Walls *sp* Image Engineering Inc.
☆ Brandon Adams, Everett McGill, Wendy Robie, A. J. Langer, Ving Rhames, Sean Whalen, Bill Cobbs, Kelly Jo Minter, Jeremy Roberts
'This revival of the plot-driven, exhausting, funny-pointed, suspense-horror picture is a welcome change.' – *Kim Newman, Sight and Sound*

The People vs. Larry Flynt ***
US 1996 130m Technicolor Panavision
Columbia TriStar/Ixtlan/Phoenix (Oliver Stone, Janet Yang, Michael Hausman)
A poor Kentucky boy grows up to be a successful publisher of porn magazines, and takes his fight to protect his business and freedom of speech to the Supreme Court.
Biopic of the publisher of Hustler *that also manages to be a witty, engaging portrait of the extremes and excesses – sexual, religious, judicial and political – of modern American society.*
w Scott Alexander, Larry Karaszewski *d* Milos Forman *ph* Philippe Rousselot *m* Thomas Newman *pd* Patrizia von Brandenstein *ed* Christopher Tellefsen
☆ *Woody Harrelson, Courtney Love, Edward Norton*, James Cromwell, Crispin Glover, James Carville, Brett Harrelson, Donna Hanover
'That Forman has found the raucous, satirical side of Larry Flynt's story doesn't surprise us; that he has uncovered its pathos, and something that could even be considered its patriotism, is a stunning achievement.' – *David Ansen, Newsweek*
'Makes it OK to take your brain to the movies again. Not just OK, but necessary; you'll need all the skepticism and relish for irony that you can muster.' – *Joe Morgenstern, Wall Street Journal*
'For all its virtues of writing, direction and performance, the film still leaves a brackish taste in the mouth and seems very much less than wholly satisfactory.' – *Derek Malcolm, Guardian*
† Larry Flynt himself appears as the judge who sentenced him early in his career to 25 years' imprisonment on charges of obscenity and links to organized crime.
Milos Forman; Woody Harrelson

People Will Talk
US 1935 60m bw
Paramount
Mr and Mrs Wilton try to patch up their daughter's failing marriage.
Slight domestic comedy with popular leads.
w Herbert Fields, Sophie Kerr, F. Hugh Herbert *d* Alfred Santell
☆ Charles Ruggles, Mary Boland, Leila Hyams, Dean Jagger, Edward Brophy
'Strictly light summer fare and not solid enough to stand alone.' – *Variety*

People Will Talk **
US 1951 110m bw
TCF (Darryl F. Zanuck)
A surgeon's unorthodox psychological methods cause jealousy among his colleagues, especially when he falls in love with a pregnant patient.
Oddly entertaining jumble of melodrama, comedy, romance, speeches and a little mystery, all quite typical of its director.
wd Joseph L. Mankiewicz *play* Dr Praetorius *by* Curt Goetz *ph* Milton Krasner *md* Alfred Newman
☆ Cary Grant, Jeanne Crain, Finlay Currie, Hume Cronyn, Walter Slezak, Sidney Blackmer, Basil Ruysdael
'A picture so mature and refreshingly frank as to hold that an erring young woman might be rewarded with a wise and loving mate is most certainly a significant milestone in the moral emancipation of American films.' – *New York Times*

'The Most Fabulous Fun Show Ever On The Screen! So Hilarious! So Heartwarming! You'll Glow All Over!'
Pepe
US 1960 195m Eastmancolor Cinemascope
Columbia/George Sidney (Jacques Gelman)
A Mexican peasant in Hollywood gets help from the stars.
Feeble and seemingly endless extravaganza in which the boring stretches far outnumber the rest, and few of the guests have anything worthwhile to do.
w Dorothy Kingsley, Claude Binyon *d* George Sidney *ph* Joe MacDonald *md* Johnny Green *ed* Viola Lawrence, Al Clark
☆ Cantinflas, Dan Dailey, Shirley Jones, Ernie Kovacs, Jay North, William Demarest, Michael Callan, Maurice Chevalier, Bing Crosby, Richard Conte, Bobby Darin, Sammy Davis Jnr, Jimmy Durante, Zsa Zsa Gabor, Judy Garland and also Hedda Hopper, Joey Bishop, Peter Lawford, Janet Leigh, Jack Lemmon, Kim Novak, André Previn, Donna Reed, Debbie Reynolds, Greer Garson, Edward G. Robinson, Cesar Romero, Frank Sinatra, Billie Burke, Tony Curtis, Dean Martin, Charles Coburn
'A joyous production crammed with delightful entertainment.' – *New York Daily News*
Joe MacDonald; Johnny Green; song 'Faraway Part of Town' (*m*André Previn, *ly* Dory Langdon); editing

Pépé le Moko **
France 1936 90m bw
Paris Film
A Parisian gangster lives in the Algerian casbah where the police can't get at him; but love causes him to emerge and be shot.
Romantic melodrama modelled on the American gangster film but with a decided poetic quality of its own: the Americans promptly paid it the compliment of remaking it as the not-too-bad Algiers.
w Henri Jeanson, Roger d'Ashelbe *novel* Roger d'Ashelbe (Henri La Barthe) *d Julien Duvivier* *ph* Jules Kruger *m* Vincent Scotto *ad* Jacques Krauss
☆ *Jean Gabin*, Mireille Ballin, Gabriel Gabrio, Lucas Gridoux
'One of the most compelling of all French films.' – *New Yorker, 1977*
'Perhaps there have been pictures as exciting on the thriller level ... but I cannot remember one which has succeeded so admirably in raising the thriller to a poetic level.' – *Graham Greene*

Pepi, Luci, Bom
Spain 1980 80m colour
Metro/Figaro (Pepon Corominas)
original title: *Pepi, Luci, Bom y otras chicas del montón*
A woman raped by a policeman takes her revenge by encouraging his wife to form a lesbian relationship with a sadistic singer.
Almodóvar's first full-length feature attempts to shock and surprise with a kitsch mix of sex, cruelty and eccentricity.
wd Pedro Almodóvar *ph* Paco Femenia *ed* Pepe Salcedo
☆ Carmen Maura, Félix Rotaeta, Olvido 'Alaska' Gara, Eva Siva, Diego Alvarez, Pedro Almodóvar
'The roots of Almodóvar's down-and-dirty, intentionally amoral and often disgusting films are abundant in *Pepi, Luci, Bom*.' – *Variety*

Perceval Le Gallois
France 1978 140m colour Panavision
Les Films du Losange/Barbet Schroeder/FR3/ARD/SSR/RAI/Gaumont (Margaret Menegoz)
A naïve Welsh youth becomes a knight at the court of King Arthur and meets the Fisher King.
This is less a film than an interesting, though not engrossing, illustrated accompaniment, against stylized backgrounds, to a long medieval poem.
wd Eric Rohmer *poem* Chrétien de Troyes *ph* Nestor Almendros *m* Guy Robert *ad* Jean-Pierre Kohut-Svelko *ed* Cecile Decugis
☆ Fabrice Luchini, André Dussollier, Solange Boulanger, Catherine Schroeder, Francisco Orozco, Deborah Nathan, Pascale Ogier
'Combines real people and real horses with toy castles and small, stylized trees, and the effect is just the opposite of what Rohmer could have wanted: it's cute. And it's cute for only a short time because nothing can be cute for a long time.' – *Stanley Kauffmann*

Percy
GB 1971 103m Eastmancolor
Anglo EMI/Welbeck (Betty E. Box)
After an unfortunate accident, a young man undergoes a successful penis transplant, and sets out to discover who the donor was.
Barrage of phallic jokes, some quite funny, but mostly as witless as the whole idea.
w Hugh Leonard *novel* Raymond Hitchcock *d* Ralph Thomas *ph* Ernest Steward *m* Ray Davies
☆ Hywel Bennett, Elke Sommer, *Denholm Elliott*, Britt Ekland, Cyd Hayman

Percy's Progress
GB 1974 101m Eastmancolor
EMI (Betty E. Box)
US title: *It's Not the Size that Counts*
A chemical causes impotence in all males except the owner of the first transplanted penis.
Percy *dug deep, but this is really the bottom of the barrel.*
w Sid Colin *d* Ralph Thomas *ph* Tony Imi *m* Tony Macauley
☆ Leigh Lawson, Elke Sommer, Denholm Elliott, Judy Geeson, Harry H. Corbett, Vincent Price, Adrienne Posta, Julie Ege, James Booth

Perdita Durango
Spain/Mexico 1997 126m colour 'Scope
Sogetel/Lolafilms/Mirador/Canal+/Imcine (Andres Vicente Gomez)
A whore teams up with a drug dealer for a life of crime and murder.
Energetic, sex-obsessed thriller that would have benefited by being much shorter; it falls short of the mythic status it aims for.
w Barry Gifford, Jorge Guerricaechevarria, David Trueba, Alex de la Iglesia *novel* 59 Degrees and Raining: The Story of Perdita Durango *by* Barry Gifford *d* Alex de la Iglesia *ph* Flavio Martinez Labiano *m* Simon Boswell *pd* Jose Luis Arrizabalaga, Arturo Garcia *ed* Teresa Font
☆ Rosie Perez, Javier Bardem, Harley Cross, Aimee Graham, James Gandolfini, Screamin' Jay Hawkins, Carlos Bardem, Santiago Segura, Don Stroud, Alex Cox
'A well-scripted, well-directed and mostly enjoyable story.' – *Empire*

The Perez Family
US 1995 113m DeLuxe
Film Four/Samuel Goldwyn (Michael Nozik, Lydia Dean Pilcher)
After 20 years in a Cuban jail, a former plantation owner goes to Miami to be reunited with his family, but finds a new life instead.
Uncertain domestic drama, with comic undertones, about breaking free from the past.
w Robin Swicord *novel* Christine Bell *d* Mira Nair *ph* Stuart Dryburgh *m* Alan Silvestri *pd* Mark Friedberg *ed* Robert Estrin
☆ Marisa Tomei, Alfred Molina, Chazz Palminteri, Anjelica Huston, Trini Alvarado, Celia Cruz, Diego Wallraff, Angela Lanza
'A disappointingly messy picture that seldom finds its dramatic or emotional core.' – *Variety*

'Health clubs – more sex than sweat?'
Perfect
US 1985 115m Technicolor
Columbia/Delphi III (James Bridges)
An aerobics instructor (female) meets a reporter (male) doing a story on health clubs, but it isn't love at first sight.
Nervy, unattractive drama which didn't find an audience.
w Aaron Latham, James Bridges *d* James Bridges *ph* Gordon Willis *m* Ralph Burns
☆ John Travolta, Jamie Lee Curtis, Anne de Salvo, Marilu Henner, Laraine Newman
'Guilty of the sins it condemns – superficiality, manipulation and smugness.' – *Variety*

Perfect Alibi
US 1994 96m
Rysher (Bruce Cohn Curtis)
A doctor's wealthy wife discovers that the new French au pair is not what she seems to be.
Involved, implausible thriller about uninteresting people.
wd Kevin Meyer *novel* Where's Mommy Now? *by* Rochelle Majer Krich *ph* Doyle Smith *m* Amotz Plessner *pd* Elayne Barbara Ceder *ed* David H. Lloyd
☆ Teri Garr (Laney Tolbert), Hector Elizondo (Det Ryker), Alex McArthur (Keith Bauers), Lydie Denier (Janine), Kathleen Quinlan (Melanie Bauers), Charles Martin Smith (Franklin Dupard), Anne Ramsay (Paula Simpson), Gedde Watanabe (Det Onoda), Bruce McGill (Det Spivak), Rex Linn (Bartender), Estelle Harris (Aunt Dorothy)

A Perfect Couple *
US 1979 112m DeLuxe
TCF/Lions Gate (Robert Altman)
A middle-aged Greek much dependent on his family meets a jazz singer through a dating service.
A free-speaking update of Marty, *featuring the Altman repertory company; intelligent sequences are muffled by the familiar Altman messiness of approach.*
w Robert Altman, Allan Nicholls *d* Robert Altman *ph* Edmond L. Koons *md* Tom Pierson, Tony Berg
☆ Paul Dooley, Marta Heflin, Titos Vandis, Belita Moreno, Henry Gibson, Dimitra Arliss
'Has the usual Altman assets: technical deftness, idiosyncrasy, unexpected subject. But the deftness rattles around in a vacuum, the idiosyncrasy – because unsupported in theme or dynamics – degenerates quickly into egotism, and the unexpected subject is so poorly developed that it quickly becomes sterile.' – *Stanley Kauffmann*

Perfect Day *
US 1929 20m bw
Hal Roach
Various problems delay a family's departure for a picnic.
Technically a most adept star comedy but its repetition can annoy.
w Hal Roach, Leo McCarey, H. M. Walker *d* James Parrott *ed* Richard Currier
☆ Stan Laurel, Oliver Hardy, Edgar Kennedy
† The picnic was originally to have occupied the second reel, but the departure gags swelled to occupy the entire footage.

Perfect Friday *
GB 1970 95m Eastmancolor
London Screenplays/Sunnymede (Jack Smith)
A bank manager engages aristocratic help to rob his own bank.
Middling comedy caper.
w Anthony Greville-Bell, J. Scott Forbes *d* Peter Hall *ph* Alan Hume *m* Johnny Dankworth *pd* Terence Marsh *ed* Rex Pyke
☆ Stanley Baker, Ursula Andress, David Warner, Patience Collier, T. P. McKenna, David Waller, Joan Benham, Julian Orchard

The Perfect Furlough
US 1958 93m Eastmancolor Cinemascope
U-I (Robert Arthur)
GB title: *Strictly for Pleasure*
To help morale at a remote Arctic army unit, one of the men is selected to enjoy the perfect leave in Paris on behalf of the others.

Amiable farce which entertains while it's on but is quickly forgotten.
w Stanley Shapiro *d* Blake Edwards *ph* Philip Lathrop *m* Frank Skinner *ad* Alexander Golitzen *ed* Milton Carruth
☆ Tony Curtis, Janet Leigh, Elaine Stritch, Keenan Wynn, Troy Donahue, King Donovan, Linda Cristal

The Perfect Gentleman
US 1935 73m bw
MGM
GB title: *The Imperfect Lady*
A retired officer helps an actress make a comeback.
Genial comedy which didn't quite work well enough to make an English variety star popular on both sides of the Atlantic.
w Edward Childs Carpenter *d* Tim Whelan
☆ Cicely Courtneidge, Frank Morgan, Heather Angel, Herbert Mundin, Henry Stephenson

The Perfect Marriage
US 1946 88m bw
Paramount/Hal B. Wallis
On their tenth wedding anniversary, a happy couple have a row and start divorce proceedings.
Wispy comedy, unmemorable and rather tiresome.
w Leonard Spigelgass *play* Samson Raphaelson *d* Lewis Allen *ph* Russell Metty *m* Frederick Hollander
☆ David Niven, Loretta Young, Eddie Albert, Nona Griffith, Virginia Field, Jerome Cowan, Rita Johnson, Charles Ruggles, Nana Bryant, ZaSu Pitts
'Another film about disillusionment and reconciliation in a mansion with constant evening dress.' – *Sunday Times*

The Perfect Murder
India 1988 95m colour
Enterprise/Merchant Ivory (Wahid Chowhan)
A Bombay detective investigates an attempted murder, with a little diamond smuggling on the side.
Keating's fictional Inspector Ghote transfers poorly to the screen in a film that is more slapstick than thriller.
w Zafar Hai, H. R. F. Keating *novel* H. R. F. Keating *d* Zafar Hai *ph* Walter Lassally *m* Richard Robbins *pd* Kiran Patki, Sartaj Noorani *ed* Charles Rees
☆ Naseeruddin Shah, Stellan Skarsgard, Dalip Tahil, Madhur Jaffrey, Sakeena Jaffrey, Dinshaw Daji

A Perfect Murder
US 1998 105m Technicolor
Warner (Arnold Kopelson, Anne Kopelson, Christopher Mankiewicz, Peter Macgregor-Scott)
To kill his wealthy wife a husband hires the artist and ex-convict with whom she is having an affair.
Slick, glossy thriller that fails to involve an audience on an emotional level.
w Patrick Smith Kelly *play Dial M for Murder* by Frederick Knott *d* Andrew Davis *ph* Dariusz Wolski *m* James Newton Howard *pd* Philip Rosenberg *ed* Dennis Virkler, Dov Hoenig
☆ Michael Douglas, Gwyneth Paltrow, Viggo Mortensen, David Suchet, Sarita Choudhury, Constance Towers, Michael P. Moran, Novella Nelson
'A fast-moving, logically thought-out and beautifully crafted thriller … both psychologically and socially sharp.' – *Philip French, Observer*
'An artistic misdemeanor.' – *Variety*
† Knott's play was filmed by Alfred Hitchcock as *Dial M for Murder* (qv).

The Perfect Snob
US 1941 63m bw
Walter Morosco/TCF
A woman tosses her daughter at millionaires. The girl settles on a poor boy … who turns out to be a millionaire after all.
Predictable comedy with competent cast.
w Lee Loeb, Harold Buchman *d* Ray McCarey
☆ Charles Ruggles, Charlotte Greenwood, Lynn Bari, Cornel Wilde, Anthony Quinn, Alan Mowbray

'…They Thought He Was A "Mamma's Boy" … But When He Broke Loose! … Wow!'
The Perfect Specimen
US 1937 82m bw
Warner (Harry Joe Brown)
The grandmother of a rich young man brings him up uncontaminated by the world, but when a girl crashes her car into his fence he proves fitted to deal with the situation.
Fantasticated comedy a long way after Mr Deeds and too slow by half.
w Norman Reilly Raine, Lawrence Riley, Brewster Morse, Fritz Falkenstein, Samuel Hopkins Adams *d* Michael Curtiz *ph* Charles Rosher
☆ Errol Flynn, Joan Blondell, Hugh Herbert, Edward Everett Horton, May Robson, Dick Foran, Beverly Roberts, Allen Jenkins
'Upper bracket comedy for the family trade.' – *Variety*

The Perfect Storm *
US 2000 129m Technicolor Panavision
Warner/Baltimore Spring Creek/Radiant (Paula Weinstein, Wolfgang Petersen, Gail Katz)
The crew of a small fishing boat, the Andrea Gail, is caught in unprecedently violent storms in the North Atlantic.
There are some astonishing visual moments here – notably the small boat attempting to climb an impossibly high wave – but the crew members, each equipped with a personal crisis to fill in the gaps between the waves, are no more than stereotypes so that their elemental struggle remains uninvolving.
w Bill Wittliff *book* Sebastian Junger *d* Wolfgang Petersen *ph* John Seale *m* James Horner *pd* William Sandell *ed* Richard Francis-Bruce *sp* Industrial Light & Magic
☆ George Clooney (Billy Tyne), Mark Wahlberg (Bobby Shatford), John C. Reilly (Dale 'Murph' Murphy), Diane Lane (Christine Cotter), William Fichtner (David 'Sully' Sullivan), John Hawkes (Michael 'Bugsy' Moran), Allen Payne (Alfred Pierre), Mary Elizabeth Mastrantonio (Linda Greenlaw), Karen Allen (Melissa Brown), Cherry Jones (Edie Bailey), Bob Gunton (Alexander McAnally III), Christopher McDonald (Todd Gross), Michael Ironside (Bob Brown)
'Lies stranded in the shallows of its genre. What we're left with is the story of an adventure which people happen not to survive.' – *Adam Mars-Jones, Times*
† The film took $323m at the most office worldwide.
visual effects (Stefan Fangmeier, Habib Zargarpour, John Frazier, Walt Conti); sound (John Reitz, Gregg Rudloff, David Campbell, Keith A. Wester)
visual effects

Perfect Strangers **
GB 1945 102m bw
MGM/London Films (Alexander Korda)
US title: *Vacation from Marriage*
A downtrodden clerk and his dowdy wife go to war, and come back unrecognizably improved.
Pleasant comedy with good actors; but the turnabout of two such caricatures really strains credibility.
w Clemence Dane, Anthony Pelissier *d* Alexander Korda *ph* Georges Périnal *m* Clifton Parker
☆ Robert Donat, Deborah Kerr, Glynis Johns, Ann Todd, Roland Culver, Elliot Mason, Eliot Makeham, Brefni O'Rorke, Edward Rigby
'War is supposed to be the catalyst, the sportsman's bracer; and the film's chief weakness is its failure to show the briefly exalted couple sinking back, uncontrollably, under their peacetime stone.' – *James Agee*
'It glows with laughter and honest sentiment.' – *New York Times*
original story (Clemence Dane)

'They met by chance, and once they kissed, they knew they never should have!'
Perfect Strangers
US 1950 87m bw
Warner (Jerry Wald)
GB title: *Too Dangerous to Love*
Two jurors on a murder case fall in love.
Talkative, unlikely, and rather boring potboiler.
w Edith Sommer *play Ladies and Gentlemen* by Charles MacArthur, Ben Hecht *d* Bretaigne Windust *ph* Peverell Marley *m* Leigh Harline
☆ Ginger Rogers, Dennis Morgan, Thelma Ritter, Margalo Gillmore, Howard Freeman, Alan Reed, Paul Ford, George Chandler

Perfect Strangers: see *Blind Alley (1984)*

Perfect Understanding *
GB 1933 80m bw
Gloria Swanson British Pictures Ltd
A couple agree to marry on condition that they will never disagree with each other.
Silly comedy with a unique star combination looking acutely uncomfortable.
w Miles Malleson, Michael Powell *d* Cyril Gardner *ph* Curt Courant
☆ Gloria Swanson, Laurence Olivier, John Halliday, Nigel Playfair, Michael Farmer, Genevieve Tobin, Nora Swinburne
'Dull and talky picture, done in the uninspiring British style.' – *Variety*

The Perfect Weapon
US 1991 85m Technicolor
Paramount (Mark DiSalle, Pierre David)
A Kenpo karate expert returns home to avenge the death of his friend at the hands of the drug-dealing Korean mafia.
The usual revenge plot and the usual fight sequences of American martial arts movies are done with a small attempt at style, but otherwise it is strictly an assembly-line product.
w David C. Wilson *d* Mark DiSalle *ph* Russell Carpenter *m* Gary Chang *pd* Curtis A. Schnell *ed* Wayne Wahrman
☆ Jeff Speakman, John Dye, Mako, James Hong, Mariska Hargitay, Dante Basco, Beau Starr, Seth Sakai, Clyde Kusatsu, Cary-Hiroyuki Tagawa
† The British TV version runs for 65m.

A Perfect Weekend: see *The St Louis Kid*

The Perfect Woman *
GB 1949 89m bw
GFD/Two Cities (George and Alfred Black)
A girl changes places with her inventor uncle's robot woman.
Described as a romp, this is in fact a pretty good farce, very fast moving and well played after the usual expository start.
w George Black, Bernard Knowles, J. B. Boothroyd *play* Wallace Geoffrey, Basil Mitchell *d* Bernard Knowles *ph* Jack Hildyard *m* Arthur Wilkinson
☆ Patricia Roc, Nigel Patrick, Stanley Holloway, David Hurst, Miles Malleson, Irene Handl

A Perfect World *
US 1993 138m Technicolor Panavision
Warner/Malpaso (Mark Johnson, David Valdes)
A father–son relationship develops between an escaped convict and the seven-year-old boy he takes as a hostage.
A very American mix of male bonding, road movie and thriller that every now and then reveals a few signs of originality.
w John Lee Hancock *d* Clint Eastwood *ph* Jack N. Green *m* Lennie Niehaus *pd* Henry Bumstead *ed* Joel Cox, Ron Spang
☆ Kevin Costner, Clint Eastwood, Laura Dern, T. J. Lowther, Keith Szarabajka, Leo Burmester, Paul Hewitt, Bradley Whitford
'A somber, subtly nuanced study of an escaped con's complex relationship with an abducted boy that carries a bit too much narrative flab for its own good.' – *Variety*
'As jarring and fundamentally goofy as the movie is, it never feels like an ordinary, generic Hollywood product: at every moment, there's something to gape at – sometimes in admiration, often in disbelief.' – *Terrence Rafferty, New Yorker*

Perfectly Normal *
Canada 1990 105m colour
Palace/Bialystock & Bloom/Téléfilm Canada/BSB/Skyhost/British Screen (Michael Burns)
An ice hockey-playing brewery worker teams up with a dubious chef to open an operatic restaurant.
Bizarre comedy of eccentric lives in a small-town setting.
w Eugene Lipinski, Paul Quarrington *d* Yves Simoneau *ph* Alain Dostie *m* Richard Gregoire *pd* Anne Pritchard *ed* Ronald Sanders
☆ Robbie Coltrane, Michael Riley, Deborah Duchene, Eugene Lipinski, Jack Nichols, Elizabeth Harpur, Patricia Gage, Kenneth Welsh
'The movie is too eager to be loved, but has its moments.' – *Philip French, Observer*

Performance ***
GB 1970 105m Technicolor
Warner/Goodtimes (Donald Cammell)
A vicious gangster moves in with an ex-pop star.
Dense, Pinterish melodrama about alter egos.
w Donald Cammell *d Nicolas Roeg, Donald Cammell ph Nicolas Roeg m* Jack Nitzsche *md* Randy Newman
☆ James Fox, Mick Jagger, Anita Pallenberg, Michèle Breton, Stanley Meadows, Allan Cuthbertson
'A humourless, messy mixture of crime and decadence and drug-induced hallucination.' – *New Yorker, 1980*
'You don't have to be a drug addict, pederast, sado-masochist or nitwit to enjoy it, but being one or more of these things would help.' – *John Simon*

Perfume of the Cyclone: see *Night of the Cyclone*

Péril: see *Death in a French Garden*

Péril en la Demeure: see *Death in a French Garden*

Perilous Holiday
US 1946 89m bw
Columbia
A newly acquainted couple become involved with counterfeiters in Mexico City.
Passable comedy-crime programme filler.
w Robert Carson, Roy Chanslor *d* Edward H. Griffith
☆ Pat O'Brien, Ruth Warrick, Alan Hale, Minna Gombell

A Perilous Journey
US 1953 87m bw
Republic (W. J. O'Sullivan)
A party of women sail to the California goldfields to sell themselves into marriage.
Reasonably lively action drama.
w Richard Wormser *novel The Golden Tide* by Virgie Roe *d* R. G. Springsteen *ph* Jack Marta *m* Victor Young
☆ Vera Ralston, David Brian, Charles Winninger, Scott Brady, Virginia Grey, Ben Cooper

The Perils of Pauline
US 1934 bw serial: 12 eps
Universal
The daughter of a noted scientist seeks a deadly gas formula in Indo-China.
Semi-remake of the famous silent serial.
d Ray Taylor
☆ Evalyn Knapp, Robert Allan, James Durkin, Sonny Ray, Frank Lackteen

The Perils of Pauline *
US 1947 96m Technicolor
Paramount (Sol C. Siegel)
The career of silent serial queen Pearl White.
An agreeable recreation of old time Hollywood, with plenty of slapstick chases but a shade too much sentiment also.
w P. J. Wolfson *d* George Marshall *ph* Ray Rennahan *md* Robert Emmett Dolan
☆ Betty Hutton, John Lund, Billy de Wolfe, William Demarest, Constance Collier, Frank Faylen, William Farnum, Paul Panzer, Snub Pollard, Creighton Hale, Chester Conklin, James Finlayson, Hank Mann, Bert Roach, Francis McDonald and also Chester Clute
'People who can accept such stuff as solid gold have either forgotten a lot, or never knew first-rate slapstick when they saw it, twenty or thirty years ago, when it was one of the wonders of the world.' – *James Agee*
song 'I Wish I Didn't Love You So' (*m/ly* Frank Loesser)

Period of Adjustment
US 1962 122m bw Panavision
MGM/Marton (Lawrence Weingarten)
A Korean War veteran has the shakes and his sexual adequacy is affected, as his wife furiously discovers.
Comedy of maladjustment, tolerably witty but unsuitably widescreened.
w Isobel Lennart *play* Tennessee Williams
d George Roy Hill *ph* Paul C. Vogel *m* Lyn Murray
☆ Tony Franciosa, Jane Fonda, Jim Hutton, Lois Nettleton

Les Perles de la Couronne *
France 1937 118m bw
Serge Sandburg/Tobis
The history over four centuries of seven pearls given by Pope Clement VII to Catherine de Medici.
Generally amusing series of historical sketches in Guitry's inimitable style.
w Sacha Guitry *d* Sacha Guitry, Christian-Jaque
☆ Sacha Guitry, Renée Saint-Cyr, Lyn Harding, Percy Marmont, Arletty, Claude Dauphin, Raimu, Jean-Louis Barrault, Jacqueline Delubac
'Headed to bring in returns both at home and abroad.' – *Variety*
† The picture tried, but failed, to be intelligible without sub-titles to all language-speakers.

Permanent Midnight
US 1998 85m DeLuxe
Artisan (Jane Hamsher, Don Murphy)
A successful TV scriptwriter becomes a heroin addict, to the detriment of his relationships and career.
Based on an autobiography, a glum account of enslavement to drugs.
wd David Veloz *book* Jerry Stahl *ph* Robert Yeoman *m* Daniel Licht *pd* Jerry Fleming
ed Steven Weisberg, Cara Silverman
☆ Ben Stiller, Elizabeth Hurley, Mario Bello, Owen Wilson, Lourdes Benedicto, Cheryl Ladd, Peter Greene, Janeane Garofalo, Jerry Stahl
'Exactly the kind of affliction-of-the-week babble the talented Stahl rails against in his bestselling memoir.' – *Glenn Lovell, Variety*

Permanent Record
US 1988 91m Technicolor
Paramount (Frank Mancuso Jnr)
The unexpected suicide of a popular high school student has a traumatic effect on his friends.
Well-meaning but dull drama of teenage angst.
w Jarre Fees, Alice Liddle, Larry Ketron *d* Marisa Silver *ph* Frederick Elmes *m* Joe Strummer
pd Michel Levesque *ed* Robert Brown
☆ Keanu Reeves, Alan Boyce, Michelle Meyrink, Jennifer Rubin, Barry Corbin, Kathy Baker, Pamela Gidley, Richard Bradford

Permission to Kill
US/Austria 1975 97m Technicolor
Panavision
Warner/Sascha (Paul Mills)
British agents try to stop a communist returning home from the west.
Prolonged, confusing and boring spy melodrama in which everyone looks understandably glum.
w Robin Estridge *novel* Robin Estridge *d* Cyril Frankel *ph* Freddie Young *m* Richard Rodney Bennett
☆ Bekim Fehmiu, Dirk Bogarde, Ava Gardner, Timothy Dalton, Frederic Forrest
'Pretentious political mishmash.' – *MFB*

Permissive
GB 1970 86m colour
Shonteff Films (Jack Shulton)
A provincial girl goes to London and becomes a groupie.
Dull exploitation movie of sex and rock, with too much footage given over to uninteresting groups of the period.
w Jeremy Craig Dryden *d* Lindsay Shonteff
ph John C. Taylor *m* Forever More, Comus
ed Jackson J. Bowdell
☆ Maggie Stride, Gay Singleton, Gilbert Wynne, Debbie Bowen, Robert Daubigny, Titus Groan, Nicola Austin

'Probably because of the shoestring budget, the squalor of life on the streets comes across quite well.' – *David McGillivray, Dark Side*

Perri **
US 1957 75m Technicolor
Walt Disney (Winston Hibler)
The life of a squirrel.
Disney's first True Life Fantasy, in which live footage of animals is manipulated against artificial backgrounds to produce an effect as charming and unreal as a cartoon.
w Ralph Wright, Winston Hibler *novel* Felix Salten *d* Ralph Wright *ph* various *m* Paul Smith
Paul Smith

Persecution
GB 1974 96m Eastmancolor
Fanfare/Tyburn (Kevin Francis)
US title: *The Terror of Sheba*
aka: *The Graveyard*
A rich American woman in England is hated by her son and fearful that her murky past will be revealed.
Rich but not engrossing nonsense, somewhat à la Baby Jane, *with hazy script and stolid production.*
w Robert B. Hutton, Rosemary Wootten *d* Don Chaffey *ph* Ken Talbot *m* Paul Ferris
☆ Lana Turner, Ralph Bates, Olga Georges-Picot, Trevor Howard, Suzan Farmer, Ronald Howard, Patrick Allen
'Gives off the unmistakable odour of damp mothballs.' – *Michael Billington, Illustrated London News*

The Persecution and Assassination of Jean-Paul Marat: see *The Marat/Sade*

Persona ****
Sweden 1966 81m bw
Svensk Filmindustri (Lars-Owe Carlberg)
A nurse begins to identify with her mentally ill patient, and herself has a nervous breakdown.
Intense clinical study presented in a very complex cinematic manner which tends to obscure the main theme while providing endless fascination for cinéastes.
wd Ingmar Bergman *ph* Sven Nykvist *m* Lars Johan Werle *ad* Bibi Lindström
☆ *Liv Ullmann, Bibi Andersson*, Margaretha Krook, Gunnar Björnstrand
'Reactions have ranged from incomprehension to irritation with what is dismissed as a characteristic piece of self-indulgence on Bergman's part – Bergman talking to himself again.' – *David Wilson, MFB*
'A puzzling, obsessive film that Bergman seems not so much to have worked out as to have torn from himself.' – *New Yorker, 1977*

Personal Affair
GB 1953 83m bw
Rank/Two Cities (Anthony Darnborough)
A schoolmaster and his neurotic wife run into trouble when a girl pupil develops a crush on him.
Preposterous domestic drama making much ado about nothing.
w Lesley Storm *play* Lesley Storm *d* Anthony Pelissier *ph* Reg Wyer *m* William Alwyn
☆ Leo Genn, Gene Tierney, Glynis Johns, Pamela Brown

Personal Best
US 1982 122m Technicolor
Warner (Robert Towne)
A female Olympic track star has a lesbian relationship.
So what, is the response to two numbing hours of tedium.
wd Robert Towne *ph* Michael Chapman *m* Jack Nitzsche
☆ Mariel Hemingway, Scott Glenn, Patrice Donnelly, Kenny Moore, Jim Moody
'There's an undercurrent of flabbergasted awe in this celebration of women's bodies, and everything in the movie is physically charged.' – *Pauline Kael, New Yorker*

Personal Choice: see *Beyond the Stars*

Personal Column: see *Lured*

Personal Column: see *Pièges (1939)*

Personal Maid's Secret
US 1935 60m bw
Warner/Bryan Foy
A maid's financial tips keep her master and mistress solvent.
Modest comedy which was well liked at the time.
w F. Hugh Herbert, Lillie Hayward *story* Lillian Day *d* Arthur Greville Collins
☆ Ruth Donnelly, Anita Louise, Warren Hull, Margaret Lindsay, Frank Albertson, Arthur Treacher

Personal Property *
US 1937 84m bw
MGM (John W. Considine Jnr)
GB title: *The Man in Possession*
An American widow in England, in financial straits, falls for the bailiff sent to keep an eye on her.
Moderate star comedy which still amuses.
w Hugh Mills, Ernest Vajda *play* The Man in Possession by H. M. Harwood *d* W. S. Van Dyke II
ph William Daniels *m* Franz Waxman
☆ Jean Harlow, Robert Taylor, Reginald Owen, Una O'Connor, Henrietta Crosman, E. E. Clive, Cora Witherspoon, Barnett Parker
'Harmless boudoir farce, for the undergraduates.' – *Variety*

Personal Services *
GB 1987 105m Eastmancolor
Zenith (Tim Bevan)
Adventures of a London madam.
Rather astonishing study of British attitudes to sex; not for Aunt Edna, but with a fair measure of interest for many.
w David Leland *d* Terry Jones *ph* Roger Deakins
ed George Akers
☆ *Julie Walters*, Alec McCowen, Shirley Stelfox, Danny Schiller, Victoria Hardcastle

Personal Velocity: Three Portraits *
US 2001 86m colour
Optimum/IFC/InDigEnt/Goldheart/Blue Magic (Gary Winick, Lemore Syvan, Alexis Alexanian)
Three short films: a woman takes her three children and leaves her abusive husband; a copy editor realises she must excise her husband from her life; a young woman picks up a hitchhiker with unexpected consequences.
A portmanteau movie in which women take actions that change their lives, though whether for the better or worse is open to debate; sharp performances get the most out of the material.
wd Rebecca Miller *short stories* Rebecca Miller
ph Ellen Kuras *m* Michael Rohaytn *pd* Judy Becker *ed* Sabine Hoffman
☆ Jon Ventimiglia (Narrator), Kyra Sedgwick (Delia), David Warshofsky (Kurt), Brian Tarantina (Pete), Parker Posey (Greta), Tim Guinee (Lee), Wallace Shawn (Mr Gelb), Joel de la Fuente (Thavi), Fairuza Balk (Paula), Lou Taylor Pucci (Kevin), Seth Gilliam (Vincent), David Patrick Kelly (Peter), Patti D'Urbanville (Celia)
'Often saddled with excruciating political and emotional correctness and earnestly imagined blue collar/rural settings. Miller's creative-writing-school prose is preserved in a droning voiceover.' – *Peter Bradshaw, Guardian*
'Artistic and moving, with a lovely moment of clarity and insight as the pay-off in each life lesson. Its literary origin is undisguised, with extensive and effective use of narration.' – *Angie Errigo, Empire*

'She's the woman behind the killer behind the gun!'
Persons in Hiding *
US 1939 71m bw
Paramount
A bored girl absconds with gangsters and becomes a public enemy.
Interesting programmer which led to several sequels using the same book as source; this one was vaguely inspired by the story of Bonnie and Clyde.
w William R. Lipman, Horace McCoy *book* J. Edgar Hoover *d* Louis King *ph* Harry Fischbeck
m Boris Morros
☆ Patricia Morison, J. Carrol Naish, Lynne Overman, William Henry, Helen Twelvetrees, William Frawley

'Strong supporter for the duals ... will depend entirely on rep of J. Edgar Hoover to attract.' – *Variety*
'A little on the tame side, but distinguished by the presence of a crooked and merciless heroine.' – *Graham Greene*

Persons Unknown *
Italy 1958 105m bw
Lux/Vides/Cinecittà (Franco Cristaldi)
original title: *I Soliti Ignoti*
US title: *Big Deal on Madonna Street*
Adventures of a gang of incompetent thieves, who get arrested more often than they get away, and finally, elaborately drill through a wall into the bank ... only to find it's the wrong wall and they are in another room of the same flat.
Spoof black comedy working up to an elaborate take-off of Rififi; *a great success in Italy and the USA, mildly received elsewhere.*
w Age Scarpelli, Suso Cecchi d'Amico, Mario Monicelli *d* Mario Monicelli *ph* Gianni di Venanzo *m* Piero Umiliani
☆ Vittorio Gassman, Renato Salvatori, Toto, Marcello Mastroianni, Memmo Carotenuto, Carla Gravina, Rossana Rory

Persons Unknown
US 1996 99m Foto-Kem
Metro/Tartan/Guild/Promark/Spectacor/Videal (David Lancaster)
A crooked ex-cop helps two sisters who are being hunted down by Colombian drug dealers.
A downbeat thriller, set among sleazy two-timers; only occasional moments elevate it out of the ordinary.
w Craig Smith *d* George Hickenlooper
ph Richard Crudo *m* Ed Tomney *pd* Jerry Fleming *ed* Suzanne Pettit
☆ Joe Mantegna, Kelly Lynch, Naomi Watts, J. T. Walsh, Xander Berkeley, Jon Favreau
'For those who like their thrillers hard-boiled, *Persons Unknown* is about as tough as it gets.' – *Jake Hamilton, Empire*

'It's never too late for true love.'
Persuasion *
GB 1995 102m colour
BBC-TV/WGBH/Boston and Millesime/France2 (Fiona Finlay)
A naval officer and the woman who was persuaded to reject his proposal some years before get a second chance at romance.
A lively but coarse adaptation that strives too hard to avoid gentility and to add action to a largely static, domestic drama.
w Nick Dear *novel* Jane Austen *d* Roger Michell
ph John Daly *m* Jeremy Sams *pd* William Dudley
ed Kate Evans
☆ Amanda Root (Anne Elliot), Ciaran Hinds (Captain Wentworth), Susan Fleetwood, Corin Redgrave, Fiona Shaw, John Woodvine, Samuel West, Phoebe Nicholls, Judy Cornwell
'A Jane Austen movie that is never pretty and only occasionally charming; instead it is troubled, astringent and touched with melancholy – not unlike the novel.' – *Anthony Lane, New Yorker*
† The film was originally made for BBC-TV and later given a cinema release.

La Perversa Caricia De Satan: see *The Devil's Kiss*

The Pest
US 1997 82m DeLuxe
Columbia TriStar/Bubble Factory (Sid, John and Bill Sheinberg)
A con man tries a multitude of disguises to escape from a gang of Scottish crooks, and a big-game hunter who plans to hunt him.
A cartoon-style comic variation on The Most Dangerous Game, *featuring frenetic gags that depend for their humour on flatulence and vomit.*
w David Bar Katz *d* Paul Miller *ph* Roy H. Wagner *m* Kevin Kiner *pd* Rodger E. Maus
ed Ross Albert, David Rawlins
☆ John Leguizamo, Jeffrey Jones, Edoardo Ballerini, Freddy Rodriguez, Tommy Townsend, Aries Spears, Joe Morton, Charles Hallahan

Pet Sematary
US 1989 103m Technicolor Panavision
UIP/Paramount (Richard P. Rubinstein)

A doctor and his family move into a house near a burial ground where the dead can be brought back to life.
Turgid horror, lacking in suspense and excitement.
w Stephen King *novel* Stephen King *d* Mary Lambert *ph* Peter Stein *m* Elliot Goldenthal *pd* Michael Z. Hanan *ed* Michael Hill, Daniel Hanley
☆ Dale Midkiff, Fred Gwynne, Denise Crosby, Brad Greenquist, Michael Lombard, Miko Hughes, Blaze Berdahl
'If all the usual excesses of the genre are well exercised, King's old-dark-house clichés have come up with far more edge and shine than he deserved.' – *Philip Strick, MFB*

'Raise some hell.'
Pet Sematary Two
US 1992 102m DuArt
Paramount (Ralph S. Singleton)

A father and son move to a new house, next to a cemetery where the dead can be resurrected.
Nasty little shocker, with no redeeming features.
w Richard Outten *novel* Stephen King *d* Mary Lambert *ph* Russell Carpenter *m* Mark Governor *pd* Michelle Minch *ed* Tom Finan *sp* Peter Chesney, Steve Johnson
☆ Edward Furlong, Anthony Edwards, Clancy Brown, Jared Rushton, Darlanne Fluegel, Jason McGuire, Sarah Trigger, Lisa Waltz
'About 50% better than its predecessor, which is to say it's not very good at all.' – *Variety*
'A complete waste of time.' – *Nigel Floyd, The Dark Side*

Pétain
France 1992 133m colour
Gala/Mod/France 2 (Jacques Kirsner)

In 1940, the ageing Marshall Pétain becomes the leader of France; in Vichy, he makes peace with the invading German army and, under the influence of Laval, collaborates with the Nazis.
Mundane biopic that plods through the facts without making them seem particularly relevant.
w Jean-Pierre Marchand *book* Marc Ferro *d* Jean Marboeuf *ph* Dominique Bouilleret *m* Georges Garvarentz *pd* Jerome Clément *ed* Anne-France Lebrun
☆ Jacques Dufilho, Jean Yanne, Jean-Pierre Cassel, Jean-Claude Dreyfus, Antoinette Moya, Julie Marboeuf, Ludwig Haas (Hitler)
'A major accomplishment. Taboo-breaking and ideologically irreproachable pic about Vichy and its legacy is a clear and nuanced – and long overdue – view of crucial French history. Unfailingly cinematic, intelligently structured and beautifully cast, pic is essential viewing for Gallic auds and deserves to be shown everywhere.' – *Variety*
'The film plods along, serenely untroubled by anything that would justify its 133 minutes. Quiet days in Vichy indeed.' – *Sheila Johnston, Independent*

'The story of a jazz-man of the wide-open 20s ... caught in the crossfire of its blazing .38s!'
Pete Kelly's Blues *
US 1955 95m Warnercolor Cinemascope
(Warner) Mark VII Ltd (Jack Webb)

Jazz musicians in the twenties get involved with gangsters.
Minor cult film, mainly for the score; dramatically it is not exactly compelling.
w Richard L. Breen *d* Jack Webb *ph* Harper Goff *m* Sammy Cahn, Ray Heindorf, Arthur Hamilton, Matty Matlock
☆ Jack Webb, Edmond O'Brien, Janet Leigh, Peggy Lee, Andy Devine, *Ella Fitzgerald*, Lee Marvin, Martin Milner
'Concerned with striking attitudes and establishing an atmosphere rather than developing anything very coherent in the way of narrative ... one remains aware of an over-deliberate straining after effect.' – *Penelope Houston*
Peggy Lee

'Honeymoon's over – time to get married!'
Pete 'n Tillie *
US 1972 100m Technicolor Panavision
Universal (Julius J. Epstein)
The tragi-comic marriage of two eccentrics.
Curious: plain drama treated as comedy, with surprisingly satisfactory results, but not an example to be followed.
w Julius J. Epstein *novel Witch's Milk* by Peter de Vries *d* Martin Ritt *ph* John Alonzo *m* John T. Williams
☆ *Walter Matthau, Carol Burnett*, Geraldine Page, René Auberjonois, Barry Nelson, Henry Jones
'For the most part an amusing, moving, sentimental comedy. The wisecracks stay on this side of human possibility – that is, we don't feel, as we do so often with Neil Simon, that the characters have private gag writers in their homes.' – *Stanley Kauffmann*
Julius J. Epstein; Geraldine Page
Walter Matthau

'The most beautiful romance in all modern literature!'
Peter Ibbetson *
US 1935 85m bw
Paramount (Louis D. Lighton)
Childhood sweethearts meet again as adults, are separated when he is imprisoned for her husband's murder, but are reunited in heaven.
Downright peculiar romantic fantasy, even more oddly cast, but extremely well produced.
w Vincent Lawrence, Waldemar Young, Constance Collier *novel* George du Maurier *d* Henry Hathaway *ph* Charles Lang *m* Ernst Toch
☆ Gary Cooper, Ann Harding, Ida Lupino, John Halliday, Douglass Dumbrille, Virginia Weidler, Dickie Moore, Doris Lloyd
'In a day and a world hard-boiled and realistic Paramount hopes to sell a picture about dreams and beauty and love. It just isn't in the cards.' – *Variety*
'A triumph of surrealist thought.' – *André Breton*
'One of the world's ten best films.' – *Luis Buñuel*
Ernst Toch

Peter Pan ***
US 1953 76m Technicolor
Walt Disney

Three London children are taken into fairyland by a magic flying boy who cannot grow up.
Solidly crafted cartoon version of a famous children's play; not Disney's best work, but still miles ahead of the competition.
d Wilfred Jackson, Clyde Geronimi, Hamilton Luske *m* Oliver Wallace *supervisor* Ben Sharpsteen
☆ Featuring the voices of Bobby Driscoll, Kathryn Beaumont, Hans Conried, Bill Thompson, Heather Angel
'A painful travesty.' – C. A. Lejeune

Peter Rabbit and the Tales of Beatrix Potter:
see *Tales of Beatrix Potter*

Peter the Great *
USSR 1937 96m bw
Lenfilm
The rise to power of the famous autocrat.
Standard Russian first feature with plenty of action and striking composition, but not really memorable.
w Alexei Tolstoy, Vladimir Petrov *d* Vladimir Petrov
☆ Nikolai Simonov, Nikolai Cherkassov, Alla Tarasova, M. Zharov
'Surprisingly strong: a cinch in Russian-languagers.' – *Variety*

'A comedy about love, friendship and other natural disasters.'
Peter's Friends **
GB 1992 101m Technicolor
Entertainment/Renaissance/Samuel Goldwyn/Channel 4 (Kenneth Branagh)

A decade after they left university, a group of former friends get together for a New Year's reunion at a country mansion.
A British variation on The Big Chill *that is a good deal chillier, with a cast too familiar from innumerable television comedies to be entirely convincing in their roles.*
w Martin Bergman, Rita Rudner *d* Kenneth Branagh *ph* Roger Lanser *m* Gavin Greenaway *pd* Tim Harvey *ed* Andrew Marcus
☆ Kenneth Branagh, Alphonsia Emmanuel, Stephen Fry, Hugh Laurie, Phyllida Law, Alex Lowe, Rita Rudner, Tony Slattery, Imelda Staunton, Emma Thompson, Richard Briers
'Well written, beautifully performed and highly entertaining.' – *Derek Malcolm, Guardian*
'A lot more work is called for all round before these likeable people produce something worthy to be called disposable film entertainment.' – *Adam Mars-Jones, Independent*
'Awful, with glimpses of wit. The script is hopelessly schematic: one long, drawing-room chat in which people dish each other, then leave the room so they can be talked about.' – *Richard Corliss, Time*

The Peterville Diamond
GB 1942 85m bw
Warner (A. H. Salomon)
A bored wife revives her husband's interest by cultivating the advances of a jewel thief.
Modest comedy-drama, smoothly presented: the same play formed the basis of Dieterle's Jewel Robbery.
w Brock Williams, Gordon Wellesley *play Jewel Robbery* by Ladislas Fodor *d* Walter Forde *ph* Basil Emmott *md* Jack Beaver
☆ Anne Crawford, Donald Stewart, Renee Houston, Oliver Wakefield, Charles Heslop, William Hartnell, Felix Aylmer, Charles Victor

Pete's Dragon
US 1977 127m Technicolor
Walt Disney (Ron Miller, Jerome Courtland)

In Maine in 1900, a nine-year-old boy escapes from grasping foster-parents with his pet dragon, which no one but himself can see.
A kind of juvenile rewrite of Harvey. *The dragon is drawn (rather poorly) and the human characters are not exactly three-dimensional. A long way from* Mary Poppins.
w Malcolm Marmorstein *story* Seton I. Miller, S. S. Field *d* Don Chaffey *ph* Frank Phillips *md* Irwin Kostal *ch* Onna White *animation* Ken Anderson *songs* Al Kasha, Joel Hirschhorn
☆ Sean Marshall, Mickey Rooney, Jim Dale, Helen Reddy, Red Buttons, Shelley Winters, Jim Backus, Joe E. Ross, Ben Wrigley
'For a Disney film it's terribly badly made, in parts so clumsy that it looks like the work of the Burbank Amateur Camera Club.' – *Barry Took, Punch*
music; song 'Candle on the Water'

La Petite Bande **
France 1983 91m colour
Squirrel/Gaumont-Stand'Art/FR3/Hamster Productions (Denis Mermet)
A gang of English children stow away to France where they cause mayhem and save the world from a gang of wicked adults before ending up on a desert island.
Lively and subversive entertainment intended for children.
w Gilles Perrault, Michel Déville, Yan Appas, Joan Népami *d* Michel Déville *ph* Claude Lecompte *m* Edgar Cosma *pd* Michel Guyot, Régis Des Plas *ed* Raymonde Guyot
☆ Andrew Chandler, Hélène Dassule, Nicole Palmer, Hamish Scrimgeour, Katherine Scrimgeour, Nicolas Sireau, Rémi Usquin, Valérie Gauthier

La Petite Voleuse *
France 1988 109m Fujicolour
Pathé/Orly Films/Renn Productions/Ciné Cinq/Les Films du Carrosse/Sedif (Jean-José Richer)
A young girl becomes the lover and accomplice of a thief.
Moderately engaging account of a defiant, amoral outlaw determined to make her own way in the world.
w François Truffaut, Claude de Givray *d* Claude Miller *ph* Dominique Chapuis *ad* Jean-Pierre Kohut Svelko *ed* Albert Jurgenson
☆ Charlotte Gainsbourg, Didier Bazace, Simon de la Brosse, Raoul Billerey, Chantal Banlier, Nathalie Cardone, Clotilde de Bayser

Les Petites Filles Modèles
France 1971 88m Eastmancolor
Plan-Film/Studio du Dragon/Labrador/Tanagra (Louis Duchesne)

aka: *Good Little Girls*
The amorous adventures of a wealthy aristocratic widow and her two nubile daughters.
Lively comic carry-on, updating a novel about well-brought-up young girls behaving badly.
w François de Bernis *novel* Comtesse de Ségur *d* Jean-Claude Roy *ph* Claude Saunier *m* Maurice Lecoeur *ed* Florence Eymon
☆ Jessica Dorn, Marie-Georges Pascal, Cathy Reghin, Sylvie Lafontaine, Michèle Girardon, Bella Darvi, Béatrice Arnac, François Guerin, Dominique Paturel (narrator)
'This crudely unsubtle adaptation, which reduces the story to the level of a mild exploitation picture, full of coy nudity and *doubles entendres*, and made without any grace or humour.' – *John Gillett, MFB*

The Petrified Forest **
US 1936 83m bw
Warner (Henry Blanke)

Travellers at a way station in the Arizona desert are held up by gangsters.
Rather faded melodrama (it always was), which is important to Hollywood for introducing such well used figures as the poet idealist hero and the gangster anti-hero, and for giving Bogart his first meaty role. Otherwise, the settings are artificial, the acting theatrical, the development predictable and the dialogue pretentious.
w Charles Kenyon, Delmer Daves *play* Robert E. Sherwood *d* Archie Mayo *ph* Sol Polito *md* Leo F. Forbstein
☆ *Leslie Howard*, Bette Davis, *Humphrey Bogart*, Genevieve Tobin, Dick Foran, Joe Sawyer, Porter Hall, Charley Grapewin
ALAN SQUIER (LESLIE HOWARD): 'Let there be killing. All this evening I've had a feeling of destiny closing in.'
JACKIE (JOE SAWYER): 'Now, just behave yourself and nobody'll get hurt. This is Duke Mantee, the world-famous killer, and he's hungry.'
'Marquee draft should offset the philosophic meanderings which minimize appeal.' – *Variety*
'Drama slackens under the weight of Mr Sherwood's rather half-baked philosophy.' – *Alistair Cooke*
'There is good dramatic material here, but Mr Sherwood doesn't see his play as certain things happening, but as ideas being expressed, "significant" cosmic ideas ... Life itself, which crept in during the opening scene, embarrassed perhaps at hearing itself so explicitly discussed, crept out again, leaving us only with the symbols, the too pasteboard desert, the stunted cardboard studio trees.' – *Graham Greene*
† Remade as *Escape in the Desert* (qv).

Petticoat Fever
US 1936 80m bw
MGM (Frank Davis)
A girl and her stuffy fiancé crash land their plane in sub-Arctic Labrador and are helped by a wireless operator who has not seen a woman for two years.
Pert, slightly unusual comedy which comes off pretty well.
w Harold Goldman *play* Mark Reed *d* George Fitzmaurice *ph* Ernest Haller *m* William Axt
☆ Robert Montgomery, Myrna Loy, Reginald Owen, Winifred Shotter

The Petty Girl
US 1950 88m Technicolor
Columbia (Nat Perrin)
GB title: *Girl of the Year*
A calendar artist takes a staid college professor as his model, and causes a scandal.
Witless comedy musical which barely lingers in the memory.
w Nat Perrin *story* Mary McCarthy *d* Henry Levin *ph* William Snyder *m* George Duning *songs* Harold Arlen, Johnny Mercer
☆ Robert Cummings, Joan Caulfield, Melville Cooper, Elsa Lanchester, Audrey Long, Mary Wickes, Frank Orth

Petulia ☆
US 1968 105m Technicolor
Warner/Petersham (Raymond Wagner)

A doctor's life is disrupted by his meeting and loving a kooky girl who has family problems.
Swinging London melodrama which happens to be set in San Francisco. All very flashy, and occasionally arresting or well acted, but adding up to nothing.
w Lawrence B. Marcus *novel* Me and the Arch Kook Petulia by John Haase *d* Richard Lester *ph* Nicolas Roeg *m* John Barry
☆ George C. Scott, Julie Christie, Richard Chamberlain, Joseph Cotten, Arthur Hill, Shirley Knight, Kathleen Widdoes, Pippa Scott
'A sad and savage comment on the ways we waste our time and ourselves in upper-middle-class America.' – *Richard Schickel*
'A soulless, arbitrary, attitudinizing piece of claptrap.' – *John Simon*

Peur sur la Ville: see *Night Caller*

'Everybody in this town hides behind plain wrappers!'
Peyton Place ☆☆
US 1957 157m DeLuxe Cinemascope
TCF (Jerry Wald)

Sex, frustration and violence ferment under the placid surface of a small New England town.
Well-made film of what was at the time a scandalous bestseller, one of the first to reveal those nasty secrets of 'ordinary people'.
w John Michael Hayes *novel* Grace Metalious *d* Mark Robson *ph* William Mellor *m* Franz Waxman
☆ Lana Turner, Arthur Kennedy, Hope Lange, Lee Philips, Lloyd Nolan, Diane Varsi, Russ Tamblyn, Terry Moore, Barry Coe, David Nelson, Betty Field, Mildred Dunnock, Leon Ames, Lorne Greene
best picture; John Michael Hayes; Mark Robson; William Mellor; Lana Turner; Arthur Kennedy; Hope Lange; Diane Varsi; Russ Tamblyn

Phaedra ☆
US/Greece 1961 116m bw
UA/Melinafilm (Jules Dassin)
A tycoon's wife falls in love with her stepson.
Ludicrous, awesomely folly-filled attempt to modernize and sex up Greek tragedy.
wd Jules Dassin *ph* Jacques Natteau *m* Mikis Theodorakis
☆ Melina Mercouri, Anthony Perkins, Raf Vallone, Elizabeth Ercy
'Unfortunately unforgettable.' – *John Simon*

'If this one doesn't scare you ... you're already dead!'
Phantasm
US 1979 90m Technicolor
Avco Embassy

A 16-year-old has nightmares which seem to come true.
Cleverly assembled horror comic with many nasty moments. Not for the squeamish, and with no real merit except the power to frighten.
wd Don Coscarelli (who was 20 at the time) *ph* Don Coscarelli *ed* Don Coscarelli
☆ Michael Baldwin, Bill Thornbury, Reggie Bannister, Angus Scrimm

Phantasm II
US 1988 97m colour
Guild/Starway International (Roberto A. Quezada)

A creature from another dimension who brings corpses back to life is thwarted by a teenager and his old adversary.
In the nine years separating this sequel from the original, its director has retained his ability to shock but still cannot tell a story convincingly.
wd Don Coscarelli *ph* Dayn Okada *m* Fred Myrow, Christopher L. Stone *pd* Philip J. C. Duffin *ed* Peter Teschner
☆ James Le Gros, Reggie Bannister, Angus Scrimm, Paula Irvine, Samantha Phillips, Kenneth Tigar, Ruth C. Engel, Mark Anthony Major, Rubin Kushner
'A slick-looking but uninvolving, uncertain picture.' – *MFB*

The Phantom
US/Australia 1996 100m DeLuxe
Paramount/Ladd Company/Village Roadshow (Robert Evans, Alan Ladd Jnr)

A pirate's plan to make himself dictator of America by obtaining three skulls with supernatural powers is thwarted by a masked hero.
A limp action movie featuring a dull super-hero, this is below-par Saturday matinée stuff.
w Jeffrey Boam *comic strip* Lee Falk *d* Simon Wincer *ph* David Burr *m* David Newman *pd* Paul Peters *ed* O. Nicholas Brown, Bryan H. Carroll
☆ Billy Zane, Kristy Swanson, Treat Williams, Catherine Zeta Jones, James Remar, Jon Teney, Cary-Hiroyuki Tagawa, Patrick McGoohan, Bill Smitrovich, Samantha Eggar
'Brings a light touch to appealingly old-fashioned action material, creating a fast-moving yarn.' – *Variety*

The Phantom Baron: see *Le Baron Fantôme*

The Phantom Carriage: see *Thy Soul Shall Bear Witness*

The Phantom Fiend: see *The Lodger*

Phantom Killer
US 1942 57m bw
A. W. Hackel/Monogram
A young district attorney uncovers an ingenious criminal ruse by twin brothers.
Better-than-average crime filler.
w Karl Brown *d* William Beaudine
☆ Dick Purcell, Joan Woodbury, John Hamilton, Warren Hymer, J. Farrell MacDonald, Mantan Moreland

Phantom Lady ☆☆
US 1944 87m bw
Universal (Joan Harrison)
A man is accused of murder and his only alibi is a mysterious lady he met in a bar.
Odd little thriller which doesn't really hold together but is made for the most part with great style.
w Bernard C. Schoenfeld *novel* William Irish *d* Robert Siodmak *ph* Woody Bredell *m* Hans Salter
☆ Franchot Tone, Alan Curtis, Ella Raines, Elisha Cook Jnr, Fay Helm, Andrew Tombes

The Phantom Light
GB 1935 76m bw
Gaumont British/Gainsborough (Jerome Jackson)
A new keeper takes over at a remote Welsh lighthouse which is reputed to be haunted.
An old-fashioned and stagey melodrama, a sort of seafaring Ghost Train, *which defeats the director's best efforts to create something more realistic.*
w Ralph Smart, J. Jefferson Farjeon, Austin Melford *play* The Haunted Light by Evadne Price, Joan Roy Byford *d* Michael Powell *ph* Roy Kellino *md* Louis Levy *ad* A. Vetchinsky *ed* D. N. Twist
☆ Binnie Hale, Gordon Harker, Donald Calthrop, Milton Rosmer, Ian Hunter, Herbert Lomas

Phantom Love: see *Ai No Borei*

Phantom of 42nd Street
US 1945 58m bw
PRC/Mooney-Herman
A young Broadway star is suspected when her uncle is murdered backstage.
Lightweight but amiable mystery.
w Milton Raison *d* Albert Herman
☆ Dave O'Brien, Kay Aldridge, Alan Mowbray, Frank Jenks, Jack Mulhall

Phantom of Crestwood ☆
US 1932 77m bw
RKO (David O. Selznick)

Murder strikes when a blackmailer assembles her victims.
Lively mystery with spoof elements.
w Bartlett Cormack, J. Walter Ruben *d* J. Walter Ruben *ph* Henry Gerrard *m* Max Steiner
☆ Ricardo Cortez, H. B. Warner, Anita Louise, Karen Morley, Pauline Frederick, Robert McWade, Skeets Gallagher
'Below the deluxe classification it should give a good account of itself.' – *Variety*

The Phantom of Liberty ☆☆☆
France 1974 104m Eastmancolor
Fox-Rank/Greenwich (Serge Silberman)

original title: *Le Fantôme de la Liberté*
Surrealist episodes in the lives of various loosely linked individuals that range from a firing squad in 1808 to modern-day Paris where a dead woman phones her brother to offer him consolation and the police prepare to suppress a revolt.
A hit and miss affair in its treatment of middle-class hypocrisies, often funny, but sometimes no more than bizarre, although you keep watching, just to see what happens next.
w Luis Buñuel, Jean-Claude Carrière *d* Luis Buñuel *ph* Edmond Richard *ad* Pierre Guffroy *ed* Hélène Plemiannikov
☆ Monica Vitti, Jean-Claude Brialy, Michel Piccoli, Jean Rochefort, Adolfo Celi, Michel Lonsdale, Adriana Asti, Bernard Verley, Maxence Mailfort, Muni, Philippe Brigaud
'A magnificent film ... one of Buñuel's masterpieces.' – *Tom Milne, Sight and Sound*
'Buñuel has a great spare, tonic style, but the domesticated surrealism of this picture has no sting and no after-effect. The film drifts out of your head before it's over.' – *Pauline Kael, New Yorker*

Phantom of Paris
US 1931 73m bw
MGM
A magician proves by a complex plan that he did not kill his fiancée's father.
Unusual but tortuous thriller which fails to thrill.
w Bess Meredyth, John Meehan, Edwin Justus Mayer *d* John S. Robertson
☆ John Gilbert, Leila Hyams, Ian Keith, C. Aubrey Smith, Lewis Stone, Jean Hersholt
'It isn't Gilbert that makes the picture, it makes itself. Merits above-average gross.' – *Variety*

Phantom of the Opera ☆☆☆
US 1925 94m (24 fps) bw (Technicolor sequence) silent
Universal

A disfigured man in a mask abducts the prima donna of the Paris Opera House to his lair in the sewers below.
Patchy but often splendid piece of Grand Guignol which not only provided its star with a famous role but was notable for its magnificent visual style.
w Raymond Schrock, Elliott Clawson *novel* Gaston Leroux *d* Rupert Julian *ph* Charles Van Enger, Virgil Miller *ad* Dan Hall
☆ Lon Chaney, Mary Philbin, Norman Kerry, Gibson Gowland
'The greatest inducement to nightmare that has yet been screened.' – *Variety*
† The chase was directed by Edward Sedgwick.
†† In 1930 an 89m talkie version was issued with approximately 35% dialogue which had been recorded by the surviving actors, and some new footage.

The Phantom of the Opera ☆
US 1943 92m Technicolor
Universal (George Waggner)

A shy violinist, obsessed with a chorus girl, haunts the sewers of the opera house after he is disfigured by having acid thrown in his face by a jealous rival.
This version of the familiar story is more decorous and gentlemanly than most, with much attention paid to the music, but it certainly has its moments.
w Erich Taylor, Samuel Hoffenstein *d* Arthur Lubin *ph* Hal Mohr, W. Howard Greene *m* Edward Ward *ad* John B. Goodman, Alexander Golitzen
☆ Claude Rains, Nelson Eddy, Susanna Foster, Edgar Barrier, Leo Carrillo, J. Edward Bromberg, Jane Farrar, Hume Cronyn
'A grand and gaudy entertainment.' – *Manchester Guardian*
Hal Mohr, W. Howard Greene; John B. Goodman, Alexander Golitzen; Edward Ward

Phantom of the Opera
GB 1962 90m Technicolor
U-I/Hammer (Anthony Hinds)

A disfigured composer lurks beneath an opera house with his hunchbacked assistant and kidnaps the singer he loves to coach her in a leading role.
Stodgy remake with the accent on shock. Its box-office failure was attributed to treating the phantom too sympathetically.
w John Elder (Anthony Hinds) *d* Terence Fisher *ph* Arthur Grant *m* Edwin Astley *md* John Hollingsworth *ad* Bernard Robinson, Don Mingaye *ed* Alfred Cox
☆ Herbert Lom, Edward de Souza, Heather Sears, Thorley Walters, Michael Gough, Ian Wilson, Martin Miller, John Harvey, Miriam Karlin
'The only shock is that the British, who could have had a field day with this antique, have simply wafted it back with a lick and a promise.' – *New York Times*

Phantom of the Opera
US 1989 93m colour
Castle Premier/21st Century/Breton Film (Harry Alan Towers)

Struck on the head, a singer finds herself back in Victorian England, where she falls under the influence of a disfigured musical genius who has sold his soul to the devil.
Undistinguished variation on a familiar story, cashing in on the popularity of the actor who plays 'Freddy' in the Nightmare On Elm Street *series.*
w Duke Sandefur, Gerry O'Hara *d* Dwight H. Little *ph* Elemer Ragalyi *m* Misha Segal *ad* Tivadar Bertalan *ed* Charles Bornstein
☆ Robert Englund, Jill Schoelen, Alex Hyde-White, Bill Nighy, Terence Harvey, Stephanie Lawrence, Nathan Lewis, Peter Clapham

Phantom of the Paradise ☆
US 1974 91m Movielab
TCF/Pressman Williams (Edward R. Pressman)

A modern satirical remake of *Phantom of the Opera* in rock opera terms, set in a pop music palace.
Not bad in spots, but it doesn't really know where it's going.
wd Brian de Palma *ph* Larry Pizer *m* Paul Williams *pd* Jack Fisk
☆ Paul Williams, William Finley, Jessica Harper, George Memmoli, Gerrit Graham
'Too broad in its effects and too bloated in style to cut very deeply as a parody ... closer to the anything goes mode of a *Mad* magazine lampoon.' – *Richard Combs*
Paul Williams

'It Strikes, Vanishes, Then Lunges Out Again And Again!'
'Nothing like it was ever known before...let's hope nothing like its terror will ever happen again!'
Phantom of the Rue Morgue
US 1954 84m Warnercolor 3-D
Warner (Henry Blanke)
In old Paris, a killer of pretty girls turns out to be an ape.
Dull revamping of a rather dull story, with boring characters and little horror.
w Harold Medford, James R. Webb *story* Murders in the Rue Morgue by Edgar Allan Poe *d* Roy del Ruth *ph* Peverell Marley *m* David Buttolph *md* Ray Heindorf *ad* Bertram Tuttle *ed* James C. Moore
☆ Karl Malden (Dr Maraio), Claude Dauphin (Inspector Bonnard), Steve Forrest (Prof. Paul Dupin), Patricia Medina (Jeanette Bouvere), Allyn McLerie (Yvonne), Dolores Dorn (Camille), Anthony Caruso (Jacques), Veola Vonn (Arlette), Merv Griffin (Georges Brevert)

The Phantom President ☆
US 1932 78m bw
Paramount
A fast-talking quack doubles for a lacklustre presidential candidate.
A likely but in fact unsuccessful film début for a famous Broadway star: many points of interest.
w Walter de Leon, Harlan Thompson *d* Norman Taurog *ph* David Abel *songs* Richard Rodgers, Lorenz Hart
☆ George M. Cohan, Claudette Colbert, Jimmy Durante, George Barbier, Sidney Toler, Jameson Thomas, Paul Hurst, Alan Mowbray

'A lot of smart stuff is packed into the footage … should do well without threatening to rate itself a smash.' – *Variety*

'For anyone who cares about American theatrical history, it's an indispensable record of Cohan's style.' – *New Yorker, 1978*

Phantom Ship: see *The Mystery of the Marie Celeste*

The Phantom Strikes: see *The Gaunt Stranger*

The Phantom Tollbooth

US 1969 89m Metrocolor
MGM/Animation/Visual Arts (Abe Levitow, Les Goldman)

A bored young boy, oblivious to his surroundings, is transported into a world of the imagination, where words and numbers battle for supremacy.
A witty, literate children's story, depending on wordplay, becomes a conventional animated film, constraining the antic imagination of Chuck Jones.
w Chuck Jones, Sam Rosen *novel* Norton Juster *d* Chuck Jones, Abe Levitow (animation); David Monahan (live action) *ph* Lester Shorr *m* Dean Elliott *m/ly* Norman Gimbel, Lee Pockriss, Paul Vance *pd* Maurice Noble *ed* Jim Faris
☆ Butch Patrick and also the voices of Mel Blanc, Daws Butler, Candy Candido, Hans Conried, June Foray, Patti Gilbert

'Chuck Jones and Abe Levitow have approached Juster with an appalling condescension – manifested partly in the snail's pace and constant over-emphasis, and partly in the sickening cuteness, reminiscent of Disney at his worst.' – *Tom Milne, MFB*

Phar Lap

Australia 1983 118m colour Panavision
TCF/Michael Edgley International (John Sexton)

GB title: *Phar Lap – Heart of a Nation*
The story of a crack racehorse which was the talk of the world in the early thirties but died of a mysterious disease.
The film, though adequately textured, won't win any races.
w David Williamson *d* Simon Wincer *ph* Russell Boyd *m* Bruce Rowland
☆ Tom Burlinson, Martin Vaughan, Judy Morris, Celia de Burgh, Ron Liebman, Vincent Ball

'The day the earth was turned into a cemetery!'

Phase IV *

GB 1973 84m Technicolor
Paramount/Alced (Paul B. Radin)

In the Arizona desert, ants attack a scientific installation.
Oddly effective if repulsive science fiction; the ants are all the more unpleasant because they stay the normal size.
w Mayo Simon *d Saul Bass* *ph* Dick Bush *m* Brian Gascoigne
☆ Nigel Davenport, Lynne Frederick, Michael Murphy, Alan Gifford

'Sin City of Alabama!'

The Phenix City Story *

US 1955 100m bw
Allied Artists (Sam Bischoff, David Diamond)
A young lawyer fights the racketeers who control his town.
Goodish example of the semi-documentary melodramas of small-town corruption which swarmed out of Hollywood following the Kefauver investigations.
w Crane Wilbur, Dan Mainwaring *d Phil Karlson* *ph* Harry Neumann *m* Harry Sukman
☆ Richard Kiley, *Edward Andrews*, John McIntire, Kathryn Grant

Phenomena: see *Creepers*

'Some Things In Life Just Can't Be Explained.'

Phenomenon

US 1996 124m Technicolor Panavision
Buena Vista/Touchstone (Barbara Boyle, Michael Taylor)

A dim-witted mechanic becomes a genius after he is knocked out by seeing a bright light in the sky.
Sentimental weepie with the message that it's good to conform.
w Gerald DiPego *d* Jon Turteltaub *ph* Phedon Papamichael *m* Thomas Newton *pd* Garreth Stover *ed* Bruce Green
☆ John Travolta, Kyra Sedgwick, Forest Whitaker, Jeffrey DeMunn, Robert Duvall, Richard Kiley, Brent Spiner

'Suggests that, in late-20th-century America, to work at gaining knowledge is to be weird – a freak to be feared. The film would be unbearable were Travolta not so consistently charming.' – *Ken Tucker, Entertainment Weekly*

'Don't Say it. See it!'

Phffft

US 1954 91m bw
Columbia (Fred Kohlmar)

The title refers to the sound of an expiring match; the story tells of a couple who get divorced and try to find out what they have been missing.
Champagne comedy with no bubbles.
w George Axelrod *d* Mark Robson *ph* Charles Lang *m* Frederick Hollander
☆ Jack Lemmon, Judy Holliday, Kim Novak, Jack Carson, Luella Gear, Donald Randolph, Donald Curtis, Merry Anders

'At best, moderate entertainment.' – *Saturday Review*

'The director was miscast.' – *George Axelrod*

'No One Would Take On His Case … Until One Man Was Willing To Take On The System.'

Philadelphia **

US 1993 125m Technicolor
TriStar/Clinca Estetico (Edward Saxon, Jonathan Demme)

A successful homosexual lawyer with AIDS sues his firm for unfair dismissal after he is sacked for 'an attitude problem'.
A feel-good film about AIDS, set within a standard Hollywood courtroom drama; it is well made and absorbing, given its limits.
w Ron Nyswaner *d* Jonathan Demme *ph* Tak Fujimoto *m* Howard Shore *pd* Kristi Zea *ed* Craig McKay
☆ Tom Hanks, Denzel Washington, Jason Robards, Mary Steenburgen, Antonio Banderas, Ron Vawter, Robert Ridgely, Charles Napier, Joanne Woodward

'An ideal film for people who have never known anyone with AIDS … extremely well-made message picture.' – *Variety*

'The film ultimately becomes a documentary on the ravages of AIDS – and on the masochistic machismo of Method acting.' – *Richard Corliss, Time*

'A heartbreakingly mediocre film. It's dishonest, it's often legally, medically and politically inaccurate, and it breaks my heart that I must say it's simply not good enough and I'd rather people not see it at all.' – *Larry Kramer*

Tom Hanks; song 'Streets of Philadelphia' (*m/ly* Bruce Springsteen)
Ron Nyswaner; song 'Philadelphia' (*m/ly* Neil Young); make-up

The Philadelphia Experiment *

US 1984 101m CFI color
New World/Cinema Group (Joel B. Michaels, Douglas Curtis)

Seamen on a 1943 destroyer fall through a time warp into 1984, and have one hell of a job getting back.
Science fiction, Outer Limits/Final Countdown *style; quite watchable, and technically proficient, but the claim that it was based on an actual incident seems a bit tall.*
w William Gray, Michael Janover *book* William I. Moore, Charles Berlitz *d* Stewart Raffill *ph* Dick Bush *m* Ken Wannberg *ad* Chris Campbell *ed* Neil Travis, William Hoy
☆ Michael Paré, Nancy Allen, Eric Christmas, Bobby Di Cicco, Louise Latham

The Philadelphia Experiment 2

US 1993 97m colour
Trimark (Mark Levinson, Doug Curtis)

An experiment goes wrong and a modern bomber-plane goes through the space-time continuum into a place of dictatorship and concentration camps.
Undemanding action fare that does little with its science-fiction elements.
w Kevin Rock, Nick Paine *d* Stephen Cornwell *ph* Ronn Schmidt *m* Gerald Couriet *pd* Armin Ganz *ed* Nina Gilberti *sp* Frank Ceglia
☆ Brad Johnson, Marjean Holden, Gerrit Graham, James Greene, Geoffrey Blake, Cyril O'Reilly, John Christian Grass

'An old idea, passably reworked.' – *Sight and Sound*

† The film was released direct to video in Britain.

'Uncle Leo's bedtime story for you older tots! The things they do among the playful rich – oh, boy!'

The Philadelphia Story ****

US 1940 112m bw
MGM (Joseph L. Mankiewicz)

A stuffy heiress, about to be married for the second time, turns human and returns gratefully to number one.
Hollywood's most wise and sparkling comedy, with a script which is even an improvement on the original play. Cukor's direction is so discreet you can hardly sense it, and all the performances are just perfect.
w Donald Ogden Stewart *play Philip Barry*
d George Cukor *ph* Joseph Ruttenberg *m Franz Waxman* *ad* Cedric Gibbons
☆ *Katharine Hepburn, Cary Grant, James Stewart, Ruth Hussey, Roland Young, John Halliday, Mary Nash, Virginia Weidler, John Howard, Henry Daniell*

'There are just not enough superlatives sufficiently to appreciate this show.' – *Hollywood Reporter*

'An exceptionally bright job of screenplay writing … though films like this do little to advance the art of motion pictures, they may help to convince some of the more discerning among cultural slugabeds that when movies want to turn their hand to anything, they can turn it.' – *Otis Ferguson*

† Cary Grant donated his salary to war relief.
Donald Ogden Stewart; James Stewart
best picture; George Cukor; Katharine Hepburn; Ruth Hussey

Philo Vance

The smooth sleuth created by S. S. Van Dine was a popular film hero of the thirties, for several different companies and with several different actors. As a series it was very variable indeed.
1929 The Canary Murder Case (Paramount: William Powell), The Greene Murder Case (Paramount: William Powell)
1930 The Bishop Murder Case (MGM: Basil Rathbone), The Benson Murder Case (Paramount: William Powell)
1933 The Kennel Murder Case (qv) (Warner: William Powell)
1934 The Dragon Murder Case (Warner: Warren William)
1935 The Casino Murder Case (MGM: Paul Lukas)
1936 The Garden Murder Case (MGM: Edmund Lowe)
1937 Night of Mystery (Paramount: Grant Richards), The Scarab Murder Case (British: Wilfrid Hyde-White)
1939 The Gracie Allen Murder Case (Paramount: Warren William), Calling Philo Vance (Warner: James Stephenson)
1947 Philo Vance Returns (PRC: William Wright), Philo Vance's Gamble (PRC: Alan Curtis), Philo Vance's Secret Mission (PRC: Alan Curtis)

Der Philosoph

West Germany 1988 83m colour
Mainline/Moana Film Produktion (Rudolf Thome)
aka: *Three Women in Love*
A writer finds three women to love and look after him.
Updating of Greek myth to male fantasy.
wd Rudolf Thome *ph* Reinhold Vorschneider *m* Hanno Rinne *ad* Eve Schaenen *ed* Dörte Völz-Mannarell
☆ Johannes Herrschmann, Adriana Altaras, Friederike Tiefenbacher, Claudia Matschulla, Jürgen Wink, Werner Gerber, Anton Rey

Phobia

Canada 1980 90m colour
Borough Park (Zale Magder)

Five volunteer phobics, released from jail for experiments, are killed one by one.
Unprepossessing whodunnit with horror touches but none of the style one might expect from its director.
w Lew Lehman, Jimmy Sangster, Peter Bellwood *d* John Huston *ph* Reginald H. Morris *m* Andre Gagnon
☆ Paul Michael Glaser, John Colicos, Susan Hogan, Alexandra Stewart, David Bolt

'The androids on Titus 4 have taken over the asylum.'

Phoenix

US 1995 96m colour
Triad (Jimmy Lifton, Dan Bates, Troy Cook)

An élite team, sent down to a mining planet to deal with revolting androids, discovers that things are not what they seem.
Unoriginal action movie with dull dialogue, clichéd characters and a predictable plot.
w Jimmy Lifton, Troy Cook *d* Troy Cook *ph* T. Alexander *m* Lisa Bloom *pd* James Scanlon *ed* Paulette Renée Victor *sp* Stargate Films
☆ Brad Dourif, Billy Drago, Stephen Nichols, Denice Duff, Peter Murnik, William Sanderson, Robert Gossett, Betsy Soo

'Your life is on the line.'

Phone Booth *

US 2002 80m DeLuxe Panavision
TCF/Fox 2000 (Gil Netter, David Zucker)

A publicity agent is trapped in a telephone booth by a sniper who threatens to kill him if he hangs up.
A B feature in all but name: short, claustrophobic and moderately tense.
w Larry Cohen *d* Joel Schumacher *ph* Matthew Libatique *m* Harry Gregson-Williams *pd* Andrew Laws *ed* Mark Stevens
☆ Colin Farrell (Stu Shepard), Kiefer Sutherland (The Caller), Forest Whitaker (Captain Ramey), Radha Mitchell (Kelly Shepard), Katie Holmes (Pamela McFadden), Richard T. Jones (Sergeant Cole)

'A half-hour TV slot, or even a short, might have proved the best format for this simple and surprise-deficient tale.' – *Todd McCarthy, Variety*

Phone Call from a Stranger

US 1952 96m bw
TCF (Nunnally Johnson)

Of four airplane acquaintances, only one survives a crash; he visits the families of the others.
Four stories with an unlikely link. (The compendium craze, which had started in 1948 with Quartet, *was now straining itself.) Nothing to remember except Miss Davis.*
w Nunnally Johnson *d* Jean Negulesco *ph* Milton Krasner *m* Franz Waxman
☆ *Bette Davis*, Gary Merrill, Michael Rennie, Shelley Winters, Keenan Wynn, Evelyn Varden, Warren Stevens, Craig Stevens

'A cinematic party line on which several conversations are going at once, none of them coming across very distinctly.' – *Time*

Phörpa: see *The Cup*

The Photograph *

Greece/France 1986 120m colour
Two expatriate Greeks living in Paris encourage each other's hopes for the future with tragic results.
Dour, skilfully made film of people unable to alter the trajectory of their lives.
wd Nicos Papatakis *ph* Aris Stavrou *m* Christodoulos Chalaris
☆ Aris Retsos, Christos Tsangas

'Another World … As Close As The Beat Of Your Heart.'

Photographing Fairies *

GB 1997 104m Technicolor
Entertainment/Starry Night/Polygram (Michele Camarda)

A photographic expert, devastated by the death of his wife and his experiences in the First World War, investigates photographs of fairies taken by two young girls and concludes that they are genuine.
An odd, obsessive film, about love and death and how people cope with loss; while not entirely successful, it has its moments.
w Nick Willing, Chris Harrald *novel* Steve Szilagyi *d* Nick Willing *ph* John de Borman

m Simon Boswell *pd* Laurence Dorman *ed* Sean Barton
☆ Toby Stephens, Ben Kingsley, Emily Woof, Frances Barber, Philip Davis, Rachel Shelley, Edward Hardwicke (Sir Arthur Conan Doyle), Hannah Bould

'The cinematic equivalent of the well-made play, the made-for-television film. It's intriguing, occasionally moving, but to magnify its impact it would be better seen on the smaller screen.' – *Nick Kimberley, Sight and Sound*

† The story of the Cottingley Fairies was also the basis for another film, *Fairytale: A True Story* (qv).
†† The script for the film is said to have gone through 23 drafts.

Physical Evidence

US 1988 99m colour
Rank/Columbia (Martin Ransohoff)

An ex-cop, accused of murder, begins to have doubts about the female lawyer hired to defend him.
Dull thriller with an unnecessarily convoluted plot.
w Bill Phillips *story* Steve Ransohoff, Bill Phillips *d* Michael Crichton *ph* John A. Alonzo *m* Henry Mancini *pd* Dan Yarhi *ed* Glenn Farr
☆ Burt Reynolds, Theresa Russell, Ned Beatty, Kay Lenz, Ted McGinley, Tom O'Brien, Kenneth Welsh, Ray Baker, Ken James, Michael P. Moran

'The whole exercise, while never quite collapsing, contrives to look and sound peculiarly futile.' – *Philip Strick, MFB*

'Faith in chaos.'

Pi **

US 1998 85m bw
Live Entertainment/Truth & Soul/Harvest/Plantain/Protozoa (Eric Watson)

An obsessive mathematician seeks to find a number that will explain the universe.
Gripping, clever theological and psychological thriller, which is less about explanations than observing varieties of monomania in action.
wd Darren Aronofsky ph Matthew Libatique *m* Clint Mansell *pd* Matthew Marraffi *ed* Oren Sach
☆ Sean Gullette, Mark Margolis, Ben Shenkman, Pamela Hart, Stephen Pearlman, Samia Shoaib

'If his film leaves one unsatisfied, it's still remarkable to what extent Aronofsky has rendered the cerebral kinetically intense. The film's imaginative, diverse images create a mind's-eye urban claustrophobia; such intensity may exhaust over 85 minutes' course, but it's never less than impressive.' – *Dennis Harvey, Variety*

Il Piacere: see *The Pleasure*

'Music was his passion. Survival was his masterpiece.'

The Pianist ***

France/Poland/Germany/GB 2002 148m colour
Pathé/RP/Heritage/Babelsberg/Runteam (Roman Polanski, Robert Benmussa, Alain Sarde)

In Warsaw after the Nazi invasion, a Jewish pianist escapes from the ghetto and goes into hiding in a ruined part of the city.
A moving, dispassionate account of survival, based on a true story, and told in the style of 1950s war movie with often searing imagery. It becomes digressive and over-long, but still retains a haunting power.
w Ronald Harwood book Wladyslaw Szpilman *d Roman Polanski ph Pawel Edelman m* Wojciech Kilar *pd* Allan Starski *ed* Hervé de Luze *cos* Anna B. Sheppard
☆ *Adrien Brody* (Wladyslaw Szpilman), Thomas Kretschmann (Captain Wilm Hosenfeld), Frank Finlay (The father), Maureen Lipman (The mother), Emilia Fox (Dorota), Ed Stoppard (Henryk), Julia Rayner (Regina), Jessica Kate Meyer (Halina), Ruth Platt (Janina)

'Polanski has never directed better. Life in the Warsaw ghetto under the Germans is put before us with a kind of terrible patience.' – *Stanley Kaufmann, New Republic*

'Surprisingly lacks a feeling of personal urgency and insight that would have made it a distinctive, even unique contribution to the considerable number of films that deal with the war in general and Holocaust in particular.' – *Todd McCarthy, Variety*

† It won the Palme D'Or at the Cannes Film Festival.
picture; Ronald Harwood; Roman Polanski; Adrien Brody
Pawel Edelman; Anna B. Sheppard; Hervé de Luze
film; Roman Polanski

La Pianiste

France/Austria 2001 130m colour
Artificial Eye/Wega/MK2/Alain Sarde/Arte (Veit Heiduschka)

aka: *The Piano Teacher*

A talented piano teacher relieves the tensions of her life by voyeurism, self-mutilation and a sado-masochistic affair with one of her students.
A gifted director and actress go astray in this intense, unlovely drama: if it has a point, it is that sex and music make unreasonable demands on those who take them seriously.
wd Michael Haneke *novel* Elfriede Jelinek *ph* Christian Berger *pd* Christoph Kanter *ed* Monika Willi, Nadine Muse
☆ Isabelle Huppert (Erika Kohut), Annie Girardot (The Mother), Benoit Magimel (Walter Klemmer), Anna Sigalevitch (Anna Schober), Susanne Lothar (Mrs Schober), Udo Samel (Dr Blonskij)

'Misguided and hilariously awful.' – *Times*

'There can be no doubt of Haneke's extraordinary ability to generate scenes of nerve-jangling disquiet and intimately unpleasant trauma. He can simply put you in a place you don't want to be, and keep you there.' – *Peter Bradshaw, Guardian*

† Benoit Magimel won the best actor award, and Isabel Huppert the best actress award at the Cannes Film Festival in 2001.

The Piano ****

Australia 1993 120m Eastmancolor
Entertainment/CIBY 2000/Jan Chapman

A mute Scottish widow travels with her young daughter for an arranged marriage to a landowner in New Zealand, where she is forced to leave her most-treasured possession, her piano, on a beach.
A complex drama of lust, love and a woman emerging from an emotional silence in a repressive community into a self-determined and fulfilled life; beautifully photographed and impeccably acted, it is powerful and moving.
wd Jane Campion ph Stuart Dryburgh m Michael Nyman pd Andrew McAlpine ed Veronika Jenet
☆ *Holly Hunter, Harvey Keitel*, Sam Neill, *Anna Paquin*, Kerry Walker, Genevieve Lemon, Tungla Baker, Ian Mune

'A riveting excursion into 19th-century sexuality, a movie that takes the conventions of the Gothic romance and refracts them through a dark contemporary lens.' – *David Ansen, Newsweek*

'Not since the early days of cinema, when audiences trampled over each other towards the exit to avoid the train emerging from the screen, could I imagine the medium of film to be so powerful.' – *Lizzie Francke, Sight and Sound*

'An emotionally devastating tour de force, both heart-rending and heart-warming.' – *Film Review*

† The film shared the *Palme d'Or* as best film, and Holly Hunter won the award as best actress, at the Cannes Film Festival in 1993.
Holly Hunter; Anna Paquin; Jane Campion (as writer)
best picture; Jane Campion (as director); Stuart Dryburgh; Veronika Jenet; costume design (Janet Patterson)
Holly Hunter; Andrew McAlpine

The Piano Teacher: see *La Pianiste*

Piatka z Ulicy Barskiej: see *Five Boys from Barska Street*

Piccadilly *

GB 1929 105m (24 fps) bw silent
BIP (E. A. Dupont)

A club owner's fiancée is accused of killing his Chinese mistress.
Sub-Edgar Wallace melodrama, no longer watchable with a straight face.
w Arnold Bennett *d* E. A. Dupont *ph* Werner Brandes
☆ Gilda Gray, Anna May Wong, Jameson Thomas, Cyril Ritchard, Ellen Pollock, Charles Laughton, Debroy Somers and his Band
† Sound added in 1930.

Piccadilly Incident *

GB 1946 102m bw
ABP (Herbert Wilcox)

During World War II, a girl believed drowned returns from the front to find her husband remarried.
The Enoch Arden theme again, and the first of the Wilcox-Neagle 'London' films, though untypically a melodrama with a sad ending. Efficient enough for its chosen audience.
w Nicholas Phipps *d* Herbert Wilcox *ph* Max Greene *m* Anthony Collins
☆ Anna Neagle, Michael Wilding, Michael Laurence, Frances Mercer, Coral Browne, A. E. Matthews, Edward Rigby, Brenda Bruce
† Michael Wilding was cast only after Rex Harrison and John Mills had proved unavailable.

Piccadilly Jim *

US 1936 100m bw
MGM (Harry Rapf)

A cartoonist helps his father to marry by making the bride's stuffy family objects of ridicule.
Amiable comedy with a diverting London setting.
w Charles Brackett, Edwin Knopf *novel* P. G. Wodehouse *d* Robert Z. Leonard *ph* Joseph Ruttenberg *m* William Axt
☆ Robert Montgomery, Madge Evans, Frank Morgan, Billie Burke, Eric Blore, Robert Benchley, Ralph Forbes, Cora Witherspoon, E. E. Clive

Piccadilly Third Stop

GB 1960 90m bw
Rank/Sydney Box/Ethiro (Norman Williams)

A smooth crook seduces the daughter of an eastern ambassador in London to gain entry to the embassy and rob it.
Boring and rather unpleasant thriller partly redeemed by a final chase through the Underground.
w Leigh Vance *d* Wolf Rilla *ph* Ernest Steward *m* Philip Green
☆ Terence Morgan, Yoko Tani, John Crawford, William Hartnell, Mai Zetterling, Dennis Price, Ann Lynn

Pick a Star

US 1937 76m bw
MGM/Hal Roach

An innocent girl in Hollywood achieves stardom with the help of a publicity man.
Perfectly awful Cinderella story with interesting glimpses behind the studio scenes and (if you can wait that long) a couple of good Laurel and Hardy sequences.
w Richard Flournoy, Arthur Vernon Jones, Thomas J. Dugan *d* Edward Sedgwick *ph* Norbert Brodine *m* Marvin Hatley, Arthur Morton *ed* William Terhune
☆ Rosina Lawrence, Jack Haley, Patsy Kelly, Mischa Auer, *Stan Laurel, Oliver Hardy*, Charles Halton, Lyda Roberti

'Part farce, part comedy, part musical and three parts dull.' – *Variety*

Pick Up

US 1933 80m bw
B. P. Schulberg/Paramount

A girl released from jail picks up with a truck driver, but her crooked husband reappears.
Sob story of the Peg's Paper type; a yawn.
w S. K. Lauren, Agnes Leahy, Vina Delmar *d* Marion Gering
☆ Sylvia Sidney, George Raft, William Harrigan, Lillian Bond

'Good title and cast, weakish film.' – *Variety*

Pick Up

US 1951 78m bw
Columbia (Hugo Haas)

A lonely middle-aged man falls for a tart who is interested only in his money.
Modest variation on The Blue Angel, *the first of several second features made by Haas to feature himself as a second Emil Jannings. They got progressively more maudlin.*
wd Hugo Haas ph Paul Ivano *m* Harold Byrns
☆ Hugo Haas, Beverly Michaels, Allan Nixon, Howland Chamberlin

The Pick-Up Artist

US 1987 81m colour
TCF (David L. Macleod)

A smug, compulsively womanizing teacher falls for the daughter of an alcoholic in trouble with gangsters.
A romantic comedy short on laughs and romance; what excites the director is gambling, which is no fun either.
wd James Toback *ph* Gordon Willis *m* Georges Delerue *pd* Paul Sylbert *ed* David Bretherton, Angelo Corrao
☆ Molly Ringwald, Robert Downey Jnr, Dennis Hopper, Harvey Keitel, Danny Aiello, Mildred Dunnock, Victoria Jackson, Bob Gunton, Frederick Koehler

'Full of spangly good humor. In its own irrepressible way it's sustained. It's not heady enough, not a lift-off, but it's bright and convivial, like the sound of the sixties girl groups on the track. It keeps you laughing.' – *Pauline Kael*

Picking Up The Pieces

US 2000 120m colour
Kushner Locke/Comala/Ostensible (Paul L. Sandberg)

Religious fervour grips a Mexican village, where miracles occur after the discovery of a dismembered hand, which is part of the body of an adulterous wife who has been butchered by her Texan husband.
Dismal and witless farce, in which its miscast actors, mostly at odds with their roles and the ramshackle script, flounder helplessly and hopelessly.
w Bill Wilson *d* Alfonso Arau *ph* Vittorio Storaro *m* Ruy Folguera *pd* Denise Pizzini *ed* Michael R. Miller *cos* Marilyn Matthews
☆ Woody Allen (Tex Cowley), David Schwimmer (Leo Jerome), Maria Gracia Cucinotta (Desi), Cheech Marin (Mayor Machado), Kiefer Sutherland (Bobo), Lou Diamond Phillips (Officer Alonso), Alfonso Arau (Dr Amado), Fran Drescher (Sister Frida), Elliott Gould (Father LaCage), Sharon Stone (Candy), Andy Dick (Father Buñuel), Joseph Gordon-Levitt (Flaco)

'A tawdry misfire of the lowest order.' – *Stephen Oxman, Variety*

The Pickle

US 1993 100m Technicolor/bw
Columbia (Paul Mazursky)

A middle-aged, once admired film director returns from France for the premiere of a science-fiction movie he made for the money, about farm boys who fly a giant cucumber to another planet.
Sour and self-referential movie about Hollywood; it's a measure of its failure that the deliberately banal excerpts from the sf movie are more entertaining than the soul-searchings of its central character.
wd Paul Mazursky *ph* Fred Murphy *m* Michel Legrand *pd* James Bissell *ed* Stuart Papp
☆ Danny Aiello, Dyan Cannon, Clotilde Courau, Shelley Winters, Barry Miller, Jerry Stiller, Chris Penn, Little Richard, Jodi Long, Rebecca Miller, Ally Sheedy

'Aims for comedy and poignance that never come, and feels wearily disenchanted and out of touch.' – *Todd McCarthy, Variety*

Pickpocket **

France 1959 80m bw
Lux

A lonely, compulsive pickpocket is redeemed through love.
Based on the themes of Dostoevsky's Crime and Punishment, *an austere but moving and complex drama, notable for its scenes of thievery.*
wd Robert Bresson *ph* Léonce-Henry Burel *m* Jean-Bapiste Lully *ed* Raymond Lamy
☆ Martin Lassalle, Marika Green, Pierre Leymarie, Jean Pelegri, Pierre Etaix, Kassagi, Dolly Scal, César Gattegno

'The style of the film is characteristic of the director. It is one of persistent concentration: the camera will not be deflected from its close stare at the silent face, the tense figure in the foreground. But this time the method defeats itself. In rejecting every irrelevant action, in ruthlessly refining away every decoration, Bresson has thrown away the motives as well.' – *Dilys Powell*

Pickup Alley: see *Interpol*

'Anybody's back seat will do – as long as he's going her way!'

Pickup on 101
US 1972 93m Movielab
AIP

A lady hitchhiker picks up with an old hobo and an unemployed rock 'n' roller.
Sentimental rather than sensational is this small drama which starts slowly and goes nowhere.
w Anthony Blake d John Florea ph Brick Marquard m Stu Phillips
☆ Lesley Warren, Jack Albertson, Martin Sheen, Michael Ontkean

Pickup on South Street **
US 1953 80m bw
TCF (Jules Schermer)

A pickpocket steals a girl's wallet and finds himself up to his neck in espionage.
Over-rich mixture of crime, violence and anti-communism, smartly made without being very interesting.
wd *Samuel Fuller* story Dwight Taylor ph Joe MacDonald m Leigh Harline ad Lyle R. Wheeler, George Patrick ed Nick de Maggio
☆ Richard Widmark, Jean Peters, *Thelma Ritter*, Richard Kiley
† Remade 1968 as *Capetown Affair*.
Thelma Ritter

The Pickwick Papers *
GB 1952 115m bw
George Minter (Bob McNaught)

Various adventures of the Pickwick Club culminate in Mrs Bardell's suit for breach of promise.
Flatly conceived and loosely constructed Dickensian comedy; good humour and lots of well-known faces do not entirely atone for lack of artifice.
wd Noel Langley ph Wilkie Cooper m Antony Hopkins ad Fred Pusey
☆ *James Hayter, James Donald*, Donald Wolfit, Hermione Baddeley, Hermione Gingold, Kathleen Harrison, *Nigel Patrick*, Alexander Gauge, Lionel Murton
'As welcome as the sun in the morning and as British as a cup of tea.' – *Daily Mirror*

'A town – a stranger – and the things he does to its people! Especially its women!'

Picnic ***
US 1955 113m Technicolor Cinemascope
Columbia (Fred Kohlmar)

A brawny wanderer causes sexual havoc one summer in a small American town.
Seminal melodrama setting new directions for Hollywood and illustrating the side of life the Hardy family never showed. Generally quite compulsive despite some overacting.
w Daniel Taradash *play William Inge* d Joshua Logan ph *James Wong Howe* m George Duning pd Jo Mielziner ad William Flannery ed Charles Nelson, William A. Lyon
☆ *William Holden*, Kim Novak, Rosalind Russell, *Susan Strasberg*, Arthur O'Connell, Cliff Robertson, Betty Field, Verna Felton, Reta Shaw
'Mr Logan's idea of an outing in the corn country includes a choir of at least a hundred voices, a camera so alert that it can pick up the significance of the reflection of a Japanese lantern in a pool (futility, wistfulness, the general transience of life, as I get it) and a sound track let loose in the most formidable music I've heard in my time at the movies.' – *New Yorker*
art direction; editing
best picture; Joshua Logan; George Duning; Arthur O'Connell

'A recollection of evil...'

Picnic at Hanging Rock ****
Australia 1975 115m Eastmancolor
Picnic Productions/Australia Film Corporation (Hal and Jim McElroy)

In 1900, schoolgirls set out for a picnic; some disappear and are never found.
A film that ventures successfully into the mystic and bravely offers no answer to its central puzzle, just a question that continues to haunt the mind. Whether you want to regard it as a parable of sexual awakening or of colonial repression, it successfully retains its own mystery.
w Cliff Green *novel* Joan Lindsay d Peter Weir ph Russell Boyd m Bruce Smeaton
☆ Rachel Roberts, Dominic Guard, Helen Morse, Jacki Weaver, Vivean Gray, Kirsty Child
'Atmospherically vivid, beautifully shot, and palpably haunting.' – *Michael Billington, Illustrated London News*
'If this film had a rational and tidy conclusion, it would be a good deal less interesting. But as a tantalizing puzzle, a tease, a suggestion of forbidden answer just out of earshot, it works hypnotically and very nicely indeed.' – *Roger Ebert*
Russell Boyd

'Hawaii, 1918. She left Japan for a man she had never met, in a new world she could not imagine ... America.'

Picture Bride
US 1995 95m Foto-Kem
Artificial Eye/Thousand Cranes/Miramax (Lisa Onodera, Cellin Glick)

An 18-year-old Japanese woman comes gradually to love the middle-aged man in Hawaii that she is tricked into marrying.
Effective domestic drama along predictable lines.
w Kayo Hatta, Mari Hatta d Kayo Hatta ph Claudio Rocha m Mark Adler pd Paul Guncheon ed Lynzee Klingman, Mallory Gottlieb
☆ Youki Kudoh, Akaira Takayama, Tamlyn Tomita, Cary-Hiroyuki Tagawa, Toshiro Mifune, Yoko Sugi
'However predictable the story-line, the film-makers succeed in making us care about the characters right from the start.' – *Philip Kemp, Sight and Sound*

Picture Mommy Dead
US 1966 88m Pathécolor
Embassy/Berkeley (Bert I. Gordon)

A girl who has been hospitalized following the death of her mother in a fire returns home to find, apparently, that her father's new wife is trying to kill her.
Twist-ending shocker with tired stars, from the tag end of the Baby Jane cycle.
w Robert Sherman d Bert I. Gordon ph Ellsworth Fredericks m Robert Drasnin
☆ Don Ameche, Martha Hyer, Zsa Zsa Gabor, Susan Gordon, Maxwell Reed, Signe Hasso, Wendell Corey

The Picture of Dorian Gray ***
US 1945 110m bw (Technicolor inserts)
MGM (Pandro S. Berman)

A Victorian gentleman keeps in the attic a picture of himself, which shows his age and depravity while he stays eternally young.
Elegant variation on Dr Jekyll and Mr Hyde, presented in portentous style which suits the subject admirably.
wd *Albert Lewin novel* Oscar Wilde ph Harry Stradling m Herbert Stothart ad Cedric Gibbons, Hans Peters
☆ *George Sanders, Hurd Hatfield*, Donna Reed, Angela Lansbury, Peter Lawford
SIR HENRY (GEORGE SANDERS): 'If I could get back my youth, I'd do anything in the world – except get up early, take exercise or be respectable.'
SIR HENRY: 'I apologize for the intelligence of my remarks, Sir Thomas, I had forgotten that you were a Member of Parliament.'
DORIAN (HURD HATFIELD): 'If only the picture could change and I could be always what I am now. For that, I would give anything. Yes, there's nothing in the whole world I wouldn't give. I'd give my soul for that.'
'Respectful, earnest, and, I'm afraid, dead.' – *James Agee*
'Loving and practised hands have really improved Wilde's original, cutting down the epigrammatic flow ... and rooting out all the preciousness which gets in the way of the melodrama.' – *Richard Winnington*
Harry Stradling
Angela Lansbury; art direction

'Kate always lived her life by the rules ... some rules were meant to be broken.'

Picture Perfect
US 1997 100m Technicolor
TCF/3 Arts (Erwin Stoff)

In order to succeed in her job, a female advertising executive pretends to be engaged to a man she briefly met.
Slight, enervated romantic comedy that might have made a passable half-hour television sitcom.
w Arleen Sorkin, Paul Slansky, Glenn Gordon Caron d Glenn Gordon Caron ph Paul Sarossy m Carter Burwell pd Larry Fulton ed Robert Reitano
☆ Jennifer Aniston, Jay Mohr, Kevin Bacon, Olympia Dukakis, Illeana Douglas, Kevin Dunn, Faith Prince, Anne Twomey
'Too ineffectual to tickle either the funnybone or the heartstrings.' – *Variety*

The Picture Show Man *
Australia 1977 98m Eastmancolor
Limelight (Joan Long)
Adventures of a travelling picture show troupe in the 1920s.
Agreeably nostalgic incidents, not very dramatically connected.
w Joan Long d John Power ph Geoffrey Burton m Peter Best
☆ Rod Taylor, John Meillon, John Ewart, Harold Hopkins, Judy Morris, Patrick Cargill

The Picture Snatcher *
US 1933 77m bw
Warner
An ex-racketeer just out of prison becomes a scandal photographer.
Lively star vehicle, interesting for period detail.
w Allen Rivkin, P. J. Wolfson d Lloyd Bacon ph Sol Polito md Leo F. Forbstein
☆ James Cagney, Ralph Bellamy, Patricia Ellis, Alice White, Ralf Harolde, Robert Emmett O'Connor, Robert Barrat
'A vulgar but generally funny collection of blackouts.' – *Time*
'Fast, snappy, tough and packed with action.' – *New York Herald Tribune*
† Remade 1947 as *Escape from Crime*, with Richard Travis.

Pidä Huivista Kiinni, Tatjana: see *Take Care of Your Scarf, Tatjana*

Pie in the Sky
US 1995 95m Foto-Kem
New Line (Denise Shaw, Allan Mindel)

Boy obsessed with traffic meets girl, loses girl, gets girl.
An offbeat romantic comedy about an unlikely couple; it attempts to overwhelm with its charm, which proves resistible well before the end.
wd Bryan Gordon ph Bernd Heinl m Michael Convertino pd Linda Pearl ed Colleen Halsey
☆ Josh Charles, Anne Heche, Peter Riegert, Christine Ebersole, Wil Wheaton, Christine Lahti, John Goodman, Bob Balaban
'For all its manifest flaws (structural, directional and dramatic), it serves as a cheeky reminder of how formulaic and orthodox most Hollywood teen romance flicks are.' – *Sight and Sound*

A Piece of the Action
US 1977 135m Metrocolor
Warner/First Artists/Verdon (Melville Tucker)

Crooks are blackmailed into helping rebellious adolescents.
A black version, at immense length, of the hoodlum comedies in which the Dead End Kids so often featured. Not badly made, but out of date without being nostalgic.
w Charles Blackwell story Timothy March d Sidney Poitier ph Don Morgan m Curtis Mayfield
☆ Sidney Poitier, James Earl Jones, Bill Cosby, Denise Nicholas, Hope Clarke, Tracy Reed, Jason Evers, Marc Lawrence

The Pied Piper **
US 1942 86m bw
TCF (Nunnally Johnson)
An elderly man who hates children finds himself smuggling several of them out of occupied France.
Smart, sentimental, occasionally funny war adventure.
w Nunnally Johnson *novel* Nevil Shute d Irving Pichel ph Edward Cronjager m Alfred Newman
☆ *Monty Woolley*, Anne Baxter, Roddy McDowall, Otto Preminger, J. Carrol Naish, Lester Matthews, Jill Esmond, Peggy Ann Garner
best picture; Edward Cronjager; Monty Woolley

The Pied Piper
GB 1971 90m Eastmancolor
Panavision
Sagittarius/Goodtimes (David Puttnam, Sanford Lieberson)
In 1349 a strolling minstrel rids Hamelin of a plague of rats.
Paceless, slightly too horrific, and generally disappointing fantasy, especially from this director; poor sets and restricted action.
w Jacques Demy, Mark Peploe, Andrew Birkin d Jacques Demy ph Peter Suschitsky m Donovan pd Assheton Gorton
☆ Donovan, Donald Pleasence, Michael Hordern, Jack Wild, Diana Dors, John Hurt

Pièges
France 1939 120m bw
Speva (Michel Safra)
US title: *Personal Column*
aka: *Snares*
A dancer acts as a decoy to trap a serial killer murdering women who answer lonely hearts advertisements.
A thriller that finds it hard to accommodate murders and leave room for its debonair singing star.
w Jacques Companeez, Ernest Neuville, Simon Gantillon d Robert Siodmak m Michelet ad G. Wakhevitch ed Yvonne Martin
☆ Maurice Chevalier, Pierre Renoir, Marie Déa, Erich von Stroheim, Jean Temerson, André Brunot
† This was Siodmak's last French film before he left for Hollywood. It was remade in Hollywood in 1947 as *Lured* (qv), directed by Douglas Sirk.

Pier 13: see *Me and My Gal (1932)*

Pierre of the Plains
US 1942 66m bw
MGM
Adventures of a cheerful trapper in Canada's northwest territory.
Unashamed second-feature version of a play which its producer, Edgar Selwyn, had written in 1907 and which had been filmed in 1918 (as Hearts of the Wild*) and in 1922 (as* Over the Border*). (Selwyn was the man who once merged with Goldfish to form Goldwyn, a name which Goldfish then kept.)*
w Bertram Millhauser, Lawrence Kimble d George B. Seitz
☆ John Carroll, Ruth Hussey, Bruce Cabot, Reginald Owen, Henry Travers, Evelyn Ankers

Pierrot Le Fou **
France/Italy 1968 110m Eastmancolor
Techniscope
Rome/Paris/SNC (Reneé Pigneres, Gerard Beytout)

Bored by his marriage, a Frenchman leaves his wife at a party and takes off with an old flame, now involved in gun-running and crime.
A pulp thriller re-told in terms of farce and artifice, and a playful and enjoyably intellectual romp through pop culture, though it is difficult to take it as seriously as its maker intended.
wd Jean-Luc Godard *novel Obsession* by Lionel White ph Raoul Coutard m Antoine Duhamel ad Pierre Guffroy ed Françoise Colin
☆ *Jean-Paul Belmondo, Anna Karina*, Dirk Sanders, Raymond Devos, Graziella Galvani
'Godard has reached a stage at which self-confidence and self-indulgence join hands to lead him into a disaster area.' – *Dilys Powell*
'Purports to be against a world of advertising and conspicuous consumption; yet what it offers as an alternative, the mindless, feckless, and finally feelingless relationship of its hero and heroine, is at least as repugnant.' – *John Simon*

The Pigeon that Took Rome
US 1962 101m bw Panavision
Paramount/Llenroc (Melville Shavelson)
American undercover agents are smuggled into Rome during the German occupation.
Heavy-going war comedy-drama with bright sequences countered by too little wit and too many voluble Italians.

wd Melville Shavelson *novel* The Easter Dinner by Donald Downes *ph* Daniel Fapp *m* Alessandro Cicognini
☆ Charlton Heston, Elsa Martinelli, Brian Donlevy, Harry Guardino, Baccaloni

Pigeons
US 1970 87m Movielab
Saturn/Lois Holland Callaway/Plaza (Richard Lewis)
aka: *The Sidelong Glances of a Pigeon Kicker*
A Princeton graduate turned New York taxi driver thinks himself superior to all those he meets.
Dim would-be satirical drama making fun of conformity. With its pretentious and unlikeable protagonist, the fun is flat when it should be fizzy. Its style derives from the cycle of dull 'swinging London' movies, probably because of its British director.
w Ron Whyte *novel* David Boyer *d* John Dexter *ph* Urs Furrer *m* Pat Williams, Lee Holdridge, Edd Kaleroff, Chris Dedrick, Warren Marley *ad* Manny Gerard *ed* John Oettinger
☆ Jordan Christopher, Jill O'Hara, Robert Walden, William Redfield, Kate Reid, Lois Nettleton, Riggs O'Hara, Boni Enten, David Doyle, Elaine Stritch, Melba Moore, Pat Ast

Pigskin Parade
US 1936 93m bw
TCF (Bogart Rogers)
GB title: *Harmony Parade*
A country farmer becomes a college football hero.
Livelier-than-average college comedy.
w Harry Tugend, Jack Yellen, William Conselman *d* David Butler *ph* Arthur Miller *m/ly* Sidney Mitchell, Lew Pollack *md* David Buttolph
☆ Stuart Erwin, Patsy Kelly, Jack Haley, Johnny Downs, Betty Grable, Arline Judge, Dixie Dunbar, Judy Garland, Tony Martin, Elisha Cook Jnr
♫ 'You're Slightly Terrific'; 'You Do the Darndest Things Baby'; 'Texas Tornado'; 'It's Love I'm After'
Academy Award nomination: Stuart Erwin

The Pilgrim *
US 1923 38m approx (24 fps) bw silent
First National/Charles Chaplin
An escaped convict disguises himself as a minister and does a few good deeds.
Star comedy with more sentiment than laughter.
wd Charles Chaplin *ph* Rollie Totheroh
☆ Charles Chaplin, Edna Purviance, Kitty Bradbury, Mack Swain

Pilgrimage *
US 1933 95m bw
Fox
A selfish mother sees the error of her ways when she makes a post-war journey to her son's grave.
Strong character study, put across with style.
w Dudley Nichols, Philip Klein, Barry Conners *story* I. A. R. Wylie *d* John Ford
☆ *Henrietta Crosman*, Heather Angel, Norman Foster, Marian Nixon, Maurice Murphy, Charley Grapewin, Hedda Hopper
'A natural for residential clienteles: mother love from a new angle.' – *Variety*

Pillars of the Sky
US 1956 95m Technicolor Cinemascope
U-I (Robert Arthur)
GB title: *The Tomahawk and the Cross*
An Indian scout and a missionary help bring peace between cavalry and Indians.
Modest Western, adequately done.
w Sam Rolfe *novel* Frontier Fury by Will Henry *d* George Marshall *ph* Harold Lipstein *m* Joseph Gershenson *ad* Alexander Golitzen, Bill Newberry *ed* Milton Carruth
☆ Jeff Chandler, Dorothy Malone, Ward Bond, Keith Andes, Lee Marvin, Sydney Chaplin, Michael Ansara, Willis Bouchey

The Pillow Book **
GB/Netherlands/France 1995 126m colour
Film Four/Kasander & Wigman/Alpha/Woodline (Kees Kasander)
A Japanese woman with a fetish for being written upon takes an elaborate revenge on the homosexual publisher who humiliated her father.
A complex narrative that gives a sexual edge to the act of writing, it is ravishing to watch, especially in its split-screen recreations of pleasures listed in The Pillow Book of Sei Shonagon, *but too often seems little more than an elaborate literary conceit.*
wd Peter Greenaway *ph* Sacha Vierny *pd* Wilbert van Dorp, Andree Putman *ed* Chris Wyatt, Peter Greenaway
☆ Vivian Wu, Yoshi Oida, Ken Ogata, Hideko Yoshida, Ewan McGregor, Judy Ongg, Ken Mitsuishi
'Decidely not everyone's cup of sake, but for Greenaway fans and filmgoers willing to be seduced by a mature and richly decorative slice of Asian culture, *The Pillow Book* will be a treat, albeit at times a demanding one.' – *David Stratton, Variety*

Pillow of Death
US 1945 66m bw
Universal
A lawyer is suspected when his wife is murdered.
First fumbling story in the Inner Sanctum series, of which the title sequence was always the most entertaining portion.
w George Bricker *d* Wallace Fox
☆ Lon Chaney Jnr, Brenda Joyce, J. Edward Bromberg, Rosalind Ivan, Clara Blandick

Pillow Talk **
US 1959 110m Eastmancolor
Cinemascope
Universal/Arwin (Ross Hunter, Martin Melcher)
Two people who can't stand each other fall in love via a party line.
Slightly elephantine romantic comedy which nevertheless contains a number of funny scenes and was notable for starting off the Hudson–Day partnership and a run of similar comedies which survived the sixties.
w Stanley Shapiro, Maurice Richlin, Russell Rouse, Clarence Greene *d* Michael Gordon *ph* Arthur E. Arling *m* Frank de Vol *ad* Richard H. Riedel *ed* Milton Carruth
☆ *Doris Day, Rock Hudson, Tony Randall, Thelma Ritter*, Nick Adams, Julia Meade, Allen Jenkins, Marcel Dalio, Lee Patrick
Academy Award: Stanley Shapiro, Maurice Richlin, Russell Rouse, Clarence Greene
Academy Award nomination: Frank de Vol; Doris Day; Thelma Ritter; art direction

Pillow to Post
US 1945 96m bw
Warner (Alex Gottlieb)
A girl poses as a soldier's wife to get a hotel room.
*World War II comedy on a familiar theme (*The More the Merrier, Standing Room Only, The Doughgirls*, etc). Uninspired.*
w Charles Hoffman *play* Pillar to Post by Rose Simon Kohn *d* Vincent Sherman *ph* Wesley Anderson *m* Frederick Hollander
☆ Ida Lupino, Sydney Greenstreet, William Prince, Stuart Erwin, Ruth Donnelly, Barbara Brown, Frank Orth

The Pilot *
US 1979 92m colour
Summit/New Line
A once great pilot insists on working despite an alcohol problem.
Not enough meat on the story bones is enough to ground this dismal drama, but the air scenes look terrific and the actors seem to believe in what they're doing.
wd Cliff Robertson *novel* Robert P. Davis *ph* *Walter Lassally* *m* John Addison
☆ *Cliff Robertson*, Frank Converse, Diane Baker, Gordon MacRae, Dana Andrews, Milo O'Shea

Pimpernel Smith **
GB 1941 121m bw
British National (Leslie Howard)
US title: *Mister V*
aka: *The Fighting Pimpernel*
A professor of archaeology goes into war-torn Europe to rescue refugees.
The Scarlet Pimpernel *unassumingly and quite effectively brought up to date, with memorable scenes after a slow start.*
w Anatole de Grunwald, Roland Pertwee, Ian Dalrymple *d* Leslie Howard *ph* Max Greene *m* John Greenwood
☆ *Leslie Howard, Mary Morris, Francis L. Sullivan*, Hugh McDermott, Raymond Huntley, Manning Whiley, Peter Gawthorne, David Tomlinson
'Funny, touching, imaginative, and enormously exciting.' – C. A. Lejeune
'Just an amusing piece of hokum.' – *Leslie Howard*

A Pin for the Butterfly *
GB/Czechoslovakia 1994 113m colour
Heureka/Channel 4/British Screen/Skreba (James Crawford)
Life in the 50s under a Stalinist regime, as seen through the eyes of a young girl, who, unlike the adults around her, tries to tell the truth.
An uneven drama that begins in an exaggerated and grotesque style before settling for a more absorbing account of compromise and betrayal.
wd Hannah Kodicek *ph* Ivan Slapeta *m* Ilona Sekacz *pd* Jiri Matolin *ed* Kant Pan
☆ Joan Plowright, Ian Bannen, Hugh Laurie, Imogen Stubbs, Ian Hogg, Florence Hoath
'In a market crammed with bloody vengeance tales and erotica, *Pin* deserves points for its seriousness of purpose and willingness to make a tough family film.' – *Variety*

Pin Up Girl
US 1944 83m Technicolor
TCF (William Le Baron)
A Washington secretary becomes a national celebrity when she meets a navy hero.
Adequate star flagwaver, mildly interesting for its new streamlined set designs.
w Robert Ellis, Helen Logan, Earl Baldwin *story* Libbie Block *d* H. Bruce Humberstone *ph* Ernest Palmer *md* Emil Newman, Charles Henderson *ch* Hermes Pan *ad* James Basevi, Joseph C. Wright *songs* James V. Monaco, Mack Gordon
☆ Betty Grable, John Harvey, Martha Raye, Joe E. Brown, Eugene Pallette, Dave Willock, Charles Spivak and his Orchestra
'A spiritless blob of a musical, and a desecration of a most inviting theme.' – *Bosley Crowther*

Pink Cadillac *
US 1989 122m Technicolor
Warner/Malpaso (David Valdes)
A bounty hunter goes in search of a mother who has disappeared with her baby and a pink Cadillac containing $250,000 belonging to a bunch of neo-Nazis.
Amiable, if somewhat aimless, comedy with unsubtle performances.
w John Eskow *d* Buddy Van Horn *ph* Jack N. Green *m* Steve Dorff *pd* Edward C. Carfagno *ed* Joel Cox
☆ Clint Eastwood, Bernadette Peters, Timothy Carhart, John Dennis Johnston, Michael Des Barres, Geoffrey Lewis

Pink Floyd The Wall *
GB 1982 95m Metrocolor
MGM/Tin Blue/Goldcrest (Alan Marshall)
A washed-up pop star finds his life a mixture of fact and fiction, of reality and animation.
Dislikeable self-pitying dirge, accompanied by animation which will not be to everybody's taste but is sometimes brilliantly arranged.
w Roger Waters *d* Alan Parker *ph* Peter Biziou *m* Roger Waters *animation designer* Gerald Scarfe
☆ Bob Geldof, Christine Hargreaves, James Laurenson, Eleanor David, Kevin McKeon, Bob Hoskins
'A vacuous, bombastic and humourless piece of self-indulgence.' – *Steve Jenkins, MFB*
'Roger Waters flounders in woman-hating self-pity; Gerald Scarfe turns up particularly weedy examples of his animated savagery; and Alan Parker revels in the chance to make a feature-length TV commercial.' – *Sight and Sound*

The Pink Jungle
US 1968 104m Techniscope
Universal/Cherokee (Stan Margulies)
A photographer and his model are stranded in a South American village and become involved in a diamond hunt.
Curious mixture of adventure and light comedy that works only in patches.
w Charles Williams *novel* Snake Water by Alan Williams *d* Delbert Mann *ph* Russell Metty *m* Ernie Freeman
☆ James Garner, Eva Renzi, George Kennedy, Nigel Green, Michael Ansara, George Rose
'Another backlot cheapie.' – *Robert Windeler*

'A unique experience in visual fantasy.'
Pink Narcissus
US 1971 102m colour
Smerpix/Les Folies des Hommes
A young hustler, trying to escape the sordid reality of his life, imagines a series of mainly masturbatory homosexual encounters: as a matador, a Roman slave, a harem boy in the tent of a sheik, a wood nymph, and as his own, ageing client.
A once-notorious gaudily coloured exploitation film aimed at gay audiences which is very much of its time, being almost a definitive example of camp and kitsch. It received its first large-scale British showing in a grainy video release in 1993.
w Anonymous *d* Anonymous *ph* Anonymous *md* Martin Jay Sadoff, Gary Goch *ed* Martin Jay Sadoff
☆ Bobby Kendall
'We are expected to be drooling, aroused, captivated – and weak enough to approve this celebration of the bottomless Narcissistic pit – instead of damning it as the oafish indulgence it really is. One would care less if it were content to be pornography, but instead it operates smugly within the "decadent" underground style of Anger et al.' – *Shock Xpress*
† Although the film and the video release list the producer, director and writer as anonymous, some prints credit 'Jim Bidgood' as director.

The Pink Panther **
US 1963 113m Technirama
UA/Mirisch (Martin Jurow)
An incompetent *Sûreté* inspector is in Switzerland on the trail of a jewel thief called The Phantom.
Sporadically engaging mixture of pratfalls, Raffles, *and* Monsieur Hulot, *all dressed to kill and quite palatable for the uncritical.*
w Maurice Richlin, Blake Edwards *d* Blake Edwards *ph* Philip Lathrop *m* Henry Mancini *ad* Fernando Carrere *animation* De Patie-Freleng
☆ David Niven, Peter Sellers, Capucine, Claudia Cardinale, Robert Wagner, Brenda de Banzie, Colin Gordon
† Peter Ustinov had been offered the role of Clouseau first, but backed out. Inspector Clouseau later became a cartoon character and also provoked six sequels: *A Shot in the Dark, Inspector Clouseau, The Return of the Pink Panther, The Pink Panther Strikes Again, The Revenge of the Pink Panther* and *Son of the Pink Panther.*
Academy Award nomination: Henry Mancini

The Pink Panther Strikes Again *
GB 1976 103m DeLuxe Panavision
United Artists/Amjo (Blake Edwards)
After a nervous breakdown, Chief Inspector Dreyfus builds up a vast criminal organization devoted to the extermination of Inspector Clouseau.
Zany pratfall farce with signs of over-confidence since the success of The Return of the Pink Panther. *But some gags are funny, despite a rather boring star.*
w Frank Waldman, Blake Edwards *d* Blake Edwards *ph* Harry Waxman *m* Henry Mancini
☆ Peter Sellers, Herbert Lom, Colin Blakely, Leonard Rossiter, Lesley-Anne Down, Burt Kwouk
Academy Award nomination: song 'Come To Me' (*m* Henry Mancini, *ly* Don Black)

Pink String and Sealing Wax *
GB 1945 89m bw
Ealing (Michael Balcon)
In 1880 Brighton, a publican's wife plans to have her husband poisoned.
Unusual, carefully handled period crime melodrama which needed a slightly firmer grip.
w Diana Morgan, Robert Hamer *play* Roland Pertwee *d* Robert Hamer *ph* Richard S. Pavey *m* Norman Demuth
☆ Googie Withers, Mervyn Johns, Gordon Jackson, Sally Ann Howes, Mary Merrall, John Carol, Catherine Lacey, Garry Marsh

The Pink Telephone
France 1975 93m colour
Gaumont International/Les Productions 2000 (Alain Poire)
aka: *Le Téléphone Rose*
An old-fashioned, provincial businessman becomes involved with an expensive Parisian call-girl.

Satire on big business, sexual politics and middle-aged angst that runs out of steam before the end.
w Francis Véber *d* Edouard Molinaro *ph* Gérard Hameline *m* Vladimir Cosma *pd* Robert Sussfeld, Michel Choquet *ed* Robert and Monique Isnardon
☆ Mireille Darc, Pierre Mondy, Michel Lonsdale, Daniel Ceccaldi, Françoise Prevost, Gérard Hérold

'She passed for white!'
Pinky **
US 1949 102m bw
TCF (Darryl F. Zanuck)
In the American South, a Negro girl who passes for white has romantic problems.
Rather blah problem picture which seemed brave at the time; a highly professional piece of work nevertheless.
w Philip Dunne, Dudley Nichols *novel* *Quality* by Cid Ricketts Summer *d Elia Kazan ph* Joe *MacDonald m* Alfred Newman
☆ Jeanne Crain, Ethel Barrymore, Ethel Waters, William Lundigan, Basil Ruysdael, Nina Mae McKinney, Frederick O'Neal, Evelyn Varden
'It has about as much daring as a cheese-mite. It is careful to affront no particular section of the public, to draw no particular conclusion, to outrage no particular code of cinema ethics, to challenge no particular box-office convention.' – C. A. *Lejeune*
Jeanne Crain; Ethel Barrymore; Ethel Waters

'Out of a dream world into yours!'
Pinocchio ****
US 1940 77m Technicolor
Walt Disney
The blue fairy breathes life into a puppet, which has to prove itself before it can turn into a real boy.
Charming, fascinating, superbly organized and streamlined cartoon feature without a single second of boredom.
m/ly Leigh Harline, Ned Washington, Paul J. Smith supervisors Ben Sharpsteen, Hamilton Luske
☆ voices of: Dickie Jones, Christian Rub, *Cliff Edwards*, Evelyn Venable, Walter Catlett, Frankie Darro
'A film of amazing detail and brilliant conception.' – *Leonard Maltin*
'A work that gives you almost every possible kind of pleasure to be got from a motion picture.' – *Richard Mallett, Punch*
'The limits of the animated cartoon have been blown so wide open that some of the original wonder of pictures has been restored.' – *Otis Ferguson*
Leigh Harline, Ned Washington, Paul J. Smith (m); song 'When You Wish Upon a Star' (*m* Leigh Harline, *ly* Ned Washington)

Pinocchio and the Emperor of the Night
US 1987 90m colour
Palace/Filmation (Lou Scheimer)
Pinocchio continues his adventures as a real boy.
Sugary confection that cannot stand comparison with Disney's classic.
w Robby London *d* Hal Sutherland *m* Anthony Marinelli, Brian Banks *songs* Will Jennings, Barry Mann, Steve Tyrell
☆ Featuring the voices of Ed Asner, Lana Beeson, Tom Bosley, Linda Gary, Scott Grimes, James Earl Jones, Rickie Lee Jones, Don Knotts

Pioneer Builders: see *The Conquerors*

Pippi in the South Seas (dubbed)
Sweden/Germany 1974 100m Movielab
Beta/Iduna/K B Nordart (Olle Nordemar)
Pippi, a girl with superhuman strength, sets off with two friends to rescue her father who has been captured by pirates.
An atrocious children's film, cheap and shoddy and so badly dubbed as to be unwatchable.
novel Astrid Lindgren *d* Olle Hellbom *ph* Kalle Bergholm *m* George Riedel *ed* Jan Persson, Jutte Schweden
☆ Inger Nilsson, Maria Persson, Par Sundberg, Alfred Schieske, Wolfgang Volz, Nikolaus Schilling

Pippi Longstocking
Sweden/Germany/Canada 1997 78m colour
Optimum/Nelvana/TFC/Iduna (Hasmi Giakoumis, Merle-Anne Ridley)
Thieves try to steal the gold belonging to the strongest girl in the world, who sets up home alone while waiting for the return of her sea-faring father.
Yet another dud film made from a favourite children's book, with substandard animation and a dull story.
w Catherine Stackelberb, Ken Sobol, Frank Nissen *books* Astrid Lindgren *d* Clive Smith *m* Anders Berglund *ad* Clive Powsey *ed* Noda Tsamardos
☆ Featuring voices of: Melissa Altro, Catherine O'Hara, Dave Thomas, Gordon Pinsent, Wayne Robson, Carole Pope, Richard Binsley, Rick Jones
'Here, Pippi's dislike of conformity, attractive on the printed page, seems selfish and tiresome rather than spirited.' – *Sight and Sound*

'Lost River Lake was a thriving resort – until they discovered...'
Piranha *
US 1978 92m Metrocolor
New World (Roger Corman, Jeff Schechtman, Jon Davison)
A mad doctor's stock of man-eating fish is accidentally released into the local rivers.
Slightly spoofy thriller with a high death rate and a better than usual script. On the whole, an improvement on Jaws.
w John Sayles *d Joe Dante ph* Jamie Anderson *m* Pino Donaggio *sp* Jon Berg
☆ Bradford Dillman, Heather Menzies, Kevin McCarthy, Bruce Gordon, Barbara Steele, Keenan Wynn, Dick Miller

'They bred the ultimate killing machine ... Now you're not safe OUT of the water!'
Piranha II: The Spawning
Italy/US 1982 94m Technicolor
Columbia/Chako (Chako van Leevwew, Jeff Schechtman)
aka: *Piranha II: Flying Killers*
Holiday-makers are attacked by mutant flying fish.
Feeble low-budget sequel, the first feature of a director who went on to make more successful action movies, including Terminator *and* Terminator 2.
w H. A. Milton *d* James Cameron *ph* Roberto D'Ettore Piazzoli *m* Steve Powder *ed* Robert Silvi
☆ Tricia O'Neil, Steve Marachuk, Lance Henriksen, Ricky G. Paull, Ted Richert, Leslie Graves

The Pirate **
US 1948 102m Technicolor
MGM (Arthur Freed)
In a West Indian port, a girl imagines that a wandering player is a famous pirate, who in fact is her despised and elderly suitor.
Minor MGM musical with vivid moments and some intimation of the greatness shortly to come; all very set-bound, but the star quality is infectious.
w Albert Hackett, Frances Goodrich *play* S. N. Behrman *d* Vincente Minnelli *ph* Harry Stradling *m/ly* Cole Porter *md* Lennie Hayton
☆ *Gene Kelly, Judy Garland*, Walter Slezak, Gladys Cooper, Reginald Owen, George Zucco, *the Nicholas Brothers*
'Most of the considerable artistry that has gone into this production collides head-on with artiness or is spoiled by simpler kinds of miscalculation.' – *James Agee*
'A $5,000,000 Hollywood picture that was unspeakably wretched, the worst that money could buy.' – *Cole Porter*
♫ 'Mack the Black'; 'Nina'; 'You Can Do No Wrong'; 'Be a Clown'; 'Love of My Life'
Lennie Hayton

The Pirate Movie
Australia 1982 105m Colorfilm
Fox/Joseph Hamilton International
A girl dreams herself back into *The Pirates of Penzance* but changes some of the details.
Galumphing fantasy which suggests that Australian film-makers had better stick to Botany Bay, Gallipoli *and sheep shearing.*
w Trevor Farrant *d* Ken Annakin *ph* Robin Copping *pd* Tony Woollard *ed* Kenneth W. Zemke
☆ Kristy McNichol, Christopher Atkins, Ted Hamilton, Bill Kerr, Maggie Kirkpatrick, Garry Macdonald
'The slapstick and the swordplay are as ineptly choreographed as the production numbers.' – *Kim Newman, MFB*

Pirates
France/Tunisia 1986 124m Eclaircolor Panavision
Cannon/Carthago/Accent Dominco (Tarak Ben Ammar)
A British buccaneer, cast adrift on a raft, is taken aboard a Spanish galleon and causes mayhem.
A disaster from a director who should never be allowed to attempt comedy. This one is revolting when it is not a crashing bore.
w Gerard Brach, Roman Polanski *d* Roman Polanski *ph* Witold Sobocinski *m* Philippe Sarde
☆ Walter Matthau, Damien Thomas, Richard Pearson, Roy Kinnear, Ferdy Mayne, Charlotte Lewis
† The galleon, which cost 8 million dollars, was not wasted. It was given to the municipality of Cannes and became a tourist attraction.
costumes (Anthony Powell)

Pirates of Blood River *
GB 1961 84m Technicolor Hammerscope
Hammer (Anthony Nelson Keys)
Pirates in search of gold terrorize a Huguenot settlement.
Land-locked blood and thunder for tough schoolboys.
w John Hunter, John Gilling *d* John Gilling *ph* Arthur Grant
☆ Christopher Lee, Andrew Keir, Kerwin Mathews, Glenn Corbett, Peter Arne, Oliver Reed, Marla Landi, Michael Ripper

The Pirates of Penzance
GB 1982 112m Technicolor Panavision
Universal (Joseph Papp, Timothy Burrill)
An adaptation of the Gilbert and Sullivan operetta in the form of the Joseph Papp Broadway revival.
What was tolerably pretty and witty on the stage is a great bore on wide film.
wd Wilford Leach *ph* Douglas Slocombe *m* Gilbert and Sullivan *pd* Elliott Scott *ed* Anne V. Coates
☆ Kevin Kline, Angela Lansbury, Linda Ronstadt, George Rose, Tony Azito, Rex Smith
'Not the slightest trace of imagination.' – *MFB*
'Anyone who thinks Gilbert and Sullivan indestructible should see this.' – *Observer*

Pirates of Tortuga
US 1961 97m DeLuxe Cinemascope
Sam Katzman/TCF
In the 17th-century Caribbean, a privateer is ordered by the king to go undercover and rout Sir Henry Morgan.
Listless swashbuckler with inferior talent.
w Melvin Levy, Jesse L. Lasky Jnr, Pat Silver *d* Robert D. Webb
☆ Ken Scott, Dave King, Letitia Roman, John Richardson, Robert Stephens, Edgar Barrier

Pirates of Tripoli
US 1955 72m Technicolor
Columbia (Sam Katzman)
A pirate captain comes to the aid of an oriental princess.
More akin to the Arabian Knights than Blackbeard, but not bad for a double-biller.
w Allen March *d* Felix Feist *ph* Henry Freulich *md* Mischa Bakaleinikoff
☆ Paul Henreid, Patricia Medina, Paul Newland, John Miljan, Lillian Bond

Pisma Myortovovo Cheloveka: see *Letters from a Dead Man*

A Pistol for Ringo *
Italy/Spain 1965 99m colour
PCM/Balcàzar (Alberto Pugliese, Luciano Ercoli)
original title: *Una Pistola per Ringo*
A wandering gunman goes to the aid of a Texan family whose ranch has been taken over by Mexican bandits.
Above-average spaghetti Western, much influenced by the work of John Ford and Howard Hawks.
wd Duccio Tessari *ph* Francisco Marin *m* Ennio Morricone *ad* Juan Alberto Soler *ed* Lucia Quaglia
☆ Giuliano Gemma, Fernando Sancho, Hally Hammond (Lorella de Luca), Nieves Navarro, Antonio Casas, Jorge Martin
† It was followed by a sequel, *The Return of Ringo* (qv).

Pistola di Deo: see *God's Gun*

The Pit and the Pendulum *
US 1961 85m Pathécolor Panavision
AIP/Alta Vista (Roger Corman)
Lovers plan to drive her brother mad; he responds by locking them in his torture chamber.
The centrepiece only is borrowed from Poe; the rest is lurid but mostly ineffective. Still, its commercial success started the Poe cycle of the sixties.
w Richard Matheson *d* Roger Corman *ph* Floyd Crosby *m* Les Baxter
☆ Vincent Price, Barbara Steele, John Kerr
'As in *House of Usher*, the quality of the film is its full-blooded feeling for Gothic horror – storms and lightning, mouldering castles and cobwebbed torture chambers, bleeding brides trying to tear the lids from their untimely tombs.' – *David Robinson*

Pitch Black
US 2000 108m colour
UIP/Gramercy/Interscope (Tom Engelman)
After their spaceship crashes on an unknown planet, the survivors, who include a hardened killer, find that it is too hot to move except at night, when the place is crawling with fierce creatures.
Essentially a 'B' movie with a few pretensions, this delivers its shocks efficiently enough, but is otherwise in need of a better script and a bigger budget.
w Jim Wheat, Ken Wheat, David Twohy *d* David Twohy *ph* David Eggby *m* Graeme Revell *pd* Graham 'Grace' Walker *ed* Rick Shaine *sp* Patrick Tatopoulos
☆ Radha Mitchell (Fry), Vin Diesel (Riddick), Cole Hauser (Johns), Keith David (Imam), Lewis Fitz-Gerald (Paris), Claudia Black (Shazza), Rhiana Griffith (Jack), John Moore (Zeke), Simon Burke (Owens)
'Mildly scary but not particularly engaging on any other level.' – *Emanuel Levy, Variety*

Pitfall
US 1948 85m bw
Samuel Bischoff
An insurance investigator proves easy prey for a grasping woman.
Modest suspenser, quite efficiently made.
w Jay Dratler *novel* Jay Dratler *d* André de Toth *ph* Harry Wild *md* Louis Forbes
☆ Dick Powell, Lizabeth Scott, Jane Wyatt, Raymond Burr, John Litel, Byron Barr, Ann Doran

Pittsburgh
US 1942 91m bw
Universal (Charles K. Feldman)
A coal miner's daughter has two loves, all of them trying to improve their social status as Pittsburgh becomes a world centre of steel production.
Routine melodrama ending as a flagwaver, and allowing none of its stars any opportunity.
w Kenneth Gamet, Tom Reed *d* Lewis Seiler *ph* Robert de Grasse *m* Hans Salter
☆ Marlene Dietrich, Randolph Scott, John Wayne, Frank Craven, Louise Allbritton, Shemp Howard, Ludwig Stossel, Thomas Gomez

Pixote **
Brazil 1981 127m colour
Palace/Embrafilme
A 10-year-old living on the streets of São Paulo tries to survive by pimping, drug-dealing and murder.
Grim and sensational exposé of a social problem, using actual homeless children to add to its reality.
w Hector Babenco, Jorge Duran *novel* *Infancia dos Mortos* by José Louzeiro *d Hector Babenco*

ph Rodolfo Sanches *m* John Neschling *ad* Clovis Bueno *ed* Luiz Elias
☆ Fernando Ramos da Silva, Jorge Julião, Gilberto Moura, Edilson Lino, Zenildo Oliveira Santos, Claudio Bernardo, Marilia Pera, José Nilson Dos Santos

The Pizza Triangle: see *Jealousy Italian Style*

'They do it in the name of love!'
A Place for Lovers
US 1969 102m colour
MGM
A dying American fashion designer retires to her Italian villa and has a high old time with an Italian engineer.
Incomparably crass tearjerker which seems eager to offer too many morals about life and love and art.
w Peter Baldwin, Ennio de Concini, Tonino Guerra, Julian Halevy (Julian Zimet), Cesare Zavattini *story* Brunello Rondi *d* Vittorio de Sica
☆ Faye Dunaway, Marcello Mastroianni, Caroline Mortimer, Karin Engh
'The most God-awful piece of pseudo-romantic slop I've ever seen.' – *Roger Ebert, Chicago Sun Times*
'The worst movie I have seen all year and possibly since 1926.' – *Charles Champlin, L.A. Times*
'The five scriptwriters who supposedly worked on the film must have spent time enough at the watercooler to flood a camel.' – *Time*
† Screenwriter Zimet wrote under a pseudonym because of the blacklist.

'Seldom has the screen so captured the fire and fever of today's youth! Seldom has a film boasted three such exciting star performances!'
A Place in the Sun **
US 1951 122m bw
Paramount/George Stevens
A poor young man, offered the chance of a rich wife, allows himself to be convicted and executed for the accidental death of his former fiancée.
Overblown, overlong and over-praised melodrama from a monumental novel of social guilt; sometimes visually striking, this version alters the stresses of the plot and leaves no time for sociological detail. A film so clearly intended as a masterpiece could hardly fail to be boring.
w Michael Wilson, Harry Brown *novel An American Tragedy* by Theodore Dreiser *d George Stevens ph William C. Mellor m* Franz Waxman *ad* Hans Dreier, Walter Tyler *ed* William Hornbeck
☆ Montgomery Clift, Elizabeth Taylor, Shelley Winters, Anne Revere, Keefe Brasselle, Fred Clark, Raymond Burr, Frieda Inescort, Shepperd Strudwick, Kathryn Givney, Walter Sande
'An almost incredibly painstaking work ... mannered enough for a very fancy Gothic murder mystery. This version gives the story a modern setting, but the town is an arrangement of symbols of wealth, glamour and power versus symbols of poor, drab helplessness – an arrangement far more suitable to the thirties than to the fifties.' – *Pauline Kael*
Academy Award: script; George Stevens; William C. Mellor; Franz Waxman; editing
Academy Award nomination: best picture; Montgomery Clift; Shelley Winters

A Place of One's Own **
GB 1944 92m bw
GFD/Gainsborough (R. J. Minney)
In Edwardian times, an old house is taken over by an elderly couple, and their young companion is possessed by the spirit of a murdered girl.
Charming little ghost story, not quite detailed enough to be totally effective.
w Brock Williams *novel* Osbert Sitwell
d Bernard Knowles *ph Stephen Dade m* Hubert Bath *md* Louis Levy
☆ James Mason, Barbara Mullen, Margaret Lockwood, Dennis Price, Helen Haye, Michael Shepley, Dulcie Gray, Moore Marriott
'A fine piece of work ... gripping, marvellous, outstanding, eerie, perky, beautiful, lovely and different.' – C. A. Lejeune
'One comes away with an impression of elegance which has not so far been frequent in the British cinema.' – *Dilys Powell*

Place Vendôme **
France/Belgium/GB 1998 118m colour Technovision
Artificial Eye/TF1/l'Etang/Alhena/Angel's Co. (Alain Sarde)
The alcoholic widow of a near-bankrupt jeweller tries to protect the business from its importunate creditors.
Elegant, intriguing French thriller that provides Deneuve with probably her best role for years, as a pressured woman recovering her dignity and abilities.
w Jacques Fieschi, Nicole Garcia *d* Nicole Garcia *ph* Laurent Dailland *m* Richard Robbins *ad* Thierry Flamand *ed* Luc Barnier, Francoise Bonnot *cos* Nathalie du Roscoat, Elisabeth Tavernier
☆ *Catherine Deneuve* (Marianne), Jean-Pierre Bacri (Jean-Pierre), Emmanuelle Seigner (Nathalie), Jacques Dutronc (Battistelli), Bernard Fresson (Vincent Malivert), François Berléand (Eric Malivert), Philippe Clévenot (Kleiser)
'A rhinestone rather than a gem, this is a drama that looks sophisticated and deep, but proves hollow.' – *Angie Errigo, Empire*

Places in the Heart
US 1984 111m Technicolor
Tri-Star/Delphi (Arlene Donovan)
In 1935 Texas, the sheriff's widow struggles to maintain the family farm.
All-American saga with asides including the Ku Klux Klan; though based on the author's recollections of childhood, it all seems predictable.
wd Robert Benton *ph* Nestor Almendros *m* John Kander *pd* Gene Callahan
☆ Sally Field, Lindsay Crouse, Ed Harris, Amy Madigan, John Malkovich, Danny Glover
'Basically just another calculated tug at the heartstrings.' – *Tom Milne, MFB*
Academy Award: Sally Field; original screenplay
Academy Award nomination: best picture; John Malkovich (supporting actor); Lindsay Crouse (supporting actress); direction

Plaff! Or Too Afraid of Life *
Cuba 1988 92m colour
Metro/ICAIC (Ricardo Avila)
original title: *Desmasiado Miedo A La Vida, O Plaff*
A superstitious mother tries to get rid of her scientific daughter-in-law.
Deliberately ramshackle political comedy – the beginning of the film is kept to the end – which is not without a certain surrealist charm.
w Daniel Chavarría, Juan Carlos Tabío *d* Juan Carlos Tabío *ph* Julio Valdés *ad* Raúl Oliva *ed* Roberto Bravo, Osvaldo M. Donatien
☆ Daisy Granados, Thais Valdés, Luis Alberto Garcia, Raúl Pamares, Alicia Bustamente, Jorge Cao
'A wittily cynical exercise in alienation which oozes awkwardness and provokes uncomfortable laughter.' – *MFB*

La Plage des Enfants Perdus: see *The Beach of Lost Children*

The Plague Dogs
GB/US 1982 103m Technicolor
Nepenthe Productions
Two dogs escape from a research laboratory and are in danger of infecting the country with a deadly virus.
Misguided and woefully overlong attempt to preach a message through a cartoon. Like Watership Down, *it needs the printed word and is deflected by the inevitably cuddly look of the animated animals.*
wd Martin Rosen *novel* Richard Adams
☆ Featuring the voices of John Hurt, James Bolam, Christopher Benjamin, Judy Geeson, Barbara Leigh-Hunt

The Plague of the Zombies *
GB 1965 91m Technicolor
Hammer (Anthony Nelson Keys)
A voodoo-practising Cornish squire raises zombies from the dead and uses them to work his tin mine.
They don't explain why he didn't simply hire the living; apart from that this is Hammer on its better side, with a charming elderly hero and good suspense sequences.
w Peter Bryan *d* John Gilling *ph* Arthur Grant *m* James Bernard
☆ *André Morell, John Carson,* Diane Clare, Brook Williams, Jacqueline Pearce, Alex Davion, Michael Ripper
'Visually the film is splendid ... the script manages several offbeat strokes.' – *MFB*

Plain Clothes
US 1988 98m CFI color
Paramount (Richard Wechsler, Michael Manheim)
After his brother is accused of murdering a teacher, a cop, who is suspended from the force, decides to go undercover as a high-school student to find the real killer.
An occasionally amusing comedy, though it is doubtful whether there are enough laughs, or even smiles, to make watching it worthwhile.
w A. Scott Frank *d* Martha Coolidge *ph* Daniel Hainey *m* Scott Wilk *pd* Michel Levesque *ed* Patrick Kennedy, Edward Abroms
☆ Arliss Howard, Suzy Amis, George Wendt, Diane Ladd, Seymour Cassel, Larry Pine, Jackie Gayle, Abe Vigoda, Robert Stack

'Grandest love story ever told!'
The Plainsman **
US 1936 113m bw
Paramount/Cecil B. de Mille
The life of Wild Bill Hickok and his friends Buffalo Bill and Calamity Jane.
Standard big-scale 30s Western; narrative lumpy, characters idealized, spectacle impressive, technical credits high.
w Waldemar Young, Lynn Riggs, Harold Lamb *d Cecil B. de Mille ph* Victor Milner, George Robinson *m* George Antheil *md* Boris Morros
☆ Gary Cooper, James Ellison, Jean Arthur, Charles Bickford, Helen Burgess, Porter Hall, Paul Harvey, Victor Varconi
'It should do all right for business, ranging from big to good, possibly irregular in spots.' – *Variety*
'Certainly the finest western since *The Virginian*; perhaps the finest western in the history of the film.' – *Graham Greene*
† The story was remade as a TV movie in 1966, with Don Murray.

The Plainsman and the Lady
US 1946 84m bw
Republic
In 1847, the Pony Express is threatened by stagecoach owners.
Moderate Western for family consumption.
w Richard Wormser *d* Joseph Kane
☆ William Elliott, Gail Patrick, Vera Ralston, Joseph Schildkraut

Le Plaisir *
France 1952 97m bw
Stera/CCFC
Three stories by Guy de Maupassant, about the search for pleasure: 'Le Masque', 'La Maison Tellier', 'Le Modèle'.
Stylish but rather subdued compendium, with no highlights to stay in the memory.
w Jacques Natanson, Max Ophüls *d* Max Ophüls *ph* Christian Matras, Philippe Agostini *m* Joe Hajos *ad* Max Ophuls
☆ Claude Dauphin, Gaby Morlay; Madeleine Renaud, Danielle Darrieux, Ginette Leclerc, Jean Gabin, Pierre Brasseur; Simone Simon, Daniel Gélin
'An attractive theme tune, good performances, and the pleasure itself of virtuosity.' – *Gavin Lambert, MFB*
Academy Award nomination: art direction

'There comes a time in every man's life when he just can't believe his eyes!'
Plan 9 from Outer Space
US 1958 79m bw
Wade Williams Productions (Edward D. Wood Jnr)
aka: *Grave Robbers from Outer Space*
Space people try to resurrect the Earth's dead and turn them against the world.
Inept mini-budgeter often hailed as the worst film ever made. It is certainly among the most boring.
wd Edward D. Wood Jnr *ph* William C. Thompson *md* Gordon Zahler *ad* Tom Kemp *sp* Charles Duncan
☆ Bela Lugosi, Tor Johnson, Gregory Walcott, Mona McKinnon, Vampira, Lyle Talbot
SAMPLE DIALOGUE: 'One thing's sure, Inspector Clay's dead. Murdered. And somebody's responsible.'
† Lugosi died after four days of shooting and is mostly represented by a double, who keeps his cape up so that it covers his face.

Planes, Trains and Automobiles *
US 1987 93m colour
UIP/Paramount (John Hughes)
An advertising executive, trying to get home for Thanksgiving, finds many obstacles hampering his progress, including an insufferable companion.
Cheerful farce that allows some room for characterization.
wd John Hughes *ph* Don Peterman *m* Ira Newborn *pd* John W. Corso *ed* Paul Hirsch
☆ Steve Martin, John Candy, Michael McKean, Kevin Bacon, Dylan Baker, Carol Bruce, Olivia Burnette, Diana Douglas, William Windom

'Somewhere in the universe, there must be something better than man!'
Planet of the Apes ***
US 1968 119m DeLuxe Panavision
TCF/Apjac (Mort Abrahams)
Astronauts caught in a time warp land on a planet which turns out to be Earth in the distant future, when men have become beasts and the apes have taken over.
Stylish, thoughtful science fiction which starts and finishes splendidly but suffers from a sag in the middle. The ape make-up is great.
Sequels, in roughly descending order of interest, were:
1969 Beneath the Planet of the Apes
1970 Escape from the Planet of the Apes
1972 Conquest of the Planet of the Apes
1973 Battle for the Planet of the Apes.
A TV series followed in 1974, and a cartoon series in 1975.
w Michael Wilson, Rod Serling novel Monkey Planet by Pierre Boulle *d Franklin Schaffner ph Leon Shamroy m* Jerry Goldsmith *ad* William Creber, Jack Martin Smith *ed* Hugh S. Fowler *sp L.B. Abbott, John Chambers, Art Cruickshank, Emil Kosa Jnr*
☆ *Charlton Heston,* Roddy McDowall, *Kim Hunter,* Maurice Evans, James Whitmore, James Daly, Linda Harrison
'One of the most telling science fiction films to date.' – *Tom Milne*
† John Chambers was awarded an honorary Oscar for 'outstanding make-up achievement'.
Academy Award: make-up (John Chambers)
Academy Award nomination: Jerry Goldsmith; costumes (Morton Haack)

'Rule the planet.'
Planet of the Apes
US 2001 120m DeLuxe Panavision
TCF/Zanuck Co. (Richard D. Zanuck)
An astronaut goes forward in time to a world where talking apes rule over a slave population of humans.
Burton claimed this was a 're-imagining' of the original movie; with its glum hero and turgid action, all it demonstrates is the poverty of his imagination.
w William Broyles Jnr, Lawrence Konner, Mark Rosenthal *novel* Pierre Boulle *d* Tim Burton *ph* Philippe Rousselot *m* Danny Elfman *pd* Rick Heinrichs *ed* Chris Lebenzon *sp* Rick Baker; ILM
☆ Mark Wahlberg (Captain Leo Davidson), Tim Roth (Thade), Helena Bonham Carter (Ari), Michael Clarke Duncan (Attar), Paul Giamatti (Limbo), Estella Warren (Daena), Cary-Hiroyuki Tagawa (Krull), David Warner (Sandar), Kris Kristofferson (Karubi), Erick Avari (Tival)
'A film whose knuckles scrape along the ground, when it should be swinging through the trees.' – *Peter Bradshaw, Guardian*
'A bad let down after the wait for it, ridiculous without being witty enough and laboured without achieving suspense.' – *Alexander Walker, London Evening Standard*
† It cost around $100m to make and took more than $180m at the US box-office.

The Planter's Wife
GB 1952 91m bw
Rank/Pinnacle (John Stafford)
US title: *Outpost in Malaya*
original title: *White Blood*
Malaya under the terrorists. A wife is planning to leave but changes her mind after she and her husband defend their home in a siege.
Superficial studio-bound melodrama unworthy of its subject but a good star vehicle.
w Peter Proud, Guy Elmes *d* Ken Annakin
ph Geoffrey Unsworth *m* Allan Gray
☆ Claudette Colbert, Jack Hawkins, Ram Gopal, Jeremy Spenser, Tom Macauley, Helen Goss

Platform
Hong Kong/Japan/France/Nethlands/Switzerland
2000 155m colour
Artificial Eye/Hu-Tong/T-Mark/Artcam/Office Kitano/ Bandai (Li Kit-ming, Shozo Ichiyama)
original title: *Zhantai*
A theatrical troupe in a remote Chinese province experience cultural changes in the decade that began in 1979.
From Maoist plays to performances of Western rock, the movie charts shifts in Chinese society, but does so in such a distanced way, mainly viewing the action in static long-shot, that it becomes difficult to be involved in what ought to be interesting times.
wd Jia Zhang-ke *ph* Yu Lik-wai *m* Yoshihiro Hanno *ad* Qiu Sheng *ed* Kong Jing-lei
☆ Wang Hong-wei (Minliang), Zhao Tao (Ruijuan), Liang Jing-dong (Chang Jun), Yang Tian-yi (Zhong Pin), Wang Bo (Yao Eryong)
'It takes itself to the very limit of unwatchability. And, very often, two or three shattering steps beyond.' – *Peter Bradshaw, Guardian*
† The film was originally shown at the Venice Film Festival in a version running for 195m.

Platinum Blonde *
US 1931 92m bw
Columbia
A newspaper reporter falls for an heiress.
Limp romantic comedy with interesting performances: the film which established Jean Harlow.
w Robert Riskin, Jo Swerling *story* Harry E. Chandler, Doug Churchill *d* Frank Capra
ph Joseph Walker
☆ *Robert Williams*, Loretta Young, Jean Harlow, Halliwell Hobbes, Reginald Owen
'A programmer that fully entertains, is laughy and represents what cast, dialogue and direction can do with a lean story.' – *Variety*

Platinum High School
US 1960 96m bw
MGM (Red Doff)
GB title: *Rich, Young and Deadly*
A father investigates his son's death at a military academy for rich juvenile delinquents.
Hilarious serial-like melodrama with the worm turning to some effect.
w Robert Smith *d* Charles Haas *ph* Russell Metty *m* Van Alexander
☆ Mickey Rooney, Dan Duryea, Terry Moore, Warren Berlinger, Yvette Mimieux, Conway Twitty, Elisha Cook Jnr, Richard Jaeckel

'The first casualty of war is innocence.'
Platoon **
US 1986 120m CFI color
Hemdale/Arnold Kopelson
Experiences of infantrymen during the Vietnam war.
Not badly done in the style of Bataan *(plus brutality and gore). One would have thought it too late to do it at all, but the American public made it a box-office hit.*
wd Oliver Stone *ph* Robert Richardson
m Georges Delerue *ed* Claire Simpson
☆ Tom Berenger, Willem Dafoe, Charlie Sheen, Forest Whitaker, Francesco Quinn
'It is fundamentally an entirely formulaic war movie, more "artistic" than many of its genre but true to conventions in both characters and narrative.' – *Judith Williamson, New Statesman*
best picture; Oliver Stone as director; Claire Simpson
Tom Berenger, Willem Dafoe; Oliver Stone for original screenplay; Robert Richardson
Oliver Stone (as director)

Play Dirty *
GB 1969 118m Technicolor Panavision
UA/Lowndes (Harry Saltzman)
During World War II, a squad of ex-criminals is given the job of destroying an enemy oil depot in North Africa.
Small-scale Dirty Dozen *with would-be ironic twists; well made entertainment for the stout-hearted.*
w Lotte Colin, Melvyn Bragg *d* André de Toth
ph Edward Scaife *m* Michel Legrand
☆ Michael Caine, Nigel Davenport, Nigel Green, Harry Andrews, Bernard Archard, Daniel Pilon

Play It Again Sam *
US 1972 86m Technicolor Panavision
Paramount/APJAC/Rollins-Joffe (Arthur P. Jacobs)
A neurotic film critic is abandoned by his wife and seeks fresh companionship, with help from the shade of Humphrey Bogart.
Random comedy for star fans, mainly quite lively and painless.
w Woody Allen *play* Woody Allen *d* Herbert Ross *ph* Owen Roizman *m* Billy Goldenberg
☆ Woody Allen, Diane Keaton, Jerry Lacy, Susan Anspach

Play It as It Lays
US 1972 94m Technicolor Panavision
Universal
An unsuccessful actress takes stock of her wrecked life.
With-it melodrama which audiences preferred to be without.
w Joan Didion, John Gregory Dunne *novel* Joan Didion *d* Frank Perry
☆ Anthony Perkins, Tuesday Weld, Tammy Grimes, Adam Roarke, Ruth Ford

Play It Cool
GB 1962 81m bw
Independent Artists/Coronado (David Deutsch)
An unsuccessful rock group, twisting around London's clubs, saves an heiress from the clutches of an unscrupulous singer.
A slight, unsubtle comedy hampered by a lack of memorable songs, and intended to showcase the talents of Britain's best Elvis-styled rocker, which do not extend to acting; other singers featured include Helen Shapiro, Bobby Vee, Danny Williams, Shane Fenton and the Fentones, and Jimmy Crawford.
w Jack Henry *d* Michael Winner *ph* Reginald Wyer *m* Norrie Paramor *m/ly* Norrie Paramor, Richard B. Rowe, Bernard Jewry, Norman Newell, Ron Fraser, Bob Barratt, Larry Parnes *ad* Lionel Couch *ed* Tristam Cones
☆ Billy Fury, Michael Anderson Jnr, Dennis Price, Richard Wattis, Ray Brooks, Maurice Kaufman, Peter Barkworth, Max Bacon, Lionel Blair

'Two Best Friends Take A Shot At Hitting It Big.'
Play It To The Bone
US 1999 124m Technicolor Panavision
Buena Vista/Touchstone/Shanghai'd (Stephen Chin)
Two friends, unsuccessful Los Angeles boxers, get a last chance to make good in Las Vegas, fighting one another.
Episodic account of a couple of would-be contenders that goes nowhere; it is understandably cynical about professional boxing, but at the same time suggests its participants are to be admired.
wd Ron Shelton *ph* Mark Vargo *m* Alex Wurman *pd* Claire Jenora Bowin *ed* Paul Seydor, Patrick Flannery *cos* Kathryn Morrison
☆ Antonio Banderas (Cesar Dominguez), Woody Harrelson (Vince Boudreau), Lolita Davidovich (Grace Pasic), Tom Sizemore (Joe Domino), Lucy Liu (Lia), Robert Wagner (Hank Goody), Richard Masur (Artie), Willie Garson (Cappie Caplan), Cylk Cozart (Rudy), Jack Carter (Dante Solomon)
'The characters are coarse, but the film itself is coarser, as well as overlong and poorly written.' – *Philip French, Observer*

Play Me Something
GB 1989 72m bw/colour
BFI/Film Four International/Scottish Film Production Fund/Grampian TV (Kate Swan)
On a small Scottish island, a group of passengers waiting for a plane listen to a story about an Italian peasant leaving his village to go to Venice.
An intellectual endeavour that never quite comes alive on the screen.
w John Berger, Timothy Neat *story* Once in Europe by John Berger *d* Timothy Neat *ph* Chris Cox *m* Jim Sutherland *ad* Annette Gillies
ed Russell Fenton
☆ Lucia Lanzarini, Charlie Barron, John Berger, Hamish Henderson, Tilda Swinton, Stewart Ennis, Robert Carr, Liz Lochhead

'The scream you hear may be your own!'
Play Misty for Me *
US 1971 102m Technicolor
Universal/Malpaso (Robert Daley)
A radio disc jockey is pestered by a girl who turns out to be homicidally jealous.
Smartly made if over-extended psycho melodrama with good suspense sequences and a fair quota of shocks.
w Jo Heims, Dean Riesner *d* Clint Eastwood
ph Bruce Surtees *m* Dee Barton
☆ Clint Eastwood, Jessica Walter, Donna Mills, John Larch

The Playboy: see *Kicking the Moon Around*

'Maurice brings a new kind of love to you!'
Playboy of Paris
US 1930 82m bw
Paramount
A waiter inherits a million but finds he can't leave his job, so he becomes a playboy by night only.
Rather rickety star vehicle which demands attention only when he is on screen.
w Percy Heath *play* The Little Café by Tristan Bernard *d* Ludwig Berger
☆ *Maurice Chevalier*, Frances Dee, O. P. Heggie, Stuart Erwin, Eugene Pallette
'Light, amusing farce story doesn't help and may hurt ... Chevalier's the only draw.' – *Variety*

'In a small community, love is never a private affair.'
The Playboys *
GB 1992 109m Technicolor
Samuel Goldwyn/Green Umbrella (William P. Cartlidge, Simon Perry)
In an Irish village in the 1950s, the alcoholic local policeman and a strolling player both fall in love with an unmarried mother.
A soap opera-style narrative of thwarted love, of interest mainly for its performances.
w Shane Connaughton, Kerry Crabbe *d* Gillies MacKinnon *ph* Jack Conroy *m* Jean-Claude Petit
pd Andy Harris *ed* Humphrey Dixon
☆ Albert Finney, Aidan Quinn, Robin Wright, Milo O'Shea, Alan Devlin, Niamh Cusack, Niall Buggy, Adrian Dunbar
'A heartbreak tragedy wrapped up inside an ingratiating comedy.' – *Alexander Walker, London Evening Standard*

The Player ****
US 1992 124m DeLuxe
Guild/Avenue (David Brown, Michael Tolkin, Nick Wechsler)
A Hollywood studio executive gets away with murder.
A deft and dazzling satire on the film industry – witty, surprising and intelligent.
w Michael Tolkin *novel* Michael Tolkin *d* Robert Altman *ph* Jean Lepine *m* Thomas Newman
pd Stephen Altman *ed* Geraldine Peroni
☆ Tim Robbins, Greta Scacchi, Fred Ward, Whoopi Goldberg, Peter Gallagher, Brion James, Cynthia Stevenson, Vincent D'Onofrio, Dean Stockwell, Richard E. Grant, Sydney Pollack
'The movie has the exhilarating nonchalance of the director's seventies classics, and its tone is volatile, elusive: with breathtaking assurance, it veers from psychological-thriller suspense to goofball comedy to icy satire.' – *Terrence Rafferty, New Yorker*
† The film featured more than 60 stars playing themselves, including Harry Belafonte, James Coburn, Peter Falk, Teri Garr, Angelica Huston, Jack Lemmon, Nick Nolte, Burt Reynolds, Julia Roberts, Susan Sarandon, Rod Steiger and Bruce Willis.
Robert Altman; Michael Tolkin; Geraldine Peroni
Robert Altman; Michael Tolkin

Players: see *The Club*

Players
US 1979 120m Metrocolor
Paramount (Robert Evans)
A pro tennis player is trained for top stardom by a sculptress with a mysterious past.
Entirely uninvolving romantic drama stretched around a Wimbledon match; slickness does not compensate for a gaping hole at the centre.
w Arnold Schulman *d* Anthony Harvey
ph James Crabe *m* Jerry Goldsmith *pd* Richard Sylbert
☆ Ali MacGraw, Dean-Paul Martin, Maximilian Schell, Pancho Gonzalez

The Players Club
US 1998 104m DeLuxe
New Line (Patricia Charbonnet)
A single mother works as a stripper to pay her way through college.
Energetic, uneven drama with a comic tone and an uncertain attitude towards sex and gender.
wd Ice Cube *ph* Malik Sayeed *m* Hidden Faces
pd Dina Lipton *ed* Suzanne Hines
☆ Lisa Raye, Bernie Mac, Monica Calhoun, A. J. Johnson, Ice Cube, Alex Thomas, Jamie Foxx, Chrystale Wilson, Adele Givens, Larry McCoy
'A messy but lively B-movie that recalls the more spirited comedic dramas of the '70s blaxploitation era.' – *Joe Leydon, Variety*

Playgirl
US 1954 85m bw
Universal-International
A small-town girl becomes a good-time girl in the big city.
Totally unsurprising melodrama.
w Robert Blees *d* Joseph Pevney *ph* Carl Guthrie
m Joseph Gershenson
☆ Shelley Winters, Barry Sullivan, Colleen Miller, Gregg Palmer, Richard Long, Kent Taylor

The Playgirl and the War Minister: see *The Amorous Prawn*

'To live and love in LA.'
Playing By Heart
US 1998 121m DeLuxe Panavision
Buena Vista/Miramax/Intermedia/Morpheus/Hyperion (Willard Carroll, Meg Liberman, Tom Wilhite)
In Los Angeles, a group of loosely-connected people look for love.
Garrulous romantic drama that never quite conveys true emotion.
wd Willard Carroll *ph* Vilmos Zsigmond *m* John Barry *pd* Melissa Stewart *ed* Pietro Scalia
☆ Gillian Anderson (Meredith), Angelina Jolie (Joan), Madeleine Stowe (Gracie), Anthony Edwards (Roger), Ryan Phillippe (Keenan), Gena Rowlands (Hannah), Sean Connery (Paul), Dennis Quaid (Hugh), Ellen Burstyn (Mildred), Jay Mohr (Mark), Jon Stewart (Trent), Patricia Clarkson (Allison), Nastassja Kinski (Melanie)
'A rather wearisome and sentimental film, with uneven acting.' – *Peter Bradshaw, Guardian*

Playing God
US 1997 94m DeLuxe
Blue Dolphin/Touchstone/Beacon (Marc Abraham, Laura Bickford)
A disgraced, drug-addicted surgeon goes to work for a gangster.
A lugubrious central performance sinks this sluggish, predictable thriller.
w Mark Haskell Smith *d* Andy Wilson
ph Anthony B. Richmond *m* Richard Hartley
pd Naomi Shohan *ed* Louise Rubacky
☆ David Duchovny, Timothy Hutton, Angelina Jolie, Michael Massee, Peter Stormare, Andrew Tiernan, Gary Dourdan, John Hawkes
'This trashy thriller aspires to flip black comedy but manages only moments of unintentional hilarity.' – *Liese Spencer, Sight and Sound*

Playmates *
US 1941 96m bw
RKO (Cliff Reid)
For the sake of a lucrative radio contract, John Barrymore agrees to turn bandleader Kay Kyser into a Shakespearian actor.

Barrymore's last film is a weird comedy concoction, awesome in its waste of his talents but fairly funny in a high school kind of way.
w James V. Kern *d* David Butler *ph* Frank Redman *songs* James Van Heusen, Johnny Burke
☆ *Kay Kyser and his Band, John Barrymore*, Ginny Simms, Lupe Velez, May Robson, Patsy Kelly, Peter Lind Hayes, George Cleveland

Playtime *
France 1968 152m Eastmancolor 70mm
Specta Films (René Silvera)
Hulot and a group of American tourists are bewildered by life in an airport, a business block and a restaurant.
Incredibly extended series of sketches, none of which is devastatingly funny. The irritation is that the talent is clearly there but needs control.
w Jacques Tati, Jacques Lagrange *d* Jacques Tati *ph* Jean Badal, Andreas Winding *m* Francis Lemarque *pd* Eugène Roman
☆ *Jacques Tati*, Barbara Dennek, Jacqueline Lecomte, Henri Piccoli
'Tati still seems the wrong distance from his audience: not so far that we cannot see his gifts, not close enough so that they really touch.' – *Stanley Kauffmann*
'How sad that the result of all this, though it includes a great deal of intermittent pleasure, comes at times so dangerously close to boredom.' – *Brenda Davies, MFB*
'A series of brilliant doodles by an artist who has earned the right to indulge himself on such a scale.' – *Alexander Walker*

Plaza Suite *
US 1971 114m Technicolor
Paramount (Howard B. Koch)
Three sketches set in the same suite at New York's Plaza Hotel, with Walter Matthau appearing in all three but in different character.
A highly theatrical entertainment which was bound to seem flattened on the screen, but emerges with at least some of its laughs intact.
w Neil Simon *play* Neil Simon *d* Arthur Hiller *ph* Jack Marta *m* Maurice Jarre
☆ *Walter Matthau*, Maureen Stapleton, Barbara Harris, Lee Grant, Louise Sorel
† In the play, Maureen Stapleton played all three female roles.

'Nothing is as simple as black and white.'
Pleasantville **
US 1998 124m DeLuxe/bw
New Line/Larger Than Life (Gary Ross, Jon Kilik, Robert J. Degus, Steven Soderbergh)
Two colourful teenagers of the 90s are sucked back through the television into the black-and-white, hygienic world of a 50s sitcom.
Engaging fantasy that makes fun of the repressions and restrictions of the past, takes pleasure in the uncertainties of living, and uses special effects with wit.
wd Gary Ross *ph* John Lindley *m* Randy Newman *pd* Jeannine Oppewall *ed* William Goldenberg
☆ Tobey Maguire, Jeff Daniels, Joan Allen, William H. Macy, J. T. Walsh, Don Knotts, Reese Witherspoon
'A provocative, complex and surprisingly anti-nostalgic parable wrapped in the beguiling guise of a commercial high-concept comedy.' – *Joe Leydon, Variety*
Randy Newman; Jeannine Oppewall; Judianna Makovsky (costumes)

Please Believe Me
US 1950 87m bw
MGM (Val Lewton)
An English girl inherits an American ranch and is chased by a millionaire, a con man and a lawyer.
Dullsville comedy which failed to establish its star in America.
w Nathaniel Curtis *d* Norman Taurog *ph* Robert Planck *m* Hans Salter
☆ Deborah Kerr, Robert Walker, Mark Stevens, Peter Lawford, James Whitmore, Spring Byington

Please Don't Eat the Daisies
US 1960 111m Metrocolor Panavision
MGM (Joe Pasternak)
The family of a drama critic move to the country.
Thin, obvious comedy, all dressed up but with nowhere to go.
w Isobel Lennart *book* Jean Kerr *d* Charles Walters *ph* Robert Bronner *m* David Rose
☆ Doris Day, David Niven, Janis Paige, Spring Byington, Patsy Kelly, Richard Haydn, Jack Weston, John Harding, Margaret Lindsay

Please Sir
GB 1971 101m Eastmancolor
Rank/LWI/Leslie Grade (Andrew Mitchell)
The masters and pupils of Fenn Street school go on an annual camp.
Grossly inflated, occasionally funny big-screen version of the TV series.
w John Esmonde, Bob Larbey *d* Mark Stuart *ph* Wilkie Cooper *m* Mike Vickers
☆ *John Alderton, Deryck Guyler*, Joan Sanderson, Noel Howlett, Eric Chitty, Richard Davies

Please Teacher
GB 1937 75m bw
Associated British
An heir tries to find his bequest in the country house he has sold as a girls' school.
Cheerful star farce with songs.
wd Stafford Dickens *musical* K. R. G. Browne, R. P. Weston
☆ Bobby Howes, René Ray, Vera Pearce, Wylie Watson, Bertha Belmore, Lyn Harding
'Plenty of laughs.' – *Variety*

Please Turn Over
GB 1959 87m bw
Beaconsfield/Anglo Amalgamated
A teenager writes a sexy best-seller clearly featuring her family and friends.
Acceptable but uninspired comedy from a West End success.
w Norman Hudis *play Book of the Month* by Basil Thomas *d* Gerald Thomas *ph* Ted Scaife *m* Bruce Montgomery
☆ Ted Ray, Jean Kent, Leslie Phillips, Joan Sims, Julia Lockwood, Charles Hawtrey, Lionel Jeffries

The Pleasure (dubbed)
Italy 1985 94m colour
Filmirage
original title: *Il Piacere*
In 30s Venice a woman models herself on her dead mother in order to lose her virginity to her mother's aristocratic lover.
Dreary sub-pornographic nonsense, with the cast appearing as bored as its likely spectators.
w Homerus S. Zweitag, Clyde Anderson *d* Joe D'Amato (Aristide Massaccesi) *ph* Aristide Massaccesi *m* Cluster *ad* Italo Focacci *ed* Franco Alessandre
☆ Steve Wyler, Laura Gemser, Isabelle Andréa Guzon, Marco Mattioli, Lillie Carati
† The version released in British cinemas ran for 90m.

The Pleasure Garden
GB/Germany 1925 74m approx (24 fps) bw silent
Gainsborough/Emelka (Michael Balcon, Erich Pommer)
A chorus girl marries a rich colonial who goes native.
Boring melodrama with a few touches typical of its director, whose first film it is.
w Eliot Stannard *novel* Oliver Sandys *d* Alfred Hitchcock *ph* Baron Ventigmilia
☆ Virginia Valli, John Stuart, Miles Mander, Carmelita Geraghty

The Pleasure of His Company
US 1961 114m Technicolor
Paramount/Perlberg-Seaton
An ageing playboy arrives unexpectedly in San Francisco for his daughter's wedding.
Tame family comedy, very flatly adapted from the stage; dressed to kill, but with no narrative or cinematic drive.
w Samuel Taylor *play* Samuel Taylor, Cornelia Otis Skinner *d* George Seaton *ph* Robert Burks *m* Alfred Newman
☆ Fred Astaire, Lilli Palmer, Debbie Reynolds, Charles Ruggles, Tab Hunter, Gary Merrill, Harold Fong
'Smart comedy in its most diluted form.' – *MFB*

'Do Men Deserve Everything They Get?'
The Pleasure Principle
GB 1991 100m Metrocolor
Palace/Psychology News (David Cohen)
A medical journalist, divorced from his lesbian wife, tries to keep three affairs on the go at once.
Flaccid farce of sexual misadventures, performed with perfunctory interest.
wd David Cohen *ph* Andrew Spellar *m* Sonny Southon *pd* Cecilia Brereton *ed* Joe McAllister
☆ Peter Firth, Lynsey Baxter, Haydn Gwynne, Lysette Anthony, Sara Mair-Thomas, Ian Hogg, Francesca Folan, Liam McDermott
'A refreshing light comedy that simply asks its audience to lie back and enjoy.' – *Variety*
'It does not stimulate as it simulates and is essentially a throwback to those sleazy British soft-core comedies of the mid-Seventies.' – *Philip French, Observer*
† The film was made for £200,000, which its producer-director borrowed from his bank.

The Pleasure Seekers
US 1964 107m DeLuxe Cinemascope
TCF (David Weisbart)
Three girls in Madrid find boyfriends.
Dim remake of Three Coins in the Fountain*, adequate but unstimulating on all levels.*
w Edith Sommer *d* Jean Negulesco *ph* Daniel L. Fapp *m* Lionel Newman, Alexander Courage
☆ Ann-Margret, Tony Franciosa, Carol Lynley, Gene Tierney, Brian Keith, Gardner McKay, Isobel Elsom
Lionel Newman, Alexander Courage

'Detective Jerry Black has made a promise he can't break, to catch a killer he can't find.'
The Pledge **
US 2000 123m DeLuxe 'Scope
Warner/Morgan Creek/Franchise/Clyde Is Hungry (Michael Fitzgerald, Sean Penn, Elie Samaha)
A retired cop is obsessed by a promise he made to a mother: to find the man who raped and killed her child.
Bleak drama of a man's disintegration in his quest for justice and order in a world of chance.
w Jerzy Kromolowski, Mary Olson-Kromolowski *novel* Friedrich Dürrenmatt *d* Sean Penn *ph* Chris Menges *m* Hans Zimmer, Klaus Badelt *pd* Bill Groom *ed* Jay Cassidy
☆ Jack Nicholson (Jerry Black), Patricia Clarkson (Margaret Larsen), Benicio Del Toro (Toby Jay Wadenah), Dale Dickey (Strom), Aaron Eckhart (Stan Krolak), Costas Mandylor (Monash Deputy), Helen Mirren (Doctor), Robin Wright Penn (Lori), Vanessa Redgrave (Annalise Hansen), Mickey Rourke (Jim Olstand), Sam Shepard (Eric Pollack), Lois Smith (Helen Jackson), Harry Dean Stanton (Floyd Cage)
'Penn fulfills the promises of his first two pictures. He never takes a false directorial step.' – *Stanley Kaufmann, New Republic*
'A compelling drama, part psychological thriller, part parable, part tragedy.' – *Peter Bradshaw, Guardian*

Plein Soleil **
France/Italy 1960 115m colour
Paris/Panitalia/Titanus (Robert and Raymond Hakim)
aka: *Purple Noon*
aka: *Lust for Evil*
Hired to bring a rich friend back home to his father, a young wastrel decides to kill him instead and assume his identity.
Sparkling variation on an American film noir, glowing in the Mediterranean sun and maintaining suspense as well as a sense of sexual ambiguity.
w René Clément, Paul Gégauff *novel The Talented Mr Ripley* by Patricia Highsmith *d* René Clément *ph* Henri Decaë *m* Nino Rota *ad* Paul Bertrand *ed* Françoise Javet
☆ *Alain Delon*, Marie Laforêt, Maurice Ronet, Elvire Popesco, Erno Crisa, Frank Latimore, Bill Kearns
'All it has going for it is this sensuous kicky atmosphere: you feel as if you're breathing something beautiful and rotten.' – *Pauline Kael*
† Highsmith's novel was remade in 2000 by Anthony Minghella under its original title, *The Talented Mr Ripley* (qv).

Plenty *
US 1985 124m Technicolor Panavision
TCF/RKO/Edward R. Pressman
After World War II, the career of a neurotic society woman has parallels with the problems of western Europe.
Heavy-going allegory which should have stayed on the stage.
w David Hare *play* David Hare *d* Fred Schepisi *ph* Ian Baker *m* Bruce Smeaton *pd* Richard MacDonald *ed* Peter Honess
☆ Meryl Streep, Charles Dance, Tracey Ullman, John Gielgud, Sting, Ian McKellen, Sam Neill
'The press tell us that this film is an allegory of the fall of the British Empire. No wonder it is dreary!' – *Quentin Crisp*

The Plot Against Harry
US 1969 81m bw
Electric/Contemporary/King Screen (Robert Young, Michael Roemer)
Out of jail on parole, a gangster finds that business and his family are not what they were.
Put on the shelf for twenty years before its eventual release and hailed by some as a comic masterpiece, it turns out to be a moderately amusing movie that shows its age.
wd Michael Roemer *ph* Robert Young *m* Frank Lewin *ad* Howard Mandel *ed* Maurice Schell
☆ Martin Priest, Ben Lang, Maxine Woods, Henry Nemo, Jacques Taylor, Jean Leslie, Ellen Herbert, Sandra Kazan
'Harry's wit looks less deadpan than stone dead.' – *Kevin Jackson, Independent*

The Plot Thickens
US 1936 69m bw
RKO/William Sistrom
A murder proves to be connected with an art swindle.
Another minor case for Hildegarde Withers.
w Clarence Upson Young, Jack Townley *novel* Stuart Palmer *d* Ben Holmes
☆ James Gleason, ZaSu Pitts, Owen Davis Jnr, Louise Latimer

The Plot to Kill Roosevelt: see *Teheran*

The Plough and the Stars *
US 1936 72m bw
RKO (Cliff Reid, Robert Sisk)
In 1916, a Dublin marriage is threatened by the husband's appointment as commander of the citizen army.
Rather elementary film version of the play about the Troubles; interesting for effort rather than performance, and for the talent involved.
w Dudley Nichols *play* Sean O'Casey *d* John Ford *ph* Joseph August *m* Roy Webb
☆ Barbara Stanwyck, Preston Foster, Barry Fitzgerald, Denis O'Dea, Eileen Crowe, F. J. McCormick, Arthur Shields, Una O'Connor, Moroni Olsen, J. M. Kerrigan, Bonita Granville
'Skilfully made but not impressive as a money entry.' – *Variety*

The Ploughman's Lunch ***
GB 1983 107m colour
Goldcrest/Greenpoint/AC & D (Simon Relph, Ann Scott)
Media people find their cynicism deepened after the Falklands War.
Tough and intelligent, with nice observation and twists of detail.
w Ian McEwan *d* Richard Eyre *ph* Clive Tickner *m* Dominic Muldowney
☆ Jonathan Pryce, Tim Curry, Rosemary Harris, Frank Finlay, Charlie Dore, David de Keyser, Nat Jackley
'You don't have to agree with it, but you can't ignore it.' – *Daily Mail*
'It quietly and persuasively suggests that we get precisely the media we deserve.' – *Guardian*

Plovec: see *The Swimmer*

The Plow that Broke the Plains **
US 1936 28m bw
Resettlement Administration Film Unit

The story of how overcultivation of America's Great Plains resulted in the Dust Bowl.
Classic documentary which inevitably means less now than it did at the time but is still an impressive counterpoint to The Grapes of Wrath.
wd Pare Lorenz *m* Virgil Thomson

Pluck of the Irish: see *Great Guy*

Plucking the Daisy (dubbed) *
France 1956 100m bw
EGE/Hoche

original title: *En Effeuillant la Marguerite*
aka: *Mam'selle Striptease*
A general's daughter is forced to become a striptease performer in order to raise some much-needed money.
Pleasing comedy, designed to show off the body of Brigitte Bardot, at which it succeeds admirably.
w Marc Allégret, Roger Vadim *d* Marc Allégret *ph* Louis Page *m* Paul Misraki *ad* Alexandre Trauner *ed* Suzanne de Troeve
☆ Brigitte Bardot, Daniel Gélin, Robert Hirsch, Darry Cowl, Nadine Tallier, Mischa Auer

Plunder *
GB 1930 98m bw
Herbert Wilcox/British and Dominions
Two society friends turn jewel thieves to help an heiress.
Primitive talkie version of a Ben Travers farce which veered towards melodrama but had a successful stage revival at the National Theatre in 1978; valuable as a record of the original performances.
w W. P. Lipscomb *d* Tom Walls *ph* Freddie Young
☆ Tom Walls, Ralph Lynn, Robertson Hare, Winifred Shotter, Sydney Lynn, Ethel Coleridge
'Just a photographic record of the stage success.' – *Variety*

Plunder of the Sun *
US 1953 81m bw
Warner (Robert Fellows)
Various criminal elements seek buried treasure among the Mexican Aztec ruins.
Interestingly located, well made, unconvincingly scripted melodrama, yet another borrowing from The Maltese Falcon.
w Jonathan Latimer *novel* David Dodge *d* John Farrow *ph* Jack Draper *m* Antonio D. Conde
☆ Glenn Ford, Diana Lynn, Francis L. Sullivan, Patricia Medina, Sean McClory, Douglass Dumbrille, Eduardo Noriega

The Plunderers
US 1948 87m bw
Republic
An undercover cavalry officer becomes friends with an outlaw who saves his life.
Routine Western, just about watchable.
w Gerald Geraghty, Gerald Drayson Adams *d* Joseph Kane
☆ Rod Cameron, Ilona Massey, Adrian Booth

The Plunderers
US 1960 94m bw
Allied Artists/August (Joseph Pevney)
In the old west, four juvenile delinquents take over a town.
The Wild One *in period dress. Nothing in particular.*
w Bob Barbash *d* Joseph Pevney *ph* Eugene Polito *m* Leonard Rosenman
☆ Jeff Chandler, John Saxon, Ray Stricklyn, Roger Torrey, Dee Pollock, Marsha Hunt, Dolores Hart, Jay C. Flippen, James Westerfield

'They rob the rich and ... that's it.'
Plunkett & Macleane
GB 1999 101m Technicolor
Polygram/Working Title/Arts Council (Tim Bevan, Eric Fellner, Rupert Harvey)

In 18th-century London, a highwayman teams up with a penurious aristocrat to rob the rich.
A period romp with all the class and style of a Carry On movie, though its humour is on a lower level; crass, anachronistic and trivial, it has the narrative coherence of a pop video.
w Robert Wade, Neil Purvis, Charles McKeown *screenplay* Selwyn Roberts *d* Jake Scott *ph* John Mathieson *m* Craig Armstrong *pd* Norris Spencer *ed* Oral Norrie Ottey
☆ Robert Carlyle, Jonny Lee Miller, Liv Tyler, Ken Stott, Michael Gambin, Alan Cumming, Iain Robertson, Tommy Flanagan, Stephen Walters, James Thornton, Terence Rigby
'Was this film part of some new experiment to test the lower limits of audience expectation to see how little we would accept, and how much its makers could get away with? Talk about daylight robbery.' – *Tom Shone, Sunday Times*

La Plus Longue Nuit du Diable: see *The Devil's Nightmare*

Pluto Nash: see *The Adventuires of Pluto Nash*

Plymouth Adventure *
US 1952 105m Technicolor
MGM (Dore Schary)

The Pilgrim Fathers sail from Plymouth on the *Mayflower* and spend their first months ashore on the coast of America.
Well-meaning schoolbook history, totally unconvincing and very dull despite obvious effort all round. One or two of the actors have their moments.
w Helen Deutsch *novel* Ernest Gebler *d* Clarence Brown *ph* William Daniels *m* Miklos Rozsa
☆ Spencer Tracy, Gene Tierney, Van Johnson, Leo Genn, Dawn Addams
'It demonstrates how Hollywood can dull down as well as jazz up history.' – *Judith Crist, 1973*

Pocahontas
US 1995 81m Technicolor
Buena Vista/Walt Disney (James Pentecost)

Pocahontas falls in love with the British settler Captain John Smith and saves him from death.
Bad history, indifferent animation, dull songs, and an unexciting story all combine to produce a poor film, a disappointment after Disney's recent return to top form, though it still drew the crowds at the box-office and Disney stores.
w Carl Binder, Susannah Grant, Philip Lazebnik *idea* Mike Gabriel *d* Mike Gabriel, Eric Goldberg *m* Hawk Pope *m/ly* Alan Menken, Stephen Schwartz *md* Danny Troob, David Friedman *ad* Michael Giaimo *ed* H. Lee Patterson
☆ Featuring the voices of: Irene Bedard, Judy Kuhn, Mel Gibson, David Ogden Stiers, John Kassir, Russell Means, Christian Bale, Linda Hunt, Danny Mann, Billy Connolly
'Disney's fable of an arcadian American history wrecked by incursions from the Old World is obviously a means of allaying a bad conscience, while voicing xenophobic resentments about corrupt Europeans.' – *Roy Porter, Sunday Times*
'Pleasant to look at, and it will probably satisfy very small kiddies, but virtually everything in the movie is as generic as the two hygienic lovers.' – *Owen Gleiberman, Entertainment Weekly*
'The dullest Disney animation for years.' – *Empire*
† Twelve people contributed to the film's story.
†† The film took more than $317m at the box-office worldwide.
††† In real life Pocahontas was 12 when she met the 27-year-old Smith. She became the wife of a member of her tribe before leaving him when she converted to Christianity to marry John Rolfe, who took her and their son to England, where she died of smallpox.
Alan Menken (score and music), Stephen Schwartz (lyrics); song 'Colors of the Wind' (*m/ly* Alan Menken, Stephen Schwartz)

Pocket Money
US 1972 100m Technicolor
First Artists/Coleytown (John Foreman)

Two slow-thinking Arizona cowboys try to make money herding cattle.
Peculiar modern Western comedy drama which doesn't work.
w Terrence Malick *novel* *Jim Kane* by J. K. S. Brown *d* Stuart Rosenberg *ph* Laszlo Kovacs *m* Alex North
☆ Paul Newman, Lee Marvin, Strother Martin, Kelly Jean Peters, Wayne Rogers

Pocketful of Miracles
US 1961 136m Technicolor Panavision
UA/Franton (Frank Capra)

Kindly gangsters help an old apple seller to persuade her long lost daughter that she is a lady of means.
Boring, overlong remake of Lady for a Day, *showing that Capra's touch simply doesn't work on the wide screen, that his themes are dated anyway, and that all the fine character actors in Hollywood are a liability unless you find them something to do.*
w Hal Kanter, Harry Tugend *story* Damon Runyon *scenario* *Robert Riskin* *d* Frank Capra *ph* Robert Bronner *m* Walter Scharf
☆ Bette Davis, Glenn Ford, Hope Lange, Arthur O'Connell, Peter Falk, Thomas Mitchell, Edward Everett Horton, Sheldon Leonard, Barton MacLane, Jerome Cowan, Fritz Feld, Snub Pollard, David Brian, Ann-Margret, John Litel and also Jay Novello, Willis Bouchey, George E. Stone, Mike Mazurki, Jack Elam, Mickey Shaughnessy, Peter Mann, Frank Ferguson
'The effect is less one of whimsy than of being bludgeoned to death with a toffee apple.' – *Peter John Dyer*
'The story has enough cracks in it for the syrup to leak through.' – *Playboy*
title song (*m* James Van Heusen, *ly* Sammy Cahn); Peter Falk

Poetic Justice
US 1993 109m Technicolor
Columbia TriStar (Steve Nicolaides, John Singleton)

In South Central Los Angeles, a poetry-writing beautician, upset by the murder of her boyfriend, becomes involved with a mailman and his young daughter.
A disappointing second film from the director of Boyz N The Hood, *much closer to a conventional soap opera and with a clumsy and contrived narrative.*
wd John Singleton *ph* Peter Lyons Collister *m* Stanley Clarke *pd* Keith Brian Burns *ed* Bruce Cannon
☆ Janet Jackson, Tupac Shakur, Regina King, Joe Torry, Tyra Ferrell, Roger Guenveur Smith, Maya Angelou, Billy Zane, Lori Petty
'The film still deals too much in stereotypes to be convincing, and can't get away from the fact that it needs a stronger storyline than this to be properly effective.' – *Derek Malcolm, Guardian*

Poet's Pub
GB 1949 79m bw
GFD/Aquila (Donald B. Wilson)
A rowing blue takes over a Tudor inn and discovers a priceless jewelled gauntlet, the wearer of which is kidnapped during the performance of a pageant.
Very thin, naïve treatment of a whimsical novel. The last film to use the Independent Frame process.
w Diana Morgan *novel* Eric Linklater *d* Frederick Wilson *ph* George Stretton *m* Clifton Parker
☆ Derek Bond, Rona Anderson, Barbara Murray, Leslie Dwyer, Joyce Grenfell

Poil de Carotte ***
France 1932 94m bw
Legrand Majestic/Marcel Vandal-Charles Delac
aka: *The Redhead*
A red-haired boy, neglected by his father and tormented by his mother, attempts suicide.
A moving and unsentimental account of childhood, notable for the performances of Baur and Lynen as father and son.
wd *Julien Duvivier* *story* Jules Renard *ph* Armand Thirard *m* Alexandre Tansman *ed* Marthe Poncin
☆ *Harry Baur, Robert Lynen*, Catherine Fonteney, Louis Gouthier, Simone Aubry, Maxime Fromiot, Colette Segall, Christiane Dor
† The British censors banned the film for a time and in America it was restricted to adult audiences. Duvivier had made a silent version of the story in 1925. There were less successful remakes by Paul Mesnier in 1951 and Henri Graziani in 1973.

Point Blank *
US 1967 92m Metrocolor Panavision
MGM/Judd Bernard, Irwin Winkler

A gangster takes an elaborate revenge on his cheating partner.
Extremely violent gangster thriller, well shot on location and something of a cult, but with irritating pretentiousness and obscure plot points.
w Alexander Jacobs, David Newhouse, Rafe Newhouse *novel* *The Hunter* by Richard Stark *d* John Boorman *ph* *Philip Lathrop* *m* Johnny Mandel
☆ Lee Marvin, Angie Dickinson, Keenan Wynn, Carroll O'Connor, Lloyd Bochner, Michael Strong, John Vernon, Sharon Acker
'The fragmentation was necessary to give the characters and the situation ambiguity, to suggest another meaning beyond the immediate plot.' – *John Boorman*
† *The Outfit* (qv) is a kind of sequel/reprise.

'Every Friendship Has Its Limits. Every Man Has His Breaking Point. Together They Take Adventure Past The Point Of No Return.'
Point Break
US 1991 122m DeLuxe
TCF/Largo/Tapestry (Peter Abrams, Robert L. Levy)

An FBI agent goes undercover among Californian surfers and skydivers to investigate a series of bank robberies.
Ridiculous thriller, with convoluted and unbelievable plot and a great deal of masculine posturing.
w W. Peter Iliff *d* Kathryn Bigelow *ph* Donald Peterman *m* Mark Isham *pd* Peter Jamison *ed* Howard Smith, Scott Conrad, Burt Lovitt
☆ Patrick Swayze, Keanu Reeves, Gary Busey, Lori Petty, John McGinley, James Le Gros, John Philbin, Bojesse Christopher, Julian Reyes
'Acts like a huge, nasty wave, picking up viewers for a few major thrills but ultimately grinding them into the sand via overkill and absurdity.' – *Variety*

'The Government Gave Her A Choice. Death. Or Life As An Assassin. Now, There's No Turning Back.'
Point of No Return
US 1993 108m Technicolor Panavision
Warner (Art Linson)

GB title: *The Assassin*
A drug addict captured by the police during a robbery is given a choice between dying or becoming a government assassin.
A remake of the French movie Nikita *which apes the original in virtually every respect, yet fails to match it in interest; it says much about Hollywood, and American attitudes to subtitles, that such a pointless exercise should ever have been carried out.*
w Robert Getchell, Alexandra Seros *d* John Badham *ph* Michael Watkins *m* Hans Zimmer, Nick Glennie-Smith *pd* Philip Harrison *ed* Frank Morriss
☆ Bridget Fonda, Gabriel Byrne, Dermot Mulroney, Miguel Ferrer, Harvey Keitel, Olivia D'Abo, Richard Romanus, Geoffrey Lewis
'A soulless, efficiently slavish remake.' – *Variety*

'The Film That Shocked America! Denounced As "Obscene" and "Pornographic" by the Moral Majority.'
Poison *
US 1990 85m colour/bw
Mainline/Bronze Eye (Christine Vachon)

Three stories are interwoven: 'Hero', in which a seven-year-old boy kills his father and flies away; 'Homo', in which a jealous prisoner rapes another; 'Horror', in which a doctor creates a serum containing the sex drive, drinks it and becomes a monster.
Cleverly dealing with deviance, sexual and social, and inspired by the work of Jean Genet, it ranges in style from the risible to the repugnant.
wd Todd Haynes *ph* Maryse Alberti *m* James Bennett *pd* Sarah Stollman *ed* James Lyons, Todd Haynes
☆ 'Hero': Edith Meeks, Millie White, Buck Smith, Anne Giotta;, 'Homo': Scott Renderer, James Lyons, John R. Lombardi, Tony Pemberton, Andrew Harpending, Tony Gigante;', 'Horror': Larry Maxwell, Susan Norman, Al Quagliata, Michelle Sullivan
'A provocative look at societal outcasts and twisted behavior that can be read in ways both artistic and political.' – *Variety*
'A whole that is often uneven but, in less than 90 minutes, says more about desire and transgression than most more straightforward

movies on that theme.' – *Derek Malcolm, Guardian*

Poison Ivy
US 1992 89m colour
New Line (Andy Ruben)
A teenage schoolgirl decides she wants the father of her best friend, which means getting rid of his invalid wife.
A heady brew of incest, lesbianism, drunkenness and death which quickly goes flat.
w Katt Shea Ruben, Andy Ruben *d* Katt Shea Ruben *ph* Phedon Papamichael *m* Aaron Davies *pd* Virginia Lee *ed* Gina Mittleman
☆ Drew Barrymore, Sara Gilbert, Tom Skerritt, Cheryl Ladd
'Will make audiences itch to get out of the theater and into the open.' – *Variety*
'The film, distinguished by a complete absence of thrills, is too turgid even to qualify as camp.' – *Stephen Farber, Movieline*

Poison Pen *
GB 1939 79m bw
ABP (Walter C. Mycroft)
A village community is set at odds by a writer of vindictive anonymous letters.
Effective minor drama, with good location atmosphere.
w Doreen Montgomery, William Freshman, N. C. Hunter, Esther McCracken *play* Richard Llewellyn *d* Paul Stein
☆ *Flora Robson*, Reginald Tate, Robert Newton, Ann Todd, Geoffrey Toone, Belle Chrystal, Edward Chapman, Edward Rigby
'Sordid theme makes it doubtful film fare.' – *Variety*
'A lamentably artificial piece.' – *Richard Mallett, Punch*

'One boy can save the world.'
Pokémon 2: The Power of One
Japan 2000 81m DeLuxe
Pikachu Project '99-Shogakukan/4Kids (Norman J. Grossfeld, Choji Yoshikawa, Yukako Matsusako, Takemoto Mori)
A Pokémon collector upsets the balance of nature by his greed.
Another instalment of crude animation and an incomprehensible story; for fans only.
w Takeshi Shudo *d* Kunihiko Yuyama *ph* Hisao Shirai *m* Ralph Schuckett, John Loeffler *ad* Katsuyoshi Kanemura *ed* Jay Film
☆ voices of: Veronica Taylor, Rachael Lillis, Addie Blaustein, Eric Stuart, Ed Paul, Michelle Goguen, Eric Rath, Neil Stewart, Ikue Otani
'This film will astonish and insult you with its staggeringly poor animation.' – *Peter Bradshaw, Guardian*

'This Spring The Unknown Spells Adventure'
Pokémon 3 the Movie: Spell of the Unown (dubbed)
Japan 2001 73m colour
Warner/Pikachu/Shogakukan/4Kids (Norman J. Grossfeld, Choji Yoshikawa, Yukako Matsusako, Takemoto Mori)
A professor's daughter summons up an imaginary monster to replace her father, who has been kidnapped by an abstract entity that has turned his home into crystal.
Trying to follow the convoluted narrative of a Pokemon movie is enough to give any adult a severe headache; unfortunately the only distraction offered to non-believers is substandard animation.
w Takeshi Shudo, Hideki Sonoda *d* Kunihiko Yuyama *ph* Hisao Shirai *m* Ralph Schuckett *ad* Katsuyoshi Kanemura *ed* Jay Film, Toshio Henmi
☆ voices of: Veronica Taylor, Rachael Lillis, Eric Stuart, Ikue Otani, Maddie Blaustein, Amy Birnbaum, Dan Green, Stan Hart
'It's doubtful that the franchise can be sustained much longer as its original fans have left for fresher anime thrills.' – *Robert Koehler, Variety*

Pokémon: The First Movie
Japan/US 1999 75m DeLuxe
Warner/Pikachu Project '98-Shogakukan/4Kids (Norman J. Grossfeld, Choji Yoshikawa, Tomoyuki Igarashi, Takemoto Mori)
A Pokémon trainer is invited to a championship match on an island, and discovers that it is a trap set by Mewto, a rogue Pokémon who plans to rule the world.
A critic-proof movie: the millions of Pokémon collectors will love it; all others will cringe from a poorly animated, incomprehensible, confusing story featuring oddly unpleasant creatures (and that's just the strangely-drawn human participants).
w Takeshi Shudo (English adaptation: Norman J. Grossfeld, Michael Haigney, John Touhey) *characters created by* Satoshi Tajiri *d* Kunihiko Yuyama (English adaptation d Michael Haigney) *ph* Hisao Shirai *m* Ralph Schuckett, John Loeffle *ed* Toshio Henmi,Yutaka Ito
☆ Featuring voices of: Veronica Taylor, Philip Bartlett, Rachael Lillis, Eric Stuart, Addie Blaustein, Ikue Otani
'Humourless, boring, impenetrable and with animation of such staggeringly low quality that it constitutes an insult to cinemagoers of all ages.' – *Peter Bradshaw, Guardian*
† The film took more than $85.5m at the US box office.

Pokjaniye, Monanieba: see *Repentance*

Pokolenie: see *Generation*

Pola X
France/Germany/Japan/Switzerland 1999 134m colour
Pathé/Arena/Pola/Théo/France2/Pandora/EuroSpace/Vega (Bruno Pesery)
A wealthy young novelist gives up his privileged life after he becomes involved with a homeless immigrant who claims to be his father's illegitimate daughter.
A romantic melodrama that risks absurdity and achieves it; it cannot long sustain its level of hysteria about the horrors of modern life.
w Leos Carax, Lauren Sedofsky, Jean-Pol Fargeau *novel* *Pierre, or, the Ambiguities* by Herman Melville *d* Leos Carax *ph* Eric Gautier *m* Scott Walker *ad* Laurent Allaire *ed* Nelly Quettier *cos* Esther Walz
☆ Guillaume Depardieu (Pierre), Katerina Golubeva (Isabelle), Catherine Deneuve (Marie), Delphine Chuillot (Lucie), Petruta Catana (Razerka), Mihaella Silaghi (Little Girl), Laurent Lucas (Thibault), Patachou (Marguerite)
'An often intriguing, sometimes hypnotic work, but one that quickly starts to unravel in the final hour as it becomes clear there's not much beneath the emperor's clothes.' – *Derek Elley, Variety*

Police *
France 1985 113m colour Panavision
Artificial Eye/Gaumont/TF1
A tough and bigoted cop, investigating Tunisian drug-dealers, falls for a suspect.
Well-directed thriller, filmed in documentary style, that was a box-office hit in France, though it offers nothing that has not been seen before.
w Catherine Breillat, Sylvie Danton, Jacques Fieschi, Maurice Pialat *d* Maurice Pialat *ph* Luciano Tovoli *m* Henryk Mikolaj Gorecki *ad* Constantin Mejinksy *ed* Yann Dedet, Helene Viard, Nathalie Letrosne
☆ Gérard Depardieu, Sophie Marceau, Richard Ancanina, Pascale Rocard, Sandrine Bonnaire, Franck Karoul, Jonathan Leina

'Call them what you like. Just don't call them when you're in trouble!'
Police Academy
US 1984 96m Technicolor
Paul Maslansky/Ladd Company/Warner Brothers
The mayor of an American city lifts all restrictions on entry to the police force.
Appallingly unfunny series of snippets about police training, like an American Carry On with few jokes leading to a punch line and occasional resorting to dirty bits.
w Neal Israel, Pat Proft, Hugh Wilson *d* Hugh Wilson
☆ Steve Guttenberg, Kim Cattrall, G. W. Bailey, Bubba Smith, Donovan Scott, George Gaynes
'Hit or miss comic juvenilia ... pure popcorn fantasy fodder.' – *Paul Taylor, MFB*

Police Academy 2: Their First Assignment
US 1985 87m Technicolor
Warner/Ladd (Paul Maslansky)
The new recruits foil attempts from an ambitious lieutenant to take over command.
An unambitious and dull sequel.
w Barry Blaustein, David Sheffield *d* Jerry Paris *ph* James Crabe *m* Robert Folk *pd* Trevor Williams *ed* Bob Wyman
☆ Steve Guttenberg, Bubba Smith, David Graf, Michael Winslow, Art Metrano, Marion Ramsey, George Gaynes

Police Academy 3: Back in Training
US 1986 82m colour
Warner (Paul Maslansky)
Rival police academies vie for survival.
Plodding comedy that recycles a few familiar, unfunny routines.
w Gene Quintano *d* Jerry Paris *ph* Robert Saad *m* Robert Folk *pd* Trevor Williams *ed* Bud Malin
☆ Steve Guttenberg, Bubba Smith, David Graf, Michael Winslow, Marion Ramsey, Leslie Easterbrook, George Gaynes, Bobcat Goldthwait, Art Metrano

Police Academy 4: Citizens on Patrol
US 1987 87m colour
Warner (Paul Maslansky)
A police commandant attempts to involve ordinary people in law enforcement.
A feeble comedy that makes it impossible to understand the apparent popularity of this turgid series.
w Gene Quintano *d* Jim Drake *ph* Robert Saad *m* Robert Folk *pd* Trevor Williams *ed* David Rawlins
☆ Steve Guttenberg, Bubba Smith, David Graf, Michael Winslow, Sharon Stone, Leslie Easterbrook, Bobcat Goldthwait, George Gaynes
'Carries the banner of tasteless humor ... to new heights of insipidness.' – *Variety*

Police Academy 5: Assignment: Miami Beach
US 1988 90m colour
Warner (Paul Maslansky)
Cops on holiday in Miami help foil a gang of jewel thieves.
Witlessness reaches a new low in a comedy devoid of laughs.
w Stephen J. Curwick *d* Alan Myerson *ph* Jim Pergola *m* Robert Folk *pd* Trevor Williams *ed* Hubert de la Bouillerie
☆ Matt McCoy, Janet Jones, George Gaynes, G. W. Bailey, Rene Auberjonois, Bubba Smith, David Graf, Michael Winslow, Leslie Easterbrook

Police Academy 6: City Under Siege
US 1989 84m Technicolor
Warner (Paul Maslansky)
The police squad track down a criminal mastermind responsible for a massive crime wave.
Farcical, broadly acted comedy that does raise an occasional smile.
w Stephen J. Curwick *d* Peter Bonerz *ph* Charles Rosher Jnr *m* Robert Folk *pd* Tho E. Azzari *ed* Hubert de la Bouillerie
☆ Bubba Smith, David Graf, Michael Winslow, Leslie Easterbrook, Marion Ramsey, Lance Kinsey, Matt McCoy, Bruce Mahler, G. W. Bailey, George Gaynes, Kenneth Mars

Police Academy 7: Mission to Moscow
US 1994 83m colour
Warner (Paul Maslansky)
Members of the Police Academy go to Moscow to deal with the Russian mafia's plans to take over the world.
Witless romp that is by far the worst of the series, and they don't come any worse than that.
w Randolph Davis, Michele S. Chodos *d* Alan Metter *ph* Ian Jones *m* Robert Folk *pd* Frederic Weiler *ed* Denise Hill, Suzanne Hines
☆ George Gaynes, Michael Winslow, David Graf, Leslie Easterbrook, G. W. Bailey, Charlie Schlatter, Christopher Lee, Ron Perlman, Claire Forlani
'An inept, geriatric romp that's for completists only.' – *Variety*
† The film flopped at the box-office.

Police Dog
GB 1955 70m bw
Westridge (Harold Huth)
A policeman trains a stray to become a police dog and tracks down the thief who murdered his friend.
Semi-documentary on the theme that our police dogs are wonderful; Christopher Lee makes a brief appearance as a frightened constable.
wd Derek Twist *ph* Cedric Williams *md* Bretton Byrd *ad* Duncan Sutherland *ed* Gordon Pilkington
☆ Joan Rice, Tim Turner, Sandra Dorne, Charles Victor, Nora Gordon, Cecil Brock, John Le Mesurier, James Gilbert, Christopher Lee, Rex III

Police Force: see *Police Story (1985)*

Police Story (dubbed) *
Hong Kong 1985 85m colour
Golden Harvest/Paragon (Leonard Ho)
original title: *Jingcha Gushi*
US title: *Police Force*
A cop is given the task of guarding a witness who is the girlfriend of a drug-dealing gangster.
Standard cops and robbers martial arts mayhem, enlivened by some spectacular stunts and chases.
w Edward Tang *d* Jackie Chan *ph* Cheung Yiu Joe *m* Kevin Bassingson *ad* Oliver Wong *ed* Peter Cheung
☆ Jackie Chan, Brigitte Lin, Maggie Cheung, Cho Yuen, Bill Tung, Kenneth Tong
† The film was cut by 15 minutes for its release on video cassette.

Police Story II (dubbed)
Hong Kong 1988 92m colour
Golden Harvest/Paragon (Leonard Ho)
Demoted to traffic cop, a former detective is re-instated to combat a gang extorting money from big business.
The mixture as before: elaborately choreographed fights and broad comedy, but lacking the set-pieces of the first film.
w Jackie Chan, Edward Tang *d* Jackie Chan *ph* Cheung Yiu Joe, Lee Yau Tong *m* Michael Lai *pd* Oliver Wong *ed* Peter Cheung
☆ Jackie Chan, Maggie Cheung, Bill Tung, Lam Kwok Hung, Charles Chao, Cho Yuen

Police Story III: Supercop
Hong Kong 1992 93m colour
Golden Way (Willie Chan, Tang King-Sung)
An undercover Hong Kong cop infiltrates a gang of drug smugglers with the aid of the Chinese police and a glamorous inspector.
Some spectacular stunts add interest to a familiar story, which is given an extra topical twist with its references to the takeover of Hong Kong by mainland China.
w Tang King-Sung, Ma Mei-Ping, Lee Wei-Yee *d* Stanley Tong *ph* Lam Kwok-Wah *m* Lee Chung Sing *ad* Oliver Wong *ed* Cheung Yaeo-Chung, Cheung Kai Fei
☆ Jackie Chan, Michelle Yeaoh, Maggie Cheung, Tsang Kong, Yuen Wah, Lo Lieh
'An okay adventure.' – *Variety*

The Polish Bride **
Netherlands 1998 90m
Artificial Eye/Motel/IJswater/VPRO (Marc Bary, Ilana Netiv, Jeroen Beker, Frans van Gestel)
original title: *De Poolse Bruid*
A farmer shelters a fugitive Polish woman, on the run from her brutal employers.
A spare film, of affection developing between two isolated people amid a flat landscape. The dialogue is minimal, but much is conveyed by simple gestures; it yields quiet pleasures.
w Kees van de Hulst *d* Karim Traidia *ph* Jacques Laureys *m* Fons Merkies *ad* Anne Winterink *ed* Chris Teerink

☆ Jaap Spijkers (Henk Woldring), Monic Hendricks (Anna), Rudi Falkenhagen (Father), Roef Ragas (Son), Hakim Traidia (Postman), Soraya Traidia (Krystyna)

'The surprise is how tightly all-of-a-piece it is, and, from the first to the last shot, how totally absorbing.' – *Alexander Walker, London Evening Standard*

Polish Wedding

US 1998 107m DeLuxe

Fox Searchlight/Lakeshore (Tom Rosenberg, Julia Chasman, Geoff Stier)

Tensions erupt in a large working-class Polish family in Detroit when the only daughter becomes pregnant.

Boisterous comic drama, full of a forced vitality and soap opera situations; its cast tries hard to elevate it above triteness.

wd Theresa Connelly *ph* Guy Dufaux *m* Luis Bacalov *pd* Kara Lindstrom *ed* Curtiss Clayton, Suzanne Fenn

☆ Lena Olin, Gabriel Byrne, Claire Danes, Adam Trese, Mili Avital, Daniel Lapaine, Steven Petrarca, Jeffrey Nordling, Ramsey Krull, Rade Serbedzija

'A movie of gratifying small moments, some of which are hilariously funny and charged with healthy eroticism.' – *Emanuel Levy, Variety*

The Politic Flapper: see *The Patsy*

Politics

US 1931 71m bw

MGM

Two small-town women get into politics to fight racketeers.

Scrappy star comedy which probably seemed funnier at the time.

w Robert E. Hopkins, Wells Root, Zelda Sears, Malcolm Stuart Boylan *d* Charles F. Reisner

☆ Marie Dressler, Polly Moran, Roscoe Ates, Karen Morley, William Bakewell, John Miljan

'Loaded with technical faults, but it has too many laugh moments to fail to sock the b.o.' – *Variety*

Pollock **

US 2000 122m colour

Columbia TriStar/Brant-Allen/Zeke Films/Ed Harris, Fred Berner Films

Biopic of artist Jackson Pollock from his early struggles, his success as an action painter, and untimely death.

Pollock's life, as a man who embraced painting, women and drink wuth great passion, suits this formulaic movie approach to the artist as tormented genius; an abrasive script and committed performances lift it above the ordinary.

w Barbara Turner, Susan J. Emshwiller *book* Jackson Pollock: *An American Saga* by Steven Naifeh, Gregory White Smith *d* Ed Harris *ph* Lisa Rinzler *m* Jeff Beal *pd* Mark Friedberg *ed* Kathryn Himoff

☆ Ed Harris (Jackson Pollock), Marcia Gay Harden (Lee Krasner), Amy Madigan (Peggy Guggenheim), Jennifer Connelly (Ruth Kligman), Jeffrey Tambor (Clement Greenberg), Bud Cort (Howard Putzel), John Heard (Tony Smith), Val Kilmer (William DeKooning)

'Admirable. It reminds us that great art isn't about creating beauty out of misty-eyed Hallmark moments but about discovering and communicating messy truths that spill all over the place, just like the lives of the artists driven to uncover them.' – *Stephen Holden, New York Times*

Marcia Gay Harden

Ed Harris

Polly Fulton: see *BF's Daughter*

Polly of the Circus

US 1932 72m bw

MGM (Paul Bern)

A trapeze artiste falls for the local minister, but incurs disapproval from his bishop.

Elementary romance reminiscent of silent drama.

w Carey Wilson *play* Margaret Mayo *d* Alfred Santell *ph* George Barnes *m* William Axt

☆ Marion Davies, Clark Gable, C. Aubrey Smith, Raymond Hatton, David Landau, Maude Eburne, Guinn Williams, Ray Milland

'Frail entertainment with both leads miscast.' – *Variety*

Pollyanna *

US 1960 134m Technicolor

Walt Disney (George Golitzen)

A 12-year-old orphan girl cheers up the grumps of the small town where she comes to live.

Well cast but overlong and rather humourless remake of a children's classic from an earlier age.

wd David Swift *novel* Eleanor Porter *ph* Russell Harlan *m* Paul Smith *ad* Carroll Clark, Robert Clatworthy

☆ Hayley Mills, Jane Wyman, Karl Malden, Nancy Olson, Adolphe Menjou, Donald Crisp, Agnes Moorehead, Richard Egan, Kevin Corcoran, James Drury, Reta Shaw, Leora Dana

'Even Hayley Mills can neither prevent one from sympathizing with the crusty aunts, hermits, vicars and hypochondriacs who get so forcibly cheered up, nor from feverishly speculating whether films like this don't run the risk of inciting normally kind and gentle people into certain excesses of violent crime – child murder, for instance.' – *MFB*

special award to Hayley Mills for 'the most outstanding juvenile performance'

'It knows what scares you!'

Poltergeist **

US 1982 114m Metrocolor Panavision

MGM/SLM (Steven Spielberg)

Suburban life is disrupted when through her TV set a young girl releases unpleasant forces from the cemetery over which the modern estate was built.

Skilful but dramatically thin and sometimes rather nasty horror movie in which the producer's hand seems often to have controlled the director's. Misjudgment must be the reason that it was not the huge success intended.

w Steven Spielberg, Michael Grais, Mark Victor *d* Tobe Hooper *ph* Matthew F. Leonetti *m* Jerry Goldsmith *ed* Michael Kahn

☆ JoBeth Williams, Craig T. Nelson, Beatrice Straight, Dominique Dunne, Oliver Robbins

music, visual effects (Richard Edlund, Michael Wood, Bruce Nicholson)

Poltergeist II

US 1986 90m Metrocolor Panavision

MGM-UA/Freddie Fields/Victor-Grais

The family from *Poltergeist* is in for more trouble when Grandma dies and they begin receiving phone messages from the other side.

More pointless spine-shivering: good technical effects but no message of any kind, not even entertainment.

w Mark Victor, Michael Grais *d* Brian Gibson *ph* Andrew Laszlo *pd* Ted Haworth

☆ JoBeth Williams, Craig T. Nelson, Heather O'Rourke, Oliver Robins, Julian Beck

'He's found her.'

Poltergeist III

US 1988 98m Astrocolor

UIP/MGM-UA (Barry Bernardi)

A young child living in Chicago is haunted by an evil ghost who takes her and others into another dimension.

Lacklustre sequel, with only the occasional effective shock to recommend it.

w Gary Shearman, Brian Taggert *d* Gary Shearman *ph* Alex Nepomniaschy *m* Joe Renzetti *pd* Paul Eads *ed* Ross Albert

☆ Tom Skerritt, Nancy Allen, Heather O'Rourke, Zelda Rubinstein, Lara Flynn Boyle, Kip Wentz, Richard Fire

Polyester

US 1981 86m colour Odorama

New Line (John Waters)

A Baltimore housewife with a dysfunctional family finds true love elsewhere.

Camp comedy, where the fun, such as it is, lies in the exaggerated performances.

wd John Waters *ph* David Insley *m* Chris Stein, Michael Kamen *ad* Vincent Paranio *ed* Charles Roggero

☆ Divine, Tab Hunter, Edith Massey, Mink Stole, David Samson, Joni Ruth White, May Garlington, Stiv Bators, Ken King, Hans Kramm

Ponette *

France 1996 97m colour

Les Films Alain Sarde/Rhône-Alpes Cinéma

A four-year-old girl tries to come to terms with the death of her mother in a car crash.

An unsettling film, partly because of doubts over the methods used to extract such an astonishing, emotional, tearful performance from its young protagonist, but also because of the harshness it exhibits – all the adults behave inappropriately – and its final lurch into banal fantasy.

wd Jacques Doillon *ph* Caroline Champetier *m* Philippe Sarde *ad* Henri Berthon *ed* Jacqueline Lecompte

☆ *Victoire Thivisol*, Marie Trintignant, Claire Nebout, Xavier Beauvois, Matiaz Bureau Caton, Delphine Schiltz, Léopoldine Serre, Luckie Royer, Carla Ibled, Antoine du Merle

'A magical, poetic and, at times, surreal psychological study of a child's emotional landscape.' – *Helen Van Kruyssen, Film Review*

† Victoire Thivisol won the best actress award at the Venice Film Festival in 1996.

Pontiac Moon

US 1994 107m DeLuxe

Paramount (Robert Schaffel, Youssef Vahabzadeh)

In 1969, a teacher, worried about his agoraphobic wife's effect on his young son, decides to drive him on a 1,776-mile journey, which will bring his Pontiac car's mileage up to 238,857 miles, the distance to the moon, and so celebrate the Apollo landing and moonwalk.

Flimsy road movie that settles for easy sentimentality.

w Finn Taylor, Jeffrey Brown *d* Peter Medak *ph* Thomas Kloss *m* Randy Edelman *pd* Jeffrey Beecroft *ed* Anne V. Coates

☆ Ted Danson, Mary Steenburgen, Ryan Todd, Eric Schweig, Cathy Moriarty, Max Gail, Lisa Jane Persky

'Inane whimsy.' – *Sight and Sound*

Pontius Pilate

Italy/France 1961 100m Technicolor

Glomer Film/Lux (Enzo Merolle)

original title: *Ponzio Pilato*

Pontius Pilate runs into political and personal problems while trying to govern Israel.

Pilate's love-life is given prominence over Jesus's trial and crucifixion, although both receive standard Italian sword-and-sandals treatment to reduce them to banality. Barrymore doubles as Judas and Jesus (who is seen only from the back).

w Gino de Santis, Ivo Perilli, Oreste Biancoli, Gian Paolo Callegari, Guglielmo Santangelo, Josette France, Guy Elmes *d* Irving Rapper *ph* Massimo Dallamano *m* A. Francesco Lavagnino

☆ Jean Marais, Jeanne Crain, Basil Rathbone, Letitia Roman, John Drew Barrymore, Massimo Serato

Pony Express *

US 1953 101m Technicolor

Paramount (Nat Holt)

In 1860 Buffalo Bill Cody and Wild Bill Hickok are sent to establish pony express stations across California.

Standard Western which tells a factual tale adequately if rather slowly.

w Charles Marquis Warren *d* Jerry Hopper *ph* Ray Rennahan *m* Paul Sawtell

☆ Charlton Heston, Forrest Tucker, Rhonda Fleming, Jan Sterling

Pony Soldier

US 1952 82m Technicolor

TCF (Samuel G. Engel)

GB title: *MacDonald of the Canadian Mounties*

The Mounties settle the hash of Canadian Indian renegades who have been causing trouble on the American border.

Mediocre outdoor adventure.

w John C. Higgins *d* Joseph M. Newman *ph* Harry Jackson *m* Alex North

☆ Tyrone Power, Cameron Mitchell, Robert Horton, Thomas Gomez, Penny Edwards, *Adeline de Walt Reynolds*

Ponzio Pilato: see *Pontius Pilate*

Pookie: see *The Sterile Cuckoo*

Pool of London

GB 1950 85m bw

Ealing (Michael Relph)

A smuggling sailor gets involved in murder.

Routine semi-documentary police thriller with locations in London docks decorating a standard piece of thick ear.

w Jack Whittingham, John Eldridge *d* Basil Dearden *ph* Gordon Dines *m* John Addison

☆ Bonar Colleano, Susan Shaw, Earl Cameron, Renée Asherson, Moira Lister, Max Adrian, James Robertson Justice, Joan Dowling

'Done with such imagination, humour and visual attractiveness as to hold the pleased attention of all who like to use their eyes and their ears.' – *Richard Mallett, Punch*

De Poolse Bruid: see *The Polish Bride*

'A love story about a girl, the man she is living for, and the man she is living with.'

Poor Cow *

GB 1967 101m Eastmancolor

Anglo Amalgamated/Vic/Fenchurch (Joe Janni)

The dismal life of a young London mother who lives in squalor with her criminal husband.

Television-style fictional documentary determined to rub one's nose in the mire. Innovative and occasionally striking but not very likeable.

w Nell Dunn, Ken Loach *novel* Nell Dunn *d* Ken Loach *ph* Brian Probyn *m* Donovan

☆ *Carol White*, Terence Stamp, John Bindon, Kate Williams, Queenie Watts

'A superficial, slightly patronizing excursion into the nether realms of social realism.' – *Jan Dawson*

Poor Little Rich Girl *

US 1936 79m bw

TCF (Darryl F. Zanuck)

A child is separated from her father and joins a radio singing act.

Pleasing star vehicle with all the expected elements, adapted from a Mary Pickford vehicle of 1917.

w Sam Hellman, Gladys Lehman, Harry Tugend *d* Irving Cummings *ph* John Seitz *songs* Mack Gordon, Harry Revel

☆ *Shirley Temple*, Jack Haley, Alice Faye, Gloria Stuart, Michael Whalen, Sara Haden, Jane Darwell, Claude Gillingwater, Henry Armetta

'Too cool for words.'

Pootie Tang

US 2001 81m DeLuxe

Paramount/MTV/Alphaville/3 Arts (Chris Rock, David Gale, Ali LeRoi, Cotty Chubb)

Adventures of a street-wise superhero who talks in a black vernacular no one can understand.

Based on a TV sketch, this is humour that doesn't travel far, particularly in such a ramshackle vehicle as this.

wd Louis C. K. *ph* Willy Kurant *m* QD3, Prince Paul *pd* Amy Silver *ed* Doug Abel, David Lewis Smith

☆ Lance Crouther (Pootie Tang), Jennifer Coolidge (Ireenie), Wanda Sykes (Biggie Shorty), Robert Vaughn (Dick Lecter), Chris Rock (J. B.), Dave Attell (Frank), Reg E. Cathey (Dirty Dee), J. B. Smoove (Trucky)

'You watch in puzzlement: How did this train wreck happen? How was this movie assembled out of such ill-fitting pieces? Who thought it was funny? Who thought it was finished? For that matter, was it finished?' – *Roger Ebert, Chicago Sun-Times*

'Has the distinction of being one of the most amateurish features ever released by a major studio.' – *Todd McCarthy, Variety*

Pop Always Pays
US 1940 65m bw
RKO/Bert Gilroy
Pop promises to match his future son-in-law's savings, but runs into a business slump.
Minor comedy which accelerates into frantic farce, but the star was always funnier at two-reel length.
w Charles E. Roberts *d* Leslie Goodwins *ph* Jack MacKenzie *md* Paul Sawtell
☆ Leon Errol, Dennis O'Keefe, Adele Pearce, Walter Catlett, Marjorie Gateson, Tom Kennedy

Pope Joan
GB 1972 132m Eastmancolor Panavision
Big City Productions/Kurt Unger
aka: *The Devil's Impostor*
The legend of a ninth-century German semi-prostitute who discovered a vocation to preach and was made Pope.
Uninspiring pageant, brutish and rather silly, full of would-be medieval sensationalism.
w John Briley *d* Michael Anderson *ph* Billy Williams *m* Maurice Jarre *pd* Elliott Scott
☆ Liv Ullmann, Trevor Howard, Olivia de Havilland, Maximilian Schell, Keir Dullea, Robert Beatty, Franco Nero, Patrick Magee

'In the tradition of the great religious epics, *Ben Hur, The Greatest Story Ever Told* and *91/2 Weeks*, comes a film that breaks all Ten Commandments and a few laws of nature.'

The Pope Must Die
GB 1991 99m colour
Palace/Michael White/Miramax/British Film/Film Four (Stephen Woolley)
US title: *The Pope Must Diet*
Through an error, a former car mechanic, rock singer and inept priest becomes Pope and tries to clean up a Vatican infiltrated by the Mafia.
Farcical and misfiring comedy, a poor attempt at a parody of gangster films.
w Peter Richardson, Pete Richens *d* Peter Richardson *ph* Frank Gell *m* Anne Dudley, Jeff Beck *pd* John Ebden *ed* Katharine Wenning
☆ Robbie Coltrane, Beverly D'Angelo, Herbert Lom, Alex Rocco, Paul Bartel, Balthazar Getty, William Hootkins, Robert Stephens, Annette Crosbie, Steve O'Donnell, John Sessions

The Pope of Greenwich Village
US 1984 120m Metrocolor
MGM-UA/Koch-Kirkwood (Benjy Rosenberg)
In New York, Charlie and his cousin Paulie become thieves and fall foul of the Mafia.
Back again to the mean streets of the east side, but with nothing at all new to add to the scores of indistinguishable real-life melodramas of this kind.
w Vincent Patrick *novel* Vincent Patrick *d* Stuart Rosenberg *ph* John Bailey *m* Dave Grusin *pd* Paul Sylbert
☆ Eric Roberts, Mickey Rourke, Daryl Hannah, Geraldine Page, Kenneth McMillan, Tony Musante, M. Emmet Walsh, Burt Young
Geraldine Page (supporting actress)

Popeye
US 1980 114m colour
Paramount/Disney (Robert Evans)
Popeye returns to Sweethaven in search of the father who abandoned him.
Lamentable attempt by an ill-chosen director to humanize and sentimentalize a celebrated cartoon character who doesn't get into the expected physical action until the film is nearly over.
w Jules Feiffer, from characters created by E. C. Segar *d* Robert Altman *ph* Giuseppe Rotunno *m/ly* Harry Nilsson *pd* Wolf Kroeger
☆ Robin Williams, Shelley Duvall, Ray Walston, Paul Dooley
'The picture doesn't come together, and much of it is cluttered, squawky, and eerily unfunny.' – *Pauline Kael, New Yorker*

Popi *
US 1969 113m DeLuxe
UA/Leonard Films (Herbert B. Leonard)
Adventures of a cheerful inhabitant of New York's Puerto Rican ghetto.
Ethnic comedy-drama of the kind that has since found its way in abundance into American TV series. Very competently done for those who like it, e.g. Puerto Ricans.
w Tina and Lester Pine *d* Arthur Hiller *ph* Ross Lowell *m* Dominic Frontière
☆ Alan Arkin, Rita Moreno, Miguel Alejandro, Ruben Figuero
'An appropriately disenchanted view of an immigrant's struggling ambitions in the Promised Land.' – *Richard Combs*

Popiol y Diament: see *Ashes and Diamonds*

Poppy *
US 1936 74m bw
Paramount (Paul Jones)
An itinerant medicine-seller sets up his stall in a small town where his daughter falls in love with the mayor's son.
Clumsily but heavily plotted vehicle for W. C. Fields, who as usual has great moments but seems to rob the show of its proper pace.
w Waldemar Young, Virginia Van Upp *play* Dorothy Donnelly *d* A. Edward Sutherland *ph* William Mellor *m* Frederick Hollander
☆ *W. C. Fields*, Rochelle Hudson, Richard Cromwell, Granville Bates, Catherine Doucet, Lynne Overman, Maude Eburne
'Antique hokum trussed up for a Fields vehicle.' – *Literary Digest*
'To watch Mr Fields, as Dickensian as anything Dickens ever wrote, is a form of escape for poor human creatures: we who are haunted by pity, by fear, by our sense of right and wrong, who are tongue-tied by conscience, watch with envious love this free spirit robbing the gardener of ten dollars, cheating the country yokels by his own variant of the three-card trick, faking a marriage certificate, and keeping up all the time, in the least worthy and the most embarrassing circumstances, his amazing flow of inflated sentiments.' – *Graham Greene, The Spectator*

Porgy and Bess *
US 1959 138m Technicolor Todd-AO
Columbia/Samuel Goldwyn
A slum girl falls in love with a crippled beggar.
Negro opera about the inhabitants of Catfish Row; full of interest for music lovers, but not lending itself very readily to screen treatment.
w N. Richard Nash *play* Porgy by DuBose and Dorothy Heyward *libretto* DuBose Heyward *d* Otto Preminger *ph* Leon Shamroy *m* George Gershwin *md* André Previn, Ken Darby *ch* Hermes Pan *ly* DuBose Heyward, Ira Gershwin
☆ Sidney Poitier, Dorothy Dandridge, Sammy Davis Jnr, Pearl Bailey, Brock Peters, Diahann Carroll, Clarence Muse
† Diahann Carroll's vocals were dubbed by Loulie Jean Norman, Dorothy Dandridge's by Adele Addison, and Sidney Poitier's by Robert McFerrin.
André Previn, Ken Darby
Leon Shamroy

'Bold! blunt! blustering! the battle picture without equal!'

Pork Chop Hill *
US 1959 97m bw
United Artists/Melville/Lewis Milestone
The Americans in Korea take a vital hill but the colonel in command finds it difficult to hold.
Ironic war film with vivid spectacle separated by much talk.
w James R. Webb *d Lewis Milestone ph Sam Leavitt* *m* Leonard Rosenman *pd* Nicolai Remisoff
☆ Gregory Peck, Harry Guardino, George Shibata, Woody Strode, James Edwards, Rip Torn, George Peppard, Barry Atwater, Robert Blake

Porky's
Canada 1982 98m colour
Melvin Simon/Astral Bellevue Pathé/Porky's Productions/ (Don Carmody, Bob Clark)
In Florida in the early fifties, high school boys try to get into a local brothel.
Ghastly teenage goings-on taking cinema bad taste just about as far as it will get.
wd Bob Clark *ph* Reginald H. Morris *m* Carl Zittrer, Paul Zaza *pd* Reuben Freed
☆ Dan Monahan, Mark Herrier, Wyatt Knight, Roger Wilson, Kim Cattrall, Art Hindle, Wayne Maunder, Alex Karras, Nancy Parsons
'It is difficult to say which is the more depressing: the technical expertise with which this mind-numbing tripe has been put together, or its great success at the US box office.' – *Jo Imeson, MFB*
'One of those movies that makes you weep for the state of the contemporary commercial cinema – and, even more, for the gullibility of the public that pays to see it.' – *Margaret Hinxman, Daily Mail*
† *Porky's 2* followed in 1983 and was even worse. 1985 brought *Porky's Revenge*, about which there is nothing to be said.

Le Pornographe
France/Canada 2001 111m colour
Metro Tartan/Haut & Court/In Extremis (Carole Scotta)
aka: *The Pornographer*
A retired pornographic film maker returns to work in order to sort out his life.
Gloomy, pretentious, solemn and extremely boring, this is the sort of production that gives arthouse films a bad name.
wd Bertrand Bonello *ph* Josée Deshaies *m* Laurie Markovitch *ad* Romain Denis *ed* Fabrice Rouaud *cos* Romane Bohringer
☆ Jean-Pierre Léaud (Jacques), Jérémie Renier (Joseph), Dominique Blanc (Jeanne), Thibault De Montalembert (Richard), André Marcon (Louis), Catherine Mouchet (Olivia Riochet)
'A laboured affair, lacking humour and insight.' – *Philip French, Observer*
† The BBFC cut some 11 seconds from the British release.

The Pornographer: see *Le Pornographe*

The Pornographer
US 1999 86m colour
Integrity (Doug Atchison)
A 25 year-old sex-obsessed legal executive who is a failure with women decides to make his own pornographic movies.
Risibly simple-minded cautionary tale that is unconvincing on every level.
wd Doug Atchison *ph* Christopher Mosio *m* Warner David Jansen *pd* Dan Haberkorn
☆ Michael DeGood (Paul Ryan), Craig Wasson (Spano), Monique Parent (Charise), Katheryn Cain (Kate), Todd Feder (Randy), Marjorie Harris (Teresa), Kelly Stone (Natalie), George Hertzberg (Tom)
'Extremely naive... a film that has little new to say.' – *Emanuel Levy, Variety*

Porridge *
GB 1979 93m Eastmancolor
Black Lion/Witzend
US title: *Doing Time*
Two convicts at Slade Prison become unwilling participants in a break-out.
Genial expansion of a successful TV series to the big screen; alas, as usual the material is stretched to snapping point, and the welcome irony of the original becomes sentimentality. Still, the film is a valuable record of memorable characters.
w Dick Clement, Ian La Frenais *d* Dick Clement *ph* Bob Huke *md* Terry Oates
☆ *Ronnie Barker, Richard Beckinsale, Fulton Mackay, Brian Wilde, Peter Vaughan,* Geoffrey Bayldon, Julian Holloway

Port Afrique
GB 1956 92m Technicolor
David E. Rose/Columbia
In Morocco, an American pilot solves the shooting of his wife.
Tropical variation on The Maltese Falcon *and* The Blue Dahlia*; not much cop on its own account.*
w Frank Partos, John Cresswell *novel* Bernard Victor Dyer *d* Rudolph Maté *ph* Wilkie Cooper *m* Malcolm Arnold
☆ Phil Carey, Pier Angeli, Dennis Price, Eugene Deckers, James Hayter, Rachel Gurney, Anthony Newley

Port of Call *
Sweden 1948 99m bw
Svensk Filmindustri
original title: *Hamnstad*
A sailor who quits the sea begins an affair with a lonely and unhappy girl recently released from reform school.
A tough and perceptive drama of class, conventions and relationships, particularly a destructive one between mother and daughter, shot in a documentary style against a background of docks.
wd Ingmar Bergman *story* Olle Länsberg *ph* Gunnar Fischer *m* Erland von Koch *ad* Nils Svenwall *ed* Oscar Rosander
☆ Nine Christine Jönsson, Bengt Eklund, Berta Hall, Mimi Nelson, Birgitta Valberg, Sif Ruud, Else Merete Heiberg

Port of New York *
US 1949 82m bw
Eagle Lion (Aubrey Schenck)
A woman narcotics smuggler determines to betray her colleagues to the authorities.
Good routine semi-documentary thick ear, notable for an early appearance by Yul Brynner as villain-in-chief.
w Eugene Ling *d* Laslo Benedek *ph* George E. Diskant *m* Sol Kaplan
☆ Scott Brady, Richard Rober, K. T. Stevens, Yul Brynner

Port of Seven Seas *
US 1938 81m bw
MGM (Henry Henigson)
Love on the Marseilles waterfront.
Stagey Hollywoodization of Pagnol's Marius trilogy: some vigour shows through.
w Preston Sturges *d* James Whale *ph* Karl Freund *m* Franz Waxman
☆ Wallace Beery, Frank Morgan, Maureen O'Sullivan, John Beal, Jessie Ralph, Cora Witherspoon
'Genuine and touching drama ... strong solo biller.' – *Variety*

Port of Shadows: see *Quai des Brumes*

Porte des Lilas *
France/Italy 1957 95m bw
Filmsonor/Rizzoli (Jacques Plante)
aka: *Gate of Lilacs*
A gangster on the run shelters in a poor quarter of Paris, but his treachery is his undoing.
Atmospheric comedy-drama put across with the expected style but providing very little to smile at.
w René Clair, Jean Aurel *novel La Grande Ceinture* by René Fallet *d* René Clair *ph* Robert Le Fèbvre *m* Georges Brassens
☆ Pierre Brasseur, Georges Brassens, Henri Vidal, Dany Carrel, Raymond Bussières, Amedée, Alain Bouvette

Les Portes de la Nuit *
France 1946 106m bw
Pathé Cinema
aka: *Gates of Night*
Various people in post-war Paris are drawn into a pattern woven by Destiny – who appears as a melancholy tramp.
A polished piece of post-war gloom, and the archetype of all films noirs of the period. The beginning, also, of its director's decline.
w Jacques Prévert *d Marcel Carné ph* Philippe Agostini *m* Joseph Kosma *ad* Alexander Trauner
☆ Pierre Brasseur, Yves Montand, Nathalie Nattier, Serge Reggiani, Jean Vilar, Saturnin Fabre, Mady Berry, Dany Robin
† One of the few films to have been based on a ballet – *Le Rendezvous* by Prévert. Oddly enough its realistic scenes of daily life are among its most successful elements.

Les Portes Tournantes: see *The Revolving Doors*

'From the pages of Faith Baldwin's greatest story comes this tense, moving drama of a woman who faced the world, alone, for love...'

Portia on Trial *
US 1937 83m bw
Republic
GB title: *The Trial of Portia Merriman*
A lady lawyer uses her skills in the courtroom to right the personal wrongs done to her years before.
Efficient tearjerker, Madame X *style, and one of the comparatively big productions Republic occasionally tried.*
w Sam Ornitz, E. E. Paramore Jnr *novel* Faith Baldwin *d* George Nicholls Jnr *m* Alberto Colombo
☆ Frieda Inescort, Walter Abel, Neil Hamilton, Heather Angel, Ruth Donnelly, Barbara Pepper, Clarence Kolb
'A distinguished production: exploitation required to overcome title and no-name handicap.' – *Variety*
Alberto Colombo

Portnoy's Complaint
US 1972 101m Technicolor Panavision
Warner/Chehnault (Ernest Lehman)
A young New York Jewish boy has mother and masturbation problems.
Foolhardy attempt to film a fashionably sensational literary exercise; one of Hollywood's last attempts – thank goodness – to be 'with it'.
wd Ernest Lehman *novel* Philip Roth *ph* Philip Lathrop *m* Michel Legrand
☆ Richard Benjamin, Karen Black, Lee Grant, Jack Somack, Jill Clayburgh, Jeannie Berlin
'The spectator is forced into the doubly uncomfortable position of a voyeur who can't actually see anything.' – *Jan Dawson*

Portrait from Life
GB 1948 90m bw
GFD/Gainsborough (Antony Darnborough)
US title: *The Girl in the Painting*
In an art gallery, a German professor recognizes a portrait as that of his daughter, lost during the war in Germany, and after a search discovers her to have been an amnesiac under the protection of a leading Nazi.
Tolerable melodrama with similarities to The Seventh Veil *(the girl has to choose between four men).*
w Frank Harvey Jnr, Muriel and Sydney Box *d* Terence Fisher *ph* Jack Asher *m* Benjamin Frankel
☆ Mai Zetterling, Robert Beatty, Guy Rolfe, Herbert Lom, Patrick Holt

Portrait in Black *
US 1960 113m Eastmancolor
U-I/Ross Hunter
An elderly shipping tycoon is murdered by his wife and doctor, but they are blackmailed.
Absurd old-fashioned melodrama of dark doings among the idle rich. Quite entertaining for addicts.
w Ivan Goff, Ben Roberts *d* Michael Gordon *ph* Russell Metty *m* Frank Skinner *ad* Richard H. Riedel *ed* Milton Carruth
☆ Lana Turner, Anthony Quinn, Richard Basehart, Anna May Wong, Lloyd Nolan, Sandra Dee, John Saxon, Ray Walston, Virginia Grey
'Connoisseurs of the higher tosh should find it irresistible.' – *Penelope Houston*

Portrait in Smoke: see *Wicked as They Come*

Portrait of a Hitman: see *Jim Buck*

The Portrait of a Lady *
GB/US 1996 144m Technicolor Panavision
Polygram/Propaganda (Monty Montgomery, Steve Golin)
In Europe in the 1870s, an American heiress makes an unhappy marriage.
Cool and uninvolving version of a classic novel which never quite gets to grips with its drama of a woman who unexpectedly loses her independence to a domineering husband, not helped by the miscasting of its central roles.
w Laura Jones *novel* Henry James *d* Jane Campion *ph* Stuart Dryburgh *m* Wojciech Kilar *pd* Janet Patterson *ed* Veronika Jenet
☆ Nicole Kidman, John Malkovich, Martin Donovan, Barbara Hershey, Mary-Louise Parker, Shelley Winters, Richard E. Grant, Shelley Duvall, Viggo Mortensen, Christian Bale, John Gielgud
'Like a Merchant Ivory movie where there's nothing you'd want to buy; it's one of those movies where I want Pauly Shore to suddenly run on-screen and start rubbing himself against someone.' – *Libby Gelman-Waxner, Premiere*
Barbara Hershey; Jane Patterson (costumes)

Portrait of a Mobster
US 1961 108m bw
Warner
The career of twenties gangster Dutch Schultz.
Over-familiar, warmed over racketeering stuff with no particular edge or style.
w Howard Browne *d* Joseph Pevney *ph* Eugene Polito *m* Max Steiner
☆ Vic Morrow, Leslie Parrish, Peter Breck, Ray Danton (Legs Diamond), Norman Alden, Ken Lynch
† Danton also played the title role in *The Rise and Fall of Legs Diamond (qv).*

Portrait of a Sinner: see *The Rough and the Smooth*

Portrait of Alison *
GB 1955 84m bw
Anglo-Amalgamated/Insignia (Frank Godwin)
aka: *Postmark for Danger*
A journalist dies while investigating an international smuggling ring, and his brother takes up the case.
Solidly carpentered mystery with all the twists expected from this source.
w Guy Green, Ken Hughes *radio serial* Francis Durbridge *d* Guy Green *ph* Wilkie Cooper *m* John Veale
☆ Robert Beatty, Terry Moore, William Sylvester, Josephine Griffin, Geoffrey Keen, Allan Cuthbertson, Henry Oscar

Portrait of Clare
GB 1950 98m bw
ABPC (Leslie Landau)
In 1900, a woman looks back on her three marriages.
High school novelette for easily pleased female audiences.
w Leslie Landau, Adrian Arlington *novel* Francis Brett Young *d* Lance Comfort *ph* Günther Krampf *ad* Don Ashton
☆ Margaret Johnston, Richard Todd, Robin Bailey, Ronald Howard, Mary Clare, Marjorie Fielding, Anthony Nicholls, Lloyd Pearson

Portrait of Jennie ***
US 1948 86m bw (tinted sequence)
David O. Selznick
GB title: *Jennie*
A penniless artist meets a strange girl who seems to age each time he sees her; they fall in love and he discovers that she has long been dead, though she finally comes to life once more during a sea storm like the one in which she perished.
A splendid example of the higher Hollywood lunacy: a silly story with pretensions about life and death and time and art, presented with superb persuasiveness by a first-class team of actors and technicians.
w Peter Berneis, Paul Osborn, Leonard Bernovici *novel* Robert Nathan *d William Dieterle ph Joseph August m Dimitri Tiomkin, after Debussy ad* J. McMillan Johnson *ed* William Morgan, Gerald Wilson
☆ *Jennifer Jones, Joseph Cotten, Ethel Barrymore,* David Wayne, Lillian Gish, Henry Hull, Florence Bates
PROLOGUE: 'Since time began man has looked into the awesome reaches of infinity and asked the eternal questions: What is time? What is life? What is space? What is death? Through a hundred civilizations, philosophers and scientists have come together with answers, but the bewilderment remains ... Science tells us that nothing ever dies but only changes, that time itself does not pass but curves around us, and that the past and the future are together at our side for ever. Out of the shadows of knowledge, and out of a painting that hung on a museum wall, comes our story, the truth of which lies not on our screen but in your hearts.'
JENNIE'S SONG: 'Where I come from, nobody knows ... And where I'm going, everything goes ... The wind blows The sea flows ... And nobody knows...'
EBEN (JOSEPH COTTEN): 'I want you, not dreams of you.'
JENNIE (JENNIFER JONES): 'There is no life, my darling, until you love and have been loved. And then there is no death.'
'Easily the Selznick masterpiece, rich in superb performances, tasteful direction and superb photography.' – *Motion Picture Herald*
'One of the most exquisite fantasy films ever made ... a milieu rich in visual and aural imagery ... a sensuous evocation of time and timelessness.' – *Cinefantastique*
'Though the story may not make sense, the pyrotechnics, joined to the dumbfounded silliness, keep one watching.' – *New Yorker, 1976*
special effects
Joseph August

'Auteur. Couturier. Actor. Author. Shopper. Friend.'
'Whatever they do, they do with style.'
Portraits Chinois
France/GB 1996 123m colour
Film Four/IMA/U&GC/France2/Polar (Georges Benyoun)
An English fashion designer in Paris loses her boyfriend and her job to a newcomer.
The tangled love lives of twentysomethings, in which art is shown as mirroring life, something this slight movie significantly fails to do.
w Martine Dugowson, Peter Chase *d* Martine Dugowson *ph* Antoine Roch *m* Peter Chase *ad* Pierre Guffroy *ed* Martine Barraque, Noëlle Boisson
☆ Helena Bonham Carter, Romane Bohringer, Marie Trintignant, Elsa Zylberstein, Yvan Attal, Sergio Castellitto, Jean-Philippe Ecoffey, Jean-Claude Brialy
'A smart look at the way we live. Sassy as hell and funny in a covert way, it's terrific.' – *Marianne Gray, Film Review*

The Poseidon Adventure **
US 1972 117m DeLuxe Panavision
TCF/Kent (Irwin Allen)
A luxury liner is capsized, and trapped passengers have to find their way to freedom via an upside down world.
Tedious disaster movie which caught the public fancy and started a cycle. Spectacular moments, cardboard characters, flashes of imagination.
w Stirling Silliphant, Wendell Mayes *novel* Paul Gallico *d* Ronald Neame *ph* Harold Stine *m* John Williams *pd* William Creber
☆ Gene Hackman, Ernest Borgnine, Shelley Winters, Red Buttons, Carol Lynley, Leslie Nielsen, Arthur O'Connell, Pamela Sue Martin, Roddy McDowall, Eric Shea, Jack Albertson, Stella Stevens
'The script is the only cataclysm in this waterlogged *Grand Hotel.*' – *New Yorker*
† See also: *Beyond the Poseidon Adventure.*
song 'The Morning After' (*m/ly* Al Kasha, Joel Hirschhorn)
Harold Stine; John Williams; Shelley Winters
Gene Hackman

Posse **
US 1975 93m Technicolor Panavision
Paramount/Bryna (Kirk Douglas)
A US marshal seeking higher office vows to capture a railroad bandit, but the tables are smartly turned.
Unusual minor Western, quite pleasing in all departments and neither mindless nor violent.
w William Roberts, Christopher Knopf d Kirk Douglas ph Fred Koenekamp *m* Maurice Jarre
☆ Kirk Douglas, Bruce Dern, Bo Hopkins, James Stacy, Luke Askew, David Canary

'The untold story of the wild west.'
Posse
GB/US 1993 111m Technicolor
Rank/Polygram/Working Title (Preston Holmes, Jim Steel)
In the 1890s, a group of black cowboys defeat the Ku Klux Klan and other dastardly whites.
An undistinguished Western in the Italian manner, but lacking style and substance.
w Sy Richardson, Dario Scardapane *d* Mario Van Peebles *ph* Peter Menzies Jnr *m* Michel Colombier *pd* Catherine Hardwicke *ed* Mark Conte, Seth Flaum
☆ Mario Van Peebles, Stephen Baldwin, Charles Lane, Tiny Lister, Big Daddy Kane, Billy Zane, Blair Underwood, Melvin Van Peebles, Tone Loc, Isaac Hayes
'Races through its paces with little attention to nuance or characterization, but its action, hip attitude, and cool cast should score with youthful general auds as well as blacks.' – *Variety*

Posse from Hell
US 1961 89m Technicolor
Universal-International
Four killers escape from jail and take over a town.
Moderate Western programmer with more violence than usual.
w Clair Huffaker *novel* Clair Huffaker *d* Herbert Coleman *ph* Clifford Stine *m* Joseph Gershenson
☆ Audie Murphy, John Saxon, Zohra Lampert, Vic Morrow, Robert Keith

Possessed *
US 1931 76m bw
MGM
A factory girl goes to New York in search of riches.
Reasonably gutsy Depression melodrama which moves at a fair pace.
w Lenore Coffee *play* The Mirage by Edgar Selwyn *d* Clarence Brown *ph* Oliver T. Marsh
☆ Joan Crawford, Clark Gable, Wallace Ford, Skeets Gallagher, Frank Conroy, Marjorie White, John Miljan
'Lots of luxury; lots of charm; lots of smooth talk about courage and marriage and what women want.' – *James R. Quirk*

'You'll be possessed by its love madness!'
Possessed *
US 1947 108m bw
Warner (Jerry Wald)
An emotionally unstable nurse marries her employer but retains a passionate love for an engineer whom she kills when he does not respond.
Extremely heavy, almost Germanic, flashback melodrama with everyone tearing hammer and tongs at the rather ailing script. Fun if you're in that mood, and an interesting example of the American film noir *of the forties.*
w Silvia Richards, Ranald MacDougall *novel* One Man's Secret by Rita Weiman *d Curtis Bernhardt ph Joseph Valentine m* Franz Waxman
☆ *Joan Crawford,* Raymond Massey, Van Heflin, Geraldine Brooks, Stanley Ridges, John Ridgely, Moroni Olsen
'Acting with bells on.' – *Richard Winnington*
'Miss Crawford performs with the passion and intelligence of an actress who is not content with just one Oscar.' – *James Agee*
Joan Crawford

Possession
France/West Germany 1981 127m colour
Olianne/Marianne/Soma (Marie-Laure Reyre)
An unhappy woman leaves her husband and lover and gives birth to a monster.
Extraordinary horror movie pitched at a level of hysteria and, with its setting of a divided Berlin, no doubt is intended as an allegory, though of what, among the blood and gore, attitudinizing and demented performances, is anybody's guess.
wd Andrzej Zulkawski *ph* Bruno Nuytten *m* Andrzej Korzynski, Art Phillips *ad* Holger Gross *sp* Carlo Rambaldi
☆ Isabelle Adjani, Sam Neill, Margit Carstensen, Heinz Bennent, Johanna Hofer, Michael Hogben, Shaun Lawton
† It was released in the US in a 97m version.
†† Isabelle Adjani was adjudged best actress in the French equivalent of the Oscars in 1982.

'The past will connect them. The passion will possess them.'
'Human passion is the ultimate mystery.'

Possession
US/GB 2002 102m Technicolor
Warner/Baltimore/Spring Creek/Contagious (Paula Weinstein, Barry Levinson)

Two academics become attracted to one another as they discover a secret and tragic affair between two Victorian writers.
Inert adaptation of a complex novel, too genteel in tone to convey either the rivalries and excitements of literary discovery or the overpowering emotions of hidden love.
w David Henry Hwang, Laura Jones, Neil LaBute *novel* A. S. Byatt *d* Neil LaBute *ph* Jean Yves Escoffier *m* Gabriel Yared *pd* Luciana Arrighi *ed* Claire Simpson
☆ Gwyneth Paltrow (Maud Bailey), Aaron Eckhart (Roland Michell), Jeremy Northam (Randolph Henry Ash), Jennifer Ehle (Christabel LaMotte), Lena Headey (Blanche Glover), Toby Stephens (Fergus Wolfe), Tom Hickey (Blackadder), Trevor Eve (Cropper), Tom Hollander (Euan), Graham Crowden (Sir George), Anna Massey (Lady Bailey)
'One of the stupidest, most badly acted and clumsily directed films I have ever seen. And did I mention *boring*.' – *Peter Bradshaw Guardian*
'I was wooed by its sexy romanticism all the way through to the mysterious and beautiful coda.' – *Johnathan Rosenbaum, Chicago Reader*

The Possession of Joel Delaney
US 1971 108m Eastmancolor
ITC/Haworth (George Justin)

A wealthy New York divorcee tries to save her brother from death at the hands of a Puerto Rican occult group who believe in ritual murder and demonic possession.
Unpleasant, frightening and overlong horror film with some kind of message struggling to get out but precious little entertainment value.
w Matt Robinson, Grimes Grice *novel* Ramona Stewart *d* Waris Hussein *ph* Arthur J. Ornitz *m* Joe Ragoso
☆ Shirley MacLaine, Perry King, Lisa Kohane, David Elliott
'Some see the film as a political allegory; I see it as a piece of political tosh.' – *Michael Billington, Illustrated London News*

Possible Worlds **
Canada 2000 92m colour
Momentum/In Extremis Images/East Side (Sandra Cunningham, Bruno Jobin)

A man, who may be dead, appears to live in several different worlds at the same time, with differing relationships with the same woman.
A puzzle of a film that begins promisingly, with the discovery of a corpse without a brain, but then develops into a movie without much sense.
w John Mighton, Robert Lepage *play* John Mighton *d* Robert Lepage *ph* Jonathan Freeman *m* Ron Proulx *pd* François Seguin *ed* Susan Shipton
☆ Tilda Swinton (Joyce), Tom McCamus (George Barber), Sean McCann (Inspector Berkley), Gabriel Gascon (Scientist), Rick Miller (Williams)
'A pile-up of pretentious illustrations about the nature of consciousness and the multiplicity of personality' – *Alexander Walker*

Postcards from America *
US/GB 1995 93m colour
Islet/Channel 4/Normal (Christine Vachon, Craig Paul)

Adapted from two semi-autobiographical books by an artist and writer who died from AIDS in 1992, this fragmentary work concentrates on a loveless childhood with a violent father and adult years as a petty thief and hustler.
A highly stylized, episodic account of a man's remembrance of his search for affection and love and finding only disappointment and disease; the approach emphasizes the alienation of not only the protagonist, but of his audience.
wd Steve McLean *novels* Close to the Knives and Memories that Smell Like Gasoline by David Wojnarowicz *ph* Ellen Kuras *m* Stephen Endelman *pd* Thérèse Deprez *ed* Elizabeth Gazzara
☆ James Lyons, Michael Tighe, Olmo Tighe, Michael Imperiolo, Michael Ringer, Maggie Low

'Having a wonderful time, wish I were here.'

Postcards from the Edge *
US 1990 101m Technicolor
Columbia (Mike Nichols, John Calley)

A drug-addicted actress is forced to live with her unstable mother, an ageing film star.
Entertaining parade of Hollywood egos, enjoyable providing you do not take it seriously.
w Carrie Fisher *novel* Carrie Fisher *d* Mike Nichols *ph* Michael Ballhaus *m* Carly Simon *pd* Patrizia von Brandenstein *ed* Sam O'Steen
☆ Meryl Streep, Shirley MacLaine, Dennis Quaid, Gene Hackman, Richard Dreyfuss, Rob Reiner, Mary Wickes, Conrad Bain, Annette Bening, Simon Callow
'Packs a fair amount of emotional wallop in its dark-hued comic take on a chemically dependent Hollywood mother and daughter.' – *Variety*
Meryl Streep; original song 'I'm Checkin' Out' (m/ly Shel Silverstein)

'A shy postman didn't stand a chance with the island's most beautiful woman until the great poet of love gave him the courage to follow his dreams ... and the words to win her heart.'

Il Postino **
Italy/France 1994 100m Eastmancolor
Buena Vista/Cecchi Gori/Tiger/Pentafilm/Mediterraneo/Blue Dahlia/Canal

aka: *The Postman*
An Italian postman is inspired by the exiled Chilean poet Pablo Neruda to woo and win a beautiful woman.
A gentle comedy that gains a great deal from Troisi's contained performance, which illumines the sometimes clumsy narrative, so that it becomes genuinely moving despite its obvious manipulation.
w Anna Pavignano, Michael Radford, Furio Scarpelli, Giacomo Scarpelli, Massimo Troisi *novel* Il Postino di Neruda by Antonio Skarmeta *d* Michael Radford *ph* Franco di Giacomo *m* Luis Enrique Bacalov *pd* Lorenzo Baraldi *ed* Roberto Perpignani
☆ *Massimo Troisi*, Philippe Noiret, Maria Grazia Cucinotta, Linda Moretti, Renato Scarpa, Anna Bonaiuto, Bruno Alessandro
'A tender and wistful comedy.' – *Kenneth Turan, Los Angeles Times*
† Massimo Troisi died of a heart attack within days of finishing the film.
Luis Enrique Bacalov
best picture; Michael Radford; Massimo Troisi; screenplay adaptation
best foreign-language film; Michael Radford

The Postman: see *Il Postino (1994)*

The Postman
US 1997 177m Technicolor Panavision
Warner/Tig (Jim Wilson, Steve Tisch, Kevin Costner)

In 2013, after a world war, a man tries to keep scattered communities together by setting up a postal service.
An apocalyptic Western, lost in a wilderness of its own making.
w Eric Roth, Brian Helgeland *novel* David Brin *d* Kevin Costner *ph* Stephen Windon *m* James Newton Howard *pd* Ida Random *ed* Peter Boyle
☆ Kevin Costner, Will Patton, Larenz Tate, Olivia Williams, James Russo, Daniel von Bargen, Tom Petty, Scott Bairstow
'A rare epic film that is actually about something.' – *Variety*
'This lacks both the visual and verbal stimuli to keep you watching for three hours.' – *David Eimer, Empire*
† The film cost $80m and took around $17.4m at the US box-office.

The Postman Always Rings Twice *
US 1946 113m bw
MGM (Carey Wilson)

A guilty couple murder her husband but get their come-uppance.
Pale shadow of Double Indemnity, *efficient but not interesting or very suspenseful.*
w Harry Ruskin, Niven Busch *novel* James M. Cain *d* Tay Garnett *ph* *Sidney Wagner* *m* George Bassman
☆ Lana Turner, John Garfield, Cecil Kellaway, Hume Cronyn, Leon Ames, Audrey Totter, Alan Reed
'It was a real chore to do *Postman* under the Hays Office, but I think I managed to get the sex across.' – *Tay Garnett*

'You will feel the heat!'
'Their love was a war that destroyed!'

The Postman Always Rings Twice *
US 1981 121m Metrocolor
Lorimar/Northstar International (Charles Mulvehill, Bob Rafelson)

A remake of the above with more heavy breathing and some table-ending.
Not otherwise any better, but an interesting measure of the times.
w David Mamet *novel* James M. Cain *d* Bob Rafelson *ph* Sven Nykvist *m* Michael Small *pd* George Jenkins *ed* Graeme Clifford
☆ Jack Nicholson, Jessica Lange, John Colicos, Michael Lerner, John P. Ryan, Anjelica Huston
'Too cheerless to be erotic, too charmless to be titillating.' – *Margaret Hinxman, Daily Mail*

Postman's Knock *
GB 1961 88m bw
MGM (Ronald Kinnoch)
A village postman is transferred to London, finds life and work bewildering, but captures some crooks and ends up a hero.
Mildly amusing star vehicle rising to good comic climaxes.
w John Briley, Jack Trevor Story *d* Robert Lynn *ph* Gerald Moss *m* Ron Goodwin
☆ Spike Milligan, Barbara Shelley, Wilfrid Lawson

Postmark for Danger: see *Portrait of Alison*

'The only way to trap a serial killer is to know what he feels, what he thinks and when he'll strike again.'

Postmortem
US 1997 105m Foto-Kem
Imperial/Filmwerks/Wild Side (Gary Schmoeller, Tom Karnowski)

A depressed, heavy-drinking, best-selling author, a former San Francisco homicide detective, moves to Glasgow, where his help is sought in catching a serial killer.
Downbeat thriller, shot in sickly hues of blue, green and orange, and noteworthy only for lacking its director's usual action-packed, explosive manner.
w John Lowry Lamb, Robert McDonnell *d* Albert Pyun *ph* George Mooradian *m* Tony Riparetti *pd* Pat Campbell *ed* Natasha Gjurokovic
☆ Charles Sheen, Michael Halsey, Ivana Milicevic, Stephen McCole, Gary Lewis

Il Posto: see *The Job*

Pot Luck *
GB 1936 71m bw
Gainsborough (Michael Balcon)
A Scotland Yard inspector enlists the aid of department store staff to recover a stolen Chinese vase.
Surprisingly not from a stage original, this action farce gets better as it goes along and finds time for a quick spoof of The Old Dark House.
w Ben Travers *d* Tom Walls *ph* Roy Kellino, Arthur Crabtree *md* Louis Levy
☆ Tom Walls, Ralph Lynn, Robertson Hare, Diana Churchill, Gordon James, Martita Hunt
'There is too much melodrama, too little Hare, and, of course, as always to my mind, too much Lynn, too much of the scaly tortoise face and hollow imbecility.' – *Graham Greene*

Pot o' Gold
US 1941 87m bw
Globe/James Roosevelt

GB title: *The Golden Hour*
A radio giveaway show finds work for idle musicians.
Thin Capraesque comedy which needed more determined handling.
w Walter de Leon *d* George Marshall *ph* Hal Mohr *md* Lou Forbes
☆ James Stewart, Paulette Goddard, Horace Heidt, Charles Winninger, Mary Gordon, Frank Melton, Jed Prouty

Pote tin Kyriaki: see *Never on Sunday*

Potemkin: see *The Battleship Potemkin*

Potomok Chingis-Khana: see *Storm over Asia*

Poulet au Vinaigre: see *Cop au Vin*

Pourquoi Pas Moi?
France/Spain/Switzerland 1998 94m colour
Millivres/Elzevir/M6/Glozel/Maestranza/Sogedasa/Alhena (Marie Masmonteil, Caroline Adrian)

Three gay friends decide to come out to their parents at a country house weekend.
An amusing camp comedy that climaxes with the Virgin Mary singing along to a Patsy Cline song.
wd Stéphane Giusti *ph* Antoine Roch *pd* Rosa Ros *ed* Catherine Schwartz
☆ Amira Casar (Camille), Julie Gayet (Eva), Bruno Putzulu (Nico), Alexandra London (Ariane), Carmen Chaplin (Lili), Johnny Hallyday (José), Marie-France Pisier (Irene), Brigitte Roüan (Josepha), Assumpta Serna (Diane), Elli Medeiros (Malou), Vittoria Scognamiglio (Sara), Jean-Claude Dauphin (Alain), Joan Crosas (Tony)
'Amiable but predictable, chic but superficial.' – *Empire*

Powaqqatsi *
US 1988 97m colour
Cannon/Golan-Globus (Mel Lawrence, Godfrey Reggio, Lawrence Taub)

Montage of images of back-breaking labour in the Third World.
A sequel to Koyaanisqatsi, *silent apart from the hypnotic score, its beautifully composed images detract from the undignified labour it shows.*
w Godfrey Reggio, Ken Richards *d* Godfrey Reggio *ph* Graham Berry, Leonidas Zourdoumis *m* Philip Glass *ed* Iris Cahn, Alton Walpole

Powder
US 1995 112m Technicolor
Buena Vista/Hollywood/Caravan (Roger Birnbaum, Daniel Grodnik)

When an old man dies, locals discover the existence of his freakish grandson, a hairless, white-skinned boy with strange powers and a powerful intellect.
A familiar story of a misunderstood teenager, tricked out with some hocus-pocus of mysterious powers, and undermined by its sentimentality.
wd Victor Salva *ph* Jerzy Zielinski *m* Jerry Goldsmith *pd* Waldemar Kalinowski *ed* Dennis M. Hill
☆ Mary Steenburgen, Sean Patrick Flanery, Lance Henriksen, Jeff Goldblum, Brandon Smith, Bradford Tatum, Susan Tyrrell
'Features some fine performances, an imaginative premise and a couple of go-for-broke emotional scenes. But the muddled script plays like a first draft, the continuity is jagged and the climax is a cop-out of sappy mysticism.' – *Joe Leydon, Variety*

Power: see *Jew Suss (1934)*

The Power *
US 1967 109m Metrocolor Cinemascope
MGM/George Pal
Scientists researching into human endurance are menaced by one of their number who has developed the ability to kill by will power.
Interesting but finally unexciting and exasperating science fiction which badly lacks a gimmick one can actually see.
w John Gay *novel* Frank M. Robinson *d* Byron Haskin *ph* Ellsworth Fredericks *m* Miklos Rozsa
☆ Michael Rennie, George Hamilton, Suzanne Pleshette, Nehemiah Persoff, Earl Holliman, Arthur O'Connell, Aldo Ray, Barbara Nichols, Yvonne de Carlo, Richard Carlson, Gary Merrill, Ken Murray, Miiko Taka, Celia Lovsky
'The movie takes itself very seriously. We don't have to.' – *Robert Windeler*

Power
US 1986 111m Technicolor
TCF/Lorimar/Polar (Reene Schisgal, Mark Tarlov)
A political PR man takes on an industrialist of dubious background.
Slick and punchy but somewhat unnecessary investigation of corruption in the media, an American version of The Ploughman's Lunch.
w David Himmelstein *d* Sidney Lumet
ph Andrzej Bartkowiak *m* Cy Coleman *pd* Peter Larkin *ed* Andrew Mondsheim
☆ Richard Gere, Julie Christie, Gene Hackman, Kate Capshaw, Denzel Washington, E. G. Marshall, Beatrice Straight, Fritz Weaver, Michael Learned

The Power and the Glory *
US 1933 76m bw
Fox (Jesse L. Lasky)
The flashback story of a tycoon who rose from nothing and was corrupted by power.
Often noted as a forerunner of Citizen Kane, *this is in fact a disappointing film with a very thin script and a general sense of aimlessness. 'Presented in narratage' meant that the characters voice their unspoken thoughts. Most interesting for its credits.*
w Preston Sturges *d* William K. Howard
ph James Wong Howe
☆ Spencer Tracy, Colleen Moore, Ralph Morgan, Helen Vinson
'Débuting at two dollars on Broadway. Not two dollars but decidedly above-average film fare. Packs plenty of appeal, even with a not too punch marquee cast.' – *Variety*

The Power and the Prize *
US 1956 98m bw Cinemascope
MGM (Nicholas Nayfack)
An ambitious company executive is criticized by his president for wanting to marry a European refugee, but the other executives support him.
Unconvincing big business fairy tale which passes the time competently enough, though Taylor is a humourless hero.
w Robert Ardrey *novel* Howard Swiggett
d Henry Koster *ph* George Folsey *m* Bronislau Kaper
☆ Robert Taylor, Elisabeth Mueller, Mary Astor, Burl Ives, Charles Coburn, Cedric Hardwicke

'He's had to fight all his life. Now he's fighting for theirs.'
The Power of One
US 1991 127m Technicolor
Warner (Arnon Milchan)
In South Africa in the 1930s, an English boy, who witnesses the brutality of the Afrikaners and is taught boxing by a black prisoner, decides to dedicate his life to the cause of racial equality.
Sentimental and unconvincing account of an African childhood, with Rocky-like moments thrown in for good measure.
w Robert Mark Kamen *novel* Bryce Courtenay
d John G. Avildsen *ph* Dean Semler *m* Hans Zimmer, Lebo M *pd* Roger Hall *ed* John G. Avildsen
☆ Stephen Dorff, John Gielgud, Armin Mueller-Stahl, Morgan Freeman, Guy Witcher, Simon Fenton
'Crude, patronising and mawkish, sure, but rescued by excellent performances, beautiful landscape photography, and hard-to-argue-with themes of natural justice, delivered with a punch.' – *Angie Errigo, Empire*

Power of the Press
US 1943 63m bw
Columbia
The owner of a New York paper kills to maintain its isolationist line.
Hard-hitting melodrama which overdoes the propaganda.
w Samuel Fuller, Robert D. Andrews *d* Lew Landers
☆ Lee Tracy, Guy Kibbee, Otto Kruger, Gloria Dickson

Power Play
GB/Canada 1978 109m colour
Robert Cooper/Canada United Kingdom (Christopher Dalton)
In a mythical country, a tank commander joins the leaders of a coup d'état only to doublecross them.
Uninteresting mixture of violent action and verbosity.
wd Martyn Burke *ph* Ousama Rawi *m* Ken Thorne
☆ Peter O'Toole, David Hemmings, Donald Pleasence, Barry Morse

The Power Within
US 1995 97m colour
PM (Joseph Merhi, Richard Pepin)
A high-school student is all that prevents a vicious thief from obtaining an ancient ring that will give him immense power.
Violent, childish, teenage wish fulfilment about a nerd who takes on the bad guys.
w Jacobsen Hart, Scott McAboy *d* Art Camacho
ph Ken Blakey *m* Jim Halfpenny *pd* Chris Blocker *ed* Chris Worland
☆ Ted Jan Roberts (Stan), Karen Valentine (Clyda), Keith Coogan (Eric), John O'Hurley (Lt Cabrell), Gerald Okamura (Yung), Tracy Lindsey (Sandy), P. J. Soles (Mrs Applegate), Ed O'Ross (Deriva), Jacob Parker (Deke), William Zabka (Raymond Vonn)

'Saving the world before bedtime!'
Powerpuff Girls *
US 2002 74m colour
Warner/Cartoon Network (Donna Castricone)
When a scientist's experiment to make the perfect girl goes wrong, he creates instead three bug-eyed girls with superpowers.
A TV favourite among the very young transfers to the big screen. Its relentless energy is wearing after a while, but it will appeal to its many fans – though it's possibly less entertaining than an average TV episode.
w Charlie Bean, Lauren Faust, Craig McCracken, Paul Rudish, Don Shank *d* Craig McCracken
ad Mike Moon *ed* Rob DeSales
☆ voices of: Catherine Cavadini (Blossom), Tara Strong (Bubbles), E.G. Daily (Buttercup), Roger L. Jackson (Mojo Jojo), Tom Kane (Professor Utonium), Tom Kenny (Mayor/Narrator)
'What's really so appealing about the characters is their resemblance to everyday children. They're wildly energetic, competitive and (sometimes dangerously) impulsive. But they also learn from their mistakes, and their instincts are good.' – *Stephen Holden, New York Times*

The Powers Girl
US 1942 92m bw
UA/Charles R. Rogers
GB title: *Hello Beautiful*
Girls come to New York to become models for John Robert Powers.
Extremely thin and forgettable musical.
w Edwin Moran, Harry Segall *book* John Robert Powers *d* Norman Z. McLeod *ph* Stanley Cortez *md* Louis Silvers
☆ George Murphy, Anne Shirley, Carole Landis, Alan Mowbray (John Robert Powers), Dennis Day, Benny Goodman and his Orchestra, Mary Treen

Powwow Highway
GB 1988 91m Technicolor
Handmade (Jan Wieringa)
A militant American Indian leaves the reservation with his simple friend to make a long journey to rescue his sister, imprisoned on a trumped-up drugs charge.
Rambling road movie that comes to the conclusion that it is morally justifiable for the exploited to lie, cheat and steal.
w Janet Heaney, Jean Stawarz *novel* David Seals
d Jonathan Wacks *ph* Toyomichi Kurita *m* Barry Goldberg *pd* Cynthia Sowder *ed* Hilarie Roope
☆ A. Martinez, Gary Farmer, Joanelle Nadine Romero, Geoff Rivas, Roscoe Born, Wayne Waterman, Margo Kane, Amanda Wyss, Sam Vlanos
'Settles for the affirmations of the buddy movie, without achieving either a consistently manic tone or a convincing balance between character, humour and suspense.' – *Farrah Anwar, MFB*

'Falling in love is the trickiest spell of all.'
Practical Magic
US 1998 105m Technicolor
Warner/Village Roadshow/Di Novi/Fortis
Two young witches deal with an ancient curse that any man who falls in love with them will die.
Like one of those spells where you throw everything into a cauldron and stir hopefully, this has ingredients of a feminist tract, a romantic comedy, a thriller, and domestic drama; nothing works.
w Robin Swicord, Akiva Goldsman, Adam Brooks *novel* Alice Hoffman *d* Griffin Dunne
ph Andrew Dunn *m* Alan Silvestri *pd* Robin Standefer *ed* Elizabeth Kling, Craig McKay
sp Cinesite Digital Studios
☆ Sandra Bullock, Nicole Kidman, Dianne Wiest, Stockard Channing, Aidan Quinn, Goran Visnic, Evan Rachel Wood, Alexandra Astrip, Mark Feuerstein
'A chick movie with multiple personality disorder.' – *Angie Errigo, Empire*

Practically Yours
US 1944 89m bw
Paramount (Mitchell Leisen)
A war hero comes back after being supposed dead, and finds himself with a fiancée he never met.
Silly romantic comedy which never gets going.
w Norman Krasna *d* Mitchell Leisen *ph* Charles Lang Jnr *m* Victor Young
☆ Claudette Colbert, Fred MacMurray, Gil Lamb, Cecil Kellaway, Robert Benchley, Rosemary de Camp, Tom Powers, Jane Frazee
'It's a one-joke story, that's the problem with it.' – *Mitchell Leisen*

'It Started With A Kiss.'
Prague *
GB/France 1991 89m Eastmancolor
Winstone/BBC/Constellation/UGC Hachette-Premiere/British Screen/Canal (Christopher Young)
A Scot goes to Prague in search of a wartime newsreel that will reveal information about his mother and her family.
Moderately interesting account of a shared European past that illumines the present, but lacking narrative drive.
wd Ian Sellar *ph* Darius Khondji *m* Jonathan Dove *pd* Jiri Matolin *ed* John Bloom
☆ Alan Cumming, Sandrine Bonnaire, Bruno Ganz, Raphael Meiss, Henri Meiss, Hana Gregorova
'A decent Euro-movie that makes good use of the idea of film as collective memory.' – *Philip French, Observer*
'Comes across like a collection of ideas for a Euro co-production to be lensed in a photogenic city rather than an accomplished vital picture.' – *Variety*

Prancer *
US 1989 102m Film House colour
Orion/Nelson/Cineplex Odeon (Raffaella de Laurentiis)
The eight-year-old daughter of a widowed, taciturn, near-bankrupt farmer takes care of an injured reindeer which she believes belongs to Father Christmas.
Pleasing family drama that for the most part avoids cuteness and sentimentality.
w Greg Taylor *d* John Hancock *ph* Misha Suslov *m* Maurice Jarre *pd* Chester Kaczenski *ed* Dennis O'Connor
☆ Sam Elliott, Rebecca Harrell, Cloris Leachman, Rutanya Alda, Abe Vigoda, Ariana Richards, Michael Constantine

A Prayer for the Dying
GB 1987 107m Metrocolor
Peter Snell/Samuel Goldwyn Co
An ex-IRA gunman feels unable to silence a priest witness of a killing, and confesses his sins instead.
Convoluted melodrama which kills its chances as a thriller by striving to say something meaningful.
w Edmund Ward, Martin Lynch *novel* Jack Higgins *d* Mike Hodges (who disowned the version released) *m* Bill Conti
☆ Mickey Rourke, Bob Hoskins, Alan Bates, Sammi Davis, Christopher Fulford

Prayer of the Rollerboys
US 1990 94m colour
First Independent/Gaga/Fox Lorber/Academy/JVC/TV Tokyo (Robert Mickelson)
In a future bankrupt America, a youth, working undercover for the police, infiltrates a vicious gang of young, skating drug dealers.
Dull, paranoid science fiction aimed at a teenage audience.
w W. Peter Iliff *d* Rick King *ph* Phedon Papamichael *m* Stacy Widelitz *pd* Thomas A. Walsh *ed* Daniel Loewenthal
☆ Corey Haim, Patricia Arquette, Christopher Collet, J. C. Quinn, Julius Harris, Devin Clark, Mark Pellegrino, Morgan Weisser
'Offers blood-pumping entertainment in a pulpy, cartoonish mode.' – *Variety*

The Preacher's Wife
US 1996 124m Technicolor
Buena Vista/Touchstone/Samuel Goldwyn
An angel helps sort out the troubled marriage of a preacher.
Bland and gruesomely sentimental comedy that is out of touch with the modern world, and lacks the charm to persuade an audience otherwise; its sole point seems to have been to sell the soundtrack songs by Houston.
w Nat Maudlin, Allan Scott *d* Penny Marshall
ph Miroslav Ondricek *m* Hans Zimmer *pd* Bill Groom *ed* Stephen A. Rotter, George Bowers
☆ Denzel Washington, Whitney Houston, Courtney B. Vance, Gregory Hines, Jenifer Lewis, Loretta Devine, Lionel Ritchie
'Marshall's marshmallow world and her heavy-handedness in trying so hard to win your approval every step of the way simply grate on the nerves.' – *Alan Jones, Film Review*
† It is a remake of *The Bishop's Wife* (qv), directed by Henry Koster in 1947 and starring Cary Grant.
Hans Zimmer

Preaching to the Perverted
GB 1997 100m Fujicolour
Victor/Cyclops (Stuart Urban)
The young aide to a campaigning, puritanical politician infiltrates a London sex club run by an American dominatrix.
Fetishistic images predominate in this coarse and dispiriting satire that may appeal to masochists: certainly, watching it is torture.
wd Stuart Urban *ph* Sam McCurdy *m* Maya and Magnus Fiennes *pd* James Hendy *ed* Julian Rodd
☆ Guinevere Turner, Christien Anholt, Tom Bell, Julie Graham, Julian Wadham, Ricky Tomlinson, Georgina Hale, Sue Johnston, Roger Lloyd Pack, Keith Allen
'The film's impact is blunted by the decision to downplay its serious intent in favour of a comic approach which aims at satire, but swiftly descends into *Carry On* territory.' – *Sheila Johnston, Screen International*
† The credits include 'Ms Turner's Nipple Double', 'Ms Turner's Tongue Double', 'Ms Graham's Bottom Double' and 'Mr Anholt's Nipple Double', as well as the statement: 'The Producers wish to point out that no animals were improperly treated during the making of this motion picture; however, all the submissives were.'

Precinct 45: Los Angeles Police: see *The New Centurions*

Pred dozdot: see *Before the Rain*

Predator
US 1987 107m DeLuxe
TCF/Lawrence Gordon/Joel Silver/John Davis
An allied military rescue team gets into trouble in South America.
Lethargic action thriller with unpleasant moments.
w Jim and John Thomas *d* John McTiernan
ph Donald McAlpine, Leon Sanchez *m* Alan Silvestri *pd* John Vallone *ed* John F. Link, Mark Helfrich
☆ Arnold Schwarzenegger, Carl Weathers, Bill Duke, Elpidia Carrillo, Jesse Ventura

'Silent. Invisible. Invincible.'
'He's Coming To Town With A Few Days To Kill.'
Predator 2
US 1990 108m DeLuxe
Fox/Lawrence Gordon/Joel Silver/John Davis

A heavily armed alien killer visits Earth.
Violent and gore-filled, filmed in a frenetic style that soon wearies.
w Jim Thomas, John Thomas *d* Stephen Hopkins *ph* Peter Levy *m* Alan Silvestri *pd* Lawrence G. Paull *ed* Mark Goldblatt
☆ Danny Glover, Gary Busey, Ruben Blades, Maria Conchita Alonso, Bill Paxton, Kevin Peter Hall
'In terms of overall excitement, it outdoes its first safari in start-to-finish hysteria.' – *Variety*

Prefontaine
US 1997 107m Technicolor
Buena Vista/Hollywood (Irby Smith, Jon Lutz, Mark Doonan, Peter Gilbert)

Biopic of the record-breaking American athlete who died young.
Documentary-style movie that never quite gets to grips with the charismatic track star, who liked to run from the front but never had the time to live up to his own high expectations.
w Steve James, Eugene Corr *d* Steve James *ph* Peter Gilbert *m* Mason Daring *pd* Carol Winstead Wood *ed* Peter Frank
☆ Jared Leto (Steve Prefontaine), R. Lee Ermey (Bill Bowerman), Ed O'Neill (Bill Dellinger), Amy Locane (Nancy Alleman), Lindsay Crouse (Elfriede Prefontaine), Laurel Holloman (Elaine Finley), Breckin Meyer (Pat Tyson), Brian McGovern (Mac Wilkins), Kurtwood Smith (Curtis Cunningham), Peter Anthony Jacobs (Ray Prefontaine)
'The film never strays sufficiently beyond the straight-line narrative to allow the potential character relationships to breathe or take on much resonance.' – *Todd McCarthy, Variety*
† *Without Limits* (qv), another biopic of Prefontaine, was released in 1998.

Prehistoric Women: see *Slave Girls*

Prelude to a Kiss
US 1992 106m DuArt
TCF (Michael Gruskoff, Michael I. Levy)

After his bride kisses a mysterious old man at her wedding, her husband discovers that she has become a stranger to him.
An oddly uncompelling romantic fantasy; charm is laid on with a trowel, but it is otherwise thin and unconvincing.
w Craig Lucas *play* Craig Lucas *d* Norman René *ph* Stefan Czapsky *m* Howard Shore *pd* Andrew Jackness *ed* Stephen A. Rotter
☆ Alec Baldwin, Meg Ryan, Kathy Bates, Ned Beatty, Patty Duke, Sydney Walker, Stanley Tucci
'Back in the 1930s or '40s, this sort of sophisticated, literary-oriented treatment of a simple romantic idea would have been the norm. Today's general audiences, however, may be put off by the quick-witted talk and mildly confused by the central device.' – *Todd McCarthy, Variety*
† The play ran on Broadway in 1990, with Alec Baldwin playing the same role. Alec Guinness was originally offered the role of the old man. It was released direct to video in Britain in 1994.

Prelude to Fame
GB 1950 88m bw
Rank/Two Cities (Donald B. Wilson)
The health of a child musical prodigy is endangered by an ambitious woman who pushes him to the top.
Banal drama with classical music, generally overacted by the adults.
w Robert Westerby, Bridget Boland *story* Young Archimedes by Aldous Huxley *d* Fergus McDonell *ph* George Stretton *ad* Fred Pusey *ed* Sid Hayers
☆ *Jeremy Spenser*, Guy Rolfe, Kathleen Ryan, Kathleen Byron, James Robertson Justice, Henry Oscar, Rosalie Crutchley

Prelude to War ***
US 1943 53m bw
US Signal Corps (Frank Capra)
First in the Why We Fight series.
A brilliant assemblage of newsreel, diagrams, and March of Time techniques which pointed a new way for documentary.
'There isn't a dull second.' – *Variety*

The Premature Burial
US 1961 81m Eastmancolor Panavision
AIP (Roger Corman)

A man afraid of being buried alive suffers just that fate, but later comes to and wreaks revenge on his tormentors.
Gloomy Gothic horror based vaguely on Edgar Allan Poe: the ultimate in graveyard ghoulishness.
w Charles Beaumont, Ray Russell *d* Roger Corman *ph* Floyd Crosby *m* Ronald Stein *ad* Daniel Haller
☆ Ray Milland, Heather Angel, Hazel Court, Richard Ney, Alan Napier, John Dierkes

Premiere
GB 1938 71m bw
ABPC
The principal backer of a stage show is shot during the first performance.
Slightly unusual mystery drama.
w F. McGrew Willis *d* Walter Summers *ph* Otto Kanturek *m* Peter Fenn
☆ John Lodge, Judy Kelly, Joan Marion, Hugh Williams, Edmund Breon, Steven Geray, Edward Chapman

'It's Halloween Night All Over Again ... Be Warned.'
The Premonition
Sweden 1992 114m colour
Svensk Filmindustri (Waldemar Bergendahl)

original title: *Svart Lucia*
aka: *Black Lucia*
A girl's dreams of sex and death, which she records in her diary, begin to come true on the longest night of the year.
A psychological thriller with voyeuristic overtones, stronger on disturbing images than narrative interest; it owes much to American examples, from Hitchcock to Carpenter.
w Carina Rydberg, Rumle Hammerich *d* Rumle Hammerich *ph* Jens Fischer *m* Jacob Groth *pd* Gert Wibe *ed* Camilla Skousen
☆ Tova Magnusson, Lars Green, Agneta Ekmanner, Figge Norling, Björn Kjellman, Liv Alsterland, Malin Berghagen, Niklas Hjulström
'More interested in atmosphere than action, with character insights instead of suspense, this isn't going to satisfy fans of Freddy and Jason.' – *Kim Newman, Empire*

Préparez Vous Mouchoirs: see *Get Out Your Handkerchiefs*

Present Arms: see *Leathernecking*

Presenting Lily Mars *
US 1943 104m bw
MGM (Joe Pasternak)
A girl from the sticks hits it big on Broadway.
No, the plot wasn't new, but some of the numbers were nice.
w Richard Connell, Gladys Lehman *novel* Booth Tarkington *d* Norman Taurog *ph* Joseph Ruttenberg *md* George Stoll
☆ Judy Garland, Van Heflin, Fay Bainter, Richard Carlson, Marta Eggerth, Spring Byington, Bob Crosby and his band, Tommy Dorsey and his band
♫ 'Presenting Lily Mars'; 'Is It Really Love?'; 'Tom Tom the Piper's Son'; 'Tovaritch'; 'Russian Rhapsody'; 'Kulebiaka'; 'Where There's Music'; 'Every Little Movement'; Three O'Clock in the Morning'; 'Broadway Rhythm'; 'Think of Me'

The President Vanishes
US 1934 80m bw
Walter Wanger (Paramount)
GB title: *Strange Conspiracy*
The president of the US agrees to drop out of sight for a few days, pretending to have been kidnapped, so that his country will not be drawn into a European war.
Reasonably intriguing political fantasy with good production and performances.
w Lynn Starling, Carey Wilson, Cedric Worth *novel* anonymous *d* William A. Wellman
☆ Arthur Byron, Janet Beecher, Paul Kelly, Peggy Conklin, Rosalind Russell, Sidney Blackmer, Walter Kingsford, Charley Grapewin, Edward Arnold
'Provocative topical meller, but likely to be spotty.' – *Variety*

The President's Analyst *
US 1967 104m Technicolor Panavision
Paramount/Panpiper (Stanley Rubin)

A psychiatrist who has been asked to treat the president is pursued by spies of every nationality.
Wild political satirical farce which finally unmasks as its chief villain the telephone company. Laughs along the way, but it's all rather too much.
wd *Theodore J. Flicker* *ph* William A. Fraker *m* Lalo Schifrin *pd* Pato Guzman
☆ James Coburn, Godfrey Cambridge, Severn Darden, Joan Delaney, Pat Harrington, Eduard Franz, Will Geer
'Free-wheeling, outrageous and very funny, laced with a sophisticated zaniness that is sheer delight.' – *Judith Crist*

The President's Lady *
US 1953 96m bw
TCF (Sol C. Siegel)
An account of the early career of Andrew Jackson, a lawyer whose frail wife died shortly after he became president.
Well-produced political historical romance.
w John Patrick *novel* Irving Stone *d* Henry Levin *ph* *Leo Tover* *m* *Alfred Newman* *ad* Lyle Wheeler, Leland Fuller
☆ Charlton Heston, Susan Hayward, John McIntire, Fay Bainter, Carl Betz
'History plays a curious second fiddle to love's old sweet song.' – *New York Times*
Academy Award nomination: art direction

The Presidio
US 1988 98m Technicolor Panavision
UIP/Paramount (D. Constantine Conte)

An army officer and a former cop, who are old adversaries, investigate a murder at an army base.
Tame and uninvolving action movie.
w Larry Ferguson *d* Peter Hyams *ph* Peter Hyams *m* Bruce Broughton *pd* Albert Brenner *ed* James Mitchell, Diane Adler, Beau Barthel-Blair
☆ Sean Connery, Mark Harmon, Meg Ryan, Jack Warden, Mark Blum, Dana Gladstone, Jenette Goldstein, Marvin J. McIntyre, Don Calfa, John DiSanti

Presque Rien
France/Belgium 2001 97m Telecipro
Peccadillo/Lancelot/Man's Films/Arte France/RTBF (Jean-Christophe Colson, Cecile Amillat, Christian Tison)

GB and US title: *Come Undone*
A teenage student recalls his despair over his first summer love affair with another youth.
Slight account, reticent to the point of inscrutability, of the rehabilitation of a sensitive boy over an unhappy love.
w Sebastien Lifshitz, Stephane Bouquet *d* Sebastien Lifshitz *ph* Pascal Poucet *m* Perry Blake *pd* Roseanna Sacco *ed* Yann Dedet
☆ Jeremie Elkaim (Mathieu), Stephane Rideau (Cedric), Marie Matheron (Annick), Dominique Reymond (Mother), Laetitia Legrix (Sarah), Nils Ohlund (Pierre), Rejane Kerdaffrec (Psychiatrist)
'Perhaps the greatest achievement… of this modest masterpiece is that a film that looks so incomplete should be so technically and emotionally accomplished.' – *Paul Julian Smith, Sight & Sound*

Press for Time
GB 1966 102m Eastmancolor
Rank/Ivy/Titan (Robert Hartford Davis, Peter Newbrook)

The prime minister's grandson is a newspaper seller, and is quietly promoted to be a journalist in a seaside town where it is thought he can do no harm.
The star's last comedy in his original style; competent but nothing special.
w Norman Wisdom, Eddie Leslie *novel* Yea Yea Yea by Angus McGill *d* Robert Asher *ph* Peter Newbrook *m* Mike Vickers
☆ Norman Wisdom, Derek Bond, Angela Browne, Derek Francis, Noel Dyson, Peter Jones, David Lodge

Pressure Point *
US 1962 89m bw
UA/Larcas/Stanley Kramer

A black prison psychiatrist has longstanding trouble with a violent racist inmate.
Curious, quite compelling case history, told in pointless and confusing flashback; sharply made and photographed, melodramatically acted.
w Hubert Cornfield, S. Lee Pogostin *d* *Hubert Cornfield* *ph* *Ernest Haller* *m* Ernest Gold
☆ *Sidney Poitier, Bobby Darin*, Peter Falk, Carl Benton Reid

Prestige
US 1932 71m bw
RKO
A woman follows her fiancé to a Malayan prison colony where he is on the staff, and finds he has become an alcoholic.
Tediously stilted romantic melodrama which seems at least twice as long as its actual running time.
w Francis Edward Faragoh *novel* *Lips of Steel* by Harry Hervey *d* Tay Garnett *ph* Lucien Andriot *md* Arthur Lange
☆ Ann Harding, Melvyn Douglas, Adolphe Menjou, Guy Bates Post, Clarence Muse

'Attraction. Desire. Deception. Murder. No one is ever completely innocent.'
Presumed Innocent **
US 1990 127m DuArt
Warner/Mirage (Sydney Pollack, Mark Rosenberg)

A public prosecutor is accused of murdering a colleague.
Gripping courtroom drama in which very little is what it seems.
w Frank Pierson, Alan J. Pakula *novel* Scott Turow *d* *Alan J. Pakula* *ph* Gordon Willis *m* John Williams *pd* George Jenkins *ed* Evan Lottman
☆ Harrison Ford, Brian Dennehy, Raul Julia, Bonnie Bedelia, Paul Winfield, Greta Scacchi, John Spencer, Joe Grifasi, Sab Shimono, Jesse Bradford
'A demanding, disturbing javelin of a courtroom murder mystery.' – *Variety*

'The fashion world laid bare.'
Prêt-à-Porter
US 1994 133m Technicolor Panavision
Buena Vista/Miramax (Robert Altman)

aka: *Ready to Wear*
Journalists and fashion designers converge upon Paris for the week of ready-to-wear fashion shows.
About as revealing of the cut-throat world of the fashion business as the Emperor's new clothes, this wastes a great many talents on a ramshackle affair, connected neither to the fantasy nor the reality of the world it depicts; it needed a much stronger narrative structure to knit together its disparate elements.
w Robert Altman, Barbara Shulgasser *d* Robert Altman *ph* Pierre Mignot, Jean Lépine *m* Michel Legrand *pd* Stephen Altman *ed* Geraldine Peroni
☆ Anouk Aimée, Lauren Bacall, Kim Basinger, Michael Blanc, Sophia Loren, Marcello Mastroianni, Anne Canovas, Jean-Pierre Cassel, Rossy de Palma, François Cluzet, Rupert Everett, Teri Garr, Richard E. Grant, Sally Kellerman, Ute Lemper and also Linda Hunt, Lyle Lovett, Stephen Rea, Tim Robbins, Julia Roberts, Jean Rochefort, Tracey Ullman, Forest Whitaker
'A flaccid mess, missing its easy targets. It is also undiluted Altman – a movie that sums up his attitude toward actors, audiences, the press, humanity. When one hears the word contempt, one thinks of Robert Altman.' – *Richard Corliss, Time*
'A supremely slack satire on the fashion business.' – *Adam Mars-Jones, Independent*

Pretty Baby *
US 1950 92m bw
Warner (Harry Kurnitz)

A girl finds it easier to get a seat on the subway if she is carrying a (dummy) baby, but gets into complications when she meets a baby food king.

Silly but quite pleasant comedy variation on Bachelor Mother.
w Everett Freeman, Harry Kurnitz *d* Bretaigne Windust *ph* Peverell Marley *m* David Buttolph
☆ Betsy Drake, Edmund Gwenn, Dennis Morgan, Zachary Scott, William Frawley

Pretty Baby **
US 1978 109m Metrocolor
Paramount (Louis Malle)

A 12-year-old girl grows up in a New Orleans brothel in the 1910s.
A teasing exploration of adult hypocrisies as seen through the eyes of a child, beautifully composed in the manner of French paintings of the period.
w Polly Platt, Louis Malle *d* Louis Malle *ph* Sven Nykvist *md* Jerry Wexler
☆ Keith Carradine, Susan Sarandon, Brooke Shields, Francis Faye, Antonio Fargas
'The picture is too rotten to be worth much of a fuss; it's worth just enough attention to show why it's rotten.' – *Stanley Kauffmann*
Jerry Wexler

Pretty in Pink
US 1986 96m Technicolor
Paramount (Lauren Shuler-Donner)

A pretty girl from the wrong side of the tracks begins to find herself when she goes to a classy high school.
Slick but not very interesting look at the insecurities of American adolescents.
w John Hughes *d* Howard Deutch *ph* Tak Fujimoto *m* Michael Gore
☆ Molly Ringwald, Harry Dean Stanton, Jon Cryer, Andrew McCarthy, Annie Potts

Pretty Ladies
US 1925 70m (24 fps) bw silent
MGM
The husband of a Broadway actress leaves her for a chorus girl.
Heavy-going melodrama with a star who later turned comedienne and a couple of stars-to-be playing bits.
w Adela Rogers St Johns *d* Monta Bell
☆ ZaSu Pitts, Tom Moore, Norma Shearer, Lilyan Tashman, Conrad Nagel, George K. Arthur, Myrna Loy, Joan Crawford

Pretty Maids All in a Row
US 1971 95m Metrocolor
MGM (Gene Roddenberry)
High school girl students are being murdered by their guidance counsellor.
Uneasy murder comedy with few laughs, casting its star as a most unlikely villain. An interesting if unsuccessful attempt to be different.
w Gene Roddenberry *novel* Francis Pollini *d* Roger Vadim *ph* Charles Rosher *m* Lalo Schifrin
☆ Rock Hudson, Angie Dickinson, Telly Savalas, Roddy McDowall, Keenan Wynn

Pretty Poison *
US 1968 89m DeLuxe
TCF/Lawrence Turman/Mollino (Marshal Backlar, Noel Black)

A psychotic arsonist enlists the aid of a teenager but soon discovers she is kinkier than he and has murder in mind.
Bizarre black comedy-melodrama, quite successfully mixed and served.
w Lorenzo Semple Jnr *novel* *She Let Him Continue* by Stephen Geller *d* Noel Black *ph* David Quaid *m* Johnny Mandel
☆ *Anthony Perkins, Tuesday Weld,* Beverly Garland, John Randolph, Dick O'Neill, Clarice Blackburn

Pretty Polly
GB 1967 102m Techniscope
Universal/George W. George, Frank Granat
US title: *A Matter of Innocence*
On a world tour with her vulgar aunt, a timid maiden finds romance in Singapore.
Slight romantic fable decked out with travel guide backgrounds and at odds with the cynicism of the short story from which it originates.
w Keith Waterhouse, Willis Hall *story* Noël Coward *d* Guy Green *ph* Arthur Ibbetson *m* Michel Legrand
☆ Hayley Mills, Trevor Howard, Shashi Kapoor, Brenda de Banzie, Dick Patterson, Peter Bayliss, Patricia Routledge, Dorothy Alison
'It came and went this winter, leaving a slight trace of camphor and old knitting needles.' – *Wilfrid Sheed*

Pretty Village Pretty Flame ***
Serbia 1996 129m colour 'Scope
Guild Pathé/Cobra/RTV/MCRC (Goran Bjelogrlic, Dragan Bjelogrlic, Nikola Kojo, Milko Josifov)

original title: *Lepa Sela Lepo Gore*
Two friends from boyhood, one Serbian, the other Muslim, find themselves on opposite sides in a civil war.
An angry, bitter film about the madness of the conflict that overwhelmed Yugoslavia, shifting back and forth in time to illumine the lives of those caught up in the craziness.
w Vanja Bulic, Srdan Dragojevic, Nikola Pejakovic *d* Srdan Dragojevic *ph* Dusan Joksimovic *m* Aleksandar Sasa Habic *pd* Milenko Jeremic *ed* Petar Markovic
☆ Dragan Bjelogrlic, Nikola Kojo, Dragan Maksimovic, Velimir Bata Zivojlinovic, Zoran Cvijanovic, Milorad Mandic, Dragan Petrovic
'It's enough to know this one has plenty of action, a witty script, buckets of blood, a couple of sex scenes and is pretty darned good.' – *Jake Hamilton, Empire*

Pretty Woman *
US 1990 119m Technicolor
Buena Vista/Touchstone (Arnon Milchan, Steven Reuther)

A wealthy workaholic asset stripper picks up a hooker and invites her to spend a week with him.
Shameless Hollywood concoction of romance and glossy fantasy that was an immense popular success in 1990, proving that there remains an insatiable demand for escapist fairy tales.
w J. F. Lawton *d* Garry Marshall *ph* Charles Minsky *m* James Newton Howard *pd* Albert Brenner *ed* Priscilla Nedd
☆ Richard Gere, Julia Roberts, Ralph Bellamy, Jason Alexander, Laura San Giacomo, Hector Elizondo
'Despite its obvious flaws, Garry Marshall's sentimental pic hits the right emotional targets to shape up as a monster hit.' – *Variety*
Julia Roberts

'The Extraterrestrial Triangle'
Prey
GB 1977 85m Eastmancolor
Supreme/Tymar (Terence Marcel, David Wimbury)

An alien, who likes to eat the flesh of humans, takes over the body of a young man and is invited to stay the night by two lesbians, one of whom is a murderer.
Absurd mix of sexploitation and science fiction, treated with the utmost seriousness by director and cast.
w Max Cuff *story* Quinn Donoghue *d* Norman J. Warren *ph* Derek V. Brown *m* Ivor Slaney *ad* Hayden Pearce *ed* Alan Jones
☆ Glory Annen, Sally Faulkner, Barry Stokes, Sandy Chinney, Eddie Stacey
'Shabby low-budget exploitation pic with a ludicrous storyline.' – *Sight and Sound*
† The version released in the British cinemas was cut to 83m.

A Price above Rubies
US 1998 116m DeLuxe
Film4/Miramax (Lawrence Bender, John Penotti)

An Orthodox Jewish wife feels oppressed by the Brooklyn community she inhabits, and seeks freedom elsewhere.
An earnest soap opera with a feminist slant, as a woman seeks her identity in a male-dominated world.
wd Boaz Yakin *ph* Adam Holender *m* Lesley Barber *pd* Dan Leigh *ed* Arthur Coburn
☆ Renee Zellweger, Christopher Eccleston, Glenn Fitzgerald, Allen Payne, Julianna Margulies, Kathleen Chalfant, Edie Falco, John Randolph, Kim Hunter, Jackie Ryan, Shelton Dane
'It's an awful big dung-heap to wade through for those small gems.' – *Ceri Thomas, Total Film*

'For every dream there is a sacrifice.'
Price of Glory
US 2000 117m DeLuxe
Metrodome/New Line (Moctesuma Esparza, Robert Katz, Arthur E. Friedman)

A former boxer forces his three sons into the sport in the hope that they will achieve the success denied him.
Dull, plodding drama that cannot sustain interest in the sport or the family dynamics.
w Phil Berger *d* Carlos Avila *ph* Affonso Beato *m* Joseph Julian Gonzalez *pd* Robb Wilson King *ed* Gary Karr
☆ Jimmy Smits (Arturo Ortega), Jon Seda (Sonny Ortega), Clifton Collins Jnr (Jimmy Ortega), Maria del Mar (Rita Ortega), Sal Lopez (Hector Salmon), Louis Mandylor (Davey Lane), Danielle Camastra (Mariella Cruz), Ron Perlman (Nick Everson)
'Not particularly well acted, it overstays its welcome and proves simultaneously predictable as a sports film and unconvincing as family drama.' – *Lawrence Van Gelder, New York Times*

Prick up Your Ears **
GB 1987 108m Eastmancolor
Zenith/Civilhand (Andrew Brown)

The life and violent death of Joe Orton, playwright.
Raunchy homosexual saga of a writer who became a cult figure with the sophisticated; treatment full of vigour for those who can take the pace.
w Alan Bennett *biography* John Lahr *d* Stephen Frears *ph* Oliver Stapleton *m* Stanley Myers *pd* Hugo Luczyc-Wyhowski
☆ Gary Oldman, Alfred Molina, Vanessa Redgrave, Wallace Shawn, Julie Walters, James Grant

'Five charming sisters on the gayest, merriest manhunt that ever snared a bewildered bachelor! Girls! take a lesson from these husband hunters!'
Pride and Prejudice ***
US 1940 116m bw
MGM (Hunt Stromberg)

An opinionated young lady of the early 19th century wins herself a rich husband she had at first despised for his pride.
A pretty respectable version of Jane Austen's splendid romantic comedy, with a generally excellent cast; full of pleasurable moments.
w Aldous Huxley, Jane Murfin *play* Helen Jerome *novel* *Jane Austen* *d* *Robert Z. Leonard* *ph* Karl Freund *m* Herbert Stothart *ad* Cedric Gibbons, Paul Groesse
☆ *Laurence Olivier, Greer Garson, Edmund Gwenn, Mary Boland, Melville Cooper, Edna May Oliver,* Karen Morley, Frieda Inescort, Bruce Lester, Edward Ashley, Ann Rutherford, Maureen O'Sullivan, E. E. Clive, Heather Angel, Marsha Hunt
'The most deliciously pert comedy of old manners, the most crisp and crackling satire in costume that we can remember ever having seen on the screen.' – *Bosley Crowther*
'Animated and bouncing, the movie is more Dickens than Austen; once one adjusts to this, it's a happy and carefree viewing experience.' – *New Yorker, 1980*
art direction

The Pride and the Passion *
US 1957 131m Technicolor
Vistavision
UA/Stanley Kramer

In 1810 Spain a British naval officer helps Spanish guerrillas, by reactivating an old cannon, to win their fight against Napoleon.
Stolid, miscast adventure spectacle, its main interest being the deployment of the gun across country by surging throngs of peasants.
w Edna and Edward Anhalt *novel* *The Gun* by C. S. Forester *d* Stanley Kramer *ph* *Franz Planer* *m* Georges Antheil
☆ Cary Grant, Sophia Loren, Frank Sinatra, Theodore Bikel, John Wengraf, Jay Novello, Philip Van Zandt
'The whirr of the cameras often seems as loud as the thunderous cannonades. It evidently takes more than dedication, cooperative multitudes and four million dollars to shoot history in the face.' – *Time*

Pride of Kentucky: see *The Story of Seabiscuit*

The Pride of St Louis
US 1952 93m bw
TCF (Jules Schermer)

The life of baseball star Dizzy Dean, who injured himself and became a commentator.
Sporting biopic of clearly restricted interest; modestly well done.
w Herman J. Mankiewicz *d* Harmon Jones *ph* Leo Tover *m* Arthur Lange
☆ Dan Dailey, Joanne Dru, Richard Haydn, Richard Crenna, Hugh Sanders
original story (Guy Trosper)

Pride of the Bowery
US 1941 61m bw
Savoy/Monogram/Banner (Sam Katzman)

The East Side Kids go to a Civilian Conservation Corps camp, so that Muggsy can train for a boxing championship; but, in trying to help a friend, he is accused of theft.
One of the Kids' less comic and more earnest efforts, emphasizing good works rather than their usual high spirits.
w George Plympton *story* Steven Clensos, William Lively *d* Joseph H. Lewis *ph* Robert Kline *md* Lange and Porter *ed* Robert Golden
☆ Leo Gorcey, Bobby Jordan, Kenneth Howell, Mary Ainslee, Bobby Stone, Donald Haines, David Gorcey, Sunshine Sammy Morrison, Kenneth Harlan, Nick Stuart, Lloyd Ingraham

Pride of the Marines *
US 1945 120m bw
Warner (Jerry Wald)
GB title: *Forever in Love*
The story of Marine Al Schmid, blinded while fighting the Japanese.
Over-dramatic, sudsy biopic which is well enough mounted to carry quite an impact in the flagwaving Hollywood style.
w Albert Maltz *d* Delmer Daves *ph* Peverell Marley *m* Franz Waxman
☆ *John Garfield,* Eleanor Parker, Dane Clark, John Ridgely, Rosemary de Camp, Ann Doran, Warren Douglas, Tom D'Andrea
'Long drawn out and never inspired, but very respectably honest and dogged.' – *James Agee*
Albert Maltz

'The most wonderful story America ever took to its heart!'
The Pride of the Yankees *
US 1942 128m bw
Samuel Goldwyn

The story of baseball star Lou Gehrig, who died of amytropic lateral sclerosis at the height of his powers.
Standard sporting biopic ending on Gehrig's famous speech to the crowd; emotion covers the film's other deficiencies.
w Jo Swerling, Herman J. Mankiewicz *story* Paul Gallico *d* Sam Wood *ph* Rudolph Maté *m* Leigh Harline *pd* William Cameron Menzies *ed* Daniel Mandell
☆ Gary Cooper, Teresa Wright, Babe Ruth, Walter Brennan, Dan Duryea, Elsa Janssen, Ludwig Stossel, Virginia Gilmore
'A simple, tender, meticulous and explicitly narrative film ... a real saga of American life, homey, humorous, sentimental, and composed in patient detail.' – *New York Times*
† In order to show Cooper batting left-handed, the prints were reversed for these sequences. Elsewhere in the movie, he is right-handed.
Daniel Mandell
best picture; script; Paul Gallico; Rudolph Maté; Leigh Harline; Gary Cooper; Teresa Wright

'In A World Of Rituals, In A Place Of Secrets, A Man Must Choose Between Keeping The Faith And Exposing The Truth.'
'One man is about to challenge two thousand years of tradition.'

Priest **

GB 1994 109m colour
Electric/BBC/Polygram (George Faber, Josephine Ward)

A young Catholic priest goes to work in a working-class Liverpool parish where his faith and his ability to deal with problems are tested and his homosexuality is made public.
Powerful drama examining the attitudes of the Catholic hierarchy to sexuality and social ills which is didactic and sometimes lacking in logic – the young priest, priggish and disapproving of sexual activity, cruises a gay bar for a pick-up with the accustomed ease of an habitué of such places – but compelling viewing, nevertheless.
w Jimmy McGovern *d* Antonia Bird *ph* Fred Tammes *m* Andy Roberts *pd* Raymond Langhorn *ed* Susan Spivey
☆ *Linus Roache, Tom Wilkinson,* Cathy Tyson, Robert Carlyle, James Ellis, Lesley Sharp, Robert Pugh, Christine Tremarco
'Can only be really recommended to people who have never heard the phrases "piss off" and "out of my diocese" in the same sentence, and are anxious to rectify the omission.' – *Adam Mars-Jones, Independent*
'What the film delivers is naked emotion and a powerful sense of drama that often strays into melodrama. What it fails to do is make you think, since it's so intent on telling us what to think itself.' – *Derek Malcolm, Guardian*
† The US Catholic League for Religious and Civil Rights condemned the film as 'designed to stick it to the Catholic Church' and attempted to prevent its distribution. French Catholics also attempted to have it banned.

'Their extravagant romance was more tempestuous than anything he wrote!'

Priest of Love

GB 1981 125m colour
Ronceval/Milesian (Stanley J. Seeger)

The last years of D. H. Lawrence, when his books were banned and he was seeking warmer climes to help his TB.
An extremely disappointing film, seeming to consist of aimless travelling by fractious people who never have anything interesting to say. Stilted in all departments.
w Alan Plater *d* Christopher Miles *ph* Ted Moore *m* Joseph James
☆ *Ian McKellen,* Janet Suzman, Helen Mirren, Penelope Keith, Jorge Rivero, John Gielgud
'Miles has assigned himself a missionary role but he is just not up to the task.' – *Jill Forbes, MFB*

The Priest's Wife (dubbed)

Italy/France 1970 106m Technicolor
Warner/Champion/ECF (Carlo Ponti)
original title: *La Moglie del Prete*
A pop singer seduces a priest who attempts to save her from suicide.
Dreary treatment of the topical theme of celibacy.
w Ruggero Maccari, Bernardino Zapponi *d* Dino Risi *ph* Alfio Contini *m* Armando Trovaioli *ad* Gianni Polidori *ed* Alberto Gallitti
☆ Sophia Loren, Marcello Mastroianni, Venantino Venantini, Jacques Stany, Pippo Starnazza
'Vulgar, fence-sitting charade.' – *John Gillett, MFB*
† The film was cut to 103m on its British release.

Prima della Rivoluzione: see *Before the Revolution*

'Sooner or later a man who wears two faces forgets which one is real.'

Primal Fear

US 1996 129m DeLuxe
UIP/Paramount/Rysher (Gary Lucchesi)

A slick lawyer defends a shy choirboy accused of murdering an archbishop.
An implausible thriller with a twist at its end, but one that diminishes all that has gone before, so that an audience is more likely to feel cheated than surprised.
w Steve Shagan, Ann Biderman *novel* William Diehl *d* Gregory Hoblit *ph* Michael Chapman *m* James Newton Howard *pd* Jeannine Oppewall *ed* David Rosenbloom
☆ Richard Gere, Laura Linney, John Mahoney, Alfre Woodard, Frances McDormand, Edward Norton, Terry O'Quinn, Andre Braugher
'This frail thriller has a clean, unfussed-over look – which is about all one can say for it.' – *Peter Matthews, Sight and Sound*
Edward Norton

'What Went Down On The Way To The Top.'

Primary Colors **

US 1998 143m DeLuxe 'Scope
Universal/Mutual/Icarus (Mike Nichols)

A manipulative and womanizing governor from a Southern state, aided by his tough-talking wife, runs for the job of President of the United States.
A tart, knowing account of American politics, based on a bestselling novel that was itself based on Bill Clinton's first presidential campaign; it both entertains and, in its exposure of the backstage mechanics of massaging public opinion, appals.
w Elaine May *novel* Anonymous (Joe Klein) *d* Mike Nichols *ph* Michael Ballhaus *m* Ry Cooder *pd* Bo Welch *ed* Arthur Schmidt
☆ John Travolta, Emma Thompson, Billy Bob Thornton, Adrian Lester, Maura Tierney, Paul Guilfoyle, Larry Hagman, Kathy Bates, Diane Ladd, Caroline Aaron, Mykelti Williamson
'Frequently funny, wonderfully performed, eerily evocative of recent history and gratifyingly blunt in its assessment of what it takes to get to the top in modern American politics, pic also lacks something crucial at its center that prevents it from being an entirely credible portrait of its subject.' – *Todd McCarthy, Variety*
Kathy Bates; Elaine May
Elaine May

Prime Cut

US 1972 91m Technicolor Panavision
Cinema Center (Joe Wizan)

A Kansas gangster incurs the wrath of his Chicago bosses, and a hired killer is sent to eliminate him.
Gory cat-and-mouse chase melodrama with no interest save its excesses.
w Robert Dillon *d* Michael Ritchie *ph* Gene Polito *m* Lalo Schifrin
☆ Gene Hackman, Lee Marvin, Angel Tompkins, Sissy Spacek

The Prime Minister *

GB 1941 109m bw
Warner (Max Milder)
Episodes in the life of Disraeli.
Modestly budgeted historical pageant notable only for performances.
w Brock Williams, Michael Hogan *d* Thorold Dickinson *ph* Basil Emmott
☆ *John Gielgud,* Diana Wynyard, Will Fyffe, Stephen Murray, Owen Nares, Fay Compton (Queen Victoria), Lyn Harding, Leslie Perrins

The Prime of Miss Jean Brodie *

GB 1969 116m DeLuxe
TCF (Robert Fryer)

A sharp-minded Edinburgh schoolmistress of the thirties is a bad influence on her more easily-swayed pupils.
Interesting but slackly handled and maddeningly played character drama.
w Jay Presson Allen *novel* Muriel Spark *d* Ronald Neame *ph* Ted Moore *m/ly* Rod McKuen *pd* John Howell
☆ Maggie Smith, Robert Stephens, Pamela Franklin, Celia Johnson, Gordon Jackson, Jane Carr
'The novel lost a good deal in its stage simplification, and loses still more in its movie reduction of that stage version.' – *John Simon*
Maggie Smith
song 'Jean' (*m/ly* Rod McKuen)
Maggie Smith; Celia Johnson

The Primrose Path

US 1940 92m bw
RKO (Gregory La Cava)

The youngest of a family of shanty-town prostitutes falls in love with an honest hamburger stand proprietor.
Downright peculiar melodrama for its day and age, and not very entertaining either, spending most of its time being evasive.
w Allan Scott, Gregory La Cava *play* Robert Buckner, Walter Hart *novel* *February Hill* by *Victoria Lincoln* *d* Gregory La Cava *ph* Joseph H. August *m* Werner Heymann
☆ Ginger Rogers, Joel McCrea, Marjorie Rambeau, Henry Travers, Miles Mander, Queenie Vassar, Joan Carroll
'The story isn't good enough, the direction isn't sincere enough, to give any pain to the lumps in the throat which its designers obviously had in mind.' – *Richard Mallett, Punch*
Marjorie Rambeau

'In One Thrill-Packed Night You'll Live The Adventures Of A Lifetime!'

The Prince and the Pauper *

US 1937 118m bw
Warner (Robert Lord)

In Tudor London, young Edward VI changes places with a street urchin who happens to be his double.
Well-produced version of a famous story; it never quite seems to hit the right style or pace, but is satisfying in patches.
w Laird Doyle *novel* Mark Twain *d* William Keighley *ph* Sol Polito *m* *Erich Wolfgang Korngold*
☆ Errol Flynn (Miles Hendon), Claude Rains (Earl of Hertford), Billy Mauch (Tom Canty), Bobby Mauch (Prince Edward), Henry Stephenson (Duke of Norfolk), Barton MacLane (John Canty), Alan Hale (Captain of the Guard), Eric Portman (1st Lord), Montagu Love (Henry VIII), Lionel Pape, Halliwell Hobbes, Fritz Leiber
'Lavish but not convincing. Doubtful box office: the commercial aspect seems wholly concerned in the timeliness of a Coronation sequence and the name of Errol Flynn. It is not enough.' – *Variety*

The Prince and the Pauper *

Panama 1977 121m Technicolor Panavision
International Film Production/Ilya and Alexander Salkind (Pierre Spengler)

US title: *Crossed Swords*
Young Edward VI changes place with a beggar, who helps to expose a traitor.
Moderately well-made swashbuckler with an old-fashioned air, not really helped by stars in cameo roles or by the poor playing of the title roles.
w George MacDonald Fraser *novel* Mark Twain *d* Richard Fleischer *ph* Jack Cardiff *m* Maurice Jarre *pd* Anthony Pratt *ad* Tony Pratt *ed* Ernest Walter
☆ Mark Lester, Oliver Reed, Raquel Welch, Ernest Borgnine, George C. Scott, Rex Harrison, David Hemmings, Charlton Heston (Henry VIII), Harry Andrews, Murray Melvin, Julian Orchard

The Prince and the Showgirl *

GB 1957 117m Technicolor
Warner/Marilyn Monroe Productions (Laurence Olivier)

In London for the 1911 coronation, a Ruritanian prince picks up a chorus girl and they come to understand and respect each other.
Heavy-going comedy, rich in production values but weak in dramatic style and impact.
w Terence Rattigan *play* *The Sleeping Prince* by Terence Rattigan *d* Laurence Olivier *ph* Jack Cardiff *m* Richard Addinsell *pd* Roger Furse *ad* Carmen Dillon
☆ Laurence Olivier, Marilyn Monroe, Sybil Thorndike, Richard Wattis, Jeremy Spenser, Esmond Knight, Rosamund Greenwood, Maxine Audley
† Colin Clark's book *The Prince, the Showgirl and Me* is an entertaining account of the behind-the-screen story of the making of the film, as seen from the viewpoint of its 3rd assistant director.

Prince of Darkness

US 1987 101m colour
Guild/Alive (Larry Franco)

Scientists are called in by a priest to deal with a canister containing the spirit of Satan.
Risible horror that never arouses any interest.
w Martin Quatermass (John Carpenter) *d* John Carpenter *ph* Gary B. Kibbe *m* John Carpenter, Alan Howarth *pd* Daniel Lomino *ed* Steve Mirkovich
☆ Donald Pleasence, Victor Wong, Lisa Blount, Dennis Dun, Jameson Parker, Susan Blanchard, Anne Howard, Ann Yen, Ken Wright

'The Power Is Real. The Story Is Forever. The Time Is Now.'

The Prince of Egypt **

US 1998 97m colour
DreamWorks (Penney Finkelman Cox, Sandra Rabins)

In Ancient Egypt, the baby Moses escapes death, is adopted by the Queen, and grows up to lead the Israelites from slavery.
An animated feature that mistakenly apes the epic spectacle of a Cecil B. de Mille – while a real cast of thousands or vast sets may appeal, the effect is diminished when drawn, since anything is possible with pencil and paper. For a rival to Disney, it sticks very close to that studio's prevailing style of pop musicals.
w Philip LaZebnik *d* Brenda Chapman, Steve Hickner, Simon Wells *m* Hans Zimmer *m/ly* Stephen Schwartz *pd* Darek Gogol *ed* Nick Fletcher
☆ Featuring the voices of: Val Kilmer, Ralph Fiennes, Michelle Pfeiffer, Sandra Bullock, Jeff Goldblum, Danny Glover, Patrick Stewart, Helen Mirren, Steve Martin, Martin Short
'Epic storytelling on the grandest scale. Big imagery, big themes, big emotions – all met head-on and accomplished triumphantly within a film that is in essence a live action movie – more precisely, a Steven Spielberg live action movie – writ cartoon.' – *Ian Freer, Empire*
song 'When You Believe' (*m/ly* Stephen Schwartz)
Stephen Schwartz, Hans Zimmer

'A saga of scoundrels in a century of infamy!'

Prince of Foxes *

US 1949 107m bw
TCF (Sol. C. Siegel)
A wandering adventurer in medieval Italy gets mixed up with the Borgias.
Good-looking historical fiction with a slight edge to it.
w Milton Krims *novel* Samuel Shellabarger *d* Henry King *ph* Leon Shamroy *m* Alfred Newman
☆ Tyrone Power, Orson Welles, Wanda Hendrix, Felix Aylmer, Everett Sloane, Katina Paxinou, Marina Berti
'Plot, counterplot, action and vengeance.' – MFB
'This pretentious chapter of pseudo-history never rises above the merely spectacular, hovers mostly around the conventionally banal, and descends once to the unpardonably crude.' – *Richard Mallett, Punch*
Leon Shamroy

Prince of Jutland

Denmark/France/Germany/Netherlands/GB 1994 107m colour
Allarts/Ariane/Woodline/Eurimages/Roses/Kenneth Madsen

A prince avenges the death of his father.
Given the talents involved, a disappointing version of the story of Hamlet, based on the original legend from The Exploits of the Danes, *written early in the 13th century by the secretary to the Archbishop of Lund.*
w Gabriel Axel, Erik Kjersgard *book* Saxo Grammaticus *d* Gabriel Axel *ph* Henning Kristiansen *m* Per Norgaard *pd* Sven Wichmann *ed* Jean-François Naudon
☆ Gabriel Byrne, Helen Mirren, Christian Bale, Tony Haygarth, Steven Waddington, Freddie Jones, Brian Cox, Kate Beckinsale
'Looks like a made-for-TV film, meandering from the mildly diverting to the mundane.' – *Sight and Sound*

The Prince of Pennsylvania *

US 1988 93m Technicolor
Palace/New Line Cinema (Joan Fishman)

A rebellious teenager has problems with his father.
Sensitive, downbeat tale of a boy's alienation from his family that avoids easy conclusions.
wd Ron Nyswaner *ph* Frank Prinzi *m* Thomas Newman *pd* Tony Corbett *ed* William Scharf
☆ Fred Ward, Keanu Reeves, Bonnie Bedelia, Amy Madigan, Jeff Hayenga, Tracey Ellis, Joseph de Lisi, Jay O. Sanders, Kari Keegan

Prince of Pirates
US 1953 80m Technicolor
Columbia (Sam Katzman)
A young prince of the Netherlands turns pirate when his brother allies with the Spanish invader.
Fast-moving costume potboiler with lavish use of action scenes from Joan of Arc.
w John O'Dea, Samuel Newman *d* Sidney Salkow *ph* Henry Freulich *md* Mischa Bakaleinikoff
☆ John Derek, Barbara Rush, Carla Balenda, Whitfield Connor, Edgar Barrier

Prince of Players *
US 1955 102m DeLuxe Cinemascope
TCF (Philip Dunne)
Episodes in the life of actor Edwin Booth, brother of the man who killed Abraham Lincoln.
Earnest but ham-fisted biopic more notable, as a Hollywood entertainment, for its dollops of straight Shakespeare than for any dramatic interest.
w Moss Hart *book* Eleanor Ruggles *d* Philip Dunne *ph* Charles G. Clarke *m* Bernard Herrmann
☆ Richard Burton, Eva Le Gallienne, Maggie McNamara, John Derek, Raymond Massey, Charles Bickford, Elizabeth Sellars, Ian Keith

Prince of Shadows: see *Beltenebros*

Prince of the City *
US 1981 167m Technicolor
Warner/Orion (Jay Presson Allen)
A New York policeman on the drug beat is induced to inform on his corrupt colleagues.
Punishingly long police semi-documentary based on real events and apparently filmed with a political motive. Excellent acting and production detail do not prevent the enterprise from seeming like a half-speed version of Serpico.
w Jay Presson Allen, Sidney Lumet *book* Robert Daley *d* Sidney Lumet
☆ *Treat Williams*, Jerry Orbach, Don Billett, Richard Foronjy, Carmine Caridi, Kenny Marino
screenplay

Prince of Thieves
US 1948 72m bw
Sam Katzman/Columbia
Robin Hood saves a nobleman's intended from Baron Tristram.
Tatty second-feature version of a legendary figure.
w Maurice Tombragel *d* Howard Bretherton
☆ Jon Hall, Patricia Morison, Alan Mowbray, Michael Duane, Adele Jergens

'A story about the memories that haunt us, and the truth that sets us free.'
The Prince of Tides **
US 1991 132m Technicolor
Columbia/Barwood/Longfellow (Barbra Streisand, Andrew Karsch)
A married psychiatrist falls in love with the unhappy brother of her catatonic patient.
Excellent performances enliven a lushly romantic melodrama.
w Pat Conroy, Becky Johnston *novel* Pat Conroy *d* Barbra Streisand *ph* Stephen Goldblatt *m* James Newton Howard *pd* Paul Sylbert *ed* Don Zimmerman
☆ Barbra Streisand, *Nick Nolte*, *Blythe Danner*, *Kate Nelligan*, Jeroen Krabbé, Melinda Dillon, George Carlin, Jason Gould, Brad Sullivan
'Has a passion seldom found in contempo US films and a quality not usually associated with Barbra Streisand – self-effacement.' – *Variety*
'This phoney overblown movie ... is the king of soaps.' – *Philip French, Observer*
film; Nick Nolte; Kate Nelligan; Pat Conroy, Becky Johnston; Stephen Goldblatt; James Newton Howard; Paul Sylbert

Prince Valiant *
US 1954 100m Technicolor Cinemascope
TCF (Robert L. Jacks)
The son of the exiled king of Scandia seeks King Arthur's help against the usurper, and becomes involved in a court plot.
Agreeable historical nonsense for teenagers, admittedly and sometimes hilariously from a comic strip.
w Dudley Nichols *comic strip* Hal Foster *d* Henry Hathaway *ph* Lucien Ballard *m* Franz Waxman
☆ Robert Wagner, James Mason, Debra Paget, Janet Leigh, Sterling Hayden, Victor McLaglen, Donald Crisp, Brian Aherne, Barry Jones, Primo Carnera

Prince Valiant
US/GB/Ireland/Germany 1997 91m colour Super 35
Entertainment/Paramount/Constantin/Lakeshore/Legacy (Carsten Lorenz)
The adventures of Prince Valiant, Sir Gawain's royal squire, against the Vikings in the time of King Arthur.
A lively, old-fashioned medieval romp, in appropriate comic-book style, but one that may not have much appeal these days.
w Michael Frost Beckner, Anthony Hickox, Carsten Laurenz *comic strip* Harold R. Foster *d* Anthony Hickox *ph* Roger Lanser *m* David Bergeaud *pd* Crispian Sallis *ed* Martin Hunter
☆ Stephen Moyer, Katherine Heigl, Thomas Kretschmann, Edward Fox, Udo Kier, Warwick Davis, Gavan O'Herlihy, Ben Pullen, Walter Gotell, Zach Galligan, Chesney Hawkes, Joanna Lumley, Ron Perlman, Anthony Hickox

The Prince Who Was a Thief
US 1951 88m Technicolor
U-I (Leonard Goldstein)
An Arabian Nights prince is lost as a baby and brought up by thieves, but finally fights back to his rightful throne.
Given the synopsis, any viewer can write the script himself. Standard eastern Western romp.
w Gerald Drayson Adams, Aeneas Mackenzie *story* Theodore Dreiser *d* Rudolph Maté *ph* Irving Glassberg *m* Hans Salter
☆ Tony Curtis, Piper Laurie, Everett Sloane, Jeff Corey

The Princess *
Hungary 1982 113m bw
Cinegate/Tarsulas Studio/Mafilm (Pal Erdoss)
original title: *Adj Király Katonát!*
A 15-year-old girl moves to Budapest to discover that life is tougher than she expected.
Downbeat, documentary-style examination of a teenager facing a succession of disappointments; the film, though, manages to suggest that there is hope for the future.
w Istvan Kardos *d* Pál Erdöss *ph* Ferenc Pap, Lajos Koltai, Gabor Szabo *pd* Andras Gyurki *ed* Klara Majoros
☆ Erika Ozda, Andrea Szendrei, Denes Diczhazi, Arpad Toth, Juli Nyako, Lajos Soltis

The Princess and the Goblin
GB/Hungary 1992 111m colour
Entertainment/Siriol/Pannonia/SC4/NHK Enterprises (Robin Lyons)
A miner's son saves a princess from being kidnapped by goblins.
Uninteresting animated feature, with a dull fairy-tale plot dully executed.
w Robin Lyons *novel* George MacDonald *d* József Gémes *ph* Arpad Lessecry, Gyergy Verga, Ede Pagner, Nick Smith, Pete Turner, Steve Turner, Andreas Klawsz *m* István Lerch *ed* Magda Hap
☆ Featuring the voices of: Joss Ackland, Claire Bloom, Roy Kinnear, Sally Ann Marsh, Rik Mayall, Peggy Mount, Peter Murray, Victor Spinetti, Mollie Sugden
'A potentially charming medieval cartoon let down by so-so technique and unimaginative plotting.' – *Variety*

The Princess and the Pirate *
US 1944 94m Technicolor
Samuel Goldwyn (Don Hartman)
An impostor is on the run from a vicious pirate.
Typical star costume extravaganza with fewer laughs than you'd expect.
w Don Hartman, Melville Shavelson, Everett Freeman *d* David Butler *ph* William Snyder, Victor Milner *m* David Rose *ad* Ernst Fegte
☆ Bob Hope, Virginia Mayo, Victor McLaglen, Walter Slezak, Walter Brennan, Marc Lawrence, Hugo Haas, Maude Eburne
'From start to finish, Hope dominates the action with well-timed colloquial nifties.' – *Variety*
David Rose; Ernst Fegte

The Princess and the Warrior: see *Der Krieger und die Kaiserin*

The Princess Bride *
US 1987 98m DeLuxe
Act III (Andrew Scheinmann, Rob Reiner)
Grandfather tells a fairy tale of good and evil.
Rather strained fantasy with occasional bright moments.
w William Goldman *novel* William Goldman *d* Rob Reiner *ph* Adrian Biddle *m* Mark Knopfler *pd* Norman Garwood
☆ Cary Elwes, Mandy Patinkin, Chris Sarandon, Christopher Guest, Peter Falk, Wallace Shawn
song 'Storybook Love'

'She was everything they dreamed of ... And nothing they expected.'
Princess Caraboo *
US 1994 97m colour
Entertainment/Beacon/TriStar/J&M/Longfellow/Artisan (Andy Karsch, Simon Bosanquet)
In the early 18th century, a woman found wandering in Devon claims to be a Javanese princess who has escaped from pirates and is taken up by the aristocracy.
A moderately entertaining comedy of identity that has its basis in fact and is blessed with a better cast than it deserves, even if their performances are well below their best.
w Michael Austin, John Wells *d* Michael Austin *ph* Freddie Francis *m* Richard Hartley *pd* Michael Howells *ed* George Akers
☆ Phoebe Cates, Jim Broadbent, Wendy Hughes, Kevin Kline, John Lithgow, Stephen Rea, Peter Eyre, Roger Lloyd Pack, John Sessions, John Lynch
'Delve deeper into this period meringue and the whole concoction deflates into fluffy nothingness.' – *Colin Brown, Screen International*

Princess Charming
GB 1934 78m bw
Gainsborough
A Ruritanian revolution forces a princess to escape in disguise.
Light operetta with an intriguing cast.
w L. DuGarde Peach, Arthur Wimperis, Lauri Wylie *play* *Alexandra* by F. Martos *d* Maurice Elvey *ph* Max Greene *songs* Ray Noble, Max Kester
☆ Evelyn Laye, Yvonne Arnaud, George Grossmith, Max Miller, Henry Wilcoxon, Ivor Barnard, Francis L. Sullivan
'Still just below the peak of excellence for which Hollywood is noted.' – *Variety*

The Princess Comes Across *
US 1936 76m bw
Paramount (Arthur Hornblow Jnr)
A starstruck Brooklyn girl makes a transatlantic liner voyage disguised as a princess, and finds herself involved in a murder mystery.
Zany comedy thriller with plenty of jokes.
w Walter de Leon, Francis Martin, Frank Butler, Don Hartman, Philip MacDonald *novel* Louis Lucien Rogger *d* William K. Howard *ph* Ted Tetzlaff *m* Phil Boutelje
☆ *Carole Lombard*, Fred MacMurray, Alison Skipworth, Douglass Dumbrille, William Frawley, Porter Hall, George Barbier, Lumsden Hare, Sig Rumann, Mischa Auer, Tetsu Komai

'She rocks. She rules. She reigns.'
The Princess Diaries
US 2001 114m Technicolor
Buena Vista/Walt Disney/Brownhouse (Whitney Houston, Debra Martin Chase, Mario Iscovich)
Told that she is in reality princess of a tiny European country, an American teenager has a royal makeover by her grandmother.
Ghastly comedy, so vapid and ridiculous that it is hard to believe that it was ever made, or released.
w Gina Wendkos *novel* Meg Cabot *d* Garry Marshall *ph* Karl Walter Lindenlaub *m* John Debney *pd* Mayne Berke *ed* Bruce Green
☆ Julie Andrews (Queen Clarisse Renaldi), Anne Hathaway (Mia Thermopolis), Hector Elizondo (Joe), Heather Matarazzo (Lilly Moscovitz), Mandy Moore (Lana Thomas), Caroline Goodall (Helen), Robert Schwartzman (Michael Moscovitz), Erik Von Detten (Josh Bryant)
'What a very silly film! Even technically it is deficient.' – *Derek Malcolm, Guardian*
'Has all the political sophistication of a Barbie doll.' – *Christopher Tookey, Daily Mail*

Princess of the Nile
US 1954 71m Technicolor
TCF
An Egyptian princess of the middle ages leads her country against the invasion of a bedouin prince.
Lethargic costume piece with hopelessly miscast actors.
w Gerald Drayson Adams *d* Harmon Jones *ph* Lloyd Ahern *m* Lionel Newman
☆ Debra Paget, Michael Rennie, Jeffrey Hunter, Dona Drake, Edgar Barrier, Jack Elam, Lee Van Cleef

Princess O'Hara
US 1935 79m bw
Universal
In her father's memory a girl steals the racehorse he loved.
Sentimental comedy from Damon Runyon, later remade for Abbott and Costello as It Ain't Hay. *Not up to much in either version.*
w Doris Malloy, Harry Clork *d* David Burton
☆ Jean Parker, Chester Morris, Leon Errol, Vince Barnett, Henry Armetta, Ralph Remley, Clara Blandick
'Poor construction limits this one's chances ... not likely to go above average grosses.' – *Variety*

Princess O'Rourke
US 1943 94m bw
Warner (Hal B. Wallis)
An ace pilot falls for a princess and causes diplomatic complications.
Very thin wartime comedy with a propaganda ending involving Franklin Roosevelt.
wd Norman Krasna *ph* Ernest Haller *m* Frederick Hollander
☆ Olivia de Havilland, Robert Cummings, Charles Coburn, Jack Carson, Jane Wyman, Harry Davenport, Gladys Cooper, Minor Watson, Curt Bois
Norman Krasna (as writer)

Princesse de l'Erotisme: see *Virgin among the Living Dead*

Il Principe Di Homburg *
Italy 1996 85m Eastmancolor
Filmalbatross/Istituto Luce (Pier Giorgio Bellocchio)
aka: *The Prince of Homburg*
A headstrong cavalry commander is condemned to death for disobeying orders.
Intriguing psychological drama, somewhat underpowered in this version; its theme—that discipline and obedience matter more than individual liberty—lacks popular appeal.
wd Marco Bellocchio *play* Heinrich von Kleist *ph* Giuseppe Lanci *m* Carlo Crivelli *md* Rinaldo Muratori *pd* Giantito Burchiellaro *ed* Francesca Calvelli
☆ Andrea Di Stefano, Barbara Bobulova, Toni Bertorelli, Anita Laurenzi, Fabio Camilli, Gianluigi Fogacci, Italo Dall'Orto, Bruno Corazzari

La Prise de Pouvoir par Louis XIV: see *The Rise of Louis XIV*

Prison: see *The Devil's Wanton*

Prison
US 1988 103m colour
Entertainment/Empire (Irwin Yablans)
The spirit of a long-dead prisoner returns for revenge against the prison's new governor.
Energetic horror movie, re-animating all the clichés of prison dramas.
w C. Courtney Joyner *story* Irwin Yablans *d* Renny Harlin *ph* Michael Ballhaus *m* Richard Band, Christopher Stone *pd* Phillip Duffin *ed* Ray Lovejoy
☆ Viggo Mortensen, Chelsea Field, Lane Smith, Lincoln Kilpatrick, Tom Everett, Ivan Kane

Prison Farm
US 1938 69m bw
Paramount
A girl denounces her boyfriend when he is wanted for robbery and murder.
Good example of this studio's tour of criminals and penal institutions.
w Eddie Welch, Robert Yost, Stuart Anthony d Louis King ph Harry Fishbeck md Boris Morros ed Edward Dmytryk
☆ Lloyd Nolan, Shirley Ross, John Howard, J. Carrol Naish, Porter Hall, Anna Q. Nilsson, Esther Dale, May Boley
'First-rate entertainment despite lightweight star names.' – *Variety*

Prison without Bars
GB 1938 80m bw
Columbia/London Films (Arnold Pressburger)
The newest inmate of a reform school for girls vies with the superintendent for the love of the doctor.
Basically paperback trash, this film of a notorious original was shot in three languages, but the English version at least omitted the lesbianism, except by implication. Cinematically it was without style.
w Hans Wilhelm, Margaret Kennedy, Arthur Wimperis play *Prison sans Barreau* by Gina Kaus, E. and O. Eis, Hilde Koveloff d Brian Desmond Hurst ph Georges Périnal m John Greenwood ad Vincent Korda ed Charles Crichton
☆ Edna Best, Corinne Luchaire, Barry K. Barnes, Mary Morris, Lorraine Clewes, Martita Hunt, Glynis Johns

The Prisoner *
GB 1955 91m bw
(Columbia) Facet/London Independent Producers (Vivian A. Cox)
In a European totalitarian state, a Cardinal is tortured and brainwashed.
Virtually a two-character talkpiece from an offbeat play which should have stayed in the theatre.
w Bridget Boland play Bridget Boland d Peter Glenville ph Reg Wyer m Benjamin Frankel
☆ Alec Guinness, Jack Hawkins, Wilfrid Lawson, Kenneth Griffith, Ronald Lewis, Raymond Huntley

'An undercover cop. An investigation. A mistake ... he's dead meat.'
The Prisoner (dubbed) *
Hong Kong 1991 91m colour
Golden Harvest/Blaine & Blake (Jimmy Wang Yu)
An episodic film set in a tough prison ruled by thuggish warders, where an undercover cop is sent to discover the assassin of his elderly mentor, a prisoner keeps escaping to see his young son, and a gangster arrives to murder the man who accidentally killed his brother.
Interlocking plots give this downbeat martial arts movie a greater narrative appeal than most of its kind, though its morality is hardly endearing and Jackie Chan fans may be disappointed that he plays only a minor role, despite his star billing.
w Fu Li, Yeh Yuen Chin d Chu Yen Ping m Fu Lap ad Cheung Sau Ping ed Chow Tak Yeung
☆ Jackie Chan, Andy Lau, Samo Hung, Tony Leung, Jimmy Wang Yu, Ko Chuen Hsiung, Tao Chung Hwa
'Surprisingly good entertainment.' – *Impact*
'Unsurprising but enjoyable chop-sockey fodder.' – *Sight and Sound*

Prisoner of Rio
Brazil 1988 105m colour
Palace/Doisirmaos Producioes (Klaus Pagh, Michael Lunderskoff)
A British policeman goes to Brazil to bring back to justice one of the Great Train Robbers.
Special pleading on behalf of Ronald Biggs, one of the thieves involved in the robbery in 1963, which even he may find embarrassing to watch.
w Lech Majewski, Ronald Biggs, Julia Frankel d Lech Majewski ph George Mooradian m Luis Bonfa, Hans Zimmer, Luciano Perrone ad Oscar Ramos ed Darren Kloomok
☆ Steven Berkoff, Paul Freeman, Peter Firth, Florinda Bolkan, Jose Wilker, Zeze Mota, Desmond Llewelyn, Breno Mello

'And you think you've got problems?'
The Prisoner of Second Avenue *
US 1975 98m Technicolor Panavision
Warner (Melvin Frank)
A New York clerk and his wife are driven to distraction by the problems of urban living.
Gloomier-than-usual (from this author) collection of one-liners which almost turns into a psychopathic melodrama and causes its amiable leading players to overact horrendously.
w Neil Simon play Neil Simon d Melvin Frank ph Philip Lathrop m Marvin Hamlisch
☆ Jack Lemmon, Anne Bancroft, Gene Saks, Elizabeth Wilson

The Prisoner of Shark Island **
US 1936 95m bw
TCF (Darryl F. Zanuck)
The story of the doctor who treated the assassin of President Lincoln.
Well-mounted historical semi-fiction with excellent detail.
w Nunnally Johnson d John Ford ph Bert Glennon md Louis Silvers
☆ *Warner Baxter*, Gloria Stuart, Joyce Kay, Claude Gillingwater, Douglas Wood, Harry Carey, Paul Fix, John Carradine
'Strong film fare for men; will have to be sold for femme appeal.' – *Variety*
'A powerful film, rarely false or slow, maintaining the relentless cumulative pressure, the logical falling of one thing into another, until the audience is included in the movement and carried along with it in some definite emotional life that is peculiar to the art of motion pictures at its best.' – *Otis Ferguson*

Prisoner of the Cannibal God: see *La Montagna del Dio Cannibale*

Prisoner of the Mountains **
Russia/Kazakhstan 1996 99m colour
Metro/Tartan/Karavan/BG (Boris Giller, Sergei Bodrov)
original title: *Kavkazskii Plennik*
In the Caucasus, two Russian soldiers escape from their Muslim captors, who want to exchange them for a prisoner held by the Russians.
An engaging and tragic account of growing respect and affection across ethnic divides by people trapped in a conflict they simply wish to survive.
w Arif Aliev, Sergei Bodrov, Boris Giller d Sergei Bodrov m Leonid Desiatnikov pd Valerii Kostrin ed Olga Grinshpun, Vera Kruglova, Alan Baril
☆ Oleg Men'shikov, Sergei Bodrov Jnr, Susanna Mekhralieva, Dzhemal Sikharulidze, Alesandr Bureev, Valentina Fedotova, Aleksei Zharkov
'A powerful war story, with confused loyalties and moral codes at its centre.' – *Film Review*
🏆 foreign language film

Prisoner of the Volga
Italy/France 1959 102m Eastmancolor
Fidès/Transmonde/Rialto (Arnaldo Genoino)
original title: *I Battellieri del Volga*
aka: *The Boatmen*
A cavalry officer discovers that his newly married wife is pregnant as the result of having been raped by his commanding officer.
Revenge melodrama of an unremarkable kind.
w Mario Damiani, Arnaldo Genoino screenplay Salka Viertel, Al Lyx d Viktor Tourjansky, Arnaldo Genoino ph Mario Montuori m Norbert Glanzberg ed Roberto Cinquini
☆ John Derek, Elsa Martinelli, Dawn Adams, Gert Frobe, Charles Vanel, Ingmar Zeisberg, Rik Battaglia, Feodor Chaliapin Jnr

Prisoner of War
US 1954 81m bw
MGM (Henry Berman)
Life in a communist prison camp in Korea.
Sensational propaganda, reduced to comic strip level.
w Allen Rivkin d Andrew Marton ph Robert Planck m Jeff Alexander
☆ Ronald Reagan, Steve Forrest, Dewey Martin, Oscar Homolka, Robert Horton, Paul Stewart, Henry Morgan, Stephen Bekassy
'It presents its catalogue of horrors in a manner unworthy of the cause it attempts to uphold.' – *John Gillett*

'The Immortal Lovers All The World Loves!'
The Prisoner of Zenda ****
US 1937 101m bw
David O. Selznick
An Englishman on holiday in Ruritania finds himself helping to defeat a rebel plot by impersonating the kidnapped king at his coronation.
A splendid schoolboy adventure story is perfectly transferred to the screen in this exhilarating swashbuckler, one of the most entertaining films to come out of Hollywood.
w John Balderston, Wells Root, Donald Ogden Stewart novel Anthony Hope d John Cromwell ph James Wong Howe m Alfred Newman ad Lyle Wheeler
☆ *Ronald Colman, Douglas Fairbanks Jnr*, Madeleine Carroll, David Niven, Raymond Massey, Mary Astor, C. *Aubrey Smith*, Byron Foulger, Montagu Love
'The most pleasing film that has come along in ages.' – *New York Times*
'One of those rare movies that seem, by some magic trick, to become more fascinating and beguiling with each passing year.' – *John Cutts, 1971*
† Previously filmed in 1913 and 1922.
🏆 Alfred Newman; Lyle Wheeler

The Prisoner of Zenda *
US 1952 100m Technicolor
MGM (Pandro S. Berman)
A costly scene-for-scene remake which only goes to show that care and discretion are no match for the happy inspiration of the original.
w John Balderston, Noel Langley, Donald Ogden Stewart d Richard Thorpe ph Joseph Ruttenberg m *Alfred Newman*
☆ Stewart Granger, James Mason, Deborah Kerr, Robert Coote, Robert Douglas, Jane Greer, Louis Calhern, Francis Pierlot, Lewis Stone
† Donald Ogden Stewart, blacklisted during the 50s, had his name restored to the writing credits in 1999.

The Prisoner of Zenda
US 1979 108m Technicolor
Universal (Walter Mirisch)
Palpably uneasy version of the above which teeters between comedy and straight romance, with barely a moment of real zest creeping in. The star is way off form in both roles.
w Dick Clement, Ian La Frenais d Richard Quine ph Arthur Ibbetson m Henry Mancini pd John J. Lloyd
☆ Peter Sellers, Lynne Frederick, Lionel Jeffries, Elke Sommer, Gregory Sierra, Stuart Wilson, Jeremy Kemp, Catherine Schell, Simon Williams, Norman Rossington, John Laurie
'Flatly directed, leadenly unfunny.' – *Paul Taylor, MFB*

Prisoners of the Casbah
US 1953 78m Technicolor
Columbia (Sam Katzman)
An Eastern princess and her lover take refuge from the evil Grand Vizier in the Casbah, a haven for outcasts.
Inept sword and sandal actioner; you can almost smell the Turkish delight.
w DeVallon Scott d Richard Bare ph Henry Freulich md Mischa Bakaleinikoff
☆ Gloria Grahame, Cesar Romero, Turhan Bey, Nestor Paiva

'All women take to men who have the appearance of wickedness!'
The Private Affairs of Bel Ami *
US 1946 119m bw
UA/David L. Loew (Ray Heinz)
In 1890s Paris, a career journalist climbs to fame over the ruined lives of his friends.
Tame and stuffy adaptation of an incisive novel, rather poorly produced.
wd Albert Lewin novel Guy de Maupassant ph Russell Metty m Darius Milhaud
☆ George Sanders, Angela Lansbury, Ann Dvorak, Frances Dee, John Carradine, Hugo Haas, Marie Wilson, Albert Basserman, Warren William

Private Angelo
GB 1949 106m bw
Pilgrim (Peter Ustinov)
An Italian soldier hates war and spends World War II on the run from both sides.
Listless satirical comedy that just isn't funny enough.
w Peter Ustinov, Michael Anderson novel Eric Linklater d Peter Ustinov ph Erwin Hillier
☆ Peter Ustinov, Godfrey Tearle, Robin Bailey, Maria Denis, Marjorie Rhodes, James Robertson Justice, Moyna McGill

Private Benjamin
US 1980 110m Technicolor
Warner/Hawn-Myers-Shyer-Miller
A well-heeled Jewish widow, at a crossroads in her life, joins the army.
Half-assed attempt at combining slapstick, character study, sentiment, sex and a recruiting poster. Some funny moments don't really make it worth sitting through.
w Nancy Meyers, Charles Shyer, Harvey Miller d Howard Zieff ph David M. Walsh m Bill Conti
☆ Goldie Hawn, Eileen Brennan, Armand Assante, Robert Webber, Sam Wanamaker, Barbara Barrie, Harry Dean Stanton
🏆 screenplay; Goldie Hawn; Eileen Brennan (supporting actress)

Private Buckaroo
US 1942 68m bw
Universal
The difficulties of putting on shows for soldiers.
Slaphappy second feature worth preserving for the talent.
w Edmund Kelso, Edward James d Edward F. Cline ph Woody Bredell md Harry James ch John Mattison ad Jack Otterson ed Milton Carruth
☆ The Andrews Sisters, Harry James and his Orchestra, Joe E. Lewis, Donald O'Connor, Peggy Ryan, Huntz Hall, Ernest Truex, Shemp Howard

A Private Conversation ***
USSR 1983 96m colour
Contemporary/Mosfilm
original title: *Bez Svidetelei*
aka: *Without Witnesses*
A party hack visits his ex-wife for an evening of recrimination and raking over the past.
A two-character movie in the limited setting of a small flat, but one that succeeds in its searing portrait of a failed marriage and a wasted life.
w Nikita Mikhalkov, Sofia Prokofieva, Ramiz Fataliev play Sofia Prokofieva d Nikita Mikhalkov ph Pavel Lebeshev m Eduard Artemiev ad Alexander Adabashian, Igor Makarov, Alexander Samulekin
☆ Mikhail Ulyanov, Irina Kupchenko

The Private Files of J. Edgar Hoover *
US 1978 112m Movielab
AIP/Larco (Larry Cohen)
The supposedly true facts of the career of the longtime head of the FBI.
Unreliable exposé with some interesting bits.
wd Larry Cohen ph Paul Glickman m Miklos Rozsa
☆ Broderick Crawford, José Ferrer, Michael Parks, Ronee Blakley, Rip Torn, Celeste Holm, Dan Dailey, Raymond St Jacques, Howard Da Silva, June Havoc, John Marley, Andrew Duggan, Lloyd Nolan

A Private Function ***
GB 1984 94m colour
Handmade (Mark Shivas)
In 1947 Yorkshire, a doctor and his family secretly fatten an unlicensed pig.
Sharply-detailed comedy typical of its author, but less likeable than many.
w Alan Bennett d Malcolm Mowbray ph Tony Pierce-Roberts m John Du Prez pd Stuart Walker ed Barrie Vince
☆ Michael Palin, Maggie Smith, Denholm Elliott, Richard Griffiths, Tony Haygarth, *Liz Smith*, John Normington
BAFTA: Maggie Smith; Liz Smith (supporting actress); Denholm Elliott (supporting actor)

Private Hell 36 *

US 1954 81m bw

Filmakers

Two cops on a robbery trail find the loot and keep it for themselves.

Predictable but stylish film noir, still moderately watchable.

w Collier Young, Ida Lupino *d Don Siegel*
ph Burnett Guffey *m* Leith Stevens

☆ Ida Lupino, Steve Cochran, Howard Duff, Dean Jagger, Dorothy Malone

Private Izzy Murphy

US 1926 80m approx (24 fps) bw silent

Warner

A Jewish boy loves a Catholic girl.

Dreary variant on Abie's Irish Rose, popular enough for a 1927 sequel called Sailor Izzy Murphy.

w Philip Lonergan *d* Lloyd Bacon

☆ George Jessel, Patsy Ruth Miller, Vera Gordon

Private Lessons

US 1981 87m Metrocolor

Barry & Enright (R. Ben Efraim)

When his father goes away on business, a rich 15-year-old boy is left in the care of a seductive housekeeper and a crooked chauffeur.

Tedious mixture of schoolboy smut and feeble comedy.

w Dan Greenburg *novel Philly* by Dan Greenburg *d* Alan Myerson *ph* Jan de Bont *ad* Linda Pearl *ed* Fred Chulack

☆ Sylvia Kristel, Howard Hesseman, Eric Brown, Patrick Piccininni, Ed Begley Jnr, Pamela Bryant, Meredith Baer, Dan Greenburg

Private Life *

USSR 1982 104m colour

Contemporary/Mosfilm

original title: *Chastnaya Zhizn*

A businessman, retiring in his fifties, discovers that he has drifted away from his wife and children.

Perceptive, occasionally ponderous, study of a man in crisis.

w Anatoly Grebnyev, Yuli Raizman *d* Yuli Raizman *ph* Nikolai Olonovsky *ad* Tatyana Lapshina

☆ Mikhail Ulyanov, Iya Savvina, Irina Gubanova, Tatyana Dogileva, Aleksei Blokhin, Elena Sanayeva, Liliya Gritsenko

best foreign film

The Private Life of Don Juan

GB 1934 90m bw

London Films (Alexander Korda)

In 17th-century Spain, the famous lover fakes death and makes a comeback in disguise.

Lacklustre frolic by an overage star through dismal sets. The production was meant to extend the success of The Private Life of Henry VIII, *but totally failed to do so.*

w Lajos Biro, Frederick Lonsdale *play* Henri Bataille *d* Alexander Korda *ph* Georges Périnal *m* Ernst Toch

☆ Douglas Fairbanks, Merle Oberon, Binnie Barnes, Benita Hume, Joan Gardner, Melville Cooper, Athene Seyler, Owen Nares

'Technically it has so much in its favour that it's too bad it doesn't promise solid b.o. attraction.' – *Variety*

'One of those ideas that never really take off.' – *New Yorker, 1977*

'The things I do for England!'

The Private Life of Henry VIII ***

GB 1933 97m bw

London Films (Alexander Korda)

How Henry beheaded his second wife and acquired four more.

This never was a perfect film, but certain scenes are very funny and its sheer sauciness established the possibility of British films making money abroad, as well as starting several star careers. It now looks very dated and even amateurish in parts.

w Lajos Biro, *Arthur Wimperis d* Alexander Korda *ph* Georges Périnal *m* Kurt Schroeder

☆ *Charles Laughton, Elsa Lanchester*, Robert Donat, Merle Oberon, Binnie Barnes, Franklin Dyall, Miles Mander, Wendy Barrie, Claud Allister, Everley Gregg

'Among the best anywhere and by far the top British picture ... figures a sock entry, especially for the best houses.' – *Variety*

Charles Laughton

best picture

The Private Life of Sherlock Holmes ***

GB 1970 125m DeLuxe Panavision

UA/Phalanx/Mirisch/Sir Nigel (Billy Wilder)

A secret Watson manuscript reveals cases in which Sherlock Holmes became involved with women.

What started as four stories is reduced to two, one brightly satirical and the other no more than a careful and discreet recreation, with the occasional jocular aside, of the flavour of the stories themselves. A very civilized and pleasing entertainment except for the hurried rounding-off which is a let-down.

w Billy Wilder, I. A. L. Diamond d Billy Wilder *ph* Christopher Challis *m* Miklos Rozsa *ad Alexander Trauner ed* Ernest Walter

☆ *Robert Stephens, Colin Blakely*, Genevieve Page, Clive Revill, Christopher Lee, Catherine Lacey, Stanley Holloway

'Affectionately conceived and flawlessly executed.' – *NFT, 1974*

'Wilder's least embittered film, and by far his most moving. Great.' – *Time Out, 1984*

Private Lives *

US 1931 82m bw

MGM (Albert Lewin)

Ex-marrieds desert their intended new spouses to try each other again.

An essentially theatrical comedy, and a great one, seems somewhat slow-witted on film.

w Hans Kraly, Richard Schayer *play* Noël Coward *d* Sidney Franklin *ph* Ray Binger

☆ Norma Shearer, Robert Montgomery, Reginald Denny, Una Merkel, Jean Hersholt

'Stars are a big asset to this parlour comedy which will amuse the women more than the men.' – *Variety*

'For polish, few comedies of the thirties can equal this early alliance of cinema and stage.' – *John Baxter, 1968*

The Private Lives of Elizabeth and Essex **

US 1939 106m Technicolor

Warner (Robert Lord)

reissue title: *Elizabeth the Queen*

Elizabeth I falls in love with the Earl of Essex, but events turn him into a rebel and she has to order his execution.

Unhistorical history given the grand treatment; a Hollywood picture book, not quite satisfying dramatically despite all the effort.

w Norman Reilly Raine, Aeneas Mackenzie *play Elizabeth the Queen* by Maxwell Anderson *d* Michael Curtiz *ph* Sol Polito, W. Howard Greene *m* Erich Wolfgang Korngold *ad* Anton Grot

☆ *Bette Davis, Errol Flynn*, Olivia de Havilland, Donald Crisp, Vincent Price, Alan Hale, Henry Stephenson, Henry Daniell, Leo G. Carroll, Nanette Fabray, Robert Warwick, John Sutton

'Solid box office material, with fine grosses and holdovers indicated ... in all technical departments, picture has received topnotch investiture.' – *Variety*

'A rather stately, rigorously posed and artistically technicolored production.' – *Frank S. Nugent*

Sol Polito, W. Howard Greene; Erich Wolfgang Korngold; Anton Grot

The Private Navy of Sergeant O'Farrell

US 1968 92m Technicolor

Hope Enterprises (John Beck)

After World War II, military personnel congregate on an island which has been by-passed by hostilities.

Nothing much wrong with the plot, but at this time in his career Hope seemed unable to do anything right, and the film was barely released.

wd Frank Tashlin *ph* Alan Stensvold *m* Harry Stikman

☆ Bob Hope, Gina Lollobrigida, Phyllis Diller, Jeffrey Hunter, Mylene Demongeot, Henry Wilcoxon

Private Number

US 1936 80m bw

TCF (Raymond Griffith)

GB title: *Secret Interlude*

A wealthy young man keeps a secret of his marriage to a housemaid.

Warmed-over class melodrama previously filmed in 1930 as Common Clay. *Adequate within its lights.*

w Gene Markey, William Conselman *play Common Clay* by Cleves Kinkead *d* Roy del Ruth *ph* Peverell Marley *m* Louis Silvers

☆ Loretta Young, Robert Taylor, Basil Rathbone, Patsy Kelly, Marjorie Gateson, Paul Harvey, Monroe Owsley, John Miljan

'He turned on everyone who tuned in!'

Private Parts

US 1997 109m DeLuxe

Paramount/Rysher (Ivan Reitman)

New York radio personality Howard Stern tells how, although he wants to be loved by everyone, he is always misunderstood.

Unlikable, self-regarding biopic of a notorious 'shock jock', famed for his outrageousness, though there's little evidence of it in this anodyne confection, in which he is about as abrasive as cotton wool; he limits himself to a few farting jokes and a great deal of mock humility.

w Len Blum, Michael Kalesniko *book* Howard Stern *d* Betty Thomas *ph* Walt Lloyd *m* Van Dyke Parks *pd* Charles Rosen *ed* Peter Teschner

☆ Howard Stern, Robin Quivers, Mary McCormack, Fred Norris, Paul Giamatti, Gary Dell'Abate, Jackie Martling, Carol Alt

'The Stern on display here wants to go Hollywood and so has turned in a bland cookie-cutter biopic about a vulnerable, misunderstood young man eager to make it in showbiz.' – *Mark Steyn, Spectator*

Private Potter

GB 1962 89m bw

MGM/Ben Arbeid

A young soldier is court-martialled for cowardice but claims he had a vision of God.

Stilted morality play, unpersuasively made and acted.

w Ronald Harwood *TV play* Ronald Harwood *d* Caspar Wrede *ph* Arthur Lavis *m* George Hall

☆ Tom Courtenay, Mogens Wieth, Ronald Fraser, James Maxwell, Ralph Michael, Brewster Mason

The Private Secretary

GB 1935 70m bw

Twickenham

A clerical gentleman is duped into protecting a rich young idler from his creditors.

Moderately effective filming of a popular stage farce from a German original.

w Arthur Macrae, George Broadhurst, H. Fowler Mear *play* Van Moser *d* Henry Edwards

☆ Edward Everett Horton, Barry Mackay, Judy Gunn, Oscar Asche, Sydney Fairbrother, Alastair Sim, Michael Shepley

The Private War of Major Benson

US 1955 105m Technicolor Cinemascope

U-I (Howard Pine)

A soldier with outspoken views is sent to cool off as commander of a military academy run by an order of nuns.

Cute and sentimental nonsense with unlikely situations, a martinet becoming soft-centred and a happy-ever-after finale.

w William Roberts, Richard Alan Simmons *d* Jerry Hopper *ph* Harold Lipstein *m* Henry Mancini, Herman Stein *md* Joseph Gershenson *ad* Robert Boyle, Alexander Golitzen *ed* Ted J. Kent

☆ Charlton Heston, Julie Adams, Tim Hovey, William Demarest, Tim Considine, Sal Mineo, Nana Bryant, Milburn Stone, Mary Field

original story (Bob Mosher, Joe Connelly)

The Private Wore Skirts: see *Never Wave at a WAC*

'She loved a man who did not exist – except in her own private world!'

Private Worlds *

US 1935 84m bw

Paramount (Walter Wanger)

Romance among the doctors at a mental hospital.

Melodrama treated with what was at the time unexpected seriousness.

w Lynn Starling *novel* Phyllis Bottome *d* Gregory La Cava *ph* Leon Shamroy *m* Heinz Roemheld

☆ Claudette Colbert, Charles Boyer, Joel McCrea, Joan Bennett, Helen Vinson, Esther Dale, Samuel S. Hinds

'Fine but not too artistic production ... woman's picture of fair b.o. potentialities.' – *Variety*

Claudette Colbert

A Private's Affair

US 1959 92m DeLuxe Cinemascope

TCF (David Weisbart)

Three army recruits form a close harmony trio and get into various scrapes.

Thin service comedy for the 'new' youth audience.

w Winston Miller *d* Raoul Walsh *ph* Charles G. Clarke *m* Cyril Mockridge

☆ Sal Mineo, Christine Carere, Barry Coe, Barbara Eden, Gary Crosby, Terry Moore, Jim Backus, Jessie Royce Landis

Privates on Parade *

GB 1982 113m colour

Handmade (Simon Relph)

Farcical and serious incidents in the lives of an army concert party in 1948 Singapore.

Rather heavy-going comedy with much bad language and an overdose of effeminacy; on the whole no funnier than It Ain't Half Hot, Mum.

w Peter Nichols *play* Peter Nichols *d* Michael Blakemore *ph* Ian Wilson *m* Denis King

☆ *John Cleese, Denis Quilley*, Michael Elphick, Nicola Pagett, Bruce Payne, Joe Melia

Private's Progress ***

GB 1956 97m bw

British Lion/Charter (Roy Boulting)

An extremely innocent young national serviceman is taught a few army dodges and becomes a dupe for art thieves.

Celebrated army farce with satirical pretensions; when released it had something to make everyone in Britain laugh.

w Frank Harvey, John Boulting novel Alan Hackney *d John Boulting ph* Eric Cross *m* John Addison

☆ *Ian Carmichael*, Terry-Thomas, Richard Attenborough, *Dennis Price*, Peter Jones, William Hartnell, Thorley Walters, Ian Bannen, Jill Adams, Victor Maddern, Kenneth Griffith, Miles Malleson, *John Le Mesurier*

Prividenie, Kotoroe ne Vozvrashchaetsya: see *The Ghost That Never Returns*

Privilege *

GB 1967 103m Technicolor

Universal/Worldfilm/Memorial (John Heyman)

The publicity campaign for a pop star turns him into a religious messiah.

Rather hysterical fable for our time, undeniably forceful in spots and yawnful in others.

w Norman Bogner *story* Johnny Speight *d Peter Watkins ph* Peter Suschitsky *m* Mike Leander

☆ Paul Jones, Jean Shrimpton, Mark London, Max Bacon, Jeremy Child, James Cossins, Victor Henry

'Everything in it goes wrong, and one can do little but catalogue the failures.' – *MFB*

Privileged *

GB 1982 96m Technicolor

ITC/The Oxford Film Company (Richard Stevenson)

Oxford undergraduates rehearsing *The Duchess of Malfi* become involved in sexual intrigues which result in suicide.

Highly unusual because made and funded by the students themselves, this melodrama has vivid patches but generally lacks a professional eye.

w Michael Hoffman, David Woollcombe, Rupert Walters *d* Michael Hoffman *ph* Fiona Cunningham Reid *m* Rachel Portman *ad* Peter Schwabach *ed* Derek Goldman

☆ Robert Woolley, Diana Katis, Hugh Grant, Victoria Studd, James Wilby

Le Prix du Danger: see *The Prize of Peril*

The Prize ***
US 1963 135m Metrocolor Panavision
MGM/Roxbury (Pandro S. Berman)

In Stockholm during the Nobel Prize awards, a drunken American author stumbles on a spy plot.
Whatever the original novel is like, the film is a Hitchcock pastiche which works better than most Hitchcocks: suspenseful, well characterized, fast moving and funny from beginning to end.
w Ernest Lehman *novel* Irving Wallace *d* Mark Robson *ph* William Daniels *m* Jerry Goldsmith
☆ *Paul Newman*, Elke Sommer, *Edward G. Robinson*, Diane Baker, Kevin McCarthy, *Leo G. Carroll*, Micheline Presle

A Prize of Arms
GB 1961 105m bw
British Lion/Interstate (George Maynard)
An ex-army officer and an explosives expert plan to steal an army payroll.
Standard, pacy caper melodrama offering nothing at all new.
w Paul Ryder *d* Cliff Owen *ph* Gilbert Taylor *m* Robert Sharples
☆ Stanley Baker, Tom Bell, Helmut Schmid, John Phillips

A Prize of Gold
GB 1955 100m Technicolor
Columbia/Warwick (Phil C. Samuel)
An American army sergeant in Berlin decides to steal a cargo of Nazi loot.
Routine caper thriller with sentimental leanings.
w Robert Buckner, John Paxton *novel* Max Catto *d* Mark Robson *ph* Ted Moore *m* Malcolm Arnold
☆ Richard Widmark, Mai Zetterling, Nigel Patrick, George Cole, Donald Wolfit, Andrew Ray, Joseph Tomelty, Karel Stepanek

The Prize of Peril
France/Yugoslavia 1983 88m Eastmancolor
Brent Walker/Swanie Productions/ TF1/UGC/Top 1/ Avala (Norbert Saada)
original title: *Le Prix du Danger*
A man volunteers to enter a TV contest, where the prize goes to the person who can survive being hunted across Paris by armed killers.
An interesting idea, badly executed.
w Yves Boisset, Jean Curtelin *story* Robert Sheckley *d* Yves Boisset *ph* Pierre-William Glenn *m* Vladimir Cosmo *ad* Aleksandar Milovic *ed* Michelle David
☆ Gérard Lanvin, Michel Piccoli, Marie-France Pisier, Bruno Cremer, Andréa Ferréol, Jean Rougerie, Jean-Claude Dreyfus

The Prizefighter and the Lady
US 1933 102m bw
MGM (Hunt Stromberg)
GB title: *Every Woman's Man*
A boxer falls for a high-class gangster's girl.
Plodding romantic melodrama, popular because it starred a real boxer.
w John Meehan, John Lee Mahin *d* W. S. Van Dyke *ph* Lester White *m* David Snell
☆ Myrna Loy, Max Baer, Otto Kruger, Walter Huston, Jack Dempsey, Primo Carnera
'Freak Max Baer starrer, a picture that entertains in high-pressure manner.' – *Variety*
Academy Award nomination: original story (Frances Marion)

Prizzi's Honor *
US 1985 129m DeLuxe
ABC/John Foreman
Male and female hired killers for Mafia families fall in love but are assigned to 'hit' each other.
Critically lauded but puzzling and unsatisfactory black comedy which takes far too long to get going, is muddled in narrative, and leaves an unpleasant taste.
w Richard Condon, Janet Roach *novel* Richard Condon *d* John Huston *ph* Andrzej Bartkowiak *m* Alex North *pd* Dennis Washington *ed* Rudi and Kaja Fehr
☆ *Jack Nicholson*, *Kathleen Turner*, Robert Loggia, William Hickey, John Randolph, *Anjelica Huston*
'Certainly one of the most curious films to kick off the summer season by an American major.' – *Variety*
Academy Award: Anjelica Huston (supporting actress)
Academy Award nomination: best picture; direction; Jack Nicholson; William Hickey; adapted screenplay; editing
BAFTA: adapted screenplay

Problem Child
US 1990 81m DeLuxe
UIP/Universal/Imagine Entertainment (Robert Simonds)
A badly behaved boy is adopted by a small-town couple.
Broadly played, predictable comedy of mayhem and misunderstandings.
w Scott Alexander, Larry Karaszewski *d* Dennis Dugan *ph* Peter Lyons Collister *m* Miles Goodman *pd* George Costello *ed* Daniel Hanley, Michael Hill
☆ John Ritter, Jack Warden, Michael Oliver, Gilbert Gottfried, Amy Yasbeck, Michael Richards, Peter Jurasik, Charlotte Akin
'Universal took a step in the right direction by whittling it down to just 81 minutes but didn't go far enough. The studio should have excised another 75 minutes and released this unbelievable mess as a short.' – *Variety*

'Now, Junior has a brand new friend. He's bad. She's worse.'
Problem Child 2
US 1991 91m DeLuxe
UIP/Universal/Imagine (Robert Simonds)
An ill-behaved boy decides that his father should marry the mother of his friend, a badly behaved girl.
Nasty-minded, witless slapstick with an anal fixation.
w Scott Alexander, Larry Karaszewski *d* Brian Levant *ph* Peter Smokler *m* David Kitay *pd* Maria Caso *ed* Lois Freeman-Fox, Robert P. Seppey
☆ John Ritter, Michael Oliver, Jack Warden, Laraine Newman, Amy Yasbeck, Ivyann Schwan, Gilbert Gottfried, Paul Wilson
'No seam of bad taste is left unmined as the screenwriters sink to impossibly low depths in pursuit of anything vaguely resembling a laugh.' – *Mark Salisbury, Empire*

Le Procès: see *The Trial*

Procès de Jeanne d'Arc **
France 1962 65m bw
Agnès Delahaie
aka: *The Trial of Joan of Arc*
Joan of Arc is tried for heresy at the University of Paris and, under pressure from the English, burned at the stake.
An austere, almost ritualistic retelling of the trial, based on the actual documents and eye-witness accounts; its non-judgmental approach, letting the drama speak for itself, is ultimately more moving and engrossing than the usual sensationalist approaches.
wd Robert Bresson *ph* Léonce-Henry Burel *m* Francis Seyrig *ad* Pierre Charbonnier *ed* Germaine Artus
☆ Florence Carrez, Jean-Claude Fourneau, Roger Honorat, Marc Jacquier, Jean Gillibert, Michel Herubel, André Régnier, Arthur Le Bau
'Little good can be said about Bresson's catatonic *Trial of Joan of Arc*.' – *John Simon*
'Terse, spare, and oddly perfunctory.' – *Pauline Kael*
† The film won the Special Jury Prize at the Cannes Film Festival of 1962.

The Prodigal
US 1931 76m bw
MGM
The scion of a Southern plantation becomes a tramp.
Pleasant minor musical with a star who never really caught on.
w Bess Meredyth, Wells Root *d* Harry Pollard
☆ Lawrence Tibbett, Esther Ralston, Roland Young, Cliff Edwards, Purnell Pratt, Hedda Hopper, Stepin Fetchit
'Between average and good … should top the normal gross.' – *Variety*

'The story of woman's beauty and man's temptation!'
The Prodigal
US 1955 115m Eastmancolor Cinemascope
MGM (Charles Schnee)
The son of a Hebrew farmer falls for the high priestess of a pagan cult.
Wildly apocryphal 'biblical' story of obvious expensiveness but no merit.
w Maurice Zimm *d* Richard Thorpe *ph* Joseph Ruttenberg *m* Bronislau Kaper
☆ Lana Turner, Edmund Purdom, Louis Calhern, James Mitchell, Walter Hampden, Francis L. Sullivan, Joseph Wiseman, Audrey Dalton, Taina Elg, Neville Brand, Cecil Kellaway
'A few lines of dialogue derive from the Bible; the rest is pure Hollywood, but Hollywood in its mood of sham solemnity when even the unintentional jokes are not funny.' – *MFB*
'A costume stinker … it should have played Disneyland!' – *Lana Turner*

The Prodigal Son (dubbed)
Hong Kong 1981 90m colour
Paragon (Raymond Chow)
A spoilt, rich young man, determined to become a kung fu master, attaches himself to a fighter who is also the star of a Chinese opera troupe, with fatal results for many.
By Western standards, an unsettling mix of broad comedy and bloody violence, but done with some style.
w Samo Hung, Wong Bing Yiu *d* Samo Hung *ph* Lau Kwun Wai *m* Frankie Chan, Chan Pui Lap *ad* Chien Sum *ed* Cheung Yiu Chung
☆ Samo Hung, Yuen Biao, Frankie Chan, Lam Chen Ying, Chung Fat, Dick Wai, Wai Pak, Chan Lung

The Producers *
US 1968 88m Pathécolor
Avco /Springtime/Crossbow (Sidney Glazier)
A Broadway producer seduces elderly widows to obtain finance for his new play, sells 25,000 per cent in the expectation that it will flop, and is horrified when it succeeds.
Dismally unfunny satire except for the play itself, Springtime for Hitler, which is neatly put down. This has, however, become a cult film, so that criticism is pointless.
wd Mel Brooks *ph* Joseph Coffey *m* John Morris
☆ Zero Mostel, Gene Wilder, Kenneth Mars, Estelle Winwood, Renee Taylor, Dick Shawn
'Over and over again promising ideas are killed off, either by over-exposure or bad timing.' – *Tom Milne*
'An almost flawless triumph of bad taste, unredeemed by wit or style.' – *Arthur Schlesinger Jnr*
Academy Award: Mel Brooks (as writer)
Academy Award nomination: Gene Wilder

Profession: Reporter: see *The Passenger*

The Professional
France 1981 111m colour
Les Films Ariane/Cerito (Alain Belmondo)
original title: *Le Professionnel*
A French hitman, betrayed by his superiors, escapes from an African prison to seek revenge by carrying out his original assignment.
Routine action adventure, influenced by spaghetti Westerns; it has its occasional moments, including a car chase around the steps of Paris.
w Georges Lautner, Jacques Audiard, Michel Audiard *novel* *Death of a Thin-Skinned Animal* by Patrick Alexander *d* Georges Lautner *ph* Henri Decae *m* Ennio Morricone *ad* Eric Moulard *ed* Michelle David
☆ Jean-Paul Belmondo, Jean Desailly, Marie-Christine Descouard, Cyrielle Claire, Robert Hossein, Elisabeth Marconi, Jean-Louis Richard, Michel Beaune

The Professional: see *Leon (1994)*

A Professional Gun: see *The Mercenary*

Professional Soldier
US 1936 75m bw
TCF (Darryl F. Zanuck)
A kidnapper befriends the young prince who is his victim.
Predictable, polished family film.
w Gene Fowler, Howard Ellis Smith *story* Damon Runyon *d* Tay Garnett *ph* Rudolph Maté *m* Louis Silvers
☆ Victor McLaglen, Freddie Bartholomew, Constance Collier, Gloria Stuart, Michael Whalen
'Some of the sequences are amusing; some of the action is very fast. But fundamentally the story is not believable.' – *Variety*

Professional Sweetheart
US 1933 70m bw
RKO (Merian C. Cooper)
GB title: *Imaginary Sweetheart*
A radio 'purity girl' seeks some real life romance.
Modestly smart comedy of no lasting merit.
w Maurine Watkins *d* William Seiter *ph* Edward Cronjager *m* Max Steiner
☆ Ginger Rogers, Betty Furness, Gregory Ratoff, Sterling Holloway, Frank McHugh, ZaSu Pitts, Allen Jenkins, Norman Foster, Edgar Kennedy, Franklin Pangborn
'After a fast start this radio satire loses a lot of ground … but comedy's there all the way.' – *Variety*

The Professionals **
US 1966 123m Technicolor Panavision
Columbia/Pax (Richard Brooks)
Skilled soldiers of fortune are hired by a millionaire rancher to get back his kidnapped wife.
Strong-flavoured star Western with good suspense sequences.
wd Richard Brooks *novel* *A Mule for the Marquesa* by Frank O'Rourke *ph* Conrad Hall *m* Maurice Jarre
☆ *Burt Lancaster*, Lee Marvin, Robert Ryan, Jack Palance, Ralph Bellamy, Claudia Cardinale, Woody Strode
'After the *Lord Jim* excursion, it is good to see Brooks back on his own professional form, filming the tight, laconic sort of adventure which usually seems to bring out the best in Hollywood veterans.' – *Penelope Houston*
'It has the expertise of a cold old whore with practised hands and no thoughts of love.' – *Pauline Kael, 1968*
Academy Award nomination: Richard Brooks (as writer and as director); Conrad Hall

Professor Beware *
US 1938 93m bw
Paramount
A staid professor finds himself on the run across America in pursuit of an Egyptian artefact.
Slow-starting comedy with only moments of the comedian at his best.
w Delmer Daves, Jack Cunningham *story* Crampton Harris, Francis M. and Marian B. Cockrell *d* Elliott Nugent *ph* Archie Stout
☆ Harold Lloyd, Phyllis Welch, Raymond Walburn, Lionel Stander, William Frawley, Thurston Hall, Cora Witherspoon, Sterling Holloway
'Both Lloyd and the audience are out of breath after 3000 miles cross country, but most of it is exhaustion from laughing.' – *Variety*

Professor Mamlock **
USSR 1938 100m bw
Lenfilm
The leading surgeon of a Berlin hospital is driven to attempt suicide because he is a Jew.
Ironic in all kinds of ways, this quite devastating film was a unique attack by one government on a neighbouring one.
w Friedrich Wolf, Adolph Minkin, Herbert Rappaport *d* Adolph Minkin, Herbert Rappaport
☆ Sergei Mezhinski, E. Nikitina, Oleg Zhakov, Nina Shaternikova, Vasili Merkuriev
'An arresting picture which is sure to arouse strenuous comment.' – *Variety*
'The theme of a story should never be expressed so plainly; argument is valueless in fiction unless it is dramatic and individualized.' – *Graham Greene, The Spectator*

Profondo Rosso: see *Deep Red*

Profundo Carmesi: see *Deep Crimson*

Progeny
US 1998 100m colour
Fries (Jack F. Murphy, Henry Seggerman)
A Californian doctor fears that his wife is going to give birth to an alien baby.
Slow-paced psychological horror with some gruesome moments; after a long, dull opening, it becomes more interesting and suspenseful.
w Aubrey Solomon, Stuart Gordon *d* Brian Yuzna *ph* James Hawkinson *m* Steven Morrell *pd* Anthony Tremblay *ed* Christopher Roth, Harry B. Miller III *sp* make-up: Anthony C. Ferrante; visual fx: Marcus Keys; creature: Screaming Mad George
☆ Arnold Vosloo, Jillian McWhirter, Brad Dourif, Lindsay Crouse, Wilford Brimley, Willard E. Pugh, David Wells

The Program
US 1993 114m colour
Buena Vista/Touchstone/Samuel Goldwyn (Samuel Goldwyn Jnr)
A college coach, faced with losing his job unless his team improves, recruits some dubious new players.
The problems of college football have never seemed less interesting; the movie retains a slight anthropological interest for audiences outside North America.
w David S. Ward, Aaron Latham *d* David S. Ward *ph* Victor Hammer *m* Michel Colombier *pd* Albert Brenner *ed* Paul Seydor, Kimberly Ray
☆ James Caan, Halle Berry, Omar Epps, Craig Sheffer, Kristy Swanson, Andrew Benrubi, Duane Davis, Andrew Bryniarski, J. Leon Pridgen II

Il Proiezionista: see *The Inner Circle*

Project A *
Hong Kong 1984 108m colour
Golden Harvest (Leonard K. C. Ho)
In 1903 a Chinese coastguard quits the force in order to track down pirates that his superiors tolerate.
One of the better kung-fu movies, mixing humour with spectacular stunts and frenetically choreographed fights.
wd Jackie Chan
☆ Jackie Chan, Samo Hung, Li Hai Sheng, Yuan Baio

Project A-Ko (dubbed)
Japan 1986 120m colour
Soeishinsha/APPP (Kazufumu Nomura)
While aliens try to kidnap her, a 16-year-old girl with superhuman powers fights a rival for the friendship of another girl.
Bizarre animated parody of high-tech science fantasy and high-school romance.
w Yuji Moriyama, Katsuhiko Nishijima, Tomoko Kawasaki *d* Katsuhiko Nishijima *ph* Takafumi Arai *m* Richie Zito, Joey Carbone, Toji Akasaka *ad* Shinji Kimura
☆ Featuring the voices of: Stacey Gregg, Denica Fairman, Julia Brahms, Marc Smith, Jay Benedict, Lisa Ross

Project M 7: see *The Net*

Project X *
US 1968 97m Technicolor
Paramount/William Castle
In the year 2118, a man is scientifically induced to think he lives in the 1960s so that he can recover a lost secret.
Fearsomely complex science fiction, cheaply made but on the whole intriguingly imagined.
w Edmund Morris *novel* Leslie P. Davies *d* William Castle *ph* Harold Stine *m* Van Cleave
☆ Christopher George, Greta Baldwin, Henry Jones, Monte Markham, Harold Gould

Project X
US 1987 108m DeLuxe
TCF (Walter F. Parkes, Lawrence Lasker)
A pilot rebels when he is assigned a new job teaching chimps to fly and then discovers the real purpose of the project.
An odd little film that raises questions about the morality of experimenting on animals and then retreats into fantasy instead of confronting them. Some attractive performances from the apes hardly compensate.
w Stanley Weiser *d* Jonathan Kaplan *ph* Dean Cundey *m* James Horner *pd* Lawrence G. Paull *ed* O. Nicholas Brown
☆ Matthew Broderick, Helen Hunt, Bill Sadler, Johnny Ray McGhee, Jonathan Stark, Robin Gammell, Stephen Lang, Jean Smart

The Projected Man
GB 1966 90m Technicolor Techniscope
Compton (John Croydon, Maurice Foster)
A scientist working on a matter transmitter experiments on himself and turns monster.
Low-budget shocker with a narrative that owes more than a little to The Fly; *the acting and direction are ponderous at best, and the subplot, involving love and jealousy, is uninteresting.*
w John C. Cooper, Peter Bryan *story* Frank Quattrocchi *d* Ian Curteis *ph* Stanley Pavey *m* Kenneth V. Jones *ad* Peter Mullins *ed* Derek Holding *sp* Flo Nordhoff, Robert Hedges, Mike Hope
☆ Mary Peach, Norman Wooland, Derek Farr, Bryant Haliday, Ronald Allen, Tracey Crisp, Derrick de Marney, Sam Kydd, Gerard Heinz

'Don't go there alone!'
Promenons-Nous Dans Les Bois
France 2000 90m colour
Canal+/Fidelelite/Glozel/Cofimage/Gimages/Images6 (Olivier Delbosc, Marc Missonnier)
GB title: *Deep in the Woods*
An aristocrat invites a troupe of young actors to his remote chateau in order to stage a performance of *Red Riding Hood* for his grandson; then the killings begin…
Glib, glossy and gory horror that is derivative of recent Hollywood teen slasher movies.
w Annabelle Perrichon, Lionel Delplanque *d* Lionel Delplanque *ph* Denis Rouden *m* Jérôme Coullet *pd* Arnaud de Moléron *ed* Pomme Zhed
☆ Clotilde Courau (Sophie), Clément Sibony (Matthieu), Vincent Lecoeur (Wilfried), Alexia Stresi (Jeanne), Maud Buquet (Mathilde), François Berléand (Axel de Fersen), Denis Lavant (Stéphane)
'Despite its enthusiastic and liberal doses of gore and naked flesh, Delplanque's crude feature debut fails to either excite or scare.' – *Chris Wiegand, Boxoffice*

The Promise
GB 1969 98m Eastmancolor
Commonwealth United/Howard and Wyndham
Two young men and a girl share a flat after the 1942 siege of Leningrad; thirteen years later, their dreams of life considerably modified, they meet again and change partners.
Talky and too carefully budgeted screen version of a somewhat pretentious play.
w Michael Hayes *play* Aleksei Arbuzov *d* Michael Hayes *ph* Brendan Stafford *m* Iwan Williams *pd* William McCrow
☆ Ian McKellen, John Castle, Susan Macready, Mary Jones, David Mettheim

The Promise
US 1979 97m Technicolor Panavision
Universal (Fred Weintraub, Paul Heller)
GB TV title: *Face of a Stranger*
A young man fails to recognize his lost love when her face has been rebuilt after an accident.
Rambling teenage variation on Random Harvest, *not very well done and about forty years behind its proper times.*
w Garry Michael White *d* Gilbert Cates *ph* Ralph Woolsey *m* David Shire
☆ Kathleen Quinlan, Stephen Collins, Beatrice Straight, Laurence Luckinbill, William Prince
'Appalling romantic tushery by any standards.' – *Tom Milne, MFB*
song 'I'll Never Say Goodbye' (*m*David Shire, *ly*Alan and Marilyn Bergman)

The Promise *
Germany/France 1994 110m Eastmancolor
Artificial Eye/Bioskop/Odessa/MH/WDR (Eberhard Junkersdorf)
original title: *Das Versprechen*
Lovers are separated for more than 20 years by the Berlin Wall.
Slow-moving, intermittently engaging, small-scale drama of the effect of the Cold War on individual lives.
w Peter Schneider, Margarethe von Trotta *idea* Francesco Laudadio *d* Margarethe von Trotta *ph* Franz Rath *m* Jürgen Knieper *pd* Martin Dostal *ed* Suzanne Baron
☆ Meret Becker, Corinna Harfouch, Anian Zollner, August Zirner, Susann Ugé, Eva Mattes, Jean-Yves Gaultier
'Plods doggedly through the bitter years, underlining its metaphorical points heavy-handedly.' – *George Perry*

Promise at Dawn
US/France 1970 102m DeLuxe
Avco/Nathalie (Jules Dassin)
The boyhood of novelist Romain Gary and the last years of his fearsome Russian Jewish actress mother with whom he traipses around Europe.
Scrappy star vehicle and unnecessary biopic in a variety of indulgent styles.
w Jules Dassin *play* *First Love* by Samuel Taylor *d* Jules Dassin *ph* Jean Badal *m* Georges Delerue
☆ Melina Mercouri, Assaf Dayan

Promise Her Anything
GB 1966 97m Technicolor
Seven Arts (Stanley Rubin)
A mail order movie maker falls for a young French widow in the next flat.
Scatty comedy set in Greenwich Village and aiming in vain for a kind of frantic bohemian charm, with a baby as deus ex machina.
w William Peter Blatty *d* Arthur Hiller *ph* Douglas Slocombe *m* Lyn Murray
☆ Warren Beatty, Leslie Caron, Hermione Gingold, Lionel Stander, Robert Cummings, Keenan Wynn, Cathleen Nesbitt
'Good-natured bounce the picture has, but the going gets mighty bumpy and frantic in this harmless story.' – *New York Times*

Promised Land
US 1988 103m colour
Vestron/Wildwood/Oxford Film Company
Two high-school friends meet a couple of years later, when one is a cop and the other a robber.
Atmospheric, downbeat tale of thwarted hopes.
wd Michael Hoffman *ph* Ueli Steiger, Alexander Gruszynski *m* James Newton Howard *pd* Eugenio Zanetti *ed* David Spiers
☆ Kiefer Sutherland, Meg Ryan, Jason Gedrick, Tracy Pollan, Googy Gress, Deborah Richter

Promises in the Dark
US 1979 115m Metrocolor
Warner/Orion (Jerome Hellman)
A young girl dies of cancer.
Depressing and not particularly well done case history, a curious enterprise in view of the hundreds of television movies relentlessly exploring the same field.
w Loring Mandel *d* Jerome Hellman *ph* Adam Holender *m* Leonard Rosenman
☆ Marsha Mason, Ned Beatty, Susan Clark, Michael Brandon, Kathleen Beller, Paul Clemens

The Promoter: see *The Card*

'Before Love Comes Trust. Before Trust Comes…'
Proof **
Australia 1991 90m colour
Artificial Eye/House & Moorhouse Films/Australian Film Commission/Film Victoria (Lynda House)
A blind photographer spurns the love of his housekeeper and forms a friendship with a restaurant worker who describes his photographs to him.
A complex story of betrayal that was a notable debut for its director.
wd Jocelyn Moorhouse *ph* Martin McGrath *m* Not Drowning, Waving *pd* Patrick Reardon *ed* Ken Sallows
☆ Hugo Weaving, Genevieve Picot, Heather Mitchell, Jeffrey Walker, Daniel Pollock, Frankie J. Holden, Frank Gallacher, Saskia Post
'An imaginative ethical and psychological drama that is as gripping as a thriller.' – *Philip French, Observer*
'One of this or any year's most confident and original writer-director debuts … a breakthrough in concept and technique.' – *Alexander Walker, London Evening Standard*

Proof of Life
US/GB 2000 135m Technicolor Panavision
Warner/Castle Rock/Bel-Air/Anvil (Taylor Hackford, Charles Mulvehill)
After her husband is kidnapped in South America, a wife hires an ex-SAS officer to negotiate his release.
A movie that fails to make an audience care for the people involved, for all its attempts to update Casablanca *with its repressed romance and world-weary airs.*
w Tony Gilroy *Vanity Fair article* *Adventures in the Ransom Trade* by William Prochnau *book* *Long March to Freedom* by Thomas Hargrove *d* Taylor Hackford *ph* Slawomir Idzak *m* Danny Elfman *pd* Bruno Rubeo *ed* John Smith, Sheldon Kahn *cos* Ruth Myers
☆ Meg Ryan (Alice Bowman), Russell Crowe (Terry Thorne), David Morse (Peter Bowman), Pamela Reed (Janis Goodman), David Caruso (Dino), Anthony Heald (Ted Fellner), Stanley Anderson (Jerry), Gottfried John (Eric Kessler), Alun Armstrong (Wyatt), Michael Kitchen (Ian Havery), Margo Martindale (Ivy)
'A complete no-brainer.' – *Guardian*
'A disappointingly routine thriller that prefers to lean on tired Hollywood conventions rather than to explore fresh dramatic and stylistic territory.' – *Todd McCarthy, Variety*

'It lives. Don't move. Don't breathe. There's nowhere to run. It will find you.'
Prophecy
US 1979 102m Movielab Panavision
Paramount (Robert L. Rosen)
In rural Maine, mercury poisoning produces huge animal mutants.
Unpleasant ecological shocker with no particular talent in evidence.
w David Seltzer *d* John Frankenheimer *ph* Harry Stradling Jnr *m* Leonard Rosenman *pd* William Craig Smith
☆ Talia Shire, Robert Foxworth, Armand Assante, Richard Dysart

The Prophecy
US 1995 96m colour
Neo Motion (Joel Soisson)
aka: *God's Army*
A former priest turned detective discovers that the angel Gabriel is revolting against God and, to help with strategy, is seeking the soul of a dead general that has been hidden in a living girl.
Bizarre low-budget chase thriller that is enjoyable in an over-the-top way; it's helpful to discover that bad angels wear black leather trousers.
wd Gregory Widen *ph* Bruce D. Johnson, Richard Clabaugh *m* David C. Williams *pd* Clark Hunter *ed* Sonny Baskin *sp* Jor van Kline
☆ Christopher Walken, Elias Koteas, Eric Stoltz, Virginia Madsen, Moriah Snyder, Amanda Plummer, Viggo Mortensen, Adam Goldberg
'An occult freakshow so inert it seems to have been pasted together out of stock footage.' – *Owen Gleiberman, Entertainment Weekly*

'Their mistake was trusting her.'
The Proposal
US 1999 91m colour
Curb/Front Street (Carole Curb Nemoy/Mike Curb, Harvey Kahn)
A paranoid undercover cop investigating a ruthless gangster reluctantly accepts a female partner when he needs to pretend to be married.
A slow-paced thriller with not many thrills and an inevitable romance; it never achieves any feeling of place or reality.
w Maurice Hurley *d* Richard Gale *ph* Curtis Petersen *m* Joseph Conlan *pd* Ilya Obretenov *ed* Richard Benwick, Pamela Benwuck
☆ Jennifer Esposito (Susan Reese), Nick Moran (Terry Martin), Stephen Lang (Simon Bacig), William B. Davis (Agent Frank Gruning), Michael Kopsa (Zack Mallette), Alex Daikun (Jimmy), Brian Jensen (Ray), Mark Acheson (Jules), Ted Kozma (Jojo), Jerry Walliser (Ice)

'One man gave up everything he owned. The other, everything he believed in.'

The Proposition

US 1998 110m Technicolor

Polygram/Interscope (Ted Field, Diane Nabatoff, Scott Kroopf)

In Boston in the 30s, a man falls in love with the wife of an impotent lawyer after he is hired to impregnate her.

A lurid melodrama of sudden deaths, overwhelming passions and a priest behaving badly, it hovers on the edge of risibility.

w Rick Ramage *d* Lesli Linka Glatter *ph* Peter Sova *m* Stephen Endelman *pd* David Brisbin *ed* Jacqueline Cambas

☆ Kenneth Branagh, Madeleine Stowe, William Hurt, Neil Patrick Harris, Robert Loggia, Josef Sommer, Blythe Danner, David Byrd

'*The Proposition* is an offer most people will be able to refuse.' – *Todd McCarthy, Variety*

The Proprietor

GB/France/Turkey/US 1996 113m Fujicolour

Warner/Merchant Ivory/Ognon/Fez (Humbert Balsan, Donald Rosenfeld)

A Jewish writer returns from New York to buy a hotel in Paris as a means of investigating her past and her mother's death at the hands of the Nazis.

Unsuccessful and meandering exploration of multi-culturalism; it never quite comes into focus, whether dealing with highbrow or with popular culture.

w Jean-Marie Besset, George Trow, Andrew Litvak *d* Ismail Merchant *ph* Larry Pizer *m* Richard Robbins *pd* Bruno Santini, Kevin Thompson *ed* William Webb

☆ Jeanne Moreau, Sean Young, Sam Waterston, Christopher Cazenove, Nell Carter, Jean-Pierre Aumont, Austin Pendleton

'For once, even Moreau's magic is not enough to save a film.' – *George Perry*

Proshchanie: see *Farewell*

Prosperity

US 1932 90m bw

MGM

Mothers-in-law disagree about the marriage of their children.

Reliable comedy of the Depression, marking the last teaming of its popular stars.

w Eve Greene, Zelda Sears *d* Sam Wood

☆ *Marie Dressler, Polly Moran*, Anita Page, Norman Foster, Henry Armetta

'Sure-fire money picture ... could stand a little cutting but on the whole it's a workmanlike production.' – *Variety*

Prospero's Books **

Netherlands/France/Italy 1991 120m colour

Palace/Allarts/Cinea/Camera One/Penta/Elsevier Vendex/Film Four/VPRO/Canal Plus/NHK (Kees Kasander, Denis Wigman)

Abandoned with his daughter on an island, the former Duke of Milan invokes a storm to wreck the ship carrying those who betrayed him and so regain his dukedom.

A free and exuberant adaptation of Shakespeare, using the techniques of High Definition Television and computer technology to create dense, rich, bookish images and with Gielgud speaking virtually all of the verse. It may be best watched on video, where you can rewind the film or freeze-frame images to take it all in.

wd Peter Greenaway *play* *The Tempest* by William Shakespeare *ph* Sacha Vierny *m* Michael Nyman *pd* Ben van Os, Jan Roelfs *ed* Marina Bodbyl

☆ John Gielgud, Michael Clark, Michel Blanc, Erland Josephson, Isabelle Pasco, Tom Bell, Kenneth Cranham, Mark Rylance, Gérard Thoolen, Pierre Bokma, Michiel Romeyn

'An intellectually and erotically rampaging meditation on the arrogance and value of the artistic process.' – *Variety*

'A remarkable feast, taking in the video revolution at one level and a highly literate interpretation of Shakespeare at another. Nothing quite like it has been seen before, let alone from a British director.' – *Derek Malcolm, Guardian*

Prostitute

GB 1980 96m colour

Kestrel (Tony Garnett)

A provincial tart moves into the West End.

Downbeat, supposedly realistic documentary drama which ends up being depressing but not in the least titillating.

wd Tony Garnett *ph* Charles Stewart *m* The Gangsters

☆ Eleanor Forsythe, Kate Crutchley, Kim Lockett, Nancy Samuels

'There's something funny going on in the world of diplomacy!'

Protocol

US 1984 96m Technicolor

Warner (Anthea Sylbert)

A cocktail waitress thwarts an assassination and becomes a career diplomat.

Star comedy with Something to Say and not much to laugh at; a step down even from Private Benjamin.

w Buck Henry *d* Herbert Ross *ph* William A. Fraker *m* Basil Poledouris *pd* Bill Malley *ed* Paul Hirsch

☆ Goldie Hawn, Chris Sarandon, Gail Strickland, Richard Romanus, André Gregory, Cliff de Young

Prototype

US 1992 94m colour

Filmtown (Gian-Carlo Scandiuzzi, Phillip Roth)

In Los Angeles in the 21st century, a cripple is transformed into an indestructible cybernetic robot in order to eliminate the last of the Omegas, human beings altered to become the new leaders of civilization.

Post-apocalyptic science fiction, cheap in every respect, indifferently acted and where the future looks much like the present, only dirtier and with no-smoking rules relaxed.

wd Phillip Roth *ph* Mark W. Gray *m* Emilio Kauderer *ed* Daniel Lawrence

☆ Lane Lenhart, Robert Tossberg, Brenda Swanson, Paul Coulj, Mitchell Cox, Sebastien Scandiuzzi

'Dingy visuals, murky scripting, vague characters and a lack of actual action render the whole thing remarkably unexciting.' – *Empire*

The Proud and Profane

US 1956 112m bw Vistavision

Paramount (William Perlberg)

In the Pacific War a Roman Catholic widow falls for a tough lieutenant colonel. ('My pleasure is physical; my men call me The Beast.')

Unlikely romantic melodrama with a certain amount of plain speaking, otherwise routine.

wd George Seaton *novel* *The Magnificent Bastards* by Lucy Herndon Crockett *ph* John F. Warren *m* Victor Young *ad* Hal Pereira, A. Earl Hedrick

☆ William Holden, Deborah Kerr, Thelma Ritter, Dewey Martin, William Redfield

art direction

The Proud and the Beautiful

France 1953 90m bw

C.I.C.C./Chrysaor/Iena/Reforma (Louis Wipf, Felipe Subervielle)

original title: *Les Orgueilleux*

aka: *The Proud Ones*

In a small Mexican town, a drunken doctor is redeemed by the love of a tourist unexpectedly detained by the sudden death of her husband from a contagious disease.

Ineffably silly, poorly acted and unconvincing romance.

w Jean Aurenche, Yves Allegret *novel* *L'Amour Rédempteur* by Jean-Paul Sartre *d* Yves Allégret *ph* Alex Phillips *m* Paul Misraki *ad* Gunther Gerszo *ed* Claude Nicole

☆ Michele Morgan, Gérard Philipe, Victor Manuel Mendoza, Carlos Lopez Moctezuma, Michele Cordoue, Andre Toffel, Arturo Soto Rangel

Jean-Paul Sartre

The Proud Ones: see *The Proud and the Beautiful (1953)*

The Proud Ones

US 1956 94m Eastmancolor Cinemascope

TCF (Robert L. Jacks)

A marshal cleans up a crooked town despite the hazards of his own physical disability and a deputy who hates him.

Entertaining though rather foolishly scripted Western.

w Edmund North, Joseph Patracca *d* Robert D. Webb *ph* Lucien Ballard *m* Lionel Newman

☆ Robert Ryan, Jeffrey Hunter, Virginia Mayo, Robert Middleton

'One has only to look at a first-rate Western to recognise the makeshift quality of *The Proud Ones*.' – *Dilys Powell*

The Proud Ones *

France 1980 118m Eastmancolor

Gala/Production Bela/TF1 (Georges de Beauregard)

original title: *Le Cheval d'Orgueil*

In the early years of the century, a young boy grows up in a peasant community in Brittany.

Lovingly observed and glossy exercise in nostalgia, ravishing to look at, but somewhat stilted.

w Daniel Boulanger, Claude Chabrol *book* Pierre-Jakez Helias *d* Claude Chabrol *ph* Jean Rabier *m* Pierre Jansen *ad* Hilton McConnico *ed* Monique Fardoulis

☆ Jacques Dufilho, Bernadette Lesache, François Cluzet, Ronan Hubert, Paul Leperson, Pierre Le Rumeur, Michel Blanc

The Proud Rebel

US 1958 103m Technicolor

MGM/Sam Goldwyn Jnr

After the Civil War, a Southerner wanders the Yankee states in search of a doctor to cure his mute son; he falls for a lady farmer and his son finds his voice at a crucial moment.

Pretty dim family Western for pretty dim families; everything happens precisely according to plan.

w Joseph Patracca, Lillie Hayward *d* Michael Curtiz *ph* Ted McCord *m* Jerome Moross

☆ Alan Ladd, Olivia de Havilland, David Ladd, Dean Jagger, Cecil Kellaway, Harry Dean Stanton, Henry Hull, John Carradine, James Westerfield

The Proud Valley *

GB 1939 76m bw

Ealing (Sergei Nolbandov)

A black stoker helps unemployed Welsh miners reopen their pits.

Neat little propaganda drama.

w Roland Pertwee, Louis Golding, Jack Jones *d* *Pen Tennyson* *ph* Roy Kellino, Glen MacWilliams *m* Ernest Irving

☆ *Paul Robeson*, Edward Chapman, Edward Rigby, *Rachel Thomas*, Simon Lack, Clifford Evans, Allan Jeayes

'The direction of the quiet documentary scenes is good, but Mr Pen Tennyson, who may have been handicapped by an undistinguished cast and a wobbly script, seems ill at ease with drama.' – *Graham Greene, The Spectator*

Providence *

France/Switzerland 1977 107m Eastmancolor

Action Film/Société Française de Production/FR3/Citel (Philippe Dussart)

A famous writer, dying, spends a painful night in unpleasant and sometimes fantastic recollections of his sons and their women; but the reality, when they come to lunch next day, is somewhat different.

Despite its cast and other credits, this is a repellent and not too well acted study in the lack of communication, told at undue length and in turgid colour.

w David Mercer *d* Alain Resnais *ph* Ricardo Aronovich *m* Miklos Rozsa *ad* Jacques Saulnier

☆ *John Gielgud*, Dirk Bogarde, Ellen Burstyn, David Warner, Elaine Stritch

'The movie is peculiarly fastidious and static: you feel as if it were going to dry up and blow away.' – *New Yorker*

La Provinciale: see *A Girl from Lorraine*

The Prowler *

US 1950 92m bw

Horizon (Sam Spiegel)

A discontented wife thinks she sees a prowler and calls a cop; they have an affair and murder her husband.

Another variant on Double Indemnity *and* The Postman Always Rings Twice; *the script is terse and the actors well-handled.*

w Hugo Butler *d* *Joseph Losey* *ph* Arthur Miller *m* Lyn Murray

☆ Van Heflin, Evelyn Keyes, John Maxwell, Katharine Warren

'A film in which the spectator is repelled by the characters, finds in them no curiosity of nature to overcome his repugnance, and is therefore indifferent to their fate; and I call that a nauseating film.' – *Dilys Powell*

'A rivetingly cool, clean thriller.' – *NFT, 1973*

Prudence and the Pill *

GB 1968 92m DeLuxe

TCF/Kenneth Harper, Ronald Kahn

A girl borrows her mother's contraceptive pills and replaces them with aspirin, causing no end of complications.

Self-consciously naughty sex comedy with a long dénouement and some stiff patches to affect one's enjoyment of the brighter moments.

w Hugh Mills *play* Hugh Mills *d* Fielder Cook *ph* Ted Moore *m* Bernard Ebbinghouse

☆ David Niven, Deborah Kerr, Edith Evans, Keith Michell, Robert Coote, Irina Demick, Joyce Redman, Judy Geeson

'Everybody winds up pregnant to clutter the earth, apparently, with people as obnoxious as their progenitors.' – *Judith Crist*

Przesluchnie: see *Interrogation*

Psyche 59

GB 1964 94m bw

Columbia/Troy/Schenck (Philip Hazelton)

A wife recovers from blindness after realizing that her husband is in love with her sister.

Pretentious melodrama with stuffy dialogue, pompous direction and irritating characters.

w Julian Halevy (Julian Zimet) *novel* Françoise de Ligneris *d* Alexander Singer *ph* Walter Lassally *m* Kenneth V. Jones

☆ Patricia Neal, Curt Jurgens, Samantha Eggar, Ian Bannen, Beatrix Lehmann

† Screenwriter Zimet wrote under a pseudonym because he was blacklisted at the time.

Psychic Killer

US 1975 90m

Avco Embassy (Mardi Rustam)

A man released from an asylum kills those who put him there by the power of his mind.

Low-budget exploitation movie that draws heavily on Hitchcock, even if it substitutes heavy-handedness for his teasing style.

w Mike Angel, Greydon Clark, Raymond Danton *d* Raymond Danton *ph* Herb Pearl *m* William Kraft *ad* Joel Leonard *ed* Mike Brown

☆ Jim Hutton, Paul Burke, Julie Adams, Nehemiah Persoff, Neville Brand, Aldo Ray, Della Reese, Rod Cameron

'The screen's master of suspense moves his camera into the icy blackness of the unexplained!'

'Don't give away the ending – it's the only one we have!'

Psycho ****

US 1960 109m bw

Shamley/Alfred Hitchcock

At a lonely motel vicious murders take place and are attributed to the manic mother of the young owner.

Curious shocker devised by Hitchcock as a tease and received by most critics as an unpleasant horror piece in which the main scene, the shower stabbing, was allegedly directed not by Hitchcock but by Saul Bass. After enormous commercial success it achieved classic status over the years; despite effective moments of fright, it has a childish plot and script, and its interest is that of a tremendously successful confidence trick, made for very little money by a TV crew.

w Joseph Stefano *novel* Robert Bloch *d* *Alfred Hitchcock (and Saul Bass)* *ph* John L. Russell *m* *Bernard Herrmann* *ad* Joseph Hurley, Robert Clatworthy

☆ *Anthony Perkins*, Vera Miles, John Gavin, Janet Leigh, John McIntire, Martin Balsam, Simon Oakland

'Probably the most visual, most cinematic picture he has ever made.' – *Peter Bogdanovich*

'I think the film is a reflection of a most unpleasant mind, a mean, sly, sadistic little mind.' – *Dwight MacDonald*

† When asked by the press what he used for the blood in the bath, Mr Hitchcock said: 'Chocolate sauce.'

†† This is the whole text of Hitchcock's trailer, in which he audaciously wandered round the sets and practically gave away the entire plot: Here we have a quiet little motel, tucked away off the main highway, and as you see perfectly harmless looking, whereas it has now become known as the scene of a crime ... This motel also has an adjunct, an old house which is, if I may say so, a little more sinister looking. And in this house the most dire, horrible events took place. I think we can go inside because the place is up for sale – though I don't know who would buy it now. In that window in the second floor, the one in front, that's where the woman was first seen. Let's go inside. You see, even in daylight this place looks a bit sinister. It was at the top of these stairs that the second murder took place. She came out of that door there and met the victim at the top. Of course in a flash there was the knife, and in no time the victim tumbled and fell with a horrible crash ... I think the back broke immediately it hit the floor. It's difficult to describe the way ... the twisting of the ... I won't dwell on it. Come upstairs. Of course the victim, or should I say victims, hadn't any idea of the kind of people they'd be confronted with in this house. Especially the woman. She was the weirdest and the most ... well, let's go into her bedroom. Here's the woman's room, still beautifully preserved. And the imprint of her body on the bed where she used to lie. I think some of her clothes are still in the wardrobe. (He looks, and shakes his head.) Bathroom. This was the son's room but we won't go in there because his favourite spot was the little parlour behind the office in the motel. Let's go down there. This young man ... you have to feel sorry for him. After all, being dominated by an almost maniacal woman was enough to ... well, let's go in. I suppose you'd call this his hideaway. His hobby was taxidermy. A crow here, an owl there. An important scene took place in this room. There was a private supper here. By the way, this picture has great significance because ... let's go along into cabin number one. I want to show you something there. All tidied up. The bathroom. Oh, they've cleaned all this up now. Big difference. You should have seen the blood. The whole place was ... well, it's too horrible to describe. Dreadful. And I tell you, a very important clue was found here. (Shows toilet.) Down there. Well, the murderer, you see, crept in here very slowly – of course, the shower was on, there was no sound, and ...

Music wells up fiercely, shower curtain swishes across, blackout.

Voice: The picture you must see from the beginning – or not at all.

Janet Leigh's book *Psycho: Behind the Scenes of the Classic Thriller* (1995) chronicles the making of the film.

Alfred Hitchcock; John L. Russell; Janet Leigh; art direction

'A New Vision Of The Most Frightening Movie Experience Of All Time.'

Psycho

US 1998 104m DeLuxe

Universal/Imagine (Brian Grazer, Gus Van Sant)

A mother's boy murders a woman who visits his isolated motel.

A genuine curiosity, though, unfortunately, not a very interesting one: a remake of Hitchcock's thriller that hardly deviates from the original, except that it is in colour, the acting is inferior, and the content is a little tired.

w Josef Stefano *novel* Robert Bloch *d* Gus Van Sant *ph* Chris Doyle *m* Bernard Herrmann, Danny Elfman *pd* Tom Foden *ed* Amy Duddleston

☆ Vince Vaughn, Julianne Moore, Viggo Mortensen, William H. Macy, Anne Heche

'This version isn't a sacrilege – it's just pointless.' – *Anthony Quinn, Independent*

'However low-yield the shift in meaning Van Sant accomplishes proves to be, it's enough to justify the experiment: same film, different meaning. Where Hitchcock's Norman is conclusively Other, Van Sant's is one of us.' – *Gavin Smith, Sight and Sound*

'It's 22 years later and Norman Bates is coming home!'

Psycho 2 *

US 1983 113m Technicolor

Universal/Oak (Hilton A. Green)

Despite protests from the sister of one of his victims, Norman Bates is released after 22 years in a mental institution ... and the murders begin again.

A reasonably inventive sequel, if on the gory side. It probably holds the record for the longest delayed follow-up.

w Tom Holland *d* Richard Franklin *ph* Dean Cundey *m* Jerry Goldsmith *pd* John W. Corso

☆ Anthony Perkins, Vera Miles, Meg Tilly, Robert Loggia, Dennis Franz

'It's all very well having your tongue in your cheek, but it helps to have a brain in your head.' – *Sunday Times*

Psycho 3

US 1986 93m colour

Universal/Hilton A. Green

A suicidal novice flees after unwittingly causing the death of another nun, and takes refuge at the Bates Motel.

More variations on the original Psycho murders, with invention wearing a bit thin by now.

w Charles Edward Pogue *d* Anthony Perkins *ph* Bruce Surtees *m* Carter Burwell *pd* Henry Bumstead *ed* David Blewitt

☆ Anthony Perkins, Diana Scarwid, Jeff Fahey, Roberta Maxwell

Psycho Sex Fiend: see *Scream ... and Die!*

Psycho-Circus: see *Circus of Fear*

Psychomania

GB 1972 91m Technicolor

Benmar (Andrew Donally)

A Hells Angels motor cyclist commits suicide and returns from the dead an invulnerable monster.

Arrant nonsense of the macabre sort, sometimes irresistibly amusing.

w Armand d'Usseau *d* Don Sharp *ph* Ted Moore *m* David Whitaker

☆ George Sanders, Nicky Henson, Beryl Reid, Robert Hardy

The Psychopath

GB 1966 83m Techniscope

Paramount/Amicus (Milton Subotsky)

Men are found dead in London, each with a doll beside him.

Complicated horror thriller in which the actors go further over the top the more the plot winds down.

w Robert Bloch *d* Freddie Francis *ph* John Wilcox *m* Philip Martell

☆ Patrick Wymark, Margaret Johnston, John Standing, Alexander Knox, Judy Huxtable, Don Borisenko, Thorley Walters, Colin Gordon

Puberty Blues

Australia 1982 81m Eastmancolor

Panavision

Limelight

Teenage girls aim to become beach groupies.

Both repellent and boring, this mindless sex movie has little more to offer than the beach extravaganzas of the sixties.

w Margaret Kelly *novel* Kathy Lette, Gabrielle Carey *d* Bruce Beresford *ph* Donald McAlpine *pd* David Copping

☆ Nell Schofield, Jad Capelja, Geoff Rhoe, Tony Hughes, Sandy Paul

Public Access

US/Japan 1993 87m DeLuxe

Cinemabeam (Kenneth Kokin, Adam Ripp)

A new broadcaster in town begins a telephone chat show that causes intense controversy.

An interesting film that promises more than it delivers: it hovers tensely on the edge of revelation for most of its length, but then ends disappointingly.

w Christopher McQuarrie, Michael Feit Dougan, Bryan Singer *d* Bryan Singer *ph* Bruce Douglas Johnson *m* John Ottman *pd* Jan Sessler *ed* John Ottman

☆ Ron Marquette, Dina Brooks, Burt Williams, Larry Maxwell, Charles Kavanaugh, Brandon Boyce

'Serious-minded and bounces around some provocative ideas, but is vague about such important matters as key story points, motivation and overriding theme.' – *Todd McCarthy, Variety*

'It's an arresting beginning, shot in a baroque style that defies a puny budget.' – *Adam Mars-Jones, Independent*

Public Deb Number One

US 1940 80m bw

TCF

A waiter spanks a spoiled society girl at a communist rally, and accepts a job which makes him a capitalist.

Lively comedy packed with familiar faces.

w Karl Tunberg, Darrell Ware *d* Gregory Ratoff

☆ Brenda Joyce, George Murphy, Ralph Bellamy, Elsa Maxwell, Mischa Auer, Charles Ruggles, Maxie Rosenbloom, Berton Churchill, Franklin Pangborn, Hobart Cavanaugh, Lloyd Corrigan, Elisha Cook Jnr

'Drama that hurls a mighty challenge to all humanity!'

Public Enemy ***

US 1931 84m bw

Warner

GB title: *Enemies of the Public*

Two slum boys begin as bootleggers, get too big for their boots, and wind up dead.

Although it doesn't flow as a narrative, this early gangster film still has vivid and startling scenes and was most influential in the development of the urban American crime film.

w Harvey Thew *story* Kubec Glasmon, John Bright *d William Wellman ph Dev Jennings* *m* David Mendoza

☆ *James Cagney*, Edward Woods, Jean Harlow, Joan Blondell, Beryl Mercer, Donald Cook, Mae Clarke, Leslie Fenton

'Roughest, most powerful and best gang picture to date. So strong as to be repulsive in some aspects, plus a revolting climax. No strong cast names but a lot of merit.' – *Variety*

'The real power of The Public Enemy lies in its vigorous and brutal assault on the nerves and in the stunning acting of James Cagney.' – *James Shelley Hamilton*

'A postscript said that the producers wanted to "depict honestly an environment that exists today in certain strata of American life, rather than glorify the hoodlum or the criminal". The film had a different effect: Cagney was playful and dynamic, and so much more appealing than the characters opposed to him that audiences rooted for him in spite of themselves.' – *Martin Quigley Jnr, 1970*

'What not many people know is that right up to two days before shooting started, I was going to play the good guy, the pal. Edward Woods played it in the end.' – *James Cagney*

Kubec Glasmon, John Bright

Public Enemy's Wife

US 1936 78m bw

Warner (Sam Bischoff)

GB title: *G-Man's Wife*

A girl agrees to marry an escaped convict so that the FBI can track him down.

Lower-berth gangster thrills culminating in a chase climax; neatly enough done.

w Abem Finkel, Harold Buckley *story* David O. Selznick, P. J. Wolfson *d* Nick Grinde *ph* Ernest Haller

☆ Pat O'Brien, Margaret Lindsay, Robert Armstrong, Cesar Romero, Dick Foran, Dick Purcell

† Remade as *Bullets for O'Hara* (1942).

The Public Eye: see *Follow Me*

'Murder. Scandal. Crime. No matter what he was shooting, Bernzy never took sides he only took pictures ... Except once.'

The Public Eye

US 1992 99m colour

UIP/Universal (Sue Baden-Powell)

A tabloid newspaper photographer becomes involved with a beautiful woman who runs a night-club and is in trouble with the Mafia.

A modern attempt at a film noir set in the 1940s that works only intermittently.

wd Howard Franklin *ph* Peter Suschitzky *m* Mark Isham *pd* Marcia Hinds-Johnson *ed* Evan Lottman *sp* Industrial Light and Magic

☆ Joe Pesci, Barbara Hershey, Stanley Tucci, Jerry Adler, Jared Harris, Richard Riehle, Bryan Travis Smith

'Never quite takes off, either as romantic melodrama or as a consideration of one very eccentric man's means of self-expression.' – *Vincent Canby, New York Times*

† The film was based in part on the New York photographer Weegee, whose book of photographs of the seamier side of life inspired the movie *The Naked City* (qv).

Public Hero Number One

US 1935 89m bw

MGM (Lucien Hubbard)

A G-man goes undercover to track down the Purple Gang.

Moderate thick ear dating from the time when studios tried to smother public outcry against gangster films by presenting the cop as the hero.

w Wells Root *d* J. Walter Ruben *ph* Gregg Toland

☆ Chester Morris, Jean Arthur, Joseph Calleia, Lionel Barrymore, Paul Kelly, Lewis Stone, Paul Hurst

'Rates with the best of the G-men pictures.' – *Variety*

'The best picture on criminal life I've seen.' – *Otis Ferguson*

'Knowing where to draw the line'

Puckoon

GB/Ireland/Germany 2002 83m Technicolor

Guerilla/MPB/Y2K/Insight/Distinguished Features (Ken Tuohy, Terence Ryan)

In 1924, a small village is divided by the border between the Irish Republic and Northern Ireland, which cuts through the pub and the church.

Valiant attempt to bring to the screen Spike Milligan's surreal humour, but it's watered down into the usual Irish whimsy.

wd Terence Ryan *novel* Spike Milligan *ph* Peter Hannan *m* Richard Hartley, Pol Brennan *pd* John Bunker *ed* Dermot Diskin

☆ Sean Hughes (Dan Madigan), Elliott Gould (Dr Goldstein), Daragh O'Malley (Father Rudden), John Lynch (O'Brien), Griff Rhys Jones (Col Stokes), Nickolas Grace (Foggerty), B. J. Hogg (Rafferty), David Kelly (O'Toole), Milo O'Shea (Sgt McGillikuddie), Freddie Jones (Sir John Meredith), Richard Attenborough (Writer-Director)

'There's a lot to enjoy in this tall tale.' – *David Stratton, Variety*

Puerto Escondido

Italy 1993 125m colour

Mayfair/Pentafilm/Colorado (Maurizio Totti, Mario and Vittorio Cecchi Gori)

A Milanese bank manager drops out and goes to Mexico after seeing a policeman murder a colleague and then try to kill him, but his troubles follow him.

Amiable comedy, but one that never comes close to making any point, other than a vague approval of escapism.

w Enzo Monteleone, Diego Abatantuono, Gabriele Salvatores *d* Gabriele Salvatores *ph* Italo Petriccione *m* Mauro Pagani, Federico de Robertis *ad* Marco Belluzzu, Alejandro Olmas *ed* Nino Baragli

☆ Diego Abatantuono, Valeria Golino, Claudio Bisio, Renato Carpentieri, Antonio Catania

'So drawn out it will take a very mellow-minded viewer not to lose patience with the cartoonish characters and their unconnected adventures.' – *Variety*

Pufnstuf
US 1970 98m Technicolor
Universal/Krofft Enterprises
A dejected boy is led by his talking flute on a talking boat to Living Island, full of strange but friendly animals in fear of an incompetent witch.
Amalgam of a TV series using life-size puppets to project a mildly pleasing variation on The Wizard of Oz, *without quite achieving the right blend of wit and charm.*
w John Fenton Murray, Si Rose *d* Hollingsworth Morse *ph* Kenneth Peach *m* Charles Fox *ad* Alexander Golitzen
☆ Jack Wild, Billie Hayes, Martha Raye, Mama Cass

I Pugni in Tasca: see *Fists in the Pocket*

Pulp *
GB 1972 95m colour
UA/Klinger-Caine-Hodges (Michael Klinger)
An ex-funeral director now living in the Mediterranean as a successful pulp fiction writer gets involved with gangsters and weirdos.
Occasionally funny pastiche which sorely lacks shape and is sustained by guest appearances and zany ideas.
wd Mike Hodges *ph* Ousama Rawi *m* George Martin
☆ Michael Caine, *Mickey Rooney*, Lizabeth Scott, Lionel Stander, Nadia Cassini, Al Lettieri, Dennis Price
'Various eccentrics act out their "turns", but never quite lift a light comedy-thriller through the more playful and productive inversions of parody.' – *Richard Combs*

Pulp Fiction ***
US 1994 153m DeLuxe Panavision
Buena Vista/Miramax/A Band Apart/Jersey (Lawrence Bender)
Four interlocking stories with unexpected twists involve a gangster, his two hitmen, his wife, a mysterious briefcase, and a boxer who refuses to throw a fight after being paid to do so.
Clever, witty, violent celebration of junk culture, drawing rather too heavily on past thrillers but blessed with some excellent performances which crackle with menace.
w Quentin Tarantino, Roger Avary *d Quentin Tarantino* *ph* Andrzej Sekula *pd* David Wasco *ed* Sally Menke
☆ *John Travolta, Samuel L. Jackson, Uma Thurman*, Harvey Keitel, Tim Roth, Amanda Plummer, Ving Rhames, Maria de Madeiros, Eric Stoltz, Rosanna Arquette, Christopher Walken, Bruce Willis
'Tarantino's adrenaline rush of an American melodrama is a brash dare to Hollywood filmmakers in their current slough of timidity. Let's see, he says, if you can be this smart about going this far.' – *Time*
'A spectacularly entertaining piece of pop culture.' – *Todd McCarthy, Variety*
'A very funky, American sort of pop masterpiece, improbable, uproarious, with bright colors and danger and blood right on the surface.' – *David Denby, New York*
† In a poll conducted by the *Sunday Times* in April 1995, its readers voted it the seventh-best film of all time, and Tarantino the seventh-best director, ahead of Martin Scorsese, Orson Welles and Stanley Kubrick but behind David Lean, Alfred Hitchcock, Michael Curtiz, Billy Wilder and Francis Ford Coppola.
Quentin Tarantino, Roger Avary (screenplay)
best picture; Quentin Tarantino; John Travolta; Samuel L. Jackson; film editing
Quentin Tarantino, Roger Avary; Samuel L. Jackson

Pulse
US 1988 95m DeLuxe
Columbia/Aspen (Patricia A. Stallone)
Visiting his father, a small boy discovers that there is a malevolent force affecting the electrical equipment in the home.
Tepid thriller, a tame variation on Poltergeist.
wd Paul Golding *ph* Peter Lyons Collister *m* Jay Ferguson *pd* Holger Gross *ed* Gib Jaffe
☆ Joey Lawrence, Cliff de Young, Roxanne Hart, Charles Tyner, Myron Healey

Pummaro
Italy 1990 102m Video Lux
Numero Uno/RAI/Cineuropa '92 (Claudio Bonivento)
A Ghanaian studying to be a doctor travels around Italy looking for his brother, who, after working in Naples, is on the run from the police and the Camorra.
A bleak, episodic account of the lives of immigrant workers and the dispossessed, which modulates into a melodramatic interracial romance; drama is too often replaced by earnestness.
w Sandro Petraglia, Stefano Rulli, Michele Placido *d* Michele Placido *ph* Vilko Filac *m* Lucio Dalla, Mauro Malavasi *ad* Lorenzo Baraldi *ed* Ruggero Mastroianni
☆ Thywill A. K. Amenya, Pamela Villoresi, Jacqueline Williams, Gerardo Scala, Nicola di Pinto, Franco Interlenghi

Pump Up the Volume *
US 1990 105m
New Line/SC Entertainment (Rupert Harvey, Sandy Stern)
A discontented student starts his own pirate radio station.
Loud and raucous and aimed at an audience that reveres rebellion and rock music.
wd Allan Moyle *ph* Walt Lloyd *md* Nicole Freegard *pd* Bruce Bolander *ed* Wendy Bricmont, Ric Keeley, Kurt Hathaway
☆ Christian Slater, Ellen Greene, Annie Ross, Samantha Mathis, Scott Paulin
'It could appeal not only to '90s teens, but to sympathetic young adults who remember the stormy passage through adolescence.' – *Variety*

Pumping Iron **
US 1976 81m colour
White Mountain Films (George Butler, Jerome Gary)
Documentary on body-builders' contest for the title of Mr Olympia.
Well-observed study in competitiveness and obsession that first brought Arnold Schwarzenegger to the general attention.
book *Pumping Iron* by Charles Gaines, George Butler *d* George Butler, Robert Fiore *ph* Robert Fiore *m* Michael Small *ed* Larry Silk, Geof Bartz
☆ Arnold Schwarzenegger, Louis Ferrigno, Natty and Victoria Ferrigno, Mike Katz, Franco Columbu

Pumping Iron II: The Women *
US 1984 107m colour
Blue Dolphin/Cinecom (George Butler)
Documentary on a 1983 contest and its preliminaries in Las Vegas, with the male judges trying to decide at what point musculation ceases to be feminine.
Enjoyable and sometimes witty, though it has an air of contrivance about it.
w Charles Gaines, George Butler *book* *Pumping Iron II: The Unprecedented Women* by Charles Gains, George Butler *d* George Butler *ph* Dyanna Taylor *m* David McHugh, Michael Montes *ed* Paul Barnes, Susan Crutcher, Jane Kurson
☆ Lori Bowen, Carla Dunlop, Bev Francis, Rachel McLish, Kris Alexander, Lydia Cheng

The Pumpkin Eater ***
GB 1964 118m bw
Columbia/Romulus (James Woolf)
A compulsive mother (of eight children) finds her third marriage rocking when she gets evidence of her husband's affairs.
Brilliantly made if basically rather irritating kaleidoscope of vivid scenes about silly people, all quite recognizable as sixties Londoners; very well acted.
w Harold Pinter *novel* Penelope Mortimer *d Jack Clayton* *ph Oswald Morris* *m* Georges Delerue
☆ *Anne Bancroft, Peter Finch, James Mason*, Maggie Smith, Cedric Hardwicke, Richard Johnson, Eric Porter
'There never was a film so rawly memorable.' – *Evening Standard*
'It is solid, serious, intelligent, stylish. It is also, for the most part, quite dead.' – *The Times*
'It plays like a house afire.' – *Time*
Anne Bancroft
Anne Bancroft; Oswald Morris

Pumpkinhead *
US 1988 86m Technicolor
UA (Howard Smith, Richard C. Weinman)
aka: *Vengeance: The Demon*
A farmer summons an earth demon to destroy the teenagers who accidentally kill his son and finds that he gets more than he expected.
Effective and chilling little shocker, gaining much from the intensity of Henriksen's performance and from its superior monster.
w Mark Patrick Carducci, Gary Gerani *poem* Ed Justin *d* Stan Winston *ph* Bojan Bazelli *m* Richard Stone *pd* Cynthia Kay Charette *ed* Marcus Manton *sp* Alec Gillis, Richard Landon, Shane Patrick Mahan, John Rosengrant, Tim Woodruff Jnr
☆ Lance Henriksen, Jeff East, John DiAguino, Kimberly Ross, Joel Hoffman, Cynthia Bain, Kerry Remsen
'An elegant and unforgettable tale of backwoods terror that will keep you enthralled.' – *John McCarty, Splatter Movie Guide*
† A dull sequel, *Pumpkinhead II* (aka *The Revenge of Pumpkinhead II: Blood Wings*), followed in 1993, directed by Jeff Burr and starring Ami Dolenz and Andrew Robinson; it was released on video.

The Punch and Judy Man *
GB 1962 96m bw
(ABP) Macconkey (Gordon L. T. Scott)
A seashore children's entertainer tries and fails to establish himself as an important citizen.
Melancholy comedy of failure which did not please its star's adherents and indeed just missed the style it was seeking.
w Philip Oakes, Tony Hancock *d* Jeremy Summers *ph* Gilbert Taylor *m* Derek Scott, Don Banks
☆ Tony Hancock, Sylvia Syms, Ronald Fraser, Barbara Murray, John Le Mesurier, Hugh Lloyd

Punch-Drunk Love *
US 2002 95m colour Panavision
Columbia/Revolution/New Line (Joanne Sellar, Daniel Lupi, Paul Thomas Anderson)
A depressed and sometimes violent dealer in novelty toilet products finds his romance threatened byy the owner of a phone-sex business.
This curious combination of lowbrow comic with mass appeal and offbeat director works in fits and starts, but is unlikely to satisfy admirers of either or even, if such there be, both.
'Essentially a one-trick pony that, hampered by an undeveloped script, ultimately pulls up lame.' – *J. Hoberman, Village Voice*
'It's very cute, very weird and madly diverting. Anderson has a firm grip on Sandler's dangerous essence and draws it out in an astonishing performance.' – *Angie Errigo, Empire*

'Dying's easy. Comedy's hard'
Punchline *
US 1988 122m DeLuxe
Columbia TriStar (Daniel Melnick, Michael Rachmil)
A housewife and aspiring stand-up comedienne is helped by another comedian with personality problems.
A serious look at the business of being funny.
wd David Seltzer *ph* Reynaldo Villalobos *m* Charles Gross *pd* Jack Degovia *ed* Bruce Green
☆ Sally Field, Tom Hanks, John Goodman, Mark Rydell, Kim Greist, Paul Mazursky, Pam Matteson

'Is there a limit to revenge?'
The Punisher
Australia 1989 90m Eastmancolor
Castle Premier/New World International/Marvel Entertainment (Robert Mark Kamen)
A former policeman, who lives in the sewers, takes revenge on the gangsters who killed his family.
Undistinguished, excessively violent action movie based on a comic-book character.
w Robert Mark Kamen, Boaz Yakin *d* Mark Goldblatt *ph* Ian Baker *m* Dennis Dreith *pd* Norma Moriceau *ed* Tim Wellburn
☆ Dolph Lundgren, Louis Gossett Jnr, Jeroen Krabbe, Kim Miyori, Bryan Marshall, Nancy Everhard, Barry Otto, Brian Rooney, Zoshka Mizak, Todd Boyce

The Punk and the Princess
GB 1993 96m Technicolor
Feature Film/Videodrome/M2 (Mike Sarne, Robin Mahoney)
aka: *The Punk*
A young punk leaves home and falls in love with a wealthy American actress.
An odd little fable, vaguely updating Romeo and Juliet, *which strings together a series of incidents of interest to its presumed audience – rows with parents and pub fights predominating – and does not bother with characterization or motivation.*
wd Mike Sarne *novel* *The Punk* by Gideon Sams *ph* Alan M. Trow *m* Claudia Sarne, Charlie Creed-Miles, Nigel Powell *ed* Gwyn Jones, Matthew Salkeld
☆ Charlie Creed-Miles, Vanessa Hadaway, David Shawyer, Jess Conrad, Yolanda Mason, Jacqueline Skarvellis, Peter Miles
'Featuring some of the most unforgivably trite "street" dialogue, contrived working-class relationships and one-dimensional performances from its two leads, it's difficult to see, post-*Slacker* generation, exactly where its appeal might lie.' – *Karen McLuskey, Empire*
† The film is based on a novel written by a 14-year-old.

Puppet Master
US 1990 90m colour
Full Moon (Hope Perello)
Four psychics who go to investigate strange happenings at an isolated hotel find themselves being attacked by living puppets.
A twist on the Frankenstein story, with some clever special effects adding a little interest to the usual slasher narrative.
w Joseph G. Collodi *story* Charles Band, Kenneth J. Hall *d* David Schmoeller *ph* Sergio Salvati *m* Richard Band *pd* John Myhre *ed* Tom Meshelski *sp* David Allen Productions
☆ Paul Le Mat, Irene Miracle, Matt Roe, Kathryn O'Reilly, Robert Frates, Merrya Small, William Hickey

Puppet Master II
US 1991 88m DeLuxe
Full Moon (David DeCoteau, John Schouweiler)
Puppets who have been brought to life, each with their own special weapon, stalk and slay a group of psychic researchers staying in a supposedly haunted hotel.
All that distinguishes this sequel from the original is the addition of some new puppets with different and gory ways of killing. They, unlike the remainder of the cast, are effectively animated.
w David Pabian *story* Charles Band *d* David Allen *ph* Thomas F. DeNove *m* Richard Band *pd* Kathleen Coates *ed* Peter Teschner, Bert Glatstein *sp* David Allen, David Barton, Steve Neill
☆ Elizabeth MacClellan, Collin Bernsen, Gregory Webb, Charlie Spradling, Steve Welles, Jeff Weston, Nita Talbot
'Gruesome thrills.' – *Variety*

The Puppet Masters *
US 1994 108m Technicolor
Hollywood Pictures (Ralph Winter)
aka: *Robert A. Heinlein's The Puppet Masters*
Parasitical aliens, who share the same mind, invade the Earth and begin to take over the population.
Slick low-budget science-fiction thriller, done with a little style and more intelligence than usual, though the three Invasion of the Bodysnatchers *movies have made the narrative somewhat familiar.*
w Ted Elliott, Terry Rossio, David S. Goyer *novel* Robert A. Heinlein *d* Stuart Orme *ph* Clive Tickner *m* Colin Towns *pd* Daniel A. Lomino *ed* William Goldenberg
☆ Donald Sutherland, Eric Thal, Julie Warner, Keith David, Will Patton, Richard Belzer, Marshall Bell, Yaphet Kotto
'A thoroughly undistinguished if inoffensive telling of Heinlein's classic tale.' – *Variety*
'Deliriously entertaining.' – *Sight and Sound*
† The film was released direct to video in Britain.

Puppet on a Chain *

GB 1970 98m Technicolor
Big City (Kurt Unger)

An American Interpol agent hunts down drug smugglers in Amsterdam.
Sadistic adventure thriller, a toughened version of James Bond, climaxing in a splendid boat chase through Amsterdam.
w Alistair MacLean, Don Sharp, Paul Wheeler *novel* Alistair MacLean *d* Geoffrey Reeve, Don Sharp *ph* Jack Hildyard, Skeets Kelly *m* Piero Piccioni
☆ Sven Bertil Taube, Barbara Parkins, Patrick Allen, Alexander Knox, Vladek Sheybal
'One suspects that a marionette also sat in for Alistair MacLean.' – *Judith Crist*

'There is always someone pulling the strings.'

The Puppetmaster **

Taiwan 1993 142m colour
Electric Pictures/Nian Dai (Qiu Fusheng)

original title: *Hsimeng Rensheng*
A Chinese boy grows to manhood and becomes a celebrated puppeteer during the 50-year occupation of Taiwan by the Japanese, which finished at the end of the Second World War.
An austere biopic, narrated by the 84-year-old Li Tienlu himself, exploring with restraint the life of an actor and puppetmaster during interesting times. The often motionless camera, the long takes and the lack of close-ups frame the action in a theatrical way, celebrating a life full of harshness, and an ancient and vanishing culture, without nostalgia.
w Wu Nianzhen, Zhu Tianwen *story* Li Tienlu *d* Hou Hsiao-Hsien *ph* Lee Pingbin *m* Chen Mingzhang, Zhang Hongda *pd* Zhan Hongzhi *ed* Liao Qingsong
☆ Li Tienlu, Lim Giong, Chen Kuizhong
'Those not attuned to Hou's distanced, controlled style will be turned off; enthusiasts, however, will relish its greater refinement, painterly visuals and deeply humanistic style.' – *Derek Elley, Variety*
'Stubbornly sluggish and as serious as a final-term dissertation.' – *Empire*

Pure Country

US 1992 112m Technicolor
Warner/Jerry Weintraub

A country singer grows tired of showbiz trappings and tries to return to his roots.
Rambling and pleasant enough meander through an urban jungle and a rural paradise, though only likely to interest fans of its star.
w Rex McGee *d* Christopher Cain *ph* Richard Bowen *m* Steve Dorff *pd* Jeffrey Howard *ed* Jack Hofstra
☆ George Strait, Lesley Ann Warren, Isabel Glasser, Kyle Chandler, John Doe, Rory Calhoun, Molly McClure
'An effective vehicle for amiable country star George Strait.' – *Variety*

The Pure Hell of St Trinian's *

GB 1960 94m bw
British Lion/Hallmark/Tudor (Frank Launder, Sidney Gilliat)
After the girls burn down St Trinian's, a dubious headmaster offers to create a new school for them.
Bright comedy performances from some of the best character actors add a gloss to familiar material.
w Frank Launder, Sidney Gilliat, Val Valentine *d* Frank Launder *ph* Gerald Gibbs *m* Malcolm Arnold *ad* Wilfred Shingleton *ed* Thelma Connell
☆ Cecil Parker, Joyce Grenfell, George Cole, Thorley Walters, Irene Handl, Eric Barker, Dennis Price, Raymond Huntley, Julie Alexander, John Le Mesurier, Liz Fraser, George Benson, Michael Ripper, Nicholas Phipps, Sidney James

Pure Luck

US 1991 96m DeLuxe
Universal/Silver Lion (Lance Hool, Sean Daniel)

A cop and his hapless assistant go to Mexico in search of a missing accident-prone heiress.
Broad and unsubtle comedy that relies for its humour on obvious and mistimed slapstick; it never rises above well-intentioned mediocrity.
w Herschel Weingrod, Timothy Harris *d* Nadia Tass *ph* David Parker *m* Jonathan Sheffer, Danny Elfman *pd* Peter Wooley *ed* Billy Weber
☆ Martin Short, Danny Glover, Sheila Kelley, Sam Wanamaker, Scott Wilson, Harry Shearer, Jorge Russek
† It is a remake of the French *Le Chevre*, directed by François Veber.

'They're a couple of zeros short of a grand.'

Purely Belter *

GB 2000 99m DeLuxe
Film4/Mumbo Jumbo (Elizabeth Karlsen)
Two young fans of Newcastle United football team dream of having season tickets to the team's games.
Pleasing comedy of youthful aspirations that strives too hard for a feel-good finale.
wd Mark Herman *novel* *The Season Ticket* by Jonathan Tulloch *ph* Andy Collins *m* Ian Broudie, Michael Gibbs *pd* Don Taylor *ed* Michael Ellis
☆ Chris Beattie (Gerry McCarten), Greg McLane (Sewell), Charlie Hardwick (Mrs McCarten), Jody Baldwin (Gemma), Kerry Ann Christiansen (Bridget), Tracy Whitwell (Clare), Roy Hudd (Mr Sewell), Tim Healy (Mr McCarten), Kevin Whatley (Mr Caird), Alan Shearer (Himself)
'Watchable, easy-going and at times genuinely moving stuff.' – *Empire*

The Purple Gang

US 1960 85m bw
Allied Artists
In Detroit during prohibition a gang of juvenile delinquents becomes as powerful as the gangsters.
Unpleasant detail mars this cops-and-robbers subject; twenty years later it would have been even more of a shocker, but it's bad enough as it is.
w Jack DeWitt *d* Frank McDonald *ph* Ellis Carter *m* Paul Dunlap
☆ Robert Blake, Barry Sullivan, Elaine Edwards, Marc Cavell, Jody Lawrance, Susie Marquette, Paul Dubov

'The "Inside Japan" Story Of Yanks Bombing Tokyo ... Taken Jap Prisoners ... Put On Trial For "Murder"!'

The Purple Heart *

US 1944 99m bw
TCF (Darryl F. Zanuck)

American prisoners of war in Japan are tried and executed.
Relentlessly sombre flagwaver, extremely persuasively presented.
w Jerome Cady, Darryl F. Zanuck *d* Lewis Milestone *ph* Arthur Miller *m* Alfred Newman
☆ Dana Andrews, Richard Conte, Farley Granger, Kevin O'Shea, Sam Levene, Don Barry, Richard Loo
'It is unusually edged, well organized and solidly acted. But I feel extremely queasy watching fiction – especially persuasive fiction – which pretends to clarify facts that are not clear, and may never become so.' – *James Agee*

Purple Heart Diary

US 1951 73m bw
Columbia (Sam Katzman)
GB title: *No Time for Tears*
Entertainers tour war zones and bring various comforts.
Sentimental piece which the USO picked up as useful propaganda.
w William Sackheim *d* Richard Quine *ph* William Whitley *m* Ross Di Maggio
☆ Frances Langford, Ben Lessy, Tony Romano, Judd Holdren

Purple Hearts

US 1984 116m Technicolor Panavision
Warner/The Ladd Company (Sidney J. Furie)

In Vietnam, a naval surgeon falls for a nurse but the course of true romance is interrupted by the war.
Conventional war heroics with time out for a trite love story; it gets sillier as it goes on.
w Rick Natkin, Sidney J. Furie *d* Sidney J. Furie *ph* Jan Kiesser *m* Robert Folk *ad* Francisco Balangue *ed* George Grenville
☆ Ken Wahl, Cheryl Ladd, Stephen Lee, Annie McEnroe, Paul McCrane, Cyril O'Reilly, David Harris, R. Lee Ermey, Drew Snyder

The Purple Mask

US 1955 82m Technicolor Cinemascope
U-I (Howard Christie)
In 1802 Paris the Royalist resistance to Napoleon is led by the mysterious Purple Mask, who also disguises himself as a foppish dandy.
Cheeky rewrite of The Scarlet Pimpernel, *with plenty of gusto but not much style.*
w Oscar Brodney *d* H. Bruce Humberstone *ph* Irving Glassberg *m* Joseph Gershenson *ad* Alexander Golitzen, Eric Orbom *ed* Ted J. Kent
☆ Tony Curtis, Dan O'Herlihy, Colleen Miller, Gene Barry, Angela Lansbury, George Dolenz, John Hoyt
'Sir Percy, one feels, would have personally conducted this lot to the guillotine.' – *MFB*

The Purple Monster Strikes

US 1945 bw serial: 15 eps
Republic

A Martian kills a great scientist and enters his body.
Early example of unpleasant aliens, a precursor of It Came from Outer Space *and* Invasion of the Body Snatchers.
d Spencer Bennet, Fred Brannon
☆ Dennis Moore, Linda Stirling, Roy Barcroft

Purple Noon: see *Plein Soleil*

Purple People Eater

US 1988 91m colour
MPCA/Vertex (Brad Krevoy, Steve Stabler)
A purple one-eyed alien helps a lonely boy learn confidence by forming a rock group and helping elderly people threatened with eviction from their homes.
Feeble kids' film based on a witless novelty hit of the late 50s; an embarrassment for all those involved.
wd Linda Shayne *ph* Peter Deming *m* Dennis Dreith *pd* Stephen Greenberg *ed* Cari Ellen Coughlin *song* Sheb Wooley
☆ Ned Beatty, Shelley Winters, Neil Patrick Harris, Peggy Lipton, James Houghton, John Brumfield, Chubby Checker, Little Richard, Sheb Wooley

The Purple Plain *

GB 1954 100m Technicolor
GFD/Two Cities (John Bryan)
During the Burma campaign, a Canadian squadron leader regains his shattered nerves during an arduous trek across country.
Psychological study and eastern adventure combined; not the best of either, but a potent crowd-puller.
w Eric Ambler *novel* H. E. Bates *d* Robert Parrish *ph* Geoffrey Unsworth *m* John Veale
☆ Gregory Peck, Maurice Denham, Win Min Than, Lyndon Brook, Brenda de Banzie, Bernard Lee, Anthony Bushell, Ram Gopal

The Purple Rose of Cairo *

US 1984 82m DeLuxe
Orion/Jack Rollins-Charles H. Joffe (Robert Greenhut)

In the thirties, a film-struck woman is confronted in reality by the hero of her dreams.
Amusing but slight comedy: several good jokes, but in sum no more than an elongated sketch.
wd Woody Allen *ph* Gordon Willis *m* Dick Hyman *pd* Stuart Wurtzel *ed* Susan E. Morse
☆ Mia Farrow, Jeff Daniels, Danny Aiello, Dianne Wiest, Van Johnson, Zoe Caldwell, John Wood, Milo O'Shea
best picture, original screenplay

Pursued *

US 1947 101m bw
(Warner) United States (Milton Sperling)

A revenge-seeking cowboy accidentally causes a tragedy in his adopted family.
Glum, good-looking revenge Western.
w Niven Busch *d* Raoul Walsh *ph* James Wong Howe *m* Max Steiner
☆ Robert Mitchum, Teresa Wright, Judith Anderson, Dean Jagger, Alan Hale, Harry Carey Jnr

Pursuit

US 1935 73m bw
Lucien Hubbard-Ned Marin/MGM
A child is kidnapped, and several people want the reward for restoring him.
Rather frantic chase thriller with insufficient variety.
w Wells Root, Lawrence G. Blochman *d* Edwin L. Marin
☆ Chester Morris, Sally Eilers, Scotty Beckett, Henry Travers, C. Henry Gordon, Dorothy Peterson, Harold Huber

The Pursuit of D. B. Cooper

US 1981 100m Metrocolor
Polygram (Daniel Wigutow, Michael Taylor)

A skyjacker bails out with his loot and is chased by various people after the reward.
Fantasy variation on a real case which was never solved; of no interest whatever despite the talent involved.
w Jeffrey Alan Fiskin *book* *Free Fall* by J. D. Reed *d* Roger Spottiswoode (also John Frankenheimer, Buzz Kulik) *ph* Harry Stradling Jnr *m* James Horner *pd* Preston Ames
☆ Robert Duvall, Treat Williams, Kathryn Harrold, Ed Flanders, Paul Gleason, R. G. Armstrong
'Doubtless a law-enforcement ploy to lure the skyjacker out of hiding: surely after seeing this mess he will want to surface and sue somebody.' – *Variety*

The Pursuit of Happiness

US 1934 75m bw
Paramount (Arthur Hornblow Jnr)
In 1776 Connecticut a Puritan maid falls for a Hessian soldier.
Mildly pleasing romantic comedy centring on the ancient practice of 'bundling' in which betrothed couples might sleep together fully clothed.
w Stephen Morehouse Avery, Jack Cunningham, J. P. McEvoy, Virginia Van Upp *play* Lawrence Langner, Armina Marshall *d* Alexander Hall *ph* Karl Struss
☆ Francis Lederer, Joan Bennett, Charles Ruggles, Mary Boland, Walter Kingsford, Minor Watson
'A comedy that will entertain and merits business.' – *Variety*

The Pursuit of Happiness *

US 1970 98m Eastmancolor
Columbia/TA Films/Norton-Simon (David Susskind)

A New York college dropout is sent to prison after a hit and run accident.
Smooth, watchable but empty youth movie.
w Sidney Carroll, George L. Sherman *d* Robert Mulligan *ph* Dick Kratina *m* Dave Grusin
☆ Michael Sarrazin, Barbara Hershey, Robert Klein, Ruth White, E. G. Marshall, Arthur Hill

Pursuit of the Graf Spee: see *The Battle of the River Plate*

Pursuit to Algiers

US 1945 65m bw
Universal (Roy William Neill)
Sherlock Holmes guards the young king of Ruritania on a sea voyage.
After an amiably lunatic first reel, this settles down as one of the dullest of the series, but it never entirely taxes the patience.
w Leonard Lee *d* Roy William Neill *ph* Paul Ivano *m* Hans Salter *md* Edgar Fairchild
☆ Basil Rathbone, Nigel Bruce, Martin Kosleck, Marjorie Riordan, Rosalind Ivan, John Abbott, Frederic Worlock, Morton Lowry

Pusher *

Denmark 1996 110m colour
Metrodome/Balboa (Henrik Danstrup)

In Copenhagen, a heroin dealer is prepared to cheat anyone in order to pay off his debt to a local gangster.
A week in the life of a loser, a tough and gritty account of a trapped, petty criminal going round in ever-diminishing circles, fiercely directed.
w Nicolas Winding Refn, Jens Dahl *d* Nicolas Winding Refn *ph* Morten Soborg *m* various *pd* Kim Lovetand Julebaek *ed* Anne Osterud
☆ Kim Bodnia, Zlatko Buric, Laura Drasbaek, Slavko Labovic, Mads Mikkelsen, Peter Anderson, Vanja Bajicic

'Brutal, upsetting and impressive in its refusal to tart itself up with the modish tricks of Quentin Tarantino or Abel Ferrara. There are no cute monologues here. No one has the time to indulge in existential reveries.' – *Richard Williams, Guardian*

Pushing Tin **

US 1999 124m DeLuxe Super 35
TCF/Fox 2000, Regency (Art Linson)

Rivalry develops between a top, long-established New York air-traffic controller and a newcomer.
Often engrossing social comedy set in a fascinating environment, with two men giving each other, and their wives, a bumpy ride; unfortunately it crash-lands half-an-hour before it ends.
w Glen Charles, Les Charles *article* *Something's Got to Give* by Darcy Frey *d* Mike Newell
ph Gale Tattersall *m* Anne Dudley *pd* Bruno Rubeo *ed* Jon Gregory
☆ John Cusack (Nick Falzone), Billy Bob Thornton (Russell Bell), Cate Blanchett (Connie Falzone), Angelina Jolie (Mary Bell), Tina Leary (Vicki Lewis), Kurt Fuller (Barry Plotkin), Matt Ross (Ron Hewitt), Jerry Grayson (Leo Morton), Michael Willis (Pat Feeney)

'An adherence to the conventions of slick Hollywood comedy-drama goes down as smoothly as a bout of clear air turbulence.' – *Simon Braund, Empire*

'One of the most consistently enjoyable US films of the year.' – *Andrew O'Hehir, Sight and Sound*

Pushover *

US 1954 91m bw
Columbia (Jules Schermer)

An honest policeman involves himself in murder for loot.
Another variation on Double Indemnity, *smoothly carpentered as the first appearance of newly-groomed star Kim Novak. The events of a night were familiar and watchable.*
w Roy Huggins *novels* *The Night Watch* by Thomas Walsh, *Rafferty* by William S. Ballinger *d* Richard Quine *ph* Lester B. White *m* Arthur Morton
☆ Fred MacMurray, Kim Novak, Phil Carey, Dorothy Malone, E. G. Marshall

Puss och Kram: see *Hugs and Kisses*

Pussycat Alley: see *The World Ten Times Over*

Pussycat, Pussycat, I Love You

US 1970 100m DeLuxe
UA/Three Pictures (Jerry Bresler)

A sex-mad writer tells a doctor how he lost his wife to a film-star.
Tedious chase comedy that goes nowhere in particular.
wd Rod Amateau *ph* Tonino Delli Colli *m* Lalo Schifrin *ad* Toni Sarzi-Braga *ed* Larry Heath
☆ Ian McShane, Anna Calder-Marshall, Severn Darden, Joyce Van Patten, John Gavin, Beba Loncar

'The gags, both visual and verbal, strain and creak, giving the impression of being made up on the spur of the moment.' – *David McGillivray, MFB*

Putney Swope *

US 1969 85m bw/Eastmancolor
Contemporary/Herald

A black adman takes over an agency, renaming it Truth and Soul Inc. and staffing it with black militants.
Anarchic, intermittently funny comedy, stuffed with jokes at the expense of most institutions.
wd Robert Downey *ph* Gerald Cotts *m* Charley Cuva *ad* Gary Weist *ed* Bud Smith
☆ Arnold Johnson, Antonio Fargas, Laura Greene, Eric Krupnik, Pepi Hermine, Ruth Hermine

'Visual graffiti of this order don't merit public exposure.' – *David Wilson, MFB*

Puttin' on the Ritz

US 1930 88m bw (colour sequence)
UA/Joseph M. Schenck (John W. Considine Jnr)

A has-been vaudevillian gets a second chance but succumbs to the demon rum.
Primitive early musical melodrama valuable only as an example of the work of its star.
w John W. Considine Jnr *d* Edward Sloman
ph Ray June *ad* William Cameron Menzies
☆ Harry Richman, Joan Bennett, James Gleason, Aileen Pringle, Lilyan Tashman, Purnell Pratt

'Entertaining backstage story with ultra production values.' – *Variety*

Putting Pants on Philip *

† US 1927 20m bw silent
Hal Roach

A respectable man meets his randy Scottish nephew who wears nothing under his kilt.
Early star comedy, allegedly their first as a team but before their more recognizable characteristics had developed. Not at all bad in its way, though developing into one long chase.
w H. M. Walker *d* Clyde Bruckman
☆ Laurel and Hardy, Sam Lufkin, Harvey Clark

Puzzle of a Downfall Child

US 1970 104m Technicolor
Universal/Newman-Foreman

Fantasy reminiscences of a top fashion model.
Pretentious, fashionable, seemingly interminable collage of sex and high living.
w Adrien Joyce (Carole Eastman) *d* Jerry Schatzberg *ph* Adam Holender *m* Michael Small
☆ Faye Dunaway, Barry Primus, Viveca Lindfors, Barry Morse, Roy Scheider

Pygmalion ****

GB 1938 96m bw
Gabriel Pascal

A professor of phonetics takes a bet that he can turn a Cockney flower seller in six months into a lady who can pass as a duchess.
Perfectly splendid Shavian comedy of bad manners, extremely well filmed and containing memorable lines and performances; subsequently turned into the musical My Fair Lady *(qv). One of the most heartening and adult British films of the thirties.*
w Anatole de Grunwald, W. P. Lipscomb, Cecil Lewis, Ian Dalrymple *play* *Bernard Shaw*
d *Anthony Asquith, Leslie Howard* *ph* Harry Stradling *m* *Arthur Honegger* *ad* Laurence Irving *ed* David Lean
☆ *Leslie Howard* (Henry Higgins), *Wendy Hiller* (Eliza Doolittle), *Wilfrid Lawson* (Alfred Doolittle), *Scott Sunderland* (Colonel Pickering), *Marie Lohr* (Mrs Higgins), *David Tree* (Freddy Eynsford-Hill), *Esmé Percy* (Count Aristid Karpathy), *Everley Gregg* (Mrs Eynsford-Hill), *Jean Cadell* (Mrs Pearce)

HIGGINS (LESLIE HOWARD): 'Yes, you squashed cabbage leaf, you disgrace to the noble architecture of these columns, you incarnate insult to the English language, I can pass you off as the Queen of Sheba.'

HIGGINS: 'Where the devil are my slippers, Eliza?'

'Ought to have big potentialities in the US, with some cutting ... An introductory title briefly gives the source of the play, which was Shakespeare's *Pygmalion*.' (!) – *Variety*

'An exhibition of real movie-making – of a sound score woven in and out of tense scenes, creating mood and tempo and characterization.' – *Pare Lorentz*

'Every possible care has been taken in the presentation of what may well prove to have a significant effect on future British film production, for it is live, human entertainment, flawlessly presented and making an obvious appeal to all kinds of audiences.' – *The Cinema*

Academy Award: Bernard Shaw; Ian Dalrymple, Cecil Lewis, W. P. Lipscomb
Academy Award nomination: best picture; Leslie Howard; Wendy Hiller

Pyjama Girl: see *The Pajama Girl Case*

Pyrates

US 1991 95m colour
Rank/Act III/Mixed Breed (Jonathan Furie)

The passion of two lovers is so incendiary that they literally set the world alight.
Odd and risible little movie, with a great deal of uninteresting chat about love.
wd Noah Stern *ph* Janusz Kaminski *m* Peter Himmelman *pd* Sherman Williams *ed* Gib Jaffe
☆ Kevin Bacon, Kyra Sedgwick, Bruce Martyn Payne, Kristin Dattilo

'Warning: This is only a love story. Do not try this at home.'

A Pyromaniac's Love Story

US 1995 94m Technicolor
Buena Vista/Hollywood (Mark Gordon)

After the neighbourhood baker's shop burns down, many people confess to starting the fire.
Genial, gently farcical fable of love that becomes too whimsical for its own good.
w Morgan Ward *d* Joshua Brand *ph* John Schwartzman *m* Rachel Portman *pd* Dan Davis *ed* David Rosenbloom
☆ William Baldwin, John Leguizamo, Sadie Frost, Erika Eleniak, Michael Lerner, Mike Starr, Julio Oscar Mechoso, Joan Plowright, Armin Mueller-Stahl, Richard Crenna

Q & A *
US 1990 132m Technicolor
Virgin/Regency/Odyssey (Arnon Milchan, Burtt Harris)

An inexperienced assistant D.A. investigates the killing of a Puerto Rican crook by a veteran policeman and uncovers widespread corruption.
Increasingly ponderous and predictable drama of an innocent struggling in a moral quicksand.
wd Sidney Lumet *novel* Judge Edwin Torres *ph* Andrezej Bartkowiak *m* Ruben Blades *pd* Philip Rosenberg *ed* Richard Cirincione
☆ Nick Nolte, Timothy Hutton, Armand Assante, Patrick O'Neal, Lee Richardson, Luis Guzman, Charles Dutton, Jenny Lumet, Paul Calderon
'One is left reflecting sadly on the miscalculations ... that make a film which opens with the bang of a superb first half gradually tail away to a whimper.' – *Tom Milne, MFB*

Q Planes **
GB 1939 82m bw
Harefield/London Films (Irving Asher, Alexander Korda)

US title: *Clouds over Europe*
A secret ray helps spies to steal test aircraft during proving flights.
Lively comedy thriller distinguished by a droll leading performance.
w Ian Dalrymple, Brock Williams, Jack Whittingham, Arthur Wimperis *d* Tim Whelan *ph* Harry Stradling *md* Muir Mathieson
☆ Ralph Richardson, Laurence Olivier, Valerie Hobson, George Merritt, George Curzon, Gus McNaughton, David Tree
'A bright vigorous little picture, and Mr Richardson's Major is the brightest thing in it. You should see it. You'll like it. It has savour.' – C. A. *Lejeune*

Q – The Winged Serpent **
US 1982 93m colour Panavision
Larco/Larry Cohen

aka: *The Winged Serpent*
An ex-con on the run finds a monstrous Aztec god, a flying serpent, nesting in the spire of the Chrysler building.
Quirky, above-average horror film with flashes of brightness.
wd Larry Cohen ph Fred Murphy *m* Robert O. Ragland *ed* Armand Lebowitz
☆ *Michael Moriarty*, Candy Clark, David Carradine, Richard Roundtree, James Dixon

Qiu Ju Da Guansi: see *The Story of Qiu Ju*

Qiuyue: see *Autumn Moon*

Quackser Fortune Has a Cousin in the Bronx *
US 1970 90m Eastmancolor
UMC (John H. Cushingham)

An Irish layabout strikes up an acquaintance with an American student.
Likeable if plotless Dublin comedy, pleasantly photographed.
w Gabriel Walsh *d* Waris Hussein *ph* Gil Taylor *m* Michael Dress *ad* Herbert Smith *ed* Bill Blunden
☆ Gene Wilder, Margot Kidder, Eileen Colgan, Seamus Ford, May Ollis, Liz Davis, Caroline Tully, David Kelly

Quadrophenia
GB 1979 120m Eastmancolor
Brent-Walker/Polytel (Roy Baird, Bill Curbishley)

A drama of bitter rivalry between Mods and Rockers on the Brighton beaches in 1964.
What passed for a successful musical at the end of the seventies is typified by this violent, screaming and wholly unattractive amalgam of noise, violence, sex and profanity.
w Dave Humphries, Martin Stellman, Franc Roddam *d* Franc Roddam *ph* Brian Tufano *m* The Who *md* John Entwistle, Pete Townshend *pd* Simon Holland *ed* Mike Taylor
☆ Phil Daniels, Mark Wingett, Philip Davis, Leslie Ash, Garry Cooper, Toyah Wilcox, Sting

Quai des Brumes ***
France 1938 89m bw
Rabinovitch

US title: *Port of Shadows*
An army deserter rescues a girl from crooks but is killed before they can escape.
Artificial, set-bound, but at the time wholly persuasive melodrama which became one of the archetypal French films of the thirties, its doomed lovers syndrome not being picked up by Hollywood until after World War II.
w Jacques Prévert novel Pierre MacOrlan *d Marcel Carné ph Eugen Schüfftan m Maurice Jaubert ad Alexander Trauner*
☆ *Jean Gabin, Michèle Morgan, Michel Simon, Pierre Brasseur*
'Unity of space, time and action give the film a classical finish.' – *Georges Sadoul*
'The sort of powerful and joyless film that the French do so well – a study in foetid atmosphere, in which the one beauty is its uncompromising honesty.' – C. A. *Lejeune*
† The plot was in fact almost identical with that of *Pépé le Moko*. The romantic pessimism of these films, plus *Le Jour Se Lève*, so suited the mood of France that Vichy officials later said: 'If we have lost the war it is because of *Quai des Brumes*.'

Quai des Orfèvres *
France 1947 105m bw
Majestic
A music hall artiste is accused of murdering the man he took to be seducing his mistress.
The equivalent of many a British Scotland Yard thriller, but a good one, with excellent acting, atmosphere and suspense.
w Henri-Georges Clouzot, Jean Ferry *novel Légitime Défense* by Stanislas-André Steeman *d Henri-Georges Clouzot ph* Armand Thirard *m* Francis Lopez
☆ *Louis Jouvet*, Bernard Blier, Suzy Delair, Pierre Larquey, Simone Rennant
'The wonder of *Quai des Orfèvres* is the way Clouzot has pricked it with life.' – *Guardian*
'A stunningly well made entertainment.' – *New Yorker, 1982*

'Two love experts in a daring game of hearts!'
Quality Street *
US 1937 84m bw
RKO (Pandro S. Berman)

When an officer returns from the Napoleonic wars, he does not recognize his sweetheart, whose beauty has faded, so she masquerades as her own capricious niece.
Fairly successful attempt to capture on screen the essence of Barrie whimsy; everyone tries hard, anyway.
w Mortimer Offner, Allan Scott *play* J. M. Barrie *d* George Stevens *ph* Robert de Grasse *m* Roy Webb
☆ Katharine Hepburn, Franchot Tone, Fay Bainter, Eric Blore, Cora Witherspoon, Estelle Winwood, Florence Lake, Joan Fontaine
'Hepburn and Tone unable to instil any life, and little entertainment, into this old-timer from legit ... one for the bonnet and shawl trade.' – *Variety*
'It is strictly a self-propelled picture, tearing breathlessly, even hysterically, through Barrie's quizzical account of a man-hunt ... But we were exhausted by the intensity of Miss Hepburn's concentration on it. Her Phoebe needs a neurologist far more than a husband. Such flutterings and jitterings and twitchings, such hand-wringings and mouth-quiverings, such runnings-about and eyebrow-raisings have not been on the screen in many a moon.' – *Frank Nugent, New York Times*
'Actually quite repulsive.' – *Katharine Hepburn*
† Previously made by MGM in 1927 (silent), with Marion Davies and Conrad Nagel; directed by Sidney Franklin.
Roy Webb

Quante Volte... Quella Notte (dubbed)
Italy/Germany 1972 90m colour
Delfino/Hape (Zeljko Kunkera, Claudio Rainis)
aka: *Four Times That Night*
Four people tell what happened after a playboy picked up a girl.
Italian fluff that copies Rashomon *with its central conceit of the same event seen from differing viewpoints, but is mainly concerned with undressing its female star, a former Miss Italy.*
w Mario Moroni, Carl Ross, Guido Leoni *d* Mario Bava *ph* Antonio Rinaldi *m* Lallo Gori *pd* Andrea Crisanti *ed* Otello Colangeli
☆ Daniela Giordano, Brett Halsey, Dick Randall, Valeria Sabel, Michael Hinz, Rainer Basedow, Pascale Petit, Brigitte Skay, Calisto Calisti

Quantez
US 1957 80m Eastmancolor Cinemascope
Universal-International
Robbers hiding for the night in a frontier town become involved in an Indian attack.
Curious, slow-paced attempt to redo The Gunfight *with inferior materials; not a profitable experience.*
w R. Wright Campbell *d* Harry Keller *ph* Carl Guthrie *m* Herman Stein
☆ Fred MacMurray, Dorothy Malone, James Barton, Sydney Chaplin, John Gavin, John Larch, Michael Ansara

Quantrill's Raiders
US 1958 68m DeLuxe Cinemascope
Allied Artists (Ben Schwalb)
A Southern agent seeks the help of Quantrill's gang to attack an army arsenal at Lawrence, Kansas, and regrets it.
Uninteresting, conventional Western with a flimsy narrative and dull characterization.
w Polly James *d* Edward Bernds *ph* William Whitley *m* Marlin Skiles *ad* David Milton *ed* William Austin
☆ Steve Cochran, Diane Brewster, Leo Gordon, Gale Robbins, Will Wright, Kim Charney, Myron Healey

The Quare Fellow
GB 1962 90m bw
BLC/Bryanston (Anthony Havelock-Allan)

Life in a Dublin prison when two men are to be hanged, as experienced by a new young warder.
Watered-down version of a rumbustious stage tragi-comedy, with not much but the gloom left.
wd Arthur Dreifuss *play* Brendan Behan *ph* Peter Hennessey *m* Alexander Faris
☆ Patrick McGoohan, Sylvia Syms, Walter Macken, Dermot Kelly, Hilton Edwards

Quartet ***
GB 1948 120m bw
GFD/Gainsborough (Anthony Darnborough)

Four stories introduced by the author.
This entertaining production began the compendium fashion (Full House, Phone Call from a Stranger, etc.) *and is fondly remembered, though all the stories had softened endings and the middle two did not work very well as drama. Subsequent Maugham compilations were* Trio *and* Encore *(both qv).*
The Facts of Life:
d Ralph Smart *ph* Ray Elton with *Basil Radford, Naunton Wayne, Mai Zetterling, Jack Watling,* James Robertson Justice
The Alien Corn:
d Harold French *ph* Ray Elton with Dirk Bogarde, Françoise Rosay, Raymond Lovell, Honor Blackman, Irene Browne
The Kite:
d Arthur Crabtree *ph* Ray Elton with *George Cole,* Hermione Baddeley, Susan Shaw, Mervyn Johns, Bernard Lee
The Colonel's Lady:
d Ken Annakin *ph* Reg Wyer with *Cecil Parker, Linden Travers, Nora Swinburne,* Ernest Thesiger, Felix Aylmer, Henry Edwards, Wilfrid Hyde-White
w R. C. Sherriff stories W. Somerset Maugham
m John Greenwood

Quartet *
GB/France 1981 101m GTC colour
TCF/Merchant Ivory (Ismail Merchant, Jean Pierre Mahot de la Querantonnais)

In 1927 Paris, a convict's wife finds herself part of a *ménage à trois.*
Slow-moving, good-looking study of characters in a milieu; as usual with films from this stable, it has nothing to please the majority.
w Ruth Prawer Jhabvala *novel* Jean Rhys *d* James Ivory *ph* Pierre Lhomme *m* Richard Robbins
☆ Isabelle Adjani, Maggie Smith, Alan Bates, Anthony Higgins

'See women defiled by monsters from outer space! Men turned killers by mysterious power more incredible than anything today's science or fiction ever imagined!'
Quatermass and the Pit **
GB 1967 97m Technicolor
Hammer/Anthony Nelson Keys

US title: *Five Million Years to Earth*
Prehistoric skulls are unearthed during London Underground excavations, and a weird and deadly force makes itself felt.
The third film of a Quatermass serial is the most ambitious, and in many ways inventive and enjoyable, yet spoiled by the very fertility of the author's imagination: the concepts are simply too intellectual to be easily followed in what should be a visual thriller. The climax, in which the devil rears over London and is 'earthed', is satisfactorily harrowing.
w Nigel Kneale TV serial Nigel Kneale *d Roy Ward Baker ph* Arthur Grant *m* Tristram Cary
☆ *Andrew Keir, James Donald, Barbara Shelley,* Julian Glover, Duncan Lamont, Edwin Richfield, Peter Copley

'You Can't Escape It! Nothing Can Destroy It! It's Coming For You From Space To Wipe All Living Things From The Face Of The Earth! Can It Be Stopped?'

The Quatermass Experiment **
GB 1955 82m bw
Exclusive/Hammer (Anthony Hinds)
US title: *The Creeping Unknown*
When a rocketship returns from space, two of its three crew members have disappeared and the third is slowly taken over by a fungus which thrives on blood.
Intelligent science fiction based on a highly successful BBC TV serial; the film version is generally workmanlike despite its obvious low budget.
w Richard Landau, Val Guest *serial Nigel Kneale* *d* Val Guest *ph* Jimmy Harvey
☆ Brian Donlevy, Jack Warner, Margia Dean, *Richard Wordsworth*, David King Wood, Thora Hird, Gordon Jackson

Quatermass II **
GB 1957 85m bw
Hammer (Anthony Hinds)
US title: *Enemy from Space*
A research station operating under military secrecy is supposed to be making synthetic foods, but is in fact an acclimatization centre for invaders from outer space.
Simplified version of a TV serial, a bit stodgy in the talk scenes, but building into sequences of genuine alarm and based on an idea of lingering persuasiveness.
w Nigel Kneale, Val Guest *serial Nigel Kneale* *d Val Guest* *ph* Gerald Gibbs *m* James Bernard
☆ Brian Donlevy, John Longden, Sidney James, Bryan Forbes, William Franklyn, Charles Lloyd Pack, Percy Herbert, Tom Chatto

Quatre Aventures de Reinette et Mirabelle: see *Four Adventures of Reinette and Mirabelle*

Les Quatre Cents Coups: see *The Four Hundred Blows*

Quattro Passi fra le Nuvole: see *Four Steps in the Clouds*

Que He Hecho Yo Para Merecer Esto?: see *What Have I Done to Deserve This?*

Que la Bête Meure ***
France/Italy 1969 110m colour
La Boétie/Rizzoli (André Génovés)
US title: *This Man Must Die*
aka: *The Beast Must Die; Killer!*
A father decides to find and murder the hit-and-run driver who killed his young son.
A complex and engrossing psychological study that ignores the thriller aspects of the story to concentrate on relationships of love and hatred, with a memorable performance from Yanne as an uncouth villain.
w Paul Gégauff *novel The Beast Must Die* by Nicholas Blake *d* Claude Chabrol *ph* Jean Rabier *m* Pierre Jansen, Brahms *ad* Guy Littaye *ed* Jacques Gaillard
☆ Michel Duchaussoy, Caroline Cellier, Jean Yanne, Anouk Ferjac, Marc di Napoli, Maurice Pialat, Jean-Louis Maury, Louise Chevalier, Guy Marly

'The movie is so attenuated and unhurried that it dies on the screen.' – *Pauline Kael*

Quebec
US 1951 85m Technicolor
Paramount
The wife of the loyalist governor of Quebec is in love with the leader of the rebels.
Ho-hum period actioner with some pretty backgrounds and not much personality.
w Alan Le May *d* George Templeton *ph* W. Howard Greene *m* Van Cleave
☆ Corinne Calvet, John Barrymore Jnr, Barbara Rush, Patric Knowles, John Hoyt, Arnold Moss

'She's so excitingly good when she's so wonderfully bad!'

Queen Bee *
US 1955 95m bw
Columbia (Jerry Wald)
A wealthy woman has a compulsion to dominate everyone around her.
Claustrophobic Southern-set melodrama obviously created for its star.
wd Ranald MacDougall *novel* Edna Lee *ph* Charles Lang *m* George Duning *md* Morris Stoloff
☆ *Joan Crawford*, Barry Sullivan, Betsy Palmer, John Ireland, Lucy Marlow, William Leslie, Fay Wray
Charles Lang

Queen Christina ***
US 1933 101m bw
MGM (Walter Wanger)
The queen of 17th-century Sweden, distressed at the thought of a political marriage, goes wandering through her country in men's clothes and falls in love with the new Spanish ambassador.
The star vehicle par excellence, *superb to look at and one of its star's most fondly remembered films. Historically it's nonsense, but put across with great style.*
w Salka Viertel, H. M. Harwood, S. N. Behrman *d Rouben Mamoulian* *ph William Daniels* *m Herbert Stothart*
☆ *Greta Garbo*, John Gilbert, Ian Keith, Lewis Stone, C. Aubrey Smith, Reginald Owen, Elizabeth Young

ANTONIO (JOHN GILBERT): 'It's all a question of climate. You cannot serenade a woman in a snowstorm. All the graces in the art of love – elaborate approaches that will make the game of love amusing – can only be practised in those countries that quiver in the heat of the sun.'

CHRISTINA (GRETA GARBO): 'I have been memorizing this room. In the future, in my memory, I shall live a great deal in this room.'

'The shortcomings, such as they are, are so far overshadowed by the potency of the premier satellite, the sterling support, the Mamoulian montage and the Behrman crisp dialogue that they're relatively unimportant; for Christina is cinch b.o.' – *Variety*

'Garbo, as enchanting as ever, is still enveloped by her unfathomable mystery.' – *Photoplay*

'An unending series of exceptional scenes.' – *Modern Screen*

† The leading male role was announced in turn for Leslie Howard, Franchot Tone, Nils Asther, Bruce Cabot and Laurence Olivier: Garbo turned them all down.

Queen Elizabeth *
France 1912 35m approx (24 fps) bw silent
Histrionic Film
original title: *Les Amours de la Reine Elisabeth*
Scenes from the life of the queen.
Abysmally boring now, this film is important in several ways. It is our best record of Sarah Bernhardt. It was immensely successful throughout the world. It made cinema interesting to all classes, not just the hoi polloi. It made the fortunes of Adolph Zukor, who bought it cheaply and went on to found Paramount Pictures. (Bernhardt is said to have remarked to him: 'You have put me in pickle for all time!')
w Eugène Moreau *d* Henri Desfontaines, Louis Mercanton
☆ Sarah Bernhardt, Lou Tellegen

Queen Kelly **
US 1928 100m approx (24 fps) bw silent
United Artists/Gloria Productions/Joseph Kennedy
A convent girl goes to the bad, is ill-used by a prince, becomes a white slave in Africa but finally inherits a fortune.
Sexually-oriented extravaganza, the last great folly of its director but never finished by him. Various versions exist: in all of them individual scenes are more entertaining than the whole. Extracts were shown in Sunset Boulevard.
wd Erich von Stroheim *ph* Gordon Pollock, Paul Ivano, Ben Reynolds. *m* Adolf Tandler *ad* Harry Miles
☆ Gloria Swanson, Walter Byron, Seena Owen

† The version released on video in 1994 is the European version of 1931, which runs for 115m.

Queen Margot: see *La Reine Margot*

Queen of Atlantis: see *L'Atlantide*

Queen of Destiny: see *Sixty Glorious Years*

Queen of Hearts *
GB 1936 80m bw
ATP (Basil Dean)
A working girl poses as a socialite and wins a matinée idol.
Stalwart romantic comedy with its star slightly more glamorized than usual.
w Clifford Grey, H. F. Maltby, Douglas Furber, Anthony Kimmins, Gordon Wellesley *d* Monty Banks *ph* John W. Boyle *md* Ernest Irving *ad* J. Elder Wills
☆ *Gracie Fields*, John Loder, Enid Stamp Taylor, Fred Duprez, Edward Rigby, Hal Gordon

Queen of Hearts *
GB 1989 112m colour
Enterprise/TVS Films/Nelson Entertainment/Film Four International/Telso International (John Hardy)
A ten-year-old, part of a large and happy Italian family living in London, watches while his father risks everything by gambling.
Odd and ultimately unsatisfactory mix of fantasy and reality, contrasting Italian warmth and British cool to the detriment of both.
w Tony Grisoni *d* Jon Amiel *ph* Mike Southon *m* Michael Convertino *pd* Jim Clay *ed* Peter Boyle
☆ Vittorio Duse, Joseph Long, Anita Zagaria, Eileen Way, Vittorio Amandola, Roberto Scateni, Stefano Spagnoli, Alec Bregonzi

Queen of Outer Space
US 1958 79m DeLuxe Cinemascope
Allied Artists (Ben Schwalb)
The man-hating Queen of Venus is thwarted in her plans to destroy the Earth with a powerful ray by astronauts who crash-land on the planet.
Ludicrously inept science fiction that borrows from Flight to Mars, World without End *and* Forbidden Planet *for many of its props and special effects. No film that casts a heavily accented Zsa Zsa Gabor as a Venusian scientist in sequins, silk and gold high heels can have been intended as entirely serious, but most of the laughter is at the expense of the acting, dialogue and aliens, who look as if they have just stepped out of a chorus line.*
w Charles Beaumont *story* Ben Hecht *d* Edward Bernds *ph* William Whitley *m* Marlin Skiles *ad* David Milton *ed* William Austin
☆ Zsa Zsa Gabor, Eric Fleming, Dave Willock, Laurie Mitchell, Lisa Davis, Patrick Waltz, Paul Birch, Barbara Darrow, Marilyn Buferd

The Queen of Spades **
GB 1948 96m bw
ABP/World Screen Plays (Anatole de Grunwald)
A Russian officer tries to wrest from an ancient countess the secret of winning at cards, in return for which he has sold his soul to the devil; but she dies of fright and haunts him.
Disappointingly slow-moving but splendidly atmospheric recreation of an old Russian story with all the decorative stops out; the chills when they come are quite frightening, the style is impressionist and the acting suitably extravagant.
w Rodney Ackland, Arthur Boys *novel* Alexander Pushkin *d Thorold Dickinson* *ph Otto Heller* *m Georges Auric* *ad Oliver Messel*
☆ *Anton Walbrook, Edith Evans*, Ronald Howard, Yvonne Mitchell, Mary Jerrold

'The photography is adventurous, the cutting imaginative and the sets startling.' – *Evening Standard*

'It is fine to come across such distinguished filmcraft.' – *Evening News*

The Queen of Spies: see *Joan of Ozark*

'All She Wants Is Hell On Earth.'

Queen of the Damned
US/Australia 2002 101m Technicolor
Warner/Village Roadshow/NPV/Material (Jorge Saralegui)
A vampire rock singer angers his fellow creatures by calling them to come out of hiding, and awakens their destructive queen.
Feeble and listless movie that offers nothing in the way of satisfaction.
w Scott Abbott, Michael Petroni *novels The Vampire Chronicles* by Anne Rice *d* Michael Rymer *ph* Ian Baker *m* Richard Gibbs, Jonathan Davis *pd* Graham 'Grace' Walker *ed* Dany Cooper *sp* Bob McCarron
☆ Stuart Townsend (Lestat), Aaliyah (Akasha), Marguerite Moreau (Jesse Reeves), Vincent Perez (Marius), Paul McGann (David Talbot), Lena Olin (Maharet), Christian Manon (Mael), Claudia Black (Pandora), Bruce Spence (Khayman)

'It isn't great entertainment or camp, but pic sets its ambitions so low, it can't help partially delivering on them.' – *Scott Foundas, Variety*

Queen of the Mob *
US 1940 61m bw
Paramount
A murderess and her three sons are captured by the FBI.
Pacy crime melodrama from the Persons in Hiding *series, based on the exploits of Ma Barker.*
w Horace McCoy, William Lipman *d* James Hogan *ph* Theodor Sparkuhl
☆ *Blanche Yurka*, Ralph Bellamy, Jack Carson, Richard Denning, Paul Kelly, J. Carrol Naish, Jeanne Cagney, William Henry, James Seay, Hedda Hopper

Queen of the Nile: see *Nefertite, Queen of the Nile*

Queen of the Road
Australia 1984 96m colour
JNP (James Davern)
A daughter inherits trouble when she takes over her father's truck haulage business.
A dull comedy of mishap and misadventure, interspersed with country and western songs and relying for the most part on the old joke (though it may be new to Australia) that women are poor drivers.
w Tom Mitchell *d* Bruce Best *ph* Joseph Pickering *m* Mike Perjanik *ad* Michael Ralph *ed* Zsolt Kollanyi
☆ Joanne Samuel, Amanda Muggleton, Shane Worthington, Jonathan Sweet, Chris Hession

The Queen's Guards
GB 1960 112m Technicolor Cinemascope
TCF/Imperial (Michael Powell)
Reminiscences during trooping the colour of father and son guardsmen.
Incredibly old-fashioned family melodrama complete with skeleton in family closet; despite its date it has a decidedly pre-war air, except that it might have been more smartly done then.
w Roger Milner *d* Michael Powell *ph* Gerald Turpin *m* Brian Easdale
☆ Raymond Massey, Daniel Massey, Robert Stephens, Ursula Jeans, Judith Stott, Elizabeth Shepherd, Duncan Lamont, Ian Hunter, Jack Watling

'This flagwaving museum piece would be distressing if it weren't so inept … [the actors] battle manfully with dialogue and characters as dated as a Crimean cavalry charge. The film could scarcely be taken as a tribute to the Guards except, just possibly, by elderly aunts in Cheltenham.' – *MFB*

The Queen's Husband: see *The Royal Bed*

Queens Logic *
US 1991 116m DeLuxe
New Visions (Stuart Oken, Russ Smith)
Friends from boyhood offer each other support and succour at a moment of marital crisis.
Energetically acted domestic drama that covers familiar ground but does so in an enjoyably high-spirited manner.
w Tony Spiridakis *story* Tony Spiridakis, Joseph W. Savino *d* Steve Rash *ph* Amir Mokri *m* Joe Jackson *pd* Edward Pisoni *ed* Patrick Kennedy

☆ Kevin Bacon, Linda Fiorentino, John Malkovich, Joe Mantegna, Ken Olin, Tony Spiridakis, Tom Waits, Chloe Webb, Jamie Lee Curtis

'This deadpan midlife crisis comedy-drama is undeniably compulsive in its simplified TV fashion, thanks to a cleverly worked script and some heartening acting.' – *John Lyttle, Independent*

Queimada!

France/Italy 1968 132m DeLuxe
PEA/PPA (Alberto Grimaldi)

aka: *Burn!*

A diplomat is sent to a Caribbean island to break the Portuguese sugar monopoly and becomes involved with revolutionaries.

An indigestible attempt to combine adventure with the film of ideas; very tedious.

w Franco Solinas, Giorgio Arlorio *d* Gillo Pontecorvo *ph* Marcello Gatti *m* Ennio Morricone

☆ Marlon Brando, Renato Salvatori, Norman Hill, Evaristo Marquez

'Theirs was a time of love and violence!'

Quentin Durward *

GB 1955 101m Eastmancolor Cinemascope
MGM (Pandro S. Berman)
aka: *The Adventures of Quentin Durward*

An elderly English lord sends his nephew to woo a French lady on his behalf; but the boy falls in love with her himself.

Haphazardly constructed and produced, but quite enjoyable, period romp, with a bold black villain and several rousing set-pieces including a final set-to on bell ropes.

w Robert Ardrey *novel* Sir Walter Scott *d* Richard Thorpe *ph* Christopher Challis *m* Bronislau Kaper *ed* Ernest Walter

☆ Robert Taylor, Kay Kendall, Robert Morley, Alec Clunes, Marius Goring, Wilfrid Hyde-White, Ernest Thesiger, *Duncan Lamont*, Harcourt Williams, Laya Raki, George Cole

Querelle

West Germany/France 1982 108m Eastmancolor
Planet/Albatross/Gaumont

A homosexual sailor has a mystical quest which involves murder.

Overheated fantasy which may have something to say to gays, but not much to other audiences.

wd Rainer Werner Fassbinder *book* Jean Genet *ph* Xaver Schwarzenberger *m* Peer Raben

☆ Brad Davis, Franco Nero, Jeanne Moreau, Laurent Malet

The Quest

US 1996 95m DeLuxe 'Scope
Universal/MDP (Moshe Diamant)

A petty thief takes part in a martial arts championship in Tibet in the 20s.

Trivial martial arts flick, serving up the same old narrative as usual; this time it is woodenly directed as well as acted.

w Steve Klein, Paul Mones *story* Frank Dux, Jean-Claude Van Damme *d* Jean-Claude Van Damme *ph* David Gribble *m* Randy Edelman *pd* Steve Spence *ed* John F. Link, William J. Meshover

☆ Jean-Claude Van Damme, Roger Moore, James Remar, Janet Gunn, Jack McGee, Aki Aleong, Abdel Qissi, Louis Mandylor

'Dull stuff, except perhaps for martial-arts fanatics.' – *George Perry*

Quest for Camelot

US 1998 86m Technicolor
Warner (Dalisa Cooper Cohen)

GB title: *The Magic Sword: Quest for Camelot*

The daughter of a murdered knight goes in search of King Arthur's sword Excalibur, which has been stolen and lost in a magic forest.

Like Mulan, *this is one of the current cycle of animated movies with heroines who take on male roles; maybe boys no longer watch cartoons, which in this case is the sensible option.*

w Kirk de Micco, William Schifrin, Jacqueline Feather, David Seidler *novel The King's Damosel* by Vera Chapman *d* Frederick Du Chau *ph* Mark Dinicola *m* Patrick Doyle *pd* Steve Pilcher *ed* Stanford C. Allen

☆ Featuring the voices of: Jessalyn Gilsig (sung by Andrea Corr), Cary Elwes (sung by Bryan White), Gary Oldman, Eric Idle, Don Rickles, Jane Seymour, Celine Dion, Pierce Brosnan (sung by Steve Perry), Bronson Pinchot, Jaleel White, Gabriel Byrne, John Gielgud

🏆 song 'The Prayer' (*m* Carole Bayer Sager, David Foster, *l* Carole Bayer Sager, David Foster, Tony Renis, Alberto Testa)

Quest for Fire

Canada/France 1981 100m Bellevue-Pathé Panavision
ICC/Cine Trail/Belstar/Stephan (Michael Gruskoff)

Eighty thousand years ago, a primitive tribe uses the discovery of fire to defeat its enemies.

Scientifically cosseted but sometimes unintentionally funny attempt to make us care about the problems of primitive man. Lively sequences are separated by longueurs.

w Gérard Brach *novel La Guerre du Feu* by J. H. Rosny *d* Jean-Jacques Annaud *ph* Claude Agostini *m* Philippe Sarde *pd* Guy Comtois, Brian Morris *special language* Anthony Burgess *body movement* Desmond Morris

☆ Everett McGill, Ron Perlman, Rae Dawn Chong, Nameer El-Kadi

'He had seen her, felt her touch, knew she existed...'

Quest for Love *

GB 1971 90m Eastmancolor
Rank/Peter Rogers Productions (Peter Eton)

After an explosion during an experiment, a young physicist finds himself living a different life, in love with a dying girl; returning to normal, he finds the girl and saves her.

Pleasing variation on Berkeley Square, *quite well staged and played.*

w Terence Feely *story Random Quest* by John Wyndham *d* Ralph Thomas *ph* Ernest Steward *m* Eric Rogers

☆ Tom Bell, Joan Collins, Denholm Elliott, Laurence Naismith, Lyn Ashley

A Question of Adultery

GB 1958 84m bw
Eros/Connaught Place/Raymond Stross

When a husband is discovered to be sterile, his wife suggests artificial insemination, but when she seems to have a lover he institutes divorce proceedings.

Opportunist melodrama from the headlines. Not even interesting then.

w Anne Edwards *play Breach of Marriage* by Dan Sutherland *d* Don Chaffey *ph* Stephen Dale *m* Philip Green

☆ Julie London, Anthony Steel, Basil Sydney, Donald Houston, Anton Diffring, Andrew Cruickshank, Conrad Phillips, Kynaston Reeves

A Question of Silence *

Netherlands 1982 96m colour
C.O.W./Sigma Films (Matthijs van Heijningen)
original title: *De Stilte Rond Christine M*

A lawyer, defending three women who commit a gratuitous act of murder of a male boutique owner, claims that their action is the result of masculine oppression.

Stylish feminist thriller that skilfully wraps its propagandist message.

wd Marleen Gorris *ph* Frans Bromet *m* Lodewijk de Boer, Martijn Hasebos *ad* Harry Ammerlaan *ed* Hans van Dongen

☆ Edda Barends, Nelly Frijda, Henriette Tol, Cox Habbema, Eddy Brugman, Hans Croiset, Erik Plooyer

'The Wild West Just Got A Little Wilder'

The Quick and the Dead *

US 1995 108m Technicolor
Columbia TriStar (Joshua Donen, Allen Shapiro, Patrick Markey)

Gunmen and one vengeful woman congregate in a Western town run by a psychotic killer for a gunfighting contest in which the winner is the last man left alive.

The Western genre taken to a logical conclusion: as a succession of quick-draw contests; the influence here is Sergio Leone, to which the director adds his trademark convulsive camerawork.

w Simon Moore *d* Sam Raimi *ph* Dante Spinotti *m* Alan Silvestri *pd* Patrizia von Brandenstein *ed* Pietro Scalia

☆ Gene Hackman, Sharon Stone, Leonardo DiCaprio, Russell Crowe, Tobin Bell, Roberts Blossom, Lance Henriksen, Pat Hingle, Gary Sinise, Woody Strode

'Take it as parody or take it seriously, the effect is the same: extreme boredom.' – *Geoff Brown, The Times*

'The definitive postmodern, postfeminist, post-what-have-you western – for what it's worth.' – *Premiere*

Quick Before It Melts

US 1964 97m Metrocolor Panavision
MGM/Biography (Douglas Lawrence, Delbert Mann)

A journalist is sent to cover a naval enterprise in the Antarctic, and gets a scoop despite his shyness.

Noisy service comedy with precious little plot.

w Dale Wasserman *novel* Philip Benjamin *d* Delbert Mann *ph* Russell Harlan *m* David Rose

☆ George Maharis, Robert Morse, Anjanette Comer, James Gregory, Howard St John, Janine Gray, Michael Constantine

'The combination of romantic dalliance, service high jinks and hectic journalism remains uniformly flat all through.' – *MFB*

Quick Change

US 1990 88m DuArt Panavision
Warner/Devoted (Robert Greenhut, Bill Murray)

Two men and a woman stage a flawless bank robbery and then have trouble making their getaway from New York.

Farcical comedy taken at a decorous pace and with the joke of an escalating series of disasters too often mistimed to produce any amusement.

w Howard Franklin *novel* Jay Cronley *d* Howard Franklin, Bill Murray *ph* Michael Chapman *m* Randy Edelman *ad* Speed Hopkins *ed* Alan Heim

☆ Bill Murray, Geena Davis, Randy Quaid, Jason Robards, Bob Elliott, Kimberleigh Aarn, Ron Ryan, Brian McConnachie, Jack Gilpin

The Quick Gun

US 1964 88m Techniscope
Admiral/Columbia

A gunfighter gets an icy welcome when he returns home to claim his father's farm.

Standard Western with the hero redeemed and elected sheriff at the end.

w Robert E. Kent *d* Sidney Salkow *ph* Lester Shorr *m* Richard La Salle

☆ Audie Murphy, Merry Anders, James Best, Ted de Corsia, Walter Sande, Frank Ferguson

Quick Let's Get Married

US 1965 100m colour
Golden Eagle (William Marshall)
aka: *The Confession, Seven Different Ways*

The voice of a sneak thief in a ruined church is taken by an unwed mother as a miracle.

Downright peculiar mishmash wasting interesting stars; an independent production by Rogers and husband in Jamaica.

w Allan Scott *d* William Dieterle *ph* Robert Bronner *m* Michael Colicchio

☆ Ginger Rogers, Ray Milland, Barbara Eden, Walter Abel, Cecil Kellaway, Elliott Gould, Michael Ansara, David Hurst

Quick Millions **

US 1931 69m bw
Fox

An ambitious truck driver becomes a ruthless racketeer.

Fast-moving, otherwise naïve early gangster melodrama notable for Tracy's first star performance.

w Courteney Terrett, Rowland Brown, John Wray *d Rowland Brown* *ph* Joseph August

☆ Spencer Tracy, Marguerite Churchill, Sally Eilers, Robert Burns, John Wray, George Raft

'This film is in the money. Ranks with the best of the gangster items.' – *Variety*

Quicker than the Eye

France/Switzerland 1989 92m Fujicolour
Condor/Crocodile/SRG/ZDF/ORF/Paul-Boris Lobadowsky/William Hartman (Peter-Christian Fueter)
original title: *Passe-Passe*

In Switzerland, a gang of ruthless assassins, hired to kill the president of an African country, plan to use an American magician as their cover.

Uninteresting and uninvolving thriller, with a cast coasting through the convolutions of the plot.

w Joseph Morhaim, Nicolas Gessner *novel* Claude Cueni *d* Nicolas Gessner *ph* Wolfgang Treu *m* George Garvarentz *pd* Max Stubenrauch *ed* Daniela Roderer

☆ Ben Gazzara, Mary Crosby, Jean Yanne, Robert Linesol, Catherine Jarrett, Eb Lottimer, Wolfram Berger, Dinah Hinz, Ivan Desny

The Quiet American **

US 1957 122m bw
UA/Figaro (Joseph L. Mankiewicz)

An American in Saigon has naïve ideas for ending the war; he saves the life of a journalist who for various reasons becomes jealous and is duped into betraying the American to the communists.

Semi-successful excursion into the territory of Graham Greene, who as in Brighton Rock *has allowed his ironic ending to be totally re-emphasized, here making the film anti-communist instead of anti-American.*

wd Joseph L. Mankiewicz novel Graham Greene *ph* Robert Krasker *m* Mario Nascimbene

☆ *Michael Redgrave, Audie Murphy, Claude Dauphin*, Giorgia Moll, Bruce Cabot, Fred Sadoff, Richard Loo

🏆 Michael Caine

'In war, the most powerful weapon is seduction.'

The Quiet American ***

US/Germany 2002 101m Atlab Panavision
Buena Vista/Mirage/Saga/IMF (William Horberg, Staffan Ahrenberg)

In Vietnam in the early 50s, a tired and cynical British journalist and an idealistic American agent clash over love and politics.

True to the spirit of Greene's novel, one that seems to have become more than ever relevant, this film superbly captures its account of political and personal betrayal, the danger of do-gooders and the corruption of spirit that weariness with the world can bring.

w Christopher Hampton, Robert Schenkkan *d Phillip Noyce* *ph* Christopher Doyle *m* Craig Armstrong *pd* Roger Ford *ed* John Scott *cos* Norma Moriceau

☆ *Michael Caine* (Thomas Fowler), Brendan Fraser (Alden Pyle), Do Thi Hai Yen (Phuong), Rade Sherbedgia (Inspector Vigot), Tzi Ma (Hinh), Robert Stanton (Joe Tunney), Holmes Osborne (Bill Granger), Pham Thi Mai Hoa (Phuong's Sister), Quang Hai (The General)

'Greene's lifelong concern with moral ambiguity gives this film a texture and complexity that movies don't usually achieve.' – *Kenneth Turan, Los Angeles Times*

'Reveals itself to be not so much a historical allegory as an Iliad of the heart. It's sad and smart and beautiful and true.' – *Shawn Levy, Oregonian*

Quiet Days in Clichy

France/Italy/Germany 1989 100m colour
ItalFrance (Lawrence Schiller)

original title: *Jours Tranquilles à Clichy*

An elderly American writer recalls the sexual encounters of his youth.

Curiously passionless and unconvincing movie set in an art director's idea of decadent pre-war Paris, not helped by the casting of the bland McCarthy as Miller; it is better on politics than sex.

w Ugo Leonzio, Claude Chabrol *novel* Henry Miller *d* Claude Chabrol *ph* Jean Rabier *m* Matthieu Chabrol, Luigi Ceccarelli, Jean-Michel Bernard *ad* Marco Dentici *ed* Monique Fardoulis

☆ Andrew McCarthy, Nigel Havers, Barbara de Rossi, Stephanie Cotter, Isolde Barth, Eva Grimaldi, Anna Galiena, Stephane Audran, Elide Melli

The Quiet Earth **
New Zealand 1985 94m colour
Cinepro/Pillsbury Films (Sam Pillsbury, Don Reynolds)
After an experiment goes disastrously wrong, a suicidal scientist wakes to discover that he appears to be the only person left alive in the world.
An intriguing and often witty exercise in apocalyptic science fiction, with an unconventional approach.
w Bill Baer, Bruno Lawrence, Sam Pillsbury *novel* Craig Harrison *d* *Geoff Murphy* *ph* James Bartle *m* John Charles *pd* Josephine Ford *ed* Michael Horton
☆ Bruno Lawrence, Alison Routledge, Peter Smith

The Quiet Man ***
US 1952 129m Technicolor
Republic/Argosy (John Ford, Merian C. Cooper)
An Irish village version of *The Taming of the Shrew*, the tamer being an ex-boxer retired to the land of his fathers and in need of a wife. Archetypal John Ford comedy, as Irish as can be, with everything but leprechauns and the Blarney Stone on hand.
Despite some poor sets the film has a gay swing to it, much brawling vigour and broad comedy, while the actors all give their roistering best.
w Frank Nugent story Maurice Walsh *d John Ford ph Winton C. Hoch, Archie Stout m Victor Young*
☆ *John Wayne, Maureen O'Hara, Barry Fitzgerald, Victor McLaglen, Ward Bond,* Mildred Natwick, Francis Ford, Arthur Shields, Eileen Crowe, Sean McClory, Jack MacGowran

'Ford's art and artifice ... are employed to reveal a way of life – stable, rooted, honourable, purposeful in nature's way, and thereby rhythmic. Everyone is an individual, yet everyone and everything has a place.' – *Henry Hart, Films in Review*

Academy Award: John Ford; Winton C. Hoch, Archie Stout
Academy Award nomination: best picture; Frank Nugent; Victor McLaglen

A Quiet Place to Kill: see *Paranoia*

Quiet Please, Murder *
US 1943 70m bw
TCF (Ralph Dietrich)
Nazis and art thieves cause a high death rate in a public library.
Unusual, stylish second feature.
wd John Larkin ph Joe MacDonald *m* Arthur Lange *md* Emil Newman
☆ George Sanders, Kurt Katch, Gail Patrick, Richard Denning, Lynne Roberts, Sidney Blackmer, Byron Foulger

SAMPLES OF QUIRKY DIALOGUE: PATRICK TO SANDERS: 'How many butterflies did you torture since lunch, hoping one would turn on you?'

SANDERS: 'I am a punishment in your life. Your conscience demands it. The unconscious instinct to punish ourselves sometimes becomes self-destructive. The way we live is a constant threat to our own security. We love it. Giving and taking pain.'

PATRICK: 'You hate because you fear love – and the thought of desiring.'

Quiet Wedding ***
GB 1940 80m bw
Paramount/Conqueror (Paul Soskin)
Middle-class wedding preparations are complicated by family guests.
A semi-classic British stage comedy is admirably filmed with a splendid cast.
w Terence Rattigan, Anatole de Grunwald play Esther McCracken d Anthony Asquith
☆ Margaret Lockwood, Derek Farr, *A. E. Matthews, Marjorie Fielding, Athene Seyler, Peggy Ashcroft,* Margaretta Scott, Frank Cellier, Roland Culver, Jean Cadell, David Tomlinson, Bernard Miles

'A completely unpretentious and charming film, the components of which are as delicately balanced as the mechanism of a watch.' – *New York Times*

'No subtlety of glance, movement or dialogue has been missed, no possible highlight omitted.' – *MFB*

† Production was halted five times when bombs fell on the studio.
†† Remade as *Happy is the Bride* (qv).

Quiet Weekend
GB 1946 92m bw
Associated British (Warwick Ward)
The Royds spend a weekend at their country cottage and get involved with poachers.
Trivial and poorly-made sequel, not up to the standard of Quiet Wedding *as a comic study of British types.*
w Victor Skutezky *play* Esther McCracken *d* Harold French *ph* Eric Cross
☆ Derek Farr, Marjorie Fielding, George Thorpe, Frank Cellier

Quigley Down Under
US 1990 120m colour Panavision
UIP/Pathé (Stanley O'Toole, Alexandra Rose)
In 1860s Australia, an American hired gun is outlawed after quarrelling with his employer, a violent British cattle rancher.
Apart from its outback setting, a conventional and unoriginal Western, given perfunctory treatment.
w John Hill *d* Simon Wincer *ph* David Eggby *m* Basil Poledouris *pd* Ross Major *ed* Peter Burgess
☆ Tom Selleck, Laura San Giacomo, Alan Rickman, Chris Haywood, Ron Hadrick, Tony Bonner, Jerome Ehlers, Conor McDermottroe, Roger Ward, Ben Mendelsohn, Steve Dodd

'Potters along for two hours juggling cardboard figures and contrived situations that might have strayed in from some Hollywood potboiler of the 50s.' – *Geoff Brown, MFB*

† The script was originally written in the 1970s for Steve McQueen.

The Quiller Memorandum *
GB 1966 105m Eastmancolor Panavision
Rank/Ivan Foxwell/Carthay
A British secret service man is sent to Berlin to combat a neo-Nazi organization.
Disappointingly thin but smooth and watchable spy story.
w Harold Pinter *novel The Berlin Memorandum* by Adam Hall (Elleston Trevor) *d* Michael Anderson *ph Erwin Hillier m* John Barry
☆ George Segal, Max von Sydow, Alec Guinness, Senta Berger, George Sanders, Robert Helpmann, Robert Flemyng

'In disposing of most of the storyline Pinter has virtually thrown out the baby with the bathwater; all that remains is a skeleton plot which barely makes sense and is totally lacking in excitement.' – *Brenda Davies*

'Harold Pinter wrote the screenplay and for each word of dialogue there has to be a separate scene involving several different camera angles, which is perhaps why they asked him to do it as the story is pretty thin.' – *J. A., Illustrated London*

'Meet the Marquis de Sade. The pleasure is all his.'
Quills *
US 2000 123m DeLuxe
TCF/Fox Searchlight/Industry Entertainment/Walrus/Hollywood Partners (Julia Chasman, Nick Wechsler, Peter Kaufman)
The Marquis de Sade, incarcerated in Charenton asylum, defies all attempts to prevent him from writing.
A fantasia on de Sade as an icon of subversion and victim of institutional repression, given a spurious power by the quality of the acting.
w Doug Wright *play* Doug Wright *d* Philip Kaufman *ph* Rogier Stoffers *m* Stephen Warbeck *pd* Martin Childs *ed* Peter Boyle *cos* Jacqueline West
☆ Geoffrey Rush (Marquis de Sade), Kate Winslet (Madeleine), Joaquin Phoenix (Coulmier), Michael Caine (Royer-Collard), Billie Whitelaw (Madame LeClerc), Patrick Malahide (Delbene), Amelia Warner (Simone), Jane Menelaus (Renee Pelagie), Stephen Moyer (Prouix)

'A botch, crude in its ironies and its debate.' – *Adam Mars-Jones, Times*

'The film's basic trouble is not the departure from fact, it is the intrinsic conflict between the movie-ness of the screenplay and the frenzied anti-cliché directorial style.' – *Stanley Kauffmann, New Republic*

† In reality, at the time De Sade was imprisoned in Charenton, he was extremely fat and had already written his greatest works. The asylum's director Coulmier, the role played by Joaquin Phoenix, was four feet tall and deformed. De Sade died in his sleep.

Academy Award nomination: Geoffrey Rush; art direction (Martin Childs, Jill Quertier); Jacqueline West

The Quince Tree Sun **
Spain 1992 137m Eastmancolor
Artificial Eye/Maria Moreno
original title: *El Sol del Membrillo*
aka: *Dream of Light*
Painter Antonio López meticilously prepares a canvas and his subject: a tree of yellow, ripening quinces in the morning sun. The documentary then follows his progress through ten weeks, struggling against the fading light and unsympathetic weather, reminiscing and talking to friends, eventually abandoning his original oil painting and making a drawing instead.
A slow but absorbing examination of the process of artistic creation.
d Victor Erice *ph* Javier Aguirresarobe, Angel Luis Fernéndez *m* Pascal Gaigne *ed* Juan Ignacio San Mateo

'What might have proven a poignant statement on life and art unfortunately runs so long impact is diluted.' – *Variety*

Quingchun Ji: see *Sacrificed Youth*

Quintet
US 1979 118m DeLuxe
TCF/Lions Gate (Robert Altman)
In an icebound city of the future, citizens play a death game and a survivor hunts down a killer who plays for real.
Dismayingly pretentious claptrap which did its star's career no good at all.
w Frank Barhydt, Robert Altman, Patricia Resnick *d* Robert Altman *ph* Jean Boffety *m* Tom Pierson *pd* Leon Ericksen
☆ Paul Newman, Vittorio Gassman, Fernando Rey, Bibi Andersson, Brigitte Fossey, Nina Van Pallandt

'I find it mysterious, exciting, tenacious.' – *Dilys Powell, Punch*

'Paralyzingly stupid.' – *Stanley Kauffmann*

'Fifty million people watched, but no one saw a thing.'
Quiz Show **
US 1994 132m Technicolor
Buena Vista/Hollywood/Wildwood/Baltimore (Robert Redford, Michael Jacobs, Julian Krainin, Michael Nozik)
In the 50s, the producers of TV's most popular quiz show fix the results in search of higher ratings and are exposed.
A smart and gripping drama of media corruption, based on fact and revealing inequities of class and culture that retain their power today.
w Paul Attanasio book Remembering America: A Voice from the Sixties by Richard N. Goodwin *d Robert Redford ph* Michael Ballhaus *m* Mark Isham *pd* Jon Hutman *ed* Stu Linder
☆ John Turturro, Ralph Fiennes, Rob Morrow, *Paul Scofield*, David Paymer, Hank Azaria, Christopher McDonald, Griffin Dunne, Mira Sorvino, Martin Scorsese

'It hums along like a well-constructed farce, and its crazy momentum carries it over the bumps of social significance.' – *Terrence Rafferty, New Yorker*

'Something that's fast becoming a rarity: an entertaining, funny, intelligent studio picture.' – *Sheila Johnston, Independent*

Academy Award nomination: best picture; Robert Redford; Paul Scofield; Paul Attansio
BAFTA: Paul Attansio

'In making this film, MGM feel privileged to add something of permanent value to the cultural treasure house of mankind...'
'Ancient Rome is going to the dogs, Robert Taylor is going to the lions, and Peter Ustinov is going crazy!'
Quo Vadis **
US 1951 171m Technicolor
MGM (Sam Zimbalist)
A Roman commander under Nero falls in love with a Christian girl and jealous Poppea has them both thrown to the lions.
Spectacular but stagey and heavy-handed Hollywood version of a much-filmed colossus which shares much of its plot line with The Sign of the Cross. *Three hours of solemn tedium with flashes of vigorous acting and a few set-pieces to take the eye; but the sermonizing does not take away the bad taste of the emphasis on physical brutality.*
w John Lee Mahin, S. N. Behrman, Sonya Levien *novel* Henryk Sienkiewicz *d* Mervyn Le Roy *ph* Robert Surtees, William V. Skall *m* Miklos Rozsa *ad* Cedric Gibbons, Edward Carfagno, William Horning *ed* Ralph E. Winters
☆ Robert Taylor, Deborah Kerr, *Peter Ustinov, Leo Genn, Patricia Laffan,* Finlay Currie, Abraham Sofaer, Marina Berti, Buddy Baer, Felix Aylmer, Nora Swinburne, Ralph Truman, Norman Wooland

Academy Award nomination: best picture; Robert Surtees, William V. Skall; Miklos Rozsa; Peter Ustinov; Leo Genn; art direction; editing

RPM (Revolutions Per Minute)
US 1970 97m colour
Columbia/Stanley Kramer

At an American college, a middle-aged professor teaches liberal ideas.
Dim, thankfully forgotten addition to the Strawberry Statement *cycle.*
w Erich Segal *d* Stanley Kramer *ph* Michel Hugo, Perry Botkin Jnr *m* Barry de Vorzon
☆ Anthony Quinn, Ann-Margret, Gary Lockwood, Paul Winfield, Alan Hewitt

RX Murder
GB 1958 85m bw Cinemascope
TCF
aka: *Family Doctor*
The doctor of a small seaside resort has had four wives die on him. Could it be murder?
Modest mystery with an obvious outcome.
wd Derek Twist *novel The Deeds of Dr Deadcert* by Joan Fleming *ph* Arthur Grant *m* John Wooldridge
☆ Marius Goring, Rick Jason, Lisa Gastoni, Mary Merrall, Vida Hope, Phyllis Neilson-Terry, Frederick Leister, Nicholas Hannen

'Three years ago Rabbit Angstrom ran out to buy his wife cigarettes. He hasn't come back yet…'
Rabbit, Run
US 1970 94m Technicolor Panavision
Warner (Howard Kreitsek)
A man leaves his pregnant wife for a prostitute.
Uninteresting sex melodrama without any of the wit which distinguishes the book; hard to sit through.
w Howard B. Kreitsek *novel* John Updike *d* Jack Smight *ph* Philip Lathrop *m* Ray Burton, Brian King
☆ James Caan, Anjanette Comer, Arthur Hill, Jack Albertson, Carrie Snodgress

Rabbit Test
US 1978 84m colour
Avco Embassy (Edgar Rosenberg)

A man becomes pregnant.
Dreary and tasteless film, the nadir of comedy.
w Jay Redack, Joan Rivers *d* Joan Rivers *ph* Lucien Ballard *m* Peter Carpenter, Mike Post *ad* Robert Kinoshita *ed* Stanford C. Allen
☆ Billy Crystal, Joan Prather, Alex Rocco, Doris Roberts, Edward Ansara, Imogene Coca, Jane Connell, Keene Curtis, Roddy McDowall, Sheree North, Joan Rivers

The Rabbit Trap *
US 1959 76m bw
UA/Canon (Harry Kleiner)
A hardworking draughtsman finally defies his boss and completes his holiday with his family.
Watchable minor drama just about marking the end of Hollywood's infatuation with TV plays which had begun with Marty; *the moral and family problems of ordinary people were beginning to prove a shade lacking in excitement.*
w J. P. Miller TV play J. P. Miller *d Philip Leacock ph* Irving Glassberg *m* Jack Marshall *ad* Edward Carrere *ed* Ted J. Kent
☆ *Ernest Borgnine, Bethel Leslie*, David Brian, Kevin Corcoran, June Blair, Christopher Dark

'A Daring Escape. An Epic Journey. The True Story Of 3 Girls Who Walked 1500 Miles To Find Their Way Home…'
Rabbit-Proof Fence ***
Australia/GB 2002 94m Atlab Panavision
Buena Vista/AFFC/Hanway (Phillip Noyce, Christine Olsen, John Winter)

In the early 30s, three young girls of mixed race escape after they are taken away from their aboriginal mother and sent to a special school to be trained as servants for whites.
Engrossing true story of fierce determination, shot against a spare desert landscape; it is a startling insight into the human cost of an Australian government policy that continued until the 1970s.
w Christine Olsen *book Follow the Rabbit-Proof Fence* by Doris Pilkington Garimara *d* Phillip Noyce *ph* Christopher Doyle *m* Peter Gabriel *pd* Roger Ford *ed* John Scott, Veronika Jenet
☆ Everlyn Sampi (Molly Craig), Tianna Sansbury (Daisy Craig), Laura Monaghan (Gracie Fields), David Gulpilil (Moodoo), Kenneth Branagh (A. O. Neville), Deborah Mailman (Mavis), Jason Clarke (Constable Riggs), Ningali Lawford (Molly's Mother)
'Bold in concept and inspirational in intent.' – *David Stratton, Variety*
'It has real beauty and feeling.' – *Anthony Quinn, Independent*

'Pray it doesn't happen to you.'
Rabid
Canada 1976 91m colour
Alpha/Cinepix/Dibar/Famous Players (Dan Goldberg)

aka: *Rage*
After extensive intestinal surgery, a woman develops a taste for human blood, infecting her victims with a form of rabies.
Gory though stylish horror about predatory sexuality that features a star of pornographic movies and has gained a cult following.
wd David Cronenberg *ph* René Verzier *m* Ivan Reitman *ad* Claude Marchand *ed* Jean Lafleur *sp* Art Griswold
☆ Marilyn Chambers, Frank Moore, Joe Silver, Howard Ryshpan, Patricia Gage, Susan Roman

Rabid Grannies
Belgium/US 1988 88m colour
Troma/Star Pictures Nr 1 (James Desert, Jonathan Rambert)

Two elderly aunts (there is not a granny to be seen) invite their family to a birthday celebration and, under demonic influence, proceed to murder them.
Exceptionally silly and unpleasant, gore-filled horror.
wd Emmanuel Kervyn *ph* Hugo Labye *m* Pierre-Damien Castelain, Jean-Bruno Castelain *pd* Luc Bertrand *ed* Philippe Ravoet
☆ Elie Lison, Catherine Aymerie, Jacques Mayar, Françoise Moens, Robert du Bois, Florine Elslande, Guy Van Riet, Françoise Lamoureux

Race for the Yankee Zephyr
New Zealand/Australia 1981 108m Eastmancolor Panavision
Enterprise/Hemdale/Pact/First City (David Hemmings, Antony I. Ginnane, John Barnett)

Adventurers discover an American aircraft wrecked in 1944, and argue over the loot without knowing that it contains a 50-million-dollar payroll.
Very moderate adventure story distinguished only by good locations.
w Everett de Roche *d* David Hemmings *ph* Vincent Monton *m* Brian May
☆ Ken Wahl, Lesley Ann Warren, Donald Pleasence, George Peppard, Bruno Lawrence, Robert Bruce

Race Gang: see *The Green Cockatoo*

Race with the Devil
US 1975 88m DeLuxe
TCF/Saber/Maslansky (Wes Bishop)

Holidaymakers witness a black mass and are pursued by the diabolists.
Silly melodrama which resolves into a wild car chase and much violence.
w Lee Frost, Wes Bishop *d* Jack Starrett *ph* Robert Jessup *m* Leonard Rosenman
☆ Peter Fonda, Warren Oates, Loretta Swit, Lara Parker, R. G. Armstrong

'Why do you need a woman when death is your mistress every afternoon?'
'A love story that hurtles full speed across the barriers of convention!'
The Racers
US 1955 112m DeLuxe Cinemascope
TCF (Julian Blaustein)
GB title: *Such Men Are Dangerous*
A Monte Carlo Rally contestant is financed by an attractive lady gambler.
Routine racing car melodrama, totally unmemorable but impersonally efficient.
w Charles Kaufman *novel* Hans Ruesch *d* Henry Hathaway *ph* Joe MacDonald *m* Alex North
☆ Kirk Douglas, Bella Darvi, Gilbert Roland, Cesar Romero, Lee J. Cobb, Katy Jurado, Charles Goldner, George Dolenz

Rachel and the Stranger *
US 1948 92m bw
RKO (Richard H. Berger)

A widowed farmer first feels real love for the new wife he bought when an attractive stranger seems likely to take her away from him.
Modestly appealing romantic drama in a Western setting.
w Waldo Salt *stories Rachel; Neighbor Sam* by Howard Fast *d* Norman Foster *ph* Maury Gertsman *m* Roy Webb *m/ly* Roy Webb, Waldo Salt *md* Constantin Bakaleinikoff *ad* Albert S. D'Agostino, Walter E. Keller, Jack Okey *ed* Les Milbrook *cos* Edith Head
☆ Loretta Young (Rachel), Robert Mitchum (Jim Fairways), William Holden (Big Davey Harvey), Gary Gray (Little Davey), Tom Tully (Parson Jackson), Sara Haden (Mrs Jackson), Frank Ferguson (Mr Green), Walter Baldwin (Callus)
♫ Just Like Me; Oh He, oh Hi, oh Ho; Summer Song; Along Came A Tall Dark Stranger; Foolish Pride; Rachel

The Rachel Papers
GB 1989 95m colour
Virgin/Initial Film and Television/Longfellow Pictures (Andrew S. Karsch)

A would-be Oxford University student has an on-and-off affair with an American girl.
Bungled attempt at a contemporary comedy of manners.
wd Damian Harris *novel* Martin Amis *ph* Alex Thomson *m* Chaz Jankel, David Storrs *pd* Andrew McAlpine *ed* David Martin
☆ Dexter Fletcher, Ione Skye, Jonathan Pryce, James Spader, Bill Paterson, Shirley Anne Field, Michael Gambon, Lesley Sharp, Jared Harris, Aubrey Morris

Rachel, Rachel **
US 1968 101m Eastmancolor
Warner/Kayos (Paul Newman)

Events in the life of a middle-aged schoolmistress in a small New England town.
Appealing and freshly observed study of a limited personality in a small community.
w Stewart Stern novel A Jest of God by Margaret Laurence *d Paul Newman ph Gayne Rescher m* Jerome Moross
☆ *Joanne Woodward*, Estelle Parsons, James Olson, Kate Harrington, Donald Moffat, Geraldine Fitzgerald, Bernard Barrow
'It could all very easily degenerate into a woman's weepy; and the fact that it doesn't is due largely to Newman's refusal to treat Manawaka as another Peyton Place.' – *Jan Dawson*
'It tends to verge on dullness, but something always saves it.' – *John Simon*
best picture; Stewart Stern; Joanne Woodward; Estelle Parsons

Rachel River
US 1987 90m DuArt
American Playhouse/Marx/Smolan (Timothy Marx)

A radio journalist tries to cope with an impoverished life in a small Minnesota town with her two children and an unhelpful ex-husband.
Unpretentious, folksy drama dealing with everyday happenings in an undemandingly nostalgic manner.
w Judith Guest *stories* Carol Bly *d* Sandy Smolan *ph* Paul Elliott *m* Arvo Pärt *pd* David Wasco *ed* Susan Crutcher
☆ Pamela Reed, Viveca Lindfors, Zeljko Ivanek, James Olson, Craig T. Nelson, Alan North, Jo Henderson, Jon DeVries

Racing with the Moon
US 1984 108m Movielab
Paramount/Jaffe-Lansing (Alain Bernheim, John Kohn)

In 1942 California, two young men await induction into the Marines and say goodbye to their girlfriends.
Disappointing flashback by people who fail to capture the spirit of the time, and replace it by conventional boy–girl teenage antics.
w Steven Kloves *d* Richard Benjamin *ph* John Bailey *m* Dave Grusin *pd* David L. Snyder
☆ Sean Penn, Elizabeth McGovern, Nicolas Cage, John Karlen, Max Showalter

The Rack
US 1956 100m bw
MGM (Arthur M. Loew Jnr)
A veteran of the Korean War is courtmartialled for collaborating with the enemy under torture.
Dullish courtroom melodrama overstretched from a TV play.
w Stewart Stern *play* Rod Serling *d* Arnold Laven *ph* Paul Vogel *m* Adolph Deutsch
☆ Paul Newman, Walter Pidgeon, Edmond O'Brien, Lee Marvin, Cloris Leachman, Wendell Corey

The Racket *
US 1951 88m bw
RKO/Edmund Grainger

Police break up the empire of a powerful gangster.
Oddly timed and rather weak remake of the 1928 film; glossy but very old-fashioned in treatment.
w William Wister Haines *play* Bartlett Cormack *d* John Cromwell *ph* George E. Diskant *md* Constantin Bakaleinikoff
☆ Robert Ryan, Robert Mitchum, Ray Collins, Lizabeth Scott, William Talman

Racket Busters
US 1938 71m bw
Warner (Samuel Bischoff)
A gangster aiming to take over a trucking enterprise is opposed by the special prosecutor's office.
Routine cops and robbers, still very watchable but also forgettable.
w Robert Rossen, Leonardo Bercovici *d* Lloyd Bacon *ph* Arthur Edeson *m* Adolph Deutsch
☆ George Brent, Humphrey Bogart, Gloria Dickson, Allen Jenkins, Walter Abel, Penny Singleton, Henry O'Neill

Rackety Rax
US 1932 65m bw
Fox
Gangster methods are applied to college football.
Stiff burlesque which didn't transfer well from the printed page.
w Ben Markson, Lou Breslow *novel* Joel Sayre
d Alfred Werker
☆ Victor McLaglen, Greta Nissen, Nell O'Day, Alan Dinehart, Allen Jenkins

Radio City Revels
US 1938 90m bw
RKO
A songwriter can work only in his sleep.
A wisp of plot is the peg for a very moderate revue.
w Matt Brooks, Eddie Davis, Anthony Veiller, Mortimer Offner *d* Ben Stoloff *ph* J. Roy Hunt *md* Victor Baravalle *ch* Hermes Pan
☆ Bob Burns, Jack Oakie, Kenny Baker, Victor Moore, Ann Miller, Milton Berle, Helen Broderick, Jane Froman, Buster West, Richard Lane
'Should do well at b.o., but no smash.' – *Variety*

Radio Days **
US 1987 85m DuArt
Orion (Robert Greenhut)
At the beginning of World War II, families near New York are affected by what they hear on the radio.
Shapeless montage of funny bits, best appreciated by those who lived through the time at somewhere near the place.
wd Woody Allen *ph* Carlo di Palma *pd* Santo Loquasto *ed* Susan E. Morse *m/ed* Dick Hyman
☆ Mia Farrow, Dianne Wiest, Seth Green, Julie Kavner, Josh Mostel, Michael Tucker, Wallace Shawn
'One of his most purely entertaining pictures.' – *Daily Variety*
best original screenplay; art direction (Speed Hopkins)
Santo Loquasto

'Powered By Imagination.'
Radio Flyer
US 1992 113m Technicolor Panavision
Columbia/Stonebridge Entertainment (Lauren Schuler-Donner)
A father tells his sons how, when he was young, he and his small brother decided to build a flying machine in an attempt to escape from their increasingly violent stepfather.
An uneasy mix of fantasy and reality that remains stolidly earthbound.
w David Mickey Evans *d* Richard Donner *ph* Laszlo Kovacs *m* Hans Zimmer *ad* J. Michael Riva *ed* Stuart Baird, Dallas Puett
☆ Lorraine Bracco, John Heard, Elijah Wood, Joseph Mazello, Adam Baldwin, Ben Johnson, Tom Hanks (uncredited)
'A film one would like to like more.' – *Variety*
† Originally, David Mickey Evans was assigned to direct with Rosanna Arquette playing the mother, but that production was abandoned. The film was released direct to video in Britain.

Radio On
GB 1979 101m bw
BFI/Road Movies (Keith Griffiths)
A disc-jockey in a biscuit factory makes a haphazard journey from London to Bristol to discover the circumstances of his brother's death.
Inconsequential road movie that can barely summon up any interest in its characters; it is much influenced by the films of Wim Wenders, who was its associate producer.
wd Christopher Petit *ph* Martin Schafer *ad* Susannah Buxton *ed* Anthony Sloman
☆ David Beames, Lisa Kreuzer, Sandy Ratcliff, Andrew Byatt, Sue Jones, Sting
'For all its German and American antecedents, however, *Radio On* remains peculiarly English in its concerns and atmosphere. It is in fact one of the most distinguished attempts by a native film-maker to contain all those influences and emerge with a firm sense of its own identity.' – *Richard Combs*

Radio Parade of 1935
GB 1934 96m bw (colour sequence)
BIP (Walter C. Mycroft)
US title: *Radio Follies*
Amateur talent makes it big for a radio station.
Historically interesting revue which unfortunately requires its comic lead to play straight.
w Jack Davies, Paul Perez, Arthur Woods, James Bunting *d* Arthur Woods *ph* Claude Friese-Greene
☆ Will Hay, Helen Chandler, Clifford Mollison, Davy Burnaby, The Western Brothers, Alfred Drayton, Lily Morris, Nellie Wallace, Clapham and Dwyer, Claude Dampier, Ronald Frankau, Ted Ray, Beryl Orde, Stanelli

Radio Stars on Parade
US 1945 69m bw
RKO/Ben Stoloff
Agents fix up a show despite threats from gangsters.
Slim excuse for a revue including talent popular at the time.
w Robert E. Kent, Monte Brice *d* Leslie Goodwins
☆ Wally Brown, Alan Carney, Frances Langford, Don Wilson, Tony Romano, Rufe Davis, Sheldon Leonard, Ralph Edwards, Skinnay Ennis and his band

Radioland Murders
US 1994 108m Rank Colour
Universal/Lucasfilm (Rick McCallum, Fred Roos)
In 1939, a series of murders disrupts the opening night of a new radio network and an attempt by a writer to win back his estranged wife.
Fitfully engaging exercise in nostalgia, but as easy to switch off as it is to switch on.
w Willard Huyck, Gloria Katz, Jeff Reno, Ron Osborn *story* George Lucas *d* Mel Smith *ph* David Tattersall *m* Joel McNeely *pd* Gavin Bocquet *ed* Paul Trejo
☆ Mary Stuart Masterson, Brian Benben, Ned Beatty, George Burns, Brion James, Michael McKean, Christopher Lloyd, Scott Michael Campbell, Stephen Tobolowsky, Corbin Bernsen, Michael Lerner, Bobcat Goldthwait
'A well-intentioned but annoying shrill exercise virtually devoid of romance, suspense or wit.' – *Brian Lowry, Variety*

Rafferty and the Gold Dust Twins
US 1975 92m Technicolor Panavision
Warner/Gruskoff-Venture-Linson
A drifter encounters two female vagrants who force him at gunpoint to drive them to New Orleans and get him into various adventures.
Indulgent and unattractive 'road' movie which despite occasional amusing incident gets nowhere very slowly.
w John Kaye *d* Dick Richards *ph* Ralph Woolsey *m* Artie Butler
☆ Alan Arkin, Sally Kellerman, MacKenzie Phillips, Alex Rocco, Charlie Martin Smith, Harry Dean Stanton, John McLiam

Raffles *
US 1930 72m bw
UA/Samuel Goldwyn
A gentleman thief decides to go straight, but then agrees to carry out a final robbery to save a suicidal schoolfriend from disgrace.
Colman's performance adds a touch of elegance to a staid but still entertaining, wittily scripted light-hearted drama.
w Sidney Howard *novel The Amateur Cracksman* by E. W. Hornung *d* Harry D'Abbadie D'Arrast, George Fitzmaurice *ph* George S. Barnes, Gregg Toland *ad* W. Cameron Menzies, Park French *ed* Stuart Heisler
☆ Ronald Colman, Kay Francis, David Torrence, Frederick Kerr, Bramwell Fletcher, John Rogers, Wilson Benge, Alison Skipworth, Frances Dade
† The film's on-screen credits do not include the name of its director. Harry D'Arrast was fired by Goldwyn because he was playing the scenes too fast for the producer's liking and was replaced by Fitzmaurice. The film made a profit of $200,000.

Raffles *
US 1939 72m bw
Samuel Goldwyn
Raffles the famous cricketer is also a compulsive and daring amateur thief.
Slight, modernized version of the turn-of-the-century stories; very palatable, but it could have been better.
w John Van Druten, Sidney Howard *novel Raffles the Amateur Cracksman* by E. W. Hornung *d* Sam Wood *ph* Gregg Toland *m* Victor Young
☆ David Niven, Olivia de Havilland, Dudley Digges, May Whitty, Douglas Walton, Lionel Pape, E. E. Clive, Peter Godfrey
'Fair remake … moderate b.o. potential.' – *Variety*
† This was virtually a scene-for-scene remake of the 1930 Goldwyn version starring Ronald Colman, Kay Francis and Alison Skipworth. It was written by Sidney Howard and George Fitzmaurice.

Rag Doll
GB 1960 67m bw
Mancunian (Tom Blakeley)
US title: *Young, Willing and Eager*
A 17-year-old runs away to Soho, where she gets a job as a waitress in a shady club and falls in love with a singer.
A melodramatic cautionary tale, given a little life by the playing of some expert character actors propping up the young leads.
w Brock Williams, Derry Quinn *d* Lance Comfort *ph* Basil Emmott *m* Martin Slavin *ad* John Earl *ed* Peter Pitt
☆ Jess Conrad, Christina Gregg, Hermione Baddeley, Kenneth Griffith, Patrick Magee, Patrick Jordan, Michael Wynne

Ragan
Spain 1968 90m Movielab
Westside International (Sidney Pink)
An American pilot, a former mercenary, is hired to help overthrow the government of a small country.
Glossy but dull thriller, a low-budget, low-talent attempt at a Bond-style entertainment.
w Howard Berk, Sidney Pink *d* Gilbert Lee Kay *ph* Antonio Macasoli *m* Nico Fidenco, G. Dell'orso *ed* Tony Ramirez
☆ Ty Hardin, Antonella Lualdi, Gustavo Rojo, Jack Stewart, Rossella Como, Joe Caffarell, Dick Palace

La Ragazza dal Pigiama Giallo: see *The Pajama Girl Case*

Rage
US 1966 103m Technicolor
Columbia/Joseph M. Schenck/Cinematografico Jalisco (Gilberto Gazcon)
A drunken doctor finds a new will to live during a difficult journey to avert a rabies epidemic.
Pattern melodrama with no surprises, but gripping most of the way.
w Teddi Sherman, Gilberto Gazcon, Fernando Mendez *d* Gilberto Gazcon *ph* Rosalio Solano *m* Gustavo Cesar Carreon
☆ Glenn Ford, Stella Stevens, David Reynoso, Armando Silvestre

Rage
US 1972 99m DeLuxe Panavision
Warner (Fred Weintraub)
A father takes revenge when his son dies after a chemical warfare accident.
Well-meaning but turgid and boring melodrama.
w Philip Friedman, Dan Kleinman *d* George C. Scott *ph* Fred Koenekamp *m* Lalo Schifrin
☆ George C. Scott, Richard Basehart, Martin Sheen, Barnard Hughes, Stephen Young
'Sluggish, tired and tiring.' – *Variety*

Rage at Dawn
US 1955 86m Technicolor
RKO/Nat Holt
Detectives stage a fake train robbery to attract the evil Reno brothers.
Very moderate Western programmer.
w Horace McCoy *d* Tim Whelan *ph* Ray Rennahan *m* Paul Sawtell
☆ Randolph Scott, Forrest Tucker, J. Carrol Naish, Mala Powers, Edgar Buchanan, Ray Teal

'Looks Can Kill.'
The Rage: Carrie 2
US 1999 101m DeLuxe/bw
MGM/UA/Red Bank (Paul Monash)
A teenage girl who is humiliated at school discovers that she has appalling telekinetic powers.
A sequel that recycles the original movie with no understanding of what made it effective.
w Rafael Moreu *d* Katt Shea *ph* Donald M. Morgan *m* Danny P. Harvey *pd* Peter Jamison *ed* Richard Nord
☆ Emily Bergl, Jason London, Dylan Bruno, J. Smith-Cameron, Amy Irving, Zachery Ty Bryan, John Doe, Gordon Clapp, Rachel Blanchard, Charlotte Ayanna, Justin Urich
'An uninspired update with video cameras, sexual frankness, margaritas and tattoos.' – *Anita Gates, New York Times*
'Abysmal' – *Variety*

A Rage in Harlem **
GB 1991 108m DeLuxe
Palace/Miramax (Stephen Woolley, Kerry Boyle)
In 1950s Harlem, a gullible undertaker's assistant gives refuge to a gangster's mistress with a trunkful of gold.
Lively, entertaining, fast-paced tongue-in-cheek thriller.
w John Toles-Bey, Bobby Crawford *novel* Chester Himes *d* Bill Duke *ph* Toyomichi Kurita *m* Elmer Bernstein *pd* Steven Legler *ed* Curtis Clayton
☆ Forest Whitaker, Gregory Hines, Robin Givens, Zakes Mokae, Danny Glover, Badja Djola, John Toles-Bey, Ron Taylor, Samm-Art Williams
'Many will be turned off by the excessive bloodshed, but the fine cast keeps the pic watchable.' – *Variety*
'Enjoyable though it is, Bill Duke's mix of brisk action, sexy innuendo and cameo-studded comedy takes considerable liberties with the spirit of Himes' Harlem.' – *Jonathan Romney, Sight and Sound*

Rage in Heaven
US 1941 82m bw
MGM (Gottfried Reinhardt)
An unstable millionaire becomes jealous of his wife and arranges his own death so that her supposed lover will be suspected.
Stilted melodrama with the stars more or less at sea.
w Christopher Isherwood, Robert Thoeren *novel* James Hilton *d* W. S. Van Dyke II *ph* Oliver T. Marsh *m* Bronislau Kaper
☆ Robert Montgomery, Ingrid Bergman, George Sanders, Lucile Watson, Oscar Homolka, Philip Merivale, Matthew Boulton, Aubrey Mather
'Nothing happens but the obvious, and that only after a long and confused struggle.' – *Otis Ferguson*
† Directors Robert Sinclair and Richard Thorpe also worked on the film, which was sabotaged by Robert Montgomery giving a deliberately monotonous performance because he felt affronted by not being consulted over the script. The writers added a speech by a psychiatrist commenting on the listlessness of Montgomery's character in order to explain his acting.

The Rage of Paris *
US 1938 78m bw
Universal (B. G. de Sylva)
Confidence tricksters invest their money in a French girl who is out to nail a millionaire.
If memory serves right, an amusingly amoral trifle in the best style of its year.
w Bruce Manning, Felix Jackson *d* Henry Koster
☆ Danielle Darrieux, Douglas Fairbanks Jnr, Louis Hayward, Mischa Auer, Helen Broderick, Harry Davenport, Samuel S. Hinds, Mary Martin
'Smart comedy of first-run calibre … a finished and polished job.' – *Variety*

'The names and the places didn't matter – only when!'
A Rage to Live
US 1965 101m bw Panavision
UA/Mirisch (Lewis J. Rachmil)
The unhappy college and married life of a nymphomaniac.
Well made but deliberately 'daring' case history which becomes too obvious and silly.
w John T. Kelley *novel* John O'Hara *d* Walter Grauman *ph* Charles Lawton *m* Nelson Riddle
☆ Suzanne Pleshette, Bradford Dillman, Ben Gazzara, Peter Graves, Bethel Leslie, James Gregory, Ruth White
'Stuff like this needs the exuberance of grand opera; sadly, all it gets here is a blue note.' – *MFB*

Raggedy Ann and Andy *
US 1977 85m Movielab Panavision
Lester Osterman (Richard Horner)
Toys come to life and have their own adventures while their owner is absent.
Attractive fully animated cartoon feature in which only the central story is lacking in pace and humour.
w Patricia Thackray, Max Wilk *stories* Johnny Gruelle *d* *Richard Williams* *m* Joe Raposo

Raggedy Man
US 1981 94m Technicolor
Universal/William D. Wittliff, Burt Weissbourd
In 1944, a small-town switchboard operator and her two children are protected by a mysterious stranger.
Curious and quite unnecessary melodrama of some skill but very dubious appeal.
w William D. Wittliff *d* Jack Fisk *ph* Ralf Bode *m* Jerry Goldsmith *ed* Edward Warschilka
☆ Sissy Spacek, Eric Roberts, Sam Shepard, William Sanderson, Tracey Walter, R. G. Armstrong
'Despite the casual, unhurried pace of the film, it doesn't seem to observe much.' – *Richard Combs, MFB*

The Raggedy Rawney *
GB 1987 103m Technicolor
Virgin/HandMade (Bob Weis)
An army deserter disguises himself as a woman and joins a group of wandering gypsies.
Downbeat rural tale, providing cold comfort.
w Bob Hoskins, Nicole de Wilde *d* Bob Hoskins *ph* Frank Tidy *m* Michael Kamen *pd* Jiri Matolin *ed* Alan Jones
☆ Bob Hoskins, Dexter Fletcher, Zoe Nathenson, Zoe Wanamaker, David Hill, Ian Dury, Ian McNeice, Veronica Clifford, Gawn Grainger, Jim Carter

Raging Bull ****
US 1980 119m bw/colour
UA/Chartoff-Winkler
The rise to fame of an unlikeable middle-weight boxer, based on the autobiography of Jake La Motta.
Tough, compelling, powerfully made ringside melodrama. A poll of American critics voted it the best movie of the 1980s.
w Paul Schrader, Mardik Martin *d* *Martin Scorsese* *ph* Michael Chapman *m* from library sources *pd* Gene Rudolf
☆ Robert DeNiro, Cathy Moriarty, Joe Pesci, Frank Vincent, Nicholas Colasanto
'Scorsese makes pictures about the kind of people you wouldn't want to know.' – *Variety*
'A bravura display of cinematic skill.' – *Daily Mail*
editing (Thelma Schoonmaker); Robert DeNiro
best film; best direction; Cathy Moriarty; Joe Pesci; Michael Chapman
editing

The Raging Moon *
GB 1970 111m Technicolor
EMI (Bruce Cohn Curtis)
aka: *Long Ago Tomorrow*
A love affair develops between two inmates of a home for the physically handicapped.
Appealing romantic drama which nearly became a big commercial success.
wd *Bryan Forbes* *novel* Peter Marshall *ph* Tony Imi *m* Stanley Myers
☆ *Malcolm McDowell*, *Nanette Newman*, Georgia Brown, Bernard Lee, Gerald Sim, Michael Flanders

The Raging Tide
US 1951 93m bw
U-I (Aaron Rosenberg)
A San Francisco gangster stows away on a fishing trawler and redeems himself when he perishes saving the life of a fisherman.
Fearfully old-fashioned seafaring melodrama, rather well made.
w Ernest K. Gann *novel* *Fiddler's Green* by Ernest K. Gann *d* George Sherman *ph* *Russell Metty* *m* Frank Skinner *ad* Hilyard Brown, Bernard Herzbrun *ed* Ted J. Kent
☆ Richard Conte, Charles Bickford, Shelley Winters, Stephen McNally, Alex Nicol, Jesse White, John McIntire

Raging Waters: see *Green Promise*

Una Ragione per Vivere e Una per Morire: see *A Reason to Live, a Reason to Die*

The Ragman's Daughter
GB 1972 94m Technicolor
TCF/Penelope (Harold Becker)
A Nottingham layabout falls in love with an exciting middle-class girl; they fail to overcome parental opposition and she is killed in a road accident.
Wispy drama framed in pointless flashbacks; done on the cheap, it never seems to get anywhere and even fails to use its locations to advantage.
w Alan Sillitoe *story* Alan Sillitoe *d* Harold Becker *ph* Michael Seresin *m* Kenny Clayton
☆ Simon Rouse, Victoria Tennant, Patrick O'Connell, Leslie Sands

'What a time it was, an incredible time, a good time, a bad time...'
Ragtime *
US 1981 155m Technicolor Todd-AO
Ragtime/Sunley (Dino de Laurentiis)
Just before World War I, various Americans are affected by world events, and a chapter of accidents turns a placid Negro into a revolutionary.
The fascinating patchwork of the novel has been virtually abandoned in favour of its least interesting episode, which is even further drawn out by the decision to bring on the aged James Cagney as a comic turn not in the novel. The early sequences show what might have been.
w Michael Weller *novel* E. L. Doctorow *d* Milos Forman *ph* *Miroslav Ondricek* *m* Randy Newman *ad* John Graysmark, Patrizia von Brandenstein, Anthony Reading
☆ James Olson, Mary Steenburgen, James Cagney, Pat O'Brien, Elizabeth McGovern, *Howard E. Rollins Jnr*, Brad Dourif, Moses Gunn, Kenneth McMillan, Donald O'Connor
'It's limp ... it always seems to be aiming about halfway toward the effects that Doctorow achieved in his literary extravaganza.' – *New Yorker*
'The book, despite its defects, was funny, radical and angry. The film, despite its virtues, is solemn, liberal and passive.' – *Sunday Times*
† The film cost 32 million dollars and took eleven.
screenplay; Miroslav Ondricek; Randy Newman; Elizabeth McGovern (supporting actress); Howard E. Rollins Jnr; art direction; song 'One More Hour'

The Raid *
US 1954 83m Technicolor
TCF (Robert L. Jacks)
In 1864 six confederate soldiers escape from a union prison, and from a Canadian refuge carry out a revenge raid on a small Vermont town.
Interesting little action drama, crisply characterized and plotted, and based on a historical incident.
w Sydney Boehm *story* *Affair at St Albans* by Herbert Ravenal Sass *d* *Hugo Fregonese* *ph* *Lucien Ballard* *m* Roy Webb
☆ Van Heflin, Anne Bancroft, Richard Boone, Lee Marvin, Tommy Rettig, Peter Graves, Douglas Spencer, Will Wright, John Dierkes

Raid on Rommel
US 1971 99m Technicolor
Universal (Harry Tatelman)
In North Africa during World War II, a British officer releases prisoners of war and leads them in an assault on Tobruk.
Dispirited low-budget actioner apparently first intended for television.
w Richard Bluel *d* Henry Hathaway *ph* Earl Rath *m* Hal Mooney
☆ Richard Burton, John Colicos, Clinton Greyn, Wolfgang Preiss

The Raiders: see *Riders of Vengeance (1952)*

The Raiders
US 1964 75m Technicolor
Revue/Universal
Cattle drovers enlist the aid of famous Western characters to persuade the railroad company to extend its line through dangerous country.
Slightly oddball Western with endearing moments amid the miscalculations.
w Gene L. Coon *d* Herschel Daugherty *ph* Bud Thackery *m* Morton Stevens
☆ Robert Culp (Wild Bill Hickok), Judi Meredith (Calamity Jane), James McMullan (Buffalo Bill Cody), Brian Keith, Alfred Ryder, Simon Oakland

Raiders of the Lost Ark ***
US 1981 115m Metrocolor Panavision
Paramount/Lucasfilm (Frank Marshall)
In the thirties, an American archaeologist and explorer beats the Nazis to a priceless artefact, the magical box containing fragments of the stones on which God wrote his laws.
Commercially very successful, this attempted wrap-up of the Saturday morning serials of two generations ago spends a great deal of money and expertise on frightening us rather than exciting us; in Dolby sound the experience is horrendous. Second time round, one can better enjoy the ingenious detail of the hero's exploits and ignore the insistence on unpleasantness; still, there are boring bits in between, and the story doesn't make a lot of sense.
w Lawrence Kasdan *d* *Steven Spielberg* *ph* Douglas Slocombe *m* John Williams *pd* *Norman Reynolds*
☆ Harrison Ford, Karen Allen, Ronald Lacey, Paul Freeman, John Rhys-Davies, Denholm Elliott
'Both de trop and not enough.' – *Sight and Sound*
'Children may well enjoy its simple-mindedness, untroubled by the fact that it looks so shoddy and so uninventive.' – *Observer*
'Kinesthetically, the film gets to you, but there's no exhilaration, and no surge of feeling at the end.' – *Pauline Kael, New Yorker*
'An out of body experience, a movie of glorious imagination and breakneck speed that grabs you in the first shot, hurtles you through a series of incredible adventures, and deposits you back in reality two hours later – breathless, dizzy, wrung-out, and with a silly grin on your face.' – *Roger Ebert*
† Tom Selleck was the first choice for the lead, but was tied up with his TV series *Magnum*.
†† It was followed by two sequels: *Indiana Jones and the Temple of Doom* and *Indiana Jones and the Last Crusade* (qqv).
editing (Michael Kahn); visual effects
best picture; Steven Spielberg; Douglas Slocombe; John Williams
Norman Reynolds

Railroaded *
US 1947 72m bw
Charles F. Reisner/Eagle Lion
A detective is on the trail of a ruthless mobster.
A new post-war toughness was evident in this sharply made second feature.
w John C. Higgins, Gertrude Walker *d* Anthony Mann *ph* Guy Roe *m* Alvin Levin
☆ John Ireland, Sheila Ryan, Hugh Beaumont, Jane Randolph, Ed Kelly, Charles D. Brown

Rails into Laramie
US 1954 81m Technicolor
Universal-International
Railway construction is hampered in Laramie by a salon keeper who keeps the workers too happy.
Solid co-feature Western, quite enjoyable.
w D. D. Beauchamp, Joseph Hoffman *d* Jesse Hibbs *ph* Maury Gertsman *m* Frederick Herbert, Arnold Hughes *md* Joseph Gershenson *ed* Ted J. Kent
☆ John Payne, Dan Duryea, Mari Blanchard, Barton MacLane, Harry Shannon, Lee Van Cleef, Joyce MacKenzie, Ralph Dumke

'A film for adults to take their children, too!'
The Railway Children ***
GB 1970 108m Technicolor
EMI (Robert Lynn)
Three Edwardian children and their mother move into Yorkshire when their father is imprisoned as a spy, and have adventures on the railway line while helping to prove his innocence.
Fresh and agreeable family film with many pleasing touches to compensate for its meandering plot.
wd *Lionel Jeffries* *novel* E. Nesbit *ph* *Arthur Ibbetson* *m* Johnny Douglas
☆ Dinah Sheridan, William Mervyn, Jenny Agutter, Bernard Cribbins, Iain Cuthbertson, Gary Warren, Sally Thomsett
'There are passages in Mr Jeffries' deliberately nostalgic film which may appeal more to sensitive parents than to their bloodthirsty offspring. But everybody, I hope, will enjoy the playing.' – *Dilys Powell*

Rain *
US 1932 92m bw
UA/Art Cinema Corporation (Joseph Schenck)
Stranded passengers in Pago Pago during an epidemic include a prostitute and a missionary who lusts after her.
Early talkie version of a much filmed story; interesting but not very entertaining now that the sensational aspects have worn off.
w Maxwell Anderson *play* John Colton, Clemence Randolph *story* *W. Somerset Maugham* *d* Lewis Milestone *ph* Oliver T. Marsh *m* Alfred Newman
☆ Joan Crawford, Walter Huston, William Gargan, Beulah Bondi, Matt Moore, Guy Kibbee, Walter Catlett
'A b.o. disappointer. Only the play's rep and Joan Crawford's personal pull will save it.' – *Variety*
† Other versions: *Sadie Thompson* (1928) with Gloria Swanson; *Miss Sadie Thompson* (1953) (qv).

Rain Man **
US 1988 133m DeLuxe
UIP/United Artists/Guber-Peters (Mark Johnson)
A fast-talking salesman discovers, on his father's death, that he has an autistic elder brother.
An intelligent road movie, but one that does not move far enough from more conventional buddy-buddy movies.
w Ronald Bass, Barry Morrow *d* *Barry Levinson* *ph* John Seale *m* Hans Zimmer *pd* Ida Random *ed* Stu Linder, Thomas R. Moore
☆ Dustin Hoffman, Tom Cruise, Valeria Golino, Jerry Molen, Jack Murdock, Michael D. Roberts, Ralph Seymour, Lucinda Jenney, Bonnie Hunt
best picture; best director; best original screenplay; Dustin Hoffman
best original score; best cinematography; best film editing; best art direction

Rain or Shine *
US 1930 90m bw
Columbia (Harry Cohn)
A circus performer puts on a one-man show in an attempt to stop it from closing.
A musical comedy translated to the screen without its songs as a showcase for the acrobatic, slack-wire and juggling talents of its star, a Broadway comedian famous for his wide smile and nonsense patter.
w Jo Swerling, Dorothy Howell *musical comedy* James Gleason, Maurice Marks *d* Frank Capra *ph* Joe Walker *md* Bakaleinikoff *ed* Maurice Wright
☆ Joe Cook, Louise Fazenda, Joan Peers, William Collier Jnr, Tom Howard

The Rain People
US 1969 101m Technicolor
Warner/American Zoetrope (Bart Patton, Ronald Colby)
A depressed housewife leaves home, drives across country, and picks up a mentally retarded hitch-hiker who tries to protect her.
Slow, pretentious character drama which strains after art but only presents an unedifying study of failure.
wd Francis Ford Coppola *ph* Wilmer Butler *m* Ronald Stein
☆ Shirley Knight, James Caan, Robert Duvall, Tom Aldredge, Marya Zimmet
'The rain people are people made of rain and when they cry they disappear because they cry themselves away.' – *sample dialogue*

The Rainbow *
GB 1988 111m Technicolor
Vestron (Ken Russell)

Determined to be independent, a farmer's daughter rejects her lover to go to university.
Over-simplified version of the novel, but watchable enough.
w Ken Russell, Vivian Russell *novel* D. H. Lawrence *d* Ken Russell *ph* Billy Williams *m* Carl Davis *pd* Luciana Arrighi *ed* Peter Davies
☆ Sammi Davis, Paul McGann, Amanda Donohoe, Christopher Gable, David Hemmings, Glenda Jackson, Dudley Sutton, Jim Carter, Judith Paris, Ken Colley

Rainbow
GB/Canada 1995 101m
Technicolor/bw Digital High Definition
First Independent/Winchester (Rainbow)/Filmline/Screen Partners (Robert Sidaway, Nicolas Clermont)

Children steal gold from a rainbow, which causes colour to drain from the world with disastrous results.
Heavy-handed, didactic children's film that strives for a fairy-tale quality, but too frequently falls flat.
w Ashley Sidaway, Robert Sidaway *d* Bob Hoskins *ph* Freddie Francis *m* Alan Reeves *pd* Claude Paré *ed* Ray Lovejoy
☆ Bob Hoskins, Dan Aykroyd, Saul Rubinek, Jacob Tierney, Willy Lavenda, Jonathan Schuman, Eleanor Misrahi
'It would be hard to find a more charmless fable than this leaden patience-tester which gets everything wrong from the whimsical atmosphere striven for to the light touch so desperately needed to make the completely hopeless humour work.' – *Alan Jones, Film Review*
† It is the first film to be shot in Digital High Definition video.

'The siren of the sarongs is calling you!'
Rainbow Island
US 1944 95m Technicolor
Paramount (I. D. Leshin)
A white girl brought up by her doctor father on a Pacific island is pursued by three sailors escaping from the Japanese.
Cheerful spoof of the sarong cycle with the star seeing the joke; otherwise a silly service farce with South Sea trimmings.
w Walter de Leon, Seena Owen, Arthur Phillips *d* Ralph Murphy *ph* Karl Struss *m* Roy Webb *songs* Burton Lane, Ted Koehler
☆ Dorothy Lamour, Eddie Bracken, Gil Lamb, Barry Sullivan, Forrest Orr, Anne Revere, Reed Hadley, Marc Lawrence

The Rainbow Jacket
GB 1954 99m Technicolor
Ealing (Michael Relph)
A boy jockey is blackmailed into losing a big race.
Disappointing racecourse drama which packs in all the expected ingredients.
w T. E. B. Clarke *d* Basil Dearden *ph* Otto Heller *m* William Alwyn
☆ Kay Walsh, Bill Owen, Edward Underdown, Robert Morley, Wilfrid Hyde-White, Charles Victor, Honor Blackman, Sidney James
'Probably the best racing film ever made.' – C. A. Lejeune

Rainbow on the River
US 1936 83m bw
Sol Lesser (RKO)
After the Civil War, an orphan is brought up by a Black mammy and later discovered to be rich.
Sentimental drama with songs from its boy star; not much, but popular.
w Earle Snell, William Hurlbut *story* Mrs C. V. Jamison *d* Kurt Neumann
☆ Bobby Breen, May Robson, Charles Butterworth, Louise Beavers, Alan Mowbray, Benita Hume, Henry O'Neill
'Phoney and over-sugared sentimentality.' – *Variety*

Rainbow round My Shoulder
US 1952 78m Technicolor
Columbia
A society girl breaks into show business.
Agreeable light musical for the easily pleased.
w Blake Edwards, Richard Quine *d* Richard Quine
☆ Frankie Laine, Billy Daniels, Charlotte Austin, Arthur Franz, Ida Moore, Lloyd Corrigan

Raining Stones **
GB 1993 91m colour
First Independent/Parallax/Channel 4 (Sally Hibbin)

An unemployed Catholic father tries to raise the money to buy a communion dress for his seven-year-old daughter.
A realistic drama about working-class lives, absorbing, richly detailed and welcome as one of the few British films of recent years to concern itself with contemporary, everyday life and its problems.
w Jim Allen *d* Ken Loach *ph* Barry Ackroyd *m* Stewart Copeland *pd* Martin Johnson *ed* Jonathan Morris
☆ Bruce Jones, Julie Brown, Gemma Phoenix, Ricky Tomlinson, Tom Hickey, Mike Fallon, Ronnie Ravey, Lee Brennan
'The film contains more truth and humor than many a large-screen picture, and is sure to captivate audiences who seek it out.' – *Variety*

The Rainmaker
US 1956 121m Technicolor Vistavision
Paramount/Hal B. Wallis (Paul Nathan)

In 1913 Kansas, a fake rainmaker has more success melting the heart of a confirmed spinster.
Such a whimsical play is too talky to make a good movie, especially as the actors are over-age, their performances are mannered, the dialogue seems interminable and the production is too stagey.
w N. Richard Nash *play* N. Richard Nash *d* Joseph Anthony *ph* Charles Lang Jnr *m* Alex North
☆ Katharine Hepburn, Burt Lancaster, Wendell Corey, Lloyd Bridges, Earl Holliman, Cameron Prud'homme, Wallace Ford
Alex North; Katharine Hepburn

The Rainmaker: see *John Grisham's The Rainmaker (1997)*

The Rainmakers
US 1935 79m bw
RKO
Fake rainmakers are chased by midwestern farmers to California, where they get involved in an irrigation scheme.
Slow-paced comedy with a train chase finale which comes too late.
w Grant Garrett, Leslie Goodwins *d* Fred Guiol
☆ Bert Wheeler, Robert Woolsey, Dorothy Lee, Berton Churchill, George Meeker
'May appeal mildly to their fans, but won't make new business.' – *Variety*

The Rains Came ***
US 1939 103m bw
TCF (Harry Joe Brown)
High-class parasites in India during the Raj redeem themselves when a flood disaster strikes.
Wholly absorbing disaster spectacular in which the characterization and personal plot development are at least as interesting as the spectacle, and all are encased in a glowingly professional production.
w Philip Dunne, Julien Josephson *novel* Louis Bromfield *d* Clarence Brown *ph* Arthur Miller *m* Alfred Newman *ed* Barbara McLean *sp* Fred Sersen
☆ Myrna Loy, George Brent, Tyrone Power, Brenda Joyce, Maria Ouspenskaya, Joseph Schildkraut, H. B. Warner, Nigel Bruce, Mary Nash, Jane Darwell, Marjorie Rambeau, Henry Travers
'A big box-office picture with the advantage of a new locale.' – *Variety*
'It would be difficult to improve on the direction, the outbreak of the monsoon, a curtain billowing in the breeze, a lamp casting the shadow of lattice work against white silk, servants scattering for cover…' – *Charles Higham, 1972*
'Slick Hollywood film-making at its professional best.' – *Channel 4, 1982*
† Myrna Loy was third choice after Dietrich and Lamarr; Brent second choice after Ronald Colman.
Alfred Newman; editing

The Rains of Ranchipur
US 1955 104m Eastmancolor
Cinemascope
TCF (Frank Ross)
Dismal remake of *The Rains Came*, with bored actors and inferior production, all the character of the original being wiped out by badly processed wide-screen spectacle.
w Merle Miller *d* Jean Negulesco *ph* Milton Krasner *m* Hugo Friedhofer
☆ Lana Turner, Fred MacMurray, Richard Burton, Joan Caulfield, Eugenie Leontovich, Michael Rennie

Raintree County
US 1957 166m Technicolor Panavision (Camera 65)
MGM (David Lewis)

During the Civil War a Southern belle gets the man she thinks she wants, but subsequently finds life as a schoolmaster's wife boring.
Dreary attempt by MGM to out-do Gone with the Wind, *with neither characters nor plot one third as interesting and the production values merely expensive.*
w Millard Kaufman *novel* Ross Lockridge *d* Edward Dmytryk *ph* Robert Surtees *m* Johnny Green *ad* William A. Horning, Urie McCleary
☆ Montgomery Clift, Elizabeth Taylor, Eva Marie Saint, Nigel Patrick, Lee Marvin, Rod Taylor, Agnes Moorehead, Walter Abel, Jarma Lewis, Tom Drake, Gardner McKay, Rhys Williams
Johnny Green; Elizabeth Taylor; art direction

Raise Ravens *
Spain 1975 115m colour
Elias Querejeta

original title: *Cria Cuervos*
aka: *Cria!*
A woman remembers her life as a child, when she may have caused the death of her philandering father.
Elliptical story of childhood and of women trapped in a world dominated by men; it is never less than watchable, but its meaning, possibly obliquely political, remains obscure.
wd Carlos Saura *ph* Teo Escamilla *m* Federico Mompoli *ad* Rafael Palmero *ed* Pablo G. del Amo
☆ Geraldine Chaplin, Monica Randall, Florinda Chico, Ana Torrent, Conchi Perez, Maite Sanchez, Josefina Diaz, German Cobos, Hector Alterio, Mirta Miller
'Saura has succeeded in conjuring up, with many nice touches, a picture of childhood which is finely balanced between reality and sentimentality.' – *John Pym, MFB*
† The film won the Special Jury Prize at the 1976 Cannes Film Festival.

'China, 1920's. One master, four wives … One fate.'
Raise the Red Lantern **
Hong Kong 1991 125m Eastmancolor
Palace/Era/China Film (Chiu Fu-Sheng)

original title: *Dahong Denglong Gaogao Gua*
A young woman, who has become the fourth wife of a rich merchant, finds herself in competition with his other wives for her husband's favour.
Cool study of sexual politics and the subjugation of women.
w Ni Zhen *story* Su Tong *d* Zhang Yimou *ph* Zhao Fei *m* Zhao Jiping *ad* Cao Jiuping, Dong Huamiao *ed* Du Yuan
☆ Gong Li, Ma Jingwu, He Caifei, Cao Cuifeng, Jin Shuyuan, Kong Li, Ding Weimin, Cui Zhigang, Chu Xiao
best foreign film
best foreign film

Raise the Roof
GB 1930 77m bw
BIP
An actress is bribed to sabotage a touring show.
Early talkie which retains surprising freshness.
w Walter Summers, Philip MacDonald *d* Walter Summers
☆ Betty Balfour, Maurice Evans, Jack Raine, Sam Livesey, Ellis Jeffreys
† Credited as the first British musical.

Raise the Titanic!
US 1980 122m DeLuxe
Lord Grade/Martin Starger (William Frye)

Assorted Americans try to recover rare minerals from the wreck of the ship which sank in the North Atlantic in 1912.
Heavy-going exploiter with little action and even less plot.
w Adam Kennedy, Eric Hughes *novel* Clive Cussler *d* Jerry Jameson *ph* Matthew F. Leonetti *m* John Barry *pd* John F. DeCuir *second unit ph* Rex Metz *underwater ph* Bob Steadman
☆ Jason Robards, Richard Jordan, Alec Guinness, David Selby, Anne Archer, J. D. Cannon
'Hits new depths hitherto unexplored by the worst of Lew Grade's overloaded ark melodramas. This one wastes a potentially intriguing premise with dull scripting, a lacklustre cast, laughably phony trick work and clunky direction that makes *Voyage of the Damned* seem inspired by comparison.' – *Variety*
'The longer it all goes on, the more one hopes that, if they ever do raise the *Titanic*, they'll heave the film overboard to replace it.' – *Guardian*
'Right boat, wrong direction!' – *Michael McKean*
† The film cost $40m and took $7m. As Sir Lew Grade commented, 'It would have been cheaper to lower the Atlantic.'

A Raisin in the Sun *
US 1961 128m bw
Columbia/Paman – Doris (David Susskind, Philip Rose)

The life of a struggling black family in a cramped Chicago flat.
Earnest but claustrophobic play-on-film which long outstays its welcome but contains good performances.
w Lorraine Hansberry *play* Lorraine Hansberry *d* Daniel Petrie *ph* Charles Lawton Jnr *m* Laurence Rosenthal
☆ Sidney Poitier, Ruby Dee, Claudia McNeil, Diana Sands, Ivan Dixon, John Fiedler, Lou Gossett

Raising a Riot
GB 1955 90m Technicolor
British Lion/Wessex (Ian Dalrymple, Hugh Perceval)
With his wife away, a naval officer tries to cope with his three lively children while staying with his elderly father in a derelict windmill.
Sentimental domestic comedy that goes for easy laughs and misses most of them.
w Ian Dalrymple, Hugh Perceval *novel* Alfred Toombs *d* Wendy Toye *ph* Christopher Challis *m* Bruce Montgomery *md* Muir Mathieson *ad* Joseph Bato *ed* Albert Rule
☆ Kenneth More, Shelagh Fraser, Ronald Squire, Olga Lindo, Jan Miller, Nora Nicholson, Lionel Murton, Mandy, Gary Billings, Fusty Bentine, Robin Brown

Raising Arizona *
US 1987 94m DuArt
Circle Films/TCF

In the American heartlands, a petty crook falls for the lady cop who regularly checks him into jail.
Zany collection of incidents which scarcely welds itself into a story but offers a few laughs along the way.
w Ethan and Joel Coen *d* Joel Coen *ph* Barry Sonnenfeld *m* Carter Burwell
☆ Nicolas Cage, Holly Hunter, Trey Wilson, John Goodman, William Forsythe

'When Jenny cheated on her husband, he didn't just leave … he split.'
Raising Cain
US 1992 92m colour
UIP/Universal (Gale Anne Hurd)

A psychologist develops multiple personalities, including that of a murderous twin brother.
Risible thriller, stuffed full of shock moments that hamper the narrative flow, and growing increasingly ridiculous throughout; it fails to repay its huge debt to Peeping Tom and to Hitchcock.
wd Brian de Palma *ph* Stephen H. Burum *m* Pino Donaggio *pd* Doug Kraner *ed* Paul Hirsch, Bonnie Koehler, Robert Dalva
☆ John Lithgow, Lolita Davidovich, Steven Bauer, Frances Sternhagen, Gregg Henry, Tom Bower, Mel Harris, Teri Austin, Gabrielle Carteris

'Scandalously prodigal with its loose ends and red herrings, and scandalously unfair with its narrative let-outs.' – *Sight and Sound*

'A superficial, often risible, exercise in pure aesthetics that's likely to turn off mainstream audiences, spelling a fast flop.' – *Variety*

Raising the Wind
GB 1961 91m colour
GHW/Anglo Amalgamated (Peter Rogers)
US title: *Roommates*
Misadventures of students at a music academy.
A Carry On in all but name, from the same stable; good moments among the dross.
w Bruce Montgomery *d* Gerald Thomas *ph* Alan Hume *m* Bruce Montgomery
☆ James Robertson Justice, Leslie Phillips, Kenneth Williams, Sidney James, Paul Massie, Liz Fraser, Eric Barker, Jennifer Jayne, Geoffrey Keen, Esma Cannon

The Rake's Progress *
GB 1945 123m bw
GFD/Individual (Frank Launder, Sidney Gilliat)
US title: *Notorious Gentleman*
The career of a cheerful ne'er-do-well playboy of the thirties.
The road to ruin played for light comedy, with silly endpapers in which, quite out of character, the rake becomes a war hero. Generally good production, witty script.
w Frank Launder, Sidney Gilliat *story* Val Valentine *d* Sidney Gilliat *ph* Wilkie Cooper *m* William Alwyn *pd* David Rawnsley
☆ Rex Harrison, Lilli Palmer, Margaret Johnston, Godfrey Tearle, Griffith Jones, Guy Middleton, Jean Kent, Marie Lohr, Garry Marsh, David Horne, Alan Wheatley

'Bright, witty and finished.' – *Richard Winnington*

† In the American version Harrison crowned the Martyrs' Memorial not with a chamber pot but with a top hat.

Rally Round the Flag Boys
US 1958 106m DeLuxe Cinemascope
TCF (Leo McCarey)
A small community protests at the siting nearby of a missile base.
Raucous service and sex comedy which becomes frenetic without ever being very funny.
w Claude Binyon, Leo McCarey *novel* Max Shulman *d* Leo McCarey *ph* Leon Shamroy *m* Cyril Mockridge
☆ Paul Newman, Joanne Woodward, Joan Collins, Jack Carson, Dwayne Hickman, Tuesday Weld, Gale Gordon, Murvyn Vye

'She has been quite promiscuous since early childhood. She has absolutely no control over her sexual impulses. Miss Rosebud has arrived!'
Rambling Rose **
US 1991 112m DuArt/DeLuxe
Guild/Carolco (Renny Harlin)
During the Depression, a boy becomes infatuated with a sexually-free young woman who comes to work at his home.
Gripping domestic drama that gains from its period setting.
w Calder Willingham *novel* Calder Willingham *d* Martha Coolidge *ph* Johnny E. Jensen *m* Elmer Bernstein *pd* John Vallone *ed* Steven Cohen
☆ Laura Dern, Robert Duvall, Diane Ladd, Lukas Haas, John Heard, Kevin Conway, Robert Burke, Lisa Jakub, Evan Lockwood, Matt Sutherland

'A quiet, unassertive picture, very literary in the memories it evokes, full of universal insights into family life, and performed with delicacy by all concerned.' – *Philip French, Guardian*

Laura Dern; Diane Ladd

Rambo: First Blood Part Two
US 1985 92m Technicolor Panavision
Anabasis Investments NV/Buzz Feitshans
A special ops veteran is sent to spring POWs in Vietnam.
Absurdly overwrought comic strip action which shamefully caught the mood of America at the time of its release.
w Sylvester Stallone, James Cameron *d* George Pan Cosmatos *ph* Jack Cardiff *m* Jerry Goldsmith
☆ Sylvester Stallone, Richard Crenna, Charles Napier, Julia Nickson, Steven Berkoff

'One mounting fireball ... risible production, comic book heroics.' – *Variety*

Rambo III
US 1988 101m Technicolor
Columbia TriStar/Carolco (Buzz Feitshans)
Rambo invades Afghanistan to rescue a friend captured by the Soviet forces.
More ludicrously melodramatic heroics, with Stallone as a one-man army defeating the massed forces of the enemy.
w Sylvester Stallone, Sheldon Lettich *d* Peter MacDonald *ph* John Stanier *m* Jerry Goldsmith *pd* Bill Kenney *ed* James Symons, Andrew London, O. Nicholas Brown, Edward Warschilka
☆ Sylvester Stallone, Richard Crenna, Marc de Jonge, Kurtwood Smith, Spiros Focas, Sasson Gabai

† Russel Mulcahy began directing the film but left after a few days. It was the most expensive film made to that date, costing in excess of $60 million.

Ramona
US 1936 90m Technicolor
TCF (Sol M. Wurtzel)
A half-breed girl and an Indian chief's son combat the greed of white pioneers.
Old-fashioned, stuffy adventure romance, much filmed in silent days.
w Lamar Trotti *novel* Helen Hunt Jackson *d* Henry King *ph* William Skall, Chester Lyons *m* Alfred Newman
☆ Loretta Young, Don Ameche, Kent Taylor, Pauline Frederick, Jane Darwell, Katherine de Mille, Victor Kilian, John Carradine

Rampage
US 1963 98m Technicolor
Warner Seven Arts/Talbot (William Fadiman)
Two white hunters love the same girl; one releases a tiger to harm the other, but it escapes.
Silly, unconvincing, old-style melodrama in which even the animals seem to overact.
w Robert Holt, Marguerite Roberts *novel* Alan Caillou *d* Phil Karlson *ph* Harold Lipstein *m* Elmer Bernstein
☆ Robert Mitchum, Jack Hawkins, Elsa Martinelli, Sabu, Emile Genest

The Ramparts We Watch *
US 1940 87m bw
RKO/Louis de Rochemont
A typical American family exemplifies the need for military preparedness.
A feature acted by amateurs, produced by the March of Time unit; interesting rather than influential, as it still took Pearl Harbor to bring the Americans into the war.
w Robert Richards, Cedric B. Worth *d* Louis de Rochemont

'It enters the fray with frankness in its favour.' – *Variety*

'A woman is soft and warm ... and deadlier than steel!'
Ramrod
US 1947 94m bw
(MGM) Enterprise (Harry Sherman)
A predatory lady ranch owner hires a tough foreman and her ruthlessness causes several deaths and a stampede.
Ho-hum minor Western with fading stars.
w Jack Moffitt, Graham Baker, Cecile Kramer *story* Luke Short *d* André de Toth *ph* Russell Harlan *m* Adolph Deutsch *pd* Lionel Banks *ed* Sherman A. Rose
☆ Veronica Lake, Joel McCrea, Preston Foster, Charles Ruggles, Donald Crisp, Arleen Whelan, Lloyd Bridges

Ran ****
Japan 1985 161m colour
Herald-Ace/Nippon-Herald/Greenwich (Masato Hara, Serge Silberman)
A Japanese version of *King Lear*, with three sons instead of three daughters.
Predictable bloodshed and tremendous style are evident in this oriental epic from a master hand at the age of 75.
w Akira Kurosawa, Hideo Oguni, Masato Ide *d Akira Kurosawa ph Takao Saito m* Toru Takemitsu
☆ Tatsuya Nakadai, Satoshi Terao, Jinpachi Nezu, Daisuke Ryu

'Prepare to be astonished ... a towering achievement in any language.' – *People*

costumes (Emi Wada)
direction, photography, art direction
best foreign film

Rancho De Luxe
US 1974 95m DeLuxe
UA/EK (Anthony Ray)
Cheerful cattle rustlers go on a binge and end up in prison.
Modern anti-everything Western; it's anti-entertainment as well.
w Thomas McGuane *d* Frank Perry *ph* William A. Fraker *m* Jimmy Buffett
☆ Sam Waterston, Jeff Bridges, Elizabeth Ashley, Charlene Dallas, Clifton James, Slim Pickens

'Where anything goes ... for a price!'
Rancho Notorious
US 1952 89m Technicolor
RKO/Fidelity (Howard Welsch)
A cowboy seeking revenge for his girlfriend's murder follows a clue to a lonely ranch run by a saloon singer.
Curious Western which seems to have been intended as another Destry Rides Again *but is made in a hard inflexible style which prevents it from appealing.*
w Daniel Taradash *d* Fritz Lang *ph* Hal Mohr *m* Hugo Friedhofer *md* Emil Newman
☆ Marlene Dietrich, Arthur Kennedy, Mel Ferrer, Gloria Henry, William Frawley, Jack Elam

'Every quality you might ask of a western is in lavish supply – except entertainment value.' – *Alton Cook*

'Those In The Know, Know.'
Rancid Aluminium
GB 2000 91m colour Super 35
Entertainment/Fiction Factory (James Hawes, Mike Parker, Mike Thomas)
When his close friend inherits the family business, an envious accountant decides to take over the company with the financial aid of Russian gangsters.
Rancid it is, so bad that it won't even become a cult movie.
w James Hawes *d* Ed Thomas *ph* Tony Imi *m* John Hardy *pd* Hayden Pearce *ed* Chris Lawrence
☆ Joseph Fiennes (Sean Deeny), Rhys Ifans (Pete Thompson), Tara Fitzgerald (Masha), Sadie Frost (Sarah), Stephen Berkoff (Mr Kant), Keith Allen (Dr Jones), Dani Behr (Charlie), Andrew Howard (Trevor), Nick Moran (Harry), Barry Foster (Doctor)

'A stupid, unfunny and self-satisfied film that should be avoided at all costs.' – *Cosmo Landesman, Sunday Times*

'By universal consent, it is the worst film ever made in the UK. People who have seen it belong to an exclusive club. They cannot speak about the film, they simply shudder at its mention.' – *Jacques Perretti, Guardian*

The Randolph Family: see *Dear Octopus*

Random Harvest ***
US 1942 126m bw
MGM (Sidney Franklin)
A shell-shocked officer in the 1914–18 war escapes from an asylum, marries a music hall singer and is idyllically happy until a shock makes him remember that he is the head of a noble family. His wife, whom he does not now remember, dutifully becomes his secretary and years later another shock brings memory and happiness back.
A silly enough story works remarkably well in this rather splendid, no holds barred, roses round the door romance in Hollywood's best style with incomparable stars. A triumph of the Peg's Paper syndrome, and hugely enjoyable because it is done so enthusiastically.
w Claudine West, George Froeschel, Arthur Wimperis *novel* James Hilton *d Mervyn Le Roy ph* Joseph Ruttenberg *m* Herbert Stothart *ad* Cedric Gibbons, Randall Duell
☆ *Ronald Colman, Greer Garson*, Susan Peters, Philip Dorn, Reginald Owen, Henry Travers, Margaret Wycherly, Bramwell Fletcher, Arthur Margetson

'I would like to recommend this film to those who can stay interested in Ronald Colman's amnesia for two hours and who could with pleasure eat a bowl of Yardley's shaving soap for breakfast.' – *James Agee*

'A strangely empty film ... its characters are creatures of fortune, not partisans in determining their own fates.' – *Bosley Crowther, New York Times*

'It is cast with pearly players in every part. Its pedigreed plot is savoured with just the right mixture of ups and downs, ecstasy and well-bred anguish, implausibility and psyche. And it moves towards its climax with the measured tread and nicely timed emotional bumps of a Hearst Cosmopolitan serial. It is perhaps the clearest example of the year of how a studio possessing lion's shares of movie-making capital and ingratiating talent can mate these two to synthesize a magnificent neuter, which will predictably bring in vast box office returns with which to produce more neuters.' – *John McManus, PM*

best picture; script; Mervyn Le Roy; Herbert Stothart; Ronald Colman; Susan Peters; art direction

'In a perfect world, they never would have met.'
Random Hearts
US 1999 133m DeLuxe
Columbia/Rastar/Mirage (Sydney Pollack, Marykay Powell)
When his wife is killed in a plane crash, a cop discovers that she was with her lover, and goes to meet the widow of the man with whom she was having an affair.
Run-of-the-mill romance of an odd couple, thrown together by chance; it is difficult to summon up much interest in their doings.
w Kurt Luedtke, Darryl Ponicsan *novel* Warren Adler *d* Sydney Pollack *ph* Philippe Rousselot *m* Dave Grusin *pd* Barbara Ling *ed* William Steinkamp
☆ Harrison Ford (Dutch Van Den Broeck), Kristin Scott Thomas (Kay Chandler), Charles S. Dutton (Alcee), Bonnie Hunt (Wendy Judd), Dennis Haysbert (Det George Beaufort), Sydney Pollack (Carl Broman), Richard Jenkins (Truman Trainor), Paul Guilfoyle (Dick Montoya), Susanna Thompson (Peyton Van Den Broeck), Peter Coyote (Cullen Chandler), Dylan Baker (Richard Judd)

'An ideal rainy day matinee attraction for well-to-do ladies of a certain age.' – *Todd McCarthy, Variety*

'Dismal.' – *Times*

Randy Rides Alone
US 1934 53m bw
Monogram/Lone Star (Paul Malvern)
An undercover agent unmasks a murdering outlaw, who is disguised as a dumb storekeeper, Matt the Mute. He also gets the girl.
Quickie Western with some of the trappings of a detective story, including secret hiding places and a portrait whose eyes move.
w Lindsley Parsons *d* Harry Fraser *ph* Archie Stout *ed* Carl Pierson
☆ John Wayne, Alberta Vaughn, George Hayes, Yakima Canutt, Earl Dwire

Rangers of Fortune
US 1940 79m bw
Paramount (Dale Van Every)
Three amiable gun-runners clean up a south-west town.
Good reliable Western with star appeal.
w Frank Butler *d* Sam Wood
☆ Fred MacMurray, Albert Dekker, Gilbert Roland, Patricia Morison, Joseph Schildkraut, Dick Foran, Betty Brewer

Ranghe Khoda: see *The Colour of Paradise*

Rango
US 1931 70m bw
Paramount
An old man and a boy in Sumatra go about their business of killing tigers.
Faded semi-documentary by the man who was about to direct King Kong.
wd Ernest B. Schoedsack
☆ Claude King, Douglas Scott

Rangoon: see *Beyond Rangoon*

'He faced a decision that someday may be yours to make!'
Ransom *
US 1955 104m bw
MGM (Nicholas Nayfack)
A rich man takes desperate measures to rescue his son from a kidnapper.
Solid but overlong suspenser, virtually a vehicle for a star at his twitchiest and most dogged.
w Cyril Hume, Richard Maibaum *d* Alex Segal *ph* Arthur E. Arling *m* Jeff Alexander
☆ Glenn Ford, Donna Reed, Leslie Nielsen, Juano Hernandez, Robert Keith

Ransom *
GB 1975 98m Eastmancolor
Lion International (Peter Rawley)
aka: *The Terrorists*
A British ambassador to Scandinavia is kidnapped by terrorists and a Norwegian security chief gives chase.
Topical but unconvincing action thriller with unfamiliar detail; builds up to exciting sequences but is quickly forgotten.
w Paul Wheeler *d* Caspar Wrede *ph* Sven Nykvist *m* Jerry Goldsmith
☆ Sean Connery, Ian McShane, Norman Bristow, John Cording, Isabel Dean, William Fox, Robert Harris

'Someone Is Going To Pay.'
Ransom *
US 1996 120m Technicolor
Buena Vista/Touchstone (Brian Grazer, Scott Rudin, B. Kipling Hagopian)
Realizing that his kidnapped son is unlikely to be returned to him alive, a millionaire offers the ransom money as a reward for the capture of the criminals.
A moderately tense psychological thriller, competently made but only passably interesting.
w Richard Price *story* Alexander Ignon *d* Ron Howard *ph* Piotr Sobocinski *m* James Horner *pd* Michael Corenblith *ed* Dan Hanley, Michael Hill
☆ Mel Gibson, Rene Russo, Gary Sinise, Delroy Lindo, Lili Taylor, Liev Schreiber, Evan Handler, Donnie Wahlberg, Dan Hedaya
'A crackerjack thriller with some unusually tasty plot twists.' – *Todd McCarthy, Variety*
'Watchable, made with a highly professional gloss, has a decent performance from a major star, and is pretty forgettable.' – *Derek Malcolm, Guardian*
† It is a remake of the 1956 film written by Cyril Hume and Richard Maibum, starring Glenn Ford, Donna Reed and Leslie Nielsen, and directed by Alex Segal, who had previously directed it as a TV play.

Rapa Nui *
US 1994 107m Technicolor Panavision
Entertainment/Majestic/Tig/Newcomm (Kevin Costner, Jim Wilson)
In the 1680s, on what was later known as Easter Island, antagonism between warring clans and the island's two classes – nobles and labourers – flares during a dangerous annual race in which young men swim through shark-infested waters to bring back an egg from a nearby island.
Unconvincing, exotic epic which dithers between being a conventional love story and a conventional ecological fable; it looks splendid but is let down by its often banal dialogue and varying styles of acting.
w Tim Rose Price, Kevin Reynolds *d* Kevin Reynolds *ph* Stephen Windon *m* Stewart Copeland *pd* George Liddle *ed* Peter Boyle
☆ Jason Scott Lee, Esai Morales, Sandrine Holt, George Henare, Zac Wallace, Nathaniel Lees, Eru Potaka-Dewes, Pete Smith, Rawiri Paratene
'Looks very much like an act of cinematic folly, a wacky anthropological adventure staged on a grand scale and filmed in obviously difficult and inhospitable circumstances. It's more of a guilty pleasure than a satisfying movie experience.' – *Variety*
'Almost no movie last year was more unintentionally funny, nor more wrongheaded.' – *Stephen Rebello, Movieline*
† The movie, despite its lack of expensive stars, cost more than $20m. Filming on the remote Easter Island was, said Kevin Reynolds, 'a nightmare'.

Rape Me: see *Baise-Moi*

The Rape of Malaya: see *A Town Like Alice*

Rapid Fire
US 1992 95m DeLuxe
TCF (Robert Lawrence)
After a Chinese college student is witness to a mob murder he has no alternative but to help the FBI bust two international drugs rings.
Cliché-ridden action movie whose only point of interest is that it stars Bruce Lee's son, although he has yet to acquire his father's charisma.
w Alan McElroy *story* Cindy Cirile, Alan McElroy *d* Dwight H. Little *ph* Ric Waite *m* Christopher Young *pd* Ron Foreman *ed* Gib Jaffe
☆ Brandon Lee, Powers Boothe, Nick Mancuso, Raymond J. Barry, Kate Hodge, Tzi Ma, Tony Longo, Michael Paul Chan, Dustin Nguyen
'A clumsily plotted, clumsily choreographed and clumsily acted attempt at combining a hard-nosed cop thriller with an old-fashioned martial arts fable.' – *Geoffrey Macnab, Sight and Sound*

Rapture
US/France 1965 104m bw
International Classics/TCF (Christian Ferry)
A mentally unstable girl has a tragic romance with a fugitive murderer.
Gloomy all the way, and if it's art it needs explaining.
w Stanley Mann *novel* Rapture in My Rags *by* Phyllis Hastings *d* John Guillermin *ph* Marcel Grignon
☆ Patricia Gozzi, Dean Stockwell, Melvyn Douglas, Gunnel Lindblom

The Rapture **
US 1991 100m DeLuxe
Electric/New Line/Wechsler/Tenenbaum/Parker
Tiring of her empty and promiscuous life, a telephone operator turns to fundamentalist religion and, claiming she has received a message from God, heads for the desert with her young daughter to await the Second Coming.
A clever and thought-provoking movie which overturns expectations – the apparently mad and neurotic turn out to be right in their predictions – but finally seems to side with an individual's right to justice at all costs.
wd Michael Tolkin *ph* Bojan Bazelli *m* Thomas Newman *pd* Robert Standefer *ed* Suzanne Fenn
☆ Mimi Rogers, David Duchovny, Patrick Bauchau, Kimberly Cullum, Terri Hanauer, Dick Anthony Williams, James Le Gros
'The film is long on empathy, short on insight.' – *Philip French, Observer*
'A complex and intellectual horror story tackling a thorny subject in a manner simply guaranteed to offend almost everyone at some point.' – *Kim Newman, Empire*

The Rare Breed
US 1966 97m Technicolor Panavision
Universal (William Alland)
An English bull is taken by its woman owner to St Louis to breed with American longhorns, and various frictions are caused among the ranchers.
Amusing Western idea which misses fire by not coming down firmly as either drama or comedy; it does however pass the time amiably enough.
w Ric Hardman *d* Andrew V. McLaglen *ph* William H. Clothier *m* Johnny Williams
☆ James Stewart, Maureen O'Hara, Brian Keith, Juliet Mills, Don Galloway, David Brian, Jack Elam, Ben Johnson

Rascals
US 1938 77m bw
TCF
A rich young man and a girl suffering from amnesia join a gypsy troupe.
Absurdly cast and plotted semi-musical with a certain liveliness to keep it going.
w Robert Ellis, Helen Logan *d* H. Bruce Humberstone
☆ Jane Withers, Borrah Minevitch and his Rascals, Robert Wilcox, Rochelle Hudson, Steffi Duna
'In the main amusing and entertaining.' – *Variety*

Rashomon ****
Japan 1951 83m bw
Daiei (Jingo Minoura)
aka: *In the Woods*
In medieval Japan, four people have different versions of a violent incident when a bandit attacks a nobleman in the forest.
Indescribably vivid in itself, and genuinely strange (one of the versions is told by a ghost), Rashomon *reintroduced Japanese films to the world market and was remade (badly) in Hollywood as* The Outrage.
wd Akira Kurosawa *story* Inside a Bush *by* Ryunosuke Akutagawa *ph* Kazuo Matsuyama *m* Takashi Matsuyama *ad* H. Motsumoto
☆ Toshiro Mifune, Machiko Kyo, Masayuki Mori, Takashi Shimura
'A masterpiece, and a revelation.' – *Gavin Lambert, MFB*
best foreign film
art direction

Raskolnikov *
Germany 1923 80m approx (24 fps) bw silent
Neumann (Robert Wiene)
A student kills a pawnbroker and is hounded by a police inspector until he confesses.
Interesting adaptation of Crime and Punishment *with some of the expressionist aspects of the same director's* The Cabinet of Dr Caligari.
wd Robert Wiene *ph* Willy Godberger *ad* Andre Andreyev
☆ Gregory Khmara, Michael Tarkhanov, Pavel Pavlov, Vera Toma

Rasputin: see *Agony*

Rasputin and the Empress *
US 1932 133m bw
MGM (Irving Thalberg)
GB title: *Rasputin the Mad Monk*
The story of the last years of the Russian court, when a sinister monk gained influence over the empress.
An unhappy film which was besieged by lawsuits and never generated much drama of its own despite starring the three Barrymores, who all seemed to be acting in separate rooms. Production values are the most impressive thing about it.
w Charles MacArthur *d* Richard Boleslawski *ph* William Daniels *m* Herbert Stothart *ad* Cedric Gibbons, Alexander Toluboff *ed* Tom Held
☆ John Barrymore (Prince Paul Chegodieff), Ethel Barrymore (Empress Alexandra), Lionel Barrymore (Rasputin), Diana Wynyard (Natasha), Ralph Morgan (Emperor Nikolai), C. Henry Gordon (Grand Duke Igot), Edward Arnold (Doctor), Jean Parker, Gustav von Seyffertitz, Anne Shirley
† The lawsuit was by Prince Youssoupoff (portrayed as Chegodieff), who claimed that although he did kill Rasputin his wife was never raped. He was awarded one million dollars.
Charles MacArthur

Rasputin the Mad Monk: see *Rasputin and the Empress (1932)*

Rasputin the Mad Monk
GB 1966 92m DeLuxe CinemaScope
Warner-Pathé/Hammer/7 Arts (Anthony Nelson-Keys)
A recapitulation of well-known events with fictional trimmings.
Dreary excuse for its star to go berserk.
w John Elder *d* Don Sharp *ph* Michael Reed *m* Don Banks *pd* Bernard Robinson *ed* James Needs, Roy Hyde
☆ Christopher Lee, Barbara Shelley, Richard Pasco, Francis Matthews, Renee Asherson

The Rat *
GB 1937 72m bw
Herbert Wilcox/Imperator
A Parisian thief takes the blame for murder, but is saved by the socialite who loves him.
Rather smart talkie version of a well-worn theatrical hit, previously filmed in 1925 as a silent, with Ivor Novello as star.
w Hans Rameau, Marjorie Gaffney, Miles Malleson and Romney Brent *play* Ivor Novello, Constance Collier *d* Jack Raymond
☆ Anton Walbrook, Ruth Chatterton, Rene Ray, Beatrix Lehmann, Felix Aylmer, Mary Clare

Le Rat des Villes et le Rat des Champs **
France 1927 14m bw
Tobis Klangfilm
A country rat visits Paris and finds life too hectic for his rural tastes.
Witty exercise in stop-motion animation, brilliantly done for its time and notable for its ballet danced by two rats.
wd Ladislaw Starewicz *m* Georges Tzipine *ad* Jacques Natanson
† The film has been released on video with the feature-length *The Tale of the Fox* (qv) and four other shorts under the title *Ladislaw Starewicz: Selected Films.*

The Rat Race *
US 1960 105m Technicolor
Paramount/Perlberg-Seaton
A young jazz musician and a dance hall hostess share a flat and face the adversities of New York.
A kind of sour fairy tale of the big city which has neither enough jokes nor enough incident but purveys the kind of charm that grows on one despite oneself.
w Garson Kanin *play* Garson Kanin *d* Robert Mulligan *ph* Robert Burks *m* Elmer Bernstein
☆ Tony Curtis, Debbie Reynolds, Jack Oakie, Kay Medford, Don Rickles
'The New Yorkers of *The Rat Race* – noisy soft-hearted landlady, philosophical bartender, backchatting taxi driver – are as familiar as the settings of shabby apartment house and quiet little bar across the street. Film makers no longer need to invent here – they simply move in for a few weeks.' – *Penelope Houston*

Rat Race
US 2001 112m DeLuxe Panavision
Paramount/Fireworks/Alphaville/Zucker (Jerry Zucker, Janet Zucker, Sean Daniel)
Las Vegas smalltime gamblers race to be the first to find $2m hidden in a railway station in New Mexico, not realising that other gamblers are betting on the outcome of their race.
A chase movie in the style of It's A Mad, Mad, Mad, Mad World, *and even more mean-spirited.*
w Andy Breckman *d* Jerry Zucker *ph* Thomas Ackerman *m* John Powell *pd* Gary Frutkoff *ed* Tom Lewis
☆ Rowan Atkinson (Enrico Pollini), John Cleese (Donald Sinclair), Whoopi Goldberg (Vera Baker), Cuba Gooding Jnr (Owen Templeton), Seth Green (Duane Cody), Jon Lovitz (Randy Pear), Breckin Meyer (Nick Schaffer), Kathy Najimy (Bev Pear)
'Chooses to rehash the worst aspect of *Mad, Mad World*, downgrading the experience from mindless to dreadful.' – *Elvis Mitchell, New York Times*
'Rowdy, bouncy, and acceleratingly funny.' – *Lisa Schwarzbaum, Entertainment Weekly*

Ratboy
US 1986 104m Technicolor
Warner/Malpaso
A half-rodent alien gets the anticipated rough treatment when he visits Earth.
Clint Eastwood's favourite co-star was given leave to make the film of her choice, but the choice is inexplicable in the wake of so many other E.T. *imitations.*
w Rob Thompson *d* Sondra Locke *ph* Bruce Surtees *m* Lennie Niehaus
☆ Sondra Locke, Robert Townsend, Christopher Hewett, Larry Hankin

Ratcatcher **
GB/France 1999 93m colour
Pathé (Gavin Emerson)
In 1970s Glasgow, a boy feels guilty about causing the death of a friend by drowning, and dreams of moving from his tenement slum to a new housing estate on the edge of the city.
Glum drama of family life enlivened by a lyrical visual approach.
wd Lynne Ramsay *ph* Alwin Küchler *m* Rachel Portman *pd* Jane Morton *ed* Lucia Zucchetti
☆ William Eadie (James), Tommy Flanagan (Da), Mandy Matthews (Ma), Michelle Stewart (Ellen), Lynne Ramsay Jnr (Anne Marie), Leanne Mullen (Margaret Anne), John Miller (Kenny), Jackie Quinn (Mrs Quinn)
'A must-see: a wonderful film from a brilliant director.' – *Peter Bradshaw, Guardian*
Lynne Ramsay (best newcomer)

Rationing
US 1943 93m bw
MGM (Orville Dull)
A small-town shopkeeper is frustrated by wartime restrictions.
Amiable comedy for established stars.
w William Lipman, Grant Garrett, Harry Ruskin *d* Willis Goldbeck
☆ Wallace Beery, Marjorie Main, Donald Meek, Howard Freeman, Connie Gilchrist

Raton Pass
US 1951 84m bw
Warner (Saul Elkins)
GB title: *Canyon Pass*
A greedy wife swindles her husband out of his share in their ranch.
Unusual Western melodrama; quite entertaining.
w Tom Blackburn, James Webb *d* Edwin L. Marin *ph* Wilfred M. Cline *m* Max Steiner
☆ Dennis Morgan, Patricia Neal, Steve Cochran, Scott Forbes, Dorothy Hart

Rattle of a Simple Man
GB 1964 95m bw
Sydney Box (William Gell)
A shy football supporter in London spends the night with a tart for a bet.
Archetypal farcical situation with sentiment added to string it out to twice its proper length. Production values modest but adequate.
w Charles Dyer *play* Charles Dyer *d* Muriel Box *ph* Reg Wyer *m* Stanley Black
☆ Harry H. Corbett, *Diane Cilento*, Thora Hird, Charles Dyer

'The Edgar Allan Poe Mystery Show!'
The Raven *
US 1935 61m bw
Universal
A doctor obsessed by Poe-inspired torture devices transforms a gangster on the run into a hideous mutant.
Silly but quite effective horror film with memorable sequences.
w David Boehm *d* Lew Landers *ph* Charles Stumar *md* Gilbert Kurland
☆ *Bela Lugosi, Boris Karloff*, Samuel S. Hinds, Irene Ware, Lester Matthews
'Maintains Universal's high batting average with the shockers ... should come through with nice grosses.' – *Variety*

The Raven: see *Le Corbeau (1943)*

The Raven *
US 1963 86m Pathécolor Panavision
AIP/Alta Vista (Roger Corman)
Two 15th-century conjurors fight a deadly duel of magic.
The rather splendid duel is a long time coming; the preliminaries are largely confined to chat in a single set, and the random jokes do not quite atone for the boredom.
w Richard Matheson *d* Roger Corman *ph* Floyd Crosby *m* Les Baxter
☆ *Vincent Price, Peter Lorre, Boris Karloff*, Hazel Court, Jack Nicholson
'Edgar Allan Poe might turn over in his grave at this nonsensical adaptation of his immortal poem, but audiences will find the spooky goings-on a cornpop of considerable comedic dimensions.' – *Variety*

Ravenous
US 1999 100m DeLuxe 'Scope
TCF/Fox 2000/ (Adam Fields, David Heyman)
In the mid-19th century, an isolated army outpost is commanded by a cannibal who initiates others in the addictive eating of human flesh.
Grisly drama that veers between black comedy and horror while remaining an unappetizing stew.
w Ted Griffin *d* Antonia Bird *ph* Anthony B. Richmond *m* Michael Nyman, Damon Albarn *pd* Bryce Perrin *ed* Neil Farrell
☆ Guy Pearce, Robert Carlyle, Jeremy Davies, Jeffrey Jones, John Spencer, Stephen Spinella, Neal McDonough, David Arquette
'A bigger mystery than anything in the plot is why fine actors like Guy Pearce and Robert Carlyle chose this shoddy vehicle as a showcase.' – *Stephen Farber, Movieline*
† Directors Milcho Manchevski and Raja Gosnell both worked on the film before Antonia Bird became involved.

Raw Courage
US 1984 90m colour
Adams Apple/Sandy Howard (Ronny Cox, Robert L. Rosen)
aka: *Courage*
Three long-distance runners are attacked by a fanatical group of would-be soldiers in the New Mexican desert.
A land-locked, brain-dead variation on Deliverance*, notably short on thrills.*
w Ronny Cox, Mary Cox *d* Robert L. Rosen *ph* F. Pershing Flynn *m* Johnny Harris *pd* Don Nunley *ed* Steven Polivka
☆ Ronny Cox, Art Hindle, M. Emmet Walsh, Tim Maier, Lois Chiles, William Russ, Lisa Sutton

Raw Deal
US 1948 78m bw
Reliance/Eagle Lion
A convict is helped by his girlfriend to escape, and the police chase them across country.
Fairly violent crime melodrama which holds the attention.
w Leopold Atlas, John C. Higgins *d* Anthony Mann
☆ Dennis O'Keefe, Claire Trevor, Marsha Hunt, John Ireland, Raymond Burr

Raw Deal
US 1986 106m Technicolor JDC Wide Screen
De Laurentiis/International (Martha Schumacher)
An ex-FBI man is recruited to infiltrate Chicago's biggest mob.
Violent crime hokum with momentary amusements.
w Gary M. DeVore, Norman Wexler *d* John Irvin *ph* Alex Thomson *m* Cinemascore
☆ Arnold Schwarzenegger, Kathryn Harrold, Sam Wanamaker, Paul Shenar, Ed Lauter, Darren McGavin, Joe Regalbuto
'Comic book crime meller suffers from an irredeemable script' – *Variety*

Raw Edge
US 1956 76m Technicolor
Universal-International (Albert Zugsmith)
A rancher's workers plan to kill him.
Tense, fairly adult Western.
w Harry Essex, Robert Hill *d* John Sherwood *ph* Maury Gertsman *ad* Alexander Golitzen
☆ Rory Calhoun, Yvonne de Carlo, Mara Corday, Rex Reason, Neville Brand

'Kill... Or Be Killed.'
Raw Justice
US 1994 95m Image Transform colour
West Side (David Winters)
aka: *Good Cop Bad Cop*
An ex-cop is hired to tail an innocent man framed for murder, and discovers that a killer is after both of them.
Cliché-ridden thriller that recycles the corniest images and dumbest dialogue from every bad cop movie ever made.
wd David A. Prior *ph* Carlos Gonzalez *m* William Stromberg, Lennie Moore, David Keith *ed* Tony Malanowski
☆ David Keith (Mace), Robert Hays (Mitch McCullum), Pamela Anderson (Sarah), Leo Rossi (Atkins), Charles Napier (Stiles), Javi Mulero (Gordo), Stacy Keach (Jenkins)

Raw Meat: see *Death Line*

Raw Wind in Eden
US 1958 93m Eastmancolor Cinemascope
U-I (William Alland)
A model is stranded on a Sardinian island, and falls in love with a mysterious American who turns out to be a disillusioned millionaire.
Wish-fulfilment woman's picture with the occasional relief of a smart line.
w Elizabeth and Richard Wilson *d* Richard Wilson *ph* Enzo Serafin *m* Hans Salter
☆ Esther Williams, Jeff Chandler, Carlos Thompson, Rossana Podesta, Eduardo de Filippo, Rik Battaglia

'He's Pure Evil. Pure Power. Pure Terror.'
Rawhead Rex
US 1987 86m colour
Empire/Alpine/Paradise/Green Man (Kevin Attew, Don Hawkins)
In Ireland a farmer unwittingly releases a primitive demon, which immediately goes on the rampage.
Ineffectual, low-budget horror.
w Clive Barker *d* George Pavlou *ph* John Metcalfe *ad* Lee Huntingford *ed* Andy Horvitch
☆ David Dukes, Kelly Piper, Ronan Wilmot, Niall Toibin, Heinrich von Schellendoft, Niall O'Brian

Rawhide **
US 1950 86m bw
TCF (Samuel G. Engel)
TV title: *Desperate Siege*
Four escaped convicts terrorize a stagecoach stop.
Good suspense Western with excellent technical credits.
w Dudley Nichols d Henry Hathaway ph Milton Krasner *m* Sol Kaplan
☆ Tyrone Power, Susan Hayward, Hugh Marlowe, Jack Elam, Dean Jagger, George Tobias, Edgar Buchanan, Jeff Corey

The Rawhide Years
US 1956 85m Technicolor
Universal International (Stanley Rubin)
A poor but honest riverboat gambler clears himself of a murder charge with the aid of a con man.
Run-of-the-mill but amiable-enough Western, with Curtis more convincing as a card sharp than as a cowboy.
w Earl Felton, Robert Presnell Jnr, D. D. Beauchamp *novel* Norman A. Fox *d* Rudolph Maté *ph* Irving Glassberg *m* Frank Skinner, Hans J. Salter *md* Joseph Gershenson *ad* Alexander Golitzen, Richard H. Riedel *ed* Russell Schoengarth
☆ Tony Curtis (Ben), Colleen Miller (Zoe), Arthur Kennedy (Rick Harper), William Demarest (Brand Comfort), William Gargan (Marshal Sommers), Peter Van Eyck (Andre Boucher), Minor Watson (Matt Comfort), Donald Randolph (Carrico), Robert Wilke (Neal)

Raye Makhfi: see *Secret Ballot*

Le Rayon Vert: see *The Green Ray*

Razorback
Australia 1984 95m colour Panavision
UAA/Western (Hal McElroy)
In a small outback town a man is tried for the murder of his grandson, actually carried off by a wild boar.
Grim images of Australian life pepper this cross between Jaws *and the dingo baby case. Not, as they say, for the squeamish.*
w Everett de Roche *novel* Peter Brennan *d* Russell Mulcahy *ph* Dean Semler *m* Iva Davies *pd* Bryce Walmsley *ed* William Anderson
☆ Gregory Harrison, Arkie Whiteley, Bill Kerr, Chris Haywood

'Between love and hatred there is a line as sharp as a razor's edge!'
The Razor's Edge *
US 1946 146m bw
TCF (Darryl F. Zanuck)
A well-to-do young man spends the years between the wars first idling, then looking for essential truth.
The novel was an empty parable with amusing trimmings. In the film the trimmings seem less amusing, but the presentation is glossy.
w Lamar Trotti *novel* W. Somerset Maugham *d* Edmund Goulding *ph* Arthur Miller *m* Alfred Newman *ad* Richard Day, Nathan Juran
☆ Tyrone Power, Gene Tierney, *Clifton Webb, Herbert Marshall*, John Payne, Anne Baxter, Lucile Watson, Frank Latimore, Elsa Lanchester, Fritz Kortner
'I like Somerset Maugham when he's looking through keyholes or down cracks, not at vistas.' – *Richard Winnington*
'Almost as irresistibly funny and terrible as *The Fountainhead*.' – *Pauline Kael, 70s*
† Maugham has a different source for his title, in the shape of an Oriental proverb, probably invented: 'The sharp edge of a razor is difficult to pass over; thus the wise say that the path to salvation is hard.'
Anne Baxter
best picture; Clifton Webb; art direction

The Razor's Edge
US 1984 128m colour
Columbia (Robert P. Marucci, Harry Benn)
A man searches for the meaning of life.
An unlikely remake which came into being because the star persuaded the studio to do it, then failed in his attempt to convey the necessary spirituality. As for the rest, the time is out of joint (except for Denholm Elliott).
w John Byrum, Bill Murray *d* John Byrum *ph* Peter Hannan *m* Jack Nitzsche *pd* Philip Harrison *ed* Peter Boyle
☆ Bill Murray, Denholm Elliott, Theresa Russell, Catherine Hicks, James Keach, Peter Vaughan, Faith Brook

'Death is just the beginning!'
Re-Animator
US 1985 86m DeLuxe
Entertainment/Empire International (Brian Yuzna)
When a crazy scientist brings people back to life, they come back violent.
Gross and grisly horror comic which amused some critics.
w Dennis Paoli, William J. Norris, Stuart Gordon *story Herbert West – Re-animator* by H. P. Lovecraft *d* Stuart Gordon *ph* Mac Ahlberg, Stephen Sealy *m* Richard Band *ad* R. A. Burns, Charles Nixon *ed* Lee Percy
☆ Jeffrey Combs, Bruce Abbott, Barbara Crampton, David Gale
'For those with a strong sense of humour, and a stomach stronger still.' – *Sunday Times*
'A cheap smell of excess.' – *Observer*

'Date. Mate. Re-animate.'
Re-Animator 2
US 1989 96m colour
Medusa/Wildstreet (Paul White, Keith Walley, Hidetaka Konno)
aka: *Bride of Re-Animator*
A scientist, building himself a woman from spare parts, is attacked by the re-animated remnants of his previous experiments.
The mixture much as before, and gaining nothing from the repetition.
w Woody Keith, Rick Fry *story* H. P. Lovecraft *d* Brian Yuzna *ph* Rick Fichter *m* Richard Band *pd* Philip J. C. Duffin *ed* Peter Teschner
☆ Bruce Abbott, Claude Earl Jones, Fabiana Udenio, David Gale, Kathleen Kinmont, Jeffrey Combs, Mel Stewart, Michael Strasser, Irene Forrest
'Yet another example of a sequel that is content to rehash all the ingredients of the first film without ever gelling in the way that made the original work.' – *MFB*

Reach for Glory *
GB 1962 86m bw
Columbia/Blazer (John Kohn, Jud Kinberg)
During World War II, evacuee boys play war games and a German refugee is accidentally killed.
Grim and unpalatable parable, competently rather than excitingly made.
w John Rae *novel* *The Custard Boys* by John Rae *d* Philip Leacock *ph* Bob Huke *m* Bob Russell
☆ Kay Walsh, Harry Andrews, Michael Anderson Jnr, Oliver Grimm, Alexis Kanner, Martin Tomlinson, Richard Vernon

Reach for the Sky *
GB 1956 135m bw
Rank/Pinnacle (Daniel M. Angel)
Douglas Bader loses both legs in a 1931 air crash, learns to walk on artificial limbs and flies again in World War II.
Box-office exploitation of one man's personal heroism, adequately but not inspiringly put together with many stiff upper lips and much jocular humour.
wd Lewis Gilbert *book* Paul Brickhill *ph* Jack Asher *m* John Addison
☆ *Kenneth More* (Douglas Bader), Muriel Pavlow (Thelma Bader), Lyndon Brook (Johnny Sanderson), Lee Patterson (Stan Turner), Alexander Knox (Mr Joyce), Dorothy Alison, Sydney Tafler, Howard Marion Crawford
'It is least successful in what should be exciting action.' – *Dilys Powell*
British film

Reaching for the Moon
US 1931 90m bw
United Artists (Douglas Fairbanks)
On a transatlantic liner, a new cocktail has a sensational effect on a mild-mannered hero.
Very flimsy comedy with songs and some athletic stunts for its hero.
wd Edmund Goulding *ph* Ray June *song* Irving Berlin
☆ Douglas Fairbanks, Bebe Daniels, Edward Everett Horton, Claud Allister, Jack Mulhall, Bing Crosby
'Not a smash entry, but should do moderately and perhaps a little better than that.' – *Variety*

'You'll love them as much as they love each other!'
Reaching for the Sun
US 1941 90m bw
Paramount
A clam digger who needs an outboard motor goes to work in a Detroit car plant.
Easygoing comedy, too muted to recommend itself widely.
w W. L. River *novel* Wessel Smitter *d* William Wellman
☆ Joel McCrea, Ellen Drew, Eddie Bracken, Albert Dekker

Read My Lips: see *Sur Mes Lèvres*

'They're Headed For The Big Time...Face First!'
Ready to Rumble
US 2000 107m Technicolor
Warner/Bel Air/Outlaw/Tollin/Robbins (Bobby Newmyer, Jeffrey Silver)
Two World Championship Wrestling fans decide to revive the career of a defeated champion.
Braindead movie that is even less entertaining than wrestling itself, and as crude and overblown in its approach.
w Steven Brill *d* Brian Robbins *ph* Clark Mathis *m* George S. Clinton *pd* Jaymes Hinkle *ed* Ned Bastille, Cindy Mollo
☆ David Arquette (Gordie Boggs), Oliver Platt (Jimmy King), Scott Caan (Sean Dawkins), Bill Goldberg (Himself), Rose McGowan (Sasha), Diamond Dallas Page (Himself), Richard Lineback (Mr Boggs), Chris Owen (Isaac), Steve 'Sting' Borden (Himself), Joe Pantoliano (Titus Sinclair), Martin Landau (Sal)
'Truly atrocious, lame-brained comedy.' – *Steve Grant, Sunday Times*

'Sing! Swing! Youth Has Its Fling!'
Ready Willing and Able
US 1937 93m bw
Warner (Samuel Bischoff)
Two songwriters import an English leading lady for their new show.
Lightweight star musical with no outstanding qualities except a number in which girls dance on the keys of a huge typewriter.
w Sig Herzig, Jerry Wald, Warren Duff *d* Ray Enright *ph* Sol Polito *ch* Bobby Connolly *songs* Johnny Mercer, Richard Whiting
☆ Ruby Keeler, Ross Alexander, Lee Dixon, Wini Shaw, Jane Wyman, Allen Jenkins
'Too many numbers and a slow script.' – *Variety*
Bobby Connolly

The Real Blonde *
US 1997 105m colour
Paramount/Lakeshore (Marcus Viscidi, Tom Rosenberg)
Two struggling actors in troubled relationships make good at work and home.
Enjoyable satire on such easy targets as fashion photographers and TV soap opera stars.
wd Tom DiCillo *ph* Frank Prinzi *m* Jim Farmer *pd* Christopher A. Nowak *ed* Camilla Toniolo
☆ Matthew Modine, Catherine Keener, Daryl Hannah, Maxwell Caulfield, Elizabeth Berkley, Marlo Thomas, Bridgette Wilson
'Winds up a cartoonish satire on a cartoonish world – form and content in perfect unison.' – *Xan Brooks, Sight and Sound*

Real Genius
US 1985 104m Metrocolor Panavision
TriStar/Delphi III (Brian Grazer)
A 15-year-old scientific prodigy joins a think-tank of whizz kids who are being unwittingly exploited by the military.
Slickly directed youth movie that abandons any seriousness in favour of anarchic slapstick comedy; its message appears to be that too much intelligence is bad for you.
w Neal Israel, Pat Proft, Peter Torokvei *d* Martha Coolidge *ph* Vilmos Zsigmond *m* Thomas Newman *pd* Josan F. Russo *ed* Richard Chew
☆ Val Kilmer, Gabe Jarret, Michelle Meyrink, William Atherton, Patti D'Arbanville, Robert Prescott

'Always outnumbered! Never outfought!'
'One of the most stunning dramas of love and courage ever brought to the screen!'
The Real Glory *
US 1939 96m bw
Samuel Goldwyn
Soldiers of fortune help the American Army to quell a terrorist uprising in the Philippines just after the Spanish-American War.
Well made Gunga Dinnery.
w Jo Swerling, Robert R. Presnell *d* Henry Hathaway *ph* Rudolph Maté *m* Alfred Newman *ad* James Basevi
☆ Gary Cooper, David Niven, Broderick Crawford, Andrea Leeds, Reginald Owen, Kay Johnson, Russell Hicks, Vladimir Sokoloff
'Moro uprisings, guerrilla warfare, cholera epidemics, and fancy exhibitions of inhuman cruelty are the frame against which an innocuous melodramatic yarn is told.' – *Variety*
'The same sort of picture as Gunga Din.' – *Richard Mallett, Punch*
'Recommended to adolescents of all ages.' – *New Statesman*
'In times like these, we question the wisdom of rattling the bones in Yankee imperialism's closet.' – *Daily Worker*

The Real Howard Spitz *
GB/Canada 1997 101m colour
The Mob/Metrodome/Images/TMN (Paul Brooks, Christopher Zimmer)
A child-hating author finds success when he writes a book about a cow detective with the aid of a young girl in search of her father.
Pleasant children's film with a light, comic touch.
w Jurgen Wolff *d* Vadim Jean *ph* Glen Macpherson *m* David A. Hughes, John Murphy *pd* Chris Townsend *ed* Pia Di Ciaula
☆ Kelsey Grammer, Amanda Donohoe, Joseph Rutten, Patrick McKenna, Genevieve Tessier, Kay Tremblay
'A worthy small-scale alternative to summer heavyweights.' – *Empire*

Real Life *
US 1979 99m colour
Paramount (Penelope Spheeris)
A self-centred film-maker moves in with an average family in order to make a documentary about them.
Clever satire on a certain style of television programme, but the joke is over-stretched.
w Albert Brooks, Monica Johnson, Harry Shearer *d* Albert Brooks *ph* Eric Saarinen *m* Mort Lindsay *ad* Linda Marder, Linda Spheeris *ed* David Finfer
☆ Albert Brooks, Charles Grodin, Frances Lee McCain, J. A. Preston, Matthew Tobin, Jennings Lang

Real Life
GB 1983 92m colour
Entertainment/The Real Life Partnership (Mike Dinseen)
An estate agent's assistant with a vivid imagination becomes involved in thefts.
Clumsy, witless comedy which quickly bores.
w Francis Megahy, Bernie Cooper *d* Francis Megahy *ph* Peter Jessop *m* David Mindel *pd* John White *ed* Peter Delfgou
☆ Rupert Everett, Cristina Raines, Norman Beaton, Warren Clarke, Isla Blair, James Faulkner
'Try as one may to look sympathetically on this brand of independent British venture, the resolute lack of wit or style wipes the indulgent smile from one's lips early on, and it never returns.' – *Guardian*

'She's the only one who can break into a bank that holds $18m, but it's not for the money.'
The Real McCoy
US 1993 101m Technicolor
Capella (Martin Bregman, Willi Baer, Michael S. Bregman)
A reluctant cat burglar is forced to rob a bank by a gangster who kidnaps her young son.
There is nothing original here, merely a competent director and cast going through familiar routines with moderate enthusiasm.
w William Davies, William Osborne *d* Russell Mulcahy *ph* Denis Crossan *m* Brad Fiedel *pd* Kim Colefax *ed* Peter Honess
☆ Kim Basinger, Val Kilmer, Terence Stamp, Gailard Sartain, Zach English, Raynor Scheine
'Provides scant suspense, and the final bank job doesn't blaze any trails for anyone who's seen caper movies. Similarly, the payoff may satisfy the undemanding, but most viewers will have seen it coming a mile off.' – *Variety*

Real Men
US 1987 96m Metrocolor
United Artists (Martin Bregman)
An unpredictable CIA agent recruits a timid insurance clerk to deliver a message to friendly aliens while rival agents attempt to kill them both.
Dim though frenetic comedy that provides nothing but tedium.
wd Dennis Feldman *ph* John A. Alonzo *m* Miles Goodman *ad* William J. Cassidy, James Allen *ed* Malcolm Campbell, Glenn Farr
☆ James Belushi, John Ritter, Barbara Barrie, Bill Morey, Isa Andersen, Gale Barle, Mark Herrier

'Real women take chances, have flaws, embrace life...'
Real Women Have Curves *
US 2002 93m colour
Optimum/HBO (George LaVoo, Effie T. Brown)
In Los Angeles, an 18 year-old Mexican-American girl has to choose between family pressure to get a job or following her dream of studying at Columbia University.
Some attractive performances grace an otherwise mundane domestic drama, the outcome of which is never in doubt.
ph Jim Denault *m* Emma Garcia De Mantilla *pd* Brigitte Broch *ed* Sloane Klevin
☆ America Ferrera (Ana), Lupe Ontiveros (Carmen), Ingrid Oliu (Estela), George Lopez (Mr Guzman), Brian Sites (Jimmy)
'Effervescent and satisfying, a crowd pleaser that does not condescend.' – *Elvis Mitchell, New York Times*

'A Comedy About Love In The '90s.'
Reality Bites *
US 1994 99m colour
Universal/Jersey (Danny DeVito, Michael Shamberg)
Four friends, newly graduated, try to survive in the real world in Houston; one makes a video documentary of their lives and becomes emotionally involved with another, an articulate rock musician, and with an ambitious TV executive.
Up-to-the-minute details of life among the recently 20, but so timely in its references it already seems old-fashioned; its love story is very familiar, though it may seem new to the recently adult.
w Helen Childress *d* Ben Stiller *ph* Emmanuel Lubezki *m* Karl Wallinger *pd* Sharon Seymour *ed* Lisa Churgin
☆ Winona Ryder, Ethan Hawke, Ben Stiller, Janeane Garofalo, Steve Zahn, Swoosie Kurtz, Joe Don Baker, John Mahoney, Harry O'Reilly, Barry Sherman
'Patchy stuff at the best of times and irritatingly off-the-wall at its worst. Reality only occasionally bites, and then with none too sharp teeth.' – *Derek Malcolm, Guardian*
'The old, old love triangle tangle, dressed by Gap and styled by MTV.' – *Angie Errigo, Empire*

'Man against terrifying monster – in the most spectacular underwater scenes ever filmed!'
Reap the Wild Wind **
US 1942 124m Technicolor
Paramount/Cecil B. de Mille
Seafaring salvage engineers fight over a Southern belle.
Georgia-set period adventure; intended as another Gone with the Wind, *it simply doesn't have the necessary, but on its level it entertains solidly, climaxing with the famous giant squid fight.*
w Alan le May, Jesse Lasky Jnr, Charles Bennett *d* *Cecil B. de Mille* *ph* Victor Milner, Dewey Wrigley, William V. Skall *m* Victor Young *ad* Hans Dreier, Roland Anderson
☆ Ray Milland, John Wayne, *Paulette Goddard*, Raymond Massey, Robert Preston, Lynne Overman, Susan Hayward, Charles Bickford, Walter Hampden, Louise Beavers, Martha O'Driscoll, Hedda Hopper
'The essence of all his experience, the apogee of all his art, and as jamfull a motion picture as has ever played two hours upon a screen.' – *Howard Barnes, New York Herald Tribune*
† The underwater scenes were filmed in the Santa Monica Pan Pacific Marine Museum, which had a pool 100 feet long and 50 feet wide. The 50-foot giant squid was operated by a 24-button electronic keyboard
photography; art direction

Rear Window ****
US 1954 112m Technicolor
Paramount/Alfred Hitchcock
A news photographer, confined to his room by a broken leg, sees a murder committed in a room on the other side of the court.
Artificial but gripping suspenser of an unusual kind; with such restricted settings, all depends on the script and the acting, and they generally come up trumps.
w John Michael Hayes *novel* Cornell Woolrich *d* *Alfred Hitchcock* *ph* Robert Burks *m* Franz Waxman
☆ James Stewart, Grace Kelly, Raymond Burr, Judith Evelyn, Wendell Corey, Thelma Ritter
John Michael Hayes; Alfred Hitchcock; Robert Burks

A Reason to Live, a Reason to Die (dubbed)
Italy/France/Spain 1972 96m colour Scope
K-Tel/Sancrosiap-Terza/Europrodis/Atlantida/Corona (Michael Billingsley)
original title: *Una Ragione per Vivere e Una per Morire*
In the American Civil War, a Union colonel recruits seven desperadoes, all due to be executed, for a daring raid to recapture a Confederate fort.
An unexciting cut-rate variation on The Dirty Dozen.
w Tonino Valerii, Ernesto Gastaldi *d* Tonino Valerii *ph* Alejandro Ulloa *m* Riz Ortolani *ed* Franklin Boll
☆ James Coburn, Telly Savalas, Bud Spencer (Carlo Pedersoli), Ralph Goodwin, Joseph Mitchell, Robert Burton, William Spofford
'A colourless, perfunctory gloss on a text that the director and scriptwriters might assume their audiences to know by heart.' – *MFB*
† The film was cut to 91m on its British release.

A Reasonable Man *
South Africa/France 1999 103m colour
Pandora/Moviworld/AME/M-Net (Paul Raleigh, Gavin Hood)
A white lawyer is forced to reconsider his values when he defends a Zulu herd-boy who killed a baby that he thought was an evil spirit..
Effective courtroom drama, though it raises more questions than it answers.
wd Gavin Hood *ph* Buster Reynolds *m* Neill Solomon *pd* Robert Van der Coolwijk *ed* Avril Beukes
☆ Gavin Hood (Sean Raine), Nigel Hawthorne (Judge Wendon), Janine Eser (Jennifer Raine), Nandi Nyembe (Sangoma Rachel Ndlovu), Ian Roberts (Chris Van Rooyen), Vusi Kunen (Prosecutor Linde), Ken Gampu (Headman), Graham Hopkins (Professor MacKenzie), Loyiso Gxwala (Sipho)

Rebecca ****
US 1940 130m bw
David O. Selznick
The naïve young second wife of a Cornish landowner is haunted by the image of his glamorous first wife Rebecca.
The supreme Hollywood entertainment package, set in Monte Carlo and Cornwall, with generous helpings of romance, comedy, suspense, melodrama and mystery, all indulged in by strongly-drawn characters, and directed by the English wizard from a novel which sold millions of copies. It really couldn't miss, and it didn't.
w Robert E. Sherwood, Joan Harrison novel Daphne du Maurier *d Alfred Hitchcock ph George Barnes m Franz Waxman ad Lyle Wheeler ed Hal C. Kern*
☆ *Laurence Olivier, Joan Fontaine, George Sanders, Judith Anderson, Nigel Bruce, Gladys Cooper, Florence Bates, Reginald Denny, C. Aubrey Smith,* Melville Cooper, Leo G. Carroll, Leonard Carey
NARRATOR: 'Last night I dreamed I went to Manderley again...'
FAVELL (GEORGE SANDERS) TO MRS DE WINTER: 'I say, marriage with Max is not exactly a bed of roses, is it?'
MRS DANVERS (JUDITH ANDERSON): 'You're overwrought, madam. I've opened a window for you. A little air will do you good. Why don't you go? Why don't you leave Manderley? He doesn't need you. He's got his memories. He doesn't love you – he wants to be alone again with *her*. You've nothing to stay for. You've nothing to live for, have you, really? Look down there. It's easy, isn't it? Why don't you? Go on, go on. Don't be afraid...'
MAXIM (LAURENCE OLIVIER): 'You thought I loved Rebecca? You thought that? I hated her. Oh, I was carried away by her – enchanted by her, as everyone was – and when I was married, I was told I was the luckiest man in the world. She was so lovely, so accomplished, so amusing. "She's got the three things that really matter in a wife," everyone said, "breeding, brains and beauty." And I believed them completely. But I never had a moment's happiness with her. She was incapable of love, or tenderness, or decency.'
'A carefully considered trying out of the superior technical resources now at Hitchcock's disposal.' – *George Perry, 1965*
'Hitchcock fans will have to put up with a surprising lack of the characteristic Hitchcock improvisations in the way of salty minor personages and humorous interludes, and satisfy themselves with a masterly exhibition of the Hitchcock skill in creating suspense and shock with his action and his camera.' – *National Board of Review*
'Riveting and painful – a tale of fear and guilt, class and power.' – *Time Out, 1988*
'Hitch kept me off balance, much to his own delight ... he would constantly tell me that no one thought I was very good except himself.' – *Joan Fontaine*
† Original casting thoughts, all rejected, were Ronald Colman, William Powell and Leslie Howard for Maxim; Anne Baxter, Margaret Sullavan, Loretta Young, Vivien Leigh and Olivia de Havilland (for the second Mrs de Winter).
best picture; George Barnes
script; Alfred Hitchcock; Franz Waxman; Laurence Olivier; Joan Fontaine; Judith Anderson; Lyle Wheeler; Hal C. Kern

Rebecca of Sunnybrook Farm
US 1932 75m bw
Fox
A rural glad girl wins over her dour aunt and reforms an atheist.
Routine sound remake of the children's classic in a 1921 silent version in which Mary Pickford starred.
w S. N. Behrman, Sonya Levien *novel* Kate Douglas Wiggin and Charlotte Thompson *d* Alfred Santell
☆ Marian Nixon, Ralph Bellamy, Mae Marsh, Louise Closser Hale, Alan Hale, Charlotte Henry

Rebecca of Sunnybrook Farm
US 1938 80m bw
TCF (Raymond Griffith)
A child performer becomes a pawn in the fight to exploit her talents on radio.
Unrecognizable revamping of a famous story makes a very thin star vehicle.
w Karl Tunberg, Don Ettlinger *novel* Kate Douglas Wiggin and Charlotte Thompson *d* Allan Dwan *ph* Arthur Miller *m* Arthur Lange *songs* various
☆ Shirley Temple, Randolph Scott, Jack Haley, Gloria Stuart, Phyllis Brooks, Helen Westley, Slim Summerville, Bill Robinson
'More fitting title would be *Rebecca of Radio City* ... a weak story, indifferently directed and acted.' – *Variety*

Rebecca's Daughters *
GB/Germany 1991 97m colour
Mayfair/Palace/Rebecca's Daughters/Astralma Erste Filmproduktions/Delta/BBC Wales/British Screen (Chris Sievernich)
In the 19th century, Welsh farmers form gangs dressed in women's clothes to protest against unfair toll-gate charges imposed by the local aristocracy.
Ramshackle caper, ripely performed and occasionally amusing.
w Guy Jenkin, Karl Francis *story* based on a screenplay by Dylan Thomas *d* Karl Francis *ph* Russ Walker *m* Rachel Portman *pd* Ray Price *ed* Roy Sharman
☆ Peter O'Toole, Paul Rhys, Joely Richardson, Keith Allen, Simon Dormandy, Dafydd Hywel, Sue Roderick
'An irresistible period romp.' – *Variety*

The Rebel *
GB 1960 105m Technicolor
Associated British (W. A. Whitaker)
US title: *Call Me Genius*
A suburban businessman goes to Paris to become an artist.
A kind of farcical The Moon and Sixpence, *insufficiently well tailored to the requirements of a very specialized comic, but occasionally diverting none the less.*
w Alan Simpson, Ray Galton *d* Robert Day *ph* Gilbert Taylor *m* Frank Cordell
☆ *Tony Hancock*, George Sanders, Paul Massie, Margit Saad, Grégoire Aslan, Dennis Price, Irene Handl, Mervyn Johns, Peter Bull, John Le Mesurier, Nanette Newman, Oliver Reed, John Wood
'The more prosaic the setting, the funnier Hancock seems; transplanted into a conventionally silly screen art world, he is submerged among the other grotesques.' – *Penelope Houston*

Rebel
Australia 1985 89m colour
Village Roadshow (Phillip Emanuel)
In wartime Sydney, a singer shelters a deserter from the US Marines.
Dim romance, punctuated by some dull song and dance routines.
w Michael Jenkins, Bob Herbert *play No Names, No Pack Drill* by Bob Herbert *d* Michael Jenkins *ph* Peter James *m* Chris Neal *m/ly* Peter Best *pd* Brian Thomson *ed* Michael Honey
☆ Matt Dillon, Debbie Byrne, Bryan Brown, Bill Hunter, Ray Barrett, Julie Nihill

Rebel in Town
US 1956 78m bw
Bel Air/UA
A bank robber accidentally kills a small boy and is hunted down by the father.
Surprisingly stark Western with no particular merit.
w Danny Arnold *d* Alfred Werker *ph* Gordon Avil *m* Les Baxter
☆ John Payne, John Smith, Ruth Roman, J. Carrol Naish, Ben Cooper

The Rebel Nun: see *Flavia the Heretic*

Rebel Rousers
US 1969 78m colour
Paragon International (Martin B. Cohen)
An architect and his pregnant lover are terrorized by a gang of bikers in a small Arizona town.
Typical low-budget biker movie, lacking any originality but peopled by actors who went on to better films later.
w Abe Polsky, Michael Kars, Martin B. Cohen *d* Martin B. Cohen *ph* Leslie Kouvacs, Glen Smith *m* William Loose *ed* Thor Brooks
☆ Cameron Mitchell, Diane Ladd, Bruce Dern, Jack Nicholson, Harry Dean Stanton, Neil Burstyn, Lou Procopo, Earl Finn, Phil Carey

The Rebel Son
GB 1939 90m bw
London Films Omnia (E. C. Molinier, Charles David)
A Tartar leader's son falls in love with the daughter of the opposing leader.
Resistible grafting of the Romeo and Juliet story into the barbarians of the Steppes, with much carousing and threatened violence surrounding a good central performance. It includes much footage from a 1936 French film, Taras Bulba, *directed by Alexis Granowsky.*
w Adrian Brunel *story* Gogol *d* Alexis Granowsky, Adrian Brunel *ph* Franz Planer, Bernard Browne
☆ Harry Baur, Patricia Roc, Roger Livesey, Anthony Bushell, Joan Gardner
'After half an hour the joke had gone on long enough and I left. A man in the audience was remarking slowly, with some of Dr Johnson's weight, "I am still wondering what the reason for the existence of this film can be".' – *Graham Greene, The Spectator*

'The bad boy from a good family!'
Rebel without a Cause **
US 1955 111m Warnercolor Cinemascope
Warner (David Weisbart)
The adolescent son of a well-to-do family gets into trouble with other kids and the police.
The first film to suggest that juvenile violence is not necessarily bred in the slums, this somewhat dreary melodrama also catapulted James Dean to stardom as the prototype fifties rebel.
w Stewart Stern story Nicholas Ray *d* Nicholas Ray *ph* Ernest Haller *m* Leonard Rosenman
☆ *James Dean*, Natalie Wood, Jim Backus, Sal Mineo, Ann Doran, Dennis Hopper
original story (Nicholas Ray); Natalie Wood; Sal Mineo

Rebound
US 1931 88m bw
RKO-Pathé
A woman tries to forgive her husband when he is jilted by a girlfriend.
A sophisticated stage comedy presented with the minimum of alteration.
w Horace Jackson *play* Donald Ogden Stewart *d* Edward H. Griffith
☆ Ina Claire, Robert Williams, Robert Ames, Myrna Loy, Hedda Hopper, Louise Closser Hale
'A splendidly made picture which will delight smart audiences.' – *Variety*

'Saving The World One Playground At A Time.'
Recess: School's Out
US 2000 83m Technicolor
Buena Vista/Disney (Paul Germain, Joe Ansolabehere, Stephen Swofford)
School kids foil a plan to make it winter all year long.
Based on a TV show that Britain is thankfully spared, this is a dull story, simply animated and unlikely to keep the restive young quiet for more than a few minutes.
w Jonathan Greenberg *story* Joe Ansolabehere, Paul Germain, Greenberg *d* Chuck Sheetz *m* Denis M. Hannigan *ad* Eric Keyes *ed* Nancy Frazen, Tony Mizgalski
☆ voices of: Rickey D'Shon Collins, Jason Davis, Ashley Johnson, Andy Lawrence, Courtland Mead, Pam Segall, Dabney Coleman, Robert Goulet, James Woods
'The animation is remedial; the script lacks pep.' – *Guardian*

'The biggest musical show of the century, with a throbbing love story as exciting as its title!'
Reckless
US 1935 96m bw
MGM (David O. Selznick)
A theatrical agent loves the glamorous star he represents, but she marries a drunken millionaire.
Remarkably flat backstage melodrama with music, based on the life of Libby Holman.
w P. J. Wolfson *d* Victor Fleming *ph* George Folsey *md* Edward Ward *songs* various
☆ Jean Harlow, William Powell, Franchot Tone, May Robson, Ted Healy, Nat Pendleton, Rosalind Russell, Henry Stephenson
'Several sets of dramatic premises are established and then permitted to wander aimlessly, making the 93 minutes seem much longer than that.' – *Variety*

Reckless Kelly
Australia 1993 94m Eastmancolor Panavision
Warner/Yahoo Serious
A modern Ned Kelly battles to save his home from bankers and greedy developers.
A rambling but enjoyable anti-British comedy.
w Yahoo Serious, David Roach, Warwick Ross, Lulu Serious *d* Yahoo Serious *ph* Kevin Hayward *m* Tommy Tycho *ed* David Roach, Robert Gibson, Antony Gray
☆ Yahoo Serious (Ned Kelly), Melora Hardin, Alexei Sayle, Hugo Weaving, Tracy Mann, Kathleen Freeman
'Full of ideas and nonsense but short on genuine laughs and zest.' – *Variety*
† The British video release ran for 76m.

The Reckless Moment *
US 1949 82m bw
Columbia (Walter Wanger)
A woman accidentally kills her daughter's would-be seducer, and is then trailed by a blackmailer.
Uninteresting melodrama electrified by Ophuls's direction, which might have been applied to something more worthwhile.
w Henry Garson, R. W. Soderborg *novel The Blank Wall* by Elizabeth Sanxay Holding *d Max Ophüls ph* Burnett Guffey *m* Hans Salter *md* Morris Stoloff
☆ *Joan Bennett*, James Mason, Geraldine Brooks, Henry O'Neill, Shepperd Strudwick
'Swift, sure narrative and solidly pleasurable detail.' – *Richard Winnington*
† It was remade in 2001 as *The Deep End (qv)*.

The Reckoning **
GB 1969 108m Technicolor
Columbia/Ronald Shedlo (Hugh Perceval)
A tough London executive with a Liverpool-Irish background has a brutal streak and a self-destructive urge, but goes on narrowly averting misfortune.

Interesting melodrama of a man disgusted with both bourgeois and working-class values; slickly made and fast-moving.
w John McGrath *novel* The Harp That Once by Patrick Hall *d* Jack Gold *ph* Geoffrey Unsworth *m* Malcolm Arnold
☆ Nicol Williamson, Rachel Roberts, Paul Rogers, Zena Walker, Ann Bell, Gwen Nelson, J. G. Devlin

Recollections of the Yellow House
Portugal 1989 119m colour
Invicta (João Pedro Bénard, Joaquim Pinto)
original title: *Recordacões da Casa Amarela*
Life in a Lisbon boarding house, where a middle-aged voyeur and fetishist goes slowly mad.
Despite its billing as 'a Portuguese comedy', a drawn-out, downbeat movie that strives too hard for significance.
wd João César Monteiro *ph* José Antonio Loureiro *m* Schubert, Vivaldi *ad* Luis Monteiro *ed* Helena Alvez, Claudio Martinez
☆ Manuela de Freitas, João César Monteiro, Sabina Sacchi, Teresa Calado, Ruy Furtado, Henrique Viana, Luis Miguel Cintra

Recordacões da Casa Amarela: see *Recollections of the Yellow House*

'Trust. Betrayal. Deception. In the C.I.A. nothing is what it seems.'
The Recruit *
US 2003 115m Technicolor Panavision
Buena Vista/Touchstone/Spyglass (Roger Birnbaum, Jeff Apple, Gary Barber)
A new undercover agent falls for a a female recruit and then is told by his mentor to investigate her for stealing a CIA computer virus.
Despite an oft repeated mantra 'nothing is what it seems', a half-alert audience will be ahead of the agents in working out the villain of this paranoid thriller that begins well before succumbing to the usual conspiracy theories.
w Roger Towne, Kurt Wimmer, Mitch Glazer *d* Roger Donaldson *ph* Stuart Dryburgh *m* Klaus Badelt *pd* Andrew McAlpine *ed* David Rosenbloom
☆ Al Pacino (Walter Burke), Colin Farrell (James Clayton), Bridget Moynahan (Layla), Gabriel Macht (Zack), Karl Pruner (Dennis Slayne), Eugene Lipinski (Husky Man)
'The whole picture may be hokey, but the first part is agreeably so, the second part not. At the very least, one comes away with a new appreciation of the difficulty of inner-office romance at the CIA.' – *Todd McCarthy, Variety*
'Truly abysmal.' – *Guardian*

The Red Badge of Courage **
US 1951 69m bw
MGM (Gottfried Reinhardt)
A youth called up during the Civil War gets his first taste of battle.
Fresh, poetic, but dramatically unsatisfactory filming of a classic American novel. The story of its production is fascinatingly told in Picture, *a book by Lillian Ross.*
wd John Huston *novel* Stephen Crane *ph* Harold Rosson *m* Bronislau Kaper
☆ Audie Murphy, Bill Mauldin, Douglas Dick, Royal Dano, John Dierkes, Andy Devine, Arthur Hunnicutt

Red Ball Express
US 1952 83m bw
U-I (Aaron Rosenberg)
A supply column runs from the Normandy beachhead to Patton's army on the outskirts of Paris.
Standard war adventure, not too convincingly mounted but providing the usual excitements.
w John Michael Hayes *d* Budd Boetticher *ph* Maury Gertsman
☆ Jeff Chandler, Sidney Poitier, Alex Nicol, Judith Braun, Hugh O'Brian, Jack Kelly, Jack Warden

The Red Balloon ****
France 1955 34m Technicolor
Films Montsouris
A lonely boy finds a balloon which becomes his constant companion and finally lifts him to the skies.
Absorbing and quite perfectly timed fantasy, one of the great film shorts.
wd Albert Lamorisse *ph* Edmond Sechan *m* Maurice Le Roux
☆ Pascal Lamorisse
Academy Award: best original screenplay

The Red Baron: see *Von Richthofen and Brown*

The Red Beret
GB 1953 88m Technicolor
Warwick (Irving Allen, Albert R. Broccoli)
US title: *Paratrooper*
In 1940, an American with a guilt complex joins the British paratroopers.
Routine war action flagwaver; good battle scenes, rubbish in between.
w Richard Maibaum, Frank Nugent *book* Hilary St George Saunders *screen adaptation* Sy Bartlett *d* Terence Young *ph* John Wilcox *m* John Addison *md* Muir Mathieson *ad* Edward Carrick *ed* Gordon Pilkington *cos* Julie Harris
☆ Alan Ladd (Canada), Susan Stephen (Penny Gardner), Leo Genn (Major Snow), Harry Andrews (RSM), Donald Houston (Taffy), Anthony Bushell (General Whiting), Patric Doonan (Flash), Stanley Baker (Breton), Lana Morris (Pinky), Tim Turner (Rupert), Michael Kelly (Dawes), Anton Diffring (The Pole), Thomas Heathcote (Alf), Carl Duering (Rossi), Harry Locke (Medical Orderly) and also Michael Balfour (American Sergeant)

Red Canyon
US 1949 82m Technicolor
Universal (Leonard Goldstein)
A cowboy drifter sets out to corral a famous wild stallion.
Old-fashioned family Western.
w Maurice Geraghty *novel* Zane Grey *d* George Sherman *ph* Irving Glassberg *m* Walter Scharf
☆ Howard Duff, George Brent, Ann Blyth, Edgar Buchanan, John McIntire, Chill Wills, Jane Darwell, Lloyd Bridges

The Red Circle (dubbed) *
France/Italy 1970 102m colour
Corona (Robert Dorfmann)
original title: *Le Cercle Rouge*
An ex-convict teams up with a criminal on the run and a former police marksman to steal jewels from a shop equipped with a high-tech security system.
Dark, grim thriller with downbeat ending, enlivened by the central set-piece of the robbery itself.
wd Jean-Pierre Melville *ph* Henri Decae *m* Eric de Marsan *ad* Theo Meurisse
☆ Alain Delon, André Bourvil, Gian-Maria Volonte, Yves Montand, Paul Crauchet, François Périer

Red Corner
US 1997 122m DeLuxe
MGM (Jon Avnet, Jordan Kerner, Charles B. Mulvehill, Rosalie Swedlin)
While trying to set up a television satellite deal in China, an American lawyer is framed for murder.
Unconvincing mix of courtroom thriller and action-man antics, despite its footage secretly shot in Beijing.
w Robert King *d* Jon Avnet *ph* Karl Walter Lindenlaub *m* Thomas Newman *pd* Richard Sylbert *ed* Peter E. Berger
☆ Richard Gere, Bai Ling, Bradley Whitford, Byron Mann, Peter Donat, Robert Stanton, Tsai Chin, James Hong
'A ludicrous but humourless anti-Chinese diatribe thriller ... self important tosh.' – *Angie Errigo, Empire*

The Red Danube
US 1950 119m bw
MGM (Carey Wilson)
In occupied Vienna, citizens are being returned to Russia against their will.
Tedious and silly Red-baiting cold war charade.
w Gina Kaus, Arthur Wimperis *novel* Vespers in Vienna by Bryan Marshall *d* George Sidney *ph* Charles Rosher *m* Miklos Rozsa *ad* Cedric Gibbons, Hans Peters
☆ Ethel Barrymore, Walter Pidgeon, Janet Leigh, Peter Lawford, Francis L. Sullivan, Angela Lansbury, Louis Calhern, Melville Cooper
Academy Award nomination: art direction

Red Dawn
US 1984 114m Metrocolor
MGM-UA/Valkyrie (Buzz Feitshans, Barry Beckerman)
Russians lead a violent invasion into Colorado and are wiped out by the locals.
Ludicrous and somewhat dangerous Cold War throwback with little entertainment value to commend it. Violent teenage nonsense.
w Kevin Reynolds, John Milius *d* John Milius *ph* Ric Waite *m* Basil Poledouris *pd* Jackson de Govia *ed* Thom Noble
☆ Patrick Swayze, C. Thomas Howell, Lea Thompson, Charlie Sheen, Darren Dalton, Jennifer Grey, Ben Johnson, Harry Dean Stanton, Ron O'Neal, Vladek Sheybal, Powers Boothe

The Red Desert *
Italy/France 1964 116m Eastmancolor
Duemila/Federiz (Angelo Rizzoli)
original title: *Il Deserto Rosso*
A wife suffers from depression, and a brief affair with her husband's friend doesn't help.
Elongated character study, very talkative but rather decoratively designed with the same subtle use of colour in an urban landscape as was seen later in Blow Up.
w Michelangelo Antonioni, Tonino Guerra *d* Michelangelo Antonioni *ph* Carlo di Palma *m* Giovanni Chionetti
☆ Monica Vitti, Richard Harris, Carlos Chionetti
'The beauty is stationary, painterly; and the arresting image precisely arrests and retards the already moribund thrust of the film.' – *John Simon*
'Boredom in Ravenna, and it seeps into the viewer's bones.' – *Pauline Kael, New Yorker, 1984*

'Before the Silence, there was the Dragon.'
Red Dragon *
US/Germany 2002 124m DeLuxe Panavision
Universal/MGM (Dino De Laurentiis, Martha De Laurentiis)
An FBI agent seeks the help of a imprisoned murderer, a former psychiatrist, to help him catch a serial killer.
A remake that didn't need to be made, other than as a source of profit and to allow Hopkins to perform his gustatory routine as Hannibal Lecter; it's slickly done, but might have been better left undone.
w Ted Tally *novel* Thomas Harris *d* Brett Ratner *ph* Dante Spinotti *m* Danny Elfman *pd* Kristi Zea *ed* Mark Helfrich
☆ Anthony Hopkins (Hannibal Lecter), Edward Norton (Will Graham), Ralph Fiennes (Francis Dolarhyde), Harvey Keitel (Jack Crawford), Emily Watson (Reba McClane), Mary-Louise Parker (Molly Graham), Philip Seymour Hoffman (Freddy Lounds), Anthony Heald (Dr Chilton), Bill Duke (Police Chief)
'An intense, unnerving experience.' – *Todd McCarthy, Variety*
'*Red Dragon's* formula is so risible and rote by now that the natural reaction to scenes of peril, torture, and suffering is flippant laughter.' – *Michael Atkinson, Village Voice*
† The novel was first filmed in 1986 as *Manhunter (qv)*, directed by Michael Mann.
†† It took $93m at the US box-office.

'He treated her rough – and she loved it!'
Red Dust ***
US 1932 86m bw
MGM (Hunt Stromberg)
On a rubber plantation in Indo-China, the overseer is pursued by his engineer's bride but himself falls for a stranded prostitute.
Vigorous romantic melodrama with echoes of Rain; *remade as* Congo Maisie *(1940) and* Mogambo *(1954).*
w John Lee Mahin *play* Wilson Collison *d* Victor Fleming *ph* Harold Rosson
☆ Clark Gable, Jean Harlow, Mary Astor, Gene Raymond, Donald Crisp, Tully Marshall, Forrester Harvey
'Lots of pash, sex and undress ... an exhib's delight and a cinch for fancy takings. Done so expertly it almost overcomes the basic script shortcomings.' – *Variety*
'Gable and Harlow have full play for their curiously similar sort of good-natured toughness.' – *Time*
† The Gable role was first announced for John Gilbert.
†† Scenes showing the shooting of *Red Dust* are included in *Bombshell*.

'An Explosive Love Story'
Red Firecracker, Green Firecracker **
China/Hong Kong 1993 115m colour
Electric/Yung/Xi'an Studio/Beijing Salon (Chan Chun-Keung, Yong Naiming)
original title: *Paoda Shuang Deng*
An artist begins an affair with a young woman who is also head of a thriving family business, making fireworks – but before he can marry her, he has to compete in a firework contest with a rival suitor.
An enjoyably exotic story of romance and thwarted love, colourful and exciting and visually arresting.
w Da Ying *novel* Feng Jicai *d* He Ping *ph* Yang Lun *m* Zhao Jiping *ad* Qian Yunxiu *ed* Yuan Hong
☆ Ning Jing, Wu Gang, Zhao Xiaorui, Gao Yang, Xu Zhengyum, Zhao Liang
'A beguilingly mad tale of illicit passion and sacrifice.' – *Lizzie Francke, Guardian*

Red Garters **
US 1954 91m Technicolor
Paramount (Pat Duggan)
Various familiar types congregate in the Western town of Paradise Lost, and settle matters by the Code of the West.
Amusing Western musical spoof slightly deadened by its pretty but finally boring theatrically stylized scenery. Songs are catchy, performances good natured.
w Michael Fessier *d* George Marshall *ph* Arthur E. Arling *m* Joseph J. Lilley *ad* Hal Pereira, Roland Anderson *songs* Jay Livingston, Ray Evans
☆ Rosemary Clooney, Guy Mitchell, Gene Barry, Jack Carson, Pat Crowley, Cass Daley, Frank Faylen, Reginald Owen
'A musical of considerable freshness and gaiety.' – *MFB*
Academy Award nomination: art direction

Red Headed Woman *
US 1932 74m bw
MGM (Albert Lewin)
A shopgirl marries the boss but is rejected in his social circles.
Unconvincing but occasionally entertaining melodrama.
w Anita Loos *novel* Katharine Brush *d* Jack Conway *ph* Harold Rosson
☆ Jean Harlow, Chester Morris, Lewis Stone, Leila Hyams, Una Merkel, Henry Stephenson, Charles Boyer, May Robson
'Gingery treatment of a controversial subject that is bound to engage femme interest.' – *Variety*

Red Heat *
US 1988 104m Technicolor
Columbia TriStar/Carolco/Lone Wolf/Oak (Walter Hill, Gordon Carroll)
A Russian and a Chicago cop team up against an international gang of drug smugglers.
Fast-moving action movie, but one that offers only a minor variation on the standard plot of ill-assorted partners.
w Harry Kleiner, Walter Hill, Troy Kennedy Martin *d* Walter Hill *ph* Matthew F. Leonetti *pd* John Vallone *ed* Freeman Davies, Carmel Davies, Donn Aron
☆ Arnold Schwarzenegger, James Belushi, Peter Boyle, Ed O'Ross, Larry Fishburne, Gina Gershon, Richard Bright, J. W. Smith, Brent Jennings

The Red House *
US 1947 100m bw
(UA) Thalia (Sol Lesser)
A moody farmer's guilty obsession with an old house in the woods is that he murdered his parents in it.
Psycho-like suspense melodrama, too extended for comfort and too restricting for the actors, but effective in spurts.
wd Delmer Daves *novel* George Agnew Chamberlain *ph* Bert Glennon *m* Miklos Rozsa

☆ Edward G. Robinson, Judith Anderson, Lon McCallister, Allene Roberts, Rory Calhoun, Julie London, Ona Munson

The Red Inn *
France 1951 95m bw
Memnon
original title: *L'Auberge Rouge*
In 1833, stagecoach travellers stay at a remote inn, where the owners intend to rob and murder them.
Extreme black farce which manages to be pretty funny for those who can take this kind of thing: even the survivors of the night's massacre fall down a ravine.
w *Jean Aurenche, Pierre Bost* *d* Claude Autant-Lara *ph* André Bac *m* René Cloërc *ad* Max Douy
☆ *Fernandel*, Françoise Rosay, Carette, Grégoire Aslan

Red Kiss: see *Rouge Baiser*

The Red Light
US 1949 83m bw
UA/Pioneer (Roy Del Ruth)
An industrialist tracks down his brother's murderer.
Competent routine detection piece with engaging clues.
w George Callahan, Charles Grayson *story* This Guy Gideon by Donald Barry *d* Roy Del Ruth *ph* Bert Glennon *m* Dimitri Tiomkin *ad* F. Paul Syles *ed* Richard Heermance
☆ George Raft, Virginia Mayo, Raymond Burr, Gene Lockhart, Henry Morgan, Arthur Franz, Barton MacLane, Ken Murray

Red Line 7000
US 1965 110m Technicolor
Paramount/Laurel (Howard Hawks)
The career and loves of a stock car racer.
Very routine romantic actioner full of the director's favourite situations but failing to find any fresh slant.
w George Kirgo *d* Howard Hawks *ph* Milton Krasner *m* Nelson Riddle
☆ James Caan, Laura Devon, Gail Hire, Charlene Holt, John Robert Crawford
'Vulgar, witless and outrageously ponderous.' – *Bosley Crowther, New York Times*
'I just messed it up. It's as simple as that.' – *Howard Hawks*

Red Lips: see *Sadisterotica*

The Red Menace
US 1949 87m bw
Republic
GB title: *The Enemy Within*
A discontented war veteran is preyed on by communists.
An odd piece of anti-Red propaganda to come from an action studio, but it had some effect on thinking at the time.
w Albert DeMond, Gerald Geraghty *d* R. G. Springsteen *ph* John MacBurnie *m* Nathan Scott
☆ Robert Rockwell, Hanne Axman, Shepard Menken
'It waves the flag at the proper times and is an okay melodrama on other points.' – *Variety*
† The cast was deliberately chosen from unknowns.

Red Mountain
US 1951 84m Technicolor
Paramount/Hal B. Wallis
A Confederate captain joins Quantrell's Raiders but is horrified by their brutality.
Fast-moving action Western.
w John Meredyth Lucas, George W. George, George F. Slavin *d* William Dieterle *ph* Charles Lang Jnr *m* Franz Waxman
☆ Alan Ladd, Lizabeth Scott, Arthur Kennedy, John Ireland, Jeff Corey, James Bell

'Not A Sound. Not A Warning. Not A Chance. Not Alone.'
Red Planet
US 2000 106m Technicolor Panavision
Warner/Village Roadshow/NPV (Mark Canton, Bruce Berman, Jorge Saralegui)
In 2050, a small band of astronauts run into trouble after they land on Mars to prepare the planet for colonisation.
Dreary science-fiction, with the actors inhibited by their space-suits; nothing interesting happens very slowly.
w Chuck Pfarrer, Jonathan Lemkin *d* Antony Hoffman *ph* Peter Suschitzky *m* Graeme Revell *pd* Owen Paterson *ed* Robert K. Lambert, Dallas S. Puett
☆ Val Kilmer (Gallagher), Carrie-Anne Moss (Bowman), Tom Sizemore (Burchenal), Benjamin Bratt (Santen), Simon Baker (Pettengil), Terence Stamp (Chantilas)
'As dull and arid as a hike through the desert, which is essentially what the film documents.' – *Todd McCarthy, Variety*

'The World Torn Asunder By A Threat From Outer Space!'
Red Planet Mars
US 1952 87m bw
UA/Donald Hyde, Anthony Veiller
Americans and Russians both tune in to Mars and learn that it is a powerful Christian planet; the news causes first panic, then a religious revival and a determination to live more harmoniously on Earth.
Lunatic farrago that has to be seen to be believed.
w Anthony Veiller, John L. Balderston *d* Harry Horner *ph* Joseph Biroc *m* Mahlon Merrick *md* David Chudnow *ad* Charles D. Hall
☆ Herbert Berghof, Peter Graves, Andrea King, Marvin Miller

The Red Pony
US 1949 88m Technicolor
Republic (Lewis Milestone)
When his pet pony dies after an illness, a farmer's son loses faith in his father.
Sincere but rather obvious little fable which although capably made does not make inspiring film drama.
w John Steinbeck *d* Lewis Milestone *ph* Tony Gaudio *m* Aaron Copland *pd* Nicolai Remisoff
☆ Myrna Loy, Robert Mitchum, Peter Miles, Louis Calhern, Shepperd Strudwick, Margaret Hamilton

Red River **
US 1948 133m bw
UA/Monterey (Howard Hawks)
How the Chisholm Trail was developed as a cattle drive.
Brawling Western, a bit serious and long drawn out but with splendid action sequences.
w Borden Chase, Charles Schnee *d* *Howard Hawks* *ph* *Russell Harlan* *m* *Dimitri Tiomkin* *ed* *Christian Nyby*
☆ *John Wayne, Montgomery Clift*, Joanne Dru, Walter Brennan, Coleen Gray, John Ireland, Noah Beery Jnr, Harry Carey Jnr
† It was remade as a TV film in 1988, directed by Richard Michaels and starring James Arness, Bruce Boxleitner and Gregory Harrison.
original story (Borden Chase); editing

'Death is a $10,000 Bullet.'
Red Rock West *
US 1992 98m DeLuxe
Rank/Red Rock (Sigurjon Sighvatsson, Steve Golin)
A drifter who arrives in a small town is mistaken for a hitman and hired by both a husband and a wife to kill the other.
Enjoyable, blackly comic thriller with plenty of twists and turns.
w John Dahl, Rick Dahl *d* John Dahl *ph* Marc Reshovsky *m* William Olvis *pd* Robert Pearson *ed* Scott Chestnut
☆ Nicolas Cage, Lara Flynn Boyle, Dennis Hopper, J. T. Walsh, Craig Reay, Vance Johnson, Robert Apel
'Though it vaguely resembles a droll Buñuel construction, it owes more to the hard-boiled thrillers of the 1940s, albeit with a very large tongue-in-cheek quotient.' – *Variety*
'Very entertaining, doesn't detain you long, and has total confidence in its cinematic convictions.' – *Derek Malcolm, Guardian*

Red Salute *
US 1935 78m bw
Reliance (Edward Small)
aka: *Runaway Daughter*
GB title: *Arms and the Girl*
A college girl with communist leanings takes a cross country trip with an American soldier.
Odd little romantic comedy modelled on It Happened One Night; *it was picketed for its inconsequential attitude to politics.*
w Humphrey Pearson, Manuel Seff *d* Sidney Lanfield *ph* Robert Planck
☆ Barbara Stanwyck, Robert Young, Hardie Albright, Cliff Edwards, Ruth Donnelly, Gordon Jones, Henry Kolker
'Tepid comedy romance wrapped up in a preachment against campus agitators who oppose militarism.' – *Variety*

Red Scorpion
US 1989 102m DeLuxe
Shapiro Glickenhaus (Jack Abramoff)
A Russian agent's assignment is to assassinate the leader of a group of African terrorists.
Incompetent action movie that staggers from one dull moment to another with a complete lack of conviction.
w Arne Olsen *d* Joseph Zito *ph* João Fernandes *m* Jay Chattaway *pd* Ladislav Wilheim *ed* Daniel Loewenthal *sp* John Evans; make-up: Tom Savini
☆ Dolph Lundgren, M. Emmet Walsh, Al White, T. P. McKenna, Carmen Argenziano, Alex Cohen, Brion James

Red Scorpion 2
US 1994 90m colour
August/Northwood (Robert Malcolm)
A government agent recruits an élite group of soliders to recover the legendary spear of destiny, which is in the possession of a neo-fascist businessman and his gang of violent skinheads.
Frenetic action film, drawing some of its inspiration from The Dirty Dozen, *though it operates on a far lower level.*
w Troy Bolotnick, Barry Victor *d* Michael Kennedy *ph* Curtis Petersen *m* George Blondheim *pd* Brent Thomas *ed* Gary Zubeck
☆ Matt McColm, John Savage, Jennifer Rubin, Michael Ironside, Michael Covert, Real Andrews, George Touliatos
'Contains almost non-stop fights, explosions, shooting and general mayhem, certainly enough to keep the action crowd moderately happy.' – *Variety*

The Red Shoes ****
GB 1948 136m Technicolor
GFD/The Archers (Michael Powell, Emeric Pressburger)
A girl student becomes a great ballet star but commits suicide when torn between love and her career.
Never was a better film made from such a penny plain story so unpersuasively written and performed; the splendour of the production is in the intimate view it gives of life backstage in the ballet world with its larger-than-life characters. The ballet excerpts are very fine, and the colour discreet; the whole film is charged with excitement.
wd *Michael Powell, Emeric Pressburger* *ph* *Jack Cardiff* *m* *Brian Easdale* *pd* *Hein Heckroth* *ed* *Reginald Mills*
☆ *Anton Walbrook, Moira Shearer*, Marius Goring, Robert Helpmann, Albert Basserman, Frederick Ashton, Leonide Massine, Ludmilla Tcherina, Esmond Knight
'In texture, like nothing the British cinema has ever seen.' – *Time Out, 1981*
Brian Easdale; Hein Heckroth
best picture; original story (Michael Powell, Emeric Pressburger); editing

Red Skies of Montana
US 1952 99m Technicolor
TCF (Samuel G. Engel)
aka: *Smoke Jumpers*
Tension among firefighting crews in the mountains of Montana.
Adequate, routine action melodrama with semi-documentary touches.
w Harry Kleiner *d* Joseph M. Newman *ph* Charles G. Clarke *m* Sol Kaplan
☆ Richard Widmark, Jeffrey Hunter, Constance Smith, Richard Boone, Richard Crenna

'A man's desperation – a woman's passion – a boy's awakening – a girl's desire!'
Red Sky at Morning
US 1970 113m Technicolor
Universal/Hal Wallis
During World War II the family of an officer on active service find life in New Mexico not what they've been used to.
Peyton Place by any other name, well produced but of little real interest.
w Marguerite Roberts *novel* Richard Bradford *d* James Goldstone *ph* Vilmos Zsigmond *m* Billy Goldenberg
☆ Claire Bloom, Richard Thomas, Richard Crenna, Catherine Burns, Desi Arnaz Jnr, John Colicos, Harry Guardino

Red Sonja
US 1985 89m Metrocolor
MGM-UA/Thorn EMI (Christian Ferry)
In the times of sword and sorcery, Sonja avenges her sister's death and deposes an evil queen.
Absolute comic strip nonsense: even the monsters look mechanical.
w Clive Exton, George MacDonald Fraser *stories* Robert E. Howard *d* Richard Fleischer *ph* Giuseppe Rotunno *m* Ennio Morricone *pd* Danilo Donati *ed* Frank J. Urioste
☆ Brigitte Nielsen, Arnold Schwarzenegger, Sandahl Bergman, Paul Smith, Ronald Lacey

Red Sorghum ***
China 1987 92m Eastmancolor
Palace/Xi'an Film Studio (Li Changqing)
original title: *Hong Gaoliang*
A man recalls his grandparents' love affair and violent times.
Exuberant tragi-comic folk tale, told with immense panache.
w Chen Jianyu, Zhu Wei, Mo Yan *d* Zhang Yimou *ph* Gu Changwei *m* Zhao Jiping *ad* Yang Gang *ed* Du Yuan
☆ Gong Li, Jiang Wen, Teng Rujun, Liu Ji, Qian Ming, Ji Chunhua, Zhai Chunhua
'A rough, proletarian belch of a film, a gleeful assertion of peasant vitality, founded on amoral (but fully justified) acts of transgression' – *Tony Rayns, MFB*

The Red Squirrel **
Spain 1993 114m colour
Sogetel (Ricardo Garcia Arrojo)
original title: *La Ardilla Roja*
A suicidal rock musician invents a new identity as her lover for a woman who crashes her motorcycle and, as a result, apparently loses her memory.
An intriguing playful comedy of identity and commitment, memory and imagination, directed with a light touch.
wd *Julio Medem* *ph* Gonzalo Fernandez Berridi *m* Alberto Iglesias *ed* Maria Elena Sainz de Rozas
☆ Emma Suarez, Nancho Novo, Maria Barranco, Karra Elejalde, Carmelo Gomez, Cristina Marcos, Monica Molina, Ana Gracia
'A pleasingly complex film – it's a love story, a mystery, a comedy – which is an unnerving, thought-provoking mix of the commonplace and the surreal, the sinister and the comic.' – *Yvette Huddleston, Empire*

Red Sun
France/Italy/Spain 1971 108m Eastmancolor
Corona/Oceania/Balcazar (Robert Dorfman)
In 1870 Arizona, an outlaw is forced to accompany a Japanese samurai to recover a ceremonial sword which his partner has stolen.
Unusual but generally ineffective Western with a fashionable international cast.
w Laird Koenig, D. B. Petitclerc, W. Roberts, L. Roman *d* Terence Young *ph* Henri Alekan *m* Maurice Jarre
☆ Charles Bronson, Toshiro Mifune, Alain Delon, Ursula Andress, Capucine
'A nice exotic item ruined by suburban direction.' – *Sight and Sound*

Red Sundown
US 1956 81m Technicolor
Universal-International (Albert Zugsmith)
A gunslinger becomes a deputy and tames a lawless town.
Elementary Western action piece, not unentertaining.
w Martin Berkeley *story* Black Trail by Lewis B. Patten *d* Jack Arnold *ph* William Snyder *m* Hans J. Salter
☆ Rory Calhoun, Martha Hyer, Dean Jagger, Robert Middleton, James Millican, Grant Williams

'Who is killing the serial killers?'
Red Team
Canada 1999 90m colour
Flashpoint/Regent (Paul Colichman, Mark R. Harris)
video title: *The Crimson Code*
An FBI agent discovers that an elite team within the agency is killing serial killers instead of bringing them to trial.
Predictable by-the-numbers paranoid drama, short of thrills or suspense.
w Alex Metcalf *d* Jeremy Haft *ph* Ian Elkin *m* Ken Williams *ad* Gord Wilding *ed* Neila Benson
☆ Patrick Muldoon (Jason Chandler), Cathy Moriarty (Stephanie Dobson), C. Thomas Howell (J.B. Gaines), David Millbern (Reed), David Beecroft (Garcia), Tim Thomerson (William Heywood), Fred Ward (Randall Brooks)

The Red Tent *
Italy/USSR 1970 121m Technicolor
Paramount/Vides/Mosfilm (Franco Cristaldi)
The story of General Nobile's ill-fated 1928 expedition by dirigible to the Arctic.
Stiffly-conceived international spectacular with one striking sequence but not much good cheer.
w Ennio de Concini, Richard Adams *d* Mikhail Kalatozov *ph* *Leonid Kalashnikov* *m* Ennio Morricone
☆ Peter Finch, Sean Connery, Hardy Kruger, Claudia Cardinale, Mario Adorf, Massimo Girotti

Red Tomahawk
US 1967 80m Technicolor
A. C. Lyles/Paramount
The small town of Deadwood is caught up in the aftermath of Little Big Horn.
Talkative Western filled with old faces, as is this producer's wont.
w Steve Fisher *d* R. G. Springsteen *ph* W. Wallace Kelley *m* Jimmie Haskell
☆ Howard Keel, Joan Caulfield, Broderick Crawford, Scott Brady, Wendell Corey, Richard Arlen, Tom Drake

The Red Violin *
Canada/Italy 1998 130m colour
Film4/New Line/Téléfilm Canada/Rhombus Media/Mikado/Sidecar (Niv Fichman)
A violin, which was the last work of a master craftsman, travels through various hands until the present time, when it is the star attraction in an auction.
An episodic movie on the power of music that holds the interest for the most part, though a romantic and miscast interlude in England nearly ruins the pleasure it provides.
w Don McKellar, François Girard *d* François Girard *ph* Alain Dostie *m* *John Corigliano* *pd* François Séguin *ed* Gaëtan Huot
☆ Samuel L. Jackson, Don McKellar, Carlo Cecchi, Irene Grazioli, Jean-Luc Bideau, Christoph Koncz, Jason Flemyng, Greta Scacchi, Sylvia Chang, Liu Zi Feng, Colm Feore, Monique Mercure

> 'Fails on a number of counts, mostly because the individual stories aren't very gripping.' – *David Stratton, Variety*

John Corigliano

Red Wagon
GB 1933 107m bw
BIP (Walter C. Mycroft)
Passions mount in a travelling circus. Gypsies and jealousies are the ingredients of a melodrama aimed at the international market.
It failed.
w Roger Burford, Edward Knoblock, Arthur Woods *novel* Lady Eleanor Smith *d* Paul Stein *ph* Jack Cox *md* Kurt Schroeder *ed* Leslie Norman
☆ Charles Bickford, Raquel Torres, Greta Nissen, Don Alvarado, Anthony Bushell, Paul Graetz, Jimmy Hanley, Frank Pettingell, Francis L. Sullivan

Redbeard *
Japan 1965 165m bw Tohoscope
Toho-Kurosawa
original title: *Akahige*
Problems of a 19th-century doctor. Almost a Japanese version of *The Citadel*: Kurosawa himself called it 'a monument to goodness in man'.
Rather heavy-going, but sporadically compelling.
w Masato Ide, Hideo Oguni, Akira Kurosawa *novel* Shugoro Yamamoto *d* Akira Kurosawa *ph* A. Nakai, T. Saito *m* M. Sato
☆ Toshiro Mifune, Yuzo Kayama

> 'A three-hour excursion into nineteenth-century hospital soap opera; a mediocre enough script, but beautifully directed and flawlessly acted.' – *John Simon*

Redemption
US 1930 82m bw
MGM
A man thought dead commits suicide rather than interrupt his wife's new life.
Elaborate but unsuccessful talkie début of a waning star; very hard going.
w Dorothy Farnum, Edwin Justus Mayer *novel* *The Living Corpse* by Leo Tolstoy *d* Fred Niblo
☆ John Gilbert, Renee Adoree, Eleanor Boardman, Conrad Nagel

The Redhead: see *Poil de Carotte*

The Redhead from Wyoming
US 1953 81m Technicolor
Universal-International (Leonard Goldstein)
An ambitious businessman provokes a range war so that he can become governor of Wyoming and the state's biggest cattle-rustler.
Energetic drama, with the fiery O'Hara as a saloon-owner trying to keep the peace between warring factions; it is let down by the script's reliance on over-familiar situations.
w Polly James, Herb Meadow *d* Lee Sholem *ph* Winton Hoch *md* Joseph Gershenson *ad* Bernard Herzbrun, Hilyard Brown *ed* Milton Carruth *cos* Edward Stevens
☆ Maureen O'Hara (Kate Maxwell), Alex Nicol (Stan Blaine), William Bishop (Jim Averell), Robert Strauss ('Knuckles' Hogan), Alexander Scourby (Reece Duncan), Palmer Lee (Hal Jessup), Jack Kelly (Sandy), Jeanne Cooper (Myra), Dennis Weaver (Matt Jessup), Stacy Harris (Chet Jones)

Redneck
Italy/GB 1972 87m colour
Crawford/CIAC/Sterle (Michael Lester, Silvio Narizzano)
original title: *Senza Ragione*
Two crooks on the run steal a car and discover that it contains a teenage boy.
Dull chase film that wanders around the Italian countryside to little effect.
w Win Wells, Masolino D'Amico *story* Rafael Sanchez Campoy *d* Silvio Narizzano *ph* Giorgio Tonti *m* Maurizio Catalano *ad* Arrigo Equini *ed* Thom Noble
☆ Franco Nero, Telly Savalas, Mark Lester, Ely Galleani, Duilio Del Prete, Maria Michi

'Not since *Gone with the Wind* has there been a great romantic epic like it!'
Reds ***
US 1981 196m Technicolor
Paramount (Warren Beatty)
The last years of John Reed, an American writer who after stormy romantic vicissitudes goes with his wife to Russia and writes *Ten Days That Shook the World*.
Interminably long but full of quality, this immensely detailed work was a most unlikely project to succeed in the eighties, but its very strangeness enabled it to break even.
w Warren Beatty, Trevor Griffiths *d* *Warren Beatty* *ph* *Vittorio Storaro* *m* Stephen Sondheim *pd* *Richard Sylbert*
☆ Warren Beatty, Diane Keaton, Edward Herrmann, Jerzy Kosinski, Jack Nicholson, Maureen Stapleton, Paul Sorvino
Warren Beatty (as director); Vittorio Storaro; Maureen Stapleton (supporting actress)
best picture; screenplay; editing (Dede Allen, Craig McKay); Warren Beatty (as actor); Diane Keaton; Jack Nicholson
best supporting actor (Jack Nicholson); best supporting actress (Maureen Stapleton)

Reducing
US 1931 73m bw
MGM
The proprietress of a beauty parlour sends for an old family servant to help her.
Loosely plotted comedy consisting largely of slapstick in a Turkish bath.
w Willard Mack, Beatrice Banyard *d* Charles F. Reisner
☆ Marie Dressler, Polly Moran, Anita Page, Lucien Littlefield, Sally Eilers

> 'Rough and tumble hoke comedy addressed to the banana peel sense of humour.' – *Variety*

Reed – México Insurgente **
Mexico 1971 106m bw
Salvador Lopez/Ollin y Asociados
Reporting the Mexican revolution in 1913, American journalist John Reed learns to identify with the oppressed.
A low-key documentary-style account of Reed's conversion to political action, eschewing mock-heroics and enhanced by sepia photography.
wd Paul Leduc *ph* Alexis Grivas
☆ Claudio Obregón, Ernesto Gómez Cruz, Eduardo López Rojas, Juan Angel Martinez, Carlos Castañón

Reefer and the Model *
Ireland 1988 93m Technicolor
Metro/Berber Films (Lelia Doolan)
A former IRA man, his trawler-owning friends, and a pregnant girl he picks up, attempt a bank robbery to raise money.
Raffishly enjoyable thriller, though its attempt to explain the political context of modern Ireland lacks resonance.
wd Joe Comerford *ph* Breffni Byrne *m* Johnny Duhan *pd* John Lucas *ed* Sé Merry
☆ Ian McElhinney, Eve Watkinson, Carol Scanlan, Birdy Sweeney, Sean Lawlor, Ray McBride

Reefer Madness
US 1936 67m bw
Motion Picture Ventures/G & H (George A. Hirliman)
aka: *The Burning Question*
aka: *Tell Your Children*
Clean-cut kids tread the downward path to fast cars, sex and murder after smoking marijuana.
Direly made, low-budget, unsophisticated, sensational exposé that reveals much about attitudes of the period; as a film its value is nil, though the maniacal acting may provide some amusement.
w Arthur Hoerl, Paul Franklin *story* Lawrence Meade *d* Louis Gasnier *ph* Jack Greenhalgh *md* Abe Meyer *ad* Robert Priestley *ed* Carl Pierson
☆ Dorothy Short, Kenneth Craig, Lillian Miles, Dave O'Brien, Thelma White, Carleton Young, Warren McCullom, Pat Royale, Joseph Royale
† The film opens with the foreword: 'The motion picture you are about to witness may startle you. It would not have been possible, otherwise, to sufficiently emphasize the frightful toll of the new drug menace which is destroying the youth of America in alarmingly-increasing numbers. Marihuana is that drug – a violent narcotic – an unspeakable scourge – The Real Public Enemy Number One! Its first effect is sudden, violent, uncontrollable laughter; then come dangerous hallucinations – space expands – time slows down, almost stands still … fixed ideas come next, conjuring up monstrous extravagances – followed by emotional disturbances, the total inability to direct thoughts, the loss of all power to resist physical emotions … leading finally to acts of shocking violence … ending often in incurable insanity. In picturing its soul-destroying effects no attempt was made to equivocate. The scenes and incidents, while fictionalized for the purposes of this story, are based upon actual research into the results of Marihuana addiction. If their stark reality will make you *think*, will make you aware that something *must be done* to wipe out this ghastly menace, then the picture will not have failed in its purpose … Because the dreaded Marihuana may be reaching forth next for your son or daughter … or *yours* … or *YOURS!*'

'He took them hostage. They drove him crazy.'
The Ref
US 1994 93m Technicolor
Buena Vista/Touchstone/Don Simpson/Jerry Bruckheimer (Ron Bozman, Richard LaGravenese, Jeff Weiss)
GB title: *Hostile Hostages*
At Christmas, a bad-tempered cat burglar on the run takes hostage an argumentative yuppie couple whose marriage is in difficulties.
Misfiring black comedy; what might have been a bracing alternative to It's a Wonderful Life, *a sort of* What a Lousy Existence, *too often leaves a sour taste, although it has a few moments.*
w Richard LaGravenese, Marie Weiss *d* Ted Demme *ph* Adam Kimmel *m* David A. Stewart *pd* Dan Davis *ed* Jeffrey Wolf
☆ Denis Leary, Judy Davis, Kevin Spacey, Robert J. Steinmiller Jnr, Glynis Johns, Richard Bright, Raymond J. Barry

> 'Unrelenting rough language, bitter, caustic humor and unbearable grotesqueries in place of characters seem unlikely elements to generate feel-good numbers for Simpson-Bruckheimer's first production for Disney.' – *Variety*

'It's all part of the American Dream.'
The Reflecting Skin
GB 1990 95m Technicolor
Virgin/Fugitive Features/BBC Films/British Screen/Zenith (Dominic Anciano, Ray Burdis)
A young boy suspects a strange woman of having killed his friends.
Grotesque, death-obsessed movie, directed at a somnambulistic pace, though it found admirers at several film festivals.
wd Philip Ridley *ph* Dick Pope *m* Nick Bicat *ad* Rick Roberts *ed* Scott Thomas
☆ Viggo Mortensen, Lindsay Duncan, Jeremy Cooper, Sheila Moore, Duncan Fraser, David Longworth, Robert Koons, David Bloom

> 'The film strains for poetic resonance: a puffed-up frog trying to pass as a prince.' – *Independent*
> 'This is American Grand Guignol orchestrated by a foreigner with a frightening idea of how the mysteries of the adult world seem to the highly imaginative but still relatively innocent young.' – *Guardian*

Reflection of Fear
US 1971 90m Eastmancolor
Columbia (Howard B. Jaffe)
A retarded teenage girl kills her mother and her grandmother.
Psycho thriller of little interest or suspense.
w Edward Hume, Lewis John Carlino *novel* *Go to Thy Deathbed* by Stanton Forbes *d* William A. Fraker *ph* Laszlo Kovacs *m* Fred Myrow
☆ Robert Shaw, Mary Ure, Signe Hasso, Sondra Locke, Mitch Ryan

Reflections in a Golden Eye *
US 1967 108m Technicolor
Warner Seven Arts (Ray Stark)
Repressions at a peacetime army camp in Georgia. A private soldier rides nude on horseback, a major has the hots for him, the major's wife has an affair with their neighbour, whose wife has cut off her nipples with garden shears.
A film as idiotic as its story line, but smoothly marshalled so that at least it's more amusing than boring.
w Chapman Mortimer, Gladys Hill *novel* Carson McCullers *d* *John Huston* *ph* *Aldo Tonti* *m* Toshiro Mayuzumi *pd* Stephen Grimes
☆ Marlon Brando, Elizabeth Taylor, Brian Keith, Julie Harris, Robert Forster, Zorro David

> 'One feels trapped in a huge overheated hothouse containing nothing but common snapdragons. Pedestrian, crass, and uninvolving to the point of repellence.' – *John Simon*
> 'Nothing more than nutty people and pseudo porn.' – *Judith Crist*

The Reformer and the Redhead *
US 1950 90m bw
MGM (Norman Panama, Melvin Frank)
A small-town reform candidate abandons his crooked protector and wins under his own steam, helped by the daughter of the zoo superintendent.
Scatty sub-Capra comedy with a lightweight script but good production and playing.
wd Norman Panama, Melvin Frank *ph* Ray June *m* David Raksin
☆ Dick Powell, June Allyson, Cecil Kellaway, David Wayne, Ray Collins, Robert Keith, Marvin Kaplan

'Somewhere in America a woman is being terrorized by a major domestic appliance.'
'Just when you thought it was safe to go back into the kitchen.'
The Refrigerator
US 1991 86m colour
Avenue D (Christopher Oldcorn)
Two newlyweds move from Ohio to New York and rent an apartment with a carnivorous refrigerator.
Camp horror movie, satirizing suburban domesticity and consumerism, but done without any wit or style.
w Nicholas Jacobs, Christopher Oldcorn, Philip Dolin *d* Nicholas Jacobs *ph* Paul Gibson *m* Don Peterkofsky, Adam Roth, Chris Burke *pd* Therese Deprez *ed* P. J. Pesce, Suzanne Pillsbury, Christopher Oldcorn, Nicholas Jacobs
☆ David Simonds, Julia McNeal, Phyllis Sanz, Angel Caban, Nena Segal, Jaime Rojo, Alex Trisano
'Smart, quirky horror spoof. Slick-looking production delivers its thrills with enough laughs to promise a cult following.' – *Variety*

Regain: see *Harvest*

Regalo di Natale: see *Christmas Present*

Regarde les Hommes Tomber: see *See How They Fall*

Regarding Henry
US 1991 108m Technicolor
UIP/Paramount (Scott Rudin, Mike Nichols)
A tough lawyer, who loses most of his faculties in a shooting, becomes a much nicer person as he recovers.
Sentimental fable that fails to convince.
w Jeffrey Abrams *d* Mike Nichols *ph* Giuseppe Rotunno *m* Hans Zimmer *pd* Tony Walton *ed* Sam O'Steen
☆ Harrison Ford, Annette Bening, Bill Nunn, Mikki Allen, Donald Moffat, Aida Linares, Elizabeth Wilson, Robin Bartlett, Bruce Altman, Rebecca Miller

Regeneration **
GB/Canada 1997 110m colour
Artificial Eye/Norstar/Telefilm Canada/SFPF/GFF (Allan Scott, Peter R. Simpson)
In 1917, in order to nullify his growing opposition to the war, the poet Siegfried Sassoon is sent to a Scottish psychiatric hospital treating shell-shocked officers.
Excellently acted, sensitively directed drama of the impact of war; but there is a stilted quality to the script that keeps it earthbound.
w Allan Scott *novel* Pat Barker *d* Gillies MacKinnon *ph* Glen MacPherson *m* Mychael Danna *pd* Andy Harris *ed* Pia di Ciaula
☆ Jonathan Pryce, James Wilby (Siegfried Sassoon), Jonny Lee Miller, Stuart Bunce (Wilfred Owen), Tanya Allen, John Neville
'Dignified but uninvolving.' – *Variety*

'A Couple... A Secret... A Nightmare.'
Regina Roma
Germany/Italy 1982 86m colour
Genesis/Bognor/Curiator Spiritus/Galia (David Amiri, Serge Roux)
video title: *Regina*
When her son brings home the shy girl he wants to marry, his mother tries to break up the romance.
Curious over-heated domestic drama that was Ava Gardner 's last movie, one that was hardly released. The direction is tentative and the acting variable.
w Pierre Rey *d* Jean-Yves Prate *ph* Serge Haignere *m* Lorin Maazel *ed* Roberto Silvi
☆ Ava Gardner (Mama), Ray Sharkey (Cary), Anna Karina (Regina), Anthony Quinn (Papa)

La Règle du Jeu ***
France 1939 113m bw
La Nouvelle Edition Française (Claude Renoir)
aka: *The Rules of the Game*
A count organizes a weekend shooting party which results in complex love intrigues among servants as well as masters.
Celebrated satirical comedy with a uniquely bleak outlook.
w Jean Renoir, Carl Koch d Jean Renoir ph Jean Bachelet, Alain Renoir *m* Joseph Kosma, Roger Desormières *ad* Eugène Lourié, Max Douy *ed* Marguerite Renoir, Marthe Huguet
☆ *Marcel Dalio*, Nora Gregor, Jean Renoir, Mila Parély, Julien Carette, Gaston Modot, Roland Toutain
'It is a question of panache, of preserving a casual indifference to the workings of fate.' – *The Times*
'How brilliantly Renoir focuses the confusion! The rather fusty luxury of the chateau, the constant mindless slaughter of wild animals, the minuets of adultery and seduction, the gavottes of mutual hatred or mistrust...' – *Basil Wright, 1972*
† The film was originally banned as indicting the corruption of France, and during the war the negative was destroyed during an air raid; but eventually a full version was pieced together from various materials.

'Fight Fire With Fire.'
Reign of Fire
US 2002 101m Technicolor Panavision
Buena Vista/Touchstone/Spyglass (Richard D. Zanuck, Lili Fini Zanuck, Gary Barber, Roger Birnbaum)
In the near future, an American rallies a small group of survivors in a Britain devastated by fire-breathing dragons that emerged from a new tunnel under London.
Muscle-bound heroics dominate in this B feature, which is all brawn and no brain.
w Gregg Chabot, Kevin Peterka, Matt Greenberg *d* Rob Bowman *ph* Adrian Biddle *m* Edward Shearmur *pd* Wolf Kroeger *ed* Thom Noble *sp* Richard R. Hoover
☆ Christian Bale (Quinn), Matthew McConaughey (Denton Van Zan), Izabella Scorupco (Alex), Gerald Butler (Creedy), Scott James Moutter (Jared Wilke), David Kennedy (Eddie Stax), Alexander Siddig (Ajay), Ned Dennehy (Barlow), Alice Krige (Karen Abercromby)
'Mesmerizing junk.' – *New Yorker*
'A slick, sleek and periodically scary piece of work.' – *Joe Leydon, Variety*

Reign of Terror: see *The Black Book*

The Reincarnation of Peter Proud
US 1974 104m Technicolor
Avco Embassy/Bing Crosby (Frank P. Rosenberg)
A history professor is troubled by recurring dreams of his former existence.
Hysterical psychic melodrama which pretty well ruins its own chances by failing to explain its plot.
w Max Ehrlich *novel* Max Ehrlich *d* J. Lee-Thompson *ph* Victor J. Kemper *m* Jerry Goldsmith
☆ Michael Sarrazin, Jennifer O'Neill, Margot Kidder, Cornelia Sharpe, Paul Hecht
'It may well be the silliest approach to the subject in any medium ... all flashbacks trampling the action with the finesse of a rogue elephant.' – *Tom Milne*

'The Trap Is Set. The Game Is On.'
Reindeer Games
US 2000 104m DeLuxe Panavision
Buena Vista/Dimension (Marty Katz, Bob Weinstein, Chris Moore)
GB title: *Deception*
A petty crook becomes involved with a beautiful woman and a gang of murderous but incompetent thieves.
Fast-paced thriller that despite the occasional striking moment (five dead Santa Clauses lying in the snow) has little to recommend it; its narrative twists grow increasingly silly.
w Ehren Kruger *d* John Frankenheimer *ph* Alan Caso *m* Alan Silvestri *pd* Barbara Dunphy *ed* Tony Gibbs, Michael Kahn *cos* May Routh
☆ Ben Affleck (Rudy Duncan), Gary Sinise (Gabriel), Charlize Theron (Ashley), Dennis Farina (Jack Bangs), James Frain (Nick), Donal Logue (Pug), Danny Trejo (Jumpy), Isaac Hayes (Zook), Gordon Tootoosis (Old Governor), Dana Stubblefield (The Alamo), Clarence Williams III (Merlin)
'A breathlessly paced potboiler that's a "thriller" in name only.' – *Todd McCarthy, Variety*
'It's not a really bad movie, just so mediocre–the visual equivalent of aeroplane food.' – *Cosmo Landesman, Sunday Times*
† The film cost $36m and took $23m at the US box-office.

'She was the daughter of a King, the sister of a King, the wife of a King ... and the lover of an enemy.'
La Reine Margot **
France/Germany/Italy 1994 162m colour
Guild/Renn/France 2/DA/NEF/Degeto/RCS
In 1572, the sister of the Catholic King of France reluctantly agrees to marry the Protestant Duke of Navarre, an event that leads to the Saint Bartholomew's Day Massacre of Protestants and causes turmoil in the kingdom.
Engagingly vivid account of power struggles on personal, political and religious levels, involving bloodshed, poison, lust and betrayal.
w Danièle Thompson, Patrice Chereau *novel* Alexandre Dumas *d Patrice Chéreau ph Philippe Rousselot m* Goran Bregovic *pd* Richard Peduzzi, Olivier Radot *ed* François Gédiger, Hélène Viard
☆ Isabelle Adjani, Daniel Auteuil, Jean-Hugues Anglade, Vincent Perez, Virna Lisa, Dominique Blanc, Pascal Greggory, Asia Argento, Jean-Claude Brialy
'A tempestuous, lavish and intelligently thought-out account of the Saint Bartholomew's Day Massacre and its aftermath, marinated in gore and lovingly trimmed with the finest brocade.' – *Jonathan Romney, Guardian*
costume design

Reise der Hoffnung: see *Journey of Hope*

The Reivers *
US 1969 111m Technicolor Panavision
Cinema Center/Duo/Solar (Irving Ravetch)
In Mississippi at the turn of the century a hired hand borrows the new family auto for a trip into Memphis with the grandson of the family and a black stablehand.
Pleasant but insubstantial yarn of more gracious days; most attractive to look at, it entertains gently without ever reaching a point.
w Irving Ravetch, Harriet Frank Jnr *novel* William Faulkner *d* Mark Rydell *ph Richard Moore m* John Williams
☆ Steve McQueen, Sharon Farrell, Will Geer, Rupert Crosse, Mitch Vogel, Michael Constantine, Juano Hernandez, Clifton James
John Williams; Rupert Crosse

'A Comedy Of Discriminating Taste And Dirty Little Secrets.'
'A family comedy in a class of its own.'
Relative Values
GB/US 2000 87m colour
Alliance Atlantis/Midsummer/IOMFC (Christopher Millburn)
An English countess is concerned when her son arrives at the family estate with his unsuitable fiancée, a Hollywood actress.
A play that was old-fashioned when it first arrived on the stage makes an even more old-fashioned film that is well-enough done but somewhat pointless; its impeccable construction provides some amusement.
w Paul Rattigan, Michael Walker *play* Noël Coward *d* Eric Styles *ph* Jimmy Dibling *m* John Debney *pd* Humphrey Jaeger *ed* Caroline Limmer *cos* Nic Ede
☆ Julie Andrews (Felicity), Sophie Thompson (Moxie), Edward Atterton (Nigel), Jeanne Tripplehorn (Miranda Frayle), William Baldwin (Don Lucas), Colin Firth (Peter), Stephen Fry (Crestwell), Anwen Carlisle (Alice), Gaye Brown (Lady Hayling), Michael Culkin (Lord Ludmurrey), Katy Stephens (Caroline), Stephanie Beacham (Elizabeth)
'Individual performances and Coward's neatly turned dialogue just about make the pic go the distance, triumphing over unimaginative direction and an awkward screenplay.' – *Derek Elley, Variety*

Relentless
US 1948 93m Technicolor
Columbia (Eugene B. Rodney)
A cowboy framed for murder must clear himself before the posse catches up with him.
Brisk Western copy of The 39 Steps.
w Winston Miller *d* George Sherman *ph* Edward Cronjager *m* Marlin Skiles
☆ Robert Young, Marguerite Chapman, Willard Parker, Barton MacLane, Will Wright

Relentless
US 1989 93m Foto-Kem
New Line (Howard Smith)
The son of a disgraced LA cop turns serial killer.
A formulaic thriller with occasional moments that lift it out of the very mundane.
w Jack T. D. Robinson *d* William Lustig *ph* James Lemmo *m* Jay Chattaway *pd* Gene Abel *ed* David Kern
☆ Judd Nelson, Robert Loggia, Meg Foster, Leo Rossi, Patrick O'Brien, Ken Lerner, Mindy Seeger

'Some Things Are Best Left Undiscovered.'
The Relic
US 1997 110m DeLuxe Panavision
Paramount/Cloud Nine/Pacific Western (Sam Mercer, Gale Anne Hurd)
Crates shipped from the Brazilian jungle to a Chicago museum contain a brain-eating monster.
A standard monster movie, done with a certain amount of relish but no originality.
w Amy Jones, John Raffo, Rick Jaffa *novel* Douglas Preston, Lincoln Child *d* Peter Hyams *ph* Peter Hyams *m* John Debney *pd* Philip Harrison *ed* Steven Kemper *sp* Stan Winston; VIFX
☆ Penelope Ann Miller, Tom Sizemore, Linda Hunt, James Whitmore, Clayton Rohner, Chi Muoi Lo, Lewis Van Bergen
'A B-movie shocker in an expensive suit.' – *George Perry*

The Reluctant Astronaut
US 1967 101m Technicolor
Universal (Edward J. Montagne)
By a series of accidents a man with vertigo becomes an astronaut.
Feeble vehicle for a comedian briefly popular.
w Jim Fritzell, Everett Greenbaum *d* Edward J. Montagne *ph* Rexford Wimpey *m* Vic Mizzy
☆ Don Knotts, Leslie Nielsen, Joan Freeman, Jesse White, Jeanette Nolan, Arthur O'Connell

The Reluctant Débutante *
US 1958 96m Metrocolor Cinemascope
MGM/Avon (Pandro S. Berman)
A noble couple have difficulty in steering their American-educated daughter through the intricacies of the London season.
A slight but pleasing British comedy has become a rather strident example of lend-lease, but still affords minor pleasures.
w William Douglas Home *play* William Douglas Home *d* Vincente Minnelli *ph* Joseph Ruttenberg *md* Eddie Warner *ad* Jean d'Aubonne
☆ Rex Harrison, Kay Kendall, Sandra Dee, Peter Myers, Angela Lansbury, John Saxon, Diane Clare

The Reluctant Dragon **
US 1941 72m Technicolor
Walt Disney
A tour of the Disney Studios affords some glimpses of how cartoons are made.
*Amiable pot-pourri of cartoon shorts (*Baby Weems, How to Ride a Horse *and the title story) linked by a studio tour of absorbing interest.*
w various *d* Alfred Werker (live action), various
☆ *Robert Benchley*, Frances Gifford, Nana Bryant

Reluctant Heroes *
GB 1951 80m bw
Byron (Henry Halstead)

Comedy of national servicemen and their misdemeanours.
Simple-minded army farce which was popular for years as play and film.
w Colin Morris *play* Colin Morris *d* Jack Raymond *ph* James Wilson
☆ *Brian Rix*, Ronald Shiner, Derek Farr, Christine Norden, Larry Noble

The Reluctant Widow
GB 1950 91m bw
Rank/Two Cities (Gordon Wellesley)
During the Napoleonic wars a governess is co-opted as a spy.
Thin romantic drama which despite nice art direction never really sparks into life.
w Gordon Wellesley, J. B. Boothroyd *novel* Georgette Heyer *d* Bernard Knowles *ph* Jack Hildyard *ad Carmen Dillon*
☆ Jean Kent, Guy Rolfe, Kathleen Byron, Paul Dupuis, Lana Morris, Julian Dallas, Peter Hammond, Andrew Cruickshank

The Remains of the Day **
GB/US 1993 134m Technicolor
Columbia/Merchant Ivory (Ishmail Merchant, Mike Nichols, John Calley)

A butler comes to realize that his lifelong respect for, and loyalty to, his aristocratic master was misplaced.
An artful, nicely composed study in repressed emotions, stiff upper lips and class attitudes; in the final analysis, though, it seems no more than P. G. Wodehouse re-played as tragedy.
w Ruth Prawer Jhabvala *novel* Kazuo Ishiguro *d* James Ivory *ph* Tony Pierce-Roberts *m* Richard Robbins *pd* Luciana Arrighi *ed* Andrew Marcus
☆ *Anthony Hopkins*, Emma Thompson, James Fox, Christopher Reeve, Peter Vaughan, Hugh Grant, Michel Lonsdale, Tim Piggot-Smith, Patrick Godfrey
'Continuously absorbing, but lacks the emotional resonance that would have made it completely satisfying.' – *Variety*
'This luxuriously mounted and often brilliantly engineered adaptation … could well be the producer and director team Merchant Ivory's most comprehensive success. It unquestionably deserves to be.' – *Derek Malcolm, Guardian*
Anthony Hopkins; Emma Thompson; James Ivory; best picture; Ruth Prawer Jhabvala; Richard Robbins; Luciana Arrighi; costume design (Jenny Beavan, John Bright)
Anthony Hopkins

Remains to Be Seen
US 1953 88m bw
MGM (Arthur Hornblow Jnr)
The manager of an apartment house finds a dead body, and before the police arrive someone sticks a knife into it.
Flabby comedy-thriller giving the cast little to work on.
w Sidney Sheldon *play* Howard Lindsay, Russel Crouse *d* Don Weis *ph* Robert Planck *md* Jeff Alexander
☆ June Allyson, Van Johnson, Angela Lansbury, Louis Calhern, John Beal, Dorothy Dandridge

'By thunderation, I'll show America how to get tough!'
The Remarkable Andrew *
US 1942 80m bw
Paramount (Richard Blumenthal)
A young municipal bookkeeper is framed by local politicians but helped by the ghost of Andrew Jackson and friends.
Pleasant, rather faded, whimsical comedy which also managed to be propaganda for the war effort.
w Dalton Trumbo *d* Stuart Heisler *ph* Theodor Sparkuhl *m* Victor Young
☆ William Holden, Ellen Drew, Brian Donlevy, Rod Cameron, Richard Webb, Porter Hall, Frances Gifford, Nydia Westman, Montagu Love
'About all that comes through in the juxtaposition of these lithograph characters over modern Shale City is Franklin's delight over the electric light and Jackson's alarm over the radio.' – *John McManus, PM*

The Remarkable Mr Kipps: see *Kipps*

The Remarkable Mr Pennypacker
US 1958 87m Technicolor Cinemascope
TCF (Charles Brackett)
A Pennsylvania businessman leads two lives with two separate families.
Feeble and obvious period comedy of bigamy; very few laughs.
w Walter Reisch *play* Liam O'Brien *d* Henry Levin *ph* Milton Krasner *m* Leigh Harline
☆ Clifton Webb, Dorothy McGuire, Charles Coburn, Ray Stricklyn, Jill St John, Ron Ely, David Nelson

Rembrandt ****
GB 1936 85m bw
London Films (Alexander Korda)

Episodes in the life of the 17th-century painter.
Austerely comic, gently tragic character piece, superbly staged and photographed, with a great performance at its centre.
w Lajos Biro, June Head, Carl Zuckmayer d Alexander Korda ph Georges Perinal, Richard Angst m Geoffrey Toye
☆ *Charles Laughton*, Elsa Lanchester, Gertrude Lawrence, Edward Chapman, Walter Hudd, Roger Livesey, Herbert Lomas, Allan Jeayes, Sam Livesey, Raymond Huntley, John Clements
'Never exciting, and only partly believable … a feature film without a story plot.' – *Variety*
'Amazingly full of that light which the great master of painting subdued to his supreme purpose.' – *James Agate*
'The film is ruined by lack of story and continuity: it has no drive. Like *The Private Life of Henry the Eighth* it is a series of unrelated tableaux.' – *Graham Greene*

Remember?
US 1939 83m bw
MGM (Milton Bren)
A newly married couple do not get on, so a friend gives them a potion which makes them lose their memories and fall in love all over again.
Silly, witless comedy which did no good for anyone concerned.
w Corey Ford, Norman Z. McLeod *d* Norman Z. McLeod *ph* George Folsey *m* Edward Ward
☆ Robert Taylor, Greer Garson, Lew Ayres, Billie Burke, Reginald Owen, George Barbier, Henry Travers, Richard Carle, Laura Hope Crews, Halliwell Hobbes, Sig Rumann
'Many bright episodes contrast with some bumpy and over-dialogued stretches.' – *Variety*

Remember Last Night? **
US 1936 80m bw
Universal
Socialites with hangovers find that murder was committed during their party.
Ingenious but overlong mixture of styles: farce, Thin Man *comedy, murder mystery, satire, fantasy. Very well worth looking at.*
w Harry Clork, Dan Totheroh, Doris Malloy *novel The Hangover Murders* by Adam Hobhouse *d* James Whale *ph* Joseph Valentine *m* Franz Waxman *ed* Ted J. Kent
☆ Robert Young, Edward Arnold, Arthur Treacher, Constance Cummings, Robert Armstrong, Sally Eilers, Reginald Denny, Ed Brophy, Jack La Rue, Gustav von Seyffertitz, Gregory Ratoff
'It will be hard to sell because it is hard to understand … the basic story can scarcely be followed, while the superficial gloss of phoney sophistication neither fits a narrative in which four murders and two suicides are recorded, nor carries conviction of itself.' – *Variety*
'Parodying the detective thriller in a dazzling cascade of gags, this brilliant divertissement eventually takes off into pure surrealism.' – *Tom Milne, MFB, 1974*

Remember Me?
GB 1997 81m Metrocolor
Film Four/Talisman (Alan Shallcross, Alan Wright)

A suburban couple's life is turned upside down when they are visited by the wife's former boyfriend, a charmer who is being hounded by his creditors.
A limp sitcom that looks and sounds as if it were quick-frozen in the 50s and now partially thawed out.
w Michael Frayn *d* Nick Hurran *ph* David Odd *m* Michael Kamen, Ed Shearmur *pd* Christopher Bradshaw *ed* John Wilson
☆ Robert Lindsay, Rik Mayall, Imelda Staunton, Brenda Blethyn, James Fleet, Haydn Gwynne, Natalie Walker, Tim Matthews
'It's a disaster: a prehistoric burial mound of farcical clichés beyond even this talented cast's power to excavate.' – *Alexander Walker, London Evening Standard*

Remember My Name *
US 1978 94m DeLuxe
Columbia/Lion's Gate (Robert Altman)
After twelve years in prison, a woman takes calm revenge on the man who allowed her to take the blame for his crime.
Basically reminiscent of a Barbara Stanwyck vehicle of the forties, this interesting film is finally too concerned to strike on all levels, including satire, social awareness and fashionable pessimism.
wd Alan Rudolph *ph* Tak Fujimoto *ed* Thomas Walls, William A. Sawyer *songs* Alberta Hunter
☆ Geraldine Chaplin, Anthony Perkins, Moses Gunn, Berry Berenson, Jeff Goldblum

Remember That Face: see *The Mob*

Remember the Day *
US 1941 86m bw
TCF (William Perlberg)
An elderly schoolteacher recollects her past life.
Pleasant sentimental drama, very well mounted.
w Tess Schlesinger, Frank Davis, Allan Scott *play* Philo Higley *d* Henry King *ph* George Barnes *m* Alfred Newman
☆ Claudette Colbert, John Payne, Shepperd Strudwick, Jane Seymour, Anne Revere, Frieda Inescort
'For those who like wghat is popularly known as "a good cry" this hour-and-a-half of undiluted sob-stuff will please.' – *James Agate*

Remember the Night *
US 1940 94m bw
Paramount (Mitchell Leisen)
An assistant district attorney takes a lady shoplifter home with him for Christmas.
Eccentric but winning blend of comedy, romance and drama, deftly mixed by master chefs.
w Preston Sturges d Mitchell Leisen ph Ted Tetzlaff *m* Frederick Hollander
☆ Barbara Stanwyck, Fred MacMurray, Beulah Bondi, Elizabeth Patterson, Sterling Holloway, Paul Guilfoyle, Willard Robertson
'Rarely has such a theme been so smoothly advanced and so pleasantly played out to so sensible and credible a conclusion.' – *New York Times*

'History is written by the winners.'
Remember the Titans
US 2000 113m Technicolor Panavision
Buena Vista/Walt Disney/Technical Black (Jerry Bruckheimer, Chad Oman)

In Virginia in the 1970s, a new black coach makes his racially-integrated high-school football team into champions and eases racial tensions in the community.
Deeply sentimental and shamelessly manipulative drama, based on a true story but so platitudinous in its telling that any feeling for the period or in its truth is soon lost.
w Gregory Allen Howard *d* Boaz Yakin *ph* Philippe Rousselot *m* Trevor Rabin *pd* Deborah Evans *ed* Michael Tronick *cos* Judy Ruskin Howell
☆ Denzel Washington (Herman Boone), Will Patton (Bill Yoast), Donald Faison (Petey Jones), Wood Harris (Julius 'Big Ju' Campbell), Ryan Hurst (Gerry Bertier), Ethan Suplee (Lewis Lastik), Nicole Ari Parker (Carol Boone), Hayden Panettiere (Sheryl Yoast), Kip Pardue (Ronnie 'Sunshine' Bass), Craig Kirkwood (Jerry 'The Rev' Harris), Kate Bosworth (Emma Hoyt)
'An earnest, bombastic feelgood movie in which the issue of racial harmony is treated as rougly being equal in importance to the holy game of football.' – *Peter Bradshaw, Guardian*
'The movie is heartfelt, yes, and I was moved by it, but it plays safe.' – *Roger Ebert*

Remembrance
GB 1982 117m Eastmancolor
Channel 4/Colin Gregg
Young sailors in Plymouth enjoy a last night's leave before a six-month tour of duty with the NATO forces.
A few slices of what in the eyes of film-makers passes for realism these days: boozing, violence and bad language. The film seems to make no point and certainly doesn't entertain, though the components are slickly enough assembled.
w Hugh Stoddart *d* Colin Gregg *ph* John Metcalfe *m* various pop performances *ed* Peter Delfgou
☆ John Altman, Al Ashton, Martin Barrass, Nick Dunning, Sally Jane Jackson, David John, Peter Lee-Wilson, Kenneth Griffith
'A clear and disheartening case of ambition exceeding grasp.' – *Geoff Brown, MFB*

Remo Williams: The Adventure Begins
US 1985 121m DeLuxe
Orion/Dick Clark, Larry Spiegel, Mel Bergman

GB title: *Remo: Unarmed and Dangerous*
A New York cop is recruited by the CIA to learn martial arts which will help him to fight an evil arms manufacturer.
Po-faced and oddly unlikeable, this elaborate adventure movie never really finds a style, and is dislocated by a middle section in which our hero is taught by an elderly Korean.
w Christopher Wood *novels Destroyer series by Richard Sapir, Warren Murphy d* Guy Hamilton *ph* Andrew Laszlo *m* Craig Safan *pd* Jackson de Govia
☆ Fred Ward, Joel Grey, Wilford Brimley, J. A. Preston, Charles Cioffi, Kate Mulgrew, George Coe

Remorques *
France 1941 80m bw
MAIC
US title: *Stormy Waters*
A tugboat captain falls in love with a mysterious woman but remains faithful to his invalid wife.
Effective, minor, romantic melodrama.
w Jacques Prévert, André Cayatte *novel* Roger Vercel *d* Jean Grémillon *ph* Armand Thirard, Louis Née *m* Roland Manuel
☆ Jean Gabin, Michèle Morgan, Madeleine Renaud, Fernand Ledoux

Renaissance Man
US 1994 129m Technicolor
Guild/Cinergi (Sara Colleton, Elliot Abbott, Robert Greenhut)

An out-of-work ad-man is employed to teach some of the army's dimmest recruits and gives them a sense of self-esteem.
Soft-centred comedy that marches along predictable tracks and has little to do with the realities of teaching or army service; as recruiting propaganda, it no doubt serves a purpose.
w Jim Burnstein *d* Penny Marshall *ph* Adam Greenberg *m* Hans Zimmer *pd* Geoffrey Kirkland *ed* George Bowers, Battle Davis
☆ Danny DeVito, Gregory Hines, James Remar, Cliff Robertson, Stacey Dash, Lillo Brancato Jnr, Kadeem Hardison, Richard T. Jones, Mark Wahlberg
'Warm-hearted humanism is glopped all over *Renaissance Man* in the hopes we won't notice that the story makes no sense.' – *Richard Schickel, Time*
† Mark Wahlberg is better known as rapper Marky Mark.

Rendez-Vous **
France 1985 83m colour
Cannon/T Films/A2 (Alain Terzian)

A provincial actress, trying for success in Paris, becomes involved with a self-destructive actor.
Stylish drama of young hopefuls that won the best director award at the Cannes Film Festival in 1985.
w André Téchiné, Olivier Assayas *d* André Téchiné *ph* Renato Berta *m* Philippe Sarde *pd* Jean-Pierre Kohut Svelko *ed* Martine Giordano
☆ Juliette Binoche, Lambert Wilson, Wadeck Stanczak, Jean-Louis Trintignant, Dominique Lavanant

Rendez-vous in Paris *
France 1995 98m colour
Artificial Eye/Mayfair/Compagnie Eric Rohmer/Canal (Françoise Etchegaray)
Three tales of meetings: in the first, a law student discovers that her boyfriend is seeing another woman; in the second, a man tries to persuade a woman to leave her lover for him; in the third, an artist, showing a tourist around Paris, is attracted by a woman in one of the galleries
Three casual accounts of accidental meetings between men and women and the impossibility of successful relationships between them; the stories are deceptively slight, conveying more than at first appears
wd Eric Rohmer *ph* Diane Baratier *ed* Mary Stephen
☆ Clara Beller, Antoine Basler, Mathias Megard, Judith Chancel, Malcolm Conrath
'Far from his greatest, but still has his familiar gracenotes.' – *Sunday Times*

Rendezvous
US 1935 106m bw
MGM (Lawrence Weingarten)
A decoding expert breaks an enemy spy ring.
Agreeable light romantic comedy drama with an espionage plot.
w Bella and Samuel Spewack *novel* *Black Chamber* by Herbert Yardley *d* William K. Howard *ph* William Daniels *m* William Axt
☆ William Powell, Rosalind Russell, Binnie Barnes, Lionel Atwill, Cesar Romero, Samuel S. Hinds, Henry Stephenson, Frank Reicher
'Another chill-and-chuckle play aiming at the *Thin Man* trade and scoring a bull's-eye.' – *Variety*

Rendezvous 24
US 1946 70m bw
TCF (Sol M. Wurtzel)
American secret agents track down post-war Nazis who are working on atomic explosions from a remote base in the Harz mountains.
Routine thick ear despite claims of timeliness; as such, quite tolerable.
w Aubrey Wisberg *d* James Tinling
☆ William Gargan, Maria Palmer, Pat O'Moore, David Leonard, Kurt Katch, Herman Bing

Rendezvous at Midnight
US 1935 60m bw
Universal
A police commissioner investigates the murder of his predecessor.
Modest mystery co-feature which wastes time up front on a fashion show.
w Gladys Unger *play* *The Silver Fox* by Gaetano Sazlo *d* Christy Cabanne
☆ Ralph Bellamy, Valerie Hobson, Catherine Doucet, Irene Ware, Helen Jerome Eddy
'The woeful lack of action drags it down.' – *Variety*

Rendezvous de Juillet **
France 1949 110m bw
UGC-SNEG (René G. Vuattoux)
A group of young people in post-war St Germain-des-Prés plan an expedition to the Congo.
Highly likeable series of impressions of interesting people, a little indeterminate and possibly dated now, but in its time extremely fresh and vital.
wd Jacques Becker *ph* Claude Renoir *m* Jean Wiener, Mezz Mezzrow
☆ Daniel Gelin, Maurice Ronet, Brigitte Auber, Pierre Trabaud, Nicole Courcel

Les Rendezvous du Diable **
France 1958 80m colour
Union Générale Cinématographique/Jacques Constant/Haroun Tazieff
aka: *Volcano*
Adventures of a Belgian volcanologist.
Daring exploits on the rims of the world's most active volcanoes, including Etna and Stromboli in eruption. Fascinating footage is urbanely presented.
m Marius-François Gaillard *wd/ph* *Haroun Tazieff*
'Beauty blends with horror, romantic grandeur with fear.' – *MFB*

Rendezvous with Annie
US 1946 89m bw
Republic
An American soldier in England goes absent without leave to see his wife in New York, an exploit which later nearly loses him a fortune.
An engaging comedy idea filmed with insufficient wit, this gets by on charm.
w Mary Loos, Richard Sale *d* Allan Dwan
☆ Eddie Albert, Faye Marlowe, C. Aubrey Smith

Réne La Canne *
France/Italy 1977 98m Telecolor
Président/Rizzoli (Jacques-Eric Strauss)
During the Second World War a French policeman and a thief defy the Germans; after it, they find themselves in friendly rivalry.
Broad and sometimes blackish farce which amuses mainly by the expert and stylized comedy performances of the two male leads.
w Jacques Rouffio, Francis Girod *novel* Roger Borniche *d* Francis Girod *ph* Aldo Tonti *m* Ennio Morricone *ad* Jean-Jacques Caziot *ed* Eva Zora
☆ Gérard Depardieu, Sylvia Kristel, Michel Piccoli, Stefano Patrizi, Riccardo Garrone, Jacques Jouanneau, Jean Rigaux, Orchidea de Santis, Venantino Venantini, Valerie Mairesse, Jean Carmet

Renegade
Italy 1987 90m colour
Paloma/Cinecitta (Lucio Bompani)
A modern-day itinerant cowboy promises to look after the knowing 14-year-old son of an imprisoned friend.
Comic Western that ambles in an easy-going, unmemorable manner from one mild joke, usually involving a punch-up, to another. Its only novelty is that, instead of the cavalry, Hells Angels ride to the rescue.
w Mark Barboni *d* E. B. Clucher (Enzo Barboni) *ph* Alfio Contini *m* Mauro Paoluzzi *pd* Carlo Simi *ed* Eugene Alabiso
☆ Terence Hill (Mario Girotti), Robert Vaughn, Ross Hill, Norman Bowler, Beatrice Palme, Lisa Ann Rubin, Donal Hodson

Renegade
US 1993 95m Foto-Kem
Cannell Entertainment
An ex-cop turned bounty hunter joins an organization that stages fights to the death in order to discover what happened to his brother, who disappeared 17 years earlier.
Risible action adventure with muscle-bound acting and dialogue, and padded out with some irrelevant scenes of love-making between extras.
w Stephen J. Cannell, Nick Corea *d* Ralph Hemecker, R. Marvin *ph* Kenneth L. Gibb *m* Roger Neill *ad* Michel Levesque *ed* John W. Carr, Skip Robinson
☆ Lorenzo Lamas, Branscombe Richmond, Kathleen Kinmont, Charles Napier, Madison Mason, Stephen J. Cannell, Marjean Holden, Danny Wells, Mitchell Ryan, Martin Kove

Renegade Girls: see *Caged Heat*

Renegades
US 1930 84m bw
Fox
A disgraced French officer becomes a hero of the Foreign Legion.
Satisfying romantic melodrama of its period.
w Jules Furthman *novel* André Armandy *d* Victor Fleming
☆ Warner Baxter, Myrna Loy, Bela Lugosi, Noah Beery, C. Henry Gordon, Gregory Gaye
'Everyone in the picture dies in the last few feet.' – *Variety*

Renegades
US 1946 88m Technicolor
Columbia
An outlaw's son tries in vain to go straight.
Unsurprising but efficient bill-topping Western of its day.
w Melvin Levey, Francis Faragoh *d* George Sherman
☆ Evelyn Keyes, Larry Parks, Willard Parker, Edgar Buchanan

Renegades
US 1989 105m colour
Virgin/Morgan Creek/Interscope Communications (David Madden)
A cop and an Indian team up to recover a stolen sacred lance.
Run-of-the-mill action movie in which nothing memorable occurs.
w David Rich *d* Jack Sholder *ph* Phil Meheux *m* Michael Kamen *pd* Carol Spier *ed* Caroline Biggerstaff
☆ Kiefer Sutherland, Lou Diamond Phillips, Jami Gertz, Rob Knepper, Bill Smitrovich, Peter MacNeill

Reno
US 1939 72m bw
RKO
As Reno becomes a great city for gambling and divorce, a lawyer becomes a gambling hall proprietor.
Mildly interesting romantic drama in a flashback format.
w John Twist, Ellis St Joseph *d* John Farrow
☆ Richard Dix, Gail Patrick, Anita Louise, Paul Cavanagh, Laura Hope Crews, Louis Jean Heydt, Hobart Cavanaugh, Charles Halton
'Capable handling of an interesting story against a colourful background.' – *Variety*

Rent-a-Cop
US 1988 96m colour
Kings Road (Raymond Wagner)
A tough policeman, who loses his job when a drug arrest goes wrong, teams up with a prostitute to track down a vicious killer.
Dull and violent thriller, in which Reynolds's laid-back cop and Minnelli's hyper-active hooker fail to achieve any noticeable rapport.
w Dennis Shryack, Michael Blodgett *d* Jerry London *ph* Giuseppe Rotunno *m* Jerry Goldsmith *pd* Tony Masters *ed* Robert Lawrence
☆ Burt Reynolds, Liza Minnelli, James Remar, Richard Masur, Dionne Warwick, Bernie Casey, Robby Benson, John Stanton

Rentadick
GB 1972 94m Eastmancolor
Rank/Paradine/Virgin (Ned Sherrin)
Incompetent private eyes become involved in the battle for a deadly nerve gas.
Ineffective crazy comedy which never takes shape, preferring to aim barbs of satire in all directions.
w John Wells, John Fortune *d* Jim Clark *ph* John Coquillon *m* Carl Davis
☆ James Booth, Richard Briers, Julie Ege, Donald Sinden

Repeat Performance *
US 1947 93m bw
Eagle Lion/Aubrey Schenck
People in trouble find they can repeat the previous year.
Adequate flashback fantasy, very dated now.
w Walter Bullock *d* Alfred L. Werker *ph* Lew O'Connell *m* George Antheil
☆ Louis Hayward, Joan Leslie, Tom Conway, Richard Basehart, Virginia Field

Repentance ***
USSR 1984 155m colour
Cannon/Sovexportfilm/Gruziafilm
original title: *Pokjaniye, Monanieba*
A woman explains to a court why she keeps exhuming the body of the town's long-serving and much respected mayor.
A bleak and blackly humorous account of a society's complicity in a rule of terror; Abuladze uses dreams and other non-realistic techniques to create a biting allegory of the corruption of a society by Stalinism.
w Nana Djanelidze, Tengiz Abuladze, Rezo Kveselava *d* *Tengiz Abuladze* *ph* Mikhail Agranovich *m* Nana Djanelidze *pd* Georgy Mikeladze *ed* Guliko Omadze
☆ *Avtandil Makharadze*, Ia Ninidze, Merab Ninidze, Zeinab Botsvadze, Ketevan Abuladze, Edisher Giorgobiani, Kakhi Kavsadze, Nino Zakariadze
† The film did not receive a release until 1987. It was the third part of a trilogy that began with *The Plea* (1968) and *The Wishing Tree* (1976).

'Kill Or Be Replaced.'
The Replacement Killers
US 1998 86m Technicolor Panavision
Columbia/WCG (Brad Grey, Bernie Brillstein)
A Chinese hitman, hired by an Asian gangster in New York to kill the young son of a cop, becomes a target himself when he decides that it is one death too many.
A not-too-successful attempt to make an American star out of a Hong Kong one, which is not helped by his rudimentary grasp of English, and action sequences that are less effective than those of his home-grown movies.
w Ken Sanzel *d* Antoine Fuqua *ph* Peter Lyons Collister *m* Harry Gregson-Williams *pd* Naomi Shohan *ed* Jay Cassidy
☆ Chow Yun-Fat, Mira Sorvino, Michael Rooker, Jürgen Prochnow, Kenneth Tsang, Til Schweiger, Danny Trejo
'This mechanical effort is studied rather than heartfelt and will disappoint aficionados and thwart potential fans.' – *Leonard Klady, Variety*

'Pros on strike. Everyday guys get to play.'
The Replacements
US 2000 118m Technicolor
Warner/Bel Air (Dylan Sellers)
When his millionaire American footballers go on strike, their team owner recruits a retired coach to find a team of replacement players.
Lowbrow, slapstick comedy that does not travel well outside the USA.
w Vince McKewin *d* Howard Deutch *ph* Tak Fujimoto *m* John Debney *pd* Dan Bishop *ed* Bud Smith, Seth Flaum *cos* Jill Ohanneson
☆ Keanu Reeves (Shane Falco), Gene Hackman (Jimmy McGinty), Orlando Jones (Clifford Franklin), Jon Favreau (Bateman), Brooke Langton (Annabelle Farrell), Rhys Ifans (Nigel Gruff), Jack Warden (Edward O'Neil), Faizon Love (Jamal), Michael 'Bear' Taliferro (Andre), Ace Yonamine (Fumiko), Troy Winbush (Walter Cochran), Keith David (Lindell)
'Most of the smooth moves come from a well-thumbed playbook, and no key player bothers to go outside the lines while tackling his stereotypical role.' – *Joe Leydon, Variety*

Repo Man *
US 1984 92m DeLuxe
Universal/Edge City (Peter McCarthy, Jonathan Wacks)
A repossessor of cars finds himself on the run from all manner of dangers.
Nightmarish film noir with nods to many predecessors and some elements of black fantasy.
wd Alex Cox *ph* Robby Müller *m* Tito Larriva, Steven Hufsteter
☆ Harry Dean Stanton, Emilio Estevez, Tracey Walter, Olivia Barash, Sy Richardson, Susan Barnes
'The saltiest, sweetest, most sublimely sleazy tickle in the Los Angeles ribs. If it doesn't convulse you with belly laughs, then you're a stiff.' – *Carrie Rickey, Boston Herald*

Report from the Aleutians **
US 1943 45m colour
US Signal Corps
American forces live under tough conditions on a group of Arctic islands from which they raid Japanese bases.
Simple and somewhat overlong, but still one of the better US documentaries to come out of World War II.
wd and narrated by John Huston; additional narration by Walter Huston

Report to the Commissioner
US 1974 112m Metrocolor
UA/M. J. Frankovich
GB title: *Operation Undercover*
A policeman's son follows in father's footsteps but finds life around Times Square dismaying.
Realistic, concerned crime melodrama with nothing very new to say.
w Abby Mann, Ernest Tidyman *novel* James Mills *d* Milton Katselas *ph* Mario Tosi *m* Elmer Bernstein
☆ Michael Moriarty, Yaphet Kotto, Susan Blakely, Hector Elizondo, Tony King, Michael McGuire

'A clear also-ran in the police thriller stakes.' – *Verina Glaessner*

'A bit too full of sweat and frenzy.' – *Michael Billington, Illustrated London News*

Repossessed
US 1990 84m CFI color
Guild/First Class films (Steve Wizan)

Attempting an exorcism on television, a priest struggles to control a demon intent on possessing the entire viewing audience.
Raucous parody of The Exorcist, *crammed with jokes, most of them juvenile.*
wd Bob Logan *ph* Michael D. Margulies
m Charles Fox *pd* Shay Austin *ed* Jeff Freeman
☆ Linda Blair, Ned Beatty, Leslie Nielsen, Anthony Starke, Thom J. Sharp, Lana Schwab

'Clunking, but the jokes are just about numerous enough to stifle the groans.' – *Sight and Sound*

Reprieve: see *Convicts Four*

The Reptile *
GB 1966 90m Technicolor
Warner-Pathé/Hammer (Anthony Nelson-Keys)

A Cornish village is terrified by several mysterious and unpleasant deaths; it turns out that the daughter of the local doctor, victim of a Malayan sect, periodically turns into a deadly snake.
Silly horror story most effectively filmed as a mixture of chills, detection and good characterization.
w John Elder d John Gilling ph Arthur Grant
m Don Banks *pd* Bernard Robinson *ed* James Needs, Roy Hyde
☆ Noel Willman, Jennifer Daniel, Ray Barrett, Jacqueline Pearce, Michael Ripper, John Laurie, Marne Maitland

Repulsion **
GB 1965 105m bw
Compton/Tekli (Gene Gutowski)

A Belgian manicurist in London is driven by pressures into neurotic withdrawal; terrified above all by sex, she locks herself up in her gloomy flat and murders her boyfriend and landlord when they try to approach her.
Weird, unmotivated but undeniably effective Grand Guignol in the form of a case history; little dialogue, which is just as well as the director at that time clearly had no ear for the language.
w Roman Polanski, Gerard Brach *d Roman Polanski ph Gilbert Taylor m* Chico Hamilton
☆ *Catherine Deneuve*, Ian Hendry, John Fraser, Patrick Wymark, Yvonne Furneaux

'An unashamedly ugly film, but as a lynx-eyed view of a crumbling mind it is a masterpiece of the macabre.' – *Daily Mail*

Reputation: see *Lady with a Past*

Requiem for a Dream **
US 2000 102m DeLuxe
Artisan/Thousand Words (Eric Watson, Palmer West)

Like her ineffectual, junkie son, a Coney Island mother becomes hooked on drugs.
Grim, unrelenting drama of desolation and despair, in which the energy comes from a visual style that effectively mimics the disjointed and distorted effects of drug-taking.
w Hubert Selby Jnr, Darren Aronofsky
novel Hubert Selby Jnr *d* Darren Aronofsky
ph Matthew Libatique *m* Clint Mansell (string quartets performed by Kronos Quartet) *pd* James Chinlund *ed* Jay Rabinowitz *cos* Laura Jean Shannon
☆ Ellen Burstyn (Sara Goldfarb), Jared Leto (Harry Goldfarb), Jennifer Connelly (Marion Silver), Marlon Wayans (Tyrone C. Love), Christopher McDonald (Tappy Tibbons), Louise Lasser (Ada), Keith David (Little John), Sean Gullette (Arnold the Shrink)

'It's technically striking filmmaking, to be sure, but what it's presenting is nothing that many people will want to look at.' – *Todd McCarthy, Variety*

'A bleak tour de force of technique.' – *Adam Mars-Jones, Times*

Ellen Burstyn

Requiem for a Heavyweight *
US 1962 87m bw
Columbia (David Susskind)
GB title: *Blood Money*
The last bouts of a prizefighter who will not realize his career is over.
Tough, effective melodrama, extremely well acted.
w Rod Serling TV play Rod Serling *d Ralph Nelson ph Arthur J. Ornitz m* Laurence Rosenthal
☆ Anthony Quinn, *Jackie Gleason, Mickey Rooney*, Julie Harris, Stan Adams, Madame Spivy, Jack Dempsey, Cassius Clay

Requiem for a Vampire (dubbed)
France 1971 95m colour
Les Films A.B.C. (Jean Rollin)

original title: *Requiem pour un Vampire*
aka: *Virgins and Vampires*
Two young gun-toting girls on the run from killers take refuge in a ruined chateau where vampires live.
Stylish, dreamlike fantasy, with little dialogue, intermingled with scenes of sex and sadism that have no connection to the main narrative; the music is unpleasantly obtrusive.
wd Jean Rollin *ph* Renan Polles *m* Pierre Raph *ed* Michel Patient
☆ Marie-Pierre Castel, Mireille D'Argent, Philippe Gasté, Dominique, Louise Dhour, Paul Bisciglia

'You will get more out of this if you abandon all foolish misconceptions of discovering a coherent plotline and any form of characterisation. Rollin makes these things up as he goes along and to enjoy them you have to get into the same "anything goes" spirit. I always find a stiff drink helps fortify the critical faculties.' – *The Dark Side*

† The British video release runs for 78m.

Requiem for Dominic: see *Requiem für Dominic*

Requiem für Dominic **
Austria 1990 90m
Terra Film/OFF/ORF (Norbert Blecha)

aka: *Requiem for Dominic*
An exiled Romanian scientist returns to his home town of Timisoara to investigate the death of a friend accused of mass murder.
Based on a true story and filmed where the events happened, the documentary style thriller achieves a horrific truth by incorporating actual footage of the accused man as he lay dying.
w Michael Kohlmeier, Felix Mitterer *d* Robert Dorhelm *ph* Hans Selikovsky *m* Harald Kloser *ed* Ingrid Koller
☆ Felix Mitterer, Viktoria Schubert, August Schmolzer, Angelica Schutz, Antonia Rados, Nikolas Vogel, Georg Hoffman-Ostenhorf, Werner Prinz, Georg Metzenrad

'The most remarkable political thriller since Z ... nail-biting cinema' – *Variety*

Requiescant: see *Kill and Pray*

La Resa dei Conti: see *The Big Gundown*

The Rescue
US 1988 98m colour
Touchstone/Silver Screen Partners III (Laura Ziskin)

A group of American teenagers in South Korea set out to rescue their fathers, imprisoned in North Korea as spies.
Ludicrous film, of a quite stupifying banality, which even its intended audience of gung-ho 13-year-olds are likely to treat with the derision it deserves.
w Jim Thomas, John Thomas *d* Ferdinand Fairfax *ph* Russell Boyd *m* Bruce Broughton *pd* Maurice Cain *ed* David Holden, Carroll Timothy O'Meara
☆ Kevin Dillon, Christine Harnos, Marc Price, Ned Vaughn, Ian Giatti, Charles Haid, Edward Albert, Mel Wong

The Rescuers *
US 1977 77m Technicolor
Walt Disney (Ron Miller)

The Mouse Rescue Aid Society volunteers to bring back a girl lost in a swamp.
Feature-length cartoon which, while by no means as bad as some of Disney's very routine seventies product, still seems light years away from his classics of the thirties.
w Larry Clemmons, Ken Anderson
stories Margery Sharp *d* Wolfgang Reitherman, John Lounsbery, Art Stevens *m* Artie Butler
☆ Featuring the voices of Bob Newhart, Eva Gabor, Geraldine Page, Joe Flynn, Jim Jordan, John McIntire

'The people who really need rescuing are the Disney animators and cameramen.' – *Time Out*

'It's no *Snow White* but there are long moments when its inventiveness and skill are entirely captivating. I have only this one lingering doubt: if you are going to put this amount of effort into a movie shouldn't you have more at the end than a snappy collection of 330,000 drawings and a bill for six million dollars?' – *Barry Took, Punch*

song 'Someone's Waiting for You' (*m* Sammy Fain, *ly* Carol Conners, Ayn Robbins)

The Rescuers Down Under **
US 1990 77m Technicolor
Warner/Walt Disney/Silver Screen Partners IV (Thomas Schumacher)

The mouse Rescue Aid Society goes to help a trapped eagle and a boy in Australia.
Slick, lively and enjoyable animated feature, an improvement on the original.
w Jim Cox, Karey Kirkpatrick, Byron Simpson, Joe Ranft *d* Hendel Butoy, Mike Gabriel *m* Bruce Broughton *ad* Maurice Hunt *ed* Michael Kelly, Mark Hester
☆ Featuring the voices of Bob Newhart, Eva Gabor, John Candy, Tristan Rogers, Adam Ryen, George C. Scott, Wayne Robson, Douglas Seale, Frank Walker, Peter Firth, Billy Barty

'Comes on like an Indiana Jones movie which has been reconceived as animation and then proceeded to push back that medium's technical boundaries.' – *Sight and Sound*

Reserved for Ladies: see *Service for Ladies*

'Let's go to work.'
Reservoir Dogs ***
US 1991 99m colour
Rank/Live America/Dog Eat Dog (Lawrence Bender)

While one of their number bleeds to death after a bungled robbery, the rest of the gang, hiding out in a warehouse, try to discover what went wrong.
Brilliant, if sometimes repellent, gangster movie; notably violent, it is also a tense and exciting examination of male egos on a collision course.
wd Quentin Tarantino ph Andrzej Sekula
pd David Wasco *ed* Sally Menks
☆ *Harvey Keitel*, Tim Roth, Michael Madsen, Chris Penn, Steve Buscemi, Lawrence Tierney, Randy Brooks, Kirk Baltz, Eddie Bunker, Quentin Tarantino

'An astute mix of wit and cynicism which washes down its melodramatic excesses with sly satire on the blood-and-guts elements of the crime movie, this is a film of considerable acuity and power.' – *Kim Newman, Sight and Sound*

'Undeniably juicy, with its salty talk and gunplay, film is nihilistic but not resonantly so, giving it no meaning outside the immediate story and characters. Pic is impressive, but impossible to love.' – *Variety*

'No one should go to see *Reservoir Dogs* without prior thought. But what they will see is a riveting treatment on the theme of betrayal set in an urban wasteland that murders hope and makes redemption virtually impossible.' – *Derek Malcolm, Guardian*

† Quentin Tarantino has acknowledged that the film was influenced by Hong Kong director Ringo Lam's *City on Fire*, as well as by Stanley Kubrick's *The Killing* and Joseph Sargent's *The Taking of Pelham 123*.

'A secret experiment. A deadly virus. A fatal mistake.'
Resident Evil
GB/Germany/France 2002 100m colour
Pathé/Screen Gems/Constantin/New Legacy/Davis/Impact (Bernd Eichinger, Samuel Hadida, Jeremy Bolt, Paul W. S. Anderson)

A virus turns workers in a vast, underground laboratory into flesh-eating zombies.
Frenetic, frantic, mindless action movie that offers much less enjoyment than the computer game on which it is based.
wd Paul W. S. Anderson *ph* David Johnson
m Marco Beltrami, Marilyn Manson *pd* Richard Bridgland *ed* Alexander Berner
☆ Milla Jovovich (Alice), Michelle Rodriguez (Rain), Eric Mabius (Matt), James Purefoy (Spence), Colin Salmon (One), Martin Crewes (Kaplan), Michaela Dicker (Red Queen)

'The movie has a frantic staccato style that is more game-oriented than cinematic. The action begins immediately, and there's no letup from the pounding barrage.' – *Stephen Holden, New York Times*

Restless: see *The Beloved*

'Torn from the blazing pages of Texas history!'
The Restless Breed
US 1957 81m Eastmancolor by Pathé
National Pictures (Edward L. Alperson)

The son of a secret service agent arrives in a frontier town to avenge his father's death.
Standard star Western full of expected elements.
w Steve Fisher *d* Allan Dwan *ph* John Boyle
m Edward L. Alperson Jnr
☆ Scott Brady, Anne Bancroft, Jay C. Flippen, Jim Davis, Rhys Williams

Restless Natives
GB 1985 89m Technicolor
Thorn EMI/Oxford Film Company (Rick Stevenson)

Two young idlers set up as modern highwaymen, robbing American visitors on coach tours; to their surprise, they become a tourist attraction.
Irritatingly patchy and amoral comedy which wastes a potentially interesting idea.
w Ninian Dunnett *d* Michael Hoffman
ph Oliver Stapleton *m* Stuart Adamson
pd Adrienne Atkinson *ed* Sean Barton
☆ Vincent Friell, Joe Mullaney, Teri Lally, Ned Beatty, Robert Urquhart

The Restless Years
US 1959 86m bw Cinemascope
Universal-International
A small-town dressmaker tries to prevent her daughter from discovering that she is illegitimate.
Antediluvian sudser with second-string talent.
w Edward Anhalt *play Teach Me How to Cry* by Patricia Joudry *d* Helmut Kautner
☆ John Saxon, Sandra Dee, Margaret Lindsay, Luana Patten, Virginia Grey

Restoration *
US 1996 118m colour
Buena Vista/Segue/Avenue/Oxford Film Company (Cary Brokaw, Andy Paterson, Sarah Ryan Black)

A young doctor falls out of favour with Charles II when he agrees to an unconsummated marriage with one of the king's mistresses but then desires her.
A sumptuous costume drama of one man's redemption, set against the excesses of the 1660s and such events as the Plague and the Great Fire of London. Underlying it, though, is a puritanical dislike of sex. (And, in reality, Charles II was happy to share his many mistresses with all-comers.)
w Rupert Walters *novel* Rose Tremain *d* Michael Hoffman *ph* Oliver Stapleton *m* James Newton Howard *pd Eugenio Zanetti ed* Garth Craven
☆ Robert Downey Jnr, Sam Neill, David Thewlis, Polly Walker, Meg Ryan, Ian McKellen, Hugh Grant, Ian McDiarmid, Mary Macleod

Eugenio Zanetti; costume design (James Acheson)

Resurrected *
GB 1989 92m colour
Hobo/St Pancras Films/Film Four International/British Screen (Tara Prem, Adrian Hughes)
A soldier believed killed in the Falklands War turns up alive after the fighting is over and is accused of being a deserter.
Effective and dramatic examination of patriotism and the aftermath of battle.
w Martin Allen *d* Paul Greengrass *ph* Ivan Strasburg *m* John Keane *pd* Chris Burke *ed* Dan Rae
☆ David Thewlis, Tom Bell, Rita Tushingham, Michael Pollitt, Rudi Davies, William Hoyland, Ewan Stewart, Christopher Fulford, David Lonsdale

Resurrection
US 1931 81m bw
Universal
In 1870s Russia, a peasant girl is seduced by a prince and bears his child.
Unremarkable version of a much-filmed melodrama.
w Finis Fox *novel* Leo Tolstoy *d* Edwin Carewe *ph* Robert B. Kurrle, Al Green *m* Dimitri Tiomkin
☆ Lupe Velez, John Boles, Nance O'Neil, William Keighley, Rose Tapley
† See also: *We Live Again.*

Resurrection
US 1980 103m Technicolor
Universal (Renee Missel, Howard Rosenman)
A woman who has escaped death in a car crash finds herself miraculously able to heal others.
Curious modern parable with nowhere to go; even religious reactionaries may find it rather boring.
w Lewis John Carlino *d* Daniel Petrie *ph* Mario Tosi *m* Maurice Jarre
☆ Ellen Burstyn, Sam Shepard, Richard Farnsworth, Eva LeGallienne, Roberts Blossom, Clifford David
Ellen Burstyn; Eva LeGallienne (supporting actress)

'Be afraid. For he is coming.'
Resurrection
US 1999 108m DeLuxe
Interlight/Baldwin/Cohen/Resurrection (Howard Baldwin, Christopher Lambert, Patrick Choi, Nile Niami)
A Chicago detective goes after a serial killer who is removing body parts from his victims in order to reconstruct the body of Christ in time for Easter.
Slickly-made, gruesome thriller that recycles familiar elements – a maverick cop traumatised by a private grief, a clever, obsessional killer given to macabre rituals – as it languishes in the shadow of Seven.
w Brad Mirman *d* Russell Mulcahy *ph* Jonathan Freeman *m* James McGrath *pd* Tim Boyd *ed* Gordon McClellan
☆ Christopher Lambert (John Prudhomme), Barbara Tyson (Sara Prudhomme), Rick Fox (Scholfield), Leland Orser (Det. Andrew Hollinsworth), David Cronenberg (Father Rousell), Jonathan Potts (Det. Moltz), Peter Macneill (Captain Whippley), Philip Williams (Rousch)

'Get right to the source of the fear.'
Resurrection Man *
GB 1998 102m Rank Colour
Polygram/Revolution (Andrew Eaton)
In Belfast in the mid-70s, a psychopath leads a gang of Loyalists on a Catholic killing spree.
Grim and bloody portrait of a born killer who is as much influenced by James Cagney's gangster antics as by any political convictions; the film, too, is shackled by movie conventions.
w Eoin McNamee *novel* Eoin McNamee *d* Marc Evans *ph* Pierre Aim *m* David Holmes, Gary Burns, Keith Tenniswood *pd* Mark Tildesley *ed* John Wilson
☆ Stuart Townsend, Geraldine O'Rawe, James Nesbitt, Brenda Fricker, John Hannah, James Ellis, Sean McGinley, Derek Thompson, Zara Turner, B. J. Hogg
'The film leaves you with a feeling of having been on an occasionally unguided tour of an abattoir.' – *Richard Falcon, Sight and Sound*

Le Retour de Martin Guerre: see *The Return of Martin Guerre*

Le Retour du Grand Blond: see *Return of the Tall Blond*

Retreat, Hell!
US 1952 95m bw
(Warner) United States (Milton Sperling)
Adventures of a Marine unit in the Korean War.
Standard war film.
w Milton Sperling, Ted Sherdeman *d* Joseph H. Lewis *ph* Warren Lynch *m* William Lava
☆ Frank Lovejoy, Richard Carlson, Anita Louise, Russ Tamblyn

Retribution
US 1988 108m colour
Medusa/Unicorn/Renegade (Guy Magar)
A shy artist is possessed by the vengeful spirit of a murderer.
Gory, predictable and fussily frenetic horror movie.
w Guy Magar, Lee Wasserman *d* Guy Magar *ph* Gary Thieltges *m* Alan Howarth *pd* Robb Wilson King *ed* Guy Magar
☆ Dennis Lipscomb, Leslie Wing, Suzanne Snyder, Jeff Pomerantz, George Murdock, Pamela Dunlap, Susan Peretz

Return from the Ashes *
GB 1965 104m bw Panavision
UA/Mirisch (J. Lee-Thompson)
A woman returns from Dachau to find that her husband is living with her step-daughter and that they plan to murder her.
Broken-backed thriller melodrama, the first half of which is quite irrelevant to the second. The whole is modestly inventive for those who don't mind a mixture of Enoch Arden, Psycho *and* Dial M for Murder *with a touch of the concentration camps and a background of post-war misery.*
w Julius J. Epstein *novel* Hubert Monteilhet *d* J. Lee-Thompson *ph* Christopher Challis *m* Johnny Dankworth
☆ *Ingrid Thulin*, Maximilian Schell, Samantha Eggar, Herbert Lom

Return from the River Kwai
GB 1988 101m colour
Rank/Screenlife Establishment (Kurt Unger)
An American pilot teams up with a British officer to try to prevent the Japanese taking prisoners of war back to Japan.
Rambling adventure movie that has no connection, other than its title, with The Bridge on the River Kwai.
w Sargon Tamini, Paul Mayersberg *book* Joan Blair, Clay Blair Jnr *d* Andrew V. McLaglen *ph* Arthur Wooster *m* Lalo Schifrin *pd* Michael Stringer *ed* Alan Strachan
☆ Edward Fox, Denholm Elliott, Christopher Penn, Tatsuya Nakadai, George Takei, Nick Tate, Timothy Bottoms, Michael Dante, Richard Graham

Return from Witch Mountain
US 1978 93m Technicolor
Walt Disney (Ron Miller, Jerome Courtland)
A brother and sister from outer space come back to Earth for a vacation and are used by crooks for their own purposes.
Acceptable sequel to Escape from Witch Mountain, *with improved special effects.*
w Malcolm Marmorstein *d* John Hough *ph* Frank Phillips *m* Lalo Schifrin *sp* Eustace Lycett, Art Cruickshank, Danny Lee
☆ Bette Davis, Christopher Lee, Ike Eisenmann, Kim Richards, Jack Soo

Return Home
Australia 1989 90m colour
Musical Films/Film Victoria/Australian Film Commission (Cristina Pozzan)
Unhappy with his life, a successful insurance broker returns to his home town to visit his brother who runs a garage.
Amiable domestic drama that comes to few conclusions slowly.
wd Ray Argall *ph* Mandy Walker *ad* Kerith Holmes *ed* Ken Sallows
☆ Dennis Coard, Frankie J. Holden, Ben Mendelsohn, Micki Camilleri

The Return of a Man Called Horse *
US 1976 125m DeLuxe Panavision
UA/Sandy Howard/Richard Harris
The English nobleman of *A Man Called Horse* goes back to the West to save his adopted Indian tribe from extinction.
Another 'realistic' action adventure with torture highlights; nicely made, but not for the squeamish.
w Jack de Witt *d* Irvin Kershner *ph* Owen Roizman *m* Laurence Rosenthal
☆ Richard Harris, Gale Sondergaard, Geoffrey Lewis, Bill Lucking, Jorge Luke
'Maintains a tidy balance between nausea and boredom.' – *Judith Crist*
† At 17 minutes, this pre-title sequence must be the longest so far.

Return of a Stranger
GB 1937 69m bw
Sun/Premier
US title: *The Face Behind the Scar*
A chemist's elopement with his boss's daughter runs into problems when he is accused of murder.
Stilted melodrama, both in performance and direction; too often it suggests a view from the stalls of a provincial repertory theatre.
w Reginald Long, Akos Tolnay *play* Rudolf Lothar *d* Victor Hanbury *ph* James Wilson *m* Jack Beaver *ad* Jack Hallward, Philip Balcombe *ed* Ralph Thomas
☆ Ellis Jeffreys, Athole Stewart, Cecil Ramage, Griffith Jones, Rosalyn Boulter, Sylvia Marriot, James Harcourt, Tarver Penna

The Return of Bulldog Drummond
GB 1934 71m bw
BIP
Drummond forms a society to oust crooked foreigners from Britain.
Thin Drummond exploit with traces of the original Fascism.
wd Walter Summers *novel The Black Gang* by 'Sapper' *ph* Jack Parker *ad* John Mead
☆ Ralph Richardson, Ann Todd, Francis L. Sullivan, Claud Allister, Joyce Kennedy, Pat Aherne

The Return of Captain Invincible
Australia 1982 91m Eastmancolor Panavision
Seven Keys/Willarra
An American superhero is discovered in the back streets of Sydney, a down-and-out drunk; but his skills are needed for the fight against Mr Midnight.
Occasionally agreeable spoof which for most of its length is too frantic.
w Steven E. de Souza, Andrew Gaty *d* Philippe Mora
☆ Alan Arkin, Christopher Lee, Kate Fitzpatrick, Bill Hunter, Michael Pate, John Bluthal

The Return of Count Yorga
US 1971 97m Movielab
AIP/Peppertree (Michael Macready)
Count Yorga falls in love with an orphan while killing most of the orphanage's other inhabitants.
A second instalment that is as amateurish as the first, though also suffering from the belief that a great deal of screaming is automatically scary; its tempo remains so somnambulistic that it is closer to a zombie movie than a conventional tale of vampires.
w Bob Kelljan, Yvonne Wilder *d* Bob Kelljan *ph* Bill Butler *m* Bill Marx *ed* Fabien Tordjmann, Laurette Odney
☆ Robert Quarry, Mariette Hartley, Roger Perry, Yvonne Wilder, Tom Toner, Rudy DeLuca, Philip Frame, George Macready, Walter Brooke

The Return of Dr X *
US 1939 62m bw
Warner (Bryan Foy)
A modern vampire terrorizes the city.
Minor thriller which doesn't get going till the last reel; only notable for Bogart's appearance as the monster. Nothing to do with Dr X.
w Lee Katz *novel The Doctor's Secret* by William J. Makin *d* Vincent Sherman *ph* Sid Hickox *m* Bernhard Kaun
☆ Dennis Morgan, Rosemary Lane, Wayne Morris, Humphrey Bogart, Olin Howland, John Litel

The Return of Dracula *
US 1958 77m bw
UA/Gramercy (Jules V. Levy, Arthur Gardner)
GB title: *The Fantastic Disappearing Man*
A European vampire makes his way to an American small town in the guise of a refugee Iron Curtain painter.
Quite nicely made low-budget horror film with a good balance of the supernatural and the ordinary.
w Pat Fielder *d Paul Landres ph* Jack MacKenzie *m* Gerald Fried
☆ *Francis Lederer*, Norma Eberhardt, Ray Stricklyn, Jimmy Baird, John Wengraf

The Return of Frank James *
US 1940 92m Technicolor
TCF (Darryl F. Zanuck)
A sequel to *Jesse James* (qv).
Moody, nicely photographed Western in which Jesse's brother avenges his murder.
w Sam Hellman *d Fritz Lang ph* George Barnes, William V. Skall *m* David Buttolph
☆ Henry Fonda, Gene Tierney, Jackie Cooper, Henry Hull, John Carradine, J. Edward Bromberg, Donald Meek, Eddie Collins, George Barbier
'I doubt if any character was ever as lily white as that of Frank James here, but that is a present from the Hays Office to you, and anyway the part is played by Henry Fonda. Durn if I don't like that boy.' – *Otis Ferguson*

The Return of Martin Guerre *
France 1982 123m Fujicolour
Palace/Marcel Dassault/SFP
original title: *Le Retour de Martin Guerre*
In the 16th century, a man comes to a French village claiming to be the one who left his wife and child eight years before. Complaints are laid that he is an impostor ...
Mildly intriguing story which falls apart because one is never sure where the film's sympathies lie.
w Jean-Claude Carrière, Daniel Vigne *d* Daniel Vigne *ph* André Neau *m* Michel Portal *ad* Alain Negre *ed* Denise de Casabianca
☆ Gérard Depardieu, Nathalie Baye, Sylvie Meda, Maurice Barrier
'By far the most enigmatic film seen in London this year.' – *Sunday Times*
'A plodding, confusing narrative that neither does proper justice to the story nor really teases out the complex historical, moral and psychological issues which it raises.' – *Observer*

The Return of Monte Cristo *
US 1946 92m bw
Columbia/Edward Small-Grant Whytock
GB title: *Monte Cristo's Revenge*
The grandson of the original count is framed and sent to Devil's Island, but escapes.
Very tolerable action romp of its time, with a fair troupe of actors enjoying themselves.
w George Bruce, Alfred Neumann, Kurt Siodmak *d* Henry Levin *ph* Charles Lawton Jnr *m* Lucien Moraweck
☆ Louis Hayward, Barbara Britton, George Macready, Una O'Connor, Henry Stephenson, Steve Geray, Ray Collins, Ludwig Donath, Ivan Triesault

The Return of October
US 1948 89m Technicolor
Columbia
GB title: *A Date with Destiny*
A girl's inheritance is contested on the grounds that she thinks a horse is the reincarnation of her Uncle Willie.
Thin whimsy which leaves its stars with egg on their faces.
w Norman Panama, Melvin Frank *d* Joseph H. Lewis *ph* William Snyder *m* George Duning
☆ Glenn Ford, Terry Moore, Dame May Whitty, James Gleason, Albert Sharpe

The Return of Peter Grimm
US 1935 82m bw
RKO
A strong-minded family man returns as a ghost to see how his family is getting on without him.
Fairly satisfying fantasy with good performances.
w Francis Edward Faragoh *play* David Belasco *d* George Nicholls Jnr
☆ Lionel Barrymore, Helen Mack, Edward Ellis, Donald Meek
'Sombre fantasy ... pretty dull and boresome.' – *Variety*
† Previously filmed in 1926 with Alec B. Francis and Janet Gaynor.

The Return of Ringo (dubbed) **
Italy/Spain 1965 96m Eastmancolor
Golden Era/Mediterranee/Rizzoli/Balcàzar (Alberto Pugliese, Luciano Ercoli)
original title: *Il Ritorno di Ringo*
Returning home after the Civil War, a man discovers that the town, including his family and home, have been taken over by a Mexican bandit.
Superior spaghetti Western that allows room for character development among the usual baroque touches.
w Duccio Tessari, Fernando Di Leo *d* Duccio Tessari *ph* Francisco Marin *m* Ennio Morricone *ad* Juan Alberto Soler *ed* Lucia Quaglia
☆ Giuliano Gemma, Fernando Sancho, Hally Hammond (Lorella de Luca), Nieves Navarro, Antonio Casas, Pajarito, Jorge Martin
† The movie was a sequel to *A Pistol for Ringo* (qv).

Return of Sabata (dubbed)
Italy/France/West Germany 1971 88m Technicolor Techniscope
UA/PEA/Artistes Associés/Artemis (Alberto Grimaldi)
original title: *E Tornato Sabata ... Hai Chiuso un'Altra Volta*
The gunfighter Sabata is double-crossed by an old friend in his search for gold but emerges victorious as usual.
Almost a repeat of the original film, except that it now lacks the element of surprise and has little else to offer.
w Renato Izzo, Gianfranco Parolini *d* Frank Kramer (aka Gianfranco Parolini) *ph* Sandro Mancori *m* Marcello Giombini *ad* Luciano Puccini *ed* Gianfranco Parolini, Salvatore Aventario
☆ Lee Van Cleef (Sabata), Reiner Schöne (Clyde), Annabella Incontrera (Maggie), Gianni Rizzo (Jeremy Sweeney), Gianpiero Albertini (McIntock), Pedro Sanchez (aka Ignazio Spalla) (Bronco), Nick Jordan (aka Aldo Canti) (Angel), Jacqueline Alexandre (Jackie)
'Fairly run-of-the-mill Spaghetti Western, with the usual quota of menacing close-ups and modish camera angles.' – *Alistair Whyte, MFB*
† The film was a sequel to *Sabata* (qv). It was originally released in Italy at 107m.

Return of Superfly
US 1990 95m colour
Crash Pictures (Sig Shore, Anthony Wisdom)
A former drug-dealer decides to destroy his old gang.
Dull and violent sequel that hits a new low.
w Anthony Wisdom *d* Sig Shore *ph* Anghel Decca *m* Curtis Mayfield *pd* Jeremie Frank *ed* John Mullen
☆ Nathan Purdee, Margaret Avery, Leonard Thomas, Christopher Curry
'Shore brings no style or humor to a routine portrayal of New York's drug underground.' – *Variety*

Return of the Ape Man: see *The Ape Man*

The Return of the Bad Men
US 1948 90m bw
RKO (Nat Holt)
A farmer tries to reform the female leader of a terrorist outlaw gang, but she is killed in a bank raid.
Standard, well-shot Western which contrives to introduce a number of well-known historical bandits.
w Charles O'Neal, Jack Natteford, Luci Ward *d* Ray Enright *ph* J. Roy Hunt *m* Roy Webb *md* Constantin Bakaleinikoff
☆ Randolph Scott, Robert Ryan, Anne Jeffreys, Jacqueline White, Steve Brodie

'Riding to greater glory as the gay O. Henry hero!'
The Return of the Cisco Kid
US 1939 70m bw
TCF (Kenneth MacGowan)
The Kid escapes a Mexican firing squad into Arizona and defeats swindlers.
Modest Western with plenty of zip.
w Milton Sperling *d* Herbert I. Leeds
☆ Warner Baxter, Lynn Bari, Cesar Romero, Henry Hull, Kane Richmond, C. Henry Gordon, Robert Barrat
'Substantial fare for adventure audiences.' – *Variety*

The Return of the Corsican Brothers: see *Bandits of Corsica*

Return of the Dragon: see *The Way of the Dragon*

The Return of The Evil Dead
Spain 1973 91m Eastmancolor
London International/Ancla Century (Roman Plana)
original title: *El Ataque de los Muertos sin Ojos*
Devil-worshipping Knights Templar, blinded and killed by villagers in the Middle Ages, rise from their graves to slaughter the locals and a visiting American.
Gruesome but dull horror movie, one of a series featuring the dead Knights.
wd Amando de Ossorio *ph* Miguel F. Mila *m* Tony Abril *ed* Joseph Anthony
☆ Tony Kendal, Fernando Sancha, Esther Rey, Lone Fleming, Frank Blake

'Blood-Curdling Giant Fly-Creature Runs Amok!'
'Scream At The Human Terror Created By Atoms Gone Wild!'
'Scream At Ghastly Fly Monster As He Keeps A Love Tryst!'
'Scream At The Desperate Search For The Fly With A Heart Of A Man!'
Return of the Fly
US 1959 80m bw
TCF (Bernard Glasser)
The son of the original fly man meets the same fate as his father.
Cheerless follow-up.
wd Edward Bernds *ph* Brydon Baker *m* Paul Sawtell, Bert Shefter
☆ Vincent Price, Brett Halsey, John Sutton, David Frankham, Dan Seymour

Return of the Jedi *
US 1983 132m DeLuxe Panavision
TCF/Lucasfilm (Howard Kazanjian)
aka: *Star Wars: Episode VI – Return of the Jedi*
'Episode 6' of the *Star Wars* serial: our heroes combat Darth Vader and Jabba the Hutt.
More expensive fantasy for the world's children of all ages, especially the undemanding ones.
w Lawrence Kasdan, George Lucas *d* Richard Marquand *ph* Alan Hume *m* John Williams *pd* Norman Reynolds
☆ Mark Hamill, Harrison Ford, Carrie Fisher, Billy Dee Williams, Anthony Daniels, Peter Mayhew, Kenny Baker
'I admire the exquisite skill and talent which have been poured into these films, while finding the concepts behind these gigantic video games in the sky mindlessly tedious.' – *Margaret Hinxman, Daily Mail*
'An impersonal and rather junky piece of moviemaking.' – *Pauline Kael, New Yorker*
'Only the effects are special.' – *Sight and Sound*
Academy Award nomination: John Williams; art direction

'They're back – and they're hungry!'
The Return of The Living Dead
US 1985 90m DeLuxe
Tom Fox/Hemdale/Orion
The army is called in to repel a zombie onslaught.
Cult horror movie hailed by some as a black comedy, but likely to repel most audiences.
wd Dan O'Bannon *story* Rudy Ricci, John Russo, Russell Streiner *ph* Jules Brenner *m* Matt Clifford *pd* William Stout *ed* Robert Gordon
☆ Clu Gulager, James Karen, Don Calfa, Thom Mathews

'Back From The Dead And Hungry For More.'
Return of The Living Dead III
US 1993 105m Foto-Kem
Trimark/Bandai Visual/Ozla (Gary Schmoeller, Brian Yuzna)
A youth who spies on an experiment to revive the dead decides to bring his girlfriend back to life when she is killed in a motorcycle accident.
A Romeo and Juliet for the splatter generation: an extremely gory movie of flesh-eating zombies, aimed unerringly at the teens and twenties with its narrative of young love gone awry; it is slickly done, though its scenes with blood-spattered, mutilated bodies and decaying corpses are not for the squeamish.
w John Penney *d* Brian Yuzna *ph* Gerry Lively *m* Barry Goldberg *pd* Anthony Tremblay *ed* Christopher Roth *sp* Steve Johnson, Tim Ralston, Kevin Brennan, Christopher Nelson, Wayne Toth
☆ Mindy Clarke, J. Trevor Edmond, Kent McCord, Sarah Douglas, James T. Callahan, Mike Moroff, Sal Lopez, Basil Wallace
'A pedestrian and gruesome, but never really scary, story.' – *Variety*
'The best of the series so far, with a back-to-basics story that goes for solid scares rather than splatter spoofery ... one of the best zombie movies since the glory days of George Romero.' – *The Dark Side*
† The film was released direct to video in Britain in an uncut version. For the American cinema release, which runs for 97m, some of the bloodier scenes were removed.

Return of The Living Dead Part II
US 1987 89m Photolab
Guild/Lorimar/Greenfox (Tom Fox)
Brain-eating zombies attack a small town.
Dismal horror movie, unable to raise chills or laughs.
wd Ken Widerhorn *ph* Robert Elswit *m* J. Peter Robinson, Vladimir Horunzhy *ad* Dale Allan Pelton *ed* Charles Bornstein
☆ James Karen, Thom Mathews, Dana Ashbrook, Marsha Dietlein, Suzanne Snyder, Philip Bruns, Michael Kenworthy, Thor Van Lingen, Jason Hogan
'The film is typical of the juvenile, enervating would-be comic approach adopted by too many horror movies in the late 80s.' – *Kim Newman, MFB*

Return of the Magnificent Seven: see *Return of the Seven*

The Return of the Musketeers
GB/France/Spain 1989 101m colour
Entertainment/Timoth Burrill Productions/Fildebroc-Cine 5/Iberoamericana (Pierre Spengler)
The daughter of Milady de Winter vows vengeance on the Musketeers who were responsible for her mother's execution.
A sequel to The Four Musketeers, *it is a lacklustre affair of four middle-aged failures attempting to redeem themselves.*
w George MacDonald Fraser *novel* *Vingt Ans Après* by Alexandre Dumas *d* Richard Lester *ph* Bernard Lutic *m* Jean-Claude Petit *pd* Gil Parrondo *ed* John Victor Smith
☆ Michael York, Oliver Reed, Frank Finlay, C. Thomas Howell, Kim Cattrall, Geraldine Chaplin, Roy Kinnear, Christopher Lee, Philippe Noiret, Richard Chamberlain, Eusebio Lazaro, Alan Howard, Jean-Pierre Cassel
'*The Return* should never have been made.' – *Christopher Lee*

The Return of the Pink Panther *
GB 1974 113m DeLuxe Panavision
UA/Jewel/Pimlico/Mirisch/Geoffrey (Blake Edwards)
When the Pink Panther diamond – national treasure of the Eastern state of Lugash – is once again stolen, bungling Inspector Clouseau is called in.
Rehash of jokes from The Pink Panther *(qv), not bad in parts but a rather tedious whole.*
w Frank Waldman, Blake Edwards *d* Blake Edwards *ph* Geoffrey Unsworth *m* *Henry Mancini*
☆ *Peter Sellers*, Christopher Plummer, Herbert Lom, Catherine Schell, Peter Arne, Peter Jeffrey, Grégoire Aslan, David Lodge, Graham Stark
'The film never comes fully to the boil, but simmers in a series of self-contained, self-destructing little set pieces.' – *Richard Combs*
'The first film in history to be upstaged by its own credit titles.' – *Benny Green, Punch*

The Return of the Scarlet Pimpernel *
GB 1937 94m bw
London Films (Alexander Korda, Arnold Pressburger)
Sir Percy Blakeney saves his wife and other French aristos from the guillotine.
Predictable, stylish revolutionary romance, much thinner in plot and performance than its predecessor.
w Lajos Biro, Arthur Wimperis, Adrian Brunel *d* Hans Schwarz *ph* Mutz Greenbaum *m* Arthur Benjamin
☆ Barry K. Barnes, Sophie Stewart, Margaretta Scott, James Mason, *Henry Oscar*, Francis Lister, Anthony Bushell

Return of the Seven
US 1966 95m Technicolor Panavision
UA/Mirisch/CB (Ted Richmond)
aka: *Return of the Magnificent Seven*
The seven gunmen, slightly reconstituted, fight again to rescue some kidnapped farmers.
The mixture as before (see The Magnificent Seven*); adequate but scarcely inspired.*
w Larry Cohen *d* Burt Kennedy *ph* Paul Vogel *m* Elmer Bernstein
☆ Yul Brynner, Robert Fuller, Julian Mateos, Warren Oates, Claude Akins, Virgilio Teixeira, Emilio Fernandez, Jordan Christopher, Fernando Rey
Academy Award nomination: Elmer Bernstein

The Return of the Soldier *
GB 1982 102m Technicolor
Brent Walker/Barry R. Cooper (Ann Skinner, Simon Relph)
In 1916, a shellshocked soldier returns home, able to remember his old sweetheart but not his wife.
Overcast and heavy-handed treatment of a classy novella.
w Hugh Whitemore *novel* Rebecca West *d* Alan Bridges *ph* Stephen Goldblatt *m* Richard Rodney Bennett *pd* Luciana Arrighi
☆ Alan Bates, Ann-Margret, Julie Christie, Glenda Jackson, Jeremy Kemp, Edward de Souza, Frank Finlay, Jack May, Ian Holm
'The film has nowhere to go except into rhetorical bluster about class distinctions.' – *Tom Milne, MFB*

Return of the Swamp Thing
US 1989 85m DeLuxe
Medusa/Lightyear Entertainment/J & M Entertainment (Benjamin Melniker, Michael E. Uslan)
A mad scientist is thwarted from using his step-daughter in genetic experiments by a vegetable monster.
Ineffectual and relentlessly jokey approach to a comic-book hero.
w Derek Spencer, Grant Morris *d* Jim Wynorski *ph* Zoran Hochstatter *m* Chuck Cirino *pd* Robb Wilson King *ed* Leslie Rosenthal
☆ Louis Jourdan, Heather Locklear, Sarah Douglas, Dick Durock, Joey Sagal, Ace Mask, Chris Doyle, Daniel Taylor

Return of the Tall Blond *
France 1974 89m colour
Fox-Rank/Gaumont/De la Gueville (Alain Poiré, Yves Robert)
original title: *Le Retour du Grand Blond*
A violinist is once again caught up in rivalry between the police and the secret service.
Enjoyable, gently humorous sequel that lives up to the original.
w Francis Veber, Yves Robert *d* Yves Robert *ph* René Mathelin *m* Vladimir Cosma *pd* Guy Blanc *ed* Ghislaine Desjonquières, Françoise London
☆ Pierre Richard, Mireille Darc, Jean Carmet, Jean Rochefort, Michel Duchaussoy, Paul Le Person, Colette Castel
'The film never loses its light-hearted humour.' – *MFB*
† A sequel to *Le Grand Blond avec une Chaussure Noire*.

The Return of the Terror
US 1934 65m bw
Warner
A scientist feigns insanity to avoid prosecution for murder, and escapes to his old sanatorium, where murder strikes again.
Barnstorming murder mystery borrowing its title and nothing else from Edgar Wallace.
w Eugene Solow, Peter Milne *d* Howard Bretherton
☆ John Halliday, Mary Astor, Lyle Talbot, Frank McHugh, Irving Pichel, J. Carrol Naish
'Formula mystery, but speedy.' – *Variety*

'Terrifying! Paralysing! Horrifying!'
The Return of the Vampire *
US 1943 69m bw
Columbia (Sam White)
Dracula reappears amid the London blitz.
Surprisingly well made and complexly plotted horror film; it looks good and only lacks humour. The wolf man, however, is a regrettable intrusion.
w Griffin Jay *d* Lew Landers *ph* John Stumar, L. J. O'Connell *m* Mario Castelnuovo-Tedesco *md* Morris Stoloff
☆ *Bela Lugosi*, Nina Foch, Frieda Inescort, Miles Mander, Matt Willis, Roland Varno, Ottola Nesmith

Return to Glennascaul *
Eire 1951 23m bw
Dublin Gate Theatre
Orson Welles gives a man a lift and is told a gentle ghost story.
Neither very satisfying nor very well done, this little film deserves a niche in history because of the talents involved. It was apparently made during one of the many intervals in the filming of Othello.
wd Hilton Edwards *narrator* Orson Welles
short film

Return to Macon County
US 1975 89m Movielab
AIP/Macon Service Company (Eliot Schick)
In the fifties, two wandering youths pick up a waitress and have serious trouble with a manic policeman in America's unfriendliest area.
Slam-bang sequel to Macon County Line, *rather unintentionally comic.*
wd Richard Compton *ph* Jacques Marquette *m* Robert O. Ragland
☆ Nick Nolte, Don Johnson, Robin Mattson, Robert Viharo

'A comedy straight from the heart.'
Return to Me
US 2000 113m DeLuxe
MGM/JLT (Jennie Lew Tugend)
A widower discovers that the waitress he is dating had a heart transplant from his dead wife.
Slight and sentimental romantic comedy that trundles along in an obvious way to its feel-good ending.
w Bonnie Hunt, Don Lake *d* Bonnie Hunt *ph* Laszlo Kovacs *m* Nicholas Pike *pd* Brent Thomas *ed* Garth Craven *cos* Lis Bothwell
☆ David Duchovny (Bob Rueland), Minnie Driver (Grace Briggs), Carroll O'Connor (Marty O'Reilly), Robert Loggia (Angelo Pardipillo), Bonnie Hunt (Megan Dayton), David Alan Grier (Charlie Johnson), Joely Richardson (Elizabeth Rueland), Eddie Jones (Emmett McFadden), James Belushi (Joe Dayton), Marianne Muellerleile (Sophie), William Bronder (Wally Jatczak)
'Harmless but unexciting confection.' – *Variety*

'Faith, trust and pixie dust.'
Return to Never Land *
US 2002 72m Technicolor
Buena Vista/Walt Disney (Christopher Chase, Michelle Robinson, Dan Rounds)
The daughter of Wendy, who only half-believes her mother's tales of Peter Pan, is kidnapped by Captain Hook and taken to Never Land.
Another of Disney's sequels to better films of half a century ago; it's lively enough, but seems sadly dated.
w Temple Mathews, Carter Crocker *d* Robin Budd, Donovan Cook *m* Joel McNeely *ad* Wendell Luebbe *ed* Anthony F. Rocco
☆ voices of: Harriet Owen (Jane/Young Wendy), Blayne Weaver (Peter Pan), Corey Burton (Captain Hook), Jeff Bennett (Smee/Pirates), Kath Soucie (Wendy), Andrew McDonough (Danny)
'A bright and energetic animated comedy, with all the slick polish we expect from Disney, but it's not much more.' – *Roger Ebert, Chicago Sun-Times*

Return to Oz
US 1985 110m Technicolor
Walt Disney/Silver Screen Partners (Paul Maslansky)
Dorothy has traumas because of her Oz experiences, and suffers further nightmares under shock treatment.
A weird way to treat a children's classic, the result being a movie which appealed strongly to nobody except, possibly, the producer. The Disney people should have known better.
w Walter Murch, Gill Dennis *d* Walter Murch *ph* David Watkin *m* David Shire
☆ Fairuza Balk, Jean Marsh, Nicol Williamson, Piper Laurie, Matt Clark, Emma Ridley
'Astonishingly sombre, melancholy, and sadly unengaging.' – *Variety*
'Without musical numbers this narrative seems a perilously thin journey with no particular purpose.' – *Time Out*

Return to Paradise *
US 1953 109m Technicolor
UA/Aspen (Theron Warth)
A peace seeker settles on a tiny South Sea island and leaves when his wife dies; he returns after World War II with his daughter.
Curious idyll, slow but not displeasing.
w Charles Kaufman *novel* James Michener *d* Mark Robson *ph* Winton Hoch *m* Dimitri Tiomkin
☆ Gary Cooper, Barry Jones, Roberta Haynes, Moira MacDonald

'Give up three years of their lives or give up the life of their friend. They have eight days to decide.'
Return to Paradise
US 1998 111m colour
Polygram/Propaganda/Tetragram (Alain Bernheim, Steve Golin)
Two American men, who discover that their friend is about to be executed for drug offences in Malaysia, have to choose between letting him die or returning to testify, and facing possible imprisonment themselves.
A drama of total predictability; it raises moral issues only to avoid resolving them.
w Wesley Strick, Bruce Robinson *screenplay* Pierre Jolivet, Olivier Schatzky *d* Joseph Ruben *ph* Reynaldo Villalobos *m* Mark Mancina *pd* Bill Groom *ed* Andrew Mondshein, Craig McKay
☆ Vince Vaughn, Anne Heche, Joaquin Phoenix, David Conrad, Vera Farmiga, Nick Sandow, Jada Pinkett Smith
'Disappointingly conventional treatment of an intriguing story that could have used either more narrative zing or greater thematic complexity.' – *Todd McCarthy, Variety*
† It is a remake of the 1989 French film *Force Majeure* (qv).

Return to Peyton Place *
US 1961 122m DeLuxe Cinemascope
TCF/API (Jerry Wald)
Constance Mackenzie's daughter writes a novel about Peyton Place and falls in love with the publisher.
More closets are unlocked, more skeletons fall out; for addicts, the sequel does not disappoint, and it's all very glossy.
w Ronald Alexander *d* José Ferrer *ph* Charles G. Clarke *m* Franz Waxman
☆ Jeff Chandler, Carol Lynley, Eleanor Parker, Mary Astor, Robert Sterling, Luciana Paluzzi, Brett Halsey, Tuesday Weld
'Enough soap suds to pollute the Mississippi along with the mind.' – *Judith Crist, 1973*

Return to Snowy River
Australia 1988 97m colour Panavision
Burrowes Film Group/Hoyts
aka: *The Man from Snowy River Part II*
aka: *The Untamed*
Returning home with a herd of horses, a restless young rancher finds that he is resented by the more conventional settlers, who plan to dispossess him of his land.
Stolid sequel to a local success; an uninspired drama which does not have much to offer other than a great many horses.
w John Dixon, Geoff Burrowes *d* Geoff Burrowes *ph* Keith Wagstaff *m* Bruce Rowland *pd* Leslie Binns *ed* Gary Woodyard
☆ Tom Burlinson, Sigrid Thornton, Brian Dennehy, Nicholas Eadie, Bryan Marshall, Mark Hembrow, Rhys McConnochie, Peter Cummins

Return to the Blue Lagoon
US 1991 98m Technicolor
Columbia TriStar/Price (William A. Graham)
A mother, her daughter and an orphaned boy are washed up on a desert island; the girl and boy grow to adulthood and fall in love.
A sequel that, once it has disposed of the adult, is virtually a remake of the 1980 version and no better the second time around.
w Leslie Stevens *novel* *The Garden of God* by Henry de Vere Stacpoole *d* William A. Graham *ph* Robert Steadman *m* Basil Poledouris *pd* Jon Dowding *ed* Ronald J. Fagan
☆ Milla Jovovich, Brian Krause, Lisa Pelikan, Courtney Phillips

Reuben, Reuben *
US 1982 101m CFI color
Saltair/Taft (Walter Shenson)
A drunken British poet upsets a New England community.
Oddball comedy at which one laughs without much enthusiasm.
w Julius J. Epstein *play* *Spofford* by Herman Shumlin *novel* *Peter de Vries* *d* Robert Ellis Miller *ph* Peter Stein *m* Billy Goldenberg *pd* Peter Larkin
☆ *Tom Conti*, Kelly McGillis, Robert Blossom, Cynthia Harris, Joel Fabiani
Tom Conti; adaptation

Reunion
US 1936 83m bw
Darryl Zanuck/TCF
GB title: *Hearts in Reunion*
When a doctor retires, the townsfolk reunite him with many of the children he has brought into the world.
Tiresome second attempt to cash in on the Dionne Quintuplets, who make several appearances.
w Sam Hellman, Gladys Lehman, Sonya Levien *d* Norman Taurog
☆ Jean Hersholt, Rochelle Hudson, Helen Vinson, Slim Summerville, J. Edward Bromberg, Sara Haden
'Too episodic to command interest or supply suspense.' – *Variety*
† A sequel to *The Country Doctor*.

Reunion
France/West Germany/GB 1989 110m colour
Rank/Les Films Ariane/FR3/NEF/CLG/TAC (Anne Françoise)
original title: *L'Ami Retrouvé*
Returning to Germany as an old man, a Jewish lawyer recalls a schoolboy friendship destroyed by the Nazis' anti-Semitism.
Minimally scripted, ploddingly directed and lacking in emotional weight.
w Harold Pinter *novel* *Reunion* by Fred Uhlman *d* Jerry Schatzberg *ph* Bruno de Keyzer *m* Philippe Sarde *pd* Alexandre Trauner *ed* Martine Barraque
☆ Jason Robards, Christien Anholt, Samuel West, Françoise Fabian, Maureen Kerwin, Barbara Jefford, Dorothea Alexander, Frank Baker, Tim Barker
'A tedious re-exploration of already over-charted territory.' – *Tom Milne, MFB*

'We're all whores and pimps. Some of us just get a better corner to work!'
The Reunion
US 1998 84m bw/colour
Asylum/Esquire (Paul Corvino, Leticia Gomez, Dallas Hartnett)
Remembering the manner in which he was humiliated at school eighteen years earlier, at a class re-union a man takes his former tormentors hostage in order to get revenge.
Claustrophobic psychological thriller in which a small group of people are forced to examine their past and present behaviour; its dramatic contrivances never quite convince and it lacks tension.
w Paul Corvino *d* Larry Eudene *ph* Pat Capone *m* Kirsten Vogelsang *pd* Zeljka Pavlinovic *ed* Robert Fitzgerald, Glenn Conte *cos* Deirdra Govan
☆ Timothy Devlin (Louis Witkowski), Mimi Langeland (Caroline Coleman), Jack Mulcahy (Hal Coleman), Elizabeth P. McKay (Felicia Witowski), Patrick Ferraro (Joey Tucci), Kristopher Medina (Standard), Leila Sbitani (Ashley), Edouard DeSoto (Santiago)
† The film won an award as best thriller, and Timothy Devlin as best actor, at the New York International Independent Film & Video Festival in 1998.

Reunion in France
US 1942 104m bw
MGM (Joseph L. Mankiewicz)
GB title: *Mademoiselle France*
A selfish Parisian dress designer gradually realizes that her world has changed when the Nazis invade and she is asked to help an American flyer.
Action flagwaver which tries also to be a woman's picture and goes pretty soppily about it.
w Jan Lustig, Marvin Borowsky, Marc Connelly *story* Ladislas Bus-Fekete *d* Jules Dassin *ph* Robert Planck *m* Franz Waxman
☆ Joan Crawford, John Wayne, Philip Dorn, Reginald Owen, Albert Basserman, John Carradine, Ann Ayars, J. Edward Bromberg, Henry Daniell, Moroni Olsen, Howard da Silva
'Miss Crawford isn't making all the sacrifices implied in the script ... Dressing like a refugee is certainly not in her contract.' – *New York Herald Tribune*

Reunion in Vienna *
US 1933 100m bw
MGM
A long-exiled nobleman tries to take up an old romance even though the lady is married.
Lacklustre adaptation of a play which must have style; the performances remain interesting.
w Ernest Vajda, Claudine West *play* Robert E. Sherwood *d* Sidney Franklin *ph* George Folsey *m* William Axt
☆ *John Barrymore*, Diana Wynyard, Frank Morgan, May Robson, Eduardo Ciannelli, Una Merkel, Henry Travers
'Unlikely money film outside a few of the larger cities.' – *Variety*
George Folsey

Reveille With Beverly *
US 1943 78m bw
Columbia (Sam White)
A girl disc jockey runs a programme for soldiers.
Thin excuse for a musical, but the result was pretty popular.
w Howard J. Green, Jack Henley, Albert Duffy *d* Charles Barton
☆ Ann Miller, William Wright, Dick Purcell, Franklin Pangborn, Tim Ryan, Larry Parks

Revelation
GB 2001 109m DeLuxe 'Scope
Miracle/Romulus/Cyclops Vision (Jonathan Woolf, Stuart Urban)
A millionaire tycoon and his son search for a box containing the nails from Christ's crucifixion, chased by a satanist who plans to use it to create an anti-Christ.
Deliriously bizarre occult thriller that will confuse the brain but may tickle the funny-bone.
wd Stuart Urban *idea* Frank Falco *ph* Sam McCurdy *m* Edmund Butt *pd* James Merifield *ed* Julian Rodd
☆ Terence Stamp (Magnus Martel), James D'Arcy (Jake Martel), Natasha Wightman (Mira), Udo Kier (The Grand Master), Liam Cunningham (Father Ray Connolly), Ron Moody (Sir Isaac Newton), Derek Jacobi (The Librarian), Heathcote Williams (The Tourist), Celia Imrie (Harriet Matrel)
'Curiously watchable despite its lackluster dialogue, acting by numbers and frequent disregard for normal continuity.' – *Derek Elley, Variety*

Revenge
GB 1971 89m Eastmancolor
Rank/Peter Rogers Productions (George H. Brown)
When children are raped and murdered in a north country town, two men take the law into their own hands.
Crude melodrama set in Cold Comfort Farm country; efficient but unrewarding.
w John Kruse *d* Sidney Hayers *ph* Ken Hodges *m* Eric Rogers

☆ Joan Collins, Sinead Cusack, James Booth, Ray Barrett, Kenneth Griffith

Revenge: see *Blood Feud (1979)*

Revenge
US 1989 124m DeLuxe Panavision
Columbia TriStar/Raster (Hunt Lowry, Stanley Rubin)
Left for dead by a jealous husband, a former pilot seeks revenge and reunion with his lover.
Brutal, shallow thriller that is too predictable to be enjoyable.
w Jim Harrison, Jeffrey Fiskin *novel* Jim Harrison *d* Tony Scott *ph* Jeffrey Kimball *m* Jack Nitzsche *pd* Michael Seymour, Benjamin Fernandez *ed* Chris Lebenzon, Michael Tronick
☆ Kevin Costner, Anthony Quinn, Madeleine Stowe, Tomas Milian, Joaquin Martinez, James Gammon, Jesse Corti, Sally Kirkland, Miguel Ferrer

Revenge Is My Destiny
US 1971 95m colour
Gold Key (Toby Ross)
A one-eyed hero returns from Vietnam to discover that his hated wife is missing; he goes looking for her.
Drab thriller with less than adequate script, direction and performances.
w Mardik Martin *d* Joseph Adler *ph* Ares Parshalis Demertzis *m* Stu Phillips, Richard Markowitz *ad* Paul Moore *ed* Joseph Adler, Charles Carrubba
☆ Chris Robinson, Sidney Blackmer, Elisa Ingram, Joe E. Ross, John Lodge, Patricia Rainier, Willie Pastrano

Revenge of Billy the Kid
GB 1992 87m Colour
Powerhouse Pictures/Montage (Tim Dennison)
A carnivorous monster, the offspring of a goat and a farmer, kills off his father's family.
Grotesque and disgusting low-budget horror comedy, obsessed with rape, bestiality and the nastier bodily functions. A credit for 'Flatulence Artists' sets the tone.
w Tim Dennison, Jim Groom, Richard Matthews *d* Jim Groom *ph* David Read *m* Tony Flynn
☆ Michael Balfour, Samantha Perkins, Jackie D. Broad, Trevor Peake, Bryan Heeley, Norman Mitchell, Dean Williamson, Michael Ripper
'Amateurish horror spoof made on a tiny budget and with even less wit or intelligence.' – *Sight and Sound*

'If you go alone – you'll find yourself running all the way home!'
The Revenge of Frankenstein
GB 1958 89m Technicolor
Columbia/Hammer (Anthony Hinds)
Baron Frankenstein evades the guillotine and makes a new creature with the brain of a homicidal dwarf.
Dullish horror farrago with a few indications of quirkish humour.
w Jimmy Sangster, Hurford Janes *d* Terence Fisher *ph* Jack Asher *m* Leonard Salzedo *pd* Bernard Robinson *ed* James Needs, Alfred Cox
☆ *Peter Cushing*, Michael Gwynn, Oscar Quitak, Francis Matthews, Eunice Gayson, John Welsh, Lionel Jeffries, Richard Wordsworth, Charles Lloyd Pack, John Stuart, Arnold Diamond
† This second Hammer Frankenstein set the tone for the rest; see *The Curse of Frankenstein*.

Revenge of the Blood Beast: see *She Beast*

Revenge of the Dead: see *Night of the Ghouls*

Revenge of the Gladiators: see *Fire over Rome*

Revenge of the Nerds
US 1984 90m DeLuxe
TCF/Interscope (Ted Field, Peter Samuelson)
College freshmen decide to fight back when they are evicted from their dormitories and mocked by the football team and rejected by the fraternities.
Raucous comedy for the intellectually challenged.
w Steve Zacharias, Jeff Buhai *story* Tim Metcalfe, Miguel Tejada-Flores *d* Jeff Kanew *ph* King Baggot *m* Thomas Newman *pd* James L. Schoppe *ed* Alan Balsam
☆ Robert Carradine, Anthony Edwards, Ted McGinley, Bernie Casey, Julia Montgomery, John Goodman
† It was followed by two lesser sequels: *Revenge of the Nerds II: Nerds in Paradise*, directed by Joe Roth in 1987; *Revenge of the Nerds III: The Next Generation*, directed for TV by Roland Mesa in 1992.

Revenge of the Pink Panther
US 1978 98m Technicolor Panavision
UA/Blake Edwards
Inspector Clouseau tracks down a drug-smuggling industrialist.
Feeble addition to a series which was always too pleased with itself.
w Frank Waldman, Ron Clark, Blake Edwards *d* Blake Edwards *ph* Ernie Day *m* Henry Mancini
☆ Peter Sellers, Herbert Lom, Robert Webber, Dyan Cannon, Burt Kwouk, Paul Stewart, Robert Loggia, Graham Stark

Revenge of the Vampire: see *Mask of Satan*

Revenge of the Zombies
US 1943 61m bw
Lindsley Parsons/Monogram
A Nazi scientist in Mexico tries to convert an army of the dead for Hitler's use.
Unpersuasive horror cheapie.
w Edmund Kelso, Van Norcross *d* Steve Sekely
☆ John Carradine, Robert Lowery, Gale Storm, Veda Ann Borg, Mantan Moreland

The Revengers
US 1972 108m DeLuxe Panavision
Cinema Center/Martin Rackin
A rancher gathers a posse to hunt down the Indians who have allegedly murdered his wife and family.
Standard major Western with a dismal script which echoes The Dirty Dozen *and* The Wild Bunch*: sometimes repulsive, seldom exciting.*
w Wendell Mayes *d* Daniel Mann *ph* Gabriel Torres *m* Pino Calvi
☆ William Holden, Ernest Borgnine, Susan Hayward, Woody Strode, Roger Hanin

The Revengers' Comedies
GB/France 1997 82m Technicolor
J&M/BBC/Arts Council/France 2/Artisan/IMA (Simon Bosanquet)
Two suicidal strangers agree to take revenge on each other's nemesis.
Despite the efforts of an accomplished cast, this is a lumpy comedy of a dull man who finds himself ill-at-ease in eccentric, upper-middle-class society.
wd Malcolm Mowbray *plays* Alan Ayckbourn *ph* Romain Winding *m* Alexandre Desplat *pd* Stuart Walker *ed* Barrie Vince
☆ Sam Neill, Helena Bonham-Carter, Kristin Scott Thomas, Rupert Graves, Martin Clunes, Steve Coogan, John Wood, Liz Smith, Anita Dobson, Charlotte Coleman

Reversal of Fortune ★★
US 1990 111m Technicolor
Warner/Shochiku Fuji/Sovereign Pictures/Edward R. Pressman, Oliver Stone
A European aristocrat, found guilty of attempting to murder his wealthy American wife, hires a brilliant lawyer to mount an appeal against the sentence.
Based on a true story, it combines the appeal of court-room drama with a prurient curiosity about the lives of the very rich.
w Nicholas Kazan *book* Alan Dershowitz *d* Barbet Schroeder *ph* Luciano Tovoli *m* Mark Isham *pd* Mel Bourne *ed* Lee Percy
☆ Glenn Close, Jeremy Irons, Ron Silver, Annabella Sciorra, Uta Hagen, Fisher Stevens, Christine Baranski, Jack Gilpin, Stephen Mailer
'A classy piece of filmmaking.' – *Variety*
Jeremy Irons
Barbet Schroeder; Nicholas Kazan

The Revolt of Job ★★
Hungary 1983 98m colour
Mafilm Tarsulas Filmstudio/Hungarian TV/ZDF
original title: *Jób Lázadása*
A young Christian orphan is adopted by a Jewish farmer and his wife, who fear the coming of the Nazis.
Touching, understated film, told from the perspective of the child, which gives a freshness and poignancy to a familiar theme.
w Katalin Petényi, Imre Gyöngyössi, Barna Kabay *d* Imre Gyöngyössi, Barna Kabay *ph* Gábor Szabó *m* Zoltán Jeney
☆ Ference Zenthe, Hédi Temessy, Gábor Fehér, Péter Rudolf, Leticia Cano, Gregor Henry
best foreign-language film

The Revolt of Mamie Stover
US 1956 93m Eastmancolor Cinemascope
TCF (Buddy Adler)
A dance hall girl leaves San Francisco for Honolulu, makes money there but reforms for love of a rich novelist.
Absurdly bowdlerized and boring film version of a novel about a sleazy prostitute; hardly worth making at all in this form, especially as the cast seems well capable of a raunchier version.
w Sydney Boehm *novel* William Bradford Huie *d* Raoul Walsh *ph* Leo Tover *m* Hugo Friedhofer
☆ Jane Russell, Agnes Moorehead, Richard Egan, Joan Leslie

The Revolt of the Praetorians (dubbed)
Italy 1964 90m Technicolor Techniscope
FIA
original title: *La Rivolta dei Pretoriani*
The leader of the Praetorian guard doubles as the Red Wolf, the masked leader of a revolt against the vicious and autocratic rule of the emperor Domitian.
Typical undistinguished sword-and-sandals historical romp.
w Gianpaolo Callegari *d* Alfonso Brescia *ph* Pierludovico Pavoni *m* Carlo Franci *ad* Piervittorio Marchi *ed* Nella Nannuzzi
☆ Richard Harrison, Moira Orfei, Giuliano Gemma, Piero Lulli, Aldo Cecconi, Paola Pitti
† The film's American star, Richard Harrison, turned down the lead in *A Fistful of Dollars*, which went to Clint Eastwood instead.

Revolution
US 1985 125m Technicolor
Warner/Goldcrest/Viking (Irwin Winkler)
A trapper becomes involved in the American War of Independence and with the aristocratic daughter of a loyalist.
A mouse of a movie, despite its epic pretensions; the narrative has been swallowed by incoherent set-pieces and the period setting falters under the Method acting of its star.
w Robert Dillon *d* Hugh Hudson *ph* Bernard Lutic *m* John Corigliano *pd* Assheton Gorton *ed* Stuart Baird
☆ Al Pacino, Donald Sutherland, Nastassja Kinski, Joan Plowright, Dave King, Steven Berkoff, John Wells, Annie Lennox, Dexter Fletcher, Richard O'Brien
'Hudson has thrown what doubtless started as a perfectly straightforward script to the winds and marched off in search of images that would somehow galvanise the whole show into life. But as his camera stumbles through the smoke, fire, and mobs of expensively costumed extras it's clear he's not going to find them.' – *David Ehrenstein*

The Revolutionary
US 1970 101m Technicolor
(UA) Pressman-Williams (Edward R. Pressman)
Episodes in the life of a revolutionary, from distributing leaflets to attempted assassination.
A rather casual study of one man's radicalism, in no particular time or place; no doubt of great interest to other revolutionaries.
w Hans Königsberger *d* Paul Williams *ph* Brian Probyn *m* Michael Small
☆ Jon Voight, Jennifer Salt, Robert Duvall

The Revolving Doors
France/Canada 1988 102m colour
Gala/Malofilm/Canal Plus (René Malo, Francyne Morin)
original title: *Les Portes Tournantes*
A dying woman recalls her earlier life, marriage and musical ambitions.
Slight but quite enjoyable bout of nostalgia, heavy on period charm.
w Jacques Savoie, Francis Mankiewicz *d* Francis Mankiewicz *ph* Thomas Vamos *m* François Dompierre *ad* Anne Pritchard *ed* André Corriveau
☆ Monique Spaziani, Gabriel Arcand, Miou-Miou, François Methe, Jacques Penot, Françoise Faucher, Jean-Louis Roux, Remy Girard, Charles Reiner
'This lumbering tale of thwarted mother-love seems even more bereft of sense than sensibility.' – *Derek Malcolm, Guardian*

The Reward
US 1965 92m DeLuxe Cinemascope
TCF/Aaron Rosenberg
A mixed group of adventurers set out across the desert to capture a murderer; but thieves fall out.
Pretentious and talky melodrama which quickly scuttled its director's chances in Hollywood. Little action, obvious outcome, attractive Death Valley locations.
w Serge Bourgignon, Oscar Mullard *novel* Michael Barrett *d* Serge Bourgignon *ph Joe MacDonald* *m* Elmer Bernstein
☆ Max von Sydow, Efrem Zimbalist Jnr, Yvette Mimieux, Gilbert Roland, Emilio Fernandez, Henry Silva

'Emotions clash in a crescendo of drama!'
Rhapsody
US 1954 116m Technicolor
MGM (Lawrence Weingarten)
A wealthy woman affects the lives of two quite different musicians, each of whom has his weakness.
Tedious romantic drama which vainly attempted a smart veneer but boasted a splendid musical soundtrack.
w Fay and Michael Kanin *novel Maurice Guest* by Henry Handel Richardson *d* Charles Vidor *ph* Robert Planck *md* Johnny Green, Bronislau Kaper *piano* Claudio Arrau *violin* Michael Rabin
☆ Elizabeth Taylor, Vittorio Gassman, John Ericson, Louis Calhern, Michael Chekhov, Barbara Bates, Celia Lovsky, Richard Hageman

Rhapsody in August ★
Japan 1990 97m colour
Palace/Shochiku/Akira Kurosawa
original title: *Hachigatsu-no-Kyoshikyoku*
A grandmother, prompted by her grandchildren and a visit from her Japanese-American nephew, recalls the death of her husband when the atomic bomb was dropped on Nagasaki.
A small-scale but ponderous plea for an understanding of the past.
wd Akira Kurosawa *novel Nabe-no-Naka* by Kiyoko Murata *ph* Takao Saito, Masaharu Ueda *m* Shinichiro Ikebe *ad* Yoshiro Muraki *ed* Akira Kurosawa
☆ Richard Gere, Sachiko Murasé, Hisashi Igawa, Narumi Kayashima, Tomoko Ohtakara, Mitsunori Isaki, Toshié Negishi, Choichiro Kawarasaki, Hidetaka Yoshioka, Mié Suzuki

Rhapsody in Blue ★★
US 1945 139m bw
Warner (Jesse L. Lasky)
The life story of composer George Gershwin.
No more trustworthy on factual matters than other Hollywood biopics of its era, this rather glum saga at least presented the music and the performers to excellent advantage.
w Howard Koch, Elliot Paul *story* Sonya Levien *d Irving Rapper* *ph Sol Polito (musical numbers: Ernest Haller, Merritt B. Gerstad)* *md* Leo Forbstein, Max Steiner *ch* Le Roy Prinz *ad* Anton Grot, John Hughes
☆ *Robert Alda*, Joan Leslie, Alexis Smith, Charles Coburn, Julie Bishop, *Albert Basserman, Oscar Levant, Herbert Rudley*, Rosemary de Camp, Morris Carnovsky, *Al Jolson, Paul Whiteman*, George White, Hazel Scott

'With no story at all, this two-hour concert of Gershwin music would be well worth the price of admission' – *Daily Mail*

† Joan Leslie's songs were dubbed by Louanne Hogan.

Ray Heindorf, Max Steiner

Rhinestone

US 1984 111m DeLuxe
TCF/Howard Smith, Marvin Worth

A night-club singer bets her obnoxious employer that she can turn a cab driver into a star.
Crude and witless Pygmalion variation with unsympathetic leads.
w Phil Alden Robinson, Sylvester Stallone *d* Bob Clark *ph* Timothy Galfas *m* Dolly Parton
☆ Dolly Parton, Sylvester Stallone, Richard Farnsworth, Ron Leibman, Tim Thomerson

'You'd have thought we all got together and decided how we could fastest ruin our careers.' – *Sylvester Stallone*

Rhino

US 1964 91m Metrocolor
MGM/Ivan Tors (Ben Chapman)

A scientist working with white rhinos is joined by an unscrupulous big game hunter.
Inoffensive African adventure.
w Art Arthur, Arthur Weiss *d* Ivan Tors *ph* Sven Persson, Lamar Boren *m* Lalo Schifrin
☆ Harry Guardino, Robert Culp, Shirley Eaton

Rhinoceros

US 1974 101m Eastmancolor
AFT/American Express/Cinevision/Ely Landau

In an American town, an alcoholic clerk is horrified to see his friends all turning into rhinoceroses.
An unsuccessful absurdist play about the pressures of conformity has become a somewhat absurd movie, though there is a little pleasure to be found in the comic interaction of Mostel and Wilder.
w Julian Barry *play* Eugene Ionesco *d* Tom O'Horgan *ph* James Crabe *m* Galt MacDermot *pd* Jack Martin Smith *ed* Bud Smith
☆ Gene Wilder, Zero Mostel, Karen Black, Joe Silver, Robert Weil, Marilyn Chris, Lou Cutell

Rhodes: see *Rhodes of Africa*

Rhodes of Africa *

GB 1936 91m bw
Gaumont (Geoffrey Barkas)

US title: *Rhodes*
A rough-hewn diamond miner becomes Prime Minister of Cape Colony.
Heavy-going but generally interesting historical drama shot on location.
w Michael Barringer, Leslie Arliss, Miles Malleson *book* Sarah Millin *d* Berthold Viertel *ph* Bernard Knowles *m* Hubert Bath
☆ Walter Huston, Oscar Homolka, Basil Sydney, Peggy Ashcroft, Frank Cellier, Bernard Lee, Lewis Casson

'One of the better English-made pictures ... should do all right even if it doesn't get the women.' – *Variety*

'Solid, worthy, humourless, it unrolls its eleven well-bred reels with all the technical advantages of 1936.' – *Graham Greene*

Rhubarb

US 1951 94m bw
Paramount (Perlberg-Seaton)

A millionaire leaves his fortune, including a baseball team, to a wild ginger cat, which means problems for his publicity agent.
Typical scatty farce of the early fifties, held together by the splendid performance of the disdainful feline in the title role rather than by any special merit in the handling.
w Dorothy Reid, Francis Cockrell *novel* H. Allen Smith *d* Arthur Lubin *ph* Lionel Lindon *m* Van Cleave
☆ Ray Milland, Jan Sterling, Gene Lockhart, William Frawley

Rhubarb

GB 1969 37m Technicolor
ABPC/Avalon

Various village notables congregate on the golf course.
Virtually silent comedy (nobody says anything but 'rhubarb') which could have been very funny with better jokes. A TV remake in 1979 was however much worse.
wd Eric Sykes
☆ Harry Secombe, Eric Sykes, Jimmy Edwards, Hattie Jacques, Gordon Rollins, Graham Stark, Kenneth Connor

Rhythm of the Islands

US 1943 60m bw
Universal (Bernard Burton)

A rather dull South Sea island sets itself up to attract tourists.
Moderate musical programmer, one of many from this studio during the war.
w Oscar Brodney, M. M. Musselman *d* Roy William Neill
☆ Allan Jones, Jane Frazee, Andy Devine, Ernest Truex, Marjorie Gateson, Mary Wickes

'Acceptably fulfils its purpose of providing an hour's diverting footage for dual support in the general runs.' – *Variety*

Rhythm on the Range *

US 1936 87m bw
Paramount (Benjamin Glazer)

A hired hand saves the boss's daughter when she is kidnapped by local badmen.
Easy-going musical comedy with a Western background, later remade as Pardners *(qv).*
w John C. Moffett, Sidney Salkow, Walter de Leon, Francis Martin *d* Norman Taurog *ph* Karl Struss *songs* various
☆ *Bing Crosby*, Martha Raye, Frances Farmer, Bob Burns, Lucile Watson, Samuel S. Hinds, George E. Stone, Warren Hymer

'Bing Crosby as a cowboy; Bing Crosby crooning a prize bull to sleep on a freight car; Bing Crosby more than ever like Walt Disney's Cock Robin; it needs some stamina to be a film reviewer.' – *Graham Greene*

Rhythm on the River *

US 1940 90m bw
Paramount (William Le Baron)

A song writer employs 'ghosts' to produce his music and lyrics; they discover this fact and go into business for themselves.
Cheerful musical with strong billing.
w Dwight Taylor, Billy Wilder, Jacques Théry *d* Victor Schertzinger *ph* Ted Tetzlaff *m* Johnny Burke, James V. Monaco
☆ *Bing Crosby, Mary Martin, Basil Rathbone, Oscar Levant*, Oscar Shaw, Charley Grapewin, William Frawley

song 'Only Forever'

Rhythm Romance: see *Some Like It Hot (1939)*

Rhythm Serenade

GB 1943 87m bw
Columbia British (Ben Henry)

During the Second World War, a teacher who starts a day nursery so that mothers can work in a munitions factory falls in love with a commando recovering from a breakdown.
Sentimental little flag-waver with a few songs thrown in.
w Basil Woon, Marjorie Deans *d* Gordon Wellesley *ph* Erwin Hillier, Geoffrey Faithfull *md* Harry Bidgood *ad* George Provis *ed* Alan Jaggs
☆ Vera Lynn, Peter Murray-Hill, Julien Mitchell, Charles Victor, Jimmy Jewel, Ben Warris, Irene Handl, Jimmy Clitheroe, Joan Kemp Welch

Rhythm Thief

US 1994 88m bw
Film Crash (Jonathan Starch)

A hustler who makes a living on the streets selling bootleg tapes is pursued by violent punk rockers and a girl who was in a mental home with his mother.
There is talent on show here, but in the unloveliest of settings and among blank, alienated, strung-out, drugged denizens of the streets, whose horizons are limited to getting through the day.
w Matthew Harrison, Christopher Grimm *d* Matthew Harrison *ph* Howard Krupa *m* Danny Brenner, Hugh O'Donovan, John L. Horn, Kevin Okerlund *ad* Daniel Fisher *ed* Matthew Harrison
☆ Jason Andrews, Eddie Daniels, Kevin Corrigan, Kimberly Flynn, Sean Hagerty, Mark Alfred, Christopher Cooke, Bob McGrath

'No-budget New York item gets stronger as it moves confidently forward, weaving together the lives of some very desperate Lower East Siders before reaching a quietly devastating close.' – *Ken Eisner, Variety*

† The film was shot in 11 days.

Rice People *

Cambodia/France 1994 130m colour
Gala/JBA/Thelma/La Sept/TSR (Jacques Bidou)
original title: *Neak Sre*
aka: *Les Gens de la Rizière*

When her husband dies suddenly, the wife of a Cambodian rice farmer tries to tend the crops as well as looking after her seven daughters.
Elegantly shot, low-key drama that can be rewarding if you submit to its slow, seasonal rhythms.
w Rithy Panh, Eve Deboise *novel Ranju Sepanjang Jalan* by Shahnon Ahmad *d* Rithy Panh *ph* Jacques Bouquin *m* Marc Marder *ad* Nhean Chamnaul *ed* Andrée Davanture, Marie-Christine Rougerie
☆ Peng Phan, Mom Soth, Chhim Naline, Va Simorn, Meas Daniel, Phang Chamroeun, Sophy Sodany, Muong Danyda

'Hard to enthuse about so much noble suffering. But it's occasionally fascinating, all the same, as a window on a very different world.' – *Sheila Johnston, Independent*

'From the very beginning, they knew they'd be friends to the end. What they didn't count on was everything in between!'

Rich and Famous

US 1981 117m Metrocolor
MGM/Jaquet/William Allyn

Two girlfriends meet again years after college; one has become a famous highbrow novelist, and with her help the other becomes a lowbrow one.
Unattractively sexed-up remake of Old Acquaintance, *with even more talk than the original, and much less style.*
w Gerald Ayres *d* George Cukor *ph* Don Peterman, Peter Eco *m* Georges Delerue *pd* Jan Scott *ed* John F. Burnett
☆ Candice Bergen, Jacqueline Bisset, David Selby, Hart Bochner, Steven Hill, Meg Ryan

'A sadly dispiriting occasion ... a jumbled conflation of *The Group* and a female version of *Carnal Knowledge*.' – *Tim Pulleine, MFB*

† The director was 82 when the film was shot, which must be some kind of record.

Rich and Strange *

GB 1931 83m bw
BIP (John Maxwell)

US title: *East of Shanghai*
A young couple come into money and take a trip around the world.
Slight, agreeable early talkie with a few Hitchcock touches.
w Alma Reville, Val Valentine, Alfred Hitchcock *novel* Dale Collins *d Alfred Hitchcock ph* Jack Cox, Charles Martin *m* Hal Dolphe
☆ Henry Kendall, Joan Barry, Percy Marmont, Betty Amann, Elsie Randolph

'Hitchcock, being Britain's D. W. Griffith, according to the press agents around here, usually gets a rave as his pictures take the screen. Here's one where the admirers will have difficulty knowing what to say.' – *Variety*

'Perhaps his bravest failure.' – *George Perry, 1965*

The Rich Are Always with Us

US 1932 73m bw
Warner (Sam Bischoff)

A socialite determines on a divorce but her new love is annoyed by her concern for her ex-husband.
Cocktail drama of a kind which totally disappeared from the screen.
w Austin Parker *novel* E. Pettit *d* Alfred E. Green *ph* Ernest Haller *m* W. Franke Harling
☆ Ruth Chatterton, George Brent, John Miljan, Bette Davis, Adrienne Dore, Mae Madison, Robert Warwick

'Chiefly a femme picture ... the title's appropriateness is as obscure as the wisdom of so metaphoric a label for a flicker.' – *Variety*

The Rich Full Life: see *Cynthia*

Rich in Love

US 1992 105m DeLuxe Panavision
UPI/MGM (Richard D. Zanuck/Lili Fini Zanuck)

A teenage schoolgirl tries to keep the family together as her father begins to disintegrate after her mother leaves home suddenly, and her pregnant sister arrives with her new husband.
Meandering domestic drama, an attempt at a character study which fails because its participants distinctly lack character, cleaving only to the obvious and expected.
w Alfred Uhry *novel* Josephine Humphreys *d* Bruce Beresford *ph* Peter James *m* Georges Delerue *pd* John Stoddart *ed* Mark Warner
☆ Albert Finney, Jill Clayburgh, Kathryn Erbe, Kyle MacLachlan, Piper Laurie, Ethan Hawke, Suzy Amis, Alfre Woodard

'It could play on television tomorrow, and no-one would find anything amiss, save perhaps the ratings dropping precipitously as the audience drifted away in search of something more than genteel good taste.' – *John Harkness, Sight and Sound*

Rich Kids

US 1979 96m Technicolor
Lion's Gate/UA (George W. George, Michael Hausman)

An adolescent boy and girl are mildly corrupted by the behaviour of their parents.
Spasmodically interesting comedy-drama which seems ill at ease among the rich and alternates between exploitation, satire and whimsy.
w Judith Ross *d* Robert M. Young *ph* Ralf D. Bode *m* Craig Doerge
☆ Trini Alvarado, Jeremy Levy, Kathryn Walker, John Lithgow, Terry Kiser, David Selby

Rich Man, Poor Girl

US 1938 72m bw
MGM

Consternation takes a white-collar family when a millionaire takes a fancy to one of its daughters.
Unexciting comedy-drama vaguely modelled on You Can't Take It With You.
w Joseph Fields, Jerome Chodorov *play* Edith Ellis *d* Reinhold Schünzel
☆ Lew Ayres, Ruth Hussey, Robert Young, Don Castle, Guy Kibbee, Lana Turner, Rita Johnson

'Lightweight in marquee strength but should build through word of mouth.' – *Variety*

Rich Man's Folly

US 1931 80m bw
Paramount

A rich man has no time for his children.
Curious updating of Dickens's Dombey and Son; *not really a success.*
w Grover Jones, Edward Paramore Jnr *d* John Cromwell *ph* David Abel
☆ George Bancroft, Frances Dee, Robert Ames, Juliette Compton, Dorothy Peterson

'Splendid cast and serviceable product anywhere.' – *Variety*

The Rich Man's Wife

US 1996 94m Technicolor
Buena Vista/Hollywood/Caravan (Roger Birnbaum, Julie Bergman Sender)

An unhappily married woman discovers that her lover had her husband killed by an unstable stranger.
Predictable thriller, told in flashback, that never carries conviction.
wd Amy Holden Jones *ph* Haskell Wexler *m* John Frizzell, James Newton Howard *pd* Jeannine Oppewall *ed* Wendy Greene Bricmont
☆ Halle Berry, Christopher McDonald, Clive Owen, Peter Greene, Charles Hallahan, Frankie Faison, Clea Lewis

'A lady-and-the-psycho yarn so generic it might have been constructed by computer printout.' – *Godfrey Cheshire, Variety*

Rich, Young and Deadly: see *Platinum High School*

Rich, Young and Pretty
US 1951 95m Technicolor
MGM (Joe Pasternak)

A Texas rancher takes his young daughter to Paris, where she meets her real mother.
Moderate musical.
w Dorothy Cooper, Sidney Sheldon *d* Norman Taurog *ph* Robert Planck *m* Nicholas Brodszky *ch* Nick Castle *ly* Sammy Cahn
☆ Danielle Darrieux, Wendell Corey, Jane Powell, Fernando Lamas, Vic Damone
song 'Wonder Why'(m Nicholas Brodszky, *ly* Sammy Cahn)

Richard III ***
GB 1955 161m Technicolor Vistavision
London Films (Laurence Olivier)

Shakespeare's play about Richard Crookback, his seizure of the throne and his defeat at Bosworth.
Theatrical but highly satisfying filming of a splendidly melodramatic view of history. Interesting but not fussy camera movement, delightful sets (followed by a disappointingly 'realistic' battle) and superb performances.
w William Shakespeare (adapted by Laurence Olivier, Alan Dent, with additions) *d Laurence Olivier ph* Otto Heller *m William Walton pd Roger Furse ad Carmen Dillon*
☆ *Laurence Olivier*, Claire Bloom, *Ralph Richardson, Cedric Hardwicke*, Stanley Baker, Alec Clunes, John Gielgud, Mary Kerridge, Pamela Brown, Michael Gough, Norman Wooland, Helen Haye, Patrick Troughton, Clive Morton, Andrew Cruickshank
'Wherever the play was loose-jointed or ill-fitting, Sir Laurence has been its tinker and its tailor, but never once its butcher.' – *Paul Dehn, News Chronicle*
Laurence Olivier
film; British film; Laurence Olivier

'I can smile ... and murder while I smile.'
Richard III ***
GB 1995 105m Technicolor
UA/British Screen/First Look (Liza Katselas Pare, Stephen Bayly)

In a fascist England of the 30s, the King's younger brother murders his way to the throne and attempts to hold it as civil war rages.
A fast-moving, pared-down version of Shakespeare that remains true to much of the play's poetry, concentrating on political manoeuvre and successfully translating the action to a modern setting.
w Ian McKellen play William Shakespeare *stage production Richard Eyre d Richard Loncraine ph* Peter Biziou *m* Trevor Jones *pd Tony Burrough ed* Paul Green
☆ *Ian McKellen*, Annette Bening, Jim Broadbent, Robert Downey Jnr, Nigel Hawthorne, Kristin Scott Thomas, Maggie Smith, John Wood, Adrian Dunbar, Dominic West
'A superb political thriller in an England that is a subtly distorting mirror of reality – or a reality adjacent to our own.' – *Peter Holland, TLS*
'A fast, exuberant, violent ride.' – *Variety*
Tony Burrough; costume design (Shuna Harwood)

Richer than the Earth: see *The Whistle at Eaton Falls*

The Richest Girl in the World
US 1934 80m bw
RKO (Pandro S. Berman)
A millionairess changes places with her secretary to find a man who will love her for herself.
Rose-coloured romance, remade in 1944 as Bride by Mistake.
w Norman Krasna *d* William A. Seiter *ph* Nick Musuraca *md* Max Steiner
☆ Miriam Hopkins, Joel McCrea, Fay Wray, Henry Stephenson, Reginald Denny, Beryl Mercer
'Eighty minutes of unerring entertainment ... a pip picture for Miriam Hopkins.' – *Variety*
Norman Krasna

'Five buddies, one butler, and a dog on an adventure so big ... Even the world's richest kid can't afford to miss it.'
Richie Rich
US 1994 95m colour
Warner/Silver Pictures/Davis Entertainment (Joel Silver, John Davis)

A wealthy 12-year-old, aided by his poorer friends, saves his parents when they are threatened by a murderous employee.
Unexceptional entertainment aimed at a young audience; it might keep them quiet for half an hour or so.
w Tom S. Parker, Jim Jennewein *story* Neil Tolkin, based on characters appearing in Harvey Comics *d* Donald Petrie *ph* Don Burgess *m* Alan Silvestri *pd* James Spencer *ed* Malcolm Campbell
☆ Macaulay Culkin, John Larroquette, Edward Herrmann, Jonathan Hyde, Christine Ebersole, Michael McShane
'Decently crafted but oddly charmless.' – *Variety*

'He's a cop accused of murder. The only person who knows he's innocent is the psycho who wants him dead.'
'This is one case that's going to be settled out of court.'
Ricochet
US 1991 102m colour
First Independent/Summit/Silver (Joel Silver, Michael Levy)

Seeking revenge, a murderer sets out to frame the one-time cop, now an assistant district attorney, who put him inside.
Depressingly violent and unpleasant thriller.
w Steven E. de Souza *story* Fred Dekker, Menno Meyjes *d* Russell Mulcahy *ph* Peter Levy *m* Alan Silvestri *pd* Jay Hinkle *ed* Peter Honess
☆ Denzel Washington, John Lithgow, Ice T, Kevin Pollak, Lindsay Wagner, Mary Ellen Trainor, Josh Evans, Victoria Dillard
'If you don't flinch when power tools are being abused and can swallow ridiculous plot points if more dynamite action is only a minute away, then this is a good bet for an entertaining night out.' – *Kim Newman, Empire*

The Riddle of the Sands *
GB 1978 102m Eastmancolor Panavision
Rank/Worldmark (Drummond Challis)

In 1901 a British yachtsman in the North Sea hits upon a German trial invasion.
Rather too placid adaptation of a semi-classic adventure story in which too little happens to make a rousing action film; points of interest along the way, though.
w Tony Maylam, John Bailey *novel* Erskine Childers *d* Tony Maylam *ph* Hazel Peiser *m* Howard Blake
☆ Michael York, Simon MacCorkindale, Jenny Agutter, Alan Badel, Jurgen Andersen

The Riddle of the Stinson *
Australia 1988 95m colour
Kennedy Miller (Terry Hayes, George Miller, Doug Mitchell)
In 1937, a farmer goes to the rescue of survivors of a plane crash in inaccessible country.
A pleasant period picture, based on fact and told in direct and simple manner.
w Tony Morphett *d* Chris Noonan *ph* Geoffrey Simpson *m* Jim Conway, Colin Watson *pd* Owen Paterson *ed* Frans Vandenburgh
☆ Norman Kaye, Richard Roxburgh, Helen O'Connor, Esben Storm, Huw Williams, Susan Lyons

Ride a Crooked Mile *
US 1938 70m bw
Paramount (Jeff Lazarus)
An ex-Cossack cattle hijacker is disappointed when jailed to find that his son will not help him escape.
Lively crime melodrama with an unusual twist.
w Ferdinand Reyher, John C. Moffitt *d* Alfred E. Green
☆ Akim Tamiroff, Leif Erickson, Frances Farmer, Lynne Overman, John Miljan, Vladimir Sokoloff
'Fine melodrama, handicapped by lack of cast strength and so-so title.' – *Variety*

Ride a Crooked Trail
US 1958 88m Eastmancolor Cinemascope
Universal-International (Howard Pine)
A crook takes refuge in a small town and becomes its honest marshal.
One we've heard before, and seen better done.
w Borden Chase *d* Jesse Hibbs *ph* Harold Lipstein
☆ Audie Murphy, Walter Matthau, Gia Scala, Henry Silva

The Ride Back *
US 1957 79m bw
UA/Associates and Aldrich (William Conrad)
A lawman arrests an outlaw wanted for murder, but has the problem of getting him back to base.
Slightly offbeat low-budget Western, well enough done if it had to be done at all.
w Anthony Ellis *d* Allen H. Miner *ph* Joseph Biroc *m* Frank de Vol
☆ Anthony Quinn, William Conrad, George Trevino, Lita Milan

Ride beyond Vengeance
US 1966 100m Technicolor
Columbia/Tiger/Goodson/Todman/Sentinel/Fenady
A young Westerner, accused of cattle rustling and branded, vows revenge.
Dourly brutal but studio-bound and very padded Western; if there is any entertainment value it doesn't emerge for more than a few moments.
w Andrew J. Fenady *novel The Night of the Tiger* by Al Dewlen *d* Bernard McEveety *ph* Lester Shorr *m* Richard Markowitz
☆ Chuck Connors, Michael Rennie, Kathryn Hays, Claude Akins, Bill Bixby, Paul Fix, Gary Merrill, Joan Blondell, Gloria Grahame, Ruth Warrick, Arthur O'Connell, Frank Gorshin, James MacArthur
† Probably intended as a TV movie and found too violent.

Ride Clear of Diablo
US 1954 80m Technicolor
Universal-International (John W. Rogers)
A young man seeking vengeance on his father's murderer becomes deputy to a sheriff hired to kill him too.
Lively enough star Western.
w George Zuckerman *d* Jesse Hibbs *ph* Irving Glassberg *m* Joseph Gershenson
☆ Audie Murphy, Dan Duryea, Susan Cabot, Abbe Lane, Russell Johnson, Paul Birch, Jack Elam

Ride 'Em Cowboy
US 1941 82m bw
Universal (Alex Gottlieb)

Two hot dog vendors find themselves working on an Arizona dude ranch.
Slick but routine comedy star vehicle with no outstanding sequences.
w True Boardman, John Grant *d* Arthur Lubin *ph* John W. Boyle *m* Frank Skinner *songs* Don Raye, Gene de Paul
☆ Bud Abbott, Lou Costello, Dick Foran, Anne Gwynne, Samuel S. Hinds, Richard Lane, Johnny Mack Brown, Ella Fitzgerald

Ride Him Cowboy
US 1932 55m bw
Warner

GB title: *The Hawk*
A cowboy saves Duke, a temperamental horse, from being shot for murder, tames the beast and tracks down the real killer.
Enjoyable, fast-moving low-budget Western, the first in which Wayne displayed star quality.
w Scott Mason *story* Kenneth Perkins *d* Fred Allen
☆ John Wayne, Ruth Hall, Otis Harlan, Henry B. Walthall, Harry Gribbon, Duke
† The film was a remake of the silent *The Unknown Cavalier*, made in 1926 and starring Ken Maynard.

Ride in the Whirlwind *
US 1965 82m colour
Jack H. Harris/Proteus (Jack Nicholson, Monte Hellman)

Three cowhands are mistaken for outlaws by a vengeful posse.
Grim and talkative Western about lives trapped by circumstance.
w Jack Nicholson *d* Monte Hellman *ph* Gregory Sandor *m* Robert Drasnin *ad* James Campbell
☆ Cameron Mitchell, Millie Perkins, Jack Nicholson, Katherine Squire, George Mitchell, Rupert Crosse, Harry Dean Stanton

Ride Lonesome
US 1959 73m Eastmancolor Cinemascope
Columbia
A bounty hunter catches a killer as bait to trap the criminal's brother against whom he plots vengeance.
Mildly suspenseful Western, rather lost on the wide screen.
w Burt Kennedy *d* Budd Boetticher *ph* Charles Lawton Jnr *m* Heinz Roemheld
☆ Randolph Scott, Karen Steele, Pernell Roberts, James Best, James Coburn, Lee Van Cleef

Ride Out for Revenge
US 1957 79m bw
Bryna/UA (Norman Retchin)
Gold is discovered on land to which the army is moving Indians, and this causes second thoughts.
Low-key, rather brooding Western which aims to be different.
w Norman Retchin *d* Bernard Girard *ph* Floyd Crosby *m* Leith Stevens
☆ Rory Calhoun, Lloyd Bridges, Gloria Grahame, Joanne Gilbert, Vince Edwards

Ride the High Country **
US 1962 94m Metrocolor Cinemascope
MGM (Richard E. Lyons)

GB title: *Guns in the Afternoon*
Two retired lawmen help transport gold from a mining camp to the bank, but one has ideas of his own.
Thoughtful Western graced by ageing star presences; generally well done.
w N. B. Stone Jnr *d Sam Peckinpah ph* Lucien Ballard *m* George Bassman
☆ *Joel McCrea, Randolph Scott*, Edgar Buchanan, Mariette Hartley, James Drury
'A nice little conventional unconventional Western.' – *Stanley Kauffmann*

'The movie that rocked the debutantes – down to their last martini!'
Ride the High Iron
US 1957 74m bw
Columbia (William Self)

A war veteran gets into the seamier side of public relations.
Curious little urban melodrama with a high moral tone, like a cut-price Sweet Smell of Success.
w Milton Gelman *d* Don Weis *ph* Joe Novak *m* Melvyn Leonard
☆ Don Taylor, Raymond Burr, Sally Forrest
† Originally made for TV.

Ride the Man Down
US 1952 90m Trucolor
Republic
The death of a rancher sets off a bitter fight for his lands.
Flat and uninteresting Western melodrama.
w Mary McCall Jnr *story* Luke Short *d* Joseph Kane *ph* Jack Marta *m* Ned Freeman
☆ Brian Donlevy, Ella Raines, Rod Cameron, Forrest Tucker, Barbara Britton, James Bell, Chill Wills, J. Carrol Naish, Jim Davis

Ride the Pink Horse *
US 1947 101m bw
U-I (Joan Harrison)
An ex-serviceman visits a New Mexican town in search of the gangster who killed his buddy.
Dour, complex melodrama with a certain amount of style but not enough substance.
w Charles Lederer *novel* Dorothy B. Hughes *d* Robert Montgomery *ph* Russell Metty *m* Frank Skinner
☆ Robert Montgomery, Wanda Hendrix, Andrea King, Thomas Gomez, Fred Clark, Art Smith
'One of a kind: no one in his right mind would imitate it.' – *Pauline Kael, 70s*
Thomas Gomez

Ride the Wild Surf
US 1964 101m Eastmancolor
Columbia/Jana (Jo and Art Napoleon)
Surf riders go to Hawaii and find romance.
Pleasant, overlong, open air fun and games.
w Jo and Art Napoleon *d* Don Taylor *ph* Joseph Biroc *m* Stu Phillips
☆ Fabian, Shelley Fabares, Tab Hunter, Barbara Eden

The Ride to Hangman's Tree
US 1967 90m Technicolor
Universal (Howard Christie)
Three bandits never quite manage to reform.
Easy-going Western, played on the light side in a vein later developed in Butch Cassidy and the Sundance Kid.
w Luci Ward, Jack Natteford, William Bowers *d* Alan Rafkin *ph* Gene Polito *m* Frank Skinner *md* Joseph Gershenson *ad* Alexander Golitzen, John F. McCormack *ed* Gene Palmer
☆ Jack Lord, James Farentino, Don Galloway, Melodie Johnson, Richard Anderson

Ride, Vaquero
US 1953 90m Anscocolor
MGM (Stephen Ames)
Ranchers settling in New Mexico after the Civil War cause some natives to turn bandit; one of them has a mysterious American associate called Rio.
Very mildly interesting Western with the stars rather swamping a humourless script.
w Frank Fenton *d* John Farrow *ph* Robert Surtees *m* Bronislau Kaper
☆ Robert Taylor, Ava Gardner, Howard Keel, Anthony Quinn, Charlita

'In a No-man's Land between North and South, You didn't fight for the Blue or the Grey... You fought for your friends and family.'
Ride With The Devil **
US 1999 138m DeLuxe Panavision
Entertainment/Universal/Good Machine (Ted Hope, Robert Colesberry, James Schamus)
In Missouri in the 1860s, a youth goes with his friends to join the Southern irregular forces and participates in the massacre of the Kansas town of Lawrence.
Dour, beautifully photographed semi-western, a harsh drama of idealism corrupted and redeemed; it ably shows the futility of war, as both sides commit atrocities and betrayals, but might have benefitted from a maturer point of view than that of its youthful participants.
w James Schamus *novel* *Woe to Live On* by Daniel Woodrell *d* Ang Lee *ph* Frederick Elmes *m* Mychael Danna *pd* Mark Friedberg *ed* Tim Squyres *cos* Marit Allen
☆ Skeet Ulrich (Jack Bull Chiles), Tobey Maguire (Jake Roedel), Jewel (Sue Lee Shelley), Jeffrey Wright (Daniel Holt), Simon Baker (George Clyde), Jonathan Rhys Meyers (Pitt Mackeson), James Caviezel (Black John), Thomas Guiry (Riley Crawford), Tom Wilkinson (Orton Brown), Jonathan Brandis (Cave Wyatt), Matthew Faber (Turner Rawls), Stephen Mailer (Babe Hudspeth), John Ales (Quantrill)
'A masterpiece that is also one of the finest films touching on the Civil War.' – *Philip French, Observer*
'The focus is diffused among too many characters, some of them so poorly defined as to be indistinguishable.' – *Stephen Farber, Movieline*

Le Rideau Cramoisi: see *The Crimson Curtain*

Rider from Tucson
US 1950 60m bw
RKO (Herman Scholm)
Two rodeo performers ride to Colorado to be at a friend's wedding and find that they must first rescue his bride-to-be.
Standard second-feature Western that jogs along in an unmemorable manner.
w Ed Earl Repp *d* Lesley Selander *ph* Nicholas Musuraca *m* Paul Sawtell *ad* Albert S. D'Agostino, Walter E. Keller *ed* Robert Swink
☆ Tim Holt, Richard Martin, Elaine Riley, Douglas Fowley, Veda Ann Borg, Robert Shayne

Rider on the Rain
France/Italy 1969 119m colour
Joseph E. Levine, Serge Silberman
original title: *Passager de la Pluie*
A woman shoots her rapist and then tries to conceal the crime.
Routine, fairly implausible thriller that owes much to Hitchcock.
w Sebastien Japrisot *d* René Clément *ph* Andreas Winding *m* Francis Lai *ad* Pierre Guffroy
☆ Charles Bronson, Marlène Jobert, Annie Cordy, Jill Ireland, Gabriele Tinti, Jean Gaven, Jean Piat, Corinne Marchand

Riders in the Sky
US 1949 70m bw
Columbia/Gene Autry (Armand Schaefer)
A former investigator for a county attorney, who decides to become a rancher, finds himself pitted against the ruthless boss of a small town.
Built around a hit song (for Vaughn Monroe), a leisurely minor Western of no particular interest.
w Gerald Geraghty *story* Herbert A. Woodbury *d* John English *ph* William Bradford *md* Mischa Bakaleinikoff *ad* Harold MacArthur *ed* Henry Batista
☆ Gene Autry, Champion, Pat Buttram, Gloria Henry, Mary Beth Hughes, Robert Livingston, Steve Darrell, Alan Hale Jnr, Tom London

Riders of Destiny
US 1933 54m bw
Monogram/Lone Star (Paul Malvern)
An undercover agent goes West to investigate small ranchers being swindled out of their water rights.
A dramatically crude and inert Western, with Wayne looking decidedly uncomfortable when strumming a guitar on horseback as the heroic 'Singin' Sandy'.
wd Robert N. Bradbury *ph* Archie Stout *ed* Carl Pierson
☆ John Wayne, Cecilia Parker, Forrest Tucker, George Hayes, Al St John, Heinie Conklin, Yakima Canutt, Earl Dwire
† Wayne's singing was dubbed by Jack Kirk.

Riders of the Purple Sage
US 1931 58m bw
Fox
A rootin', tootin' cowboy traps a villain and weathers a stampede and an avalanche.
Good standard Western previously filmed in 1918 with William Farnum and in 1925 with Tom Mix. This version was premièred on the wide screens of the period.
novel Zane Grey *d* Hamilton McFadden
☆ George O'Brien, Marguerite Churchill, Noah Beery, Yvonne Pelletier, Stanley Fields
'Still a good Western and okay outside the de luxers.' – *Variety*

Riders of Vengeance
US 1952 80m Technicolor
Universal-International (William Alland)
GB title: *The Raiders*
During the California gold rush, a prospector takes revenge on a local dictator.
Standard Western themes against a colourful background.
w Polly James, Lillie Hayward *d* Lesley Selander *ph* Carl Guthrie
☆ Richard Conte, Barbara Britton, Viveca Lindfors, Hugh O'Brian, Morris Ankrum, William Reynolds, Dennis Weaver

Riders to the Stars *
US 1954 81m Color Corporation
UA/Ivan Tors
Rocket scientists investigate the problems of cosmic bombardment.
Enjoyably straightforward science fiction with no monsters or political problems; it has decided historic interest as a record of what scientists in 1954 thought rocket travel would be like.
w Curt Siodmak *d* Richard Carlson *ph* Stanley Cortez *m* Harry Sukman
☆ Richard Carlson, Herbert Marshall, William Lundigan, Dawn Addams, Martha Hyer, Robert Karnes, Lawrence Dobkin

Ridicule **
France 1996 103m colour
Electric/Epithète/Cinéa/France 3 (Gilles Legrand, Frédérick Brillion/Philippe Carcassonne)
In the 1780s, a minor aristocrat arrives at the court of Louis XVI at Versailles seeking help to improve his peasants' lives, only to discover that the only quality valued is the exercise of wit.
Enjoyable period extravaganza on the power of language to make and break careers, and a portrait of a corrupt culture in its final decadence.
w Remi Waterhouse, Michel Fessler, Eric Vicaut *d* Patrice Leconte *ph* Thierry Arbogast *m* Antoine Duhamel *pd* Ivan Maussion *ed* Joëlle Hache
☆ Fanny Ardant, Charles Berling, Bernard Giraudeau, Judith Godrèche, Jean Rochefort, Carlo Brandt
'Resplendent and terrific entertainment.' – *Film Review*
foreign-language film
foreign film

'It's a rootin', tootin', six-gun shootin' musicalallapalooza!'
Riding High
US 1943 88m Technicolor
Paramount (Fred Kohlmar)
GB title: *Melody Inn*
A burlesque queen goes home to Arizona and helps ranchers by performing at a dude ranch.
Dim formula musical with exuberance but neither wit nor style.
w Walter de Leon, Arthur Phillips, Art Arthur *play* *Ready Money* by James Montgomery *d* George Marshall *ph* Karl Struss, Harry Hallenberger *md* Victor Young
☆ Dorothy Lamour, Dick Powell, Victor Moore, Gil Lamb, Cass Daley, Bill Goodwin, Rod Cameron, Glenn Langan, Andrew Tombes, Tim Ryan, Douglas Fowley, Milt Britton and his Band

Riding High *
US 1950 112m bw
Paramount (Frank Capra)
An easygoing racing man forsakes the chance of wealth to train his beloved horse for the Imperial Derby.
The director's familiar ingredients – farce, sentimentality, fast cutting, nice people and a lot of noise – seem a shade too tried and tested in this remake of his 1934 success Broadway Bill. *Despite the cast, the result is only moderately entertaining.*
w Robert Riskin *d* Frank Capra *ph* George Barnes, Ernest Laszlo *m* James Van Heusen *ly* Johnny Burke
☆ Bing Crosby, Coleen Gray, Charles Bickford, Raymond Walburn, James Gleason, Oliver Hardy, Frances Gifford, William Demarest, Ward Bond, Clarence Muse, Percy Kilbride, Harry Davenport, Margaret Hamilton, Douglass Dumbrille, Gene Lockhart

'The story of a girl who did everything wrong, but got everything right.'
Riding In Cars With Boys
US 2001 DeLuxe
Columbia/Gracie (James L. Brooks, Julie Ansell, Richard Sakai, Sara Colleton, Laurence Mark)
A woman rises above the troubles in her life – marriage at 15 to a feckless drug addict who gets her pregnant – to become a novelist.
Domestic drama of redemption, based on a true story, but never seeming more than fraudulent uplift.
w Morgan Upton Ward *book* Beverly Donofrio *d* Penny Marshall *ph* Miroslav Ondricek *m* Hans Zimmer, Heitor Pereira *pd* Bill Groom *ed* Richard Marks, Lawrence Jordan *cos* Cynthia Flynt
☆ Drew Barrymore (Beverly Donofrio), Steve Zahn (Ray Hasek), Brittany Murphy (Fay Forrester), Adam Garcia (Jason Donofrio), Lorraine Bracco (Mrs Donofrio), James Woods (Mr Donofrio), Sara Gilbert (Tina), Desmond Harrington (Bobby)
'It's almost sinister, this remorseless diminution of human experience to the acceptable contours of a punch-line.' – *Peter Matthews, Sight & Sound*
'A film with honesty, sincerity and a great big heart.' – *Rex Reed, New York Observer*

Riding Shotgun
US 1954 75m Warnercolor
Warner
A shotgun stagecoach guard carries on a long vendetta against an outlaw.
Routine Western excitements, played mainly indoors.
w Tom Blackburn *d* André de Toth *ph* Bert Glennon *m* David Buttolph
☆ Randolph Scott, Wayne Morris, Joan Weldon, Joe Sawyer, James Millican, Charles Bronson, James Bell

Rien Ne Va Plus
France/Switzerland 1997 106m colour
Artificial Eye/MK2/TF1/CAB/CDE
A couple of confidence tricksters have a love-hate relationship with one another.
Casual, slightly comic movie that Chabrol has called autobiographical, though he must have led a more interesting life than the ones that he here puts on the screen.
wd Claude Chabrol *ph* Eduardo Serra *m* Matthieu Chabrol *ad* Françoise Benoît-Fresco *ed* Monique Fardoulis
☆ Isabelle Huppert, Michel Serrault, François Cluzet, Jean-François Balmer, Jackie Berroyer, Jean Benguigui, Mony Dalmes, Thomas Chabrol
'There's little mystery, and surprisingly little humanity either, in a film that's finally as dead and dated as the wretched pop *chanson* that ends it.' – *Jonathan Romney, Sight and Sound*

Riff Raff *
US 1935 90m bw
MGM (Irving Thalberg)
A con man and his wife end up on the wrong side of the law.
Modest comedy drama that never quite sparks.
w Frances Marion, H. W. Haneman, Anita Loos *d* J. Walter Ruben *ph* Ray June *m* Edward Ward
☆ Jean Harlow, Spencer Tracy, Joseph Calleia, Una Merkel, Mickey Rooney, Victor Kilian, J. Farrell MacDonald
'It ain't art, but it's box office.' – *Variety*

Riff Raff *
US 1947 80m bw
RKO (Nat Holt)
A dying man hands a Panama City con man a map to valuable oil deposits, and various shady people are after it.
Rather heavy but well made comedy-drama with some striking scenes.
w Martin Rackin *d* Ted Tetzlaff *ph* George E. Diskant *m* Roy Webb
☆ Pat O'Brien, Walter Slezak, Anne Jeffreys, Percy Kilbride, Jerome Cowan

'Those that live on the edge sometimes fall.'
Riff-Raff **
GB 1990 95m colour
BFI/Parallax (Sally Hibbin)
Labourers on a building site take revenge on their employers when one of them is killed in an accident.
Successful blend of wit and naturalism, although the overlapping dialogue in many regional accents can be hard to follow at times.
w Bill Jesse *d* Ken Loach *ph* Barry Ackroyd *m* Stewart Copeland *pd* Martin Johnson *ed* Jonathan Morris
☆ Robert Carlyle, Emer McCourt, Jimmy Coleman, George Moss, Ricky Tomlinson, David Finch, Richard Belgrave, Ade Sapara, Derek Young, Bill Moores
'A wonderfully entertaining account of life on the margins in London that combines laughter and tears, delivering its message in an intimate and subtle way.' – *Screen International*
† The film was turned down by Britain's major distributors. It received a limited release after winning an award as the best European film of the year and receiving the International Critics Prize at the Cannes Film Festival.

Rififi **
France 1955 116m bw
Indus/Pathé/Prima
original title: *Du Rififi chez les Hommes*
After an elaborate raid on a jewellery store, thieves fall out and the caper ends in bloodshed.

A film with much to answer for, in the form of hundreds of imitations showing either detailed accounts of robberies (Topkapi, Gambit) or gloomy looks at the private lives of criminals. At the time it seemed crisp and exciting, and the 25-minute silent robbery sequence is quite something.
w René Wheeler, Jules Dassin, Auguste le Breton *novel* Auguste le Breton *d Jules Dassin*
ph Philippe Agostini *m* Georges Auric
☆ *Jean Servais*, Carl Mohner, Robert Manuel, Marie Sabouret, Perlo Vita (Jules Dassin)

'I sometimes ask myself whether so much of the film is silent because of my own lack of French.' – *Jules Dassin*

† Several 'sequels' were made using the word *rififi* (criminal argot for 'trouble') in the title, but in plot terms they were entirely unrelated.

The Rift: see *La Grieta*

Riget: see *The Kingdom*

The Right Approach
US 1961 92m bw Cinemascope
TCF (Oscar Brodney)
A Hollywood opportunist tries to make it as a star.
A potentially witty Hollywood story is sabotaged by a style which is as naïve as it is dismal; and Mr Vaughan's hopes of stardom unfairly ended right here.
w Fay and Michael Kanin *play* Garson Kanin *d* David Butler *ph* Sam Leavitt *m* Dominic Frontière
☆ Frankie Vaughan, Martha Hyer, Juliet Prowse, Gary Crosby, David MacLean, Jesse White, Jane Withers

Right Cross
US 1950 90m bw
MGM (Armand Deutsch)
A boxing champion injures his hand and has to abandon his career.
Rather dull sporting melodrama with a Mexican background, saved by good production values.
w Charles Schnee *d* John Sturges *ph* Norbert Brodine *m* David Raksin
☆ Dick Powell, June Allyson, Lionel Barrymore, Ricardo Montalban

The Right Stuff *
US 1983 193m Technicolor
Warner/Ladd (Irwin Winkler, Robert Chartoff)
Test pilots are recruited and trained as astronauts.
A reasonably factual account of the Mercury programme: extremely well made but somehow too brash and inhuman to provide much entertainment. An unexpected commercial flop.
wd Philip Kaufman *book* Tom Wolfe *ph* Caleb Deschanel *m* Bill Conti *pd* Geoffrey Kirkland *ed* Glenn Farr, Lisa Fruchtman, Stephen A. Rotter, Douglas Stewart, Tom Rolf
☆ Sam Shepard, Scott Glenn, Ed Harris, Dennis Quaid, Fred Ward, Barbara Hershey, Kim Stanley, Veronica Cartwright
Bill Conti; editing; sound; sound editing
best picture; Sam Shepard; Caleb Deschanel

The Right to Live
US 1935 75m bw
Warner
GB title: *The Sacred Flame*
Someone in the family mercifully kills a crippled war hero.
Uninspired rendering of Somerset Maugham's play The Sacred Flame, *previously filmed under its own title in 1929 (with Pauline Frederick, Henrietta Crosman).*
w Ralph Block *d* William Keighley
☆ George Brent, Colin Clive, Josephine Hutchinson, Peggy Wood, C. Aubrey Smith, Leo G. Carroll, Halliwell Hobbes

The Right to Love *
US 1930 79m bw
Paramount
A mother has a strong affinity with her illegitimate daughter who is a missionary on the other side of the world.
Curious mystic melodrama which adds a twist to the popular mother-love devices. Technically it introduced the Bell light valve which improved sound reproduction, and also the Dunning process which improved the presentation of dual roles. (The star played mother and daughter.)
w Zoe Akins *novel* Brook Adams by Susan Glaspell *d* Richard Wallace *ph* Charles Lang
☆ *Ruth Chatterton*, Paul Lukas, David Manners, Irving Pichel, George Baxter

'A profound and thoughtful romantic drama treated with utmost refinement of sophistication and still possessing elements which will appeal to the broadest kind of screen audience.' – *Variety*

Charles Lang

The Right to Love: see *Brainwashed (1972)*

Rikky and Pete
Australia 1988 107m colour
UA/Cascade (Nadia Tass, David Parker)
An irresponsible, cop-hating inventor and his sister, a singer and geologist, leave home and head for a remote mining town, pursued by an obsessive policeman.
Unsuccessful comedy, over-elaborate and heavy-handed with its jokes, and seemingly uncertain as to its point.
w David Parker *d* Nadia Tass *ph* David Parker *m* Eddie Rayner *m/ly* Philip Judd *pd* Josephine Ford *ed* Ken Sallows
☆ Stephen Kearney, Nina Landis, Tetchie Agbayani, Bill Hunter, Bruno Lawrence, Bruce Spence, Lewis Fitz-Gerald, Dorothy Alison

The Ring: see *Ringu*

The Ring *
GB 1927 116m approx bw
BIP (John Maxwell)
Two boxers vie for the love of a woman.
Early Hitchcock that shows his already developed skill for deft story-telling; it was the first of his films to reveal his individuality as a director.
w Alfred Hitchcock, Alma Reville, Eliot Stannard *d* Alfred Hitchcock *ph* John J. Cox *ad* C. Wilfred Arnold
☆ Carl Brisson, Lilian Hall Davis, Ian Hunter, Forrester Harvey, Harry Terry, Gordon Harker, Billy Wells

'Succeeds in that very rare accomplishment of being the purest film art and a fine popular entertainment.' – *Evening News*

† The version released on video runs for 73m.

The Ring
US 1952 79m bw
King Brothers
A young Mexican becomes a prizefighter in the hope of winning greater respect for Mexican-Americans.
Well-meant low-budget programmer.
w Irving Shulman *d* Kurt Neumann *ph* Russell Harlan *m* Herschel Burke Gilbert
☆ Gerald Mohr, Lalo Rios, Rita Moreno, Robert Arthur

'Before you die, you see the ring.'
The Ring
US 2002 115m Eastmancolor
DreamWorks (Walter F. Parkes, Laurie MacDonald)
A reporter investigates the death of teenagers who died a week after watching a videotape and receiving a phone call.
A remake of the Japanese movie Ringu (qv) that at least produced a slight other-wordly frisson in its story of a vengeful ghost; translated to an American setting, it seems no more than feeble.
w Ehren Kruger *novel* Koji Suzuki *d* Gore Verbinski *ph* Bojan Bazelli *m* Hans Zimmer *pd* Tom Duffield *ed* Craig Wood
☆ Naomi Watts (Rachel Keller), Martin Henderson (Noah), David Dorfman (Aidan), Brian Cox (Richard Morgan), Jane Alexander (Dr Grasnik), Lindsay Frost (Ruth), Amber Tamblyn (Katie), Rachael Bella (Becca), Daveigh Chase (Samara)

'This incoherent mess…contemptible catchpenny.' – *Alexander Walker, London Evening Standard*

'Comes across in muted fashion, with uninvolving characters and lack of genuine excitement or fright creating a second-rate, second-hand feel.' – *Todd McCarthy, Variety*

† The film cost around $45m and took more than $128m at the US box office.

Ring 0: The Birthday: see *Ringu 0: Basudei*

The Ring 2: see *Ringu 2*

Ring of Bright Water *
GB 1969 107m Technicolor
Palomar/Brightwater (Joseph Strick)
A civil servant buys a pet otter and moves to a remote cottage in the western Highlands.
Disneyesque fable for animal lovers, from a bestselling book.
w Jack Couffer, Bill Travers *book* Gavin Maxwell *d* Jack Couffer *ph* Wolfgang Suschitsky *m* Frank Cordell
☆ Bill Travers, Virginia McKenna, Peter Jeffrey, Roddy McMillan, Jameson Clark

Ring of Fear
US 1954 88m Warnercolor Cinemascope
Warner/Wayne-Fellows (Robert M. Fellows)
A homicidal maniac returns to the circus where he used to work and causes various 'accidents.'
Tediously predictable circus melodrama with a curious but not very likeable cast.
w Paul Fix, Philip MacDonald, James Edward Grant *d* James Edward Grant *ph* Edwin DuPar *m* Emil Newman, Arthur Lange
☆ Clyde Beatty, Pat O'Brien, Mickey Spillane, Sean McClory, Marian Carr, John Bromfield, Pedro Gonzalez Gonzalez, Emmett Lynn

Ring of Fire
US 1961 90m Metrocolor
MGM/Andrew and Virginia Stone
An Oregon sheriff is kidnapped by teenage delinquents but manages to lead them into both a police trap and a forest fire.
Outdoor action thriller with a plot which is ludicrously unconvincing in detail, though the fire scenes impress.
wd Andrew L. Stone *ph* William H. Clothier *m* Duane Eddy
☆ David Janssen, Joyce Taylor, Frank Gorshin, Joel Marston

Ring of Spies *
GB 1963 90m bw
British Lion (Leslie Gilliatt)
US title: *Ring of Treason*
How the Portland spy ring was tracked down.
Documentary drama, rather less intriguing, somehow, than the actual facts; but the sheer thought of spies in the suburbs keeps interest going.
w Frank Launder, Peter Barnes *d* Robert Tronson *ph* Arthur Lavis
☆ Bernard Lee, Margaret Tyzack, David Kossoff, Nancy Nevinson, William Sylvester

Ring of Treason: see *Ring of Spies*

Ring Up the Curtain: see *Broadway to Hollywood*

The Ringer *
GB 1952 78m bw
BL/London (Hugh Perceval)
A dangerous criminal known only as The Ringer threatens to kill the crooked lawyer responsible for his sister's death.
Artful old-fashioned mystery, quite well restaged, and in fact the best extant example of filmed Wallace.
w Val Valentine *play and novel* Edgar Wallace *d* Guy Hamilton *ph* Ted Scaife *m* Malcolm Arnold
☆ *Donald Wolfit*, Mai Zetterling, Herbert Lom, Greta Gynt, William Hartnell, Norman Wooland
† The play was also filmed in 1931 with Patric Curwen, Franklin Dyall and Gordon Harker; and in 1938 as *The Gaunt Stranger* (qv).

'Thanksgiving is about sharing … blow by blow.'
Ringmaster
US 1998 90m DeLuxe
Artisan/Kushner-Locke (Steve Stabler, Gary Goldstein, Jerry Springer, Brad Jenkel, Gina Rugolo-Judd)
Fans of a trashy TV talk show petition to appear on the programme, to expose the sexual misbehaviour of those close to them.
With the host of a trashy TV talk show playing a similar fictional creation, this seems a completely redundant movie; it is certainly not a watchable one.
w John Bernstein *d* Neil Abramson *ph* Russell J. Lyster *m* Kennard Ramsey *pd* Dorian Vernacchio, Deborah Raymond *ed* Suzanne Hines
☆ Jerry Springer, Jaime Pressly, William McNamara, Molly Hagan, John Capodice, Wendy Raquel Robinson, Michael Jai White, Michael Dudikoff

'As Springer well knows, however, you can't go broke overestimating the bad taste of the American public, so perhaps paying customers do exist who will find this feature funner 'n' a lesbian mud-wrestling match.' – *Dennis Harvey, Variety*

Ringo and His Golden Pistol (dubbed)
Italy 1966 88m Eastmancolor
MGM/Sanson (Joseph Fryd)
original title: *Johnny Oro*
A Mexican bounty hunter is chased across the border to a small law-abiding town by bandits and Apaches seeking revenge.
Stylish spaghetti Western, though its invincible hero comes near to being a bore.
w Adriano Bolzoni, Franco Rossetti *d* Sergio Corbucci *ph* Riccardo Pallottini *m* Carlo Savina *ad* Carlo Simi *ed* Otello Colangeli
☆ Mark Damon, Valeria Fabrizi, Franco Derosa, Giulia Rubini, Loris Loddi, Ettore Manni
† For its US release, the name of the original was changed to take advantage of the success of Duccio Tessari's *A Pistol for Ringo* (qv).

Rings on Her Fingers *
US 1942 85m bw
TCF (Milton Sperling)
The front girl for a couple of confidence tricksters falls in love with their first victim.
Lively comedy which drags into drama in its second half.
w Ken Englund *d* Rouben Mamoulian *ph* George Barnes *m* Cyril Mockridge
☆ Gene Tierney, Henry Fonda, Laird Cregar, Spring Byington, Shepperd Strudwick, Frank Orth, Henry Stephenson, Marjorie Gateson

Ringside Maisie
US 1941 96m bw
MGM (J. Walter Ruben)
GB title: *Cash and Carry*
A showgirl becomes involved with a reluctant boxer and his manager.
Bright, slight comedy that slides unconvincingly into melodrama and never recovers.
w Mary C. McCall Jnr *d* Edwin L. Marin *ph* Charles Lawton *m* David Snell *ad* Cedric Gibbons
☆ Ann Sothern, George Murphy, Robert Sterling, Virginia O'Brien, Natalie Thompson, Margaret Moffat, Maxie Rosenbloom

Ringu *
Japan 1998 98m colour
Kadokawa/Pony Canyon/Imagica/Asmik-Ace/Omega (Shinya Kawai, Takashige Ichise, Takenori Sento)
GB title: *The Ring*
A TV reporter investigates the death of a schoolgirl, who died after watching a video and then receiving a mysterious phone message; when the reporter watches the video, she also gets a phone call…
A ghost story that was a big hit in Japan, though it seems too mild to create the same effect elsewhere.
w Hiroshi Takahashi *novel* Koji Suzuki *d* Hideo Nakata *ph* Junichiro Hayashi *m* Kinji Kawai *pd* Iwao Saito *ed* Nobuyuki Takahashi
☆ Nanako Matsushima (Reiko Asakawa), Miki Nakatani (Mai Takano), Hiroyuki Sanada (Ryuji Takayama), Yuko Takeuchi (Tomoko Oishi), Hitomi Sato (Masami Kurahashi), Yoichi Numata (Takashi Yamamura), Yutaka Matsushige (Yoshino), Katsumi Muramatsu (Koichi Asakawa), Rikiya Otaka (Yoichi Asakawa), Masako (Shizuko Yamamura)

'Riveting amalgam of modern urban myth and ancient eastern legend.' – *Mark Kermode, Sight & Sound*

Ringu 0: Basudei
Japan 2001 99m colour
Toho/Asmik Ace/Ring 0 (Shinji Ogawa, Masao Nagai, Takashige Ichise)
GB title: *Ring 0: The Birthday*
A reporter investigates a young woman with strange psychic powers who leaves a trail of death behind her.

Effective prequel to the first two films in the Ring cycle, conjuring up an atmosphere of dread.
w Hiroshi Takahashi *novels* Koji Suzuki *d* Norio Tsuruta *ph* Takahide Shibanushi *ad* Osamu Yamaguchi *ed* Hiroshi Sunaga *sp* Hajime Matsumoto, Nobuaki Sugiki
☆ Yukie Nakama (Sadako), Seiichi Tanabe (Toyama), Kumiko Aso (Etsuko Tachihara), Yoshiko Tanaka (Akiko Miyaji)
'Wraps up the whole story without delivering the skin-crawling psycho-horror of the initial, and best, movie.' – *Derek Elley, Variety*

Ringu 2
Japan 1999 92m colour
Kadokawa Shoten (Masato Hara)
GB title: *The Ring 2*
Investigations continue into a mysterious videotape that brings death to those who watch it.
A sequel that is likely to confuse those who haven't seen the first, and superior, movie; this is less effective, merely tidying up, and cashing in on, the original.
w Hiroshi Takahashi *novel* Koji Suzuki *d* Hideo Nakata *ph* Hideo Yamamoto *m* Kenji Kawai *ed* Nobuyuki Takahashi *sp* Hajime Matsumoto
☆ Miki Nakatani (Mai), Daisuke Ban (Dr Heihachiro Ikuma), Nanako Matsushima (Reiko Asakawa), Kyoko Fukada (Kanae Sawaguchi), Kenjiro Ishimaru (Omuta), Hiroyuki Sanada (Ryuji Takayama), Yoichi Numata (Takashi Yamamura), Hitomi Sato (Masami Kurahashi)
'A few moments of shock and a reasonably sustained creepy atmosphere do not compensate for the lackadaisical plotting.' – *Neil Norman, London Evening Standard*

Rio
US 1939 78m bw
Universal
A crooked financier escapes from Devil's Island to join his wife in Rio, only to find she has been unfaithful.
Modest but well made melodrama.
w Stephen Morehouse Avery, Frank Partos, Edwin Justus Mayer, Aben Kandel, Jean Negulesco *d* John Brahm *ph* Hal Mohr *m* Frank Skinner *md* Charles Previn
☆ Basil Rathbone, Victor McLaglen, Sigrid Gurie, Robert Cummings, Leo Carrillo, Billy Gilbert, Irving Bacon, Irving Pichel
'A fair programmer with a blend of romance and adventure ... should stand up satisfactorily as a top dualler in most situations.' – *Variety*

Rio Bravo **
US 1959 141m Technicolor
Warner/Armada (Howard Hawks)
A wandering cowboy and a drunken sheriff hold a town against outlaws.
Cheerfully overlong and slow-moving Western in which everybody, including the director, does his thing. All very watchable for those with time to spare, but more a series of revue sketches than an epic.
w Jules Furthman, Leigh Brackett *d* Howard Hawks *ph* Russell Harlan *m* Dimitri Tiomkin
☆ *John Wayne, Dean Martin,* Ricky Nelson, Angie Dickinson, Walter Brennan, Ward Bond, John Russell, Pedro Gonzalez-Gonzalez, Claude Akins, Harry Carey Jnr, Bob Steele
'After we finished we found we could have done it a lot better ... and that's why we went ahead and made *El Dorado*.' – *Howard Hawks*
† More or less remade in 1966 as *El Dorado* and in 1970 as *Rio Lobo*.

Rio Conchos *
US 1964 107m DeLuxe Cinemascope
TCF (David Weisbart)
Two thousand rifles are stolen from an army command post and traced to the hide-out of a former Confederate colonel who wants to continue the Civil War.
Good standard Western which shares much of its story line with The Comancheros.
w Clair Huffaker, Joseph Landon *novel* Clair Huffaker *d* Gordon Douglas *ph* Joe MacDonald *m* Jerry Goldsmith
☆ *Richard Boone, Edmond O'Brien,* Stuart Whitman, Tony Franciosa

Rio Grande *
US 1950 105m bw
Republic/Argosy (John Ford, Merian C. Cooper)
A Cavalry unit on the Mexican border in the 1880s conducts a vain campaign against marauding Indians.
Thin Ford Western on his favourite theme, with too many pauses for song, too many studio sets, and too little plot. Aficionados, however, will find much to admire.
w James Kevin McGuinness *story* James Warner Bellah *d* John Ford *ph* Bert Glennon *m* Victor Young
☆ John Wayne, Maureen O'Hara, Ben Johnson, Claude Jarman Jnr, Harry Carey Jnr, Chill Wills, J. Carrol Naish, Victor McLaglen

Rio Lobo *
US 1970 114m Technicolor
Cinema Center (Howard Hawks)
A Union colonel near the end of the Civil War recovers a gold shipment and exposes a traitor.
Rambling Western with traces of former glory, enjoyable at least for its sense of humour.
w Leigh Brackett, Burton Wohl *d* Howard Hawks *ph* William Clothier *m* Jerry Goldsmith *pd* Robert Smith *ed* John Woodcock
☆ John Wayne (Capt. Cord McNally), Jorge Rivero (Lt Pierre Cordona), Jennifer O'Neill (Shasta), *Jack Elam* (Phillips), Victor French (Ketcham), Chris Mitchum (Tuscarora), Mike Henry (Sheriff Hendricks), Sherry Lansing (Amelita), Susana Dosamantes (Maria Carmen)
'Too peevish to qualify as tragic, and only occasionally funny.' – *Jonathan Rosenbaum, Chicago Reader*
'Hawks' direction is as listless as the plot.' – *Variety*
'I didn't think it was any good.' – *Howard Hawks*

Rio Rita
US 1929 135m bw and Technicolor
RKO (William Le Baron)
Romance on a ranch near the Mexican border.
Very early talkie version of a popular Broadway operetta of the twenties; historical interest only.
w Luther Reed, Russell Mack *book* Guy Bolton, Fred Thomson, as produced by Florenz Ziegfeld *d* Luther Reed *ph* Robert Kurrk, Lloyd Knechtel *md* Victor Baravalle *songs* Harry Tierney, Joe McCarthy
☆ Bebe Daniels, John Boles, Bert Wheeler, Robert Woolsey, Dorothy Lee, Don Alvarado, George Renavent

Rio Rita
US 1942 91m bw
MGM (Pandro S. Berman)
Flat-footed remake bringing in Nazi spies.
Poor comedy even by Abbott and Costello standards.
w Richard Connell, Gladys Lehman *d* S. Sylvan Simon *ph* George J. Folsey *m* Herbert Stothart
☆ Bud Abbott, Lou Costello, John Carroll, Kathryn Grayson, Tom Conway, Barry Nelson

Riot
US 1968 98m Technicolor
Paramount/William Castle
While the warden is away, thirty-five convicts take over a state penitentiary and are violently subdued.
Strikingly bloody melodrama set in an actual prison in Arizona; well made, but less entertaining than Cagney and Raft used to be.
w James Poe *novel* Frank Elli *d* Buzz Kulik *ph* Robert B. Hauser *m* Christopher Komeda
☆ Gene Hackman, Jim Brown, Ben Carruthers, Mike Kellin, Gerald O'Loughlin, Clifford David

Riot in Cell Block Eleven *
US 1954 80m bw
Allied Artists/Walter Wanger
In a big American prison three convicts seize their guards, free the other prisoners and barricade themselves in their block.
Socially concerned low-budgeter, quite nicely made and persuasive of the need for prison reform.
w Richard Collins d Don Siegel ph Russell Harlan *m* Herschel Burke Gilbert
☆ Neville Brand, *Emile Meyer,* Frank Faylen, Leo Gordon, Robert Osterloh, Paul Frees, Don Keefer
'As a compassionate, angry, unsensational account of an episode of violence it makes considerably more impact than many of the overblown melodramas currently in fashion.' – *Penelope Houston*

Les Ripoux: see *Le Cop*

Ripoux contre ripoux: see *Le Cop 2*

Riptide *
US 1934 90m bw
MGM (Irving Thalberg)
A British diplomat weds a Manhattan chorus girl, but she later falls for an old flame.
Elegantly set, star-packed drawing-room drama which somehow didn't click.
wd Edmund Goulding *ph* Ray June *m* Herbert Stothart
☆ Norma Shearer, Robert Montgomery, Herbert Marshall, Mrs Patrick Campbell, Skeets Gallagher, Ralph Forbes, Lilyan Tashman, Helen Jerome Eddy, George K. Arthur, Halliwell Hobbes
'Has all the earmarks of box office ... a commendable job all round.' – *Variety*

The Rise and Fall of Legs Diamond
US 1960 101m bw
Warner/United States (Milton Sperling)
The career of a New York hoodlum of the twenties.
Inspired, like King of the Roaring Twenties, *by the TV success of* The Untouchables, *this was part of a brief attempt by Warner to recapture its pre-war gangster image. Alas, stars and style were equally lacking.*
w Joseph Landon *d* Budd Boetticher *ph* Lucien Ballard *m* Leonard Rosenman
☆ Ray Danton, Karen Steele, Elaine Stewart, Jesse White, Simon Oakland, Robert Lowery, Warren Oates, Judson Pratt

The Rise and Rise of Michael Rimmer
GB 1970 101m Technicolor
Warner/David Frost (Harry Fine)
An efficiency expert takes over an advertising agency and is soon an MP, a cabinet minister, and PM.
Satirical comedy which quickly goes overboard and is only occasionally funny; it does, however, mark the final death throes of the swinging sixties, and the changeover to Monty Python.
w Peter Cook, John Cleese, Kevin Billington, Graham Chapman *d* Kevin Billington *ph* Alex Thomson *m* John Cameron
☆ Peter Cook, John Cleese, Arthur Lowe, Denholm Elliott, Ronald Fraser, Vanessa Howard, George A. Cooper, Harold Pinter, James Cossins, Roland Culver, Dudley Foster, Julian Glover, Dennis Price, Ronnie Corbett

The Rise of Catherine the Great: see *Catherine the Great*

The Rise of Helga: see *Susan Lenox, Her Fall and Rise*

The Rise of Louis XIV **
France 1966 100m Eastmancolor
ORTF (Pierre Gout)
original title: *La Prise de Pouvoir par Louis XIV*
The young King of France asserts his power through the use of fashion, style and spectacle.
A complex study of power, shot in a direct, semi-documentary manner, with much use of a zoom lens.
w Jean Gruault *story* Philippe Erlanger *d* Roberto Rossellini *ph* Georges Leclerc, Jean-Louis Picavet *ad* Maurice Valay *ed* Armand Ridel
☆ Jean-Michel Patte, Raymond Jourdan, Silvagni, Katharine Renn, Dominique Vincent, Pierre Barrat
'Even the fact that it was made as a spectacular for French television does not quite justify its singular vapidity and pointlessness.' – *John Simon*
† The film was first shown on French TV before being given a cinema release.

Rising Damp
GB 1980 98m colour
ITC/Black Lion (Roy Skeggs)
The amorous and conniving landlord of a slum boarding house develops a passion for one of his tenants.
A useful reminder of a TV sitcom worth remembering, but handicapped by restriction of action, paucity of plot and the overlength usual in film versions of such things, not to mention the premature death of its original co-star Richard Beckinsale.
w Eric Chappell *d* Joe McGrath *ph* Frank Watts *m* David Lindup
☆ Leonard Rossiter, Frances de la Tour, Don Warrington, Denholm Elliott, Christopher Strauli

'Unforgettably John Ford's finest film!'
The Rising of the Moon
Eire 1957 81m bw
Warner/Four Provinces (Lord Killanin)
Three Irish short stories.
Curiously dull John Ford portmanteau with the Abbey players.
w Frank Nugent *stories* Frank O'Connor, Malcolm J. McHugh, Lady Gregory *d* John Ford *ph* Robert Krasker *m* Eamonn O'Gallagher *narrator* Tyrone Power
☆ Maureen Connell, Eileen Crowe, Cyril Cusack, Maureen Delany, Donal Donnelly, Frank Lawton, Edward Lexy, Jack MacGowran, Denis O'Dea, Jimmy O'Dea, Noel Purcell

'A collision of East and West. A conspiracy of seduction and murder. A battle between tradition and power. Business is war.'
Rising Sun
US 1993 129m DeLuxe
TCF (Peter Kaufman)
Two cops, one an expert in Japanese culture, investigate the murder of a prostitute in the boardroom of a Japanese corporation's new Los Angeles headquarters.
Turgid thriller, revealing paranoid feelings about the Japanese in America but not much else to engage the interest.
w Philip Kaufman, Michael Crichton, Michael Backes *novel* Michael Crichton *d* Philip Kaufman *ph* Michael Chapman *m* Toru Takemitsu, Richard Marriott *pd* Dean Tavoularis *ed* Stephen A. Rotter, William S. Scharf
☆ Sean Connery, Wesley Snipes, Harvey Keitel, Cary-Hiroyuki Tagawa, Kevin Anderson, Mako, Ray Wise, Stan Egi, Stan Shaw, Tia Carrere, Steve Buscemi
'The myth in *Rising Sun* is that found in most late 20th-century boysy genre films – the battle to prove white (or sometimes these days, black) male superiority in a world in which extreme male violence is constant, natural, and inevitable ... one sits in the cinema feeling spattered by something false and degrading' – *Marilyn French*
'Even if the director was keen on doing a thriller exercise, his creative instincts don't seem to have been fully ignited.' – *Variety*

Risky Business
US 1939 67m bw
Universal
A crusading radio columnist tracks down a kidnapper.
Tolerable crime programmer.
w Charles Grayson from a previous script by William Anthony McGuire *d* Arthur Lubin
☆ George Murphy, Dorothea Kent, Eduardo Ciannelli, Leon Ames, El Brendel, John Wray
'It will garner nice business in city spots, where they like their melodrama realistic.' – *Variety*

'Joel was a perfectly ordinary high-school virgin with two perfectly ordinary obsessions: SEX and MONEY'
Risky Business
US 1983 99m Technicolor
Tisch-Avnet/Geffen
A 17-year-old is left in charge of his parents' house and fills it with pimps and prostitutes ... a lucrative business.
Would-be outrageous teenage comedy which is pretty well made but soon wears out its welcome.
wd Paul Brickman *ph* Reynaldo Villalobos, Bruce Surtees *m* Tangerine Dream *pd* William J. Cassidy *ed* Richard Chew

☆ Tom Cruise, Rebecca de Mornay, Joe Pantoliano, Richard Masur, Bronson Pinchot, Curtis Armstrong, Nicholas Pryor

Riso Amaro: see *Bitter Rice*

Rita, Sue and Bob Too *
GB 1987 95m Eastmancolor
Mainline/Umbrella/British Screen/Film Four (Sandy Lieberson)

Schoolgirl babysitters are introduced to sex by their employer on the way home.
Raunchy yet appealing study of British attitudes to sex, in the tradition of Letter to Brezhnev.
w Andrea Dunbar *plays* The Arbour *and* Rita, Sue And Bob Too *by Andrea Dunbar* *d* Alan Clarke *ph* Ivan Strasburg *m* Michael Kamen *pd* Len Huntingford *ed* Stephen Singleton
☆ Michelle Holmes, Siobhan Finneran, George Costigan, Lesley Sharp

'The secrets some men keep can be killers.'
Rites of Passage *
US 1999 92m FotoKem
World International (J. Todd Harris, Pierre David)

A heated family confrontation in a remote lakeside cabin between a father and his two sons, one of them gay, is interrupted by two escaped prisoners.
An intense drama on masculine identity and attitudes that is overwhelmed by the contrivances of its thriller-like narrative.
wd Victor Salva *ph* Don E. Fauntleroy *m* Bennett Salvay *pd* William J. Perretti *ed* Ed Marx
☆ Dean Stockwell (Del Farraday), Jason Behr (Campbell Farraday), Robert Glen Keith (D.J. Farraday), Jaimz Woolvett (Red), James Remar (Frank)
'Constantly wavers across a line between dead seriousness and hyperbolic near-silliness.' – *Dennis Harvey, Variety*

Il Ritorno di Ringo: see *The Return of Ringo*

Los Ritos Sexuales del Diablo: see *Black Candles*

Ritual dos Sadicos
Brazil 1969 91m bw/colour
Fotocena (José Mojica Marins, Giorgio Attili, George Michel Serkeis)

aka: *O Despertar da Besta*
aka: *Awakening of the Beast*
Four drug addicts watch a film featuring the horror figure Coffin Joe and, after apparently taking LSD, experience the horrors of their existence.
Cheap, incoherent, misogynistic, self-aggrandising exploitation movie, done in a documentary style as a TV talk show debate, which provides an excuse to show grainy sex and nudity.
w José Mojica Marins, Rubens F. Lucchetti *d* José Mojica Marins *ph* Giorgio Attili *ad* Graveto *ed* Luis Elias
☆ José Mojica Marins, Sérgio Hingst, Ozualdo Candeias, Andreia Bryan, Lurdes Ribas, Mário Lima, Annik Malvil, Itala Nandi
† The film was banned by the Brazilian censors.

The Ritz *
US 1976 90m Technicolor
Warner/Courtyard (Denis O'Dell)

A comedy of mistaken identities in a gay New York turkish bath.
An adaptation of a stage success which doesn't seem nearly as funny as it thinks it is; but some of it does work.
w Terrence McNally *play* Terrence McNally *d* Richard Lester *ph* Paul Wilson *m* Ken Thorne *pd* Phillip Harrison
☆ *Jack Weston*, Rita Moreno, Jerry Stiller, Kaye Ballard, Bessie Love, George Coulouris, F. Murray Abraham, Treat Williams

The River *
India 1951 87m Technicolor
Oriental/International/Theatre Guild (Kenneth McEldowney)

Episodes in the life of a small English community living on the banks of the Ganges.
A slight and surprising work from this director, superbly observed and a pleasure to watch but dramatically very thin.
w Rumer Godden, Jean Renoir *novel* Rumer Godden *d Jean Renoir* *ph Claude Renoir* *m* M. A. Partha Sarathy *pd Eugene Lourié*
☆ Nora Swinburne, Esmond Knight, Arthur Shields, Adrienne Corri
† Renoir's assistant was Satyajit Ray.

The River
US 1984 122m Technicolor
Universal/Edward Lewis

The Garveys battle flood waters to save the family farm.
Old-fashioned rural drama, at times reminiscent of Way Down East *plus a dash of symbolism. A surprise in 1984, and not a very pleasant one, despite or because of its political awareness.*
w Robert Dillon, Julian Barry *d* Mark Rydell *ph* Vilmos Zsigmond *m* John Williams *pd* Charles Rosen *ed* Sidney Levin
☆ Mel Gibson, Sissy Spacek, Shane Bailey, Becky Jo Lynch, Scott Glenn, Billy Green Bush
Academy Award nomination: Sissy Spacek; photography; music; sound

The River *
Taiwan 1997 115m colour
BFI/Central (Hsu Li-Kong, Chiu Shun-Ching)

original title: *Heliu*
In Taipei, a youth becomes ill after playing the part of a drowned corpse in a movie and seeks treatment in vain.
A downbeat account of a family emotionally distant from one another; nothing much happens for most of the film, and audiences will either go with the slow-moving flow or find its lack of resolution intensely irritating.
w Tsai Ming-Liang, Yang Pi-Ying, Tsai Yi-Chun *d* Tsai Ming-Liang *ph* Lao Pen-Jung *pd* Tony Lan *ed* Chen Sheng-Chang, Lei Chen-Ching
☆ Miao Tian, Li Kangsheng, Lu Xiaolin, Ann Hui, Chen Xiangqi
'It's a film that requires a tremendous amount of patience and concentration from the viewer, taking its leave from inaction, not movement. Occasionally tiresome, meaning is very much left to personal interpretation.' – *James Mottram, Film Review*
† The film won the Silver Bear at the Berlin Film Festival.

River of No Return *
US 1954 91m Technicolor Cinemascope
TCF (Stanley Rubin)

During the California gold rush a widower and his 10-year-old son encounter a saloon singer with a gold claim.
Cheerful, clichéd star Western designed to exploit the splendours of early Cinemascope, and very adequate for this purpose.
w Frank Fenton *d* Otto Preminger *ph* Joseph LaShelle *m* Cyril Mockridge *md* Lionel Newman
☆ Robert Mitchum, Marilyn Monroe, Tommy Rettig, Rory Calhoun, Murvyn Vye

The River Rat
US 1984 93m Technicolor
Paramount/Sundance/Larson Rickman (Bob Larson)

During a river journey on a raft to escape from a dishonest parole officer, a just-released convict tries to form a relationship with the young daughter he has never known.
A domestic drama that is never more than moderately effective.
wd Tom Rickman *ph* Jan Kiesser *m* Mike Post *pd* John J. Lloyd *ed* Dennis Virkler
☆ Tommy Lee Jones, Nancy Lea Owen, Brian Dennehy, Martha Plimpton

A River Runs through It *
US 1992 123m Technicolor
Guild/Allied Filmmaker/Columbia (Robert Redford, Patrick Markey)

Two brothers, whose relationship with each other is often troubled, find shared pleasure in fly-fishing.
A soothingly nostalgic movie, often graceful but more often sluggish.
w Richard Friedenberg *story* Norman Maclean *d* Robert Redford *ph* Philippe Rousselot *m* Mark Isham *pd* Jon Hutman *ed* Lynzee Klingman, Robert Estrin
☆ Craig Sheffer, Brad Pitt, Tom Skerritt, Brenda Blethyn, Emily Lloyd, Edie McClurg, Stephen Shellen, Nicole Burdette, Susan Traylor
'Old-fashioned, literary and restrained … but its concerns are too refined, gentle and, finally, unexciting to stir the masses.' – *Variety*
'Cool, allusive and, in the best sense, poetic movie, rich in unforced metaphors and feelings.' – *Richard Schickel, Time*
'As a film, it has all the virtues except tension, which is unfortunately like saying that a watch would be a good timekeeper if the mainspring wasn't bust.' – *Adam Mars-Jones, Independent*
Academy Award: Philippe Rousselot
Academy Award nomination: Richard Friedenberg; Mark Isham

'The vacation is over.'
The River Wild *
US 1994 111m DeLuxe Panavision
UIP/Turman-Foster (David Foster, Lawrence Turman)

A family on a white-water rafting expedition is forced to help armed robbers escape their pursuers.
Predictable action drama, made with some skill but too obvious in its plotting to create much suspense.
w Denis O'Neill *d* Curtis Hanson *ph* Robert Elswit *m* Jerry Goldsmith *pd* Bill Kenney *ed* Joe Hutshing, David Brenner
☆ Meryl Streep, Kevin Bacon, David Strathairn, Joseph Mazzello, John C. Reilly, Benjamin Bratt
'So formulaic that the picture is never more than moderately exciting; you can see round every bend in this river.' – *Terrence Rafferty, New Yorker*
'Streep goes down-market and down-river … The things Hollywood stars have to do to get back into the mainstream sometimes.' – *Derek Malcolm, Guardian*

Riverboat Rhythm
US 1946 65m bw
RKO
A Mississippi riverboat captain is financially embarrassed.
Very mild comedy with the star in dual roles.
w Robert Faber, Charles Roberts *d* Leslie Goodwins
☆ Leon Errol, Walter Catlett, Glenn Vernon, Marc Cramer, Jonathan Hale, Joan Newton

The River's Edge
US 1956 87m Eastmancolor Cinemascope
TCF (Benedict Bogeaus)
A fugitive bank robber forces a farmer to guide him over the mountains into Mexico.
Sluggish open-air character melodrama.
w Harold J. Smith *d* Allan Dwan *ph* Harold Lipstein *m* Lou Forbes
☆ Ray Milland, Anthony Quinn, Debra Paget, Byron Foulger

River's Edge **
US 1986 99m Metrocolor
Palace/Hemdale (Sarah Pillsbury, Midge Sanford)

After a teenager murders his girlfriend, his friends wonder what action they should take.
A gripping drama of teenage alienation.
w Neal Jimenez *d* Tim Hunter *ph* Frederick Elmes *m* Jurgen Knieper *pd* John Muto *ed* Howard Smith, Sonya Sones
☆ Crispin Glover, Keanu Reeves, Ione Skye, Daniel Roebuck, Dennis Hopper, Joshua Miller
'An unusually downbeat and depressing youth pic.' – *Variety*
'This brilliant, messy little picture, another triumph for the independent film movement, should cause people to argue and celebrate for years – argue over how it could have been done better, celebrate that it was done at all.' – *David Denby, New York*

River's End
US 1930 74m bw
Warner
A Mountie dies chasing his man, who then impersonates him.
Popular, contrived, outdoor thriller, previously filmed in 1922 with Lewis Stone, and subsequently in 1940 with Dennis Morgan (this version became known as Double Identity*).*
w Charles Kenyon *story* James Oliver Curwood *d* Michael Curtiz
☆ Charles Bickford, Evalyn Knapp, J. Farrell MacDonald, ZaSu Pitts, David Torrence

La Rivière du Hibou: see *Incident at Owl Creek*

'Evil rises to new heights'
Les Rivières Pourpres
France 2000 103m colour
Legende/Gaumont/TF1/Canal+ (Alain Goldman)

GB and US title: *The Crimson Rivers*
Two detectives investigating different crimes discover that they are after the same crypto-Nazi perpetrator.
Gruesomely ludicrous and overwrought thriller in thrall to the worst excesses of Hollywood movies.
w Jean-Christophe Grange, Mathieu Kassovitz *d* Mathieu Kassovitz *ph* Thierry Arbogast *m* Bruno Coulais *ad* Thierry Flamand *ed* Maryline Monthieux *cos* Sandrine Follet, Julie Mauduech
☆ Jean Reno (Pierre Niemans), Vincent Cassel (Max Kerkerian), Nadia Fares (Fanny Ferreira), Dominique Sanda (Sister Andrée), Karim Belkhadra (Capt. Dahmane), Jean-Pierre Cassel (Dr Cherneze)
'A breathtaking exercise in the macabre… even when the movie is perfect nonsense, it's so voluptuous that you're grateful to be watching it anyway.' – *Roger Ebert*

The Road: see *La Strada*

Road Agent
US 1941 69m bw
Universal
Three cowboys are released from jail so that they can capture an outlaw gang.
Feeble 'B'-movie Western with a couple of forgettable songs thrown in.
w Morgan Cox, Arthur Strawn, Maurice Tombragel *story* Sherman Lowe, Arthur St Clare *d* Charles Lamont *ph* Jerome Ash *md* H. J. Salter *ad* Jack Otterson *ed* Frank Gross
☆ Dick Foran, Leo Carillo, Andy Devine, Anne Gwynne, Samuel S. Hinds, Richard Davis, Anne Nagel, Morris Ankrum

The Road Back **
US 1937 105m bw
Universal (James Whale)
After World War I, German soldiers go home to problems and disillusion.
A major work, intended as a sequel to All Quiet on the Western Front. *Despite impressive sequences, it doesn't quite reach inspiring heights.*
w R. C. Sherriff, Charles Kenyon *novel* Erich Maria Remarque *d James Whale* *ph John Mescall, George Robinson* *m* Dimitri Tiomkin *ad* Charles D. Hall *ed* Ted J. Kent
☆ Richard Cromwell, John King, Slim Summerville, Andy Devine, Barbara Read, Louise Fazenda, Noah Beery Jnr, Lionel Atwill, John Emery, Etienne Girardot, Spring Byington, Laura Hope Crews
'Big and frequently effective, but a let-down in toto … does not compare with *All Quiet* in quality or power.' – *Variety*
'They call it an all-star cast and that means there isn't a single player of any distinction to be picked out of the herd … It might be funny if it wasn't horrifying. This is America seeing the world in its own image.' – *Graham Greene*
† The film is said to have been extensively reshot after protests from the German consul in Los Angeles. No 35mm negative now exists, as it reverted to Remarque and was lost.

Road Games
Australia 1981 110m colour
Avco Embassy/Barber International/Quest (Richard Franklin)

A long-distance truck-driver unwittingly picks up a murderer on the run.
Tolerable but overlong road thriller.
w Everett de Roche *d* Richard Franklin *ph* Vincent Monton *m* Brian May *pd* John Dowding *ed* Edward McQueen-Mason
☆ Stacy Keach, Jamie Lee Curtis, Marion Edwards, Grant Page

Road Gang
US 1936 60m bw
First National
GB title: *Injustice*
Penal corruption and brutality in a Southern state is exposed by the *Chicago Sun*.
A rough ride over familiar ground.
w Abem Finkel, Dalton Trumbo, Harold Buckley *d* Louis King
☆ Donald Woods, Carlyle Moore Jnr, Kay Linaker, Harry Cording, Marc Lawrence

The Road Home
US 1989 116m colour
Rank/Orion (Howard Rosenman, Thomas Baer)
aka: *Lost Angels*
A rebellious youth is sent to a private institution for the problem children of the wealthy.
Confused and unconvincing picture of teenage traumas.
w Michael Weller *d* Hugh Hudson *ph* Juan Ruiz-Anchia *m* Philippe Sarde *pd* Assheton Gorton *ed* David Gladwell
☆ Donald Sutherland, Adam Horovitz, Amy Locane, Don Bloomfield, Celia Weston, Graham Beckel, Patricia Richardson, Ron Frazier, Joseph d'Angerio
'What is wrong with it, apart from a rather overblown style which is never hard-edged enough, is the depiction of the rebellion itself which seems too predicated on adult perfidy to be entirely true.' – *Derek Malcolm, Guardian*

The Road Home ★★
China 2000 89m bw/colour
Columbia/Guangxi Film Studio/Beijing New Picture (Zhao Yu)
original title: *Wo De Fu Qin Mu Qin*
Returning home for the funeral of his father, a businessman remembers his parents' courtship.
Simply told, a straightforward romance, a story of patience and fidelity, that also reasserts the worth of traditional values over crass materialism.
w Bao Shi *novel* Remembrance by Bao Shi *d* Zhang Yimou *ph* Hou Yong *m* San Bao *ad* Cao Jiuping *ed* Zhai Ru *cos* Dong Huamiao
☆ Zhang Ziyi (Young Zhao Di), Sun Honglei (Luo Yusheng), Zheng Hao (Luo Changyu), Zhao Yuelin (Old Zhao Di), Li Bin (Grandmother), Chang Guifa (Old Mayor), Sung Wencheng (Mayor), Liu Qi (Old Carpenter Xia), Ji Bo (Carpenter Xia), Zhang Zhongxi (Crockery Repairman)
'At heart just another shallow and sentimental love story.' – *Cosmo Landesman, Sunday Times*
'Deeply engaging, directed and performed with sweetness and humanity.' – *Peter Bradshaw, Guardian*

Road House ★
US 1948 95m bw
TCF (Edward Chodorov)
A road house owner is jealous of his manager and frames him for murder.
Dated but watchable film noir of its era, with all characters cynical or homicidal.
w Edward Chodorov *d* Jean Negulesco *ph* Joseph LaShelle *m* Cyril Mockridge
☆ Richard Widmark, Ida Lupino, Cornel Wilde, Celeste Holm

Road House ★
US 1989 114m DeLuxe Panavision
UIP/United Artists/Star Partners II/Silver Pictures (Joel Silver)
A kung fu expert, who is hired to clean up a saloon, incurs the enmity of a local racketeer.
Rowdy action movie that provides unthinking enjoyment.
w David Lee Henry, Hilary Henkin *d* Rowdy Herrington *ph* Dean Cundey *ad* William J. Durrell Jnr *ed* Frank J. Urioste, John F. Link
☆ Patrick Swayze, Kelly Lynch, Sam Elliott, Ben Gazzara, Marshall Teague, Julie Michaels, Red West, Sunshine Parker, Jeff Healey
'Very nearly a perfect exploitation movie.' – *MFB*

Road Kill
US 1993 93m DeLuxe
RicMar/Faultline (T. Michael, Rebecca Taylor, Marcie Lestz Jastrow, Richard Jastrow)
A failing LA film student persuades his neighbour, a female assassin, to let him make a documentary about her final assignment in Miami.
Quirky low-budget thriller.
wd Matthew Leutwyler *ph* Steven Gainer *m* Mark Bonilla *pd* Grant Fenning *ed* Matthew Leutwyler
☆ Jennifer Rubin (Blue), Erik Palladino (Alex), Billy Jayne (Lars), Tony Denison (Mr Z), Jon Polito (Jelly), Richard Portnow (Mr Charboneau), Brian Vander Ark (Joey)
'Pic's humorous awareness of its poor-cousin status on the paid-assassin food chain proves sufficiently disarming to permit enjoyment of its inventive, oddball riffs on familiar material.' – *Todd McCarthy*

The Road Killers: see *Roadflower*

Road Show ★
US 1941 86m bw
Hal Roach
A young man wrongly committed to an insane asylum escapes with another inmate and joins a travelling circus.
Engaging scatty comedy on familiar Roach lines which suffers from lame pacing but manages some likeable moments.
w Arnold Belgard, Harry Langdon, Mickell Novak *novel* Eric Hatch *d* Gordon Douglas *ph* Norbert Brodine *m* George Stoll
☆ John Hubbard, Adolphe Menjou, Carole Landis, Patsy Kelly, George E. Stone

Road to Bali ★
US 1952 91m Technicolor
Paramount (Harry Tugend)
In and around the South Seas, with colour making the sets obvious and the gags only tediously funny.
The team's zest was also flagging.
w Frank Butler, Hal Kanter, William Morrow *d* Hal Walker *ph* George Barnes *md* Joseph J. Lilley *songs* Johnny Burke, Jimmy Van Heusen
☆ Bob Hope, Bing Crosby, Dorothy Lamour, Murvyn Vye, Peter Coe

The Road to Corinth: see *La Route de Corinthe*

The Road to Denver
US 1955 90m Trucolor
Republic
An honest ranch hand gets into trouble when he tries to help his lawless brother.
Uninspired Western which just about passes the time.
w Horace McCoy, Allen Rivkin *story* Bill Gulick *d* Joseph Kane *ph* Reggie Lanning *m* R. Dale Butts
☆ John Payne, Lee J. Cobb, Skip Homeier, Mona Freeman, Ray Middleton, Andy Clyde, Lee Van Cleef

'They came for the gold. They stayed for the adventure.'
The Road to El Dorado ★
US 2000 89m Technicolor
DreamWorks (Bonne Radford, Brooke Breton)
In 1519, two conmen, who are seeking the golden city of El Dorado, are taken for Gods after they are washed up on the shores of Mexico.
An animated film very much in the Disney mould and tipping its hat to the Bing Crosby-Bob Hope Road comedies of the 40s, but lacking both a memorable story and hummable songs.
w Ted Elliott, Terry Rossio *d* Eric Bergeron, Don Paul *m* Hans Zimmer, John Powell *m/ly* Elton John, Tim Rice *pd* Christian Schellewald *ed* John Carnochan, Dan Molina, Vicki Hiatt
☆ voices of: Kevin Kline (Tulio), Kenneth Branagh (Miguel), Rosie Perez (Chel), Armand Assante (Tzekel), Edward James Olmos (Chief), Elton John (Narrator)
'A movie that misfires at every turn.' – *Empire*

The Road to Frisco: see *They Drive by Night*

The Road to Glory ★
US 1936 103m bw
TCF (Darryl F. Zanuck)
Adventures of a French regiment in World War I.
Meticulously produced war movie which bears comparison with All Quiet on the Western Front.
w Joel Sayre, William Faulkner *d* *Howard Hawks* *ph* *Gregg Toland* *m* Louis Silvers
☆ *Fredric March, Warner Baxter,* Lionel Barrymore, June Lang, Gregory Ratoff, Victor Kilian, John Qualen, Julius Tannen, Leonid Kinskey

Road to Hong Kong
GB 1962 91m bw
UA/Melnor (Melvin Frank)
Curious, slightly dismal-looking attempt to continue the series in a British studio and on a low budget.
A few good gags, but it's all very tired by now, and the space fiction plot makes it seem more so.
w Norman Panama, Melvin Frank *d* Norman Panama *ph* Jack Hildyard *m* Robert Farnon *pd* Roger Furse
☆ Bob Hope, Bing Crosby, Dorothy Lamour, Joan Collins, Robert Morley, Walter Gotell, Felix Aylmer, David Niven, Frank Sinatra, Dean Martin, Jerry Colonna, Peter Sellers

The Road to Hope: see *Il Cammino della Speranza*

The Road to Life ★
USSR 1930 100m bw
Mejrabpom
Moscow street children are rounded up and reformed.
A kind of Russian prequel to the Dead End Kids, *presented with much style.*
wd Nikolai Ekk
☆ Mikhail Zharov, Maria Gonfa, Tsifan Kyrla
'Judged purely as entertainment the film recedes quickly, as do most Russian films.' – *Variety*

'Where the human wreckage of the seven seas foregather, this powerful tale of love and intrigue is told!'
Road to Mandalay
US 1926 77m (24 fps) bw silent
MGM
Two eastern planters quarrel over a girl.
Potboiling star vehicle.
w Elliott Clawson, Herman Mankiewicz *d* Tod Browning
☆ Lon Chaney, Lois Moran, Owen Moore, Henry B. Walthall

Road to Morocco ★
US 1942 83m bw
Paramount (Paul Jones)
Two shipwrecked Americans are taken to an Arab princess, who is determined to marry one of them to lift an ancient curse.
Hollywood Arab palaces, topical gags and talking camels provide a little amusement..
w Frank Butler, Don Hartman *d* David Butler *ph* William C. Mellor *md* Victor Young *songs* Johnny Burke, Jimmy Van Heusen
☆ Bob Hope, Bing Crosby, Dorothy Lamour, Anthony Quinn, Dona Drake
'A bubbly spontaneous entertainment without a semblance of sanity.' – *Variety*
'It would be difficult to find a screen pantomime with better wartime credentials.' – *Kine Weekly*
'This is the screwiest picture I've ever been in.' – *Camel*
script

'Every Father Is A Hero To His Son.'
Road to Perdition ★★
US 2002 116m Technicolor Panavision
TCF/DreamWorks (Richard D. Zanuck, Dean Zanuck, Sam Mendes)
After his wife and son are killed, a Chicago hitman plans revenge while going on the run to save the life of his surviving son.
Visually splendid crime thriller, with a balletic finale in the rain; but the approach is too ponderous to be entirely engaging and Hanks makes an unconvincing killer.
w David Self *graphic novel* Max Allan Collins, Richard Piers Rayner *d* Sam Mendes *ph* Conrad L. Hall *m* Thomas Newman *pd* Dennis Gassner *ed* Jill Bilcock
☆ Tom Hanks (Michael Sullivan), Paul Newman (John Rooney), Jude Law (Maguire), Jennifer Jason Leigh (Annie Sullivan), Stanley Tucci (Frank Nitti), Daniel Craig (Connor Rooney), Tyler Hoechlin (Michael Sullivan Jnr), Liam Aiken (Peter Sullivan), Dylan Baker (Alexander Rance), Ciaran Hinds (Finn McGovern)
'A solemnly beautiful art concept – which is not quite the same thing as a great movie.' – *David Denby, New Yorker*
'A wonderful movie – powerfully moving, majestically thrilling, a consummate work of movie-making art.' – *Jonathan Ross, Daily Mirror*
'Rarely do you see a film that takes on so many big themes and has so little of substance to say about any of them.' – *Cosmo Landesman, Sunday Times*
Conrad L. Hall
Paul Newman; Thomas Newman; Dennis Gassner (with Nancy Haigh); sound (Scott Millan, Bob Beemer, John Pritchett); sound editing (Scott Hecker)
Conrad L. Hall; Dennis Gassner

The Road to Reno
US 1938 69m bw
Universal
A rancher won't give his wife the divorce she thinks she wants.
Combination comedy, drama, romance and horse opera which doesn't gel.
w Roy Chanslor, Adele Comandini, Brian Marlow *novel* I. A. R. Wylie *d* S. Sylvan Simon
☆ Randolph Scott, Hope Hampton, Glenda Farrell, Helen Broderick, Alan Marshal, Samuel S. Hinds

Road to Rio ★★
US 1947 100m bw
Paramount (Daniel Dare)
Guest stars are given their head, plot intrudes again in the shape of a hypnotized heiress, and the style is more constrained (but still funny).
w Edmund Beloin, Jack Rose *d* Norman Z. McLeod *ph* Ernest Laszlo *md* Robert Emmett Dolan *songs* Johnny Burke, Jimmy Van Heusen
☆ Bob Hope, Bing Crosby, Dorothy Lamour, Gale Sondergaard, Frank Faylen, the Wiere Brothers, the Andrews Sisters
'Enough laughs to pass the time easily and to remind you how completely, since sound came in, the American genius for movie comedy has disintegrated.' – *James Agee*
Robert Emmett Dolan

Road to Ruin
US/France 1992 90m colour
Chrysalide/Canal+/Movie Group/RTBF (Monique Annaud)
After he pretends to be poor in order to test a model's love for him, a millionaire businessman is bankrupted by his partner and sets out to regain his fortune and the woman's love.
Slick, glossy, extremely shallow romantic comedy that prefers implausibility to reality.
w Eric Anjou *story* Richard Gitelson, Eric Freiser *d* Charlotte Brandstrom *ph* Jean-Yves Le Mener *m* John Goldstein *ad* Bertrand Seitz *ed* Michele Robert-Lauliac
☆ Peter Weller, Carey Lowell, Michel Duchaussoy, Nathalie Auffret

The Road to Salina
France/Italy 1971 96m colour Panavision
Robert Dorfmann
original title: *Quando il Sola Scotta*
The proprietress of a roadside café recognizes a drifter as her long-lost son.
Boring emotional drama stymied by the multi-language problem.
w Georges Lautner, Pascal Jardin, Jack Miller *novel* Maurice Cury *d* Georges Lautner *ph* Maurice Fellons *m* Bernard Gérard, Ian Anderson
☆ Rita Hayworth, Mimsy Farmer, Robert Walker Jnr, Ed Begley, Sophie Hardy

Road to Singapore
US 1931 70m bw
Warner
A doctor's wife is caught with her lover, and her life falls to pieces.
Tensions among the oriental upper crust: very dated and not very convincing.
w J. Grubb Alexander *play* Roland Pertwee *d* Alfred E. Green
☆ William Powell, Louis Calhern, Doris Kenyon, Marian Marsh, Alison Skipworth

Road to Singapore *
US 1940 84m bw
Paramount (Harlan Thompson)
Two rich playboys swear off women until they quarrel over a Singapore maiden.
The first Hope-Crosby-Lamour 'road' picture is basically a light romantic comedy and quite forgettable; the series got zanier as it progressed.
w Don Hartman, Frank Butler *story* Harry Hervey *d* Victor Schertzinger *ph* William C. Mellor *m* Victor Young
☆ Bing Crosby, Bob Hope, Dorothy Lamour, Charles Coburn, Judith Barrett, Anthony Quinn, Jerry Colonna
'A deft blend of romance and comedy, songs and fisticuffs.' – *Picture Show*
'Two of the most congenially harmonized performances caught by the camera in recent years.' – *Motion Picture Herald*
† The script was originally designed for Fred MacMurray and Jack Oakie, who weren't available; then for Burns and Allen, who turned it down.

Road to Utopia **
US 1945 89m bw
Paramount (Paul Jones)
The Klondike gold rush, with all the previous gag styles in good order, capped by a cheeky epilogue and constant explanatory narration by Robert Benchley.
w Norman Panama, Melvin Frank *d* Hal Walker *ph* Lionel Lindon *m* Leigh Harline *songs* Johnny Burke, Jimmy Van Heusen
☆ Bob Hope, Bing Crosby, Dorothy Lamour, Douglass Dumbrille, Hillary Brooke, Jack La Rue
Norman Panama, Melvin Frank

'A Comedy Of The Heart And Other Organs.'
The Road to Wellville *
US 1994 120m Technicolor
J&M/Beacon/Dirty Hands (Alan Parker, Armyan Bernstein, Robert Colesberry)
In the early 1900s, a couple whose marriage is in difficulties visit a famous sanatarium, run by Dr Kellogg, in a town full of get-rich-quick merchants hoping to cash in on the fad for healthy living and invented foods, such as cornflakes.
A film quite unlike any other in its exuberant account of the quirky methods of the health industry; Hopkins brings toothy menace to the role of Kellogg, but the screenplay fatally softens the darkly satirical tone of its source, bringing it closer in spirit to a Carry On movie.
wd Alan Parker *novel* T. Coraghessen Boyle *ph* Peter Biziou *m* Rachel Portman *pd* Brian Morris *ed* Gerry Hambling
☆ Anthony Hopkins, Bridget Fonda, Matthew Broderick, John Cusack, Dana Carvey, Michael Lerner, Colm Meaney, John Neville, Lara Flynn Boyle
'Amusing without being particularly funny, and not especially involving in terms of its characters or melodrama, Alan Parker's unzipped cereal comedy is more something to gape at in wonderment, so persistently odd and unusual are its setting and tone.' – *Todd McCarthy, Variety*
'One of the most intricately tiresome movies ever made.' – *David Denby, New York*
'Like its hero, it's possessed of an awesome oddity that is finally rather endearing. In an era of Big Mac movies, the occasional nut cutlet can come as a tonic relief.' – *Sheila Johnston, Independent*
'It just didn't work. It was a terrible movie but I don't think it's anyone's fault.' – *Matthew Broderick*

Road to Zanzibar **
US 1941 92m bw
Paramount (Paul Jones)
The trio on safari in Africa, with *Hellzapoppin* gags breaking in and an anything-goes atmosphere.
w Frank Butler, Don Hartman *d* Victor Schertzinger *ph* Ted Tetzlaff *m* Victor Young *songs* Johnny Burke, Jimmy Van Heusen
☆ Bob Hope, Bing Crosby, Dorothy Lamour, Una Merkel, Eric Blore, Luis Alberni, Douglass Dumbrille
'The funniest thing I've seen on the screen in years. Years.' – *Otis Ferguson*

'The Greatest College Tradition Of All.'
Road Trip
US 2000 94m Technicolor
DreamWorks/Montecito (Daniel Goldberg, Joe Medjuck)
After a student videotapes sex with an acquaintance and accidentally mails it to his girlfriend, he sets out with three friends to recover it.
Tasteless and dislikeable youth comedy.
w Todd Phillips, Scot Armstrong *d* Todd Phillips *ph* Mark Irwin *m* Mike Simpson *pd* Clark Hunter *ed* Sheldon Kahn *cos* Peggy Stamper
☆ Breckin Meyer (Josh), Seann William Scott (E.L.), Amy Smart (Beth), Paulo Costanzo (Rubin), D.J. Qualls (Kyle), Rachel Blanchard (Tiffany), Anthony Rapp (Jacob), Fred Ward (Earl Edwards), Tom Green (Barry), Andy Dick (Motel Clerk), Ethan Suplee (Ed)
'A pretty broad, crude, charmless movie.' – *Peter Bradshaw, Guardian*

The Road Warrior: see *Mad Max 2*

Roadblock *
US 1951 73m bw
RKO (Lewis J. Rachmil)
An insurance investigator plans a million-dollar robbery after falling for a woman who wants a rich life.
Minor film noir, about the corruption of an honest man, with slick dialogue ('Happiness can't buy you money') and an effective finale along the Los Angeles riverbed.
w Steve Fisher, George Bricker *story* Richard Landau, Geoffrey Homes *d* Harold Daniels *ph* Nicholas Musuraca *m* Paul Sawtell *md* Constantin Bakaleinikoff *ad* Albert D'Agostino, Walter E. Keller *ed* Robert Golden
☆ Charles McGraw, Joan Dixon, Lowell Gilmore, Louis Jean Heydt, Milburn Stone, Joseph Crehan

'The highway to hell.'
Roadflower
US 1993 89m DeLuxe Panavision
Miramax/Silver Lion (John Flock, Lance Hool)
video title: *The Road Killers*
On a remote Nevada desert road, a mild-mannered man is left for dead and his family kidnapped by a violent psychopath and his retarded accomplices.
Nasty, meretricious thriller, with a turgid script, which requires everyone to behave very stupidly; the cast compensate by overacting.
w Tedi Sarafian *d* Deran Sarafian *ph* James L. Carter *m* Les Hooper *pd* Jonathan Carlson *ed* Peck Prior
☆ Christopher Lambert (Jack), Craig Sheffer (Cliff), David Arquette (Bobby), Josh Brolin (Tom), Michelle Forbes (Helen), Michael Greene (Sherrif Hodes), Alexondra Lee (Ashley), Christopher McDonald (Glen), John Pyper-Ferguson (Hauser), Richard Sarafian (Trucker), Adrienne Shelly (Red)

Roadhouse 66
US 1984 90m colour
Atlantic (Scott M. Rosenfelt, Mark Levinson)
A motorist and his down-at-heel hitchhiker are stuck in a small town when their car breaks down.
Uninteresting drama, lacking verve and originality.
w Galen Lee, George Simpson *d* John Mark Robinson *ph* Tom Ackerman *m* Gary Scott *pd* Chester Kaczenski *ed* Jay Lash Cassidy
☆ Willem Dafoe, Judge Reinhold, Karen Lee, Kate Vernon, Stephen Elliott

Roadhouse Nights *
US 1930 71m bw
Paramount
A reporter exposes a gangster operating from a country night-club.
Experimental mingling of elements which later become very familiar.
w Garrett Fort *story* Ben Hecht *d* Hobart Henley *ph* William Steiner
☆ Helen Morgan, Charles Ruggles, Fred Kohler, Jimmy Durante, Fuller Mellish Jnr

Roadkill: see *Joy Ride*

Roadside Prophets
US 1992 96m CFI color
Electric/New Line (Peter McCarthy, David Swinson)
A biker sets off across country to scatter the ashes of his friend in a place where he had been happy.
A punkish road movie, mainly peopled by the sort of eccentrics you would take back-roads to avoid; an Easy Rider for the 90s it isn't.
wd Abbe Wool *story* David Swinson *ph* Tom Richmond *m* Pray For Rain, John Doe *pd* J. Rae Fox *ed* Nancy Richardson
☆ John Doe, David Anthony Marshall, Adam Horovitz, Barton Heyman, John Cusack, Jennifer Balgobin, Ellie Raab, David Carradine, Timothy Leary, Arlo Guthrie
'With its unfashionable adherence to the idealism of 60s drop-out cinema and occasional deadpan belly laughs, this is well worth travelling along with for an hour and a half.' – *Kim Newman, Empire*

Roald Dahl's Matilda
US 1996 100m Technicolor
Columbia TriStar/Jersey (Danny DeVito, Michael Shamberg, Stacey Sher, Liccy Dahl)
aka: *Matlida*
The precocious daughter of horrid parents uses her powers of telekinesis to frighten her headmistress.
Sour little black comedy, celebrating childish wish-fulfilment; adults may find it tough going.
w Nicholas Kazan, Robin Swicord *novel* Roald Dahl *d* Danny DeVito *ph* Stefan Czapsky *m* David Newman *pd* Bill Brzeski *ed* Lynzee Klingman, Brent White
☆ Danny DeVito, Rhea Perlman, Embeth Davidtz, Pam Ferris, Mara Wilson, Paul Reubens, Tracey Walter, Brian Levinson
'This is strongish stuff, funny and bitter in turn and not entirely softened by its feel-good ending.' – *Derek Malcolm, Guardian*

Roar *
US 1981 102m colour Panavision
Noel Marshall/Banjiro Uemura
A research biologist lives in the African bush with assorted wild animals. He is expecting his family, but they arrive a day early when he is out …
A rather silly story takes in some of the most remarkable animal photography on record, and there is a sub-plot involving villainous game hunters.
wd Noel Marshall *ph* Jan de Bont *m* Dominic Frontière
☆ Noel Marshall, Tippi Hedren, and family
† The Marshalls live with their 150 lions and other wild animals in a ranch near Los Angeles. During production the film, which eventually cost 17 million dollars, was halted by flood, fire, epidemic and injury.

Roar of the Dragon
US 1932 70m bw
Radio
Passengers in a Chinese river boat are menaced by bandits.
Curious water-set version of Shanghai Express, *with a good cast its best recommendation.*
w Howard Estabrook *story* George Kibbee Turner, Merian C. Cooper, Jane Bigelow *d* Wesley Ruggles *ph* Edward Cronjager *md* Max Steiner
☆ Richard Dix, Edward Everett Horton, Gwili Andre, ZaSu Pitts, Arline Judge, Dudley Digges, C. Henry Gordon

'The land of the free gone wild! The heyday of the hotcha! The shock-crammed days G-men took ten whole years to lick!'
The Roaring Twenties ***
US 1939 106m bw
Warner (Hal B. Wallis)
A World War I veteran returns to New York, innocently becomes involved in bootlegging, builds up an empire and dies in a gang war.
Among the last of the Warner gangster cycle, this was perhaps the best production of them all, despite the familiar plot line: stars and studio were in cracking form.
w Jerry Wald, Richard Macaulay, Richard Rossen *story* Mark Hellinger *d* *Raoul Walsh, Anatole Litvak* *ph* *Ernest Haller* *m* Heinz Roemheld
☆ James Cagney, Humphrey Bogart, Priscilla Lane, Jeffrey Lynn, Gladys George, Frank McHugh, Paul Kelly, Elizabeth Risdon
† The James Cagney character was based on Larry Fay, who was Texas Guinan's partner, and Gladys George is clearly Guinan herself.
†† Walsh replaced Litvak as director during filming.

'Honour made him a man. Courage made him a hero. History made him a legend.'
Rob Roy **
US 1995 139m DeLuxe
UIP/UA/Talisman (Peter Broughan, Richard Jackson)
In the early 1700s, Rob Roy McGregor turns outlaw rather than act dishonourably, as the English demand.
Enjoyably old-fashioned adventure among the heather, though it is the villains who get the best lines.
w Alan Sharp *d* Michael Caton-Jones *ph* Karl Walter Lindenlaub *m* Carter Burwell *pd* Assheton Gorton *ed* Peter Honess
☆ Liam Neeson, Jessica Lange, John Hurt, *Tim Roth*, Eric Stoltz, Andrew Keir, Brian Cox, Brian McCardie, Gilbert Martin, Vicki Masson
'Gives more pleasure than you think you might get, despite its length and empty patches. It's an epic that at least tries for some sort of authenticity and rises to the main occasion with some bravura.' – *Derek Malcolm, Guardian*
'Profoundly mediocre.' – *Empire*
Tim Roth
Tim Roth

Rob Roy the Highland Rogue
GB 1953 81m Technicolor
Walt Disney (Perce Pearce)
After the defeat of the clans in the 1715 rebellion, their leader escapes and after several adventures is granted a royal pardon.
A kind of Scottish Robin Hood, so stiffly acted and made that it might as well – or better – be a cartoon.
w Lawrence E. Watkin *d* Harold French *ph* Guy Green *m* Cedric Thorpe Davie
☆ Richard Todd, Glynis Johns, James Robertson Justice, Michael Gough, Finlay Currie, Geoffrey Keen, Archie Duncan

Robbers' Roost
US 1955 82m DeLuxe
UA (Leonard Goldstein)
An honest cowboy is employed by cattle rustlers and strives to clear his name.
Fair Western programmer.
w John O'Dea, Sidney Salkow, Maurice Geraghty *novel* Zane Grey *d* Sidney Salkow *ph* Jack Draper *m* Paul Dunlap
☆ George Montgomery, Richard Boone, Sylvia Findley, Bruce Bennett, Peter Graves, Warren Stevens, William Hopper

Robbery *
GB 1967 113m Eastmancolor
Joseph E. Levine/Oakhurst (Michael Deeley, Stanley Baker)
Criminals conspire to rob the night mail train from Glasgow.
Heavy-going fictionalized account of the famous train robbery of 1963; best seen as standard cops and robbers, with some good chase sequences.
w Edward Boyd, Peter Yates, George Markstein *d* *Peter Yates* *ph* Douglas Slocombe *m* Johnny Keating

☆ Stanley Baker, James Booth, Frank Finlay, Joanna Pettet, Barry Foster, William Marlowe, Clinton Greyn, George Sewell

Robbery under Arms
GB 1957 99m Eastmancolor
Rank (Joe Janni)

In 19th-century Australia, two farming brothers join the notorious outlaw Captain Starlight.
Howlingly dull film version of a semi-classic adventure novel; a rambling story with no unity of viewpoint is saved only by excellent photography.
w Alexander Baron, W. P. Lipscomb *novel* Rolf Boldrewood *d* Jack Lee *ph* *Harry Waxman* *m* Matyas Seiber
☆ Peter Finch, David McCallum, Ronald Lewis, Maureen Swanson, Jill Ireland, Laurence Naismith, Jean Anderson

Robbery under Arms
Australia 1985 141m colour
Jock Blair/South Australia Film Corporation

Adventures of two young followers of the highwayman Captain Starlight.
Uninteresting cut-down of a TV mini-series; earlier versions were made in 1907, 1911, 1920 and 1957 (above).
w Graeme Koetsveld, Tony Morphett *novel* Rolf Boldrewood *d* Ken Hannam, Donald Crombie
☆ Sam Neill, Steven Vidler, Christopher Cummins, Liz Newman, Ed Devereaux

'The miracle story of all time!'
The Robe **
US 1953 135m Technicolor Cinemascope
TCF (Frank Ross)

Followers and opponents of Jesus are affected by the robe handed down by him at his crucifixion.
The first film in Cinemascope was, surprisingly, a biblical bestseller, but the crowded Roman sets hid most of the flaws in the process. The film itself was competent and unsurprising in the well-tried Sign of the Cross *manner.*
w Philip Dunne, Albert Maltz *adaptation* Gina Kaus *novel Lloyd C. Douglas* *d* Henry Koster *ph Leon Shamroy* *m* Alfred Newman *ad* Lyle Wheeler, George W. Davis
☆ Richard Burton, Jean Simmons, Michael Rennie, *Victor Mature*, Jay Robinson, Torin Thatcher, Dean Jagger, Richard Boone, Betta St John, Jeff Morrow, Ernest Thesiger, Dawn Addams
'The film, then, is the usual vulgarising stuff; and to judge CinemaScope on this evidence would be unfair. The weaknesses of the system are obvious.' – *Dilys Powell*
† Tyrone Power was originally cast in the Burton role, and Burt Lancaster in Mature's.
†† Screenwriter Albert Maltz was excluded from the film's original credits because he was blacklisted at the time.
art direction
best picture; Leon Shamroy; Richard Burton

Robert A. Heinlein's The Puppet Masters: see *The Puppet Masters*

Roberta *
US 1935 105m bw (Technicolor sequence)
RKO (Pandro S. Berman)

An American inherits a Parisian fashion house.
Thin and remarkably flatly-handled musical romance of the old school, charged only by the occasional appearances in supporting roles of Astaire and Rogers, then on the brink of stardom.
w Jane Murfin, Sam Mintz, Allan Scott *play* Otto Harbach *book Alice Duer Miller* by *Gowns by Roberta* *d* William A. Seiter *ph* Edward Cronjager *m Jerome Kern* *md* Max Steiner *ch* Fred Astaire *ad* Van Nest Polglase
☆ Irene Dunne, *Fred Astaire*, *Ginger Rogers*, Randolph Scott, Helen Westley, Claire Dodd, Victor Varconi, Torben Meyer
'Musical picture-making at its best – fast, smart, good-looking and tuneful.' – *Variety*
† Remade as *Lovely to Look At* (qv).
song 'Lovely to Look At' (*m* Jerome Kern, *ly* Dorothy Fields, Jimmy McHugh)

Roberto Succo **
France 2001 125m colour
Artificial Eye/Agat/CIE/Diaphana/Ex Nihilo/ France3/ Gimages (Gilles Sandoz, Patrick Sobelman)

An Italian who murdered his parents escapes from a hospital for the criminally insane and begins a two-year spree of rape and murder.
Cool thriller, based on a true story, of a mad killer on the loose, with a chilling performance from the non-professional Cassetti in the title role. Although it was condemned in France for glamourising Succo, its approach is objective and detached, and thus all the more horrific.
wd Cedric Kahn *book Je te tue: Histoire vraie de Roberto Succo* by Pascal Froment *ph* Pascal Marti *m* Julien Civange *pd* François Abelanet *ed* Yann Dedet
☆ Stefano Cassetti (Kurt), Isild Le Besco (Lea), Patrick Dell'Isola (Thomas), Vincent Deneriaz (Denis), Vincent Deneriaz (Denis), Aymeric Chauffert (Delaunay), Viviana Aliberti (Swiss schoolteacher), Estelle Perron (Celine)
'Succo is a tyrant without portfolio, a mini-megalomaniac rantingly presiding over his mental landscape. He is a revolting and very unglamorous villain in one of the most compelling films of the year.' – *Peter Bradshaw, Guardian*

Robin and Marian *
US 1976 107m Technicolor
Columbia/Rastar (Dennis O'Dell)

Robin Hood returns from the Crusades and finds conditions in Britain depressing; he finally conquers the Sheriff but dies in the attempt.
A kind of serious parody of medieval life, after the fashion of The Lion in Winter *but much glummer; in fact, nothing to laugh at at all.*
w James Goldman *d* Richard Lester *ph* David Watkin *m* John Barry *pd* Michael Stringer
☆ Sean Connery, Audrey Hepburn, Robert Shaw, Ronnie Barker, Nicol Williamson, Richard Harris, Denholm Elliott, Kenneth Haigh, Ian Holm, Bill Maynard, Esmond Knight, Peter Butterworth
'Surface realism only hides a core of mush, suddenly revealed when the hero and heroine settle down for love-making in a field of corn.' – *Geoff Brown*
'Whimsical jokiness is a bit hard to reconcile with the final plunge into sacrificial romance.' – *Michael Billington, Illustrated London News*

Robin and the Seven Hoods *
US 1964 123m Technicolor Panavision
Warner/PC (Howard W. Koch, William H. Daniels)

A spoof of the Robin Hood legend set in gangland Chicago of the twenties.
Too flabby by far to be as funny as it thinks it is, this farrago of cheerful jokes has effective moments and lively routines, but most of them are nearly swamped by flat treatment and the wide screen.
w David Schwartz *d* Gordon Douglas *ph* William H. Daniels *m* Nelson Riddle *songs* Sammy Cahn, James Van Heusen
☆ Frank Sinatra, Dean Martin, Bing Crosby, Sammy Davis Jnr, Peter Falk, Barbara Rush, Edward G. Robinson, Victor Buono, Barry Kelley, Jack La Rue, Allen Jenkins, Sig Rumann, Hans Conried
Nelson Riddle; song 'My Kind of Town' (*m* James Van Heusen, *ly* Sammy Cahn)

Robin Hood **
US 1922 127m approx (24 fps) bw silent
Douglas Fairbanks

Robin Hood combats Prince John and the Sheriff of Nottingham.
An elaborate version of the legend which featured some of Hollywood's most celebrated sets and allowed the star to perform a selection of exhilarating stunts.
w Douglas Fairbanks *d* Allan Dwan *ph* Arthur Edeson *ad* Wilfrid Buckland, Irvin J. Martin
☆ Douglas Fairbanks, Wallace Beery, Alan Hale, Enid Bennett
'The high water mark of film production. It did not grow from the bankroll, it grew from the mind.' – *R. E. Sherwood*
'A story book picture, as gorgeous and glamorous a thing in innumerable scenes as the screen has yet shown ... thrilling entertainment for the whole family group.' – *National Board of Review*
† See also *The Adventures of Robin Hood* and *The Story of Robin Hood and his Merrie Men.*

Robin Hood
US 1973 83m Technicolor
Walt Disney (Wolfgang Reitherman)

Alarmingly poor cartoon feature with all the characters 'played' by animals; songs especially dim and treatment quite lifeless.
w Larry Clemmons, Ken Anderson, others *d* Wolfgang Reitherman
☆ Featuring the voices of Brian Bedford, Peter Ustinov, Terry-Thomas, Phil Harris, Andy Devine, Pat Buttram
song 'Love' (*m* George Bruns, *ly* Floyd Huddleston)

Robin Hood
US 1991 104m colour
TCF/Working Title (Sarah Radclyffe, Tim Bevan)

Condemned for saving a poacher, a Saxon nobleman, Robert Hode, becomes the outlaw Robin Hood.
Dully facetious re-telling of a familiar tale.
w Mark Allen Smith, John McGrath *d* John Irvin *ph* Jason Lehel *m* Geoffrey Burgon *pd* Austen Spriggs *ed* Peter Tanner
☆ Patrick Bergin, Uma Thurman, Jurgen Prochnow, Edward Fox, Jeroen Krabbé, Owen Teale, David Morrissey, Alex North, Gabrielle Reidy
'The film increasingly comes to resemble a 1960s Hammer cheapie.' – *Sight and Sound*

Robin Hood: Men in Tights
US 1993 102m DeLuxe
TCF/Brooksfilms/Gaumont (Mel Brooks)

Robin Hood escapes from prison in the Holy Land to return to England and fight against the tyranny of the Sheriff of Rottingham with the help of his merry men, including Will Scarlett O'Hara and Rabbi Tuckman.
An uninventive parody of Kevin Costner's commercially successful outing as the outlaw of Sherwood Forest; the Costner version is the funnier.
w Mel Brooks, J. David Shapiro, Evan Chandler *d* Mel Brooks *ph* Michael D. O'Shea *m* Hummie Mann *pd* Roy Forge Smith *ed* Steven E. Rivkin *cos* Dodie Shepard
☆ Cary Elwes, Richard Lewis, Roger Rees, Amy Yasbeck, Tracey Ullman (Latrine), Mel Brooks, Dom DeLuise, Dick Van Patten, Isaac Hayes, Patrick Stewart
'A return to the wild anarchic scatological comedies that made Mel Brooks a marquee name around the world.' – *Variety*
'Doesn't so much lampoon *Prince of Thieves* as try to rise on its jerkin-tails – what is it that he thinks he is adding when he takes off a film?' – *Adam Mars-Jones*
'To say it's feeble would be to give it the benefit of quite a few doubts. It's very feeble indeed.' – *Derek Malcolm*

Robin Hood of El Dorado *
US 1936 86m bw
MGM
Joaquin Murieta turns bandit to avenge himself on the men who killed his wife.
Whitewashed biopic of a notorious Western desperado, played mainly for action and light relief.
w William Wellman, Melvin Levy, Joseph Calleia *d* William Wellman
☆ Warner Baxter, Bruce Cabot, Margo, Eric Linden, J. Carrol Naish, Ann Loring

Robin Hood: Prince of Thieves *
US 1991 143m Technicolor
Warner/Morgan Creek (John Watson, Pen Densham, Richard B. Lewis)

Returning from the Crusades to discover that his father has been killed by the Sheriff of Nottingham, Robin of Locksley becomes an outlaw to get his revenge.
A glum version, with little sense of community among the outlaws and an odd mix of acting styles. But it found great favour with the public, becoming one of the most commercially successful films of the year.
w Pen Densham, John Watson *d* Kevin Reynolds *ph* Douglas Milsome *m* John Blakeley *pd* John Graysmark *ed* Peter Boyle
☆ Kevin Costner, Morgan Freeman, Mary Elizabeth Mastrantonio, Christian Slater, Alan Rickman, Sean Connery (uncredited), Geraldine McEwan, Michael McShane, Brian Blessed, Michael Wincott, Nick Brimble
song '(Everything I Do) I Do For You' (*m*Michael Kamen, *ly*Bryan Adams, Robert John Lange)
Alan Rickman

Robinson Crusoe: see *The Adventures of Robinson Crusoe*

Robinson Crusoe and the Tiger
Mexico 1969 110m Eastmancolor
Avant/Avco Embassy
Simple but extremely handsome version of the famous story, with the addition of a tiger which Crusoe takes as a pet.
w Mario Marzac, Rene Cardona Jnr *novel* Daniel Defoe *d* Rene Cardona Jnr *ph* Alex Phillips, Luis Medina *m* Raul Lavista
☆ Hugo Stieglitz, Ahui

Robinson Crusoe on Mars **
US 1964 110m Techniscope
Paramount/Devonshire (Aubrey Schenck)

An astronaut lands on Mars and learns to survive until rescue comes.
Remarkably close to Defoe (Man Friday being a refugee in an interplanetary war) this is an absorbing, entertaining and well-staged piece of science fiction, strikingly shot in Death Valley.
w Ib Melchior, John C. Higgins *d Byron Haskin* *ph Winton C. Hoch* *m* Van Cleave *ad* Hal Pereira, Arthur Lonergan *sp Lawrence Butler*
☆ Paul Mantee, Adam West, Vic Lundin
'Here comes a pleasant surprise, a piece of science fiction based on valid speculation ... modest yet provocative.' – *Time*

Robinson Crusoeland
France/Italy 1950 98m bw
Sirius/Franco-London/Fortezza

aka: *Atoll K*
aka: *Escapade; Utopia*
Stan and Ollie inherit an island in the Pacific, but uranium is discovered on it.
Laurel and Hardy's last film is a dispiriting mess, and the less said about it the better.
w John Klorer, Frederick Kohner, Rene Wheeler, Pierro Tellini *d* Leo Joannon, John Berry *ph* Armand Thirard, Louis Née *m* Paul Misraki *ad* Roland Quignon *ed* Raymond Isnardon
☆ Stan Laurel, Oliver Hardy, Suzy Delair, Max Elloy

Robinson in Space *
GB 1997 81m colour
BBC/BFO/Koninck (Keith Griffiths)

A man is commissioned to make a study of the problem of present-day Britain.
A film that consists of a sequence of carefully framed shots of Britain's less enticing sights – run-down factories, motorways and the detritus of industrial life – with an oblique commentary, on the relationship between the narrator and the man he accompanies on his travels, which gains its effect by often having little direct connection with what is shown.
wd Patrick Keiller *ph* Patrick Keiller *ed* Larry Sidor
☆ Paul Scofield (narrator)
'Like leafing through a picture album with someone bombarding you with facts over your shoulder.' – *Derek Elley, Variety*
† The film is a continuation of the director's *London* (qv).

'Part man. Part machine. All cop.'
Robocop ***
US 1987 103m DuArt
Rank/Orion (Arne Schmidt)

Detroit in the future: a badly injured cop is reconstructed by science, and defeats the forces of evil.
Gleefully dark vision of the future, directed with flair, although the violence goes over the top towards the end. It gained a best director award at the Sitges Film

Festival and a special award for excellence at the 16th Fantasy Film Festival at Avoriaz.
w Edward Neumeier, Michael Miner *d Paul Verhoeven ph* Jost Vacano *m* Basil Poledouris *pd* William Sandell *ed* Frank J. Urioste
☆ Peter Weller, Nancy Allen, Ronny Cox, Kurtwood Smith, Dan O'Herlihy, Miguel Ferrer
'The greatest science-fiction film since Metropolis' – *Ken Russell*
'A comic book film that's definitely not for kids.' – *Daily Variety*
'Very violent and very funny.' – *Time Out*
'Essentially, it's just a hipper, more bam-bam version of the law-and-order hits of the seventies ... The picture keeps telling you that its brutishness is a terrific turn-on, and maybe it is if you're hooked on Wagnerian sci-fi comic books.' – *Pauline Kael, New Yorker*
Academy Award nomination: editing (Frank J. Urioste)

Robocop 2
US 1990 118m DuArt
Rank/Orion (Jon Davison)
Robocop goes into battle against Robocop 2, a vicious cyborg with the brain of a criminal drug-addict.
Stupefyingly frenetic sequel with none of the panache or wit of the original.
w Frank Miller, Walon Green *d* Irvin Kershner *ph* Mark Irwin *m* Leonard Rosenman *pd* Peter Jamison *ad* Pam Marcotte *ed* William Anderson
☆ Peter Weller, Nancy Allen, Dan O'Herlihy, Belinda Bauer, Tom Noonan, Gabriel Damon, Felton Perry, Willard Pugh
'The level of constant violence, with noisy sound effects, explosions and hundreds of thousands of rounds fired by automatic weaponry, is at first arresting but ultimately numbing and boring.' – *Variety*
'If you like to stagger away from a film feeling numb and slightly sick, this one's for you.' – *Empire*

Robocop 3
US 1993 104m DuArt
Orion (Patrick Crowley)
Robocop is caught in a fight between a controlling Japanese corporation and the poor it is trying to evict to build a new city.
Inspiration is sadly lacking here in a film aimed at an audience of early teens; all that can be said in its favour is that it contains less violence than its predecessor.
w Frank Miller, Fred Dekker *d* Fred Dekker *ph* Gary B. Kibbe *m* Basil Poledouris *pd* Hilda Stark *ed* Bert Lovitt *sp* Jeff Jarvis
☆ Robert John Burke, Nancy Allen, Rip Torn, John Castle, Jill Hennessy, Mako, Robert DoQui
'A cluttered, nasty exercise that seems principally intent on selling action figures.' – *Variety*
† A *Robocop* television series followed in 1994.

Rocco and His Brothers **
Italy/France 1960 180m bw
Titanus/Les Films Marceau (Goffredo Lombardo)
A peasant family moves into Milan, and each of its five brothers has his problems.
Massive portmanteau of realistic stories, a bit hard to take despite its undoubted brilliance.
w Luchino Visconti, Suso Cecchi d'Amico, Vasco Pratolini *d Luchino Visconti ph* Giuseppe Rotunno *m* Nino Rota
☆ Alain Delon, Renato Salvatori, Annie Girardot, Katina Paxinou, Roger Hanin, Paolo Stoppa, Suzy Delair, Claudia Cardinale
'Joins the band of films which, these last months, have given one new hope for the cinema.' – *Dilys Powell*

'Alcatraz. Only one man has ever broken out. Now five million lives depend upon two men breaking in.'
The Rock
US 1996 136m Technicolor Panavision
Buena Vista/Hollywood (Don Simpson, Jerry Bruckheimer)
A top agent and a convict combine forces to break into Alcatraz, where a renegade general threatens to destroy San Francisco.
Ludicrously over-the-top thriller, filmed and edited in frenetic bursts of action for those with short attention spans; the narrative lacks logic, with explosions used to distract attention from its shortcomings.
w David Weisberg, Douglas S. Cook, Mark Rosner *d* Michael Bay *ph* John Schwartzman *m* Nick Glennie-Smith, Hans Zimmer *pd* Michael White *ed* Richard Francis-Bruce *sp* Dream Quest Images
☆ Sean Connery, Nicolas Cage, Ed Harris, Michael Biehn, William Forsythe, David Morse, John Spencer, John C. McGinley
'Hollywood appears to have developed a new definition of the comedy thriller: not a thriller that's also funny, but one with a plot so stupid that it can only be played for laughs.' – *John Wrathall, Sight and Sound*
'The movie is so relentless and assaultive it runs roughshod over its own characters.' – *Owen Gleiberman, Entertainment Weekly*
† The film was among the box-office successes of 1996, taking more than $134m at the US box-office and a further $195m worldwide.
†† Apart from the credited screenwriters, Dick Clement and Ian La Frenais worked on Connery's dialogue, and Jonathan Hensleigh, Aaron Sorkin and Quentin Tarantino also contributed to the script.
Academy Award nomination: sound

Rock a Bye Baby
US 1958 107m Technicolor Vistavision
Paramount (Jerry Lewis)
A film star asks her devoted schoolday admirer to look after her triplets by a secret marriage.
Tasteless jazzing-up of The Miracle of Morgan's Creek *by talents distinctly unsympathetic.*
wd Frank Tashlin *ph* Haskell Boggs *m* Walter Scharf
☆ Jerry Lewis, Marilyn Maxwell, Reginald Gardiner, Salvatore Baccaloni, Hans Conried, Isobel Elsom, James Gleason, Ida Moore, Connie Stevens

Rock All Night
US 1957 65m bw
AIP (Roger Corman)
Two gangsters hide out in a pub and hold its customers hostage.
Talky, cheap rock movie, with some occasionally bright dialogue, and a single set in which heavy drinkers philosophise and listen to a few indifferent musical numbers; at least, it doesn't take itself too seriously.
w Charles B. Griffith *wd* Richard Corman *story* David P. Harmon *ph* Floyd Crosby *md* Buck Ram *ad* Robert Kinoshita *ed* Frank Sullivan
☆ Dick Miller, Russell Johnson, Abby Dalton, Jeanne Cooper, Robin Morse, Mel Welles, Richard Cutting, Chris Alcaide, Jonathan Haze, Bruno Ve Sota, The Platters, The Blockbusters, Nora Hayes
♫ I'm Sorry; He's Mine; Rock All Night; I Wanna Rock Now; Rock and Roll Guitar; The Great Pretender; I Guess I Won't Hang Around Here Any More

Rock around the Clock *
US 1956 74m bw
Columbia (Sam Katzman)
A band playing a new form of music – rock 'n' roll – becomes a nationwide sensation.
A cheap second feature with guest artists, this cheerful little movie deserved at least a footnote in the histories because it spotlights the origins and the leading purveyors of rock 'n' roll. It also caused serious riots in several countries. A sequel in 1957, Don't Knock the Rock, *was merely cheap.*
w Robert E. Kent, James B. Gordon *d* Fred F. Sears *ph* Benjamin H. Kline
☆ Bill Haley and the Comets, the Platters, Little Richard, Tony Martinez and his Band, Freddie Bell and the Bellboys, Johnny Johnston, Alan Freed, Lisa Gaye, Alix Talton

Rock Hudson's Home Movies **
US 1992 63m video
Mark Rappaport
A semi-documentary, in which an actor playing the role of Rock Hudson comments on film clips of the real Hudson, looking at his performances from a gay perspective.
A witty deconstruction of Hudson's masculine and heterosexual screen image and the constraints and evasions of Hollywood movies in the 1950s and 60s.
wd Mark Rappaport ph Mark Daniels *ed* Mark Rappaport
☆ Eric Farr (Rock Hudson)
'Shatters the false image of the movies so completely that you wonder how it ever lasted so long.' – *Premiere*

Rock 'n' Roll Cop
Hong Kong 1994 90m colour
Sky Point
original title: *Sang Gong Yatho Tungchap Fan*
Two incompatible cops – a guitar-playing loner from Hong Kong and an uptight disciplinarian from mainland China – combine forces to go after a violent gang that divides its time between the two territories.
Frenetically violent action movie, frequently incoherent and often unpleasantly sadistic, that looks forward to the absorption of Hong Kong into China in 1997; despite the heroics, both police forces here seem remarkably incompetent at catching criminals.
w Lou Bing *d* Che Kirk Wong *ph* Ko Tsiu-lam *m* Tsung Ding-yat *ad* Eddie Ma *ed* Kam Ma
☆ Anthony Wong, Wu Hsing-Kuo, Yu Wing-kwong, Carrie Ng, Chan Ming-tsing
'The action sequences deliver.' – *Variety*

Rock 'n' Roll High School *
US 1979 93m colour
New World (Michael Finnell)
High-school students rebel against an oppressive principal.
A tongue-in-cheek, sometimes self-conscious update of a 1950s rock movie, retaining and enjoying every cliché.
w Russ Dvonch, Joseph McBride, Richard Whitley *story* Allan Arkush, Joe Dante *d* Allan Arkush *ph* Dean Cundey *m* The Ramones *ad* Marie Kordus *ed* Larry Bock, Gail Werbin
☆ P. J. Soles, Vincent Van Patten, Clint Howard, Dey Young, Mary Woronov, Paul Bartel, Dick Miller, Grady Sutton

Rock Rock Rock
US 1957 83m bw
Vanguard (Max J. Rosenberg, Milton Subotsky)
Two girls are rivals for the love of a high-school rock singer.
Poorly written and ineptly acted low-budget movie exploiting the popularity of rock 'n' roll. It consists mainly of a series of performances that have nothing to do with the narrative, which are either by second-string performers – the appalling Ivy Schulman, Cirino and The Bowties, Jimmy Cavallo and His House Rockers, The Three Chuckles, The Moonglows – or better ones such as Chuck Berry, The Flamingos, Frankie Lymon and LaVern Baker performing second-rate material.
w Milton Subotsky *d* Will Price *ph* Morris Hartzband *md* Milton Subotsky *ad* Paul M. Heller *ed* Blandine Hafela
☆ Tuesday Weld, Teddy Randazzo, Jacqueline Kerr, Ivy Schulman, Alan Freed, Fran Manfred, Jack Collins, Carol Moss
† Rock singer Johnny Burnette (1934–64) is featured in his only screen performance.
†† Connie Francis dubbed Tuesday Weld's two songs.

'The story of a wannabe who got to be.'
Rock Star
US 2001 105m Technicolor Super 35
Warner/Bel-Air/Maysville (Robert Lawrence, Toby Jaffe)
A photocopier repairman, who sings in a heavy metal tribute band, is hired to replace the rock singer he imitates.
Although based on a true story, this has little sense of reality about it, and is merely an uninteresting update of the familiar showbiz tale of the understudy who becomes a star.
w John Stockwell *d* Stephen Herek *ph* Ueli Steiger *m* Trevor Rabin *m/ly* Sammy Hagar, Peter Beckett, Steve Plunkett, Twiggy Ramirez, Desmond Childs, Jay Popoff, Jeremy Topan, Brian Vander Ark *pd* Mayne Berke *ed* Trudy Ship
☆ Mark Wahlberg (Chris Cole), Jennifer Aniston (Emily Poule), Jason Flemyng (Bobby Beers), Timothy Olyphant (Rob), Timothy Spall (Mats), Dominic West (Kirk Cuddy), Dagmara Dominczyk (Tania), Matthew Glave (Joe Jnr)
'Hits all the trite notes.' – *Rolling Stone*
'Every rock'n'roll cliché is here.' – *Observer*

Rock-a-Doodle
GB 1990 74m Technicolor
Rank/Goldcrest/Sullivan Bluth (Don Bluth, Gary Goldman, John Pomeroy, Robert Enrietto)
A farmboy, transformed into a cat by a wicked owl, travels to the big city to persuade a rock-singing rooster to return home and make the sun shine again.
Excellent animation is rendered pointless by a poor and confusing narrative.
w David N. Weiss *story* Don Bluth, David N. Weiss, John Pomeroy, T. J. Kuenster, David Steinberg, Gary Goldman *d* Don Bluth *m* Robert Folk, T. J. Kuenster *pd* David Goetz *ed* Bernard Caputo, Fiona Trayler, Lisa Dorney, Joe Gall
☆ Featuring the voices of Phil Harris, Glen Campbell, Eddie Deezen, Kathryn Holcomb, Toby Scott Ganger, Stan Ivar, Christian Hoff, Jason Marin, Christopher Plummer, Sandy Duncan

Rockabye
US 1932 70m bw
Radio
A great actress who has scratched her way up is unhappy because of frustrated mother love.
One of many tearjerkers of its type produced in the first three years of the thirties: it doesn't travel well across the decades.
w Jane Murfin, Kubec Glasmon *play* Lucia Bronder *d* George Cukor
☆ Constance Bennett, Joel McCrea, Paul Lukas, Walter Pidgeon, Jobyna Howland, Walter Catlett
'Moderate grosser, best for the neighbourhood mats.' – *Variety*

Rockers
Jamaica 1978 100m colour
Jesse Burton Stone (Patrick Hulsey)
A hard-up Rastafarian reggae drummer plans an elaborate revenge when big-city gangsters steal the motorbike that was going to make his fortune.
There's an air of authenticity about this slight and often charming narrative of life on the streets of Jamaica, frequently interrupted for music, but it is also casual to the point of amateurishness.
wd Theodoros Bafaloukos *ph* Peter Sova *m* Kiddus-I, Jacob Miller and the Inner Circle, Burning Spear, Gregory Isaacs, Peter Tosh, Rockers All Stars *ad* Lilly Kilvert *ed* Susan Steinberg
☆ Leroy (Horsemouth) Wallace, Richard Hall, Monica Craig, Marjorie Norman, Jacob Miller, Gregory Isaacs, Winston Rodney, Frank Dowding
† The credits include 'Keeper of The Peace'.

The Rocket Man
US 1954 79m bw
TCF
A visitor from outer space gives a magic ray gun to an orphan boy and tells him to use it only for good.
Elementary fantasy with amusing moments.
w Lenny Bruce, Jack Henley *d* Oscar Rudolph *ph* John F. Seitz *m* Lionel Newman
☆ Charles Coburn, George 'Foghorn' Winslow, Spring Byington, Anne Francis, John Agar

Rocket to the Moon: see *Cat Women of the Moon*

The Rocketeer
US 1991 108m Technicolor Panavision
Walt Disney/Silver Screen Partners IV (Lawrence Gordon, Charles Gordon, Lloyd Levin)
In 1938 a racing pilot finds a one-man rocket pack which he uses to foil a Nazis' attempt at world domination.
Tame attempt at a period adventure that never gets off the ground.
w Danny Bilson, Paul de Meo *graphic novel Dave Stevens d* Joe Johnston *ph* Hiro Narita *m* James Horner *pd* Jim Bissell *ed* Arthur Schmidt *sp* Jon G. Belyeu
☆ Bill Campbell, Jennifer Connelly, Alan Arkin, Timothy Dalton, Paul Sorvino, Terry O'Quinn, Ed Lauter, James Handy
'This high-octane, high-flying, live-action comic strip has been machine-tooled into agreeable lightweight summer fare.' – *Variety*

'He's just taking up space.'

Rocketman
US 1997 93m Technicolor
Buena Vista/Walt Disney/Caravan (Roger Birnbaum)

An accident-prone spaceship designer goes to Mars as part of a two-man, one-woman and a chimpanzee team.
A mix of fart jokes, slapstick and science-fiction heroics, so silly that it raises the occasional smile.
w Craig Mazin, Greg Erb *d* Stuart Gillard *ph* Steven Poster *m* Michael Tavera *pd* Roy Forge Smith *ed* William D. Gordean
☆ Harland Williams (Fred Z. Randall), Jessica Lundy (Julie Ford), William Sadler ('Wild Bill' Overbeck), Jeffrey DeMunn (Paul Wick), James Pickens Jnr (Ben Stevens), Don Lake (Flight Surgeon), Peter Onorati (Gary Hackman), Beau Bridges (Bud Nesbitt), William Arthur Jenkins (Mission Controller), Ken Farmer (Mission Controller), Raven (Ulysses)
'A dimwitted juvenile comedy.' – *New York Times*

Rockets Galore
GB 1958 94m Technicolor
Rank (Basil Dearden)
US title: *Mad Little Island*
The Scottish island of Todday resists the installation of a rocket-launching site.
Amiable but disappointingly listless sequel to Whisky Galore.
w Monja Danischewsky *novel* Compton Mackenzie *d* Michael Relph *ph* Reg Wyer *m* Cedric Thorpe Davie
☆ Jeannie Carson, Donald Sinden, Roland Culver, Noel Purcell, Ian Hunter, Duncan Macrae, Jean Cadell, Carl Jaffe, Gordon Jackson, Catherine Lacey

Rocketship X-M *
US 1950 79m bw
Lippert (Kurt Neumann)

An expedition to the moon lands by accident on Mars.
The first post-war space adventure is sheer hokum, quite likeable for its cheek though not for its cheap sets.
wd Kurt Neumann *ph* Karl Struss *m* Ferde Grofe
☆ Lloyd Bridges, Osa Massen, John Emery, Hugh O'Brian
'The message of *Rocketship X-M* is clear: never take a lady as your fuel expert on a trip into interstellar space.' – *C. A. Lejeune*

The Rocking Horse Winner *
GB 1949 90m bw
Rank/Two Cities (John Mills)

A boy discovers he can predict winners while riding an old rocking horse; his mother's greed has fatal results.
A very short story is fatally over-extended and becomes bathetic; but the production is solid and the film deserves a mark for trying.
wd Anthony Pelissier *story* D. H. Lawrence *ph* Desmond Dickinson *m* William Alwyn *ad* Carmen Dillon
☆ John Mills, Valerie Hobson, John Howard Davies, Ronald Squire, Hugh Sinclair, Cyril Smith
'Fails as an interpretation of D. H. Lawrence. But as a skilful piece of narrative with excellent technical qualities it is well worth a visit.' – *Dilys Powell, Britain Today*

'His whole life was a million-to-one shot!'

Rocky ***
US 1976 119m Technicolor
UA/Chartoff-Winkler (Gene Kirkwood)

A slightly dimwitted Philadelphia boxer makes good.
Pleasantly old-fashioned comedy-drama with rather unattractive characters in the modern manner. Despite the freshness, on the whole Marty is still preferable.
w Sylvester Stallone *d John G. Avildsen ph* James Crabe *m* Bill Conti
☆ *Sylvester Stallone*, Burgess Meredith, Talia Shire, Burt Young, Carl Weathers, Thayer David
best picture; John G. Avildsen
Sylvester Stallone (as writer); song 'Gonna Fly Now' (*m* Bill Conti, *ly* Carol Connors, Ayn Robbins); Sylvester Stallone (as actor); Burgess Meredith; Talia Shire; Burt Young

The Rocky Horror Picture Show ***
GB 1975 100m Eastmancolor
TCF (Michael White)

A couple, whose car breaks down on a dark and stormy night, take refuge in an old, dark mansion where a mad scientist is trying to make the perfect man.
A spoof of horror and science-fiction movies, based on a hit musical, and notable mainly for the high-energy performance of Tim Curry, repeating his stage success as a transvestite transsexual from Transylvania.
w Richard O'Brien, Jim Sharman *play The Rocky Horror Show* by Richard O'Brien *d* Jim Sharman *ph* Peter Suschitzky *m* Richard O'Brien *pd* Brian Thomson *ed* Graeme Clifford
☆ Tim Curry, Susan Sarandon, Barry Bostwick, Richard O'Brien, Patricia Quinn, Little Nell, Jonathan Adams, Peter Hinwood, Meatloaf, Charles Gray
'A self-consciously slick rendition of the original material, shorn of the song reprises, staged and performed with evident delight in having larger and more lavish sets to move around in.' – *Tony Rayns, MFB*
'A quite wonderful mixture of spoof horror and sci-fi.' – *Empire*
† The film was a failure on its first release but later became a cult phenomenon at midnight screenings, with audiences dressed as the characters and chanting their dialogue.

Rocky II
US 1979 119m Technicolor
UA/Irwin Winkler, Robert Chartoff

After success comes failure; then Rocky marries his sweetheart and works for another big fight.
Over-inflated but under-nourished sequel with absolutely nothing new to offer.
wd Sylvester Stallone *ph* Bill Butler *m* Bill Conti
☆ Sylvester Stallone, Talia Shire, Burt Young, Carl Weathers, Burgess Meredith

'A Fighter. A Lover. A Legend. The Greatest Challenge.'

Rocky III
US 1982 99m Technicolor
United Artists/Chartoff-Winkler (James D. Brubaker)

Rocky is challenged by a brutal slugger who beats him at the first match …
Unnecessary regurgitation of bits and pieces from the first two Rocky movies.
wd Sylvester Stallone *ph* Bill Butler *m* Bill Conti *pd* William J. Cassidy *ed* Don Zimmerman, Mark Warner
☆ Sylvester Stallone, Talia Shire, Burt Young, Burgess Meredith, Carl Weathers, Tony Burton, Mr T, Hulk Hogan
'The time has surely come for Rocky Balboa to take the final count.' – *Tom Milne, MFB*
'The first Rocky was primitive in a relatively innocent way. This picture is primitive too, but it's also shrewd and empty and inept.' – *New Yorker*
original song 'Eye of the Tiger' by Jim Peterik and Frankie Sullivan III

Rocky IV
US 1985 91m Metrocolor
MGM/UA/Winkler-Chartoff

Rocky takes on a Russian champion.
Hilarious, hysterical, would-be allegorical, this is the pits; but it took a lot of money.
wd Sylvester Stallone *ph* Bill Butler *m* Vince DiCola, Bill Conti *pd* Bill Kenney *ed* Don Zimmerman, John W. Wheeler
☆ Sylvester Stallone, Dolph Lundgren, Carl Weathers, Talia Shire, Burt Young, Brigitte Nielsen
'Ludicrous rubbish, but efficient with it.' – *Shaun Usher, Daily Mail*

Rocky Mountain
US 1950 83m bw
Warner (William Jacobs)
A Confederate horseman gets involved in an Indian war.
Routine star Western with unusual tragic ending.
w Winston Miller, Alan le May *d* William Keighley *ph* Ted McCord *m* Max Steiner
☆ Errol Flynn, Patrice Wymore, Scott Forbes, Guinn Williams, Slim Pickens

Rocky Mountain Mystery
US 1935 64m bw
Paramount
An engineer solves a number of murders at a radium mine.
Routine whodunnit in an unfamiliar setting. Mrs Leslie Carter provides a rare screen appearance, and just as well to judge from her performance
w Edward E. Paramore Jnr *novel Golden Dreams* by Zane Grey *d* Charles Barton
☆ Randolph Scott, Charles Chic Sale, Mrs Leslie Carter, Kathleen Burke, Ann Sheridan
'Good entertainment in spite of minor shortcomings.' – *Variety*

'Where does a champion go when he takes off the gloves?'

Rocky V
US 1990 104m DeLuxe
UIP/United Artists/Star Partners III (Robert Chartoff, Irwin Winkler)

Rocky, suffering, unsurprisingly, from brain-damage, takes on a young protégé.
The series continues its steep, downward spiral into insipid nonsense.
w Sylvester Stallone *d* John G. Avildsen *ph* Steven Poster *m* Bill Conti *pd* William J. Cassidy *ed* John G. Avildsen, Michael N. Knue
☆ Sylvester Stallone, Talia Shire, Burt Young, Sage Stallone, Burgess Meredith, Tommy Morrison, Richard Gant, Tony Burton
† Stallone's original ending had Rocky dying in his moment of final triumph.

Roger & Me **
US 1989 90m DuArt
Warner/Dog Eat Dog Films/Michael Moore

A journalist attempts to interview the chairman of General Motors about his decision to close its factory in the town where the company began and so put thousands of people out of work.
Entertaining, blackly comic (though not always accurate) documentary on the human cost of big business.
wd Michael Moore *ph* Christopher Beaver, John Prusak, Kevin Rafferty, Bruce Schermer *ed* Wendy Stanzler, Jennifer Beman
'A fascinating account of blue collar life unable to come to terms with the clouding of the American Dream they are perpetually adjured to believe in.' – *Derek Malcolm, Guardian*

Roger Touhy, Gangster
US 1944 73m bw
TCF
GB title: *The Last Gangster*
An associate of Al Capone is finally cornered by the FBI.
Unsurprising, competent cops-and-robbers melodrama, based more or less on fact.
w Crane Wilbur, Jerry Cady *d* Robert Florey
☆ Preston Foster, Victor McLaglen, Lois Andrews, Kent Taylor, Anthony Quinn, Henry Morgan

Rogue Cop
US 1954 92m bw
MGM (Nicholas Nayfack)
A police detective is on the payroll of a crime syndicate.
Uncompelling star melodrama.
w Sydney Boehm *novel* William P. McGivern *d* Roy Rowland *ph* John Seitz *m* Jeff Alexander
☆ Robert Taylor, George Raft, Janet Leigh, Steve Forrest, Anne Francis
'Another of the sour, disillusioned crime stories which have recently been coming into fashion.' – *Penelope Houston*
John Seitz

'Renegade Justice!'

Rogue Force
US 1998 90m colour
New City/Triple Peak (Alan Schechter)

aka: *Counterforce*
An FBI agent and a female cop team up to investigate a gang of disaffected cops who are murdering pornographers and gangsters.
Loud and implausible action movie that indulges in overkill; its fascination with the tactics of SWAT teams overwhelms what might have been a nervy drama.
w Rick Bloggs, Alan Schechter *d* Martin Kunert *ph* Adam Kane *m* Patrick Griffin *pd* Scott Swank *ed* Kert Vander Meulen
☆ Michael Rooker (Special Agent Matt Cooper), Robert Patrick (Sgt Jake Macilroy), Diane DiLascio (Detective Helen Simms), Louis Mandylor (Officer Peter Roth), James Kisicki (Frank), Darnell Suttles (Detective Westbrook), Charles Brown (Santana), Jeff Blanchard (FBI Tactician)

The Rogue Song *
US 1930 115m Technicolor
MGM (Lionel Barrymore)
A bandit wins the hand of a Russian princess.
Primitive early sound operetta, not salvaged by a few Laurel and Hardy scenes added as an afterthought.
w Frances Marion, John Colton *operetta Gypsy Love* by *Franz Lehár, Robert Bodansky d* Lionel Barrymore, Hal Roach *ph* Percy Hilburn, C. Edgar Schoenbaum *m* Dimitri Tiomkin *ed* Margaret Booth
☆ Lawrence Tibbett, Catherine Dale Owen, Florence Lake, Judith Vosselli, Nance O'Neil, Stan Laurel, Oliver Hardy
'Slow unto dullness outside of Tibbett's singing; Laurel and Hardy names draw but their comedy is very weak.' – *Variety*
† No print is known to exist, but in 1980 the sound track was issued on record.
Lawrence Tibbett

'He'll risk everything to beat the system!'

Rogue Trader
GB/US 1998 101m colour
Pathé/Granada/Newmarket/David Paradine (James Dearden, Paul Raphael, Janette Day)

An English merchant banker, working in Singapore, gains a reputation as a financial genius while losing millions of dollars.
A biopic, of a man who ruined one of London's most venerable merchant bankers, that should have made a perfect morality play on modern day values, but instead settles for a tabloid approach that explains and illumines nothing.
wd James Dearden *book Rogue Trader: How I Brought Down Barings Bank and Shook the Financial World* by Nicholas Leeson and Edward Whitley *ph* Jean-François Robin *m* Richard Hartley *pd* Alan MacDonald *ed* Catherine Creed
☆ Ewan McGregor (Nick Leeson), Anna Friel (Lisa Leeson), Yves Beneyton (Pierre Bonnefoy), Betsy Brantley (Brenda Granger), Caroline Langrishe (Ash Lewis), Nigel Lindsay (Ron Baker), Tim McInnerney (Tony Hawes), Irene Ng (Bonnie Lee), Lee Ross (Danny Argyropoulos), Simon Shepherd (Peter Norris), John Standing
'Truly awful.' – *Guardian*

Rogue's March
US 1953 84m bw
MGM (Leon Gordon)
A British army officer is unjustly accused of espionage but becomes a hero in India.
Victorian comedy adventure set on a never-never frontier. Not much.
w Leon Gordon *d* Allan Davis *ph* Paul C. Vogel *m* Alberto Colombo
☆ Peter Lawford, Richard Greene, Janice Rule, Leo G. Carroll, John Abbott, Patrick Aherne

Rogues of Sherwood Forest *
US 1950 80m Technicolor
Columbia (Fred M. Packard)
Robin Hood's son helps the barons to force the signing of Magna Carta.
Satisfactory action adventure.
w George Bruce *d* Gordon Douglas *ph* Charles Lawton Jnr *m* Heinz Roemheld, Arthur Morton
☆ John Derek, Diana Lynn, George Macready, Alan Hale, Paul Cavanagh, Lowell Gilmore, Billy House

Rogues' Regiment
US 1948 86m bw
Universal-International (Robert Buckner)
An intelligence man joins the French Foreign Legion in Saigon to track down an ex-Nazi.
Keen but rather muddled actioner.
w Robert Buckner *d* Robert Florey *ph* Maury Gertsman *m* Daniele Amfitheatrof

☆ Dick Powell, Marta Toren, Vincent Price, Stephen McNally

Le Roi de Coeur: see *King of Hearts*

Rojin Z: see *Roujin Z*

Roller Boogie
US 1979 103m colour
United Artists (Bruce Cohn Curtis)

With the help of an expert roller-skater, a poor little rich girl foils a crooked businessman who is trying to take over the local roller disco.
A silly and trivial attempt to cash in on a teenage craze, with much skating to unmemorable songs; it has nothing to recommend it, least of all the leading performances.
w Barry Schneider *story* Irwin Yablans *d* Mark L. Lester *ph* Dean Cundey *m* Bob Esty *m/ly* Bob Esty, Michele Aller, Michael Brooks *ad* Keith Michl *ed* Howard Kunin
☆ Linda Blair, Jim Bray, Beverly Garland, Roger Perry, James Van Patten, Kimberly Beck, Sean McClory, Mark Goddard

Rollerball *
US 1975 129m Technicolor Scope
UA/Norman Jewison

In the 21st century an ultra-violent game is used to release the anti-social feelings of the masses.
A one-point parable, and an obvious point at that, is stretched out over more than two hours of violence in which the rules of the game are not even explained. A distinctly unlikeable film.
w William Harrison *d* Norman Jewison *ph* Douglas Slocombe *md* André Previn *pd* John Box
☆ James Caan, John Houseman, Ralph Richardson, Maud Adams, John Beck, Moses Gunn
'A classic demonstration of how several millions of dollars can be unenjoyably wasted.' – *Jonathan Rosenbaum*
John Box

'Get In The Game.'
Rollerball
US 2002 98m DeLuxe Panavisionê
MGM (Charles Roven, Beau St Clair, John McTiernan)

In 2005, an American athlete gets involved in a violent sport where the only rule is survival.
Loud, incoherent, near-incomprehensible, totally inept remake.
w Larry Ferguson, John Pogue *story and screenplay* William Harrison *d* John McTiernan *ph* Steve Mason *m* Eric Serra *ch* Marty Kudelka, Teresa Estinosa *pd* Norman Garwood, Dennis Bradford *ed* John Wright *sp* Pixel Magic, Panopoly, Riot, digital.art.media, Pacific Title and Art Studio
☆ Chris Klein (Jonathan), Jean Reno (Petrovich), LL Cool J (Marcus Ridley), Rebecca Romijn-Stamos (Aurora), Naveen Andrews (Sanjay), Oleg Taktarov (Denekin), David Hemblen (Serokin), Janet Wright (Coach Olga)
'Chaos on wheels, a hysterically edited jumble that defies belief at nearly every juncture.' – *Robert Koehler, Variety*
'This oddly scrambled new version eventually falls apart so badly you feel embarrassed for the people who made it.' – *Jonathan Foreman, New York Post*

Rollercoaster
US 1977 118m Technicolor Panavision Sensurround
Universal (Jennings Lang)

A saboteur blows up rollercoasters if his blackmail demands are not met.
Limp, unsuspenseful, would-be spectacular in which a stalwart cast struggles with inane dialogue and situations.
w Richard Levinson, William Link *d* James Goldstone *ph* David M. Walsh *m* Lalo Schifrin
☆ George Segal, Timothy Bottoms, Richard Widmark, Susan Strasberg, Harry Guardino, Henry Fonda

Rolling Thunder
US 1977 94m DeLuxe
AIP (Norman T. Herman)

A former prisoner of war in Vietnam seeks revenge on the killers of his wife and son.
Moderate action thriller, although its use of the Vietnam War seems opportunistic rather than apposite.
w Heywood Gould, Paul Schrader *d* John Flynn *ph* Jordan Cronenweth *m* Barry DeVorzon *ad* Steve Burger *ed* Frank P. Keller
☆ William Devane, Tommy Lee Jones, Linda Haynes, Lisa Richards, Dabney Coleman, James Best

Rollover
US 1981 115m Technicolor Panavision
Orion/IPC (Bruce Gilbert)

The widow of a murdered bank president exposes various kinds of financial chicanery on an international scale.
So complexly plotted as to be virtually unintelligible, this slick romantic melodrama was caviare to the general despite its stars.
w David Shaber *d* Alan J. Pakula *ph* Giuseppe Rotunno, William Garroni *m* Michael Small
☆ Jane Fonda, Kris Kristofferson, Hume Cronyn, Josef Sommer, Bob Gunton

Roma: see *Fellini's Roma*

Roma, Città Aperta: see *Open City*

Le Roman de Renard: see *The Tale of the Fox*

Le Roman d'un Tricheur *
France 1936 83m bw
Cinéas
aka: *The Story of a Cheat*
A reformed elderly cardsharp writes his memoirs.
First person singular comedy, a tour de force in which only the narrator speaks, the rest use pantomime only.
wd Sacha Guitry *ph* Marcel Lucien
☆ Sacha Guitry, Marguerite Moreno, Serge Grave

Roman Holiday **
US 1953 118m bw
Paramount (William Wyler)

A princess on an official visit to Rome slips away incognito and falls in love with a newspaperman.
Wispy, charming, old-fashioned romantic comedy shot in Rome and a little obsessed by the locations; one feels that a studio base would have resulted in firmer control of the elements. The stars, however, made it memorable.
w Ian McLellan Hunter, John Dighton *d* William Wyler *ph* Franz Planer, Henri Alekan *m* Georges Auric *ad* Hal Pereira, Walter Tyler *ed* Robert Swink
☆ Gregory Peck, Audrey Hepburn, Eddie Albert, Hartley Power, Harcourt Williams
'While Capra, or in a different way Lubitsch, could have made something wholly enjoyable from it, it would seem that Wyler's technique is now too ponderously inflexible for such lightweight material.' – *MFB*
† Dalton Trumbo, then a blacklisted writer, was the actual author of the original story, although Ian McLellan Hunter received the credit for it.
original story (Ian McLellan Hunter); Audrey Hepburn; costumes (Edith Head)
picture; script; William Wyler; Franz Planer, Henri Alekan; Eddie Albert; art direction; editing
Audrey Hepburn

Roman Scandals **
US 1933 93m bw
Samuel Goldwyn

A troubled young man dreams himself back in ancient Rome.
Musical farce which is not only pretty entertaining on its own account but remains interesting for a number of reasons; as its star's best vehicle, for its Depression bookends, as a spoof on The Sign of the Cross *and the inspiration of scores of other comedies in which the heroes dreamed themselves back into other times. Note also the musical numbers, the chariot race finale, and the rare appearance of Ruth Etting.*
w William Anthony McGuire, George Oppenheimer, Arthur Sheekman, Nat Perrin *story* George S. Kaufman, Robert E. Sherwood *d* Frank Tuttle *ph* Gregg Toland *m* Alfred Newman *ch* Busby Berkeley *chariot sequence* Ralph Cedar *songs* Harry Warren *(m)*, Al Dubin, L. Wolfe Gilbert *(ly)*
☆ Eddie Cantor, Gloria Stuart, Ruth Etting, Edward Arnold, Alan Mowbray, Verree Teasdale
'An extraordinary rigmarole containing everything from chariot races to a torch song.' – *Time*

The Roman Spring of Mrs Stone *
GB 1961 104m Technicolor
Warner Seven Arts/AA (Louis de Rochemont)

A widowed American actress in Rome begins to drift into lassitude and moral decline.
Vivien Leigh gets degraded again in this rambling novella complete with mysterious dark stranger waiting at the end. Nice to look at, and occasionally compelling, but unsuccessful as a whole.
w Gavin Lambert *novel* Tennessee Williams *d* José Quintero *ph* Harry Waxman *m* Richard Addinsell *pd* Roger Furse *ad* Herbert Smith
☆ Vivien Leigh, Warren Beatty, Lotte Lenya, Jeremy Spenser, Coral Browne, Ernest Thesiger
'The slightly sweet smell of decay hovers over everything. Although its very subject matter limits this film and smothers it slightly, it is quietly and sincerely made.' – *New York Herald Tribune*
Lotte Lenya

Romance *
US 1930 76m bw
MGM

A clergyman falls in love with the opera singer mistress of an industrialist.
Simple-minded romantic drama with the star not at her best; but an interesting example of 'high class' romance of the time.
w Bess Meredyth, Edwin Justus Mayer *play* Edward Sheldon *d* Clarence Brown *ph* William Daniels
☆ Greta Garbo, Lewis Stone, Gavin Gordon, Elliott Nugent, Clara Blandick, Florence Lake, Henry Armetta
'A first-run hit of the sort that won't miss.' – *Variety*
Clarence Brown; Greta Garbo

Romance **
France 1999 99m colour
Blue Light/Flach/CB/ARTE (Jean-François Lepetit)

Frustrated by her partner's refusal to make love to her, a schoolteacher embarks on a series of affairs.
A movie that caused controversy because of its scenes of explicit sexual activity, some of which involved the well-endowed porn star Siffredi; otherwise it is one of those films, typical of France, in which a woman's search for sexual emancipation causes her to be abused by men. Finally, it becomes a twisted drama of revenge.
wd Catherine Breillat *ph* Yorgos Arvanitis *m* Raphael Tidas, DJ Valentin *pd* Frédérique Belvaux *ed* Agnès Guillemot
☆ Caroline Ducey (Marie), Sagamore Stévenin (Paul), François Berléand (Robert), Rocco Siffredi (Paolo), Reza Habouhossein (Man on stairs), Fabien de Jomaron (Claude), Emma Colberti (Charlotte), Ashley Wanninger (Ashley)
'What makes the film as a whole so odd is that the sexual acts are the only realistic things in it. If this is a landmark in cinema, it's strangely stranded.' – *Adam Mars-Jones, Times*

Romance and Riches: see *The Amazing Quest of Ernest Bliss*

Romance for Three: see *Paradise for Three*

Romance in Flanders
GB 1937 73m bw
Franco-London/British Lion
US title: *Romance on the Western Front*
Two sergeants fall for a Belgian farmer's daughter; she marries the one she doesn't love, thinking the other is dead.
Rose-coloured romantic hokum, of no sustaining interest.
w Harold Simpson *book* Mario Fort, Ralph E. Vanloc *d* Maurice Elvey
☆ Paul Cavanagh, Marcelle Chantal, Garry Marsh, Olga Lindo, Alastair Sim

Romance in Manhattan
US 1934 78m bw
RKO

A New York girl helps a Czech immigrant to find work in the metropolis.
Slim, sentimental movie novelette without a touch of sophistication.
w Jane Murfin, Edward Kaufman *d* Stephen Roberts
☆ Ginger Rogers, Francis Lederer, Arthur Hohl, J. Farrell MacDonald, Eily Malyon, Donald Meek

Romance in the Dark
US 1938 78m bw
Paramount
A famous baritone helps a singing servant to get famous.
Musical romance for the carriage trade, with apparently more comedy asides than were originally intended.
w Frank Partos, Anne Morrison Chapin *d* H. C. Potter
☆ Gladys Swarthout, John Boles, John Barrymore, Claire Dodd, Fritz Field, Curt Bois
'Biz will be good, if no wow. Boles and Barrymore will give some tug to the tide against the turnstiles.' – *Variety*

Romance is Sacred: see *The King and the Chorus Girl*

Romance of a Horse Thief
US/Yugoslavia 1971 100m Technicolor
Allied Artists/Jadran/Emmanuel L. Wolf (Gene Gutowski)

In a Polish village in 1904 there is dismay when horses are commandeered by Cossacks for service in the Russo-Japanese war.
Nostalgic Jewish drama which ends up rather like Fiddler on the Roof *without the music.*
w David Opatoshu, based on his father Joseph's novel *d* Abraham Polonsky *ph* Piero Portalupsisic *m* Mort Shuman
☆ Yul Brynner, Eli Wallach, Jane Birkin, Oliver Tobias, Lainie Kazan, David Opatoshu

The Romance of Rosy Ridge
US 1947 103m bw
MGM (Jack Cummings)
After the Civil War, farmers make their own peace.
Mild period romance with everything settled by a betrothal.
w Lester Cole *novel* Mackinlay Kantor *d* Roy Rowland *ph* Sidney Wagner *m* George Bassman
☆ Van Johnson, Thomas Mitchell, Janet Leigh, Selena Royle, Marshall Thompson, Dean Stockwell
'Rustic charm spread through it like molasses.' – *Douglas Eames*

Romance on the High Seas *
US 1948 99m Technicolor
Warner (Alex Gottleib, George Amy)

GB title: *It's Magic*
Various romances mesh on an ocean voyage.
Lightweight musical which introduces Doris Day and generally manages to keep afloat.
w Julius J. and Philip G. Epstein, I. A. L. Diamond *d* Michael Curtiz *ph* Elwood Bredell *m* Ray Heindorf *songs* Jule Styne, Sammy Cahn
☆ Jack Carson, Janis Paige, Don Defore, Doris Day, Oscar Levant, S. Z. Sakall, Eric Blore, Franklin Pangborn, Fortunio Bonanova
Ray Heindorf; song 'It's Magic' (*m* Jule Styne, *ly* Sammy Cahn)

Romancing the Stone *
US 1984 106m DeLuxe Panavision
TCF/El Corazon (Michael Douglas)

A best-selling lady romance novelist gets more than she bargained for when she tries to find her kidnapped sister in Colombia.
Spoof adventure thriller which takes too long to get going and then finds it has nowhere to go. But commercial…
w Diane Thomas *d* Robert Zemeckis *ph* Dean Cundey *m* Alan Silvestri *pd* Lawrence G. Paull *ed* Donn Cambern, Frank Morriss
☆ Michael Douglas, Kathleen Turner, Danny DeVito, Zack Norman, Alfonso Arau

'The picture has a bravura opening and a jolly kind of movement, but it becomes too slambang.' – *Pauline Kael, New Yorker*
Donn Cambern, Frank Morriss

Romanoff and Juliet *
US 1961 103m Technicolor
U-I/Pavla (Peter Ustinov)
Both Americans and Russians woo the tiny country of Concordia, and war threatens while the ambassadors' children fall in love.
Despite the author's wit this pattern comedy became something of a bore as a stylized stage piece, and the film is not smartly enough handled to be anything but a yawn; the humour never becomes cinematic.
wd Peter Ustinov *play* Peter Ustinov *ph* Robert Krasker *m* Mario Nascimbene *ad* Alexander Trauner
☆ Peter Ustinov, Sandra Dee, John Gavin, Akim Tamiroff, Tamara Shayne, John Phillips, Alix Talton, Peter Jones

The Romantic Age
GB 1949 86m bw
Pinnacle – Rank
US title: *Naughty Arlette*
A precocious French student sets her cap at the art teacher.
Fluffy farce in which all the adults behave like children; not well regarded.
w Edward Dryhurst, Peggy Barwell *novel* Serge Weber *d* Edmond T. Gréville *ph* Hone Glendining *m* Charles Williams
☆ Mai Zetterling, Hugh Williams, Margot Grahame, Petula Clark, Carol Marsh, Raymond Lovell, Paul Dupuis

Romantic Comedy
US 1983 102m Metrocolor
MGM-UA/Taft Entertainment/The Mirisch Corporation (Walter Mirisch, Morton Gottlieb)
A Broadway playwright and a New England schoolteacher have a creative partnership that is more personal than professional.
Tedious film version of a play which wallows in autobiography.
w Bernard Slade *play* Bernard Slade *d* Arthur Hiller *ph* David M. Walsh *m* Marvin Hamlisch *pd* Alfred Sweeney
☆ Dudley Moore, Mary Steenburgen, Frances Sternhagen, Janet Eilber, Robyn Douglass, Ron Leibman
'When a movie's production notes wax lyrical about the pile of the living room carpet, one senses that they're in trouble.' – *Nick Roddick, MFB*

The Romantic Englishwoman *
GB 1975 116m Eastmancolor
Dial/Meric-Matalon (Daniel M. Angel)
A discontented woman, holidaying at Baden Baden, falls in love with a stranger while her husband completes a novel on the same theme.
Almost as ambiguous as Last Year in Marienbad, *this annoying film wastes good actors in a script which hovers uncertainly between fantasy, melodrama and reality, intending one supposes to make humourless and obvious comparisons between romance and life.*
w Tom Stoppard, Thomas Wiseman *novel* Thomas Wiseman *d* Joseph Losey *ph* Gerry Fisher *m* Richard Hartley
☆ Glenda Jackson, Michael Caine, Helmut Berger, Marcus Richardson, Kate Nelligan, René Kolldehoff, Michel Lonsdale
'The central trio bite off their lines, play deviously with hypocrisies and humiliations, and seem slightly aware that they're creations by artifice out of artificiality.' – *Penelope Houston*
'An itsy-bitsy, fragmented film that seems less than the sum of its parts.' – *Michael Billington, Illustrated London News*

Rome Adventure
US 1962 119m Warnercolor
Warner
GB title: *Lovers Must Learn*
A pretty American librarian goes to Rome to learn about love, and does.
Sluggish and overstretched travelogue with dollops of arch romance; hard to take.
wd Delmer Daves *novel* Irving Fineman *ph* Charles Lawton Jnr *m* Max Steiner
☆ Suzanne Pleshette, Troy Donahue, Angie Dickinson, Rossano Brazzi, Constance Ford, Chad Everett

Rome Express ***
GB 1932 94m bw
Gaumont (Michael Balcon)
Thieves and blackmail victims are among the passengers on an express train.
Just a little faded now as sheer entertainment, this remains the prototype train thriller from which The Lady Vanishes, Murder on the Orient Express *and a hundred others are all borrowed; it also spawned a myriad movies in which strangers are thrown together in dangerous situations. Technically it still works very well, though the script needs modernizing.*
w Clifford Grey, Sidney Gilliat, Frank Vosper, Ralph Stock *d* Walter Forde *ph* Gunther Krampf
☆ *Conrad Veidt*, Gordon Harker, Esther Ralston, Joan Barry, Harold Huth, Cedric Hardwicke, Donald Calthrop, Hugh Williams, Finlay Currie, Frank Vosper, Muriel Aked, Eliot Makeham
HARKER: 'Discretion is the better part of Wagons Lits.'
'A first class craftsman's job.' – *Basil Wright*
'Technically, and in a sense intellectually speaking, this film puts Forde into Class A1.' – *Cinema Quarterly*
† Remade 1948 as *Sleeping Car to Trieste* (qv).

'The greatest love drama, the mightiest entertainment of our time.'
Romeo and Juliet *
US 1936 127m bw
MGM (Irving Thalberg)
Hollywood Shakespeare with a super production and a rather elderly cast.
Not entertaining in the strict sense, but full of interest.
w Talbot Jennings *d* George Cukor *ph* William Daniels *m* Herbert Stothart *ad* Cedric Gibbons, Frederic Hope, Edwin B. Willis
☆ Leslie Howard, Norma Shearer, John Barrymore, Basil Rathbone, Edna May Oliver, Henry Kolker, C. Aubrey Smith, Violet Kemble-Cooper, Robert Warwick, Virginia Hammond, Reginald Denny, Ralph Forbes, Andy Devine, Conway Tearle
'Unimaginative, coarse-grained, a little banal, it is frequently saved – by Shakespeare – from being a bad film.' – *Graham Greene*
'It is impossible to realize how bad this film was unless you reflect on how good it might have been.' – *Alberto Cavalcanti*
† Fredric March, Robert Donat and Robert Montgomery all refused the lead before Leslie Howard accepted.
best picture; Norma Shearer; Basil Rathbone; art direction

Romeo and Juliet
GB 1954 138m Technicolor
Rank/Verona (Joe Janni, Sandro Ghenzi)
Good-looking but extremely boring version shot on Italian locations with quite unacceptable leads.
wd Renato Castellani *ph* Robert Krasker *m* Roman Vlad
☆ Laurence Harvey, Susan Shentall, Aldo Zollo, Enzo Fiermonte, Flora Robson, Mervyn Johns, Sebastian Cabot, Lydia Sherwood, Giulio Garbinetti, Nietta Zocchi, Bill Travers, Norman Wooland, John Gielgud (Prologue speaker)

Romeo and Juliet *
GB 1968 152m Technicolor
Paramount/BHE/Verona/Dino de Laurentiis (Anthony Havelock-Allan, John Brabourne, Richard Goodwin)
The with-it version for modern youngsters.
Unfortunately the admirably rapid style does not suit the verse, and long before the much-deferred end the thing becomes just as tiresome as the other versions.
w Franco Brusati, Masolino D'Amico *d* Franco Zeffirelli *ph* Pasquale de Santis *m* Nino Rota
☆ Leonard Whiting, Olivia Hussey, John McEnery, Michael York, Pat Heywood, Milo O'Shea, Paul Hardwick, Natasha Parry, Antonio Pierfederici, Esmeralda Ruspoli, Bruce Robinson, Roberto Bisacco, Laurence Olivier as prologue speaker
'A large gold watch should be tossed to Zeffirelli for his part in reversing the movies' reputation for emasculating the classics.' – *Newsweek*
Pasquale de Santis; costumes (Danilo Donati)
best picture; Franco Zeffirelli

Romeo and Juliet: see *William Shakespeare's Romeo and Juliet (1996)*

Romeo in Pajamas: see *Parlor, Bedroom and Bath*

Romeo Is Bleeding
US 1993 108m DeLuxe
Rank/Polygram/Working Title (Hilary Henkin)
A cop, who takes bribes from the crooks he investigates while trying to keep his wife and his mistress happy, is assigned to protect a sexy hitwoman on the run from his gangster friends; it proves to be a recipe for mayhem.
Hectic, delirious thriller in which violence takes precedence over character and plot.
w Hilary Henkin *d* Peter Medak *ph* Dariusz Wolski *m* Mark Isham *pd* Stuart Wurtzel *ed* Walter Murch
☆ Gary Oldman, Lena Olin, Annabella Sciorra, Juliette Lewis, Roy Scheider, David Proval, Will Patton
'This heavy dose of ultra-violent neo-noir gives Gary Oldman a face-first trip through the gutter that would make Mickey Rourke drool, but the far-fetched plotting eventually goes so far over the top that pic flirts with inventing a new genre of film noir camp.' – *Variety*

'The Word On The Street Is...'
Romeo Must Die
US 2000 115m Technicolor
Warner (Joel Silver, Jim Van Wyck)
A former cop escapes from a Hong Kong jail and goes to America to avenge the death of his brother, who was killed in a gang war.
Some spectacular moments of martial arts combat are not enough to save this dull and confused action movie.
w Eric Bernt, John Jarrell *story* Mitchell Kapner *d* Andrzej Bartkowiak *ph* Glen MacPherson *m* Stanley Clarke, Timbaland *pd* Michael Bolton *ed* Derek G. Brechin *martial arts sup* Corey Yuen
☆ Jet Li (Han Sing), Aaliyah (Trish O'Day), Isaiah Washington (Mac), Russell Wong (Kai), DMX (Silk), Delroy Lindo (Isaak O'Day), Henry O (Ch'u Sing), D. B. Woodside (Colin), Edoardo Ballerini (Vincent Roth), Jon Kit Lee (Po Sing), Anthony Anderson (Maurice)
'Dire... will have thousands of despairing cinemagoers attempting to karate-chop themselves to death in the auditorium.' – *Peter Bradshaw, Guardian*

Romero
US 1989 105m DeLuxe
Warner/Paulist Pictures (Ellwood E. Kieser)
An apolitical priest is transformed by events into an archbishop who vigorously opposes El Salvador's government-sanctioned death squads.
Low-key biopic that tends to pussyfoot around its subject.
w John Sacret Young *d* John Duigan *ph* Geoff Burton *m* Gabriel Yared *ad* Francisco Magallon *ed* Frans Vandenburg
☆ Raul Julia, Richard Jordan, Ana Alicia, Eddie Velez, Alejandro Bracho, Tony Plana, Harold Gould, Lucy Reina

Rommel, Desert Fox: see *The Desert Fox*

Romper Stomper *
Australia 1992 92m Eastmancolor
Seon/Australian Film Commission/Film Victoria (Daniel Scharf, Ian Pringle)
In Melbourne, Nazi-loving skinheads battle with a Vietnamese gang.
A violent excursion into Australian low-life and one that refrains from any implied comment on the anti-social action it presents.
wd Geoffrey Wright *ph* Ron Hagen *m* John Clifford White *pd* Steven Jones-Evans *ed* Bill Murphy
☆ Russell Crowe, Daniel Pollock, Jacqueline McKenzie, Alex Scott, Leigh Russell
'Swiftly turns into another from the seemingly endless conveyor belt of debut moviemakers who use street violence as their calling card and a hand-held camera to conceal their other deficiencies of talent, imagination or personal vision.' – *Alexander Walker, London Evening Standard*
'Art house patrons are likely to be turned off by the brutally depicted violence and dominant antisocial behaviour ... Pic is well acted and directed with a certain slickness, but rarely has there been such a disturbing, essentially misconceived pic.' – *Variety*

Romuald et Juliette *
France 1989 112m colour
Gala/Cinéa/Eniloc/FR3 (Jean-Louis Piel, Philippe Carcassonne)
A managing director, whose business is being sabotaged by disgruntled colleagues, is saved by his cleaner.
Amusing comedy of ineffectual men and strong women.
wd Coline Serreau *ph* Jean-Noël Ferragut *ad* Jean-Marc Stehle *ed* Catherine Renault
☆ Daniel Auteuil, Firmine Richard, Pierre Vernier, Maxime Leroux, Gilles Privat, Muriel Combeau, Catherine Salviat

Romy and Michele's High School Reunion
US 1997 91m Technicolor
Buena Vista/Bungalow 78 (Laurence Mark)
Two flatmates in their 20s, who have missed out on success, decide to go to their high-school reunion and pretend to be rich and famous.
A movie about humiliation at school and undeserved success after which is too rooted in American rituals and manners to mean much anywhere else.
w Robin Schiff *d* David Mirkin *ph* Reynaldo Villalobos *m* Steve Bartek *pd* Mayne Berke *ed* David Finfer
☆ Mira Sorvino, Lisa Kudrow, Janeane Garofalo, Alan Cumming, Julia Campbell, Mia Cottet, Kristen Bauer
'Desperately uncertain in tone and able to generate only sporadic laughs, pic decks out its meager story of revenge and comeuppance with a vulgar, flashy shimmer that will no doubt attract teenage girls.' – *Todd McCarthy, Variety*

La Ronde ***
France 1950 100m bw
Sacha Gordine
In 1900 Vienna, an elegant compère shows that love is a merry-go-round: prostitute meets soldier meets housemaid meets master meets married woman meets husband meets midinette meets poet meets actress meets officer meets prostitute meets soldier ...
Superb stylized comedy with a fine cast, subtle jokes, rich decor and fluent direction; not to mention a haunting theme tune.
w Jacques Natanson, Max Ophüls *novel* Arthur Schnitzler *d* *Max Ophüls* *ph* Christian Matras *m* Oscar Straus
☆ *Anton Walbrook*, Simone Signoret, Serge Reggiani, Simone Simon, Daniel Gélin, Danielle Darrieux, Fernand Gravey, Odette Joyeux, Jean-Louis Barrault, Isa Miranda, Gérard Philipe
'One of the most civilized films to have come from Europe in a long time.' – *Gavin Lambert, MFB*
'A film that drags on and on by what seems like geometric progression.' – *John Simon, 1968*
Jacques Natanson, Max Ophuls (script)
film

La Ronde
France 1964 110m Eastmancolor
Franscope
Robert and Raymond Hakim
Vulgarization of the above, reset in Paris in 1913.
The lack of a compère vastly reduces the number of jokes.
w Jean Anouilh *d* Roger Vadim *ph* Henri Decaë *m* Michel Magne
☆ Marie Dubois, Claude Giraud, Anna Karina, Jean-Claude Brialy, Jane Fonda, Maurice Ronet, Catherine Spaak, Bernard Noel, Francine Bergé, Jean Sorel

'Loyalty Is Bought. Betrayal Is A Way Of Life...'
Ronin
US 1998 121m DeLuxe Panavision
UA/FGM (Frank Mancuso Jnr)
Six undercover agents, who are recruited to steal a briefcase by Irish revolutionaries, betray one another.
Involved and implausible thriller, though there's some pleasure to be gained from watching the cast out-tough one another.
w J. D. Zeik, Richard Weisz (David Mamet)
d John Frankenheimer ph Robert Fraisse m Elia Cmiral pd Michael Z. Hanan ed Tony Gibbs
☆ Robert de Niro, Jean Réno, Natascha McElhone, Stellan Skarsgard, Sean Bean, Skipp Sudduth, Michael Lonsdale, Jan Triska, Jonathan Pryce
'Can be watched as appreciatively for its hard-boiled performances as for its visceral excitement.' – *Janet Maslin, New York Times*

Rooftops
US 1989 95m DeLuxe
Fox/New Vision/Koch Company (Howard W. Koch)
Teenagers living on the roofs of an old tenement building combine to fight a vicious drug dealer.
Uninteresting teen movie, involving unlikeable characters.
w Terence Brennan story Allan Goldstein
d Robert Wise ph Theo Van de Sande
m Michael Kamen pd Jeannine C. Oppewall
ed William Reynolds
☆ Jason Gedrick, Troy Beyer, Eddie Velez, Tisha Campbell, Alexis Cruz, Allen Payne, Steve Love, Rafael Baez, Jaime Tirelli
'Words fail me where this absurd piece of tuppence-coloured fantasy is concerned.' – *Derek Malcolm, Guardian*

Rookery Nook **
GB 1930 107m bw
British and Dominions (Herbert Wilcox)
A nervous husband on holiday tries to hide a runaway girl who has asked for protection against her stepfather.
Primitive talkie technique cannot entirely conceal the brilliance of the original Aldwych farce team in their most enduring vehicle.
w *Ben Travers* play *Ben Travers* d Tom Walls
ph Dave Kessan
☆ Ralph Lynn, Tom Walls, Robertson Hare, Winifred Shotter, Mary Brough, Ethel Coleridge, Griffith Humphreys, Margot Grahame
'As a talker it is the best specimen so far made on this side.' – *Variety*

'He took a new kid and made a hero out of him.'
The Rookie
US 1990 121m Technicolor
Warner/Malpaso (Howard Kazanjian, Steven Siebert, David Valdes)
Ageing cop teaches his new young partner how to act tough.
Dreary, amoral and cliché-ridden slog through all-too-familiar territory.
w Boaz Yakin, Scott Spiegel d Clint Eastwood
ph Jack N. Green m Lennie Niehaus ed Joel Cox
☆ Clint Eastwood, Charlie Sheen, Raul Julia, Sonia Braga, Tom Skerritt, Lara Flynn Boyle, Pepe Serna, Marco Rodriguez, Pete Randall
'Overlong, sadistic and stale even by the conventions of the buddy pic genre.' – *Variety*
'Clint Eastwood has forgotten how to make popular entertainment.' – *Philip French, Observer*

'It's never too late to believe in your dreams.'
The Rookie
US 2002 127m Technicolor Panavision
Buena Vista/Walt Disney/Gran Via (Gordon Gray, Mark Ciardi, Mark Johnson)
In Texas, a baseball coach is persuaded by the success of his high school team to try for the major league.
Deft, sentimental tale of winners that seems too good to be true, though it is apparently based on fact.
w Mike Rich d John Lee Hancock ph John Schwartzman m Carter Burwell pd Barry Robison ed Eric L. Beason
☆ Dennis Quaid (Jim Morris), Rachel Griffiths (Lorri Morris), Jay Hernandez (Joaquin 'Wack' Campos), Beth Grant (Olline), Angus T. Jones (Hunter), Brian Cox (Jim Snr), Rick Gonzalez (Rudy Bonilla), Chad Lindberg (Joe David West)
'An unapologetically emotional film that doesn't make you gag, one that manages to be sentimental without turning into a shameless wallow.' – *Kenneth Turan, Los Angeles Times*
'Demonstrates that a skillful movie need not be good.' – *Roger Ebert, Chicago Sun-Times*

Rookie of the Year
US 1993 103m Technicolor
TCF (Robert Harper)
A young boy, who can throw a ball at great speed after an accident to his arm, becomes a pitcher for the Chicago Cubs baseball team, turning them from losers to winners.
A soft-centred wish-fulfilment fantasy for young baseball fans that offers little to those not enraptured by the sport.
w Sam Harper d Daniel Stern ph Jack N. Green
m Bill Conti pd Steven Jordan ed Donn Cambern, Raja Gosnell
☆ Gary Busey, Thomas Ian Nicholas, Albert Hall, Amy Morton, Dan Hedaya, Eddie Bracken, Daniel Stern, Bruce Altman, John Candy (uncredited)
'Rife with humor and sentimentality but is just one run away from the game-winning score.' – *Variety*

Rookies
US 1927 75m (24 fps) bw silent
MGM
Army adventures of a tough sergeant and a bumbling recruit.
Popular comedy of its day which established a new team of Dane and Arthur.
w Byron Morgan d Sam Wood
☆ Karl Dane, George K. Arthur, Marceline Day, Louise Lorraine, Tom O'Brien

Rookies: see *Buck Privates (1941)*

Rookies Come Home: see *Buck Privates Come Home*

Room at the Top ***
GB 1958 117m bw
Remus (John and James Woolf)
An ambitious young clerk causes the death of his real love but manages to marry into a rich family.
Claimed as the first British film to take sex seriously, and the first to show the industrial north as it really was, this melodrama actually cheats on both counts but scene for scene is vivid and entertaining despite a weak central performance.
w *Neil Paterson* novel John Braine d *Jack Clayton*
ph *Freddie Francis* m Mario Nascimbene
☆ Laurence Harvey, *Simone Signoret*, Heather Sears, Donald Wolfit, Ambrosine Philpotts, Donald Houston, Raymond Huntley, John Westbrook, Allan Cuthbertson, Hermione Baddeley, Mary Peach
'A drama of human drives and torments told with maturity and precision.' – *Stanley Kauffmann*
Academy Award: Neil Paterson; Simone Signoret
Academy Award nomination: picture; Jack Clayton; Laurence Harvey; Hermione Baddeley
BAFTA: film; British film; Simone Signoret

Room for One More
US 1952 95m bw
Warner (Henry Blanke)
aka: *The Easy Way*
A married couple adopt several underprivileged children.
Slightly mawkish family movie redeemed by star performances.
w Jack Rose, Melville Shavelson d Norman Taurog ph Robert Burks m Max Steiner
☆ Cary Grant, Betsy Drake, Lurene Tuttle, Randy Stuart, George Winslow

A Room for Romeo Brass *
GB 1999 87m Technicolor
Alliance Atlantis/BBC/Arts Council/Company /Big Arty (George Faber, Charles Pattinson)
The rapport between two 13-year-old boys, next door neighbours in a working-class Nottingham suburb, is threatened when one of them is befriended by a unbalanced adult.
At times an engaging, well-observed study of childhood and domestic disruptions, but hampered by the increasing implausibility of the central relationships.
w Paul Fraser, Shane Meadows d Shane Meadows
ph Ashley Rowe m Nick Hemming pd Crispian Sallis ed Paul Tothill
☆ Andrew Shim (Romeo Brass), Ben Marshall (Knock Knock), Paddy Considine (Morell), Frank Harper (Joe Brass), Julia Ford (Sandra Woolley), James Higgins (Bill Woolley), Vicky McClure (Ladine Brass), Ladene Hall (Carol Brass), Bob Hoskins (Steven Laws)
'For much of the time, the movie is a chucklesome portrait of fractionally offbeat types, dryly observed and not straying far from the British realist tradition.' – *Derek Elley, Variety*

The Room of Words
Italy 1989 97m Kodak Color
Filmirage/Wind Film
Anaïs Nin falls in love with writer Henry Miller and his wife June.
Inept on every level, lacking any sense of period or place (despite a streetcar named Desire) and concentrating on artfully shot lesbian love scenes. It is also saddled with an obtrusive and unsympathetic score and the near incomprehensible English of Martine Brochard as Anaïs Nin.
w Franco Molè play Franco Molè d Joe D'Amato
ph Giancarlo Ferrando m Gianni Silano
ed Kathleen Stratton
☆ Martine Brochard, David Brandon, Linda Carol, Ron Gural, Colette de La Croix

Room Service *
US 1938 78m bw
RKO (Pandro S. Berman)
Penniless theatricals find ways of staying in a hotel until they can find a backer.
Claustrophobic Broadway farce unsuitably adapted for the Marx Brothers, who are constrained by having to play characters with a passing resemblance to human beings.
w Morrie Ryskind play John Murray, Allen Boretz
d William A. Seiter ph Russell Metty m Roy Webb
☆ Groucho Marx, Chico Marx, Harpo Marx, Lucille Ball, *Donald MacBride*, Frank Albertson, Ann Miller, Philip Loeb
'A natural for the box office ... the change of pace is a good idea.' – *Variety*
'It should also be noted ... that there is a scene in which a turkey is chased around a room. Not everybody will care for this.' – *MFB*
† Remade as *Step Lively* (qv).

Room to Rent
GB/France 2000 95m colour
UIP/Film Consortium/Canal+/IMA (Ildiko Kemeny)
About to be deported from Britain, a young Egyptian would-be screenwriter works in odd jobs and is offered marriage by a Marilyn Monroe impersonator and by an elderly blind woman.
Slight whimsy that ignores the realities of immigrant life for a parade of English eccentricity.
w Khaled Al Haggar, Amanda Mackenzie Stuart
d Khaled Al Haggar ph Romain Winding m Safy Boutella pd Eli Bo ed John Richards
☆ Said Taghmaoui (Ali), Juliette Lewis (Linda), Rupert Graves (Mark), Anna Massey (Sarah Stevenson), Clementine Celarie (Vivienne), Karim Belkhadra (Ahmed)
'Competently made, but totally without edge.' – *Alexander Walker*
† The film was banned in Egypt.

A Room with a View ***
GB 1985 115m colour
Merchant Ivory/Goldcrest (Ismail Merchant)
An innocent Edwardian girl travelling in Italy has her eyes opened to real life and romance.
Competent, unexciting equivalent of a television classic mini-series which so perfectly filled a need as to become a runaway commercial success.
w Ruth Prawer Jhabvala novel E. M. Forster
d *James Ivory* ph Tony Pierce-Roberts m Richard Robbins pd Gianna Quaranta, Brian Ackland-Snow ed Humphrey Dixon
☆ Maggie Smith, Denholm Elliott, Helena Bonham Carter, Julian Sands, Daniel Day-Lewis, Simon Callow, Judi Dench, Rosemary Leach, Rupert Graves
'Quality-starved filmgoers will welcome it.' – *Variety*
Academy Award: art direction; adapted screenplay; costumes (Jenny Beavan, John Bright)
Academy Award nomination: James Ivory as director; Tony Pierce-Roberts; best picture; Maggie Smith; Denholm Elliott
BAFTA: best picture; production design; Maggie Smith; Judi Dench

Roommates
US 1995 108m Technicolor
Buena Vista/Polygram/Interscope (Ted Field, Scott Kroopf, Robert W. Cort)
A young doctor learns the important lessons of life through his grandfather, a retired baker, who moves in with him.
Low-key domestic soap opera, strong on charm but outstaying its welcome.
w Max Apple, Stephen Metcalfe d Peter Yates
ph Mike Southon m Elmer Bernstein pd Dan Bishop ed John Tintori
☆ Peter Falk, D. B. Sweeney, Julianne Moore, Jan Rubes, Frankie Faison, Noah Fleiss, Joyce Reehling, Ellen Burstyn
'Goes down painlessly but hasn't much flavor or substance.' – *Variety*

Rooney *
GB 1958 88m bw
Rank (George H. Brown)
Adventures of a bachelor Irish dustman.
Moderately charming, though unconvincing, Dublin comedy.
w Patrick Kirwan novel Catherine Cookson
d George Pollock ph Christopher Challis
m Philip Green
☆ John Gregson, Barry Fitzgerald, Muriel Pavlow, June Thorburn, Noel Purcell, Marie Kean, Liam Redmond, Jack MacGowran, Eddie Byrne

Rooster Cogburn *
US 1975 108m Technicolor
Panavision
Universal (Paul Nathan)
An elderly marshal after a gang of outlaws is helped by the Bible-thumping daughter of a priest.
Disappointing Western too obviously patterned after True Grit *and* The African Queen. *Having had the idea for outrageous star casting, the producers obviously decided erroneously that the film would make itself.*
w Martin Julien d Stuart Millar ph Harry Stradling Jnr m Laurence Rosenthal
☆ John Wayne, Katharine Hepburn, Anthony Zerbe, Richard Jordan, John McIntire, Strother Martin
'Like one of those infuriating exhibition bouts in which two resilient old pros bob, weave and spar without ever landing any punches.' – *Michael Billington, Illustrated London News*
† 'Martin Julien' allegedly covers the writing talents of Hal Wallis, his wife Martha Hyer, and some friends.

The Root of All Evil
GB 1946 110m bw
GFD/Gainsborough (Harold Huth)
A jilted woman becomes unscrupulous in business in order to get even with her ex-boyfriend.
Incredible farrago with a star ill at ease.
wd Brock Williams novel J. S. Fletcher
ph Stephen Dade m Bretton Byrd md Louis Levy
ad John Bryan ed Charles Knott
☆ Phyllis Calvert (Jackie Farnish), Michael Rennie (Charles Mortimer), John McCallum (Joe Bartle), Moore Marriott (Scholes), Brefni O'Rorke (Farnish), Hazel Court (Rushie Farnish), Rory McDermot (Overthwaite), Arthur Young (George Grice), Hubert Gregg (Albert Grice), Diana Decker (Pam), George Carney (Bowser), Reginald Purdell (Perkins), George Merritt (Landlord)

The Roots of Heaven *
US 1958 125m Eastmancolor
Cinemascope
TCF/Darryl F. Zanuck
A white man in central Africa dedicates himself to prevent the slaughtering of elephants.
Curiously patchy version of a novel which was a strange choice for filming; so many side issues are

introduced that at times it takes on the look of another jolly safari adventure.
w Romain Gary, Patrick Leigh-Fermor
novel Romain Gary d John Huston ph Oswald Morris m Malcolm Arnold
☆ Trevor Howard, Juliette Greco, Errol Flynn, Eddie Albert, Orson Welles, Paul Lukas, Herbert Lom, Grégoire Aslan, Friedrich Ledebur, Edric Connor
'The Huston who did *Sierra Madre* would have lighted his cigar with this script.' – *Stanley Kauffmann*

Roozi Khe Zan Shodam **
Iran 2000 78m colour
Artificial Eye/Mohsen Makhmalbaf
aka: *The Day I Became A Woman*
Three stories about women's existence on the island of Kish: a girl reaches the age of nine, and, now she is a woman, can no longer play with boys; a cyclist taking part in a race ignores demands from her husband, father, village elders, and brothers that she stop; a old woman spends a fortune buying everything she has ever wanted.
Powerful drama about female oppression, ranging from the social to the surreal; no definite conclusion is reached in any of the stories, but they are told with passion and humour.
w Mohsen Makhmalbaf, Marziyeh Meshkini
d Marziyeh Meshkini ph Ebrahim Ghafori, Mohammad Ahmadi m Ahmad Reza Darvishi
ad Akbar Meshkini ed Maysam Makhmalbaf, Shahrzad Poya
☆ Fatemeh Cherag Akhar (Hava), Shabnam Toloui (Cyclist), Azizeh Sedighi (Elderly Woman)
'The film is not a very exciting one but it has a purity of vision and lyricism that should reward all discerning film-goers.' – *James Cameron-Wilson, Film Review*

Rope **
US 1948 80m Technicolor
Transatlantic (Sidney Bernstein, Alfred Hitchcock)
Two homosexuals murder a friend for the thrill of it and conceal his body in a trunk from which they serve cocktails to a party including his father and girlfriend.
An effective piece of Grand Guignol on the stage, this seemed rather tasteless when set in a New York skyscraper, especially when the leading role of the investigator was miscast and Hitch had saddled himself with the ten-minute take, a short-lived technique which made the entire action (set in one room) cinematically continuous (and dizzy-making). Of considerable historic interest, nevertheless.
w Arthur Laurents play Patrick Hamilton
d Alfred Hitchcock ph Joseph Valentine, William V. Skall md Leo F. Forbstein theme Francis Poulenc
☆ James Stewart, John Dall, Farley Granger, Joan Chandler, Cedric Hardwicke, Constance Collier, Edith Evanson, Douglas Dick
'It was a limiting use of the medium, and parts of the film are unbearably tedious.' – *George Perry, 1965*

'A mighty story of savage greed and sultry love!'
Rope of Sand *
US 1949 105m bw
Paramount (Hal B. Wallis)
Various factions seek hidden diamonds in a prohibited South African area.
Ham-fisted adventure story which suggests at times that a violent parody of Casablanca *was intended. The stars carry it through.*
w Walter Doniger d William Dieterle ph Charles Lang m Franz Waxman
☆ Burt Lancaster, Paul Henreid, Claude Rains, Peter Lorre, Corinne Calvet, Sam Jaffe

Rosa Luxemburg **
West Germany 1986 112m colour
Bioskop/Pro-Jekt/Regina Ziegler/Bärenfilm (Eberhard Junkersdorf)
Biopic of the Polish-born socialist revolutionary and martyr (1871–1919) who was involved in political activity in Germany, including founding its Communist party, imprisoned for her activities, and murdered by the militia in Berlin.
Impressive, well-acted account, from a feminist viewpoint, of an impassioned life, based on Rosa Luxemburg's own writings, which limits its historical perspective but brings into sharp focus her own beliefs and feelings in reaction to the events of her time.
wd Margarethe von Trotta ph Franz Rath
m Nicolas Economou ad Bernd Lepel, Karel Vacek ed Dagmar Hirtz
☆ Barbara Sukowa, Daniel Olbrychski, Otto Sander, Doris Schade, Hannes Jaenicke, Adelheid Arndt, Jürgen Holtz
'Often comes close to a conventional bio-pic which traces a star's career from success to tragic decline.' – *MFB*
† Barbara Sukowa's performance won her the award for best actress at the Cannes Film Festival in 1986.

'The entertainment world is ablaze!'
Rosalie *
US 1937 118m bw
MGM (William Anthony McGuire)
A college football hero falls for an incognito Balkan princess.
Ambitious light musical with a wispy plot but satisfying numbers.
w William Anthony McGuire play William Anthony McGuire, Guy Bolton d W. S. Van Dyke ph Oliver T. Marsh m Herbert Stothart
songs Cole Porter
☆ Nelson Eddy, Eleanor Powell, Frank Morgan, Ray Bolger, Ilona Massey, Reginald Owen, Edna May Oliver, Jerry Colonna
'The most lavish, ornate, tinselled and glittering production which has come from Hollywood.' – *Variety*

Rosalie Goes Shopping
West Germany 1989 93m colour
Mainline/Pelemele (Percy Adlon, Eleonore Adlon)
A German housewife, living in Arizona with her large family, uses credit card frauds to keep them supplied with the good things of life.
Slight comedy of consumerism that relies too heavily on the charm of its performers.
w Percy Adlon, Eleonore Adlon, Christopher Doherty d Percy Adlon ph Bernd Heinl
ad Stephen Lineweaver ed Heiko Hinders
☆ Marianne Sägebrecht, Brad Davis, Judge Reinhold, William Harlander, Erika Blumberger, Patricia Zehentmayr, John Hawkes, Alex Winter, Courtney Kraus

The Rosary Murders
US 1987 105m colour
Laurel-Mihalich/Samuel Goldwyn
In Detroit, murders are committed by someone with a grudge against the Catholic Church.
Lax thriller with a priest detective.
w Elmore Leonard, Fred Walton d Fred Walton
☆ Donald Sutherland, Charles Durning, Josef Sommer, Belinda Bauer

'She gave ... and gave ... and gave ... until there was nothing left to give!'
The Rose
US 1979 134m DeLuxe
TCF (Tony Ray)
Drink and drugs cause the decline and death of a famous rock singer.
An unattractive, hysterical, foul-mouthed show business biopic roughly based on Janis Joplin, this does afford an undisciplined night-club talent a role to get her teeth into.
w Bill Kerby, Bo Goodman d Mark Rydell
ph Vilmos Zsigmond md Paul A. Rothchild
pd Richard MacDonald
☆ *Bette Midler*, Alan Bates, Frederic Forrest, Harry Dean Stanton, Barry Primus
Frederic Forrest; Bette Midler

The Rose and the Sword: see *Flesh and Blood (1985)*

The Rose Garden
US/West Germany 1989 112m Eastmancolor
MGM/Pathé/CCC/Cannon/ZDF/FFA/FKT/BMI (Artur Brauner, Yoram Globus, Christopher Pearce)
aka: *Der Rosengarten*
A female lawyer with marital problems defends a concentration camp survivor who attacked an elderly man at an airport, but refuses to explain why.
Some powerful performances give a little impetus to this drama of a Nazi atrocity, and state complicity in a cover-up; the problem is that its mix of thriller and courtroom confrontation lacks reality, despite the factual basis of its narrative.
w Paul Hengge d Fons Rademakers ph Gernot Roll m Egisto Macchi pd Jan Schlubach ed Kees Linthorst
☆ Liv Ullmann (Gabriele), Maximilian Schell (Aaron), Peter Fonda (Herbert), Jan Niklas (Paessler), Hanns Zischler (Eckert), Kurt Hübner (Krenn), Georg Matischika (Brinkmann), Gila Almagor (Ruth), Katerina Lena Müller (Tina), Nicolaus Sombart (Judge)

Rose Marie *
US 1936 113m bw
MGM (Hunt Stromberg)
A Canadian Mountie gets his man – and a lady.
Backwoods romance from a stage success, filmed mostly on location and quite successfully.
w Frances Goodrich, Albert Hackett, Alice Duer Miller play Otto Harbach, Oscar Hammerstein II d W. S. Van Dyke ph William Daniels m Rudolf Friml md Herbert Stothart songs various
☆ Nelson Eddy, Jeanette MacDonald, James Stewart, Reginald Owen, Allan Jones, Gilda Gray, George Regas, Alan Mowbray, Robert Greig, Una O'Connor, David Niven, Herman Bing
'An operatic honey with MacDonald and Eddy for the tungstens.' – *Variety*
† Previously filmed in 1928 – and see below.

Rose Marie
US 1954 115m Technicolor Cinemascope
MGM (Mervyn Le Roy)
Dull remake with stodgy handling and poor sets.
w Ronald Millar d Mervyn Le Roy ph Paul C. Vogel md Georgie Stoll ch Busby Berkeley
☆ Howard Keel, Ann Blyth, Fernando Lamas, Bert Lahr, Marjorie Main, Ray Collins

Rose of the Rancho
US 1935 83m bw
Paramount (William LeBaron)
Spanish settlers in California fight landgrabbers.
Romantic musical with interesting if seldom-used talent.
w Frank Partos, Charles Brackett, Arthur Sheekman, Nat Perrin, Harlan Thompson, Brian Hooker play Richard Walton Tully, David Belasco d Marion Gering
☆ John Boles, Gladys Swarthout, Willie Howard, Charles Bickford, Herb Williams, H. B. Warner
'A fandango mustang meller ... a tango version of a bronc opera.' – *Variety*

'Song by song ... scene by scene ... the thrill grows greater!'
Rose of Washington Square **
US 1939 86m bw
TCF (Darryl Zanuck)
Tribulations of a Broadway singer in love with a worthless husband.
Revamping of the Fanny Brice story; smartly done, but the material interpolated for Jolson is what makes the film notable.
w Nunnally Johnson story John Larkin, Jerry Horwin d Gregory Ratoff ph Karl Freund
m Louis Silvers songs various
☆ Alice Faye, Tyrone Power, *Al Jolson*, *Hobart Cavanaugh*, William Frawley, Joyce Compton, Louis Prima and his band
'This is Jolson's picture ... the rest is also-ran.' – *Variety*
'Jolson's singing is something for the memory book.' – *New York Times*
† Fanny Brice sued TCF for 75,000 dollars for invasion of privacy; the defendants settled.

'The boldest story of love you have ever been permitted to see!'
The Rose Tattoo
US 1955 117m bw Vistavision
Paramount/Hal B. Wallis
A Sicilian woman on the gulf coast is tormented by the infidelity of her dead husband, but a brawny truckdriver makes her forget him.
Heavily theatrical material, unsuited to the big screen for all the powerful acting (or perhaps because of it).
w John Michael Hayes play Tennessee Williams
d Daniel Mann ph James Wong Howe m Alex North ad Hal Pereira, Tambi Larsen ed Warren Low
☆ Anna Magnani, Burt Lancaster, Marisa Pavan, Ben Cooper, Virginia Grey, Jo Van Fleet
James Wong Howe; Anna Magnani; art direction
picture; Alex North; Marisa Pavan; editing
Anna Magnani

Roseanna McCoy
US 1949 89m bw
Samuel Goldwyn
In old Virginia the Hatfields and the McCoys continue their feud with tragic results.
Hillbilly Romeo and Juliet saga, a shade too cornfed despite the credits.
w John Collier d Irving Reis ph Lee Garmes
m David Buttolph
☆ Joan Evans, Farley Granger, Charles Bickford, Raymond Massey, Richard Basehart, Aline MacMahon

'A romantic comedy about the things we do for love'
Roseanna's Grave
US/GB 1996 98m Technicolor Panavision
Polygram/Fine Line/Spelling (Paul Trijbits, Alison Owen, Dario Poloni)
aka: *For Roseanna*
As the last plots in the graveyard of an Italian town are filled, a husband is anxious to secure one for his dying wife by ensuring that everyone else stays alive.
Moribund comedy that dithers between sentimentality and farce, and finally settles for soft-centred romance.
w Saul Turteltaub d Paul Weiland ph Henry Braham m Trevor Jones pd Rod McLean
ed Martin Walsh
☆ Jean Reno (Marcello), Mercedes Ruehl (Roseanna), Polly Walker (Cecilia), Mark Frankel (Antonio), Luigi Diberti, Roberto della Casa, Giovanni Pallavicino, Jorge Krimer
'A lightweight movie that constantly finds itself balancing between genuine whimsy and forced comedy.' – *Bob McCabe, Empire*

Les Roseaux Sauvages **
France 1993 102m colour
Gala/Ima/Alain Sarde
aka: *The Wild Reeds*
In the early 60s, as the Algerian War comes to an end, provincial French schoolboys experiment with sex and political action.
A stylish evocation of adolescence, sensitively handled.
w André Techiné, Gilles Taurand, Olivier Massart
d André Techiné ph Jeanne Lapoirie pd Pierre Soula ed Martine Giordano
☆ Elodie Bouchez, Gael Morel, Stephane Rideau, Frederic Gorny, Michele Moretti
'Politics and post-pubescent sex are the interlocking elements in this well-crafted and sober study of provincial French youth in the early 1960s.' – *Alexander Walker, London Evening Standard*

Rosebud
US 1975 126m Eastmancolor Panavision
UA/Otto Preminger
Five girls of wealthy families are kidnapped by the Palestine Liberation Army.
Overlong topical suspenser which goes awry by not being very suspenseful, and by packing in too many irrelevant satirical jibes.
w Erik Lee Preminger novel Joan Hemingway, Paul Bonnecarrere d Otto Preminger ph Denys Coop m Laurent Petitgirard titles Saul Bass
☆ Peter O'Toole, Richard Attenborough, Cliff Gorman, Claude Dauphin, John V. Lindsay, Peter Lawford, Raf Vallone, Adrienne Corri

Roseland *
US 1977 103m colour
Cinema Shares/Merchant Ivory (Ismail Merchant)
Generation after generation, the lonely and the loving come to a New York ballroom.
Pleasantly intentioned slice-of-life drama which is rather slackly written and handled, with unprofessionalism showing through at several points.
w Ruth Prawer Jhabvala d James Ivory ph Ernest Vincze m Michael Gibson
☆ Geraldine Chaplin, Teresa Wright, Lou Jacobi, Don de Natale, Louise Kirkland, Helen Gallagher,

Joan Copeland, Conrad Janis, Lilia Skala, Christopher Walken

'Typically discreet and dull film from Merchant-Ivory ... what one might call over-decorous.' – *Time Out, 1984*

Roselyne and the Lions **

France 1989 137m colour

Palace/Cargo Films/Gaumont (Jean-Jacques Beineix)

original title: *Roselyne et les Lions*

Two trainee lion tamers fall in love and run away to join a circus.

Charming, dreamlike boy-meets-girl romance.

w Jean-Jacques Beineix, Jacques Forgeas, Thierry Le Portier *d* Jean-Jacques Beineix *ph* Jean-François Robin *m* Reinhardt Wagner *ad* Carlos Conti *ed* Marie Castro-Brechignac, Annick Baly, Danielle Fillios, Oswald Bargero

☆ Isabelle Pasco, Gérard Sandoz, Philippe Clevenot, Gunter Meisner, Wolf Harnisch, Gabriel Monnet, Jacques Le Carpentier, Dimitro Furdui

Rosemary's Baby **

US 1968 137m Technicolor

Paramount/William Castle

After unwittingly becoming friendly with diabolists, an actor's wife is impregnated by the Devil.

Seminal gothic melodrama which led in due course to the excesses of The Exorcist*; in itself well done in a heavy-handed way, the book being much more subtle.*

wd Roman Polanski *novel Ira Levin ph* William Fraker *m* Krzysztof Komeda *pd* Richard Sylbert *ed* Sam O'Steen, Bob Wyman *sp* Farciot Edouart

☆ *Mia Farrow* (Rosemary Woodhouse), John Cassavetes (Guy Woodhouse), Ruth Gordon (Minnie Castevet), Sidney Blackmer (Roman Castevet), Patsy Kelly (Laura-Louise), Ralph Bellamy (Dr Sapirstein), Maurice Evans (Hutch), Angela Dorian (Terry Fionoffrio), Elisha Cook (Mr Nicklas), Charles Grodin (Dr Hill)

'It may not be for the very young, and perhaps pregnant women should see it at their own risk.' – *Motion Picture Herald*

'Tension is sustained to a degree surpassing Alfred Hitchcock at his best.' – *Daily Telegraph*

† William Castle, the producer, is glimpsed outside a phone booth.

†† A TV sequel followed: *Look What Happened to Rosemary's Baby*.

Ruth Gordon

Roman Polanski (as writer)

Rosencrantz and Guildenstern Are Dead *

US 1990 118m Technicolor

Hobo/Brandenburg (Michael Brandman, Emanuel Azenburg)

Two courtiers are summoned to Elsinore by the King of Denmark to discover why Prince Hamlet is behaving so strangely.

A celebrated stage play, and gloss on Shakespeare, transfers awkwardly to the screen.

wd Tom Stoppard *play* Tom Stoppard *ph* Peter Biziou *m* Stanley Myers *pd* Vaughan Edwards *ed* Nicolas Gaster

☆ Gary Oldman, Tim Roth, Richard Dreyfuss, Joanna Roth, Iain Glen, Donald Sumpter, Joanna Miles, Ljubo Zecevic, Ian Richardson, Sven Medvesck

'Stoppard's adaptation, at a shade under two hours, is too long, too slow, and ponderous when it is trying to be humorous.' – *Sight and Sound*

Rosetta ***

Belgium/France 1999 94m colour

Artificial Eye/Les Films du Fleuve/RTBF/ARP (Luc and Jean-Pierre Dardenne, Michele and Laurent Petin)

In a Belgian industrial town, a young unemployed woman, living on a caravan site with her alcoholic mother, dreams of leading a normal life.

Intense, gritty drama concentrating almost entirely on a woman's desperate search for some small acceptance from a hostile world; it gains immeasurably from its unforced central performance.

wd Luc and Jean-Pierre Dardenne *ph* Alain Marcoen *m* Jean-Pierre Cocco *ad* Igor Gabriel *ed* Marie-Hélène Dozo

☆ *Emilie Dequenne* (Rosetta), Fabrizio Rongione (Riquet), Anne Yernaux (Rosetta's mother), Olivier Gourmet (Boss)

'A stunning and remarkable achievement... It is a film whose grace and lyricism has earned it, simply, the status of classic: something of real greatness.' – *Peter Bradshaw, Guardian*

'An unforgiving piece of hard-boiled cinéma-vérité...desperately moving and desperately depressing.' – *James Christopher, Times*

† At the 1999 Cannes Film Festival, the film won the Palme d'Or, and Emilie Dequenne was awarded the prize for best actress.

'In 1923, a black town was burned to the ground, its people hunted and murdered because of a lie. This film is for them.'

Rosewood **

US 1997 140m Technicolor Panavision

Warner/Peters/New Deal

In 1923, a white lynch mob in a small Florida town goes on the rampage against the prosperous black population on the basis of a false rumor of rape.

Based on a true story, the movie begins impressively as an indictment of racial bigotry and intolerance, but its later reliance on stereotypical situations dissipates much of its power.

w Gregory Poirier *d* John Singleton *ph* Johnny E. Jensen *m* John Williams *pd* Paul Sylbert *ed* Bruce Cannon *cos* Ruth E. Carter

☆ Jon Voight (Jon Wright), Ving Rhames (Mann), Don Cheadle (Sylvester Carrier), Bruce McGill (Duke), Loren Dean (James Taylor), Esther Rolle (Aunt Sarah), Elise Neal (Scrappie), Sheriff Walker (Michael Rooker), Robert Patrick (Lover), Catherine Keller (Fanny Taylor), Akusua Busia (Jewel), Paul Benjamin (James Carrier), Badja Djola (John Bradley), Jaimz Woolvett (Deputy Earl)

'A well-made film that tells a gripping, important story.' – *Roger Ebert, Chicago Sun-Times*

Rosie

US 1967 98m Techniscope

Universal/Ross Hunter (Jacque Mapes)

A rich woman spends wildly and her daughters try to have her committed to safeguard their inheritance.

Hopelessly muddled comedy drama which flits from one mood to the other without making a success of either.

w Samuel Taylor *play* Ruth Gordon *French original Les Joies de la Famille* by *Philippe Heriat* *d* David Lowell Rich *ph* Clifford Stine *m* Lyn Murray

☆ Rosalind Russell, Brian Aherne, Sandra Dee, Vanessa Brown, Audrey Meadows, James Farentino, Leslie Nielsen, Margaret Hamilton, Reginald Owen, Juanita Moore, Virginia Grey

'A mawkish mixture of *Auntie Mame* and *King Lear*.' – *MFB*

Rosie Dixon, Night Nurse

GB 1877 88m colour

Columbia (Davina Belling, Clive Parsons)

A student nurse discovers that hospital doctors expect her to give her all on the job.

Dismal, witless farce with the emphasis on titillation.

w Christopher Wood, Justin Cartwright *novel Confessions of a Night Nurse* by Rosie Dixon *d* Justin Cartwright *ph* Alex Thomson *m* Ed Welch *pd* Albert Witherick *ed* Geoffrey Foot

☆ Debbie Ash (Rosie), Caroline Argyle (Penny), Beryl Reid (Matron), John Le Mesurier (Sir Archibald), Arthur Askey (Arkwright), Liz Fraser (Mrs Dixon), John Junkin (Mr Dixon), Lance Percival (Jake Fletcher), Bob Todd (Buchanan), Christopher Ellison (Quint), Peter Mantle (Richmond), Ian Sharp (MacSweeney), Jeremy Sinden (Fishlock), David Timson (Geoffrey), Leslie Ash (Natalie) and also Harry Towb (Phillips)

Rosie the Riveter

US 1944 75m bw

Armand Schaefer/Republic

GB title: *In Rosie's Room*

Warplant workers have to share rooms in a boarding house.

Easy-going wartime comedy.

w Jack Townley, Aleen Leslie *story* Dorothy Curnow Handley *d* Joseph Santley

☆ Jane Frazee, Frank Albertson, Vera Vague, Frank Jenks, Lloyd Corrigan, Frank Fenton, Maude Eburne, Carl 'Alfalfa' Switzer

Rote Lippen: see *Sadisterotica*

Rotten to the Core

GB 1965 88m bw Panavision

BL-Tudor (Roy Boulting)

Ex-convicts plan an army payroll robbery.

Routine caper comedy, unsuitably widescreened, with a few good jokes along the way.

w Jeffrey Dell, Roy Boulting, John Warren, Len Heath *d* John Boulting *ph* Freddie Young *m* Michael Dress *ad* Alex Vetchinsky *ed* Teddy Darvas

☆ Anton Rodgers (The Duke), *Thorley Walters* (Chief Constable), Eric Sykes (Hunt), Kenneth Griffith (Lenny), Charlotte Rampling (Sara Capell), Ian Bannen (Lt Vine), Avis Bunnage (Countess de Wett (Matron)), Dudley Sutton (Jelly), Peter Vaughan (Sir Henry Capell), Victor Maddern (Anxious O'Toole), James Beckett (Scapa)

† The original title, *Rotten to the Corps*, was more apt but plainly seemed too subtle.

Rouge **

Hong Kong 1987 93m colour

ICA/Golden Harvest/Golden Way (Jackie Chan)

original title: *Yanzhi Kou*

More than 50 years after she killed herself in the mid-30s, the ghost of a courtesan enlists the aid of a journalist to search for the lover with whom she made a suicide pact.

An exotic, bitter-sweet romance of a lost past and its contrast with a radically altered present, acted with style and directed with visual panache.

w Lee Bihua, Qiu-Dai Anping *novel* Lee Bihua *d* Stanley Kwan *ph* Bill Wong *m* Michael Lai *ad* Piao Ruomu, Horace Ma *ed* Peter Cheung

☆ Anita Mui, Leslie Cheung, Alex Man, Emily Chu, Irene Wan, Patrick Tse, Wang Yu

'Seems assured of its status as a classic.' – *Tony Rayns, Sight and Sound*

Rouge Baiser *

France/Germany 1985 112m Fujicolour

Stephan/A2/Farena/C&H/Aldo Lado

aka: *Red Kiss*

A 15-year-old Jewish girl growing up in 50s Paris has her faith in Communism shaken but begins to appreciate the power of love.

One of the rare films to take politics seriously, as it follows one person's disillusionment with ideology.

w Vera Belmont, Guy Konopnicki, David Milhaud *d* Vera Belmont *ph* Raymond Suarez *m* Jean-Marie Senia *ed* Martine Giordano

☆ Charlotte Valandrey, Lambert Wilson, Marthe Keller, Laurent Terzieff, Gunther Lamprecht, Laurent Arnal, Elsa Lunghini

Le Rouge et le Noir *

France/Italy 1954 170m approx

Eastmancolor

Franco London/Documento

aka: *Scarlet and Black*

A carpenter's son becomes a private tutor, seduces his master's wife and is sent to study for the priesthood ...

Massive attempt to conquer an unfilmable novel. Some enjoyable scenes and décor are the best it can offer.

w Jean Aurenche, Pierre Bost, Claude Autant-Lara *novel* Stendhal *d* Claude Autant-Lara *ph* Michel Kelber *m* René Cloërc *ad* Max Douy

☆ Gérard Philipe, Danielle Darrieux, Antonella Lualdi, Jean Martinelli

The Rough and the Smooth

GB 1959 99m bw

Renown (George Minter)

US title: *Portrait of a Sinner*

An archaeologist about to marry the niece of a press lord falls for a mysterious nymphomaniac.

Preposterous melodrama about unreal people; its very excesses become enjoyable for those who can stay the course.

w Audrey Erskine-Lindop, Dudley Leslie *novel* Robin Maugham *d* Robert Siodmak *ph* Otto Heller *m* Douglas Gamley *md* Muir Mathieson

☆ Tony Britton, Nadja Tiller, William Bendix, Natasha Parry, Norman Wooland, Donald Wolfit, Tony Wright, Adrienne Corri, Joyce Carey

'The script is never even on nodding terms with life, and tries to make up for this deficiency by a candidly explosive vocabulary which gives the production a weirdly old-fashioned air.' – *MFB*

Rough Company: see *The Violent Men*

Rough Cut

US 1980 112m Movielab

Paramount/David Merrick

A retiring Scotland Yard inspector spars with a jewel thief and finally changes sides.

Dated comedy which required a much lighter touch in all departments.

w Francis Burns *novel Touch the Lion's Paw* by Derek Lambert *d* Don Siegel *ph* Frederick Young *m* Nelson Riddle, from Duke Ellington themes *pd* Ted Haworth

☆ Burt Reynolds, Lesley-Anne Down, David Niven, Timothy West, Patrick Magee, Joss Ackland

'All surface smartness without a single structural idea.' – *Richard Combs, MFB*

Rough Diamonds

Australia 1994 88m colour

ITC/Forest Home/AFFC/Film Queensland/Beyond/Southern Star (Damien Parer)

A rancher and a country and western singer fall in love after she helps him win an award with his champion bull.

Dreary little star vehicle for Donovan, though even his fans may have difficulty in staying awake until the end.

w Donald Crombie, Christopher Lee *d* Christopher Lee *ph* John Stokes *pd* Georgina Greenhill *ed* Wayne Le Clos

☆ Jason Donovan, Angie Milliken, Peter Phelps, Max Cullen, Jocelyn Gabriel, Hayley Toomey, Kit Taylor, Lee James

'Probably pitched at undemanding early teens but it's hard to tell; it's the sort of film where jolly banjo music breaks out whenever a fist fight does.' – *Jonathan Romney, Guardian*

'Donovan fans will probably enjoy this fluff, and they are welcome to it.' – *Sheila Johnston, Independent*

Rough Magic

GB/France 1995 105m Technicolor

TCF/UGC/Recorded Picture (Laurie Parker, Delan Baldwin)

A reporter, hired by a millionaire to find his missing fiancée, who has magic powers, tracks her down to Mexico and falls in love with her.

An odd fantasy, in which a fire-breathing heroine vomits up her heart and turns an adversary into a sausage; its absurdities do not hold the attention for long.

w Robert Mundy, William Brookfield, Clare Peploe *novel Miss Shumway Waves a Wand* by James Hadley Chase *d* Clare Peploe *ph* John J. Campbell *m* Richard Hartley *pd* Waldemar Kalinowski *ed* Suzanne Fenn

☆ Bridget Fonda, Russell Crowe, Jim Broadbent, D. W. Moffet, Paul Rodriguez, Euva Anderson

'A peculiar and often uncomfortable mixture of romantic caper, farce and film noir.' – *Empire*

Rough Night in Jericho

US 1967 97m Technicolor Techniscope

Universal (Martin Rackin)

A stagecoach man rids a cattle town of a villain.

Totally uninteresting star Western with glum performances.

w Sidney Boehm, Marvin H. Albert *novel The Man in Black* by Marvin H. Albert *d* Arnold Laven *ph* Russell Metty *m* Don Costa *ad* Alexander Golitzen, Frank Arrigo *ed* Ted J. Kent

☆ George Peppard (Dolan), Dean Martin (Alex Flood), Jean Simmons (Molly Lang), John McIntire (Ben Hickman), Slim Pickens (Yarbrough), Don Galloway (Jace), Brad Weston (Torrey)

Rough Shoot *

GB 1952 86m bw

Raymond Stross

US title: *Shoot First*

A retired US officer in Dorset thinks he has shot a poacher – but the dead man is a spy, and someone else shot him.

Minor Hitchcock-style thriller with a climax in Madame Tussaud's. Generally efficient and entertaining.

w Eric Ambler novel Geoffrey Household *d Robert Parrish ph* Stan Pavey *md* Hans May

☆ Joel McCrea, Evelyn Keyes, Marius Goring, Roland Culver, Frank Lawton, Herbert Lom

Rough, Tough and Ready
US 1945 64m bw
Alexis Thurn-Taxis/Columbia
Two members of the Army engineers' port repair service fall out over a girl.
A faint echo of the old Flagg and Quirt comedies.
w Edward T. Lowe *d* Del Lord
☆ Victor McLaglen, Chester Morris, Veda Ann Borg, Jean Rogers

Roughly Speaking *
US 1945 117m bw
Warner (Henry Blanke)
Oddball, overlong domestic drama about father's wild and impractical schemes.
w Louise Randall Pierson *book* Louise Randall Pierson *d* Michael Curtiz *ph* Joseph Walker *m* Max Steiner
☆ Rosalind Russell, Jack Carson, Robert Hutton, Jean Sullivan, Alan Hale, Donald Woods, Andrea King, Ray Collins, Kathleen Lockhart

Roughshod
US 1949 88m bw
RKO (Richard H. Berger)
Two cowboys journeying to California with a herd of horses come up against villains intent on revenge.
Likeable old-fashioned Western.
w Geoffrey Homes, Hugo Butler *d* Mark Robson *ph* Joseph F. Biroc *m* Roy Webb
☆ Robert Sterling, Gloria Grahame, Claude Jarman Jnr, John Ireland, Jeff Donnell, Martha Hyer

Roujin Z *
Japan 1991 80m colour
Manga/Tokyo Theaters/TV Ashahi/Sony (Yasuhito Nomura, Yasuku Kazama, Yoshiaki Motoya)
▣
original title: *Rojin Z*
A robotic bed becomes possessed by the spirit of the dead wife of an elderly man chosen to test it and develops a will of its own.
An odd, satirical animated film, written by the creator of Akira, about the effect of technology and the dangers of militarism. The animation is sometimes poor, but the themes give it an interest beyond anime's usual teenage audience.
w Katsuhiro Otomo *d* Kiroyuki Kitakubo *m* Fumi Itakura *ad* Hiroshi Sasaki *ed* Eiko Nishiide
☆ Featuring the voices of Allan Wagner, Toni Barry, Barbara Barnes, Adam Henderson, Jana Carpenter, Ian Thompson
'Shot through with wry humour, genuine tenderness and inventive action.' – *Manga Mania*

Round Midnight **
France 1986 133m Eastmancolor
Warner/Little Bear/PECF (Irwin Winkler)
▣ ▬ ◎ ♫
A black American jazz musician spends his last days in Paris.
A jazz buff's tribute to Bud Powell and Lester Young; acclaimed by the critics but essentially a film for minorities.
w Bertrand Tavernier, David Rayfiel *d Bertrand Tavernier ph* Bruno de Keyzer *m Herbie Hancock md Herbie Hancock pd* Alexandre Trauner
☆ *Dexter Gordon*, François Cluzet, Gabrielle Haker, John Berry, Martin Scorsese
🏆 Herbie Hancock
🏅 Dexter Gordon

The Rounders
US 1965 85m Metrocolor Panavision
MGM (Richard E. Lyons)
▬
Two modern cowboys mean to settle down but never get around to it.
Pale comedy Western which never gets going.
wd Burt Kennedy *novel* Max Evans *ph* Paul C. Vogel *m* Jeff Alexander
☆ Henry Fonda, Glenn Ford, Chill Wills, Sue Ane Langdon, Edgar Buchanan
'One of those utterly relaxed comedies that make ideal entertainment because there's tender loving care every step of the way and no sweat.' – *Judith Crist*

Rounders
US 1998 121m DeLuxe 'Scope
Buena Vista/Miramax/Spanky (Joel Stillerman, Ted Demme)
▣ ▬ ◎ ♫
The ups and downs, in love and cards, of a young poker player.
A romantic thriller on predictable lines that is unable to make playing cards seem a life-or-death situation.
w David Levien, Brian Koppelman *d* John Dahl *ph* Jean-Yves Escoffier *m* Christopher Young *pd* Rob Pearson *ed* Scott Chestnut
☆ Matt Damon, Edward Norton, John Turturro, Famke Janssen, Gretchen Moll, John Malkovich, Martin Landau
'As dull and mechanical as poker itself is to the uninitiated.' – *Edward Yardley, Sight and Sound*

Roustabout
US 1964 101m Techniscope
Hal B. Wallis
▣ ▬ ◎
A wandering tough guy joins a travelling carnival.
Dreary star vehicle momentarily salvaged by its co-star.
w Allan Weiss, Anthony Lawrence *d* John Rich *ph* Lucien Ballard *m* Joseph L. Lilley
☆ Elvis Presley, Barbara Stanwyck, Sue Ane Langdon, Joan Freeman, Leif Erickson

La Route de Corinthe *
France/Italy/Greece 1967 90m Eastmancolor
La Boëtie/CGFC/Orion (André Génovés)
▣
aka: *The Road to Corinth*
The wife of a secret agent, accused of killing her husband in Greece, goes in search of the real killer.
Engaging, lightweight thriller, a parody of the espionage genre, which is stylishly shot against some superb Greek locations.
w Claude Brûlé, Daniel Boulanger *novel* Claude Rank *d* Claude Chabrol *ph* Jean Rabier *m* Pierre Jansen *ed* Jacques Gaillard
☆ Jean Seberg, Maurice Ronet, Christian Marquand, Michel Bouquet, Saro Urzi, Antonio Passalia, Claude Chabrol
'Flimsy, forgettable stuff.' – *Sight and Sound*

A Row of Crows: see *A Climate for Killing*

Rowing with the Wind *
Spain/Norway 1987 94m colour
Ditirambo (Andres Vincente Gomez)
Mary Shelley recalls her elopement with Shelley, their meeting with Byron and her creation of Frankenstein.
A glossy death-haunted romantic melodrama, with Frankenstein's monster popping up throughout as a reminder of mortality; a few startling images, such as a meeting between a giraffe and a cardinal in a Venetian palace, spice the familiar story.
wd Gonzalo Suarez *ph* Carlos Suarez *m* Alejandro Masso *ad* Wolfgang Burman *ed* José Salcedo
☆ Hugh Grant, Lizzy McInnerny, Valentine Pelka, Elizabeth Hurley, José Luis Gomez, Virginia Mataix, Ronan Vibert, José Carlos Rivas, Bibi Andersen
† Other films on a similar theme include *Gothic*, *Haunted Summer* and *Frankenstein Unbound* (qqv).

Roxanne *
🚶 US 1987 107m DeLuxe
Columbia/Michael Rachmil, Daniel Melnick
▣ ▬ ◎ ◎ ♫
An ugly man writes love letters for his friend ... but true love will find a way.
Zany modernization of Rostand's Cyrano de Bergerac, *funny in spots but way overlong.*
w Steve Martin *d* Fred Schepisi *ph* Ian Baker *m* Bruce Smeaton *pd* Jack DeGovia
☆ Steve Martin, Daryl Hannah, Rick Rossovich, Shelley Duvall, John Kapelos, Fred Willard, Michael J. Pollard

'The low down story of a high class gal!'
Roxie Hart **
US 1942 72m bw
TCF (Nunnally Johnson)
A twenties showgirl confesses for the sake of publicity to a murder of which she is innocent.
Crowded Chicago burlesque which now seems less funny than it did but is full of smart moments.
w Nunnally Johnson play Chicago by Maurine Watkins *d William Wellman ph Leon Shamroy m* Alfred Newman
☆ Ginger Rogers, George Montgomery, *Adolphe Menjou*, Lynne Overman, Nigel Bruce, Spring Byington, Sara Allgood, William Fawley
'A masterpiece of form, of ensemble acting, of powerhouse comedy and scripting.' – *NFT, 1974*
'Why then, am I not in the aisles all the time? Is it possible that Ginger Rogers, by overplaying the brainless little creature, destroys some of the plausibility and therefore some of the fun? Maybe; I can offer no other explanation of my moments of repose, straight-faced and in my stall.' – *Dilys Powell*
† The play was also filmed in 1927 under its original title, with Phyllis Haver.

Royal African Rifles
🚶 US 1954 75m Cinecolor
Allied Artists
GB title: *Storm over Africa*
In British East Africa in 1914, a lieutenant tracks down a consignment of stolen guns.
Mini-budgeted Boy's Own Paper *heroics; quite enjoyable on its level.*
w Dan Ullman *d* Lesley Selander *ph* Ellis Carter *m* Paul Dunlap
☆ Louis Hayward, Veronica Hurst, Michael Pate, Angela Greene, Steve Geray, Bruce Lester

The Royal Bed
US 1931 74m bw
RKO
GB title: *The Queen's Husband*
The king and queen of a European country lead their own private lives.
Insufficient wit graces this would-be daring romantic drama from a Broadway hit.
w J. Walter Ruben *play The Queen's Husband* by Robert E. Sherwood *d* Lowell Sherman
☆ Mary Astor, Lowell Sherman, Nance O'Neil, Anthony Bushell, Robert Warwick

Royal Cavalcade
GB 1935 104m bw
BIP
A chronicle of the events of the reign of King George V.
Thoroughly embarrassing jubilee tribute, of historical interest only.
w Marjorie Deans, Val Gielgud, Eric Maschwitz, Holt Marvel *d* Marcel Varnel, Thomas Bentley, Herbert Brenon, Norman Lee, Walter Summers, Will Kellino *ph* Brian Langley, Leslie Rowson, Phil Grindrod, Jack Cox, Horace Wheddon *md* Idris Lewis
☆ Marie Lohr, Hermione Baddeley, Esme Percy, John Mills, Reginald Gardiner, Syd Walker, Seymour Hicks, Owen Nares, Matheson Lang, George Robey, Florrie Forde, many others

A Royal Divorce
GB 1938 85m bw
Herbert Wilcox/Imperator
Napoleon Bonaparte in 1809 marries a widow whose reputation isn't exactly spotless.
Heavy comedy or light drama, take your pick; not exactly riveting as either.
w Miles Malleson *novel Josephine* by Jacques Thery *d* Jack Raymond
☆ Pierre Blanchar, Ruth Chatterton, Frank Cellier, Carol Goodner, George Curzon, John Laurie, Jack Hawkins

The Royal Family of Broadway *
US 1930 82m bw
Paramount
GB title: *Theatre Royal*
The off-stage escapades of a famous family of actors.
Fairly funny lampoon of the Barrymores, primitively staged and very talky but still entertaining for those in the joke.
w Herman J. Mankiewicz, Gertrude Purcell *play* George S. Kaufman, Edna Ferber *d* George Cukor, Cyril Gardner *ph* George Folsey
☆ *Fredric March*, Henrietta Crosman, Ina Claire, Mary Brian, Charles Starrett, Frank Conroy
'Lionel does not come into the burlesque at all, and I can quite believe that he is the most damaged of the entire family.' – *James Agate*
'Stagebound and awkward, but great fun anyway.' – *New Yorker, 1977*
🏅 Fredric March

Royal Flash
🚶 GB 1975 118m Technicolor
TCF/Two Roads (David V. Picker, Denis O'Dell)
▬
A Victorian bully and braggart has various adventures in Europe and Ruritania.
A rather unsatisfactory romp which takes pot shots at every 19th-century person and object in the encyclopaedia, but is never as funny as it intends to be.
w George Macdonald Fraser *novel* George Macdonald Fraser *d* Richard Lester *ph* Geoffrey Unsworth *m* Ken Thorpe *pd* Terence Marsh
☆ Malcolm McDowell, Oliver Reed, Alan Bates, Florinda Bolkan, Britt Ekland, Lionel Jeffries, Tom Bell, Joss Ackland, Leon Greene, Richard Hurndall, Alastair Sim, Michael Hordern

Royal Flush: see *Two Guys from Milwaukee*

The Royal Hunt of the Sun
GB 1969 121m Technicolor
Security Pictures (Eugene Frenke, Philip Yordan)
◎
How the Spanish soldier Pizarro on his South American trek overcame the Inca god-king Atahualpa.
Deadly literal rendering with nothing to replace the play's theatrical splendour, resembling nothing so much as an opera without the music.
w Philip Yordan *play* Peter Shaffer *d* Irving Lerner *ph* Roger Barlow *m* Marc Wilkinson
☆ Robert Shaw, Christopher Plummer, Nigel Davenport, Michael Craig, Leonard Whiting, Andrew Keir, James Donald, Percy Herbert, Alexander Davion

A Royal Scandal
US 1945 94m bw
TCF (Ernst Lubitsch)
GB title: *Czarina*
The illicit loves of Catherine the Great.
Censored romps around some chilly court sets; very few moments of interest, and none of the style of the silent version Forbidden Paradise.
w Edwin Justus Mayer *play* Lajos Biro, Melchior Lengyel *d* Otto Preminger *ph* Arthur Miller *m* Alfred Newman
☆ Tallulah Bankhead, Charles Coburn, Anne Baxter, William Eythe, Vincent Price, Mischa Auer, Sig Rumann, Vladimir Sokoloff
'Nothing is one-tenth well enough done, and all the laughs are played for at their cheapest, far down the ramp.' – *James Agee*

'Family Isn't A Word... It's A Sentence.'
The Royal Tenenbaums *
US 2001 Technicolor Panavision
Buena Vista/Touchstone/American Empirical (Wes Anderson, Barry Mendel, Scott Rudin)
▣ ▬ ◎ ◎ ♫
A disgraced lawyer attempts to return to his family of precocious geniuses fallen on hard times.
The fun here lies in the details – dalmatian-spotted mice, battered taxicabs, the elegant pages of an imaginary book – rather than in the disjointed narrative, which sets the scene deftly and then collapses.
w Wes Anderson, Owen Wilson *d* Wes Anderson *ph* Robert Yeoman *m* Mark Mothersbaugh *pd* David Wasco *ed* Dylan Tichenor *cos* Karen Patch
☆ Gene Hackman (Royal Tenenbaum), Anjelica Huston (Etheline Tenenbaum), Ben Stiller (Chas Tenenbaum), Gwyneth Paltrow (Margot Tenenbaum), Luke Wilson (Richie Tenenbaum), Owen Wilson (Eli Cash), Danny Glover (Henry Sherman), Bill Murray (Raleigh St Clair), Seymour Cassel (Dusty), Kumar Pallana (Pagoda), Alec Baldwin (Narrator)
'Merely fiddles around with its people and their eccentricities for a while, apparently in the belief that just to be fey is enough.' – *Stanley Kaufmann, New Republic*
'Sweet and funny, doggedly oddball if bordering precious.' – *J. Hoberman, Village Voice*
🏅 Wes Anderson, Owen Wilson (screenplay)

Royal Wedding
US 1951 93m Technicolor
MGM (Arthur Freed)
▣ ▬ ◎ ◎ ◎
GB title: *Wedding Bells*
Journalists congregate in London for the royal wedding.
Thin musical with acceptable numbers.

w Alan Jay Lerner *d* Stanley Donen *ph* Robert Planck *md* Johnny Green *songs* Alan Jay Lerner, Burton Lane
☆ Fred Astaire, Jane Powell, Sarah Churchill, Peter Lawford, Keenan Wynn
song 'Too Late Now' (*m* Burton Lane, *ly* Alan Jay Lerner)

Ruba al Prossimo Tua: see *A Fine Pair*

Ruby
US 1992 DeLuxe
Rank/Propaganda (Sigurjon Sighvatsson, Steve Golin)
A shady night-club owner kills Lee Harvey Oswald, assassin of President Kennedy, in order to expose a plot by the Mafia and the CIA to murder the President.
Muddled, small-scale, mainly fictional conspiracy movie that confuses the issues it attempts to explain.
w Stephen Davis *play* Love Field by Stephen Davis *d* John MacKenzie *ph* Phil Meheux *m* John Scott *pd* David Brisbin *ed* Richard Trevor
☆ Danny Aiello, Sherilyn Fenn, Frank Orsatti, Jeffrey Nordling, Jane Hamilton, Maurice Bernard, Joe Viterelli, Robert S. Telford

Ruby and Rata
New Zealand 1990 113m colour
Preston-Laing/NZFC
An uneasy relationship develops between an elderly woman and her tenant, an unemployed would-be rock singer with a small son.
Uninteresting domestic drama, presumably intended as a comedy.
w Graeme Tetley *d* Gaylene Preston *ph* Leon Narbey *m* Jonathan Crayford *pd* Robert Gillies *ed* Paul Sutorius
☆ Yvonne Lawley, Vanessa Rare, Lee Mete-Kingi, Simon Barnett

Ruby Cairo
US 1992 111m Technicolor
Entertainment/Majestic (Lloyd Phillips)
After her husband is reported killed in a car crash, his hard-up wife discovers that he had a fortune hidden in bank accounts across the world.
Dull thriller, which doubles as an attractive travelogue.
w Robert Dillon, Michael Thomas *d* Graeme Clifford *ph* Laszlo Kovacs *m* John Barry *pd* Richard Sylbert *ed* Caroline Biggerstaff
☆ Andie MacDowell, Liam Neeson, Viggo Mortensen, Jack Thompson, Paul Spencer, Chad Power, Monica Mikala
'An old-fashioned Yank-in-Europe mystery-adventure that squanders an interesting cast.' – *Variety*
'Nothing but a plot and the plot nothing but predictable.' – *Sight and Sound*

'Dangerous ... destructive ... deadly to love!'
Ruby Gentry
US 1952 82m bw
Joseph Bernhard/King Vidor
A tempestuous girl, brought up as a boy in the Carolina swamps, has a love-hate relationship with a local aristocrat, revenges herself on the people who scorn her, loses her lover in a swamp shooting, and becomes a sea captain.
Richly absurd sex melodrama typical of its director and star yet not very entertaining.
w Silvia Richards *d* King Vidor *ph* Russell Harlan *m* Heinz Roemheld *ad* Dan Hall
☆ Jennifer Jones, Charlton Heston, Karl Malden, Josephine Hutchinson

Ruby in Paradise
US 1993 114m DuArt
Mainline/Ruby in Paradise/A Full Crew/Say Yea
A young woman leaves home to seek life and love and ends up in an out-of-season holiday resort.
A deliberately small-scale movie, focussing its attention on minor matters and the frequently dull intricacies of everyday living.
wd Victor Nuñez *ph* Alex Vlacos *m* Charles Engstrom *pd* John Iacovelli *ed* Victor Nuñez
☆ *Ashley Judd*, Todd Field, Bentley Mitchum, Allison Dean, Dorothy Lyman, Betsy Douds, Felicia Hernandez, Sharon Lewis

'Very well played, very well set and directed with a sharp eye for detail.' – *Derek Malcolm, Guardian*

'Two hippies come back from 1969 to get the bad news...'
Rude Awakening
US 1989 101m Technicolor
Rank (Aaron Russo)
Two hippies return to New York after twenty years in Central America.
Weak ecological and political farce.
w Neil Levy, Richard LaGravenese *d* Aaron Russo, David Greenwalt *ph* Tom Sigel *m* Jonathan Elias *pd* Mel Bourne *ed* Paul Fried
☆ Cheech Marin, Eric Roberts, Julie Hagerty, Robert Carradine, Buck Henry, Louise Lasser, Cindy Williams

Rude Boy
UK 1980 120m colour
Michael White/Buzzy (Jack Hazan, David Mingay)
An unemployed young South Londoner becomes a roadie for the rock group The Clash at the time of their 'rock against racism' tour...
Uneasy mix of documentary footage and fictional story, interspersed with performances from the Clash; it does provide a flavour of the times.
w David Mingay, Ray Gange, Jack Hazan *d* Jack Hazan, David Mingay *m* Joe Strummer, Mick Jones
☆ Ray Gange (Rude Boy), Joe Strummer (Himself), Mick Jones (Himself), Paul Simonon (Himself), Nicky Headon (Himself)

Rudy
US 1993 116m Technicolor
Columbia TriStar (Robert N. Fried, Cary Woods)
An undersized youth is determined to play football for the University of Nötre Dame.
Based on a true story, a likeable, though predictable and overly sentimental, story of success against the odds.
w Angelo Pizzo *d* David Anspaugh *ph* Oliver Wood *m* Jerry Goldsmith *pd* Robb Wilson King *ed* David Rosenbloom
☆ Sean Astin, Ned Beatty, Charles Dutton, Lili Taylor, Jason Miller, Robert Prosky, Greta Lind, Jon Favreau
'A film that hits all the right emotional buttons, it's an intelligent, sentimental drama that lifts an audience to its feet cheering.' – *Leonard Klady, Variety*
'Appears to confirm the basic premise of the American dream – that you can do anything if you try hard enough. Its appeal is almost incomprehensible out of America.' – *Nick Hasted, Sight and Sound*

Rudyard Kipling's Jungle Book: see *The Jungle Book (1942)*

Rudyard Kipling's Jungle Book *
US 1994 111m Technicolor
Buena Vista/Walt Disney (Edward S. Feldman, Raju Patel)
The adventures of Mowgli, an Indian boy brought up by jungle animals.
Enjoyable children's adventure, closer to Indiana Jones than to Kipling, but with enough action and animals to keep it interesting.
w Stephen Sommers, Ronald Yanover, Mark D. Geldman *d* Stephen Sommers *ph* Juan Ruiz Anchia *m* Basil Poledouris *pd* Allan Cameron *ed* Bob Ducsay
☆ Jason Scott Lee, Cary Elwes, Lena Headey, Sam Neill, John Cleese, Jason Flemyng, Stefan Kalipha, Ron Donachie
'An engrossing, bloodthirsty family fable that's an edge-of-the-seater for all over-tens.' – *Tom Hutchinson, Film Review*

Rudyard Kipling's The Second Jungle Book: Mowgli and Baloo
US 1997 88m FotoKem Technovision
TriStar/MDP (Raju Patel)
aka: *The Second Jungle Book: Mowgli and Baloo*
aka: *Jungle Book 2: Mowgli and Baloo*
In India, in 1890, a ten-year-old wolf boy is chased through the jungle by apes and by hunters from Barnum's circus.
Low budget, unmemorable adventure with occasional moments of charm, though the comic relief, in the form of a cowardly Indian trickster, is hard to take.
w Bayard Johnson, Matthew Horton *stories* The Second Jungle Book; Kaa's Hunting by Rudyard Kipling *d* Duncan McLachlan *ph* Adolfo Bartoli *m* John Scott *pd* Errol Kelly *ed* Marcus Manton *sp* Cinemagic
☆ Roddy McDowall (King Murphy), Bill Campbell (Harrison), Jamie Williams (Mowgli), David Paul Francis (Chuchundra), Gulshan Grover (Buldeo), Dyrk Ashton (Karait)

Rue Cases Nègres **
France 1983 106m Fujicolour
Artificial Eye/Orion Classics/Su Ma Fa/Orca/NEF Diffusion (Jean-Luc Ormieres)
US title: *Sugar Cane Alley*
aka: *Black Shack Alley*
In Martinique in the 1930s, a woman sacrifices herself so that her grandson can escape from poverty through education.
Moving and evocative account of colonial life, tinged with nostalgia but marked by some full-blooded performances.
wd Euzhan Palcy *novel* Joseph Zobel *ph* Dominique Chapuis *m* Groupe Malavoi *ad* Hoang Thanh At, Romul Eloise *ed* Marie-Joseph Yoyotte
☆ Garry Cadenat, Darling Legitimus, Douta Seck, Joby Bernabe, Francisco Charles, Marie-Jo Descas, Marie-Ange Farot

Rue de l'Estrapade *
France 1953 95m bw
Cinephonic/SGGC/Filmsonor
aka: *Françoise Steps Out*
A young Parisienne suspects her husband of having an affair.
Lightly likeable domestic comedy in the vein of Edouard et Caroline, *but not quite up to its standard.*
w Annette Wademant *d* Jacques Becker *ph* Marcel Grignon *m* Georges Van Parys, Marguerite Monnot
☆ Louis Jourdan, Anne Vernon, Daniel Gelin, Jean Servais, Micheline Dax

'Five comedy stars in a five-star comedy!'
Ruggles of Red Gap **
US 1935 90m bw
Paramount (Arthur Hornblow Jnr)
A British butler has a startling effect on the family of an American rancher who takes him out west.
A famous comedy which seemed hilarious at the time but can now be seen as mostly composed of flat spots; the performances however are worth remembering.
w Walter de Leon, Harlan Thompson, Humphrey Pearson *novel* Harry Leon Wilson *d* Leo McCarey *ph* Alfred Gilks
☆ *Charles Laughton, Mary Boland, Charles Ruggles, ZaSu Pitts, Roland Young*, Leila Hyams, James Burke, Maude Eburne, Lucien Littlefield
'Plenty of marquee strength, and dynamite on the inside. An A1 comedy.' – *Variety*
'A sane, witty, moving and quite unusual picture of Anglo-American relations.' – *C. A. Lejeune*
'The most heart-warming comedy of the season ... there is about it a sympathetic and even a patriotic quality which is touching.' – *Literary Digest*
'The archetypal film they don't make any more, partly because comedy has now grown too raucous to favour the quiet drollery of players like Charlie Ruggles and Mary Boland, partly because even McCarey himself had trouble after the thirties separating sentiment from sentimentality.' – *Time Out, 1980*
† Remade as *Fancy Pants* (qv).
best picture

'France never had a chance!'
The Rugrats in Paris: The Movie *
US/Germany 2000 79m DeLuxe
Paramount/Nickelodeon (Arlene Klasky, Gabor Csupo)
A gang of kids wreak havoc in Paris, accompanying the father of one of them, who is attempting to repair a robot dinosaur in a Japanese theme park.
Lively infantile fun at the expense of Disney that will please the many fans of the little monsters' TV series, though adults may weary before the end.
w J. David Stem, David N. Weiss, Jill Gorey, Barbara Herndon, Kate Boutilier *d* Stig Bergqvist, Paul Demeyer *m* Mark Mothersbaugh *pd* Dima Malanitchev *ed* John Bryant
☆ voices of: E.G. Daily (Tommy Pickles), Christine Cavanaugh (Chuckie Finster), Michael Bell (Drew Pickles), Susan Sarandon (Coco LaBouche), Cheryl Chase (Angelica Pickles), Julia Kato (Kira Watanabe), Jack Riley (Stu Pickles), Melanie Chartof (Didi Pickles), Tara Charendoff (Dil Pickles), Kath Soucie (BettyLil/Phil Deville), John Lithgow (Jean-Claude), Lisa McClowry (Princess), Debbie Reynolds (Lulu Pickles), Mako (Mr Yamaguchi)
'A sequel that proves to be superior on every level to the first effort.' – *Variety*

The Rugrats Movie **
US 1999 79m DeLuxe
Paramount/Nickelodeon (Arlene Klasky, Gabor Csupo)
A gang of small children, attempting to return the new baby brother of their leader to hospital, become lost in a forest which is full of unfriendly animals.
Fast-moving, lively animated feature, based on a TV series, that takes to extremes an infant's-eye view of the adult world.
w David N. Weiss, J. David Stem *d* Norton Virgien, Igor Kovalyov *m* Mark Mothersbaugh *ad* Dima Malanitchev *ed* John Bryant
☆ Featuring the voices of: E. G. Daily, Christine Cavanaugh, Kath Soucie, Cheryl Case, Tara Charendoff, Melanie Chartoff, Jack Riley, Joe Alaskey, Phil Proctor, Cree Summer, Michael Bell, Tress MacNeille, Busta Rhymes, Whoopi Goldberg, David Spade
'Witty, sophisticated and, in its depiction of very young children as a wild bunch with bad attitude and faces like over-boiled potatoes, it's hard to fault.' – *Alexander Walker, London Evening Standard*

Rulers of the Sea *
US 1939 96m bw
Paramount (Frank Lloyd)
Problems surround the first steamship voyage across the Atlantic.
Well-made period action drama.
w Talbot Jennings, Frank Cavett, Richard Collins *d* Frank Lloyd *ph* Theodor Sparkuhl, Archie Stout *m* Richard Hageman
☆ Douglas Fairbanks Jnr, Margaret Lockwood, Will Fyffe, Montagu Love, George Bancroft, Mary Gordon, Alan Ladd
'Timely in content and grand for exploitation. In the British Empire it will be greeted as inspirational entertainment.' – *Variety*

'There Are No Rules.'
Rules of Attraction *
US/Germany 2002 110m DeLuxe
Icon/Lions Gate/Kingsgate/Roger Avary (Greg Shapiro)
A rich young man partakes of, and deals in, drugs and sex at a New England college.
A story of callow students indulging in fleshly pleasures; tricked out with a narrative that goes backwards (as sometimes does the film) and other gimmicks, it's like experiencing the day after the night before in a hungover flashback.
wd Roger Avary *novel* Brett Easton Ellis *ph* Robert Brinkman *m* tomandandy *pd* Sharon Seymour *ed* Sharon Rutter
☆ James Van Der Beek (Sean Bateman), Ian Somerhalder (Paul Denton), Shannyn Sossamon (Lauren Hynde), Jessica Biel (Lara), Kip Pardue (Victor), Thomas Ian Nicholas (Mitchell), Kate Bosworth (Kelly), Fred Savage (Marc), Eric Stoltz (Mr Lance Lawson), Clifton Collins Jnr (Rupert),

Faye Dunaway (Mrs Denton), Swoosie Kurtz (Mrs Jared)

'Sex, drugs and rack 'n' ruin; pretty people doing nasty things to one another…honestly, what more could you want in a movie?' – *Richard Corliss, Time*

'The harder the movie tries to shock, the shriller it rings. Too much of the time, its tone suggests the harangue of a spoiled brat trying to fluster Mommy and Daddy by waving snapshots from the orgy room.' – *Stephen Holden, New York Times*

'A hero should never have to stand alone.'

Rules of Engagement

US/Germany 2000 127m CFI Panavision

Paramount/Seven Arts (Richard D. Zanuck, Scott Rudin)

An American army officer is tried for murder after he orders his men to fire on demonstrators beseiging the US Embassy in the Yemen.

Jingoistic court-room drama of the kind to give patriotism a bad name, with a screenplay that keeps its thumb firmly jammed on the scales of justice.

w Stephen Gaghan *story* James Webb *d* William Friedkin *ph* Nicola Pecorini, William Fraker *m* Mark Isham *pd* Robert Laing *ed* Augie Hess *sp* Digital Domain *cos* Gloria Gresham

☆ Tommy Lee Jones (Col Hays Hodges), Samuel L. Jackson (Col Terry Childers), Guy Pearce (Maj Mark Biggs), Bruce Greenwood (National Security Adviser William Sokal), Blair Underwood (Capt Lee), Philip Baker Hall (Gen H. Lawrence Hodges), Anne Archer (Mrs Mourain), Ben Kingsley (Ambassador Mourain), Mark Feuerstein (Capt Tom Chandler), Dale Dye (Major Gen Perry)

'What the film argues, without ever articulating it, is that the life of a US marine is more valuable than that of some "raghead" protester.' – *Anthony Quinn, Independent*

'This shrill, belligerent, reactionary nonsense is lazily plotted, grotesquely dishonest, and dripping with a creepy strain of Islamophobia.' – *Peter Bradshaw, Guardian*

The Rules of the Game: see *La Règle du Jeu*

The Ruling Class *

GB 1972 155m DeLuxe

Keep Films (Jules Buck, Jack Hawkins)

The fetishistic Earl of Gurney is succeeded by his mad son Jack who believes he is God.

An overlong satirical play with brilliant patches is hamfistedly filmed but boasts some bright performances. The hits are as random as the misses, however.

w Peter Barnes *play* Peter Barnes *d* Peter Medak *ph* Ken Hodges *m* John Cameron

☆ Peter O'Toole, Harry Andrews, *Arthur Lowe, Alastair Sim*, Coral Browne, Michael Bryant

'This irritating and unsatisfying film is worth being irritated and unsatisfied by.' – *Stanley Kauffmann*

Peter O'Toole

'This is the dance of love!'

Rumba *

US 1935 71m bw

Paramount (William Le Baron)

A society girl has a yen for a Broadway hoofer.

Streamlined star vehicle which attempts to recapture the success of Bolero *(qv).*

w Howard J. Green *d* Marion Gering *ph* Ted Tetzlaff

☆ *Carole Lombard, George Raft*, Margo, Lynne Overman, Monroe Owsley, Iris Adrian, Gail Patrick, Samuel S. Hinds, Jameson Thomas

Rumble Fish

US 1983 94m bw (with colour inserts)

Universal/Zoetrope (Fred Roos, Douglas Claybourne)

A Tulsa teenager survives local gang violence and while working in a petshop sees himself in the rumble fish, which fights even its own image in a glass.

Glum piece of self-absorption by a director going rapidly downhill.

wd Francis Ford Coppola *novel* S. E. Hinton *ph* Stephen H. Burum *m* Stewart Copeland *pd* Dean Tavoularis *ed* Barry Malkin

☆ Matt Dillon, Mickey Rourke, Diane Lane, Dennis Hopper, Diana Scarwid

Rumble in the Bronx

Hong Kong 1995 105m colour

Golden Harvest (Leonard K. C. Ho)

In New York, a Hong Kong cop helps a Chinese woman whose supermarket is threatened by a biker gang.

Moderate martial arts action with a few comic moments; the film is calculated to appeal to Western audiences, though Chan always seems at his best on his home ground.

w Edward Tang *story* Stanley Tong, Ma Mei-ping *d* Stanley Tong *ph* Jingle Ma *m* J. Peter Robinson *ad* Oliver Wong *ed* Peter Cheung

☆ Jackie Chan, Anita Mui, Bill Tung, Yip Fong-wa, Bai Cheun-wai

'An enjoyable comedy-actioner whose ooh-aah moments are mostly confined to the last few reels.' – *Variety*

Run

US 1990 91m Technicolor

Buena Vista/Hollywood (Raymond Wagner)

An accident-prone law student is hunted by crooked cops and robbers when he accidentally causes the death of a gangster's son.

Inane thriller, with a less than sympathetic protagonist, that amounts to little more than a series of car chases and crashes.

w Dennis Shryack, Michael Blodgett *d* Geoff Burrowes *ph* Bruce Surtees *m* Phil Marshall *pd* John Willett *ed* Jack Hofstra

☆ Patrick Dempsey (Charlie Farrow), Kelly Preston (Karen Landers), Ken Pogue (Halloran), James Kidnie (Sammy), Sean McCann (Marv)

Run for Cover *

US 1955 92m Technicolor Vistavision

Paramount (William H. Pine)

An ex-convict becomes innocently involved in a train robbery.

Adequate star Western.

w William C. Thomas *story* Harriet Frank Jnr, Irving Ravetch *d* Nicholas Ray *ph* Daniel Fapp *md* Howard Jackson

☆ *James Cagney*, Viveca Lindfors, John Derek, Jean Hersholt, Grant Withers, Ernest Borgnine, Jack Lambert

Run for the Sun

US 1956 99m Technicolor Superscope

UA/Russ-Field (Harry Tatelman)

Crashlanding in the Mexican jungle, a disillusioned author and a lady journalist find themselves at the mercy of renegade Nazis.

Tame remake of The Most Dangerous Game *with Count Zaroff replaced by Lord Haw-Haw. Sluggish plot development mars the action.*

w Dudley Nichols, Roy Boulting *d* Roy Boulting *ph* Joseph LaShelle *m* Fred Steiner

☆ Richard Widmark, Jane Greer, Trevor Howard, Peter Van Eyck

A Run for Your Money *

GB 1949 83m bw

Ealing (Leslie Norman)

Welsh Rugby supporters have various adventures on their one day in London.

Slight, bright, British chase comedy with characterizations as excellent as they are expected.

w Richard Hughes, Charles Frend, Leslie Norman *d* Charles Frend *ph* Douglas Slocombe *m* Ernest Irving

☆ *Alec Guinness*, Meredith Edwards, Moira Lister, Donald Houston, Hugh Griffith, Clive Morton, Joyce Grenfell

Run Lola Run ***

Germany 1998 80m colour

Columbia TriStar/Bavaria/German Independents/X Filme/ (Stefan Arndt)

original title: *Lola Rennt*

A girl has 20 minutes in which to save her boyfriend from death, after he loses a bag of money belonging to a drug dealer.

Exhilarating, speedy thriller which provides three alternative versions of events, depending on tiny incidents which precipitate different consequences; it's a witty demonstration of the vagaries of cause and effect and the unpredictability of life.

wd Tom Tykwer *ph* Frank Griebe *m* Tom Tykwer, Johnny Klimek, Reinhold Hei *ad* Alexander Manasse *ed* Mathilde Bonnefoy

☆ Franka Potente (Lola), Moritz Bleibtreu (Manni), Herbert Knaup (Lola's Father), Armin Rohde (Mr Schuster), Joachim Krol (Nortbert von Au), Nina Petri (Jutta Hansen), Heino Ferch (Ronnie)

'That Tykwer maintains our flow of empathy while demonstrating and exploiting the potential of interactive cinema manqué is, in itself, an awesome achievement.' – *Richard Falcon, Sight and Sound*

'This stylish, hugely likeable bit of adrenaline-pumped Euro-nonsense should shatter the illusions of those convinced that all subtitled fare is musty, wordy and dull.' – *Caroline Westbrook, Empire*

'A Rebel's Hate … A Woman's Undying Love!'

Run of the Arrow *

US 1957 85m Technicolor RKOscope

Global (Samuel Fuller)

An ex-Civil War soldier is captured by Indians and accepted by them, but sickened by their violence.

Bloody little Western in the accustomed Fuller vein.

wd Samuel Fuller *ph* Joseph Biroc *m* Victor Young

☆ Rod Steiger, Sarita Montiel, Charles Bronson, Tim McCoy, Ralph Meeker

'Just an ordinary cavalry-Indian film, conspicuous for a lot of raw blood-letting.' – *Bosley Crowther*

'Sometimes, the most daring step to freedom is out the front door.'

The Run of the Country

GB/Ireland 1995 108m Technicolor Panavision

Rank/Castle Rock/One Two Nine (Peter Yates, Ruth Boswell)

An Irish policeman in a small town near the border with Northern Ireland has problems with his teenage son.

A domestic drama that skirts round the Irish troubles but uses them as a backdrop to an unilluminating account of young love and its aftermath.

w Shane Connaughton *novel* Shane Connaughton *d* Peter Yates *ph* Mike Southon *m* Cynthia Millar *pd* Mark Geraghty *ed* Paul Hodgson

☆ Albert Finney, Matt Keeslar, Victoria Smurfit, Anthony Brophy, David Kelly, Dearbhla Molloy

'A bog-standard rite-of-passage film.' – *Sheila Johnston, Independent*

A Run on Gold: see *Midas Run*

Run Silent Run Deep *

US 1958 93m bw

UA/Hecht-Hill-Lancaster (William Schorr)

Antagonisms flare up between the officers of a US submarine in Tokyo Bay during World War II

Competent, unsurprising war actioner trading on its stars.

w John Gay *d* Robert Wise *ph* Russell Harlan *m* Franz Waxman

☆ Clark Gable, Burt Lancaster, Jack Warden, Brad Dexter, Nick Cravat, Joe Maross, H. M. Wynant

'Mostly good sea fights. Otherwise it's damn the torpedoes, half speed ahead.' – *Time*

Run Wild, Run Free *

GB 1969 98m Technicolor

Columbia/Irving Allen (John Danischewsky)

A mute boy living on Dartmoor gains self-confidence through the love of animals.

Rather vaguely developed family film with agreeable sequences.

w David Rook *novel* The White Colt by David Rook *d* Richard C. Sarafian *ph* Wilkie Cooper *m* David Whitaker

☆ John Mills, Sylvia Syms, Mark Lester, Bernard Miles, Gordon Jackson, Fiona Fullerton

The Runaround *

US 1946 100m bw

Universal (Joseph Gershenson)

Two rival detectives are hired to find a missing heiress.

Peripatetic comedy on the lines of It Happened One Night; *unexpectedly enjoyable.*

w Arthur T. Horman, Sam Hellman *d* Charles Lamont *ph* George Robinson *m* Frank Skinner *ad* Robert Clatworthy, Jack Otterson *ed* Ted J. Kent

☆ Rod Cameron, Broderick Crawford, Ella Raines, Samuel S. Hinds, Frank McHugh, George Cleveland

Runaway

US 1984 100m Metrocolor Panavision

Tri-Star/Michael Crichton (Michael Rachmil)

An electronics wizard sets a half-perfected robot on the rampage.

Simple-minded comedy-melodrama which feels as though it ought to have been played entirely for laughs.

wd Michael Crichton *ph* John A. Alonzo *m* Jerry Goldsmith *pd* Douglas Higgins *ed* Glenn Farr

☆ Tom Selleck, Cynthia Rhodes, Gene L. Simmons, Kirstie Alley, Stan Shaw

'Catch her if you can.'

Runaway Bride *

US 1999 116m Technicolor Panavision

Paramount/Touchstone/Interscope/Lakeshore (Ted Field, Tom Rosenberg, Scott Kroopf, Robert Cort)

A sacked newspaper columnist goes to find the thrice-bolting bride who cost him his job.

A romantic comedy in search of a better script; this one manages to make both of its protagonists unsympathetic.

w Josann McGibbon, Sara Parriott *d* Garry Marshall *ph* Stuart Dryburgh *m* James Newton Howard *pd* Mark Friedberg *ed* Bruce Green *cos* Albert Wolsky

☆ Julia Roberts (Maggie Carpenter), Richard Gere (Ike Graham), Joan Cusack (Peggy Flemming), Hector Elizondo (Fisher), Rita Wilson (Ellie), Paul Dooley (Walter), Christopher Meloni (Bob Kelly), Donal Logue (Brian Norris)

'Director Garry Marshall specialises in this kind of schmaltz. This time, though, the trademark warm glow only highlights the script's awesome deficiences.' – *Andrew O'Hagan, Daily Telegraph*

'An ultracommercial mainstream romantic comedy that delivers all the laughs and smiles it intends to.' – *Todd McCarthy, Variety*

† The film grossed more than $155m at the US box-office.

The Runaway Bus *

GB 1954 78m bw

Eros/Conquest-Guest (Val Guest)

Passengers at London Airport are fogbound, and a relief bus driver takes some of them to Blackbushe. Incognito among them are robbers and detectives…

Vaguely plotted variation on The Ghost Train, *with fair production, a good smattering of jokes, and a hilarious view of a great airport in its earlier days.*

wd Val Guest *ph* Stan Pavey *m* Ronald Binge

☆ Frankie Howerd, Margaret Rutherford, George Coulouris, Petula Clark, Terence Alexander, Toke Townley, Belinda Lee

Runaway Daughter: see *Red Salute*

'Once it starts, nothing can stop it!'

Runaway Train *

US 1985 111m Rank Colour

Cannon/Northbrook (Menahem Golan, Yoram Globus)

Prison breakers escape into the Alaskan wilderness and commandeer a train which can't stop.

Violent, foul-mouthed melodrama with no interest beyond breathtaking photography of the speeding train. Its general pretentiousness, perhaps, is also something to experience.

w Djordje Milicevic, Paul Zindel, Edward Bunker, from screenplay by Akira Kurosawa *d* *Andrei Konchalovsky* *ph* *Alan Hume* *m* Trevor Jones *pd* Stephen Marsh

☆ Jon Voight, Eric Roberts, Rebecca DeMornay, Kyle T. Heffner

'The most exciting epic since *The Road Warrior*.' – *Variety*

'Nervy, exciting violence; immaculate, metallic camerawork; unstoppable pace.' – *Sight and Sound*

Jon Voight; Eric Roberts (supporting actor); editing

The Runner
Iran 1984 94m colour
Electric/Studio of the Voice and Portrait of the Islamic Revolution of Iran (Fatholah Dalili)
original title: *Dawandeh*
A 13-year-old orphan makes his living on the streets of a Gulf port while learning to outdistance his peers.
Unsparing but repetitious account of childhood poverty.
w Amir Naderi, Behruz Gharibpur *d* Amir Naderi *ph* Firuz Malekzadeh *pd* Gholam Reza Ramezani *ed* Bahram Beyza'i
☆ Majid Nirumand, Musa Torkizadeh, A. Gholamzadeh, Reza Ramezani

The Runner Stumbles
US 1979 110m CFI color
Melvin Simon Productions (Stanley Kramer)
In the mid-twenties, a Catholic priest is accused of the murder of a nun for whom he had felt a strong romantic attraction.
Musty exhumation of a genuine case which has little dramatic interest and even less wider significance. Good acting does not atone.
w Milan Stiff *play* Milan Stiff *d* Stanley Kramer *ph* Laszlo Kovacs *m* Ernest Gold *pd* Alfred Sweeney Jnr
☆ Dick Van Dyke, Kathleen Quinlan, Maureen Stapleton, Ray Bolger, Tammy Grimes, Beau Bridges

'The reanimated corpse of middlebrow Hollywood pretension ... funereal pacing, portentous low angles and symbolic overkill.' – *Paul Taylor, MFB*

Runners
GB 1983 106m colour
Goldcrest (Barry Hanson)
Distraught parents try to trace their missing children in London.
Heavy-going realistic drama with apparent inner meanings which are not brought to the surface.
w Stephen Poliakoff *d* Charles Sturridge *ph* Howard Atherton *m* George Fenton *pd* Arnold Chapkis
☆ James Fox, Kate Hardie, Jane Asher, Eileen O'Brien, Ruti Simon

Running
Canada 1979 103m colour
Universal (Robert Cooper, Ronald Cohen)
A man in his 30s who has failed in his work and marriage decides that he can succeed as an Olympic marathon runner.
Slight drama with rather too much footage of our hero running through city streets to the accompaniment of syrupy music to maintain any interest in its conventional and sentimental narrative.
wd Steven Hilliard Stern *ph* Laszlo George *m* André Gagnon *pd* Roy Forge Smith *ed* Kurt Kirschler
☆ Michael Douglas, Susan Anspach, Lawrence Dane, Eugene Levy, Charles Shamata, Philip Akin, Jim McKay

Running Brave
US 1983 106m colour
ITC/Englander Productions
A young Sioux from the reservation faces the pressures of the white world and becomes an Olympic runner.
The terrible punning title is the best thing in this very predictable piece of do-goodery, which would just about have passed muster as a TV movie.
w Henry Bean, Shirl Hendryx *d* D. S. Everett *ph* François Protat *m* Mike Post *pd* Carol Spier *ed* Tony Lower, Earle Herden
☆ Robby Benson, Pat Hingle, Claudia Cron, Jeff McCracken

'This is in essence a propaganda film for the American way, masked as a piece of liberal sentiment, and I distrust it thoroughly.' – *Observer*

Running Cool
US 1993 106m colour
Paramount (Beverly Sebastian)
Two bikers go to help a wildlife-loving friend in a small South Carolina town, whose swampland is threatened by the reckless son of a ruthless developer.
Overlong, cliché-ridden action movie with an environmental message, providing you can accept that 400 bikers improve an environment.
w Ferd & Beverly Sebastian *d* Ferd Sebastian *ph* Ferd Sebastian *m* Robert Etoll *ed* Ralph Clemente
☆ Andrew Divoff, Tracy Sebastian, Dedee Pfeiffer, James Gammon, Paul Gleason, Arlen Dean Snyder, Bubba Baker

'Time is running out for him!'
The Running Man *
GB 1963 103m Technicolor Panavision
Columbia/Peet (Carol Reed, John R. Sloan)
A private airline pilot fakes an accident and disappears, leaving his wife to collect the insurance and meet him in Spain.
Flabby, expensive suspenser; both plot and character take a back seat to scenic views.
w John Mortimer *novel* *The Ballad of the Running Man* by Shelley Smith *d* Carol Reed *ph* Robert Krasker *m* William Alwyn
☆ Laurence Harvey, Alan Bates, Lee Remick, Felix Aylmer, Eleanor Summerfield, Allan Cuthbertson

'There seems to be something about the panoramic screen that seduces film-makers into filling it with irrelevant local colour and drawing the whole proceedings out to a length that matches its width.' – *Brenda Davies*

The Running Man
US 1987 101m colour
Rank/Braveworld (Tim Zinnemann, George Linder)
In the future, a convict, framed on a murder charge, takes part in a TV game show in which he is hunted through Los Angeles by expert killers.
Fast-moving action movie, full of violence and some dubious jokes.
w Steven E. de Souza *novel* Stephen King *d* Paul Michael Glaser *ph* Thomas Del Ruth *m* Harold Faltermeyer *pd* Jack T. Collis *ed* Mark Roy Warner, Edward A. Warschilka, John Wright
☆ Arnold Schwarzenegger, Maria Conchita Alonso, Yaphet Kotto, Jim Brown, Jesse Ventura, Erland Van Lidth, Marvin J. McIntyre, Mick Fleetwood, Richard Dawson

Running on Empty
US 1988 116m Technicolor
Warner/Lorimar/Double Play (Amy Robinson, Griffin Dunne)
A teenager, whose parents are long-time political activists on the run from the FBI, tries to live his own life as a budding musician.
Mundane family drama that fails to illuminate the problems it describes.
w Naomi Foner *d* Sidney Lumet *ph* Gerry Fisher *m* Tony Mottola *pd* Philip Rosenberg *ed* Andre Mondshein
☆ Christine Lahti, River Phoenix, Judd Hirsch, Jonas Abry, Martha Plimpton, Ed Crowley, L. M. Kit Carson, Steven Hill, Augusta Dabney, David Margulies

best original screenplay; River Phoenix

Running Scared
GB 1972 98m Technicolor Panavision
Paramount/Wigan/Hemmings/O'Toole (Gareth Wigan)
A university student is generally condemned for allowing his friend to commit suicide; eventually he takes his own life.
Depressing and rather pointless exercise in death wish complicated by a doomed love affair.
w Clive Exton, David Hemmings *novel* Gregory MacDonald *d* David Hemmings *ph* Ernest Day *m* Michael J. Lewis
☆ Robert Powell, Gayle Hunnicutt, Barry Morse, Stephanie Bidmead, Edward Underdown, Maxine Audley, Georgia Brown

Running Scared
US 1986 106m Metrocolor Panavision
MGM-UA/Turman-Foster (Peter Hyams)
Accident-prone Chicago cops nevertheless succeed in getting their man.
Crime comedy-melodrama of a type seen far too often before.
w Gary DeVore, Jimmy Huston *d* Peter Hyams *ph* Peter Hyams *m* Rod Temperton *pd* Albert Brenner
☆ Gregory Hines, Billy Crystal, Steven Bauer, Joe Pantoliano, Tracy Reed, Darlanne Fluegel

La Rupture *
Belgium/France/Italy 1970 125m Eastmancolor
Contemporary/Films de la Boetie (André Genoves)
aka: *The Breakup*
A mother who wants custody of her young son after she divorces her drug-addicted husband finds herself in conflict with her ruthless and powerful father-in-law.
Enjoyable thriller in which innocence triumphs over experience.
wd Claude Chabrol *novel* Charlotte Armstrong *ph* Jean Rabier *m* Pierre Jansen
☆ Stéphane Audran, Jean-Pierre Cassel, Michel Bouquet, Jean-Claude Drouot, Annie Cordy, Jean Carmet, Michel Duchaussoy, Catherine Rouvel

'The director, who can indubitably be very subtle if he chooses, is pleased this time to wallow in the obvious, but to do so with a fine cinematic judgement.' – *Gordon Gow, Films and Filming*

'How far do they go before they've gone too far?'
Rush *
US 1992 120m DeLuxe Panavision
MGM/Zanuck (Richard D. Zanuck)
In the 1970s two undercover narcotics cops become drug addicts.
Unrelenting, though skilfully made, tale of degradation and despair.
w Pete Dexter *book* Kim Wozencraft *d* Lili Fini Zanuck *ph* Kenneth MacMillan *m* Eric Clapton *pd* Paul Sylbert *ed* Mark Warner
☆ Jason Patric, Jennifer Jason Leigh, Sam Elliott, Max Perlich, Gregg Allman, Tony Frank

'Downbeat nature of this addiction saga may be too intense and draining for general audiences, but resounding implications of the subject are bound to touch a nerve.' – *Variety*

'The Fastest Hands in the East versus the Biggest Mouth in the West.'
Rush Hour *
US 1998 98m DeLuxe
New Line (Arthur Sarkissian, Roger Birnbaum, Jonathan Glickman)
A Chinese detective joins a disgraced LA cop in tracking down a master criminal.
A movie designed to package Chan for US audiences, in which it succeeds, providing some sharply written exchanges along with his usual blend of comedy, fights and extraordinary stunts.
w Jim Kouf, Ross Lamanna *d* Brett Ratner *ph* Adam Greenberg *m* Lalo Schifrin *pd* Robb Wilson King *ed* Mark Helfrich
☆ Jackie Chan, Chris Tucker, Tom Wilkinson, Elizabeth Peña, Philip Baker Hall, Mark Rolston, Tzi Ma, Rex Linn, Ken Leung, Chris Penn, Julia Hsu

'A frankly formulaic but raucously entertaining action comedy.' – *Joe Leydon, Variety*

'Get Ready For A Second Rush!'
Rush Hour 2 *
US 2001 90m DeLuxe Panavision
Entertainment/New Line (Arthur Sarkissian, Roger Birnbaum, Jay Stern, Jonathan Glickman)
In Hong Kong, an American and a Chinese cop go after a gangster who has bombed the US consulate.
Amiable sequel that makes little demands on its audience, other than lie back and enjoy the fights and racial bickering between the two leads.
w Jeff Nathanson *d* Brett Ratner *ph* Matthew F. Leonetti *m* Lalo Schifrin *pd* Terence Marsh *ed* Mark Helfrich
☆ Jackie Chan (Lee), Chris Tucker (Carter), John Lone (Ricky Tan), Zhang Ziyi (Hu Li), Roselyn Sanchez (Isabella), Harris Yulin (Agent Sterling), Alan King (Steven Reign), Kenneth Tsang (Captain Chin)

'The very model of the limber, transnational Hollywood action comedy.' – *Robert Koehler, Variety*

'All's fair when love is war.'
Rushmore *
US 1998 93m DeLuxe Panavision
Buena Vista/Touchstone/American Empirical (Barry Mendel, Paul Schiff)
A precocious 15-year-old student and a wealthy businessman compete for the attentions of a school teacher.
Quirky comedy of adolescent ambition and adult resignation that has its moments, but loses its way long before the end.
w Wes Anderson, Owen Wilson *d* Wes Anderson *ph* Robert Yeoman *m* Mark Mothersbaugh *pd* David Wasco *ed* David Moritz
☆ Jason Schwartzman (Max Fischer), Bill Murray (Herman Blume), Olivia Williams (Rosemary Cross), Seymour Cassel (Bert Fischer), Brian Cox (Dr Guggenheim), Mason Gamble (Dirk Calloway), Sara Tanaka (Margaret Yang), Stephen McCole (Magnus Buchan), Ronnie McCawley (Ronny Blume), Keith McCawley (Donny Blume), Connie Nielsen (Mrs Calloway), Kim Terry (Mrs Blume)

'A genre-defying marvel, switching between outrageous humour and genuine pathos at a moment's notice.' – *Peter Bradshaw, Guardian*

'Made to be treasured: it feels like an immediate American classic.' – *Richard Kelly, Sight and Sound*

The Russia House *
US 1990 123m Technicolor
UIP/Pathé Entertainment (Paul Maslansky, Fred Schepisi)
A publisher, acting as a go-between for western intelligence and a Soviet scientist, finds life complicated by love.
Intelligent but sluggish thriller with few surprises.
w Tom Stoppard *novel* John Le Carré *d* Fred Schepisi *ph* Ian Baker *m* Jerry Goldsmith *pd* Richard MacDonald *ad* Roger Cain *ed* Peter Honess
☆ Sean Connery, Michelle Pfeiffer, Roy Scheider, James Fox, John Mahoney, Michael Kitchen, J. T. Walsh, Ken Russell, David Threlfall, Klaus Maria Brandauer

'An absorbing but muted yarn of romance and political intrigue.' – *Variety*

'The first live-action one-take feature film ever made.'
Russian Ark **
Russia/Germany 2002 99m colour
Artificial Eye/Hermitage Bridge/Egoli Tossell (Andrei Deriabin, Jens Meurer, Karsten Stoter)
An unseen ghost and a French diplomat from the 19th century wander through time around the Hermitage gallery in St Petersburg, encountering famous figures from the past and present and examining the paintings.
Technically, a virtuoso performance as the video camera glides through 33 rooms, eavesdropping on history and taking in more than 2,000 actors in period costumes, including a ballroom scene with full orchestra and the floor crowded with dancers – all filmed in one long take. There is a dreamlike quality to the action, though it can be difficult to discover precisely what is happening; in the end, it resembles a superlative son et lumière, a tourist's eye view of pre-revolutionary Russian history.
w Anatoly Nikiforov, Alexander Sokurov, Boris Khaimsky, Svetlana Proskurina *d* Alexander Sokurov *ph* *TilmanButtner* *m* Sergei Yevtushenko *pd* Yelena Zhukova, Natalia Kochergina *ed* Sergey Ivanov
☆ Sergei Dreiden (The Marquis), Maria Kuznetsova (Catherine the Great), Leonid Mozgovoy (Spy), David Giorgobiani (Orbeli), Alexander Chaban (Boris Piotrovsky), Maxim Sergeyev (Peter the Great)

'By the time of the closing shot – twists of fog rising like spectres from a leaden sea – even the most stubborn viewer will be lying back in a state of happy hypnosis.' – *Anthony Lane, New Yorker*

'A magnificent conjuring act, an eerie historical mirage evoked in a single sweeping wave of the hand.' – *Stephen Holden, New York Times*

'As pageant it's impressive, but as drama it's lightweight, and the trance one falls into may not be entirely inspired by awe.' – *Anthony Quinn, Independent*

Russian Roulette
US 1975 90m Eastmancolor
ITC/Elliott Kastner/Bulldog

Real and fake secret agents shoot it out when the Russian premier is about to visit Vancouver.
Fast-moving but impossible to follow location thriller which resolves itself into a series of chases.
w Tom Ardies, Stanley Mann, Arnold Margolin *novel Kosygin is Coming* by Tom Ardies *d* Lou Lombardo *ph* Brian West *m* Michael J. Lewis
☆ George Segal, Gordon Jackson, Denholm Elliott, Cristina Raines, Richard Romanus, Louise Fletcher, Nigel Stock

'A stale, mechanical espionage caper that wastes its star.' – *Kevin Thomas*

'Why the crazy title? If we told you, you'd only laugh!'
The Russians Are Coming, The Russians Are Coming *
US 1966 126m DeLuxe Panavision
UA/Mirisch (Norman Jewison)

Russian submariners make a forced landing on a Connecticut holiday island and cause panic.
'Daring' cold war comedy which turns out to be of the most elementary and protracted nature, saved from boredom only by a few cameos.
w William Rose *novel The Off-Islanders* by Nathaniel Benchley *d* Norman Jewison *ph* Joseph Biroc *m* Johnny Mandel
☆ Carl Reiner, Eva Marie Saint, Alan Arkin, John Phillip Law, Paul Ford, Tessie O'Shea, Brian Keith, Jonathan Winters, Theodore Bikel, Ben Blue

'Rather amiable, though the film, like its title, seems to repeat most things twice.' – *Sight and Sound*

best picture; William Rose; Alan Arkin

Russicum
Italy 1987 112m colour Cinemascope
Columbia TriStar/TigerCinematographica/RAI/Mario Cecchi Gori, Vittorio Cecchi Gori

Investigating the death of an American nun in Rome, a diplomat discovers a plot to prevent the Pope visiting Russia.
Dull, lifeless thriller in which it becomes difficult to discover who is doing what to whom.
w Valerio Riva, Robert Balchus, Pasquale Squitieri *novel I Mertedi del Diavolo* by Enzo Russo *d* Pasquale Squitieri *ph* Giuseppe Tinelli *m* Renato Serio *ad* Emilio Baldelli *ed* Mauro Bonanni
☆ F. Murray Abraham, Treat Williams, Danny Aiello, Rita Rusic, Luigi Montini, Robert Balchus, Nigel Court, Leopoldo Mastelloni, Rossano Brazzi

'Clearly destined to drop straight into the dustiest oubliette in film history.' – *Tom Milne, MFB*

Rustler's Rhapsody *
US 1985 88m Metrocolor Panavision
Paramount/Impala/Tesauro (David Giler, Walter Hill)

A 'B' Western hero of 1940s movies copes with a more modern and colourful world where life is no longer a matter of simple black and white.
An affectionate parody of cowboy clichés, though the joke begins to wear thin before the final shoot-out.
wd Hugh Wilson *ph* José Luis Alcaine *m* Steve Dorff *pd* Gil Parrondo *ed* John Victor Smith
☆ Tom Berenger, G. W. Bailey, Marilu Henner, Fernando Rey, Andy Griffith, Sela Ward

'Love betrayed them – power destroyed them!'
Ruthless *
US 1948 104m bw
Eagle Lion/Arthur S. Lyons

A conniver breaks several lives on his way to the top.
Rich melodrama with some entertaining moments.
w S. K. Lauren, Gordon Kahn *novel Prelude to Night* by Dayton Stoddert *d* Edgar G. Ulmer *ph* Bert Glennon *m* Werner Janssen
☆ Zachary Scott, Sydney Greenstreet, Diana Lynn, Louis Hayward, Martha Vickers, Lucille Bremer, Edith Barrett, Raymond Burr, Dennis Hoey

'Beginning pictures at the end
Is, I'm afraid, the modern trend.
But I'd find *Ruthless* much more winning
If it could end at the beginning.' – C. A. *Lejeune*

Ruthless People *
US 1986 93m DeLuxe
Touchstone/Silver Screen Partners II/Wagner-Lancaster

Comic kidnappers find they have on their hands a troublesome woman whose husband won't pay for her return.
Raucous comedy which packs a few good laughs before wearing out its welcome.
w Dale Launer *d* Jim Abrahams, David and Jerry Zucker *ph* Jan DeBont *m* Michel Colombier
☆ Danny DeVito, Bette Midler, Judge Reinhold, Helen Slater, Anita Morris, Bill Pullman

Ryan's Daughter **
GB 1970 206m Metrocolor Panavision 70
MGM/Faraway (Anthony Havelock-Allan)

1916 Ireland: a village schoolmaster's wife falls for a British officer.
A modestly effective pastoral romantic melodrama, stretched on the rack of its director's meticulous film-making technique and unnecessarily big budget. A beautiful, impressive, well-staged and well-acted film but not really four hours' worth of drama.
w Robert Bolt *d* David Lean *ph* Frederick A. Young *m* Maurice Jarre *pd* Stephen Grimes (who created an entire village)
☆ Sarah Miles, Robert Mitchum, Chris Jones, John Mills, Trevor Howard, Leo McKern

'Instead of looking like the money it cost to make, the film feels like the time it took to shoot.' – *Alexander Walker*

'Gush made repectable by millions of dollars tastefully wasted.' – *Pauline Kael*

Frederick A. Young; John Mills
Sarah Miles

S

SER ★
USSR 1989 75m colour
Artificial Eye/Mosfilm (Victor Trakhtenberg)
aka: *Freedom is Paradise*
A boy escapes from reform school to find his father who is also a prisoner.
Simple, understated and gripping account of the dispossessed.
wd Sergei Bodrov *ph* Yuri Skirtladze
m Alexander Raskatov *pd* Velery Kostrin
ed Valentina Kulagina
☆ Volodya Kozyrev, Alexander Bureyev, Svetlana Gaitan, Vitautas Tomkus
'It may not be too great a hope to see in its spare approach a hitherto under-explored way forward for Russian, or even Soviet, cinema.' – *Verina Glaessner, MFB*

S.F.W. ★
US 1994 96m Eastmancolor
Rank/A&M/Propaganda (Dale Pollock)
A fast-food chef becomes a celebrity because of his cool reaction to surviving being taken hostage by a terrorist group: 'So fucking what?'
Sharp and cynical drama of empty lives and the media that consume them.
w Danny Rubin, Jefery Levy *d* Jefery Levy
ph Peter Deming *m* Graeme Revell *pd* Eve Cauley *ed* Lauren Zuckerman
☆ Stephen Dorff, Reese Witherspoon, Jake Busey, Joey Lauren Adams, Pamela Gidley, David Barry Gray
'Levy's message creaks with typical Generation X griping. But as contrived as it may be, he hits many of the right buttons.' – *Empire*

S.I.S. – Extreme Justice: see *Extreme Justice*

SLC Punk!
US/Australia 1999 98m colour Panavision
Columbia TriStar/Beyond/Blue Tulip (Sam Maydew, Peter Ward)
In Salt Lake City, a clever student gives up being a punk to go to Harvard.
Aimless movie, directed in a frenetic style, of failed rebellion and middle-class conformity, with an unsympathetic protagonist who won't stop talking.
wd James Merendino *ph* Greg Littlewood
pd Charlotte Malmloff *ed* Esther P. Russel
☆ Matthew Lillard (Stevo), Michael Goorjian (Bob), Annabeth Gish (Trish), Jennifer Lien (Sandy), Christopher McDonald (Father), Devon Sawa (Sean), Jason Segel (Mike), Summer Phoenix (Brandy), James Duval (John the Mod), Til Schweiger (Mark), Adam Pascal (Eddie), Chiara Barzini (Jennifer), Kevin Breznahan (Chris)
'Thematically barren, visually bland and stylistically bland, *SLC Punk!* is, no bones about it, a bad movie.' – *Rupert Laight, Film Review*

S.O.B.
US 1981 121m Metrocolor Panavision
Lorimar/Geoffrey (Blake Edwards, Tony Adams)
A Hollywood director goes bananas when his much-touted epic is a fiasco, and decides to remake it as a sex picture.
Tasteless, vulgar and unfunny comedy, with everybody shouting at once and most of the jokes about vomiting, farting and funerals. Julie Andrews, who is made to bare her breasts, could surely use it as grounds for divorce.
wd Blake Edwards *ph* Harry Stradling Jnr
m Henry Mancini
☆ Julie Andrews, Richard Mulligan, *Robert Preston*, William Holden, Robert Vaughn, Robert Webber, Larry Hagman, Shelley Winters, Marisa Berenson, Loretta Swit, Craig Stevens, Robert Loggia
'One feels that this in-house comedy was in some way intended as a purge and not an entertainment.' – *John Pym, MFB*
'At best the humour is cheap and at worst unnecessarily vulgar.' – *Margaret Hinxman, Daily Mail*
† S.O.B., it seems, stands no longer for Son of a Bitch but for Standard Operational Bullshit.

SOS Iceberg ★
US 1933 117m bw
Universal
A young scientist seeks to recover the records of the lost Wegener expedition to the Arctic.
At the time this was a spectacular semi-documentary, but it did no business.
w Tom Reed, Edwin H. Knopf *d* Tay Garnett
☆ Rod la Rocque, Leni Riefenstahl, Sepp Rist, Gibson Gowland
† The production was begun in Berlin and taken over by Universal when the producers ran out of money.

SOS Pacific ★
GB 1959 91m bw
Rank/Sydney Box (John Nasht, Patrick Filmer-Sankey)
Survivors of a Pacific plane crash await rescue on a small island which is the site of an imminent H-bomb test.
Satisfactory open-air thick ear with strongly deployed types and a suspense climax.
w Robert Westerby *d* Guy Green *ph* Wilkie Cooper *m* Georges Auric
☆ Eddie Constantine, Pier Angeli, John Gregson, Richard Attenborough, Eva Bartok, Clifford Evans, Jean Anderson, Cec Linder

S.W.9: see *South West Nine*

S1m0ne
US 2002 117m DeLuxe Panavision
Entertainment/New Line (Andrew Niccol)
aka: *Simone*
A washed-up film director finds himself overwhelmed by his own secret creation, a computer-generated actress who becomes a superstar.
A variation on the Frankenstein myth, about a man pursued by a monster he has made: we have to take on trust Simone's qualities as what we see on screen has little star appeal, but it has some fun at Hollywood's self-absorption and fear of the future.
wd Andrew Niccol *ph* Edward Lachman
m Carter Burwell *pd* Jan Roelfs *ed* Paul Rubell
☆ Al Pacino (Viktor Taransky), Catherine Keener (Elaine Christian), Pruitt Taylor Vince (Max Sayer), Jay Mohr (Hal Sinclair), Jason Schwartzman (Milton), Stanley Anderson (Frank Brand), Evan Rachel Wood (Lainey Christian), Daniel Von Bargen (Chief Detective), Rachel Roberts (Simone)
'Such a tedious Hollywood farce, so unpleasantly glib and relentlessly shallow, that Pacino's excessive performance is not even the worst thing about it.' – *Kenneth Turan, Los Angeles Times*
'Funny, smart, improbably successful satire on contemporary celebrity obsessions, the waning summer's most delirious comedy.' – *Richard Shickel, Time*

Saadia
US 1953 87m Technicolor
MGM (Albert Lewin)
A young French doctor in the Sahara has trouble with the local witch doctor.
Pretentious and ill-considered multi-national romance from the champion of Omar's Rubaiyat.
wd Albert Lewin *novel* *Echec au Destin* by Francis D'Autheville *ph* Christopher Challis
m Bronislau Kaper
☆ Cornel Wilde, Mel Ferrer, Rita Gam, Michel Simon, Wanda Rotha, Cyril Cusack, Marcel Poncin, Peter Bull

Sabata (dubbed) ★
Italy 1969 106m Technicolor Techniscope
UA/PEA/Delphos (Alberto Grimaldi)
original title: *Ehi, Amico ... C'e Sabata, Hai Chiuso*
An inventive bounty hunter attempts to find the brains behind a bank robbery.
Stylish over-the-top spaghetti Western.
w Gianfranco Parolini, Renato Izzo *d* Frank Kramer (Gianfranco Parolini) *ph* Sandro Mancori
m Marcello Giombini *ad* Carlo Simi
ed Edmondo Lozzi
☆ Lee Van Cleef, William Berger, Franco Ressel, Linda Veras, Pedro Sanchez (Ignazio Spalla), Gianni Rizzo
'A certain cold-blooded ingenuity provides a substitute for inspiration in this colourful but extended anthology of Italian Western clichés.' – *Richard Combs, MFB*
† The film was followed by two sequels, *The Bounty Hunters* and *Return of Sabata* (qqv).

Sabotage ★★★
GB 1936 76m bw
Gaumont British (Michael Balcon, Ivor Montagu)
US title: *A Woman Alone*
The proprietor of a small London cinema is a dangerous foreign agent.
Unattractively plotted but fascinatingly detailed Hitchcock suspenser with famous sequences and a splendidly brooding melodramatic atmosphere.
w Charles Bennett, Ian Hay, Helen Simpson, E. V. H. Emmett *novel* *The Secret Agent* by Joseph Conrad *d* *Alfred Hitchcock* *ph* Bernard Knowles
md Louis Levy
☆ *Oscar Homolka, Sylvia Sidney*, John Loder, Desmond Tester, Joyce Barbour, Matthew Boulton
'Tightly packed, economical, full of invention and detail.' – *NFT, 1961*
'The cleverest picture Alfred Hitchcock has made since the arrival of the talkies. It is also, to me, the least likeable of them all ... Discreet directors don't kill schoolboys and dogs in omnibuses. Believe me, it isn't done.' – *C. A. Lejeune*

Sabotage
Canada 1996 99m colour
Imperial/Applecreek (Andy Emilio)
An FBI agent and a bodyguard discover corruption and cover-ups when they investigate the murder of a senator.
Routine action fodder, with a typically paranoid plot that makes little sense but provides opportunities for gunfights and explosions.
w Rick Filon, Michael Stokes *d* Tibor Takacs
ph Curtis Petersen *m* Guy Zerafa *pd* Ian Hall
ed Craig Nisker
☆ Mark Dasascos, Carrie Anne Moss, Graham Greene, Tony Todd, John Neville, Heidi Von Palleske, James Purcell

Saboteur ★★★
US 1942 108m bw
Universal (Frank Lloyd, Jack H. Skirball)
A war worker unjustly suspected of sabotage flees across the country and unmasks a spy ring.
Flawed Hitchcock action thriller, generally unsatisfactory in plot and pace but with splendid sequences at a ball, in Radio City Music Hall, and atop the Statue of Liberty.
w Peter Viertel, Joan Harrison, Dorothy Parker *story* Alfred Hitchcock *d* *Alfred Hitchcock*
ph Joseph Valentine *m* Frank Skinner
md Charles Previn
☆ Robert Cummings, Priscilla Lane, Otto Kruger, Alan Baxter, Alma Kruger, *Norman Lloyd*
'It throws itself forward so rapidly that it allows slight opportunity for looking back.' – *New York Times*
'The drama of a nation stirred to action, of a people's growing realization of themselves and their responsibilities.' – *Motion Picture Herald*
† Hitchcock wanted for the three leading roles Gary Cooper, Barbara Stanwyck and Harry Carey, but all refused or were unavailable.

'World War II espionage adventure and human lives have never before been combined so explosively!'
The Saboteur, Code Name Morituri ★
US 1965 122m bw
TCF/Arcola/Colony (Aaron Rosenberg)
aka: *Morituri*
aka: *The Saboteur*
In 1942 a German pacifist working for the allies is actually a German spy.
Dreary as a whole, suspenseful in snatches, this shipboard melodrama is full of irrelevancies and is in any case played much more seriously than the matter demands.
w Daniel Taradash *novel* Werner Jeorg Kosa
d Bernhard Wicki *ph* Conrad Hall *m* Jerry Goldsmith
☆ Yul Brynner, Marlon Brando, Trevor Howard, Janet Margolin
Academy Award nomination: Conrad Hall

The Sabre and the Arrow: see *Last of the Comanches*

Sabre Jet
US 1953 96m Cinecolor
Krueger Productions/UA
A US Air Force colonel in Korea has trouble with his career-hunting wife as well as with the enemy.
Propaganda cheapie with a few stirring aerial moments.
w Dale Eunson, Katherine Albert *d* Louis King
ph Charles Van Enger *m* Herschel Burke Gilbert
☆ Robert Stack, Coleen Gray, Richard Arlen, Julie Bishop, Leon Ames, Amanda Blake

Sabrina ★
US 1954 113m bw
Paramount (Billy Wilder)
GB title: *Sabrina Fair*
The chauffeur's daughter is wooed by both her brother employers.
Superior comedy, rather uneasily cast.
w Billy Wilder *play* Samuel Taylor *d* Billy Wilder *ph* Charles Lang Jnr *m* Frederick Hollander *ad* Hal Pereira, Walter Tyler
ed Arthur Schmidt *cos* *Edith Head*
☆ Humphrey Bogart (Linus Larrabee), William Holden (David Larrabee), Audrey Hepburn (Sabrina Fairchild), Walter Hampden (Oliver Larrabee), John Williams (Thomas Fairchild), Martha Hyer (Elizabeth Tyson), Joan Vohs (Gretchen Van Horn), Marcel Dalio (Baron)
'This is never less than a glittering entertainment, but somehow a certain measure of lead has found its way into the formula.' – *Time*
† Cary Grant was sought for the role played by Bogart.
Academy Award: Edith Head
Academy Award nomination: Billy Wilder (as writer and director); Charles Lang Jnr; Audrey Hepburn; art direction

'You are cordially invited to the most surprising merger of the year.'

Sabrina
US 1995 127m DeLuxe
UIP/Paramount/Constellation/Mirage/Sandollar (Sydney Pollack, Scott Rudin)

A chauffeur's daughter is loved by both a playboy and his workaholic millionaire brother.
A waste of effort for all concerned: the story seems tired, the performances are inferior, the romance and comedy have been dissipated, and there is very little left to engage the attention, other than to wonder why anyone should want to remake the Wilder version.
w Barbara Benedek, David Rayfiel *play* Samuel Taylor *d* Sydney Pollack *ph* Giuseppe Rotunno *m* John Williams *pd* Brian Morris *ed* Frederic Steinkamp
☆ Harrison Ford, Julia Ormond, Greg Kinnear, Nancy Marchand, John Wood, Richard Crenna, Angie Dickinson, Lauren Holly, Fanny Ardant
'Has plenty of innocent pleasure to impart in a time when movies tend to appeal to our basic instincts, and satisfyingly fills in the emotional holes left by the original.' – *Ian Nathan, Empire*
John Williams; song 'Moonlight' (*m* John Williams, *ly* Alan and Marilyn Bergman)

Sabrina Fair: see *Sabrina*

The Sacred Flame: see *The Right to Live*

The Sacrifice *
Sweden 1986 149m Eastmancolor/bw
Swedish Film Institute/SVT2/Film Four/Argos/Sandrew/Josephson & Nykvist (Katinka Farago)

original title: *Offret*
A writer, who dreams that a nuclear war has begun, promises God that he will renounce his home, his family and speech if the world can return to normal.
A brilliantly filmed but obscure and confusing parable that does not easily yield its meaning.
wd Andrei Tarkovsky *ph* Sven Nykvist *m* J. S. Bach, folk music *ad* Anna Asp *ed* Andrei Tarkovsky, Michel Leszczlylowski
☆ Erland Josephson, Susan Fleetwood, Valerie Mairesse, Allan Edwall, Gudrún Gísladóttir, Sven Wollter, Filippa Franzén
best foreign film

Sacrificed Youth *
China 1985 96m colour
Artificial Eye/Peking Youth Studio (Zhao Yamin)
original title: *Quingchun Ji*
During the Cultural Revolution, a young student is sent from her family in the city to work on a remote farm.
Touching, quietly elegant account of a girl growing to adulthood.
wd Zhang Nuanxin *story* There Was That Beautiful Place by Zhang Manling *ph* My Deyuan, Deng Wei *m* Liu Suola, Qu Xiaosong *pd* Li Yonxin, Wang Yanjin *ed* Zhao Qihua
☆ Li Fengxu, Feng Yuanzheng, Song Tao, Guo Jianguo, Yu Da

The Sad Sack
US 1957 98m bw Vistavision
Paramount (Paul Nathan)

Adventures of an army misfit.
Resistible star comedy.
w Edmund Beloin, Nate Monaster *cartoon* George Baker *d* George Marshall *ph* Loyal Griggs *m* Walter Scharf
☆ Jerry Lewis, David Wayne, Phyllis Kirk, Peter Lorre, Joe Mantell, Gene Evans, George Dolenz, Liliane Montevecchi, Shepperd Strudwick

Saddle the Wind *
US 1958 84m Metrocolor Cinemascope
MGM (Armand Deutsch)
A reformed gunman's young brother gets into bad company.
Modestly effective, humourless Western drama.
w Rod Serling *d* Robert Parrish *ph* George J. Folsey *m* Elmer Bernstein *ad* William J. Horning, Malcolm Brown *ed* John McSweeney Jnr
☆ Robert Taylor, John Cassavetes, Julie London, Donald Crisp, Charles McGraw, Royal Dano, Richard Erdman

Saddle Tramp
US 1950 76m Technicolor
Universal-International
A wandering cowboy adopts four orphan children and after various adventures marries the eldest of them.
Mild family Western for star-fanciers.
w Harold Shumate *d* Hugo Fregonese *ph* Charles Boyle *m* Joseph Gershenson
☆ Joel McCrea, Wanda Hendrix, John Russell, John McIntire, Jeanette Nolan, Russell Simpson

Sadie McKee *
US 1934 88m bw
MGM (Lawrence Weingarten)

A maid at various times loves her master, a young ne'er-do-well, and a middle-aged millionaire.
Solidly carpentered millgirl's romance of the period.
w John Meehan *story* Vina Delmar *d* Clarence Brown *ph* Oliver T. Marsh *m* William Axt
☆ *Joan Crawford*, Franchot Tone, Gene Raymond, Edward Arnold, Esther Ralston, Jean Dixon, Leo Carrillo, Akim Tamiroff
'The stuff the fans cry for.' – *Hollywood Reporter*

Sadie Thompson *
US 1928 95m (24 fps) bw silent
Gloria Swanson

In the South Seas, a fire-and-brimstone missionary is attracted to a prostitute.
Steamy, much-filmed melodrama (see Rain, Miss Sadie Thompson*). This version has long been unavailable for revaluation.*
w C. Gardner Sullivan *story* Rain by W. Somerset Maugham *d* Raoul Walsh *ph* George Barnes, Robert Kurrle *ad* William Cameron Menzies
☆ *Gloria Swanson*, Lionel Barrymore, Blanche Frederici, Charles Lane, Florence Midgley, Raoul Walsh
'It's stirring and ironic and funny. You couldn't ask more.' – *Photoplay*
George Barnes; Gloria Swanson

Sadisterotica (dubbed)
Germany/Spain 1967 80m colour
Aquila/Montana (Adrian Hoven)

aka: *Red Lips*
aka: *Rote Lippen*
A female private detective, hired to find a missing woman, discovers that her disappearance is linked to a reclusive artist.
Ridiculous thriller, poorly acted and directed, and badly dubbed; the disjointed narrative may be caused by cuts to remove some of its moments of nudity or could be due to the director's usual incompetence.
w Luis Revenga, Jesús Franco *d* Jesús Franco *ph* Jorge Herrero, Franz Hofer *m* Jerry Van Rooyen *ad* Carlos Viudes, Graf Pilati
☆ Janine Renault, Rossana Yanni, Chris Howland, Alexander Engel, Marcello Arriota, Manuel Otero, Adrian Hoven

Safar é Ghandehar **
Iran/France 2001 85m colour
ICA/Bac/Mohsen Makhmalbaf

aka: *Kandahar*
An exiled Afghanistan journalist returns to the country to seek her suicidal sister, who is tired of life under the Taliban.
Impassioned semi-documentary of the oppression of women and the hazards of life under a rigid Muslim regime in a country long torn apart by war; its surreal tone, though, sometimes jars.
wd Mohsen Makhmalbaf *ph* Ebrahim Ghafouri *m* M. R. Darvishi *ed* Mohsen Makhmalbaf
☆ Niloufar Pazira (Nafas), Hassan Tantai (Tabib Sahid), Sadou Teymouri (Khak), Hayatalah Hakimi (Hayat)
'The dubbing is poor; the non-professional performances are stiff and monotonously declarative… but it communicates a certain urgency and at times a powerful sense of the absurd.' – *J. Hoberman, Village Voice*

Safari
GB 1956 91m Technicolor Cinemascope
Warwick (Adrian Worker)
A white hunter falls in love with the wife of his employer and luckily the latter is killed by the Mau Mau.
Feeble adventure story exploiting political tensions.
w Anthony Veiller *d* Terence Young *ph* John Wilcox, Fred Ford, Ted Moore *m* William Alwyn
☆ Victor Mature, Janet Leigh, Roland Culver, John Justin, Earl Cameron, Liam Redmond, Orlando Martins

'In the 21st Century Nobody Is…'

Safe **
US 1995 118m colour
Metro Tartan/American Playhouse/Chemical/Good Machine/Kardana/Channel 4/Arnold Semler (Christine Vachon, Lauren Zalaznick)

A house-proud housewife begins to develop allergies to most aspects of modern life and moves to a New Age desert refuge for the chemically sensitive.
A studiously detached account of the effects on an individual of a mysterious ailment, which may simply be life itself; beneath its placid surface, it packs an unexpected power.
wd Todd Haynes *ph* Alex Nepomniaschy *m* Ed Tomney *pd* David Bomba *ed* James Lyons
☆ Julianne Moore, Xander Berkeley, Dean North, Julie Burgess, Ronnie Farer, Jodie Markell
'The film's neutral tone isn't easy, but it makes for a movie that is exceptional in both style and content and it addresses pressing problems with very considerable intelligence and skill.' – *Derek Malcolm, Guardian*

Safe Conduct: see *Laissez-Passer*

Safe Men
US 1998 88m Technicolor
UIP/Andell/Blue Guitar (Andrew Hauptman, Ellen Bonfman, Jeffrey Clifford, Jonathan Cohen)

Gangsters recruit two layabouts, mistaking them for expert safe-breakers.
A jokey blend of crime caper and romantic comedy, lightweight but occasionally amusing.
wd John Hamburg *ph* Michael Barrett *m* Theodore Shapiro *pd* Anthony Gasparro *ed* Suzanne Pillsbury, Scott Smith
☆ Sam Rockwell, Steve Zahn, Mark Ruffalo, Josh Pais, Paul Giamatti, Michael Schmidt, Christina Kirk, Harvey Fierstein, Michael Lerner
'Tepid tangle of half-baked buffoonery.' – *Alan Jones, Film Review*

Safe Passage
US 1994 96m DeLuxe
Entertainment/Pacific Western (Gale Anne Hurd)

Six sons and their estranged father gather at their mother's home when they fear that their brother, a Marine, may have been killed in an explosion in the Sinai Desert.
A domestic drama that follows a familiar and well-trodden path, really never rising above the level of soap opera, though the cast do their best to make it all seem fresh and original.
w Deena Goldstone *novel* Ellyn Bache *d* Robert Allan Ackerman *ph* Ralf Bode *m* Mark Isham *pd* Dan Bishop *ed* Rick Shaine
☆ Susan Sarandon, Sam Shepard, Robert Sean Leonard, Sean Astin, Marcia Gay Harden, Nick Stahl, Jason London, Matt Keeslar, Philip Bosco
'Aside from a few nicely tetchy scenes, there is nothing in this lugubrious film worth committing to.' – *Geoff Brown, The Times*

The Safecracker
GB 1958 96m bw
MGM/Coronado (David E. Rose)
A safecracker is released to help in a commando raid during World War II.
One-twelfth of a dirty dozen, with a long indecisive lead-up and not much pull as drama or comedy.
w Paul Monash *story* Rhys Davies *d* Ray Milland *ph* Gerald Gibbs *m* Richard Rodney Bennett *ed* Ernest Walter
☆ Ray Milland, Barry Jones, Jeanette Sterke, Victor Maddern, Ernest Clark, Cyril Raymond, Melissa Stribling

Safety Last ***
US 1923 70m (24 fps) bw silent
Harold Lloyd

A small-town boy goes to the big city and to impress his girlfriend enters a contest to climb a skyscraper.
Marvellous star comedy which set a new standard not only in sight gags but in the comedy-thrill stunts which became Lloyd's stock-in-trade.
w Harold Lloyd, Sam Taylor, Tim Whelan, Hal Roach *d* Sam Taylor, Fred Newmeyer *ph* Walter Lundin
☆ *Harold Lloyd*, Mildred Davis, Noah Young

The Saga of Anatahan
Japan 1953 90m bw
Daiwa
During the Pacific war, castaways on a remote island kill each other for the sake of one woman.
A curious footnote to its director's career, this mannered film is entirely in Japanese with English commentary, and does not recommend itself to western audiences.
m Akira Ifukube *wd/ph* Josef von Sternberg

The Saga of Hemp Brown
US 1958 80m colour CinemaScope
Universal (Gordon Kay)
A blameless cavalry lieutenant, dishonourably discharged from the army, sets out to track down the man who caused his disgrace.
Unoriginal western in which the confrontation between hero and villain is re-staged several times to diminishing effect.
w Bob Williams *story* Bernard Girard *d* Richard Carlson *ph* Philip Lathrop *m* Joseph Gershenson *ad* Alexander Golitzen, Robert E. Smith *ed* Tony Martinelli
☆ Rory Calhoun (Hemp Brown), Beverly Garland (Mona Langley), John Larch (Jed Givens), Russell Johnson (Hook), Fortunio Bonanova (Serge Bolanos), Allan Lane (Sheriff), Morris Ankrum (Bo Slauter)

Sagebrush Trail
US 1933 58m bw
Monogram/Lone Star (Paul Malvern)

Falsely imprisoned for murder, a cowboy escapes from jail to discover the real killer.
Routine Western with the occasional spectacular stunt.
w Lindsley Parsons *d* Armand Schaefer *ph* Archie Stout *ed* Carl Pierson
☆ John Wayne, Nancy Shubert, Lane Chandler, Yakima Canutt, Henry Hall, Wally Wales, Bob Burns

Sahara **
US 1943 97m bw
Columbia (Harry Joe Brown)

During the retreat from Tobruk a group of men of mixed nationality find water for themselves and harass the Nazis.
Good, simple war actioner with a realistic feel and strong characters deployed in melodramatic situations.
w John Howard Lawson, Zoltan Korda *story* Philip MacDonald *d* *Zoltan Korda* *ph* Rudolph Maté *m* Miklos Rozsa
☆ Humphrey Bogart, Bruce Bennett, Lloyd Bridges, Rex Ingram, J. Carrol Naish, Dan Duryea, Kurt Kreuger
'It borrows, chiefly from the English, a sort of light-alloy modification of realism which makes the traditional Hollywood idiom seem as obsolete as a minuet.' – *James Agee*
'The tank keeps rolling, picking up strays along the way until it has a full Hollywood ethnic complement.' – *Pauline Kael, 70s*
Rudolph Maté; J. Carrol Naish

Sahara
US 1984 111m Metrocolor
MGM-UA/Cannon (Menahem Golan, Yoram Globus)

In the 1920s, an heiress who competes in a trans-Sahara rally in a car made by her father's company is kidnapped by a lecherous Arab sheik.
Laughably bad and unoriginal romantic adventure, given a perfunctory treatment by all concerned.
w James R. Silke *d* Andrew V. McLaglen *ph* David Gurfinkel, Armando Nannuzzi *m* Ennio Morricone *ad* Luciano Spadoni *ed* Michael Duthie
☆ Brooke Shields, Lambert Wilson, Horst Buchholz, John Rhys-Davies, Ronald Lacey, John Mills, Steve Forrest
'Lamentably low on excitement, laughs and passion.' – *Variety*

Said O'Reilly to McNab
GB 1937 83m bw
Gainsborough
US title: *Sez O'Reilly to McNab*
A rich Scot is afflicted by an Irish con man.
Lively ethnic comedy, a good vehicle for two stars.
w Leslie Arliss, Marriott Edgar *story* Howard Irving Young *d* William Beaudine *ph* Arthur Crabtree
☆ Will Mahoney, Will Fyffe, Ellis Drake, Sandy McDougal
'Most hinterland exhibs have the quakes and headaches when it comes time on their sked to play a British film, but here's one, if sold along American lines, which may be found acceptable to the patrons in most places.' – *Variety*

'It's dynamite – when these two come together in the powderkeg city of the Far East!'
Saigon
US 1947 93m bw
Paramount (P. J. Wolfson)
Veteran airmen in Saigon are offered half a million to help in a robbery.
Tired studio-set star actioner.
w P. J. Wolfson, Arthur Sheekman *d* Leslie Fenton *ph* John Seitz *m* Robert Emmett Dolan
☆ Alan Ladd, Veronica Lake, Douglas Dick, Wally Cassell, Luther Adler, Morris Carnovsky, Mikhail Rasumny

Saigon
US 1988 102m colour
Fox (Alan Barnette)
aka: *Off Limits*
Two cops in Saigon track down a mass murderer of Vietnamese prostitutes.
Violent thriller for those with a boredom threshold as high as the body count.
w Christopher Crowe, Jack Thibeau *d* Christopher Crowe *ph* David Gribble *m* James Newton Howard *pd* Dennis Washington *ed* Douglas Ibold
☆ Willem Dafoe, Gregory Hines, Fred Ward, Amanda Pays, Scott Glenn, Kay Tong Lim, David Alan Grier

Saikaku Ichidai Onna: see *The Life of Oharu*

Sail a Crooked Ship
US 1961 88m bw
Columbia/Philip Barry Jnr
A shipowner unwittingly takes on a crew of crooks intending to use the boat as a getaway after a bank robbery.
Flimsy comedy sustained by a star comedian.
w Ruth Brooks Flippen, Bruce Geller *novel* Nathaniel Benchley *d* Irving Brecher *ph* Joseph Biroc *m* George Duning
☆ Robert Wagner, *Ernie Kovacs*, Dolores Hart, Carolyn Jones, Frank Gorshin

Sailing Along
GB 1938 90m bw
Gaumont-British (Michael Balcon)
A girl barge hand meets an impresario and becomes a dancing star.
Rather deadly British musical romance with the star not at her best, the supporting talents wasted, and a generally heavy hand in evidence.
wd Sonnie Hale *ph* Glen MacWilliams *m/ly* Arthur Johnston, Maurice Sigler *ad* Alfred Junge
☆ Jessie Matthews, Roland Young, Barry Mackay, Jack Whiting, Noel Madison, Alastair Sim, Athene Seyler, Frank Pettingell

Sailor Beware
US 1952 103m bw
Paramount/Hal B. Wallis
Martin and Lewis in the navy.
Unlovable star antics.
w James Allardice, Martin Rackin *play* Kenyon Nicholson, Charles Robinson *d* Hal Walker *ph* Daniel L. Fapp *m* Joseph J. Lilley
☆ Dean Martin, Jerry Lewis, Corinne Calvet, Marion Marshall, Robert Strauss, Leif Erickson

Sailor Beware! *
GB 1956 80m bw
Romulus (Jack Clayton)
US title: *Panic in the Parlor*
A young sailor has trouble with his mother-in-law-to-be.
Plain but adequate film version of a successful lowbrow stage farce about an archetypal female dragon.
w Philip King, Falkland L. Cary *play* Philip King, Falkland L. Cary *d* Gordon Parry *ph* Douglas Slocombe *m* Peter Akister
☆ *Peggy Mount* (Emma Hornett), *Esma Cannon* (Edie Hornett), *Cyril Smith* (Henry Hornett), Shirley Eaton (Shirley Hornett), Ronald Lewis (Albert Tufnell), Joy Webster (Daphne), Gordon Jackson (Carnoustie Bligh), Thora Hird (Mrs Lack), Geoffrey Keen (Rev Purefoy), Jack MacGowran (Toddy)
'It's the music-hall mother-in-law joke inflated to gigantic proportions.' – *Times*

The Sailor from Gibraltar
GB 1967 89m bw
Lopert (Oscar Lewenstein, Neil Hartley)
A mysterious woman searching for her lost lover meets a man determined to abandon his mistress.
A dry and unimaginative movie, with a good cast seemingly all at sea.
w Christopher Isherwood, Don Magner, Tony Richardson *novel* Marguerite Duras *d* Tony Richardson *ph* Raoul Coutard *m* Antoine Duhamel *ad* Marilena Aravantinou *ed* Anthony Gibbs
☆ Jeanne Moreau, Ian Bannen, Vanessa Redgrave, Zia Moyheddin, Hugh Griffith, Orson Welles, Eleanor Bron, John Hurt

Sailor of the King: see *Single-Handed*

The Sailor Takes a Wife
US 1945 91m bw
MGM
A sailor on leave gets married and finds he has acquired a few problems.
Rather self-consciously cute sentimental comedy, proficiently staged.
w Anne Chapin, Whitfield Cook *play* Chester Erskine *d* Richard Whorf
☆ June Allyson, Robert Walker, Reginald Owen, Hume Cronyn, Eddie Anderson, Audrey Totter, Gerald Oliver Smith

'He gave his soul to the sea and his heart to a woman! Their love will arouse you – their story will disturb you – the ending will startle you!'
'Like the act of love, this film must be experienced from beginning to end!'
The Sailor Who Fell from Grace with the Sea
GB 1976 105m Technicolor
AVCO/Sailor Company (Martin Poll)
A precocious boy interferes with his widowed mother's affair with a sailor by castrating the latter.
Weird and unattractive sex fantasy set in Dartmouth of all places and not helped by tiresome sex scenes.
wd Lewis John Carlino *novel* Gogo No Eiko by Yukio Mishima *ph* Douglas Slocombe *m* John Mandel
☆ Sarah Miles, Kris Kristofferson, Jonathan Kahn, Margo Cunningham, Earl Rhodes
'This everyday tale of torture, scopophilia, copulation, masturbation, dismemberment and antique dealing deserves to be traded back to the Japs and made required viewing for timorous kamikaze pilots.' – *Benny Green, Punch*

The Sailor's Return
GB 1978 100m colour
Euston Films
A Victorian seaman returns to his native village with a black bride, and opens a pub.
Lame-paced and highly predictable yarn of prejudice and doomed love, assembled with almost no cinematic flair.
w James Saunders *novel* David Garnett *d* Jack Gold
☆ Tom Bell, Shope Sodeinde, Elton Charles, Mick Ford, Clive Swift
† As a theatrical film it found no takers, and in GB was first shown on television in 1980.

Sailors Three **
GB 1940 86m bw
Ealing (Culley Forde)
US title: *Three Cockeyed Sailors*
Drunken sailors capture a German battleship by mistake.
Low service comedy which keeps moving, is brightly played and reaches a good standard. Sequel: Fiddlers Three (qv).
w Angus Macphail, John Dighton, Austin Melford *d* Walter Forde *ph* Gunther Krampf *md* Ernest Irving
☆ Tommy Trinder, Claude Hulbert, Michael Wilding, Carla Lehmann, Jeanne de Casalis, James Hayter, John Laurie

The Saint
Leslie Charteris's famous character, the reformed British gentleman crook who becomes a Robin Hood of crime, has been most popular in the long-running sixties TV series starring Roger Moore.
The film series (qqv) which featured him never seemed to hit quite the right note, and now seem slow. All were made for RKO, who later switched allegiance to THE FALCON (qv).
1938 The Saint in New York
1939 The Saint Strikes Back, The Saint in London
1940 The Saint's Double Trouble, The Saint Takes Over
1941 The Saint in Palm Springs, The Saint's Vacation, The Saint Meets the Tiger
1953 The Saint's Return (US: The Saint's Girl Friday)
Louis Hayward played the role in the first and last; Hugh Sinclair in Vacation and Tiger; George Sanders in the rest. In 1997, Val Kilmer starred in a big-budget remake, *The Saint* (qv), though the alienated character he portrayed bore little resemblance to Charteris's original.

The Saint
US 1997 116m Rank Colour
Paramount/Rysher (David Brown, Robert Evans, William J. MacDonald, Mace Neufeld)
A millionaire crook, sent to obtain a formula for cheap energy, falls in love with the female research scientist who discovered it.
An action adventure that commits the unforgivable sin of being dull. There are attempts to reposition Charteris's suave hero as a man with a troubled past, in the manner of the modern version of Batman, and to turn him into another James Bond. Both fail, for while Kilmer's Saint is described as 'a master of disguise', he seems more a ham actor in search of a role.
w Jonathan Hensleigh, Wesley Strick *d* Phillip Noyce *ph* Phil Meheux *m* Graeme Revell *pd* Joseph Nemec III *ed* Terry Rawlings
☆ Val Kilmer, Elisabeth Shue, Rade Serbedzija, Valery Nikolaev, Henry Goodman, Alun Armstrong, Michael Byrne, Evgeny Lazarev, Irena Apeximova, Lev Prigunov, Charlotte Cornwell
'One unholy mess.' – *Sunday Times*
'With his array of comic voices and false moustaches, Kilmer would be more suited to a summer season at the Southend Cliffs Pavilion than a Hollywood movie.' – *Ryan Gilbey, Independent*

St Benny the Dip
US 1951 79m bw
Danzigers
GB title: *Escape If You Can*
Gamblers learn to escape the law by dressing as priests, but circumstance converts them to good works.
Unfunny comedy notable only for its cast.
w John Roeburt *d* Edgar G. Ulmer *ph* Don Malkames *m* Robert Stringer
☆ Freddie Bartholomew, Roland Young, Dick Haymes, Lionel Stander, Nina Foch

'The passion burns deep!'
St Elmo's Fire
US 1985 108m Metrocolor
Columbia/Lauren Shuler
A group of college graduates drift apart as realities impinge on their lives.
Nobody explained why audiences should want to interest themselves in such a group of objectionable people; and they didn't.
w Joel Schumacher, Carl Kurlander *d* Joel Schumacher *ph* Stephen H. Burum *m* David Foster
☆ Rob Lowe, Demi Moore, Andrew McCarthy, Judd Nelson, Ally Sheedy, Emilio Estevez, Mare Winningham, Martin Balsam

The Saint in London
US 1939 72m bw
RKO (William Sistrom)
The Saint exposes a gang of forgers.
Amiable thriller, with Sanders coasting along on his charm.
w Lynn Root, Frank Fenton *story* The Million Pound Day by Leslie Charteris *d* John Paddy Carstairs *ph* Claude Friese-Greene *m* Harry Acres *ad* Wilfred Arnold *ed* Douglas Robertson
☆ George Sanders, Sally Gray, David Burns, Gordon McLeod, Athene Seyler, Henry Oscar, John Abbott, Ballard Berkeley

The Saint in New York *
US 1938 71m bw
RKO (William Sistrom)
New York police ask the Saint for help in dealing with a crime wave.
Slick, enjoyable programmer, the success of which led to the series of films featuring the Saint, though Hayward only returned to the role for the last film in the sequence.
w Charles Kaufman, Mortimer Offner *novel* Leslie Charteris *d* Ben Holmes *ph* Joseph August, Frank Redman *ad* Van Nest Polglase, Perry Ferguson *ed* Harry Marker
☆ Louis Hayward, Kay Sutton, Sig Rumann, Jonathan Hale, Jack Carson, Paul Guilfoyle, Frederick Burton, Ben Welden

The Saint in Palm Springs
US 1941 65m bw
RKO (Howard Benedict)
The Saint, wanted for murder and in possession of some rare stamps, turns the tables on a criminal gang.
Undistinguished time-waster, with cast and director showing only scant enthusiasm for their tasks.
w Jerry Cady *story* Leslie Charteris *d* Jack Hively *ph* Harry Wild *m* Roy Webb *ad* Van Nest Polglase *ed* George Hively
☆ George Sanders, Wendy Barrie, Jonathan Hale, Paul Guilfoyle, Linda Hayes, Ferris Taylor, Harry Shannon, Eddie Dunn

'He's clean! He's mean! He's the go-between!'
St Ives
US 1976 93m Technicolor
Warner (Pancho Kohner, Stanley Canter)
An ex-police reporter gets involved in a complex murder puzzle.
Soporific suspenser with every tired situation in the book.
w Barry Beckerman *novel* The Procane Chronicle by Oliver Bleeck *d* J. Lee- Thompson *ph* Lucien Ballard *m* Lalo Schifrin
☆ Charles Bronson, Harry Guardino, John Houseman, Jacqueline Bisset, Maximilian Schell, Harris Yulin, Dana Elcar, Elisha Cook Jnr
'Much cross-cutting of the sort where the only events you care less about than the ones you cut from are the ones you cut to.' – *John Simon*

'People make love for so many crazy reasons – why shouldn't money be one of them?'
Saint Jack
US 1979 115m colour
New World/Shoals Creek/Playboy/Copa de Oro (Roger Corman)
An American wanderer in Singapore finds his metier as a pimp.
Whimsical, loquacious black comedy which failed to set its wavering director back on the firm ground he needed.
w Peter Bogdanovich, Howard Sackler, Paul Theroux *novel* Paul Theroux *d* Peter Bogdanovich *ph* Robby Muller *m* various
☆ Ben Gazzara, Denholm Elliott, James Villiers, Joss Ackland, Rodney Bewes, Mark Kingston, Lisa Lu, George Lazenby, Peter Bogdanovich

Saint Joan
GB 1957 110m bw
Wheel (Otto Preminger)
Glumly assembled screen version of the brilliantly argumentative play about the Maid of Orleans.
Plenty of talent, but neither wit nor style.
w Graham Greene *play* Bernard Shaw *d* Otto Preminger *ph* Georges Périnal *m* Mischa Spoliansky *pd* Roger Furse
☆ Jean Seberg, Anton Walbrook, Richard Widmark, John Gielgud, Felix Aylmer, Harry Andrews, Richard Todd

St Louis Blues *
US 1939 92m bw
Paramount (Jeff Lazarus)
A Broadway musical star finds new fame down south.
Moderate star entertainment with good guest artists.
w John C. Moffitt, Malcolm Stuart Boylan, Frederick Hazlitt Brennan *d* Raoul Walsh *ph* Theodor Sparkuhl *songs* Frank Loesser, Burton Lane
☆ Dorothy Lamour, Lloyd Nolan, Tito Guizar, Jerome Cowan, Jessie Ralph, William Frawley, the King's Men, Matty Melneck and his Orchestra
'It doesn't quite jell but will suffice as passable divertissement.' – *Variety*

St Louis Blues
US 1958 93m bw VistaVision
Paramount (Robert Smith)
W. C. Handy, son of a black Memphis preacher, becomes a blues composer.
Unsurprising biopic with some good music and the usual strained plot about father's disapproval of the new music.
w Robert Smith, Ted Sherdeman *d* Allen Reisner *ph* Haskell Boggs *md* Nelson Riddle
☆ Nat King Cole, Eartha Kitt, Pearl Bailey, Cab Calloway, Mahalia Jackson, Ruby Dee, Juano Hernandez, Ella Fitzgerald

The St Louis Kid
US 1934 67m bw
Warner (Sam Bischoff)
GB title: *A Perfect Weekend*
A hot-headed truck driver takes the side of milk farmers in a trade dispute.
Modest star action comedy with a fair amount to amuse.
w Seton I. Miller, Warren Duff *story* Frederick Hazlitt Brennan *d* Ray Enright *ph* Sid Hickox *md* Leo F. Forbstein *ad* Jack Okey *ed* Clarence Kolster
☆ James Cagney, Patricia Ellis, Hobart Cavanaugh, Spencer Charters, Addison Richards
'Jimmy in another slugger role, with results this time not so satisfactory.' – *Variety*

St Martin's Lane *
GB 1938 85m bw
Mayflower (Erich Pommer)
US title: *Sidewalks of London*
A middle-aged busker falls in love with a brilliant girl dancer who becomes a star.
Well-made romantic drama with star performances and interesting theatrical background.
w Clemence Dane *d* Tim Whelan *ph* Jules Kruger *m* Arthur Johnston
☆ Charles Laughton, Vivien Leigh, Rex Harrison, Tyrone Guthrie, Larry Adler, Gus MacNaughton
'In its choice of subject, its overwhelming interest in character and its introspective, uncompromising treatment, it is experimental in a courageous fashion.' – *Film Weekly*

The Saint Meets the Tiger
US 1943 70m bw
RKO
The Saint is pitted against a resourceful gangster and gold smuggler.
Feeble little thriller with Sinclair proving an inadequate substitute for Sanders in the title role.
w Leslie Arliss, Wolfgang Wilhelm, James Seymour *novel* Meet the Tiger by Leslie Charteris *d* Paul L. Stein *ph* Robert Krasker *ad* Paul Sheriff *ed* Ralph Kemplen
☆ Hugh Sinclair, John Slater, Gordon McLeod, Clifford Evans, Wylie Watson, Charles Victor

The Saint of Fort Washington
US 1993 108m Technicolor
(David V. Picker, Nessa Hyams)
Two homeless people, a young schizophrenic drifter and a black Vietnam veteran, help each other survive on the streets.
A well-meaning but bland piece of escapism, romanticizing the dispossessed.
w Lyle Kessler *d* Tim Hunter *ph* Frederick Elmes *m* James Newton Howard *pd* Stuart Wurtzel *ed* Howard Smith
☆ Danny Glover, Matt Dillon, Rick Aviles, Nina Siemaszko, Joe Seneca, Ving Rhames
'The sort of worthy project big-name stars tackle to earn artistic and social brownie points between megabuck sequels.' – *Kim Newman, Empire*

The Saint Strikes Back
US 1939 67m bw
RKO (Robert Sisk)
The Saint goes to San Francisco to save the father of a female friend from being framed for murder.
Enjoyable minor thriller, which made the most of Sanders's world-weary charm.
w John Twist *novel* Angels of Doom by Leslie Charteris *d* John Farrow *ph* Frank Redman *md* Roy Webb *ad* Van Nest Polglase, Albert S. D'Agostino *ed* Jack Hively
☆ George Sanders, Barry Fitzgerald, Wendy Barrie, Jonathan Hale, Jerome Cowan, Edward Gargan

The Saint Takes Over
US 1940 69m bw
RKO (Howard Benedict)
The Saint comes to the aid of his friend, Inspector Fernack, who has been framed by crooked gamblers.
Pleasant, fast-moving, though undistinguished, little thriller.
w Lynn Root, Frank Fenton *d* Jack Hively *ph* Frank Redman *md* Roy Webb *ad* Van Nest Polglase *ed* Desmond Marquette
☆ George Sanders, Wendy Barrie, Jonathan Hale, Paul Guilfoyle, Morgan Conway

The St Valentine's Day Massacre
US 1967 99m DeLuxe Panavision
TCF/Los Altos (Roger Corman)
The twenties gang war between Al Capone and Bugs Moran.
The director's first big studio film is disappointing; stagey, poorly developed, unconvincing-looking and overacted.
w Howard Browne *d* Roger Corman *ph* Milton Krasner *m* Fred Steiner *md* Lionel Newman
☆ Jason Robards Jnr, George Segal, Ralph Meeker, Jean Hale, Clint Ritchie, Joseph Campanella, Richard Bakalyan, David Canary, Bruce Dern, Harold J. Stone, Kurt Kreuger, John Agar, Alex D'Arcy

'You'll love every illegal inch of 'em!'
The Sainted Sisters
US 1948 89m bw
Paramount (Richard Maibaum)
Two New York con girls find themselves taken in by the inhabitants of the small town in which they are hiding out.
Unfunny period comedy which misses on all cylinders.
w Harry Clork *d* William D. Russell *ph* Lionel Lindon *m* Van Cleave
☆ Veronica Lake, Joan Caulfield, Barry Fitzgerald, William Demarest, George Reeves, Beulah Bondi, Chill Wills, Darryl Hickman
'Lake, Caulfield, and a swarm of clichés, pleasantly kidded in a manner derived from Preston Sturges.' – *James Agee*

Saints and Sinners
GB 1948 85m bw
London Films/BLPA (Leslie Arliss)
An ex-convict comes back to his home town to prove that those who condemned him were fools or knaves.
Curious slice of Irish whimsy mixed with Ealing comedy; not very satisfactory.
w Paul Vincent Carroll, Leslie Arliss *d* Leslie Arliss *ph* Osmond Borradaile *m* Philip Green *ad* Wilfred Shingleton *ed* David Newhouse
☆ Kieron Moore, Christine Norden, Sheila Manahan, Michael Dolan, Maire O'Neill, Noel Purcell

The Saint's Double Trouble
US 1940 68m bw
RKO (Cliff Reid)
The Saint discovers that a jewel thief is his double.
Lacklustre thriller that fails to make much of Sanders playing both sides of the law.
w Ben Holmes *story* Leslie Charteris *d* Jack Hively *ph* J. Roy Hunt *md* Roy Webb *ed* Theron Warth
☆ George Sanders, Helene Whitney, Jonathan Hale, Bela Lugosi, Thomas W. Ross

The Saint's Girl Friday: see *The Saint's Return*

The Saint's Return
GB 1954 73m bw
RKO/Royal/Hammer (Anthony Hinds, Julian Lesser)
US title: *The Saint's Girl Friday*
The Saint goes after a gang of gamblers who have murdered a former girlfriend.
Effective programmer, though the concept was beginning to seem more than a little dated and old-fashioned.
w Allan MacKinnon *d* Seymour Friedman *ph* Walter Harvey *m* Ivor Slaney *ad* J. Elder Wills *ed* James Needs
☆ Louis Hayward, Naomi Chance, Sydney Tafler, Charles Victor, Jane Carr, Harold Lang, Diana Dors
† The US release ran for 68m.

The Saint's Vacation
US 1941 60m bw
RKO (William Sistrom)
Holidaying in Switzerland, the Saint outwits spies searching for a secret code.
Moderate thriller, though missing the piquancy that Sanders's personality added to the routine nature of the enterprise.
w Leslie Charteris, Jeffrey Dell *novel* Getaway by Leslie Charteris *d* Leslie Fenton *ph* Bernard Knowles *md* Bretton Byrd *ad* Paul Sheriff *ed* Al Barnes
☆ Hugh Sinclair, Sally Gray, Cecil Parker, Arthur Macrae, Leueen MacGrath, Felix Aylmer, Ivor Barnard

La Saison des Hommes **
France/Tunisia 2000 123m colour
ICA/Losange/Maghrebfilms Carthage/Arte France (Margaret Menegoz, Mohamed Tlatli)
aka: *The Season of Men*
A wife asserts her independence from her overbearing husband by returning to the abandoned family home with her unhappy daughters and autistic son.
Deft interweaving of past and present gives shape and bulk to this drama of women escaping from male dominance and finding their own satisfactions.
w Moufida Tlatli, Nouri Bouzid *d* Moufida Tlatli *ph* Youssef Ben Youssef *m* Anouar Brahem *pd* Khaled Joulak, Claude Bennys *ed* Isabelle Devinck
☆ Rabiaa Ben Abdallah (Aicha), Sabah Bouzouita (Zeineb), Ghalia Ben Ali (Meriem), Hend Sabri (Emna), Ezzedine Gennoun (Said), Mouna Noureddine (Matriarch)
'A relentless cri du coeur eviscerating a sexual ethos so repressive that at least one woman is nearly driven crazy by a gut-gnawing mixture of fear, shame and desire.' – *Stephen Holden, New York Times*

Saiyu-ki: see *Alakazam the Great*

Salaam Bombay! **
India/France/GB 1988 114m colour
Mainline/Mirabai Films/NFDC/Cadrage/La SEPT/Channel 4 (Mira Nair)
Street life in an Indian city among pimps, prostitutes, drug peddlers and addicts, as seen by a tea-boy abandoned by his mother.
Poignant, well-observed narrative of small treacheries and smaller hope, acted by a mainly amateur cast.
w Sooni Taraporevala *d* Mira Nair *ph* Sandi Sissel *m* L. Subramaniam *pd* Mitch Epstein *ed* Barry Alexander Brown
☆ Shafiq Syed, Raghubir Yadav, Nana Patekar, Irshad Hasni, Aneeta Kanwar, Hansa Vithal
'A notable debut.' – *MFB*

Le Salaire de la Peur: see *The Wages of Fear*

The Salamander
US/GB/Italy 1981 101m colour
Grade/William R. Foreman (Paul Maslansky)
A colonel in army intelligence thwarts a fascist takeover of Italy.
Lurid melodrama with an inane script.
w Robert Katz, Rod Serling *novel* Morris West *d* Peter Zinner *ph* Marcello Gatti *m* Jerry Goldsmith *pd* Giantito Burchiellaro *ed* Claudio Cutry
☆ Franco Nero, Anthony Quinn, Martin Balsam, Sybil Danning, Christopher Lee, Cleavon Little, Paul Smith, John Steiner, Claudia Cardinale, Eli Wallach

'For this woman men would commit every sin … every sacrilege.'
Salambo
Italy 1959 95m DeLuxe Cinemascope
Fidès/Stella
aka: *The Loves of Salammbo*
The love affair between the daughter of a Carthaginian general and the leader of a mercenary army does not run smoothly.
A cut-price epic with an inadequate central performance.
w John Blamy, Barbara Schmers *novel* Salammbo by Gustave Flaubert *d* Sergio Grieco *ph* Piero Portalupi *m* Alexandre Derenevsky
☆ Jeanne Valérie, Edmund Purdom, Jacques Sernas, Arnoldo Foà, Kamala Devi, Charles Fawcett, Ricardo Garrone
† After the fiasco of *Cleopatra*, 20th Century-Fox abandoned its plans to produce a film of Flaubert's novel starring Gina Lollobrigida, and instead bought the rights to this production, which it released in 1962 in a version cut to 72m.

Salem's Lot: The Movie *
US 1979 112m colour Panavision
Warner/Serendipity Productions (Richard Kobritz)
A writer returns to his small hometown to discover that it is being taken over by vampires.
Effective horror movie, cut from a 200 minute two-part TV mini-series.
w Paul Monash *novel* Stephen King *d* Tobe Hooper *ph* Jules Brenner *m* Harry Sukman *pd* Mort Rabinowitz *ed* Carol Sax, Tom Pryor
☆ David Soul, *James Mason*, Lance Kerwin, Bonnie Bedelia, Lew Ayres, Julie Cobb, Elisha Cook, George Dzundza, Ed Flanders, Kenneth McMillan

Salesman **
US 1969 95m bw
Maysles Films
A team of salesmen, urged on by their aggressive manager, sell Bibles door to door to Catholics mostly reluctant to buy.
Fascinating cinema-verité documentary, especially in the contrast between the sales convention, with its sanctimonious hyperbole, and the actual experiences on the road.
d Albert and David Maysles, Charlotte Zwerin *ph* Albert Maysles *ed* David Maysles, Charlotte Zwerin
'The film tries to be at once tough and sentimental, mocking and sympathetic … They have stumbled onto something much bigger than they realize: a condemnation – however fragmented, fortuitous, and even inept – of the human condition, of man himself; but also of a society plagued by superstition, idiotic competitiveness, and stultifying materialism.' – *John Simon*

Sally
US 1930 90m Technicolor
Warner
A waitress makes it to the lights of Broadway.
Lightweight musical play, previously filmed in 1925 with Colleen Moore and Leon Errol, here the basis of an elaborate colour production with its original star, who however did not take too kindly to the camera.

w Waldemar Young *play* Guy Bolton, Jerome Kern *d* John Francis Dillon *ph* Dev Jennings, E. E. Schoenbaum *ch* Larry Ceballos *ad* Jack Okey
☆ Marilyn Miller, Joe E. Brown, Alexander Gray, T. Roy Barnes, Pert Kelton, Ford Sterling
Jack Okey

Sally and St Anne
US 1952 90m bw
U-I (Leonard Goldstein)
When an Irish-American family is threatened with eviction, the daughter appeals to St Anne for help.
Whimsical comedy, quite nimbly performed.
w James O'Hanlon, Herb Meadow *d* Rudolph Maté *ph* Irving Glassberg *m* Frank Skinner
☆ Ann Blyth, Edmund Gwenn, Hugh O'Brian, John McIntire, Jack Kelly

Sally in Our Alley *
GB 1931 77m bw
ATP/Basil Dean
Poor girl loves wounded soldier.
Early talkie drama with music which made Gracie Fields a star and gave her a theme song.
w Miles Malleson, Archie Pitt, Alma Reville *play* *The Likes of 'Er* by Charles McEvoy *d* Maurice Elvey *ph* Robert G. Martin, Alex Bryce
☆ Gracie Fields, Ian Hunter, Florence Desmond, Ivor Barnard
'The songs are just numbers, the general standard nothing to shout about.' – *Variety*

Sally, Irene and Mary
US 1938 86m bw
TCF (Gene Markey)
Three girls try to break into show business.
Simple-minded romantic comedy-musical, well enough done.
w Harry Tugend, Jack Yellen *d* William A. Seiter *ph* Peverell Marley *md* Arthur Lange
☆ Alice Faye, Tony Martin, Fred Allen, Jimmy Durante, Gregory Ratoff, Joan Davis, Marjorie Weaver, Gypsy Rose Lee
'Palatable light entertainment that is no Pulitzer prizer but prize b.o.' – *Variety*

Sally of the Sawdust
US 1925 78m (24 fps) bw silent
Paramount/United Artists
A circus juggler and faker tries to prevent his daughter from discovering that she is adopted.
Silent version of the stage hit Poppy, *remade under its own title in 1936 (qv). In both versions W. C. Fields takes over the whole show (not to one's entire satisfaction) and the director's name in this case should not lead one to expect a film of significance, as he seems to have been glad of the work.*
w Forrest Halsey *play* Dorothy Donnelly *d* D. W. Griffith
☆ W. C. Fields, Carol Dempster, Alfred Lunt, Effie Shannon, Erville Alderson

Salmonberries
Germany 1991 95m DeLuxe
Electric/PeleMele (Eleonore Adlon)
A mysterious and parentless young woman is attracted to a middle-aged German woman, working as a librarian in a small Alaskan mining town.
A somewhat glum and claustrophobic account of thwarted lives.
w Percy Adlon, Felix O. Adlon *d* Percy Adlon *ph* Tom Sigel *m* Bob Telson *pd* Amadeus Capra *ed* Conrad Gonzalez
☆ k. d. lang, Rosel Zech, Chuck Connors, Jane Lind, Oscar Kawagley, Wolfgang Steinberg, Christel Merian
'An exhaustingly slow-moving tale which makes for trying viewing.' – *Empire*

Salo: see *120 Days of Sodom*

Salome
US 1923 80m (24 fps) bw silent
Nazimova
Almost unendurable as an entertainment, this stylized silent provided a famous role for its star against backgrounds in Aubrey Beardsley style, and is much illustrated in film histories. The *New Yorker* commented on a 1980 revival: 'The movie looks better in stills than when one actually sees it, but a folly like this should probably be experienced.'
play Oscar Wilde *drawings* Aubrey Beardsley *d* Charles Bryant *ad* Natacha Rambova *cos* Natacha Rambova
☆ Nazimova, Mitchell Lewis, Nigel de Brulier

'The supreme screen achievement of our time!'
Salome
US 1953 103m Technicolor
Columbia/Beckworth (Buddy Adler)
Princess Salome of Galilee eludes her licentious stepfather, falls in love with a secret Christian, and leaves home when her dancing fails to save the life of John the Baptist.
Distorted biblical hokum with an interesting cast frozen into unconvincing attitudes.
w Harry Kleiner, Jesse Lasky Jnr *d* William Dieterle *ph* Charles Lang *m* George Duning *md* Daniele Amfitheatrof *ad* John Meehan
☆ Rita Hayworth, Charles Laughton, Stewart Granger, Judith Anderson, Cedric Hardwicke, Alan Badel, Basil Sydney, Maurice Schwartz, Rex Reason, Arnold Moss
'Pomp and splendour are paraded across the screen as a background to the story's combination of sex and religion.' – *Variety*

Salome Where She Danced *
US 1945 90m Technicolor
Universal (Walter Wanger, Alexander Golitzen)
During the Austro-Prussian war a dancer is suspected of being a spy and flees to Arizona, where she affects the lives of the citizenry.
Absurdly plotted and stiffly played romantic actioner whose sheer creakiness made it a minor cult film.
w Laurence Stallings *story* Michael J. Phillips *d* Charles Lamont *ph* Hal Mohr, W. Howard Green *m* Edward Ward
☆ Yvonne de Carlo, Rod Cameron, Albert Dekker, David Bruce, Walter Slezak, Marjorie Rambeau, J. Edward Bromberg, Abner Biberman, John Litel, Kurt Katch
'I gratefully salute it as the funniest dead-pan parody I have ever seen.' – *James Agee*

Salome's Last Dance
GB 1987 90m Technicolor
Vestron/Jolly Russell Productions (Penny Corke)
Oscar Wilde watches a production of his banned play, *Salome*, acted by prostitutes in a brothel.
Coarse and clumsy treatment, all excess and no moderation, though some found it entertaining.
wd Ken Russell *play* *Salome* by Oscar Wilde *ph* Harvey Harrison *md* Richard Cooke, Ray Beckett *ad* Michael Buchanan *ed* Timothy Gee
☆ Glenda Jackson, Stratford Johns, Nickolas Grace, Douglas Hodge, Imogen Millais-Scott, Denis Lill, Ken Russell
'An outstanding film marking a new career bent for film-maker Russell.' – *Variety*

Salon Kitty
France/Germany/Italy 1978 127m colour
TCF/Coralta/S.R.L./Cinema Seven (Giulio Barigia, Ermanno Donati)
In 1939, a Nazi army officer takes over a Berlin brothel and installs spying devices and prostitutes loyal to the party to report on their clients.
A voyeuristic movie with a gloating nastiness about it that is thoroughly dislikeable.
w Ennio de Concini, Maria Pia Fusco, Tinto Brass *d* Tinto Brass *ph* Silvano Ippoliti *m* Fiorenzo Caspi *pd* Ken Adam *ed* Luciana di Russo, Fiorenza Muller
☆ Helmut Berger, Ingrid Thulin, Teresa Ann Savoy, Bekim Fehmiu, John Ireland, Tina Aumont

Saloon Bar *
GB 1940 76m bw
Ealing (Michael Balcon)
A murder is solved during an evening in a pub.
Amusing, well-made little suspenser from a West End success.
w Angus MacPhail, John Dighton *play* Frank Harvey *d* Walter Forde *ph* Ronald Neame *md* Ernest Irving
☆ *Gordon Harker*, Elizabeth Allen, Mervyn Johns, Joyce Barbour, Anna Konstam, Judy Campbell, Norman Pierce, Alec Clunes, Felix Aylmer, Mavis Villiers, Torin Thatcher, O. B. Clarence
'The detail has been sought lovingly and with exactitude … this is a modest and endearing film.' – *New Statesman*

Salsa
US 1988 99m TVC Color
Cannon/Menahem Golan, Yoram Globus
A motor mechanic is determined to become the best salsa dancer.
A few energetic dance routines break up a weak narrative and some sub-standard acting.
w Boaz Davidson, Tomas Benitez, Shepherd Goldman *story* Boaz Davidson, Eli Tabor *d* Boaz Davidson *ph* David Gurfinkel *pd* Mark Hastings *ed* Alain Jakubowicz
☆ Robby Rosa, Rodney Harvey, Magali Alvarado, Miranda Garrison, Moon Orona, Angela Alvarado, Loyda Ramos, Valente Rodriguez

Salt and Pepper
GB 1968 101m DeLuxe
UA/Chrislaw/Tracemark (Milton Ebbins)
Soho night-club proprietors solve a murder.
Infuriating throwaway star vehicle set in the dregs of swinging London. The two stars teamed up again in an even worse film, One More Time *(1970).*
w Michael Pertwee *d* Richard Donner *ph* Ken Higgins *m* Johnny Dankworth
☆ Sammy Davis Jnr, Peter Lawford, Michael Bates, Ilona Rodgers, John Le Mesurier, Graham Stark, Ernest Clark

Salt on Our Skin
Germany/France/Canada 1992 106m colour
Warner/Neue Constantin/Torii/Telescene/RTL Plus/Canal (Bernd Eichinger, Martin Moszkowicz)
A sophisticated half-French woman remembers a youthful love affair in Scotland with the son of a local farmer, which she resumed a decade later.
A dull romantic drama of minimal interest and credibility.
w Andrew Birkin, Bee Gilbert *novel* *Les Vaisseaux du Coeur* by Benoîte Groult *d* Andrew Birkin *ph* Dietrich Lohmann *m* Klaus Doldinger *pd* Jean-Baptiste Tard, Robert Laing *ed* Dagmar Hirtz
☆ Greta Scacchi, Vincent D'Onofrio, Anais Jeanneret, Hanns Zischler, Barbara Jones, Rolf Illic, Petra Berndt, László Kish, Claudine Auger
'An old-fashioned weepie.' – *Variety*

Salt to the Devil: see *Give Us This Day*

'If You're Looking For The Truth, You've Come To The Wrong Place.'
The Salton Sea
US 2002 103m Technicolor
Warner/Castle Rock/Darkwoods/Humble Journey (Frank Darabont, Eriq LaSalle, Ken Aguado, Butch Robinson)
A jazz musician doubles as a drug addict and dealer and police informer in order to discover the identity of his wife's killer.
Sleazy movie that enjoys its descent into the gutter, which here is full of grotesque characters and incidents, including a noseless dealer who recreates the Kennedy assassination with the aid of pigeons in model cars.
w Tony Gayton *d* D. J. Caruso *ph* Amir Mokri *m* Thomas Newman *pd* Tom Southwell *ed* Jim Page *cos* Karyn Wagner
☆ Val Kilmer (Danny/Tom), Vincent D'Onofrio (Pooh-Bear), Adam Goldberg (Kujo), Luis Guzman (Quincy), Doug Hutchison (Morgan), Anthony LaPaglia (Garcetti), Glenn Plummer (Bobby), Peter Sarsgaard (Jimmy The Finn), Deborah Kara Unger (Colette), Chandra West (Liz), B. D. Wong (Bubba), R. Lee Ermey (Verne Plummer), Shirley Knight (Nancy Plummer), Bo (Meat Loaf)
'It's not clear when and how watching women getting brutalized and seeing a starved, rabid badger taking realistic swipes at a terrified man's private parts added up to mass entertainment, but that's the world we're living in now.' – *Kenneth Turan, Los Angeles Times*
'An edgy, triple-twist neo-noir thriller with a brutally cynical sense of humor and an erotically charged atmosphere of danger.' – *Joe Leydon, San Francisco Examiner*
† It was released direct to video in Britain.

Saltwater *
Ireland/GB/Spain 1999 96m colour
Artificial Eye/Treasure (Robert Walpole)
As their own lives go awry, the two sons of an Irish-Italian café-owner try to come to the aid of their debt-ridden father.
Pleasing, if unambitious, feature debut from a noted Irish playwright, investigating masculine attitudes, especially in their relationships with women.
wd Conor McPherson *ph* Oliver Curtis *m* Plague Monkeys, Carol Keogh, Donal O'Mahony *pd* Luana Hanson *ed* Emer Reynolds *cos* Kathy Strachan
☆ Peter McDonald (Frank Beneventi), Brian Cox (George Beneventi), Conor Mullen (Dr Raymond Sullivan), Laurence Kinlan (Joe Beneventi), Brendan Gleeson ('Simple' Simon McCurdie), Eva Birthistle (Deborah McCeever), Valerie Spelman (Carmel Beneventi), David O'Rourke (Damien Fitzgibbon), Caroline O'Boyle (Tara), Gina Moxley (Sgt Duggan)
'An affable, pawky comedy.' – *Sight and Sound*

Salty O'Rourke
US 1945 100m bw
Paramount/E. D. Leshin
A racetrack con man is reformed by a schoolteacher.
Very moderate and overlong star vehicle.
w Milton Holmes *d* Raoul Walsh *ph* Theodor Sparkuhl *m* Robert Emmett Dolan
☆ Alan Ladd, Gail Russell, William Demarest, Bruce Cabot, Spring Byington, Stanley Clements
Milton Holmes

Saludos Amigos *
US 1943 43m Technicolor
Walt Disney
Donald Duck has various South American adventures with a parrot named Joe Carioca.
Basically a naïve implementation of the good neighbour policy, but with flashes of brilliant animation and some mingling of live-action with cartoon.
production supervisor Norman Ferguson
'Self-interested, belated ingratiation embarrasses me, and Disney's famous cuteness, however richly it may mirror national infantilism, is hard on my stomach.' – *James Agee*
music (Edward H. Plumb, Paul J. Smith, Charles Wolcott); title song (*m*Charles Wolcott, *ly*Ned Washington)

Salut Cousin! *
France/Belgium/Algeria/Luxembourg 1996 100m colour
Les Films Du Roseau/JBA/La Sept/Artémis/RTFB/Flashback/Samsa/Clea (Jacques Bidou)
The adventures of an Algerian innocent, who visits his cousin, a would-be singer, in Paris.
An engaging fable of an immigrant community, of would-be sophisticates adrift in a big city.
w Merzak Allouache, Caroline Thivel *d* Merzak Allouache *ph* Pierre Aim, Georges Diane *m* Safy Boutella *ad* Olivier Raoux *ed* Denise de Casabianca
☆ Gad el Maleh, Mess Hattou, Magaly Berdy, Ann-Gisel Glass, Jean Beguigui, Xavier Maly, Cheik Doukoure, Mohamed Ourdache

Salut l'Artiste (dubbed) **
France/Italy 1973 97m Eastmancolor
Gaumont/De La Guéville/Euro-Internazionale (Alain Poiré, Yves Robert)
GB title: *The Bit Player*
After his mistress walks out, an unsuccessful actor tries to return to his wife and children but finds life too complicated.
Adroit and witty comedy, performed with insouciant skill.
w Jean-Loup Dabadie, Yves Robert *d* Yves Robert *ph* Jean Penzer *m* Vladimir Cosma *ad* Theo Meurisse *ed* Ghislaine Desjonquières
☆ Marcello Mastroianni, Françoise Fabian, Jean Rochefort, Carla Gravina, Xavier Gelin, Evelyne Buyle

Salute for Three
US 1943 75m bw
Paramount
An all-girl orchestra opens a canteen for servicemen.

Modest, middling propaganda musical with minimum talents.
w Davis Anderson, Curtis Kenyon, Hugh Wedlock Jnr and Howard Snyder d Ralph Murphy
☆ Betty Jane Rhodes, Macdonald Carey, Dona Drake and her orchestra, Marty May, Lorraine and Rognan

Salute John Citizen
GB 1942 98m bw
British National (Wallace Orton)
A clerk and his family suffer cheerfully through the blitz.
Modest, competent propaganda piece.
w Clemence Dane, Elizabeth Baron novel *Mr Bunting at War* by Robert Greenwood d Maurice Elvey ph James Wilson
☆ Edward Rigby, Stanley Holloway, George Robey, Mabel Constanduros, Jimmy Hanley, Dinah Sheridan, Peggy Cummins, Stewart Rome

The Salute of the Jugger
Australia 1989 91m Technicolor
Virgin/Handistrom/Kamisha Corporation/Kings Road Entertainment
In the future, a group of outcasts challenges a big city team to a violent sports contest.
Derivative and pallid low-budget science fiction movie of little interest.
wd David Peoples ph David Eggby m Todd Boekelheide pd John Stoddart ed Richard Francis-Bruce
☆ Rutger Hauer, Delroy Lindo, Anna Katarina, Vincent Phillip D'Onofrio, Gandhi McIntyre, Justin Monju, Aaron Martin, Joan Chen

Salute to the Marines
US 1943 101m Technicolor
MGM (John Considine Jnr)
A sergeant-major struggles to get his family out of the Philippines when the Japs attack.
Recruiting poster heroics with comedy interludes.
w Wells Root, George Bruce story Robert Andrews d S. Sylvan Simon ph Charles Schoenbaum, W. Howard Green m Lennie Hayton
☆ Wallace Beery, Fay Bainter, Marilyn Maxwell, William Lundigan, Keye Luke, Reginald Owen, Ray Collins, Noah Beery, Russell Gleason

Salvador *
US 1986 123m colour
Hemdale/Gerald Green, Oliver Stone
Adventures of an American photo-journalist in Central America.
Drama torn from the headlines; it should perhaps have stayed there, as few people proved to be interested in paying to see it. One cannot, however, deny its brilliant if superficial technical command.
w Oliver Stone, Richard Boyle d Oliver Stone ph Robert Richardson m Georges Delerue
☆ James Woods, James Belushi, Michael Murphy, John Savage
'As raw, difficult, compelling, unreasonable, reckless and vivid as its protagonist.' – *Variety*
§ best original screenplay; James Woods

The Salvation Hunters **
US 1925 65m (24 fps) bw silent
Academy Photoplays (Josef von Sternberg, George K. Arthur)
Among the mud flats of San Pedro, a boy wins his girl from a brute.
Mini-budgeted minor classic whose very artiness and pretentiousness were keys to its director's later development.
wd *Josef von Sternberg* ph Josef von Sternberg, Edward Gheller
☆ George K. Arthur, Georgia Hale, Bruce Guerin
'Audience reaction was: even our lives are not so drab as this, and if they are we don't want to know about it. Asked to comment on the failure of a film he had praised so highly, Chaplin said, "Well, you know I was only kidding. They all take everything I say so seriously. I thought I'd praise a bad picture and see what happened."' – *Richard Griffith and Arthur Mayer, The Movies*

Salvation Nell
US 1931 83m bw
Tiffany
A wronged girl sinks lower and lower until she joins the Salvation Army.
One thinks it must have been meant as a spoof, but apparently not.
w Selma Stein, Walter Woods play Edward Sheldon d James Cruze
☆ Helen Chandler, Ralph Graves, Sally O'Neil, Jason Robards, Dewitt Jennings
'It probably will be livelier in the States, where the Mme Cloquette scene is not cut out.' – *Variety*

Salvatore Giuliano *
Italy 1961 125m bw
Lux/Vides/Galatea (Franco Cristaldi)
The bullet-ridden body of key Sicilian Mafia leader Giuliano triggers flashbacks to his complex and brutal career.
Vivid, sometimes obscure, politically oriented melodrama based on fact. Undoubtedly a local classic, but not an easy film to appreciate.
w Francesco Rosi, Suso Cecchi d'Amico, Enzo Provenzale, Franco Solinas d *Francesco Rosi* ph Gianni di Venanzo m Piero Piccioni
☆ Frank Wolff, Salvo Randone, Federico Zardi
'Epic reportage in the twentieth-century manner of a society reminiscent of some backward corner of the nineteenth century.' – *Peter John Dyer, MFB*

The Salzburg Connection
US 1972 93m DeLuxe Panavision
TCF (Ingo Preminger)
An American lawyer on holiday in Salzburg finds himself suspected by spies of both sides.
Turgid, routine action thriller with attractive locations.
w Oscar Millard novel Helen MacInnes d Lee H. Katzin ph Wolfgang Treu md Lionel Newman
☆ Barry Newman, Anna Karina, Klaus-Maria Brandauer, Karen Jensen, Wolfgang Preiss
'So dull you can't tell the CIA agents from the neo-Nazis or double agents – or the inept actors from the blocks and stones in the handsome Austrian locales.' – *Judith Crist*

Sam Whiskey
US 1969 96m DeLuxe
UA/Brighton (Jules Levy, Arthur Gardner, Arnold Laven)
An itinerant gambler is paid to recover a fortune in gold bars from the bottom of a Colorado river.
Easy-going but rather slackly handled Western.
w William W. Norton d Arnold Laven ph Robert Moreno m Herschel Burke Gilbert
☆ Burt Reynolds, Clint Walker, Ossie Davis, Angie Dickinson, Rick Davis, William Schallert

Samba Traoré
Burkina Faso/France 1992 85m colour
De La Plaine/De L'Avenir/Waka/A2 (Christophe Chesson, Joseph Traoré)
After robbing a petrol station, a man returns to his village and marries, but cannot escape the consequences of his act.
A pleasant but undramatic tale of strong women and weak men, told in a leisurely fashion.
w Idrissa Ouédraogo, Jacques Arhex, Santiago Amigoréna d Idrissa Ouédraogo ph Pierre Laurent Chenieux, Mathieu Vadepied m Faton Cahen, Lamine Konté ad Yves Brover ed Joelle Dufour
☆ Bakary Sangaré, Mariam Kaba, Irene Tassembedo, Abdoulaye Komboudri, Moumouri Compaoré, Sibidou Ouédraogo

Same Old Song
France/Switzerland/Italy/GB 1997 122m colour
Pathé/Arena/Camera One/France 2/Vega/Greenpoint Films (Bruno Pesery)
original title: *On Connaît la Chanson*
Six characters in search of love and luxury apartments.
Claiming inspiration from the work of English playwright Dennis Potter, this has the cast expressing their feelings by lip-synching to popular songs or, at any rate, songs popular in France; it gives a little lift to an otherwise conventional romantic comedy.
w Agnes Jaoui, Jean-Pierre Bacri d Alain Resnais ph Renato Berta m Bruno Fontaine ad Jacques Saulnier ed Hervé de Luze
☆ Pierre Arditi, Sabine Azema, Jean-Pierre Bacri, André Dussollier, Agnes Jaoui, Lambert Wilson, Jane Birkin, Jean-Paul Roussillon
'A comedy that's amiable enough but nothing exceptional.' – *Philip Kemp, Sight and Sound*

'The story of the longest-run date in the history of non-marriage!'
Same Time, Next Year *
US 1978 119m colour
Universal/Walter Mirisch, Robert Mulligan
An illicit affair is carried on for twenty-five years, the couple confining themselves to one annual meeting in a hotel.
Careful film version of a smash Broadway comedy; the flimsiness of the premise is well concealed, but it remains a one-set play.
w Bernard Slade play Bernard Slade d Robert Mulligan ph Robert Surtees m Marvin Hamlisch pd Henry Bumstead
☆ *Ellen Burstyn, Alan Alda*
§ Bernard Slade; Robert Surtees; Ellen Burstyn; song 'The Last Time I Felt Like This' (m Marvin Hamlisch, ly Alan and Marilyn Bergman)

Sammy and Rosie Get Laid *
GB 1987 100m colour
Cinecom/Film Four (Tim Bevan, Sarah Radclyffe)
A young Pakistani accountant in London is confused by the return of his long-lost father, and vice versa.
Those who liked the harsh conflicts of My Beautiful Laundrette *will get similar frissons from this; others will be as confused as the characters.*
w Hanif Kureishi d Stephen Frears ph Oliver Stapleton m Stanley Myers ed Mick Audsley
☆ Shashi Kapoor, Claire Bloom, Ayub Khan Din, Frances Barber, Roland Gift
'This is a film standing on important territory, confronting important issues, and trying to say important things. But its supreme failure as a film is that, frankly, I don't give a damn whether Sammy and Rosie get laid.' – *Judith Williamson, New Statesman*

Sammy Going South *
GB 1963 128m Eastmancolor Cinemascope
Bryanston (Hal Mason)
US title: *A Boy Ten Feet Tall*
A 10-year-old boy is orphaned in Port Said and hitch-hikes to his aunt in Durban.
Disappointing family-fodder epic in which the mini-adventures follow each other too predictably.
w Denis Cannan novel W. H. Canaway d Alexander Mackendrick ph Erwin Hillier m Tristram Cary
☆ Fergus McClelland, Edward G. Robinson, Constance Cummings, Harry H. Corbett

'A story as timeless and tumultuous as the violent age it spreads before you!'
Samson and Delilah
US 1949 128m Technicolor
Paramount/Cecil B. de Mille
Delilah, rejected by religious strong man Samson, cuts his hair and delivers him to his enemies.
Absurd biblical hokum, stodgily narrated and directed, monotonously photographed and edited, and notable only for the 30-second destruction of the temple at the end.
w Jesse L. Lasky Jnr, Fredric M. Frank d Cecil B. de Mille ph George Barnes m Victor Young ad Hans Dreier, Walter Tyler
☆ Hedy Lamarr, Victor Mature, Angela Lansbury, George Sanders, Henry Wilcoxon, Olive Deering, Fay Holden, Russ Tamblyn
'To ignore so enormous, over-coloured, over-stuffed, flamboyant an "epic" would be almost as absurd as taking it seriously.' – *Richard Mallett, Punch*
'Perhaps de Mille's survival is due to the fact that he decided in his movie nonage to ally himself with God as his co-maker and get his major scripts from the Bible, which he has always handled with the proprietary air of a gentleman fondling old love letters.' – *New Yorker*
art direction
§ George Barnes; Victor Young

The Samurai ***
France 1967 95m colour
Filmel/CICC/Fida (Raymond Borderie, Eugene Lepicier)
original title: *Le Samourai*
US title: *The Godson*
A hired assassin who lives by a code of self-sufficiency betrays himself by falling in love with the woman who witnessed his murder of a night-club owner.
Moodily atmospheric, engrossing, low-key thriller with minimal dialogue, shot in tones of greys and blues.
wd Jean-Pierre Melville ph Henri Decaë m François de Roubaix pd Georges Casati ad François de Lamothe ed Monique Bonnot, Yo Maurette
☆ Alain Delon, François Périer, Nathalie Delon, Caty Rosier, Jacques Le Roy, Michel Boisrond, Robert Favart
† A dubbed version released in Britain in 1971 ran for 86m.

San Antone
US 1952 90m bw
Republic
During the Civil War a Texas rancher antagonizes an army lieutenant.
Very routine, competent Western without any moment of inspiration.
w Steve Fisher novel *Golden Herd* by Curt Carroll d Joseph Kane ph Bud Thackery m R. Dale Butts
☆ Rod Cameron, Forrest Tucker, Arleen Whelan, Katy Jurado, Rodolfo Acosta

San Antonio *
US 1945 109m Technicolor
Warner (Robert Buckner)
A cowboy incurs the jealousy of a saloon owner.
Typically thinly plotted Warner star Western which works well enough sequence by sequence, climaxing with a fight in the deserted Alamo.
w Alan le May, W. R. Burnett d David Butler ph Bert Glennon m Max Steiner ad Ted Smith
☆ Errol Flynn, Alexis Smith, Paul Kelly, Victor Francen, S. Z. Sakall, John Litel, Florence Bates, Robert Shayne, Monte Blue, Robert Barrat
§ song 'Some Sunday Morning' (mRay Heindorf, M. K. Jerome, lyTed Koehler); Ted Smith

San Demetrio London *
GB 1943 105m bw
Ealing (Robert Hamer)
In 1940, the survivors of a crippled tanker bring it back home.
Rather flat and dated propaganda piece which seemed much more vivid at the time.
w Robert Hamer, Charles Frend story F. Tennyson Jesse d Charles Frend ph Ernest Palmer, Roy Kellino m John Greenwood
☆ Walter Fitzgerald, Mervyn Johns, Ralph Michael, Robert Beatty, Charles Victor, Frederick Piper, Gordon Jackson
'In many ways a model for war films.' – *Dilys Powell*

San Diego I Love You *
US 1944 83m bw
Universal (Michael Fessier, Ernest Pagano)
A family travels to San Diego to promote father's inventions.
Pleasing, easy-come-easy-go comedy full of memorable incident and characterization.
w Michael Fessier, Ernest Pagano d Reginald Le Borg ph Hal Mohr m Hans Salter
☆ Louise Allbritton, Edward Everett Horton, Jon Hall, Eric Blore, *Buster Keaton*, Irene Ryan

'She fell in love with the toughest guy on the toughest street in the world!'
San Francisco ****
US 1936 117m bw
MGM (John Emerson, Bernard Hyman)
The loves and career problems of a Barbary Coast saloon proprietor climax in the 1906 earthquake.
Incisive, star-packed, superbly-handled melodrama which weaves in every kind of appeal and for a finale has some of the best special effects ever conceived.
w *Anita Loos* story Robert Hopkins d *W. S. Van Dyke* ph *Oliver T. Marsh* m Edward Ward md *Herbert Stothart* montage *John Hoffman* title song Bronislau Kaper

☆ *Clark Gable, Spencer Tracy, Jeanette MacDonald, Jack Holt, Jessie Ralph,* Ted Healy, Shirley Ross, Al Shean, Harold Huber

'Prodigally generous and completely satisfying.' – *Frank S. Nugent*

best picture; Robert Hopkins; W. S. Van Dyke; Spencer Tracy

San Francisco Docks
US 1940 64m bw
Marshall Grant/Universal

A man accused of killing a crooked politician proves he didn't do it.
Curiously pretentious melodrama with suggestions of Group Theater style; not for the action buffs, or anybody else.
w Stanley Crea Rubin, Edmund L. Hartmann *d* Arthur Lubin
☆ Burgess Meredith, Irene Hervey, Raymond Walburn, Barry Fitzgerald, Robert Armstrong, Lewis Howard

'Between the sea and the Sierras stood the brawling gateway to gold!'
The San Francisco Story *
US 1952 90m bw
Warner/Fidelity-Vogue (Howard Welsch)

In 1856, a wanderer bound for China stops in San Francisco to get involved in politics.
Lively melodrama with good period feel.
w D. D. Beauchamp *novel* Richard Summers *d* Robert Parrish *ph* John Seitz *m* Paul Dunlap *md* Emil Newman
☆ Joel McCrea, Yvonne de Carlo, Sidney Blackmer, Florence Bates

San Quentin *
US 1937 70m bw
Warner (Sam Bischoff)

A convict's sister loves the warden.
Standard tough prison melodrama, competently done.
w Peter Milne, Humphrey Cobb *story* John Bright, Robert Tasker *d* Lloyd Bacon *ph* Sid Hickox *m* Heinz Roemheld, David Raksin
☆ Pat O'Brien, Ann Sheridan, Humphrey Bogart, Barton MacLane, Joseph Sawyer, Veda Ann Borg

'Fairly good appeal but will need pushing.' – *Variety*

Sanctuary
US 1960 90m bw Cinemascope
TCF (Richard D. Zanuck)

The governor's daughter is seduced by a bootlegger, and her life goes from one tragedy to another.
Confused adaptation of unadaptable material, full of pussyfoot daring but little sense.
w James Poe *novel* William Faulkner *d* Tony Richardson *ph* Ellsworth Fredericks *m* Alex North
☆ Lee Remick, Bradford Dillman, Yves Montand, Odetta, Harry Townes, Howard St John, Reta Shaw, Strother Martin

'This is the story of the men on the USS *San Pablo* who disturbed the sleeping dragon of China as the world watched in breathless terror.'
The Sand Pebbles *
US 1966 193m DeLuxe Panavision
TCF/Argyle/Solar (Robert Wise)

In 1926 an American gunboat patrolling the Yangtze river gets involved with Chinese warlords.
Confused action blockbuster with Vietnam parallels for those who care to pick them up; pretty thinly stretched entertainment despite the tons of explosive.
w Robert Anderson *novel* Richard McKenna *d* Robert Wise *ph* Joseph MacDonald *m* Jerry Goldsmith
☆ Steve McQueen, Candice Bergen, Richard Attenborough, Richard Crenna, Marayat Andriane, Mako, Larry Gates, Simon Oakland

'If it had been done twenty years ago, it would have been fast and unpretentious, with some ingeniously faked background shots ... and we would never have asked for larger historical meanings.' – *Pauline Kael*

best picture; Joseph MacDonald; Jerry Goldsmith; Steve McQueen; Mako

Sanders: see *Death Drums along the River*

Sanders of the River *
GB 1935 98m bw
London (Alexander Korda)

US title: *Bosambo*
Problems of a British colonial servant in keeping peace among the tribes.
Much-caricatured African adventure of the very old school, helped by Robeson's personality.
w Lajos Biro, Jeffrey Dell *stories* Edgar Wallace *d* Zoltan Korda *ph* Georges Perinal, Osmond Borrodaile, Louis Page *m/ly* Mischa Spoliansky, Arthur Wimperis *md* Muir Mathieson *ed* Charles Crichton
☆ *Leslie Banks, Paul Robeson,* Nina Mae McKinney, Robert Cochran, Martin Walker, Richard Grey

'It will interest those who are sincerely interested in the cinema as an art form, but it will suffer the hazards of all pioneers.' – *Variety*

† The film's opening credits included the description: 'Africa ... Tens of millions of natives under British rule, each tribe with its own chieftain, governed and protected by a handful of white men whose everyday work is an unsung saga of courage and efficiency. One of them was Commissioner Sanders.'

The Sandlot
US 1993 101m colour
TCF/Island World

GB title: *The Sandlot Kids*
In the early 60s, an 11-year-old boy makes new friends with kids playing baseball in a sandlot and passes a personal test of courage by retrieving a valuable ball from a fearsome dog.
Pleasant, undemanding entertainment for the young, a nostalgic evocation of an idealized time.
w David Mickey Evans, Robert Gunter *d* David Mickey Evans *ph* Anthony B. Richmond *m* David Newman *pd* Chester Kaczenski *ed* Michael A. Stevenson
☆ Tom Guiry, Mike Vitar, Patrick Renna, Marty York, Chauncey Leopardi, Denis Leary, Karen Allen, James Earl Jones, Art La Fleur

'It leaves the odd impression of not only starring 12-year-olds, but being made by one.' – *Nick Hasted, Sight and Sound*

Sandokan against the Leopard of Sarawak
Italy 1964 94m Eastmancolor Totalscope
Liber (Ottavio Poggi)

Three years after recovering his kingdom of Sarawak, Sandokan rescues his bride-to-be after she is kidnapped by the ambitious son of the former ruler.
A gaudy, plodding, low-brow adventure, short on thrills and likely to irritate many with its insistence that men have stronger wills than women.
w Deriso Arpad, Luigi Capuano *novel* Emilio Salgari *d* Luigi Capuano *ph* Adalberto Albertini *m* Carlo Rustichelli *ad* Giancarlo Bartolini Salimbeni, Ernest Kronberg *ed* Antonietta Zita
☆ Ray Danton, Guy Madison, Franca Bettoja, Mario Petri, Alberto Farnese, Mino Doro, Giulio Marchetti, Aldo Bufi-Landi

† It was a sequel to *Sandokan Fights Back* (qv).

Sandokan Fights Back
Italy/West Germany 1964 96m colour
Liber/Eichberg (Ottavio Poggi)

A Malaysian pirate discovers that he is the rightful Rajah of Sarawak and decides to regain his kingdom.
Inept and trivial adventure, devoid of thrills.
w Arpad de Riso, Luigi Capuano *novel* Emilio Salgari *d* Luigi Capuano *ph* Adalberto Albertini *ed* Antonietta Zita
☆ Ray Danton, Guy Madison, Franca Bettoja, Mino Doro

† It was followed by a sequel, *Sandokan against the Leopard of Sarawak* (qv).

Sandokan the Great
Italy/France/Spain 1963 114m Techniscope
Filmes/CCF/Ocean

The son of the Sultan of Borneo wages jungle war against the oppressive British.
A curious mixture of Tarzan and Robin Hood, this character appeared in several adventures before expiring; the first chapter is the best, or least worst.
w Fulvio Gicca, Umberto Lenzi *novel* Emilio Salgari *d* Umberto Lenzi *ph* Aurelio Gutierrez Larraya, Angelo Lotti *m* Giovanni Fusco
☆ Steve Reeves, Genevieve Grad, Rik Battaglia, Andrea Bosic

The Sandpiper
US 1965 116m Metrocolor Panavision
MGM/Filmways (John Calley)

An artist lives with her illegitimate son in a Monterey beach shack; when she is forced to send the boy to school he attracts the attention of the minister in charge.
Absurd novelettish love story basically copied from The Garden of Allah; *pretty seascapes are the most rewarding aspect.*
w Dalton Trumbo, Michael Wilson *d* Vincente Minnelli *ph* Milton Krasner *m* Johnny Mandel
☆ Elizabeth Taylor, Richard Burton, Eva Marie Saint, Charles Bronson, Robert Webber

'Straight Louisa May Alcott interlarded with discreet pornographic allusions.' – *John Simon*

'Sex-on-the-sand soap opera.' – *Robert Windeler*

song 'The Shadow of Your Smile' (mJohnny Mandel, lyPaul Francis Webster)

'My name is Stryker. Sgt John M. Stryker. You're gonna be my squad!'
Sands of Iwo Jima *
US 1949 109m bw
Republic (Edmund Grainger)

During World War II in the Pacific, a tough sergeant of marines moulds raw recruits into fighting men but is himself shot by a sniper.
Celebrated star war comic, still quite hypnotic in its flagwaving way.
w Harry Brown, James Edward Grant *d* Allan Dwan *ph* Reggie Lanning *m* Victor Young *ed* Richard L. Van Enger
☆ *John Wayne,* John Agar, Adele Mara, Forrest Tucker, Arthur Franz, Julie Bishop, Richard Jaeckel

'The battle sequences are terrifyingly real ... but the personal dramatics make up a compendium of war-picture clichés.' – *Variety*

'Say what you like about the sentimental flavour of war pictures such as this, there's no denying they keep you in your seat.' – *Richard Mallett, Punch*

Harry Brown (original story); John Wayne; editing

Sands of the Desert
GB 1960 92m Technicolor
Associated British

A diminutive travel agent goes out to investigate a desert holiday camp which has suffered from sabotage.
Limp star comedy with poor studio work and meandering script.
wd John Paddy Carstairs *ph* Gilbert Taylor *m* Stanley Black
☆ Charlie Drake, Peter Arne, Sarah Branch, Raymond Huntley, Peter Illing, Harold Kasket

Sands of the Kalahari
GB 1965 119m Technicolor Panavision
Pendennis (Cy Endfield, Stanley Baker)

Survivors of a plane crash trek across the desert and are menaced by baboons and each other.
Hysterical melodrama with predictable heebie-jeebies by all concerned and the baddie finally left to the mercy of the monkeys. For hardened sensationalists.
wd Cy Endfield *novel* William Mulvihill *ph* Erwin Hillier *m* Johnny Dankworth
☆ Stanley Baker, Stuart Whitman, Harry Andrews, Susannah York, Theodore Bikel, Nigel Davenport, Barry Lowe

The Sandwich Man *
GB 1966 95m Eastmancolor
Rank/Titan (Peter Newbrook)

In the course of a walking day around London a sandwich man encounters many of his eccentric acquaintances.
Spurned when it was first released, this comedy variety show, mostly in mime, can now be seen to be of a kind popularized by TV, and may have been simply ahead of its time. It certainly seems funnier than it did.
w Michael Bentine, Robert Hartford-Davis *d* Robert Hartford-Davis *ph* Peter Newbrook *m* Mike Vickers
☆ Michael Bentine, Dora Bryan, Suzy Kendall, Norman Wisdom, Harry H. Corbett, Bernard Cribbins, Ian Hendry, Stanley Holloway, Alfie Bass, Diana Dors, Ron Moody, Wilfrid Hyde-White, Donald Wolfit, Max Bacon, Fred Emney and also Frank Finlay, Peter Jones, Michael Medwin, Ronnie Stevens, John Le Mesurier, Sydney Tafler, John Junkin, Warren Mitchell

Sandy Gets Her Man
US 1940 65m bw
Universal (Burt Kelly)

A councilman's baby gets involved in the rival claims of police and fire departments for the best funding.
Rather complex excuse for a slight family comedy.
w Sy Bartlett, Jane Storm *d* Otis Garrett, Paul Gerard Smith
☆ Baby Sandy, Stuart Erwin, Edgar Kennedy, Una Merkel, William Frawley, Edward Brophy

Sandy Is a Lady
US 1940 62m bw
Universal (Burt Kelly)

A baby is responsible for her father's promotion.
Third of a series featuring the gurgling infant introduced in East Side of Heaven. *(The others:* Little Accident, Unexpected Father, Sandy Gets Her Man.*) This one is an excuse for slapstick comedy situations.*
w Charles Grayson *d* Charles Lamont
☆ Baby Sandy, Butch and Buddy, Eugene Pallette, Nan Grey, Tom Brown, Mischa Auer, Billy Gilbert, Edgar Kennedy

Sandy Takes a Bow: see *Unexpected Father*

Le Sang d'un Poète: see *The Blood of a Poet*

Sang Gong Yatho Tungchap Fan: see *Rock'N'Roll Cop*

Sangaree
US 1953 95m Technicolor 3-D
Paramount/Pine-Thomas

Trouble ensues when a plantation owner wills his wealth to the son of a slave.
Period skulduggery rather hammily presented.
w David Duncan *novel* Frank G. Slaughter *d* Edward Ludwig *ph* Lionel Lindon, W. Wallace Kelley *m* Lucien Cailliet
☆ Fernando Lamas, Arlene Dahl, Patricia Medina, Francis L. Sullivan, Charles Korvin, Tom Drake, John Sutton, Willard Parker, Lester Matthews

Sanger Fran Andra Vaningen ***
Sweden/France/Denmark/Norway/Germany 2000 99m colour
ICA/Roy Andersson/Sveriges TV/Danmarks Radio/Norsk Rikskringkasting/Arte France/SPDP/Essential/Easy/ZDF/La Sept (Lisa Alwert)

aka: *Songs From the Second Floor*
In a European city, financial experts fiddle with unlikely solutions to an economic crisis, while individuals suffer.
An extraordinary work, a surrealist satire on modern society that proceeds by discontinuous scenes, filmed in a vividly individual way; there is no other film quite like it.
wd Roy Andersson *ph* Istvan Borbas, Jesper Klevenas *m* Benny Andersson *ed* Roy Andersson *cos* Leontine Arvidsson
☆ Lars Nordh (Kalle), Stefan Larsson (Stefan), Torbjörn Fahlström (Pelle Wigert), Sten Andersson (Lasse), Lucio Vucino (Magician), Hanna Eriksson (Mia), Peter Roth (Tomas), Tommy Johansson (Uffe), Sture Olsson (Sven)

'Rapidly wears out its welcome after the first few reels to finish up as a perplexing objet d'art.' – *Derek Elley, Variety*

'Here is a film to try the patience of the non-believer, but astonish everyone else. Some might find it a curate's egg of strangeness. But it's one of the Fabergé variety.' – *Peter Bradshaw, Guardian*

'Audacious, offensive, original.' – *Roger Ebert*

Sango Malo *
Cameroon/Burkina Faso 1991 93m colour
Les Films Terre Africaine/Cameroun Radio and TV/FODIC/DIPROCI (Emmanuel Toko)
An idealistic schoolteacher in his first job angers village leaders and his punitive and conservative headmaster by ignoring traditional ways and putting the emphasis on practical education.
A tough and complex view of Cameroonian village life, in which there are no heroes.
wd Bassek Ba Kobhio *novel* Sango Malo – Le Maître du Canton by Bassek Ba Kobhio *ph* Joseph Guerin *m* Francis Bebey *ad* François Bollo *ed* Marie-Jeanne Kanyala
☆ Jérome Bolo, Marcel Mvondo II, Edwige Ntongon è Zock, Jean Minguele, Jimmy Biyong, Henriette Fenda
'Offers a valuable look at the harsh realities of life in this little-seen land. But despite a relatively lively script, pic is unable to sustain its initially fast pace.' – *Variety*

Sangre de Virgenes
Argentina 1967 72m Eastmancolor
Associated Argent (Oreste Trucco)
aka: *Blood of the Virgins*
On a dark and stormy night, tourists take refuge in a deserted farmhouse that is said to be haunted.
Low budget soft-core porn masquerading as a vampire movie; by any standards, it is inept and extremely dull.
wd Emilio Vieyra *ph* Anibal Gonzales Paz *m* Victor Buchino *ed* Oscar Ronet *sp* Martin Best
☆ Ricardo Bauleo, Gloria Prat, Raoul Monroy, Walter Kliche, Susan Beltran, Mitlon Ghio, Mariella Albano, Jiustin Martin

Sanjuro **
Japan 1962 96m bw Tohoscope
Toho/Kurosawa (Tomoyuki Tanaka, Ryuzo Kikushima)
original title: *Tsubaki Sanjuro*
A ronin, or wandering samurai, inspires some young and rebellious warriors to fight against corruption.
Deftly enjoyable drama, spiced with wit and humanity, and tinged with sadness for its lone and homeless hero.
w Ryuzo Kikushima, Hideo Oguni, Akira Kurosawa *novel* Shugoro Yamamoto *d* Akira Kurosawa *ph* Fukuzo Koizumi *m* Masaru Sato *ad* Yoshio Muraki
☆ *Toshiro Mifune*, Tatsuya Nakadai, Yuzo Kayama, Akihiko Hirata, Kunie Tanaka
'The most autumnal of Kurosawa's Japanese Westerns.' – *Nigel Andrews*
† Despite the change in name, the ronin played by Mifune is the same character who appeared in the earlier *Yojimbo* (qv).

Sans Lendemain *
France 1940 83m bw
Gregor Rabinovitch/Cine Alliance
A night-club hostess with a mysterious past is troubled when an old lover turns up.
Moody melodrama in the Quai des Brumes *tradition.*
w Jean Wilhelm, Max Colpet *d* *Max Ophüls*
☆ Edwige Feuillère, Georges Rigaud, Georges Lannes, Paul Azais

Sans Toit ni Loi: see *Vagabonde*

Sansho the Bailiff ***
Japan 1954 132m bw
Daiei (Masaichi Nagata)
original title: *Sansho dayu*
In medieval Japan, a provincial governor is exiled for trying to protect the peasants from exploitation; following him seven years later, his wife is forced into prostitution and his son and daughter bought as slaves by the ruthless Sansho.
A tough tale of oppression and injustice, sacrifice and redemption, told simply but with great skill, the beauty of its images alleviating some of the narrative's harshness, but not its power.
w Fuji Yahiro, Yoshikata Yoda *novel* Ogai Mori *d* Kenji Mizoguchi *ph* *Kazuo Miyagawa* *m* Fumio Hayasaka *ad* Kasaku Ito *ed* Mitsuji Miyata
☆ Eitaro Shindo, Kinuyo Tanaka, Yoshiaki Hanayagi, Kyoko Kagawa, Akitaka Kono, Keiko Enami, Masahiko Kato
† The film was awarded a Silver Lion at the Venice Film Festival in 1955.

Santa Claus
GB 1985 112m Rank Colour Panavision
Alexander Salkind (Ilya Salkind, Pierre Spengler)
An old woodcutter is given immortality by the elves and turned into Santa Claus; in modern times, he goes to New York to rescue a discontented elf from the clutches of a demon toymaker.
Utterly charmless treatment of an extremely vague legend, with the two halves entirely failing to coalesce and the level of invention low throughout.
w David Newman *d* Jeannot Szwarc *ph* Arthur Ibbetson *m* Henry Mancini *pd* Anthony Pratt *ed* Peter Hollywood
☆ David Huddleston, Dudley Moore, John Lithgow, Judy Cornwell, Christian Fitzpatrick, Burgess Meredith
'For children of all ages, but it skews best towards infancy or senility.' – *Variety*

The Santa Clause
US 1994 95m colour
Buena Vista/Walt Disney (Brian Reilly, Jeffrey Silver, Robert Newmyer)
When Santa Claus falls off the roof of his house, an advertising executive takes over and discovers he is stuck with the job.
A pleasant though far from hilarious comedy that seems uncertain whether it's intended for kids or adults and is unlikely to prove memorable for either audience.
w Leonard Benvenuti, Steve Rudnick *d* John Pasquin *ph* Walt Lloyd *m* Michael Convertino *pd* Carol Spier *ed* Larry Bock
☆ Tim Allen, Judge Reinhold, Wendy Crewson, Eric Lloyd
'Allen can mug with the best of them, but his straight material is found wanting. Like a latter-day Bob Hope, he can't transcend his popular persona.' – *Denis Seguin, Screen International*

The Santa Clause 2
2002 104m Technicolor
Buena Vista
American adman-turned-Santa-Claus discovers that he must find a wife before Christmas Eve and returns from the North Pole in search of one.
Amiable, eminently forgettable comedy of suburban life.
w Don Rhymer, Cinco Paul, Ken Daurio, EdDecter, John J. Strauss *story* Leo Benvenuti, Steve Rudnick *d* Michael Lembeck *ph* Adam Greenberg *m* George S. Clinton *pd* Tony Burrough *ed* David Finfer
☆ Tim Allen (Scott Calvin/Santa/Toy Santa), Elizabeth Mitchell (Carol), David Krumholtz (Bernard), Eric Lloyd (Charlie Calvin), Judge Reinhold (Neil Miller), Wendy Crewson (Laura Miller), Spencer Breslin (Curtis), Liliana Mumy (Lucy Miller)
'You might find the syllables bah, hum, and bug dancing on your lips.' – *Peter Bradshaw, Guardian*

Santa Fe
US 1951 89m Technicolor
Columbia (Harry Joe Brown)
After the Civil War, the eldest of four westbound brothers tries to prevent the others from becoming outlaws.
Regulation star Western, with action sequences a little under par.
w Kenneth Gamet *d* Irving Pichel *ph* Charles Lawton Jnr *m* Paul Sawtell
☆ Randolph Scott, Jerome Courtland, Janis Carter, Peter Thompson, John Archer, Warner Anderson, Roy Roberts

Santa Fe Passage
US 1955 89m Trucolor
Republic
An Indian-hating scout with a bad record is hired to transport arms to Santa Fe.
Rough-and-ready brawling Western with very little going for it.
w Lillie Hayward *d* William Witney *ph* Bud Thackery *m* R. Dale Butts
☆ John Payne, Rod Cameron, Faith Domergue, Slim Pickens, Leo Gordon

'The thundering story that challenges all filmdom to match its excitement!'
Santa Fe Trail **
US 1940 110m bw
Warner (Robert Fellows)
A cavalry officer is responsible for the final capture of John Brown.
The most solemn Western from star or studio has impressive patches amid routine excitements.
w Robert Buckner *d* *Michael Curtiz* *ph* Sol Polito *m* Max Steiner *ad* John Hughes *ed* George Amy
☆ Errol Flynn (Jeb Stuart), Olivia de Havilland ('Kit Carson' Holliday), Raymond Massey (John Brown), Ronald Reagan (George Custer), Alan Hale (Tex Bell), Van Heflin (Rader), Gene Reynolds (Jason Brown), Henry O'Neill (Cyrus Holliday), William Lundigan (Bob Holliday), Guinn 'Big Boy' Williams (Windy Brody), Alan Baxter (Oliver Brown), John Litel (Martin), Moroni Olsen (Robert E. Lee), Ward Bond (Townley)

'Forget everything you have ever seen!'
Santa Sangre
Italy 1989 123m colour
Mainline/Produzioni Intersound (Claudio Argento)
An armless, but far from harmless, mother forces her demented son to use his arms and hands as substitutes for her own, severed by her jealous husband.
Phantasmagoria of images of death and mutilation that, despite their occasional visual flamboyance, signify very little.
w Robert Leoni, Alejandro Jodorowsky, Claudio Argento *d* Alejandro Jodorowsky *ph* Daniele Nannuzzi *m* Simon Boswell *pd* Alejandro Luna *ed* Mauro Bonanni
☆ Axel Jodorowsky, Blanca Guerra, Guy Stockwell, Thelma Tixou, Sabrina Dennison, Adan Jodorowski, Faviola Elenka Tapia, Teo Jodorowsky

Santee
US 1972 93m colour
Vagabond (Deno Paoli, Edward Platt)
A boy goes west to find his father and befriends the bounty hunter who has killed him.
Personable, violent Western with adequate style and performances.
w Brand Bell *d* Gary Nelson *ph* Donald Morgan *m* Don Randi
☆ Glenn Ford, Michael Burns, Dana Wynter, Jay Silverheels, Harry Townes, John Larch

Santiago
US 1956 92m Warnercolor Cinemascope
Warner (Martin Rackin)
GB title: *The Gun Runner*
A Mississippi paddle-boat sets out for Cuba with a consignment of guns for the rebels.
Stiff period actioner of no particular merit.
w Martin Rackin, John Twist *d* Gordon Douglas *ph* John Seitz *m* David Buttolph
☆ Alan Ladd, Rossana Podesta, Lloyd Nolan, Chill Wills, Paul Fix, L. Q. Jones, Frank de Kova

The Saphead *
US 1920 70m (24 fps) bw silent
Metro/Buster Keaton
A shy young man reads a manual on how to win the modern girl.
Interesting early star comedy: quite winning in its way, but without the spectacular moments which were a feature of his later films.
w June Mathis *play* The New Henrietta by Winchell Smith, Victor Mapes *d* Herbert Blache *ph* Harold Wenstrom
☆ Buster Keaton, Beula Booker, William H. Crane, Irving Cummings

Sapphire **
GB 1959 92m Eastmancolor
Rank/Artna (Michael Relph)
Scotland Yard solves the murder of a black music student.
Efficient police thriller with a strong race angle.
w Janet Green *d* Basil Dearden *ph* Harry Waxman *m* Philip Green
☆ Nigel Patrick, Michael Craig, Yvonne Mitchell, Paul Massie, Bernard Miles, Olga Lindo, Earl Cameron, Gordon Heath, Robert Adams
'A dandy murder mystery – taut, tantalizing and beautifully done.' – *Judith Crist, 1980*
British film

Saps at Sea
US 1940 60m bw
Hal Roach
Ollie needs a rest after working in a horn factory, so he and Stan take a boating holiday but are kidnapped by a gangster.
Disappointing star comedy with gags too few and too long drawn out.
w Charles Rogers, Harry Langdon, Gil Pratt, Felix Adler *d* Gordon Douglas *ph* Art Lloyd *m* Marvin Hatley
☆ Stan Laurel, Oliver Hardy, James Finlayson, Dick Cramer, Ben Turpin

Saraband: see *Saraband for Dead Lovers*

Saraband for Dead Lovers *
GB 1948 96m Technicolor
Ealing (Michael Relph)
US title: *Saraband*
The tragic love affair of Konigsmark and Sophie Dorothea, wife of the Elector of Hanover who later became George I of England.
Gloomy but superb-looking historical love story; it just misses being a memorable film.
w John Dighton, Alexander Mackendrick *novel* Helen Simpson *d* Basil Dearden, Michael Relph *ph* Douglas Slocombe *m* Alan Rawsthorne *ad* Jim Morahan, William Kellner, Michael Relph
☆ Stewart Granger, Joan Greenwood, Françoise Rosay, Flora Robson, Peter Bull
'Suspense, romance, interest and excitement in full measure.' – *MFB*
art direction

The Saracen Blade
US 1954 76m Technicolor
Columbia (Sam Katzman)
In the 13th century a young Italian crusader devotes himself to avenging the murder of his father.
Cut-price swashbuckler full of unintentional laughs and therefore quite watchable.
w DeVallon Scott, George Worthing Yates *novel* Frank Yerby *d* William Castle *ph* Henry Freulich *m* Mischa Bakaleinikoff
☆ Ricardo Montalban, Betta St John, Rick Jason, Carolyn Jones, Michael Ansara

'The Sound of Freedom.'
'Her story will move you. Her struggle will change you. Her spirit will inspire you.'
Sarafina!
South Africa 1992 116m Agfacolor
Warner/Ideal/Distant Horizon/Videovision/Ariane/VPI/BBC (Anant Singh, David M. Thompson)
A South African schoolgirl in Soweto realizes she has to fight for freedom, following the example of her history teacher and her mother – and learning from her own experiences when she is imprisoned and tortured.
An odd mix of musical and near-documentary realism that obstinately fails to comes to life on the screen.
w William Nicholson, Mbongeni Ngema *musical* Mbongeni Ngema *d* Darrell James Roodt *ph* Mark Vincente *m* Stanley Myers *ch* Michael Peters, Mbongeni Ngema *ed* Peter Hollywood, Sarah Thomas
☆ Leleti Khumalo, Whoopi Goldberg, Miriam Makeba, John Kani, Dumisani Diamini, Mbongeni Ngema, Sipho Kunene
'If one is prepared to forgive it its large measure of amateurishness and naivety, and is braced for the distress inherent in the subject matter, this can be cautiously recommended as a vivid testament to the unacceptable circumstances in which too many children grow up.' – *Angie Errigo, Empire*

Sarah and Son
US 1930 85m bw
Paramount (David O. Selznick)
A widow seeks the baby her husband took away from her.

Mother love saga; soppy but with good credits.
w Zoe Akins *novel* Timothy Shea *d* Dorothy Arzner *ph* Charles Lang
☆ Ruth Chatterton, Fredric March, Fuller Mellish Jnr, Gilbert Emery, Doris Lloyd
'Madame X with a slightly varied theme. Photography and recording par.' – *Variety*
Ruth Chatterton

Saratoga *
US 1937 102m bw
MGM (Bernard H. Hyman)
A bookmaker helps the daughter of a horse breeder.
Forgettable racetrack drama notable chiefly as the last film of Jean Harlow who died before it was completed.
w Anita Loos, Robert Hopkins *d* Jack Conway *ph* Ray June *m* Edward Ward
☆ Clark Gable, Jean Harlow, Lionel Barrymore, Frank Morgan, Walter Pidgeon, Una Merkel, Cliff Edwards, George Zucco, Jonathan Hale
'Glib, forthright, knowing and adroit.' – *Time*
'Surefire box office, and tastefully produced.' – *Variety*

'Their times were violent – and so was their love!'
Saratoga Trunk *
US 1943 135m bw
Warner (Hal B. Wallis)
A notorious woman comes back to New Orleans and falls for a cowboy helping a railroad combine against their rivals.
Curious, unsatisfactory, miscast and overlong film version of a bestseller; there are enjoyable sequences, but it simply fails to come alive.
w Casey Robinson *novel* Edna Ferber *d* Sam Wood *ph* Joseph St Amaad *m* Max Steiner
☆ Ingrid Bergman, Gary Cooper, Flora Robson, Jerry Austin, Florence Bates, John Warburton, John Abbott, Curt Bois, Ethel Griffies
'It lacks a logical pattern of drama and character … a piece of baggage labelled solely for the stars.' – *Bosley Crowther*
Flora Robson

Sarraounia *
Burkina Faso 1986 121m Fujicolour Technovision
Les Films Soleil (Med Hondo)
An African warrior queen resists white colonization of her country.
Based on actual events in the 1890s in what is now Nigeria, an ambitious, if flawed, attempt at an epic of repression and power politics.
w Med Hondo, Abdoulaye Mamani, Abdoul War *book* Abdoulaye Mamani *d* Med Hondo *ph* Guy Famechon *m* Pierre Akendengue *pd* Jacques D'Ovidio *ed* Marie-Therese Boiché
☆ Ai Keïta, Jean-Roger Milo, Feodor Atkine, Didier Sauvegrain, Roger Mirmont, Luc-Antoine Diquaro, Jean-Pierre Castaldi, Tidjani Ouedraogo
'An alternative to mainstream cinema which is both exhilarating and accessible … cinema-goers will be surprised how much they enjoy it.' – *Judith Williamson, New Statesman*

Sartana
Italy/West Germany 1968 97m Telecolor Paris-Etoile/Widescreen (Aldo Addobbati)
A mysterious stranger thwarts the plans of gangs of ruthless killers and gains a fortune in gold.
Uninteresting spaghetti Western with an invulnerable hero, notable only for its high body count and its contrived yet clichéd details, ranging from an eccentric coffin-maker to a cackling villain, deaths accompanied by the sound of a tinkling, musical watch, and a gunfighter who shoots a four-barrelled pistol.
w Renato Izzo, Gianfranco Parolini, Werner Hauff *story* Luigi de Santis, Fabio Piccioni, Adolfo Cagnacci *d* Frank Kramer (Gianfranco Parolini) *ph* Sandro Mancori *m* Piero Piccioni *ad* Giorgio Desideri *ed* Edmundo Lozzi
☆ John Garko (Gianni Garko), William Berger, Sydney Chaplin, Klaus Kinski, Gianni Rizzo, Fernando Sancho, Andrew Scott, Carlo Tamberlani, Franco Pesce, Heidi Fisher

Saskatchewan
US 1954 87m Technicolor
U-I (Aaron Rosenberg)
GB title: *O'Rourke of the Royal Mounted*
A mountie helps the lady survivor of an Indian attack.
Standard star actioner.
w Gil Doud *d* Raoul Walsh *ph* John Seitz *m* Hans Salter
☆ Alan Ladd, Shelley Winters, J. Carrol Naish, Hugh O'Brian, Robert Douglas, Richard Long, Jay Silverheels

The Satan Bug *
US 1965 114m DeLuxe Panavision
UA/Mirisch/Kappa (John Sturges)
At a top-secret desert research station, one scientist is a traitor, and a deadly virus has been stolen for use by a mad millionaire.
Slow-moving, portentous, gadget-filled actioner which looks good but seldom stimulates.
w James Clavell, Edward Anhalt *novel* Alistair MacLean *d* John Sturges *ph* Robert Surtees *m* Jerry Goldsmith
☆ George Maharis, Richard Basehart, Anne Francis, Dana Andrews, Ed Asner

Satan Met a Lady *
US 1936 74m bw
Warner (Henry Blanke)
Various crooks and a private detective pursue a rare artifact.
Perversely rewritten version of The Maltese Falcon *(qv). Fascinating but not really successful.*
w Brown Holmes *d* William Dieterle *ph* Arthur Edeson *m* Leo F. Forbstein
☆ Bette Davis, Warren William, Alison Skipworth, Arthur Treacher, Wini Shaw, Marie Wilson, Porter Hall
'One lives through it in constant expectation of seeing a group of uniformed individuals appear suddenly from behind the furniture and take the entire cast into protective custody.' – *Bosley Crowther*

Satan Never Sleeps
US/GB 1962 126m DeLuxe Cinemascope
TCF/Leo McCarey
GB title: *The Devil Never Sleeps*
In the late forties in China, Catholic missionaries defy the communists.
Failed anti-Red imitation of Inn of the Sixth Happiness *with the priests from* Going My Way. *Has to be seen to be believed.*
w Claude Binyon, Leo McCarey *d* Leo McCarey *ph* Oswald Morris *m* Richard Rodney Bennett
☆ Clifton Webb, William Holden, France Nuyen, Weaver Lee, Athene Seyler, Martin Benson
'For all its superficial smirk of piety, this is just a prurient, soft-soapy and holy water version of the spicy story about the lonely missionary and the beautiful native girl.' – *Time*

The Satanic Rites of Dracula
GB 1973 88m Technicolor
Hammer (Roy Skeggs)
US title: *Count Dracula and His Vampire Bride*
When vampires infest London, a property speculator proves to be Dracula himself.
Intriguingly plotted screamer with more mystery than horror.
w Don Houghton *d* Alan Gibson *ph* Brian Probyn *m* John Cacavas *ad* Lionel Couch *ed* Chris Barnes *sp* Les Bowie
☆ Peter Cushing, Christopher Lee, Michael Coles, William Franklyn, Freddie Jones, Richard Vernon, Patrick Barr
'Shot with the kind of flashy anonymity that one expects of a TV series.' – *David Pirie, MFB*

Satan's Skin: see *Blood on Satan's Claw*

'Never told till now! The world's most guarded secret!'
Satellite in the Sky
GB 1956 85m Warnercolor Cinemascope
Warner/Tridelta/Danziger
A rocketship is ordered to lose a tritonium bomb in space, but the device attaches itself to the side of the ship.
Boringly talkative low-budget science fiction with ideas beyond its station but not enough talent to put them over.
w John Mather, J. T. McIntosh, Edith Dell *d* Paul Dickson *ph* Georges Périnal *m* Albert Elms
☆ Kieron Moore, Lois Maxwell, Donald Wolfit, Bryan Forbes, Jimmy Hanley, Alan Gifford

Satisfaction
US 1988 96m DeLuxe
TCF/NBC (Aaron Spelling, Alan Greisman)
aka: *The Girls of Summer*
A rock band – three women, one man – win a summer residency and find romance, or sex, at a smart club.
Inconsequential teen drama providing no entertainment and sub-standard rock.
w Charles Purpura *d* Joan Freeman *ph* Thomas Del Ruth *m* Michel Colombier *ed* Joel Goodman
☆ Justine Bateman, Liam Neeson, Trini Alvarado, Scott Coffey, Britta Phillips, Julia Roberts, Debbie Harry

'Will they go all the way?'
Satreelex
Thailand 2000 104m colour
ICA/Tai Entertainment
GB and US title: *The Iron Ladies*
Tired of rejection, some Thai transsexuals, transvestites and gay men form a volleyball team that wins the national championships.
Based on a true story of the volleyball champions of 1996, this deliriously camp account is played for easy laughs, and may amuse audiences in an indulgent mood.
w Visuthichai Boonyakarinjana, Jira Maligool, Yongyoot Thongkongtoon *d* Yongyoot Thongkongtoon *ph* Jira Maligool *m* Wild at Heart *ad* Narucha Vijitvarit *ed* Sunit Assavinikul
☆ Chaichan Nimpoonsawas (Jung), Sahaparp Virakamin (Mon), Giorgio Maiocchi (Nong), Gokgorn Benjathikul (Pia), Jessdaporn Pholdee (Chai), Siridhana Hongsophon (Coach Bee), Ekachai Burnanapanit (Wit)
'A giddy feel-good comedy…as flimsy and manipulative as the shallowest Hollywood fantasy.' – *Stephen Holden, New York Times*
† The film became the second highest-grossing Thai film so far.

Saturday Island
GB 1951 102m Technicolor
Coronado (David E. Rose)
US title: *Island of Desire*
In 1943 a supply boat is torpedoed and a Canadian nurse finds romance on a desert island with a US marine and a one-armed RAF pilot.
Unlikely, conversational, old-fashioned love story.
wd Stuart Heisler *novel* Hugh Brooke *ph* Oswald Morris *m* William Alwyn
☆ Linda Darnell, Tab Hunter, Donald Gray

Saturday Night and Sunday Morning ****
GB 1960 89m bw
Bryanston/Woodfall (Harry Salzman, Tony Richardson)
A Nottingham factory worker is dissatisfied with his lot, gets into trouble through an affair with a married woman, but finally settles for convention.
Startling when it emerged, this raw working-class melodrama, with its sharp detail and strong comedy asides, delighted the mass audience chiefly because of its strong central character thumbing his nose at authority. Matching the mood of the times, and displaying a new attitude to sex, it transformed British cinema and was much imitated.
w Alan Sillitoe *novel* Alan Sillitoe *d* Karel Reisz *ph* Freddie Francis *m* Johnny Dankworth
☆ *Albert Finney*, Shirley Anne Field, *Rachel Roberts*, Bryan Pringle, Norman Rossington, Hylda Baker
'Here is a chance for our own new wave.' – *Evening Standard*
† Warwickshire never showed the film because the producers refused to delete two love scenes. David Kingsley of British Lion said: 'We are not prepared to agree that a film of outstanding importance and merit should be re-edited by the Mrs Grundys of the Warwickshire County Council. It is fortunate for the world that Warwickshire's greatest and often bawdy son, William Shakespeare, was not subject in his day to the restrictions of prim and petty officialdom.'
best British film; Albert Finney; Rachel Roberts

Saturday Night at the Palace *
South Africa 1987 90m colour
Intertrade (Robert Davies)
An embittered, unemployed white vents his anger on the black manager of an all-night diner.
Tough drama of racial antagonism, based on a true story, with a slow start and a rousing, if overly theatrical, conclusion.
w Paul Slabolepszy, Bill Flynn *play* Paul Slabolepszy *d* Robert Davies *ph* Robert Davies *ad* Wayne and Sandy Attrill *ed* Lena Farugia, Carla Sandrock
☆ Bill Flynn, John Kani, Paul Slabolepszy

Saturday Night Fever ***
US 1977 119m Movielab
Paramount/Robert Stigwood (Milt Felsen)
Italian roughnecks in Brooklyn live for their Saturday night disco dancing, and one of them falls in love with a girl who makes him realize there are better things in life.
Foul-mouthed, fast-paced slice of life which plays like an updated version of Marty *except that all the characters seem to have crawled from under stones. The slick direction, fast editing and exciting dance numbers do something to take away the sour taste.*
w Norman Wexler *story* Nik Cohn *d* *John Badham* *ph* Ralf D. Bode *m* David Shire *pd* Charles Bailey *ed* David Rawlins *songs* Barry, Robin and Maurice Gibb (and others), performed by the Bee Gees
☆ *John Travolta*, Karen Lynn Gorney, Barry Miller, Joseph Cali, Paul Pape, Bruce Ornstein
'A stylish piece of contemporary anthropology, an urban safari into darkest America, a field study of the mystery cults among the young braves and squaws growing up in North Brooklyn.' – *Alan Brien, Sunday Times*
John Travolta

Saturday Night Out
GB 1963 96m bw
Compton-Tekli
Five sailors spend an overnight leave in London.
Portmanteau drama in which all elements are equally uninteresting.
w Donald and Derek Ford *d* Robert Hartford-Davis *ph* Peter Newbrook *m* Robert Richards
☆ Bernard Lee, Heather Sears, John Bonney, Francesca Annis, Erika Remberg, Colin Campbell, David Lodge

Saturday's Children
US 1940 101m bw
Warner (Henry Blanke)
An impractical young inventor marries an ambitious young woman, but depressed finances lead to discord.
Glum, dated rehash of a 1929 silent; watchable but not compelling.
w Julius J. and Philip G. Epstein *play* Maxwell Anderson *d* Vincent Sherman *ph* James Wong Howe
☆ John Garfield, Claude Rains, Anne Shirley, Lee Patrick, George Tobias, Roscoe Karns, Elizabeth Risdon, Berton Churchill
† The story was also made in 1935 as *Maybe It's Love*, with Ross Alexander, Henry Travers and Gloria Stuart; William McGann directed without flair.

Saturday's Hero
US 1951 110m bw
Columbia (Sidney Buchman)
GB title: *Idols in the Dust*
A poor boy wins a football scholarship but finds his value to the college is purely commercial and he isn't given time to learn anything.
A spirited attack on the American sporting system, but a dull and overlong film.
w Millard Lampell, Sidney Buchman *novel* *The Hero* by Millard Lampell *d* David Miller *ph* Lee Garmes *m* Elmer Bernstein
☆ John Derek, Donna Reed, Sidney Blackmer, Alexander Knox, Elliott Lewis, Howard St John

Saturn 3
GB 1980 87m colour
ITC/Transcontinental (Stanley Donen)
A maniac builds a robot on a remote space station, and they both go berserk.

Rather unpleasant blend of space fiction, horror and suspense, with some nasty detail and a general feeling that the actors wish they were elsewhere.
w Martin Amis *story* John Barry *d* Stanley Donen *ph* Billy Williams *m* Elmer Bernstein *pd* Stuart Craig
☆ Kirk Douglas, Farrah Fawcett, Harvey Keitel, Ed Bishop

Satyricon *
Italy/France 1969 129m DeLuxe Panavision
UA/PAA/PEA (Alberto Grimaldi)
aka: *Fellini Satyricon*
Sexual adventures of a Roman student.
Garish, sporadically enjoyable sketches on a very thin thread of plot: a more benevolent version of the usual Fellini nightmare.
w Federico Fellini, Bernardino Zapponi
d Federico Fellini *ph* Giuseppe Rotunno *m* Nino Rota, Ilhan Mimaroglu, Tod Dockstader, Andrew Rudin *pd* Danilo Donati
☆ Martin Potter, Hiram Keller, Salvo Randone, Max Born
'A picaresque satire in fragments ... a series of tableaux which carry the poetry visually at the price of coherence.' – *Mike Wallington, MFB*
'Part of the gradual decomposition of what once was one of the greatest talents in film history ... a gimcrack, shopworn nightmare.' – *John Simon*
Federico Fellini (as director)

Le Sauvage
France/Italy 1978 107m Eastmancolor
Lira/PAI (Raymond Danon)
A business executive has opted out of life to be alone on a desert island, but on his last night in the city accidentally helps a runaway heiress who follows him.
A promising and amusing start is squandered in the tedious island sequences of this patchy romantic comedy, which does however leave one with a sense of freshness and optimism rare in the cinema of the seventies.
w Jean-Paul Rappeneau, Elizabeth Rappeneau, Jean-Loup Dabadie *d* Jean-Paul Rappeneau *ph* Pierre Lhomme *m* Michel Legrand
☆ Yves Montand, Catherine Deneuve, Luigi Vannucchi, Dana Wynter

Sauve Qui Peut (La Vie) *
France/Switzerland 1980 87m colour
Sara/MK2/Saga/Sonimage/CDIC/ZDF/SSR/ORF
aka: *Slow Motion*
US title: *Every Man for Himself*
The lives of three people cross: a country girl who becomes a prostitute in the city, a woman leaving the city for a rural life, and her lover, who is not sure where he wants to be.
Godard's return to more commercial cinema is intermittently interesting, but lacks the challenge and playfulness of his best work.
w Anne-Marie Miéville, Jean-Claude Carrière *d* Jean-Luc Godard *ph* William Lubtchansky, Renato Berta, Jean-Bernard Menoud *m* Gabriel Yared *ad* Romain Goupil *ed* Anne-Marie Miéville, Jean-Luc Godard
☆ Isabelle Huppert, Jacques Dutronc, Nathalie Baye, Roland Amstutz, Anna Baldaccini, Fred Personne

The Savage
US 1952 95m Technicolor
Paramount (Mel Epstein)
A white boy grows up with Indians and later suffers from divided loyalties.
Solemn, rather tedious but well produced Western.
w Sydney Boehm *novel* L. L. Foreman *d* George Marshall *ph* John F. Seitz *m* Paul Sawtell
☆ Charlton Heston, Susan Morrow, Peter Hanson, Joan Taylor, Richard Rober, Don Porter

The Savage Eye *
US 1959 68m bw
City Film Corporation (Ben Maddow, Joseph Strick, Sidney Meyers)
An unhappily married young woman takes a jaundiced view of life around her in Los Angeles.
The wisp of plot is merely an excuse to present a documentary exposé of the seamier side of life in America's most eccentric city, with its faith healers and revellers. Much of it is fascinating, though the film is not a cohesive whole and the would-be poetic commentary falls on its face.
ph Jack Couffer, Haskell Wexler, Helen Levitt *m* Leonard Rosenman *wd/ed* Ben Maddow, Joseph Strick, Sidney Meyers
☆ Barbara Baxley, Gary Merrill, Herschel Bernardi
'The picture is funny, pathetic, cruel, terrible; and it is worth going miles to see.' – *Dilys Powell, Sunday Times*

Savage Hearts
GB 1996 111m colour
August/Wavepower Navigation/Bratton (Keith Hayley)
Told she has six months to live, a young woman steals £2m from an aristocratic drug dealer and goes on a spending spree, aided and hampered by a con man and a prostitute.
Drearily incompetent thriller, poorly acted, scripted and directed; the narrative twists and turns without going anywhere interesting.
wd Mark Ezra *ph* James Aspinall *m* Dominic Crawford-Collins, Basil Moore-Asfouri *pd* Jenny Chartres *ed* Andrea MacArthur
☆ Jamie Harris, Maryam D'Abo, Myriam Cyr, Richard Harris, Stephen Marcus, Angus Deayton, Jerry Hall, Julian Fellowes

The Savage Innocents
GB/France/Italy 1960 107m SuperTechnirama 70
Joseph Janni/Magic Film/Playart/Gray Films (Maleno Malenotti)
aka: *Ombre Bianchi*
Trials of an Eskimo and his wife in Canada's frozen north.
Conscientious, determined and very boring account of Eskimo life played by actors talking pidgin English. Not a success despite the magnificent photography.
w Nicholas Ray *novel* *Top of the World* by Hans Ruesch *d* Nicholas Ray, Baccio Bandini *ph* Aldo Tonti, Peter Hennessy *m* Angelo Lavagnino
☆ Anthony Quinn, Yoko Tani, Marie Yang, Peter O'Toole, Carlo Justini, Anna May Wong, Lee Montague, Ed Devereaux
† The Anna May Wong in the cast is not the famous silent star.

'Don't Bother To Hide ... He's Already Inside.'
The Savage Intruder
US 1973 90m Movielab
Congdon Films (Donald Wolfe)
A former Hollywood star hires as a nurse a psychopathic killer who dismembers middle-aged women.
Gruesome thriller, which borrows from Night Must Fall *and* Sunset Boulevard *and is inept when it is not unpleasant.*
wd Donald Wolfe *ph* John A. Morrill *m* Stu Phillips *pd* Norman Houlé *ed* Hatwig Deeb
☆ Miriam Hopkins, John David Garfield, Gale Sondergaard, Florence Lake, Lester Matthews, Riza Royce, Joe Besser, Minta Durfee, Virginia Wing
† The film was cut to 85m for its British video release.

Savage Islands
New Zealand 1983 94m colour
Paramount (Lloyd Phillips, Rob Whitehouse)
On the morning of his execution, a pirate recalls rescuing a beautiful Englishwoman from a rival brigand.
Standard adventure fare, given a slight novelty by being set in the era of steam warships.
w John Hughes, David Odell *story* Lloyd Phillips *d* Ferdinand Fairfax *ph* Tony Imi *m* Trevor Jones *pd* Maurice Cain *ed* John Shirley
☆ Tommy Lee Jones, Michael O'Keefe, Max Phipps, Jenny Seagrove, Bruce Allpress, Grant Tilley

Savage Messiah *
GB 1972 103m Metrocolor
MGM/Russ-Arts (Ken Russell)
The life together (1910–14) of the 18-year-old painter Gaudier and 38-year-old Sophie Brzeska.
Intense, fragmentary art film about two eccentrics; would have better suited TV.
w Christopher Logue *book* H. S. Ede *d* Ken Russell *ph* Dick Bush *m* Michael Garrett *pd* Derek Jarman
☆ Dorothy Tutin, Scott Anthony, Helen Mirren, Lindsay Kemp, Michael Gough, John Justin

'1986. Passion, Rage, Liberty and Love.'
Savage Nights *
France 1992 126m colour
Banfilm Ter/La Sept/Erre/Canal/Sofinergie II/CNC (Nella Banfi)
original title: *Les Nuits Fauves*
A bisexual cameraman begins an affair with a 17-year-old girl without telling her he is HIV positive; she finds it impossible to share him with others.
A rawly emotional film about sex, love and death and rootless, excitement-seeking young people, often hysterical in tone and curiously uninvolving.
wd Cyril Collard *novel* *Les Nuits Fauves* by Cyril Collard *ph* Manuel Téran *m* Cyril Collard and others *ed* Lise Beaulieu
☆ Cyril Collard, Romane Bohringer, Carlos Lopez, Corine Blue, Claude Winter, René-Marc Bini, Maria Schneider, Clémentine Célarié
'The movie finally confounds everyone's best intentions, including the audience's. It is both sensational and sentimentalized. It ricochets from one lurid fresco to another.' – *Richard Corliss, Time*
† Cyril Collard died of AIDS in 1993, four days before his film won French César awards for best film, best first film, best female newcomer (Romane Bohringer) and best editing.

Savage Pampas
Spain/Argentina/US 1967 108m Eastmancolor Superpanorama
Jaime Prados-Dasa-Sam Bronston
In 19th-century Argentina the commander of an isolated fort finds that a bandit is bribing his men to desert.
Densely plotted semi-Western, sometimes good to look at but slow and lugubrious.
w Hugo Fregonese, John Melson *d* Hugo Fregonese *ph* Marcel Berenguer *m* Waldo de los Rios
☆ Robert Taylor, Ron Randell, Ty Hardin, Rosenda Monteros, Marc Lawrence

Savage Princess: see *Aan*

Savage Sam *
US 1962 104m Technicolor
Walt Disney (Bill Anderson)
The youngest son of a homesteading family has a troublesome dog which redeems itself by tracking down Apaches.
Folksy boy-and-dog Western, good of its kind, with adequate suspense and scenery.
w Fred Gipson, William Tunberg *d* Norman Tokar *ph* Edward Colman *m* Oliver Wallace
☆ Brian Keith, Tommy Kirk, Kevin Corcoran, Dewey Martin, Jeff York
'A cadet edition of the best of Ford.' – *MFB*

Savage Wilderness
US 1956 98m Technicolor Cinemascope
Columbia (William Fadiman)
GB title: *The Last Frontier*
An Indian-hating fort commander puts himself and his charges in jeopardy.
Standard Western with good performances and excellent action scenes.
w Philip Yordan, Russell S. Hughes *novel* *The Gilded Rooster* by Richard Emery Roberts *d* Anthony Mann *ph* William Mellor *m* Leigh Harline
☆ Victor Mature, *Robert Preston*, Guy Madison, Anne Bancroft, James Whitmore, Peter Whitney

Savages
US 1972 106m colour
Angelika/Merchant-Ivory (Joseph Saleh)
Forest wanderers take over a deserted mansion and begin to feel its civilizing influence.
Mild fable which needed a Buñuel to do it justice; a few lively moments.
w George Swift Trow, Michael O'Donoghue *d* James Ivory *ph* Walter Lassally *m* Joe Raposo
☆ Lewis J. Stadlen, Anne Francine, Thayer David, Salome Jens, Neil Fitzgerald
'Adds up to a disappointing and indigestible blend of flip anthropological metaphor, sophomoric gags and intentional or unintentional visual nods to other directors.' – *Nigel Andrews, MFB*

Savannah Smiles
US 1983 107m CFI
Embassy/Hal Clifford/Mark Miller, Donald J. Williams (Clark L. Paylow)
An escaped convict and his partner inadvertently kidnap a millionaire's young daughter
Tedious and clumsy romp, in which a strong willed child turns the tables on two hardened criminals.
w Mark Miller *d* Pierre De Moro *ph* Stephen W. Gray *m* Ken Sutherland *pd* Charles Sewart *ed* Eva Ruggiero
☆ Mark Miller (Alvie), Donovan Scott (Boots), Bridgette Andersen (Savannah), Peter Graves (Harland Dobbs), Chris Robinson (Richard Driscoll), Michael Parks (Lt Savage), Barbara Stanger (Joan Driscoll), Pat Morita (Father O'Hara), Philip Abbott (Chief Pruitt)

'The Only Person You Need To Be Is Yourself.'
Save The Last Dance
US 2001 112m DeLuxe
Paramount/MTV (Robert W. Cort, David Madden)
A white girl who wants to be a ballet dancer moves to a new school in Chicago, where she learns to love hip-hop and the black youth who shows it to her.
A 'teen romance with a little grit and a modicum of charm that went down well with its target audience.
w Duane Adler, Cheryl Edwards *d* Thomas Carter *ph* Robbie Greenberg *m* Mark Isham *ch* Fatima, Randy Duncan *pd* Paul Eads *ed* Peter E. Berger
☆ Julia Stiles (Sara), Sean Patrick Thomas (Derek), Kerry Washington (Chenille), Fredro Starr (Malakai), Terry Kinney (Roy), Bianca Lawson (Nikki), Vince Green (Snookie), Garland Whitt (Kenny)
'The setup promises clichés, but the development is intelligent, the characters are more complicated than we expect, and the ending doesn't tie everything up in a predictable way.' – *Roger Ebert, Chicago Sun-Times*
'The film has a lot of surface complication but no attention span; it's a centimeter deep.' – *Elvis Mitchell, New York Times*

'Juggle the books. Set fire to the factory. Supply women for the clients. Harry Stoner will do anything to get one more season.'
Save the Tiger *
US 1973 100m Movielab
Paramount/Jalem/Filmways/Cirandinha (Steve Shagan)
A middle-aged businessman regrets the slack morality of modern America.
Self-adulatory drama which really has little point but gets a few marks for meaning well and for vivid scenes.
w Steve Shagan *d* John G. Avildsen *ph* Jim Crabe *m* Marvin Hamlisch
☆ *Jack Lemmon, Jack Gilford*, Laurie Heineman, Norman Burton, Thayer David
'A scathing indictment of the US, of materialism, war, marriage – the works. Wordy, literate and deeply felt.' – *NFT, 1974*
'Not a very good movie but it's rather a brave one, a serious-minded examination of some of the least interesting aspects of the failed American Dream.' – *Vincent Canby, New York Times*
Jack Lemmon
Steve Shagan; Jack Gilford

Saving Grace
US 1986 112m Technicolor Technovision
Columbia/Embassy (Herbert F. Solow)
A Pope escapes from office to meet the real people.
The trouble with this movie is, he learns nothing by doing so.
w Joaquin Montana *novel* Celia Gittelson *d* Robert M. Young *ph* Reynaldo Villalobos
☆ Tom Conti, Fernando Rey, Erland Josephson, Giancarlo Giannini, Donald Hewlett
'More sleeping draught than balm for the spirits.' – *Sight and Sound*

'Take the high road to a comedy that truly lights up.'
Saving Grace
GB 1999 94m DeLuxe
TCF/Portman/Sky/Wave/Homerun (Mark Crowdy)

A hard-up widow resorts to growing marijuana to make ends meet.
Genial comedy that stretches its one joke, of genteel drug dealers and users, further than it can go.
w Craig Ferguson, Mark Crowdy *d* Nigel Cole *ph* John de Borman *m* Mark Russell *pd* Eve Stewart *ed* Alan Strachan
☆ Brenda Blethyn (Grace), Craig Ferguson (Matthew), Martin Clunes (Dr Bamford), Tcheky Karyo (Jacques), Jamie Forman (China), Bill Bailey (Vince), Valerie Edmond (Nicky), Tristan Sturrock (Harvey), Clive Merrison (Quentin), Leslie Phillips (Vicar), Diana Quick (Honey), Phyllida Law (Margaret)
'We're left with a promising idea for a comedy, which arrives at some laughs but never finds its destination.' – *Roger Ebert*
'A spiritedly daft and droll gem of straight-faced lunacy...harvests a bumper crop of laughs.' – *Joe Leydon, Variety*

'The mission is a man.'
Saving Private Ryan ***
US 1998 169m Technicolor
Paramount/Amblin/Mutual (Steven Spielberg, Ian Bryce, Mark Gordon, Gary Levinsohn)

After surviving the D-Day landings, eight soldiers are sent on a special mission to bring back a private, the only survivor of four brothers, who is somewhere behind enemy lines.
Two battles, the opening sequence on the Omaha beach and a later one in a ruined town, are virtuoso demonstrations of the director's art; in between, though, the film settles for a standard platoon-in-peril routine familiar from other war movies.
w Robert Rodat *d Steven Spielberg ph Janusz Kaminski m* John Williams *pd* Tom Sanders *ed Michael Kahn*
☆ Tom Hanks, Edward Burns, Tom Sizemore, Jeremy Davies, Vin Diesel, Adam Goldberg, Barry Pepper, Giovanni Ribisi, Matt Damon, Dennis Farina, Ted Danson, Harve Presnell, Harrison Young
'As powerful, devastating, memorable and moving as movies get.' – *Ian Freer, Empire*
'One of the greatest war movies ever made.' – *James Cameron-Wilson, Film Review*
† The film took more than $460m at the box-office worldwide.
Steven Spielberg; Janusz Kaminski; Michael Kahn; sound; sound effects editing
best picture; Tom Hanks; Robert Rodat; John Williams; Tom Sanders; make-up
visual effects; sound

'2 Best Friends + 1 Girlfriend = War'
Saving Silverman
US/Australia/Canada 2001 90m DeLuxe Super 35
Columbia TriStar/Village Roadshow/NPV/Original (Neal H. Moritz)

GB title: *Evil Woman*
Two friends kidnap the uptight fiancée of their oldest buddy so that he will be reunited with his childhood sweetheart, who plans to become a nun.
Tired, trivial movie about the members of a Neil Diamond tribute band, with even an appearance by Diamond himself, which is about as funny as it gets.
w Hank Nelken, Greg DePaul *d* Dennis Dugan *ph* Arthur Albert *m* Mike Simpson *pd* Michael Bolton *ed* Debra Neil-Fisher
☆ Jason Biggs (Darren Silverman), Steve Zahn (Wayne), Jack Black (J. D.), Amanda Peet (Judith), R. Lee Ermey (Coach), Amanda Detmer (Sandy), Neil Diamond (Himself), Lillian Carlson (Mother Superior)
'It manages to be nasty, cynical and dull at the same time.' – *Peter Bradshaw, Guardian*
'Really stinks. No, really. It's bad. Awful.' – *Desson Howe, Washington Post*
† The movie was budgeted at around $22m; it took less than $20m at the US box office.

'Hope is worth fighting for.'
'He's fighting a war he doesn't believe in, hoping to find something he does.'
Savior
US 1998 103m DeLuxe Panavision
First Independent/Initial Entertainment (Oliver Stone, Janet Yang)

An American mercenary, fighting for the Serbians in Bosnia, helps deliver the baby of a woman raped by Muslims and tries to get them both to safety, while threatened by both sides in the civil war.
Topical and melodramatic war movie that simplifies a complex situation in order to make an obvious point.
w Robert Orr *d* Peter Antonijevic *ph* Ian Wilson *m* David Robbins *pd* Vladislav Lasic *ed* Ian Crafford, Gabriella Cristiani
☆ Dennis Quaid, Nastassja Kinski, Stellan Skarsgard, Natasa Ninkovic, Sergej Trifunovic, Nebojsa Glogovac, Vesna Trivalic
'Grim but engrossing pic ... has little going for it commercially but is an impressive addition to the war-as-existential-battlefield genre that dates back to the '50s.' – *Derek Elley, Variety*

Saviour of the Soul
Hong Kong 1992 90m colour
Team Work (Andy Lau)

In the 21st century, a city soldier tries to protect the woman he loves from a ruthless criminal, Silver Fox, who has supernatural powers.
A movie in comic-book style, with little in the way of comprehensible narrative; it relies instead on immature notions of romantic love, and outbursts of spectacular, well-choreographed and violent action to compensate for its paper-thin characterizations.
w Kar-Wai Wong *d* Yuen Kwai, David Lai
☆ Andy Lau, Anita Mui, Aaron Kwok
'*The Water Margin* is crossed with manga and *Blade Runner* in this imaginative sci-fi action movie.' – *Sight and Sound*
† The English subtitles are often in a language all their own: 'We'll treat him some nutrious soup'; 'It's useless to have force, but should have brain!'; and 'I think you are guest so I give you some face.'

Sawdust and Tinsel *
Sweden 1953 95m bw
Svensk Filmindustri

aka: *The Naked Night*
original title: *Gycklarnas Afton*
The owner of a travelling circus leaves his mistress for his separated wife, and is challenged to fight by the mistress's new lover.
Powerfully-made yet rather pointless melodrama about unpleasant people.
wd Ingmar Bergman ph Sven Nykvist *m* Karl-Birger Blomdahl
☆ Harriet Andersson, Ake Grönberg, Hasse Ekman, Annika Tretow
'One of the extremely rare instances of a film's elements all blending perfectly.' – *John Simon*

Sax Rohmer's The Blood of Fu Manchu
GB/Germany/Spain 1969 92m colour
Udastex (Harry Alan Towers)
aka: *Fu Manchu and the Kiss of Death*
US title: *Kiss and Kill*
Fu Manchu infects ten beautiful women with a deadly poison and sends them out into the world to kill his enemies by kissing them.
Feeble and inchorent adventure; despite Lee's top billing he pops up only occasionally as a passive figure, with the action depending upon the rest of the mostly inadequate cast and its cackling villains.
w Peter Welbeck (Harry Alan Towers) *d* Jess Franco *ph* Manuel Merino *m* Daniel White *ed* Alan Morrison
☆ Christopher Lee (Fu Manchu), Tsai Chin (Lin Tang), Maria Rohm (Ursula), Howard Marion Crawford (Dr Petrei), Frances Kahn (Carmen), Isaura De Oliveira (Yuma), Richard Greene (Nayland Smith), Gotz George (Carl), Ricardo Palacios (Sanco), Shirley Eaton
'Fundamentally, the weakness of the series was lack of trust in Sax Rohmer.' – *Christopher Lee*

The Saxon Charm
US 1948 88m bw
Universal (Joseph Sistrom)
A Broadway impresario dominates the lives of those around him.
Rather heavy-going comedy drama which could have done with more malicious wit; allegedly based on Jed Harris.
wd Claude Binyon *novel* Frederick Wakeman *ph* Milton Krasner *m* Walter Scharf
☆ Robert Montgomery, Susan Hayward, John Payne, Audrey Totter, Henry Morgan, Harry von Zell, Cara Williams, Chill Wills, Heather Angel

'To know Lloyd Dobler is to love him. Diane Court is about to know Lloyd Dobler.'
Say Anything... *
US 1989 100m DeLuxe
TCF (Polly Platt)

A student whose ambition it is to become a kick-boxer dates a beautiful and brainy girl, to the distress of her father.
Better than average teenage romance, deft and sometimes witty.
wd Cameron Crowe *ph* Laszlo Kovacs *m* Richard Gibbs, Anne Dudley, Nancy Wilson *pd* Mark Mansbridge *ed* Richard Marks
☆ John Cusack, Ione Skye, John Mahoney, Lili Taylor, Amy Brooks, Pamela Segall, Jason Gould, Joan Cusack, Lois Chiles
'One of the best films of 1989 – a film that is really about something, that cares deeply about the issues it contains – and yet it also works wonderfully as a funny, warmhearted romantic comedy.' – *Roger Ebert*

'My husband has a memory that you can never share – he can remember me when I was nineteen'
Say Hello to Yesterday
GB 1970 92m Eastmancolor
Josef Shaftel (William Hill)

A middle-aged married woman goes to London for shopping and is pursued by a strange young man whom she allows to seduce her.
Unattractive 'with it' romantic drama with a swinging London setting, a long way after Brief Encounter.
w Alvin Rakoff, Peter King *d* Alvin Rakoff *ph* Geoffrey Unsworth *m* Riz Ortolani
☆ Jean Simmons, Leonard Whiting, *Evelyn Laye*, John Lee, Jack Woolgar

Say It in French
US 1938 67m bw
Paramount
A golf champion marries a French girl, but on his return, in order to help his father's finances, has to pretend to be marrying a rich girl, so his wife pretends to be a maid.
Thin comedy which has a job to sustain its short running time.
w Frederick Jackson *play* Jacques Deval *d* Andrew L. Stone
☆ Ray Milland, Olympe Bradna, Irene Hervey, Janet Beecher, Mary Carlisle, Holmes Herbert, Erik Rhodes
'The harder it strives for hare-brained badinage, the more laboured it becomes.' – *Variety*

Say It Isn't So
US 2001 96m DeLuxe
TCF/Conundrum (Bobby Farrelly, Bradley Thomas, Peter Farrelly)

An orphan makes love to a hairdresser and then discovers that she may be his sister.
Infantile comedy that does its feeble best to shock with gross jokes; even its target adolescent audience must by now be tiring of such witless, poorly constructed stuff.
w Peter Gaulke, Gerry Swallow *d* J. B. Rogers *ph* Mark Irwin *m* Mason Daring *pd* Sidney J. Bartholomew Jnr *ed* Larry Madaras *cos* Lisa Jensen
☆ Chris Klein (Gilly Noble), Heather Graham (Jo Wingfield), Orlando Jones (Dig McCaffey), Sally Field (Valdine Wingfield), Richard Jenkins (Walter Wingfield), John Rothman (Larry Falwell), Jack Plotnick (Leon Pitofsky), Eddie Cibrian (Jack Mitchelson)
'Heavy-handed comedy of the very worst kind. Has the gross-out teen sex comedy bubble burst? On this evidence, please God, say it is so...' – *Chris Hewitt, Empire*
'An uninspired dud.' – *New York Times*

Say It with Flowers (A Human Story) *
GB 1934 71m bw
Real Art (Julius Hagen)
Traders in a London street market rally round when a flower-seller becomes too ill to work.
A mix of music-hall jokes and a documentary on Cockney life which, for all its caricatures, reveals more about the everyday life of its time than many more ambitious films. It has not only acquired the fascination of a social document but also gives a rare glimpse of several music-hall performers: Charles Coburn (singing 'The Man Who Broke the Bank at Monte Carlo'), Marie Kendall (singing 'Did Your First Wife Ever Do That?' and 'Just Like the Ivy'), and Florrie Forde (reprising her hits 'Lassie from Lancashire', 'Has Anybody Here Seen Kelly?', 'Hold Your Hand Out Naughty Boy', 'Oh, Oh Antonio' and 'Down at the Old Bull and Bush').
w H. Fowler Mear *story* William Orton *d John Baxter ph* Sydney Blythe *md* Colin Wark *ad* James A. Carter *ed* Michael C. Chorlton
☆ Mary Clare, Ben Field, George Carney, Mark Daly, Edgar Driver, Freddie Watts, Edwin Ellis, Wilson Coleman

Say It with Songs
US 1929 89m bw
Warner

A radio singer accidentally kills a man and is jailed for manslaughter.
Miscalculated star vehicle with a few good moments among the sentiment and melodrama.
w Darryl F. Zanuck, Joseph Jackson, Harvey Gates *d* Lloyd Bacon *ph* Lee Garmes
☆ Al Jolson, Davey Lee, Marian Nixon, Fred Kohler, Holmes Herbert
† Though Jolson was paid half a million dollars to do it, the film was a tremendous flop. The songs were again by De Sylva, Brown and Henderson, but 'Little Pal' was not another 'Sonny Boy'.

Say One for Me
US 1959 117m DeLuxe Cinemascope
TCF/Bing Crosby (Frank Tashlin)
Adventures of a parish priest in New York's theatrical quarter.
Unconvincing, unattractive imitation of Going My Way *which counters bad taste with religiosity.*
w Robert O'Brien *d* Frank Tashlin *ph* Leo Tover *md* Lionel Newman *songs* Sammy Cahn, James Van Heusen
☆ Bing Crosby, Robert Wagner, Debbie Reynolds, Ray Walston, Les Tremayne, Connie Gilchrist, Frank McHugh, Joe Besser, Sebastian Cabot
'Tasteless and disturbing.' – *Variety*
Lionel Newman

'I am not allowed to love. But I will love you if that is your desire!'
Sayonara **
US 1957 147m Technirama
Goetz Pictures-Pennebaker (William Goetz)

An American air force major in Tokyo after the war falls in love with a Japanese actress.
A lush travelogue interrupted by two romances, one tragic and one happy. A great success at the time, though mainly of interest to Americans; now vaguely dated.
w Paul Osborn *novel* James A. Michener *d* Joshua Logan *ph Ellsworth Fredericks m* Franz Waxman *ad* Ted Haworth *ed* Arthur P. Schmidt, Philip W. Anderson
☆ Marlon Brando, Miyoshi Umeki, Miiko Taka, Red Buttons, Ricardo Montalban, Patricia Owens, Kent Smith, Martha Scott, James Garner
Miyoshi Umeki; Red Buttons; art direction
best picture; Paul Osborn; Joshua Logan; Ellsworth Fredericks; Marlon Brando; editing

Scalawag
US/Italy 1973 93m Technicolor
Bryna/Inex-Oceania (Anne Douglas)
Mexico 1840: a one-legged pirate and a boy try to trace a hidden treasure.
Flagrant reworking of Treasure Island, *heavily overdone by stars and rhubarbing extras alike.*
w Albert Maltz, Sid Fleischman *d* Kirk Douglas *ph* Jack Cardiff *m* John Cameron
☆ Kirk Douglas, Mark Lester, Neville Brand, Don Stroud, Lesley-Anne Down, Phil Brown

The Scalphunters *
US 1968 102m DeLuxe Panavision
UA/Bristol/Norlan (Levy-Gardner-Laven)
An old cowboy and a black ex-slave track down a gang who kill Indians for their scalps.
Vigorous, aimless, likeable comedy Western with the emphasis on brawling.
w William Norton *d* Sydney Pollack *ph* Duke Callaghan, Richard Moore *m* Elmer Bernstein
☆ *Burt Lancaster*, *Ossie Davis*, Telly Savalas, Shelley Winters, Nick Cravat, Paul Picerni
'It is the sort of frolic where bodies litter the ground, but you know they'll get up and draw their pay. And where even a villain can crack a joke without losing face.' – *Robert Ottaway*

The Scamp
GB 1957 90m bw
Minter/Renown (James H. Lawrie)
A couple decide to adopt a lovable but mischievous boy.
Amiable minor film, a vehicle for a child actor who had made an impression in Smiley (qv) the year before, a success he was never to recapture.
wd Wolf Rilla *play* Charlotte Hastings *ph* Freddie Francis *m* Francis Chagrin *ad* Elven Webb *ed* Bernard Gribble
☆ Colin Petersen, Richard Attenborough, Dorothy Alison, Terence Morgan, Jill Adams, Sam Kydd, Margaretta Scott, Geoffrey Keen, Charles Lloyd Pack

Scandal *
GB 1988 115m Fujicolour
Palace/Miramax/British Screen (Stephen Woolley)
A showgirl's sexual relationships with a leading British politician and a Russian diplomat cause a major upset.
Leaden account of the British scandal of the 1960s involving Christine Keeler, osteopath Stephen Ward and John Profumo, a Conservative Minister.
w Michael Thomas *d* Michael Caton-Jones *ph* Mike Molloy *m* Carl Davis *pd* Simon Holland *ed* Angus Newton
☆ John Hurt, Joanne Whalley-Kilmer, Ian McKellen, Bridget Fonda, Leslie Phillips, Britt Ekland, Daniel Massey, Roland Gift, Jeroen Krabbé

Scandal at Scourie
US 1953 90m Metrocolor
MGM (Edwin H. Knopf)
The wife of the Protestant reeve of a Scottish-Canadian Protestant community adopts a Catholic child.
Sentimental whimsy with no holds barred, but with rather jaded acting and production.
w Norman Corwin, Leonard Spigelgass, Karl Tunberg *d* Jean Negulesco *ph* Robert Planck *m* Daniele Amfitheatrof
☆ Greer Garson, Walter Pidgeon, Agnes Moorehead, Arthur Shields, Philip Ober, Donna Corcoran

A Scandal in Paris *
US 1946 100m bw
UA/Arnold Pressburger
aka: *Thieves' Holiday*
Adventures of Vidocq, a 19th-century rogue who became Paris chief of police.
The actors look uneasy in their costumes, and the sets are cardboard, but there is fun to be had from this light comedy-drama.
w Ellis St Joseph *d* Douglas Sirk *ph* Guy Roe *m* Hanns Eisler
☆ George Sanders, Signe Hasso, Carole Landis, Akim Tamiroff, Gene Lockhart

Scandal Sheet
US 1931 77m bw
Paramount
A newspaper editor with principles prints scandal involving his wife.
Dated star drama.
w Vincent Lawrence, Max Marcin *d* John Cromwell
☆ George Bancroft, Kay Francis, Regis Toomey, Clive Brook

Scandal Sheet
US 1939 67m bw
Columbia
A ruthless publisher sacrifices himself to save his son.
Uninteresting star quickie.
w Joseph Carole *d* Nick Grinde
☆ Otto Kruger, Ona Munson, Edward Norris

Scandal Sheet
US 1952 81m bw
Columbia (Edward Small)
GB title: *The Dark Page*
An editor has to allow his star reporter to expose a murderer – himself.
Obvious, reasonably holding melodrama with familiar characters.
w Ted Sherdeman, Eugene Ling, James Poe *novel* Samuel Fuller *d* Phil Karlson *ph* Burnett Guffey *m* George Duning
☆ Broderick Crawford, John Derek, Donna Reed, Rosemary de Camp, Henry O'Neill, Henry Morgan

Scandal Street
US 1938 63m bw
Paramount
The arrival in a small town of an innocent young girl causes gossip which leads to murder.
Satisfactory mini-drama for the easily pleased.
w Bertram Millhauser, Eddie Welch *story* Vera Caspary *d* James Hogan
☆ Lew Ayres, Louise Campbell, Roscoe Karns, Porter Hall, Virginia Weidler, Edgar Kennedy, Elizabeth Patterson
'A curiously beguiling little hodge-podge.' – *Variety*

Le Scandale: see *The Champagne Murders*

Scandalous!
GB 1984 92m Technicolor
Hemdale/Raleigh/Angeles Cinema Investors (Arlene Sellers, Alex Winitsky)
A TV reporter becomes involved with two con artists, who seem to have some connection with the murder of his wife.
Frantic black comedy which never even begins to be funny.
w Rob Cohen, John Byrum *d* Rob Cohen *ph* Jack Cardiff *m* Dave Grusin *pd* Peter Mullins
☆ Robert Hays, John Gielgud, Pamela Stephenson, M. Emmet Walsh, Nancy Wood, Jim Dale

Scandalous John
US 1971 117m Technicolor
Walt Disney (Bill Walsh)
The elderly owner of a derelict ranch resists all efforts to close him up.
Unsatisfactory Disney attempt to capture a more adult audience than usual; overlong, repetitious and dreary.
w Bill Walsh, Don da Gradi *novel* Richard Gardner *d* Robert Butler *ph* Frank Phillips *m* Rod McKuen
☆ Brian Keith, Alfonso Arau, Michele Carey, Rick Lenz, Henry Morgan, Simon Oakland

Scanner Cop
Canada 1993 94m FotoKem
Image (Pierre David)
When ordinary citizens begin to murder policemen, a young cop applies his dangerous telepathic abilities to solve the crime.
An attempt to take the Scanner series away from horror into another action genre and a more character-driven narrative; it is unfortunate that the characters on display are not very interesting.
w George Saunders, John Bryant *story* Pierre David *d* Pierre David *ph* Jacques Haitkin *m* Louis Febre *pd* Deborah Richmond, Dorian Vernacchio *ed* Julian Semilian *sp* John Carl Buechler; Magical Media *cos* Yana Syrkin
☆ Daniel Quinn (Samuel Stazlak), Darlanne Fluegel (Dr Joan Alden), Richard Grove (Cdr Peter Harrigan), Mark Rolston (Lt Brown), Hilary Shepard (Zena), James Horan (Melvin), Gary Hudson (Damon Pratt), Cyndi Pass (Sara Kopek), Luca Bercovici (Dr Krench), Christopher Kriesa (Riley), Brion James (Dr Hampton), Richard Lynch (Glock)

'Their thoughts can kill!'
Scanners
Canada 1980 103m Eastmancolor
Filmplan International (Claude Heroux)
Certain people are found to be telepathic 'scanners' able to lock at will into other people's nervous systems. This has the occasional result of blowing apart the other people's heads.
Overlong science fiction which concentrates on the nastier elements.
wd David Cronenberg *ph* Mark Irwin *m* Howard Shore
☆ Jennifer O'Neill, Patrick McGoohan, Stephen Lack, Lawrence Dane, Michael Ironside

Scanners II: The New Order
Canada 1991 104m colour
Malofilm (René Malo)
A corrupt police chief attempts to use people with frightening telepathic powers for his own ends.
Effective sequel with several exploding heads.
w B. J. Nelson *d* Christian Duguay *ph* Rodney Gibbons *m* Marty Simon *pd* Richard Tassé *ed* Yves Langlois *sp* Michael Smithson
☆ David Hewlett, Yvan Ponton, Deborah Raffin, Isabelle Majias, Raoul Trujillo, Tom Butler, Vlasta Vrana
'A first class imitation of the mind-blowing original.' – *Variety*

Scanners III: The Takeover
Canada 1992 101m colour
Republic/Malofilm (Rene Malo)
An experimental drug turns a female scanner into a power-hungry killer.
The intriguing notion of the first film has now become an excuse for a horror movie indistinguishable from, and no more distinguished than, a hundred others.
w B. J. Nelson, Julie Richard, David Preston, Christian Duguay *d* Christian Duguay *ph* Hughes de Haeck *m* Marty Simon *pd* Michael Joy *ed* Yves Langlois *sp* Mike Maddi
☆ Liliana Komorowska, Valerie Valois, Steve Parrish, Colin Fox, Daniel Pilon, Michel Perron, Harry Hill
'A technically slick, relatively mindless thriller.' – *Variety*

The Scapegoat *
GB 1959 92m bw
MGM/Du Maurier-Guinness (Dennis Van Thal)
A quiet bachelor on a French holiday is tricked into assuming the identity of a lookalike aristocrat who wants to commit a murder.
Disappointing adaptation of a good story, with much evidence of re-cutting and an especially slack middle section.
w Gore Vidal, Robert Hamer *novel* Daphne du Maurier *d* Robert Hamer *ph* Paul Beeson *m* Bronislau Kaper
☆ Alec Guinness, Bette Davis, Irene Worth, Nicole Maurey, Pamela Brown, Geoffrey Keen
'A disaster.' – *Daphne du Maurier*

The Scar
US 1948 83m bw
Eagle-Lion (Bryan Foy, Paul Henreid)
aka: *Hollow Triumph*
A fugitive kills his psychoanalyst double and takes his place, but is caught for the double's crimes.
Cheap suspense thriller with no suspense and no surprises.
w Daniel Fuchs *novel* Murray Forbes *d* Steve Sekely *ph* John Alton *m* Sol Kaplan
☆ Joan Bennett, Paul Henreid, Eduard Franz, Leslie Brooks, John Qualen, Mabel Paige, Herbert Rudley

Scaramouche **
US 1952 115m Technicolor
MGM (Carey Wilson)
A young man disguises himself as an actor to avenge the death of his friend at the hands of a wicked marquis.
Cheerful swashbuckler set in French revolutionary times, first filmed in the twenties with Ramon Novarro. MGM costume production at somewhere near its best.
w Ronald Millar, George Froeschel *novel* Rafael Sabatini *d* George Sidney *ph* Charles Rosher *m* Victor Young *ad* *Cedric Gibbons*, *Hans Peters*
☆ Stewart Granger, Mel Ferrer, Eleanor Parker, Janet Leigh, Henry Wilcoxon, Nina Foch, Lewis Stone, Robert Coote, Richard Anderson
† The sword fight, at 6½ minutes, is credited with being the longest in cinema history.

Scarecrow *
US 1973 112m Technicolor Panavision
Warner (Robert M. Sherman)
Two of the world's losers hitch-hike across America.
Well-shot but eventually dreary parable of friendship, a pedestrian Easy Rider.
w Garry Michael White *d* Jerry Schatzberg *ph* Vilmos Zsigmond *m* Fred Myrow
☆ Gene Hackman, Al Pacino
'Here's a picture that manages to abuse two American myths at once – the Road and the Male Pair.' – *Stanley Kauffmann*

The Scarecrow *
New Zealand 1981 88m colour
Oasis/New Zealand National Film Unit (Rob Whitehouse)
In a small town in the early fifties, a strange chain of events is set in motion by the disappearance of six chickens.
A curious mix of sinister atmosphere which seems mystical and sinister events which are all too real. Interesting but unsatisfying, both as a murder mystery and as a study in evil.
w Michael Heath, Sam Pillsbury *novel* Ronald Hugh Morrieson *d* Sam Pillsbury *ph* James Bartle *m* Schtung
☆ John Carradine, Tracy Mann, Jonathan Smith, Daniel McLaren, Denise O'Connell, Anne Flannery

'They're making a spook-tacle of themselves!'
Scared Stiff
US 1953 108m bw
Paramount (Hal B. Wallis)
Night-club entertainers get involved with a girl who has inherited a spooky castle off the Cuban coast.
Stretched-out remake of The Ghost Breakers; *the last half hour, being closest to the original, is the most nearly funny.*
w Herbert Baker, Walter de Leon, Ed Simmons, Norman Lear *d* George Marshall *ph* Ernest Laszlo *md* Joseph J. Lilley
☆ Dean Martin, Jerry Lewis, Lizabeth Scott, Carmen Miranda, George Dolenz, Dorothy Malone, William Ching, Jack Lambert

Scared to Death
US 1947 65m Cinecolor
Golden Gate
A corpse explains how it came to be dead.
Eccentric mystery set in a sanatorium presided over by a mad doctor; the green-tinged colour adds to the atmosphere.
w Walter Abbott *d* Christy Cabanne *ph* Marcel Le Picard *m* Carl Hoefle *ad* Harry Reif *ed* George McGuire
☆ Bela Lugosi, Douglas Fowley, Joyce Compton, George Zucco, Nat Pendleton, Angelo Rossitto, Molly Lamont
† It was released on DVD together with *Devil Bat* (qv).

The Scarf
US 1951 86m bw
UA/Gloria (I. G. Goldsmith)
A man escapes from a lunatic asylum and proves himself innocent of the crime for which he was committed.
Glum and pretentious murder mystery with a pictorial style to match its flowery dialogue.
wd E. A. Dupont *ph* Franz Planer *m* Herschel Burke Gilbert
☆ John Ireland, Mercedes McCambridge, Emlyn Williams, James Barton, Lloyd Gough, Basil Ruysdael

'I'm going to run the whole works. There's only one law: do it first, do it yourself, and keep doing it!'

Scarface **
US 1932 99m bw
Howard Hughes
aka: *The Shame of a Nation*
The life and death of a Chicago gangster of the twenties.
Obviously modelled on Al Capone, with an incestuous sister thrown in, this was perhaps the most vivid film of the gangster cycle, and its revelling in its own sins was not obscured by the subtitle, The Shame of a Nation.
w Ben Hecht, Seton I. Miller, John Lee Mahin, W. R. Burnett, Fred Pasley *novel* Armitage Trail
d Howard Hawks ph Lee Garmes, L. W. O'Connell
m Adolph Tandler, Gus Arnheim
☆ *Paul Muni, Ann Dvorak, George Raft,* Boris Karloff, Osgood Perkins, Karen Morley, C. Henry Gordon, Vince Barnett, Henry Armetta, Edwin Maxwell
'Presumably the last of the gangster films, on a promise, it is going to make people sorry that there won't be any more. Should draw wherever it can play.' – *Variety*
'More brutal, more cruel, more wholesale than any of its predecessors.' – *James Shelley Hamilton*
'Because it was so close to the actual events, it possesses a kind of newsreel quality which cannot be recaptured or imitated. It vibrates with the impact of things that were real and deeply felt.' – *National Film Theatre programme, 1961*
† On original release added scenes showed Tony tried, convicted and hanged, though since Muni is never seen, it appears that they were an afterthought made when he was not available.

'He loved the American Dream. With a vengeance.'

Scarface
US 1983 170m Technicolor Panavision
Universal (Martin Bregman)
Absurdly brutalized version of the above, with detailed violence and a superabundance of foul language. Scarface has now become an emigré Cuban, and the film seems to want to make a political statement.
w Oliver Stone *d* Brian de Palma *ph* John A. Alonzo *m* Giorgio Moroder
☆ Al Pacino, Steven Bauer, Michelle Pfeiffer, Mary Elizabeth Mastrantonio, Robert Loggia, Paul Shenar, Harris Yulin

The Scarface Mob *
US 1958 96m bw
Desilu (Quinn Martin)
Al Capone's empire thrives while he is in Alcatraz, and prohibition agent Eliot Ness recruits a tough squad to fight the gangsters.
Though released theatrically, this was in effect a pilot film for the successful TV series The Untouchables, *well enough done within its limits.*
w Paul Monash *novel The Untouchables* by Eliot Ness *d* Phil Karlson *ph* Charles Straumer
m Wilbur Hatch
☆ Robert Stack, Neville Brand, Keenan Wynn, Barbara Nichols, Joe Mantell, Pat Crowley, Bruce Gordon, Paul Picerni, Abel Fernandez

Scarlet and Black: see *Le Rouge et le Noir*

Scarlet Angel
US 1952 81m Technicolor
U-I (Leonard Goldstein)
A saloon hostess presents herself to a wealthy family as their dead son's wife.
Modest, satisfactorily plotted picture with action interludes.
w Oscar Brodney *d* Sidney Salkow *ph* Russell Metty *md* Joseph Gershenson *ad* Robert Clatworthy, Bernard Herzbrun *ed* Ted J. Kent
☆ Yvonne de Carlo, Rock Hudson, Richard Denning, Henry O'Neill, Amanda Blake

The Scarlet Blade *
GB 1963 82m Technicolor Hammerscope
Hammer (Anthony Nelson-Keys)
US title: *The Crimson Blade*
In 1648, a Cromwellian colonel plans to hang every royalist rebel.
Adequate swashbuckler.
wd John Gilling ph Jack Asher m Gary Hughes
pd Bernard Robinson *ed* John Dunsford
☆ Lionel Jeffries, Oliver Reed, Jack Hedley, June Thorburn, Duncan Lamont

The Scarlet Buccaneer: see *Swashbuckler*

The Scarlet Claw **
US 1944 74m bw
Universal (Roy William Neill)
Grisly revenge murders take place in the fog-bound Canadian village of Le Mort Rouge.
Possibly the best of the modernized Sherlock Holmes series, with a plot hastily borrowed from The Hound of the Baskervilles.
w Edmund L. Hartmann, Roy William Neill
d Roy William Neill ph George Robinson *m* Hans Salter *md* Paul Sawtell
☆ Basil Rathbone, Nigel Bruce, Miles Mander, Gerald Hamer, Paul Cavanagh, Kay Harding, Arthur Hohl

The Scarlet Coat
US 1955 99m Eastmancolor Cinemascope
MGM (Nicholas Nayfack)
During the American War of Independence, an American officer deserts to the British in order to unmask a traitor.
Rather talky historical actioner with too much time spent on friendship and romance.
w Karl Tunberg *d* John Sturges *ph* Paul C. Vogel
m Conrad Salinger
☆ Cornel Wilde, Michael Wilding, George Sanders, Anne Francis, Robert Douglas, Bobby Driscoll, John McIntire

Scarlet Dawn *
US 1932 76m bw
Warner (Hal Wallis)
During the Russian revolution, an exiled aristocrat loves a serving maid.
Heavy-going romantic drama distinguished by stylish direction and sets.
w Niven Busch, Erwin Gelsey, Douglas Fairbanks Jnr *novel Revolt* by Mary McCall Jnr *d William Dieterle ph* Ernest Haller *ad Anton Grot*
☆ Douglas Fairbanks Jnr, Nancy Carroll, Lilyan Tashman, Guy Kibbee, Sheila Terry, Frank Reicher
'The story starts off to get somewhere but fails to arrive.' – *Variety*

'Based on a private diary of Catherine the Great!'
'The screen's reigning beauty in a wild pageant of barbaric splendour!'
'A cavalcade of fury led by a woman of fire!'

The Scarlet Empress ***
US 1934 109m bw
Paramount
A fantasia on the love life of Catherine the Great.
A marvellous, overwhelming, dramatically insubstantial but pictorially brilliant homage to a star; not to everyone's taste, but a film to remember.
w Manuel Komroff *d Josef von Sternberg ph Bert Glennon md* W. Franke Harling, John M. Leipold, Milan Roder *ad Hans Dreier, Peter Ballbusch, Richard Kollorsz cos Travis Banton*
☆ *Marlene Dietrich, John Lodge, Sam Jaffe,* Louise Dresser, C. Aubrey Smith, Gavin Gordon, Jameson Thomas
'She's photographed behind veils and fishnets, while dwarfs slither about and bells ring and everybody tries to look degenerate.' – *New Yorker, 1975*
'A ponderous, strangely beautiful, lengthy and frequently wearying production.' – *Mordaunt Hall, New York Times*

The Scarlet Hour
US 1955 93m bw Vistavision
Paramount (Michael Curtiz)
A bored wife persuades her lover to turn thief; her husband misconstrues the situation and is accidentally killed.
Complex suspenser designed to introduce new talent; rather too smooth, and pretty boring.
w Rip van Ronkel, Frank Tashlin, Meredyth Lucas
d Michael Curtiz *ph* Lionel Lindon *m* Leith Stevens
☆ Carol Ohmart, Tom Tryon, James Gregory, Jody Lawrance, E. G. Marshall, Elaine Stritch

The Scarlet Letter *
US 1926 90m (24 fps) bw silent
MGM/Jury
In Puritan New England, the mother of an illegitimate child wears the scarlet A (for adulteress) for years rather than reveal that her lover was the village priest.
Celebrated 17th-century melodrama, quite powerfully made in the best silent tradition, but of little intrinsic interest for modern audiences.
w Frances Marion *novel* Nathaniel Hawthorne
d Victor Sjostrom *ph* Henrik Sartov *ad* Cedric Gibbons
☆ Lillian Gish, Lars Hanson, Karl Dane, Henry B. Walthall
† Other versions include the following: US 1910, US 1911, US 1913, US 1917, US 1920, GB 1922, US 1934, Germany 1971, US (TV) 1979.

The Scarlet Letter
US 1934 70m bw
Darmour/Majestic
A lightened version with an attempt at comedy relief.
Not in any way remarkable.
w Leonard Fields, David Silverstein *d* Robert G. Vignola
☆ Colleen Moore, Hardie Albright, Henry B. Walthall, William Farnum, Alan Hale

'When intimacy is forbidden and passion is a sin, love is the most defiant crime of all.'

The Scarlet Letter
US 1995 135m Technicolor
Entertainment/Hollywood/Lightmotive/Allied Stars/Cinergi/Moving Pictures (Roland Joffé, Andrew G. Vajna)
In 17th-century Massachusetts, a settler's wife gives birth to an illegitimate daughter but refuses to name the father of her child.
Hilariously bad period drama, loosely based on Hawthorne's original, with little sense of history or decorum; it respresents Hollywood at its most crass and unthinking.
w Douglas Day Stewart *novel* Nathaniel Hawthorne *d* Roland Joffé *ph* Alex Thomson
m John Barry *pd* Roy Walker *ed* Thom Noble
☆ Demi Moore, Gary Oldman, Robert Duvall, Robert Prosky, Edward Hardwicke, Joan Plowright, Roy Dotrice, Dana Ivey, Lisa Joliff-Andoh
'A campy period piece of pseudo-erotica. It should wear a brand mark all right – but not the letter "A" (for adulteress, and the accompanying spiritual penance). More appropriate would be the letter "V" (for video, which is its only hope of earthly salvation).' – *Alexander Walker*
'Provides all the usual incidental pleasures to be had from Hollywood's frequent bear hugs with great literature – unmappable migrations of thees and thines, an extra with an arrow through his neck who simply will not drop out of sight until he has caught the camera's eye, and – my favourite, this – a proud young Indian beauty with bikini marks. Absolute bliss.' – *Tom Shone, Sunday Times*
'A ponderously overstuffed package. Moore brandishes her scarlet letter snootily, as if she'd been forced to wear something from last year's fashion collections.' – *Owen Gleiberman, Entertainment Weekly*
† The film was not given a press show when it opened in Britain.

The Scarlet Pimpernel ***
GB 1934 98m bw
London Films (Alexander Korda)
In the early days of the French revolution, an apparently foppish Englishman leads a daring band in rescuing aristocrats from the guillotine.
First-class period adventure with a splendid and much imitated plot, strong characters, humour and a richly detailed historical background.
w Robert E. Sherwood, Sam Berman, Arthur Wimperis, Lajos Biro *novel* Baroness Orczy
d Harold Young ph Harold Rosson *m* Arthur Benjamin
☆ *Leslie Howard, Merle Oberon, Raymond Massey,* Nigel Bruce, Bramwell Fletcher, Anthony Bushell, Joan Gardner, Walter Rilla
'Excellent British import that will do business.' – *Variety*
'One of the most romantic and durable of all swashbucklers.' – *New Yorker, 1976*
'A triumph for the British film world.' – *Sunday Times*
† Some scenes were directed by Alexander Korda, others by Rowland Brown, whom Korda replaced after a few days.
†† The story was remade as *The Elusive Pimpernel* (qv); in 1982 in a TV version starring Anthony Andrews, and in 1998 in a TV version starring Richard E. Grant. See also *The Return of the Scarlet Pimpernel.*

'I've been wanting to laugh in your face ever since I met you. You're old and ugly and I'm sick of you – sick, sick, sick!'

Scarlet Street **
US 1945 103m bw
Universal/Diana (Fritz Lang)
A prostitute is murdered by her client and her pimp is executed for the crime.
Daring but rather gloomy Hollywood melodrama, the first in which a crime went unpunished (though the culprit was shown suffering remorse). Interesting and heavily Teutonic, but as entertainment not a patch on the similar but lighter The Woman in the Window, *which the same team had made a year previously.*
w Dudley Nichols *play La Chienne* by George de la Fouchardière (filmed by Jean Renoir in 1932)
d Fritz Lang ph Milton Krasner *m* Hans Salter
ad Alexander Golitzen, John B. Goodman
ed Arthur Hilton
☆ Edward G. Robinson (Christopher Cross), Joan Bennett (Kitty March), Dan Duryea (Johnny Prince), Jess Barker (Janeway), Margaret Lindsay (Millie), Rosalind Ivan (Adele Cross), Samuel S. Hinds (Charles Pringle), Arthur Loft (Dellarowe)
'The director unerringly chooses the right sound and image to assault the spectator's sensibilities.' – C. A. Lejeune

The Scarlet Thread
GB 1950 84m bw
Nettlefold/Butcher
Jewel thieves take refuge in a Cambridge college.
Flabby melodrama featuring emergent young talent.
w A. R. Rawlinson *play* A. R. Rawlinson, Moie Charles *d* Lewis Gilbert *ph* Geoffrey Faithfull
m Kenneth D. Morrison
☆ Kathleen Byron, Laurence Harvey, Sydney Tafler, Arthur Hill, Dora Bryan

The Scarlet Tunic
GB 1998 91m Fujicolour
Indy/Scarlet/Bigger Picture/Scorpio (Zygi Kamasa, Daniel Figuero)
An English farmer's daughter falls for a handsome German cavalry officer, who is planning to desert from his regiment.
A mundane period romantic drama, worthy but dull.
w Mark Jenkins, Colin Clements, Stuart St Paul *story The Melancholy Hussar of the German Legion* by Thomas Hardy *d* Stuart St Paul *ph* Malcolm McLean *m* John Scott *pd* Richard Elton *ed* Don Fairservice
☆ Jean-Marc Barr, Emma Fielding, Simon Callow, Jack Shepherd, John Sessions, Lynda Bellingham, Thomas Lockyer
'A nicely made film with no surprises.' – *Guardian*
† The film was made for £500,000.

Scars of Dracula
GB 1970 96m Technicolor
Hammer/EMI (Aida Young)
A young man on the run finds himself an unwitting guest of Count Dracula.
Overpadded vampire saga, its few effective moments stemming directly from the original novel.
w John Elder *d* Roy Ward Baker *ph* Moray Grant
m James Bernard *ad* Scott MacGregor *ed* James Needs
☆ Christopher Lee, Dennis Waterman, Christopher Matthews, Jenny Hanley, Patrick Troughton, Michael Gwynn, Bob Todd

'No mercy. No shame. No sequel.'

Scary Movie

US 2000 88m DeLuxe

Dimension/Wayans Bros/Gold-Miller and Brad Grey (Eric L. Gold, Lee R. Mayes)

A killer murders high school students.

With more scriptwriters than jokes, this smuttily feeble spoof of the Scream series of horror movies inexplicably found a mass audience for its tired routines.

w Shawn Wayans, Marlon Wayans, Buddy Johnson, Phil Beauman, Jason Friedberg, Aaron Seltzer *d* Keenen Ivory Wayans *ph* Francis Kenny *m* David Kitay *ad* Lawrence F. Pevec *ed* Mark Helfrich *cos* Darryle Johnson

☆ Shawn Wayans (Ray), Marlon Wayans (Shorty), Cheri Oteri (Gail Hailstorm), Shannon Elizabeth (Buffy), Anna Faris (Cindy Campbell), Jon Abrahams (Bobby), Lochlyn Munro (Greg), Regina Hall (Brenda), Dave Sheridan (Doofy), Dan Joffre (Kenny)

'The grossest manistream Hollywood movie of the year and will be an instant must-see for the biggest cinema-going demographic in the world – the teenage boy.' – *Mike Goodridge, Screen International*

'A spoof this bad, that *is* scary.' – *Times*

† The film cost $20m to make and took $157m at the US box office and another $120m in the rest of the world.

'No More Mercy. No More Shame. No More Sequels – Honest! – We Lied.'

Scary Movie 2

US 2001 83m DeLuxe

Buena Vista/Miramax/Dimension/Wayans Bros (Eric L. Gold)

A psychology professor invites his class to spend a weekend in a haunted house.

A movie with more writers than jokes, which, apart from an Exorcist spoof, are recycled from the first feeble effort; this is even feebler, if that were possible.

w Shawn Wayans, Marlon Wayans, Alyson Fouse, Greg Grabiansky, Dave Polsky, Michael Anthony Snowden, Craig Wayans *d* Keenen Ivory Wayans *ph* Steven Bernstein *pd* Cynthia Charette *ed* Peter Teschner, Tom Nordberg, Richard Pearson

☆ Shawn Wayans (Ray), Marlon Wayans (Shorty), Anna Faris (Cindy), Regina Hall (Brenda), Chris Masterson (Buddy), Kathleen Robertson (Theo), David Cross (Dwight), James Woods (Father McFeely), Tim Curry (The Professor), Tori Spelling (Alex), Chris Elliott (Hanson)

'Never less than pitiful.' – *Andrew Pulver, Guardian*

Scattergood Baines

US 1941 69m bw

RKO

The new owner of a small-town hardware store takes an interest in his fellow men.

First of several second features featuring the exploits of a likeable busybody.

w Michael L. Simmons, Edward T. Lowe *stories* Clarence Budington Kelland *d* Christy Cabanne

☆ *Guy Kibbee*, Carol Hughes, John Archer, Emma Dunn

† The succeeding episodes were as follows: *Scattergood Pulls the Strings*, 1941; *Scattergood Meets Broadway*, 1941; *Scattergood Rides High*, 1942; *Scattergood Survives a Murder*, 1942; *Cinderella Swings It*, 1943.

Scavenger Hunt

US 1979 116m DeLuxe

TCF/Melvin Simon

A rich man leaves a fortune to the member of his family who can collect most of the useless objects in a list provided.

Depressing cheapjack imitation of Kramer's It's a Mad Mad Mad Mad World, *which itself was not free from fault.*

w Steven A. Vail, Henry Harper *d* Michael Schultz *ph* Ken Lamkin *m* Billy Goldenberg

☆ Richard Benjamin, James Coco, Scatman Crothers, Cloris Leachman, Cleavon Little, Roddy McDowall, Robert Morley, Richard Mulligan, Tony Randall, Dirk Benedict, Vincent Price

'Loud, obnoxious, and above all unfunny.' – *Variety*

Lo Sceicco Bianco: see *The White Sheik*

A Scene at the Sea *

Japan 1991 101m colour

ICA/Totsyu/Office Kitano (Masayuki Mori, Takio Yoshida)

original title: *Ano Natsu, Ichiban Shizukana Umi*

A deaf and dumb garbage collector tries to become a champion surfer, with the aid of his girlfriend, who is also a deaf-mute.

A restrained, heartfelt movie of momentary redemption; it is austere throughout, and its ambiguous ending leaves a sense of loss.

wd Takeshi Kitano *ph* Katsumi Yanagishima *m* Joe Hishaishi *ed* Takeshi Kitano

☆ Kurodo Maki, Hiroko Oshima, Sabu Kawahara

'A 'miniature' with huge emotional and even philosophical resonance.' – *Tony Rayns, Sight and Sound*

Scener Ur Ett äktenskap: see *Scenes from a Marriage*

Scenes from a Mall

US 1990 87m DuArt Panavision

Warner/Touchstone/Silver Screen Partners IV (Paul Mazursky)

Preparing to celebrate their sixteenth wedding anniversary, a Los Angeles couple confess their recent affairs while on a shopping spree.

An unsuccessful comic teaming in a wordy celebration of conspicuous consumption.

w Roger L. Simon, Paul Mazursky *d* Paul Mazursky *ph* Fred Murphy *m* Marc Shaiman *pd* Pato Guzman *ed* Stuart Pappé

☆ Bette Midler, Woody Allen, Bill Irwin, Daren Firestone, Rebecca Nickels, Paul Mazursky

Scenes from a Marriage ***

Sweden 1973 168m colour

Cinematograph (Ingmar Bergman)

original title: *Scener Ur Ett äktenskap*

After ten years of marriage, a husband announces to his wife that he is leaving her because he has fallen in love with someone else; over the next ten years they continue to meet and examine their relationship.

Bergman edited the film into feature length from six 50-minute episodes made for television, and the structure of the original remains, with each episode given its own title, moving from Innocence and Panic, *with an apparently happy marriage on display, to* In the Middle of the Night in a Dark House Somewhere in the World, *with the couple, by now remarried to other partners, seeking solace with each other. The time-span gives the characters room to develop: the husband from complacency to wry understanding, the wife from subservience to individuality. It is an unsparing and detailed examination of a relationship, marked by more pain than pleasure, but reaching a hopeful conclusion; it is also, despite its claustrophobic style, of a succession of close-ups of talking heads, rivetting cinema.*

wd Ingmar Bergman ph Sven Nykvist *m* none *ad* Björn Thulin *ed* Siv Lundgren

☆ *Liv Ullmann, Erland Josephson*, Bibi Andersson, Jan Malmsjö, Gunnel Lindblom, Anita Wall

'Shows how habit and conciliatory effort erode communication. But it is ultimately an optimistic film, suggesting that beyond the hell of a return to zero, the knowledge of one's absolute separateness from others can lead through despair to a glowing fulfilment.' – *Jan Dawson, MFB*

Scenes from the Class Struggle in Beverly Hills

US 1989 103m CFI color

Rank/North Street Films/Cinecom Entertainment (Amir J. Malin, Ira Deutchman)

Two servants bet that they can seduce the other's mistress, both of whom have sexual problems of their own.

Bed-hopping black-tinged comedy that never goes quite far enough to be funny.

w Bruce Wagner *story* Paul Bartel, Bruce Wagner *d* Paul Bartel *ph* Steven Fierberg *m* Stanley Myers *pd* Alex Tavoularis *ed* Alan Toomayan

☆ Jacqueline Bisset, Ray Sharkey, Mary Woronov, Robert Beltran, Ed Begley Jnr, Wallace Shawn, Arnetia Walker, Paul Bartel, Paul Mazursky, Rebecca Schaeffer

'Col. Frank Slade has a very special plan for the weekend. It involves travel, women, good food, fine wine, the tango, chauffeured limousines and a loaded forty-five. And he's bringing Charlie along for the ride.'

Scent of a Woman *

US 1992 157m DeLuxe

UIP/Universal/City Lights (Martin Brest)

A blind former soldier shows a high-school student how to enjoy life.

Sentimental drama showcasing a flamboyant over-the-top performance from Pacino.

w Bo Goldman *d* Martin Brest *ph* Donald E. Thorin *m* Thomas Newman *pd* Angelo Graham *ed* William Steinkamp

☆ Al Pacino, Chris O'Donnell, James Rebhorn, Gabrielle Anwar, Philip S. Hoffman, Richard Venture

'Essentially a two-character piece that goes on nearly an hour too long, Martin Brest's latest boasts good writing, filmmaking and performances, but far too much of each.' – *Variety*

† The film was suggested by the Italian movie *Profumo di Donna*, directed in 1974 by Dino Risi from the novel *Il Buio e il Miele* by Giovanni Arpino.

Al Pacino

Best picture; Martin Brest; Bo Goldman

The Scent of Green Papaya **

France 1993 104m colour

Artificial Eye/Lazennec/La Sept/Canal

original title: *Mùi Du Du Xanh*

In Saigon in the 50s, a young village girl grows up as she works as a maid for a family where the mother struggles to bring up her sons in the absence of their father.

Gentle, well-observed domestic drama, crafted with care and visual style.

wd Tran Anh Hung *ph* Benoît Delhomme *m* Tiêt Ton-That *ad Alain Nègre ed* Nicole Dedieu, Jean-Pierre Roques

☆ Yên-Khê Tran Nu, Man San Lu, Thi Lôc Truong, Anh Hoa Nguyen, Hoa Hôi Vuong, Ngoc Trung Tran

'Although visually more rigorous, Hung's movie in some ways recalls the early works of Indian helmer Satyajit Ray in its portrayal of childhood dreams and the invisible walls between kids and adults.' – *Variety*

'Marries nature and artifice, taking the graceful shape of an Oriental character that grows, like a cherry tree, into ever larger meaning as pen-strokes are slowly added.' – *Kathleen Murphy, Film Comment*

best foreign film

'First they moved (1895)! Then they talked (1927)! Now they smell!'

Scent of Mystery *

US 1959 125m Technicolor Cinerama (70mm)

Cinerama/Mike Todd Jnr

aka: *Holiday in Spain*

An Englishman on holiday in Spain protects a mysterious girl.

More of a travelogue than a thriller, but worth a note as the cinema's first 'smellie'. A process called Smell-o-Vision released appropriate odours throughout the auditorium...

w William Rose *d* Jack Cardiff *ph* John von Kotze *m* Mario Nascimbene

☆ Denholm Elliott, Peter Lorre, Beverly Bentley, Paul Lukas, Liam Redmond, Leo McKern, Peter Arne, Mary Laura Wood, Elizabeth Taylor

† The first film to credit its providers of shoe polish.

Scent of Passion (dubbed)

Italy 1990 84m Telecolor

Film 90

A choreographer, dissatisified by his relationships with dancers, decides to find a woman he can mould to his taste and picks up a vagrant from the streets.

Glossy, silly and empty movie that uses the trappings of culture – the work of a classic writer and the ballet – for a great deal of macho posturing and, by the women, breast-baring; not so much a vision of Gautier's belief in art for art's sake as an example of soft porn for money's sake.

w Leandro Lucchetti *novel Violette* by Theophile Gautier *d* Pasquale Fanetti *ph* (uncredited) *m* Donimak, Lindok *ad* Vlado Perkovic *ed* Cesare Bianchini

☆ Malú, Angeles Lopez Barea, Giancarlo Teodori, Zvonco Zrncic, Suada Herak, Melita Turisic, Mircea Hurdubea

Die Schaukel: see *The Swing*

'The List Is Life. The Man Was Real. The Story Is True.'

Schindler's List ****

US 1993 195m bw/colour

Universal/Amblin (Steven Spielberg, Gerald R. Molen, Branko Lustig)

During the Second World War, an Austrian businessman persuades the Nazis to let him use Jewish slave labour in his factory; and then, with the money he earns, bribes a brutal SS commandant to save 1,100 Jews from the concentration camps.

A brilliantly realized, fiercely controlled and restrained treatment of a true story, using monochrome photography for the most part to achieve a documentary feel; harsh and compassionate, it avoids sentimentality until the end. It marks not only a notable achievement, but Spielberg's coming of age as an adult film-maker.

w Steven Zaillian novel Thomas Keneally *d Steven Spielberg ph Janusz Kaminski m* John Williams *pd Allan Starski ed Michael Kahn*

☆ *Liam Neeson, Ben Kingsley, Ralph Fiennes*, Caroline Goodall, Jonathan Sagalle, Embeth Davidtz, Malgosha Gebel, Shmulik Levy, Mark Ivanir

'Evinces an artistic rigor and unsentimental intelligence unlike anything the world's most successful filmmaker has demonstrated before.' – *Variety*

'The elevated downer of the decade.' – *Richard Corliss, Time*

'He captures images of experience that most of us thought we would never see represented adequately on the screen. This is by far the finest, fullest dramatic (i.e. nondocumentary) film ever made about the Holocaust.' – *Terrence Rafferty, New Yorker*

'Indiana Jones in the Cracow Ghetto.' – *Will Tremper, Die Welt*

best film; Steven Spielberg; Steven Zaillian; Janusz Kaminski; Michael Kahn; John Williams; Allan Starski

Liam Neeson; Ralph Fiennes; costume design (Anna Biedrzycka-Sheppard); make-up

best film; adapted screenplay; Steven Spielberg; Ralph Fiennes; Janusz Kaminski; John Williams

'Schizophrenia...When the left hand doesn't know who the right hand is killing.'

Schizo

GB 1976 109m Technicolor

Columbia-Warner/Pete Walker

aka: *Amok*

aka: *Blood of the Undead*

A series of bloody murders result when a famous ice-skater announces that she is to be married.

An unsuccessful attempt at a slick and surprising thriller; the twist in the plot is obvious from the beginning.

w David McGillivray *d* Peter Walker *ph* Peter Jessop *m* Stanley Myers *ad* Chris Burke *ed* Alan Brett

☆ Lynne Frederick, John Leyton, Stephanie Beacham, John Fraser, Jack Watson, Queenie Watts, John McEnery, Colin Jeavons

'Deprived of any support from the script this time, Pete Walker's direction, all thump, scream and cut as shadows lurk and doorknobs turn – with each cliché heralded by a triumphant tremolo or bass boom from the score – reduces the whole thing to risible absurdity.' – *Tom Milne, MFB*

Die Schlangengrube und das Pendel: see *The Blood Demon*

School for Husbands

GB 1937 71m bw

Wainwright (Richard Wainwright)

A romantic novelist annoys the husbands of his adoring fans.

Would-be champagne comedy which bubbles pretty well for most of its length.
w Frederick Jackson, Gordon Aherry, Austin Melford *play* Frederick Jackson *d* Andrew Marton *ph* Phil Tannura
☆ Rex Harrison, Henry Kendall, Romney Brent, Diana Churchill, June Clyde

The School for Scandal
GB 1930 73m Raycol Colour
Albion Film Syndicate
Two brothers have characters opposite to their appearances.
Doomed attempt to film the famous 18th-century comedy of manners.
w Jean Jay *play* Richard Brinsley Sheridan *d* Maurice Elvey
☆ Madeleine Carroll, Basil Gill, Henry Hewitt, Ian Fleming
'Its value in the States looks like exactly nothing.' – *Variety*

School for Scoundrels *
GB 1960 94m bw
ABP/Guardsman (Hal E. Chester)
A failure reports to the College of One-Upmanship and his life is transformed.
Amusing trifle, basically a series of sketches by familiar comic actors.
w Patricia Mayes, Hal E. Chester *books* Stephen Potter *d* Robert Hamer *ph* Erwin Hillier *m* John Addison
☆ *Ian Carmichael, Alastair Sim,* Terry-Thomas, Janette Scott, Dennis Price, Peter Jones, Edward Chapman, John Le Mesurier
† Cyril Frankel directed some scenes uncredited after Hamer was too drunk to continue.

School for Secrets
GB 1946 108m bw
Rank/Two Cities (George H. Brown, Peter Ustinov)
US title: *Secret Flight*
The boffins who invented radar find themselves in a little war action of their own.
An unsatisfactory entertainment which, with the best intentions, shuffles between arch comedy, character drama, war action and documentary, doing less than justice to any of these aspects.
wd Peter Ustinov *ph* Jack Hildyard *m* Alan Rawsthorne
☆ Ralph Richardson, Raymond Huntley, Richard Attenborough, Marjorie Rhodes, John Laurie, Ernest Jay, David Tomlinson, Finlay Currie

School for Unclaimed Girls: see *The Smashing Bird I Used to Know*

School Ties *
US 1992 107m DeLuxe
Paramount (Stanley R. Jaffe, Sherry Lansing)
In the mid-1950s a Jewish boy conceals his religion when he wins a scholarship to an exclusive school rife with anti-Semitism.
A slickly directed, well-acted, moderately gripping drama.
w Dick Wolf, Darryl Ponicsan *d* Robert Mandel *ph* Freddie Francis *m* Maurice Jarre *pd* Jeannine Claudia Oppewall *ed* Jerry Greenberg, Jacqueline Cambas
☆ Brendan Fraser, Matt Damon, Chris O'Donnell, Randall Batinkoff, Andrew Lowery, Amy Locane, Ed Lauter
'Gives a multifaceted, nuanced look at the roots of prejudice and self-denial.' – *Variety*

Das Schreckliche Mädchen: see *The Nasty Girl*

Schtonk!
Germany 1992 111m colour
Artificial Eye/Bavarian Film/WDR (Gunter Rohrbach, Helmut Dietl)
A forger decides to fake Hitler's diaries to sell to a collector of Nazi memorabilia and enlists the aid of a journalist.
The heavy-handed farcical treatment of an hilarious true story provides little amusement, although it was a great success in its home country.
w Helmut Dietl, Ulrich Limmer *d* Helmut Dietl *ph* Xaver Schwarzenberger *m* Konstantin Wecker *ad* Götz Weidner, Benedikt Herforth *ed* Tanja Schmidbauer
☆ Götz George, Uwe Ochsenknecht, Christiane Hörbiger, Rolf Hoppe, Dagmar Manzel, Veronica Ferres, Rosemarie Fendel
'This crude, overacted account of the Hitler diaries scandal is largely of sociological interest, an occasion for sporadic chuckles rather than sustained laughter.' – *Philip French, Observer*
foreign language film

Schweik's New Adventures
GB 1943 84m bw
Eden Films
An unassuming Czechoslovakian writer gently kids the Nazi occupiers and manages to save some of his friends from the concentration camp.
Curious English attempt to film a popular Czechoslovakian character; it made mildly effective wartime propaganda, though few went to see it.
w Karel Lamac, Con West *novel* Jaroslav Hasek *d* Karel Lamac
☆ Lloyd Pearson, George Carney, Julien Mitchell, Richard Attenborough, Margaret McGrath

Schwestern oder die Balance des Glücks: see *Sisters or the Balance of Happiness*

Sciuscià: see *Shoeshine*

'Throughout The Ages, One Hero Has Cowered Above The Rest.'
Scooby-Doo
US 2002 86m Technicolor
Warner/Mosaic Media (Charles Roven, Richard Suckle)
Members of a defunct crime-fighting gang re-united to discover who is brain-washing tourists on Spooky Island.
A live-action version of the TV cartoons about amateur detectives and their cowardly dog that always seemed over-stretched in a running time of half-an-hour. The movie version is over-stretched in half that time.
w James Gunn *characters created by* Hanna-Barbera Prods *d* Raja Gosnell *ph* David Eggby *m* David Newman *pd* Bill Boes *ed* Kent Beyda *sp* Peter Crosman
☆ Freddie Prinze Jnr (Fred), Sarah Michelle Gellar (Daphne), Matthew Lillard (Shaggy), Linda Cardellini (Velma), Rowan Atkinson (Mondavarious), Isla Fisher (Mary Jane), Miguel A. Nunez Jnr (Voodoo Maestro), Steven Grives (N'Goo Tuana)
'Incredibly leaden and unutterably boring.' – *Peter Bradshaw, Guardian*
'Get out your pooper-scoopers.' – *Peter Travers, Rolling Stone*

Scorchers
US 1991 82m colour
Rank/Goldcrest/FilmWorks (Morrie Eisenman, Richard Hellman)
In a sleazy bar, a prostitute sorts out a wife's marital problems while nearby a newly-wed couple have troubles of their own.
Risibly decadent movie, set in a town of misfits.
wd David Beaird *play* David Beaird *ph* Peter Deming *m* Carter Burwell *pd* Bill Eigenbrodt *ed* David Garfield
☆ Faye Dunaway, Denholm Elliott, James Earl Jones, Emily Lloyd, Jennifer Tilly, James Wilder, Anthony Geary, Leland Crooke, Luke Perry
'An uncomfortable mix of melodrama, sentimentality and failed farce.' – *Empire*

Scorching Winds: see *Garm Hava*

'There are no partners in crime.'
The Score *
US/Germany 2001 124m DeLuxe Panavision
Pathé/Mandalay/Horseshoe Bay (Gary Foster, Lee Rich)
A veteran thief is persuaded by his old partner and a cocky newcomer to do one last robbery.
A stellar cast render this familiar narrative watchable, but do little to lift it above the ordinary.
w Kario Salem, Lem Dobbs, Scott Marshall Smith *d* Frank Oz *ph* Rob Hahn *m* Howard Shore *pd* Jackson De Govia *ed* Richard Pearson *cos* Aude Bronson-Howard
☆ Robert De Niro (Nick), Edward Norton (Jack/Brian), Marlon Brando (Max), Angela Bassett (Diane), Gary Farmer (Burt), Paul Soles (Danny)
'If you're not too demanding, it's an easy film to go along with: an "old times' sake" caper, and doubly welcome for its avoidance of violence.' – *Alexander Walker, London Evening Standard*

'When Scorpio wants you, there is nowhere to hide!'
Scorpio
US 1972 114m Technicolor
UA/Scimitar (Walter Mirisch)
CIA agents doublecross each other.
Incredibly complex spy thriller in which it's difficult to know, or care, who's following whom. The brutalities, however, are capably staged.
w David W. Rintels, Gerald Wilson *d* Michael Winner *ph* Robert Paynter *m* Jerry Fielding
☆ Burt Lancaster, Alain Delon, Paul Scofield, John Colicos, Gayle Hunnicutt, J. D. Cannon
'Strictly zoom and thump.' – *Sight and Sound*
'Relying on moments of violence for effect, Winner directs with typically crass abandon.' – *Time Out, 1984*

'Warrior. Legend. King.'
The Scorpion King
US 2002 91m FotoKem Panavision
Universal/WWF/Alphaville (Stephen Sommers, Sean Daniel, James Jacks, Kevin Misher)
In ancient times, the leader of a band of assassins, who is hired to overthrow a local tyrant, decides to become king himself.
Thick slice of witless, incoherent Hollywood hokum, starring a ponderously muscular wrestler whose sobriquet fits his approach to acting.
w Stephen Sommers, William Osborne, David Hayter *d* Chuck Russell *ph* John R. Leonetti *m* John Debney *pd* Ed Verreaux *ed* Michael Tronick, Greg Parsons *sp* CFX/Das Werk
☆ The Rock (The Scorpion King/Mathayus), Steven Brand (Memnon), Michael Clarke Duncan (Balthazar), Kelly Hu (Sorceress), Bernard Hill (Philos), Grant Heslov (Arpid), Peter Facinelli (Takmet), Ralf Moeller (Thorak), Branscombe Richmond (Jesup), Roger Rees (King Pheron), Sherri Howard (Queen Isis)
'It's like having several garbage cans clogged with stale pizza, lukewarm cola, soggy French fries and greasy, ketchup-stained napkins emptied over your head.' – *Stephen Holden, New York Times*
'Crude and prosaic, a storming-the-cardboard-castle potboiler with reasonably vigorous sword fights served up every 15 minutes or so, like commercials.' – *Owen Gleiberman, Entertainment Weekly*

Scorsese x 4: see *The Big Shave, ItalianAmerican, It's Not Just You Murray!, What's A Nice Girl Like You Doing in a Place Like This?*

'Protection Is The Job, Justice Is The Goal, Death Is The Price.'
La Scorta **
Italy 1993 92m Technicolor
Claudio Bonivento
aka: *The Escort*
Following the assassination by the Sicilian Mafia of a judge, a team of carabinieri is assigned to protect his replacement.
Tough, timely and suspenseful thriller about political corruption in Italy, based on truth and close in style to American gangster movies.
w Graziano Diana, Simona Izzo *d Ricky Tognazzi* *ph* Alessio Gelsini *m* Ennio Morricone *ad* Mariangela Capuano *ed* Carla Simoncelli
☆ Claudio Amendola, Enrico Lo Verso, Carlo Cecchi, Ricky Memphis, Tony Sperandeo, Francesca D'Aloja, Angelo Infanti, Leo Gullotta
'This finds a gripping, even uplifting, human story inside its depiction of oppressive and omnipresent evil.' – *Kim Newman, Empire*

Scotch on the Rocks: see *Laxdale Hall*

Scotland Yard
US 1941 68m bw
TCF (Sol M. Wurtzel)
The Nazis capture a London banker and use his double to turn funds over to them.
Outlandish spy melodrama which certainly keeps the interest.
w Samuel G. Engel, John Balderston *play* Deniston Clift *d* Norman Foster *ph* Virgil Miller *m* Emil Newman
☆ Nancy Kelly, Edmund Gwenn, Henry Wilcoxon, John Loder, Melville Cooper, Gilbert Emery, Norma Varden

Scotland Yard Investigator
US 1945 68m bw
Republic (George Blair)
Frenchmen attempt to steal the Mona Lisa from its wartime home in the National Gallery.
Very passable programme filler with stalwart actors enjoying themselves.
w Randall Faye *d* George Blair
☆ Sir Aubrey Smith, Erich von Stroheim, Stephanie Bachelor, Forrester Harvey, Richard Fraser, Frederick Worlock

Scott of the Antarctic **
GB 1948 111m Technicolor
Ealing (Sidney Cole)
After long preparation, Captain Scott sets off on his ill-fated 1912 expedition to the South Pole.
The stiff-upper-lip saga par excellence*; inevitable knowledge of the end makes it pretty downbeat, and the actors can only be sincere; but the snowscapes, most of them artificial, are fine.*
w Ivor Montagu, Walter Meade, Mary Hayley Bell *d* Charles Frend *ph* Geoffrey Unsworth, Jack Cardiff, Osmond Borradaile *m* Ralph Vaughan Williams
☆ John Mills, James Robertson Justice, Derek Bond, Harold Warrender, Reginald Beckwith, Kenneth More, James McKechnie, John Gregson

The Scoundrel **
US 1935 74m bw
Paramount (Ben Hecht, Charles MacArthur)
A famous writer dies; his ghost comes back to find the meaning of love.
Unique thirties supernatural melodrama with barbs of dated wit despatched by a splendid cast. Nonsense, but great nonsense.
wd Ben Hecht, Charles MacArthur *ph* Lee Garmes *m* George Antheil
☆ *Noël Coward, Alexander Woollcott,* Julie Haydon, Stanley Ridges, Eduardo Ciannelli
'Good Hotel Algonquin literati stuff, but not for the Automat trade.' – *Variety*
'An unmistakable whiff from a gossip column world which tries hard to split the difference between an epigram and a wisecrack.' – *William Whitebait*
'Practically flawless drama. It's arty, but if this is art, let us have more of it.' – *Photoplay*
'An impudent work ... but there are brains in it, and observation, and even a kind of stunted poetry.' – *Observer*
† Helen Hayes and Edna Ferber made cameo appearances.
original story

The Scoundrel *
France/Italy/Rumania 1971 100m Eastmancolor
Cinecenta/Gaumont/Rizzoli/BFP (Alain Poiré)
original title: *Mariés de L'An Deux*
The adventures in the 1790s of a Frenchman who returns from America to divorce his wife and then decides he wants to stay married.
Enjoyable and hectic swashbuckling period romp in which true love triumphs after a great number of death-defying moments.
w Jean-Paul Rappeneau, Claude Sautet, Maurice Clavel, Daniel Boulanger *d* Jean-Paul Rappeneau *ph Claude Renoir* *m* Michel Legrand *ad* Alexandre Trauner, Will Holt *ed* Pierre Gillette
☆ Jean-Paul Belmondo, Marlène Jobert, Michel Auclair, Sami Frey, Laura Antonelli, Pierre Brasseur

Scram! *

US 1932 20m bw

Hal Roach

Two vagrants are ordered out of town but by a series of misadventures are found drunk with the judge's wife.

Generally sprightly star comedy culminating in a marathon laughing session.

w H. M. Walker *d* Ray McCarey *ed* Richard Currier

☆ Stan Laurel, Oliver Hardy, Arthur Housman, Rychard Cramer, Vivien Oakland

Scream *

US 1996 110m CFI color Panavision

Buena Vista/Miramax/Dimension (Cary Woods, Cathy Konrad)

A serial killer with an extensive knowledge of horror movies begins to murder teenage girls.

A knowing romp through the conventions of slasher movies, but one that also manages to scare as well; it is most likely to appeal to those familiar with the genre, who will appreciate its parodies.

w Kevin Williamson *d* Wes Craven *ph* Mark Irwin *m* Marco Beltrami *pd* Bruce Alan Miller *ed* Patrick Lussier *sp* Frank Seglia; make-up: Robert Kurtzman, Greg Nicotero, Howard Berger

☆ Drew Barrymore, Neve Campbell, Skeet Ulrich, Courteney Cox, Rose McGowan, David Arquette

'An ingeniously unsettling tribute to the splatterific teen horror films of the '80s.' – *Owen Gleiberman, Entertainment Weekly*

'Just about every effect in the picture is predictable.' – *Herschell Gordon Lewis*

'Someone has taken their love of *sequels* one step too far.'

Scream 2 *

US 1997 120m Foto-Kem Panavision

Miramax/Dimension/Konrad (Cathy Konrad, Marianne Maddalena)

Attending the première of a movie based on their experiences with a serial killer, two students become the first victims of a copycat murderer.

Another dose of knowing, self-referential horror movie lore that finally twists back on itself with a killer who claims to have been corrupted by movies; it's very ingenious, but it's still junk.

w Kevin Williamson *d* Wes Craven *ph* Peter Deming *m* Marco Beltrami *pd* Robert Ziembicki *ed* Patrick Lussier

☆ David Arquette, Neve Campbell, Courteney Cox, Sarah Michelle Gellar, Jamie Kennedy, Jerry O'Connell, Jada Pinkett, Liev Schreiber, David Warner, Laurie Metcalf

'Visceral, witty and appropriately redundant, the sequel has a winning commercial recipe that's certain to cook up excellent returns in all areas.' – *Leonard Klady, Variety*

'The Third and Final chapter in the trilogy that made you laugh, and made you Scream.'

Scream 3

US 2000 116m DeLuxe

Buena Vista/Konrad (Cathy Konrad, Kevin Williamson, Marianne Maddalena)

The cast of a horror film *Stab 3* are killed off one by one.

A sequel so self-referential that audiences who have not seen the first two movies in the series will be at a loss to understand what is happening; but, then those who didn't see the earlier Screams will want to miss this one, too.

w Ehren Kruger *d* Wes Craven *ph* Peter Deming *m* Marco Beltrami *pd* Bruce Alan Miller *ed* Patrick Lussier

☆ David Arquette (Dewey Riley), Neve Campbell (Sidney Prescott), Courteney Cox Arquette (Gale Weathers), Patrick Dempsey (Mark Kincaid), Scott Foley (Roman Bridger), Lance Henriksen (John Milton), Matt Keeslar (Tom Prinze), Jenny McCarthy (Jenny McCarthy), Emily Mortimer (Angelina Tyler), Parker Posey (Jennifer Jolie), Deon Richmond (Tyson Fox), Liev Schreiber (Cotton Weary), Heather Matarazzo (Martha Meeks), Carrie Fisher (Bianca Burnette), Kevin Smith (Silent Bob) and also Roger Corman

'So tediously knowing that it ceases to be an entertainment. It becomes simply an extended raft of film references, as chilling as a draughty lavatory seat and as sexy as number crunching.' – *James Christopher, Times*

Scream ... and Die!

GB 1973 99m Eastmancolor

Variety/Blackwater (Diana Daubeney)

aka: *Psycho Sex Fiend*

A model fears that she may be murdered after witnessing an unidentifiable man in black stab a girl to death in a remote country mansion.

Trivial thriller that sets out to titillate, but fails miserably.

w Derek Ford *d* Joseph Larraz (José Ramón Larraz) *ph* Trevor Wrenn *m* Terry Warr *ad* John Hoesli *ed* Roy Deverell

☆ Andrea Allan, Karl Lanchbury, Maggie Walker, Peter Forbes-Robertson, Judy Matheson, Annabella Wood, Alex Leppard

'At heart just another sexploitation film posing as a thriller.' – *Tom Milne, MFB*

'Triple distilled horror ... as powerful as a vat of boiling acid!'

Scream and Scream Again *

GB 1969 94m Eastmancolor

AIP/Amicus (Milton Subotsky, Max J. Rosenberg)

Murders are traced to superhuman composite beings created by a mad scientist.

Energetic and well-staged though rather humourless shocker.

w Christopher Wicking *novel The Disorientated Man* by Peter Saxon *d* Gordon Hessler *ph* John Coquillon *m* David Whittaker *ad* Don Mingaye

☆ Vincent Price, Christopher Lee, Peter Cushing, Alfred Marks, Anthony Newlands, David Lodge, Peter Sallis

Scream, Blacula, Scream

US 1973 96m Movielab

Gala/AIP (Joseph T. Naar)

A 19th-century African vampire is brought back to life.

Routine horror movie of little interest, a lacklustre sequel to Blacula *(qv).*

w Joan Torres, Raymond Koenig, Maurice Jules *d* Bob Kelljan *ph* Isidore Mankofsky *m* Bill Marx *ad* Alfeo Bocchicchio *ed* Fabian Tordjmann *sp* Jack de Bron

☆ William Marshall, Pam Grier, Don Mitchell, Michael Conrad, Richard Lawson, Lynne Moody, Beverly Gill, Bernie Hamilton

'Will excite only the most undemanding audiences.' – *MFB*

Scream for Help

US 1984 90m colour

Miracle/Lorimar/Videoform (Michael Winner)

A teenager becomes convinced that her stepfather is trying to murder her mother.

Crude splatter movie which the director presumably undertook as a joke.

w Tom Holland *d* Michael Winner *ph* Robert Paynter, Dick Kratina *m* Howard Blake *ad* Tony Reading *ed* Christopher Barnes

☆ Rachael Kelly, David Brooks, Marie Masters, Rocco Sisto, Lolita Lorre

'Over the moronic characterization, daft dialogue, inept performances and opportunistic camerawork, music has been poured like a constant stream of cold gravy, making a sound that on occasion resembles, not inappropriately, a growling stomach.' – *Philip Strick, MFB*

Scream of Fear: see *Taste of Fear*

Scream of Stone *

Germany/France/Canada 1991 105m colour

SERA/A2/Les Films Stock/ZDF/Canal Plus/Telefilm Canada/Lucky Red/RAI2 (Walter Saxer)

A young climber challenges an older one to tackle the most difficult mountain in the world in Patagonia.

Spectacular photography compensates for a muddled narrative about obsessive people.

w Hans-Ulrich Klenner, Walter Saxer *story* Reinhold Messner *d* Werner Herzog *ph* Rainer Klausmann, Herbert Raditschnig *m* Ingram Marshall, Alan Lamb *pd* Juan Santiago *ed* Suzanne Baron

☆ Vittorio Mezzogiorno, Mathilda May, Stefan Glowacz, Brad Dourif, Donald Sutherland

'While it does feature some spectacular mountain photography in an area of the world few will ever see first-hand, the dramatic and psychological aspects remain so obscure as to become silly.' – *Variety*

Screamers *

US/Canada/Japan 1996 107m colour

Triumph/Fuji Eight/Fries/Allegro (Tom Berry, Franco Battista)

In 2078, on the planet Sirius 6B, an alliance of mine-workers and scientists invents killer robots to win a war against a corrupt and authoritarian mining corporation.

Paranoid science fiction, bleak in tone but interesting in its speculations about intelligent machines and violent people; judging by the soundtrack song, rock music will regress in the future.

w Dan O'Bannon, Miguel Tejada-Flores *story Second Variety* by Philip K. Dick *d* Christian Duguay *ph* Rodney Gibbons *m* Normand Corbeil *pd* Perri Gorrara *ed* Yves Langlois *sp* Ernest Faring; Richard Ostiguy

☆ Peter Weller, Roy Dupuis, Jennifer Rubin, Andy Lauer, Ron White, Charles Powell, Liliana Komorowska

† Dick's original story, published in 1953, was set on Earth, with a war between UN forces and the Soviet Union.

The Screaming Dead: see *Dracula – Prisoner of Frankenstein*

Screaming Mimi

US 1958 79m bw

Sage/Columbia (Harry Joe Brown, Robert Fellows)

After being sexually assaulted a dancer comes to believe she has committed murder ... and later we learn that she has.

Sub-Freudian melodrama on the comic strip level.

w Robert Blees *book* Frederic Brown *d* Gerd Oswald *ph* Burnett Guffey *md* Mischa Bakaleinikoff

☆ Anita Ekberg, Phil Carey, Harry Townes, Gypsy Rose Lee, Romney Brent, Alan Gifford, Red Norvo

'Everyone gets it in the end.'

Screwed

US 2000 81m DeLuxe

Universal (Robert Simonds)

A servant's plan to kidnap and ransom his employer's pet dog goes disastrously wrong.

Broad and slapstick comedy by a cast with no obvious talent for the genre.

wd Scott Alexander, Larry Karaszewski *ph* Robert Brinkman *m* Michael Colombier *pd* Mark Freeborn *ad* Sandi Tanaka *ed* Michael Jablow

☆ Norm Macdonald (Willard Fillmore), Dave Chappelle (Rusty P. Hayes), Elaine Stritch (Miss Crock), Danny DeVito (Grover Cleaver), Daniel Benzali (Detective Tom Dewey), Sherman Hemsley (Chip Oswald), Sarah Silverman (Hillary), Malcolm Stewart (Roger)

'A confusedly misconceived hybrid of interracial buddy comedy and imitation Marx Brothers farce.' – *Stephen Holden, New York Times*

Scrooge *

GB 1935 78m bw

Twickenham (Julius Hagen)

A miser reforms after ghosts haunt him on Christmas Eve.

Acceptable unambitious version with interesting performances.

w Seymour Hicks, H. Fowler Mear *novel* Charles Dickens *d* Henry Edwards *ph* Sidney Blythe, William Luff

☆ Seymour Hicks (Ebenezer Scrooge), Donald Calthrop (Bob Cratchit), Athene Seyler, Oscar Asche, Barbara Everest, Maurice Evans, C. V. France, Marie Ney

† Seymour Hicks starred in a silent version in 1913.

Scrooge ***

GB 1951 86m bw

Renown (Brian Desmond Hurst)

US title: *A Christmas Carol*

By far the best available version of the classic parable; casting, art direction, pace and general handling are as good as can be.

w Noel Langley *d Brian Desmond Hurst ph* C. Pennington-Richards *m* Richard Addinsell

☆ *Alastair Sim*, Mervyn Johns, Kathleen Harrison, Jack Warner, Michael Hordern, Hermione Baddeley, George Cole, Miles Malleson

Scrooge *

GB 1970 113m Technicolor Panavision

Cinema Center/Waterbury (Robert H. Solo)

Dim musical version, darkly coloured and quite lost on the wide screen; but it has its macabre moments of trick photography.

d Ronald Neame *ph* Oswald Morris *pd* Terry Marsh *w/m/ly* Leslie Bricusse

☆ Albert Finney, Michael Medwin, Alec Guinness, Edith Evans, Kenneth More, David Collings, Laurence Naismith, Kay Walsh

† Richard Harris and Rex Harrison were both sought before Finney was signed.

song 'Thank You Very Much' (*m/ly* Leslie Bricusse); original score; art direction; costume design (Margaret Furse)

Scrooged *

US 1988 101m Technicolor

Paramount/Mirage (Richard Donner, Art Linson)

Updated version of Dickens's *A Christmas Carol*, centring on the president of a New York television company.

Energetic and sometimes genuinely scary seasonal entertainment for modern kids.

w Mitch Glazer, Michael O'Donoghue *d* Richard Donner *ph* Michael Chapman *m* Danny Elfman *pd* J. Michael Riva

☆ Bill Murray, Karen Allen, John Forsythe, Robert Mitchum, John Houseman, Lee Majors

Scrubbers

GB 1982 93m Eastmancolor

Handmade (Don Boyd)

Sensational events in a girls' borstal.

Wild-eyed melodrama which seems to serve no sort of purpose and is certainly not entertaining.

w Roy Minton, Jeremy Watt, Mai Zetterling *d* Mai Zetterling *ph* Ernest Vincze *m* Michael Hurd

☆ Amanda York, Chrissie Cotterill, Elizabeth Edmonds, Kate Ingram, Honey Bane, Eva Motley

Scudda Hoo, Scudda Hay

US 1948 98m Technicolor

TCF (Walter Morosco)

GB title: *Summer Lightning*

A farmer's son is less interested in girls than in the welfare of his two mules.

Antediluvian rural romance for the simple-minded.

wd F. Hugh Herbert *novel* George Agnew Chamberlain *ph* Ernest Palmer *m* Cyril Mockridge

☆ June Haver, Lon McCallister, Walter Brennan, Anne Revere, Natalie Wood, Robert Karnes, Henry Hull, Tom Tully, Marilyn Monroe

Scum *

GB 1979 97m Eastmancolor

GTO/Berwick Street Films (Clive Parsons, Davina Belling)

Injustices in a Borstal institution lead to a riot.

Gorily overstated view of boys' prison life from the inside, with the camera gloating over each violent close-up. (The original TV play had been made, then banned, by the BBC.)

w Roy Minton *d* Alan Clarke *ph* Phil Meheux *ad* Judith Lang *ed* Mike Bradsell

☆ Ray Winstone, Mick Ford, Julian Firth, John Blundell

The Sea: see *El Mar*

The Sea Bat

US 1930 69m bw

MGM

Mexican fishermen compete to kill a deadly sting-ray.

The Jaws of its time; box-office hokum.

w Bess Meredyth and John Howard Lawson *d* Wesley Ruggles

☆ Charles Bickford, Raquel Torres, Nils Asther, John Miljan, Gibson Gowland, Boris Karloff

The Sea Beast *
US 1926 125m approx bw silent
Warner
In this version of *Moby Dick*, Ahab gets to settle down at the end with his lady love.
Memorable sea scenes and a star performance.
w Bess Meredyth *d* Millard Webb
☆ *John Barrymore*, Dolores Costello, George O'Hara, Mike Donlin, Sam Baker

The Sea Chase *
US 1955 117m Warnercolor Cinemascope
Warner (John Farrow)
In 1939 a German freighter tries to make it from Sydney harbour back to Germany.
Unusual but not very compelling naval melodrama, chiefly because the leads are miscast.
w James Warner Bellah, John Twist *novel* Andrew Geer *d* John Farrow *ph* William Clothier *m* Roy Webb
☆ John Wayne, Lana Turner, David Farrar, Lyle Bettger, Tab Hunter, James Arness, Dick Davalos, John Qualen
'A film compounded of monotonously familiar ingredients.' – *Penelope Houston*

Sea Devils
US 1937 88m bw
RKO
Exploits of the ice patrols of the US Coast Guard.
Flagwaving action hokum for popular stars.
w Frank Wead, John Twist, P. J. Wolfson *d* Ben Stoloff *ph* J. Roy Hunt, Joseph August *md* Roy Webb
☆ Victor McLaglen, Preston Foster, Ida Lupino, Donald Woods

Sea Devils
GB 1953 90m Technicolor
Coronado (David E. Rose)
Spies prevent Napoleon's invasion of England.
Cheerful, forgettable swashbuckler.
w Borden Chase *d* Raoul Walsh *ph* Wilkie Cooper *m* Richard Addinsell
☆ Yvonne de Carlo, Rock Hudson, Maxwell Reed, Denis O'Dea, Michael Goodliffe, Bryan Forbes, Ivor Barnard, Arthur Wontner

Sea Fury
GB 1958 97m bw
Rank (Benjamin Fisz)
Rivalry strikes up between an old and a young sailor on tugboats plying between Spain and England.
Shapeless, leery melodrama with strong performances and an exciting storm-at-sea climax.
w John Kruse, Cy Endfield *d* Cy Endfield *ph* Reg Wyer *m* Philip Green
☆ Stanley Baker, Victor McLaglen, Luciana Paluzzi, Grégoire Aslan, Francis de Wolff, David Oxley, Rupert Davies, Robert Shaw

'They stand side by side. Young and old. Rich and poor. They gather together for a single purpose. Survival.'
The Sea Gull *
GB 1968 141m Technicolor
Warner/Sidney Lumet
Loves and hates on a 19th-century Russian estate.
Rather heavily star-studded, but certainly proficient film version of a Chekhov favourite.
w Moura Budberg *play* Anton Chekhov *d* Sidney Lumet *ph* Gerry Fisher *m* none *pd* Tony Walton
☆ James Mason, Simone Signoret, Vanessa Redgrave, David Warner, Harry Andrews, Ronald Radd, Eileen Herlie, Kathleen Widdoes, Denholm Elliott, Alfred Lynch
'The camera cannot capture the hollowness of space, the oppressive immovableness of a seemingly harmless enclosure, stasis settling on everything like a fine, corrosive dust.' – *John Simon*

'If you miss it, you will owe yourself an apology!'
The Sea Hawk ***
US 1940 122m bw
Warner (Hal B. Wallis, Henry Blanke)
Elizabeth I encourages one of her most able captains to acts of piracy against the Spanish.
Wobbly-plotted but stirring and exciting seafaring actioner, with splendid battle and duel scenes.
w Seton I. Miller, Howard Koch *d Michael Curtiz ph Sol Polito m Erich Wolfgang Korngold ad Anton Grot*
☆ *Errol Flynn*, Flora Robson, Brenda Marshall, *Henry Daniell*, Claude Rains, Donald Crisp, Alan Hale, Una O'Connor, James Stephenson, Gilbert Roland, William Lundigan
'Endless episodes of court intrigue tend to diminish the effect of the epic sweep of the high seas dramatics.' – *Variety*
Erich Wolfgang Korngold; Anton Grot

'A man who loved as ruthlessly as he ruled. A woman whose indiscretions cost a lifetime of happiness!'
The Sea of Grass
US 1947 131m bw
MGM (Pandro S. Berman)
A cattle tycoon is so obsessed by his work that he alienates his family.
Brooding, overlong semi-Western with an unexpected cast.
w Marguerite Roberts, Vincent Lawrence *novel* Conrad Richter *d* Elia Kazan *ph Harry Stradling m* Herbert Stothart
☆ Spencer Tracy, Katharine Hepburn, Melvyn Douglas, Phyllis Thaxter, Robert Walker, Edgar Buchanan, Harry Carey, Ruth Nelson, James Bell
'In spite of all the sincerity and talent involved, an epically dreary film.' – *Time*
'The only film I ever made that I'm truly ashamed of.' – *Elia Kazan*

Sea of Lost Ships
US 1953 85m bw
Republic
The US Coast Guard saves a passenger ship from an iceberg.
Scrappy, semi-documentary account punctuated by rough action highlights.
w Steve Fisher *d* Joseph Kane *ph* Reggie Lanning *m* R. Dale Butts
☆ Walter Brennan, John Derek, Wanda Hendrix, Richard Jaeckel, Barton MacLane, Darryl Hickman

Sea of Love **
US 1989 112m DeLuxe Panavision
Universal (Martin Bregman, Louis A. Stroller)
A New York cop, suffering a mid-life crisis, falls in love with the chief suspect of a series of murders of men advertising in lonely hearts columns.
Effective urban thriller, though the emphasis is more on the romance than in discovering whodunnit.
w Richard Price *d* Harold Becker *ph* Ronnie Taylor *m* Trevor Jones *pd* John Jay Moore *ed* David Bretherton
☆ Al Pacino, Ellen Barkin, John Goodman, William Hickey, Michael Rooker, Richard Jenkins

Sea of Sand *
GB 1958 98m bw
Rank/Tempean (Robert Baker, Monty Berman)
US title: *Desert Patrol*
Just before Alamein an Eighth Army desert group plans to destroy one of Rommel's last petrol dumps.
Good standard war suspenser.
w Robert Westerby *d* Guy Green *ph* Wilkie Cooper *m* Clifton Parker
☆ Richard Attenborough, John Gregson, Vincent Ball, Percy Herbert, Michael Craig, Barry Foster, Andrew Faulds, Dermot Walsh

Sea of Silence: see *La Mer Cruelle*

The Sea Shall Not Have Them
GB 1954 93m bw
Eros/Daniel M. Angel
Survivors of a seaplane crash await rescue in a dinghy.
Rather dim computerized compendium of flashback mini-dramas.
w Lewis Gilbert, Vernon Harris *d* Lewis Gilbert *ph* Stephen Dade *m* Malcolm Arnold
☆ Dirk Bogarde, Michael Redgrave, Bonar Colleano, Jack Watling, Anthony Steel, Nigel Patrick, James Kenney, Sydney Tafler, George Rose

The Sea Wall: see *This Angry Age*

'One of the most challenging stories of faith ever told! What happened out there ... in the surging vastness of the Indian Ocean?'
Sea Wife
GB 1957 82m DeLuxe Cinemascope
TCF/Sumar (André Hakim)
Survivors of a shipwreck near Singapore in 1942 are rescued, not before the bosun has fallen in love with the only lady, not knowing she is a nun.
Flashbacked, uncertain, intermittently effective film of a popular minor novel.
w George K. Burke *novel Sea Wyf* by J. M. Scott *d* Bob McNaught *ph* Ted Scaife *m* Kenneth V. Jones, Leonard Salzedo
☆ Richard Burton, Joan Collins, Basil Sydney, Cy Grant

The Sea Wolf **
US 1941 90m bw
Warner (Henry Blanke)
Survivors of a ferry crash in San Francisco Bay are picked up by a psychopathic freighter captain who keeps them captive.
Much filmed action suspenser which in this version looks great but overdoes the talk.
w Robert Rossen *novel* Jack London *d Michael Curtiz ph Sol Polito m Erich Wolfgang Korngold*
☆ *Edward G. Robinson, Alexander Knox*, Ida Lupino, John Garfield, Gene Lockhart, Barry Fitzgerald, Stanley Ridges, David Bruce, Howard da Silva
'A Germanic, powerful work almost devoid of compromise.' – *Charles Higham, 1972*
† Other versions appeared in 1913, with Hobart Bosworth; in 1920, with Noah Beery; in 1925, with Ralph Ince; in 1930, with Milton Sills; in 1950 (as *Barricade*, turned into a Western), with Raymond Massey; in 1958 (as *Wolf Larsen*), with Barry Sullivan; and in 1975 (Italian), as *Wolf of the Seven Seas*, with Chuck Connors.

The Sea Wolves *
GB/US/Switzerland 1980 122m Eastmancolor
Richmond-Lorimar-Varius (Euan Lloyd)
In 1943, elderly British territorials living in India dispose of a Nazi transmitter in neutral Goa.
Mildly larkish Boy's Own Paper adventure with a somewhat geriatric air; an interesting 1980 throwback to the films of 1950.
w Reginald Rose *novel Boarding Party* by James Leasor *d* Andrew McLaglen *ph* Tony Imi *m* Roy Budd
☆ Gregory Peck, Roger Moore, Trevor Howard, David Niven, Barbara Kellerman, Patrick Macnee, Patrick Allen, Bernard Archard, Faith Brook, Martin Benson, Allan Cuthbertson, Kenneth Griffith, Donald Houston, Glyn Houston, Percy Herbert and also Patrick Holt, Terence Longdon, John Standing, Michael Medwin
'As a genre – the arterio-sclerotic war movie – it'll never catch on.' – *Time Out*
† The film was dedicated to Earl Mountbatten after his assassination.

Seagulls over Sorrento
GB 1954 92m bw
MGM (John Boulting)
US title: *Crest of the Wave*
Life on a naval research station on a small Scottish island.
A long-running British service comedy has been Americanized to little effect, but it remains just about watchable.
w Frank Harvey, Roy Boulting *play* Hugh Hastings *d* Roy Boulting *ph* Gilbert Taylor *m* Miklos Rozsa
☆ Gene Kelly, John Justin, Bernard Lee, Sidney James, Jeff Richards, Patric Doonan, Patrick Barr

Seal Island: see *The Living Desert*

Sealed Cargo *
US 1951 90m bw
RKO (Warren Duff)
In 1943, an American fishing-boat captain, sailing to Newfoundland, becomes suspicious of the captain of a wrecked schooner he discovers.
Enjoyable and atmospheric wartime thriller, maintaining its sense of mystery and suspense to the end.
w Dale Van Every, Oliver H. P. Garrett, Roy Huggins *novel The Gaunt Woman* by Edmund Gilligan *d* Alfred Werker *ph* George E. Diskant *m* Roy Webb *pd* J. McMillan Johnson *ad* Albert S. D'Agostino *ed* Ralph Dawson
☆ Dana Andrews, Carla Balenda, Claude Rains, Philip Dorn, Onslow Stevens, Skip Homeier, Eric Feldary, J. M. Kerrigan, Arthur Shields, Morgan Farley

Sealed Lips: see *After Tonight*

'What is the truth about fraternization?'
Sealed Verdict
US 1948 83m bw
Paramount (Robert Fellows)
An American officer in Germany falls in love with the ex-girlfriend of a Nazi war criminal.
Routine melodrama, as boring as it sounds.
w Jonathan Latimer *novel* Lionel Shapiro *d* Lewis Allen *ph* Leo Tover *m* Hugo Friedhofer
☆ Ray Milland, Florence Marly, Broderick Crawford, John Hoyt, John Ridgely, Ludwig Donath

Seance on a Wet Afternoon *
GB 1964 121m bw
Rank/Allied Film Makers (Richard Attenborough, Bryan Forbes)
A fake medium persuades her husband to kidnap a child so that she can become famous by revealing its whereabouts in a trance.
Overlong character melodrama in which the suspense is better than the psychopathology. A mannered performance from the lady, a false nose from the gentleman, and a general air of gloom.
wd Bryan Forbes ph Gerry Turpin *m* John Barry
☆ Kim Stanley, Richard Attenborough, Nanette Newman, Patrick Magee
'Not only a psychological suspense thriller but also a top-notch crime-and-detection tale and, above all, a horror film.' – *Judith Crist*
Kim Stanley
Richard Attenborough

The Search *
US/Switzerland 1948 105m bw
MGM/Praesens Film (Lazar Wechsler)
An American soldier in Germany cares for a war orphan.
Vivid semi-documentary post-war drama which falls down in its elementary dramatics but sent audiences home wiping away tears.
w Richard Schweizer, David Wechsler, Paul Jarrico *d Fred Zinnemann ph Emil Berna m* Robert Blum
☆ Montgomery Clift, Aline MacMahon, Ivan Jandl, Wendell Corey
'Far and away the most touching film we have seen for years.' – C. A. Lejeune
original story (Richard Schweizer, David Wechsler); Ivan Jandl (special award for outstanding juvenile performance)
script; Fred Zinnemann; Montgomery Clift

'You never saw so many skins you'd like to touch!'
Search for Beauty
US 1934 77m bw
Paramount
A physical culture magazine sponsors an international contest for beauties of both sexes.
Mildly amusing extravaganza staking its popularity on girls in bathing dress.
w Claude Binyon, Sam Hellman, Frank Butler and others *play* Schuyler E. Gray, Paul R. Milton *d* Erle C. Kenton
☆ Larry 'Buster' Crabbe, Ida Lupino, Toby Wing, James Gleason, Robert Armstrong, Gertrude Michael, Roscoe Karns
'A couple of years ago so many girls in abbreviated dress would have been enough for one picture ... but they've seen massed pulchritude quite often lately, so the girls here are just trimmings.' – *Variety*

The Search for Bridey Murphy *
US 1956 84m bw Vistavision
Paramount (Pat Duggan)
A Colorado businessman and amateur hypnotist finds a lady neighbour so good a subject that he is able to delve into her previous incarnation as a long-dead Irish peasant.
Adequately presented with alienation effects, but mainly consisting of two-shots and fuzzy flashbacks, this treatment of an actual case (subsequently

discredited) works up to a fine pitch of frenzy when the subject seems unable to come back from her previous life.*
wd Noel Langley *book* Morey Bernstein *ph* John F. Warren *m* Irvin Talbot
☆ Teresa Wright, Louis Hayward, Kenneth Tobey, Nancy Gates, Richard Anderson

'He had to find her ... he had to find her...'
The Searchers ★★★★
US 1956 119m Technicolor Vistavision
Warner/C. V. Whitney (Merian C. Cooper)
A Confederate war veteran tracks down the Indians who have slaughtered his brother and sister-in-law and carried off their daughter.
Disturbing Western of obsession and racism which has become Ford's most influential film, in which Wayne gives his most ambiguous performance, being no longer a simple gung-ho hero, but a tormented loner out of step with his society. Its themes of loss and reconciliation are echoed in many films that followed.
w Frank S. Nugent *novel* Alan le May *d* John Ford *ph* Winton C. Hoch *m* Max Steiner
☆ John Wayne, Jeffrey Hunter, Natalie Wood, Vera Miles, Ward Bond, John Qualen, Henry Brandon, Antonio Moreno
'You can read a lot into it, but it isn't very enjoyable.' – *Pauline Kael, 70s*

Searching for Bobby Fischer
US 1993 110m DeLuxe
Paramount/Mirage (Scott Rudin, William Horberg)
GB title: *Innocent Moves*
A father discovers that his seven-year-old son is a chess prodigy.
An off-beat film that concentrates on the father–son relationship, although it does attempt the impossible of making chess games visually exciting and accessible to non-players.
wd Steven Zaillian *book* Fred Waitzkin *ph* Conrad L. Hall *m* James Horner *pd* David Gropman *ed* Wayne Wahrman
☆ Joe Mantegna, Max Pomeranc, Ben Kingsley, Joan Allen, Laurence Fishburne, Michael Nirenberg, Robert Stephens, David Paymer
'Earnest and well-acted.' – *Variety*
🏆 Conrad L. Hall

'What strange power could drive this man from the lips of the woman he married to the arms of the woman he loved?'
The Searching Wind ★
US 1946 107m bw
Paramount (Hal B. Wallis)
Affairs of an American diplomat in Europe during the thirties.
Earnest melodrama which would have been better timed six years earlier. Excellent production, though.
w Lillian Hellman *play* Lillian Hellman *d* William Dieterle *ph* Lee Garmes *m* Victor Young *ad* Hans Drier, Franz Bachelin
☆ Robert Young, Sylvia Sidney, Ann Richards, Douglas Dick, Dudley Digges, Albert Basserman, Dan Seymour

The Seashell and the Clergyman ★
France 1928 30m approx (24 fps) bw silent
(Producer unknown)
A clergyman is afflicted by sexual torments.
Celebrated surrealist short with memorable images and a great deal of confusion.
w Antonin Artaud *d* Germaine Dulac *ph* Paul Guichard
☆ Alix Allin
† In GB the film was banned by the censor with the famous comment: 'It is so cryptic as to have no apparent meaning. If there is a meaning, it is doubtless objectionable.'

Seaside Swingers: see *Every Day's a Holiday*

The Season of Men: see *La Saison des Hommes*

Season of Passion: see *Summer of the Seventeenth Doll*

Season of the Witch
US 1973 89m colour
Latent Image (Nancy M. Romero)
aka: *Jack's Wife*
aka: *Hungry Wives*
A housewife, bored by the sameness of her domestic routine, turns to witchcraft, which leads in turn to murder.
A low-budget satirical take on the horrors of suburbia, often imaginatively photographed and edited, but fatally sabotaged by its rudimentary acting and frequently naïve script.
wd George A. Romero *ph* George A. Romero *m* Steve Gorn *ed* George A. Romero
☆ Jan White, Ray Laine, Anne Muffly, Joedda McClain, Virginia Greenwald, Bill Thunhurst, Neil Fisher, Shirlee Strasser
'A strange experimental film, with an unmistakeable (but amateurish) aura of Bergman.' – *David Pirie, Time Out*
† The British video release in 1994 ran for 104m.

The Seaweed Children: see *Malachi's Cove*

Sebastian
GB 1968 100m Eastmancolor
Paramount/Maccius (Herb Brodkin, Michael Powell)
An Oxford professor and code expert is appointed to the secret service.
Mildly spoofy spy yarn: style but not much substance.
w Gerald Vaughan-Hughes *story* Leo Marks *d* David Greene *ph* Gerry Fisher *m* Jerry Goldsmith *pd* Wilfred Shingleton
☆ Dirk Bogarde, John Gielgud, Lilli Palmer, Susannah York, Janet Munro, Margaret Johnston, Nigel Davenport, Ronald Fraser
'One of the problems with this kind of movie is the enormous pressure put on the audience to have a good time over practically nothing.' – *Renata Adler*

Sebastian
Norway/Sweden 1995 84m colour
Mefistofilm/Miramar/Nordisk (Peter Vennerod, Hansi Mandoki, Lars Kolvig)
A 16-year-old boy has problems coming to terms with his homosexuality.
A no-problem movie, about a boy whose lifestyle is accepted without many qualms by those around him; the lack of real conflict leads to blandness.
w Svend Wam, Peter Vennerod, Hansi Mandoki, Per Källberg *novel* Svart Cayal by Per Knutsen *d* Svend Wam *ph* Per Källberg *m* various *ad* Crispin Gerholt *ed* Einar Egeland
☆ Hampus Björck, Nicolai Cleve Broch, Ewa Fröling, Helge Jordal, Rebecka Hamse, Lena Olander

Sebastiane ★
GB 1976 86m colour
Megalovision/Cinegate/Disctac (James Waley, Howard Malin)
Sebastian, a soldier and former favourite banished to a remote outpost by the Emperor Diocletian, is executed by his commander when he refuses his sexual advances.
Unusual semi-improvised feature in which the dialogue is in Latin with English subtitles. It was the first British film to deal openly with homosexual desire.
w Derek Jarman, James Waley *d* Derek Jarman, Paul Humfress *ph* Peter Middleton *m* Brian Eno *pd* Derek Jarman *ed* Paul Humfress
☆ Leonardo Treviglio, Barney James, Neil Kennedy, Richard Warwick, Donald Dunham, Ken Hicks, Lindsay Kemp
'The most promising sign of new film life in independent narrative cinema in this country in many, many years.' – *Tony Rayns, MFB*

Second Best
GB/US 1994 105m Technicolor
Warner/Regency/Alcor/Fron/Monarchy (Sarah Radclyffe)
An introverted Welsh postman adopts a young boy with problems.
Small-scale domestic drama of male bonding that remains too inert to engage attention.
w David Cook *novel* David Cook *d* Chris Menges *ph* Ashley Rowe *m* Simon Boswell *pd* Michael Howells *ed* George Akers
☆ William Hurt, Chris Cleary Miles, Keith Allen, Prunella Scales, Jane Horrocks, Alan Cumming, John Hurt, Alfred Lynch, Doris Hare, Nerys Hughes, Jodhi May
'So modest in its aim and achievement that it will be exceedingly difficult to drum up much audience interest in seeing it.' – *Variety*

Second Best Bed
GB 1938 74m bw
Capitol
A magistrate is suspected of adultery.
Cheerful star comedy with a touch of sophistication.
w Ben Travers *d* Tom Walls *ph* Jack Cox *md* Van Phillips
☆ Tom Walls, Jane Baxter, Veronica Rose, Carl Jaffe, Greta Gynt

The Second Best Secret Agent in the Whole Wide World: see *Licensed to Kill*

Second Chance
US 1953 82m Technicolor 3-D
RKO (Edmund Grainger)
In South America, a professional killer stalks a gangster's moll.
Comic strip antics with a climax on a stalled cable car.
w Oscar Millard, Sydney Boehm *story* D. M. Marshman Jnr *d* Rudolph Maté *ph* William Snyder *m* Roy Webb
☆ Robert Mitchum, Linda Darnell, Jack Palance, Reginald Sheffield, Roy Roberts

Second Chorus
US 1940 84m bw
Paramount (Boris Morros)
Two trumpeters and their lady manager hit Broadway.
Mild musical.
w Elaine Ryan, Ian Mclellan Hunter, Frank Cavett *d* H. C. Potter *ph* Theodor Sparkuhl *m* Artie Shaw *songs* various
☆ Fred Astaire, Burgess Meredith, Paulette Goddard, Charles Butterworth, Artie Shaw and his Band, Frank Melton, Jimmy Conlin
🏆 Artie Shaw; song 'Love of my Life' (*m* Artie Shaw, *ly* Johnny Mercer)

Second Class Mail
GB 1984 4m colour
NFTS
A woman sends away by mail order for an inflatable husband.
A delightful joke, told at the perfect length.
wd Alison Snowden
🏆 animated short

'The greatest combination of talent ever gathered in one show!'
Second Fiddle
US 1939 86m bw
TCF (Gene Markey)
A Minnesota skating schoolteacher goes to Hollywood and becomes a star.
Routine star vehicle.
w Harry Tugend *d* Sidney Lanfield *ph* Leon Shamroy *md* Louis Silvers *songs* Irving Berlin
☆ Sonja Henie, Tyrone Power, Edna May Oliver, Rudy Vallee, Mary Healy, Lyle Talbot, Alan Dinehart
🏆 song 'I Poured My Heart into a Song' (*m/ly*Irving Berlin)

The Second Greatest Sex
US 1955 87m Technicolor Cinemascope
U-I (Albert J. Cohen)
Western women emulate Lysistrata to stop their men from feuding.
Flat attempt to cash in on Seven Brides for Seven Brothers; some good acrobatic dancing but no style.
w Charles Hoffman *d* George Marshall *ph* Wilfrid M. Cline *md* Joseph Gershenson *ch* Lee Scott
☆ Jeanne Crain, George Nader, Bert Lahr, Kitty Kallen, Paul Gilbert, Keith Andes, Mamie Van Doren, Tommy Rall

Second Honeymoon
US 1937 79m bw
TCF (Raymond Griffith)
A man tries to win back his ex-wife.
Moderate star romantic comedy.
w Kathryn Scola, Darrell Ware *story* Philip Wylie *d* Walter Lang *ph* Ernest Palmer *m* David Buttolph
☆ Tyrone Power, Loretta Young, Stuart Erwin, Claire Trevor, Marjorie Weaver, Lyle Talbot, J. Edward Bromberg

The Second Mrs Tanqueray
GB 1952 75m bw
Vandyke (Roger Proudlock)
A Victorian society widower marries a notorious lady.
Stiff-backed penny-pinching version of an interestingly antiquated play.
play Arthur Wing Pinero *d* Dallas Bower *ph* Gerald Gibbs
☆ Pamela Brown, Hugh Sinclair, Ronald Ward, Virginia McKenna, Andrew Osborn

Second Skin: see *Segunda Piel*

Second Thoughts
US 1982 98m Movielab
Turman-Foster/EMI
A lady lawyer gets into complex trouble when she bails out her inconsiderate lover from a Santa Fe jail.
An absurd series of situations is played for drama rather than comedy, and the feminist flag is frequently waved. The result is an unlikeable muddle.
w Steve Brown *d* Lawrence Turman *ph* King Baggot *m* Henry Mancini
☆ Lucie Arnaz, Craig Wasson, Ken Howard, Anne Schedeen
'Alternately dull and risible.' – *Chris Auty, MFB*

The Second Time Around
US 1961 99m DeLuxe Cinemascope
TCF/Cummings/Harman (Jack Cummings)
In 1912 Arizona, a widow stands for sheriff and has plenty of choice for a husband.
Light-hearted Western fun mixed with family sentimentality.
w Oscar Saul, Cecil Van Heusen *novel* Richard Emery Roberts *d* Vincent Sherman *ph* Ellis W. Carter *m* Gerald Fried
☆ Debbie Reynolds, Steve Forrest, Andy Griffith, Juliet Prowse, Thelma Ritter, Ken Scott, Isobel Elsom
'Keep a lemon handy for sucking to ward off an attack of the terminal cuteies.' – *Judith Crist, 1973*

The Second Victory
GB 1986 112m Rank Colour
Lelaleuka/J and M (Gerald Thomas)
In Austria after World War II, British occupation forces try to keep order in face of unrest following the murder of a sergeant.
Curiously timed return to the Third Man era, with a plotline unlikely to appeal to modern filmgoers; technical resources adequate rather than inspired.
w Morris West *novel* Morris West *d* Gerald Thomas
☆ Anthony Andrews, Helmut Griem, Max von Sydow, Mario Adorf, Birgit Doll

The Second Woman
US 1950 91m bw
United Artists/Cardinal (Mort Briskin)
GB title: *Ellen*
An architect, apparently paranoic, is proved to be the victim of a revenge plot.
Tolerable semi-star melodrama with a deliberate film noir look.
w Robert Smith *d* James V. Kern *ph* Hal Mohr *md* Nat Finston
☆ Robert Young, Betsy Drake, John Sutton, Florence Bates, Morris Carnovsky, Henry O'Neill

The Second-Floor Mystery
US 1930 56m bw
Warner
Correspondents through an agony column find themselves enmeshed in mystery and murder.
Burlesque whodunnit which seemed a smart trick at the time.
w Joseph Jackson *novel* The Agony Column by Earl Derr Biggers *d* Roy del Ruth
☆ Loretta Young, Grant Withers, H. B. Warner, Claire McDowell, John Loder

Seconds **

US 1966 106m bw

Paramount/Joel/Gibraltar (Edward Lewis)

A secret organization sells a special service to the jaded rich; apparent death followed by physical rejuvenation.

An intriguing half-hour is followed by a glum new life for our hero, capped by a horrifying finale in which, dissatisfied, he learns he is to become one of the corpses necessary to the organization's continuance.

w Lewis John Carlino *novel* David Ely *d* John Frankenheimer *ph* James Wong Howe *m* Jerry Goldsmith *titles* Saul Bass

☆ Rock Hudson, *John Randolph*, *Will Geer*, Salome Jens, Jeff Corey, Richard Anderson, Murray Hamilton, Wesley Addy

'A really horrifying piece of science fiction that burns its way into your mind like a gnawing headache.' – *Sunday Express*

'An ending that is one of the most terrifying episodes I have ever seen on the screen.' – *Daily Express*

James Wong Howe

Le Secret *

France 2000 107m colour

Optimum/Bagheera/France3/Diaphana (François Marquis)

aka: *The Secret*

A married encyclopedia saleswoman decides to have an affair with a visiting American dancer.

Engaging account of an impulsive, intense relationship with nowhere to go, one that hints at past, and future, disappointments.

w Virginie Wagon, Erick Zonca *d* Virginie Wagon *ph* Jean-Marc Fabre *m* Mercury Rev, Chuck Berry *pd* Brigitte Brassart *ed* Yannick Kergoat

☆ Anne Coesens (Marie), Michel Bompoil (François), Tony Todd (Bill), Quentin Rossi (Paul), Jacqueline Jehanneuf (Marie's mother)

'A powerful, impossible-to-forget picture.' – *Variety*

'A nursery crime of epic proportions...'

The Secret Adventures of Tom Thumb **

GB 1993 60m colour

Bolex Brothers/BBC Bristol/La Sept/Manga/Lumen (Richard 'Hutch' Hutchison)

A freakish tiny child, taken from his parents to a laboratory full of mutants, escapes into a rubbish dump inhabited by small people much like himself.

A squalid, predatory and unlovely universe is brilliantly created using a mix of live action, pixilation and stop-motion animation. The images are of decay and dissolution and disturbing in their detail (a laboratory technician's rubber gloves covered in bristles, a crucified Father Christmas, a man catching and eating a moth). The overall effect is of a wayward originality.

wd Dave Borthwick ph Dave Borthwick, Frank Passingham *m* John Paul Jones, Startled Insects *pd* Dave Borthwick *ed* Dave Borthwick

☆ Nick Upton, Deborah Collard, Frank Passingham, John Schofield, Mike Gifford, Robert Heath, George Brandt

'Brilliantly achieved but not one for the delectation of the feelgood brigade.' – *Derek Malcolm, Guardian*

The Secret Agent **

GB 1936 83m bw

Gaumont British (Michael Balcon, Ivor Montagu)

A reluctantly recruited spy is ordered to kill a man.

Unsatisfactory in casting and writing, this Hitchcock suspenser nevertheless has many typically amusing moments.

w Charles Bennett *play* Campbell Dixon *story* Ashenden by *Somerset Maugham d Alfred Hitchcock ph* Bernard Knowles *md* Louis Levy

☆ John Gielgud, Robert Young, *Peter Lorre*, Madeleine Carroll, Percy Marmont, Lilli Palmer, Florence Kahn

'As uncommon as it is unsentimentally cruel.' – *Peter John Dyer, 1964*

'Many sequences which show Hitchcock at his very best: the fake funeral, the murder on the mountainside, the riverside café, and the climax in a chocolate factory.' – *NFT, 1961*

'How unfortunate it is that Mr Hitchcock, a clever director, is allowed to produce and even to write his own films, though as a producer he has no sense of continuity and as a writer he has no sense of life. His films consist of a series of small "amusing" melodramatic situations: the murderer's button dropped on the baccarat board; the strangled organist's hands prolonging the notes in the empty church; the fugitives hiding in the bell tower when the bell begins to swing. Very perfunctorily he builds up to these tricky situations ... and then drops them.' – *Graham Greene*

'Hitch said he was offering me Hamlet in modern dress. But when we came to make it, all the psychological interest was dissipated.' – *John Gielgud*

The Secret Agent

GB 1996 95m Technicolor

Fox/Capitol (Norma Heyman)

aka: *Joseph Conrad's The Secret Agent*

In Victorian London, a double agent is ordered by his Russian masters to commit a terrorist act: blowing up the Greenwich Observatory.

Wan, drably understated version of Conrad's novel of small-time revolutionaries.

wd Christopher Hampton *novel* Joseph Conrad *ph* Denis Lenoir *m* Philip Glass *pd* Caroline Amies *ed* George Akers

☆ Bob Hoskins, Patricia Arquette, Gérard Depardieu, George Spelvin, Jim Broadbent, Christian Bale, Eddie Izzard, Elizabeth Spriggs, Peter Vaughan, Julian Wadham, Robin Williams (uncredited)

'Appropriately gloomy and grim, but these are not qualities that will recommend it to most audiences.' – *Variety*

† Conrad's novel was also filmed by Alfred Hitchcock as *Sabotage* (qv).

The Secret Agent Club

US 1996 90m Foto-Kem

Marquee/Starlight/Secret Agent/Hit (Brian Shuster, James Ian Lifton)

A gang of kids led by the son of a secret agent defeat the baddies who steal a deadly laser gun.

Dismal action film for a young audience, which tones down the violence somewhat, but remains as morally dubious as its adult counterparts.

w Rory Johnson *d* John Murlowski *ph* S. Douglas Smith *m* Jan Hammer *pd* James Scanlon *ed* Leslie Rosenthal

☆ Hulk Hogan, Richard Moll, Matthew McCurley, Edward Albert, Lyman Ward, James Hong, Barry Bostwick, Lesley-Anne Down

'A film with few pretentions to quality and scant interest in stimulating or engaging grown-ups.' – *Sight and Sound*

Secret Ballot **

Iran/Italy/Canada/Switzerland 2001 105m colour

Artificial Eye/Fabrica/Payam/SharmshirRAI/RTSI (Marco Muller, Babak Payami)

original title: *Raye Makhfi*

On the island of Kish a female election agent orders a soldier to accompany her to collect the scattered inhabitants' votes.

Gentle, absurdist comedy of isolation and male-female tensions, thyough its attitude to the democratic process is more ambivalent and sometimes mocking.

wd Babak Payami *idea* Mohsen Makhmalbaf *ph* Farzad Jodat *m* Michael Galasso *pd* Mandana Masoudi *ed* Babak Karimi

☆ Nassim Abdi (Girl), Cyrus Abidi (Soldier)

'A precious bit of ethnographic essence for moviegoers who can appreciate political irony for its own sake.' – *Andrew Sarris, New York Observer*

'Behind a locked door – the relentless evil of his past!'

Secret Beyond the Door

US 1948 98m bw

Universal/Walter Wanger (Fritz Lang)

An heiress marries a moody millionaire with a death fixation, and comes to think of herself as his next potential victim.

Silly melodrama with much chat and little suspense.

w Silvia Richards *story* Rufus King *d* Fritz Lang *ph* Stanley Cortez *m* Miklos Rozsa

☆ Joan Bennett, Michael Redgrave, Anne Revere, Barbara O'Neil, Natalie Schafer, Paul Cavanagh

'A dog-wagon *Rebecca* with a seasoning of psychiatrics.' – *Otis L. Guernsey Jnr*

'Lang gets a few wood-silky highlights out of this sow's ear, but it is a hopeless job and a worthless movie.' – *James Agee*

The Secret Bride

US 1935 63m bw

Warner

GB title: *Concealment*

A District Attorney is secretly married to the daughter of the politician he is trying to convict.

Dismal melodrama, tritely scripted.

w Tom Buckingham, F. Hugh Herbert, Mary McCall Jnr *play Concealment* by Leonard Ide *d* William Dieterle *ph* Ernest Haller

☆ Barbara Stanwyck, Warren William, Glenda Farrell, Grant Mitchell, Arthur Byron, Henry O'Neill, Douglass Dumbrille

'Fast moving melodrama, well above average.' – *Variety*

Secret Ceremony

GB 1969 109m Eastmancolor

Universal/World Films/Paul M. Heller (John Heyman, Norman Priggen)

A prostitute mothers a young girl with a strange past.

Nuthouse melodrama for devotees of the director.

w George Tabori *short story* Marco Denevi *d* Joseph Losey *ph* Gerry Fisher *m* Richard Rodney Bennett

☆ Elizabeth Taylor, Robert Mitchum, Mia Farrow, Pamela Brown, Peggy Ashcroft

'This piece of garbage is so totally ridiculous that I can't imagine why anyone would want to be in it, let alone see it.' – *Rex Reed*

Secret Command

US 1944 92m bw

Columbia (Phil L. Ryan)

An ex-foreign correspondent goes undercover at a shipyard to track down saboteurs.

Routine wartime thick ear.

w Roy Chanslor *story The Saboteurs* by John and Ward Hawkins *d* A. Edward Sutherland *ph* Franz Planer *m* Paul Sawtell

☆ Pat O'Brien, Carole Landis, Chester Morris, Ruth Warrick, Barton MacLane, Tom Tully, Wallace Ford, Howard Freeman

Secret Défense

France/Switzerland/Italy 1997 173m colour

Artificial Eye/La Sept/T&C (Martine Marignac, Christian Lambert)

A scientist's investigation into the death of her father leads to more deaths, accidental and deliberate.

An overlong, over-complicated thriller of tangled relationships.

w Pascal Bonitzer, Emmanuelle Cuau, Jacques Rivette *d* Jacques Rivette *ph* William Lubtchansky *m* Hesperion XX *ad* Manu de Chavigny *ed* Nicole Lubtchansky

☆ Sandrine Bonnaire, Jerzy Radziwilowicz, Laure Marsac, Grégoire Colin, Bernadette Giraud, Micheline Herzog, Sara Louis, Mark Saporta

'Patience is needed to watch the film and some may argue is not rewarded by the conclusion. My reply: watch more the unfurling than the answer.' – *James Mottram, Film Review*

Secret Flight: see *School for Secrets*

The Secret Four: see *The Four Just Men (1939)*

The Secret Four: see *Kansas City Confidential (1952)*

Secret Friends

GB 1991 97m Metrocolor

Feature/Whistling Gypsy/Film Four (Rosemarie Whitman)

On a train journey an artist hovers between dreams and reality as he imagines that his wife is a killer and that he has murdered his mistress.

Confusing account of a mid-life crisis in which it is difficult to separate fantasy from real life and hardly worth the effort of working out which is which.

wd Dennis Potter *novel Ticket to Ride* by Dennis Potter *ph* Sue Gibson *m* Nicholas Russell-Pavier *pd* Gary Williamson *ed* Clare Douglas

☆ Alan Bates, Gina Bellman, Frances Barber, Tony Doyle, Joanna David, Colin Jeavons, Rowena Cooper

'A tough ride for a very small return: the cramped and narcissistic anguish of a middle-aged male as seen in Potter passim.' – *Sheila Johnston, Independent*

'It is time that Potter pulled the communication cord on this particular train of thought.' – *Jonathan Romney, Sight and Sound*

The Secret Fury

US 1950 86m bw

RKO (Jack H. Skirball, Bruce Manning)

A successful pianist is deliberately driven insane by her fiancé.

Derivative melodrama of no great interest.

w Lionel House *d* Mel Ferrer *ph* Leo Tover *m* Roy Webb *md* Constantin Bakaleinikoff

☆ Claudette Colbert, Robert Ryan, Jane Cowl, Paul Kelly, Philip Ober, Elizabeth Risdon, Doris Dudley

The Secret Game: see *Les Jeux Interdits*

The Secret Garden *

US 1949 92m bw (Technicolor sequence)

MGM (Clarence Brown)

An orphan girl goes to stay with her moody uncle and brightens up the lives of those around her.

Subdued, richly produced, rather likeable Victorian fable with the same moral as The Bluebird *and* The Wizard of Oz: *happiness is in your own back yard.*

w Robert Ardrey *novel* Frances Hodgson Burnett *d* Fred M. Wilcox *ph* Ray June *m* Bronislau Kaper

☆ Margaret O'Brien, Herbert Marshall, Gladys Cooper, Elsa Lanchester, Dean Stockwell, Brian Roper

'Uneven, but oddly and unexpectedly interesting.' – *Richard Mallett, Punch*

'Let's have more pictures in this kindly vein.' – *Picturegoer*

'The timeless tale of a special place where magic, hope and love grow.'

The Secret Garden **

US 1993 101m Technicolor

Warner/American Zoetrope (Fred Fuchs, Fred Roos, Tom Luddy)

A young, lonely, orphaned girl, sent to live with her aristocratic uncle, helps her invalid cousin back to life.

A charming version of the classic children's story, deftly made, though its appeal may be too tame for today's audiences.

w Caroline Thompson *novel* Frances Hodgson Burnett *d* Agnieszka Holland *ph* Roger Deakins *m* Zbigniew Preisner *pd* Stuart Craig *ed* Isabelle Lorente

☆ Maggie Smith, Kate Maberly, Heydon Prowse, Andrew Knott, Laura Crossley, John Lynch, Walter Sparrow, Irene Jacob

'Executed to near perfection in all artistic departments, this superior adaptation of the perennial favorite novel will find its core public among girls but should prove satisfying enough to a range of audiences.' – *Variety*

The Secret Heart

US 1946 97m bw

MGM (Edwin H. Knopf)

A widow has problems with her emotionally disturbed daughter.

Old-fashioned woman's picture.

w Whitfield Cook, Anne M. Chapin *story* Rose Franken, William Brown Meloney *d* Robert Z. Leonard *ph* George Folsey *m* Bronislau Kaper

☆ Claudette Colbert, Walter Pidgeon, June Allyson, Robert Sterling, Marshall Thompson, Elizabeth Patterson, Richard Derr, Patricia Medina

'"There are three things you can't hide," says Walter Pidgeon in one of his bantering moments; "love, smoke, and a man riding a camel." I would add a fourth – that old MGM touch.' – *Richard Winnington*

Secret Interlude: see *Private Number (1936)*

Secret Interlude: see *The View From Pompey's Head (1955)*

'The daring plan – the staggering odds – the incredible five!'

The Secret Invasion
US 1964 98m DeLuxe Panavision
UA/San Carlos (Gene Corman)
During World War II five convicted criminals become commandos.
Cut price Dirty Dozen, quite well made and exciting.
w R. Wright Campbell *d* Roger Corman *ph* Arthur E. Arling *m* Hugo Friedhofer
☆ Stewart Granger, Raf Vallone, Henry Silva, Mickey Rooney, Edd Byrnes, William Campbell, Peter Coe

The Secret Laughter of Women *
GB 1998 99m Rank Film colour
Optimum/Paragon/HandMade/ECF/BSkyB/Arts Council/Elba (O.O. Sagay, Jon Slan)
In France, a successful, married science-fiction writer begins a tenative romance with an exiled Nigerian single mother, who is also courted by her priest who insists that Satan is white.
A romantic comedy that provides some pleasure in its depiction of a culture clash between Africans and English; otherwise it relies on its protagonists behaving in unbelievable ways.
w O.O. Sagay *d* Peter Schwabach *ph* Martin Fuhrer *m* Yves Laferriere *pd* Christopher J. Bradshaw *ed* Michael Pacek *cos* Louise Stjernsward
☆ Colin Firth (Matthew Field), Nia Long (Nimi Da Silva), Dan Lett (John), Joke Silva (Nene), Ariyon Bakare (Reverend Fola), Joy Elias-Rilwan (Mama Fola), Hakeem Kae-Kazim (Doctor Ade), Bella Enahoro (Madame Rosa), Oluwafisayo Roberts (Sammy), Rakie Ayola (Talking Drum), Caroline Goodall (Jenny Field), Ellen Thomas (Bitter Leaf), Thomas Baptiste (Papa Fola)
'Rambling and slight it may be. But it's also surprisingly endearing.' – *James Christopher, Times*

The Secret Life of an American Wife **
US 1968 92m DeLuxe
TCF/Charlton (George Axelrod)
A bored suburban housewife sets out to seduce a movie star.
Sympathetic comedy of sixties suburban manners.
wd George Axelrod ph Leon Shamroy *m* Billy May
☆ Walter Matthau, Anne Jackson, Patrick O'Neal, Edy Williams
'Both a first-class satire on American mores and a compassionate study of wish-fulfilment.' – *NFT, 1970*

The Secret Life of Sergei Eisenstein **
Italy/GB 1987 58m bw/colour
Polivideo/SSR-RTSI/BFI
Documentary on the life and work of the great Russian director.
Told in the first person, and drawing on Eisenstein's own words, this is a revealing portrait of a revolutionary artist in a hurry, one that gains from using excerpts from the films to illustrate the events of his life.
w Gian Carlo Bertelli, Pier Marco De Santi *writings of* Sergei M.Eisenstein *d* Gian Carlo Bertelli *m* Graziano Mandozzi *ed* Pedro Del Rey
☆ Paul Vaughan (Narrator)

The Secret Life of Walter Mitty **
US 1947 110m Technicolor
Samuel Goldwyn
A mother's boy dreams of derring-do, and eventually life catches up with fiction.
This pleasantly remembered star comedy, though it never had much to do with Thurber, can now be seen to have missed most of its opportunities, though the nice moments do tend to compensate.
w Ken Englund, Everett Freeman *story* James Thurber *d* Norman Z. McLeod *ph* Lee Garmes *m* David Raksin
☆ *Danny Kaye*, Virginia Mayo, Boris Karloff, Florence Bates, Fay Bainter, *Thurston Hall*, Ann Rutherford, Gordon Jones, Reginald Denny

Secret Meeting: see *Marie Octobre*

Secret Mission
GB 1942 94m bw
GFD/Marcel Hellman/Excelsior
During World War II four British Intelligence officers are landed in occupied France to discover the truth about German defences.
Stilted war suspenser.
w Anatole de Grunwald, Basil Bartlett, Terence Young *d* Harold French *ph* Bernard Knowles *m* Mischa Spoliansky
☆ Hugh Williams, Carla Lehmann, James Mason, Roland Culver, Nancy Price, Michael Wilding, Percy Walsh

Secret Motive: see *The London Blackout Murders*

The Secret of Blood Island
GB 1964 84m Technicolor
U-I/Hammer (Anthony Nelson Keys)
A girl parachutist secret agent is smuggled into a Japanese POW camp and out again.
Absurd blood and thunder, almost perversely enjoyable – but not quite.
w John Gilling *d* Quentin Lawrence *ph* Jack Asher *m* James Bernard
☆ Barbara Shelley, Jack Hedley, Charles Tingwell, Bill Owen, Lee Montague

The Secret of Convict Lake *
US 1951 83m bw
TCF (Frank P. Rosenberg)
In the 1870s, escaped convicts take over a California town.
Brooding, snowy, set-bound Western melodrama; predictable but watchable.
w Oscar Saul *d* Michael Gordon *ph* Leo Tover *m* Sol Kaplan *md* Lionel Newman
☆ Glenn Ford, Gene Tierney, Ann Dvorak, Ethel Barrymore, Zachary Scott, Barbara Bates, Cyril Cusack, Jeanette Nolan, Ruth Donnelly

The Secret of Madame Blanche
US 1933 85m bw
MGM
The woman who takes the blame for murder committed by a young man is the mother he never knew.
Or, Madame X unofficially revisited: all-stops-out melodrama very typical of its time.
w Frances Goodrich, Albert Hackett *play The Lady* by Martin Brown *d* Charles Brabin
☆ Irene Dunne, Phillips Holmes, Lionel Atwill, Douglas Walton, Jean Parker, Una Merkel

The Secret of My Success
GB 1965 105m Metrocolor Panavision
MGM/Andrew and Virginia Stone
A village policeman follows his mother's dictum that he should not think ill of others, and accidentally goes from success to success.
Flabby portmanteau comedy full of in-jokes and flat-footed farce; satire is not evident.
wd Andrew L. Stone *ph* David Boulton *m* Lucien Cailliet and others *md* Roland Shaw
☆ James Booth, Lionel Jeffries, *Amy Dalby*, Stella Stevens, Honor Blackman, Shirley Jones, Joan Hickson

The Secret of My Success *
US 1987 110m DeLuxe
Universal/Rastar (Herbert Ross)
A country cousin in New York is determined to hit the big time.
An amiable melange of familiar situations with just a touch of Midnight Cowboy and a sharp edge to some of the writing; but not enough to keep its star at the top.
w Jim Cash, Jack Epps, A. J. Carothers *d* Herbert Ross *ph* Carlo Di Palma *m* David Foster
☆ Michael J. Fox, Helen Slater, Richard Jordan, Margaret Whitton, John Pankow, Christopher Murney
'A bedroom farce with a leaden touch, a corporate comedy without teeth.' – *Daily Variety*

The Secret of Nimh *
US 1982 82m Technicolor
Aurora/Don Bluth
Forced out of her cosy field, a widowed mouse seeks the help of Nicodemus, king of the rat pack.
Animated cartoon by Disney artists who rejected that company's declining standards and set up their own factory. Alas, though they have the skills, the narrative they have chosen needed refining.
w Don Bluth, John Pomeroy, Gary Foldman, Will Finn *novel Mrs Frisby and the Rats of Nimh* by Robert C. O'Brien *d* Don Bluth *m* Jerry Goldsmith
☆ Featuring the voices of: Elizabeth Hartman, Derek Jacobi, Dom DeLuise, John Carradine, Peter Strauss, Aldo Ray, Edie McClurg, Wil Wheaton
'Vintage techniques are proudly invoked, but the story desperately needs loving care.' – *Sight and Sound*

'Between Land And Sea There Is A Place Where Myths Are Real...'

The Secret of Roan Inish
US 1993 102m DuArt
Metro Tartan/Skerry/Jones Entertainment (John Sloss, Glenn R. Jones, Peter Newman)
In Ireland, a young girl persuades her family to move to a seal-haunted island off the Donegal coast, where their ancestors once lived.
A Celtic myth, of loss and salvation, told with some sensitivity; but it is likely to leave modern audiences unmoved.
wd John Sayles *novel Secret of the Ron Mor Skerry* by Rosalie K. Fry *ph* Haskell Wexler *m* Mason Daring *pd* Adrian Smith *ed* John Sayles
☆ Mick Lally, Eileen Colgan, John Lynch, Jeni Courtney, Richard Sheridan, Cillian Byrne
'Hard to get through even as myth and even harder to contemplate as a contribution to any relevant form of Irish culture.' – *Derek Malcolm, Guardian*

The Secret of St Ives
US 1949 76m bw
Columbia
During the Napoleonic War, a French prisoner-of-war escapes from Edinburgh Castle, only to be accused of murder.
Modest swashbuckler with a somewhat lacklustre atmosphere.
w Eric Taylor *story* Robert Louis Stevenson *d* Phil Rosen *ph* Henry Freulich *m* Mischa Bakaleinikoff
☆ Richard Ney, Vanessa Brown, Henry Daniell, Aubrey Mather

The Secret of Santa Vittoria *
US 1969 140m Technicolor Panavision
UA/Stanley Kramer
In 1945 an Italian village hides its wine from the occupying Germans.
Expected, exhausting epic comedy with everyone talking at once.
w William Rose, Ben Maddow *novel* Robert Crichton *d* Stanley Kramer *ph* Giuseppe Rotunno *m* Ernest Gold
☆ Anthony Quinn, Anna Magnani, Virna Lisi, Hardy Kruger, Sergio Franchi, Renato Rascel
'A brainless farrago of flying rolling pins and rotten vegetables, filled with the kind of screaming, belching, eye-rolling fictional Italians only Stanley Kramer could invent.' – *Rex Reed*
Ernest Gold

The Secret of Stamboul
GB 1936 93m bw
Wainwright
reissue title: *The Spy in White*
An English adventurer foils a Turkish revolution.
Pale rendering of a full-blooded best-seller.
w Richard Wainwright, Howard Irving Young, Noel Langley *novel The Eunuch of Stamboul* by Dennis Wheatley *d* Andrew Marton
☆ Valerie Hobson, Frank Vosper, James Mason, Kay Walsh, Peter Haddon

The Secret of the Blue Room
US 1933 66m bw
Universal
An heiress's three suitors all volunteer to spend the night in the haunted room of her mansion.
Murderous malarkey without the courage of its convictions.
w William Hurlbut *d* Kurt Neumann
☆ Lionel Atwill, Gloria Stuart, Paul Lukas, Edward Arnold, Onslow Stevens, Robert Barrat, Elizabeth Patterson
'Americanization of a German mystery yarn which ought to do well in the smaller spots.' – *Variety*
† Remade in 1938 as *The Missing Guest* and in 1944 as *Murder in the Blue Room.*

The Secret of the Incas
US 1954 101m Technicolor
Paramount (Mel Epstein)
Various adventurers seek a priceless Inca jewel.
Boys' Own Paper yarn which sounds a good deal more exciting than it is: too much talk and a few choice studio backcloths drop the tension alarmingly, and the script lacks humour and conciseness.
w Ranald MacDougall, Sydney Boehm *story Legend of the Incas* by Sydney Boehm *d* Jerry Hopper *ph* Lionel Lindon *m* David Buttolph *ad* Hal Pereira, Tambi Larsen *ed* Eda Warren
☆ Charlton Heston, Robert Young, Thomas Mitchell, Nicole Maurey, Yma Sumac, Glenda Farrell, Michael Pate

The Secret of the Loch
GB 1934 80m bw
ABFD/Bray Wyndham
A diver thinks he finds a prehistoric monster in Loch Ness.
Mildly amusing exploitation item following the 1934 rebirth of interest in the old legend.
w Charles Bennett, Billie Bristow *d* Milton Rosmer *ph* Jimmy Wilson *m* Peter Mendoza
☆ Seymour Hicks, Nancy O'Neil, Gibson Gowland, Frederick Peisley, Rosamund John, Ben Field

'Run for your life! You must find the secret before it finds you!'

The Secret Partner *
GB 1961 91m bw
MGM (Michael Relph)
A blackmailing dentist is visited by a mysterious hooded stranger who forces him to rob one of his businessman victims.
Complex puzzle thriller, neatly made in sub-Hitchcock style.
w David Pursall, Jack Seddon *d* Basil Dearden *ph* Harry Waxman *m* Philip Green
☆ Stewart Granger, Haya Harareet, Bernard Lee, Hugh Burden, Melissa Stribling, Norman Bird, Conrad Phillips

The Secret People *
GB 1951 96m bw
Ealing (Sidney Cole)
European refugees in London during the thirties become members of a ring of anarchists.
Downbeat political melodrama which pleased neither the masses nor the highbrows, despite plaudits for sensitive direction and performances.
w Thorold Dickinson, Wolfgang Wilhelm *d Thorold Dickinson ph* Gordon Dines *m* Roberto Gerhard
☆ Valentina Cortese, Serge Reggiani, Audrey Hepburn, Charles Goldner, Megs Jenkins, Irene Worth, Athene Seyler, Reginald Tate
'The tension and power of the film make it one of the most remarkable British productions for some time.' – *Penelope Houston*
'That *Secret People*, despite the creative agonies recorded by Mr Lindsay Anderson [in a book on the making of the film] should turn out to be a confused, unco-ordinated spy thriller concealing a tentative message deep down below some strained effects of style is another tragedy of British film hopes.' – *Richard Winnington*

Secret Places
GB 1984 98m Eastmancolor
Rank/Skreba/Virgin (Simon Relph, Ann Skinner)
At the beginning of the Second World War an English schoolgirl forms a close relationship with another boarder, a refugee from Germany.
Psychological drama that is too sensitive for its own good, so that it seems more attenuated than intense.
wd Zelda Barron *novel* Janice Elliott *ph* Peter MacDonald *m* Michel Legrand *ed* Laurence Mery-Clark
☆ Marie-Therese Relin, Tara MacGowran, Claudine Auger, Jenny Agutter, Cassie Stuart, Anne-Marie Gwatkin, Klaus Barner, Sylvia Coleridge

The Secret Rapture *
GB 1993 96m colour
Oasis/Greenpoint/Channel 4 (Simon Relph)
Following the death of their father, two sisters become deadly rivals.
An only partially successful adaptation of a stage play, one that softens the political aspects of the original to concentrate on the personal, a melodramatic study of self-destruction.
w David Hare *play* David Hare *d* Howard Davies *ph* Ian Wilson *m* Richard Hartley *pd* Barbara Gosnold *ed* George Akers
☆ Juliet Stevenson, Joanne Whalley-Kilmer, Penelope Wilton, Alan Howard, Neil Pearson, Robert Stephens, Hilton McRae, Robert Glenister
'A relentless, humourless movie – and one that ultimately fails to move.' – *Robin Brooks, Empire*

Secret Service
US 1931 67m bw
RKO
During the Civil War a Yankee officer goes behind enemy lines and falls in love with a Southern girl.
Sluggish romantic adventure.
w Bernard Schubert *play* William Gillette *d* J. Walter Ruben
☆ Richard Dix, Shirley Grey, William Post Jnr, Gavin Gordon
'Dix does a good character. It's all the picture has.' – *Variety*

Secret Service of the Air
US 1939 61m bw
Warner
A government agent tracks down smugglers.
Serial-like thrills and comedy, adequately presented.
w Raymond Schrock *d* Noel Smith
☆ Ronald Reagan, Eddie Foy Jnr, John Litel, Ila Rhodes, James Stephenson
'No marquee names, but a better than average story of its kind.' – *Variety*

A Secret Sin: see *The Locusts*

The Secret Six *
US 1931 83m bw
MGM
A syndicate of businessmen finance two reporters to get evidence against a gang of bootleggers.
Solidly carpentered gangster thriller.
w Frances Marion *d* George Hill *ph* Harold Wenstrom
☆ Wallace Beery, Lewis Stone, Clark Gable, John Mack Brown, Jean Harlow, Marjorie Rambeau, Paul Hurst, Ralph Bellamy, John Miljan
'A gangster talker too rough, crude and familiar. In big cities it may pull the roughneck trade ... but the vocalized expression for it will be adverse.' – *Variety*

'It's not who you con – it's how you do it!'
The Secret War of Harry Frigg
US 1967 109m Techniscope
Universal/Albion (Hal E. Chester)
In 1943 a private engineers the escape of five captured generals.
Unattractive war comedy; slow, uninventive and overlong.
w Peter Stone, Frank Tarloff *d* Jack Smight *ph* Russell Metty *m* Carlo Rustichelli
☆ Paul Newman, *John Williams*, Sylva Koscina, Andrew Duggan, Tom Bosley, Charles D. Gray, Vito Scotti, James Gregory

The Secret Ways *
US 1961 112m bw
U-I/Heath (Richard Widmark)
An American reporter is recruited to rescue a scholar from communist Hungary.
Pretentious Iron Curtain melodrama, quite good to look at but overlong and no Third Man.
w Jean Hazelwood *novel* Alistair MacLean *d* Phil Karlson *ph* Max Greene *m* Johnny Williams
☆ Richard Widmark, Sonja Ziemann, Charles Regnier, Walter Rilla, Howard Vernon, Senta Berger

Secret Wedding **
Argentina/Netherlands 1989 95m colour
Allarts/Cogurccio/Cinéphile (Lujan Pflaum)
original title: *Boda Secreta*
Returning home after 13 years unjustly imprisoned in Buenos Aires, a man discovers that no one is prepared to recognize him, not even the woman he loves.
A gripping tale of political persecution, underscored by an unhappy romance.
wd Alejandro Agresti *ph* Ricardo Rodriguez *m* Paul Michael Van Brugge *pd* Juan Collini *ed* Rene Wiegmans
☆ Tito Haas, Mirtha Busnelli, Sergio Poves Campos, Nathan Pinzon, Flora Bloise, Elio Marchi

'A comedy for everybody who's been tied up at work.'
Secretary **
US 2002 111m colour
Metro Tartan/SloughPond/Double A/Twopoundbag (Steven Shainberg, Andrew Fierberg, Amy Hobby)
A troubled secretary begins a sado-masochistic sexual relationship with her new boss.
A quirky romantic story that isn't as painful as it sounds; there is a wry wit about its odd couple and their pleasures.
w Erin Cressida Wilson *story* Mary Gaitskill *d* Steven Shainberg *ph* Steven Fierberg *m* Angelo Badalamenti *pd* Amy Danger *ed* Pam Wise, Jay Rabinowitz
☆ James Spader (E. Edward Grey), Maggie Gyllenhaal (Lee Holloway), Jeremy Davies (Peter), Patrick Bauchau (Dr Twardon), Stephen McHattie (Burt Holloway), Oz Perkins (Jonathan), Jessica Tuck (Tricia O'Connor), Amy Locane (Lee's Sister), Lesley Ann Warren (Joan Holloway)
'In its own sick way, this has fervour and warped, erotic rapture. And it's very funny.' – *Peter Bradshaw, Guardian*
† The leading role was turned down by, among others, Claire Danes, Kate Hudson, Juliette Lewis, Sarah Polley, Christina Ricci and Reese Witherspoon.

Secrets *
US 1933 85m bw
UA (Mary Pickford)
A pioneering couple sticks together despite the husband's infidelities.
Curiously mixed-up star vehicle, part romantic comedy, part Western, part sob-stuff. Interesting rather than entertaining.
w Frances Marion *play* Rudolf Besier, May Edgington *d* Frank Borzage
☆ Mary Pickford, Leslie Howard, C. Aubrey Smith, Blanche Friderici, Doris Lloyd, Ned Sparks
'Singularly uneven ... but at least the story is given fine production and interesting playing.' – *Variety*.
'You can be sure you won't make any mistake by taking the family to see it.' – *Photoplay*
† Norma Talmadge starred in a 1923 silent version.

Secrets
Australia/New Zealand 1992 91m colour/bw
Victorian International/Avalon/NFU (Michael Pattinson)
In 1964, at the beginning of the Beatles' tour of Australia, five teenagers become trapped in the basement of the group's hotel.
A 'teen movie stretched beyond its limits; the director does not seem to know what to do with his ill-assorted group, once they are stuck in a cramped setting, other than let them talk too much.
w Jan Sardi *d* Michael Pattinson *ph* David Connell *m* Dave Dobbyn *pd* Kevin Leonard-Jones *ed* Peter Carrodus
☆ Beth Champion, Malcolm Kennard, Dannii Minogue, Willa O'Neill, Noah Taylor
'Pleasurable low-key entertainment.' – *Variety*

Secrets and Lies ***
GB 1995 141m Metrocolor
Film Four/CiBy 2000/Thin Man/Channel 4 (Simon Channing-Williams)
A successful black woman goes in search of her real mother, and discovers that she is white, unmarried and working-class.
Deft and sometimes moving portrait of a family finding redemption through the sharing of its secrets, though some of the performances teeter on the edge of caricature; it was much admired, particularly away from Britain, where audiences gave it less attention than it deserved.
wd Mike Leigh *ph* Dick Pope *m* Andrew Dickson *pd* Alison Chitty *ed* Jon Gregory
☆ *Timothy Spall*, Phyllis Logan, *Brenda Blethyn*, Claire Rushbrook, *Marianne Jean-Baptiste*, Elizabeth Berrington, Michele Austin, Lee Ross
'A beautifully constructed sentimental melodrama, with none of the rough edges that Mike Leigh has insisted on in the past. The only mystery is that Leigh should have come up with so classic a humanist product after proclaiming for so long that things could never be so simple.' – *Adam Mars-Jones, Independent*
'The movie, for all its appeal, is naggingly sanctimonious. It's *Guess Who's Coming to Dinner* for the culturally correct '90s.' – *Owen Gleiberman, Entertainment Weekly*
† It won the Palme d'Or, and Brenda Blethyn received the best actress award, at the Cannes Film Festival in 1996.
best picture; Mike Leigh (as writer and director); Brenda Blethyn; Marianne Jean-Baptiste
best British film; Mike Leigh (as writer); Brenda Blethyn

Secrets of a Secretary
US 1931 76m bw
Paramount
A social secretary discovers that her ex-husband is blackmailing her employer's daughter.
Peg's Paper *romance of a heroine who rises above her many problems.*
w Dwight Taylor, Charles Brackett *d* George Abbott
☆ Claudette Colbert, Herbert Marshall, George Metaxa, Mary Boland, Berton Churchill

Secrets of a Soul **
Germany 1926 95m (24 fps) bw silent
UFA/Hans Neumann
A chemist develops a knife phobia, has hallucinations, and tries to cut his wife's throat.
A lesson in elementary psychology which was innovatory at the time and survives as cinema for its stylish and impressionist use of visual techniques.
w Colin Ross, Hans Neumann, G. W. Pabst *d* G. W. Pabst *ph* Guido Seeber, Curt Oertel, Robert Lach
☆ Werner Krauss, Jack Trevor, Ruth Weyher, Pawel Pawlow

Secrets of an Actress
US 1938 70m bw
Warner
A star actress falls for one of her backers, a married architect.
High-life suffering of a familiar kind: it satisfied the Peg's Paper *audience.*
w Milton Krims, Rowland Leigh, Julius J. Epstein *d* William Keighley
☆ Kay Francis, George Brent, Ian Hunter, Gloria Dickson, Isabel Jeans, Peggy Singleton
'Miss Francis may be able to live up to all requirements except an acrobatic dance on the toes, but it's no use hitching race horses to milk wagons.' – *Variety*

Secrets of G32: see *Fly By Night*

Secrets of Scotland Yard
US 1944 68m bw
Republic (George Blair)
A British secret service man is impersonated by his Nazi twin brother.
Likeable absurdities with a strong cast.
w Denison Clift *novel* Room 40, O.B. by Denison Clift *d* George Blair
☆ C. Aubrey Smith, Edgar Barrier, Stephanie Bachelor, Lionel Atwill, Henry Stephenson, John Abbott, Walter Kingsford, Martin Kosleck

Secrets of the French Police
US 1932 55m bw
RKO
The Sûreté tracks down a hypnotist and murderer.
Rather wildly-imagined suspenser with points of interest.
w Samuel Ornitz, Robert Tasker *d* A. Edward Sutherland
☆ Gwili André, Frank Morgan, Gregory Ratoff, Murray Kinnell, John Warburton
'Hodge-podge of melodramatics ... hardly enough for the de luxers.' – *Variety*

Secrets of the Heart **
Spain/France/Portugal 1997 108m colour
Metrodome/Aiete/Ariane/DMVB/Fabrica de Imagens (Imanol Uribe, Andres Santana)
In Spain in the early 1960s, two boys dare each other to explore a deserted house, and also seek answers to the family secrets that seem to haunt the adults.
A sensitive child's-eye-view of adult desires and passions, made with skill and understanding.
wd Montxo Armendariz *ph* Javier Aguirresarobe *m* Bingen Mendizabal *pd* Felix Murcia *ed* Rori Sainz de Rozas *cos* Josune Lasa
☆ Andoni Erburu (Javi), Carmelo Gomez (Uncle), Charo Lopez (Aunt Maria), Silvia Munt (Mother), Vicky Pena (Aunt Rosa), Alvaro Nagore (Juan), Inigo Garces (Carlos)
'Ultimately suffers from its all too familiar subject, while the palpable sense of discovery becomes little more than a palpable sense of boredom.' – *Bob McCabe, Empire*
foreign film

Secrets of the Phantom Caverns
GB 1984 90m colour
Adams Apple (Sandy Howard, Robert D. Bailey)
aka: *What Waits Below*
Anthropologists and soldiers exploring a cave system in Latin America discover a lost albino tribe living underground.
Totally inept fantasy from beginning to end.
w Christy Marx, Robert Vincent O'Neil *story* Ken Barnett *d* Don Sharp *ph* Virgil Harper *m* Michael Rubini, Denny Jaeger *ad* Stephen Marsh *ed* John R. Bowey
☆ Robert Powell, Lisa Blount, Richard Johnson, Anne Heywood, A. C. Weary, Timothy Bottoms

Secrets of the Underground
US 1943 70m bw
Republic
The proprietor of a fashionable gown shop is a Nazi agent.
Nifty second feature on predictable wartime lines.
w Robert Tasker, Geoffrey Homes *d* William Morgan
☆ John Hubbard, Virginia Grey, Lloyd Corrigan, Miles Mander, Ben Welden

Secrets of Women: see *Waiting Women*

'Satan has chosen his victims. The battle with evil has begun.'
The Sect *
Italy 1991 115m Technicolor
Penta/ADC (Mario and Vittorio Cecchi Gori, Dario Argento)
original title: *La Setta*
A schoolteacher becomes accidentally involved with a group of devil worshippers who practise ritual human sacrifice.
Elegant, eerie and suspenseful horror with some gruesome moments.
w Dario Argento, Giovanni Romoli, Michele Soavi *d* Michele Soavi *ph* Raffaele Mertes *m* Pino Donaggio *pd* M. Antonello Geleng *ed* Franco Fraticelli
☆ Kelly Curtis, Herbert Lom, Tomas Arana, Maria Angela Giordano, Michel Adatte, Carla Cassola, Angelika Maria Boeck, Giovanni Lombardo Radice, Niels Gullov
'Soavi's dreamlike direction and enticing eye for design lend an air of gravitas to an otherwise workaday storyline, while a few choice moments of grisly gore ensure that diehard horror fans will not be disappointed.' – *Sight and Sound*

Sedmikrasky: see *Daisies*

'There are many ways to be seduced. Fame ... power ... love!'
The Seduction of Joe Tynan *
US 1979 107m Technicolor
Universal (Martin Bregman)
A young senator alienates his wife when he sacrifices his principles for advancement.
Fairly arresting political character drama with strong narrative and acting.

w Alan Alda *d* Jerry Schatzberg *ph* Adam Holender *m* Bill Conti
☆ Alan Alda, Barbara Harris, Meryl Streep, *Melvyn Douglas*, Rip Torn, Carrie Nye, Charles Kimbrough

The Seduction of Julia: see *Adorable Julia*

Seduction: The Cruel Woman
West Germany 1985 84m colour
Out on a Limb/Hyäne (Elfi Mikesch, Monika Treut)
original title: *Verführung: die Grausame Frau*
A dominatrix displays varieties of sado-masochistic sex in public and private.
Elegant, subversive film of limited appeal which ignores more normal sexuality for exotic and fetishistic variations, but the subject is treated with an obsessiveness that can seem risible to those who do not share its concerns.
wd Elfi Mikesch, Monika Treut *novel Venus in Furs* by Leopold von Sacher-Masoch *ph* Elfi Mikesch *m* Maran Gosov *ad* Manfred Blösser, Klaus Weinrich *ed* Renata Merck
☆ Mechthild Grossmann, Udo Kier, Sheila McLaughlin, Carola Regnier, Peter Weibel, Georgette Dee
'A dark and disturbing movie.' – *Sight and Sound*

See America Thirst
US 1930 71m bw
Universal
Two hoboes become involved with rum runners.
Poorly constructed talkie début for a silent comedian who never made it.
w Edward Luddy, Vin Moore, C. J. Horwin *d* W. J. Craft
☆ Harry Langdon, Slim Summerville, Bessie Love, Mitchell Lewis, Stanley Fields
'Direction shows silent technique throughout, and is unmindful of the talkie advent. Rub is that this system got reversed in the important sequences.' – *Variety*

See Here Private Hargrove *
US 1944 102m bw
MGM (George Haight)
Adventures of a raw recruit in the US army.
Standard transcription of a humorous bestseller which did its best to make the war painless for Americans.
w Harry Kurnitz *book* Marion Hargrove *d* Wesley Ruggles *ph* Charles Lawton *m* David Snell
☆ Robert Walker, Donna Reed, Robert Benchley, Keenan Wynn, Bob Crosby, Ray Collins, Chill Wills, Grant Mitchell
† Sequel 1945: *What Next, Corporal Hargrove?*

See How They Fall **
France 1993 100m colour 'Scope
MIHK/Bloody Mary/France3/CEC (Didier Haudepin)
original title: *Regarde les Hommes Tomber*
A crippled con man teaches criminal ways to an amoral young protégé who betrays him.
Dark, deftly made thriller with more than a hint of Jean Genet about it in its concentration on homosexual desire, degradation and death.
w Alain Le Henry, Jacques Audiard *novel Triangle* by Terry White *d* Jacques Audiard *ph* Gérard Sterin *m* Alexandre Desplat *pd* Jacques Rouxel *ed* Juliette Welfling
☆ Jean-Louis Trintignant, Jean Yanne, Mathieu Kassovitz, Bulle Ogier, Christine Pascal, Yvon Back

See How They Run
GB 1955 84m bw
Winwell (BL)
A country vicarage gets lively when several miscreants pretend to be the vicar.
Reliable stage farce which doesn't get the laughs on screen.
w Leslie Arliss, Roy Miller, Val Valentine *play* Philip King *d* Leslie Arliss *ph* Ken Talbot *m* John Bath
☆ Ronald Shiner, Greta Gynt, James Hayter, Wilfrid Hyde-White, Dora Bryan, Richard Wattis, Viola Lyel

See My Lawyer
US 1945 67m bw
Universal
Comedians try to get out of a night-club commitment by insulting the customers.
Thin vehicle for a team that wasn't going anywhere: too many variety acts got in their way.
w Edmund L. Hartmann, Stanley Davis *d* Edward F. Cline
☆ Ole Olsen, Chic Johnson, Grace McDonald, Franklin Pangborn, Alan Curtis, Noah Beery Jnr, Ed Brophy

See No Evil: see *Blind Terror*

See No Evil, Hear No Evil
US 1989 102m Technicolor
Columbia TriStar (Marvin Worth)
Suspected of murder, two friends, one deaf and the other blind, go in pursuit of the real killer.
Halting comedy that is not worth watching.
w Earl Barret, Arne Sultan, Eliot Wald, Andrew Kurtzman, Gene Wilder *d* Arthur Hiller *ph* Victor J. Kemper *m* Stewart Copeland *pd* Robert Gundlach *ed* Robert C. Jones
☆ Richard Pryor, Gene Wilder, Joan Severance, Kevin Spacey, Alan North, Anthony Zerbe, Louis Giambalvo, Kirsten Childs

'The Smart One Isn't Wearing Any Pants.'
See Spot Run
US/Australia 2001 97m Technicolor
Warner/Village Roadshow/NPV (Robert Simonds, Tracey Trench, Andrew Deane)
A slow-witted postman babysits a six-year-old boy and adopts an FBI dog on the run from gangsters.
A comedy with more writers than jokes, dumb, dim and witless.
w George Gallo, Gregory Poirier, Chris Faber, Danny Baron *adaptation* Stuart Gibbs, Craig Titley *d* John Whitesell *ph* John Bartley *m* John Debney *pd* Mark Freeborn *ed* Cara Silverman
☆ David Arquette (Gordon), Michael Clarke Duncan (Agent Murdoch), Leslie Bibb (Stephanie), Joe Viterelli (Gino), Angus T. Jones (James), Steven R. Schirripa (Arliss), Anthony Anderson (Benny), Paul Sorvino (Sonny), Bob (Agent 11)
'Seldom have movie co-stars been ordered to stoop so low in a film's sorry quest for laughs.' – *Variety*

See You in Hell Darling: see *An American Dream*

See You in the Morning
US 1988 119m Metrocolor
Warner/Lorimar (Alan J. Pakula)
A divorced psychiatrist begins an affair with an insecure widow with two young children.
Enjoyable, though hardly memorable, study of confused relationships.
wd Alan J. Pakula *ph* Donald McAlpine *m* Michael Small *pd* George Jenkins *ed* Evan Lottman
☆ Jeff Bridges, Alice Krige, Farrah Fawcett, Drew Barrymore, Lukas Haas, David Dukes, Frances Sternhagen, George Hearn, Theodore Bikel, Macaulay Culkin

Seed
US 1931 96m bw
Universal
A husband leaves his family to become a novelist, but returns ten years later.
Long-drawn-out domestic drama whose few virtues have not weathered the years.
w Gladys Lehman *novel* Charles G. Norris *d* John Stahl *ph* Jackson Rose *ed* Ted J. Kent
☆ John Boles, Genevieve Tobin, Lois Wilson, Raymond Hackett, Bette Davis, ZaSu Pitts
'Good woman's picture that will strike generous b.o. anywhere.' – *Variety*

'She never doubted his innocence. Now she'll pay for his freedom.'
Seeds of Doubt
Canada 1996 DeLuxe
Libra/Split Image (Craig Pryce)
A journalist campaigns for the release of an artist she claims was wrongly convicted of murder; after gaining his release, she begins an affair with him, and the killings begin again.
Dull thriller in which the audience is likely to be several steps ahead of the police in solving the crimes.
w David Wiechorek *d* Peter Foldy *ph* Thom Best *m* Barron Abramovitch *pd* Jennifer Carroll *ed* David Ransley
☆ Peter Coyote (Henry Dexter), Alberta Watson (Jennifer Kingsley), Joe Lando (Raymond Crawford), Colin Fox (David Golden), Frank Moore (Lester Crowley), Brooke Johnson (Mary Grimes), David Storch (Vincent Grimes), Tony Rosato (Nick Brand)

The Seekers
GB 1954 90m Eastmancolor
GFD/Fanfare (George H. Brown)
US title: *Land of Fury*
In 1820 a British sailor and his family emigrate to New Zealand.
Stilted epic which never gains the viewer's sympathy or interest.
w William Fairchild *d* Ken Annakin *ph* Geoffrey Unsworth *m* William Alwyn
☆ Jack Hawkins, Glynis Johns, Inia Te Wiata, Noel Purcell, Kenneth Williams, Laya Raki

Seemabadha: see *Company Limited*

Seems Like Old Times *
US 1980 102m Metrocolor
Columbia/Ray Stark
An innocently involved bank robber takes refuge with his ex-wife, a lady lawyer married to the district attorney.
Nostalgic farce which doesn't quite live up to the old skills and often bogs down in talk. Funny moments, though.
w Neil Simon *d* Jay Sandrich *ph* David M. Walsh *m* Marvin Hamlisch *pd* Gene Callahan *ed* Michael A. Stevenson
☆ Goldie Hawn, Chevy Chase, Charles Grodin, Robert Guillaume, Harold Gould, George Grizzard

Il Segno di Zorro: see *The Mark of Zorro (1963)*

Segunda Piel
Spain 1999 106m colour Panavision
Gala/Lolafilms/Via Digital/ Antena 3 (Andres Vicente Gomez)
aka: *Second Skin*
In Madrid, a wife discovers that her husband is having an affair with another man.
Bland drama of adultery, with an undeveloped and uninteresting character at its centre.
w Angeles Gonzalez-Sinde *d* Gerardo Vera *ph* Julio Madurga *m* Roque Banos *ad* Ana Alvargonzalez *ed* Nick Wentworth
☆ Javier Bardem (Diego), Jordi Molla (Alberto), Ariadna Gil (Elena), Cecilia Roth (Eva), Javier Albala (Rafa), Mercedes Sampietro (Elena's Mother), Adrian Sac (Manuel)
'The movie is quiet, modest and sympathetic almost to a fault; its scenes of emotional discord, accompanied by a swooning, sniffling score, seem best suited to cable television.' – A. O. Scott, *New York Times*

Sei Donne per l'Assassino: see *Blood and Black Lace*

Sei Sei Vivo, Spara!: see *Django, Kill!*

Seize the Day *
US 1986 93m colour
Learning in Focus (Chiz Schultz)
In the mid-50s a salesman who quits his job meets rejection and disillusion at every turn.
A movie faithful to the book, but its relentless portrait of a man's disintegration and humiliation is much less easy to bear on the screen than it was on the page.
w Ronald Ribman *novel* Saul Bellow *d* Fielder Cook *ph* Eric Van Haren Noman *m* Elizabeth Swados *pd* John Robert Lloyd *ed* Sidney Katz, Rachel Igel
☆ Robin Williams, Joseph Wiseman, Jerry Stiller, Glenne Headly, William Hickey, Tony Roberts, Tom Aldredge
† The film was made for TV. Saul Bellow has a walk-on role as a man in a hotel corridor.

Sélect Hotel
France 1996 82m colour
MIHK/Climax (Francisco Guiterrez)
Some denizens of a Parisian flophouse – a drug-addicted prostitute, her thieving brother and pimp – go about their miserable lives.
A depressing portrait of hopeless lives, lived on the edge of danger, which are viewed with sympathy and a disdain for conventional existence.
wd Laurent Bouhnik *ph* Gilles Henry *m* Jérôme Coullet *ad* Isabelle Millet *ed* Jacqueline Mariani, Clémence Bielov
☆ Julie Gayet, Jean-Michel Fête, Serge Blumental, Sabine Bail, Eric Aubrahn, Emmannuelle Rozes, Michel Gondoin
'Hardly a comfortable night at the pictures, this is an extraordinarily powerful but utterly draining piece of cinema.' – *Giala Murray, Empire*

'The story of a girl who had the spirit to believe in a dream and the courage to make it come true.'
Selena
US 1997 127m Technicolor
Warner/Q (Moctesuma Esparza, Robert Katz)
Biopic of the short life of the Mexican-American singer, who was murdered in 1995 just as she was on the brink of international stardom.
A bland drama that does not deviate from a familiar, stereotyped, showbiz format; its appeal will be mainly to fans of the singer, though it is enlivened by Jennifer Lopez's performance.
wd Gregory Nava *ph* Edward Lachman *m* Dave Grusin *pd* Cary White *ed* Nancy Richardson
☆ Jennifer Lopez (Selena Quintanilla), Edward James Olmos (Abraham Quintanilla), Jon Seda (Chris Perez), Constance Marie (Marcela Quintanilla), Jacob Vargas (Abie Quintanilla), Lupe Ontiveros (Yolanda Saldivar), Jackie Guerra (Suzette Quintanilla), Rebecca Lee Meza (Young Selena)

A Self-Made Hero ***
France 1995 106m colour
Artificial Eye/Alicélo/Lumière/France 3/M6/Initial (Patrick Godeau)
original title: *Un Héros Très Discret*
After the liberation of France, a cowardly and simple-minded fantasist reinvents himself as a hero of the Resistance.
Sharply political comedy of assumed identity and innocence – imagine a cross between Candide and Captain of Kopenick – which casts a beady and entertaining eye over French attitudes to the recent past.
w Alain Le Henry, Jacques Audiard *novel* Jean-François Deniau *d* Jacques Audiard *ph* Jean-Marc Fabre *m* Alexandre Desplat *ad* Michel Vandestien *ed* Juliette Welfling
☆ Mathieu Kassovitz, Anouk Grinberg, Sandrine Kiberlain, Jean-Louis Trintignant, Albert Dupontel, Nadia Barentin, Bernard Bloch
'Half comic and half in deadly earnest – a political film seemingly determined to cause offence by questioning both orthodox history and those who made it.' – *Derek Malcolm, Guardian*

The Selling of America: see *Beer*

The Sellout
US 1951 82m bw
MGM (Nicholas Nayfack)
A newspaper exposes a corrupt administration.
Competent melodrama with no surprises.
w Charles Palmer *d* Gerald Mayer *ph* Paul Vogel *m* David Buttolph
☆ Walter Pidgeon, John Hodiak, Audrey Totter, Thomas Gomez, Everett Sloane, Cameron Mitchell, Karl Malden, Paula Raymond

The Sellout
GB/Italy 1975 102m colour
Warner/Oceanglade/Amerifilm (Josef Shaftel)
Russians and Americans lure a double agent to Jerusalem in order to eliminate him.
Unsmiling spy melodrama with a complex plot, a bagful of clichés and some unnecessarily unpleasant violence.
w Judson Kinberg, Murray Smith *d* Peter Collinson *ph* Arthur Ibbetson *m* Mike Green, Colin Frechter

☆ Richard Widmark, Oliver Reed, Gayle Hunnicutt, Sam Wanamaker, Vladek Sheybal, Ori Levy, Assaf Dayan

La Semana del Asesino: see *Cannibal Man*

Semi-Tough *

US 1977 107m DeLuxe
UA/David Merrick

The manager's daughter decides between two star members of a football team.
Rambling satiric comedy which takes jabs at various states of mind in America today, notably the fashionable forms of self-help therapy. Much of it comes off quite well.
w Walter Bernstein *novel* Dan Jenkins
d Michael Ritchie *ph* Charles Rosher Jnr *m* Jerry Fielding
☆ Burt Reynolds, Kris Kristofferson, Jill Clayburgh, Bert Convy, Robert Preston, Lotte Lenya, Roger E. Mosley

Seminole

US 1953 86m Technicolor
Universal-International (Howard Christie)
A West Point graduate goes to Florida to make peace with the Indians.
Slightly unusual but not very interesting semi-Western with the usual clichés.
w Charles K. Peck Jnr *d* Budd Boetticher
ph Russell Metty *md* Joseph Gershenson
☆ Rock Hudson, Anthony Quinn, Barbara Hale, Richard Carlson, Hugh O'Brian, Russell Johnson, Lee Marvin, James Best

The Senator Was Indiscreet *

US 1947 95m bw
U-I (Nunnally Johnson)
GB title: *Mr Ashton Was Indiscreet*
A foolish politician determines to become president and hires a press agent.
Satirical political farce which hurls its shafts wide and doesn't seem to mind how few of them hit.
w Charles MacArthur *story* Edwin Lanham
d George S. Kaufman *ph* William Mellor
m Daniele Amfitheatrof
☆ William Powell, Ella Raines, Peter Lind Hayes, Ray Collins, Arleen Whelan, Allen Jenkins, Hans Conried, Charles D. Brown

Send Me No Flowers *

US 1964 100m Technicolor
U-I/Martin Melcher (Harry Keller)
A hypochondriac mistakenly thinks he is dying and tries to provide another spouse for his wife.
A timeworn farcical situation is handled in the glossy Doris Day manner; it all starts quite brightly but gradually fizzles out.
w Julius Epstein *play* Norman Barrasch, Carroll Moore *d* Norman Jewison *ph* Daniel Fapp
m Frank de Vol *ad* Alexander Golitzen, Robert Clatworthy
☆ Doris Day, Rock Hudson, Tony Randall, Paul Lynde, Clint Walker, Hal March, Edward Andrews

The Seniors

US 1977 87m Metrocolor
CSI (Stanley Shapiro, Carter de Haven)
Four college students discover a way to become rich by making prostitution respectable.
Exploitative comedy, mixing teenage wish-fulfilment with black but unfunny farce.
w Stanley Shapiro *d* Rod Amateau *ph* Robert Jessup *ed* Guy Scarpitta
☆ Jeffrey Byron, Gary Imhoff, Dennis Quaid, Lou Richards, Rocky Flintermann, Priscilla Barnes, Alan Reed

La Señora *

Spain 1987 103m colour
ICA/Virginia (Jonni Bassiner)
Sexually frustrated by a loveless marriage, an aristocratic woman finds temporary happiness with her gardener.
Moderately engrossing melodrama of sex and class.
w Jordi Cadena, Silvia Tortosa *novel* Antoni Mus
d Jordi Cadena *ph* José G. Galisteo *m* J. M. Pagan *pd* Joseph Maria Espada *ed* Amat Carreras
☆ Silvia Tortosa, Hermann Bonnin, Luis Merlo, Fernando Guillén-Cuervo, Jeaninne Mestre, Alfonso Guirao

Sensation

GB 1936 67m bw
BIP (Walter Mycroft)
A village barmaid is murdered and only our reporter hero sees the wider implications.
Presentable murder mystery.
w Dudley Leslie, Marjorie Deans, William Freshman *play* *Murder Gang* by Basil Dean, George Munro *d* Brian Desmond Hurst
ph Walter Harvey
☆ John Lodge, Diana Churchill, Francis Lister, Joan Marion, Margaret Vyner, Athene Seyler, Richard Bird
'The genuine situation is lost in false trials, in an absurd love story, in humour based on American films, and in the complete unreality of the "murder gang".' – *Graham Greene*

Sensations of 1945

US 1944 87m bw
Andrew L. Stone
Father and son disagree over the handling of their publicity agency.
Slim plot holds together a ragbag of variety acts, some quite choice.
w Dorothy Bennett *d* Andrew L. Stone
ph Peverell Marley, John Mescall *md* Mahlon Merrick
☆ Eleanor Powell, W. C. Fields, Sophie Tucker, Dennis O'Keefe, Eugene Pallette, C. Aubrey Smith, Lyle Talbot, Dorothy Donegan, Cab Calloway and his band, Woody Herman and his band
Mahlon Merrick

Sense and Sensibility ***

GB/US 1995 136m Technicolor
Columbia/Mirage (Lindsay Doran)
Two sisters hope for suitable husbands when they, their younger sister and widowed mother lose their home and money and are forced to move into a small cottage.
A high-spirited romance that is a joy to watch; Emma Thompson's casting as Elinor (who is a 19-year-old in the book) slightly undermines Austen's intent, but does not reduce the pleasure the film provides.
w Emma Thompson *story* Jane Austen *d Ang Lee*
ph Michael Coulter *m* Patrick Doyle *pd* Luciana Arrighi *ed* Tim Squyres
☆ Emma Thompson, Alan Rickman, *Kate Winslet*, Hugh Grant, James Flett, Harriet Walter, Gemma Jones, Elizabeth Spriggs, Robert Hardy, Greg Wise, *Hugh Laurie*, Imelda Staunton, Imogen Stubbs, Emile François
'Luminously brings to life Austen's vision of the dance of the sexes. The final romantic epiphany is a stunner, at once rapturous and funny.' – *Owen Gleiberman, Entertainment Weekly*
'It is still a pleasant shock to see a film so divested of precious charm in favour of humour, dramatic force and the kind of romance that isn't merely sentimental.' – *Derek Malcolm, Guardian*
† It won the Golden Bear as the best film at the 1996 Berlin Film Festival.
Emma Thompson (adapted screenplay)
best picture; Emma Thompson (as actress); Kate Winslet; Michael Coulter; Patrick Doyle; costume design (Jenny Beavan, John Bright)
best film; Emma Thompson (as actress); Kate Winslet

'A Secret Experiment... With Hilarious Side Effects!'
Senseless

US 1998 93m DeLuxe
Mandeville/Gold/Miller (David Hoberman)
A college student is the subject of an experiment that enhances his five senses.
Madcap comedy with a succession of hit-or-miss gags; most miss.
w Greg Erb, Craig Mazin *d* Penelope Spheeris
ph Daryn Okada *m* Yello *pd* Peter Jamison
ed Ross Albert
☆ Marlon Wayans (Darryl Witherspoon), David Spade (Scott Thorpe), Matthew Lillard (Tim LaFlour), Brad Dourif (Dr Wheedon), Tamara Taylor (Janice), Rip Torn (Randall Tyson), Richard McGonagle (Robert Bellweather), Esther Scott (Denise Witherspoon)
'Fairly fast-moving but essentially a collection of slipshod scenes.' – *USA Today*

Senso *

Italy 1953 115m Technicolor
Lux
aka: *The Wanton Countess (cut version)*
In 1866 Venice a noblewoman falls in love with an officer of the invading Austrian army, but finally denounces him.
The melodramatic plot is less important than the portrait of a period, for this is an expensive film in the grand style, often breathtaking to look at.
w Luchino Visconti, Suso Cecchi d'Amico and others *story* Camilla Botto *d Luchino Visconti*
ph G. R. Aldo, *Robert Krasker* *m* Anton Bruckner
ad Ottavio Scotti
☆ Alida Valli, Farley Granger, Massimo Girotti, Christian Marquand

The Sensualist

Japan 1992 54m colour
Ren Usami, Tsunemasa Hatano, Zuza Hagiwara
A merchant, whose life is dedicated to lust, aids a tailor who has wagered his manhood on bedding a courtesan at their first meeting.
A rarity: an animated film intended for an adult audience. The images, based on traditional Japanese woodcuts, are attractive; the inconsequential narrative less so.
w Eiichi Yamamoto *novel* Saikaku Ihara *d* Yukio Abe *ph* Minoru Fujita *m* Keiju Ishikawa
ad Yukio Abe *ed* Kenichi Takashima

Sentimental Journey

US 1946 94m bw
TCF (Walter Morosco)
An actress who knows she is dying arranges for a little orphan girl to take her place in her husband's affections.
Hollywood's most incredible three- handkerchief picture; nicely made, but who dared to write it?
w Samuel Hoffenstein, Elizabeth Reinhardt
story Nelia Gardner White *d* Walter Lang
ph Norbert Brodine *m* Cyril Mockridge
☆ Maureen O'Hara, John Payne, William Bendix, Cedric Hardwicke, Glenn Langan, Mischa Auer, Connie Marshall, Kurt Kreuger
'In twenty years of filmgoing I can't remember being so slobbered at: the apotheosis of the weepie.' – *Richard Winnington*
'It may not be for the critics, but who are critics? Just a lot of Joes, with passes.' – *Variety*
† Remade as *The Gift of Love* (qv).

'Doomed to guard the gates of Hell forever!'
The Sentinel

US 1976 92m Technicolor
Universal/Jeffrey Konvitz
A disturbed girl in an old apartment house is haunted by walking corpses: the house turns out to be the gateway to hell and she its appointed sentinel.
Vulgarly modish rip-off of several fashionable themes, notably Rosemary's Baby *and* The Exorcist.
w Michael Winner, Jeffrey Konvitz *novel* Jeffrey Konvitz *d* Michael Winner *ph* Dick Kratina
m Gil Melle
☆ Chris Sarandon, Cristina Raines, Martin Balsam, John Carradine, José Ferrer, Ava Gardner, Arthur Kennedy, Burgess Meredith, Sylvia Miles, Deborah Raffin, Eli Wallach, Jerry Orbach
'Moral or ironic points are hard to discern in the eye-wrenching flux of a Michael Winner movie, which drifts and zooms across its polished people and places in a continual caressing motion, as crudely excitatory as any sex movie when the climaxes are approaching.' – *Richard Combs, MFB*
'A man with a face that looks like chicken giblets, a naked whore with a mouse on her thigh, a cat devouring a canary and Sylvia Miles in a tight leotard – these are some of the highlights of *The Sentinel*, a perfect film for those who like to slow down and look at traffic accidents.' – *Janet Maslin, Newsweek*

Senza Ragione: see *Redneck*

Seom *

South Korea 2000 89m colour
Metro Tartan/CJ Entertainment/Myung (Lee Eun)
GB title: *The Isle*
A fugitive who killed his wife and her lover hides out on a remote island with the aid of a mysterious mute prostitute.
A strange fable of sexual jealousy and violent lust, where lovers literally reel each other in on fishing lines
wd Kim Ki-duk *ph* Hwang Suh-shik *ad* Kim Ki-duk *ed* Kyung Min-ho
☆ Seoh Jung (Hee-Jin), Kim Yu-seok (Hyun-Shik), Park Sung-hee (Eun-A), Jang Hang-sun (Middle-aged man), Jo Jae-hyun (Mang Chee)
'A gross-out movie in art-house clothing.' – *Richard Falcon, Sight and Sound*
'A gorgeously restrained, apocalyptically horrifying pas de deux that's notorious for precipitating fainting spells and vomit seizures at press screenings.' – *Michael Atkinson, Village Voice*

Separate Beds: see *The Wheeler Dealers*

Separate Lives

US 1995 101m colour
Interscope/Trimark (Mark Amin, Diane Nabatoff, Guy Reidel)
A psychology professor with a split personality fears she may have committed a murder.
Dully derivative thriller, offering nothing that has not been done rather better in the past.
w Steven Pressfield *d* David Madden *ph* Kees Van Oostrum *m* William Olvis *pd* Bernt Capra
ed Janice Hampton
☆ James Belushi, Linda Hamilton, Vera Miles, Elisabeth Moss, Drew Snyder, Mark Lindsay Chapman, Marc Poppel, Elizabeth Arlen
'A thinly plotted and tiresomely formulaic drama.' – *Variety*

Separate Tables **

US 1958 98m bw
UA/Hecht-Hill-Lancaster (Harold Hecht)
Emotional tensions among the boarders at a British seaside guest house.
The genteel melodramas seem less convincing on the Hollywood screen than they did on the London stage, but the handling is thoroughly professional.
w Terence Rattigan, John Gay *play* Terence Rattigan *d* Delbert Mann *ph* Charles Lang
m David Raksin
☆ Burt Lancaster, Rita Hayworth, *David Niven*, Deborah Kerr, *Wendy Hiller*, *Gladys Cooper*, *Cathleen Nesbitt*, *Felix Aylmer*, Rod Taylor, Audrey Dalton, *May Hallatt*
David Niven; Wendy Hiller
best picture; script; Charles Lang; David Raksin; Deborah Kerr

La Séparation *

France 1994 88m colour
Guild/Renn/France2/DA/MCV/Canal (Claude Berri)
An unmarried couple, who have a young child, begin to drift apart.
A buttoned-up account of the breakdown of a relationship, given intensity by the acting of its two protagonists.
w Dan Franck, Christian Vincent *novel* Dan Franck *d* Christian Vincent *ph* Denis Lenoir
m Bach *ad* Christian Vallerin *ed* François Ceppi
☆ Isabelle Huppert, Daniel Auteuil, Jerôme Deschamps, Karin Viard, Laurence Lerel, Louis Vincent, Nina Morato

Seppuku: see *Hara Kiri*

September

US 1987 83m DuArt/DeLuxe
Orion (Jack Rollins, Charles H. Joffe)
Enclosed family drama: Allen in his melancholy Bergman mode.
wd Woody Allen *ph* Carlo Di Palma *m* various
ad Speed Hopkins *ed* Susan E. Morse
☆ Denholm Elliott, Dianne Wiest, Mia Farrow, Elaine Stritch, Sam Waterston
'The debts to Chekhov are everywhere.' – *Variety*

September Affair
US 1950 104m bw
Paramount (Hal B. Wallis)

Two married people fall in love and a plane crash in which they are reported dead gives them their chance.
Turgid romantic melodrama, not very well made despite the background tour of Capri; what made it a hit was the playing of the old Walter Huston record of the title song.
w Robert Thoeren *d* William Dieterle *ph* Charles B. Lang *m* Victor Young
☆ Joseph Cotten, Joan Fontaine, Françoise Rosay, Jessica Tandy, Robert Arthur, Jimmy Lydon
'A smooth surface mirrors the film's essential superficiality.' – *Penelope Houston*

September Storm
US 1960 110m DeLuxe Cinemascope 3-D
TCF/Alco (Edward L. Alperson)
A New York model and two adventurers search for sunken treasure off an uncharted Mediterranean island.
Thin actioner originally intended to marry 3-D and Cinemascope, but failed to do so.
w W. R. Burnett *novel* *The Girl in the Red Bikini* by Steve Fisher *d* Byron Haskin *ph* Jorge Stahl Jnr, Lamar Boren *m* Edward L. Alperson Jnr
☆ Joanne Dru, Mark Stevens, Robert Strauss

Sequestro di Persona: see *Island of Crime*

Sequoia
US 1934 73m bw
MGM
A girl living in the High Sierras defends wild animals from hunters.
Refreshingly unusual outdoor drama with good location photography.
w Ann Cunningham, Sam Armstrong, Carey Wilson *d* Chester Franklin *ph* Chester Lyons
☆ Jean Parker, Russell Hardie, Samuel S. Hinds, Paul Hurst
'It was unlikely that either Miss Parker or the deer would eat the puma, but I hung on hoping that the puma would eat the deer or Miss Parker.' – *James Agate*

Serena
GB 1962 62m bw
Butcher's (John I. Phillips)
A Scotland Yard detective investigating a murder discovers that the victim is not who he thought it was.
A neat but somewhat plodding mystery with a clever twist at the end.
w Reginald Hearne, Edward and Valerie Abraham *d* Peter Maxwell *ph* Stephen Dade *m* John Gregory *ad* George Provis *ed* Allan Morrison
☆ Patrick Holt, Emrys Jones, Honor Blackman, Bruce Beeby, John Horsley, Vi Stevens, Gerry Duggan, Benedicta Leigh, Wally Patch

Serenade: see *Broadway Serenade (1939)*

Serenade
US 1956 121m Warnercolor
Warner (Henry Blanke)
A vineyard worker becomes a successful opera singer and is desired by two women.
Cliché success story with plot taking second place to singing.
w Ivan Goff, Ben Roberts, John Twist *novel* James M. Cain *d* Anthony Mann *ph* Peverell Marley *md* Ray Heindorf *songs* *Nicholas Brodszky (m), Sammy Cahn (ly)*
☆ Mario Lanza, Joan Fontaine, Sarita Montiel, Vincent Price, Joseph Calleia, Harry Bellaver, Vince Edwards, Silvio Minciotti

'Fate–the best matchmaker there is.'
'Can Once In A Lifetime Happen Twice?'
Serendipity
US 2001 90m DeLuxe
Buena Vista/Tapestry (Simon Fields, Peter Abrams, Robert L. Levy)
As the date of his marriage looms, a man goes in search of a woman he met briefly years before.
Amiable but empty romantic comedy, so full of coincidence that it becomes risible.
w Marc Klein *d* Peter Chelsom *ph* John De Borman *m* Alan Silvestri *pd* Caroline Hanania *ed* Christopher Greenbury
☆ John Cusack (Jonathan Trager), Kate Beckinsale (Sara Thomas), Molly Shannon (Eve), Jeremy Piven (Dean Kansky), John Corbett (Lars Hammond), Bridget Moynahan (Halley Buchanan), Eugene Levy (Bloomingdale's Salesman)
'Will serve as an excellent gauge of any viewer's tolerance level for schmaltzy contrivance and manipulation.' – *Todd McCarthy, Variety*

The Sergeant
US 1968 108m Technicolor
Warner/Robert Wise (Richard Goldstone)
France, 1952. In a dreary army camp, a tough army sergeant with a guilt complex is brought face to face with his own homosexuality.
Well-made but very ponderous and limited melodrama which could have been told in half the time.
w Dennis Murphy *play* Dennis Murphy *d* John Flynn *ph* Henri Persin *m* Michel Mayne
☆ Rod Steiger, John Phillip Law, Frank Latimore, Ludmila Mikael

Sgt Bilko
US 1996 94m DeLuxe
Universal/Imagine/Entertainment (Brian Grazer)
Sergeant Bilko outsmarts an old rival, an army major.
Dull and miscast comedy, one that only makes the original television series seem, in retrospect, better than it was.
w Andy Breckman *d* Jonathan Lynn *ph* Peter Sova *m* Alan Silvestri *pd* Lawrence G. Paull *ed* Tony Lombardo
☆ Steve Martin, Dan Aykroyd, Phil Hartman, Glenne Headly, Daryl Mitchell, Max Casella, Eric Edwards, Dan Ferro
'This misconceived venture could just give a laugh or two to those who have never seen the original, but those who have may curse the day Martin was born.' – *Derek Malcolm, Guardian*
'A terrible film ... has no visual wit, a pathetically scrappy script and the usual "pop-noodle" soundtrack of disparate songs. Oh, and Dan Aykroyd's Colonel Hall is as much an insult to Paul Ford's magnificent creation as this whole episode is a piss-stain on Phil Silver's pedestal.' – *Kim Newman, Sight and Sound*
† The original TV series was first titled *You'll Never Get Rich*, then was known as *The Phil Silvers Show*, running from 1955 to 1959, and retitled *Sgt Bilko* when it was syndicated. Created by Nat Hiken, who named its hero after his favourite baseball player, Steve Bilko, it starred Phil Silvers as Bilko, supported by Paul Ford as his commanding officer and Elisabeth Fraser as his girlfriend.

'The funniest foul-up of the space age!'
Sergeant Deadhead
US 1965 89m CFI color
AIP (James H. Nicholson, Samuel Z. Arkoff)
An army sergeant is accidentally sent into orbit and undergoes a personality change.
Clumsy comedy partially redeemed by its supporting players.
w Louis M. Heyward *d* Norman Taurog *ph* Floyd Crosby *m* Les Baxter
☆ Frankie Avalon, Deborah Walley, Fred Clark, Cesar Romero, Eve Arden, Gale Gordon, Buster Keaton, Harvey Lembeck, John Ashley

Sergeant Madden
US 1939 78m bw
MGM (J. Walter Ruben)
A policeman's son becomes a gangster.
Routine crime melodrama with sentimental trimmings, quite untypical of its director.
w Wells Root *story* *A Gun in His Hand* by William A. Ulman *d* Josef von Sternberg *ph* John Seitz *m* William Axt
☆ Wallace Beery, Tom Brown, Alan Curtis, Laraine Day, Fay Holden, Marc Lawrence, Marion Martin
'Good programme drama, geared to supply strong support in the key duals.' – *Variety*

Sgt Pepper's Lonely Hearts Club Band
US 1978 111m Technicolor
Panavision
Universal/Robert Stigwood (Dee Anthony)
A family band finds a new sound despite the activities of villains.
Oddball hotch-potch of middle-aged comedy and youth nostalgia with an American small-town setting. Some moments please, but most of it simply doesn't gel.
w Henry Edwards *d* Michael Schultz *ph* Owen Roizman *m* various (mostly the Beatles) *pd* Brian Eatwell
☆ Peter Frampton, Barry Gibb, Robin Gibb, Maurice Gibb, George Burns, Frankie Howerd, Donald Pleasence, Paul Nicholas, Sandy Farina, Alice Cooper, Steve Martin, Earth Wind and Fire
'Another of those films which serve as feature-length screen advertising for an album.' – *Variety*

Sergeant Rutledge *
US 1960 111m Technicolor
Warner/John Ford (Willis Goldbeck, Patrick Ford)
In 1881 a black army sergeant is on trial for rape and murder, but his defence counsel reveals the real culprit.
Flashback Western; not the director's best, but generally of some interest.
w James Warner Bellah, Willis Goldbeck *d* John Ford *ph* Bert Glennon *m* Howard Jackson
☆ Woody Strode, Jeffrey Hunter, Constance Towers, Willis Bouchey, Billie Burke, Carleton Young, Juano Hernandez, Mae Marsh

Sergeant Steiner
West Germany 1979 115m Eastmancolor
Panavision
Palladium/Rapidfilm (Arlene Sellers, Alex Winitsky)
aka: *Breakthrough*
The German sergeant hero of *Cross of Iron* survives the Western Front and involvement in an anti-Hitler conspiracy.
Somewhat bloodless though interesting sequel to an exceptionally nasty war film, with an international cast aiming at better box-office.
w Tony Williamson *d* Andrew McLaglen *ph* Tony Imi *m* Peter Thomas
☆ Richard Burton, Robert Mitchum, Curt Jurgens, Rod Steiger, Helmut Griem, Michael Parks

Sergeant York **
US 1941 134m bw
Warner (Jesse L. Lasky)
The story of a gentle hillbilly farmer who became a hero of World War I.
Standard real-life fiction given the big treatment; a key Hollywood film of its time in several ways.
w Abem Finkel, Harry Chandler, Howard Koch, John Huston *d* *Howard Hawks* *ph* *Sol Polito* *m* *Max Steiner* *ad* *John Hughes* *ed* *William Holmes*
☆ Gary Cooper, Joan Leslie, Walter Brennan, George Tobias, David Bruce, Stanley Ridges, Margaret Wycherly, Dickie Moore, Ward Bond
'I hardly think the effect is any different from that of a parade, with colours and a band; it is stirring and it is too long; there are too many holdups and too many people out of step, and your residue of opinion on the matter is that it will be nice to get home and get your shoes off.' – *Otis Ferguson*
'It has all the flavour of true Americana, the blunt and homely humour of backwoodsmen and the raw integrity peculiar to simple folk.' – *Bosley Crowther, New York Times*
Gary Cooper
best picture; script; Howard Hawks; Sol Polito; Max Steiner; Walter Brennan; Margaret Wycherly; John Hughes; William Holmes

Sergeants Three
US 1961 112m Technicolor Panavision
(UA) Essex-Claude (Frank Sinatra)
Just after the Civil War three cavalry sergeants, with the help of an ex-slave bugler, dispose of some hostile Indians.
High-spirited but exhausting parody of Gunga Din, with bouts of unfunny bloodthirstiness separated by tedious slabs of dialogue.
w W. R. Burnett *d* John Sturges *ph* Winton Hoch, Carl Guthrie *m* Billy May
☆ Frank Sinatra, Dean Martin, Peter Lawford, Sammy Davis Jnr, Joey Bishop, Henry Silva, Ruta Lee
'The participants have a better time than the onlookers.' – *Judith Crist, 1973*

Serial *
US 1980 91m Movielab
Paramount/Sidney Beckerman
Well-heeled Californians in a high suburban community go in for various cults and fashions.
Amusing satire on everything from Peyton Place to Bob and Carol and Ted and Alice. Just a little late in coming, that's all.
w Rich Eustis, Michael Elias *novel* Cyra McFadden *d* Bill Persky *ph* Rexford Metz *m* Lalo Schifrin
☆ Martin Mull, Tuesday Weld, Jennifer McAllister, Sam Chew Jnr, Sally Kellerman, Nita Talbot, Bill Macy, Christopher Lee, Pamela Bellwood, Peter Bonerz, Tom Smothers

'A loving mother. A caring wife. A model citizen. So what's the problem?'
Serial Mom *
US 1994 89m Technicolor
Guild/Savoy/Polar (John Fiedler, Mark Tarlov)
A devoted home-loving wife and mother becomes famous after she murders everyone who upsets her by not behaving as she expects.
Mildly amusing one-sick-joke movie, given a little spark by Turner's comic turn as the killer mother.
wd John Waters *ph* Robert M. Stevens *m* Basil Poledouris *pd* Vincent Peranio *ed* Janice Hampton, Erica Huggins
☆ *Kathleen Turner*, Sam Waterston, Ricki Lake, Matthew Lillard, Mary Jo Catlett, Patricia Hearst, Mink Stole, Suzanne Somers (herself)
'There is something insubstantial about Waters' satire of sit-com suburbia.' – *Kim Newman, Sight and Sound*

'Real People In Real Danger'
Series 7: The Contenders **
US 2000 87m colour
Film4/USA/Blow Up/Killer/Open City (Jason Kliot, Joana Vicente, Christine Vachon, Katie Roumel)
In a national lottery for a TV programme, five people are chosen for a contest which only one of them can survive.
Slick, engaging thriller, updating a satirical notion explored by writer Robert Sheckley in The Seventh Victim some 40 years ago, and gaining topicality with the current craze for 'reality TV'.
wd Daniel Minahan *ph* Randy Drummond *m* Girls Against Boys *pd* Gideon Ponte *ed* Malcolm Jamieson
☆ Brooke Smith (Dawn), Glenn Fitzgerald (Jeff), Marylouise Burke (Connie), Richard Venture (Franklin), Michael Kaycheck (Tony), Merritt Wever (Lindsay), Angelina Phillips (Doria), Nada Despotovich (Michelle)
'Effectively satiric while still developing and sustaining a rooting interest in its invented story over the course of a smart, short running time.' – *Todd McCarthy, Variety*

Serious Charge
GB 1959 99m bw
Alva (Mickey Delamar)
A small-town troublemaker, accused by his priest of being responsible for the death of a young girl, amuses himself by accusing the priest of making homosexual advances.
A sensational play of its time makes a dull film despite earnest performances.
w Guy Elmes, Mickey Delamar *play* Philip King *d* Terence Young *ph* Georges Périnal *m* Leighton Lucas
☆ Anthony Quayle, Andrew Ray, Sarah Churchill, Irene Browne, Percy Herbert, Cliff Richard

The Serpent
France/Italy/Germany 1974 124m colour
Films La Boetie (Henri Verneuil)
A top KGB official defects to the West.
Complicated, humourless, multi-lingual spy capers.

w Henri Verneuil, Gilles Perrault *novel* Pierre Nord *d* Henri Verneuil *ph* Claude Renoir *m* Ennio Morricone
☆ Yul Brynner, Henry Fonda, Dirk Bogarde, Philippe Noiret, Farley Granger, Virna Lisi

The Serpent and the Rainbow
US 1987 98m DuArt
UIP/Universal (David Ladd, Doug Claybourne)

A scientist travels to Haiti to investigate zombies.
Standard horror film, designed to shock, in which it succeeds.
w Richard Maxwell, A. R. Simoun *book* Wade Davis *d* Wes Craven *ph* John Lindley *m* Brad Fiedel *pd* David Nichols *ed* Glenn Farr
☆ Bill Pullman, Cathy Tyson, Zakes Mokae, Paul Winfield, Brent Jennings, Conrad Roberts, Badja Djola, Theresa Merritt, Michael Gough

The Serpent's Egg *
West Germany/US 1977 120m Eastmancolor
Rialto-Dino de Laurentiis

An American trapeze artist has a hard time in Berlin at the time of Hitler's rise to power.
More of a curate's egg, really, with a poor leading performance and too many lapses into nastiness, but much incidental interest of the kind one associates with the director.
wd Ingmar Bergman *ph* Sven Nykvist *m* Rolf Wilhelm *pd* Rolf Zehetbauer
☆ David Carradine, Liv Ullmann, Gert Frobe, James Whitmore, Heinz Bennent
'A crackpot tragedy: everything is strained, insufficient, underfelt.' – *New Yorker*

'She hunts to mate and mates to kill.'
Serpent's Lair
US 1995 90m DeLuxe
Kushner-Locke/WarnerVision/Castel (Vlad Paunescu)

A businessman is seduced by an irresistible and sexually voracious succubus.
Risible exploitation movie, barely competent on any level.
w Marc Rosenberg *d* Jeffrey Reiner *ph* Feliks Parnell *m* Vinny Golia *pd* Stuart Blatt *ed* Virginia Katz
☆ Jeff Fahey, Lisa B., Heather Medway, Anthony Palermo, Kathleen Noone, Jack Kehler, Patrick Bauchau, Taylor Nichols

Serpico *
US 1973 130m Technicolor
Paramount/Artists Entertainment Complex/Dino de Laurentiis (Martin Bregman)

A New York cop reveals police corruption and is eventually forced to leave the country.
A harrowing true story played with authentic gloom and violence.
w Waldo Salt, Norman Wexler *book* Peter Maas *d* Sidney Lumet *ph* Arthur J. Ornitz *m* Mikis Theodorakis
☆ Al Pacino, John Randolph, Jack Kehoe, Biff McGuire
'There's nothing seriously wrong with *Serpico* except that it's unmemorable, and not even terribly interesting while it's going on.' – *Stanley Kauffmann*
script; Al Pacino

The Servant **
GB 1963 116m bw
Elstree/Springbok (Joseph Losey, Norman Priggen)

A rich, ineffectual young man is gradually debased and overruled by his sinister manservant and his sexy 'sister'.
Acclaimed in many quarters on its first release, this downbeat melodrama now seems rather naïve and long drawn out; its surface gloss is undeniable, but the final orgy is more risible than satanic.
w Harold Pinter *novel* Robin Maugham *d* Joseph Losey *ph* *Douglas Slocombe* *m* Johnny Dankworth
☆ *Dirk Bogarde, James Fox, Sarah Miles,* Wendy Craig, Catherine Lacey, Richard Vernon
'Moodily suggestive, well acted, but petering out into a trickle of repetitious unmeaningful nastiness.' – *John Simon*
Dirk Bogarde; James Fox; Douglas Slocombe

Service De Luxe *
US 1938 85m bw
Universal
Adventures of the members of a super-secretarial agency.
Very tolerable but uninspired comedy which doesn't really allow its acting talent full rein.
w Gertrude Purcell, Leonard Spigelgass *d* Rowland V. Lee *ph* George Robinson *ad* Jack Otterson *ed* Ted J. Kent
☆ Constance Bennett, Vincent Price, Charles Ruggles, Helen Broderick, Mischa Auer, Halliwell Hobbes
'A speedy comedy-drama ... will hold its own as a leadoff attraction in the keys.' – *Variety*

Service for Ladies
GB 1932 93m bw
Paramount (Alexander Korda)
US title: *Reserved for Ladies*
A waiter has a way with his rich lady clients.
Tenuous satirical comedy, a variation on the American silent The Grand Duchess and the Waiter.
w Eliot Crawshay-Williams, Lajos Biro *novel* *The Head Waiter* by Ernst Vajda *d* Alexander Korda *m* Percival Mackey *ad* Alfred Junge *ed* Harold Young
☆ Leslie Howard, George Grossmith, Benita Hume, Elizabeth Allan, Morton Selten, Cyril Ritchard, Martita Hunt, Merle Oberon
'Too talky and English for general American consumption.' – *Variety*

'The One Thing That Could Bring Them Together Is Revenge.'
Serving Sara
US/Germany 2002 99m DeLuxe
Paramount/Mandalayl/Ilusion/Halsted

A subpoena server double-crosses a Texan millionaire when he is sent to serve divorce papers on the man's unsuspecting wife.
Farcical chase comedy with a coarse line in jokes and little else to recommend it.
w Jay Scherick, David Ronn *d* Reginald Hudlin *ph* Robert Brinkmann *m* Marcus Miller *pd* Rusty Smith *ed* Jim Miller
☆ Matthew Perry (Joe Tyler), Elizabeth Hurley (Sara Moore), Bruce Campbell (Gordon Moore), Amy Adams (Kate), Vincent Pastore (Tony), Cedric the Entertainer (Ray Harris), Jerry Stiller (Milton the Cop)
'Little more than a mall movie designed to kill time.' – *Robert Koehler, Variety*

Set It Off *
US 1996 122m DeLuxe
Entertainment/New Line/Peak (Dale Pollock, Oren Koules)

In Los Angeles, four women with money and other troubles become bank robbers.
Tough action film in a blaxploitation style updated with female bonding; quite fun in its regressive way.
w Kate Lanier, Takashi Bufford *d* F. Gary Gray *ph* Marc Reshovsky *m* Christopher Young *pd* Robb Wilson-King *ed* John Carter *sp* Tom Bellissimo
☆ Jada Pinkett, *Queen Latifah,* Vivica A. Fox, John C. McGinley, Kimberly Elise, Blair Underwood, Anna Maria Horsford
'Applies a gender twist to the familiar formula of hold-ups, car chases and shootouts, but makes many sacrifices to plausibility.' – *George Perry*

The Set Up ***
US 1949 72m bw
RKO (Richard Goldstone)

An ageing boxer refuses to pull his last fight, and is beaten up by gangsters.
One of the most brilliant little films noirs of the late forties; thoroughly studio-bound, yet evoking a brilliant feeling for time and place. Photography, direction, editing, acting are all of a piece.
w Art Cohn *poem* Joseph Moncure March *d* *Robert Wise* *ph* *Milton Krasner* *md* Constantin Bakaleinikoff
☆ *Robert Ryan,* Audrey Totter, George Tobias, Alan Baxter, Wallace Ford

La Setta: see *The Sect*

The Settlement
Australia 1983 100m colour
Queensland Film Corporation/Robert Bruning
In Queensland in the 1950s, two drifters outrage locals when they set up house with a prostitute.
Small, enjoyable movie, with the accent on character and humour.
w Ted Roberts *d* Howard Rubie *ph* Ernest Clark *m* Sven Libaek *ad* John Watson *ed* Henry Dangar
☆ Bill Kerr, John Jarratt, Lorna Lesley, Tony Barry, Katy Wild, David Downer, Elaine Cusick, Alan Cassell

Seul contre Tous *
France 1998 81m colour 'Scope
Alliance/Cinémas de la Zone/Lovestreams/CNC (Gaspar Noé)
aka: *I Stand Alone*
An unemployed butcher beats up his pregnant mistress and returns to his haunts in the slums of Paris to seek work, and to be reunited with the mute daughter he abandoned.
Bleak study in alienation that uses shock tactics – sudden pans or zooms and a percussive soundtrack, a warning towards the end that you have 30 seconds to leave the cinema – to keep its audience alert. It is impressive in demonstrating how much can be achieved with minimal means, but the ending is a cop-out, and, like Zola, Noé piles up the malignancies until they become unintentionally funny.
wd Gaspar Noé *ph* Dominique Colin *ed* Lucille Hadzihalilovic, Gasper Noé
☆ Philippe Nahon, Frankye Pain, Blandine Lenoir, Martine Audrain
'Probes as relentlessly into the psychology of nihilism as any movie has ever attempted.' – *Stephen Holden, New York Times*
'An ultra-widescreen slice of jaundice that creates its own unrelentingly tawdry, hermetic universe.' – *Lisa Nesselson, Variety*
† Excerpts from a pornographic film being watched by the protagonist were shown blurred in the UK version.

'Seven deadly sins. Seven ways to die.'
Seven ***
US 1995 127m DeLuxe Panavision
Entertainment/New Line (Arnold Kopelson, Phyllis Carlyle)

A detective nearing retirement and his temperamental young replacement track down a serial killer who is working his way through the seven deadly sins.
A tense, involving thriller that rises above the somewhat predictable schematics of its screenplay and its central situation to reach a surprisingly downbeat conclusion; it depicts the city as a paradise lost, and its inhabitants as mostly beyond redemption.
w Andrew Kevin Walker *d* *David Fincher* *ph* Darius Khondji *m* Howard Shore *pd* Arthur Max *ed* Richard Francis-Bruce
☆ Brad Pitt, *Morgan Freeman,* Richard Roundtree, R. Lee Ermey, John C. McGinley, Julie Araskog, Kevin Spacey, Gwyneth Paltrow
'Dark, grim and terrific ... this weirdly off-kilter suspenser goes well beyond the usual police procedural or killer-on-the-rampage yarn.' – *Todd McCarthy, Variety*
Richard Francis-Bruce

Seven Angry Men *
US 1954 90m bw
Allied Artists (Vincent M. Fennelly)
In Kansas, John Brown determines to abolish slavery by violence.
Low-budget, intensely felt little biopic of the celebrated 19th-century fanatic and his sons.
w Daniel B. Ullman *d* Charles Marquis Warren *ph* Ellsworth Fredericks *m* Carl Brandt
☆ Raymond Massey, Jeffrey Hunter, Larry Pennell, Debra Paget, Leo Gordon, John Smith, James Best, Dennis Weaver

Seven Beauties *
Italy 1975 115m Technicolor
Medusa (Lina Wertmuller, Giancarlo Giannini, Arrigo Colombo)

original title: *Pasqualino Settebellezze*
An incorrigible survivor manages to get through the rigours of World War II and scarcely notices the damage to his honour.
Candide-like mixture of farce and satire with the addition of a good deal of unpleasantness. Less meaningful abroad than on its home ground.
wd Lina Wertmüller *ph* Tonino Delli Colli *m* Enzo Jannacci
☆ Giancarlo Giannini, Fernando Rey, Shirley Stoler, Piero di Iorio
'A stunning piece of work. Wertmüller proves here more brilliantly than before she is a somewhat erratic but individual, strong, fierce talent.' – *Stanley Kauffmann*
Lina Wertmüller (as writer and as director); best foreign film; Giancarlo Giannini

'I now pronounce you – men and wives!'
Seven Brides for Seven Brothers **
US 1954 104m Anscocolor Cinemascope
MGM (Jack Cummings)

In the Old West, seven hard-working brothers decide they need wives, and carry off young women from the villages around.
Disappointingly studio-bound Western musical, distinguished by an excellent score and some brilliant dancing, notably the barn-raising sequence.
w Frances Goodrich, Albert Hackett *story* *Sobbin' Women* by Stephen Vincent Benet *d* *Stanley Donen* *ph* George Folsey *m* Adolph Deutsch, Saul Chaplin *ch* *Michael Kidd* *ed* Ralph E. Winters *songs* *Johnny Mercer, Gene de Paul*
☆ Howard Keel, Jane Powell, Jeff Richards, Russ Tamblyn, Tommy Rall, Howard Petrie, Marc Platt, Jacques d'Amboise, Matt Mattox
'It does have a plot, it does have imagination, it fairly explodes into life, and many discerning people will find the dance arrangements – exact, insidious, acrobatic, graceful, slipped in as if they were a natural development of the story – wildly exciting.' – *C. A. Lejeune*
Adolph Deutsch, Saul Chaplin
best picture; script; George Folsey; editing

Seven Chances **
US 1925 69m (24 fps) bw silent
Buster Keaton/Joseph M. Schenck

A meek young man finds that he is to inherit seven million dollars if he is married within a few hours.
Slim and rather slow comedy which builds to a fine climax as the hero is pursued first by hordes of women and then by rolling boulders.
w Clyde Bruckman, Jean Havez, Joseph A. Mitchell *play* Roi Cooper Megrue *d* Buster Keaton *ph* Elgin Lessley, Byron Houck
☆ *Buster Keaton,* Ruth Dwyer, Ray Barnes, Snitz Edwards
† The rocks sequence, which makes the film, was added only after a disappointing sneak preview.

'The sword and the cross battle for California's soul!'
Seven Cities of Gold *
US 1955 103m DeLuxe Cinemascope
TCF (Robert D. Webb, Barbara McLean)

In 1796, a Spanish expedition sets out from Mexico to annex California, but with it goes Father Junipero Serra ...
A semi-historical, semi-religious Western which ends up not being much of anything but has interesting sequences.
w Richard L. Breen, John C. Higgins *novel* Isabelle Gibson Ziegler *d* Robert D. Webb *ph* Lucien Ballard *m* Hugo Friedhofer
☆ Michael Rennie, Richard Egan, Anthony Quinn, Rita Moreno, Jeffrey Hunter, Eduardo Noriega, John Doucette

Seven Days in May ***
US 1964 120m bw
Seven Arts/Joel/John Frankenheimer (Edward Lewis)

An American general's aide discovers that his boss intends a military takeover because he considers the President's pacifism traitorous.
Absorbing political mystery drama marred only by the unnecessary introduction of a female character. Stimulating entertainment.
w *Rod Serling* *novel* Fletcher Knebel, Charles W. Bailey II *d* *John Frankenheimer* *ph* *Ellsworth Fredericks* *m* Jerry Goldsmith
☆ *Kirk Douglas,* Burt Lancaster, *Fredric March,* Ava Gardner, Martin Balsam, *Edmond O'Brien,* George Macready, John Houseman
'A political thriller which grips from start to finish.' – *Penelope Houston*

'It is to be enjoyed without feelings of guilt, there should be more movies like it, and there is nothing first class about it.' – *John Simon*

'In the best tradition of the suspense thriller, with the ultimate thrill our awareness of its actual potential.' – *Judith Crist*

'An entertainment, in Graham Greene's sense of the word, and an intelligent one.' – *MFB*

† In 1994, it was remade as a TV movie, *The Enemy Within*, starring Forest Whitaker and Sam Waterston.

Edmond O'Brien

Seven Days Leave
US 1929 83m bw
Paramount (Louis D. Lighton)
GB title: *Medals*
A London charlady 'adopts' a soldier, and both their lives are changed.
Sentimental melodrama which suited the times and confirmed Cooper's stardom.
w John Farrow, Dan Totheroh *play* The Old Lady Shows Her Medals by J. M. Barrie *d* Richard Wallace *ph* Charles Lang
☆ Gary Cooper, Beryl Mercer, Daisy Belmore, Nora Cecil, Tempe Piggott, Arthur Hoyt, Basil Radford

Seven Days Leave
US 1942 87m bw
RKO (Tim Whelan)
In order to inherit a hundred thousand dollars, a soldier must marry within a week.
Cheerful frivolity featuring radio stars of the time.
w William Bowers, Ralph Spence, Curtis Kenyon, Kenneth Earl *d* Tim Whelan *ph* Robert de Grasse *md* Roy Webb *songs* Frank Loesser, Jimmy McHugh
☆ Lucille Ball, Victor Mature, Harold Peary, Mary Cortes, Ginny Simms, Ralph Edwards, Peter Lind Hayes, Marcy McGuire, Wallace Ford

Seven Days to Noon **
GB 1950 94m bw
London Films (Roy Boulting)
A professor engaged on atomic research threatens to blow up London unless his work is brought to an end.
Persuasively understated suspense piece which was subsequently much copied, so that it now seems rather obvious.
w Frank Harvey, Roy Boulting, Paul Dehn, James Bernard d John Boulting ph Gilbert Taylor *m* John Addison
☆ *Barry Jones, Olive Sloane, André Morell, Joan Hickson*, Sheila Manahan, Hugh Cross, Ronald Adam, Marie Ney

'A first rate thriller that does not pretend to a serious message, but yet will leave a query in the mind.' – *Richard Winnington*

'A film of great tension and excitement with a climax that is reached after breathless suspense.' – *Star*

Paul Dehn, James Bernard (motion picture story)

The Seven Deadly Sins *
France/Italy 1952 150m bw
Franco London/Costellazione
The master of ceremonies introduces seven stories and an epilogue.
Among the most successful compendiums of its kind, partly because of cast and credits and partly because it came when French naughtiness was appealing to a wide international audience.
w Jean Aurenche, Pierre Bost, Roberto Rossellini, Leo Joannon, Carlo Rim, Diego Fabbri, Liana Ferri, Eduardo de Filippo, Charles Spaak, Turi Vaselle, René Wheeler *d* Eduardo de Filippo, Jean Dréville, Yves Allégret, Roberto Rossellini, Carlo Rim, Claude Autant-Lara, Georges Lacombe
☆ Gérard Philipe, Isa Miranda, Eduardo de Filippo, Noel-Noel, Louis de Funès, Viviane Romance, Frank Villard, Henri Vidal, Michèle Morgan, Françoise Rosay

Seven Different Ways: see *Quick Let's Get Married*

Seven Faces of Dr Lao *
US 1964 100m Metrocolor
MGM/George Pal
An elderly Chinaman with a penchant for spectacular disguise solves the problems of a Western desert town.
A pleasant idea and excellent production are submerged in a sloppily sentimental and verbose script.
w Charles Beaumont *novel* The Circus of Dr Lao by Charles G. Finney *d* George Pal *ph* Robert Bronner *m* Leigh Harline *make-up* William Tuttle
☆ *Tony Randall*, Arthur O'Connell, John Ericson, Barbara Eden, Noah Beery Jnr, Lee Patrick, Minerva Urecal, John Qualen

Seven Footsteps to Satan
US 1929 70m bw
Warner
A rich recluse plays an elaborate and macabre joke on his niece and nephew.
Richly-designed but dramatically disappointing haunted house spoof.
w Richard Bee *d* Benjamin Christensen
☆ Thelma Todd, Creighton Hale, Sheldon Lewis, Ivan Christie, Sojin

Seven Golden Men *
Italy/France/Spain 1965 91m Eastmancolor
Atlantica/PUF/Asfilm/Warner
Seven master criminals plot to rob a bank of its gold.
Simple-minded but slickly handled caper story with many visual pleasures.
wd Marco Vicario
☆ Rossana Podesta, Philippe Leroy, Gastone Moschin, Gabriele Tinti
† A sequel, *Seven Golden Men Strike Again*, was less successful.

Seven Hills of Rome
US/Italy 1957 104m Technirama
MGM/Titanus (Lester Welch)
An American singer in Italy is pursued by the fiancée with whom he has quarrelled.
Thin travelogue with several halts for the star to sing; production very patchy.
w Art Cohn, Giorgio Prosperi *d* Roy Rowland *ph* Tonino Delli Colli *md* George Stoll
☆ Mario Lanza, Renato Rascel, Marisa Allasio, Peggie Castle

711 Ocean Drive *
US 1950 102m bw
Columbia (Frank N. Seltzer)
A wireless expert is drawn into the bookie racket.
Overlong but vigorous crime exposé melodrama with excellent location sequences, notably a climax on Hoover Dam.
w Richard English, Francis Swann *d Joseph M. Newman ph* Franz Planer *m* Sol Kaplan
☆ Edmond O'Brien, Joanne Dru, Otto Kruger, Don Porter, Sammy White, Dorothy Patrick, Barry Kelley, Howard St John

Seven Keys to Baldpate *
US 1935 69m bw
RKO
A novelist retiring to a lonely inn for inspiration finds it full of criminals and damsels in distress.
An old theatrical warhorse with a trick ending, also filmed in 1929 (with Richard Dix; Variety *said 'it all happens like a synopsis of what might have occurred') and in 1947 with Philip Terry. There was also a horror variation in 1982,* House of the Long Shadows *(qv). None was as satisfying as a good stage production.*
play George M. Cohan *story Earl Derr Biggers d* William Hamilton, Edward Killy *ph* Robert de Grasse
☆ Gene Raymond, Margaret Callahan, Eric Blore, Grant Mitchell, Moroni Olsen, Henry Travers

'Too much conversation and too little action.' – *Variety*

† The 1935 version at least will be found to have lost its trick ending, without which it ends lamely. A curious executive decision.

The Seven Little Foys *
US 1955 95m Technicolor Vistavision
Paramount (Jack Rose)
The story of a family vaudeville act.
Routine showbiz biopic, a little heavy on the syrup.
w Melville Shavelson, Jack Rose *d* Melville Shavelson *ph* John F. Warren *md* Joseph J. Lilley
☆ Bob Hope, Milly Vitale, George Tobias, Angela Clarke, Herbert Heyes, *James Cagney* (George M. Cohan)
† Milly Vitale's singing was dubbed by Viola Vonn.
script

Seven Men from Now
US 1956 78m Warnercolor
Batjac (Andrew V. McLaglen, Robert E. Morrison)
A sheriff seeks revenge when his wife is killed by bandits.
Good Western programmer.
w Burt Kennedy *d* Budd Boetticher *ph* William H. Clothier *m* Henry Vars
☆ Randolph Scott, Gail Russell, Lee Marvin, Walter Reed, Don Barry, John Larch

Seven Miles from Alcatraz
US 1942 62m bw
RKO (Herman Schlom)
Prison escapees take over an offshore lighthouse.
Compact melodrama with the lifers heroically catching spies.
w Joseph Krumgold, John D. Klorer *d* Edward Dmytryk
☆ James Craig, Bonita Granville, Frank Jenks, Cliff Edwards, George Cleveland, Tala Birell, John Banner

The Seven Minutes
US 1971 102m DeLuxe
TCF (Russ Meyer)
A bookseller is arrested for distributing an obscene novel, and many people are unexpectedly involved in the court case.
A fascinating piece of old-fashioned hokum, full of 'daring' words and cameo performances.
w Richard Warren Lewis *novel* Irving Wallace *d* Russ Meyer *ph* Fred Mandl *m* Stu Phillips
☆ Wayne Maunder, Marianne MacAndrew, Yvonne de Carlo, Phil Carey, Jay C. Flippen, Edy Williams, Lyle Bettger, Ron Randell, David Brian, Charles Drake, John Carradine, Harold J. Stone

Seven Nights in Japan
GB/France 1976 104m Eastmancolor
EMI-Marianne (Lewis Gilbert)
The heir to the British throne has shore leave in Tokyo and falls in love with a geisha.
Tediously daring romance with a banal script which seems over impressed by its own barely-existent controversial qualities.
w Christopher Wood *d* Lewis Gilbert *ph Henri Decaë m* David Hentschel
☆ Michael York, Hidemi Aoki, James Villiers, Peter Jones, Charles Gray

The Seven Per Cent Solution
US 1976 114m Technicolor
Universal (Herbert Ross)
Dr Watson lures Sherlock Holmes to Vienna so that Professor Freud can cure him of persecution complex and cocaine addiction.
Drearily serious spoof with only a glimmer of the required style and a totally miscast Holmes.
w Nicholas Meyer *novel* Nicholas Meyer *d* Herbert Ross *ph* Oswald Morris *m* John Addison *pd* Ken Adam
☆ Nicol Williamson, Robert Duvall, Alan Arkin, Vanessa Redgrave, Laurence Olivier, Jeremy Kemp, Samantha Eggar, Joel Grey, Charles Gray, Georgia Brown, Regine

'Sorrily botched all-star extravaganza.' – *Sight and Sound*

'Comes into the category of hit and myth ... A heavyweight spoof in which Sherlock Holmes is placed under hypnosis by Sigmund Freud. The audience is then placed under hypnosis by director Herbert Ross.' – *Michael Billington, Illustrated London News*

script

The Seven Samurai ****
Japan 1954 155m bw
Toho (Shojiro Motoki)
original title: *Shichi-nin no Samurai*
16th-century villagers hire samurai to defend their property against an annual raid by bandits.
Superbly strange, vivid and violent medieval adventure which later served as the basis for the Western The Magnificent Seven *and the science-fiction film* Battle Beyond the Stars.
w Akira Kurosawa, Shinobu Hashimoto, Hideo Oguni *d Akira Kurosawa ph* Asaichi Nakai *m* Fumio Hayasaka *ad* Takashi Matsuyama
☆ *Toshiro Mifune*, Takashi Shimura, Kuninori Kodo

'It is as sheer narrative, rich in imagery, incisiveness and sharp observation, that it makes its strongest impact ... It provides a fascinating display of talent, and places its director in the forefront of creative film-makers of his generation.' – *Gavin Lambert, Sight and Sound*

'This, on the surface, is a work of relentless, unmitigated action, as epic as any film ever made, and, again on the surface, sheer entertainment. Yet it is also an unquestionable triumph of art.' – *John Simon*

art direction

Seven Seas to Calais
US/Italy 1962 103m Eastmancolor Cinemascope
MGM/Adelphia (Paolo Moffa)
In 1577, Sir Francis Drake follows the Spanish treasure route.
Ho-hum swashbuckler with a background of schoolboy history.
w Filippo Sanjust *d* Rudolph Maté *ph* Giulio Gianini *m* Franco Mannino
☆ Rod Taylor, Keith Michell, Irene Worth, Anthony Dawson, Basil Dignam

Seven Sinners *
GB 1936 70m bw
Gaumont (Michael Balcon)
US title: *Doomed Cargo*
Gunrunners wreck trains to cover traces of murder.
Fascinatingly dated comedy suspenser with excellent sub-Hitchcock sequences, the whole thing having a strong flavour of The 39 Steps.
w Frank Launder, Sidney Gilliat, L. DuGarde Peach, Austin Melford *play* The Wrecker by Arnold Ridley, Bernard Merivale *d Albert de Courville ph* Mutz Greenbaum (Max Greene)
☆ Edmund Lowe, Constance Cummings, Thomy Bourdelle, Henry Oscar, Felix Aylmer, Allan Jeayes, O. B. Clarence

Seven Sinners *
US 1940 86m bw
Universal (Joe Pasternak)
GB title: *Café of Seven Sinners*
A cabaret singer is deported from several South Sea islands for causing too many fights among the naval officers.
Ho-hum hokum with an amiable cast and a good-natured final free-for-all.
w John Meehan, Harry Tugend *d* Tay Garnett *ph* Rudolph Maté *m* Frank Skinner *ad* Jack Otterson *ed* Ted J. Kent
☆ Marlene Dietrich, John Wayne, Albert Dekker, Broderick Crawford, Mischa Auer, Billy Gilbert, Oscar Homolka, Anna Lee, Samuel S. Hinds

'Nothing to worry about, unless you happen to be in the theatre, watching it go from fairly good to worse than worse.' – *Otis Ferguson*

Seven Sweethearts
US 1942 98m bw
MGM (Joe Pasternak)
Seven daughters must marry in sequence, eldest first.
Period musical frou-frou inspired by Pride and Prejudice. *So light it almost floats.*
w Walter Reisch, Leo Townsend *d* Frank Borzage *ph* George Folsey *m* Franz Waxman
☆ Kathryn Grayson, Marsha Hunt, Van Heflin, Cecilia Parker, S. Z. Sakall, Peggy Moran, Isobel Elsom, Diana Lewis, Donald Meek, Louise Beavers

Seven Thieves *
US 1960 102m bw Cinemascope
TCF (Sidney Boehm)
An elderly crook conceives a last plan to rob the Monte Carlo casino.
Routine caper story, efficiently presented with some humour.
w Sydney Boehm *novel Lions at the Kill* by Max Catto *d* Henry Hathaway *ph* Sam Leavitt *m* Dominic Frontière

☆ Edward G. Robinson, Rod Steiger, Joan Collins, Eli Wallach, Michael Dante, Alexander Scourby, Berry Kroeger, Sebastian Cabot

'Christ, it was supposed to be a fun film, and Steiger is far, far from having a sense of humour.' – *Henry Hathaway*

Seven Thunders
GB 1957 100m bw
Rank (Daniel M. Angel)
US title: *The Beasts of Marseilles*
In wartime Marseilles, escaped POWs are helped by a doctor who turns out to have sinister intent.
Slow chiller which telegraphs its surprises but gets by on good production values.
w John Baines *novel* Rupert Croft-Cooke *d* Hugo Fregonese *ph* Wilkie Cooper *m* Antony Hopkins
☆ James Robertson Justice, Stephen Boyd, Kathleen Harrison, Anna Gaylor, Tony Wright, Eugene Deckers, Rosalie Crutchley

Seven Waves Away
GB 1956 95m bw
Columbia/Copa (John R. Sloan)
US title: *Abandon Ship*
After the sinking of a luxury liner, the officer in charge of a lifeboat has to make life or death decisions.
Initially gripping but finally depressing open sea melodrama derived from Souls at Sea *and later remade for TV as* The Last Survivors*.*
wd Richard Sale *ph* Wilkie Cooper *m* Arthur Bliss
☆ Tyrone Power, Mai Zetterling, Lloyd Nolan, Stephen Boyd, Moira Lister, James Hayter, Marie Lohr, Moultrie Kelsall, Noel Willman, Gordon Jackson, Clive Morton, John Stratton

'Eventually one is bludgeoned into a grudging admiration for the film's staying power.' – *Peter John Dyer*

'It jabs at your entrails with a cold unrelenting spear.' – *New York Times*

Seven Ways from Sundown
US 1960 87m Eastmancolor
Universal-International
A Texas Ranger befriends an outlaw, but has twinges of conscience.
Straightforward character Western with the inevitable shootout finale.
w Clair Huffaker *d* Harry Keller
☆ Audie Murphy, Barry Sullivan, Venetia Stevenson, John McIntire, Kenneth Tobey

'Love, lust, courage and cowardice! Faith, fury and sacrifice!'

Seven Women *
US 1966 100m Metrocolor Panavision
MGM/John Ford/Bernard Smith
In 1935, an isolated Chinese mission staffed by American women is overrun by bandits.
Dusty melodrama which might have appealed in the thirties but was quite out of tune with the sixties. Well enough made and acted, but a strange choice for Ford's last film.
w Janet Green, John McCormick *story* Chinese Finale by Norah Lofts *d* John Ford *ph* Joseph LaShelle *m* Elmer Bernstein
☆ Anne Bancroft, Flora Robson, Margaret Leighton, Sue Lyon, Mildred Dunnock, Betty Field, Anna Lee, Eddie Albert, Mike Mazurki, Woody Strode, Irene Tsu

The Seven Year Itch *
US 1955 105m DeLuxe Cinemascope
TCF (Charles K. Feldman, Billy Wilder)
A married man has a fling with the girl upstairs.
An amusing theatrical joke, with dream sequences like revue sketches, is really all at sea on the big screen, especially as the affair remains unconsummated, but direction and performances keep the party going more or less.
w Billy Wilder, George Axelrod *play* George Axelrod *d* *Billy Wilder* *ph* Milton Krasner *m* Alfred Newman
☆ *Tom Ewell*, *Marilyn Monroe*, Sonny Tufts, Evelyn Keyes, Robert Strauss, Oscar Homolka, Marguerite Chapman, Victor Moore

'We didn't really make a very good picture.' – *George Axelrod*

Seven Years in Tibet *
US 1997 139m Technicolor Panavision
Entertainment/Mandalay/Reperage and Vanguard/Applecross (Jean-Jacques Annaud, John H. Williams, Iain Smith)
Escaping from a British prisoner-of-war camp in India, an Austrian mountaineer makes it through the Himalayas to the forbidden Tibetan city of Lhasa, where he becomes friends with the Dalai Lama.
Uninvolving epic that looks much better than it sounds.
w Becky Johnston *book* Heinrich Harrer *d* Jean-Jacques Annaud *ph* Robert Fraisse *m* John Williams *pd* At Hoang *ed* Noëlle Boisson
☆ Brad Pitt, David Thewlis, B. D. Wong, Mako, Danny Denzongpa, Victor Wong, Ingeborga Dapkunaite, Jamyang Jamsho Wangchuk

'A glossy, good-natured travelogue with modest philosophical pretensions.' – *Mark Kermode, Sight and Sound*

'They take the third degree one step further!'

The Seven-Ups
US 1973 103m DeLuxe
TCF/Philip D'Antoni
Gangsters are hunted down by a secret force of the New York police.
Formulary realistic rough stuff in the wake of The French Connection*.*
w Albert Ruben, Alexander Jacobs *d* Philip D'Antoni *ph* Urs Furrer *m* *Don Ellis*
☆ Roy Scheider, Victor Arnold, Jerry Leon, Tony Lo Bianco, *Richard Lynch*

1732 Høtten
Norway/GB 1999 99m colour
United Media/Norsk/Merkurfilm (Tom Remlov)
aka: *Bloody Angels*
A detective meets with hostility when he goes to a small town to investigate the murder of a teenager suspected of raping and killing a girl with Down's syndrome.
Bleak drama of casual killing as icy at heart as its snowbound setting.
w Kjetil Indegaard *d* Karin Julsrud *ph* Philip Ogaard *m* Kjetil Bjerkestrand, Magne Furuholmen *ed* Sophie Hesselberg
☆ Reidar Sørensen (Nicholas Ramm), Gaute Skjegstad (Niklas Hartmann), Trond Høvik (Holger), Laila Goody (Victoria), Stig Henrik Hoff (Dwayne Karlson), Simon Norrthon (Cato)

'Crisply made crime thriller that makes excellent use of wintry locations in rural Norway... filled with sardonic humor and sharp observation.' – *David Stratton, Variety*

1776 *
US 1972 141m Eastmancolor Panavision
Columbia/Jack L. Warner
The thirteen American colonies prepare to declare their independence of Great Britain.
Plain, low-key filming of the successful Broadway musical showing the domestic lives of the historical figures concerned. Splendid moments alternate with stretches of tedium.
w Peter Stone *play* Peter Stone *d* Peter Hunt *ph* Harry Stradling Jnr *m/ly* Sherman Edwards *md* Ray Heindorf *ad* George Jenkins
☆ William Daniels, Howard da Silva, Ken Howard, Donald Madden, Blythe Danner
Harry Stradling Jnr

Seventh Cavalry
US 1956 75m Technicolor
Columbia (Harry Joe Brown)
An officer accused of cowardice volunteers to bring back General Custer's body after Little Big Horn.
Lively co-feature with a good traditional action climax.
w Peter Packer *story* Glendon F. Swarthout *d* Joseph H. Lewis *ph* Ray Rennahan *m* Mischa Bakaleinikoff
☆ Randolph Scott, Barbara Hale, Jay C. Flippen, Jeanette Nolan, Frank Faylen

The Seventh Cross **
US 1944 112m bw
MGM (Pandro S. Berman)
Seven Germans escape from a concentration camp, and the Nazis threaten to execute them all. Just one escapes.
Impressive melodrama, brilliantly limiting its escape/suspense story to studio sets. Old style Hollywood production at its best; but a rather obviously contrived story.
w Helen Deutsch *novel* Anna Seghers *d* *Fred Zinnemann* *ph* *Karl Freund* *m* Roy Webb *ad* *Cedric Gibbons*, *Leonid Vasian*
☆ *Spencer Tracy*, Signe Hasso, Hume Cronyn, Jessica Tandy, Agnes Moorehead, Felix Bressart, George Macready, George Zucco
Hume Cronyn

The Seventh Curse
Hong Kong 1986 93m colour
Paragon (Leonard K. C. Ho)
A doctor seeks a cure for a deadly curse put upon him by a sorcerer after he saves a woman in Thailand from being sacrificed to a living skeleton.
Risible fantasy that begins as a violent action movie before it settles for a delirious mix of horror and science fiction, with low-budget monsters, lashings of gore and not much sense.
w I. Kuang *d* Lan Wei-tsang
☆ Chow Yun-Fat, Chin Siu Ho, Maggie Cheung, Dick Wei, Elvis Tsui

The Seventh Dawn
GB 1964 123m Technicolor
UA/Holden/Charles K. Feldman (Karl Tunberg)
In the early fifties a Malayan rubber planter finds that his best friend is a leading terrorist.
Doom-laden romantic adventure drama with a lot of suffering and too little entertainment value.
w Karl Tunberg *novel* *The Durian Tree* by Michael Keon *d* Lewis Gilbert *ph* Freddie Young *m* Riz Ortolani
☆ William Holden, Tetsuro Tamba, Capucine, Susannah York, Michael Goodliffe, Allan Cuthbertson, Maurice Denham

'Echoes of *The Ugly American*, *Love Is a Many-Splendored Thing*, and many another adventure East of Sumatra, with every character running absolutely true to form.' – *MFB*

'An interminable melange of political, racial and romantic clichés, with performances and dialogue as overripe as the jungle setting.' – *Judith Crist, 1973*

Seventh Day, Eighth Night **
Czechoslovakia 1969 108m bw
Filmowe Studio Barrandov (Vera Kadlecova)
original title: *Den Sedmy – Osma Noc*
Following the disappearance of the station master, a village is panicked into believing that it is facing danger from an unknown enemy.
Savage, black political farce of intimidation and betrayal that was withheld for several years by the Czech authorities.
w Zdenek Mahler, Evald Schorm *d* Evald Schorm *ph* Vaclav Hanus *m* Jan Klusak *pd* Karel Lier
☆ Jaroslav Wagner-Kleuka, Jan Kacer, Jana Markova, Kveta Fialova, Ljuba Skorepova, Josef Bek

'Lovers Who Lift Your Heart To The Skies ... In The Tenderest Romance Of Our Time!'

Seventh Heaven **
US 1927 93m approx (24 fps) bw silent
Fox (William Fox)
A Paris sewer worker shelters a street waif, marries her and after idyllic happiness goes off to war, returning blinded.
All softness, sweetness and light, a very typical – and attractive – film of its director and a big influence on Hollywood's European period.
w Benjamin Glazer *play* Austin Strong *d* *Frank Borzage* *ph* Ernest Palmer, J. A. Valentine *ad* Harry Oliver
☆ *Janet Gaynor*, *Charles Farrell*, Gladys Brockwell, David Butler
Benjamin Glazer; Frank Borzage; Janet Gaynor
best picture; Harry Oliver

Seventh Heaven *
US 1937 102m bw
TCF (Raymond Griffith)
Dewy-eyed remake; the mood is antediluvian but the production impresses.
w Melville Baker *d* *Henry King* *ph* *Merritt Gerstad* *md* Louis Silvers *ad* *William Darling*
☆ James Stewart, Simone Simon, Jean Hersholt, Gale Sondergaard, J. Edward Bromberg, Gregory Ratoff, John Qualen, Victor Kilian, Sig Rumann, Mady Christians

'A romance that can stand another telling ... the older element will join in making it a bracer for the box office.' – *Variety*

The Seventh Seal ****
Sweden 1957 95m bw
Svensk Filmindustri (Allan Ekelund)
original title: *Det Sjunde Inseglet*
Death comes for a knight, who challenges him to a game of chess while he tries to show illustrations of goodness in mankind: but Death takes them all away in the end.
A modestly budgeted minor classic which, because of its international success and its famous shots, is seldom analysed in detail. It is kept going by its splendid cinematic feel and its atmosphere is that of a dark world irrationally sustained by religion.
wd *Ingmar Bergman* *ph* *Gunnar Fischer* *m* Erik Nordgren
☆ *Max von Sydow*, *Bengt Ekerot*, Gunnar Bjornstrand, Nils Poppe, Bibi Andersson, Gunnel Lindblom

'The most extraordinary mixture of beauty and lust and cruelty, Odin-worship and Christian faith, darkness and light.' – *Alan Dent, Illustrated London News*

'You know where they dance along the horizon? We'd packed up for the evening and were about to go home. Suddenly I saw a cloud, and Fischer swung his camera up. Some actors had gone, so grips had to stand in. The whole scene was improvised in ten minutes flat.' – *Ingmar Bergman*

The Seventh Sign
US 1988 95m colour
Columbia Tri-Star/Interscope (Ted Field, Robert Cort)
A pregnant mother fears that the birth of her baby will signal the end of the world.
Apocalyptic thriller that is too silly to be enjoyable on any level.
w Clifford Green, Ellen Green *d* Carl Schultz *ph* Juan Ruiz-Anchia *m* Jack Nitzsche *pd* Stephen Marsh *ed* Caroline Biggerstaff
☆ Jürgen Prochnow, Demi Moore, Michael Biehn, Peter Friedman, John Taylor, John Heard

The Seventh Sin
US 1957 94m bw Cinemascope
MGM (David Lewis)
A faithless wife accompanies her bacteriologist husband to fight a Chinese cholera epidemic, and regains her self-respect.
Tatty remake of a Garbo vehicle which was dated even in 1934. (See The Painted Veil*.)*
w Karl Tunberg *novel* *The Painted Veil* by Somerset Maugham *d* Ronald Neame *ph* Ray June *m* Miklos Rozsa
☆ Eleanor Parker, Bill Travers, George Sanders, Jean-Pierre Aumont, Françoise Rosay

The Seventh Veil **
GB 1945 94m bw
Theatrecraft/Sydney Box/Ortus
A concert pianist is romantically torn between her psychiatrist, her guardian, and two other fellows.
A splendid modern melodrama in the tradition of Jane Eyre *and* Rebecca*; it set the seal of moviegoing approval on psychiatry, classical music, and James Mason, and it is the most utter tosh.*
w *Muriel and Sydney Box* *d* Compton Bennett *ph* Reg Wyer *m* *Benjamin Frankel*
☆ *James Mason*, *Ann Todd*, *Herbert Lom*, Albert Lieven, Hugh McDermott, Yvonne Owen, David Horne, Manning Whiley

'An example of the intelligent, medium-priced picture made with great technical polish which has represented for Hollywood the middle path between the vulgar and the highbrow.' – *Spectator*

'A popular film that does not discard taste and atmosphere.' – *Daily Mail*

'A rich, portentous mixture of Beethoven, Chopin, Kitsch and Freud.' – *Pauline Kael, 1968*

'An odd, artificial, best sellerish kind of story, with reminiscences of *Trilby* and *Jane Eyre* and all their imitations down to *Rebecca*.' – *Richard Mallett, Punch*

'Maybe, with a few veils stripped away, all of us have a fantasist inside who gobbles up this sadomasochistic sundae.' – *Pauline Kael, 70s*
Muriel and Sydney Box

The Seventh Victim *
US 1943 71m bw
RKO (*Val Lewton*)

A girl goes to New York in search of her sister, who is under the influence of Satanists.
Much praised but in effect rather boring little thriller, with rather stately acting and ponderous direction and dialogue. Censorship made the plot so obscure that it's difficult to follow.
w Charles O'Neal, De Witt Bodeen *d* Mark Robson *ph* Nicholas Musuraca *m* Constantin Bakaleinikoff
☆ Kim Hunter, Tom Conway, Jean Brooks, Hugh Beaumont, Erford Gage, Isabel Jewell, Evelyn Brent
'It is the almost oppressive mood, the romantic obsession with death-in-life, which dominates the film.' – *NFT, 1973*
† Note the use in the first scene of the staircase from *The Magnificent Ambersons*.

The Seventh Voyage of Sinbad *
US 1958 89m Technicolor
Columbia/Morningside (Charles Schneer)

Sinbad seeks a roc's egg which will restore his fiancée from the midget size to which an evil magician has reduced her.
Lively fantasy with narrative drive and excellent effects.
w Kenneth Kolb *d* Nathan Juran *ph* Wilkie Cooper *m* Bernard Herrmann *sp* *Ray Harryhausen*
☆ Kerwin Mathews, Kathryn Grant, Torin Thatcher, Richard Eyer, Alec Mango

Several Interviews on Personal Problems **
USSR 1979 94m colour
Gruziafilm
original title: *Neskolko Intervyu Po Lichnyam Voprosam*
A busy journalist spends her time sorting out other people's problems while failing to solve her own domestic difficulties.
Interspersed with interviews with Soviet women on their lives, it provides a compassionate, witty look at the situation of women in Russia.
w Zaira Arsenishvili, Erlom Akhvlediani, Lana Gogoberidze *d* Lana Gogoberidze *ph* Nugzar Erkomaishvili *m* Gia Kanchell
☆ Sofiko Chiaureli, Gia Badridze, Ketevan Orakhelashvili, Janri Lolashvili, Salome Kancheli, Ketevan Bochorishvili, Noutsa Alexi-Meskhshvili

A Severed Head *
GB 1970 98m Technicolor
Columbia/Winkast (Alan Ladd Jnr)
A wine merchant has a long-standing affair which he thinks is secret, but is annoyed when his wife tries the same game.
Unwisely boisterous screen version of a slyly academic novel; tolerably sophisticated for those who don't know the original.
w Frederic Raphael *novel* Iris Murdoch *d* Dick Clement *ph* Austin Dempster *m* Stanley Myers *pd* Richard Macdonald
☆ Lee Remick, Richard Attenborough, Ian Holm, Claire Bloom, Jennie Linden, Clive Revill

Severed Ties
US 1991 90m colour
Fangoria Films (Christopher Webster)

A mad, mother-dominated scientist grows himself a new arm from plasma taken from a serial killer and a lizard, with predictable results.
Unbelievably cheap, would-be comic horror, by far the worst film its two stars have ever made (and they have appeared in some appalling ones), devoid of style or invention, and taking its plot from half a dozen better movies.
w John Nystrom, Henry Dominic *story* Damon Santostefano, David A. Casci *d* Damon Santostefano *ph* Geza Sincovics *m* Daniel Licht *pd* Don Day *ed* Richard Roberts *sp* KNB Effects
☆ Oliver Reed, Elke Sommer, Garrett Morris, Johnny Legend, Denise Wallace, Roger Perkovich, Bekki Vallin, Billy Morrisette
'Combo of grotesque gore effects and over-the-top acting is a winning one.' – *Variety*

Sex and Lucia *
Spain 2001 129m colour
Metro Tartan/Sogecine/Alicia (Fernando Bovaira, Enrique Lopez Lavigne)

aka: *Lucia y El Sexo*
After her novelist-lover disappears, a waitress visits an island he knew and forms relationships with friends and lovers from his earlier life.
A steamy, overtly sexual movie, married to a sometimes incoherent narrative, all flashbacks and coincidences, that may or may not be the creation of the writer at the centre of a confusion of love affairs; it's best to lie back and think of very little to gain the maximum enjoyment.
wd Julio Medem *ph* Kiko de la Rica *m* Alberto Iglesias *ad* Montse Sanz *ed* Ivan Aledo
☆ Paz Vega (Lucia), Tristan Ulloa (Lorenzo), Najwa Nimri (Elena), Daniel Freire (Carlos/Antonio), Elena Anaya (Belen), Silvia Llanos (Luna), Javier Camara (Pepe)
'The kind of trifle that date nights were invented for.' – *Kenneth Turan, Los Angeles Times*
'Medem strains madly for cosmic alliances, fairy-tale imagery, and fated coincidences, but he triumphs only with two hot bodies, a cluttered apartment, and a Shower Massage.' – *Michael Atkinson, Village Voice*

Sex and the Single Girl
US 1964 114m Technicolor
Warner/Richard Quine/Reynard (William T. Orr)

A journalist worms his way into the life of a lady sexologist in order to unmask her – but guess what.
Coy sex comedy with noise substituting for wit and style, all pretence being abandoned in a wild chase climax.
w Joseph Heller, David R. Schwartz *book* Helen Gurley Brown *d* Richard Quine *ph* Charles Lang Jnr *m* Neal Hefti
☆ Natalie Wood, Tony Curtis, Henry Fonda, Lauren Bacall, Mel Ferrer, Fran Jeffries, Edward Everett Horton, Otto Kruger
'For those willing to devote two hours of their lives to a consideration of Natalie Wood's virginity.' – *Judith Crist, 1973*

Sex and the Vampire: see *Le Frisson des Vampires*

sex, lies and videotape **
US 1989 100m CFI color
Virgin/Outlaw Productions (Robert Newmyer, John Hardy)

An old college friend, who likes to videotape interviews with women about their sexual experiences, visits a couple whose marriage is in difficulties.
Witty, intelligent conversation piece that won the Palme D'Or for best film at the Cannes Film Festival.
wd Steven Soderbergh *ph* Walt Lloyd *m* Cliff Martinez *ad* Joanne Schmidt *ed* Steve Soderbergh
☆ James Spader, Andie MacDowell, Peter Gallagher, Laura San Giacomo, Ron Vawter
best original screenplay

Sex Life in a Convent: see *Behind Convent Walls*

The Sex Life of a Female Private Eye: see *Big Zapper*

'His fantasy was a great idea, until she liked it... a lot.'
The Sex Monster
US 1999 97m colour
Trimark/Sun-Lite (Jack Binder, Scott Stephens)

An LA businessman persuades his wife to try three-in-a-bed and lives to regret it.
A thin farce of a man who gets both more, and less, than he bargained for.
wd Mike Binder *ph* Keith Smith *pd* Katie Lipsitt *ed* Lee Grubin *cos* Caroline B. Marx
☆ Mariel Hemingway (Laura Barnes), Mike Binder (Marty Barnes), Renee Humphrey (Didi), Taylor Nichols (Billy), Missy Crider (Diva), Stephen Baldwin (Murphy), Christopher Lawford (Dave Pembroke), Joanna Heimbold (Evie Pembroke), Kevin Pollak (Dr Berman)
'A cheesy, obvious farce that is funnier than it has any right to be.' – *Todd McCarthy, Variety*

Sex: The Annabel Chong Story **
US/Canada 1999 87m
Metrodome/Coffee House/Omni/Greycat (Hugh F. Curry, Dave Whitten, Gough Lewis)

Grace Quek, a student at the University of Southern California works in pornographic films under the name of Annabel Chong and sets a new record by having sex with 251 men in ten hours, while being filmed for a video *The World's Biggest Gang Bang*. Later, her record is broken by another porn star who has sex with 300 men.
Disturbing documentary, and not so much for its content as for its portrait of a self-deluded and, by the end, unhappy woman who allows herself to be exploited in the belief that her actions will empower her and make her free.
d Gough Lewis *ph* Jim Michaels, Kelly Morris, Gough Lewis, Tony Morone *m* Peter Mundinger *ed* Kelly Morris
☆ Grace Quek/Annabel Chong
'This is art cinema that gets into bed with porn but keeps one foot on the floor.' – *Linda Ruth Williams, Sight and Sound*

The Sex Thief
GB 1973 89m Eastmancolor
LMG/Ocarina/Drumbeat/Rainbow (Michael Style, Teddy White)

A writer turns cat burglar by night, making love to the women he robs.
Low-budget sex quickie, better acted and with brighter dialogue than average for the genre.
w Edward Hyde (Michael Armstrong) *d* Martin Campbell *ph* Grenville Middleton *m* Mike Vickers *ad* Anthony Noble *ed* Rex Graves
☆ David Warbeck, Diane Keen, Terence Edmond, Linda Coombes, Michael Armstrong, Christopher Neil, Christopher Biggins, James Aubrey
'Tawdry, ridiculous fare, only marginally redeemed by its own self-mocking humour.' – *Sight and Sound*

Sextette *
US 1978 91m Metrocolor
Briggs and Sullivan (Warren G. Toub)

The honeymoon of a Hollywood film star is interrupted by her previous husbands.
An amazing last stab at her old métier by an 86-year-old ex-star. It doesn't work, of course, and most of it is embarrassing, but the attempt is in itself remarkable.
w Herbert Baker *play* Mae West *d* Ken Hughes *ph* James Crabe *m* Artie Butler
☆ Mae West, Tony Curtis, Ringo Starr, Dom DeLuise, Timothy Dalton, George Hamilton, Alice Cooper, Rona Barrett, Walter Pidgeon, George Raft

Sexton Blake and the Hooded Terror
GB 1938 70m bw
George King
A millionaire is unmasked as the head of a criminal gang.
Rather unyielding series melodrama, chiefly interesting for the casting of Tod Slaughter as Blake's Moriarty.
w A. R. Rawlinson *d* George King *ph* H. M. Glendining *md* Jack Beaver *ad* Philip Bawcombe *ed* John Seabourne
☆ George Curzon, Tod Slaughter, Greta Gynt, Charles Oliver, David Farrar, Tony Sympson
TERROR: 'You little fool! Don't you realise that the game is up? The Black Quorum has seen through your treacheries. I alone can save you from their revenge!'
GIRL: 'I'd rather die.'
† Other Sexton Blake movies, all cheaply made by British independents, include six 1928 two-reelers starring Langhorne Burton: *Sexton Blake and the Bearded Doctor* and *Sexton Blake and the Mademoiselle*, both 1935, both with Curzon; *Meet Sexton Blake* and *The Echo Murders*, both 1943, both with David Farrar; and *Murder on Site Three*, 1963 with Geoffrey Toone.

The Sexual Life of the Belgians 1950–1978 *
Belgium 1994 63m colour
Metro Tartan/Transatlantic (Jan Bucquoy)

original title: *La Vie Sexuelle des Belges 1950–1978*
The sexual experiences of a Flemish man, from babyhood to a failed marriage and what appears to be his most enjoyable relationship, with an inflatable doll.
An odd little comedy of repression and release that claims to be autobiographical; it is subversive in a downbeat way.
wd Jan Bucquoy *ph* Michel Baudour *m* Francis de Smet *pd* Nathalie André, Nicole Lenoir *ed* Matyas Veress
☆ Jean-Henri Compère, Noé Francq, Isabelle Legros, Sophie Schneider, Pascale Binneri, Michele Shor
'There's a wonderful sense of abandon to this light, titillating comedy.' – *Empire*

'Sometimes It's Hard To Say No.'
Sexy Beast *
GB/Spain/US 2000 88m DeLuxe Super 35
FilmFour/Recorded Picture/Fox Searchlight (Jeremy Thomas)

A London thief who has retired with his wife to an easy life on the Costa del Sol is summoned back to do one last job by a vicious gangster.
Enjoyable thriller that immediately creates an atmosphere of ill-defined menace; but clumsy construction and odd, surreal episodes detract from its overall impact.
w Louis Mellis, David Scinto *d* Jonathan Glazer *ph* Ivan Bird *m* Roque Baños *pd* Jan Houllevigue *ed* John Scott, Sam Sneade
☆ Ray Winstone (Gary 'Gal' Dove), Ben Kingsley (Don 'Malky' Logan), Ian McShane (Teddy Bass), Amanda Redman (Deedee), Cavan Kendall (Jackie), Alvaro Monje (Enrique), James Fox (Harry), Darkie Smith (Stan Higgins)
'One of the most purely enjoyable films I've seen for a long time.' – *Peter Bradshaw, Guardian*
'An elaborate riff on not very much' – *Variety*
Ben Kingsley

Sh! The Octopus
US 1937 54m bw
First National
Lamebrain detectives fight a giant octopus in a lighthouse.
Footling remake of The Gorilla *(qv).*
w George Bricker *d* William McGann *ph* Arthur Todd *ed* Clarence Kolster
☆ Hugh Herbert, Allen Jenkins, Marcia Ralston, John Eldredge, George Rosener
'This bit of grist for the double-feature mills is so feeble even the actors seem embarrassed.' – *Variety*

Shack Out on 101 *
US 1955 80m bw
AA/William F. Broidy

A waitress at a café near a research establishment unmasks two spies.
Modest suspenser which seemed at the time to have some fresh and realistic attitudes.
w Ed and Mildred Dein *d* *Ed Dein* *ph* *Floyd Crosby* *m* Paul Dunlap
☆ Frank Lovejoy, Lee Marvin, Keenan Wynn, Terry Moore, Whit Bissell

Shadey
GB 1985 106m colour
Larkspur/Otto Plashkes
A bankrupt car mechanic will do almost anything to finance his sex change operation.
Weird, utterly unprovoked and unmotivated black comedy which confounded all comers.
w Snoo Wilson *d* Philip Saville *ph* Roger Deakins *m* Colin Towns
☆ Anthony Sher, Billie Whitelaw, Patrick Macnee, Leslie Ash, Bernard Hepton, Larry Lamb, Katherine Helmond

The Shadow
GB 1933 74m bw
UA/Real Art (Julius Hagen)
A police hunt for a murderous blackmailer leads to the Chief Commissioner's house.
Old-fashioned whodunnit that looks like a stage production transferred intact to the screen.

w H. Fowler Mear, Terence Egan, Donald Stuart *d* George A. Cooper *ph* Sydney Blythe *ad* James A. Carter *ed* Jack Harris
☆ Henry Kendall, Elizabeth Allan, Felix Aylmer, John Turnbull, Cyril Raymond

'The Glamour. The Mystery. The Danger.'
The Shadow
US 1994 107m DeLuxe
UIP (Martin Bregman, Willi Baer)
In the 30s, a former criminal-turned-vigilante with psychic powers battles in New York against a descendant of Genghis Khan who plans to destroy the city and rule the world.
A dim attempt to revive a forgotten hero of pulp fiction, radio and a little-regarded cinema serial of the 40s; the period setting looks good but the story is thin and the result forgettable.
w David Koepp *d* Russell Mulcahy *ph* Stephen H. Burum *m* Jerry Goldsmith *pd* Joseph Nemec III *ed* Peter Honess
☆ Alec Baldwin, Penelope Ann Miller, John Lone, Peter Boyle, Ian McKellen, Tim Curry, Jonathan Winters, Sab Shimono
'A helpful how-to guide for Hollywood producers who are looking to make expensive bad movies.' – *Mo Ryan, Cinescape*

Shadow Conspiracy
US 1997 103m Technicolor Panavision
Buena Vista/Hollwyood/Cinergi (Terry Collis)
A White House aide is the only person who can save the President from assassination.
Risibly silly chase movie that fails to do more than amuse by its presumption.
w Adi Hasak, Ric Gibbs *d* George P. Cosmatos *ph* Buzz Feitshans IV *m* Bruce Broughton *pd* Joe Alves *ed* Robert A. Ferretti
☆ Charlie Sheen, Donald Sutherland, Linda Hamilton, Stephen Lang, Ben Gazzara, Nicholas Turturro, Sam Waterston, Henry Strozier, Theodore Bikel, Gore Vidal
'One of those misfires that is so bad it's funny.' – *Variety*

Shadow in the Sky
US 1951 78m bw
MGM (William H. Wright)
A shell-shocked marine moves from a psychiatric hospital to live with his sister.
Low-key drama, plainly but quite well done, though of little continuing interest.
w Ben Maddow *d* Fred M. Wilcox *ph* George Folsey *m* Bronislau Kaper
☆ Ralph Meeker, Nancy Davis, James Whitmore, Jean Hagen

Shadow Makers
US 1989 127m Technicolor
UIP/Paramount (Tony Garnett)
aka: *Fat Man and Little Boy*
The army and scientists clash when working on a project to develop the first atom bomb.
A significant moment in history is rendered mundane in a damp squib of a film.
w Bruce Robinson, Roland Joffe *d* Roland Joffé *ph* Vilmos Zsigmond *m* Ennio Morricone *pd* Gregg Fonseca *ed* Françoise Bonnot
☆ Paul Newman, Dwight Schultz, Bonnie Bedelia, John Cusack, Laura Dern, Ron Frazier, John C. McGinley, Natasha Richardson, Ron Vawter

'The Good Guys Don't Always Wear Black.'
The Shadow Men
US 1997 91m colour
Promark/Spectacor (Steve Beswick)
After a family report an experience with a UFO they are menaced by pale men dressed entirely in black.
A low-budget, low-enterprise reworking of themes from Men in Black *and the TV series* The X Files, *with small rewards.*
w Eric Miller, Justin Stanley *d* Timothy Bond *ph* Frank Byers *pd* Cecil Gentry *ed* Barry Zetlin
☆ Eric Roberts, Sherilyn Fenn, Dean Stockwell

Shadow of a Doubt ***
US 1943 108m bw
Universal (Jack H. Skirball)
A favourite uncle comes to visit his family in a small Californian town. He is actually on the run from police, who know him as the Merry Widow murderer.
Hitchcock's quietest film is memorable chiefly for its depiction of small-town life; but the script is well written and keeps the suspense moving slowly but surely.
w Thornton Wilder, Sally Benson, Alma Reville story Gordon McDonell *d Alfred Hitchcock ph* Joe Valentine *m* Dimitri Tiomkin *ad* Robert Boyle, John B. Goodman *ed* Milton Carruth
☆ Joseph Cotten, Teresa Wright, Hume Cronyn, Macdonald Carey, Patricia Collinge, Henry Travers, Wallace Ford
'Some clever observation of rabbity white-collar life which, in spite of a specious sweetness, is the best since *It's a Gift*.' – *James Agee*
† Remade in 1959 as *Step Down to Terror*, with Charles Drake.
†† A lacklustre TV version was made in 1991, starring Mark Harmon and directed by Karen Arthur.
original story

A Shadow of a Doubt **
France 1992 106m colour CinemaScope
CIBY 2000/TF1 (Patrick Lancelot)
original title: *L'Ombre du Doute*
An 11-year-old girl claims that her father is sexually abusing her, but he denies it and his wife believes him.
Complex, emotionally charged film that catches the confusion of a child caught between reality and fantasy, in a situation too difficult for her to deal with; it tackles its difficult subject-matter without sensationalism, concentrating on the love-hate relationship between father and daughter and its repercussions on other members of the family.
w Aline Issermann, Martine Fadier-Nisse, Frederique Gruyer *d* Aline Issermann *ph* Darius Khondji *m* Reno Isaac *ad* Cyr Boitard *ed* Hervé Schneid
☆ Mireille Perrier, Alain Bashung, Sandrine Blancke, Emmanuelle Riva, Michel Aumont, Luis Issermann, Roland Bertin, Dominique Lavanant, Thierry L'hermitte
'This sensitive and emotionally powerful film does an extremely good job with material that has a good many pitfalls.' – *Derek Malcolm, Guardian*

Shadow of a Man
GB 1954 69m bw
New Realm (Edwin J. Fancey)
In Hastings, police investigate the death of an unpleasant drunk, while two men vie for the affections of his widow.
Clumsy, melodramatic and inadequate whodunnit that betrays its theatrical origins in every mismanaged scene.
w Paul Erikson, Michael McCarthy *play* Paul Erikson *d* Michael McCarthy *ph* Geoffrey Faithfull *m* Jackie Brown *ad* Ivan King *ed* Monica Kimick
☆ Paul Carpenter (Gene Landers), Rona Anderson (Linda Bryant), Jane Griffiths (Carol Seaton), Tony Quinn (Inspector Gates), Ronald Leigh-Hunt (Norman Farrel), Bill Nagy (Paul Bryant), Jack Taylor (Sgt McBride), Robert O'Neil (Max)

Shadow of Doubt
US 1935 71m bw
MGM
An actress suspected of murder is cleared by the efforts of her fiancé's aunt.
Routine mystery with a strong part for a new character actress from England.
w Wells Root, Arthur Somers Roche *d* George B. Seitz
☆ Ricardo Cortez, Virginia Bruce, *Constance Collier*, Arthur Byron, Isabel Jewell, Regis Toomey, Edward Brophy
'Passable murder mystery.' – *Variety*

Shadow of Fear
GB 1963 60m bw
Butcher's (John I. Phillips)
An American oilman, returning to London from Baghdad, is caught up in espionage.
Mundane and stupid programmer, ploddingly directed.
w Ronald Liles, James O'Connolly *story* Decoy, Be Damned by T. F. Fotherby *d* Ernest Morris *ph* Walter J. Harvey *m* Martin Slavin *ad* Wilfred Arnold *ed* Henry Richardson
☆ Paul Maxwell, Clare Owen, Anita West, John Sutton, John Arnatt, Eric Pohlmann, Alan Tilvern, Reginald Marsh

Shadow of the Cat
GB 1961 79m bw
U-I/BHP (Jon Penington)
A cat appears to wreak vengeance on those who murdered its mistress.
Tolerable old dark house shocker with an amusing theme not too well sustained.
w George Baxt *d* John Gilling *ph* Alec Grant *m* Mikis Theodorakis
☆ André Morell, William Lucas, Barbara Shelley, Conrad Phillips, Alan Wheatley, Vanda Godsell, Richard Warner, Freda Jackson

Shadow of the Eagle
GB 1950 92m bw
Valiant (Anthony Havelock-Allan)
In 1770, a Russian envoy to Venice falls for the princess he is supposed to kidnap.
Limp swashbuckler based on a deservedly shadowy corner of European history.
w Doreen Montgomery, Hagar Wilde *d* Sidney Salkow *ph* Erwin Hillier *m* Hans May
☆ Richard Greene, Valentina Cortese, Greta Gynt, Binnie Barnes, Charles Goldner, Walter Rilla

Shadow of the Vampire **
GB/US 2000 93m DeLuxe
Metrodome/Lions Gate/Saturn/Long Shot/BBC/Delux (Nicolas Cage, Jeff Levine)
About to shoot *Nosferatu*, his rip-off of *Dracula*, film director F.W. Murnau hires a real vampire, Max Schreck, for the leading role.
An unusual and enjoyable fang-in-cheek twist on vampire and silent movie legend that also manages to be a critique of the film business: it is the director who emerges as the true monster.
w Steven Katz *d* E. Elias Merhige *ph* Lou Bogue *m* Dan Jones *pd* Assheton Gorton *ed* Chris Wyatt *cos* Caroline de Vivaise
☆ John Malkovich (F.W. Murnau), *Willem Dafoe* (Max Schreck), Cary Elwes (Fritz Wagner), John Aden Gillet (Henrick Galeen), Eddie Izzard (Gustav von Wangerheim), Udo Kier (Albin Grau), Catherine McCormack (Greta Schroeder), Ronan Vibert (Wolfgang Muller)
'The movie often meanders from comedy to terror to chin-stroking intellectualism. Yet though it's often frustrating, the movie lingers in the mind like an especially intense dream.' – A.O. Scott, *New York Times*
Willem Dafoe; make-up (Ann Buchanan, Amber Sibley)

Shadow of the Wolf
Canada/France 1993 112m Sonolab Color Cinemascope
Vision/Transfilm/Eiffel/Canal (Claude Leger)
aka: *Agaguk*
In the 1930s, an Eskimo, banished for his hatred of white men, becomes an outcast who has to learn to fend for himself.
Simple-minded rites-of-passage drama of a man pitted against the elements.
w Rudy Wurlitzer, Evan Jones, David Milhaud *novel* Yves Theriault *d* Jacques Dorfmann *ph* Billy Williams *m* Maurice Jarre *pd* Wolf Kroeger *ed* Françoise Bonnot
☆ Lou Diamond Phillips, Toshiro Mifune, Jennifer Tilly, Bernard-Pierre Donnadieu, Donald Sutherland
'Pic is too simple-minded and clichéd for adults, but probably too rough for kids.' – *Variety*
† The film, which cost around $30 million, was the most expensive Canadian production so far. It was released direct to video in Britain.

The Shadow on the Window
US 1957 73m bw
Columbia (Jonie Taps)
Three teenage thugs break into a lonely house, murder its owner and hold a girl hostage.
Routine crime programmer, rather boringly unravelled.
w Leo Townsend, David Harmon *d* William Asher *ph* Kit Carson *m* George Duning
☆ Betty Garrett, Phil Carey, John Barrymore Jnr, Corey Allen, Gerald Saracini

Shadow Warrior: see *Kagemusha*

'He thought that magic only existed in books, and then he met her.'
Shadowlands ***
GB 1993 131m colour Scope
UIP/Showlands/Spelling/Pirce/Savoy (Richard Attenborough, Brian Eastman)
The emotionally repressed C. S. Lewis, Oxford don and famous writer of children's books and works of popular theology, enters into a marriage of convenience with an American woman, whom he grows to love, only to learn that she has terminal cancer.
Impeccably acted and directed drama of emotional risk and the pain and joy it can bring.
w William Nicholson *play* William Nicholson *d Richard Attenborough ph* Roger Pratt *m* George Fenton *pd* Stuart Craig *ed* Lesley Walker
☆ *Anthony Hopkins, Debra Winger*, John Wood, Edward Hardwicke, Joseph Mazzello, Julian Fellowes, Roddy Maude-Roxby, Michael Denison, Peter Firth
'A mature film for grown-ups.' – *Variety*
'Reticent is the word for Richard Attenborough's film version. But that's a virtue, not a defect, when the setting is English academia (no one has more persuasively captured its manners) and your subject is mortality.' – *Richard Corliss, Time*
'The picture isn't actually very good; it's just a tearjerker with clumsy interpolations of theology.' – *Terrence Rafferty, New Yorker*
'A beautifully crafted movie that gleams like a newly-made antique.' – *Philip French, Observer*
† William Nicholson first wrote the story as a play for BBC TV and then adapted it for the stage before it became a film. Despite Hopkins's Welsh accent, Lewis was an Ulsterman, born in Belfast.
Debra Winger; William Nicholson

Shadows *
US 1959 81m bw
Cassavetes/Cassel/Maurice McEndree
Two blacks and their sister find their identities in Manhattan.
16mm realistic drama which began a new and essentially dreary trend of grainily true-life pictures with improvised dialogue and little dramatic compression.
w the cast *d* John Cassavetes *ph* Erich Kollmar *m* Charles Mingus
☆ Ben Carruthers, Lelia Goldoni, Hugh Hurd, Rupert Crosse, Anthony Ray
'I don't so much object to its mindlessness as to its formlessness, regardless of the practical excuses that may be advanced for its rambling incoherence.' – *William S. Pechter*
'A picture of startling immediacy and shocking power.' – *Robert Hatch, Nation*
'We were improvising ... every scene was very simple. They were predicated on people having problems that were overcome with other problems. At the end of the scene another problem would come in and overlap.' – *John Cassavetes*

Shadows and Fog *
US 1991 86m bw
Columbia TriStar/Orion (Jack Rollins, Charles Joffe)
In a town where a circus has come to visit, a timid individual is forced by his neighbours to join vigilantes trying to trap a murderer.
An occasionally witty excursion into the world of German expressionist movies of the 20s.
wd Woody Allen *ph* Carlo Di Palma *m* Kurt Weill *pd* Santo Loquasto *ed* Susan E. Morse
☆ Woody Allen, Mia Farrow, John Malkovich, Madonna, Donald Pleasence, Lily Tomlin, Jodie Foster, Kathy Bates, John Cusack, Kate Nelligan, Julie Kavner, Fred Gwynne

'Is Allen confronting his inability to treat history, or anything else, as tragedy rather than farce? The film is a serious joke, possibly reflecting on German re-unification, and it has an unpleasant aftertaste.' – *Philip French, Observer*

Shadows of our Forgotten Ancestors *
USSR 1964 100m bw/colour
Dovzhenko Film Studios

original title: *Teni Zabytykh Predkov*
A youth falls in love with the daughter of the rich landowner who killed his father.
A story of a doomed love, told in the form of a folk-tale, episodic and highly coloured.
w Sergo Paradjanov, Ivan Chendei d Sergo Paradjanov ph Y. Ilyenko m M. Sorik
☆ Ivan Nikolaichuk, Larisa Kadochnikova, Tatiana Bestayeva, Spartak Bagashvili

Shadows of the Peacock
Australia 1987 94m colour
Laughing Kookaburra (Jane Scott)

After discovering her husband's infidelity, a politician's wife asserts her independence by going to Thailand and falling for a Balinese dancer.
Slight, bitter-sweet romance, acted and directed at a somnambulistic pace.
w Jan Sharp, Anne Brooksbank d Phillip Noyce ph Peter James m William Motzing pd Judith Russell ed Frans Vandenburg
☆ Wendy Hughes, John Lone, Rod Mullinar, Peta Toppano, Steven Jacobs, Gillian Jones

Shady Lady
US 1945 90m bw
Universal
An elderly cardsharp is persuaded to help the district attorney nab others of his kind.
Poorish comedy which offers its star little support.
w Curt Siodmak, Gerald Geraghty and M. M. Musselman d George Waggner
☆ Charles Coburn, Ginny Simms, Robert Paige, Martha O'Driscoll, Alan Curtis

Shaft *
US 1971 100m Metrocolor
MGM/Shaft Productions (Joel Freeman)

A black private eye finds himself at odds with a powerful racketeer.
Violent, commercial action thriller which spawned two sequels and a tele-series as well as stimulating innumerable even more violent imitations.
w Ernest Tidyman, John D. F. Black d Gordon Parks ph Urs Furrer m Isaac Hayes
☆ Richard Roundtree, Moses Gunn, Charles Cioffi, Christopher St John
'Relentlessly supercool dialogue, all throwaway colloquialisms and tough Chandlerian wisecracks.' – *MFB*
title song (m/ly Isaac Hayes)
Isaac Hayes (musical score)

'Still The Man.'
Shaft
US 2000 98m DeLuxe Panavision
Paramount (Scott Rudin, John Singleton)

A black cop quits in disgust over the treatment given to a murder suspect, who is wealthy and white, but continues his investigation.
Quite why anyone should wish to remake Gordon Parks' blaxploitation hit twenty-nine years later is difficult to understand, particularly as the result is a mess: a shrill and violent movie with little to offer.
w Richard Price, John Singleton, Shane Salerno novel Ernest Tidyman d John Singleton ph Donald E. Thorin m David Arnold, Isaac Hayes pd Patrizia Von Brandenstein ed John Bloom, Antonia Van Drimmelen cos Ruth Carter
☆ Samuel L. Jackson (John Shaft), Vanessa Williams (Carmen Vasquez), Jeffrey Wright (Peoples Hernandez), Christian Bale (Walter Wade Jnr), Busta Rhymes (Rasaan), Dan Hedaya (Jack Roselli), Toni Collette (Diane Palmieri), Richard Roundtree (Uncle John Shaft), Ruben Santiago-Hudson (Jimmy Groves), Josef Sommer (Curt Fleming), Lynne Thigpen (Carla Howard), Philip Bosco (Walter Wade Snr), Lee Tergesen (Luger), Mekhi Phifer (Trey Howard)
'Ends up looking cheaper than any big-budget Hollywood entertainment should.' – *Andrew O'Hehir, Sight and Sound*
'The action set-pieces look decidedly shop-worn… It's not an unmitigated disaster, but it is a disappointment.' – *Simon Braund, Empire*

Shaft in Africa
US 1973 112m Metrocolor Panavision
MGM/Shaft Productions (Roger Lewis)
Shaft is kidnapped by an Ethiopian emir who wants him to track down a gang of slavers.
More miscellaneous violence, rather shoddily assembled, with a few good jokes.
w Stirling Silliphant d John Guillermin ph Marcel Grignon m Johnny Pate ad John Stoll ed Max Benedict
☆ Richard Roundtree, Frank Finlay, Vonetta McGee

Shaft's Big Score!
US 1972 105m Metrocolor Panavision
MGM/Shaft Productions (Richard Lewis, Ernest Tidyman)

Shaft avenges the death of a friend and comes up against the numbers racket.
Violent footage and an incomprehensible plot. No one, least of all the director, shows any interest in the narrative, which is ignored for a succession of action-packed set-pieces, finally settling down into a long chase sequence, in which our hero can dispose of all the villains without anyone trying to make sense of the plot.
w Ernest Tidyman d Gordon Parks ph Urs Furrer m Gordon Parks ad Emanuel Gerard ed Harry Howard
☆ Richard Roundtree, Moses Gunn, Joseph Mascolo, Kathy Imrie, Wally Taylor, Julius W. Harris, Drew Bundini Brown
'Self-conscious, contrived, ambitious and sluggish.' – *Variety*

Shag
GB 1988 100m colour
Palace/Hemdale (Stephen Woolley, Julia Chasman)

Four girls go to the beach for fun and boys.
Set in the 1960s, it is an attempt, successful enough in its inane way, to revive the style of the teen movies of the time.
w Robin Swicord, Lanier Laney, Terry Sweeney d Zelda Barron ph Peter MacDonald pd Buddy Cone ed Laurence Mery Clark
☆ Phoebe Cates, Scott Coffey, Bridget Fonda, Annabeth Gish, Page Hannah, Robert Rusler, Tyrone Power III, Jeff Yagher

The Shaggy DA
US 1976 92m Technicolor
Walt Disney (Ron Miller)

A magic ring enables a young lawyer to become a talking dog and thus expose corruption.
Rather feeble sequel to The Shaggy Dog, *with overtones of Watergate.*
w Don Tait d Robert Stevenson ph Frank Phillips m Buddy Baker sp Eustace Lycett, Art Cruickshank, Danne Lee
☆ Dean Jones, Tim Conway, Suzanne Pleshette, Jo Anne Worley, Vic Tayback, Keenan Wynn, Dick Van Patten

The Shaggy Dog *
US 1959 101m bw
Walt Disney (Bill Walsh)

A small boy turns into a big shaggy dog and catches some crooks.
Simple-minded, overlong Disney comedy for kids and their indulgent parents; good laughs in the chase scenes.
w Bill Walsh, Lillie Hayward novel *The Hound of Florence* by Felix Salten d Charles Barton ph Edward Colman m Paul Sawtell
☆ Fred MacMurray, Jean Hagen, Tommy Kirk, Cecil Kellaway, Annette Funicello, Tim Considine, Kevin Corcoran, Alexander Scourby

Shake Hands with Murder
US 1944 61m bw
American Productions/PRC
Bailbondsmen get involved in murder.
Tolerable little mystery for the bottom of the bill.
w John T. Neville, Martin Mooney d Albert Herman ph Robert Cline md Lee Zahler
☆ Frank Jenks, Iris Adrian, Douglas Fowley, Jack Raymond

Shake Hands with the Devil *
Eire 1959 110m bw
UA/Troy/Pennebaker (Michael Anderson)

In 1921 Dublin a surgeon is the secret leader of the IRA, and comes to cherish violence as an end rather than a means.
Downbeat action melodrama, politically very questionable but well made.
w Ivan Goff, Ben Roberts novel Rearden Connor d Michael Anderson ph Erwin Hillier m William Alwyn
☆ James Cagney, Glynis Johns, Don Murray, Dana Wynter, Michael Redgrave, Sybil Thorndike, Cyril Cusack, Niall MacGinnis, Richard Harris, Ray McAnally, Noel Purcell

Shake, Rattle & Rock!
US 1956 75m bw
AIP (James H. Nicholson, Samuel Z. Arkoff)
A small-town disc jockey demands a public trial after a vigilante committee is set up to ban rock 'n' roll.
Enjoyable-enough exploitation movie in a familiar groove, notable for the musical performances of Joe Turner ('Lipstick, Powder And Paint') and Fats Domino ('Ain't That A Shame', 'I'm In Love Again'), and Margaret Dumont, Groucho Marx's old adversary, as a killjoy.
w Lou Rusoff d Edward L. Cahn ph Frederick E. West m Alexander Courage ad Don Ament ed Robert S. Eisen, Charles Gross Jnr
☆ Touch Connors, Lisa Gaye, Sterling Holloway, Raymond Hatton, Paul Dubov, Douglass Dumbrille, Clarence Kolb, Margaret Dumont, Frank Jenks, Percy Helton, Tommy Charles, Fats Domino, Annita Ray, Joe Turner

The Shakedown
GB 1959 92m bw
Rank/Alliance/Ethiro (Norman Williams)
A Soho vice boss photographs prominent people in compromising situations and blackmails them.
A semi-remake set in the squalid London so beloved of film makers at the time, before it became 'swinging'. Of no interest or entertainment value.
w Leigh Vance d John Lemont ph Brendan J. Stafford m Philip Green
☆ Terence Morgan, Hazel Court, Donald Pleasence, Bill Owen, Robert Beatty, Harry H. Corbett, Gene Anderson, Eddie Byrne

Shakedown: see *Blue Jean Cop (1988)*

Shaker Run
New Zealand 1985 90m colour
Laurelwood/Aviscom/Mirage (Igo Kantor, Larry Parr)

Two American stunt car drivers help a girl who for the best political reasons has stolen a deadly virus.
Harebrained excuse for car chases against beautiful scenery; quite exhausting.
w James Kouf Jnr, Henry Fownes, Bruce Morrison d Bruce Morrison ph Kevin Hayward m Stephen McCurdy
☆ Cliff Robertson, Leif Garrett, Lisa Harrow, Shane Briant

'A comedy about the greatest love story *almost* never told.'
Shakespeare in Love ***
US 1998 113m DeLuxe
UIP/Miramax/Universal/Bedford Falls (David Parfitt, Donna Gigliotti, Harvey Weinstein, Edward Zwick, Mark Norman)

Shakespeare, suffering writer's block over his new work, *Romeo and Ethel, the Pirate's Daughter*, is inspired when he falls in love with a cross-dressing heiress.
If movies be the food of love, then there's an excess of it in this delightful romantic comedy, a clever romp that makes witty use of theatrical conventions and Shakespeare's own works; it is not only in love with love, but with the power of theatre.
w *Marc Norman, Tom Stoppard* d *John Madden* ph *Richard Greatrex* m *Stephen Warbeck* pd *Martin Childs* ed *David Gamble*
☆ *Gwyneth Paltrow*, Joseph Fiennes, *Geoffrey Rush*, Colin Firth, Ben Affleck, *Judi Dench*, Rupert Everett, Simon Callow, Jim Carter, Martin Clunes, Antony Sher, Imelda Staunton, Tom Wilkinson, Mark Williams
'A ripely emotional comedy fantasia.' – *David Denby, New Yorker*
'A great success, bawdy, silly, handsome, brainy and energetic.' – *Ian Nathan, Empire*
† The day after the Oscar ceremony, its US box-office income increased by 42 per cent.
†† Judi Dench, winner of the Oscar as best supporting actress, was on-screen for eight minutes.
††† Daniel Day-Lewis and Julia Roberts were the first choices for the roles played by Joseph Fiennes and Gwyneth Paltrow.
best picture; Gwyneth Paltrow; Judi Dench; Marc Norman, Tom Stoppard; Stephen Warbeck; Martin Childs; Sandy Powell (costumes)
John Madden; Geoffrey Rush; Richard Greatrex; David Gamble; make-up; sound
best film; Judi Dench; Geoffrey Rush; David Gamble

Shakespeare Wallah *
India 1965 125m bw
Merchant Ivory (Ismail Merchant)

A troupe of English actors find their Indian tour interrupted by romance.
Interesting but sluggish drama on an unusual subject. Not by any means a classic, but it set off this partnership on an enduring wave of critical acclaim and public indifference.
w Ruth Prawer Jhabvala, James Ivory d James Ivory ph Subrata Mitra m Satyajit Ray
☆ Felicity Kendal, Shashi Kapoor, Laura Liddell, Geoffrey Kendal, Madhur Jaffrey, Utpal Dutt
'Touched by brilliance, marked throughout by grace, it is a quiet film that allows one to perceive the ironies and the poignancy of a time of transition.' – *Judith Crist*

Shakha Proshakha: see *Branches of the Tree*

The Shakiest Gun in the West
US 1967 101m Techniscope
Universal (Edward J. Montagne)

A cowardly dentist becomes a Western hero.
Dreary farce, an unsubtle remake of The Paleface.
w Jim Fritzell, Everett Greenbaum d Alan Rafkin ph Andrew Jackson m Vic Mizzy
☆ Don Knotts, Barbara Rhoades, Jackie Coogan, Don Barry

'Sex. Love. Marriage. Infidelity. Happiness. Success. Friendship. Trust. Babies. Work. Deadlines. Parents. Dreams. Money. Hopes. Fears. Secrets. Growing Up. Hanging Out. Hanging In.'
Shaking the Tree
US 1990 107m Astor Color
Hobo/Reality (Robert J. Wilson)

The lives of a group of old schoolfriends go through changes as they gather for a Christmas reunion.
Tedium sets in early in this examination of the dull lives of uninteresting people.
w Duane Clark, Steven Wilde d Duane Clark ph Ronn Schmidt m David E. Russo ed Martin L. Bernstein
☆ Arye Gross, Gale Hansen, Doug Savant, Steven Wilde, Courteney Cox, Christina Haag
'Lackluster tale of four childhood buddies generates little interest despite competent technical credits all-around and some nice acting turns. The who-cares factor is simply too high.' – *Variety*

Shalako
GB 1968 118m Technicolor Franscope
Kingston/Dimitri de Grunwald (Euan Lloyd)

New Mexico, 1880: a cowboy acts as guide to European aristocratic big game hunters, but the Indians become annoyed and attack.
A cute idea is given routine treatment; though packed with stars, the action never becomes very exciting despite incidental brutalities.
w J. J. Griffith, Hal Hopper, Scot Finch novel Louis L'Amour d Edward Dmytryk ph Ted Moore m Robert Farnon
☆ Sean Connery, Brigitte Bardot, Jack Hawkins, Stephen Boyd, Peter Van Eyck, Honor Blackman, Eric Sykes, Alexander Knox, Woody Strode, Valerie French

Shall We Dance? **
US 1937 116m bw
RKO (Pandro S. Berman)
Dancing partners pretend to be married but are not; until they both get the same idea.
A light musical which was full of good things but nevertheless began the decline of Astaire-Rogers films; repetition was obvious, as was ostentation for its own sake, and the audience was expecting too much.
w Allan Scott, Ernest Pagano *d* Mark Sandrich *ph* David Abel *m/ly George and Ira Gershwin* *md* Nathaniel Shilkret *ad* Van Nest Polglase
☆ *Fred Astaire, Ginger Rogers,* Edward Everett Horton, Eric Blore, Harriet Hoctor, Jerome Cowan, Ketti Gallian, Ann Shoemaker
'Another holdover musical in the Astaire-Rogers string … it has everything it needs on production.' – *Variety*
song 'They Can't Take That Away From Me'

'He's An Overworked Accountant. She's An Accomplished Dancer. Passion Is About To Find Two Unlikely Partners.'
Shall We Dance? **
Japan 1995 119m colour
Buena Vista/Altamura/Daiei/NTV/Hakuhodo/Nippon Shuppan (Yasuyoshi Tokuma)
An office worker, bored by his job and his marriage, joins a ballroom dancing class.
Charming comedy that makes the familiar seem extraordinarily exotic.
wd Masayuki Suo *ph* Naoki Kayano *m* Yoshikazu Suo *pd* Kyoko Heya *ed* Junichi Kikuchi
☆ Koji Yakusho, Tamiyo Kusakari, Naoto Takenaka, Eriko Watanabe, Akira Emoto, Yu Tokui, Hiromasa Taguchi, Reiko Kasamura, Hideko Hara
'An enormously sweet-tempered comedy.' – *Alexander Walker*
† It became the most successful Japanese film shown in the USA.

'What's a little murder between friends?'
Shallow Grave **
GB 1994 92m colour
Rank/Figment/Channel 4/Glasgow Film Fund (Andrew Macdonald)
Three flatmates, who discover that their new tenant has died leaving a suitcase full of money, decide to dispose of the body and keep the cash.
Energetic, fast-moving thriller that maintains its breathless pace to the end and is done with great panache, almost enough to overlook its faults of unconvincing character shifts, unlikely plot developments and its final burst of insufficiently motivated and gratuitous violence.
w John Hodge *d Danny Boyle* *ph* Brian Tufano *m* Simon Boswell *pd* Kave Quinn *ed* Masahiro Hirakubo
☆ Kerry Fox, Christopher Eccleston, Ewan McGregor, Ken Stott, Keith Allen, Colin McCredie
'A British thriller of great assurance and fair accomplishment.' – *Adam Mars-Jones, Independent*
'A masterpiece of creepy terror.' – *Stephen Farber, Movieline*
best British film

'The Biggest Love Story Ever Told.'
Shallow Hal
US 2001 114m DeLuxe
TCF/Conundrum (Bradley Thomas, Charles B. Wessler, Bobby Farrelly, Peter Farrelly)
A man who judges women on their looks is hypnotised to see only inner beauty, and falls for a 300 lb woman.
A movie that has its cake and eats it several times over, gorging on fat jokes and then adding a syrup of sentimentality to excuse them.
w Sean Moynihan, Bobby Farrelly, Peter Farrelly *d* Bobby Farrelly, Peter Farrelly *ph* Russell Carpenter *m* Ivy *pd* Sidney J. Bartholomew Jnr *ed* Christopher Greenbury *cos* Pamela Withers
☆ Gwyneth Paltrow (Rosemary), Jack Black (Hal), Jason Alexander (Mauricio), Joe Viterelli (Steve Shanahan), Rene Kirby (Walt), Bruce McGill (Reverend Larson), Tony Robbins (Tony Robbins), Susan Ward (Jill)
'Has enough amusing and endearing moments to put it over as a reasonably commercial date movie.' – *Todd McCarthy, Variety*
'A one-gag film of unplumbable vulgarity. Physical disability is mocked and knocked all through, then hypocritically discounted to permit a happy ending.' – *Alexander Walker, London Evening Standard*

Shame **
Australia 1987 94m Eastmancolor
Metro/Barron Films/UAA Films (Damien Parer, Paul D. Barron)
A female lawyer uncovers a series of rapes in a small town.
Powerful indictment of male bonding and aggression.
w Beverly Blankenship, Michael Brindley *d* Steve Jodrell *ph* Joseph Pickering *m* Mario Millo *pd* Phil Peters *ed* Kerry Regan
☆ Deborra-Lee Furness, Tony Barry, Simone Buchanan, Gillian Jones, Peter Aanensen, Margaret Ford, David Franklin, Bill McClusky

The Shame of a Nation: see *Scarface*

Shampoo *
US 1975 110m Technicolor
Columbia/Persky-Bright/Vista (Warren Beatty)
A Beverly Hills hairdresser seduces his most glamorous clients.
Ugly little sex farce with few laughs but much dashing about and bad language. Its setting on election eve 1968 has made some people think it a political satire.
w Robert Towne, Warren Beatty *d* Hal Ashby *ph* Laszlo Kovacs *m* Paul Simon
☆ Warren Beatty, Julie Christie, Lee Grant, Goldie Hawn, Jack Warden, Tony Bill, Jay Robinson, Carrie Fisher, Brad Dexter
'It has the bursting-with-talent but fuzziness-of-effect aspect of a movie made by a group of friends for their own amusement.' – *Richard Combs*
Lee Grant
script; Jack Warden

Shamus
US 1972 98m Eastmancolor
Columbia/Robert M. Weitman
A private eye is hired by a wealthy man to recover stolen jewels and find a murderer.
A forties retread with seventies violence; junky stuff, with a few laughs for buffs who can spot the in-jokes.
w Barry Beckerman *d* Buzz Kulik *ph* Victor J. Kemper *m* Jerry Goldsmith
☆ Burt Reynolds, Dyan Cannon, John Ryan, Joe Santos, Giorgio Tozzi, Ron Weyland
'Very hectic, very vividly New York and as idiotic as Reynolds' physical resiliency.' – *Judith Crist*

Shane ***
US 1953 118m Technicolor
Paramount (George Stevens)
A mysterious stranger helps a family of homesteaders.
Archetypal family Western, but much slower and statelier than most, as though to emphasize its own quality, which is evident anyway.
w A. B. Guthrie Jnr *novel* Jack Schaefer *d George Stevens* *ph* Loyal Griggs *m* Victor Young
☆ *Alan Ladd,* Jean Arthur, Van Heflin, *Jack Palance,* Brandon de Wilde, Ben Johnson, Edgar Buchanan, Emile Meyer, Elisha Cook Jnr, John Dierkes
'A kind of dramatic documentary of the pioneer days of the west.' – *MFB*
'Westerns are better when they're not too self-importantly self-conscious.' – *New Yorker, 1975*
'Stevens managed to infuse a new vitality, a new sense of realism into the time-worn story through the strength and freshness of his visuals.' – *Arthur Knight*
Loyal Griggs
best picture; A. B. Guthrie Jnr; George Stevens; Jack Palance; Brandon de Wilde

Shangai Joe (dubbed)
Italy/West Germany 1974 96m colour
CBA/Divina (Ennio Onorati)
A Chinese stranger protects peasants and townspeople from a crooked businessman and his gang.
Spaghetti Western with the added ingredient of martial arts; together with its broadly comic tone, the combination results in rather too many slapstick punch-ups.
w Bitto Albertini, Carlo Alberto Alfieri *story* Mariano Caiano, Luigi Russo *d* Bitto Albertini *ph* Pier Luigi Santi *m* Mario Chiara *ad* Riccardo Domenici *ed* Fausto Ulisse
☆ Klaus Kinski, Cheen Lie, Karin Field, Tommy Polgar, Claudio Giorgi, Paolo Casella, Tom Felleghy, Fortunato Rena

Shanghai
US 1935 77m bw
(Paramount)
A visiting American lady falls in love with a half caste.
Romantic drama programmer.
w Gene Towne, Graham Baker, Lynn Starling *d* James Flood *ph* James Van Trees
☆ Loretta Young, Charles Boyer, Warner Oland, Alison Skipworth, Fred Keating, Charles Grapewin, Walter Kingsford

Shanghai Express ***
US 1932 84m bw
Paramount
A British officer and his old flame meet on a train which is waylaid by Chinese bandits.
Superbly pictorial melodrama which set the pattern for innumerable train movies to come, though none matched its deft visual quality and few sketched in their characters so neatly. Plot and dialogue are silent style, but refreshingly so.
w Jules Furthman *d Josef von Sternberg* *ph Lee Garmes* *m* W. Franke Harling *ad Hans Dreier*
☆ *Marlene Dietrich,* Clive Brook, Warner Oland, Anna May Wong, Eugene Pallette, Lawrence Grant, Louise Closser Hale, Gustav von Seyffertitz
LILY (MARLENE DIETRICH): 'It took more than one man to change my name to Shanghai Lily.'
'Good programme picture bolstered by the Dietrich name … Excellent camerawork overcomes really hoke melodramatic story.' – *Variety*
'A limited number of characters, all meticulously etched, highly atmospheric sets and innumerable striking photographic compositions.' – *Curtis Harrington, 1964*
Lee Garmes
best picture; Josef von Sternberg

'Shanghai. Where Almost Anything Can Happen … And Does!'
The Shanghai Gesture *
US 1941 90m bw
Arnold Pressburger (Albert de Courville)
The proprietress of a Shanghai gambling casino taunts her ex-husband by showing him his daughter in a state of degradation; but he proves that the girl is her daughter also.
An ancient theatrical shocker was completely bowdlerized and chopped into nonsense for the screen; but the director's hand showed in the handling of the vast casino set.
w Josef von Sternberg, Geza Herczeg, Karl Vollmoeller, Jules Furthman *play* John Colton *d Josef von Sternberg* *ph* Paul Ivano *m* Richard Hageman *ad Boris Leven*
☆ *Ona Munson, Victor Mature, Walter Huston,* Gene Tierney, Albert Basserman, Phyllis Brooks, Maria Ouspenskaya, Eric Blore, Ivan Lebedeff, Mike Mazurki
'The effect of a descent into a maelstrom of iniquity.' – *Curtis Harrington, 1962*
'In spite of all the changes necessitated by the Hays Office, seldom have decadence and sexual depravity been better suggested on the screen.' – *Richard Roud, 1966*
'Hilariously, awesomely terrible.' – *New Yorker, 1977*
Richard Hageman; Boris Leven

Shanghai Madness
US 1933 63m bw
Fox
A naval officer is cashiered in Shanghai and gets mixed up with Communists.
Weakish melodrama which goes the long way round to a happy ending.
w Frederick Hazlitt Brennan, Austin Parker, Gordon Wellesley *d* John G. Blystone
☆ Spencer Tracy, Fay Wray, Ralph Morgan, Eugene Pallette, Herbert Mundin
'Okay generally but in big spots will need stage support.' – *Variety*

'The Classic Western Gets A Kick In The Pants.' 'Western Action. Eastern Flavour. Won Ton Of Adventure.'
Shanghai Noon *
US/Hong Kong 2000 110m Technicolor Panavision
Buena Vista/Touchstone/Spyglass/Jackie Chan Films (Roger Birnbaum, Gary Barber, Jonathan Glickman)
In Nevada, an imperial guard and an incompetent outlaw team up to rescue a kidnapped Chinese princess.
Engaging mix of martial arts and comedy that will pass an agreeable hour or two; its slicker wit is a welcome change to Chan's more usual slapstick comedy.
w Alfred Gough, Miles Millar *d* Tom Dey *ph* Dan Mindel *m* Randy Edelman *pd* Peter J. Hampton *ed* Richard Chew
☆ Jackie Chan (Chon Wang), Owen Wilson (Roy O'Bannon), Lucy Liu (Princess Pei Pei), Brandon Merrill (Indian Wife), Roger Yuan (Lo Fong), Xander Berkeley (Van Cleef), Walton Goggins (Wallace), P. Adrien Dorval (Blue), Rafael Baez (Vasquez), Jason Connery (Andrews), Russell Badger (Sioux Chief)
'This enjoyable East-meets-Western likely will succeed on its own terms as a sure-fire, long-legged crowd-pleaser.' – *Joe Leydon, Variety*

Shanghai Surprise
GB 1986 97m Technicolor
HandMade/Vista/John Kohn
A lady missionary hires an adventurer to track down a stack of opium before it falls into the wrong hands.
Astonishingly abysmal adventure romance set rather uncertainly in the 1937 Orient. Nothing matches the so-called talents involved.
w John Kohn, Robert Bentley *novel Faraday's Flowers* by Tony Kenrick *d* Jim Goddard *ph* Ernest Vincze *m* George Harrison, Michael Kamen
☆ Madonna, Sean Penn, Paul Freeman, Richard Griffiths
'A silly little trifle which wouldn't even have passed muster as a 1930s programmer.' – *Variety*

'In 1930's Shanghai violence was not the problem. It was the solution.'
Shanghai Triad **
Hong Kong 1995 108m colour
Electric/Shanghai Studio/Alpha/UGC-Images/La Sept (Jean-Louis Piel)
original title: *Yao a Yao Yao dao Waipo Qiao*
In the 30s, a young country boy goes to work for a gangster's mistress and becomes a witness to a power struggle involving another gang member and a rival triad.
A skilled and colourful account of corruption and betrayal, which avoids on-screen violence for the most part in order to concentrate on its devastating aftermath.
w Bi Feiyu *novel Gang Law* by Li Xiao *d Zhang Yimou* *ph* Lu Yue *m* Zhang Guangtian *pd* Cao Jiuping *ed* Du Yuan
☆ *Gong Li,* Li Baotian, Wang Xiaoxiao, Li Xuejian, Sun Chun, Fu Biao, Chen Shu, Liu Jiang
'Oozes a confidence that carries the viewer almost without pause to its shocking climax and ironic close.' – *Derek Elley, Variety*
Lu Yue

Shaolin Martial Arts (dubbed)
Hong Kong 1987 112m colour Shaw Scope
Shaw Brothers/Chang's Film Co. (Run Run Shaw)
Followers of the Shaolin school of kung-fu, feared as rebels, are threatened with extinction by the

authorities, with the aid of the rival Manchu faction and their two invincible fighters.
Period action film, somewhat staid and old-fashioned by present-day standards but moderately entertaining, with its succession of grumpy, taciturn old men teaching the young how to fight.
w I Kuang, Chang Cheh *d* Chang Cheh
ph Kung Mu-To *ed* Kuo Ting-Hung
☆ Fu Sheng, Chi Kuan-Chun, Chen I-Ling, Liu Chia Hui, Tang Yen Tsan, Li Chen-Piao, Liang Chia-Jen, Wang Lung-Wei

Shark
US/Mexico 1969 88m Eastmancolor
Heritage/Cinematografica Calderon
A gunrunner in the Sudan becomes involved with unscrupulous divers after wrecks.
Tepid adventure yarn allegedly damaged by recutting but showing very little sign of original talent.
w Samuel Fuller, John Kingsbridge *novel His Bones Are Coral* by Victor Canning *d* Samuel Fuller *ph* Raul Martinez Solares *m* Rafael Moroyoqui
☆ Burt Reynolds, Arthur Kennedy, Barry Sullivan, Silvia Pinal, Enrique Lucero

'There's Blood In The Water.'
Shark Attack
US 1999 100m colour
Nu Image/Nu World (Mandy Branch)
A marine biologist investigates mysterious deaths from sharks in an African port.
Jaws on Valium, a tired, badly-acted drama.
w Scott Devine, William Hooke *d* Bob Misiorowski *ph* Lawrence Sher *m* Serge Colbert *pd* David Varod *ed* Gerard Jakubowicz
☆ Casper Van Dien (Steven McKray), Ernie Hudson (Laurence Rhodes), Bentley Mitchum (Dr Miles Craven), Jennifer McShane (Corinne DeSantis), Tony Caprari (Mani), Chris Olley (Police Chief)

The Sharkfighters
US 1956 72m Technicolor Cinemascope
(UA) Formosa (Samuel Goldwyn Jnr)
To save the lives of flyers forced down into the sea, navy scientists experiment with a shark repellent.
Straightforward semi-documentary with suspenseful action sequences.
w Lawrence Roman, John Robinson *d* Jerry Hopper *ph* Lee Garmes *m* Jerome Moross
☆ Victor Mature, Karen Steele, James Olson, Claude Akins

Shark's Treasure *
US 1974 95m DeLuxe
UA/Symbol (Cornel Wilde)
Treasure hunters seek buried gold in the Caribbean where sharks abound.
Fairly thrilling action hokum.
wd Cornel Wilde *ph* Jack Atcheler, Al Giddings *m* Robert O. Ragland
☆ Cornel Wilde, Yaphet Kotto, John Neilson, David Canary, Cliff Osmond
'Wilde maintains his reputation for making the most likeable bad movies around.' – *Tom Milne*

'Some cops are good at opening a case. Sharky knows how to finish one.'
Sharky's Machine
US 1981 120m Technicolor
Warner/Orion/Deliverance (Hank Moonjean)
A vice squad policeman builds up a new team.
Exceptionally violent cop thriller on the lines of Dirty Harry.
w Gerald Di Pego *novel* William Diehl *d* Burt Reynolds *ph* William A. Fraker *md* Al Capps
☆ Burt Reynolds, Vittorio Gassman, Brian Keith, Charles Durning, Earl Holliman, Bernie Casey, Henry Silva, Rachel Ward

Sharpshooters
US 1938 63m bw
TCF
Adventures of a newsreel cameraman who saves a young prince from kidnapping.
Serial-like action and comedy very palatably blended: the first of a short series.
w Robert Ellis, Helen Logan *d* James Tinling
☆ Brian Donlevy, Lynn Bari, Wally Vernon, John King, Douglass Dumbrille, C. Henry Gordon, Sidney Blackmer

'A standard programmer to entertain, and a natural for the juve trade.' – *Variety*

Shatter
GB 1974 90m colour
Hammer (Michael Carreras, Vee King Shaw)
US title: *Call Him Mr Shatter*
A professional assassin is marked for death by his former employer in Hong Kong.
Botched attempt to combine a thriller with the style of a kung fu movie.
w Don Houghton *d* Michael Carreras *ph* Brian Probyn, John Wilcox, Roy Ford *m* David Lindup *ed* Eric Boyd-Perkins
☆ Stuart Whitman, Ti Lung, Peter Cushing, Anton Diffring, Lily Li

'Murder Is Never An Accident.'
Shattered *
US 1991 98m Technicolor
Palace/Capella/Davis Entertainment (Wolfgang Petersen, John Davis, David Korda)
Recovering from a car crash that left him with no memory and facial injuries that required plastic surgery, a property developer hires a private eye to discover more about his past.
Clever, unsettling mystery that keeps an audience guessing until the end.
wd Wolfgang Petersen *novel The Plastic Nightmare* by Richard Neely *ph* Laszlo Kovacs *m* Angelo Badalamenti *pd* Gregg Fonseca *ed* Hannes Nikel, Glenn Farr
☆ Tom Berenger, Greta Scacchi, Bob Hoskins, Joanne Whalley-Kilmer, Corbin Bernsen, Debi A. Monahan, Bert Robario, Scott Getlin, Kellye Nakahara
'A solidly entertaining plot-driven thriller which, although it requires an initial act of faith from its audience, rewards them with an intelligent, satisfying mystery.' – *Nigel Floyd, Sight and Sound*

'Fear can hold you prisoner. Hope can set you free.'
The Shawshank Redemption *
US 1994 142m Technicolor
Rank/Castle Rock (Niki Marvin)
A banker, wrongly imprisoned for 20 years, and a murderer serving a life sentence revenge themselves on the prison warden who exploits them.
A melodrama of wasted lives and male bonding with a twist ending, more enjoyable for the performances than the narrative, which veers unpredictably between toughness and sentimentality.
wd Frank Darabont *novel* Stephen King
ph Roger Deakins *m* Thomas Newman
pd Terence Marsh *ed* Richard Francis-Bruce
☆ Tim Robbins, Morgan Freeman, Bob Gunton, William Sadler, Clancy Brown, James Whitmore, Gil Bellows, Mark Rolston, Jeffrey DeMunn
'The movie burns with dubious ardor. No one could disagree with its point of view. No one is likely to be much interested either.' – *David Denby, New York*
'An extremely satisfying entertainment.' – *Entertainment Weekly*
best picture; Morgan Freeman; Frank Darabont; cinematography; film editing; Thomas Newman

'Young and beautiful for 500 years – and wicked every one of them!'
She *
US 1935 89m bw
RKO (Merian C. Cooper)
Ancient papers lead a Cambridge professor and his friends to the lost city where dwells a queen who cannot die – until she falls in love.
The producers have the right spirit for this Victorian fantasy, but tried too hard to emulate the mood of their own King Kong, *and it was a mistake to transfer the setting from Africa to the Arctic. One for connoisseurs, though.*
w Ruth Rose, Dudley Nichols *novel* H. Rider Haggard *d* Irving Pichel, Lansing G. Holden *ph* J. Roy Hunt *m* Max Steiner *ch* Benjamin Zemach
☆ Randolph Scott, Nigel Bruce, Helen Gahagan
'Beautiful production, but story dubious for discriminating adults.' – *Variety*
'To an unrepentant Haggard fan it does sometimes seem to catch the thrill as well as the childishness of his invention.' – *Graham Greene*
'A spectacle of magnificent proportions with the decadent effluvium of the tomb period.' – *Photoplay*
'The stagey décor of Kor is in the art deco style of Radio City Music Hall, and you keep expecting the Rockettes to turn up.' – *Pauline Kael, 70s*
Benjamin Zemach

She
GB 1965 105m Technicolor
Hammerscope
ABP/Hammer (Michael Carreras, Aida Young)
Explorers discover a lost city ruled by an immortal queen.
Flat, uninventive and tedious remake which reverts to Africa but does nothing else right; it ignores the essential Cambridge prologue and all suggestions of fantasy.
w David T. Chantler *novel* H. Rider Haggard *d* Robert Day *ph* Harry Waxman *m* James Bernard *ad* Robert Jones, Don Mingaye *ed* James Needs, Eric Boyd-Perkins
☆ Peter Cushing (Major Horace Holly), Ursula Andress (Ayesha), Christopher Lee (Billali), John Richardson (Leo Vincey), Bernard Cribbins (Job), André Morell (Haumei), Rosenda Monteros (Ustane)

She Beast
Italy 1965 76m Eastmancolor 'Scope
Leith (Paul M. Maslansky)
original title: *La Sorella di Satana*
aka: *Sister of Satan/Revenge of the Blood Beast*
The spirit of a witch killed in the eighteen century possesses the body of an Englishwoman on her honeymoon in Transylvania.
A powerful opening, set in the past, gives way to a modern horror comedy, which is uncertain in tone and hampered by its low budget.
w Michael Byron (Michael Reeves) *d* Michael Reeves *ph* G. Gengarellli *m* Ralph Ferraro *ed* Nera Omri
☆ Barbara Steele, John Karlsen, Ian Ogilvy, Mel Welles, Jay Riley, Richard Watson, Ed Randolph, Peter Grippe, Lucrezia Love, Tony Antonelli

She Couldn't Say No
US 1952 89m bw
RKO (Robert Sparks)
GB title: *Beautiful But Dangerous*
An heiress returns to the town of her childhood to distribute anonymous gifts to those who had helped her.
Moderate Capraesque comedy which doesn't quite come off.
w D. D. Beauchamp, William Bowers, Richard Flournoy *d* Lloyd Bacon *ph* Harold J. Wild *m* Roy Webb
☆ Jean Simmons, Robert Mitchum, Arthur Hunnicutt, Edgar Buchanan, Wallace Ford, Raymond Walburn

She Couldn't Take It *
US 1935 89m bw
Columbia (B. P. Schulberg)
A rich old reprobate meets a gangster in prison and puts him in charge of his rebellious family.
Little-known crazy comedy with touches of melodrama; not a success, but with interesting elements.
w Gene Towne, Oliver H. P. Garrett *story* Graham Baker *d* Tay Garnett *ph* Leon Shamroy
☆ George Raft, Joan Bennett, Walter Connolly, Billie Burke, Lloyd Nolan, Wallace Ford, Alan Mowbray, Donald Meek

The She Creature
US 1956 77m bw
AIP/Golden State (Alex Gordon)
An evil hypnotist regresses his subject back through time to summon up a murderous prehistoric monster from the sea.
Unusual B movie that concentrates less on the monster and more on its exploitation by a corrupt businessman.
w Lou Rusoff *story* Jerry Zigmond *d* Edward L. Cahn *ph* Frederick E. West *m* Ronald Stein *ad* Don Ament *ed* Ronald Sinclair
☆ Chester Morris, Tom Conway, Cathy Downs, Lance Fuller, Ron Randell, Frieda Inescort, Marla English

She Didn't Say No!
GB 1958 97m Technicolor
GW Films (Sergei Nolbandov)
A young Irish widow has five illegitimate children, each by a different father.
Coyly daring comedy full of stage Oirishisms and obvious jokes, a few of which work.
w T. J. Morison, Una Troy *novel We Are Seven* by Una Troy *d* Cyril Frankel *ph* Gilbert Taylor *m* Tristram Cary
☆ Eileen Herlie, Jack MacGowran, Perlita Neilson, Niall MacGinnis, Ian Bannen

She Done Him Wrong ***
US 1933 68m bw
Paramount (William Le Baron)
A lady saloon keeper of the Gay Nineties falls for the undercover cop who is after her.
As near undiluted Mae West as Hollywood ever came: fast, funny, melodramatic and pretty sexy; also a very atmospheric and well-made movie.
w Mae West play Diamond Lil by Mae West (with help on the scenario from Harry Thew, John Bright) *d Lowell Sherman ph* Charles Lang *songs Ralph Rainger (m), Leo Robin (ly)*
☆ *Mae West, Cary Grant,* Owen Moore, Gilbert Roland, Noah Beery, David Landau, Rafaela Ottiano, Rochelle Hudson, Dewey Robinson
'Only alternative to a strong drawing cast, nowadays if a picture wants business, is strong entertainment. This one has neither.' – *Variety*
best picture

She Freak
US 1967 87m colour
David F. Friedman
aka: *Alley of Nightmares*
A waitress leaves a diner, joins a carnival, marries a freak-show operator and ends up as a sideshow attraction.
Cheap and feeble exploitation movie that takes what little inspiration it has from Tod Browning's Freaks *(qv); much of the film was shot without sound and, despite its brevity, is padded out with a great many irrelevant shots of fairground activities.*
w David F. Friedman *d* Byron Mabe *ph* Bill Troiano *m* Billy Allen *ed* Byron Mabe
☆ Claire Brennen, Lee Raymond, Lynn Courtney, Bill McKinney, Claude Smith, Ben Moore, Felix Silla, Bill Bagdad

She Gets Her Man *
US 1945 73m bw
Universal (Warren Wilson)
A country girl in New York tracks down a blowgun murderer.
Disarming mystery farce which tries every slapstick situation known to gag writers, and gets away with it.
w Warren Wilson, Clyde Bruckman *d* Erle C. Kenton *ph* Jerry Ash
☆ *Joan Davis,* William Gargan, Leon Errol, Milburn Stone, Russell Hicks

She Got Her Man: see *Maisie (Maisie Gets Her Man)*

She Has What It Takes
US 1943 66m bw
Colbert Clark/Columbia
A small-time singer masquerades as the long-lost daughter of a famous stage star.
An excuse for musical padding, for indulgent audiences.
w Paul Yawitz *d* Charles Barton
☆ Jinx Falkenburg, Tom Neal, Constance Worth, Joe King, The Radio Rogues, The Vagabonds

She Killed in Ecstasy
West Germany 1970 86m colour
Cinerama/Tele-Cine (Rudolph Herzog Jnr)
original title: *Sie Tötete in Ekstase*
The widow of a doctor, who killed himself after being struck off for experimenting on human embryos, takes revenge on those responsible for his expulsion.
A rarity from this director: a movie with an almost coherent narrative; unfortunately, it is an uninteresting

one, being merely a peg on which to hang a few unimaginatively shot scenes of female nudity.
wd Frank Hollman (Jesús Franco) *ph* Manuel Merino *m* Manfred Hübler, Siegfried Schwab *ed* Clarissa Ambach
☆ Horst Tappert, Susann Korda, Fred Williams, Paul Müller, Howard Vernon, Ewa Stroemberg

She Knew All the Answers
US 1941 84m bw
Charles R. Rogers/Columbia
Prevented by his uncle from marrying a playboy, a chorine falls for the uncle.
Mildly merry comedy which came and went without being noticed.
w Harry Segall, Kenneth Earl, Curtis Kenyon *story* Jane Allen *d* Richard Wallace
☆ Joan Bennett, Franchot Tone, John Hubbard, Eve Arden, William Tracy

She Learned about Sailors
US 1934 82m bw
Fox
In Shanghai, a couple get married so that they will be permitted to leave; back home, they're not sure they want an annulment.
Mild comedy with music.
w William Conselman, Henry Johnson *story* Randall H. Faye *d* George Marshall
☆ Alice Faye, Lew Ayres, Harry Green, Frank Mitchell, Jack Durant

'The hi-de-hi of higher education!'
She Loves Me Not *
US 1934 85m bw
Paramount (Benjamin Glazer)
A showgirl murder witness takes refuge in a men's college.
Larky musical farce later remade as True to the Army *and* How to be Very Very Popular; *this first version is perhaps the most nearly amusing.*
w Ben Glazer *play* Howard Lindsay *novel* Edward Hope *d* Elliott Nugent *ph* Charles Lang *songs* various
☆ Bing Crosby, Miriam Hopkins, Kitty Carlisle, Edward Nugent, Lynne Overman, Henry Stephenson, Warren Hymer, George Barbier
Academy Award nomination: song 'Love in Bloom' (*m*Ralph Rainger, *ly*Leo Robin)

She Married an Artist
US 1938 78m bw
Columbia
A wife becomes jealous of her husband's models.
Very mild romantic comedy.
w Avery Strakosch, Delmer Daves, Gladys Lehman *d* Marion Gering
☆ John Boles, Frances Drake, Albert Dekker

She Married Her Boss
US 1935 90m bw
Columbia
A secretary marries her boss and finds herself taken for granted.
Pleasant but rather thin romantic comedy with amiable stars.
w Sidney Buchman *d* Gregory La Cava *ph* Leon Shamroy
☆ Claudette Colbert, Melvyn Douglas, Raymond Walburn, Edith Fellows, Jean Dixon, Katherine Alexander

She Played with Fire: see *Fortune is a Woman*

She Shall Have Murder
GB 1950 90m bw
Concanen/IFD
A law clerk helps to solve the murder of an elderly client.
Old-fashioned light comedy whodunnit, the equivalent of reading a Crime Club thriller.
w Allan Mackinnon *novel* Delano Ames *d* Daniel Birt *ph* Robert Navarro *m* Eric Spear
☆ Rosamund John, Derrick de Marney, Mary Jerrold, Felix Aylmer, Joyce Heron, Beatrice Varley

She Shall Have Music
GB 1935 91m bw
Twickenham (Julius Hagen)
A band leader helps prevent dirty doings at sea.
A story that is no more than an excuse for a series of dull production numbers by Jack Hylton's Band and assorted singers.
w H. Fowler Mear, Arthur Macrae *story* Paul England *d* Leslie Hiscott *ph* Sydney Blythe, William Luff *ad* James Carter
☆ Claude Dampier, June Clyde, Jack Hylton

She Wanted a Millionaire
US 1932 74m bw
Fox
A girl spurns her childhood sweetheart for a rich man who turns out to be dangerous.
Curious comedy-melodrama which confuses its watchers.
w Sonya Levien *story* William Anthony McGuire *d* John G. Blystone
☆ Joan Bennett, Spencer Tracy, James Kirkwood, Una Merkel, Dorothy Peterson

'Beauty or beast? Woman or monster?'
She Wolf of London
US 1946 61m bw
Universal
GB title: *The Curse of the Allenbys*
A girl thinks she must be the family werewolf.
Risibly inept semi-horror melodrama with a highly implausible solution and poor production.
w George Bricker *d* Jean Yarbrough
☆ June Lockhart, Don Porter, Sara Haden, Lloyd Corrigan, Dennis Hoey, Martin Kosleck

She Wore a Yellow Ribbon **
US 1949 103m Technicolor
RKO/Argosy (John Ford, Merian C. Cooper)
Problems of a cavalry officer about to retire.
Fragmentary but very enjoyable Western with all Ford ingredients served piping hot.
w Frank Nugent, Laurence Stallings *story* James Warner Bellah *d John Ford ph Winton C. Hoch* *m* Richard Hageman
☆ *John Wayne*, Joanne Dru, John Agar, Ben Johnson, Harry Carey Jnr, Victor McLaglen, Mildred Natwick, George O'Brien, Arthur Shields
Academy Award: Winton C. Hoch

She Wouldn't Say Yes
US 1945 87m bw
Columbia
A lady psychiatrist falls for the subject of an experiment.
Star comedy vehicle which falls rather flat.
w Laszlo Gorog, William Thiele, Virginia Van Upp, John Jacoby, Sarett Tobias *d* Alexander Hall
☆ Rosalind Russell, Lee Bowman, Charles Winninger, Adele Jergens

She Wrote the Book
US 1946 72m bw
Universal
A lady professor imagines herself to be the glamorous femme fatale heroine of a lurid novel.
Adventures of a female Walter Mitty; one of the star's better comedies.
w Warren Wilson, Oscar Brodney *d* Charles Lamont
☆ Joan Davis, Mischa Auer, Jack Oakie, Kirby Grant, John Litel, Gloria Stuart, Thurston Hall

She-Devil
US 1989 99m DuArt
Rank/Orion (Jonathan Brett, Susan Seidelman)
An unattractive housewife takes her revenge when her husband leaves her for a glamorous romantic novelist.
Unsuccessful and bland adaptation of the sour comedy of the original.
w Barry Strugatz, Mark R. Burns *novel The Life and Loves of a She-Devil* by Fay Weldon *d* Susan Seidelman *ph* Oliver Stapleton *m* Howard Shore *pd* Santo Loquasto *ed* Craig McKay
☆ Meryl Streep, Roseanne Barr, Ed Begley Jnr, Sylvia Miles, Linda Hunt, Elisebeth Peters, Bryan Larkin, A. Martinez

'Guts As Hard As The Steel Of Their 'Hogs'!'
She-Devils On Wheels
US 1968 83m colour
Mayflower Pictures/Herschell Gordon Lewis
A gang of female bikers indulge in sex and violence, including the decapitation of a rival male biker.
Ineptly written, poorly acted, photographed and directed – a sort of inferior home movie – it reveals that a cult reputation is not necessarily an indication of talent.
w Louise Downe *d* Herschell Gordon Lewis *ph* Roy Collodi *m* Larry Wellington *pd* Robert Enrietto *ed* Richard Brinkman
☆ Betty Connell, Nancy Lee Noble, Christie Wagner, Rodney Bedell

The She-Wolf
US 1931 90m bw
Universal
A woman gets rich but neglects her children.
Talkative filmed play, almost redeemed by its star performance.
w Winifred Dunn *play Mother's Millions* by Winifred Dunn *d* James Flood
☆ May Robson, James Hall, Lawrence Gray, Frances Dade

'When paradise became a battleground, she led the fight for survival!'
Sheena, Queen of the Jungle
US 1984 115m Metrocolor
Panavision
Columbia/Delphi II (Paul Aratow)
Orphaned when her explorer parents are killed, a white girl is raised by an African tribe.
Female Tarzan stuff from a comic strip, smoothly made but too rough and slightly too sexy for the family audience which must have been intended.
w David Newman, Lorenzo Semple Jnr *d* John Guillermin *ph* Pasqualino de Santis *m* Richard Hartley
☆ Tanya Roberts, Ted Wass, Donovan Scott

The Sheep Has Five Legs *
France 1954 96m bw
Raoul Ploquin
original title: *Le Mouton a Cinq Pattes*
A town seeking publicity tries to bring together the five quintuplet grandsons of its oldest inhabitant.
Mildly saucy star vehicle which was in fact most notable for introducing Fernandel to an international audience.
w Albert Valentin *d* Henri Verneuil *ph* Armand Thirard *m* Georges Van Parys
☆ Fernandel, Françoise Arnoul, Delmont, Paulette Dubost, Louis de Funès
Academy Award nomination: original story

The Sheepman *
US 1958 91m Metrocolor Cinemascope
MGM (Edmund Grainger)
A tough sheep farmer determines to settle in a cattle town.
Easy-going Western with humorous moments.
w William Bowers, James Edward Grant *d* George Marshall *ph* Robert Bronner *m* Jeff Alexander
☆ Glenn Ford, Shirley MacLaine, Leslie Nielsen, Mickey Shaughnessy, Edgar Buchanan
Academy Award nomination: script

'When an Arab sees a woman he wants, he takes her!' – *ancient Arabian proverb*
'A photoplay of tempestuous love between a madcap English beauty and a bronzed Arab chief!'
The Sheik *
US 1921 73m (24 fps) bw silent
Famous Players-Lasky/George Melford
An English heiress falls for a desert chieftain.
Archetypal romantic tosh which set the seal on Valentino's superstardom.
w Monte M. Katterjohn *novel* E. M. Hull *d* George Melford *ph* William Marshall
☆ *Rudolph Valentino*, Agnes Ayres, Adolphe Menjou, Walter Long, Lucien Littlefield
† *Son of the Sheik*, released in 1926, was even more popular.

The Sheik Steps Out
US 1937 68m bw
Republic (Herman Schlom)
A modern sheik has a riotous time in the big city.
Uninventive spoof of the Valentino myth.
w Adele Buffington, Gordon Kahn *d* Irving Pichel *ph* Jack Marta *md* Alberto Colombo
☆ Ramon Novarro, Lola Lane, Gene Lockhart, Kathleen Burke, Stanley Fields

> 'Novarro in a comeback start. An action picture of the desert for the lower half of the duals.' – *Variety*

She'll Be Wearing Pink Pajamas
GB 1985 90m Eastmancolor
Virgin/Pink Pajamas/Film Four International (Tara Prem, John Goldschmidt)
Women go on an outdoor survival course.
Basically an excuse for a lot of female nattering; it might have seemed more appealing under a more sensible title.
w Eva Hardy *d* John Goldschmidt *ph* Clive Tickner *m* John Du Prez *pd* Colin Pocock *ed* Richard Key
☆ Julie Walters, Anthony Higgins, Jane Evers, Janet Henfrey, Paula Jacobs

She'll Have to Go
GB 1962 90m bw
Anglo-Amalgamated/Asher Brothers
US title: *Maid to Murder*
Two brothers plan to murder the woman who has inherited their home; when they meet her, both decide to marry her.
A ponderous farce: instead of the needed lightness of touch, there is a great deal of mugging from its cast, who are all determined to let the audience know it's meant to be funny.
w Ian Stuart Black, John Waterhouse *play We Must Kill Toni* by Ian Stuart Black *d* Robert Asher *ph* Jack Asher *m* Philip Green *ed* Gerry Hambling
☆ Bob Monkhouse, Alfred Marks, Hattie Jacques, Anna Karina, Dennis Lotis, Clive Dunn, Peter Butterworth, Graham Stark, Hugh Lloyd, Harry Locke

'A woman's dangerous and erotic journey beneath...'
The Sheltering Sky **
GB/Italy 1990 138m Technicolor
Technovision
Palace/Sahara Company/TAO Film/Recorded Picture Company/Aldrich Group (Jeremy Thomas)
An American couple wander through North Africa in search of themselves.
Austere, stunningly photographed movie that yields rewards if approached on its own terms.
w Mark Peploe, Bernardo Bertolucci *novel* Paul Bowles *d* Bernardo Bertolucci *ph* Vittorio Storaro *m* Ryuichi Sakamoto, Richard Horowitz *pd* Gianni Silvestri *ed* Gabriella Cristiani
☆ Debra Winger, John Malkovich, Campbell Scott, Jill Bennett, Timothy Spall, Eric Vu-An, Amina Annabi, Philippe Morier-Genoud, Paul Bowles

> 'It refuses to indulge those who believe movies should be easy and edifying, with characters worth snuggling up to.' – *Richard Corliss, Time*

Shenandoah **
US 1965 105m Technicolor
Universal (Robert Arthur)
How the American Civil War affected the lives of a Virginia family.
Surprisingly hard-centred and moving semi-Western for the family; excellent performances and well-controlled mood.
w James Lee Barrett d Andrew V. McLaglen *ph* William Clothier *m* Frank Skinner *md* Joseph Gershenson
☆ *James Stewart*, Rosemary Forsyth, Doug McClure, Glenn Corbett, Katharine Ross, Philip Alford

Shepherd of the Hills *
US 1941 98m Technicolor
Paramount/Jack Moss
Ozarkian backwoodsmen enjoy their lifestyle except for the intrusions of the revenue men and a mysterious stranger.
Early colour adaptation of a long-favourite American story, deliberately styled for rural audiences.
w Grover Jones, Stuart Anthony *novel* Harold Bell Wright Jnr *d* Henry Hathaway *ph* Charles Lang Jnr, W. Howard Greene *m* Gerard Carbonara
☆ John Wayne, Betty Field, Harry Carey, Beulah Bondi, James Barton, Samuel S. Hinds, Marjorie Main, Ward Bond, Marc Lawrence, John Qualen, Fuzzy Knight

Shergar
GB/US 2000 93m DeLuxe
Nu Image/Blue Rider/Morlaw/IoMFC (Brian Agnew, Jeff Geoffray, Walter Josten)
A stable lad cares for a famous racehorse kidnapped by the IRA and runs away with the animal when the IRA ordered it killed.
A fiction based on the factual disappearance of Shergar in 1983; it never breaks into a gallop.
wd Denis C. Lewiston *ph* David Lewis *m* John Scott *pd* Brian Ackland-Snow *ed* Alan Strachan
☆ Ian Holm (Joseph Maguire), David Warner (Garritty), Mickey Rourke (Gavin O'Rourke), Andrew Connolly (Concannon), Laura Murphy (Kate), Tom Walsh (Kevin Doherty), Alan Barker (Elliott Smyth), Billy Boyle (Carrigan)
'There's something almost endearing about the film's eager embrace of every available narrative cliché.' – *Philip Kemp, Sight and Sound*
† The film was shot in 1998.

The Sheriff of Fractured Jaw
GB 1958 103m Eastmancolor Cinemascope
TCF/Daniel M. Angel
A London gunsmith in the old west accidentally becomes a hero.
Tame, predictable comedy with a clear lack of invention.
w Arthur Dales (Howard Dimsdale) *story* Jacob Hay *d* Raoul Walsh *ph* Otto Heller *m* Robert Farnon
☆ Kenneth More, Jayne Mansfield, Robert Morley, Ronald Squire, David Horne, Henry Hull, Eynon Evans, Bruce Cabot, William Campbell
† Howard Dimsdale wrote the script under a pseudonym because of the blacklist.

Sherlock Holmes
The innumerable Sherlock Holmes films are noted in *Filmgoer's Companion*, and in this volume the appropriate films are listed under their own titles including the modernized dozen made in the forties by Universal, starring Basil Rathbone as Holmes and Nigel Bruce as Watson. These followed on from Fox's two period pieces, *The Hound of the Baskervilles* and *The Adventures of Sherlock Holmes* (qv). The series started and ended somewhat lamely but several of the episodes remain highly enjoyable, for performances and dialogue rather than plot or pacing. All but the first were directed by Roy William Neill.
1942 Sherlock Holmes and the Voice of Terror (*d* John Rawlins, with Reginald Denny, Thomas Gomez), Sherlock Holmes and the Secret Weapon (L)* (with Lionel Atwill as Moriarty)
1943 Sherlock Holmes in Washington (V)* (with Henry Daniell, George Zucco), Sherlock Holmes Faces Death (V, L)** (with Halliwell Hobbes, Dennis Hoey)
1944 Sherlock Holmes and the Spider Woman (V)** (with Gale Sondergaard, Dennis Hoey), The Scarlet Claw** (with Gerald Hamer), The Pearl of Death** (with Miles Mander, Dennis Hoey, Rondo Hatton)
1945 The House of Fear* (with Aubrey Mather, Dennis Hoey), The Woman in Green (L)* (with Henry Daniell as Moriarty), Pursuit to Algiers (with Martin Kosleck)
1946 Terror by Night (V)* (with Alan Mowbray), Dressed to Kill (GB title: Sherlock Holmes and the Secret Code (V); with Patricia Morison)

Sherlock Holmes *
US 1932 68m bw
Fox
Moriarty brings Chicago gangsters into London.
Interesting but rather unsatisfactory Holmes adventure.
w Bertram Milhauser *d* William K. Howard *ph* George Barnes
☆ Clive Brook, Reginald Owen, Ernest Torrence, Miriam Jordan, Alan Mowbray, Herbert Mundin
'Old-fashioned artificial stage play with modern trimmings that only muddle it. The interpolated modern gangster angle will mystify the mugs who go for underworld and it's a late day to offer the Conan Doyle thing straight to educated clienteles.' – *Variety*

Sherlock Holmes: see *The Adventures of Sherlock Holmes (1939)*

Sherlock Holmes and the Secret Code: see *Dressed to Kill (1946)*

Sherlock Holmes and the Secret Weapon *
US 1942 68m bw
Universal (Howard Benedict)
Sherlock Holmes saves a stolen bombsight from Nazi agents.
Slightly stiff modernized Holmes story with amusing ingredients.
w Edward T. Lowe, W. Scott Darling, Edmund L. Hartmann, vaguely based on The Dancing Men *by Sir Arthur Conan Doyle* *d* Roy William Neill *ph* Les White *m* Frank Skinner
☆ Basil Rathbone (Sherlock Holmes), Nigel Bruce (Dr Watson), Lionel Atwill (Moriarty), Dennis Hoey, Karen Verne, William Post Jnr, Mary Gordon

Sherlock Holmes and the Spider Woman: see *Spider Woman*

Sherlock Holmes and the Voice of Terror
US 1942 65m bw
Universal (Howard Benedict)
Sherlock Holmes unmasks a Lord Haw Haw in the war cabinet.
Fairly risible first entry in the modernized series, with a Hollywood view of London and a singular haircut for the star.
w Lynn Riggs *story* *His Last Bow* by Sir Arthur Conan Doyle *d* John Rawlins *ph* Woody Bredell *m* Frank Skinner
☆ Basil Rathbone, Nigel Bruce, Hillary Brooke, Reginald Denny, Evelyn Ankers, Montagu Love, Thomas Gomez, Mary Gordon

Sherlock Holmes: Dressed to Kill: see *Dressed to Kill (1946)*

Sherlock Holmes Faces Death **
US 1943 68m bw
Universal (Roy William Neill)
Weird murders occur in a convalescent home for retired officers.
One of the better entries in this rather likeable modernized series; fairly close to the original story except that the events don't make a lot of sense.
w Bertram Millhauser *story* *The Musgrave Ritual* by Sir Arthur Conan Doyle *d* Roy William Neill *ph* Charles Van Enger *m* Hans Salter
☆ Basil Rathbone, Nigel Bruce, Hillary Brooke, Milburn Stone, Halliwell Hobbes, Arthur Margetson, Dennis Hoey, Gavin Muir, Frederic Worlock, Olaf Hytten, Gerald Hamer, Mary Gordon, Vernon Downing

Sherlock Holmes in Washington *
US 1943 70m bw
Universal (Howard Benedict)
Sherlock Holmes flies west and prevents Nazi spies from grabbing a microfilmed document concealed in a match folder.
Moderate adventure in the modernized series, with a good beginning and end but a sag in the middle.
w Bertram Millhauser, Lynn Riggs *d* Roy William Neill *ph* Lester White *m* Frank Skinner
☆ Basil Rathbone, Nigel Bruce, Henry Daniell, George Zucco, Marjorie Lord, John Archer, Gavin Muir

Sherlock Junior **
US 1924 45m (24 fps) bw silent
Metro/Buster Keaton (Joseph M. Schenck)
A film projectionist, unjustly accused of stealing a watch, has dreams of being a great detective.
Fast-moving, gag-filled comedy which ranks among its star's best.
w Clyde Bruckman, Jean Havez, Joseph Mitchell *ph* Elgin Lessley, Byron Houck *d/ed* Buster Keaton
☆ *Buster Keaton*, Kathryn McGuire, Ward Crane, Joseph Keaton

'There's more to attraction than meets the eye.'
She's All That
US 1999 96m DeLuxe
Miramax/Tapestry/Film Colony (Peter Abrams, Robert L. Levy, Richard N. Gladstein)
Smarting after losing his girlfriend, a high school student bets that he can make even the unlikiest girl into the prom queen.
Familiar variation on Pygmalion, the sort of tale that has been a staple of romantic comedies for generations; all that happens here is that it is combined with equally familiar high-school clichés.
w R. Lee Fleming Jnr *d* Robert Iscove *ph* Francis Kenny *m* Stewart Copeland *pd* Charles Breen *ed* Casey O Rohrs
☆ Freddie Prinze Jnr (Zack Siler), Rachael Leigh Cook (Laney Boggs), Matthew Lillard (Brock Hudson), Paul Walker (Dean Sampson), Jodi Lyn O'Keefe (Taylor Vaughan), Kevin Pollak (Wayne Boggs), Anna Paquin (Mackenzie Siler), Kieran Culkin (Simon Boggs), Elden Henson (Jesse Jackson), Usher Raymond (Campus D.J.), Kimberly 'Lil' Kim' Jones (Alex), Gabrielle Union (Katie), Dule Hill (Preston Harrison)
'Feels like it could have been made by a team of septuagenarians from the glory days of American Intl. Pictures. The overall mood is one of condescension to the milieu, the material and teen filmgoers.' – *Godfrey Cheshire, Variety*

She's Got Everything
US 1937 70m bw
RKO
A young woman in debt meets a stuffed shirt coffee planter.
Mild comedy which never seems to jell despite the talent assembled.
w Harry Segall, Maxwell Shane *d* Joseph Santley
☆ Ann Sothern, Gene Raymond, Victor Moore, Helen Broderick, Parkyakarkus, Billy Gilbert

She's Gotta Have It
US 1986 84m bw/colour
40 Acres And A Mule Filmworks (Shelton J. Lee)
Three men woo the same woman.
Smart, but ultimately tiresome, comedy as the men explain one-by-one and then together why each would make the perfect lover.
wd Spike Lee *ph* Ernest Dickerson *m* Bill Lee *pd* Wynn Thomas *ed* Spike Lee
☆ Tracy Camilla Johns, Tommy Redmon Hicks, John Canada Terrell, Raye Dowell, Joie Lee, Spike Lee

She's Out of Control
US 1989 95m CFI color
Columbia TriStar/Weintraub Entertainment (Stephen Deutsch)
A widower follows the advice of a psychiatrist in trying to control the sex life of his teenage daughter.
Lifeless and singularly witless comedy.
w Seth Winston, Michael J. Nathanson *d* Stan Dragoti *ph* Donald Peterman *m* Alan Silvestri *pd* David L. Snyder *ed* Dov Hoenig
☆ Tony Danza, Catherine Hicks, Wallace Shawn, Dick O'Neill, Ami Dolenz, Laura Mooney, Derek McGrath, Dana Ashbrook
'The movie begins shakily and ends feebly, but, in between, is often sharp and funny.' – *Philip French, Observer*

'The story of one outrageous woman. Caught between two men. Both of them certain of one thing...'
She's So Lovely
US/France 1997 97m colour
Miramax/Clyde is Hungry/Hachette (Rene Cleitman)
A wife and mother is forced to choose between her husband and her violent former husband, who has been released from a mental institution after ten years.
An unconvincing triangular love story with overheated performances; the script was written more than 20 years ago and it shows its age.
w John Cassavetes *d* Nick Cassavetes *ph* Thierry Arbogast *m* Joseph Vitarelli *pd* David Wasco *ed* Petra Van Oefflen
☆ Sean Penn, Robin Wright Penn, John Travolta, Harry Dean Stanton, Debi Mazar, James Gandolfini, Gena Rowlands, Kelsey Mulrooney
'A vastly uneven, only intermittently enjoyable film.' – *Variety*

'A film about love, marriage, happiness ... and the little distractions in between.'
She's the One *
US 1996 96m DeLuxe Panavision
TCF/Good Machine/Marlboro (Ted Hope, James Schamus, Edward Burns)
Two brothers with marital problems come to blows before they resolve their troubles.
Much in the vein of Burns's first film, The Brothers McMullen *(qv), this explores the interaction between members of a family, in which women provide the catalyst for some soul-searching.*
wd Edward Burns *ph* Frank Prinzi *m* Tom Petty *pd* William Barclay *ed* Susan Graef
☆ Jennifer Aniston, Maxine Bahns, Edward Burns, Cameron Diaz, John Mahoney, Mike McGlone, Anita Gillette
'While it is never quite as funny or sassy as its credentials promise, it still makes for an easy-going diversion.' – *Empire*

'She shakes the student body like it's never been shook before!'
She's Working Her Way through College
US 1952 101m Technicolor
Warner (William Jacobs)
A burlesque queen goes to college and brings out the beast in an English professor.
Limp and vulgar musical remake of a well-liked play and film; just about gets by as a lowbrow timekiller.
w Peter Milne *play* *The Male Animal* by James Thurber, Elliott Nugent *d* H. Bruce Humberstone *ph* Wilfrid Cline *md* Ray Heindorf *ch* Le Roy Prinz *ad* Charles H. Clarke *ed* Clarence Kolster *songs* Sammy Cahn, Vernon Duke
☆ Virginia Mayo, Ronald Reagan, Don Defore, Gene Nelson, Phyllis Thaxter, Patrice Wymore
† Sequel 1953: *She's Back on Broadway.*
♫ 'I'll Be Loving You'; 'Love Is Still For Free'; 'The Stuff That Dreams Are Made Of'

Shichi-nin no Samurai: see *Seven Samurai*

Shidi Chuma: see *The Young Master*

Shiloh
US 1996 93m colour
Utopia/Carl Borack/Zeta (Zane W. Levitt, Dale Rosenbloom)
A young boy takes care of a runaway beagle, owned by a cruel hunter.
Amiable, predictable tale of puppy love.
wd Dale Rosenbloom *novel* Phyllis Reynolds Naylor *ph* Frank Byers *m* Joel Goldsmith *pd* Amy Ancona *ed* Mark Westmore
☆ Michael Moriarty, Rod Steiger, Blake Heron, Scott Wilson, Bonnie Bartlett, Ann Dowd

Shine ***
Australia/GB 1996 105m Cinevex
Buena Vista/AFFC/Momentum/SAFC/Film Victoria (Jane Scott)
A promising classical pianist, dominated by his anxious and repressive father, suffers a mental breakdown, from which he is eventually rescued by an unexpected love.
Moving, superbly acted drama of tragedy and redemption that brilliantly evokes a man's alienation from his roots and his disintegration, as well as his re-emergence into the world.
w Jan Sardi *story* Scott Hicks *d Scott Hicks* *ph Geoffrey Simpson* *m* David Hirschfelder *pd* Vicki Niehus *ed* Pip Karmel
☆ *Geoffrey Rush, Armin Mueller-Stahl, Noah Taylor*, Lynn Redgrave, Googie Withers, Sonia Todd, Nicholas Bell, John Gielgud, Chris Haywood
'A throwback to the best of old-fashioned Hollywood movies, able to move an audience without insulting it in the process.' – *Kenneth Turan, Los Angeles Times*
† The film is based on the life of pianist David Helfgott, who embarked on an international concert tour following the film's release, and also played at the Oscars award ceremony in 1997.
†† It won nine Australian Film Institute awards, including best picture, best director, best actor (Geoffrey Rush) and best original screenplay.
Geoffrey Rush

best picture; Scott Hicks (as director and writer); Jan Sardi; Armin Mueller-Stahl; David Hirschfelder; Pip Karmel
Geoffrey Rush

Shine on Harvest Moon *
US 1944 112m bw (Technicolor sequence)
Warner (William Jacobs)
The life and times of vaudeville singer Nora Bayes.
Standard ragtime biopic, very adequately made.
w Sam Hellman, Richard Weil, Francis Swan, James Kern *d* David Butler *ph* Arthur Edeson *md* Heinz Roemheld
☆ Ann Sheridan, Dennis Morgan, Jack Carson, Irene Manning, S. Z. Sakall, Marie Wilson, Robert Shayne

Shiner
GB 2000 99m colour 'Scope
Momentum/Wisecroft/Visionview (Geoff Reeve)
A dubious boxing promoter gets into more trouble than he can handle when his son fights for a shot at a world title.
Caine makes a convincing hard man here, and the sensibilities of London's low-life are well caught, but nothing, especially not its variation on Shakespeare's King Lear, can save the movie from its inadequate script.
w Scott Cherry *d* John Irvin *ph* Mike Molloy *m* Paul Grabowsky *pd* Austen Spriggs *ed* Ian Crafford
☆ Michael Caine (Billy 'Shiner' Simpson), Frank Spedding (Martin Landau), Frances Barber (Georgie), Claire Rushbrook (Ruth), Frank Harper (Stoney), Andy Serkis (Mel), Matthew Marsden (Eddie 'Golden Boy' Simpson), Gary Lewis (Vic)
'Brutal, hard-edged, unsqueamish…a film that's British to its back teeth. Ones that are not even Hollywood-capped.' – *Alexander Walker, London Evening Standard*

'All work and no play make Jack a dull boy…'
The Shining *
GB 1980 119m colour
Warner/Stanley Kubrick
Under the influence of a desolate hotel where murders had occurred, a caretaker goes berserk and threatens his family.
Uninteresting ghost story sparked by meticulous detail and sets but finally vitiated by overlength and an absurdly over-the-top star performance.
w Stanley Kubrick, Diane Johnson *novel* Stephen King *d* Stanley Kubrick *ph* *John Alcott* *m* Bela Bartok (on record) *pd* *Roy Walker*
☆ Jack Nicholson, Shelley Duvall, Danny Lloyd, Barry Nelson, Scatman Crothers, Philip Stone
'The truly amazing question is why a director of Kubrick's stature would spend his time and effort on a novel that he changes so much it's barely recognizable, taking away whatever originality it possessed while emphasizing its banality. The answer presumably is that Kubrick was looking for a "commercial" property he could impose his own vision on, and Warners, not having learned its lesson with Barry Lyndon, was silly enough to let him do it.' – *Variety*
'A grandiose horror tale which consumes itself, snake-like, swallowing its own tail in a series of narrowing spirals.' – *Sunday Times*

The Shining Hour
US 1938 76m bw
MGM
A night-club dancer marries a gentleman farmer, but has trouble with his family.
Overcast melodrama with insufficient basic interest in the characters.
w Ogden Nash, Jane Murfin *play* Keith Winter *d* Frank Borzage
☆ Joan Crawford, Melvyn Douglas, Margaret Sullavan, Robert Young, Fay Bainter, Allyn Joslyn, Hattie McDaniel
'A confused jumble of cross-purpose motivations and situations that fail entirely to arouse interest.' – *Variety*

'He needed to trust her with his secret. She had to trust him with her life.'
Shining Through
US 1992 132m Panavision
TCF/Peter V. Miller Investment Corp/Sandollar (Howard Rosenman, Carol Baum)
A secretary recalls how she fell in love with a lawyer and became an American spy in wartime Berlin.
Glossily romantic thriller, not only soft-centred but also coated in marshmallow.
wd David Seltzer *novel* Susan Isaacs *ph* Jan de Bont *m* Michael Kamen *pd* Anthony Pratt *ed* Craig McKay
☆ Michael Douglas (Ed Leland), Melanie Griffith (Linda Voss), Liam Neeson (Franze-Otto Dietrich), Joely Richardson (Margrete Von Eberstein), John Gielgud (Konrad Friedrichs), Francis Guinan (Andrew Berringer), Sylvia Syms (Linda's Mother), Stanley Beard (Linda's Father)
'Little more than a big, brassy Hallmark card with a World War II backdrop.' – *Variety*
'Fun, in an extravagant, hopelessly retrograde fashion.' – *Janet Maslin, New York Times*

Shinjuku Dorobo Nikki: see *Diary of a Shinjuku Thief*

Ship Ahoy
US 1942 95m bw
MGM (Jack Cummings)
On a trip to Puerto Rico, a tap dancer is enlisted as a spy.
Tepid musi-comedy.
w Harry Clork *d* Edward Buzzell *ph* Leonard Smith *md* George Stoll *ad* Merrill Pye
☆ Eleanor Powell, Red Skelton, Bert Lahr, Virginia O'Brien, William Post Jnr, James Cross

Ship Café
US 1935 65m bw
Harold Hurley/Paramount
A singing stoker wins a rich girl.
Musical star vehicle of the lower class.
w Harlan Thompson, Herbert Fields *d* Robert Florey
☆ Carl Brisson, Arline Judge, Mady Christians, William Frawley, Eddie Davis

Ship of Fools ***
US 1965 150m bw
Columbia/Stanley Kramer
In 1933 a German liner leaves Vera Cruz for Bremerhaven with a mixed bag of passengers.
Ambitious, serious, quite fascinating slice-of-life shipboard multi-melodrama. Capable mounting, memorable performances and a bravura finale erase memories of padding and symbolic pretensions.
w *Abby Mann* *novel* Katherine Anne Porter *d* *Stanley Kramer* *ph* *Ernest Laszlo* *m* *Ernest Gold*
☆ *Vivien Leigh, Simone Signoret, Oskar Werner, Heinz Ruhmann*, José Ferrer, Lee Marvin, Elizabeth Ashley, *Michael Dunn*, George Segal, Jose Greco, Charles Korvin, Alf Kjellin, Werner Klemperer, John Wengraf, Lilia Skala and also Karen Verne
GLOCKEN (MICHAEL DUNN): 'My name is Karl Glocken, and this is a ship of fools. I'm a fool. You'll meet more fools as we go along. This tub is packed with them. Emancipated ladies and ballplayers. Lovers. Dog lovers. Ladies of joy. Tolerant Jews, Dwarfs. All kinds. And who knows – if you look closely enough, you may even find yourself on board!'
'When you're not being hit over the head with the symbolism, you're being punched in the stomach by would-be inventive camera work while the music score unremittingly fills your nostrils with acrid exhalations.' – *John Simon*
'There is such wealth of reflection upon the human condition, so subtle an orchestration of the elements of love and hate, that it is not fair to tag this with the label of any other film.' – *New York Times*
Ernest Laszlo
best picture; Abby Mann; Simone Signoret; Oskar Werner; Michael Dunn

The Ship that Died of Shame
GB 1955 91m bw
Ealing (Michael Relph)
The wartime crew of a motor gunboat buy the vessel and go into postwar business as smugglers.
Thin and rather obvious melodramatic fable.
w John Whiting, Michael Relph, Basil Dearden *novel* Nicholas Monsarrat *d* Basil Dearden *ph* Gordon Dines *m* William Alwyn
☆ Richard Attenborough, George Baker, Bill Owen, Virginia McKenna, Roland Culver, Bernard Lee, Ralph Truman, John Chandos
'A sentimental fantasy tacked on to a basically conventional thriller.' – *Penelope Houston*

A Ship to India *
Sweden 1947 102m bw
Sveriges Folkbiografer (Lorens Marmstedt)
original title: *Skepp Till Indialand*
aka: *The Land of Desire*
A hunchbacked sailor, returning after seven years at sea and searching for the woman he loved, recalls how the affair began after his father, a bullying tugboat captain, brought her aboard.
Despite the movie's low-budget origins, a sombre, claustrophobic and complex study of relationships and damaged lives which builds to a hopeful ending.
wd Ingmar Bergman *play* Martin Soederhjelm *ph* Goran Strindberg *m* Erland von Koch *ad* O. A. Lundgren *ed* Tage Holmberg
☆ Holger Lowenadler (Alexander Blom), Anna Lindahl (Alice Blom), Birger Malmsten (Johannes), Gertrud Fridh (Sally), Naemi Briese (Selma), Hjordis Pettersson (Sofie)

The Ship Was Loaded: see *Carry On Admiral*

Shipbuilders
GB 1943 89m bw
British National
A cavalcade of the problems of a Clydeside tycoon in the thirties.
Plodding propaganda piece ending with masters and unions working for Britain.
w Gordon Wellesley, Stephen Potter, Reginald Pound *d* John Baxter
☆ Clive Brook, Morland Graham, Finlay Currie, Maudie Edwards

Shipmates Forever
US 1935 124m bw
Warner
An admiral's son disappoints his dad by preferring song and dance to the navy.
Very stretched light musical without any overpowering talents.
w Delmer Daves *d* Frank Borzage
☆ Dick Powell, Ruby Keeler, Lewis Stone, Ross Alexander, Eddie Acuff, Dick Foran

'Dive beneath the surface.'
The Shipping News
US 2001 111m DeLuxe Super 35
Buena Vista/Miramax (Irwin Winkler)
After the death of his promiscuous wife, a timid man finds redemption for himself and his young daughter by returning to his father's old home in Newfoundland.
Weakly-told, sentimental fable that has all the depth and interest of a small puddle.
w Robert Nelson Jacobs *novel* E. Annie Proulx *d* Lasse Hallström *ph* Oliver Stapleton *m* Christopher Young *pd* David Gropman *ed* Andrew Mondshein
☆ Kevin Spacey (Quoyle), Julianne Moore (Wavey Prowse), Judi Dench (Agnis Hamm), Cate Blanchett (Petal), Pete Postlethwaite (Tert Card), Scott Glenn (Jack Buggit), Rhys Ifans (Beaufield Nutbeem), Gordon Pinsent (Billy Pretty), Jason Behr (Dennis Buggit), Larry Pine (Bayonet Melville), Alyssa Gainer/Kaitlyn Gainer/Lauren Gainer (Bunny)
'The final product is soft at the center, a rustic cinematic greeting card.' – *Stephen Holden, New York Times*
'A movie that engrosses, hypnotizes and clings to the memory long after the final frame.' – *Rex Reed, New York Observer*
'Some novels need to be left alone. Hear that, Hollywood?' – *Peter Travers, Rolling Stone*

Ships with Wings *
GB 1941 103m bw
Ealing (S. C. Balcon)
Aircraft carriers prepare for World War II.
Historically interesting, dramatically insubstantial flagwaver.
w Sergei Nolbandov, Patrick Kirwan, Austin Melford, Diana Morgan *d* Sergei Nolbandov *ph* Max Greene, Eric Cross, Roy Kellino, Wilkie Cooper *m* Geoffrey Wright
☆ John Clements, Leslie Banks, Jane Baxter, Ann Todd, Basil Sydney, Edward Chapman, Hugh Williams, Frank Pettingell, Michael Wilding

Shipyard Sally
GB 1939 79m bw
TCF (Edward Black)
A barmaid persuades a shipyard owner to reopen.
Sub-Ealing style comedy with music which manages to bring in management and man as well as waving a flag or two.
w Karl Tunberg, Don Ettlinger *d* Monty Banks *ph* Otto Kanturek
☆ Gracie Fields, Sydney Howard, Morton Selten, Norma Varden, Oliver Wakefield
'This picture has the embarrassment of a charade where you don't know the performers well.' – *Graham Greene*

Shiqisuide Danche: see *Beijing Bicycle*

The Shiralee *
GB 1957 99m bw
Ealing (Jack Rix)
An Australian swagman leaves his wife and takes to the road with his small daughter.
Episodic character comedy-drama throwing a fairly sharp light on the Australian scene.
w Neil Paterson, Leslie Norman *novel* D'Arcy Niland *d* *Leslie Norman* *ph* Paul Beeson *m* John Addison
☆ *Peter Finch*, Dana Wilson, Elizabeth Sellars, George Rose, Russell Napier, Niall MacGinnis, Tessie O'Shea

Shirley Valentine **
US 1989 108m Technicolor
UIP/Paramount (Lewis Gilbert)
A bored housewife abandons her husband to enjoy a holiday romance in Greece.
Enjoyably old-fashioned movie, with some entertaining monologues on her narrow existence from its heroine.
w Willy Russell *play* Willy Russell *d* Lewis Gilbert *ph* Alan Hune *m* Willy Russell, George Hatzinassios *pd* John Stoll *ed* Lesley Walker
☆ *Pauline Collins*, Tom Conti, Julia McKenzie, Alison Steadman, Joanna Lumley, Sylvia Syms, Bernard Hill
Pauline Collins; song 'The Girl Who Used to be Me' (*m* Marvin Hamlisch; *l* Alan and Marilyn Bergman)
Pauline Collins

Shivers: see *The Parasite Murders*

Shoah ***
France 1985 566m colour
Aleph/Historia
Massive documentary history of the Holocaust, using survivors' testimony and some reenactment but no historical footage.
d Claude Lanzmann
† Part 1 is 274m, Part 2 292m.

Shock
US 1946 70m bw
TCF
A girl in a hotel sees a murder committed, and an elaborate plan is concocted to silence her.
Flat treatment ruins a good suspense situation.
w Eugene Ling *d* Alfred Werker *ph* Glen MacWilliams, Joe MacDonald *m* David Buttolph
☆ Vincent Price, Lynn Bari, Frank Latimore, Annabel Shaw
'Extreme improbabilities and a general lack of finish.' – *MFB*

The Shock *
France 1982 95m colour Panavision
Sara Films/T. Films (Charlotte Fraisse)
original title: *Le Choc*
A professional killer finds himself in trouble with his boss when he decides to retire.
Slick, glossy romantic thriller that is enjoyable providing you can stomach its amorality or believe that Catherine Deneuve could be the wife of a turkey farmer.
w Alain Delon, Dominique Robelet, Claude Veillot, Robin Davis *novel* *La Position du Tireur Couché* by Jean-Patrick Manchette *d* Robin Davis *ph* Pierre-William Glenn *m* Philippe Sarde *ad* Serge Douy *ed* Thierry Derocles
☆ Alain Delon, Catherine Deneuve, Philippe Leotard, Etienne Chicot, Jean-Louis Richard, Catherine Leprince, François Perrot

Shock Corridor **
US 1963 101m bw (colour sequence)
Leon Fromkess/Sam Firks (Samuel Fuller)
A journalist gets himself admitted to a mental asylum to solve the murder of an inmate.
Sensational melodrama, a cinematic equivalent of the yellow press, and on that level quite lively.
wd Samuel Fuller *ph* Stanley Cortez *m* Paul Dunlap *ad* Eugene Lourie
☆ Peter Breck, Constance Towers, Gene Evans, James Best, Hari Rhodes, Philip Ahn
'A minor masterpiece' – *Derek Malcolm, Guardian*

'Killing is easy. Getting away with it is murder'
A Shock to the System
US 1990 87m DuArt
Medusa/Corsair (Patrick McCormick)
Passed over for promotion and bored by his wife, a marketing executive turns to murder to resolve his difficulties.
Lacklustre black comedy.
w Andrew Klavan *novel* Simon Brett *d* Jan Egleson *ph* Paul Goldsmith *m* Gary Chang *pd* Howard Cummings *ed* Peter C. Frank, William A. Anderson
☆ Michael Caine, Elizabeth McGovern, Peter Riegert, Swoosie Kurtz, Will Patton, Jenny Wright, John McMartin, Barbara Baxley, Haviland Morris, Philip Moon
'A study of personal psychosis and corporate ruthlessness that is at once mordantly comic and chillingly controlled.' – *Nigel Floyd, MFB*

Shock Treatment
US 1964 94m bw
Warner (Aaron Rosenberg)
Murders are committed in a mental institution.
Tasteless thriller, not even very arresting as a yarn.
w Sydney Boehm *d* Denis Sanders *ph* Sam Leavitt *m* Jerry Goldsmith
☆ Lauren Bacall, Roddy MacDowall, Carol Lynley, Ossie Davis, Stuart Whitman, Douglass Dumbrille

'Trust me, I'm a doctor.'
Shock Treatment
GB 1982 95m Technicolor
TCF (John Goldstone)
An innocent young couple are trapped on a bizarre TV game show.
A sort of sequel to The Rocky Horror Show *(qv), featuring the same hapless hero and heroine, but lacking any spark of originality. It also failed to attract its predecessor's cult following.*
w Richard O'Brien, Jim Sharman *d* Jim Sharman *ph* Mike Molloy *m* Richard Hartley, Richard O'Brien *pd* Brian Thomson *ed* Richard Bedford
☆ Jessica Harper, Cliff de Young, Richard O'Brien, Patricia Quinn, Charles Gray, Nell Campbell, Ruby Wax, Barry Humphries, Rik Mayall

Shocker
US 1989 110m Foto-Kem
Guild/Alive Films/Carolco International (Marianne Maddalena, Barin Kumar)
The spirit of a mass murderer survives his execution.
Mundane horror, lacking any spark of originality and obviously patterned on the director's Nightmare On Elm Street.
wd Wes Craven *ph* Jacques Haitkin *m* William Goldstein *ad* Randy Moore *ed* Andy Blumenthal
☆ Michael Murphy, Peter Berg, Cami Cooper, Mitch Pileggi, John Tesh, Heather Langenkamp, Jessica Craven, Richard Brooks

The Shocking Miss Pilgrim
US 1946 85m Technicolor
TCF (William Perlberg)
In 1894 Boston, a lady typist (stenographer) fights for women's rights.
Period comedy with music; not nearly as sharp as it thinks it is.
wd George Seaton *ph* Leon Shamroy *md* David Raksin *ad* James Basevi, Boris Leven *songs* George and Ira Gershwin
☆ Betty Grable, Dick Haymes, Anne Revere, Allyn Joslyn, Gene Lockhart, Elizabeth Patterson, Arthur Shields, Elizabeth Risdon

The Shoes of the Fisherman **
US 1968 157m Metrocolor Panavision
MGM (George Englund)
After twenty years as a political prisoner, a Russian bishop becomes Pope.
Predigested but heavy-going picturization of a bestseller; big budget, big stars, big hopes. In fact a commercial dud, with plenty of superficial interest but more dramatic contrivance than religious feeling.
w John Patrick, James Kennaway *novel* Morris West *d* Michael Anderson *ph* Erwin Hillier *m* Alex North *ad* Edward Carfagno, George W. Davis *ed* Ernest Walter
☆ Anthony Quinn, David Janssen, Laurence Olivier, Oskar Werner, John Gielgud, Barbara Jefford, Leo McKern, Vittorio de Sica, Clive Revill, Paul Rogers
'A splendidly decorated curate's egg.' – *MFB*
Alex North

Shoeshine **
Italy 1946 90m bw
Alfa (Paolo W. Tamburella)
original title: *Sciuscià*
In Nazi-occupied Rome two shoeshine boys become involved in black marketeering, with tragic consequences.
Not especially rewarding to watch now, this was a key film in the development of Italian neo-realism.
w Cesare Zavattini, Sergio Amidei, Adolfo Franci, C. G. Viola *d* Vittorio de Sica *ph* Anchise Brizzi, Elio Paccara
☆ Franco Interlenghi, Rinaldo Smordoni
'It is filled in every scene with an awareness of the painful complexity of even simple evil.' – *James Agee*
special award
script

Shogun Assassin *
Japan/US 1980 86m Fujicolour Tohoscope
Facelift/Katsu (Shintaro Katsu, Hisaharu Matsubara, David Weisman)
A disgraced shogun executioner seeks revenge for the murder of his wife.
Dubbed and edited for American consumption from the first two films in a Japanese series featuring Lone Wolf, a comic-book character and the hero of the goriest martial arts films so far made, it concentrates on the violence.
w Kazuo Koike, Robert Houston, David Weisman *d* Kenji Misumi, Robert Houston *ph* Chishi Makiura *m* Hideakira Sakurai, Mark Lindsay, W. Michael Lewis *ad* Akira Naito *ed* Toshio Taniguchi, Lee Percy
☆ Tomisaburo Wakayama, Masahiro Tomikawa, Kayo Matsuo, Minoru Ohki, Shoji Kobayashi, Shia Kishida, Akhiro Tomikawa
'No one bleeds like this unless they have garden hoses for veins.' – *Roger Ebert*

Shogun Warrior
Japan 1991 105m colour
Sanyo/Sho Productions/Mayeda/Sho Kosugi
US title: *Journey of Honor*
In the 17th century a samurai travels from Japan to Spain to buy flintlock rifles to give his side the advantage in a clan war to decide the ruler of the country.
Enjoyable, action-filled romp mixing martial arts, swashbuckling, pirates, assassins and a little romance.
w Nelson Gidding, Sho Kosugi *d* Gordon Hessler *ph* John Connor *m* John Scott *pd* Adrian Gorton *ed* Bill Butler
☆ Sho Kosugi, David Essex, Kane Kosugi, Christopher Lee, Norman Lloyd, Ronald Pickup, John Rhys-Davies, Polly Walker, Dylan Kussman, Miwa Takada, Nijiko Kiyokawa, Toshiro Mifune

Shokutaku No Nai Ie: see *The Empty Table*

Shoot First: see *Rough Shoot*

Shoot the Moon *
US 1981 123m Metrocolor
MGM (Alan Marshall)
The family is affected when well-heeled parents decide to split up.
A halfway decent actors' piece which doesn't really justify its time or leave affectionate memories behind. In essence it adds nothing except noise to what was being done in this field forty years ago.
w Bo Goldman *d* Alan Parker *ph* Michael Seresin *m* no credit *pd* Geoffrey Kirkland
☆ Albert Finney, Diane Keaton, Karen Allen, Peter Weller, Dana Hill, Leora Dana
'Despite their superficial sophistication, these are immature creatures playing grown-up games which would be thought childish in Bugsy Malone.' – *Sunday Times*

Shoot the Pianist *
France 1960 80m bw Dyaliscope
Films de la Pléiade (Pierre Braunberger)
original title: *Tirez sur le Pianiste*
A bar-room piano player becomes involved with gangsters and his girlfriend is killed.
Fair copy of an American film noir, not especially interesting except for its sharp observation.
w Marcel Moussy, François Truffaut *novel* *Down There* by David Goodis *d* François Truffaut *ph* Raoul Coutard *m* Jean Constantin, Georges Delerue
☆ Charles Aznavour, Nicole Berger, Marie Dubois, Michèle Mercier, Albert Rémy
'Pictorially it is magnificent, revealing Truffaut's brilliant control over his images; emotionally, it is all a little jejune.' – *John Gillett, MFB*

Shoot the Works
US 1934 82m bw
Albert Lewis/Paramount
A band leader and a gossip columnist stage a fake feud.
Anaemic Hollywood version of a rather sharp Broadway play which in this form means less than nothing.
w Howard J. Green, Claude Binyon *play* *The Great Magoo* by Ben Hecht, Gene Fowler *d* Wesley Ruggles
☆ Jack Oakie, Ben Bernie, Dorothy Dell, Arline Judge, Alison Skipworth, Roscoe Karns, William Frawley, Paul Cavanagh, Lew Cody

Shoot to Kill
US 1988 110m colour
Touchstone/Silver Screen Partners III (Ron Silverman, Daniel Petrie Jnr)
UK title: *Deadly Pursuit*
An FBI agent and a guide track down a killer who is hiding in the mountains.
Moderately suspenseful, though unmemorable, thriller.
w Harv Zimmell, Michael Burton, Daniel Petrie Jnr *d* Roger Spottiswoode *ph* Michael Chapman *m* John Scott *pd* Richard Sylbert *ed* Garth Craven, George Bowers
☆ Sidney Poitier, Tom Berenger, Kirstie Alley, Clancy Brown, Frederick Coffin, Richard Masur, Andrew Robinson, Kevin Scannell

The Shooter
US 1994 104m Technicolor
Polygram/Adelson/Muraglia Sladek/Newmarket/Baumgarten (Paul Pompian, Silvio Muraglia)
A US marshal goes to Prague to arrest the hit-woman who killed the Cuban ambassador in New York and falls for her instead.
Risible action film with a narrative that follows familiar patterns of paranoia and conspiracy.
w Yves Andre Martin, Meg Thayer, Billy Ray *d* Ted Kotcheff *ph* Fernando Arguelles *m* Stefano Mainetti *pd* Brian Eatwell *ed* Ralph Brunjes
☆ Dolph Lundgren, Maruschka Detmers, Assumpta Serna, Gavan O'Herlihy, John Ashton, Simon Andreu
'A fairly perfunctory post-cold-war exercise with not too much thought expended on plot logic.' – *Sunday Times*

Shooters
GB/Netherlands/US 2000 95m colour
Universal/PFG/Coolbeans/Catapult (Margery Bone)
Let out of prison, a convicted killer is persuaded by his former partner to commit one more crime.
Derivative gangster movie, in which the cast posture in a macho manner and drool over guns.
w Gary Young, Andrew Howard, Louis Dempsey *d* Colin Teague, Glenn Durfort *ph* Tom Erisman *m* Kemal Ultanur *pd* Robin Tarsnane *ed* Kevin Whelan
☆ Adrian Dunbar (Max Bell), Andrew Howard (J), Louis Dempsey (Gilly), Gerard Butler (Jackie Junior), Matthew Rhys (Eddie), Emma Fielding (DI Sarah Pryce), Jason Hughes (Charlie Franklin), Ioan Gruffydd (Freddy Guns)
'Despite an ostentatiously wised-up, ironic voiceover, this film looks like a 14-year-old's saucer-eyed fantasy of how grown-up tough guys behave.' – *Peter Bradshaw, Guardian*

The Shooting
US 1966 82m DeLuxe
Santa Clara (Jack Nicholson, Monte Hellman)
An ex-bounty hunter is trailed by a hired killer.
Simplistic semi-professional Western which achieves some power despite poor technical quality and a deliberately obscure ending.
w Adrien Joyce *d* Monte Hellman *ph* Gregory Sandor *m* Richard Markowitz
☆ Warren Oates, Will Hutchins, Jack Nicholson, Millie Perkins

Shooting Fish *
GB 1997 109m Technicolor Super 35
Entertainment/Fox/Winchester/Gruber Brothers/Arts Council/Tomboy (Richard Holmes, Glynis Murray)
Two young con men who set out to cheat their way to owning a stately home find love instead.
An engagingly acted, hectic farce that loses its way and becomes increasingly desperate in its search for laughs.
w Stefan Schwartz, Richard Holmes *d* Stefan Schwartz *ph* Henry Braham *m* Stanislas Syrewicz *pd* Max Gottlieb *ed* Alan Strachan
☆ Dan Futterman, Stuart Townsend, Kate Beckinsale, Nickolas Grace, Peter Capaldi, Annette Crosbie, Jane Lapotaire, Phyllis Logan, Claire Cox
'An unashamed crowd-pleaser weakened by a third act that suffers from plot overload.' – *Derek Elley, Variety*

The Shooting Party *
GB 1984 96m Technicolor
Edenflow/Geoff Reeve (Peter Dolman)
In 1913 Sir Randolph Nettleby invites guests for a weekend at his country estate, but the coming war is foretold in their behaviour.
Mild little symbolic play which provides the expected minor pleasures.
w Julian Bond *novel* Isabel Colegate *d* Alan Bridges *ph* Fred Tammes *m* John Scott
☆ James Mason, Edward Fox, Dorothy Tutin, John Gielgud, Gordon Jackson, Cheryl Campbell, Robert Hardy

Shooting Stars *
GB 1928 80m (24 fps) bw silent
British Instructional (H. Bruce Woolf)
The wife of a film star puts real bullets in a prop gun but her lover is killed by mistake.
Late silent drama with comedy touches: its main interest lies in its behind-the-scenes background and in the emergence of a new director.
w John Orton, Anthony Asquith *d* Anthony Asquith, A. V. Bramble *ph* Karl Fisher
☆ Annette Benson, Brian Aherne, Donald Calthrop, Wally Patch, Chili Bouchier

The Shootist ***
US 1976 100m Technicolor Panavision
Paramount/Frankovich-Self

In 1901, a dying ex-gunfighter arrives in a small town to set his affairs in order.
Impressive semi-Western melodrama, very well written and acted all round; the kind of solidly entertaining and thoughtful movie one imagined they didn't make any more.
w Miles Hood Swarthout, Scott Hale *novel* Glendon Swarthout *d* Don Siegel *ph* Bruce Surtees *m* Elmer Bernstein
☆ John Wayne, Lauren Bacall, James Stewart, Ron Howard, Bill McKinney, Richard Boone, John Carradine, Scatman Crothers, Harry Morgan, Hugh O'Brian, Sheree North
'Just when it seemed that the western was an endangered species, due for extinction because it had repeated itself too many times, Wayne and Siegel have managed to validate it once more.' – *Arthur Knight*
'Watching this film is like taking a tour of Hollywood legends.' – *Frank Rich*

'Three fast guns against one determined man!'
Shootout
US 1971 94m Technicolor
Universal (Hal B. Wallis)
After seven years in prison, a bank robber seeks out his betrayer.
Routine, flatly-handled revenge Western.
w Marguerite Roberts *novel* The Lone Cowboy by Will James *d* Henry Hathaway *ph* Earl Rath *m* Dave Grusin
☆ Gregory Peck, Pat Quinn, Robert F. Lyons, Susan Tyrrell, Jeff Corey, James Gregory, Rita Gam

Shootout at Medicine Bend
US 1957 87m bw
Warner
Three ex-soldiers clean up a corrupt community.
Entertaining Western programmer.
w John Tucker Battle, D. D. Beauchamp *d* Richard Bare *ph* Carl Guthrie *m* Roy Webb *ed* Clarence Kolster
☆ Randolph Scott, James Craig, Angie Dickinson, James Garner, Gordon Jones

The Shop around the Corner **
US 1940 97m bw
MGM (Ernst Lubitsch)

In a Budapest shop, the new floorwalker and a girl who dislikes him find they are pen pals.
Pleasant period romantic comedy which holds no surprises but is presented with great style.
w Samson Raphaelson *play* Parfumerie by Miklos Laszlo *d* Ernst Lubitsch *ph* William Daniels *m* Werner Heymann
☆ James Stewart, Margaret Sullavan, Frank Morgan, Joseph Schildkraut, Sara Haden, Felix Bressart, William Tracy
'It's not pretentious but it's a beautiful job of picture-making, and the people who did it seem to have enjoyed doing it just as much as their audiences will enjoy seeing it.' – *James Shelley Hamilton*
'An agreeably bittersweet example of light entertainment.' – *Charles Higham, 1972*
'One of the most beautifully acted and paced romantic comedies ever made in this country.' – *New Yorker, 1978*
† Remade as *In the Good Old Summertime* (qv).

The Shop at Sly Corner
GB 1946 92m bw
Pennant (George King)
US title: *Code of Scotland Yard*
An antique dealer who is also a fence kills a blackmailer in order to shield his daughter.
Competent but stagey version of a West End success, giving full rein to a bravura star performance.
w Katherine Strueby *play* Edward Percy *d* George King *ph* Hone Glendinning *m* George Melachrino *ad* Bernard Robinson *ed* Manuel Del Campo
☆ Oscar Homolka (Descius Heiss), Muriel Pavlow (Margaret Heiss), Derek Farr (Robert Graham), Manning Whiley (Corder Morris), Kenneth Griffith (Archie Fellowes), Kathleen Harrison (Mrs Catt), Garry Marsh (Major Elliot), Irene Handl (Ruby Towser), Johnnie Schofield (Inspector Robinson), Diana Dors

The Shop on Main Street *
Czechoslovakia 1965 128m bw
Ceskoslovensky Film

original title: *Obchod na Korze*
aka: *The Shop on the High Street*
During the German invasion of Czechoslovakia, a well-meaning carpenter tries to shield an old Jewish lady, but his own rough treatment kills her.
A rather obvious sentimental fable, developed at too great length, but with bravura acting.
w Ladislav Grosman, Jan Kadar, Elmar Klos *d* Jan Kadar, Elmar Klos *ph* Vladimir Novotny *m* Zdenek Liska
☆ Ida Kaminska, Jozef Kroner, Hana Slivkova, Martin Holly
'Overlong, derivative, ploddingly directed.' – *John Simon*
best foreign film
Ida Kaminska

The Shop on the High Street: see *The Shop on Main Street*

'No one leaves without paying...'
Shopping
GB 1994 107m colour
Rank/Channel 4/Polygram/Kazui/WMG/Impact (Jeremy Bolt)

As soon as he leaves prison, a young thief reverts to his old ways of stealing cars, ram-raiding (smash-and-grab raids on stores using a car as a battering-ram) and taunting the police.
An unconvincing drama of urban disaffection, set in the near future and concentrating on action without much attempt at even rudimentary character portrayal; it presents no more than a collection of attitudes posing as rootless teenagers, though it does have energy.
wd Paul Anderson *ph* Tony Imi *m* Barrington Pheloung *pd* Max Gottlieb *ed* David Stiven
☆ Sadie Frost, Jude Law, Sean Pertwee, Fraser James, Sean Bean, Marianne Faithfull, Jonathan Pryce
'Though the subject is torn from the headlines, this is hardly social realism ... As an all-action carquake, this is flawed by budgetary stinginess. There is also a problem with the cast: Law and Frost look less like homeless desperadoes than slumming models.' – *Kim Newman, Empire*
'So obsessed with its own hipness that it ends up being totally embarrassing.' – *Sight and Sound*

Shopworn Angel *
US 1928 90m approx bw part-talkie
Paramount (Louis D. Lighton)
A showgirl meets a naïve young soldier off to war and forsakes her man about town.
Hard-boiled, soft-centred romantic drama remade as below and later as That Kind of Woman *(qv).*
w Howard Estabrook, Albert Shelby Le Vino *play* Private Pettigrew's Girl by Dana Burnet *d* Richard Wallace *ph* Charles Lang
☆ Nancy Carroll, Gary Cooper, Paul Lukas, Emmett King

Shopworn Angel *
US 1938 85m bw
MGM (Joseph L. Mankiewicz)
Smooth, close remake of the above.
w Waldo Salt *d* H. C. Potter *ph* Joseph Ruttenberg *m* Edward Ward *montage* Slavko Vorkapich
☆ Margaret Sullavan (Daisy Heath), James Stewart (Bill Pettigrew), Walter Pidgeon (Sam Bailey), Hattie McDaniel (Martha), Sam Levene, Nat Pendleton (Dice), Charley Grapewin (Wilson), Charles D. Brown (Mr Gonigle)

Short Circuit *
US 1986 98m Metrocolor Panavision
Rank/PSO (David Foster, Lawrence Turman)

An electric shock transforms a military robot into a creature with a mind of its own.
Amusing, if predictable comedy that owes much to E.T.
w S. S. Wilson, Brent Maddock *d* John Badham *ph* Nick McLean *m* David Shire *ad* Dianne Wager *ed* Frank Morriss
☆ Ally Sheedy, Steve Guttenberg, Fisher Stevens, Austin Pendleton, G. W. Bailey, Brian McNamara, Tim Blaney

Short Circuit 2
US 1988 110m Technicolor
Columbia TriStar (David Foster, Lawrence Turman, Gary Foster)

At large in the big city, a robot with human sensibilities is fooled into helping jewel thieves.
Ineffectual sequel, lacking in laughs and bungling the action.
w S. S. Wilson, Brent Maddock *d* Kenneth Johnson *ph* John McPherson *m* Charles Fox *pd* Bill Brodie *ed* Conrad Buff
☆ Fisher Stevens, Michael McKean, Cynthia Gibb, Jack Weston, Dee McCafferty, David Hemblen, Tim Blaney

Short Cut to Hell
US 1957 89m bw Vistavision
Paramount (A. C. Lyles)
A racketeer hires a gunman to commit a double murder, then double-crosses him.
Rough and ready remake of This Gun for Hire *(qv), less arresting than the original.*
w Ted Berkeman, Raphael Blau, W. R. Burnett *novel* A Gun for Sale by Graham Greene *d* James Cagney *ph* Haskell Boggs *md* Irvin Talbot
☆ Robert Ivers, Georgeann Johnson, William Bishop, Murvyn Vye
† Screenwriter Albert Maltz name was removed from the credits because he was blacklisted at the time.

Short Cuts ***
US 1993 188m colour Panavision
Artificial Eye/Spelling/Fine Line/Avenue (Cary Brokaw)

In Los Angeles, the lives of nine dysfunctional, suburban couples interwine.
An excellent, continually fascinating examination of people living on the edge, cut off from the truth of their emotions. The complexity of the cross-cutting between one scene and another is brilliantly achieved; what mars the film is its tendency to melodrama, particularly in its treatment of an alcoholic jazz singer and her equally disturbed cello-playing daughter.
w Robert Altman, Frank Barhydt *story* Raymond Carver *d* Robert Altman *ph* Walt Lloyd *m* Mark Isham *pd* Stephen Altman *ed* Geraldine Peroni
☆ Andie MacDowell, Bruce Davison, Jack Lemmon, Zane Cassidy, Julianne Moore, Matthew Modine, Anne Archer, Fred Ward, Jennifer Jason Leigh, Chris Penn, Joseph C. Hopkins, Josette Macario, Robert Downey Jnr, Madeleine Stowe, Tim Robbins and also Lily Tomlin, Tom Waits, Frances McDormand, Peter Gallagher, Annie Ross, Lori Singer, Lyle Lovett, Buck Henry
'Altman has used Carver's stories as a vehicle for presenting a vast panorama of life problems that are humorous, grim and absurd in equal measure. Viewer interest in the goings-on is generated not by artificial melodrama or hyped-up filmmaking technique, but by the recognition factor of the human foibles on display.' – *Todd McCarthy, Variety*
'A victory both as a summation of Altman's unflattering, but not unloving, view of American society, and an epic piece of cinema of innate daring and imagination.' – *Derek Malcolm, Guardian*
'A film with no dud line, flawed performance or slick piece of editing in all its 188 minutes ... Only at a second viewing can one fully appreciate the magnificence of the film's grand design, which is the presentation of life as a mutually shared tragi-comedy.' – *Philip French, Observer*
Robert Altman (as director)

Short Encounters *
USSR 1967 95m bw
Odessa Feature Film Studio
original title: *Korotkie Vstrechi*
Two women, one a bureaucrat, the other a young country girl, recall their love for the same man, a footloose geologist.
An innocuous love story, it was banned for 20 years by the Soviet authorities because of the attitudes it displays towards sex and social misdemeanours.
w Kira Muratova, Leonid Zhukhovitsky *d* Kira Muratova *ph* G. Kariuk *m* Oleg Karavaichuk
☆ Nina Ruslanova, Vladimir Vysotsky, Kira Muratova

A Short Film about Killing ****
Poland 1988 84m colour
Gala/Film Unit 'Tor'/Zespoly Filmowe (Ryszard Chutkowski)

original title: *Krótki Film O Zabijaniu*
A disenchanted youth who commits a bungled and motiveless murder is defended by an idealistic lawyer opposed to capital punishment.
Powerful and unremittingly bleak, but unforgettable in its condemnation of killing, whether criminal or judicial. It is one of the Decalogues, a series of films on the ten commandments made for television.
w Krzysztof Piesiewicz, Krzysztof Kieslowski *d* Krzysztof Kieslowski *ph* Slawomir Idziak *m* Zbigniew Preisner *ad* Halina Dobrowolska *ed* Ewa Small
☆ Miroslaw Baka, Krzysztof Globisz, Jan Tesarz, Zbigniew Zapasiewicz

A Short Film about Love **
Poland 1988 87m colour
Gala/Polish Film Producers' Corporation (Ryszard Chutkowski)

original title: *Krótki Film O Milosci*
A teenager spies on the sexual activities of a woman who lives opposite his flat.
Grim but gripping film on the impossibility of love.
w Krzysztof Piesiewicz, Krzysztof Kieslowski *d* Krzysztof Kieslowski *ph* Witold Adamek *m* Zbigniew Preisner *pd* Halina Dobrowolska *ed* Ewa Smal
☆ Grazyna Szapolowska, Olaf Lubaszenko, Stefania Iwinska, Piotr Machalica, Artur Barcis

Short Fuse: see *Good to Go*

'Getting killed isn't as easy as it looks'
Short Time
US 1987 102m colour
Rank/Gladden Entertainment/Touchstone (Todd Black)

Discovering he has a fatal disease and wanting to die on active service so his family can collect on his insurance policy, an ageing cop volunteers for dangerous assignments.
A comedy suffering from a terminal lack of laughs.
w John Blumenthal, Michael Berry *d* Gregg Champion *ph* John Connor *m* Ira Newborn *pd* Michael Bolton *ed* Frank Morriss
☆ Dabney Coleman, Matt Frewer, Teri Garr, Barry Corbin, Joe Pantoliano, Xander Berkeley, Rob Roy

Shot in the Dark
GB 1933 53m bw
Real Art (Julius Hagen)
A golfing rector solves the murder of an eccentric who was hated by his relatives.
A country-house melodrama of a very old-fashioned kind, moderately enjoyable as an example of English acting styles of the time.
w George Pearson, Terence Egan *novel* Gerard Fairlie *d* George Pearson *ph* Ernest Palmer *ad* James A. Carter *ed* Lister Laurance
☆ Jack Hawkins, Michael Shepley, Dorothy Boyd, O. B. Clarence, Davy Burnaby, Russell Thorndike, Margaret Yarde, A. Bromley Davenport

A Shot in the Dark *
US 1964 101m DeLuxe Panavision
UA/Mirisch/Geoffrey (Blake Edwards)

A woman is accused of shooting her lover; accident-prone Inspector Clouseau investigates.
Further adventures of the oafish, Tatiesque clodhopper from The Pink Panther*; mildly funny for those in the mood for pratfalls.*
w Blake Edwards, William Peter Blatty *d* Blake Edwards *ph* Christopher Challis *m* Henry Mancini *pd* Michael Stringer
☆ Peter Sellers, Elke Sommer, George Sanders, Herbert Lom, Tracy Reed, Graham Stark

Shotgun
US 1954 81m Technicolor
Allied Artists

A deputy marshal avenges the death of his boss.
Rather violent Western with a few unusual angles.
w Clark E. Reynolds, Rory Calhoun *d* Lesley Selander *ph* Ellsworth J. Fredricks *m* Carl Brandt

☆ Sterling Hayden, Zachary Scott, Yvonne de Carlo, Guy Prescott, Robert Wilke

Should Ladies Behave?
US 1933 90m bw
MGM
A young girl falls for her aunt's lover.
Brittle comedy of manners which transferred poorly from Broadway with a star well over the top.
w Sam and Bella Spewack *play* The Vinegar Tree by Paul Osborn *d* Harry Beaumont
☆ Alice Brady, Lionel Barrymore, Conway Tearle, Katherine Alexander, Halliwell Hobbes, Mary Carlisle

Should Married Men Go Home?
US 1928 20m bw silent
Hal Roach
Tribulations on the golf course end in a mud-slinging contest.
Goodish star slapstick, but the preliminary domestic scene is the funniest.
w Leo McCarey, James Parrott, H. M. Walker *d* James Parrott *ph* George Stevens *ed* Richard Currier
☆ Stan Laurel, Oliver Hardy, Edgar Kennedy, Kay Deslys

Shoulder Arms *
US 1918 24m (24 fps) bw silent
Charles Chaplin/First National
A soldier in the trenches dreams of winning the war single-handedly.
A comedy which meant a great deal at the time of its release but now provides precious little to laugh at.
wd Charles Chaplin *ph* Rollie Totheroh
☆ Charles Chaplin, Edna Purviance, Sydney Chaplin, Henry Bergman, Albert Austin

The Shout *
GB 1978 87m colour
Rank/Recorded Picture (Jeremy Thomas)
A man who may be mad claims that, like the old Aborigine magicians, he can kill by shouting.
Curiously gripping but ultimately pointless fable, very well done to little purpose.
w Michael Austin, Jerzy Skolimowsky *story* Robert Graves *d* Jerzy Skolimowsky *ph* Mike Molloy *m* Rupert Hine, Anthony Banks, Michael Rutherford
☆ Alan Bates, Susannah York, John Hurt, Robert Stephens, Tim Curry
'Poorly acted, incoherent and unendurably loud.' – *Pauline Kael, New Yorker*

Shout
US 1991 89m DeLuxe
Universal (Robert Simonds)
In the early 50s, a rebellious teenager, sent to a strict Texan boys' home, falls for the tough warden's daughter and learns to love rock 'n' roll, as taught by the new music teacher.
Ludicrous teen melodrama that even its target audience is likely to find condescending and immature.
w Joe Gayton *d* Jeffrey Hornaday *ph* Robert Brinkmann *m* Randy Edelman *pd* William F. Matthews *ed* Seth Flaum
☆ James Walters, John Travolta, Heather Graham, Richard Jordan, Linda Fiorentino, Scott Coffey, Glenn Quinn, Gwyneth Paltrow

Shout at the Devil *
GB 1976 147m Technicolor Panavision
Tonav (Michael Klinger)
In 1913 Zanzibar, a hard-drinking American and an old Etonian Englishman join forces to rout a brutal German commissioner who resents their poaching ivory in his territory.
The main characters are respectively repellent, effete, and just plain nasty, but the action scenes are vivid and the production is mainly notable as an expensive old-fashioned British film made at a time when there were few British films of any kind.
w Wilbur Smith, Stanley Price, Alastair Reid *novel* Wilbur Smith *d* Peter Hunt *ph* Mike Reed *m* Maurice Jarre
☆ Lee Marvin, Roger Moore, Barbara Parkins, René Kolldehoff, Ian Holm, Karl Michael Vogler, Maurice Denham, Jean Kent, Robert Lang, Murray Melvin, George Coulouris

'Elephantine plod through the action highlights of a best seller.' – *Sight and Sound*

Show Business ***
US 1944 92m bw
RKO (Eddie Cantor)
The careers of four friends in vaudeville.
Lively low-budget period musical which probably presents the best picture of what old-time vaudeville was really like; a lot of fun when the plot doesn't get in the way.
w Joseph Quillan, Dorothy Bennett *d* *Edwin L. Marin* *ph* Robert de Grasse, Vernon L. Walker *m* George Duning *md* Constantin Bakaleinikoff *ch* *Nick Castle*
☆ *Eddie Cantor, Joan Davis, George Murphy, Constance Moore*, Don Douglas, Nancy Kelly
'Bits of archaic vaudeville which give off a moderately pleasant smell of peanuts and cigar smoke.' – *James Agee*

Show Girl in Hollywood
US 1930 77m bw (colour sequence)
First National
Adventures of a New York girl on the west coast.
Comedy with music; it seems content to wallow in supposed Hollywood glamour without contributing much by way of wit or storyline.
w Harvey Thew, James A. Starr, J. P. McEvoy *d* Mervyn Le Roy
☆ Alice White, Jack Mulhall, Blanche Sweet, Ford Sterling, John Miljan, Herman Bing

The Show Goes On
GB 1937 93m bw
ATP (Basil Dean)
A mill girl becomes a star singer with the help of a dying composer.
An attempt to turn Gracie Fields into a serious performer, this was not much enjoyed by her fans.
w Austin Melford, Anthony Kimmins, E. G. Valentine *d* Basil Dean *ph* Jan Stallich
☆ Gracie Fields, Owen Nares, Edward Rigby, John Stuart, Horace Hodges, Amy Veness, Cyril Ritchard

Show Me Love: see *Fucking Amal*

A Show of Force
US 1990 93m Technicolor
Paramount/Golden Harvest (John Strong)
In 1978, a TV reporter investigates the death of two left-wingers campaigning for an independent Puerto Rico who were apparently murdered with the connivance of the FBI.
Unconvincing mix of exposé and thriller, for all its supposed basis in fact; its gloss, glibness and reliance on formula film-making render it highly suspect.
w Evan Jones, John Strong *book* Murder Under Two Flags by Anne Nelson *d* Bruno Barreto *ph* James Glennon *m* Georges Delerue *pd* William J. Cassidy *ed* Henry Richardson, Sonya Polansky
☆ Amy Irving, Andy Garcia, Lou Diamond Phillips, Robert Duvall, Kevin Spacey, Erik Estrada, Juan Fernandez

'In Vitaphone, it eclipses the sun in splendour!'
Show of Shows **
US 1929 128m Technicolor
Warner (Darryl F. Zanuck)
A big musical show put on by Warner contract artists.
Primitive early talkie, of vital historical interest but mostly photographed from a seat in the stalls.
d John G. Adolfi *ph* Barney McGill *m/ly* various *ch* Jack Haskell, Larry Ceballos
☆ Frank Fay, H. B. Warner, Monte Blue, Lupino Lane, Ben Turpin, Chester Morris, Ted Lewis and his band, Georges Carpentier, Patsy Ruth Miller, Beatrice Lillie, Winnie Lightner, Irene Bordoni, Myrna Loy, Douglas Fairbanks Jnr, John Barrymore and also Betty Compson
'Colour photography of the crudest, most garish kind, the resulting impression being that a child of seven has been let loose with a shilling box of paints.' – *James Agate*

Show People
US 1928 80m (24 fps) bw silent
MGM
A naïve young actress makes it in Hollywood.
Historically important comedy with cameo appearances by many stars of the time.
w Wanda Tuchock, Agnes Christine Johnston, Laurence Stallings *d* *King Vidor*
☆ Marion Davies, William Haines

Show Them No Mercy *
US 1935 76m bw
TCF (Raymond Griffith)
GB title: *Tainted Money*
Kidnappers are rounded up by G-men.
Lively crime thriller typical of its time.
w Kubec Glasmon, Henry Lehrman *d* George Marshall *ph* Bert Glennon *m* David Buttolph
☆ Rochelle Hudson, Cesar Romero, Bruce Cabot, Edward Norris, Edward Brophy, Warren Hymer
'Direct, surely dramatic, inevitable and full of terror.' – *Otis Ferguson*

The Show-Off
US 1934 80m bw
MGM
A girl's blundering new husband alienates his in-laws and nearly wrecks his brother-in-law's career.
Surefire satirical comedy-drama from a Broadway staple, this low-budget item gave MGM a new star.
w Herman Mankiewicz *play* George Kelly *d* Charles Riesner
☆ *Spencer Tracy*, Madge Evans, Clara Blandick, Henry Wadsworth, Grant Mitchell, Lois Wilson
† The play had been filmed twice in silent days by Paramount, and turned up again in 1946 as a Red Skelton vehicle.

Showboat ***
US 1936 110m bw
Universal (Carl Laemmle Jnr)
Lives and loves of the personnel on an old-time Mississippi showboat.
Great style and excellent performances mark this version, which still suffers from longueurs in the middle followed by the rapid passage of many years to provide a happy ending.
w Oscar Hammerstein II *book* Oscar Hammerstein II for the Broadway musical *novel* *Edna Ferber* *d* *James Whale* *ph* *John Mescall* *m/ly* *Jerome Kern, Oscar Hammerstein II* *md* Victor Baravalle *ch* LeRoy Prinz *ad* Charles D. Hall *ed* Ted J. Kent, Bernard W. Burton
☆ *Irene Dunne, Allan Jones, Helen Morgan, Paul Robeson, Charles Winninger, Hattie McDaniel*, Donald Cook, Sammy White
'For three quarters of its length good entertainment: sentimental, literary, but oddly appealing.' – *Graham Greene*
† A primitive version of *Showboat* was made in 1929, which was part-talkie with synchronised sound for the silent sequences. Once thought lost, it survives in a version that lacks some of its sound. Directed by Harry Pollard, it starred Laura La Plante and Joseph Schildkraut.
†† Before Allan Jones was cast, Walter Pidgeon, Robert Taylor, John Boles, Fredric March and Nelson Eddy were all considered.

Showboat **
US 1951 108m Technicolor
MGM (Arthur Freed)
Vigorous remake with good ensemble dancing; otherwise inferior to the 1936 version.
w John Lee Mahin, George Wells, Jack McGowan *d* George Sidney *ph* Charles Rosher *md* Conrad Salinger, Adolph Deutsch *ch* *Robert Alton*
☆ Kathryn Grayson, *Howard Keel*, Ava Gardner, William Warfield, *Joe E. Brown*, Robert Sterling, Marge Champion, Gower Champion, Agnes Moorehead
† Ava Gardner's singing was dubbed by Annette Warren.
Charles Rosher; Conrad Salinger, Adolph Deutsch

The Showdown
US 1950 86m bw
Republic
A trail boss seeks revenge on his brother's killer.
Routine Western with a touch of mystery.
w Richard Wormser and Dan Gordon *d* Darrell and Stuart McGowan *ph* Reggie Lanning *m* Stanley Wilson
☆ Wild Bill Elliott, Marie Windsor, Walter Brennan, Henry Morgan, William Ching, Rhys Williams

Showdown
US 1963 79m Technicolor
Universal
Two wandering cowboys become involved with a criminal.
Below-par Western with little action and rather boring characters.
w Bronson Howitzer *d* R. G. Springsteen *ph* Ellis Carter *m* Hans J. Salter
☆ Audie Murphy, Charles Drake, Harold J. Stone, Kathleen Crowley, Skip Homeier, L. Q. Jones, Strother Martin

Showdown
US 1972 99m Technicolor Todd-AO 35
Universal (George Seaton)
A sheriff finds that his old friend is leader of an outlaw gang.
Routine star Western adequately done.
w Theodore Taylor *d* George Seaton *ph* Ernest Laszlo *m* David Shire
☆ Rock Hudson, Dean Martin, Susan Clark, Donald Moffat, John McLiam

Showdown at Abilene
US 1956 80m Technicolor
Universal-International
A shellshocked Civil War veteran, returning home to find his girl married, reluctantly takes a job as sheriff.
Fairly lively Western remade eleven years later as Gunfight in Abilene.
w Berne Giler *novel* Gun Shy by Clarence Upson Young *d* Charles Haas
☆ Jock Mahoney, David Janssen, Martha Hyer, Lyle Bettger, Grant Williams

'One's a warrior. One's a wise ass. They're two L.A. cops going after a gang of drug lords. Feet first.'
Showdown in Little Tokyo
US 1991 77m Technicolor
Warner (Mark L. Lester, Martin E. Caan)
A cop takes revenge on the Japanese gangster who killed his parents.
Cheap, but not particularly cheerful, action nonsense, in which no one seems to have minded that the script was banal, perhaps because the money appears to have been spent on sound effects of bodies being hit and bones breaking.
w Stephen Glantz, Caliope Brattlestreet *d* Mark L. Lester *ph* Mark Irwin *m* David Michael Frank *pd* Craig Stearns *ed* Steven Kemper, Robert A. Ferretti
☆ Dolph Lundgren, Brandon Lee, Cary-Hiroyuki Tagawa, Tia Carrere, Toshiro Obata, Philip Tan
'By-the-numbers revenge stuff, although screenplay skips a lot of numbers, the better to focus on nonstop and generally unimaginative action sequences.' – *Variety*

Shower: see *Xizao*

Showgirl in Hollywood
US 1930 80m bw and Technicolor
Warner
A girl singer is spotted and trained for movie stardom.
Naïve look behind the studio scenes, historically fascinating but dramatically dull.
w Harvey Thew, James A. Starr *novel* Hollywood Girl by J. P. McEvoy *d* Mervyn LeRoy
☆ Alice White, Jack Mulhall, Blanche Sweet, Ford Sterling, John Miljan, Herman Bing

'Leave Your Inhibitions At The Door.'
Showgirls
US 1995 131m Technicolor Clairmont
Guild/United Artists/Chargeurs/Carolco (Alan Marshall, Charles Evans)
A Las Vegas stripper has ambitions to be slightly more than a lap dancer.
A prurient and voyeuristic display which its director apparently saw as an updated version of the Hollywood musical; but the routines on display are invariably tawdry, all the characters are dim, exploited and

exploitative, the script is composed of the stalest clichés, and the acting is barely competent.
w Joe Eszterhas *d* Paul Verhoeven *ph* Jost Vacano *m* David A. Stewart *pd* Allan Cameron *ed* Mark Goldblatt, Mark Helfrich
☆ Elizabeth Berkley, Kyle MacLachlan, Gina Gershon, Glenn Plummer, Robert Davi, Alan Rachins, Gina Ravera

'A very shallow and ultimately rather silly film.' – *Derek Malcolm, Guardian*

'Beyond teasing, titillation and an abundant display of female flesh in various stages of undress, there is very little reason for *Showgirls* to exist. The plot is wobbly, the acting one short step ahead of amateurish and what passes for dialogue is a mere collection of turgid lines.' – *Anna Maria Bahiana, Screen International*

'Akin to being keelhauled through a cesspool, with sharks swimming alongside.' – *Todd McCarthy, Variety*

† Only one of the 14 leading British critics, and two out of 34 critics in Chicago, New York and Los Angeles, liked the film. It received an NC-17 certificate in the US, an 18 certificate in Britain with 15 seconds cut, a 12 certificate in France, and was banned in Ireland. Paul Verhoeven recut the film for its US video release.
†† The film flopped at the US box-office, taking around $20m.

Showtime: see *Gaiety George*

'Lights. Camera. Aggravation.'
Showtime
US 2002 95m Technicolor 'Scope
Warner/Village Roadshow/NPV/Material (Jorge Saralegui, Jane Rosenthal)

Two mismatched cops – a conscientious detective and his partner, a frustrated actor – are forced to star in a reality TV show.
Tired comedy that promises to be a satire of TV's manipulative take on real life, but settles instead for being a poor excuse for an action movie that wastes its stars.
w Keith Sharon, Alfred Gough, Miles Millard *story* Jorge Saralegui *d* Tom Dey *ph* Thomas Kloss *m* Alan Silvestri *pd* Jeff Mann *ed* Billy Weber
☆ Robert De Niro (Mitch Preston), Eddie Murphy (Trey Sellars), Rene Russo (Chase Renzi), Pedro Damian (Vargas), Mos Def (Lazy Boy), Frankie R. Faison (Captain Winship), William Shatner (Himself)

'A lead-balloon caper… the jokes in this movie, if there ever were any, must now be on the cutting-room floor.' – *Owen Gleiberman, Entertainment Weekly*

'The greatest fairy tale never told.'
Shrek ***
US 2001 89m Technicolor
DreamWorks/PDI (Aron Warner, John H. Williams, Jeffrey Katzenberg)

When his swamp is occupied by exiled fairy-tale characters, an ugly, green ogre agrees to rescue a princess in return for being left alone, and falls in love with her.
Slick computer-generated animation adorns a clever and witty tale that manages both to be true to the conventions of fairy tales and to make fun of them, mainly at the expense of Disney's approach to traditional stories. The result has charm and is as polished as its gleaming animations.
w Ted Elliott, Terry Rossio, Joe Stillman, Roger S. H. Schulman *book* William Steig *additional dialogue* Cody Cameron, Chris Miller, Conrad Vernon *d* Andrew Adamson, Vicky Jenson *m* Harry Gregson-Williams, John Powell *pd* James Hegedus *ed* Sim Evan-Jones
☆ Mike Myers (Shrek), Eddie Murphy (Donkey), Cameron Diaz (Princess Fiona), John Lithgow (Lord Farquaad), Vincent Cassel (Monsieur Hood)

'An instant animated classic… It offers entertainment equally to viewers from 4 to 104.' – *Todd McCarthy, Variety*

animated feature film
Ted Elliott, Terry Rossio, Joe Stillman, Roger S. H. Schulman
Ted Elliott, Terry Rossio, Joe Stillman, Roger S. H. Schulman

The Shrieking: see *Hex*

The Shrike
US 1955 88m bw
U-I (Aaron Rosenberg)
A brilliant theatre man has a nervous breakdown because his wife is a vindictive harpy.
Theatrical two-hander, aridly filmed, of little interest except to show that both stars are capable of sustained emotional acting.
w Ketti Frings *play* Joseph Kramm *d* José Ferrer *ph* William Daniels *m* Frank Skinner *titles* Saul Bass
☆ José Ferrer, June Allyson, Joy Page, Jacqueline de Wit, Kendall Clark

'The film is unvaryingly paced, the result, one feels, of a respectable but far from invigorating honesty of purpose.' – *MFB*

Shrunken Heads
US 1994 86m Foto-Kem
Full Moon (Charles Band)

A Haitian witch doctor in America shrinks the heads of three teenagers killed by local thugs and turns them into avenging, flying monsters.
Bizarre comic horror that never quite achieves the atmosphere it needs to work.
w Matthew Bright *idea* Charles Band *d* Richard Elfman *ph* Stephen McNutt *m* Richard Band, Danny Elfman (title theme) *pd* Milo *ed* Charles Simmons *sp* Alchemy fx; Paul Gentry
☆ Meg Foster, Julius Harris, Aeryk Egan, Becky Herbst

'A promising idea ruined by shoddy production values and an inadequate script.' – *Sight and Sound*

Shuanglong Hui: see *Twin Dragons*

The Shuttered Room
GB 1967 110m Technicolor
Warner/Troy-Schenck (Philip Hazelton)

Returning to her childhood home on an island off the New England coast, a girl and her husband are subjected to terror and violence.
Stretched out suspenser which looks good and is carefully made but fails in its effort to combine the menace of teenage yobboes with that of the monster lurking upstairs.
w D. B. Ledrov, Nathaniel Tanchuck *story* H. P. Lovecraft, August Derleth *d* *David Greene* *ph* *Ken Hodges* *m* Basil Kirchin
☆ Gig Young, Carol Lynley, Flora Robson, Oliver Reed, William Devlin

Shy People *
US 1987 120m colour
Cannon/Menahem Golan, Yoram Globus

A glamorous journalist, who researches into her family, traces some isolated relatives to the bayous of Louisiana.
Off-beat melodrama that has a queasy fascination.
w Gérard Brach, Marjorie David, Andrei Konchalovsky *d* Andrei Konchalovsky *ph* Chris Menges *m* Tangerine Dream *pd* Stephen Marsh *ed* Alain Jakubowicz
☆ Jill Clayburgh, Barbara Hershey, Martha Plimpton, Merritt Butrick, John Philbin, Don Swayze, Pruitt Taylor Vince

Une Si Jolie Petite Plage *
France 1948 91m bw
CICC (Emile Darbon)
aka: *Such a Pretty Little Beach*
A murderer returns to the small seaside town where he spent his childhood, befriends the maid at the hotel, and after a few days kills himself.
A melancholy anecdote which works both as a character study and pictorially.
w Jacques Sigurd *d* Yves Allégret *ph* Henri Alekan *m* Maurice Thiriet
☆ *Gérard Philipe*, Jean Servais, *Madeleine Robinson*, Jane Marken, Carette

'Shows fine craftsmanship and is beautifully sensitive to place and atmosphere.' – *Gavin Lambert, MFB*

Si Può Fare … Amigo: see *The Big and the Bad*

Si Tous les Gars du Monde… *
France 1956 108m bw
Ariane/Filmsonor/Francinex (Alexandre Mnouchkine)
aka: *Race for Life*
When members of a French trawler crew fall ill in mid-Atlantic, amateur radio operators around the world arrange rescue.
Well-meaning realistic melodrama with a hands-across-the-sea message.
w Jacques Remy *d* Christian-Jaque *ph* Armand Thiraud *m* Georges Van Parys
☆ Andre Valmy, Jean Gaven, Doudou-Babet, Jean-Louis Trintignant

Si Tutte le Donne del Mondo: see *Kiss the Girls and Make Them Cry*

'In the battle between man and the universe…back the universe.'
Siam Sunset *
Australia/GB 1999 92m colour Panavision
Blue Dolphin/Showtime/Artists Services/AFFC (Al Clark)

A disaster-prone Englishman wins a tour of the Australian outback.
Fitfully amusing, occasionally violent comedy of a busload of misfits, with a little light romance thrown in.
w Max Dann, Andrew Knight *d* John Polson *ph* Brian Breheny *m* Paul Grabowsky *pd* Steven Jones-Evans *ed* Nicholas Beauman
☆ Linus Roache (Perry), Victoria Hill (Maree), Danielle Cormack (Grace), Ian Bliss (Martin), Roy Billing (Bill), Alan Brough (Stuart), Rebecca Hobbs (Jane), Terry Kenwrick (Arthur), Deidre Rubenstein (Celia), Peter Hosking (Roy), Victoria Eagger (Rowena), Robert Menzies (Eric), Eliza Lovell (Michelle), Choung Dao (Mr Nguyen)

'The briskly paced, visually lush film deserves to find appreciative audiences worldwide.' – *David Stratton, Variety*

'Descends into over-the-top silliness, before spontaneously combusting into utter crappiness.' – *Cosmo Landesman, Sunday Times*

Sib: see *The Apple (1997)*

Siberia
Netherlands/France 1998 87m colour
Metro Tartan/Siberia Experience/Stichting/Cineco (Clea de Koning)
In Amsterdam, two flatmates, who specialise in seducing female backpagers and stealing their money, fall out when one of them falls for a woman from Siberia.
Energetic movie about exploitative youth, which it in turn exploits, filmed in the style of a pop video.
w Robert Jan Westdijk, Jos Driessen *d* Robert Jan Westdijk *ph* Bert Pot *m* Junkie XL *ad* Anouk Damoiseaux *ed* Herman P. Koerts *cos* Ciska Nagel
☆ Hugo Metsers (Hugo), Roeland Fernhout (Goof), Vlatca Simac (Lara), Nicole Eggert (Kristy), Johnny Lion (Freddy), Jessica Stockmann (Beate), Nefeli Anthopoulou (Marina), Alessia Sorvillo (Angela), Francesca Rizzo (Kika), Syan Blake (Maggie), Katja Dreyer (Kate), Bente Jonker (Ute)

'It's impossible to overlook the smug sexism that underpins this unrepentant comedy.' – *David Parkinson, Empire*

Sibirski Tsiriulnik: see *The Barber of Siberia*

'It was not sex it was *good*!'
Sibling Rivalry
US 1990 88m colour
First Independent/Castle Rock/Nelson

Complications ensue after an unhappy wife, advised by her sister to have an affair, goes to bed with her sister's husband.
Broad farce of marital upset that causes an occasional smile.
w Martha Goldhirsh *d* Carl Reiner *ph* Reynaldo Villalobos *m* Jack Elliott *pd* Jeannine C. Oppewall *ed* Bud Molin
☆ Kirstie Alley, Bill Pullman, Carrie Fisher, Jami Gertz, Scott Bakula, Frances Sternhagen, John Randolph, Sam Elliott, Ed O'Neill, Paul Benedict

'In opting for romantic comedy rather than the black variety, the picture has grave problems of mood which are never resolved.' – *Philip French, Observer*

The Sicilian
US 1987 146m Technicolor
Fox/Gladden Entertainment (Michael Cimino, Joann Carelli)

The Sicilian bandit Salvatore Giuliano, who robs the rich in order to give to the poor, is betrayed by his own men.
Over-long and with a cast that lack authenticity as Sicilians, the movie rarely rises above incoherence.
w Steve Shagan *novel* Mario Puzo *d* Michael Cimino *ph* Alex Thomson *m* David Mansfield *pd* Wolf Kroeger *ed* Françoise Bonnot
☆ Christophe Lambert, Terence Stamp, Joss Ackland, John Turturro, Richard Bauer, Barbara Sukowa, Ray McAnally, Aldo Ray

The Sicilian Cross
Italy 1976 92m colour
Aetos (Manolo Bolognini, Luigi Borghese)
US title: *Street People*
original title: *Gli Esecutori*
A Mafia investigator and his racing-driver buddy set out to discover the person responsible for double-crossing a gang leader by hiding heroin in a crucifix sent from Sicily to the United States.
Conventional thriller, composed of shoot-outs and car chases, in which it is difficult to remember, or care, who is doing what to whom.
w Ernest Tidyman, Randal Kleiser, Gianfranco Bucceri, Roberto Leoni, Gian Franco Bucceri, Nicola Badalucco, Maurizio Lucidi *story* Gianfranco Bucceri, Roberto Leoni *d* Maurizio Lucidi *ph* Aiace Parolin *m* Luis Enriquez *ad* Gastone Carsetti *ed* Renzo Lucidi
☆ Roger Moore, Stacy Keach, Ivo Garrani, Fausto Tozzi, Ennio Balbo, Rosemarie Lindt, Ettore Manni

'The uneasy pairing of Moore and Stacy Keach suggests, however, that Maurizio Lucidi intended to enter his picture in the even less inspired Starsky and Hutch stakes.' – *MFB*

Sick: The Life and Death of Bob Flanagan, Supermasochist
US 1997 90m colour
Kirby Dick/Peter Norton/Art Matters

Documentary on Bob Flanagan, an artist and self-styled Supermasochist, who had the incurable disease cystic fibrosis and used suffering as the basis of his life, involved in a sado-masochistic relationship, and work.
Despite Flanagan's joy in life and his humour, this is a painful film to face, not only in his performances but in the final moments of his life, caught on video and still photographs; it remains a curiosity.
d Kirby Dick *ph* Jonathan Dayton, Kirby Dick, Sheree Rose, Geza Sinkovics *m* Blake Leyh *ed* Kirby Dick, Dody Dorn
☆ Bob Flanagan, Sheree Rose

Sid and Nancy
GB 1986 111m colour
Zenith/Initial (Eric Fellner)

An account of the self-destruction of the leader of a punk rock group and his American girlfriend.
Some have said stimulating, most have preferred revolting. Consensus, an example of the dregs to which cinema has been reduced.
w Alex Cox, Abbe Wool *d* Alex Cox *ph* Roger Deakins *m* The Pogues
☆ Gary Oldman, Chloe Webb, David Hayman

'The dialogue is extremely rough, the settings sordid, the theme of wasted lives depressing.' – *Variety*

'Relentlessly whingeing performances and a lengthy slide into drugs, degradation and death make this a solemnly off-putting moral tract.' – *Sight and Sound*

Siddharta
US 1972 94m Eastmancolor Panavision
Columbia-Warner/Lotus (Conrad Rooks)
A young Brahmin leaves his comfortable home to join a band of itinerant holy men.
Despite its visual charm, a dull, though faithful, version of the book.
wd Conrad Rooks *novel* Hermann Hesse *ph* Sven Nykvist *m* Hemanta Kuma *ad* Malcolm Golding *ed* Willy Kemplen
☆ Shashi Kapoor, Simi Garewal, Rommesh Sharma, Pincho Kapoor, Amrik Singh, Zul Vellani, Shanti Hiranand, Kunal Kapoor

Side by Side
GB 1975 84m Technicolor
GTO (Drummond Challis)
When a magistrate orders that one of a town's two rundown night-clubs will have to close in a month, the rival owners search for new acts to boost their chances of remaining open.
A ramshackle comedy mainly designed as a showcase for a succession of bland pop groups; in between the songs, the narrative includes, for no good reason, an old music-hall slapstick routine and some occasionally funny moments from Terry-Thomas as a seedy entrepreneur. Performances from groups such as Fox have also gained a measure of hilarity over the years.
w Garry Chambers, Ron Inkpen, Peter James, Bruce Beresford *d* Bruce Beresford *ph* Harvey Harrison *m* Hello, Mac and Katie Kisson, Bob Kerr's Whoopee Band, Desmond Dekker and the Israelites *ad* Terry Gough *ed* Ray Lovejoy
☆ Terry-Thomas, Barry Humphries, Stephanie de Sykes, Billy Boyle, Dave Mount, Frank Thornton, Jennifer Guy
'The exuberant vulgarity which characterised Bruce Beresford's Barry McKenzie movies is wholly absent from this abysmal comedy.' – *MFB*

Side Out
US 1990 100m colour
Tri-Star/Aurora/Then/Jay Wesson (Gary Foster)
A young would-be lawyer goes to California to work for his uncle, but prefers professional volleyball.
Trivial 'teen picture built around a game that may be fun to play, but is hell to watch.
w David Thoreau *d* Peter Israelson *ph* Ron Garcia *m* Jeff Lorber *pd* Dan Lomino *ed* Conrad Buff
☆ C. Thomas Howell, Peter Horton, Courtney Thorne-Smith, Harley Jane Kozak, Christopher Rydell, Terry Kiser
'Anodyne Californian whimsy which celebrates beach culture and the body beautiful.' – *Sight and Sound*

Side Street
US 1950 83m bw
MGM (Sam Zimbalist)
A petty thief finds himself involved with big-time crooks.
Well-made but rather boring crime melodrama with an excellent car chase finale.
w Sydney Boehm *d* Anthony Mann *ph* Joseph Ruttenberg *m* Lennie Hayton
☆ Farley Granger, Cathy O'Donnell, James Craig, Paul Kelly, Jean Hagen, Edmon Ryan, Paul Harvey

'It's the hottest day in the real New York.'
Side Streets
US 1998 131m Technicolor
First Independent/Merchant Ivory/Cornerstone (Bruce Weiss)
A day in the New York life of five immigrants, who are all struggling to make a living.
Ambitious but meandering account of the diversity of city life on one stifling day; but the characters stubbornly refuse to come to life.
w Lynn Nottage, Tony Gerber *d* Tony Gerber *ph* Russell Lee Fine *m* Evan Lurie *pd* Stephen McCabe *ed* Kate Williams
☆ Valeria Golino, Shashi Kapoor, Leon, Art Malik, Shabana Azmi, Mirjana Jokovic, Miho Nikaldo, Marc Tissot, John Ortiz
'Very, very long and dull.' – *Peter Bradshaw, Guardian*

Sidekicks
US 1993 100m colour
Gallery (Don Carmody)
An asthmatic teenager escapes his unhappiness by day-dreams of heroic acts at the side of his hero, Chuck Norris.
A movie for young audiences, who may be able to share the fantasies on offer.
w Don Thompson, Lou Illar *d* Aaron Norris *ph* João Fernandes *m* Alan Silvestri *pd* Reuben Freed *ed* David Rawlins, Bernard Weiser
☆ Chuck Norris, Beau Bridges, Jonathan Brandis, Mako, Julia Nickson-Soul, Joe Piscopo, Danica McKellar

Sidewalk Stories *
US 1989 97m bw
Palm (Charles Lane)
A homeless street artist looks after a little girl after her father is killed by muggers.
Whimsical, almost silent movie with deft musical accompaniment; its lightness of touch almost disguises its underlying anger on behalf of the dispossessed.
wd Charles Lane *ph* Bill Dill *m* Marc Marder *pd* Lyn Pinezich *ed* Anne Stein, Charles Lane
☆ Charles Lane, Nicole Alysia, Sandye Wilson, Darnell Williams, Trula Hoosier, Michael Baskin, George Riddick

Sidewalks of London: see *St Martin's Lane*

Sidewalks of New York *
US 1931 73m bw
MGM (Lawrence Weingarten)
The playboy owner of some tenement apartments falls in love with the daughter of one of the tenants.
Interesting rather than wholly successful early sound comedy which marked the beginning of Keaton's decline; he was not allowed full control and the comedy scenes are thinly spaced.
w George Landy, Paul Gerard Smith, Eric Hatch, Robert E. Hopkins *d* Jules White, Zion Myers *ph* Leonard Smith
☆ *Buster Keaton*, Anita Page, Cliff Edwards, Frank Rowan

'In a city of 8 million people, what are the odds the perfect two will meet?'
Sidewalks of New York
US 2001 108m Technicolor
Helkon SK/Marlboro Road Gang/APG/Newmarket (Margot Bridger, Edward Burns, Cathy Schulman, Rick Yorn)
A group of New Yorkers, recovering from failed love affairs, find their lives intertwining in their search for new partners.
Slight, occasionally amusing movie of self-centered seekers of satisfaction who talk a great deal but do not feel at all.
wd Edward Burns *ph* Frank Prinzi *ed* David Greenwald *cos* Catherine Thomas
☆ Edward Burns (Tommy), Rosario Dawson (Maria), Dennis Farina (Carpo), Heather Graham (Annie), David Krumholtz (Ben), Brittany Murphy (Ashley), Stanley Tucci (Griffin), Michael Leydon Campbell (Gio/Harry), Nadia Dajani (Hilary), Callie Thorne (Sue), Aida Turturro (Shari)
'Not just instantly forgettable, but beginning to fade from memory even as its images still play across the screen.' – *Scott Foundas, Variety*

Sie Tötete in Ekstase: see *She Killed in Ecstasy*

The Siege
US 1998 116m DeLuxe Super 35
TCF (Lynda Obst, Edward Zwick)
Martial law is declared after Arab terrorists begin to explode bombs in New York.
Hysterical political melodrama, which will leave most audiences outside the USA feeling decidedly queasy.
w Lawrence Wright, Menno Meyjes, Edward Zwick *d* Edward Zwick *ph* Roger Deakins *m* Graeme Revell *pd* Lilly Kilvert *ed* Steven Rosenblum
☆ Denzel Washington, Annette Bening, Bruce Willis, Tony Shalhoub, Sami Bouajila, David Proval
'The filmmakers peddle fear and then try to claim the moral high ground; the treatment is foolish, confused and borderline irresponsible.' – *David Denby, New Yorker*

The Siege at Red River
US 1954 86m Technicolor
TCF/Panoramic (Leonard Goldstein)
During the American Civil War a Confederate agent behind northern lines defeats a treacherous helper and escapes to the South.
Modest, generally watchable, and quite forgettable Western.
w Sydney Boehm *d* Rudolph Maté *ph* Edward Cronjager *m* Lionel Newman
☆ Van Johnson, Joanne Dru, Richard Boone, Milburn Stone, Jeff Morrow, Craig Hill

The Siege of Pinchgut
GB 1959 104m bw
Ealing (Eric Williams)
US title: *Four Desperate Men*
Escaped convicts take over a small island in Sydney harbour.
Disappointingly obvious location melodrama with routine excitements.
w Harry Watt, Jon Cleary *d* Harry Watt *ph* Gordon Dines *m* Kenneth V. Jones
☆ Aldo Ray, Heather Sears, Neil McCallum, Victor Maddern, Carlo Justini

The Siege of Sidney Street *
GB 1960 92m bw Dyaliscope
Midcentury (Robert S. Baker, Monty Berman)
An account of the anarchists who infiltrated London in 1912.
Detailed but not dramatically absorbing historical reconstruction with unsatisfactory fictional trimmings.
w Jimmy Sangster, Alexander Baron *m* Stanley Black *d/ph* Robert S. Baker, Monty Berman
☆ *Peter Wyngarde*, Donald Sinden, Nicole Berger, Kieron Moore, Leonard Sachs, Tutte Lemkow

'He used the power of the universe 2,500 years ago to destroy the Roman invaders.'
The Siege of Syracuse
Italy/France 1959 115m Eastmancolor Dyaliscope
Glomer/Galatea/Lyre (Giovanni Laterza, Armando Grottini)
original title: *L'Assedio di Siracusa*
Scientist meets slave girl, scientist loses slave girl, scientist gets slave girl while saving his city from the Romans.
Colourful epic that successfully mixes action and romance; directed with verve, it is one of the better examples of its kind.
w Pietro Francisci, Giorgio Graziosi, Ennio de Concini *d* Pietro Francisci *ph* Carlo Carlini *m* Angelo Francesco Lavagnino *pd* Ottavio Scotti *ed* Nino Baragli
☆ Rossano Brazzi (Archimedes), Tina Louise (Diana), Sylva Koscina (Clio), Enrico Maria Salerno, Gino Cervi, Alberto Farnese
† The film was released in the US in 1962 in a dubbed version that runs for 96m.

The Siege of the Saxons
GB 1963 85m Technicolor
Columbia/Ameran (Jud Kinberg)
When King Arthur is ill, the Saxons plot his overthrow but are foiled by a handsome outlaw.
Comic strip adventure with action highlights borrowed from older and better films.
w John Kohn, Jud Kinberg *d* Nathan Juran *ph* Wilkie Cooper, Jack Willis *m* Laurie Johnson
☆ Ronald Lewis, Janette Scott, Ronald Howard, Mark Dignam, John Laurie, Richard Clarke, Jerome Willis

Sierra
US 1950 83m Technicolor
Universal (Michael Kraike)
A father, accused of a crime he did not commit, hides out in the hills with his son.
Dim Western, routinely directed and with little conviction in the performances.
w Edna Anhalt, Milton Gunzburg *novel The Mountains Are My Kingdom* by Stuart Hardy *d* Alfred E. Green *ph* Russell Metty *m* Walter Scharf *ad* Bernard Herzbrun, Robert Boyle *ed* Ted J. Kent
☆ Wanda Hendrix, Audie Murphy, Dean Jagger, Burl Ives, Richard Rober, Anthony (Tony) Curtis, Sara Allgood, James Arness
'Worth its weight in manure. A really lousy western.' – *Clive Hirschhorn, The Universal Story*
† It was a remake of *Forbidden Valley* (qv).

Siesta
US 1987 100m colour
Palace/Lorimar (Gary Kurfirst)
An amnesiac skydiver, visiting her former lover in Spain, is implicated in a murder.
Pretentious, deliberately obscure movie where there is little reward for working out what is happening.
w Patricia Louisianna Knop *novel* Patrice Chaplin *d* Mary Lambert *ph* Bryan Loftus *m* Miles Davis *pd* John Beard *ed* Glen Morgan
☆ Ellen Barkin, Gabriel Byrne, Julian Sands, Isabella Rossellini, Martin Sheen, Alexei Sayle, Grace Jones, Jodie Foster

Il Sigillo di Pechino: see *The Peking Medallion*

The Sign of Four
GB 1932 75m bw
ATP
Sherlock Holmes clears up a mystery including a hidden fortune, a secret pact, revenge from the east, and a pygmy who blows poison darts through a pipe.
Very acceptable version of the famous story, previously filmed as a silent.
w W. P. Lipscomb, John Paddy Carstairs *novel* Sir Arthur Conan Doyle *d* Graham Cutts *ph* Robert de Grasse, Robert G. Martin *md* Ernest Irving
☆ Arthur Wontner, Ian Hunter, Isla Bevan, Miles Malleson, Herbert Lomas, Roy Emerton

'A picture which will proudly lead all the entertainments the world has ever seen!'
'Like a shining light – the simple faith that was mightier than a pagan empire!'
The Sign of the Cross ***
US 1932 123m bw
Paramount (Cecil B. de Mille)
In the days of Nero, a Roman officer is converted to Christianity.
A heavily theatrical play becomes one of de Mille's most impressive films, the genuine horror of the arena mingling with the debauched humour of the court. A wartime prologue added in 1943 prolongs the film without improving it.
w Waldemar Young, Sidney Buchman *play* Wilson Barrett *d Cecil B. de Mille ph Karl Struss m* Rudolph Kopp
☆ Fredric March, Elissa Landi, *Charles Laughton, Claudette Colbert*, Ian Keith, Harry Beresford, Arthur Hohl, Nat Pendleton
'A beautiful film to watch ... a triumph of popular art.' – *Charles Higham, 1972*
'However contemptible one may find de Mille's moralizing, it is impossible not to be impressed by The Sign of the Cross.' – *John Baxter, 1968*
'De Mille's bang-them-on-the-head-with-wild-orgies-and-imperilled-virginity style is at its ripest.' – *New Yorker, 1976*
'Preposterous, but the laughter dies on the lips.' – *NFT, 1974*
'This slice of "history" has it all: Laughton's implicitly gay Nero fiddling away while an impressive miniature set burns, Colbert bathing up to her nipples in asses' milk, Christians and other unfortunates thrown to a fearsome menagerie, much suggestive slinking about in Mitchell Leisen's costumes, much general debauchery teetering between the sadistic and the erotic. Not for people with scruples.' – *Geoff Brown, Time Out, 1980*
Karl Struss

Sign of the Gladiator
Italy/France/West Germany 1959 84m Eastmancolor Dyaliscope
Glomer Film/Lyre-Lux/Tele Film (Rino Merolle)
original title: *Nel Segno di Roma*
Zenobia, Queen of Syria, revolts against Roman rule but falls in love with the consul sent to destroy her.
An early, dull example of Italy's 'sword and sandal' cycle, lacking the genre's saving spectacle
w F. Thellung, F. de Feo, Sergio Leone, G. Mangione, Guido Brignone *d* Guido Brignone, Riccardo Freda (battle scenes) *ph* Luciano Trasatti *m* A. Francesco Lavagnino *ad* Ottavio Scotti *ed* Nino Baragli
☆ Anita Ekberg, Georges Marchal, Folco Lulli, Jacques Sernas, Lorella de Luca, Alberto Farnese, Chelo Alonso

'Against his ruthless pagan lusts – the power of a woman's love!'
The Sign of the Pagan
US 1954 92m Technicolor Cinemascope
U-I (Albert J. Cohen)
Attila the Hun is defeated by the Romans.
Historic horse opera, rather cheaply done.
w Oscar Brodney, Barre Lyndon *d* Douglas Sirk *ph* Russell Metty *m* Frank Skinner, Hans Salter *ad* Alexander Golitzen, Emrich Nicholson *ed* Milton Carruth, Al Clark
☆ Jeff Chandler, Jack Palance, Rita Gam, Ludmilla Tcherina, Jeff Morrow, George Dolenz, Eduard Franz, Alexander Scourby

The Sign of the Ram
US 1948 84m bw
Columbia (Irving Cummings Jnr)
A selfish invalid interferes in her family's affairs.
Stultifying melodrama in the wake of Guest in the House*, devised for the unfortunate Miss Peters who was crippled after an accident. Poor production values don't help.*
w Charles Bennett *d* John Sturges *ph* Burnett Guffey *m* Hans Salter
☆ Susan Peters, Alexander Knox, Peggy Ann Garner, May Whitty

Signal 7
US 1983 92m colour
Myron/Taylor/New Front/Alliance
Two middle-aged taxi drivers, with aspirations to be actors, reminisce about their lives and hopes.
Semi-improvised slice of life, although you wouldn't necessarily want to ride in either of the protagonists' cabs.
w Signal 7 Group (Victoria Bennett, Hildy Burns, Steve Burns, Roy Kissin, Sara Morris, Rob Nilsson, David Schickele) *d* Rob Nilsson *ph* Geoff Schaaf, Tomas Tucker *m* Andy Narell *ed* Richard Harkness
☆ Bill Ackridge, Dan Leegant

Le Signe du Lion *
France 1959 90m bw
AJYM Films/Claude Chabrol (Jean Cotet)
aka: *The Sign of Leo*
An American composer living in Paris mistakenly believes he has inherited a fortune and is reduced to penury as a result.
Rohmer's first feature, a lively slice-of-life among French bohemians, but spoiled by its unlikely ending.
w Eric Rohmer, Paul Gegauff *d* Eric Rohmer *ph* Nicolas Hayer *m* Louis Saguer *ed* Anne-Marie Cotret
☆ Jess Hahn, Michèle Girardon, Van Doude, Paul Bisciglia, Gilbert Edard, Stéphane Audran, Jean Le Poulain

La Signora della Notte: see *Lady of the Night*

Signore e Signori: see *The Birds, the Bees and the Italians*

Signpost to Murder
US 1964 74m bw Panavision
MGM/Martin (Lawrence Weingarten)
A convicted murderer escapes after ten years and a lonely wife promises to help him.
Tricksy mystery set in a never-never English village.
w Sally Benson *play* Monte Doyle *d* George Englund *ph* Paul C. Vogel *m* Lyn Murray
☆ Joanne Woodward, Stuart Whitman, Edward Mulhare, Alan Napier, Murray Matheson

'Don't See It Alone'
Signs
US 2002 106m Technicolor
Buena Vista/Touchstone/Blinding Edge (M. Night Shyamalan, Frank Marshall, Sam Mercer)
A lapsed priest regains his faith after an invasion by little green men.
Vapid supernatural thriller that fails to convince on any level, even on the basic one of suspense.
wd M. Night Shyamalan *ph* Tak Fujimoto *m* James Newton Howard *pd* Larry Fulton *ed* Barbara Tulliver *sp* ILM *cos* Ann Roth
☆ Mel Gibson (Graham Hess), Joaquin Phoenix (Merrill Hess), Cherry Jones (Officer Caroline Paski), Rory Culkin (Morgan Hess), Abigail Breslin (Bo Hess), Patricia Kalember (Colleen Hess), M. Night Shyamalan (Ray Reddy)
'A wonderful sustained slice of American gothic…top-quality entertainment.' – *Cosmo Landesman, Sunday Times*
'the untidy logic of the premise, coupled with the unoriginal plot twists, laboured ending, unbelievable dialogue and predictable concluding shot made me feel cheated and terrifically let down.' – *Jonathan Ross, Daily Mirror*
'Sitting through the last reel is significantly less charming than listening to a four-year-old with a taste for exaggeration recount his Halloween trip to the Haunted House.' – *Jessica Winter, Village Voice*

Signs of Life *
West Germany 1968 90m bw
Werner Herzog
original title: *Lebenszeichen*
During the Second World War, a German soldier, sent to a small Greek island to guard a fortress while he recovers from a wound, is maddened by the peace and boredom of the place.
A coolly dispassionate account of an individual's breakdown when faced with the apparent meaningless of existence.
wd Werner Herzog *story Der tolle Invalide auf dem Fort Ratonneau* by Achim von Arnim *ph* Thomas Mauch *m* Stavros Xarchakos *ed* Beate Mainke-Jellinghaus, Maxi Mainke
☆ Peter Brogle, Wolfgang Reichmann, Julio Pinheiro, Athina Zacharopoulou, Wolfgang von Ungern-Sternberg, Wolfgang Stumpf
'A limpidly clear meditation on life shrivelling under a self-imposed oppression.' – *Richard Combs, MFB*

The Silence *
Sweden 1963 96m bw
Svensk Filmindustri
original title: *Tystnaden*
Of two women in a large hotel in a foreign city where the military are dominant, one masturbates while the other sleeps with a barman.
Bergman may know what this was all about, but it's a certainty that no one else did: so everyone thought it must be very clever and went to see it. Superficially, as usual, it is careful and fascinating.
wd Ingmar Bergman *ph* Sven Nykvist *m* from Bach
☆ Ingrid Thulin, Gunnel Lindblom
'There is not enough forward thrust, not enough momentum to unite the specific points, the complementary but discrete images. The pearls are there, but the string is too weak to hold them.' – *John Simon*

Le Silence est d'Or *
France 1947 99m bw
Pathé/RKO Radio (René Clair)
In 1906 a comedian becomes a film producer and as a result falls into an affair with a young girl.
Somehow not an important film, but quite a delightful one, especially for its local colour and for the combination of Clair and Chevalier up to their old tricks.
wd René Clair ph Armand Thirard *m* Georges Van Parys
☆ *Maurice Chevalier*, François Périer, Marcelle Derrien

The Silence of Dean Maitland
Australia 1934 97m bw
Cinesound (Ken G. Hall)
A clergyman sires an illegitimate baby, kills the girl's father and allows another man to be convicted.
Once sensational stuff which almost caused an Australian scandal.
w Gayne Dexter, Edmund Barclay *d* Ken G. Hall
☆ John Longden, Charlotte Francis, Jocelyn Howarth, Patricia Minchin

Silence of the Hams
Italy/US 1993 81m Foto-Kem
Polygram/Thirtieth Century Wolf/Berlusconi (Ezio Greggio, Julie Corman)
A woman who steals money from her boss spends the night in a motel, where she is murdered in the shower; an FBI agent and a private eye investigate.
An inept attempt by a popular Italian television comic to cash in on the market for dumb, lazy spoofs of popular movies, though this one harks back to Hitchcock's Psycho*, with Balsam sadly parodying his original role, more than to* Silence of the Lambs.
wd Ezio Greggio *ph* Jacques Haitkin *m* Parmer Fuller *pd* Jim Newport *ed* Robert Barrere, Andy Horvitch
☆ Ezio Greggio, Dom DeLuise, Billy Zane, Joanna Pacula, Charlene Tilton, Martin Balsam, Stuart Pankin, John Astin, Phyllis Diller, Bubba Smith, Shelley Winters, Henry Silva
'Even if you smirked at the title, don't waste another second of your life.' – *Sight and Sound*
† Joe Dante, John Carpenter, John Landis and Mel Brooks also appear in cameo roles, poor things.

Silence of the Lambs ***
US 1990 118m Technicolor Panavision
Rank/Orion/Strong Heart/Demme (Edward Saxon, Kenneth Utt, Ron Bozman)
A young female FBI agent seeks the aid of an imprisoned serial killer and psychiatrist, Hannibal 'The Cannibal' Lecter, to track down another mass murderer.
Tense, exciting and sometimes gruesome thriller, suspenseful enough to make you overlook its essential absurdities. Hopkins plays the role of the devious Lecter with lip-smacking relish.
w Ted Tally *novel* Thomas Harris *d Jonathan Demme ph* Tak Fujimoto *m* Howard Shore *pd* Kristi Zea *ed* Craig McKay
☆ *Jodie Foster, Anthony Hopkins*, Scott Glenn, Ted Levine, Anthony Heald, Lawrence A. Bonney, Kasi Lemmons, Lawrence J. Wrentz, Frankie Faison, Roger Corman
HANNIBAL LECTER: 'I do wish we could chat longer, but I'm having an old friend for dinner.'
HANNIBAL LECTER: 'A census taker once tried to test me. I ate his liver with some fava beans and a nice chianti.'
'A mesmerizing thriller that will grip audiences from first scene to last.' – *Variety*
'A sombre masterpiece' – *Sight and Sound*
'An exceptionally good film, perhaps this fine director's best, in which the horror genre is elevated into the kind of cinema that can at least be argued about as a treatise for its unsettling times.' – *Derek Malcolm, Guardian*
† It was followed by *Hannibal* in 2001 and *Red Dragon (qqv)* in 2002. An earlier version of *Red Dragon* was made in 1986 as *Manhunter (qv)*.
film; Jonathan Demme; Anthony Hopkins; Jodie Foster; Ted Tally
editing; sound
Anthony Hopkins; Jodie Foster

Silence of the North
Canada 1981 94m colour
Universal (Canada) (Murray Shostak)
In 1919 a city girl is courted by a trapper and joins him in the north country.
Nicely filmed but utterly predictable romantic melodrama, based on a biography but not carrying much conviction. D. W. Griffith would have liked it.
w Patricia Louisianna Knop *book* Olive Fredrickson, Ben East *d* Allan Winton King *ph* Richard Leiterman *m* Allan MacMillan
☆ Ellen Burstyn, Tom Skerritt, Gordon Pinsent, Jennifer McKinney

'Follow his secret from bedroom to bedlam, with guns, girls and dynamite!'
The Silencers *
US 1966 103m Technicolor
Columbia/Irving Allen (Jim Schmerer)
Adventures of a sexy secret agent.
*Or, James Bond sent up rotten. Plenty of fun along the way, with in-jokes and characters like Lovey Kravezit, but the plot could have done with more attention, and the sequels (*Murderers Row, The Ambushers, Wrecking Crew*) were uncontrolled disaster areas.*
w Oscar Saul *novel* Donald Hamilton *d* Phil Karlson *ph* Burnett Guffey *m* Elmer Bernstein
☆ *Dean Martin*, Stella Stevens, Victor Buono, Daliah Lavi, Cyd Charisse, Robert Webber, James Gregory, Nancy Kovack
'The dullest, dirtiest thud excreted by the sex-and-sadism spoofs of Bondism.' – *Judith Crist*

The Silences of the Palace *
France/Tunisia 1994 127m colour
ICA/Mat/Cinetelefilms/Magfilm (Ahmed Baha, Eddine Attia, Richard Magnien)
A singer returns to the Tunisian palace where she was brought up by her mother, a servant and mistress of the king, and recalls her past life.
A leisurely, careful drama of women trapped within a social system that denies them freedom over their own lives.
wd Moufida Tlatli *ph* Youssef Ben Youssef *m* Anouar Brahem *ad* Claude Bennys, Mondher Dhrif *ed* Moufida Tlatli, Camille Cotte, Kerim Hammouda
☆ Ahmel Hedhili, Hend Sabri, Najia Ouerghi, Ghalia Lecroix, Sami Bouajila, Kamel Fazaa

'Honourable, but a little torpid – better on the textures of feudal life than storytelling.' – *Kevin Jackson, Independent*
'This is, at heart, a Stella Dallas story set in the shimmering reflections of royal life before any revolution.' – *Time*

The Silent Battle
GB 1939 84m bw
Pinebrook (Anthony Havelock-Allan)
A French agent battles revolutionaries in the Balkans.
Unconvincing spy stuff with an uncertain tone.
w Wolfgang Wilhelm, Rodney Ackland *novel* Jean Bommart *d* Herbert Mason
☆ Rex Harrison, Valerie Hobson, John Loder, Muriel Aked, John Salew, George Devine

Silent Dust *
GB 1948 82m bw
ABP/Independent Sovereign (Nat Bronsten)
A baronet builds a memorial to his son who has apparently been killed in action, but the son turns up and proves to be an absolute bounder.
Effective stage melodrama, quite neatly filmed.
w Michael Pertwee *play The Paragon* by Roland and Michael Pertwee *d* Lance Comfort *ph* Wilkie Cooper *m* Georges Auric
☆ Sally Gray, Derek Farr, Stephen Murray, Nigel Patrick, Seymour Hicks

The Silent Enemy
GB 1958 112m bw
Romulus (Bertram Ostrer)
The World War II exploits of a naval frogman in the Mediterranean.
Stereotyped naval underwater adventures, adequately presented.
wd William Fairchild *book Commander Crabb* by Marshall Pugh *ph* Egil Woxholt, Otto Heller *m* William Alwyn
☆ Laurence Harvey, John Clements, Michael Craig, Dawn Addams, Sidney James, Alec McCowen, Nigel Stock

'A Savage Crime. A Silent Witness.'
Silent Fall
US 1994 101m Technicolor
Warner/Morgan Creek (James G. Robinson)
An autistic nine-year-old is the only witness to his parents' brutal murder.
Dull thriller, silly when it is not predictable and cheap in its use of autism for such a trivial end.
w Akiva Goldsman *d* Bruce Beresford *ph* Peter James *m* Stewart Copeland *pd* John Stoddart
☆ Richard Dreyfuss, Linda Hamilton, John Lithgow, J. T. Walsh, Ben Faulkner, Liv Taylor, Zahn McClarnon
'Nothing could save this film from being mediocre at best.' – *Derek Malcolm, Guardian*
'For a thriller about the life of the mind, this one is chock-full of cheap thinking.' – *Tom Shone, Sunday Times*

The Silent Flute
US 1978 95m colour
Volare (Richard St Johns)
In a martial arts tournament, a hero is chosen to challenge the wizard Zetan.
Curiously mystical adventure allegory with an unhelpful title. Not too bad for those in the mood.
w Stirling Silliphant, Stanley Mann *d* Richard Moore *ph* Ronnie Taylor *m* Bruce Smeaton
☆ Jeff Cooper, David Carradine, Roddy McDowall, Christopher Lee, Eli Wallach

Silent Movie *
US 1976 87m DeLuxe
TCF/Crossbow (Michael Hertzberg)
An alcoholic producer gets the idea that a silent movie would be a great novelty, and tries to get stars to take part.
Fairly lively spoof with the talents concerned in variable form. The shortage of laughter made it a hit in the seventies, but at no time does it approach the Keaton or Laurel and Hardy level.
w Mel Brooks, Ron Clark, Rudy de Luca, Barry Levinson *d* Mel Brooks *ph* Paul Lohmann *m* John Morris
☆ Mel Brooks, Marty Feldman, Dom DeLuise, Bernadette Peters, Sid Caesar, Harold Gould, Fritz Feld, Harry Ritz, Henny Youngman

† *guest stars* Anne Bancroft, Paul Newman, Burt Reynolds, James Caan, Liza Minnelli, Marcel Marcea.
†† Marcel Marceau utters the only word in the movie, which is '*Non*'.

Silent Night, Evil Night: see *Black Christmas*

The Silent Partner
Canada 1978 105m colour
Carolco (Garth H. Drabinsky)
A bank teller foils an attempted raid and steals the money himself.
A suspense thriller of a familiar kind; it might have been entertaining but elects instead to be unpleasant.
w Curtis Hanson *novel Think of a Number* by Anders Bodelsen *d* Daryl Duke *ph* Stephen Katz *m* Oscar Peterson
☆ Christopher Plummer, Elliott Gould, Susannah York, Celine Lomez, Michael Kirby

The Silent Passenger
GB 1935 75m bw
Phoenix
Lord Peter Wimsey clears a man of a murder charge.
Not an unappealing presentation of Dorothy Sayers's famous detective, though he is presented as too much the silly ass and the story is weak.
w Basil Mason *story* Dorothy L. Sayers *d* Reginald Denham *ph* Jan Stallich
☆ Peter Haddon, John Loder, Mary Newland, Austin Trevor, Donald Wolfit, Leslie Perrins, Robb Wilton

Silent Running *
US 1971 90m Technicolor
Universal/Michel Gruskoff
Members of a space station crew in 2001 are space gardening to replenish nuclear-devastated Earth.
Sombre futuristic fantasy, well made but slow and muddled in development.
w Deric Washburn, Michael Cimino, Steve Bochco *d* Douglas Trumbull *ph* Charles F. Wheeler *m* Peter Schickele
☆ Bruce Dern, Cliff Potts, Ron Rifkin, Jesse Vint

Silent Scream *
GB 1989 85m
BFI/Film Four International (Paddy Higson)
Jailed for the murder of a bartender, a depressive prisoner, dying from an overdose of drugs, recalls his past life.
Based on the writings and life of Larry Winters, who was transferred to a prison where he was encouraged to be creative, the film's hallucinatory style too often obscures its intentions.
w Bill Beech, Jane Beech *d* David Hayman *ph* Denis Crossan *m* Callum McNair *pd* Andy Harris *ed* Justin Krish
☆ Iain Glen, Paul Samson, Andrew Barr, Kenneth Glenaan, Steve Hotchkiss, John Murtagh, Bobby Carlyle, Tom Watson, Julie Graham
'I felt as if someone had handed me a bag of jumbled jigsaw pieces and told me to make up my own picture.' – *Philip French, Observer*

The Silent Stranger: see *Step Down to Terror*

'Justice can never be silenced.'
Silent Tongue
US 1993 101m colour
Entertainment/Belbo/Alive (Carolyn Pfeiffer, Ludi Boeken)
A horse-dealer sets out to buy as a new wife for his son the daughter of a alcoholic quack, after her twin sister dies in childbirth; the two girls were born as the result of their father's rape of a mute Indian woman.
A portentous, heavily symbolic melodrama that might have been more effective on the stage or on the page; certainly, the ripe over-acting of the cast is no help to understanding its point.
wd Sam Shepard *ph* Jack Conroy *m* Patrick O'Hearn *pd* Cary White *ed* Bill Yahraus
☆ Richard Harris, Sheila Tousey, Alan Bates, River Phoenix, Dermot Mulroney, Tantoo Cardinal, Jeri Arredondo
'The whole thing looks like one of those moody philosophical westerns they used occasionally to make before the genre ran out of both ideas and box-office appeal.' – *Derek Malcolm, Guardian*

The Silent Touch
GB/Poland/Denmark 1992 96m colour
Mayfair/Tor/Mark Forstater
A Polish music student goes to Denmark to encourage a composer who has not written a note for 40 years to complete his work.
A curious fable about creativity, which precisely lacks that quality.
w Peter Morgan, Mark Wadlow *story* Krzysztof Zanussi, Edward Zebrowski *d* Krzysztof Zanussi *ph* Jaroslaw Zamojda *m* Wojciech Kilar *pd* Ewa Braun *ed* Mark Denys
☆ Max von Sydow, Lothaire Bluteau, Sarah Miles, Sofie Grabol, Aleksander Bardini, Peter Hesse Overgaard, Lars Lunoe
'A great score, von Sydow's performance and a number of delightful moments do not compensate for the ludicrous plot which fails to fully engage the imagination.' – *Empire*

The Silent Village **
GB 1943 35m bw
Humphrey Jennings/Ministry of Information
Harrowing depiction, by the members of a Welsh village, of what happened to the Czech population of Lidice after the assassination of Heydrich.
A chilling documentary at the time, this little classic has kept its kick.
wd Humphrey Jennings *ed* Stewart McAllister

Silent Voice: see *Amazing Grace and Chuck*

The Silent Voice: see *The Man Who Played God (1932)*

The Silent Voice: see *Paula (1952)*

The Silent Witness
US 1932 73m bw
Fox
A man confesses to murder in order to protect his son.
Solid courtroom stuff of its day, built for a new star who never quite made it.
play Jack de Leon and Jack Celestin *d* Marcel Varnel, R. L. Hough
☆ Lionel Atwill, Helen Mack, Greta Nissen, Bramwell Fletcher, Alan Mowbray
'A gripping talker that rates well above most of the creep releases.' – *Variety*

The Silent Woman
France 1989 96m colour
Antenne 2/Son et Lumière
A doctor finds her isolated country home invaded by three assassins, who plan to kill her after she witnesses their murder of a politician, and a lunatic who escapes from a nearby asylum.
Suspenseful, though silly, thriller in which the hitmen behave with surprising stupidity.
w Jean-Claude Carriere, Joyce Bunuel *d* Joyce Bunuel *m* François Breant
☆ Marie-Christine Barrault, Véronique Genest, Pierre Clementi

The Silk Hat Kid
US 1935 70m bw
Fox (Joseph Engel)
A settlement housekeeper accepts help from a racketeer.
Thin little drama, perfunctorily played.
w Edward Eliscu, Lou Breslow, Dore Schary *story* Gerald Beaumont *d* H. Bruce Humberstone
☆ Lew Ayres, Mae Clarke, Paul Kelly, Ralf Harolde, William Harrigan
'It hasn't the story nor the entertainment weight to lift it out of the double feature classification.' – *Variety*

Silk Stockings *
US 1957 116m Metrocolor Cinemascope
MGM (Arthur Freed)
A Russian composer in Paris agrees to write music for a Hollywood film; a lady commissar is sent to get him back.
Musical rewrite of Ninotchka *via a Broadway show; good moments but generally very stretched.*
w Leonard Gershe, Leonard Spigelgass *play* George S. Kaufman, Leueen McGrath, Abe Burrows *original play Melchior Lengyel* *d* Rouben Mamoulian *ph* Robert Bronner *m/ly* Cole Porter *md* André Previn
☆ Fred Astaire, Cyd Charisse, Peter Lorre, Janis Paige, George Tobias, Jules Munshin, Joseph Buloff
† Cyd Charisse's singing was dubbed by Carole Richards.
♫ 'Too Bad'; 'Paris Loves Lovers'; 'Stereophonic Sound'; 'It's a Chemical Reaction, That's All'; 'All of You'; 'Satin and Silk'; 'Without Love'; 'Fated to Be Mated'; 'Josephine'; 'Siberia'; 'Red Blues'; 'The Ritz Rock and Roll'

The Silken Affair
GB 1956 96m bw
Dragon (Fred Feldkamp)
An accountant decides to live it up, and finds himself on trial for manipulating the firm's books.
Unsatisfactory mix of comedy and fantasy, with a dim plot and virtually no comic ideas.
w Robert Lewis Taylor *d* Roy Kellino *ph* Gilbert Taylor *m* Peggy Stuart
☆ David Niven, Genevieve Page, Wilfrid Hyde-White, Ronald Squire, Beatrice Straight, Howard Marion Crawford, Dorothy Alison

Silken Skin **
France 1964 118m bw
Films du Carrosse/SEDIF
original title: *La Peau Douce*
A middle-aged married man leaves his wife for an attractive young girl, but the latter leaves him and his wife shoots him.
Carefully balanced mixture of comedy and melodrama which rings almost every possible change on the theme of adultery and does so with wit.
w François Truffaut, Jean-Louis Richard *d* François Truffaut *ph* Raoul Coutard *m* Georges Delerue
☆ Jean Desailly, Françoise Dorléac, Nelly Benedetti
'Very funny, very touching, very wise about human beings.' – *New York Herald Tribune*

Silkwood *
US 1983 131m Technicolor
ABC (Mike Nichols, Michael Hausman)
The true story, more or less, of a girl worker in a nuclear processing plant who mysteriously dies in an accident just before she is going to talk to a reporter about a safety problem.
Despite the historical interest of the case, it is too simple to merit a film of this length, which is filled with pregnant pauses and romantic asides. Nor are the actors quite so charismatic as they think they are.
w Nora Ephron, Alice Arlen *d* Mike Nichols *ph* Miroslav Ondricek *m* Georges Delerue *pd* Patrizia von Brandenstein
☆ Meryl Streep, Cher, Kurt Russell, Craig T. Nelson, Diana Scarwid, Fred Ward
'A movie with a preordained conclusion but nowhere to go … it submerges what could have been its most telling points in a kind of concentrated soap opera.' – *Richard Combs, MFB*
Meryl Streep; Cher; direction; screenplay; editing (Sam O'Steen)

Silver Bears
GB 1977 113m Technicolor
EMI/Raleigh (Arlene Sellers, Alex Winitsky)
A Las Vegas money man invests money in various European outlets and makes a killing.
Extraordinarily complex financial jape which tries the patience of all but financiers.
w Peter Stone *novel* Paul Erdman *d* Ivan Passer *ph* Anthony Richmond *m* Claude Bolling
☆ Michael Caine, Louis Jourdan, Cybill Shepherd, Stephane Audran, David Warner, Tom Smothers, Martin Balsam, Charles Gray

Silver Blaze
GB 1937 70m bw
Twickenham (Julius Hagen)
US title: *Murder at the Baskervilles*
Sherlock Holmes clears a racehorse of having killed its trainer.
Not the best of the Holmes series, but this is a very satisfying Holmes.
w Arthur Macrae, H. Fowler Mear *story* Sir Arthur Conan Doyle *d* Thomas Bentley *ph* Sydney Blythe *ad* James Carter
☆ Arthur Wontner, Ian Fleming, Lyn Harding, Judy Gunn, Lawrence Grossmith, Arthur Macrae

The Silver Brumby
Australia 1993 92m colour
Media World/AFFC (John Tatoulis, Colin J. South)
A foal grows up to become a stallion and leader of a herd of wild horses, only to be hunted by a ruthless man.
Despite some excellent photography, the slight and uninteresting narrative makes it heavy going even for horse lovers.
w John Tatoulis, Jon Stephens, Elyne Mitchell *book* Elyne Mitchell *d* John Tatoulis *ph* Mark Gilfedder *m* Tassos Ioannides *pd* Phil Chambers *ed* Peter Burgess
☆ Caroline Goodall (Elyne), Russell Crowe (The Man), Ami Daemion (Indi), Johnny Raaen (Jock)
'A superbly crafted family film for animal lovers.' – *Variety*

Silver Bullet
US 1985 95m Technicolor
Paramount/Dino de Laurentiis (Martha Schumacher)
Murders at Tarker's Mill turn out to be the work of a werewolf.
Dreary, unimaginative rendition of a theme that was more entertaining in 1941.
w Stephen King *novelette Cycle of the Werewolf* by Stephen King *d* Daniel Attias *ph* Armando Nannuzzi *m* Jay Chattaway
☆ Corey Haim, Gary Busey, Megan Follows, Everett McGill
'It's a Stephen King filmette from his novelette which may sell some tickettes but not without regrettes.' – *Variety*

'I bid you seek the lost silver cup … for sin is rising like the swollen rivers!'
'Against the broad canvas of history's mad era of splendour and seduction – here is the story of the sacred cup of silver that challenged the iron sword of tyranny – the mighty struggle to possess it – and the loves and the faith that triumphed in humanity's darkest hour!'
The Silver Chalice
US 1954 142m Warnercolor Cinemascope
Warner (Victor Saville)
Adventures of a slave freed by Luke the apostle to fashion a chalice to hold the cup used at the Last Supper.
Po-faced biblical hokum, slower and deadlier than most, with howlingly bad casting and direction. On reflection, interesting things are being attempted with limbo set design, but in this sea of boredom the attempt only raises an eyebrow.
w Lesser Samuels *novel* Thomas B. Costain *d* Victor Saville *ph* William V. Skall *m* Franz Waxman *pd* Rolf Gerard
☆ Paul Newman, Pier Angeli, Jack Palance, Virginia Mayo, Walter Hampden, Joseph Wiseman, Alexander Scourby, Lorne Greene, Michael Pate, E. G. Marshall
William V. Skall; Franz Waxman

Silver City
US 1951 90m Technicolor
Paramount (Nat Holt)
GB title: *High Vermilion*
A mining assayer helps a farmer and his daughter protect the ore found on their land.
Standard Western programmer with plenty of action
w Frank Gruber *story* Luke Short *d* Byron Haskin *ph* Ray Rennahan *m* Paul Sawtell
☆ Yvonne de Carlo, Edmond O'Brien, Barry Fitzgerald, Richard Arlen, Gladys George, Laura Elliott, Edgar Buchanan, John Dierkes

Silver City *
Australia 1984 102m Eastmancolor
Artificial Eye/Limelight Productions (Joan Long)
Arriving in Australia in 1949, a Polish woman is sent to a camp where she has an affair with another, married immigrant.
Sharp study of bigotry and hostility undercut by a limp romance.
w Sophia Turkiewicz, Thomas Keneally *d* Sophia Turkiewicz *ph* John Seale *m* William Motzing *ad* Igot Nay *ed* Don Saunders
☆ Gosia Dobrowolska, Ivar Kants, Anna Jemison, Steve Bisley, Debra Lawrance, Ewa Brok, Joel

Cohen, Tim McKenzie, Dennis Miller, Annie Byron

'Works best as a sociological study of cultural clash.' – *Brian McFarlane, Australian Cinema 1970–1985*

The Silver Cord

US 1933 74m bw

RKO (Pandro S. Berman)

A young wife threatens to leave her husband because of his excessive devotion to his mother.

Stilted version of an old theatrical warhorse.

w Jane Murfin *play* Sidney Howard *d* John Cromwell *ph* Charles Rosher

☆ Irene Dunne, Joel McCrea, Laura Hope Crews, Frances Dee, Eric Linden, Helen Cromwell

The Silver Darlings

GB 1947 84m bw

Holyrood (Carl Grune)

Hebridean islanders take to herring fishing as a last chance to avoid emigration.

Uneventful island mood piece which lacks the poetic quality which might have made it memorable.

w Clarence Elder *novel* Neil Gunn *d* Clarence Elder, Clifford Evans *ph* Francis Carver *m* Clifton Parker *md* Muir Mathieson *ad* Ivan King *ed* Max Brenner

☆ Clifford Evans (Roddy), Helen Shingler (Catrine), Carl Bernard (Angus), Norman Shelley (Hendry), Simon Lack (Don), Hugh Griffith (Packman), Stanley Jay (Bo'sun), Harry Fine (Lieutenant)

Silver Dollar *

US 1932 84m bw

Warner

A poor farmer goes to Colorado for the gold rush, strikes it rich, and learns that money doesn't bring happiness.

Packed biopic of one H. A. W. Tabor, an excellent star vehicle.

w Carl Erickson, Harvey Thew *d* Alfred E. Green *ph* James Van Trees *m* Milan Roder

☆ Edward G. Robinson, Bebe Daniels, Aline MacMahon, Jobyna Howland, Robert Warwick, Russell Simpson

'Historical subject admirably done as to its variety but not so strong on its commercial side.' – *Variety*

Silver Dream Racer

GB 1980 111m Eastmancolor Panavision

Rank/David Wickes (Rene Dupont)

A garage mechanic becomes a racing motorcyclist and is killed at the peak of success.

One wonders who can have thought there was any box-office appeal in this cliché-ridden, derivative, flashily made update of the Road to Ruin.

wd David Wickes *ph* Paul Beeson *m* David Essex

☆ David Essex, Beau Bridges, Cristina Raines, Harry H. Corbett, Lee Montague, Clarke Peters

'Watching this grotesque hotch-potch of implausible characters being shunted through improbable situations is uncannily akin to being assaulted by a non-stop stream of TV commercials.' – *Tom Milne, MFB*

The Silver Fleet *

GB 1943 87m bw

GFD/Archers (Michael Powell, Emeric Pressburger, Ralph Richardson)

In occupied Holland, a shipping magnate destroys his new U-boat and himself and his Nazi mentors with it.

Slow-starting, rather stilted melodrama which when it gets into its stride provides good acting and gripping propaganda.

wd Vernon Sewell, Gordon Wellesley *ph* Erwin Hillier

☆ *Ralph Richardson*, Esmond Knight, Googie Withers, Beresford Egan, Frederick Burtwell, Kathleen Byron

Silver Lode

US 1954 80m Technicolor

Benedict Bogeaus/RKO

A respected citizen of Silver Lode proves that the marshal who rides into town on his wedding day to accuse him of murder is a civilian bent on revenge.

Broody little Western melodrama, not half bad.

w Karen de Wolf *d* Allan Dwan *ph* John Alton *m* Louis Forbes

☆ John Payne, Dan Duryea, Lizabeth Scott, Dolores Moran, Emile Meyer, Robert Warwick

Silver Queen

US 1942 80m bw

UA/Harry Sherman

A chivalrous Western gambler rescues a girl from the wiles of a villain.

Standard romantic melodrama mainly set in saloons.

w Bernard Schubert, Cecile Kramer *d* Lloyd Bacon *ph* Russell Harlan *m* Victor Young *ad* Ralph Berger

☆ George Brent, Priscilla Lane, Bruce Cabot, Lynne Overman, Eugene Pallette, Janet Beecher, Guinn Williams, Roy Barcroft

Academy Award nomination: Victor Young; Ralph Berger

Silver River

US 1948 110m bw

Warner (Owen Crump)

A ruthless gambler becomes powerful but loses everything because of his character defects.

Meandering Western drama with a few good highlights dissipated by long chunks of character building and a rehash of the David and Bathsheba story.

w Stephen Longstreet, Harriet Frank Jnr *d* Raoul Walsh *ph* Sid Hickox *m* Max Steiner

☆ Errol Flynn, Ann Sheridan, Thomas Mitchell, Bruce Bennett, Tom D'Andrea, Barton MacLane, Monte Blue, Alan Bridge

Silver Skates

US 1942 73m bw

Monogram (Lindsley Parsons)

A touring ice revue is lapsing into debt.

Novelties on ice occupy more screen time than the story, which is just as well. Competent small-scale musical filler.

w Jerry Cady *d* Leslie Goodwins

☆ Kenny Baker, Patricia Morison, Belita, Frick and Frack

The Silver Streak *

US 1934 85m bw

RKO

A streamlined train makes its first run from Chicago to Boulder Dam, where a victim of infantile paralysis must be got into an iron lung.

Historically interesting melodrama which seldom pauses for breath.

w H. W. Hanemann, Jack O'Donnell, Roger Whately *d* Tommy Atkins *ph* J. Roy Hunt *md* Alberto Colombo

☆ Sally Blane, Charles Starrett, Hardie Albright, William Farnum, Irving Pichel, Arthur Lake, Edgar Kennedy

'Pretty absurd, yet exciting and fast ... there's scarcely a stunt known to the railroad picture formula that hasn't been employed.' – *Variety*

Silver Streak *

US 1976 113m DeLuxe

TCF/Martin Ransohoff, Frank Yablans

On a trans-continental train, a young publisher discovers a murder and is at the mercy of the culprits.

Rather like an update of a Bob Hope comedy-thriller with a whiff of sex, this amiable spoof goes on too long, brings in a second comic too late, and ends with fashionable but irrelevant violence.

w Colin Higgins *d* Arthur Hiller *ph* David M. Walsh *m* Henry Mancini *pd* Alfred Sweeney

☆ Gene Wilder, Jill Clayburgh, Richard Pryor, Patrick McGoohan, Ned Beatty, Clifton James, Ray Walston, Richard Kiel

'Nineteen-seventies performers are trapped in this fake thirties mystery comedy, which is so inept you can't even get angry.' – *New Yorker*

Silverado *

US 1985 132m Technicolor Super Techniscope

Lawrence Kasdan

In the 1880s, various pioneers try to establish a future in the west.

Interesting but not wholly successful attempt to revive in one movie various Western myths and legends; a little more conscious humour might have helped.

w Lawrence and Mark Kasdan *d* Lawrence Kasdan *ph* John Bailey *m* Bruce Broughton *pd* Ida Random *ed* Carol Littleton

☆ Kevin Kline, Scott Glenn, Kevin Costner, Danny Glover, John Cleese, Rosanna Arquette, Brian Dennehy, Linda Hunt, Jeff Goldblum

'Less like the film westerns of imagination and more like something more common. Maybe it was that way in real life.' – *Variety*

Academy Award nomination: music

Simba

GB 1955 99m Eastmancolor

GFD/Group Film (Peter de Sarigny)

An English farmer in Kenya fights the Mau Mau.

Savagely topical melodrama which tends to cheapen a tragic situation.

w John Baines *d* Brian Desmond Hurst *ph* Geoffrey Unsworth *m* Francis Chagrin

☆ Dirk Bogarde, Donald Sinden, Virginia McKenna, Basil Sydney, Marie Ney, Joseph Tomelty, Earl Cameron, Orlando Martins

Simon *

US 1980 97m Technicolor

Warner/Orion (Louis A. Stroller, Martin Bregman)

Corrupt scientists brainwash a psychology professor into thinking he's from another planet.

Solemn comic fantasy which doesn't seem to make much of a point and only superficially entertains, but is well made and well acted.

wd Marshall Brickman *ph* Adam Holender *m* Stanley Silverman *pd* Stuart Wurtzel

☆ *Alan Arkin*, Madeline Kahn, Austin Pendleton, Judy Graubart, William Finley, Fred Gwynne

Simon and Laura *

GB 1955 91m Technicolor Vistavision

GFD/Group Films (Teddy Baird)

The actors who play husband and wife in a TV series are married in reality and hate each other, a fact that shows in the live Christmas episode.

Adequate film of a reasonably sophisticated West End comedy; good lines and performances.

w Peter Blackmore *play* Alan Melville *d* Muriel Box *ph* Ernest Steward *m* Benjamin Frankel

☆ *Peter Finch, Kay Kendall, Ian Carmichael*, Alan Wheatley, Richard Wattis, Muriel Pavlow, Maurice Denham, Hubert Gregg

Simon Birch

US 1998 113m Technicolor

Buena Vista/Hollywood/Caravan (Laurence Mark, Roger Birnbaum)

A man remembers the diminutive childhood friend who caused the death of his mother and changed his life.

Maudlin tale, manipulative and melodramatic for the most part; its story of loss and redemption never convinces.

wd Mark Steven Johnson *suggested by novel* A Prayer for Owen Meany by John Irving *ph* Aaron E. Schneider *m* Marc Shaiman *pd* David Chapman *ed* David Finfer

☆ Ian Michael Smith (Simon Birch), Joseph Mazzello (Joe Wenteworth), Ashley Judd (Rebecca Wenteworth), Oliver Platt (Ben Goodrich), David Strathairn (Rev. Russell), Dana Ivey (Grandmother Wenteworth), Hildie Grove (Beatrice Winde), Jim Carrey (Adult Joe Wenteworth), Jan Hooks (Miss Leavey)

'Though routinely slick, feature grows more irksome as it goes along — the lack of any genuinely felt emotions communicated makes later melodrama come off as shameless contrivance.' – *Dennis Harvey, Variety*

† Unhappy at the adaptation, John Irving insisted that the film's credit should read 'suggested by' his novel, and that the name of his central character should be changed.

'A Haunting Story Of Earthly Reason And Divine Intervention.'

'In an unforgiving land, the fate of a forgotten village rests in his hands.'

Simon Magus

GB/France/Germany/Italy 1999 106m colour

A simple-minded outcast in a village in Silesia is used by an anti-Semitic businessman to try to prevent a land deal that would have benefited the Jewish community.

Described as a magical tale from a vanished world, this odd, slow-moving film does conjure up a long-forgotten way of life, but its intimations of an even worse future are not enough to give it point.

wd Ben Hopkins *ph* Nic Knowland *m* Deborah Mollison *pd* Angela Davies *ed* Alan Levy

☆ Noah Taylor (Simon), Stuart Townsend (Dovid Bendel), Sean McGinley (Maximillian Hase), Embeth Davidtz (Leah), Amanda Ryan (Sarah), Rutger Hauer (Count Albrecht), Ian Holm (Sirius/Boris/The Devil), Terence Rigby (Bratislav), Ursula Jones (Rebecca), Cyril Shaps (Chaim), David De Keyser (Rabbi)

'There is something rather plodding about this romantic fantasy.' – *Peter Bradshaw, Guardian*

Simon of the Desert **

Mexico 1965 45m bw

Gustavo Alatriste

original title: *Simón del Desierto*

A holy man, following the example of St Simeon Stylites by living at the top of a column in the desert, is tempted by the Devil in the shape of a woman.

Intriguing and amusing fable on the nature of goodness, though it does not come to a satisfactory conclusion.

w Luis Buñuel, Julio Alejandro *d* Luis Buñuel *ph* Gabriel Figueroa *m* Raul Lavista *ed* Carlos Savage Jnr

☆ Claudio Brook, Silvia Pinal, Enrique Alvarez Felix, Hortensia Santoveña, Francisco Reiguera, Luis Aceves Castañeda, Enrique Garcia Alvarez

'It is Buñuel at his best: stylite and stylist face each other from their respective pedestals.' – *John Simon*

† The film was intended to be at least twice as long, but many scenes, including a visit from the Emperor of Byzantium, had to be cut when the producer ran out of money. Buñuel has said that it was the reason that the film's ending is somewhat abrupt.

Simon the Swiss: see *Le Voyou*

Simone: see *S1m0ne*

'How Much Can Three Friends Share?'

Simpatico *

US/France 1999 106m DeLuxe

Alliance/Emotion/Canal (Dan Lupovitz, Timm Oberwelland, Jean-Francois Fonlupt)

A multimillionaire racehorse owner discovers that a seedy boyhood friend is about to expose their dubious past.

A muted, melancholy drama of men being overtaken and destroyed by unnecessary guilt; the acting is a pleasure to watch.

w Matthew Warchus, David Nicholls *play* Sam Shepard *d* Matthew Warchus *ph* John Toll *m* Stewart Copeland *pd* Amy Ancona *ed* Pasquale Buba

☆ Nick Nolte (Vinnie), Jeff Bridges (Carter), Sharon Stone (Rosie), Catherine Keener (Cecilia), Albert Finney (Simms), Shawn Hatosy (Young Vinnie), Liam Waite (Young Carter), Kimberly Williams (Young Rosie)

'Thoughtful and appealing entertainment.' – *Variety*

'There is no such thing as adventure and romance. There's only trouble and desire.'

Simple Men *

GB/US 1992 105m Technicolor

Metro/Zenith/American Playhouse/Fine Line/Film Four/BIM (Ted Hope, Hal Hartley)

A petty crook and his brother search for their father, a former radical baseball star who has been on the run since the 60s.

Off-beat, occasionally amusing road movie that goes nowhere very interesting. It is too determinedly eccentric to be effective, but incidental pleasures include a fight between a nun and a policeman and a sheriff desperately searching for the meaning of life.

wd Hal Hartley *ph* Michael Spiller *m* Ned Rifle *pd* Daniel Ouellette *ed* Steve Hamilton

☆ Robert Burke, William Sage, Karen Sillas, Elina Löwensohn, Martin Donovan, Mark Chandler Bailey, Chris Cooke

'Effortlessly manages to encompass social comment and satire as it oscillates between the comic and the absurd with a stylish self-confidence.' – *Mark Salisbury, Empire*

'Sometimes good people do evil things.'

A Simple Plan ***

US 1998 120m colour

Paramount/Mutual/Savoy (James Jacks, Adam Schroeder)

Outside a small Minnesota town, three friends stumble across a bag containing $4.4m dollars in a crashed plane, and decide to keep the money.

A deft, chilling thriller of corruption and greed, charting an inexorable slide from integrity to betrayal and worse.

w Scott B.Smith *novel* Scott B. Smith *d Sam Raimi ph* Alar Kivilo *m Danny Elfman pd* Patrizia von Brandenstein *ed* Arthur Coburn, Eric L. Beason

☆ Bill Paxton, *Billy Bob Thornton*, Bridget Fonda, Brent Briscoe, Gary Cole, Becky Ann Baker, Chelcie Ross, Jack Walsh

'Marvellously nuanced and beautifully acted.' – *Andrew Sarris*

Billy Bob Thornton; Scott B. Smith

'Michael McCann Is About To Find Wealth Beyond His Imagination ... A Real Family.'

A Simple Twist of Fate *

US 1994 106m Technicolor

Buena Vista/Touchstone (Ric Kidney)

A reclusive and miserly furniture-maker redeems himself when he adopts a small and abandoned girl.

A not entirely successful attempt to make the plot of Eliot's Victorian novel work in a modern setting, but it has its moments.

w Steve Martin *novel Silas Marner* by George Eliot *d* Gillies MacKinnon *ph* Andrew Dunn *m* Cliff Edelman *pd* Andy Harris *ed* Humphrey Dixon

☆ Steve Martin, Gabriel Byrne, Laura Linney, Catharine O'Hara, Stephen Baldwin, Byron Jennings, Michael des Barres, Amelia Campbell, Kellen Crosby

'A faithful, heartfelt, somber piece about family and responsibility.' – *Variety*

A Simple Wish

US 1997 90m DeLuxe

Universal/Bubble Factory (Sid Sheinberg, Bill Sheinberg, Jon Sheinberg)

An incompetent fairy godfather has problems making a child's wish come true.

Sickly whimsy that is over-reliant on special effects.

w Jeff Rothberg *d* Michael Ritchie *ph* Ralf Bode *m* Bruce Broughton *pd* Stephen Hendrickson *ed* William Scharf *sp* Greg Cannom

☆ Martin Short, Kathleen Turner, Mara Wilson, Robert Pastorelli, Amanda Plummer, Francis Capra, Ruby Dee, Teri Garr, Alan Campbell

'A case of talent adrift on an ocean of cutesy kids material.' – *Empire*

Simply Irresistible

US/Germany 1999 96m DeLuxe

TCF/Monarchy/Regency (John Fiedler, Jon Amiel, Joseph M. Carracciolo Jnr)

An indifferent cook, who suddenly produces great food with the aid of a magic crab, attracts a businessman with an interest in restaurants.

Dire and risible romantic comedy, quite bereft of any magic.

w Judith Roberts, Elisabeth Robinson *d* Mark Tarlov *ph* Robert Stevens *m* Gil Goldstein *pd* John Kàsarda, William Barclay *ed* Paul Karasick

☆ Sarah Michelle Gellar (Amanda Shelton), Sean Patrick Flanery (Tom Bartlett), Patricia Clarkson (Lois McNally), Dylan Baker (Jonathan Bendel), Larry Gilliard Jnr (Nolan Traynor), Christopher Durang (Gene O'Reilly), Betty Buckley (Aunt Stella), Olek Krupa (Valderon), Amanda Peet (Chris), Alex Draper (François)

'Simply excruciating.' – *Empire*

Sin: see *The Beloved*

Sin Compasión *

Peru/Mexico/France 1994 120m DuArt

Gala/Inca/Aramanta/CiBy 2000 (Francisco J. Lombardi)

aka: *No Mercy*

A poor, idealistic student confesses murdering a wealthy old woman and her husband to a priest.

An updated version of the original, taken at a too-leisurely pace that allows attention to slacken.

w Augusto Cabada *novel Crime and Punishment* by Feodor Dostoevsky *d* Francisco J. Lombardi *ph* Pili Flores Guerra *m* Leopoldo La Rosa *pd* Cecilia Montiel *ed* Luis Barrios

☆ Diego Bertie, Adriana Davila, Jorge Chiarella, Hernan Romero, Marcello Rivera, Mariells Trejos, Carlos Onetto

'The complicated moral universe inhabited by Dostoevsky's characters seems a long way indeed from this gallery of one-dimensionality.' – *Sight and Sound*

The Sin of Harold Diddlebock: see *Mad Wednesday*

The Sin of Madelon Claudet

US 1931 74m bw

MGM (Harry Rapf)

GB title: *The Lullaby*

A mother is separated from her illegitimate baby.

Sob stuff for a rising star: hilarious now.

w Charles MacArthur *play* Edward Knoblock *d* Edgar Selwyn

☆ Helen Hayes, Robert Young, Neil Hamilton, Lewis Stone, Marie Prevost, Cliff Edwards, Jean Hersholt, Karen Morley

'Natural sobber for women and grosses ... but you don't have to go back as far as *Madame X* to find a parallel for the plot.' – *Variety*

Helen Hayes

Sin Town

US 1942 74m bw

Universal (George Waggner)

Two confidence tricksters arrive in a Western town and solve a murder.

Members of the studio repertory company in a passable Western discarded by Marlene Dietrich.

w Gerald Geraghty, W. Scott Darling, Richard Brooks *d* Ray Enright *m* Hans Salter

☆ Constance Bennett, Broderick Crawford, Leo Carrillo, Anne Gwynne, Patric Knowles, Andy Devine, Ward Bond, Ralf Harolde

Sinbad and the Eye of the Tiger

GB 1977 113m Metrocolor

Columbia/Andor (Charles H. Schneer, Ray Harryhausen)

Sinbad frees a city from a wicked woman's spell.

Lumpish sequel to a sequel: even the animated monsters raise a yawn this time.

w Beverley Cross *d* Sam Wanamaker *ph* Ted Moore *m* Roy Budd *sp* Ray Harryhausen

☆ Patrick Wayne, Taryn Power, Jane Seymour, Margaret Whiting, Patrick Troughton

Sinbad the Sailor

US 1947 117m Technicolor

RKO (Stephen Ames)

Sinbad sets off on his eighth voyage to find the lost treasure of Alexander.

Well-staged but humourless Arabian Nights swashbuckler.

w John Twist *d* Richard Wallace *ph* George Barnes *m* Roy Webb

☆ *Douglas Fairbanks Jnr*, Walter Slezak, Maureen O'Hara, Anthony Quinn, George Tobias, Jane Greer, Mike Mazurki, Sheldon Leonard

'Is there a public for this twopence-coloured rubbish. For me, it belongs to the Christmas theatre, with a principal boy in tights.' – *Stephen Watts, Sunday Express*

Since You Went Away ***

US 1944 172m bw

David O. Selznick

When hubby is away at the war, his wife and family adopt stiff upper lips.

Elaborate flagwaving investigation of the well-heeled American home front in World War II, with everyone brimming with goodwill and not a dry eye in the place. Absolutely superbly done, if it must be done at all, and a symposium of Hollywood values and techniques of the time.

w David O. Selznick *book* Margaret Buell Wilder *d John Cromwell ph Stanley Cortez, Lee Garmes m* Max Steiner *pd William L. Pereira ad* Mark-Lee Kirk *ed* Hal C. Kern, James E. Newcom

☆ Claudette Colbert, Joseph Cotten, Jennifer Jones, Shirley Temple, Agnes Moorehead, Monty Woolley, Lionel Barrymore, Guy Madison, Robert Walker, Hattie McDaniel, Craig Stevens, Keenan Wynn, Albert Basserman, Nazimova, Lloyd Corrigan

PREFACE: 'This is the story of the unconquerable fortress – the American home, 1943.'

'A deft, valid blend of showmanship, humour, and yard-wide Americanism.' – *James Agee*

'The whole litany of that middle-class synthetic emotionalism, meticulously annotated over a decade by tough and sentimental experts, has been procured for us.' – *Richard Winnington*

'A rather large dose of choking sentiment.' – *Bosley Crowther*

'It is not an average US reality. It is an average US dream.' – *Time*

'Selznick wrote the script himself, intending his story to be moving and simple, along epic lines; the result is pedestrian in a peculiarly grandiose manner.' – *Pauline Kael, 70s*

† Jennifer Jones's marriage to Robert Walker had broken down just before shooting began, which added awkwardness to their love scenes together, especially as the ever-present Selznick was then busily courting Jones. Cinematographer George Barnes was replaced during filming.

Max Steiner

best picture; Stanley Cortez; Claudette Colbert; Jennifer Jones; Monty Woolley; art direction; editing

Sincerely Yours

US 1955 115m Warnercolor

Warner (Henry Blanke)

A concert pianist goes deaf and retires to his penthouse, but with the help of binoculars lipreads the humble folk below. Helping them anonymously gives him courage to have an operation.

Absurd updating for a modern non-star of a creaky old George Arliss vehicle The Man Who Played God.

w Irving Wallace *d* Gordon Douglas *ph* William H. Clothier *musical advisor* George Liberace

☆ Liberace, Joanne Dru, Dorothy Malone, Alex Nicol, William Demarest

'Drenched in coy bathos to the point of embarrassment.' – *Films and Filming*

'Given sufficient intoxication, you could find this movie amusing.' – *Saturday Review*

La Sindrome di Stendhal: see *The Stendhal Syndrome*

Sinful Davey

GB 1968 95m Eastmancolor Panavision

UA/Mirisch/Webb (William N. Graf)

In 1821 a young Scotsman determines to become a criminal like his father, but falls in love.

Thin imitation of Tom Jones, *highly implausible but played with some zest.*

w James R. Webb *autobiography* David Haggart *d* John Huston *ph* Ted Scaife, Freddie Young *m* Ken Thorne *pd* Stephen Grimes

☆ John Hurt, Pamela Franklin, Nigel Davenport, Ronald Fraser, Robert Morley, Maxine Audley, Noel Purcell

Sing

US 1988 98m Technicolor

Columbia TriStar (Craig Zadan)

Students at a school faced with closure organise a singing and dancing competition.

Dim, cliché-ridden movie that offers little, even for its target audience of the young and undemanding.

w Dean Pitchford *d* Richard Baskin *ph* Peter Sova *m* Jay Gruska *pd* Carol Spier *ed* Bud Smith, Jere Huggins, Scott Smith

☆ Lorraine Bracco, Peter Dobson, Jessica Steen, Louise Lasser, George DiCenzo, Patti LaBelle, Susan Peretz

'Remarkably old-fashioned.' – *MFB*

Sing and Be Happy

US 1937 67m bw

TCF (Milton H. Feld)

A young man is too irresponsible to work in his father's advertising agency.

A wisp of a plot with some wisps of music attached; nothing to remember next day.

w Ben Markson, Lou Breslow, John Patrick *d* James Tinling

☆ Tony Martin, Leah Ray, Joan Davis, Chick Chandler, Helen Westley, Allan Lane, Berton Churchill

'This musical will require plenty of exploitative pressure by exhibs.' – *Variety*

Sing As We Go ***

GB 1934 80m bw

ATP (Basil Dean)

An unemployed millgirl gets various holiday jobs in Blackpool.

A splendid, pawky star vehicle which is also the best picture we have of industrial Lancashire in the thirties. Great fun.

w J. B. Priestley, Gordon Wellesley d Basil Dean ph Robert G. Martin

☆ *Gracie Fields*, John Loder, *Frank Pettingell*, Dorothy Hyson, Stanley Holloway

'We have an industrial north that is bigger than Gracie Fields running around a Blackpool fun fair.' – C. A. *Lejeune*

Sing Baby Sing *

US 1936 87m bw

TCF (Darryl F. Zanuck)

A drunken Shakespearian actor sets his sights on a night-club singer.

Reasonably hilarious take-off on the John Barrymore-Elaine Barrie affair, with several Fox contractees fooling to the top of their bent with the help of good musical numbers.

w Milton Sperling, Jack Yellen, Harry Tugend *d* Sidney Lanfield *ph* Peverell Marley *md* Louis Silvers *songs* various

☆ Alice Faye, Adolphe Menjou, Gregory Ratoff, Patsy Kelly, Ted Healy, The Ritz Brothers, Montagu Love, Dixie Dunbar

song 'When Did You Leave Heaven?' (*m*Richard Whiting, *ly*Walter Bullock)

Sing, Boy, Sing

US 1958 91m bw Cinemascope

TCF (Henry Ephron)

A rock and roll star comes close to a nervous breakdown because of an unscrupulous manager and a revivalist grandfather.

Fairly painless vehicle for a singing star.

w Claude Binyon *d* Henry Ephron *ph* William C. Mellor *m* Lionel Newman

☆ Tommy Sands, Edmond O'Brien, John McIntire, Lili Gentle, Nick Adams, Josephine Hutchinson

Sing Me a Love Song

US 1936 78m bw

Cosmopolitan/First National

A reformed playboy starts at the bottom as a clerk in his father's department store.

Thin but mildly pleasing musical with good comedy support.

w Sig Herzig, Jerry Wald, Harry Sauber *d* Ray Enright

☆ James Melton, Patricia Ellis, *Hugh Herbert*, ZaSu Pitts, Allen Jenkins, Nat Pendleton, Ann Sheridan, Walter Catlett, Hobart Cavanaugh, Charles Halton

'Story isn't much and the dialogue fails to sparkle, yet there's a constant stream of laughs.' – *Variety*

'The god-darnedest family in the whole USA!'

Sing You Sinners **

US 1938 88m bw

Paramount (Wesley Ruggles)

The adventures of a happy-go-lucky family and their racehorse.

Cheerful family musical with amiable cast and good tunes.

w Claude Binyon *d* Wesley Ruggles *ph* Karl Struss *md* Boris Morros *songs* James V. Monaco, Johnny Burke

☆ *Bing Crosby*, Donald O'Connor, Fred MacMurray, Elizabeth Patterson, Ellen Drew, John Gallaudet

'Homespun, down to earth, and as natural as eggs for breakfast.' – *Variety*

Sing Your Worries Away

US 1941 71m bw

RKO (Cliff Reid)

A debt-ridden songwriter has a girlfriend unaware of a huge pending inheritance.

Rather ribby comedy material which adds up to very little.

w Monte Brice *d* A. Edward Sutherland

☆ Bert Lahr, Buddy Ebsen, June Havoc, Patsy Kelly, Sam Levene, Margaret Dumont

'She was back with him... as a stranger.'

Singapore

US 1947 79m bw

Universal (Jerry Bresler)

A sailor and pearl smuggler discovers that the fiancée he thought was dead is alive, but has forgotten him.

Dull story of intrigue and double-cross, flat-footedly directed.

w Seton I. Miller, Robert Thoeren *d* John Brahm *ph* Maury Gertsman *m* Daniele Amfitheatrof *md* David Tamkin *ad* Bernard Herzbrun, Gabriel Scognamillo *ed* William Hornbeck

☆ Fred MacMurray (Matt Gordon), Ava Gardner (Linda), Roland Culver (Michael Van Leyden), Richard Haydn (Chief Inspector Hewitt), Thomas Gomez (Mr Mauribus), Spring Byington (Mrs Bellows)

† It was remade as *Istanbul (qv)*.

Singapore Woman

US 1941 65m bw

Warner (Harlan Thompson)

A slightly fallen woman is redeemed by a plantation owner.

Hasty and uninteresting remake of the Bette Davis vehicle Dangerous.

w Laird Doyle *story Hard Luck Dame* by Laird Doyle *d* Jean Negulesco *ph* Ted McCord *ad* Charles Novi *ed* Everett Dodd

☆ Brenda Marshall, David Bruce, Virginia Field, Jerome Cowan, Rose Hobart, Heather Angel

Un Singe en Hiver: see *A Monkey in Winter*

The Singer Not the Song

GB 1960 132m colour Cinemascope

Rank (Roy Baker)

In an isolated Mexican town a priest defies an outlaw who oddly respects him.

Lengthy character drama with little action or humour but a great deal of moody introspection and a suggestion of homosexuality.

w Nigel Balchin *novel* Audrey Erskine Lindop *d* Roy Baker *ph* Otto Heller *m* Philip Green

☆ John Mills, Dirk Bogarde, Mylene Demongeot, John Bentley, Laurence Naismith, Eric Pohlmann

'A rewarding film, as startling as a muffled scream from the subconscious.' – *Peter John Dyer*

Singin' in the Rain ★★★★

US 1952 102m Technicolor

MGM (Arthur Freed)

When talkies are invented, the reputation of one female star shrivels while another grows.

Brilliant comic musical, the best picture by far of Hollywood in transition, with the catchiest tunes, the liveliest choreography, the most engaging performances and the most hilarious jokes of any musical.

w Adolph Green, Betty Comden ph Harold Rosson m Nacio Herb Brown md Lennie Hayton d/ch Gene Kelly, Stanley Donen ly Arthur Freed

☆ *Gene Kelly, Donald O'Connor, Debbie Reynolds, Millard Mitchell, Jean Hagen, Rita Moreno, Cyd Charisse, Douglas Fowley*

'Perhaps the most enjoyable of all movie musicals.' – *New Yorker, 1975*

Lennie Hayton; Jean Hagen

The Singing Fool ★★

US 1928 110m bw

Warner

A successful singer goes on the skids when his small son dies.

Early talkie musical, a sensation because of its star's personality, but a pretty maudlin piece of drama.

w C. Graham Baker *play* Leslie S. Barrows *d* Lloyd Bacon *ph* Byron Haskin *m/ly* Lew Brown, Ray Henderson, B. G. de Sylva *ch* Larry Ceballos

☆ *Al Jolson*, Davey Lee, Betty Bronson, Josephine Dunn, Arthur Housman

'Obvious and tedious as the climax is, when the black-faced comedian stands before the camera and sings "Sonny Boy" you know the man is greater, somehow, than the situation, the story or the movie.' – *Pare Lorentz*

The Singing Kid

US 1936 83m bw

Warner (Robert Lord)

A cocky night-club singer takes a talented juvenile under his wing.

Routine star vehicle most notable for a string of standards sung by him right after the credits.

w Warren Duff, Pat C. Flick *d* William Keighley *ph* George Barnes *md* Leo F. Forbstein *songs* E. Y. Harburg, Harold Arlen

☆ Al Jolson, Sybil Jason, Allen Jenkins, Lyle Talbot, Edward Everett Horton, Beverly Roberts, Claire Dodd

The Singing Marine

US 1937 107m bw

Warner

A marine singer wins a talent contest and success goes to his head.

Light musical of very little interest save two dance sequences by Busby Berkeley.

w Delmer Daves *d* Ray Enright

☆ Dick Powell, Doris Weston, Jane Darwell, Hugh Herbert, Lee Dixon, Dick Wesson, Allen Jenkins, Jane Wyman, Larry Adler

The Singing Musketeer: see *The Three Musketeers (1939)*

The Singing Nun

US 1966 98m Metrocolor Panavision

MGM (Jon Beck)

Adventures of a nun who takes her music to the outside world.

Icky musical drama based on a true character.

w Sally Benson, John Furia *d* Henry Koster *ph* Milton Krasner *md* Harry Sukman *songs* Soeur Sourire

☆ Debbie Reynolds, Greer Garson, Ricardo Montalban, Agnes Moorehead, Chad Everett, Katharine Ross, Ed Sullivan, Juanita Moore

Harry Sukman

The Singing Sheriff

US 1944 60m bw

Universal (Bernard W. Burton)

A New York singer inadvertently becomes sheriff of a town threatened by the gang of a crooked lawyer.

Bizarre comic minor Western, interspersed with songs and vaudeville acts, culminating in a courtroom scene in which the prosecutor sings a demand for the death penalty: 'Yeah, yeah, hang him on the hickory/Yeah, yeah, rid him of his trickery/Yeah, yeah, hang him on the hickory/We want to see him swing,' goes the chorus, in which all the court joins in.

w Henry Blankford, Eugene Conrad *story* John Grey *d* Leslie Goodwins *ph* Charles Van Enger *md* Sam Freed Jnr *ad* John B. Goodman, Abraham Grossman

☆ Bob Crosby, Fay McKenzie, Fuzzy Knight, Iris Adrian, Samuel S. Hinds, Edward Norris, Doodles Weaver, Spade Colley and his Orchestra

A Single Life

Australia 1985 108m colour

AFT (Hugh Rule)

Desperate to have a child, an unmarried woman begins an affair with her married boss.

Unsatisfactory domestic drama in which the characters' actions seem dictated solely by the whims of the authors.

w Mark Poole, John Power *d* John Power *ph* Vladimir Osherov *m* Brett Goldsmith *pd* Chris Kennedy *ed* Ian Lang

☆ Tina Bursill, Steven Jacobs, Jane Clifton, Pamela Rabe, Tony Rickards, Esben Storm

'Allie's new roommate is about to borrow a few things without asking. Her clothes. Her boyfriend. Her life.'

'Living with a roommate can be murder.'

Single White Female ★

US 1992 108m Technicolor

Columbia TriStar/Columbia (Barbet Shroeder)

A young Manhattan businesswoman finds that her new flatmate is taking over her life.

Well-done thriller, but its subject-matter is too familiar from too many recent films to cause much in the way of a frisson.

w Don Roos *novel SWF Seeks Same* by John Lutz *d* Barbet Schroeder *ph* Luciano Tovoli *m* Howard Shore *pd* Milena Canonero *ed* Lee Percy

☆ Bridget Fonda, Jennifer Jason Leigh, Steven Weber, Peter Friedman, Stephen Tobolowsky

'It is saddening to see a fine filmmaker courting the crowds by trashing his talent.' – *Geoff Brown, The Times*

Single-Handed ★

GB/US 1953 83m bw

TCF (Frank McCarthy)

US title: *Sailor of the King*

The action of a Canadian seaman, who was born as the result of an affair between a naval officer and a woman he meets on a train during the First World War, results in the destruction of a German battleship during World War II.

Deft drama of wartime action, an effective flag-waver with its theme of courage and leadership through the generations.

w Valentine Davies *novel Brown on Resolution* by C. S. Forester *d* Roy Boulting *ph* Gilbert Taylor *m* Clifton Parker *md* Muir Mathieson *ad* Alec Vetchinsky *ed* Alan Osbiston

☆ Jeffrey Hunter, Michael Rennie, Wendy Hiller, Bernard Lee, Peter Van Eyck, Victor Maddern, John Horsley, Patrick Barr, Robin Bailey

† The film was made with two endings, with the first audiences asked to vote on which they preferred: in one, the most dramatically effective, our hero dies and his mother receives his posthumous medal; in the other, he survives and unknowingly meets his father. The latter version is the most common, though prints showing both endings survive.

†† C. S. Forester's novel was first filmed in 1935 under the title *Forever England*, directed by Walter Forde with an action sequence directed by Anthony Asquith, and starring John Mills and Betty Balfour.

Singles ★

US 1992 99m Technicolor

Warner/Atkinson/Knickerbocker (Cameron Crowe, Richard Hashimoto)

The young occupants of an apartment block in Seattle fall in and out of love.

A meandering movie of singles attempting to become couples in order to occupy their empty lives; it is slight, but perceptive.

wd Cameron Crowe *ph* Ueli Steiger *m* Paul Westerberg *pd* Stephen Lineweaver

☆ Bridget Fonda, Campbell Scott, Kyra Sedgwick, Sheila Kelley, Jim True, Matt Dillon, Ally Walker, Eric Stoltz, Tom Skerritt

'The movie gets nowhere in particular, but the leading performances are immensely attractive.' – *Philip French, Observer*

'Superbly scripted, cast and scored, pic is a natural for the partner-hunting twentysomething crowd and should easily cross over to thirtysomething singles or couples primed to laugh at the dating syndrome.' – *Variety*

Singleton's Pluck: see *Laughterhouse*

The Sinister Man ★

GB 1961 60m bw

Anglo Amalgamated/Merton Park (Jack Greenwood)

The murder of an Oxford scholar is linked to archaeological relics which are coveted for political purposes.

Very tolerable minor thriller in the Edgar Wallace series: short, sharp and snappy.

w Robert Banks Stewart *d* Clive Donner *ph* Bert Mason *m* Charles Blackwell

☆ Patrick Allen, John Bentley, Jacqueline Ellis, Eric Young, Arnold Lee, John Glyn-Jones, William Gaunt, Wilfrid Brambell

'Personal! Powerful! Human! Heroic!'

Sink the Bismarck! ★★

GB 1960 97m bw Cinemascope

TCF/John Brabourne

In 1941, Britain's director of naval operations arranges the trapping and sinking of Germany's greatest battleship.

Tight little personal drama which would have been better on a standard screen, as its ships are plainly models and much of the footage stretched-out newsreel. Nevertheless, a good example of the stiff-upper-lip school.

w Edmund H. North *d* Lewis Gilbert *ph* Christopher Challis *m* Clifton Parker *md* Muir Mathieson

☆ *Kenneth More*, Dana Wynter, Karel Stepanek, Carl Mohner, Laurence Naismith, Geoffrey Keen, Michael Hordern, Maurice Denham, Esmond Knight

Sinner Take All

US 1937 74m bw

MGM (Lucien Hubbard, Sam Marx)

Members of a family are murdered one by one.

Moderate puzzler with a reporter sharing solving honours with the police.

w Leonard Lee, Walter Wise *novel Murder of a Wanton* by Whitman Chambers *d* Errol Taggart

☆ Bruce Cabot, Margaret Lindsay, Joseph Calleia, Stanley Ridges, Vivienne Osborne, Charley Grapewin, Edward Pawley, George Zucco

'Above the usual whodunit average ... able to make its way alone in the less exacting spots.' – *Variety*

Sinner's Holiday

US 1930 55m bw

Warner

A fairground barker loves the daughter of a penny arcade owner, but is framed by her brother.

Early talkie quickie using Broadway talent, and introducing James Cagney to the screen. It still has vigour if little else.

w Harvey Thew, George Rosener *play Penny Arcade* by Marie Baumer *d* John G. Adolfi *ph* Ira Morgan

☆ Grant Withers, Evalyn Knapp, James Cagney, Joan Blondell, Lucille La Verne, Warren Hymer, Noel Madison

Sinners' Holiday: see *Christmas Eve (1947)*

Sinners in Paradise

US 1938 65m bw

Universal (Ken Goldsmith)

Air travellers are wrecked on a South Sea island.

Much ado about very little, and a grave disappointment from its director.

w Lester Cole, Harold Buckley, Louis Stevens *d* James Whale

☆ Madge Evans, John Boles, Bruce Cabot, Marion Martin, Gene Lockhart, Charlotte Wynters, Nana Bryant

'Melodrama sufficiently lurid to be cut into several parts and released as a serial.' – *Variety*

Sinners in the Sun

US 1932 69m bw

Paramount

A young couple break up; each has romantic adventures, but eventually they come together again.

Blah comedy-drama with the defects of its period.

w Vincent Lawrence, Waldemar Young, Samuel Hoffenstein, Mildred Cram *d* Alexander Hall

☆ Carole Lombard, Chester Morris, Adrianne Allen, Alison Skipworth, Walter Byron, Cary Grant

'Only high-powered selling will aid a dull and poorly-handled story.' – *Variety*

The Sins of Rachel Cade

US 1961 123m Technicolor

Warner (Henry Blanke)

An American missionary nurse in the Belgian Congo falls in love with a crashed flyer and has a baby.

Romantic melodrama which starts like The Nun's Story *and ends like Peg's Paper; competent on its level.*

w Edward Anhalt *novel* Charles Mercer *d* Gordon Douglas *ph* Peverell Marley *m* Max Steiner

☆ Angie Dickinson, Roger Moore, Peter Finch, Errol John, Woody Strode, Juano Hernandez, Frederick O'Neal, Mary Wickes

Sins of Rome: see *Spartacus (1952)*

'Sometimes The Most Dangerous Journey Is Into Your Past.'

Sioux City
US 1994 100m Foto-Kem
Cabin Fever/Facet (Brian Rox, Jane Ubell)
GB video title: *Ultimate Revenge*
A Lakota Indian youth, adopted as a baby by a Jewish couple, investigates the murder of his real mother, who had invited him to visit her, and rediscovers his roots.
Dull thriller on an interesting theme of cultural identity.
w L. Virginia Browne *d* Lou Diamond Phillips *ph* James W. Wrenn *m* Christopher Lindsey *pd* Rando Schmook *ed* Christopher Rouse, Mark Fitzgerald
☆ Lou Diamond Phillips, Salli Richardson, Melinda Dillon, Ralph Waite, Bill Allen, Adam Roarke, Gary Farmer
'An undistinguished mystery-thriller that's criminally short on mystery and thrills.' – *Joe Leydon, Variety*

Sir Henry at Rawlinson End
GB 1980 71m bw
Charisma (Tony Stratton Smith)
A grossly eccentric English aristocrat lays a family ghost.
Weirdly isolated, semi-professional comedy with elements of everything from Ealing to Monty Python.
w Vivian Stanshall, Steve Roberts *radio play Vivian Stanshall d* Steve Roberts *ph* Martin Bell *m* Vivian Stanshall *pd* Alistair Bowtell *ed* Chris Rose
☆ Trevor Howard, Patrick Magee, Denise Coffey, J. G. Devlin, Vivian Stanshall

Siren of Atlantis: see *L'Atlantide*

Siren of Bagdad
US 1953 72m Technicolor
Columbia (Sam Katzman)
A travelling magician helps reinstate a deposed sultan.
Flippant oriental extravaganza aiming at the Hope-Crosby style but falling sadly short of it.
w Robert E. Kent *d* Richard Quine *ph* Henry Freulich *m* Mischa Bakaleinikoff
☆ Paul Henreid, Patricia Medina, Hans Conried, Charlie Lung

La Sirène du Mississippi: see *The Mississippi Mermaid*

'A Seductive New Comedy.'

Sirens ★
Australia/GB 1994 94m colour
Buena Vista/WGM/AFFC/British Screen/Samson/Sarah Radclyffe (Sue Milliken)
The repressed wife of an English vicar learns to lose her inhibitions when the couple visit the Australian painter Norman Lindsay and his Bohemian entourage of free-living models.
A light-hearted and lightweight summertime clash of attitudes and cultures, enjoyable without being particularly memorable.
wd John Duigan *ph* Geoff Burton *m* Rachel Portman *pd* Roger Ford *ed* Humphrey Dixon
☆ *Hugh Grant, Tara Fitzgerald*, Sam Neill, Elle Macpherson, Portia de Rossi, Kate Fischer, Pamela Rabe, Ben Mendelsohn, Mark Gerber, Tom Polson
'A deliciously sexy and hedonistic comedy of morals and manners.' – *Variety*
'The kind of attractive, fluent period film which those who swear by James Ivory will appreciate.' – *Derek Malcolm, Guardian*

Sirocco
US 1951 98m bw
Columbia/Santana (Robert Lord)
In 1925 Damascus, an American runs guns for the rebels.
Tedious romantic drama in the Casablanca vein but with none of the magic.
w A. I. Bezzerides, Hans Jacoby *novel Coup de Grâce* by Joseph Kessel *d* Curtis Bernhardt *ph* Burnett Guffey *m* George Antheil
☆ Humphrey Bogart, Marta Toren, Lee J. Cobb, Everett Sloane, Gerald Mohr, Zero Mostel, Onslow Stevens

'No Sex. No Booze. No Men. No Way.'

Sister Act ★
US 1992 100m Technicolor
Buena Vista/Touchstone/Touchwood Pacific Partners (Teri Schwartz)
A singer on the run from the Mafia takes refuge in a convent and transforms its choir.
Cheerful and modest comedy, though lacking in wit and with a plot that makes little sense. It was the surprise hit of 1992, ranking fourth at the box-office.
w Joseph Howard *d* Emile Ardolino *ph* Adam Greenberg *m* Marc Shaiman *pd* Jackson DeGovia *ed* Richard Halsey
☆ Whoopi Goldberg, Maggie Smith, Kathy Najimy, Wendy Makkena, Mary Wickes, Harvey Keitel, Bill Nunn, Robert Miranda, Richard Portnow
'The film isn't a divine comedy, and it's not satisfyingly profane either. But it generates a few laughs. It's got a good beat, and you can dance to it.' – *Michael Sragow, New Yorker*
'Offers the kind of cute, synthetic uplift usually found in television commercials and casts its nun characters as walking sight gags rather than real people.' – *Janet Maslin, New York Times*
'A truly awful film, pretending to be audacious but in fact pandering to every facile assumption in the book.' – *Derek Malcolm, Guardian*

Sister Act 2: Back in the Habit
US 1993 106m Technicolor Cinemascope
Buena Vista/Touchstone (Scott Rudin, Dawn Steel)
A Las Vegas singer agrees to dress as a nun to teach singing at a ghetto school that is in trouble.
Distressingly dire comedy, sickly and silly; it is smug and patronizing in its attitudes to the problems of inner-city life and not at all amusing.
w James Orr, Jim Cruickshank, Judi Ann Mason *d* Bill Duke *ph* Oliver Wood *m* Miles Goodman *pd* John DeCuir Jnr *ed* John Carter, Pem Herring, Stuart Pappé
☆ Whoopi Goldberg, Kathy Najimy, Barnard Hughes, Mary Wickes, James Coburn, Maggie Smith, Wendy Makkena, Lauryn Hill, Sheryl Lee Ralph
'Two trips to the convent is one too many.' – *Variety*
'If *Sister Act 2* is how Hollywood rewards success, how does it punish failure?' – *Adam Mars-Jones, Independent*
† Kathy Najimy's singing was dubbed by Andrea Robinson.

Sister Kenny ★
US 1946 116m bw
RKO (Dudley Nichols)
The career of a nurse who instigated treatment for polio.
Standard, well-done biopic.
w Dudley Nichols, Alexander Knox, Mary McCarthy *d* Dudley Nichols *ph* George Barnes *m* Alexander Tansman
☆ Rosalind Russell, Alexander Knox, Dean Jagger, Philip Merivale, Beulah Bondi, Dorothy Peterson
† From the autobiography of Australian nurse Mary Kenny: *And They Shall Walk.*
Rosalind Russell

Sister My Sister ★
GB 1994 104m colour
Arrow/Film Four/British Screen/NFH (Norma Heyman)
In France in the 30s, two sisters who work as maids in the same strict household begin an incestuous affair and start acting strangely.
Claustrophobic upstairs/downstairs tragedy, in which the only escape seems to be through violence.
w Wendy Kesselman *play My Sister in This House* by Wendy Kesselman *d* Nancy Meckler *ph* Ashley Rowe *m* Stephen Warbeck *pd* Caroline Amies *ed* David Stiven
☆ Julie Walters, Joely Richardson, Jodhi May, Sophie Thursfield
'A small-scale film with some powerful moments' – *Variety*
'A piece of cinema of almost stifling intensity and formidably acted throughout.' – *Derek Malcolm, Guardian*
† The same true-life story was the basis of Jean Genet's play *The Maids*, which was filmed in 1974 (qv).

Sister of Satan: see *She Beast*

The Sisters ★
US 1938 98m bw
Warner (Hal B. Wallis)
The marriages of three sisters from a small Montana town.
Well-made potboiler for women; it even brings in the San Francisco earthquake, and the star teaming is piquant to say the least.
w Milton Krims *novel* Myron Brinig *d* Anatole Litvak *ph* Tony Gaudio *m* Max Steiner
☆ Bette Davis, Errol Flynn, Anita Louise, Ian Hunter, Donald Crisp, Beulah Bondi, Jane Bryan, Alan Hale, Dick Foran, Henry Travers, Patric Knowles, Lee Patrick, Harry Davenport
'Worth seeing for the adroit period direction and the fragile, pop-eyed acting of Miss Bette Davis.' – *Graham Greene*

Sisters ★
US 1973 92m colour
British Lion/Pressman-Williams Enterprises (Edward R. Pressman)
GB title: *Blood Sisters*
A Siamese twin takes on the personality of her deranged and dead sister.
The plots of Alfred Hitchcock's Psycho *and* Rear Window *are both raided for this effective, if derivative, shocker.*
w Brian de Palma, Louisa Rose *d* Brian de Palma *ph* Gregory Sandor *m* Bernard Herrmann *pd* Gary Weist *ed* Paul Hirsch
☆ Margot Kidder, Jennifer Salt, Charles Durning, Bill Finley, Lisle Wilson, Barnard Hughes
'A long way from being the brilliant thriller the ads say it is, but its limp technique doesn't seem to matter to the people who want their gratuitous gore. The movie supplies it, but why is there so much gratuitous dumbness, too?' – *Pauline Kael, New Yorker*
'A distinctly uneasy blend of that brand of unprincipled exploitation that makes horror out of madness and birth abnormality.' – *MFB*

Sisters ★
US 1988 93m colour
UIP/MGM/Oxford Film Company (Andy Paterson, Mark Bentley)
US title: *Some Girls*
An American student who goes to spend Christmas with the Catholic family of his girlfriend in Quebec finds himself looking after her dying grandmother.
Mildly amusing comedy of cultural misunderstandings.
w Rupert Walters *d* Michael Hoffman *ph* Ueli Steiger *m* James Newton Howard *pd* Eugenio Zanetti *ed* David Spiers
☆ Patrick Dempsey, Jennifer Connelly, Sheila Kelley, Lance Edwards, Lila Kedrova, Florinda Bolkan, Andre Gregory, Ashley Greenfield

Sisters or The Balance of Happiness ★
West Germany 1979 95m colour
Blue Dolphin/Bioskop Film/WDR (Eberhard Junkersdorf)
original title: *Schwestern oder Die Balance des Glücks*
Two sisters, one an executive secretary, the other a biology student whom she supports and stifles, grow ever more dependent upon each other.
Troubling, claustrophobic study of damaging family relationships.
wd Margarethe von Trotta *ph* Franz Rath, Thomas Schwan *m* Konstantin Wecker *ad* Winifred Hennig *ed* Annette Dorn
☆ Jutta Lampe, Gudrun Gabriel, Jessica Fruh, Konstantin Wecker, Heinz Bennet

Sisters under the Skin
US 1934 65m bw
Columbia
An older man loses his mistress to a bohemian composer.
Surprise, surprise: and the screenplay does not enliven the situation.
w Jo Swerling, S. K. Lauren *d* David Burton
☆ Frank Morgan, Elissa Landi, Joseph Schildkraut, Doris Lloyd, Clara Blandick, Samuel S. Hinds
'Mild flicker of obvious triangle story texture.' – *Variety*

Sitcom
France 1998 79m colour
Alliance/Fidélité/Canal+ (Olivier Delbosc, Marc Missonnier)
After their father brings home a white rat, a family disintegrates; so he apparently kills them all.
A film determined to shock by its stew of seduction and incest; but it is simply silly.
wd François Ozon *ph* Yorik Le Saux *m* Eric Neveux *ad* Angelique Puron *ed* Dominique Petrot
☆ Evelyne Dandry, François Marthouret, Marina de Van, Adrien de Van, Stephane Rideau, Lucia Sanchez, Julien-Emmanuel Eyoum Deido, Jean Douchet
'This childish film is intended to shock, but is merely tedious.' – *Philip French, Observer*

Sitting Bull
US 1954 106m Eastmancolor Cinemascope
United Artists/W. R. Frank/Televoz of Mexico
Despite the massacre of Custer's men, a cavalry officer strives to establish a relationship with Sitting Bull.
Sloppy and undernourished Western epic in abysmal colour, not helped by Mexicans pretending to be Indians.
w Jack de Witt, Sidney Salkow *d* Sidney Salkow *ph* Charles Van Enger, Victor Herrera *m* Raoul Kraushaar
☆ Dale Robertson, Mary Murphy, J. Carrol Naish, Iron Eyes Cody, John Litel, William Hopper, Douglas Kennedy (Custer)

Sitting Ducks
US 1978 88m DeLuxe
Sunny Side Up (Meira Atta Dor)
Two men steal a fortune and abscond to Miami with two women who turn out to have a contract on them.
Endlessly talkative sex comedy from a practitioner who scorns built-up gags. The kind of movie that puts people off movies.
wd Henry Jaglom *ph* Paul Glickman *m* Richard Romanus
☆ Michael E. Jaglom, Zack Norman, Patrice Townsend, Irene Forrest, Richard Romanus, Henry Jaglom

Sitting in Limbo
Canada 1986 95m colour
NFBC (David Wilson, John N. Smith)
In Montreal, a black teenager discovers she is pregnant and goes to live with her caring but irresponsible boyfriend.
Low-key slice-of-life drama, focusing on the divide between single mothers and the men who father their children, and mainly notable for presenting a black working-class community not often seen in Canadian films.
w David Wilson, John N. Smith *d* John N. Smith *ph* Barry Perles, Andreas Poulsson *ed* David Wilson
☆ Pat Dillon, Fabian Gibbs, Sylvie Clarke, Debbie Grant, Compton McLean, Millicent Dillon, Ronald Lang

Sitting Pretty
US 1933 85m bw
Paramount (Charles R. Rogers)
Two songwriters strike it rich in Hollywood.
Cheerful comedy musical, interesting for its backgrounds.
w Jack McGowan, S. J. Perelman, Lou Breslow *d* Harry Joe Brown *ph* Milton Krasner *songs* Mack Gordon, Harry Revel
☆ Jack Oakie, Jack Haley, Ginger Rogers, Thelma Todd, Gregory Ratoff, Lew Cody, Harry Revel, Mack Gordon
'Should please all over.' – *Variety*

Sitting Pretty ***
US 1948 84m bw
TCF (Samuel G. Engel)
A young couple acquire a most unusual male baby sitter, a self-styled genius who sets the neighbourhood on its ears by writing a novel about it.
Out of the blue, a very funny comedy which entrenched Clifton Webb as one of Hollywood's great characters and led to two sequels, Mr Belvedere Goes to College *and* Mr Belvedere Rings the Bell *(qv).*
w F. Hugh Herbert *novel* Belvedere by Gwen Davenport *d* Walter Lang *ph* Norbert Brodine *m* Alfred Newman
☆ *Clifton Webb*, Robert Young, Maureen O'Hara, *Richard Haydn*, Louise Allbritton, Ed Begley, Randy Stuart, Larry Olsen
Academy Award nomination: Clifton Webb

Sitting Target
GB 1972 92m Metrocolor
MGM (Barry Kulick)
A violent killer escapes from jail and seeks revenge on those who 'shopped' him.
Rough, tough action thriller; passes the time for hardened addicts.
w Alexander Jacobs *novel* Lawrence Henderson *d* Douglas Hickox *ph* Ted Scaife *m* Stanley Myers *pd* Jonathan Barry
☆ Oliver Reed, Jill St John, Edward Woodward, Frank Finlay, Ian McShane, Freddie Jones, Robert Beatty

Situation Hopeless But Not Serious
US 1965 97m bw
Paramount/Castle (Gottfried Reinhardt)
In 1944, two American flyers are captured by a friendly, lonely mild-mannered German, who keeps them in his cellar and hasn't the heart to tell them when the war is over ...
Flat little comedy which leaves a talented cast no room for manoeuvre.
w Silvia Reinhardt *novel* The Hiding Place by Robert Shaw *d* Gottfried Reinhardt *ph* Kurt Hasse *m* Harold Byrne
☆ Alec Guinness, Robert Redford, Mike Connors, Anita Hoefer

Six Black Horses
US 1962 80m Eastmancolor
Universal-International (Gordon Kay)
A girl hires a gunslinger and a horse thief to escort her across Indian territory.
Rather glum Western programmer.
w Burt Kennedy *d* Harry Keller *ph* Maury Gertsman *md* Joseph Gershenson *ad* Alexander Golitzen, Robert Luthardt *ed* Aaron Stell
☆ Audie Murphy, Dan Duryea, Joan O'Brien, George Wallace, Roy Barcroft, Bob Steele, Henry Wills, Phil Chambers, Charlita Regis, Dale Van Sickel

Six Bridges to Cross
US 1955 96m bw
U-I (Aaron Rosenberg)
The criminal career of a young hoodlum in Boston in the thirties.
Public Enemy *reprise with a sentimental veneer, smooth but uninteresting.*
w Sydney Boehm *novel* They Stole Two and a Half Million Dollars and Got Away with It by Joseph F. Dineen *d* Joseph Pevney *ph* William Daniels *m* Joseph Gershenson
☆ Tony Curtis, George Nader, Julie Adams, Jay C. Flippen, Sal Mineo, Jan Merlin

'Are You Who You Think You Are?'
The 6th Day *
US 2000 124m DeLuxe
Columbia/Phoenix (Mike Medavoy, Arnold Schwarzenegger, Jon Davison)
[icons: DVD Region 2, DVD Region 1, Soundtrack]
In a future world, a helicopter pilot is forced to go on the run after he is cloned by an evil genetics tycoon.
An action film that gains from its topical theme; the violence here has been toned down in comparison to that found in Schwarzenegger's earlier movies.
w Cormac Wibberley, Marianne Wibberley *d* Roger Spottiswoode *ph* Pierre Mignot *m* Trevor Rabin *pd* James Bissell, John Willett *ed* Mark Conte, Dominique Fortin, Michel Arcand *sp* Rhythm & Hues Studios *cos* Trish Keating
☆ Arnold Schwarzenegger (Adam Gibson), Tony Goldwyn (Michael Drucker), Michael Rapaport (Hank Morgan), Michael Rooker (Robert Marshall), Sarah Wynter (Talia Elsworth), Wendy Crewson (Natalie Gibson), Rod Rowland (Wiley), Terry Crews (Vincent), Ken Pogue (Speaker Day), Colin Cunningham (Tripp), Robert Duvall (Dr Griffin Weir)
'A crisp and agreeable futuristic adventure.' – *Sight and Sound*

Six Day Bike Rider
US 1934 69m bw
Warner (Sam Bischoff)
One of life's failures impresses his girl by entering a cycling contest.
One of the star's stronger comedy vehicles.
w Earl Baldwin *d* Lloyd Bacon *ph* Warren Lynch
☆ Joe E. Brown, Maxine Doyle, Frank McHugh, Gordon Westcott

'After This Week In Paradise, They're Going To Need A Vacation.'
Six Days, Seven Nights
US 1998 101m Technicolor Panavision
Touchstone/Caravan/Northern Lights (Ivan Reitman, Wallis Nicita, Roger Birnbaum)
En route to Tahiti, a pilot makes an emergency landing and strands himself and his passenger, a New York fashion editor, on an unknown island.
A romantic comedy so obvious in its outcome that an audience can sleep through most of it without missing anything of interest.
w Michael Browning *d* Ivan Reitman *ph* Michael Chapman *m* Randy Edelman *pd* J. Michael Riva *ed* Sheldon Kahn, Wendy Greene Bricmont
☆ Harrison Ford, Anne Heche, David Schwimmer, Temuera Morrison
'Plagued with a hackneyed screenplay (which borrows from so many films you'll lose count), this lame romantic comedy falls to pieces within six minutes and seven seconds.' – *Judy Sloane, Film Review*

Six Days, Six Nights **
France 1994 98m colour
New Light/France 3 (Alexandre Arcady)
original title: *A la Folie*
An unhappily married art teacher envies her sister's success as an artist and her happy new relationship with a boxer.
Deft and intriguing drama of sibling rivalry and destructive passions.
wd Diane Kurys *ph* Fabio Conversi *m* Michael Nyman *pd* Tony Egry *ed* Luc Barnier
☆ Anne Parillaud, Béatrice Dalle, Patrick Aurignac, Bernard Verley, Alain Chabat, Jean-Claude de Goros, Marie Guillard

'For Paul, every person is a new door to a new world.'
Six Degrees of Separation **
US 1993 111m DeLuxe
MGM/Maiden Movies/New Regency (Fred Schepisi, Arnon Milchan)
A young man arrives on the doorstep of a wealthy and sophisticated New York couple claiming to be mugged and convinces them that he is a friend of their children and the son of Sidney Poitier.
Witty, complex, always engrossing study of identity and more; the key moment comes as the con man lectures his captive audience, complacent in their belief in themselves and their understanding of culture, on the death of the imagination – and fools them.
w *John Guare play* John Guare *d* *Fred Schepisi* *ph* Ian Baker *m* Jerry Goldsmith *pd* Patrizia von Brandenstein *ed* Peter Honess
☆ *Stockard Channing, Will Smith*, Donald Sutherland, Mary Beth Hurt, Bruce Davison, Heather Graham, Anthony Michael Hall, Eric Thal, Richard Masur, Ian McKellen
'This is a wonderful play about the capacity of the ever-so-slightly guilty haves to be gulled rotten by those have-nots who have yet got the wit to deceive them. But, being American, it has only the vaguest of ideas about the political implications of what it shows. Which is why the film tails off startlingly at the end, almost disappearing up its own elegant backside.' – *Derek Malcolm, Guardian*
'Always entertains, looks elegant, never mangles its source material, and gives movie audiences that rare commodity: something to think about.' – *Geoff Brown, The Times*
† The title refers to the belief that each person in the world can trace a connection by friendship or acquaintance to any other person which will involve no more than six intermediary links, that everyone is thus joined by a maximum of six degrees of separation to everyone else.

Six Hours to Live *
US 1932 78m bw
Fox
A scientist revives a diplomat for six hours so that his murderer can be traced.
Fanciful hokum set at a Geneva peace conference.
w Bradley King *story* Gordon Morris, Morton Barteaux *d* William Dieterle
☆ Warner Baxter, John Boles, Miriam Jordan, Irene Ware, George Marion
'A strong box office title which together with an aggressive sales campaign should bring picture into the money.' – *Variety*

633 Squadron *
GB 1964 94m Technicolor Panavision
UA/Mirisch (Cecil F. Ford)
In 1944 Mosquito aircraft try to collapse a cliff overhanging a munitions factory in a Norwegian fjord.
Standard war heroics with enough noise and disorder to keep most audiences hypnotized.
w James Clavell, Howard Koch *novel* Frederick E. Smith *d* Walter Grauman *ph* Ted Scaife, John Wilcox *m* *Ron Goodwin*
☆ Cliff Robertson, George Chakiris, Maria Perschy, Harry Andrews, Donald Houston, Michael Goodliffe

Six in Paris: see *Paris Vu Par...*

Six Inches Tall: see *Attack of the Puppet People*

Six Lessons from Madame La Zonga
US 1941 62m bw
Universal
A Cuban night-club proprietress causes mix-ups on a pleasure boat.
Witless vehicle for two stars popular at another studio in the Mexican Spitfire series.
w Stanley Rubin, Marion Orth, Larry Rhine, Ben Chapman *d* John Rawlins
☆ Lupe Velez, Leon Errol, William Frawley, Helen Parrish, Charles Lang, Eddie Quillan, Quinn Williams

'Their first honeymoon was so much funThey're off to have another one!'
Six of a Kind *
US 1934 69m bw
Paramount
Comic adventures of six people driving across America.
Minor comedy which doesn't come off as a whole but adequately displays the talents of its stars.
w Walter de Leon, Harry Ruskin *d* Leo McCarey *ph* Henry Sharp *m* Ralph Rainger
☆ Charles Ruggles, Mary Boland, W. C. Fields, Alison Skipworth, George Burns, Gracie Allen
'Another pleasing film ... it reminds the Englishman of Three Men in a Boat.' – *E. V. Lucas, Punch*
'Old-fashioned farce that gets a lot of laughs. Better for duals than de luxers.' – *Variety*

Six Pack
US 1982 110m DeLuxe
TCF/Lion Share (Michael Trikilis)
A loner stock car driver finds himself fathering six orphan kids.
Old-fashioned family picture built around a country singer.
w Mike Marvin, Alex Matter *d* Daniel Petrie *ph* Mario Tosi *m* Charles Fox
☆ Kenny Rogers, Diane Lane, Erin Gray, Barry Corbin

6,000 Enemies
US 1939 61m bw
MGM (Lucien Hubbard)
A district attorney is framed for a prison stretch and finds himself hated by every convict inside.
Formula support climaxing in a prison break: well enough done.
w Bertram Millhauser *d* George B. Seitz
☆ Walter Pidgeon, Rita Johnson, Paul Kelly, Nat Pendleton, Harold Huber, Grant Mitchell
'Prison meller with action aplenty.' – *Variety*

Six Weeks
US 1982 107m Metrocolor
Polygram (Peter Guber, Jon Peters)
A lady cosmetics tycoon whose ten-year-old daughter is dying of leukaemia enlists the aid of a politician to make what's left of her life a triumph.
Icky tearjerker on the lines of The Christmas Tree. *Everything is done to make it palatable, but it won't be many people's cup of bromide.*
w David Seltzer *novel* Fred Mustard Stewart *d* Tony Bill *ph* Michael D. Margulies *m* Dudley Moore *ad* Hilyard Brown *ed* Stu Linder
☆ Dudley Moore, Mary Tyler Moore, Katherine Healy, Shannon Wilcox, Bill Calvert
'Very sleek and very sickmaking.' – *Observer*
† Nick Nolte and Audrey Hepburn were originally to have starred. Sylvester Stallone also turned down the lead.

Sixteen Candles *
US 1985 95m Technicolor
Universal (Hilton A. Green)
A teenage girl, pursued by one boy and pursuing another, finds her 16th birthday being overlooked by her family.
Mildy amusing comedy of teenage life, from a 'teen's viewpoint, though reaffirming conventional family values.
wd John Hughes *ph* Bobby Byrne *m* Ira Newborn *pd* John W. Corso *ed* Edward Warschilka
☆ Molly Ringwald, Justin Henry, Michael Schoeffling, Haviland Morris, Gedde Watanabe, Anthony Michael Hall, Paul Dooley, John Cusack, Joan Cusack, Jami Gertz
'It doesn't amount to much, and it's certainly not to be confused with a work of art, but the young writer-director John Hughes has a knack for making you like the high-school-age characters better each time you hear them talk.' – *Pauline Kael, New Yorker*

Sixth Happiness *
GB 1997 98m Metrocolor
BFI/BBC/Kennedy Mellor (Tatiana Kennedy)
The autobiography of a boy born with brittle bone disease, growing older in Bombay of the 60s.
With Kanga playing a fictional version of himself from early childhood, this is a necessarily stylized, episodic account of the formative influences of a writer; the tone is lightly confessional, verging on the satirical in its portrait of people maintaining a British way of life against all odds.
w Firdaus Kanga *novel* Trying to Grow by Firdaus Kanga *d* Waris Hussein *ph* James Welland *m* Dominique Le Gendre *pd* Lynne Whiteread *ed* Laurence Méry-Clark
☆ Firdaus Kanga, Souad Faress, Khodus Wadia, Ashen Bhatti, Indira Varma, Nina Wadia, Nisha K. Nahar, Roger Hammond, Sabira Merchant
'Pic has idiosyncratic characters and situations that never come to life thanks to flat-footed execution.' – *Dennis Harvey, Variety*

'They're lifting the game to a higher level.'
The Sixth Man
US 1997 107m colour
Touchstone/Mandeville (David Hoberman)
The ghost of a dead basketball player comes to the aid of his brother's team.
Trivial comedy which for the most part seems to elevate cheating to the aim of the game; though more unforgivable than its dubious morality is its lack of genuine humour.
w Christopher Reed, Cynthia Carle *d* Randall Miller *ph* Michael Ozier *m* Marcus Miller *pd* Michael Bolton *ed* Eric Sears
☆ Marlon Wayans, Kadeem Hardison, David Paymer, Michael Michele, Kevin Dunn, Harold Sylvester, Vladimir Cuk, Travis Ford

'Dim slapstick in a cloying comedy which adds nothing new to a now moribund fornmula.' – *Sight and Sound*

The Sixth Sense ***
US 1999 107m Technicolor
Buena Vista/Hollywood/Spyglass (Frank Marshall, Kathleen Kennedy, Barry Mendel)
A child psychologist begins to treat a disturbed young boy, who can see the dead.
Spooky movie with a twist ending that changes the focus of what has gone before; it's both clever and disturbing, maintaining a haunting atmosphere that keeps its audience off-balance.
wd M. Night Shyamalan *ph* Tak Fujimoto *m* James Newton Howard *pd* Larry Fulton *ed* Andrew Mondshein *sp* make-up fx: Stan Winston Studio; visual fx: Dream Quest Images
☆ Bruce Willis (Malcolm Crowe), Toni Collette (Lynn Sear), Olivia Williams (Anna Crowe), *Haley Joel Osment* (Cole Sear), Donnie Wahlberg (Vincent Gray), Glenn Fitzgerald (Sean), Mischa Barton (Kyra Collins), Trevor Morgan (Tommy Tammisimo), Bruce Norris (Stanley Cunningham)
'Moody, low-key and semi-pretentious effort is ominous without being scary or suspenseful for most of its running time.' – *Todd McCarthy, Variety*
'A preposterous piece of work.' – *Adam Mars-Jones, Times*
† The film was a box-office success, taking more than $276m at the US box-office, and earning Willis an estimated $50m.
picture; Haley Joel Osment; Toni Collette; M. Night Shyamalan (as director); M. Night Shyamalan (as writer); Andrew Mondshein

'68
US 1988 98m colour
Entertainment/New World (Dale Djerassi, Isabel Maxwell, Steven Kovacs)
A Hungarian immigrant experiences problems with his children as he opens a restaurant in San Francisco in the mid-1960s.
The movie's background, with its emphasis on the political events of the time, overwhelms its insufficiently developed characters.
wd Steven Kovacs *ph* Daniel Lacambre *ad* Joshua Koral *ed* Cari Coughlin
☆ Eric Larsen, Robert Locke, Sandor Tecsi, Anna Dukasz, Neil Young

Sixty Glorious Years **
GB 1938 95m Technicolor
Imperator (Herbert Wilcox)
US title: *Queen of Destiny*
Scenes from the life of Queen Victoria.
A stately pageant apparently composed of material which couldn't be fitted into the previous year's black-and-white success Victoria the Great. *Fascinating, though the camerawork is not very nimble.*
w Robert Vansittart, Miles Malleson, Charles de Grandcourt *d* Herbert Wilcox *ph* Frederick A. Young
☆ Anna Neagle, Anton Walbrook, C. Aubrey Smith, Walter Rilla, Charles Carson, Felix Aylmer, Lewis Casson
'One of the most artistic and expensive films made in England.' – *Variety*
† The two films were edited together in 1943 to make a new selection called *Queen Victoria*, and in the process the original negatives were accidentally destroyed, so that both films now have to be printed from unattractive dupes.

Det Sjunde Inseglet: see *The Seventh Seal*

Skateboard
US 1977 95m Technicolor
Universal
A small-time theatrical agent in trouble builds up a professional skateboard team.
Unsatisfactory exploitation item which devotes more time to its plot than to its sport.
w Richard A. Wolf, George Gage *d* George Gage *ph* Ross Kelsay *m* Mark Snow
☆ Allen Garfield, Kathleen Lloyd, Leif Garrett, Richard Van Der Wyk

Skepp Till Indialand: see *A Ship to India*

Sketch Artist
US 1992 86m Foto-Kem
Motion Picture Corp of America (Brad Krevoy, Steve Stabler)
A police artist sketching a witness's description of a murderer finds that he has produced a drawing of his wife.
A slick little thriller, enjoyable enough on its own limited terms.
w Michael Angeli *d* Phedon Papamichael *ph* Wally Pfister *m* Mark Isham *pd* Phedon Papamichael Snr *ed* Carole Kravetz
☆ Jeff Fahey, Sean Young, Frank McRae, Tcheky Karyo, James Tolkan, Charlotte Lewis, Drew Barrymore

'Pray they never have to rescue YOU ... !'
Ski Patrol
US 1989 92m DeLuxe
Entertainment/Epic/Sarlui/Diamant/Paul Maslansky (Phillip B. Goldfine, Donald L. West)
A developer attempts to sabotage the safety record of a ski resort.
Broad farce in the style of the Police Academy *series and no funnier.*
w Steven Long Mitchell, Craig W. Van Sickle *d* Richard Correll *ph* John Stephens *m* Bruce Miller *pd* Fred Weiler *ed* Scott Wallace
☆ Roger Rose, Yvette Nipar, T. K. Carter, Leslie Jordan, Paul Feig, Sean Gregory Sullivan, Corbin Timbrook, George Lopez, Ray Walston

The Ski Raiders
US 1972 90m Technicolor Panavision
Warner (Edward L. Rissien)
aka: *Snow Job*
An alpine ski instructor devises a scheme to rob a bank.
Very medium caper thriller with a breathtaking opening sequence.
w Ken Kolb, Jeffrey Bloom *d* George Englund *ph* Gabor Pogany, Willy Bogner *m* Jacques Loussier
☆ Jean Claude Killy, Cliff Potts, Vittorio de Sica, Daniele Gaubert

Ski School
Canada 1991 88m colour
Movie Store Entertainment/Rose & Ruby (Damian Lee)
Rival groups of skiers try to sabotage each other.
Crass comedy that is mainly an excuse for ski stunts and the cavortings of skimpily clad bimbos.
w David Mitchell *d* Damian Lee *ph* Curtis Petersen, Roxanne Di Santo *m* Steven Hunter *ad* Craig MacMillan *ed* Robert Gordon
☆ Dean Cameron, Tom Breznahan, Patrick Laborteaux, Mark Thomas Miller, Darlene Vogel, Charlie Spradling

Skidoo
US 1968 98m Technicolor Panavision
Paramount/Sigma (Otto Preminger)
Active and reformed gangsters get involved with hippies and preach universal love.
Abysmal mishmash with top talent abused; clearly intended as satirical farce, but in fact one of the most woebegone movies ever made.
w Doran William Cannon *d* Otto Preminger *ph* Leon Shamroy *m* Harry Nilsson
☆ Jackie Gleason, Carol Channing, Groucho Marx, Frankie Avalon, Fred Clark, Michael Constantine, Frank Gorshin, John Phillip Law, Peter Lawford, Burgess Meredith, George Raft, Cesar Romero, Mickey Rooney
'Unspeakable.' – *Michael Billington, Illustrated London News*

Skin & Bone
US 1995 110m Foto-Kem
Film Research (Claudia Hoover, Gardner Monks)
Hopeful Hollywood actors work as male prostitutes for an escort agency, satisfying the fantasies of their clients.
A relentlessly downbeat slice of violent low life, dimly photographed.
wd Everett Lewis *ph* Fernando Arguelles *m* Geoff Harper, Mark Jan Wlodarkiewicz *ed* Everett Lewis
☆ B. Wyatt, Alan Boyce, Nicole Dillenberg, Garret Scullin, Chad Kula, Susannah Melvoin
'This 16mm production offers hardly any incentives to viewing: one must continually peer through a smog of blurry, underlit cinematography to make out the rudiments of the images, and long stretches of dialogue are rendered semi-inaudible by the traffic noise.' – *Peter Matthews, Sight and Sound*

Skin Deep
US 1989 101m Technicolor Panavision
Braveworld/Fox/Morgan Creek/BECO (Tony Adams)
A best-selling author devotes his time to booze and women.
Shallow comedy too much in love with its unprepossessing hero.
wd Blake Edwards *ph* Isidore Mankofsky *pd* Rodger Maus *ed* Robert Pergament
☆ John Ritter, Vincent Gardenia, Alyson Reed, Joel Brooks, Julianne Phillips, Chelsea Field, Peter Donat, Don Gordon, Nina Foch
'Edwards' undeniable personal obsessions are winding up as bland, uniform, nothing-in-particular films like this.' – *Kim Newman, MFB*

The Skin Game
GB 1932 85m bw
BIP (John Maxwell)
A landowner hates his self-made neighbour.
Stiff picturization of a well-known stage play.
w Alfred Hitchcock, Alma Reville *play* John Galsworthy *d* Alfred Hitchcock *ph* Jack Cox
☆ Edmund Gwenn, John Longden, Jill Esmond, C. V. France, Helen Haye, Phyllis Konstam, Frank Lawton

The Skin Game *
US 1971 102m Technicolor Panavision
Warner/Cherokee (Harry Keller)
A white and a black con man have near escapes in many a Western town.
Amusing comedy Western with good pace and a few shafts of wit.
w Peter Stone, Richard Alan Simmons *d* Paul Bogart *ph* Fred Koenekamp *m* David Shire
☆ James Garner, Lou Gossett, Susan Clark, Brenda Sykes, Ed Asner, Andrew Duggan, Henry Jones, Neva Patterson

Skin of Man, Heart of Beast *
France 1999 98m colour
ICA/Why Not/Arte France/Canal+ (Pascal Caucheteux)
original title: *Peau d'Homme, Couer De Bête*
Antagonisms arise with his two siblings when a brutal brother returns to the family home after a 15 year absence.
An unblinking portrait of dysfunctional masculinity as seen through children's eyes.
w Hélène Angel, Agnès de Sacy *d* Hélène Angel *ph* Isabelle Razavet *m* Philippe Miller, Martin Wheler *ad* Mathieu Menut *ed* Laurent Rouan, Eric Renault
☆ Serge Riaboukine (Francky), Bernard Blancan (Coco), Pascal Cervo (Alex), Maaike Jansen (Marthe), Cathy Hinderchied (Aurelie), Virginie Guinand (Christelle), Jean-Louis Richard (Tac Tac), Guilaine Londez (Annie)
'Although it leaves you with a knot in your stomach, its power is undercut by its own head-banging obviousness.' – *Stephen Holden, New York Times*

Skinheads
US 1988 93m colour
Greydon Clark
aka: *Skinheads: The Second Coming of Hate*
A gang of neo-Nazis hunt down a couple who witnessed their slaughter of a café owner and her customers.
Unpleasant low-budget shocker, badly written, hammily acted and dully directed. Despite his star billing, Connors sensibly makes a brief appearance.
w David Reskin, Greydon Clark *d* Greydon Clark *ph* Nicholas von Sternberg *m* Dan Slider *ad* Doug Abrahamson *ed* Travis Clark
☆ Chuck Connors, Barbara Bain, Brian Brophy, Jason Culp, Elizabeth Sagal

Skippy *
US 1931 88m bw
Paramount
The young son of a local health inspector makes friends in the slums.
Standard, blameless family entertainment.
w Joseph L. Mankiewicz, Norman McLeod *comic strip* Percy Crosby *d* Norman Taurog *ph* Karl Struss
☆ *Jackie Cooper*, Robert Coogan, Mitzi Green, Jackie Searl, Willard Robertson
'A great kid talker, but not for kids only ... if there is such a thing as being 100% inhuman, only then is it possible for anyone to dislike *Skippy* as entertainment.' – *Variety*
Norman Taurog
best picture; script; Jackie Cooper

Skirts Ahoy
US 1952 105m Technicolor
MGM (Joe Pasternak)
Three girls join the navy and get their men.
Musical recruiting poster, quite devoid of interest.
w Isobel Lennart *d* Sidney Lanfield *ph* William Mellor *m* Harry Warren *ch* Nick Castle *ly* Ralph Blane
☆ Esther Williams, Vivian Blaine, Joan Evans, Barry Sullivan, Keefe Brasselle, Dean Miller, Debbie Reynolds, Bobby Van, Billy Eckstine

Skrivanci Na Niti: see *Larks on a String*

'When The Skull Strikes You'll Scream!'
The Skull
GB 1965 83m Techniscope
Paramount/Amicus (Milton Subotsky)
The skull of the Marquis de Sade haunts two antiquarians.
Clodhopping horror with very visible wires.
w Milton Subotsky *story* Robert Bloch *d* Freddie Francis *ph* John Wilcox *m* Elisabeth Lutyens
☆ Peter Cushing, Christopher Lee, Patrick Wymark, Jill Bennett, Nigel Green, Michael Gough, George Coulouris

Skullduggery
US 1969 105m Technicolor Panavision
Universal (Saul David)
Archaeologists and adventurers clash on a trek in New Guinea.
Fashionable oddball adventure about the discovery of an unspoiled primitive tribe; the elements don't jell.
w Nelson Gidding *d* Gordon Douglas *ph* Robert Moreno *m* Oliver Nelson
☆ Burt Reynolds, Susan Clark, Roger C. Carmel, Paul Hubschmid, Chips Rafferty, Alexander Knox, Edward Fox, Wilfrid Hyde-White, Rhys Williams

'Getting in is easy...getting out is a killer.'
The Skulls
US 2000 107m DeLuxe
Universal/Original/Newmarket (Neal H. Moritz, John Pogue)
A working-class student at an Ivy League university joins a powerful secret society and suspects its members are guilty of murder.
Bland conspiracy drama that plays like a bad TV movie.
w John Pogue *d* Rob Cohen *ph* Shane Hurlbut *m* Randy Edelman *pd* Bob Ziembicki *ed* Peter Amundson *cos* Marie-Sylvie Deveau
☆ Joshua Jackson (Luke McNamara), Paul Walker (Caleb Mandrake), Hill Harper (Will Beckford), Leslie Bibb (Chloe), Christopher McDonald (Martin Lombard), Steve Harris (Detective Sparrow), William Peterson (Ames Levitt), Craig T. Nelson (Litten Mandrake)
'It's nightmarishly bad...Confoundingly clichéd, abrasively overdone, over-the-top on every level.' – *Michael Wilmington, Chicago Tribune*

Sky Bandits
GB 1986 93m Rank Colour
London Front Ltd (Richard Herland)
aka: *Gunbus*
Adventures of World War I flyers.
An attempt at a light-hearted Hell's Angels. *It misfires on all cylinders.*
w Thom Keyes *d* Zoran Perisic *ph* David Watkin *m* Alfie Kabilje *pd* Tony Woollard *ed* Peter Tanner
☆ Scott McGinnis, Jeff Osterhage, Ronald Lacey, Miles Anderson, Valerie Steffen, Ingrid Held, Adrian Dunbar

Sky Bride
US 1932 75m bw
Paramount
An aerial barnstormer loses his nerve after an accident.
Formula melodrama with aerobatics.
w Joseph L. Mankiewicz, Agnes Brand Leahy, Grover Jones *d* Stephen Roberts
☆ Richard Arlen, Jack Oakie, Virginia Bruce, Robert Coogan, Charles Starrett
'Lack of romantic interest is somewhat of a handicap to a conventional air plot with a suspensive finish.' – *Variety*

Sky Devils
US 1931 89m bw
Caddo/Howard Hughes
Two draft dodgers find themselves heroes of the Army Air Corps in World War I France.
Little-seen but unremarkable adventure comedy in the Flagg and Quirt tradition.
w Joseph Moncure March, Edward Sutherland *d* A. Edward Sutherland *ph* Tony Gaudio *md* Alfred Newman *ch* Busby Berkeley
☆ Spencer Tracy, William Boyd, Ann Dvorak, George Cooper, Billy Bevan, Forrester Harvey
'A hodge-podge of all the laugh war stuff ... and how they want something to laugh about right now. Psychologically and in a material way, it should do nicely.' – *Variety*

Sky Full of Moon
US 1952 73m bw
MGM (Sidney Franklin Jnr)
A rodeo cowboy wins money and a showgirl in Las Vegas.
Ambling comedy with an agreeable air of innocence.
wd Norman Foster *ph* Ray June *m* Paul Sawtell
☆ Carleton Carpenter, Jan Sterling, Keenan Wynn

Sky Giant
US 1938 80m bw
RKO (Robert Sisk)
Romance and adventure at a flying school.
Unremarkable melodrama with expected heroics.
w Lionel Houser *d* Ken Landers
☆ Richard Dix, Joan Fontaine, Chester Morris, Harry Carey, Paul Guilfoyle
'Good for the lighter weight first run houses and the upper berth of double deckers.' – *Variety*

Sky Pirates
Australia 1986 89m Colorfilm Panavision
John Lamond Motion Pictures (John Lamond, Michael Hirsh)
A pilot foils a crazed squadron leader attempting to obtain the three parts of an ancient stone that will provide him with unlimited power.
Silly and thrill-free adventure with an over-complicated narrative which amounts to no more than a feeble imitation of the Indiana Jones movies.
w John Lamond *d* Colin Eggleston *ph* Garry Wapshott *m* Brian May *pd* Kristian Fredrickson *ed* John Lamond, Michael Hirsh *sp* Dennis Nicholson
☆ John Hargreaves, Meredith Phillips, Max Phipps, Bill Hunter, Simon Chilvers, Alex Scott

'He'll try anything once ... even if it's impossible!'
Sky Riders *
US 1976 91m DeLuxe Todd-AO 35
TCF (Terry Morse Jnr)
In Athens, the family of an American businessman is kidnapped by terrorists and rescued by hang-gliders led by a soldier of fortune.
Old-fashioned actioner with new-fashioned political concern.
w Jack de Witt, Stanley Mann, Garry Michael White, Hall T. Sprague, Bill McGaw *d* Douglas Hickox *ph* Ousama Rawi *m* Lalo Schifrin
☆ James Coburn, Susannah York, Robert Culp, Charles Aznavour, Werner Pochath, Kenneth Griffith, Harry Andrews

Sky West and Crooked
GB 1965 102m Eastmancolor
Rank/John Mills (Jack Hanbury)
US title: *Gypsy Girl*
A mentally retarded girl falls in love with a gypsy.
Eccentric rural melodrama with echoes of Cold Comfort Farm *and* Les Jeux Interdits. *Interesting, but scarcely a runaway success.*
w Mary Hayley Bell, John Prebble *d* John Mills *ph* Arthur Ibbetson *m* Malcolm Arnold
☆ Hayley Mills, Ian McShane, Laurence Naismith, *Geoffrey Bayldon*, Annette Crosbie, Norman Bird
'Behind the overwhelming feyness of it all lurk assumptions which in cold blood look almost sinister.' – *MFB*

Skyjacked *
US 1972 101m Metrocolor Panavision
MGM/Walter Seltzer
A Boeing 707 on a flight from Los Angeles to Minneapolis is forced by a mad bomber to fly to Moscow.
Shamelessly hackneyed aeroplane adventure with quite enjoyable elements.
w Stanley R. Greenberg *novel Hijacked* by David Harper *d* John Guillermin *ph* Harry Stradling Jnr *m* Perry Botkin Jnr
☆ Charlton Heston, Yvette Mimieux, James Brolin, Claude Akins, Jeanne Crain, Rosey Grier, Walter Pidgeon, Leslie Uggams

Skylark
US 1941 94m bw
Paramount (Mark Sandrich)
A wife decides on her fifth anniversary that she is tired of being secondary to her husband's career, and needs a fling.
Formula matrimonial comedy; plenty of talent but no sparkle.
w Z. Myers *play* Samson Raphaelson *d* Mark Sandrich *ph* Charles Lang *m* Victor Young
☆ Claudette Colbert, Ray Milland, Brian Aherne, Binnie Barnes, Walter Abel, Grant Mitchell, Mona Barrie, Ernest Cossart

The Sky's the Limit
GB 1937 79m bw
Jack Buchanan
A sacked aircraft designer suddenly finds himself in demand.
Amiable star musical.
w Jack Buchanan, Douglas Furber *d* Lee Garmes and Jack Buchanan
☆ Jack Buchanan, Mara Loseff, William Kendall, David Hutcheson, H. F. Maltby, Athene Seyler, Sara Allgood

The Sky's the Limit *
US 1943 89m bw
RKO (David Hempstead)
A flyer on leave meets and falls for a news photographer.
Thin musical with incidental compensations.
w Frank Fenton, Lynn Root *d* Edward H. Griffith *ph* Russell Metty *m* Leigh Harline *md* Leo F. Forbstein
☆ *Fred Astaire*, Joan Leslie, *Robert Benchley*, Robert Ryan, Elizabeth Patterson
† Joan Leslie's singing was dubbed by Sally Sweetland.
Leigh Harline; song 'My Shining Hour' (*m* Harold Arlen, *ly* Johnny Mercer)

Skyscraper Souls
US 1932 100m bw
MGM
In an office building, several personal dilemmas interlock.
Portmanteau drama in the Grand Hotel *mould, and quite comparable.*
w C. G. Sullivan, Elmer Harris *book* Faith Baldwin *d* Edgar Selwyn
☆ Warren William, Maureen O'Sullivan, Verree Teasdale, Gregory Ratoff, Jean Hersholt, Norman Foster, Anita Page, George Barbier, Wallace Ford, Hedda Hopper
'The usual portentous jumble about nothing in particular.' – *James Agate*

Slab Boys *
GB 1997 97m Technicolor
Channel 4/Skreba/Wanderlust (Simon Relph, Lauren Lowenthal)
In 50s Scotland, three working-class teenagers mixing paints in a carpet factory dream of a better life.
An interesting attempt to find an appropriate visual style for two plays that worked better on the stage; the power and passion are too often dissipated and the result has the quaintness of a period piece.
wd John Byrne *plays The Slab Boys and Cuttin' a Rug by John Byrne* *ph* Seamus McGarvey *m* Jack Bruce *pd* Luana Hanson *ed* John Macdonnell
☆ Robin Lang, Duncan Ross, Russell Barr, Bill Gardiner, Louise Berry, Anna Massey, Tom Watson, Moray Hunter, David O'Hara
'A whole lot of energy and visual design going nowhere special.' – *Variety*

Slacker **
US 1991 97m colour
Feature/Detour (Richard Linklater)
In Austin, Texas, young people wandering the streets confide to the camera their odd beliefs and attitudes, including the avoidance of careers.
Leisurely, lackadaisical feature of oddballs that exerts a certain bemused fascination.
wd Richard Linklater *ph* Lee Daniel *m* Buffalo Gals, Triangle Mallet Apron, The Texas Instruments *ad* Debbie Pastor *ed* Scott Rhodes
☆ Richard Linklater, Rudy Basquez, Jean Caffeine, Jan Hockey, Stephan Hockey, Mark James
'A film of quirky, unpredictable and oddly poetic charm.' – *Philip Kemp, Sight and Sound*
'One of the freshest independent films to come along in some time, but because of its non-narrative, non-characterization approach, film won't be to all tastes.' – *Variety*

'Higher Education Just Hit A New Low.'
Slackers
US 2002 87m Technicolor
Momentum/Screen Gems/Alliance Atlantis (Neal H. Moritz, Erik Feig)
An unlovely youth blackmails three friends, who are cheating their way through exams, to get him a date with the school's most popular girl.
Crude, anything goes comedy with some moments to embarrass the audience, if not the cast; it is best to look away when Mamie Van Doren is on-screen.
w David H. Steinberg *d* Dewey Nicks *ph* James Bagdonas *m* Joey Altruda, Venus Brown & Printz Board, Justin Stanley *pd* William Arnold *ed* Tara Timpone
☆ Devon Sawa (Dave), Jason Schwartzman (Ethan), James King (Angela), Jason Segel (Sam), Michael Maronna (Jeff), Mamie Van Doren (Mrs Van Graaf), Joe Flaherty (Mr Leonard), Leigh Taylor Young (Valerie Patton), Cameron Diaz (Movie Star)
'A dirty movie. Not a sexy, erotic, steamy or even smutty movie, but a just plain dirty movie. It made me feel unclean' – *Roger Ebert, Chicago Sun-Times*
'The movie, which suffers from a severe case of attention deficit disorder, is so lazy and slipshod it confuses the mere flashing of kinky soft-core imagery with naughty fun.' – *Stephen Holden, New York Times*
'I laughed until I was thoroughly ashamed of myself.' – *Joe Leydon, San Francisco Examiner*

Slade: see *Jack Slade*

Slam *
US 1998 100m colour
Trimark/Off Line (Henri Kessler, Marc Levin, Richard Stratton)
Thrown into prison, a black poet uses his art to persuade others that violence solves nothing.
Earnest drama, in a semi-documentary style, on the power of rap to change macho attitudes.
w Richard Stratton, Marc Levin, Sonja Sohn, Saul Williams *d* Marc Levin *ph* Marc Benjamin *ed* Emir Luis
☆ Saul Williams, Sonja Sohn, Bonz Malone
'Emotionally powerful and technically innovative.' – *Variety*

Slam Dunk Ernest
US 1995 92m colour
Emshell (George Horie, Stacy Williams)
A dimwitted handyman becomes a basketball wizard when he puts on some magic shoes.
Dimwitted, heavy-handed slapstick comedy of little appeal.
w John R. Cherry III, Daniel Butler *d* John Cherry *ph* David Geddes *m* Mark Adler *pd* Chris August *ed* Craig Bassett, Chris Ellis
☆ Jim Varney, Cylk Cozart, Miguel A. Nunez Jnr, Lester Barrie, Colin Lawrence, Richard Leacock, Jay Brazeau, Kareem Abdul-Jabbar
† The film was released direct to video.

'An erotic thriller. It's *not* about dancing'
Slamdance
US 1987 99m colour
Zenith Productions/Island Pictures (Rupert Harvey, Barry Opper)
A newspaper cartoonist is framed for a murder by a corrupt cop.
Silly, convoluted mish-mash of a thriller.
w Don Opper *d* Wayne Wang *ph* Amie Mokri *m* Mitchell Froom *pd* Eugenio Zanetti *ed* Lee Percy
☆ Tom Hulce, Mary Elizabeth Mastrantonio, Virginia Madsen, Millie Perkins, Don Opper, Adam Ant, John Doe, Robert Beltran, Judith Barsi, Harry Dean Stanton

Slander
US 1956 81m bw
MGM (Armand Deutsch)
Revelations about a film star in a scandal magazine lead to blackmail and murder.
Unlikely melodrama, routinely assembled, based on the Confidential Magazine lawsuits.
w Jerome Weidman *d* Roy Rowland *ph* Harold J. Marzerati *m* Jeff Alexander
☆ Van Johnson, Ann Blyth, Steve Cochran, *Marjorie Rambeau*, Harold J. Stone

'No French People Were Harmed In The Making Of This Film.'
Slap Her, She's French
Germany/US 2001 92m
Winchester/Constantin/Bandeira/Film 2 (Beau Flynn, Jonathan King, Matthias Emcke)
At a small Texan high school, a power struggle erupts between the school's most popular girl and a French exchange student.
Lamentable teen comedy, bereft of laughs and clinging to national stereotypes in its vain hope to amuse.
w Lamar Damon, Robert Lee King *d* Melanie Mayron *ph* Charles Minsky *m* David Michael Frank *pd* Anne Stuhler, Roswell Hamrick *ed* Marshall Harvey *cos* Julia Caston
☆ Piper Perabo (Genevieve LePlouff), Jane McGregor (Starla Grady), Trent Ford (Ed Mitchell), Michael McKean (Monsieur Duke), Julie White (Bootsie Grady), Brandon Smith (Arnie Grady), Jesse James (Randolph Grady)
'Yet one more celebration of dumbness, turn-of-the-century-style, and rarely laugh-out-loud.' – *Derek Elley, Variety*
† The film's original director Evan Dunsky left after a week's shooting.

Slap Shot *
US 1977 124m Technicolor
Universal/Robert J. Wunsch, Stephen Friedman
The wily player-coach of a fading ice hockey team finds ways, including dirty play, of keeping it going.
Violent, foul-mouthed comedy which works as it goes but leaves a bad taste in the mouth.
w Nancy Dowd *d* George Roy Hill *ph* Victor Kemper, Wallace Worsley *md* Elmer Bernstein
☆ Paul Newman, Michael Ontkean, Lindsay Crouse, Jennifer Warren, Strother Martin
'Fast, noisy, profane ... gets you laughing, all right, but you don't necessarily enjoy yourself.' – *New Yorker*
'Both indulgent and moralizing, the self-consciously racy script ends up looking merely opportunistic.' – *Time Out*

Slattery's Hurricane
US 1949 87m bw
TCF (William Perlberg)
Loves of a storm-spotting pilot with the US Weather Bureau in Florida.
Forgettable programmer with good storm sequences.
w Herman Wouk, Richard Murphy *novel* Herman Wouk *d* André de Toth *ph* Charles G. Clarke *m* Cyril Mockridge
☆ Richard Widmark, Linda Darnell, Veronica Lake, John Russell, Gary Merrill, Walter Kingsford

Slaughter
US 1972 90m DeLuxe Todd-AO 35
AIP/Slaughter United (Monroe Sachson)
A black Vietnam veteran hunts down the underworld syndicate which killed his mother and father.
Hectic crime yarn with a pitilessly violent hero and not enough style to relieve the unappetizing monotony.
w Mark Hanna, Don Williams *d* Jack Starrett *ph* Rosanio Solano *m* Luchi de Jesus
☆ Jim Brown, Rip Torn, Don Gordon, Cameron Mitchell
'The cast perform their trigger-happy tasks with all the passionate conviction of a team of well-oiled robots.' – *Jan Dawson*

Slaughter on Tenth Avenue
US 1957 103m bw
U-I (Albert Zugsmith)
The New York DA's office investigates union murders on the docks.
Uninteresting imitation of On the Waterfront.
w Lawrence Roman *novel The Man Who Rocked the Boat* by William J. Keating, Richard Carter *d* Arnold Laven *ph* Fred Jackman *m* Richard Rodgers
☆ Richard Egan, Jan Sterling, Dan Duryea, Julie Adams, Walter Matthau, Charles McGraw, Sam Levene, Mickey Shaughnessy, Harry Bellaver

Slaughter Trail
US 1951 78m Cinecolor
RKO (Irving Allen)
Three outlaws cause trouble between white man and Indian.
Rough-hewn Western strung together by verses of a ballad.
w Sid Kuller *d* Irving Allen *ph* Jack Greenhalgh *ad* George Van Marter *ed* Fred Allen
☆ Brian Donlevy, Gig Young, Virginia Grey, Andy Devine, Robert Hutton

Slaughterhouse Five *
US 1972 104m Technicolor
Universal/Vanadas (Paul Monash)
A suburban optometrist has nightmare space/time fantasies involving Nazi POW camps and a strange futuristic planet.
Interesting but infuriating anti-war fantasy for intellectuals.
w Stephen Geller *novel* Kurt Vonnegut Jnr *d* George Roy Hill *ph* Miroslav Ondricek *m* J. S. Bach, performed by Glen Gould *pd Henry Bumstead*
☆ Michael Sacks, Ron Leibman, Eugène Roche, Sharon Gans, Valerie Perrine, Sorrell Booke, John Dehner
'A lot of good makings in this picture; but very little is made.' – *Stanley Kauffmann*

Slaughter's Big Rip-Off
US 1973 93m Movielab Todd-AO 35
AIP (Monroe Sachson)
Still on the run from gangsters who have killed his best friend, Slaughter violently disposes of a number of adversaries.
More routine black violence, a rampage of senseless brutality against sunny Los Angeles backgrounds.
w Charles Johnson *d* Gordon Douglas *ph* Charles Wheeler *m* James Brown, Fred Wesley
☆ Jim Brown, Ed MacMahon, Brock Peters, Don Stroud

Slave Girl
US 1947 79m Technicolor
U-I (Michael Fessier, Ernest Pagano)
In the early 1800s, a diplomat is sent to Tripoli to ransom sailors held by the power-mad potentate.
Criticism would be superfluous; when the film was finished it was obviously so bad that executives ordered the addition of a talking camel and other Hellzapoppin*-type jokes in order to turn it into a comedy.*
w Michael Fessier, Ernest Pagano *d* Charles Lamont *ph* George Robinson, W. Howard Greene *m* Milton Rosen
☆ George Brent, Yvonne de Carlo, Albert Dekker, Broderick Crawford, Lois Collier, Andy Devine, Carl Esmond, Arthur Treacher

Slave Girls
GB 1968 74m Technicolor Cinemascope
Hammer (Aida Young)
US title: *Prehistoric Women*
A hunter seeking white rhinoceros finds himself in a lost valley ruled by a tribe of women.
Feebly preposterous comic strip farrago without the saving grace of humour.
w Henry Younger (Michael Carreras) *d* Michael Carreras *ph* Michael Reed *m* Carlo Martelli *ad* Robert Jones *ed* Jim Needs, Roy Hyde
☆ Michael Latimer, Martine Beswick, Edina Ronay, Carol White

'The Highest Love ... The Lowest Men The Seven Seas Have Ever Known.'
Slave Ship **
US 1937 100m bw
TCF (Darryl F. Zanuck)
An American slave captain decides to become respectable but finds a mutiny on his hands.
Well-made adventure movie in the old tradition, a model of studio production.
w Sam Hellman, Lamar Trotti, Gladys Lehman *novel* George S. King *story William Faulkner* *d* Tay Garnett *ph* Ernest Palmer *m* Alfred Newman
☆ Wallace Beery, Warner Baxter, Elizabeth Allen, Mickey Rooney, George Sanders, Jane Darwell, Joseph Schildkraut, Arthur Hohl, Minna Gombell, Billy Bevan, Francis Ford, Edwin Maxwell, J. Farrell MacDonald, Paul Hurst, Holmes Herbert
'Plenty of action and de luxe scenic trimmings ... good box office blood and thunder.' – *Variety*

Slave Women of Corinth: see *Aphrodite, Goddess of Love*

Slaves
US 1969 110m Eastmancolor
Slaves Company/Theatre Guild/Walter Reade (Philip Langner)
In 1850 Kentucky a slave stands up for his rights and plans escape.
Well-meaning but muddled and old-fashioned melodrama, hardly well enough done to raise comparison with Gone with the Wind.
wd Herbert J. Biberman *ph* Joseph Brun *m* Bobby Scott
☆ Stephen Boyd, Ossie Davis, Dionne Warwick, Shepperd Strudwick, Nancy Coleman, David Huddleston, Gale Sondergaard

Slaves of New York
US 1989 125m Technicolor
Columbia TriStar/Hendler-Merchant Ivory/Ismail Merchant, Gary Hendler
Trendy young artists and fashion designers in New York fall in and out of love.
Inconsequential movie that is unable to get to grips with its insubstantial characters.
w Tama Janowitz *stories* Tama Janowitz *d* James Ivory *ph* Tony Pierce-Roberts *m* Richard Robbins *pd* David Gropman *ed* Katherine Wenning
☆ Bernadette Peters, Madeleine Potter, Adam Coleman Howard, Nick Corri, Charles McCaughan, Jonas Abry, Tama Janowitz

Slayground
GB 1983 89m Technicolor
EMI/Jennie and Co. (John Dark, Gower Frost)
A rich man hires an assassin to track down a criminal who accidentally killed his daughter.
One of those tedious and violent films in which the criminal wins out; slickness seems to make it worse.
w Trevor Preston *novel* Richard Stark *d* Terry Bedford *ph* Stephen Smith, Herb Wagreich *m* Colin Towns *pd* Keith Wilson
☆ Peter Coyote, Mel Smith, Billie Whitelaw, Philip Sayer, Bill Luhrs
'A disappointingly lame front runner for the new EMI stable.' – *Philip Strick, MFB*

Sleep My Love *
US 1948 96m bw
UA/Mary Pickford (Charles 'Buddy' Rogers, Ralph Cohn)
A man plots to murder his wife, but is foiled.
Thin suspenser, rather splendidly photographed in the expressionist manner.
w St Clair McKelway, Leo Rosten *novel* Leo Rosten *d Douglas Sirk ph Joseph Valentine* *m* Rudy Schrager
☆ Claudette Colbert, Don Ameche, Robert Cummings, Rita Johnson, George Coulouris, Hazel Brooks, Keye Luke, Raymond Burr

'After all, what are friends for?'
Sleep with Me *
US 1994 94m Foto-Kem
First Independent/August/Paribas/Revolution (Michael Steinberg, Roger Hedden, Eric Stoltz)
A couple who have been living together decide to get married; then the wife has a brief affair with their best friend.
An episodic film about self-obsessed young people in social settings, with each section written by a different hand; it offers little that is fresh, apart from Tarantino's monologue on the gay subtext of Top Gun, *but there are moments of nice observation along the way.*
w Duane Dell'Amico, Roger Hedden, Neal Jimenez, Joe Keenan, Rory Kelly, Michael Steinberg *d* Rory Kelly *ph* Andrzej Sekula *m* David Lawrence *pd* Randy Eriksen *ed* David Moritz
☆ Eric Stoltz, Meg Tilly, Craig Sheffer, Todd Field, Dean Cameron, Susan Traylor, Thomas Gibson, Adrienne Shelly, Quentin Tarantino
'A comedy so laid back that at times it faces atrophy.' – *Sheila Johnston, Independent*

'A love story about two people who hate each other!'
Sleeper **
US 1973 88m DeLuxe
UA/Jack Rollins, Charles Joffe (Jack Grossberg)
A health food store owner is deep frozen after an operation and wakes two hundred years in the future.
Predictable star vehicle with an agreeable string of bright gags.
w Woody Allen, *Marshall Brickman* *d* Woody Allen *ph* David M. Walsh *m* Woody Allen *pd* Dale Hennesy
☆ Woody Allen, Diane Keaton, John Beck, Mary Gregory
'Verbal and visual gags rain down like hailstones.' – *Michael Billington, Illustrated London News*

The Sleepers: see *Little Nikita*

'Four friends made a mistake that changed their lives forever.'
Sleepers
US 1996 147m Technicolor
Polygram/Warner/Propaganda/Baltimore (Barry Levinson, Steve Golin)
With the aid of a journalist and a lawyer, two petty gangsters get away with the murder of a sadistic guard who abused the four of them when they were teenagers in a reform home.
Allegedly based on a true incident, this nevertheless has the insubstantiality of pulp fiction, as just another example of the modern cycle of unexceptional, amoral vigilante thrillers.
wd Barry Levinson *book* Lorenzo Carcaterra *ph* Michael Ballhaus *m* John Williams *pd* Kristi Zea *ed* Stu Linder
☆ Kevin Bacon, Robert DeNiro, Dustin Hoffman, Bruno Kirby, Jason Patric, Brad Pitt, Brad Renfro, Ron Eldard, Billy Crudup, Vittorio Gassman, Minnie Driver
'Stylish, lurid, yet insubstantial film.' – *Sight and Sound*
♫ John Williams

The Sleeping Beauty *
US 1959 75m Technirama 70
Walt Disney (Ken Peterson)
A wicked queen casts a spell on a beautiful princess and puts her to sleep.
Rather stodgy, unwisely Cinemascoped feature cartoon of the old legend; very fashionable and detailed, but somehow lifeless.
d Clyde Geronimi *md* George Bruns *pd* Don da Gradi, Ken Anderson
☆ Featuring the voices of Mary Costa, Bill Shirley, Eleanor Audley, Verna Felton, Barbara Jo Allen, Barbara Luddy
'The drawings on the whole suggest a combination of *New Yorker*, comic horror strip and chocolate box – the special Disney chocolate box assortment with hard centres and soft centres.' – *C. A. Lejeune*
♫ George Bruns

Sleeping Car
GB 1933 82m bw
Gaumont (Michael Balcon)
A woman on the run pretends to marry a sleeping car attendant, then finds they really are married.
Artificial comedy with interesting cast from London stage.
w Franz Schultz *d* Anatole Litvak *ph* Günther Krampf, Glen MacWilliams
☆ Madeleine Carroll, Ivor Novello, Laddie Cliff, Kay Hammond, Claud Allister, Stanley Holloway
'A gay comedy, with a wealth of laughter.' – *Sunday Pictorial*
'An unhappy attempt at farce.' – *Madeleine Carroll*

The Sleeping Car Murders *
France 1965 95m bw Cinemascope
PECF (Julien Derode)
original title: *Compartiment Tueurs*
When the overnight express from Marseilles reaches Paris, a girl is found dead in the sleeping car.
Rather long-winded whodunnit with an unlikely solution: a good pace helps, however, as do skilful borrowings from American police films of the forties.
wd Costa-Gavras *novel* Sebastien Japrisot *ph* Jean Tournier *m* Michel Magne
☆ Yves Montand, Simone Signoret, Pierre Mondy, Catherine Allégret, Jacques Pérrin, Jean-Louis Trintignant, Michel Piccoli

Sleeping Car to Trieste *
GB 1948 95m bw
GFD/Two Cities (George H. Brown)
Spy melodrama, a slow-starting but generally entertaining remake of *Rome Express* (qv).
w Allan Mackinnon *d* John Paddy Carstairs *ph* Jack Hildyard *m* Benjamin Frankel
☆ *Albert Lieven*, Jean Kent, David Tomlinson, David Hutcheson, Rona Anderson, Paul Dupuis, Finlay Currie, *Alan Wheatley*, Derrick de Marney, Grégoire Aslan, Hugh Burden

The Sleeping Cardinal
GB 1931 84m bw
Twickenham (Julius Hagen)
Sherlock Holmes exposes a smuggling ring.
Slow-paced but interesting adaptation, vaguely based on The Empty House.
w Cyril Twyford, H. Fowler Mear *stories* Sir Arthur Conan Doyle *d* Leslie Hiscott
☆ Arthur Wontner, Ian Fleming, Norman McKinnel, Jane Welsh, Louis Goodrich

The Sleeping City **
US 1950 85m bw
U-I (Leonard Goldstein)
A policeman disguises himself as a medical student to learn more about a murder in a general hospital.
A location melodrama of modest excellence.
w Jo Eisinger d George Sherman ph William Miller *m* Frank Skinner
☆ Richard Conte, Richard Taber, Coleen Gray, John Alexander, Peggy Dow, Alex Nicol

The Sleeping Tiger
GB 1954 89m bw
Anglo-Amalgamated/Insignia (Victor Hanbury)
A psychiatrist overpowers a criminal and takes him home as a guinea pig; the criminal then falls in love with the psychiatrist's wife.
Turgid and unconvincing melodrama, a thoroughgoing bore.
w Derek Frye (Harold Buchman, Carl Foreman) *novel* Maurice Moiseiwitsch *d* Joseph Losey *ph* Harry Waxman *m* Malcolm Arnold
☆ Dirk Bogarde, Alexander Knox, Alexis Smith, Hugh Griffith, Maxine Audley, Glyn Houston, Billie Whitelaw
'There is a splendour about this film, which has one of the most absurdly extravagant plots on record, and never flinches from it.' – *Gavin Lambert*
† The script was written under a pseudonym because of the blacklist.

'She changed her name. Her looks. Her life. All to escape the most dangerous man she's ever met. Her husband.'

Sleeping with the Enemy
US 1990 99m DeLuxe
TCF (Leonard Goldberg)

In order to leave her violent husband, a wife fakes her own death and takes a new identity.
Uninvolving thriller that is never original enough to overcome its predictability.
w Ronald Bass novel Nancy Price d Joseph Ruben ph John W. Lindley m Jerry Goldsmith pd Doug Kraner ed George Bowers
☆ Julia Roberts, Patrick Bergin, Kevin Anderson, Elizabeth Lawrence, Kyle Secor, Claudette Nevins, Tony Abatemarco, Marita Geraghty, Harley Venton
'A glossy combination of secondhand showing-off-Julia scenes from Pretty Woman and secondhand scares from The Stepfather.' – *Pauline Kael, New Yorker*

'What if someone you never met, someone you never saw, someone you never knew was the only someone for you?'

Sleepless in Seattle *
US 1993 105m Technicolor
TriStar (Gary Foster)

After his mother dies, an eight-year-old boy confides to a radio phone-in that he wants to find someone for his father to marry; the call is heard by an intrigued journalist, worried about her engagement to a dull man.
Enjoyable romantic comedy, although its overall tone is excessively sweet.
w Nora Ephron, David S. Ward, Jeff Arch d *Nora Ephron* ph Sven Nykvist m Marc Shaiman pd Jeffrey Townsend ed Robert Reitano
☆ *Tom Hanks, Meg Ryan*, Ross Malinger, Rita Wilson, Victor Garber, Tom Riis Farrell, Carey Lowell, Bill Pullman
'This shamelessly romantic comedy ... delivers ample warmth and some explosively funny moments.' – *Variety*
Nora Ephron, David S. Ward, Jeff Arch; song 'A Wink and a Smile' (m Marc Shaiman, ly Ramsey McLean)

Sleepwalkers
US 1992 89m Technicolor
Columbia TriStar/Columbia/ION (Mark Victor, Michael Grais, Nabeel Zahid)

A mother and son, shape-shifting monsters, move into a new community.
Ridiculous horror, lacking suspense, sense or the slightest ability to shock or scare.
w Stephen King d Mick Garris ph Rodney Charters m Nicholas Pike pd John DeCuir Jnr ed O. Nicholas Brown sp Apogee Productions
☆ Brian Krause, Mädchen Amick, Alice Krige, Jim Haynie, Cindy Pickett, Ron Perlman, Lyman Ward, Dan Martin, John Landis, Joe Dante, Stephen King, Clive Barker, Tobe Hooper
'Piffle.' – *Sheila Johnston, Independent*
'This technically proficient, surprisingly gory but utterly nonsensical movie is billed as the first screenplay written by horror novelist Stephen King expressly for the screen. Unfortunately, this hardly rates as a recommendation.' – *Nigel Floyd, Sight and Sound*

'Heads will roll.'

Sleepy Hollow *
US 1999 105m DeLuxe
Paramount/Mandalay/American Zoetrope (Scott Rudin, Adam Schroeder)

An effete New York constable goes to a village to solve a series of beheadings by a mysterious figure.
This is yet another 'B' movie with pretensions, a big-budget Hammer-styled horror. It succeeds only on the level of design and atmosphere; the narrative creaks, and the performances tend to eccentricity for no good purpose.
w Andrew Kevin Walker, Kevin Yagher d Tim Burton ph *Emmanuel Lubezki* m Danny Elfman pd *Rick Heinrichs* ed Chris Lebenzon sp Industrial Light & Magic; Kevin Yagher cos *Colleen Atwood*
☆ Johnny Depp (Ichabod Crane), Christina Ricci (Katrina Van Tassel), Miranda Richardson (Lady Van Tassel/Crone), Michael Gambon (Baltus Van Tassel), Caspar Van Dien (Brom Van Brunt), Jeffrey Jones (Rev Steenwyck), Christopher Lee (Burgomaster), Richard Griffiths (Magistrate Philipse), Ian McDiarmid (Doctor Lancaster), Michael Gough (Notary Hardenbrook), Christopher Walken, Lisa Marie, Steven Waddington (Killian), Claire Skinner (Beth Killian), Alun Armstrong (High Constable)
'As beautifully crafted a film as anyone could ever hope to see.' – *Todd McCarthy, Variety*
'A film with no theatrical core and no integrity in the writing, acting or storytelling. The jokes aren't funny. The tone is uncertain. It invokes nothing real or fantastic.' – *Mick LaSalle, San Francisco Chronicle*
Rick Heinrichs
Emmanuel Lubezki; Colleen Atwood
Rick Heinrichs, Colleen Atwood

The Slender Thread *
US 1965 98m bw
Paramount/Athene (Stephen Alexander)

A volunteer social worker tries to prevent a woman from committing suicide while police track her down from their phone conversations.
Acceptable star melodrama, curiously artificially styled.
w Stirling Silliphant d *Sydney Pollack* ph Loyal Griggs m Quincy Jones
☆ *Anne Bancroft, Sidney Poitier*, Steven Hill, Telly Savalas

'Think of the crime ... then go one step further ... If it was murder, where's the body? If it was for a woman, which woman? If it's only a game, why the blood?'

Sleuth **
GB 1972 139m colour
Palomar (Morton Gottlieb)

A successful thriller writer invents a murder plot which rebounds on himself.
Well-acted version of a highly successful piece of stage trickery; despite hard work all round it seems much less clever and arresting on the screen, and the tricks do show.
w *Anthony Shaffer* play Anthony Shaffer d Joseph L. Mankiewicz ph Oswald Morris m John Addison
☆ *Laurence Olivier, Michael Caine*
Joseph L. Mankiewicz; John Addison; Laurence Olivier; Michael Caine

Sliding Doors *
GB/US 1998 108m Technicolor
Paramount/Miramax (Sydney Pollack, Philippa Braithwaite, William Horberg)

Two possible lives unfold for a public relations executive: in one, she misses the train that would have taken her home in time to discover her boyfriend in their bed with his former girlfriend; in the other, she catches the train.
A formally clever, occasionally charming romance; the problem is that instead of one not very interesting existence, we witness two.
wd Peter Howitt ph Remi Adfarasin m David Hirschfelder pd Maria Djurokovic ed John Smith
☆ Gwyneth Paltrow, John Hannah, John Lynch, Jeanne Tripplehorn, Zara Turner, Douglas McFerran, Paul Brightwell, Nina Young, Virginia McKenna
'Pulls off the rare fusion of a clever, almost philosophical conceit with a comedy-drama which packs a satisfying emotional punch.' – *Demetrious Matheou, Premiere*
'You're watching two things at the same time: a great idea for a film, and the actual film unfolding in front of you. Who knows? In another life, it could have been great.' – *Tom Shone, Sunday Times*

A Slight Case of Murder ***
US 1938 85m bw
Warner (Sam Bischoff)
When a beer baron tries to go legitimate his colleagues attempt to kill him, but end up shooting each other.
Amusing black farce, remade to less effect as Stop, You're Killing Me *(qv).*
w Earl Baldwin, Joseph Schrank play Damon Runyon, Howard Lindsay d *Lloyd Bacon* ph Sid Hickox m M. K. Jerome, Jack Scholl
☆ *Edward G. Robinson*, Jane Bryan, Willard Parker, *Ruth Donnelly*, Allen Jenkins, John Litel, Harold Huber, Edward Brophy, Bobby Jordan
'Nothing funnier has been produced by Hollywood for a long time ... a mirthful and hilarious whimsy.' – *Variety*
'The complications crazily mount, sentiment never raises its ugly head, a long nose is made at violence and death.' – *Graham Greene*

Slightly French
US 1948 81m bw
Columbia (Irving Starr)
A film director in trouble passes off a Bowery-born carnival dancer as an exotic French star.
Rather tedious comedy which lively performances can't sustain.
w Karen de Wolf d Douglas Sirk m George Duning
☆ Dorothy Lamour, Don Ameche, Janis Carter, Jeanne Manet, Willard Parker

'Her heart belongs to daddy, and she calls everybody daddy!'

Slightly Honorable
US 1940 85m bw
UA/Walter Wanger (Tay Garnett)

Lawyer partners set out to break a crime syndicate.
Fair crime thriller which can't decide whether it's comedy or drama.
w John Hunter Lay, Robert Tallman, Ken Englund novel *Send Another Coffin* by F. G. Presnell d Tay Garnett ph Merritt Gerstad m Werner Janssen
☆ Pat O'Brien, Broderick Crawford, Edward Arnold, Eve Arden, Claire Dodd, Ruth Terry, Bernard Nedell, Alan Dinehart, Douglass Dumbrille, Ernest Truex
'The story skips along without deftness between serious drama and comedy, and winds up in the aggregate as a whatisit.' – *Variety*

Slightly Scarlet
US 1930 72m bw
Paramount
Two jewel thieves outwit a malicious mastermind.
Somewhat effete comedy-drama in a long bygone style.
w Howard Estabrook, Joseph L. Mankiewicz, Percy Heath d Louis Gasnier, Edwin H. Knopf
☆ Clive Brook, Evelyn Brent, Paul Lukas, Eugene Pallette, Helen Ware, Virginia Bruce, Henry Wadsworth, Claud Allister
'Fair general programme feature.' – *Variety*

Slightly Scarlet
US 1956 92m Technicolor Superscope (RKO)

The mayor's secretary loves the leader of a criminal gang.
Competent but uninteresting crime romance.
w Robert Blees novel James A. Cain d Allan Dwan ph John Alton m Louis Forbes
☆ Arlene Dahl, John Payne, Rhonda Fleming, Kent Taylor, Ted de Corsia
'So complicated that it is difficult to sort out which characters are supposed to be sympathetic.' – *MFB*

Slim
US 1937 85m bw
Warner
Electric linesmen argue about their work and their women.
A reworking of Tiger Shark *which itself later became* Manpower*; competent action stuff.*
w William Wister Haines d Ray Enright
☆ Pat O'Brien, Margaret Lindsay, Henry Fonda, Stuart Erwin, J. Farrell MacDonald, Jane Wyman
'A comedy drama which will do all right without setting off fireworks.' – *Variety*

Slim Carter
US 1957 82m Eastmancolor
Universal-International
A playboy is signed up by a Hollywood studio and required to change his image.
Curious sentimental comedy which might have worked with stronger casting.
w Montgomery Pittman d Richard H. Bartlett ph Ellis Carter m Herman Stein
☆ Jock Mahoney, Julie Adams, Tim Hovey, William Hopper, Ben Johnson, Barbara Hale

Sling Blade **
US 1996 136m CFI color
Miramax/Shooting Gallery (Brandon Rosser, David L. Bushell)

A simple-minded man goes to live with a widow and her unhappy son in a small Southern town, after leaving the mental hospital where he was incarcerated for 25 years for murdering his mother and her lover.
Slow-paced tragedy, notable for some fine, detailed performances, and marred by its remorseless predictability.
wd Billy Bob Thornton ph Barry Markowitz m Daniel Lanois pd Clark Hunter ed Hughes Winborne
☆ Billy Bob Thornton, Dwight Yoakam, J. T. Walsh, John Ritter, Lucas Black, Natalie Canderday, Robert Duvall, Jim Jarmusch
† The film began as a short, *Some Call It a Sling Blade*, which was directed by George Hickenlooper.
Billy Bob Thornton (as writer)
Billy Bob Thornton (as actor)

'A Tale Of Exploration, Imagination, And Inspiration.'

The Slingshot **
Sweden 1993 101m colour
Columbia TriStar/AB/SVT Kanal/Nordisk/SFI (Waldemar Bergendahl)

original title: *Kådisbellan*
A Jewish boy, the son of a crippled socialist, grows up in Stockholm in the 1920s, trying to make money by selling slingshots made from scrap metal and condoms, which his mother sells under the counter in her tobacconist shop, and taking revenge on his sadistic teacher.
A wry and charming story of childhood, family life and resilience, filmed with exuberance, capturing the past in loving detail.
wd *Åke Sandgren* novel Roland Schutt ph Goran Nilsson m Bjorn Isfalt pd Lasse Westfelt ed Grete Moldrup
☆ Jesper Salen, Stellan Skarsgard, Basia Frydman, Niclas Olund, Ernst-Hugo Jaregard, Reine Brynolifsson
'This is the sort of film that has little real dramatic flow or narrative drive, but relies instead on its slightly picaresque characters and a certain sad but not unfunny charm to carry it through.' – *Derek Malcolm, Guardian*
† It won the Swedish Academy award as best picture.

'You'll forget every love story you ever saw – or sang to!'

The Slipper and the Rose *
GB 1976 146m Technicolor
Panavision
Paradine Co-Productions (David Frost, Stuart Lyons)

The story of Cinderella.
The elements are charming, but the treatment is fussy yet uninventive and the film is immensely overlong and lacking in magic and wit. Alas, not the renaissance of the family film that was hoped for.
w Bryan Forbes, Robert and Richard Sherman d Bryan Forbes ph Tony Imi pd *Ray Simm* songs Robert and Richard Sherman
☆ *Richard Chamberlain*, Gemma Craven, Kenneth More, Michael Hordern, Edith Evans, Annette Crosbie, Margaret Lockwood, *Christopher Gable*, Julian Orchard, Lally Bowers, John Turner
'The tunes, I'm afraid, go in one ear and out the other; and, as Dr Johnson said of *Paradise Lost*, no man wished it a minute longer.' – *Michael Billington, Illustrated London News*
music; song 'He Danced with Me'

Slipstream
GB 1989 102m Eastmancolor
Entertainment/Entertainment Film Productions (Gary Kurtz)

In a post-holocaust future, an android learns human feelings while being hunted by a policeman and woman.
Futuristic chase movie, a little lacking in imagination.
w Tony Kayden story Bill Bauer d Steven M. Lisberger ph Frank Tidy m Elmer Bernstein pd Andrew McAlpine ed Terry Rawlings
☆ Mark Hamill, Bob Peck, Bill Paxton, Kitty Aldridge, Eleanor David, Ben Kingsley, F. Murray Abraham, Robbie Coltrane

Slither *
US 1972 96m Metrocolor
MGM/Talent Associates/Jack Sher

An ex-con, some gangsters, and a few mobile homes are involved in a chase across California for some hidden loot.
Wackily with-it comedy-thriller ranging from violence to slapstick, the former always undercut into the latter. Pretty funny, once you get the idea.
w W. D. Richter *d* Howard Zieff *ph* Laszlo Kovacs *m* Tom McIntosh
☆ James Caan, Peter Boyle, Sally Kellerman, Louise Lasser

'You Like To Watch *Don't You*.'
Sliver
US 1993 108m DeLuxe
Paramount (Robert Evans)

A woman moves into an apartment block where the tenants are being murdered and discovers that its owner maintains a video surveillance of every room in the building.
A voyeuristic thriller, no doubt intended to be erotic but only succeeding in being dull.
w Joe Eszterhas *novel* Ira Levin *d* Phillip Noyce *ph* Vilmos Zsigmond *m* Howard Shire *pd* Paul Sylbert *ed* Richard Francis-Bruce, William Hoy
☆ Sharon Stone, William Baldwin, Tom Berenger, Polly Walker, Colleen Camp, Amanda Foreman, Martin Landau, C. C. H. Pounder
'All flash and no sizzle.' – *Variety*

Slow Dancing in the Big City
US 1978 110m Technicolor
UA/CIP (Michael Levee, John G. Avildsen)
A New York newspaper columnist is affected by a dying eight-year-old drug addict and an ailing girl ballet dancer.
Warner in the 30s might have got away with this corn, but in 1978, played against a realistic backdrop, it seems merely silly and indigestible, its title as pretentious as its use of four-letter words.
w Barra Grant *d* John G. Avildsen *ph* Ralf D. Bode *m* Bill Conti
☆ Paul Sorvino, Anne Ditchburn, Nicolas Coster, Anita Dangler
'The earnestness and shamelessness of the director are so awesome that if the picture fails as romance, it succeeds as camp.' – *New Yorker*

Slow Motion: see *Sauve Qui Peut (La Vie)*

'Take it from Vivian ... the biggest problem in the country isn't money or drugs. It's breasts.'
Slums of Beverly Hills
US 1998 90m DeLuxe
Fox Searchlight/South Fork (Michael Nozik, Stan Wlodkowski)

In the mid-70s, an adolescent girl observes her hard-up single father's attempts to maintain a family life in Beverly Hills.
Coarse, semi-autobiographical comedy that resembles a TV sitcom with ideas above its station.
wd Tamara Jenkins *ph* Tom Richmond *m* Rolfe Kent *pd* Dena Roth *ed* Pamela Martin
☆ Alan Arkin, Marisa Tomei, Natasha Lyonne, Kevin Corrigan, Eli Marienthal, David Krumholtz, Jessica Walter, Carl Reiner, Rita Moreno
'Everything is delivered with such a heavy hand that you want to grab the movie and its makers by the shoulders and give them all a good shake.' – *James Cameron-Wilson, Film Review*

Sma Ulykker: see *Minor Mishaps*

Smack and Thistle *
GB 1990 90m Technicolor
Channel 4/Working Title (Sarah Cellan Jones, Alison Jackson)
A former convict, chased by police and gangsters after he gains possession of an MP's stolen briefcase containing details of shady deals, falls in love with an upper-class heroin addict.
A fast-paced thriller, with a little romance thrown in, acted and directed with verve.
wd Tunde Ikoli *ph* Peter Sinclair *m* Colin Towns *pd* Hugo Luczyc-Wyhowski *ed* Angus Newton
☆ Charlie Cain, Rosalind Bennett, Patrick Malahide, Connie Booth, Rudolph Walker, John Elmes, James Saxon, Geoffrey Palmer, Trevor Laird, Thomas Craig

The Small Back Room **
GB 1949 106m bw
London Films/The Archers

US title: *Hour of Glory*
A bomb expert with a lame foot and a drink problem risks his life dismantling a booby bomb and returns to his long-suffering girlfriend.
Rather gloomy suspense thriller with ineffective personal aspects but well-made location sequences and a fascinating background of boffins at work in post-war London.
wd Michael Powell, Emeric Pressburger *novel* Nigel Balchin *ph* Christopher Challis *m* Brian Easdale
☆ David Farrar, Kathleen Byron, Jack Hawkins, Leslie Banks, Robert Morley, Cyril Cusack
'The film as a whole can be recommended as unusually adult entertainment, notable for some admirable writing and acting.' – *Campbell Dixon*
'An exceptionally well-told story.' – *Dilys Powell*

Small Change *
France 1976 105m Eastmancolor
Films du Carosse/Artistes Associés (Marcel Berbert, Roland Thenot)

original title: *L'Argent de Poche*
Linked incidents affecting a class of small boys in provincial France.
Competent if rather ordinary little portmanteau which one can't imagine adults actually paying to see.
w François Truffaut, Suzanne Schiffman
d François Truffaut *ph* Pierre-William Glenn
m Maurice Jaubert
☆ Geory Desmouceaux, Philippe Goldman, Claudio Deluca
'Aside from the arrant sentimentality of much of Truffaut's text, the picture is depressed by the self-imitation of his film-making: the opening iris-in, the wipes. His eye for color has never been worse.' – *Stanley Kauffmann*

A Small Circle of Friends
US 1980 112m Technicolor
United Artists

Adventures of Harvard men at the end of the sixties.
Comedy, sex, politics and melodrama are all ploughed into this tiresome and predictable mixture.
w Ezra Sacks *d* Rob Cohen *ph* Michael Butler *m* Jim Steinman
☆ Brad Davis, Karen Allen, Jameson Parker, Shelley Long, John Friedrich
'Sacks' recreation of his college days relies on a mistaken belief that an audience will love his characters as much as they love each other.' – *John Pym, MFB*

Small Faces **
GB 1995 108m colour
Guild/BBC/Glasgow Film Fund/Skyline (Billy MacKinnon, Steve Clark-Hall)

In the 60s, three Glaswegian brothers become involved in gang warfare.
An involving, toughly humorous drama of dawning maturity, high spirited and rooted in reality.
w Billy MacKinnon, Gillies MacKinnon *d* Gillies MacKinnon *ph* John de Borman *m* John Keane *pd* Zoe Macleod *ed* Scott Thomas
☆ Ian Robertson, Joseph McFadden, J. S. Duffy, Laura Fraser, Garry Sweeney, Clare Higgins, Kevin McKidd, Mark McConnochie
'Consummately crafted, surprisingly delicately acted by its young cast, it surely stands alongside Bill Douglas's trilogy and Bill Forsyth's *Gregory's Girl* as one of the great Scottish evocations of youth.' – *Geoffrey Macnab, Sight and Sound*

Small Hotel
GB 1957 59m bw
Associated British/Welwyn (Robert Hall)
An elderly head waiter at the Jolly Fiddler resists the area manager's attempts to get rid of him.
Mild entertainment enlivened by some expert comedy performances from Harker, Handl and Loder.
w Wilfred Eades *play* Rex Frost *d* David MacDonald *ph* Norman Warwick *md* Louis Levy *ad* Terence Verity *ed* Seymour Logie
☆ Gordon Harker, Marie Lohr, John Loder, Irene Handl, Francis Matthews, Billie Whitelaw, Ruth Trouncer, Frederick Schiller, Derek Blomfield, Janet Munro

The Small Miracle: see *Never Take No for an Answer*

Small Soldiers *
US 1998 110m Technicolor Panavision
UPI/DreamWorks/Universal/Amblin (Mike Finnell, Colin Wilson)

Prototypes of toy soldiers, equipped with a redundant military microprocessor, come to life and besiege a family.
A quirky satire on militarism and big business, overwhelmed by its own technological prowess in creating lifelike toys that caricature a liking for violence.
w Gavin Scott, Adam Rifkin, Ted Elliott, Terry Rossio *d* Joe Dante *ph* Jamie Anderson *m* Jerry Goldsmith *pd* William Sandell *ed* Marshall Harvey, Michael Thau
☆ Kirsten Dunst, Gregory Smith, Jay Mohr, Phil Hartman, Kevin Dunn, Denis Leary, David Cross, Ann Magnuson, Wendy Schaal, Alexandra Wilson, Dick Miller, Robert Picardo and also the voices of: Tommy Lee Jones, Frank Langella, Ernest Borgnine, Jim Brown, Bruce Dern, George Kennedy, Clint Walker, Christopher Guest, Sarah Michelle Gellar, Christina Ricci
'While pic's sense of a toy store turned upside down, courtesy of dazzling f/x, will draw young viewers, ultimately the film's mean-spiritedness and serious underpinnings will turn off its core audience.' – *Leonard Klady, Variety*

Small Time
US 1991 88m bw
Panorama (Norman Loftis)

A petty criminal tries to survive among the crooks, hustlers and prostitutes of Harlem.
Gritty, downbeat drama of a doomed life, filmed in a documentary style.
wd Norman Loftis *ph* Michael C. Miller
m Arnold Bieber *pd* Nancy Evangelista *ed* Marc Cohen
☆ Richard Barboza, Carolyn Kinebrew, Scott Ferguson, Keith Allen, Jane Williams

'They took a bite out of crime.'
Small Time Crooks *
US 2000 94m Technicolor
DreamWorks/Sweetland (Jean Doumanian)

A former convict tries to rob a bank but strikes it rich in the cookie business.
Allen's return to the broader comedy of his first films is only partly successful; there's an unpleasant snobbery about the jokes aimed at the nouveau riche and those who patronise and exploit them.
wd Woody Allen *ph* Zhao Fei *pd* Santo Loquasto *ed* Alisa Lepselter
☆ Woody Allen (Ray Winkler), Tracey Ullman (Frenchy Winkler), Tony Darrow (Tommy), Hugh Grant (David), George Grizzard (George Blint), Jon Lovitz (Benny), Elaine May (May), Michael Rapaport (Denny), Elaine Stritch (Chi Chi Potter)
'It would be hard to imagine more of a non-event.' – *Adam Mars-Jones, Times*
'Feels like the kind of halfway decent film Allen can make without breaking sweat.' – *Peter Bradshaw, Guardian*

Small Town Girl *
US 1936 90m bw
MGM (Hunt Stromberg)
A girl traps a handsome stranger into offering marriage when he's drunk, then sets out to win him when he's sober.
Thin but adequate romantic comedy, a good example of MGM's production line of the mid-thirties, with established star and character players helping upcoming talents.
w John Lee Mahin, Edith Fitzgerald *novel* Ben Ames Williams *d* William A. Wellman *ph* Oliver Marsh, Charles Rosher *m* Edward Ward
☆ Janet Gaynor, Robert Taylor, James Stewart, Binnie Barnes, Frank Craven, Elizabeth Patterson, Lewis Stone, Andy Devine, Isabel Jewell, Charley Grapewin, Robert Greig, Agnes Ayres

Small Town Girl *
US 1952 93m Technicolor
MGM (Joe Pasternak)

Musical remake of the above.
Willing hands make the most of it, but the songs are not the best.
w Dorothy Cooper, Dorothy Kingsley *d* Leslie Kardos *ph* Joseph Ruttenberg *md* André Previn *ch* Busby Berkeley *songs* Leo Robin, Nicholas Brodszky
☆ Jane Powell, Farley Granger, *Bobby Van*, Ann Miller, Robert Keith, Billie Burke, S. Z. Sakall, Fay Wray, Nat King Cole
song 'My Flaming Heart'

A Small Town in Texas
US 1976 96m colour
AIP

An ex-convict returns to his home town seeking revenge on those who framed him.
Unpleasant shock thriller with much violence.
w William Norton *d* Jack Starrett *ph* Robert Jessup *m* Charles Bernstein
☆ Susan George, Timothy Bottoms, Bo Hopkins, Art Hindle

The Small Voice *
GB 1948 83m bw
British Lion/Constellation (Anthony Havelock-Allan)
US title: *Hideout*
Escaped convicts hold up a playwright and his wife in their country cottage.
Gripping, well-characterized version of a very well worn plot.
w Derek Neame, Julian Orde *novel* Robert Westerby *d* Fergus McDonell *ph* Stan Pavey
☆ James Donald, Valerie Hobson, Howard Keel, David Greene, Michael Balfour, Joan Young

The Small World of Sammy Lee
GB 1962 107m bw
Bryanston/Seven Arts/Ken Hughes (Frank Godwin)
A small-time Soho crook tries desperately to raise money to pay off threatening bookies.
Overlong 'realist' comedy-melodrama based on a TV play and filled with low-life 'characters'; vivid but cursed with a tedious hero.
wd Ken Hughes *TV play* Ken Hughes
ph Wolfgang Suschitsky *m* Kenny Graham
ad Seamus Flannery
☆ Anthony Newley, Julia Foster, Robert Stephens, Wilfrid Brambell, Warren Mitchell, Miriam Karlin, Kenneth J. Warren

The Smallest Show on Earth *
GB 1957 81m bw
British Lion/Launder and Gilliat (Michael Relph)
US title: *Big Time Operators*
Two young marrieds inherit a decayed cinema and make it pay.
Amiable caricature comedy with plenty of obvious jokes and a sentimental attachment to old cinemas but absolutely no conviction, little plot, and a very muddled sense of the line between farce and reality.
w William Rose, John Eldridge *d* Basil Dearden *ph* Douglas Slocombe *m* William Alwyn
☆ Bill Travers, Virginia McKenna, Margaret Rutherford, Bernard Miles, Peter Sellers, Leslie Phillips, Francis de Wolff

Smalltime
GB 1996 60m colour
BFI/Big Arty (Shane Meadows)

Two petty crooks – 'we rob from the rich and sell it to the poor, half-price' – attempt to carry out a big robbery in a run-down suburb of a northern city.
A low-budget slice of low life, about a bunch of losers who use a supermarket trolley as their getaway vehicle; entertaining, and occasionally perceptive, in a desultory way.
wd Shane Meadows *ph* Helene Whitehall
m Gavin Clarke *ed* David Wilson
☆ Mat Hand, Dena Smiles, Shane Meadows, Gena Kawecka, Jimmy Hynd, Leon Lammond, Tim Cunningham, Dominic Dillon

Smalltime Obsession *
UK 2000 118m colour
Guerilla/Solo/Seventh Twelfth (Piotr Szopiak)

In a South London Polish community, a youth has to decide between taking over his father's shop or following his friends into a life of crime.
Interesting thriller, rooted in a particular community, but one that tries to pack in so much that it loses its focus.

wd Piotr Szkopiak *ph* Niels Reedtz Johansen *m* Martin Bell *pd* Vince Raj *ed* Piotr Szkopiak
☆ Alex King (Michael), Juliette Caton (Ali), Jason Merrells (Chris), Oliver Young (Steve), Richard Banks (John), Kirsten Parker (Jackie), Andrew Tiernan (Mr Page), Geoff Lawson (Geordie), Giles Ward (Pope), Jurek Jarosz (Mr Korczynski), Teresa Nowakowska (Mrs Korczynski)
'There's some interesting material here, but it's spread way too thin to hold attention on the big screen.' – *Derek Elley, Variety*

Smart Blonde *
US 1936 57m bw
Warner
A female reporter beats the cops to the solution of a murder.
Slick second feature, first in the Torchy Blane series.
w Don Ryan, Kenneth Gamet, Frederick Nebel *d* Frank McDonald
☆ Glenda Farrell, Barton MacLane, Wini Shaw, Craig Reynolds, Addison Richards, Jane Wyman
'Fairly well paced with gunplay, an amount of smart talk, but no mountings to mention.' – *Variety*

Smart Girl
US 1935 78m bw
Paramount (Walter Wanger)
Girls left orphaned and penniless get their men – each other's.
Very mild comedy.
w Frances Hyland, Wilson Collison *d* Aubrey Scotto
☆ Ida Lupino, Kent Taylor, Gail Patrick, Joseph Cawthorn, Sidney Blackmer, Pinky Tomlin

Smart Girls Don't Talk
US 1948 81m bw
Warner
A society girl rats on her gangster boyfriend after her brother has been killed.
Flatly handled underworld melodrama, as uninteresting as its cast.
w William Sackheim *d* Richard Bare *ph* Ted McCord *m* David Buttolph *ad* Stanley Fleischer *ed* Clarence Kolster
☆ Virginia Mayo, Bruce Bennett, Robert Hutton, Richard Rober, Tom D'Andrea

'A fool in love! A sap for women!'
Smart Money
US 1931 67m bw
Warner
A gambler hits the big time but finally goes to jail.
Rather ordinary crime drama, a distinct letdown for its star after Little Caesar.
w Kubec Glasmon, John Bright *story* Lucien Hubbard, Joseph Jackson *d* Alfred E. Green *ph* Robert Kurrie
☆ Edward G. Robinson, James Cagney, Evalyn Knapp, Ralf Harolde, Noel Francis, Margaret Livingston, Boris Karloff, Billy House
'It will have no trouble upholding its title at the box office.' – *Variety*
† This film marks the only teaming of Robinson and Cagney.
🏅 Lucien Hubbard, Joseph Jackson

Smart Woman
US 1948 93m bw
Monogram (Hal E. Chester)
A crafty lady lawyer becomes romantically involved with a crusading district attorney.
What to Monogram was a high-class production would have been a very routine programmer from anyone else.
w Alvah Bessie, Louis Morheim, Herbert Margolis *d* Edward A. Blatt *ph* Stanley Cortez *m* Louis Gruenberg *md* Constantin Bakaleinikoff
☆ Constance Bennett, Brian Aherne, Barry Sullivan, Michael O'Shea, James Gleason, Otto Kruger, Isobel Elsom, Taylor Holmes, John Litel

Smash and Grab
GB 1937 76m bw
GFD/Jack Buchanan
US title: *Larceny Street*
A detective's wife helps him track down a criminal mastermind.
Agreeable star comedy.
w Ralph Spence *d* Tim Whelan *ph* Roy Clark, Henry Harris
☆ Jack Buchanan, Elsie Randolph, Arthur Margetson, Antony Holles, Zoe Wynn, Edmund Willard, David Burns

Smash Palace *
New Zealand 1981 108m colour
Aardvark Films
The owner of a car-wrecking business goes to pieces when his wife leaves him.
Downbeat character study of the kind of psychopath who doesn't arouse much sympathy; but the film is well mounted.
wd Roger Donaldson *ph* Graeme Cowley *m* Sharon O'Neill
☆ Bruno Lawrence, Anna Jemison, Keith Aberdein, Greer Robson
'May be the most melodramatic but also the most acutely motivated film yet about divorce.' – *Richard Schickel, Time*

Smash-up, The Story of a Woman
US 1947 113m bw
Universal-International (Walter Wanger)
GB title: *A Woman Destroyed*
The story of a lady alcoholic.
Tedious distaff side of The Lost Weekend.
w John Howard Lawson *d* Stuart Heisler *ph* Stanley Cortez *m* Daniele Amfitheatrof *ad* Alexander Golitzen *ed* Milton Carruth
☆ Susan Hayward, Lee Bowman, Eddie Albert, Marsha Hunt, Carl Esmond, Carleton Young, Charles D. Brown
🏅 original story (Dorothy Parker, Frank Cavett); Susan Hayward

The Smashing Bird I Used to Know
GB 1969 95m colour
Titan (Peter Newbrook)
aka: *School for Unclaimed Girls*
aka: *House of Unclaimed Women*
A schoolgirl suffering from guilt over the death of her father is sent to a remand home after stabbing her mother's lecherous boyfriend.
Sensationalist treatment of a trite story.
w John Peacock *d* Robert Hartford-Davis *ph* Peter Newbrook *m* Bobby Richards *ad* Bruce Grimes *ed* Don Deacon
☆ Madeline Hinde, Renee Asherson, Dennis Waterman, Patrick Mower, Faith Brook, Janina Faye, David Lodge, Maureen Lipman, Derek Fowlds, Megs Jenkins

Smashing the Money Ring
US 1939 57m bw
First National/Warner (Bryan Foy)
The Secret Service investigates gambling ships.
Fast-moving serial-like action.
w Anthony Coldeway, Raymond Schrock *d* Terry Morse
☆ Ronald Reagan, Eddie Foy Jnr, Margot Stevenson, Charles D. Brown

Smashing the Rackets
US 1938 69m bw
RKO (B. P. Fineman)
An FBI agent turned special prosecutor cleans up the city.
Lively 'B' movie with a sensational, tabloid approach, though its campaign against slot machines dates it somewhat.
w Lionel Hauser *story* Forrest Davis *d* Lew Landers *ph* Nicholas Musuraca *md* Frank Tours *pd* Van Nest Polglase *ed* Harry Marker
☆ Chester Morris, Frances Mercer, Rita Johnson, Bruce Cabot, Edward Pawley, Joseph de Stefani, Kay Sutton, Ben Welden

Smashing Time
GB 1967 96m Eastmancolor
Paramount/Partisan/Carlo Ponti (Ray Millichip)
Two north country girls have farcical adventures in swinging London, including paint squirting and pie throwing.
Horrendous attempt to turn two unsuitable actresses into a female Laurel and Hardy; plenty of coarse vigour but no style or sympathy.
w George Melly *d* Desmond Davis *ph* Manny Wynn *m* John Addison
☆ Rita Tushingham, Lynn Redgrave, Ian Carmichael, Anna Quayle, Michael York, Irene Handl, Jeremy Lloyd

Smile ***
US 1975 113m DeLuxe
UA (Michael Ritchie)
A bird's eye view of the Young Miss America pageant in a small California town.
A witty series of sketches in the form of a drama-documentary or satirical mosaic. Highly polished fun for those who can stay the course.
w Jerry Belson d Michael Ritchie ph Conrad Hall *m* various
☆ Bruce Dern, Barbara Feldon, Michael Kidd, Geoffrey Lewis, Nicholas Pryor
'A beady, precise, technically skilful movie.' – *Michael Billington, Illustrated London News*

A Smile Like Yours
US 1997 98m DeLuxe
Paramount/Rysher (David Kirkpatrick, Tony Amatullo)
Without discussing it with her husband, a wife tries hard to have a baby.
Somnolent attempt at a romantic comedy, in which it is difficult to feel much sympathy for either of the leading characters.
w Kevin Meyer, Keith Samples *d* Keith Samples *ph* Richard Bowen *m* William Ross *pd* Garreth Stover *ed* Wayne Wahrman
☆ Greg Kinnear, Lauren Holly, Joan Cusack, Jay Thomas, Jill Hennessy, Christopher McDonald, Donald Moffat, France Nuyen, Marianne Muellerleile
'Flat and formulaic, this painfully charmless romantic comedy is destined to disappear quickly after its halfhearted theatrical release.' – *Joe Leydon, Variety*
† Shirley MacLaine appears uncredited.

Smiles of a Summer Night ***
Sweden 1955 105m bw
Svensk Filmindustri
original title: *Sommarnattens Leende*
A country lawyer meets again a touring actress who was once his mistress, and accepts an invitation for him and his young wife to stay at her mother's country home for a weekend.
Comedy of high period manners with an admirable detached viewpoint and elegant trappings. It later formed the basis of Stephen Sondheim's A Little Night Music, *a stage musical which was later filmed.*
wd Ingmar Bergman ph Gunnar Fischer *m* Erik Nordgren *ad* P.A. Lundgren *ed* Oscar Rosander
☆ *Gunnar Bjornstrand* (Fredrik Egerman), Eva Dahlbeck (Desirée Armfeldt), Ulla Jacobsson (Anne Egerman), Harriet Andersson (Petra), Margit Carlqvist (Charlotte Malcolm), Naima Wifstrand (Madame Armfeldt), Jarl Kulle (Count Carl-Magnus Malcolm)

Smiley *
GB 1956 97m Technicolor
Cinemascope
TCF/London Films (Anthony Kimmins)
An adventurous Australian boy has various adventures and finally gets the bicycle he wants.
An open-air 'William'-type story for children, quite nicely made and generally refreshing. Smiley Gets a Gun *was a less effective sequel.*
w Moore Raymond, Anthony Kimmins *novel* Moore Raymond *d* Anthony Kimmins *ph* Ted Scaife, Russ Wood *m* William Alwyn
☆ Colin Petersen, Ralph Richardson, Chips Rafferty, John McCallum

Smiley Gets a Gun
Australia 1958 90m Technicolor
Cinemascope
Canberra Films
Smiley is promised a rifle if he can keep out of trouble.
Unexceptional sequel.
w Anthony Kimmins, Rex Rienits *d* Anthony Kimmins *ph* Ted Scaife *m* Wilbur Sampson
☆ Keith Calvert, Bruce Archer, Sybil Thorndike, Chips Rafferty

Smilin' Through *
US 1932 97m bw
MGM (Irving Thalberg)
Three generations of complications follow when a Victorian lady is accidentally killed by a jealous lover on her wedding day.
Archetypal sentimental romantic drama, wholly absorbing to the mass audience and extremely well done; originally a 1922 Norma Talmadge vehicle.
w Ernest Vajda, Claudine West, Donald Ogden Stewart, J. B. Fagan *play* Jane Cowl, Jane Murfin *d* Sidney Franklin *ph Lee Garmes m* William Axt
☆ Norma Shearer, Leslie Howard, Fredric March, O. P. Heggie, Ralph Forbes, Beryl Mercer
'A big women's picture of tear-drawing power, done with satisfying sincerity by a cast which spells money.' – *Variety*
'A sensitive and beautiful production distinguished by excellent settings and rich photography.' – *New York Mirror*
🏅 best picture

Smilin' Through *
US 1941 100m Technicolor
MGM (Victor Saville)
Flat but adequate remake of the above.
w Donald Ogden Stewart, John Balderston *d* Frank Borzage *ph* Leonard Smith *m* Herbert Stothart
☆ Jeanette MacDonald, Gene Raymond, Brian Aherne, Ian Hunter, Frances Robinson, Patrick O'Moore

Smiling Along: see *Keep Smiling*

The Smiling Ghost
US 1941 71m bw
Warner
A girl reporter solves a haunted house mystery.
Moderate comedy chiller with plenty going on.
w Kenneth Gamet *d* Lewis Seiler *ph* Arthur Todd
☆ Alexis Smith, Wayne Morris, Brenda Marshall, Alan Hale, Willie Best, David Bruce, Helen Westley, Richard Ainley

'His intimate and roguish romance will break your heart – with love and laughter!'
The Smiling Lieutenant **
US 1931 88m bw
Paramount (Ernst Lubitsch)
A Viennese guards officer leaves his mistress to become consort to a visiting princess.
A sophisticated soufflé in Lubitsch's best style, naughty but quite nice, with visual effects largely replacing dialogue.
w Ernest Vajda, Samson Raphaelson *operetta A Waltz Dream d Ernst Lubitsch ph* George Folsey *m* Oscar Straus *md* Adolph Deutsch
☆ *Maurice Chevalier*, Miriam Hopkins, Claudette Colbert, Charles Ruggles, George Barbier, Elizabeth Patterson
'Will delight smart audiences and figures to be liked well enough by the average fan. A good but not a smash picture.' – *Variety*
'All the shrewd delights that were promised in *The Love Parade* all realized with an economy and sureness that give it a luster which no other American-made comedy satire has achieved. One must look to *Le Million* to find its peer.' – *Richard Watts, New York Post*
🏅 best picture

'Snow covers everything ... except the truth.'
Smilla's Feeling for Snow *
Germany/Denmark/Sweden 1997 121m colour Panavision
TCF/Constantin/Greenland/Bavaria (Bernd Eichinger, Martin Moszkowicz)
In Copenhagen, a woman investigates the apparently accidental death of her neighbour's young son.
A stilted thriller based on a bestselling book; it never quite settles down to deliver on its promise.
w Ann Biderman *novel Miss Smilla's Feeling for Snow* by Peter Hoeg *d* Bille August *ph* Jörgen Persson *m* Harry Gregson-Williams *pd* Anna Asp *ed* Janus Billeskov-Jansen
☆ Julia Ormond, Gabriel Byrne, Richard Harris, Vanessa Redgrave, Robert Loggia, Jim Broadbent, Mario Adorf, Bob Peck, Tom Wilkinson, Emma Croft, Peter Capaldi
'An exceedingly sleek and handsome thriller.' – *Variety*

Smithereens *
US 1982 90m colour
Susan Seidelman
Obsessed with becoming manager of a punk rock band, a young girl in New York drifts through a series of unsatisfactory encounters.
Unblinking account of empty lives, well done but ultimately depressing.
w Susan Seidelman, Ron Nyswaner, Peter Askin *d* Susan Seidelman *ph* Chirine El Khadem *m* Glenn Mercer, Bill Million *pd* Franz Harland *ed* Susan Seidelman
☆ Susan Berman, Brad Rinn, Richard Hell, Roger Jet

Smoke *
US 1995 112m DuArt
Miramax/Nippon (Greg Johnson, Peter Newman, Hisami Kuriowa, Kenzo Hurikoshi)
The interlinked lives of customers who frequent a Brooklyn cigar store.
Pleasantly anecdotal and articulate account of lives shifted and altered by chance and coincidence, the way lives are.
w Paul Auster *d* Wayne Wang *ph* Adam Holender *m* Rachel Portman *pd* Kalina Ivanov *ed* Maisie Hoy
☆ William Hurt, Harvey Keitel, Forest Whitaker, Harold Perrineau Jnr, Victor Argo, Erica Gimpel, Clarice Taylor, Malik Yoba, Mary Ward, Jared Harris
'Plenty of smoke but not a great deal of fire.' – *Variety*
† As filming finished, another film in the same style, *Blue in the Face* (qv), was quickly made, also featuring Keitel as the cigar store owner.

Smoke Jumpers: see *Red Skies of Montana*

Smoke Signal
US 1955 88m Technicolor
U-I (Howard Christie)
A small band of cavalry, together with their prisoner, an officer accused of treason and murder, attempt to escape maurauding Indians by travelling down a dangerous, uncharted river.
A Western that abandons dry land for boats, but still manages to tell a familiar story of redemption and romance.
w George F. Slavin, George W. George *d* Jerry Hopper *ph* Clifford Stine *md* Joseph Gershenson *ad* Alexander Golitzen, Richard H. Riedel *ed* Milton Carruth
☆ Dana Andrews, Piper Laurie, Rex Reason, Milburn Stone, William Talman, Douglas Spencer, Gordon Jones, William Schallert

Smokey and the Bandit *
US 1977 97m Technicolor
Universal/Rastar (Robert L. Levy)
A Georgia bootlegger on a mission picks up a girl in distress and is chased by her irate sheriff fiancé.
Frantic chase comedy full of car crashes and low lines: a surprise box-office smash.
w James Lee Barrett, Charles Shyer, Alan Mandel *d* Hal Needham *ph* Bobby Byrne *m* Bill Justis, Jerry Reed, Art Feller
☆ Burt Reynolds, Jackie Gleason, Sally Field, Jerry Reed, Mike Henry, Pat McCormick, Paul Williams

Smokey and the Bandit II
US 1980 101m Technicolor
Universal/Rastar/Mort Engelberg
GB title: *Smokey and the Bandit Ride Again*
A trucker is hired to take a pregnant elephant to the Republican convention.
More mindless chasing and crashing, with even less wit than before and rather more wholesale destruction.
w Jerry Belson, Brock Yates *d* Hal Needham *ph* Michael Butler *md* Snuff Garrett
☆ Burt Reynolds, Jackie Gleason, Sally Field, Jerry Reed, Dom DeLuise, Paul Williams

Smokey and the Bandit III
US 1983 88m Technicolor
Mort Engelberg/Universal
Sheriff Justice mistakes an innocent driver for his old enemy.
A rather random car chase movie, obviously the last of a short line.
w Stuart Birnbaum, David Dashev *d* Dick Lowry *ph* James Pergola *m* Larry Cansler *ad* Ron Hobbs *ed* Byron Brandt, David Blewitt, Christopher Greenbury
☆ Jackie Gleason, Jerry Reed, Mike Henry, Pat McCormick, Burt Reynolds (cameo)
'A patchwork of arbitrary mayhem.' – *Variety*

Smokey and the Bandit Ride Again: see *Smokey and the Bandit II*

Smokey and the Goodtime Outlaws
US 1978 88m CFI color
Howco (Tommy Amato)
Two dim-brained country singers go to Nashville in search of fame.
A stupefying mix of car chases, bar-room brawls and country-and-western music, put together with little evidence of sense or style.
w Frank Dobbs, Bob Walsh *story* Jesse Turner *d* Alex Grasshoff *m* Mauro Bruno *ed* Geoffrey Rowland
☆ Jesse Turner, Dennis Fimple, Slim Pickens, Diane Sherill, Marcie Barkin, Hope Summers, Don Sherman

Smoking/No Smoking **
France 1993 146m colour
Mainline/Arena/Camera One/France 2 (Bruno Persey, Michel Seydoux)
Happenings to do with love and death in a Yorkshire village, the outcome of which is dependent upon whether or not the wife of the local headmaster decides to give up smoking.
An unusual and engaging cinematic experience, based on a sequence of eight plays which each had two possible endings. Here the two films, which can be watched in any order, provide 12 varying conclusions, dependent upon earlier actions, but each ending in a graveyard. Yorkshire has never looked quite as it does in this French studio re-creation, but the film does provide for some virtuoso acting from its two stars, who play 17 parts between them.
w Jean-Pierre Bacri, Agnes Jaoui *play Intimate Exchanges* by Alan Ayckbourn *d* Alain Resnais *ph* Renato Berta *m* John Pattison *pd* Jacques Saulnier *ed* Albert Jurgenson
☆ Sabine Azéma, Pierre Arediti
'Just about perfect within the boundaries it sets itself.' – *Variety*

Smoky
US 1946 87m Technicolor
TCF (Robert Bassler)
An especially independent horse virtually runs the ranch on which he lives.
Family saga of the great outdoors, well enough assembled.
w Dwight Cummins, Lillie Hayward, Dorothy Yost *novel* Will James *d* Louis King *ph* Charles Clarke *m* David Raksin *md* Emil Newman
☆ Fred MacMurray, Anne Baxter, Burl Ives, Bruce Cabot, Esther Dale
† The story was also made by Fox in 1933 with Victor Jory, and in 1966 with Fess Parker.

Smooth Talk
US 1985 92m colour
Nepenthe/American Playhouse/Goldcrest (Martin Rosen)
A mixed-up 15-year-old girl has a dangerous encounter with a mildly psychopathic male.
Unattractive scenario about thoroughly dislikeable people.
w Tom Cole *story* Joyce Carol Oates *d* Joyce Chopra *ph* James Glennon *m* Bill Payne, Russ Kunkel, George Massenburg *md* James Taylor *pd* David Wasco *ed* Patrick Dodd
☆ Treat Williams, Laura Dern, Mary Kay Place, Levon Helm

The Smugglers: see *The Man Within*

Smultronstället: see *Wild Strawberries*

SNAFU
US 1945 85m bw
Columbia
GB title: *Welcome Home*
Middle-class parents rescue their difficult 15-year-old son from the army, then wish they hadn't.
Predictable, well-greased comedy of a rebellious teenager.
w Louis Solomon, Harold Buchman *play* Louis Solomon, Harold Buchman *d* Jack Moss *ph* Franz Planer *m* Paul Sawtell
☆ Robert Benchley, Vera Vague, Conrad Janis, Nanetta Parks
† The title can be bowdlerized as 'Situation Normal, All Fouled Up'.

'A Shocking Movie From The World's Most Sensational Director!'
Snake Eyes
US 1993 104m DeLuxe
Rank/Cecchi Gori/Maverick (Mary Kane)
aka: *Dangerous Game*
A film director making a movie about a marriage on the rocks, with an abusive husband who berates and beats his wife for abandoning their sex- and drug-filled life, discovers that reality begins to mirror the fiction.
A confused film that swiftly disappears up its own pretensions; it has the air of a semi-improvised piece, but the relentless soul-searchings of the characters, and their identification with the roles they play, seem hardly worthwhile when the film they are making is even worse than the 'reality' the audience is watching; self-indulgent is a polite way of describing the result.
w Nicholas St John *d* Abel Ferrara *ph* Ken Kelsch *m* Joe Delia *pd* Alex Tavoularis *ed* Anthony Redman
☆ Harvey Keitel, Madonna, James Russo, Nancy Ferrara, Reilly Murphy
'As long as you go with it, it seduces you into playing along with its circuit of sex, drugs, anger, confusion, fear and deception. If you let go, it becomes easy to ask why you should bother watching these brittle, self-engrossed people whose unmitigated self-disgust is not simply depressing but irritating.' – *Amanda Lipman, Sight and Sound*
'Another abrasive, confrontational downer likely to appeal only to a marginal audience.' – *Variety*

'Believe everything except your eyes.'
Snake Eyes *
US 1998 99m DeLuxe Panavision
Buena Vista/DeBart (Brian de Palma)
A corrupt cop investigates the shooting of a senior politician at a championship boxing match.
An implausible thriller on the theme of surveillance, with broad acting and some impressive directorial flourishes that keep the adrenalin flowing.
w David Koepp *d* Brian de Palma *ph* Stephen H. Burum *m* Ryuichi Sakamoto *pd* Anne Pritchard *ed* Bill Pankow *sp* Industrial Light & Magic
☆ Nicolas Cage, Gary Sinise, John Heard, Carla Gugino, Stan Shaw, Kevin Dunn, Michael Rispoli, Joel Fabiani, Luis Guzman, David Anthony Higgins
'Wispy threads of dramatic plausibility and character involvement unravel completely by the time of the incredibly silly final reel.' – *Todd McCarthy, Variety*

The Snake Pit **
US 1948 108m bw
TCF (Anatole Litvak, Robert Bassler)
A girl becomes mentally deranged and has horrifying experiences in an institution.
A headline-hitting film which made a stirring plea for more sympathetic treatment of mental illness. Very well made, and arrestingly acted, but somehow nobody's favourite movie.
w Frank Partos, Millen Brand *novel* Mary Jane Ward *d Anatole Litvak* *ph* Leo Tover *m* Alfred Newman
☆ *Olivia de Havilland*, Leo Genn, Mark Stevens, Celeste Holm, Glenn Langan, Leif Erickson, Beulah Bondi, Lee Patrick, Natalie Schafer
'A film of superficial veracity that requires a bigger man than Litvak; a good film with bad things.' – *Herman G. Weinberg*
† The British censor insisted on a foreword explaining that everyone in the film was an actor and that conditions in British mental hospitals were unlike those depicted.
best picture; script; Anatole Litvak; Alfred Newman; Olivia de Havilland

Snares: see *Pièges*

Snatch *
GB/US 2000 103m DeLuxe
Columbia/Ska (Matthew Vaughn)
Groups of London crooks try to retrieve a valuable diamond stolen by an American thief from an Antwerp jeweler.
Chaotic and hectic thriller involving American, Russian and English low-life, Irish gypsies and dodgy boxing promoters; the narrative moves quickly without getting out of the morass, while Brad Pitt goes over the top in a parody of his Fight Club role.
wd Guy Ritchie *ph* Tim Maurice-Jones *m* John Murphy *pd* Hugo Luczyc-Wyhowski *ed* John Harris, Les Healey
☆ Benicio Del Toro (Franky Four Fingers), Dennis Farina (Avi), Vinnie Jones (Bullet Tooth Tony), Brad Pitt (Mickey O'Neil), Rade Sherbedgia (Boris the Blade), Jason Statham (Turkish), Alan Ford (Brick Top), Mike Reid (Doug the Head), Robbie Gee (Vinny), Lennie James (Sol), Ewen Bremner (Mullet), Jason Flemyng (Darren), Stephen Graham (Tommy)
'One of the very best films of the year.' – *Film Review*

'We could tell you what it's about. But then, of course, we would have to kill you.'
Sneakers **
US 1992 125m DeLuxe
UIP/Universal (Walter F. Parkes, Lawrence Lasker)
A group of oddball experts is hired to recover from a criminal mastermind an electronic device that can penetrate the government's most secure computer systems.
Enjoyable caper that pleasantly passes a couple of hours.
w Phil Alden Robinson, Lawrence Lasker, Walter F. Parkes *d* Phil Alden Robinson *ph* John Lindley *m* James Horner *pd* Patrizia von Brandenstein *ed* Tom Rolf
☆ Robert Redford, Dan Aykroyd, Ben Kingsley, Mary McDonnell, River Phoenix, Sidney Poitier, David Strathairn, James Earl Jones, Stephen Tobolowsky
'The mainstream pleasures it affords should appeal to just about all audience segments, save perhaps ultra-sophisticates and low-brow teens.' – *Variety*
'This isn't really a serious film. It's over-stretched and under-characterised, but watchable for all that if you don't find the techno aspects too depressing.' – *Derek Malcolm, Guardian*

The Sniper **
US 1952 87m bw
Columbia/Stanley Kramer (Edna and Edward Anhalt)
A psychopath kills a succession of blondes with a high-powered rifle.
Semi-documentary police drama which was quite startling and influential when released but seems quite routine now.
w Harry Brown *d Edward Dmytryk* *ph* Burnett Guffey *m* George Antheil
☆ *Adolphe Menjou*, Arthur Franz, Gerald Mohr, Richard Kiley, Frank Faylen, Marie Windsor
original story (Edna and Edward Anhalt)

Sniper *
US 1993 98m colour
Columbia TriStar/Baltimore (Robert L. Rosen)
An experienced Marine sniper is joined by a novice on a dangerous assignment in Panama.
Familiar ingredients are expertly mixed to create a tense action picture.
w Michael Frost Beckner, Crash Leyland *d* Luis Llosa *ph* Bill Butler *m* Gary Chang *pd* Herbert Pinter *ed* Scott Smith
☆ Tom Berenger, Billy Zane, J. T. Walsh, Aden Young, Ken Radley, Reinaldo Arenas, Carlos Alvarez, Roy Edmonds
'An expertly directed, yet ultimately unsatisfying psychological thriller.' – *Variety*

Snitch
US 1998 93m colour
Filmline/Phoenician/Clinica Estetico/Tribeca/Spanky/Apostle (Joel Stillerman, Ted Demme, Jim Serpico, Nicolas Clermont, Elie Samaha)
aka: *Noose*
In Boston, a group of petty crooks discover that there is no honour among thieves.

Gritty drama of dead-end lives, well enough acted but inconsequential.
w Mike Armstrong d Ted Demme ph Adam Kimmel pd Ruth Ammon ed Jeffrey Wolf
☆ Denis Leary, Jason Barry, Billy Crudup, John Diehl, Greg Dulli, Noah Emmerich, Ian Hart, Famke Janssen, Colm Meaney, Martin Sheen, Jean Tripplehorn

The Snorkel
GB 1958 90m bw
Columbia/Hammer (Michael Carreras)
A man murders his wife and is given away by his observant young stepdaughter.
Tenuous suspenser which outstays its welcome.
w Peter Myers, Jimmy Sangster, Anthony Dawson d Guy Green ph Jack Asher ad John Stoll ed James Needs, Bill Lenney
☆ Peter Van Eyck, Betta St John, Mandy Miller, William Franklyn, Grégoire Aslan

'Roads closed. Schools shut. Rules were made to be frozen!'
Snow Day
US 2000 89m DeLuxe
Paramount/Nickelodeon (Albie Hecht, Julia Pistor)
A failing weather forecaster and his dysfunctional family have their problems solved during an unexpected fall of snow.
Amiable, unexceptional comedy of family troubles and 'teen love.
w Will McRobb, Chris Viscardi d Chris Koch ph Robbie Greenberg m Steve Bartek pd Leslie McDonald ed David Finfer
☆ Chris Elliott (Snowplowman), Mark Webber (Hal Brandston), Jean Smart (Laura Brandston), Schuyler Fisk (Lane Leonard), Iggy Pop (Mr Zellweger), Pam Grier (Tina), Chevy Chase (Tom Brandston), John Schneider (Chad Symmonz), Zena Grey (Natalie Brandston), Claire Bonner (Emmanuelle Chriqui)
'A family film that's about as fluffy as fresh powder…mixes a cast of familiar faces with bright new talent in an unremarkable, innocuous package.' – *Lael Loewenstein, Variety*

'Get ready for mush hour!'
Snow Dogs
US 2002 99m Technicolor
Buena Vista/Walt Disney/Galapagos (Jordan Kerner)
Discovering that he was adopted, a dentist goes to Alaska to discover more about his roots.
Lighweight, slapstick comedy of the sort that Disney made in the '60s and then wisely abandoned.
w Jim Kouf, Tommy Swerdlow, Michael Goldberg, Mark Gibson, Philip Halprin suggsted by *Winterdance: The Fine Madness of Running the Iditarod* by Gary Paulsen d Brian Levant ph Thomas Ackerman m John Debney pd Stephen Lineweaver ed Roger Bondelli
☆ Cuba Gooding Jnr (Ted Brooks), James Coburn (Thunder Jack), Sisqo (Dr Rupert Brooks), Nichelle Nichols (Amelia Brooks), M. Emmet Walsh (George), Graham Greene (Peter Yellowbear), Brian Doyle-Murray (Ernie), Joanna Bacalso (Barb), Jean-Michel Pare (Olivier), Michael Bolton (Himself)
'Remarkably inept…The pratfalls are so uninventive that they inspire more pity than hilarity.' – *A. O. Scott, New York Times*

Snow Falling On Cedars *
US 1999 126m Alpha Cine Lab Panavision
Universal/Harry J. Ufland/Ron Bass (Kathleen Kennedy, Frank Marshall, Harry J. Ufland, Ron Bass)
In the 1940s, soon after the end of the Second World War, a reporter living in an island community intervenes in the trial of a Japanese-American for the murder of a local fisherman.
A slow-moving drama of smalltown racial prejudice that lingers on landscapes as much as on the individuals caught up in a courtroom drama of a familiar kind.
w Ron Bass, Scott Hicks novel David Guterson d Scott Hicks ph Robert Richardson m James Newton Howard pd Jeannine Oppewall ed Hank Corwin
☆ Ethan Hawke (Ishmael Chambers), James Cromwell (Judge Fielding), Richard Jenkins (Sheriff Art Moran), James Rebhorn (Alvin Hooks), Sam Shepard (Arthur Chambers), Eric Thal (Carl Heine Jnr), Max von Sydow (Nels Gudmundsson), Youki Kudoh (Hatsue Miyamoto), Rick Yune (Kazuo Miyamoto)
'The cinematic equivalent of an arty coffee-table book. It is so busy illustrating the story (with elaborate flashbacks and montage sequences) that it forgets to be dramatic.' – *Stephen Holden, New York Times*
† The film cost around $45m and took $13m at the US box office.
Robert Richardson

Snow Job: see *The Ski Raiders*

Snow Treasure
US 1968 95m Eastmancolor
Sagittarius (Irving Jacoby)
In Nazi-occupied Norway a teenage boy finds gold hidden in the snow; an underground agent helps him get it to safety.
Curiously undernourished but attractively made adventure film.
w Irving Jacoby, Peter Hansen novel Marie McSwigan d Irving Jacoby ph Sverre Bergli m Egil Monn-Iversen
☆ James Franciscus, Paul Anstad, Paoul Oyen, Randi Borch

Snow White: A Tale of Terror
GB/US 1996 100m colour
Polygram/Interscope (Tom Engelman)
A young girl takes refuge with seven gold miners when her wicked stepmother, jealous of her beauty, tries to kill her.
An interesting attempt to take the familiar story of Snow White back to its Gothic and grotesque roots; unfortunately, it is not successful, just something to frighten the children.
w Tom Szollosi, Deborah Serra story The Brothers Grimm d Michael Cohn ph Mike Southon m John Ottman pd Gemma Jackson ed Ian Crafford
☆ Sigourney Weaver, Sam Neill, Gil Bellows, Taryn Davis, David Conrad, Brian Glover, Monica Keena, Anthony Brophy, Frances Cuka
'Cloaked thickly with an oppressive, unsettling atmosphere, the film succeeds by drawing deep, fearful uncertainty from its ambiguity.' – *Darren Bignall, Empire*

Snow White and the Seven Dwarfs ****
US 1937 82m Technicolor
Walt Disney
Disney's first feature cartoon, a mammoth enterprise which no one in the business thought would work. The romantic leads were wishy-washy but the splendid songs and the marvellous comic and villainous characters turned the film into a worldwide box-office bombshell which is almost as fresh today as when it was made.
w Ted Sears, Otto Englander, Earl Hurd, Dorothy Ann Blank, Richard Creedon, Dick Richard, Merrill de Maris, Webb Smith, from the fairy tale by the brothers Grimm m Frank Churchill, Leigh Harline, Paul Smith supervising d David Hand songs *Larry Morey, Frank Churchill*
☆ Featuring the voices of Adriana Caselotti, Harry Stockwell, Lucille La Verne, Billy Gilbert
'The first full-length animated feature, the turning point in Disney's career, a milestone in film history, and a great film.' – *Leonard Maltin*
'Sustained fantasy, the animated cartoon grown up.' – *Otis Ferguson*
'The sort of film that happens once in a generation. It is as necessary a part of our film upbringing as *The Birth of a Nation* or *The Jazz Singer*. Crude, tentative, and born of compromise it may be, but it is still history in the making.' – *C. A. Lejeune*
† Adriana Caselotti (1916–97) was the voice of Snow White, chosen after 150 teenagers, including Deanna Durbin, had auditioned for the role. Snow White's appearance was based on dancer Marjorie Belcher, who was later better known as Marge Champion.
Special Award to Walt Disney for 'a significant screen innovation'. He was given one Oscar and seven miniature statuettes.
Frank Churchill, Leigh Harline, Paul Smith

Snow White and the Three Clowns: see *Snow White and the Three Stooges*

Snow White and the Three Stooges *
US 1961 107m DeLuxe
Cinemascope
(TCF) Chanford (Charles Wick)
GB title: *Snow White and the Three Clowns*
The old story retold as a vehicle for a champion skater and three veteran clowns.
Surprisingly tolerable as a holiday attraction, once you get over the shock.
w Noel Langley, Elwood Ullman d Walter Lang ph Leon Shamroy m Lyn Murray ad Jack Martin Smith, Maurice Ransford
☆ Carol Heiss, Moe Howard, Larry Fine, Joe de Rita, Edson Stroll, Patricia Medina, Guy Rolfe, Buddy Baer, Edgar Barrier

Snowball Express
US 1972 99m Technicolor
Walt Disney (Ron Miller)
An insurance accountant inherits a dilapidated skiing hotel in the Colorado Rockies.
Uninspired family comedy with slapstick on the snow slopes.
w Don Tait, Jim Parker, Arnold Margolin novel *Château Bon Vivant* by Frankie and John O'Rear d Norman Tokar ph Frank Phillips m Robert F. Brunner
☆ Dean Jones, Nancy Olson, Henry Morgan, Keenan Wynn, Mary Wickes, Johnny Whittaker
'As wholesome and bland as that old American favourite the peanut butter and jelly sandwich.' – *MFB*

Snowbound
GB 1948 87m bw
GFD/Gainsborough
Various people congregate at a ski hut in the Swiss Alps; all are after buried Nazi loot.
A rather foolish story which provides little in the way of action but at least assembles a fine crop of character actors.
w David Evans, Keith Campbell novel *The Lonely Skier* by Hammond Innes d David MacDonald ph Stephen Dade ad George Provis, Maurice Carter ed Charles Knott
☆ Robert Newton, Dennis Price, Herbert Lom, Stanley Holloway, Marcel Dalio, Mila Parely, Guy Middleton

'Out of one masterpiece, another has been created!'
The Snows of Kilimanjaro **
US 1952 117m Technicolor
TCF (Darryl F. Zanuck)
A hunter lies wounded in Africa and while waiting for help looks back over his life and loves.
Hollywood version of a portable Hemingway, with reminiscences of several novels stirred into a lush and sprawling mix of action and romance, open spaces and smart salons. A big popular star film of its time, despite constricted and unconvincing characters.
w Casey Robinson story Ernest Hemingway d *Henry King* ph Leon Shamroy m Bernard Herrmann ad Lyle Wheeler, John DeCuir
☆ Gregory Peck, Susan Hayward, Ava Gardner, Hildegard Neff, Leo G. Carroll, Torin Thatcher, Marcel Dalio
'A naïve kind of success story with a conventional boy-meets-lots-of-girls plot.' – *Karel Reisz*
'The succinct and vivid qualities associated with Hemingway are rarely evoked, and what has been substituted is for the most part meandering, pretentious and more or less maudlin romance.' – *Newsweek*
Leon Shamroy; art direction

So Big *
US 1932 80m bw
Warner (Lucien Hubbard)
A schoolteacher marries a farmer, has trouble with her son, falls in love with a sculptor.
Watchable, superficial, top-talented adaptation of a best-seller, first filmed in 1925 with Colleen Moore.
w J. Grubb Alexander, Robert Lord novel Edna Ferber d William Wellman ph Sid Hickox m W. Franke Harling
☆ *Barbara Stanwyck*, George Brent, Dickie Moore, Guy Kibbee, Bette Davis, Hardie Albright
'Too long getting started, and only has moments towards the end … somewhat of a bore for the major part of its footage.' – *Variety*

So Big
US 1953 101m bw
Warner (Henry Blanke)
By the time this inflated remake came along, the story was just too corny despite careful production.
w John Twist d Robert Wise ph Ellsworth Fredericks m Max Steiner
☆ Jane Wyman, Sterling Hayden, Richard Beymer, Nancy Olson, Steve Forrest, Elisabeth Fraser, Martha Hyer

So Bright the Flame: see *The Girl in White*

So Close to Life **
Sweden 1958 84m bw
Nordisk Tonefilm
original title: *Nära Livit*
aka: *Brink of Life*
In a maternity ward of a Stockholm hospital, three women reach a turning point in their lives.
A bleak and austere drama of life and death and the randomness of existence, given vigour and intensity by the acting of the women at its centre.
w Ingmar Bergman, Ulla Isaksson story *Det vängila, värdiga* by Ulla Isaksson d Ingmar Bergman ph Max Wilén ad Bibi Lindström ed Carl-Olov Skeppstedt
☆ *Eva Dahlbeck, Ingrid Thulin, Bibi Andersson, Barbro Hiort af Ornäs*, Erland Josephson, Max von Sydow, Gunnar Sjöberg
† Ingmar Bergman won the award as best director, and Eva Dahlbeck, Ingrid Thulin, Bibi Andersson and Barbro Hiort af Ornäs were collectively awarded the best actress prize at the 1958 Cannes Film Festival.

So Dark the Night *
US 1946 71m bw
Columbia
A detective tracks down a murderer whom he finds to be himself.
Smart second feature with a likeable leading performance.
w Aubrey Wisberg, Martin Berkeley, Dwight Babcock d Joseph H. Lewis ph Burnett Guffey m Hugo Friedhofer
☆ *Steven Geray*, Ann Codee, Micheline Cheirel

So Dear to My Heart *
US 1948 84m Technicolor
Walt Disney
Life on a country farm in 1903
Live action nostalgia with a few cartoon segments; well enough done, but mainly appealing to well brought up children.
w John Tucker Battle novel *Midnight and Jeremiah* by Sterling North d Harold Schuster ph Winton C. Hoch m Paul Smith
☆ Burl Ives, Beulah Bondi, Harry Carey, Luana Patten, Bobby Driscoll
song 'Lavender Blue' (m Eliot Daniel, ly Larry Morey)

So Ends Our Night *
US 1941 120m bw
UA (David L. Loew, Albert Lewin)
Refugees from Nazi Germany are driven from country to country and meet persecution everywhere.
Worthy but rather drab and unfocused melodrama from the headlines.
w Talbot Jennings novel *Flotsam* by Erich Maria Remarque d John Cromwell ph William Daniels m Louis Gruenberg
☆ Fredric March, Margaret Sullavan, Glenn Ford, Frances Dee, Anna Sten, Erich von Stroheim, Joseph Cawthorn, Leonid Kinskey, Alexander Granach, Sig Rumann
'It ought to be a great picture but it isn't.' – *Archer Winsten, New York Post*
Louis Gruenberg

So Evil My Love *
GB 1948 100m bw
Paramount (Hal B. Wallis)
A missionary's widow is enticed into a life of crime and immorality by a scoundrelly artist.
Curious Victorian melodrama with a Wildean flavour; doesn't quite come off.
w Leonard Spigelgass, Ronald Millar novel Joseph Shearing d Lewis Allen ph Max Greene m Victor Young, William Alwyn
☆ Ray Milland, Ann Todd, Geraldine Fitzgerald, Leo G. Carroll, Raymond Huntley, Martita Hunt,

Moira Lister, Raymond Lovell, Muriel Aked, Finlay Currie, Hugh Griffith

'There's only one thing that can keep them apart – the seven-foot thing she's married to!'

So Fine

US 1981 91m Technicolor
Warner/Lobell – Bergman (Mike Lobell)

A professor of literature trying to save his father from gangsters becomes involved in strange adventures.
Weirdly titled action comedy which tries to be far too clever for its own good.
wd Andrew Bergman *ph* James A. Contner *m* Ennio Morricone
☆ Ryan O'Neal, Jack Warden, Mariangela Melato, Richard Kiel, Fred Gwynne, Mike Kellin
'A visual insult, crudely lighted and framed, and jumping out at you.' – *Pauline Kael, New Yorker*

So Goes My Love

US 1946 88m bw
U-I (Jack H. Skirball, Bruce Manning)
GB title: *A Genius in the Family*
The domestic life of inventor Hiram Maxim.
Formula period family film with pleasant moments.
w Bruce Manning, James Clifden *d* Frank Ryan *ph* Joseph Valentine *m* Hans Salter *ad* Lionel Banks *ed* Ted J. Kent
☆ Myrna Loy, Don Ameche, Rhys Williams, Bobby Driscoll, Richard Gaines

'For Harriet, the honeymoon was her best yet. For Charles, it was a pain in the neck.'

So I Married an Axe Murderer

US 1993 92m Technicolor
TriStar/Fried/Woods Films

A poet suspects that his newly married wife, a butcher, is a serial killer of husbands.
Slight and slightly amusing comedy, parodying Hitchcock with some sophistication and moderate success.
w Robbie Fox *d* Thomas Schlamme *ph* Julio Macat *m* Bruce Broughton *pd* John Graysmark *ed* Richard Halsey, Colleen Halsey
☆ Mike Myers, Nancy Travis, Anthony LaPaglia, Amanda Plummer, Brenda Fricker, Matt Doherty, Charles Grodin, Phil Hartman
'A hip slice of life about the dilemma of marital commitment with just a pinch of Hitchcock providing a cutting edge. Fueled by an anarchic style and a winning cast, it looks like an appealing commercial prospect.' – *Variety*
'An inconsequential, light-hearted black comedy populated by San Francisco eccentrics.' – *Philip French, Observer*

So Little Time

GB 1952 88m bw
ABP/Mayflower (Aubrey Baring, Maxwell Setton)
In occupied Belgium an aristocratic lady falls in love with a Nazi colonel.
Doomed love story with musical accompaniment; tolerable but slow.
w John Cresswell *d* Compton Bennett *ph* Oswald Morris *m* Robert Gill
☆ Marius Goring, Maria Schell, Gabrielle Dorziat, Barbara Mullen

So Long at the Fair *

GB 1950 86m bw
Rank/Gainsborough/Sydney Box (Betty E. Box)
During the 1889 Paris Exposition a girl books into a hotel with her brother, and next day finds that he has totally disappeared and his existence is denied by all concerned.
Straightforward version of an old yarn which has turned up in such varied forms as The Lady Vanishes *and* Bunny Lake is Missing. *This modest production is pleasant enough but badly lacks drive.*
w Hugh Mills, Anthony Thorne *d* Terence Fisher, Anthony Darnborough *ph* Reginald Wyer *m* Benjamin Frankel *ad* Cedric Dawe
☆ Jean Simmons, Dirk Bogarde, David Tomlinson, Marcel Poncin, Cathleen Nesbitt, Honor Blackman, Betty Warren, Felix Aylmer, André Morell

'A foxhole was her honeymoon hotel!'
'The first great story of our women at the fighting front!'

So Proudly We Hail *

US 1943 125m bw
Paramount (Mark Sandrich)
The self-sacrifice of war nurses in the Pacific.
Fairly harrowing and well-meant but studio-bound and unconvincing flagwaver.
w Allan Scott *d* Mark Sandrich *ph* Charles Lang *m* Miklos Rozsa
☆ Claudette Colbert, Paulette Goddard, Veronica Lake, George Reeves, Barbara Britton, Walter Abel, Sonny Tufts, John Litel
'Probably the most deadly accurate picture ever made of what war looks like through the lenses of a housewives' magazine romance.' – *James Agee*
'The stars are devotedly, almost gallantly, deglamorized and dishevelled but they cannot escape the smell of studio varnish.' – *Richard Winnington*
Allan Scott; Charles Lang; Paulette Goddard

'The flower of southern chivalry dewed with the shining glory of a woman's tears!'

So Red the Rose *

US 1935 82m bw
Paramount (Douglas MacLean)
The life of a Southern family during the Civil War.
Quiet, pleasing historical romance.
w Laurence Stallings, Maxwell Anderson, Edwin Justus Mayer *novel* Stark Young *d* King Vidor *ph* Victor Milner *m* W. Franke Harling
☆ Margaret Sullavan, Randolph Scott, Walter Connolly, Elizabeth Patterson, Janet Beecher, Robert Cummings
'Certain to go better in the Dixie belt than north, but okay on average.' – *Variety*

So This Is London

GB 1939 89m bw
TCF
An American magnate visits his English rival, and romance springs up between their children.
Brightish comedy with a fair scattering of funny lines.
w William Conselman, Ben Travers, Tom Phipps, Douglas Furber *d* Thornton Freeland *ph* Otto Kanturek
☆ Robertson Hare, Alfred Drayton, George Sanders, Berton Churchill, Fay Compton, Carla Lehmann, Stewart Granger, Ethel Revnell, Gracie West

So This Is Love

US 1953 101m Technicolor
Warner (Henry Blanke)
GB title: *The Grace Moore Story*
Events leading up to Grace Moore's debut at the Metropolitan Opera in 1928.
Acceptable musical biopic full of the usual Hollywood contrivances.
w John Monks Jnr *autobiography* Grace Moore *d* Gordon Douglas *ph* Robert Burks *md* Ray Heindorf, Max Steiner *ch* Le Roy Prinz *ad* Edward Carrere
☆ Kathryn Grayson, Merv Griffin, Joan Weldon, Walter Abel, Rosemary de Camp, Jeff Donnell, Douglas Dick, Mabel Albertson, Fortunio Bonanova

So This Is New York *

US 1948 78m bw
Enterprise/Stanley Kramer
In 1919 some country cousins who have come into money have a big time in the gay city.
Curious, sporadically effective, silent-style comedy which doesn't quite come off.
w Carl Foreman, Herbert Baker *novel* The Big Town by Ring Lardner *d* Richard Fleischer *ph* Jack Russell *m* Dimitri Tiomkin
☆ Henry Morgan, Rudy Vallee, Hugh Herbert, Bill Goodwin, Virginia Grey, Dona Drake, Leo Gorcey

So This Is Paris

US 1954 96m Technicolor
U-I (Albert J. Cohen)

Three American sailors on leave in Paris meet girls and help war orphans.
Very thin imitation of On the Town, *bogged down by sentimentality and lack of sparkle. The musical numbers, however, are not bad.*
w Charles Hoffman *d* Richard Quine *ph* Maury Gertsman *md* Joseph Gershenson *ch* Gene Nelson, Lee Scott
☆ Tony Curtis, Gloria de Haven, Gene Nelson, *Corinne Calvet*, Paul Gilbert, Mara Corday, Allison Hayes

So Well Remembered *

GB 1947 114m bw
RKO/Alliance (Adrian Scott)

The ambitious daughter of a mill-owner marries a rising politician but almost ruins his life.
Rather routine treatment of a three-decker north country novel; humdrum incident and unsympathetic characters, but full of minor British virtues.
w John Paxton *novel* James Hilton *d* Edward Dmytryk *ph* Frederick A. Young *m* Hanns Eisler *ad* L. P. Williams *ed* Douglas Robertson
☆ John Mills (George Boswell), Martha Scott (Olivia), Trevor Howard (Whiteside), Patricia Roc (Julie), Richard Carlson (Charles), Reginald Tate (Mangin), Beatrice Varley (Annie), Frederick Leister (Channing), Ivor Barnard (Spivey), Juliet Mills (Baby Julie)
'The occasional slackness of narrative is atoned for by a strongly communicated sense of place: the mean streets shining with rain, the sullen suffocated houses.' – *Dilys Powell, Sunday Times*

Soak the Rich *

US 1935 74m bw
Paramount (Ben Hecht, Charles MacArthur)
A rebellious rich girl is cured when she is rescued from kidnapping.
Smartly written social comedy-melodrama.
wd Ben Hecht, Charles MacArthur *ph* Leon Shamroy
☆ Walter Connolly, John Howard, Mary Taylor, Lionel Stander, Ilka Chase
'Hecht and MacArthur have not been very successful in their attempts to gauge public opinion ... inadequate entertainment.' – *Variety*

Soapdish *

US 1991 97m Technicolor
UIP/Paramount (Aaron Spelling, Alan Greisman)

A jealous co-star tries to sabotage the popularity of America's most popular star of a daily soap-opera.
Fitfully amusing parody of a TV soap, but one that failed to find much of an audience.
w Robert Harling, Andrew Bergman *d* Michael Hoffman *ph* Ueli Steiger *m* Alan Silvestri *pd* Eugenio Zanetti *ed* Garth Craven
☆ Sally Field, Kevin Kline, Robert Downey Jnr, Whoopi Goldberg, Carrie Fisher, Cathy Moriarty, Teri Hatcher, Paul Johansson, Elisabeth Shue, Garry Marshall
'An amiable comedy with enough one-liners to keep the chuckles coming regularly.' – *Sight and Sound*

'He's a goal crazy mutt with some winning moves and he's on his way to the championship!'

Soccer Dog: The Movie

US 1998 98m FotoKem Panavision
Watershed (John H. Brister)

A lonely, orphaned boy teams up with a runaway dog to form a winning combination on the soccer field.
Slow-paced, uninteresting variation on Air Bud *(qv) with some heavy-handed humour; even the dog is ordinary.*
w Daniel Forman *d* Tony Giglio *ph* Christopher Duddy *m* Victoria Dolceamore *pd* Nanette Vanderbilt *ed* Alan Z. McCurdy
☆ James Marshall (Alden), Olivia D'Abo (Elena), Jeremy Foley (Clay), Sam McMurray (Coach Shaw), Billy Drago (The Dog Catcher), Kyle Gibson (Vince), Evan Cohen (Sonny), Brocker Way (Berger)

Social Register

US 1934 71m bw
Columbia (William de Mille)
A chorus girl fights the prejudices of her in-laws to be.
Dull and obvious romantic drama mainly notable for its cast, and for the star who failed to make a comeback.
w Clara Beranger, Anita Loos, John Emerson *d* Marshall Neilan
☆ Colleen Moore, Charles Winninger, Pauline Frederick, Alexander Kirkland, Robert Benchley, Ross Alexander
'Good players lost in a trite story.' – *Variety*

'It's all about fitting in.'

Society

US 1989 99m colour
Medusa/Society Productions/Wild Street Pictures (Keith Walley)

A student discovers that his wealthy parents and friends are shape-shifting monsters who devour the poor.
Weird allegory of class warfare that contains stomach-turning special effects.
w Woody Keith, Rick Fry *d* Brian Yuzna *ph* Rick Fichter *m* Mark Ryder, Phil Davies *pd* Mathew C. Jacobs *ed* Peter Teschner *sp* Screaming Mad George
☆ Bill Warlock, Devin DeVasquez, Evan Richards, Ben Meyerson, Charles Lucia, Connie Danese, Patrice Jennings
'One of the most extraordinary genre debuts of the 80s.' – *MFB*

Society Doctor

US 1935 63m bw
MGM (Lucien Hubbard)
GB title: *After Eight Hours*
A doctor's modern ideas incur hostility: he goes into private practice, but returning to the hospital is wounded by a gangster and supervises his own operation under spinal anaesthetic.
Melodramatic hokum with most attention going to the second male lead, the young and rising Robert Taylor.
w Sam Marx, Michael Fessier *novel* The Harbor by Theodore Reeves *d* George B. Seitz *ph* Lester White *m* Oscar Radin
☆ Chester Morris, Virginia Bruce, Robert Taylor, Billie Burke, Raymond Walburn, Henry Kolker, William Henry

Society Girl

US 1932 72m bw
Fox
A prizefighter falls for a society girl.
Weak melodrama whose best scenes are in the ring.
w Charles Benhan, Elmer Harris *play* John Larkin Jnr *d* Sidney Lanfield
☆ James Dunn, Spencer Tracy, Peggy Shannon, Walter Byron, Marjorie Gateson
'Falls short of first-rate classification.' – *Variety*

Society Lawyer

US 1939 77m bw
MGM (John W. Considine Jnr)
A lawyer is embarrassed by the gratitude of a racketeer.
Tolerable co-feature with class production.
w Frances Goodrich, Albert Hackett, Leon Gordon, Hugo Butler *d* Edwin L. Marin
☆ Walter Pidgeon, Virginia Bruce, Leo Carrillo, Eduardo Ciannelli, Lee Bowman, Herbert Mundin
'Fairish murder mystery with sophisticated background. For duals.' – *Variety*

Sodom and Gomorrah

Italy/France 1963 154m colour
Titanus/S. N. Pathé (Goffredo Lombardo, Joseph E. Levine)

Lot and the Hebrews become involved in a Helamite plan to take over the rich sinful cities of Sodom and Gomorrah.
Dreary biblical blood-and-thunder; an international muddle, tedious in the extreme outside a few hilariously misjudged moments.
w Hugo Butler, Giorgio Prosperi *d* Robert Aldrich *ph* Silvano Ippoliti, Cyril Knowles *m* Miklos Rozsa *ad* Ken Adam
☆ Stewart Granger, Stanley Baker, Pier Angeli, Anouk Aimée, Rossana Podesta

Sofie *

Denmark/Norway/Sweden 1992 152m colour
Arrow/Nordisk/Norsk/Svensk Filmindustri (Lars Kolvig)

In Copenhagen in the 1890s, a Jewish woman is forced by her family to reject her non-Jewish admirer and move away from the city to marry a cousin who goes slowly mad.
A well-acted, long domestic saga that follows changing attitudes across three generations, from Sofie's parents,

anxious to be anonymous in a larger society while preserving their own way of life, to Sofie, wanting to break away but unable to do so, to her son, who rejects the old traditions; it is nevertheless at its most affecting when depicting the pleasures of Sofie's parents rather than the miseries of her own mismatch.
w Liv Ullmann, Peter Poulsen *novel* Mendel Philipsen and Son by Henri Nathansen *d* Liv Ullmann *ph* Jörgen Persson *pd* Peter Hoimark *ed* Grete Moldrup
☆ Karen-Lise Mynster, Ghita Norby, Erland Josephson, Jesper Christensen, Torben Zeller, Henning Moritzen, Stig Hoffmeyer, Kirsten Rolffes
'Lurches regrettably towards the gratuitous miserablism of Bergmanesque stereotype.' – *Sight and Sound*

'The movie with the 6 best Sellers in one!'
Soft Beds, Hard Battles
GB 1973 107m colour
Rank/Charter (John Boulting)
US title: *Undercovers Hero*
Inhabitants of a Paris brothel help to win World War II.
Ragbag of poor sketches and dirty jokes, with the star in several ineffective roles including Hitler.
w Leo Marks, Roy Boulting *d* Roy Boulting *ph* Gil Taylor *m* Neil Rhoden
☆ Peter Sellers, Lila Kedrova, Curt Jurgens, Gabriella Licudi, Jenny Hanley

Soft Deceit
Canada 1994 91m colour
Chesler/Perlmutter (Lewis B. Chester, T. A. Baird, Jorge Montesi)
A female special agent offers to spring a master thief from prison in an attempt to recover the $6m he stole from the Catholic Church.
Slick, trivial, pulp thriller, with softboiled dialogue and a narrative that is predictably implausible.
w Jorge Montesi, Roy Sallows *d* Jorge Montesi *ph* Philip Linzey *m* Ian Thomas *pd* Harold Thrasher *ed* George Roulston
☆ Patrick Bergin, Kate Vernon, John Wesley Shipp, Gwynyth Walsh, Nigel Bennett, Ted Dykstra, Damir Andrei

'A Motorvated Comedy.'
'They're going to make it. Nothing will stop them now...'
Soft Top, Hard Shoulder *
GB 1992 95m colour
Feature/Road Movie Productions (Richard Holmes)
An unsuccessful Scottish artist living in London has 36 hours to drive to Glasgow in his ancient car so that he can share in the family fortune; on the way he picks up a female hitch-hiker.
Amiable, soft-centred road movie with an affection for eccentricity.
w Peter Capaldi *d* Stefan Schwartz *ph* Henry Braham *m* Chris Rea *pd* Sonja Klaus *ed* Derek Trigg
☆ Peter Capaldi, Frances Barber, Catherine Russell, Jeremy Northam, Richard Wilson, Peter Ferninando, Simon Callow, Phyllis Logan
'The initial novelty of this particular roadshow ultimately pales.' – *Empire*

Soigne Ton Gauche *
France 1937 12m bw
Cady (Fred Orain)
A boxing training session in a village ends in chaos.
A gentle short comedy from Tati, revealing his pleasure in the eccentric details of life.
w Jean Marie Huard *d* René Clément *m* Jean Yatove
☆ Jacques Tati, Max Martell, Robur Cliville
† It was released on video together with *L'école des Facteurs* and *Cours du Soir* under the title *Tati Shorts*.

Sol Madrid
US 1968 90m Metrocolor Panavision
MGM/Gershwin-Kastner (Hall Bartlett)
GB title: *The Heroin Gang*
An undercover narcotics agent is assigned to track down an elusive Mafia executive.
Humdrum, predictable, brutishly violent international crime caper.
w David Karp *novel* Fruit of the Poppy by Robert Wilder *d* Brian G. Hutton *ph* Fred Koenekamp *m* Lalo Schifrin
☆ David McCallum, Telly Savalas, Stella Stevens, Ricardo Montalban, Rip Torn, Pat Hingle, Paul Lukas, Perry Lopez, Michael Ansara

Solamente Nero: see *The Bloodstained Shadow*

Solange Du da bist: see *As Long as You're Near Me*

Solar Crisis
US/Japan 1992 107m DeLuxe
Trimark/Gakken/NHK (Richard Edlund, James Nelson, Morris Morishima)
A power-crazed industrialist plans to sabotage Earth's last hope: a spaceship carrying an anti-matter bomb to the sun in order to prevent a massive flare from burning up the planet.
Dire science-fiction extravaganza; the banality of the plot is exceeded only by the stupidity of the dialogue.
w Joe Gannon, Crispan Bolt *novel* Takeshi Kawata *d* Alan Smithee (Richard Sarafian) *ph* Russ Carpenter *m* Maurice Jarre, Michael Boddicker *pd* George Jenson *ed* Richard Trevor *sp* Neil Krepela
☆ Tim Matheson, Charlton Heston, Peter Boyle, Annabel Schofield, Corin 'Corky' Nemec, Tetsuya Bessho, Jack Palance, David Ursin, Brenda Bakke, Paul Williams (voice)
† The movie cost $35 million. It was released direct to video in Britain.

Solar Warriors
US 1986 94m colour
MBM/Brooksfilms (Irene Walzer, Jack Frost Sanders)
US title: *Solarbabies*
In a future world where water is scarce, a gang of roller-skating teenagers rebel against authority with the aid of a mystic ball.
Ludicrous science fiction adventure that lacks invention, style and plausibility.
w Walon Green, Douglas Anthony Metrov *d* Alan Johnson *ph* Peter MacDonald *m* Maurice Jarre *pd* Anthony Pratt *ed* Conrad Buff
☆ Richard Jordan, Jami Gertz, Jason Patric, Lukas Haas, James Le Gros, Claude Brooks, Peter DeLuise, Sarah Douglas, Charles Durning

Solarbabies: see *Solar Warriors*

'The planet where nightmares come true...'
Solaris ***
USSR 1972 165m Sovcolor 'Scope
Mosfilm
A psychologist is sent to investigate the many deaths in a space station orbiting a remote planet.
Heavy-going but highly imaginative space fiction in which the menaces are ghosts materialized from the subjects' guilty pasts. The technology is superbly managed, but the whole thing is rather humourless.
w Andrei Tarkovsky, Friedrich Gorenstein *novel* Stanislaw Lem *d* Andrei Tarkovsky *ph* Vadim Yusov *m* Eduard Artemyev *ad* Mikhail Romadin
☆ Natalya Bondarchuk (Harey), Donatas Banionis (Kris), Yuri Yarvet (Snaut), Anatoli Sonlonitsin (Sartorius)

'There are some places man is not ready to go.'
Solaris *
US 2002 98m DeLuxe Panavision
TCF/Lightstorm (James Cameron, Rae Sanchini, Jon Landau)
Called to a remote space-station to discover what has happened to its crew, a psychologist is seemingly re-united with his dead wife.
Austere meditation on the difficulties of loving and the attractions of death; shorter than Tarkovsky's version, Soderbergh concentrates on a central relationship in such a cool manner that all emotion is lost.
wd Steven Soderbergh *novel* Stanislaw Lem *ph* Peter Andrews (Steven Soderbergh) *m* Cliff Martinez *pd* Philip Messina *ed* Mary Ann Bernard *sp* Cinesite; Rhythm & Hues
☆ George Clooney (Dr Chris Kelvin), Natascha McElhone (Rheya), Jeremy Davies (Snow), Viola Davis (Dr Helen Gordon), Ulrich Tukur (Gibarian)
'An investigation of primal emotions approached in an entirely cerebral manner.' – *Todd McCarthy, Variety*
'As elegant, moody, intelligent, sensuous, and sustained a studio movie as we are likely to see this season.' – *J. Hoberman, Village Voice*

Solas **
Spain 1999 98m colour
Artificial Eye/Maestranza/Via Digital (Antonio P. Perz)
aka: *Alone*
An elderly mother finds it hard to adjust to city life when she goes to stay with her unhappy, pregnant, single daughter.
Slow but affecting drama of the hostility of big cities, the disappearance of traditional values, and of two generations of women suffering at the hands of uncaring men.
wd Benito Zambrano *ph* Tote Trenas *m* Antonio Meliveo *ad* Lala Obrero *ed* Fernando Pardo
☆ María Galiana (Madre), Ana Fernandez (María), Carlos Alvarez (Vecino), Antonio Dechent (Doctor), Paco De Osca (Father), Juan Fernandez (Juan), Miguel Alcíbar (El Gordo)
'Skilful, emotionally complex and ultimately life-affirming slice of kitchen sink drama.' – *Jim Smith, Film Review*

'Left for dead on a remote planet for obsolete machines and people, a fallen hero has one last battle to fight.'
Soldier
US 1998 95m Technicolor
Warner/Morgan Creek/Impact (Jerry Weintraub)
In a rigidly controlled future a discarded soldier, replaced by swifter cyborgs, protects a peace-loving community from obliteration.
Brutal science-fiction, set in a harsh world, with Russell looking grim at all times and uttering only a few monosyllables throughout; the emphasis is on action, as he wages a single-handed war against the modern fighting machines that have replaced him.
w David Webb Peoples *d* Paul Anderson *ph* David Tattersall *m* Joel McNeely *pd* David L. Snyder *ed* Martin Hunter *sp* Ed Jones
☆ Kurt Russell (Todd), Jason Scott Lee (Caine 607), Connie Nielsen (Mace), Michael Chiklis (Jimmy Pig), Jason Isaacs (Col Mekum), Sean Pertwee (Mace), Gary Busey (Church)
'Pic's nonstop mayhem should draw enough indiscriminate action fans to launch this one; thereafter, derivative heroics and done-to-death post-apocalyptic setting will spell a fast slide.' – *Glenn Lovell, Variety*

The Soldier and the Lady *
US 1937 85m bw
RKO (Pandro S. Berman)
GB title: *Michael Strogoff*
In Napoleonic times, a messenger from the Czar sees more trouble than he expected.
Mildly ambitious swashbuckler from a story much remade in Europe; the elements jelled quite well in the Hollywood fashion.
w Mortimer Offner, Anthony Veiller, Anne Morrison Chapin *novel* Jules Verne *d* George Nicholls Jnr *ph* Joseph H. August
☆ Anton Walbrook, Elizabeth Allan, Akim Tamiroff
'Spectacle film lacking strength and names. Will have its troubles.' – *Variety*
† Exteriors were taken from a German/French film of 1936, *Courier to the Czar* (*Der Kurier des Zaren*), also starring Anton Walbrook.

'Stained with the blood of the innocent!'
Soldier Blue *
US 1970 114m Technicolor Panavision
Avco (Gabriel Katzka, Harold Loeb)
A paymaster's detachment of the US cavalry is attacked by Indians seeking gold, and two white survivors trek through the desert.
Extremely violent 'anti-violence' Western with a particularly nauseating climax following clichés all the way. From a director with pretensions.
w John Gay *novel* Arrow in the Sun by Theodore V. Olsen *d* Ralph Nelson *ph* Robert Hauser *m* Roy Budd
☆ Candice Bergen, Peter Strauss, Donald Pleasence
'One is more likely to be sickened by the film itself than by the wrongs it tries to right.' – *Tom Milne*

Soldier in the Rain
US 1963 87m bw
AA/Cedar/Solar (Martin Jurow)
Two army sergeants have wild plans for their demob, but one dies.
Curious sentimental tragi-comedy which misfires on all cylinders.
w Blake Edwards, Maurice Richlin *novel* William Goldman *d* Ralph Nelson *ph* Philip Lathrop *m* Henry Mancini
☆ Steve McQueen, Jackie Gleason, Tuesday Weld, Tony Bill, Tom Poston, Ed Nelson, John Hubbard

Soldier of Fortune *
US 1955 96m DeLuxe Cinemascope
TCF (Buddy Adler)
When a photographer disappears in Red China, his wife comes to Hong Kong to institute a search, enlists the aid of an amiable smuggler.
Cheerful Boy's Own Paper adventure romance with attractive locations and some silly anti-Red dialogue.
w Ernest K. Gann *novel* Ernest K. Gann *d* Edward Dmytryk *ph* Leo Tover *m* Hugo Friedhofer
☆ Clark Gable, Susan Hayward, Gene Barry, Alex D'Arcy, Michael Rennie, Tom Tully, Anna Sten, Russell Collins, Leo Gordon
'A very good adventure film but not one of the Gable smashes.' – *Hollywood Reporter*

Soldier of Fortune (dubbed)
Italy/France 1976 90m colour
Mondial/Cite/J. Leitienne/Labrador/Impexci
original title: *Il Soldata di Ventura*
A wandering Italian soldier and his small troop defeat an invading French army.
Comic epic, a good-natured, though undistinguished, romp through the past.
w Castellano, Pipolo, Franco Verucci, Pasquale Festa Campanile *d* Pasquale Festa Campanile *ph* Marcello Masciocchi *m* Guido and Maurizio de Angelis *ad* Pier Luigi Pizzi *ed* Mario Morra
☆ Bud Spencer (Carlo Pedersoli), Franco Agostini, Enzo Cannavale, Frederic de Pasquale, Jacques Dufilho, Andrea Ferreol

'The city of lights. A famous American author and the decade that changed a generation ... forever.'
A Soldier's Daughter Never Cries *
GB 1998 127m Technicolor
Capitol/Merchant Ivory/British Screen (Ismail Merchant)
In the mid-60s, an unhappy young girl grows up in Paris and the USA.
Based on a semi-autobiographical novel by the daughter of writer James Jones, this is a rewarding domestic drama of an out-of-the-ordinary family, coping with their status as outsiders.
w James Ivory, Ruth Prawer Jhabvala *novel* Kayle Jones *d* James Ivory *ph* Jean-Marc Fabre *m* Richard Robbins *pd* Jacques Bufnoir, Pat Garner *ed* Noëlle Boisson
☆ Kris Kristofferson, Barbara Hershey, Leelee Sobieski, Jesse Bradford, Anthony Roth Costanzo, Dominique Blanc, Jane Birkin, Virginie Ledoyen, Samuel Gruen, Luisa Conlon, Isaac de Bankole
'Nicely mounted, superbly acted picture, which should appeal to the art crowd that has supported Merchant Ivory productions over the last two decades.' – *Emanuel Levy, Variety*

Soldiers of Innocence
South Korea 1989 103m colour
ASCO/Cinevest/CineKor (Dennis H. Christen, Eun Kyong Soe)
A US sergeant, who stays behind while his company retreats, takes shelter in a church where two nuns are attemtping to protect children caught up in the Korean war.
Ineffectual melodrama that has little sense of reality about it.
w Dennis H. Christen, Han Woo Jung *d* Han Woo Jung *ph* Ok Hyun Shin *m* Bob Dee *pd* Jong Moon Kim, Sang Tae Lee *ed* Soon Doke Park
☆ Dennis Christen (Sgt Collins), Susan Richardson (Sister Anne), Eun Kyong Soe, Yong

Nam Ahn, Greta Blackburn, Hyokee Moon, Gary Wood (Capt Buzz Waters)

Soldiers of the King
GB 1933 80m bw
Gainsborough (Michael Balcon)
A guards lieutenant causes trouble when he wants to marry a music hall star.
Sprightly star vehicle with all talents in good form.
w J. O. C. Orton, Jack Hulbert, W. P. Lipscomb *story* Douglas Furber *d* Maurice Elvey *ph* Leslie Rowson *md* Louis Levy
☆ Cicely Courtneidge, Edward Everett Horton, Anthony Bushell, Frank Cellier, Dorothy Hyson, Leslie Sarony

A Soldier's Story *
US 1984 101m Metrocolor
Columbia/Delphi (Norman Jewison, Patrick Palmer)
In 1944 Louisiana, a hated sergeant at a small army post is shot dead.
Investigative melodrama on the old lines of Boomerang; *quite watchable and well acted.*
w Charles Fuller *play* Charles Fuller *d* Norman Jewison *ph* Russell Boyd *m* Herbie Hancock *pd* Walter Scott Herndon *ed* Caroline Biggerstaff, Mark Warner
☆ Howard E. Rollins Jnr (Capt. Davenport), Adolph Caesar (Sgt Waters), Art Evans (Pvt. Wilkie), David Alan Grier (Cpl Cobb), David Harris (Pvt Smalls), Denzel Washington (Pfc Peterson), Patti LaBelle (Big Mary), Wings Hauser (Lt Byrd)
best picture; Adolph Caesar (supporting actor); adapted screenplay

A Soldier's Tale
US 1988 94m colour
Mirage/Atlantic (Larry Parr)
A sergeant in the British Army tries to protect a young woman accused of being a collaborator by the French Resistance.
Bleak wartime drama of love and lust that never quite convinces.
w Grant Hindin Miller, Larry Parr *novel* M. K. Joseph *d* Larry Parr *ph* Alun Bollinger *m* John Charles *pd* Ivan Maussion *ed* Mike Horton
☆ Gabriel Byrne, Marianne Basler, Paul Wyett, Maurice Garrel, Benoit Regent, Jacques Mathou, Judge Reinhold

Soldiers Three
US 1951 87m bw
MGM (Pandro S. Berman)
Adventures of three roistering British officers on the North-West Frontier.
A kind of unofficial remake of Gunga Din *without the title character; one suspects it was meant seriously and found to be so bad that the only way out was strenuously to play it for laughs.*
w Marguerite Roberts, Tom Reed, Malcolm Stuart Boylan *d* Tay Garnett *ph* William Mellor *m* Adolph Deutsch
☆ Stewart Granger, David Niven, Robert Newton, Walter Pidgeon, Cyril Cusack, Greta Gynt, Frank Allenby, Robert Coote, Dan O'Herlihy
'Kipling fans will probably have a fit but my guess is that it will have most people in fits of laughter.' – *Daily Mail*

Il sole anche di notte: see *Night Sun*

The Solid Gold Cadillac **
US 1956 99m bw
Columbia (Fred Kohlmar)
A very minor stockholder upsets the crooked board of a large corporation.
Vaguely Capraesque comedy which begins brightly but peters out; performances sustain passing interest.
w Abe Burrows *play* George S. Kaufman, Howard Teichmann *d* Richard Quine *ph* Charles Lang *m* Cyril Mockridge *ad* Ross Bellah
☆ *Judy Holliday*, Paul Douglas, *John Williams*, *Fred Clark*, Hiram Sherman, Neva Patterson, Ralph Dumke, Ray Collins, Arthur O'Connell
art direction

'What would happen if your lover could read your mind?'
Solitaire for Two
GB 1994 106m Eastmancolor
Entertainment/Solitaire (Gary Sinyor, Richard Holmes)
A psychologist dates a woman who is able to read the minds of the men around her, who all seem to be thinking the same thing.
A botched romantic comedy, with neither the wit nor the cast to carry off its underdeveloped central conceit.
wd Gary Sinyor *ph* Henry Braham *m* David A. Hughes, John Murphy *pd* Carmel Collins *ed* Ewa J. Lind
☆ Mark Frankel, Amanda Pays, Roshan Seth, Jason Isaacs, Maryam D'Abo, Annette Crosbie
'A still-born attempt at a latter-day Hawksian comedy.' – *Variety*

The Solitaire Man *
US 1933 68m bw
MGM
Crooks doublecross each other on a Paris-London aeroplane.
Smart little comedy with top talent.
w James Kevin McGuinness *play* Bella and Samuel Spewack *d* Jack Conway
☆ Herbert Marshall, Elizabeth Allan, Mary Boland, Lionel Atwill, May Robson, Ralph Forbes
'Diverting crook melodrama in the drawing room manner ... a lot better than the grosses it will probably get.' – *Variety*

I Soliti Ignoti: see *Persons Unknown*

'Part Man. Part Machine. Total Weapon.'
Solo
US/Mexico 1996 94m Technicolor
Triumph/Orpheus/Kinema/Van Peebles (Joseph Newton Cohen, John Flock)
The US army decides to destroy the perfect android soldier after he develops a conscience about killing.
Dull action movie that borrows from The Terminator *and* The Seven Samurai *without creating any excitement of its own.*
w David L. Corley *novel* *Weapon* by Robert Mason *d* Norberto Barba *ph* Christopher Walling *m* Christopher Franke *pd* Markus Canter *ed* Scott Conrad
☆ Mario Van Peebles (Solo), Barry Corbin (General Clyde Haynes), William Sadler (Colonel Madden), Adrien Brody (Bill Stewart), Seidy Lopez (Agela), Jaime Gomez (Lorenzo), Abraham Verduzco (Miguel)
'Not one fight is memorable, and the set looks recycled from an Indiana Jones theme park. "So low" is right.' – *Susan Wloszczyna, USA Today*

'Their tragedy was to fall in love.'
Solomon and Gaenor *
GB 1998 104m DeLuxe
Film4/S4C/Arts Council/APT (Sheryl Crown)
In the early 1900s, a Jewish salesman and a Welsh woman fall in love, to the dismay of both their families.
A sometimes moving story of star-crossed lovers encountering racial prejudices.
wd Paul Morrison *ph* Nina Kellgren *m* Ilona Sekacz *pd* Hayden Pearce *ed* Kant Pan
☆ Ioan Gruffudd, Nia Roberts, Sue Jones Davies, William Thomas, Mark Lewis Jones, Maureen Lipman, David Horovitch, Cyril Shaps
'Beautifully photographed and confidently directed, with powerful and affecting performances.' – *Peter Bradshaw, Guardian*
foreign film

'Only once in 3000 years – anything like it!'
Solomon and Sheba
US 1959 142m Super Technirama 70
UA/Edward Small (Ted Richmond)
When David names his younger son as heir, his older son plots revenge.
Dullish biblical spectacle, alternating between pretentiousness and cowboys and Indians.
w Anthony Veiller, Paul Dudley, George Bruce *story* Crane Wilbur *d* King Vidor *ph* Frederick A. Young *m* Mario Nascimbene *ad* Richard Day, Alfred Sweeney
☆ Yul Brynner, Gina Lollobrigida, George Sanders, Marisa Pavan, David Farrar, John Crawford, Laurence Naismith, Alejandro Rey, Harry Andrews
'Penance is due.' – *Hollis Alpert*
'Watch out it doesn't put you to sleep.' – *New York Times*

Sombrero
US 1953 103m Technicolor
MGM (Jack Cummings)
Two Mexican villages feud over the burial place of a famous poet.
Rather self-consciously unusual musical which never catches fire but certainly keeps one watching its incredible mixture of music and melodrama.
w Norman Foster, Josefina Niggli *novel* *A Mexican Village* by Josefina Niggli *d* Norman Foster *ph* Ray June *m* Leo Arnaud
☆ Ricardo Montalban, Pier Angeli, Yvonne de Carlo, Nina Foch, Cyd Charisse, Rick Jason, Jose Greco, Thomas Gomez, Kurt Kasznar, Walter Hampden, John Abbott
'Staggering is the only word for the hokum of this extraordinary film.' – *Gavin Lambert*

Some Call It Loving
US 1973 103m Technicolor
Pleasant Pastures/James B. Harris
A young man buys a 'sleeping beauty' at a fair but is sorry when he wakes her up.
Fashionable fantasy, amplified from a slender, winning short story.
wd James B. Harris *story* *Sleeping Beauty* by John Collier *ph* Mario Tosi *m* Richard Hazard
☆ Zalman King, Carol White, Tisa Farrow, Richard Pryor, Veronica Anderson

Some Came Running
US 1958 136m Metrocolor Cinemascope
MGM/Sol C. Siegel
A disillusioned writer returns after service to his home town and takes up with a gambler and a prostitute.
Strident and rather pointless melodrama with solid acting and production values.
w John Patrick, Arthur Sheekman *novel* James Jones *d* Vincente Minnelli *ph* William H. Daniels *m* Elmer Bernstein
☆ Frank Sinatra, Dean Martin, Shirley MacLaine, Martha Hyer, Arthur Kennedy, Nancy Gates, Leora Dana
song 'To Love and Be Loved' (*m* James Van Heusen, *ly* Sammy Cahn); Shirley MacLaine; Martha Hyer; Arthur Kennedy

Some Girls: see *Sisters*

Some Girls Do
GB 1969 93m Eastmancolor
Rank/Ashdown (Betty E. Box)
Bulldog Drummond traces the sabotage of a supersonic airliner to a gang of murderous women.
Abysmal spoof melodrama in the swinging sixties mould; a travesty of a famous character.
w David Osborn, Liz Charles-Williams *d* Ralph Thomas *ph* Ernest Steward *m* Charles Blackwell
☆ Richard Johnson, Daliah Lavi, Beba Loncar, James Villiers, Sydne Rome, Robert Morley, Maurice Denham, Florence Desmond, Ronnie Stevens

Some Kind of a Nut
US 1969 89m DeLuxe
UA/Mirisch/TFT/DFI (Walter Mirisch)
When a bank teller grows a beard because of an unsightly bee sting, he is thought to be flouting authority and his whole life changes.
Laboured, cliché-ridden anti-establishment comedy, a waste of the talent involved.
wd Garson Kanin *ph* Burnett Guffey, Gerald Hirschfeld *m* Johnny Mandel
☆ Dick Van Dyke, Angie Dickinson, Rosemary Forsyth, Zohra Lampert, Elliott Reid, Dennis King

Some Kind of Hero
US 1981 97m Movielab
Paramount (Howard W. Koch)
After six years as a prisoner of the Vietcong, an army veteran returns home to find his life no bed of roses.
Weird mixture of comedy and melodrama which simply doesn't jell, especially when it tries to get earnest.
w James Kirkwood, Robert Boris *novel* James Kirkwood *d* Michael Pressman *ph* King Baggot *m* Patrick Williams *ad* James L. Schoppe *ed* Christopher Greenbury
☆ Richard Pryor, Margot Kidder, Ray Sharkey, Ronny Cox, Lynne Moody, Olivia Cole

Some Kind of Wonderful
US 1987 95m Technicolor Panavision
Paramount (John Hughes)
Girl meets boy, boy meets another girl, boy loses girl, boy gets first girl.
Teen romance pandering to its target audience: all adults are stupid and repressive, and maturity and wisdom are to be found among the young. Its appeal will be limited to the immature.
w John Hughes *d* Howard Deutch *ph* Jan Kiesser *m* Stephen Hague, John Musser *pd* Josan Russo *ed* Bud Smith, Scott Smith
☆ Eric Stoltz, Mary Stuart Masterson, Craig Sheffer, John Ashton, Lea Thompson, Elias Koteas, Maddie Corman

'The killer-diller of all swing shows!'
Some Like It Hot
US 1939 65m bw
Paramount (William C. Thomas)
TV reissue title: *Rhythm Romance*
A sideshow owner runs out of money.
Very mild comedy, one of several which helped to establish Hope's star potential.
w Lewis R. Foster *play* Wilkie C. Mahoney, Ben Hecht, Gene Fowler *d* George Archainbaud *ph* Karl Struss
☆ Bob Hope, Shirley Ross, Una Merkel, Gene Krupa, Richard Denning
'Turned out deliberately to catch the jitterbug devotees ... will satisfy moderately.' – *Variety*
† The play, *The Great Magoo*, was previously filmed in 1934 as *Shoot the Works*.

Some Like It Hot ****
US 1959 122m bw
UA/Mirisch (Billy Wilder)
Two unemployed musicians accidentally witness the St Valentine's Day Massacre and flee to Miami disguised as girl musicians.
A milestone of film comedy which keeps its central situation alive with constant and fresh invention; its wit, combined with a sense of danger, has rarely been duplicated and never equalled.
w *Billy Wilder*, *I. A. L. Diamond* *d* *Billy Wilder* *ph* Charles Lang Jnr *m* Adolph Deutsch *ad* Ted Howarth
☆ *Jack Lemmon*, *Tony Curtis*, *Marilyn Monroe*, *Joe E. Brown*, George Raft, Pat O'Brien, Nehemiah Persoff, George E. Stone, Joan Shawlee
'A comedy set in the Prohibition era, with transvestism, impotence, role confusion, and borderline inversion – and all hilariously innocent, though always on the brink of really disastrous double-entendre.' – *Pauline Kael*
'Most of the time Billy Wilder's new piece – a farce blacker than is common on the American screen – whistles along at a smart, murderous pace.' – *Dilys Powell*
'Hectic slapstick, smartass movie parodies, sexist stereotyping, crass one-liners, and bad taste galore.' – *Time Out, 1984*
script; Billy Wilder (as director); Charles Lang Jnr; Jack Lemmon; art direction
Jack Lemmon

Some Like It Sexy
GB 1969 89m Eastmancolor
Donwin (Donovan Winter)
aka: *Come Back Peter*
A butcher's boy dreams of a series of sexual conquests, changing his personality to suit each woman.
Dull, though slickly made, exploitation film, which could have done with more variation in its interminable scenes of unadventurous love-making.
wd Donovan Winter *ph* Ian D. Struthers, Gus Coma *ed* Donovan Winter
☆ Christopher Matthews, Yolande Turner, Valerie St Hélène, Annabel Leventon, Penny Riley, Erika Bergmann, Maddy Smith, Mary and Madeleine Collinson, Nicola Pagett
† The version released in the cinemas ran for 65m.

Some Mother's Son
US/Ireland 1996 112m colour
Rank/Castle Rock/Turner/Hell's Kitchen (Jim Sheridan, Arthur Lappin, Edward Burke)

In Northern Ireland, a schoolteacher is drawn into political activism when her son is arrested by the British and put in prison, where, following the lead of Bobby Sands, he is among those who go on hunger strike.
A bleak drama, based on the events in 1981 when ten men starved themselves to death; that reality overwhelms this fiction, which does no more than recreate the tragedy through the reactions of two mothers.
w Terry George, Jim Sheridan *d* Terry George *ph* Geoffrey Simpson *m* Bill Whelan *pd* David Wilson *ed* Craig McKay
☆ Helen Mirren, Fionnula Flanagan, Aiden Gillen, David O'Hara, John Lynch, Tom Hollander, Tim Woodward, Ciaran Hinds
'The action is dominated by the realities of domestic violence, prison life and a prolonged hunger strike, all of which rate as box office negatives.' – *Todd McCarthy, Variety*

Some People
GB 1962 93m Eastmancolor
Vic Films (James Archibald)
Troublesome teenage factory workers are helped by a church organist and become model citizens.
Bland propaganda for the Duke of Edinburgh's Award scheme for young people, quite acceptably presented, with pop music ad lib.
w John Eldridge *d* Clive Donner *ph* John Wilcox *m* Ron Grainer
☆ Kenneth More, Ray Brooks, Annika Wells, David Andrews, Angela Douglas, David Hemmings, Harry H. Corbett

Some Voices *
GB 2000 101m colour
FilmFour/Dragon/British Screen (Damian Jones)
Released from psychiatric hospital, a schizophrenic causes problems to his brother and a woman he becomes involved with.
Unambitious small-scale drama concentrating on a fractured relationship between the two brothers; despite the creditable performances, it would seem best suited for the TV movie 'disease of the week' spot.
w Joe Penhall *play* Joe Penhall *d* Simon Cellan Jones *ph* David Odd *m* Adrian Johnston *pd* Zoe MacLeod *ed* Elen Pierce Lewis *cos* James Keast
☆ Daniel Craig (Ray), David Morrissey (Pete), Kelly Macdonald (Laura), Julie Graham (Mandy), Peter McDonald (Dave)
'Definitely worth seeing, showcases some terrific British talent, and only fails to make the four-star grade by a whisker.' – *Mark Wyman, Film Review*

Some Will, Some Won't
GB 1969 90m Technicolor
ABP/Transocean (Giulio Zampi)

In order to inherit under an eccentric will, four people have to perform tasks out of character.
Thin remake of Laughter in Paradise *(qv); funny moments extremely few.*
w Lew Schwartz *d* Duncan Wood *ph* Harry Waxman *m* Howard Blake
☆ Ronnie Corbett, Thora Hird, Michael Hordern, Leslie Phillips, Barbara Murray, James Robertson Justice, Dennis Price, Wilfrid Brambell, Eleanor Summerfield, Arthur Lowe

Somebody Killed Her Husband
US 1978 96m Movielab
Columbia/Melvin Simon (Martin Poll)
The title tells what happened when an unhappily married young mother falls in love.
Very thin suspense comedy which starts as it ends, uncertainly.
w Reginald Rose *d* Lamont Johnson *ph* Andrew Laszlo, Ralf D. Bode *m* Alex North *pd* Ted Haworth
☆ Farrah Fawcett-Majors, Jeff Bridges, John Wood, Tammy Grimes, John Glover, Patricia Elliott

Somebody Loves Me
US 1952 97m Technicolor
Paramount/Perlberg-Seaton
First successful in San Francisco at earthquake time, Blossom Seeley climbs to Broadway success with her partner Benny Fields, then retires to become his wife.
Adequate, unsurprising star musical of the second or third rank.
wd Irving Brecher *ph* George Barnes *songs* Jay Livingston, Ray Evans
☆ Betty Hutton, Ralph Meeker, Robert Keith, Adele Jergens, Billie Bird, Sid Tomack, Ludwig Stossel

'She Was Worth Living For ... Worth Killing For...'
Somebody to Love *
US 1994 103m Foto-Kem
Entertainment/Lumiere/Initial (Lila Cazes)

A dancer in a sleazy Los Angeles club, who hopes to become a film star, has problems with the men in her life.
Confused and unfocused drama of showbiz hopefuls whose ambitions are greater than their talents; there are occasional pleasures to be had.
w Sergei Bodrov, Alexandre Rockwell *d* Alexandre Rockwell *ph* Robert Yeoman *m* Mader *pd* J. Rae Fox *ed* Elena Maganini
☆ Rosie Perez, Harvey Keitel, Anthony Quinn, Michael DeLorenzo, Steve Buscemi, Sam Fuller, Stanley Tucci
'Rarely fires on more than one cylinder at a time.' – *Variety*
† The film was inspired by Fellini's *Cabiria* (qv) and the character played by Giulietta Masina.

Somebody Up There Likes Me *
US 1956 112m bw
MGM (Charles Schnee)

An East Side kid with reform school experience becomes middleweight boxing champion of the world.
A sentimental fantasia on the life of Rocky Graziano, expertly blending violence, depression, prizefight sequences and fake uplift.
w Ernest Lehman *d* Robert Wise *ph* Joseph Ruttenberg *m* Bronislau Kaper *ad* Cedric Gibbons, Malcolm F. Brown *ed* Albert Akst
☆ Paul Newman, Pier Angeli, Everett Sloane, Eileen Heckart, Sal Mineo, Joseph Buloff, Harold J. Stone, Robert Loggia
Academy Award: Joseph Ruttenberg; art direction
Academy Award nomination: editing

Someone at the Door
GB 1936 74m bw
BIP (Walter Mycroft)
The new owner of a spooky house invents a murder which seems to come true.
Derivative but quite amusing comedy thriller.
w Jack Davies, Marjorie Deans *play* Dorothy and Campbell Christie *d* Herbert Brenon *ph* Bryan Langley
☆ Billy Milton, Aileen Marson, Noah Beery, Edward Chapman, Hermione Gingold, John Irwin
† Remade in 1950 with Michael Medwin, Yvonne Owen and Garry Marsh; directed by Francis Searle; for Hammer.

Someone Behind the Door
France 1971 97m colour
Miracle/Lira Film/Comaccio/SNC (Raymond Danon)

original title: *Quelqu'un derrière la Porte*
aka: *Two Minds for Murder*
A brain surgeon takes a psychopathic patient home and tries to make him commit murder.
Adequate but somehow unexciting suspenser.
w Mark Boehm, Jacques Robert *novel* Jacques Robert *d* Nicolas Gessner *ph* Pierre Lhomme *m* Georges Garvarentz
☆ Charles Bronson, Anthony Perkins, Jill Ireland, Henri Garcia

Someone Else's America *
France/Germany/GB 1995 93m Fujicolour
Film Four/Mact/Intrinsica/Lichtblick/Stefi 2 (Antonie de Clermont-Tonnerre, David Rose, Helga Bähr)
original title: *L'Amérique des autres*
In Brooklyn, a struggling Spanish bar-owner helps the family of his best friend, illegal immigrants who arrive unexpectedly from Montenegro.
A ramshackle film, set in the gap between life as it is at the bottom of the heap and the American dream, which has a few telling moments.
w Gordan Mihic *d* Goran Paskaljevic *ph* Yorgos Arvanitis *m* Andrew Dickson *ad* Wolf Seesselberg *ed* William Diver
☆ Tom Conti, Miki Manojlovic, Maria Casarès, Zorka Manojlovic, Sergej Trifunovic, Jose Ramon Rosario, Lanny Flaherty
'Sentimental, eccentric and quietly funny.' – *Sight and Sound*

'A Story About The One That Got Away And The One She Never Saw Coming.'
Someone Like You
US 2001 97m DeLuxe
TCF/Fox 2000 (Lynda Obst)

GB title: *Animal Attraction*
After an unhappy love affair, a TV researcher moves into a flat with a womanising colleague and develops a theory that men are programmed to be unfaithful.
Illogical romantic comedy that fails to deliver on its promises and offers no compensating surprises.
w Elizabeth Chandler *novel* *Animal Husbandry* by Laura Zigman *d* Tony Goldwyn *ph* Anthony B. Richmond *m* Rolfe Kent *pd* Dan Leigh *ed* Dana Congdon *cos* Ann Roth, Michelle Maitlin
☆ Ashley Judd (Jane Goodale), Greg Kinnear (Ray Brown), Hugh Jackman (Eddie Alden), Marisa Tomei (Liz), Ellen Barkin (Diane Roberts), Catherine Dent (Alice), Peter Friedman (Stephen), Laura Regan (Evelyn)
'A romantic comedy as lamely generic as its title...leaves no stone unturned in its attempt to be as conventional and predictable as possible.' – *Todd McCarthy, Variety*

Someone to Love *
US 1987 105m DeLuxe
ICA/International Rainbow/Jagfilm (M. H. Simonsons)

On Valentine's Day, a director throws a party for his single and divorced friends and questions them on camera about their attitudes to love and relationships.
Little more than a succession of turns by various actors and actresses, but intermittently interesting and notable for Welles's final appearance on film, bringing it to an end with a shout of 'Cut!'
wd Henry Jaglom *ph* Hanania Baer *ed* Henry Jaglom
☆ Orson Welles, Henry Jaglom, Andrea Marcovicci, Michael Emil, Sally Kellerman, Oja Kodar, Stephen Bishop, Dave Frishberg

Someone to Watch Over Me *
US 1987 106m DeLuxe
Columbia/Thierry de Ganay

A New York cop falls for the witness he must protect from a vicious killer.
Lively thriller with slick technicalities.
w Howard Franklin *d* *Ridley Scott* *ph* Steven Poster *m* Michael Kamen *pd* Jim Bissell
☆ Tom Berenger, Mimi Rogers, Lorraine Bracco, Jerry Orbach, John Rubinstein, Andreas Katsulas
'Stylish and romantic ... manages to triumph over several hard-to-swallow plot developments.' – *Daily Variety*

Something about Love
Canada 1988 93m colour
Allegro/NFBC (Franco Battista, Tom Berry, Stefan Wodoslawsky)
A Hollywood producer returns home to reconcile with his father, who is suffering from Alzheimer's disease.
Mundane domestic drama that never gets to grips with its subject.
w Tom Berry, Stefan Wodoslawsky *d* Tom Berry *ph* Rodney Gibbons *m* Lou Forestieri *ad* Guy Lalande *ed* Franco Battista
☆ Stefan Wodoslawsky, Jan Rubes, Jennifer Dale, Ron James, Leonore Zann, Diana Reis

Something Big
US 1971 108m Technicolor
Cinema Center/Stanmore and Penbar (Andrew V. McLaglen)
A retiring cavalry colonel has a last battle with his old enemy.
Wry serio-comic Western in the Ford tradition.
w James Lee Barrett *d* Andrew V. McLaglen *ph* Harry Stradling Jnr *m* Marvin Hamlisch *ad* Alfred Sweeney *ed* Robert Simpson
☆ Dean Martin (Joe Baker), Brian Keith (Colonel Morgan), Honor Blackman (Mary Anna Morgan), Carol White (Dover), Ben Johnson (Jesse Bookbinder), Albert Salmi (Johnny Cobb), Denver Pyle (Junior Frisbee)

Something for Everyone *
US 1970 110m colour
National General (John Flaxman)

GB title: *Black Flowers for the Bride*
A young con man insinuates himself into the household of a widowed Austrian countess.
Unusual black comedy which doesn't quite come off.
w Hugh Wheeler *novel* *The Cook* by Harry Kressing *d* Harold Prince *ph* Walter Lassally *m* John Kander
☆ Angela Lansbury, Michael York, Anthony Corlan, Heidelinde Weis
'Nothing much for anyone, actually.' – *New Yorker*

Something for the Birds
US 1952 81m bw
TCF (Samuel G. Engel)
An elderly fraud is of help to a Washington girl trying to save a bird sanctuary.
Derivative, competent but slightly boring political whimsy on Capra lines.
w I. A. L. Diamond, Boris Ingster *d* Robert Wise *ph* Joseph LaShelle *m* Sol Kaplan
☆ Edmund Gwenn, Victor Mature, Patricia Neal, Larry Keating, Christian Rub

Something for the Boys
US 1944 87m Technicolor
TCF (Irving Starr)
A Southern plantation is turned into a retreat for army wives.
Modest musical, vaguely based on a Broadway success.
w Robert Ellis, Helen Logan, Frank Gabrielson *musical comedy* Cole Porter, Herbert and Dorothy Fields *d* Lewis Seiler *ph* Ernest Palmer *m* Cyril Mockridge *title song* Cole Porter *other songs* Harold Adamson, Jimmy McHugh
☆ Carmen Miranda, Michael O'Shea, Vivian Blaine, Phil Silvers, Sheila Ryan, Perry Como, Glenn Langan, Cara Williams

Something in the Wind
US 1947 89m bw
U-I (Joseph Sistrom)
A lady disc jockey is mistaken for her aunt, who has been seeing too much for the heirs' liking of a wealthy old man.
Poorish star musical comedy.
w Harry Kurnitz, William Bowers *d* Irving Pichel
☆ Deanna Durbin, Donald O'Connor, John Dall, Charles Winninger, Helena Carter

Something Money Can't Buy
GB 1952 82m bw
Rank/Vic (Joe Janni)
After World War II a young couple find civilian life difficult and dreary, but finally start a catering and secretarial business.
Weakly contrived comedy which makes nothing of its possibilities and is limply handled all round.
w Pat Jackson, James Landsdale Hodson *d* Pat Jackson *ph* C. Pennington-Richards *m* Nino Rota
☆ Patricia Roc, Anthony Steel, A. E. Matthews, Moira Lister, David Hutcheson, Michael Trubshawe, Diane Hart, Charles Victor, Henry Edwards

Something of Value
US 1957 113m bw
MGM (Pandro S. Berman)

A young African with many English friends is initiated into the Kikuyu.
An attempt to see all sides in the case of the African ritual murders of the fifties; bloodthirsty and unconvincing as well as dull.
wd Richard Brooks *novel* Robert Ruark *ph* Russell Harlan *m* Miklos Rozsa
☆ Rock Hudson, Sidney Poitier, Dana Wynter, Wendy Hiller, Robert Beatty, Juano Hernandez, William Marshall, Walter Fitzgerald, Michael Pate

'Believe in Love. Believe in Life. Believe in Yourself. Believe in Miracles.'

Something to Believe In
GB/Germany 1997 113m colour 'Scope
Warner/Grade/Kirch (John Hough)
A female croupier, given two months to live, goes to Italy in search of a miracle cure, and falls in love with a concert pianist.
Risibly sentimental weepie, extraordinarily old-fashioned in its attitudes and approach.
w John Goldsmith, John Hough *d* John Hough *ph* Tony Pierce Roberts *m* Lalo Schifrin *pd* Nello Giorgetti *ed* Peter Tanner
☆ William McNamara, Maria Pitillo, Tom Conti, Maria Schneider, Ian Bannen, Robert Wagner, Jill St John, Roddy McDowall
'Simply defies credulity.' – *Guardian*
'A movie this stupid could change your life forever.' – *Independent*

Something to Hide
GB 1971 99m Eastmancolor
Avton (Michael Klinger)
A civil servant has a row with his wife, kills her and buries her body on the Isle of Wight.
Unpleasant and uninteresting melodrama demanding a hysterical performance from its star. Pleasant photography is its only asset.
wd Alastair Reid *novel* Nicholas Monsarrat *ph* *Wolfgang Suschitzky* *m* Roy Budd, Jack Fishman
☆ Peter Finch, Colin Blakely, John Stride, Shelley Winters, Linda Hayden, Harold Goldblatt

Something to Live For
US 1952 89m bw
Paramount (George Stevens)
A commercial artist member of Alcoholics Anonymous falls for a dipsomaniac actress but refuses to break up his marriage.
Glossy romantic melodrama with some style but no depth; the casting makes it seem like a sequel to The Lost Weekend.
w Dwight Taylor *d* George Stevens *ph* George Barnes *m* Victor Young
☆ Ray Milland, Joan Fontaine, Teresa Wright, Richard Derr, Douglas Dick
'The victory over alcohol becomes a somewhat woebegone business.' – *Penelope Houston*
† Completed in 1950, but not released until later.

Something to Shout About
US 1943 93m bw
Columbia (Gregory Ratoff)
A press agent tries to get rid of an untalented star.
Tolerable musical comedy.
w Fred Shiller, Lou Breslow, Edward Eliscu, George Owen *d* Gregory Ratoff *md* Morris Stoloff *songs* Cole Porter
☆ Don Ameche, Janet Blair, William Gaxton, Perry Como
Morris Stoloff; song 'You'd Be So Nice to Come Home To'

Something to Sing About *
US 1937 90m bw
Grand National (Zion Myers)
A New York bandleader decides to take a fling at Hollywood.
Lightweight but reasonably pleasing musical, made by the star as an independent during a rift with his studio, Warner.
w Austin Parker *ph* John Stumar *md* Constantin Bakaleinikoff *d/songs* Victor Schertzinger
☆ *James Cagney*, Evelyn Daw, Mona Barrie, William Frawley, Gene Lockhart
'A first-class comedy with music; will please everywhere.' – *Variety*
Victor Schertzinger

Something to Talk About
US 1995 106m Technicolor
Warner/Spring Creek (Anthea Sylbert, Paula Weinstein)
A wife discovers that her husband has been having an affair and throws him out of the house; her mother-in-law follows her example.
Vacuous and glossy romantic comedy which emphasizes that the wealthy also suffer, though in greater comfort than the rest of us.
w Callie Khouri *d* Lasse Hallström *ph* Sven Nykvist *m* Hans Zimmer, Graham Preskett *pd* Mel Bourne *ed* Mia Goldman
☆ Julia Roberts, Dennis Quaid, Robert Duvall, Gena Rowlands, *Kyra Sedgwick*, Brett Cullen, Haley Aull, Muse Watson
'Bland one moment and barbed the next ... dithers on like compulsive conversationalists who take twice as long as necessary to say what they want to say.' – *Variety*

Something Wicked This Way Comes *
US 1983 95m Technicolor
Walt Disney/Bryna (Peter Vincent Douglas)
A sinister carnival with a power over time and age visits a small town in Illinois.
A curious departure for the Disney studio is this grim fairy tale from a novel which was probably intractable. In the cinema, this is the sort of film very lucky to find an audience despite its good qualities.
w Ray Bradbury *novel* Ray Bradbury *d* Jack Clayton *ph* Stephen H. Burum *m* James Horner *pd* Richard MacDonald
☆ Jason Robards, Jonathan Pryce, Diane Ladd, Pam Grier, Royal Dano, Vidal Peterson, Shawn Carson

Something Wild
US 1961 112m bw
(UA) Prometheus (George Justin)
A girl's life and attitudes change after she is raped, and she moves in with a garage mechanic.
A bit of a wallow, with much method acting but no clear analysis of the central relationship.
w Jack Garfein, Alex Karmel *novel* *Mary Ann* by Alex Karmel *d* Jack Garfein *ph* Eugene Schufftan *m* Aaron Copland *ad* Richard Day
☆ Carroll Baker, Ralph Meeker, Mildred Dunnock, Charles Watts, Martin Kosleck, Jean Stapleton

Something Wild
US 1986 113m colour
Orion/Religioso Primitiva Du Art (Jonathan Demme, Kenneth Utt)
Two irresponsible young people find themselves on the run from police and criminals.
Unremarkable melodrama with trendy musical trappings.
w E. Max Frye *d* Jonathan Demme *ph* Tak Fujimoto *m* John Cale, Laurie Anderson
☆ Jeff Daniels, Melanie Griffith, Ray Liotta, Margaret Colin

Sometimes a Great Notion *
US 1971 114m Technicolor Panavision
Universal/Newman-Foreman
GB title: *Never Give an Inch*
In a small Oregon township, trouble is caused by an independent family of lumberjacks.
Freewheeling but unsatisfactorily eccentric comedy-melodrama which never quite jells but has flashes of individuality.
w John Gay *novel* Ken Kesey *d* *Paul Newman* *ph* Richard Moore *m* Henry Mancini
☆ Paul Newman, Henry Fonda, Lee Remick, Michael Sarrazin, Richard Jaeckel, Linda Lawson, Cliff Potts
song 'All His Children' (mHenry Mancini, lyAlan and Marilyn Bergman); Richard Jaeckel

Somewhere I'll Find You *
US 1942 108m bw
MGM (Pandro S. Berman)
Brother war correspondents quarrel over a girl and later find her in Indo-China smuggling Chinese babies to safety.
Absurd but satisfactory star vehicle of the second rank, with the theme designed to prepare America for war.
w Marguerite Roberts *story* Charles Hoffman *d* Wesley Ruggles *ph* Harold Rosson *m* Bronislau Kaper
☆ Clark Gable, Lana Turner, Robert Sterling, Patricia Dane, Reginald Owen, Lee Patrick, Charles Dingle, Rags Ragland, William Henry

Somewhere in England
GB 1940 79m bw
Mancunian (John E. Blakeley)
High jinks among army recruits staging a show.
One of a series of misshapen and badly made regional comedies which afflicted British cinemas in the forties and should be mentioned for their immense popularity, their new-style vulgarity (later to be refined by the Carry On series) and their highly popular stars.
w Arthur Mertz, Roney Parsons *d* John E. Blakeley *ph* Geoffrey Faithfull
☆ *Frank Randle, Harry Korris, Robbie Vincent*, Winki Turner, Dan Young
† Subsequently released, or allowed to escape, between 1941 and 1949 were *Somewhere in Camp*, *Somewhere on Leave*, *Somewhere in Civvies* and *Somewhere in Politics*.

Somewhere in France: see *The Foreman Went to France*

Somewhere in Sonora
GB 1933 58m bw
Warner
A cowboy goes to the aid of his friend, whose son has been kidnapped by an outlaw gang.
John Wayne once more steps into Ken Maynard's boots in a remake of the silent star's unremarkable 1927 Western.
w Joe Roach *novel* *Somewhere South in Sonora* by Will L. Comfort *d* Mack V. Wright
☆ John Wayne, Henry B. Walthall, Shirley Palmer, Paul Fix, Ann Faye, Billy Franey, Ralph Lewis, Frank Rice, J. P. McGowan

Somewhere in the Night *
US 1946 111m bw
TCF (Anderson Lawler)
An amnesiac war veteran tries to discover his true identity and discovers he is a crook with much-wanted information.
Overlong suspenser with a tentative film noir *atmosphere. A few nice touches partly atone for a tediously conversational plot.*
w Howard Dimsdale, Joseph L. Mankiewicz *story* *The Lonely Journey* by Marvin Borowsky *d* Joseph L. Mankiewicz *ph* Norbert Brodine *m* David Buttolph
☆ John Hodiak, Nancy Guild, Lloyd Nolan, Richard Conte, Josephine Hutchinson, Fritz Kortner

Somewhere in Time *
US 1980 104m Technicolor
Universal/Rastar (Stephen Deutsch)
A playwright falls in love with the photograph of an actress, and finds a way back in time to meet her.
Rather a charming variation on Berkeley Square, *but hardly a theme to do well in the hardnosed eighties.*
w Richard Matheson *novel* *Bid Time Return* by Richard Matheson *d* Jeannot Szwarc *ph* Isidore Mankofsky *m* John Barry *pd* Seymour Klate *ed* Jeff Gourson *cos* *Jean-Pierre Dorleac*
☆ Christopher Reeve (Richard Collier), Christopher Plummer (W. F. Robinson), Jane Seymour (Elise McKenna), Teresa Wright (Laura Roberts), Bill Erwin (Arthur), George Voskovec (Dr Gerald Finney), Susan French (Older Elise), John Alvin (Arthur's Father)
'A charming, witty, passionate romantic drama.' – *Variety*
Jean-Pierre Dorleac

Somewhere on Leave
GB 1942 96m bw
Mancunian/F. W. Baker and John E. Blakeley
New recruits in the Army go to spend a weekend in a stately home.
Low-budget comedy that switches from some low comedy music-hall routines and anarchic acrobatic fun from Randle to a stilted, badly acted romance by the young leads; it has a few amusing moments.
w Roney Parsons, Anthony Toner *d* John E. Blakeley *ph* Geoffrey Faithfull *m* A. W. Stanbury *md* Percival Mackey *ad* W. J. Hemsley *ed* E. Richards
☆ Frank Randle, Harry Korris, Dan Young, Robbie Vincent, Toni Lupino, Pat McGrath, Tonie Edgar Bruce

Somewhere Tomorrow
US 1983 87m colour
Blue Marble (Robert Wiemer, Glenn Kershaw)
After watching *Topper* on TV, a girl falls in love with the ghost of a boy killed in a plane crash.
Forgettable teenage romance, over-sentimental for all but the very sweet-toothed.
wd Robert Wiemer *ph* Glenn Kershaw *m* Paul Baillargeon *ad* Richard Hoover, Ruth Ammon *ed* Peter Hammer
☆ Sarah Jessica Parker, Nancy Addison, Tom Shea, Rick Weber, Paul Bates

Sommaren med Monika: see *Summer with Monika*

Sommarlek: see *Summer Interlude*

Sommarnattens Leende: see *Smiles of a Summer Night*

Sommersby
US/France 1993 113m Technicolor
Warner/Regency/Canal (Arnon Milchan, Steven Reuther)
After the American Civil War, a man who returns home after a gap of seven years is suspected of being an impostor.
Lush costume piece that never comes to terms with the ambiguity of its story.
w Nicholas Meyer, Sarah Kernochan *d* Jon Amiel *ph* Philippe Rousselot *m* Danny Elfman *pd* Bruno Rubeo *ed* Peter Boyle
☆ Richard Gere, Jodie Foster, Bill Pullman, James Earl Jones, Lanny Flaherty, William Windom, Wendell Wellman, Brett Kelley
'Fails to generate any sense of tragedy or passion, preferring to remain at a distance to the story, mistaking seriousness for profundity and aloofness for sophistication.' – *Jason Drake, Sight and Sound*
† It is a remake of the French film *The Return of Martin Guerre* (qv).

The Son: see *Le Fils*

Son of a Gunfighter
US/Spain 1964 90m Metrocolor
Cinemascope
Zurbano/MGM (Lester Welch)
A young Westerner stalks the outlaw responsible for his mother's death.
Tolerable international Western.
w Clarke Reynolds *d* Paul Landres *ph* Manuel Berenguer *md* Frank Barber
☆ Russ Tamblyn, Kieron Moore, James Philbrook, Fernando Rey

Son of Ali Baba
US 1952 75m Technicolor
U-I (Leonard Goldstein)
A cadet of the military academy outwits a wicked caliph.
Routine Arabian Nights hokum.
w Gerald Drayson Adams *d* Kurt Neumann *ph* Maury Gertsman *m* Joseph Gershenson
☆ Tony Curtis, Piper Laurie, Susan Cabot, Victor Jory

Son of Blob: see *Beware! The Blob*

Son of Captain Blood
Italy/Spain 1962 95m Eastmancolor
Dyaliscope
CCM/BP/Harry Joe Brown
Captain Blood's son routs his father's enemies.
Lively swashbuckler with the original star's son rather unhappily cast.
w Mario Caiano *d* Tulio Demicheli *ph* Alejandro Ulloa *m* Angelo Francesco Lavagnino
☆ Sean Flynn, Ann Todd, Jose Nieto, John Kitzmiller

Son of Dr Jekyll
US 1951 77m bw
Columbia
Dr Jekyll's son worries about developing a split personality, but discovers that his father's supposed friend Dr Lanyon is the spanner in the works.
Irresistibly silly elaboration of a famous story; no thrills but several good unintentional laughs.
w Mortimer Braus, Jack Pollexfen *d* Seymour Friedman *ph* Henry Freulich *m* Paul Sawtell
☆ Louis Hayward, Alexander Knox, Jody Lawrance, Lester Matthews, Paul Cavanagh, Gavin Muir, Rhys Williams

'Searing the screen with new terror!'
Son of Dracula *
US 1943 80m bw
Universal (Ford Beebe)

A mysterious stranger named Alucard, with a penchant for disappearing in puffs of smoke, turns up on a Southern plantation.
Stolid series entry with a miscast lead; nicely handled moments.
w Eric Taylor *d* *Robert Siodmak* *ph* *George Robinson* *m* Hans Salter
☆ Lon Chaney Jnr, Louise Allbritton, Robert Paige, Samuel S. Hinds, Evelyn Ankers, Frank Craven, J. Edward Bromberg
† The title cheats: he isn't the son of, but the old man himself ...

Son of Flubber
US 1963 100m bw
Walt Disney

An inventor tries out a rain-making machine that goes wrong.
Mildly silly comedy with a couple of amusing moments.
d Robert Stevenson *ph* Edward Colman
m George Bruns
☆ Fred MacMurray, Nancy Olson, Keenan Wynn, Tommy Kirk, Ed Wynn, Charlie Ruggles, Leon Ames, William Demarest, Paul Lynde
† It was a sequel to *The Absent-Minded Professor* (qv).

'The black shadows of the past bred this half-man, half-demon!'
Son of Frankenstein ***
US 1939 99m bw
Universal (Rowland V. Lee)

The old baron's son comes home and starts to dabble, with the help of a broken-necked and vindictive shepherd.
Handsomely mounted sequel to Bride of Frankenstein *and the last of the classic trio. The monster is less interesting, but there are plenty of other diversions, including the splendid if impractical sets.*
w *Willis Cooper* *d* *Rowland V. Lee* *ph* *George Robinson* *m* *Frank Skinner* *ad* *Jack Otterson*
ed Ted J. Kent
☆ *Basil Rathbone*, *Boris Karloff*, *Bela Lugosi*, *Lionel Atwill*, Josephine Hutchinson, Donnie Dunagan, Emma Dunn, *Edgar Norton*, Lawrence Grant
'Rather strong material for the top keys, picture will still garner plenty of bookings in the secondary first runs along the main stem.' – *Variety*
'The slickness of production gives a kind of refinement to the horrific moments and a subtlety to the suspense.' – *Film Weekly*

Son of Fury *
US 1942 102m bw
TCF (William Perlberg)
An 18th-century Englishman is deprived of his inheritance, flees to a South Sea island but comes back seeking restitution.
Elaborate costumer which suffers from loss of suspense during the central idyll. Much to enjoy along the way.
w Philip Dunne *novel* *Benjamin Blake* by Edison Marshall *d* *John Cromwell* *ph* Arthur Miller
m Alfred Newman
☆ Tyrone Power, Gene Tierney, George Sanders, Frances Farmer, Roddy McDowall, John Carradine, Elsa Lanchester, *Dudley Digges*, Harry Davenport, Halliwell Hobbes
† Remade as *Treasure of the Golden Condor* (qv).

Son of Godzilla
Japan 1967 86m colour
Toho Company (Tomoyuki Tanaka)

Intrepid scientists, experimenting with the weather on a remote island, battle against back projections of spiders and a giant mantis as a motherless son is born to Godzilla.
Standard monster hokum, with actors in rubber suits trampling on model buildings.
w Shinichi Sekizawa, Kazue Shiba *d* Jun Fukuda
ph Kazuo Yamada *m* Masaru Sato *ad* Takeo Kita
ed Ryohei Fujii
☆ Tadeo Takashima, Bibari Maeda, Akira Kubo, Akihiko Hirata, Kenji Sahara, Yoshio Tsuchiya

Son of Kong *
US 1933 69m bw
RKO (Merian C. Cooper)

After Kong has wrecked New York, producer Carl Denham flees from his creditors and finds more monsters on the old island.
Hasty sequel to the splendid King Kong; *the results were so tame and unconvincing that the film was sold as a comedy, but it does have a few lively moments after four reels of padding.*
w Ruth Rose *d* Ernest B. Schoedsack *ph* Eddie Linden, Vernon Walker, J. O. Taylor *m* Max Steiner *sp* *Willis O'Brien*
☆ Robert Armstrong, Helen Mack, Frank Reicher, John Marston, Victor Wong
'The sequel to and wash-up of the King Kong theme, consisting of salvaged remnants from the original production ... the punch is no longer there.' – *Variety*

Son of Lassie
US 1945 100m Technicolor
MGM (Samuel Marx)

A dog follows its young master to the war and helps settle the hash of a few Nazis.
Silly dog story, the first sequel to Lassie Come Home; *far too slow to start with, then packed with serial-like action.*
w Jeanne Bartlett *d* S. Sylvan Simon *ph* Charles Schoenbaum *m* Herbert Stothart
☆ Peter Lawford, Donald Crisp, June Lockhart, Nigel Bruce, Leon Ames, Nils Asther
'Good old sentimental hokum.' – *Variety*

Son of Monte Cristo *
US 1940 102m bw
(UA)

The masked avenger who quashes a dictatorship in 1865 Lichtenstein is none other than the son of Edmond Dantes.
Cheerful swashbuckler of the second class.
w George Bruce *d* Rowland V. Lee *ph* George Robinson *m* Edward Ward *ad* John DuCasse Schulze
☆ Louis Hayward, Joan Bennett, George Sanders, Florence Bates, Lionel Royce, Montagu Love, Clayton Moore, Ralph Byrd
art direction

Son of Paleface *
US 1952 95m Technicolor
(Paramount) Bob Hope (Robert L. Welch)

A tenderfoot and a government agent compete for the attentions of a lady bandit.
Gagged-up sequel to The Paleface; *much of the humour now seems self-conscious and dated in the* Road *tradition which it apes, but there are still moments of delight.*
w Frank Tashlin, Joseph Quillan, Robert L. Welch
d Frank Tashlin *ph* Harry J. Wild *m* Lyn Murray
☆ Bob Hope, Roy Rogers, Jane Russell, Trigger, Douglass Dumbrille, Harry von Zell, Bill Williams, Lloyd Corrigan
song 'Am I in Love' (*m/ly* Jack Brooks)

Son of Robin Hood
GB 1958 77m Eastmancolor
Cinemascope
TCF/Argo (George Sherman)
Robin's daughter joins with the Regent's brother to overthrow the Black Duke.
Empty-headed romp, more or less in the accepted tradition.
w George George, George Slavin *d* George Sherman *ph* Arthur Grant *m* Leighton Lucas
☆ David Hedison, June Laverick, David Farrar, Marius Goring, Philip Friend, Delphi Lawrence, George Coulouris, George Woodbridge

'Where The Wicked Are Bold...And The Bold Are Beautiful Women!'
Son of Sinbad *
US 1955 88m Technicolor
Superscope
RKO (Robert Sparks)

Sinbad and Omar Khayyam are imprisoned by the Caliph but escape with the secret of green fire.
Arabian Nights burlesque, mainly quite bright, with the forty thieves played by harem girls.
w Aubrey Wisberg, Jack Pollexfen *d* Ted Tetzlaff
ph William Snyder *m* Victor Young
md Constantin Bakaleinikoff *ch* Olga Lynn
ad Albert s. D'Agostino, Walter E. Keller
ed Roland A. Gross *cos* Michael Woulfe
☆ Dale Robertson (Sinbad), Vincent Price (Omar Khayyam), Sally Forrest (Amcer), Lili St Cyr (Nerissa), Mari Blanchard (Kristina), Leon Askin (Khalif), Jay Novello (Jiddah), Raymond Greenleaf (Simon)
† Kim Novak is among the starlets playing the forty thieves.

'Clumsy has a colour all its own.'
Son of the Pink Panther
US 1993 93m DeLuxe
MGM/UA/Filmauro (Tony Adams)

A French policeman, the illegitimate son of Inspector Clouseau, hinders the investigation of the kidnapping of a princess by terrorists.
Benigni, a natural clown with splendidly fractured English, was an ideal choice, if one had to be made, to take over the role of a bumbling policeman in the Pink Panther *series – but that had already become lacking in inspiration during Peter Sellers's time and now its condition is terminal; even natural clowns need good material.*
w Blake Edwards, Steve Sunshine, Madeline Sunshine *d* Blake Edwards *ph* Dick Bush
m Henry Mancini *pd* Peter Mullins *ed* Robert Pergament
☆ Roberto Benigni, Herbert Lom, Debrah Farentino, Claudia Cardinale, Robert Davi, Burt Kwouk, Graham Stark, Oliver Cotton, Anton Rodgers
'A tired pastiche of recycled sketches and gags.' – *Variety*

'An eye feast of virile action, colourful settings and glowing climaxes!'
The Son of the Sheik *
US 1926 74m (24 fps) bw silent
(UA)

Ahmed protects a dancing girl from a band of renegades.
Tongue-in-cheek desert romp which was probably its star's best film. He plays a dual role of father and son.
w Frances Marion, George Marion Jnr, Frederick Gresac *d* George Fitzmaurice *m* (1934 sound version) Jack Ward
☆ Rudolph Valentino, Vilma Banky, Agnes Ayres
'The very picture for which the world's wife, mother and daughter have been waiting!' – *Louella Parsons*
'We expect every fan in the country to be saying: It is Rudy's best. We can never forget him.' – *Photoplay*

Son-in-Law
US 1993 95m Technicolor
Buena Vista/Hollywood Pictures (Michael Rotenberg, Peter M. Lenkov)

A girl takes her Californian boyfriend home to the family farm for Thanksgiving.
A sickly, oversweet comedy featuring an antic, unfunny comedian caught in direly predictable situations.
w Fax Bahr, Adam Small, Shawn Schepps
story Patrick J. Clifton, Susan McMartin, Peter Lenkov *d* Steve Rash *ph* Peter Deming
m Richard Gibbs *pd* Joseph T. Garrity *ed* Dennis M. Hill
☆ Pauly Shore, Carla Gugino, Lane Smith, Cindy Pickett, Mason Adams, Patrick Renna, Dennis Burkley
'You'd have to dig way back to the likes of Sleep 'n' Eat and the Bowery Boys' Huntz Hall to find a moron-funnyman persona as irksome as Pauly Shore's.' – *Variety*

Sonatine
Canada 1983 92m colour
Corporation Image/M & M (Pierre Gendron)
Two teenage girls form tentative relationships with older men before joining in a public suicide pact.
Trite tale of teenagers unable to make contact with a wider world than themselves.
wd Micheline Lanctôt *ph* Guy Dufaux
m François Lanctôt *ed* Louise Surprenant
☆ Pascale Bussieres, Marcia Pilote, Pierre Fauteux, Kliment Dentchev

Sonatine *
Japan 1993 93m colour
ICA/Bandai/Shochiku Dai-ichi Kogyo (Masayuki Mori, Hisao Nabeshima, Takio Yoshida)

A violent Tokyo gangster, sent to intervene in a gang war in Okinawa, realizes that he has made a mistake and, after relaxing at the seaside with his gang, faces a final showdown.
An odd gangster movie, violent and downbeat, but also veering away from the genre into casual moments of fun and games.
wd Takeshi Kitano *ph* Katsumi Yanagishima
m Joe Hisaishi *ad* Osamu Sasaki *ed* Takeshi Kitano
☆ 'Beat' Takeshi (Takeshi Kitano), Aya Kokumai, Tetsu Watanabe, Masanobu Katsumura, Susumu Terashima, Ren Ohsugi, Tonbo Zushi, Kenichi Yajima
'Pic's combo of dry humor, sudden bursts of violence, and world-weary romanticism will take a while to build for first-time viewers of Kitano's movies, and the jigsaw of plot and characters only takes recognisable shape about halfway in.' – *Variety*

Söndags Barn: see *Sunday's Children*

A Song Is Born *
US 1948 113m Technicolor
Samuel Goldwyn

A young academic, one of a group of professors researching the history of music, becomes involved with a nightclub singer.
Flat remake of Ball of Fire *(qv), graced by an array of top-flight musical talent.*
w Harry Tugend *d* Howard Hawks *ph* Gregg Toland *m* Hugo Friedhofer *md* Emil Newman
songs Don Raye, Gene de Paul
☆ Danny Kaye, Virginia Mayo, Hugh Herbert, Steve Cochran, Felix Bressart, J. Edward Bromberg, Mary Field, Ludwig Stossel, Louis Armstrong, Charlie Barnet, Benny Goodman, Lionel Hampton, Tommy Dorsey, Mel Powell

Song o' My Heart
US 1930 85m bw
Fox
A professional singer looks after the orphaned children of his former love.
A thin story is the excuse for a great tenor to sing eleven songs.
w Tom Barry, J. J. McCarthy *d* Frank Borzage
☆ *John McCormack*, Maureen O'Sullivan, John Garrick, J. M. Kerrigan, Alice Joyce
'A simple tale charmingly told ... sitting through it is no hardship.' – *Variety*

'We're going to see Jennifer Jones again in...'
The Song of Bernadette **
US 1943 156m bw
TCF (William Perlberg)

A peasant girl has a vision of the Virgin Mary at what becomes the shrine of Lourdes.
Hollywood religiosity at its most commercial; but behind the lapses of taste and truth is an excellent production which was phenomenally popular and created a new star.
w George Seaton *novel* Franz Werfel *d* *Henry King* *ph* *Arthur Miller* *m* *Alfred Newman* *ad* *James Basevi*, *William Darling* *ed* *Barbara McLean*
☆ *Jennifer Jones*, William Eythe, Charles Bickford, Vincent Price, Lee J. Cobb, Gladys Cooper, Anne Revere, Roman Bohnen, Patricia Morison, Aubrey Mather, Charles Dingle, Mary Anderson, Edith Barrett, Sig Rumann
PROLOGUE: 'For those who believe in God, no explanation is necessary. For those who do not believe in God, no explanation is possible.'
'A tamed and pretty image, highly varnished, sensitively lighted, and exhibited behind immaculate glass, the window at once of a shrine and of a box office.' – *James Agee*
'It contains much to conciliate even the crustiest and most prejudiced objector.' – *Richard Mallett, Punch*
Arthur Miller; Alfred Newman; Jennifer Jones; James Basevi, William Darling
best picture; George Seaton; Henry King; Charles Bickford; Gladys Cooper; Anne Revere; Barbara McLean

Song of Ceylon **
GB 1934 40m bw
Ceylon Tea Board (John Grierson)
A pictorial, almost sensuous, but not very informative documentary in four sections: 'The Buddha', 'The Virgin Island', 'The Voices of Commerce', 'The Apparel of a God'. Its influence was immense.
m Walter Leigh *wd/ph* *Basil Wright*

Song of Freedom *
GB 1936 80m bw
Hammer (J. Fraser Passmore)
A black London docker becomes an opera singer, then goes to Africa to free the tribe of which he has discovered himself to be the head.
A weird fable but a good star vehicle and a surprisingly smart production for the time.
w Fenn Sherie, Ingram d'Abbes, Michael Barringer, Philip Lindsay *d* J. Elder Wills *ph* Eric Cross
☆ *Paul Robeson*, Elizabeth Welch, George Mozart, Esmé Percy
'The direction is distinguished but not above reproach, the story is sentimental and absurd, and yet a sense stays in the memory of an unsophisticated mind fumbling on the edge of simple and popular poetry.' – *Graham Greene*

Song of India
US 1949 77m bw
Columbia (Albert S. Rogell)
An Indian prince protects his land against a big game hunter.
Not much singing, but lots of animals and a fight with knives: tolerable programme filler.
w Art Arthur, Kenneth Perkins *d* Albert S. Rogell
☆ Sabu, Gail Russell, Turhan Bey, Anthony Caruso, Aminta Dyne, Fritz Leiber

Song of Love *
US 1947 118m bw
MGM (Clarence Brown)
The story of Clara and Robert Schumann and their friend Johannes Brahms.
Dignified musical biopic which unfortunately falls into most of the pitfall clichés of the genre. Dull it may be, but it looks good and the music is fine.
w Ivan Tors, Irmgard von Cube, Allen Vincent, Robert Ardrey *d* Clarence Brown *ph* Harry Stradling *md* Bronislau Kaper *ad* Cedric Gibbons *piano* Artur Rubinstein
☆ Katharine Hepburn, Paul Henreid, Robert Walker, Henry Daniell, Leo G. Carroll, Elsa Janssen, Gigi Perreau
'This is how Brahms and the Schumanns might very possibly have acted if they had realized that later on they would break into the movies.' – *Time*

Song of Norway *
US 1970 141m DeLuxe Super Panavision 70
ABC/Andrew and Virginia Stone
A fantasia on the life of Grieg.
Multinational hodgepodge, mostly in the Sound of Music *style but with everything from cartoons to Christmas cracker backgrounds. Quite watchable, and the landscapes are certainly splendid.*
wd Andrew Stone *play* Homer Curran *stage musical Milton Lazarus (book), Robert Wright, George Forrest (m/ly)* *ph* Davis Boulton *md* Roland Shaw *ad* William Albert Havemeyer *ed* Virginia Lively Stone
☆ Toralv Maurstad, Florence Henderson, Christina Schollin, Frank Porretta, Harry Secombe, Edward G. Robinson, Robert Morley, Elizabeth Larner, Bernard Archard, Oscar Homolka, Richard Wordsworth

Song of Russia
US 1944 107m bw
MGM (Joe Pasternak)
An American symphony conductor is in Russia when hostilities begin, and watches the citizens' war effort with admiration.
A terrible big-budget film which followed the wartime propaganda line but five years later was heavily criticized by the Unamerican Activities Committee (for the wrong reasons).
w Paul Jarrico, Richard Collins *d* Gregory Ratoff *ph* Harry Stradling *m* Herbert Stothart
☆ Robert Taylor, Susan Peters, John Hodiak, Robert Benchley, Felix Bressart, Michael Chekhov, Darryl Hickman
'Film makers have evolved a new tongue – the broken accent deriving from no known language to be used by foreigners on all occasions.' – *Richard Winnington*
'MGM performs the neatest trick of the week by leaning over backward in Russia's favour without once swaying from right to left.' – *Newsweek*

Song of Scheherezade
US 1947 107m Technicolor
Universal (Edward Kaufman)
In 1865 naval cadet Rimsky-Korsakov falls in love with a dancer.
Yet another composer takes a drubbing in this dull and unconvincing hodgepodge.
wd Walter Reisch *ph* Hal Mohr, William V. Skall *md* Miklos Rozsa *ch* Tilly Losch *ad* Jack Otterson
☆ Yvonne de Carlo, Jean-Pierre Aumont, Brian Donlevy, Eve Arden, Charles Kullman, John Qualen, Richard Lane, Terry Kilburn

'One of the world's great love stories comes to the star who can make it live!'
Song of Songs *
US 1933 89m bw
Paramount (Rouben Mamoulian)
A German peasant girl falls for a sculptor but marries a lecherous baron.
Pretentious romantic nonsense, made fairly palatable by the director's steady hand.
w Leo Birinsky, Samuel Hoffenstein *play* Edward Sheldon *novel Das hohe Lied by Herman Sudermann* *d* Rouben Mamoulian *ph* Victor Milner *m* Karl Hajos, Milan Rodern *ad* Hans Dreier
☆ Marlene Dietrich, Brian Aherne, Lionel Atwill, Alison Skipworth, Hardie Albright
'An ornate and irresistible slice of outright hokum.' – *Peter John Dyer, 1966*

'From the moment she heard this strange, compelling music of love – she was lost!'
Song of Surrender
US 1949 93m bw
Paramount (Richard Maibaum)
In turn-of-the-century New England, a sophisticated visitor from New York falls for the wife of the museum curator.
Ho-hum romantic drama, well enough presented.
w Richard Maibaum *d* Mitchell Leisen *ph* Daniel L. Fapp *m* Victor Young
☆ Wanda Hendrix, Claude Rains, Macdonald Carey, Andrea King, Henry Hull, Elizabeth Patterson, Art Smith

Song of the Islands *
US 1942 75m Technicolor
TCF (William Le Baron)
On a South Sea island, the daughter of an Irish beachcomber falls for the son of an American cattle king.
Wispy musical with agreeable settings and lively songs.
w Joseph Schrank, Robert Pirosh, Robert Ellis, Helen Logan *d* Walter Lang *ph* Ernest Palmer *md* Alfred Newman *songs* various
☆ Betty Grable, Victor Mature, Jack Oakie, Thomas Mitchell, *Hilo Hattie*, Billy Gilbert, George Barbier

Song of the Open Road
US 1944 93m bw
UA (Charles R. Rogers)
A dissatisfied child movie star goes off to help volunteers to save a tomato crop.
Thin youth drama enlivened by a putting-on-a-show finale.
w Albert Mannheimer *d* S. Sylvan Simon
☆ Jane Powell, Bonita Granville, Jackie Moran, W. C. Fields, Edgar Bergen and Charlie McCarthy, Sammy Kaye and his orchestra
Charles Previn (music direction); song 'Too Much in Love' (*m*Walter Kent, *ly*Kim Gannon)

Song of the Road *
GB 1937 73m bw
UK Films
Laid off when the firm they work for goes over to lorries, a man and his cart-horse travel through a Britain that is becoming mechanized, looking for work.
Sentimental, idealized account of a country at peace with itself and its institutions; it has a gentle charm in its narrative of a simple, honourable man putting the world to rights.
d John Baxter
☆ Bransby Williams, Ernest Butcher, Muriel George, Davy Burnaby, Tod Slaughter, John Turnbull

Song of the South *
US 1946 94m Technicolor
Walt Disney (Perce Pearce)
On a long-ago Southern plantation, small boys listen to the Brer Rabbit stories from an elderly black servant.
Too much Uncle Remus and not enough Brer Rabbit, we fear, but children liked it. The cartoons were actually very good.
w Dalton Raymond *d* Harve Foster, Wilfred Jackson *ph* Gregg Toland *m* Daniele Amfitheatrof, Paul J. Smith, Charles Wolcott *cartoon credits* various
☆ Ruth Warrick, Bobby Driscoll, James Baskett, Luana Patten, Lucile Watson, Hattie McDaniel
'The ratio of live to cartoon action is approximately two to one, and that is the ratio of the film's mediocrity to its charm.' – *Bosley Crowther*
song 'Zip-a-Dee-Do-Dah' (*m* Allie Wrubel, *ly* Ray Gilbert); James Baskett (special award)
Daniele Amfitheatrof, Paul J. Smith, Charles Wolcott

A Song to Remember **
US 1944 113m Technicolor
Columbia (Louis F. Edelman)
The life and death of Chopin and his liaison with George Sand.
Hilarious classical musical biopic which was unexpectedly popular and provoked a flood of similar pieces. As a production, not at all bad, but the script...
w Sidney Buchman *d* Charles Vidor *ph* Tony Gaudio, Allan M. Davey *md* Miklos Rozsa, Morris Stoloff *ad* Lionel Banks, Van Nest Polglase *ed* Charles Nelson *piano José Iturbi*
☆ Cornel Wilde, Merle Oberon, Paul Muni, Stephen Bekassy, Nina Foch, George Coulouris, Sig Arno, Howard Freeman, George Macready
'It is the business of Hollywood to shape the truth into box-office contours.' – *Richard Winnington*
'This glorious picture is a major event in film history.' – *Hollywood Reporter*
'As infuriating and funny a misrepresentation of an artist's life and work as I have seen.' – *James Agee*
original story (Ernst Marischka); Tony Gaudio, Allen M. Davey; Miklos Rozsa, Morris Stoloff; Cornel Wilde; Charles Nelson

Song without End
US 1960 142m Eastmancolor Cinemascope
Columbia (William Goetz)
The life and loves of Franz Liszt.
What worked at the box-office for Chopin failed disastrously for Liszt; famous people are turned into papier mâché dullards. Again, the production is elegance itself.
w Oscar Millard *d* Charles Vidor, George Cukor *ph* James Wong Howe *md* Morris Stoloff, Henry Sukman *ad Walter Holscher* *piano* Jorge Bolet
☆ Dirk Bogarde, Capucine, Genevieve Page, Patricia Morison, Ivan Desny, Martita Hunt, Lyndon Brook, Alex Davion (Chopin)
Morris Stoloff, Henry Sukman

Songs From the Second Floor: see *Sanger Fran Andra Vaningen*

Songwriter
US 1984 94m Metrocolor
Tri-Star (Sydney Pollack)
Adventures of a country-music duo.
Very moderate entertainment which gives the impression of stars doing their own thing.
w Bud Shrake *d* Alan Rudolph *ph* Matthew Leonetti *m* Kris Kristofferson *pd* Joel Schiller *ed* Stuart Pappe
☆ Willie Nelson, Kris Kristofferson, Melinda Dillon, Rip Torn, Lesley Ann Warren, Richard C. Sarafian
Kris Kristofferson (for music)

Sono Otoko Kyobo ni Tsuki: see *Violent Cop*

Sons *
US 1989 88m DuArt
Pacific (Marc Toberoff)
Three warring brothers take their father, unable to speak or walk after a stroke, to Normandy to find the Frenchwoman he loved when he was a soldier during the Second World War.
Meandering, episodic movie of sibling conflicts with a few flashes of insight and originality.
w Alexandre Rockwell, Brandon Cole
d Alexandre Rockwell *ph* Stefan Czapsky
m Mader *pd* Virginia Fields *ed* Jay Freund
☆ William Forsythe, D. B. Sweeney, Robert Miranda, Samuel Fuller, Stéphane Audran, Judith Godreche, William Hickey, Jennifer Beals, Shirley Stoller, Bernard Fresson

'The first experiences of a young man in the mysteries of woman!'
Sons and Lovers ***
GB 1960 103m bw Cinemascope
TCF/Company of Artists/Jerry Wald
A Nottingham miner's son learns about life and love.
Well-produced and generally absorbing, if unsurprising, treatment of a famous novel.
w Gavin Lambert, T. E. B. Clarke *novel* D. H. Lawrence *d Jack Cardiff* *ph Freddie Francis* *m* Mario Nascimbene *ad* Tom Morahan
☆ *Dean Stockwell, Trevor Howard, Wendy Hiller*, Mary Ure, Heather Sears, William Lucas, Donald Pleasence, Ernest Thesiger
'An album of decent Edwardian snapshots.' – *Peter John Dyer*
'A rare, remarkable and courageous film.' – *Daily Herald*
Freddie Francis
best picture; script; Jack Cardiff; Trevor Howard; Mary Ure; art direction

Sons o' Guns
US 1936 79m bw
Warner
A Broadway dancer in uniform finds himself accidentally enlisted and sent to France.
Among the better comedies of this star.
w Julius J. Epstein, Jerry Wald *d* Lloyd Bacon
☆ Joe E. Brown, Joan Blondell, Eric Blore, Wini Shaw, Robert Barrat

The Sons of Katie Elder *
US 1965 122m Technicolor Panavision
Paramount/Hal B. Wallis (Paul Nathan)
At Katie Elder's funeral, her four troublesome wandering sons find themselves on the verge of further trouble.
Sluggish all-star Western with predictable highlights.
w Allan Weiss, William H. Wright, Harry Essex *d* Henry Hathaway *ph* Lucien Ballard *m* Elmer Bernstein
☆ John Wayne, Dean Martin, Michael Anderson Jnr, Earl Holliman, Martha Hyer, Jeremy Slate, James Gregory, George Kennedy, Paul Fix

Sons of the Desert ****
US 1934 68m bw
Hal Roach
GB title: *Fraternally Yours*
Stan and Ollie want to go to a Chicago convention, but kid their wives that they are going on a cruise for health reasons.
Archetypal Laurel and Hardy comedy, unsurpassed for gags, pacing and sympathetic characterization.
w Frank Craven, Byron Morgan *d William A. Seiter* *ph* Kenneth Peach *m/ly* Marvin Hatley *ed* Bert Jordan
☆ *Stan Laurel, Oliver Hardy, Charley Chase*, Mae Busch, Dorothy Christie, Lucien Littlefield
'Funny all the way through.' – *New York Times*

Sons of the Musketeers: see *At Sword's Point*

Sons of the Sea
GB 1939 82m Dufaycolor
British Consolidated
Life at the Royal Naval College in Dartmouth.
Simple-minded recruiter with a top dressing of spy stuff: naïve but well liked at the time.
w Gerald Elliott, Maurice Elvey, D. William Woolf, George Barraud *d* Maurice Elvey
☆ Leslie Banks, Mackenzie Ward, Kay Walsh, Simon Lack, Cecil Parker, Ellen Pollock, Nigel Stock

The Son's Room: see *La Stanza del Figlio*

Sophie's Choice *
US 1982 157m Technicolor
Universal/AFD/ITC/Keith Barish
In 1947, a Polish girl who has been in a concentration camp finds that her past still haunts her in New York.
Glum romantic drama about guilt and retribution, long and uncinematic as well as rather poorly done; but its intentions are doubtless honourable.
wd Alan J. Pakula *novel* William Styron *ph* Nestor Almendros *m* Marvin Hamlisch *pd* George Jenkins *ed* Evan Lottman
☆ Meryl Streep, Kevin Kline, Peter MacNicol, Rita Karin, Stephen D. Newman, Josh Mostel
'Handsome, doggedly faithful and astoundingly tedious.' – *Variety*
'Not boring, simply unilluminating. By the end, only one question remains: why did Pakula have to make this movie?' – *Sight and Sound*
Meryl Streep
screenplay (adaptation); cinematography; costume design; music

Sophie's Place: see *Crooks and Coronets*

Sorcerer
US 1977 121m Technicolor
Universal/Film Properties International (William Friedkin)
GB title: *Wages of Fear*
Volunteers are needed to drive nitro-glycerine to an outpost in the South American jungle.
Why anyone should have wanted to spend twenty million dollars on a remake of The Wages of Fear, *do it badly, and give it a misleading title is anybody's guess. The result is dire.*
w Walon Green *novel* Georges Arnaud (and the film by Henri-Georges Clouzot) *d* William Friedkin *ph* John M. Stephens, Dick Bush *m* Tangerine Dream, Keith Jarrett, Charlie Parker *pd* John Box
☆ Roy Scheider, Bruno Cremer, Francisco Rabal, Amidou, Ramon Bieri
sound

The Sorcerers
GB 1967 85m Eastmancolor
Tigon/Curtwel/Global (Patrick Curtis, Tony Tenser)
An old couple find a way of regaining their youth through hypnotizing a young man to do their bidding.
Rather slight but oddly memorable horror film, with an elegant old lady becoming the real monster.
w Michael Reeves, Tom Baker, John Burke *d* Michael Reeves *ph* Stanley Long *m* Paul Ferris
☆ Boris Karloff, *Catherine Lacey*, Ian Ogilvy, Elizabeth Ercy, Victor Henry, Susan George, Meier Tzelniker

Les Sorcières de Salem: see *The Witches of Salem*

La Sorella di Satana: see *She Beast*

Sorok Pervyi: see *The Forty First*

Sorority Girl
US 1957 61m bw
AIP/Sunset (Roger Corman)
A poor little rich college girl feels alienated from her mother and her contemporaries.
Corman's campus exploitation movie is positively middle-aged in its stodgy approach, with a cast that looks far too old and a script mouldering with aged clichés.
w Ed Waters *story* Leo Lieberman *d* Roger Corman *ph* Monroe P. Askins *m* Ronald Stein *ed* Charles Gross Jnr
☆ Susan Cabot, Dick Miller, Barboura O'Neill, June Kenney, Barbara Crane, Fay Baker, Jeanne Wood, Joan Lora

Sorrell and Son
GB 1933 97m bw
B and D/Herbert Wilcox
When his wife leaves them, a man devotes his life to his worthless son.
Fair picturization of a popular novel.
w Lydia Hayward *novel* Warwick Deeping *d* Jack Raymond *ph* Cyril Bristow
☆ H. B. Warner, Hugh Williams, Winifred Shotter, Margot Grahame, Donald Calthrop, Louis Hayward
'Insufficient in action for the average American screen devotee.' – *Variety*
† H. B. Warner played the same role in the silent version of 1927.

Sorrowful Jones
US 1949 88m bw
Paramount (Robert L. Welch)
A racetrack tout unofficially adopts an orphan girl.
Heavy-going sentimental comedy peopled by comic gangsters, a remake of Little Miss Marker *with the emphasis changed.*
w Melville Shavelson, Edmund Hartmann, Jack Rose *story* Damon Runyon *d* Sidney Lanfield *ph* Daniel L. Fapp *m* Robert Emmett Dolan
☆ Bob Hope, Lucille Ball, William Demarest, Bruce Cabot, Thomas Gomez, Tom Pedi, Houseley Stevenson, Mary Jane Saunders

The Sorrows of Satan *
US 1926 115m approx bw silent
Famous Players/Paramount
A struggling writer accepts success in the form of a fortune offered to him by a prince who is in fact Satan.
Smooth Faust derivative with a few choice scenes of special effects.
w Forrest Halsey, John Russell, George Hull *novel* Marie Corelli *d* D. W. Griffith (who didn't want to do it)
☆ Adolphe Menjou, Ricardo Cortez, Lya de Putti, Carol Dempster, Ivan Lebedeff

Sorry, Wrong Number **
US 1948 89m bw
Paramount (Hal B. Wallis, Anatole Litvak)
A bedridden neurotic woman discovers she is marked for murder and tries to summon help.
Artificial but effective suspenser, extended from a radio play.
w Lucille Fletcher *play* Lucille Fletcher *d* Anatole Litvak *ph* Sol Polito *m* Franz Waxman *ed* Warren Low
☆ Barbara Stanwyck, Burt Lancaster, Ann Richards, Wendell Corey, Ed Begley, Harold Vermilyea, Leif Erickson, William Conrad
'The people who made it ... have tried to do just one thing – to thrill. This they have triumphantly done.' – *James Monahan*
Barbara Stanwyck

Sorted
GB 2000 102m colour
Metrodome/Jovy Junior (Fabrizio Chiesa, Mark Crowdy)
A lawyer comes to London to investigate the death of his brother and discovers his involvement with drug-dealing in clubland.
Slick but empty thriller, with a predictable plot and cardboard characters.
w Nick Villiers *screenplay* Christian Spurrier, Malcolm Campbell *story* Alex Jovy *d* Alex Jovy *ph* Mike Southon *m* Guy Farley *pd* Eve Stewart *ed* Justin Krish *cos* Ffion Elinor
☆ Matthew Rhys, Sienna Guillory, Tim Curry, Fay Masterson, Jason Donovan, Steven Marcus, Kelly Brook, Sebastian Knapp
'About as enjoyable as an aspirin sandwich.' – *Dan Jolin, Total Film*

Soshun: see *Early Spring*

Sotto Gli Occhi Dell'Assassino: see *Tenebrae*

Le Souffle au Coeur ***
France/Italy/West Germany 1971 118m colour
NEF/Marianne Films/Video Films/Seitz (Maurice Urbain)
US title: *Murmur of the Heart*
aka: *Dearest Love*
Recovering from an illness at a spa, a 15-year-old boy overcomes his sexual problems after sleeping, almost inadvertently, with his mother.
A witty and observant study of middle-class attitudes to love, sex and adolescent traumas, with incest forming a minor theme.
wd Louis Malle *ph* Ricardo Aronovich *m* Gaston Frèche, Sidney Bechet, Henri Renaud, Charlie Parker *pd* Jean-Jacques Caziot, Philippe Turlure *ed* Suzanne Baron
☆ Léa Massari, Benoit Ferreux, Daniel Gelin, Michel Lonsdale, Ave Ninchi, Gila von Weitershausen
Louis Malle (writer)

Soul Food
US 1997 114m DeLuxe
TCF (Tracey E. Edmonds, Robert Teitel)
A family group, of three sisters and their husbands, begins to disintegrate when their mother sickens and dies.
An unimaginative, familiar domestic drama, set around a ritual of Sunday lunches, in which squabbling siblings are finally reconciled.
wd George Tillman *ph* Paul Elliott *m* Wendy Melvoin, Lisa Coleman *pd* Maxine Shepard *ed* John Carter
☆ Vanessa L. Williams, Vivica A. Fox, Nia Long, Michael Beach, Mekhi Phifer, Brandon Hammond, Jeffrey D. Sams, Gina Ravera, Irma P. Hall, Carl Wright
'A rich tapestry of characters and stories deftly woven together to create an engaging and satisfying drama. Colourful, observant and refreshingly free from cliché.' – *James Cameron-Wilson, Film Review*

Soul in the Hole *
US 1995 99m colour
Metrodome/Asphalt (Lilibert Foster)
In Brooklyn in 1993, an amateur coach leads his street basketball team to some famous victories.
An interesting documentary on a street culture that offers a means of escape from the ghetto.
d Danielle Gardner *ph* Paul Gibson *ed* Melissa Neidich
☆ Kenny Jones, Ed Smith, Gary Sims, Javone Moore, Braheen Cotton, Charles Jones, Dennis Miller

The Soul Kiss: see *A Lady's Morals*

Soul Man
US 1986 101m Technicolor Panavision
New World (Steve Tisch)
A white student tans his skin to win a black scholarship to law school.
Despite its premise, basically a farce of mistaken identities rather than a treatment of racism.
w Carol Black *d* Steve Miner *ph* Jeffrey Jur *m* Tom Scott *pd* Greg Fonseca *ed* David Finfer
☆ C. Thomas Howell, Rae Dawn Chong, Arye Gross, Melora Hardin, James B. Sikking, Leslie Nielsen, James Earl Jones

The Soul of a Monster
US 1944 61m bw
Columbia (Ted Richmond)
A rich man is saved from death by a female hypnotist, who keeps him under her spell.
Unusual but not very interesting thriller.
w Edward Dein *d* Will Jason
☆ Rose Hobart, George Macready, Jim Bannon, Jeanne Bates

'The World of the Dead and the World of the Living... are about to Collide.'
Soul Survivors
US 2001 85m DeLuxe
Momentum/Artisan (Neal H. Moritz, Stokely Chaffin)
Following a car crash, a college student is haunted by her boyfriend, who died in the accident.
A 'teen variation on Jacob's Ladder that never gets off the ground.
wd Steve Carpenter *ph* Fred Murphy *m* Daniel Licht *pd* Larry Fulton *ed* Janice Hampton, Todd Ramsay
☆ Melissa Sagemiller (Cassie), Casey Affleck (Sean), Wes Bentley (Matt), Eliza Dushku (Annabel), Angela Featherstone (Raven), Luke Wilson (Father Jude), Allen Hamilton (Dr Haverston), Ken Moreno (Hideous Dancer), Carl Paoli (Deathmask)
'A horror movie without horror, a spook pic without spookiness and a metaphysical drama without the slightest spiritual tug.' – *Robert Koehler, Variety*

'Out of the secret annals of the sea comes the strangest story ever told!'
Souls at Sea *
US 1937 93m bw
Paramount (Henry Hathaway)
In a 19th-century shipwreck an intelligence officer must save himself, and his mission, at the cost of other lives, and is courtmartialled.
A lively seafaring melodrama produced on a fairly impressive scale.
w Grover Jones, Dale Van Every *d* Henry Hathaway *ph* Charles Lang Jnr *m* Milan Roder, W. Franke Harling *md* Boris Morros *ad* Hans Dreier, Roland Anderson
☆ Gary Cooper, George Raft, Frances Dee, Henry Wilcoxon, Harry Carey, Olympe Bradna, Robert Cummings, Porter Hall, George Zucco, Virginia Weidler, Joseph Schildkraut, Gilbert Emery
'First rate slave ship adventure.' – *Variety*
Milan Roder, W. Franke Harling; art direction

The Sound and the Fury
US 1959 117m Eastmancolor Cinemascope
TCF/Jerry Wald
A once proud Southern family has sunk low in finance and moral stature, and a stern elder son tries to do something about it.
Heavy melodrama with performances to match.
w Irving Ravetch, Harriet Frank Jnr *novel* William Faulkner *d* Martin Ritt *ph* Charles G. Clarke *m* Alex North
☆ Yul Brynner, Joanne Woodward, Margaret Leighton, Stuart Whitman, Ethel Waters, Jack Warden, Françoise Rosay, John Beal, Albert Dekker
'A fourth carbon copy of Chekhov in Dixie.' – *Stanley Kauffmann*

The Sound Barrier **
GB 1952 118m bw
London Films (David Lean)
US title: *Breaking the Sound Barrier*
An aircraft manufacturer takes risks with the lives of his family and friends to prove that the sound barrier can be broken.
Riveting, then topical, melodrama with splendid air sequences; a bit upper crust, but with well-drawn characters.
w Terence Rattigan d David Lean ph Jack Hildyard m Malcolm Arnold
☆ *Ralph Richardson, Nigel Patrick,* Ann Todd, John Justin, Dinah Sheridan, Joseph Tomelty, Denholm Elliott
'The most exciting film about the air that has ever been produced anywhere.' – *Daily Express*
'A peacetime film as exciting as any wartime one.' – *Sunday Dispatch*
Terence Rattigan
film; British film; Ralph Richardson

The Sound of Fury: see *Try and Get Me*

The Sound of Music ***
US 1965 172m DeLuxe Todd-AO
TCF/Argyle (Robert Wise)
In 1938 Austria, a trainee nun becomes governess to the Trapp family, falls in love with the widower father, and helps them all escape from the Nazis.
Slightly muted, very handsome version of an enjoyably old-fashioned stage musical with splendid tunes.
w Ernest Lehman *book* Howard Lindsay, Russel Crouse *d Robert Wise ph Ted McCord m/ly Richard Rodgers, Oscar Hammerstein II md Irwin Kostal pd Boris Leven*

☆ *Julie Andrews*, *Christopher Plummer*, Richard Haydn, Eleanor Parker, *Peggy Wood*, Anna Lee, Marni Nixon

'The success of a movie like *The Sound of Music* makes it even more difficult for anyone to try to do anything worth doing, anything relevant to the modern world, anything inventive or expressive.' – *Pauline Kael*, *New Yorker*

'This last, most remunerative and least inspired, let alone sophisticated, of the Rodgers and Hammerstein collaborations is square and solid sugar. Calorie-counters, diabetics and grown-ups from eight to eighty had best beware.' – *Judith Crist*

'...sufficient warning to those allergic to singing nuns and sweetly innocent children.' – *John Gillett*

† Christopher Plummer's singing was dubbed by Bill Lee, and Peggy Wood's by Margery McKay.

best picture; Robert Wise; Irwin Kostal

Ted McCord; Julie Andrews; Peggy Wood

Sound Off

US 1952 83m Supercinecolor
Columbia (Jonie Taps)

An entertainer is recruited into the army and has predictable difficulties.
Dishevelled service farce with funny moments.
w Blake Edwards, Richard Quine *d* Richard Quine *ph* Ellis Carter *m* George Duning *md* Morris Stoloff
☆ *Mickey Rooney*, Anne James, Sammy White, John Asher, Gordon Jones

Sounder *

US 1972 105m DeLuxe Panavision
TCF/Radnitz-Mattel (Robert B. Radnitz)

During the 30s Depression, black sharecroppers in the deep South endure various tribulations.
Well made liberated family movie ... but not very exciting.
w Lonnie Elder III *novel* William H. Armstrong *d* Martin Ritt *ph* John Alonzo *m* Taj Mahal
☆ *Paul Winfield*, *Cicely Tyson*, Kevin Hooks, Carmen Mathews, James Best, Taj Mahal
best picture; Lonnie Elder III; Paul Winfield; Cicely Tyson

Le Soupirant: see *The Suitor*

Sour Grapes *

US 1998 91m Technicolor
Columbia/Castle Rock (Laurie Lennard)

Two cousins fall out after one wins a fruit-machine jackpot with money lent to him by the other.
An intermittently amusing, extended TV sitcom that is visually uninspiring but saved by some clever writing.
wd Larry David *ph* Victor Hammer *pd* Charles Rosen *ed* Priscilla Nedd-Friendly
☆ Steven Weber, Craig Bierko, Matt Keeslar, Karen Sillas, Robyn Peterman, Viola Harris, Orlando Jones, Jennifer Leigh Warren, Richard Gant, James MacDonald, Sonya Eddy, Philip Baker Hall, Ann Guilbert

'Catch it fast, because it bears all the hallmarks of a future cult classic.' – *Alan Jones*, *Film Review*

Soursweet **

GB 1988 111m colour
Curzon/First Film/British Screen/Zenith/Film Four International (Roger Randall-Cutler)

A Chinese couple living in London start their own small restaurant.
Affecting drama of immigrant life.
w Ian McEwan *novel* Timothy Mo *d* Mike Newell *ph* Michael Garfath *m* Richard Hartley *pd* Adrian Smith *ed* Mick Audsley
☆ Sylvia Chang, Danny An-Ning, Jodi Long, Speedy Choo, Han Tan, Soon-Teck Oh, William Chow

Sous le Ciel de Paris Coule la Seine

France 1951 111m bw
Regina Filmsonor (Pierre O'Connell and Arys Nisotti)

The adventures of a variety of characters during a day in Paris.
The director is back on his multi-story band wagon, but in this case the stories are undeveloped and the handling less than interesting.
w René Lefèvre, Julien Duvivier *d* Julien Duvivier *ph* Nicholas Hayer *m* Jean Wiener
☆ Brigitte Auber, Jean Brochard, René Blancard, Paul Frankeur, Sylvie

'A hotchpotch of familiar story devices, camera tricks and picturesque characterizations and settings, bundled together with an old hand's facility.' – *MFB*

Sous Le Sable **

France 2000 96m colour
Fidelite/Euro Space/Haut &Court,/Arte France

aka: *Under the Sand*

After her husband disappears, presumed drowned, on their holiday, a university teacher refuses to accept the fact of his death.
Engrossing, emotionally restrained study in grief, loss and guilt; it leaves open the question of whether its central character, an intellectual sometimes unaware of what is happening around her, is haunted, unhinged or ultimately reconciled to the truth.
w François Ozon, Emmanuele Bernheim, Marina De Van, Marcia Romano *d* François Ozon *ph* Jeanne Lapoirie, Antoine Heberle *m* Philippe Rombi *ad* Sandrine Canaux *ed* Laurence Bawedin
☆ *Charlotte Rampling* (Marie Drillon), Bruno Cremer (Jean Drillon), Jacques Nolot (Vincent), Alexandra Stewart (Amanda), Pierre Vernier (Gerard), Andrée Tainsy (Suzanne)

'An intriguing piece, in which Ozon's direction preserves a mood of eerie, reticent calm.' – *Peter Bradshaw*, *Guardian*

Sous le Soleil de Satan: see *Under Satan's Sun*

Sous les Toits de Paris *

France 1930 92m bw
Tobis (Frank Clifford)

A Parisian street singer falls in love with a girl, fights her lover, and proves himself innocent of theft.
Surprisingly serious and darkly lit little comedy-drama which, while well enough directed, hardly seems to merit its classic status.
wd *René Clair* *ph* Georges Périnal *m* Armand Bernard *pd* Lazare Meerson
☆ Albert Préjean, Pola Illery, Gaston Modot, Edmond Gréville

'Real film fare of quality ... a talker which is intelligible to any country.' – *Variety*

'It is far more movie than talkie, which exercises the imagination and rests the ear.' – *National Board of Review*

South **

GB 1919 81m bw silent
BFI

Documentary of Sir Ernest Shackleton's expedition to the Antarctic in 1914, when the crew of 28 and 70 dogs were marooned for nine months after their ship was first trapped, and then destroyed, by the sea ice.
Beautifully restored by the National Film and Television Archive, a fascinating report on an ill-fated journey, with some remarkable photography.
† Presenting a wonderful and true story of British pluck, self-sacrifice and indomitable courage displayed by a small party of men who set forth on a voyage of discovery into the hitherto unexplored lands and uncharted seas of the great Antarctic Continent.

The South **

Spain/France 1983 94m colour
Connoisseur/Television EspanolaChloe/Elias Querejeta
original title: *El Sur*

A woman recalls her childhood in the late 1950s and her relationship with her unhappy father.
Delicate, poetic account of a child's view of adult experience.
w Jose Luis Lopez Linares *story* Adelaida Garcia Morales *d* *Victor Erice* *ph* Jose Luis Alcaine *ad* Antonio Belizon *ed* Pablo G. Del Amo
☆ Omero Antonutti, Lola Cardona, Aurore Clement, Sonsoles Arangueren, Iciar Bollain, Rafaela Aparicio, Germaine Montero, Maria Caro

South **

Argentina/France 1988 127m colour
Cinesur/Pacific/Canal (Sabina Sigler)
original title: *Sur*

Released after five years, a political prisoner wanders the streets of his home town accompanied by the ghosts of his past.
Dream, fantasy, past and present merge into a powerful, elegaic account of tyranny and oppression, hope and despair.
wd Fernando Solanas *ph* Felix Monti *m* Astor Piazzolla *pd* Fernando Solanas *ed* Juan Carlos Macias, Pablo Mari
☆ Susu Pecoraro, Miguel Angel Sola, Philippe Leotard, Lito Cruz, Ulises Dumont
† The film won Solanas the award for best director at the Cannes Film Festival in 1988.

South American George

GB 1941 93m bw
Ben Henry/Columbia

An unsuccessful singer poses as a South American opera star.
Not among the star's best.
w Leslie Arliss, Norman Lee, Austin Melford *d* Marcel Varnel *ph* Arthur Crabtree
☆ George Formby, Linden Travers, Enid Stamp-Taylor, Jacques Brown, Felix Aylmer

South Central *

US 1992 99m DeLuxe
Ixtlan/Monument/Enchantment (Janet Yang, William B. Steakley)

GB title: *South Central L.A.*

A black hoodlum, imprisoned for murder, discovers that his 10-year-old son has joined his old gang.
A well-acted but over-earnest account of a man's attempt to redeem his violent past.
wd Steve Anderson *book* *Crips* by Donald Bakeer *ph* Charlie Lieberman *m* Tim Truman *pd* David Brian Miller, Marina Kieser *ed* Steve Nevius
☆ Glenn Plummer, Byron Keith Minns, LaRita Shelby, Kevin Best, Christian Coleman, Starletta Dupois, Ivory Ocean, Carl Lumbly

'Speaks eloquently to black kids desperately in need of straight talk. A profoundly moving story ... It has the power to save lives.' – *Variety*

South of Algiers

GB 1952 95m Technicolor
ABP/Mayflower (Aubrey Baring, Maxwell Setton)
US title: *The Golden Mask*

Archaeologists and thieves search the Sahara for a priceless mask.
Schoolboy adventure story with a straightforward plot and plenty of local colour.
w Robert Westerby *d* Jack Lee *ph* Oswald Morris *m* Robert Gill
☆ Van Heflin, Wanda Hendrix, Eric Portman, Charles Goldner, Jacques François, Jacques Brunius, Alec Mango, Marne Maitland

'A thousand thundering terrific thrills in a fight-swept tropic paradise!'

South of Pago Pago

US 1940 96m bw
(UA) Edward Small (Erle C. Kenton)

Greedy white men seek riches in pearls by cheating and overworking the natives.
Slightly unfamiliar backgrounds and a fair supply of two-fisted action gave this romantic adventure drama plenty of box-office pull.
w George Bruce *d* Alfred E. Green *ph* John Mescall *m* Edward Ward
☆ Victor McLaglen, Jon Hall, Frances Farmer, Olympe Bradna, Gene Lockhart, Douglass Dumbrille, Francis Ford

South of St Louis

US 1948 88m Technicolor
Warner (Milton Sperling)

Before the Civil War starts, Southern farmers are plagued by Union guerrillas.
Pretty good Western with plenty of action.
w Zachary Gold and James R. Webb *d* Ray Enright *ph* Karl Freund *m* Max Steiner *ad* Leo K. Kuter *ed* Clarence Kolster
☆ Joel McCrea, Zachary Scott, Victor Jory, Douglas Kennedy, Dorothy Malone, Alexis Smith, Alan Hale

'Distinguished by the fact that all the good men wear bells on their spurs in contradistinction to the bad men. This determines character without benefit of acting, as well as making a jolly noise.' – *C. A. Lejeune*

South of Suez

US 1940 85m bw
Warner

A diamond miner falls for the daughter of a man he is accused of murdering.
Watchable melodrama with pleasing actors.
w Barry Trivers *d* Lewis Seiler
☆ George Brent, Brenda Marshall, George Tobias, James Stephenson, Lee Patrick, Eric Blore, Cecil Kellaway

South of Tahiti

US 1941 75m bw
Universal
GB title: *White Savage*

Four adventurers drift ashore on a tropical island.
Penny-pinching hokum without even the colour to make it watchable.
w Gerald Geraghty *d* George Waggner
☆ Brian Donlevy, Maria Montez, Broderick Crawford, Andy Devine, Henry Wilcoxon, H. B. Warner

South Pacific **

US 1958 170m Technicolor Todd-AO
Magna/S. P. Enterprises (Buddy Adler)

In 1943 an American navy nurse on a South Pacific island falls in love with a middle-aged French planter who becomes a war hero.
Overlong, solidly produced film of the musical stage hit, with great locations, action climaxes and lush photography (also a regrettable tendency to use alarming colour filters for dramatic emphasis).
w Paul Osborn, Richard Rodgers, Oscar Hammerstein II, Joshua Logan *stories* *Tales of the South Pacific* by James A. Michener *d* Joshua Logan *ph* *Leon Shamroy* *m/ly* *Richard Rodgers*, *Oscar Hammerstein II* *md* Alfred Newman, Ken Darby *ch* Le Roy Prinz
☆ Mitzi Gaynor, Rossano Brazzi, Ray Walston, John Kerr, France Nuyen, Juanita Hall

'What a monstrous visual riot! What a din!' – *C. A. Lejeune*

† Rossano Brazzi's singing was dubbed by Giorgio Tozzi, John Kerr's by Bill Lee and Juanita Hall's by Muriel Smith, even though she had sung the role of Bloody Mary in the Broadway production.
Leon Shamroy; Alfred Newman, Ken Darby

South Park: Bigger Longer & Uncut **

US 1999 81m DeLuxe
Paramount/Warner/Comedy Central/Scott Rudin/Trey Parker/Matt Stone (Trey Parker, Matt Stone)

After schoolkids sneak into an R-rated movie, featuring two foul-mouthed Canadian comedians, their mothers campaign for a war against Canada.
With humour often as crude as the animation, this is nevertheless a deft and witty demolition of many aspects of modern life, aimed particularly at all those who maintain double standards or tell others what to do and how to behave.
w Trey Parker, Matt Stone, Pam Brady *d* Trey Parker *m* Marc Shaiman *m/ly* Trey Parker, Marc Shaiman *ed* John Venzon
☆ Featuring voices of: Matt Stone, Trey Parker, Mary Kay Bergman, Isaac Hayes, George Clooney, Brent Spiner, Minnie Driver, Eric Idle

'The funniest, most risk-taking, most incisive movie of the summer.' – *Lisa Schwarzbaum*, *Entertainment Weekly*

'The most impressively vicious and nasty-minded film satire of the year.' – *Andrew Pulver*, *Guardian*

♫ Mountain Town; Uncle Fucka; Wendy's Song; It's Easy Mmmkay; Hell Isn't Good; Blame Canada; Kyle's Mom's a Bitch; What Would Brian Boitano Do?; Up There; I Can Change; I'm Super; Eyes of a Child
song 'Blame Canada' (m/l Trey Parker, Marc Shaiman)

South Riding **

GB 1937 91m bw
London Films (Alexander Korda, Victor Saville)

A schoolmistress in a quiet Yorkshire dale exposes crooked councillors and falls for the depressed local squire.
Dated but engrossing multi-drama from a famous novel; a good compact piece of film-making.

w Ian Dalrymple, Donald Bull *novel* Winifred Holtby *d* Victor Saville *ph* Harry Stradling *m* Richard Addinsell
☆ Ralph Richardson, Edna Best, Edmund Gwenn, Ann Todd, Glynis Johns, John Clements, Marie Lohr, Milton Rosmer, Edward Lexy
'Another artistic Korda film … lacking in a story of popular appeal.' – *Variety*
'A convincing and dramatic picture of English provincial life.' – *Film Weekly*

South Sea Sinner
US 1949 88m bw
Universal-International
GB title: *East of Java*
On a South Sea island, a fugitive from justice is blackmailed by a café owner.
Hackneyed elements are strung together without much flair in this routine melodrama.
w Joel Malone, Oscar Brodney *d* H. Bruce Humberstone *ph* Maury Gertsman *m* Walter Scharf *ad* Bernard Herzbrun, Richard H. Riedel *ed* Ted J. Kent
☆ Macdonald Carey, Shelley Winters, Luther Adler, Helena Carter, Frank Lovejoy, Art Smith, Liberace

South Sea Woman
US 1953 99m bw
Warner (Sam Bischoff)
Adventures of a fight-loving marine in the Pacific war.
Unlovable mixture of brawling, romancing and war-winning.
w Edwin Blum *play* William M. Rankin *d* Arthur Lubin *ph* Ted McCord *m* David Buttolph *ed* Clarence Kolster
☆ Burt Lancaster, Virginia Mayo, Chuck Connors, Arthur Shields, Barry Kelley, Leon Askin

South West Nine *
GB/Ireland 2001 98m DeLuxe
Fruit Salad/Irish Screen (Allan Niblo)
aka: *S.W.9*
A disparate group of people gather in London's Brixton, where a local drug dealer is staging a rave in a derelict church to pay off his debts.
Portrait of the alienated young in a multi-ethnic, working-class community – from poor little rich squatters, to anarchists, sneak thieves, addicts and dealers. Despite the accuracy of observation, the narrative itself is under-nourished.
w Richard Parry, Steve North *d* Richard Parry *ph* Graham Fowler *m* David Bradnum *pd* Rob Lunn *ed* Christine Pancott
☆ Wil Johnson (Freddy), Stuart Laing (Jake), Mark Letheren (Mitch), Amelia Curtis (Kit), Orlessa Edwards (Helen), Nicola Stapleton (Sal), Frank Harper (Douser)
'A comedy-thriller with its own two-way get-out clause: the "comedy" excusing the absence of plausible thrills, and the "thriller" acting as an alibi for the lack of laughs.' – *Peter Bradshaw, Guardian*
'Defines the temper of our age as vividly as Derek Jarman's *Jubilee* did all of 23 years ago.' – *Alexander Walker, London Evening Standard*

'It's The Land Of Hospitality… Unless You Don't Belong.'
Southern Comfort ****
US 1981 106m DeLuxe
EMI/Phoenix/Cinema Group Venture (David Giler)
National Guardsmen on a routine exercise into swampland find themselves involved in a life-and-death struggle with the Cajun inhabitants.
Brilliant, compelling, tightly-constructed thriller that manages also to be an allegory of American involvement in Vietnam.
w Michael Kane, Walter Hill, David Giler *d* Walter Hill *ph* Andrew Laszlo *m* Ry Cooder
☆ Keith Carradine, Powers Boothe, Fred Ward, Franklyn Seales, T. K. Carter, Lewis Smith
'As an action director Walter Hill has a dazzling competence. Southern Comfort comes across with such immediacy that it had a near-hypnotic hold on me and I felt startled – brought up short – when it ended.' – *Pauline Kael, New Yorker*

'Africa explodes with a thousand surprises!'
The Southern Star *
GB/France 1968 105m Techniscope
Columbia/Eurofrance/Capitole (Roger Duchet)
In French West Africa in 1912, a penniless American finds a huge diamond which several crooks are after.
Quite a likeable adventure romp, with good suspense sequences and convincing jungle settings.
w David Pursall, Jack Seddon *novel* Jules Verne *d* Sidney Hayers *ph* Raoul Coutard *m* Georges Garvarentz
☆ George Segal, Ursula Andress, Orson Welles, Ian Hendry, Michael Constantine, Johnny Sekka, Harry Andrews

A Southern Yankee *
US 1948 90m bw
MGM (Paul Jones)
GB title: *My Hero*
During the Civil War a Southern bellboy masquerades as a spy and finds himself behind enemy lines.
A rather feeble reworking of Buster Keaton's The General, *with some excellent gags supervised by the master himself.*
w Harry Tugend *d* Edward Sedgwick *ph* Ray June *m* David Snell
☆ Red Skelton, Brian Donlevy, Arlene Dahl, George Coulouris, Lloyd Gough, John Ireland, Minor Watson, Charles Dingle

'She was his woman! And he was her man! That's all they had to fight with – against the world, the flesh, and the devil!'
The Southerner ***
US 1945 91m bw
(UA)
Problems of penniless farmers in the deep South.
Impressive, highly pictorial outdoor drama, more poetic than The Grapes of Wrath *and lacking the acting strength.*
wd Jean Renoir *novel* Hold Autumn in Your Hand by George Sessions Perry *ph* Lucien Andriot *m* Werner Janssen *ad* Eugene Lourie
☆ Zachary Scott, Betty Field, Beulah Bondi, J. Carrol Naish, Percy Kilbride, Blanche Yurka, Norman Lloyd
'I cannot imagine anybody failing to be spellbound by this first successful essay in Franco-American screen collaboration.' – *Richard Winnington*
'You can smell the earth as the plough turns it up; you can sense the winter and the rain and the sunshine.' – *C. A. Lejeune*
† Some sources state that the script was by William Faulkner.
Jean Renoir (as director); Werner Janssen

'Dreams are the only thing worth fighting for.'
Southpaw *
Ireland/GB 1998 80m colour
Channel4/IFB/Treasure (Paddy Breathnach, Robert Walpole)
aka: *Southpaw: The Francis Barrett Story*
Two years in the life of an Irish amateur boxer, from a travelling family in Galway, who qualifies for the Atlanta Olympics in 1996.
Interesting documentary of a personable young man overcoming obstacles and prejudice to become a local hero.
d Liam McGrath *ph* Cian De Buitlear *m* Dario Marianelli *ed* James E. Dalton
☆ Francis Barrett, Chick Gillen, Tom Humphries, Colum Flynn, Nicolas Cruz Hernandez, Gerry Callan, Jim McGee, Eamonn Hunt (narrator)
'An easy film to warm to.' – *Sight and Sound*
† The documentary ends with Barrett hoping to compete in the Sydney Olympics of 2000. Instead, he turned professional, beginning his career in London.

Southwest to Sonora: see *The Appaloosa*

Souvenir
GB 1987 93m Technicolor
Curzon/Fancy Free/Geoff Reeve Pictures (Tom Reeve, James Reeve)
An elderly German living in New York returns to the French town where he was involved in a massacre of the inhabitants during the Second World War.
Unsuccessful and heavy-handed, it never comes close to exploring the themes of guilt and individual responsibility that it raises.
w Paul Wheeler *novel* The Pork Butcher by David Hughes *d* Geoffrey Reeve *ph* Fred Tammes *m* Tony Kinsey *pd* Morley Smith *ed* Bob Morgan
☆ Christopher Plummer, Catherine Hicks, Michael Lonsdale, Christopher Cazenove, Lisa Daniely, Jean Badin, Patrick Bailey
'Could be a bad joke about the type of international co-production which is made because the money, rather than the audience, can be found for it.' – *MFB*

Soylent Green *
US 1973 97m Metrocolor Panavision
MGM (Walter Seltzer, Russell Thatcher)
In 2022, the population of New York exists in perpetual heat on synthetic foods; a policeman hears from his elderly friend about an earlier time when things were better.
Lively futuristic yarn with a splendid climax revealing the nature of the artificial food; marred by narrative incoherence and by direction which fails to put plot points clearly across.
w Stanley R. Greenberg *novel* Make Room, Make Room by Harry Harrison *d* Richard Fleischer *ph* Richard H. Kline *m* Fred Myrow
☆ Charlton Heston, Edward G. Robinson, Leigh Taylor-Young, Chuck Connors, Brock Peters, Joseph Cotten

The Space Children
US 1958 71m bw VistaVision
Paramount (William Alland)
Children at a rocket testing site sabotage equipment on the instructions of a strange pulsating object.
Naïve moral fable, not badly done on its level.
w Bernard Schoenfeld *d* Jack Arnold *ph* Ernest Laszlo *m* Van Cleave
☆ Adam Williams, Peggy Webber, Michel Ray, Jackie Coogan

'Space Will Never Be The Same.'
Space Cowboys *
US/Australia 2000 129m Technicolor Panavision
Warner/Village Roadshow/ Pictures/Clipsal/Malpaso/Mad Chance (Clint Eastwood, Andrew Lazar)
An ageing, retired airforce pilot recruits a team of his contemporaries to go into space to repair a communications satellite.
Affable action movie that gives some familiar actors a chance to strut their stuff and play slightly comic variations on their usual roles.
w Ken Kaufman, Howard Klausner *d* Clint Eastwood *ph* Jack N. Green *m* Lennie Niehaus *pd* Henry Bumstead *ed* Joel Cox *sp* Industrial Light & Magic
☆ Clint Eastwood (Frank Corvin), Tommy Lee Jones (Hawk Hawkins), Donald Sutherland (Jerry O'Neill), James Garner (Tank Sullivan), James Cromwell (Bob Gerson), Marcia Gay Harden (Sara Holland), William Devane (Eugene Davis), Loren Dean (Ethan Grace), Courtney B. Vance (Roger Hines), Barbara Babcock (Barbara Corvin), Rade Sherbedgia (General Vostov), Blair Brown (Dr Anne Caruthers)
'A movie for those who prefer Budweiser and Jack Daniel's to summer wine.' – *Philip French, Observer*
'Just about passes muster as an action adventure, but as an advert for old age it's pretty hard to take.' – *Adam Mars-Jones, Times*
sound editing (Alan Robert Murray and Bub Asman)

Space Jam
US 1996 87m Technicolor
Warner (Ivan Reitman, Joe Medjuck, Daniel Goldberg)
After Bugs Bunny and other Looney Tunes characters are kidnapped by aliens, basketball star Michael Jordan comes to the rescue.
An unlovely mix of live action and animation, climaxing in a basketball game, which might have been passable had it been 80 minutes shorter. It is little more than a long commercial that, in the process, diminishes its cartoon stars, erasing their quirky individuality in favour of a bland and hectic banality.
w Leo Benvenuti, Steve Rudnick, Timothy Harris, Herschel Weingrod *d* Joe Pytka *ph* Michael Chapman *m* James Newton Howard *pd* Geoffrey Kirkland *ed* Sheldon Kahn
☆ Michael Jordan, Wayne Knight, Theresa Randle and also the voices of: Billy West, Bradley Baker, Danny DeVito
'Cute, rambunctious, generally amusing rather than outright funny, this clever mix of live action, highlighted by the unequaled skills of basketball superstar Michael Jordan, and animated Looney Tunes antics will be a must-see for kids.' – *Todd McCarthy, Variety*
'A lazy, cynical attempt to pitch the Warners characters (and the merchandising derived from them) at pre-teen black, or black-identified, punters. It's a hugely dispiriting film.' – *Jonathan Romney, Sight and Sound*
† The film was based on a commercial for Nike sneakers.

Space Master X-7
US 1958 71m bw Regalscope
Twentieth Century Fox (Bernard Glasser)
A space probe returns from Mars carrying a deadly fungus.
Dull science fiction, done on the cheap in a documentary style that fails to provide any much-needed urgency; the alien growth resembles an inanimate length of grey felt.
w George Worthing Yates, Daniel Mainwaring *d* Edward Bernds *ph* Brydon Baker *m* Josef Zimanich *ad* Harry Reif *ed* John F. Link
☆ Bill Williams, Lyn Thomas, Robert Ellis, Paul Frees, Rhoda Williams, Joan Barry, Carol Varga, Moe Howard

Space Raiders
US 1983 82m colour
Millennium (Roger Corman)
A space mercenary promises to help return a 10-year-old stowaway to his home planet.
Low-budget Star Wars *rip-off for juvenile audiences, incorporating footage from* Battle beyond the Stars.
wd Howard R. Cohen *ph* Alec Hirschfeld
☆ Vince Edwards, David Mendenhall, Patsy Pease, Thom Christopher, Dick Miller

Space Truckers
US/Ireland 1996 96m Technicolor
Goldcrest/Peter Newman/Interal/Mary Breen-Farrelly
A maverick space trucker discovers that he is carrying a cargo of killer robots to take over the Earth.
Pulp science fiction of a very old-fashioned kind, done with tongue in cheek; not that that makes it any more enjoyable.
w Ted Mann *d* Stuart Gordon *ph* Mac Ahlberg *m* Colin Towns *pd* Simon Murton *ed* John Victor Smith *sp* Brian Johnson, Paul Gentry; bio-mechanicals: Screaming Mad George
☆ Dennis Hopper, Stephen Dorff, Debi Mazar, George Wendt, Vernon Wells, Barbara Crampton, Shane Rimmer, Charles Dance
'Amiable latenight trash.' – *Variety*

Spaceballs
US 1987 96m Metrocolor
MGM/UA (Mel Brooks, Ezra Swerdlow)
A ruthless race is out to steal the air supply from the planet Druidia.
Flabby spoof of Star Wars, *without any funny ideas.*
w Mel Brooks, Thomas Meehan, Ronny Graham *d* Mel Brooks *ph* Nick McLean *m* John Morris *pd* Terence Marsh *ed* Conrad Buff IV
☆ Mel Brooks, John Candy, Rick Moranis, Bill Pullman, Daphne Zuniga, Dom DeLuise, John Hurt
'At its worst, it displays a colossal ego at work and humour better left to home movies.' – *Daily Variety*

SpaceCamp
US 1986 107m DeLuxe Panavision
TCF/ABC (Patrick Bailey, Walter Coblenz)
Five teenagers attending a NASA summer camp are accidentally launched into space.
Tolerable entertainment for ten-year-olds, who may enjoy its empowerment of the young, and will be willing to overlook the ordinary special effects that include a rather irritating robot.

w Clifford Green, Ellen Green, Casey T. Mitchell *story* Patrick Bailey, Larry B. Williams *d* Harry Winer *ph* William A. Fraker *m* John Williams *pd* Richard MacDonald *ed* John W. Wheeler, Timothy Board
☆ Kate Capshaw, Lea Thompson, Kelly Preston, Larry B. Scott, Leaf Phoenix, Tate Donovan, Tom Skerritt, Barry Primus, Terry Quinn

Spaced Invaders

US 1989 100m CFI color
Medusa/Smart Egg Pictures (Luigi Cingolani)

A spaceship load of inept Martians mistakenly try to conquer the Earth.
Inane spoof of the current cycle of science fiction films.
w Patrick Read Johnson, Scott Alexander *d* Patrick Read Johnson *ph* James L. Carter *m* David Russo *pd* Tony Tremblay *ed* Seth Gaven, Daniel Bross
☆ Douglas Barr, Royal Dano, Ariana Richards, J. J. Anderson, Gregg Berger, Fred Applegate, Patrika Darbo

'The first movie that puts *you* in outer space.'
Spacehunter: Adventures in the Forbidden Zone

US 1983 90m Metrocolor 3-D
Columbia/Delphi (Don Carmody, Andre Link, John Dunning)

In the 22nd century, a spaceship salvage expert lands on a long-forgotten planet to rescue three Earthwomen from the tyrants of Graveyard City.
Mindless and rather unattractive space fantasy, far less likeable than Flash Gordon.
w David Preston, Edith Rey, Dan Goldbert, Len Blum *d* Lamont Johnson *ph* Frank Tidy *m* Elmer Bernstein *pd* Jackson de Govia
☆ Peter Strauss, Molly Ringwald, Ernie Hudson, Andrea Marcovicci, Michael Ironside

The Spaceman and King Arthur

GB 1979 93m Technicolor
Walt Disney
US title: *Unidentified Flying Oddball*
An astronaut and his robot accidentally land themselves back at the court of King Arthur.
Mindless but occasionally funny rewrite of Mark Twain's A Connecticut Yankee.
w Don Tait *d* Russ Mayberry *ph* Paul Beeson *m* Ron Goodwin
☆ Dennis Dugan, Jim Dale, Ron Moody, Kenneth More, John Le Mesurier, Rodney Bewes, Robert Beatty

Spaceways

GB 1953 76m bw
Exclusive/Hammer (Michael Carreras)
A scientist is suspected of killing his wife and her lover and sending their bodies into space in Britain's first satellite.
Trite marital drama in a science-fiction setting, interesting only for its belief that the 1960s would bring the first manned space station.
w Paul Tabori, Richard Landau *play* Charles Eric Maine *d* Terence Fisher *ph* Reginald Wyer *md* Ivor Slaney *ad* J. Elder Wills *ed* Maurice Rootes *sp* The Trading Post
☆ Howard Duff, Eva Bartok, Alan Wheatley, Philip Leaver, Michael Medwin, Andrew Osborn, Cecile Chevreau

La Spada e la Croce: see *The Sword and the Cross*

The Spaniard's Curse

GB 1958 74m bw
Independent Film Distributors/Wentworth (Roger Proudlock)
A man wrongly convicted of murder pronounces an old Spanish death curse on the judge, prosecuting counsel, foreman of the jury and the killer.
A neat, well-plotted little thriller.
w Kenneth Hyde, Ralph Kemplen, Roger Proudlock *story* Edith Pargeter *d* Ralph Kemplen *ph* Arthur Grant *m* Lambert Williamson *pd* Tony Masters *ed* Stanley Hawkes
☆ Tony Wright, Lee Patterson, Michael Hordern, Susan Beaumont, Ralph Truman, Henry Oscar, Brian Oulton, Olga Dickie, Roddy Hughes, Joe Gibbons

Spanish Affair

US 1958 92m Technicolor Vistavision
Paramount/Nomad (Bruce Odlum)
An American architect in Madrid falls in love with his interpreter and is pursued by her lover.
Curiously plotless excuse for a travelogue, lushly photographed but not exactly gripping.
w Richard Collins *d* Don Siegel *ph* Sam Leavitt *m* Daniele Amfitheatrof
☆ Richard Kiley, Carmen Sevilla, Jose Guardiola

Spanish Fly

GB 1975 86m Technicolor
EMI (Peter James, Gerald Flint-Shipman)

An Englishman in Majorca tries to improve a purchase of local wine by putting an aphrodisiac in it, with predictable results.
Crude, tatty comedy by people who should know better.
w Robert Ryerson *d* Bob Kellett *ph* Jack Atcheler *m* Ron Goodwin
☆ Terry-Thomas, Leslie Phillips, Graham Armitage, Frank Thornton, Sue Lloyd

The Spanish Gardener

GB 1956 97m Technicolor Vistavision
Rank (John Bryan)
The British consul in Spain is annoyed when his young son develops a strong friendship with the gardener.
Slow, understated study in human relationships which doesn't come off; any sexual relevance is well concealed.
w Lesley Storm, John Bryan *novel* A. J. Cronin *d* Philip Leacock *ph* Christopher Challis *m* John Veale
☆ Dirk Bogarde, Michael Hordern, Jon Whiteley, Cyril Cusack, Geoffrey Keen, Maureen Swanson, Lyndon Brook, Josephine Griffin, Bernard Lee, Rosalie Crutchley

The Spanish Main *

US 1945 101m Technicolor
RKO (Robert Fellows)

In the Caribbean, the fiancée of the Spanish viceroy is kidnapped by a pirate who determines to tame her before marrying her.
Slightly tongue-in-cheek pirate hokum; generally good value for the easily amused.
w George Worthing Yates, Herman J. Mankiewicz *d* Frank Borzage *ph* George Barnes *m* Hanns Eisler *md* Constantin Bakaleinikoff
☆ Paul Henreid, Maureen O'Hara, Binnie Barnes, Walter Slezak, John Emery, Barton MacLane, J. M. Kerrigan, Nancy Gates, Fritz Leiber, Jack La Rue, Mike Mazurki, Victor Kilian
George Barnes

The Spanish Prisoner **

US 1997 112m Technicolor Panavision
Sweetland (Jean Doumanian)

A paranoid scientist does not know whom to trust, among colleagues, friends and FBI, with his valuable formula.
A clever, intriguing game of double-cross and treble bluff that keeps the audience, as well as its characters, guessing throughout.
wd David Mamet *ph* Gabriel Beristain *m* Carter Burwell *pd* Tim Galvin *ed* Barbara Tulliver
☆ Campbell Scott, Rebecca Pidgeon, Steve Martin, Ricky Jay, Ben Gazzara, Felicity Huffman, Ed O'Neill

> 'Ingenious but glassily unengaging, like watching a game of chess at a distance of 100 metres.' – *Tom Shone, Sunday Times*

> 'Mamet plays his genre games with such elegant wit that no one should pine for the usual battering from galactic explosions.' – *Geoff Brown, The Times*

'A Darkly Humorous Suburban Tale Creeping Beyond Normality...'
Spanking the Monkey **

US 1995 106m colour
Metro Tartan/Buckeye/Swelter

A medical student is told by his father, a commercial traveller, that he must spend the summer looking after his mother, who has broken a leg in a suicide attempt.
Deft, witty and assured account of confused family relationships and a young man's search for his sexual identity, which leads to an incestuous relationship; it is an often dark work, but one about survivors.
wd David O. Russell *ph* Michael Mayers *m* David Carbonara *pd* Susan Block *ed* Pamela Martin
☆ Jeremy Davies, *Alberta Watson*, Benjamin Hendrickson, Carlo Gallo, Matthew Puckett, Judette Jones

> 'A thought provoking movie that should not be allowed to disappear beneath this year's Dredds and Batmans.' – *Empire*

† The film won the Audience Award at the 1994 Sundance Film Festival.

Spare a Copper *

GB 1940 77m bw
Ealing
A police war reservist catches saboteurs.
One of the last good Formby comedies, with everything percolating as it should.
w Roger MacDougall, Austin Melford, Basil Dearden *d* John Paddy Carstairs *ph* Bryan Langley *m* Louis Levy
☆ George Formby, Dorothy Hyson, Bernard Lee, John Warwick, John Turnbull, George Merritt

Spare the Rod

GB 1961 93m bw
British Lion/Bryanston/Weyland (Victor Lyndon)
At an East End school, a novice master wins the confidence of tough pupils.
A British Blackboard Jungle, *paving the way for* To Sir with Love; *not exciting on its own account.*
w John Cresswell *novel* Michael Croft *d* Leslie Norman *ph* Paul Beeson *m* Laurie Johnson
☆ Max Bygraves, Geoffrey Keen, Donald Pleasence, Richard O'Sullivan, Betty McDowall, Eleanor Summerfield, Mary Merrall

'Her passion was a caged bird waiting to be set free...'
Sparrow

Italy 1993 106m colour
Rank/Polygram/Nippon (Mario Cecchi Gori, Vittorio Cecchi Gori)

Sent home because of a plague threatening the convent, a nun preparing for her final vows meets and falls in love with a young student.
A moody, period melodrama of a doomed love, given an operatic treatment and hindered by the fact that its leading characters cannot portray the emotional upheavals required of them.
wd Franco Zeffirelli *novel* *A Sparrow's Tale* by Giovanni Verga *ph* Ennio Guarnieri *m* Claudio Cappani, Alessio Vlad *ed* Richard Marden
☆ Angela Bettis, Sinead Cusack, Johnathon Schaech, Vanessa Redgrave, John Castle, Valentina Cortese, Frank Finlay, Pat Heywood, Denis Quilley

> 'Dramatic, grand in scope, and tragic in its tale of unfulfilled love and lives. Unfortunately the plot is almost tortuously slow, and the film ends up neither emotionally nor intellectually gripping.' – *Karen Regelman, Variety*

Sparrows Can't Sing

GB 1962 94m bw
Elstree/Carthage (Donald Taylor)

Returning after two years at sea, a sailor searches for his wife and threatens vengeance on her lover.
Relentlessly caricatured Cockney comedy melodrama, too self-conscious to be effective, and not at all likeable anyway.
w Stephen Lewis, Joan Littlewood *d* Joan Littlewood *ph* Max Greene *m* James Stevens
☆ James Booth, Barbara Windsor, Roy Kinnear, Avis Bunnage, George Sewell, Barbara Ferris, Murray Melvin, Arthur Mullard

Spartaco: see *Spartacus (1952)*

'Behold the splendor and fury of a city made with pleasure.'
Spartacus

Italy 1952 92m bw
RKO/Consorzio Spartacus

original title: *Spartaco*
aka: *Spartacus the Gladiator; Sins of Rome*
After he rejects the advances of the daughter of a Roman general, a Thracian slave becomes a gladiator, and leads a revolt against Rome.
A version that substitutes a love affair and action for historical accuracy; it has good performances and splendid photography to recommend it.
w Jean Ferry, Mario Bori *d* Riccardo Freda *ph* Gabor Rogany *m* Renzo Rossellini
☆ Massimo Girotti, Lumilla Tcherina, Gianni Maria Canale, Yves Vincent, Vittorio Sanipoli, Carlo Ninchi
† The US version ran for 71m.

Spartacus **

US 1960 196m Super Technirama 70
U-I/Bryna (Edward Lewis)

The slaves of ancient Rome revolt and are quashed.
Long, well-made, downbeat epic with deeper than usual characterization and several bravura sequences.
w Dalton Trumbo *novel* Howard Fast *d* *Stanley Kubrick* *ph* *Russell Metty* *m* Alex North *pd* Alexander Golitzen *ed* Robert Lawrence
☆ Kirk Douglas, Laurence Olivier, Charles Laughton, Tony Curtis, Jean Simmons, Peter Ustinov, John Gavin, Nina Foch, Herbert Lom, John Ireland, John Dall, Charles McGraw, Woody Strode

> 'Everything is depicted with a lack of imagination that is truly Marxian.' – *Anne Grayson*

> 'A lot of first-rate professionals have pooled their abilities to make a first-rate circus.' – *Stanley Kauffmann*

> 'One comes away feeling rather revolted and not at all ennobled.' – *Alan Dent, Illustrated London News*

† The movie's original director, Anthony Mann, was replaced by Kubrick after a fortnight's shooting.
Russell Metty; Peter Ustinov; art direction
Alex North; editing

Spartacus the Gladiator: see *Spartacus (1952)*

'Born In Darkness. Sworn To Justice.'
Spawn

US 1997 97m DeLuxe
Entertainment/New Line/Todd McFarlane (Clint Goldman)

An assassinated special agent is brought back to life with supernatural powers on condition that he leads the Devil's army to take over the world.
Exceptionally dreary, noisy nonsense that shows the cinema of mindless sensation at its worst: it makes little narrative sense, displays no imagination in its repetitive action sequences, and is peopled by uninteresting characters.
w Alan McElroy *comic book* Todd McFarlane *d* Mark A.Z. Dippé *ph* Guillermo Navarro *m* Graeme Revell *pd* Philip Harrison *ed* Michael N. Knue *sp* Robert Kurtzman, Gregory Nicotero, Howard Berger; ILM
☆ John Leguizamo, Michael Jai White, Martin Sheen, Theresa Randle, Melinda Clarke, Miko Hughes, Sydni Beaudoin, Nicol Williamson, D. B. Sweeney

> 'Gives you the pleasurably junky sensation of living inside an apocalyptic videogame.' – *Owen Glieberman, Entertainment Weekly*

> 'If you're looking for a movie to restore your faith in superhero film-making, this sure as hell isn't the one.' – *Jason Caro, Film Review*

'A love story stormy as raging Arctic seas!'
Spawn of the North **

US 1938 110m bw
Paramount (Albert Lewin)
In 1890s Alaska, American fishermen combat Russian poachers.
Solidly carpentered all-star action melodrama, a sizzler of its day. Remade 1953 as Alaska Seas.
w Talbot Jennings, Jules Furthman *d* *Henry Hathaway* *ph* *Charles Lang* *m* Dimitri Tiomkin
☆ George Raft, Henry Fonda, Dorothy Lamour, *John Barrymore*, Akim Tamiroff, Louise Platt, Lynne Overman, Fuzzy Knight, Vladimir Sokoloff, Duncan Renaldo, John Wray

> 'The visual features are so realistic and terrifying that audiences will find complete satisfaction in the production.' – *Variety*

> 'This film has something which the cinema of bygone days used to supply as a matter of course – action and thrills, the quickened pulse and the lump in the throat.' – *Basil Wright*

'Rousing old-fashioned spectacle.' – *New York Times*
Special Award for special effects

Spawn of the Slithis
US 1978 86m Movielab
Paul Fabian/Stephen Traxler
A teacher of journalism investigates deaths in the neighbourhood and discovers a monster lurking in the local canals.
Low-budget shocker that is also bereft of originality or talent.
wd Stephen Traxler *ph* Robert Caramico *m* Steve Zuckerman *ad* Catherine Deeter *ed* Robert M. Ross
☆ Alan Blanchard, J. C. Claire, Dennis Lee Falt, Mello Alexandria, Win Condict

Speak Easily *
US 1932 83m bw
MGM (Lawrence Weingarten)
A professor inherits a Broadway musical and falls for the lure of the bright lights.
Interesting Keaton talkie at the point of his decline.
w Ralph Spence, Laurence E. Johnson *novel* *Footlights* by Clarence Budington Kelland *d* Edward Sedgwick *ph* Harold Wentstrom
☆ Buster Keaton, Jimmy Durante, Hedda Hopper

Speaking Parts
Canada 1989 92m colour
Recorded Releasing/Ego Film Arts/Telefilm Canada/Ontario Film Development Company/Academy Pictures/Film Four International
A screenwriter and a hotel maid both fall in love with a gigolo who wants to be an actor.
Curious and ultimately unsatisfactory triangular drama of personalities who connect with each other mainly through the medium of video.
wd Atom Egoyan *ph* Paul Sarossy *m* Mychael Danna *ad* Linda Del Rosario *ed* Bruce McDonald
☆ Michael McManus, Arsinee Khanjian, Gabrielle Rose, Tony Nardi, David Hemblen, Patricia Collins

Special Agent
US 1935 74m bw
Cosmopolitan/Warner
A special investigator pretends to be a newspaperman.
Routine rough stuff, quite watchable.
w Laird Doyle, Abem Finkel *d* William Keighley *ph* Sid Hickox *md* Leo F. Forbstein *ad* Esdras Hartley *ed* Clarence Kolster
☆ Bette Davis, George Brent, Ricardo Cortez, Jack La Rue, Henry O'Neill, J. Carrol Naish
'Indifferent entertainment but Bette Davis may help.' – *Variety*

Special Delivery
US 1976 99m DeLuxe
TCF/Bing Crosby Productions (Richard Berg)
Three disabled Vietnam veterans rob a bank, and the consequences are complicated.
Unremarkable suspenser which takes itself too seriously.
w Don Gazzaniga *d* Paul Wendkos *ph* Harry Stradling Jnr *m* Lalo Schifrin
☆ Bo Svenson, Cybill Shepherd, Michael C. Gwynne, Vic Tayback, Sorrell Booke, Jeff Goldblum

'Killing Is His Profession. Revenge Is Her Goal. Together They Take On The Battle Against The Underworld Of Miami.'
The Specialist
US 1994 110m Technicolor
Warner (Jerry Weintraub)
A woman seeking revenge infiltrates the gang that murdered her parents and hires an expert in explosives to kill them.
Trashily risible action movie, with the two stars kept far apart for much of the picture, for reasons that only become apparent when they are together.
w Alexandra Seros *suggested by* 'The Specialist' novels by John Shirley *d* Luis Llosa *ph* Jeffrey L. Kimball *m* John Barry *pd* Walter P. Martishius *ed* Jack Hofstra
☆ Sylvester Stallone, Sharon Stone, James Woods, Rod Steiger, Eric Roberts, Mario Ernesto Sanchez, Sergio Dore Jnr
'A pretty silly film. And it is capped by a sex scene involving Stone and Sylvester Stallone that has to be seen to be disbelieved.' – *Derek Malcolm, Guardian*
'Cheesecake meets beeake.' – *New Yorker*

'Two decades ago we sent a message to space. This is the reply...'
Species *
US 1995 108m DeLuxe Panavision
UIP/MGM (Fred Mancuso Jnr, Dennis Feldman)
Scientists chase a half-human, half-alien girl who escapes from an experimental laboratory, concerned that she intends to mate and breed.
Enjoyable, fast-moving science-fiction thriller; it offers nothing new but presents a familiar tale with some style.
w Dennis Feldman *d* Roger Donaldson *ph* Andrzej Bartkowiak *m* Christopher Young *pd* John Muto *ed* Conrad Buff *sp* visual effects: Richard Edlund; 'Sil' design: H. R. Giger
☆ Ben Kingsley, Michael Madsen, Alfred Molina, Forest Whitaker, Marg Helgenberger, Natasha Henstridge, Michelle Williams
'Think of it as *Beach Blanket Alien* – sure, it's dopey, but it's a guilty-pleasure pig-out.' – *Premiere*

Species II
US 1998 93m DeLuxe
UIP/MGM/FGM (Frank Mancuso Jnr)
A woman who is part alien tracks down an astronaut on a killing spree who has returned from Mars infected with alien DNA.
A sequel that rings a few welcome changes on the original, and offers more fast-paced entertainment.
w Chris Brancato *d* Peter Medak *ph* Matthew F. Leonetti *m* Edward Shearmur *pd* Miljen Kreka Kljakovic *ed* Richard Nord *sp* Steve Johnson
☆ Michael Madison, Natasha Henstridge, Marg Helgenberger, Mykelti Williamson, George Dzundza, James Cromwell, Myriam Cyr, Sarah Wynter
'A carnival of the absurdly gruesome.' – *Philip Strick, Sight and Sound*

The Speckled Band
GB 1931 80m bw
B and D/Herbert Wilcox
Sherlock Holmes saves an heiress from a horrible death.
Limp and overstretched version of Conan Doyle's story, interesting only for the actors.
w W. P. Lipscomb *d* Jack Raymond *ph* Freddie Young
☆ Raymond Massey (Sherlock Holmes), Athole Stewart (Dr Watson), Lyn Harding (Dr Rylott), Angela Baddeley, Nancy Price

The Specter of the Rose *
US 1946 90m bw
Republic (Ben Hecht)
A schizophrenic ballet dancer lives his role and nearly murders his wife.
A rather hilarious bid for culture: hard to sit through without laughing, but unique.
wd Ben Hecht *ph* Lee Garmes *m* Georges Antheil
☆ Viola Essen, Ivan Kirov, Michael Chekhov

The Spectre of Edgar Allan Poe
US 1972 86m Eastmancolor
Doverton/Cintel (Mohy Quandour)
Poe visits an asylum where his beloved Lenore has been taken to recover from being buried alive and finds himself in a nightmare world of murder and monsters.
An intriguing notion is quickly done to death in an unimaginative production.
wd Mohy Quandour *story* Kenneth Hartford, Denton Foxx *ph* Robert Birchall *m* Allen D. Allen *ed* Abbas Amin *sp* Byrd Holland
☆ Robert Walker, Mary Grover, Cesar Romero, Tom Drake, Carol Ohmart

Speechless
US 1994 99m DeLuxe
MGM/Forge (Renny Harlin, Geena Davis)
Two speech writers for rival candidates in a senatorial contest fall for each other.
Pleasant but unmemorable romantic comedy, cynical about politics and sentimental about love.
w Robert King *d* Ron Underwood *ph* Don Peterman *m* Marc Shaiman *pd* Dennis Washington *ed* Richard Francis-Bruce
☆ Michael Keaton, Geena Davis, Christopher Reeve, Bonnie Bedelia, Ernie Hudson, Charles Martin Smith, Gailard Sartain, Ray Baker, Mitchell Ryan
'Never achieves the madcap hilarity of the '40s romantic comedies it seeks to emulate, and some of the dramatic moments feel a bit forced.' – *Brian Lowry, Variety*

Speed ***
US 1994 115m DeLuxe Panavision
TCF (Mark Gordon)
A mad bomber attempts to hold a city to ransom by planting a bomb on a bus which will explode if the vehicle's speed drops below 50 mph.
A fast, adrenalin-pumping action-packed thriller that achieves a high level of suspense; it works brilliantly well for the most part, even if the good guys cause more destruction than the bad, although it goes off the rails towards the end.
w Graham Yost *d* *Jan de Bont* *ph* Andrzej Bartkowiak *m* Mike Mancina *pd* Jackson de Govia *ed* John Wright
☆ Keanu Reeves, Dennis Hopper, Sandra Bullock, Joe Morton, Jeff Daniels, Alan Ruck, Glenn Plummer, Richard Lineback, Beth Grant, Hawthorne James, Carlos Carrasco
'A non-stop actioner that rarely pauses to take a breath. While highly derivative and mechanical in planning and execution, this high-octane thrillathon boasts more twists, turns and obstacles than the most hazardous video arcade road raceway.' – *Variety*
sound (Gregg Landaker, Steve Maslow, Bob Beemer, David R. R. MacMillan); sound effects editing (Stephen Hunter Flick)
editing
editing

'Rush Hour Hits The Water.'
Speed 2 – Cruise Control
US 1997 125m DeLuxe Panavision
TCF/Blue Tulip (Jan de Bont)
A psychotic computer expert sabotages a cruise liner, whose passengers include a Los Angeles cop and his girlfriend.
A sequel so contrived and artificial that it swiftly sinks with all hands.
w Randall McCormick, Jeff Nathanson, Jan de Bont *d* Jan de Bont *ph* Jack N. Green *m* Mark Mancina *pd* Joseph Nemec III *ed* Alan Cody *sp* ILM; Rhythm and Hues
☆ Sandra Bullock, Jason Patric, Willem Dafoe, Temuera Morrison, Brian McCardie, Christine Firkins, Michael G. Hagerty, Colleen Camp, Lois Chiles, Bo Svenson
'Has no real logic, or characters or dramatic tension.' – *Derek Malcolm, Guardian*
'Suffers from a slender script, a tedious first reel and a routine villain.' – *Variety*
† It grossed more than $48m in the US, and $105m elsewhere.

Speed Zone
US/Canada 1989 95m Film House colour
Orion/Ruddy-Morgan/Entcorp (Murray Shostak)
aka: *Cannonball Fever*
When a police chief tries to stop the Cannonball Run by arresting the drivers, substitutes take over.
Dreary comedy, consisting of crude slapstick, tiresome car chases and cardboard characterizations; a few jokes might have helped.
w Michael Short *d* Jim Drake *ph* François Protat, Robert Saad *m* David Wheatley *ed* Michael Economou
☆ Melody Anderson, Peter Boyle, Donna Dixon, John Candy, Eugene Levy, Tim Matheson, Smothers Brothers, Shari Belafonte, Joe Flaherty, Matt Frewer, Mimi Kuzyk, Jamie Farr, Don Lake, Alyssa Milano, John Schneider and also Brooke Shields, Michael Spinks, Lee Van Cleef
† It is a sort of sequel to *The Cannonball Run* and *Cannonball Run II* (qqv).

Speedy **
US 1928 90m approx bw silent
Paramount (Harold Lloyd)
A young man saves his girl's grandfather's trolley car business.
One of its star's most stylish comedies, and his last silent film, with a trolley car ride for climax.
w John Grey, Lex Neal, Howard Emmett Rogers, Jay Howe *d* *Ted Wilde* *ph* Walter Lundin
☆ *Harold Lloyd*, Ann Christy, Bert Woodruff, Brooks Benedict, Babe Ruth
Ted Wilde

The Spell of Amy Nugent: see *Spellbound (1940)*

The Spellbinder
US 1939 68m bw
RKO
A criminal lawyer full of tricks finds himself on trial for murder.
Contrived courtroom drama tailored to its star.
w Thomas Lennon, Joseph A. Fields *d* Jack Hively
☆ Lee Tracy, Barbara Read, Patric Knowles, Allan Lane, Morgan Conway
'Average supporter for duals.' – *Variety*

Spellbinder
US 1988 99m colour
MGM/Indian Neck (Joe Wizan, Brian Russell)
A Los Angeles lawyer rescues a girl from a beating and finds himself confronting a murderous cult of devil worshippers.
Dreary occult drama, lacking any trace of magic, black or otherwise, and with a twist in the plot that will come as no surprise to anyone who has watched The Wicker Man.
w Tracy Tormé *d* Janet Greek *ph* Adam Greenberg *m* Basil Poledouris *pd* Rodger Maus *ed* Steve Mirkovich
☆ Timothy Daly, Kelly Preston, Audra Lindley, Cary-Hiroyuki Tagawa, Diana Bellamy, Anthony Crivello, Rick Rossovich

Spellbound
GB 1940 82m bw
Pyramid Amalgamated (R. Murray Leslie)
aka: *Passing Clouds*
US title: *The Spell of Amy Nugent*
A young man is in despair when his fiancée dies, and nearly goes mad when a medium materializes her from the dead.
Very odd, very naïve, but somehow rather winning.
w Miles Malleson *novel* *The Necromancers* by Robert Benson *d* John Harlow *ph* Walter Harvey
☆ Derek Farr, Vera Lindsay, Frederick Leister, Hay Petrie, Diana King, Felix Aylmer

Spellbound **
US 1945 111m bw
David O. Selznick
The new head of a mental institution is an impostor and an amnesiac; a staff member falls in love with him and helps him recall the fate of the real Dr Edwardes.
Enthralling and rather infuriating psychological mystery; the Hitchcock touches are splendid, and the stars shine magically, but the plot could have stood a little more attention.
w Ben Hecht, Angus MacPhail *novel* *The House of Dr Edwardes* by Francis Beeding *d* *Alfred Hitchcock* *ph* *George Barnes* *m* *Miklos Rozsa* *ad* James Basevi *dream sequence* Salvador Dali
☆ *Ingrid Bergman, Gregory Peck, Leo G. Carroll, Michael Chekhov*, Rhonda Fleming, John Emery, Norman Lloyd, Steve Geray
'Just about as much of the id as could be safely displayed in a Bergdorf Goodman window.' – *James Agee*
'Glossily produced and wildly improbable.' – *George Perry, 1965*
'Bergman's apple-cheeked sincerity has rarely been so out of place as in this confection whipped up by jaded chefs.' – *New Yorker, 1976*
Miklos Rozsa
best picture; Alfred Hitchcock; George Barnes; Michael Chekhov

Spencer's Mountain *
US 1963 121m Technicolor Panavision
Warner (Delmer Daves)

Life in rural America in the thirties with a poor quarry worker and his family of nine.
Sentimental rose-tinted hokum which later became TV's The Waltons. *Expertly concocted, Hollywood style.*
wd Delmer Daves *novel* Earl Hamner Jnr
ph Charles Lawton, H. F. Koenekamp *m* Max Steiner *ad* Carl Anderson *ed* David Wages
cos Marjorie Best
☆ Henry Fonda, Maureen O'Hara, James MacArthur, Donald Crisp, Wally Cox, Mimsy Farmer, Lillian Bronson
'Outstanding for its smirking sexuality, its glorification of the vulgar, its patronizing tone, its mealymouthed piety.' – *Judith Crist*

Spendthrift
US 1936 80m bw
Paramount
A millionaire playboy runs out of cash.
Mild romantic comedy.
w Raoul Walsh, Bert Hanlon *story* Eric Hatch
d Raoul Walsh *ph* Leon Shamroy *md* Boris Morros
☆ Henry Fonda, Pat Paterson, Mary Brian, George Barbier, Ed Brophy

Speriamo Che Sia Femmina: see *Let's Hope It's A Girl*

Spetters **
Netherlands 1980 115m Eastmancolor
Embassy/VSE (Joop Van Den Ende)

In a small town, three young men, two of them hoping to win a motor-cross biking championship, are all involved with a blonde sex siren who serves food from a mobile kitchen.
High energy melodrama, full of sex and violence, but eminently watchable.
w Gerard Soeteman *d* Paul Verhoeven *ph* Jöst Vacano *m* Ton Scherpenzeel *ad* Dick Schillemans *ed* Ine Schenkkan
☆ Hans Van Tongeren, Renee Soutendijk, Toon Agterberg, Maarten Spanjer, Marianne Boyer, Hugo Metsers, Kittye Courbois, Rutger Hauer, Jeroen Krabbé

'Terror Can Fill Any Space.'
Sphere
US 1998 133m Monaco Film Lab Arriflex
Warner/Baltimore/Constant/Punch (Michael Crichton, Andrew Wald, Barry Levinson)

A team of scientists investigate a mysterious alien sphere discovered on the ocean floor.
Like most American science-fiction movies of the 90s, this is merely an excuse for characters to explore their own inner space in an attempt to come to terms with themselves.
w Stephen Hauser, Paul Attanasio *story* Michael Crichton *d* Barry Levinson *ph* Adam Greenberg
m Elliot Goldenthal *pd* Norman Reynolds
ed Stu Linder *adaptation* Kurt Wimmer
☆ Dustin Hoffman, Sharon Stone, Samuel L. Jackson, Peter Coyote, Liev Schreiber, Queen Latifah, Marga Gomez
'An empty shell.' – *Variety*

The Sphinx
US 1933 63m bw
Monogram

A murderer uses his deaf mute brother as an alibi.
Mildly ingenious low-budget thriller.
w Albert DeMond *d* Phil Rosen
☆ Lionel Atwill, Sheila Terry, Theodore Newton, Paul Hurst, Luis Alberni
'Fair returns are probable if dated properly.' – *Variety*

Sphinx
US 1980 118m Technicolor Panavision
Warner/Orion (Stanley O'Toole)

Archaeologists in modern Cairo find clues to an ancient treasure.
Expensive penny dreadful which lurches about from comedy to horror but is often well worth looking at.
w John Byrum *novel* Robin Cook *d* Franklin J. Schaffner *ph* Ernest Day *m* Michael J. Lewis
pd Terence Marsh
☆ Lesley-Anne Down, Frank Langella, Maurice Ronet, John Gielgud, Vic Tablian, Martin Benson, John Rhys-Davies
'A glossily-packaged exercise in random-selection box-office formulae.' – *Jo Imeson, MFB*

Spiceworld the Movie
GB 1997 92m Technicolor
Polygram/Icon/Fragile (Uri Fruchtman, Barnaby Thompson)

A week in the life of a pop group as they prepare for a concert at the Albert Hall.
Brash, lively movie aimed at the many fans of the Spice Girls, but one that is unlikely to convert others to the cause.
w Kim Fuller, Jamie Curtis *d* Bob Spiers
ph Clive Tickner *m* Paul Hardcastle
pd Grenville Horner *ed* Andrea MacArthur
☆ The Spice Girls (Mel B., Emma, Mel C., Geri, Victoria), Richard E. Grant, Alan Cumming, George Wendt, Claire Rushbrook, Mark McKinney, Richard O'Brien, Roger Moore, Barry Humphries, Meatloaf, Stephen Fry, Richard Briers, Bill Paterson
'A bright and breezy movie that's as timely but evanescent as the Cool Britannia culture it celebrates.' – *Derek Elley, Variety*

Spicy Rice: see *Dragon's Food*

The Spider
US 1931 65m bw
Fox
A theatre magician traps a killer.
Rather flat transcription of a play which in its original form took every advantage of the audience and other elements.
play Fulton Oursler, Lowell Brentano *d* William Cameron Menzies, Kenneth MacKenna
☆ Edmund Lowe, Howard Phillips, Lois Moran, George E. Stone, El Brendel

The Spider
GB 1939 81m bw
Admiral Films (Victor M. Greene)
A theatrical agent kills his partner on a train.
Barely competent murder thriller.
w Kenneth Horne, Reginald Long *novel* Henry Holt *d* Maurice Elvey
☆ Derrick de Marney, Diana Churchill, Cecil Parker, Jean Gillie, Frank Cellier, Allan Jeayes

'The only thing worse than losing your mind... is finding it again.'
Spider *
Canada/GB/Japan/France 2002 98m colour
Helkon SK/Davis/AIN/Grosvenor Park (David Cronenberg, Samuel Hadida, Catherine Bailey)

A terrible past and an uncertain present merge in the confused mind of a schizophrenic who has been released from a mental institution after twenty years.
Fiennes gives a compelling performance as a shambling man lost in a trauma of sex and violence, but nothing outside his skewed vision is shown so that the result becomes as confused as his mind.
w Patrick McGrath *novel* Patrick McGrath
d David Cronenberg *ph* Peter Suschitzky
m Howard Shore *pd* Andrew Sanders *ed* Ronald Sanders
☆ *Ralph Fiennes* (Spider), Miranda Richardson (Yvonne/Mrs. Cleg/Mrs. Wilkinson), Gabriel Byrne (Bill Cleg), Bradley Hall (Young Spider), Lynn Redgrave (Mrs Wilkinson), John Neville (Terrence), Gary Reineke (Freddy), Philip Craig (John)
'Spider is not a pulse-quickening experience, but Fiennes's art makes it engrossing.' – *Stanley Kaufmann, New Republic*
'The movie is well made and acted, but it lacks dimension because it essentially has only one character, and he lacks dimension.' – *Roger Ebert, Chicago Sun-Times*

The Spider and the Fly
GB 1949 95m bw
GFD/Maxwell Setton, Aubrey Baring
In 1913 a Parisian safecracker constantly outwits an inspector of the Sûreté, but war brings changes.
Coldly ironic comedy drama which really, regrettably, doesn't work.
w Robert Westerby *d* Robert Hamer *ph* Geoffrey Unsworth *m* Georges Auric
☆ Eric Portman, Guy Rolfe, Nadia Gray, George Cole, Edward Chapman, John Carol, Maurice Denham
'Not sufficiently exciting for a thriller, not quite sharp enough for a real drama of character.' – *Gavin Lambert, MFB*

'The Seductive Innocence of Lolita! The Savage Hunger of a Black Widow!'
Spider Baby
US 1964 80m bw
Admit One (Gil Lasky, Paul Monka)

aka: *The Liver Eaters*
A chauffeur takes care of the family whose members degenerate into cannibals as they grow older.
A low-budget horror with a cult reputation for its general ineptitude, which extends to Chaney singing the rock 'n' roll title song.
wd Jack Hill *ph* Alfred Taylor *m* Ronald Stein
ad Ray Storey *ed* Elliot Fayad
☆ Lon Chaney Jnr, Carol Ohmart, Quinn Redeker, Mantan Moreland, Beverly Washburn, Mary Mitchell, Jill Banner, Sid Haig
'A sort of more perverse *Addams Family*, with genuinely grotesque humour and a unique cheesiness.' – *Kim Newman, Nightmare Movies*

Spider Woman **
US 1944 62m bw
Universal (Roy William Neill)

aka: *Sherlock Holmes and the Spider Woman*
A female Moriarty kills her victims with spiders so that she can collect on their insurance policies.
Lively episode in the modernized series, which packs in several suspenseful episodes borrowed from a variety of Conan Doyle originals.
w Bertram Millhauser *d* Roy William Neill
ph Charles Van Enger *m* Hans Salter
☆ *Basil Rathbone* (Sherlock Holmes), *Nigel Bruce* (Dr Watson), *Gale Sondergaard* (Andrea Spedding), Dennis Hoey (Lestrade), Vernon Downing (Norman Locke), Alec Craig (Radlik), Mary Gordon (Mrs Hudson), Arthur Hohl (Gilflower)

The Spider Woman Strikes Back
US 1946 59m bw
Universal (Howard Welsch)
An innocent girl is used as decoy by a conniving female criminal.
Boring crime filler, scarcely a worthy sequel to Spider Woman.
w Eric Taylor *d* Arthur Lubin *ph* Paul Ivano
md Milton Rosen
☆ Gale Sondergaard, Brenda Joyce, Rondo Hatton, Milburn Stone, Kirby Grant, Hobart Cavanaugh

'With great power comes great responsibility.'
Spider-Man *
US 2002 121m DeLuxe
Columbia TriStar/Marvel (Laura Ziskin, Ian Bryce)

A high school wimp is bitten by a genetically-altered spider and turns into the superhero Spider-Man, just in time to battle against a mad scientist, who remakes himself as the Green Goblin.
Critic-proof, comic-book entertainment that will trap large audiences with its spin of romance and action, though it could have done with a better (that is, badder) villain.
w David Koepp *comic book* Stan Lee, Steve Ditko
d Sam Raimi *ph* Don Burgess *m* Danny Elfman
pd Neil Spisak *ed* Bob Murawski, Arthur Coburn
sp John Dykstra
☆ Tobey Maguire (Spider-Man/Peter Parker), Willem Dafoe (Green Goblin/Norman Osborn), Kirsten Dunst (Mary Jane Watson), James Franco (Harry Osborn), Cliff Robertson (Ben Parker), Rosemary Harris (May Parker), J. K. Simmons (J. Jonah Jameson), Flash Thompson (Joe Manganiello)
'A perfectly serviceable early-summer popcorn picture that will satisfy its core teen constituency and not displease general viewers looking for some disposable entertainment.' – *Todd McCarthy, Variety*
'A canny franchise escapade; it gets the job done. But it also leaves you hungry for something more, and I don't necessarily mean the next episode.' – *Owen Gleiberman, Entertainment Weekly*
† It set a new record by taking $115m at the US box-office in its first three days.
visual effects (John Dykstra, Scott Stokdyk, Anthony LaMolinara, John Frazier); sound (Kevin O'Connell, Greg P. Russell, Ed Novick)

The Spider's Stratagem *
Italy 1970 97m Eastmancolor
Radiotelevisione Italiana/Red Film (Giovanni Bertolucci)

original title: *Strategia del Ragno*
Revisiting the village in the Po valley where his father was murdered by fascists in 1936, our gradually disillusioned hero learns that his father was really a traitor executed by his own men.
Elaborately mysterious puzzle play for intellectuals, with infinite shades of meaning which few will bother to explore. The atmosphere, however, is superbly caught.
w Bernardo Bertolucci, Eduardo de Gregorio, Marilu Parolini *story* *The Theme of the Traitor and the Hero* by Jorge Luis Borges *d* Bernardo Bertolucci *ph* Vittorio Storaro, Franco di Giacomo
☆ Giulio Brogi, Alida Valli, Tino Scotti, Pino Campanini

Der Spiegel Ayna: see *The Mirror*

The Spies: see *Les Espions*

Spies Like Us
US 1985 109m Technicolor
Warner (Brian Grazer, George Folsey Jnr)

Bumbling bureaucrats are mistakenly chosen for a spy mission.
Inept attempts at humour fall flat throughout this dreary venture, which is as though Hope and Crosby had set out on the road to Morocco without a script.
w Dan Aykroyd, Lowell Ganz, Babaloo Mandel
d John Landis *ph* Robert Paynter *m* Elmer Bernstein *pd* Peter Murton *ed* Malcolm Campbell
☆ Chevy Chase, Dan Aykroyd, Steve Forrest, Donna Dixon, Bruce Davison, William Prince, Bernie Casey

Spies of the Air
GB 1939 77m bw
British National (John Corfield)
A test pilot turns out to be an enemy agent.
Moderate programmer with an engaging cast.
w A. R. Rawlinson, Bridget Boland *play* *Official Secrets* by Jeffrey Dell *d* David MacDonald
☆ Barry K. Barnes, Roger Livesey, Joan Marion, Basil Radford, Felix Aylmer, John Turnbull, Henry Oscar

The Spikes Gang
US 1974 96m DeLuxe
UA/Mirisch/Duo/Sanford (Walter Mirisch)
Three boys shelter a bank robber and join his gang.
Doom-laden, violent Western with a few comic lines.
w Irving Ravetch, Harriet Frank Jnr *novel* *The Bank Robber* by Giles Tippette *d* Richard Fleischer
ph Brian West *m* Fred Karlin
☆ Lee Marvin, Gary Grimes, Ron Howard, Charles Martin Smith, Arthur Hunnicutt, Noah Beery Jnr

Spin of a Coin: see *The George Raft Story*

La Spina Dorsale del Diavolo: see *The Deserter*

Spinout
US 1966 93m Metrocolor Panavision
MGM/Euterpe (Joe Pasternak)

GB title: *California Holiday*
A carefree touring singer agrees to drive an experimental car in a road race.
Mild star musical which at least stays in the open air.
w Theodore J. Flicker, George Kirgo *d* Norman Taurog *ph* Daniel L. Fapp *md* Georgie Stoll
☆ Elvis Presley, Shelley Fabares, Carl Betz, Cecil Kellaway, Diane McBain, Deborah Walley, Jack Mullaney, Will Hutchins, Una Merkel

Spinster: see *Two Loves*

The Spiral Road
US 1962 145m Eastmancolor
U-I (Robert Arthur)

In 1936 Java, an atheist medical man fights a leprosy epidemic and eventually becomes a missionary.
A long slog through jungle/religious clichés, with a hilariously miscast star and an almost Victorian script.
w John Lee Mahin, Neil Paterson *novel* Jan de Hartog *d* Robert Mulligan *ph* Russell Harlan *m* Jerry Goldsmith
☆ Rock Hudson, Burl Ives, Geoffrey Keen, Gena Rowlands, Will Kuluva, Neva Patterson, Philip Abbott

The Spiral Staircase ***
US 1945 83m bw
RKO (Dore Schary)

A small town in 1906 New England is terrorized by a psychopathic killer of deformed girls.
Archetypal old dark house thriller, superbly detailed and set during a most convincing thunderstorm. Even though the identity of the villain is pretty obvious, this is a superior Hollywood product.
w Mel Dinelli novel Some Must Watch by Ethel Lina White d Robert Siodmak ph Nicholas Musuraca m Roy Webb ad Albert S. D'Agostino, Jack Okey
☆ *Dorothy McGuire*, George Brent, Kent Smith, Ethel Barrymore, Rhys Williams, Rhonda Fleming, Gordon Oliver, Sara Allgood, James Bell
'A nice, cosy and well-sustained atmosphere of horror.' – *C. A. Lejeune*
Ethel Barrymore

The Spiral Staircase
GB 1975 89m Technicolor
Warner/Raven (Peter Shaw)

Modernized remake of the above using virtually the same script, and apparently determined to prove how badly it can be presented.
w Andrew Meredith *d* Peter Collinson *ph* Ken Hodges *m* David Lindup
☆ Jacqueline Bisset, Christopher Plummer, Sam Wanamaker, Mildred Dunnock, Gayle Hunnicutt, Sheila Brennan, Elaine Stritch, John Ronane, Ronald Radd, John Phillip Law
'I don't think this needless remake is going to set anyone's flesh creeping, except at the vulgar flashiness of the whole enterprise.' – *Michael Billington, Illustrated London News*

The Spirit Is Willing
US 1966 100m Technicolor
Paramount/William Castle
A family finds that its holiday home is haunted by the ghosts of a *crime passionel*.
Overlong, overplayed and witless farce with virtually no opportunity well taken.
w Ben Starr *novel The Visitors* by Nathaniel Benchley *d* William Castle *ph* Hal Stine *m* Vic Mizzy
☆ Sid Caesar, Vera Miles, John McGiver, Cass Daley, John Astin, Mary Wickes, Jesse White

Spirit of Culver
US 1939 89m bw
Universal
A boy grows up at Culver Military Academy.
Very humdrum flagwaver combined with a last attempt to maintain stardom for two child performers.
w Nathanael West, Whitney Bolton *d* Joseph Santley
☆ Jackie Cooper, Freddie Bartholomew, Tim Holt, Henry Hull, Andy Devine, Gene Reynolds
'Mild entertainment for duals and kids.' – *Variety*

The Spirit of St Louis *
US 1957 135m Warnercolor Cinemascope
Warner (Leyland Hayward)

In 1927 Charles Lindbergh flies a specially constructed plane 3,600 miles nonstop New York to Paris in 33½ hours.
Impeccably in its period, this needlessly Cinemascoped reconstruction can scarcely avoid dull patches since for long stretches its hero is on screen solo apart from a fly, and his monologues become soporific.
w Billy Wilder, Wendell Mayes *book* Charles Lindbergh *d* Billy Wilder *ph* Robert Burks, Peverell Marley *m* Franz Waxman
☆ James Stewart, Murray Hamilton, Marc Connelly

The Spirit of the Beehive *
Spain 1973 98m Eastmancolor
Elias Querejeta

original title: *El Espíritu de la Colmene*
In 1940 in a remote village, two children see a travelling film show of Frankenstein, and their imaginations run riot; or do they?
Sensitive story of childish imagination, reminiscent of Jeux Interdits *and yet very much its own vision.*
w Francisco J. Querejeta *d* Victor Erice *ph* Luis Cuadrado *m* Luis de Pablo
☆ Fernando Fernan Gomez, Teresa Gimpera, Ana Torrent, Isabel Telleria

Spirit of the People: see *Abe Lincoln in Illinois*

'Some legends can never be tamed.'
Spirit: Stallion of the Cimarron *
US 2002 84m Technicolor 'Scope
DreamWorks (Mireille Soria, Jeffrey Katzenberg)

In the 1800s in the Old West, a horse grows up to value his freedom and resist capture by the cavalry.
Simple sentimental tale of horses and Indians with little dialogue but lots of simple, sentimental songs and some nature-loving animation.
w John Fusco *d* Kelly Asbury, Lorna Cook *m* Hans Zimmer *m/ly* Bryan Adams *pd* Kathy Altieri *ed* Nick Fletcher
☆ voices of: Matt Damon (Spirit), James Cromwell (The Colonel), Daniel Studi (Little Creek)
'Gooey animation for pony club fanatics.' – *James Christopher, Times*
'The whole thing is horribly close to Bambi, which doesn't cut it in 2002.' – *Peter Bradshaw, Guardian*
animated feature

Spirits of the Dead: see *Histoires Extraordinaires*

The Spiritualist: see *The Amazing Dr X*

Spite Marriage *
US 1929 77m (24 fps) bw silent
MGM/Buster Keaton (Lawrence Weingarten)

A tailor's assistant loves an actress, who marries him to spite someone else.
For a Keaton comedy from his great period, this is remarkably thin on invention, and its pleasures, though undeniable, are minor.
w Richard Schayer, Lew Lipton *d* Edward Sedgwick *ph* Reggie Lanning
☆ Buster Keaton, Dorothy Sebastian, Edward Earle, Leila Hyams

Spitfire *
US 1934 88m bw
RKO (Pandro S. Berman)

An Ozark mountain girl believes herself to be a faith healer and is driven from the community.
Curious star melodrama with effective moments.
w Jane Murfin *play Trigger* by Lula Vollmer *d* John Cromwell *ph* Edward Cronjager *m* Max Steiner
☆ Katharine Hepburn, Robert Young, Ralph Bellamy, Martha Sleeper, Louis Mason
'The veins of the story carry thin milk rather than heavy corpuscles.' – *Variety*
'The picture would suggest that Katharine Hepburn is condemned to elegance, doomed to be a lady for the rest of her natural life, and that her artistry does not extend to the interpretation of the primitive or the uncouth. That her producers have not bothered to give her a scenario of any interest or quality is another aspect of the situation.' – *New Yorker*

Spitfire: see *The First of the Few (1942)*

The Spitfire Grill
US 1996 117m DeLuxe
Rank/Turner/Castle Rock/Gregory/Mendocino (Forrest Murray)

aka: *Care of the Spitfire Grill*
The new waitress at a small-town diner, who served time for manslaughter, precipitates change and tragedy among the locals.
A minor melodrama among the dispossessed, soft at its centre, but strongly performed.
wd Lee David Zlotoff *ph* Robert Draper *m* James Horner *pd* Howard Cummings *ed* Margie Goodspeed
☆ Alison Elliott, Ellen Burstyn, Marcia Gay Harden, Will Patton, Kieran Mulroney, Gailard Sartain, John M. Jackson
'This view of café-society is too maudlin for its own good.' – *Tom Hutchinson, Film Review*

Spivs: see *I Vitelloni*

'She was the woman of his dreams. She had large dark eyes, a beautiful smile, and a great pair of fins.'
Splash! *
US 1984 110m Technicolor
Touchstone/Buena Vista (Brian Grazer)

A New York wholesaler on holiday off Cape Cod falls in love with a mermaid.
A kind of updated and mildly sexed-up Miranda: *occasionally funny but far too long.*
w Lowell Ganz, Babaloo Mandel, Bruce Jay Friedman, Brian Grazer *d* Ron Howard *ph* Don Peterman *m* Lee Holdridge
☆ Tom Hanks, Daryl Hannah, Eugene Levy, John Candy, Dody Goodman, Shecky Greene, Richard B. Shull, Howard Morris
'A typically Disney subject trying to be grown up.' – *Kim Newman, MFB*
'The picture is frequently on the verge of being more wonderful than it is ... more lyrical, a little wilder.' – *Pauline Kael, New Yorker*
screenplay

Splendor
US 1935 77m bw
Samuel Goldwyn
The son of a once-wealthy Park Avenue family marries a poor girl.
Dated romantic drama.
w Rachel Crothers *play* Rachel Crothers *d* Elliott Nugent *ph* Gregg Toland *md* Alfred Newman
☆ Joel McCrea, Miriam Hopkins, Helen Westley, Katherine Alexander, David Niven, Paul Cavanagh, Billie Burke, Arthur Treacher
'An unusually good production, but probably too quiet for the lesser spots.' – *Variety*
'A model of dramatic exposition, but it suffers from inaction and its theme is too commonplace.' – *New York Times*

Splendor **
Italy/France 1988 99m Cinecitta
Warner/Cecchi Gori/Tiger Cinematografica/Studio El/Gaumont/Generale d'Images/RAI (Mario Cecchi Gori, Vittorio Cecchi Gori)
A bankrupt small-town cinema owner remembers past glories.
Charming, gently nostalgic lament for movies as a communal experience.
wd Ettore Scola *ph* Luciano Tovoli *m* Armando Trovaioli *ad* Luciano Ricceri *ed* Francesco Malvestito
☆ Marcello Mastroianni, Massimo Troisi, Marina Vlady, Paolo Panelli, Pamela Villoresi, Giacomo Piperno, Massimo Bartocini

'Most pictures end in a theatre. This picture ends late at night in your heart.'
Splendor in the Grass *
US 1961 124m Technicolor
Warner/NBI (Elia Kazan)

Adolescent love in a small Kansas town in the twenties.
Impressive though curiously unmemorable addition to a nostalgic young sex cycle which was already played out; production and performances well up to scratch.
w William Inge *d* Elia Kazan *ph* Boris Kaufman *m* David Amram
☆ Natalie Wood, Warren Beatty, Pat Hingle, Audrey Christie, Barbara Loden, Zohra Lampert, Sandy Dennis
'Less like a high-school version of *Summer and Smoke* than [like] an Andy Hardy story with glands.' – *Stanley Kauffmann*
William Inge
Natalie Wood

Splinters
GB 1929 82m bw
B and D (Herbert Wilcox)
Soldiers at the front in 1915 form a concert party.
Easy-going crowd-pleaser of its time.
w W. P. Lipscomb *d* Jack Raymond *ph* David Kesson *m* Carroll Gibbons
☆ Nelson Keyes, Sydney Howard, Lew Lake, Hal Jones, Reg Stone
† Sequels, of roughly the same standard, included *Splinters in the Navy*, 1931, and *Splinters in the Air*, 1937; both with Sidney Howard.

The Split
US 1968 90m Metrocolor Panavision
MGM/Spectrum (Robert Chartoff, Irwin Winkler)
A black criminal plans to rob the Los Angeles Coliseum during a football match.
Busy, brutal crime thriller, well enough done but totally unsympathetic.
w Robert Sabaroff *novel The Seventh* by Richard Stark *d* Gordon Flemyng *ph* Burnett Guffey *m* Quincy Jones
☆ Jim Brown, Diahann Carroll, Ernest Borgnine, Julie Harris, Gene Hackman, Jack Klugman, Warren Oates, James Whitmore, Donald Sutherland

Split Image *
US 1982 111m Metrocolor Panavision
Polygram Pictures (Ted Kotcheff)
A normal middle-class college athlete becomes involved with a religious cult.
Effective melodrama about brainwashing.
w Scott Spencer, Robert Kaufman, Robert Mark Kamen *d* Ted Kotcheff *ph* Robert Jessup *m* Bill Conti *pd* Wolf Kroeger *ed* Jay Kamen
☆ Michael O'Keefe, Karen Allen, James Woods, Elizabeth Ashley, Brian Dennehy, Ronnie Scribner, Michael Sacks, Peter Fonda

Split Second
US 1953 85m bw
RKO (Edmund Grainger)
An escaped convict hides out with four hostages in an Arizona ghost town which has been cleared in preparation for an atom bomb test.
Routine suspenser.
w William Bowers, Irving Wallace *d* Dick Powell *ph* Nicholas Musuraca *m* Roy Webb
☆ Stephen McNally, Alexis Smith, Jan Sterling, Keith Andes, Arthur Hunnicutt, Paul Kelly, Richard Egan, Robert Paige

Split Second
GB 1991 90m Eastmancolor
Entertainment/Challenge/Muse (Laura Gregory)

In 2008, in a flooded London, a cop goes after a serial killer who turns out to be a monster.
A gallant, if misguided, attempt to revive the man-in-a-rubber-suit school of horror movies.
w Gary Scott Thompson *d* Tony Maylam *ph* Clive Tickner *m* Stephen Parsons, Francis Haines *pd* Chris Edwards *ed* Dan Rae
☆ Rutger Hauer, Kim Cattrall, Neil Duncan, Michael J. Pollard, Alun Armstrong, Peter Postlethwaite, Ian Dury, Roberta Eaton, Tony Steedman
'An extremely stupid monster film, boasting enough violence and special effects to satisfy less discriminating vid fans.' – *Variety*

Splitface: see *Dick Tracy*

Splitting Heirs
GB 1993 87m Technicolor
UIP/Prominent Features (Simon Bosanquet, Redmond Morris)

A city businessman, adopted by a Pakistani family, discovering that he, and not his best friend, is really the heir to the Dukedom of Bournemouth, decides to murder his rival.
Sad and trivial comedy, consisting of ineptly performed knockabout routines.
w Eric Idle *d* Robert Young *ph* Tony Pierce-Roberts *m* Michael Kamen *pd* John Beard *ed* John Jympson

☆ Eric Idle, Rick Moranis, Barbara Hershey, Catherine Zeta Jones, John Cleese, Sadie Frost, Stratford Johns, Brenda Bruce, William Franklyn, Jeremy Clyde, Eric Sykes

'Breezy but lightweight comedy.' – *Variety*

'The pace and cheerful inanity of the picture may go some way to excusing its lack of wit and subtlety.' – *Geoffrey Macnab, Sight and Sound*

The Spoilers *
US 1930 86m bw
Paramount (Lloyd Sheldon)

In Alaska during the gold rush, crooked government officials begin despoiling the richest claims.

Early talkie version of a famous brawling saga.

w Bartlett Cormack, Agnes Brand Leahy *novel* Rex Beach *d* Edward Carewe *ph* Harry Fischbeck

☆ Gary Cooper, William 'Stage' Boyd, Betty Compson, Kay Johnson, Harry Green, Slim Summerville

'Fair for a week in the de luxers, but made to order for the neighbourhoods and grinds everywhere.' – *Variety*

The Spoilers **
US 1942 87m bw
Universal (Frank Lloyd)

Two adventurers in the Yukon quarrel over land rights and a saloon entertainer.

Well-packaged mixture of saloon brawls, romance and adventure, much filmed as a silent.

w Lawrence Hazard, Tom Reed *d* Ray Enright *ph* Milton Krasner *m* Hans Salter *ad* Jack Otterson, John B. Goodman *ed* Clarence Kolster

☆ Marlene Dietrich, Randolph Scott, John Wayne, Margaret Lindsay, Harry Carey, Richard Barthelmess, George Cleveland, Samuel S. Hinds

'All concerned have kept their tongues firmly in their cheeks.' – *New York Times*

art direction

The Spoilers *
US 1955 82m Technicolor
U-I (Ross Hunter)

Adequate, unmemorable remake of the above.

w Oscar Brodney, Charles Hoffman *d* Jesse Hibbs *ph* Maury Gertsman *m* Joseph Gershenson

☆ Anne Baxter, Jeff Chandler, Rory Calhoun, Barbara Britton, Carl Benton Reid, Ray Danton, John McIntire, Raymond Walburn, Wallace Ford

Spoklenci slasti: see *Conspirators of Pleasure*

Spontaneous Combustion
US 1990 108m colour
Taurus (Jim Rogers)

The son of parents subjected to nuclear experiments discovers that he can set people on fire.

Direly ridiculous horror, a wet blanket of a movie, depressing and unimaginative.

w Tobe Hooper, Howard Goldberg *d* Tobe Hooper *ph* Levie Isaacks *m* Graeme Revell *ed* David Kern

☆ Brad Dourif, Cynthia Bain, Jon Cypher, William Prince, Dey Young, Melinda Dillon, John Landis

'Silly beyond belief ... a horror pic that literally goes up in flames.' – *Variety*

Spooks Run Wild
US 1941 65m bw
Monogram/Banner (Sam Katzman)

The East Side Kids are sent, against their will, to summer camp, where a killer is on the prowl.

Lively haunted-house comedy, with Lugosi providing a parody of his Count Dracula.

w Carl Foreman, Charles R. Marion, Jack Henley *d* Phil Rosen *ph* Marcel Le Picard *ed* Robert Golden

☆ Bela Lugosi, Leo Gorcey, Bobby Jordan, Huntz Hall, Sunshine Sammy Morrison, Dave O'Brien, David Gorcey, Angelo Rossitto

Spoorloos: see *The Vanishing*

Sport of a Nation: see *The All-American*

The Sport of Kings
GB 1931 98m bw
Gainsborough (Michael Balcon)

A strict JP inherits a bookie business.

Heavy-going adaptation of a stage comedy warhorse, which nevertheless paved the way for many screen farces of the thirties.

w Angus MacPhail *play* Ian Hay *d* Victor Saville *ph* Freddie Young

☆ Leslie Henson, Gordon Harker, Hugh Wakefield, Dorothy Boyd

Sporting Blood
US 1931 80m bw
MGM

A horse passes through various hands and finally wins the Kentucky Derby.

Unremarkable programme fodder.

w Charles Brabin, Wanda Tuchock, Willard Mack *story* Horseflesh by Frederick Hazlitt Brennan *d* Charles Brabin

☆ Clark Gable, Ernest Torrence, Madge Evans, Lew Cody, Marie Prevost

'Racetrack romance with a different twist and only name Clark Gable.' – *Variety*

Sporting Love
GB 1937 68m bw
British Lion/Hammer

Two owners of a bankrupt racing stable try to kidnap their prize horse which has been mortgaged.

Thin musical farce from a stage success.

w Fenn Sherie, Ingram D'Abbes *play* Stanley Lupino *d* J. Elder Wills *ph* Eric Cross

☆ Stanley Lupino, Laddie Cliff, Henry Carlisle, Edna Peel, Bobbie Comber

Spot: see *Dogpound Shuffle*

'It's the business.'

Spotswood *
Australia 1991 95m colour
Feature/Meridian/Smiley (Richard Brennan, Timothy White)

An English time-and-motion expert investigates a ramshackle shoe factory.

Pleasant comedy in the Ealing tradition of the little man against uncaring bureaucracy.

w Max Dann, Andrew Knight *d* Mark Joffe *ph* Ellery Ryan *m* Ricky Fataar *pd* Chris Kennedy *ed* Nicholas Beauman

☆ Anthony Hopkins, Ben Mendelsohn, Alwyn Kurts, Bruno Lawrence, Angela Punch McGregor, Russell Crowe, Toni Collette

'Glides along with a dry wit, a keen visual sense and a kindly heart.' – *Geoff Brown, The Times*

Spring and Port Wine
GB 1970 101m Technicolor
EMI/Memorial (Michael Medwin)

A Lancashire family runs into trouble when stern father insists that teenage daughter should eat a meal she refuses.

A popular old-fashioned stage comedy which simply doesn't work on film, partly from being set in a too-real town (Bolton) and partly because of a miscast lead.

w Bill Naughton *play* Bill Naughton *d* Peter Hammond *ph* Norman Warwick *m* Douglas Gamley *pd* Reece Pemberton

☆ James Mason, Diana Coupland, Susan George, Rodney Bewes, Hannah Gordon, Adrienne Posta, Arthur Lowe

Spring in Park Lane **
GB 1948 92m bw
Imperadio/Herbert Wilcox

A diamond merchant's niece falls for a footman who just happens to be an impoverished lord in disguise.

Flimsy but highly successful romantic comedy which managed to get its balance right and is still pretty entertaining, much more so than its sequel Maytime in Mayfair.

w Nicholas Phipps play Come Out of the Kitchen by Alice Duer Miller *d Herbert Wilcox ph* Max Greene *m* Robert Farnon

☆ *Anna Neagle, Michael Wilding, Tom Walls, Nicholas Phipps*, Peter Graves, Marjorie Fielding, *Nigel Patrick*, Lana Morris

'A never-failing dream of Olde Mayfaire and its eternally funny butlers and maids, its disguised lords and ladies.' – *Richard Winnington*

'A gag comedy which absolutely sparkles.' – *Picture Show*

'The best comedy any British studio has produced for more years than I care to remember.' – *News of the World*

Spring Madness
US 1938 66m bw
MGM

The romance of a Harvard man and a student in the nearby women's college.

Very thin comedy material, stretched to its tearing point.

w Edward Chodorov *play* Spring Dance by Philip Barry *d* S. Sylvan Simon

☆ Maureen O'Sullivan, Lew Ayres, Ruth Hussey, Burgess Meredith, Joyce Compton

Spring Meeting
GB 1940 93m bw
ABPC

In Ireland, an impecunious widow wants her son to marry the daughter of an old flame.

Staid film version of a comedy whose characters turned up again in Treasure Hunt.

w Walter C. Mycroft, Norman Lee *play* M. J. Farrell, John Perry *d* Walter C. Mycroft

☆ Nova Pilbeam, Basil Sydney, Henry Edwards, Sarah Churchill, Michael Wilding, *Margaret Rutherford*, Enid Stamp Taylor, Hugh McDermott

Spring Parade *
US 1940 89m bw
Universal (Joe Pasternak)

A single baker's assistant falls for a prince.

Pleasing, artificial Austrian frou-frou with star and support in good escapist form.

w Bruce Manning, Felix Jackson *story* Ernst Marischka *d* Henry Koster *ph* Joseph Valentine *m* Robert Stolz *md* Charles Previn *ch* Larry Ceballos

☆ *Deanna Durbin*, Robert Cummings, S. Z. Sakall, Mischa Auer, Henry Stephenson, Anne Gwynne, Butch and Buddy

Joseph Valentine; Charles Previn; song 'Waltzing in the Clouds' (*m* Robert Stolz, *ly* Gus Kahn)

Spring Reunion
US 1956 79m bw
UA/Bryna (Jerry Bresler)

College classmates fall in love all over again at a reunion fifteen years later.

Romantic fiction for the middle-aged, performed with bare competence.

wd Robert Pirosh *ph* Harold Lipstein *m* Herbert Spencer, Earle Hagen

☆ Betty Hutton, Dana Andrews, Jean Hagen, Robert Simon, James Gleason, Laura La Plante, Irene Ryan

Spring Symphony
West Germany 1983 103m colour
Blue Dolphin/Allianz Filmproduktion/Peter Schamoni
original title: *Frühlingssinfonie*

Biopic of the love affair between the composer Robert Schumann and the pianist Clara Wieck.

Glossy and stolid plod through a decade that relies on the music to maintain interest.

wd Peter Schamoni *ph* Gerard Vandenberg *m* Schumann *pd* Alfred Hirschmeier *ed* Elfi Tillack

☆ Nastassja Kinski, Herbert Grönemeyer, Rolf Hoppe, André Heller, Bernhard Wicki, Gidon Kremer, Edda Seippel

Spring Tonic
US 1935 55m bw
Fox

An escaped tigress causes various farcical episodes.

Comedy extravaganza on modest lines, like a stretched-out two-reeler.

w Patterson McNutt, H. W. Hanemann *play* Man Eating Tiger by Ben Hecht, Rose Caylor *d* S. Sylvan Simon

☆ Lew Ayres, Claire Trevor, Walter Woolf King, ZaSu Pitts, Jack Haley, Tala Birell, Sig Rumann

'Hodge-podge of hokum that offers no hope to distraught exhibitors.' – *Variety*

'The gun ... the girl ... they made one man the equal of five!'

Springfield Rifle
US 1952 93m Warnercolor
Warner (Louis E. Edelman)

A Union officer gets himself cashiered, joins the Confederates as a spy, and unmasks a traitor.

Stolid Civil War Western with Grade-A production but not much individuality.

w Charles Marquis Warren, Frank Davis *d* André de Toth *ph* Edwin DuPar *m* Max Steiner

☆ Gary Cooper, Phyllis Thaxter, David Brian, Lon Chaney Jnr, Paul Kelly, Phil Carey, James Millican, Guinn Williams

Springtime for Henry
US 1935 73m bw
Fox (Jesse L. Lasky)

A rich man makes a vocation of woman chasing.

Modest version of a play which was toured for many years with Edward Everett Horton in the lead.

w Keene Thompson, Frank Tuttle *play* Benn W. Levy *d* Frank Tuttle

☆ Otto Kruger, Nancy Carroll, Nigel Bruce, Heather Angel, Herbert Mundin

'Farcical intent, but only a few snickers.' – *Variety*

Springtime in the Rockies
US 1942 91m Technicolor
TCF (William LeBaron)

Romances blossom on a mountain holiday.

Flimsily-plotted, studio-bound, absolutely routine musical.

w Walter Bullock, Ken Englund *story* Philip Wylie *d* Irving Cummings *ph* Ernest Palmer *md* Alfred Newman *songs* Mack Gordon, Harry Warren

☆ Betty Grable, John Payne, Carmen Miranda, Edward Everett Horton, Cesar Romero, Charlotte Greenwood, Frank Orth, Harry James and his Music Makers

Spy 13: see *Operator 13*

Spy for a Day
GB 1939 71m bw
Two Cities (Mario Zampi)

A farm hand is discovered to be the exact double of a spy.

The only screen vehicle for this 'gormless' comedian, and not a bad one.

w Anatole de Grunwald, Hans Wilhelm, Emeric Pressburger, Ralph Block, Tommy Thompson *story* Stacy Aumonier *d* Mario Zampi *ph* Bernard Knowles *m* Nicholas Brodszky *ed* David Lean

☆ Duggie Wakefield, Paddy Browne, Jack Allen, Albert Lieven, Nicholas Hannen, Gibb McLaughlin

'It's not how you play the GAME...It's how the GAME plays you.'

Spy Game
Germany/US/Japan/France 2001 126m
DeLuxe Panavision
Universal/Beacon (Douglas Wick/Marc Abraham)

On his last day at work, a veteran CIA agent decides to ignore orders in order to save the life of a younger protegee who faces death in a Chinese prison.

Slick, fast-moving spy movie with a paranoid flavour and a sentimental ending.

w Michael Frost Beckner, David Arata *d* Tony Scott *ph* Dan Mindel *m* Harry Gregson-Williams *pd* Norris Spencer, Chris Seagers, Nina Ruscio *ed* Christian Wagner *cos* Louise Frogley

☆ Robert Redford (Nathan Muir), Brad Pitt (Tom Bishop), Catherine McCormack (Elizabeth Hadley), Stephen Dillane (Charles Harker), Larry Bryggman (Troy Folger), Michael Paul Chan (Vincent Vy Ngo), Marianne Jean-Baptiste (Gladys Jennip), Ken Leung (Li), David Hemmings (Harry Duncan), Amidou (The Sheik's Doctor), Charlotte Rampling (Anne Cathcart)

'The movie provides a vehicle for macho romanticism, a fantasy of danger and derring-do for the deskbound... The problem lies in the calculating pretentiousness of using human misery to make shallow entertainment seem serious.' – *A. O. Scott, New York Times*

'A follow-the-dots bore with only one mild diversion: the opportunity to watch Mr Redford and Mr Pitt try to underplay each other.' – Rex Reed

Spy Hard
US 1996 81m Technicolor
Buena Vista/Hollywood (Rick Friedberg, Doug Draizin, Jeffrey Konvitz)
Special agent WD-40 is assigned to defeat a mad general who threatens to blow up the world.
This scrapes the bottom of a genre that is now beyond satirizing and no longer funny in itself; a ragbag of feeble jokes ineffectually aimed at the Bond films, it doesn't even attempt to hit its target.
w Rick Friedberg, Dick Chudnow, Jason Friedberg, Aaron Seltzer *d* Rick Friedberg *ph* John R. Leonetti *m* Bill Conti *pd* William Creber *ed* Eric Sears
☆ Leslie Nielsen, Nicollette Sheridan, Charles Durning, Marcia Gay Harden, Barry Bostwick, John Ales, Andy Griffith, Mason Gamble
'They should have called it *Dire Hard*.' – *Film Review*
† Those appearing in cameo roles include Dr Joyce Brothers, Ray Charles, Roger Clinton, Robert Culp, Robert Guillaume, Hulk Hogan, Pat Morita and Mr T.

The Spy in Black **
GB 1939 82m bw
Harefield/Alexander Korda (Irving Asher)
US title: *U-Boat 29*
In the Orkneys in 1917, German spies don't trust each other.
Unusual romantic melodrama which provided an unexpectedly interesting romantic team.
w Emeric Pressburger, Roland Pertwee novel J. Storer Clouston *d Michael Powell ph* Bernard Browne *m* Miklos Rozsa
☆ *Conrad Veidt, Valerie Hobson*, Hay Petrie, Helen Haye, Sebastian Shaw, Marius Goring, June Duprez, Athole Stewart, Cyril Raymond

Spy in the Pantry: see *Ten Days in Paris*

The Spy in White: see *The Secret of Stamboul*

'Real Spies...only smaller.'
Spy Kids *
US 2001 88m CFI color
Buena Vista/Miramax/Dimension/Troubleshooter (Robert Rodriguez, Elizabeth Avellan)
The children of two spies become spies themselves to save their parents and the world from a madman and his robots.
Hyperactive sub-James Bond fantasy for children, full of gadgetry and gimmicks and a few jokes for adults.
wd Robert Rodriguez *ph* Guillermo Navarro *m* Danny Elfman, Gavin Greenaway, Heitor Pereira, John Debney, Robert Rodriguez, Los Lobos *pd* Cary White *ed* Robert Rodriguez *sp* Robert Kurtzman, Gregory Nicotero, Howard Berger
☆ Antonio Banderas (Gregorio Cortez), Carla Gugino (Ingrid Cortez), Alexa Vega (Carmen Cortez), Daryl Sabara (Juni Cortez), Alan Cumming (Fegan Floop), Tony Shalhoub (Alexander Minion), Teri Hatcher (Ms Gradenko), Cheech Marin (Felix Gumm), Robert Patrick (Mr Lisp), Danny Trejo (Machete)
'Unashamedly brilliant, a fast and furious fusion of hip references, cute action, dynamic visuals and sheer delight.' – *Bob McCabe, Empire*

'Huge New Adventure – Slightly Larger Spies'
Spy Kids 2: Island of Lost Dreams *
US 2002 99m DeLuxe
Buena Vista/Dimension/Troublemaker (Elizabeth Avellan, Robert Rodriguez)
Two rival couples of child spies compete to save the world from a mad scientist.
Another helping of mini-James Bonds, done with considerable verve and enjoyment.
wd Robert Rodriguez *ph* Robert Rodriguez *m* Robert Rodriguez, John Debney *pd* Robert Rodriguez *ed* Robert Rodriguez *sp* Robert Rodriguez, Daniel Leduc
☆ Antonio Banderas (Gregorio Cortez), Carla Gugino (Ingrid Cortez), Alexa Vega (Carmen Cortez), Daryl Sabara (Juni Cortez), Steve Buscemi (Romero), Mike Judge (Donnagan), Danny Trejo (Machete), Cheech Marin (Felix Gumm), Ricardo Montalban (Grandfather)

'Children will not feel embarrassed to take their parents and guardians to see it.' – *Philip French, Observer*

Spy of Napoleon
GB 1936 101m bw
JH Productions
A dancer saves Louis Napoleon from assassination.
Solidly mounted period piece without much sense of humour.
w L. DuGarde Peach, Frederick Merrick, Harold Simpson *novel* Baroness Orczy *d* Maurice Elvey *ph* Curt Courant *md* W. L. Trytel
☆ Richard Barthelmess, Dolly Haas, Frank Vosper, Francis L. Sullivan, Lyn Harding, Henry Oscar

'Brace yourself for greatness!'
The Spy Who Came in from the Cold **
GB 1965 112m bw
Paramount/Salem (Martin Ritt)
A British master spy is offered a chance to get even with his East German opponent by being apparently sacked, disillusioned, and open for recruitment.
The old undercover yarn with trimmings of such sixties malaises as death wish, anti-establishmentism and racial problems. As a yarn, quite gripping till it gets too downbeat, but very harshly photographed.
w Paul Dehn, Guy Trosper *novel* John Le Carré *d* Martin Ritt *ph* Oswald Morris *m* Sol Kaplan *pd* Hal Periera, Tambi Larsen, Edward Marshall
☆ Richard Burton, Claire Bloom, *Oskar Werner*, Peter Van Eyck, Sam Wanamaker, Rupert Davies, George Voskovec, Cyril Cusack, Michael Hordern, Robert Hardy, Bernard Lee, Beatrix Lehmann
Academy Award nomination: Richard Burton; Hal Periera, Tambi Larsen, Edward Marshall
BAFTA: British film; Oswald Morris; Richard Burton; art direction

The Spy Who Loved Me
GB 1977 125m Eastmancolor Panavision
UA/Eon (Albert R. Broccoli)
James Bond and a glamorous Russian spy combine forces to track down and eliminate a megalomaniac shipping magnate with an undersea missile base.
Witless spy extravaganza in muddy colour, with the usual tired chases and pussyfoot violence but no new gimmicks except a seven-foot villain with steel teeth.
w Christopher Wood, Richard Maibaum *novel* Ian Fleming *d* Lewis Gilbert *ph* Claude Renoir *m* Marvin Hamlisch *pd* Ken Adam
☆ Roger Moore, Barbara Bach, Curt Jurgens, Richard Kiel, Caroline Munro, Walter Gotell, Bernard Lee, Lois Maxwell, George Baker, Desmond Llewelyn, Edward de Souza, Sydney Tafler
'The film, bearing no relation to its nominal source, seems to do nothing more than anthologize its forerunners.' – *Tim Pulleine, MFB*
Academy Award nomination: Marvin Hamlisch; song 'Nobody Does It Better' (*m*Marvin Hamlisch, *ly*Carole Bayer Sager)

The Spy with a Cold Nose
GB 1966 93m Eastmancolor
Paramount/Associated London/Embassy (Robert Porter)
A fashionable vet is blackmailed by MI5 into inserting a radio transmitter into a bulldog.
Rather painful, overacted and overwritten farce full of obvious jokes masquerading as satire.
w Ray Galton, Alan Simpson *d* Daniel Petrie *ph* Kenneth Higgins *m* Riz Ortolani
☆ *Lionel Jeffries*, Laurence Harvey, Daliah Lavi, Eric Sykes, Eric Portman, Colin Blakely, Denholm Elliott, Robert Flemyng, Paul Ford, Bernard Lee, June Whitfield, Bernard Archard

The Spy with My Face
US 1966 86m Metrocolor
MGM/Arena (Sam Rolfe)
Enemy spies use a double of Napoleon Solo in an attempt to take over the world.
An extended version of an episode from the television series The Man from U.N.C.L.E., *no better than the others in the series and more confusing than most.*
w Clyde Ware, Joseph Calvelli *ph* Fred Koenekamp *m* Morton Stevens *ad* George W. Davis, Merrill Pye *ed* Joseph Dervin
☆ Robert Vaughn, David McCallum, Leo G. Carroll, Michael Evans, Sharon Farrell

Spylarks: see *The Intelligence Men*

S*P*Y*S
GB 1974 100m Technicolor
Dymphana/C-W/American Film Properties (Irwin Winkler, Robert Chartoff)
Clumsy CIA agents in Paris come across a list of KGB agents in China.
Surprisingly dull and unfashionable parade of comic spy clichés; the talents involved obviously intended something closer to M*A*S*H.
w Malcolm Marmorstein, Lawrence J. Cohen, Fred Freeman *d* Irvin Kershner *ph* Gerry Fisher *m* John Scott
☆ Elliott Gould, Donald Sutherland, Zouzou, Joss Ackland, Kenneth Griffith, Vladek Sheybal
'Seems to have arrived several years too late to find its true niche.' – *Sight and Sound*

Squadron Leader X
GB 1942 100m bw
RKO (Victor Hanbury)
A Nazi hero poses as a British pilot but has difficulty getting back home.
Tall war story with dreary romantic trimmings.
w Wolfgang Wilhelm, Miles Malleson *d* Lance Comfort *ph* Mutz Greenbaum (Max Greene)
☆ Eric Portman, Ann Dvorak, Walter Fitzgerald, Barry Jones, Henry Oscar, Beatrice Varley

The Squall
US 1929 105m bw
First National
A Hungarian gypsy girl attracts all the male members of a farming family, and causes trouble.
Perfectly awful melodrama made worse by early sound techniques.
w Bradley King *play* Jean Bart *d* Alexander Korda
☆ Myrna Loy, Alice Joyce, Loretta Young, Richard Tucker, Carroll Nye, ZaSu Pitts, Harry Cording

The Square Circle *
India 1996 103m Eastmancolor
Blue Dolphin/Gateway (Pravesh Sippy)
original title: *Daayraa*
A beautiful young girl, escaping from a gang of kidnappers, disguises herself as a man and journeys back to her village with the help of a transvestite busker.
A curiosity, but an interesting one – a melodrama about gender, sexual differences and identity done in a crowd-pleasing style.
w Timeri N. Murari, Chitra Palekar, Shashank Shanker, Amol Palekar, Kamlesh Pande *story* Timeri N. Murari *d* Amol Palekar *ph* Debu Deodhar *m* Anand-Milind *pd* Prem Pillai *ed* Waman Bhosle
☆ Nirmal Pandey, Sonali Kulkarni, Faiyyaz, Rekha Sahay, Nina Kulkarni, Hyder Ali
'A welcome and controversial diversion from the hundreds of popular Bollywood movies released each year.' – *Empire*

Square Dance *
GB 1986 112m Metrocolor
NBC/Michael Nesmith/Island (Daniel Petrie)
An awkward 13-year-old girl in rural Texas leaves her gruff grandfather for a visit to the mother she dislikes.
Unremarkable but cohesive family drama which most will feel they have seen before.
w Alan Hines *novel* Alan Hines *d* Daniel Petrie *ph* Jacek Laskus *m* Bruce Broughton *pd* Jan Scott *ed* Bruce Green
☆ Jason Robards, Jane Alexander, Winona Ryder, Rob Lowe, Deborah Richter

The Square Jungle
US 1955 85m bw
U-I (Albert Zugsmith)
A conceited boxer gets his come-uppance.
Tailor-made studio co-feature.
w George Zuckerman *d* Jerry Hopper *ph* George Robinson *m* Heinz Roemheld
☆ Tony Curtis, Ernest Borgnine, Pat Crowley, Jim Backus, Paul Kelly

The Square Peg *
GB 1958 89m bw
Rank (Hugh Stewart)
An army recruit finds he is the double of a German general.
Slam-bang star slapstick, shorter than usual and with a few jokes that can't fail.
w Jack Davies *d* John Paddy Carstairs *ph* Jack Cox *m* Philip Green
☆ *Norman Wisdom*, Honor Blackman, Edward Chapman, Campbell Singer, Hattie Jacques, Brian Worth, Terence Alexander

The Square Ring *
GB 1953 83m bw
Ealing (Michael Relph)
One night at a boxing stadium.
An assortment of anecdotes does not constitute one of Ealing's best films, but the competence level is high.
w Robert Westerby, Peter Myers, Alec Grahame *play* Ralph Peterson *d* Basil Dearden *ph* Otto Heller *md* Dock Mathieson *ad* Jim Morahan *ed* Peter Bezencenet
☆ Jack Warner, Robert Beatty, Maxwell Reed, Bill Owen, Joan Collins, Kay Kendall, Bernadette O'Farrell, Eddie Byrne, Sid James, Alfie Bass

The Squaw Man
US 1931 106m bw
MGM (Cecil B. de Mille)
GB title: *The White Man*
An Indian maiden saves the life of a British aristocrat, bears his child and commits suicide.
Third outing for a hoary miscegenation drama filmed in 1914 with Dustin Farnum and Red Wing, and in 1918 with Elliott Dexter and Ann Little. This talkie version sank without trace.
w Lucien Hubbard, Lenore Coffee *play* Edwin Milton Royle *d* Cecil B. de Mille *ph* Harold Rosson *m* Herbert Stothart
☆ Warner Baxter, Lupe Velez, Charles Bickford, Eleanor Boardman, Roland Young, Paul Cavanagh, Raymond Hatton
'Should be generally fair b.o. in the smaller localities and perhaps not so hot for the diffident big-town show shoppers.' – *Variety*

The Squeaker *
GB 1937 77m bw
UA/Denham Productions (Alexander Korda)
US title: *Murder on Diamond Row*
A dangerous diamond fence is unmasked by a discredited policeman.
Typical Edgar Wallace who-is-it, performed with old-fashioned bravura.
w Edward O. Berkman, Bryan Wallace *novel* Edgar Wallace *d* William K. Howard *ph* Georges Périnal *m* Miklos Rozsa *ad* Vincent Korda *ed* Russell Lloyd
☆ Edmund Lowe, Sebastian Shaw, Ann Todd, Tamara Desni, Alastair Sim, Robert Newton, Allan Jeayes, Stewart Rome
† Previously filmed in 1930, directed by Edgar Wallace for British Lion; with Percy Marmont, Eric Maturin, Anne Grey and Nigel Bruce.

The Squeeze
GB 1977 107m Technicolor
Warner/ Martinat (Stanley O'Toole)
An alcoholic ex-cop rescues his ex-wife from kidnappers.
Sleazy action thriller which despite efficient production goes over the top in its search for unpleasant detail.
w Leon Griffiths *novel* David Craig *d* Michael Apted *ph* Dennis Lewiston *m* David Hentschel
☆ Stacy Keach, David Hemmings, Stephen Boyd, Edward Fox, Carol White, Freddie Starr
'It provides action and moral ambiguity enough to stock a Don Siegel thriller.' – *Richard Combs, MFB*

Squibs *
GB 1935 77m bw
Twickenham
A Cockney flowergirl wins a sweepstake.
Acceptable sound version of a series of rather naïve silents which pleased the crowds in the early twenties with the same star: they were Squibs, Squibs MP, Squibs' Honeymoon *and* Squibs Wins the Calcutta Sweep.
w Michael Hogan, H. Fowler Mear *play* Clifford Seyler, George Pearson *d* Henry Edwards

☆ *Betty Balfour*, Gordon Harker, Stanley Holloway, Margaret Yarde, Michael Shepley

Squirm
US 1976 92m Movielab
AIP/The Squirm Company (Edgar Lansbury, Joseph Beruh)

A power cable cut in a storm turns worms into maneaters.
Revolting shocker with a few funny moments for those who can take it.
wd Jeff Lieberman *ph* Joseph Mangine *m* Robert Prince
☆ John Scardino, Patricia Pearcy, R. A. Dow, Jean Sullivan

Stablemates
US 1938 89m bw
MGM
A broken-down vet saves a stableboy's racehorse.
Sentimental comedy vehicle for two masters of the surreptitious tear.
w Reginald Owen, William Thiele *d* Sam Wood
☆ Wallace Beery, Mickey Rooney, Margaret Hamilton, Minor Watson, Marjorie Gateson

Stacy's Knights
US 1983 95m colour
Crown/American Twist/Golden Gators (JoAnn Locktov, Freddy Sweet)

A female blackjack player sets out to revenge her partner's death.
Mediocre thriller that owes its occasional television screenings to the fact that its cast includes Costner in his first leading role.
w Michael Blake *d* Jim Wilson *ph* Raoul Lomas *m* Norton Buffalo *ad* Florence Fellman *ed* Bonnie Koehler
☆ Andra Millen, Kevin Costner, Eve Lilith, Mike Reynolds, Ed Semenza, Don Hackstaff

Stage Door ***
US 1937 93m bw
RKO (Pandro S. Berman)

Life in a New York theatrical boarding house for girls.
Melodramatic, sharply comedic, always fascinating slice of stagey life from a Broadway hit; the performances alone make it worth preserving.
w Morrie Ryskind, Anthony Veiller play Edna Ferber, *George S. Kaufman d Gregory La Cava ph* Robert de Grasse *m* Roy Webb *ad* Van Nest Polglase
☆ *Katharine Hepburn, Ginger Rogers*, Adolphe Menjou, Gail Patrick, Constance Collier, Andrea Leeds, Lucille Ball, Samuel S. Hinds, Jack Carson, Franklin Pangborn, Eve Arden

'It is a long time since we have seen so much feminine talent so deftly handled.' – *Otis Ferguson*
'Zest and pace and photographic eloquence.' – *Frank S. Nugent, New York Times*
'A rare example of a film substantially improving on a stage original and a remarkably satisfying film on all levels.' – *NFT, 1973*
'One of the flashiest, most entertaining comedies of the 30s, even with its tremolos and touches of heartbreak.' – *Pauline Kael, 70s*

best picture; script; Gregory La Cava; Andrea Leeds

'48 stars plus a great love story!'
Stage Door Canteen *
US 1943 132m bw
Sol Lesser (Barnett Briskin)

How the stars in New York entertained the armed forces during World War II.
Nothing as a film, mildly interesting as sociology and for some rarish appearances.
w Delmer Daves *d* Frank Borzage *ph* Harry Wild *m* Freddie Rich *pd* Harry Horner
☆ Cheryl Walker, Lon McCallister, Judith Anderson, Tallulah Bankhead, Ray Bolger, Katharine Cornell, Helen Hayes, George Jessel, Alfred Lunt, Harpo Marx, Yehudi Menuhin, Elliott Nugent, Cornelia Otis Skinner, Ethel Waters, May Whitty and also William Demarest, Gracie Fields, Katharine Hepburn, Gertrude Lawrence, Ethel Merman, Merle Oberon, Johnny Weissmuller, Edgar Bergen, Jane Cowl, Lynn Fontanne, Paul Muni, Gypsy Rose Lee, George Raft, etc; Count Basie, Benny Goodman, Xavier Cugat, Guy Lombardo, Kay Kyser and their bands

'A nice harmless picture for the whole family, and a goldmine for those who are willing to go to it in the wrong spirit.' – *James Agee*

Freddie Rich; song 'We Mustn't Say Goodbye' (*m* James V. Monaco, *ly* Al Dubin)

Stage Fright *
GB 1950 110m bw
Warner/ABPC (Alfred Hitchcock)

A man is on the run for a backstage murder, and his girlfriend takes a job as maid to the great star he says is responsible.
Creaky Hitchcock thriller in which you can see all the joins and the stars seem stuck in treacle; but a few of the set-pieces work well enough.
w Whitfield Cook *novel Man Running* by Selwyn Jepson *d* Alfred Hitchcock *ph* Wilkie Cooper *m* Leighton Lucas
☆ Marlene Dietrich, Jane Wyman, Richard Todd, Alastair Sim, Michael Wilding, Sybil Thorndike, Kay Walsh, Miles Malleson

Stage Mother
US 1933 85m bw
MGM
The mother of a young actress is not above sacrificing her daughter for financial gain.
Wisecracking comedy-romance, rather similar to the later Gypsy.
w John Meehan, Bradford Ropes *novel* Bradford Ropes *d* Charles Brabin
☆ Alice Brady, Maureen O'Sullivan, Franchot Tone, Phillips Holmes, Ted Healy, C. Henry Gordon

'Packed with colour, not a little s.a., and certain of adequate b.o. attention.' – *Variety*

Stage Struck
US 1936 95m bw
Warner (Robert Lord)
Young people put on a show and become instant hits.
Dim musical oddly shorn of production numbers.
w Tom Buckingham, Pat C. Flick, Robert Lord *ph* Byron Haskin *m* Leo F. Forbstein *d/ch* Busby Berkeley *songs* Harold Arlen, E. Y. Harburg
☆ Dick Powell, Joan Blondell, Jeanne Madden, the Yacht Club Boys, Warren William, Frank McHugh

Stage Struck **
US 1957 95m Technicolor
RKO (Stuart Millar)

A young actress comes to New York intent on stardom …
Careful, slightly arid remake of Morning Glory *marred by a tiresome central performance; good theatrical detail.*
w Ruth and Augustus Goetz *play* Zoe Akins *d Sidney Lumet ph Franz Planer m* Alex North *ad* Kim Edgar Swados
☆ Susan Strasberg, Henry Fonda, Herbert Marshall, *Joan Greenwood*, Christopher Plummer

Stage to Thunder Rock
US 1964 89m Techniscope
Paramount/A.C. Lyles
An ageing sheriff takes a bank robber back to jail by stagecoach.
Acceptable lower-berth Western with the producer's usual roster of half-forgotten character actors.
w Charles Wallace *d* William F. Claxton *ph* W. Wallace Kelley *m* Paul Dunlap
☆ Barry Sullivan, Marilyn Maxwell, Scott Brady, Keenan Wynn, Allan Jones, Lon Chaney Jnr, John Agar, Wanda Hendrix, Anne Seymour, Robert Lowery

Stagecoach ****
US 1939 99m bw
(UA)

Various Western characters board a stagecoach in danger from an Indian war party.
What looked like a minor Western with a plot borrowed from Maupassant's Boule de suif, *became a classic by virtue of the firm characterization, restrained writing, exciting climax and the scenery of Monument Valley. Whatever the reasons, it damn well works.*
w Dudley Nichols story Stage to Lordsburg by Ernest Haycox *d John Ford ph* Bert Glennon *m* Richard Hageman, W. Frank Harling, John Leopold, Leo Shuken, Louis Gruenberg *md* Boris Morros *ad* Alexander Toluboff *ed* Otho Lovering, Dorothy Spencer
☆ *Claire Trevor, John Wayne, Thomas Mitchell, George Bancroft*, Andy Devine, *Berton Churchill*, Louise Platt, *John Carradine, Donald Meek*, Tim Holt, Chris-Pin Martin

'It displays potentialities that can easily drive it through as one of the surprise big grossers of the year.' – *Variety*
'The basic western, a template for everything that followed.' – *John Baxter, 1968*
'Grand Hotel on wheels.' – *New Yorker, 1975*
'A motion picture that sings a song of camera.' – *Frank S. Nugent, New York Times*

music; Thomas Mitchell
best picture; John Ford; Bert Glennon; art direction; editing

Stagecoach
US 1966 114m DeLuxe Cinemascope
TCF/Martin Rackin

Absolutely awful remake of the above; costly but totally spiritless, miscast and uninteresting.
w Joseph Landon *d* Gordon Douglas *ph* William H. Clothier *m* Jerry Goldsmith
☆ Ann-Margret, Alex Cord, Bing Crosby, Van Heflin, Slim Pickens, Robert Cummings, Stefanie Powers, Michael Connors, Red Buttons, Keenan Wynn

The Stagecoach Kid
US 1949 63m bw
RKO (Herman Schlom)
In order to escape to the big city, a rancher's daughter disguises herself as a cowboy but then falls in love with a stagecoach owner.
Light-hearted Western, a pleasant if unmemorable programme-filler.
w Norman Houston *d* Lew Landers *ph* Nicholas Musuraca *m* Paul Sawtell *ad* Albert D'Agostino, Feild Gray *ed* Les Millbrook
☆ Tim Holt, Richard Martin, Jeff Donnell, Joe Sawyer, Thurston Hall, Carol Hughes, Robert Bray

Stagecoach to Dancer's Rock
US 1958 72m bw
Universal/Gray-Mac (Earl Bellamy)
Passengers on a long-distance stagecoach are abandoned in the desert when it is thought that one of them has smallpox.
Unusual minor Western, though it goes full gallop into melodrama rather than the character study it set out to be; Landau is here heavily under the influence of the Method approach to acting.
w Kenneth Darling *d* Earl Bellamy *ph* Ed Fitzgerald *m* Franz Steininger *ad* Leslie Thomas *ed* Budd Small
☆ Warren Stevens, Martin Landau, Jody Lawrance, Don Wilbanks, Del Moore, Bob Anderson, Judy Dan, Rand Brooks, Gene Roth

Staggered *
GB 1994 95m Technicolor
Entertainment/Big Deal (Philippa Braithwaite)

Following a stag party, a toy demonstrator wakes up to find himself naked on a Scottish island, with three days to get home before his wedding.
Sporadically amusing, episodic movie that has its moments; it often borders on the obvious, but the acting and direction display a good sense of comic timing.
w Paul Alexander, Simon Braithwaite *d* Martin Clunes *ph* Simon Kossoff *m* Peter Brewis *pd* Iain Andrews *ed* Peter Delfgou
☆ Martin Clunes, Michael Praed, Sarah Winman, Sylvia Syms, Virginia McKenna, Griff Rhys Jones, Michael Medwin, John Forgeham, Anna Chancellor

'Sitcom-style humor, peopled by a large gallery of British eccentrics. Produces a steady flow of mild gags, but doesn't build a proper head of steam to go the distance as a feature.' – *Derek Elley, Variety*

Staircase *
US/France 1969 101m DeLuxe Panavision
TCF/Stanley Donen
The problems of two ageing homosexual hairdressers.
Unsatisfactorily opened-out and over-acted version of an effective two-hander play. Oddly made in France, so that the London detail seems all wrong.
w Charles Dyer *play* Charles Dyer *d* Stanley Donen *ph* Christopher Challis *m* Dudley Moore
☆ Richard Burton, Rex Harrison, Cathleen Nesbitt, Beatrix Lehmann

'The shape is smashed … no longer a graceful duet, it becomes a waddling tale, spattered with ugliness, that falls into the biggest sentimental trap for homosexual material: it pleads for pity.' – *Stanley Kauffmann*

Stairway to Heaven: see *A Matter of Life and Death*

Stakeout
US 1987 115m DeLuxe
Touchstone (Jim Kouf, Cathleen Summers)

One of two Seattle cops engaged in a long stakeout falls in love with a suspect.
Ho-hum policier with insufficient plot for its length.
w Jim Kouf *d* John Badham *ph* John Seale *m* Arthur B. Rubinstein *pd* Philip Harrison *ed* Tom Rolf, Michael Ripps
☆ Richard Dreyfuss, Emilio Estevez, Madeleine Stowe, Aidan Quinn, Dan Lauria

Stakeout on Dope Street *
US 1958 83m bw
Warner (Andrew J. Fenady)
Three young men find a briease containing heroin and are attacked by the gangsters who lost it.
Lively little crime morality, uneven but worth a look.
w Irwin Schwartz, Irvin Kershner, Andrew J. Fenady *d Irvin Kershner ph Mark Jeffrey m* Richard Markowitz
☆ Yale Wexler, Jonathan Haze, Morris Miller, Abby Dalton

Stalag 17 **
US 1953 120m bw
Paramount (Billy Wilder)

Comedy and tragedy for American servicemen in a Nazi prisoner-of-war camp.
High jinks, violence and mystery in a sharply calculated mixture; an atmosphere quite different from the understated British films on the subject.
w Billy Wilder, Edwin Blum play Donald Bevan, Edmund Trzinski *d* Billy Wilder *ph* Ernest Laszlo *m* Franz Waxman
☆ William Holden, Don Taylor, Otto Preminger, *Robert Strauss*, Harvey Lembeck, Richard Erdman, Peter Graves, Neville Brand, Sig Rumann

'A facility for continuous rapid-fire action which alternately brings forth the laughs and tingles the spine.' – *Otis L. Guernsey Jnr*
'Raucous and tense, heartless and sentimental, always fast-paced, it has already been assigned by critics to places on their lists of the year's ten best movies.' – *Life*

William Holden
Billy Wilder (as director), Robert Strauss

Stalingrad **
Germany 1992 138m colour
Entertainment/Royal/Bavaria/BA/Perathon (Joseph Vilsmaier, Hanno Huth, Günter Rohrbach)

German soldiers try to escape the horrors of war during and after the battle for Stalingrad.
An impressive, downbeat account, from the viewpoint of a lieutenant and his troop, of an attempt to survive the depredations of the harsh Russian winter and of their own officers.
w Johannes Heide, Jürgen Büsche, Joseph Vilsmaier *d* Joseph Vilsmaier *ph* Joseph Vilsmaier *m* Norbert J. Schneider *pd* Wolfgang Hundhammer, Jindrich Goetz *ed* Hannes Nikel
☆ Dominique Horwitz, Jochen Nickel, Sebastian Rudolph, Thomas Kretschmann, Martin Benrath, Dana Vavrova

'A unique movie in that it sticks so closely to its foot soldier heroes, enabling us to see very clearly what happens when a mad leader pushes them too far and too fast.' – *Derek Malcolm, Guardian*

Stalker *
USSR 1979 161m colour/bw
Mosfilm Unit 2
In the centre of an industrial wasteland there appears a mysterious zone where all normal laws of life are suspended.
Part political allegory, part personal fantasy, all very fascinating but rather hard tack for anybody in search of entertainment.
w Arkady Strugatsky, Boris Strugatsky *story* Arkady Strugatsky, Boris Strugatsky *ph* Aleksandr Knyazhinsky *m* Eduard Artemyev *d/pd* *Andrei Tarkovsky*
☆ Aleksandr Kaidanovsky, Anatoly Solonitsin, Nikolai Grinko, Alisa Freindlikh

The Stalker
US 1992 85m Foto-Kem
Concorde/New Horizons (Mike Elliott)
In the aftermath of a San Francisco earthquake a woman finds herself imprisoned by her neighbourhood psychopath.
Typical product of Roger Corman's company, exploitative and topical, competent but uninspired.
w Mark Evan Schwartz *story* Rob Kerchner *d* Louis Morneau *ph* Mark Parry *m* Nigel Holton *pd* Stuart Blatt *ed* Glenn Garland
☆ Steve Railsback, Erika Anderson, Eb Lottimer, Burton Gilliam, Dick Miller

The Stalking Moon *
US 1968 109m Technicolor Panavision
National General/Stalking Moon Company (Alan J. Pakula)
An ageing scout escorts home a white woman who has escaped from the Indians, and kills a murderous Apache.
Slow, thoughtful Western with effective moments.
w Alvin Sargent *novel* Theodore V. Olsen *d* Robert Mulligan *ph* Charles Lang *m* Fred Karlin
☆ Gregory Peck, Eva Marie Saint, Robert Forster, Frank Silvera

Stallion Road
US 1947 97m bw
Warner (Alex Gottlieb)
An outbreak of anthrax threatens a racing stable.
Routine romantic drama with sporting background.
w Stephen Longstreet *d* James V. Kern *ph* Arthur Edeson *m* Frederick Hollander
☆ Ronald Reagan, Alexis Smith, Zachary Scott, Peggy Knudsen, Patti Brady, Harry Davenport, Frank Puglia
'The film, so free and fluent as long as it is talking horses, becomes curiously trite and turgid over the business of mating humans.' – *C. A. Lejeune, Observer*

Stamboul Quest
US 1934 88m bw
MGM (Walter Wanger)
During World War I, Germany's most notorious lady spy falls for an American medical student.
Modest variation on the true story twice filmed as Fraülein Doktor*; standard Hollywood values.*
w Herman J. Mankiewicz *d* Sam Wood *ph* James Wong Howe *m* Herbert Stothart
☆ Myrna Loy, George Brent, Lionel Atwill, C. Henry Gordon, Douglass Dumbrille, Mischa Auer

Stampeded: see *The Big Land*

Stan and George's New Life
Australia 1990 104m colour
Lea/AFC/Margot McDonald, Brian McKenzie
Bored with his life, and his quarrelling parents, a 40-year-old Melbourne barber gets a new job as a clerk in the weather bureau, where he marries into another dysfunctional family.
Drab drama of drabber lives, so low-key as to be virtually comatose.
w Brian McKenzie, Deborah Cox *d* Brian McKenzie *ph* Ray Argall *m* Michael Atkinson *ad* Daryl Mills *ed* Edward McQueen-Mason
☆ Paul Chubb, John Bluthal, Julie Forsyth, Margaret Ford, Roy Baldwin, Bruce Alexander, Beverly Gardiner, Shapoor Baltiwallia

Stand Alone
US 1985 90m Metrocolor
Texas Star (Leon Williams)
A grandfather, a hero in the Second World War, is targeted by professional gangsters after he witnesses a murder in his local diner.
Dull and implausible drama, slow-moving, uninvolving and faintly risible.
w Roy Carlson *d* Alan Beattie *ph* Tom Richmond, Tim Suhrstedt *m* David Richard Campbell *ad* Pam Warner *ed* Fabien Tordjmann
☆ Charles Durning, Pam Grier, James Keach, Bert Remsen, Barbara Sammeth, Lu Leonard, Luis Contreras, Willard Pugh, Bob Tzudiker

Stand and Deliver **
US 1988 104m Foto-Kem
Warner/American Playhouse (Tom Musca)
A maths teacher at a tough high school persuades his class of violent pupils that education is an asset.
Based on facts, the engaging story wins out over the rudimentary cinematic style.
w Ramon Menendez, Tom Musca *d* Ramon Menendez *ph* Tom Richmond *m* Craig Safan *ad* Milo *ed* Nancy Richardson
☆ *Edward James Olmos*, Lou Diamond Phillips, Rosana de Soto, Andy Garcia, Ingrid Oliu, Karla Montana, Vanessa Marquez, Mark Eliot
Edward James Olmos

The Stand at Apache River
US 1953 77m Technicolor
Universal-International (William Alland)
Apaches attack a reservation when the army won't listen to reason.
Conventional Western with sympathy for the Indians.
w Arthur Ross *d* Lee Sholem *ph* Charles Boyle *m* Frank Skinner
☆ Stephen McNally, Julie Adams, Hugh Marlowe, Hugh O'Brian, Jack Kelly

Stand by for Action
US 1943 109m bw
MGM (Robert Z. Leonard, Orville O. Dull)
GB title: *Cargo of Innocents*
A Harvard graduate learns the realities of war on an old destroyer.
Studio-bound war heroics slurping into sentiment.
w George Bruce, Herman J. Mankiewicz, John L. Balderston *d* Robert Z. Leonard *ph* Charles Rosher *m* Lennie Hayton
☆ Robert Taylor, Charles Laughton, Brian Donlevy, Walter Brennan, Marilyn Maxwell, Henry O'Neill

Stand by Me *
US 1986 89m Technicolor/DeLuxe
Columbia/Act III
A boys' gang finds the body of a missing teenager.
Less macabre than its source would suggest, the film is mostly concerned with the friendships and tensions within the group; nostalgia for 50s childhood is nicely conveyed.
w Raynold Gideon, Bruce A. Evans *story* The Body by Stephen King *d* Rob Reiner *ph* Thomas Del Ruth *m* Jack Nitzsche *pd* Dennis Washington
☆ Wil Wheaton, River Phoenix, Corey Feldman, Jerry O'Connell, Kiefer Sutherland, Richard Dreyfuss
screenplay

Der Stand Der Dinge: see *The State of Things*

Stand Easy: see *Down among the Z Men*

'Hail! The conquering hero comes!'
Stand In *
US 1937 90m bw
Walter Wanger
An efficiency expert is sent to save a Hollywood studio from bankruptcy.
Amusing satire which could have done with sharper scripting and firmer control but is pleasantly remembered.
w Gene Towne, Graham Baker *serial* Clarence Budington Kelland *d* Tay Garnett *ph* Charles G. Clarke *m* Heinz Roemheld
☆ *Leslie Howard, Joan Blondell*, Humphrey Bogart, Alan Mowbray, Marla Shelton, C. Henry Gordon, Jack Carson, Tully Marshall
'A joyous and nonsensical Hollywood fantasia.' – *Spectator*

Stand Up and Be Counted *
US 1971 99m Eastmancolor
Columbia/Mike Frankovich
An international woman journalist returns to Denver and becomes involved in women's lib.
A glamoured-up flirtation with a fashionable theme, quite nicely done but instantly dated – and sociologically interesting.
w Bernard Slade *d* Jackie Cooper *ph* Fred Koenekamp *m* Ernie Wilkins
☆ Jacqueline Bisset, Stella Stevens, Steve Lawrence, Gary Lockwood, *Loretta Swit*, Lee Purcell, Madlyn Rhue

Stand Up and Cheer *
US 1934 80m bw
Fox (Winfield Sheehan)
The new US Secretary of Amusement attempts to shake the country's Depression blues by staging a mammoth revue.
Naïve propaganda, but the whole world was swept away to cloud nine – by Shirley Temple.
w Ralph Spence, Will Rogers, Philip Klein *d* Hamilton McFadden *ph* Ernest Palmer *md* Arthur Lange
☆ Warner Baxter, Madge Evans, Nigel Bruce, Stepin Fetchit, Frank Melton, Lila Lee, Ralph Morgan, James Dunn, *Shirley Temple*, John Boles, George K. Arthur
'Its intrinsic merits do not quite match its pretentiousness.' – *Variety*
'Impossible to file it away in an ordinary drawer marked "Stinkers". This one is extra, it is super, and it butters itself very thickly with the most obvious sort of topical significance.' – *Otis Ferguson*
† The original title was *Fox Follies*.

'They Built a New America with Glory and Guns … They were MEN that Women Could Love!'
Stand Up and Fight *
US 1938 99m bw
MGM (Mervyn Le Roy)
A Southern aristocrat comes into conflict with a stagecoach operator used as transportation for stolen slaves.
Superior star action piece with plenty of vigorous brawls.
w James M. Cain, Jane Murfin, Harvey Ferguson *d* *W. S. Van Dyke II* *ph* Leonard Smith *m* William Axt
☆ Wallace Beery, Robert Taylor, Florence Rice, Helen Broderick, Charles Bickford, Barton MacLane, Charley Grapewin, John Qualen
'An action thriller that will please the muggs more than the dames … should prove strong at the b.o.' – *Variety*

Stand Up Virgin Soldiers
GB 1977 90m Technicolor
Warner/Greg Smith/Maidenhead
More sexual adventures of National Servicemen in Singapore in 1950.
The Virgin Soldiers *had a certain authenticity behind the fooling; this is a bawdy romp, and not a very efficient one.*
w Leslie Thomas *novel* Leslie Thomas *d* Norman Cohen *ph* Ken Hodges *m* Ed Welch
☆ Nigel Davenport, Robin Askwith, George Layton, Robin Nedwell, Warren Mitchell, John Le Mesurier, Edward Woodward, Irene Handl

'The hilarious story of what a girl will do to get her boss a bed in Washington!'
Standing Room Only *
US 1944 83m bw
Paramount (Paul Jones)
Hotel rooms being hard to find in wartime Washington, a resourceful secretary hires out herself and her boss as a servant couple.
Moderate romantic farce with a few good laughs.
w Darrell Ware, Karl Tunberg *d* Sidney Lanfield *ph* Charles Lang *m* Robert Emmett Dolan
☆ Paulette Goddard, Fred MacMurray, Edward Arnold, Roland Young, Hillary Brooke, Porter Hall, Clarence Kolb, Anne Revere

Stanley & Iris
US 1989 105m DuArt
UIP/MGM/Star Partners II (Arlene Sellers, Alex Winitsky)
A cook who loses his job because he is illiterate is taught to read by a sympathetic widow.
Dull, heavy-handed and sentimental, not even its stars can save it from tedium.
w Harriet Frank Jnr, Irving Ravetch *novel* Union Street by Pat Barker *d* Martin Ritt *ph* Donald McAlpine *m* John Williams *pd* Joel Schiller *ed* Sidney Levin
☆ Jane Fonda, Robert DeNiro, Swoosie Kurtz, Martha Plimpton, Harley Cross, Jamey Sheridan, Feodor Chaliapin

Stanley and Livingstone ***
US 1939 101m bw
TCF (Kenneth MacGowan)
An American journalist goes to Africa to find a lost Victorian explorer.
A prestige picture which played reasonably fair with history and still managed to please the masses.
w Philip Dunne, Julien Josephson *d* *Henry King* *ph* *George Barnes* *m* David Raksin, David Buttolph, Cyril Mockridge, Alfred Newman *ad* Thomas Little
☆ *Spencer Tracy*, Cedric Hardwicke, Richard Greene, Nancy Kelly, Walter Brennan, Charles Coburn, Henry Hull, Henry Travers, Miles Mander, Holmes Herbert
'Sound, worthy, interesting.' – *Richard Mallett, Punch*
'Most of the film consists of long shots of stand-ins moving across undistinguished scenery … Mr Tracy is always a human being, but Sir Cedric is an elocution lesson, a handclasp.' – *Graham Greene*
'Holds box office promise for socko biz … it's absorbing and adventurous drama.' – *Variety*

Stanno Tutti Bene **
Italy 1990 125m colour
Erre/Ariane (Angelo Rizzoli)
aka: *Everybody's Fine*
An elderly Sicilian decides to visit his five adult children living in various parts of Italy and finds that the reality does not live up to his expectations for them.
Bitter-sweet tale of muddling through life, elegantly acted and directed.
w Giuseppe Tornatore, Tonino Guerra *d* Giuseppe Tornatore *ph* Blasco Giurato *m* Ennio Morricone *ad* Andrea Crisanti *ed* Mario Morra
☆ *Marcello Mastroianni*, Michele Morgan, Marino Cenna, Roberto Nobile, Valeria Cavali, Norma Martelli
'Liberally sprinkled with ideas that provide the viewer with periodic payoffs and laughs.' – *Variety*

La Stanza del Figlio ***
Italy/France 2001 87m colour
Momentum/Sacher/Bac/Canal+/RAITelepiu (Angelo Barbagallo, Nanni Moretti)
aka: *The Son's Room*
An apparently happy middle-class family begins to fall apart when the teenage son dies in an accident.
Moving, often humorous, low-key drama of love and loss that achieves its ends without ostentation, but with undeniable truth and power.
w Linda Ferri, Nanni Moretti, Heidrun Schleef *d* *Nanni Moretti* *ph* Giuseppe Lanci *m* Nicola Piovani *ad* Giancarlo Basili *ed* Esmeralda Calabria
☆ Nanni Moretti (Giovanni), Laura Morante (Paola), Jasmine Trinca (Irene), Giuseppe Sanfelice (Andrea), Silvio Orlando (Oscar), Claudia Della Seta (Raffaella), Stefano Accorsi (Tommaso), Sofia Vigliar (Arianna)
'A measured, decorous, at times pat film that manages to be quietly moving because it touches on something real.' – *Kenneth Turan, Los Angeles Times*
'Superbly acted, refreshingly direct and blessed with an ingenious, unexpected final act.' – *Peter Bradshaw, Guardian*
† It won the Palme D'Or at the Cannes Film Festival in 2001

'When the star fades, the woman is born!'
'The story of every woman who ever climbed the stairway to the stars – and found herself at the bottom looking up!'

The Star *

US 1952 91m bw
TCF/Bert E. Friedlob

A once famous Hollywood star is financially and psychologically on her uppers.
A movie apparently tailor-made for its star turns out to be a disappointingly plotless wallow.
w Katherine Albert, Dale Eunson *d* Stuart Heisler *ph* Ernest Laszlo *m* Victor Young
☆ *Bette Davis*, Sterling Hayden, Natalie Wood, Warner Anderson, Minor Watson
† The role was originally designed for Joan Crawford.
Bette Davis

Star! **

US 1968 194m DeLuxe Todd-AO
TCF/Robert Wise (Saul Chaplin)

Revue artist Gertrude Lawrence rises from poverty to international stardom and a measure of happiness.
Elephantiasis finally ruins this patient, detached, generally likeable recreation of a past theatrical era. In the old Hollywood style, it would probably have been even better on a smaller budget; but alas the star would still have been ill at ease with the drunken termagant scenes.
w William Fairchild *d* *Robert Wise* *ph* Ernest Laszlo *md* Lennie Hayton *ch* Michael Kidd *pd* Boris Leven
☆ Julie Andrews (Gertrude Lawrence), Richard Crenna (Richard Aldrich), Michael Craig (Sir Anthony Spencer), *Daniel Massey* (Noël Coward), John Collin, Robert Reed, Bruce Forsyth, Beryl Reid, Jenny Agutter
† Short version: *Those Were the Happy Days*.
†† The film cost 14 million and took four.
Ernest Laszlo; Lennie Hayton; title song (*m* James Van Heusen, *ly* Sammy Cahn); Daniel Massey

Star 80

US 1983 103m Technicolor
Warner/Ladd (Wolfgang Glattes, Kenneth Utt)

The murder by her husband of Dorothy Stratten, the *Playboy* centrefold model.
Unappetizing recounting, made less palatable by flashy direction, of a story with no possible moral.
wd Bob Fosse *ph* Sven Nykvist *m* Ralph Burns *pd* Tony Walton *ed* Alan Heim
☆ Mariel Hemingway (Dorothy Stratten), Eric Roberts (Paul Snider), Cliff Robertson (Hugh Hefner), Carroll Baker (Dorothy's mother), Roger Rees (Aram Nicholas), Lisa Gordon (Eileen), David Clennon (Geb), Josh Mostel (Private detective)
'A mishmash of embarrassments.' – *Tom Milne, MFB*
'Obviously intended as a cautionary tale for our times, with the beautiful dreamers and ruthless schemers peopling a colour supplement world of success.' – *Sight and Sound*

The Star Chamber

US 1983 109m DeLuxe Panavision
TCF/Frank Yablans

Judges get together to retry defendants who have been unjustly freed, and then have them executed by hired assassins.
A bit hard to swallow; also overlong and rather unpleasant.
w Roderick Taylor, Peter Hyams *d* Peter Hyams *ph* Richard Hannah *m* Michael Small *pd* Bill Malley
☆ Michael Douglas, Hal Holbrook, Yaphet Kotto, Sharon Gless, James B. Sikking, Joe Regalbuto
'Michael Winner territory with a veneer of conscience.' – *Sight and Sound*
'Small-screen material suffering from crippling inflation.' – *Steve Jenkins, MFB*

Star Dust *

US 1940 85m bw
TCF (Kenneth MacGowan)
A talent scout discovers a new Hollywood star.
Light, amusing studio comedy, a pleasing addition to Hollywood mythology.
w Robert Ellis, Helen Logan *d* Walter Lang *ph* Peverell Marley *m* David Buttolph
☆ Linda Darnell, John Payne, Roland Young, Charlotte Greenwood, William Gargan, Mary Beth Hughes, Donald Meek, Jessie Ralph

Star in the Dust

US 1956 80m Technicolor
Universal (Albert Zugsmith)
A new sheriff tries to keep the peace between farmers and ranchers when a gunman hired by the cattlemen is condemned to death.
Effective minor Western with its characters caught up in conflicting emotions, though its final resolution is a little hurried.
w Oscar Brodney *novel* *Law Man* by Lee Leighton *d* Charles Haas *ph* John L. Russell Jnr *m* Frank Skinner *md* Joseph Gershenson *ad* Alexander Golitzen, Alfred Sweeney *ed* Ray Snyder
☆ John Agar (Sheriff Bill Jorden), Mamie Van Doren (Ellen Ballard), Richard Boone (Sam Hall), Coleen Gray (Nellie Mason), Leif Erickson (George Ballard), James Gleason (Orval Jones), Randy Stuart (Nan Hogan), Terry Gilkyson (Music Man), Paul Fix (Mike MacNamara), Harry Morgan (Lew Hogan), Stuart Randall (Jess Ryman), Robert Osterloh (Rigdon)

A Star Is Born ***

US 1937 111m Technicolor
David O. Selznick

A young actress meets Hollywood success and marries a famous leading man, whose star wanes as hers shines brighter.
Abrasive romantic melodrama which is also the most accurate study of Hollywood ever put on film.
w *Dorothy Parker, Alan Campbell, Robert Carson* *story* William A. Wellman, based partly on 'What Price Hollywood' (1932) (qv) *d* *William A. Wellman* *ph* *W. Howard Greene* *m* Max Steiner
☆ *Janet Gaynor, Fredric March, Adolphe Menjou, Lionel Stander*, Andy Devine, May Robson, Owen Moore, Franklin Pangborn
'One of those rare ones which everyone will want to see and talk about … disproves the tradition that good pictures can't be made with a Hollywood background.' – *Variety*
'Good entertainment by any standards.' – *Frank S. Nugent, New York Times*
'A peculiar sort of masochistic self-congratulatory Hollywood orgy.' – *New Yorker, 1975*
'The first colour job that gets close to what colour must eventually come to: it keeps the thing in its place, underlining the mood and situation of the story rather than dimming everything else out in an iridescent razzle-dazzle.' – *Otis Ferguson*
original story; Special Award to W. Howard Greene for colour photography
best picture; script; William A. Wellman; Janet Gaynor; Fredric March

'Fate raised her to fame – and killed the man she loved!'

A Star Is Born **

US 1954 181m Technicolor Cinemascope
Warner/Transcona (Sidney Luft)

A young actress marries the ageing, alcoholic star who helps her to become a success.
Musical version of the 1937 movie, which begins very strongly and has two splendid performances, but suffers in the second half from a lack of writing strength and heavy post-production cutting. The numbers add very little except length.
w Moss Hart *d* *George Cukor* *ph* Sam Leavitt *md* *Ray Heindorf* *ad* Malcolm Bert, Gene Allen, Irene Sharaff
☆ *Judy Garland, James Mason*, Charles Bickford, Jack Carson, Tommy Noonan, Amanda Blake, Lucy Marlow
'Maintains a skilful balance between the musical and the tear jerker.' – *Penelope Houston*
'By far the best of all the films about life behind the cameras, the lights, the wind-machines, and the cocktail bars of Hollywood.' – *Dilys Powell*
† Cary Grant and Humphrey Bogart were both sought before James Mason was signed.
†† Ronald Haver's book *A Star Is Born* (1988) is an account of the making of the film and its 1983 restoration.
♫ 'Born in a Trunk'; 'Gotta Have Me Go With You'; 'Here's What I'm Here For'; 'It's a New World'; 'Someone At Last'; 'The Man That Got Away'
Ray Heindorf; song 'The Man that Got Away' (*m* Harold Arlen, *ly* Ira Gershwin); Judy Garland; James Mason; art direction

A Star Is Born *

US 1976 140m Metrocolor
Warner/Barwood/First Artists (Barbra Streisand, Jon Peters)

Interminable remake set in the pop world amid screaming crowds and songs at high decibel level; also an insufferable piece of showing off by the star. But some of the handling has style.
w John Gregory Dunne, Joan Didion, Frank Pierson *d* Frank Pierson *ph* Robert Surtees *md* Paul Williams *pd* Polly Platt
☆ Barbra Streisand, Kris Kristofferson, Paul Mazursky, Gary Busey
'A clear case for the monopolies commission.' – *Michael Billington, Illustrated London News*
'A bore is starred.' – *Village Voice*
song 'Evergreen'.(*m* Barbra Streisand, *ly* Paul Williams)
Robert Surtees; Roger Kellaway (music underscoring)

Star Kid

US 1998 101m Foto-Kem
Entertainment/Trimark (Jennie Lew Tugend)

A young boy finds an alien cybersuit – a sort of living armour – which he wears first to punish his bullies, and then to protect the Earth from attack by a monster robot.
Pleasant, infantile science fiction of a familiar kind, offering harmless fantasies for the young.
wd Manny Coto *ph* Ronn Schmidt *m* Nicholas Pike *pd* C. J. Strawn *ed* Bob Ducsay
☆ Joseph Mazello, Joey Simmrin, Alex Daniels, Arthur Burghardt, Brian Simpson, Richard Gilliland
'Should strike a responsive chord with pre-adolescent boys.' – *Variety*

The Star Maker *

US 1939 94m bw
Paramount (Charles R. Rogers)
A songwriter makes the big time by organizing kid acts.
Pleasant minor musical based on the career of Gus Edwards.
w Frank Butler, Don Hartman, Arthur Caesar *d* Roy del Ruth *ph* Karl Struss
☆ Bing Crosby, Louise Campbell, Linda Ware, Ned Sparks, Laura Hope Crews, Janet Waldo, Walter Damrosch
'A rollicking filmusical, first-class entertainment.' – *Variety*

Star of Midnight *

US 1935 90m bw
RKO (Pandro S. Berman)

A New York attorney solves the disappearance of a leading lady.
Wisecracking, debonair murder mystery modelled on The Thin Man.
w Howard J. Green, Anthony Veiller, Edward Kaufman *d* Stephen Roberts *ph* J. Roy Hunt *m* Max Steiner
☆ William Powell, Ginger Rogers, Paul Kelly, Gene Lockhart, Ralph Morgan, Leslie Fenton, J. Farrell MacDonald
'Too bad the title isn't more attractive, but the picture is excellent otherwise and should be a snappy grosser.' – *Variety*
'It is all suavity and amusement, pistol shots and cocktails.' – *Graham Greene*
'One of the best sophisticated comedy-mysteries in a period full of such films.' – *NFT, 1973*

The Star Packer

US 1934 60m bw
Monogram/Lone Star (Paul Malvern)

Investigating the murders of his three predecessors, a new sheriff and his Indian aide uncover the identity of an outlaw known as The Shadow.
Wayne as usual gets his man and the girl in a low-budget Western full of action and some novel stunts.
wd Robert N. Bradbury *ph* Archie Stout *ed* Carl Pierson
☆ John Wayne, Verna Hillie, George Hayes, Yakima Canutt, Billy Franey, Ed Parker, Earl Dwire, Tom Lingham

The Star Said No: see *Callaway Went Thataway*

The Star Spangled Girl

US 1971 92m colour
Paramount (Howard W. Koch)
A sweet old-fashioned girl is fought for by two young radicals.
Unamusingly 'with it' comedy from an unsuccessful play.
w Arnold Margolin, Jim Parker *play* Neil Simon *d* Jerry Paris *ph* Sam Leavitt *m* Charles Fox
☆ Sandy Duncan, Tony Roberts, Todd Susman, Elizabeth Allen

Star Spangled Rhythm ***

US 1942 99m bw
Paramount (Joseph Sistrom)

The doorman of Paramount Studios pretends to his sailor son that he is a big producer.
Frenetic farce involving most of the talent on Paramount's payroll and culminating in an 'impromptu' show staged for the navy. A good lighthearted glimpse of wartime Hollywood.
w Harry Tugend *d* George Marshall *ph* Leo Tover, Theodor Sparkuhl *md* Robert Emmett Dolan *songs* Johnny Mercer, Harold Arlen
☆ *Betty Hutton*, Eddie Bracken, *Victor Moore, Walter Abel*, Anne Revere, Cass Daley, Gil Lamb, Macdonald Carey, Bob Hope, Bing Crosby, Paulette Goddard, Veronica Lake, Dorothy Lamour, Vera Zorina, Fred MacMurray and also Ray Milland, Lynne Overman, Franchot Tone, Dick Powell, *Walter Dare Wahl and Co, Cecil B. de Mille, Preston Sturges*, Alan Ladd, Rochester, Katherine Dunham, Susan Hayward
† Veronica Lake's singing was dubbed by Martha Mears.
Robert Emmett Dolan; song 'That Old Black Magic' (*m* Harold Arlen, *ly* Johnny Mercer)

'Resistance Is Futile.'

Star Trek: First Contact *

US 1996 110m DeLuxe
Paramount (Rick Berman)

Captain Jean-Luc Picard takes his Starship *Enterprise* back through time, chasing the Borg, a hive lifeform that wants to conquer the Earth by preventing the first contact with friendly aliens.
One for the fans, though it provides more action and excitement, as well as a hint of alien sex, than most of the series.
w Brannon Braga, Ronald D. Moore, Rick Berman *d* Jonathan Frakes *ph* Matthew F. Leonetti *m* Jerry Goldsmith *pd* Herman Zimmerman *ed* John W. Wheeler *sp* Industrial Light and Magic; make-up: Michael Westmore
☆ Patrick Stewart, Jonathan Frakes, Brent Spiner, LeVar Burton, Michael Dorn, Gates McFadden, Alfre Woodard, James Cromwell, Alice Krige
'A smashingly exciting sci-fi adventure.' – *Variety*
'A cheesy B-movie with a second-rate cast and plot and effects only marginally more special than the TV shows.' – *Screen International*
Michael Westmore, Scott Wheeler, Jake Garber (make-up)

Star Trek: Generations *

US 1994 118m DeLuxe
UIP/Paramount (Rick Berman)

A mad scientist is willing to destroy worlds and ally with the Klingons to return to a strange joy-bringing ribbon of energy known as the Nexus.
A movie that will be remembered, if it is remembered, for marking the death of Captain Kirk and the arrival of Picard and other new cast members from the latest TV incarnation of the programme; what it really needs, if it is to appeal to more than the converted, is a better script.
w Ronald D. Moore, Brannon Braga, Rick Berman *d* David Carson *ph* John A. Alonzo *m* Dennis McCarthy *pd* Herman Zimmerman *ed* Peter Berger
☆ Patrick Stewart, William Shatner, Malcolm McDowell, Jonathan Frakes, Brent Spiner, LeVar Burton, Michael Dorn, Gates McFadden, Marina

Sirtis, James Doohan, Walter Koenig, Whoopi Goldberg

'Addressed primarily at cultists, and is not especially well plotted or directed.' – *Sheila Johnston, Independent*

Star Trek III: The Search for Spock

US 1984 105m Metrocolor
Panavision
Paramount/Cinema Group Venture (Harve Bennett)

Admiral Kirk discovers that Spock is not dead but has been reborn as a Vulcan child …

Very silly, empty and unamusing follow-up.

w Harve Bennett *d* Leonard Nimoy *ph* Charles Correll *m* James Horner

☆ William Shatner, DeForest Kelley, James Doohan, Walter Koenig, Nichelle Nichols, Robert Hooks, Leonard Nimoy

'The Battle For Paradise Has Begun.'

Star Trek Insurrection

US 1998 105m colour 'Scope
Paramount (Rick Berman)

Captain Jean-Luc Picard discovers that the Federation is behaving unfairly towards a peaceful long-lived race, who face genocide.

A simple tale, of the sort that filled half an hour or less of television time, is here tricked out with special effects and rather more action; but it's still an example of more resulting in less.

w Michael Piller *d* Jonathan Frakes *ph* Matthew F. Leonetti *m* Jerry Goldsmith *pd* Herman Zimmerman *ed* Peter E. Berger *sp* make-up designer: Michael Westmore; Terry Frazee

☆ Patrick Stewart, Jonathan Frakes, Brent Spiner, LeVar Burton, Michael Dorn, Gates McFadden, Martina Sirtis, F. Murray Abraham, Donna Murphy, Anthony Zerbe, Gregg Henry, Daniel Hugh Kelly, Michael Welch

'Little more than a glorified television episode.' – *New York Times*

Star Trek IV: The Voyage Home *

US 1986 119m Technicolor
Panavision
Paramount/Harve Bennett

GB title: *The Voyage Home: Star Trek IV*

The *Enterprise* crew is called home to face trial for mutiny: they find a very alien world.

The best of the series: it isn't saying much, but at least there are shreds of wit in the script.

w Harve Bennett, Steve Meerson, Peter Krikes, Nicholas Meyer *d* Leonard Nimoy *ph* Don Peterman *m* Leonard Rosenman *pd* Jack T. Collis *ed* Peter E. Berger

☆ William Shatner, Leonard Nimoy, De Forrest Kelley, James Doohan, George Takei, Walter Koenig, Jane Wyatt, Catherine Hicks

Don Peterman; Leonard Rosenman

'A Generation's Final Journey… Begins'

Star Trek: Nemesis

US 2002 117m DeLuxe Panavision
Paramount (Rick Berman)

Captain Picard fights a clone of himself in a battle to save the Earth.

Dull, dull, dull. The cast seem unable to summon up much interest in a script feeble enough to put this series into a suspended animation for all time.

w John Logan *d* Stuart Baird *ph* Jeffrey L. Kimball *m* Jerry Goldsmith *pd* Herman Zimmerman *ed* Dallas Puett *sp* Digital Domain; make-up: Michael Westmore *cos* Bob Ringwood

☆ Patrick Stewart (Jean-Luc Picard), Jonathan Frakes (William Riker), Brent Spiner (Data/B-4), Levar Burton (Geordi La Forge), Michael Dorn (Worf), Marina Sirtis (Deanna Troi), Gates McFadden (Beverly Crusher), Tom Hardy (Shinzon), Ron Perlman (Viceroy)

'This will test fan loyalty to destruction.' – *Peter Bradshaw, Guardian*

'Supposed to be edge-of-the-seat stuff, and in a way, for me, it was. My head had come to rest, quite comfortably, on that very spot.' – *Anthony Quinn, Independent*

'The human adventure is just beginning!'

Star Trek: The Motion Picture

US 1979 132m Metrocolor
Panavision
Paramount (Gene Roddenberry)

In the 23rd century, Admiral Kirk resumes command of the *Enterprise* to combat an alien force.

And a surprisingly boring one. Vast sets and big-screen solemnity hardly make this more enjoyable than some of the TV episodes which got more tricks and philosophical fun into one-third of the length.

w Harold Livingston, Alan Dean Foster *d* Robert Wise *ph* Richard H. Kline, Richard Yuricich *m* Jerry Goldsmith *pd* Harold Michelson *ed* Todd Ramsey

☆ William Shatner, Leonard Nimoy, De Forrest Kelley, Stephen Collins, Persis Khambatta

Jerry Goldsmith; visual effects (Douglas Trumbull, John Dykstra and others); art direction

'At the end of the universe lies the beginning of vengeance!'

Star Trek: The Wrath of Khan

US 1982 114m Movielab
Panavision
Paramount (Harve Bennett)

The crew of the starship *Enterprise* counter the wiles of an evil genius on a distant planet.

Comic strip capers a long way from the controlled intelligence of some episodes of the TV series; but more entertaining than the first movie.

w Jack B. Sowards *d* Nicholas Meyer *ph* Gayne Rescher *m* James Horner *pd* Joseph R. Jennings

☆ William Shatner, Leonard Nimoy, Ricardo Montalban, De Forrest Kelley, Ike Eisenmann

'A pitiful snack for the eyes with some unappetizing crumbs left over for the mind to chew on.' – *Philip Strick, MFB*

Star Trek V: The Final Frontier

US 1989 107m Technicolor
Panavision
UIP/Paramount (Harve Bennett)

Captain Kirk goes in search of a legendary planet, said to be inhabited by God.

Mystic moments, tamely rendered, that indicate it is long after the time when the series should have been laid to rest.

w David Loughery *story* William Shatner, Harve Bennett, David Loughery *d* William Shatner *ph* Andrew Laszlo *m* Jerry Goldsmith *pd* Herman Zimmerman *ed* Peter Berger

☆ William Shatner, Leonard Nimoy, DeForest Kelley, James Doohan, Walter Koenig, Nichelle Nichols, George Takei, David Warner, Laurence Luckinbill

'The battle for peace has begun.'

Star Trek VI: The Undiscovered Country **

US 1991 110m Technicolor
UIP/Paramount (Ralph Winter, Steven-Charles Jaffe)

Mr Spock attempts to solve the murder of a Klingon peace delegate after Captain Kirk and Dr McCoy are convicted of the crime.

The last voyage of the original crew of the Starship Enterprise turns out to be their finest hour and fifty minutes.

w Nicholas Meyer, Denny Martin Flynn *story* Leonard Nimoy, Lawrence Konner, Mark Rosenthal *d* Nicholas Meyer *ph* Hiro Narita *m* Cliff Eidelman *pd* Herman Zimmerman *ed* Ronald Roose, William Hoy *sp* Industrial Light and Magic

☆ William Shatner, Leonard Nimoy, DeForest Kelley, James Doohan, Walter Koenig, George Takei, Christian Slater, Kim Cattrall, Mark Lenard, Christopher Plummer, David Warner

'A lumbering and self-indulgent picture, dragged down at every turn by the weight of twenty-five years of illogical mediocrity, as if the series' notional science-fiction aspects pre-empted the need for characters, stories or a universe that made any dramatic sense.' –*Kim Newman, Sight and Sound*

'There are no signs of waning energy here, not even in an *Enterprise* crew that looks ever more ready for intergalactic rocking chairs.' – *Janet Maslin, New York Times*

Star Wars ****

US 1977 121m Technicolor
Panavision
TCF/Lucasfilm (Gary Kurtz)

aka: *Star Wars IV: A New Hope*

A rebel princess in a distant galaxy escapes, and with the help of her robots and a young farmer overcomes the threatening forces of evil.

Flash Gordon rides again, but with timing so impeccably right that the movie became a phenomenon and one of the top grossers of all time. Good harmless fun, put together with style and imagination.

wd George Lucas *ph* Gilbert Taylor *m* John Williams *pd* John Barry *ed* Paul Hirsch, Marcia Lucas, Richard Chew *sp* Rick Baker, John Dykstra

☆ Mark Hamill (Luke Skywalker), Harrison Ford (Han Solo), Carrie Fisher (Princess Leia Organa), Peter Cushing (Grand Moff Tarkin), Alec Guinness (Obi-Wan Kenobi), Anthony Daniels (See Threepio), Kenny Baker (Artoo-Detoo), Dave Prowse (Darth Vader), Phil Brown (Owen Lars)

'A great work of popular art, fully deserving the riches it has reaped.' – *Time*

'Acting in this movie I felt like a raisin in a giant fruit salad. And I didn't even know who the coconuts or the canteloups were.' – *Mark Hamill*

'He intended his film, Lucas confesses, for a generation growing up without fairy tales. His target audience was fourteen years and younger … It was a celebration, a social affair, a collective dream, and people came again and again, dragging their friends and families with them.' – *Les Keyser, Hollywood in the Seventies*

'The loudness, the smash and grab editing and the relentless pacing drive every idea from your head, and even if you've been entertained you may feel cheated of some dimension – a sense of wonder, perhaps.' – *New Yorker, 1982*

'Heartless fireworks ignited by a permanently retarded director with too much clout and cash.' – *Time Out, 1984*

† The voice of Darth Vader was supplied by the uncredited James Earl Jones.

†† The film was re-released in 1997, with its sound remixed and digital technology used to improve battle sequences and the size of the city of Mos Eisley. Some unused footage from the original was added, together with computer animation, to show a meeting between Han Solo and Jabba the Hutt. It took more than $46m in the first week of its re-release, and became the first film to gross more than $400m at the US box-office.

John Williams; John Barry; editing; costumes (John Mollo); visual effects (John Stears, John Dykstra and others); sound

best picture; script; direction; Alec Guinness

John Williams

'A Jedi Shall Not Know Anger. Nor Hatred. Nor Love.'

Star Wars: Episode II – Attack of the Clones *

US 2002 143m DeLuxe Panavision
TCF/Lucasfilm (Rick McCallum)

War breaks out between the Republic and secessionists, while the force of the Jedi diminishes and the dark side grows stronger.

Much computer-generated invention goes to waste here – the battle scenes are so perfunctorily done that it's hard to know which side is which – its chocolate-box romance is dull, and most of the performances are duller; only in a gladiatorial arena does the movie attain an epic excitement.

w George Lucas, Jonathan Hales *d* George Lucas *ph* David Tattersall *m* John Williams *pd* Gavin Bocquet *ed* Ben Burtt *sp* Industrial Light & Magic *cos* Trisha Biggar

☆ Ewan McGregor (Obi-Wan Kenobi), Natalie Portman (Padme), Hayden Christensen (Anakin Skywalker), Christopher Lee (Count Dooku), Samuel L. Jackson (Mace Windu), Yoda (Frank Oz (voice)), Ian McDiarmid (Supreme Chancellor Palpatine), Pernilla August (Shmi Skywalker), Temuera Morrison (Jango Fett), Jimmy Smits (Senator Bail Organa), Jack Thompson (Cliegg Lars), Anthony Daniels (C-3PO), Kenny Baker (R2-D2)

'The really fun stuff is a long time coming, and it only confirms your suspicion that "Attack of the Clones" is just for kids. Once upon a time – in "The Empire Strikes Back", directed by Irvin Kershner – the tale had stirring mythic undertones that spoke to every generation.' – *David Anson, Newsweek*

'A technological exercise that lacks juice and delight.' – *Roger Ebert, Chicago Sun-Times*

'It is not really much of a movie at all, if by movie you mean a work of visual storytelling about the dramatic actions of a group of interesting characters.' – *A. O. Scott, New York Times*

Star Wars: Episode I – The Phantom Menace **

US 1999 116m DeLuxe
TCF/Lucasfilm (Rick McCallum)

Jedi knights come to the aid of the young queen of a peaceful planet, who is invaded by a powerful trade federation.

Having started the saga in the middle of things with the original Star Wars, there's a lot of static exposition here to explain what came after. The human actors tend to play supporting roles to the often dazzling special effects and computer-generated creatures; at times it seems little more than an illustrated toy catalogue for the 12-year-olds at which it is aimed. It is also the most critic-proof movie ever made.

wd George Lucas *ph* David Tattersall *m* John Williams *pd* Gavin Bocquet *ed* Paul Martin Smith *sp* ILM

☆ Liam Neeson, Ewan McGregor, Natalie Portman, Jake Lloyd, Pernilla August, Frank Oz, Ian McDiarmid, Oliver Ford Davies, Hugh Quarshie, Ahmed Best, Samuel L. Jackson, Ray Park, Peter Serafinowicz, Ralph Brown, Terence Stamp and also Brian Blessed, Sofia Coppola

'It is neither captivating nor transporting, for it lacks any emotional pull, as well as the sense of wonder and awe that marks the best works of sci-fi/fantasy.' – *Todd McCarthy, Variety*

'Brimming with dazzling special effects but short on dramatic focus.' – *John Hazleton, Screen International*

† The film set new records by taking $28.5m at the US box-office on its first day. It went on to take $430.4m in the US and a total of $920m around ther world.

sound (Gary Rydstrom, Tom Johnson, Shawn Murphy, John Midgley); sound effects editing (Ben Burtt, Tom Bellfort); visual effects (John Knoll, Dennis Muren, Scott Squires, Rob Coleman)

Star Wars: Episode V – The Empire Strikes Back: see *The Empire Strikes Back*

Star Wars: Episode VI – Return of the Jedi: see *Return of the Jedi*

The Star Witness *

US 1931 68m bw
Warner

An old man witnesses a crime and is threatened by gangsters.

Pacy melodrama with good performances.

w Lucien Hubbard *d* William Wellman *ph* James Van Trees

☆ Walter Huston, Chic Sale, Grant Mitchell, Frances Starr, Sally Blane

'Plenty of action, laughs, and a tear.' – *Variety*

Lucien Hubbard

Starcrash

US 1979 92m Metrocolor
Columbia/AIP/Film Enterprise (Nat Wachsberger, Patrick Wachsberger)

A spaceship pilot and her navigator are released from prison to find a kidnapped boy and, with the aid of a robot, defeat an evil dictator who wants to rule their world.

Science-fiction hokum of the silly kind, directed at a breathless pace and influenced by Star Wars, for its plot, and Barbarella, for its sex appeal.

w Luigi Cossi, Nat Wachsberger, R. A. Dillon *d* Lewis Coates (Luigi Cozzi) *ph* Roberto D'Ettorre Piazzoli, Paul Beeson *m* John Barry *pd* Aurelio Crugnola *ed* Sergio Montanari *sp* Armando Valcauda, Germano Natali, Ron Hays

☆ Marjoe Gortner, Caroline Munro, Christopher Plummer, David Hasselhoff, Robert Tessier, Joe Spinell, Nadia Cassini, Judd Hamilton, Hamilton Camp

'Show me a boy who never wanted to be a rock star – and I'll show you a liar'

Stardust

GB 1974 111m Technicolor
EMI/Goodtimes (David Puttnam, Sandy Lieberson)

The rise and fall of a pop singer.
Unappetizing rehash of Road to Ruin, *pop music style.*
w Ray Connolly *d* Michael Apted *ph* Tony Richmond *md* Dave Edmunds, David Puttnam
☆ David Essex, Adam Faith, Larry Hagman, Marty Wilde, Rosalind Ayres

Stardust Memories *

US 1980 88m bw
UA/Jack Rollins, Charles H. Joffe (Robert Greenhut)

An increasingly melancholy comedian attends a retrospective of his work and is plagued by real and imaginary fears.
A plainly autobiographical work which, while amusing and moving in spots, makes it doubtful that the writer/director/star can even now shake off his obsessions.
wd Woody Allen *ph* Gordon Willis *m* Dick Hyman
☆ Woody Allen, Charlotte Rampling, Jessica Harper, Marie-Christine Barrault, Tony Roberts, Helen Hanft
'Its posturing pyrotechnics seem more the symptom of a crisis than its controlled expression.' – *Gilbert Adair, MFB*

Stargate

US 1994 120m DeLuxe
Guild/Canal/Centropolis/Carolco (Joel B. Michaels, Oliver Eberle, Dean Devlin)

An Egyptologist discovers a gateway to another world where an alien intelligence rules over a slave kingdom of inhabitants descended from the ancient Egyptians; the American military goes through to bring them democracy and the atom bomb.
An old-fashioned gung-ho space opera, recycling threadbare themes, which unexpectedly found favour with the public.
w Roland Emmerich, Dean Devlin *d* Roland Emmerich *ph* Karl Walter Lindenlaub *m* David Arnold *pd* Holger Gross *ed* Michael Duthie, Derek Brechin *sp* Kleiser-Walczak Construction Company, Cinema Research Corporation, Available Light; creature effects: Patrick Tatopoulos
☆ Kurt Russell, James Spader, Jaye Davidson, Viveca Lindfors, Alexis Cruz, Mili Avital, Leon Rippy, John Diehl
'The movie, which does have a sort of cheeky energy, goes into narrative and cliché overload once the spacemen start exploring the unnamed planet – shall we call it Lucasland – where they set down.' – *Richard Schickel, Time*
'What this juvenile adventure has in spades is special effects and picturesque locations. What it lacks is an emotional link to make the Saturday afternoon he-man posturing palatable, or at least bearable.' – *Leonard Klady, Variety*

Starlift

US 1951 102m bw
Warner (Robert Arthur)
Movie stars entertain at Travis Air Base, where the boys are constantly leaving for Korea.
Insipid musical with even more insipid romantic interludes.
w John Klorer, Karl Kamb *d* Roy del Ruth *ph* Ted McCord *md* Ray Heindorf
☆ Janice Rule, Dick Wesson, Richard Webb, Howard St John, Doris Day, Gordon MacRae, Virginia Mayo, Gene Nelson, Ruth Roman, James Cagney, Gary Cooper, Phil Harris, Louella Parsons, Randolph Scott, Jane Wyman

Starlight Hotel *

New Zealand 1987 90m
Recorded Releasing/Challenge Film Corp/NZ Film Commission (Finola Dwyer, Larry Parr)

Two runaways – one a rebellious child, the other a suspected murderer – team up on the road.
Slight but engaging story, with good period detail.
w Grant Hinden-Miller *novel* *The Dream Monger* *d* Sam Pillsbury *ph* Warrick Attewell *m* Andrew Hayes, Morton Wilson *pd* Mike Becroft *ad* Roger Guise *ed* Michael Horton
☆ Peter Phelps, Greer Robson, Marshall Napier, Alice Fraser

The Starmaker *

Italy 1994 107m Technicolor Panavision
TCF/Cecchi Gori/Tiger/Sciarlò (Vittorio Cecchi Gori, Rita Cecchi Gori)

original title: *L'Uomo delle Stelle*
In Sicily in the mid-50s, a travelling con man offers townspeople the chance of stardom if they give him money to make a screen test.
A road movie about people's dreams and disappointments, too schematic to be entirely successful.
w Fabio Rinaudo, Giuseppe Tornatore
d Giuseppe Tornatore *ph* Dante Spinotti
m Ennio Morricone *pd* Francesco Bronzi
ed Massimo Quaglia
☆ Sergio Castellitto, Tizana Lodato, Leopoldo Trieste, Nicola di Pinto, Franco Scaldati
'A gorgeously produced tourism commercial for the Italian island, this threadbare tale of a cocky con man's painful comeuppance has very little heart and, consequently, conjures few real emotions.' – *David Rooney, Variety*

Starman

US 1984 115m MGM Color
Columbia/Delphi (Larry J. Franco)

An alien arrives in Wisconsin and takes human form, falling in love with the widow of the man he impersonates.
Derivative but eccentric science-fiction fantasy with lapses of narrative and a general attempt to make the love story predominant over the hardware.
w Bruce A. Evans, Raynold Gideon *d* John Carpenter *ph* Donald M. Morgan *m* Jack Nitzsche *pd* Daniel Lomino *ed* Marion Rothman
☆ Jeff Bridges, Karen Allen, Charles Martin Smith, Richard Jaeckel, Robert Phalen, Tony Edwards
Jeff Bridges

Staroye i Novoye: see *The General Line*

Stars and Bars

US 1988 94m DuArt/DeLuxe
Columbia (Sandy Lieberson)

Cliché Englishman's encounters with stereotyped Americans in search for long-lost Renoir painting.
w William Boyd *novel* William Boyd *d* Pat O'Connor *ph* Jerzy Zielinski *m* Stanley Myers *pd* Leslie Dilley, Stuart Craig *ed* Michael Bradsell
☆ Daniel Day-Lewis, Harry Dean Stanton, Martha Plimpton, Joan Cusack
'Unhappy mixture of farce and misdirected satire.' – *Variety*

Stars and Stripes Forever *

US 1952 89m Technicolor
TCF (Lamar Trotti)

GB title: *Marching Along*
In the 1890s John Philip Sousa, a bandmaster who wants to write ballads, finds success as a writer of marches.
Low-key musical biopic with predictably noisy numbers.
w Lamar Trotti *autobiography* John Philip Sousa *d* Henry Koster *ph* Charles G. Clarke *md* Alfred Newman
☆ Clifton Webb, Debra Paget, Robert Wagner, Ruth Hussey, Finlay Currie, Roy Roberts, Lester Matthews

The Stars Are Singing

US 1952 99m Technicolor
Paramount (Irving Asher)
A Polish refugee girl illegally enters the US and becomes an opera star.
Painless Cinderella fantasy in which everybody sings.
w Liam O'Brien *d* Norman Taurog *ph* Lionel Lindon *md* Victor Young
☆ Anna Maria Alberghetti, Lauritz Melchior, Rosemary Clooney, Fred Clark, Mikhail Rasumny
♫ Come-On-A-My-House; Haven't Got a Worry; I Do! I Do! I Do!; Lovely Weather for Ducks; My Heart Is Home; My Kind of Day.

The Stars Fell on Henrietta

US 1995 110m Technicolor Panavision
Warner/Malpaso/Butcher's Run (Clint Eastwood, David Valdes)

A woman remembers her childhood in the mid-30s, and the arrival of an eccentric, penniless wildcatter, who was convinced that there was oil on land belonging to her father, a poor Texan farmer.
Pleasant but unremarkable period drama of one man's determined struggle against constant humiliation, and his effect on the lives of others.
w Philip Railsback *d* James Keach *ph* Bruce Surtees *m* David Benoit *pd* Henry Bumstead *ed* Joel Cox
☆ Robert Duvall, Aidan Quinn, Frances Fisher, Brian Dennehy, Lexi Randall, Kaytlyn Knowles, Francesca Ruth Eastwood, Billy Bob Thornton, Victor Wong
'A muted character piece of modest ambition and achievement.' – *Todd McCarthy, Variety*

Stars in My Crown *

US 1950 89m bw
MGM (William H. Wright)
A two-gun parson brings peace to a Tennessee town after the Civil War.
Sentimental family Western, quite pleasantly made and performed.
w Margaret Fitts *novel* Joe David Brown
d Jacques Tourneur *ph* Charles Schoenbaum
m Adolph Deutsch
☆ Joel McCrea, Ellen Drew, Dean Stockwell, Juano Hernandez, James Mitchell, Lewis Stone, Alan Hale, Amanda Blake

The Stars Look Down **

GB 1939 110m bw
Grafton (Isadore Goldschmidt)

The son of a coal miner struggles to become an MP.
Economically but well made social drama from a popular novel, with good pace and backgrounds.
w J. B. Williams, A. J. Cronin *novel* A. J. Cronin
d Carol Reed *ph* Max Greene *m* Hans May
☆ Michael Redgrave, Margaret Lockwood, Edward Rigby, Emlyn Williams, Nancy Price, Allan Jeayes, Cecil Parker, Linden Travers
'Dr Cronin's mining novel has produced a very good film – I doubt whether in England we have ever produced a better.' – *Graham Greene*
'A splendidly directed portrait of those who burrow for the black diamond in England's northland ... the picture is mounted with exactness of detail and technique.' – *Variety*

Stars over Broadway

US 1935 89m bw
Warner (Sam Bischoff)
Agent turns hotel porter into radio star.
Unremarkable musical, with unusual talent.
w Jerry Wald, Julius J. Epstein, Pat C. Flick
d William Keighley *ph* George Barnes *md* Leo F. Forbstein *ch* Busby Berkeley, Bobby Connolly *songs* Harry Warren, Al Dubin
☆ James Melton, Jane Froman, Pat O'Brien, Jean Muir, Frank McHugh, Marie Wilson, Frank Fay
'A far from inspired backstage yarn with pleasant dialogue and fancy trimmings.' – *Variety*

'Since his existence, man has ruled the Earth. In the future, the rules will change.'

Starship Troopers **

US 1997 129m Technicolor
Buena Vista/TriStar/Touchstone (Jon Davison, Alan Marshall)

In the future, when the miltary rule an Earth facing an invasion from giant bug-like aliens, a group of friends become soldiers to fight the creatures on their own planet.
An uneasy and ambivalent movie: it attempts to subvert the intention of Heinlein's novel, which praises the notion of a military élite, yet remains true to the original's enjoyment of violent battles and military superiority; the cast suggest that individuality is a luxury the future cannot afford.
w Ed Neumeier *novel* Robert A. Heinlein *d* Paul Verhoeven *ph* Jost Vacano *m* Basil Poledouris *pd* Allan Cameron *ed* Mark Goldblatt, Caroline Ross *sp* Phil Tippett, Scott E. Anderson, Alec Gillis, John Richardson
☆ Caspar Van Dien, Dina Meyer, Denise Richards, Jake Busey, Neil Patrick Harris, Clancy Brown, Seth Gilliam, Patrick Muldoon, Michael Ironside, Rue McClanahan
'A spectacularly gung-ho sci-fi epic that delivers two hours of good, nasty fun.' – *Todd McCarthy, Variety*
'Would Paul Verhoeven kindly stop making movies?' – *Tom Shone, Sunday Times*
'The crowning achievement of Paul Verhoeven's film-making career to date.' – *Andrew O'Hehir, Sight and Sound*
† Robert Heinlein had to change publishers in order to get *Starship Troopers* published in 1959; the book was intended for a juvenile audience.
†† The film took around $55m at the US box-office.
visual effects

Starstruck

Australia 1982 102m colour
Palm Beach Pictures (David Elfick, Richard Brennan)

In a bid to keep open the family pub, a teenage boy makes a star of his young cousin.
Youth musical that does no more than transfer the usual backstage clichés to a punk and working-class setting.
w Stephen MacLean *d* Gillian Armstrong
ph Russell Boyd *md* Mark Moffat *pd* Brian Thomson *ed* Nicholas Beauman
☆ Jo Kennedy, Ross O'Donovan, Margo Lee, Max Cullen, Pat Evison, John O'May, Ned Lander

Start Cheering

US 1938 78m bw
Columbia

An actor's agent has problems when his potential star decides to go to college.
Fairly amusing low-budget musical with some surprises.
w Eugene Solow, Richard E. Wormser, Philip Rapp, Corey Ford *d* Albert S. Rogell
☆ Jimmy Durante, Walter Connolly, Joan Perry, Charles Starrett, the Three Stooges, Hal Leroy, Ernest Truex, Gertrude Niesen, Raymond Walburn, Broderick Crawford
'Longer on entertainment satisfaction than many of the more formidable pricers.' – *Variety*

Start the Revolution without Me *

US 1969 90m Technicolor
Warner/Norbud (Norman Lear)

Two sets of twins get mixed up at the court of Louis XVI.
Historical spoof of the kind subsequently made familiar by Mel Brooks; the script might have suited Abbott and Costello better than these two actors.
w Fred Freeman, Lawrence J. Cohen *d* Bud Yorkin *ph* Jean Tournier *m* John Addison
☆ Donald Sutherland, Gene Wilder, Hugh Griffith, Jack MacGowran, Billie Whitelaw, Victor Spinetti, Ewa Aulin

Starting Over *

US 1979 106m Movielab
Paramount/Century Associates (Alan J. Pakula, James L. Brooks)

A divorced man nearly goes back to his wife but finally plumps for a nursery school teacher.
Plain-speaking sex comedy-drama with accomplished stars giving rather more than the script is worth.
w James L. Brooks *novel* Dan Wakefield *d* Alan J. Pakula *ph* Sven Nykvist *m* Marvin Hamlisch *pd* George Jenkins
☆ Burt Reynolds, Jill Clayburgh, Candice Bergen, Charles Durning, Austin Pendleton
Jill Clayburgh, Candice Bergen

'The rise and fall of the American dream.'

Startup.com *

US 2001 108m colour
Artificial Eye/Pennebaker Hegedus Films/Noujaim (D.A. Pennebaker)

Documentary on two school friends who raise $50m to set up in New York an Internet company that failed.
Interesting account of the bursting of one Internet bubble, though too often the cameras stay outside the rooms where the crucial talks take place. It throws a sidelight on US corporate culture: even cutting-edge companies are given over to the chanting of slogans and the singing of company songs.

d Jehane Noujaim, Chris Hegedus *ph* Jehane Noujaim *ed* Chris Hegedus, Jehane Noujaim, Erez Laufer

'Acquires the fascination of another Titanic retelling—a movie in which you chew your popcorn and wait almost gleefully for the iceberg that will take these overweeners down.' – *David Edelstein, Slate*

'When A Film Crew Came To Waterford Fremont, They Shot First And Asked Questions Later.'

State and Main *

US 2000 106m

Redbus/Fine Line/Filmtown/El Dorado (Sarah Green)

A small New England town is invaded by a Hollywood film crew, complete with ineffectual writer, bad-tempered director, temperamental actress and a star with a liking for underage girls.

Crisp dialogue enlivens an unexpectedly soft-centered comedy of self-interest.

wd David Mamet *ph* Oliver Stapleton *m* Theodore Shapiro *pd* Gemma Jackson *ed* Barbara Tulliver

☆ Alec Baldwin (Bob Barrenger), William H. Macy (Walt Price), Sarah Jessica Parker (Claire Wellesley), Philip Seymour Hoffman (Joseph Turner White), Rebecca Pidgeon (Ann Black), Charles Durning (Mayor George Bailey), David Paymer (Marty Rossen), Patti LuPone (Sherry Bailey), Julia Stiles

'A surprisingly unpolished piece of work that plays as though it were written for the stage and only slightly modified for the screen' – *Stephen Holden, New York Times*

State Fair **

US 1933 98m bw

Fox (Winfield Sheehan)

Dad wants his prize pig to win at the fair, but the younger members of his family have romance in mind.

Archetypal family film, much remade but never quite so pleasantly performed.

w Paul Green, Sonya Levien *novel* Phil Stong *d* Henry King *ph* Hal Mohr *md* Louis de Francesco

☆ Will Rogers, Janet Gaynor, Lew Ayres, Sally Eilers, Norman Foster, Louise Dresser, Frank Craven, Victor Jory, Hobart Cavanaugh

'A pungent, good-humoured motion picture.' – *Pare Lorentz*

'Vigour, freshness and sympathy abound in its admittedly idealized fantasy treatment of small-town life.' – *Charles Higham, 1972*

best picture; script

State Fair **

US 1945 100m Technicolor

TCF (William Perlberg)

TV title: *It Happened One Summer*

The adventures of an Iowa hog farmer and his family at the annual State Fair.

Musical remake of the 1933 movie with an amiable cast and a rousing score.

w Oscar Hammerstein II d Walter Lang *ph* Leon Shamroy *m/ly Richard Rodgers, Oscar Hammerstein II md* Alfred Newman *ad* Lyle Wheeler, Lewis Creber *ed* J. Watson Webb

☆ *Charles Winninger*, Jeanne Crain, Dana Andrews, Vivian Blaine, Dick Haymes, Fay Bainter, Frank McHugh, Percy Kilbride, Donald Meek

'Surely the sort of theme that clamours for movie treatment. But no, say Twentieth Century Fox: let's make the fair look like a night club. Let's look around for stars of pristine nonentity. Let's screw the camera down to the studio floor. The result, "an epic that sings to the skies ... with glorious, glamorous new songs".' – *Richard Winnington*

'Comes pretty close to being another Oklahoma.' – *Motion Picture Herald*

† Jeanne Crain's songs were dubbed by Louanne Hogan.

song 'It Might As Well Be Spring'

Alfred Newman

State Fair

US 1962 118m DeLuxe

Cinemascope

TCF (Charles Brackett)

Dullsville modernized version, condescending towards the rurals and peopled by unattractive youngsters.

w Richard Breen *d* José Ferrer *ph* William C. Mellor *md* Alfred Newman

☆ Pat Boone, Alice Faye, Tom Ewell, Pamela Tiffin, Ann-Margret, Bobby Darin, Wally Cox

State of Grace

US 1990 134m DeLuxe Panavision

Rank/Cinehaus/Orion (Ned Dowd, Randy Ostrow, Ron Rotholz)

In New York, an undercover cop returns to the district where he grew up in order to infiltrate an Irish gang that is about to make a deal with the Mafia.

Dull and plodding gangster movie.

w Dennis McIntyre *d* Phil Joanou *ph* Jordan Cronenweth *m* Ennio Morricone *pd* Patrizia von Brandenstein, Doug Kraner *ed* Claire Simpson

☆ Sean Penn, Ed Harris, Gary Oldman, Robin Wright, John Turturro, John C. Reilly, R. D. Call, Joe Vitorelli, Burgess Meredith, Deirdre O'Connell

'One of the more intriguing American thrillers of the year if only because it turns out to be dripping with old-fashioned romanticism as well as new-fangled violence.' – *Derek Malcolm, Guardian*

State of the Union ***

US 1948 110m bw

MGM/Liberty Films (Frank Capra)

GB title: *The World and His Wife*

An estranged wife rejoins her husband when he is running for president.

Brilliantly scripted political comedy which unfortunately goes soft at the end but offers stimulating entertainment most of the way.

w Anthony Veiller, Myles Connolly *play* Howard Lindsay, Russel Crouse *d Frank Capra ph* George J. Folsey *m* Victor Young

☆ *Spencer Tracy, Katharine Hepburn, Adolphe Menjou, Van Johnson*, Angela Lansbury, Lewis Stone, Howard Smith, Raymond Walburn, Charles Dingle

'A triumphant film, marked all over by Frank Capra's artistry.' – *Howard Barnes*

The State of Things *

US/Portugal 1982 120m bw

Artificial Eye/Road Movies/Pro-Ject/ZDF/Musidora/ Film International (Chris Sievernich)

original title: *Der Stand Der Dinge*

A film director tracks down in Los Angeles the producer who abandoned him and his film crew in Portugal.

A sort of B movie about the making of a B movie and a reflection on the meaning of cinema, within the loose format of a thriller.

w Wim Wenders, Robert Kramer *d* Wim Wenders *ph* Henri Alekan, Martin Schafer, Fred Murphy *m* Jurgen Knieper *ad* Ze Branco *ed* Barbara von Weitershausen, Peter Przygodda

☆ Isabelle Weingarten, Rebecca Pauly, Patrick Bauchau, Paul Getty III, Samuel Fuller, Roger Corman, Allen Goorwitz

State Secret **

GB 1950 104m bw

British Lion/London (Frank Launder, Sidney Gilliat)

US title: *The Great Manhunt*

In a Ruritanian country, spies pursue a surgeon, the only man who knows that the dictator is dead.

Hitchcockian chase comedy-thriller which is well detailed and rises to the heights on occasion.

wd Sidney Gilliat *novel Appointment with Fear* by Roy Huggins *ph* Robert Krasker *m* William Alwyn *ed* Thelma Myers

☆ *Douglas Fairbanks Jnr, Glynis Johns, Herbert Lom, Jack Hawkins*, Walter Rilla, Karel Stepanek, Carl Jaffe

'An admirably fast-moving diversion in the Hitchcock tradition.' – *Richard Mallett, Punch*

'One of the best thrillers a British studio (any studio, for that matter) has made for years.' – *Leonard Mosley*

State's Attorney *

US 1932 79m bw

RKO

GB title: *Cardigan's Last Case*

A prosecuting counsel nearly pays the penalty for arrogance.

Good star melodrama.

w Rowland Brown, Gene Fowler *d* George Archainbaud

☆ John Barrymore, Jill Esmond, William Boyd, Helen Twelvetrees

'Good programme box office stuff if not particularly smashing.' – *Variety*

Static

US 1986 93m colour

Necessity Films (Amy Ness)

An unemployed young man invents a device for displaying images of heaven on a television set, but he is the only one able to see them.

A desultory variation on the fable of the Emperor's new clothes, in which it is assumed that eccentricity is interesting and amusing; here, it isn't.

w Keith Gordon, Mark Romanek *d* Mark Romanek *ph* Jeff Jur *pd* Cynthia Sowder *ed* Emily Paine

☆ Keith Gordon, Amanda Plummer, Bob Gunton, Lily Knight, Barton Heyman, Reathel Bean

Station Six Sahara

GB 1962 101m bw

British Lion/CCC/Artur Brauner (Victor Lyndon)

Five men working on a remote Saharan pipeline quarrel over the favours of an American girl whose car crashes nearby.

Raging old-fashioned melodrama with the courage of its lack of convictions.

w Bryan Forbes, Brian Clemens *d* Seth Holt *ph* Gerald Gibbs *m* Ron Grainer

☆ Carroll Baker, Ian Bannen, Peter Van Eyck, Denholm Elliott, Mario Adorf, Jorg Felmy, Biff McGuire

Station West

US 1948 91m bw

RKO (Robert Sparks)

A saloon queen is the secret head of a gang of gold robbers.

Predictable but well-made Western patterned after Destry Rides Again.

w Frank Fenton, Winston Miller *novel* Luke Short *d* Sidney Lanfield *ph* Harry J. Wild *m* Heinz Roemheld

☆ Dick Powell, Jane Greer, Agnes Moorehead, Burl Ives, Tom Powers, Gordon Oliver, Steve Brodie, Guinn Williams, Raymond Burr, Regis Toomey

'The face was his ... the body was his ... but suddenly, Hello, Charlie!'

The Statue

GB 1970 89m Eastmancolor

Cinerama/Josef Shaftel (Anis Nohra)

A languages professor is embarrassed when his sculptress wife makes an immense nude statue of him – with someone else's private parts.

Strained phallic comedy which doesn't even make the most of its one joke.

w Alec Coppel, Denis Norden *d* Rod Amateau *ph* Piero Portalupi *m* Riz Ortolani

☆ David Niven, Virna Lisi, Robert Vaughn, Ann Bell, John Cleese, Hugh Burden

Stay Away Joe

US 1968 102m Metrocolor Panavision

MGM (Douglas Lawrence)

An Indian rodeo rider returns to his reservation, makes several romantic conquests, and helps a government rehabilitation scheme.

Thin if surprising vehicle for a singing star; all rather tedious.

w Michael A. Hoey *novel* Dan Cushman *d* Peter Tewkesbury *ph* Fred Koenekamp *m* Jack Marshall

☆ Elvis Presley, Burgess Meredith, Joan Blondell, Katy Jurado, Thomas Gomez, Henry Jones, L. Q. Jones

Stay Hungry

US 1976 102m DeLuxe

UA/Outov (Harold Schneider, Bob Rafelson)

The heir to an Alabama estate annoys the locality by assembling a curious bunch of friends and making unexpected use of his money.

Rather obvious and pointless fable; well made but not very stimulating.

w Charles Gaines, Bob Rafelson *novel* Charles Gaines *d* Bob Rafelson *ph* Victor Kemper *m* Bruce Langhorne, Byron Berline

☆ Jeff Bridges, Sally Field, Arnold Schwarzenegger, R. G. Armstrong, Robert Englund, Roger E. Mosley

'The picture isn't just unsatisfying, it's a mess.' – *Stanley Kauffmann*

Stay Tuned

US 1992 87m Technicolor

Warner/Morgan Creek (James G. Robinson)

A couple are trapped in a cable television system run by the Devil.

An unsuccessful send-up of obsessive television viewing, mainly because it picks targets, such as Wayne's World, *that are beyond parody.*

w Tom S. Parker, Jim Jennewein *d* Peter Hyams *ph* Peter Hyams *m* Bruce Broughton *pd* Philip Harrison *ed* Peter E. Berger *sp* Rhythm and Hues Inc.

☆ John Ritter, Pam Dawber, Jeffrey Jones, David Thom, Heather McComb, Bob Dishy

'High class trash ... redeemed by a manic script, good special effects and production values.' – *Sheila Johnston, Independent*

'A picture with nothing for everybody.' – *Variety*

'It's five years later for Tony Manero. The fever still burns!'

Staying Alive

US 1983 96m Metrocolor

Paramount/Robert Stigwood/Cinema Group Venture (Sylvester Stallone)

Tony Manero becomes a Broadway dancer.

Fragile sequel to Saturday Night Fever, *with some of its frenetic quality but none of its impact.*

w Sylvester Stallone, Norman Wexler *d* Sylvester Stallone *ph* Nick McLean *m* Johnny Mandel, Robin Garb, others *pd* Robert Boyle

☆ John Travolta, Cynthia Rhodes, Finola Hughes, Steve Inwood, Julie Bovasso

'By turns exhilarating and absurd.' – *Nick Roddick, MFB*

'Stallone doesn't bother much with character, scenes or dialogue. He just puts the newly muscle-plated Travolta in front of the camera, covers him with what looks like oil slick, and goes for the whambams.' – *Pauline Kael, New Yorker*

Staying Together

US 1989 91m CFI color

Hemdale (Joseph Fuery)

Three brothers growing up in a small town experience the pangs of requited love.

Exuberant but corny tale of family relationships.

w Monte Merrick *d* Lee Grant *ph* Dick Bush *m* Miles Goodman *pd* Stuart Wurtzel *ed* Katherine Wenning

☆ Sean Astin, Stockard Channing, Melinda Dillon, Jim Haynie, Levon Helm, Dinah Manoff, Dermot Mulroney, Tim Quill

'Whips up the clichés and homilies of American small-town melodrama without adding the slightest spice.' – *Geoff Brown, MFB*

'A tale of kidnapping, computer fraud and Morris Minors.'

The Steal

GB 1994 91m Eastmancolor

Warner/Poseidon (Gary Kurtz, Barbara Stone)

An English lawyer and an American computer hacker join forces to rob a corrupt bank.

A bungled attempt to revive the style of Ealing comedy, with little imagination and no attempt to update the genre to match changing social conditions.

wd John Hay *ph* Ronnie Taylor *m* Barry Kirsch *pd* Phil Robertson *ed* David Martin

☆ Alfred Molina, Helen Slater, Peter Bowles, Dinsdale Landen, Stephen Fry, Bryan Pringle, Patricia Hayes, Heathcote Williams

'Frighteningly inept and almost completely lacking in humour or thrills.' – *Empire*

Steal Big, Steal Little

US 1995 134m Technicolor
TCF/Chicago Pacific (Andrew Davis, Fred Caruso)

Twins, one good, one bad, quarrel over the estate left by their adopted mother.
Appalling comedy that gets sillier by the minute, so that by its long-drawn-out conclusion, it is beyond belief; it receives the performances it deserves.
w Andrew Davis, Lee Blessing, Jeanne Blake, Teresa Tucker-Davies *d* Andrew Davis *ph* Frank Tidy *m* William Olvis *pd* Michael Haller *ed* Don Brochu, Tina Hirsch
☆ Andy Garcia, Alan Arkin, Rachel Ticotin, Joe Pantoliano, Holland Taylor, Ally Walker, David Ogden Stiers

'With its slapstick morality and cartoon characterisations, what this vastly unentertaining dud resembles most is an interminable episode of *The Dukes of Hazzard*, complete with the corpulent judges, their weak-minded sidekicks and gold-hearted crooks.' – *Liese Spencer, Sight and Sound*

'The Most Beautiful Place To Be Is Love.'

Stealing Beauty *

Italy/France/GB 1995 118m Technicolor
TCF/Fiction Cinematografica/Recorded Picture/UGC (Jeremy Thomas)

A 19-year-old American girl visits her dead mother's artistic expatriate friends in Italy, determined to discover the identity of her biological father, and to lose her virginity.
Much inconsequential talk, determined ogling of Liv Tyler and languorous perambulations in the Tuscan landscape make for a pretty, but empty, film.
w Susan Minot *story* Bernardo Bertolucci *d* Bernardo Bertolucci *ph* Darius Khondji *m* Richard Hartley *pd* Gianni Silvestri *ed* Pietro Scalia
☆ Sinead Cusack, Jeremy Irons, Jean Marais, Donal McCann, D. W. Moffett, Stefania Sandrelli, Rachel Weisz, Liv Tyler, Carlo Cecchi, Joseph Fiennes, Jason Flemyng

'A richly satisfying chamber piece that is both literary and utterly contemporary.' – *Variety*
'The film is all taste and texture and nothing else. It melts in your mouth and fades from the screen like yesterday's gossip.' – *Tom Shone, Sunday Times*

Stealing Heaven

GB/Yugoslavia 1988 115m colour
Rank/Amy International/Jadran (Simon McCorkindale)

The dying Heloise recalls her love-affair with Abelard.
Pasteboard reproduction of medieval life and love.
w Chris Bryant *novel* Marion Meade *d* Clive Donner *ph* Mikael Salomon *m* Nick Bicat *pd* Voytek Roman *ed* Michael Ellis
☆ Derek de Lint, Kim Thompson, Denholm Elliott, Bernard Hepton, Kenneth Cranham, Patsy Byrne, Cassie Stuart, Philip Locke, Rachel Kempson, Angela Pleasence, Yvonne Bryceland, Mark Jax

Stealing Home

US 1988 98m Technicolor
Warner/Mount (Thom Mount, Hank Moonjean)

Returning home after the suicide of the woman he loved as a youth, a failed baseball player recalls their relationship.
Drab little domestic drama of unfulfilled hopes and desires.
wd Steven Kampmann, Will Aldis *ph* Bobby Byrne *m* David Foster *pd* Vaughan Edwards *ed* Antony Gibbs
☆ Mark Harmon, Blair Brown, Jonathan Silverman, Harold Ramis, William McNamara, Richard Jenkins, John Shea, Jodie Foster, Helen Hunt

Steamboat Bill Jnr *

US 1928 71m (24 fps) bw silent
UA/Buster Keaton/Joseph Schenck

A student takes over his father's old Mississippi steamboat, and wins the daughter of his rival.
Rather flat comedy redeemed by a magnificent cyclone climax.
w Carl Harbaugh, Buster Keaton *d* Charles Riesner *ph* J. Devereaux Jennings, Bert Haines
☆ *Buster Keaton*, Ernest Torrence, Marion Byron

Steamboat Round the Bend *

US 1935 80m bw
TCF (Sol M. Wurtzel)

A Mississippi steamboat captain defeats his rival and finds evidence to clear his nephew of a murder charge.
Rather heavily-scripted star vehicle which sacrifices fun for atmosphere but is often good to look at.
w Dudley Nichols, Lamar Trotti *novel* Ben Lucien Burman *d John Ford* *ph* George Schneiderman *md* Samuel Kaylin
☆ Will Rogers, Anne Shirley, Eugene Pallette, John McGuire, Irvin S. Cobb, Berton Churchill, Stepin Fetchit, Roger Imhof, Raymond Hatton

'Will Rogers' final picture ... in the money despite a drab theme.' – *Variety*

Steaming

GB 1985 95m colour
Paul Mills/World Film Services/Columbia

Women in a rundown steam bath confide in each other.
Excessively dreary talk piece which apparently seemed crisper on the stage.
w Patricia Losey *play* Nell Dunn *d* Joseph Losey (his last film) *ph* Chris Challis
☆ Vanessa Redgrave, Sarah Miles, Diana Dors, Patti Love, Brenda Bruce

'It cannot be denied that it is very British. The humor is coarse and the outlook grim. It is the work of Nell Dunn and is a shameless feminist and socialist treatise. Whether these qualities rank as vices or virtues is, of course, a matter of taste.' – *Quentin Crisp*

Steel

US 1979 101m Movielab
Columbia/Panzer/Davis/Fawcett-Majors (Lee Majors)

When a construction boss is killed, his daughter vows to complete his last project.
Flashy, foul-mouthed, but basically old-fashioned hokum climaxing in a race to complete before foreclosure.
w Leigh Chapman *d* Steve Carver *ph* Roger Shearman *m* Michel Colombier *pd* Ward Preston
☆ Lee Majors, Jennifer O'Neill, Art Carney, George Kennedy, Harris Yulin, Terry Kiser, Richard Lynch, Albert Salmi

Steel

US 1997 97m Technicolor
Warner (Quincy Jones, David Salzman, Joel Simon)

A former army weapons expert devises a steel suit so that he can keep the streets free from teenage hoodlums.
Tepid, preachy action film, missing by miles its target audience of the young.
wd Kenneth Johnson *characters created by* Louise Simonson, Jon Bogdanove *ph* Mark Irwin *m* Mervyn Warren *pd* Gary Wissner *ed* John F. Link
☆ Shaquille O'Neal, Annabeth Gish, Judd Nelson, Richard Roundtree, Irma P. Hall, Ray J., Charles Napier

'Too broad and episodic to attract anything other than the most undemanding crowd.' – *Leonard Klady, Variety*

The Steel Bayonet

GB 1957 85m bw Hammerscope
UA/Hammer (Michael Carreras)

During the assault on Tunis a battle-weary platoon holds a farm against enemy attack.
Dreary cliché-ridden war melodrama, peopled by all the usual types.
w Howard Clewes *d* Michael Carreras *ph* Jack Asher *m* Leonard Salzedo *ad* Ted Marshall *ed* Bill Lenny
☆ Leo Genn, Kieron Moore, Michael Medwin, Robert Brown, Michael Ripper, John Paul, Bernard Horsfall

Steel Magnolias *

US 1989 117m Technicolor
Columbia TriStar/Rastar/Ray Stark

A group of women, who gather in a small-town beauty parlour, face up to life's vicissitudes.
Slickly made, sentimental account of marriage and motherhood that provides some meaty roles for the assembled actresses.
w Robert Harling *play* Robert Harling *d* Herbert Ross *ph* John A. Alonzo *m* Georges Delerue *pd* Gene Callahan, Edward Pisoni *ed* Paul Hirsch
☆ Sally Field, Dolly Parton, Shirley MacLaine, Daryl Hannah, Olympia Dukakis, Julia Roberts, Tom Skerritt, Sam Shepard

'A lush, excruciatingly elongated emotional wallow.' – *Tom Milne, MFB*

Julia Roberts

Steel Town

US 1952 84m Technicolor
U-I (Leonard Goldstein)

A steel president's nephew joins the company as a furnace hand.
Routine drama with an unusual background.
w Gerald Drayson Adams, Lou Breslow *d* George Sherman *ph* Charles P. Boyle *m* Joseph Gershenson *ad* Robert Clatworthy, Bernard Herzbrun *ed* Ted J. Kent
☆ Ann Sheridan, John Lund, Howard Duff, James Best, Nancy Kulp

The Steel Trap *

US 1952 85m bw
TCF/Thor (Bert E. Friedlob)

An assistant bank manager steals half a million dollars from the vault but is troubled by conscience and manages to put it back before the loss is discovered.
Solidly competent little suspenser with plenty of movement.
wd Andrew Stone *ph* Ernest Laszlo *m* Dimitri Tiomkin
☆ Joseph Cotten, Teresa Wright, Jonathan Hale, Walter Sande

Steelyard Blues

US 1972 92m Technicolor
Warner/S. B. Productions (Tony Bill, Michael and Julia Phillips)

An ex-con and his call-girl friend are an embarrassment to his DA brother.
Bits and pieces of anti-establishment comedy are tacked on to a thin plot; a few of them work.
w David S. Ward *d* Alan Myerson *ph* Laszlo Kovacs, Steven Larner *m* Nick Gravenites
☆ Donald Sutherland, Jane Fonda, Peter Boyle, Howard Hesseman

Stella

US 1990 109m colour
Rank/Samuel Goldwyn Company/Touchstone (David V. Picker)

A waitress makes sacrifices so that her illegitimate daughter can escape from the working class.
Outmoded soap opera that fails to achieve the tears provoked by the two earlier film versions.
w Robert Getchell *novel* *Stella Dallas* by Olive Higgins Prouty *d* John Erman *ph* Billy Williams *m* John Morris *pd* James Hulsey *ed* Jerrold L. Ludwig, Bud Molin, Lisa M. Citron
☆ Bette Midler, John Goodman, Trini Alvarado, Stephen Collins, Marsha Mason, Eileen Brennan, Linda Hart

'Bette Midler deserves better than this heap of cornball slush.' – *John Coldstream, Daily Telegraph*

Stella Dallas *

US 1925 110m approx (24 fps) bw silent
Samuel Goldwyn

An uncouth woman loses both husband and daughter.
Standard weepie complete with 'out into the cold cold snow' ending, but handled here with tact and discretion. A seminal film of its time.
w Frances Marion *novel* Olive Higgins Prouty *d* Henry King *ph* Arthur Edeson
☆ Belle Bennett, Ronald Colman, Lois Moran, Jean Hersholt, Douglas Fairbanks Jnr, Alice Joyce

'A sad film, but sad with the curious quality of sadness that leaves only happiness in its train. We, watching it, are happy to be so sad. We find here a vicarious courage; a fidelity and a generous understanding that by proxy become ours.' – C. A. *Lejeune*

Stella Dallas *

US 1937 106m bw
Samuel Goldwyn

Fashionable remake with excellent talent; 1937 audiences came to sneer and stayed to weep.
w Victor Heerman, Sarah Y. Mason *d King Vidor* *ph* Rudolph Maté *m* Alfred Newman
☆ Barbara Stanwyck, John Boles, Anne Shirley, Barbara O'Neil, Alan Hale, Marjorie Main, Tim Holt

'A tear-jerker of A ranking. There are things about the story that will not appeal to some men, but no one will be annoyed or offended by it. And the wallop is inescapably there for femmes.' – *Variety*

† Goldwyn's premier choices for the lead were Ruth Chatterton and Gladys George.

Barbara Stanwyck; Anne Shirley

Stella Does Tricks *

GB 1996 99m Metrocolor
BFI/Channel 4/Compulsive/Sidewalk (Adam Barker)

A Scottish teenage prostitute in London manages to escape from her abusive pimp and begins a relationship with a heroin addict.
Austerely truthful film of masculine exploitation, of people trapped in a cycle of deprivation; it is not without a bleak humour.
w A. L. Kennedy *d* Coky Giedroyc *ph* Barry Ackroyd *m* Nick Bicat *pd* Lynne Whiteread *ed* Budge Tremlett
☆ Kelly Macdonald, James Bolam, Hans Matheson, Ewan Stewart, Lindsay Henderson

The Stendhal Syndrome

Italy 1996 119m Technicolor
Medusa/Cine 2000 (Dario Argento, Giuseppe Colombo)

original title: *La Sindrome di Stendhal*

A serial killer repeatedly rapes the female detective investigating him, who has the habit of fainting when confronted by great works of art.
Risible thriller that becomes increasingly silly; although its quota of gore is low by its director's standards, it has some unpleasant moments.
wd Dario Argento *inspired by La Sindrome di Stendhal* by Graziella Magherini *ph* Giuseppe Rotunno *m* Ennio Morricone *ad* Antonello Geleng *ed* Angelo Nicolini *sp* Sergio Stivaletti
☆ Asia Argento, Thomas Kretschmann, Marco Leonardi, Luigi Diberti, Paolo Bonacelli, Julien Lambroschini, John Quentin

'The film that finally proves beyond any reasonable argument that Dario Argento has finally lost it.' – *The Dark Side*

Step by Step *

US 1946 62m bw
RKO (Sid Rogell)

The FBI gives chase to a young couple who may or may not have stolen government plans.
Trim second feature melodrama with nice touches.
w Stuart Palmer *d* Phil Rosen
☆ Lawrence Tierney, Anne Jeffreys, Lowell Gilmore, George Cleveland, Jason Robards

Step Down to Terror

US 1959 76m bw
U-I (Joseph Gershenson)

GB title: *The Silent Stranger*

A man returns to his home town and is discovered to be a psychopathic killer on the run.
Dismal reworking of Shadow of a Doubt; *strictly second feature stuff.*
w Mel Dinelli, Czenzi Ormonde, Chris Cooper *d* Harry Keller *ph* Russell Metty *m* Joseph Gershenson
☆ Charles Drake, Colleen Miller, Rod Taylor, Josephine Hutchinson, Jocelyn Brando

Step Lively *

US 1944 88m bw
RKO (Robert Fellows)

Gleaming musical remake of *Room Service* (qv); all very efficient if witless.

w Warren Duff, Peter Milne *d* Tim Whelan *ph* Robert de Grasse *md* Constantin Bakaleinikoff *ad* Albert S. D'Agostino, Carroll Clark *songs* Jule Styne, Sammy Cahn
☆ Frank Sinatra, George Murphy, Adolphe Menjou, Gloria de Haven, Anne Jeffreys, Walter Slezak, Eugene Pallette
art direction

Step Lively, Jeeves
US 1937 69m bw
TCF (John Stone)
Two confidence tricksters attempt to persuade an English valet that he is heir to the fortune of Sir Francis Drake.
Broad and raucous farce with a gullible Jeeves who bears little resemblance to P. G. Wodehouse's creation of the imperturbable gentleman's gentleman.
w Frank Fenton, Lynn Root *story* Frances Hyland *d* Eugene Forde *ph* Daniel Clark *md* Samuel Kaylin *ad* Duncan Cramer *ed* Fred Allen
☆ Arthur Treacher, Patricia Ellis, Robert Kent, Alan Dinehart, George Givot, Helen Flint, Franklin Pangborn

Stepfather: see *Beau-Père (1981)*

The Stepfather
US 1986 88m CFI color
Jay Benson/Vista/New World
A teenage girl discovers that her new stepfather is a psychopath who may make her his victim.
Well enough done but rather obvious suspenser on the lines of Love from a Stranger.
w Donald E. Westlake *story* Brian Garfield *d* Joseph Ruben *ph* John Lindley *m* Patrick Moraz
☆ Terry O'Quinn, Jill Schoelen, Shelley Hack, Charles Lanyer
'A one-joke movie, but the joke is wonderfully subversive ... It's not the culture's violence that drives people mad, but its fake harmony – especially the sunny world of TV sitcoms, where every crisis is handily resolved.' – *David Edelstein, Village Voice*

'There's Something You Should Know About My Past.'
Stepfather II
US 1989 86m colour
ITC (Darin Scott, William Burr)
A mass murderer escapes from an asylum and sets up as a psychiatrist so that he can discover a ready-made family to take over.
A limp sequel that lacks suspense and offers no more than a predictable re-run of the original.
w John Auerbach *d* Jeff Burr *ph* Jacek Laskus *m* Jim Manzie, Pat Regan *pd* Byrnadette Disanto *ed* Pasquale A. Buba
☆ Terry O'Quinn, Meg Foster, Caroline Williams, Jonathan Brandis, Henry Brown, Mitchell Laurance
† It was followed by a made-for-TV movie, *Stepfather III*, which provided little variation on the original plot.

The Stepford Wives *
US 1974 115m TVC Color
Fadsin/Palomar (Edgar J. Sherick)
A new wife in a commuter village outside New York finds all her female friends too good to be true ... because their husbands have had them replaced by computerized models.
An attractive idea which needs a much lighter and pacier touch but entertains in patches and shows agreeable sophistication.
w William Goldman *novel* Ira Levin *d* Bryan Forbes *ph* Owen Roizman *m* Michael Small *pd* Gene Callahan
☆ Katharine Ross, Paula Prentiss, Nanette Newman, Peter Masterson, Patrick O'Neal, Tina Louise, William Prince
'It was hard to tell Katharine Ross playing a robot from Katharine Ross playing a normal housewife.' – *Les Keyser, Hollywood in the Seventies*
'The first women's lib gothic – hardly the landmark the world had been waiting for.' – *Pauline Kael, New Yorker*

Stephen King's IT
US 1990 180m colour
Lorimar (Matthew O'Connor)
Childhood friends gather after 30 years to rid their home town of a murderous evil spirit.
Overlong, indifferently acted, predictably scripted TV mini-series transferred to video.
w Lawrence D. Cohen, Tommy Lee Wallace *novel* IT by Stephen King *d* Tommy Lee Wallace *ph* Richard Leiterman *m* Richard Bellis *pd* Douglas Higgins *ed* Robert F. Shugrue, David Blangsted
☆ Harry Anderson, Dennis Christopher, Richard Masur, Annette O'Toole, Tim Reid, John Ritter, Richard Thomas, Tim Curry, Olivia Hussey

Stephen King's Thinner
US 1996 92m DeLuxe
Paramount/Spelling (Richard P. Rubinstein, Mitchell Galin)
An overweight lawyer, who is cursed by a gypsy king after he has run over his daughter, begins to get thinner and thinner ...
Tedious little fable that claims to be about 'moral culpability', but simply shows its makers' lack of understanding and imagination.
w Tom Holland, Michael McDowell *novel* Stephen King *d* Tom Holland *ph* Kees Van Oostrum *m* Daniel Licht *pd* Laurence Bennett *ed* Marc Laub *sp* Greg Cannom
☆ Robert John Burke, Joe Mantegna, Michael Constantine, Lucinda Jenney, Kari Wuhrer, John Horton, Stephen King
'There's nothing particularly fresh in this routinely crafted, banally scripted and directed effort.' – *Leonard Klady, Variety*

Stepkids: see *Big Girls Don't Cry ... They Get Even*

'Be There For The Joy. Be There For The Tears. Be There For Each Other.'
Stepmom
US 1998 124m Technicolor Panavision
Columbia/1492 (Wendy Finerman, Chris Columbus, Mark Radcliffe, Michael Barnathan)
A divorced mother is scornful of her ex-husband's new girlfriend until she is diagnosed with cancer and needs help.
It is sometimes difficult to imagine what Hollywood scriptwriters would do without a terminal illness to fall back on: it provides opportunity for sentimentality, redemption, reconciliation and big gestures, all of which are too much in evidence here.
w Gigi Levangie, Jessie Nelson, Steven Rogers, Karen Leigh Hopkins, Ron Bass *d* Chris Columbus *ph* Donald M. McAlpine *m* John Williams *pd* Stuart Wurtzel *ed* Neil Travis
☆ Julia Roberts, Susan Sarandon, Ed Harris, Jena Malone, Liam Aiken, Lynn Whitfield, Darrell Larson, Mary Louise Wilson
'Tears are jerked with strenuously sincere calculation ... which sees some very talented thesps working over the most mawkish conventions as if they were freshly minted ... not a single cliché of the modern feel-good tragic melodrama genre has gone unturned, resulting in a soggy heart-tugger.' – *Todd McCarthy, Variety*

Steppin' in Society
US 1945 72m bw
Republic (Joseph Bercholtz)
A judge is caught in a storm and takes refuge in a low club frequented by criminals.
Uncertain comedy which never really works.
w Bradford Ropes *novel* Marcel Arnac *d* Alexander Esway
☆ Edward Everett Horton, Gladys George, Ruth Terry, Robert Livingston, Jack La Rue, Lola Lane

'Your dreams are just a step away.'
Stepping Out
US 1991 110m Technicolor
UIP/Paramount (Lewis Gilbert)
A tap-dance teacher attempts to prepare a class of amateurs for a charity performance.
Mundane and old-fashioned drama that lacks precision.
w Richard Harris *play* Richard Harris *d* Lewis Gilbert *ph* Alan Hume *m* Peter Matz *ch* Danny Daniels *pd* Peter Mullins *ed* Humphrey Dixon
☆ Liza Minnelli, Shelley Winters, Robyn Stevan, Jane Krakowski, Bill Irwin, Ellen Greene, Sheila McCarthy, Andrea Martin, Julie Walters, Carol Woods, Luke Reilly

'The man, the music, the murder.'
Stepping Razor Red X *
Canada 1992 92m Fujicolour
Feature Film/SC Entertainment (Edgar Egger)
Documentary on the life and violent death, in 1987, of Jamaican Rastafarian reggae singer Peter Tosh, using some concert performances and tapes he recorded, which he intended to use as the basis of his autobiography, to be called *Red X*, after the cross in red ink he saw after his name on official documents, showing where he should put his signature, but which he interpreted as indicating that he was being singled out.
Interesting, if inconclusive, investigation of the reasons for Tosh's murder: was it a robbery or a politically motivated hit? Tosh's own, often bitter, paranoid and rambling commentary, couched in apocalyptical language, adds another layer of mystification.
wd Nicholas Campbell *ph* Edgar Egger *ed* Trevor Ambrose
'For all the stridency of his ideas and of his music, Peter Tosh remains a phantom beyond this film's grasp.' – *Sight and Sound*

Steptoe and Son
GB 1972 98m Technicolor
EMI/Associated London Films (Aida Young)
Harold gets married, mislays his wife but thinks he is a father.
Strained attempt to transfer the TV rag-and-bone comedy (which in the US became Sanford and Son*) to the big screen. Not the same thing at all.*
w Ray Galton, Alan Simpson *d* Cliff Owen *ph* John Wilcox *m* Roy Budd, Jack Fishman
☆ Wilfrid Brambell, Harry H. Corbett, Carolyn Seymour, Arthur Howard, Victor Maddern
† *Steptoe and Son Ride Again*, which followed in 1973, was even more crude and out of character.

Steptoe and Son Ride Again
GB 1973 99m Technicolor
MGM/EMI/Associated London Films (Aida Young)
Sent out to buy a new horse, Harold spends the family savings on a greyhound that won't run.
Dim, coarse comedy that long overstays its welcome.
w Ray Galton, Alan Simpson *d* Peter Sykes *ph* Ernie Steward *m* Roy Budd, Jack Fishman, Ron Grainer *ad* Bernard Sarron *ed* Bernard Gribble
☆ Wilfrid Brambell, Harry H. Corbett, Diana Dors, Milo O'Shea, Neil McCarthy, Bill Maynard, George Tovey, Sam Kydd, Yootha Joyce, Henry Woolf, Geoffrey Bayldon, Frank Thornton
'Retains the trappings but none of the subtlety or intimacy of the original TV series ... sacrificed to the demands of the basic British screen comedy with its emphasis on lavatories, booze, breasts and (curiously enough) the hilarity of death.' – *Clyde Jeavons, MFB*

The Sterile Cuckoo
US 1969 107m Technicolor
Paramount/Boardwalk (Alan J. Pakula)
GB title: *Pookie*
A talkative but insecure college girl has her first sexual adventures.
Rather tiresome comedy drama with good scenes; general handling far too restrained.
w Alvin Sargent *novel* John Nicholson *d* Alan J. Pakula *ph* Milton Krasner *m* Fred Karlin
☆ Liza Minnelli, Tim McIntire, Wendell Burton, Austin Green, Sandra Faison
song 'Come Saturday Morning' (*m* Fred Karlin, *ly* Dory Previn); Liza Minnelli

Stevie *
US/GB 1978 102m Technicolor
First Artists/Grand Metropolitan (Robert Enders)
An account of the uneventful life of poetess Stevie Smith, lived out mainly in a London suburb under the fear of death.
Claustrophobic showcase for a whimsical lady; interesting for some specialized audiences.
w Hugh Whitemore *play* Hugh Whitemore *d* Robert Enders *ph* Freddie Young *m* Marcus Gowers
☆ Glenda Jackson, *Mona Washbourne*, Trevor Howard, Alec McCowen

Stick
US 1985 109m Technicolor
Universal/Jennings Lang (Robert Daley)
A hardboiled ex-con goes to Miami's low-life district in search of the man who killed his friend.
Wearisome crime melodrama with too many pauses for the hero's self-examination.
w Elmore Leonard, Joseph C. Stinson *novel* Elmore Leonard *d* Burt Reynolds *ph* Nick McLean *m* Barry de Vorzon, Joseph Conlan
☆ Burt Reynolds, Candice Bergen, George Segal, Charles Durning
'Plot is of the convoluted kind beloved by exhibitors since patrons can wander out for popcorn and come back without missing anything.' – *Variety*

The Stick Up
GB 1977 101m colour
Backstage (Elliott Kastner, Danny O'Donovan)
In Devon in 1935, an American gives a lift to a café waitress and finds she is a thief on the run.
Numbingly peculiar comedy melodrama which tries too hard to have any chance of succeeding.
wd Jeffrey Bloom *ph* Michael Reed *m* Michael J. Lewis
☆ David Soul, Pamela McMyler, Johnny Wade, Michael Balfour
'The worst film of this or possibly any year.' – *Barry Took, Punch*

'Playing the Shots. Covering the Angles. Waiting for the Big Break.'
Stickmen
New Zealand 2001 96m
Portman/NZFC/Film2/Stick (Michelle Turner)
Three friends try to save the closure of their favourite bar by entering a pool tournament run by gangsters.
Unoriginal comedy thriller under the influence of Lock, Stock and Two Smoking Barrels.
w Nick Ward *d* Hamish Rothwell *ph* Nigel Bluck *m* House of Downtown *pd* Neville Stevenson *ed* Owen Ferrier-Kerr
☆ Robbie Magasiva (Jack), Scott Wills (Wayne), Paolo Rotondo (Thomas), Simone Kessell (Karen), Anne Nordhaus (Sara), John Leigh (Dave), Enrico Mammarella (Daddy), Kirk Torrance (Holden)
'A lot less to it than meets the eye... A waste of an attractive young cast bursting with energy.' – *Sight and Sound*

Sticky Fingers
US 1988 88m DuArt
Virgin/Hightop/Spectrafilm (Catlin Adams, Melanie Mayron)
Two struggling musicians spend a fortune left with them for safe keeping by a drug dealer.
Lacklustre comedy without enough wit to keep it alive.
w Catlin Adams, Melanie Mayron *d* Catlin Adams *ph* Gary Thieltges *m* Gary Chang *ed* Bob Reitano
☆ Helen Slater, Melanie Mayron, Danitra Vance, Eileen Brennan, Carol Kane, Loretta Devine, Stephen McHattie, Christopher Guest

Stiff Upper Lips
GB 1997 94m Metrocolor
Cavalier/Impact/Chrysalis/Yorkshire (Jeremy Bolt, Gary Sinyor)
An upper-class girl, who falls for a working-class boy, is taken by her aunt on trips to Italy and India.
A joke-stuffed send-up of Merchant Ivory's period dramas that occasionally raises a smile or three.
w Paul Simpkin, Gary Sinyor, Stephen Deitch, Richard Sparks *d* Gary Sinyor *ph* Simon Archer *m* David A. Hughes, John Murphy *pd* Mike Grant *ed* Peter Hollywood
☆ Peter Ustinov, Prunella Scales, Georgina Cates, Samuel West, Sean Pertwee, Brian Glover, Frank Finlay, Robert Portal, Richard Braine
'Terrible even as pastiche.' – *Gaby Wood, Guardian*

'It Will Scare The Hell Into You.'
Stigmata
US 1999 103m colour
MGM (Frank Mancuso)

A Catholic priest investigates when an irreligious Pittsburg hairdresser shows the weeping wounds of Christ on her hands and feet.
A good-looking, though irredeemably silly, horror movie that follows somewhat wanly in the footsteps of The Exorcist.
w Tom Lazarus, Rick Ramage *d* Rupert Wainwright *ph* Jeffrey L. Kimball *m* Billy Corgan, Elia Cmiral, Mike Garson *pd* Waldemar Kalinowski *ed* Michael R. Miller, Michael J. Duthie *sp* make-up: Ve Neill
☆ Patricia Arquette (Frankie Paige), Gabriel Byrne (Father Kiernan), Jonathan Pryce (Cardinal Houseman), Nia Long (Donna Chadway), Thomas Kopache (Father Durning), Rade Sherbedgia (Marion Petrocelli), Enrico Colantoni (Father Dario), Dick Latessa (Father Delmonico), Portia de Rossi (Jennifer Kelliho), Patrick Muldoon (Steven), Ann Cusack (Dr Reston)
'Whips up an entertaining hysteria of stylistic overkill, tittersome dialogue and giddily outlandish situations.' – *David Rooney, Variety*

Stiletto
US 1969 99m Berkeley-Pathé
Avco/Harold Robbins (Norman Rosemont)
A wealthy playboy racing driver is in fact a Mafia executioner.
Dreary, violent, fashionable Mafioso melodrama with international jet set trimmings.
w A. J. Russell *novel* Harold Robbins *d* Bernard Kowalski *ph* Jack Priestley *m* Sid Ramin
☆ Alex Cord, Britt Ekland, Barbara McNair, Patrick O'Neal, Joseph Wiseman, John Dehner, Eduardo Ciannelli, Roy Scheider
'Cardboard characters crumpled by a script which deals exclusively in clichés.' – *Sight and Sound*

Stiletto Dance
US 2001 97m colour
TVA/Chesler/Perlmutter (Robert Wertheimer)
GB title: *Gangsta's Paradise*
In Buffalo, NY, undercover cops become hired killers after they infiltrate a Russian gang planning to sell nuclear equipment.
Uninteresting drama, marked by gratuitous violence and cliché-ridden dialogue and situations.
w Alfonse Ruggiero *d* Mario Azzopardi *ph* Pierre Jodoin *m* Gary Koftinoff *pd* Paola Ridolfi *ed* Glenn Berman
☆ Eric Roberts (Kit Adrian), Romano Orzari (Jay Flowers), Shawn Doyle (Anton Seaberg), Lucie Laurier (Lena), Yaphet Kotto (Captain Rick Sands), Brett Porter (Rolfe), Justin Louis (James Launcher)

'100 watts too loud. 50 pills too many. 20 years too late?'
Still Crazy **
GB/US 1998 95m colour
Columbia (Amanda Marmot)
After 21 years away, a rock group of the 70s gets together again for a concert appearance.
Amiable comedy that pokes gentle fun at ageing rockers and their followers.
w Dick Clements, Ian La Frenais *d* Brian Gibson *ph* Ashley Rowe *m* Clive Langer *pd* Max Gottlieb *ed* Peter Boyle
☆ Stephen Rea, Billy Connolly, Jimmy Nail, Timothy Spall, Bill Nighy, Juliet Aubrey, Helena Bergström, Hans Matheson, Phil Daniels, Frances Barber, Phil Davis
'Though cinematically unadventurous, this is brilliantly observed and perfectly pitched. Every scene is a joy, every line one to remember.' – *Neil Jeffries, Empire*

Still of the Night *
US 1982 91m Technicolor
MGM/UA (Arlene Donovan)
A psychiatrist finds himself in danger when one of his patients is murdered.
Hitchcock-style mystery melodrama with the villain fairly well concealed ... but somehow not very entertaining. The actors all take their characters too seriously.
w Robert Benton, David Newman *d* Robert Benton *ph* Nestor Almendros *m* John Kander *pd* Mel Bourne
☆ Roy Scheider, Meryl Streep, Jessica Tandy, Sara Botsford, Josef Sommer, Joe Grifasi
'A lifeless and frustrating muddle.' – *Steve Jenkins, MFB*

De Stilte Rond Christine M: see *A Question of Silence*

'All it takes is a little confidence!'
The Sting ***
US 1973 129m Technicolor
Universal/Richard Zanuck, David Brown (Tony Bill, Michael S. Phillips)
In twenties Chicago, two con men stage an elaborate revenge on a big time gangster who caused the death of a friend.
Bright, likeable, but overlong, unconvincingly studio-set and casually developed comedy suspenser cashing in on star charisma but riding to enormous success chiefly on its tinkly music and the general lack of simple entertainment.
w David S. Ward *d George Roy Hill ph* Robert Surtees *m* Scott Joplin (arranged by Marvin Hamlisch) *ad* Henry Bumstead
☆ Paul Newman, *Robert Redford*, Robert Shaw, Charles Durning, Ray Walston, Eileen Brennan
'A visually claustrophobic, mechanically plotted movie that's meant to be a roguishly charming entertainment.' – *New Yorker*
'It demonstrates what can happen when a gifted young screenwriter has the good fortune to fall among professionals his second time out.' – *Judith Crist*
'A testament to the value of blue eyes and bright smiles.' – *Les Keyser, Hollywood in the Seventies*
best picture; David S. Ward; George Roy Hill; Marvin Hamlisch
Robert Surtees; Robert Redford

'The con is on – place your bets!'
The Sting 2
US 1983 102m Technicolor
Universal (Jennings Lang)
Lonnegan plots his revenge on the two who stung him in twenties Chicago.
Boring reprise of an overrated movie: though efficiently made, it never catches fire, and the cast is indisputably a second team.
w David S. Ward *d* Jeremy Paul Kagan *ph* Bill Butler *m* Lalo Schifrin *pd* Edward C. Carfagno
☆ Jackie Gleason, Mac Davis, Karl Malden, Oliver Reed, Bert Remsen, Teri Garr
'The vivid minor characters have been squeezed into lifelessness by the python-like plot.' – *Tom Milne, MFB*
Lalo Schifrin

Stingaree
US 1934 76m bw (colour sequence)
RKO (Pandro S. Berman)
An Australian outlaw of the eighties falls for a rancher's daughter.
Unexciting but unobjectionable piece of Robin Hoodery.
w Becky Gardiner *stories* E. W. Hornung *d* William A. Wellman *ph* James Van Trees *m* Max Steiner
☆ Irene Dunne, Richard Dix, Mary Boland, Conway Tearle, Andy Devine, Henry Stephenson, Una O'Connor, Reginald Owen, Snub Pollard, George Barraud
'Should bring medium results. It does not promise to rise to greater heights.' – *Variety*

Stir Crazy
US 1980 111m Metrocolor
Columbia/Hannah Weinstein
Two New Yorkers heading for California to try their luck are wrongly convicted of a bank robbery but plan escape from prison.
Extended farce giving rather too free rein to its stars' potential for mugging, and polishing up every prison gag in the book.
w Bruce Jay Friedman *d* Sidney Poitier *ph* Fred Schuler *m* Tom Scott *pd* Alfred Sweeney
☆ Gene Wilder, Richard Pryor, Georg Stanford Brown, JoBeth Williams

'In every mind there is a door that has never been opened.'
Stir of Echoes *
US 1999 99m colour
TCF/Artisan
After he has been hypnotised, a man begins to experience visions and sees the ghost of a murdered child.
Muddled supernatural thriller that is at its best when concentrating on the normal: the relationship of an unfulfilled working-class man, who is finding it difficult to cope with life, and his concerned wife.
wd David Koepp *novel* Richard Matheson *ph* Fred Murphy *m* James Newton Howard *pd* Nelson Coates *ed* Jill Savitt
☆ Kevin Bacon (Tom Witzky), Kathryn Erbe (Maggie Witzky), Illeana Douglas (Lisa), Liza Weil (Debbie Kozac), Kevin Dunn (Frank McCarthy), Conor O'Farrell (Harry Damon), Jennifer Morrison (Samantha), Zachary David Cope (Jake Witzky), Lisa Lewis (Debbie's Mother), Eddie Bo Smith Jnr (Neil the Cop)
'You can do a lot worse on a Friday night than this.' – *Peter Bradshaw, Guardian*

A Stitch in Time
GB 1963 94m bw
Rank (Hugh Stewart)
A butcher's boy goes into hospital and falls for a nurse.
Thin star slapstick; all one can say is that it's marginally preferable to Jerry Lewis.
w Jack Davies *d* Robert Asher *ph* Jack Asher *m* Philip Green
☆ Norman Wisdom, Edward Chapman, Jerry Desmonde, Jeanette Sterke, Jill Melford

Stockade
US 1990 97m colour
Entertainment/Movie Group/Northern Lights Media Corporation (Richard Davis)
US title: *Count a Lonely Cadence*
A young soldier, sent to the stockade for brawling, is persecuted by a bigoted sergeant in charge.
Uninvolving prison drama.
w Dennis Shryack, Martin Sheen *novel Count a Lonely Cadence* by Gordon Weaver *d* Martin Sheen *ph* Richard Leiterman *m* Georges Delerue *pd* Ian Thomas *ed* Martin Hunter
☆ Charlie Sheen, Martin Sheen, F. Murray Abraham, Larry Fishburne, Blu Mankuma, Michael Beach, Harry Stewart
'Predictably staged, glossily performed, erratically edited, and seems unable to conceal a mood of smug optimism.' – *Philip Strick, MFB*

The Stolen Children **
Italy/France 1992 114m Technicolor
Mayfair/Erre/Alia/RAIDUE/Arena/Vega (Angelo Rizzoli, Stefano Munafo)
original title: *Il Ladro di Bambini*
A young cop travels across Italy to a children's home with an 11-year-old girl, forced to become a prostitute by her mother, and her younger brother.
Tough and compassionate movie that refuses to sensationalize its subject-matter, of adult and official indifference to the sufferings of the young.
w Sandro Petraglia, Stefano Rulli, Gianni Amelio *d Gianni Amelio ph* Tonino Nardi, Renato Tafuri *m* Franco Piersanti *pd* Andrea Crisanti *ed* Simona Paggi
☆ Enrico Lo Verso, Valentina Scalici, Giuseppe Ieracitano, Renato Carpentieri, Vitalba Andrea, Grignani, Massimo de Lorenzo
'Classical humanist cinema, almost in the neo-realist tradition.' – *Derek Malcolm, Guardian*
'Quiet, honest, admirably acted.' – *Philip French, Observer*

Stolen Face
GB 1952 72m bw
Exclusive/Hammer (Michael Hinds)
Via plastic surgery a girl criminal is given another face, which produces a different kind of trouble.
Quickie melodrama which proved fairly popular because of its Hollywood stars.
w Martin Berkeley, Richard Landau *d* Terence Fisher *ph* Walter Harvey *m* Malcolm Arnold
☆ Paul Henreid, Lizabeth Scott, André Morell, John Wood, Susan Stephen, Mary Mackenzie, Arnold Ridley

Stolen Harmony
US 1935 79m bw
Paramount
An ex-con becomes a saxophonist with a band and is suspected of a robbery.
Tedious mix-up of mayhem and music.
w Leon Gordon, Harry Ruskin, Claude Binyon, Lewis Foster *d* Alfred Werker
☆ George Raft, Ben Bernie, Grace Bradley, Iris Adrian, Lloyd Nolan, Ralf Harolde
'Once under way it provides some exciting entertainment; but the poor beginning isn't easily tossed off.' – *Variety*

Stolen Hearts: see *Two If by Sea*

'Its surprise finish will lift you to amazing emotional peaks!'
Stolen Heaven
US 1931 72m bw
Paramount
A boy and girl decide to commit suicide after spending the twenty thousand dollars they've stolen, but neither can go through with it.
A very silly idea, ineptly presented.
w Dana Burnet *d* George Abbott
☆ Nancy Carroll, Phillips Holmes, Louis Calhern, Edward Keane
'It will range down from moderate figures.' – *Variety*

Stolen Heaven
US 1938 88m bw
Paramount
Two jewel thieves in love are harboured on the run by an old concert pianist.
Sentimental melodrama which almost works, with its backing of classical piano pieces.
w Eve Greene, Frederick Jackson, Andrew L. Stone *d* Andrew L. Stone
☆ Gene Raymond, Olympe Bradna, Lewis Stone, Glenda Farrell, Porter Hall, Douglass Dumbrille
'Pleasing entertainment all the way.' – *Variety*

Stolen Holiday
US 1937 82m bw
Warner
A model marries a fortune hunter to protect him from the law.
Slightly unusual romantic drama based on the career of Alexander Stavisky.
w Casey Robinson *d* Michael Curtiz
☆ *Claude Rains*, Kay Francis, Ian Hunter, Alison Skipworth, Charles Halton, Alex D'Arcy

Stolen Hours
GB 1963 97m DeLuxe
UA/Mirisch/Barbican (Denis Holt)
An American divorcee with only a year to live falls in love with her surgeon.
Tired remake of Dark Victory*; pleasant Cornish backgrounds.*
w Jessamyn West *d* Daniel Petrie *ph* Harry Waxman *m* Mort Lindsey
☆ Susan Hayward, Michael Craig, Diane Baker, Edward Judd, Paul Rogers

Stolen Kisses *
France 1968 91m Eastmancolor
Films du Carrosse/Artistes Associés (Marcel Berbert)
original title: *Baisers Volés*
An ineffective young man can find neither work nor love.
A pleasing, rather sad little comedy which has almost the feel of a Keaton; but one is not quite sure at the end what its creator intended.
w François Truffaut, Claude de Givray, Bernard Revon *d* François Truffaut *ph* Denys Clerval *m* Antoine Duhamel
☆ Jean-Pierre Léaud, Delphine Seyrig, Michel Lonsdale, Claude Jade
best foreign film

A Stolen Life *
GB 1939 91m bw
(Paramount) Orion (Anthony Havelock-Allan)
In Brittany, a woman deceives her husband by exchanging identities with her dead twin.
An actress's showcase, quite satisfactorily mounted.
w Margaret Kennedy, George Barraud *novel* Karel J. Benes *d* Paul Czinner *ph* Philip Tannura *m* William Walton

☆ Elisabeth Bergner, Michael Redgrave, Wilfrid Lawson, Richard Ainley, Mabel Terry-Lewis, Clement McCallin

A Stolen Life *
US 1946 107m bw
Warner (Bette Davis)
A twin assumes her sister's identity to be with the man she loves.
Enjoyable if slightly disappointing remake of the British 1939 movie with New England backgrounds.
w Catherine Turney *d* Curtis Bernhardt *ph* Sol Polito, Ernest Haller *m* Max Steiner
☆ Bette Davis, Glenn Ford, Dane Clark, Walter Brennan, Charles Ruggles, Bruce Bennett, Peggy Knudsen, Esther Dale
'A distressingly empty piece of show-off.' – *Bosley Crowther*
'What I'm waiting for is a film about beautiful identical quintuplets who all love the same man.' – *Richard Winnington*

'Drugs, Sex And Murder.'
Stone Cold
US 1992 92m DeLuxe
Columbia TriStar/Stone Group/Mace Neufeld/Yoram Ben Ami/Walter Doniger
A cop goes undercover in Mississippi to investigate a gang of violent bikers who have gone on a killing spree.
Standard action-movie stuff, but done with a little flair, despite its overblown climax.
w Walter Doniger *d* Craig R. Baxley *ph* Alexander Gruszynski *m* Sylvester Levay *pd* John Mansbridge, Richard Johnson *ed* Mark Helfrich, Larry Bock, Edward A. Warschilka Jnr
☆ Brian Bosworth, Lance Henriksen, William Forsythe, Arabella Holzbog, Sam McMurray, Richard Gant, David Tress
'Strictly six-pack fodder.' – *Empire*

Stone Cold Dead
Canada 1979 97m Bellevue-Pathé
Ko-Zak (George Mendeluk, John Ryan)
A tough cop investigates the serial murders of prostitutes.
Beginning with a death, by gunshot in a shower, by a killer who photographs his victims, it attempts a few variations on very familiar themes but fails to establish any rhythm of its own; it also takes much suspension of disbelief to accept Paul Williams as a successful pimp.
wd George Mendeluk *novel* *The Sin Sniper* by Hugh Garner *ph* Dennis Miller *m* Paul James Zaza *ed* Martin Pepler
☆ Richard Crenna, Paul Williams, Linda Sorensen, Belinda J. Montgomery, Monique Mercure, George Chuvalo, Jennifer Dale, Frank Moore

'Take away his badge and he'd top the Ten Most Wanted list!'
The Stone Killer *
US 1973 96m Technicolor
Columbia/Dino de Laurentiis (Michael Winner)
A brutal Los Angeles police detective takes on the Mafia.
Fast-moving amalgam of chases and violence with a downbeat hero.
w Gerald Wilson *novel* *A Complete State of Death* by John Gardner *d* Michael Winner *ph* Richard Moore *m* Roy Budd
☆ Charles Bronson, Martin Balsam, Ralph Waite, David Sheiner, Norman Fell
'Film-making as painting by numbers.' – *Sight and Sound*
'Keeps turning into exciting cinema, crude, often funny and sometimes quite brilliantly idiomatic. It may come as close to inspired primitivism as we are likely to get in the movies these days.' – *Roger Greenspun, New York Times*

'Between maleness and femaleness there is fabulousness.'
Stonewall *
GB 1996 98m Technicolor
Metro Tartan/BBC (Christine Vachon, Ruth Caleb)
A gay man becomes radicalized when he moves from his small town to New York and eventually riots against the police when they raid the Stonewall bar, a seminal moment in the movement for homosexual liberation.
An engaging, low-budget drama of a revolt against oppression, often camp in style, with its focus on drag artistes, and celebrating an unexpected victory.
w Rikki Beadle Blair *book* Martin Duberman *d* Nigel Finch *ph* Chris Seager *m* Michael Kamen, Pat Seymour *pd* Therese DePrez *ed* John Richards
☆ Guillermo Diaz, Frederic Weller, Brendan Corbalis, Duane Boutté, Bruce MacVittie, Peter Ratray, Dwight Ewell, Matthew Faber
'The logistical problems of shooting a gay historical epic for peanuts must have been nightmarish; but, with all due sympathy, the fact remains, the filmmakers haven't solved them.' – *Peter Matthews, Sight and Sound*
'Its energy is positively blithe.' – *Adam Mars-Jones, Independent*

The Stooge
US 1952 100m bw
Paramount/Hal B. Wallis
In 1930 a conceited song and dance man fails to realize that his moronic stooge is the act's real attraction.
Typical, and particularly resistible, Martin and Lewis concoction: whenever one thinks of laughing, a dollop of sentimentality comes along and promptly quashes the idea.
w Fred Finklehoffe, Martin Rackin *d* Norman Taurog *ph* Daniel L. Fapp *m* Joseph J. Lilley
☆ Dean Martin, Jerry Lewis, Polly Bergen, Marie McDonald, Eddie Mayehoff, Marion Marshall, Richard Erdman

Stop Me Before I Kill: see *The Full Treatment*

Stop! Or My Mom Will Shoot
US 1992 87m DeLuxe
UIP/Universal/Northern Lights (Ivan Reitman, Joe Medjuck, Michael C. Gross)
The mother of a Los Angeles cop helps him solve a murder and get back together with his girlfriend.
Lamentable comedy, a failed attempt to extend Stallone's narrow range.
w Blake Snyder, William Osborne, William Davies *d* Roger Spottiswoode *ph* Frank Tidy *m* Alan Silvestri *pd* Charles Rosen *ed* Mark Conte, Lois Freeman-Fox
☆ Sylvester Stallone (Sgt Joe Bomowski), Estelle Getty (Tutti Bomowski), JoBeth Williams (Lt Gwen Harper), Roger Rees (Parnell), Martin Ferrero (Paulie), Gailard Sartain (Munroe), Dennis Burkley (Mitchell), John Wesley (Tony), Al Fann (Lou), Ella Joyce (McCabe), J. Kenneth Campbell (Ross)
'One of those Hollywood films in which the flimsiest of plots buckles under the most obvious of concepts.' – *Lizzie Franke, Sight and Sound*

Stop You're Killing Me
US 1953 86m Warnercolor
Warner (Louis F. Edelman)
At the end of prohibition a beer baron decides to go straight, but finds his house filled with the corpses of rival gangsters.
Frantic remake of A Slight Case of Murder *with a few musical numbers added; all rather messy.*
w James O'Hanlon *d* Roy del Ruth *ph* Ted McCord *md* Ray Heindorf
☆ Broderick Crawford, Claire Trevor, Virginia Gibson, Bill Hayes, Sheldon Leonard, Joe Vitale, Howard St John, Henry Morgan, Margaret Dumont

Stopover Tokyo
US 1957 100m Eastmancolor Cinemascope
TCF (Walter Reisch)
An American spy in Tokyo seeks to capture a communist undercover man.
Sprawling espionage stuff with frequent halts for scenic tours.
w Richard L. Breen, Walter Reisch *novel* John P. Marquand *d* Richard L. Breen *ph* Charles G. Clarke *m* Paul Sawtell
☆ Robert Wagner, Joan Collins, Edmond O'Brien, Ken Scott, Larry Keating

Storia di una Monaca di Clausura: see *Story of a Cloistered Nun*

Stories from a Flying Trunk
GB 1979 88m Technicolor
EMI/Sands (John Brabourne, Richard Goodwin)
Three Hans Andersen stories are performed by stop frame animation and by ballet dancers dressed as vegetables.
Lugubrious attempt to repeat the success of Tales of Beatrix Potter; *moments to make one smile, but on the whole a depressing experience.*
wd Christine Edzard *ph* Robin Browne, Brian West *m* Gioacchino Rossini
☆ Murray Melvin, Ann Firbank, Johanna Sonnex, Tasneem Maqsood

The Stork Club
US 1945 98m bw
Paramount (B. G. de Sylva)
A night-club hat-check girl saves an elderly millionaire from drowning.
Very light comedy with music, a great ad for a once famous night haunt.
w B. G. de Sylva, John McGowan *d* Hal Walker *ph* Charles Lang Jnr *md* Robert Emmett Dolan
☆ Betty Hutton, Barry Fitzgerald, Don Defore, Robert Benchley, Bill Goodwin, Iris Adrian, Mary Young, Mikhail Rasumny

The Storm
US 1930 76m bw
Universal
An orphan girl left with a trapper becomes an object of jealousy between him and his partner.
Old-fashioned outdoor melodrama, previously filmed in 1916 and 1922. Not really talkie material.
w Wells Root *play* Langdon McCormick *d* William Wyler
☆ Lupe Velez, Paul Cavanagh, William Boyd, Alphonse Ethier
'A fairly good programmer ... the fight is a pip.' – *Variety*

The Storm
US 1938 79m bw
Universal (Ken Goldsmith)
Tensions lead to violence among shipboard radio operators.
Lively action melodrama culminating in a storm at sea.
w Daniel Moore, Hugh King, Theodore Reeves *d* Harold Young
☆ Charles Bickford, Barton MacLane, Preston Foster, Tom Brown, Nan Grey, Andy Devine, Frank Jenks
'Good enough for the duals, but too weak for solo billing.' – *Variety*

Storm at Daybreak
US 1932 80m bw
MGM
A fanciful reconstruction of events leading up to the Sarajevo assassination which precipitated World War I.
Unlikely melodrama with stars forced to overact; still, a rich and historically interesting slice of ham.
w Bertram Millhauser *play* Sandor Hunyady *d* Richard Boleslawski
☆ Walter Huston, Kay Francis, Nils Asther, Phillips Holmes, Eugene Pallette, C. Henry Gordon, Jean Parker
'A good cast unwisely spent on weak material: doubtful as a grosser.' – *Variety*

Storm Boy **
Australia 1976 87m colour
South Australian Film Corp (Matt Carroll)
A young boy, living in an isolated beachside shack with his misanthropic father, rears a pelican as a pet.
A pleasantly modest drama about a boy growing up and learning to come to terms with death and adult behaviour.
w Sonia Borg *novel* *Storm Boy* by Colin Thiele *d* Henri Safran *ph* Geoff Burton *m* Michael Carlos *ad* David Copping *ed* G. Turney-Smith
☆ Peter Cummins, David Gulpilil, Greg Rowe, Judy Dick, Tony Allison
'A beautifully crafted film for children.' – *MFB*

'Who really set the town aflame?'
Storm Center
US 1956 87m bw
Columbia/Phoenix (Julian Blaustein)
A small-town librarian is dismissed when she refuses to remove a communist book from the shelves.
Formula anti-McCarthy melodrama originally designed for Mary Pickford's comeback; not very absorbing and rather dingily produced.
w Daniel Taradash, Elick Moll *d* Daniel Taradash *ph* Burnett Guffey *m* George Duning
☆ Bette Davis, Brian Keith, Kim Hunter, Paul Kelly, Joe Mantell

Storm Fear
US 1955 88m bw
UA/Theodora (Cornel Wilde)
Three fugitives from justice hide in a mountain cabin, but all meet violent deaths.
Gloomy, strenuous melodrama, partly shot outdoors.
w Horton Foote *novel* Clinton Seeley *d* Cornel Wilde *ph* Joseph LaShelle *m* Elmer Bernstein
☆ Cornel Wilde, Jean Wallace, Dan Duryea, Lee Grant, Steven Hill, Dennis Weaver

Storm in a Teacup *
GB 1937 87m bw
Alexander Korda/Victor Saville
A national sensation ensues when a Scottish provost fines an old lady for not licensing her dog, and she refuses to pay.
Early Ealing-type comedy, a bit emaciated by later standards.
w Ian Dalrymple, Donald Bull *play* *Sturm im Wasserglass* by Bruno Frank *d* Ian Dalrymple, Victor Saville *ph* Max Greene *m* Frederic Lewis
☆ Vivien Leigh, Rex Harrison, Cecil Parker, Sara Allgood, Ursula Jeans, Gus McNaughton, Arthur Wontner

Storm over Africa: see *Royal African Rifles*

Storm over Asia *
USSR 1928 93m approx (24 fps) bw silent
Mezhrabpomfilm
original title: *Potomok Chingis-Khana*
aka: *The Heir to Genghis Khan*
A Mongolian trapper is discovered to be descended from Genghis Khan and made puppet emperor of a Soviet province.
Curious yarn without much discernible point though with the usual patches of propagandizing. It certainly looks good.
w Osip Brik *d* V. I. Pudovkin *ph* A. L. Golovnya
☆ I. Inkizhinov, Valeri Inkizhinov, A. Dedintsev
'Fetid with propaganda and thematically ridiculous to any semi-intelligent audience. The more illiterate a man is in these Russian blurbs, the better his chances to make a name for himself in the Red World.' – *Variety*

Storm over Lisbon
US 1944 86m bw
Republic (George Sherman)
An international spy mastermind runs a Lisbon night-club and sells documents to the highest bidder.
Feeble copy of Casablanca.
w Doris Gilbert, Dane Lussier *d* George Sherman *ph* John Alton *m* Walter Scharf
☆ Vera Hruba Ralston, Erich von Stroheim, Richard Arlen, Eduardo Ciannelli, Otto Kruger, Robert Livingston, Mona Barrie, Frank Orth

Storm over the Andes
US 1935 82m bw
Universal (Maurice Pivar)
An American flyer helps Bolivia against Paraguay.
Thick-ear melodrama about a forgotten local war; soundly made of its kind.
w Eliot Gibbons, Laclede Christy, Frank Wead, Al de Mond, Eve Greene *d* Christy Cabanne
☆ Jack Holt, Antonio Moreno, Mona Barrie, Gene Lockhart, Grant Withers

Storm over the Nile
GB 1955 107m Technicolor Cinemascope
Independent/London (Zoltan Korda)
Feeble remake of *The Four Feathers* (qv), using most of that film's action highlights stretched out to fit the wide screen.
w R. C. Sherriff *d* Terence Young *ph* Ted Scaife, Osmond Borradaile *m* Benjamin Frankel
☆ Anthony Steel, Laurence Harvey, Ronald Lewis, Ian Carmichael, James Robertson Justice, Mary Ure, Geoffrey Keen, Jack Lambert, Ferdy Mayne, Michael Hordern
'The material appears not so much dated as fossilized within its period.' – *Penelope Houston*

Storm over Tibet
US 1951 87m bw
Columbia/Summit (Ivan Tors, Laslo Benedek)
An explorer steals a holy mask which brings bad luck.
Slight adventure yarn ingeniously built around an old German documentary.
w Ivan Tors, Sam Mayer *d* Andrew Marton
ph George E. Diskant, Richard Angst *m* Arthur Honegger
☆ Rex Reason, Diana Douglas, Myron Healey

Storm over Wyoming
US 1950 60m bw
RKO (Herman Schlom)
Two cowboys intervene in a range war between a rancher and a sheepman.
Fast-moving but standard stuff, with an over-familiar, no-surprises plot.
w Ed Earl Repp *d* Lesley Selander *ph* J. Roy Hunt *m* Paul Sawtell *ad* Albert S. D'Agostino, Feild Gray *ed* Robert Swink
☆ Tim Holt, Richard Martin, Noreen Nash, Richard Powers (Tom Keene), Betty Underwood, Bill Kennedy

Storm Warning *
US 1950 93m bw
Warner (Jerry Wald)
A New York model goes south to visit her sister, and finds that her brother-in-law is an oversexed brute and a Ku Klux Klan killer.
Heavy melodrama disguised as a social document; sufficiently arresting for its purposes.
w Daniel Fuchs, Richard Brooks *d* Stuart Heisler
ph Carl Guthrie *m* Daniele Amfitheatrof
ed Clarence Kolster
☆ Ginger Rogers, Doris Day, *Steve Cochran*, Ronald Reagan, Hugh Sanders, Raymond Greenleaf, Ned Glass

Stormy
US 1935 67m bw
Universal (Henry MacRae)
Stable-boy meets horse, stable-boy loses horse, stable-boy gets horse, and girl.
A simple-minded, sentimental story for horse-lovers, though directed with sufficient energy to maintain interest; there are, for a 'B' movie, some spectacular scenes of wild horses.
w Ben Grauman Kohn, George Plympton
story Cherry Wilson *d* Louis Friedlander (Lew Landers) *ph* Richard Fryer *md* Heinz Roemheld
ad Ralph Berger *ed* Murray Seldeen
☆ Noah Beery Jnr, Jean Rogers, J. Farrell MacDonald, Raymond Hatton, Walter Miller, Fred Kohler, James Burtis, The Arizona Wranglers, Rex ('King of Wild Horses')
† The film opens with the statement: 'In the belief that in every heart abides the love of beauty in all things of the Universe, I dedicate this picture to my fellowmen of all nations. We have tried here to capture nature at her finest and manhood at its best. Set in the Painted Desert, of Arizona, "Stormy" combines for young and old the wonders of nature and the glory of human courage.'

Stormy Monday
GB 1987 93m colour
Palace/Moving Picture Company/Film Four International/Atlantic Entertainment/British Screen (Nigel Stafford-Clark)
An American gangster tries to put a Newcastle club-owner out of business.
Dull and implausible thriller of uninteresting characters.
wd Mike Figgis *ph* Roger Deakins *m* Mike Figgis
pd Andrew McAlpine *ed* Dave Martin
☆ Melanie Griffith, Tommy Lee Jones, Sting, Sean Bean, James Cosmo, Mark Long, Brian Lewis
'An obscure, uninvolving and lethargic movie.' – *Kim Newman, MFB*

Stormy Waters: *see Remorques*

Stormy Weather
GB 1935 74m bw
Gainsborough (Michael Balcon)
A top executive foils a blackmail racket in Chinatown.
Very presentable vehicle for the Aldwych team of farceurs.
w Ben Travers *play* Ben Travers *d* Tom Walls
ph Philip Tannura *md* Louis Levy
☆ Tom Walls, Ralph Lynn, Robertson Hare, Yvonne Arnaud, Gordon James, Graham Moffatt

Stormy Weather ***
US 1943 77m bw
TCF (Irving Mills)
A backstage success story lightly based on the career of Bill Robinson.
Virtually a high-speed revue with all-black talent, and what talent! The production is pretty slick too.
w Frederick Jackson, Ted Koehler *d Andrew Stone*
ph Leon Shamroy, Fred Sersen md Benny Carter
ch Clarence Robinson
☆ *Bill Robinson, Lena Horne, Fats Waller, Ada Brown, Cab Calloway*, Katherine Dunham and her Dancers, Eddie Anderson, Flournoy Miller, *The Nicholas Brothers*, Dooley Wilson
'A first-rate show, a spirited divertissement ... a joy to the ear.' – *New York Times*
♫ 'There's No Two Ways about Love'; 'That Ain't Right'; 'Ain't Misbehavin''; 'Diga Diga Doo'; 'I Can't Give You Anything but Love'; 'Geechee Joe'; 'Stormy Weather'; 'My, My, Ain't That Somethin'?'

The Story of a Cheat: *see Le Roman d'un Tricheur*

Story of a Cloistered Nun (dubbed)
Italy 1973 90m colour
PAC Consorziate (Tonino Cervi)
original title: *Storia di una Monaca di Clausura*
aka: *Diary of a Cloistered Nun*
In the 1600s, an aristocratic young woman is forced to become a nun when she refuses to marry the man chosen for her.
Turgid period drama, devoid of dramatic interest, with occasional interludes of unerotic love-making.
w Domenico Paolella, Antonio Cervi
d Domenico Paolella *ph* Armando Nannuzzi
m Piero Piccioni *ad* Pietro Filippone *ed* Amedeo Giomini
☆ Catherine Spaak, Suzy Kendall, Eleonora Giorgi, Martine Brochard, Ann Odessa, Antonio Falsi, Umberto Orsini
† The print quality of the British video release is poor.

Story of a Love Story
France/Italy 1973 110m colour
Franco-London/FLF/Robert Bradford/Euro International (Jud Kinberg)
aka: *Impossible Object*
A married middle-aged writer who finds it difficult to distinguish fiction from fact indulges in an affair with a woman whose husband is aware of her infidelity.
Meandering and rarely interesting account of the varieties of love; it lacks conviction and passion.
w Nicholas Mosley *novel Impossible Object* by Nicholas Mosley *d* John Frankenheimer
ph Claude Renoir *m* Michel Legrand
pd Alexandre Trauner *ed* Albert Jurgenson
☆ Alan Bates, Dominique Sanda, Michel Auclair, Evans Evans, Paul Crauchet, Lea Massari, Vernon Dobtcheff
† The film never received a cinema release.

The Story of a Woman
US/Italy 1969 101m Technicolor
Universal/Westward (Leonardo Bercovici)
A Swedish girl pianist in Rome falls in love with a fashionable doctor, then back in Sweden meets an American diplomat.
Intermezzo-type romantic drama with colour supplement trappings. Tolerable of its kind.
wd Leonardo Bercovici *ph* Piero Portalupi
m John Williams
☆ Robert Stack, Bibi Andersson, James Farentino, Annie Girardot, Frank Sundstrom

The Story of Adèle H *
France 1975 98m Eastmancolor
Films du Carrosse/Artistes Associés (Marcel Berbert, Claude Miller)
In 1863, the daughter of Victor Hugo follows her lover to Nova Scotia.
Surprisingly slow and stilted version of a true story, though with a few of the expected subtleties.
w François Truffaut, Jean Gruault, Suzanne Schiffman *d* François Truffaut *ph* Nestor Almendros *m* Maurice Jaubert
☆ Isabelle Adjani, Bruce Robinson, Sylvia Marriott
🎖 Isabelle Adjani

'America's most thrilling story! Of love so great and faith so strong that it inspired this man to endure ridicule, privation and hunger – to achieve the miracle of wings for the human voice!'
The Story of Alexander Graham Bell **
US 1939 97m bw
TCF (Kenneth MacGowan)
GB title: *The Modern Miracle*
The inventor of the telephone marries a deaf girl.
Acceptable history lesson with dullish principals but excellent production.
w Lamar Trotti *d* Irving Cummings *ph* Leon Shamroy *m* Louis Silvers
☆ Don Ameche, Henry Fonda, Loretta Young, Charles Coburn, Gene Lockhart, Spring Byington, Bobs Watson
'Production will need teasing to get the women.' – *Variety*

The Story of Dr Ehrlich's Magic Bullet: see *Dr Ehrlich's Magic Bullet*

The Story of Dr Wassell *
US 1944 140m Technicolor
Paramount/Cecil B. de Mille
The adventures of a naval doctor who heroically saved men during the Pacific war.
Long, slogging, glamorized account of real events which is typical de Mille and very unconvincing physically, but keeps one watching simply as a story.
w Alan le May, Charles Bennett *book* James Hilton *d* Cecil B. de Mille *ph* Victor Milner, William Snyder *m* Victor Young
☆ Gary Cooper, Laraine Day, Signe Hasso, Dennis O'Keefe, Carol Thurston, Carl Esmond, Paul Kelly, Stanley Ridges
'The director has taken a true story of heroism ... and jangled it into a cacophony of dancing girls, phoney self-sacrifice and melodramatic romance.' – *Howard Barnes*
'To be regretted beyond qualification. It whips the story into a nacreous foam of lies whose speciousness is only the more painful because Mr de Mille is so obviously free from any desire to alter the truth except for what he considers to be its own advantage.' – *James Agee*
'Close to the last word in honest understanding and convincing production.' – *Motion Picture Herald*

The Story of Esther Costello *
GB 1957 103m bw
Columbia/Romulus (James Woolf)
US title: *The Golden Virgin*
A blind Irish deaf mute girl is adopted by an American socialite and her plight becomes an international cause.
Rich melodrama develops from this unlikely premise and the star enjoys it hugely.
w Charles Kaufman *novel* Nicholas Monsarrat
d David Miller *ph* Robert Krasker *m* Georges Auric
☆ *Joan Crawford, Heather Sears*, Rossano Brazzi, Ron Randell, Lee Patterson, Fay Compton, John Loder, Denis O'Dea, Sidney James, Maureen Delany
'A regular little *Titus Andronicus*, it abounds in fraud, embezzlement, suicide, murder and rape; all it wants is somebody baked in a pie.' – *Dilys Powell*
Heather Sears

The Story of GI Joe **
US 1945 108m bw
(UA) Lester Cowan (David Hall)
aka: *War Correspondent*
Journalist Ernie Pyle follows fighting men into the Italian campaign.
Slow, convincing, sympathetic war film with good script and performances; not by any means the usual action saga.
w Leopold Atlas, Guy Endore, Philip Stevenson
book Ernie Pyle *d William A. Wellman ph Russell Metty m* Ann Ronell, Louis Applebaum
☆ *Burgess Meredith, Robert Mitchum*, Freddie Steele, Wally Cassell, Jimmy Lloyd, Jack Reilly
'It is humorous, poignant and tragic, an earnestly human reflection of a stern life and the dignity of man.' – *Thomas M. Pryor*
'A tragic and eternal work of art.' – *James Agee*
'One of the best films of the war.' – *Richard Mallett, Punch*
🎖 script; music score; song 'Linda' (*m/ly* Ann Ronell); Robert Mitchum

The Story of Gilbert and Sullivan *
GB 1953 109m Technicolor
British Lion/London Films (Frank Launder, Sidney Gilliat)
US title: *The Great Gilbert and Sullivan*
In 1875 a young composer named Arthur Sullivan and a librettist named William Gilbert come together under the auspices of Rupert D'Oyly Carte and write the Savoy Operas.
Light, accurate, well-cast and well-produced Victorian musical which somehow fails to ignite despite the immense talent at hand.
w Sidney Gilliat, Leslie Bailey *d* Sidney Gilliat
ph Christopher Challis *md* Sir Malcolm Sargent
pd Hein Heckroth
☆ Robert Morley, Maurice Evans, Peter Finch, Eileen Herlie, Dinah Sheridan, Isabel Dean, Wilfrid Hyde-White, Muriel Aked
'It is like a sound radio scrapbook, combined with a television passing show. It is bright, swift and bitty; faintly sentimental, enormously good-natured.' – C. A. Lejeune

The Story of Louis Pasteur ***
US 1936 85m bw
Warner/Cosmopolitan (Henry Blanke)
How the eminent 19th-century French scientist overcomes obstacles in finding cures for various diseases.
Adequate biopic which caused a sensation and started a trend; some of the others were better but this was the first example of Hollywood bringing schoolbook history to box-office life.
w Sheridan Gibney, Pierre Collings *d William Dieterle ph* Tony Gaudio *m* Bernhard Kaun, Heinz Roemheld
☆ *Paul Muni*, Josephine Hutchinson, Anita Louise, Donald Woods, Fritz Leiber, Henry O'Neill, Porter Hall, Akim Tamiroff, Walter Kingsford
'Probably limited b.o. but a creditable prestige picture.' – *Variety*
'What should be vital and arresting has been made hollow and dull ... we are tendered something that is bright and stagey for something out of life.' – *Otis Ferguson*
'More exciting than any gangster melodrama.' – *C. A. Lejeune*
original story; screenplay; Paul Muni
🎖 best picture

'Men and their women from the beginning of creation! Never so vast an undertaking!'
The Story of Mankind
US 1957 100m Technicolor
Warner/Cambridge (Irwin Allen)
A heavenly tribunal debates whether to allow man to destroy himself, and both the Devil and the Spirit of Man cite instances from history.
Hilarious charade, one of the worst films ever made, but full of surprises, bad performances, and a wide range of stock shots.
w Irwin Allen, Charles Bennett *book* Hendrik Van Loon *d* Irwin Allen *ph* Nicholas Musuraca
m Paul Sawtell
☆ Ronald Colman, Vincent Price, Cedric Hardwicke, the Marx Brothers, Hedy Lamarr, Agnes Moorehead, Reginald Gardiner, Peter Lorre, Virginia Mayo, Charles Coburn, Francis X. Bushman
'A poor excuse to use a batch of available actors in some of the weirdest casting ever committed.' – *Newsweek*
'The script was bad to begin with and it worsened with daily changes. I remember one puzzled visitor asking Ronnie Colman, "Is this picture based on a book?", and he replied in that beautiful soft diction of his, "Yes. But they're only using the notes on the dust jacket."' – *Vincent Price*

The Story of Qiu Ju ***
China/Hong Kong 1992 100m colour
Sil-Metropole/Beijing Film Academy Youth Film Studio (Ma Fung Kwok)

The pregnant wife of a peasant appeals to higher authorities to force the village headman to apologize for injuring her husband.
Less flamboyant than the director's previous films, this takes a documentary-style approach to the story of a woman determined that principles must be upheld whatever the cost.
w Liu Heng *novel* Chen Yuanbin *d* Zhang Yimou *ph* Chi Xiaoning, Yu Xiaoqun *m* Zhao Jiping *ad* Cao Jiuping *ed* Du Yuan
☆ Gong Li, Lei Laosheng, Liu Peiqi, Yang Liuchun

'This simple, repetitive tale has a mesmerizing quality able to hook audiences from beginning to end.' – *Variety*

† The film won the Golden Lion award for best film and Gong Li won the award for best actress at the 1992 Venice Film Festival.

The Story of Robin Hood and his Merrie Men
GB 1952 84m Technicolor
Walt Disney (Perce Pearce)

When Prince John starts a ruthless taxation campaign, Robert Fitzooth turns outlaw.
Fairly competent but quite forgettable version of the legend, softened for children.
w Lawrence E. Watkin *d* Ken Annakin *ph* Guy Green *m* Clifton Parker
☆ Richard Todd, Joan Rice, James Hayter, Hubert Gregg, James Robertson Justice, Martita Hunt, Peter Finch

The Story of Ruth
US 1960 132m DeLuxe Cinemascope
TCF (Samuel G. Engel)

Ruth becomes the favourite of a pagan king but eventually flees to Israel.
Tedious, portentous bible-in-pictures, of virtually no interest or entertainment value.
w Norman Corwin *d* Henry Koster *ph* Arthur E. Arling *m* Franz Waxman
☆ Elana Eden, Peggy Wood, Viveca Lindfors, Stuart Whitman, Tom Tryon, Jeff Morrow, Thayer David, Eduard Franz

The Story of Seabiscuit
US 1949 98m Technicolor
Warner (William Jacobs)

GB title: *Pride of Kentucky*
The success story of a racehorse.
Blue grass vapidities, the kind of family entertainment that drove the families away.
w John Taintor Foote *d* David Butler *ph* Wilfrid Cline *md* David Buttolph
☆ Shirley Temple, Barry Fitzgerald, Lon McCallister, Rosemary de Camp, Donald McBride, Pierre Watkin

The Story of Shirley Yorke
GB 1948 92m bw
Nettlefold
A nobleman tries to blame his wife's nurse for her death by poison.
Lethargic version of a play previously filmed as Lord Camber's Ladies (qv).
w A. R. Rawlinson, Maclean Rogers and Kathleen Butler *play The Case of Lady Camber* by H. A. Vachell *d* Maclean Rogers
☆ Derek Farr, Dinah Sheridan, Margaretta Scott, John Robinson, Barbara Couper, Valentine Dyall

The Story of Temple Drake *
US 1933 71m bw
Paramount (Ben Glazer)
A neurotic Southern flapper is abducted by gangsters, and likes it.
Deliberately shocking melodrama of its time, restructured from a notorious book later filmed under its own title. Very dated, but interesting.
w Oliver H. P. Garrett *novel Sanctuary* by William Faulkner *d* Stephen Roberts *ph* Karl Struss
☆ *Miriam Hopkins*, Jack La Rue, William Gargan, William Collier Jnr, Irving Pichel, Guy Standing, Elizabeth Patterson, Florence Eldridge

'Under Haysian ban the title of the novel can't be ballyhooed, but any whispering campaign about this is the picture's best b.o. asset. It has little else to commend it.' – *Variety*

The Story of Three Loves
US 1953 122m Technicolor
MGM (Sidney Franklin)

Three love stories concerning the passengers on a transatlantic liner.
Three bits of old-fashioned kitsch, one tragic, one whimsical, one melodramatic, all rather slow and dull though well produced.
w John Collier, Jan Lustig, George Froeschel *d* Gottfried Reinhardt, Vincente Minnelli *ph* Charles Rosher, Harold Rosson *m* Miklos Rozsa *ad* Cedric Gibbons, Preston Ames, Edward Carfagno, Gabriel Scognamillo
☆ Ethel Barrymore, James Mason, Moira Shearer, Pier Angeli, Leslie Caron, Kirk Douglas, Farley Granger, Agnes Moorehead, Zsa Zsa Gabor
art direction

The Story of Us
US 1999 94m DeLuxe
Warner/Castle Rock (Rob Reiner, Alan Zweibel, Jessie Nelson)

After 15 years of marriage and two children, a writer and his wife, a crossword compiler, decide to try a trial separation.
There's little sign of strain in the relationship Reiner shows us, so the ending will come as no surprise; but there's hardly any sign of pleasure, either, so the story is of the soporific bedtime sort.
w Alan Zweibel, Jessie Nelson *d* Rob Reiner *ph* Michael Chapman *m* Eric Clapton, Mark Shaiman *pd* Lilly Kilvert *ed* Robert Leighton, Alan Edward Bell
☆ Bruce Willis (Ben Jordan), Michelle Pfeiffer (Katie Jordan), Rob Reiner (Stan), Tim Matheson (Marty), Rita Wilson (Rachel), Paul Reiser (Dave), Julie Hagerty (Liza), Colleen Rennison (Erin), Jake Sandvig (Josh), Jayne Meadows (Dot), Tom Poston (Harry), Betty White (Lillian), Red Buttons (Arnie)

'As an ode to the ups and downs of middle-aged marriage, this arthritic suburban story is enough to make single people want to file for divorce.' – *Janet Maslin, New York Times*

The Story of Vernon and Irene Castle **
US 1939 93m bw
RKO (George Haight, Pandro S. Berman)

The story of a husband and wife dance team who had their first success in Paris and became influential international celebrities before he was killed as a flyer in World War I.
Pleasant understated musical with very agreeable dance sequences and a firm overall style. The last of the main stream of Astaire–Rogers musicals.
w Richard Sherman, Oscar Hammerstein II, Dorothy Yost *books* Irene Castle *d* H. C. Potter *ph* Robert de Grasse *md* Victor Baravalle *ch* Hermes Pan *ad* Van Nest Polglase
☆ *Fred Astaire, Ginger Rogers*, Edna May Oliver, Walter Brennan, Lew Fields, Etienne Girardot, Donald MacBride

'One of the best Astaire-Rogers musicals ... a wealth of nostalgic appeal.' – *Variety*

† The title was devised and insisted on by Mrs Castle.

The Story of Will Rogers
US 1950 109m Technicolor
Warner (Robert Arthur)
A wild west performer becomes a Ziegfeld star and pop philosopher.
Bland, unshaped biopic of one of American show business's best loved figures, who died in an air crash in 1935.
w Frank Davis, Stanley Roberts *d* Michael Curtiz *ph* Wilfrid M. Cline *md* Victor Young
☆ Will Rogers Jnr, Jane Wyman, James Gleason, Eddie Cantor (as himself), Carl Benton Reid

The Story on Page One
US 1960 123m bw Cinemascope
TCF/Company of Artists (Jerry Wald)
A lawyer undertakes the defence of a woman who with her lover is charged with the murder of her husband.
Long-drawn-out and not very interesting courtroom drama, performed and presented with some style.
wd Clifford Odets *ph* James Wong Howe *m* Elmer Bernstein
☆ Rita Hayworth, Tony Franciosa, Gig Young, Mildred Dunnock, Hugh Griffith, Sanford Meisner, Alfred Ryder

Storytelling **
US 2001 87m DeLuxe
Entertainment/Killer Films/Good Machine (Ted Hope, Christine Vachon)

Fiction: a creative writing student writes a story, about her seduction by the course's teacher, which her fellow student dismiss; *Nonfiction*: a would-be documentary director makes a film about a rich teenager and his dysfunctional family.
Part apologia for Solondz's own satiricial methods, part an investigation of the purpose of stories and their relationship with truth, and the way reality can be manipulated, this is a clever, sardonic, if somewhat heartless, pleasure.
w Todd Solondz *ph* Frederick Elmes *m* Belle & Sebastian, Nathan Larson *pd* James Chinlund *ed* Alan Oxman
☆ Selma Blair (Vi), Leo Fitzpatrick (Marcus), Aleksa Palladino (Catherine), Robert Wisdom (Gary Scott), Noah Fleiss (Brady Livingston), Paul Giamatti (Toby Oxman), John Goodman (Marty Livingston), Julie Hagerty (Fern Livingston), Lupe Ontiveros (Consuelo), Jonathan Osser (Mikey Livingston), Franka Potente (Editor)

'Worth taking seriously, a task only slightly impeded by the fact that it's awfully funny. And I do mean awfully.' – *A. O. Scott, New York Times*
'It's bile, pure and simple. Solondz has devolved from an interesting filmmaker with a wicked sensibility to a bitter, monotonous solipsist bent on convincing the world that growing up in the suburbs is poopy.' – *Shawn Levy, Oregonian*

'A candidate's private moment can all too quickly become public record.'
Storyville
US 1992 113m CFI color
Spelling/Davis (David Roe, Edward R. Pressman)

A rich young lawyer running for Congress and trying to discover why his father killed himself finds himself caught up in scandal and murder.
Overheated and muddled story of corruption with a narrative that depends on its central character behaving extremely stupidly throughout; an audience with any sense will keep well away.
w Mark Frost, Lee Reynolds *novel Juryman* by Frank Galbally and Robert Macklin *d* Mark Frost *ph* Ron Garcia *m* Carter Burwell *pd* Richard Hoover *ed* B. J. Sears
☆ James Spader, Joanne Whalley-Kilmer, Jason Robards, Charlotte Lewis, Michael Warren, Michael Parks, Chuck McCann, Charlie Haid, Chino Fats Williams, Woody Strode, Jeff Perry, Piper Laurie

'A straightforward and lacklustre potboiler, composed of disparate elements with little dynamic coherence.' – *Sight and Sound*

Stowaway *
US 1936 86m bw
TCF (Earl Carroll, Harold Wilson)

The orphan daughter of a Shanghai missionary stows away on an American pleasure ship.
Very good star vehicle in which Shirley performs some of her best musical numbers.
w William Conselman, Arthur Sheekman, Nat Perrin *d* William A. Seiter *ph* Arthur Miller *md* Louis Silvers *songs* Mack Gordon, Harry Revel
☆ *Shirley Temple*, Robert Young, Alice Faye, Eugene Pallette, Helen Westley, Arthur Treacher, J. Edward Bromberg, Astrid Allwyn

'No exhib worrying necessary for this one.' – *Variety*

Stowaway Girl: see *Manuela*

La Strada ***
Italy 1954 94m bw
Ponti/de Laurentiis

aka: *The Road*
A half-witted peasant girl is sold to an itinerant strong man and ill-used by him.
Curious attempt at a kind of poetic neo-realism, saved by style and performances.
w Federico Fellini, Ennio Flaiano, Tullio Pinelli *d Federico Fellini ph* Otello Martelli *m* Nino Rota
☆ Giulietta Masina, Anthony Quinn, Richard Basehart
best foreign film
script

Straight on Till Morning
GB 1972 96m Technicolor
EMI/Hammer (Roy Skeggs)

A Liverpool girl in London meets a dangerous psychotic.
Unattractive suspenser, wildly directed.
w Michael Peacock *d* Peter Collinson *ph* Brian Probyn *m* Roland Shaw
☆ Rita Tushingham, Shane Briant, Tom Bell, Annie Ross, James Bolam

Straight out of Brooklyn
US 1991 83m colour
Artificial Eye/Blacks N'Progress/American Playhouse (Matty Rich)

Determined to escape the poverty that has engulfed his hard-working mother and drunken father, a young black man persuades his friends to rob some local hoodlums.
Interesting first feature of ghetto life from a teenaged director.
wd Matty Rich *ph* John Rosnell *m* Harold Wheeler *ad* Walter Meade *ed* Jack Haigis
☆ George T. Odom, Ann D. Sanders, Lawrence Gilliard Jnr, Barbara Sanon, Reana E. Drummond, Matty Rich, Mark Malone

'Not a glittering debut, but it does have a low-budget, first-time energy which sets it apart from much mainstream work.' – *Michael O'Pray, Sight and Sound*
'Rudimentary in every way, from writing to acting to camerawork, and covers all-too-familiar ground with no particular flair.' – *Variety*

Straight, Place and Show *
US 1938 66m bw
TCF
GB title: *They're Off*
Three pony-ride proprietors impersonate Russian jockeys to save a race.
Lively, unpretentious vehicle for three zanies, with a further bonus in its lead singer.
w M. M. Musselman, Allen Rivkin *play* Damon Runyon, Irving Caesar *d* David Butler
☆ The Ritz Brothers, Ethel Merman, Richard Arlen, Phyllis Brooks, George Barbier, Sidney Blackmer

The Straight Story ***
France/US 1999 111m FotoKem 'Scope
Buena Vista/Les Films Alain Sarde/Canal+/Picture Factory (Alain Sarde, Mary Sweeney, Neal Edelstein)

An elderly widower makes a 300 mile trip to see his ailing brother on the only transport available to him, a lawn mower.
A gentle, folksy road movie that takes its time but establishes a mood of quiet enjoyment for simple pleasures, mixed with a little regret for some past events; Farnsworth epitomises a man who knows his own worth and that of the others he meets on his journey.
w John Roach, Mary Sweeney d David Lynch ph Freddie Francis m Angelo Badalamenti *pd* Jack Fisk *ed* Mary Sweeney
☆ *Richard Farnsworth* (Alvin Straight), Sissy Spacek (Rose), Jane Galloway Heitz (Dorothy), Everett McGill (Tom the Dealer), Jennifer Edwards-Hughes (Brenda), John Farley (Thorvald), John Lordan (Priest), Harry Dean Stanton (Lyle)

'A lyrical poem to America's vast land and country folks.' – *Emanuel Levy, Variety*
'This must be the strangest road movie ever made, but it is also one of the most lovable.' – *Adam Mars-Jones, Times*
Richard Farnsworth

'Dreams do come true … sometimes.'

Straight Talk
US 1992 91m Technicolor
Warner/Hollywood/Sandollar (Robert Chartoff, Fred Berner)

An Arkansas dance teacher goes to Chicago to become a TV agony aunt.
Mundane romantic comedy tailored to the personality of Dolly Parton.
w Craig Bolotin, Patricia Resnick *d* Barnet Kellman *ph* Peter Sova *m* Brad Fiedel *pd* Jeffrey Townsend *ed* Michael Tronick
☆ Dolly Parton, James Woods, Griffin Dunne, Michael Madsen, Deirdre O'Connell, John Sayles, Teri Hatcher, Spalding Gray, Jerry Orbach, Philip Bosco
'Glib but sunny romantic comedy … should be a B.O. winner.' – *Variety*

Straight Time
US 1978 114m Technicolor
Warner/First Artist/Sweetwall (Stanley Beck, Tim Zinnemann)

A psychotic parolee fails to go straight.
Unappetizing social melodrama with an irresolute leading performance.
w Alvin Sargent, Edward Bunker, Jeffrey Boam *novel* No Beast So Fierce by Edward Bunker *d* Ulu Grosbard *ph* Owen Roizman *m* David Shire
☆ Dustin Hoffman, Theresa Russell, Gary Busey, Harry Dean Stanton
'One leaves the theatre hoping the character will die painfully and slowly in a hail of bullets.' – *Variety*

'Just keep saying to yourself – it's only a film, it's only a film!'

Strait Jacket
US 1963 92m bw
Columbia/William Castle

A woman who murdered her faithless husband with an axe is released twenty years later, and more axe murders occur.
Dull and unattractive shocker in which all concerned lean over backwards to conceal the trick ending.
w Robert Bloch *d* William Castle *ph* Arthur E. Arling *m* Van Alexander
☆ Joan Crawford, Diane Baker, Leif Erickson, Howard St John, Rochelle Hudson, George Kennedy

Stranded
US 1935 73m bw
Warner
A woman working for Traveller's Aid meets an old school beau.
Much ado about nothing, the kind of movie that loses stars their reputations.
w Delmer Daves, Carl Erickson, Frank Wead, Ferdinand Reyher *d* Frank Borzage
☆ Kay Francis, George Brent, Patricia Ellis, Donald Woods, Robert Barrat, Barton MacLane
'Limited chances.' – *Variety*

Stranded
Canada 1991 88m colour
Libra/Erin (Christian Bruyere)
A woman trying to save her marriage goes to stay with her husband in an isolated lighthouse, near where her sister died mysteriously.
Cheap, nasty and stupid thriller, of no conceivable interest to anyone.
w Boon Collins, Stanley Park, Dan Vining, Deborah Wakeham *story* Daniel D. Williams *d* Paul Tucker *ph* Tobias Schliessler *m* Michael Conway Baker *pd* Richard Wilcox *ed* Jana Fritsch
☆ Deborah Wakeham, Ryan Michael, Stephen E. Miller, Blu Mankuma, Gabrielle Rose, Ric Reid
† The copyright notice on the credits is apposite: 'Erin Features No. 1 Ltd. in Bankruptcy'.

Stranded in Paris: see *Artists and Models Abroad*

The Strange Adventure of David Gray: see *Vampyr*

The Strange Affair
GB 1968 106m Techniscope
Paramount (Howard Harrison, Stanley Mann)
A young London policeman finds that his superiors are almost as corrupt as the villains.
Stylishly made melodrama of despair, with a sexy nymphet heroine straight from swinging London. It all leaves a sour taste in the mouth.
w Stanley Mann *novel* Bernard Toms *d* David Greene *ph* Alex Thomson *m* Basil Kirchin
☆ Michael York, Jeremy Kemp, Susan George, Jack Watson, George A. Cooper

The Strange Affair of Uncle Harry
US 1945 82m bw
Universal (Joan Harrison)

aka: *Uncle Harry*
A man henpecked by his two sisters plans to murder one of them.
Stilted melodrama from an uninspired stage original, with a cop-out dream ending tacked on.
w Stephen Longstreet, Keith Winter *play* Thomas Job *d* Robert Siodmak *ph* Woody Bredell *m* Hans Salter
☆ George Sanders, Geraldine Fitzgerald, Ella Raines, Sara Allgood, Moyna MacGill, Samuel S. Hinds, Harry von Zell, Ethel Griffies

Strange Bargain
US 1949 68m bw
RKO (Sid Rogell)

A lowly bookkeeper finds himself accomplice in an insurance swindle.
Watchable second feature suspenser.
w Lillie Hayward *d* Will Price *ph* Harry J. Wild
☆ Jeffrey Lynn, Henry Morgan, Martha Scott, Katherine Emery, Richard Gaines, Henry O'Neill

Strange Bedfellows
US 1965 99m Technicolor
U-I/Panama-Frank (Melvin Frank)
An American executive in London nearly divorces his fiery Italian wife.
Frantic sex comedy with picture postcard background; fatiguing rather than funny, but with minor compensations.
w Melvin Frank, Michael Pertwee *d* Melvin Frank *ph* Leo Tover *m* Leigh Harline
☆ Rock Hudson, Gina Lollobrigida, Gig Young, Edward Judd, Howard St John, Arthur Haynes, Dave King, Terry-Thomas
'The grind of predictable situations is further afflicted by considerable lapses in taste.' – *MFB*

Strange Boarders ★
GB 1938 79m bw
GFD/Gainsborough (Edward Black)
A police detective postpones his honeymoon to book into a boarding house and discover which of the guests is a spy.
Quite engaging comedy-thriller in the Hitchcock mould, with entertaining performances and incidents.
w A. R. Rawlinson, Sidney Gilliat *novel* The Strange Boarders of Paradise Crescent by E. Phillips Oppenheim *d* Herbert Mason *ph* Jack Cox
☆ Tom Walls, Renee Saint-Cyr, Leon M. Lion, Googie Withers, C. V. France, Ronald Adam, Irene Handl, George Curzon, Martita Hunt

Strange Brew
US 1983 90m colour
MGM (Louis M. Silverstein)

Two dim-witted, beer-swilling Canadian brothers visit the Elsinore brewery in search of free drinks and, with the aid of some lunatics, thwart a plan to take over the world.
Offbeat but unamusing comedy, based on two characters from the SCTV Network television comedy series and borrowing much of its plot from Hamlet.
w Rick Moranis, Dave Thomas, Steven de Jarnatt *d* Dave Thomas, Rick Moranis *ph* Steven Poster *m* Charles Fox *pd* David L. Snyder *ed* Patrick McMahon
☆ Dave Thomas, Rick Moranis, Max von Sydow, Paul Dooley, Lynne Griffin, Angus MacInnes, Tom Harvey, Douglas Campbell

Strange Cargo ★
US 1940 105m bw
MGM (Joseph L. Mankiewicz)

Eight convicts escape from Devil's Island and are influenced by a Christ-like fugitive.
One of Hollywood's occasional lunacies; one doubts whether even the author knew the point of this cockamamy parable, but it was well produced and acted.
w Lawrence Hazard *novel* Not Too Narrow, Not Too Deep by Richard Sale *d* Frank Borzage *ph* Robert Planck *m* Franz Waxman
☆ Clark Gable, Joan Crawford, Ian Hunter, Peter Lorre, Paul Lukas, Albert Dekker, J. Edward Bromberg, Eduardo Ciannelli, Frederick Worlock
'Even the most hardened mystics may blush.' – *New Yorker, 1978*

The Strange Case of Clara Deane
US 1932 60m bw
Paramount
A young mother is unjustly convicted of a crime which she didn't commit and bids a tearful farewell to her child …
Hilariously inept and theatrical rendering of a very outmoded play.
w Max Marcin *play* Arthur M. Brillant *d* Louis Gasnier, Max Marcin
☆ Wynne Gibson, Pat O'Brien, Frances Dee, Dudley Digges
'Strictly for the minors where the clientele is elderly and naive.' – *Variety*

The Strange Case of Doctor RX
US 1942 66m bw
Universal
A mysterious murderer eliminates criminals whom the law can't touch.
Inept semi-horror which wastes a good cast, as did the same author's Night Monster.
w Clarence Upson Young *d* William Nigh
☆ Lionel Atwill, Patric Knowles, Anne Gwynne, Samuel S. Hinds, Shemp Howard, Mona Barrie, Paul Cavanagh, Mantan Moreland

Strange Confession: see *The Imposter*

Strange Conquest: see *The Crime of Dr Hallet*

Strange Conspiracy: see *The President Vanishes*

'You know you want it.'

Strange Days ★
US 1995 145m DeLuxe Panavision
UIP/Lightstorm (James Cameron, Steven-Charles Jaffe)

On the eve of the millennium, in the urban war zone that is Los Angeles in 1999, a former cop, who peddles an illegal form of virtual reality to eager customers, searches for his girlfriend, who has left him for a vicious gangster.
A thunderous, over-emphatic thriller of the near-future, when entertainment consists of experiencing other people's reality, from rape to murder; but under all the flash and frenetic activity is a narrative that was old when the world was much younger.
w James Cameron, Jay Cocks *d* Kathryn Bigelow *ph* Matthew F. Leonetti *m* Graeme Revell *pd* Lilly Kilvert *ed* Howard Smith *sp* Digital Domain
☆ Ralph Fiennes, Angela Bassett, Juliette Lewis, Tom Sizemore, Vincent D'Onofrio, Michael Wincott, Glenn Plummer
'Has a dazzling atmosphere of grunge futurism, but beneath its dark satire of audiovisual decadence lurks a naggingly conventional underworld thriller.' – *Owen Gleiberman, Entertainment Weekly*
'Terrifically hyped-up style will thrill many buffs, sci-fi and head trip elements will appeal to techies, and rough action and heavy racial angle will find a following among young ethnic viewers.' – *Todd McCarthy*

The Strange Death of Adolf Hitler ★
US 1943 74m bw
Universal (Ben Pivar)
A stage impressionist murders the Führer and takes his place, steering Germany deliberately into losing the war.
One of the more eccentric curios of World War II, especially from a mundane studio like Universal. Once one recovers from the shock of its existence, the thing is moderately well done. See also The Magic Face.
w Fritz Kortner *d* James Hogan *ph* Jerome Ash *m* Hans Salter *ad* John B. Goodman *ed* Milton Carruth
☆ *Ludwig Donath*, Gale Sondergaard, Fritz Kortner, George Dolenz

The Strange Door ★
US 1951 81m bw
U-I (Ted Richmond)

A young nobleman, passing through the one-way door of a castle, finds himself the prisoner of a madman.
Torture-chamber suspenser, adequately if rather tediously developed, with most of its interest reposing in the cast.
w Jerry Sackheim *story* The Sire de Maletroit's Door by Robert Louis Stevenson *d* Joseph Pevney *ph* Irving Glassberg *m* Hans Salter
☆ Charles Laughton, Boris Karloff, Michael Pate, Sally Forrest, Richard Stapley, Alan Napier

Strange Evidence
GB 1932 71m bw
Paramount/London Films (Alexander Korda)
When an invalid dies, his adulterous wife is suspected.
Mildly interesting quickie whodunnit.
w Miles Malleson *story* Lajos Biro *d* Robert Milton *ph* Robert Martin *ed* Stephen Harrison
☆ Leslie Banks, Carol Goodner, George Curzon, Frank Vosper, Norah Baring, Diana Napier

Strange Holiday
US 1945 61m bw
General Motors/Elite Pictures (Arch Oboler)
A man back from holiday discovers that American Nazis have taken over the country.
Over-talkative fantasy which barely scraped a release, especially since it was made in 1940 but not offered until five years later.
wd Arch Oboler *ph* Robert Surtees *m* Gordon Jenkins
☆ Claude Rains, Gloria Holden, Milton Kibbee, Bobbie Stebbins, Barbara Bate, Martin Kosleck

Strange Incident: see *The Ox Bow Incident*

'A woman suspected! A woman desired! A woman possessed!'
'The film in which you hear the characters think!'

Strange Interlude ★★
US 1932 110m bw
MGM (Irving Thalberg)

GB title: *Strange Interval*
Problems of an unfulfilled wife and her lover.
Surprising film version of a very heavy modern classic, complete with asides to the audience; very dated now, but a small milestone in Hollywood's development.
w Bess Meredyth, C. Gardner Sullivan *play* Eugene O'Neill *d* Robert Z. Leonard *ph* Lee Garmes
☆ Norma Shearer, Clark Gable, May Robson, Alexander Kirkland, Ralph Morgan, Robert Young, Maureen O'Sullivan, Henry B. Walthall
'Chiefly a reserved seat attraction, dubious for general release appeal' – *Variety*
'A cinematic novelty to be seen by discerning audiences.' – *Film Weekly*
'More exciting than a thousand "action" movies.' – *Pare Lorentz*

Strange Interval: see *Strange Interlude*

Strange Intruder
US 1957 78m bw
AA (Lindsley Parsons)
A psychopathic ex-POW menaces the children of his dead friend's wife.
Gloomy second feature melodrama, rather well presented.
w David Evans, Warren Douglas *novel* Helen Fowler *d* Irving Rapper *ph* Ernest Haller *m* Paul Dunlap
☆ Edmund Purdom, Ida Lupino, Ann Harding, Jacques Bergerac, Carl Benton Reid

Strange Invaders *
US 1983 93m DeLuxe
EMI/Orion/Michael Laughlin (Walter Coblenz)

An Illinois town is taken over by beings from outer space.
Patchy but often amusing take-off of the Invasion of the Body Snatchers *genre.*
w William Condon, Michael Laughlin *d* Michael Laughlin *ph* Louis Horvath, Zoltan Vidor *m* John Addison *pd* Susanna Moore
☆ Paul Le Mat, Nancy Allen, Diana Scarwid, Michael Lerner, Louise Fletcher, Fiona Lewis, Kenneth Tobey
'Isn't so much a spoof of '50s sci-fi formulae as it is a running commentary on styles of cultural awareness.' – *Richard T. Jameson, Seattle Weekly*

Strange Lady in Town
US 1955 118m Warnercolor Cinemascope
Warner (Mervyn Le Roy)
Adventures of a woman doctor in 1880 Santa Fe.
Quaint Western drama which is never any more convincing than its star.
w Frank Butler *d* Mervyn Le Roy *ph* Harold Rosson *m* Dimitri Tiomkin
☆ Greer Garson, Dana Andrews, Cameron Mitchell, Lois Smith, Walter Hampden

'Fate drew them together and only murder can part them!'
'Whisper her name!'
The Strange Love of Martha Ivers **
US 1946 116m bw
Paramount/Hal B. Wallis

A murderous child becomes a wealthy woman with a spineless lawyer husband; the melodrama starts when an ex-boyfriend returns to town.
Irresistible star melodrama which leaves no stone unturned; compulsive entertainment of the old school.
w Robert Rossen *d* Lewis Milestone *ph* Victor Milner *m* Miklos Rozsa
☆ Barbara Stanwyck, Van Heflin, Kirk Douglas, Lizabeth Scott, Judith Anderson, Roman Bohnen
'Exciting nonsense.' – *James Agate*
original story (Jack Patrick)

The Strange Love of Molly Louvain
US 1932 72m bw
Warner
A young mother has gone to the bad through men.
Hoary melodrama which the cast seem forever on the point of sending up.
w Maurine Watkins, Erwin Gelsey *play* The Tinsel Girl by Maurine Watkins *d* Michael Curtiz
☆ Lee Tracy, Ann Dvorak, Richard Cromwell, Guy Kibbee, Leslie Fenton, Frank McHugh
'A lightweight yarn which never takes a toehold to deliver a sock.' – *Variety*

The Strange Mr Gregory
US 1945 63m bw
Monogram (Louis Berkoff)
In pursuit of a murder fraud, a magician feigns his own death and poses as his brother.
Complex but watchable little crime thriller.
w Myles Connolly, Charles S. Belden *d* Phil Rosen
☆ Edmund Lowe, Jean Rogers, Don Douglas, Frank Reicher, Robert Emmett Keane

The Strange One *
US 1957 99m bw
Columbia/Sam Spiegel
GB title: *End as a Man*
A sadistic cadet causes trouble at a Southern military college.
A weird and unsavoury but rather compelling melodrama which unreels like a senior version of Tom Brown's Schooldays.
w Calder Willingham *novel* End as a Man by Calder Willingham *d* Jack Garfein *ph* Burnett Guffey *m* Kenyon Hopkins
☆ Ben Gazzara, George Peppard, Mark Richman, Pat Hingle, Arthur Storch, Paul Richards, Geoffrey Horne, James Olson
'The film's brilliance is in its persuasive depiction of a highly controversial, artificially organized world; its failure is to make any dramatic statement about it.' – *MFB*

The Strange Ones: see *Les Enfants Terribles*

A Strange Place to Meet: see *Drôle D'Endroit pour une Rencontre*

Strange Planet **
Australia 1999 96m colour
Redbus/AFFC/Strange Planet/Premium/Showtime/NSW Film & TV (Stavros Kazantzidis, Anastasia Sideris)
Three young women, who share a house, and three young men, partners in a law firm, all look for love in Sydney.
Engaging comedy, which follows six people from one New Year's Eve to another, though the two sets of friends do not meet each other for most of the year; there is a happy ending, though judging by the relationships that have gone before, it's likely to be a temporary one.
w Emma-Kate Croghan, Stavros Kazantzidis *d* Emma-Kate Croghan *ph* Justin Brickle *pd* Annie Beauchamp *ed* Ken Sallows
☆ Claudia Karvan (Judy), Naomi Watts (Alice), Tom Long (Sally), Aaron Jeffrey (Joel), Felix Williamson (Neil), Hugo Weaving (Steven), Marshall Napier (Robert)
'An immensely likable romantic comedy.' – *Variety*

The Strange Woman
US 1946 100m bw
UA/Hunt Stromberg (Jack Chertok)

A scheming woman plays with the lives of three men.
Star wish-fulfilment; otherwise a hammy costume piece.
w Herb Meadows *novel* Ben Ames Williams *d* Edgar G. Ulmer *ph* Lucien Andriot *m* Carmen Dragon
☆ Hedy Lamarr, George Sanders, Louis Hayward, Gene Lockhart, Hillary Brooke

'Shock by incredible shock this ravaging death overruns the earth ... menacing mankind with overwhelming chaos.'
'When men of different planets unite to combat the most loathsome peril the universe has ever known!'
Strange World of Planet X
GB 1957 75m bw
Eros Films (George Maynard)

US title: *Cosmic Monsters*
A mad scientist's experiments with magnetic fields cause insects to mutate into huge creatures with a taste for human flesh.
Risible science fiction with a great deal too much talk and the feeblest monsters to be found in any of the giant insect movies of the period.
w Paul Ryder *novel* Rene Ray *d* Gilbert Gunn *ph* Joe Ambor *m* Robert Sharples *ad* Bernard Sarron *ed* Francis Bieber
☆ Forrest Tucker, Gaby André, Martin Benson, Alec Mango, Wyndham Goldie, Hugh Latimer

The Stranger *
US 1946 95m bw
International (Sam Spiegel)

An escaped Nazi criminal marries an American woman and settles in a Connecticut village.
Highly unconvincing and artificial melodrama enhanced by directorial touches, splendid photography and no-holds-barred climax involving a church clock.
w Anthony Veiller *story* Victor Trivas *d* Orson Welles *ph* Russell Metty *m* Bronislau Kaper
☆ Edward G. Robinson, Orson Welles, Loretta Young, Philip Merivale, Richard Long, Konstantin Shayne
'Some striking effects, with lighting and interesting angles much relied on.' – *Bosley Crowther*
'A film of confused motivations and clumsy effects.' – *Basil Wright, 1972*
Victor Trivas

The Stranger: see *The Intruder (1961)*

The Stranger
US/Argentina 1987 83m DeLuxe
Columbia/Tusitala/Michael Nolin (Hugo Lamonica)

aka: *Mortifero*
Fleeing from witnessing three brutal murders, a woman crashes her car and forgets her identity; then the killers track her down ...
Awkward thriller, acted with no great conviction, and only occasionally suspenseful or entertaining.
w Dan Gurskis *d* Adolfo Aristarain *ph* Horacio Maira *m* Craig Safan *pd* Abel Facello *ed* Eduardo Lopez
☆ Bonnie Bedelia, Peter Riegert, Barry Primus, David Spielberg, Ricardo Darin, Julio de Grazia, Cecilia Roth, Marcos Woinski

The Stranger: see *Agantuk (1991)*

The Stranger: see *Butterfly Legend (1999)*

A Stranger among Us: see *Close to Eden*

Stranger at My Door
US 1956 85m bw
Republic (Sidney Picker)
A gunman takes refuge in the house of a preacher who tries to convert him.
Odd, sentimental little Western morality play, not badly presented.
w Barry Shipman *d* William Witney *ph* Bud Thackery *m* Dale Butts
☆ Macdonald Carey, Skip Homeier, Patricia Medina, Louis Jean Heydt

The Stranger Came Home
GB 1954 80m bw
Exclusive/Hammer (Michael Carreras)
US title: *The Unholy Four*
After being assaulted in the Far East, a financier loses his memory and does not return home until three years later, when murder ensues.
Muddled mystery quickie, only notable as the film which persuaded its star to retire.
w Michael Carreras *novel* Stranger at Home by George Sanders *d* Terence Fisher *ph* James Harvey *m* Ivor Slaney *ed* Bill Lenney
☆ Paulette Goddard, William Sylvester, Patrick Holt, Paul Carpenter, Russell Napier, Alvys Maben

The Stranger In Between: see *Hunted*

A Stranger in My Arms
US 1958 88m bw Cinemascope
U-I (Ross Hunter)
A test pilot falls in love with his dead friend's widow and helps her face up to her in-laws.
Dreary romantic drama.
w Peter Berneis *novel* And Ride a Tiger by Robert Wilder *d* Helmut Kautner *ph* William Daniels *m* Joseph Gershenson
☆ June Allyson, Jeff Chandler, Mary Astor, Sandra Dee, Charles Coburn, Conrad Nagel, Peter Graves

A Stranger in Town
US 1943 67m bw
MGM (Robert Sisk)
A supreme court judge on vacation finds himself sorting out crooked local politicians.
Interesting second feature with good cast and production values.
w Isobel Lennart, William Koslenko *d* Roy Rowland
☆ Frank Morgan, Richard Carlson, Jean Rogers, Porter Hall, Robert Barrat, Donald MacBride, Andrew Tombes, John Hodiak

A Stranger Is Watching
US 1981 92m Metrocolor
MGM-UA (Sidney Beckerman)

A small girl is terrified by the psychopath who raped and murdered her mother.
Unpleasant thriller in the modern manner.
w Earl Mac Rauch, Victor Miller *novel* Mary Higgins Clark *d* Sean S. Cunningham
☆ Kate Mulgrew, Rip Torn, James Naughton, Shawn Van Schreiber

The Stranger Left No Card **
GB 1952 23m bw
British Lion/Meteor (George Arthur)
A weirdly dressed eccentric comes to a small town and is accepted by the townspeople; but his real purpose is murder.
Smart little trick film which as a novelty has not been surpassed.
w Sidney Carroll *d* Wendy Toye *ph* Jonah Jones *md* Muir Mathieson
☆ Alan Badel, Cameron Hall, Eileen Way

Stranger on the Prowl
Italy/US 1952 82m bw
UA/CPCT (Noel Calef)
Italian title: *Imbarco a Mezzanotte*
GB title: *Encounter*
In an Italian port, a stranger helps a boy but is shot by the police.
Ineffective melodrama, a sad comedown for its star.
w Andrea Forzano (Ben Barzman) *story* Noel Calef *d* Andrea Forzano (Joseph Losey) *ph* Henri Alekan *m* G. C. Sonzogno *ad* Antonio Valente *ed* Thelma Connell
☆ Paul Muni, Joan Lorring, Vittorio Manunta, Aldo Silvani
† Both director and scriptwriter worked under a pseudonym owing to Hollywood's black-listing.

Stranger on the Third Floor *
US 1940 64m bw
RKO (Lee Marcus)

A reporter finds that he was wrong in the well-intentioned testimony which helps convict an innocent man for murder.
Stylish B feature with a striking dream scene and a curious fleeting performance by Lorre as the real murderer.
w Frank Partos *d* Boris Ingster *ph* Nicholas Musuraca *m* Roy Webb
☆ Margaret Tallichet, Peter Lorre, John McGuire, Charles Waldron, Elisha Cook Jnr, Charles Halton, Ethel Griffies

Stranger than Paradise *
US/Germany 1984 90m bw
Grokenberger/Cinesthesia/ZDF (Sara Driver)

The small adventures in America of a young Hungarian immigrant, her cousin and his friend.
Filmed in bleached-out black and white and not edited in the conventional sense – each take is shown complete and followed by a brief blackout before the next shot is shown – it focuses upon grungey lives in which nothing happens – and if it should, no one would notice; but it exerts a slight charm by its very waywardness.
wd Jim Jarmusch *ph* Tom DiCillo *m* John Lurie *ed* Jim Jarmusch, Melody London
☆ John Lurie, Eszter Balint, Richard Edson, Cecillia Stark
'To think *Stranger than Paradise* was a knockout of a movie you'd have to tune in to its minimalism so passively that you lowered your expectations. The film is so hemmed in that it has the feel of a mousy East European comedy; it's like a comedy of sensory deprivation.' – *Pauline Kael, New Yorker*
'Full of a quirky character and irony that makes its central theme of American alienation seem extremely entertaining.' – *Derek Malcolm, Guardian*

A Stranger Walked In: see *Love from a Stranger*

'For him death has two faces – and he faces them both, alone!'
The Stranger Wore a Gun
US 1953 83m Technicolor 3-D
Columbia

An honest adventurer finds that the man who once saved his life has become a stagecoach robber.
Routine Western with many objects hurled at the audience to show off the 3-D process.
w Kenneth Gamet *novel* John M. Cunningham *d* André de Toth *ph* Lester White *md* Mischa Bakaleinikoff
☆ Randolph Scott, George Macready, Claire Trevor, Joan Weldon, Lee Marvin, Ernest Borgnine, Alfonso Bedoya

Strangers: see *Voyage to Italy*

Strangers All
US 1935 70m bw
RKO
A mother tries to keep the peace while her three unsuccessful sons – a shopkeeper, an actor and a political activist – quarrel about the worth of their callings and her daughter abandons her wealthy fiancé to marry a lawyer.
Sentimental family comedy-drama, enjoyable enough in its old-fashioned way if somewhat abrupt in its sudden ending.

w Milton Krims *play* Marie M. Bercovici
d Charles Vidor *ph* John W. Boyle *md* Roy Webb
ad Van Nest Polglase *ed* Jack Hively
☆ May Robson, Preston Foster, Florine McKinney, William Bakewell, James Bush, Samuel Hinds, Leon Ames

The Stranger's Hand
GB 1953 85m bw
Independent Film Producers/John Stafford, Peter Moore
aka: *Mano della Straniero*
A schoolboy is due to meet his father in Venice, but the father is kidnapped by enemy agents.
Rather tentative suspense thriller with a vague plot which seems to defeat an excellent cast.
w Guy Elmes, Giorgio Bassani *story* Graham Greene *d* Mario Soldati *ph* Enzo Serafin *m* Nino Rota
☆ Trevor Howard, Richard O'Sullivan, Francis L. Sullivan, Alida Valli, Eduardo Ciannelli, Richard Basehart, Stephen Murray

Strangers in Good Company: see *The Company of Strangers*

Strangers in Love
US 1932 68m bw
Paramount
A ne'er-do-well has some difficulties when he tries to step into his dead twin's shoes.
Predictable comedy-melodrama, quite well acted.
w Grover Jones, William Slavens McNutt *play* *The Shorn Lamb* by William J. Locke *d* Lothar Mendes
☆ Fredric March, Kay Francis, Stuart Erwin, Juliette Compton, George Barbier, Sidney Toler
'All the qualities that bespeak wide appeal.' – *Variety*

Strangers May Kiss
US 1931 82m bw
MGM
A sophisticated wife takes love and fidelity lightly.
Dated romantic drama.
w John Meehan *novel* Ursula Parrott *d* George Fitzmaurice *ph* William Daniels
☆ Norma Shearer, Robert Montgomery, Neil Hamilton, Marjorie Rambeau, Irene Rich
'Outstanding money picture. It'll sell itself.' – *Variety*

'It begins with the scream of a train whistle – and ends with screaming excitement!'
Strangers on a Train ***
US 1951 101m bw
Warner (Alfred Hitchcock)
A tennis star is pestered on a train by a psychotic who wants to swap murders, and proceeds to carry out his part of the bargain.
This quirky melodrama has the director at his best, sequence by sequence, but the story is basically unsatisfactory. It makes superior suspense entertainment, however.
w Raymond Chandler, Czenzi Ormonde *novel* Patricia Highsmith *d* *Alfred Hitchcock* *ph* *Robert Burks* *m* *Dimitri Tiomkin* *md* Ray Heindorf
☆ Farley Granger, *Robert Walker*, Ruth Roman, Leo G. Carroll, Patricia Hitchcock, *Marion Lorne*, Howard St John, Jonathan Hale, Laura Elliot
BRUNO (ROBERT WALKER): 'Some people are better off dead – like your wife and my father, for instance.'
'You may not take it seriously, but you certainly don't have time to think about anything else.' – *Richard Mallett, Punch*
'The construction seems a little lame, but Hitch takes delight in the set pieces.' – *Time Out, 1985*
† Remade 1970 as *Once You Kiss A Stranger*.
Robert Burks

The Stranger's Return
US 1933 89m bw
MGM
An old farmer disapproves of his granddaughter's affair with a married man.
An American view of Cold Comfort Farm *country, too heavy to click at the box-office.*
w Brown Holmes, Phil Stong *d* King Vidor
☆ Lionel Barrymore, Miriam Hopkins, Franchot Tone, Beulah Bondi, Stuart Erwin, Irene Hervey

Strangers When We Meet *
US 1960 117m Technicolor Cinemascope
Columbia/Bryna (Richard Quine)
A successful architect starts an affair with a beautiful married neighbour.
Beverly Hills soap opera with lots of romantic suffering in luxury. Lumpy but generally palatable.
w Evan Hunter *novel* Evan Hunter *d* Richard Quine *ph* Charles Lang Jnr *m* George Duning
☆ Kirk Douglas, Kim Novak, *Ernie Kovacs, Walter Matthau*, Barbara Rush, Virginia Bruce, Helen Gallagher, Kent Smith

The Strangler
US 1963 80m bw
AA
An obese lab technician murders nurses who help his hated mother.
Modest, lively shocker.
w Bill S. Ballinger *d* Burt Topper *ph* Jacques Marquette *m* Marlin Skiles
☆ Victor Buono, David McLean, Ellen Corby, Diane Sayer

The Stranglers of Bombay
GB 1960 80m bw MegaScope
Columbia/Hammer (Anthony Nelson-Keys)
In 1826 travellers are waylaid and sacrificially killed by a cult of stranglers.
Semi-historical parade of atrocities, repellent but scarcely exciting.
w David Z. Goodman *d* Terence Fisher *ph* Arthur Grant *m* James Bernard *ad* Bernard Robinson, Don Mingaye *ed* James Needs, Alfred Cox
☆ Guy Rolfe, Allan Cuthbertson, Andrew Cruickshank, Marne Maitland, Jan Holden, George Pastell, Paul Stassino

Strapless
GB 1988 100m Technicolor
Virgin/Granada/Film Four International (Rick McCallum)
Two sisters assert their independence after unsatisfactory relationships with men.
Uneasy blend of unbelievable romance and politics.
wd David Hare *ph* Andrew Dunn *m* Nick Bicat *pd* Roger Hall *ed* Edward Marnier
☆ Blair Brown, Bruno Ganz, Bridget Fonda, Alan Howard, Michael Gough, Hugh Laurie, Suzanne Burden, Rohan McCullough

Strategic Air Command
US 1955 114m Technicolor Vistavision
Paramount (Samuel J. Briskin)
A baseball player is recalled to air force duty.
Sentimental flagwaver featuring the newest jets of the fifties.
w Valentine Davies, Beirne Lay Jnr *d* Anthony Mann *ph* William Daniels *m* Victor Young
☆ James Stewart, June Allyson, Frank Lovejoy, Barry Sullivan, Alex Nicol, Bruce Bennett, Jay C. Flippen, James Millican, James Bell
original story (Beirne Lay Jnr)

The Stratton Story
US 1949 106m bw
MGM (Jack Cummings)
An amateur baseball enthusiast becomes a famous professional, but suffers an accident which involves the amputation of a leg.
Mild sentimental biopic, well made but not very interesting.
w Douglas Morrow, Guy Trosper *d* Sam Wood *ph* Harold Rosson *m* Adolph Deutsch
☆ James Stewart, June Allyson, Frank Morgan, Agnes Moorehead, Bill Williams
† Van Johnson and Donna Reed were originally cast in the leading roles.
original story (Douglas Morrow)

Strauss's Great Waltz: see *Waltzes from Vienna*

'The knock at the door meant the birth of one man and the death of seven others!'
Straw Dogs
GB 1971 118m Eastmancolor
Talent Associates/Amerbroco (Daniel Melnick)
In a Cornish village, a mild American university researcher erupts into violence when taunted by drunken villagers who commit sustained assaults on himself and his wife.
Totally absurd, poorly contrived, hilariously overwritten Cold Comfort Farm *melodrama with farcical violence.*
w David Zelag Goodman, Sam Peckinpah *novel* *The Siege of Trencher's Farm* by Gordon M. Williams *d* Sam Peckinpah *ph* John Coquillon *m* Jerry Fielding *pd* Ray Simm
☆ Dustin Hoffman, Susan George, Peter Vaughan, David Warner, T. P. McKenna, Colin Welland
'Before the end you will have gasped and shuddered through an orgy of detailed rape, slaughter, arson and wanton destruction.' – *Cecil Wilson, Daily Mail*
'A magnificent piece of red-raw, meaty entertainment.' – *Ernest Betts, The People*
Jerry Fielding

'Distant Dreams and Passionate Lovers.'
Strawberry and Chocolate **
Cuba/Mexico/Spain 1993 111m colour
Metro Tartan/ICAIC/IMC/Telemadrid/Co. Tabasco (Miguel Mendoza)
original title: *Fresa y Chocolate*
In Havana, a naïve and conformist university student, a Communist Party member, reluctantly becomes friends with a cultured homosexual, who is persecuted for his subversive views.
The first Cuban film to show homosexuality in a positive way is also concerned with more important matters than being gay; it is a playful attack on hidebound attitudes and prejudices and on a revolution that has gone stale, and a passionate plea for cultural diversity.
w Senel Paz *novel* *El Lobo, el Bosque y el Hombre Nuevo* by Senel Paz *d* Tomás Gutiérrez Alea, Juan Carlos Tabío *ph* Mario Garcia Joya *m* José Maria Vitier *ad* Orlando Gonzalez *ed* Miriam Talavera, Osvaldo Donatien
☆ *Jorge Perugorria*, Vladimir Cruz, Mirta Ibarra, Francisco Gattorno, Joel Angelino, Marilyn Solaya
'This new comedy from Cuba is a gem. Filled with malicious swipes against the Castro regime, it's a provocative but very humane comedy about sexual opposites.' – *David Stratton, Variety*
† Juan Carlos Tabio helped with the direction when Alea became ill with cancer.
best foreign language film

The Strawberry Blonde **
US 1941 97m bw
Warner (William Cagney)
A dentist in turn-of-the-century Brooklyn wonders whether he married the right woman.
Pleasant period comedy drama, a remake of One Sunday Afternoon *(qv).*
w Julius J. and Philip G. Epstein *d* Raoul Walsh *ph* *James Wong Howe* *m* Heinz Roemheld
☆ *James Cagney*, Olivia de Havilland, *Rita Hayworth, Alan Hale*, George Tobias, Jack Carson, Una O'Connor, George Reeves
'It not only tells a very human story, it also creates an atmosphere, recreates a period.' – *New York Sun*
'A blithe, sentimental, turn-of-the-century buggy ride.' – *Time*
Heinz Roemheld

The Strawberry Statement
US 1970 109m Metrocolor
MGM/Robert Chartoff, Irwin Winkler
Student rebels occupy a university administration building.
One of a short-lived group of student anti-discipline films of the early seventies, and about the most boring.
w Israel Horovitz *novel* James Simon Kunen *d* Stuart Hagmann *ph* Ralph Woolsey *m* Ian Freebairn Smith
☆ Bruce Davison, Kim Darby, Bud Cort, Murray MacLeod

Streamers
US 1983 118m Movielab
Rank/Streamers International (Robert Altman, Nick J. Mileti)
Tensions mount at a training camp for the 83rd Airborne Division.
Claustrophobic photographed play about generally worthless people.
w David Rabe *play* David Rabe *d* Robert Altman *ph* Pierre Mignot *pd* Wolf Kroeger *ed* Norman Smith
☆ Matthew Modine, Michael Wright, Mitchell Lichtenstein, David Alan Grier, Guy Boyd, George Dzundza

'A thing of beauty is a joy for ever...'
Street Angel *
US 1928 101m bw part-talkie
Fox
An unwilling prostitute becomes a circus artiste.
A sentimental and tawdry tale becomes a vehicle for good typical work by director and stars.
w Marion Orth *play* *Lady Cristallinda* by Monckton Hoffe *d* *Frank Borzage* *ph* Ernest Palmer, Paul Ivano *ad* Harry Oliver
☆ Janet Gaynor, Charles Farrell, Henry Armetta, Guido Trento
Janet Gaynor
Ernest Palmer; Harry Oliver

Street Corner
GB 1953 94m bw
Rank/LIP/Sydney Box (William MacQuitty)
US title: *Both Sides of the Law*
Days in the lives of the women police of Chelsea.
Patter-plotted female Blue Lamp*; just about watchable.*
w Muriel and Sydney Box *d* Muriel Box *ph* Reg Wyer *m* Temple Abady
☆ Rosamund John, Anne Crawford, Peggy Cummins, Terence Morgan, Barbara Murray, Sarah Lawson, Ronald Howard, Eleanor Summerfield, Michael Medwin

Street Fighter
US 1994 102m DeLuxe
UIP/Capcom (Edward R. Pressman, Kenzo Tsujimoto)
Street fighters set out to rescue hostages held by a mad dictator.
A popular video game is transferred to the screen with all its slam-bang excitement missing; it is presumably aimed at an easily satisfied audience of kids too young to play the game.
wd Steven E. de Souza *ph* William A. Fraker *m* Graeme Revell *pd* William Creber *ed* Dov Hoenig, Anthony Redman, Robert F. Shugrue, Ed Abroms, Donn Aron
☆ Jean-Claude Van Damme, Raul Julia, Kylie Minogue, Damian Chapa, Ming-Na Wen, Simon Callow, Roshan Seth, Wes Studi, Byron Mann
'Noisy, overblown and effects-laden and lacks sustained action or engaging characters.' – *Variety*
'I enjoyed making it but when I saw it, it was so bad both my wife and I walked out.' – *Roshan Seth*

Street Fleet: see *D. C. Cab*

Street Gang
US 1982 90m TVC Color Panavision
Film Ventures/Vigilante (William Lustig, Andrew Garroni)
aka: *Vigilante*
After his son is killed by a Puerto Rican gang, a factory worker joins a vigilante group to clean up the streets.
An unpleasant movie of rough justice that follows in the footsteps of Death Wish.
w Richard Vetere *d* William Lustig *ph* James Lemmo *m* Jay Chattaway *pd* Mischa Petrow *ed* Lorenzo Marinelli
☆ Robert Forster, Fred Williamson, Richard Bright, Rutanya Alda, Willie Colon, Joe Spinell, Carol Lynley, Woody Strode, Joseph Carberry

Street of Chance
US 1930 78m bw
Paramount (David O. Selznick)
A New York gambler gets his come-uppance.
Dullish family melodrama with gangsters as dei ex machina.

w Howard Estabrook, Lenore Coffee *d* John Cromwell *ph* Charles Lang
☆ William Powell, Kay Francis, Regis Toomey, Jean Arthur
'Strong exploitation can cinch this one. Strongly hints at recent murder of well-known gambler.' – *Variety*
script

'Where women came to forget – one man came to remember!'

Street of Chance *
US 1942 74m bw
Burt Skelly/Sol C. Siegel/Paramount
An amnesia case discovers that he is wanted for murder.
The plot was fairly original at the time, and the treatment maintains interest.
w Garrett Fort *story* Cornell Woolrich *d* Jack Hively
☆ Burgess Meredith, Claire Trevor, Sheldon Leonard, Jerome Cowan, Frieda Inescort, Louise Platt

Street of Shadows
GB 1953 84m bw
Anglo Amalgamated/Merton Park (William H. Williams)
US title: *Shadow Man*
A Soho club-owner and his society girlfriend become mixed up in murder when the corpse of his mistress is discovered in his office.
Run-of-the-mill melodramatic thriller, with a better cast than it deserves.
wd Richard Vernon *novel* *The Creaking Chair* by Laurence Meynell *ph* Phil Grindrod *m* Eric Spear
☆ Cesar Romero, Kay Kendall, Simone Silva, Edward Underdown, Victor Maddern, John Penrose, Eileen Way, Bill Travers

Street of Shame *
Japan 1956 85m bw
Daiei (Masaichi Nagata)
original title: *Akasen Chitai*
Stories of women in a Tokyo brothel.
Unremarkable material executed with the style expected of the director.
w Masashige Narusawa *d* Kenji Mizoguchi *ph* Kazuo Miyagawa *m* Toshiro Mayazumi
☆ Machiko Kyo, Ayako Wakao, Aiko Mimasu

Street of Women
US 1932 59m bw
Warner
A property developer is torn between his wife and his mistress.
Choppily developed drama which starts haltingly and gets nowhere.
w Mary McCall Jnr *novel* Polan Banks *d* Archie Mayo
☆ Kay Francis, Alan Dinehart, Roland Young, Marjorie Gateson, Gloria Stuart
'Just a programme picture.' – *Variety*

Street People: see *Sicilian Cross*

Street Scene *
US 1931 80m bw
Samuel Goldwyn
In a New York slum street on a hot summer night, an adulterous woman is shot by her husband.
Slice-of-life drama from an influential play; never much of a film, and very dated.
w Elmer Rice *play* Elmer Rice *d* King Vidor *ph* George Barnes *m* Alfred Newman
☆ Sylvia Sidney, William Collier Jnr, Max Mantor, David Landau, Estelle Taylor, Russell Hopton
'Whenever the camera starts to focus on two or three characters, the plot thickens and *Street Scene* flies out the window; petty domestic tragedy supplants the original slice-of-life conception.' – *National Board of Review*
'As a commercial proposition it will cause talk and reap honours, but whether it will prove an exceptional box office attraction remains to be seen.' – *Variety*

The Street Singer
GB 1937 85m bw
British National
A musical comedy star is mistaken for a beggar by a girl with whom he falls in love.
Rather tiresome star vehicle.
w Reginald Arkell *d* Jean de Marguenat *md* Lew Stone
☆ Arthur Tracy, Margaret Lockwood, Arthur Riscoe, Hugh Wakefield

Street Smart
US 1987 95m TVC Color
Cannon (Menahem Golan, Yoram Globus)
A top journalist turns in a story that gets him involved with pimps and prostitutes.
Unpersuasive crime melodrama in which the star seems surprised to find himself.
w David Freeman *d* Jerry Schatzberg *ph* Adam Holender *m* Robert Irving *pd* Dan Leigh *ed* Priscilla Nedd
☆ Christopher Reeve, Kathy Baker, Mimi Rogers, Jay Patterson, Andre Gregory, Morgan Freeman
Morgan Freeman

The Street with No Name *
US 1948 93m bw
TCF (Samuel G. Engel)
An FBI man goes undercover to unmask a criminal gang.
The oldest crime plot in the world, applied with vigour to the documentary realism of The House on 92nd Street *and built around the Kiss of Death psychopathic character created by Richard Widmark.*
w Harry Kleiner *d* William Keighley *ph* Joe MacDonald *m* Lionel Newman
☆ Richard Widmark, Mark Stevens, Lloyd Nolan, Barbara Lawrence, Ed Begley
† Remade 1955 as *House of Bamboo*.

A Streetcar Named Desire **
US 1951 122m bw
Warner/Elia Kazan (Charles K. Feldman)
A repressed Southern widow is raped and driven mad by her brutal brother-in-law.
Reasonably successful, decorative picture from a highly theatrical but influential play; unreal sets and atmospheric photography vaguely Sternbergian.
w Tennessee Williams *play* Tennessee Williams *d* *Elia Kazan* *ph* *Harry Stradling* *m* Alex North *ad* Richard Day
☆ *Vivien Leigh, Marlon Brando, Kim Hunter, Karl Malden*
† Two television versions followed, one in 1984 starring Ann-Margret and Treat Williams, and one in 1994 starring Jessica Lange and Alec Baldwin.
Vivien Leigh; Kim Hunter; Karl Malden
best picture; Tennessee Williams; Elia Kazan; Harry Stradling; Alex North; Marlon Brando; Richard Day
Vivien Leigh

The Streetfighter: see *Hard Times*

Streets of Fire
US 1984 94m Technicolor
Universal/RKO/Hill-Gordon-Silver (Lawrence Gordon, Joel Silver)
A rock singer is kidnapped and a professional trouble shooter takes on the job of recovery.
Violent melodrama with an unsuccessful comic strip approach which fails to raise the material into the realm of myth.
w Walter Hill, Larry Gross *d* Walter Hill *ph* Andrew Laszlo *m* Ry Cooder *pd* John Vallone *ed* Freeman Davies, Michael Ripps
☆ Michael Paré, Diane Lane, Rick Moranis, Amy Madigan, Willem Dafoe

Streets of Gold *
US 1986 95m DeLuxe
TCF/James G. Robinson/Ufland-Roth
A disenchanted immigrant finds an unexpected road to success as a boxing coach for two streetwise kids.
Unappealing variation on the Rocky movies, good to look at but devoid of content.
w Heywood Gould, Richard Price, Tom Cole *d* Joe Roth *ph* Arthur Albert *m* Jack Nitzsche *pd* Marcos Flaksman *ed* Richard Chew
☆ Klaus Maria Brandauer, Adrian Pasdar, Wesley Snipes, Angela Molina

Streets of Laredo
US 1949 92m Technicolor
Paramount (Robert Fellows)
Two of three bandit friends become Texas Rangers.
Adequate star Western, a remake of The Texas Rangers.
w Charles Marquis Warren *d* Leslie Fenton *ph* Ray Rennahan *m* Victor Young
☆ William Holden, William Bendix, Macdonald Carey, Mona Freeman

Streets of New York
US 1939 72m bw
Monogram
The teenage owner of a newsstand studies law at night school.
Unconvincing street-life drama, an obvious vehicle for a boy star.
w Robert Andrews *d* William Nigh
☆ Jackie Cooper, Martin Spellman, George Cleveland, Dick Purcell
'Should do all right if not pointed too high.' – *Variety*

The Streetwalker: see *La Marge*

Strictly Ballroom ***
Australia 1992 94m Eastmancolor
Rank/M&A/Australian Film Finance Corp (Tristam Miall)
A would-be champion ballroom dancer, who incurs the wrath of the establishment by improvising his own steps, searches for a new partner in tune with his ideas.
Exuberant, charming, witty romance acted and directed with style and verve.
w Baz Luhrmann, Craig Pearce *play* N.I.D.A. stage production devised by its original cast *story* *Baz Luhrmann*, *Andrew Bovell* *d* *Baz Luhrmann* *ph* Steve Mason *m* David Hirschfelder *ch* John 'Cha Cha' O'Connell, Paul Mercurio *pd* Catherine Martin *ed* Jill Bilcock
☆ *Paul Mercurio*, Tara Morice, Bill Hunter, Pat Thomson, Gia Carides, Peter Whitford, Barry Otto, John Hannan, Sonia Kruger, Kris McQuade, Antonio Vargas, Armonia Benedito
'Bright, breezy and immensely likable musical-comedy.' – *Variety*
David Hirschfelder; Catherine Martin

Strictly Confidential: see *Broadway Bill*

Strictly Dishonourable
US 1951 94m bw
MGM (Melvin Frank, Norman Panama)
A young girl falls in love with a rakish Italian opera star; he is such a sentimentalist that he marries her.
Emasculated sentimental version of the sharp Preston Sturges comedy.
wd Norman Panama, Melvin Frank *ph* Ray June *m* Lennie Hayton
☆ Ezio Pinza, Janet Leigh, Millard Mitchell, Maria Palmer
† Previously filmed in 1931 by Universal, with Paul Lukas, Sidney Fox and Lewis Stone.

Strictly for Pleasure: see *The Perfect Furlough*

Strictly Unconventional: see *The Circle*

Strike ***
USSR 1924 70m approx (24 fps) bw silent
Goskino/Proletkult
A 1912 strike of factory workers is brutally put down by the authorities.
Brilliant propaganda piece with superbly cinematic sequences.
wd *Sergei M. Eisenstein* *ph* Edouard Tissé, Vassili Khvatov
☆ Grigori Alexandrov, Maxim Strauch, Mikhail Gomarov

Strike It Rich: see *Loser Takes All*

Strike Me Pink *
US 1935 104m bw
Samuel Goldwyn
A timid amusement park owner is threatened by crooks.
Acceptable star comedy with music..
w Frank Butler, Walter de Leon, Francis Martin *d* Norman Taurog *ph* Gregg Toland, Merritt Gerstad *m* Alfred Newman *songs* Harold Arlen, Lew Brown
☆ Eddie Cantor, Sally Eilers, Ethel Merman, William Frawley, Parkyakarkus
'At the box office both here and abroad the take will be big.' – *Variety*

Strike Up the Band *
US 1940 120m bw
MGM (Arthur Freed)
A high-school band takes part in a nationwide radio contest.
Rather tiresomely high-spirited musical with the stars at the top of their young form.
w Fred Finklehoffe, John Monks Jnr *ph* Ray June *m* Roger Edens *d/ch* Busby Berkeley *ly* Arthur Freed
☆ *Judy Garland, Mickey Rooney*, Paul Whiteman and his Orchestra, June Preisser, William Tracy, Larry Nunn
♫ 'Our Love Affair'; 'Do the Conga'; 'Heaven Will Protect the Working Girl'; 'Nobody'; 'Nell of New Rochelle'; 'Drummer Boy'; 'Strike Up the Band'
Georgie Stoll, Roger Edens; song 'Our Love Affair' (m/ly Roger Edens, Georgie Stoll)

'They shouldn't have put him in the water, if they didn't want him to make waves.'

Striking Distance
US 1993 102m Technicolor
Columbia (Arnon Milchan, Tony Thomopoulos, Hunt Lowry)
A hard-drinking maverick cop tracks down the serial killer who murdered his father.
An unoriginal mix of car chases, tough cops and fist fights providing undemanding entertainment for the unthinking.
w Rowdy Herrington, Martin Kaplan *d* Rowdy Herrington *ph* Mac Ahlberg *m* Brad Fiedel *pd* Greg Fonseca *ed* Pasquale Buba, Mark Helfrich
☆ Bruce Willis, Sarah Jessica Parker, Dennis Farina, Tom Sizemore, Brion James, Robert Pastorelli, Timothy Busfield, John Mahoney
'An OK action movie until it sinks under the weight of implausible plotting and over-the-top direction.' – *Brian Lowry, Variety*

The Strip *
US 1951 85m bw
MGM (Joe Pasternak)
A band drummer is accused of the murder of a racketeer.
Minor mystery melodrama intriguingly set on Sunset Strip, with jazz accompaniment.
w Allen Rivkin *d* Leslie Kardos *ph* Robert Surtees *m* George Stoll
☆ Mickey Rooney, Sally Forrest, William Demarest, James Craig, Kay Brown, Louis Armstrong, Earl Hines, Jack Teagarden
song 'A Kiss To Build a Dream On (m/ly Bert Kalmar, Harry Ruby, Oscar Hammerstein II)

'Today's army needs men of courage – honesty – integrity – ambition. Instead, they got John Winger...'

Stripes
US 1981 106m Metrocolor
Columbia (Ivan Reitman, Dan Goldberg)
Sergeant Hulka tries to train a platoon of misfit volunteers.
Ancient army wheezes dressed up with fashionable black comedy and sex, but no funnier than Carry On Sergeant.
w Len Blum, Dan Goldberg, Harold Ramis *d* Ivan Reitman *ph* Bill Butler *m* Elmer Bernstein
☆ Bill Murray, Harold Ramis, Warren Oates, P. J. Soles, John Larroquette, Sean Young

The Stripper *
US 1963 95m bw Cinemascope
TCF (Jerry Wald)
GB title: *Woman of Summer*
An ageing beauty queen returns to her Kansas hometown and has an affair with a 19-year-old garage hand.
Downbeat character melodrama typical of its time and its author; competent but sterile and rather tedious.
w Meade Roberts *play A Loss of Roses* by William Inge *d Franklin Schaffner ph* Ellsworth Fredericks *m* Jerry Goldsmith
☆ *Joanne Woodward*, Richard Beymer, *Claire Trevor*, Carol Lynley, Robert Webber, Louis Nye, Gypsy Rose Lee, Michael J. Pollard

Stripper *
US 1986 90m colour
Arnon Milchan/Visionaire (Jerome Gary, Geof Bartz, Melvyn J. Estrin)
Strippers congregate in Las Vegas in 1984 to compete for the Golden G-string Award.
Interesting and saddening documentary on strippers, who talk of their art and pride in what they are doing, before performing their dispiriting routines in tacky clubs.
d Jerome Gary *ph* Edward Lachman *m* Buffy Sainte-Marie, Jack Nitzsche *ed* Geof Bartz, Bob Eisenhardt, Lawrence Silk

'Some people get into trouble ... No matter what they wear.'
Striptease
US 1996 117m Technicolor
Rank/Castle Rock/Turner (Mike Lobell)
Investigating a murder involving a corrupt Congressman, a detective enlists the help of a single mother, who is working as a stripper to gain custody of her child.
Unsuccessful adaptation of a slick, witty thriller, fatally compromised by the casting of Demi Moore, whose requirements as a star run counter to the demands of the narrative.
wd Andrew Bergman *novel* Carl Hiaasen *ph* Stephen Goldblatt *m* Howard Shore *pd* Mel Bourne *ed* Anne V. Coates
☆ Demi Moore, Burt Reynolds, Armand Assante, Ving Rhames, Robert Patrick, Paul Guilfoyle, Jerry Grayson, Rumer Willis
'Sub-soft porn masquerading as a television custody drama – with jokes. Unfortunately it has no idea of how to bring off this generic *ménage à trois*.' – *Linda Ruth Williams, Sight and Sound*

Striptease Lady: see *Lady of Burlesque*

Stroker Ace
US 1983 96m Technicolor Panavision
Universal/Warner (Hank Moonjean)
A top racing car driver is sponsored by the owner of a chain of fast-food restaurants.
Tediously leering comedy, with Reynolds repeating his over-familiar role as a macho ladies' man.
w Hugh Wilson, Hal Needham *novel Stand On It* by William Neely, Robert K. Ottum *d* Hal Needham *ph* Nick McLean *m* Al Capps *ad* Paul Peters *ed* Carl Kress, William Gordean
☆ Burt Reynolds, Ned Beatty, Jim Nabors, Parker Stevenson, Loni Anderson

Stromboli
Italy 1949 107m bw
RKO/Be-Ro (Roberto Rossellini)
A Lithuanian refugee accepts the protection of marriage to an Italian fisherman, but resents the barrenness and hostility of her life, especially when the local volcano erupts.
Sloppy melodrama with pretensions, interesting but not even attractive to the eye.
w Roberto Rossellini and others *d* Roberto Rossellini *ph* Otello Martelli *m* Renzo Rossellini
☆ Ingrid Bergman, Mario Vitale, Renzo Cesana
† The international version was cut to 81m.

'From the coolest city on the planet comes the hippest film of the year.'
Strong Language
GB 1999 80m bw/colour
Rumleyvision (Simon Rumley)
A group of twenty- and thirty-something Londoners discuss their lives, loves, likes and dislikes, and the event that links them together.
Fuzzily photographed confessions from a disparate group, given to the sort of monologues a barman might overhear on a bad night.
wd Simon Rumley *ph* Armando Smit *m* David Conway, Laurence Elliot-Potter *pd* Joanna Cross *ed* Simon Rumley, Sasha Austen, Rick Moore
☆ David Groves (Narrator), Paul Tonkinson (Danny), Tania Emery (Zoe), Stuart Laing (Mark), Ricci Harnett (Nathan), Kelly Marcell (Phillipa), Robyn Lewis (Corinne), Julie Rice (Tatty), Al Nedjari (Peter), Ruth Purser (Jane)
'Absorbing and revealing as it heads to its conclusion and carves another notch in British cinema's innovative bedpost.' – *Film Review*

The Strong Man *
US 1926 75m approx (24 fps) bw (colour sequence) silent
First National/Harry Langdon
A war veteran returns and searches the city for his female penfriend.
Quite charming star comedy, probably Langdon's best.
w Frank Capra, Arthur Ripley, Hal Conklin, Robert Eddy *d* Frank Capra *ph* Elgin Lessley, Glenn Kershner
☆ *Harry Langdon*, Gertrude Astor, Tay Garnett

Stronger than Desire
US 1939 82m bw
MGM
A lawyer's wife gets into trouble and lets him try an innocent man for her crime.
Fast remake of Evelyn Prentice; *a good half-bill.*
w David Hertz, William Ludwig *d* Leslie Fenton
☆ Walter Pidgeon, Virginia Bruce, Ann Dvorak, Lee Bowman, Rita Johnson, Ilka Chase

Stronger than Fear: see *Edge of Doom*

The Strongest Man in the World
US 1976 92m Technicolor
Walt Disney (Bill Anderson)
An accident in a science lab gives a student superhuman strength.
Formula comedy for older children.
w Joseph L. McEveety, Herman Groves *d* Vincent McEveety *ph* Andrew Jackson *m* Robert F. Brunner
☆ Kurt Russell, Joe Flynn, Eve Arden, Cesar Romero, Phil Silvers, Dick Van Patten, Harold Gould, William Schallert, James Gregory, Roy Roberts, Fritz Feld, Raymond Bailey, Eddie Quillan, Burt Mustin

Strongroom *
GB 1961 80m bw
Bryanston/Theatrecraft (Guido Coen)
Two car breakers plan a once-for-all bank robbery but get involved with potential murder when their hostages get locked in.
Suspenseful second feature with gloss and pace.
w Max Marquis, René Harris *d Vernon Sewell ph* Basil Emmott *m* Johnny Gregory
☆ Colin Gordon, Ann Lynn, Derren Nesbitt, Keith Faulkner

Stroszeck *
West Germany 1977 108m colour
Werner Herzog/ZDF
A crook, a prostitute and a friend move from Germany to what they hope will be the freedom of a mobile home in the United States; but everything goes wrong and they part company.
A simple narrative – described as 'a ballad' by its director – of a failed search for individuality and the exchange of one prison for another.
wd Werner Herzog *ph* Thomas Mauch, Ed Lachmann, Wolfgang Knigge, Stefano Guidi *m* Chet Atkins, Sonny Terry *ed* Beate Mainka-Jellinghaus
☆ Bruno S, Eva Mattes, Clemens Scheitz, Burkhard Driest, Alfred Edel, Norbert Grupe

The Struggle *
US 1931 88m bw
UA/D. W. Griffith
A New Yorker goes to the bad on bootleg liquor.
The director's last film reveals many of his old skills allied to a Victorian tract.
w Anita Loos, John Emerson *d* D. W. Griffith *ph* Joseph Ruttenberg
☆ Hal Skelly, Zita Johann, Charlotte Wynters, Jackson Halliday
'A dull and sodden rendering with old-time ranting and little drama ... just dull when it isn't in the highest degree maudlin.' – *Dwight MacDonald*
† It was based on *The Drunkard* by Emile Zola.
†† The picture failed and was re-released as *Ten Nights in a Bar-room*.

Stryker
US/Philippines 1983 86m colour
New World/Cirio H. Santiago
In a world turned to desert by nuclear holocaust, gangs battle for water (though guns, ammunition, petrol and leatherwear remain in apparently endless supply).
Cheap and incompetent rip-off of Mad Max *(qv).*
w Howard R. Cohen *d* Cirio H. Santiago *ph* Ricardo Remias *m* Ed Gatchalian, Susan Justin *pd* Pol Dimalanta *ed* Rudy Cabrales
☆ Steve Sandor, Andria Savio, William Ostrander, Michael Lane, Julie Gray, Monique St Pierre, Ken Metcalfe

Stuart Little **
US 1999 92m DeLuxe
Columbia/Franklin/Waterman (Douglas Wick)
Promising their young son a little brother, a New York couple adopt a mouse, which annoys the family cat.
Clever, occasionally witty children's movie, seamlessly marrying live action and animation.
w M. Night Shyamalan, Greg Brooker *book* E.B. White *d* Rob Minkoff *ph* Guillermo Navarro *m/ly* Alan Silvestri *pd* Bill Brzeski *ed* Tom Finan *sp* John Dykstra; Jerome Chen
☆ Geena Davis (Mrs. Little), Hugh Laurie (Mr Little), Jonathan Lipnicki (George Little), Brian Doyle-Murray (Cousin Edgar), Estelle Getty (Grandma Estelle), Julia Sweeney (Mrs. Keeper), Dabney Coleman (Dr Beechwood) and also voices of: Michael J. Fox (Stuart Little), Nathan Lane, Chazz Palminteri, Steve Zahn, Jim Doughan, David Alan Grier, Jennifer Tilly, Bruno Kirby
'Sustains a lovely balance between enchantment and playfulness.' – *Stephen Holden, New York Times*
visual effects (John Dykstra, Jerome Chen, Henry F. Anderson III, Eric Allard)

'A Little Goes A Long Way'
Stuart Little 2 *
US 2002 78m DeLuxe
Columbia (Lucy Fisher, Douglas Wick)
A mouse, who is the adopted child of a New York couple, becomes involved with a bird.
Lively children's movie, full of innocent, good-hearted fun.
w Bruce Joel Rubin *story* Douglas Wick *novel Stuart Little* by E. B. White *d* Rob Minkoff *ph* Steven Poster *m* Alan Silvestri *pd* Bill Brzeski *ed* Priscilla Nedd Friendly
☆ Geena Davis (Mrs Little), Hugh Laurie (Mr Little), Jonathan Lipnicki (George Little), Anna Hoelck/Ashley Hoelck (Martha Little), Marc John Jefferies (Will), voices of: Michael J. Fox (Stuart Little), Nathan Lane (Snowbell), Melanie Griffith (Margalo), James Woods (Falcon), Steve Zahn (Monty)
'Aimed squarely at moppets with piddling attention spans.' – *Variety*

'You'll laugh because it's not your family. You'll cry because it is.'
Stuart Saves His Family
US 1995 95m colour
Paramount/Constellation (Lorne Michaels, Trevor Albert)
A self-help guru has to help himself when his public access TV show is cancelled and his family takes to drink and drugs.
Based on a Saturday Night Live sketch, this would be overstretched at a quarter of its length; it is the kind of maudlin movie that loses its audience in its first simpering thirty seconds and never gets it back.
w Al Franken *book I'm Good Enough, I'm Smart Enough, and Doggone It, People Like Me, Daily Affirmations with Stuart Smalley* by Al Franken *d* Harold Ramis *ph* Lauro Escorel *m* Marc Shaiman *pd* Joseph T. Garrity *ed* Pembroke Herring, Craig Herring
☆ Al Franken (Stuart Smalley), Laura San Giacomo (Julia), Vincent D'Onofrio (Donnie), Shirley Knight (Stuart's Mom), Harris Yulin (Stuart's Dad), Lesley Boone (Jodie), John Link Graney (Kyle), Julia Sweeney (Mea C)
'It isn't good enough, it isn't smart enough, and, doggone it, most people won't like *Stuart Saves His Family*.' – *Joe Leydon, Variety*

The Stud
GB 1978 90m colour
Brent Walker/Artoc (Edward D. Simons)
A millionaire's wife installs her lover as manager of a discotheque, but he becomes bored and wants a place of his own.
Life among the unpleasant rich. A surprise box-office success, richly undeserved.
w Jackie Collins *novel* Jackie Collins *d* Quentin Masters *ph* Peter Hannan *m* Biddu
☆ Joan Collins, Oliver Tobias, Sue Lloyd, Mark Burns, Doug Fisher, Walter Gotell
'Watching it is rather like being buried alive in a coffin stuffed with back numbers of *Men Only*.' – *Alan Brien*

The Student Prince
US 1954 107m Anscocolor Cinemascope
MGM (Joe Pasternak)
A prince studies in Heidelberg and falls for a barmaid.
Ruritanian operetta, lumpishly filmed, with Mario Lanza providing only the voice of the hero as he got too fat to play the part.
w William Ludwig, Sonya Levien *play Old Heidelberg* by Wilhelm Meyer-Foerster *operetta Dorothy Donnelly d* Richard Thorpe *ph* Paul C. Vogel *m Sigmund Romberg md* George Stoll
☆ Edmund Purdom, Ann Blyth, John Williams, Edmund Gwenn, S. Z. Sakall, John Ericson, Louis Calhern, Betta St John, Evelyn Varden
† Without the music, the play had been filmed at MGM in 1926, with Ramon Novarro and Norma Shearer under Ernst Lubitsch's direction.

Student Tour
US 1934 80m bw
MGM
A professor of philosophy chaperones a world tour by collegiates.
Very thin comedy yarn with songs.
w Ralph Spence, Philip Dunne *d* Charles F. Reisner
☆ Jimmy Durante, Charles Butterworth, Maxine Doyle, Phil Regan, Douglas Fowley, Betty Grable, Nelson Eddy
'Long, slow, and of mild entertainment appeal.' – *Variety*

The Studio Murder Mystery
US 1929 62m bw
Paramount
An actor is murdered on a film set.
Primitive talkie comedy mystery now interesting only for its studio backgrounds.
w Frank Tuttle *serial* the Edingtons *d* Frank Tuttle
☆ Neil Hamilton, Florence Eldridge, Warner Oland, Eugene Pallette, Fredric March, Doris Hill, Chester Conklin

Studs Lonigan
US 1960 95m bw
Longridge (Philip Yordan)
The growing up of an unlettered Chicago Irishman in the twenties.
Rough-and-ready version of a celebrated novel, not a bad try but insufficiently detailed to be any kind of classic.
w Philip Yordan *novel* James T. Farrell *d* Irving Lerner *ph* Arthur Feindel *m* Jerry Goldsmith

☆ Christopher Knight, Jack Nicholson, Frank Gorshin

A Study in Scarlet
US 1933 71m bw
KBS

Sherlock Holmes solves a mysterious murder.
Rather emaciated version of a spirited yarn.
w Robert Florey *story* Sir Arthur Conan Doyle *d* Edwin L. Marin
☆ Reginald Owen, Warburton Gamble, Anna May Wong, June Clyde, Alan Dinehart, Alan Mowbray
'Okay for secondary houses.' – *Variety*

A Study in Terror *
GB 1965 95m Eastmancolor
Compton-Tekli/Sir Nigel (Henry E. Lester)

Sherlock Holmes discovers the identity of Jack the Ripper.
A reasonably good Holmes pastiche marred by a surfeit of horror and over-riotous local colour; quite literate, but schizophrenic.
w Donald and Derek Ford *novel* Ellery Queen *d* James Hill *ph* Desmond Dickinson *m* John Scott *ad* Alex Vetchinsky
☆ John Neville, Donald Houston, John Fraser, Robert Morley, Cecil Parker, Anthony Quayle, Barbara Windsor, Adrienne Corri, Judi Dench, Frank Finlay, Barry Jones, Kay Walsh, Georgia Brown

The Stuff
US 1985 93m Technicolor
New World (Paul Kurta)

A monstrous yogurt-like goo eats people from the inside out.
Messy comedy-horror without benefit of much plotline.
wd Larry Cohen *ph* Paul Glickman *m* Anthony Guefen
☆ Michael Moriarty, Andrea Marcovicci, Paul Sorvino, Scott Bloom, Danny Aiello, Alexander Scourby

The Stunt Man *
US 1980 129m Metrocolor
Melvin Simon (Richard Rush)

A Vietnam veteran on the run from the police finds refuge as a star stunt man for a sinister film director.
Overlong, curious, but sometimes compelling melodrama which entertains on the surface while its actual aims are harder to fathom.
w Lawrence B. Marcus *novel* Paul Brodeur *d Richard Rush ph* Mario Tosi *m* Dominic Frontière
☆ Peter O'Toole, Steve Railsback, Barbara Hershey, Allen Goorwitz, Alex Rocco, Sharon Farrell
'It's like one of those sets of Chinese boxes, each one with another box inside, growing smaller and smaller until finally there is nothing left at all.' – *Roger Ebert*
screenplay; Richard Rush; Peter O'Toole

Stunts *
US 1977 90m colour
New Line (Raymond Lafaro, William Panzer)

The brother of a murdered stuntman takes his place in order to investigate the death.
Slick action thriller which capitalizes on the attraction of daring stunts.
w Barney Chen, Dennis Johnson *story* Michael Harpster, Raymond Lafaro, Robert Shaye *d* Mark L. Lester *ph* Bruce Logan *m* Michael Kamen *ed* Corky Ehlers
☆ Robert Forster, Fiona Lewis, Joanna Cassidy, Darrell Fetty, Bruce Glover, James Luisi

The Stupids
US 1995 94m Technicolor
Rank/Savoy/New Line/Imagine (Leslie Belzberg)

The dim father of a dimmer family tries to discover who is stealing his garbage.
Based on the characters from a successful series of children's books, this manages to be no more than a succession of crudely laborious slapstick jokes.
w Brent Forrester *books* James Marshall, Henry Allard *d* John Landis *ph* Manfred Guthe *m* Christopher Stone *pd* Phil Dagort *ed* Dale Beldin
☆ Tom Arnold, Jessica Lundy, Bug Hall, Alex McKenna, Mark Metcalf, Matt Keeslar, Christopher Lee
'Not quite bad enough to be laughable.' – *Derek Malcolm, Guardian*
† Directors making mercifully brief appearances include Mick Garris, David Cronenberg, Costa-Gavras, Robert Wise, Atom Egoyan, Norman Jewison and Gillo Pontecorvo.

Su Zhou He: see *Suzhou River*

The Subject Was Roses *
US 1968 107m Metrocolor
MGM (Edgar Lansbury)
A young war veteran finds he can't communicate with his parents, and vice versa.
Photographed play notable for its performances.
w Frank D. Gilroy *play* Frank D. Gilroy *d* Ulu Grosbard *ph* Jack Priestley
☆ *Patricia Neal, Jack Albertson*, Martin Sheen, Don Saxon, Elaine Williams
Jack Albertson
Patricia Neal

Submarine Command
US 1951 87m bw
Paramount (John Farrow, Joseph Sistrom)
A submarine officer who considers himself a coward becomes a hero in Korea.
Very routine soul-searching actioner.
w Jonathan Latimer *d* John Farrow *ph* Lionel Lindon *m* David Buttolph
☆ William Holden, Don Taylor, Nancy Olsen, William Bendix, Moroni Olson, Peggy Webber

Submarine D1
US 1937 93m bw
Cosmopolitan/Warner
Adventures of recruits to the naval submarine service.
Standard flagwaver of no intrinsic interest.
w Frank Wead, Warren Duff, Lawrence Kimble *d* Lloyd Bacon
☆ Pat O'Brien, George Brent, Wayne Morris, Frank McHugh, Doris Weston, Ronald Reagan, Henry O'Neill, Regis Toomey, Broderick Crawford
'An instructive and illuminating document ... film waves its own flag, the best on earth, and with some exhibitor push it should do business.' – *Variety*

'Youth ... Eager, Vital ... Offers Its Life ... Glorifies Its Ardent Love ... In The Greatest Adventure Of The Great War!'
Submarine Patrol
US 1938 93m bw
TCF (Darryl Zanuck)
Recruits learn to handle sub-chasing boats at Annapolis.
Cheerful propaganda comedy-drama with familiar faces on hand and some good thrill sequences.
w Rian James, Darrell Ware, Jack Yellen *book* Ray Milholland *d* John Ford
☆ Richard Greene, Nancy Kelly, Preston Foster, George Bancroft, Slim Summerville, John Carradine, Henry Armetta, Warren Hymer, Elisha Cook Jnr, E. E. Clive, Ward Bond, George E. Stone
'Surefire film entertainment directed by a veteran who knows all the tricks.' – *Variety*

Submarine X-1
GB 1967 90m Eastmancolor
UA/Mirisch (John C. Champion)
A submarine commander in World War II trains men to attack the *Lindendorf* in midget submarines.
Belated quota quickie, routine in every department.
w Donald S. Sanford, Guy Elmes *story* John C. Champion, Edmund North *d* William Graham *ph* Paul Beeson *m* Ron Goodman *ad* Bill Andrews *ed* John S. Smith
☆ James Caan (Commander Bolton), Norman Bowler (Sub Lt Pennington), David Sumner (Lt Davies), Rupert Davies (Vice Admiral Redmayne), William Dysart (Lt Gogan), Brian Grellis (CPO Barquist), Paul Young (Leading Seaman Quentin), John Kelland (Sub Lt Willis)

Submarine Zone: see *Escape to Glory*

'Doing What Is Right... Could Cost Him Everything.'
The Substance of Fire
US 1996 97m colour
Miramax (Jon Robin Baitz, Randy Finch, Ron Kastner)

A holocaust survivor loses control of his mind and publishing business in a dispute with his children, opposed to his overbearing and controlling ways.
Wordy, and not particularly illuminating, drama about a man who loves books more than people.
w Jon Robin Baitz *play* Jon Robin Baitz *d* Daniel Sullivan *ph* Robert Yeoman *m* Joseph Vitarelli *pd* John Lee Beatty *ed* Pamela Martin
☆ Tony Goldwyn (Aaron Geldhart), Sarah Jessica Parker (Sarah Geldhart), Ron Rifkin (Isaac Geldhart), Gil Bellows (Val Chenard), Ronny Graham (Louis Foukold), Elizabeth Franz (Miss Barzakian), Debra Monk (Martha Hackett), Roger Rees (Max), Eric Bogosian (Gene Byck), Timothy Hutton (Martin Geldhart)
'Goes through all the motions with proper style and casting but is curiously devoid of emotional impact.' – *Lisa Nesselson, Variety*

The Substitute
US 1996 103m Foto-Kem
Live Entertainment/Dinamo/H2 (Morrie Eisenman, Jim Steele)

When his girlfriend, a teacher, is beaten up by drug dealers involved with her school, a commando-turned-mercenary substitutes for her and sorts out the trouble with the aid of some old friends.
Proficiently made but empty drama composed of third-hand and fourth-rate elements that hardly warrant repetition: a deprived school, young hoodlums, large men with big guns, and a narrative with more holes in it than its many dead. The explosive finale illustrates the maxim that in order to save the school, it was necessary to destroy it.
w Roy Frumkes, Rocco Simonelli, Alan Ormsby *d* Robert Mandel *ph* Bruce Surtees *m* Gary Chang *pd* Ron Foreman *ed* Alex Mackie
☆ Tom Berenger, Ernie Hudson, Diane Venora, Glenn Plummer, Marc Anthony, Raymond Cruz, Cliff de Young, Richard Brooks, William Forsythe
'A throwback to the mid-80s, when many films as tawdry as this used to get a cinema release.' – *Sight and Sound*

Subterfuge
GB 1968 86m Eastmancolor
Rank/Intertel (Peter Snell)

In London a CIA agent becomes involved with the wife of a British double-agent.
A routine retread of standard spy stories, crippled by its inexplicable narrative.
w David Whitaker *d* Peter Graham Scott *ph* Roy Garner, Albert Tolley *m* Cyril Ornadel *ad* Ron Fouracre *ed* Bill Lewthwaite
☆ Gene Barry, Joan Collins, Richard Todd, Tom Adams, Suzanna Leigh, Michael Rennie, Marius Goring, Colin Gordon
'A sad waste of several very capable players.' – *Brenda Davies, MFB*

'We are the new Bohemians!'
The Subterraneans
US 1960 89m Metrocolor Cinemascope
MGM (Arthur Freed)
The love affairs of San Francisco bohemians.
A boring oddity with lashings of eccentric behaviour and sexual hang-ups; MGM venturing very timidly outside its field.
w Robert Thom *novel* Jack Kerouac *d* Ranald MacDougall *ph* Joseph Ruttenberg *m* André Previn
☆ George Peppard, Leslie Caron, Janice Rule, Roddy McDowall, Anne Seymour, Jim Hutton

'He's an intergalactic Super Hero whose quest is to rid the Universe of evil-doers and combat the forces of darkness ... But sometimes you gotta come down to Earth.'
Suburban Commando
US 1991 90m DeLuxe
Entertainment/New Line (Howard Gottfried)

An alien bounty-hunter takes a holiday on Earth and lodges with a suburban family.
Amiable, juvenile, low-brow comedy of no particular originality or distinction.
w Frank Capello *d* Burt Kennedy *ph* Patrick J. Swovelin *pd* Ivo Cristante, C. J. Strawn *ed* Sonny Baskin *sp* creature effects: Steve Johnson's XFX Productions
☆ Hulk Hogan, Christopher Lloyd, Shelley Duvall
'A sort of sickly lovechild of *Star Wars* (whose effects are reproduced on the cheap, and whose music is repeatedly plagiarized) and *Kindergarten Cop*.' – *Adam Mars-Jones, Independent*

Suburbia *
US 1983 99m colour
Suburbia Productions (Bert Dragin)

aka: *The Wild Side*
A gang of rebellious teenagers leave home to set up their own community, arousing the antagonism of their parents.
Uncompromising account of unlovely LA punks and unlovelier adults that makes something personal out of standard teen-rebellion material.
wd Penelope Spheeris *ph* Timothy Suhrstedt *m* Alex Gibson *ad* Randy Moore *ed* Ross Albert
☆ Chris Pederson, Bill Coyne, Jennifer Clay, Timothy Eric O'Brien, Wade Walston, Mike B. The Flea, Maggie Ehrig, Grant Miner, Christina Beck

SubUrbia **
US 1996 121m Technicolor
Carlton/Castle Rock/Detour

The return of a rock star to his home town precipitates a crisis among the three high-school friends he left behind.
Set in the car park of a convenience store, among disaffected twenty-or-so-year-olds, a darkly compelling take on stranded lives being thrown away.
w Eric Bogosian *play* Eric Bogosian *d* Richard Linklater *ph* Lee Daniel *m* Sonic Youth *pd* Catherine Hardwicke *ed* Sandra Adair
☆ Jayce Bartok, Amie Carey, Nicky Katt, Ajay Naidu, Parker Posey, Giovanni Ribisi, Samia Shoaib, Dina Spybey, Steve Zahn
'Truly great film-making combined with a truly great play.' – *Alan Jones, Film Review*

'An underground story where lives intertwine.'
Subway
France 1985 104m colour CinemaScope
Gaumount/Films du Loup/TSF/TFI

An eccentric hero on the run from thugs takes refuge overnight in the Paris Metro.
Oddball melodrama with more style than substance.
w Luc Besson and others *d* Luc Besson *ph* Carlo Varini *m* Eric Serra *ad* Alexandre Trauner
☆ Christophe Lambert, Isabelle Adjani, Richard Bohringer

Subway in the Sky
GB 1958 87m bw
Orbit (John Temple-Smith, Patrick Filmer-Sankey)
A Berlin cabaret star finds her landlady's ex-husband, a deserter, hiding in her apartment and sets out to prove his innocence of drug smuggling.
Tedious photographed play with precious few points of dramatic interest.
w Jack Andrews *play* Ian Main *d* Muriel Box *ph* Wilkie Cooper *m* Mario Nascimbene
☆ Hildegarde Neff, Van Johnson, Katherine Kath, Cec Linder, Albert Lieven, Edward Judd

Success at Any Price
US 1934 74m bw
RKO
A young man climbs to great business heights by crushing those around him, then attempts suicide when the crash comes.
Slackly handled drama with an unsympathetic hero.
w John Howard Lawson, Howard J. Green *d* J. Walter Ruben
☆ Douglas Fairbanks Jnr, Genevieve Tobin, Frank Morgan, Colleen Moore, Edward Everett Horton, Nydia Westman, Henry Kolker
'Episodic, unreasonable and anything but audience proof.' – *Variety*

Success Is the Best Revenge
GB/France 1984 91m Technicolor
De Vere/Gaumont (Jerzy Skolimowski)

A Polish theatre director in London stages a symbolic show but alienates his son.
Another study of Polish exiles to follow Moonlighting, *but this time with surrealist elements.*

w Jerzy Skolimowski, Michael Lyndon *d* Jerzy Skolimowski *ph* Mike Fash *m* Stanley Myers, Hans Zimmer
☆ Michael York, Joanna Szczerbic, Michael Lyndon, Jerry Skol, Michel Piccoli, John Hurt, Anouk Aimée, Jane Asher

A Successful Calamity
US 1931 75m bw
Warner
A millionaire discovers the true worth of his family when he pretends to be poor.
Good star vehicle which pleases despite its predictability.
w Maude Howell, Julien Josephson and Austin Parker *play* Clare Kummer *d* John G. Adolfi
☆ George Arliss, Mary Astor, Evalyn Knapp, Grant Mitchell, William Janney

Succubus (dubbed)
West Germany 1967 91m colour
Border/Trans American/Aquila (Adrian Hoven)
original title: *Necronomicon – Geträumte Stünden*
aka: *Necronomicon*
A mysterious woman, who performs a night-club act that involves sex and sadism, is haunted by a past she cannot quite remember and fantasizes scenes of love-making and death.
An unholy mix of cut-rate surrealism, pretentious dialogue and incomprehensible narrative which has a vague connection with the legend of Faust; it will not bear close examination.
w Pier A. Caminneci *d* Jess (Jesús) Franco *ph* Robert Gaffron *m* Friedrich Gulda *md* Jerry Van Rooyen *ad* Karl Heinz Mannchen *ed* Frizzi Schmidt
☆ Janine Reynaud, Jack Taylor, Howard Vernon, Nathalie Nort, Michel Lemoine, Pier A. Caminneci, Adrian Hoven
'An absurdly hit-or-miss affair, with scenes that have a certain bizarre appeal (shop window dummies coming to life) juxtaposed with others of crushing banality.' – *David McGillivray, MFB*
† The British release was cut to 81m.

Such a Gorgeous Kid Like Me: see *Une Belle Fille Comme Moi*

Such a Long Journey *
Canada/GB 1998 113m colour
Optimum/Long Journey/Amy (Paul Stephens, Simon McCorkindale)
In Bombay during the 1970s, a Parsi bank clerk copes with family and other problems.
This saga of one man losing control of his life provides some intermittently interesting moments before it gives way to melodrama and sentimentality.
w Sooni Taraporevala *novel* Rohinton Mistry *d* Sturla Gunnarsson *ph* Jan Kiesser *m* Jonathan Goldsmith *pd* Nitin Desai *ed* Jeff Warren
☆ Om Puri (Ghulam), Roshan Seth (Gustad Noble), Naseeruddin Shah (Jimmy Bilimoria), Sam Dastor (Dinshawji), Kurush Deboo (Tehmul), Vrajesh Hirjee (Sohrab Noble), Shazneed Damania (Roshan Noble), Ranjit Chowdhry (pavement artist), Soni Razdan (Dilnavaz Noble)
'Heartfelt, humane and comic.' – *Empire*

Such a Pretty Little Beach: see *Une Si Jolie Petite Plage*

Such Good Friends *
US 1971 102m Movielab
Paramount/Sigma (Otto Preminger)
A successful man has a mysterious illness and his wife enlists help from his friends.
Satirical parable which alternates between sex comedy and medical exposé; generally heavy-going but with good moments.
w Elaine May *novel* Lois Gould *d* Otto Preminger *ph* Gayne Rescher *m* Thomas Z. Shepard
☆ Dyan Cannon, James Coco, Jennifer O'Neil, Nina Foch, Laurence Luckinbill, Ken Howard, Burgess Meredith, Louise Lasser, Sam Levene, Rita Gam, Nancy Guild

Such Men Are Dangerous
US 1930 83m bw
Fox
A crooked financier undergoes plastic surgery and leads a new life.
Phoney melodrama with slow pace and unconvincing details.
w Ernest Vajda, Elinor Glyn *d* Kenneth Hawks
☆ Warner Baxter, Catherine Dale Owen, Albert Conti, Hedda Hopper, Claud Allister, Bela Lugosi
'Will bore intelligent fans and impress even the gullible with its implausibilities.' – *Variety*

Such Men Are Dangerous: see *The Racers (1955)*

Such Women Are Dangerous
US 1934 81m bw
Fox
Through circumstances an innocent man about town is accused of murder.
Mild drama which fails through slack handling.
w Jane Storm, Oscar M. Sheridan *story* *Odd Thursday* by Vera Caspary *d* James Flood
☆ Warner Baxter, Rosemary Ames, Rochelle Hudson, Mona Barrie, Herbert Mundin, Henrietta Crosman
'Just fair screen amusement.' – *Variety*

Sudba Cheloveka: see *Destiny of a Man*

'Action Goes Into Overtime.'
Sudden Death *
US 1995 110m DeLuxe Panavision
Universal/Signature/Baldwin Cohen (Moshe Diamant, Howard Baldwin)
A fire marshal deals with a gang who take the Vice-President hostage and demand a $1.7 billion ransom during an ice-hockey game.
Fast-paced action movie; it is mindless entertainment, but efficiently delivers the requisite thrills and spills.
w Gene Quintano *story* Karen Baldwin *d* Peter Hyams *ph* Peter Hyams *m* John Debney *pd* Philip Harrison *ed* Steven Kemper
☆ Jean-Claude Van Damme, Powers Boothe, Raymond J. Barry, Whittni Wright, Ross Malinger, Dorian Harewood, Kate McNeil, Michael Gaston
'A whipcord-taut actioner that's bigger and better than its main star.' – *Variety*
'Tripe, but hard not to enjoy' – *Empire*

Sudden Fear **
US 1952 111m bw
RKO/Joseph Kaufman
A playwright heiress finds that her husband is plotting to kill her.
Archetypal star suspenser, glossy and effectively climaxed.
w Lenore Coffee, Robert Smith *d* *David Miller* *ph* *Charles Lang Jnr* *m* Elmer Bernstein
☆ *Joan Crawford, Jack Palance*, Gloria Grahame, Bruce Bennett, Mike Connors
Charles Lang Jnr; Joan Crawford; Jack Palance

'Go on – make his day!'
Sudden Impact
US 1983 117m Technicolor
Warner/Malpaso (Clint Eastwood)
San Francisco detective Harry Callahan goes after a lady killer of men who raped her.
Unattractive and overlong cop show featuring an increasingly tired Dirty Harry.
w Joseph C. Stinson *d* Clint Eastwood *ph* Bruce Surtees *m* Lalo Schifrin *pd* Edward Carfagno
☆ Clint Eastwood, Sondra Locke, Pat Hingle, Bradford Dillman, Paul Drake
'Eastwood presumably takes credit for such gems of authorial self-awareness as replacing the orang-outang of the *Which Way* films, with a farting dog.' – *Paul Taylor, MFB*
'To all those cowboy movies we saw in our youth, all those TV westerns and cop dramas and war movies, Dirty Harry has brought a great simplification: A big man, a big gun, a bad guy, and instant justice.' – *Roger Ebert*

Sudden Terror: see *Eyewitness (1970)*

Suddenly *
US 1954 75m bw
UA/Robert Bassler
Gunmen take over a suburban house and plan to assassinate the President who is due to pass by.
Moderately effective minor suspenser with rather too much psychological chat.
w Richard Sale *d* Lewis Allen *ph* Charles G. Clarke *m* David Raksin
☆ *Frank Sinatra*, Sterling Hayden, James Gleason, Nancy Gates, Kim Charney

'What she doesn't know about spring – neither does Cupid!'
Suddenly It's Spring
US 1947 87m bw
Paramount (Claude Binyon)
A WAC captain comes home to find that her husband wants a divorce.
Tired romantic comedy with no fizz at all.
w Claude Binyon *d* Mitchell Leisen *ph* Daniel L. Fapp *m* Victor Young
☆ Paulette Goddard, Macdonald Carey, Fred MacMurray, Arleen Whelan, Lillian Fontaine, Frank Faylen, Victoria Horne

Suddenly Last Summer *
GB 1959 114m bw
Columbia/Horizon (Sam Spiegel)
A homosexual poet's young cousin goes mad when she sees him raped and murdered by beach boys.
Arty flashback talk-piece from a one-act play, padded out with much sub-poetic mumbo jumbo; it takes too long to get to the revelation, which is ambiguously presented anyway.
w Gore Vidal *play* Tennessee Williams *d* Joseph L. Mankiewicz *ph* *Jack Hildyard* *m* Buxton Orr, Malcolm Arnold *pd* *Oliver Messel*
☆ *Katharine Hepburn*, Elizabeth Taylor, Montgomery Clift, Albert Dekker, Mercedes McCambridge, Gary Raymond
'A short play turns into a ludicrous, lumbering horror movie.' – *New Yorker, 1978*
'I loathe this film, I say so candidly. To my mind it is a decadent piece of work, sensational, barbarous and ridiculous.' – *C. A. Lejeune, Observer*
'A wholly admirable rendering into film of a work at once fascinating and nauseating, brilliant and immoral.' – *Arthur Knight*
Katharine Hepburn; Elizabeth Taylor; art direction

'Driven By The Love Of Two Women ... He Tore Continents Apart That Ships Might Sail The Desert!'
Suez *
US 1938 104m bw
TCF (Gene Markey)
The career of French engineer Ferdinand de Lesseps, who built the Suez Canal.
Superbly mounted but rather undramatic fictionalized biopic.
w Philip Dunne, Julien Josephson *story* Sam Duncan *d* Allan Dwan *ph* Peverell Marley *m* David Raksin, David Buttolph, Cyril Mockridge *md* Louis Silvers
☆ Tyrone Power, Annabella, Loretta Young, J. Edward Bromberg, Joseph Schildkraut, Henry Stephenson, Sidney Blackmer, Maurice Moscovich, Sig Rumann, Nigel Bruce, Miles Mander, George Zucco, Leon Ames, Rafaela Ottiano
'It's a big film in its attempt, but it misses out on its epic aims.' – *Variety*
Peverell Marley; Louis Silvers

Sugar Cane Alley: see *Rue Cases Nègres*

Sugar Hill
US 1994 123m DeLuxe
TCF/Beacon/South Street (Rudy Langlais, Gregory Brown)
Two brothers, successful drug dealers in Harlem, have a gang war on their hands, but one of them decides to give up the life that has made them rich because he has fallen in love with an actress.
Trite melodrama with flashbacks – to the death of his mother from an overdose of heroin, the shooting of his drug-dealing father by gangsters, and to his own academic prowess – designed to elicit sympathy for its guilt-ridden, thuggish protagonist; but he remains a blank and uninteresting one.
w Barry Michael Cooper *d* Leon Ichaso *ph* Bojan Bazelli *m* Terence Blanchard *pd* Michael Helmy *ed* Gary Carr
☆ Wesley Snipes, Michael Wright, Theresa Randle, Leslie Uggams, Larry Joshua, Sam Bottoms, Joe Dallesandro, Clarence Williams III, Abe Vigoda, Ernie Hudson
'At every level, this is a film falling short of conviction.' – *Sight and Sound*

Sugarbaby **
West Germany 1984 87m colour
Electric/Pelemele film/BMI/Bayerischen Rundfunks (Eleonore Adlon)
original title: *Zuckerbaby*
A fat woman pursues a handsome, married train driver whom she loves.
Enjoyable and witty romantic comedy.
wd Percy Adlon *ph* Johanna Heer *m* Dreier, Franz Erlmeier, Fritz Köstler, Paul Würges Combo *pd* Matthias Heller *ed* Jean-Claude Piroue
☆ Marianne Sägebrecht, Eisi Gulp, Toni Berger, Manuela Denz, Will Spindler, Hans Stadlbauer

Sugarfoot
US 1951 80m Technicolor
Warner
TV title: *Swirl of Glory*
Two men meet on a train for Prescott, Arizona, and each determines to make the town his own.
Unusual but fatally sluggish Western.
w Russell Hughes *novel* Clarence Budington Kelland *d* Edwin L. Marin *ph* Wilfred Cline *m* Max Steiner *ed* Clarence Kolster
☆ Randolph Scott, Raymond Massey, Adele Jergens, S. Z. Sakall, Robert Warwick, Arthur Hunnicutt

'The true story of a girl who took on all of Texas ... and almost won.'
Sugarland Express *
US 1974 110m Technicolor Panavision
Universal (Richard Zanuck, David Brown)
A convict's wife persuades him to escape because their baby is being adopted, and they inadvertently leave behind them a trail of destruction, ending in tragedy.
Mainly comic adventures with a bitter aftertaste, very stylishly handled.
w Hal Barwood, Matthew Robbins *d* *Steven Spielberg* *ph* Vilmos Zsigmond *m* John Williams
☆ Goldie Hawn, Ben Johnson, Michael Sacks, William Atherton
'*Ace in the Hole* meets *Vanishing Point*.' – *Sight and Sound*

The Suicide Club: see *Trouble for Two*

Suicide Squadron: see *Dangerous Moonlight*

Suite 16
GB/Belgium 1994 100m colour
Feature Film/Corsan/Theorema (Paul Breuls)
A wealthy voyeur in a wheelchair hires a young gigolo to seduce a woman and kill her while he listens.
A slick but hollow account of decadence and power, not far removed from the staple of Soho cinema clubs in its emphasis on sex.
w Charles Higson, Lise Mayer *d* Dominique Deruddere *ph* Jean-François Robin *m* Walter Hus *ed* Kant Pan
☆ Pete Postlethwaite, Antonie Kamerling, Geraldine Pailhas, Tom Jansen, Bart Siegers
'A pretty silly film from a director who has enough talent to stop farting about with semi-porn.' – *Derek Malcolm, Guardian*

The Suitor *
France 1962 85m bw
CAPAC
original title: *Le Soupirant*
A nervous young man makes several attempts to get married.
The most successful feature of Pierre Etaix, a student of Tati: his jokes are more polished but in the end his own personality seems rather lacking.
w Pierre Etaix, Jean-Claude Carrière *d* Pierre Etaix *ph* Pierre Levant *m* Jean Paillaud
☆ *Pierre Etaix*, Laurence Lignères, France Arnell

The Sullivans *
US 1944 111m bw
TCF (Sam Jaffe)
reissue title: *The Fighting Sullivans*
Five sons of the same family are killed in World War II.
Inspirational true story which had a wide appeal.

w Mary C. McCall Jnr d Lloyd Bacon ph Lucien Andriot m Alfred Newman
☆ Anne Baxter, Thomas Mitchell, Selena Royle, Edward Ryan, Trudy Marshall, John Campbell, James Cardwell, John Alvin, George Offerman Jnr, Roy Roberts
original story (Jules Schermer, Edward Doherty)

'There's no speed limit and no brake When Sullivan travels with Veronica Lake!'
Sullivan's Travels **
US 1941 90m bw
Paramount (Paul Jones)
A Hollywood director tires of comedy and goes out to find real life.
Marvellously sustained tragi-comedy which ranges from pratfalls to the chain gang and never loses its grip or balance.
wd *Preston Sturges* ph *John Seitz* m *Leo Shuken*
☆ *Joel McCrea*, *Veronica Lake*, *Robert Warwick*, William Demarest, Franklin Pangborn, Porter Hall, Byron Foulger, Eric Blore, Robert Greig, Torben Meyer, *Jimmy Conlin*, Margaret Hayes
DEDICATION: 'To all the funny men and clowns who have made people laugh.'
'A brilliant fantasy in two keys – slapstick farce and the tragedy of human misery.' – *James Agee*
'The most witty and knowing spoof of Hollywood movie-making of all time.' – *Film Society Review*
'A deftly sardonic apologia for Hollywood make-believe.' – *New York Times*
'Reflecting to perfection the mood of wartime Hollywood, it danced on the grave of thirties social cinema.' – *Eileen Bowser, 1969*

'27,000 nuclear weapons. One is missing.'
The Sum of All Fears
US 2002 124m DeLuxe Panavision
Paramount (Mace Neufeld)
An American secret agent prevents a nuclear war between the US and Russia.
Bombastic hokum that uses the destruction of Boston by nuclear bomb solely to show off the gung-ho attitude of its hero, dourly played by the uncharismatic Affleck; it never recovers from this miscalculation.
w Paul Attanasio, Daniel Pyne novel Tom Clancy d Phil Alden Robinson ph John Lindley m Jerry Goldsmith pd Jeannine Oppewall ed Neil Travis sp Rhythm & Hues
☆ Ben Affleck (Jack Ryan), Morgan Freeman (DCI William Cabot), James Cromwell (President Fowler), Liev Schreiber (John Clark), Bridget Moynahan (Dr Cathy Muller), Alan Bates (Dressler), Ciaran Hinds (President Nemerov), Philip Baker Hall (Defense Secretary Becker), Ron Rifkin (Secretary of State Owens), Colm Feore (Olson)
'One whale of an exciting action blockbuster.' – *Rex Reed, New York Observer*
'Trite espionage thriller without the thrills but with a lingering measure of nausea.' – *Michael Atkinson, Village Voice*

'Not your typical father and son story.'
The Sum of Us
Australia 1994 95m colour
Southern Star/AFFC (Hal McElroy)
A widowed father and his gay son both search for other relationships.
Engaging performances are not enough to compensate for the longeurs in this small-scale, earnest and sentimental drama of male bonding and homophobia.
w David Stevens play David Stevens d Kevin Dowling, Geoff Burton ph Geoff Burton m Dave Faulkner pd Graham (Grace) Walker ed Frans Vandenburg
☆ Jack Thompson, Russell Crowe, John Polson, Deborah Kennedy

Summer: see *The Green Ray*

A Summer Affair *
France 1977 84m Eastmancolor Panavision
Gala/Renn Productions/Société Française de Production (Pierre Grunstein)
original title: *Un Moment D'égarement*
aka: *One Wild Moment*
A middle-aged man begins an affair with his best friend's teenage daughter when the two families go on holiday together.
Occasionally witty examination of the generation gap.
wd Claude Berri ph André Neau m Michel Stelio ed Jacques Witta
☆ Jean-Pierre Marielle, Victor Lanoux, Christine Dejoux, Agnes Soral, Martine Sarcey
† In 1984, the film was remade by Stanley Donen as *Blame It On Rio*.

'Bold ideas ... bolder people!'
Summer and Smoke
US 1961 118m Technicolor Panavision
Paramount/Hal B. Wallis
In a small Mississippi town in 1916, the minister's spinster daughter nurses an unrequited love for the local rebel.
Wearisome screen version, in hothouse settings, of a pattern play about earthly and spiritual love.
w James Poe, Meade Roberts play Tennessee Williams d Peter Glenville ph Charles Lang Jnr m Elmer Bernstein ad Walter Tyler
☆ Geraldine Page, Laurence Harvey, Una Merkel, John McIntire, Pamela Tiffin, Rita Moreno, Thomas Gomez, Casey Adams, Earl Holliman, Lee Patrick, Malcolm Atterbury
Elmer Bernstein; Geraldine Page; Una Merkel

A Summer at Grandpa's **
Taiwan 1984 102m colour
Marble Road (Chang Hwa-Kuen)
original title: *Tung-Tung-te chia-ch'i*
When his mother becomes seriously ill, a 12-year-old boy is sent with his small sister to stay with his grandfather in the country.
An episodic film of some charm, in part nostalgic for the idle pleasures of a holiday, and in part a comment on the world of adults as seen through the eyes of the disinterested young. The family is the bedrock of society, remarks a notary marrying a reluctant couple, but the family depicted here seems on the point of disintegration, surviving only by absorbing some antisocial behaviour.
w Chu Tien-Wen, Hou Hsiao-Hsien d Hou Hsiao-Hsien ph Chen K'un'hou m Edward Yang
☆ Wang Qiguang, Zhou Shengli, Gu Jun, Mei Fang, Lin Xiuling

'live fast., die young'
Summer City
Australia 1977 83m colour
Avalon Films (Phil Avalon)
aka: *Coast of Terror*
Four friends set out for a weekend of surfing and fun.
Disjointed, semi-improvised movie celebrating an intensely masculine culture of booze and birds, of interest only as a glimpse of Gibson's inauspicious beginning.
w Phil Avalon d Christopher Fraser ph Jerry Marek m Phil Butkis pd Jann Harris ed David Stiven
☆ John Jarratt (Sandy), Phil Avalon (Robbie), Steve Bisley (Boo), Mel Gibson (Scollop), James Elliott (Caroline's Father), Debbie Forman (Caroline), Abigail (Woman in Pub), Ward 'Pally' Austin (Himself)
'It was never finished. All the leading actors fell into a serious argument with the producer and refused to continue working on the project. I never expected to see it on the screen.' – *Christopher Fraser, IMDB*
'An abomination.' – *Mel Gibson*
† Mel Gibson was paid $20 for his role.

Summer Holiday **
US 1948 92m Technicolor
MGM (Arthur Freed)
Life for a small-town family at the turn of the century.
Musical version of a famous play: excellent individual numbers, warm playing and sympathetic scenes, but a surprising lack of overall style.
w Frances Goodrich, Albert Hackett, Ralph Blane play *Ah Wilderness* by Eugene O'Neill d *Rouben Mamoulian* ph *Charles Schoenbaum* md Lennie Hayton ch *Charles Walters* songs Harry Warren, Ralph Blane
☆ *Walter Huston*, Mickey Rooney, Frank Morgan, Agnes Moorehead, Butch Jenkins, Selena Royle, Marilyn Maxwell, Gloria de Haven, Anne Francis
† The film was finished in 1946 and held back because it seemed unlikely to succeed.

Summer Holiday *
GB 1962 109m Technicolor Cinemascope
ABP/Ivy (Kenneth Harper)
Four young London Transport mechanics borrow a double-decker bus for a continental holiday.
Pacy, location-filmed youth musical with plenty of general appeal.
w Peter Myers, Ronnie Cass d *Peter Yates* ph John Wilcox md Stanley Black
☆ *Cliff Richard*, Lauri Peters, Melvyn Hayes, Una Stubbs, Teddy Green, Ron Moody, Lionel Murton, David Kossoff

Summer Interlude *
Sweden 1950 97m bw
Svensk Filmindustri (Alan Ekelund)
original title: *Sommarlek*
A prima ballerina remembers a happy summer she spent with a boy who was tragically killed.
Melancholy romance quite typical of its creator but with less density of meaning than usual.
w Ingmar Bergman, Herbert Grevenius d Ingmar Bergman ph Gunnar Fischer, Bengt Jarnmark m Erik Nordgren
☆ Maj-Britt Nilsson, Birger Malmsten, Alf Kjellin

Summer Lightning: see *Scudda Hoo, Scudda Hay*

Summer Lovers
US 1982 98m Technicolor Panavision
Orion (Mike Moder)
A young man on holiday on a Greek island persuades his girlfriend that he needs a local girl as well.
A movie with little dialogue and less intelligence, just attractive locations, through which the three principals romp inanely to bubble-gum music. It might just pass muster on the level of a tourist brochure.
wd Randal Kleiser ph Timothy Galfas, Dimitri Papaconstandis m Basil Poledouris pd Bruce Weintraub ed Robert Gordon
☆ Peter Gallagher, Daryl Hannah, Valerie Quennessen, Barbara Rush, Carole Cook

Summer Madness: see *Summertime*

Summer Magic *
US 1963 104m Technicolor
Walt Disney (Ron Miller)
Children help their widowed mother in 1912 Boston.
Amiable remake of Mother Carey's Chickens, *irreproachably presented.*
w Sally Benson d James Neilson ph William Snyder m Buddy Baker songs the Sherman Brothers
☆ Hayley Mills, Burl Ives, Dorothy McGuire, Darren McGavin, Deborah Walley, Una Merkel, Eddie Hodges, Michael J. Pollard

Summer Manoeuvres: see *Les Grandes Manoeuvres*

Summer of '42 *
US 1971 103m Technicolor
Warner/Mulligan-Roth (Richard Alan Roth)
Adolescents make sexual explorations on a New England island in 1942.
Well-observed indulgence in the new permissiveness.
w Herman Raucher d Robert Mulligan ph Robert Surtees m Michel Legrand
☆ Jennifer O'Neill, Gary Grimes, Jerry Houser, Oliver Conant, Lou Frizzell
Michel Legrand
Herman Raucher; Robert Surtees
Michel Legrand

The Summer of Aviya *
Israel 1988 95m colour
Mutual/HSA (Eitan Evan, Gila Almagor)
original title: *Hakayitz Shel Aviya*
A young girl's unhappy relationship with her disturbed mother comes to a head during a summer holiday.
Affecting, semi-autobiographical account of suffering in the aftermath of the Second World War.
w Eli Cohen, Gila Almagor, Chaim Buzaglo novel Gila Almagor d Eli Cohen ph David Gurfinkel m Shem-Tov Levi ad Yoram Shayer ed Tova Ne'eman
☆ Gila Almagor, Kaipo Cohen, Eli Cohen, Marina Rosetti, Avital Dicker, Dina Avrech
'Eli Cohen transforms the horror and trauma of the past and its excesses into a measured, assured and humane expression of what can be achieved in the face of evil.' – *MFB*

'NYC '77. Disco In The Clubs. Panic In The Streets.'
Summer of Sam *
US 1999 142m Technicolor
Downtown/Touchstone/40 Acres and a Mule (Jon Kilik, Spike Lee)
A gang of Italian-Americans in the Bronx try to solve the mystery of a serial killer in the neighbourhood, during the hot summer of 1977.
The point of this shapeless ensemble piece seems to be a remark by a black woman that if the killer known as the Son of Sam had been black, there would have been riots in New York. Otherwise, it deals in minor panic and mishaps among stereotypical would-be mobsters; but not even the period detail is right.
w Victor Colicchio, Michael Imperioli, Spike Lee d Spike Lee ph Ellen Kuras m Terence Blanchard pd Therese DePrez ed Barry Alexander Brown cos Ruth E. Carter
☆ John Leguizamo (Vinny), Adrien Brody (Ritchie), Mira Sorvino (Dionna), Jennifer Esposito (Ruby), Anthony LaPaglia (Det Lou Petrocelli), Bebe Neuwirth (Gloria), Patti LuPone (Helen), Ben Gazarra (Luigi), Joe Lisi (Tony Olives), Michael Badalucco (Son of Sam), Michael Rispoli (Joe T), John Savage (Simon), Spike Lee (John Jeffries)
'A great little movie that has real heart and intelligence.' – *Cosmo Landesman, Sunday Times*
'An enormously energetic, flavourful film.' – *Kim Newman, Empire*

Summer of the Seventeenth Doll
US/Australia 1959 94m bw
UA/Hecht-Hill-Lancaster (Leslie Norman)
US title: *Season of Passion*
Two cane-cutters on their annual city lay-off have woman trouble.
Miscast and unsatisfactory rendering of a good play; the humour has evaporated.
w John Dighton play Ray Lawler d Leslie Norman ph Paul Beeson m Benjamin Frankel
☆ Ernest Borgnine, John Mills, Angela Lansbury, Anne Baxter, Vincent Ball

A Summer Place
US 1959 130m Technicolor
Warner (Delmer Daves)
Romantic summer adventures of teenagers and their elders on an island off the coast of Maine.
Sex among the idle rich: a routine piece of Hollywood gloss, bowdlerized from a bestseller.
wd Delmer Daves novel Sloan Wilson ph Harry Stradling m Max Steiner
☆ Richard Egan, Dorothy McGuire, Sandra Dee, Arthur Kennedy, Troy Donahue, Constance Ford, Beulah Bondi

Summer Rental
US 1985 93m colour
Paramount (George Shapiro)
An accident-prone air traffic controller takes his family on a holiday where everything goes wrong.
Broad, lively comedy that relies too heavily on the skills and charm of Candy, though he almost manages to carry the picture.
w Jeremy Stevens, Mark Reisman d Carl Reiner ph Ric Waite m Alan Silvestri pd Peter Wooley ed Bud Molin
☆ John Candy, Richard Crenna, Rip Torn, Karen Austin, Kerri Green, Joey Lawrence, Aubrey Jene, John Larroquette

Summer School
US 1987 98m Technicolor
Paramount (George Shapiro, Howard West)
A reluctant sports teacher, forced to give lessons in remedial English to even more reluctant students at summer school, makes a deal with his class.
Slight comedy that may amuse teenagers with nothing better to do with their time.

w Jeff Franklin, Stuart Birnbaum, David Dashev *d* Carl Reiner *ph* David M. Walsh *m* Danny Elfman *pd* David L. Snyder *ed* Bud Molin
☆ Mark Harmon, Kirstie Alley, Robin Thomas, Patrick Laborteaux, Courtney Thorne Smith, Dean Cameron, Gary Reilly

Summer Stock *
US 1950 109m Technicolor
MGM (Joe Pasternak)
GB title: *If You Feel Like Singing*
A theatre troupe takes over a farm for rehearsals, and the lady owner gets the bug.
Likeable but halting musical with the star's weight problems very obvious.
w George Wells, Sy Gomberg *d* Charles Walters *ph* Robert Planck *m/ly* Saul Chaplin, Harry Warren, Mack Gordon *md* Johnny Green *ch* Nick Castle
☆ Judy Garland, Gene Kelly, Gloria de Haven, Carleton Carpenter, Eddie Bracken, Phil Silvers, Hans Conried
† June Allyson was to have starred, but became pregnant.
♫ 'If You Feel Like Singing, Sing'; 'Dig-Dig-Dig-Dig for Your Dinner'; 'Mem'ry Island'; 'You, Wonderful You'; 'Friendly Star'; 'All For You'; 'Happy Harvest Howdy Neighbor'; 'Heavenly Music'

Summer Storm *
US 1944 106m bw
(UA)
In 1912 Russia, a provincial judge falls for a local mancatcher.
One of Hollywood's occasional aberrations, an attempt to do something very European in typical west coast style. An interesting failure.
w Rowland Leigh *story The Shooting Party* by Anton Chekhov *d* Douglas Sirk *ph* Archie Stout *md* Karl Hajos
☆ George Sanders, Linda Darnell, *Edward Everett Horton*, Anna Lee, Hugo Haas, John Philiber, Sig Rumann, André Charlot

'There are bits of acting and photography which put it as far outside the run of American movies as it laudably tries to be. But most of it had for me the sporty speciousness of an illustrated drugstore classic.' – *James Agee*

Karl Hajos

A Summer Story
GB 1988 97m colour
Warner/ITC (Danton Rissner)
A lawyer recalls his love for a working-class country girl.
Stiff upper lip romance, pretty to look at but providing little else.
w Penelope Mortimer *story The Apple Cart* by John Galsworthy *d* Piers Haggard *ph* Kenneth MacMillan *m* Georges Delerue *pd* Leo Austin *ed* Ralph Sheldon
☆ James Wilby, Imogen Stubbs, Ken Colley, Sophie Ward, Susannah York, Jerome Flynn

Summer Vacation 1999
Japan 1988 90m Eastmancolor
New Century/CBS-Sony (Yutaka Okada, Eiji Kishi)
original title: *1999 – Nen No Natsu Yasumi*
Three adolescent boys spending the summer at an otherwise deserted school think their friend has returned from the dead when they are joined by a fourth boy who exactly resembles him.
Slow-moving, self-consciously poetic and finally ridiculous tale of repressed love and teenage angst, not helped by the fact that the boys are played by girls.
w Rio Kishida *d* Shusuke Kaneko *ph* Kenji Takama *m* Yuriko Nakamura *ad* Shu Yamaguchi
☆ Eri Miyajima, Tomoko Otakara, Miyuki Nakano, Rie Mizuhara

Summer Wishes, Winter Dreams *
US 1973 88m Technicolor
Columbia/Rastar (Jack Brodsky)
A neurotic New York housewife goes to pieces when her mother dies but finds a new understanding of her husband when she accompanies him on a trip to the World War II battlefields.
Menopausal melodrama, well observed but disappointingly wispy and underdeveloped.
w Stewart Stern *d* Gilbert Cates *ph* Gerald Hirschfeld *m* Johnny Mandel
☆ *Joanne Woodward*, Martin Balsam, Sylvia Sidney, Dori Brenner, Win Forman
Joanne Woodward; Sylvia Sidney
Joanne Woodward

Summer with Monika *
Sweden 1952 97m bw
Svensk Filmindustri (Allan Ekelund)
original title: *Sommaren med Monika*
A wild, restless girl defies her parents and goes off with her boyfriend for an island holiday. Her subsequent pregnancy and motherhood don't in the least suit her, and the father is left alone with the baby.
Probably truthful but rather glum and unsophisticated drama of young love; not among Bergman's most interesting films.
wd Ingmar Bergman *novel* Per Anders Fogelstrom *ph* Gunnar Fischer *m* Erik Nordgren
☆ Harriet Andersson, Lars Ekborg

Summerfield
Australia 1977 91m Eastmancolor
Clare Beach/AFC/Victorian Film (Patricia Lovell)
A new schoolteacher arrives in an isolated community to find he faces hostility from the locals and a mystery concerning the fate of his predecessor.
A slick mystery story, although too slow and predictable to be engrossing.
w Cliff Green *d* Ken Hannam *ph* Mike Molloy *m* Bruce Smeaton *ad* Graham Walker *ed* Sara Bennett
☆ Nick Tate, John Waters, Elizabeth Alexander, Michelle Jarman, Charles Tingwell, Geraldine Turner

A Summer's Tale: see *Conte d'été*

Summertime ***
US 1955 99m Eastmancolor
London Films/Lopert Productions (Ilya Lopert)
GB title: *Summer Madness*
An American spinster has a holiday in Venice and becomes romantically involved.
Delightful, sympathetic travelogue with dramatic asides, great to look at and hinging on a single superb performance.
w David Lean, H. E. Bates *play The Time of the Cuckoo* by Arthur Laurents *d David Lean ph Jack Hildyard m* Sandro Cicognini
☆ *Katharine Hepburn*, Rossano Brazzi, Isa Miranda, Darren McGavin, Mari Aldon, André Morell

'The eye is endlessly ravished.' – *Dilys Powell*

David Lean; Katharine Hepburn

Summertree
US 1971 88m Eastmancolor
Warner/Bryna (Kirk Douglas)
A bored student learns about life and becomes a Vietnam casualty.
Well-made, rather tedious character study; good social observation.
w Edward Hume, Stephen Yafa *play* Ron Cowen *d* Anthony Newley *ph* Richard C. Glouner *m* David Shire
☆ Michael Douglas, Brenda Vaccaro, Jack Warden, Barbara Bel Geddes

The Sun Also Rises **
US 1957 129m Eastmancolor
Cinemascope
TCF (Darryl F. Zanuck)
In Paris after World War I an impotent journalist meets a nymphomaniac lady of title, and they and their odd group of friends have various saddening adventures around Europe.
Not a bad attempt to film a difficult novel, though Cinemascope doesn't help and the last half hour becomes turgid. The Last Flight (qv) conveyed the same atmosphere rather more sharply.
w Peter Viertel *novel* Ernest Hemingway *d Henry King ph* Leo Tover *m* Hugo Friedhofer
☆ Tyrone Power, Ava Gardner, *Errol Flynn*, Eddie Albert, Mel Ferrer, Robert Evans, Juliette Greco, Gregory Ratoff, Marcel Dalio, Henry Daniell

The Sun Never Sets
US 1939 98m bw
Universal (Rowland V. Lee)
Two brothers in the African colonial service prevent a munitions baron from plunging the world into war.
Stiff upper lip melodrama, very dated.
w W. P. Lipscomb *d* Rowland V. Lee *ph* George Robinson *m* Frank Skinner *md* Charles Previn *ad* Jack Otterson, Richard H. Riedel *ed* Ted J. Kent
☆ Basil Rathbone, Douglas Fairbanks Jnr, Virginia Field, Lionel Atwill, Barbara O'Neil, C. Aubrey Smith, Melville Cooper

'Confusing script and poor direction relegate this to lower duals ... brightest thing is the title.' – *Variety*

The Sun Shines Bright **
US 1953 92m bw
Republic/Argosy (John Ford, Merian C. Cooper)
Forty years after the Civil War, the judge of a Kentucky town still has trouble quelling the Confederate spirit.
Mellow anecdotes of time gone by, scrappily linked but lovingly polished; a remake of a Will Rogers vehicle Judge Priest.
w Laurence Stallings *stories* Irwin S. Cobb *d John Ford ph Archie Stout m Victor Young*
☆ Charles Winninger, Arleen Whelan, John Russell, Stepin Fetchit, Milburn Stone, Grant Withers, Russell Simpson

'Passages of quite remarkable poetic feeling ... alive with affection and truthful observation.' – *Lindsay Anderson*

Sun Valley Serenade *
US 1941 86m bw
TCF (Milton Sperling)
The band manager at an Idaho ice resort takes care of a Norwegian refugee.
Simple-minded musical which still pleases because of the talent involved.
w Robert Ellis, Helen Logan *d* H. Bruce Humberstone *ph* Edward Cronjager *m* Emil Newman *songs* Mack Gordon, Harry Warren
☆ Sonja Henie, *Glenn Miller and his Orchestra*, John Payne, *Milton Berle*, Lynn Bari, Joan Davis, *The Nicholas Brothers*, Dorothy Dandridge
Edward Cronjager; Emil Newman; song 'Chattanooga Choo-Choo' (*m* Harry Warren, *ly* Mack Gordon)

Suna no Onna: see *Woman of the Dunes*

Sunbonnet Sue
US 1945 89m bw
Monogram/Scott R. Dunlap
In the 1890s, a Park Avenue matron objects to her niece singing in a Bowery saloon.
Old-fashioned family movie for the innocent-minded.
w Paul Gerard Smith, Bradford Ropes *d* Ralph Murphy
☆ Gale Storm, Phil Regan, Minna Gombell, George Cleveland, Raymond Hatton, Alan Mowbray
Edward J. Kay (music)

Sunburn
GB/US 1979 98m Technicolor
Hemdale/Bind Films (David Korda)
An insurance investigator hires a model to act as his wife while he trails a suspected murderer in Acapulco.
All sun and skin and swirling cameras, this entire movie is a seventies cliché, but it provides some fitful amusement.
w John Daly, Stephen Oliver, James Booth *novel The Bind* by Stanley Ellin *d* Richard C. Sarafian *ph* Alex Phillips Jnr *m* John Cameron
☆ Farrah Fawcett, Charles Grodin, Art Carney, Joan Collins, William Daniels, John Hillerman, Eleanor Parker, Keenan Wynn

The Sunchaser
US 1996 122m Technicolor Panavision
Warner/Monarchy/Regency (Arnon Milchan, Michael Cimino, Larry Spiegel)
An ambitious doctor is kidnapped by a teenage convict, dying from cancer, and forced to travel to Arizona to find a Navajo medicine man.
Heavily symbolic road movie, travelling through photogenic landscapes but imbued with a second-hand mysticism.
w Charles Leavitt *d* Michael Cimino *ph* Doug Milsome *m* Maurice Jarre *pd* Victoria Paul *ed* Joe D'Augustine
☆ Woody Harrelson, Jon Seda, Anne Bancroft, Alexandra Tydings, Matt Mulhern, Talisa Soto, Richard Bauer, Victor Aaron

'A conceptually bold tale marked, in its execution, both by visceral intensity and dramatic sloppiness.' – *Variety*

'It's about three decent people. They will break your heart!'
Sunday, Bloody Sunday ***
GB 1971 110m DeLuxe
UA/Vectia (Joseph Janni)
A young designer shares his sexual favours equally between two loves of different sexes, a Jewish doctor and a lady executive.
Stylishly made character study with melodramatic leanings, rather self-conscious about its risky subject but, scene by scene, both adult and absorbing, with an overpowering mass of sociological detail about the way we live.
w Penelope Gilliatt d John Schlesinger ph Billy Williams m Ron Geesin *pd* Luciana Arrighi
☆ *Glenda Jackson, Peter Finch*, Murray Head, Peggy Ashcroft, Maurice Denham, Vivian Pickles, Frank Windsor, Tony Britton, Harold Goldblatt

'This is not a story about the loss of love, but about its absence.' – *Roger Ebert*

Penelope Gilliatt; John Schlesinger; Glenda Jackson; Peter Finch
best picture; John Schlesinger; Peter Finch; Glenda Jackson

'Their eyes met! Their lips questioned! Their arms answered!'
Sunday Dinner for a Soldier *
US 1944 86m bw
TCF (Walter Morosco)
A poor family living on a derelict Florida houseboat scrape together enough money to invite a soldier for a meal.
Sentimental little flagwaving romance, quite sympathetically presented and agreeably underacted.
w Wanda Tuchock, Melvin Levy *d* Lloyd Bacon *ph* Joe MacDonald *m* Alfred Newman
☆ Anne Baxter, John Hodiak, Charles Winninger, Anne Revere, Connie Marshall, Chill Wills, Bobby Driscoll, Jane Darwell

'Simple, true and tender, the best propaganda America has put out in the current year.' – *Richard Winnington*

Sunday in August: see *Domenico d'Agosto*

Sunday in New York *
US 1963 105m Metrocolor
MGM/Seven Arts (Everett Freeman)
Complications in the love life of a brother and sister, each of whom thinks the other is very moral.
Fresh, fairly adult sex comedy with New York backgrounds.
w Norman Krasna *play* Norman Krasna *d* Peter Tewkesbury *ph* Leo Tover *m* Peter Nero
☆ Cliff Robertson, Rod Taylor, Jane Fonda, Robert Culp, Jo Morrow, Jim Backus

Sunday in the Country
Canada 1975 92m colour Panavision
Quadrant/Impact (David M. Perlmutter)
A righteous farmer decides to take the law into his own hands when three gun-happy bank robbers arrive at his home.
Uninteresting, brutal rural melodrama, done without finesse, and with both Pollard and Borgnine providing over-the-top performances that emphasize the pervading lack of reality; a sentimental title song is no help, either.
w Robert Maxwell, John Trent *story* David Main *d* John Trent *ph* Marc Champion *m* William McCauley, Paul Hoffert *ad* James Milton Parcher *ed* Tony Lower
☆ Ernest Borgnine, Michael J. Pollard, Hollis McLaren, Cec Linder, Louis Zorich, Vladimir Valenta, Al Waxman, Tim Henry, Murray Westgate

Sunday in the Country **
France 1984 94m Eastmancolor
Sara Films/Films A2/Little Bear (Alain Sarde)
original title: *Un Dimanche à la Campagne*
An elderly artist enjoys a Sunday visit from his family.
Delightful, slight and moving sketch for a drama, which gives nothing but pleasure yet is hard to recapture.
w Bertrand and Colo Tavernier *novella Pierre Bost d Bertrand Tavernier ph Bruno de Keyzer*
m Gabriel Fauré
☆ Louis Ducreux, Sabine Azema, Michel Aumont, Geneviève Mnich, Monique Chaumette, Claude Winter

Sunday Too Far Away
Australia 1977 94m colour
South Australian Film Corporation
Itinerant sheep shearers become involved in an industrial dispute.
Almost the archetypal Australian outback movie, good to look at but hard to care about.
w John Dingwall *d* Ken Hannam
☆ Jack Thompson, Max Cullen, Reg Lye, John Ewart

Sundays and Cybèle *
France 1962 110m bw Franscope
Terra/Fides/Orsa/Trocadéro (Romain Pinès)
original title: *Cybèle ou les Dimanches de Ville d'Avray*
An amnesiac ex-pilot strikes up a friendship with an abandoned 12-year-old girl, but the relationship is misunderstood and ends in tragedy.
A fashionable film of its time which now has little to offer: its director's reputation sagged alarmingly when he went to Hollywood.
w Serge Bourgignon, Antoine Tudal
novel Bernard Echasseriaux *d* Serge Bourgignon
ph Henri Decaë *m* Maurice Jarre
☆ Hardy Kruger, Nicole Courcel, Patricia Gozzi, Daniel Ivernel
'Studied charm and a creakingly melodramatic dénouement take the place of any serious attempt to probe the characters or situation ... the film is so busily preoccupied with being as attractive, visually and sentimentally, as it possibly can, that it never has time to consider what it is being attractive about.' – *Tom Milne, MFB*
'Uneven but highly meritorious ... a near-triumph of the intelligently mobile camera.' – *John Simon*
best foreign film
script; Maurice Jarre

Sunday's Children **
Sweden 1992 120m colour
Sandrews (Katinka Farago)
original title: *Söndags Barn*
During a summer holiday, an eight-year-old boy observes the difficulties of his parents' marriage; as a middle-aged man, he is forced to confront his relationship with his father.
Perceptive, delicately observed study of the tensions within family relationships, full of repressed emotion; it is a sort of sequel to The Best Intentions *(qv).*
w Ingmar Bergman *d* Daniel Bergman *ph* Tony Forsberg *m* Rune Gustafsson *pd* Sven Wichmann *ed* Darek Hodor
☆ Thommy Berggren, Lena Endre, Henrik Linnros, Jacob Leygraf, Anna Linnros, Malin Ek, Birgitta Valberg, Börje Ahlstedt
'Daniel Bergman gives this rambling memoir a shimmering, lyrical clarity, and his direction of the actors is extraordinary.' – *Terrence Rafferty, New Yorker*

Sundown
US 1941 91m bw
Walter Wanger
The adopted daughter of an Arab trader assists British troops in Africa during World War II.
Artificial-looking romantic actioner with good cast.
w Barre Lyndon *d* Henry Hathaway *ph* Charles Lang *m* Miklos Rozsa *ad* Alexander Golitzen
☆ Gene Tierney, Bruce Cabot, George Sanders, Harry Carey, Joseph Calleia, Cedric Hardwicke, Carl Esmond, Reginald Gardiner
'I can never resist bosh if it is delirious enough.' – *James Agate, Tatler*
Charles Lang; Miklos Rozsa; Alexander Golitzen

The Sundowners **
GB/Australia 1960 133m Technicolor
Warner (Gerry Blatner)
In the twenties an Irish sheepdrover and his family travel from job to job in the Australian bush.
Easygoing, often amusing but lethargically developed family film with major stars somewhat ill at ease. Memorable sequences.
w Isobel Lennart *novel* Jon Cleary *d Fred Zinnemann ph* Jack Hildyard *m* Dimitri Tiomkin
☆ Robert Mitchum, Deborah Kerr, *Glynis Johns, Peter Ustinov,* Michael Anderson Jnr, Dina Merrill, *Wylie Watson,* Chips Rafferty
'For all Zinnemann's generous attention to character, the hints of longing, despair and indomitable spirit, the overall impression remains one of sheer length and repetition and synthetic naturalism.' – *Richard Winnington*
best picture; Isobel Lennart; Fred Zinnemann; Deborah Kerr; Glynis Johns

'In a world gone mad – a love story!'
Sunflower
France/Italy 1970 101m Technicolor
Champion/Concordia
A man and wife are separated during World War II.
Sudsy romantic drama, partly shot in Moscow but with no other redeeming feature.
w Tonino Guerra, Cesare Zavattini, Georgiy Mdivani *d* Vittorio de Sica *m* Henry Mancini
☆ Sophia Loren, Marcello Mastroianni, Lyudmila Savelyeva
Henry Mancini

Sunny *
US 1930 81m bw
Warner
A showgirl falls for a rich young man.
Tinny early musical notable for its star.
w Humphrey Pearson, Henry McCarthy *musical play Otto Harbach, Oscar Hammerstein II, Jerome Kern d* William A. Seiter *ph* Ernest Haller
☆ Marilyn Miller, Lawrence Grey, Jack Donahue, Mackenzie Ward, O. P. Heggie

Sunny *
US 1941 97m bw
RKO/Imperator (Herbert Wilcox)
Adequate remake of the above.
w Sig Herzig *d* Herbert Wilcox *ph* Russell Metty
m Anthony Collins
☆ Anna Neagle, Ray Bolger, John Carroll, Edward Everett Horton, Frieda Inescort, Grace and Paul Hartman
Anthony Collins

Sunny Side Up *
US 1929 115m bw ('Multicolor' sequence)
Fox
A slum girl falls for the son of a rich Southampton family.
Typical early musical of the softer kind; rewarding for those who can project themselves back.
d David Butler *ph* Ernest Palmer *w/m/ly B. G. de Sylva, Lew Brown, Ray Henderson*
☆ Janet Gaynor, Charles Farrell, El Brendel, Marjorie White, Sharon Lynn

Sunnyside *
US 1919 27m approx (24 fps) bw silent
First National/Charles Chaplin
The overworked odd job man at a country hotel has a pastoral dream.
Very mildly funny star comedy which was intended as a satire on the D. W. Griffith/Charles Ray type of rural drama then popular. It doesn't work in this vein either.
wd Charles Chaplin *ph* Rollie Totheroh
☆ Charles Chaplin, Edna Purviance, Tom Wilson, Albert Austin, Henry Bergman

Sunrise **
US 1927 97m (24 fps) bw silent
Fox
A villager in love with a city woman tries to kill his wife but then repents and spends a happy day with her.
Lyrical melodrama, superbly handled: generally considered among the finest Hollywood productions of the twenties.
w Carl Mayer *novel A Trip to Tilsit* by Hermann Sudermann *d* F. W. Murnau *ph* Karl Struss, Charles Rosher *m* (sound version) Hugo Riesenfeld *ad* Rochas Gliese
☆ Janet Gaynor, George O'Brien, Margaret Livingston
OPENING TITLE: 'This story of a man and his wife is of nowhere and everywhere, you might hear it anywhere and at any time.'
'It is filled with intense feeling and in it is embodied an underlying subtlety ... exotic in many ways for it is a mixture of Russian gloom and Berlin brightness.' – *Mordaunt Hall, New York Times*
'Not since the earliest, simplest moving pictures, when locomotives, fire engines and crowds in streets were transposed to the screen artlessly and endearingly, when the entranced eye was rushed through tunnels and over precipices on runaway trains, has there been such joy in motion as under Murnau's direction.' – *Louise Bogan, The New Republic*
'The story is told in a flowing, lyrical German manner that is extraordinarily sensual, yet perhaps too self-conscious, too fable-like, for American audiences.' – *Pauline Kael, 70s*
Karl Struss, Charles Rosher; Janet Gaynor; Unique and Artistic Picture
Rochas Gliese

Sunrise at Campobello *
US 1960 143m Technicolor
Warner/Dore Schary
The early life of Franklin Roosevelt, including his battle against polio and return to politics.
Static filming of a rather interesting Broadway success and of a memorable performance.
w Dore Schary *play* Dore Schary *d* Vincent J. Donehue *ph* Russell Harlan *m* Franz Waxman
ad Edward Carrere
☆ *Ralph Bellamy,* Greer Garson, Ann Shoemaker, Hume Cronyn, Jean Hagen
Greer Garson; art direction

Sunset
US 1988 107m Technicolor Panavision
Columbia/Tri-Star/ML Delphi (Tony Adams)
In Hollywood as an adviser to a studio making a film of his life, Wyatt Earp teams up with cowboy star Tom Mix to solve a murder.
A comedy-thriller that misfires.
wd Blake Edwards *story* Rod Amateau
ph Anthony B. Richmond *m* Henry Mancini
pd Rodger Maus *ed* Robert Pergament
☆ Bruce Willis, James Garner, Malcolm McDowell, Mariel Hemingway, Kathleen Quinlan, Jennifer Edwards, Patricia Hodge, Richard Bradford, M. Emmet Walsh, Joe Dallesandro

'It happened in Hollywood ... a love story ... a drama real and ruthless, tender and terrifying!'
Sunset Boulevard ***
US 1950 110m bw
Paramount (Charles Brackett)
A luckless Hollywood scriptwriter goes to live with a wealthy older woman, a slightly dotty and extremely possessive relic of the silent screen.
Incisive melodrama with marvellous moments but a tendency to overstay its welcome; the first reels are certainly the best, though the last scene is worth waiting for and the malicious observation throughout is a treat.
w Charles Brackett, Billy Wilder, D. M. Marshman Jnr d Billy Wilder ph John F. Seitz m Franz Waxman ed Arthur Schmidt, Doane Harrison
☆ *Gloria Swanson, William Holden, Erich von Stroheim, Fred Clark, Nancy Olson,* Jack Webb, Lloyd Gough, *Cecil B. de Mille,* H. B. Warner, Anna Q. Nilsson, Buster Keaton, Hedda Hopper
'That rare blend of pungent writing, expert acting, masterly direction and unobtrusively artistic photography which quickly casts a spell over an audience and holds it enthralled to a shattering climax.' – *New York Times (T.M.P.)*
'Miss Swanson's performance takes her at one bound into the class of Boris Karloff and Tod Slaughter.' – *Richard Mallett, Punch*
'A weird, fascinating motion picture about an art form which, new as it is, is already haunted by ghosts.' – *Otis L. Guernsey Jnr, New York Herald Tribune*
'The most intelligent film to come out of Hollywood for years; lest the idea of intelligence in the cinema should lack allure, let me say that it is also one of the most exciting.' – *Dilys Powell*
† Montgomery Clift was to have played the role taken by William Holden, but decided against it at the last moment, because his real-life affair with an older woman, Libby Holman, was too close to the situation in the film.
script; Franz Waxman
best picture; Billy Wilder (as director); John F. Seitz; Gloria Swanson; William Holden; Erich von Stroheim; Nancy Olson; editing

Sunset Grill
US 1992 103m Foto-Kem
New Line/Movie Group (Faruque Ahmed)
An alcoholic ex-cop uncovers a trade in body parts when he investigates the murder of his estranged wife.
Bloody, over-ambitious thriller with a complex back-story that manages to dissipate most of the suspense and muddle of the narrative.
w Marcus Wright, Faruque Ahmed *story* Chip Walter *d* Kevin Connor *ph* Douglas Milsome
m Ken Thorne *pd* Yuda Ako *ed* Barry Peters
☆ Peter Weller, Lori Singer, Stacy Keach, Alexandra Paul, John Rhys-Davies, Michael Anderson Jnr

Sunset in Vienna
GB 1937 73m bw
Herbert Wilcox
US title: *Suicide Legion*
An Italian cavalry officer finds that his wife's brother is a spy, and shoots him.
Dated romantic melodrama with music.
w Florence Tranter *d* Norman Walker
☆ Lilli Palmer, Tullio Carminati, John Garrick, Geraldine Hislop

'Three generations. One dream.'
Sunshine *
Austria/Canada/Germany/Hungary 1999 180m colour
Alliance/ISL/Kinowelt/Screen Ventures/DOR (Robert Lantos, Andras Hamori)
A Hungarian-Jewish family in Budapest survives through more than a hundred turbulent years, including periods of Austrian, Nazi and Stalinist domination.
A movie with an epic sweep, in which Fiennes plays three roles of successive heads of the family, men eager for success even if it means compromising religion and morality; unfortunately, the detailed narrative exposition tends to overwhelm any character development.
w István Szabó, Israel Horovitz *d* István Szabó
ph Lajos Koltai *m* Maurice Jarre *ad* Atilla Kovacs *ed* Dominique Fortin, Michael Arcand
cos Pedro Moreno
☆ Ralph Fiennes (Ignatz Sonnenschein/Adam Sors/Ivan Sors), Rosemary Harris (Valerie Sors), Rachel Weisz (Greta Sors), Jennifer Ehle (Valerie Sonnenschein), Molly Parker (Hannah Wippler Sors), Deborah Kara Unger (Carola), James Frain (Gustave Sonnenschein), John Neville (Gustave Sors), Miriam Margolyes (Rose Sonnenschein), David de Keyser (Emmanuel Sonnenschein), Mark Strong (Istvan Sors), William Hurt (Andor Knorr), Bill Paterson (Minister of Justice), Rudiger Vogler (General Jakofalvy)
'The resulting dish is slightly stolid. Near the end of our epic journey we learn, "the purpose of life is... life itself", and the sense of anti-climax is palpable.' – *Julian Graffy, Sight and Sound*

'For the price of a movie, you'll feel like a million!'
The Sunshine Boys *
US 1975 111m Metrocolor
MGM/Rastar (Ray Stark)
Two feuding old vaudeville comedians come together for a television spot, and ruin it.
Over-extended sketch in which one main role is beautifully underplayed, the other hammed up, and the production lacks any kind of style. The one-liners are good, though.
w Neil Simon *play* Neil Simon *d* Herbert Ross
ph David M. Walsh *md* Harry V. Lojewski

☆ Walter Matthau, *George Burns*, Richard Benjamin, Carol Arthur

'It's just shouting, when it needs to be beautifully timed routines.' – *New Yorker*

'They feud with ill-matched resources, and the movie's visual delights vanish with the title sequence.' – *Sight and Sound*

† George Burns stepped in when Jack Benny became ill and died.

†† In 1996 it was remade as a TV film starring Peter Falk and Woody Allen.

George Burns

Neil Simon; Walter Matthau

'Take a vacation with John Sayles'

Sunshine State ***

US 2002 141m CFI

Columbia/Sony Classics/Anarchists' Convention (Maggie Renzi)

Residents of a small Florida seaside town resist attempts by property companies to redevelop the town.

A sprawling account of some unsatisfactory lives, of dreams gone wrong and futures to be avoided, that also manages to reflect the problems and momentary pleasures of a larger society.

wd John Sayles *ph* Patrick Cady *m* Mason Daring *pd* Mark Ricker *ed* John Sayles

☆ Edie Falco (Marly Temple), Angela Bassett (Desiree Perry), Jane Alexander (Delia Temple), Ralph Waite (Furman Temple), James McDaniel (Reggie), Timothy Hutton (Jack Meadows), Mary Alice (Eunice Stokes), Bill Cobbs (Dr Lloyd), Mary Steenburgen (Francine Pickney), Miguel Ferrer (Lester)

'If there's a more acute film about 'community' in America, it's yet to be made.' – *James Christopher, Times*

'You can feel the heat that ignites this gripping tale, and the humor and humanity that root it in feeling.' – *Peter Travers, Rolling Stone*

Sunshine Susie

GB 1931 87m bw

Gainsborough

A banker pretends to be a clerk in order to court a typist.

Viennese-set comedy which worked at the time but quickly dated.

w Angus MacPhail, Robert Stevenson, Victor Saville, Noel Wood-Smith *play The Private Secretary* by Franz Schultz *d* Victor Saville

☆ Renate Muller, Jack Hulbert, Owen Nares, Morris Harvey, Sybil Grove

Sunstruck

Australia 1972 92m Eastmancolor

Immigrant (Jack Neary, James Grafton)

A shy Welsh schoolmaster emigrates to the Australian outback.

Simple-minded, uninspired, predictable family comedy for star fans.

w Stan Mars *d* James Gilbert *ph* Brian West *m* Peter Knight

☆ Harry Secombe, Maggie Fitzgibbon, John Meillon, Dawn Lake

Suor Omicidi: see *Killer Nun*

Suor Omicidi: see *The Killer Nun*

'The judge sentenced slumlord Louis Kritski to six months in his own building. He would have been better off in jail.'

The Super

US 1991 85m colour

Largo/JVC (Charles Gordon)

A New York landlord is forced to live in one of his slum properties.

A misfiring movie, comic when it should be serious, and sentimental the rest of the time.

w Sam Simon *d* Rod Daniel *ph* Bruce Surtees *m* Miles Goodman *pd* Kristi Zea *ed* Jack Hofstra

☆ Joe Pesci, Vincent Gardenia, Madolyn Smith-Osborne, Ruben Blades, Stacey Travis, Carole Shelley, Paul Benjamin

'A lesson, perhaps, that those movies that fail to get a theatrical release do, with the occasional exception, deserve the direct-to-video treatment.' – *Empire*

† The film was released direct to video in Britain.

The Super Cops

US 1974 94m Metrocolor

St Regis Films/UA

Two New York cops are suspended for breaking too many rules, but wage their private war on crime.

Low-life crime melodrama which plays effectively enough as a lighter-hearted Serpico.

w Lorenzo Semple Jnr *book* L. H. Whittemore *d* Gordon Parks *ph* Dick Kratina *m* Jerry Fielding

☆ Ron Leibman, David Selby, Sheila Frazier, Pat Hingle, Dan Frazer

Super Fuzz: see *Supersnooper*

'This Ain't No Game.'

Super Mario Brothers

US 1993 104m Technicolor

Entertainment/Lightmotive/Allied/Cinergi (Jake Eberts, Roland Joffé)

The Mario brothers, two plumbers, rescue a princess from a universe in another dimension, where reptilian humanoids, descended from dinosaurs, plan to rule both worlds.

An attempt to transfer a best-selling Nintendo video game to the screen; it doesn't work.

w Parker Bennett, Terry Runté, Ed Solomon, based on characters and concept created by Shigeru Miyamato, Takashi Tezuka *d* Rocky Morton, Annabel Jankel *ph* Dean Semler *m* Alan Silvestri *pd* David L. Snyder *ed* Caroline Ross *sp* Christopher Francis Woods, Patrick Tatopoulos

☆ Bob Hoskins, John Leguizamo, Dennis Hopper, Samantha Mathis, Fisher Stevens, Richard Edson, Rona Shaw, Dana Kaminski, Lance Henriksen

'There are plenty of gags, but not one laugh.' – *Variety*

'One and a half square miles of plywood went into the making of *Super Mario Brothers*, and that was just for the performances.' – *Sight and Sound*

'Altered State Police'

Super Troopers

US 2001 103m colour

TCF/Jersey Shore/Cataland/Broken Lizard (Richard Perello)

In a Vermont town, a group of state troopers try to porove they are better cops than the local police force.

Broken Lizard, an American troupe, display their lack of comic skills while wasting the talents of rather better actors in this lazy, crude comedy.

w Broken Lizard *d* Jay Chandrasekhar *ph* Joaquin Baca-Asay *m* 38 Special *pd* Ben Conable *ed* Jacob Craycroft, Jumbulingam, Kevin Heffernan

☆ Jay Chandrasekhar (Thorny), Kevin Heffernan (Farva), Steve Lemme (Mac), Paul Soter (Foster), Erik Stolhanske (Rabbit), Brian Cox (Capt. John O'Hagan), Daniel Von Bargen (Chief Grady), Marisa Coughlan (Ursula)

'I can't quite recommend it—it's too patched together—but I almost can; it's the kind of movie that makes you want to like it.' – *Roger Ebert, Chicago Sun-Times*

'Bad and tasteless. You laugh neither with it nor at it but rather sit counting the minutes while the movie laughs, for no good reason, at itself.' – *A. O. Scott, New York Times*

Superdad

US 1974 95m Technicolor

Walt Disney

A lawyer is determined to rule the life of his teenage daughter.

Bumbling farce with frenzied and unattractive characters.

w Joseph L. McEveety *d* Vincent McEveety *ph* Andrew Jackson *m* Buddy Baker

☆ Bob Crane, Barbara Rush, Kurt Russell, Joe Flynn, Kathleen Cody

Superfly

US 1972 98m Technicolor

Warner (Sig Shore)

The New York adventures of black cocaine peddlers.

'Sensational' comedy with violence in which the pushers exit laughing. Tedious and deplorable.

w Philip Fenty *d* Gordon Parks Jnr *ph* James Signorelli *m* Curtis Mayfield

☆ Ron O'Neal, Carl Lee, Sheila Frazier

'It suggests that New York is now nothing more than a concrete junkieyard.' – *Philip Strick*

Supergirl *

GB 1984 124m colour Panavision

Cantharus/Ilya Salkind (Timothy Burrill)

A Krypton power source falls into the hands of a power-hungry witch, and Supergirl is sent to retrieve it.

Playful comic strip spectacular which entertains in Wizard of Oz *style for most of its way but was savaged by the critics.*

w David Odell *d* Jeannot Szwarc *ph* Alan Hume *m* Jerry Goldsmith *pd* Richard MacDonald

☆ Helen Slater, Faye Dunaway, Peter O'Toole, Mia Farrow, Brenda Vaccaro, Peter Cook, Simon Ward, Marc McClure, Hart Bochner, David Healy

The Supergrass

GB 1985 105m colour

Recorded Releasing

The police unwisely believe that a boaster can lead them to a drug ring.

For those who enjoy the somewhat remote satirical humour of Channel 4's The Comic Strip.

w Pete Richens, Peter Richardson *d* Peter Richardson *ph* John Metcalfe *m* Keith Tippett

☆ Adrian Edmondson, Jennifer Saunders, Peter Richardson, Dawn French, Keith Allan, Robbie Coltrane, Alexei Sayle

Superman

US 1948 bw serial: 15 eps

Columbia

The man from Krypton who poses as mild-mannered Clark Kent combats The Spider Lady.

The subject makes this serial fairly lively – livelier in fact than the multi-million-dollar 1978 film.

d Spencer Bennet, Thomas Carr

☆ Kirk Alyn, Noel Neill, Tommy Bond, Carol Forman, George Meeker

'You'll believe a man can fly!'

Superman

US/GB 1978 142m colour Panavision

Warner/Alexander Salkind (Pierre Spengler)

A baby saved from the planet Krypton when it explodes grows up as a newspaperman and uses his tremendous powers to fight evil and support the American way.

Long, lugubrious and only patchily entertaining version of the famous comic strip, with far too many irrelevant preliminaries and a misguided sense of its own importance.

w Mario Puzo, David Newman, Robert Benton, Leslie Newman *d* Richard Donner *ph* Geoffrey Unsworth *m* John Williams *pd* John Barry *ed* Stuart Baird *sp* various

☆ *Christopher Reeve*, Marlon Brando, Margot Kidder, Jackie Cooper, Glenn Ford, Phyllis Thaxter, Trevor Howard, Gene Hackman, Ned Beatty, Susannah York, Valerie Perrine

'Though one of the two or three most expensive movies made to date, it's cheesy-looking, and the plotting is so hit or miss that the story never seems to get started; the special effects are far from wizardly and the editing often seems hurried and jerky just at the crucial points.' – *New Yorker*

'It gives the impression of having been made in panic – in fear that style or too much imagination might endanger its approach to the literal-minded.' – *Pauline Kael, New Yorker*

'The epitome of supersell.' – *Les Keyser, Hollywood in the Seventies*

† Reprehensible records were set by Brando getting three million dollars for a ten-minute performance (and then suing for a share of the gross); and by the incredible 7½-minute credit roll at the end.

†† Tiny roles were played by Noel Neill, who was Lois Lane in the TV series, and by Kirk Alyn, who was Superman in two serials.

John Williams; editing; sound; visual effects

Superman II

US 1980 127m Technicolor Panavision

Warner/Alexander Salkind (Pierre Spengler)

Three renegade Kryptonians threaten Earth with a space bomb.

Half the first episode was devoted to a creaky and unnecessary setting up of plot and characters. This sequel is all the better for diving straight into action, but a classic it isn't, even of the comic strip kind.

w Mario Puzo, David Newman, Leslie Newman *d* Richard Lester *ph* Geoffrey Unsworth, Robert Paynter *m* Ken Thorne

☆ Christopher Reeve, Gene Hackman, Ned Beatty, Jackie Cooper, Sarah Douglas, Margot Kidder, Valerie Perrine, Susannah York, Terence Stamp, Jack O'Halloran, E. G. Marshall

Superman III

GB 1983 125m colour Panavision

Dovemead/Cantharus (Pierre Spengler)

Synthetic Kryptonite warps Superman's character, but his conscience is reawakened by a plea from a small boy.

Sometimes humorous but overwritten and overacted variation on a tired theme. The special effects are the thing, but there's too much padding in between.

w David Newman, Leslie Newman *d* Richard Lester *ph* Robert Paynter *m* Ken Thorne *pd* Peter Murton *ed* John Victor Smith

☆ Christopher Reeve (Clark Kent/Superman), Richard Pryor (Gus Gorman), Jackie Cooper (Perry White), Marc McClure (Jimmy Olsen), Annette O'Toole (Lana Lang), Annie Ross (Vera Webster), Pamela Stephenson (Lorelei Ambrosia), Robert Vaughn (Ross Webster), Margot Kidder (Lois Lane), Graham Stark (Blind man)

Superman IV: The Quest for Peace

GB 1987 89m colour JDC widescreen

Cannon

Superman determines that the world shall lay down its nuclear arms.

Stolid dialogue and poor technicalities are evident throughout what will surely be the last of the series.

w Lawrence Konner, Mark Rosenthal, Christopher Reeve *d* Sidney J. Furie

☆ Christopher Reeve (Clark Kent/Superman), Gene Hackman, Jackie Cooper, Marc McClure, Sam Wanamaker, Mariel Hemingway, Margot Kidder

'Her heart cried out for love – yet her hands reached out to destroy!'

Supernatural *

US 1933 67m bw

Paramount (Victor and Edward Halperin)

A girl is possessed by the soul of a dead murderess.

Mad doctor nonsense, interestingly but not very successfully styled.

w Harvey Thew, Brian Marlow *d* Victor Halperin *ph* Arthur Martinelli

☆ Carole Lombard, H. B. Warner, Randolph Scott, Vivienne Osborne, Alan Dinehart

'A 65-minute ghost story that dies after the first half-hour.' – *Variety*

'In The Farthest Reaches Of Space Something Has Gone Terribly Wrong.'

'Terror Times Infinity.'

Supernova

US 2000 90m DeLuxe Super 35

MGM/Screenland/Hammerhead (Ash R. Shah, Daniel Chuba, Jamie Dixon)

The crew of a deep-space medical-rescue ship answer a distress call from a mine on a distant planet and discover that they have an alien aboard.

Dreary and confusing science-fiction story that recycles Alien *to little effect.*

w David Campbell Wilson *story* William Malone *d* Thomas Lee (Walter Hill) *ph* Lloyd Ahern II *m* David Williams *pd* Marek Dobrowolski *ed* Michael Schweitzer, Melissa Kent *sp* makeup fx: Patrick Tatopoulos *cos* Bob Ringwood

☆ James Spader (Nick Vanzant), Angela Bassett (Kaela Evers), Robert Forster (A.J. Marley), Lou Diamond Phillips (Yerzy Penalosa), Peter Facinelli (Karl Larson), Robin Tunney (Danika Lund), Wilson Cruz (Benj Sotomejor), Eddie Rice Jnr (Flyboy), Vanessa Marshall (Sweetie)

'An intriguing and frequently gripping deep space thriller with considerable sexual edge.' – *James Cameron-Wilson, Film Review*
† Director Walter Hill had his name removed from the credits because of 'creative differences' with the producers. Francis Ford Coppola was an uncredited editor.
†† The film cost $65m.

Supersnooper
Italy/US 1981 94m Technicolor
Columbia/Trans-Cinema TV (Maximilian Wolkoff)
aka: *Super Fuzz*
A Miami cop develops superhuman powers after being exposed to radiation.
Stolid comedy with poor special effects.
w Sergio Corbucci, Sabatino Giuffini *d* Sergio Corbucci *ph* Silvano Ippoliti *m* La Bionda *pd* Marco Dentici *ed* Eugene Ballaby
☆ Terence Hill (Mario Girotti), Ernest Borgnine, Joanne Dru, Marc Lawrence, Julie Gordon, Lee Sandman

Supervixens
US 1975 105m colour
Films International/September 19 (Russ Meyer)
Accused of the murder of his girlfriend, a garage mechanic goes on the run, pursued by a homicidal cop.
Inept, amateurish wallow in Meyer's simple-minded world of big-breasted nymphomaniacs and cuckolded men; film is, unfortunately, not one of Meyer's interests, but merely a means to what obsesses him.
wd Russ Meyer *ph* Russ Meyer *m* William Loose *ad* Michael Levesque *ed* Russ Meyer
☆ Shari Eubank, Charles Napier, Uschi Digard, Charles Pitts, Henry Rowland, Christy Hartburg, Sharon Kelly

Support Your Local Gunfighter
US 1971 92m DeLuxe
UA/Cherokee/Brigade (Bill Finnegan)
A con man jumps a train at a small mining town and is mistaken for a dreaded gunfighter.
Disappointing sequel to the following; just a couple of good jokes.
w James Edward Grant *d* Burt Kennedy *ph* Harry Stradling Jnr *m* Jack Elliott, Allyn Ferguson
☆ James Garner, Suzanne Pleshette, Joan Blondell, Jack Elam, Chuck Connors, Harry Morgan, Marie Windsor, Henry Jones, John Dehner

Support Your Local Sheriff **
US 1968 92m Technicolor
UA/Cherokee (William Bowers)
Gold is found near a Western village, and the resulting influx of desperate characters causes problems for the sheriff.
Amusing comedy, drawing on many Western clichés.
w William Bowers d Burt Kennedy ph Harry Stradling Jnr *m* Jeff Alexander
☆ *James Garner*, Joan Hackett, Walter Brennan, Jack Elam, Henry Morgan, Bruce Dern, Henry Jones
'It rejuvenates a stagnating genre by combining just the right doses of parody and affectionate nostalgia.' – *Jan Dawson*

Suppose They Gave a War and Nobody Came
US 1969 114m DeLuxe
Engel – Auerbach/ABC (Fred Engel)
Three accident-prone PROs try to give the army a good name in a town which wishes it would go away; they eventually cause panic by arriving at a dance in a tank.
Muddled farce which may have hoped to be satire.
w Don McGuire, Hal Captain *d* Hy Averback *ph* Burnett Guffey *m* Jerry Fielding
☆ Tony Curtis, Brian Keith, Ernest Borgnine, Ivan Dixon, Suzanne Pleshette, *Tom Ewell*, Bradford Dillman, Arthur O'Connell, Robert Emhardt, John Fiedler, Don Ameche

El Sur: see *The South*

Sur: see *South*

'She taught him good manners, he taught her bad ones.'
Sur Mes Lèvres ***
France 2001 118m colour
Pathé/Sedif/Cine b/France 2 (Jean-Louis Livi, Philippe Carcassonne)
GB and US title: *Read My Lips*
A hard-of-hearing secretary, who can lip-read, becomes involved with a petty criminal and they take advantage of each other's abilities.
Clever thriller of a manipulative woman's descent into darkness and self-realisation.
w Tonino Benacquista, Jacques Audiard *d* Jacques Audiard *ph* Mathieu Vadepied *m* Alexandre Desplat *ad* Michel Barthelemy *ed* Juliette Welfling
☆ Vincent Cassel (Paul Angeli), Emmanuelle Devos (Carla Behm), Olivier Gourmet (Marchand), Olivia Bonamy (Annie), Olivier Perrier (Masson), Bernard Alane (Morel), Céline Samie (Josie Marchand), David Saracino (Richard Carambo)
'A breathless and rather audacious study in the sexiness of a nonsexual relationship.' – *David Denby, New Yorker*
'To be viewed and treasured for its extraordinary intelligence and originality as well as its lyrical variations on the game of love.' – *Andrew Sarris*

The Sure Thing
US 1985 94m DeLuxe
Roger Birnbaum/Monument/Embassy
Two uneasy couples travel west to California for Christmas.
Slightly unsettling youth comedy which, in the form of It Happened One Night, *seems to be saying that friendship is more important than sex.*
w Steven L. Bloom, Jonathan Roberts *d* Rob Reiner *ph* Robert Elswit *m* Tom Scott
☆ John Cusack, Daphne Zuniga, Anthony Edwards, Boyd Gaines, Tim Robbins, Lisa Jane Persky, Viveca Lindfors
'Two sounds clash: old wine being poured into new bottles, and familiar barrels being scraped.' – *Philip French, Observer*

Surf Ninjas
US 1993 87m DeLuxe
Entertainment/New Line (Ezven Kolar)
Two Californian surfers discover that they are the rightful heirs to an island kingdom in the South China Sea, ruled by an evil dictator.
Jokey action film aimed at an audience too young to enjoy the real thing.
w Dan Gordon *d* Neal Israel *m* David Kitay *pd* Michael Novotny *ed* Tom Walls
☆ Leslie Nielsen, Ernie Reyes Jnr, Rob Schneider, Tone Loc, John Karlen, Ernie Reyes Snr, Kelly Hu
'Brain-dead though this film is, it has a certain goofy charm that's almost endearing.' – *Sight and Sound*

The Surfer
Australia 1988 94m colour
Night Flight (James M. Vernon, Frank Shields)
When a beach bum investigates the killing of a friend, he finds himself framed for murder, and embroiled with gangsters, crooked politicians and cops.
Low-budget thriller, directed with a certain nervy style but running out of energy before the end.
w David Marsh *story* Frank Shields *d* Frank Shields *ph* Michael Edols *m* Davood Tabrizi *ed* Greg Bell
☆ Gary Day, Gosia Dobrowolska, Rod Mullinar, Tony Barry, Gerard Maguire, Kris McQuade, Stephen Leeder

The Surgeon: see *Exquisite Tenderness*

Surprise Package
GB 1960 100m bw
Columbia/Stanley Donen
An American gangster is deported to the same Mediterranean island as an exiled European king, whose crown gets stolen.
Flat and feeble comedy which defeats its stars.
w Harry Kurnitz *novel* Art Buchwald *d* Stanley Donen *ph* Christopher Challis *m* Benjamin Frankel
☆ Yul Brynner, Noël Coward, Mitzi Gaynor, Bill Nagy, Eric Pohlmann, George Coulouris, Warren Mitchell

Surrender
US 1931 69m bw
Fox
A French soldier in a German prison camp falls in love with a German girl at the nearby castle.
Flabby drama which seems constantly about to make symbolic points.
w S. N. Behrman, Sonya Levien *play* Axelle by Pierre Benoit *d* William K. Howard
☆ Warner Baxter, Leila Hyams, Ralph Bellamy, C. Aubrey Smith, William Pawley, Alexander Kirkland
'Anaemic picture product, not for A houses in big towns.' – *Variety*

Surrender
US 1987 95m TVC Color
Cannon (Aaron Spelling, Alan Greisman)
A writer with a history of unsatisfactory relationships with women falls for an artist who has had similar experiences with men.
Lacklustre attempt at a romantic comedy, taken at a snail's pace and with dialogue that fails to sparkle.
wd Jerry Belson *ph* Juan-Ruiz Anchia *m* Michel Colombier *pd* Lilly Kilvert *ed* Wendy Greene Bricmont
☆ Sally Field, Michael Caine, Steve Guttenberg, Peter Boyle, Jackie Cooper, Julie Kavner, Louise Lasser

Surrounded by Women: see *Between Two Women*

Survive
Mexico/US 1976 86m Technicolor
EMI/Robert Stigwood-Allan Carr/Conacine/Productora Filmica (Rene Cardona Jnr)
After a plane crash high in the Andes, surviving members of a rugby team resort to cannibalism in order to survive.
Unpleasant low-budget film, based on a true story and concentrating on the grislier aspects.
wd Rene Cardona Snr (English adaptation Martin Sherman) *book* Clay Blair Jnr *ph* Luis Medina *m* Gerald Fried *ad* A. L. de Guevara *ed* Marshall M. Borden
☆ Hugo Stiglitz, Norma Lazareno, Luz Aguilar, Fernando Larranaga, Lorenzo de Rodas, Luz Ma
'In its original form this low budget Mexican production clearly had little to offer: a sketchy script, feeble performances and scenes cloaked in fog which conveniently disguised polystyrene snow. Having been doctored in America for universal consumption, and fitted out with Dragnet-style commentary and limply banal dialogue, it is quite unbearable.' – *David McGillivray, MFB*
† The event was also the basis of the 1992 Hollywood movie *Alive* (qv).

Surviving Picasso
US/GB 1996 125m Technicolor
Warner/Merchant Ivory (Ismail Merchant, David L. Wolper)
Françoise Gilot, an art student, becomes the mistress of Picasso and bears him two children before their relationship founders.
Dull biopic that wades through all the usual clichés of artistic life without once suggesting that it is dealing with characters of flesh and blood.
w Ruth Prawer Jhabvala *book Picasso: Creator and Destroyer* by Arianna Stassinopolous Huffington *d* James Ivory *ph* Tony Pierce-Roberts *m* Richard Robbins *pd* Luciana Arrighi *ed* Andrew Marcus
☆ Anthony Hopkins, Natascha McElhone, Julianne Moore, Joss Ackland, Peter Eyre, Jane Lapotaire, Joseph Maher, Bob Peck, Diane Venora, Joan Plowright
'A winner.' – *Variety*
'A film for middle-aged, middle-class people who know nothing about art.' – *Tracey Emin, Neon*

Surviving the Game
US 1994 96m DeLuxe
New Line/David Permut
A homeless man turns the tables on six wealthy men who hunt him for sport.
This is yet another remake of Richard Connell's The Most Dangerous Game *– and one that lacks drive or suspense as it strolls through very familiar territory.*
w Eric Bernt *d* Ernest Dickerson *ph* Bojan Bazelli *m* Stewart Copeland *pd* Christiaan Wagener *ed* Sam Pollard
☆ Ice T, Rutger Hauer, Gary Busey, Charles S. Dutton, F. Murray Abraham, John C. McGinley, William McNamara, Jeff Corey
'Threadbare chase movie, which almost makes surviving the screening its own endurance test.' – *Variety*

The Survivors
US 1983 102m Metrocolor
Columbia-Delphi-Rastar-William Sackheim
An executive and a gas station attendant, both potential victims of a hit man, take refuge in the snowy mountains of Vermont.
Bewilderingly unfocused black comedy with some pleasant barbs along the way.
w Michael Leeson *d* Michael Ritchie *ph* Billy Williams *m* Paul Chihara *pd* Gene Callahan *ed* Richard A. Harris
☆ Walter Matthau, Robin Williams, Jerry Reed, James Wainwright, Kristen Vigard, Annie McEnroe

Susan and God *
US 1940 117m bw
MGM (Hunt Stromberg)
GB title: *The Gay Mrs Trexel*
A flighty society woman gets religion but fails to practise what she preaches.
Unusual comedy-drama for MGM to tackle, but a fairly successful one for high-class audiences.
w Anita Loos play Rachel Crothers *d* George Cukor *ph* Robert Planck *m* Herbert Stothart
☆ Joan Crawford, Fredric March, Ruth Hussey, John Carroll, Rita Hayworth, Nigel Bruce, Bruce Cabot, Rita Quigley, Rose Hobart, Constance Collier, Gloria de Haven, Marjorie Main
'It's not a good comedy, but it has a certain fascination, because the theme is such an odd one for Hollywood to have attempted at all.' – *Pauline Kael, 70s*

'Thrill to them together!'
Susan Lenox, Her Fall and Rise *
US 1931 76m bw
MGM (Paul Bern)
GB title: *The Rise of Helga*
A farm girl flees to the city when her father tries to marry her off to a brute.
Moderate star melodrama with the star somewhat miscast.
w Wanda Tuchock novel David Graham Phillips *d* Robert Z. Leonard *ph* William Daniels
☆ Greta Garbo, Clark Gable, Jean Hersholt, John Miljan, Alan Hale
'A torrid romance that will fascinate the femmes.' – *Variety*
'If you like your romance spread thick, your passions strong and your Garbo hot, don't miss this.' – *Photoplay*
† The author of the book had been shot by a crank who disapproved of his treatment of women.

Susan Slade
US 1961 116m Technicolor
Warner (Delmer Daves)
An engineer brings his family back to San Francisco from Chile, and his teenage daughter runs into problems of the heart.
Stilted, busy sudser.
wd Delmer Daves *novel* Doris Hume *ph* Lucien Ballard *m* Max Steiner
☆ Connie Stevens, Troy Donahue, Dorothy McGuire, Lloyd Nolan, Brian Aherne, Natalie Schafer, Grant Williams, Bert Convy, Kent Smith

Susan Slept Here
US 1954 98m Technicolor
RKO (Harriet Parsons)
The Hollywood scriptwriter of a film about youth problems agrees to look after a delinquent teenage girl.
Skittish, would-be piquant comedy; quite unattractive.
w Alex Gottlieb *d* Frank Tashlin *ph* Nicholas Musuraca *md* Leigh Harline *songs* Jack Lawrence, Richard Myers

☆ Dick Powell, Debbie Reynolds, Anne Francis, Glenda Farrell, Alvy Moore, Horace MacMahon
song 'Hold My Hand'

Susannah of the Mounties *
US 1939 78m bw
TCF (Kenneth MacGowan)

A little girl who is the only survivor of a wagon train massacre is looked after by the Canadian Mounties.
Adequate star action romance, Shirley's last real success.
w Robert Ellis, Helen Logan *d* William A. Seiter *ph* Arthur Miller *md* Louis Silvers
☆ Shirley Temple, Randolph Scott, Margaret Lockwood, J. Farrell MacDonald, Maurice Moscovich, Moroni Olsen, Victor Jory
'Strictly for the juvenile trade ... illogical situations make it no more than a moderate fairy tale.' – *Variety*

Susan's Plan
US 1998 85m Foto-Kem
Kushner-Locke (Leslie Belzberg, Brad Wyman, John Landis)

A nursery teacher and her salesman lover hire two incompetents to kill her former husband so she can collect on his insurance.
Fast-paced but dreary farce, too bland in its approach to get any amusement from its theme of murder and greed.
wd John Landis *ph* Ken Kelsch *m* Peter Bernstein *pd* Stuart Blatt *ed* Nancy Morrison
☆ Nastassja Kinski, Billy Zane, Michael Biehn, Rob Schneider, Lara Flynn Boyle, Carl Ballantine, Thomas Haden Church, Bill Duke, Lisa Edelstein, Sheree North, Dan Aykroyd

'His was a strange secret! Hers was a strange love!'
The Suspect *
US 1944 84m bw
Universal (Islin Auster)
A henpecked husband kills his wife and is blackmailed.
Efficient studio-bound suspenser with theatrically effective acting.
w Bertram Millhauser *novel* James Ronald *d* Robert Siodmak *ph* Paul Ivano *m* Frank Skinner
☆ *Charles Laughton*, *Henry Daniell*, Rosalind Ivan, Ella Raines, Molly Lamont, Dean Harens
'High marks for tension, local colour, story.' – *William Whitebait*

Suspect *
GB 1960 81m bw
British Lion/The Boulting Brothers
Government research chemists find a traitor in their midst.
Entertaining but fairly routine spy melodrama, shot on an experimental low budget but confined to lower berth bookings.
w Nigel Balchin *novel* *Sort of Traitors* by Nigel Balchin *d* Roy and John Boulting *ph* Max Greene *md* John Wilkes
☆ Tony Britton, Virginia Maskell, Peter Cushing, Ian Bannen, Raymond Huntley, Donald Pleasence, Thorley Walters, Spike Milligan, Kenneth Griffith
'A better standard of second feature film is badly needed, but the way to do it is not by making pictures which look as though they have strayed from TV.' – *Penelope Houston*

'No matter the cost. No matter the danger. They will find the truth.'
Suspect *
US 1987 121m colour
Columbia/Tri-Star (Daniel A. Sherkow)

A public defender, with the aid of a member of the jury, uncovers high-level corruption when she defends a deaf-mute tramp accused of murder.
Despite its many implausibilities, a thriller that engages the attention.
w Eric Roth *d* Peter Yates *ph* Billy Williams *m* Michael Kamen *pd* Stuart Wurtzel *ed* Ray Lovejoy *cos* Rita Ryack
☆ Cher, Dennis Quaid, Liam Neeson, John Mahoney, Joe Mantegna, Philip Bosco, E. Katherine Kerr, Fred Melamed, Lisbeth Bartlett, Paul D'Amato

Suspected Person
GB 1943 78m bw
Associated British
Thieves fall out and are tracked by police.
Slightly bitter crime drama which adequately filled half a bill.
wd Lawrence Huntington
☆ Clifford Evans, Patricia Roc, David Farrar, Robert Beatty

'Unmasking a beautiful woman's secret and unholy desires!'
Suspense
US 1946 103m bw
Monogram (Maurice and Frank King)
A tough guy crashes an ice palace and makes a play for the boss's skating star wife.
Heavy melodrama with skating interludes; remarkably similar in plot to the more famous Gilda. *Chiefly remarkable as Monogram's most expensive film.*
w Philip Yordan *d* Frank Tuttle *ph* Karl Struss
☆ Belita, Barry Sullivan, Albert Dekker, Bonita Granville, Eugene Pallette, George E. Stone, Leon Belasco

Suspicion **
US 1941 99m bw
RKO (Alfred Hitchcock)

A sedate young girl marries a playboy, and comes to suspect that he is trying to murder her.
Rather artificial and stiff Hitchcock suspenser, further marred by an ending suddenly switched to please the front office. Full of the interesting touches one would expect.
w Samson Raphaelson, Alma Reville, Joan Harrison *novel* *Before the Fact* by Francis Iles *d* *Alfred Hitchcock* *ph* Harry Stradling *m* Franz Waxman
☆ *Joan Fontaine*, Cary Grant, Nigel Bruce, Cedric Hardwicke, May Whitty, Isabel Jeans, Heather Angel, Leo G. Carroll
'The fact that Hitchcock throws in a happy end during the last five minutes, like a conjuror explaining his tricks, seems to me a pity; but it spoils the film only in retrospect, and we have already had our thrills.' – *William Whitebait, New Statesman*
Joan Fontaine
best picture; Franz Waxman

Suspicious River
Canada 2000 93m colour
Metro Tartan/Suspicious (Michael Okulitch, Raymond Massey)
A motel receptionist, who also provides sex to customers, begins an affair with a man who rapes her.
A depressing drama in two parts, interspersing a woman's current humiliations with her relationship to her younger self, observing similar abuses in her own family; but it remains hermetic and unilluminating.
wd Lynne Stopkewich *novel* Laura Kasischke *ph* Gregory Middleton *m* Don MacDonald *pd* Don MacAulay *ed* Allan Lee
☆ Molly Parker (Leila Murray), Callum Keith Rennie (Gary Jensen), Joel Bissonette (Rick Schmidt), Deanna Milligan (Millie), Mary Kate Welsh (Young girl)
'A succession of heavy-handed symbols (the title among them) and it fails equally as a case history, as a moral fable or as a pitiful account of a woman's destruction.' – *Philip French, Observer*

'The only thing more terrifying than the last twelve minutes of this film is the first eighty!'
'Once you've seen it you will never again feel safe in the dark!'
Suspiria **
Italy 1976 97m Eastmancolor Technovision
Seda Spettacoli (Claudio Argento)

A young American dance student arrives at dead of night at a continental academy where murder is the order of the day.
Psycho *meets* The Exorcist, *with no holds barred: a genuinely scary thriller with gaudy visuals and a screaming sound track. A pyrotechnic display for those who can take it.*
w Dario Argento, Daria Nicolodi *d* *Dario Argento* *ph* Luciano Tovoli *m* Dario Argento, Goblin
☆ Jessica Harper, Alida Valli, Joan Bennett, Stefania Casini, Udo Kier
'Thunderstorms and explicitly grotesque murders pile up as Argento happily abandons plot mechanics to provide a bravura display of his technical skill.' – *Time Out*

Sutter's Gold
US 1936 75m bw
Universal
During the California gold rush an immigrant has to fight for his rights when a strike starts on his land.
Patchily arresting Western which by costing much more than it should started the exit of Carl Laemmle from the chairman's office.
w Jack Kirkland, Walter Woods and George O'Neil *d* James Cruze
☆ Edward Arnold, Lee Tracy, Binnie Barnes, Katherine Alexander, Addison Richards, Montagu Love, John Miljan
† Most of the action footage was reused in a 1939 quickie, *Mutiny on the Blackhawk*.

'A thriller where nothing is black and white.'
Suture *
US 1993 96m bw
ICA/Scott McGehee, David Siegel

A poor man suffering from amnesia after being injured in an explosion is mistaken for his wealthy half-brother and assumes his personality.
A stylish thriller, less concerned with the mechanics of a crime than questions of identity. Its main trick, as irritating as it is clever, is to have the two physically similar half-brothers played by very dissimilar actors, one white and the other black.
wd Scott McGehee, David Siegel *ph* Greg Gardiner *m* Cary Berger *pd* Kelly McGehee *ed* Lauren Zuckerman
☆ Dennis Haysbert, Mel Harris, Sab Shimono, Michael Harris, Dina Merrill
'An exceedingly smart and elegant American indie feature in a very unusual vein.' – *Variety*

Suzhou River **
China/Germany/Netherlands/Japan/France 2000 83m colour
Artificial Eye/Coproduction Office/Essential/Dream Factory (Nai An, Philippe Bober)

original title: *Su Zhou He*
A motorcycle courier, who loses the girl he loves through an act of betrayal, meets a nightclub dancer years later who he is convinced is the same woman.
Hitchcock's Vertigo *has been shanghai'd and transformed into a delicate tale of double identity, love and loss.*
wd Lou Ye *ph* Wang Yu *m* Jorg Lemberg *ad* Li Zhuoyi *ed* Karl Riedl
☆ Zhou Xun (Moudan/Meimei), Jia Hongsheng (Mardar), Yao Anlian (Boss), Nai An (Mada), Hua Zhongkai (Lao B)
'A seductive and atmospheric conundrum that works pleasingly as an exercise in storytelling.' – *Lizzie Franke, Sight and Sound*

Suzy *
US 1936 95m bw
MGM (Maurice Revnes)

A French air ace of World War I marries an American showgirl; they then find that her former husband, thought dead, is still alive.
Proficient star comedy-drama with romance, action, comedy and a complex plot. A showcase for its stars.
w Dorothy Parker, Alan Campbell, Horace Jackson, Lenore Coffee *novel* Herbert Gorman *d* George Fitzmaurice *ph* Ray June *m* William Axt
☆ Jean Harlow, Cary Grant, Franchot Tone, Benita Hume, Lewis Stone
song 'Did I Remember' (*m*Walter Donaldson, *ly*Harold Adamson)

Svart Lucia: see *The Premonition*

Svengali **
US 1931 81m bw
Warner
In 1890s Paris, a hypnotist turns a girl into a great opera singer but she does not reciprocate his love.
Victorian fantasy melodrama with a great grotesque part for the star and interesting artwork.
w J. Grubb Alexander *novel* *Trilby* by George du Maurier *d* *Archie Mayo* *ph* Barney McGill *ad* Anton Grot
☆ *John Barrymore*, Marian Marsh, Luis Alberni, Lumsden Hare, Donald Crisp, Paul Porcasi
'A slow and old-fashioned melodrama.' – *Variety*
'Barrymore never needed occult powers to be magnetic, but interest flags when he's offscreen.' – *New Yorker, 1978*
Barney McGill; Anton Grot

Svengali
GB 1954 82m Eastmancolor
Renown/Alderdale (Douglas Pierce)

Flatulent remake which does have the virtue of following the original book illustrations but is otherwise unpersuasive.
wd Noel Langley *ph* Wilkie Cooper *m* William Alwyn *ad* *Fred Pusey*
☆ Donald Wolfit, Hildegarde Neff, Terence Morgan, Derek Bond, Paul Rogers, David Kossoff, Hubert Gregg, Noel Purcell, Alfie Bass, Harry Secombe

S.W.A.L.K.: see *Melody*

Swallows and Amazons
GB 1974 92m Eastmancolor
EMI/Theatre Projects (Richard Pilbrow)
In the twenties four children have adventures in the Lake District.
Mild family film, great to look at but lacking in real excitement or style.
w David Wood *novel* Arthur Ransome *d* Claude Whatham *ph* Denis Lewiston *m* Wilfred Josephs
☆ Virginia McKenna, Ronald Fraser, Simon West, Sophie Neville, Zanna Hamilton, Stephen Grendon
'I have never read the Arthur Ransome classic but, if it is as dull as the film, I doubt I ever will ... Everyone is frightfully prissy and well behaved.' – *Ken Russell, Fire over England*

The Swamp: see *La Ciénaga*

Swamp Fire
US 1946 68m bw
Paramount/Pine-Thomas
The rehabilitation of a war veteran bar pilot in the treacherous waters at the mouth of the Mississippi.
Routine romantic melo, notable only as its star's only screen appearance in long trousers.
w Geoffrey Homes *d* William Pine
☆ Johnny Weissmuller, Buster Crabbe, Virginia Grey, Carol Thurston, Edwin Maxwell, Pedro de Cordoba

Swamp Thing
US 1981 91m Technicolor
UA/Swamp Films (Benjamin Melniker, Michael E. Uslan)

A scientist, turned by accident into a cross between a man and a plant, battles against an evil colleague who wants to take over the world.
Less a horror pic, or a big-screen comic strip, more a sentimental story of vegetable love, it is about as interesting as watching grass grow.
wd Wes Craven *ph* Robin Goodwin *m* Harry Manfredini *ad* David Nichols, Robb Wilson King *ed* Richard Bracken *sp* William Munns
☆ Louis Jourdan, Adrienne Barbeau, Ray Wise, David Hess, Nicholas Worth, Don Knight
† It was followed by a sequel, *Return of The Swamp Thing* (qv).

Swamp Water **
US 1941 90m bw
TCF (Irving Pichel)
GB title: *The Man Who Came Back*
A fugitive holds out for years in the Okefenokee swamp, and affects the lives of the local township.
A strange little story, not very compelling as drama but with striking photography and atmosphere. Remade more straightforwardly as Lure of the Wilderness *(qv).*
w Dudley Nichols *story* Vereen Bell *d* *Jean Renoir* *ph* *Peverell Marley* *m* David Buttolph
☆ Walter Huston, Walter Brennan, Anne Baxter, Dana Andrews, Virginia Gilmore, John Carradine, Eugene Pallette, Ward Bond, Guinn Williams
'So bad it's terrific.' – *Otis Ferguson*

The Swan *
US 1956 108m Eastmancolor
Cinemascope
MGM (Dore Schary)

In 1910 Hungary, a girl of noble stock is groomed to marry the crown prince.
Interesting chiefly for a typical Hollywood reaction to a news event; about to lose their top star to a real life prince, MGM dusted off this old and creaky property for her last film. The star cast can't make much of it and the treatment is very heavy.
w John Dighton *play* Ferenc Molnar *d* Charles Vidor *ph* Robert Surtees *m* Bronislau Kaper *ad* Cedric Gibbons, Randall Duell
☆ Grace Kelly, Alec Guinness, Louis Jourdan, Agnes Moorehead, Jessie Royce Landis, Brian Aherne, Leo G. Carroll, *Estelle Winwood*, Robert Coote
'Balancing between artificial comedy and a no less artificial romantic theme, the film ultimately requires considerably greater finesse and subtlety in the handling.' – *Penelope Houston*

The Swan Princess
US 1994 90m Technicolor
Columbia TriStar/International Nest/Rich Animal (Richard Rich, Jared F. Brown)

A wicked magician kidnaps a princess and turns her into a swan to force her to marry him.
Pleasant but unmemorable animated film, much in the Disney manner – its director is a former Disney animator – but lacking both charm and polish.
w Brian Nissen *d* Richard Rich *m* Lex de Azevedo *m/ly* David Zippel, Lex de Azevedo *ad* Mike Hodgson, James Coleman *ed* James Koford, Armetta Jackson-Hamlett
☆ Featuring the voices of: Jack Palance, Howard McGillin, Michelle Nicastro, John Cleese, Steven Wright, Steve Vinovich, Mark Harelik, James Arrington, Sandy Duncan
'Given the essential sentiment of the genre, it's decent value for the kids – not too frightening but possessed at least with a sense of magic and mystery in its better moments.' – *Derek Malcolm, Guardian*

Swanee River **
US 1939 84m Technicolor
TCF (Darryl F. Zanuck)
The life and loves of Stephen Foster.
Attractive, unsurprising family film in rich early colour, sparked by Jolson as E. P. Christy.
w John Taintor Foote, Philip Dunne *d* Sidney Lanfield *ph* Bert Glennon *md* Louis Silvers
☆ Don Ameche, *Al Jolson*, Andrea Leeds, Felix Bressart, Russell Hicks
'An unimpressive story: will hit profitable but not big b.o.' – *Variety*
Louis Silvers

'A murder ... A lie ... A secret shared.'
Swann *
GB/Canada 1996 95m colour
Guild/Shaftesbury/Greenpoint/Majestic/Norstar (Ann Scott, Christina Jennings)
In a small Canadian town, an American feminist arrives to research the life of a local poet, whose reputation is guarded by the librarian.
Teasing biographical mystery, given a heavy-handed treatment that obscures some of its meaning.
w David Young *novel* Carol Shields *d* Anna Benson Gyles *ph* Gerald Packer *m* Richard Rodney Bennett *pd* John Dondertman *ed* Robin Sales
☆ *Miranda Richardson, Brenda Fricker*, Michael Ontkean, David Cubitt, Sean McCann, John Neville, Sean Hewitt
'A gripping, affecting, deeply-felt film, wittily and compassionately scripted and superbly acted.' – *Philip Kemp, Sight and Sound*

Swann in Love **
France 1983 111m colour
Gaumont/FR3/SFPC/Bioskop/Films du Losange (Margaret Menegoz)

original title: *Un Amour de Swann*
An elegant Jew in 19th-century Paris society becomes obsessed by a beautiful demi-mondaine.
Reasonably successful attempt to film part of an unfilmable book. Comparisons with Letter from an Unknown Woman *are inevitable.*
w Peter Brook, Jean-Claude Carrière, Marie-Hélène Estienne, from the works of Marcel Proust *d Volker Schlöndorff ph* Sven Nykvist *m* Hans Werner Henze
☆ *Jeremy Irons*, Ornella Muti, Alain Delon, Fanny Ardant, Marie-Christine Barrault, Anne Bennent
'A film of more taste than vision.' – *Gilbert Adair, MFB*
'If you've read the original, forget it.' – *Volker Schlöndorff*
'A failure, maybe, but one that deserves to be seen.' – *Observer*

The Swarm
US 1978 116m Technicolor Panavision
Warner (Irwin Allen)

African killer bees menace the US.
Very obvious all-star disaster movie with risible dialogue. A box-office flop, probably because several TV movies had already tackled the same subject.
w Stirling Silliphant *novel* Arthur Herzog *d* Irwin Allen *ph* Fred J. Koenekamp *m* Jerry Goldsmith *sp* L. B. Abbott, Van Der Veer, Howard Jensen
☆ Michael Caine, Katharine Ross, Richard Widmark, Richard Chamberlain, Olivia de Havilland, Fred MacMurray, Ben Johnson, Lee Grant, José Ferrer, Patty Duke Astin, Slim Pickens, Bradford Dillman, Henry Fonda, Cameron Mitchell
'You could pass it all off as a sick joke, except that it cost twelve million dollars, twenty-two million bees, and several years of someone's life.' – *Guardian*
'The story is of a banality matched only by the woodenness of the acting.' – *Barry Took, Punch*

Swashbuckler *
US 1976 101m Technicolor
Panavision
Universal/Elliott Kastner (Jennings Lang)

GB title: *The Scarlet Buccaneer*
Rival pirates help a wronged lady.
Uninspired reworking of some old Errol Flynn ideas; the idea was pleasant, but the old style is sadly lacking.
w Jeffrey Bloom *d* James Goldstone *ph* Philip Lathrop *m* John Addison *pd* John Lloyd
☆ Robert Shaw, James Earl Jones, Peter Boyle, Geneviève Bujold, Beau Bridges, Geoffrey Holder
'This tacky pastepot job can't make up its mind whether it's serious, tongue-in-cheek, satirical, slapstick, burlesque, parody or travesty; but be assured it is all of the above.' – *Variety*
'The talented cast is left to play living statues, immobilized by dumb dialogue and awkward action.' – *Judith Crist*

Swedenhielms
Sweden 1935 90m bw
Svensk Filmindustri
A brilliant but spendthrift scientist, who has equally extravagant children, hopes that their troubles can be ended by his winning the Nobel Prize.
A domestic saga that never quite escapes from its theatrical origins; a superior soap opera kept buoyant by its performances.
w Stina Bergman *play* Hjalmar Bergman *d* Gustav Molander *ph* Ake Dahlquist *m* Eric Bengtson
☆ Gösta Ekman, Björn Berglund, Hakan Westergren, Tutta Rolf, Ingrid Bergman, Sigurd Wallen, Nils Eriksson, Karin Swanström

Sweeney! *
GB 1976 89m Technicolor
EMI/Euston (Ted Childs)

Scotland Yard's Flying Squad investigates a suicide and uncovers an elaborate political blackmail scheme.
Enjoyable big screen version of a pacy, violent TV cop show.
w Ranald Graham *d* David Wickes *ph* Dusty Miller *m* Denis King
☆ John Thaw, Dennis Waterman, Barry Foster, Ian Bannen, Colin Welland, Michael Coles, Joe Melia

Sweeney 2
GB 1978 108m Technicolor
Euston Films (Ted Childs)

The flying squad discovers that a series of armed bank robberies is being committed by a gang of expatriates who return from a luxurious Malta development for each caper.
Silly, sluggish and violent extension of thin material which would scarcely have made a good one-hour TV episode. There isn't even an exciting climax.
w Troy Kennedy Martin *d* Tom Clegg *ph* Dusty Miller *m* Tony Hatch *ad* Bill Alexander *ed* Chris Burt
☆ John Thaw (Insp Jack Regan), Dennis Waterman (Sgt George Carter), Barry Stanton (Big John), Denholm Elliott (Jupp), Nigel Hawthorne (Dilke), John Flanagan (Willard), David Casey (Goodyear), Georgina Hale (Switchboard girl), Lewis Fiander (Gorran), Derrick O'Connor (Llewlyn), Anna Gael (Mrs Hill)

Sweeney Todd, the Demon Barber of Fleet Street *
GB 1936 68m bw
George King

A barber kills his customers and makes them into 'mutton pies' for sale at the shop next door.
Decent version of a famous old melodrama; stilted as film-making, but preserving a swaggering star performance.
w Frederick Hayward, H. F. Maltby *play* George Dibdin-Pitt *d* George King *ph* Jack Parker *ad* Percy Bell *ed* John Seabourne
☆ Tod Slaughter, Bruce Seton, Eve Lister, Stella Rho, Ben Soutten, Johnny Singer, Eve Lister

Sweepings *
US 1933 77m bw
RKO
An ambitious Chicago merchant finds that his sons do not wish to emulate him.
Curious family melodrama based on fact; interesting but not exactly inspiring.
w Lester Cohen *novel* Lester Cohen *d* John Cromwell *ph* Edward Cronjager *m* Max Steiner
☆ Lionel Barrymore, Alan Dinehart, Eric Linden, William Gargan, Gloria Stuart, Gregory Ratoff
'Nothing to interest the women and a subject too sombre to interest the men.' – *Variety*

Sweet Adeline
US 1934 85m bw
Warner (Edward Chodorov)

In the 1890s, the daughter of a beer garden owner attracts the attention of a composer and becomes a Broadway star.
Unexceptionable, and quite forgotten, adaptation of a pleasant, old-fashioned Broadway musical.
w Erwin S. Gelsey *play* Jerome Kern, Oscar Hammerstein II, Harry Armstrong, Dick Gerard *d* Mervyn Le Roy *ph* Sol Polito *m/ly* Jerome Kern, Oscar Hammerstein II *ch* Bobby Connolly *ad* Robert Haas
☆ Irene Dunne, Donald Woods, Ned Sparks, Hugh Herbert, Wini Shaw, Louis Calhern, Nydia Westman, Joseph Cawthorn
'As a production in the bigtime musical class, but strictly on merit it rates no better than fair.' – *Variety*

Sweet and Lowdown **
US 1999 95m Technicolor
Columbia TriStar/Sweetland/Magnolia (Jean Doumanian)

In the 1930s, a self-obsessed jazz guitarist enjoys fame and misfortune.
Done in the style of a biopic, this is a delightfully inventive comedy, in love with the period and its music and able to communicate that emotion to its audience; the central performances of Penn, as the musician destructive of himself and others, and Samantha Morton, as his mute admirer, are excellent.
wd Woody Allen ph Zhao Fei m Dick Hyman *pd* Santo Loquasto *ed* Alisa Lepselter *cos* Laura Cunningham Bauer
☆ *Sean Penn* (Emmet Ray), *Samantha Morton* (Hattie), Uma Thurman (Blanche), Brian Markinson (Bill Shields), Anthony LaPaglia (Al Torrio), Gretchen Mol (Ellie), Vincent Guastaferro (Sid Bishop), John Waters (Mr Haynes), Constance Schulman (Hazel), Kellie Overbey (Iris)
'Woody Allen's most delightful film in perhaps ten years.' – *Angie Errigo, Empire*
† Howard Alden dubbed Sean Penn's guitar playing.
Sean Penn; Samantha Morton

'A Promise Of Heaven. A Journey Into Hell.'
Sweet Angel Mine
GB/Canada 1996 88m colour
Optimum/HandMade/Mass Productions/ImagexBritish Screen/Telefilm Canada/NSFDC/Statescreen/Picture Palace (Sam Taylor, Christopher Zimmer)

A Londoner, who goes to Novia Scotia to search for his long-lost father, stumbles across a remote farm occupied by three women.
Feeble horror with unconvincing characters, far-fetched narrative contrivances, and, after its slow-moving first half, a frenetic, gruesome finale.
w Sue Maheu, Tim Willocks *screenplay Love's Executioners* by Tim Willocks *d* Curtis Radclyffe *ph* Witold Stok *m* John McCarthy *pd* Maria Djurkovic *ed* Anne Sopel
☆ Oliver Milburn (Paul), Margaret Langrick (Rauchine), Anna Massey (Mother), Alberta Watson (Megan)
'Isn't bad enough to be real fun and isn't good enough to convince on any level except the plain silly.' – *Derek Elley, Variety*

'He used love like most men use money!'
Sweet Bird of Youth *
US 1962 120m Metrocolor Cinemascope
MGM/Roxbury (Pandro S. Berman)

A Hollywood drifter brings an ageing glamour star back to his home town, but runs into revenge from the father of a girl he had seduced.
Emasculated version of an overwrought play with the author's usual poetic squalor; comatose patches alternate with flashes of good acting and diverting dialogue, but the wide screen and heavy colour don't direct the attention.
wd Richard Brooks *play* Tennessee Williams *ph* Milton Krasner *m* Harold Gellman *md* Robert Armbruster
☆ Paul Newman, Geraldine Page, *Ed Begley*, Mildred Dunnock, Rip Torn, Shirley Knight, Madeleine Sherwood
Ed Begley
Geraldine Page; Shirley Knight

'Love is what it's all about!'
Sweet Charity *
US 1969 149m Technicolor Panavision 70
Universal (Robert Arthur)

A New York taxi dancer dreams of love.
A revue-type musical bowdlerized from Fellini's Le notti di Cabiria *accords ill with real New York locations, especially as its threads of plot come to nothing; but behind the camera are sufficient stylists to ensure striking success with individual numbers.*
w Peter Stone *play* Neil Simon *d Robert Fosse ph Robert Surtees m* Cy Coleman *md* Joseph Gershenson *ly* Dorothy Fields
☆ *Shirley MacLaine*, Ricardo Montalban, John McMartin, *Chita Rivera*, Paula Kelly, Stubby Kaye, Sammy Davis Jnr
'The kind of platinum clinker designed to send audiences flying towards the safety of their television sets.' – *Rex Reed*
Cy Coleman (as music director)

Sweet Dreams
US 1985 115m Technicolor
Tri-Star/HBO/Silver Screen (Bernard Schwartz)

The effect on her marriage of the rise to success of folk singer Patsy Cline.
Pleasant, muted, unremarkable modern biopic.
w Robert Getchell *d* Karel Reisz *ph* Robbie Greenberg *m* Charles Gross
☆ Jessica Lange, Ed Harris, Ann Wedgeworth, David Clennon, James Staley
Jessica Lange

'The Story Of Two Women's Struggle For Survival, Self-Respect And Hard Currency.'

Sweet Emma, Dear Böbe *
Hungary 1992 78m Eastmancolor
Objektiv/Manfred Durniok Filmproduktion (Lajos Ovari, Gabriella Groz)
original title: *édes Emma, Drága Böbe – Vazlatok, Aktok*
Two young female teachers move to Budapest to work, sharing a tatty room together.
A well-made, engrossing study of glum lives.
w István Szabó, Andrea Veszits *d* István Szabó *ph* Lajos Koltai *m* Richard Schumann *pd* Attila Kovacs *ed* Eszter Kovacs
☆ Johanna Ter Steege, Eniko Börcsök, Peter Andorai
'The realities of day-to-day life in post-Communist Hungary are vividly brought to life in this compassionate, memorable film. Though the settings and narrative are understandably bleak, the treatment throbs with life and love, resulting in a most satisfying film.' – *Variety*
'The best movie to date about the way ordinary Central Europeans are experiencing the cataclysmic changes following the collapse of Communism.' – *Philip French, Observer*

Sweet Hearts Dance
US 1988 101m Technicolor
Columbia TriStar/Bright Star/Tri-Star ML Delphi Premier Productions (Jeffrey Lurie)
A small-town couple experience marital problems.
A drama of small incidents that never builds into a coherent whole.
w Ernest Thompson *d* Robert Greenwald *ph* Tak Fujimoto *m* Richard Gibbs *pd* James Allen *ed* Robert Florio, Janet Bartells
☆ Don Johnson, Susan Sarandon, Jeff Daniels, Elizabeth Perkins, Kate Reid, Justin Henry, Holly Marie Combs, Heather Coleman

The Sweet Hereafter ***
Canada 1997 112m colour Panavision
Electric/Speaking Parts/Alliance/Ego (Camelia Frieberg, Atom Egoyan)
A lawyer arrives in a small town to persuade parents, who are grieving over the deaths of 14 children killed in a school bus accident, to let him represent them.
A complex and compelling retelling of a tragic event, flashing back and forward in time to present the details of intertwined lives on the brink of disaster.
wd Atom Egoyan *novel* Russell Banks *ph* Paul Sarossy *m* Mychael Danna *pd* Philip Barker *ed* Susan Shipton
☆ Ian Holm, Maury Chaykin, Gabrielle Rose, Peter Donaldson, Bruce Greenwood, David Hemblen, Brooke Johnson, Arsinée Khanjian
'The cumulative impact is, by this director's standards, disappointingly uni-dimensional and almost banal.' – *Sheila Johnston, Screen International*
'A film of great scrupulousness and restraint, with few false notes.' – *Richard Williams, Guardian*
Atom Egoyan (as director and as writer)

'Sometimes What You're Looking For Is Right Where You Left It.'

Sweet Home Alabama
US 2002 109m Technicolor Panavision
Buena Vista/Touchstone (Neal H. Moritz, Stokely Chaffin)
A Manhattan fashion designer re-discovers small-town values when she returns to her Alabama home to divorce her husband so that she can marry a New York socialite.
Sugary confection that promises to be a sophisticated screwball comedy but turns into a romance in love with the simple life.
w C. Jay Cox *story* Douglas J. Eboch *d* Andy Tennant *ph* Andrew Dunn *m* George Fenton *pd* Clay A. Griffith *ed* Troy Takaki, Tracey Wadmore-Smith *cos* Sophie de Rakoff Carbonell
☆ Reese Witherspoon (Melanie Carmichael), Josh Lucas (Jake), Patrick Dempsey (Andrew), Candice Bergen (Kate), Mary Kay Place (Pearl Smooter), Fred Ward (Earl Smooter), Jean Smart (Stella Kay), Ethan Embry (Bobby Ray)
'As predictable as the menu for a Southern picnic and not nearly as tasty.' – *Todd McCarthy, Variety*
† The movie cost $18m and took more than $127m at the US box-office.

Sweet Kitty Bellairs
US 1930 60m Technicolor
Warner
A romance of stagecoach days set in Bath.
A decided curiosity to come from this studio in Little Caesar days, and not a successful one.
w Hermann Harrison *play* David Belasco *novel* Agnes and Egerton Castle *d* Alfred E. Green
☆ Claudia Dell, Ernest Torrence, Walter Pidgeon, June Collyer, Perry Askam, Lionel Belmore, Flora Finch
'Artistic achievement, but weak on fan pull.' – *Variety*

Sweet Liberty
US 1986 107m colour
Universal/Martin Bregman
A college professor is disgusted as he watches the Hollywood filming of his historical novel.
A good idea surprisingly wasted: the plot turns to tedium before the half-way mark.
wd Alan Alda *ph* Frank Tidy *m* Bruce Broughton *pd* Ben Edwards *ed* Michael Economou
☆ Alan Alda, Michael Caine, Michelle Pfeiffer, Lillian Gish, Bob Hoskins, Saul Rubinek, Lois Chiles, Lise Hilboldt

The Sweet Life: see *La Dolce Vita*

Sweet Lorraine *
US 1987 91m colour
Autumn Pictures (Steve Gomer)
The owner of a rundown hotel in the Catskills has her granddaughter spend the summer working for her.
Gentle and charming film, strong on character.
w Michael Zettler, Shelly Altman *d* Steve Gomer *ph* Rene Ohashi *m* Richard Robbins *pd* David Gropman *ed* Laurence Solomon
☆ Maureen Stapleton, Trini Alvarado, Lee Richardson, John Bedford Lloyd, Freddie Roman

Sweet Music
US 1934 100m bw
Warner
An orchestra leader and a girl singer spar a lot but finally make it up.
The slimmest of stories stretches over a few good numbers and some snappy dialogue; but it's all too long.
w Jerry Wald, Carl Erickson and Warren Duff *d* Alfred E. Green
☆ Rudy Vallee, Ann Dvorak, Ned Sparks, Helen Morgan, Allen Jenkins, Alice White, Robert Armstrong

Sweet November
US 1968 113m Technicolor
Warner Seven Arts (Jerry Gershwin, Elliott Kastner)
An English tycoon in New York meets a girl who takes a new lover every month because she hasn't long to live.
Irritating exercise in eccentric sentimentality, not helped by twitchy stars.
w Herman Raucher *d* Robert Ellis Miller *ph* Daniel L. Fapp *m* Michel Legrand
☆ Anthony Newley, Sandy Dennis, Theodore Bikel, Burr de Benning

'She Just Needed A Month To Change His Life Forever.'

Sweet November
US 2001 119m Technicolor
Warner/Bel Air/3 Arts (Erwin Stoff, Deborah Aal, Steven Reuther, Elliott Kastner)
A harassed, conventional advertising executive falls for a free-spirited woman, suffering from a fatal disease, who takes a new lover every month.
Soft-centered weepie romance, a remake of the Sandy Dennis-Anthony Newley movie of the 60s; time has not improved the story, nor does this more attractive cast raise it above the mundane.
w Kurt Voelker *screenplay* Herman Raucher *d* Pat O'Connor *ph* Edward Lachman *m* Christopher Young *pd* Naomi Shohan *ed* Anne V. Coates *cos* Shay Cunliffe
☆ Keanu Reeves (Nelson Moss), Charlize Theron (Sara Deever), Jason Isaacs (Chaz), Greg Germann (Vince), Liam Aiken (Abner), Lauren Graham (Angelica), Michael Rosenbaum (Brandon), Robert Joy (Raeford Dunne), Ray Baker (Buddy Leach), Frank Langella (Edgar Price)
'The woozy weightlessness of the story has a near-narcotic effect. You can almost feel the brain cells dying.' – *A. O. Scott, New York Times*

Sweet Revenge: see *Dandy the All-American Girl*

The Sweet Ride
US 1967 110m DeLuxe Panavision
TCF (Joe Pasternak)
Surfers and drop-outs on a California beach have woman trouble.
Teenage melodrama, well produced but abysmal of content.
w Tom Mankiewicz *novel* William Murray *d* Harvey Hart *ph* Robert B. Hauser *m* Pete Rugolo
☆ Jacqueline Bisset, Tony Franciosa, Michael Sarrazin, Bob Denver, Michael Wilding

Sweet Rosie O'Grady *
US 1943 79m Technicolor
TCF (William Perlberg)
A *Police Gazette* reporter tries to uncover the past of a musical comedy star.
Pleasant 1890s musical with plenty of zest but a lack of good numbers. A typical success of the war years.
w Ken Englund *d* Irving Cummings *ph* *Ernest Palmer* *ch* Hermes Pan *ad* *James Basevi, Joseph C. Wright* *songs* Mack Gordon, Harry Warren
☆ *Betty Grable*, Robert Young, Adolphe Menjou, Reginald Gardiner, Virginia Grey, Phil Regan, Sig Rumann, Hobart Cavanaugh, Alan Dinehart
† Remake of *Love Is News*; remade as *That Wonderful Urge*.

'It's you and Liam, against the world.'

Sweet Sixteen **
GB/Germany/Spain 2002 106m colour
Icon/Scottish Screen/BBC/Diaphana/BIM/Cineart/ARD/DegetoWDRSixteen/Road Movies/Tornasol/Alta (Rebecca O'Brien)
In Greenock, a teenager becomes a drug dealer so that he can get a place where he can live with his mother when she comes out of prison.
Grim story of crime offering the only hope of escape from a poverty-striken environment; the specificity of the setting and the performances make it more than special pleading.
w Paul Laverty *d* Ken Loach *ph* Barry Ackroyd *m* George Fenton *pd* Martin Johnson *ed* Jonathan Morris
☆ Martin Compston (Liam), William Ruane (Pinball), Annmarie Fulton (Chantelle), Michelle Abercromby (Suzanne), Michelle Coulter (Jean), Gary McCormack (Stan), Tommy McKee (Rab)
'If you leave the cinema feeling winded, then it must be counted a success. If you also leave feeling obscurely grateful, then that might be because you won't have to watch another Ken Loach film in a while.' – *Anthony Quinn, Independent*
'Loach's latest adheres so closely to his long-established narrative pattern – overdetermined case study crowned with a morbid jolt – that viewers might underestimate its wit, empathy, and careful characterizations.' – *Jessica Winter, Village Voice*

'This is the story of J.J. – but not the way he wants it told!'

Sweet Smell of Success ****
US 1957 96m bw
UA/Norma/Curtleigh (James Hill)
A crooked press agent helps a megalomaniac New York columnist break up his sister's romance.
Moody, brilliant, Wellesian melodrama put together with great artificial style; the plot matters less than the photographic detail and the skilful manipulation of decadent characters, bigger than life-size.
w Clifford Odets, Ernest Lehman *d* *Alexander Mackendrick* *ph* *James Wong Howe* *m* *Elmer Bernstein* *ad* Edward Carrere
☆ Burt Lancaster, *Tony Curtis*, Martin Milner, Sam Levene, Susan Harrison, Barbara Nichols, *Emile Meyer*
'A sweet slice of perversity, a study of dollar and power worship.' – *Pauline Kael*

Sweet Sweetback Baad Asssss Song **
US 1971 97m CFI color
Yeah
A black boy grows up in a brothel to become a womanizer and cop-killer.
Seminal, anarchic, anti-establishment movie that led to the blaxploitation boom of the 70s and beyond; it is fuelled by a righteous anger.
wd Melvin Van Peebles *ph* Bob Maxwell *m* Melvin Van Peebles *ed* Melvin Van Peebles
☆ Melvin Van Peebles, Rhetta Hughes, Simon Chuckster, John Amos, Hubert Scales, John Dullaghan, West Gale, Mario Van Peebles
'A slight, pale escape drama about a black man.' – *Vincent Canby, New York Times*
'Perhaps not the classic which some critics have proclaimed it, this is still an effective counterblast against racist violence and stereotyping.' – *Sight and Sound*
† Before listing individual performers, the credits begin: 'Starring The Black Community and Brer Soul.' The film is dedicated 'to all the Brothers and Sisters who have had enough of The Man'.

Sweet William
GB 1980 90m Eastmancolor
Kendon
A London girl discovers that her American lover is constantly unfaithful.
A situation in search of a story makes this slight piece with its wry observations rather less memorable than the average TV play.
w Beryl Bainbridge *novel* Beryl Bainbridge *d* Claude Whatham *ph* Les Young *md* Marcus Dods *pd* Eileen Diss
☆ Sam Waterston, Jenny Agutter, Anna Massey, Daphne Oxenford, Arthur Lowe, Geraldine James

'Foregt Mr Right, where's Mr Right Now!'

The Sweetest Thing
US 2002 88m DeLuxe
Columbia (Cathy Konrad)
Woman finds man, woman loses man, woman gets man.
Ghastly romantic comedy with coarse jokes and coarser acting.
w Nancy M. Pimenthal *d* Roger Kumble *ph* Anthony B. Richmond *m* Edward Shearmur *pd* John Gary Steele *ed* Wendy Greene Bricmont, David Rennie
☆ Cameron Diaz (Christina Walters), Christina Applegate (Courtney), Selma Blair (Jane), Thomas Jane (Peter), Jason Bateman (Roger), Parker Posey (Judy)
'Deeply misjudged, awe-inspiringly humourless girlpower romp' – *Peter Bradshaw, Guardian*
'One of the flattest, stupidest, unfunniest sex comedies – as well as one of the worst all-round pictures – I've ever seen.' – *Charles Taylor, Salon.com*

Sweetheart of the Campus
US 1941 64m bw
Columbia (Jack Fier)
GB title: *Broadway Ahead*
A college principal objects to Ozzie Nelson's band playing at a nearby night spot.
Evanescent musical filler.
w Robert D. Andrews, Edmund Hartmann *d* Edward Dmytryk *ph* Franz F. Planer *md* M. W. Stoloff *ad* Lionel Banks *ed* William Lyon
☆ Ruby Keeler, Ozzie Nelson, Harriet Hilliard, Gordon Oliver, Don Beddoe, Kathleen Howard

Sweethearts **
US 1938 120m Technicolor
MGM (Hunt Stromberg)
Two stars of the musical stage never stop fighting each other.
The lightest and most successful of the MacDonald/Eddy musicals, with an excellent script, production and cast.
w *Dorothy Parker, Alan Campbell* *d* *W. S. Van Dyke* *ph* Oliver Marsh, Allen Davey *m* Victor Herbert *md* Herbert Stothart
☆ *Jeanette MacDonald, Nelson Eddy*, Frank Morgan, Ray Bolger, Florence Rice, Mischa Auer, Fay Holden, Reginald Gardiner, Herman Bing,

Allyn Joslyn, Raymond Walburn, Lucile Watson, Gene Lockhart

'It will disappoint because of length, and general lethargy and sameness of production values.' – *Variety*

Special Award to Oliver Marsh and Allen Davey for 'colour photography'

Herbert Stothart

Sweetie **

Australia 1989 100m colour
Electric/Arena Film (John Maynard)

A woman with marital problems is visited by her unbalanced but exuberant sister.
Deliberately off-balance movie that explores the dynamic of family relationships and stifled lives.
w Gerard Lee, Jane Campion *d* Jane Campion *ph* Sally Bongers *m* Martin Armiger *ad* Peter Harris *ed* Veronika Haussler
☆ Genevieve Lemon, Karen Colston, Tom Lycos, Jon Darling, Dorothy Barry, Michael Lake, Andre Pataczek, Jean Hadgraft

Swell Guy

US 1946 86m bw
Mark Hellinger/Universal-International

A war correspondent comes home to visit his family but turns out to be something of a heel.
Ironical drama which deserved better casting and handling.
w Richard Brooks *play* *The Hero* by Gilbert Emery *d* Frank Tuttle
☆ Sonny Tufts, Ann Blyth, Ruth Warrick, William Gargan, John Litel, Thomas Gomez, Millard Mitchell, Mary Nash

Swept Away

GB/Italy/US 2002 89m DeLuxe
Screen Gems/Ska/CODI SpA (Matthew Vaughn)

After they are marooned on a desert island, a spoilt, wealthy socialite is forced into a subservient role by a lowly Italian sailor.
A vapid remake of an Italian movie on a subject that was first, and rather better, done by J. M. Barrie in The Admirable Crichton. *There's no wit or humour to be found in this treatment, just a great deal of posturing.*
wd Guy Ritchie *screenplay* *Swept Away by an Unusual Destiny in the Blue Sea of August* by Lina Wertmuller *ph* Alex Barber *m* Michel Colombier *pd* Russell de Rozario *ed* Eddie Hamilton
☆ Madonna (Amber), Adriano Giannini (Giuseppe), Jeanne Tripplehorn (Marina), Bruce Greenwood (Anthony), Elizabeth Banks (Debi), David Thornton (Michael), Michael Beattie (Todd), Yorgo Voyagis (Captain)

'The Vera Hruba Ralston of her time, Madonna has persisted in making movies despite all evidence that this is one medium in which no one wants to see or hear her.' – *Dennis Harvey, Variety*

'At no point should anyone mistake this for an actual movie. This is an extended beach video that will leave no one swept away.' – *Desson Howe, Washington Post*

† Wertmuller's movie starred Giancarlo Giannini in the role played here by his son Adriano.
†† The film cost some $10m to make and took around $600,000 at the US box-office.
††† It was released direct to video in Britain.

Swept from the Sea: see *Amy Foster*

'Obsession. Betrayal. Revenge. Some girls have all the fun.'

Swimfan

US 2002 85m DeLuxe Panavision
Icon/Greenstreet/Cobalt/Further (John Penotti, Allison Lyon Segan, Joe Caracciolo Jnr)

A girl turns vengeful after she has a one-night stand with a swimming champion.
Trite revenge drama that is a teen version of Fatal Attraction, *notable only for its immaturity.*
w Charles Bohl, Phillip Schneider *d* John Polson *ph* Giles Nuttgens *m* Louis Febre, John Debney *pd* Kalina Ivanov *ed* Sarah Flack
☆ Jesse Bradford (Ben), Erika Christensen (Madison), Shiri Appleby (Amy), Kate Burton (Carla), Clayne Crawford (Josh), Kia Joy Goodwin (Rene), Dan Hedaya (Coach Simkins)

'A chiller resolutely without chills, in which even the pool water always seems heated. And inasmuch as the pic never owns up to its own trashiness, it's not even enjoyable camp.' – *Scott Foundas, Variety*

'They had the pools – but he had their wives!'

The Swimmer *

US 1968 94m Technicolor
Columbia/Horizon/Dover (Frank Perry, Roger Lewis)

A man clad only in trunks swims his way home via the pools of his rich friends, and arrives home to find that his success is a fantasy.
Strange but compelling fable, too mystifying for popular success, about the failure of the American dream. Annoyingly inexplicit, but well made and sumptuously photographed in a variety of Connecticut estates.
w *Eleanor Perry* *short stories* John Cheever *d* Frank Perry, Sydney Pollack *ph* *David L. Quaid* *m* Marvin Hamlisch
☆ *Burt Lancaster*, Janice Rule, Kim Hunter, Diana Muldaur, Cornelia Otis Skinner, Marge Champion

The Swimmer **

USSR 1981 105m bw/colour
Gruzia Film
original title: *Plovec*

A middle-aged man invades a film set to recount the exploits of his father and grandfather, famous swimmers who were cheated of their success.
The film's subtitle provides an indication of the contents: 'Twenty-two little stories from the life of three swimmers', but not the charm. It was banned by the Soviets for a time, presumably because of its celebration of individuality.
wd Irakli Kvirikadze *ph* Turam Tugshi *m* Teimuraz Bakuradze
☆ Elgudza Burduli, Ruslan Mikaberidze, Baadur Tsuladze, Guram Pirtskhalava, Nana Kvachantiradze, Gia Lezhava, Imedo Kahkiani

Swimming to Cambodia **

US 1987 87m colour Panavision
Mainline/Cinecom International/The Swimming Co (R. A. Shafransky)

An actor who played a bit part in *The Killing Fields* reminisces about his experiences in Thailand.
Witty and fascinating one-man show, skilfully filmed.
w Spalding Gray *d* Jonathan Demme *ph* John Bailey *m* Laurie Anderson *pd* Sandy McLeod *ed* Carol Littleton
☆ Spalding Gray

'Life is not a movie.'

Swimming with Sharks *

US 1995 93m colour
Starlight/Cineville/Neofight/Mama'z Boy (Steve Alexander, Joanne Moore)

A new assistant to a tyrannical film studio executive turns the tables on his boss.
Tart black comedy on Hollywood excesses, one that enjoys the monsters it puts on display.
wd George Huang *ph* Steven Finestone *m* Tom Heil, Marco d'Ambrosio *pd* Veronika Merlin, Cecil Gentry *ed* Ed Marx
☆ *Kevin Spacey*, Frank Whaley, Benicio del Toro, Michelle Forbes, T. E. Russell, Roy Dotrice, Matthew Flynt

'A small, catty addendum to the cinema of office drudgery.' – *Tom Shone, Sunday Times*

The Swindlers: see *Il Bidone*

The Swing **

West Germany 1983 133m colour
Pelemele Film/Roxy/Pro-Ject (Percy Adlon)
original title: *Die Schaukel*

In the 1930s an elderly novelist recalls her childhood with her exuberant brothers and sisters and improvident mother and father.
Charming and humorous evocation of family life.
wd Percy Adlon *novel* Annette Kolb *d* Percy Adlon *ph* Jürgen Martin *m* Peer Raben
☆ Anja Jaenicke, Rolf Illig, Christine Kaufmann, Lena Stolze, Joachim Bernhard, Susanne Herlet

Swing

US 1998 98m CFI color
Entertainment/Kushner-Locke/Alpine (Su Lim, Louise Rosner)

In Liverpool, an ex-convict who learned to play the saxophone inside tries to form a swing band.
Dire would-be comedy that makes its many clichés seem even more dated than swing itself.
wd Nick Mead *ph* Ian Wilson *m* Ian Devaney *pd* Richard Bridgland *ed* Norman Buckley
☆ Hugo Speer (Martin Luxford), Lisa Stansfield (Joan Woodcock), Tom Bell (Sid Luxford), Rita Tushingham (Mags Luxford), Alexei Sayle (Mighty Mac), Paul Usher (Liam Luxford), Danny McCall (Andy), Clarence Clemons (Jack), Tom Georgeson (Uncle Matty)

'The film, a light comedy, is clearly not meant to be deep, but its laziness makes it seem excessively shallow.' – *Edward Porter, Sunday Times*

Swing Fever

US 1943 80m bw
MGM

A bandleader uses hypnotism to train a boxer.
Witless farrago with sprightly musical numbers.
w Nat Perrin, Warren Wilson *d* Tim Whelan
☆ Kay Kyser and his band, Marilyn Maxwell, Nat Pendleton, William Gargan, Lena Horne

Swing High Swing Low **

US 1937 97m bw
Paramount (Arthur Hornblow Jnr)

A talented trumpeter goes on a bender but is rescued by his wife.
Backstage comedy-drama, a beautifully cinematic version of a very tedious story also filmed as Dance of Life *(1929) and* When My Baby Smiles at Me *(1948).*
w Virginia Van Upp, Oscar Hammerstein II *play* *Burlesque* by George Manker Walters, Arthur Hopkins *d* *Mitchell Leisen* *ph* Ted Tetzlaff *m* Victor Young *md* Boris Morros
☆ Carole Lombard, Fred MacMurray, Charles Butterworth, Jean Dixon, Dorothy Lamour, Harvey Stephens, Franklin Pangborn, Anthony Quinn

'No reason to believe it won't jam 'em at the gate ... it's a cinch for the younger trade, and will satisfy general audience standards.' – *Variety*

'Enough concentrated filmcraft to fit out half a dozen of those gentlemen who are always dashing around in an independent capacity making just the greatest piece of cinema ever.' – *Otis Ferguson*

Swing Kids

US 1993 114m Technicolor
Buena Vista/Hollywood (Mark Gordon, John Bard Manulis)

In Germany during the rise of the Nazis, a group of young men is trapped between the attractions of American swing music and the Hitler Youth.
An extremely peculiar movie, which makes little attempt at a period authenticity, apart from its music, and seems unlikely to appeal to any audience, least of all the young.
w Jonathan Marc Feldman *d* Thomas Carter *ph* Jerzy Zielinski *m* James Horner *pd* Allan Cameron *ed* Michael R. Miller
☆ Robert Sean Leonard, Christian Bale, Frank Whaley, Barbara Hershey, Kenneth Branagh, Tushka Bergen, David Tom, Julia Stemberger

'Apart from its appealing young cast and period score, it has precious little to entice audiences.' – *Variety*

Swing Shift

US 1984 100m Technicolor
Warner/Lantana/Hawn-Sylbert/Jerry Bick

During World War II, in her husband's absence at war, a woman factory hand has an affair with a co-worker.
Surprisingly dreary romantic drama on a subject which could at least have had a livelier surface despite the lack of surprise in what passes for plot.
w 'Rob Morton' (Ron Nyswaner, Bo Goldman, Nancy Dowd) *d* Jonathan Demme *ph* Tak Fujimoto *m* Patrick Williams *pd* Peter Jamison *ed* Craig McKay
☆ Goldie Hawn, Kurt Russell, Christine Lahti, Fred Ward, Ed Harris

'Bland, muddled and inconclusive.' – *Steve Jenkins, MFB*

Christine Lahti (supporting actress)

Swing, Teacher, Swing: see *College Swing*

Swing Time **

US 1936 103m bw
RKO (Pandro S. Berman)

A dance team can't get together romantically because he has a commitment to a girl back home.
Satisfactory but unexciting musical vehicle for two stars at the top of their professional and box-office form.
w Howard Lindsay, Allan Scott *d* George Stevens *ph* David Abel *md* Nathaniel Shilkret *ch* Hermes Pan *songs* Jerome Kern, Dorothy Fields
☆ *Fred Astaire*, *Ginger Rogers*, Victor Moore, Helen Broderick, Eric Blore, Betty Furness, George Metaxa
♫ 'Pick Yourself Up'; 'A Fine Romance'; 'Never Gonna Dance'; 'The Way You Look Tonight'.

song 'The Way You Look Tonight'

Hermes Pan

Swing Your Lady *

US 1937 77m bw
Warner (Sam Bischoff)

A promoter gets involved in the problems of a hillbilly wrestler.
Minor comedy with some laughs.
w Joseph Schrank, Maurice Leo *story* *Toehold on Artemus* by H. R. Marsh *d* Ray Enright *ph* Arthur Edeson *m* Adolph Deutsch
☆ Humphrey Bogart, Louise Fazenda, Nat Pendleton, Frank McHugh, Penny Singleton, Allen Jenkins, Ronald Reagan, The Weaver Brothers and Elviry

'A comedy of not immense proportions, it is nevertheless a rollicking, considerably different laugh-piece which should do from average to good business everywhere.' – *Variety*

The Swinger

US 1966 81m Technicolor
Paramount/George Sidney

When a girl writer's wholesome stories are rejected, she pretends to have a naughty past.
With-it comedy which audiences preferred to be without.
w Lawrence Roman *d* George Sidney *ph* Joseph Biroc *m* Marty Paich
☆ Ann-Margret, Tony Franciosa, Robert Coote, Yvonne Romain, Horace MacMahon, Nydia Westman

'A hectically saucy mixture of lechery, depravity, perversion, voyeurism and girlie magazines ... a heavy, witless pudding.' – *MFB*

'Get a nightlife.'

Swingers *

US 1996 96m DeLuxe
Miramax/Independent/Alfred Shay (Victor Simpkins)

Hung up on a failed love affair, a struggling comedian hopes for success in Hollywood, and parties with his friends.
Slick and very knowing movie about a bunch of losers; it is sometimes amusing, but its superficiality soon becomes wearing.
w Jon Favreau *d* Doug Liman *ph* Doug Liman *m* Justin Reinhardt *pd* Brad Halvorson *ed* Stephen Mirrione
☆ Jon Favreau, Vince Vaughn, Ron Livingston, Patrick Van Horn, Alex Desert, Deena Martin, Katherine Kendall, Heather Graham

'Engaging, refreshingly human in its humor and becomingly modest in its aspirations, this hip look at being out of it announces some promising new talent.' – *Todd McCarthy, Variety*

'So loaded with goodies that cinema-goers cannot really afford to miss it.' – *Marianne Gray, Film Review*

The Swinging Maiden: see *The Iron Maiden*

Swirl of Glory: see *Sugarfoot*

The Swiss Conspiracy

US/Germany 1975 88m colour
Baveria Atelier/Durham (Maurice Silverstein)

When a blackmailer threatens to reveal the secret accounts of its wealthy clients, a Swiss bank hires an American former agent to investigate.
Dreary thriller, in which acting, direction and writing conspire to be as uninteresting as possible.
w Norman Klenman, Philip Saltzman, Michael Stanley *d* Jack Arnold *ph* W. P. Hassenstein

m Klaus Doldinger pd Rolf Zehetbauer
ed Murray Jordan
☆ David Janssen, Senta Berger, John Ireland, John Saxon, Anton Diffring, Arthur Brauss, Elke Sommer, Ray Milland

The Swiss Family Robinson
US 1940 93m bw
(RKO)
A shipwrecked family builds a new home on a desert island.
Pleasing low-budgeter.
w Gene Towne, Graham Baker, Walter Ferris
novel Johann Wyss d Edward Ludwig
ph Nicholas Musuraca
☆ Thomas Mitchell, Edna Best, Freddie Bartholomew, Tim Holt, Terry Kilburn
'In outlook, dialogue and manner it is frankly old-fashioned.' – *MFB*

The Swiss Family Robinson *
GB 1960 126m Technicolor
Panavision
Walt Disney (Bill Anderson, Basil Keys)
Quite pleasing comedy adventure from the children's classic.
w Lowell S. Hawley d Ken Annakin ph Harry Waxman m William Alwyn
☆ *John Mills*, Dorothy McGuire, James MacArthur, Tommy Kirk, Kevin Corcoran, Janet Munro, Sessue Hayakawa, Cecil Parker

Swiss Miss *
US 1938 73m bw
(MGM)
Two mousetrap salesmen in Switzerland run into trouble with a cook, a gorilla and two opera singers.
Operetta style vehicle which constrains its stars, since their material is somewhat below vintage anyway. Not painful to watch, but disappointing.
w James Parrott, Felix Adler, Charles Nelson
d John G. Blystone ph Norbert Brodine
m/ly Phil Charig, Arthur Quenzer md Marvin Hatley ed Bert Jordan
☆ Stan Laurel, Oliver Hardy, Walter Woolf King, Della Lind, Eric Blore
'Story, production, acting and direction suggest a revival of early sound filmusicals presented with stage technique.' – *Variety*

The Swissmakers
Switzerland 1978 108m Eastmancolor
Lyssy/Rex/Willora/Schoch/Ecco
Cases of a department investigating applicants for naturalization.
Amusing satirical comedy which presumably has more bite in its home territory.
w Rolf Lyssy, Christa Maerker d Rolf Lyssy
ph Fritz Maeder m Jonas Haefeli
☆ Walo Luond, Emil Steinberger, Beatrice Kessler

'For a ladykiller like Steve there was a fate worse than death: when he got to heaven they sent him back ... with some modifications ... It's tough being a woman in a man's world.'
Switch
US 1991 103m Technicolor Panavision
Columbia TriStar/Odyssey-Regency/HBO/Cinema Plus/LP/Beco (Tony Adams)
Murdered by old flames, a male chauvinist is sent back to Earth as a woman and told that he can live again if he can find a woman who likes him.
Bizarre farce that relies on the most obvious of sex-change jokes.
wd Blake Edwards ph Dick Bush m Henry Mancini pd Rodger Maus ed Robert Pergament
☆ Ellen Barkin, Jimmy Smits, JoBeth Williams, Lorraine Bracco, Tony Roberts, Perry King, Bruce Martyn Payne, Lysette Anthony, Victoria Mahoney
'A talented cast is wasted on a witless script.' – *Sunday Telegraph*

'The hunter is tracking the killer. But the killer is setting the trap.'
Switchback
US 1997 118m DeLuxe Panavision
Paramount/Rysher/Pacific Western (Gale Anne Hurd)
An FBI agent searches for a serial killer, whose activities are causing problems to a Texan sheriff facing re-election.
A thriller that never quite comes to life; it might have worked better as a Western.
wd Jeb Stuart ph Oliver Wood m Basil Poledouris pd Jeff Howard ed Conrad Buff
☆ Dennis Quaid, Danny Glover, Jared Leto, R. Lee Ermey, Ted Levine, William Fichtner, Leo Burmester
'A standard thriller with a couple of novel touches.' – *Variety*

Switchblade Sisters
US 1975 89m Eastmancolor
Miramax/Rolling Thunder/Johnny Legend (John Prizer)
aka: *The Jezebels*
A tough new girl in town becomes leader of a female gang.
Slick, violent exploitation movie of a familiar kind.
w F. X. Maier d Jack Hill ph Stephen Katz
m Medusa, Chuck Day, Richard Person
pd Robinson Royce, B. B. Neel ed Mort Tubor
☆ Robbie Lee, Joanne Nail, Monica Gayle, Asher Brauner, Chase Newhart, Marlene Clark, Kitty Bruce, Don Stark, Kate Murtagh
'Pic simply doesn't have a keen enough action or satiric edge to hold its head above water in the current marketplace.' – *Variety, 1996*
† The film was rereleased in the US in 1996 through Quentin Tarantino's distribution company.

The Switchboard Operator *
Yugoslavia 1969 70m bw
Avala
original title: *Ljubavni Slucaj*
US title: *Love Affair, or the Case of the Missing Switchboard Operator; aka: The Tragedy of a Switchboard Operator*
In Yugoslavia, an affair between a Hungarian-born post office worker and a Turkish rat-catcher ends in tragedy.
A collage that deftly mixes documentary, with a commentary from a sexologist and a criminologist, and fiction, with an account of a liaison that goes wrong, in which impulse and accident are as important as intent.
wd Dusan Makavejev ph Aleksander Petkovic
m Dusan Aleksic ad Vladislav Lazic ed Katarina Stojanovic
☆ Eva Ras, Slobodan Aligrudic, Ruzica Sokic, Miodrag Andric, Aleksander Kostic, Zivojin Aleksic
'Experimental, vividly performed, this is comic, tender fare, with a surprisingly dark undertow.' – *Sight and Sound*

Switching Channels *
US 1988 105m colour
Rank (Martin Ransohoff)
A television reporter, leaving to be married, agrees to undertake one last assignment.
The third remake of The Front Page, *this does not match the classic* His Girl Friday, *which, like this version, changed the sex of the hero, but it provides some amusement.*
w Jonathan Reynolds play *The Front Page* by Ben Hecht, Charles MacArthur d Ted Kotcheff
ph François Protat m Michel Legrand pd Anne Pritchard ed Thom Noble
☆ Kathleen Turner, Burt Reynolds, Christopher Reeve, Ned Beatty, Henry Gibson, George Newbern, Al Waxman, Ken James

'Leopold and Loeb. The Perfect Crime. A Deadly Love Affair.'
Swoon *
US 1992 80m bw
Argos Films (Tom Kalin, Christine Vachon)
In Chicago in 1924, two young middle-class homosexual Jews kidnap and kill a young boy as a demonstration of their criminal abilities.
An undeniably stylish account of the murders and murderers which may be closer to the real events and the couple's motivations than either of the other movie versions, Rope *or* Compulsion, *but which is less effective as a film.*
w Tom Kalin, Hilton Als d Tom Kalin ph Ellen Kuras m James Bennett ed Tom Kalin
☆ Daniel Schlachet, Craig Chester, Ron Vawter, Michael Kirby, Michael Stumm, Valda Z. Drabla, Natalie Stanford
'Kalin suggests that the couple internalised the homophobia and anti-Semitism around them into a pathological self-loathing but he doesn't show that process: his heroes seem simply born to be bad.' – *Sheila Johnston, Independent.*
'A determined attempt to reclaim a pair of notorious murderers on behalf of the gay community.' – *Philip French, Observer*
'Tom Kalin's brilliant debut feature presents history as you've always dreamed it might be: with personal, social and political perspectives all refracted through each other, and with a burning sense of the need to know and understand more, and better.' – *Tony Rayns*

The Sword and the Cross
Italy 1960 93m Technicolor
Liber Films (Ottavio Poggi)
original title: *La Spada e la Croce*
aka: *Mary Magdalene*
In Jerusalem, Mary Magdalene, mistress of the High Priest's nephew, is kidnapped by Barabbas, falls in love with a Roman officer, is converted to Christianity, and witnesses her brother Lazarus being raised from the dead, as well as the crucifixion of Christ.
The scriptwriters' inventive way with the Bible is not matched by the acting or direction, which plod along familiar ways, showing more interest in profane than sacred love; Jesus has a walk-on role.
w Ottavio Poggi, Alessandro Continenza d Carlo Ludovico Bragaglia ph Marcello Masciocchi
m Roberto Nicolosi ed Renato Cinquini
☆ Yvonne de Carlo, Jorge Mistral, Rossana Podesta, Massimo Serato, Mario Girotti
† The film is shown on TV in a dubbed version.

The Sword and the Rose
GB 1952 91m Technicolor
Walt Disney (Perce Pearce)
The romantic problems of young Mary Tudor.
Unhistorical charade not quite in the usual Disney vein, and not very good.
w Lawrence E. Watkin novel *When Knighthood Was in Flower* by Charles Major d Ken Annakin
ph Geoffrey Unsworth m Clifton Parker
☆ Richard Todd, Glynis Johns, James Robertson Justice, Michael Gough, Jane Barrett, Peter Copley, Rosalie Crutchley, Jean Mercure, D. A. Clarke-Smith

The Sword and the Sorcerer
US 1982 99m DeLuxe
Sorcerer Productions/Group One/Brandon Chase
A tyrant wins an idyllic kingdom with the help of an evil sorcerer; young Prince Talon gets it back.
Medieval magic and violence, laid on with a shovel; hopefully the last attempt to start an ill-fated cycle.
w Tom Karnowski, Albert Pyun, John Stuckmeyer
d Albert Pyun ph Joseph Mangine m David Whitaker
☆ Lee Horsley, Kathleen Beller, Simon MacCorkindale, George Maharis, Richard Lynch

Sword in the Desert
US 1949 100m bw
Robert Arthur/Universal
During World War II, Jewish refugees are smuggled to the Palestine coast.
Dim topical melodrama with an anti-British slant which caused international embarrassment.
w Robert Buckner d George Sherman ph Irving Glassberg m Frank Skinner
☆ Dana Andrews, Marta Toren, Jeff Chandler, Stephen McNally, Philip Friend

The Sword in the Stone **
US 1963 80m Technicolor
Walt Disney (Ken Peterson)
In the Dark Ages, a young forest boy named Wart becomes King Arthur.
Feature cartoon with goodish sequences but disappointingly showing a flatness and economy of draughtsmanship.
w Bill Peet novel *The Once and Future King* by T. H. White d Wolfgang Reitherman m George Bruns songs The Sherman Brothers
♫ George Bruns

Sword of Ali Baba
US 1965 81m Technicolor
Universal
Ali Baba is forced from the royal court to become a king of thieves.
Cut-rate programme filler utilizing great chunks of Ali Baba and the Forty Thieves *(twenty-one years older), with one actor, Frank Puglia, playing the same role in both films.*
w Edmund Hartmann, Oscar Brodney d Virgil Vogel ph William Margulies m Frank Skinner
☆ Peter Mann, Jocelyn Lane, Peter Whitney, Gavin McLeod

Sword of Lancelot: see *Lancelot and Guinevere*

The Sword of Monte Cristo
US 1951 80m Supercinecolor
Edward L. Alperson
Virtuous rebels and a villainous minister all seek the fabulous treasure of Monte Cristo.
Rubbishy sequel apparently shot in somebody's back garden by people only recently acquainted with film techniques.
wd Maurice Geraghty ph Jack Greenhalgh
m Raoul Kraushaar
☆ George Montgomery, Paula Corday, Berry Kroeger, Robert Warwick, William Conrad

Sword of Sherwood Forest
GB 1960 80m Technicolor
Megascope
Columbia/Hammer/Yeoman (Richard Greene, Sidney Cole)
Robin Hood reveals the villainy of the Sheriff of Nottingham and the Earl of Newark.
This big-screen version of a popular TV series makes a rather feeble addition to the legend, but the actors try hard.
w Alan Hackney d Terence Fisher ph Ken Hodges m Alan Hoddinott
☆ Richard Greene, Peter Cushing, Richard Pasco, Niall MacGinnis, Jack Gwillim, Sarah Branch, Nigel Green

Sword of the Valiant
GB 1984 101m Fujicolour JDC
Wide Screen
Cannon (Michael Kagan, Philip M. Breen)
In the mythical middle ages, squire Gawain takes on a challenge from the magical Green Knight.
An unsatisfactory mixture of realism, fantasy and deadly seriousness. Spoofing might have worked better.
w Stephen Weeks, Philip M. Breen, Howard C. Pen d Stephen Weeks ph Freddie Young, Peter Hurst m Ron Geesin pd Maurice Fowler, Derek Nice ed Richard Marden, Barry Peters
☆ Miles O'Keeffe, Sean Connery, Trevor Howard, Leigh Lawson, Cyrielle Claire, Peter Cushing, Ronald Lacey, Lila Kedrova, John Rhys-Davies, Douglas Wilmer, Wilfrid Brambell

'Log on. Hack in. Go anywhere. Steal everything.'
Swordfish
US 2001 99m Technicolor Panavision
Warner/Village Roadshow/NPV/Silver (Joel Silver, Jonathan D. Krane)
A computer hacker is hired by a dubious secret agent and bank robber to rob government funds.
Loud and overwrought action thriller that dispenses with logic and characterisation.
w Skip Woods d Dominic Sena ph Paul Cameron m Christopher Young pd Jeff Mann
ed Stephen Rivkin cos Ha Nguyen
☆ John Travolta (Gabriel Shear), Hugh Jackman (Stanley Jobson), Halle Berry (Ginger), Don Cheadle (Agent Roberts), Vinnie Jones (Marco), Sam Shepard (Senator Reisman), Drea de Matteo (Melissa), Rudolf Martin (Axl Torvalds), Zach Grenier (A.D.), Camryn Grimes (Holly)
'This is the definition of empty (and empty-headed) entertainment, willing to stoop to any level to goose a weary and jaded audience.' – *Glen Whipp, Los Angeles Daily News*

Swords of Blood: see *Cartouche*

The Swordsman
US 1947 80m Technicolor
Columbia
A young 18th-century Scot tries to end a family feud so that he can marry the girl of his choice.
Amiable costume programmer, quite forgettable but mostly enjoyable while it's on.

w Wilfred Petitt *d* Joseph H. Lewis *ph* William Snyder *m* Hugo Friedhofer
☆ Larry Parks, Ellen Drew, George Macready

Sylvia
US 1964 115m bw
Paramount/Joseph E. Levine (Martin H. Poll)
A millionaire with a mysterious fiancée hires a detective to discover the truth about her past.
Improbable story of a high-minded prostitute, sluggishly narrated and variably acted.
w Sydney Boehm *novel* E. V. Cunningham *d* Gordon Douglas *ph* Joseph Ruttenberg *m* David Raksin
☆ Carroll Baker, George Maharis, Peter Lawford, Joanne Dru, Ann Sothern, Viveca Lindfors, Edmond O'Brien, Aldo Ray
'Maharis manages to suggest that he might be worth watching in a role worth acting in a movie worth making. Sylvia wasn't.' – *Judith Crist*

Sylvia **
New Zealand 1985 98m colour
Southern Light/Cinepro (Don Reynolds, Michael Firth)
In New Zealand, a wife of a headmaster at a village school encounters official opposition to her innovative methods of teaching Maori children to read.
An effective and moving low-key account, though full of repressed sexual feelings, based on the life and autobiographical books of writer Sylvia Ashton Warner.
w Michael Quill, F. Fairfax, Michael Firth *books* Teacher *and* I Passed This Way by Sylvia Ashton Warner *d* Michael Firth *ph* Ian Paul *m* Leonard Rosenman *pd* Gary Hansen *ed* Michael Horton
☆ Eleanor David, Nigel Terry, Tom Wilkinson, Mary Regan, Martyn Sanderson, Terence Cooper, David Letch, Sarah Peirse

Sylvia and the Ghost *
France 1944 93m bw
Ecran Français/André Paulvé
original title: *Sylvie et la Fantôme*
A sixteen-year-old girl lives in her father's castle and is friendly with the ghost of a man killed in a duel fought for love of her grandmother.
Melancholy comedy which despite some charming moments somehow misses the expected style which would have made it a minor classic.
w Jean Aurenche *play* Alfred Adam *d* Claude Autant-Lara *ph* Philippe Agostini *m* René Cloerc
☆ Odette Joyeux, François Périer, Jacques Tati, Louis Salou, Jean Desailly
'A charming film, written, handled and acted with wit, feeling and a beautiful lightness of touch.' – *Gavin Lambert*

'She's a boy! It's Mr Hepburn to you!'
Sylvia Scarlett *
US 1935 94m bw
RKO (Pandro S. Berman)
A girl masquerades as a boy in order to escape to France with her crooked father.
Strange, peripatetic English comedy-adventure which failed to ring any bells but preserves aspects of interest.
w Gladys Unger, John Collier, Mortimer Offner *novel* Compton Mackenzie *d* George Cukor *ph* Joseph August *m* Roy Webb
☆ Katharine Hepburn, Cary Grant, Edmund Gwenn, Brian Aherne, Lennox Pawle
'A story that's hard to believe. Dubious entertainment for the public.' – *Variety*
'It seems to go wrong in a million directions, but it has unusually affecting qualities.' – *New Yorker, 1978*
'A sprawling and ineffective essay in dramatic chaos.' – *Richard Watts Jnr, New York Herald Tribune*
'A tragic waste of time and screen talent.' – *Eileen Creelman, New York Sun*
'A much more polished comedy than most, and consistently engaging.' – *Winston Burdett, Brooklyn Daily Eagle*

Sylvie et la Fântome: see *Sylvia and the Ghost*

Sympathy for the Devil: see *One Plus One*

La Symphonie Fantastique *
France 1947 90m bw
L'Atelier Français
The life of Hector Berlioz.
Stately but uninspired biopic chiefly notable for its leading performance.
w J. P. Feydeau, H. A. Legrand *d* Christian-Jaque
☆ *Jean-Louis Barrault*, Renée Saint-Cyr, Jules Berry, Bernard Blier

La Symphonie Pastorale *
France 1946 105m bw
Les Films Gibe
A Swiss pastor takes in an orphan child who grows up to be a beautiful girl and causes jealousy between himself and his son.
Curious mountain tragedy, a great visual pleasure with its symbolic use of snow and water.
w Jean Delannoy, Jean Aurenche *novel* André Gide *d* Jean Delannoy *ph* Armand Thirard *m* Georges Auric
☆ Pierre Blanchar, Michèle Morgan

Symphony of Six Million
US 1932 94m bw
RKO (Pandro S. Berman)
GB title: *Melody of Life*
A doctor drags himself from New York's slums to Park Avenue, but feels guilty and demoralized when he can't save the life of his own father.
Monumental tearjerker, not badly done.
w Bernard Schubert, J. Walter Ruben *novel* Fannie Hurst *d* Gregory La Cava *ph* Leo Tover *m* Max Steiner
☆ Irene Dunne, Ricardo Cortez, Gregory Ratoff, Anna Appel, Noel Madison, Julie Haydon
'Picture of Jewish home life in the familiar Hurst style ... a good-looking picture without strongly marked cast names.' – *Variety*

Symptoms *
GB 1974 91m Eastmancolor
SF/Finiton (Jean Dupuis)
aka: *The Blood Virgin*
A woman living in a remote and decaying mansion begins to show signs of madness.
Creepy thriller with lesbian undertones, stylishly directed.
w Joseph Larraz, Stanley Miller *d* Joseph Larraz (José Ramón Larraz) *ph* Trevor Mann *m* John Scott *ad* Kenneth Bridgeman *ed* Brian Smedley-Aston
☆ Angela Pleasence, Peter Vaughan, Lorna Heilbron, Nancy Nevinson, Ronald O'Neil, Raymond Huntley
'Works more on the level of atmosphere than of ideas, but its psychological perceptions are unusually sophisticated for genre cinema.' – *David Pirie, MFB*
† The film was cut to 80m on its British cinema release.

Synanon
US 1965 106m bw
Columbia/Richard Quine
GB title: *Get Off My Back*
Stories of the inmates of a voluntary Californian institution for the rehabilitation of drug addicts.
Well-intentioned but rather dreary case histories, unconvincingly dramatized. The house and its leader subsequently came in for much press criticism.
w Ian Bernard, S. Lee Pogostin *d* Richard Quine *ph* Harry Stradling *m* Neal Hefti
☆ Edmond O'Brien (Chuck Dederich), Chuck Connors, Stella Stevens, Alex Cord, Eartha Kitt, Richard Conte, Barbara Luna
'The real drug addicts who appear in the background are plumpish, greyish and utterly ordinary; but the fictional ones are glamorously handsome, and lead lives which are full of throbbing emotion and upset.' – *Tom Milne, MFB*

Syncopation *
US 1942 88m bw
RKO/William Dieterle (Charles F. Glett)
The career of a young trumpeter parallels the development of jazz.
Somewhat disappointing musical considering the talents involved.
w Philip Yordan, Frank Cavett, Valentine Davies *d* William Dieterle
☆ Jackie Cooper, Adolphe Menjou, Bonita Granville, Connee Boswell, the Hall Johnson Choir, Benny Goodman, Harry James, Gene Krupa, Charlie Barnet
† Bonita Granville's piano playing was performed by Stan Wrightsman, and Jackie Cooper's cornet was dubbed by Bunny Berigan.

The System
US 1953 90m bw
Warner (Sam Bischoff)
A crime leader is softened by love, and allows himself to be convicted.
Strange nonsense inspired by the Kefauver investigations into American society; neither edifying nor entertaining.
w Jo Eisinger *story* Investigation by Edith and Samuel Grafton *d* Lewis Seiler *ph* Edwin DuPar *m* David Buttolph *ed* Clarence Kolster
☆ Frank Lovejoy, Joan Weldon, Bob Arthur, Paul Picerni, Don Beddoe

The System
GB 1964 90m bw
British Lion/Bryanston/Kenneth Shipman
US title: *The Girl-Getters*
Seaside layabouts have a system for collecting and sharing rich girl visitors, but one of the latter traps the leader at his own game.
Adequate sexy showcase for some looming talents; all very unattractive, but smoothly directed in a number of imitated styles.
w Peter Draper *d* *Michael Winner* *ph* *Nicolas Roeg* *m* Stanley Black
☆ Oliver Reed, Jane Merrow, Barbara Ferris, Julia Foster, Ann Lynn, Guy Doleman, Andrew Ray, David Hemmings, John Alderton, Derek Nimmo, Harry Andrews
'A modest, skilful, charming, inconsequential, and fairly dishonest little picture, to be enjoyed and deprecated in roughly equal measure.' – *John Simon*

T

'The year is 2020. He's mostly human. He's totally invincible ... until now.'

TC 2000

Canada 1993 90m colour
Shapiro Glickenhaus/Film One (Jalal Merhi)

In the future, when criminal gangs control a polluted world and the rich live in a heavily protected underground environment, a former cop saves the world for more dumb movies like this.
A dim rip-off of Robocop *with elements of* Blade Runner, *done without wit or style, featuring a scantily clad female cyborg and an illogical narrative; even when outnumbered, the cop's preferred method of law enforcement is kick-boxing.*
wd T. J. Scott *story* J. Stephen Maunder, Richard M. Samuels *ph* Curtis Petersen *m* Varouje *ad* Jasna Stefanovic *ed* Reid Dennison
☆ Bolo Yeung, Jalal Merhi, Billy Blanks, Bobbie Phillips, Matthias Hues, Ramsay Smith, Gregory Philpott, Harry Mok, Kelly Gallant

'Visit the future where love is the ultimate crime!'

THX 1138 *

US 1970 95m Technicolor/scope
Warner/American Zoetrope (Francis Ford Coppola, Lawrence Sturhahn)

In a future society, computer programmed and emotionless, an automated human begins to break the rules.
Orwellian science fiction; a thoughtful, rather cold affair which is always good to look at.
w George Lucas, Walter Murch *d George Lucas* *ph* Dave Meyers, Albert Kihn *m* Lalo Schifrin
☆ Robert Duvall, Donald Pleasence, Don Pedro Colley, Maggie McOmie, Ian Wolfe

T. R. Baskin

US 1971 89m Technicolor
Paramount (Peter Hyams)
GB title: *A Date with a Lonely Girl*
A businessman in Chicago meets an unhappy girl who tells him her story of loneliness and lack of communication.
Intolerable self-pitying mishmash with no place to go.
w Peter Hyams *d* Herbert Ross *ph* Gerald Hirschfeld *m* Jack Elliott
☆ Candice Bergen, Peter Boyle, James Caan, Marcia Rodd, Erin O'Reilly

T-Men *

US 1947 96m bw
Eagle Lion (Aubrey Schenck)
Treasury Department detectives trail a gang of counterfeiters.
Tough, well-made crime melodrama which still packs a punch in the traditional vein.
w John C. Higgins *d* Anthony Mann *ph* John Alton *m* Paul Sawtell
☆ Dennis O'Keefe, Alfred Ryder, Mary Meade, Wallace Ford, June Lockhart, Charles McGraw, Jane Randolph, Art Smith

Table for Five

US 1983 124m DeLuxe
CBS/Voight-Schaffel (Robert Schaffel)
A divorced husband takes his children on a European holiday and has to tell them that their mother has been killed.
Slow, sentimental domestic drama with attractive travel backgrounds, like a TV movie writ large.
w David Seltzer *d* Robert Lieberman *ph* Vilmos Zsigmond *m* John Morris *pd* Robert F. Boyle
☆ Jon Voight, Richard Crenna, Marie-Christine Barrault, Millie Perkins, Roxana Zal, Robby Kiger, Son Hoang Bui, Maria O'Brien
'A family problem picture resolutely updated for the eighties.' – *Robert Brown, MFB*

Taboo: see *Gohatto*

Tabu *

US 1931 80m bw
Colorart Synchrotone
The life of a young Tahitian pearl fisherman.
The plot is used only to bring together the elements of a superb travelogue, but the conflicts between the aims of the two directors are clearly seen.
wd F. W. Murnau, Robert Flaherty *ph* Floyd Crosby, Robert Flaherty *m* Hugo Riesenfeld
'Never more than interesting ... it is not going to set anything on fire.' – *Variety*
Floyd Crosby

Tacones Lejanos: see *High Heels*

Ta'Det Som En Mand, Frue!: see *Take It Like a Man, Ma'am*

Taffin

GB 1988 96m colour
Vestron (Peter Shaw)
A debt collector battles with crooked developers who want to build a chemical plant in an Irish village.
Dull thriller that never rises above the mundane.
w David Ambrose *d* Francis Megahy *ph* Paul Beeson *m* Stanley Myers, Hans Zimmer *pd* William Alexander *ed* Rodney Holland, Peter Tanner
☆ Pierce Brosnan, Alison Doody, Ray McAnally, Jeremy Child, Patrick Bergin, Alan Stanford

Tagebuch einer Verliebten: see *The Diary of a Married Woman*

Tagebuch einer Verlorenen: see *Diary of a Lost Girl*

Taggart

US 1965 85m Technicolor
Universal
A young Western squatter avenges his parents' murder but finds himself pursued by three professional gunslingers.
Tough adult Western, quite well made.
w Robert Creighton Williams *novel* Louis L'Amour *d* R. G. Springsteen *ph* William Margulies *m* Herman Stein
☆ Tony Young, Dan Duryea, Dick Foran, Emile Meyer, Elsa Cardenas, Jean Hale, David Carradine

Tai Chi Master: see *Twin Warriors*

Tai Ji Zhang San Feng: see *Twin Warriors*

Tai-Pan

US 1986 127m Technicolor JDC Widescreen
Dino de Laurentiis (Raffaella de Laurentiis)
Various problems afflict the leader of the European community in Canton and Hong Kong.
19th-century soap opera with 18th-century plotting and dialogue.
w John Briley, Stanley Mann *novel* James Clavell *d* Daryl Duke *ph* Jack Cardiff *m* Maurice Jarre *pd* Tony Masters
☆ Bryan Brown, Joan Chen, John Stanton, Tim Guinee, Bill Leadbitter, Russell Wong
'Underneath all the gloss the film isn't really about anything.' – *Variety*
'With some movies, you're forever checking your watch. With *Tai-Pan*, you'll be checking your calendar.' – *People*
'Miniseries kitsch which shortchanges on dramatic spectacle.' – *Sight and Sound*

Taiheiyo Hitoribochi: see *Alone on the Pacific*

Tail Spin

US 1938 83m bw
TCF (Harry Joe Brown)
The interwoven private lives of lady civilian air pilots.
Predictable romantic goings on; a tear, a smile, a song, etc.
w Frank Wead *d* Roy del Ruth *ph* Karl Freund *m* Louis Silvers
☆ Alice Faye, Constance Bennett, Joan Davis, Nancy Kelly, Charles Farrell, Jane Wyman, Kane Richmond, Wally Vernon, Harry Davenport
'Story zooms and flutters to create many slow spots in between the spectacular flying sequences.' – *Variety*

'In a place this treacherous, what a good spy needs is a spy of his own.'

The Tailor of Panama **

US/Ireland 2001 109m DeLuxe Panavision
Columbia/Merlin (John Boorman)
A disgraced MI5 agent is banished to Panama, where he recruits a self-invented Savile Row tailor to provide him with the information he needs to revive his career.
Deft and derisive thriller, about the self-justifying fantasists of the espionage business, that acknowledges its debt to Graham Greene's Our Man in Havana. *It gains from Brosnan's performance as a sleazy, womanising spy who might imagine that he was James Bond.*
w Andrew Davies, John Le Carré, John Boorman *novel* John Le Carré *d* John Boorman *ph* Philippe Rousselot *m* Shaun Davey *pd* Derek Wallace *ed* Ron Davis
☆ Pierce Brosnan (Andy Osnard), Geoffrey Rush (Harry Pendel), Jamie Lee Curtis (Louisa Pendel), Brendan Gleeson (Mickie Abraxas), Catherine McCormack (Francesca), Leonor Varela (Marta), Harold Pinter (Uncle Benny), Daniel Radcliffe (Mark Pendel), Lola Boorman (Sarah Pendel), David Hayman (Luxmore), Mark Margolis (Rafi Domingo), Martin Ferrero (Teddy), John Fortune (Ambassador Maltby)
'Classy, articulate and richly humorous.' – *Variety*
'With the performers in riotous full swing and the images such a treat for the eyes, you're hard-pressed to dislike the movie, even when it – like Panama City – goes up in flames.' – *Desson Howe, Washington Post*

Tainted Money: see *Show Them No Mercy*

Take a Giant Step

US 1958 100m bw
UA/Sheila/Hecht-Hill-Lancaster (Julius J. Epstein)
A young black person brought up in a white town feels ill at ease and runs into adolescent troubles.
Well-meaning racial drama with good detail but no real feeling.
w Louis S. Peterson, Julius J. Epstein *d* Philip Leacock *ph* Arthur Arling *m* Jack Marshall
☆ Johnny Nash, Estelle Hemsley, Ruby Dee, Frederick O'Neal, Ellen Holly, Pauline Meyers, Beah Richards, Royce Wallace

Take a Girl Like You

GB 1970 101m Eastmancolor
Columbia/Albion (Hal E. Chester)
A north country girl comes to teach in London and has man trouble.
Old-fashioned novelette with sex trimmings and neither zest nor humour.
w George Melly *novel* Kingsley Amis *d* Jonathan Miller *ph* Dick Bush *m* Stanley Myers
☆ Hayley Mills, Oliver Reed, Noel Harrison, Sheila Hancock, John Bird, Aimi MacDonald

Take a Letter, Darling **

US 1942 94m bw
Paramount (Fred Kohlmar)
GB title: *Green-Eyed Woman*
A woman executive hires a male secretary.
Smartish romantic comedy.
w Claude Binyon *d* Mitchell Leisen *ph* John Mescall *m* Victor Young *ad* Hans Dreier, Roland Anderson
☆ Rosalind Russell, Fred MacMurray, Macdonald Carey, Constance Moore, Cecil Kellaway, Charles Arnt, Kathleen Howard, Dooley Wilson
John Mescall; Victor Young; art direction

Take Care of My Little Girl

US 1951 93m Technicolor
TCF (Julian Blaustein)
A university freshwoman gets into trouble with her sorority.
Ho-hum exposé of college conventions, of routine interest at best.
w Julius J. and Philip G. Epstein *novel* Peggy Goodwin *d* Jean Negulesco *ph* Harry Jackson *m* Alfred Newman
☆ Jeanne Crain, Mitzi Gaynor, Dale Robertson, Jean Peters, Jeffrey Hunter
'As is customary in college pictures, it appears that Tri U recruits most of its strength from the chorus.' – *Penelope Houston*

Take Care of Your Scarf, Tatjana *

Finland/Germany 1994 62m bw
ICA/Sputnik/Pandora/Suomen Elokvasäätiö/Yleisradio/TV-1/Marianne Möller/Eila Werning (Aki Kaurismäki)
original title: *Pidä Huivista Kiinni, Tatjana*
In the mid-60s, two dour and immature Finnish men give a lift to two Russian women, who are looking for love but are willing to settle for less.
A quirky, downbeat road movie about the difficulties of communication between the sexes, which can be taken either as tragedy or comedy, depending on your mood and point of view.
w Aki Kaurismäki, Sakke Järvenpää *d* Aki Kaurismäki *ph* Timo Salminen *ad* Kari Laine, Markku Pätilä, Jukka Salmi *ed* Aki Kaurismäki
☆ Kati Outinen, Matti Pellonpää, Kirsi Tykkyläinen, Mato Valtonen, Elina Salo
'Deserves to find an audience, because beneath the offhand, casual approach is a moving and funny film about relationships.' – *Variety*

Take Her, She's Mine *

US 1963 98m DeLuxe Cinemascope
TCF (Henry Koster)
A lawyer protects his teenage daughter from boys and causes.
Routine Hollywood family comedy with some laughs and an agreeable cast.
w Nunnally Johnson *play* Phoebe and Henry Ephron *d* Henry Koster *ph* Lucien Ballard *m* Jerry Goldsmith
☆ James Stewart, Sandra Dee, Robert Morley, Audrey Meadows, Philippe Forquet, John McGiver

Take It Easy

France 1971 90m colour
Adel Productions (Alain Delon)
original title: *Doucement les Basses*
A Catholic priest, a former organist, living in an isolated village, is visited by his wife, who he thought had died eight years earlier, and discovers she is now running a bordello.
A broad comedy that fails to extract much fun from its situation.
w Pascal Jardin *d* Jacques Deray *ph* Jean-Jacques Tarbes *m* Claude Bolling *ad* François de Lamotne *ed* Paul Cayatte
☆ Alain Delon, Paul Meurisse, Nathalie Delon, Julien Guiomar, Paul Préboist, André Bollet, Serge Davri

Take It Like a Man, Ma'am *
Denmark 1975 96m colour
Rīde Sīster (Ilse M. Haugaard, Trine Hedman, Annelise Hovinand)
original title: *Ta'Det Som En Mand, Frue!*
A bored middle-aged housewife dreams of the sexual roles being reversed.
Mildly enjoyable feminist movie.
wd Elisabeth Rygard, Mette Knudsen, Li Vilstrup *ph* Katia Forbert Petersen, Judy Irola, Lene Fog-Moller, Leni Schou *m* Nina Larsen, Gudrun Steen-Andersen, Maria Marcus *ed* Ann-Lis Lund
☆ Tove Maës, Bertha Quistgard, Asta Esper Andersen, Birgit Brüel, Alf Lassen

Take It or Leave It
US 1944 68m bw
TCF
A sailor enters a quiz show to raise money for his expectant wife.
Thin link for a string of old movie clips which form the questions; all from Fox films of course.
w Harold Buchman, Snag Werris, Mac Benoff *d* Ben Stoloff
☆ Phil Baker, Phil Silvers, Edward Ryan, Marjorie Massow
† Performers shown in film clips include Shirley Temple, the Ritz Brothers, Betty Grable, Alice Faye, Sonja Henie, and Al Jolson.

Take Me High
GB 1973 90m Technicolor
EMI (Kenneth Harper)
A bank manager helps an unsuccessful restaurant to launch a new hamburger.
Jaded youth musical with no dancing but some zip and bounce to commend it to mums and dads if not to its intended young audience.
w Christopher Penfold *d* David Askey *ph* Norman Warwick *m/songs* Tony Cole
☆ Cliff Richard, Debbie Watling, Hugh Griffith, George Cole, Anthony Andrews, Richard Wattis

Take Me Out to the Ball Game **
US 1949 93m Technicolor
MGM (Arthur Freed)
GB title: *Everybody's Cheering*
A woman takes over a baseball team and the players are antagonistic.
Lively, likeable 1890s comedy musical which served as a trial run for On the Town *and in its own right is a fast-moving, funny, tuneful delight with no pretensions.*
w Harry Tugend, George Wells d Busby Berkeley ph George Folsey *md* Adolph Deutsch *songs Betty Comden, Adolph Green, Roger Edens*
☆ *Gene Kelly* (Eddie O'Brian), Frank Sinatra (Dennis Ryan), Esther Williams (K.C. Williams), *Betty Garrett* (Shirley Delwyn), Jules Munshin (Nat Goldberg), Edward Arnold (Joe Lorgan), Richard Lane (Michael Gilhuly), Tom Dugan (Slappy Burke)

Take Me to Town
US 1953 81m Technicolor
U-I (Ross Hunter)
The three sons of a backwoods widower import a vaudeville artiste as their new mother.
Old-fashioned family schmaltz containing every known cliché professionally stitched into the plot.
w Richard Morris *d* Douglas Sirk *ph* Russell Metty *m* Joseph Gershenson *ad* Hilyard Brown, Alexander Golitzen, Bernard Herzbrun *ed* Milton Carruth
☆ Ann Sheridan, Sterling Hayden, Philip Reed, Lee Patrick, Lee Aaker, Harvey Grant, Dusty Henley

Take My Life **
GB 1947 79m bw
GFD/Cineguild (Anthony Havelock-Allan)
A man is suspected of murdering an ex-girlfriend, and his wife journeys to Scotland to prove him innocent.
Hitchcock-style thriller with excellent detail and performances.
w Winston Graham, Valerie Taylor *d Ronald Neame ph Guy Green m* William Alwyn *md* Muir Mathieson *pd* John Bryan *ad* Wilfred Shingleton *ed* Geoffrey Foot
☆ Hugh Williams (Nicholas Talbot), Greta Gynt (Philippa Shelley), Marius Goring (Sidney Flemming), Francis L. Sullivan (Prosecuting Counsel), Rosalie Crutchley (Elizabeth Rusman), Henry Edwards (Inspector Archer), Ronald Adam (Deaf Man), Maurice Denham (Defending Counsel)
'An extremely confident and exciting British thriller, with a story no less plausible than the average made infinitely more plausible by the smooth narrative style.' – *Dilys Powell, Sunday Times*

Take My Tip
GB 1937 74m bw
Gaumont-British (Michael Balcon)
Lord Pilkington gets his revenge on a confidence trickster when they meet at a Dalmatian hotel.
Reasonably lively comedy musical adapted for the stars.
w Sidney Gilliat, Michael Hogan, Jack Hulbert *d* Herbert Mason *ph* Bernard Knowles *songs* Sam Lerner, Al Goodhart, Al Hoffman
☆ Jack Hulbert, Cicely Courtneidge, Frank Cellier, Harold Huth, Frank Pettingell, Robb Wilton, H. F. Maltby

Take One False Step *
US 1949 94m bw
U-I (Chester Erskine)
An innocent middle-aged man who has befriended a girl is hunted by the police when she is murdered.
Fairly absorbing and well-cast chase thriller in a minor key.
w Irwin Shaw, Chester Erskine *story Night Call* by Irwin and David Shaw *d* Chester Erskine *ph* Franz Planer *m* Walter Scharf
☆ *William Powell*, Shelley Winters, Marsha Hunt, Dorothy Hart, James Gleason, Felix Bressart, Art Baker, Sheldon Leonard

Take the High Ground
US 1953 101m Anscocolor
MGM (Dore Schary)
A tough sergeant trains army conscripts for action in Korea.
Very routine flagwaver.
w Millard Kaufman *d* Richard Brooks *ph* John Alton *m* Dimitri Tiomkin
☆ Richard Widmark, Karl Malden, Carleton Carpenter, Elaine Stewart, Russ Tamblyn, Jerome Courtland, Steve Forrest, Robert Arthur
Millard Kaufman

Take the Money and Run
US 1968 85m Technicolor
Palomar (Charles H. Joffe)
A social misfit becomes a bungling crook.
A torrent of middling visual gags, not the star's best vehicle.
wd Woody Allen *ph* Lester Shorr *m* Marvin Hamlisch
☆ Woody Allen, Janet Margolin, Marcel Hillaire

Take the Stage: see *Curtain Call at Cactus Creek*

Take This Job and Shove It
US 1981 106m colour
Avco Embassy/Cinema Group (Greg Blackwell)
A thrusting business executive discovers his social conscience when he returns to his home town to take over a run-down brewery.
Unoriginal but affable corn-belt comedy affirming small-town values.
w Barry Schneider *story* Jeffrey Bernini, Barry Schneider, from a song by David Allan Coe *d* Gus Trikonis *ph* James Devis *m* Billy Sherrill *ad* Jim Dultz *ed* Richard Belding
☆ Robert Hays, Barbara Hershey, David Keith, Art Carney, Tim Thomerson, Eddie Albert, Penelope Milford, Charlie Rich, Martin Mull

Takhte Siah: see *Blackboards*

Taking Care of Business
US 1990 108m Technicolor
Warner/Hollywood Pictures/Silver Screen Partners IV (Geoffrey Taylor)
GB title: *Filofax*
A thief assumes the identity of an advertising executive whose Filofax he acquires.
Slow-moving comedy that fails to get much mileage from its tired central idea.
w Jill Mazursky, Jeffrey Abrams *d* Arthur Hiller *ph* David M. Walsh *m* Stewart Copeland *pd* Jon Hutman *ed* William Reynolds
☆ James Belushi, Charles Grodin, Anne DeSalvo, Loryn Locklin, Stephen Elliott, Hector Elizondo, Veronica Hamel
'Hiller brings his usual dogged persistence to bear, but it would take an alchemist's touch to turn *Filofax* into comic gold.' – *Geoff Brown, Sight and Sound*

The Taking of Pelham 123 *
US 1974 104m Technicolor Panavision
UA/Palomar/Palladium (Gabriel Katzka, Edgar J. Scherick)
Four ruthless gunmen hold a New York subway train to ransom and have an ingenious plan for escape.
Entertaining crime caper made less enjoyable by all the fashionable faults – the script is deliberately hard to follow and full of four letter words, the sound track hard to hear, and the visuals ugly.
w Peter Stone *novel* John Godey *d* Joseph Sargent *ph* Owen Roizman *m* David Shire
☆ Walter Matthau, Robert Shaw, Martin Balsam, Hector Elizondo, Earl Hindman, James Broderick
'Full of noise and squalling and dirty words used for giggly shock effects.' – *New Yorker*

Taking Off ***
US 1971 92m Movielab
Universal (Alfred W. Crown, Michael Hausman)
Suburban parents seek their errant daughter among the hippies, and gradually lose their own inhibitions.
Slight, formless, but amusing revue-style comment by a Czech director on the American scene.
w Milos Forman, John Guare, Jean-Claude Carrière, John Klein *d Milos Forman ph* Miroslav Ondricek
☆ Lynn Carlin, Buck Henry, Linnea Heacock

Tale of a Vampire
GB/Japan 1992 102m colour
State Screen/Tsuburaya Ezio/Furama (Simon Johnson)
A vampire in London is tracked down by the husband of his lost lover.
Slow-moving and gory account of an obsessive love.
w Shimako Sato, Jane Corbett *d* Shimako Sato *ph* Zubin Mistry *m* Julian Joseph *pd* Alice Normington *ed* Chris Wright *sp* Dave Watkins
☆ Julian Sands, Suzanna Hamilton, Kenneth Cranham, Marian Diamond, Michael Kenton, Catherine Blake, Mark Kempner, Nik Myers
'A flawed but impressive debut from a talent which deserves to be nurtured.' – *Mark Kermode, Sight and Sound*
'Is nailed to the floor by anaemic perfs from its two leads and a script that's all tease and no bite. Pic may build a small cult following among genre buffs but won't score many general converts.' – *Variety*

A Tale of Five Cities
GB 1951 99m bw
Grand National (Alexander Paal)
US title: *A Tale of Five Women*
An amnesiac American seeks clues to his past in Rome, Vienna, Paris, Berlin and London.
Tedious pattern drama remarkable only for its then untried cast.
w Patrick Kirwan, Maurice J. Wilson *d* Montgomery Tully *ph* Gordon Lang *m* Hans May
☆ Bonar Colleano, Gina Lollobrigida, Barbara Kelly, Lana Morris, Anne Vernon, Eva Bartok

A Tale of Five Women: see *A Tale of Five Cities*

A Tale of Springtime: see *Conte de Printemps*

The Tale of the Fox ***
France 1931 65m bw
BFI/Wladyslaw Starewicz (Louis Nalpas, Roger Richebé)
original title: *Le Roman de Renard*
A cunning fox defeats all the other animals that unite to attack him.
A brilliant animated film, which with its British release in 1994 helped bring belated recognition to a master of the art.
w Ladislaw Starewicz, Irène Starewicz, Jean Nohain, Antoinette Nordmann *d* Ladislaw Starewicz *m* Vincent Scotto *pd* Wladyslaw Starewicz *ed* Laura Séjourné
☆ Featuring the voices of Claude Dauphin, Romain Bouquet, Sylvain Itkine, Léon Larive, Robert Seller, Edy Debray, Nicolas Amato

'His love challenged the flames of revolution!'
A Tale of Two Cities **
US 1935 121m bw
MGM (David O. Selznick)
A British lawyer sacrifices himself to save another man from the guillotine.
Richly detailed version of the classic melodrama, with production values counting more than the acting.
w W. P. Lipscomb, S. N. Behrman *novel* Charles Dickens *d Jack Conway ph* Oliver T. Marsh *m* Herbert Stothart *ed* Conrad A. Nervig
☆ Ronald Colman, Elizabeth Allan, Basil Rathbone, Edna May Oliver, Blanche Yurka, Reginald Owen, Henry B. Walthall, Donald Woods, Walter Catlett, H. B. Warner, Claude Gillingwater, Fritz Leiber
'A screen classic ... technically it is about as flawless as possible ... it has been made with respectful and loving care.' – *Variety*
'A prodigiously stirring production ... for more than two hours it crowds the screen with beauty and excitement.' – *New York Times*
† Originally prepared at Warner for Leslie Howard.
best picture; editing

A Tale of Two Cities *
GB 1958 117m bw
Rank (Betty E. Box)
Modest but still costly remake with good moments but a rather slow pace.
w T. E. B. Clarke *d* Ralph Thomas *ph* Ernest Steward *m* Richard Addinsell
☆ Dirk Bogarde, Dorothy Tutin, Christopher Lee, Athene Seyler, Rosalie Crutchley, Ernest Clark, Stephen Murray, Paul Guers, Donald Pleasence, Ian Bannen, Cecil Parker, Alfie Bass
'Serviceable rather than imaginative.' – *MFB*

A Talent for Loving
US 1969 101m colour
Paramount (Walter Shenson)
Two generations of an international jet-setting family have woman trouble.
Little-seen melodrama apparently disowned by those who made it.
novel Richard Condon *d* Richard Quine
☆ Richard Widmark, Cesar Romero, Topol, Genevieve Page

Talent for the Game
US 1991 91m Technicolor
Paramount (Martin Elfand)
When a billionaire buys the team, a baseball scout tries to save his job by discovering a star pitcher.
Slow-moving drama that begins as an exposé of exploitation and corruption in sport before settling for a sentimental story of triumph against the odds.
w David Himmelstein, Tom Donnelly, Larry Ferguson *d* Robert M. Young *ph* Curtis Clark *m* David Newman *pd* Jeffrey Howard *ed* Arthur Coburn
☆ Edward James Olmos, Lorraine Bracco, Jamey Sheridan, Terry Kinney, Jeff Corbett

'How Far Would You Go To Become Someone Else?'
The Talented Mr Ripley **
US 1999 139m DeLuxe
Paramount/Miramax/Mirage/Timnick (William Horberg, Tom Sternberg)
Hired by a wealthy man to bring back his playboy son from Italy, a poor youth decides to kill him and assume his identity instead.
Glamorous thriller of class warfare and homosexual obsession, often engrossing but much too long.
wd Anthony Minghella *novel* Patricia Highsmith *ph* John Seale *m* Gabriel Yared *pd* Roy Walker *ed Walter Murch cos* Ann Roth, Gary Jones
☆ Matt Damon (Tom Ripley), *Jude Law* (Dickie Greenleaf), Gwyneth Paltrow (Marge Sherwood), Cate Blanchett (Meredith Logue), Philip Seymour Hoffman (Freddie Miles), Jack Davenport (Peter Smith-Kingsley), James Rebhorn (Herbert Greenleaf), Sergio Rubini (Inspector Roverini),

Philip Baker Hall (Alvin MacCarron), Rosario Fiorello (Fausto), Stefania Rocca (Silvana)

'It ends up as a dismayingly unthrilling thriller and bafflingly unconvincing character study.' – *Peter Bradshaw, Guardian*

'There are diabolically smart surprises wherever you care to look in this glittering thriller.' – *Janet Maslin, New York Times*

† Highsmith's novel was first filmed in 1960 by René Clément under the title *Plein Soleil* (qv).

Jude Law; Anthony Minghella (as writer); Gabriel Yared; Roy Walker; Ann Roth, Gary Jones

Jude Law

Tales from the Crypt *

GB 1972 92m Eastmancolor

Metromedia/Amicus (Milton Subotsky)

Five people get lost in catacombs and are shown the future by a sinister monk who turns out to be Satan.

Fair ghoulish fun; a quintet of stories with a recognizable Amicus link.

w Milton Subotsky *comic strips* William Gaines *d* Freddie Francis *ph* Norman Warwick *m* Douglas Gamley

☆ Ralph Richardson, Geoffrey Bayldon, Peter Cushing, Joan Collins, Ian Hendry, Robin Phillips, Richard Greene, Barbara Murray, Roy Dotrice, Nigel Patrick, Patrick Magee

Tales from the Crypt: Demon Knight

US 1995 92m DeLuxe

UIP/Universal (Gilbert Adler)

A servant of the Devil attempts to obtain a key, protected by a Demon Knight, that will allow evil to triumph on Earth.

Comic-book horror, done with a modicum of style, though its episodic approach allows predictability to seep in.

w Ethan Reiff, Cyrus Voris, Mark Bishop *d* Ernest Dickerson *ph* Rick Bota *m* Ed Shearmur *pd* Christiaan Wagener *ed* Stephen Lovejoy *sp* Available Light; Scott Coulter; make-up: Todd Masters

☆ Billy Zane, William Sadler, Jada Pinkett, Brenda Bakke, C. C. H. Pounder, Dick Miller, Thomas Haden Church, John Schuck

'A fang-in-cheek horror thriller that likely will please fans and turn off non-devotees.' – *Variety*

Tales from the Crypt Presents Bordello of Blood

US 1996 87m DeLuxe

Universal (Gilbert Adler)

A preacher sets up a vampire-staffed brothel beneath a cemetery.

Derivative, tongue-in-cheek and gore-all-over-the-floor horror, aimed at an adolescent audience.

w A. L. Katz, Gilbert Adler *story* Bob Gale, Robert Zemeckis *d* Gilbert Adler *ph* Tom Priestly *m* Chris Boardman *pd* Gregory Melton *ed* Stephen Lovejoy

☆ Dennis Miller, Erika Eleniak, Angie Everhart, Chris Sarandon, Corey Feldman, Aubrey Morris, Phil Fondacaro, William Sadler, Whoopi Goldberg (uncredited)

'Another cheesy goulash of smart-alecky humor and full-bore gore, spiced with more shots of topless lovelies than you'd find in a '60s sexploitation flick.' – *Joe Leydon, Variety*

Tales from the Darkside: The Movie

US 1991 93m Technicolor

Columbia TriStar/Paramount (Richard P. Rubinstein, Mitchell Galin)

Facing being roasted in an oven for dinner, a small boy postpones the event by telling stories.

Bloody anthology of horrific anecdotes that fails to cohere.

Wraparound Story:

w Michael McDowell *d* John Harrison *ph* Robert Draper *m* Donald A. Rubinstein *pd* Ruth Ammon *sp* Dick Smith *ed* Harry B. Miller III with Deborah Harry, Matthew Lawrence

Lot 249:

w Michael McDowell *story* Arthur Conan Doyle *d* John Harrison *ph* Robert Draper *m* Pat Regan *pd* Ruth Ammon *sp* Dick Smith *ed* Harry B. Miller III with Christian Slater, Robert Sedgwick, Steve Buscemi, Donald Van Horn, Michael Deak

Cat from Hell:

w George Romero *story* Stephen King *d* John Harrison *ph* Robert Draper *m* Chaz Jankel *pd* Ruth Ammon *sp* Dick Smith *ed* Harry B. Miller III with David Johansen, Paul Greene, William Hickey

Lover's Vow:

w Michael McDowell *d* John Harrison *ph* Robert Draper *m* John Harrison *pd* Ruth Ammon *sp* Dick Smith *ed* Harry B. Miller III with James Remar, Ashton Wise, Philip Lenkowsky, Rae Dawn Chong

'The rending of flesh that punctuates each episode is so extravagantly disgusting that the senses are quickly stirred not to admiration but to apathy.' – *Philip Strick, Sight and Sound*

Tales of Beatrix Potter **

GB 1971 90m Technicolor

EMI (Richard Goodwin)

US title: *Peter Rabbit and the Tales of Beatrix Potter*

Children's stories danced by the Royal Ballet in animal masks.

A charming entertainment for those who can appreciate it, though hardly the most direct way to tell these stories.

w Richard Goodwin, Christine Edzard *d* Reginald Mills *ph* Austin Dempster *m* John Lanchbery *ch Frederick Ashton pd* Christine Edzard *masks Rotislav Doboujinsky*

The Tales of Hoffman **

GB 1951 127m Technicolor

British Lion/London/Michael Powell, Emeric Pressburger

The poet Hoffman, in three adventures, seeks the eternal woman and is beset by eternal evil.

Overwhelming combination of opera, ballet, and rich production design, an indigestible hodgepodge with flashes of superior talent.

wd Michael Powell, Emeric Pressburger *ph* Christopher Challis *m Jacques Offenbach md* Sir Thomas Beecham (with the Royal Philharmonic Orchestra) *pd Hein Heckroth*

☆ Robert Rounseville, Robert Helpmann, Pamela Brown, Moira Shearer, Frederick Ashton, Leonide Massine, Ludmilla Tcherina, Ann Ayars, Mogens Wieth

'The most spectacular failure yet achieved by Powell and Pressburger, who seem increasingly to dissipate their gifts in a welter of aimless ingenuity.' – *Gavin Lambert*

'An art director's picnic: I marvelled without being enthralled.' – *Richard Mallett, Punch*

'Enchanting, a labour of love.' – *Sunday Telegraph*

'It echoes the peak of the Victorian spirit.' – *Time*

art direction

Tales of Manhattan **

US 1942 118m bw

TCF (Boris Morros, Sam Spiegel)

Separate stories of a tail coat, which passes from owner to owner.

The stories are all rather disappointing in their different veins, but production standards are high and a few of the stars shine. A sequence starring W. C. Fields was deleted before release.

w Ben Hecht, Ferenc Molnar, Donald Ogden Stewart, Samuel Hoffenstein, Alan Campbell, Ladislas Fodor, Laslo Vadnay, Laszlo Gorog, Lamar Trotti, Henry Blankfort *d* Julien Duvivier *ph* Joseph Walker *m* Sol Kaplan

☆ Charles Boyer, Rita Hayworth, Thomas Mitchell;, Ginger Rogers, Henry Fonda, Cesar Romero, Gail Patrick, Roland Young;, *Charles Laughton*, Elsa Lanchester, Victor Francen, Christian Rub, Edward G. Robinson, George Sanders, James Gleason and also Paul Robeson, Ethel Waters, Eddie Anderson

† Duvivier was clearly chosen to make this film because of his success with the similar *Carnet de Bal*; he and Boyer went on to make the less successful *Flesh and Fantasy* on similar lines.

Tales of Mystery and Imagination: see *Histoires Extraordinaires*

Tales of Ordinary Madness

Italy/France 1981 108m Eastmancolor

English version

23 Giugno/Ginis (Jacqueline Ferreri)

A drunken poet is obsessed by sex but can't find a happy relationship with his women.

Outlandish, episodic wallow, mostly on Venice beach in California. Not for maiden aunts, and probably not for anyone else either.

w Marco Ferreri and others *book Erections, Ejaculations, Exhibitions and Tales of Ordinary Madness* by Charles Bukowski *d* Marco Ferreri *ph* Tonino Delli Colli *m* Philippe Sarde

☆ Ben Gazzara, Ornella Muti, Susan Tyrrell, Tanya Lopert, Katia Berger

'By turns repellent, naive and risible.' – *Sight*

Tales of Terror *

US 1962 90m Pathécolor Panavision

AIP (Roger Corman)

'Morella': a dying girl discovers the mummified body of her mother. 'The Black Cat': a henpecked husband kills his wife and walls up the body. 'The Facts in the Case of M Valdemar': an old man is hypnotized at the moment of death.

Tolerable short story compendium, rather short on subtlety and style.

w Richard Matheson *stories* Edgar Allan Poe *d* Roger Corman *ph* Floyd Crosby *m* Les Baxter

☆ Vincent Price, Peter Lorre, Basil Rathbone, Debra Paget

Tales of the Taira Clan *

Japan 1955 108m Eastmancolor

Daiei

original title: *Shin Heike Monogatari*

In the mid-1100s, an ambitious samurai becomes involved in the struggle for power between two royal courts and armed monks.

Deft, colourful, though stately, period movie of a seminal moment in Japanese history, when military power became paramount, that successfuly combines personal and dynastic dramas.

w Yoshikata Yoda, Masahige Narusawa, Kyuichi Tsuji *novel* Eiji Yoshikawa *d* Kenji Mizoguchi *ph* Kazuo Miyagawa *m* Fumio Hayasaka

☆ Raizo Ichikawa, Ichijiro Oya, Tatsuya Ishiguro, Michiyo Kogure, Eijiro Yanagi, Naritoshi Hayashi, Eitaro Shindo, Ichiro Sugau

'An orgy of the damned!'

Tales That Witness Madness

GB 1973 90m colour

Paramount/Amicus (Milton Subotsky, Norman Priggen)

Five ghostly tales linked by an old bookshop.

Extreme example of the Amicus compendiums.

w Jay Fairbank *d* Freddie Francis *ph* Norman Warwick *m* Bernard Ebbinghouse

☆ Jack Hawkins, Donald Pleasence, Georgia Brown, Donald Houston, Suzy Kendall, Peter McEnery, Joan Collins, Michael Jayston, Kim Novak, Michael Petrovitch, Mary Tamm

Talk About a Lady

US 1946 71m bw

Columbia

A country cousin comes to town and makes good.

Easy-going musical filler, better than some.

w Richard Weil, Ted Thomas *d* George Sherman

☆ Jinx Falkenburg, Forrest Tucker, Joe Besser, Trudy Marshall, Richard Lane, Stan Kenton and his orchestra

Talk About a Stranger *

US 1952 65m bw

MGM (Richard Goldstone)

In a small town, gossip is unjustly aroused over a mysterious stranger who is suspected of various crimes.

Unusual though rather naïve second feature, directed for more than its worth.

w Margaret Fitts *novel* Charlotte Armstrong *d* David Bradley *ph* John Alton *m* David Buttolph

☆ George Murphy, Nancy Davis, Lewis Stone, Billy Gray, Kurt Kasznar

Talk of the Devil

GB 1936 78m bw

B and D

An impersonator pins a crooked deal on a magnate, who kills himself.

Glum drama chiefly notable as the first film to be shot at Pinewood Studios.

w Carol Reed, George Barraud, Anthony Kimmins *d* Carol Reed

☆ Ricardo Cortez, Sally Eilers, Basil Sydney, Randle Ayrton, Charles Carson

The Talk of the Town ***

US 1942 118m bw

Columbia (George Stevens, Fred Guiol)

A girl loves both a suspected murderer and the lawyer who defends him.

Unusual mixture of comedy and drama, delightfully handled by three sympathetic stars.

w Irwin Shaw, Sidney Buchman d George Stevens ph Ted Tetzlaff *m* Frederick Hollander *ad* Lionel Banks, Rudolph Sternad *ed* Otto Meyer

☆ Ronald Colman, Cary Grant, Jean Arthur, Edgar Buchanan, Glenda Farrell, Charles Dingle, Emma Dunn, Rex Ingram

'A rip-roaring, knock-down-and-drag-out comedy about civil liberties.' – *John T. McManus*

'Well tuned and witty, at its best when it sticks to the middle ground between farce and melodrama. The chief fault of the script is its excessive length and the fact that a standard lynching mob climax is followed by a prolonged anti-climax.' – *Newsweek*

'I can't take my lynching so lightly, even in a screwball. Still, I am all for this kind of comedy and for players like Arthur and Grant, who can mug more amusingly than most scriptwriters can write.' – *Manny Farber*

'Did the authors think they were writing a Shavian comedy of ideas? The ideas are garbled and silly, but the people are so pleasant that the picture manages to be quite amiable and high-spirited.' – *Pauline Kael, 70s*

'I knew it was going to come off all along: it didn't have that element of hazard in it. It was more of an understood flight with a take-off time and an arrival time and not too much headwind.' – *George Stevens*

† Two endings were filmed: the eventual choice of mate for Miss Arthur was determined by audience reaction at previews.

best picture; original story (Sidney Harmon); script; Ted Tetzlaff; Frederick Hollander; art direction; Otto Meyer

Talk Radio **

US 1988 109m DeLuxe

Fox/Cineplex Odeon/Ten-Four Productions (Edward R. Pressman, A. Kitman Ho)

Billed as 'the man you love to hate', the host of a radio talk-show, whose private life is a mess, courts trouble by abusing his listeners.

Powerful, virulent near-monologue of a mind at the end of its tether, filmed in an appropriately restless style.

w Eric Bogosian, Oliver Stone *play* Eric Bogosian, Ted Savinar *book Talked to Death: The Life and Murder of Alan Berg by Stephen Singular d* Oliver Stone *ph* Robert Richardson *m* Stewart Copeland *pd* Bruno Rubeo *ed* David Brenner, Joe Hutshing

☆ *Eric Bogosian*, Alec Baldwin, Ellen Greene, Leslie Hope, John C. McGinley, John Pankow, Michael Wincott

Talk to Her **

Spain 2002 113m colour 'Scope

Pathé/El Deseo/Antena 3 (Agustin Almódóvar)

original title: *Hable con Ella*

Two men bond in hospital while caring for two women who are in a comatose state.

Much praised international success, though some will find its depiction of masculine desire and female passivity more than a little creepy.

wd Pedro Almódóvar *ph* Javier Aguirresarobe *m* Alberto Iglesias *ch* Pina Bausch *ed* Jose Salcedo

☆ Javier Camara (Benigno), Dario Grandinetti (Marco), Rosario Flores (Lydia), Leonor Watling (Alicia), Geraldine Chaplin (Katerina), Mariola Fuentes (Nurse)

'Beautiful (sometimes sublimely so), daring (sometimes outrageously so), seriously crazed and terrifically funny.' – *Joe Morgenstern, Wall Street Journal*

'Affects some people very deeply, while others, like me, find it high-grade kitsch… there's something almost fetishistic about the way he savors the immutability of the women. It's as if they had become comatose so that the two men could be soul mates.' – *Peter Rainer, New York*

Pedro Almódvar (as writer)

Pedro Almódovar (as director)

foreign film; Pedro Almódvar (as writer)

The Tall Blond Man with One Black Shoe: see *Le Grand Blond avec une Chaussure Noire*

The Tall Guy
GB 1989 92m Eastmancolor
Virgin/LWT/Working Title (Tim Bevan)
The stooge to a sadistic comedian tries for stardom on his own.
Lamentably unfunny comedy, ponderously directed.
w Richard Curtis *d* Mel Smith *ph* Adrian Biddle *m* Peter Brewis *pd* Grant Hicks *ed* Dan Rae
☆ Jeff Goldblum, Emma Thompson, Rowan Atkinson, Geraldine James, Emil Wolk, Kim Thomson, Harold Innocent, Anna Massey

The Tall Headlines
GB 1952 100m bw
Grand National/Raymond Stross
aka: *The Frightened Bride*
A family is affected when the eldest son is executed for murder.
Glum, boring, badly cast, badly written and generally inept melodrama.
w Audrey Erskine Lindop, Dudley Leslie *novel* Audrey Erskine Lindop *d* Terence Young *ph* C. M. Pennington-Richards *m* Hans May
☆ Flora Robson, Michael Denison, Mai Zetterling, Jane Hylton, André Morell, Dennis Price, Mervyn Johns, Naunton Wayne
'A falsity which will surely surprise even those familiar with the conventions of British middle-class cinema.' – *Lindsay Anderson*

Tall in the Saddle
US 1944 87m bw
RKO (Robert Fellows)
The newly-arrived ranch foreman finds that his boss has been murdered.
Quite a watchable, and forgettable, mystery Western.
w Michael Hogan, Paul J. Fix *d* Edwin L. Marin *ph* Robert de Grasse *m* Roy Webb *md* Constantin Bakaleinikoff
☆ John Wayne, Ella Raines, Ward Bond, George 'Gabby' Hayes, Audrey Long, Elizabeth Risdon, Don Douglas, Paul Fix, Russell Wade

Tall Man Riding
US 1955 83m Warnercolor
Warner
An adventurer feuds with a rancher but in the end marries his daughter.
Unremarkable star Western.
w Joseph Hoffman *d* Lesley Selander *ph* Wilfred Cline *m* Paul Sawtell
☆ Randolph Scott, Robert Barrat, Dorothy Malone, Peggie Castle, John Dehner

The Tall Men *
US 1955 122m DeLuxe Cinemascope
TCF (William A. Bacher, William B. Hawks)
After the Civil War, two Texans head north for the Montana goldfields.
Solid star Western.
w Sydney Boehm, Frank Nugent *novel* Clay Fisher *d* Raoul Walsh *ph* Leo Tover *m* Victor Young
☆ Clark Gable, Jane Russell, Robert Ryan, Cameron Mitchell, Juan Garcia, Harry Shannon, Emile Meyer
'A big action feast and value for anyone's money.' – *Newsweek*

Tall Story
US 1960 91m bw
Warner/Mansfield (Joshua Logan)
A college basketball player faces various kinds of trouble when he marries.
Dislikeable campus comedy with leading players miscast.
w Julius J. Epstein *novel The Homecoming Game* by Howard Nemoor *d* Joshua Logan *ph* Ellsworth Fredericks *m* Cyril Mockridge
☆ Anthony Perkins, Jane Fonda, Ray Walston, Anne Jackson, Marc Connelly, Murray Hamilton, Elizabeth Patterson

The Tall Stranger
US 1957 83m DeLuxe Cinemascope
Allied Artists
Cared for by wagon train pioneers after being mysteriously shot, a rancher tries to help them settle.
Fair star Western with some tough action.
w Christopher Knopf *story* Louis L'Amour *d* Thomas Carr *ph* Wilfred Cline *m* Hans J. Salter
☆ Joel McCrea, Virginia Mayo, Barry Kelley, Michael Ansara, Whit Bissell

The Tall T *
US 1957 78m Technicolor
Columbia/Scott-Brown (Harry Joe Brown)
Three bandits hold up a stagecoach and take a hostage, but are outwitted by a rancher.
Good small-scale suspense Western with plenty of action and a blood-spattered finale.
w Burt Kennedy *d* Budd Boetticher *ph* Charles Lawton Jnr *m* Heinz Roemheld
☆ Randolph Scott, Richard Boone, Maureen O'Sullivan, Arthur Hunnicutt, Skip Homeier, John Hubbard, Henry Silva

Tall Tale
US 1995 96m Technicolor Panavision
Buena Vista/Walt Disney/Caravan (Joe Roth, Roger Birnbaum)
A boy trying to save the family farm enlists the aid of legendary heroes Pecos Bill, Paul Bunyan and John Henry.
Pleasant children's fable, though it hasn't the quality to lift it beyond the mundane.
w Steven L. Bloom, Robert Rodat *d* Jeremiah Chechik *ph* Janusz Kaminski *m* Randy Edelman *pd* Eugenio Zanetti *ed* Richard Chew
☆ Patrick Swayze, Oliver Platt, Roger Aaron Brown, Nick Stahl, Scott Glenn, Stephen Lang, Jared Harris, Catherine O'Hara, Burgess Meredith (uncredited)
'A lavishly produced, robustly entertaining Old West fantasy.' – *Variety*

The Tall Target **
US 1951 78m bw
MGM (Richard Goldstone)
A discredited police officer tries to stop the assassination of Abraham Lincoln on a train to Washington.
Lively period suspenser with excellent attention to detail and much of the attraction of The Lady Vanishes. *The plot slightly relaxes its hold before the end.*
w George Worthing Yates, Art Cohn d Anthony Mann ph Paul C. Vogel ad Cedric Gibbons, Eddie Imazu
☆ *Dick Powell, Adolphe Menjou,* Paula Raymond, Marshall Thompson, *Ruby Dee,* Richard Rober, Will Geer, Florence Bates
'An intelligent minor picture which makes good use of its material.' – *MFB*

Tallinn Pimeduses: see *Darkness in Tallinn*

Ta'm e Guilass: see *A Taste of Cherry*

Tam-Lin
GB 1971 106m Technicolor Panavision
Winkast (Jerry Gershwin, Elliott Kastner)
aka: *The Devil's Widow*
aka: *The Ballad of Tam-Lin*
A sinister, beautiful, middle-aged widow has a diabolic influence on the bright young people she gathers around her.
Self-indulgent melodrama which might have worked with a shorter running time and a tighter script; as it was, it sank almost without trace.
w William Spier *poem* Robert Burns *d* Roddy McDowall *ph* Willy Williams *m* Stanley Myers
☆ Ava Gardner, Ian MacShane, Richard Wattis, Cyril Cusack, Stephanie Beacham, David Whitman, Fabia Drake, Sinead Cusack, Joanna Lumley, Jenny Hanley

Tamahine
GB 1962 95m Technicolor Cinemascope
ABP (John Bryan)
The headmaster of a boys' school is visited by his glamorous half-caste Polynesian cousin.
Simple-minded school comedy with predictable situations.
w Denis Cannan *novel* Thelma Niklaus *d* Philip Leacock *ph* Geoffrey Unsworth *m* Malcolm Arnold
☆ John Fraser, Nancy Kwan, Dennis Price, Derek Nimmo, Justine Lord, James Fox, Coral Browne, Michael Gough, Allan Cuthbertson

The Tamarind Seed *
GB 1974 125m Eastmancolor Panavision
Jewel/Lorimar/Pimlico (Ken Wales)
While holidaying in Barbados, a British widow falls for a Russian military attaché.
Old-fashioned romance which turns into a mild spy caper. A well-heeled time-passer.
wd Blake Edwards *novel* Evelyn Anthony *ph* Frederick A. Young *m* John Barry *ad* Harry Pottle *ed* Ernest Walter
☆ Julie Andrews, Omar Sharif, Sylvia Syms, Dan O'Herlihy, Anthony Quayle, Oscar Homolka
'A painless timekiller, but one wishes Miss Andrews didn't always give the impression that she had just left her horse in the hallway.' – *Michael Billington, Illustrated London News*

The Taming of the Shrew *
US 1929 68m bw
United Artists/Pickford/Elton
A condensed version of the play which did not do much in its day for its stars' then declining reputations, but can now be watched with a fair measure of enjoyment.
w William Shakespeare, 'with additional dialogue by Sam Taylor' *d* Sam Taylor *ph* Karl Struss *pd* William Cameron Menzies, Laurence Irving
☆ Douglas Fairbanks, Mary Pickford, Edwin Maxwell, Joseph Cawthorn, Clyde Cook, Dorothy Jordan
† A 'widescreen' version was issued in 1976.

'In the war between the sexes, there always comes a time to surrender unconditionally!'
The Taming of the Shrew *
US 1967 122m Technicolor Panavision
Columbia/Royal/FAI (Richard McWhorter)
Petruchio violently tames his shrewish wife.
Busy version of one of Shakespeare's more proletarian comedies; the words in this case take second place to violent action and rioting colour.
w Suso Cecchi d'Amico, Paul Dehn, Franco Zeffirelli *d Franco Zeffirelli ph* Oswald Morris, Luciano Trasatti *m* Nino Rota
☆ *Richard Burton, Elizabeth Taylor,* Michael York, Michael Hordern, Cyril Cusack, Alfred Lynch, Natasha Pyne, Alan Webb, Victor Spinetti
'As entertainment *Kiss Me Kate* is infinitely better but then Cole Porter was a real artist and Burton is a culture vulture.' – *Wilfrid Sheed*
'The old warhorse of a comedy has been spanked into uproarious life.' – *Hollis Alpert*

Tammy: see *Tammy and the Bachelor*

Tammy and the Bachelor *
US 1957 89m Technicolor Cinemascope
U-I (Ross Hunter)
GB title: *Tammy*
A backwoods tomboy falls for a stranded flyer.
Whimsical romance for middle America, which started Hollywood's last series of proletarian family appeal before the family was entirely forsaken for four letter words.
w Oscar Brodney *stories* Cid Ricketts Summer *d* Joseph Pevney *ph* Arthur E. Arling *m* Frank Skinner *md* Joseph Gershenson *ad* Bill Newberry, Richard H. Riedel *ed* Ted J. Kent
☆ Debbie Reynolds, Walter Brennan, Leslie Nielsen, Mala Powers, Fay Wray, Sidney Blackmer, Mildred Natwick
song 'Tammy' (m/ly Ray Evans, Jay Livingston)

Tammy and the Doctor
US 1963 88m Eastmancolor
U-I/Ross Hunter
Tammy leaves her riverboat to accompany an old lady who needs an operation in the big city.
More artless family fodder.
w Oscar Brodney *d* Harry Keller *ph* Russell Metty *m* Frank Skinner *ad* Alexander Golitzen, George Webb *ed* Milton Carruth
☆ Sandra Dee, Peter Fonda, Macdonald Carey, Beulah Bondi, Margaret Lindsay, Reginald Owen, Adam West
'The aura of simple religion and naïve philosophy remains singularly charmless.' – *MFB*

Tammy Tell Me True
US 1961 97m Eastmancolor
U-I (Ross Hunter)
Tammy gets a college education and charms all comers.
Sugar-coated sequel to the original.
w Oscar Brodney *d* Harry Keller *ph* Clifford Stine *m* Percy Faith
☆ Sandra Dee, John Gavin, Charles Drake, Virginia Grey, *Beulah Bondi,* Julia Meade, Cecil Kellaway, Edgar Buchanan
'The heroine appears to be not so much old-fashioned as positively retarded.' – *MFB*

Tampopo **
Japan 1986 117m colour Panavision
Itami Productions/New Century Producers (Juzo Itami, Yashushi Tamaoki, Seigo Hosogoe)
Encouraged by a truck driver, a woman learns to become the best of noodle cooks.
Witty, affectionate, episodic celebration of food as nourishment, pleasure and aid to sexual enjoyment, contained within a parody of film genres, notably the Western.
wd Juzo Itami *ph* Masaki Tamura *m* Kinihiko Murai *ad* Takeo Kimura *ed* Akira Suzuki
☆ Tsutomu Yamazaki, Nobuko Miyamoto, Koji Yakuso, Ken Watanabe, Rikiya Yasouka

Tanganyika
US 1954 81m Technicolor
Universal-International
A 1900 settler finds that the African colony of his choice is terrorized by a murderer.
Curious blend of outdoor action and who-is-it; not at all bad.
w Richard Alan Simmons and William Sackheim *d* André de Toth *ph* Maury Gertsman *m* Joseph Gershenson
☆ Van Heflin, Howard Duff, Ruth Roman, Jeff Morrow, Joe Comadaore

Tangier
US 1946 74m bw
Universal-International
A dancer hunts for the Nazi war criminal responsible for her father's death.
You can tell returns had been bad from the fact that the queen of Technicolor was sentenced to monochrome, and in a two-bit Casablanca.
w M. M. Musselman, Monty Collins *d* George Waggner
☆ Maria Montez, Kent Taylor, Robert Paige, Sabu, Preston Foster, Louise Albritton, Reginald Denny, J. Edward Bromberg

'A comedy that keeps women hopping.'
Tango ***
France 1993 90m colour
Cinea/Hachette Premiere/TF1/Zoulou (Henri Brichetti)
A woman-hating judge arranges the murder of his nephew's wife by a husband he acquitted of killing his wife and her lover.
An outrageous black comedy and a witty examination of masculine and feminine attitudes to life. Style, and sprightly acting, carry the day.
w Patrice Leconte, Patrick Dewolf *d* Patrice Leconte *ph* Eduardo Serra *m* Angelique and Jean-Claude Nachon *ad* Ivan Maussion *ed* Genevieve Winding
☆ *Philippe Noiret, Richard Bohringer,* Thierry Lhermitte, Miou Miou, Judith Godreche, Carole Bouquet, Jean Rochefort
'A deliciously dark comedy.' – *Variety*

Tango *
Argentina/Spain/France/Germany 1998 115m colour
Metrodome/Pandora/Sono/Alama Ata (Luis A. Scalella, Carlos L. Mentasti, Juan C. Codazzi)
A theatre director, rehearsing his new show about the tango, begins to fall for the girlfriend of his backer, who becomes the star of the musical.

More a dance drama than a straightforward narrative, this combines reality and performance, rehearsal with documentary; it's a beguiling mix for the most part.
wd Carlos Saura *ph* Vittorio Storaro *m* Lalo Schifrin *ad* Emilio Basaldua *ed* Julia Juaniz
☆ Miguel Angel Sola (Mario Suarez), Cecilia Narova (Laura Fuentes), Mia Maestro (Elena Flores), Juan Carlos Copes (Carlos Nebbia), Carlos Rivarola (Ernesto Landi), Sandra Ballesteros (Maria Elman), Oscar Cardoza Ocampo (Daniel Stein), Martin Seefeld (Andres Castro)

'A film with plenty of sole but not much soul.' – *Empire*

foreign language film

Tango & Cash
US 1989 101m Technicolor Panavision
Warner/Jon Peters, Peter Guber

Two cops, one suave, the other dishevelled, are jailed on a false murder charge but escape to get their revenge.
Deliberately stylized, over-the-top action movie that never touches reality at any point and provides some unintentional amusement.
w Randy Feldman *d* Andrei Konchalovsky *ph* Donald E. Thorin *m* Harold Faltermeyer *pd* J. Michael Riva *ed* Hubert de La Bouillerie, Robert Ferretti
☆ Sylvester Stallone, Kurt Russell, Jack Palance, Teri Hatcher, Michael J. Pollard, Brion James, Geoffrey Lewis, James Hong, Robert Z'Dar

The Tango Lesson
GB/France/Argentina/Japan/Germany 1997 102m bw/colour
Artificial Eye/Adventure/OKCK/PIE/MDF/Imagica/Pandora/Cinema Projects/Sigma (Christopher Sheppard)

A British film director becomes obsessed with the tango and takes lessons from an Argentinian expert, but insists that she become the lead dancer.
A playful film about dance, which blurs the line between fact and fiction; ultimately, it means more to its director and star than to any audience.
wd Sally Potter *ph* Robby Müller *m* Sally Potter, Fred Frith *ch* Pablo Veron *pd* Carlos Conti *ed* Harvé Schneid
☆ Sally Potter, Pablo Veron, Gustavo Naveira, Fabian Salas, David Toole, Carolina Lotti

'In one and the same film, she's revived the Hollywood musical and taken by storm a tenaciously protected male citadel of the dance world.' – *Alexander Walker, London Evening Standard*
'A monumentally humourless, self-regarding picture.' – *Philip French, Observer*

Tank
US 1984 113m Metrocolor
Lorimar/Universal (Irwin Yablans)

A retired army sergeant lovingly restores an old tank and uses it to secure justice for his wrongly imprisoned son.
Fairly lively if predictable American fantasy in which one just man stands up against the uncaring and/or corrupt mob.
w Dan Gordon *d* Marvin Chomsky *ph* Don Birnkrant *m* Lalo Schifrin *pd* Bill Kenney
☆ James Garner, Shirley Jones, C. Thomas Howell, Mark Herrier, Dorian Harewood, G. D. Spradlin

'Further dispiriting evidence of the new reactionary spirit of Reagan's America.' – *Tom Milne, MFB*

Tank Commando: see *Tank Commandos*

Tank Commandos
US 1959 79m bw
AIP (Burt Topper)
GB title: *Tank Commando*
In Italy in 1944, a US Army demolition unit destroy an underwater bridge to prevent the Germans reinforcing their troops.
Low-budget war movie that tries for both sentimentality and melodrama and misses its targets; its death-roll is high but uninvolving because its characters never come to life.
wd Burt Topper *ph* John Nickolaus Jnr *m* Ronald Stein *ad* Dan Haller *ed* Ronald Sinclair, Asa Clark
☆ Donato Farretta, Robert Barron, Maggie Lawrence, Wally Campo, Leo V. Metranga, Jack Sowards, Anthony Rich, Larry Hudson, Maria Monay

'In 2033, justice rides a tank and wears lip gloss.'
Tank Girl
US 1994 104m DeLuxe
United Artists/Trilogy (Richard B. Lewis, Pen Densham, John Watson)

In the future, when the world has been devastated by collision with a comet and there is a continuous drought, Tank Girl, with the aid of mutant dogs and kangaroos, battles against a madman trying to monopolize the water supplies.
A muddled attempt to transfer the British comic strip by Alan Martin and Jamie Hewlett to the screen. It is all flash and no substance or narrative, lacking in imagination and presenting a future that is more familiar than most pasts; brief cartoon interludes suggest that an animated approach might have been more successful.
w Tedi Sarafian *d* Rachel Talalay *ph* Gale Tattersall *m* Graeme Revell *pd* Catherine Hardwicke *ed* James R. Symons
☆ Lori Petty, Ice T, Naomi Watts, Don Harvey, Reg E. Cathey, Scott Coffey, Malcolm McDowell, Jeff Kober

'It is not a movie, really, but a rock soundtrack with a bit of plot hanging on for dear life.' – *Tom Shone, Sunday Times*
'If Tank Girl were real she would have shot everyone rather than let this be released in her name.' – *Leslie Felperin*
'The script left much to be desired – like a plot.' – *Malcolm McDowell*

† The title role was originally to have been played by Emily Lloyd.

Tank Malling
GB 1988 109m Metrocolor
Cineplex/Parkfield Pictures/Pointlane Films (Glen Murphy, Jamie Foreman)
An investigative reporter is framed for murder.
Trivial thriller with a confusing plot and a silly denouement.
w James Marcus, Mick Southworth *d* James Marcus *ph* Jason Lehel *m* Rick Fenn, Nick Mason *pd* Geoffrey Sharpe, Chris Cook *ed* Brian Peachey
☆ Ray Winstone, Jason Connery, Amanda Donohoe, Glen Murphy, Marsha Hunt, Peter Wyngarde, John Conteh, Terry Marsh, Nick Berry

The Tanks Are Coming
US 1951 90m bw
Warner
A tough sergeant learns humility during the race to Berlin.
Tedious war drama which tries in vain to interest us in non-characters.
w Robert Hardy Andrews *story* Samuel Fuller *d* D. Ross Lederman, Lewis Seiler *ph* Edwin DuPar *m* William Lava
☆ Steve Cochran, Paul Picerni, Mari Aldon, Harry Bellaver, Philip Carey

'This Guy Knows What Women *Really* Want!'
The Tao of Steve
US 2000 88m Technicolor
Entertainment/Good Machine/Thunderhead (Anthony Bregman)

An overweight teacher with seductive gifts falls for an old classmate.
Amiable, slender romantic comedy, though its charm soon evaporates.
w Duncan North, Greer Goodman, Jenniphr Goodman *d* Jenniphr Goodman *ph* Teodoro Maniaci *m* Joe Delia *pd* Rosario Provenza *ed* Sarah Gartner
☆ Donal Logue (Dex), Greer Goodman (Syd), Kimo Wills (Dave), David Aaron Baker (Rick), Nina Jaroslaw (Maggie), Ayelet Kaznelson (Beth), John Hines (Ed)

'A wish-fulfilment fantasy for slobs.' – *James Christopher, Times*
'This perfectly agreeable and straightforward picture sparks a goodly number of laughs.' – *Todd McCarthy, Variety*

Tap *
US 1989 101m Technicolor Panavision
Braveworld/Fox/Morgan Creek/BECO (Tony Adams)

A tap-dancer turned jewel-thief is persuaded to put on his dancing shoes again.
Its slight narrative is bolstered by an enjoyable celebration of the dying art of tap.
wd Nick Castle *ph* David Gribble *m* James Newton Howard *pd* Patricia Norris *ed* Patrick Kennedy
☆ Gregory Hines, Suzzanne Douglas, Sammy Davis Jnr, Savion Glover, Joe Morton, Dick Anthony Williams, Sandman Sims, Bunny Briggs, Steve Condos

Tap Roots
US 1948 109m Technicolor
Universal-International (Walter Wanger)
A Southern family tries to remain neutral in the Civil War.
Minor Gone with the Wind *saga, quite expensively produced but not very exciting.*
w Alan le May *novel* James Street *d* George Marshall *ph* Winton C. Hoch, Lionel Lindon *m* Frank Skinner
☆ Susan Hayward, Van Heflin, Boris Karloff, Julie London, Whitfield Connor

Tape *
US 2001 86m colour
InDigEntTape Prods (Gary Winick, Alexis Alexanian, Anne Walker-McBay)

In a motel room, a film director is confronted by an old high school friend over his treatment of a girl they both dated ten years previously.
A videotaped play that does not quite become cinematic, despite Linklater's ever-mobile camera, but registers through strong performances.
w Stephen Belber *play* Stephen Belber *d* Richard Linklater *ph* Maryse Alberti *pd* Stephen J. Beatrice *ed* Sandra Adair
☆ Ethan Hawke (Vince), Robert Sean Leonard (Johnny), Uma Thurman (Amy)

'Picture a typical student film with its arty angles, bad lighting and pretentious observations.' – *Rita Kempley, Washington Post*
'Made me believe that its events could happen to real people more or less as they appear on the screen, and that is its most difficult accomplishment.' – *Roger Ebert, Chicago Sun-Times*

Taps
US 1981 126m DeLuxe
TCF/Stanley Jaffe

Cadets at a military academy go on strike when the site is sold for development, and violence ensues.
Rather uninteresting moral fable, comparable with the British If. *The moral attitudes are worked out on entirely predictable lines.*
w Darryl Ponicsan, Robert Mark Kamen *novel Father Sky* by Devery Freeman *d* Harold Becker *ph* Owen Roizman *m* Maurice Jarre
☆ Timothy Hutton, George C. Scott, Ronny Cox, Sean Penn, Tom Cruise, Brendan Ward

'Even science was stunned!'
Tarantula
US 1955 80m bw
U-I (William Alland)

Scientists working on an artificial food become grossly misshapen, and an infected spider escapes and grows to giant size.
Moderate monster hokum with the desert setting which became a cliché; the grotesque faces are more horrific than the spider, which seldom seems to touch the ground.
w Robert M. Fresco, Martin Berkeley *d* Jack Arnold *ph* George Robinson *md* Joseph Gershenson
☆ Leo G. Carroll, John Agar, Mara Corday, Nestor Paiva

'It's a great children's picture ... particularly for bad children. It'll scare hell out of the little monsters.' – *Hollywood Reporter*

'Now! add a motion picture to the wonders of the world!'
Taras Bulba *
US 1962 124m Eastmancolor Panavision
UA/H-H/Avala (Harold Hecht)

A Cossack leader has bitter disagreements with his rebellious son.
Violent action epic based on a well-worn story; plenty of spectacular highlights.
w Waldo Salt, Karl Tunberg *novel* Nicolai Gogol *d* J. Lee-Thompson *ph* Joe MacDonald *m* Franz Waxman *pd* Edward Carrere
☆ Yul Brynner, Tony Curtis, Christine Kaufmann, Sam Wanamaker, Guy Rolfe, George Macready, Vladimir Sokoloff, Abraham Sofaer

Franz Waxman

La Tarea
Mexico 1990 85m colour
Metro/Clasa Films Mundiales (Pablo Barbachano, Francisco Barbachano)

aka: *Homework*
A husband and wife indulge in a sexual fantasy with the aid of a video camera.
Curiously uninvolving, voyeuristic movie that fails to illuminate its theme of sex in the cinema.
wd Jaime Humberto Hermosillo *ph* Toni Kuhn *m* Luis Arcaraz *ad* Laura Santa Cruz
☆ Maria Rojo, José Alonso, Xanic Zepeda, Christopher

Target
US 1985 117m Technicolor
CBS/Richard Zanuck, David Brown

When his wife is kidnapped, an ex-spy goes back into action.
Lethargic, simple-minded, and often ludicrous melodrama: the intent seems to be to pile up as many clichés of the genre as the writers can remember.
w Howard Berk, Don Petersen *d* Arthur Penn *ph* Jean Tournier *m* Michael Small
☆ Gene Hackman, Matt Dillon, Gayle Hunnicutt, Josef Sommer, Guy Boyd, Herbert Berghof

Target for Scandal: see *Washington Story*

Target for Tonight ****
GB 1941 48m bw
The Crown Film Unit

The story of a bombing raid over Germany.
Classic RAF semi-documentary, not quite so genuine as it seems since many scenes were re-created in the studio.
w Harry Watt, B. Cooper *d* Harry Watt

'It looks like a sure grosser ... one of the must-see films of 1941.' – *Variety*

Special AA

Target Harry
US 1969 81m colour
ABC/Corman Company (Gene Corman)

aka: *How to Make It*
Various criminals try to discover the whereabouts of printing plates for banknotes that have gone missing from the Royal Mint.
Low budget variation on The Maltese Falcon *with an uncharismatic cast. The director's name hides the identity of Roger Corman.*
w Bob Barbash *d* Henry Neill *ph* Patrice Pouget *m* Les Baxter *pd* Sharon Compton *ed* Monte Hellman
☆ Vic Morrow, Suzanne Pleshette, Victor Buono, Cesar Romero, Stanley Holloway, Charlotte Rampling, Michael Ansara, Katy Fraysse, Fikret Hakan

Target Zero
US 1955 93m bw
Warner (David Weisbart)
An infantry patrol in Korea is cut off behind enemy lines.
Routine battle exploits with a highly unlikely superimposed romance.
w Sam Rolfe *d* Harmon Jones *ph* Edwin DuPar *m* David Buttolph *ed* Clarence Kolster
☆ Richard Conte, Charles Bronson, Richard Stapley, Chuck Connors, L. Q. Jones, Peggie Castle

Targets *
US 1967 90m Pathécolor
Peter Bogdanovich (Paramount)

An elderly horror film star confronts and disarms a mad sniper at a drive-in movie.
Oddball melodrama apparently meant to contrast real and fantasy violence; it doesn't quite work despite effective moments, and the low budget shows.
wd Peter Bogdanovich *story* Polly Platt *ph* Laszlo Kovacs *pd* Polly Platt
☆ Boris Karloff, Tim O'Kelly, James Brown, Sandy Baron

The Tarnished Angels
US 1957 91m bw Cinemascope
U-I (Albert Zugsmith)
A reporter falls in with a self-torturing family of circus air aces.
Unsatisfactory attempt to reunite the talents of Written on the Wind; *a dull story, very boringly presented.*
w George Zuckerman *novel* Pylon by William Faulkner *d* Douglas Sirk *ph* Irving Glassberg *m* Frank Skinner *md* Joseph Gershenson
☆ Rock Hudson, Robert Stack, Dorothy Malone, Jack Carson, Robert Middleton

'Married to a man she doesn't love! Loving a man she can't have! What does life hold for this pampered beauty of the drawing rooms?'
Tarnished Lady
US 1931 80m bw
Paramount
Two society women and their lovers cross each other's paths.
Exaggerated melodrama which failed to justify the London stage reputation of its American star.
w Donald Ogden Stewart *d* George Cukor
☆ Tallulah Bankhead, Clive Brook, Phoebe Foster, Alexander Kirkland, Osgood Perkins, Elizabeth Patterson
'A poor picture that fits the straight grinds best. Heavy production but too ponderous to mean anything.' – *Variety*

Tars and Spars
US 1945 86m bw
Columbia (Milton H. Bren)
Adventures of members of the Coast Guard's touring wartime revue.
Limp musical with interesting talent.
w John Jacoby, Sarett Tobias, Decla Dunning, Barry Trivers *d* Alfred E. Green
☆ Alfred Drake, Sid Caesar, Janet Blair, Marc Platt, Jeff Donnell

The Tartars
Italy 1960 105m Technicolor Totalscope
Lux (Riccardo Gualino)
Viking settlers on the Russian steppes fight Tartar invaders.
Action-packed comic strip.
d Richard Thorpe *ph* Amerigo Genarelli *m* Renzo Rossellini
☆ Orson Welles, Victor Mature, Folco Lulli, Arnoldo Foa

Tartu: see *The Adventures of Tartu*

Tarzan

The talkie *Tarzans* (qv) began with Johnny Weissmuller and tailed off from there. (See *Filmgoer's Companion* for the silents.) The 1932 version more or less followed the original Edgar Rice Burroughs novel, and all the MGM entries had a special vivid quality about them, but subsequently the productions, usually produced under the aegis of Sol Lesser, tailed off towards the standard of the TV series of the sixties starring Ron Ely. In the 80s, John Derek revived the series as a vehicle for his wife, and Hugh Hudson promised to return to Burroughs's original, but merely added some intellectual pretension of his own. In 1998, Casper Van Dien tried unsuccessfully to make the role his own.
1929 Tarzan the Tiger
1932 Tarzan the Ape Man
1933 Tarzan the Fearless
1934 Tarzan and His Mate
1935 The New Adventures of Tarzan
1936 Tarzan Escapes
1938 Tarzan's Revenge; Tarzan and the Green Goddess
1939 Tarzan Finds a Son
1941 Tarzan's Secret Treasure
1942 Tarzan's New York Adventure
1943 Tarzan Triumphs; Tarzan's Desert Mystery
1945 Tarzan and the Amazons
1946 Tarzan and the Leopard Woman
1947 Tarzan and the Huntress
1948 Tarzan and the Mermaids
1949 Tarzan's Magic Fountain
1950 Tarzan and the Slave Girl
1951 Tarzan's Peril
1952 Tarzan's Savage Fury
1953 Tarzan and the She-Devil (aka: *Tarzan Meets the Vampire*)
1955 Tarzan's Hidden Jungle
1957 Tarzan and the Lost Safari
1958 Tarzan's Fight for Life
1959 Tarzan's Greatest Adventure
1959 Tarzan the Ape Man
1960 Tarzan the Magnificent
1962 Tarzan Goes to India
1963 Tarzan's Three Challenges
1966 Tarzan and the Valley of Gold
1967 Tarzan and the Great River
1968 Tarzan and the Jungle Boy
1981 Tarzan the Ape Man
1984 Greystoke: The Legend of Tarzan, Lord of the Apes
1998 Tarzan and the Lost City

Tarzan ***
US 1999 88m Technicolor
Buena Vista/Walt Disney (Bonnie Arnold)

An orphaned baby, adopted by a great ape, grows up to discover that he is human, and becomes king of the apes.
Clever, fast-moving animated adventure that keeps the songs in the background so that they don't hold up the action; it proves there is still plenty of life left in traditional methods of animation, though it also makes use of some exciting computer-generated effects.
w Tab Murphy, Bob Tzudiker, Noni White, David Reynolds, Jeffrey Stepakoff *story* Tarzan and the Apes by Edgar Rice Burroughs *d* Kevin Lima, Chris Buck *m* Mark Mancina *m/ly* Phil Collins *ad* Daniel St Pierre *ed* Gregory Perler
☆ Featuring voices: Tony Goldwyn, Minnie Driver, Glenn Close, Brian Blessed, Nigel Hawthorne, Lance Henriksen, Wayne Knight, Alex D. Linz, Rosie O'Donnell
'The emphasis here is on trad storytelling made wondrous, and it works.' – *Ian Nathan, Empire*
song 'You'll Be in My Heart' (m/ly Phil Collins)

Tarzan and His Mate *
US 1934 105m bw
MGM (Bernard H. Hyman)

Tarzan foils ivory poachers who are searching for the elephants' graveyard.
A slick adventure, for its time, with a carefree jungle couple and lots of lions and stampeding elephants.
w James K. McGuinness, Howard Emmett Rogers, Leon Gordon *story* Edgar Rice Burroughs *d* Cedric Gibbons *ph* Clyde DeVinna, Charles Clarke *ad* A. Arnold Gillespie *ed* Tom Held
☆ Johnny Weissmuller, Maureen O'Sullivan, Neil Hamilton, Paul Cavanagh, Forrester Harvey, William Stack
† Although Gibbons received the directorial credit, he was replaced early on by Jack Conway.
†† The Hays Office objected to the skimpy costume worn by O'Sullivan and the inference that she and Tarzan were not only living in the jungle, but also in sin. The later films turned her into a more respectable, all-American housewife with a tree-house to call home.

Tarzan and the Amazons
US 1945 76m bw
RKO/Champion (Sol Lesser)
Tarzan goes to the aid of a tribe of Amazons threatened by gold hunters, though at first they do not welcome his help.
A moderately well-done adventure, but beginning to show signs of tiredness and lack of invention.
w Hans Jacoby, Marjorie L. Pfaelzer *d* Kurt Neumann *ph* Archie Stout *md* Paul Sawtell *ad* Walter Koessler *ed* Robert O. Crandall
☆ Johnny Weissmuller, Brenda Joyce, Johnny Sheffield, Henry Stephenson, Maria Ouspenskaya, Barton MacLane, Don Douglas

Tarzan and the Great River
US/Switzerland 1967 88m
Eastmancolor Panavision
Paramount/Banner/Allfin (Sy Weintraub)
Tarzan tracks down the killers of his friend, a zoo director, with the aid of a lion and a chimpanzee.
Lacklustre adventure with an uncharismatic hero and, even by the standards of the series, stock characters and narrative.
w Bob Barbash, Lewis Reed *d* Robert Day *ph* Irving Lippman *m* William Loose *ad* Herbert Smith *ed* Anthony Carras, Edward Mann
☆ Mike Henry, Jan Murray, Manuel Padilla Jnr, Diana Millay, Rafer Johnson, Paulo Grazindo

Tarzan and the Green Goddess
US 1938 72m bw
Principal/Burroughs-Tarzan (George W. Stout, Ashton Dearholt, Edgar Rice Burroughs)

Tarzan travels to South America to ensure that a statue with strange powers is kept safe from thieves.
Dreary low-budget effort, with stilted acting and direction.
w Charles F. Royal *story* Edgar Rice Burroughs *d* Edward Kull *ph* Ernest F. Smith, Edward Kull *ad* Charles Clague *ed* Thomas Neff
☆ Herman Brix (Bruce Bennett), Ula Holt, Frank Baker, Dale Walsh, Harry Ernest, Don Castello, Lewis Sergent, Jiggs the Monkey

Tarzan and the Huntress
US 1947 72m bw
RKO (Sol Lesser)
Tarzan fights off hunters who are stealing animals to restock zoos.
Pleasant-enough time-waster, recycling familiar material with a modicum of enthusiasm.
w Jerry Gruskin, Rowland Lee *d* Kurt Neumann *ph* Archie Stout *m* Paul Sawtell *ad* McClure Capps *ed* Merrill White
☆ Johnny Weissmuller, Brenda Joyce, Johnny Sheffield, Patricia Morison, Barton MacLane, John Warburton, Cheta
† It was Johnny Sheffield's last appearance in the role of Tarzan's adopted son. Two years later, he went on to star in his own series of a dozen jungle films, as Bomba the Jungle Boy (qv).

Tarzan and the Jungle Boy
US/Switzerland 1968 90m
Eastmancolor Panavision
Paramount/Banner/Allfin (Robert Day)
Tarzan helps a journalist search for a young boy lost in the jungle seven years earlier.
A dull entry in the series, with not much action and a great deal of muscle flexing.
w Stephen Lord *d* Robert Gordon *ph* Ozen Sermet *m* William Loose *ad* Herbert Smith *ed* Milton Mann, Reg Browne
☆ Mike Henry, Alizia Gur, Ronald Gans, Rafer Johnson, Ed Johnson, Steven Bond

Tarzan and the Jungle Queen: see *Tarzan's Peril*

Tarzan and the Leopard Woman
US 1946 72m bw
RKO (Sol Lesser)
Investigating a massacre, apparently by leopards, Tarzan discovers a sinister tribe ruled by a pitiless queen.
Enjoyable hokum with camp overtones, though by this date it looked as though it was becoming increasingly difficult for Weissmuller to swing through the trees.

☆ Johnny Weissmuller, Johnny Sheffield, Brenda Joyce, Acquanetta, Edgar Barrier, Tommy Cook, Dennis Hoey

Tarzan and the Lost City
US 1998 84m Technicolor
Warner (Stanley Canter, Dieter Geissler, Michael Lake)

Tarzan abandons his wedding plans to stop an evil explorer, who is destroying the jungle and its inhabitants in a search for the city where civilization began.
Lacklustre attempt to revive the fortunes of the Ape-man, suffering from a bland hero, no imagination in the narrative or direction and no confidence in the source material.
w Bayard Johnson, J. Anderson Black *stories* Edgar Rice Burroughs *d* Carl Schenkel *ph* Paul Gilpin *m* Christopher Franke *pd* Herbert Pinter *ed* Harry Hitner
☆ Caspar Van Dien (Tarzan), Jane March (Jane), Steven Waddington (Ravens), Winston Ntshona (Mugambi), Rapulana Seiphemo (Kaya), Ian Roberts (Captain Dooley), Sean Taylor (Wilkes), Schiller (Gys De Villers)
'Comes across more like a sequel to *George of the Jungle*, but without the laughs.' – *Variety*

Tarzan and the Lost Safari
GB 1957 84m Technicolor Cinemascope
MGM/Sol Lesser (John Croydon)
Tarzan rescues the survivors of a plane crash who are threatened by a ruthless white hunter.
Effective adventure that gained from being shot on location and in colour.
w Montgomery Pittman, Lillie Hayward *d* H. Bruce Humberstone *ph* C. R. Pennington-Richards *m* Clifton Parker *ad* Geoffrey Drake *ed* William Lewthwaite
☆ Gordon Scott, Robert Beatty, Yolande Donlan, Betta St John, Wilfrid Hyde-White, George Colouris, Peter Arne, Cheta
† It was the first Tarzan movie to be shot on African locations.

Tarzan and the Mermaids
US 1948 68m bw
RKO (Sol Lesser)
Tarzan goes to the aid of a pearl diver, one of a tribe threatened by a ruthless white trader.
Lively adventure that includes a fight with an octopus and gains from the expertise of Draper and Tiomkin.
w Carroll Young *d* Robert Florey *ph* Jack Draper *md* Dimitri Tiomkin *ad* McClure Capps *ed* Merrill White
☆ Johnny Weissmuller, Brenda Joyce, Linda Christian, John Lanenz, Fernando Wagner, Edward Ashley, George Zucco
† It was Weissmuller's final appearance in the role of Tarzan, though he stayed in the jungle to make 16 low-budget movies as the white hunter Jungle Jim (qv), which he followed with a 26-episode TV series.

Tarzan and the She-Devil
US 1953 76m bw
RKO (Sol Lesser)
Tarzan is taken prisoner by ivory hunters.
A cheap and cheerless movie, with little action and much talk, incorporating stock footage.
w Karl Lamb, Carroll Young *d* Kurt Neumann *ph* Karl Struss *md* Paul Sawtell *ad* Carroll Clark *ed* Leon Barsha
☆ Lex Barker, Joyce MacKenzie, Monique Van Vooren, Raymond Burr, Tom Conway, Robert Bice, Mike Ross, Cheta

Tarzan and the Slave Girl
US 1950 73m bw
RKO (Sol Lesser)
Tarzan rescues Jane from kidnap by a tribe whose women have died in an epidemic.
An unexciting adventure, in which the chimp steals the movie from his uninvolved co-stars.
w Hans Jacoby, Arnold Belgard *d* Lee Sholem *ph* Russell Harlan *md* Paul Sawtell *ad* Harry Horner *ed* Christian Nyby
☆ Lex Barker, Vanessa Brown, Robert Alda, Hurd Hatfield, Arthur Shields, Tony Caruso, Denise Darcel, Robert Warwick, Cheta

Tarzan and the Trappers
US 1958 74m colour
Sol Lesser

Tarzan fights to save jungle creatures from ruthless trappers and treasure hunters.
Standard, undistinguished stuff, cut down from three episodes of an unsuccessful TV series.
w Frederick Schlick, Robert Leach *d* Charles Haas, Sandy Howard, H. Bruce Humberstone (uncredited) *ph* William Snyder, Alan Stensvold *md* Audrey Granville *ad* Ernst Fegte *ed* George A. Gittens
☆ Gordon Scott, Eve Brent, Rickie Sorenson, Leslie Bradley, Maurice Marsac, William Keene, Scatman Crothers

Tarzan and the Valley of Gold

US/Switzerland 1966 90m Eastmancolor Panavision
AIP/Banner/Allfin (Sy Weintraub)

Tarzan stops a ruthless crook stealing the treasure from a lost Aztec city.
Dull action with an earnest hero and little else to get excited about.
w Clair Huffaker *d* Robert Day *ph* Irving Lippman *m* Van Alexander *ad* José Rodriguez Granada *ed* Frank P. Keller
☆ Mike Henry, David Opatoshu, Manuel Padilla Jnr, Nancy Kovack, Don Megowan, Frank Brandstetter, Eduardo Noriega
† It was the first of Mike Henry's three movies as Tarzan.

Tarzan Escapes

US 1936 95m bw
MGM (Sam Zimbalist)

Tarzan is captured by a white hunter, who plans to exhibit him in Britain.
The ape-man is beginning to be tamed into a more suburban way of life in this third outing, with much of the excitement and fun missing.
w Cyril Hume, John Farrow, Karl Brown *d* Richard Thorpe *ph* Leonard Smith *ad* E. E. Sheeley *ed* W. Donn Hayes
☆ Johnny Weissmuller, Maureen O'Sullivan, John Buckler, Benita Hume, William Henry, E. E. Clive, Cheta
† Nearly all the film was reshot after lukewarm audience reaction at previews.

Tarzan Finds a Son!

US 1939 90m bw
MGM (Sam Zimbalist)

Tarzan and Jane rescue and adopt a small boy, who is the only survivor of a plane crash.
The arrival of a five-year-old boy emphasizes that the series was being redirected towards juvenile audiences; on that level, it is moderately entertaining.
w Cyril Hume *d* Richard Thorpe *ph* Leonard Smith *ad* Cedric Gibbons, Urie McCleary *ed* Frank Sullivan, Gene Ruggiero
☆ Johnny Weissmuller, Maureen O'Sullivan, John Sheffield, Ian Hunter, Henry Stephenson, Frieda Inescort, Henry Wilcoxon
† The original script had O'Sullivan, who wanted to leave the series, dying; but Burroughs refused to allow his character to be killed off.

Tarzan Goes to India

US/GB/Switzerland 1962 86m Metrocolor Cinemascope
MGM/Banner/Allfin (Sy Weintraub)

Tarzan rescues a herd of elephants from floods caused by a new dam.
In an attempt to inject a little life into the series, the locale was shifted to India, but the result was no more than a cheap imitation of Elephant Boy.
w Robert Hardy Andrews, John Guillermin *d* John Guillermin *ph* Paul Beeson *m* Ken Jones, Ravi Shankar, Panchal Jaikishan *ad* George Provis *ed* Max Benedict
☆ Jock Mahoney, Mark Dana, Leo Gordon, Simi, Feroz Khan, Murad, Jai, Gajendra (King of the Elephants)

Tarzan the Ape Man **

US 1932 99m bw
MGM

Tarzan, Lord of the Jungle, falls in love with Jane, an American girl who is searching for the fabled elephants' graveyard with her explorer father.
The first sound version of Tarzan and still the best, despite its lack of sophistication; it is a tightly edited, action-packed adventure that retains its freshness and fantasy appeal.
w Cyril Hume, Ivor Novello *novel* Edgar Rice Burroughs *d* W. S. Van Dyke *ph* Harold Rosson, Clyde DeVinna *ad* Cedric Gibbons *ed* Ben Lewis, Tom Held
☆ Johnny Weissmuller, Neil Hamilton, Maureen O'Sullivan, C. Aubrey Smith, Doris Lloyd, Forrester Harvey, Ivory Williams
† Burroughs was paid $40,000 for the rights, though MGM were prepared to go to $100,000.
†† Hume named two of the jungle tribes Jocohnnies, after Joe Cohn, head of the production department, and Gibbonies, after Cedric Gibbons.
††† Tarzan's famous yell, heard for the first time in this movie, was created by Douglas Shearer using a combination of electronic methods and Weissmuller's shout played backwards.

Tarzan the Ape Man

US 1959 82m Technicolor
MGM (Al Zimbalist)

A white hunter and his daughter discover a man raised by apes living in the African jungle.
Dire remake of the original film, incorporating tinted footage from it and earlier films.
w Robert Hill *story* Edgar Rice Burroughs *d* Joseph Newman *ph* Paul C. Vogel *m* S. Rogers *ad* Hans Peters, Malcolm Brown *ed* Gene Ruggiero
☆ Denny Miller, Joanna Barnes, Cesare Danova, Robert Douglas, Thomas Yangha

'The most exciting pair in the jungle!'

Tarzan the Ape Man

US 1981 112m Metrocolor
MGM/Svengali (Bo Derek)

A young woman goes to Africa in search of her lost father, an explorer, and also finds Tarzan.
Tedium in the jungle: Derek simpers and prepares herself for wet T-shirt competitions, Harris rants and roars, O'Keeffe looks confused, and the result is certainly the worst of the Tarzan movies and possibly the most banal film so far made; even the animals give poor performances.
w Tom Rowe, Gary Goddard *novel* Edgar Rice Burroughs *d* John Derek *ph* John Derek, Wolfgang Dickmann *ad* Alan Roderick-Jones *ed* James B. Ling
☆ Bo Derek, Miles O'Keeffe (Tarzan), Richard Harris, John Phillip Law, Wilfrid Hyde-White, Akushula Selayah, Steven Strong

'The only apparent rationale of John Derek's resolutely sexist treatment of the old yarn is a besotted desire to celebrate his wife's physical attributes in various exotic settings and erotic costumes.' – *Martyn Auty, MFB*

Tarzan the Fearless

US 1933 61m bw
Principal (Sol Lesser)

Tarzan does battle with the worshippers of the jungle god Zar, in order to reunite a woman with her father.
A cheap and undistinguished rival to MGM's superior series, edited from the first four episodes of a 12-part serial.
w Basil Dickey, George Plympton *d* Robert Hill *ph* Harry Neumann, Joseph Brotherton *md* Abe Meyer *ed* Carl Himm
☆ Buster Crabbe, Jacqueline Wells, E. Alyn Warren, Edward Woods, Philo McCullough, Matthew Betz, Frank Lackteen, Mischa Auer

Tarzan the Magnificent

US 1960 88m Technicolor
Paramount/Solar (Sy Weintraub)

Tarzan escorts a criminal through the jungle to justice.
Tedious entry in a series that had run out of ideas and imagination; it might have been better had they gone back to Burroughs's original books for inspiration.
w Berne Giler, Robert Day *d* Robert Day *ph* Ted Scaife *m* Ken Jones *ad* Ray Simm *ed* Bert Rule
☆ Gordon Scott, Jock Mahoney, Betta St John, John Carradine, Lionel Jeffries, Alexandra Stewart, Carl Cameron, Charles Tingwell, Al Mulock
† It was Scott's last movie as Tarzan. He was replaced by Mahoney, who, confusingly, plays the villain here.

Tarzan the Tiger

US 1929 bw serial: 10 eps
Universal

Tarzan rescues Jane from slave traders.
Primitive talkie serial.
d Henry McRae
☆ Frank Merrill, Natalie Kingston, Lillian Worth, Al Ferguson

Tarzan Triumphs

US 1943 78m bw
RKO (Sol Lesser)

Tarzan defends the princess of a jungle city from attacking Germans.
Tarzan joins in the war effort in this very ordinary flag-waver.
w Carroll Young, Roy Chanslor *d* William Thiele *ph* Harry Wild *md* Paul Sawtell *pd* Harry Horner *ed* Hal Kern
☆ Johnny Weissmuller, Johnny Sheffield, Frances Gifford, Stanley Ridges, Sig Rumann, Pedro de Cordoba, Cheta

Tarzan's Deadly Silence

US 1970 88m colour
National General (Leon Benson)

Tarzan is faced by a mad colonel.
Edited from the TV series starring Ely, this is dull and uninspired stuff.
w Lee Erwin, Jack A. Robinson, John Considine, Tim Considine *d* Robert L. Friend, Lawrence Dobkin *ph* Abraham Vialla *m* Walter Greene *ed* Gabriel Torres
☆ Ron Ely, Manuel Padilla Jnr, Jock Mahoney, Woody Strode, Gregorio Acosta, Rudolph Charles, Nichelle Nichols

Tarzan's Desert Mystery

US 1943 70m bw
RKO/Principal (Sol Lesser)

Tarzan battles in the Sahara desert against Nazis, Arabs and giant spiders.
One of the more unusual films in the series: a delirious, incident-packed fantasy that made little sense, but provided unexpected thrills.
w Edward T. Lowe *story* Carroll Young *d* William Thiele *ph* Harry Wild, Russ Harlan *m* Paul Sawtell *md* C. Bakaleinikoff *ad* Hans Peters *ed* Ray Lockert
☆ Johnny Weissmuller, Johnny Sheffield, Nancy Kelly, Otto Kruger, Joe Sawyer, Robert Lowery

Tarzan's Fight for Life

US 1958 86m Metrocolor
MGM (Sol Lesser)

Tarzan comes to the aid of a medical man threatened by the power of a witch doctor.
Cheap and dreadful studio-bound movie, lacking any sort of excitement.
w Thomas Hal Phillips *d* H. Bruce Humberstone *ph* William Snyder *m* Ernest Gold *ad* Ernst Fegte *ed* Aaron Stell
☆ Gordon Scott, Eve Brent, James Edwards, Carl Benton Reid, Woody Strode, Rickie Sorensen, Cheta

Tarzan's Greatest Adventure

GB 1959 85m Eastmancolor
Paramount/Solar (Sy Weintraub, Harvey Hayutin)

Tarzan pursues a ruthless boatload of killers who are in search of a diamond mine.
Brisk action-packed drama, with an effective mix of animals, explosions, villains and a little romance.
w Berne Giler, John Guillermin *story* Les Crutchfield *d* John Guillermin *ph* Ted Scaife *m* Douglas Gamley *ad* Michael Stringer *ed* Bert Rule
☆ Gordon Scott, Anthony Quayle, Sara Shane, Sean Connery, Niall MacGinnis, Scilla Gabel, Al Mulock

Tarzan's Hidden Jungle

US 1955 73m bw
RKO (Sol Lesser)

Tarzan saves the animals of the jungle from a ruthless hunter.
Moderate adventure that marked the advent of Scott in the title role.
w William Lively *d* Harold Schuster *ph* William Whitley *m* Paul Sawtell *ad* William Flannery *ed* Leon Barsha
☆ Gordon Scott, Vera Miles, Peter Van Eyck, Don Beddoe, Jester Hairston, Rex Ingram, Jack Elam, Cheta

Tarzan's Jungle Rebellion

US 1967 92m colour
National General (Steve Shagan)

Tarzan protects archaeologists who are investigating a burial ground from a hostile tribe.
Dreary little movie, cobbled together from episodes of a TV series.
w Jackson Gillis *d* William Whitney *ph* Abraham Vialla *m* Nelson Riddle *ad* José Rodriguez Granada *ed* Renn Reynolds
☆ Ron Ely, Manuel Padilla Jnr, Ulla Stromstedt, Sam Jaffe, William Marshall, Harry Lauter, Jason Evers

Tarzan's Magic Fountain *

US 1949 73m bw
RKO (Sol Lesser)

Tarzan protects a fountain of youth from raiders.
Lively adventure in the footsteps of She and Lost Horizon.
w Curt Siodmak, Harry Chandlee *d* Lee Sholem *ph* Karl Struss *m* Alexander Laszlo *ad* McClure Capps *ed* Merrill White
☆ Lex Barker, Brenda Joyce, Evelyn Ankers, Albert Dekker, Charles Drake, Alan Napier, Henry Kulky

Tarzan's New York Adventure

US 1942 71m bw
MGM (Frederick Stephani)

Tarzan and Jane go to Manhattan to rescue their kidnapped son.
A little amusement is gained from the culture clash of Tarzan in an urban jungle, but one misses animals.
w Myles Connolly, William R. Lipman *d* Richard Thorpe *ph* Sidney Wagner *md* David Snell *ad* Cedric Gibbons *ed* Gene Ruggiero
☆ Johnny Weissmuller, Maureen O'Sullivan, Johnny Sheffield, Virginia Grey, Charles Bickford, Paul Kelly, Chill Wills, Russell Hicks, Mantan Moreland, Elmo Lincoln
† The urban jungle also served as a setting for *Tarzan in Manhattan*, starring Joe Ely, which was a pilot made in 1989 for a TV series that never materialized.

Tarzan's Peril

US 1951 79m bw
RKO (Sol Lesser)
GB title: *Tarzan and the Jungle Queen*

Tarzan goes to the rescue of Jane and an embattled princess when gunrunners stir up a jungle war.
Standard stuff that gained from being filmed on location in Africa.
w Samuel Newman, Francis Swann, John Cousins *d* Byron Haskin *ph* Karl Struss *m* Michel Michelet *ad* John Meehan *ed* Jack Murray
☆ Lex Barker, Virginia Huston, George Macready, Douglas Fowley, Glen Anders, Frederick O'Neal, Dorothy Dandridge, Alan Napier

Tarzan's Revenge

US 1938 70m bw
TCF/Principal (Sol Lesser)

Tarzan rescues a woman captured by a jungle ruler.
A minor movie with an absentee hero, as the movie concentrates on the plight of champion swimmer Eleanor Holm.
w Robert Lee Johnston, Jay Vann *story* Edgar Rice Burroughs *d* D. Ross Leterman *ph* George Meehan *m* Hugo Riesenfeld *ad* Lewis J. Rachmil *ed* Gene Milford
☆ Glenn Morris, Eleanor Holm, C. Henry Gordon, Hedda Hopper, George Meeker, Corbet Morris
† Glenn Morris was the 1936 Olympic decathlon champion. It was his only appearance in the role, acting not being among his talents.

Tarzan's Savage Fury

US 1952 80m bw
RKO/Principal (Sol Lesser)

Tarzan goes into action against crocodile and diamond hunters who threaten the lives of a boy and a local tribe.
Tame episode in the series, with a feeble script and little energy in the acting.
w Cyril Hume, Hans Jacoby, Shirley White *d* Cy Endfield *ph* Karl Struss *m* Paul Sawtell *ad* Walter Keller *ed* Frank Sullivan
☆ Lex Barker, Dorothy Hart, Patric Knowles, Charles Korvin, Tommy Carlton

Tarzan's Secret Treasure

US 1941 81m bw
MGM (B. P. Fineman)

Tarzan goes to the rescue of his son, who has been kidnapped by a tribe who want to sacrifice the boy.
Enjoyable adventure that manages some suspense and excitement, if beginning to lose much of the rough magic the series possessed in its earlier days.
w Myles Connolly, Paul Gangelin *d* Richard Thorpe *ph* Clyde de Vinna *m* David Snell *ad* Cedric Gibbons *ed* Gene Ruggiero

☆ Johnny Weissmuller, Maureen O'Sullivan, John Sheffield, Reginald Owen, Barry Fitzgerald, Tom Conway, Philip Dorn, Cordell Hickman, Cheta

Tarzan's Three Challenges
US 1963 92m Metrocolor
MGM/Sy Weintraub
Tarzan escorts the heir to the Thai throne across country to protect him from his wicked uncle.
An exotic location and a slick script gave a little fresh impetus to the series.
w Berne Giler, Robert Day *d* Robert Day *ph* Ted Scaife *m* Joseph Horovitz *ad* Wilfrid Shingleton *ed* Fred Burnley
☆ Jock Mahoney, Woody Strode, Earl Cameron, Tsuruko Kobayashi, Jimmy Jamal
† Mahoney was unwell during shooting.

'It's that rare kind of movie that lights the spark that lights the heart!'
Task Force
US 1949 116m bw (Technicolor sequences)
Warner (Jerry Wald)
An admiral about to retire recalls his struggle to promote the cause of aircraft carriers.
Stilted and long-drawn-out flagwaver with too much chat and action highlights borrowed from wartime newsreel.
wd Delmer Daves *ph* Robert Burks, Wilfrid M. Cline *m* Franz Waxman
☆ Gary Cooper, Walter Brennan, Jane Wyatt, Wayne Morris, Julie London, Bruce Bennett, Stanley Ridges, Jack Holt

A Taste of Cherry **
Iran 1997 98m colour
Artificial Eye/Abbas Kiarostami
original title: *Ta'm e Guilass*
In Tehran, a middle-aged man, who plans to kill himself, seeks someone to bury him.
A teasing meditation on death and the simpler joys of life, told in a series of episodic meetings that never reach a conclusion; what matters is the journey, not the destination.
wd Abbas Kiarostami *ph* Homayon Payvar *ad* Hassan Yekta Panah *ed* Abbas Kiarostami
☆ Homayon Ershadi, Abdol Hossain Bagheri
'Filmed with the piercing intensity of a parable.' – *Variety*

A Taste of Excitement
GB 1968 99m Eastmancolor
Trio Films (George Willoughby)
An English girl holidaying on the Riviera suspects that someone is trying to kill her.
Standard frightened lady/'they won't believe me' mystery with enough twists to satisfy addicts.
w Brian Carton, Don Sharp *novel* *Waiting for a Tiger* by Ben Healey *d* Don Sharp *ph* Paul Beeson *m* Keith Mansfield
☆ Eva Renzi, David Buck, Peter Vaughan, Sophie Hardy, Paul Hubschmid, Kay Walsh

Taste of Fear **
GB 1961 82m bw
Columbia/Hammer (Jimmy Sangster)
US title: *Scream of Fear*
A crippled heiress visits her long-lost father and is haunted by his corpse.
Smartly tricked-out sub-Hitchcock screamer with sudden shocks among the Riviera settings and a plot which Hammer borrowed from Les Diaboliques *and used again and again.*
w Jimmy Sangster *d* Seth Holt *ph* Douglas Slocombe *m* Clifton Parker *ad* Tom Goswell *ed* James Needs, Eric Boyd Perkins
☆ Susan Strasberg, Ann Todd, Ronald Lewis, Christopher Lee, Leonard Sachs
'All those creaking shutters, flickering candles, wavering shadows and pianos playing in empty rooms still yield a tiny frisson.' – *Penelope Houston*
'It plays its particular brand of the three-card trick with ingenuity and without scruple.' – *The Times*

A Taste of Honey ***
GB 1961 100m bw
British Lion/Bryanston/Woodfall (Tony Richardson)
Adventures of a pregnant Salford teenager, her sluttish mother, black lover and homosexual friend.
Fascinating offbeat comedy drama with memorable characters and sharply etched backgrounds.
w Shelagh Delaney, Tony Richardson *play* Shelagh Delaney *d* Tony Richardson *ph* Walter Lassally *m* John Addison
☆ *Rita Tushingham, Dora Bryan, Murray Melvin*, Robert Stephens, Paul Danquah
'Tart and lively around the edges and bitter at the core.' – *Peter John Dyer*
'Rich, full work, directed with an unerring sense of rightness.' – *New Yorker*
best British picture; Dora Bryan; Rita Tushingham; screenplay

The Taste of Others: see *Le Goût des Autres*

Taste the Blood of Dracula
GB 1970 95m Technicolor
Warner/Hammer (Aida Young)
A depraved peer involves three Victorian businessmen in the reactivation of Dracula.
Latterday vampire saga, initially lively but mainly dreary.
w John Elder (Anthony Hinds) *d* Peter Sasdy *ph* Arthur Grant *m* James Bernard *ad* Scott MacGregor *ed* Chris Barnes
☆ Christopher Lee, Geoffrey Keen, Gwen Watford, Linda Hayden, Peter Sallis, Anthony Corlan, John Carson, Ralph Bates

'You haven't met her yet and she already hates you.'
Tatie Danielle **
France 1990 112m colour
Palace/Téléma/FR3/Les Productions du Champ Poirer/Sofica (Charles Gassot)
A malicious elderly woman creates problems when she moves in with her nephew's family.
Sharp and enjoyable black comedy.
w Florence Quentin *d* Etienne Chatiliez *ph* Philippe Welt *m* Gabriel Yared *pd* Geoffroy Larcher *ed* Catherine Renault
☆ Tsilla Chelton, Catherine Jacob, Isabelle Nanty, Neige Dolsky, Eric Pratt, Laurence Février, Virgine Pradal
'A tart comedy providing welcome Gallic relief to the saccharine Hollywood-endorsed stereotypes of the elderly as armchair dispensers of love and bromides.' – *Variety*

The Tattered Dress
US 1957 93m bw Cinemascope
U-I (Albert Zugsmith)
While conducting a murder defence, a criminal lawyer annoys a vindictive small-town sheriff, who plots revenge.
Silly melodrama which rapidly loses interest after a promising start.
w George Zuckerman *d* Jack Arnold *ph* Carl Guthrie *m* Frank Skinner
☆ Jeff Chandler, Jack Carson, Jeanne Crain, Gail Russell, George Tobias, Edward Andrews, Philip Reed

'Every great love leaves its mark!'
Tattoo
US 1980 103m Technicolor
Joseph E. Levine (Robert F. Colesberry)
A mad tattooist kidnaps a cover girl and tattoos her all over before forcing her to have sex. She kills him.
And not before time.
w Joyce Bunuel *d* Bob Brooks *ph* Arthur Ornitz *m* Barry de Vorzon *pd* Stuart Wurtzel
☆ Bruce Dern, Maud Adams, Leonard Frey, Rikke Borge
''*The Collector* crossed with *Ai No Corrida* ... a sensational package for the eighties confected from ideas half remembered from other films.' – *Mark Lefanu, MFB*

Tausend Augen: see *A Thousand Eyes*

Tawny Pipit *
GB 1944 85m bw
GFD/Two Cities (Bernard Miles)
The life of a village in wartime is disrupted when two rare birds nest in a local meadow.
Pleasant, thin little comedy, a precursor of the Ealing school.
wd Bernard Miles, Charles Saunders *ph* Eric Cross *m* Noel Mewton-Wood
☆ Bernard Miles, Rosamund John, Niall MacGinnis, Jean Gillie, Christopher Steele, Lucie Mannheim, Brefni O'Rorke, Marjorie Rhodes
'Almost unimaginably genteel.' – *James Agee*
'Not quite dry enough for the epicures nor sweet enough for the addicts.' – *C. A. Lejeune*
'Seldom does such a piece of unsophisticated charm and humour reach the screen.' – *New York Times*

Taxi!
US 1931 68m bw
Warner (Robert Lord)
Independent cab drivers defy a powerful trust.
Sassy comedy drama with plenty going on.
w Kubec Glasmon, John Bright *play* *The Blind Spot* by Kenyon Nicholson *d* Roy del Ruth *ph* James Van Trees *md* Leo Forbstein
☆ James Cagney, Loretta Young, George E. Stone, Guy Kibbee, David Landau, Leila Bennett, Matt McHugh
'As a deese, dem and dose, chip-on-the-shoulder, on-the-make example of young America the audience knows no better interpretation on the screen than that which Cagney gives it. The populace are now expectant of this player socking all and sundry including all the women in the cast.' – *Variety*
'A sordid but amusing observation on minor metropolitan endeavours.' – *Time*

Taxi
US 1952 77m bw
TCF (Samuel G. Engel)
A taxi driver helps a young mother find her husband, and falls for her himself.
Practised sentimental guff, Hollywoodized from the French film Sans Laisser d'Adresse.
w D. M. Marshman Jnr, Daniel Fuchs *d* Gregory Ratoff *ph* Milton Krasner *m* Leigh Harline
☆ Dan Dailey, Constance Smith, Neva Patterson, Blanche Yurka, Walter Woolf King

Taxi *
France 1998 89m colour Technovision
Metrodome/ARP/TF1/Canal+ (Michèle Pétin, Laurent Pétin)
Arrested for speeding, a reckless pizza delivery motorcyclist turned taxi driver is forced to help an incompetent cop attempt to catch a German gang of bank robbers, who have eluded capture with their high-speed getaways.
A hectic thriller, modelled on American gangster movies, that is irreverent about everything, particularly the police; it is fun in an uncomplicated way and has one splendid joke at the end of the final car chase.
w Luc Besson *d* Gérard Pirès *m* IAM *ad* Jean-Jacques Gernolle *ed* Véronique Lange
☆ Samy Naceri (Daniel), Frédérick Diefenthal (Emilien), Marion Cotillard (Lilly), Emma Sjöberg (Petra), Manuela Gouray (Camille), Bernard Farcy (Chief Inspector Gibert), Georges Neri (Joe)
'A one trick movie and, although it's short, you wouldn't wish it any longer.' – *Edward Porter, Sunday Times*
† It was released on video in both a dubbed and a subtitled version.
†† The film was a great commercial success in France, which resulted in a sequel, Taxi 2.

Taxi 2
France 2000 84m colour Technovision
Metrodome/Leeloo/ARP/TF1/Canal+ (Luc Besson, Michèlé Pétin, Laurent Pétin)
A high-speed taxi driver helps the French police when yakuza kidnap a Japansese minister in Marseilles.
Frenetic farce, poking fun at the police and action movies.
w Luc Besson *d* Gérard Krawczyk *ph* Gerard Sterin *m* Al Khemya *ad* Jean-Jacques Gernolle *ed* Thierry Hoss
☆ Samy Naceri (Daniel), Frédéric Diefenthal (Emilien), Emma Sjoberg (Petra), Bernard Farcy (Chief Inspector Gibert), Marion Cotillard (Lilly)
'An entertaining high-speed romp, with a happy taste of Bond movies from the camp Roger Moore era.' – *Peter Bradshaw, Guardian*
'Merde.' – *Steve Grant, Sunday Times*

The Taxi Dancer
US 1926 64m (24 fps) bw silent
MGM
A Virginia girl in the big city rises from dime-a-dance joints to the big time.
Mildly suggestive star melodrama which promises more than it gives.
w A. P. Younger and Robert Terry Shannon *d* Harry Millarde
☆ Joan Crawford, Owen Moore, Douglas Gilmore, Marc McDermott, Gertrude Astor

Taxi Driver ****
US 1976 114m Metrocolor
Columbia/Italo-Judeo (Michael and Julia Philips)
A lonely Vietnam veteran becomes a New York taxi driver and allows the violence and squalor around him to explode in his mind.
The epitome of the sordid realism of the 70s, this unlovely but brilliantly made film haunts the mind and paints a most vivid picture of a hell on earth.
w Paul Schrader d Martin Scorsese ph Michael Chapman m Bernard Herrmann
☆ *Robert DeNiro*, Jodie Foster, Cybill Shepherd, Peter Boyle, Leonard Harris, Harvey Keitel
'I don't question the truth of this material. I question Scorsese's ability to lift it out of the movie gutters into which less truthful directors have trampled it.' – *Stanley Kauffmann*
† Schrader says the story was modelled after the diaries of would-be assassin Arthur Bremer.
best picture; Bernard Herrmann; Robert DeNiro; Jodie Foster
Bernard Herrmann; Jodie Foster

Taxi to the Toilet: see *Taxi Zum Klo*

Taxi Zum Klo *
West Germany 1981 92m colour
Laurens Straub, Frank Ripploh, Horst Schier
aka: *Taxi to the Toilet*
A homosexual schoolteacher, at odds with his home-loving partner, spends his spare time cruising lavatories, bars and parks in search of sex.
A semi-autobiographical film, saved from unpleasantness by its sense of humour. Its scenes of homosexual activity in grubby lavatories, seedy apartments and at a tacky drag ball may turn off all but the similarly inclined.
wd Frank Ripploh *ph* Horst Schier *m* Hans Wittstatt *ed* Marina Runne, Mathias von Gunten
☆ Frank Ripploh, Bernd Broaderup, Orpha Termin, Peter Fahrni, Dieter Godde
'An admirable film, not least for tackling its subject with a warm sense of humour.' – *Films and Filming*

A Taxing Woman **
Japan 1987 130m colour Panavision
Itami Productions (Juzo Itami)
original title: *Marusa no onna*
A dedicated female tax inspector investigates the financial affairs of a crooked hotelier
Quirky, slyly observant comedy of greed that was a big hit in Japan.
wd Juzo Itami *ph* Yonezo Maeda
☆ Nobuko Miyamoto, Tsutomu Yamazaki, Masahiko Tsugawa, Hideo Murota, Mitsuko Sugino

'He took the flaming warpath of revenge on the side of the US Cavalry...in the greatest Indian uprising of all!'
Taza, Son of Cochise
US 1954 79m Technicolor 3-D
Universal-International
Peace-loving Taza succeeds his dad and tries not to be influenced by Geronimo.
Routine pro-Indian Western, in which the scenery overpowers the performances.
w George Zuckerman, Gerald Drayson Adams *d* Douglas Sirk *ph* Russell Metty *m* Frank Skinner *ad* Bernard Herzbrun, Emrich Nicholson *ed* Milton Carruth
☆ Rock Hudson (Taza), Barbara Rush (Oona), Gregg Palmer (Captain Burnett), Bart Roberts (Naiche), Morris Ankrum (Grey Eagle), Joseph Sawyer (Sgt Hamma), Eugene Iglesias (Chato), Richard H. Cutting (Cy Hagen), Ian McDonald (Geronimo), Jeff Chandler (Cochise)

'Years from now, when you talk about this – and you will – be kind!'
'Even the most daring story can be brought onto the screen when done with courage, honesty and good taste.'

Tea and Sympathy
US 1956 122m Metrocolor Cinemascope
MGM (Pandro S. Berman)

A sensitive teenage schoolboy is scorned by his tougher classmates, but his housemaster's wife takes him in hand …
Overblown and bowdlerized version of a quiet little Broadway play; impeccable production values, but no spark.
w Robert Anderson (and the Hays office)
play Robert Anderson *d* Vincente Minnelli
ph John Alton *m* Adolph Deutsch *ad* William A. Horning, Edward Carfagno *ed* Ferris Webster
☆ Deborah Kerr (Laura Reynolds), *John Kerr* (Tom Robinson), Leif Erickson (Bill Reynolds), Edward Andrews (Herb Lee), Darryl Hickman (Al), Norma Crane (Ellie Martin), Ollie (Dean Jones)
'…mounted for the screen as if it were a precious objet d'art in danger from rioting but miraculously saved. Besides being archaic, the film is a prodigiously silly fable, pulling the realities with which it deals dishonestly, systematically out of whack.' – *Parker Tyler*

Tea for Two *
US 1950 97m Technicolor
Warner (William Jacobs)

A nearly bankrupt financier promises his niece 25,000 dollars for her new musical show if she can say no to every question for twenty-four hours.
Tinkly, quite amusing light musical which has little to do with No No Nanette *on which it is allegedly based.*
w Harry Clork *d* David Butler *ph* Wilfrid Cline *md* Ray Heindorf *ch* Le Roy Prinz
☆ Doris Day, Gordon MacRae, Gene Nelson, Eve Arden, Billy de Wolfe, S. Z. Sakall, Bill Goodwin, Patrice Wymore

'A story of civilised disobedience.'
Tea with Mussolini *
GB/Italy 1999 116m Cinecitta
UIP/Medusa/Universal

An illegitimate Italian boy is looked after by a group of elderly English expatriates, living in Florence; when they are interned during the Second World War he helps them survive with the aid of a wealthy American.
A blandly old-fashioned, nostalgic wallow, in which its gaggle of actresses tame fascists with a withering glance, and are upstaged by the buildings and Tuscan landscapes.
w John Mortimer, Franco Zeffirelli
book Autobiography by Franco Zeffirelli *d* Franco Zeffirelli *ph* David Watkin *m* Alessio Vlad, Stefano Arnaldi *ad* Carlo Centolavigna, Gioia Fiorella Mariani *ed* Tariq Anwar
☆ Judi Dench, Joan Plowright, Maggie Smith, Cher, Lily Tomlin, Baird Wallace, Charlie Lucas, Massimo Ghini, Paolo Seganti, Paul Checquer, Tessa Pritchard
'Suffers from a fatal lack of focus and emotional center, reducing potentially involving material to a succession of individual scenes.' – *Derek Elley, Variety*
'An old queen's film, awash with a rapt savouring of stellar femininity and endearingly predictable in its casting of inept but decorative young men.' – *Andy Medhurst, Sight and Sound*
Maggie Smith

Teachers
US 1984 106m Metrocolor
MGM-UA (Aaron Russo)

A burnt-out teacher is drawn back to his ideas despite, or because of, apparent lunacy in the administration.
Wildly unconsidered black comedy which takes stabs at everything and hits nothing.
w W. R. McKinney *d* Arthur Hiller *ph* David M. Walsh *m* Sandy Gibson *pd* Richard MacDonald *ed* Don Zimmermann
☆ Nick Nolte, JoBeth Williams, Judd Hirsch, Ralph Macchio, Richard Mulligan, Allen Garfield, Royal Dano

Teacher's Pet *
US 1958 120m bw Vistavision
Paramount/Perlberg-Seaton (William Perlberg)

A tough city editor falls for a lady professor of journalism and enrols as a student.
Overlong one-joke comedy which quickly reneges on its early promise; but the principals play up divertingly.
w Fay and Michael Kanin *d* George Seaton
ph Haskell Boggs *m* Roy Webb
☆ *Clark Gable, Doris Day, Gig Young*, Mamie Van Doren, Nick Adams
Fay and Michael Kanin; Gig Young

'She Gets what She Wants. At Any Cost.'
Teacher's Pet
US 2000 92m FotoKem
Alliance Atlantis/Unapix (Richard Brandes)

aka: *Devil in the Flesh 2*
An insane, lovesick girl kills anyone who comes between her and the teacher she loves.
Dully predictable and tepid thriller that never surprises, other than in its lack of originality.
w Richard Brandes *d* Marcus Spiegel *ph* M. David Mullen *m* Steve Gurevitch *pd* Radha Mehta, Melissa Blanchard *ed* Edwin Santiago
☆ Jodi Lyn O'Keefe (Debbie Strong), Jsu Garcia (Sam Deckner), Katherine Kendall (Carla Briggs), Jeanette Brox (Laney), Christiana Frank (Sydney Hollings), Todd Robert Anderson (Deputy Toby Taylor), Bill Gratton (Sheriff Bill Taylor), Sarah Lancaster (Tracy Carley), Rel Hunt (Buddy Lyle), Todd McKee (Jim Sykes)
† The film was a sort of sequel to the similar 1998 movie *Devil in the Flesh* (qv).

The Teahouse of the August Moon *
US 1956 123m Metrocolor Cinemascope
MGM (Jack Cummings)

Okinawa 1944: a wily interpreter helps American troops succumb to the oriental way of life.
Adequate, well-acted screen version of a Broadway comedy which succeeded largely because of its theatricality. A few good jokes remain.
w John Patrick *play* John Patrick *d* Daniel Mann *ph* John Alton *m* Saul Chaplin
☆ *Marlon Brando, Glenn Ford,* Eddie Albert, *Paul Ford*, Machiko Kyo, Henry Morgan

Tears for Simon: see *Lost*

Tears of the Black Tiger
Thailand 2000 110m colour
Pathé/Film Bangkok (Nonzee Nimibutr)

original title: *Fa Talai Jone*
A peasant's son becomes a famous bandit out of his frustrated love for a rich man's daughter.
High camp melodrama, a parody of horse and soap operas, notable for its saturated colour that makes every frame look as though it were hand-tinted, and for the occasional striking image.
wd Wisit Sasanatieng *ph* Nattawat Kittikhun *m* Amornpong Methakunawut *pd* Ake Aimchuen *ed* Dusanee Puinongpho *cos* Chaiwichit Somoboon
☆ Chartchai Ngamsan (Black Tiger), Stella Malucchi (Rumpoey), Supakorn Kitsuwon (Mahesuan), Arawat Ruangvuth (Police Captain Kumjorn), Sombatl (Fai), Pairoj Jaisingha (Phya Prasit), Naiyana Sheewanun (Rumpoey's maid), Kanchit Kwanpracha (Kamnan Dua), Chamloen Sridang (Sergeant Yam)
'One man's popular retro entertainment is another man's laughable kitsch, and yet another man's knowing postmodernism. You pay your bahts at the box office and you takes your choice.' – *Philip French, Observer*

The Teckman Mystery
GB 1954 90m bw
British Lion/London Films/Corona (Josef Somlo)
An author commissioned to write the biography of a dead airman finds him very much alive and his own life in danger.
Peripatetic spy story with the twists expected of this author; all quite enjoyable.
w Francis Durbridge, James Matthews *BBC serial* Francis Durbridge *d* Wendy Toye *ph* Jack Hilyard *m* Clifton Parker
☆ Margaret Leighton, John Justin, Michael Medwin, Meier Tzelniker, Roland Culver, George Coulouris, Raymond Huntley, Duncan Lamont

Ted and Venus
US 1991 100m CFI color
Double Helix/LA Dreams (Randolf Turrow, William Talmadge)

A bearded Venice Beach poet loses control when his romantic approach to a local beauty is rejected.
Misguided whimsy that meanders all over the place without getting anywhere interesting.
w Paul Ciotti, Bud Cort *d* Bud Cort *ph* Dietrich Lohmann *m* David Robbins *pd* Lynn Christopher *ed* Katina Zinner
☆ Bud Cort, Jim Brolin, Kim Adams, Carol Kane, Woody Harrelson, Rhea Perlman, Martin Mull, Timothy Leary, Gena Rowlands

'Not every serial killer fits the profile.'
Ted Bundy
US/GB 2002 99m DeLuxe
Metro Tartan/First Look/Tartan (Hamish McAlpine, Michael Muscat)

Biopic of America's first murderer to be known as a serial killer, who was responsible for the deaths of at least 38 women.
Low budget thriller that aims for black comedy; explaining little about what turned Bundy into a multiple murderer, the movie's only purpose is to make its audience's flesh creep.
w Stephen Johnston, Matthew Bright *d* Matthew Bright *ph* Sonja Rom *m* Kennard Ramsey, Eric Colvin *pd* Chris Anthony Miller *ed* Paul Heiman *sp* Tom Savini
☆ Ted Bundy (Michael Reilly Burke), Boti Ann Bliss (Lee), Stefani Brass (Julie), Marina Black (Kate), Wayne Morse (Bob)
'The filmmakers have realized that it's a sick world out there. They've simply decided, like the best "B" movie fiends, that the best defense is ghoulish amusement.' – *Jeffrey M. Anderson, San Francisco Examiner*

Teen Agent
US 1991 88m Technicolor
Warner (Craig Zadan, Neil Meron)

aka: *If Looks Could Kill*
A student is mistaken for a CIA undercover agent and assigned to guard a top European politician.
Tired teenage copy of the James Bond formula of gags and gadgetry.
w Darren Star *story* Fred Dekker *d* William Dear *ph* Doug Milsome *m* David Foster *pd* Guy J. Comtois *ed* John F. Link, Mark Stevens
☆ Richard Grieco, Linda Hunt, Roger Rees, Robin Bartlett, Gabrielle Anwar, Geraldine James, Roger Daltrey

Teen Wolf
US 1985 91m United Color
Entertainment/Atlantic (Mark Levinson, Scott Rosenfelt)

An ineffective college basketball player finds he is a hereditary werewolf, and in his altered form becomes a star.
Bewilderingly silly teenage variation on a famous legend, good-natured but totally empty.
w Joseph Loeb III, Matthew Weisman *d* Rod Daniel *ph* Tim Suhrstedt *m* Miles Goodman *ed* Lois Freeman-Fox
☆ Michael J. Fox, James Hampton, Scott Paulin, Susan Ursitti

Teen Wolf Too
US 1987 94m colour
Entertainment/Atlantic (Kent Bateman)

A college student with a talent for boxing makes the most of the fact that he is a werewolf.
Drear comedy sequel that attempts to reprise the original with a leaden touch.
w R. Timothy Kring *story* Joseph Loeb III, Matthew Weisman *d* Christopher Leitch *ph* Jules Brenner *m* Mark Goldenberg *ad* Peg McClellan *ed* Steven Polivka, Kim Secrist, Harvey Rosenstock, Raja Gosnell
☆ Jason Bateman, Kim Darby, John Astin, Paul Sand, James Hampton, Mark Holton, Estee Chandler

Teenage Bad Girl: see *My Teenage Daughter*

Teenage Frankenstein: see *I Was a Teenage Frankenstein*

'They all talk, fight and love just one way—Dirty!'
'Under-aged… over-sexed… kick-happy… thrill-hungry… always reckless and *willing*!'
Teenage Gang Debs
US 1966 77m bw
Jode (Jerry Denby)

A young hoodlum's new girl causes his downfall and trouble among the members of his biker gang.
No-budget exploitation flick, notable only for its lack of any talent, and its reliance on the obvious.
w Hy Cahl *d* Sande N. Johnsen *ph* J. Denby *m* Steve Karmen *ed* Pat Follmer
☆ Diane Conti, Joey Naudic, John Batis, Linda Gale, Sandra Kane, Eileen Scott, Sue McManus, Robin Nolan, Linda Cambi, Lin Kennedy

'Man… Beast… Or Alien?'
Teenage Monster
US 1957 65m bw
Marquette Productions

A meteor turns a home-loving teenager into a hairy rampaging monster.
Ridiculous monster movie, inept in every respect.
w Ray Buffum *d* Jacques Marquette *ph* Taylor Byars
☆ Anne Gwynne, Gloria Castillo, Stuart Wade, Gilbert Perkins, Steven Parker, Charles Courtney

'Mean. Green. And on the screen'
Teenage Mutant Ninja Turtles *
US 1990 93m Technicolor
Virgin/Golden Harvest/Limelight (Kim Dawson, Simon Fields, David Chan)

Pizza-loving, sewer-dwelling turtles and their rat guru, mutated into half-human creatures by radioactivity, battle against a gang of teenage martial arts experts led by an evil Japanese ninja.
Comic-book mayhem brought to the screen in the frenetic style of rock videos, it took more money at the box-office than any other independent film has ever done.
w Todd W. Langen, Bobby Herbeck, from comic-book characters created by Kevin Eastman and Peter Laird *d* Steve Barron *ph* John Fenner *m* John Du Prez *pd* Roy Forge Smith *ed* William Gordean, Sally Menke, James Symons *sp* creatures designed by Jim Henson's Creature Shop
☆ Judith Hoag, Elias Koteas, Josh Pais, Michelan Sisti, Leif Tilden, David Forman, James Sato

Teenage Mutant Ninja Turtles II: The Secret of the Ooze
US 1991 87m colour
TCF/Golden Harvest (Thomas K. Gray, Kim Dawson, David Chan)

The four mutant ninja turtles go into battle against their arch-enemy Shredder and his two new monsters, a mutant dog and tortoise.
A tame sequel, seemingly aimed at the young audience that watches the anodyne animated TV cartoon versions of the four sewer-dwelling heroes.
w Todd W. Langen *d* Michael Pressman *ph* Shelly Johnson *m* John Du Prez *pd* Ray Forge Smith *ed* John Wright, Steve Mirkovich
☆ Paige Turco, David Warner, Michelan Sisti, Leif Tilden, Kenn Troum, Mark Caso, Kevin Clash, Ernie Reyes Jnr, François Chau
'If watching the first Turtles film was like chewing a good pizza, watching II is more like munching on the cardboard packaging, but – as fast food goes – even that can taste good enough in parts.' – *David Lusted, Sight and Sound*

Teenage Mutant Ninja Turtles III: The Turtles Are Back … in Time
US 1992 96m Technicolor
TCF/Golden Harvest/Clearwater (Thomas K. Gray, Kim Dawson, David Chan)

The turtles travel back to 17th-century Japan to rescue their friend.
The least of the adventures, a tired and aimless movie lacking in fun.
wd Stuart Gillard *ph* David Gurfinkel *m* John Du Prez *pd* Roy Forge Smith *ed* William D. Gordean, James R. Symons

☆ Elias Koteas, Paige Turco, Stuart Wilson, Sab Shimono, Vivian Wu, Mark Caso, Matt Hill, Jim Raposa, David Fraser, James Murray, Henry Hayashi

'A decided case of diminishing returns.' – *Variety*

Teenage Rebel

US 1956 94m bw Cinemascope

TCF (Charles Brackett)

A wealthy California woman is visited by her teenage daughter from a former marriage; the girl proceeds to make difficulties for everyone.

The first film in black-and-white Cinemascope is a tedious drama of unreal people.

w Walter Reisch, Charles Brackett *play* Edith Sommer *d* Edmund Goulding *ph* Joe MacDonald *m* Leigh Harline *ad* Lyle Wheeler, Jack Martin Smith

☆ Ginger Rogers, Michael Rennie, Mildred Natwick, Betty Lou Keim, Warren Berlinger, Louise Beavers, Irene Hervey

art direction

Teheran

GB 1947 86m bw

GFD/Pendennis (John Stafford, Steven Pallos)

US title: *The Plot to Kill Roosevelt*

A correspondent in Iran foils an assassination plot.

Low-key blood and thunder; passable time-filler.

w Akos Tolnay, William Freshman *d* William Freshman, Giacomo Gentilomo *ph* U. Arata *ad* V. Colesanti *ed* A. Lucedi

☆ Derek Farr (Pemberton Grant), Marta Labarr (Natalie), Manning Whiley (Paul Sherek), John Slater (Major Sobieski), John Warwick (Major McIntyre), Pamela Stirling (Hali), Macdonald Parke (Major Wellman), Sebastian Cabot (Caretaker)

'Your next phone call may be your last!'

Telefon *

US 1977 103m Metrocolor Panavision

MGM (James B. Harris)

A Russian agent is instructed to seek out and destroy a ring of hard liners who are opposing detente with the West.

Moderately watchable espionage capers with a slightly new twist.

w Peter Hyams, Stirling Silliphant *novel* Walter Wager *d* Don Siegel *ph* Michael Butler *m* Lalo Schifrin

☆ Charles Bronson, Lee Remick, Donald Pleasence, Tyne Daly, Alan Badel, Patrick Magee, Sheree North

The Telegraph Trail

US 1933 55m bw

Warner

An army scout ensures supplies reach the men building the first telegraph line across the West.

A lacklustre Western, with action scenes lifted from the silent The Red Raiders *made seven years earlier, though Wayne does get to wear a rather fetching fringed jacket.*

w Kurt Kempler *d* Tenny Wright

☆ John Wayne, Marceline Day, Frank McHugh, Otis Harlan, Yakima Canutt, Albert J. Smith, Clarence Geldert

Le Téléphone Rose: see *The Pink Telephone*

Television Spy

US 1939 58m bw

Paramount

Enemy agents compete for the secret of long-range television transmission.

Watchable pocket thriller, with the hero and heroine getting acquainted only by television from a 3000-mile distance.

w Horace McCoy, William R. Lipman, Lillie Hayward *d* Edward Dmytryk

☆ William Henry, Judith Barrett, William Collier Snr, Anthony Quinn, Richard Denning, John Eldredge

'It may move slowly, but it does avoid the absurdity that goes with the average film crack at television.' – *Variety*

Tell England

GB 1931 88m bw

British Instructional

US title: *The Battle of Gallipoli*

In 1914, school chums join up and mostly die at Gallipoli.

Even the most patriotic audiences ended up roaring with laughter at this stiff-upper-lip charade.

w Anthony Asquith *novel* Ernest Raymond *d* Anthony Asquith, Gerald Barkas *ph* Jack Parker, Stanley Rodwell

☆ Carl Harbord, Fay Compton, Tony Bruce, Dennis Hoey, Gerald Rawlinson, Wally Patch

'Not likely to bring in any money.' – *Variety*

Tell It to a Star

US 1945 67m bw

Republic (Walter H. Goetz)

A cigarette girl in a Florida hotel aspires to be a vocalist.

The plot sets the level: minor musical.

w John K. Butler *d* Frank McDonald

☆ Ruth Terry, Robert Livingston, Alan Mowbray, Franklin Pangborn, Isabel Randolph

Tell It to the Judge

US 1949 87m bw

Columbia (Buddy Adler)

A female candidate for judicial honours is suddenly re-attracted to her divorced husband.

Leaden farce, relying entirely on its stars.

w Nat Perrin, Devery Freeman, Roland Kibbee *d* Norman Foster *ph* Joseph Walker *m* Werner Heymann

☆ Rosalind Russell, Robert Cummings, Gig Young, Marie McDonald, Harry Davenport

Tell It to the Marines

US 1926 75m (24 fps) bw silent

MGM

A marine sergeant has an eventful time during training and in the Philippines.

Lively war action piece with a more or less straight role for its star.

w Richard Schayer *d* George Hill

☆ Lon Chaney, William Haines, Eleanor Boardman, Carmel Myers, Warner Oland

Tell Me a Riddle

US 1980 90m CFI color

Godmother/Filmways

A dying old woman, long a recluse, is reconciled with her family.

Adequate if not exciting treatment of a very downbeat subject.

w Joyce Eliason, Alev Lytle *novel* Tillie Olsen *d* Lee Grant

☆ Lila Kedrova, Melvyn Douglas, Brooke Adams, Dolores Dorn, Lili Valenty, Zalman King

Tell Me That You Love Me, Junie Moon

US 1969 113m Technicolor

Paramount/Sigma (Otto Preminger)

A disfigured girl, a homosexual paraplegic and an introvert epileptic set up house together.

Absurd tragicomedy which remains disturbingly icky in conception and execution.

w Marjorie Kellogg *novel* Marjorie Kellogg *d* Otto Preminger *ph* Boris Kaufman *m* Philip Springer

☆ Liza Minnelli, Ken Howard, Robert Moore, Kay Thompson, Leonard Frey, James Coco, Fred Williamson

'Like seeing a venerated senior citizen desperately trying to show he's in love with today by donning see-through clothes.' – *Michael Billington, Illustrated London News*

'It slushes us with sentimentality to the point past compassion.' – *Judith Crist*

Tell Me Tonight

GB/Germany 1932 91m bw

Herman Fellner-Josef Somlo/Cine Alliance

US title: *Be Mine Tonight*

An Italian tenor falls in love with a Swiss mayor's daughter, but complicates matters by pretending to be someone else.

Bilingual operetta, fondly remembered for its singing star.

w John Orton *d* Anatole Litvak

☆ *Jan Kiepura*, Sonnie Hale, Magda Schneider, Edmund Gwenn, Athene Seyler

Tell No Tales **

US 1939 68m bw

MGM (Edward Chodorov)

A managing editor seeks a big scoop to save his newspaper, and solves a kidnap-murder case.

Intriguingly written and handled second feature, with excellent pace, performance and entertainment value.

w Lionel Houser d Leslie Fenton ph Joseph Ruttenberg *m* William Axt

☆ *Melvyn Douglas*, Louise Platt, Gene Lockhart, Douglass Dumbrille, Zeffie Tilbury, Halliwell Hobbes

'Full of excellent detail, and the smallest part is a genuine character. Add these qualities to its pace and excitement and you have something well worth seeing.' – *Richard Mallett, Punch*

Tell Them Willie Boy is Here *

US 1969 97m Technicolor

Universal/Jennings Lang (Philip A. Waxman)

In 1909 an Indian turned cowboy comes up against old prejudices and is pursued into the desert after an accidental death.

Boringly predictable story of white man's guilt, very professionally made.

wd Abraham Polonsky novel Willie Boy by Harry Lawton *ph Conrad Hall m* Dave Grusin

☆ Robert Redford, Robert Blake, Katharine Ross, Susan Clark, Barry Sullivan, Charles McGraw, Charles Aidman, John Vernon

Robert Redford; Katharine Ross

Tell Your Children: see *Reefer Madness*

Telling Lies in America

US 1997 101m DeLuxe 'Scope

Banner/Kazui/Ben Myron

In Cleveland in the early 60s, a teenager finds it difficult to adjust to life at home with his immigrant Hungarian father and to a corrupt wider world working for a bribe-taking rock disc jockey.

A semi-autobiographical rites-of-passage drama that never acquires enough significance to connect to a wider audience.

w Joe Eszterhas *d* Guy Ferland *ph* Reynaldo Villalobos *m* Nicholas Pike *pd* James Gelarden *ed* Jill Savitt

☆ Kevin Bacon, Brad Renfro, Maximilian Schell, Calista Flockhart, Paul Dooley, Jonathan Rhys Meyers, Luke Wilson

'Offers little to audiences that hasn't been served up in quantity in the past.' – *Variety*

Tema: see *The Theme*

The Temp

US 1993 95m DeLuxe

Paramount/Columbus Circle (David Permut, Tom Engelman)

A temporary secretary works her way up the executive ladder.

A feeble and forgettable drama of office life.

w Kevin Falls *d* Tom Holland *ph* Steve Yaconelli *m* Frederic Talgorn *pd* Joel Schiller *ed* Scott Conrad

☆ Timothy Hutton, Lara Flynn Boyle, Dwight Schultz, Oliver Platt, Steven Weber, Colleen Flynn, Faye Dunaway

'Derivative, artificial and moronic are the first adjectives that come to mind to describe this concoction.' – *Variety*

Tempest

Italy/France/Yugoslavia 1958 123m

Technirama

(Paramount)

Adventures of a Russian ensign banished by Catherine the Great.

Expensive but sloppy epic which fails to generate much interest.

w Louis Peterson, Alberto Lattuada, Ivo Perelli *novel The Captain's Daughter* by Alexander Pushkin *d* Alberto Lattuada *ph Aldo Tonti m* Piero Piccioni

☆ Van Heflin, Geoffrey Horne, Silvana Mangano, Oscar Homolka, Viveca Lindfors, Robert Keith, Vittorio Gassman, Finlay Currie, Agnes Moorehead, Helmut Dantine, Laurence Naismith

The Tempest

GB 1980 95m Eastmancolor

Boyd's Company

A punk version of Shakespeare's play; less horrendous than might have been supposed, but far from interesting in its own right.

wd Derek Jarman *ph* Peter Middleton *m* Wavemaker

☆ Heathcote Williams, Karl Johnson, Toyah Wilcox, Peter Bull, Richard Warwick, Elisabeth Welch

'Most men dream their fantasies. Philip decided to live his!'

Tempest

US 1982 142m DeLuxe

Columbia (Paul Mazursky)

An architect leaves his unfaithful wife and takes his daughter to live on a Greek island attended only by a half-witted shepherd.

Absurd attempt to update Shakespeare; any initial amusement quickly gives way to abject boredom.

w Paul Mazursky, Leon Capetanos *d* Paul Mazursky *ph* Don McAlpine *m* Stomu Yamashta *pd* Pato Guzman

☆ John Cassavetes, Gena Rowlands, Susan Sarandon, Vittorio Gassman, Raul Julia, Jerry Hardin, Molly Ringwald, Paul Stewart

'An aura of dottiness hangs over it ... the fact remains that it is handsomely visualized and, within the limits of the material, excellently played.' – *Tim Pulleine, MFB*

Tempos dificeis, este tempo: see *Hard Times*

Temptation

US 1946 92m bw

Universal (Edward Small)

An archaeologist's wife takes to poisoning both her husband and her blackmailing lover.

Hoary Edwardian melodrama, unpersuasively restaged.

w Robert Thoeren *novel Bella Donna* by Robert Hichens *d* Irving Pichel *ph* Lucien Ballard *m* Daniele Amfitheatrof

☆ Merle Oberon, George Brent, Charles Korvin, Paul Lukas, Lenore Ulric, Arnold Moss, Ludwig Stossel, Gavin Muir, Ilka Gruning, André Charlot

Temptation Harbour

GB 1946 104m bw

ABP (Victor Skutezky)

A railway signalman finds and keeps stolen money.

Well-presented but boringly predictable melodrama with an overwrought leading performance set against yards of studio fog.

w Victor Skutezky, Frederic Gotfurt, Rodney Ackland *novel Newhaven/Dieppe* by Georges Simenon *d* Lance Comfort *ph* Otto Heller *m* Mischa Spoliansky *ad* Cedric Dawe *ed* Lito Carruthers

☆ Robert Newton (Mallinson), Simone Simon (Camelia), William Hartnell (Brown), Marcel Dalio (Dupré), Margaret Barton (Betty), Edward Rigby (Tatem), Joan Hopkins (Mrs Brown), Charles Victor (Gowshall), Kathleen Harrison (Mabel), Leslie Dwyer (Reg), Irene Handl (Mrs Gowshall), Gladys Henson (Mrs Titmuss)

The Temptations of Marianne (dubbed)

France 1972 102m Eastmancolor

Unitè Un

original title: *Les Tentations De Marianne*

aka: *I Am Sexy*

A sixteen-year-old girl living in a ski resort persuades a Parisian visitor to take her with him to the city, where she is abandoned.

Slick sexploitation movie, in which a naive girl undergoes an initiation into sexual excess before returning home, older but seemingly no wiser.

wd Francis Leroi *ph* Jean Gonnet *m* Serge Kaufman *ad* Simon Saulnier *ed* Annabelle

☆ Patricia Novarini (Marianne), Bob Asklof (Bob), Bernard Tixier (Paul), Gilles Signard (Marc), Andree Damant (Marianne's Mother), Evelyne Gaillard (Mme Bernard), Alain Quercy (M Bernard), Jean Roquel (M Heinz)

The Temptress *

US 1927 80m (24 fps) bw silent

MGM

An immoral woman drives men to disgrace, murder and suicide.

No-holds-barred melodrama which, being Garbo's second American film, fully confirmed her stardom.
w Dorothy Farnum *d* Mauritz Stiller, Fred Niblo
☆ Greta Garbo, Antonio Moreno, Lionel Barrymore, Roy D'Arcy, Marc McDermott

Temptress Moon *

Hong Kong/China 1996 116m colour
Artificial Eye/Tomson/Shanghai Film (Tong Cunlin, Hsu Feng)
original title: *Fengyue*
A successful Shanghai gigolo, ordered to seduce his wealthy sister-in-law and steal her fortune, falls in love with her instead.
A bombastic melodrama on the pains of requited and unrequited love, intermittently enjoyable.
w Shu Kei, Wang Anyi, Chen Kaige *d* Chen Kaige *ph* Christopher Doyle *m* Zhao Jiping *ad* Huang Qiagui *ed* Pei Xianzhi
☆ Leslie Cheung, Gong Li, Kevin Lin, He Seifei, Xie Tian, Zang Shi, David Wu
† Some 15 minutes from the director's Hong Kong release were cut on the orders of its US distributors Miramax, who also resubtitled it.
†† The director sacked three actresses before asking Gong Li to play the role.

'Just when he thought it was safe to go back in the water...'

'10'

US 1979 122m Metrocolor Panavision
Warner/Orion/Geoffrey (Blake Edwards, Tony Adams)
A sex-mad middle-aged composer marks his girls from one to ten according to their performance.
Randy farce which struck some, but not all, audiences as the funniest thing since sliced bread.
wd Blake Edwards *ph* Frank Stanley *m* Henry Mancini *pd* Rodger Maus
☆ Dudley Moore, Julie Andrews, Bo Derek, Robert Webber, Dee Wallace, Sam Jones
Henry Mancini; song 'It's Easy to Say' (*m* Henry Mancini, *ly* Robert Wells)

10 ***

France/Iran 2002 93m colour
ICA/MK2/Abbas Kiarostami
Conversations between a woman driver and the people to whom she gives lifts over a period of two days.
Filmmaking reduced to a minimum, with two fixed cameras in the car and no director present. Yet, it works, providing intriguing glimpses into the everday lives of ordinary people.
wd Abbas Kiarostami *ph* Abbas Kiarostami *m* Howard Blake *ed* Abbas Kiarostami
☆ Mania Akbari (Driver), Amin Maher (Amin), Roya Arabshahi, Katayoun Taleidzadeh, Mandana Sharbaf, Amene Moradi
'By the end you feel that the lives of the characters, and the complicated society they inhabit, have been illuminated.' – *A. O. Scott, New York Times*
'There's no doubt that this movie is, as the network executives say, a tough watch. But it repays the investment of attention a thousandfold.' – *Peter Bradshaw, Guardian*

Ten Cents a Dance

US 1931 75m bw
Columbia
A dance hostess is desired by a rich man but marries a ne'er-do-well.
Rubbishy story inspired by a then-popular song.
w Jo Swerling *d* Lionel Barrymore
☆ Barbara Stanwyck, Monroe Owsley, Ricardo Cortez, Sally Blane, Blanche Friderici
'It lacks the magic of fancy that makes for universal entertainment.' – *Variety*

'The mightiest dramatic spectacle of all the ages!'

The Ten Commandments **

US 1923 150m approx (24 fps) bw (part Technicolor) silent
Paramount/Famous Players-Lasky (Cecil B. de Mille)
Moses leads the Israelites into the promised land in modern San Francisco; a story of two brothers shows the power of prayer and truth.
The two halves in fact are totally disconnected; but this is a de Mille spectacular and therefore beyond reproach, while as a Hollywood milestone it cannot be denied a place in the Hall of Fame.
w Jeanie MacPherson *d* Cecil B. de Mille *ph* Bert Glennon and others (colour, Ray Rennahan)
☆ *Theodore Roberts*, Richard Dix, Rod la Rocque, Edythe Chapman, Leatrice Joy, Nita Naldi
'It will last as long as the film on which it is recorded.' – *James R. Quirk, Photoplay*

'What a story it tells! What majesty it encompasses! What loves it unveils! What drama it unfolds!'

The Ten Commandments *

US 1956 219m Technicolor Vistavision
Paramount/Cecil B. de Mille (Henry Wilcoxon)
The life of Moses and his leading of the Israelites to the Promised Land.
Popular but incredibly stilted and verbose bible-in-pictures spectacle. A very long haul along a monotonous route, with the director at his pedestrian worst.
w Aeneas Mackenzie, Jesse L. Lasky Jnr, Jack Gariss, Fredric M. Frank *d* Cecil B. de Mille *ph* Loyal Griggs *m* Elmer Bernstein *ad* Hal Pereira, Walter H. Tyler, Albert Nozaki *ed* Anne Bauchens
☆ *Charlton Heston*, Yul Brynner, Edward G. Robinson, Anne Baxter, Nina Foch, Yvonne de Carlo, John Derek, H. B. Warner, Henry Wilcoxon, Judith Anderson, John Carradine, Douglass Dumbrille, Cedric Hardwicke, Martha Scott, Vincent Price and also Debra Paget
'De Mille not only moulds religion into a set pattern of Hollywood conventions; he has also become an expert at making entertainment out of it.' – *Gordon Gow, Films and Filming*
'The result of all these stupendous efforts? Something roughly comparable to an eight-foot chorus girl – pretty well put together, but much too big and much too flashy ... What de Mille has really done is to throw sex and sand into the moviegoers' eyes for almost twice as long as anyone else has ever dared to.' – *Time*
special effects (John Fulton)
best picture; Loyal Griggs; art direction; editing; sound; costumes (Edith Head and others)

Ten Days in Paris

GB 1939 82m bw
Columbia/Irving Asher (Jerome J. Jackson)
US title: *Missing Ten Days*
aka: *Spy in the Pantry*
An amnesiac wakes up in Paris and finds he has been involved in espionage activities.
Modest, quite likeable little comedy suspenser.
w John Meehan Jnr, James Curtis *novel The Disappearance of Roger Tremayne* by Bruce Graeme *d* Tim Whelan *ph* Otto Kanturek *m* Miklos Rozsa
☆ Rex Harrison, Karen Verne, Leo Genn, Joan Marion, Antony Holles, John Abbott, Hay Petrie

Ten Days That Shook the World: see *October*

Ten Gentlemen from West Point **

US 1942 104m bw
TCF (William Perlberg)
Adventures in Indian territory, and back at West Point, of the first recruits to that military academy in the early 1800s.
Likeable mixture of comedy and flagwaving adventure, with excellent production values and a dominating performance.
w Richard Maibaum, George Seaton *d* Henry Hathaway *ph* Leon Shamroy *m* Alfred Newman
☆ *Laird Cregar*, George Montgomery, Maureen O'Hara, John Sutton, Shepperd Strudwick, Victor Francen, Harry Davenport, Ward Bond, Douglass Dumbrille, Ralph Byrd, Louis Jean Heydt
Leon Shamroy

Ten Little Indians *

GB 1966 91m bw
Tenlit (Harry Alan Towers)
Ten people, including two servants, invited to a remote house in the Austrian Alps are murdered one by one.
Fair copy of a classic whodunnit.
w Peter Yeldham, Harry Alan Towers *novel* Agatha Christie *d* George Pollock *ph* Ernest Steward *m* Malcolm Lockyer
☆ Wilfrid Hyde-White, Dennis Price, Stanley Holloway, Leo Genn, Shirley Eaton, Hugh O'Brian, Daliah Lavi, Fabian, Mario Adorf, Marianne Hoppe
† Made also in 1945 and 1975, as *And Then There Were None* (qv).

Ten Little Niggers: see *And Then There Were None (1945)*

Ten North Frederick *

US 1958 102m bw Cinemascope
TCF (Charles Brackett)
At the funeral of a local politico, his family and friends think back to the events of his life.
Small beer, but a generally adult and entertaining family drama despite a miscast lead.
wd Philip Dunne novel John O'Hara *ph* Joe MacDonald *m* Leigh Harline
☆ Gary Cooper, Geraldine Fitzgerald, Diane Varsi, Stuart Whitman, Suzy Parker, Tom Tully, Ray Stricklyn, John Emery

10.30 pm Summer

US/Spain 1966 85m Technicolor
UA/Jorill/Argos (Jules Dassin, Anatole Litvak)
The neurotic Greek wife of an Englishman travelling in Spain becomes obsessed with a murderer on the run.
Preposterously overwrought romantic melodrama.
w Jules Dassin, Marguerite Duras *novel* Marguerite Duras *d* Jules Dassin *ph* Gabor Pogany *m* Christobel Hallfter
☆ Peter Finch, Melina Mercouri, Romy Schneider, Julian Mateos

Ten Rillington Place **

GB 1971 111m Eastmancolor
Columbia/Filmways (Leslie Linder)
An account of London's sordid Christie murders of the forties.
Agreeably seedy reconstruction of a cause célèbre, carefully built around the star part of a murderous aberrant landlord. Too long, however, and finally too lacking in detail.
w Clive Exton *book* Ludovic Kennedy *d* Richard Fleischer *ph* Denys Coop *m* Johnny Dankworth *ed* Ernest Walter
☆ Richard Attenborough, *John Hurt*, Judy Geeson, Pat Heywood, Isobel Black, Geoffrey Chater, André Morell, Robert Hardy

Ten Seconds to Hell

US 1959 93m bw
UA/Hammer/Seven Arts (Michael Carreras)
Bomb disposal experts in post-war Berlin quarrel over a girl.
Boring, harsh, hollow melodrama, so artificially constructed that no one can possibly care who gets exploded.
w Robert Aldrich, Teddi Sherman *novel The Phoenix* by Lawrence Bachmann *d* Robert Aldrich *ph* Ernest Laszlo *m* Kenneth V. Jones *ed* James Needs, Henry Richardson
☆ Jack Palance, Jeff Chandler, Martine Carol, Robert Cornthwaite, Dave Willock, Wesley Addy

Ten Tall Men

US 1951 97m Technicolor
Columbia/Norma (Harold Hecht)
A Foreign Legion patrol prevents a Riff attack.
Comic strip adventures, efficiently handled.
w Roland Kibbee, Frank Davis *d* Willis Goldbeck *ph* William Snyder *m* David Buttolph
☆ Burt Lancaster, Gilbert Roland, Kieron Moore, John Dehner, Jody Lawrance, George Tobias, Mike Mazurki

10 Things I Hate about You

US 1999 97m colour
Buena Vista/Touchstone/Mad Chance/Janet Entertainment (Andrew Lazar)
A doctor refuses to let his younger daughter have dates until her older sister gets a boyfriend.
An attempt to make a teenage comedy out of Shakespeare's The Taming of the Shrew; *it doesn't work.*
w Karen McCullah Lutz, Kirsten Smith *d* Gil Junger *ph* Mark Irwin *m* Richard Gibbs *pd* Carol Winstead Wood *ed* O. Nicholas Brown
☆ Heath Ledger (Patrick Verona), Julia Stiles (Katarina Stratford), Joseph-Gordon Levitt (Cameron James), Larisa Oleynik (Bianca Stratford), David Krumholtz (Michael Eckman), Andrew Keegan (Joey Donner), Susan May Pratt (Mandella), Gabrielle Union (Chastity), Larry Miller (Walter Stratford)
'Lurches all over the map, encompassing dialogue both inspired and juvenile-tasteless. There's also middling slapstick, rampant product placement and awkward bits of earnest drama.' – *Dennis Harvey, Variety*

Ten Thousand Bedrooms

US 1956 114m Metrocolor Cinemascope
MGM (Joe Pasternak)
An American millionaire finds romance when he buys a Rome hotel.
Old-fashioned, unfunny comedy sadly lacking pace and style.
w Laslo Vadnay, Art Cohn, William Ludwig, Leonard Spigelgass *d* Richard Thorpe *ph* Robert Bronner *m* George Stoll *songs* Nicholas Brodszky, Sammy Cahn
☆ Dean Martin, Eva Bartok, Anna Maria Alberghetti, Walter Slezak, Paul Henreid, Jules Munchin, Marcel Dalio

10 to Midnight

US 1983 102m Metrocolor
Cannon/Golan-Globus (Pancho Kohner, Lance Hool)
A sexual deficient kills girls who reject him, but is tracked down and shot by a cop who is the father of one of the threatened girls.
Crude and rather nasty vigilante melodrama.
w William Roberts *d* J. Lee-Thompson *ph* Adam Greenberg *m* Robert O. Ragland *ad* Jim Freiburger *ed* Peter Lee-Thompson
☆ Charles Bronson, Lisa Eilbacher, Andrew Stevens, Gene Davis, Geoffrey Lewis
'Too slow, slick and semi-respectable to live down to its inspirations.' – *Kim Newman, MFB*

Ten Wanted Men

US 1955 80m Technicolor
Columbia/Scott-Brown (Harry Joe Brown)
A rancher and his family are besieged by bandits in a lady's house.
Rather elementary but efficient and good-looking Western programmer.
w Kenneth Gamet *story* Irving Ravetch, Harriet Frank Jnr *d* H. Bruce Humberstone *ph* Wilfred Cline *m* Paul Sawtell
☆ Randolph Scott, Jocelyn Brando, Richard Boone, Alfonso Bedoya, Donna Martell, Skip Homeier

Ten Who Dared

US 1960 92m Technicolor
Walt Disney (James Algar)
In 1869 a scientific expedition sets out to chart the Colorado River.
Tedious and unconvincing adventures.
w Lawrence E. Watkin *journal* Major John Wesley Powell *d* William Beaudine *ph* Gordon Avil *m* Oliver Wallace
☆ Brian Keith, John Beal, James Drury, R. G. Armstrong, Ben Johnson, L. Q. Jones

The Tenant

France 1976 126m Eastmancolor
Paramount/Marianne (Andrew Braunsberg)
original title: *Le Locataire*
A displaced person becomes convinced that his fellow lodgers are out to murder him.
Rather like a male version of the same director's Repulsion, *this wearisome case history shows the total dissipation of whatever talent he once had.*
w Gerard Brach, Roman Polanski *novel* Roland Topor *d* Roman Polanski *ph* Sven Nykvist *m* Philippe Sarde
☆ Roman Polanski, Melvyn Douglas, Isabelle Adjani, Shelley Winters, Jo Van Fleet, Lila Kedrova, Claude Dauphin
'It does not seem to have been designed as self-parody, but it certainly comes across that way.' – *Janet Maslin, Newsweek*
'A long-winded exercise in tedium and morbidity.' – *Kevin Thomas, LA Times*

Tender and Perverse Emanuelle (dubbed)
France 1973 75m colour
Brux Inter

After a neurotic pianist is murdered, police investigate her insanely jealous husband and many lovers.
Incompetent would-be erotic thriller, which contains a great deal of bare flesh, mainly of scenes of lesbian love-making shot in soft focus; all that can be said in its favour is that it lacks Franco's usual frenetic use of the zoom lens, but it contains most of his other faults, including poor acting and a needlessly complicated, tedious script.
w A. L. Mariaux, David Khunn (Jesús Franco) *d* J. P. Johnson (Jesús Franco) *ph* Stephen Rosenfeld, Alain Hardy *m* Daniel White *ed* Claude Gros
☆ Norma Castel, Jack Taylor, Lina Romay, Alice Arno (Marie-France Broquet), Monique Van Linden

Tender Comrade
US 1943 101m bw
RKO (David Hempstead)

Lady welders whose husbands are fighting men keep their chins up during World War II.
Dim tearjerker.
w Dalton Trumbo *d* Edward Dmytryk *ph* Russell Metty *m* Leigh Harline
☆ Ginger Rogers, Robert Ryan, Ruth Hussey, Patricia Collinge, Mady Christians, Kim Hunter, Jane Darwell

Tender Flesh: see *Welcome to Arrow Beach*

Tender Is the Night *
US 1961 146m DeLuxe Cinemascope
TCF (Henry T. Weinstein)

Adventures around Europe between the wars of a rich American psychiatrist who has married his patient.
Patchy, fairly literal transcription of a patently unfilmable novel about defiantly unreal people in what would now be the jet set. About half the result is superficially entertaining.
w Ivan Moffat *novel* F. Scott Fitzgerald *d* Henry King *ph* Leon Shamroy *m* Bernard Herrmann
☆ Jennifer Jones, Jason Robards Jnr, *Joan Fontaine, Tom Ewell*, Cesare Danova, Jill St John, Paul Lukas
title song (*m*Sammy Fain, *ly*Paul Francis Webster)

Tender Mercies *
US 1982 92m Movielab
EMI/Antron Media (Horton Foote, Robert Duvall)

An ex-alcoholic resumes his former career as a country and western singer.
Quiet, downbeat character study with scenic Texas backgrounds. Mildly impressive, but no real reason to go to the cinema.
w Horton Foote *d* Bruce Beresford *ph* Russell Boyd *m* George Dreyfus *ad* Jeannine Oppewall *ed* William Anderson
☆ Robert Duvall (Mac Sledge), Tess Harper (Rosa Lee), Betty Buckley (Dixie), Wilford Brimley (Harry), Ellen Barkin (Sue Anne), Allan Hubbard (Sonny), Lenny von Dohlen (Robert)
'It conceals its deficiencies behind heartfelt performances ... the construction is so rickety that it seems at times entirely to lack a plot.' – *Kim Newman, MFB*
Robert Duvall; Horton Foote
best picture; Bruce Beresford; song 'Over You' (Austin Roberts, Bobby Hart)

The Tender Trap *
US 1955 111m Eastmancolor
Cinemascope
MGM (Lawrence Weingarten)

A smart New York agent has a way with women which annoys his friend; but Casanova gets his come-uppance when he sets his sights on an apparently naïve young actress.
Thin comedy with agreeable moments, not helped by the wide screen.
w Julius J. Epstein *play* Max Shulman, Robert Paul Smith *d* Charles Walters *ph* Paul Vogel *m* Jeff Alexander
☆ Frank Sinatra (Charles Y. Reader), Debbie Reynolds (Julie Gillis), David Wayne (Joe McGall), Celeste Holm (Sylvia Crewes), Lola Albright (Poppy), Carolyn Jones (Helen), Jarma Lewis (Jessica), Howard St John (Mr Sayers), Joey Faye (Sol Z. Steiner), Tom Helmore (Mr Loughran), Willard Sage (Director), Marc Wilder (Ballet-Actor), Jack Boyle (Audition Dancer), James Drury (Eddie)
title song (*m* James Van Heusen, *ly* Sammy Cahn)

The Tenderfoot
US 1931 73m bw
Warner
Adventures of a cowboy in New York.
Slapstick version of George Kaufman's often-remade comedy The Butter and Egg Man; *not remarkable in any way.*
w Arthur Caesar, Monty Banks, Earl Baldwin *d* Ray Enright
☆ Joe E. Brown, Ginger Rogers, Lew Cody, Vivian Oakland, Robert Greig
'It ought to do well where they like lowdown comedy.' – *Variety*

Tenderloin
US 1928 88m bw
Warner
A dancer is accused of stealing a fortune and finds gangsters suddenly interested in her.
Primitive part-talkie (15 minutes of dialogue), unspeakably hammy to listen to though visually it had some inventiveness.
w Edward T. Lowe *story* Darryl Zanuck *d* Michael Curtiz
☆ Dolores Costello, Conrad Nagel, Mitchell Lewis, George E. Stone, Dan Wolheim

Tenderness of Wolves *
West Germany 1973 83m colour
Cinegate/Tango (Rainer Werner Fassbinder)

original title: *Zärtlichkeit der Wölfe*
In Hanover, a petty criminal seduces and kills young boys, drinking their blood and selling their bodies as meat.
A blackly comic re-telling of the true story of serial killer Fritz Haarmann, showing the influence of the company's mentor, Rainer Werner Fassbinder.
w Kurt Raab *d* Ulli Lommel *ph* Jürgen Jürges *m* Bach *ad* Kurt Raab *ed* Thea Eymèsz
☆ Kurt Raab, Jeff Roden, Margit Carstensen, Hannelore Tiefenbrunner, Wolfgang Schenck, Rainer Hauer, Rainer Werner Fassbinder, Jürgen Prochnow

Tendre Ennemie *
France 1938 66m bw
World Pictures
A woman's three dead lovers return to prevent her daughter from making a romantic mistake.
Decorative whimsy which is not among its director's best, but mildly amusing none the less.
w Max Ophuls, Kurt Alexander *play L'Ennemie* by A. P. Antoine *d Max Ophüls*
☆ Simone Berriau, Jacqueline Daix, Georges Vitray, Marc Valbel, Lucien Nat
'Story is sacrificed for camera angles ... weak even for the arties.' – *Variety*

Tendre Poulet: see *Dear Inspector*

Tenebrae (dubbed)
Italy 1982 101m colour
Anglo American/Sigma (Claudio Argento)

original title: *Sotto Gli Occhi Dell'Assassino*
US title: *Unsane*
As a thriller author promotes his latest work in Rome, there is a series of murders copying those in the book.
Gory serial killer movie with an intricate plot that confuses as much as it entertains.
w Dario Argento, George Kemp *d* Dario Argento *ph* Luciano Tovoli *m* Simonetti Pignatelli Morante *ad* Giuseppe Bassan *ed* Franco Fraticelli *sp* Giovanni Corridori
☆ John Saxon (Bulmer), Anthony Franciosa (Peter Neal), Christian Borromeo (Gianni), Mirella D'Angelo (Tilde), Veronica Lario (Jane), Ania Pieroni (Elsa), Eva Robins (Girl in dream), Carola Stagnaro (Det Altieri), Daria Nicolodi (Anne), John Steiner (Cristiano Bruni)
'One is made all the more aware of the director's inability to match visual flair with anything worth watching.' – *Philip Strick, MFB*
† Four seconds were cut from the British video release.

Teni Zabytykh Predkov: see *Shadows of Our Forgotten Ancestors*

Tennessee Johnson *
US 1943 102m bw
MGM (J. Walter Ruben)
GB title: *The Man on America's Conscience*
The rise and the problems of President Andrew Johnson.
Sincere, straightforward, well-produced historical drama which failed to set the Thames – or the Hudson – on fire.
w John Balderston, Wells Root *d* William Dieterle *ph* Harold Rosson *m* Herbert Stothart
☆ Van Heflin, Ruth Hussey, Lionel Barrymore, Marjorie Main, Regis Toomey, Montagu Love, Porter Hall, Charles Dingle, J. Edward Bromberg
'Dieterle's customary high-minded, high-polished mélange of heavy touches and intelligent performances.' – *James Agee*

Tennessee's Partner
US 1955 87m Technicolor Superscope
RKO

A gambling queen and a tenderfoot are involved in a double cross which leads to murder.
Predictable Western.
w Milton Krims, D. D. Beauchamp, Graham Baker, Teddi Sherman *story* Bret Harte *d* Allan Dwan *ph* John Alton
☆ Ronald Reagan, John Payne, Rhonda Fleming, Coleen Gray

Tension
US 1950 91m bw
MGM (Robert Sisk)
A chemist plans the perfect murder of his wife's lover, loses his nerve, then finds himself suspected when the man is murdered after all.
Disappointing suspenser which starts well but outstays its welcome.
w Allen Rivkin *d* John Berry *ph* Harry Stradling *m* André Previn
☆ Richard Basehart, Audrey Totter, Barry Sullivan, Cyd Charisse, Lloyd Gough, Tom d'Andrea

Tension at Table Rock
US 1956 93m Technicolor
RKO
When a stagecoach station owner is killed, a gunman takes care of his small son and at the same time rids a town of outlaws.
All the clichés are in this one, fairly neatly amassed in corners labelled High Noon, Hondo *and* Shane.
w Winston Miller *novel* Frank Gruber *d* Charles Marquis Warren *ph* Joseph Biroc *m* Dimitri Tiomkin
☆ Richard Egan, Dorothy Malone, Cameron Mitchell, Angie Dickinson

Tentacles
Italy 1976 102m Technicolor Technovision
Esse Cinematografica (E. F. Doria)

A deadly menace which leaves its victims as skeletons washed up on the California beach turns out to be a giant octopus ...
Dreary Jaws *rehash. Sadly there is no element of spoofing, it's all deadly serious.*
w Jerome Max, Tito Carpi, Steve Carabatsos, Sonia Molteni *d* Oliver Hellman (Sonia Assonitis) *ph* Roberto d'Ettore Piazzoli *m* S. W. Cipriani
☆ Shelley Winters, John Huston, Bo Hopkins, Henry Fonda, Claude Akins, Cesare Danova, Delia Boccardo

Les Tentations De Marianne: see *The Temptations of Marianne*

Tenth Avenue Angel
US 1948 74m bw
MGM (Ralph Wheelwright)
The little daughter of poor parents loses her faith in life.
Icky sentimental piece for a waning child star.
w Angna Enters, Craig Rice, Harry Ruskin, Eleanore Griffin *d* Roy Rowland *ph* Robert Surtees *m* Rudolph G. Kopp
☆ Margaret O'Brien, Angela Lansbury, George Murphy, Phyllis Thaxter, Rhys Williams, Warner Anderson, Audrey Totter, Connie Gilchrist

The Tenth Man
GB 1936 68m bw
BIP
A wife shows faith in her husband even though she knows him to be a crook.
Stock film version of one of Somerset Maugham's less pungent plays.
w Geoffrey Kerr, Dudley Leslie, Marjorie Deans, Jack Davies *d* Brian Desmond Hurst
☆ John Lodge, Antoinette Cellier, Aileen Marson, Clifford Evans, George Graves

The Tenth Victim
Italy/France 1965 92m Technicolor
Avco/CC Champion/Concordia (Carlo Ponti)

In the 21st century murder is legalized to avoid birth control and war, and ten killings bring a fabulous prize.
Science fiction satire which just about gets by.
w Tonino Guerra, Giorgio Salvioni, Ennio Flaiano, Elio Petri *story The Seventh Victim* by Robert Sheckley *d* Elio Petri *ph* Gianni di Venanzo *m* Piero Piccioni
☆ Ursula Andress, Marcello Mastroianni, Elsa Martinelli, Massimo Serato
'When one thinks of the number of gifted men who have labored to produce this wobbly jape, one is struck by the fact that, of all the arts, film can be the greatest waster of talents.' – *John Simon*

Tenue de Soirée *
France 1986 85m Eastmancolor
Panavision
Hachette Premiere/DD Productions/Cine Valse/
Philippe Dussart

GB title: *Evening Dress*
aka: *Menage*
A husky burglar seduces the puny husband of a couple he involves in his criminal activities.
Anti-bourgeois comedy that tries too hard to be outrageous. Michel Blanc won the award for best actor at the Cannes Film Festival in 1986 for his performance as the timid husband.
wd Bertrand Blier *ph* Jean Penzer *m* Serge Gainsbourg *pd* Theobald Meurisse *ed* Claudine Merlin
☆ Gérard Depardieu, Michel Blanc, Miou-Miou, Michel Creton, Jean-François Stevenin, Mylène Demongeot, Caroline Sihol, Jean-Yves Berteloot, Bruno Cremer
'Never has there been a picture that made it more hideously clear that, even without the intervention of the police, crime does not pay and that sexual experimentation does not reward its practitioners with happiness.' – *Quentin Crisp*

Teorema: see *Theorem*

'A business on the line. A friendship on the edge. A woman caught in the middle.'
Tequila Sunrise
US 1988 115m DeLuxe
Warner/Mount Company (Tom Shaw)

A former drug-dealer, who is being tempted to get involved in one last major deal, and his friend, an undercover narcotics cop, compete for the same girl.
Wordy thriller in which everyone goes through the motions without much enthusiasm.
wd Robert Towne *ph* Conrad L. Hall *m* Dave Grusin *pd* Richard Sylbert *ed* Claire Simpson
☆ Mel Gibson, Michelle Pfeiffer, Kurt Russell, Raul Julia, J. T. Walsh, Arliss Howard, Arye Gross, Gabriel Damon
Conrad L. Hall

Teresa **
US 1950 101m bw
MGM (Arthur M. Loew)
A soldier with mother problems brings home an Italian bride.
Careful, sensitive, intelligent variation on a problem frequently considered by films of this period (Frieda, Fräulein, Japanese War Bride).
w Stewart Stern d Fred Zinnemann ph William J. Miller *m* Louis Applebaum

☆ Pier Angeli, John Ericson, Patricia Collinge, Richard Bishop, Peggy Ann Garner, Ralph Meeker, Bill Mauldin, Rod Steiger
original story (Arthur Hayes, Stewart Stern)

Term of Trial *
GB 1962 130m bw
Romulus (James Woolf)
An unsuccessful schoolmaster is accused of rape by a nymphomaniac schoolgirl he has scorned.
Rather flabby 'adult' drama, too schematic to be really interesting despite the best that acting can do.
wd Peter Glenville *novel* The Burden of Proof by James Barlow *ph* Oswald Morris *m* Jean-Michel Demase *ad* Antony Woolard
☆ Laurence Olivier, Sarah Miles, Simone Signoret, Hugh Griffith, Terence Stamp, Roland Culver, Frank Pettingell, Thora Hird, Dudley Foster, Norman Bird

'Harry Benson is a brilliant computer scientist. For three minutes a day, he is violently homicidal.'
The Terminal Man *
US 1974 104m colour
Warner (Mike Hodges)
A man, who has a computer implanted in his brain to control his murderous tendencies, discovers he enjoys the aftermath of his violent outbursts.
A moderately intriguing, modern variation on Frankenstein, done with a clinical style, in which scientists create a human monster that they cannot control.
wd Mike Hodges *novel* Michael Crichton *ph* Richard H. Kline *ad* Fred Harpman *ed* Robert Wolfe
☆ George Segal, Joan Hackett, Richard Dysart, Jill Clayburgh, Donald Moffat, Matt Clark
'Of all the bad sci-fi movies of the 70s, this one probably has the least charm.' – *Pauline Kael, New Yorker*

Terminal Station: see *Indiscretion of an American Wife*

Terminal Velocity
US 1994 102m colour
Buena Vista/Steep Hollow/Hollywood (Scott Kroopf, Tom Engelman)
A sky-diving instructor links up with an ex-KGB agent to recover a plane-load of gold bullion.
A slick but otherwise ordinary action movie with a preening hero and a few spectacular stunts.
w David Twohy *d* Deran Sarafian *ph* Oliver Wood *m* Joel McNeely *pd* David L. Snyder *ed* Frank J. Urioste
☆ Charlie Sheen, Nastassja Kinski, James Gandolfini, Christopher MacDonald, Gary Bullock, Hans R. Howes, Melvin Van Peebles

The Terminator *
US 1984 108m CFI color
Orion/Hemdale/Pacific Western (Gale Anne Hurd)
An android from the future is sent back to the present time on a mission of extermination.
Slick, rather nasty but undeniably compelling comic book adventures.
w James Cameron, Gale Anne Hurd *d* James Cameron *ph* Adam Greenberg *m* Brad Fiedel *ed* Mark Goldblatt
☆ Arnold Schwarzenegger, Michael Biehn, Linda Hamilton, Paul Winfield, Rick Rossovich, Lance Henriksen

'It's Nothing Personal.'
Terminator 2: Judgment Day **
US 1991 135m CFI color
Guild/Carolco/Pacific Western/Lightstorm (James Cameron)
An android returns from the future to save a boy and his mother from a murderous shape-changing robot.
Thunderous, high-voltage action movie with dazzling special effects that provide a distraction from the often silly narrative.
w James Cameron, William Wisher *d* James Cameron *ph* Adam Greenberg *m* Brad Fiedel *pd* Joseph Nemec III *ed* Richard A. Harris, Mark Goldblatt, Conrad Buff *sp* Fantasy II Film Effects, Industrial Light and Magic
☆ Arnold Schwarzenegger, Linda Hamilton, Edward Furlong, Robert Patrick, Earl Boen, Joe Morton, S. Epatha Merkerson, Castulo Guerra
'A science-fiction film with verve, imagination and even a little wit.' – *Derek Malcolm, Guardian*
'A humongous, visionary parable that intermittently enthralls and ultimately disappoints. T2 is half of a terrific movie – the wrong half. For a breathless first hour, the film zips along in a textbook display of plot planting and showmanship. But then it stumbles over its own ambitions before settling for a conventional climax with a long fuse.' – *Richard Corliss, Time*
† Reportedly the most expensive film so far made, at a cost of $80–$100 million, it was the biggest box-office success of 1991, taking $112m in rentals in North America alone.
visual effects (Dennis Murren, Stan Winston, Gene Warren Jnr, Robert Skotak); make-up (Stan Winston, Jeff Dawn)
Adam Greenberg; editing

Terminus ***
GB 1961 30m bw
British Transport Films
Twenty-four hours in the life of Waterloo Station.
An excellent 'fly-on-the-wall' documentary which launched the feature film career of its director and is still both funny and moving.
wd John Schlesinger *ph* Ken Phipps, Robert Paynter *m* Ron Grainer

Terminus
France/West Germany 1986 83m colour
Fox/CAT/Films du Cheval de Fer/Initial Groupe/CLB/A2 (Anne François)
In the future, a driver takes over a computer-programmed truck from its dead owner in a dangerous race.
Virtually incomprehensible science fiction, cut from its original length of 110 minutes; even when it is understandable, it fails to grip.
w Pierre-William Glenn, Patrice Duvic *story* Alain Gillot *d* Pierre-William Glenn *ph* Jean-Claude Vicquery *m* David Cunningham *ad* Alain Challier *ed* Thierry Derocles
☆ Johnny Hallyday, Karen Allen, Jurgen Prochnow, Gabriel Damon, Julie Glenn, Louise Vincent

'Come To Laugh. Come To Cry. Come To Care. Come To Terms.'
Terms of Endearment **
US 1983 132m Metrocolor
Paramount (James L. Brooks)
An eccentric widow fends off suitors while interfering with her daughter's marriage; but all is forgiven when the daughter dies.
This shapeless film is little more than an excuse for actors and writer to show off, which they do to great excess; but parts of it are entertaining enough and it certainly impressed the Academy Award committee.
wd James L. Brooks *novel* Larry McMurtry *ph* Andrzej Bartkowiak *m* Michael Gore *pd* Polly Platt
☆ *Shirley MacLaine, Jack Nicholson, Debra Winger,* Danny DeVito, Jeff Daniels, John Lithgow
'An outsize sitcom and a crassly constructed slice of anti-feminism that contrives to rub liberal amounts of soap in the viewer's eyes.' – *Sight and Sound*
'There isn't a thing I would change.' – *Roger Ebert*
best picture; Shirley MacLaine; Jack Nicholson; direction; adaptation
John Lithgow; editing (Richard Marks); Michael Gore; art direction; Debra Winger

La Terra Trema *
Italy 1948 160m bw
Universalia
The life of a Sicilian fisherman and his family.
Seriously intended, carefully composed semi-documentary stressing the economic problems of the simple life. A commercial disaster: even the Italians couldn't understand the accents of the local actors.
wd Luchino Visconti *ph* G. R. Aldo *m* Luchino Visconti, Willy Ferrero
† The cast was drawn from the inhabitants of Aci Trezza, Sicily.

The Terra-Cotta Warrior *
Hong Kong 1990 111m Eastmancolor Panavision
Art & Talent Group (Hon Pou Chu)
A soldier encased in clay and buried with his emperor comes back to life 3,000 years later to be re-united with his lover, reincarnated as an actress.
A familiar mix of the supernatural and martial arts, performed with verve.
w Lee Bik Wah *d* Ching Tung Yee *ph* Peter Pau *m* Joseph Koo *pd* Yee Chung Man *ed* Mak Chi Shin *sp* Tsui Hark
☆ Zhang Yimou, Gong Li, Yu Yung Kang

A Terrible Beauty
GB 1960 90m bw
UA/Raymond Stross
US title: *Night Fighters*
In a north Irish village, the IRA revive their activities on the outbreak of World War II.
Heavily Oirish melodrama with a muddled message.
w Robert Wright Campbell *novel* Arthur Roth *d* Tay Garnett *ph* Stephen Dade *m* Cedric Thorpe Davie
☆ Robert Mitchum, Anne Heywood, Dan O'Herlihy, Cyril Cusack, Richard Harris, Marianne Benet

The Terror
US 1928 82m approx bw
Warner
A mysterious killer lurks in the cellars of a country house.
Primitive talkie which attempted a few new styles but showed that more were needed, also that some silent actors could not make the transfer.
w Harvey Gates *play* Edgar Wallace *novel* Edgar Wallace *d* Roy del Ruth *ph* Barney McGill
☆ May McAvoy, Edward Everett Horton, Louise Fazenda, Alec B. Francis, John Miljan, Frank Austin
'The only terrible thing about this talkie Terror is its unnatural slowness ... the characters speak as if they were dictating important letters.' – *A. P. Herbert, Punch*
'May be crude, but it is a maker of history. Something has been achieved here. A new chapter of film evolution is beginning. Today it is as foolish to argue that talking films cannot be successful as to declare that a man in London cannot possibly speak by telephone to a man in New York.' – *C. A. Lejeune*
† The first film without a single subtitle: all the credits were spoken.
†† *Return of the Terror* (US 1934) has little to do with it.

The Terror
GB 1938 73m bw
Associated British
Stilted remake of the above.
w William Freshman *d* Richard Bird
☆ Wilfrid Lawson, Arthur Wontner, Alastair Sim, Linden Travers, Bernard Lee, Henry Oscar

The Terror
US 1963 81m Pathécolor
AIP/Filmgroup (Roger Corman, Francis Ford Coppola)
A baron lives for twenty years in a creepy castle, mourning the death of his wife ...
Shoddy horror improvised over a weekend on the set of The Raven. *It looks it.*
w Leo Gordon, Jack Hill *d* Roger Corman *ph* John Nickolaus *m* Ronald Stein
☆ Boris Karloff, Jack Nicholson, Sandra Knight, Dorothy Neumann

Terror Aboard
US 1933 70m bw
Paramount
Gruesome murders occur during a pleasure cruise.
Fair murder mystery.
w Harvey Thew, Manuel Seff *d* Paul Sloane
☆ Charles Ruggles, John Halliday, Shirley Grey, Neil Hamilton, Verree Teasdale, Jack La Rue

Terror by Night *
US 1946 60m bw
Universal (Howard Benedict)
Sherlock Holmes recovers a stolen jewel and solves a murder or two aboard a speeding train.
An amusing entry in the modernized series despite some bad support acting and hilarious interposed shots of the supposed scenery between London and Edinburgh.
w Frank Gruber *d* Roy William Neill *ph* Maury Gertsman *m* Hans Salter
☆ Basil Rathbone, Nigel Bruce, Dennis Hoey, Alan Mowbray, Renee Godfrey, Billy Bevan, Mary Forbes, Frederic Worlock

Terror from the Year 5000
US 1958 74m bw
AIP (Robert J. Gurney Jnr)
GB title: *Cage of Doom*
A brash young entrepreneur who has invested in an experimental time machine inadvertently brings back a woman, disfigured by radiation, from the future.
A mix of sex and science fiction with a moral, effective enough in its low-budget way, though audiences have to wait a long time for the terror to arrive.
wd Robert J. Gurney Jnr *ph* Arthur Florman *ed* Dede Allen
☆ Ward Costello, Joyce Holden, Frederick Downs, John Stratton, Salome Jens, Fred Herrick

Terror House: see *The Night Has Eyes*

Terror in a Texas Town *
US 1958 81m bw
UA/Frank N. Seltzer
A Swedish seaman arrives in a small Western town and avenges the death of his father.
Stylish second-feature Western, a genuine sleeper which holds the interest throughout.
w Ben L. Perry *d* Joseph H. Lewis *ph* Ray Rennahan *m* Gerald Fried
☆ Sterling Hayden, Sebastian Cabot, Carol Kelly, Eugene Martin, Ned Young

Terror in the Aisles
US 1984 82m CFI color
TEM/Kaleidoscope/Universal
A compilation of fragments from mainly shock films, of no great interest even to film buffs because in most cases the scenes are wrenched out of context to fit a fatuous commentary.
w Margery Doppelt *d* Andrew Kuehn

Terror in the Haunted House
US 1958 81m bw
Howco
aka: *My World Dies Screaming*
A bride finds that her honeymoon mansion is one about which she has been having recurring nightmares.
The plot has everything, even an axe murderer, but the treatment is soporific.
w Robert C. Dennis *d* Harold Daniels *ph* Frederick E. West *m* Darrell Calker
☆ Gerald Mohr, Cathy O'Donnell, William Ching, John Qualen, Barry Bernard

Terror in the Wax Museum
US 1973 94m DeLuxe
Bing Crosby Productions/Fenady Associates (Andrew J. Fenady)
In Victorian London a waxworks owner is murdered ...
Cheaply produced murder mystery (even the waxworks can't stand still) with horror asides and a cast of elderly hams.
w Jameson Brewer *d* Georg Fenady *ph* William Jurgensen *m* George Duning
☆ Ray Milland, Broderick Crawford, Elsa Lanchester, Louis Hayward, John Carradine, Shani Wallis, Maurice Evans, Patric Knowles

Terror of Mechagodzilla: see *Monsters from an Unknown Planet*

The Terror of Sheba: see *Persecution*

'Drug-crazed assassins carrying out their hate-filled ritual murders!'
The Terror of the Tongs
GB 1961 79m Technicolor
BLC/Hammer/Merlin (Kenneth Hyman)
In 1910 Hong Kong a merchant avenges the death of his daughter at the hands of a villainous secret society.
Gory melodrama with dollops of screams, torture and vaguely orgiastic goings-on.

w Jimmy Sangster d Anthony Bushell ph Arthur Grant m James Bernard ad Bernard Robinson, Thomas Goswell ed Jim Needs, Eric Boyd-Perkins ☆ Geoffrey Toone, Christopher Lee, Yvonne Monlaur, Brian Worth, Richard Leech

The Terror of the Vampires: see *Le Frisson des Vampires*

Terror on a Train: see *Time Bomb*

Terror Train
Canada 1980 97m DeLuxe
Fox/Triple T (Harold Greenberg)
Participants in a wild party aboard a train are decimated by a mysterious psychotic.
Shocks and blood in the Carpenter tradition, adequately mounted.
w T. Y. Drake d Roger Spottiswoode ph John Alcott m John Mills-Cockle pd Glenn Bydwell ed Anne Henderson
☆ Ben Johnson, Jamie Lee Curtis, David Copperfield, Hart Bochner

The Terroriser
Taiwan/Hong Kong 1986 109m colour
ICA/Sunny Overseas Corporation/Golden Harvest (Lin Dengfei, Raymond Chow)
original title: *Kongbufenzi*
aka: *The Terrorizers*
A writer, whose marriage is going wrong, finds that life is beginning to resemble her latest novel.
Unconvincing melodrama with intellectual pretensions that makes little sense.
w Xiao Ye, Edward Yang d Edward Yang ph Zhang Zhan m Weng Xiaoliang ad Lai Mingtang ed Liao Qingsong
☆ Cora Miao, Li Liqun, Jin Shijie, Gu Baoming, Wang An, Liu Ming, You Anshun

'Her death will not be ordinary.'
The Terrorist **
India 1998 100m colour
Metro Tartan/Indian Image (A. Sriram, Abhijeeth)
In an Asian country, a young female terrorist begins to have doubts about her mission as a suicide bomber.
Intriguing movie of the making, and unmaking, of a revolutionary killer, though, in the end, it leaves too much unexplained.
w Santosh Sivan, Ravi Deshpande, Vijay Deveshwar d Santosh Sivan ph Santosh Sivan m Sonu Sisupal, Rajamani pd Shyam Sunder ed A. Skreekar Prasad
☆ Ayesha Dharkar (Malli), Vishnu Vardhan (Thyagu), Bhanu Prakash (Perumal), K. Krishna (Lover), Sonu Sisupal (Leader), Vishwas (Lotus)
'A wonder several times over. Joining a compelling tale with exquisite photography and involving acting, it's a remarkable film by any standard.' – *Kenneth Turan, Los Angeles Times*
'Not only a harrowing human drama, but also a film of devastating visual simplicity.' – *Empire*

The Terrorists: see *Ransom (1975)*

The Terrorizers: see *The Terroriser*

The Terry Fox Story
Canada 1983 97m colour
ITC/CTV (Robert Cooper)
A young man dying of cancer has a leg amputated, but still runs across Canada in aid of research.
True it may be, but dramatically this is a one-note film with endless pretty pictures of countryside and in the foreground signs of failing health.
w Edward Hume d Ralph L. Thomas ph Richard Ciupka m Bill Conti ad Gavin Mitchell ed Ron Wisman
☆ Eric Fryer, Robert Duvall, Chris Makepeace, Rosalind Chao

'My name is Angela. They 're going to kill me.'
Tesis *
Spain 1996 126m colour
Escorpion (Jose Luis Cuerda)
A film student, who is researching a thesis on audiovisual violence, discovers a video showing the murder and dismemberment of a fellow student.
Clever, unsettling film that skilfully creates a sense of suspense and unease.
w Alejandro Amenábar, Mateo Gil d Alejandro Amenábar ph Hans Burmann m Alejandro Amenábar, Mariano Marín pd Wolfgang Burmann ed María Elena Sainz de Rozas
☆ Ana Torrent (Angela), Fele Martínez (Chema), Eduardo Noriega (Bosco), Nieves Herranz (Sena), Rosa Campillo (Yolanda), Miguel Picazo (Figueroa), Xavier Elorriaga (Jorge Castro)

Tess *
France/GB 1979 180m colour
Renn-Burrill (Claude Berri)
A peasant girl tries to prove her noble heritage but finds herself with an illegitimate child.
Solid, unexciting version of the classic Wessex novel; a hard sell for 1980 audiences.
w Roman Polanski, Gerard Brach, John Brownjohn novel *Tess of the D'Urbervilles* by Thomas Hardy d Roman Polanski ph Geoffrey Unsworth, Ghislain Cloquet m Philippe Sarde pd Pierre Guffroy, Jack Stevens
☆ Nastassja Kinski, Leigh Lawson, Peter Firth, John Collin, David Markham, Richard Pearson
'It emerges without a hint of what might have drawn Polanski to the material.' – *Sight and Sound*
Geoffrey Unsworth, Ghislain Cloquet; art direction; costume design (Anthony Powell)
best film; Roman Polanski; Philippe Sarde
best photography

Tess of the Storm Country
US 1932 80m bw
Fox
A retired sea captain's daughter loves the lord of the manor.
Antiquated tushery first filmed as a Mary Pickford silent.
w S. N. Behrman, Sonya Levien, Rupert Hughes novel Grace Miller White d Alfred Santell ph Hal Mohr
☆ Janet Gaynor, Charles Farrell, Dudley Digges, June Clyde, George Meeker

Tess of the Storm Country
US 1960 84m colour Cinemascope
TCF (Everett Chambers)
A Scottish girl moves to Pennsylvania and falls for a Mennonite farmer caught up in a dispute about a chemical works polluting the land.
An old-fashioned romantic drama, with a more modern ecological subplot, it is enjoyable and pleasing to the eye, though in no way memorable.
w Charles Lang novel Grace Miller White d Paul Guilfoyle ph James Wong Howe m Paul Sawtell, Bert Shefter ad John Mansbridge ed John Bushelman
☆ Diane Baker, Jack Ging, Lee Philips, Wallace Ford, Robert F. Simon, Bert Remsen, Archie Duncan, Nancy Valentine

'They're yours ... in a heart-walloping love story!'
Test Pilot **
US 1938 118m bw
MGM (Louis D. Lighton)
A brilliant but unpredictable test pilot is helped by his wife and his self-sacrificing friend.
A big box-office star vehicle of its time, still interesting as a highly efficient product.
w Waldemar Young, Vincent Lawrence story Frank Wead d Victor Fleming ph Ray June m Franz Waxman ed Tom Held
☆ *Clark Gable, Myrna Loy, Spencer Tracy,* Lionel Barrymore, Samuel S. Hinds, Marjorie Main, Gloria Holden
'B.o. potential of above-average calibre ... could have been cut 10–15 minutes without spoiling.' – *Variety*
'The picture is so noisy with sure-fire elements – box office cast, violent excitement, glycerine tears and such – that it may be hard to keep the ear attuned to the quieter, more authentically human things in it.' – *James Shelley Hamilton*
best picture; Frank Wead; Tom Held

Testament *
US 1983 90m CFI color
Entertainment Events/American Playhouse
A small California town is hit by a nuclear attack.
Probably better than the TV movie The Day After, this was less well publicized and therefore lost out.
w John Sacret Young story Carol Amen d Lynne Littman ph Steven Poster m James Horner
☆ *Jane Alexander,* William Devane, Ross Harris, Roxana Zal, Lukas Haas, Lilia Skala, Leon Ames
'After thirty years of learning to live with the Bomb, we still lack ways of conceiving the Unthinkable.' – *Sheila Johnston, MFB*
Jane Alexander

Testament
GB 1988 80m Technicolor
Black Audio Film Collective/Channel 4 (Avril Johnson, Lina Gopaul)
Twenty years after the military coup that overthrew Nkrumah's government, a television interviewer returns to Ghana to try to interview Werner Herzog and to make sense of the past.
Part documentary, part fiction, it is too personal a film to mean much to the uncommitted.
wd John Akomfrah ph David Scott m Trevor Mathison ed Brand Thumin
☆ Tania Rogers, Evans Hunter, Emma Francis Wilson, Frank Parkes, Errol Shaker
'A richly allusive, evocative meditation on memory, history and identity, both national and personal.' – *MFB*

Le Testament d'Orphée *
France 1959 83m bw
Editions Cinégraphiques (Jean Thullier)
aka: *The Testament of Orpheus*
The poet, as an 18th-century man, dies, enters spacetime, is revived, and seeks his identity.
Rather like a melancholy madman's Alice in Wonderland, *this bizarre jumble has its fascinations but misses by a mile the arresting qualities of* Orphée.
wd Jean Cocteau ph Roland Pointoizeau m Georges Auric and others
☆ Jean Cocteau, Edouard Dermithe, Maria Casarès, François Périer, Henri Crémieux, Yul Brynner, Jean-Pierre Léaud, Daniel Gélin, Jean Marais, Pablo Picasso, Charles Aznavour

The Testament of Dr Mabuse **
Germany 1933 122m bw
Nero (Fritz Lang)
A sequel to *Dr Mabuse the Gambler*: the criminal mastermind dies in an asylum, and his assistant takes over his identity.
Fast-moving penny dreadful, alleged by its director to be a denouncing of the doctrines of Hitler, but showing little evidence of being more than a very slick entertainment.
w Thea von Harbou, Fritz Lang d Fritz Lang ph Fritz Arno Wagner m Hans Erdmann ad *Karl Vollbrecht, Emil Hassler*
☆ Rudolf Klein-Rogge, Otto Wernicke, Gustav Diessl
† On arrival in America Lang claimed that 'slogans of the Third Reich have been put into the mouths of criminals in the film'. Yet his wife, who co-scripted it, stayed behind as a confirmed Nazi.

The Testament of Orpheus: see *Le Testament d'Orphée*

La Teta y la Luna: see *The Tit and the Moon*

'Bizarre, Beautiful, Horrific...'
Tetsuo II: Bodyhammer **
Japan 1991 83m colour
ICA/Kaiju Theatre/Toshiba EMI (Fuminori Shisido, Fumio Kurokawa)
A clerk, pursuing punks who have killed his son, mutates into a metallic man with built-in weaponry.
Bizarre but eminently watchable science-fiction fable.
wd Shinya Tsukamoto ph Shinya Tsukamoto, Fumikazu Oda, Katsunori Yokoyama ad Shinya Tsukamoto ed Shinya Tsukamoto
☆ Tomoroh Taguchi, Nobu Kanaoka, Shinya Tsukamoto, Keinosuke Tomioka, Sujin Kim, Min Tanaka
'Brain-blowing ... this gruesome gore fest looks to be a solid click with the midnight crowd and metal fetishists.' – *Variety*

Tetsuo: The Iron Man *
Japan 1991 67m bw
Kaijyu
After a metal fetishist is hit by a car, the driver begins to turn into a metallic man.
Weird science-fiction fantasy, by turns surreal and nasty, but displaying an unusual visual flair by its writer-director.
wd Shinya Tsukamoto ph Shinya Tsukamoto, Kei Fujiwara m Chu Ishikawa ed Shinya Tsukamoto
☆ Tomoroh Taguchi, Kei Fujiwara, Nobu Kanaoka, Shinya Tsukamoto, Naomasa Musaka, Renji Ishibashi
'For most viewers it will be the cinematic equivalent of being run over by a car and turning into a metal blob.' – *Variety*

Tevya the Milkman *
US 1939 93m bw
Henry Ziskin
A Russian village milkman watches with awe as the pogroms begin to affect his people.
One of the best Yiddish films with the best Yiddish actor, this pleasing comedy-drama was the basis for the musical Fiddler on the Roof.
wd Maurice Schwartz story Sholem Aleichem
☆ *Maurice Schwartz,* Miriam Riselle, Rebecca Weintraub, Paula Lubelska

Tex and The Lord of the Deep
Italy 1985 96m colour
Sacis/RAI (Giocchino Marano, José M. Rodriguez, Paola Bistolfi)
original title: *Tex e il Signore degli Abissi*
Tex Willer defeats an attempt to revive the Aztec empire in Mexico.
Last decadent gasp of the spaghetti Western, managing to combine cowboys and Indians with Kit Carson, a comic book hero, a scantily clad priestess, a fat man in a fez, a mummifying weapon and a volcanic eruption.
w Giorgio Bonelli, Gianfranco Clerici, Marcello Coscia, Duccio Tessari story Giovanni L. Bonelli d Duccio Tessari ph Pietro Morbidelli m Gianni Ferrio ad Antonello Geleng, Walter Patriarca ed Mirella Mercio, Lidia Bordi
☆ Giuliano Gemma, William Berger, Carlo Mucari, Isabel Russinova, Peter Berling, Flavio Bucci

The Texan
US 1930 79m bw
Paramount (Hector Turnbull)
The Llano Kid absolves his bandit past.
Early sound Western, an interesting curiosity.
w Daniel Nathan Rubin story *The Double-Dyed Deceiver* by O. Henry d John Cromwell ph Victor Milner
☆ Gary Cooper, Fay Wray, Emma Dunn, Oscar Apfel
'Few westerns are as well made and rate as high in every particular.' – *Variety*

'Love and glory on America's last frontier!'
The Texans
US 1938 92m bw
Paramount (Lucien Hubbard)
Problems of the post-Civil War years include new railroads, the Ku Klux Klan, and the new cattle drive routes.
Formula Western with fairly well staged excitements backing a routine romantic triangle.
w Bertram Millhauser, Paul Sloane, William Wister Haines d James Hogan ph Theodor Sparkuhl m Gerard Carbonara
☆ Joan Bennett, Randolph Scott, May Robson, Walter Brennan, Robert Cummings, Raymond Hatton, Robert Barrat, Francis Ford
'Enough sweep and thrills to justify generally good business.' – *Variety*

Texas
US 1941 94m bw (released in sepia)
Columbia (Sam Bischoff)
Two veteran Civil War Southerners head for Texas to set up a cattle business.
Western vehicle for two young stars, now very ordinary-looking.
w Horace McCoy, Lewis Meltzer, Michael Blankfort d George Marshall ph George Meehan
☆ William Holden, Glenn Ford, Claire Trevor, George Bancroft, Edgar Buchanan, Don Beddoe, Andrew Tombes, Addison Richards

'While spoofing a little along the way, it observes the etiquette and tradition of an accepted cinema form. It has rough riding, cattle rustling, shooting and a story that leaves out only the Indian raid and the rescue by the US Cavalry.' – *Christian Science Monitor*

Texas across the River
US 1966 101m Techniscope
Universal (Harry Keller)
A Texan, an Indian and a Spanish nobleman on the run from jealous rivals have various adventures.
Sloppy Western which seems to have had jokes added when someone realized it wasn't good enough to be taken seriously.
w Wells Root, Harold Greene, Ben Starr *d* Michael Gordon *ph* Russell Metty *m* Frank de Vol *md* Joseph Gershenson
☆ Dean Martin, Alain Delon, Joey Bishop, Rosemary Forsyth, Tina Marquand, Peter Graves, Andrew Prine, Michael Ansara

Texas Addio
Italy/Spain 1966 92m Eastmancolor
BRC/Estela (Manolo Bolognini)
aka: *The Avenger*
A man revenges his father's death.
Fast-paced, uncomplicated spaghetti Western; not very memorable.
w Franco Rossetti, Ferdinando Baldi *d* Ferdinando Baldi *ph* Enzo Barboni *m* Anton Garcia Abril *ad* Luigi Scaccianoce *ed* Sergio Montanari
☆ Franco Nero, Cole Kitosch, José Suarez, Elisa Montes, Livio Lorenzon, Hugo Blanco, José Guardiola

Texas, Brooklyn and Heaven
US 1948 76m bw
Robert S. Golden/United Artists
GB title: *The Girl from Texas*
A Texas boy meets a Texas girl in New York; after various eccentric encounters, they end up riding the range again.
Would-be Saroyanesque dalliance with odd characters which never begins to come off and has been abruptly edited into the bargain.
w Lewis Meltzer *story* Barry Benefield *d* William Castle
☆ Guy Madison, Diana Lynn, James Dunn, Lionel Stander, Florence Bates, Michael Chekhov, Margaret Hamilton, Moyna McGill, Irene Ryan, Roscoe Karns, William Frawley

Texas Carnival
US 1951 77m Technicolor
MGM (Jack Cummings)
A fairground showman is mistaken for a millionaire and runs up debts.
Very thin comedy musical relying entirely on its stars.
w Dorothy Kingsley *d* Charles Walters *ph* Robert Planck *m* Harry Warren *ch* Hermes Pan *ly* Dorothy Fields
☆ Esther Williams, Red Skelton, Howard Keel, Ann Miller, Paula Raymond, Keenan Wynn, Tom Tully

'Who will survive and what will be left of them?'
The Texas Chainsaw Massacre *
US 1974 81m CFI color
Vortex (Tobe Hooper)
Visitors to a cemetery in rural Texas find their house occupied by a homicidal maniac.
Relentless horror thriller adapted from real events which also inspired Psycho*; its cult success led to a flood of similar slasher movies, though few reached its level of sustained terror.*
w Kim Henkel, Tobe Hooper *d* Tobe Hooper *ph* Daniel Pearl *m* Tobe Hooper, Wayne Bell
☆ Marilyn Burns, Allen Danziger, Paul A. Partain, William Vail
'An absolute must for all maniacs and blood drinkers in need of a few tips.' – *Benny Green, Punch*
'It's without any apparent purpose, unless the creation of disgust and fright is a purpose.' – *Roger Ebert*
'Remains as disturbing, suspenseful and shattering as the day it first saw the light of a drive-in screen.' – *Kim Newman, Empire, 1999*

The Texas Chainsaw Massacre Part 2
US 1986 95m TVC Color
Cannon (Menahem Golan, Yoram Globus)
A family of Sweeney Todds lives in an abandoned Alamo theme park, and woe betide the stray visitor.
Splatter shocker on predictable lines.
w L. M. Kit Carson *d* Tobe Hooper *ph* Richard Kooris *m* Tobe Hooper, Jerry Lambert *pd* Cary White *ed* Alain Jakubowicz
☆ Dennis Hopper, Caroline Williams, Bill Johnson, Jim Siedow
'This sequel is a less ruthless, more cartoonish affair, inviting audiences to cheer on the gruesome effects.' – *Kim Newman, Sight and Sound*

Texas Lady
US 1955 85m Technicolor Superscope
RKO (Nat Holt)
A lady newspaper owner runs an anti-corruption campaign.
Mild family Western.
w Horace McCoy *d* Tim Whelan *ph* Ray Rennahan *m* Paul Sawtell
☆ Claudette Colbert, Barry Sullivan, Greg Walcott, James Bell, Horace MacMahon, Ray Collins, Walter Sande, Douglas Fowley

'They wrote their story in words of fire!'
The Texas Rangers *
US 1936 95m bw
Paramount (King Vidor)
Three wandering ne'er-do-wells break up; two join the Texas Rangers and hunt down the third, who is an outlaw.
Pleasantly remembered star Western, later remade as The Streets of Laredo *(qv).*
w Louis Stevens *d* King Vidor *ph* Edward Cronjager
☆ Fred MacMurray, Jack Oakie, Lloyd Nolan, Jean Parker, Edward Ellis
† Another film called *The Texas Rangers* came from Columbia in 1952 and had a similar plot to the original; otherwise it was a shoddy piece of work in Supercinecolor, with George Montgomery and Jerome Courtland.

Texas Rangers Ride Again
US 1940 67m bw
Paramount
Modern Rangers capture cattle rustlers.
Second-feature 'sequel' with no relation to the original.
w William R. Lipman, Horace McCoy *d* James Hogan
☆ John Howard, Ellen Drew, Akim Tamiroff, May Robson, Broderick Crawford, Charley Grapewin, John Miljan, Anthony Quinn

Texas Terror
US 1935 58m bw
Monogram/Lone Star (Paul Malvern)
A sheriff who believes he was responsible for the death of an old friend discovers the real culprit.
Mediocre Western, one of the least interesting of Wayne's early efforts, lacking the action and stunts that usually raised Malvern's productions above his low-budget rivals.
wd Robert N. Bradbury *ph* William Hyer *ed* Carl Pierson
☆ John Wayne, Lucile Browne, Leroy Mason, Fern Emmett, George Hayes, Buffalo Bill Jnr, John Ince

Texas to Tokyo: see *We've Never Been Licked*

'It's not a place ... it's a state of mind'
Texasville
US 1990 125m DeLuxe
Guild/Nelson Films/Cine-Source (Barry Spikings, Peter Bogdanovich)
A middle-aged oil man faces difficulties with his wife and family and in his business.
A downbeat sequel, lacking in magic, to The Last Picture Show*, with its characters now much older and more miserable.*
wd Peter Bogdanovich *novel* Larry McMurtry *ph* Nicholas von Sternberg *pd* Phedon Papamichael *ed* Richard Fields
☆ Jeff Bridges, Cybill Shepherd, Annie Potts, Cloris Leachman, Timothy Bottoms, Eileen Brennan, Randy Quaid, Harvey Christiansen, Pearl Jones, Loyd Catlett
'Making a hash of trying to adapt McMurtry's extremely long and dense novel, Bogdanovich has simply thrown away the flesh and kept the bones.' – *Tom Milne, MFB*

Thank God It's Friday
US 1978 89m Metrocolor
Columbia/Motown/Casablanca (Rob Cohen)
Problems of a disc jockey in a Hollywood disco.
Routine youth programmer, rather like Rock Around the Clock *twenty years after.*
w Barry Armyan Bernstein *d* Robert Klane *ph* James Crabe *m* various *pd* Tom H. John
☆ Valerie Landsburg, Terri Nunn, Chick Vennera, Donna Summer, The Commodores
song 'Last Dance' (*m/ly* Paul Jabara)

Thank You All Very Much: see *A Touch of Love*

Thank You, Jeeves *
US 1936 57m bw
TCF (Sol M. Wurtzel)
A valet helps prevent his master from becoming involved in gun-running.
Competent second feature notable as Niven's first leading role; also one of the very few attempts to film Wodehouse.
w Joseph Hoffman, Stephen Gross *story* P. G. Wodehouse *d* Arthur Greville Collins *ph* Barney McGill *m* Samuel Kaylin
☆ *David Niven, Arthur Treacher*, Virginia Field, Lester Matthews, Colin Tapley

Thank You, Mr Moto
US 1938 67m bw
TCF
Mr Moto protects the tomb of Genghis Khan from unscrupulous treasure-hunters.
Slick and enjoyable small-scale thriller.
w Willis Cooper, Norman Foster *story* John P. Marquand *d* Norman Foster *ph* Virgil Miller *md* Samuel Kaylin *ad* Bernard Herzbrun, Albert Hogsett *ed* Irene Morra, Nick DeMaggio
☆ Peter Lorre, Thomas Beck, Pauline Frederick, Jayne Regan, Sidney Blackmer, Sig Rugmann, John Carradine

Thank Your Lucky Stars ***
US 1943 127m bw
Warner (Mark Hellinger)
Eddie Cantor and his double get involved in planning a patriotic show.
All-star wartime musical with some unexpected turns and a generally funny script.
w Norman Panama, Melvin Frank, James V. Kern *d* David Butler *ph Arthur Edeson* *m/ly* Frank Loesser, Arthur Schwartz *md* Leo F. Forbstein *ch* Le Roy Prinz
☆ *Eddie Cantor, Dennis Morgan, Joan Leslie, Edward Everett Horton, S. Z. Sakall*, Humphrey Bogart, Jack Carson, *Bette Davis*, Olivia de Havilland, *Errol Flynn*, John Garfield, Alan Hale, Ida Lupino, *Ann Sheridan*, Dinah Shore and also George Tobias, Spike Jones and his City Slickers, Willie Best, Hattie McDaniel
'The loudest and most vulgar of the current musicals, it is also the most fun, if you are amused when show people kid their own idiom.' – *James Agee*
'An all-star show with the conspicuous flavour of amateur night at the studio.' – *New York Times*
'Everyone had a good time making it.' – *Motion Picture Herald*
song 'They're Either Too Young or Too Old'

Thanks a Million **
US 1935 87m bw
TCF (Darryl F. Zanuck)
A crooner runs for governor.
Smart, amusing political musical.
w Nunnally Johnson *d* Roy del Ruth *ph* Peverell Marley *m* Arthur Lange *m/ly* Arthur Johnston, Gus Kahn
☆ Dick Powell, Fred Allen, Ann Dvorak, Patsy Kelly, Phil Baker, Paul Whiteman and his band, the Yacht Club Boys, Benny Baker, Raymond Walburn, Alan Dinehart
'Socko filmusical for big grosses ... an example of canny showmanship and presentation.' – *Variety*

Thanks for Everything *
US 1938 70m bw
TCF (Darryl F. Zanuck)
Mr Average American is discovered, promoted and merchandized.
Very acceptable satirical comedy of the advertising world.
w Harry Tugend *d* William A. Seiter *ph* George Meehan *m* Abe Meyer
☆ Adolphe Menjou, Jack Haley, Jack Oakie, Arleen Whelan, Tony Martin, Binnie Barnes, George Barbier
'Light and breezy, a cinch for popular audience appeal.' – *Variety*
'The funniest film I can remember seeing for many months, with something of the old Kaufman touch.' – *Graham Greene*

Thanks for the Memory *
US 1938 75m bw
Paramount (Mel Shaver)
A smart novelist has trouble with his marriage.
Light, agreeable domestic comedy on familiar lines.
w Lynn Starling *play* *Up Pops the Devil* by Frances Goodrich, Albert Hackett *d* George Archainbaud *ph* Karl Struss *m* Boris Morros
☆ Bob Hope, Shirley Ross
'Although lightweight, it will please if not exactly boff them.' – *Variety*

Thark *
GB 1932 79m bw
British and Dominion (Herbert Wilcox)
The heir to an old mansion spends a night in it to prove it is not haunted.
Very funny Aldwych farce, plainly transferred to the screen with the original stage team intact. One's only regret is that it peters out at the end.
w Ben Travers *play* Ben Travers *d* Tom Walls *ph* F. A. Young
☆ *Ralph Lynn, Tom Walls*, Robertson Hare, Mary Brough, Claude Hulbert, Gordon James
'Scream after scream of laughter of the wobbling midriff variety.' – *Variety*

That Brennan Girl
US 1946 97m bw
Republic
A young mother neglects her baby for the sake of a good time.
Absurdly padded-out moral tract.
w Doris Anderson *d* Alfred Santell
☆ Mona Freeman, James Dunn, William Marshall, June Duprez

That Certain Age *
US 1938 100m bw
Universal (Joe Pasternak)
A girl gets a crush on an older man.
Pleasant, well-cast star musical for the family.
w Bruce Manning *d* Edward Ludwig *ph* Joseph Valentine *songs* Jimmy McHugh, Harold Adamson
☆ *Deanna Durbin, Melvyn Douglas*, Jackie Cooper, Irene Rich, Nancy Carroll, John Halliday, Juanita Quigley, Jackie Searl, Charles Coleman
'Certain for top grosses and extended runs.' – *Variety*
song 'My Own'

That Certain Feeling
US 1956 102m Technicolor Vistavision
Paramount (Melvin Frank, Norman Panama)
An arrogant comic strip artist loses his touch and hires a 'ghost' – the ex-husband of his secretary/fiancée.
Arid comedy from a mild Broadway play, totally miscast and lacking any kind of interest.
w Norman Panama, Melvin Frank, I. A. L. Diamond, William Altman *play* *King of Hearts* by Jean Kerr, Eleanor Brooke *d* Norman Panama, Melvin Frank *ph* Loyal Griggs *m* Joseph J. Lilley
☆ Bob Hope, George Sanders, Eva Marie Saint, Pearl Bailey, Al Capp

'She got all the breaks – in her heart!'

That Certain Woman ☆

US 1937 91m bw

Warner (Hal B. Wallis)

A gangster's widow goes straight but runs into complex marriage trouble.

Self-sacrifice and mother love are rewarded by two convenient deaths and a happy ending in this routine romantic melodrama remade from a silent success.

wd Edmund Goulding *original screenplay The Trespasser* by *Edmund Goulding ph* Ernest Haller *m* Max Steiner

☆ Bette Davis, Henry Fonda, Ian Hunter, Anita Louise, Donald Crisp, Katherine Alexander, Mary Philips, Minor Watson

'Big-time cast in a well-made first run film.' – *Variety*

That Championship Season ☆

US 1982 108m Metrocolor

Cannon-Golan-Globus (Menahem Golan, Yoram Globus)

Five rather unlikeable middle-aged men live by recreating the glory of a team basketball victory 25 years ago.

Unimaginative film version of a play which had dramatic strength but very limited general appeal. Rather less can be said of the film, as the acting shows a lack of team spirit.

wd Jason Miller *play* Jason Miller *ph* John Bailey *m* Bill Conti *pd* Ward Preston *ed* Richard Halsey

☆ Bruce Dern, Stacy Keach, Robert Mitchum, Martin Sheen, Paul Sorvino, Arthur Franz

That Cold Day in the Park

Canada 1969 115m Eastmancolor

(Commonwealth United)

A spinster invites a lonely wandering boy into her home, makes him a prisoner and becomes possessively jealous.

A companion piece to The Collector, *rather better done for those who like morbid psychology.*

w Gillian Freeman *novel* Richard Miles *d* Robert Altman *ph* Laszlo Kovacs *m* Johnny Mandel

☆ Sandy Dennis, Michael Burns, Susanne Benton, Luana Anders, John Garfield Jnr

'About as pretentious, loathsome and stupid as a film can get.' – *John Simon*

That Dangerous Age

GB 1949 98m bw

London Films (Gregory Ratoff)

US title: *If This Be Sin*

Recovering from a breakdown, a KC discovers that his daughter wants to marry a man with whom his wife once had an affair.

Purple patch melodrama which sympathetic actors can't quite freshen up.

w Gene Markey *play Autumn* by Margaret Kennedy, Ilya Surgutchoff *d* Gregory Ratoff *ph* Georges Périnal *m* Mischa Spoliansky

☆ Roger Livesey, Myrna Loy, Peggy Cummins, Richard Greene, Elizabeth Allan, Gerard Heinz, Jean Cadell, G. H. Mulcaster

That Darn Cat! ☆

US 1965 116m Technicolor

Walt Disney (Bill Walsh, Ron Miller)

A troublesome cat inadvertently helps to trail bank robbers.

Overlong but generally pleasing small-town comedy with well-paced sequences and a fascinating feline hero.

w The Gordons, Bill Walsh *novel Undercover Cat* by The Gordons *d Robert Stevenson ph* Edward Colman *m* Bob Brunner

☆ Hayley Mills, Dean Jones, Dorothy Provine, Roddy McDowall, Neville Brand, Elsa Lanchester, William Demarest, Frank Gorshin, Grayson Hall, Ed Wynn

That Darn Cat

US 1997 89m Technicolor

Buena Vista/Walt Disney (Robert Simonds)

A girl solves the mystery of a missing woman with the aid of a cat.

Coarse and corny remake in an over-emphatic style.

w S. M. Alexander, L. A. Kareszewski *novel Undercover Cat* by Mildred and Gordon Gordon *d* Bob Spiers *ph* Jerzy Zielinski *m* Richard Kendall Gibbs *pd* Jonathan Carlson *ed* Roger Barton

☆ Christina Ricci, Doug E. Doug, Dean Jones, George Dzundza, Peter Boyle, Michael McKean, Bess Armstrong, Dyan Cannon, John Ratzenberger, Estelle Parsons

'A loud and largely charmless trifle.' – *Variety*

That Forsyte Woman ☆

US 1949 114m Technicolor

MGM (Leon Gordon)

GB title: *The Forsyte Saga*

The wife of an Edwardian man of property falls in love with her niece's fiancé.

Moderately successful American attempt to film the first part of a very British novel sequence; so genteel, however, that it becomes dull.

w Jan Lustig, Ivan Tors, James B. Williams *novel A Man of Property* by John Galsworthy *d* Compton Bennett *ph* Joseph Ruttenberg *m* Bronislau Kaper

☆ Greer Garson, *Errol Flynn*, Robert Young, Janet Leigh, Walter Pidgeon, Harry Davenport, Aubrey Mather

That Funny Feeling

US 1965 92m Technicolor

U-I (Harry Keller)

A maid pretends she lives in her boss's apartment.

Makeshift romantic comedy which barely takes the attention even while it's on.

w David R. Schwartz *d* Richard Thorpe *ph* Clifford Stine *m* Joseph Gershenson

☆ Sandra Dee, Bobby Darin, Donald O'Connor, Nita Talbot, Larry Storch, Leo G. Carroll, James Westerfield

That Girl from Paris

US 1936 105m bw

RKO (Pandro S. Berman)

A Paris opera singer falls for a swing band leader and stows away on a transatlantic liner to be near him.

Comedy-accented musical romance: not bad but not memorable.

w P. J. Wolfson, Dorothy Yost, Jane Murfin *d* Leigh Jason *ph* J. Roy Hunt *m/ly* Arthur Schwartz, Edward Heyman *md* Nathaniel Shilkret

☆ Lily Pons, Gene Raymond, Jack Oakie, Herman Bing, Lucille Ball, Mischa Auer, Frank Jenks

'When it's good it's very good, and when it's bad it's pretty awful.' – *Variety*

'Around her young heart she wore the scarlet letter of another woman's shame!'

That Hagen Girl

US 1947 83m bw

Warner (Alex Gottlieb)

A girl is convinced she is the illegitimate daughter of her teacher.

Stale teenage drama with odd anti-establishment overtones.

w Charles Hoffman *novel* Edith Kneipple Roberts *d* Peter Godfrey *ph* Karl Freund *m* Franz Waxman

☆ Shirley Temple, Ronald Reagan, Rory Calhoun, Lois Maxwell, Dorothy Peterson, Charles Kemper, Conrad Janis, Harry Davenport

'Less a film than a series of false situations.' – MFB

'They shouldn't do such things to Shirley.' – *Bosley Crowther, New York Times*

That Hamilton Woman ☆☆

US 1941 128m bw

Alexander Korda Films

GB title: *Lady Hamilton*

The affair of Lord Nelson and Emma Hamilton.

Bowdlerized version of a famous misalliance; coldly made but quite effective scene by scene, with notable performances.

w Walter Reisch, R. C. Sherriff *d* Alexander Korda *ph* Rudolph Maté *m* Miklós Rozsa *ad* Vincent Korda

☆ *Laurence Olivier, Vivien Leigh, Gladys Cooper,* Alan Mowbray, Sara Allgood, Henry Wilcoxon, Halliwell Hobbes

'All its minor graces don't somehow add up to a major achievement … It is my impression that the film would have been a better job if it had stuck more to this man Nelson and bothered less about that woman Hamilton. These are not days when we have much patience for looking at history through the eyes of a trollop. And I am not at all sure that English people, who have been fighting for two years for something they like to call an ideal, will very much care for the implication that the future died with Nelson.' – C. A. *Lejeune*

Academy Award nomination: Rudolph Maté; Vincent Korda

That Kind of Woman

US 1959 92m bw

Paramount/Ponti-Girosi

World War II remake of *Shopworn Angel* (qv); rather well made but basically dated and dull.

w Walter Bernstein *d* Sidney Lumet *ph* Boris Kaufman *m* Daniele Amfitheatrof

☆ Sophia Loren, Tab Hunter, George Sanders, Jack Warden, Barbara Nichols, Keenan Wynn

'The romantic reunion of Tab Hunter and Sophia Loren resembles nothing so much as a sea scout given a luxury liner for Christmas.' – *Peter John Dyer*

That Lady

GB 1955 100m Eastmancolor

Cinemascope

TCF/Atlanta (Sy Bartlett)

A noble widow at the court of Philip II of Spain loves a minister but incurs the king's jealous hatred.

Tepid historical romance which never flows as a film should.

w Anthony Veiller, Sy Bartlett *novel* Kate O'Brien *d* Terence Young *ph* Robert Krasker *m* John Addison

☆ Olivia de Havilland, Gilbert Roland, *Paul Scofield*, Françoise Rosay, Dennis Price, Anthony Dawson, Robert Harris, Peter Illing, Christopher Lee

'Somehow, somewhere, one feels, something went very wrong.' – *MFB*

BAFTA: Paul Scofield (newcomer)

That Lady in Ermine

US 1948 89m Technicolor

TCF (Ernst Lubitsch)

Two generations of European noblewomen learn to repel invaders.

Cheerless musical comedy which never gets started, what with the director dying during production and unsuitable stars lost in tinselly sets; the result can have appealed to no one.

w Samson Raphaelson *d* Ernst Lubitsch, Otto Preminger *ph* Leon Shamroy *m* Alfred Newman *songs* Leo Robin, Frederick Hollander

☆ Betty Grable, Douglas Fairbanks Jnr, Cesar Romero, Walter Abel, Reginald Gardiner, Harry Davenport

Academy Award nomination: song 'This is the Moment' (*m*Frederick Hollander, *ly*Leo Robin)

'When A No No Girl Meets A Go Go Man – Wham!!!'

That Lucky Touch

GB 1975 93m Technicolor

Rank/Gloria (Dimitri de Grunwald)

During NATO war games in Brussels, a lady correspondent falls for an arms dealer.

Dim romantic farce which gives the impression of emanating from a dog-eared script written for the kind of stars who no longer shine.

w John Briley *story* Moss Hart *d* Christopher Miles *ph* Douglas Slocombe *m* John Scott

☆ Roger Moore, Susannah York, Lee J. Cobb, Shelley Winters, Jean-Pierre Cassel, Raf Vallone, Sydne Rome, Donald Sinden

That Mad Mr Jones: see *The Fuller Brush Man*

That Man Bolt

US 1973 103m Technicolor

Universal (Bernard Schwarz)

Adventures of a professional black courier skilled in the martial arts.

Black Kung Fu hokum from a major company; tolerable of its debased kind.

w Quentin Werty, Charles Johnson *d* Henry Levin, David Lowell Rich *ph* Gerald Perry Finnerman *m* Charles Bernstein

☆ Fred Williamson, Bryon Webster, Miko Mayama, Teresa Graves

'Gives every indication of having been devised by a computer fed with a variety of ingredients currently thought to guarantee box office success.' – *John Raisbeck, MFB*

That Man from Rio

France/Italy 1964 120m Eastmancolor

Ariane/Artistes Associés/Dear Film/Vides (Alexander Mnouchkine, Georges Danciger)

original title: *L'Homme de Rio*

An airforce pilot finds himself helping his girlfriend in a worldwide search for stolen statuettes.

Elaborate mock thriller which is never quite as much fun as those involved seem to think. It provoked several inferior sequels.

w J. P. Rappeneau, Ariane Mnouchkine, Daniel Boulanger, Philippe de Broca *d* Philippe de Broca *ph* Edmond Séchan *m* Georges Delerue

☆ Jean-Paul Belmondo, Jean Servais, Françoise Dorléac, Adolfo Celi, Simone Renant

'Fantasy takes over, with Belmondo outdoing Fairbanks in agility, Lloyd in cliffhanging, and Bond in indestructibility.' – *Brenda Davies, MFB*

Academy Award nomination: script

That Midnight Kiss

US 1949 98m Technicolor

MGM (Joe Pasternak)

An unknown becomes a great singing star.

Simple-minded vehicle for the first appearance of Mario Lanza.

w Bruce Manning, Tamara Hovey *d* Norman Taurog *ph* Robert Surtees *m* Bronislau Kaper

☆ Kathryn Grayson, Ethel Barrymore, Jose Iturbi, Mario Lanza, Keenan Wynn, J. Carrol Naish, Jules Munshin, Thomas Gomez, Marjorie Reynolds

That Night ☆

US 1957 88m bw

Galahad (Himan Brown)

An overwhelmed TV writer has a heart attack, and recovers after a series of medical setbacks.

Impressive minor case history, hardly entertainment but quite arresting.

w Robert Wallace, Burton J. Rowles *d* John Newland *ph* Maurice Hartzband *m* Mario Nascimbene

☆ *John Beal*, Augusta Dabney, Shepperd Strudwick, Ralph Murphy

That Night

US 1992 89m Technicolor

Warner/Canal/Regency/Alcor (Arnon Milchan, Steven Reuther)

A small girl aids and abets a romance between two teenagers, a Catholic girl and the manager of a bowling alley.

An unengrossing rites-of-passage story, not helped by being told from the perspective of a knowing child.

wd Craig Bolotin *novel* Alice McDermott *ph* Bruce Surtees *m* David Newman *pd* Maher Ahmad *ed* Patricia Nedd-Friendly, Gregg London

☆ C. Thomas Howell, Helen Shaver, Juliette Lewis, Eliza Dushku, John Dossett, J. Smith-Cameron

That Night in London

GB 1933 78m bw

Paramount/London Films (Alexander Korda)

US title: *Overnight*

A bank clerk decides to steal money to have one final fling before he commits suicide.

Dim low-budget drama that wastes its star.

w Dorothy Greenhill, Arthur Wimperis *d* Rowland V. Lee *ph* Robert Martin *m* Peter Mendoza *ed* Stephen Harrison

☆ Robert Donat, Pearl Argyle, Miles Mander, Lawrence Hanray, Roy Emmerton, Graham Soutten

That Night in Rio ☆

US 1941 90m Technicolor

TCF (Fred Kohlmar)

A night-club entertainer is paid to impersonate a lookalike count, but this causes complications with the countess.

Zippy musical based on a story first used in Folies Bergère *(qv) and later in* On the Riviera *(qv).*

w George Seaton, Bess Meredyth, Hal Long *play* Rudolph Lothar, Hans Adler *d* Irving Cummings *ph* Leon Shamroy *md* Alfred Newman *songs* Mack Gordon, Harry Warren

☆ *Don Ameche*, Alice Faye, Carmen Miranda, S. Z. Sakall, J. Carrol Naish, Curt Bois, Leonid Kinskey, Maria Montez

'An eye-filling and ear-filling musical comedy extravaganza.' – *Motion Picture Herald*

That Night in Varennes: see *La Nuit de Varennes*

That Night with You
US 1945 84m bw
Universal (Michael Fessier, Ernest Pagano)
A girl singer anxious to get on tells a producer that she is his illegitimate daughter.
Mindless farce with music, its gimmick being that all the songs are set to Tchaikovsky's music. Otherwise very dull.
w Michael Fessier, Ernest Pagano *d* William A. Seiter *ph* Woody Bredell
☆ Franchot Tone, Susanna Foster, David Bruce, Louise Allbritton, Buster Keaton, Irene Ryan, Jacqueline de Wit

That Obscure Object of Desire **
France/Spain 1977 103m Eastmancolor
Greenwich/Galaxie/In Cine (Serge Silberman)
A middle-aged gentleman suffers continual humiliations from the girl he loves.
Unrecognizable remake of a novel previously filmed as a vehicle for Dietrich and Bardot. Despite the tricking out with surrealist touches (the girl is played by two different actresses) it is not one of Buñuel's best, and amuses only on the surface.
w Luis Buñuel, Jean-Claude Carrière *novel La Femme et le Pantin* by Pierre Louys *d* Luis Buñuel *ph* Edmond Richard *m* from Richard Wagner
☆ Fernando Rey, Carole Bouquet, Angela Molina, Julien Bertheau
best foreign film; script

That Old Feeling
US 1997 105m DeLuxe
Universal/Bubble Factory/Boy of the Year/All Girl (Leslie Dixon, Bonnie Bruckheimer)
A divorced couple, each with a new partner, find that they are still attracted to one another when they meet at the wedding of their daughter, who is marrying a politician campaigning on family values.
A comedy constructed as a vehicle for Bette Midler, but, like the marriages on view here, it quickly breaks down.
w Leslie Dixon *d* Carl Reiner *ph* Steve Mason *m* Patrick Williams *pd* Sandy Veneziano *ed* Richard Halsey
☆ Bette Midler, Dennis Farina, Paula Marshall, Gail O'Grady, David Rasche, Jamie Denton, Danny Nucci
'Rekindles some fond memories of the sparks ignited between vintage feuding screen couples. But it also reminds us that current demands call for films to be less corny and schematic, more heartfelt and better focused.' – *Leonard Klady, Variety*

That Riviera Touch
GB 1966 98m Eastmancolor
Rank (Hugh Stewart)
Two tourists in the south of France get mixed up with jewel thieves.
Disappointing star comedy ending in a surfboard chase.
w S. C. Green, R. M. Hills, Peter Blackmore *d* Cliff Owen *ph* Otto Heller *m* Ron Goodwin
☆ Eric Morecambe, Ernie Wise, Suzanne Lloyd, Paul Stassino, Armand Mestral

That Summer of White Roses
GB/Yugoslavia 1989 103m colour
Amy International/Jadran (Simon MacCorkindale, Mike Mihalic)
In Yugoslavia in the last summer of the Second World War, a simple-minded lifeguard, who hides a woman and child from the Germans, finds that he is treated like a collaborator after he rescues the Nazi commandant from drowning.
A wartime drama that has no sense of urgency about it, nor much sense of anything; there is no resonance about the events depicted.
w Borislav Pekic, Rajko Grlic, Simon MacCorkindale *novel Defence and the Last Days* by Borislav Pekic *d* Rajko Grlic *ph* Tomislav Pinter *m* Brane Zivkovic, Junior Campbell, Mike O'Donnell *ad* Dinka Jericevic *ed* Damir F. German
☆ Tom Conti, Susan George, Rod Steiger, Alun Armstrong, John Gill, John Sharp, Geoffrey Whitehead
'Has a fine cast that is sadly under-stretched by a narrative which oscillates uncomfortably between the whimsical and the realist.' – *Jill Forbes, MFB*

'In every life there comes a time when that dream you dream becomes that thing you do.'
That Thing You Do! *
US 1996 108m DeLuxe
TCF/Clinica Estetico (Gary Goetzman, Jonathan Demme, Edward Saxon)
In the 60s, a beat group goes from the small to the big time before breaking up.
Sanitized 60s rock for those who grooved to Forrest Gump*; nostalgia for a simpler, more innocent time (at least, as seen through Hanks's distorting lens) acts as a narrative sedative, though audiences may respond to its generalized warmth.*
wd Tom Hanks *ph* Tak Fujimoto *m* Howard Shore *m/ly* Tom Hanks, Adam Schlesinger, Mike Miccirillo *et al pd* Victor Kempster *ed* Richard Chew
☆ Tom Everett Scott, Liv Tyler, Johnathon Schaech, Steve Zahn, Ethan Embry, Tom Hanks, Chris Isaak, Kevin Pollak, Jonathan Demme
'A bland, soft-centred, house-trained puppy of a film that begs to be loved.' – *Philip French, Observer*
'A lightweight but utterly loveable affair.' – *Empire*
song 'That Thing You Do!' (m/ly Adam Schlesinger)

That Touch of Mink **
US 1962 99m Eastmancolor Panavision
U-I/Granley/Arwin/Nob Hill (Stanley Shapiro, Martin Melcher)
Bachelor tycoon pursues virginal secretary.
Jaded sex comedy (or what passed for it in nudge-nudge 1962) enlivened by practised star performances and smart timing.
w Stanley Shapiro, Nate Monaster *d* Delbert Mann *ph* Russell Metty *m* George Duning *ad* Robert Clatworthy, Alexander Golitzen *ed* Ted J. Kent
☆ *Cary Grant, Doris Day, Gig Young*, Audrey Meadows, Dick Sargent, *John Astin*, Alan Hewitt, Joey Faye
'Too often there's a hampering second-hand air about situation and joke. Throughout, the determination is to keep faith with the American sex mythology at all costs.' – *Jack Pitman, Variety*
script; art direction; sound (Walden O. Watson)

That Uncertain Feeling *
US 1941 84m bw
UA/Sol Lesser (Ernst Lubitsch)
A wife with insomnia and hiccups befriends a wacky concert pianist who proceeds to move into her home.
Although Lubitsch had made this story before, as the silent Kiss Me Again, *the elements didn't really jell in this version, which seemed silly rather than funny.*
w Donald Ogden Stewart, Walter Reisch *play Divorçons* by Victorien Sardou, Emile de Najac *d Ernst Lubitsch ph* George Barnes *m* Werner Heymann *pd* Alexander Golitzen
☆ Merle Oberon, Melvyn Douglas, Burgess Meredith, Alan Mowbray, Olive Blakeney, Harry Davenport, Eve Arden, Sig Rumann
'Gay entertainment.' – *Picture Show*
Werner Heymann

That Was Then ... This Is Now
US 1985 102m TVC Color
Paramount/Media Ventures (Gary R. Lindberg, John M. Ondov)
Urban youths growing into manhood find the world a gloomy place.
Highly resistible chunk of pessimistic philosophizing with a few fights thrown in.
w Emilio Estevez *novel* S. E. Hinton *d* Christopher Cain *ph* Juan Ruiz-Anchia *m* Keith Olsen *ad* Chester Kaczenski *ed* Ken Johnson
☆ Emilio Estevez, Craig Sheffer, Kim Delaney, Jill Schoelen, Barbara Babcock, Morgan Freeman
'God save the kids who live in an S. E. Hinton novel. They're firecrackers waiting to go off.' – *Variety*

That Way with Women
US 1947 84m bw
Warner (Charles Hoffman)
A millionaire amuses himself by playing Cupid to a young couple.
Routine remake of The Millionaire*: just about watchable.*
w Leo Townsend *d* Frederick de Cordova *ph* Ted McCord *m* Frederick Hollander
☆ Sydney Greenstreet, Dane Clark, Martha Vickers, Alan Hale, Craig Stevens, Barbara Brown

That Woman Opposite
GB 1957 83m bw
Monarch (William Gell)
US title: *City after Midnight*
In a small French town, a killer returns to silence a witness.
Slow-paced semi-mystery, reasonably well done.
wd Compton Bennett *story The Emperor's Snuff Box* by John Dickson Carr *ph* Lionel Banes *m* Stanley Black
☆ Phyllis Kirk, Dan O'Herlihy, Wilfrid Hyde-White, Petula Clark, Jack Watling, William Franklyn, Margaret Withers

That Wonderful Urge
US 1948 82m bw
TCF (Fred Kohlmar)
A newspaperman is forced into marriage with a publicity-shy heiress.
Tepid romantic comedy, a remake of Love Is News *(qv).*
w Jay Dratler *d* Robert B. Sinclair *ph* Charles Clarke *m* Cyril Mockridge
☆ Gene Tierney, Tyrone Power, Reginald Gardiner, Arleen Whelan, Lucile Watson, Gene Lockhart, Porter Hall, Taylor Holmes

That'll Be the Day *
GB 1973 91m Technicolor
EMI/Goodtimes (David Puttnam, Sanford Lieberson)
In 1958, a young drifter becomes a fairground worker, and eventually walks out on his wife and family to become a pop star.
Spirited return to British realism, with well-sketched cameos, a likeable dour viewpoint, and a cheerful pop music background.
w Ray Connolly *d* Claude Whatham *ph* Peter Suschitzky *md* Neil Aspinall, Keith Moon
☆ *David Essex*, Ringo Starr, Rosemary Leach, James Booth, Billy Fury, Keith Moon, Rosalind Ayres
'As insubstantial as one of its own attempts at a statement.' – *Tony Rayns*

That's a Good Girl *
GB 1933 83m bw
British and Dominions (Herbert Wilcox)
A man about town seeks ways of making money.
Archetypal vehicle for a debonair song and dance man.
w Douglas Furber, Donovan Pedelty, Jack Buchanan *d* Jack Buchanan *ph* Freddie Young *md* Philip Braham
☆ *Jack Buchanan*, Elsie Randolph, Dorothy Hyson, Garry Marsh, Vera Pearce, William Kendall

That's Dancin'! **
US 1985 105m Metrocolor
MGM-UA/David Niven Jnr, Jack Haley Jnr
Selections from the golden age of the movie musical, featuring the likes of Fred Astaire, Gene Kelly, Eleanor Powell, Busby Berkeley.
Fascinating compilation which made little impact at the box-office.
narrators Gene Kelly, Sammy Davis Jnr, Mikhail Baryshnikov, Liza Minnelli, Ray Bolger

'Boy! do we need it now!'
That's Entertainment **
US 1974 137m Metrocolor 70mm (blown up)/scope
MGM (Daniel Melnick, Jack Haley Jnr)
Stars introduce some of their performances and other highlights from MGM's musical past.
A slapdash compilation which was generally very big at the box-office and obviously has fascinating sequences, though the narration is sloppily sentimental and the later wide-screen sequences let down the rest.
wd Jack Haley Jnr *ph* various *m* various
☆ Fred Astaire, Gene Kelly, Elizabeth Taylor, James Stewart, Bing Crosby, Liza Minelli, Donald O'Connor, Debbie Reynolds, Mickey Rooney, Frank Sinatra, Judy Garland, Esther Williams, Eleanor Powell, Clark Gable, Ray Bolger
'While many ponder the future of MGM, none can deny that it has one hell of a past.' – *Variety*
'It is particularly gratifying to get the key sequences from certain movies without having to sit through a fatuous storyline.' – *Michael Billington, Illustrated London News*
'No other film in town offers such a harvest of undiluted joy.' – *Sunday Express*

That's Entertainment! III **
US 1994 113m DeLuxe
MGM (Bud Friedgen, Michael J. Sheridan)
Former MGM stars introduce excerpts from 30 years of the studio's musicals, ranging from *The Hollywood Revue of 1929* to *Jailhouse Rock* and *Gigi*.
Enjoyable moments from the past, with fewer show-stopping numbers than the earlier films in this series, but adding some fascinating out-takes cut from such films as Easter Parade *and* Cabin in the Sky, *contrasting the performance of Ava Gardner in* Show Boat *with what might have been had Lena Horne been allowed to play the role, and providing a glimpse of Judy Garland in the role of Annie Oakley before she was fired from* Annie Get Your Gun.
d Bud Friedgen, Michael J. Sheridan *m* Marc Shaiman *ed* Bud Friedgen, Michael J. Sheridan
☆ June Allyson, Cyd Charisse, Lena Horne, Howard Keel, Gene Kelly, Ann Miller, Debbie Reynolds, Mickey Rooney, Esther Williams

That's Entertainment Part Two **
US 1976 133m Metrocolor 70mm (blown up)/scope
MGM (Saul Chaplin, Daniel Melnick)
More moments from MGM's successes, introduced by Astaire and Kelly, with comedy and drama sequences as well as musical.
An enjoyable rummage through the past, lacking a little conherence but providing plenty of nostalgic pleasures.
d Gene Kelly *ph* various *titles* Saul Bass
☆ Fred Astaire, Gene Kelly, Jeanette MacDonald, Nelson Eddy, the Marx Brothers, Stan Laurel, Oliver Hardy, Jack Buchanan, Judy Garland, Ann Miller, Mickey Rooney, Oscar Levant, Bing Crosby, Ann Miller, Louis Armstrong

That's Life!
US 1986 102m DeLuxe Panavision
Columbia/Paradise Cove/Ubilam (Tony Adams)
An architect touching sixty, with a sick wife, pours out all his fears of old age and mortality.
Blake Edwards exposing himself again; the movie was even shot in his own house. Somewhat embarrassing to watch, and overwrought, it does have a few good moments.
w Milton Wexler, Blake Edwards *d* Blake Edwards *ph* Anthony Richmond *m* Henry Mancini
☆ Jack Lemmon, Julie Andrews, Sally Kellerman, Robert Loggia, Jennifer Edwards
song 'Life in a Looking Glass' (Mancini, Leslie Bricusse)

That's My Boy
US 1951 98m bw
Paramount/Hal B. Wallis (Cy Howard)
An athletic father tries to press his hypochondriac teenage son into the same mould.
American college comedy of no international interest.
w Cy Howard *d* Hal Walker *ph* Lee Garmes *m* Leigh Harline
☆ Dean Martin, Jerry Lewis, Eddie Mayehoff, Ruth Hussey, Polly Bergen, John McIntire

That's My Man
US 1946 98m bw
Republic (Frank Borzage)
GB title: *Will Tomorrow Ever Come?*
A racing man is reunited with his wife when their son has pneumonia.
A compendium of clichés, with everything but a title card reading Came the Dawn. *Of no real interest.*
w Steve Fisher, Bradley King *d* Frank Borzage *ph* Tony Gaudio *m* Cy Feuer
☆ Don Ameche, Catherine McLeod, Roscoe Karns, John Ridgely

That's My Wife *
US 1929 20m bw silent
Hal Roach
Stan dresses up as Ollie's wife to impress his rich uncle.
Lesser-known star comedy which well sustains its basic joke and includes some splendidly timed farce in a restaurant.
w Leo McCarey, H. M. Walker *d* Lloyd French
☆ Laurel and Hardy, Vivien Oakland, William Courtright

That's Right, You're Wrong *
US 1939 91m bw
RKO (David Butler)
A band leader gets a Hollywood contract but is hated by the studio head.
Typical of the nonsense musicals featuring Kay Kyser and his radio Kollege of Musical Knowledge. The movie background and self-spoofing made this first attempt one of the best.
w William Conselman, James V. Kern *d* David Butler *ph* Russell Metty *m* George Duning *songs* various
☆ Kay Kyser, Adolphe Menjou, Lucille Ball, Dennis O'Keefe, May Robson, Edward Everett Horton, Ish Kabibble, Ginny Simms, Roscoe Karns, Moroni Olsen, Hobart Cavanaugh, Sheilah Graham, Hedda Hopper
'Moderate entertainment which will satisfy as a bill-topper.' – *Variety*

That's the Spirit
US 1945 87m bw
Universal
A ghost comes back to tell his actress wife he didn't desert her as she thought.
Rather heavy comedy of the Here Comes Mr Jordan school.
w Michael Fessier, Ernest Pagano *d* Charles Lamont
☆ Jack Oakie, Peggy Ryan, June Vincent, Gene Lockhart, Andy Devine, Arthur Treacher, Irene Ryan, Buster Keaton

That's Your Funeral
GB 1973 82m colour
Rank/Hammer (Michael Carreras)
An undertaker mistakenly appropriates a coffin containing cannabis which belongs to a rival establishment.
Moribund comedy of contrived double-entendres that die on the lips of the cast.
w Peter Lewis *d* John Robins *ph* David Holmes *m* David Whitaker *ad* Scott MacGregor *ed* Archie Ludski
☆ Bill Fraser, Raymond Huntley, David Battley, John Ronane, Dennis Price, Sue Lloyd, Richard Wattis, Roy Kinnear
'Another nail in the British film industry's coffin, this grey comedy is depressingly unfunny even by TV spin-off standards.' – *Clyde Jeavons, MFB*

Theatre of Blood *
GB 1973 102m DeLuxe
UA/Cineman (John Kohn, Stanley Mann)
A Shakespearean actor uses appropriate murder methods on the various critics who have ridiculed his performances.
Spoof horror picture which goes too far with some sick visuals; the idea and some of the performances are fine.
w Anthony Greville-Bell *d* Douglas Hickox *ph* Wolfgang Suschitzky *m* Michael J. Lewis *pd* Michael Seymour
☆ *Vincent Price*, Diana Rigg, Ian Hendry, Harry Andrews, Coral Browne, Robert Coote, Jack Hawkins, Michael Hordern, Arthur Lowe, Robert Morley, Dennis Price, Diana Dors, Joan Hickson, Renée Asherson, Milo O'Shea and also Eric Sykes

Theatre of Death
GB 1966 91m Techniscope
Pennea (Michael Smedley-Aston)
US title: *Blood Fiend*
Vampire-like murders in Paris are eventually connected with a Grand Guignol theatre.
Dreary backstage shocker with inadequate production values.
w Roger Marshall, Ellis Kadison *d* Sam Gallu *ph* Gilbert Taylor *m* Elisabeth Lutyens
☆ Christopher Lee, Jenny Till, Lelia Goldoni, Julian Glover, Ivor Dean, Evelyn Laye

Theatre Royal: see *The Royal Family of Broadway (1930)*

Theatre Royal
GB 1943 92m bw
British National
A revue and a theatre are saved by a sentimental prop man.
Shapeless star comedy with music; not their best.
w Bud Flanagan, Austin Melford, Geoffrey Orme *d* John Baxter
☆ Bud Flanagan, Chesney Allen, Peggy Dexter, Lydia Sherwood, Horace Kenney, Marjorie Rhodes, Finlay Currie

Their Big Moment
US 1934 68m bw
RKO
Phoney mindreaders solve a murder mystery in a spooky house.
Quite good, well-organized fun of its type.
w Arthur Caesar, Marion Dix, Walter Hackett *d* James Cruze *ph* Harold Wenstrom *md* Max Steiner
☆ ZaSu Pitts, Slim Summerville, William Gaxton, Ralph Morgan, Bruce Cabot, Julie Haydon, Kay Johnson
'Should have fairly good audience strength.' – *Variety*

Their First Mistake **
US 1932 20m bw
Hal Roach
Ollie decides to improve his marriage by adopting a baby, only to find that his wife has left him.
Sublimely silly but endearing star comedy with brilliant passages of imbecilic conversation followed by well-timed farce.
w H. M. Walker *d* George Marshall *ed* Richard Currier
☆ Stan Laurel, Oliver Hardy, Mae Busch, Billy Gilbert, George Marshall

Their Purple Moment
US 1928 20m bw silent
Hal Roach
Stan and Ollie go out on the town, only to discover that Stan's wife has replaced his money with grocery coupons.
Minor star comedy with efficient but predictable restaurant scenes ending in a pie fight.
w H. M. Walker *d* James Parrott *ph* George Stevens *ed* Richard Currier
☆ Stan Laurel, Oliver Hardy, Anita Garvin, Kay Deslys, Tiny Sandford

Their Secret Affair: see *Top Secret Affair*

Thelma and Louise ***
US 1991 129m DeLuxe Panavision
UIP/Pathé Entertainment (Ridley Scott, Mimi Polk)
Two women, off together on a weekend spree, go on the run after one of them kills a man who tries to rape the other.
Timely, exuberant and off-beat feminist road movie that manages to say something interesting about the relationship between the sexes.
w Callie Khouri *d* Ridley Scott *ph* Adrian Biddle *m* Hans Zimmer *pd* Norris Spencer *ed* Thom Noble
☆ *Susan Sarandon, Geena Davis*, Harvey Keitel, Michael Madsen, Christopher McDonald, Stephen Tobolowsky, Brad Pitt
'An exhilarating feminist movie … that's designed to appeal to the outlaw lurking in all of us.' – *Philip French, Observer*
'The first important American movie to plop two women in a car and send them careering down open Western roads with the cops in wheel-spinning pursuit. And it is the first to use sexism as the motivating force for their misdeeds.' – *Richard Schickel, Time*
Callie Khouri
Ridley Scott; Geena Davis; Susan Sarandon; Adrian Biddle; editing

Thelma Jordan: see *The File on Thelma Jordan*

'Kill one and two others take its place! Don't turn your back or you're doomed! And don't tell anyone what Them are!'
Them! **
US 1954 94m bw
Warner (David Weisbart)
Atomic bomb radiation causes giant ants to breed in the New Mexico desert.
Among the first, and certainly the best, of the post-atomic monster animal cycle, this durable thriller starts with several eerie desert sequences and builds up to a shattering climax in the Los Angeles sewers. A general air of understatement helps a lot.
w Ted Sherdeman *story* George Worthing Yates *d Gordon Douglas ph Sid Hickox m* Bronislau Kaper
☆ *Edmund Gwenn*, James Whitmore, Joan Weldon, James Arness, Onslow Stevens
'I asked the editor: How does it look? And he said: Fine. I said: Does it look honest? He said: As honest as twelve foot ants can look.' – *Gordon Douglas*

Them Thar Hills **
US 1934 20m bw
Hal Roach
Stan and Ollie go camping, drink from a well full of moonshine whisky, and get drunk with another camper's wife.
Consistently funny star comedy culminating in a tit-for-tat routine which was reprised in Tit for Tat *the following year.*
w Stan Laurel, H. M. Walker *d* Charles Rogers *ph* Art Lloyd *ed* Bert Jordan
☆ Stan Laurel, Oliver Hardy, Charlie Hall, Mae Busch, Billy Gilbert

The Theme *
USSR 1979 98m colour
Mosfilm
original title: *Tema*
A depressed and famous middle-aged playwright, who has settled for easy success, returns to the town where he was born and falls in love with a woman who has refused to compromise.
A portrait of the artist as a failure, looking in vain for redemption; its theme of artistic and personal freedom upset the Soviet authorities, who banned it for eight years.
w Gleb Panfilov, Aleksander Cervinski *d* Gleb Panfilov *ph* Leonid Kalashnikov *m* Vadim Bibergan
☆ Inna Churikova, Michael Ulyanov, Stanislav Lyubshin, Evgeny Vesnik, Sergei Nikonenko
† The film won the Golden Bear at the Berlin Film Festival in 1987.

Themroc **
France 1972 110m Eastmancolor
The Other Cinema/Filmanthrope/FDL (Jean-Claude Bourlat)
A depressed worker in a dead-end job suddenly breaks free of all his restrictions, making love to his sister and demolishing the walls of his apartment.
An exuberant anti-authoritarian comedy, in which normal dialogue is replaced by an invented language of grunts and whistles.
wd Claude Faraldo *ph* Jean-Marc Ripert *ad* C. Lamarque *ed* Noun Serra
☆ Michel Piccoli, Béatrice Romand, Marilu Tolo, Francesca R. Coluzzi, Patrick Dewaere, Miou-Miou
'Succeeds in being poetic without being arty and, by using laughter as a critical tactic, in suggesting that revolution in a puritanical society ought to take a hedonistic form.' – *Jan Dawson, MFB*

Theodora Goes Wild *
US 1936 94m bw
Columbia (Everett Riskin)
A small-town girl writes a titillating bestseller.
Mildly crazy comedy which helped develop the trend for stars performing undignified antics but today seems rather slow and dated.
w Sidney Buchman story Mary McCarthy *d* Richard Boleslawski *ph* Joseph Walker *m* Morris Stoloff *ed* Otto Meyer
☆ *Irene Dunne, Melvyn Douglas*, Thomas Mitchell, Thurston Hall, Rosalind Keith, Spring Byington, Elizabeth Risdon, Nana Bryant
'The best light comedy since Mr Deeds.' – *Graham Greene*
Irene Dunne; Otto Meyer

Theodore Rex
US 1995 92m colour
New Line/J&M/Shooting Star (Richard Abramson, Sue Baden-Powell)
In the near future, when prehistoric animals have been brought back to life and made almost human, a cop teams up with a dinosaur to solve a murder.
One of those films that you cannot believe ever got made; its crassness is beyond criticism.
wd Jonathan Betuel *ph* David Tattersall *m* Robert Folk *pd* Walter Martishius *ed* Rick Shaine, Steve Mirkovich *sp* dinosaurs: Criswell Prods
☆ Whoopi Goldberg, Armin Mueller-Stahl, Juliet Landau, Bud Cort, Stephen McHattie, Richard Roundtree, George Newbern (voice), Carol Kane (voice)
'A bloated youth-appeal picture with disappointing effects and a very thin story.' – *Leonard Klady, Variety*
† The film, which cost $35m, was released direct to video in the US after unsuccessful previews in three cities. It received a cinema showing in some countries, though in Britain it was also released direct to video. Whoopi Goldberg did not want to make the picture, appearing only after the threat of legal action.

Theorem *
Italy 1968 98m Eastmancolor
Aetos Film
original title: *Teorema*
A handsome young man arrives unexpectedly to stay with a Milan industrialist and his family, gratifying their desires but leaving them tragically unhappy.
Moderately amusing fable with the presumed intent of decrying all universal panaceas, including Christianity.
wd Pier Paolo Pasolini novel Pier Paolo Pasolini *ph* Giuseppe Ruzzolini *m* Ennio Morricone
☆ Terence Stamp, Silvana Mangano, Massimo Girotti, Anne Wiazemsky, Laura Betti

'If you're going to fall, make sure there's someone to catch you.'
The Theory of Flight
South Africa/GB 1998 99m DeLuxe
Buena Vista/Distant Horizon/BBC Films (Helena Spring, Ruth Caleb, David M. Thompson, Anant Singh)
A pilot is sentenced to work as a companion to a woman suffering from motor neurone disease, who is determined to lose her virginity before she dies.
Mawkish tale of an unlikely coupling that is a pain to watch.
w Richard Hawkins *d* Paul Greengrass *ph* Ivan Strasburg *m* Rolfe Kent *pd* Melanie Allen *ed* Mark Day
☆ Helena Bonham Carter (Jane Hatchard), Kenneth Branagh (Richard), Gemma Jones (Anne), Holly Aird (Julie), Ray Stevenson (Gigolo)
'A dire experience.' – *Guardian*

There Ain't No Justice
GB 1939 83m bw
Ealing (Michael Balcon)
A young boxer refuses to throw a fight.
Minor sporting drama, well praised at the time but later forgotten.
w Pen Tennyson, James Curtis, Sergei Nolbandov *novel* James Curtis *d* Pen Tennyson *ph* Mutz Greenbaum *md* Ernest Irving
☆ Jimmy Hanley, Edward Rigby, Mary Clare, Edward Chapman, Phyllis Stanley, Michael Wilding
'The whole picture breathes timidity and refinement.' – *Graham Greene*

There Goes My Heart
US 1938 81m bw
Hal Roach
A reporter is assigned to track down a runaway heiress.
Very pale imitation of It Happened One Night.
w Jack Jevne, Eddie Moran *d* Norman Z. McLeod *ph* Norbert Brodine *m* Marvin Hatley
☆ Fredric March, Virginia Bruce, Patsy Kelly, Nancy Carroll, Eugene Pallette, Claude

Gillingwater, Arthur Lake, Harry Langdon, Etienne Girardot

'A comedy clicko … plenty of zip and zing.' – *Variety*

Marvin Hatley

There Goes the Bride
GB 1980 91m Eastmancolor
Lonsdale (Martin Schute, Ray Cooney)

A harassed advertising executive suffers hallucinations about a lifesize cardboard cut-out of a twenties flapper.
Embarrassingly witless and plotless revamp of innumerable better comedies in the Topper tradition; it has to be seen to be believed.
w Terry Marcel, Ray Cooney *play* Ray Cooney, John Chapman *d* Terry Marcel *ph* James Devis *m* Harry Robinson *pd* Peter Mullins
☆ Tom Smothers, Twiggy, Sylvia Syms, Martin Balsam, Michael Whitney, Geoffrey Sumner, Hermione Baddeley, Phil Silvers, Broderick Crawford, Jim Backus

'The whole thing would be laughable if it weren't so unfunny.' – *Gilbert Adair, MFB*

There Goes the Groom
US 1937 64m bw
RKO (Albert Lewis)
A young man comes back rich from the Alaskan gold fields and reminds an old girlfriend of her promise to marry him.
A well-played comedy which can't conceal its threadbare situations.
w S. K. Lauren, Dorothy Yost, Harold Kusell, David Garth *d* Joseph Santley
☆ Ann Sothern, Burgess Meredith, Mary Boland, Onslow Stevens, Louise Henry

There Goes the Neighborhood
US 1992 89m DeLuxe Panavision
Rank/Kings Road (Stephen Friedman)

aka: *Paydirt*
A prison psychologist and a gang of convicts go in search of a stolen fortune buried in a suburban basement.
Laboured farce with heavy-handed acting and direction which fails to raise a laugh.
wd Bill Phillips *ph* Walt Lloyd *m* David Bell *pd* Dean Tschetter *ed* Sharyn L. Ross
☆ Jeff Daniels, Catherine O'Hara, Hector Elizondo, Rhea Perlman, Judith Ivey, Harris Yulin, Jonathan Banks, Chazz Palminteri, Dabney Coleman

'A TV-inspired high concept and inept production values combine for an unappealing film sans redeeming qualities.' – *Variety*

† The film was released direct to video in Britain.

There Is Another Sun
GB 1951 95m bw
Butcher/Nettlefold (Ernest G. Roy)
US title: *Wall of Death*
A fairground boxer is led astray by an embittered Wall of Death rider.
Efficient drama, bolstered by a good cast of character actors.
w Guy Morgan *d* Lewis Gilbert *ph* Wilkie Cooper *m* Wilfred Burns *ad* George Provis *ed* Charles Hasse
☆ Maxwell Reed, Susan Shaw, Laurence Harvey, Hermione Baddeley, Leslie Dwyer, Meredith Edwards, Earl Cameron, Eric Pohlmann, Robert Adair, Dennis Vance, Harry Fowler

There Was a Crooked Man *
GB 1960 107m bw
UA/Knightsbridge (John Bryan)
An ex-safecracker outwits the crooked mayor of an industrial town.
Semi-happy attempt to humanize a knockabout clown; good supporting performances and production.
w Reuben Ship *d* Stuart Burge *ph* Arthur Ibbetson *m* Kenneth V. Jones
☆ Norman Wisdom, Andrew Cruickshank, Alfred Marks, Susannah York, Reginald Beckwith

There Was a Crooked Man *
US 1970 126m Technicolor Panavision
Warner Seven Arts (Joseph L. Mankiewicz)

In 1883 Arizona a murderer tries to escape from jail and recover hidden loot but is constantly thwarted by the sheriff who arrested him, now a warden.
Curious black comedy melodrama with lots of talent going nowhere in particular; hard to endure as a whole but with entertaining scenes.
w David Newman, Robert Benton *d* Joseph L. Mankiewicz *ph* Harry Stradling Jnr *m* Charles Strouse *ad* Edward Carrere
☆ Kirk Douglas, Henry Fonda, Hume Cronyn, Warren Oates, Burgess Meredith, John Randolph, Arthur O'Connell, Martin Gabel, Alan Hale

'This example of commercialized black comedy nihilism seems to have been an evil two-year-old, and it has been directed in the Grand Rapids style of moviemaking.' – *Pauline Kael, New Yorker*

There's a Girl in my Heart
US 1949 82m bw
Allied Artists (Arthur Dreifuss)
The attractive widow who owns a music hall finds the site in demand.
Slight, artificial but mildly pleasing musical extravaganza of the gay nineties.
w Arthur Hoerl, John Eugene Hasty *d* Arthur Dreifuss *ph* Philip Tanmura *m* Herschel Burke Gilbert
☆ Lee Bowman, Elyse Knox, Lon Chaney Jnr, Gloria Jean, Peggy Ryan, Ludwig Donath, Ray McDonald, Irene Ryan

There's a Girl in My Soup *
GB 1970 96m Eastmancolor
Columbia/Ascot (John Boulting)

A randy TV personality finds himself outplotted by a waif he picks up.
Flimsy screen version of a long-running sex comedy; some laughs, but the star is uncomfortably miscast.
w Terence Frisby *play* Terence Frisby *d* Roy Boulting *ph* Harry Waxman *m* Mike D'Abo
☆ Peter Sellers, Goldie Hawn, Tony Britton, Nicky Henson, John Comer, Diana Dors, Judy Campbell

There's Always a Woman *
US 1938 81m bw
Columbia
A private detective's wife beats him to the solution of a murder.
Amiably scatty crime comedy in the Thin Man *tradition.*
w Gladys Lehman, Wilson Collison *d* Alexander Hall
☆ Joan Blondell, Melvyn Douglas, Mary Astor, Frances Drake, Jerome Cowan, Robert Paige, Thurston Hall, Pierre Watkin

'Will provide general satisfaction as entertainment and as a grosser.' – *Variety*

There's Always Tomorrow
US 1934 86m bw
Universal
A depressed family man is cheered up by a former sweetheart.
Basically rather a dull drama, but with sincere performances which lift it.
w William Hurlbut *novel* Ursula Parrott *d* Edward Sloman
☆ Frank Morgan, Binnie Barnes, Lois Wilson, Louise Latimer, Alan Hale, Robert Taylor

'Attractive screen material, it weighs in for what looks like a favourable sprint for coin.' – *Variety.*

† Remade 1956 as *These Wilder Years*, with James Cagney and Barbara Stanwyck.

There's Always Tomorrow
US 1956 84m bw
Universal (Ross Hunter)
A married man falls for another woman.
Very flat variation on Brief Encounter, *with stars going through mechanical paces.*
w Bernard Schoenfeld *story* Ursula Parrott *d* Douglas Sirk *ph* Russell Metty *m* Herman Stein, Heinz Roemheld
☆ Barbara Stanwyck, Fred MacMurray, Joan Bennett, Pat Crowley, William Reynolds, Gigi Perreau, Jane Darwell

† Previously made by Universal in 1934 with Frank Morgan and Binnie Barnes.

There's No Business like Show Business **
US 1954 117m DeLuxe Cinemascope
TCF (Sol C. Siegel)

The life and times of a family of vaudevillians.
Mainly entertaining events and marvellous tunes make up this very Cinemascoped musical, in which the screen is usually filled with six people side by side.
w Phoebe and Henry Ephron *d* *Walter Lang* *ph* Leon Shamroy *m* Lionel Newman, Alfred Newman *m/ly* *Irving Berlin* *ad* John DeCuir, Lyle Wheeler
☆ *Ethel Merman, Dan Dailey, Marilyn Monroe, Donald O'Connor*, Johnny Ray, Mitzi Gaynor, Hugh O'Brian, Frank McHugh

'One of the saddening films which only occasionally live up to their huge promise.' – *Dilys Powell*

original story (Lamar Trotti); Lionel Newman, Alfred Newman

There's Nothing Out There *
US 1991 90m colour
Valkhn (Victor Kanefsky)
Teenagers staying in an isolated mountain cabin are threatened by an alien monster.
Mildly amusing spoof of horror and science-fiction exploitation movies.
wd Rolfe Kanefsky *ph* Ed Hershberger *m* Christopher Thomas *ed* Victor Kanefsky *sp* Scott Hart; creature design: Ken Quinn
☆ Craig Peck, Wendy Bednarz, Mark Collver, Bonnie Bowers, John Carhart III, Claudia Flores, Jeff Dachis, Lisa Grant

'Tongue-in-cheeky thriller which takes dead aim at the clichés abounding in B and C list titles.' – *Variety*

There's Only One Jimmy Grimble
GB/France 2000 105m DeLuxe
Pathé/Arts Council/Canal+ (Sarah Radclyffe, Jeremy Bolt, Alison Jackson)

An unconfident teenage footballer's game improves when he is given some 'magic boots' that belonged to a player from his favourite team of Manchester City.
Likeable, light-hearted tale of a underdog learning to cope with life's little misfortunes, but looking somewhat undernourished on the big screen.
w Simon Mayle, John Hay, Rik Carmichael *d* John Hay *ph* John de Borman *m* Simon Boswell, Alex James *pd* Michael Carlin *ed* Oral Norrie Ottey *cos* Mary Jane Reyner
☆ Robert Carlyle (Eric Wirral), Ray Winstone (Harry), Gina McKee (Donna), Lewis McKenzie (Jimmy Grimble), Ben Miller (Johnny Two Dogs), Bobby Power ('Gorgeous' Gordon Gurley), Samia Ghadie (Sara), Jane Lapotaire (Old Woman), John McArdle (Headmaster), John Henshaw (Gordon's Father)

'A congenial but dramatically muddled comedy-drama.' – *Derek Elley, Variety*

'It's difficult to imagine who will want to see it.' – *Empire*

'Be Offended. Be *Very* Offended.'
There's Something about Mary *
US 1998 118m DeLuxe
TCF (Frank Beddor, Michael Steinberg, Charles B. Wessler, Bradley Thomas)

Thirteen years after graduating, a man hires a private detective to find the girl he fancied at high school.
Broad comedy which draws attention to its tastelessness; it was among the biggest box-office successes of 1998.
w Ed Decter, John J. Strauss, Peter Farrelly, Bobby Farrelly *d* Bobby Farrelly, Peter Farrelly *ph* Mark Irwin *m* Jonathan Richman *ad* Arlan Jay Vetter *ed* Christopher Greenbury
☆ Cameron Diaz, Matt Dillon, Ben Stiller, Lee Evans, Chris Elliott, Lin Shaye, Jeffrey Tambor, Markie Post, Keith David, W. Earl Brown, Jonathan Richman

'It becomes clear that the real stars of *Mary* are the two grown men behind the camera, giggling triumphantly each time one of their actors says the word "dick".' – *Danny Leigh, Sight and Sound*

There's That Woman Again
US 1938 75m bw
Columbia
A district attorney is hampered by his meddlesome spouse.
Half-hearted follow-up to There's Always a Woman; *the* McMillan and Wife *of its day.*
w Philip G. Epstein, James Edward Grant, Ken Englund *d* Alexander Hall
☆ Melvyn Douglas, Virginia Bruce, Margaret Lindsay, Stanley Ridges, Gordon Oliver, Tom Dugan, Don Beddoe

Therese *
France 1986 91m colour
AFC/Films AZ/CNC
A 19th-century Normandy girl becomes a nun, dies at 24, and is canonized.
Straightforward, austere biographical account which weaves a curious spell.
wd *Alain Cavalier* *ph* Philippe Rousselot *m* Offenbach, Fauré
☆ Catherine Mouchet, Aurore Prieto, Sylvie Habault

These Are the Damned: see *The Damned*

These Dangerous Years
GB 1957 92m bw
Everest/Anna Neagle
US title: *Dangerous Youth*
A Liverpool teenage gang leader is called up and becomes a better guy.
Dim drama with music marking the debut of a singing star.
w John Trevor Story *d* Herbert Wilcox *ph* Gordon Dines *m* Stanley Black
☆ *Frankie Vaughan*, George Baker, Carole Lesley, Jackie Lane, Katherine Kath, Eddie Byrne, Kenneth Cope

These Foolish Things: see *Daddy Nostalgie*

These Glamour Girls
US 1939 78m bw
MGM
A drunken college student invites a dime-a-dance girl for a festive weekend with his snobbish friends.
Wincingly predictable romantic comedy-drama with no outstanding talent displayed from any quarter.
w Marion Parsonnet, Jane Hall *d* S. Sylvan Simon
☆ Lew Ayres, Lana Turner, Tom Brown, Richard Carlson, Jane Bryan, Anita Louise, Ann Rutherford, Marsha Hunt

'Silly situations and mawkish lines. A dualler.' – *Variety*

These Things Happen: see *Les Choses de la Vie*

These Thousand Hills
US 1958 96m Eastmancolor Cinemascope
TCF (David Weisbart)
A successful cattle rancher finds that his best friend is a rustler.
Large-scale but somehow unimpressive Western variant on The Virginian, *cluttered with sub-plots.*
w Alfred Hayes *novel* A. B. Guthrie Jnr *d* Richard Fleischer *ph* Charles G. Clarke *m* Leigh Harline
☆ Richard Egan, Don Murray, Stuart Whitman, Lee Remick, Albert Dekker, Harold J. Stone, Patricia Owens

These Three **
US 1936 93m bw
Samuel Goldwyn

A lying schoolgirl accuses two schoolmistresses of scandalous behaviour.
Bowdlerized version of a famous play (instead of lesbianism we have extra-marital affairs). It worked well enough at the time but now seems dated; oddly enough when the play was filmed full strength in 1962 it didn't work at all.
w Lillian Hellman *play* *The Children's Hour* by Lillian Hellman *d* William Wyler *ph* Gregg Toland *m* Alfred Newman
☆ Merle Oberon, Miriam Hopkins, Joel McCrea, *Bonita Granville*, Catherine Doucet, Alma Kruger, Marcia Mae Jones, Margaret Hamilton, Walter Brennan

'I have seldom been so moved by any fictional film … After ten minutes or so of the usual

screen sentiment, quaintness and exaggeration, one began to watch with incredulous pleasure nothing less than life.' – *Graham Greene*
Bonita Granville

These Wilder Years
US 1956 91m bw
MGM (Jules Schermer)
A wealthy industrialist returns to his home town to trace his illegitimate son.
Modest sentimental drama with practised stars.
w Frank Fenton *d* Roy Rowland *ph* George Folsey *m* Jeff Alexander
☆ James Cagney, Barbara Stanwyck, Walter Pidgeon, Betty Lou Keim, Don Dubbins, Edward Andrews

'Are you afraid of the dark? You should be.'
They
US 2002 89m colour
Entertainment/Focus/Radar/Dimension (Scott Kroopf, Tom Engelman)
aka: *Wes Craven Presents: They*
A psychology student tries to discover why her old friends are falling victim to childhood fears of monsters in the dark.
Tame horror that is derivative of better movies, such as Val Lewton's Cat People, when it is not trying to shock by loud, doom-laden sound effects.
w Brendan William Hood *d* Robert Harmon *ph* Rene Ohashi *m* Elia Cmiral *pd* Douglas Higgins *ed* Chris Peppe *sp* creature design: Patrick Tatopoulos
☆ Laura Regan (Julia), Marc Blucas (Paul), Ethan Embry (Sam), Dagmar Dominczyk (Terry), Jon Abrahams (Billy), Alexander Gould (Young Billy)
'The movie might as well have been called "Wes Craven Presents: Not a Hell of a Lot."' – *Owen Gleiberman, Entertainment Weekly*

They All Died Laughing: see *A Jolly Bad Fellow*

They All Kissed the Bride
US 1942 86m bw
Columbia (Edward Kaufman)
A woman executive falls in love with the crusading writer who is out to expose working conditions in her company.
No surprises are expected or provided in this very ho-hum romantic comedy.
w P. J. Wolfson *d* Alexander Hall *ph* Joseph Walker *m* Werner Heyman *md* Morris Stoloff
☆ Joan Crawford, Melvyn Douglas, Roland Young, Billie Burke, Allen Jenkins, Andrew Tombes, Helen Parrish, Mary Treen

They All Laughed *
US 1982 115m Movielab
Time-Life/Moon (George Morfogen, Blaine Novak)
Three agency detectives fall in and out of love in the course of their duties.
It has the air of a somewhat misshapen and Americanized La Ronde, *with added suggestions of* On the Town, *but it adds up to very little and provides only a few laughs on the way.*
wd Peter Bogdanovich *ph* Robby Muller *m* various
☆ Audrey Hepburn, Ben Gazzara, John Ritter, Dorothy Stratten, Colleen Camp, Patti Hansen, George Morfogen, Blaine Novak
'One tires of long looks that speak volumes, of endless successions of meeting cute.' – *John Pym, MFB*

They Call It Sin
US 1932 68m bw
First National
GB title: *The Way of Life*
A Kansas girl joins a New York chorus and needs to be rescued from a villainous producer.
Ho-hum romantic drama without much substance.
w Lillie Hayward, Howard Green *novel* Alberta Steadman Eagan *d* Thornton Freeland
☆ Loretta Young, George Brent, Louis Calhern, David Manners, Una Merkel
'It needs the sexy title to bolster a just so-so flicker.' – *Variety*

They Call Me Mister Tibbs!
US 1970 108m DeLuxe
UA/Mirisch (Herbert Hirshman)
A San Francisco police lieutenant suspects a crusading local minister of murder.
Flat, dispirited police melodrama with irrelevant domestic asides, a long way after In the Heat of the Night *which introduced the main character. (*The Organization *was the third and last in the so-called series.)*
w Alan R. Trustman, James R. Webb *d* Gordon Douglas *ph* Gerald Finnerman *m* Quincy Jones
☆ Sidney Poitier, Martin Landau, Barbara McNair, Anthony Zerbe, Jeff Corey, Juano Hernandez, Ed Asner

They Call Me Trinity (dubbed)
Italy 1970 100m Technicolor Techniscope
Avco/West (Italo Zingarelli)
original title: *Lo Chiamavano Trinità*
A gunman and his outlaw brother defend a Mormon settlement against a ruthless landowner.
Amiable spaghetti Western that parodies The Magnificent Seven *and ambles along in a pleasantly time-wasting way.*
wd E. B. Clucher (Enzo Barboni) *ph* Aldo Giordani *m* Franco Micalizzi *ad* Enzo Bulgarelli *ed* Giampiero Giunti
☆ Terence Hill (Mario Girotti), Bud Spencer (Carlo Pedersoli), Farley Granger, Steffen Zacharias, Dan Sturkie, Gisela Hahn
'Highly engaging.' – *Sight and Sound*
† The British release ran for 93m.
†† It was followed by a sequel, *Trinity Is Still My Name* (qv).

They Came by Night
GB 1939 72m bw
TCF
A jeweller pretends to be a crook in order to lure the men who killed his brother.
Smart little suspense yarn.
w Frank Launder, Sidney Gilliat, Michael Hogan, Roland Pertwee *d* Harry Lachman
☆ Will Fyffe, Phyllis Calvert, Anthony Hulme, George Merritt, Athole Stewart, John Glyn Jones

They Came from Beyond Space
GB 1967 85m Eastmancolor
Amicus (Max J. Rosenberg, Milton Subotsky)
Disembodied aliens take over a team of scientists investigating a mysterious fall of meteors.
Implausible science fiction, lacking flair in acting, direction and writing and not helped by the change in locale from the original to an olde-worlde English setting.
w Milton Subotsky *novel The Gods Hate Kansas* by Joseph Millard *d* Freddie Francis *ph* Norman Warwick *m* James Stevens *pd* Bill Constable *ed* Peter Musgrave
☆ Robert Hutton, Jennifer Jayne, Zia Mohyeddin, Bernard Kay, Michael Gough, Geoffrey Wallace

They Came from Within: see *Shivers*

They Came to a City *
GB 1944 77m bw
Ealing (Sidney Cole)
Assorted people find themselves outside the gates of a mysterious city.
The Outward Bound *format applied to postwar reconstruction, with characters deciding what kind of a world they want. Good talk and good acting, but not quite cinema.*
w Basil Dearden, Sidney Cole *play* J. B. Priestley *d* Basil Dearden *ph* Stan Pavey
☆ Googie Withers, John Clements, Raymond Huntley, Renée Gadd, A. E. Matthews, Mabel Terry-Lewis, *Ada Reeve*, Norman Shelley, Frances Rowe

They Came to Blow Up America
US 1943 73m bw
TCF
An FBI man of German parentage goes to Nazi Germany and trains with a group of saboteurs, who are arrested when they set foot in the US.
Tolerable propaganda potboiler.
w Aubrey Wisberg *d* Edward Ludwig
☆ George Sanders, Anna Sten, Ward Bond, Dennis Hoey, Sig Rumann, Ludwig Stossel

They Came to Cordura *
US 1959 123m Technicolor Cinemascope
Columbia/Goetz-Baroda (William Goetz)
In 1916 Mexico, six American military heroes are recalled to base, but the hardships of the journey reveal their true colours.
Watchable adventure epic, not so arresting as was intended but quite professional.
w Ivan Moffat, Robert Rossen *novel* Glendon Swarthout *d* Robert Rossen *ph* Burnett Guffey *m* Elie Siegmeister
☆ Gary Cooper, Rita Hayworth, Van Heflin, Richard Conte, Tab Hunter, Michael Callan, Dick York, Robert Keith

They Came to Rob Las Vegas *
Spain/France/Germany/Italy 1969 128m Techniscope
Warner/Isasi/Capitoli/Eichberg/Franca
Criminals ambush a security truck in the Nevada desert.
Long-winded, flashily directed, gleamingly photographed, occasionally lively, frequently violent, finally tedious caper melodrama with a multi-lingual cast.
w Antonio Isasi, Jo Eisinger *d* Antonio Isasi *ph Juan Gelpi* *m* Georges Gavarentz
☆ Jack Palance, Lee J. Cobb, Elke Sommer, Gary Lockwood, Georges Geret, Jean Servais

They Dare Not Love
US 1941 76m bw
Columbia (Sam Bischoff)
An Austrian prince flees the Nazis, but they force him to return and he has to leave his fiancée in America.
Curiously naïve romantic propaganda from this director; not at all memorable.
w Charles Bennett, Ernest Vajda *d* James Whale *ph Franz Planer* *m* Morris Stoloff
☆ George Brent, Martha Scott, Paul Lukas, Egon Brecher, Roman Bohnen, Edgar Barrier, Frank Reicher

They Died with Their Boots On **
US 1941 140m bw
Warner (Robert Fellows)
The life of General Custer and his death at Little Big Horn.
It seems it all happened because of an evil cadet who finished up selling guns to the Indians. Oh, well! The first half is romantic comedy, the second steels itself for the inevitable tragic outcome, but it's all expertly mounted and played in the best old Hollywood style.
w Wally Kline, Aeneas Mackenzie *d Raoul Walsh* *ph Bert Glennon* *m* Max Steiner
☆ *Errol Flynn*, Olivia de Havilland, Arthur Kennedy, Charles Grapewin, Anthony Quinn, Sydney Greenstreet, Gene Lockhart, Stanley Ridges, John Litel, Walter Hampden, Regis Toomey, Hattie McDaniel

They Drive by Night **
GB 1938 84m bw
Warner (Jerome Jackson)
An ex-convict is helped by lorry drivers to solve the silk stocking murders of which he is suspected.
Excellent, little-seen British suspenser of the Hitchcock school.
w Derek Twist *novel* James Curtis *d* Arthur Woods *ph* Basil Emmott
☆ *Emlyn Williams, Ernest Thesiger*, Anna Konstam, Allan Jeayes, Antony Holles, Ronald Shiner
'Dialogue, acting and direction put this picture on a level with the French cinema.' – *Graham Greene*

They Drive by Night **
US 1940 97m bw
Warner (Mark Hellinger)
GB title: *The Road to Frisco*
A truck driver loses his brother in an accident, and in an attempt to improve his lot becomes involved with a scheming murderess.
Solid melodramatic entertainment which borrows the second half of its plot from Bordertown.
w Jerry Wald, Richard Macaulay *novel Long Haul* by A. I. Bezzerides *d Raoul Walsh* *ph* Arthur Edeson *md* Adolph Deutsch
☆ George Raft, Humphrey Bogart, *Ann Sheridan, Ida Lupino*, Gale Page, Alan Hale, Roscoe Karns, John Litel, Henry O'Neill, George Tobias

They Flew Alone *
GB 1941 103m bw
RKO/Imperator (Herbert Wilcox)
US title: *Wings and the Woman*
The story of Amy Johnson and Jim Mollison, married flying pioneers of the thirties.
Adequate fictionalized history with interesting historical detail.
w Miles Malleson *d* Herbert Wilcox *ph* Frederick A. Young
☆ Anna Neagle, Robert Newton, Edward Chapman, Nora Swinburne, Joan Kemp-Welch, Charles Carson, Brefni O'Rorke

They Gave Him a Gun
US 1937 94m bw
MGM (Harry Rapf)
Despite the efforts of his friend, a war-hardened veteran turns to crime and comes to a sticky end.
Dullish moral melodrama with its stars looking as though stuck in glue.
w Cyril Hume, Richard Maibaum, Maurice Rapf *novel* William Joyce Cowan *d* W. S. Van Dyke II *ph* Harold Rosson
☆ Spencer Tracy, Franchot Tone, Gladys George, Edgar Dearing, Mary Treen, Cliff Edwards
'Meller overboard on grief. Does not sum up as having b.o. punch.' – *Variety*

They Go Boom
US 1929 20m bw
Hal Roach
Stan's nocturnal efforts to cure Ollie's cold nearly bring down the house about their ears.
Average, rather protracted star comedy.
w Leo McCarey, H. M. Walker *d* James Parrott *ph* Art Lloyd, George Stevens *ed* Richard Currier
☆ Stan Laurel, Oliver Hardy, Charlie Hall

They Got Me Covered *
US 1943 93m bw
Samuel Goldwyn
An incompetent foreign correspondent inadvertently breaks up a spy ring in Washington.
One of Hope's better and most typical comedy-thriller vehicles.
w Harry Kurnitz *d* David Butler *ph* Rudolph Maté *m* Leigh Harline
☆ *Bob Hope*, Dorothy Lamour, Otto Preminger, Lenore Aubert, Eduardo Ciannelli, Marion Martin, Donald Meek, Donald MacBride, Walter Catlett, John Abbott, Florence Bates, Philip Ahn

They Just Had to Get Married
US 1933 69m bw
Universal
A butler and maid come into money and rise in the social scale.
Rather muddled comedy for star fans.
w Gladys Lehman, H. M. Walker *play* Cyril Harcourt *d* Edward Ludwig *ph* Edward Snyder *ed* Ted J. Kent
☆ ZaSu Pitts, Slim Summerville, C. Aubrey Smith, Roland Young, Verree Teasdale, Fifi D'Orsay, Robert Greig, David Landau, Elizabeth Patterson
'Not for big town first runs, but a booker's selection for B houses or less.' – *Variety*

They Knew Mr Knight
GB 1945 93m bw
IP/GHW
A clerk and his family become rich, then poor, through listening to a speculator.
Slightly oddball domestic drama reminiscent of Priestley's Angel Pavement.
w Norman Walker, Victor MacClure *novel* Dorothy Whipple *d* Norman Walker *ph* Erwin Hillier
☆ Mervyn Johns, Alfred Drayton, Nora Swinburne, Joyce Howard, Joan Greenwood, Olive Sloane, Peter Hammond

They Knew What They Wanted **
US 1940 96m bw
RKO (Erich Pommer)
A waitress agrees by mail to marry a California-Italian vineyard owner, but is aghast when she

arrives to discover that he sent his handsome foreman's photograph.

First-rate minor drama, expertly handled by stars and production team alike.

w Robert Ardrey *play* Sidney Howard *d* Garson Kanin *ph* Harry Stradling *m* Alfred Newman

☆ *Charles Laughton, Carole Lombard, William Gargan*, Harry Carey, Frank Fay

'For dialogue, acting, background and film creation it's a honey.' – *Otis Ferguson*

† Previous versions include *The Secret Love* (1928) with Pola Negri and *A Lady to Love* (1930) with Vilma Banky (and Edward G. Robinson).

William Gargan

They Live

US 1988 94m DeLuxe Panavision

Guild/Alive Films (Larry Franco)

A labourer discovers that aliens are taking over the world, using subliminal advertising.

A standard action film with an uncertain tone, as if it started out to be something more interesting.

w Frank Armitage *story* *Eight O'Clock in the Morning* by Ray Nelson *d* John Carpenter *ph* Gary B. Kibbe *m* John Carpenter, Alan Howarth *ad* William J. Durrell Jnr, Daniel Lomino *ed* Gib Jaffe, Frank E. Jiminez

☆ Roddy Piper, Keith David, Meg Foster, George 'Buck' Flower, Peter Jason, Raymond St. Jacques, Jason Robards III

They Live by Night *

US 1948 96m bw

RKO (Dore Schary)

A young man imprisoned for an accidental killing escapes with two hardened criminals and is forced to take part in their crimes.

Well-made if basically uninteresting melodrama with a draggy romantic interest; its 'realistic' yet impressionist style drew attention on its first release, and it was remade in the seventies as Thieves Like Us *(qv).*

w Charles Schnee *novel* Edward Anderson *d Nicholas Ray ph George E. Diskant m* Leigh Harline *ed* Sherman Todd

☆ Farley Granger, Cathy O'Donnell, Howard da Silva, Helen Craig

'I recommend this film for the manner in which this love-story threads its way through the criminal scene like a white line on a dark road, and for the two wonderfully tender performances by the young principal players.' – *Paul Dehn*

They Loved Life: see *Kanal*

They Made Me a Criminal *

US 1939 92m bw

Warner (Benjamin Glazer)

When he thinks he has killed a boxing opponent, a young man flees to the West and settles on a farm.

Competent remake of The Life of Jimmy Dolan, *a tribute to the American way.*

w Sig Herzig *d* Busby Berkeley *ph* James Wong Howe *m* Max Steiner

☆ John Garfield, Claude Rains, Gloria Dickson, May Robson, Billy Halop, Bobby Jordan, Leo Gorcey, Huntz Hall, Gabriel Dell, Ann Sheridan

'Handsomely mounted and printed on sepia stock – all of which helps.' – *Variety*

They Made Me a Fugitive *

GB 1947 104m bw

Warner/Alliance (Nat Bronsten, James Carter)

US title: *I Became a Criminal*

An ex-RAF pilot is drawn into black marketeering. Framed for a killing, he escapes from Dartmoor and takes revenge on the gang leader.

Deliberately squalid thriller which began a fashion for British realism, but now seems only momentarily entertaining.

w Noel Langley *novel* *A Convict Has Escaped* by Jackson Budd *d* Alberto Cavalcanti *ph* Otto Heller *m* Marcus François Gaillard *ad* Andrew Mazzei *ed* Reginald Beck

☆ Trevor Howard (Clem Morgan), Sally Gray (Sally Connor), *Griffith Jones*, René Ray, Mary Merrall, Vida Hope, Ballard Berkeley, Phyllis Robins

'The direction and cutting, in a word, are masterly and must set up in anyone – even in one like myself who is inclined to be impatient with depravity unredeemed – an alert, uneasy, tingling excitement.' – *Alan Dent, News Chronicle*

They Met in Argentina

US 1941 76m bw

RKO (Lou Brock)

A Texas oil millionaire sends his representative to buy a horse which has been winning races in Buenos Aires.

Thin romantic comedy in pursuance of the good neighbour policy.

w Jerry Cady, Lou Brock, Harold Daniels *d* Leslie Goodwins, Jack Hively

☆ Maureen O'Hara, James Ellison, Alberto Vila, Buddy Ebsen, Robert Barrat, Joseph Buloff

They Met in Bombay *

US 1941 86m bw

MGM (Hunt Stromberg)

Jewel thieves on the run in the East fall in love.

A rather unusual romantic comedy chase which provides pretty satisfactory star entertainment.

w Edwin Justus Mayer, Anita Loos, Leon Gordon *d Clarence Brown ph* William Daniels *m* Herbert Stothart

☆ *Clark Gable, Rosalind Russell*, Peter Lorre, Reginald Owen, Jessie Ralph, Matthew Boulton, Eduardo Ciannelli, Luis Alberni

They Met in the Dark

GB 1943 104m bw

Rank (Marcel Hellman)

A Blackpool theatrical agent is really a master spy.

Elementary spy romance with a richly villainous performance from Tom Walls.

w Anatole de Grunwald, Miles Malleson, Basil Bartlett, Victor MacClure, James Seymour *novel* *The Vanishing Corpse* by Anthony Gilbert *d* Karel Lamac

☆ *Tom Walls*, Joyce Howard, James Mason, Phyllis Stanley, Edward Rigby, Ronald Ward, David Farrar

They Might be Giants *

US 1972 88m Technicolor

Universal/Paul Newman, John Foreman

A lawyer imagines he is Sherlock Holmes, and is taken in hand by Dr Mildred Watson.

Curious fantasy comedy which rather tentatively satirizes modern life and the need to retreat into unreality. Mildly pleasing entertainment for intellectuals.

w James Goldman *play* James Goldman *d* Anthony Harvey *ph* Victor Kemper *m* John Barry

☆ George C. Scott, Joanne Woodward, Jack Gilford, Lester Rawlins

They Only Kill Their Masters *

US 1972 98m Metrocolor

MGM (William Belasco)

A village police chief doggedly solves a series of murders.

Atmospheric, serio-comic murder mystery with a cast of old hands.

w Lane Slate *d* James Goldstone *ph* Michel Hugo *m* Perry Botkin Jnr

☆ James Garner, Katharine Ross, Hal Holbrook, June Allyson, Harry Guardino, Tom Ewell, Peter Lawford, Ann Rutherford, Chris Connelly, Edmond O'Brien, Art Metrano, Arthur O'Connell

They Passed This Way: see *Four Faces West*

'The lovers of *The Caine Mutiny* have a picture all their own!'

They Rode West

US 1954 84m Technicolor

Columbia

A cavalry doctor at a frontier fort gets into trouble by trying to help the Indians.

Western programmer whose sights are higher than its achievement.

w De Vallon Scott, Frank Nugent *d* Phil Karlson *ph* Charles Lawton Jnr *m* Paul Sawtell

☆ Robert Francis, Donna Reed, May Wynn, Phil Carey, Onslow Stevens, Jack Kelly

They Shall Have Music

US 1939 105m bw

Samuel Goldwyn

GB title: *Melody of Youth*

Jascha Heifetz conducts a charity concert to help a music school for slum children.

Formula family film given the best possible production.

w John Howard Lawson, Irmgard von Cube d Archie Mayo *ph* Gregg Toland *md* Alfred Newman

☆ Joel McCrea, Jascha Heifetz, Andrea Leeds, Gene Reynolds, Walter Brennan, Porter Hall, Terry Kilburn, Diana Lynn (Dolly Loehr)

'A natural for the musically minded … elemental and surefire audience appeal.' – *Variety*

Alfred Newman

'People Are The Ultimate Spectacle.'

They Shoot Horses, Don't They? ***

US 1969 129m DeLuxe Panavision

Palomar/Chartoff-Winkler-Pollack

Tragedy during a six-day marathon dance contest in the early thirties.

An unrelievedly harrowing melodrama about dreary people, confused by 'flashforwards' but full of skilled technique, entertaining detail, and one brilliant performance.

w James Poe, Robert E. Thompson *novel* Horace McCoy *d Sydney Pollack ph Philip Lathrop m* John Green *md* John Green, Albert Woodbury *pd* Harry Horner

☆ *Gig Young*, Jane Fonda, Susannah York, Michael Sarrazin, Red Buttons, Bonnie Bedelia, Bruce Dern

COMPERE (GIG YOUNG): 'There can only be one winner, folks, but isn't that the American way?'

'Although *They Shoot Horses, Don't They?* does not, as a whole, reach the domain of art, many of its aspects and an aura that lingers on establish it as a true and eminent cinematic achievement.' – *John Simon*

Gig Young

script; John Green, Albert Woodbury; Sydney Pollack; Jane Fonda; Susannah York

Susannah York

They Were Expendable *

US 1945 135m bw

MGM (John Ford)

Life in and around motor torpedo boats in the Pacific War.

Long drawn out flagwaver with some nice moments.

w Frank Wead *book* William L. White *d* John Ford *ph* Joseph H. August *m* Herbert Stothart

☆ John Wayne, Robert Montgomery, Donna Reed, Jack Holt, Ward Bond, Marshall Thompson, Leon Ames, Cameron Mitchell, Jeff York

'For what seems at least half its dogged, devoted length all you have to watch is men getting on or off PT boats and other men watching them do so. But this is made so beautiful and so real that I could not feel one foot of the film was wasted.' – *James Agee*

They Were Not Divided *

GB 1950 102m bw

Rank/Two Cities (Earl St. John)

The life of a Guards officer is paralleled with that of his American friend; they both die on a reconnaissance during the advance on Berlin.

Odd mixture of barrack room comedy, semi-documentary action, propaganda and the most appalling sentimentality. No one questioned it at the box-office, though.

wd Terence Young *ph* Harry Waxman *m* Lambert Williamson *ed* Ralph Kemplen, Vera Campbell

☆ Edward Underdown, Ralph Clanton, Helen Cherry, Stella Andrews, Michael Brennan, Michael Trubshawe, R. S. M. Brittain

'It is a rather curious experience to see a film made with all the best trappings of realism containing so many of the clichés of the studio.' – *Gavin Lambert*

'Rides off in so many directions as to be beyond toleration … an empty, fumbling and evasive film.' – *Richard Winnington*

They Were Sisters

GB 1945 115m bw

GFD/Gainsborough (Harold Huth)

The problems of three married sisters.

Flatly handled multi-melodrama, the chief attraction being 'wicked' James Mason as a sadist.

w Roland Pertwee *novel* Dorothy Whipple *d* Arthur Crabtree *ph* Jack Cox *m* Louis Levy

☆ James Mason, Phyllis Calvert, Dulcie Gray, Hugh Sinclair, Anne Crawford, Peter Murray Hill, Pamela Kellino

They Who Dare

GB 1953 107m Technicolor

British Lion/Mayflower (Aubrey Baring, Maxwell Setton)

During World War II a group of British soldiers are sent on a raiding expedition to Rhodes.

Grimmish war actioner with plenty of noise but not much holding power.

w Robert Westerby *d* Lewis Milestone *ph* Wilkie Cooper *m* Robert Gill

☆ Dirk Bogarde, Denholm Elliott, Akim Tamiroff, Gérard Oury, Eric Pohlmann, Alec Mango

They Won't Believe Me *

US 1947 95m bw

RKO (Joan Harrison)

A playboy finds himself on trial for murder because of his philandering with three women.

Unusual suspenser with Hitchcock touches; quite neatly packaged, complete with twist ending.

w Jonathan Latimer *d* Irving Pichel *ph* Harry J. Wild *m* Roy Webb

☆ Robert Young, Susan Hayward, Rita Johnson, Jane Greer, Tom Powers, Don Beddoe, Frank Ferguson

'Talk and die! Until now their lips were frozen with fear!'

They Won't Forget ***

US 1937 94m bw

Warner (Mervyn Le Roy)

The murder of a girl in a Southern town leads to a lynching.

Finely detailed social drama, a classic of American realism; harrowing to watch.

w Robert Rossen, Aben Kandel novel Death in the Deep South by Ward Greene *d Mervyn Le Roy ph* Arthur Edeson, Warren Lynch *m* Adolph Deutsch *md* Leo F. Forbstein

☆ Claude Rains, Gloria Dickson, Edward Norris, Otto Kruger, Allyn Joslyn, Linda Perry, Elisha Cook Jnr, Lana Turner, Cy Kendall, Elizabeth Risdon

'Not only an honest picture, but an example of real movie-making.' – *Pare Lorenz*

They're a Weird Mob

Australia 1966 112m colour

Williamson-Powell

An Italian journalist goes to Australia and doesn't get on at first.

Patchy comedy from a local best-seller.

w Richard Imrie (Emeric Pressburger) *novel Nino Culotta* by John O'Grady *d* Michael Powell *ph* Arthur Grant *m* Alan Bonstead

☆ Walter Chiari, Clare Dunne, Chips Rafferty, Alida Chelli, Ed Devereaux, John Meillon

They're Off: see *Straight, Place and Show*

Thicker than Water

US 1935 20m bw

Hal Roach

Ollie spends his savings on a grandfather clock which is promptly destroyed by a passing truck.

Well made but slightly tiresome star comedy, the last short ever made featuring Stan and Ollie.

w Stan Laurel *d* James W. Horne *ph* Art Lloyd *ed* Ray Snyder

☆ Stan Laurel, Oliver Hardy, Daphne Pollard, James Finlayson, Charlie Hall

The Thief *

US 1952 86m bw

Harry M. Popkin (Clarence Greene)

A nuclear physicist is on the run from the FBI, who suspect him of being a spy.

Curious attempt to produce a thriller with no dialogue whatever; parts are well done, but the strain eventually shows, as the makers are not quite clever enough to flesh out the trickery with human interest.
w Clarence Greene, Russel Rouse *d* Russel Rouse *ph* *Sam Leavitt* *m* Herschel Gilbert
☆ Ray Milland, Martin Gabel, Rita Gam, Harry Bronson, John McKutcheon
Herschel Gilbert

Thief
US 1981 123m Astrocolor
United Artists/Michael Mann/Caan Productions
GB title: *Violent Streets*
A high-class thief's professional life is contrasted with his personal problems.
And at far too great a length, with the additional problem that few people are really interested. A slick but empty melodrama.
wd Michael Mann *novel* *The Home Invaders* by Frank Hohimer *ph* Donald Thorin *m* Tangerine Dream *pd* Mel Bourne
☆ James Caan, Tuesday Weld, Willie Nelson, James Belushi
'It promises too much and delivers too little.' – *Richard Combs, MFB*

'He'll Steal Your Heart!'
The Thief ***
Russia/France 1997 97m colour
NTV Profit/Le Pont/Roissy (Igor Tolstunov)
original title: *Vor*
At the end of the Second World War, a fatherless boy gradually discovers that the soldier he and his mother love is a deserter, a cheat and a thief.
Compassionate, acutely observed study in love, betrayal and childhood disillusionment that also manages to find humour in painful situations.
wd Pavel Chukhrai *ph* Vladimir Klimov *m* Vladimir Dashkevich *pd* Victor Petrov *ed* Marina Dobrianskaja, Natalia Kucerenko
☆ Vladimir Mashkov, Ekaterina Rednikova, Misha Philipchuk, Dima Chigarev, Amalia Mordvinova, Lidia Savchenko
foreign language film

The Thief of Bagdad ***
US 1924 135m approx (24 fps) bw silent
Douglas Fairbanks
In old Bagdad, a thief uses magic to outwit the evil Caliph.
Celebrated silent version of the old fable, its camera tricks a little timeworn now but nevertheless maintaining the air of a true classic by virtue of its leading performance and driving narrative energy.
w Lotta Woods, Douglas Fairbanks *d* *Raoul Walsh* *ph* *Arthur Edeson* *m* Mortimer Wilson *ad* *William Cameron Menzies*
☆ *Douglas Fairbanks*, Snitz Edwards, Charles Belcher, Anna May Wong, Julanne Johnston, Etta Lee, Brandon Hurst, Sojin
'An entrancing picture, wholesome and compelling, deliberate and beautiful, a feat of motion picture art which has never been equalled.' – *New York Times*
'Here is magic. Here is beauty. Here is the answer to cynics who give the motion picture no place in the family of the arts ... a work of rare genius.' – *James Quirk, Photoplay*

The Thief of Baghdad ****
GB 1940 109m Technicolor
London Films (Alexander Korda)
A boy thief helps a deposed king thwart an evil usurper.
Marvellous blend of magic, action and music, the only film to catch on celluloid the overpowering atmosphere of the Arabian Nights.
w *Miles Malleson, Lajos Biro* *d* *Michael Powell, Ludwig Berger, Tim Whelan* *ph* *Georges Périnal, Osmond Borradaile* *m* *Miklos Rozsa* *ad* *Vincent Korda* *sp* *Lawrence Butler*
☆ *Conrad Veidt, Sabu*, John Justin, June Duprez, Morton Selten, Miles Malleson, *Rex Ingram*, Mary Morris
ABU (SABU): 'I'm Abu the thief, son of Abu the thief, grandson of Abu the thief, most unfortunate of ten sons with a hunger that yearns day and night...'
AGED KING (MORTON SELTEN): 'This is the Land of Legend, where everything is possible when seen through the eyes of youth.'
'The true stuff of fairy tale.' – *Basil Wright*
'Both spectacular and highly inventive.' – *NFT, 1969*
'Magical, highly entertaining, and now revalued by Hollywood moguls Lucas and Coppola.' – *Time Out, 1980*
Georges Périnal; Vincent Korda
Miklos Rozsa

The Thief of Baghdad
Italy/France 1960 100m Eastmancolor Cinemascope
Titanus/Lux
A very moderate remake in the form of an action star vehicle.
w Augusto Frassinetti, Filippo Sanjust, Bruno Vailati *d* Arthur Lubin *ph* Tonino delli Colli *m* Carlo Rustichelli
☆ Steve Reeves, Georgia Moll, Arturo Dominici

The Thief of Baghdad
GB/France 1978 102m colour
Columbia/Palm Films/Victorine (Aida Young)
A prince outwits an evil Grand Vizier to win the daughter of the Caliph of Baghdad.
Colourful but unexciting retelling of the familiar tale; made for television, it was given a theatrical release in Britain.
w A. J. Carothers, Andrew Birkin *d* Clive Donner *ph* Denis Lewiston *m* John Cameron *ad* Edward Marshall *ed* Peter Tanner
☆ Roddy McDowall, Kabir Bedi, Frank Finlay, Terence Stamp, Peter Ustinov, Marina Vlady, Pavla Ustinov, Daniel Emilfork, Ian Holm
'A sadly hangdog affair ... The general aura of disaster, in fact, is mitigated only by Terence Stamp's clever portrayal of the Wazir as a perambulating corpse.' – *MFB*
† The British video release ran for 86m.

Thief of Damascus
US 1952 78m Technicolor
Columbia/Sam Katzman
The wicked ruler of Damascus is deposed by his own general, in league with Sinbad, Aladdin, and Scheherezade.
Mindless bosh, interesting only for its liberal use of scenes from Joan of Arc; the mind boggles at the costume compromise.
w Robert E. Kent *d* Will Jason *ph* Ellis W. Carter *m* Mischa Bakaleinikoff
☆ Paul Henreid, Lon Chaney Jnr, Jeff Donnell, John Sutton, Elena Verdugo

Thief of Hearts
US 1984 100m Metrocolor Panavision
Paramount (Don Simpson, Jerry Bruckheimer)
A burglar begins an obsessive affair with a woman whose intimate diary he steals.
Plodding, glossily vacuous thriller with an over-obtrusive disco score.
wd Douglas Day Stewart *ph* Andrew Laszlo *m* Giorgio Moroder *ad* Edward Richardson *ed* Tom Rolf
☆ Steven Bauer, Barbara Williams, John Getz, George Wendt, David Caruso, Christine Ebersole

The Thief Who Came to Dinner
US 1973 105m DeLuxe
Warner/Tandem (Bud Yorkin)
A computer analyst determines to become a jewel thief.
Tedious comedy aping the Raffles school but saddled with a complex plot and listless script.
w Walter Hill *novel* Terence L. Smith *d* Bud Yorkin *ph* Philip Lathrop *m* Henry Mancini
☆ Ryan O'Neal, Jacqueline Bisset, Warren Oates, Jill Clayburgh, Charles Cioffi

Thieves: see *Les Voleurs*

Thieves
US 1977 103m Technicolor
Paramount/Brut (George Barrie)
Two married teachers fall out, and into, love.
Misfiring comedy of two talkative bores, whose whimsical ways are less than endearing.
w Herb Gardner *play* Herb Gardner *d* John Berry *ph* Arthur J. Ornitz, Andrew Laszlo *m* Jule Styne, Mike Miller, Shel Silverstein *pd* John Robert Lloyd *ed* Craig McKay *cos* Albert Wolsky, Max Solomon
☆ Marlo Thomas (Sally Cramer), Charles Grodin (Martin Cramer), Irwin Corey (Joe Kaminsky), Hector Elizondo (Man Below), Mercedes McCambridge (Street Lady), John McMartin (Gordon), Gary Merrill (Street Man), Ann Wedgeworth (Nancy), Larry Scott (Carlton), Bob Fosse (Mr Day), Norman Matlock (Mr Night)

Thieves Fall Out
US 1941 72m bw
First National/Warner
An old lady lends her grandson money to start his business, but he has to rescue her when she's kidnapped.
Fairly amusing goings-on to fill the lower half of a bill.
w Charles Grayson, Ben Markson *play* Irving Gaumont, Jack Sobel *d* Ray Enright *ph* Sid Hickox *m* Heinz Roemheld *ed* Clarence Kolster
☆ Jane Darwell, Eddie Albert, Joan Leslie, Alan Hale, William T. Orr, John Litel, Anthony Quinn, Edward Brophy

Thieves' Highway **
US 1949 94m bw
TCF (Robert Bassler)
A truck driver tracks down the racketeers who cheated and maimed his father.
Glossy, highly professional thick ear shedding a convincing light into one of America's less salubrious corners.
w A. I. *Bezzerides* *novel* *Thieves' Market* by A. I. Bezzerides *d* *Jules Dassin* *ph* *Norbert Brodine* *m* Alfred Newman
☆ Richard Conte, Valentina Cortesa, Lee J. Cobb, Jack Oakie, Millard Mitchell, Joseph Pevney, Barbara Lawrence, Hope Emerson
'You will never be able to eat an apple again without calling up visions of trickery, mayhem, vandalism and violent death.' – *New York Times*
'The action sequences are brilliantly done.' – *Daily Mail*

Thieves' Holiday: see *A Scandal in Paris*

Thieves Like Us *
US 1974 123m DeLuxe
United Artists/Jerry Bick-George Litto (Robert Eggenwiler)
Three convicts break jail, and the youngest is attracted to the daughter of the farmer who helps them escape.
Gloomy romantic melodrama, agreeably set in the thirties and feelingly acted, but otherwise inferior to the much shorter version released in the forties as They Live by Night.
w Calder Willingham, Joan Tewkesbury, Robert Altman *novel* Edward Anderson *d* Robert Altman *ph* Jean Boffety *m* various songs *ed* Lou Lombardo
☆ Keith Carradine, Shelley Duvall, John Schuck, Bert Remsen, Louise Fletcher, Tom Skerritt

The Thin Blue Line **
US 1988 101m DuArt
BFI/Third Floor/American Playhouse (Mark Lipson)
Documentary that set out, successfully, to prove the innocence of a man found guilty of the murder of a Dallas policeman in 1976.
Gripping, excellently structured investigative journalism.
d Errol Morris *ph* Stefan Czapsky, Robert Chappell *m* Philip Glass *ed* Paul Barnes
'A powerful and thrillingly strange movie.' – *Terrence Rafferty, New Yorker*

'Your eyes will open wide with wonder!'
'The picture you dreamed someday you'd see ... lovely to look at, lovelier still as you listen!'
Thin Ice *
US 1937 78m bw
TCF (Raymond Griffith)
GB title: *Lovely to Look At*
A skating instructress at an Alpine resort falls in love with a visiting prince.
Light-hearted musical vehicle for Hollywood's newest novelty – a skating star.
w Boris Ingster, Milton Sperling *novel* *Der Komet* by Attilla Orbok *d* Sidney Lanfield *ph* Robert Planck, Edward Cronjager *md* Louis Silvers *ch* Harry Losee *songs* Lew Pollack, Sidney Mitchell
☆ *Sonja Henie*, Tyrone Power, Arthur Treacher, Raymond Walburn, Joan Davis, Sig Rumann, Alan Hale, Melville Cooper
'She's a flash of winter lightning, a great combination of muscle and music, a Pavlova on ice ... production wallop is the staging of three elaborate ice ballets.' – *Variety*
Harry Losee

Thin Ice
GB 1994 92m colour
ICA/Dangerous to Know (Fiona Cunningham Reid, Martien Coucke)
A white heterosexual woman becomes the lover and skating partner of a black lesbian ice skater who wants to compete in the Gay Games in New York.
The film's subtitle – 'Passion of the Pink Rink' – says it all: it is a simple, romantic story on ice.
w Geraldine Sherman, Fiona Cunningham Reid *d* Fiona Cunningham Reid *ph* Belinda Parsons *m* Claire Van Kampen, Richard Allen, Pete Baikie *pd* Patricia Boulter *ed* Rodney Sims
☆ Charlotte Avery, Sabra Williams, James Dreyfus, Clare Higgins, Guy Williams, Barbara New, Suzanne Bertish, Ian McKellen (himself)
'A horribly fluffy, naïve thing that falls into all the 1980s clichés of gay cinema.' – *Jonathan Romney, Guardian*

'She's had it with bad boys. Now it's time to get even.'
A Thin Line between Love & Hate
US 1996 108m DeLuxe
Entertainment/New Line/Savoy (Douglas McHenry, George Jackson)
A philanderer finds himself in trouble when he breaks off an affair with a vengeful woman.
A comic variation on Fatal Attraction, *an influence acknowledged by its makers, and with an equally misogynistic tone; the result is not pleasant, especially when coupled to the self-indulgent style of its director and star.*
w Martin Lawrence, Bentley Kyle Evans, Kenny Buford, Kim Bass *d* Martin Lawrence *ph* Francis Kenny *m* Roger Troutman *pd* Simon Dobbin *ed* John Carter
☆ Martin Lawrence, Lynn Whitfield, Regina King, Bobby Brown, Della Reese, Malinda Williams, Daryl Mitchell, Roger E. Mosley
'There may be a thin line between love and hate, but the boundary separating this film and romantic comedy is as wide as the Gobi desert.' – *Stephen Amidon, Sunday Times*

'A laugh tops every thrilling moment!'
The Thin Man ***
US 1934 93m bw
MGM/Cosmopolitan (Hunt Stromberg)
In New York over Christmas, a tipsy detective with his wife and dog solves the murder of an eccentric inventor.
Fast-moving, alternately comic and suspenseful mystery drama developed in brief scenes and fast wipes. It set a sparkling comedy career for two stars previously known for heavy drama, it was frequently imitated, and it showed a wisecracking, affectionate married relationship almost for the first time.
w *Frances Goodrich, Albert Hackett* *novel* *Dashiell Hammett* *d* *W. S. Van Dyke* *ph* James Wong Howe *m* William Axt
☆ *William Powell, Myrna Loy*, Maureen O'Sullivan, Nat Pendleton, Minna Gombell, Edward Ellis, Porter Hall, Henry Wadsworth, William Henry, Harold Huber, Cesar Romero, Edward Brophy
'A strange mixture of excitement, quips and hard-boiled sentiment ... full of the special touches that can come from nowhere but the studio, that really make the feet a movie walks on.' – *Otis Ferguson*
† Sequels, on the whole of descending merit, included the following, all made at MGM with the same star duo: 1936: *After the Thin Man* (V*, L; 110m). 1939: *Another Thin Man* (V*, L; 102m). 1941: *Shadow of the Thin Man* (V*, L; 97m). 1944: *The Thin Man Goes Home* (V*, L; 100m). 1947: *Song of the Thin Man* (V*, L; 86m).
best picture; script; W. S. Van Dyke; William Powell

The Thin Red Line
US 1964 99m bw Cinemascope
Security/ACE (Sidney Harmon)

Raw recruits land on Guadalcanal and most of them are killed.
Weary, routine, realistic war drama.
w Bernard Gordon *novel* James Jones *d* Andrew Marton *ph* Manuel Berenguer *m* Malcolm Arnold
☆ Keir Dullea, Jack Warden, James Philbrook, Kieron Moore

'Every Man Fights His Own War.'
The Thin Red Line ***
US 1998 170m Technicolor Panavision
TCF/Fox 2000/Phoenix (Robert Michael Geisler, John Roberdeau, Grant Hill)

In 1943, a group of American soldiers, fighting the Japanese on Guadalcanal, are ordered to take a heavily defended position.
A ruminative war movie, with much voice-over, and often depending for its viewpoint on sound and the visual contrast between the lush landscapes and the mess the soldiers make of it. War is seen as an aberration, an intrusion on a natural paradise.
wd Terrence Malick *novel* James Jones *ph* John Toll *m* Hans Zimmer *pd* Jack Fisk *ed* Billy Weber, Leslie Jones, Saar Klein
☆ Sean Penn, Adrien Brody, Jim Caviezel, Ben Chaplin, George Clooney, John Cusack, Woody Harrelson, Elias Koteas, Jared Leto, Dash Mihok, Tim Blake Nelson, Nick Nolte, John C. Reilly, Larry Romano, John Savage and also John Travolta, Arie Verveen, Miranda Otto

'A complex, highly talented work marked by intellectual and philosophical ambitions that will captivate some critics and serious viewers as well as by an abstract nature, emotional remoteness and lack of dramatic focus that will frustrate mainstream audiences.' – *Todd McCarthy, Variety*

'The film sprawls, gets lost and occasionally delivers visual poetry, the kind that could have been greatly helped by tighter editing.' – *Janet Maslin, New York Times*

best picture; Terrence Malick (as director and writer); John Toll; Hans Zimmer; Billy Weber, Leslie Jones, Saar Klein; sound

The Thing **
US 1951 87m bw
RKO/Winchester (Howard Hawks)

GB title: *The Thing from Another World*
A US scientific expedition in the Arctic is menaced by a ferocious being they inadvertently thaw out from a spaceship.
Curiously drab suspense shocker mainly set in corridors, with insufficient surprises to sustain its length. It does, however, contain the first space monster on film, and is quite nimbly made, though it fails to use the central gimmick from its original story.
w Charles Lederer *story* Who Goes There by J. W. Campbell Jnr *d* Christian Nyby (with mysterious help, either Hawks or Orson Welles) *ph* Russell Harlan *m* Dimitri Tiomkin *ad* Albert S. D'Agostino, John Hughes *ed* Roland Gross
☆ Robert Cornthwaite (Dr Arthur Carrington), Kenneth Tobey (Capt. Pat Hendry), Margaret Sheridan (Nikki Nicholson), William Self (Cpl Barnes), Dewey Martin (Bob), James Arness (The Thing), Douglas Spencer (Ned Scott), Robert Nichols (Lt Ken Erickson)

LAST SPEECH OF FILM: 'I bring you warning – to every one of you listening to the sound of my voice. Tell the world, tell this to everyone wherever they are: watch the skies, watch everywhere, keep looking – watch the skies!'

'There seems little point in creating a monster of such original characteristics if he is to be allowed only to prowl about the North Pole, waiting to be destroyed by the superior ingenuity of the US Air Force.' – *Penelope Houston*

'A monster movie with pace, humour and a collection of beautifully timed jabs of pure horror.' – *NFT, 1967*

'Man is the warmest place to hide!'
The Thing
US 1982 109m Technicolor Panavision
Universal/Lawrence Turman, David Foster

Working in the Antarctic, a group of American scientists thaw out the frozen body of an alien.
A remake using the basis of the original story (the thing conceals itself within each of the characters in turn) but filled with revolting detail which alienated many audiences.
w Bill Lancaster *story* Who Goes There? by John W. Campbell Jnr *d* John Carpenter *ph* Dean Cundey *m* Ennio Morricone *pd* John J. Lloyd *ed* Todd Ramsay *sp* Albert Whitlock
☆ Kurt Russell (MacReady), A. Wilford Brimley (Blair), T. K. Carter (Nauls), David Clennon (Palmer), Richard Dysart (Dr Copper), Richard Masur (Clark), Keith David (Childs), Charles Hallahan (Norris), Peter Maloney, Donald Moffat

The Thing Called Love
US 1993 110m DeLuxe
Paramount (John Davis)

A young New York woman goes to Nashville to join other hopefuls trying to become country and western stars.
An insipid failure of a film, a thin drama strung out long after it has ceased to entertain.
w Carol Heikkinen *d* Peter Bogdanovich *ph* Peter James *pd* Michael Seymour *ed* Terry Stokes
☆ River Phoenix, Samantha Mathis, Dermot Mulroney, Sandra Bullock, K. T. Oslin, Trisha Yearwood, Anthony Clark, Webb Wilder, Earl Poole Ball

'It's like a home movie in more ways than one; Phoenix looks drunk or tranquillised most of the time, and shows none of the gifts he once had to burn ... The film is quite stupendously aimless, with a lousy plot and even worse dialogue.' – *Sunday Times*

'Phoenix's performance is perceivably off-kilter – at best strange in a Methody mumbo-jumbo kind of way, at worst downright creepy. Camouflaged as a greasy-haired wreck with a cobra-lidded gaze, he lurches from lucidity to functionally impaired, mumbling throughout. All of this, however, is unfair baggage with which to saddle Bogdanovich's formulaic musical drama, a film which otherwise registers as a wispy but mostly enjoyable romantic fable.' – *Matt Mueller, Empire*

† The film was released direct to video in Britain, although it also received a brief showing at the National Film Theatre. It was River Phoenix's last film to be released, though he later made *Dark Blood*, which was abandoned following his death. Bogdanovich joined the film at a relatively late stage, replacing the original director.

The Thing from Another World: see *The Thing (1951)*

'The doctor blew it – he transplanted a white bigot's head onto a soul brother's body!'
The Thing with Two Heads
US 1972 89m colour
AIP
A racist brain surgeon with terminal cancer arranges to have his head transplanted on to the body of a convict; but the convict turns out to be black.
Bad taste comedy-horror with a great many frantic action sequences. Beyond criticism.
w Lee Frost, Wes Bishop, James Gordon White *d* Lee Frost *ph* Jack Steely *m* Robert O. Ragland
☆ Ray Milland, Rosey Grier, Roger Perry, William Smith

'Every bit as preposterous as it sounds.' – *LA Times*

Things Are Looking Up
GB 1935 78m bw
Gaumont
A circus horsewoman has to pose as her schoolmistress sister.
Lively star vehicle for an oddly matched team.
w Stafford Davies, Con West *d* Albert de Courville
☆ Cicely Courtneidge, William Gargan, Max Miller, Mary Lawson, Dick Henderson, Dick Henderson Jnr, Judy Kelly, Suzanne Lenglen, Vivien Leigh

Things Are Tough All Over
US 1982 92m Metrocolor Panavision
Columbia/C & C Brown (Howard Brown)

Two layabouts are hired by Arabs to drive a limousine containing five million dollars to Las Vegas.
Dire and inane comedy, full of racist jokes.
w Cheech Marin, Thomas Chong *d* Thomas K. Avildsen *ph* Bobby Byrne *m* Gaye Delorme *pd* Richard Tom Sawyer *ed* Dennis Dolan
☆ Richard 'Cheech' Marin, Thomas Chong, Shelby Fields, Rikki Marin, Evelyn Guerrero, John Steadman, Rip Taylor

Things Change **
US 1988 100m DuArt
Columbia TriStar/Filmhaus (Michael Hausman)

An incompetent crook is given the task of guarding for a week an elderly shoemaker who has agreed to go to jail in place of the leading gangster he resembles.
Gently comic anecdote, delicately played.
w David Mamet, Shel Silverstein *d* David Mamet *ph* Juan Ruiz Anchia *m* Alaric Jans *pd* Michael Merritt *ed* Trudy Ship
☆ Don Ameche, Joe Mantegna, Robert Prosky, J. J. Johnston, Ricky Jay, Mike Nussbaum, Jack Wallace, Dan Conway

The Things of Life: see *Les Choses de la Vie*

Things to Come ****
GB 1936 113m bw
London Films (Alexander Korda)

War in 1940 is followed by plague, rebellion, a new glass-based society, and the first rocketship to the moon.
Fascinating, chilling and dynamically well-staged vignettes tracing mankind's future. Bits of the script and acting may be wobbly, but the sets and music are magnificent, the first part of the prophecy chillingly accurate, and the whole mammoth undertaking almost unique in film history.
w H. G. Wells book The Shape of Things to Come by H. G. Wells ph Georges Périnal m Arthur Bliss ad Vincent Korda sp Harry Zech, Ned Mann d/pd William Cameron Menzies
☆ *Raymond Massey*, Edward Chapman, Ralph Richardson, Margaretta Scott, Cedric Hardwicke, Sophie Stewart, Derrick de Marney, John Clements

CABAL (RAYMOND MASSEY): 'It is this or that – all the universe or nothing. Which shall it be, Passworthy? Which shall it be?'

THEOTOCOPULOS (CEDRIC HARDWICKE): 'What is this progress? What is the good of all this progress onward and onward? We demand a halt. We demand a rest ... an end to progress! Make an end to this progress now! Let this be the last day of the scientific age!'

'Successful in every department except emotionally. For heart interest Mr Wells hands you an electric switch ... It's too bad present-day film distribution isn't on a Wells 2040 basis, when the negative cost could be retrieved by button pushing. It's going to be harder than that. It's going to be almost impossible.' – *Variety*

'An amazingly ingenious technical accomplishment, even if it does hold out small hope for our race ... the existence pictured is as joyless as a squeezed grapefruit.' – *Don Herold*

'A leviathan among films ... a stupendous spectacle, an overwhelming, Dorean, Jules Vernesque, elaborated Metropolis, staggering to eye, mind and spirit, the like of which has never been seen and never will be seen again.' – *Sunday Times*

'They Can Die Quickly Or They Can Die Slowly But They Have To Die.'
Things to Do in Denver When You're Dead **
US 1995 114m CFI color
Woods Entertainment (Cary Woods)

A reformed criminal, asked by the local crime boss to carry out one last job, recruits a gang of helpers who have seen better days and bungles the mission with deadly results.
An interesting and stylish thriller, but one that is too determinedly quirky, with its gallery of eccentric gangsters, to be entirely enjoyable.
w Scott Rosenberg *d* Gary Fleder *ph* Elliot Davis *m* Michael Convertino *pd* Nelson Coates *ed* Richard Marks
☆ Andy Garcia, Christopher Lloyd, William Forsythe, Bill Nunn, Treat Williams, Jack Warden, Steve Buscemi, Fairuza Balk, Gabrielle Anwar, Christopher Walken

Think Fast, Mr Moto *
US 1937 66m bw
TCF
Mr Moto goes on a long cruise from San Francisco to Shanghai to solve a case of diamond smuggling.
Enjoyable, quick-moving comedy thriller, the first in the series featuring Peter Lorre as the mild-mannered Japanese detective skilled in disguises and at judo.
w Howard Ellis Smith, Norman Foster *story* J. P. Marquand *d* Norman Foster *ph* Harry Jackson *md* Samuel Kaylin *ad* Lewis Creber *ed* Alex Troffey
☆ Peter Lorre, Virginia Field, Thomas Beck, Sig Rumann, Murray Kinnell, John Rogers, Lotus Long, George Cooper, J. Carrol Naish

Thir13en Ghosts: see *Thirteen Ghosts (2001)*

The Third Day
US 1965 119m Technicolor Panavision
Warner (Jack Smight)
An amnesiac learns that he is a rich unpopular tycoon facing a major crisis.
Glum melodrama which suggests domestic mystery but provides only interminable chat.
w Burton Wohl, Robert Presnell Jnr *novel* Joseph Hayes *d* Jack Smight *ph* Robert Surtees *m* Percy Faith
☆ George Peppard, Elizabeth Ashley, Roddy McDowall, Herbert Marshall, Mona Washbourne, Robert Webber, Charles Drake, Sally Kellerman, Arte Johnson, Vincent Gardenia

Third Finger Left Hand
US 1940 96m bw
MGM (John W. Considine Jnr)
A lady fashion editor fends off unwanted suitors by saying she is already married, but a commercial artist trumps this card by claiming to be the long lost husband of her invention.
Cheerful but overstretched romantic comedy.
w Lionel Houser *d* Robert Z. Leonard *ph* George Folsey *m* David Snell
☆ Myrna Loy, Melvyn Douglas, Lee Bowman, Bonita Granville, Raymond Walburn, Felix Bressart, Sidney Blackmer

The Third Generation
West Germany 1979 111m colour
Tango/Pro-Ject/FDA (Harry Baer)
original title: *Die dritte Generation*
A Berlin executive becomes the victim of a gang of terrorists.
Realistic melodrama, curiously muted in its satire and its anger, watchable more as an entertainment than as a polemic.
wd Rainer Werner Fassbinder *ph* Rainer Werner Fassbinder *m* Peer Raben *ed* Juiliane Lorenz
☆ Volker Spengler, Bulle Ogier, Harry Baer, Eddie Constantine, Udo Kier, Hanna Schygulla

The Third Key: see *The Long Arm*

The Third Man ****
GB 1949 100m bw
British Lion/London Films/David O. Selznick/Alexander Korda (Carol Reed)

An unintelligent but tenacious writer of Westerns arrives in post-war Vienna to join his old friend Harry Lime, who seems to have met with an accident ... or has he?
Totally memorable and irresistible romantic thriller. Stylish from the first to the last, with inimitable backgrounds of zither music and war-torn buildings pointing up a then-topical black market story full of cynical characters but not without humour. Hitchcock with feeling, if you like.
w Graham Greene d Carol Reed ph Robert Krasker m Anton Karas ed Oswald Hafenrichter
☆ *Joseph Cotten, Trevor Howard, Alida Valli, Orson Welles, Bernard Lee, Wilfrid Hyde-White*, Ernst Deutsch, Siegfried Breuer, Erich Ponto, Paul Hoerbiger

HARRY LIME (ORSON WELLES): 'Look down there. Would you really feel any pity if one of those dots stopped moving for ever? If I offered you twenty thousand pounds for every dot that stopped, would you really, old man, tell me to keep my money, or would you calculate how many dots you could afford to spare? Free of income tax, old man, free of income tax. It's the only way to save money nowadays.'

LIME: 'In Italy for thirty years under the Borgias they had warfare, terror, murder and bloodshed, but they produced Michelangelo, Leonardo da Vinci and the Renaissance. In Switzerland, they had brotherly love; they had five hundred years of democracy and peace – and what did that produce? The cuckoo clock.'

'Sensitive and humane and dedicated, [Reed] would seem to be enclosed from life with no specially strong feelings about the stories that come his way other than that they should be something he can perfect and polish with a craftsman's love.' – *Richard Winnington*

'Reaffirms Carol Reed as our foremost film-maker and one of the best three or four in the world' – *Fred Majdalany*

'Crammed with cinematic plums which could do the early Hitchcock proud.' – *Time*

Robert Krasker
Carol Reed; editing
British film

Third Man on the Mountain

GB 1959 103m Technicolor
Walt Disney (Bill Anderson)

In 1865 a Swiss dishwasher dreams of conquering the local mountain, and befriends a distinguished mountaineer.
Handsomely photographed boys' adventure story.
w Eleanore Griffin *novel Banner in the Sky* by James Ramsay Ullman *d* Ken Annakin *ph* Harry Waxman, George Tairraz *m* William Alwyn
☆ James MacArthur, Michael Rennie, Janet Munro, James Donald, Herbert Lom, Laurence Naismith, Walter Fitzgerald, Nora Swinburne

'The story of a man searching for a killer – who might even be himself!'

The Third Secret

GB 1964 103m bw Cinemascope
TCF/Hubris (Robert L. Joseph)

A psychiatrist apparently commits suicide; a patient who has relied on his strength finds the truth by interviewing other patients.
Pretentious package of short stories, only one of which is relevant to the frame (yet another one featuring Patricia Neal was shot but discarded); full of philosophical conversations on a Thames mudbank and other absurdities, but well enough put together.
w Robert L. Joseph d Charles Crichton ph Douglas Slocombe *m* Richard Arnell
☆ Stephen Boyd, *Pamela Franklin,* Jack Hawkins, Richard Attenborough, Rachel Kempson, Diane Cilento, Paul Rogers, Freda Jackson

'An unappealing and irritatingly muddled scribble of a film, thoroughly lacking in suspense, veracity and justification.' – *MFB*

Third Time Lucky

GB 1948 91m bw
Alliance-Anglofilm (Mario Zampi)

A woman explains how her involvement with a professional gambler led to a killing.
Unconvincing drama, dully directed, of love conquering a low-life addiction.
w Gerald Butler *novel They Cracked Her Glass Slipper* by Gerald Butler *d* Gordon Parry *ph* Cedric Williams *m* Stanley Black *ad* Ivan King *ed* Giulio Zampi
☆ Glynis Johns, Dermot Walsh, Charles Goldner, Harcourt Williams, Yvonne Owen, Helen Haye, Ballard Berkeley, Harold Berens, John Stuart

The Third Voice **

US 1959 80m bw Cinemascope
TCF (Maury Dexter, Hubert Cornfield)

A woman kills her wealthy lover and an accomplice impersonates him through a series of complex negotiations.
Superstylish minor thriller, with a plot fascinating as it unfolds and a climax which is only a slight letdown.
wd Hubert Cornfield novel All the Way by Charles Williams *ph* Ernest Haller *m* Johnny Mandel
☆ *Edmond O'Brien,* Laraine Day, Julie London

Third World Cop

Jamaica 1999 98m colour
Optimum/Palm/Hawk's Nest (Carolyn Pfeiffer)

Two friends from childhood meet again in Kingston, Jamaica: one has become a policeman, the other a gangster.
Ramshackle thriller with a slight charm, when you can understand what is being said.
w Chris Browne, Suzanne Fenn, Chris Salewicz *d* Chris Browne *ph* Richard Lannaman *m* Wally Badarou, Sly & Robbie *pd* Richard Lannaman *ed* Suzanne Fenn
☆ Winston Bell (Floyd), Carl Bradshaw (One Hand), Mark Danvers (Ratty), Paul Campbell (Capone), Audrey Reid (Rita), Lenford Salmon (Not Nice)

'Resolutely local in its language and setting so you can tune into its idiosyncratic pleasures even though you've seen virtually the same stock characters in crime movies since the 40s.' – *Peter Curran, Sight and Sound*

Thirst: see *Three Strange Loves*

The Thirst of Baron Blood: see *Baron Blood*

Thirteen *

USSR 1937 90m approx bw
Mosfilm

Red Army soldiers are trekking from well to well through the desert. When help arrives only one is left.
Russian adventure film which was supposedly copied from The Lost Patrol *but itself inspired* Sahara. *Good stuff, anyway.*
w L. Prout, Mikhail Romm *d* Mikhail Romm

'In 1962 America and Russia took their nations to the brink of war and the planet to the edge of extinction...'
'You'll never believe how close we came.'

Thirteen Days **

US 2000 145m DeLuxe
New Line/Beacon (Armyan Bernstein, Peter O. Almond, Kevin Costner)

In October 1962, as the Pentagon advises air strikes and invasion, an aide looks on while President Kennedy and his closest associates deal with the threat of Soviet nuclear-missile bases being set up in Cuba.
Effective and chilling dramatisation of a pivotal moment in world history, shown as it happened at the time, with no attempt at putting the event in a wider historical context, or interest in what was happening in Moscow or the rest of the world.
w David Sel *book The Kennedy Tapes–Inside the White House During the Cuban Missile Crisis* by Ernest R. May, Philip D. Zelikow *d* Roger Donaldson *ph* Andrzej Bartkowiak *m* Trevor Jones *pd* Dennis Washington *ed* Conrad Buff *cos* Isis Mussenden
☆ Kevin Costner (Kenneth P. O'Donnell), Bruce Greenwood (John F. Kennedy), Steven Culp (Robert F. Kennedy), Dylan Baker (Robert McNamara), Michael Fairman (Adlai Stevenson), Henry Strozier (Dean Rusk), Frank Wood (McGeorge Bundy), Kevin Conway (Gen Curtis LeMay), Tim Kelleher (Ted Sorensen), Len Cariou (Dean Acheson), Bill Smitrovich (Gen Maxwell Taylor), Dakin Matthews (Arthur Lundahl), Ed Lauter (Gen Marshall Carter), Andrei Gromyko (Olek Krupa), Stephanie Romanov (Jacqueline Kennedy)

'This is realpolitik, intelligently re-enacted, but shaped by Hollywood values, not history's hindsight: a game that only two can play.' – *Alexander Walker, London Evening Standard*

'A tense and engrossing political thriller.' – *Village Voice*

† The film cost around $80m and took $34.5m at the US box-office.

Thirteen Ghosts

US 1960 88m bw (colour sequence)
Columbia/William Castle

A penniless scholar inherits a haunted house.
Childish thriller for which the audience was issued with a 'ghost viewer' (anaglyph spectacles) so that they could see the 'spirits'. The gimmick was called Illusion-O.
w Robb White *d* William Castle *ph* Joseph Biroc *m* Von Dexter
☆ Charles Herbert, Jo Morrow, Martin Milner, Rosemary de Camp, Donald Woods, Margaret Hamilton

'Terror has multiplied.'

Thirteen Ghosts

US 2001 91m Technicolor
Warner/Dark Castle (Gilbert Adler, Joel Silver, Robert Zemeckis)

aka: *Thir13en Ghosts*

A poor widower and his two children inherit a haunted house.
Tedious remake with only the architecture and some ghastly ghosts to admire.
w Neal Marshall Stevens, Richard D'Ovidio *story* Robb White *d* Steve Beck *ph* Gale Tattersall *pd* Sean Hargreaves *ed* Edward A. Warschilka, Derek G. Brechin *sp* make-up fx: Howard Berger, Gregory Nicotero, Robert Kurtzman
☆ Tony Shalhoub (Arthur Kriticos), Embeth Davidtz (Kalina), Matthew Lillard (Rafkin), Shannon Elizabeth (Kathy), Alec Roberts (Bobby), JR Bourne (Ben Moss), Rah Digga (Maggie), F. Murray Abraham (Cyrus)

'Tries to combine humor with ghostly horror but excels at neither.' – *Desson Howe, Washington Post*

'Hurtling through space, eight people live fifteen dangerous, unforgettable hours!'

Thirteen Hours by Air *

US 1936 80m bw
Paramount (E. Lloyd Sheldon)

A transcontinental plane is hijacked by an ex-convict.
Solidly carpentered minor thriller which is also an interesting record of the early days of commercial aviation.
w Bogart Rogers, Kenyon Nicholson *d Mitchell Leisen ph* Theodor Sparkuhl
☆ Fred MacMurray, Joan Bennett, ZaSu Pitts, Alan Baxter, Fred Keating, Brian Donlevy, John Howard, Ruth Donnelly, Dean Jagger

'Belongs to that rather tiresome genre, of which the formula is too familiar to excite and too unrealistic to entertain, now that the novelty of a thriller worked out in the cramped surroundings of a train, hotel or 'plane has worn off.' – *Graham Greene*

13 Rue Madeleine *

US 1947 95m bw
TCF (Louis de Rochemont)

Four trained American espionage agents locate a Nazi rocket site in France.
Semi-documentary spy stuff in the tradition of The House on 92nd Street *but rather less satisfactory despite excellent technique.*
w John Monks Jnr, Sy Bartlett *d* Henry Hathaway *ph* Norbert Brodine *m* David Buttolph *md* Alfred Newman
☆ James Cagney, Annabella, Richard Conte, Frank Latimore, Walter Abel, Melville Cooper, Sam Jaffe, Blanche Yurka

'Far and away the roughest, toughest spy chase yet gleaned from the bulging files of the OSS.' – *Time*

'I stole the plot of *The Virginian* and used it. I'd always wanted to make that story anyway.' – *Henry Hathaway*

'It carries the kick of a mule.' – *Kine Weekly*

† Rex Harrison rejected the role taken by Cagney.

The 13th Warrior *

US 1999 103m Technicolor Panavision
Buena Vista /Touchstone (John McTiernan, Michael Crichton, Ned Dowd)

An Arab poet is forced to join a band of Viking warriors bent on defeating a mysterious, marauding tribe of cannibals who are rampaging through the land.
Rollicking and gory historical romp, of a kind not seen since The Vikings; *despite its claims to be based on fact, it is not to be taken seriously.*
w William Wisher, Warren Lewis *novel Eaters of the Dead* by Michael Crichton *d* John McTiernan *ph* Peter Menzies Jnr *m* Jerry Goldsmith *pd* Wolf Kroeger *ed* John Wright
☆ Antonio Banderas (Ahmed Ibn Fahdlan), Diane Venora (Queen Weilew), Dennis Storhoi (Herger), Vladimir Kulich (Buliwyf), Omar Sharif (Melchisidek), Anders T. Andersen (Wigliff), Richard Bremmer (Skeld), Tony Curran (Weath), Mischa Hausserman (Rethel), Neil Maffin (Roneth), Asbjorn Riis (Halga), Clive Russell (Helfdane), Daniel Southern (Edgtho)

'An old-fashioned potboiler with half-baked serious intentions sprinkled about.' – *Todd McCarthy, Variety*

† The film was made in 1997, but not released for two years.

'This is where evil lurks!'

13 West Street *

US 1962 80m bw
Columbia/Ladd Enterprises (William Bloom)

An engineer is attacked on the street by teenage hoodlums and becomes obsessed by revenge.
Competent, darkly photographed, rather dislikeable little thriller, a kind of trial run for Death Wish.
w Bernard Schoenfeld, Robert Presnell Jnr *d* Philip Leacock *ph* Charles Lawton Jnr *m* George Duning
☆ Alan Ladd, Rod Steiger, Dolores Dorn, Michael Callan, Kenneth MacKenna, Margaret Hayes

Thirteen Women

US 1932 73m bw
RKO

One of thirteen boarding school graduates is trying to murder the others.
Thin mystery which wastes its cast.
w Bartlett Cormack *novel* Tiffany Thayer *d* George Archainbaud
☆ Ricardo Cortez, Irene Dunne, Myrna Loy, Jill Esmond, Florence Eldridge, Julie Haydon, Marjorie Gateson, C. Henry Gordon

The Thirteenth Chair

US 1929 85m bw
MGM

A medium holds a seance to unmask a murderer.
Effective though now very dated chiller from a Broadway hit.
w Elliott Clawson *play* Bayard Veiller *d* Tod Browning
☆ Margaret Wycherly, Bela Lugosi, Holmes Herbert, Conrad Nagel, Leila Hyams

'Playgoer type will get more enjoyment from it than the moviegoer.' – *Variety*

† The same studio remade the vehicle in 1936 with Dame May Whitty, Henry Daniell, Holmes Herbert – again – Elissa Landi and Lewis Stone; the director was George B. Seitz.

'You can go there even though it doesn't exist.'

The Thirteenth Floor

US 1999 106m colour
Columbia/Centropolis (Roland Emmerich, Ute Emmerich, Marco Webber)

A computer expert investigates the murder of his boss who appears to have been able to travel back in time, or to have inhabited a computer-generated simulation of the past.
Confusing science-fiction, involving time travel into the past and the future; the problem is, nothing very interesting happens there, or in the present.
w Josef Rusnak, Ravel Centeno-Rodriguez *novel Simulacron 3* by Daniel Galouye *d* Josef Rusnak *ph* Wedigo von Schultzendorff *ed* Henry Richardson
☆ Craig Bierko (Douglas Hall), Armin Mueller-Stahl (Hannon Fuller), Gretchen Mol (Jane Fuller), Vincent D'Onofrio (Whitney/Ashton), Dennis Haysbert (Det Larry McBain), Steven Schub (Zev Bernstein), Jeremy Roberts (Tom Jones)

'Time — and movie trends — have passed it by, while its attempts at conveying a simulated cyber-reality are an extremely mixed bag.' – *Robert Koehler, Variety*

The Thirteenth Guest

US 1932 70m bw
Monogram (M. H. Hoffman)

A haunted house, a will at midnight, and a frightened lady.
Archetypal comedy thriller, shot on Poverty Row but still watchable.
w Frances Hyland, Arthur Hoerl *novel* Armitage Trail *d* Albert Ray *ph* Harry Neumann, Tom Galligan

☆ Ginger Rogers, Lyle Talbot, J. Farrell MacDonald, James Eagles, Eddie Phillips, Erville Alderson

'For all classes of houses a positive money maker.' – *Variety*

The Thirteenth Letter *

US 1951 85m bw
TCF (Otto Preminger)

A small French-Canadian town suffers from an outbreak of poison pen letters.

Moderate transcription of a memorable French film, Le Corbeau; *in this version the events seem all too predictable and the performances dull.*

w Howard Koch *d* Otto Preminger *ph* Joseph LaShelle *m* Alex North

☆ Charles Boyer, Linda Darnell, Constance Smith, Michael Rennie, Françoise Rosay, Judith Evelyn

–30–

US 1959 96m bw
Warner/Mark VII (Jack Webb)
GB title: *Deadline Midnight*

A night in the newsroom of a paper preoccupied with scoops.

Not very dramatic, oddly titled and rather pretentious newspaper melodrama confined largely to one set.

w William Bowers *d* Jack Webb *ph* Edward Colman *m* Ray Heindorf

☆ Jack Webb, William Conrad, David Nelson, Whitney Blake, James Bell, Nancy Valentine

Thirty Day Princess *

US 1934 74m bw
Paramount (B. P. Schulberg)

An actress is hired to impersonate a princess who gets mumps while visiting New York in hope of a loan.

Modest comedy which needed a wittier script but is stylishly played.

w Preston Sturges, Frank Partos *novel* Clarence Budington Kelland *d* Marion Gering *ph* Leon Shamroy

☆ Sylvia Sidney, Cary Grant, Edward Arnold, Henry Stephenson, Vince Barnett, Edgar Norton, Lucien Littlefield

'A compact little picture which will entertain generally.' – *Variety*

Thirty Is a Dangerous Age, Cynthia

GB 1967 84m Technicolor
Columbia/Walter Shenson

A timid night-club pianist has trouble with women but sells his first musical.

Mild star vehicle for a very mild star, basically a few thin sketches, frantically overdirected.

w Dudley Moore, Joe McGrath, John Wells *d* Joe McGrath *ph* Billy Williams *m* Dudley Moore *titles* Richard Williams

☆ Dudley Moore, Eddie Foy Jnr, Suzy Kendall, John Bird, Duncan Macrae, Patricia Routledge, John Wells

The 39 Steps ****

GB 1935 81m bw
Gaumont British (Ivor Montagu)

A spy is murdered; the man who has befriended her is suspected, but eludes the police until a chase across Scotland produces the real villains.

Marvellous comedy thriller with most of the gimmicks found not only in Hitchcock's later work but in anyone else's who has tried the same vein. It has little to do with the original novel, and barely sets foot outside the studio, but it makes every second count, and is unparalleled in its use of timing, atmosphere and comedy relief.

w Charles Bennett, Ian Hay, Alma Reville novel John Buchan *d Alfred Hitchcock ph Bernard Knowles m* Hubert Bath, Jack Beaver *md* Louis Levy

☆ *Robert Donat, Madeleine Carroll,* Godfrey Tearle, Lucie Mannheim, Peggy Ashcroft, John Laurie, *Wylie Watson, Helen Haye,* Frank Cellier

'A narrative of the unexpected – a humorous, exciting, dramatic, entertaining, pictorial, vivid and novel tale told with a fine sense of character and a keen grasp of the cinematic idea.' – *Sydney W. Carroll*

'A miracle of speed and light.' – *Otis Ferguson*

'Such is the zest of the Hitchcock plot that the original point of the title was totally forgotten, and half a line had to be added at the end by way of explanation.' – *George Perry, 1965*

Thirty Seconds over Tokyo **

US 1944 138m bw
MGM (Sam Zimbalist)

How the first American attack on Japan was planned.

Sturdy World War II action flagwaver, with Tracy guesting as Colonel Dolittle.

w Dalton Trumbo *book* Ted W. Lawson, Robert Considine *d* Mervyn Le Roy *ph* Harold Rosson, Robert Surtees *m* Herbert Stothart

☆ Spencer Tracy, Van Johnson, Robert Walker, Phyllis Thaxter, Tim Murdock, Don Defore, Robert Mitchum

'All of the production involving planes and technical action is so fine that the film has the tough and literal quality of an air force documentary.' – *Bosley Crowther, New York Times*

'A big studio, big scale film, free of artistic pretensions, it is transformed by its not very imaginative but very dogged sincerity into something forceful, simple and thoroughly sympathetic.' – *James Agee*

Harold Rosson, Robert Surtees

36 Chowringhee Lane

India 1981 122m colour
Shashi Kapoor

A repressed, elderly Anglo-Indian teacher suffers a life of disappointments and defeats.

Downbeat film, made watchable by Jennifer Kendal's performance.

wd Aparna Sen *ph* Ashok Mehta *md* Vanraj Bhatia *ad* Bansi Chandragupta *ed* Bhanudas Divkar

☆ *Jennifer Kendal,* Dhritiman Chatterjee, Debashree Roy, Geoffrey Kendal, Soni Razdan

32 Caliber Killer: see *Killer Calibre 32*

32 Short Films about Glenn Gould **

Canada 1993 94m colour
Electric/Rhombus Media (Niv Fichman)

Fragmentary bio-pic and semi-documentary on the life of the reclusive and eccentric Canadian concert pianist Glenn Gould (1932–82), who gave up live performances at the age of 32, with each section accompanied by excerpts from his recordings.

A portrait of the artist as an intellectual and as an individual determined to express himself at whatever cost to himself and others, by turns fascinating and irritating – some of the sequences stop just as they begin to become interesting. Apart from scenes using actors, it also draws on interviews with those who knew him and his own experimental radio documentaries.

w François Girard, Don McKellar *d François Girard ph* Alain Dostie *m* Bach, Beethoven and others, played by Glenn Gould *ad* John Rubino *ed* Gaétan Huot

☆ Colm Feore (Glenn Gould)

'Manages to hold the watcher in its grip from start to finish.' – *Derek Malcolm, Guardian*

'A uniquely entertaining venture. One need not know Gould's artistry or be attuned to the music to respond to the material.' – *Leonard Klady, Variety*

Thirty Years of Fun **

US 1962 85m bw
Robert Youngson Productions

A compilation of silent comedy, including Chaplin's *The Floorwalker, Easy Street, The Pawnshop* and *The Rink*; Keaton's *The Balloonatic* and *Daydreams*; Langdon's *Smile Please*; and Laurel and Hardy's first meeting in *Lucky Dog*.

Not the most hilarious of the compilations, but historically important, with the usual high quality prints which Youngson alone seemed able to provide.

wd Robert Youngson film quality control Paul Guffanti

The Thirty-Nine Steps

GB 1959 93m Eastmancolor
Rank (Betty E. Box)

Just to show that stars and story aren't everything, this scene-for-scene remake muffs every opportunity for suspense or general effectiveness, and is practically a manual on how not to make a thriller.

w Frank Harvey *d* Ralph Thomas *ph* Ernest Steward *m* Clifton Parker

☆ *Kenneth More,* Taina Elg, Barry Jones, Faith Brook, Brenda de Banzie, Duncan Lamont, James Hayter, Michael Goodliffe, Reginald Beckwith

The Thirty-Nine Steps *

GB 1978 102m Eastmancolor
Rank/Norfolk International (James Kenelm Clarke)

A mining engineer grapples with spies who plan to blow up central London.

Eager-to-please remake which goes back to the original period and more or less the original story, but rather spoils itself by a cliffhanger climax on the face of Big Ben, absurdly borrowed from Will Hay's My Learned Friend.

w Michael Robson *d* Don Sharp *ph* John Coquillon *m* Ed Welch *pd* Harry Pottle

☆ *Robert Powell,* Karen Dotrice, John Mills, Eric Porter, David Warner, George Baker, Ronald Pickup, Timothy West, Donald Pickering, Andrew Keir, Robert Flemyng, Miles Anderson

Thirty-Six Hours *

US 1964 115m bw Panavision
MGM/Perlberg-Seaton/Cherokee (William Perlberg)

In 1944 an American major is kidnapped by the Nazis and after drugging is made to think that the war is over.

Well-detailed spy suspenser.

wd George Seaton *stories* Roald Dahl, Carl K. Hittleman *ph* Philip Lathrop *m* Dimitri Tiomkin

☆ James Garner, Rod Taylor, Eva Marie Saint, Werner Peters, John Banner

† The film was remade for cable TV in 1989 under the title *Breaking Point*, directed by Peter Markle and starring Corbin Bernsen and Joanna Pacula.

'What we're fighting for is bigger than you or me!'

This Above All *

US 1942 110m bw
TCF (Darryl F. Zanuck)

A surgeon's daughter on active service during World War II falls in love with a conscientious objector who is also an army deserter: he proves his bravery during an air raid.

Superior studio-set war romance.

w R. C. Sherriff *novel* Eric Knight *d* Anatole Litvak *ph* Arthur Miller *m* Alfred Newman *ad* Richard Day, Joseph Wright *ed* Walter Thompson

☆ Tyrone Power, Joan Fontaine, Thomas Mitchell, Henry Stephenson, Nigel Bruce, Gladys Cooper, Philip Merivale, Alexander Knox, Melville Cooper

'Beautiful, stimulating and occasionally powerful.' – *New York Herald Tribune*

'One of the truly great pictures to come out of this war.' – *Motion Picture Herald*

Richard Day, Joseph Wright

Arthur Miller; Walter Thompson

This Angry Age

Italy 1957 104m Technirama
Dino de Laurentiis
aka: *The Sea Wall*
original title: *La Diga sul Pacifico*

A French widow in Indo-China struggles to keep her rice fields going despite her family's waning interest.

Curious international production which suffers from the audience's lack of interest in the central situation. Moments of interest and even beauty, though.

w Irwin Shaw, René Clément, Ivo Perelli and Diego Fabbri *novel Barrage Contre le Pacifique* by Marguerite Duras *d* René Clément

☆ Silvana Mangano, Jo Van Fleet, Anthony Perkins, Alida Valli, Richard Conte, Nehemiah Persoff

This Boy's Life

US 1993 115m Technicolor
Warner (Art Linson)

In the 1950s, a teenaged boy finds life hard when his mother settles down with a violent new husband.

An escapist drama, in which a series of dramatic confrontations fail to carry the power they should.

w Robert Getchell *book* Tobias Wolff *d* Michael Caton-Jones *ph* David Watkin *m* Carter Burwell *pd* Stephen J. Lineweaver *ed* Jim Clark, Peter N. Lonsdale

☆ Robert DeNiro, Ellen Barkin, Leonardo DiCaprio, Jonah Blechman, Eliza Dushku, Chris Cooper, Carla Gugino, Zack Ansley

'Despite its admirable strengths and the fact of it being a true story, there is somehow a failure to completely connect with the fierce boy, giving his unhappy and alienating youth an unfortunate air of reality.' – *Angie Errigo, Empire*

This Could Be the Night

US 1957 104m bw Cinemascope
MGM (Joe Pasternak)

A schoolteacher becomes secretary to a gangster in his Broadway night-club.

Unlikely romantic melodrama with music, like a more solemn Guys and Dolls.

w Isobel Lennart *story* Cornelia Baird Gross *d* Robert Wise *ph* Russell Harlan *m* George Stoll

☆ Jean Simmons, Paul Douglas, Tony Franciosa, Julie Wilson, Joan Blondell, J. Carrol Naish, ZaSu Pitts

'The master of inspiring spectacle makes his first great spectacle of modern times!'

This Day and Age *

US 1933 98m bw
Paramount/Cecil B. de Mille

During a youth week, boys put a gangster on trial and by his own methods force him to confess to murder.

A curious aberration for de Mille, this fairly powerful movie was condemned in some quarters as an incitement to fascism.

w Bartlett Cormack *d* Cecil B. de Mille *ph* Peverell Marley *m* Howard Jackson, L. W. Gilbert, Abel Baer

☆ Charles Bickford, Richard Cromwell, Judith Allen, Harry Green, Ben Alexander

'A highly improbable and fantastic story but, as done by de Mille, carries more than average audience appeal.' – *Variety*

'Loaded with that power which excites emotional hysteria ... should stimulate audiences to the same pitch of enthusiasm as it did the preview crowd.' – *Motion Picture Herald*

'A strange tale from the Hollywood hills ... the technical work is beyond reproach, but the story is excessively melodramatic.' – *Mordaunt Hall, New York Times*

This Earth Is Mine

US 1959 124m Technicolor Cinemascope
U-I/Vintage (Casey Robinson, Claude Heilman)

A French-American vineyard owner in California brings out his granddaughter from England in the hope that she will consolidate his dynasty.

Solidly efficient film of a solidly efficient novel.

w Casey Robinson *novel The Cup and the Sword* by Alice Tisdale Hobart *d* Henry King *ph* Winton Hoch, Russell Metty *m* Hugo Friedhofer *ad* George W. Davis, Alexander Golitzen *ed* Ted J. Kent

☆ Jean Simmons, *Claude Rains,* Rock Hudson, Dorothy McGuire, Kent Smith, Anna Lee, Ken Scott

This England

GB 1941 84m bw
British National

Landowner and labourer express contrary views through five periods of English history.

Unintentionally hilarious charade with all concerned left with egg on their faces. With propaganda like this, it's a wonder we still won the war.

w Emlyn Williams, A. R. Rawlinson, Bridget Boland *d* David MacDonald

☆ John Clements, Emlyn Williams, Constance Cummings, Frank Pettingell, Roland Culver, Esmond Knight, Morland Graham, Leslie French

† In Scotland the film was known as *Our Heritage.*

This Gun for Hire ***

US 1942 81m bw
Paramount (Richard M. Blumenthal)

A professional killer becomes involved in a fifth columnist plot.

Efficient Americanization of one of its author's more sombre entertainments. The melodrama has an authentic edge and strangeness to it, and it established the star images of both Ladd and Lake, as well as being

oddly downbeat for a Hollywood product of this jingoistic time.
w Albert Maltz, W. R. Burnett *novel* A Gun for Sale by Graham Greene *d* Frank Tuttle *ph* John Seitz *m* David Buttolph
☆ Alan Ladd, Veronica Lake, Robert Preston, Laird Cregar, Tully Marshall, Mikhail Rasumny, Marc Lawrence
† It was remade, less effectively, as a TV movie in 1991, directed by Lou Antonio and starring Robert Wagner.

This Happy Breed **
GB 1944 114m Technicolor
GFD/Two Cities/Cineguild (Noël Coward, Anthony Havelock-Allan)

Life between the wars for a London suburban family.
Coward's domestic epic is unconvincingly written and largely miscast, but sheer professionalism gets it through, and the decor is historically interesting.
w David Lean, Ronald Neame, Anthony Havelock-Allan *play* Noël Coward *d* David Lean *ph* Ronald Neame
☆ Robert Newton, Celia Johnson, Stanley Holloway, John Mills, Kay Walsh, Amy Veness, Alison Leggatt
'Nearly two hours of the pleasure of recognition, which does not come very far up the scale of aesthetic values.' – *Richard Mallett, Punch*

This Happy Feeling
US 1958 92m Eastmancolor Cinemascope
U-I (Ross Hunter)

An ageing actor is invigorated by a mild affair with his secretary.
Flat romantic comedy: the bubbles obstinately refuse to rise.
wd Blake Edwards *play* For Love or Money by F. Hugh Herbert *ph* Arthur E. Arling *m* Frank Skinner *ad* Alexander Golitzen, Richard H. Riedel *ed* Milton Carruth
☆ Curt Jurgens, Debbie Reynolds, John Saxon, Alexis Smith, *Mary Astor, Estelle Winwood*

This is Dynamite!: see *The Turning Point*

This is Elvis *
US 1981 101m Technicolor
Warner (David L. Wolper)

The life of Elvis Presley, from his first recordings to his death.
This is part-documentary, with some interesting footage, both of Elvis's early performances and of his detractors, whose opposition to his music is unashamedly racist, and part a fictional recreation of his life. Colonel Tom Parker, Elvis's manager, acted as technical adviser, so that the only startling revelation here is Elvis's terrible taste in clothes.
wd Andrew Solt, Malcolm Leo *ph* Gil Hubbs *m* Walter Scharf *ed* Bud Friedgen
☆ David Scott, Paul Boensch III, Johnny Harra, Lawrence Koller, Rhonda Lyn, Debbie Edge, Larry Raspberry, Furry Lewis, Knox Phillips

'What They Whisper To Each Other They Mean Forever!'
This Is My Affair **
US 1937 102m bw
TCF (Kenneth MacGowan)
GB title: *His Affair*
When President McKinley is assassinated, one of his top undercover agents is suspected of being a criminal, and threatened with execution.
Jolly good romantic melodrama with excellent period trappings; Hollywood of the thirties at its routine best.
w Allen Rivkin, Lamar Trotti *d* William A. Seiter *ph* Robert Planck *md* Arthur Lange
☆ Robert Taylor, Barbara Stanwyck, Victor McLaglen, Brian Donlevy, Sidney Blackmer, John Carradine, Sig Rumann, Alan Dinehart, Douglas Fowley
'Something of a G-man story in a costume setting.' – *Variety*
'The best American melodrama of the year … admirable acting, quick and cunning direction … a sense of doom, of almost classic suspense.' – *Graham Greene*

This Is My Affair: see *I Can Get It for You Wholesale (1951)*

'It's 10 p.m. Do you know where your mother is?'
This Is My Life **
US 1992 94m DeLuxe
TCF (Lynda Obst)

A mother with two young daughters tries to make it as a stand-up comedian.
Sharply observed movie with a tough comic edge about the problems and conflicts between daughters and a working mother.
w Nora Ephron, Delia Ephron *novel* This Is Your Life by Meg Wolitzer *d* Nora Ephron *ph* Bobby Byrne *m* Carly Simon *pd* David Chapman *ed* Robert Reitano
☆ Julie Kavner, Samantha Mathis, Gaby Hoffman, Carrie Fisher, Dan Aykroyd, Bob Nelson, Marita Geraghty
'Intimate, honestly rendered film looks likely to score some emotional points with the working parents it speaks to, but a funny but frank teen sex scene may somewhat erode its potential as family fare.' – *Variety*
'Woefully unfunny. If comedy is all about timing then Ephron's directorial watch needs winding.' – *Stephen Amidon, Financial Times*

This Is My Love
US 1954 91m Technicolor
RKO
A sensitive young writer gives up everything to help her sister and crippled husband run a restaurant.
Weird, miscast melodrama which ends with Cinderella murdering the ugly sister.
w Hagar Wilde, Hugh Brooke *d* Stuart Heisler *ph* Ray June *m* Franz Waxman
☆ Linda Darnell, Faith Domergue, Dan Duryea, Rick Jason

This Is My Street
GB 1963 94m bw
Anglo-Amalgamated/Adder (Jack Hanbury)
A Battersea wife has a fling with her mother's lodger.
Unremarkable low-life drama.
w Bill MacIlwraith *novel* Nan Maynard *d* Sidney Hayers *ph* Alan Hume *m* Eric Rogers
☆ June Ritchie, Ian Hendry, Avice Landon, Meredith Edwards, Madge Ryan, John Hurt, Mike Pratt, Tom Adams

This Is Spinal Tap ****
US 1984 82m CFI color
Mainline/Embassy (Karen Murphy)

Adventures of a British heavy metal rock group on tour in America.
Witty, wickedly accurate satire that skewers the pretensions of rock musicians and their hangers-on, done in documentary style. It hits its target with total precision.
w Christopher Guest, Michael McKean, Harry Shearer, Rob Reiner *d* Rob Reiner *ph* Peter Smokler *m* Christopher Guest, Michael McKean, Harry Shearer, Rob Reiner *pd* Dryan Jones *ed* Robert Leighton
☆ Christopher Guest, Michael McKean, Harry Shearer, Rob Reiner, R. J. Parnell, David Kaff, Tony Hendra, Bruno Kirby
† It was also available on an interactive CD-ROM, which includes extra audio commentary on the film and out-takes.
†† *This Is Spinal Tap: The Official Companion*, edited by Karl French, was published by Bloomsbury in 2000.

This Is the Army **
US 1943 121m Technicolor
Warner (Jack L. Warner, Hal B. Wallis)

Army recruits put on a musical revue.
Mammoth musical flagwaver.
w Casey Robinson, Claude Binyon *d* Michael Curtiz *ph* Bert Glennon, Sol Polito *m* Ray Heindorf *ad* John Hughes, Lt. John Koenig *songs* Irving Berlin
☆ George Murphy, Joan Leslie, Irving Berlin, George Tobias, Alan Hale, Charles Butterworth, Rosemary de Camp, Dolores Costello, Una Merkel, Stanley Ridges, Ruth Donnelly, Kate Smith, Frances Langford, Gertrude Niesen, Ronald Reagan and also Joe Louis
♫ 'God Bless America'; 'This Is the Army, Mr Jones'; 'I'm Getting Tired So I Can Sleep'; 'I Left My Heart at the Stage Door Canteen'; 'Oh, How I Hate to Get Up in the Morning'; 'This Time'.
Ray Heindorf
art direction

This Is the Life
US 1944 87m bw
Universal
A young girl singer gets a crush on an older man.
Lively youth musical from better-mannered days.
w Wanda Tuchock *play* Angela Is 22 by Fay Wray, Sinclair Lewis *d* Felix Feist
☆ Donald O'Connor, Susanna Foster, Peggy Ryan, Patric Knowles, Louise Allbritton, Dorothy Peterson, Jonathan Hale

This Is the Night *
US 1932 73m bw
Paramount
A married lady with an eye for other men has an unfortunate habit of getting her dress caught in doors.
Forgotten high comedy in the Lubitsch style, but without his command.
w George Marion Jnr *play* Naughty Cinderella by Avery Hopwood *d* Frank Tuttle
☆ Lili Damita, Charles Ruggles, Roland Young, Thelma Todd, Cary Grant

This Is the Sea
US/Ireland/GB 1996 104m Technicolor Panavision
Polygram/Pembridge/Overseas (Michael Garland)
In Northern Ireland, a Protestant woman falls for a Catholic man with IRA connections.
A slight, romantic story set against the background of terrorist activity; it is not particularly rewarding, even if its heart is in the right place.
wd Mary McGuckian *ph* Des Whelan *m* Mike Scott, the Waterboys, Brian Kennedy *pd* Claire Kenny *ed* Kant Pan
☆ Richard Harris, Gabriel Byrne, John Lynch, Dearbhla Molloy, Ian McElhinney, Samantha Morton, Ross McDade
'This *Romeo and Juliet* story is a winner … deftly avoiding situations that have turned into clichés from overuse.' – *Variety*

'The supreme entertainment of our time! Two and a half years in the making!'
This Island Earth **
US 1955 86m Technicolor
U-I (William Alland)

Scientists at a mysterious research station are really visitors from a planet in outer space, to which they kidnap brilliant minds who they hope can help them.
Absorbing science fiction mystery with splendid special effects and only one mutant monster to liven the last reels.
w Franklin Coen, Edward G. O'Callaghan *novel* Raymond F. Jones *d* Joseph Newman *m* Henry Mancini, Herman Stein, Hans Salter *ad* Alexander Golitzen, Richard H. Riedel *ph/sp* Clifford Stine, David S. Horsley
☆ *Jeff Morrow*, Faith Domergue, Rex Reason, Lance Fuller, Russell Johnson, Robert Nicholas, Karl Lindt

'We women who have known love – have learned how to hate!'
This Land Is Mine *
US 1943 103m bw
RKO (Jean Renoir, Dudley Nichols)

A European village fights for freedom under occupying Nazis, and a schoolmaster becomes a hero.
Rather superfluous flagwaver with good performances wasted in a totally predictable and rather uninspiring script which gives the director little scope.
w Dudley Nichols *d* Jean Renoir *ph* Frank Redman *m* Lothar Perl
☆ Charles Laughton, Maureen O'Hara, George Sanders, Walter Slezak, Una O'Connor, Kent Smith, Philip Merivale, Thurston Hall, George Coulouris
'Directed with the same Zolaesque intensity, the same excited obsession with locomotives, the same exquisite pictorial sense, that informed La Bête Humaine.' – *Guardian*
'Dull, prolix and unamusing.' – *James Agate*
'You cannot afford to dislocate or internationalize your occupied country; or to try to sell it to Americans by making your citizens as well fed, well dressed and comfortably idiomatic as Americans; or to treat the show to the corrupted virtuosities of studio lighting and heavy ballet composition.' – *James Agee*

This Love of Ours
US 1945 90m bw
U-I (Edward Dodds)
A jealous doctor leaves his wife but years later saves her from an unhappy second marriage.
Stupid romantic melodrama with characters in whose idiotic behaviour one can take no interest. Remade as Never Say Goodbye *(qv).*
w Bruce Manning, John Klorer, Leonard Lee *play* Comè Prima Meglio di Prima by Luigi Pirandello *d* William Dieterle *ph* Lucien Ballard *m* Hans Salter
☆ Merle Oberon, Charles Korvin, Claude Rains, Carl Esmond, Jess Barker, Harry Davenport, Ralph Morgan, Fritz Leiber
'About as captivating as a funeral dirge.' – *Thomas M. Pryor, New York Times*
'A juicy example of masochistic team work … my favourite bad film in two years.' – *Richard Winnington*
Hans Salter

This Man Can't Die (dubbed)
Italy 1970 87m colour
Mercurio/Gerald Fine (Gino Rossi)
An undercover agent and his family become the target of a gang of ruthless gun-runners.
Tired spaghetti Western with a mock-Morricone score, indifferently acted and directed, and lacking any of the spectacular set-pieces that made the genre worth watching.
w Luigi Emmanuele, Gino Mangini, Gianfranco Baldanello *d* Gianfranco Baldanello *ph* Claudio Cirillo *m* Amedeo Tommasi *ad* Giorgio Giovannini *ed* Alberto Gallitti
☆ Guy Madison, Lucienne Bridou, Rik Battaglia, Peter Martell, Rosalba Neri, Steve Merrich, Anna Liotti, Giola Desideri, Alberto Dell'Acqua

This Man in Paris
GB 1939 86m bw
Pinebrook
A London reporter in Paris exposes a counterfeiting gang.
Slightly disappointing sequel to the spruce This Man Is News*; no more were made.*
w Allan McKinnon, Roger MacDougall *d* David MacDonald
☆ Barry K. Barnes, Valerie Hobson, Alastair Sim, Edward Lexy, Garry Marsh
'Five years have passed since *The Thin Man*, and this particular uxorious relationship of loving insults, hygienic sex, and raillery from twin beds is period enough for *Punch*.' – *Graham Greene*

This Man Is Dangerous
GB 1941 82m bw
Rialto
aka: *The Patient Vanishes*
A police inspector's son solves the case of a fake doctor and a mysterious nursing home.
Nostalgically innocent crime caper; still quite entertaining.
w John Argyle, Edward Dryhurst *novel* They Called Him Death by David Hume *d* Lawrence Huntington
☆ James Mason, Mary Clare, Margaret Vyner, Gordon McLeod, Frederick Valk

This Man Is Mine
US 1934 76m bw
RKO
A woman wins back her wandering playboy husband.
Tedious marital drama which might have fared better as farce.
w Jane Murfin *play* Love Flies in the Window by Anne Morrison Chapin *d* John Cromwell *ph* David Abel *md* Max Steiner
☆ Irene Dunne, Ralph Bellamy, Constance Cummings, Kay Johnson, Sidney Blackmer, Charles Starrett

This Man Is Mine
GB 1946 103m bw
Columbia
A family invites a Canadian soldier for Christmas.
Moderate heartwarmer which still exudes a patriotic sentimental glow.

w Doreen Montgomery, Nicholas Phipps, Reginald Beckwith, Mabel Constanduros, Val Valentine, David Evans *play* *A Soldier for Christmas* by Reginald Beckwith *d* Marcel Varnel
☆ Tom Walls, Glynis Johns, Jeanne de Casalis, Hugh McDermott, Nova Pilbeam, Barry Morse

This Man Is News **
GB 1938 77m bw
Paramount/Pinebrook (Anthony Havelock-Allan)
A reporter tracks down jewel thieves.
Thoroughly brisk and lively comedy-thriller on Thin Man *lines. (See* This Man in Paris.*)*
w Allan MacKinnon, Roger Macdougall, Basil Dearden d David MacDonald ph Henry Harris *md* Percival Mackey
☆ *Barry K. Barnes, Valerie Hobson, Alastair Sim,* John Warwick, Garry Marsh

This Man Must Die: see *Que la Bête Meure*

This Man Reuter: see *A Dispatch from Reuter's*

This Man's Navy
US 1945 100m bw
MGM
Two old navy men compare their sons' exploits, especially in the matter of how many submarines destroyed.
Easy-going star flagwaver.
w Borden Chase *d* William Wellman
☆ Wallace Beery, James Gleason, Tom Drake, Noah Beery, Selena Royle

This Modern Age
US 1931 68m bw
MGM
The socialite child of divorced parents goes to Paris to stay with her sophisticated mother.
Mildly daring melodrama typical of its star and year.
w Sylvia Thalberg, Frank Butler *story* Mildred Cram *d* Nick Grinde *ph* Charles Rosher
☆ Joan Crawford, Pauline Frederick, Monroe Owsley, Neil Hamilton, Hobart Bosworth, Emma Dunn

'Alva was growing up the only way she knew how!'
This Property Is Condemned *
US 1966 110m Technicolor
Paramount/Seven Arts/Ray Stark (John Houseman)
Sexual adventures of a tubercular but beautiful girl in her mother's boarding house in a Mississippi town.
The Tennessee Williams mixture as before, quite well done but almost entirely resistible.
w Francis Ford Coppola, Fred Coe, Edith Sommer *play* Tennessee Williams *d* Sydney Pollack *ph* James Wong Howe *m* Kenyon Hopkins
☆ Natalie Wood, Robert Redford, Mary Badham, Kate Reid, Charles Bronson, Jon Provost, John Harding, Alan Baxter, Robert Blake

This Rebel Age: see *The Beat Generation*

This Side of Heaven
US 1934 78m bw
MGM
A slightly whacky family gets together when father is accused of embezzlement.
Unmemorable but enjoyable domestic comedy drama.
w Zelda Sears, Eve Greene *novel* Marjorie Paradis *d* William K. Howard
☆ Lionel Barrymore, Fay Bainter, Mae Clarke, Tom Brown, Una Merkel, Mary Carlisle, Onslow Stevens
'The type of clean picture Will Hays has been telling Hollywood about.' – *Variety*

This Sporting Life ***
GB 1963 134m bw
Rank/Independent Artists (Karel Reisz)
A tough miner becomes a successful rugby player, but his inner crudeness and violence keep contentment at bay.
Skilful movie-making around an unattractive hero in dismal settings; for all the excellent detail, we do not care sufficiently for the film to become any kind of classic.
w David Storey *novel* David Storey *d Lindsay Anderson ph Denys Coop m* Roberto Gerhard
☆ *Richard Harris, Rachel Roberts,* Alan Badel, William Hartnell, Colin Blakely, Vanda Godsell, Arthur Lowe
Richard Harris; Rachel Roberts
Rachel Roberts

This Strange Passion: see *El*

This Thing Called Love *
US 1941 98m bw
Columbia (William Perlberg)
GB title: *Married But Single*
A lady executive insists on proving that marriage is best if the partners start out just good friends.
Amusing comedy which at the time seemed a little saucy, and got itself banned by the Legion of Decency.
w George Seaton, Ken Englund, P. J. Wolfson *d* Alexander Hall *ph* Joseph Walker *m* Werner Heymann *md* Morris Stoloff
☆ Rosalind Russell, Melvyn Douglas, Binnie Barnes, Allyn Joslyn, Gloria Dickson, Lee J. Cobb, Gloria Holden, Don Beddoe
'One of those laborious forties comedies in which the independent-minded woman has no common sense.' – *New Yorker, 1979*

This Time for Keeps
US 1947 105m Technicolor
MGM (Joe Pasternak)
The son of a famous singer falls in love with a swimming star.
Dim star musical with no outstanding sequences.
w Gladys Lehman *d* Richard Thorpe *ph* Karl Freund *songs* various
☆ Esther Williams, Jimmy Durante, Lauritz Melchior, Johnnie Johnston, Xavier Cugat and his Orchestra
'The money spent on this production might easily have kept Mozart and Schubert alive and busy to the age of sixty, with enough left over to finance five of the best movies ever made. It might even have been invested in a good movie musical.' – *James Agee*

This Was a Woman
GB 1948 104m bw
Excelsior
A paranoid wife, prevented from running the lives of her offspring, tries to poison her husband.
Intolerable, interminable melodrama; a stage event makes a very stagey film.
w Val Valentine *play* Joan Morgan *d* Tim Whelan *ph* Günther Krampf *m* Mischa Spoliansky
☆ Sonia Dresdel, Barbara White, Walter Fitzgerald, Cyril Raymond, Marjorie Rhodes, Emrys Jones

This Way Please
US 1937 72m bw
Paramount (Mel Shauer)
Romance backstage at a cine-variety theatre.
Uninspired musical now interesting for its sociological detail.
w Maxwell Shane, Bill Thomas, Grant Garrett, Seena Owen, Howard J. Green *d* Robert Florey
☆ Charles Buddy Rogers, Betty Grable, Ned Sparks, Jim and Marion Jordan, Porter Hall, Lee Bowman, Wally Vernon

This Week of Grace
GB 1933 92m bw
Real Art
An unemployed factory girl goes into service.
Very typical but underproduced star vehicle.
w H. Fowler Mear, Jack Marks *d* Maurice Elvey
☆ Gracie Fields, Frank Pettingell, Henry Kendall, John Stuart, Douglas Wakefield, Minnie Rayner

'Every inch a lady – till you look at the record!'
This Woman Is Dangerous
US 1952 97m bw
Warner (Robert Sisk)
A woman gangster goes blind and falls in love with her doctor.
Glossy hokum without much dramatic movement; strictly for star fans.
w Geoffrey Homes, George Worthing Yates *d* Felix Feist *ph* Ted McCord *m* David Buttolph
☆ Joan Crawford, David Brian, Dennis Morgan, Mari Aldon, Phil Carey

This Woman Is Mine
US 1941 92m bw
Universal
Fur traders fall out over a beautiful stowaway.
Fairly well-produced but unexciting period drama.
w Seton I. Miller *novel* *I, James Lewis* by Gilbert Wolff Gabriel *d* Frank Lloyd *m* Richard Hageman
☆ Franchot Tone, John Carroll, Walter Brennan, Carol Bruce, Nigel Bruce, Leo G. Carroll, Sig Rumann
Richard Hageman

This World, Then the Fireworks *
US 1997 100m DeLuxe
First Independent/Largo (Chris Hanley, Brad Wyman, Larry Gross)
A man leaves his wife to move in with his unstable mother and sister, a prostitute, and begins an affair with a policewoman, intending to swindle her.
Lurid pulp melodrama of incest, murder and madness, no more than a film noir gone fetid.
w Larry Gross *story* Jim Thompson *d* Michael Oblowitz *ph* Tom Priestley Jnr *m* Pete Rugolo *pd* Maia Javan *ed* Emma E. Hickox
☆ Billy Zane, Gina Gershon, Sheryl Lee, Rue McClanahan, Seymour Cassel, Will Patton, Richard Edson, William Hootkins
'Elegantly stylish, highly erotic, intentionally over-the-top.' – *Variety*

'Everyone's looking for a prince among the pond life.'
This Year's Love *
GB 1999 109m DeLuxe
Entertainment/Kismet/Scottish Arts Council (Michael Camarda)
A London-based Scottish couple split up on their wedding day and find consolation elsewhere.
A trendy comedy of serial affairs, where sex is treated as a fashion accessory.
wd David Kane *ph* Robert Alazraki *m* Simon Boswell *pd* Sarah Greenwood *ed* Sean Barton
☆ Kathy Burke, Jennifer Ehle, Ian Hart, Douglas Henshall, Catherine McCormack, Dougray Scott, Emily Woof
'If more time had been devoted to the supposed laughs and less to the logistics of bed-hopping the film might've lived up to its gag a minute sales pitch.' – *Lorien Haynes, Film Review*

This'll Make You Whistle *
GB 1936 78m bw
Herbert Wilcox Productions
A playboy pretends to be a crook so as to shock his unwanted fiancée's guardian.
Rather flat comedy from a stage musical; all depends on the star.
w Guy Bolton, Fred Thompson *d* Herbert Wilcox
☆ *Jack Buchanan,* Elsie Randolph, Jean Gillie, William Kendall, David Hutcheson, Antony Holles

'Little engines CAN do Big Things...'
Thomas and the Magic Railroad
US/GB 2000 86m DeLuxe
Icon/Destination/Gullane/IoMFC (Britt Allcroft, Phil Fehrle)
An evil diesel train threatens the future of steam trains and the magic kingdom where they talk to one another.
A transatlantic version of the Rev. Awdry's genteel tales of steam engines, done as a mixture of live action and simple animated models – these trains talk without moving their mouths; the result may please very small children unused to sophistication.
wd Britt Allcroft *ph* Paul Ryan *m* Hummie Mann *pd* Oleg M. Savytski *ed* Ron Wisman
☆ Peter Fonda (Burnett Stone), Mara Wilson (Lily), Alec Baldwin (Mr Conductor), Didi Conn (Stacy), Michael E. Rodgers (Junior), Cody McMains (Patch), Russell Means (Billy Twofeathers), voices of: Eddie Glen (Thomas), Neil Crone (Diesel 10/Splatter/Gordon), Colm Feore (Toby)
'Derails soon after the opening credits; the rest is an inglorious wreck of a movie.' – *Edward Lawrenson, Sight and Sound*

The Thomas Crown Affair **
US 1968 102m DeLuxe Panavision
UA/Mirisch/Simkoe/Solar (Norman Jewison)
A bored property tycoon masterminds a bank robbery and is chased by a glamorous insurance investigator.
Not so much a movie as an animated colour supplement, this glossy entertainment makes style its prime virtue, plays cute tricks with multiple images and has a famous sexy chess game, but is not above being boring for the rest of the way.
w Alan R. Trustman *d Norman Jewison ph Haskell Wexler m* Michel Legrand *ad Robert Boyle*
☆ *Steve McQueen,* Faye Dunaway, Paul Burke, Jack Weston, Yaphet Kotto
'Jewison and Wexler seem to have gone slightly berserk, piling up tricks and mannerisms until the film itself sinks out of sight, forlorn and forgotten.' – *Tom Milne*
'A glimmering, empty film reminiscent of an haute couture model – stunning on the surface, concave and undernourished beneath.' – *Stefan Kanter*
song 'The Windmills of Your Mind' (*m*Michel Legrand, *ly*Alan and Marilyn Bergman)
Michel Legrand

The Thomas Crown Affair **
US 1999 110m DeLuxe
MGM/Irish DreamTime (Pierce Brosnan, Beau St. Clair)
After a billionaire steals a Monet from New York's Metropolitan Museum of Art, he is hounded by a female insurance agent determined to snare him.
Glossy, easily enjoyable thriller that aims for sophistication; it plays a little like a James Bond movie without the big-budget stunts.
w Leslie Dixon, Kurt Wimmer *story* Alan R. Trustman *d* John McTiernan *ph* Tom Priestley *m* Bill Conti *pd* Bruno Rubeo *ed* John Wright
☆ Pierce Brosnan (Thomas Crown), Rene Russo (Catherine Banning), Denis Leary (Det Michael McCann), Ben Gazzara (Andrew Wallace), Frankie Faison (Det Paretti – Frankie Faison), Fritz Weaver (John Reynolds), Charles Keating (Golchan), Mark Margolis (Knutzhorn), Faye Dunaway (Psychiatrist)
'It's updated the older film, but not outclassed it.' – *Alexander Walker*

Thoroughbreds Don't Cry
US 1937 80m bw
MGM
Jockeys fight for the chance to ride a valuable English horse.
Ho-hum racetrack yarn significant as the first teaming of two young stars.
w Lawrence Hazard, J. Walter Ruben, Eleanore Griffin *d* Alfred E. Green
☆ Mickey Rooney, Judy Garland, Ronald Sinclair, Sophie Tucker, C. Aubrey Smith

Thoroughly Modern Millie *
US 1967 138m Technicolor
Universal (Ross Hunter)
In the twenties, a young girl comes to New York, becomes thoroughly modern, falls for her boss, and has various adventures unmasking a white slave racket centring on a Chinese laundry.
Initially most agreeable but subsequently very patchy spoof of twenties fads and films, including a Harold Lloyd thrill sequence which just doesn't work and a comedy performance from Beatrice Lillie which does. Tunes and performances are alike variable.
w Richard Morris *d* George Roy Hill *ph Russell* Metty *m* Elmer Bernstein *md* André Previn, Joseph Gershenson *ch* Joe Layton *ad* Alexander Golitzen, George Webb *songs* various
☆ *Julie Andrews,* Mary Tyler Moore, *John Gavin,* James Fox, Carol Channing, *Beatrice Lillie,* Jack Soo, Pat Morita, Anthony Dexter
'What a nice 65-minute movie is buried therein!' – *Judith Crist*
Elmer Bernstein
André Previn, Joseph Gershenson; title song (*m*James Van Heusen, *ly*Sammy Cahn); Carol Channing

Those Calloways
US 1964 131m Technicolor
Walt Disney (Winston Hibler)
Adventures of a marsh trapper and his family who live near a Maine village and try to protect wild geese from hunters.
Predictable family saga with pleasant backgrounds.

w Louis Pelletier *novel Swift Water* by Paul Annixter *d* Norman Tokar *ph* Edward Colman *m* Max Steiner
☆ Brian Keith, Vera Miles, Brandon de Wilde, Walter Brennan, Ed Wynn, Linda Evans, Philip Abbott, John Larkin, John Qualen

Those Daring Young Men in Their Jaunty Jalopies
US/Italy/France 1969 125m
Technicolor Panavision
Paramount/Dino de Laurentiis/Marianne (Ken Annakin, Basil Keys)
GB title: *Monte Carlo or Bust*
Accidents befall various competitors in the Monte Carlo Rally.
Rough-edged imitation of The Great Race *and* Those Magnificent Men in Their Flying Machines, *much feebler than either but with the waste of a big budget well in evidence.*
w Jack Davies, Ken Annakin *d* Ken Annakin *ph* Gabor Pogany *m* Ron Goodwin
☆ Peter Cook, Dudley Moore, Tony Curtis, Bourvil, Walter Chiari, Terry-Thomas, Gert Frobe, Susan Hampshire, Jack Hawkins, Eric Sykes

Those Eyes, That Mouth
France/Italy 1982 100m colour
Triumph/Columbia/Odissya/Gaumont/RAI/Enca Ferrario (Enzo Porcelli)
original title: *Gli Occhi, La Bocca*
Returning home for the funeral of his suicidal brother, a failing actor begins an affair with the dead man's pregnant fiancée.
Intense family melodrama that refers back to the director's first film, Fists in the Pocket, *but lacks the same impact.*
w Marco Bellocchio, Vincenzo Cerami *d* Marco Bellocchio *ph* Giuseppe Lanci *m* Nicola Piovani *ed* Sergio Nuti
☆ Lou Castel, Angela Molina, Emmanuelle Riva, Antonio Piovanelli, Michel Piccoli

Those Fantastic Flying Fools: see *Jules Verne's Rocket to the Moon*

Those High Grey Walls
US 1939 80m bw
Columbia
A doctor is convicted for aiding a criminal.
Modest variation on a plot used for Prisoner of Shark Island, Devil's Island, *and so on.*
w William A. Ullman, Lewis Meltzer *d* Charles Vidor *ph* John Stumar *m* Morris Stoloff
☆ Walter Connolly, Onslow Stevens, Iris Meredith, Paul Fix, Bernard Nedell, Don Beddoe
'Effective prison melodrama ... will do all right where properly booked.' – *Variety*

Those Kids from Town
GB 1941 82m bw
British National
An earl takes in a group of noisy Cockney kids evacuated from the city.
Sentimental wartime crowdpleaser, not especially good but a fairly rare record of one aspect of the war.
w Adrian Arlington *novel These Our Strangers* by Adrian Arlington *d* Lance Comfort
☆ Shirley Lenner, Jeanne de Casalis, Percy Marmont, Maire O'Neill, George Cole, Charles Victor

Those Magnificent Men in Their Flying Machines, or How I Flew from London to Paris in 25 hours and 11 Minutes **
GB 1965 133m Technicolor Todd-AO
TCF (Stan Marguilies, Jack Davies)
In 1910, a newspaper owner sponsors a London to Paris air race.
Long-winded, generally agreeable knockabout comedy with plenty to look at but far too few jokes to sustain it.
w Jack Davies, Ken Annakin *d Ken Annakin ph Christopher Challis m* Ron Goodwin *pd Tom Morahan*
☆ Sarah Miles, Stuart Whitman, Robert Morley, Eric Sykes, Terry-Thomas, James Fox, Alberto Sordi, Gert Frobe, Jean-Pierre Cassel, Karl Michael Vogler, Irina Demich, Benny Hill, Flora Robson, Sam Wanamaker, Red Skelton and also Fred Emney, Cicely Courtneidge, Gordon Jackson, John Le Mesurier, Tony Hancock, William Rushton
'There is many a likely gag, but none that survives the second or third reprise. It could have been a good bit funnier by being shorter: the winning time is 25 hours 11 minutes, and by observing some kind of neo-Aristotelian unity the film seems to last exactly as long.' – *John Simon*
script

Those Marvellous Benchley Shorts: see *Benchley*

Those Were the Days *
GB 1934 80m bw
BIP (Walter C. Mycroft)
In the 1890s, a magistrate seeks out his teenage stepson in a music hall.
Lively comedy which is valuable as giving the screen's best re-creation of an old-time music hall.
w Fred Thompson, Frank Miller, Frank Launder, Jack Jordan *play The Magistrate* by Arthur Wing Pinero *d Thomas Bentley ph* Otto Kanturek *md* Idris Lewis
☆ Will Hay, John Mills, Iris Hoey, Angela Baddeley, Claud Allister, George Graves, Jane Carr, H. F. Maltby
† Music hall acts include Gaston and Andrée, Lily Morris, G. H. Elliott, Sam Curtis, Frank Boston and Betty

Those Were the Days
US 1940 74m bw
Paramount (J. Theodore Reed)
GB title: *Good Old Schooldays*
During their 40th anniversary celebrations, a married couple look back to their courtship days at college.
Pleasant, light, nostalgic escapades.
w Don Hartman *stories* George Fitch *d* J. Theodore Reed *ph* Victor Milner
☆ William Holden, Bonita Granville, Ezra Stone, Judith Barrett, Vaughan Glazer, Lucien Littlefield, Richard Denning

Those Who Love Me Can Take The Train ***
France 1998 122m colour Panavision
Artificial Eye/Telema/Canal+/France 2/France 3/Azor (Charles Gassot)
original title: *Ceux Qui M'aiment Prendront le Train*
Mourners ponder their personal problems on the train journey from Paris to Limoges, and at the funeral of a bisexual painter who influenced their lives in one way or another.
Brilliantly choreographed study, using a hand-held camera, of a disparate group united mainly by their capacity for emotional outbursts; the performances match the intensity of the director's style.
w Danièle Thompson, Patrice Chereau, Pierre Trividic *d* Patrice Chéreau *ph* Eric Gautier *ad* Richard Peduzzi, Sylvain Chauvelot *ed* François Gedigier *cos* Caroline de Vivaise
☆ Pascal Greggory (François), Jean-Louis Trintignant (Lucien/Jean-Baptiste), Valeria Bruni-Tedeschi (Claire), Charles Berling (Jean-Marie), Bruno Todeschini (Louis), Sylvain Jacques (Bruno), Vincent Perez (Viviane), Roschdy Zem (Thierry), Dominique Blanc (Catherine), Nathan Cogan (Sami), Marie Daems (Lucie)
'Technically acute, dramatically dense, utterly compelling.' – *David Parkinson, Empire*
'Cinematically vivid and emotionally draining ensembler that makes the average Woody Allen film seem like a picnic for the well-adjusted.' – *Lisa Nesselson, Variety*

Those Wonderful Movie Cranks ***
Czechoslovakia 1978 88m colour
Barrandov (Jan Suster)
A travelling conjuror at the turn of the century introduces short cinema films into his act, and solves his woman trouble meanwhile.
Charming melancholy comedy which adds a little to art as well as to history.
w Oldrich Vlcek, Jiri Menzel *d Jiri Menzel ph* Jaromir Sofr *m* Jiri Sust
☆ Rudolf Hrusinsky, Vlasta Fabianova, Blazena Holisova

A Thousand Acres
US 1997 105m colour
Buena Vista/Touchstone/Beacon/Propaganda/Via Rosa/Prairie (Marc Abraham, Lynn Arost, Steve Golin, Kate Guinzburg, Sigurjon Sighvatsson)
An ageing farmer divides his farm between his three daughters.
A variation on King Lear, *set in America's Midwest, this is no more than a melodramatic soap opera that muddles and muddies not only Shakespeare's play, but also Smiley's novel.*
w Laura Jones *novel* Jane Smiley *d* Jocelyn Moorhouse *ph* Tak Fujimoto *m* Richard Hartley *pd* Dan Davis *ed* Maryann Brandon
☆ Michelle Pfeiffer, Jessica Lange, Jason Robards, Jennifer Jason Leigh, Colin Firth, Keith Carradine, Kevin Anderson, Pat Hingle
'What was a careful, moving novel is now a helping of Hollywood soup. Disasters strike with cartoonish regularity and mock-horror.' – *Gaby Wood, Guardian*

A Thousand and One Nights *
US 1945 92m Technicolor
Columbia (Samuel Bischoff)
Aladdin seeks his princess.
Amusing take-off on the Arabian Nights, with good jokes and music.
w Wilfrid H. Pettitt, Richard English, Jack Henley *d* Alfred E. Green *ad* Stephen Goosson, Rudolph Sternad, Ray Rennahan
☆ Cornel Wilde, Phil Silvers, Evelyn Keyes, Adele Jergens, Dusty Anderson, Dennis Hoey
art direction

A Thousand Clowns *
US 1965 115m bw
UA/Harell (Fred Coe)
A New Yorker who has abdicated from work leads a cheerful, useless life with his young nephew, but the school board have their doubts.
Imitative nonconformist comedy with frequent reminiscences of older, better plays such as You Can't Take It with You. *Good lines occasionally make themselves felt, but the overall effect is patchy, the lead is miscast, and the location montages only emphasize the basic one-room set.*
w Herb Gardner *play* Herb Gardner *d* Fred Coe *ph* Arthur J. Ornitz *m* Don Walker
☆ Jason Robards, Martin Balsam, Barry Gordon, Barbara Harris, *William Daniels*, Gene Saks
'A broad and joyous comment on the rebellions and concessions of our daily life, a mature comedy that mixes its compassion with hilarity.' – *Judith Crist*
Martin Balsam
best picture; Herb Gardner; Don Walker

A Thousand Eyes (dubbed)
West Germany 1984 92m colour
Filmverlag der Autoren/Radiant/ZDF (Michael Bittins)
original title: *Tausend Augen*
A student of marine biology, who works by night in a Hamburg strip-show to earn money to enable her to join her boyfriend in Australia, becomes an object of obsession for several men.
Slow-moving and unsatisfactory drama that takes a long time to make a scarcely perceptible point.
wd Hans-Christoph Blumenberg *ph* Martin Schäfer *m* Hubert Bartholomae *pd* Christian Bussmann *ed* Helga Borsche
☆ Barbara Rudnik, Armin Mueller-Stahl, Karin Baal, Peter Kraus, Hannelore Hoger, Mehmet Yandirer, Vera Tschechowa, Gudrun Landgrebe
† There are cameo appearances by directors Jean-Marie Straub, Wim Wenders (as a thief in a video store), George Miller and Phillip Noyce.

The Thousand Eyes of Dr Mabuse *
France/Italy/Germany 1960 103m bw
CCC/Filmkunst/Incom Criterion/Ajay
Murders in a Berlin hotel are attributed to a reincarnation of the evil Dr Mabuse.
Lively if belated sequel to the director's silent films.
w Fritz Lang, Jeinz Oskar Wuttig *d* Fritz Lang *ph* Kurt Löb *m* Bert Grund, Gerhard Becker
☆ Dawn Addams, Peter Van Eyck, Gert Frobe, Wolfgang Preiss, Werner Peters

Thousand Pieces of Gold *
US 1991 105m colour
American Playhouse/Maverick/Film Four (Nancy Kelly, Kenji Yamamoto)
During hard times, a young Chinese woman is sold by her father and sent to America to work in a brothel.
Pioneer days told from the unusual perspective of a woman and an outsider, an understated drama with a feminist subtext.
w Anne Makepeace *novel* Ruthanne Lum McCunn *d* Nancy Kelly *ph* Bobby Bukowski *m* Gary Malkin *pd* Dan Bishop *ed* Kenji Yamamoto
☆ Rosalind Chao, Dennis Dun, Michael Paul Chan, Chris Cooper

Thousands Cheer *
US 1943 126m Technicolor
MGM (Joe Pasternak)
An army base stages an all-star variety show.
Ho-hum studio extravaganza with some good numbers.
w Paul Jarrico, Richard Collins *d* George Sidney *ph* George Folsey *md* Herbert Stothart *ad* Cedric Gibbons, Daniel Cathcart *songs* various
☆ Kathryn Grayson, Gene Kelly, John Boles, Mary Astor, Jose Iturbi, Kay Kyser and his Orchestra, Lionel Barrymore, Margaret O'Brien, June Allyson, Mickey Rooney, Judy Garland, Red Skelton, Eleanor Powell, Bob Crosby and his Orchestra, Lena Horne and also Frank Morgan
'A thoroughly routine musical distinguished only by Gene Kelly with nothing to use his talents on, a terrible piece of trash by Shostakovich, and the unpleasant sight of Jose Iturbi proving he is a real guy by playing the sort of boogie woogie anyone ought to be able to learn through a correspondence course.' – *James Agee*
♫ 'Let There Be Music'; 'Daybreak'; 'Three Letters in the Mailbox'; 'I Dug a Ditch'; 'Should I Reveal'; 'The Joint is Really Jumpin''
George Folsey; Herbert Stothart; art direction

Three
GB 1969 105m DeLuxe
UA/Obelisk (Bruce Becker)
Two American students on holiday in Europe pick up an English girl to show them the sights.
An aimless road movie.
wd James Salter *story Then We Were Three* by Irwin Shaw *ph* Etienne Becker *m* Laurence Rosenthal *ad* Guy Littaye *ed* Edward Nielson
☆ Charlotte Rampling, Robie Porter, Sam Waterston, Pascale Roberts, Edina Ronay, Gillian Hills
'Ambiguous action, coolly inscrutable characters, dialogue that is little more than half-heard clichés.' – *Richard Combs, MFB*
† The film was cut to 95m on its British release.

3-4x Jugatsu: see *Boiling Point*

The Three Ages *
US 1923 80m approx bw silent
Joseph Schenck/Metro
Three stories parodying Griffith's *Intolerance*.
The star's first feature film, not his strongest, is saved by the final chases.
w Clyde Bruckman, Jean Havez, Joseph Mitchell *d* Buster Keaton, Edward F. Cline
☆ *Buster Keaton*, Wallace Beery, Margaret Leahy, Joe Roberts

Three Amigos!
US 1986 105m Technicolor
Orion (Lorne Michaels, George Folsey Jnr)
Three wimpish cowboy stars find themselves hired to defend a desert town from a bandit.
Weak take-off of The Magnificent Seven, *with performances that grate.*
w Steve Martin, Lorne Michaels, Randy Newman *d* John Landis *ph* Ronald W. Browne *m* Elmer Bernstein *pd* Richard Sawyer *ed* Malcolm Campbell
☆ Chevy Chase, Steve Martin, Martin Short, Patrice Martinez, Alfonso Arau

Three Bites of the Apple
US 1966 98m Metrocolor Panavision
MGM (Alvin Ganzer)
An English travel courier wins a lot of money in a Rome casino, and nearly loses it all.
Very dull comedy perked up by attractive locations.
w George Wells *d* Alvin Ganzer *ph* Gabor Pogany *m* Eddy Manson
☆ David McCallum, Sylva Koscina, Tammy Grimes, Harvey Korman, Aldo Fabrizi

Three Blind Mice *
US 1938 75m bw
TCF (Raymond Griffith)
Three Kansas girls in the big city seek rich husbands.
Mild comedy remade as Three Little Girls in Blue *and* How to Marry a Millionaire, *and not all that different from any of the* Gold Diggers *comedy musicals.*
w Brown Holmes, Lynn Starling *d* William A. Seiter *ph* Ernest Palmer *m* Charles Maxwell
☆ Loretta Young, Joel McCrea, David Niven, Stuart Erwin, Marjorie Weaver, Pauline Moore, Binnie Barnes, Jane Darwell, Leonid Kinskey
'More names than can be handled on the marquee … good summer entertainment.' – *Variety*

Three Brave Men *
US 1956 88m bw Cinemascope
TCF (Herbert B. Swope Jnr)
A civilian employee in the US Navy is suspended as a security risk and it takes a lawsuit to set things straight.
Semi-factual anti-McCarthy drama proving that America is a great place to live – when you're winning. Good courtroom scenes.
wd Philip Dunne *articles* Anthony Lewis *ph* Charles G. Clarke *m* Hans Salter
☆ *Ray Milland, Ernest Borgnine, Nina Foch,* Dean Jagger, Frank Lovejoy, Edward Andrews, Frank Faylen, James Westerfield, Joseph Wiseman

The Three Caballeros ***
US 1945 70m Technicolor
Walt Disney (Norman Ferguson)
A programme of shorts about South America, linked by Donald Duck as a tourist.
Rapid-fire mélange of fragments supporting the good neighbour policy, following the shorter Saludos Amigos *of 1943. The kaleidoscopic sequences and the combination of live action with cartoon remain of absorbing interest.*
w various *d* various *m* Edward Plumb, Paul J. Smith, Charles Wolcott
† Stories include Pablo the Penguin, Little Gauchito, a Mexican sequence and some adventures with Joe Carioca.
Edward Plumb, Paul J. Smith, Charles Wolcott

Three Came Home **
US 1950 106m bw
TCF (Nunnally Johnson)
In 1941 writer Agnes Newton Keith tries to escape from Borneo but is interned and ill-used by the Japanese.
Well-made, harrowing war adventure.
w Nunnally Johnson *book* Agnes Newton Keith *d Jean Negulesco ph Milton Krasner m* Hugo Friedhofer *md* Lionel Newman
☆ *Claudette Colbert,* Patric Knowles, Sessue Hayakawa, Florence Desmond, Sylvia Andrew, Phyllis Morris
'It will shock you, disturb you, tear your heart out. But it will fill you with great respect for a heroic soul.' – *New York Times*

Three Cases of Murder *
GB 1954 99m bw
British Lion/Wessex/London Films (Ian Dalrymple, Hugh Perceval)
'In the Picture': a painting comes to life. 'You Killed Elizabeth': a man suspects himself of his faithless fiancée's murder. 'Lord Mountdrago': the foreign secretary dreams of killing an MP he hates.
Unlinked compendium, in which the first and third stories are quite interesting and well done, the second very commonplace.
w Donald Wilson, Sidney Caroll, Ian Dalrymple (original stories Roderick Wilkinson, Brett Halliday, W. Somerset Maugham) *d* Wendy Toye, David Eady, George More O'Ferrall *ph* Georges Périnal *m* Doreen Carwithen
☆ Alan Badel, Hugh Pryse, Leueen MacGrath, Elizabeth Sellars, John Gregson, Emrys Jones, Orson Welles, André Morell

Three Cheers for the Irish
US 1940 100m bw
Warner (Sam Bischoff)
An Irishman's daughter causes family trouble when she falls for a Scot.
Pleasant, unpretentious but overlong romantic comedy.
w Richard Macaulay, Jerry Wald *d* Lloyd Bacon *ph* Charles Rosher *m* Adolph Deutsch
☆ Thomas Mitchell, Priscilla Lane, Dennis Morgan, Alan Hale, Virginia Grey, Irene Hervey, William Lundigan

Three Cockeyed Sailors: see *Sailors Three*

Three Coins in the Fountain **
US 1954 102m DeLuxe Cinemascope
TCF (Sol C. Siegel)
Three American girls find romance in Rome.
An enormous box-office hit, the pattern of which was frequently repeated against various backgrounds; it was actually remade in Madrid as The Pleasure Seekers. *In itself a thin entertainment, but the title song carried it.*
w John Patrick *novel* John H. Secondari *d* Jean Negulesco *ph Milton Krasner m* Victor Young
☆ Clifton Webb, Dorothy McGuire, Louis Jourdan, Jean Peters, Rossano Brazzi, Maggie McNamara, Howard St John, Kathryn Givney, Cathleen Nesbitt
Milton Krasner; title song (*m Jule Styne, ly Sammy Cahn*)
best picture

Three Colours: Blue ***
France 1993 98m Eastmancolor
Artificial Eye/MK2/CED/France 3/CAB/TOR/Canal (Marin Karmitz)
original title: *Trois Couleurs: Bleu*
A secretive woman, whose husband, a composer, and child are killed in a car crash, destroys his final work, sells all their possessions and sets out to remake her life.
The first part of a trilogy, based on the colours of the French tricolour and dealing with the theme of liberty, as experienced from the viewpoint of its enigmatic central character, for whom liberty often means a refusal to engage with the world, in order to avoid pain.
w Krzysztof Pisiewicz, Krzysztof Kieslowski *d Krzysztof Kieslowski ph Slawomir Idziak m Zbigniew Preisner ad* Claude Lenoir *ed* Jacques Witta
☆ Juliette Binoche, Benoît Régent, Florence Pernel, Charlotte Véry, Hélène Vincent, Philippe Volter, Claude Duneton, Hugues Quester, Emmanuelle Riva
'What lifts it out of the doldrums is Kieslowski's fascinating use of reflections, focusing techniques and camera angles to give the somewhat pedestrian material a profound and otherworldly East European feel.' – *Kim Newman, Empire*
† The music for the film was written first and the action was filmed to match its rhythms.

Three Colours: Red ***
France/Switzerland/Poland 1994 99m Eastmancolor
Artificial Eye/MK2/France 3/CAB/Tor (Marin Karmitz)
original title: *Trois Couleurs: Rouge*
A model confides her fears about her life to a lonely and inquisitive retired judge, who secretly arranges a meeting between her and a young lawyer.
A delicate and intricate study of coincidence and destiny, of the fragile means that link one person to the next; it is a stylish and intriguing end to an impressive trilogy.
w Krzysztof Piesiewicz, Krzysztof Kieslowski d Krzysztof Kieslowski ph Piotr Sobocinski m Zbigniew Preisner pd Claude Lenoir *ed* Jacques Witta
☆ Irene Jacob, Jean-Louis Trintignant, Jean-Pierre Lorit, Frédérique Feder, Juliette Binoche, Julie Delpy
'This is the kind of film that makes you feel intensely alive and sends you out into the streets afterwards eager to talk deeply and urgently to the person you are with.' – *Roger Ebert, Chicago Sun-Times*
'If it's true – as the helmer has announced – that this opus will be his last foray into film directing, Kieslowski retires at a formal and philosophical peak.' – *Variety*
† It is the last part of a trilogy based on the French tricolour and dealing with fraternity.
Krzysztof Kieslowski (director); Krzysztof Piesiewicz (screenplay); Piotr Sobocinski

Three Colours: White ***
France/Poland 1993 92m Eastmancolor
Artificial Eye/MK2/France 3/Cab/TOR/Canal (Marin Karmitz)
original title: *Trois Couleurs: Blanc*
A Polish hairdresser suffers a series of humiliations in Paris – he becomes impotent, his French wife divorces him and he is reduced to penury – and returns to Warsaw with the aim of becoming rich and winning back his wife.
Elegant and acid comedy of a Chaplinesque little man at large in an entrepreneurial Poland – 'home at last,' says our hero, regaining consciousness on a Warsaw rubbish dump after a nightmare trip from France.
w Krzysztof Piesiewicz, Krzysztof Kieslowski d Krzysztof Kieslowski ph Edward Klosiński *m* Zbigniew Preisner *ad* Halina Dobrowolska, Claude Lenoir *ed* Urszula Lesiak
☆ Zbigniew Zamachowski, Julie Delpy, Janusz Gajos, Jerzy Stuhr, Juliette Binoche, Florence Pernel
'Funny, bleak and, like all Kieslowski films, austerely handsome – a festival of minimalist virtuosity.' – *Time*
'A fairly straightforward black comedy that skirts pretentiousness and goes easy on the symbolism while retaining Kieslowski's eerie gift for spinning mystical narrative gold from the simplest of ingredients.' – *Lisa Nesselson, Variety*
† This second part of a trilogy, based on the colours of the French flag, deals with equality.

'Out of the inferno of war came three men and a woman – to live their lives, to strive for happiness, to seek love!'
Three Comrades **
US 1938 98m bw
MGM (Joseph L. Mankiewicz)
In twenties Germany, three friends find life hard but derive some joy from their love for a high-spirited girl who is dying of tuberculosis.
Despairing romance becomes a sentimental tearjerker with all the stops out; immaculately produced and very appealing to the masses, but prevented by censorship from being the intended indictment of Nazi Germany. The final scene in which the two surviving comrades are joined in the churchyard by their ghostly friends still packs a wallop.
w F. Scott Fitzgerald, Edward E. Paramore novel Erich Maria Remarque *d Frank Borzage ph* Joseph Ruttenberg *m* Franz Waxman
☆ *Margaret Sullavan,* Robert Taylor, Robert Young, Franchot Tone, Guy Kibbee, Lionel Atwill, Henry Hull, Charley Grapewin
'Just what Frank Borzage is trying to prove is very difficult to fathom … there must have been some reason for making this picture, but it certainly isn't in the name of entertainment.' – *Variety*
'A remarkably high combination of talents has made it all very impressive and moving – good writing, a good man at the camera, good actors, and presiding over them a good director … such unforgettable bits as the pursuit of the boy who shot Gottfried, a glimpse from under the muffling blanket of the girl's stricken face, the startling downswoop of the camera's eye upon the girl getting up from bed to remove the burden of her illness from those who love her. These are high moments in a film full of beauty.' – *National Board of Review*
'A love story, beautifully told and consummately acted, but so drenched in hopelessness and heavy with the aroma of death, of wasted youth in a world of foggy shapes and nameless menaces, that its beauty and strength are often clouded and betrayed.' – *Time*
Margaret Sullavan

'They might be the family next door – but if they were, you'd move!'
Three Cornered Moon *
US 1933 72m bw
Paramount
A newly-poor Depression family has trouble finding work.
Slightly screwball romantic comedy, a predecessor of You Can't Take It with You; *the humour now seems very faded, but it was a signpost of its day.*
w S. K. Lauren, Ray Harris *play* Gertrude Tonkonogy *d* Elliott Nugent *ph* Leon Shamroy
☆ Claudette Colbert, Mary Boland, Richard Arlen, Wallace Ford, Lyda Roberti, Tom Brown, Hardie Albright

Three Daring Daughters
US 1948 115m Technicolor
MGM (Joe Pasternak)
GB title: *The Birds and the Bees*
Three girls are dismayed to hear that their mother is remarrying.
Cheerful comedy with music, but nothing to write home about.
w Albert Mannheimer, Frederick Kohner, Sonya Levien, John Meehan *d* Fred M. Wilcox *ph* Ray June *md* Georgie Stoll
☆ Jeanette MacDonald, Jose Iturbi, Jane Powell, Ann E. Todd, Mary Elinor Donahue, Larry Adler, Edward Arnold, Harry Davenport, Moyna MacGill

'His code name is Condor. In the next twenty-four hours everyone he trusts will try to kill him.'
Three Days of the Condor **
US 1975 118m Technicolor Panavision
Paramount/Dino de Laurentiis/Wildwood (Stanley Schneider)
An innocent researcher for a branch of the CIA finds himself marked for death by assassins employed by another branch.
Entertaining New York-based thriller which shamelessly follows most of the twists of The 39 Steps. *It is just possible to follow its complexities, and the dialogue is smart.*
w Lorenzo Semple Jnr, David Rayfiel novel Six Days of the Condor by James Grady *d Sydney Pollack ph* Owen Roizman *m* Dave Grusin
☆ *Robert Redford,* Faye Dunaway, Cliff Robertson, Max von Sydow, John Houseman, Walter McGinn

Three Faces East *
US 1930 71m bw
Warner (Darryl F. Zanuck)
The butler to the British war minister is a German spy, and the German nurse sent to help him is really a British agent …
Slow, melodramatic remake of 1926 silent, later turned into a Karloff vehicle, British Intelligence *(qv).*
w Oliver H. P. Garrett, Arthur Caesar *play* Anthony Paul Kelly *d* Roy del Ruth *ph* Chick McGill
☆ Constance Bennett, Erich von Stroheim, Anthony Bushell, William Holden
'Bennett and von Stroheim guarantee a better than average week.' – *Variety*

The Three Faces of Eve **
US 1957 95m bw Cinemascope
TCF (Nunnally Johnson)
A psychiatrist discovers that a female patient has three distinct personalities: a drab housewife, a good time girl and a mature sophisticated woman.
Alistair Cooke introduces this tall tale as if he believed it; as presented, it is entertaining but not very convincing. Its box-office success was sufficient to start a schizophrenia cycle.
w Nunnally Johnson *book* Corbett H. Thigpen MD, Hervey M. Cleckley MD *d Nunnally Johnson ph Stanley Cortez m* Robert Emmett Dolan
☆ *Joanne Woodward,* Lee J. Cobb, David Wayne, Nancy Kulp, Edwin Jerome
Joanne Woodward

Three Faces West
US 1940 79m bw
Republic (Sol C. Siegel)
A dust bowl community is helped by an Austrian doctor fleeing from the Nazis, but his daughter is followed by a Nazi suitor.
Unusual modern Western, blandly told.

w F. Hugh Herbert, Joseph Moncure March, Samuel Ornitz *d* Bernard Vorhaus *ph* John Alton *m* Victor Young
☆ John Wayne, Charles Coburn, Sigrid Gurie, Roland Varno, Spencer Charters, Sonny Bupp

Three for Jamie Dawn
US 1956 81m bw
AA (Hayes Goetz)
A crooked lawyer bribes three members of a murder jury.
Minor courtroom melodrama, limply developed.
w John Klempner *d* Thomas Carr *ph* Duke Green *m* Walter Scharf
☆ Laraine Day, Ricardo Montalban, Richard Carlson, June Havoc

Three for the Road
US 1987 88m DeLuxe
Vista (Herb Jaffe, Mort Engelberg)
A presidential candidate entrusts the task of escorting his delinquent daughter to a Southern reform school to a young, ambitious aide and his friend, a would-be writer.
Dire road movie, about the sort of people that one would wish strenuously to avoid.
w Richard Martini, Tim Metcalfe, Miguel Tejada-Flores *d* Bill L. Norton *ph* Stephen L. Posey *m* Barry Goldberg *pd* Linda Allen *ed* Christopher Greenbury
☆ Charlie Sheen, Kerri Green, Alan Ruck, Sally Kellerman, Blair Tefkin, Raymond J. Barry

'One for the songs and dances! Two for the laughs and romances!'
Three for the Show *
US 1955 93m Technicolor Cinemascope
Columbia (Jonie Taps)
A married Broadway star finds that her first husband is still alive.
Adequate musical remake of Too Many Husbands *(qv); not bad, not good.*
w Edward Hope, Leonard Stern *play* *Too Many Husbands* by W. Somerset Maugham *d* H. C. Potter *ph* Arthur E. Arling *md* George Duning *ch* Jack Cole *songs* various
☆ Betty Grable, Jack Lemmon, Marge Champion, Gower Champion, Myron McCormick, Paul Harvey
'It has the inimitable zing of vacuity, and it has something more important: a fundamental lilt that travels from scene to scene and makes the picture musical even when the soundtrack is silent.' – *Time*

Three Fugitives *
US 1989 96m Metrocolor
Warner/Touchstone/Silver Screen Partners IV (Lauren Shuler-Donner)
An ex-convict, trying to reform, is forced to go on the run with an inept bank robber and his small daughter.
A chase farce that piles up the absurdities with diminishing effect.
wd Francis Veber *ph* Haskell Wexler *m* David McHugh *pd* Rick Carter *ed* Bruce Green
☆ Nick Nolte, Martin Short, Sarah Rowland Doroff, James Earl Jones, Alan Ruck, Kenneth McMillan, David Arnott, Bruce McGill

Three Girls about Town *
US 1942 71m bw
Columbia
Three sisters in New York find a corpse in their hotel bedroom.
A funny 'B' picture: fast paced and lively from start to finish.
w Richard Carroll *d* Leigh Jason *ph* Franz Planer
☆ Joan Blondell, Binnie Barnes, Janet Blair, John Howard, Robert Benchley, Eric Blore, Una O'Connor

Three Godfathers *
US 1948 106m Technicolor
MGM/Argosy (John Ford)
Three outlaws escaping across the desert take charge of an orphan baby.
'Orrible sentimental parable partly redeemed by splendid scenery.
w Laurence Stallings, Frank S. Nugent *story* Peter B. Kyne *d* *John Ford* *ph* *Winton Hoch* *m* Richard Hageman
☆ John Wayne, Pedro Armendariz, Harry Carey Jnr, Ward Bond
† The story also appeared in 1909 as *Bronco Billy and the Baby*; in 1916 as *Three Godfathers*, with Harry Carey; in 1920 as *Marked Men*, with Harry Carey; in 1929 as *Hell's Heroes*, with Charles Bickford; in 1936 as *Three Godfathers*, with Chester Morris; and in 1975 as a TV movie, *The Godchild*, with Jack Palance.
†† The film is dedicated 'to the memory of Harry Carey, bright star of the early western sky'.

Three Guys Named Mike
US 1951 90m bw
MGM (Armand Deutsch)
An accident-prone air hostess has three suitors.
Inconsequential romantic comedy which shows the effort of stretching its thin material to feature length.
w Sidney Sheldon *story* Ruth Brooks Flippen *d* Charles Walters *ph* Paul Vogel *m* Bronislau Kaper
☆ Jane Wyman, Barry Sullivan, Van Johnson, Howard Keel, Phyllis Kirk, Jeff Donnell

Three Hats for Lisa *
GB 1965 99m Eastmancolor
Seven Hills/Jack Hanbury
A docker and a taxi driver help a foreign film star to steal three typically English hats.
Minor musical, silly but good to look at.
w Leslie Bricusse, Talbot Rothwell *d* Sidney Hayers
☆ Joe Brown, Sid James, Sophie Hardy, Una Stubbs, Dave Nelson, Peter Bowles

Three Hearts for Julia
US 1943 90m bw
MGM
A reporter courts his wife all over again when she threatens to divorce him.
One of those thin romantic comedies which sent its male lead back to the theatre.
w Lionel Houser *d* Richard Thorpe
☆ Melvyn Douglas, Ann Sothern, Lee Bowman, Felix Bressart, Reginald Owen, Richard Ainley

365 Nights in Hollywood
US 1934 77m bw
Sol M. Wurtzel/Fox
A down-and-out becomes a director of a fake school of acting.
Slight and casually developed comedy-romance, with comedy interludes by Mitchell and Durant.
w William Conselman, Henry Johnson *d* George Marshall
☆ James Dunn, Alice Faye, John Bradford, Grant Mitchell
'A picture with no punch and little appeal.' – *Variety*

The 300 Spartans *
US 1962 114m DeLuxe Cinemascope
TCF (Rudolph Maté, George St George)
Sparta leads the ancient Greek states against Persia's attack at Thermopylae.
Quite a lively epic with some dignity.
w George St George *d* Rudolph Maté *ph* Geoffrey Unsworth *m* Manos Hadjidakis
☆ Richard Egan, Ralph Richardson, David Farrar, Diane Baker, Barry Coe, Donald Houston, Kieron Moore, John Crawford, Robert Brown

Three in the Attic
US 1968 90m Pathécolor
AIP-Hermes (Richard Wilson)
A college Casanova is locked in an attic by three girls who seduce him by rota until he cries for mercy.
One of the first outspoken comedies of the sexual revolution, but not a particularly funny one.
w Stephen Yafa *novel* *Paxton Quigley's Had the Course* by Stephen Yafa *d* Richard Wilson *ph* J. Burgi Contner *m* Chad Stuart
☆ Chris Jones, Yvette Mimieux, Judy Pace, Maggie Turett, Nan Martin

Three in the Cellar: see *Up in the Cellar*

'Hello, Mrs Howard, I'm a friend of Mr Howard!'
Three into Two Won't Go *
GB 1969 100m Technicolor
Universal (Julian Blaustein)
An executive has an affair with a girl hitch-hiker who later moves into his house to his wife's astonishment.
Palatable sex drama with good performances, rather flabbily written and directed.
w Edna O'Brien *novel* Andrea Newman *d* Peter Hall *ph* Walter Lassally *m* Francis Lai
☆ *Rod Steiger, Claire Bloom, Judy Geeson, Peggy* Ashcroft, Paul Rogers

Three Is a Family *
US 1944 81m bw
Sol Lesser/United Artists
A middle-aged couple find their small apartment invaded by their homeless children and grandchildren.
Quite amusing comedy on a familiar theme.
w Harry Chandlee, Marjorie L. Pfaelzer *play* Phoebe and Henry Ephron *d* Edward Ludwig
☆ Charles Ruggles, Fay Bainter, Marjorie Reynolds, Helen Broderick, Arthur Lake, Hattie McDaniel, John Philliber, Jeff Donnell, Walter Catlett, Clarence Kolb, Warren Hymer

Three Kids and a Queen
US 1935 85m bw
Universal
Three boys decide to kidnap a rich old lady, but are dismayed to find that she enjoys the experience.
Sentimental comedy which seemed to hit the right note.
w Barry Trivers, Samuel Ornitz, Harry Poppe, Chester Beecroft *d* Edward Ludwig
☆ May Robson, Frankie Darro, Billy Burrud, Billy Benedict, Charlotte Henry, Herman Bing, Henry Armetta, John Miljan, Hedda Hopper
'A cinch for box office satisfaction.' – *Variety*

'They're Deserters, Rebels And Thieves. But In The Nicest Possible Way.'
'It's Good To Be King.'
Three Kings ***
US 1999 115m Technicolor Panavision
Warner/Village Roadshow/Village-A.M Film/Coast Ridge/Atlas (Charles Roven, Paul Junger Witt, Edward L. McDonnell)
As the Gulf War ends in 1991, a group US soldiers attempt to steal Saddam Hussein's hoard of gold, buried behind Iraqi lines.
Ironic, blackly humorous drama that manages to take seriously the messy mechanics of war while staying within most of the conventions of a caper movie, and adding some unsettling photographic effects to the genre.
wd David O. Russell *story* John Ridley *ph* Newton Thomas Sigel *m* Carter Burwell *pd* Catherine Hardwicke *ed* Robert K. Lambert
☆ George Clooney (Archie Gates), Mark Wahlberg (Troy Barlow), Ice Cube (Chief Elgin), Spike Jonze (Conrad Vig), Jamie Kennedy (Walter Wogaman), Mykelti Williamson (Colonel Horn), Cliff Curtis (Amir Abdulah), Said Taghmaoui (Captain Said), Judy Greer (Cathy Daitch), Liz Stauber (Debbie Barlow)
'That most unusual of sights, the grown up, intelligent Hollywood war film.' – *Times*
'There are many clever touches, but there's something tamely conventional at the film's core.' – *Janet Maslin, New York Times*

Three Little Girls in Blue
US 1946 90m Technicolor
TCF (Mack Gordon)
Musical remake of *Three Blind Mice* (qv); adequate and quite forgettable.
w Valentine Davies *d* H. Bruce Humberstone *ph* Ernest Palmer *songs* Mack Gordon, Joseph Myrow
☆ June Haver, George Montgomery, Vivian Blaine, Celeste Holm, Vera-Ellen, Frank Latimore, Charles Smith, Charles Halton

Three Little Words *
US 1950 102m Technicolor
MGM (Jack Cummings)
The careers of songwriters Bert Kalmar and Harry Ruby.
Disappointingly ordinary musical in which two witty people are made to seem dull, and the plot allows Fred Astaire only one dance.
w George Wells *d* Richard Thorpe *ph* Harry Jackson *md* André Previn *ch* Hermes Pan *songs* *Bert Kalmar, Harry Ruby and various collaborators*
☆ Fred Astaire, Red Skelton, Vera-Ellen, Arlene Dahl, Keenan Wynn, Gale Robbins, Gloria de Haven, Phil Regan, *Debbie Reynolds*
† Vera-Ellen's singing was dubbed by Anita Ellis.
André Previn

The Three Lives of Thomasina
GB 1963 97m Technicolor
Walt Disney
In a Scottish village in 1912, a vet finds that his methods are no match for a local girl who treats animals by giving them love.
Syrupy film for children: the animals are the main interest and one of them narrates…
w Robert Westerby *novel* *Thomasina* by Paul Gallico *d* Don Chaffey *ph* Paul Beeson *m* Paul Smith
☆ Susan Hampshire, Patrick McGoohan, Karen Dotrice, Vincent Winter, Laurence Naismith, Finlay Currie, Wilfrid Brambell

Three Loves Has Nancy
US 1938 69m bw
MGM (Norman Krasna)
A jilted bride takes her time about her next selection.
Adequate star comedy.
w Bella and Sam Spewack, George Oppenheimer, David Hertz *d* Richard Thorpe *ph* William Daniels
☆ Janet Gaynor, Robert Montgomery, Franchot Tone, Guy Kibbee, Claire Dodd, Reginald Owen, Charley Grapewin, Emma Dunn, Cora Witherspoon
'This may not be the funniest picture of the season, but it's certainly one of the wackiest.' – *Variety*

The Three Maxims
GB 1937 87m bw
GFD/Pathé Consortium (Herbert Wilcox)
Two trapezists love the girl member of the team, and the situation leads to attempted murder.
Effective Paris-set treatment of a well worn theme (see Trapeze*).*
w Herman Mankiewicz *d* Herbert Wilcox *ph* Frederick A. Young, Jack Cox
☆ Anna Neagle, Tullio Carminati, Leslie Banks, Horace Hodges

'They changed her diapers – she changed their lives!'
Three Men and a Baby
US 1987 102m DeLuxe
Touchstone/Silver Screen III (Ted Field, Robert W. Cort)
Three swinging bachelors find a baby on their doorstep.
Slight comedy, given some momentum by a heroin-dealing subplot, which proved surprisingly successful with audiences thanks to energetic playing.
w James Orr, Jim Cruickshank *d* Leonard Nimoy *ph* Adam Greenberg *m* Marvin Hamlisch *pd* Peter Larkin
☆ Tom Selleck, Steve Guttenberg, Ted Danson, Nancy Travis
† Remake of the more thoughtful and elegant *Trois Hommes et un Couffin* of 1985, whose director Coline Serreau was to have directed the US version but backed out.

Three Men and a Cradle *
France 1985 107m colour
UKFD/Floch Film/Soprofilm/TF1 Films (Jean-François Lepetit)
original title: *Trois Hommes et un Couffin*
Three bachelors fall for a baby left on their doorstep by a former girl-friend.
Amusing comedy of role reversal which was remade by Hollywood as the glossier Three Men and a Baby.
wd Coline Serreau *ph* Jean-Yves Éscoffier, Jean-Jacques Bouhon *pd* Yvan Maussion *ed* Catherine Renault
☆ Roland Giraud, Michel Boujenah, André Dussollier, Philippine Leroy Beaulieu

Three Men and a Girl: see *Golden Arrow (1949)*

Three Men and a Little Lady
US 1990 100m
Touchstone/Jean François LePetit-Interscope Communications (Ted Field, Robert W. Cort)

Three bachelors prevent the mother of the child they 'adopted' marrying an Englishman.
Dire sequel to Three Men and a Baby, *notably silly in its depiction of England as a backward rural country inhabited entirely by eccentrics.*
w Charlie Peters *story* Sara Parriott, Joann McGibbon *d* Emile Ardolino *ph* Adam Greenberg *m* James Newton Howard *pd* Stuart Wurtzel *ad* David M. Haber *ed* Michael A. Stevenson
☆ Tom Selleck, Steve Guttenberg, Ted Danson, Nancy Travis, Robin Weisman, Christopher Cazenove, Sheila Hancock, Fiona Shaw
'Thinking people will be hard-pressed to find a single interesting moment in this relentlessly predictable fantasy.' – *Variety*

Three Men in a Boat
GB 1956 94m Eastmancolor
Cinemascope
Romulus (Jack Clayton)

In the 1890s, misadventures befall three men holidaying on the Thames.
Flabby burlesque of a celebrated comic novel whose style is never even approached.
w Hubert Gregg, Vernon Harris *novel* Jerome K. Jerome *d* Ken Annakin *ph* Eric Cross *m* John Addison *ad* John Howell
☆ David Tomlinson, Jimmy Edwards, Laurence Harvey, Shirley Eaton, Robertson Hare, Jill Ireland, Lisa Gastoni, Martita Hunt, A. E. Matthews, Ernest Thesiger, Adrienne Corri
† A previous version in 1933 starred William Austin, Edmond Breon and Billy Milton; directed by Graham Cutts for ATP.

Three Men on a Horse *
US 1936 85m bw
Warner (Sam Bischoff)

A timid Brooklynite finds he can always pick winners, and gangsters get interested.
Smooth New Yorkish comedy which pleased at the time.
w Laird Doyle *play* John Cecil Holm, George Abbott *d* Mervyn Le Roy *ph* Sol Polito
☆ *Frank McHugh, Sam Levene*, Joan Blondell, Guy Kibbee, Carol Hughes, Allen Jenkins, Edgar Kennedy, Eddie Anderson, Harry Davenport

The Three Mesquiteers
A three-man cowboy team who operated in popular B features at the Hopalong Cassidy level. The make-up of the team varied: the actors most often found in it were John Wayne, Max Terhune, Bob Livingston, Ray Corrigan, Bob Steele, Rufe Davis, Tom Tyler, Raymond Hatton, Duncan Renaldo and Jimmy Dodd. The first film was made for RKO, all the rest for Republic: most frequent directors were George Sherman, Mack V. Wright, Joseph Kane, John English and Lester Orlebeck.
1935 Powdersmoke Range, The Three Mesquiteers
1936 Ghost Town, Gold, Roarin' Lead
1937 Riders of the Whistling Skull, Hit the Saddle, Gunsmoke Ranch, Come On Cowboys, Range Defenders, Heart of the Rockies, The Trigger Trio, Wild Horse Rodeo
1938 The Purple Vigilantes, Call the Mesquiteers, Call of the Mesquiteers, Outlaws of Sonora, Riders of the Black Hills, Heroes of the Hills, Pals of the Saddle, Over-land Stage Raiders, Santa Fe Stampede, Red River Range
1939 The Night Riders, Three Texas Steers, Wyoming Outlaw, New Frontier, The Kansas Terrors, Cowboys from Texas
1940 Heroes of the Saddle, Pioneers of the West, Covered Wagon Days, Rocky Mountain Rangers, Oklahoma Renegades, Under Texas Skies, The Trail Blazers, Lone Star Raiders
1941 Prairie Pioneers, Pals of the Pecos, Saddlemates, Gangs of Sonora, Outlaws of the Cherokee Trail, Gauchos of El Dorado, West of Cimarron
1942 Code of the Outlaw, Riders of the Range, Westward Ho, The Phantom Plainsman, Shadows on the Sage, Valley of Hunted Men
1943 Thundering Trails, The Blocked Trail, Santa Fe Scouts, Riders of the Rio Grande

The Three Musketeers
US 1935 97m bw
RKO

See below for synopsis.
A thin and poorly handled version.
w Dudley Nichols, Rowland V. Lee *d* Rowland V. Lee
☆ Walter Abel (D'Artagnan), Paul Lukas (Athos), Moroni Olsen (Porthos), Onslow Stevens (Aramis), Margot Grahame (Milady), Heather Angel (Constance), Ian Keith (de Rochefort), Miles Mander (King), Nigel de Brulier (Richelieu)
'Ineffective and disappointing adaptation … dull entertainment.' – *Variety*

The Three Musketeers **
US 1939 73m bw
TCF (Raymond Griffith)

GB title: *The Singing Musketeer*
A burlesque of the familiar story with pauses for song.
A very satisfactory entertainment with all concerned in top form.
w M. M. Musselman, William A. Drake, Sam Hellman *d Allan Dwan ph* Peverell Marley *songs* Samuel Pokrass, Walter Bullock
☆ *Don Ameche, the Ritz Brothers*, Binnie Barnes, *Joseph Schildkraut*, Lionel Atwill, Miles Mander, Gloria Stuart, Pauline Moore, John Carradine
'Whenever the action lags, the trio take the rostrum for a slapstick specialty … moderate b.o., a topper for the key duals.' – *Variety*

The Three Musketeers ***
US 1948 125m Technicolor
MGM (Pandro S. Berman)

High-spirited version of the famous story, with duels and fights presented like musical numbers.
Its vigour and inventiveness is a pleasure to behold.
w Robert Ardrey *d George Sidney ph Robert Planck m Herbert Stothart*
☆ *Gene Kelly* (D'Artagnan), Lana Turner (Charlotte de Winter), June Allyson (Constance), Frank Morgan (Louis XIII), Van Heflin (Roberrt Athos), Angela Lansbury (Queen Anne), Vincent Price (Richelieu), Keenan Wynn, John Sutton, Gig Young (Porthos), Robert Coote (Aramis), Reginald Owen, Ian Keith, Patricia Medina
'A heavy, rough-housing mess. As Lady de Winter, Lana Turner sounds like a drive-in waitress exchanging quips with hotrodders, and as Richelieu, Vincent Price might be an especially crooked used car dealer. Angela Lansbury wears the crown of France as though she had won it at a county fair.' – *New Yorker, 1980*
🏆 Robert Planck

'A Place Of Betrayal. The Fate Of A King. A Time For Heroes.'
Three Musketeers
US 1993 105m Technicolor
Panavision
Buena Vista/Walt Disney/One For All/Caravan (Joe Roth, Roger Birnbaum)

D'Artagnan and the three musketeers save the throne of France despite the machinations of Cardinal Richelieu.
A half-hearted romp by a group of actors to whom swashbuckling is a lost art, this is simply Young Guns with swords, no more than a feeble adventure with little sense of period.
w David Loughery *novel* Alexandre Dumas *d* Stephen Herek *ph* Dean Semler *m* Michael Kamen *pd* Wolf Kroeger *ed* John F. Link
☆ Charlie Sheen, Kiefer Sutherland, Chris O'Donnell, Oliver Platt, Tim Curry, Rebecca de Mornay, Gabrielle Anwar, Paul McGann, Julie Delpy
'There should be a better reason for re-making *The Three Musketeers* than to provide a vehicle for whiskery Brat-packers whose careers are on the slide.' – *Sheila Johnston, Independent*

The Three Musketeers (The Queen's Diamonds) **
Panama 1973 107m Technicolor
Film Trust (Alex Salkind)

Jokey version with realistic blood; despite very lively highlights it wastes most of its high production cost by not giving its plot a chance; but money was saved by issuing the second half separately as *The Four Musketeers* (*The Revenge of Milady*). The latter section was less attractive.
w George MacDonald Fraser *d Richard Lester ph David Watkin m* Michel Legrand *pd Brian Eatwell*
☆ Michael York, Oliver Reed, Richard Chamberlain, Frank Finlay, Raquel Welch, Geraldine Chaplin, Spike Milligan, Faye Dunaway, Charlton Heston, Christopher Lee, Jean-Pierre Cassel
'It's one dragged-out forced laugh. No sweep, no romance, no convincing chivalric tradition to mock.' – *Stanley Kauffmann*

3 Ninjas *
US 1992 84m Technicolor
Buena Vista/Touchstone/Global Venture Hollywood (Martha Chang)

The sons of an FBI agent, taught martial arts by their grandfather, defeat an evil arms dealer.
Amiable martial arts caper that should please the pre-teens.
w Edward Emanuel *story* Kenny Kim *d* Jon Turteltaub *ph* Richard Michalak *m* Rick Marvin *pd* Kirk Petruccelli *ed* David Rennie
☆ Victor Wong, Michael Treanor, Max Elliott Slade, Chad Power, Rand Kingsley, Alan McRae, Margarita Franco, Toru Tanaka
'The gracefully choreographed spectacle of three little boys fighting hordes of evil adult ninjas is a surefire juve crowd-pleaser.' – *Variety*

'Saving The Day The Ninja Way'
3 Ninjas: High Noon at Mega Mountain
US 1997 93m colour
TriStar/Sheen (James Kang, Yoram Ben-Ami)

Four small children save the day when terrorists take hostage the occupants of a theme park.
Excessively violent, dim-witted entertainment intended for the young, but not fit for any audience.
w Sean McNamara, Jeff Phillips *d* Sean McNamara *ph* Blake T. Evans *m* John Coda *pd* Chuck Conner *ed* Annamaria Szanto
☆ Hulk Hogan (Dave Dragon), Loni Anderson (Medusa), Jim Varney (Lothar Zogg), Mathew Botuchis (Rocky Douglas), Michael O'Laskey II (Colt Douglas), James Paul Roeske II (Tum Tum Douglas), Victor Wong (Grandpa Mori), Chelsey Earlywine (Amanda Morgan-Green)
'For most moviegoers over 12, this, the fourth "Three Ninjas" movie, will be interminably boring.' – *New York Times*

3 Ninjas Kick Back
US 1994 99m Foto-Kem
TriStar/Sheen/Ben-Ami/Leeds (James Kang, Arthur Leeds, Martha Chang)

Three boys travel to Japan to help their grandfather save a ceremonial dagger from an evil businessman who hopes to find buried treasure with its help.
Dreary children's movie that is a mix of fart jokes and violent slapstick; it condescends to its audience, particularly in the bad guy's unmotivated redemption at the end.
w Mark Saltzman *screenplay* Simon Sheen *d* Charles T. Kanganis *ph* Christopher Faloona *m* Richard Marvin *pd* Hiroyuki Takatsu, Gregory Martin *ed* Jeffrey Reiner, David Rennie
☆ Victor Wong (Grandpa), Max Elliott Slade (Colt), Sean Fox (Rocky), Evan Bonifant (Tum Tum), Caroline Junko King (Miyo), Dustin Nguyen (Glam), Alan McRae (Sam), Margarita Franco (Jessica), Jason Schombing (Vinnie), Angelo Tiffe (Slam), Sab Shimono (Koga)

3 Ninjas Knuckle Up
US 1995 85m colour
TriStar/Sheen (Martha Chang)

Three brothers who excel at martial arts help defeat a corrupt businessman who is dumping toxic waste on tribal land.
Crude slapstick kiddie picture of minimal interest.
w Alex S. Kim *d* Simon S. Sheen *ph* Eugene Shlugleit *m* Gary Stevan Scott *pd* Don Day *ed* Pam Choules
☆ Victor Wong, Charles Napier, Michael Treanor, Max Elliott Slade, Chad Power, Crystle Lightning, Patrick Kilpatrick, Donald L. Shanks
'Thoroughly second-rate in all regards, with slapdash production values, cartoonish performances, by-the-numbers scripting and ridiculous martial arts fight scenes.' – *Variety*
† Made in 1992, but not released until later.

Three O'Clock High
US 1987 101m DeLuxe
Universal (David E. Vogel)

A timid high school journalist is assigned to write a profile of a thuggish new student, who challenges him to a fight.
Dull, heavy-handed comedy of adolescent life that will mean little outside America; even those who can identify with its notions of student life are likely to find it uninteresting.
w Richard Christian Matheson, Thomas Szollosi *d* Phil Joanou *ph* Barry Sonnenfeld (credited as lighting consultant) *m* Tangerine Dream, Sylvester Levay *pd* William F. Matthews *ed* Joe Ann Fogle
☆ Casey Siemaszko, Anne Ryan, Richard Tyson, Jonathan Wise, Stacey Glick, Jeffrey Tambor, Philip Baker Hall, John P. Ryan

'Just your average Girl meets Girl. Girl loses Girl. Girl hires Boy to get Girl back story. With a twist.'
Three of Hearts
US 1992 110m DeLuxe
Guild/Three of Hearts/New Line (Joel B. Michaels, Matthew Irmas)

A gigolo is hired by a lesbian to break the heart of her bisexual lover so that she will return to her.
Trite tale of sexual role-playing that pussyfoots around before coming to a predictable conclusion.
w Adam Greenman, Mitch Glazer *d* Yurek Bogayevicz *ph* Andrzej Sekula *m* Richard Gibbs *pd* Nelson Coates *ed* Dennis M. Hill, Suzanne Hines
☆ William Baldwin, Kelly Lynch, Sherilyn Fenn, Joe Pantoliano, Gail Strickland, Cec Verrell, Claire Callaway, Marek Johnson
'Shallow, contrived and less than credible. But marvellously exploiting New York's downtown world, it is a commercially slick and appealing film.' – *Variety*

The Three of Us: see *Noi Tre*

'Move over, Casanova!'
Three on a Couch
US 1966 109m Technicolor
Columbia/Jerry Lewis Productions (Jerry Lewis)
An artist tries to cure the sexual hang-ups of his psychiatrist fiancée's three female patients.
Intolerably lengthy and witless comedy.
w Bob Ross, Samuel A. Taylor, Arne Sultan, Marvin Worth *d* Jerry Lewis *ph* W. Wallace Kelley *m* Louis Brown
☆ Jerry Lewis, Janet Leigh, James Best, Mary Ann Mobley, Gila Golan, Leslie Parrish, Kathleen Freeman, Fritz Feld
'A long drag through stock situations.' – *MFB*
'Unintentionally unfunny.' – *Leonard Maltin*
'Stay on your own couch and don't bother with Jerry's.' – *Steven Scheuer*

Three on a Match *
US 1932 63m bw
Warner (Sam Bischoff)

Three schoolgirl friends meet again in the big city, after which their paths cross melodramatically.
Predictable, watchable multi-story dramatics with an ironic twist: remade in 1938 as Broadway Musketeers.
w Lucien Hubbard *d* Mervyn Le Roy *ph* Sol Polito
☆ Joan Blondell, Bette Davis, Ann Dvorak, Warren William, Grant Mitchell, Lyle Talbot, Humphrey Bogart, Glenda Farrell, Clara Blandick
'A nice picture descending to mediocrity in its final two reels.' – *Variety*

Three on a Weekend: see *Bank Holiday*

3 Ring Circus
US 1954 103m Technicolor Vistavision
Paramount/Hal B. Wallis
Ex-army veterans join a circus.
The mixture as before from Martin and Lewis: variety acts interspersed with sentiment and heavy mugging.

w Don McGuire *d* Joseph Pevney *ph* Loyal Griggs *m* Walter Scharf
☆ Dean Martin, Jerry Lewis, Joanne Dru, Zsa Zsa Gabor, Wallace Ford, Sig Rumann, Gene Sheldon, Nick Cravat, Elsa Lanchester
'I wouldn't point to *3 Ring Circus* with any great deal of pride, and neither would anyone else.' – *Joseph Pevney*

Three Sailors and a Girl
US 1953 95m Technicolor
Warner (Sammy Cahn)
A ship's funds are unofficially invested in a musical show.
Undernourished comedy musical.
w Roland Kibbee, Devery Freeman *play* *The Butter and Egg Man* by George S. Kaufman *d* Roy del Ruth *ph* Carl Guthrie *songs* Sammy Fain, Sammy Cahn
☆ Jane Powell, Gordon MacRae, Gene Nelson, Sam Levene, George Givot, Veda Ann Borg

'A haunting tale of changes, choices and second chances.'
Three Seasons
US/Vietnam 1999 109m FotoKem
Pathé/October/Open City/The Goatsingers (Jason Kliot, Joana Vicente, Tony Bu)
aka: *Ba Mua*
An American former marine searches for the daughter he left behind in Saigon after the end of the Vietnam war.
Slight, sentimental tale of loss and love, emphasising the beauty of the temples and gardens in which the action takes place.
wd Tony Bui *ph* Lisa Rinzler *m* Richard Horowitz *pd* Wing Lee *ed* Keith Reamer
☆ Don Duong (Hai), Nguyen Ngoc Hiep (Kien An), Tran Manh Cuong (Teacher Dao), Harvey Keitel (James Hager), Zoe Bui (Lan), Nguyen Huu Duoc (Woody), Diem Kieu (Singing Lotus Woman), Bui Tuong Trac (Man Who Buys Lotus Flowers)
'Never rises above mediocrity.' – *Edward Porter, Sunday Times*

Three Secrets *
US 1950 98m bw
Warner/US Pictures (Milton Sperling)
Three women wait anxiously to find out whose child survived a plane crash.
Well-made, formula woman's picture.
w Martin Rackin, Gina Kaus *d* *Robert Wise* *ph* *Sid Hickox* *m* David Buttolph
☆ Eleanor Parker, Patricia Neal, Ruth Roman, Frank Lovejoy, Leif Erickson, Ted de Corsia, Edmon Ryan, Larry Keating

The Three Sisters *
GB 1970 165m Eastmancolor
Alan Clore Films
At the turn of the century, three fatherless sisters dream of abandoning Russian provincial life for the big city.
Filmed Chekhov, better than most but still lacking cinematic vigour.
translator Moura Budberg *d* Laurence Olivier *ph* Geoffrey Unsworth *m* William Walton
☆ Laurence Olivier, Joan Plowright, Jeanne Watts, Louise Purnell, Derek Jacobi, Alan Bates, Ronald Pickup

Three Sisters **
Italy/France/Germany 1987 112m colour
Erre/Reteitalia/Bioskop/Cinémax (Angelo Rizzoli)
original title: *Paura e Amore*
In a northern university town, family certainties crumble as three sisters experience unsatisfactory love affairs, two of them with the same married man, and their brother makes an unhappy marriage.
Family drama tinged with melancholy and disappointments, a variation on Chekhov's play of frustration and despair.
w Dacia Maraini, Margerethe von Trotta *d* Margarethe von Trotta *ph* Giuseppe Lanci *m* Franco Piersanti *ad* Giantito Burchiellaro *ed* Enzo Meniconi
☆ Fanny Ardant, Greta Scacchi, Valeria Golino, Peter Simonischek, Sergio Castellito, Agnès Soral, Paolo Hendel, Jan-Paul Biczyscki

Three Smart Girls **
US 1936 86m bw
Universal (Joe Pasternak)
Three sisters bring their parents back together.
Pleasant, efficient family film which made a world star of Deanna Durbin.
w Adele Commandini, Austin Parker *story* Adele Commandini *d* Henry Koster *ph* Joseph Valentine *md* Charles Previn *ed* Ted J. Kent
☆ *Deanna Durbin*, Barbara Read, Nan Grey, Charles Winninger, Binnie Barnes, Ray Milland, Alice Brady, Mischa Auer, Ernest Cossart, Hobart Cavanaugh
'Surefire entertainment for any and all types of audiences. It also has that rare quality of making an audience feel better for having seen it.' – *Variety*
'Idiotically tuned in to happiness, but it isn't boring.' – *New Yorker, 1978*
'Clever, intelligent and witty, this delightful bit of entertainment has a genuineness which is rare.' – *Photoplay*
† Remade as *Three Daring Daughters*.
best picture; original story

Three Smart Girls Grow Up *
US 1939 87m bw
Universal (Joe Pasternak)
A girl helps her sisters to find beaus.
More of the above, quite palatable but inevitably warmed over.
w Bruce Manning, Felix Jackson *d* Henry Koster *ph* Joe Valentine *md* Charles Previn *ed* Ted J. Kent
☆ Deanna Durbin, Helen Parrish, Nan Grey, Charles Winninger, Robert Cummings, William Lundigan, Ernest Cossart, Nella Walker
'The white feminine room which the three sisters share, the quilted beds, the little furry jackets over the pajamas – the whole upholstery is so virginal that it evokes little twitters of nostalgia from the stalls. Pillow fights and first love and being sent to bed without any dinner – the awkward age has never been so laundered and lavendered and laid away.' – *Graham Greene*

Three Strange Loves *
Sweden 1949 84m bw
Svensk Filmindustri
original title: *Törst*
aka: *Thirst*
A married couple tear each other apart on a train journey from Switzerland through Germany to Sweden, while the husband's former lover suffers a breakdown and commits suicide.
Gloomy domestic drama, reminiscent of Strindberg in its depiction of a couple locked together in a struggle neither can win without destroying them both.
w Herbert Grevenius *novel* Birgit Tengroth *d* Ingmar Bergman *ph* Gunnar Fischer *m* Erik Nordgren *ad* Nils Svenwall *ed* Oscar Rosander
☆ Eva Henning, Birger Malmsten, Birgit Tengroth, Mimi Nelson, Hasse Ekman, Bengt Eklund, Gaby Stenberg, Naima Wifstrand

Three Strangers *
US 1946 92m bw
Warner (Wolfgang Reinhardt)
A sweepstake ticket brings fortune and tragedy to three ill-assorted people.
Humdrum pattern play: the stars work hard to bring a little magic to it.
w John Huston, Howard Koch *d* Jean Negulesco *ph* Arthur Edeson *m* Adolph Deutsch
☆ Sydney Greenstreet, Peter Lorre, Geraldine Fitzgerald, Joan Lorring, Robert Shayne, Marjorie Riordan, Arthur Shields

Three Stripes in the Sun
US 1955 93m bw
Columbia (Fred Kohlmar)
GB title: *The Gentle Sergeant*
After World War II, a Japanese-hating sergeant in the US occupation forces helps a poverty-stricken orphanage.
Predictable sentimentality based on fact, with good background detail.
wd Richard Murphy *articles* E. J. Kelly *ph* Burnett Guffey *m* George Duning
☆ Aldo Ray, Phil Carey, Dick York, Chuck Connors, Mitsuko Kimura

'Crime Is King'
3000 Miles to Graceland
US 2001 125m DeLuxe Panavision
Warner/Morgan Creek/Franchise/Lightstone (Demian Lichtenstein, Richard Spero, Eric Manes, Elie Samaha, Andrew Stevens)
In Las Vegas, five violent robbers, who dress as Elvis Presley impersonators, fall out over dividing their loot.
Crude, rude and hyperactive action movie that quickly wears out its welcome.
w Richard Recco, Demian Lichtenstein *d* Demian Lichtenstein *ph* David Franco *m* George S. Clinton *pd* Robert DeVico *ed* Michael Duthie, Miklos Wright
☆ Kurt Russell (Michael Zane), Kevin Costner (Murphy), Courtney Cox (Cybil Waingrow), Christian Slater (Hanson), Kevin Pollak (Federal Marshal Damitry), David Arquette (Gus), Jon Lovitz (Jay Peterson), Howie Long (Jack), Thomas Haden Church (Federal Marshal Quigley), Bokeem Woodbine (Franklin), Ice-T (Hamilton)
'One of those movies that makes you want to throw up your hands in despair, disgust, or maybe both.' – *Kenneth Turan, Los Angeles Times*
'Shouldn't be reviewed in an arts section but rather in that portion of the newspaper dedicated to atrocities, environmental disasters and hate crimes' – *Shawn Levy, Oregonian*

'All's fair in the war of love.'
Three to Tango
US 1999 98m Technicolor
Warner/Village Roadshow/Village-Hoyts/Outlaw (Bobby Newmyer, Jeffrey Silver, Bettina Sofia Viviano)
A heterosexual architect goes along with a tycoon's mistaken belief that he is gay in the hope of winning a building contract, and falls for the tycoon's mistress.
Fluffy romantic comedy of minimal interest; it fails to develop its central misundertstanding with any wit or style.
w Rodney Vaccaro, Aline Brosh McKenna *d* Damon Santostefano *ph* Walt Lloyd *m* Graeme Revell *pd* David Nichols *ed* Stephen Semel *cos* Vicki Graef
☆ Matthew Perry (Oscar Novak), Neve Campbell (Amy Post), Dylan McDermott (Charles Newman), Oliver Platt (Peter Steinberg), Cylk Cozart (Kevin Cartwright), John C. McGinley (Strauss), Bob Balaban (Decker), Deborah Rush (Lenore), Kelly Rowan (Olivia Newman), Rick Gomez (Rick), Patrick Van Horn (Zack), David Ramsey (Bill)
'A smart and sassy comedy with a playful sensibility and subtle sensitivity. It boasts clever tweaking of all kinds of sexual stereotyping.' – *Joe Leydon, Variety*
'A terrible stinker…I beg you not to see this movie.' – *Cosmo Landesman, Sunday Times*

3.10 to Yuma **
US 1957 92m bw
Columbia (David Heilwell)
A sheriff has to get his prisoner on to a train despite the threatening presence of the prisoner's outlaw friends.
Tense, well-directed but rather talky low-budget Western: excellent performances and atmosphere flesh out an unconvincing physical situation.
w Halsted Welles *story* Elmore Leonard *d* *Delmer Daves* *ph* *Charles Lawton Jnr* *m* George Duning *ad* Frank Hotaling *ed* Al Clark *cos* Jean Louis
☆ Glenn Ford (Ben Wade), *Van Heflin* (Dan Evans), Felicia Farr (Emmy), Leora Dana (Mrs Alice Evans), Henry Jones (Alex Potter), Richard Jaeckel (Charlie Prince), Robert Emhardt (Mr Butterfield)
'A vivid, tense and intelligent story about probable people, enhanced by economical writing and supremely efficient direction and playing.' – *Guardian*
'We experimented by not filling the shadows with reflected light.' – *Delmer Daves*

Three Violent People
US 1956 100m Eastmancolor Vistavision
Paramount (Hugh Brown)
Brother ranchers quarrel over the wife of one of them, an ex-saloon hostess.
Characterless 'character' Western, a long way after Duel in the Sun.
w James Edward Grant *d* Rudolph Maté *ph* *Loyal Griggs* *m* Walter Scharf
☆ Charlton Heston, Anne Baxter, *Gilbert Roland*, Tom Tryon, Bruce Bennett, Forrest Tucker, Elaine Stritch, Barton MacLane

The Three Weird Sisters
GB 1948 82m bw
British National (Louis H. Jackson)
Three old maids in a Welsh village plot to kill their rich half-brother but are swept away by a flood.
All-stops-out melodrama which doesn't quite work and is generally remembered, if at all, for the last third of its writing team.
w Louise Birt, David Evans, Dylan Thomas *novel* Charlotte Armstrong *d* Daniel Birt *ph* Ernest Palmer
☆ Nancy Price, Mary Clare, Mary Merrall, Nova Pilbeam, Raymond Lovell, Anthony Hulme

Three Wise Fools
US 1946 90m bw
MGM (William Wright)
Three crusty old gents adopt an orphan, who softens them.
Antediluvian whimsy without the expected fun, remade from a silent.
w John McDermott, James O'Hanlon *play* Austin Strong *d* Edward Buzzell *m* Bronislau Kaper
☆ Margaret O'Brien, Lionel Barrymore, Thomas Mitchell, Edward Arnold, Lewis Stone, Jane Darwell, Harry Davenport, Cyd Charisse

Three Wise Girls
US 1932 80m approx bw
Columbia
Three small-town girls gain wisdom in New York.
Three millgirls' romances for the price of one. Adequate, predictable romantic fodder of its time.
w Robert Riskin, Agnes C. Johnson *d* William Beaudine *ph* Ted Tetzlaff
☆ Jean Harlow, Mae Clarke, Walter Byron, Marie Prevost, Andy Devine, Natalie Moorhead, Jameson Thomas
'Should turn in a respectable score … Miss Harlow fails to be convincing.' – *Variety*

Three Wishes
US 1995 114m DeLuxe
Entertainment/Rysher (Gary Lucchesi, Clifford Green, Ellen Green)
In the mid-50s, a widow with two young sons runs over a dog and his owner, a tramp, and takes them home with her.
A fairy tale about getting what you wish for, oozing nostalgia and sweetness, hard to take if you are over ten years old.
w Elizabeth Anderson *story* Clifford Green, Ellen Green *d* Martha Coolidge *ph* Johnny E. Jensen *m* Cynthia Millar *pd* John Vallone *ed* Stephen Cohen
☆ Patrick Swayze, Mary Elizabeth Mastrantonio, Joseph Mazello, Seth Mumy, David Marshall Grant, Michael O'Keefe, Diane Venora
'The kind of sentimental fable that might, in the old days, have made more sense than it does now.' – *Derek Malcolm, Guardian*

Three Women *
US 1924 60m approx (24 fps) bw silent
Warner
A rake charms three women, each for a different purpose.
Subtle satirical comedy; not one of the director's masterpieces, but with enough barbs to keep one watching.
w Ernst Lubitsch, Hans Kraly *novel* *The Lilie* by Yolanthe Marees *d* *Ernst Lubitsch* *ph* Charles Van Enger
☆ Lew Cody, Pauline Frederick, May McAvoy, Marie Prevost

Three Women
US 1977 123m DeLuxe Panavision
TCF/Lion's Gate (Robert Altman)
Three women come to California for different reasons; when their problems become insurmountable they rely on each other.
Tiresomely somnambulistic multi-character drama, half a satire, half a wallow, and never an entertainment.
wd Robert Altman *ph* Charles Rosher *m* Gerald Busby

☆ Sissy Spacek, Janice Rule, Shelley Duvall, Robert Fortier, Ruth Nelson, John Cromwell, Sierra Pecheur

Three Women in Love: see *Der Philosoph*

The 3 Worlds of Gulliver
US/Spain 1959 100m Technicolor
Columbia/Morningside (Charles Schneer)
Gulliver's adventures in Lilliput and Brobdingnag.
Flat treatment of marvellous material, with all the excitement squeezed out of it and not even much pizazz in the trick photography.
w Arthur Ross, Jack Sher *d* Jack Sher *ph* Wilkie Cooper *m* Bernard Herrmann *sp* Ray Harryhausen
☆ Kerwin Mathews, Basil Sydney, Mary Ellis, Jo Morrow, June Thorburn, Grégoire Aslan, Charles Lloyd Pack, Martin Benson

The Threepenny Opera: see *Die Dreigroschenoper*

'One girl, two guys, three possibilities.'
Threesome
US 1994 93m Foto-Kem
Columbia TriStar/MPCA (Bud Krevoy, Steve Stabler)
At university, one woman and two men share a room and their sexuality.
A sophomore version of Jules et Jim, *rather too earnest and conventional about its ménage à trois.*
wd Andrew Fleming *ph* Alexander Gruszynski *m* Thomas Newman *pd* Ivo Cristante *ed* William C. Carruth
☆ Lara Flynn Boyle, Stephen Baldwin, Josh Charles, Alexis Arquette, Martha Gehman, Mark Arnold, Michele Matheson
'Satisfyingly blunt and truthful under all the pranks and sexual mischief.' – *Variety*

Thrill of a Lifetime
US 1937 72m bw
Paramount
Summer campers put on a show which goes to Broadway.
Stereotyped lower-case musical with agreeable acts.
w Seena Owen, Grant Garrett, Paul Gerard Smith *d* George Archainbaud
☆ Judy Canova, Ben Blue, the Yacht Club Boys, Eleanore Whitney, Betty Grable, Johnny Downs, Dorothy Lamour, Larry Crabbe
'Lightweight but pleasant.' – *Variety*

Thrill of a Romance
US 1945 105m Technicolor
MGM (Joe Pasternak)
A lady swimmer falls for a returning serviceman.
Empty musical vehicle with nothing memorable about it except the waste of time and money.
w Richard Connell, Gladys Lehman *d* Richard Thorpe *ph* Harry Stradling *md* George Stoll
☆ Esther Williams, Van Johnson, Lauritz Melchior, Frances Gifford, Henry Travers, Spring Byington, Tommy Dorsey

The Thrill of Brazil
US 1946 90m bw
Columbia (Sidney Biddell)
An American impresario in Brazil tries to win back his estranged wife.
Efficient but unpersuasive musical, another result of the good neighbour policy.
w Allen Rivkin, Harry Clork, Devery Freeman *d* S. Sylvan Simon
☆ Evelyn Keyes, Keenan Wynn, Ann Miller, Allyn Joslyn, Tito Guizar, Veloz and Yolanda, Felix Bressart

The Thrill of It All *
US 1963 104m Eastmancolor
U-I/Ross Hunter/Arwin (Ross Hunter, Marty Melcher)
The wife of a gynaecologist becomes an advertising model, and work pressures disrupt her marriage.
Glossy matrimonial farce which starts brightly but eventually flags and becomes exhausting. Its better jokes linger in the memory.
w Carl Reiner *d* Norman Jewison *ph* Russell Metty *m* Frank de Vol *ad* Robert Boyle, Alexander Golitzen *ed* Milton Carruth
☆ Doris Day, James Garner, Arlene Francis, Edward Andrews, Reginald Owen, ZaSu Pitts, Elliott Reid
'Pleasantly reminiscent of some of the screwball comedies of the thirties.' – *MFB*

Thrillkill
Canada 1984 87m colour
Brightstar/Manesco (Anthony Kramreither)
A woman tries to solve the murder of her sister, a computer games designer, who has hacked into banks to transfer millions to her own account.
Drearily predictable thriller, peopled by stereotypes and indifferently acted and directed.
w Anthony D'Adrea *d* Anthony D'Andrea, Anthony Kramreither *ph* John Clement *m* Tim McCauley *ad* Andrew Deskin
☆ Robin Ward (Frank), Gina Massey (Bobbie), Laura Robinson (Adrian), Diana Reis (Carly), Colleen Embree (Parrish), Kurt Reis (Schofield), Eugene Clark (Grissom), Frank Moore (Caspar)

Throne of Blood ****
Japan 1957 105m bw
Toho (Akira Kurosawa, Sojiro Motoki)
original title: *Kumonosu-Jo*
A samurai, spurred on by his wife and an old witch, murders his lord at Cobweb Castle.
A Japanese version of Macbeth *with a savage and horrifying final sequence. The whole film is a treat to look at.*
w Hideo Oguni, Shinobu Hashimoto, Ryuzo Kikushima, Akira Kurosawa *play* William Shakespeare *d* Akira Kurosawa *ph* Asaichi Nakai *m* Masaru Sato *ad* Yoshiro Muraki, Kohei Ezaki *ed* Akira Kurosawa
☆ Toshiro Mifune (Taketoki Washizu), Isuzu Yamada (Asaji, Lady Washizu), Takashi Shimura (Noriyasu Odagura), Minoru Chiaki (Yoshiaki Miki), Akira Kubo (Yoshiteru), Takamaru Sasaki (Kunimaru), Chieko Naniwa (Witch)
'Its final impression is of a man who storms into a room with an impassioned speech to deliver and then discovers that he has forgotten what he came to say.' – *Kenneth Cavander, MFB*

Through a Glass Darkly *
Sweden 1961 91m bw
Svensk Filmindustri
original title: *Såsom I En Spegel*
Four unfulfilled people on a remote island fail to communicate with each other or to understand what God is.
It sounds like a parody Bergman film, and it almost is. The same themes were carried through in Winter Light *and* The Silence.
wd Ingmar Bergman *ph* Sven Nykvist *m* Bach
☆ Harriet Andersson, Gunnar Bjornstrand, Max von Sydow, Lars Passgard
best foreign film
Ingmar Bergman (as writer)

Through Different Eyes
US 1942 65m bw
TCF
A veteran DA cites an old murder case to illustrate the dangers of circumstantial evidence.
Neat and peppy crime programme filler.
w Samuel G. Engel *d* Thomas Z. Loring
☆ Frank Craven, Donald Woods, Vivian Blaine, Mary Howard, Jerome Cowan

Throw Momma from the Train *
US 1987 88m DeLuxe
Orion (Larry Brezner)
After seeing *Strangers on a Train*, a student tries to persuade his professor to 'swap' murders.
Cheerful black comedy-cum-homage to Hitchcock.
w Stu Silver *d* Danny DeVito *ph* Barry Sonnenfeld *m* David Newman *pd* Ida Random
☆ Danny DeVito, Billy Crystal, Anne Ramsey, Kim Greist, Kate Mulgrew
'Very clever and engaging from beginning to end.' – *Variety*
Anne Ramsey

Thumb Tripping *
US 1972 94m DeLuxe
Avco (Robert Chartoff, Irwin Winkler)
A boy and a girl hitch-hiker in California have a variety of violent adventures.
Tail end of the Easy Rider fashion, with odd moments of interesting detail.
w Don Mitchell *novel* Don Mitchell *d* Quentin Masters *ph* Harry Stradling Jnr *m* Bob Thompson
☆ Michael Burns, Meg Foster, Marianna Hill, Bruce Dern

'Follow Your Heart And Nothing Is Impossible.'
Thumbelina
US/Eire 1994 87m Technicolor
Warner/Don Bluth
aka: *Don Bluth's Thumbelina*
The adventures of a tiny girl before she is reunited with her fairy prince.
A dull film that cannot stand comparison with Disney's recent animated resurgence; the animation is well done in a traditional style, but the narrative is lifeless.
w Don Bluth *d* Don Bluth, Gary Goldman *m* Barry Manilow, William Ross *pd* Rowland Wilson *ed* Thomas V. Moss
☆ Featuring Voices of Jodi Benson, Gino Conforti, Barbara Cook, Will Ryan, June Foray, Kenneth Mars, Gary Imhoff, Joe Lynch
'Highly conservative in both its story-telling and character-drawing and eventually rather a let-down.' – *Derek Malcolm, Guardian*

Thumbs Up
US 1943 67m bw
Republic (Albert J. Cohen)
An American singing star in London is passed over in favour of talent from the war factories.
Curious hands-across-the-sea filler which gives the weirdest impression of Britain at war.
w Frank Gill Jnr *d* Joseph Santley
☆ Brenda Joyce, Richard Fraser, Elsa Lanchester, Arthur Margetson, J. Pat O'Malley, Gertrude Niesen, Andre Charlot

Thunder
US 1929 90m (24 fps) bw silent
MGM
A train driver has trouble with his sons.
Almost forgotten star melodrama, his last silent one, made when his health was already failing.
w Byron Morgan, Ann Price *d* William Nigh
☆ Lon Chaney, James Murray, George Duryea, Phyllis Haver

Thunder across the Pacific: see *The Wild Blue Yonder*

Thunder Afloat
US 1939 95m bw
MGM
Rival boat owners vie for a 1918 navy contract, and the winner finds he has been trapped into enlisting.
Rumbustious Flagg-and-Quirt style comedy, good enough value for the undemanding.
w Ralph Wheelwright, Wells Root, Harvey Haislip *d* George B. Seitz
☆ Wallace Beery, Chester Morris, Virginia Grey, Douglass Dumbrille, Regis Toomey, Henry Victor, Jonathan Hale
'Timely actioner, cinch for exploitation.' – *Variety*

Thunder and Lightning
US 1977 93m DeLuxe
TCF (Roger Corman)
An independent maker of moonshine whiskey finds himself in competition with his girlfriend's father.
Action-filled comedy, mainly consisting of car and boat chases and crashes.
w William Hjortsberg *d* Corey Allen *ph* James Pergola *m* Andy Stein *ed* Anthony Redman
☆ David Carradine, Kate Jackson, Roger C. Carmel, Sterling Holloway, Ed Barth

Thunder Bay *
US 1953 102m Technicolor
U-I (Aaron Rosenberg)
An engineer is convinced that oil can be raised from the Louisiana sea-bed.
Well-produced outdoor actioner.
w Gil Doud, John Michael Hayes *d* Anthony Mann *ph* William Daniels *m* Frank Skinner
☆ James Stewart, Joanne Dru, Dan Duryea, Jay C. Flippen, Antonio Moreno, Gilbert Roland, Marcia Henderson

Thunder Below
US 1932 71m bw
Paramount
A wife loves her husband's best friend.
Dreary melodrama with a star already seen to be box-office poison.
novel Thomas Rourke *d* Richard Wallace
☆ Tallulah Bankhead, Charles Bickford, Paul Lukas
'Star as weak as story ... dull and uneventful.' – *Variety*

Thunder Birds: see *Thunderbirds*

Thunder in the City
GB 1937 88m bw
Atlantic (Akos Tolnay, Alexander Esway)
An American salesman in London helps a penniless duke promote a non-existent metal.
Mild satire on British and American idiosyncrasies, now very faded.
w Robert Sherwood, Aben Kandel, Akos Tolnay *d* Marion Gering *ph* Al Gilks *m* Miklos Rozsa
☆ Edward G. Robinson, Lulu Deste, Ralph Richardson, Nigel Bruce, Constance Collier, Arthur Wontner
'Cinch to be an important feature and satisfactory booking.' – *Variety*

Thunder in the East: see *The Battle (1934)*

Thunder in the East
US 1951 98m bw
Paramount (Everett Riskin)
When India becomes independent in 1947, an American wanting to sell arms clashes with the peace-loving chief of a principality, but the arms are needed when rebels attack.
Artificial and boring action melodrama with platitudinous conversations.
w Jo Swerling *novel* *Rage of the Vulture* by Alan Moorehead *d* Charles Vidor *ph* Lee Garmes *m* Hugo Friedhofer
☆ Alan Ladd, Charles Boyer, Deborah Kerr, Corinne Calvet, Cecil Kellaway

Thunder in the Night
US 1935 69m bw
Fox
A police captain solves the murder of a blackmailer.
Reasonably snappy mystery set in Budapest.
w Frances Hyland, Eugene Solow *play* *A Woman Lies* by Ladislas Fodor *d* George Archainbaud
☆ Edmund Lowe, Karen Morley, Paul Cavanagh, Una O'Connor, Gene Lockhart, John Qualen, Russell Hicks
'Tops average: deserves to do fairly well.' – *Variety*

Thunder in the Sun
US 1959 81m Technicolor
Seven Arts/Carollton (Clarence Greene)
In 1847 an Indian scout guides a group of Basques to California with their vines.
Overwritten and melodramatic wagon train story.
wd Russel Rouse *ph* Stanley Cortez *m* Cyril Mockridge
☆ Susan Hayward, Jeff Chandler, Jacques Bergerac, Blanche Yurka, Carl Esmond

Thunder in the Valley: see *Bob, Son of Battle*

Thunder of Battle: see *Coriolanus – Hero without a Country*

'I'll make a soldier of you, Mr McQuade – if you don't break first!'
A Thunder of Drums *
US 1961 97m Metrocolor Cinemascope
MGM (Robert J. Enders)
Trouble with Apaches at a frontier post in 1870.
Solid, unexciting first-feature Western, some way after Ford.
w James Warner Bellah *d* Joseph Newman *ph* William Spencer *m* Harry Sukman

☆ Richard Boone, George Hamilton, Arthur O'Connell, Luana Patten, Richard Chamberlain, Charles Bronson

Thunder on the Hill
US 1951 84m bw
U-I (Michael Kraike)
GB title: *Bonaventure*
In Norfolk, a nun solves a murder mystery during a flood.
Modest whodunnit with an unusual background but not much suspense.
w Oscar Saul, Andrew Solt *play Bonaventure* by Charlotte Hastings *d* Douglas Sirk *ph* William Daniels *m* Hans Salter *ad* Bernard Herzbrun, Nathan Juran *ed* Ted J. Kent
☆ Claudette Colbert, Ann Blyth, Robert Douglas, Anne Crawford, Philip Friend, Gladys Cooper, John Abbott, Connie Gilchrist, Gavin Muir

Thunder over Arizona
US 1956 75m Trucolor Naturama
Republic (Joe Kane)
Trouble in Tombstone, where a family fight to save their silver mine from a corrupt mayor and his hired guns.
A familiar cast plod along a well-trodden narrative in a pleasant but undistinguished Western.
w Sloan Nibley *d* Joseph Kane *ph* Bud Thackery *m* R. Dale Butts *ad* Walter Keller *ed* Tony Martinelli
☆ Skip Homeier, Kristine Miller, George Macready, Wallace Ford, Jack Elam, Gregory Walcott, Nacho Galindo, John Doucette

Thunder over Mexico **
US 1933 60m bw silent (with music score)
Principal Pictures
The Upton Sinclair version of the troubled Eisenstein travelogue.
Packed with moments of genius, but not really a finished film in any sense.
m Hugo Reisenfeld
'It will not get to first base either as a critic's picture, or in straight box office parlance ... beautiful, slow and dull.' – *Variety*
† See also *Time in the Sun.*

Thunder over the Plains
US 1953 82m Warnercolor
Warner
After the Civil War, a Union officer is posted with his family to the southwest territory, and finds tension.
Busy but uninvolving Western programmer with a reliable star.
w Russell Hughes *d* André de Toth *ph* Bert Grennon *m* David Buttolph
☆ Randolph Scott, Phyllis Kirk, Lex Barker, Charles McGraw, Elisha Cook Jnr, Fess Parker

Thunder Road *
US 1958 92m bw
UA/DRM (Robert Mitchum)
Hillbilly bootleggers defy a Chicago gangster.
Downbeat but actionful crime melodrama with an unusual background and plenty of car chases.
w James Arlee Phillips, Walter Wise *story* Robert Mitchum *d Arthur Ripley ph* Alan Stensvold *m* Jack Marshall
☆ Robert Mitchum, Gene Barry, Jacques Aubuchon, Keely Smith, James Mitchum

Thunder Rock ***
GB 1942 112m bw
Charter Films (John Boulting)
A journalist disgusted with the world of the thirties retires to a lighthouse on Lake Michigan and is haunted by the ghosts of immigrants drowned a century before.
Subtle adaptation of an impressive and topical anti-isolationist play, very well acted and presented.
w Jeffrey Dell, Bernard Miles *play Robert Ardrey d Roy Boulting ph* Mutz Greenbaum (Max Greene) *m* Hans May
☆ *Michael Redgrave* (David Charleston), *Lilli Palmer* (Melanie Kurtz), *Barbara Mullen* (Ellen Kirby), *James Mason* (Streeter), *Frederick Valk* (Dr Kurtz), *Frederick Cooper, Finlay Currie* (Captain Joshua), *Sybilla Binder*
'Boldly imaginative in theme and treatment.' – *Sunday Express*
'More interesting technically than anything since *Citizen Kane*.' – *Manchester Guardian*
'If I thought it wouldn't keep too many people away, I'd call it a work of art.' – *Daily Express*
'What a stimulus to thought it is, this good, brave, outspoken, unfettered picture.' – *Observer*

Thunder Run
US 1986 91m DeLuxe
Cannon/Panache (Carol Lynn)
A truck driver is hired to drive across Nevada with a load of plutonium that has been targeted by a gang of terrorists.
Dull action thriller, too concerned with adding 'teen interest to maintain any suspense or interest; when it eventually comes, the action is unoriginal and mostly risible.
w Charles Davis, Carol Heyer *story* Clifford Wenger Snr, Carol Lynn *d* Gary Hudson *ph* Harvey Genkins *m* Jay Levy *ad* Carol Heyer *ed* Burton Lee Harry, Marcus Manton
☆ Forrest Tucker, John Ireland, John Shepherd, Jill Whitlow, Wally Ward, Marilyn O'Connor, Cheryl M. Lynn, Graham Ludlow, Alan Rachins, Tom Dugan

Thunderball **
GB 1965 132m Technicolor
Panavision
UA/Eon/Kevin McClory
James Bond goes underwater.
Commercially the most successful Bond, but certainly not the best despite a plethora of action sequences.
w Richard Maibaum, John Hopkins *novel* Ian Fleming *d* Terence Young *ph Ted Moore m* John Barry
☆ Sean Connery, Adolfo Celi, Claudine Auger, Luciana Paluzzi, Rik Van Nutter, Bernard Lee, Lois Maxwell, Martine Beswick
'The screenplay stands on tiptoe at the outermost edge of the suggestive and gazes yearningly down into the obscene.' – *John Simon*
special visual effects (John Stears)

Thunderbird Six
GB 1968 90m Techniscope
UA/AP/Century 21 (Gerry and Sylvia Anderson)
International Rescue combats the Black Phantom.
Bright, suspenseful puppetoon based on the TV series.
w Gerry and Sylvia Anderson *d* David Lane *ph* Harry Oakes *m* Barry Gray *ad* Bob Bell
'Holds some charm for adults, or at least for those who enjoy playing with miniature trains.' – *MFB*

Thunderbirds
US 1952 99m bw
Republic (John H. Auer)
An Oklahoma unit covers itself in glory during World War II.
Scrappy, noisy war actioner with much newsreel footage.
w Mary McCall Jnr *d* John H. Auer *ph* Reggie Lanning *m* Victor Young
☆ John Derek, John Barrymore Jnr, Mona Freeman, Ward Bond, Gene Evans

Thunderbolt **
US 1929 94m bw
Paramount
A gangster is caught, tried, and repents.
Gloomy melodrama with interesting style and credits.
w Jules Furthman, Herman J. Mankiewicz *d Josef von Sternberg ph* Henry Gerrard
☆ George Bancroft, Fay Wray, Richard Arlen, Tully Marshall, Eugénie Besserer
George Bancroft

Thunderbolt
Hong Kong 1995 108m colour
Golden Harvest/Raymond Chow/Paragon (Chua Lam)
original title: *Piklik Fo*
A motor mechanic is forced to race against a psychotic drug-dealer after his sisters are kidnapped.
Dull action film with Jackie Chan in subdued, serious mode for most of the time, despite the silly narrative; there's only one spectacular fight scene likely to assuage fans of his usual elaborate stunts.
w Hing-Kai Chan, Gordon Chan, Wai-Chung Kwok *d* Gordon Chan *ph* Horace Wong, Jose Chan, Ardy Lam *m* Pon-Yin Leung *pd* Ivy Law *ed* Peter Cheung *Stunt director* Sammo Hung
☆ Jackie Chan (Alfred Tung), Anita Yuen (Amy Yip), Michael Wong (Steve Cannon), Thorsten Nickel (Cougar), Chor Yuen (Alfred's father), Daisy Wu (Daphne), Man Chung-Han (Sammi), Yuzo Kayama (Coach)

Thunderbolt and Lightfoot *
US 1974 115m DeLuxe Panavision
UA/Malpaso (Robert Daley)
A bank robber escapes prison, disguises himself as a preacher, befriends a young drifter, and discovers that a new building stands on the spot where the loot is hidden.
Violent melodrama reworking an ancient comedy situation; well made on its level.
wd Michael Cimino *ph* Frank Stanley *m* Dee Barton
☆ Clint Eastwood, Jeff Bridges, George Kennedy, Geoffrey Lewis, Catherine Bach
Jeff Bridges

Thundercloud: see *Colt 45*

Thunderhead, Son of Flicka *
US 1945 78m Technicolor
TCF (Robert Bassler)
More where My Friend Flicka came from.
Unexceptionable family film with excellent outdoor photography.
w Dwight Cummins, Dorothy Yost *novel* Mary O'Hara *d* Louis King *ph Charles Clarke m* Cyril Mockridge
☆ Roddy McDowall, Preston Foster, Rita Johnson, James Bell, Carleton Young

'Two Men From Different Worlds. Two Cops After The Same Killer. Together They Must Uncover The Secrets. Together They Must Discover The Truth.'
Thunderheart **
US 1992 119m DuArt
Columbia TriStar/Tribeca/Waterhorse (Robert DeNiro, Jane Rosenthal, John Fusco)
A young FBI agent, assigned to help with a murder investigation in a Sioux reservation, discovers official connivance behind the killing.
An enjoyable thriller that manages to deal with questions of identity and self-discovery along the way.
w John Fusco *d* Michael Apted *ph* Roger Deakins *m* James Horner *pd* Dan Bishop *ed* Ian Crafford
☆ Val Kilmer, Sam Shepard, Graham Greene, Fred Ward, Fred Dalton Thompson, Sheila Tousey, Chief Ted Thin Elk, John Trudell, Julius Drum, Sarah Brave
'Reasonably engrossing as a mystery-thriller despite its overburdened plot, Thunderheart succeeds most in its captivating portrayal of mystical Native American ways.' – *Variety*

Thunderpants
GB/Germany 2002 83m DeLuxe
Pathé/Sky/film Council/Mission (Graham Broadbent, Damian Jones, Pete Hewitt)
A boy who can't stop farting uses his ability to power a space-rocket
A movie on one flatulent note: it may have begun as a high concept movie but it finishes on a bum note, without a script to carry it forward.
w Phil Hughes *d* Pete Hewitt *ph* Andy Collins *m* Rupert Gregson-Williams *pd* Chris Roope *ed* Michael Parker
☆ Bruce Cook (Patrick Smash), Rupert Grint (Alan A. Allen), Simon Callow (Sir John Osgood), Stephen Fry (Sir Anthony Silk QC), Celia Imrie (Miss Rapier), Paul Giamatti (Johnson J. Johnson), Ned Beatty (Gen. Ed Sheppard), Leslie Phillips (Judge), Robert Hardy (Doctor)

Thunderstorm
GB 1955 88m bw
Hemisphere/Binnie Barnes
A Spanish fisherman rescues a mysterious girl from a derelict yacht and falls in love with her although the villagers regard her as a witch.
Heady stuff on a low budget, quite smoothly done for lovers of peasant drama.
w George St George, Geoffrey Homes (Daniel Mainwaring) *d John Guillermin ph* Manuel Berenguer *m* Paul Misraki
☆ Linda Christian, Carlos Thompson, Charles Korvin

Thursday's Child
GB 1942 81m bw
ABPC
A child from an ordinary family has success in films and it goes to her head.
Predictable domestic drama with some good moments, but rather overpraised at the time.
w Donald Macardle, Rodney Ackland *novel* Donald Macardle *d* Rodney Ackland
☆ Sally Ann Howes, Wilfrid Lawson, Kathleen O'Regan, Eileen Bennett, Stewart Granger, Felix Aylmer

Thy Soul Shall Bear Witness *
Sweden 1920 70m approx (24 fps) bw silent
Svensk Filmindustri
original title: *Korkarlen*
aka: *The Phantom Carriage*
A drunkard is knocked senseless, retraces his misspent life, hears the carriage of death approaching and returns to his family.
Old-fashioned moralistic saga which hit the right note at the time and has scenes which still impress.
wd Victor Sjostrom novel Selma Lagerlöf *ph* J. Julius Jaenzon
☆ Victor Sjostrom, Hilda Borgstrom, Astrid Holm
† Remade in France in 1939 by Julien Duvivier, as *La Charette Fantôme*, with Pierre Fresnay and Louis Jouvet; and again in Sweden in 1958 as *Korkarlen*, by Arne Mattson.

Tiara Tahiti *
GB 1962 100m Eastmancolor
Rank/Ivan Foxwell
An up-from-the-ranks colonel and an aristocratic smoothie captain continue their antipathy in peacetime Tahiti, where one is nearly murdered and the other gets his come-uppance.
Uneasy mixture of light comedy and character drama; enjoyable in parts, but flabbily assembled and muddily photographed.
w Geoffrey Cotterell, Ivan Foxwell *novel* Geoffrey Cotterell *d* William T. Kotcheff *ph* Otto Heller *m* Philip Green
☆ John Mills, James Mason, Herbert Lom, Claude Dauphin, Rosenda Monteros

'A Titled Family. A Missing Heir. A Fortune At Stake.'
The Tichborne Claimant *
GB 1998 98m colour
Redbus/Bigger Picture/Swiftcall/IoMFC (Tom McCabe)
Sent to Australia to find the missing heir to the Tichborne fortune, a black servant returns to England with an imposter whom he has coached in the role.
Mildly enjoyable romp through a famous true happening in Victorian England, one that caught the imagination of the public; the film is unlikely to enjoy such success, being ramshackle and not deft enough in its satire on the high society of the time.
w Joe Fisher *d* David Yates *ph* Peter Thwaites *m* Nicholas Hooper *pd* Brian Sykes *ed* Jamie Trevill
☆ Robert Pugh (Tichborne claimant), John Kani (Andrew Bogle Tiyonga), Stephen Fry (Sir Henry Hawkins), Robert Hardy (Lord Rivers), John Gielgud (Lord Chief Justice), Rachael Dowling (Mary Anee Costa), Paola Dionisotti (Dowager Lady Tichborne), Charles Gray (Lord Arundell), James Villiers (Uncle Henry), Anita Dobson (Fanny Orton), Dudley Sutton (Onslow Onslow)
'A fascinating, funny and very handsomely done charmer.' – *Angie Errigo, Empire*

Tick, Tick, Tick... *
US 1969 100m Metrocolor Panavision
MGM/Nelson-Barrett (Ralph Nelson, James Lee Barrett)
The first black sheriff in a Southern community has trouble with murder and rape cases.
Socially conscious suspenser, well enough made from predictable elements and leading surprisingly to an upbeat ending.
w James Lee Barrett *d* Ralph Nelson *ph* Loyal Griggs *m* Jerry Stynes
☆ Jim Brown, George Kennedy, Fredric March, Lynn Carlin, Don Stroud, Clifton James

Ticket of Leave Man
GB 1937 71m bw
George King Productions (E. M. Smedley-Ashton)
The Tiger, 'the most dangerous killer in London', falls in love with a singer.
A ponderous mid-Victorian melodrama complete with barnstorming acting, and interesting mainly as an example of an earlier form of popular entertainment faithfully translated to the screen.
w H. F. Maltby, A. R. Rawlinson *play* Tom Taylor *d* George King *ph* H. M. Glendining *md* Jack Beaver *ad* Philip Bawcombe, Jack Hallward *ed* Robert Walters
☆ Tod Slaughter, John Warwick, Marjorie Taylor, Frank Cochran, Robert Adair
† The play was first produced in 1863. A typical line of dialogue from the film preserves the flavour of the original. A policeman gloats over the grave of his adversary: 'You are avenged. And so shall perish all who fall foul of Hawkshaw the detective.'

Ticket to Heaven *
Canada 1981 108m colour
Ronald Cohen Productions
A rootless young man is taken over by a religious co-operative.
Thinly veiled attack on the Moonies, quite well handled but perhaps better as a straight documentary.
w Ralph L. Thomas, Anne Cameron *book* Moonwebs by Josh Freed *d* Ralph L. Thomas *ph* Richard Leiterman *m* Maribeth Solomon
☆ Nick Mancuso, Saul Rubinek, Meg Foster, Kim Cattrall

A Ticket to Tomahawk *
US 1950 90m Technicolor
TCF (Robert Bassler)
A stagecoach line defies the new Western railroad.
Would-be satirical Western which doesn't quite have the stamina and after some pleasing touches settles for dullness.
w Mary Loos *d* Richard Sale *ph* Harry Jackson *m* Cyril Mockridge
☆ Anne Baxter, Dan Dailey, Rory Calhoun, Walter Brennan, Charles Kemper, Connie Gilchrist, Arthur Hunnicutt, Sen Yung

Tickle Me
US 1965 90m DeLuxe Panavision
AA (Ben Schwalb)
An unemployed rodeo star accepts a job at a health ranch and helps a girl escape from villains after hidden treasure.
Wispy star vehicle with an unexpected haunted ghost town climax.
w Elwood Ullman, Edward Bernds *d* Norman Taurog *ph* Loyal Griggs *m* Walter Scharf
☆ Elvis Presley, Julia Adams, Jocelyn Lane, Jack Mullaney, Merry Anders, Connie Gilchrist

A Ticklish Affair
US 1963 95m Metrocolor Panavision
MGM/Euterpe (Joe Pasternak)
A naval commander in San Diego falls for a widow with several children.
Thin romantic comedy with too many juvenile antics.
w Ruth Brooks Flippen *d* George Sidney *ph* Milton Krasner *m* George Stoll, Robert Van Eyps
☆ Shirley Jones, Gig Young, Red Buttons, Carolyn Jones, Edgar Buchanan

'A highly strung love story...'
Tie Me Up! Tie Me Down!
Spain 1989 102m colour
Enterprise/El Deseo (Agustin Almodóvar)
original title: *¡Atame!*
A man just released from a psychiatric hospital kidnaps a drug-addicted pornographic film actress and threatens to keep her tied up until she falls in love with him.
Shallow and glib, all surface and no substance, poorly constructed and flashily photographed, it nevertheless found some vociferous admirers.
wd Pedro Almodóvar *ph* José Luis Alcaine *m* Ennio Morricone *ed* Jose Salcedo
☆ Victoria Abril, Antonio Banderas, Loles Leon, Francisco Rabal, Julieta Serrano, Maria Barranco, Rossy de Palma, Lola Cardona
'The film never stops surprising, moving with fluid momentum toward a tear-jerker ending that verges on the comic but – at least the night I saw it – left most viewers in tears.' – *David Leavitt, New York Times*

The Tie that Binds
US 1995 98m Technicolor
Polygram/Interscope (David Madden, Patrick Markey, John Morrissey, Susan Zachary)
A criminal couple who abandon their young daughter later return to reclaim her and kill those who have been caring for her.
An unprepossessing thriller, crudely directed and given over to gratuitous violence.
w Michael Auerbach *d* Wesley Strick *ph* Bobby Bukowski *m* Graeme Revell *pd* Marcia Hinds-Johnson *ed* Michael N. Knue
☆ Daryl Hannah, Keith Carradine, Moira Kelly, Vincent Spano, Julia Devin, Cynda Williams
'The drama soon turns into arrant melodrama which would be laughable were it not so violent. It's very silly and quite vicious, despite Strick's ability to crank up the tension nicely.' – *Derek Malcolm, Guardian*

Tiempo de Morir: see *Time to Die*

Tierra *
Spain 1995 125m colour Panavision
Metro/Tartan/Sogetel/Lola/Sogepaq/Canal+ (Lola Pérez)
On a Spanish farm, a mysterious man with a split personality becomes involved with a married woman and her husband's mistress.
An engrossing but confusing puzzle of a film, which may, or may not, be about the intervention of an angel in human affairs.
wd Julio Medem *ph* Javier Aguirresarobe *m* Alberto Iglesias *ad* Satur Idarreta *ed* Ivan Aledo *sp* Computer Arts and Development
☆ Carmelo Gómez, Emma Suárez, Karra Elejalde, Silke Klein, Nancho Nova, Txema Blasco, Ane Sánchez
'Deliberately obscure but brilliantly made with erotic intent. It is as clearly the work of a highly cinematic film-maker. But where it comes from and where it goes is well beyond me.' – *Derek Malcolm, Guardian*

Tiffany Jones
GB 1973 90m Eastmancolor
Hemdale/Peter Walker
A model helps a prince overthrow the dictator who deposed his father.
Comic romp in the style of a Carry On *movie with some sex appeal.*
w Alfred Shaughnessy *comic strip* Pat Tourret, Jenny Butterworth *d* Peter Walker *ph* Peter Jessop *m* Cyril Ornadel *ed* Alan Brett
☆ Anouska Hempel, Ray Brooks, Susan Sheers, Damien Thomas, Eric Pohlmann, Lynda Baron, Bill Kerr
'In the place of humour, the production has recourse to some of the more lethal devices of British farce – funny foreigners and inflated third-form puns.' – *Gareth Jones, MFB*

Tiger Bay **
GB 1959 105m bw
Rank/Wintle-Parkyn (John Hawkesworth)
A Polish seaman in Cardiff kills his faithless girlfriend and kidnaps a child who proves more than a match for him.
Generally very proficient police chase melodrama with strong characterizations: a considerable box-office success of its time.
w John Hawkesworth, Shelley Smith *d* J. Lee-Thompson *ph* Eric Cross *m* Laurie Johnson
☆ *Hayley Mills, John Mills, Horst Buchholz*, Megs Jenkins, Anthony Dawson, Yvonne Mitchell
Hayley Mills (newcomer)

Tiger by the Tail
GB 1955 85m bw
Eros/Tempean (Robert S. Baker, Monty Berman)
An American journalist in London uncovers a sinister conspiracy.
Run-of-the-mill thriller which, although sticking to the same basic narrative, emasculates its far better, more cryptic source, stripping it of character and of the genre's first anti-hero.
w John Gilling, Willis Goldbeck *novel* Never Come Back by John Mair *d* John Gilling *ph* Eric Cross *md* Stanley Black *ad* Wilfred Arnold *ed* Jack Slade
☆ Larry Parks, Constance Smith, Lisa Daniely, Cyril Chamberlain, Donald Stewart, Thora Hird, Joan Heal, Alexander Gauge, Doris Hare, Ronald Leigh-Hunt
† The novel was the only thriller written by John Mair (1913–42), who died in an RAF flying accident. It was highly praised on its publication in 1941 by, among others, George Orwell and James Agate.

Tiger Cage 2
Hong Kong 1990 91m colour
D & B (Stephen Shin)
A former cop, known as The Mad Dragon, and a female lawyer become accidentally involved with money-laundering, gangsters and murder.
Broadly comic action movie, with coarse jokes and much violence and gore, working up to a climax involving sword, fist and gunfights.
w Ip Kwong Kim *d* Yuen Wo Ping *ph* Lee Ping Bing *m* Richard Yuen
☆ Donnie Yen, Rosamund Kwan, David Wu, Robin Shou, Gary Chau, Carol Cheng

Tiger in the Sky: see *The McConnell Story*

Tiger in the Smoke *
GB 1956 94m bw
Rank (Leslie Parkyn)
Ex-commando criminals comb London for hidden loot and threaten a young girl.
Odd little melodrama with a complex plot and a different, Graham Greene-like atmosphere.
w Anthony Pelissier *novel* Marjorie Allingham *d* Roy Baker *ph* Geoffrey Unsworth *m* Malcolm Arnold
☆ Tony Wright, Muriel Pavlow, Donald Sinden, Bernard Miles, Alec Clunes, Laurence Naismith, Christopher Rhodes, Kenneth Griffith, Beatrice Varley

The Tiger Makes Out *
US 1967 94m Technicolor
Columbia/Elan (George Justin)
A middle-aged New York postman takes revenge on society by kidnapping a young girl – who rather enjoys the experience.
Semi-surrealist comedy misguidedly extended from a two-character play; frantic pace prevents more than a few effective moments.
w Murray Shisgal *play* Murray Shisgal *d* Arthur Hiller *ph* Arthur J. Ornitz *m* Milton Rogers
☆ *Eli Wallach, Anne Jackson*, Bob Dishy, David Burns, Charles Nelson Reilly
'An attractive and bemusing piece of costume jewelry – but not comparable to the real thing.' – *Judith Crist*

Tiger Man: see *The Lady and the Monster*

Tiger of the Seven Seas
Italy/France 1963 90m colour
Liber Film/Euro International (Ottavio Poggi)
aka: *La Tigre de Sette Mari*
A pirate's daughter takes over his command to revenge herself on his killer.
Mundane swashbuckler with a heroine who lacks the panache of Errol Flynn.
w Luigi Capuano, Ottavio Poggi, Arpad de Riso *d* Luigi Capuano *ph* Alvaro Mancori *m* Carlo Rustichelli
☆ Gianna Maria Canale, Anthony Steel, Grazia Maria Spina, Andrea Aureli

Tiger on the Beat
Hong Kong 1988 89m colour
Cinema City (Wellington W. Fung, Tsang Kwok Chi)
An idle, womanizing cop gets a new eager partner; they are assigned to discover who murdered some Thai drug dealers.
An odd mixture of violent and bloody action and broad comedy which is likely to have a limited appeal for most Western audiences. (At one point a villain threatens to have a kidnapped female hostage burned alive. When that threat doesn't appear to work, he adds, 'Or do you want her to get screwed by foreigners?', which has the desired effect.)
w Tsang Kwok Chi *d* Lau Kar Leung *ph* Cho On Shun, Joe Chan Kwong Hung *m* Teddy Robin Kwan *ad* Eric Lee *ed* Wong Ming Lam
☆ Chow Yun-Fat, Li Chi, Conan Lee, Ti Lung, Tsui Shui Keung, Gordon Liu, Shirley Ng, Ko Fai, Tommy Tam, John Keung, James Wong, Sun Tin Ha
† The subtitling is erratic in its use of English, as in 'My brother isn't easy to deal with, he's tear and I have mucus', and 'I suspect her bra also contains cock'.

Tiger Shark *
US 1932 80m bw
Warner
A tuna fisherman who has lost a hand to a shark marries the daughter of an old friend, finds she loves someone else, and is conveniently killed by another shark.
Vivid melodrama with a plot partly borrowed from Moby Dick *and itself partly borrowed by innumerable other Warner films including* Kid Galahad, The Wagons Roll at Night, Slim *and* Manpower.
w Wells Root *story* Tuna by Houston Branch *d Howard Hawks ph* Tony Gaudio
☆ Edward G. Robinson, J. Carrol Naish, Zita Johann
'Strong and exceedingly well played and directed sea drama.' – *Variety*

A Tiger Walks *
US 1963 91m Technicolor
Walt Disney (Ron Miller)
In a small Western town, a tiger escapes from the circus.
A splendid animal and a happy ending help to make this a pretty good film for children.
w Lowell S. Hawley *novel* Ian Niall *d* Norman Tokar *ph* William Snyder *m* Buddy Baker
☆ Sabu, Brian Keith, Vera Miles, Pamela Franklin, Kevin Corcoran, Edward Andrews, Una Merkel, Frank McHugh
'The Disney message runs true to form – grown-ups should practise what they preach and children are right about animals.' – *MFB*

Tiger Warsaw
US 1988 90m colour
Recorded Releasing/Continental Film Group/Cineplex (Amin Q. Chaudhri)
After fifteen years away, a former drug-addict, who shot his father, returns home.
Predictable and ponderous melodrama.
w Roy London *d* Amin Q. Chaudhri *ph* Robert Draper *m* Ernest Troost *pd* Tom Targownik *ed* Brian Smedley-Aston
☆ Patrick Swayze, Barbara Williams, Piper Laurie, Lee Richardson, Mary McDonnell, Bobby DiCicco

The Tiger Woman
US 1944 bw serial: 12 eps
Republic
Oil drillers are delayed by jungle people led by a strange white woman who proves to be an heiress lost as a child in a plane crash.
Ho-hum hokum.
d Spencer Bennet, Wallace Grissell
☆ Allan Lane, Linda Stirling, Duncan Renaldo, George J. Lewis, LeRoy Mason

'The system wanted them to become soldiers. One soldier just wanted to be human.'
Tigerland
US/Germany 2000 109m
TCF/Haft/New Regency/Kirch (Arnon Milchan, Steven Haft, Beau Flynn)
In a training camp for the Vietnam War, a rebellious recruit learns to be a good soldier.
Although based on the experiences of its scriptwriters, this seems second-hand goods, recycling characters and themes from better movies, and flawed by its pervasive sentimentality; the documentary-styled camerawork and attractive performances give it a little credibility.
w Ross Klavan, Michael McGruther *d* Joel Schumacher *ph* Matthew Libatique *m* Nathan Larsen *pd* Andrew Laws *ed* Mark Stevens
☆ Colin Farrell (Roland Bozz), Matthew Davis (Jim Paxton), Clifton Collins Jnr (Miter), Thomas Guiry (Cantwell), Shea Whigham (Wilson), Russell Richardson (Johnson), Cole Hauser (Sergeant Cota)
'Falls back on some of the hoariest clichés of the war movie... The difference is, the soldiers in

Tigerland never see any action – which is normally what makes the clichés worth sitting through.' – *John Wrathall, Sight and Sound*

'A classy little film worthy of comparison with any other Vietnam flick.' – *Adam Smith, Empire*

A Tiger's Tale
US 1987 97m colour
Entertainment/Atlantic (Peter Douglas)

A middle-aged woman becomes pregnant as a result of an affair with a high-school student.
Dire comedy with no visible or audible wit.
wd Peter Douglas *novel Love and Other Natural Disasters* by Allen Hanney III *ph* Tony Pierce-Roberts *m* Lee Holdridge *pd* Shay Austin *ed* David Campling
☆ Ann-Margret, C. Thomas Howell, Charles Durning, Kelly Preston, William Zabka, Ann Wedgeworth, James Noble

The Tigger Movie
US 2000 77m Technicolor
Buena Vista/Walt Disney (Cheryl Abood)

Winnie-the-Pooh and his friends of the Hundred Acre Wood help Tigger in his search for his relatives.
One of Disney's less distinguished efforts, a run-of-the-mill animated cartoon, in which the bouncy Tigger becomes a very soft and soppy toy; it may pass muster with the very young.
wd Jun Falkenstein *story* Eddie Guzelian *characters created by* A.A. Milne *m* Harry Gregson-Williams *m/ly* Richard M. Sherman, Robert B. Sherman *ad* Toby Bluth
☆ Featuring voices of: Jim Cummings, Nikita Hopkins, Ken Sansom, John Fiedler, Peter Cullen, Andre Stojka, Kath Soucie, Tom Attenborough, John Hurt

'By far the least ambitious, and certainly the least interesting, animated feature to come out of Disney in quite some time.' – *Todd McCarthy, Variety*

Tight Little Island: see *Whisky Galore*

Tight Shoes
US 1941 67m bw
Universal/Mayfair (Jules Levey)
A political grafter buys tight shoes which have a series of dramatic consequences.
Moderately witty little comedy which conveyed the Runyon flavour as well as any.
w Leonard Spigelgass, Art Arthur *story* Damon Runyon *d* Albert S. Rogell
☆ Broderick Crawford, Binnie Barnes, John Howard, Anne Gwynne, Leo Carrillo, Samuel S. Hinds, Shemp Howard

Tight Spot
US 1955 97m bw
Columbia (Lewis J. Rachmil)

A material witness in the trial of a gangster is released from prison in the custody of an attorney.
Fairly routine crime melodrama with unexciting star performances.
w William Bowers *play Dead Pigeon* by Leonard Kantor *d* Phil Karlson *ph* Burnett Guffey *m* Morris Stoloff
☆ Edward G. Robinson, Ginger Rogers, Brian Keith, Lorne Greene, Lucy Marlow, Katherine Anderson

Tightrope
US 1984 114m Technicolor
Warner/Malpaso (Clint Eastwood, Fritz Manes)

A New Orleans detective investigating a series of sex murders finds that his own impulses are none too healthy.
Boring, dimly lit and generally unappealing low life thriller.
wd Richard Tuggle *ph* Billy Bragg *m* Lennie Niehaus
☆ Clint Eastwood, Geneviève Bujold, Dan Hedaya, Alison Eastwood, Jennifer Beck

'Til There Was You
US 1997 113m Technicolor
Paramount/Lakeshore (Penney Finkelman Cox, Tom Rosenberg, Alan Poul)

Two people, who are destined to fall in love, take a long time to meet one another.
Gaudy and charmless romantic comedy; it might have worked with a lighter touch.
w Winnie Holzman *d* Scott Winant *ph* Bobby Bukowski *m* Miles Goodman, Terence Blanchard *pd* Craig Stearns *ed* Richard Marks, Joanna Cappuccilli
☆ Jeanne Tripplehorn, Dylan McDermott, Sarah Jessica Parker, Jennifer Aniston, Ken Olin, Nina Foch, Christine Ebersole, Michael Tucker, Patrick Malahide

'A sorry recipe of stale ideas and sickly sweet smiles.' – *Sight and Sound*

'A tired piece of romantic cornball fare.' – *Variety*

'Til We Meet Again
US 1940 99m bw
Warner (David Lewis)
On a ship bound from Hong Kong to San Francisco, a dying woman falls for a crook about to be executed.
Stolid remake of One Way Passage *(qv).*
w Warren Duff *story* Robert Lord *d* Edmund Goulding *ph* Tony Gaudio *m* Ray Heindorf
☆ Merle Oberon, George Brent, Frank McHugh, Pat O'Brien, Geraldine Fitzgerald, Eric Blore, Binnie Barnes, Henry O'Neill, George Reeves
† Marlene Dietrich was originally scheduled for the lead.

Tilai **
Burkina Faso/Switzerland/France 1990 81m colour
Artificial Eye/Les Films de L'Avenir/Waka Films/Rhea Films (Idrissa Ouedraogo)

Returning home after being away for two years, a man discovers that his father has married his fiancée.
An African tragedy of domestic conflicts and broken promises, told with an uncomplicated directness.
wd Idrissa Ouédraogo *ph* Jean Monsigny, Pierre Laurent Chenieux *m* Abdullah Ibrahim *ed* Luc Barnier
☆ Rasmane Ouedraogo, Ina Cisse, Roukietou Barry, Assane Ouedraogo, Sibidou Sidibe, Moumouni Ouedraogo, Mariam Barry, Seydou Ouedraogo

'There is no doubt about Idrissa Ouedraogo's cinematic mastery.' – *MFB*

Till Death Us Do Part *
GB 1968 100m Eastmancolor
British Lion/Associated London Films (Jon Pennington)

From the thirties to the sixties with loud-mouthed, bigoted Londoner Alf Garnett.
Unremarkable and frequently misguided opening-up of a phenomenally successful TV series, adapted for the US as All in the Family. *The original cast wades cheerfully enough through a bitty script; the sequel,* The Alf Garnett Saga, *defeated them.*
w Johnny Speight *d* Norman Cohen *ph* Harry Waxman *m* Wilfrid Burns
☆ Warren Mitchell, Dandy Nichols, Anthony Booth, Una Stubbs, Liam Redmond, Bill Maynard, Sam Kydd, Brian Blessed

Till Glädje: see *To Joy*

Till the Clouds Roll By **
US 1946 137m Technicolor
MGM (Arthur Freed)

The life and times of composer Jerome Kern.
Better-than-average biopic with better-than-average tunes and stars.
w Myles Connolly, Jean Holloway *d* Richard Whorf *ph* Harry Stradling, George J. Folsey *md* Lennie Hayton
☆ Robert Walker, Judy Garland, Lucille Bremer, Van Heflin, Mary Nash, Dinah Shore, Van Johnson, *June Allyson*, Tony Martin, Kathryn Grayson, *Lena Horne, Frank Sinatra, Virginia O'Brien*

'A little like sitting down to a soda fountain de luxe atomic special of maple walnut on vanilla on burnt almond on strawberry on butter pecan on coffee on raspberry sherbert on tutti frutti with hot fudge, butterscotch, marshmallow, filberts, pistachios, shredded pineapple, and rainbow sprills on top, go double on the whipped cream.' – *James Agee*

† Lucille Bremer's singing was dubbed by Trudy Erwin.
♫ 'Make Believe'; 'Can't Help Lovin' Dat Man'; 'The Last Time I Saw Paris'; 'Ol' Man River'; 'All the Things You Are'; 'How'd You Like to Spoon with Me?'; 'They Didn't Believe Me'; 'Till the Clouds Roll By'; 'Look for the Silver Lining'; 'I Won't Dance'; 'Smoke Gets in Your Eyes'; 'A Fine Romance'; 'Yesterdays'

Till the End of Time *
US 1946 105m bw
RKO (Dore Schary)

Three returning GIs find romance and problems in their small town.
Downbeat variation on The Best Years of Our Lives *with a theme tune which puts words to a Chopin Polonaise.*
w Allen Rivkin *d* Edward Dmytryk *ph* Harry J. Wild *m* Leigh Harline
☆ Dorothy McGuire, Guy Madison, Robert Mitchum

Till There Was You
Australia 1990 95m colour
Rank/Five Arrows/Ayer/Southern Star (Jim McElroy)

An American barman investigates the mysterious death of his brother in the South Pacific state of Vanuatu.
An unconvincing thriller that offers nothing but occasionally spectacular photography.
w Michael Thomas *d* John Seale *ph* Geoffrey Simpson, Robert Primes *m* Graeme Revell *pd* George Liddle, Susan Emshwiller *ed* Jill Bilcock
☆ Mark Harmon, Deborah Unger, Jeroen Krabbé, Shane Briant, Ivan Kesa

Till We Meet Again
US 1936 87m bw
Paramount (Albert Lewis)
Former sweethearts find themselves both spies, but on opposing sides during the First World War.
Unconvincing but climactically suspenseful romantic drama.
w Edwin Justus Mayer, Franklin Coen, Brian Marlow *play* Alfred Davis *d* Robert Florey *ph* Victor Milner *ad* Hans Dreier, Roland Anderson *ed* Richard Currier *cos* Edith Head
☆ Herbert Marshall (Alan Barclow), Gertrude Michael (Elsa Daranyi), Lionel Atwill (Ludwig), Rod LaRoque (Karl Schrottle), Guy Bates Post (Captain Minton), Spencer Charters (Hoffer), Frank Reicher (Von Diegel)

'She came from a woman's world – into his world of men – and danger!'
Till We Meet Again
US 1944 88m bw
Paramount (David Lewis)
A French nun helps an American aviator escape from the Nazis.
Very moderate, nicely photographed, romantic war actioner.
w Lenore Coffee *play* Alfred Maury *d* Frank Borzage *ph Theodor Sparkuhl* *m* David Buttolph
☆ Ray Milland, Barbara Britton, Walter Slezak, Lucile Watson, Konstantin Shayne, Vladimir Sokoloff, Mona Freeman

Tillie and Gus *
US 1933 61m bw
Paramount (Douglas MacLean)
Two middle-aged cardsharps return home, help their niece and nephew win an inheritance, and come first in a paddleboat race.
Jumbled comedy with good moments and a rousing climax.
w Walter de Leon, Francis Martin *d* Francis Martin *ph* Benjamin Reynolds
☆ W. C. Fields, *Alison Skipworth*, Baby Le Roy, Jacqueline Wells, Clifford Jones, Clarence Wilson, Edgar Kennedy, Barton MacLane

'Very funny in spots, but not enough spots.' – *Variety*

Tillie's Punctured Romance *
US 1914 60m approx (24 fps) bw silent
Keystone/Mack Sennett

A country maid falls for a con man who steals her money; but she finally gets her revenge.
Museum piece comedy which no longer irritates the funny bone but has clear historical interest.
w Hampton Del Ruth *play Tillie's Nightmare* by Edgar Smith *d* Mack Sennett *ph* Frank D. Williams
☆ Marie Dressler, Charles Chaplin, Mabel Normand, Mack Swain

Tillsammans ***
Sweden/Denmark/Italy 2000 106m colour
Metrodome/Memfis/Film i Vast/SVT/Zentropa/Keyfilms Roma (Lars Jonsson)

GB and US title: *Together*
In the mid '70s, a mother leaves her abusive husband and moves into a disorganised, vegetarian commune with her two children.
Delightful comedy of the problems of living together and apart, told with a warm-hearted tolerance and keen observation.
wd Lukas Moodysson *ph* Ulf Brantas *ad* Carl Johan de Geer *ed* Michal Leszczylowski, Fredrik Abrahamsen
☆ Lisa Lindgren, Mikael Nyqvist, Gustaf Hammarsten, Anja Lundqvist, Jessica Liedberg, Ola Norell, Shanti Roney, Sam Kessel

'A funny, graceful and immensely good-natured work.' – *David Kehr, New York Times*

Tilly of Bloomsbury
GB 1940 83m bw
Hammersmith
The daughter of a boarding house keeper falls for a rich young man.
Basically a millgirl's romance, remembered for one final drunk scene for the star comedian.
w Nils Hostius, Jack Marks *play* Ian Hay *d* Leslie Hiscott
☆ Sydney Howard, Jean Gillie, Henry Oscar, Athene Seyler, Michael Wilding, Kathleen Harrison, Michael Denison, Martita Hunt, Athole Stewart
† Previous versions: 1921, with Tom Reynolds and Edna Best, for Samuelson; 1931, with Sydney Howard and Phyllis Konstam, for Sterling.

Tim
Australia 1979 98m colour
Pisces Productions (Michael Pate)

A romance develops between a wealthy middle-aged spinster and a young, simple-minded builder.
Sentimental melodrama, notable only as the film that launched the career of Mel Gibson.
wd Michael Pate *novel* Colleen McCullough *ph* Paul Onorato *m* Eric Jupp *ad* John Carroll *ed* David Stiven
☆ Piper Laurie, Mel Gibson, Alwyn Kurts, Pat Evison, Peter Gwynne, Deborah Kennedy

Tim Burton's The Nightmare before Christmas: see *The Nightmare before Christmas*

Timberjack
US 1954 94m Trucolor
Republic
A young man seeks his father's killer among forest lumberjacks.
Resiliently cast action story of no great interest.
w Allen Rivkin *novel* Dan Cushman *d* Joseph Kane *ph* Jack Marta *m* Victor Young
☆ Sterling Hayden, Vera Ralston, Adolphe Menjou, David Brian, Hoagy Carmichael, Chill Wills, Jim Davis, Elisha Cook Jnr

Timbuktu
US 1958 92m bw
Imperial (Edward Small)
A gun runner quells a desert revolt in the French Sudan during World War II.
Leaden-footed melodrama full of stock characters despite its complex plot.
w Anthony Veiller, Paul Dudley *d* Jacques Tourneur *ph* Maury Gertsman *m* Gerald Fried
☆ Yvonne de Carlo, Victor Mature, George Dolenz, John Dehner, Marcia Henderson

Time after Time *
US 1980 112m Metrocolor Panavision
Warner/Orion (Herb Jaffe)
Jack the Ripper escapes via H. G. Wells's time machine from Victorian London to modern San Francisco; Wells gives chase and eventually projects him into limbo.
Amusing fantasy for those with light literary inclinations, marred by too much gore and a wandering middle section.
wd Nicholas Meyer *story* Karl Alexander, Steve Hayes *ph* Paul Lohmann *m* Miklos Rozsa *pd* Edward Carfagno
☆ Malcolm McDowell, David Warner, Mary Steenburgen, Charles Cioffi, Kent Williams

Time Bandits *
GB 1981 113m Technicolor
HandMade Films (Terry Gilliam)
A schoolboy is taken through time by a group of demonic dwarfs.
Curious tall tale in which schoolboy fantasy alternates with violence and black comedy. In general, much less funny than it intended to be, but with some hilarious moments.
w Michael Palin, Terry Gilliam *d* Terry Gilliam *ph* Peter Biziou *m* Mike Moran *pd* Millie Burns
☆ John Cleese (Robin Hood), Sean Connery (Agamemnon), Ian Holm (Napoleon), Ralph Richardson (Supreme Being), David Warner (Evil Genius), Shelley Duvall (Pansy), Katherine Helmond (Mrs Ogre), Michael Palin (Vincent), Peter Vaughan, David Rappaport

Time Flies *
GB 1944 88m bw
GFD/Gainsborough (Edward Black)
A professor invents a time machine and takes his friends back to the court of Good Queen Bess.
Very passable star farce.
w J. O. C. Orton, Ted Kavanagh, Howard Irving Young *d* Walter Forde *ph* Basil Emmott *md* Louis Levy
☆ Tommy Handley, Felix Aylmer, Evelyn Dall, George Moon, Moore Marriott, Graham Moffatt, John Salew, Olga Lindo, Stephane Grappelly

Time for Action: see *Tip on a Dead Jockey*

A Time for Drunken Horses: see *Zamani Baraye Masti Asbha*

A Time for Giving: see *Generation*

A Time for Killing
US 1967 83m Pathécolor Panavision
Columbia/Sage Western (Harry Joe Brown)
GB title: *The Long Ride Home*
Confederate prisoners escape from a Union fort and the commander sets off in pursuit.
Fairly savage Western with Something to Say about the corruption of war.
w Halsted Welles *novel* *Southern Blade* by Nelson and Shirley Wolford *d* Phil Karlson *ph* Kenneth Peach *m* Mundell Lowe
☆ Glenn Ford, George Hamilton, Inger Stevens, Max Baer, Paul Petersen, Timothy Carey, Todd Armstrong

A Time for Loving
GB 1971 104m colour
Hemdale/London Screen Plays (Mel Ferrer)
Short romantic comedies set at different times in the same Paris flat.
Portmanteau ooh-la-la, quite neat but pitifully undernourished; certainly no Plaza Suite.
w Jean Anouilh *d* Christopher Miles *ph* Andreas Winding *m* Michel Legrand *pd* Theo Meurisse *ed* Henri Lanoë
☆ Joanna Shimkus (Joan), Mel Ferrer (Dr Harrison), Britt Ekland (Josette), Philippe Noiret (Marcel), Lila Kedrova (Mme Dubillard), Robert Dhéry (Leonard), Mark Burns (Geoff), Susan Hampshire (Patricia)

Time Gentlemen Please
GB 1952 83m bw
Group Three (Herbert Mason)
A lazy tramp is the one blot on a prize-winning English village.
Artificial, thinly scripted and overlit sub-Ealing comedy with familiar characters and situations.
w Peter Blackmore *novel* *Nothing to Lose* by R. J. Minney *d* Lewis Gilbert *ph* Wilkie Cooper *m* Antony Hopkins
☆ Eddie Byrne, Hermione Baddeley, Jane Barrett, Robert Brown, Raymond Lovell, Marjorie Rhodes, Dora Bryan, Thora Hird, Sidney James, Edie Martin, Ivor Barnard, Sydney Tafler
'Quite a nice little picture.' – *Karel Reisz*

Time in the Sun ***
Mexico 1933 60m bw
Marie Seton
Unfinished fragments of Eisenstein's incomplete *Que Viva Mexico*, snippets from which were later released in various forms.
This is the longest and presumably best version, with splendidly pictorial sequences of peasant and Indian life culminating with Death Day, all skulls and fireworks. Clearly the work of a master, though if completed the film might well have been a bore.
w Marie Seton, Paul Burnford *d* *Sergei Eisenstein* *ph* Edouard Tissé

Time Limit *
US 1957 95m bw
UA/Richard Widmark, William Reynolds
During the Korean war an officer is courtmartialled for suspected collaboration.
Suspenseful talk piece from a somewhat intellectualized play.
w Henry Denker *play* Henry Denker, Ralph Berkey *d* *Karl Malden* *ph* Sam Leavitt *m* Fred Steiner
☆ Richard Widmark, Richard Basehart, Dolores Michaels, June Lockhart, Carl Benton Reid, Martin Balsam, Rip Torn
'The tightly constructed story leads logically and unfalteringly to a tense climax.' – *Lindsay Anderson*

Time Lock *
GB 1957 73m bw
Romulus (Peter Rogers)
A small boy is trapped in a bank vault just as it is being locked for the weekend.
Acceptable expansion of a Canadian TV suspenser.
w Peter Rogers *play* Arthur Hailey *d* Gerald Thomas *ph* Peter Hennessy *m* Stanley Black
☆ Robert Beatty, Betty McDowall, Vincent Winter, Lee Patterson, Alan Gifford, Robert Ayres

Time Lost and Time Remembered: see *I Was Happy Here*

'You Will Orbit into the Fantastic Future!'
The Time Machine *
US 1960 103m Metrocolor
MGM/Galaxy (George Pal)
A Victorian scientist builds a machine which after some trial and error transports him into the year 802701.
Surprisingly careful recreation of a period, and an undeniably charming machine, go for little when the future, including the villainous Morlocks, is so dull.
w David Duncan *novel* H. G. Wells *d* George Pal *ph* Paul C. Vogel *m* Russell Garcia *ad* *George W. Davis, William Ferrari* *ed* George Tomasini
☆ Rod Taylor, Yvette Mimieux, Alan Young, Sebastian Cabot, Tom Helmore, Whit Bissell, Doris Lloyd
'Gifts the screen with a fascinating, exciting photoplay that is incomparably superior to the scores of pictures of the same general theme that have been avalanched upon the public during the past decade.' – *Boxoffice*
special effects (Gene Warren, Tim Baar)

'He was searching for the answer to his past. He became a hero for the future.'
The Time Machine
US 2002 96m Technicolor Panavision
Warner/DreamWorks/Arnold Leibovit (Walter F. Parkes, David Valdes)
A scientist invents a time machine and travels to a time when humanity has developed into two species, one peace-loving, the other ape-like cannibals.
Confused and unsatisfactory version of Wells' novel, even if it is directed by his great-grandson. The narrative is used merely as a peg for special effects.
w John Logan *screenplay* David Duncan *novel* H. G. Wells *d* Simon Wells *ph* Donald M. McAlpine *m* Klaus Badelt *pd* Oliver Scholl *ed* Wayne Wahrman *sp* Digital Domain, ILM, Cinesite, Stan Winston, K.N.B. Efx *cos* Deena Appel, Bob Ringwood
☆ Guy Pearce (Alexander Hartdegen), Samantha Mumba (Mara), Mark Addy (David Philby), Sienna Guillory (Emma), Phyllida Law (Mrs Watchit), Alan Young (Flower Store Worker), Omero Mumba (Kalen), Jeremy Irons (Uber-Morlock)
'Offers protracted and repetitive scuffles rather than real excitement.' – *Kim Newman, Sight and Sound*
'One of those staggeringly well-produced, joylessly extravagant pictures that keep whooshing you from one visual marvel to the next, hastily, emptily.' – *Michael Wilmington, Chicago Tribune*
† Some sequences were directed by Gore Verbinski.
make-up (John M. Elliott Jnr, Barbara Lorenz)

A Time of Destiny
US 1988 118m colour
Rank/Columbia/Nelson Entertainment/Alive Films (Anna Thomas)
An immigrant's son swears vengeance on the GI who married his sister and inadvertently caused the death of his father.
Dull revenge drama set in the 1940s.
w Gregory Nava, Anna Thomas *d* Gregory Nava *ph* James Glennon *m* Ennio Morricone *pd* Henry Bumstead *ed* Betsy Blankett
☆ William Hurt, Timothy Hutton, Melissa Leo, Francisco Rabal, Concha Hidalgo, Stockard Channing, Megan Follows, Frederick Coffin

The Time of His Life
GB 1955 74m bw
Renown/Shaftesbury (Elizabeth Hiscott)
A former convict reluctantly returns home to his aristocratic daughter, who attempts to pass him off as a dim family servant.
Dull comedy, intended as a vehicle for the slapstick antics of its star in his role as Mr Pastry, but giving him few opportunities to shine.
wd Leslie Hiscott *story* Brock Williams *ph* Kenneth Talbot *m* Elizabeth Hiscott *md* Robin Richmond *ad* Duncan Sutherland *ed* Erwin Reiner
☆ Richard Hearne, Ellen Pollock, Richard Wattis, Robert Moreton, Frederick Leister, D'Arcy Conyers, John Downing, Anne Smith, Harry Towb

Time of Miracles *
Yugoslavia 1990 100m colour
Singidunum/Television Belgrad/Channel 4/ Metropolitan (Goran Paskaljevic)
original title: *Vrema Cuda*
In September 1945, after the village school burns down, the victorious Communists commandeer the church and whitewash over its religious murals; but the paintings reappear and a stranger arrives who apparently can raise the dead.
Intriguing, if sometimes ponderous, account of faith, belief and their interactions with reality.
w Borislav Pekic, Goran Paskaljevic *novel* Borislav Pekic *d* Goran Paskaljevic *ph* Radoslav Vladic *m* Zoran Simjanovic *ad* Miodrag Nikolic *ed* Olga Skrigin, Olga Obradov
☆ Predrag Miki Manojlovic, Dragan Maksimovic, Svetozar Cvetkovic, Mirjana Karanovic, Danilo Bata Stojkovic, Mirjana Jokovic, Ljuba Tadic

Time of the Gypsies *
Yugoslavia 1989 142m colour
Enterprise/Forum Film/Sarajevo TV (Mirza Pasic)
original title: *Dom Za Vesanje*
A young gypsy with magic powers is forced to work with a band of itinerant thieves and beggars.
Cut from a six-part television series, the film, despite some lively episodes, suffers from a disjointed narrative, though that did not prevent Kusturica being voted best director at the Cannes Film Festival.
w Emir Kusturica, Gordan Mihic *d* Emir Kusturica *ph* Vilko Filac *m* Goran Bregovic *pd* Miljen Kljakovic *ed* Andrija Zafranovic
☆ Davor Dujmovic, Bora Todorovic, Ljubica Adzovic, Husnija Hasmovic, Sinolicka Trpkova, Zabit Memedov

The Time of Their Lives *
US 1946 82m bw
Universal (Val Burton)
Revolutionary ghosts haunt a country estate.
Unusual, quite effective Abbott and Costello vehicle with the comedians not playing as a team.
w Val Burton, Walter de Leon, Bradford Ropes, John Grant *d* Charles Barton *ph* Charles Van Enger *m* Milton Rosen
☆ Bud Abbott, Lou Costello, Marjorie Reynolds, Binnie Barnes, Gale Sondergaard, John Shelton

The Time of Your Life *
US 1948 109m bw
Cagney Productions (William Cagney)
A group of lovable eccentrics spend much of their time philosophizing in a San Francisco bar.
Not really a film at all, this essence of Saroyan contains much to enjoy or to annoy. The performances are pretty good.
w Nathaniel Curtis *play* *William Saroyan* *d* H. C. Potter *ph* James Wong Howe *m* Carmen Dragon
☆ *James Cagney, William Bendix,* Wayne Morris, Jeanne Cagney, Gale Page, Broderick Crawford, *James Barton,* Ward Bond, Paul Draper, James Lydon, Richard Erdman, Natalie Schafer
'They have done so handsomely by Saroyan that in the long run everything depends on how much of Saroyan you can take.' – *Time*

Time Out: see *L'Emploi du Temps*

Time Out for Romance
US 1937 75m bw
TCF
A millionairess runs from the altar and teams up with a car factory driver.
Weakish rehash of It Happened One Night, *but the script isn't up to the intention.*
w Lou Breslow, John Patrick, Eleanore Griffin, William Rankin *d* Malcolm St Clair
☆ Claire Trevor, Michael Whalen, Joan Davis, Chick Chandler, Douglas Fowley, William Demarest, Andrew Tombes
'Just misses being able to stand on its own legs as a solo performer.' – *Variety*

Time out of Mind
US 1947 88m bw
Universal-International (Robert Siodmak)
The housekeeper's daughter finances music studies for the master's ungrateful son.
Silly romantic melodrama with few visible compensations.
w Abem Finkel, Arnold Phillips *novel* Rachel Field *d* Robert Siodmak *ph* Maury Gertsman *m* Miklos Rozsa *ad* John DeCuir, Bernard Herzbrun *ed* Ted J. Kent
☆ Phyllis Calvert, Robert Hutton, Ella Raines, Eddie Albert, Leo G. Carroll

A Time out of War *
US 1954 20m bw
Terry and Denis Sanders
Two men on opposite sides of a river during the American Civil War strike up a brief friendship.
Interesting but overpraised student piece.
wd Denis Sanders *story* *Pickets* by Robert W. Chambers *ph* Terry Sanders *m* Frank Hamilton
☆ Barry Atwater, Robert Sherry, Alan Cohen

Time Regained **
France/Italy 1999 158m colour
Gemini/France 2/Films du Lendemain/Blu Cinematografica/Madragoa (Paulo Branco)
original title: *Le Temps Retrouvé*
An ill and reclusive author recalls the events of his life, from childhood to his mingling in an aristoctratic society, and the work of fiction he dervied from it.
An elegant production that plays tricks with time and space, eliding past and present and showing events from shifting perspectives; what it cannot do is finally persuade us that its parade iof characters warrants an audience's extended attention.
w Gilles Taurand, Raúl Ruiz *novel* *Remembrance of Things Past* by Marcel Proust *d* *Raúl Ruiz* *ph* Ricardo Aronovich *m* Jorge Arriagada *pd* Bruno Beauge *ed* Denise de Casabianca *cos* Gabriella Pescucci, Caroline de Vivaise

☆ Catherine Deneuve (Odette), Emmanuelle Beart (Gilberte), Vincent Perez (Morel), John Malkovich (Charlus), Pascal Greggory (Saint-Loup), Marie-France Pisier (Madame Verdurin), Chiara Mastroianni (Albertine), Arielle Dombasle (Madame de Farcy), Marcello Mazzarella (Narrator)

'This spacious, beautifully acted, lovingly considered film is a must-see.' – *Peter Bradshaw, Guardian*

The Time, the Place and the Girl
US 1946 105m Technicolor
Warner (Alex Gottlieb)
Two night-club owners have problems.
Lightweight musical, indistinguishable from a dozen others.
w Francis Swann, Agnes Christine Johnston, Lynn Starling *d* David Butler *ph* William V. Skall *m* Arthur Schwartz
☆ Dennis Morgan, Jack Carson, Janis Paige, Martha Vickers, S. Z. Sakall, Alan Hale, Donald Woods, Angela Greene, Florence Bates
song 'A Gal in Calico' (*m*Arthur Schwartz, *ly*Leo Robin)

Time to Die **
Columbia/Cuba 1985 94m colour
Artificial Eye/Focine/ICIAC (Gabriel García Marquez)
original title: *Tiempo de Morir*
After serving an eighteen-year sentence for murder, a man returns home to find that the victim's sons are waiting to exact revenge.
Basically a Latin American Western, it grips the attention in its exploration of masculine codes of honour and duty.
w Gabriel García Marquez *d* Jorge Ali Triana *ph* Mario Garcia Joya *m* Leo Brower, Nafer Duran *pd* Patricia Bonilla *ed* Nelson Rodriquez
☆ Gustavo Angarita, Sebastian Ospina, Jorge Emilio Salazar, Maria Eugenia Davila, Lina Botero, Enrique Almirante

A Time to Kill *
US 1996 149m Technicolor Panavision
Warner/Monarchy/Regency (Arnon Milchan, Michael Nathanson, Hunt Lowry, John Grisham)
In a small Mississippi town, where the Ku Klux Klan still has power, a young lawyer defends a black father who killed the two white men arrested for the rape of his young daughter.
An old-style Hollywood melodrama, effectively staged though making little effort to explore the issues involved; it's content to endorse vigilante action providing that it's not carried out by the Klan.
w Akiva Goldsman *novel* John Grisham *d* Joel Schumacher *ph* Peter Menzies Jnr *m* Elliot Goldenthal *pd* Larry Fulton *ed* William Steinkamp
☆ Matthew McConaughey, Sandra Bullock, Samuel L. Jackson, Kevin Spacey, Oliver Platt, Charles Dutton, Brenda Fricker, Donald Sutherland, Kiefer Sutherland, Patrick McGoohan, Ashley Judd

'Just another Hollywood courtroom drama.' – *Sight and Sound*

† The film was among the financial successes of 1996, taking around $109m at the US box-office.

A Time to Live and a Time to Die: see *Le Feu Follet*

The Time to Live and the Time to Die **
Taiwan 1985 137m colour
Central Motion Pictures
original title: *Tongnian Wangshi*
A Chinese man remembers growing up in Taiwan in the 1950s and 60s as one of a large family headed by his consumptive, intellectual father and his doting, rambling grandmother who dreams of returning to the mainland.
An episodic, semi-autobiographical film of family life, reaching few conclusions, other than those brought about by death, but affording insight into the tensions of everyday living.
w Zu Tianwen, Hou Hsiao-hsien *d* Hou Hsiao-hsien *ph* Li Pingbin *m* Wu Chuchu
☆ You Anshun, Tian Feng, Mei Fang, Tang Ruyun, Xiao Ai, Xin Shufen, Hu Xiangping

A Time to Love and a Time to Die *
US 1958 132m Eastmancolor
Cinemascope
U-I (Robert Arthur)
During World War II, a German officer on his last leave solves problems at home but is killed on his return to the front.
Interesting but preachy and generally misguided attempt, by the studio which made All Quiet on the Western Front *and* The Road Back, *to repeat the dose in colour and wide screen.*
w Orin Jannings *novel* Erich Maria Remarque *d* Douglas Sirk *ph* Russell Metty *m* Miklos Rozsa *ad* Alexander Golitzen, Alfred Sweeney *ed* Ted J. Kent
☆ John Gavin, Lilo Pulver, Keenan Wynn, Jock Mahoney, Thayer David, Agnes Windeck, Erich Maria Remarque

The Time Travelers *
US 1964 84m Pathécolor
AIP/Dobie (William Redlin)
Scientists venture 107 years into the future, and on escaping find themselves in a time trap.
Ingenious and lively low-budget science fiction with a sobering ending.
wd Ib Melchior ph William Zsigmond *m* Richard La Salle
☆ Preston Foster, Phil Carey, Merry Anders, John Hoyt, Joan Woodbury

Time without Pity *
GB 1957 88m bw
Harlequin (John Arnold, Anthony Simmons)
An alcoholic arrives in London to seek new evidence which will prevent his son from being executed for murder.
Heavy-going, introspective, hysterical, downbeat melodrama which takes itself with a seriousness which is almost deadly.
w Ben Barzman *play Someone Waiting* by Emlyn Williams *d* Joseph Losey *ph* Freddie Francis *m* Tristam Cary
☆ Michael Redgrave, Alec McCowen, Leo McKern, Renée Houston, Ann Todd, Peter Cushing, Paul Daneman, Lois Maxwell, George Devine, Richard Wordsworth, Joan Plowright

'It hammers home its effects with the concentration of a heavyweight out for the kill.' – *Philip Oakes*

Timebomb
US 1991 96m colour
MGM/Raffaella (Raffaella de Laurentiis)
A watchmaker and former hitman prevents a CIA plot to assassinate a liberal politician.
Confused action adventure that updates The Manchurian Candidate *to no great effect.*
wd Avi Nesher *ph* Anthony B. Richmond *m* Patrick Leonard *pd* Greg Pruss, Curtis A. Schnell *ed* Isaac Sehayek
☆ Michael Biehn, Patsy Kensit, Tracy Scoggins, Robert Culp, Richard Jordan, Raymond St Jacques

'A throwaway B-picture.' – *Empire*

'4 Cameras. No Edits. Real Time.'
'Who Do You Want To Watch?'
Timecode **
US 2000 97m DeLuxe
Screen Gems/Red Mullet (Mike Figgis, Annie Stewart)
Actors, agents and others involved in the film business converge on the production offices of Red Mullet.
Intriguing and enjoyable experiment in which, on four split screens with the action shot in real time, the actors improvise on a story written by Figgis; emphasis switches from one quarter screen to another according to the sound levels. It works here, in a tale of shifting relationships and people pitching for jobs, because the narratives are relatively trivial and don't demand more than a divided attention.
wd Mike Figgis *ph* James Wharton O'Keefe, Tony Cucchiari, Mike Figgis, Patrick Alexander Stewart *m* Mike Figgis, Anthony Marinelli *pd* Charlotte Malmlof
☆ Xander Berkeley (Evan Watz), Golden Brooks (Onyx Richardson), Saffron Burrows (Emma), Viveka Davis (Victoria Cohen), Richard Edson (Lester Moore), Aimee Graham (Sikh Nurse), Salma Hayek (Rose), Glenne Headly (Therapist), Andrew Heckler (Auditioning Actor), Holly Hunter (Executive), Danny Huston (Randy), Kyle MacLachlan (Bunny Drysdale), Julian Sands (Quentin), Stellan Skarsgard (Alex Green), Jeanne Tripplehorn (Lauren Hathaway)

'A fascinating, sometimes exhilarating, experiment.' – *Dennis Harvey, Variety*

'They Killed His Wife Ten Years Ago. There's Still Time To Save Her.'
'Murder Is Forever ... Until Now.'
Timecop
US 1994 98m DeLuxe
UIP/Largo/JVC/Signature/Renaissance/Dark Horse (Moshe Diamant, Sam Raimi, Robert Tapert)
In an era of time travel a cop whose job is to protect the past discovers that his political boss is manipulating events in order to become President and sets out to stop him.
Over-involved science fiction that does not travel well; it both exploits and ignores the paradoxes involved in changing the past, and lacks excitement and the cheap thrills of comic books.
w Mark Verheiden, Mike Richardson, based on their comic series *d* Peter Hyams *ph* Peter Hyams *m* Mark Isham *pd* Philip Harrison *ed* Steven Kemper
☆ Jean-Claude Van Damme, Mia Sara, Ron Silver, Bruce McGill, Gloria Reuben, Jason Schombling, Scott Bellis, Scott Lawrence

'Van Damme and the movie are stiffs.' – *Michael Sragow, New Yorker*

Times Square
US 1980 113m Technicolor
EMI/Robert Stigwood
Two ill-matched teenage girls form a shabby night-club act and soon have New York by its ears.
Sometimes sharply made but generally unpleasant urban fairy story with suicide as the end, like a cross between Saturday Night Fever *and* Midnight Cowboy. *Among a number of forgettable songs is one called 'Pissing in the River'.*
w Jacob Brackman *story* Allan Moyle, Leanne Unger *d* Allan Moyle *ph* James A. Contner *m* Blue Weaver
☆ Tim Curry, Trini Alvarado, Robin Johnson, Peter Coffield, Herbert Berghof, David Margulies

Times Square Lady
US 1935 69m bw
MGM
The daughter of a Broadway hustler, being chiselled by her father's attorney, is helped by one of his employees.
Flat romantic drama designed as a test for young stars.
w Albert Cohen, Robert Shannon *d* George B. Seitz
☆ Robert Taylor, Virginia Bruce, Pinky Tomlin, Helen Twelvetrees, Isabel Jewell, Nat Pendleton, Henry Kolker, Jack La Rue

'Not sufficient heft to be important.' – *Variety*

Times Square Playboy: see *The Home Towners*

Timetable *
US 1955 79m bw
UA (Mark Stevens)
An insurance investigator is assigned to a train robbery which he actually committed himself.
Concise suspenser with good script and treatment.
w Aben Kandel *d* Mark Stevens *ph* Charles Van Enger *m* Walter Scharf
☆ Mark Stevens, Felicia Farr, King Calder, Wesley Addy

Tin Cup **
US 1996 135m Technicolor
Warner/Monarchy/Regency (Gary Foster, David Lester)
A hapless, small-town golf professional attempts to clean up his act when he falls for the girlfriend of a successful rival.
Engaging romantic comedy, ramshackle in construction but full of interesting behavourial quirks that give an individuality missing from much recent homogenized Hollywood product.
w John Norville, Ron Shelton *d* Ron Shelton *ph* Russell Boyd *m* William Ross *pd* James Bissell *ed* Paul Seydor, Kimberly Ray
☆ Kevin Costner, Rene Russo, Cheech Marin, Don Johnson, Linda Hart, Dennis Burkley, Rex Linn, Lou Myers

'Gets by on that old standby: if your film lacks a taut dramatic structure, simply provide the audience with a bunch of characters they want to hang out with, and by whatever means necessary. The sign of a good film.' – *Tom Shone, Sunday Times*

The Tin Drum ****
West Germany/France 1979 142m
Eastmancolor
UA/Franz Seitz/Bioskop/GGB 14 KG/Hallelujah/Artemis/Argos/Jadran/Film Polski
original title: *Die Blechtrommel*
Not caring for the world he is growing up in, a small boy determines to remain a child.
Brilliantly made version of a labyrinthine satire on German nationalism and the rise of the Nazis; the emphasis is sometimes on sex and scatological detail, for it is intended to be disturbing viewing, succeeding in its aim of depicting a frightening world where reason is overthrown.
w Jean-Claude Carrière, Franz Seitz, Volker Schlöndorff *novel* Günter Grass *d Volker Schlöndorff ph* Igor Luther *m* Maurice Jarre *pd* Nicos Perakis
☆ David Bennent, Mario Adorf, Angela Winkler, Daniel Olbrychski
best foreign film

Tin Men **
US 1987 112m DeLuxe
Touchstone/Silver Screen Partners II (Mark Johnson)
In 1960s Baltimore, two aluminium salesmen have a series of feuds.
A comedy enjoyable not for its plot but for its authentic period backgrounds and characters.
wd Barry Levinson ph Peter Sova *m* David Steele *pd* Peter Jamison *ed* Stu Linder
☆ *Richard Dreyfuss, Danny DeVito,* Barbara Hershey, John Mahoney, Jackie Gayle, Stanley Brock

Tin Pan Alley ***
US 1940 95m bw
TCF (Kenneth MacGowan)
During World War I and after, two dancing girls love the same composer.
Archetypal musical, full of Broadway clichés, razzmatazz and zip. Remade 1950 as I'll Get By, *not to such peppy effect.*
w Robert Ellis, Helen Logan *story* Pamela Harris *d Walter Lang ph Leon Shamroy md* Alfred Newman *ch* Seymour Felix *songs* Mack Gordon, Harry Warren
☆ *Alice Faye, Betty Grable, John Payne, Jack Oakie,* Allen Jenkins, Esther Ralston, The Nicholas Brothers, John Loder, Elisha Cook Jnr
♫ 'Moonlight Bay'; 'Honeysuckle Rose'; 'The Sheik of Araby'; 'K-K-K-Katie'.
Alfred Newman

The Tin Star *
US 1957 93m bw Vistavision
Paramount/Perlberg-Seaton
An ex-sheriff turned bounty hunter helps a new young sheriff to catch bandits.
Dignified and well-characterized Western with customary pleasures.
w Dudley Nichols story Barney Slater, Joel Kane *d Anthony Mann ph* Loyal Griggs *m* Elmer Bernstein
☆ Henry Fonda, Anthony Perkins, Betsy Palmer, Michel Ray, Neville Brand, John McIntire, Lee Van Cleef
Barney Slater, Joel Kane, Dudley Nichols

Tina: What's Love Got to Do with It: see *What's Love Got to Do with It*

'Do you have the guts to sit in this chair?'
The Tingler
US 1959 82m bw
Columbia/William Castle
Fear (it says here) can create on the spinal column a parasite removable only by screaming. A scientist isolates it and it runs amok in a silent cinema.

Ridiculous shocker with generally dull handling but effective moments.
w Robb White *d* William Castle *ph* Wilfrid Cline *m* Von Dexter
☆ Vincent Price, Judith Evelyn, Darryl Hickman, Patricia Cutts
'The sheer effrontery of this piece of hokum is enjoyable in itself.' – *MFB*

Tinpis Run
France/Belgium/Papua New Guinea 1990 94m colour
JBA/Tinpis/La Sept/RTBF/Femis/Varan/Skul Bilong Wokim Piksa (Jacques Bidou)
A tribal chief who runs a taxi service with his daughter and her boyfriend returns to his village to take part in a war against a neighbouring tribe.
Moderately entertaining anecdotal account of an unusual generation clash – between the peace-loving young and their elders.
w John Barre, Severin Blanchet, Martin Maden, Pengau Nengo *d* Pengau Nengo *ph* Martin Maden *m* Severin Blanchet, Mick Giani *ad* Thomas Gawi *ed* Andrée Davanture
☆ Rhoda Selan, Leo Konga, Oscar Wanu, Gerard Gabud
'More a travelog of the island country than a wholly satisfying dramatic film.' – *Variety*

Tip on a Dead Jockey
US 1957 99m bw
MGM (Edwin H. Knopf)
GB title: *Time for Action*
A flyer loses his nerve and turns international smuggler, but reforms.
Gloomy, pedestrian star melodrama, dully cast.
w Charles Lederer *novel* Irwin Shaw *d* Richard Thorpe *ph* George J. Folsey *m* Miklos Rozsa
☆ Robert Taylor, Dorothy Malone, Gia Scala, Martin Gabel, Marcel Dalio, Jack Lord

Tip-off Girls *
US 1938 61m bw
Paramount
Gangsters use girl employees to get tips on merchandise shipments.
Routine but watchable G-man second.
w Maxwell Shane, Robert Yost, Stuart Anthony *d* Louis King
☆ Lloyd Nolan, Mary Carlisle, J. Carrol Naish, Harvey Stephens, Roscoe Karns, Larry Crabbe, Anthony Quinn
'Excellent meller ... bristles with action, tensity and suspense.' – *Variety*

Tirez sur le Pianiste: see *Shoot the Pianist*

'Tis Pity She's a Whore **
Italy 1971 109m Technicolor
Miracle/Clesi (Silvio Clementelli)
original title: *Addio, Fratello Crudele*
A husband seeks revenge when he discovers that his wife is pregnant by her brother.
A gripping version of a Jacobean tragedy on the themes of obsessive love and jealousy.
w Giuseppe Patroni Griffi, Alfio Valdarnini, Carlo Carunchio *play* John Ford *d* Giuseppe Patroni Griffi *ph* Vittorio Storaro *m* Ennio Morricone *ad* Mario Ceroli *ed* Franco Arcalli
☆ Charlotte Rampling, Oliver Tobias, Fabio Testi, Antonio Falsi, Rik Battaglia, Angela Luce, Rino Imperio
'Magnificently expressive, as sensitive a transposition of the play as *Throne of Blood* was of *Macbeth*.' – *Tony Rayns, MFB*
'Too inclined to soft-focus ramblings through pretty countryside with characters' dubbed voices failing to match their lip movements. Odd but worthwhile.' – *Empire*
† The film was cut to 102m in its English version.

The Tit and the Moon **
Spain/France 1994 91m colour
Metro Tartan/Lolafils/Cartel/Sogepaq (Andrés Vicente Gómez)
original title: *La Teta y la Luna*
Jealous of his newborn baby brother, a young boy seeks maternal comfort from a cabaret artiste married to an impotent and flatulent performer.
Oddly engaging, often charming account of a child attempting to understand adult behaviour through his own emotional turmoil.
w Cuca Canals, Bigas Luna *d* Bigas Luna *ph* José Luis Alcaine *m* Nicola Piovani *ad* Aimé Deudé *ed* Carmen Frias
☆ Biel Duran, Mathilda May, Gérard Darmon, Miguel Poveda, Abel Folk, Genis Sanchez
'It is directed with such a sharp appreciation for childhood obsessions and with such crisp cinematic flair that it becomes a totally enchanting fairy-tale, hilarious and touching by turns.' – *Derek Malcolm, Guardian*

Tit for Tat *
US 1935 20m bw
Hal Roach
Adjoining shopkeepers violently settle an old difference.
Archetypal late star comedy: brilliant timing, but the warmth and sympathy have begun to ebb.
w Stan Laurel *d* Charles Rogers *ph* Art Lloyd *ed* Bert Jordan
☆ Stan Laurel, Oliver Hardy, Charlie Hall, Mae Busch
'A good deal of obvious slapstick and just a thread of a story turns this into only moderate comedy.' – *Box Office*
best short

'Prepare for life after Earth.'
Titan A.E.
US 2000 95m Technicolor CinemaScope
TCF (David Kirschner, Don Bluth, Gary Goldman)
In the 31st century, after the destruction of Earth by aliens, a band of humans search for a spaceship that can re-unite their race.
Had the narrative, characterisation and dialogue matched the often imaginative backgrounds and animation, this might have been the movie to break free from Disney's dominance of American animation; unfortunately, it's just an interesting failure.
w Ben Edlund, John August, Joss Whedon *story* Hans Bauer, Randall McCormick *d* Don Bluth, Gary Goldman *m* Graeme Revell *pd* Philip A. Cruden *ed* Fiona Trayler, Bob Bender
☆ voices of: Matt Damon (Cale), Drew Barrymore (Akima), Bill Pullman (Korso), John Leguizamo (Gune), Nathan Lane (Preed), Janeane Garofalo (Stith), Ron Perlman (Prof Sam Tucker), Alex D. Linz (Young Cale), Tone-Loc (Tek), Jim Breuer (The Cook)
'Will thrill every nerd on the planet.' – *James Christopher, Times*
'If CGI planets and hurtling spacecraft are not your bag, its flabby, patronising tone and tired storyline are going to get right on your wick.' – *Empire*
† Its failure at the box-office led Twentieth-Century Fox to abandon its plans for further animated films.

Titanic *
US 1953 98m bw
TCF (Charles Brackett)
Personal dramas aboard the *Titanic* in 1912 come to a head as the ship hits an iceberg.
An excellent example of studio production is squandered on a dim script which arouses no excitement.
w Charles Brackett, Walter Reisch, Richard Breen *d* Jean Negulesco *ph* Joe MacDonald *m* Sol Kaplan *ad* Lyle Wheeler, Maurice Ransford
☆ Clifton Webb, Barbara Stanwyck, Robert Wagner, Audrey Dalton, Thelma Ritter, Brian Aherne, Richard Basehart, Allyn Joslyn
script
art direction

'Nothing On Earth Could Come Between Them.'
Titanic **
US 1997 194m DeLuxe Panavision
TCF/Lightstorm (James Cameron, Jon Landau)
As the *Titanic* sails for its date with an iceberg, an independent young woman, engaged to a bullying millionaire, and travelling first class, falls for a penniless Wisconsin boy in steerage.
Said Cameron, on accepting one of the many Golden Globe awards for the film: 'So does this prove, once and for all, that size does matter?' To which there are two answers: one supplied by dialogue from the film ('Do you know of Dr Freud? His ideas about the male preoccupation with size may be of interest to you') and the other, only if you confuse quantity with quality. The recreation of the splendour and the disaster of the Titanic is brilliant, and the direction and editing often impeccable; but the dialogue is frequently risible, and the love story banal when it does not indulge in the sort of melodramatics that went out with The Perils of Pauline*, which has the effect of diminishing the many real-life tragedies that occurred. Cameron is the modern-day equivalent of the Victorian theatrical designer 'Sensation' Smith of Drury Lane: a master of spectacle, but little else.*
wd James Cameron *ph* Russell Carpenter *m* James Horner *pd* Peter Lamont *ed* Conrad Buff, James Cameron, Richard A. Harris *sp* Robert Legato, Mark Lasoff, Thomas L. Fisher, Michael Kanfer; Digital Domain
☆ Leonardo DiCaprio, *Kate Winslet*, Billy Zane, Kathy Bates, Frances Fisher, Gloria Stuart, Bill Paxton, Bernard Hill, Jonathan Hyde, Victor Garber, David Warner, Danny Nucci, Suzy Amis, Bernard Fox
'The regretful verdict here: Dead in the water.' – *Richard Corliss, Time*
'As Cameron sails his lonely craft toward greatness, he should realise he needs to bring a passenger with him. Preferably someone who can write.' – *Kenneth Turan, Los Angeles Times*
'Suggests the movie Cecil B. DeMille might have made in 1928 had he not been contemplating a more modern disaster flick about a giant dirigible. Not only is the dialogue as floridly stilted as the least literate silent-movie intertitles, but the correlation between the characters' personal lives and their impending doom is absolute.' – *J. Hoberman, Premiere*
'The daring underwater remake of *Harold and Maude*, in which an 18-year-old boy falls in love with an 80-year-old woman. The embryonic facial features of Leonardo DiCaprio (as well as the dialogue, direction and performances) render the love story not merely unconvincing, but almost offensive. Here is a little boy whose face screams "I have not lived", teaching Kate Winslet how to be a woman, giving her permission to play a part in her own life.' – *Emma Forrest, Guardian*
† The film, with its 550 computer-generated shots, was the most expensive made so far, at more than $200m, and needed to gross at least $350m to break even; Cameron forewent his salary as costs escalated, keeping only the $1.5m he received as screenwriter. It broke all box-office records around the world to become the highest-grossing film so far, taking more than $1 billion, and also equalled the record set by *Ben Hur* for winning the most Oscars. As a result, Cameron was reportedly to be recompensed with 10 per cent of the gross, which would amount to more than $100m.
†† Papers released by the Public Records Office in 1998 showed that third-class passengers were not locked below decks, as shown in the movie.
best picture; James Cameron (as director); Russell Carpenter; Peter Lamont; James Horner; Deborah Lynn Scott (costume); editing; visual effects; sound; sound effects editing; song 'My Heart Will Go On' (*m* James Horner, *ly* Will Jennings)
Kate Winslet; Gloria Stuart; make-up

Titanic Town *
GB 1998 100m colour
Pandora/BBC/British Screen/Company Pictures (George Faber, Charles Patterson)
In Belfast in the early 70s, a group of women band together to put an end to violence.
A semi-comic but ultimately downbeat account of the Irish troubles.
w Anne Devlin *novel* Mary Costello *d* Roger Michell *ph* John Daly *m* Trevor Jones *pd* Pat Campbell *ed* Kate Evans
☆ Julie Walters, Ciaran Hinds, Nuala O'Neill, James Loughran, Barry Loughran, Elizabeth Donaghy, Ciaran McMenamin, Jaz Pollock, Aingeal Grehan
'Caught in a no-man's land between gritty realism and upbeat, stylised comedy.' – *Sight and Sound*

The Titfield Thunderbolt ***
GB 1952 84m Technicolor
Ealing (Michael Truman)
When a branch railway line is threatened with closure, the villagers take it over as a private concern.
Undervalued on its release in the wake of other Ealing comedies, this now seems among the best of them as well as an immaculate colour production showing the England that is no more; the script has pace, the whole thing is brightly polished and the action works up to a fine climactic frenzy.
w T. E. B. Clarke *d* Charles Crichton *ph* Douglas Slocombe *m* Georges Auric
☆ *Stanley Holloway, George Relph*, John Gregson, Godfrey Tearle, *Edie Martin*, Naunton Wayne, Gabrielle Brune, Hugh Griffith, Sidney James, Jack MacGowran, Ewan Roberts, Reginald Beckwith

Title Shot
Canada 1979 98m Film House colour
Regenthall (Rob Iveson)
A troubled detective foils a crooked boxing manager, who will go to any lengths to make a killing.
Dull and diffuse drama, indifferently performed.
w John Saxton *story* Richard Gabourie *d* Les Rose *ph* Henri Fiks *m* Paul James Zaza *ad* Karen Bromley *ed* Ronald Sanders
☆ Tony Curtis, Richard Gabourie, Susan Hogan, Allan Royal, Robert Delbert, Natsuko Ohama

'If You Think Revenge Is Sweet, Taste This.'
'The Fall Of An Empire. The Descent Of A Man.'
Titus **
US 1999 162m DeLuxe Super 35
Fox Searchlight/Clear Blue Sky/Urania/NDF (Jody Patton, Conchita Airoldi, Julie Taymor)
A Roman general and the queen of the Goths become locked in a cycle of revenge and slaughter.
Shakespeare's bloodiest play is done in spectacular style that mixes modern and antique dress; often visually arresting and always well-spoken, it exerts an iron grip.
wd Julie Taymor *play* *Titus Andronicus* by William Shakespeare *ph* Luciano Tovoli *m* Elliot Goldenthal *pd* Dante Ferretti *ed* Françoise Bonnot *cos* Milena Canonero
☆ Anthony Hopkins (Titus Andronicus), Jessica Lange (Tamora), Alan Cumming (Saturninus), Colm Feore (Marcus), James Frain (Bassianus), Laura Fraser (Lavinia), Harry Lennix (Aaron), Angus Macfadyen (Lucius), Matthew Rhys (Demetrius), Jonathan Rhys Meyers (Chiron), Geraldine McEwan
'Since the play is hard going, credit is due for a provocative cinematic effort. Fascinating, challenging, but ugh-ly!' – *Empire*
Milena Canonero

To Be or Not to Be ****
US 1942 99m bw
Alexander Korda/Ernst Lubitsch
Warsaw actors get involved in an underground plot and an impersonation of invading Nazis, including Hitler.
Marvellous free-wheeling entertainment which starts as drama and descends through romantic comedy and suspense into farce; accused of bad taste at the time, but now seen as an outstanding example of Hollywood moonshine, kept alight through sheer talent and expertise.
w Edwin Justus Mayer *story* Ernst Lubitsch, Melchior Lengyel *d* Ernst Lubitsch *ph* Rudolph Maté *m* Werner Heymann *ad* Vincent Korda
☆ *Jack Benny, Carole Lombard*, Robert Stack, *Stanley Ridges, Felix Bressart, Lionel Atwill, Sig Rumann, Tom Dugan*, Charles Halton
TURA IN DISGUISE (JACK BENNY): 'That great, great Polish actor Joseph Tura – you must have heard of him.'
ERHARDT (SIG RUMANN): 'Ah, yes ... what he did to Shakespeare, we are now doing to Poland!'
ERHARDT (AND OTHERS): 'So they call me Concentration Camp Erhardt!'
'The comedy is hilarious, even when it is hysterically thrilling.' – *Commonweal*
'As effective an example of comic propaganda as *The Great Dictator* and far better directed.' – *Charles Higham, 1972*
'Based on an indiscretion, but undoubtedly a work of art.' – *James Agee*
'In any other medium it would be acknowledged as a classic to rank with *The Alchemist* or *A Modest Proposal*.' – *Peter Barnes*
'Lubitsch's comic genius and corrosive wit are displayed at every turn.' – *John Baxter*
'The actual business at hand ... is nothing less than providing a good time at the expense of

Nazi myth ... Lubitsch distinguishes the film's zanier moments with his customary mastery of sly humour and innuendo, and when the story calls for outright melodrama he is more than equal to the occasion.' – *Newsweek*

Werner Heymann

To Be or Not to Be

US 1983 107m DeLuxe

TCF/Brooksfilms (Mel Brooks)

Flat-footed remake of the above, with stagey sets, unconvincing acting (including the unnecessary addition of a gay dresser) and a leading comedian who won't stay still in case his lack of style should be noticed.

w Thomas Meehan, Ronny Graham *d* Alan Johnson *ph* Gerald Hirschfeld *m* John Morris *pd* Terence Marsh

☆ Mel Brooks, Anne Bancroft, Tim Matheson, Charles Durning, José Ferrer, George Gaynes, Christopher Lloyd, James Haake

Charles Durning

To Catch a Thief *

US 1955 97m Technicolor Vistavision

Paramount/Alfred Hitchcock

A famous cat burglar who has retired to the Riviera catches a thief who is imitating his old style.

Very slow, floppy and rather boring entertainment enlivened by the scenery and the odd Hitchcock touch.

w John Michael Hayes *novel* David Dodge *d* Alfred Hitchcock *ph* Robert Burks *m* Lyn Murray *ad* Hal Pereira, Joseph McMillan Johnson

☆ Cary Grant, Grace Kelly, *Jessie Royce Landis, John Williams*, Charles Vanel, Brigitte Auber

'Billed as a comedy-mystery, it stacks up as a drawn-out pretentious piece that seldom hits the comedy level.' – *Variety*

Robert Burks

art direction

'Don't let the frilly shirt fool you. This man can kill without stirring a ruffle.'

To Commit a Murder (dubbed)

France/West Germany/Italy 1967 91m Eastmancolor

Cinerama/SNEG/Gaumont/Waterview/Eichberg/Franca (Alan Poire)

original title: *Peau d'Espion*

A writer becomes involved in a plot to kidnap a nuclear scientist and take him to China.

Confused and confusing thriller, long on talk and short on action.

w Edouard Molinaro, Jacques Robert *novel Peau d'Espion* by Jacques Robert *d* Edouard Molinaro *ph* Raymond Le Moigne *m* José Berghmans *ad* Robert Clavel, Olivier Girard *ed* Robert Isnardon, Monique Isnardon

☆ Louis Jourdan, Senta Berger, Edmond O'Brien, Bernard Blier

'A sleepy espionage yarn which almost grinds to a halt at the halfway mark.' – *David McGillivray, Films and Filming*

'Ghost goes Camping!'

To Die For *

GB 1994 97m colour

TDF/London Lighthouse/British Screen (Gary Fitzpatrick)

The ghost of his lover, who died of AIDS, returns to haunt a promiscuous gay man.

An uneven film that, at times, is a witty and affecting account of a man coming to terms with himself and making peace with his past, though Slattery's comic-revue turn as an earnest council official detracts from its truth and emotional impact.

w Johnny Byrne *story* Paul McEvoy, Peter Mackenzie Litten *d* Peter Mackenzie Litten *ph* John Ward *m* Roger Bolton *ed* Jeffrey Arsenault

☆ Thomas Arklie, Ian Williams, Tony Slattery, Dillie Keane, Jean Boht, John Altman

'A film of many positive qualities that is neither smug nor sentimental. Overall, it is much more satisfying than the likes of *Philadelphia*, in which all issues readily fit into neat categories and resolutions.' – *Emanuel Levy, Variety*

'She knew what it took to get to the top. A lot of heart. And a little head.'

To Die For *

US 1995 107m Technicolor

Rank/Columbia (Laura Ziskin)

A fame-obsessed weather-woman on a local TV station describes how she got away with murdering her husband.

A deft satire on the worship of celebrity for its own sake and the way television can elevate the ordinary to heroic status, though it takes aim at an exceptionally easy target – a small-town girl – without managing to hit the bull's-eye.

w Buck Henry *novel* Joyce Maynard *d* Gus Van Sant *ph* Eric Alan Edwards *m* Danny Elfman *pd* Missy Stewart *ed* Curtiss Clayton

☆ Nicole Kidman, Matt Dillon, Joaquin Phoenix, Casey Affleck, Illeana Douglas, Dan Hedaya, Kurtwood Smith, Buck Henry, David Cronenberg, George Segal (uncredited)

'Witty, energetic and splendidly acted, this handcrafted curio will find support among the specialised, adventurous-minded audiences who have patronised the director's work in the past.' – *Todd McCarthy, Variety*

To Dorothy a Son

GB 1954 84m bw

British Lion/Welbeck/Independent (Peter rogers)

US title: *Cash on Delivery*

A composer stands to gain $2m from his former wife's uncle if he can have a son within a stipulated time.

Easy-going but stagey comedy that provides an occasional smile.

w Peter Rogers *play* Roger MacDougall *ph* Ernest Steward *m* Lambert Williamson *ad* George Provis *ed* Alfred Roome

☆ Shelley Winters (Myrtle La Mar), John Gregson (Tony Rapallo), Peggy Cummins (Dorothy Rapallo), Wilfrid Hyde-White (Mr Starke), Mona Washbourne (Nurse Appleby), Hal Osmond (Livingstone Potts), Hartley Power (Cy Daniel), Martin Miller (Brodcynsky), Nicholas Parsons (Clerk), Dorothy Bramhall (Secretary), Ronald Adam (Parsons), Alfie Bass (Cab Driver), Joan Sims (Telephonist), Charles Hawtrey (Potman)

'As long as there are lovers – this picture will live!' 'Paramount proudly brings to the screens of America one of the three great love stories of all time!'

To Each His Own **

US 1946 100m bw

Paramount (Charles Brackett)

During World War II, a middle-aged woman in London meets the soldier who is her own illegitimate and long-since-adopted son.

The woman's picture par excellence, put together with tremendous Hollywood flair and extremely enjoyable to watch.

w Charles Brackett, Jacques Théry d Mitchell Leisen *ph* Daniel L. Fapp *m Victor Young ad* Hans Dreier, Roland Anderson

☆ *Olivia de Havilland*, John Lund, Roland Culver, Mary Anderson, Philip Terry, Bill Goodwin, Virginia Welles, Virginia Horne

Olivia de Havilland

original story (Charles Brackett)

To Find a Man *

US 1971 93m Eastmancolor

Columbia/Rastar (Irving Pincus)

The spoiled daughter of a rich family becomes pregnant and is helped by a young chemist.

Quiet, well-made minor drama about maturity, with good small-town atmosphere.

w Arnold Schulman novel S. J. Wilson *d* Buzz Kulik *ph* Andy Laszlo *m* David Shire

☆ Pamela Martin, Darrell O'Connor, *Lloyd Bridges*, Phyllis Newman, Tom Ewell, Tom Bosley

To Have and Have Not **

US 1945 100m bw

Warner (Howard Hawks)

An American charter boat captain in Martinique gets involved with Nazis.

Fairly routinely made studio adventure notable for first pairing of Bogart and Bacall, as an imitation of Casablanca, *and for its consistent though not outstanding entertainment value. Remade later as* The Breaking Point *(qv) and* The Gun Runners *(qv), and not dissimilar from* Key Largo *(qv).*

w Jules Furthman, William Faulkner novel Ernest Hemingway *d Howard Hawks ph* Sid Hickox *m* Franz Waxman (uncredited) *md* Leo F. Forbstein

☆ *Humphrey Bogart, Lauren Bacall*, Walter Brennan, Hoagy Carmichael, Dolores Moran, Sheldon Leonard, Dan Seymour, Marcel Dalio

'Remarkable for the ingenuity and industry with which the original story and the individualities of Ernest Hemingway have been rendered down into Hollywood basic.' – *Richard Winnington*

'Sunlight on the lattice, sex in the corridors, a new pianist at the café, pistol shots, the fat Sureté man coming round after dark.' – *William Whitebait*

To Hell and Back

US 1955 106m Technicolor Cinemascope

U-I (Aaron Rosenberg)

The war career of America's most decorated infantryman.

Routine war story which happens to be about a fellow who later became a film star.

w Gil Doud *book* Audie Murphy *d* Jesse Hibbs *ph* Maury Gertsman *m* Joseph Gershenson

☆ *Audie Murphy*, Marshall Thompson, Charles Drake, Gregg Palmer, Jack Kelly, Paul Picerni, Susan Kohner

'The emotion is congealed and there is no real personal response to the anguish of war.' – *John Gillett*

To Joy **

Sweden 1950 98m bw

Svensk Filmindustri (Allan Ekelund)

original title: *Till Glädje*

After learning of his wife's accidental death, a provincial violinist remembers the pains and pleasures of their relationship.

A frequently bleak but essentially upbeat affirmation of survival in adversity, and of the satisfactions of maturity.

wd Ingmar Bergman *ph* Gunnar Fischer *m* Mendelssohn, Mozart, Smetana, Beethoven *ad* Nils Svenwall *ed* Oscar Rosander

☆ Maj-Britt Nilsson, Stig Olin, Victor Sjöström, Birger Malmsten, John Ekman, Margit Carlqvist, Sif Ruud

To Kill a Clown

GB 1971 104m DeLuxe

Palomar (Theodore Sills)

A painter and his wife move to a New England isle and are menaced by a crippled Vietnam veteran and his vicious dogs.

Pretentious, politically oriented rehash of The Most Dangerous Game *(qv), carefully made but too slow for suspense.*

w George Bloomfield, I. C. Rapoport *novel Master of the Hounds* by Algis Budrys *d* George Bloomfield *ph* Walter Lassally *m* Richard Hill, John Hawkins

☆ Alan Alda, Blythe Danner, Heath Lamberts, Eric Clavering

'It takes a traitor and a hero...'

To Kill A King *

GB/Germany 2003 102m Technicolor Panavision

Pathé/HanWay/FilmFour/Rockwood Edge/Future/Natural Nylon (Kevin Loader)

In England at the end of the Civil War, Oliver Cromwell and General Fairfax, leader of the parliamentary army, clash over the fate of the defeated King Charles I.

Intriguing political drama of a pivotal moment in English history; it is a little short on action and spectacle but gives space to the political debate that still resonates today.

w Jenny Mayhew *d* Mike Barker *ph* Eigil Bryld *m* Richard G. Mitchell *pd* Sophie Becher *ed* Guy Bensley

☆ Tim Roth (Oliver Cromwell), Dougray Scott (Thomas Fairfax), Rupert Everett (Charles I), Olivia Williams (Lady Anne), James Bolam (Holles), Corin Redgrave (Lord de Vere), Finbar Lynch (Cousin Henry)

'A decent and honourable film that, unfashionably in contemporary cinema, shows some interest in ideas and how they function in public life.' – *Philip French, Observer*

To Kill a Mockingbird **

US 1962 129m bw

U-I (Alan Pakula)

A lawyer in a small Southern town defends a black man accused of rape.

Familiar dollops of social conscience, very well presented with a child interest and excellent atmosphere, but a mite overlong.

w Horton Foote *novel* Harper Lee *d Robert Mulligan ph* Russell Harlan *m* Elmer Bernstein

☆ *Gregory Peck, Mary Badham*, Philip Alford, John Megna, Frank Overton, Rosemary Murphy, Ruth White, Brock Peters

† The narrator is Kim Stanley.

script; Gregory Peck

best picture; Robert Mulligan; Russell Harlan; Elmer Bernstein; Mary Badham

To Kill a Priest

France/US 1988 113m colour

J. P. Productions/FR3/Sofica Valor (Jean-Pierre Alessandri)

A militant Polish priest runs foul of the local police chief.

Vaguely based on the life and death of Father Jerzy Popieluszko, a proponent of trade unions, it fails to make explicit the political and ideological events it attempts to portray.

w Agnieszka Holland, Jean-Yves Pitoun *d* Agnieszka Holland *ph* Adam Holender *pd* Emile Ghigo *ed* Herve de Luze

☆ Christophe Lambert, Ed Harris, Joss Ackland, Tim Roth, Timothy Spall, Peter Postlethwaite, Cherie Lunghi, Joanne Whalley, David Suchet

To Live **

Hong Kong 1994 125m colour

Electric/Century/Era/Shanghai Film Studios (Chiu Fu-sheng)

original title: *Huozhe*

Thirty years in the lives of a Chinese couple living through the Communist revolution and subsequent upheavals.

An engrossing domestic saga of survival, celebrating fortitude and humour but less compelling than the director's earlier films.

w Yu Hua, Lu Wei *novel* Lu Wei *d* Zhang Yimou *ph* Lu Yue *m* Zhao Jiping *ad* Cao Jiuping *ed* Du Yuan

☆ *Ge You*, Gong Li, Niu Ben, Guo Tao, Jiang Wu, Ni Dabong

'A well-crafted but in no way earth-shaking entry in the helmer's oeuvre.' – *Variety*

best foreign film

To Live and Die in L.A.

US 1985 116m Technicolor

MGM-UA/New Century/SLM/Irving H. Levin

A secret service agent nails the counterfeiter who killed his partner.

High-gloss, foul-mouthed, hysterical crime melo, a kind of west coast French Connection.

w William Friedkin, Gerald Petievich *novel* Gerald Petievich *d* William Friedkin *ph* Robby Muller *m* Wang Chung *pd* Lilly Kilvert *ed* Scott Smith

☆ William L. Petersen, Willem Dafoe, John Pankow, Debra Feuer, Dean Stockwell, John Turturro, Darlanne Fluegel

'The intense vulgarity of the characters and virtuoso stylistic overkill will turn off mainstream audiences.' – *Variety*

To Mary with Love

US 1936 87m bw

TCF

A businessman thinks back affectionately over ten years of married life.

Harmless romantic comedy-drama.

w Richard Sherman, Howard Ellis Smith *d* John Cromwell

☆ Warner Baxter, Myrna Loy, Ian Hunter, Claire Trevor, Jean Dixon

To Our Loves *
France 1983 102m colour
Les Films Du Livradois/Gaumont/FR3 (Micheline Pialat)
original title: *A Nos Amours*
A teenage girl, whose parents are splitting up, looks for love and settles for promiscuity.
Domestic misery from a specialist in teenage angst.
w Arlette Langmann, Maurice Pialat *d* Maurice Pialat *ph* Jacques Loiseleux *ed* Yann Dedet
☆ Sandrine Bonnaire, Evelyne Ker, Dominique Besnehard, Maurice Pialat, Christophe Odent

To Please a Lady *
US 1950 91m bw
MGM (Clarence Brown)
A ruthless midget-car racer falls for the lady journalist who is hounding him.
Good action programmer with no frills.
w Barre Lyndon, Marge Decker *d* Clarence Brown *ph* Harold Rosson *m* Bronislau Kaper
☆ Clark Gable, Barbara Stanwyck, Adolphe Menjou, Will Geer, Roland Winters, Emory Parnell, Frank Jenks

'A story as fresh as the girls in their minis!'
To Sir with Love
GB 1967 105m Technicolor
Columbia (James Clavell)
A West Indian teacher comes to a tough East End school.
Sentimental non-realism patterned after The Blackboard Jungle *but much softer; its influence led to a TV situation comedy,* Please Sir.
wd James Clavell *novel* E. R. Braithwaite *ph* Paul Beeson *m* Ron Grainer
☆ Sidney Poitier, Christian Roberts, Judy Geeson, Suzy Kendall, Lulu, Faith Brook, Geoffrey Bayldon, Patricia Routledge
'The sententious script sounds as if it has been written by a zealous Sunday school teacher after a particularly exhilarating boycott of South African oranges.' – *MFB*

To Sleep with Anger **
US 1990 102m CFI color
Metro/SVS Films (Caldecott Chubb, Thomas S. Byrnes, Darin Scott)
A black family which has moved from the South to Los Angeles finds itself in trouble when an old friend visits with stories of the past.
Engrossing drama of social disintegration.
wd Charles Burnett *ph* Walt Lloyd *m* Stephen James Taylor *pd* Penny Barrett *ed* Nancy Richardson
☆ Danny Glover, Paul Butler, Mary Alice, Carl Lumbly, Vonetta McGee, Richard Brooks, Sheryl Lee Ralph, Ethel Ayler, Julius Harris
'With a whole string of superb performances, dialogue that manages the difficult trick of hitting notes both lyrical and earthy, and a magical gospel and blues score, it demonstrates Burnett's instinct for cinema every inch of the way.' – *Tom Milne, MFB*

To Telefteo Psemma: see *A Matter of Dignity*

'It's more than just a sport. It's survival.'
To the Death
US 1991 86m Agfacolor
Cannon/Distant Horizon/Tangent (Anant Singh)
A retired kick-boxing champion is lured back into the ring by a corrupt gambler who organizes private fights in which the loser is shot.
Numbingly predictable nonsense, acted and directed with the sensitivity of a boot in the face. The dialogue seems to have strayed from a Victorian melodrama.
w Greg Latter *story* Darrell James Roodt, Greg Latter *d* Darrell James Roodt *ph* Mark Vicente *m* Frank Becker *pd* David Barkham *ed* Davedd Heitner
☆ John Barrett, Michel Qissi, Robert Whitehead, Michèle Bestbier, Greg Latter
HUSBAND TO WIFE SURPRISED IN BED WITH ANOTHER MAN: 'Why? Why? Why? Oh God! I give you everything your heart desires and this is how you repay me!'

To the Devil a Daughter
GB/Germany 1976 93m Technicolor
EMI/Hammer-Terra Filmkunst (Roy Skeggs)
An occult novelist is asked to take care of a girl who has been 'promised' to a group of Satanists.
Confusingly told, high camp diabolic thriller.
w Chris Wicking *novel* Dennis Wheatley *d* Peter Sykes *ph* David Watkin *m* Paul Glass *ad* Don Picton *ed* John Trumper *sp* Les Bowie
☆ Richard Widmark, Christopher Lee, Denholm Elliott, Honor Blackman, Michael Goodliffe, Anthony Valentine, Derek Francis, Nastassja Kinski

To the Ends of the Earth **
US 1948 107m bw
Columbia (Sidney Buchman)
A government agent follows a world-wide trail after a narcotics gang.
Thoroughly riveting conventional thriller, nicely made and photographed.
w Jay Richard Kennedy *d Robert Stevenson ph Burnett Guffey m* George Duning
☆ Dick Powell, Signe Hasso, Ludwig Donath, Vladimir Sokoloff, Edgar Barrier

To the Shores of Tripoli
US 1942 82m Technicolor
TCF (Milton Sperling)
A cocky playboy becomes a tough marine.
Despite the title, this modest flagwaver with romantic trimmings never moves out of the San Diego training grounds.
w Lamar Trotti *d* H. Bruce Humberstone *ph* Edward Cronjager *m* Alfred Newman
☆ Maureen O'Hara, John Payne, Randolph Scott, Nancy Kelly, William Tracy, Maxie Rosenbloom, Henry Morgan, Russell Hicks, Minor Watson
🏆 cinematography

To the Starry Island
South Korea 1994 102m colour
Park Kwang-Su/Samsung Nices/Channel 4
A poet, returning for a funeral to the small island community where he was born, remembers the tragic wartime events of 40 years earlier.
Simply told story of rural life that takes a long time to get to the point.
w Lee Chang-Dong, Park Kwang-Su *novel* Im Chul-Woo *d* Park Kwang-Su *ph* Yoo Young-Gil *m* Song Hong-Sup *ed* Kim Hyun
☆ Ahn Sung-Ki, Moon Sung-Keun, Shim Hae-Jin, Ahn So-Young, Lee Yong-Yi, Im Chul-Woo, Kim Yong-Man, Hur June-Ho, Choi Hyung-In, Lee Kyung-Young, Myung Kae-Nam

To the Victor: see *Owd Bob (1938)*

To the Victor
US 1948 100m bw
Warner (Jerry Wald)
French collaborators stand trial for war crimes.
Glum melodrama with inadequate cast.
w Richard Brooks *d* Delmer Daves *ph* Robert Burks *m* David Buttolph
☆ Dennis Morgan, Viveca Lindfors, Bruce Bennett, Victor Francen, Dorothy Malone, Tom d'Andrea, Eduardo Ciannelli, Joseph Buloff, Luis Van Rooten, William Conrad

To Trap a Spy
US 1966 92m Metrocolor
MGM (Norman Felton)
American secret agents protect an African diplomat from being killed.
An extended version of the pilot for the television series The Man from U.N.C.L.E.; *despite it, they still went ahead with more episodes.*
w Sam Rolfe *d* Don Medford *ph* Joseph Biroc *m* Jerry Goldsmith *ad* George W. Davis, Merrill Pye *ed* Henry Berman
☆ Robert Vaughn, David McCallum, Luciana Paluzzi, Patricia Crowley, Fritz Weaver, Will Kuluva, Leo G. Carroll

To Walk With Lions
GB/Canada/Kenya 1998 108m colour Cinemascope
Kingsborough Greenlight (Pieter Kroonenburg, Julie Allan)
Lion expert George Adamson's private wildlife park in Kenya is threatened with closure by the authorities, while bandits roam nearby.
Simple-minded drama of a man at the end of his tether and life, given a little vitality by Richard Harris's performance.
w Keith Ross Leckie *d* Carl Schultz *ph* Jean Lepine *m* Alan Reeves *ad* Michael Devine *ed* Angelo Corrao
☆ Richard Harris (George Adamson), John Michie (Tony Fitzjohn), Ian Bannen (Terence Adamson), Kerry Fox (Lucy Jackson), Hugh Quarshie (Maxwell), Honor Blackman (Joy Adamson), Geraldine Chaplin (Victoria Andrecelli)
'Handsomely fills almost-empty niche of ripping yarn with both family appeal and serious adult undertones.' – *Ken Eisner, Variety*
'Stilted and didactic, this is thoroughly forgettable.' – *Edward Porter, Sunday Times*
† George and Joy Adamson's adventures with lions were the subject of two other films, *Born Free* 66, and *Living Free* 72.

To What Red Hell
GB 1929 100m bw
Strand/Twickenham
A young epileptic kills a prostitute and is protected by his mother.
Unpalatable melodrama which failed to be as significant as it wished.
w Leslie Hiscott *play* Percy Robinson *d* Edwin Greenwood *ph* Basil Emmott
☆ Sybil Thorndike, John Hamilton, Bramwell Fletcher, Janice Adair

'Attitude Is Everything'
'This Time Snipes and Swayze Face Their Toughest Enemy. Stubble.'
To Wong Foo, Thanks for Everything, Julie Newmar
US 1995 108m DeLuxe
UIP/Universal/Amblin (G. Mac Brown)
Three drag queens, driving to Los Angeles from New York, break down in a small town where they solve the locals' problems.
Tiresome comedy that seems to think it enough to dress its macho stars in women's clothing.
w Douglas Carter Beane *d* Beeban Kidron *ph* Steve Mason *m* Rachel Portman *pd* Wynn Thomas *ed* Andrew Mondshein
☆ Wesley Snipes, Patrick Swayze, John Leguizamo, Stockard Channing, Blythe Danner, Arliss Howard, Jason London, Chris Penn, RuPaul, Naomi Campbell

The Toast of New Orleans
US 1950 97m Technicolor
MGM (Joe Pasternak)
A Bayou villager becomes a star of the New Orleans opera.
Very ordinary setting for a new singing star.
w Sy Gomberg, George Wells *d* Norman Taurog *ph* William Snyder *md* George Stoll *ch* Eugene Loring
☆ Kathryn Grayson, David Niven, Mario Lanza, J. Carrol Naish, James Mitchell, Richard Hageman, Clinton Sundberg, Sig Arno
'Sheer excruciation.' – *Pauline Kael, New Yorker*
🏆 song 'Be My Love' (*m* Nicholas Brodszky, *ly* Sammy Cahn)

'The screen sensation of a decade, played by a galaxy of stars in a hell-bent world of wine and women!'
The Toast of New York **
US 1937 109m bw
RKO (Edward Small)
A 19th-century medicine showman becomes a notorious Wall Street financier.
Smart biopic of Jim Fisk; good entertainment with accomplished production.
w Dudley Nichols, John Twist, Joel Sayre *d* Rowland V. Lee *ph* Peverell Marley *m* Nathaniel Shilkret
☆ *Edward Arnold, Cary Grant,* Frances Farmer, Jack Oakie, Donald Meek, Clarence Kolb, Thelma Leeds
'Making no pretence for serious consideration as a faithful and accurate reflection of life and manners in the period it depicts, it rates as a piece of hokum aimed at the box office. It will do business.' – *Variety*

Toast of the Legion: see *Kiss Me Again (1931)*

Tobacco Road ***
US 1941 84m bw
TCF (Darryl F. Zanuck)
Poor whites in Georgia are turned off their land.
This bowdlerized version of a sensational book and play has superbly orchestrated farcical scenes separated by delightfully pictorial quieter moments: it isn't what was intended, but in its own way it's quite marvellous.
w Nunnally Johnson play Jack Kirkland *novel Erskine Caldwell d John Ford ph Arthur Miller m David Buttolph*
☆ *Charley Grapewin, Elizabeth Patterson,* Dana Andrews, Gene Tierney, *Marjorie Rambeau,* Ward Bond, William Tracy, Zeffie Tilbury, Slim Summerville, Grant Mitchell, Russell Simpson, Spencer Charters

Tobe Hooper's Night Terrors
US 1993 94m colour
Cannon/Global (Harry Alan Towers)
aka: *Tobe Hooper's Nightmare*
In Alexandria, the silly daughter of an archaeologist begins to read the work of the Marquis de Sade, has erotic fantasies and is kidnapped by his depraved descendant.
Drear, minimal-budget horror of little interest to anyone; for no particular purpose, the action cuts between the 1700s, with scenes of de Sade enjoying being tortured in prison, and the 1990s; neither setting entertains, though masochists might enjoy the movie.
w Daniel Matmor, Rom Globus *d* Tobe Hooper *ph* Amnon Solomon *m* Dov Seltzer *ad* Yossi Peled *ed* Alain Jakubowicz *sp* make-up: David B. Miller
☆ Robert Englund, Zoe Trilling, Alona Kimhi, Juliano Merr, Chandra West, William Finley
'Bilge.' – *Sight and Sound*
† Tobe Hooper took over the film when the original director, Gerry O'Hara, went to work on another movie. It was originally going to be set in the 1920s, but suitable props and locations could not be found for the Egyptian scenes, shot in Israel, so it was updated to the present day.

Tobruk
US 1967 110m Techniscope
Universal/Corman/Gibraltar (Gene Corman)
During the North African war, a British major and some German Jews try to blow up the Nazi fuel bunkers.
Routine war adventure, quite tough and spectacular but undistinguished.
w Leo V. Gordon *d* Arthur Hiller *ph* Russell Harlan *m* Bronislau Kaper *ad* Alexander Golitzen, Henry Bumstead *ed* Robert C. Jones
☆ Rock Hudson, George Peppard, Nigel Green, Guy Stockwell, Jack Watson, Liam Redmond, Leo Gordon, Norman Rossington, Percy Herbert
🏆 special effects

Toby Tyler *
US 1959 96m Technicolor
Walt Disney (Bill Walsh)
In 1910, a young orphan runs away to join a travelling circus in the midwest, and with the help of a chimp becomes a famous star.
Acceptable, predictable family fare.
w Bill Walsh, Lillie Hayward *novel* James Otis Kaler *d* Charles Barton *ph* William Snyder *m* Buddy Baker
☆ Kevin Corcoran, Henry Calvin, Gene Sheldon, Bob Sweeney, James Drury

Today It's Me, Tomorrow You! *
Italy 1968 95m Technicolor
PAC/Splendid (Franco Cucca)
original title: *Oggi a Me ... Domani a Te!*
An Indian recruits a gang of gunmen in order to take vengeance on the man who raped and murdered his wife and framed him for the crime.
Spaghetti Western in the style of The Magnificent Seven.
w Dario Argento, Tonino Cervi *d* Tonino Cervi *ph* Sergio D'Offizi *m* Angelo Francesco Lavagnini *ad* Carlo Gervasi *ed* Sergio Montanari
☆ Montgomery Ford (Brett Halsey), Bud Spencer (Carlo Pedersoli), William Berger, Tatsuya Nakadai, Wayde Preston, Stanley Gordon

Today We Live *
US 1933 113m bw
MGM (Howard Hawks)
During World War I, an aristocratic English girl and her three lovers all find themselves at the front, and two fail to return.
Stilted romantic melodrama with imposing credentials.
w Edith Fitzgerald, Dwight Taylor, William Faulkner *story Turnabout* by William Faulkner
d Howard Hawks *ph* Oliver T. Marsh
☆ Joan Crawford, Gary Cooper, Robert Young, Franchot Tone, Roscoe Karns, Louise Closser Hale, Rollo Lloyd
'One of those overly long features which would serve the purpose better in 2000 or more less feet ... but the action, the men and the Crawford name should translate into satisfying figures.' – *Variety*
† Much of the flying footage was taken from the *Hell's Angels* stock.

The Todd Killings *
US 1970 93m Technicolor Panavision
National General (Barry Shear)
In a small American town, a 23-year-old boy starts out on a rampage of rape and murder.
Violent psychological melodrama, based on fact, with inventive direction.
w Dennis Murphy, Joel Oliansky *d Barry Shear*
ph Harold E. Stine *m* Leonard Rosenman
☆ Robert F. Lyons, Richard Thomas, Belinda Montgomery, Barbara Bel Geddes, Gloria Grahame
'The most striking of the many recent film versions of the souring of the American dream.' – *Tony Rayns*

'Ever get the feeling you're being watched?'
Todo Sobre Mi Madre ***
Spain/France 1999 101m colour Panavision
Pathé/El Deseo/France2/Via Digital (Agustin Almodovar)
aka: *All About My Mother*
After the death of her teenage son, an actress and single mother goes in search of the boy's father, a transsexual prostitute.
Drawing on the themes of All About Eve *and* A Streetcar Named Desire, *this is an engrossing melodrama of love and death, the difference between real and imagined emotions, the kindness of strangers and the waywardness of life.*
wd Pedro Almodóvar ph Affonso Beato
m Alberto Iglesias *ad* Antxon Gomez *ed* Jose Salcedo
☆ *Cecilia Roth* (Manuela), Eloy Azorin (Esteban), *Marisa Paredes* (Huma Rojo), Penelope Cruz (Sister Rosa), Candela Pena (Nina), *Antonia San Juan* (La Agrado), Rosa Maria Sarda (Rosa's Mother), Toni Canto (Lola, La Pionera)
'Weaves a silky web of emotional truths wrapped up in a shimmering cascade of glossy photography, glamorous close-ups and glorious acting from the cream of Spanish cinema.' – *Alan Jones, Film Review*
foreign film
Pedro Almodovar (as director); foreign film

Together: see *Tillsammans*

Together Again
US 1944 93m bw
Columbia (Virginia Van Upp)
The widow of a New England mayor commissions a statue in his honour. The title refers to the reteaming of the stars who were so popular in *Love Affair* and *When Tomorrow Comes*, which is a sign of the lack of invention elsewhere.
A comedy without laughs.
w Virginia Van Upp, F. Hugh Herbert *d* Charles Vidor *ph* Joseph Walker *m* Werner Heymann
☆ Charles Boyer, Irene Dunne, Charles Coburn, Mona Freeman, Jerome Courtland, Elizabeth Patterson, Charles Dingle, Walter Baldwin

Tokyo Cowboy
Canada 1994 94m colour/bw
Big Space (Lodi Butler, Richard Davis)
A Japanese man goes to Canada to meet his female pen-friend and live his fantasy of becoming a cowboy.
Leisurely, almost inert, drama of small-town life, family tensions and lesbian love, interspersed with Western parodies.
w Caroline Adderson *d* Kathy Garneau
ph Kenneth Hewlett *m* Ari Wise *ed* Debra Rurak
☆ Hiromoto Ida, Christianne Hirt, Janne Mortil, Anna Ferguson, Alec Willows, Michael Ironside, Christine Lippa, Dwight McFee

Tokyo Drifter **
Japan 1966 83m colour Nikkatsu-Scope
Nikkatsu (Nakagawa Tetsuro)
original title: *Tokyo Nagaremono*
aka: *The Man from Tokyo*
A hitman goes on the run around Japan, followed by killers hired by his former boss.
An enjoyably delirious thriller in which virtually anything goes, including a parody of a bar brawl straight out of a John Wayne Western. It has an exotic appeal, together with a flamboyant visual style.
w Kawauchi Yasunori *novel* Kawauchi Yasunori
d Suzuki Seijun ph Mine Shigeyoshi *m* Kaburagi So *ad* Kimura Takeo *ed* Inoue Shinya
☆ Watari Tetsuya, Matsubara Chieko, Nitani Hideaki, Kita Ryuji, Yoshida Tsuyoshi, Esumi Hideaki, Kawachi Tamio, Cho Hiroshi
'A barrage of aestheticised violence, visual gags, incongruous songs and hairdryers and mind-warping colour effects. This is a reckless reduction of the yazuka genre to its most fundamental elements, strung together with only the most minimal regard for logic or even narrative coherence.' – *Tony Rayns*

'The Self Is The Ultimate Horror.'
Tokyo Fist **
Japan 1995 88m colour
Blue Dolphin/Kaijyu (Shinya Tsukamoto)
An insurance salesman renews his friendship with a school-friend, now a boxer, which results in beatings and the loss of his girlfriend.
A curiously cold, hard-hitting work that will not be to everyone's taste; but its account of violence within a rigid society and between the sexes has a ritualistic power.
wd Shinya Tsukamoto *ph* Shinya Tsukamoto
m Chu Ishikawa *ad* Shinya Tsukamoto
ed Shinya Tsukamoto, Konno Naoto
☆ Kahori Fujii, Shinya Tsukamoto, Kohji Tsukamoto, Naomasa Musaka, Naoto Takenaka
'It suggests that technology has taken over our psyches, and it appears both impassioned and silly at the same time.' – *Derek Malcolm, Guardian*

Tokyo Joe
US 1949 88m bw
Columbia/Santana (Robert Lord)
A former night-club owner returns to postwar Japan to reclaim his fortune and his ex-wife.
Dispirited star melodrama.
w Cyril Hume, Bertram Millhauser *d* Stuart Heisler *ph* Charles Lawton Jnr *m* George Antheil
☆ Humphrey Bogart, Florence Marly, Alexander Knox, Sessue Hayakawa, Lora Lee Michel, Jerome Courtland

Tokyo Monogatari: see *Tokyo Story*

Tokyo Nagaremono: see *Tokyo Drifter*

Tokyo Pop
US 1988 99m TVC Color
Fries/Spectrafilm/Lorimar/Kuzui (Kaz Kuzui, Joel Tuber)
A backing singer in a New York punk rock group goes to Tokyo in search of fame.
Mildly entertaining tale of cultural cross-over.
w Fran Rubel Kuzui, Lynn Grossman *d* Fran Rubel Kuzui *ph* James Hayman *m* Alan Brewer
pd Terumi Hosoishi *ed* Camilla Toniolo
☆ Carrie Hamilton, Yutaka Tadokoro, Daisuke Oyama, Hiroshi Kabayashi, Hiroshi Sugita, Satoshi Kanai.

Tokyo Story ****
Japan 1953 135m bw
Shochiku
original title: *Tokyo Monogatari*
An elderly couple, who travel to Tokyo to visit their married son and daughter, discover that their children have little time for them.
Bleak, austere and moving family drama of life's disappointments.
w Kogo Noda, Yasujiro Ozu *d Yasujiro Ozu*
ph Yuharu Atsuta *m* Kojun Saito *ad* Tatsuo Hamada *ed* Yoshiyasu Hamamura
☆ *Chishu Ryu, Chieko Higashiyama*, Setsuko Hara, Haruko Sugimura, Nobuo Nakamura, So Yamamura, Kuniko Miyake, Eijiro Tono

Tol'able David *
US 1921 80m approx (24 fps) bw silent
First National/Inspiration
A quiet farming community is disrupted by three marauding convicts, who are finally despatched by the peace-loving youngest son.
Fresh, sympathetic David-and-Goliath story which was a huge popular success on its release.
w Edmund Goulding, Henry King *novel* Joseph Hergesheimer *d Henry King ph* Henry Cronjager
☆ *Richard Barthelmess*, Gladys Hulette, Ernest Torrence, Warner Richmond
'It is sentimental in places, but not sloppy. It is bucolic, but its rusticity is not rubbed in ... it is restrained, imaginatively suggestive when not briefly literal. For all these reasons it is stimulating.' – *New York Times*
† Columbia remade the story in 1930 with Richard Cromwell, but its time had passed.

Tom and Huck
US 1996 92m Technicolor Panavision
Buena Vista/Walt Disney (Laurence Mark, John Baldecchi)
Two young witnesses to a murder attempt to clear the innocent man accused of the crime.
Blandly amiable version that manages a modicum of scares and suspense without being in any way memorable.
w Stephen Sommers, David Loughery *novel The Adventures of Tom Sawyer* by Mark Twain *d* Peter Hewitt *ph* Bobby Bukowski *m* Stephen Endelman *pd* Gemma Jackson *ed* David Freeman
☆ Jonathan Taylor Thomas, Brad Renfro, Eric Schweig, Charles Rocket, Amy Wright, Michael McShane, Marian Seldes, Rachael Leigh Cook
'Unremarkable but inoffensive.' – *Variety*

Tom and Jerry: The Movie
US 1992 84m CFI color
First Independent/Turner/WMG (Phil Roman)
Tom and Jerry, left homeless, become the best of friends.
A lacklustre cartoon, which replaces the inspired mayhem of the classic shorts with sickly sweetness.
w Dennis Marks *d* Phil Roman *m* Henry Mancini *ed* Julie Ann Gustafson
☆ Featuring the voices of Richard Kind, Dana Hill, Anndi McAfee, Henry Gibson, Tony Jay
'Though slickly animated, this first full-length pic featuring the vintage cat and mouse is misconceived from start to finish. Full of gooey sentimentality in a banal melodramatic plot.' – *Variety*

Tom and Viv *
GB/US 1994 125m Technicolor
Entertainment/Samuelson/Harvey Kass/IRS/British Screen
The unhappy marriage of the poet T. S. Eliot and his first wife, Vivienne Haigh-Wood, whose behaviour causes him increasing embarrassment.
Glossy period movie that only occasionally gets to grips with its fascinating subject-matter.
w Michael Hastings, Adrian Hodges *play* Michael Hastings *d* Brian Gilbert *ph* Martin Fuhrer
m Debbie Wiseman *pd* Jamie Leonard *ed* Tony Lawson
☆ Willem Dafoe, Miranda Richardson, Rosemary Harris, Tim Dutton, Nickolas Grace, Philip Locke
'A handsomely appointed but overly starched love story that attains real clout only in the final reel ... a well-meaning but noble failure.' – *Derek Elley*
Miranda Richardson; Rosemary Harris

Tom Brown of Culver
US 1932 79m bw
Universal
Life at a military cadet school.
Idealized propaganda, with the hero a boy subsidized by the local legion because his dead father was a war hero.
w Tom Buckingham *d* William Wyler
☆ Tom Brown, H. B. Warner, Slim Summerville, Richard Cromwell, Ben Alexander, Sidney Toler, Betty Blythe
'It will probably make acceptable film fare to other than irritated cadets.' – *Variety*

Tom Brown's Schooldays *
US 1940 86m bw
(RKO) The Play's the Thing (Brian Desmond Hurst)
Tom Brown finds life at Rugby brutal, but helps to become a civilizing influence.
Pretty lively Hollywood version of a rather unattractive semi-classic.
w Walter Ferris, Frank Cavell *novel* Thomas Hughes *d* Robert Stevenson *ph* Nicholas Musuraca *m* Anthony Collins
☆ Jimmy Lydon, Cedric Hardwicke, Billy Halop, Freddie Bartholomew, Gale Storm, Josephine Hutchinson

Tom Brown's Schooldays
GB 1951 96m bw
Talisman (George Minter)
Unexciting remake featuring one surprisingly strong performance.
w Noel Langley *d* Gordon Parry *ph* C. Pennington-Richards *m* Richard Addinsell
☆ *Robert Newton*, John Howard Davies, Diana Wynyard, Francis de Wolff, Kathleen Byron, Hermione Baddeley, James Hayter, Rachel Gurney, Amy Veness, Max Bygraves, Michael Hordern, John Charlesworth, John Forrest
'An odd mixture of the brutal and the solemnly improving.' – *Richard Mallett, Punch*

Tom, Dick and Harry **
US 1941 86m bw
RKO (Robert Sisk)
A girl daydreams about her three boyfriends, but can't make up her mind.
Brightly-handled comedy which became a minor classic but does seem to have faded a little. Remade as The Girl Most Likely *(qv).*
w Paul Jarrico d Garson Kanin ph Merritt Gerstad
m Roy Webb
☆ *Ginger Rogers, Burgess Meredith*, Alan Marshal, George Murphy, *Phil Silvers*, Joe Cunningham, Jane Seymour, Lenore Lonergan
'Foot by foot the best made picture of this year.' – *Otis Ferguson*
Paul Jarrico

Tom Horn
US 1979 97m Technicolor Panavision
Warner/Solar/First Artists (Fred Weintraub)
An ex-cavalry scout gets a job as a stock detective, is framed for murder, and allows himself to be hanged.
Curious pessimistic and unsatisfactory semi-Western in which the star was found to have lost his old charisma after being too long away.
w Thomas McGuane, Bud Shrake, from the alleged autobiography of Tom Horn *d* William Wiard *ph* John Alonzo *m* Ernest Gold
☆ Steve McQueen, Linda Evans, Richard Farnsworth, Billy Green Bush, Slim Pickens, Elisha Cook Jnr
'Imagine a film that opens up with dialogue that can't be heard at all, then proceeds to build up to a fist fight that's never seen, that cuts away to sunsets to fill in other scenes that have no dramatic point, that presents a meal where the sound of knives and forks drowns out what's being said, and you have just the beginning of what's wrong with *Tom Horn*.' – *Variety*

'The whole world loves him!'

Tom Jones ****
GB 1963 129m Eastmancolor
UA/Woodfall (Tony Richardson)

In 18th-century England a foundling is brought up by the squire and marries his daughter after many adventures.
Fantasia on Old England, at some distance from the original novel, with the director trying every possible jokey approach against a meticulously realistic physical background. Despite trade fears, the Hellzapoppin style made it an astonishing box-office success (the sex helped), though it quickly lost its freshness and was much imitated.
w John Osborne *novel* Henry Fielding *d* Tony Richardson *ph* Walter Lassally, Manny Wynn *m* John Addison *pd* Ralph Brinton
☆ Albert Finney, Susannah York, Hugh Griffith, Edith Evans, Joan Greenwood, Diane Cilento, George Devine, Joyce Redman, David Warner, Wilfrid Lawson, Freda Jackson, Rachel Kempson
'Uncertainty, nervousness, muddled method ... desperation is writ large over it.' – *Stanley Kauffmann*
'Much of the time it looks like a home movie, made with sporadic talent by a group with more enthusiasm than discipline.' – *Tom Milne*
'It is as though the camera had become a method actor: there are times when you wish you could buy, as on certain juke boxes, five minutes' silence ... Obviously a film which elicits such lyric ejaculations from the reviewers cannot be all good.' – *John Simon*
'I just felt I was being used. I wasn't involved ... I was bored most of the time.' – *Albert Finney*
† The narrator was Michael MacLiammoir.
best picture; John Osborne; Tony Richardson; John Addison
Albert Finney; Hugh Griffith; Edith Evans; Diane Cilento; Joyce Redman; production design
best picture; best British film; John Osborne

Tom Sawyer
US 1973 103m DeLuxe Panavision
UA/Readers Digest (Arthur P. Jacobs)

Reverential, rather tediously over-produced version for family audiences of the seventies, with brief songs and real Mississippi locations.
d Don Taylor *ph* Frank Stanley *md* John Williams *pd* Philip Jefferies *w/m/ly* Richard and Robert Sherman
☆ Johnnie Whitaker, Celeste Holm, Warren Oates, Jeff East, Jodie Foster
† There had been a version with Jackie Coogan in 1930. Selznick's *The Adventures of Tom Sawyer* followed in 1937. In 1939 Billy Cook was Tom Sawyer, Detective, with Donald O'Connor as Huckleberry Finn.
Richard and Robert Sherman; John Williams

Tom Thumb *
GB 1958 98m Eastmancolor
MGM/Galaxy (George Pal)

A tiny forest boy outwits a couple of thieves.
Slight musical built round the legend of a two-inch boy; good trickwork and songs make it a delightful film for children.
w Ladislas Fodor *d* George Pal *ph* Georges Périnal *m* Douglas Gamley, Kenneth V. Jones *sp* Tom Howard
☆ Russ Tamblyn, Jessie Matthews, Peter Sellers, Terry-Thomas, Alan Young, June Thorburn, Bernard Miles, Ian Wallace
† Donald O'Connor badly wanted the role, but it went to the MGM contractee.
special effects

Tomahawk
US 1951 82m Technicolor
Universal-International (Leonard Goldstein)

GB title: *Battle of Powder River*
An Indian scout helps the Sioux to get their territory rights.
Competent small-scale Western.
w Silvia Richards, Maurice Geraghty *story* Daniel Jarrett *d* George Sherman *ph* Charles P. Boyle *m* Hans J. Salter *ad* Bernard Herzbrun, Richard H. Riedel *ed* Danny B. Landres
☆ Van Heflin (Jim Bridger), Yvonne de Carlo (Julie Madden), Alex Nicol (Lt Rob Dancy), Preston Foster (Col Carrington), Jack Oakie (Sol Beckworth), Tom Tully (Dan Costello), Rock Hudson (Burt Hanna), Susan Cabot (Monahseetah)

The Tomahawk and the Cross: see *Pillars of the Sky*

The Tomb of Ligeia **
GB 1964 81m Eastmancolor Cinemascope
American International (Roger Corman)

A brooding Victorian metamorphoses his dead wife into a cat, then into the beautiful Lady Rowena.
Complex but rather fascinating horror suspenser which rejogs familiar elements into something new; the best of the Corman Poes.
w Robert Towne *story* Edgar Allan Poe *d* Roger Corman *ph* Arthur Grant *m* Kenneth V. Jones
☆ Vincent Price, Elizabeth Shepherd, John Westbrook, Oliver Johnston, Richard Johnson, Derek Francis

Tomb of the Living Dead: see *The Mad Doctor of Blood Island*

Tomboy
US 1984 92m DeLuxe
Crown International/Marimark (Marilyn Jacobs Tenser)

A female mechanic falls for a professional driver, but is determined to beat him in a race.
Unsubtle 'teen flick, an unimaginative, low-budget variation on Flashdance, which even its target audience found wanting; there are rather more shower scenes and bare breasts than the narrative requires, and the rest consists of unattractive visuals to a rock accompaniment.
w Ben Zelig *d* Herb Freed *ph* Daniel Yarussi *ad* Randy Ser *ed* Richard E. Westover
☆ Betsy Russell, Jerry Dinome, Kristi Somers, Richard Erdman, Philip Sterling, Eric Douglas, Paul Gunning, Toby Iland

Tombs of the Blind Dead (dubbed)
Spain/Portugal 1972 86m Eastmancolor
Plata/Interfilme

original title: *La Noche del Terror Ciego*
aka: *The Blind Dead*
Devil-worshipping Knights Templar, killed at the time of the Crusades, rise from their graves to kill all they encounter.
Gruesome, low-budget horror with a few original touches; it proved popular enough to spawn a few sequels.
wd Amando de Ossorio *ph* Pablo Ripoli *ad* Jaime Duarte de Brito *ed* José Antonio Rojo
☆ Cesar Burner, Lone Fleming, Joseph Thelman, Helen Harp, Rufino Ingles, Veronica Llimera, Maria Sylva
† It was followed by *The Return of the Evil Dead* (qv).

'Justice is coming.'

Tombstone *
US 1993 129m Technicolor Panavision
Entertainment/Cinergi (James Jacks, Sean Daniel, Bob Misiorowski)

After his brother is killed in Tombstone, Wyatt Earp and his friend Doc Holliday take on the lawless Clanton gang.
Vigorous retelling of the incidents that led up to the famous gunfight at the OK Corral, celebrating Earp as the archetypal Western hero.
w Kevin Jarre *d* George P. Cosmatos *ph* William A. Fraker *m* Bruce Broughton *pd* Catherine Hardwicke *ed* Frank J. Urioste, Roberto Silvi, Harvey Rosenstock
☆ Kurt Russell, Val Kilmer, Sam Elliott, Bill Paxton, Powers Boothe, Michael Biehn, Charlton Heston, Jason Priestley, Jon Tenney, Stephen Lang, Robert Mitchum (narrator)
'A tough-talking but soft-hearted tale that is entertaining in a sprawling, old-fashioned manner.' – *Variety*
† Kevin Jarre was replaced as director during shooting.

'Good men (and women) live in Tombstone – but not for long!'

Tombstone (The Town Too Tough to Die)
US 1942 80m bw
Paramount
How Wyatt Earp cleaned up the town.
Lacklustre low-budget version of a famous story.
w Albert Shelby Le Vino, Edward E. Paramore *d* William McGann
☆ Richard Dix, Frances Gifford, Kent Taylor, Edgar Buchanan, Don Castle, Victor Jory

'They couldn't get lucky if they tried.'

Tomcats
US 2001 95m
Columbia TriStar/Revolution/Eagle Cove (Alan Riche, Tony Ludwig, Paul Kurta)
In order to pay off his gambling debts, a man recruits an old flame to seduce his friend into marriage, so that he can collect on a wager they made, which will be won by the person who stays a bachelor the longest.
Vulgar adolescent comedy, full of grossly obvious ill-timed gags that fail to raise a laugh; it achieved notoriety for being the first movie, but alas probably not the last, to feature an excised cancerous testicle joke.
wd Gregory Poirier *ph* Charles Minsky *m* David Kitay *pd* Robb Wilson King *ed* Harry Keramidas *cos* Alix Friedberg
☆ Jerry O'Connell (Michael Delaney), Shannon Elizabeth (Natalie Parker), Jake Busey (Kyle Brenner), Horatio Sanz (Steve), Jaime Pressly (Tricia), Bernie Casey (Hurley), David Ogden Stiers (Dr Crawford), Travis Fine (Jan), Heather Stephens (Jill), Julia Schultz (Shelby)
'A boner-headed comedy whose sense of gross-out humor is calculated rather than inspired.' – *Todd McCarthy, Variety*
'All sex comedies have scenes in which characters are embarrassed, but I can't remember one in which women are so consistently and venomously humiliated, as if they were some kind of hateful plague.' – *Roger Ebert, Chicago Sun-Times*

Tommy *
GB 1975 108m colour
Hemdale/Robert Stigwood

A deaf, dumb and blind child is eventually cured and becomes a rock celebrity.
Mystical rock opera screened with the director's usual barrage of effects and an ear-splitting score. Of occasional interest.
w Ken Russell *opera* Pete Townshend and the Who *d* Ken Russell *ph* Dick Bush, Ronnie Taylor *m* Pete Townshend and the Who
☆ Roger Daltrey, Ann-Margret, Oliver Reed, Elton John, Eric Clapton, Keith Moon
Ann-Margret; score

Tommy Boy
US 1995 96m DeLuxe
Paramount (Lorne Michaels)

A fat and hapless perpetual student inherits the family business when his father dies and saves it from his unscrupulous stepmother with the aid of a skinny friend.
A farce that grows increasingly dim as two television comedians (from Saturday Night Live) flounder helplessly with a witless, cliché-ridden script.
w Bonnie Turner, Terry Turner *d* Peter Segal *ph* Victor J. Kemper *m* David Newman *pd* Stephen J. Lineweaver *ed* William Kerr
☆ Chris Farley, David Spade, Brian Dennehy, Bo Derek, Dan Aykroyd, Julie Warner, Sean McCann, Rob Lowe (uncredited)
'The only thing worse than contemplating the oafish antics on screen is imagining the audience of cretins for whom the film was made.' – *Alexander Walker*

The Tommy Steele Story
GB 1957 82m bw
Anglo Amalgamated/Insignia (Herbert Smith)
US title: *Rock around the World*
Tommy Steele tells journalists how he rose from being a steward in the merchant navy to singing in a Soho coffee bar and appearing in cabaret at London's fashionable Café de Paris.
Small-scale movie cashing in on Steele's then status as Britain's first rock singer. The producers don't seem to have had much faith in the drawing power of rock: there is a steel band over the titles, a calypso-styled musical commentary to the action, jazz from Humphrey Lyttleton's Band, and skiffle from Chas McDevitt and Nancy Whiskey. It also avoids the teen rebel clichés of the genre – Steele is shown as a boy who does as his parents tell him.
w Norman Hudis *d* Gerard Bryant *ph* Peter Hennessy *m/ly* Lionel Bart, Tommy Steele, Michael Pratt *ad* Eric Saw *ed* Ann Chegwidden
☆ Tommy Steele, Lisa Danieli, Hilda Fenemore, Charles Lamb, Patrick Westwood, Peter Lewiston, Cyril Chamberlain, John Boxer, Mark Daly

Tommy the Toreador
GB 1959 86m Technicolor
Fanfare/AB

A seaman takes the place of a bullfighter framed for smuggling.
Acceptable star comedy of its time.
w Nicholas Phipps, Sid Colin, Talbot Rothwell *d* John Paddy Carstairs *ph* Gilbert Taylor *m* Stanley Black *songs* Lionel Bart
☆ Tommy Steele, Sid James, Janet Munro, Pepe Nieto, Noel Purcell, Kenneth Williams, Eric Sykes

Tomorrow and Tomorrow
US 1932 73m bw
Paramount
A happily married woman suddenly falls for a foreign scientist.
Sturdy woman's picture of its day.
w Josephine Lovett *play* Philip Barry *d* Richard Wallace
☆ Ruth Chatterton, Paul Lukas, Robert Ames, Harold Minjir, Tad Alexander
'A screen play of the first grade ... reflects credit on everybody concerned in its making.' – *Variety*

Tomorrow at Ten *
GB 1962 80m bw
Mancunian (Tom Blakeley)
A crook kidnaps a small boy and locks him up with a time bomb while he makes his demands in person. When the kidnapper is killed, the police have to hunt against time.
Tense second feature, well acted and efficiently done.
w Peter Millar, James Kelly *d* Lance Comfort *ph* Basil Emmott *m* Bernie Fenton
☆ Robert Shaw, John Gregson, Alec Clunes, Alan Wheatley, Ernest Clark, Kenneth Cope

Tomorrow Is Another Day
US 1951 90m bw
Warner
An ex-convict is soon on the run for a crime he didn't commit.
Miserable melodrama apparently left over from John Garfield days.
w Guy Endore, Art Cohn *d* Felix Feist *ph* Robert Burks *m* Daniele Amfitheatrof
☆ Steve Cochran, Ruth Roman, Lurene Tuttle, Bobby Hyatt, Ray Teal

Tomorrow Is Forever *
US 1945 105m bw
RKO-International (David Lewis)

A man supposed dead in the war returns with an altered face to find his wife has remarried.
Enoch Arden rides again in a rampant woman's picture which is well enough made to be generally entertaining.
w Lenore Coffee *d* Irving Pichel *ph* Joe Valentine *m* Max Steiner
☆ Orson Welles, Claudette Colbert, George Brent, Lucile Watson, Richard Long, Natalie Wood

Tomorrow Is Too Late: see *Domani è Troppo Tardi*

Tomorrow Never Comes
Canada/GB 1977 109m colour
Rank/Classic/Montreal Trust/Neffbourne (Michael Klinger, Julian Melzack)

A jealous lover shoots a caller at his girl's beach cabana and a police siege begins.
Far from the class of Le Jour Se Lève, this is an exploitative and violent melodrama which need never have been made.
w David Pursall, Jack Seddon, Sydney Banks *d* Peter Collinson *ph* François Protat *m* Roy Budd

☆ Oliver Reed, Susan George, Raymond Burr, Stephen McHattie, John Ireland, Donald Pleasence, John Osborne, Cec Linder

Tomorrow Never Dies **
US 1997 119m DeLuxe Panavision
MGM/UA/Eon (Michael G. Wilson, Barbara Broccoli)

James Bond has two days to prevent a world war involving Britain and China.
Action-packed movie that sticks close to the usual 007 formula and has a somewhat lacklustre villain in a megalomaniacal media tycoon, but at least it delivers on its promises.
w Bruce Feirstein *d* Roger Spottiswoode *ph* Robert Elswit *m* David Arnold *pd* Allan Cameron *ed* Dominique Fortin, Michel Arcand
☆ Pierce Brosnan, Jonathan Pryce, Michelle Yeoh, Teri Hatcher, Joe Don Baker, Ricky Jay, Götz Otto, Judi Dench, Desmond Llewelyn, Vincent Schiavelli, Geoffrey Palmer

'The filmmakers have steered almost exclusively toward action, at the expense of sex, humor or the sort of jet-set and gaming-room glamour often highlighted in the series.' – *Todd McCarthy, Variety*

† The film's production was a troubled one, owing partly to the producers agreeing to have the film ready for a December release. Brosnan rejected the script after it had been rewritten; it was then rewritten again during filming by the writer of the original script; director and scriptwriter were not talking to one another, and Brosnan and Teri Hatcher were not compatible. The film cost around $90m, and took more than $308m at the box-office worldwide.

Tomorrow the World *
US 1944 86m bw
UA/Lester Cowan
A college professor adopts his orphaned German nephew, who turns out to be an ardent 12-year-old Nazi.
Adequate, predictable screen version of a once-topical play.
w Ring Lardner Jnr, Leopold Atlas *play* James Gow, Armand D'Usseau *d* Leslie Fenton *ph* Henry Sharp *m* Louis Applebaum
☆ Fredric March, Betty Field, *Skip Homeier*, Agnes Moorehead, Joan Carroll

Tom's Midnight Garden
GB/US/Japan 2000 107m Rank Film Downtown/Hyperion/IoMFC/BS24 (Adam Shapiro, Charles Salmon)
A lonely young boy discvers that he can enter a past world through his uncle's grandfather clock.
Pallid exercise in nostalgia, with lacklustre performances.
wd Willard Carroll *novel* Philippa Pearce *ph* Gavin Finney *m* Debbie Wiseman *pd* James Merifield *ed* Les Healey
☆ Greta Scacchi (Aunt Gwen), James Wilby (Uncle Alan), Joan Plowright (Mrs Bartholomew), Anthony Way (Tom), David Bradley (Abel), Penelope Wilton (Aunt Melbourne), Nigel Le Vaillant (Tom Long), Liz Smith (Mrs Willows), Florence Hoath (Young Hatty), Caroline Carver (Hatty), Mel Martin (Alice Long)

'Prissy, dated, condescending rubbish.' – *Peter Bradshaw, Guardian*

Tongnian Wangshi: see *The Time to Live and the Time to Die*

Tonight and Every Night
US 1945 92m Technicolor
Columbia (Victor Saville)

The lives and loves of London showgirls during the blitz.
Ludicrous concoction looking nothing like London and certainly nothing like the Windmill, the theatre to which it allegedly pays tribute. There are some tolerable numbers along the way.
w Lesser Samuels, Abem Finkel *play* *Heart of a City* by Lesley Storm *d* Victor Saville *ph* Rudolph Maté *md* Morris Stoloff, Marlin Skiles
☆ Rita Hayworth, Lee Bowman, Janet Blair, Marc Platt, Leslie Brooks, Dusty Anderson, Florence Bates, Ernest Cossart
† Rita Hayworth's singing was dubbed by Martha Mears.
Morris Stoloff, Marlin Skiles; song 'Anywhere' (*m*Jule Styne, *ly*Sammy Cahn)

Tonight Is Ours
US 1932 76m bw
Paramount
A Balkan princess falls for a commoner in Paris.
One of the master's less sparkling plays gets the heavy Hollywood treatment.
w Edwin Justus Mayer *play* Noël Coward *d* Stuart Walker *ph* Karl Struss
☆ Fredric March, Claudette Colbert, Alison Skipworth, Paul Cavanagh, Arthur Byron, Ethel Griffies

'Slow and talky flicker, better for the class houses.' – *Variety*

Tonight or Never
US 1931 80m bw
Samuel Goldwyn
A prima donna falls for a man she thinks is a Venetian gigolo, but he turns out to be an impresario from New York.
Flimsy comedy which turned out to be its star's last vehicle of any consequence for twenty years.
w Ernest Vajda *play* Lily Hatvany *d* Mervyn Le Roy *ph* Gregg Toland *md* Alfred Newman
☆ Gloria Swanson, Melvyn Douglas, Ferdinand Gottschalk, Robert Greig, Alison Skipworth, Boris Karloff

Tonight We Raid Calais
US 1943 70m bw
TCF
A British agent lands in occupied France to pave the way for a bombing raid.
Adequate low-budget morale booster.
w Waldo Salt *d* John Brahm *ph* Lucien Ballard
☆ John Sutton, Annabella, Lee J. Cobb, Beulah Bondi, Blanche Yurka, Howard Da Silva, Marcel Dalio

Tonight We Sing *
US 1953 109m Technicolor
TCF (George Jessel)
Sol Hurok stifles his own talent to become a great musical impresario.
Blameless uppercrust biopic, with plenty of well-staged guest talent.
w Harry Kurnitz, George Oppenheimer *d* Mitchell Leisen *ph* Leon Shamroy *md* Alfred Newman *ch* David Lichine
☆ David Wayne, Anne Bancroft, Ezio Pinza (Chaliapin), Roberta Peters, Tamara Toumanova (Pavlova), Isaac Stern (Eugene Ysaye), Jan Peerce

Tonight's the Night: see *Happy Ever After (1954)*

Tonka
US 1958 97m Technicolor
Walt Disney

A Sioux Indian tames a magnificent white horse, and after many adventures is reunited with him at Little Big Horn.
Unremarkable and overlong adventure story.
w Lewis R. Foster, Lillie Hayward *novel* *Comanche* by David Appel *d* Lewis R. Foster *ph* Loyal Griggs
☆ Sal Mineo, Phil Carey, Jerome Courtland, Rafael Campos, H. M. Wynant

Tons of Money
GB 1930 97m bw
B and D/Herbert Wilcox
An inventor poses as his own cousin, and in this guise achieves instant success.
A long-running stage farce makes a grimly overlong movie.
w Herbert Wilcox, Ralph Lynn *play* Will Evans, Arthur Valentine *d* Tom Walls *ph* F. A. Young
☆ Ralph Lynn, Yvonne Arnaud, Mary Brough, Robertson Hare, Gordon James, Madge Saunders

Tony Draws a Horse
GB 1950 91m bw
Pinnacle/GFD
How to deal with a naughty boy causes mounting disagreement in the family.
Very theatrical farce which on screen seems merely silly.
w Brock Williams *play* Lesley Storm *d* John Paddy Carstairs *ph* Jack Hildyard *m* Bretton Byrd *ed* Gerald Thomas
☆ Cecil Parker, Anne Crawford, Derek Bond, Barbara Murray, Mervyn Johns, Edward Rigby

Tony Rome *
US 1967 111m DeLuxe Panavision
TCF/Arcola/Millfield (Aaron Rosenberg)

A seedy Miami private eye runs into murder when he guards a millionaire's daughter.
Complex old-fashioned murder mystery decorated with the new amorality and fashionable violence. Tolerable for its backgrounds and professional expertise. Sequel: Lady in Cement *(qv)*.
w Richard L. Breen *novel* *Miami Mayhem* by Marvin H. Albert *d* Gordon Douglas *ph* Joe Biroc *m* Billy May
☆ *Frank Sinatra*, Jill St John, Richard Conte, Gena Rowlands, Simon Oakland, Jeffrey Lynn, Lloyd Bochner, Sue Lyon

Too Beautiful For You: see *Trop Belle Pour Toi!*

Too Busy to Work
US 1932 76m bw
Fox
A tramp goes looking for his long lost wife.
Amiable remake of one of the star's most successful silents.
w Barry Conners, Philip Klein *story* *Jubilo* by Ben Ames Williams *d* John Blystone
☆ *Will Rogers*, Marian Nixon, Dick Powell, Frederick Burton, Louise Beavers

'A homey story of programmer weight ... better than average business should be figured on.' – *Variety*

Too Dangerous to Love: see *Perfect Strangers (1950)*

Too Hot to Handle: see *The Marrying Man*

Too Hot to Handle *
US 1938 105m bw
MGM (Lawrence Weingarten)

Adventures of a scoop-seeking newsreel cameraman.
Boisterous comedy-melodrama with as many sags as highlights but generally making a cheerful star entertainment.
w Laurence Stallings, John Lee Mahin *d* Jack Conway *ph* Harold Rosson *m* Franz Waxman
☆ *Clark Gable*, Myrna Loy, Walter Connolly, Walter Pidgeon, Leo Carrillo, Johnny Hines, Virginia Weidler

'Even more than *Test Pilot* it's hoked beyond the level of credibility. But it has a driving excitement, crackling dialogue, glittering performances and inescapable romantic pull. So it's a socko audience picture and should make a parachuteful of money.' – *Variety*

'It's like an old-fashioned serial ... no one can call it dull.' – *Howard Barnes*

'Breathlessly paced, witty, and violent, this is one of the more acid comedies to have been produced by the Thirties.' – *John Baxter*

Too Hot to Handle
GB 1960 100m Eastmancolor
ABP/Wigmore (Selim Cattan)

aka: *Playgirl After Dark*
Two Soho strip club owners join forces to hunt down a blackmailer.
Rotten, hilarious British gangster film set in a totally unreal underworld and very uncomfortably cast.
w Herbert Kretzmer *d* Terence Young *ph* Otto Heller *m* Eric Spear
☆ Leo Genn, Jayne Mansfield, Karl Boehm, Danik Patisson, Christopher Lee, Patrick Holt

Too Late Blues
US 1961 100m bw
Paramount (John Cassavetes)
A jazz musician falls for a neurotic girl and has fears of going commercial.
Uninteresting professional feature from a director whose reputation was made with the amateur Shadows.
w John Cassavetes, Richard Carr *d* John Cassavetes *ph* Lionel Lindon *m* David Raksin
☆ Stella Stevens, Bobby Darin, John Cassavetes, Everett Chambers, Nick Dennis, Rupert Crosse, Vince Edwards

Too Late for Tears
US 1949 99m bw
UA/Hunt Stromberg

A lady bluebeard disposes of both husbands and boyfriends.
Silly melodrama, poorly cast.
w Roy Huggins *d* Byron Haskin *ph* William Mellor *m* Dale Butts
☆ Lizabeth Scott, Don Defore, Arthur Kennedy, Dan Duryea, Kristine Miller, Barry Kelley

Too Late the Hero *
US 1969 144m Technicolor 70mm
Associates and Aldrich/Palomar

In World War II the Japanese hold one end of a small Pacific island, British and Americans the other.
Semi-cynical, long and bloody war adventure of competence but no great merit.
w Robert Aldrich, Lukas Heller *d* Robert Aldrich *ph* Joseph Biroc *m* Gerald Fried
☆ Michael Caine, Cliff Robertson, Ian Bannen, Henry Fonda, Harry Andrews, Denholm Elliott, Ronald Fraser, Percy Herbert

Too Many Crooks *
GB 1958 87m bw
Rank/Mario Zampi

Incompetent crooks plot a kidnapping.
Agreeable farce with black edges and an excellent chase sequence.
w Michael Pertwee *d* Mario Zampi *ph* Stan Pavey *m* Stanley Black
☆ Terry-Thomas, George Cole, Brenda de Banzie, Bernard Bresslaw, Sidney James, Joe Melia, Vera Day, John Le Mesurier

Too Many Girls
US 1940 85m bw
RKO (Harry Edgington, George Abbott)

The father of a wealthy co-ed hires four football heroes to protect her.
Witless nonsense, flabbily derived from a Broadway show.
w John Twist *play* George Marion Jnr, Richard Rodgers, Lorenz Hart *d* George Abbott *ph* Frank Redman *songs* Rodgers and Hart
☆ Lucille Ball, Desi Arnaz, Richard Carlson, Ann Miller, Eddie Bracken, Frances Langford, Harry Shannon
† The film on which Ball and Arnaz first met.
†† Lucille Ball's singing was dubbed by Trudy Erwin.

Too Many Husbands *
US 1940 84m bw
Columbia (Wesley Ruggles)
GB title: *My Two Husbands*
Allegedly drowned on a boat cruise, a man turns up again after his wife has remarried.
Modest variation on a familiar theme, professional but unexciting; later remade as Three for the Show *(qv)*.
w Claude Binyon *play* *Home and Beauty* by W. Somerset Maugham *d* Wesley Ruggles *ph* Joseph Walker *m* Frederick Hollander
☆ Jean Arthur, Melvyn Douglas, Fred MacMurray, Harry Davenport, Dorothy Peterson, Melville Cooper, Edgar Buchanan

Too Many Lovers
France 1958 102m Eastmancolor
Sirius (Jacques Roitfeld)
original title: *Charmants Garçons*
A dancer is pursued by a jewel thief, a gigolo, a boxer, a wealthy businessman and several husbands.
Light romantic comedy that offers occasional amusement, as well as a couple of dances by its star.
w Charles Spaak, Dominique Fabre, Etienne Perier *d* Henri Decoin *ph* Pierre Montazel *m* Georges Van Parys *ch* Roland Petit *ad* Robert Clavel *ed* Claude Durand
☆ Zizi Jeanmaire, Daniel Gelin, Henri Vidal, François Perier, Gert Frobe

Too Much Harmony
US 1933 76m bw
Paramount
A star singer helps a promising girl to the top.
Routine light musical which filled a need.
w Harry Ruskin, Joseph L. Mankiewicz *d* A. Edward Sutherland
☆ Bing Crosby, Jack Oakie, Judith Allen, Skeets Gallagher, Lilyan Tashman, Harry Green, Ned Sparks
'Should be an easy pleaser.' – *Variety*

'Always a man! Almost any man!'
Too Much Too Soon *
US 1958 121m bw
Warner (Henry Blanke)
Young actress Diana Barrymore goes to Hollywood to look after her alcoholic father John, but mild success goes to her head and she too turns to drink.
Rather dismal and murkily photographed account of an absorbing real-life situation; one performance holds the first half together.
wd Art Napoleon *memoirs* Diana Barrymore *ph* Nicholas Musuraca, Carl Guthrie *m* Ernest Gold *ad* George James Hopkins
☆ Dorothy Malone, *Errol Flynn*, Efrem Zimbalist Jnr, Neva Patterson, Martin Milner, Ray Danton, Murray Hamilton

Too Young to Kiss
US 1951 89m bw
MGM (Sam Zimbalist)
A girl pianist poses as an infant prodigy, and falls for the impresario who wants to adopt her.
Dull conveyor belt comedy.
w Frances Goodrich, Albert Hackett *d* Robert Z. Leonard *ph* Joseph Ruttenberg *m* Johnny Green *ad* Cedric Gibbons, Paul Groesse
☆ June Allyson, Van Johnson, Gig Young, Paula Corday, Larry Keating, Hans Conried
art direction

'If this happened to your daughter, would you be to blame?'
Too Young to Love
GB 1959 89m bw
Rank/Welbeck (Herbert Smith)
A 15-year-old prostitute is brought before a Brooklyn juvenile court.
Tepid filming of a popular exploitation play of the fifties, mysteriously made in England.
w Sydney and Muriel Box *play* *Pick Up Girl* by Elsa Shelley *d* Muriel Box *ph* Gerald Gibbs *m* Bruce Montgomery
☆ *Thomas Mitchell*, Pauline Hahn, Joan Miller, Austin Willis, Jess Conrad, Bessie Love, Alan Gifford

Tootsie ****
US 1982 116m colour
Columbia/Mirage/Punch (Sydney Pollack, Dick Richards)
An out-of-work actor pretends to be a woman in order to get a job in a soap opera.
As with Genevieve *and* Whisky Galore, *an unlikely comedy subject makes an instant classic. It's all in the handling.*
w Larry Gelbart, Murray Shisgal story Don McGuire *d Sydney Pollack ph* Owen Roizman *m* Dave Grusin *pd* Peter Larkin *ed* Frederic and William Steinkamp
☆ *Dustin Hoffman*, Jessica Lange, Teri Garr, Dabney Coleman, Charles Durning, Sydney Pollack, George Gaynes
Jessica Lange
best picture; Dustin Hoffman; Teri Garr; Sydney Pollack as director; original screenplay; cinematography; editing; song, 'It Might Be You' (*m* Dave Grusin, *ly* Alan Bergman, Marilyn Bergman); sound
Dustin Hoffman

Top Banana *
US 1953 100m Color Corporation
Roadshow/Harry M. Popkin
A TV comedian invites an attractive salesgirl to join his show.
A wisp of plot is the excuse for a revue, and the interest is in the old-time burlesque acts, some of which survive the generally shoddy treatment.
w Gene Towne *d* Alfred E. Green *ph* William Bradford *m/ly* Johnny Mercer
☆ *Phil Silvers*, Rose Marie, Danny Scholl, Jack Albertson

'One's tough...one's smart'
Top Dog
US 1995 86m FotoKem
Live/Tanglewood (Andy Howard)
A maverick cop is teamed with a shaggy dog to track down racist killers.
Apparently intended as family entertainment, this deplorable movie features murder, violence, white supremacy, hit men dressed as clowns and cheap sentimentality; it is unfit for any audience.
w Ron Swanson *story* Aaron Norris, Tim Grayem *d* Aaron Norris *ph* João Fernandes *m* George S. Clinton *pd* Norm Barron *ed* Peter Schink
☆ Chuck Norris (Jake Wilder), Peter Savard Moore (Karl Koller), Clyde Kusatsu (Captain Callahan), Michele Lamar Richards (Savannah Boyette), Erik Von Detten (Matthew Swanson), Carmine Caridi (Lou Swanson), Herta Ware (Jake's Mother), Kai Wulff (Otto Dietrich), Francesco Quinn (Mark Curtains), Timothy Bottoms (Nelson Houseman)
'A routine but diverting programmer.' – *Variety*

Top Gun
US 1986 110m Metrocolor
Paramount/Don Simpson, Jerry Bruckheimer
Adventures of naval fighter pilots.
A feast of hardware and noisy music; not much story.
w Jim Cash, Jack Epps Jnr *d* Tony Scott *ph* Jeffrey Kimball *m* Harold Faltermeyer *pd* John F. DeCuir Jnr *ed* Billy Weber, Chris Lebenzon
☆ Tom Cruise, Kelly McGillis, Val Kilmer, Anthony Edwards, Tom Skerritt
'Audiences prepared to go with it will be taken for a thrilling ride in the wild blue yonder.' – *Variety*
song 'Take My Breath Away' (Giorgio Moroder, Tom Whitlock)
editors

Top Hat ****
US 1935 100m bw
RKO (Pandro S. Berman)
The path of true love is roughened by mistaken identities.
Marvellous Astaire-Rogers musical, with a more or less realistic London supplanted by a totally artificial Venice, and show-stopping numbers in a style which is no more, separated by amusing plot complications lightly handled by a team of deft farceurs.
w Dwight Taylor, Allan Scott d Mark Sandrich ph David Abel, Vernon Walker m/ly Irving Berlin ch Hermes Pan ad Van Nest Polglase, Carroll Clark
☆ *Fred Astaire, Ginger Rogers, Edward Everett Horton, Helen Broderick, Eric Blore, Erik Rhodes*
'The theatres will hold their own world series with this one. It can't miss.' – *Variety*
'In 25 years *Top Hat* has lost nothing of its gaiety and charm.' – *Dilys Powell, 1960*
best picture; song 'Cheek to Cheek'; Hermes Pan; art direction

Top Man
US 1943 74m bw
Universal
When an officer is recalled to active duty his teenage son becomes head of the family.
Lively little putting-on-a-show comedy musical which established a new young star.
w Zachary Gold *d* Charles Lamont
☆ *Donald O'Connor*, Richard Dix, Peggy Ryan, Lillian Gish, Susanna Foster, Anne Gwynne

Top o' the Morning
US 1949 100m bw
Paramount (Robert L. Welch)
Investigations follow the theft of the Blarney Stone.
More Irish whimsy from the Going My Way *stars.*
w Edmund Beloin, Richard Breen *d* David Miller *ph* Lionel Lindon *m* James Van Heusen
☆ Bing Crosby, Barry Fitzgerald, Ann Blyth, Hume Cronyn, Eileen Crowe, John McIntire

The Top of His Head
Canada 1989 110m colour
Rhombus Media/Grimthorpe Film (Niv Fichman)
A satellite-dish salesman falls in love with a performance artist who is being investigated by the police.
Disastrously pretentious romantic thriller that uses experimental effects to little purpose.
wd Peter Mettler *ph* Peter Mettler *m* Fred Frith *ad* Valanne Ridgeway, Angela Murphy *ed* Peter Mettler, Margaret Van Eerdewijk
☆ Stephen Ouimette, Gary Reineke, Christie MacFadyen, David Main, Julie Wildman, Diane Barrington, David Fox

'A Ravishing Revolution In Screen Revelry!'
Top of the Town
US 1937 86m bw
Universal
The daughter of the owner of the Moonbeam Room wants to oust the swing band and stage a symbolic ballet.
A wisp of plot supports some expensive but not especially attractive numbers in a musical variety show that was supposed to be Universal's answer to other studios' biggies.
w Brown Holmes, Charles Grayson, Lou Brock *d* Ralph Murphy
☆ George Murphy, Doris Nolan, Hugh Herbert, Gregory Ratoff, Ella Logan, Gertrude Niesen, Henry Armetta, Mischa Auer, Samuel S. Hinds, Peggy Ryan
'A bundle of mediocrity ... it neither goes nor gets anywhere.' – *Variety*

'Life Is A Gamble...Let It Ride!'
Top of the World
US 1997 95m colour
On his first day out of prison, an ex-cop is accidentally implicated in the robbery of a Las Vegas casino.
Trivial thriller that substitutes frenetic action for sense; it is no more than a stupefying succession of car crashes, explosions and gunshots.
w Bart Madison *d* Sidney J. Furie *ph* Alan Caso *m* Robert O. Ragland *pd* Aaron Osborne *ed* Alain Jakubowicz
☆ Peter Weller, Dennis Hopper, Tia Carrere, David Alan Grier, Cary-Hiroyuki Tagawa, Martin Kove, Kevin Bernhardt, Peter Coyote, Joe Pantoliano

Top Secret *
GB 1952 94m bw
ABP (Mario Zampi)
US title: *Mr Potts Goes to Moscow*
A sanitary engineer, mistaken for a spy, is kidnapped to Moscow when his blueprints are taken for atomic secrets.
Farcical satire full of chases and lavatory humour; much of it comes off nicely.
w Jack Davies, Michael Pertwee d Mario Zampi ph Stan Pavey *m* Stanley Black
☆ *George Cole, Oscar Homolka*, Nadia Gray, Frederick Valk, Wilfrid Hyde-White, Geoffrey Sumner, Ronald Adam

Top Secret!
US 1984 90m Metrocolor
Paramount/Kingsmere (Jon Davison, Hunt Lowry)
An American rock star in Germany gets involved with spies of both sides.
Dull spoof from the folks who gave us Airplane! *A very few sight gags stand out among the dross.*
w Jim Abrahams, David Zucker, Jerry Zucker, Martyn Burke *d* Jim Abrahams, David Zucker, Jerry Zucker *ph* Christopher Challis *m* Maurice Jarre *pd* Peter Lamont
☆ Val Kilmer, Lucy Gutteridge, Peter Cushing, Jeremy Kemp, Warren Clarke, Michael Gough, Omar Sharif, Christopher Villiers
'Too far over the top to retain any comic sense of the targets it sets out to lampoon. The overwhelming impression is of a *Mad* magazine strip in a particularly poor week.' – *Martyn Auty, MFB*

Top Secret Affair *
US 1956 100m bw
Warner/First National (Martin Rackin)
GB title: *Their Secret Affair*
A female news publisher tries to discredit a military diplomat but falls in love with him.
Curious comedy adaptation of a rather heavy novel, moderately skilled in all departments.
w Roland Kibbee, Allan Scott *novel Melville Goodwin USA* by John P. Marquand *d* H. C. Potter *ph* Stanley Cortez *m* Roy Webb *ad* Malcolm Bert *ed* Folmar Blangsted *cos* Charles LeMaire
☆ Kirk Douglas, Susan Hayward, Jim Backus, Paul Stewart, John Cromwell, Roland Winters, A. E. Gould Parker, Michael Fox, Frank Gerstle, Charles Lane

Topaz *
US 1969 124m Technicolor
Universal/Alfred Hitchcock
In 1962 the CIA enlists a French agent to break up a Russian spy ring.
Oddly halting, desultory and unconvincing spy thriller shot mainly in flat TV style, with just a few short sequences in its director's better manner. A measure of its unsatisfactoriness is that three different endings were shot and actually used at various points of release.
w Samuel Taylor *novel* Leon Uris *d* Alfred Hitchcock *ph* Jack Hildyard *m* Maurice Jarre *pd* Henry Bumstead *ed* William Ziegler *cos* Edith Head
☆ Frederick Stafford (Andre Devereaux), John Forsythe (Michael Nordstrom), John Vernon (Rico Parra), *Roscoe Lee Browne* (Philippe Dubois), Dany Robin (Nicole Devereaux), Karin Dor (Juanita de Cordoba), Michel Piccoli (Jacques Granville), Philippe Noiret (Henri Jarre)
'A larger, slower, duller version of the spy thrillers he used to make in the thirties.' – *New Yorker, 1975*

Topaze *
US 1933 78m bw
(RKO)
A simple schoolmaster allows himself to be exploited.
Interesting little comedy with the star playing against type: remade as Mr Topaze *(qv).*
w Ben Hecht *play* Marcel Pagnol *d* Harry d'Abbadie d'Arrast *ph* Lucien Andriot *m* Max Steiner
☆ John Barrymore, Myrna Loy, Jobyna Howland, Jackie Searl
'Okay, for metropolitan spots, but scarcely for the subsequents ... there haven't been half a dozen foreign dramas that have clicked on the screen.' – *Variety*
† In 1952 Howard Hughes announced a remake with Vincent Price, but it never happened.

Topio Stin Omichli: see *Landscape in a Mist*

Topkapi *
US 1964 119m Technicolor
UA/Filmways (Jules Dassin)
International thieves try to rob the Istanbul museum.
Light-hearted caper story which gets out of control because of the variety of styles and accents, the director's impression that his wife can do no wrong, and the general slowness and lack of wit; but there are bright moments, colourful backgrounds, and a final suspense sequence in the Rififi *manner.*
w Monja Danischewsky *novel* *The Light of Day* by Eric Ambler *d* Jules Dassin *ph Henri Alekan* *m* Manos Hadjidakis
☆ Melina Mercouri, Maximilian Schell, Peter Ustinov, Robert Morley, Akim Tamiroff, Gilles Segal, Jess Hahn
'Merely silly and boring.' – *John Simon*
Peter Ustinov

Topper **
US 1937 96m bw
(MGM) Hal Roach (Milton H. Bren)
A stuffy banker is haunted by the ghosts of his sophisticated friends the Kirbys, who are visible only to him.
Influential supernatural farce, still pretty funny and deftly acted though a shade slow to get going.
w Jack Jevne, Eric Hatch, Eddie Moran *novel The Jovial Ghosts* by Thorne Smith *d* Norman Z. McLeod *ph* Norbert Brodine *md* Arthur Morton
☆ *Cary Grant, Constance Bennett, Roland Young, Billie Burke, Alan Mowbray*, Eugene Pallette, Arthur Lake, Hedda Hopper

'How substantial the fan support will be is difficult to anticipate … None of the other films of similar theme aroused more than mild enthusiasm among a small group who patronize the arty theatres and talk about pictures in terms of art expression … Effort to excuse the story's absurdities on the theory that the intent is farce comedy does not entirely excuse the production from severe rebuke. Fact also that the living dead are always facetious may be shocking to sensibilities. Some of the situations and dialogue offend conventional good taste.' – *Variety*

Roland Young

Topper Returns **
US 1941 87m bw
Hal Roach

A girl ghost helps Topper solve her own murder.
Spirited supernatural farce which spoofs murder mysteries, spooky houses, frightened servants, dumb cops, etc, in a pacy, accomplished and generally delightful manner.
w Jonathan Latimer, Gordon Douglas, with additional dialogue by Paul Gerard Smith *d* Roy del Ruth *ph* Norbert Brodine *m* Werner Heymann
☆ *Roland Young, Joan Blondell, Eddie Anderson*, Carole Landis, Dennis O'Keefe, *H. B. Warner*, Billie Burke, *Donald McBride*, Rafaela Ottiano

'Ectoplasm runs riot and blazes a trail of hilarity from 5th Avenue to the French Riviera!'
Topper Takes a Trip *
US 1939 85m bw
Hal Roach

Ghostly Mrs Kirby helps Topper to save his wife from a Riviera philanderer.
Mildly pleasant follow-up, with a dog replacing Cary Grant who had become too expensive.
w Eddie Moran, Jack Jevne, Corey Ford *d* Norman Z. McLeod *ph* Norbert Brodine *m* Hugo Friedhofer
☆ Constance Bennett, Roland Young, Billie Burke, Alan Mowbray, Verree Teasdale, Franklin Pangborn, Alexander D'Arcy
'Dandy comedy sequel … can't miss at the b.o … the original ended up a fine money-maker … no doubt one a year about Topper would be welcomed by exhibitors.' – *Variety*

Tops is the Limit: see *Anything Goes*

'The Egos. The Battles. The Words. The Music. The Women. The Scandal. Gilbert & Sullivan & So Much More'
Topsy-Turvy ***
GB 1999 160m colour
Pathé/Thin Man/Greenlight Fund/Newmarket (Simon Channing-Williams)

The trials and tribulations behind Gilbert and Sullivan's creation of *The Mikado*.
Engrossing, witty drama of a clash between three giant egos, of writer, composer and producer, that takes time to explore the characters of those involved, as well as providing an entertaining glimpse of backstage life and rivalries within a social and political context.
wd Mike Leigh ph Dick Pope m Carl Davis, based on the works of Arthur Sullivan *md* Gary Yershon *pd Eve Stewart ed* Robin Sales *cos Lindy Hemming*
☆ *Jim Broadbent* (W.S. Gilbert), Allan Corduner (Sir Arthur Sullivan), Lesley Manville (Lucy Gilbert), Eleanor David (Fanny Ronalds), Ron Cook (Richard D'Oyly Carte), Timothy Spall (Richard Temple), Martin Savage (Grossmith), Lely (Kevin McKidd), Shirley Henderson (Leonora Braham), Jessie Bond (Dorothy Atkinson), Wendy Nottingham
'One of those films that create a mix of erudition, pageantry and delectable acting opportunities.' – *Janet Maslin, New York Times*
'An overlong, overdressed and over-indulgent re-creation of an over-familiar story.' – *Alexander Walker, London Evening Standard*
Lindy Hemming; make-up (Christine Blundell, Trefor Proud)
Mike Leigh (as writer); Eve Stewart
make-up/hair (Christine Blundell)

Tora! Tora! Tora! *
US 1970 144m DeLuxe Panavision
TCF (Elmo Williams)

A reconstruction from both sides of the events leading up to Pearl Harbor.
Immense, largely studio-bound, calcified war spectacle with much fidelity to the record but no villains and no hero, therefore no drama and no suspense.
w Larry Forrester, Hideo Oguni, Ryuzo Kikushima *d* Richard Fleischer, Ray Kellogg, Toshio Masuda, Kinji Fukasaku *ph* Charles F. Wheeler and Japanese crews *m* Jerry Goldsmith *ad* Jack Martin Smith, Yoshiro Muraki, Richard Day, Taizoh Kawashima *ed* James E. Newcomb, Pembroke J. Herring, Innoue Chikaya *sp L. B. Abbott, Art Cruickshank*
☆ Martin Balsam, Joseph Cotten, James Whitmore, Jason Robards, Edward Andrews, Leon Ames, George Macready, Soh Yamamura, Takahiro Tamura
'One of the least stirring and least photogenic historical epics ever perpetrated on the screen.' – *Gary Arnold*
special visual effects (A. D. Flowers, L. B. Abbott)
Charles F. Wheeler, Osami Furuya, Sinsaku Himeda, Masamichi Satoh; art direction; sound; editing

'She sings torch songs to daddies and lullabies to babies!'
Torch Singer
US 1933 72m bw
Paramount (Albert Lewis)
aka: *Broadway Singer*
An unwed mother supports her child by singing in night-clubs.
Banal melodrama.
w Lenore Coffee, Lynn Starling *play Mike* by Grace Perkins *d* Alexander Hall *ph* Karl Struss
☆ Claudette Colbert, Ricardo Cortez, David Manners, Lyda Roberti, Baby LeRoy, Florence Roberts, Ethel Griffies, Helen Jerome Eddy
'Unwed mother film not so forte.' – *Variety*

Torch Song
US 1953 90m Technicolor
MGM (Henry Berman, Sidney Franklin Jnr)

A temperamental musical comedy star falls for a blind pianist.
Ossified star vehicle which looks great but is too often unintentionally funny.
w John Michael Hayes, Jan Lustig *story Why Should I Cry?* by I. A. R. Wylie *d* Charles Walters *ph* Robert Planck *m* Adolph Deutsch
☆ Joan Crawford, Michael Wilding, Gig Young, Marjorie Rambeau, Henry Morgan, Dorothy Patrick
'Here is Joan Crawford all over the screen, in command, in love and in color.' – *Otis L. Guernsey Jnr*
Marjorie Rambeau

Torch Song Trilogy *
US 1988 119m Metrocolor
Palace/New Line (Howard Gottfried)

Three incidents in the life of a drag artiste: in 1971, there is an on-and-off affair with a school teacher; in 1973, a young man comes to live with him; in 1980, his mother discovers his homosexuality as an old lover moves back in.
A truncated version of a successful Broadway show, the film loses the theatricality of the original and transforms the material into a dated melodrama.
w Harvey Fierstein *play* Harvey Fierstein *d* Paul Bogart *ph* Mikael Salomon *m* Peter Matz *pd* Richard Hoover *ed* Nicholas C. Smith
☆ Harvey Fierstein, Anne Bancroft, Matthew Broderick, Brian Kerwin, Karen Young, Eddie Castrodad, Ken Page, Charles Pierce, Axel Vera

Torchy Blane
Glenda Farrell played the hard-boiled girl reporter and Barton MacLane the tough police inspector who puts up with her in seven out of the nine second features made by Warner in the late 30s. The characters were created in short stories by Frederick Nebel, and the films were mostly directed by William Beaudine or Frank McDonald.
1936 Smart Blonde
1937 Fly Away Baby, The Adventurous Blonde
1938 Blondes at Work, Torchy Blane in Panama (with Lola Lane, Paul Kelly), Torchy Gets Her Man
1939 Torchy Blane in Chinatown, Torchy Runs for Mayor, Torchy Plays with Dynamite (with Jane Wyman, Allen Jenkins)

Torment: see *Frenzy (1944)*

Torment: see *L'Enfer (1993)*

Torments: see *El*

Torn Curtain **
US 1966 119m Technicolor
Universal (Alfred Hitchcock)

A defector who is really a double agent is embarrassed when his girlfriend follows him into East Germany.
Patchy Hitchcock with some mechanically effective suspense sequences, a couple of efforts at something new, a few miscalculations, some evidence of carelessness, and a little enjoyable repetition of old situations.
w Brian Moore *d Alfred Hitchcock ph* John F. Warren *m* John Addison *pd* Hein Heckroth *ed* Bud Hoffman *cos* Edith Head
☆ Paul Newman (Professor Michael Armstrong), Julie Andrews (Sarah Sherman), *Wolfgang Kieling* (Hermann Gromek), Ludwig Donath (Professor Gustav Lindt), Lila Kedrova (Countess Kuchinska), Hans-Joerg Felmy (Heinrich Gerhard), Tamara Toumanova (Ballerina)
'The pace is plodding, the political background trite, and the actors stranded by their director's customary lack of concern with performance.' – *Time Out, 1984*

Torpedo Run *
US 1958 98m Metrocolor Cinemascope
MGM (Edmund S. Grainger)

A US submarine in World War II destroys a Japanese aircraft carrier in Tokyo Bay.
Well-staged potboiler with excellent action sequences marred slightly by excessive platitudinizing.
w Richard Sale, William Wister Haines *d* Joseph Pevney *ph* George J. Folsey
☆ Glenn Ford, Ernest Borgnine, Diane Brewster, Dean Jones

Torpedoed: see *Our Fighting Navy*

The Torrent *
US 1925 75m (24 fps) bw silent
MGM (Hunt Stromberg)
Spanish sweethearts are parted by a domineering mother, and the girl consoles herself by becoming a Paris prima donna.
Adequate emotional vehicle of its day which happened to be Garbo's first American film.
w Dorothy Farnum *novel* Vicente Blasco Ibáñez *d* Monta Bell *ph* William Daniels
☆ Ricardo Cortez, Greta Garbo, Gertrude Olmsted, Edward Connelly, Lucien Littlefield

Torrents of Spring **
Italy/France 1989 101m Technicolor
Hobo/Erre Produzione/Reteitalia/Les Films Ariane/Films A2/Curzon (Angelo Rizzoli)

A young Russian aristocrat is unfaithful to the beautiful Italian pastrycook he plans to marry.
Charming and evocative treatment of a tragic romance.
w Jerzy Skolimowski, Arcangelo Bonaccorso *novel* Ivan Turgenev *d* Jerzy Skolimowski *ph* Dante Spinotti, Witold Sobocinski *m* Stanley Myers *pd* Francesco Bronzi *ed* Cesare D'Amico, Andrzej Kostenko
☆ Timothy Hutton, Nastassja Kinski, Valeria Golino, William Forsythe, Urbano Barberini, Francesca de Sapio, Jacques Herlin
'Immensely beguiling.' – *Tom Milne, MFB*

Torrid Zone **
US 1940 88m bw
Warner (Mark Hellinger)
In Central America, a banana plantation manager is tricked by his boss into staying on, and helps a wandering showgirl as well as foiling bandits.
Enjoyable, fast-paced hokum with a plot borrowed from both The Front Page *and* Red Dust.
w Richard Macaulay, Jerry Wald *d* William Keighley *ph* James Wong Howe *m* Adolph Deutsch
☆ *James Cagney, Pat O'Brien, Ann Sheridan*, Helen Vinson, Andy Devine, Jerome Cowan, George Tobias, George Reeves

Törst: see *Three Strange Loves*

Tortilla Flat *
US 1942 106m bw
MGM (Sam Zimbalist)

The problems of poor Mexican half-breeds in California.
Expensive but unappealing variation on The Grapes of Wrath, *with none of the cast quite getting under the skin of their parts, and no sense of reality, rather that of a musical without music.*
w John Lee Mahin, Benjamin Glazer *novel* John Steinbeck *d* Victor Fleming *ph* Sidney Wagner *m* Franz Waxman
☆ Spencer Tracy, Hedy Lamarr, John Garfield, Frank Morgan, Akim Tamiroff, Connie Gilchrist, John Qualen, Sheldon Leonard, Donald Meek, Allen Jenkins, Henry O'Neill
Frank Morgan

'A comedy to arouse your appetite.'
Tortilla Soup
US 2001 103m colour
Optimum/Starz/Samuel Goldwyn (John Bard Manulis)

A Mexican-American chef finds that the lives of his three adult daughters are a recipe for disaster.
Over-seasoned fast food for the undiscriminating, this is a feeble imitation of the original.
w Tom Musca, Ramon Menendez, Vera Blasi *screenplay Eat Drink Man Woman* by Ang Lee, James Schamus, Hui-Ling Wang *d* Maria Ripol *ph* Xavier Perez Grobet *m* Bill Conti *pd* Alicia Maccarone *ed* Andy Blumenthal
☆ Hector Elizondo (Martin), Jacqueline Obradors (Carmen), Elizabeth Pena (Letitia), Tamara Mello (Maribel), Nikolai Kinski (Andy), Raquel Welch (Hortensia), Joel Joan (Antonio), Paul Rodriguez (Orlando)
'So teeth-grindingly irritating you will feel your mouth filling up with enamel powder.' – *Peter Bradshaw, Guardian*
'Warm-blooded winner with equal emphasis placed on taste buds and heartstrings.' – *Ken Eisner, Variety*

The Torture Chamber of Baron Blood: see *Baron Blood*

The Torture Chamber of Dr Sadism: see *The Blood Demon*

Torture Garden *
GB 1967 93m Technicolor
Columbia/Amicus (Milton Subotsky)

Five fairground visitors are told their future by the mysterious Dr Diablo.
Crude but effective horror portmanteau including one story about the resurrection of Edgar Allan Poe.
w Robert Bloch *d* Freddie Francis *ph* Norman Warwick *m* Don Banks, James Bernard
☆ Burgess Meredith, Jack Palance, Peter Cushing, Beverly Adams, Michael Bryant, John Standing

Total Eclipse
GB/France/Belgium 1995 110m colour
Fit-Portman-SFP-K2/Capitol/Canal (Ramsay Levi)

Two poets, Verlaine and Rimbaud, engage in a destructive love affair.
Unsuccessful attempt to dramatize a famous literary conjunction; the concentration is on their behaviour rather than the work that came out of their mutual needs, and that is not grounded in any felt experience, seeming arbitrary and without point.
w Christopher Hampton *d* Agnieszka Holland *ph* Yorgos Arvanitis *m* Jan A. P. Kaczmarek *pd* Dan Weil *ed* Isabel Lorente
☆ Leonardo DiCaprio (Rimbaud), David Thewlis (Verlaine), Romane Bohringer, Dominique Blanc
'Misbegotten … a complete botch in all respects.' – *Todd McCarthy, Variety*
'Unwatchable … The movie is filled with so many hysterical let's-trash-the-hotel-room scenes that the audience goes numb.' – *Bruce Diones, New Yorker*

'They stole his mind. Now he wants it back.'

Total Recall **
US 1990 109m Technicolor
Guild/Carolco (Buzz Feitshans, Ronald Shusett)

Following an artificially-induced dream, a labourer remembers his previous existence as a secret agent on Mars.
An over-violent, paranoid and engrossing fantasy, with more than enough twists of plot to dizzy the mind.
w Ronald Shusett, Dan O'Bannon, Gary Goldman *story We Can Remember It For You Wholesale* by Philip K. Dick *d* Paul Verhoeven *ph* Jost Vacano *m* Jerry Goldsmith *pd* William Sandell *ed* Frank J. Urioste
☆ Arnold Schwarzenegger, Rachel Ticotin, Sharon Stone, Ronny Cox, Michael Ironside, Marshall Bell, Mel Johnson Jnr, Michael Champion, Roy Brocksmith, Ray Baker, Rosemary Dunsmore, Priscilla Allen
'While the temptation is just to shrug off *Total Recall* as an excessive but exciting "no brainer", enough intelligence and artistry lie behind the numbing spectacle to also make one regret its heedless contribution to the accelerating brutality of its time.' – *Variety*
best visual effects

Totally F*ed Up ***
US 1993 80m colour
Dangerous to Know/desperate pictures/blurco musclehate (Andrea Sperling, Gregg Araki)

Episodes in the life of six gay teenagers living in Los Angeles, which end in the suicide of one of them when he feels abandoned by his friends.
A flawed but interesting exploration of the fact that a greater-than-expected number of teenage suicides are gay, done in semi-documentary style. What it most obviously reveals is that its provocative director has talent to spare.
wd/ph/ed Gregg Araki
☆ James Duval, Roko Belic, Susan Behshid, Jenee Gill, Gilbert Luna, Lance May, Alan Boyce, Craig Gilmore
'A bit of a slog around the houses of those who see themselves only as irreversibly victimized and loll around a lot complaining about it.' – *Marianne Gray, Film Review*

Toto le Héros **
Belgium/France/Germany 1991 91m colour
Electric/Ibis/Metropolis/RTBF/FRZ/ZDF/Canal Plus (Philippe Dussart, Luciano Gloor)

aka: *Toto the Hero*
A bitter old man recalls the past as he plots the murder of his childhood enemy who married the woman he loved.
Strange but largely successful mix of childhood fantasy and black and bitter comedy.
w Jaco van Dormael, Laurette Vankeerberghen, Pascal Lonhay, Didier de Neck *d* Jaco van Dormael *ph* Walther van den Ende *m* Pierre van Dormael *ad* Herbert Pouille *ed* Susana Rossberg
☆ Michel Bouquet, Jo de Backer, Thomas Godet, Gisela Uhlen, Mireille Perrier, Sandrine Blancke, Peter Böhlke, Didier Ferney, Hugo Harold Harrisson

The Touch *
Sweden/US 1970 112m Eastmancolor
ABC/Cinematograph AB (Lars/Owe Carlburg)
The wife of a provincial surgeon falls in love with an archaeologist.
Freedom versus security; the Bergman treatment is given to a familiar love story, but the expected finesse is lacking.
wd Ingmar Bergman *ph* Sven Nykvist *m* Jan Johansson
☆ *Bibi Andersson*, Elliott Gould, Max von Sydow

'When It Comes To Fame And Fortune, Heaven Knows He's Got The Touch...'

Touch *
US/France 1996 97m CFI color
Pathé/Lumière (Lila Cazès, Fida Attieh)

A salesman and a right-wing Catholic both try to exploit for their own purposes a young man who apparently has the power to heal the sick.
A surprising story of a miracle-worker, given its hard-boiled source, and one that lurches uncomfortably between irony and earnestness.
wd Paul Schrader *novel* Elmore Leonard *ph* Ed Lachman *m* David Grohl *pd* David Waso *ed* Cara Silverman
☆ Bridget Fonda, Christopher Walken, Skeet Ulrich, Tom Arnold, Gina Gershon, Lolita Davidovich, Paul Mazursky, Janeane Garafalo, Breckin Mayer, John Doe, Conchata Ferrell
'Won't quite give you a profound experience but you won't feel cheated by it either.' – *Ian Calcutt, Film Review*

Touch and Go
GB 1955 85m Technicolor
Ealing (Seth Holt)

US title: *The Light Touch*
A family has doubts about its decision to emigrate to Australia.
Very mild comedy which fails to engage sympathy because the characters don't seem real.
w William Rose *d* Michael Truman *ph* Douglas Slocombe *m* John Addison
☆ Jack Hawkins, Margaret Johnston, June Thorburn, John Fraser, Roland Culver, Alison Leggatt, James Hayter

'They had the perfect love affair. Until they fell in love!'

A Touch of Class **
GB 1973 106m Technicolor Panavision
Avco/Brut/Gordon Films (Melvin Frank)

A married American businessman in London has a hectic affair with a dress designer.
Amiable and very physical sex farce with hilarious highlights and a few longueurs between; the playing keeps it above water.
w Melvin Frank, Jack Rose *d* Melvin Frank *ph* Austin Dempster *m* John Cameron
☆ *Glenda Jackson, George Segal*, Paul Sorvino, Hildegarde Neil
'Machine-tooled junk.' – *William S. Pechter*
'Brightly performed and quite engaging until it fades into vapid variations on a one-joke theme.' – *Sight and Sound*
Glenda Jackson
best picture; script; John Cameron; song 'All That Love Went to Waste' (*m*George Barrie, *ly*Sammy Cahn)

Touch of Evil ****
US 1958 95m bw
U-I (Albert Zugsmith)

A Mexican narcotics investigator honeymooning in a border town clashes with the local police chief over a murder.
Overpoweringly atmospheric melodrama crammed with Wellesian touches, but very cold and unsympathetic, with rather restrained performances (especially his) and a plot which takes some following. Hardly the most auspicious return to Hollywood for a wanderer, but now a cult classic.
wd Orson Welles novel Badge of Evil by Whit Masterson *ph Russell Metty m* Henry Mancini
☆ Charlton Heston, Orson Welles, Janet Leigh, Marlene Dietrich, Akim Tamiroff, Joseph Calleia, Ray Collins, Dennis Weaver
'Pure Orson Welles and impure balderdash, which may be the same thing.' – *Gerald Weales, Reporter*

A Touch of Larceny *
GB 1959 92m bw
Paramount/Ivan Foxwell
A naval commander mysteriously disappears in the hope that he will be branded a traitor and can sue for libel.
Fairly amusing light comedy with lively performances.
w Roger MacDougall, Guy Hamilton, Ivan Foxwell *novel The Megstone Plot* by Andrew Garve *d* Guy Hamilton *ph* John Wilcox *m* Philip Green
☆ James Mason, Vera Miles, George Sanders, Robert Flemyng, Ernest Clark, Duncan Lamont, Peter Barkworth
'A beguilingly polished comedy, reminiscent in its style, urbanity and sheen of the sort of thing Lubitsch was doing in the 30s.' – *Daily Mail*

A Touch of Love
GB 1969 107m Eastmancolor
Amicus/Palomar (Milton Subotsky)
US title: *Thank You All Very Much*
A pregnant London student tries to get an abortion but later decides against it.
Curious bid for serious drama by horror producers; all very conscientious but rather dreary.
w Margaret Drabble *novel The Millstone* by Margaret Drabble *d* Waris Hussein *ph* Peter Suschitsky *m* Michael Dress
☆ Sandy Dennis, Ian McKellen, Michael Coles, John Standing, Eleanor Bron

A Touch of the Sun
GB 1956 80m bw
Eros/Raystro (Raymond Stross)

A hall porter is left a fortune but after living it up for a while returns to his old hotel which is on the rocks.
Limp comedy vehicle.
w Alfred Shaughnessy *d* Gordon Parry *ph* Arthur Grant *m* Eric Spear
☆ Frankie Howerd, Ruby Murray, Dorothy Bromiley, Gordon Harker, Reginald Beckwith, Richard Wattis, Dennis Price, Alfie Bass, Willoughby Goddard

A Touch of Zen ***
Taiwan 1969 180m colour
International Film (Hsia Wu Liang-fang)
original title: *Hsia Nu*
In 14th-century China, a poor 30-year-old portrait painter, who lives with his nagging mother in a derelict, haunted fort, becomes involved with the fugitive daughter of a high-ranking official murdered by a powerful enemy.
Sprawling, colourful epic with a compelling narrative and a superb visual style.
wd King Hu *story* P'u Sung-ling *ph* Hua Hui-ying *m* Wu Ta-chiang *ed* King Hu
☆ Hsu Feng, Shih Chun, Pai Ying, Tien Peng, Hsueh Han, Chiao Hung, Chang Ping-yu
† The film won the Grand Prize at the Cannes Film Festival in 1975.

Touchez pas au Grisbi *
France/Italy 1953 90m approx bw
Del Duca/Antares
aka: *Honour among Thieves*
aka: *Hands Off the Loot*
Two crooks succeed in stealing a consignment of gold, but that's only the start of their worries.
Smooth underworld hokum, with a slightly comic attitude implied if not stated.
w Jacques Becker, Maurice Griffe *novel* Albert Simonin *d* Jacques Becker *ph* Pierre Montazel *m* Jean Wiener
☆ Jean Gabin, Jeanne Moreau, Gaby Basset, Daniel Cauchy, Marilyn Buferd, Lino Ventura, René Dary

Tough Enough
US 1983 107m Technicolor
TCF/American Cinema (William F. Gilmore)

A failing country singer finds success after he enters knockout boxing competitions in order to pay his bills.
Unengrossing drama enlivened by some rough-house fight sequences, but it is not a contender.
w John Leone *d* Richard O. Fleischer *ph* James A. Contner *m* Michael Lloyd, Steve Wax *pd* Bill Kenney *ed* Dann Cahn
☆ Dennis Quaid, Carlene Watkins, Stan Shaw, Pam Grier, Warren Oates, Wilford Brimley, Bruce McGill

Tough Guys
US 1986 104m DeLuxe Panavision
Touchstone/Silver Screen/Brynal (Joe Wizan)

The last train robbers are released from prison after 30 years, and, finding that an old people's home is not for them, return to their old ways.
Slackly written caper comedy with two former stars in their seventh teaming.
w James Orr, Jim Cruickshank *d* Jeff Kanew *ph* King Baggot *m* James Newton Howard
☆ Burt Lancaster, Kirk Douglas, Charles Durning, Alexis Smith, Eli Wallach

Tough Guys Don't Dance
US 1987 108m TVC Color
Zoetrope/Cannon (Menahem Golan, Yoram Globus)

A small businessman in Massachusetts gets involved in a drugs deal.
Would-be parody of the Chandler style which works only fitfully and long outstays its welcome.
wd Norman Mailer *novel* Norman Mailer *ph* Michael Moyer, Danny Dukovny *m* Paula Erickson *pd* Armin Ganz *ed* Debra McDermot
☆ Ryan O'Neal, Isabella Rossellini, Debra Sandlund, Wings Hauser, Lawrence Tierney

Toughest Man in Arizona
US 1952 90m Trucolor
Republic (Sidney Picker)
In 1861 a US marshal falls in love with the wife of an outlaw.
Easy-going, pleasant Western aimed at the top half of a double bill.
w John K. Butler *d* R. G. Springsteen *ph* Reggie Lanning *m* Dale Butts
☆ Vaughn Monroe, Joan Leslie, Edgar Buchanan, Victor Jory, Jean Parker, Henry Morgan

Tous les matins du monde *
France 1992 115m colour
Electric/FilmParFilm/D.D./Divali/Sedif/FR3/C.N.C./Canal/Paravision (Jean-Louis Livi)

Marin Marais, a French musician and composer at the court of Louis XIV, recalls the man who taught him musical values, the austere Monsieur de Sainte Colombe, and an unhappy love affair with his teacher's daughter.
Glossy period drama, often delightful to look at and hear, but hollow-centred.
w Pascal Quignard, Alain Corneau *novel* Pascal Quignard *d* Alain Corneau *ph* Yves Angelo *m* Jordi Savall *ad* Bernard Vezat *ed* Marie-Josephe Yoyotte
☆ Gérard Depardieu, Jean-Pierre Marielle, Anne Brochet, Guillaume Depardieu, Caroline Sihol, Carole Richert, Violaine Lacroix, Nadege Teron
'A memorably audacious parable, performed with understanding and set out before us with no evident compromise. But you just have to listen to the music to realise exactly what it's about.' – *Derek Malcolm, Guardian*

Toute une Vie: see *And Now My Love*

'The most exciting screen event of all time!'

Tovarich **
US 1937 98m bw
Warner (Robert Lord)
A royal Russian husband and wife flee the revolution to Paris and take jobs as servants in an eccentric household.
A lively comedy of its time; though many of the jokes now seem obvious, the playing preserves its essential quality.
w Casey Robinson *play* Jacques Deval *play adaptation Robert E. Sherwood d* Anatole Litvak *ph* Charles Lang *m* Max Steiner
☆ *Claudette Colbert, Charles Boyer, Basil Rathbone*, Anita Louise, Melville Cooper, Isabel Jeans, Maurice Murphy, Morris Carnovsky, Gregory Gaye, Montagu Love, Fritz Feld
'A yarn of charming and finely shaded characterizations. Both humour and heart appeal spring from intimate acquaintance with the background and motives of each player. Class production, magnet for first runs.' – *Variety*

Toward the Unknown
US 1956 115m Warnercolor Warnerscope
Warner/Toluca (Mervyn Le Roy)
GB title: *Brink of Hell*
An over-age officer takes part in the X2 experiments with rocket-firing aircraft.
Humourless flagwaver, very forgettable.
w Beirne Lay Jnr *d* Mervyn Le Roy *ph* Harold Rosson *m* Paul Baron
☆ William Holden, Lloyd Nolan, Virginia Leith, Charles McGraw, Murray Hamilton, L. Q. Jones, James Garner, Paul Fix, Karen Steele

Towed in a Hole ***
US 1932 20m bw
Hal Roach
Two would-be fishermen wreck the boat they have just bought.

Brilliant star farce, filled with wonderfully lunatic dialogues and freshly conceived slapstick.
w Stan Laurel *d* George Marshall *ph* Art Lloyd *ed* Richard Currier
☆ Stan Laurel, Oliver Hardy, Billy Gilbert

'They came.They saw. They died.'
Tower of Evil
GB/US 1972 89m Technicolor
MGM-EMI/Grenadier/Fanfare (Richard Gordon)
US title: *Horror of Snape Island*
A private investigator takes his family to an island lighthouse to discover the truth about three mysterious deaths.
An unoriginal little shocker.
wd Jim O'Connolly *story* George Baxt *ph* Desmond Dickinson *m* Kenneth V. Jones *ad* Disley Jones *ed* Henry Richardson
☆ Bryant Halliday, Jill Haworth, Anna Palk, William Lucas, Anthony Valentine, Jack Watson, Derek Fowlds, Dennis Price, George Coulouris
'As much energy is expended on the self-conscious nudity and violence as on the suspense, but the dialogue and performances are anyway equally unconvincing.' – *David McGillivray, MFB*

Tower of London **
US 1939 92m bw
Universal (Rowland V. Lee)
With the help of Mord the executioner, Richard Crookback kills his way to the throne but is destroyed at Bosworth.
The Shakespearean view of history played as a horror comic: despite an overall lack of pace, spirited scenes and good performances win the day.
w Robert N. Lee *d* Rowland V. Lee *ph George Robinson m* Charles Previn
☆ *Basil Rathbone*, Boris Karloff, Barbara O'Neil, Ian Hunter, Vincent Price, Nan Grey, John Sutton, Leo G. Carroll, Miles Mander
'Spine-tingling horror picture … so strong that it may provide disturbing nightmares as aftermath.' – *Variety*

Tower of London *
US 1962 79m bw
AIP/Admiral (Gene Corman)
A variation on the same events, with Price graduating from Clarence to Crookback, and the addition of ghostly visions.
All very cheap, but occasionally vivid melodrama, despite intrusive American accents.
w Leo V. Gordon, Amos Powell, James B. Gordon *d* Roger Corman *ph* Arch Dalzell *m* Michael Anderson
☆ Vincent Price, Michael Pate, Joan Freeman, Robert Brown, Justice Eatson, Sarah Selby, Richard McCauly, Bruce Gordon

The Tower of Terror
GB 1941 78m bw
ABPC
British and German agents clash in a lighthouse tended by a mad keeper.
Lurid penny-dreadful, quite amusing in its way.
w John Argyle, John Reinhart *d* Lawrence Huntington
☆ Wilfrid Lawson, Movita, Michael Rennie, Morland Graham, George Woodbridge

'One tiny spark becomes a night of towering suspense!'
The Towering Inferno ***
US 1974 165m DeLuxe Panavision
TCF/Warner (Irwin Allen)
The world's tallest building is destroyed by fire on the night of its inauguration.
Showmanlike but relentlessly padded disaster spectacular, worth seeing for its cast of stars, its sheer old-fashioned expertise, and its special effects.
w Stirling Silliphant *novels The Tower by Richard Martin Stern, The Glass Inferno by Thomas M. Scortia, Frank M. Robinson d John Guillermin, Irwin Allen ph Fred Koenekamp, Joseph Biroc m* John Williams *pd William Creber ed* Harold F. Kress, Carl Kress *sp Bill Abbott*
☆ Paul Newman, Steve McQueen, William Holden, Faye Dunaway, Fred Astaire, Susan Blakely, Richard Chamberlain, Robert Vaughn, Jennifer Jones, O. J. Simpson, Robert Wagner
'Several generations of blue-eyed charmers act their roles as if each were under a separate bell jar.' – *Verina Glaessner*
'Each scene of someone horribly in flames is presented as a feat for the audience's delectation.' – *New Yorker*
'The combination of Grade A spectacle and B-picture characters induces a feeling of sideline detachment.' – *Michael Billington, Illustrated London News*
Academy Award: photography; song 'We May Never Love Like This Again' (m/ly Al Kasha, Joel Hirschhorn); editing
Academy Award nomination: best picture; John Williams; Fred Astaire; art direction; sound
BAFTA: John Williams; Fred Astaire

Town and Country
US 2001 DeLuxe
Entertainment/New Line/FR Production/Longfellow (Andrew Karsch, Fred Roos, Simon Fields)
An adulterous architect continues his philandering ways after his wife discovers his affairs.
Glossy, slight, uninteresting bedroom comedy.
w Michael Laughlin, Buck Henry *d* Peter Chelsom *ph* William A. Fraker *m* Rolfe Kent *pd* Caroline Hanania *ed* David Moritz, Claire Simpson
☆ Warren Beatty (Porter Stoddard), Diane Keaton (Ellie Stoddard), Andie MacDowell (Eugenie Claybourne), Garry Shandling (Griffin), Jenna Elfman (Auburn), Nastassja Kinski (Alex), Goldie Hawn (Mona), Charlton Heston (Mr Claybourne), Marian Seldes (Mrs Claybourne), Josh Hartnett (Tom Stoddard), Alice Stoddard (Tricia Vessey), Buck Henry (Suttler)
'Features a lot of talent on both sides of the camera operating in low gear.' – *Todd McCarthy, Variety*
'Without warning, it goes from inept to complete disaster, sinking from indifferent to fiasco in the blink of an eye.' – *Kenneth Turan, Los Angeles Times*
† It cost around $80m to make over a period of two years, and took around $6.8m at the US box-office.

A Town Called Bastard
GB 1971 97m Technicolor Franscope
Benmar/Zurbano (Ben Fisz)
aka: *A Town Called Hell*
Mexican revolutionaries massacre a priest and his congregation and take over the town. Ten years later a widow arrives seeking vengeance.
Sadistic Western with an opening massacre followed by twenty-two killings (count 'em). Pretty dull otherwise.
w Richard Aubrey *d* Robert Parrish *ph* Manuel Berenguer *m* Waldo de Los Rios
☆ Robert Shaw, Stella Stevens, Telly Savalas, Martin Landau, Michael Craig, Fernando Rey, Dudley Sutton

A Town Called Hell: see *A Town Called Bastard*

The Town is Quiet: see *La Ville Est Tranquille*

A Town like Alice **
GB 1956 117m bw
Rank/Vic Films (Joseph Janni)
US title: *The Rape of Malaya*
Life among women prisoners of the Japanese in Malaya, especially one who is finally reunited with her Australian lover.
Genteelly harrowing war film, formlessly adapted from the first part of a popular novel; a big commercial success of its day.
w W. P. Lipscomb, Richard Mason *novel* Nevil Shute *d* Jack Lee *ph* Geoffrey Unsworth *m* Matyas Seiber
☆ Virginia McKenna, Peter Finch, Takagi, Marie Lohr, Maureen Swanson, Jean Anderson, Renée Houston, Nora Nicholson
BAFTA: Peter Finch; Virginia McKenna

'There she lay, wearing her nylons – right around her neck!'
Town on Trial *
GB 1956 96m bw
Columbia/Marksman (Maxwell Setton)
A police inspector solves the murder of a girl after a tennis club dance in a British country town.
Straightforward murder mystery shot in Weybridge, with a wide variety of suspects having something to hide; settings and characters are quite realistic and also a little dreary.
w Ken Hughes, Robert Westerby *d* John Guillermin *ph* Basil Emmott *m* Tristram Cary
☆ John Mills, Charles Coburn, Derek Farr, Barbara Bates, Alec McCowen, Geoffrey Keen, Elizabeth Seal, Margaretta Scott, Fay Compton

The Town Went Wild
US 1945 78m bw
PRC
Feuding next-door neighbours have children in love.
Romeo and Juliet in small-town America, and none of it sharp enough.
w Bernard R. Roth, Clarence Greene, Russel Rouse *d* Ralph Murphy
☆ Freddie Bartholomew, Edward Everett Horton, James Lydon, Tom Tully, Jill Browning, Minna Gombell, Maude Eburne, Charles Halton

Town without Pity *
US/Switzerland/Germany 1961 103m bw
UA/Mirisch/Osweg/Gloria (Gottfried Reinhardt)
A German girl is raped and four American soldiers are accused; the defence counsel's wiles lead to the girl's suicide.
Dour drama with overpowering expressionist technique but not much real sympathy, interest or surprise.
w Silvia Reinhardt, George Hurdalek *novel The Verdict* by Manfred Gregor *d* Gottfried Reinhardt *ph* Kurt Hasse *m* Dimitri Tiomkin
☆ Kirk Douglas, E. G. Marshall, Christine Kaufmann, Barbara Rutting, Robert Blake, Richard Jaeckel
Academy Award nomination: title song (mDimitri Tiomkin, lyNed Washington)

The Toxic Avenger
US 1985 76m colour
Blue Dolphin/Troma/Lloyd Kaufman, Michael Herz
A retarded weakling falls into a vat of radioactive chemicals and is transformed into a monstrously ugly super-hero.
A spoof of the horror genre, but so crudely made and acted as to be even more offensive than the worst of what it mocks.
w Joe Ritter *story* Lloyd Kaufman *d* Michael Herz, Samuel Weil *ph* James London, Michael Kaufman *ed* Richard W. Haines
☆ Andree Maranda, Mitchell Cohen, Pat Ryan Jnr, Jennifer Babtist, Cindy Manion, Robert Pritchard, Gary Schneider, Mark Torgl

The Toxic Avenger, Part II
US 1989 95m TVC Color
Troma/Lloyd Kaufman, Michael Herz
A chemical company wanting to dump its dangerous waste products attempts to kill the Toxic Avenger.
A marginal improvement on the first film, but only because it could hardly be worse.
w Gay Partington Terry, Lloyd Kaufman *d* Michael Herz, Lloyd Kaufman *ph* James London *m* Christopher Demarco *ad* Alexis Grey *ed* Joseph McGirr
☆ Ron Fazio, John Altamura, Phoebe Legere, Rich Collins, Rikiya Yasuoka, Tsutomu Sekine, Mayako Katsuragi, Jessica Dublin

The Toxic Avenger Part III: The Last Temptation Of Toxie
US 1989 89m TVC Color
Troma/Lloyd Kaufman, Michael Herz
The Toxic Avenger is momentarily transformed into an upwardly mobile monster before reverting to type.
Violence, crude humour and deliberately inept acting and directing create a cinematic pollution of their own.
w Gay Partington Terry *story* Lloyd Kaufman *d* Lloyd Kaufman, Michael Herz *ph* James London *m* Barrie Guard *ad* Alex Grey *ed* Michael Schweitzer
☆ Ron Fazio, John Altamura, Phoebe Legere, Rick Collins, Lisa Gaye, Jessica Dublin, Tsutomu Sekine

The Toy
US 1983 102m colour
Columbia/Rastar (Phil Feldman)
A black janitor is hired as a toy for a millionaire's nine-year-old son.
Feeble attempt to translate a 1976 French film by Francis Veber. The few laughs are laughs of embarrassment.
w Carol Sobieski *d* Richard Donner *ph* Laszlo Kovacs *m* Patrick Williams *pd* Charles Rosen
☆ Richard Pryor, Jackie Gleason, Ned Beatty, Scott Schwartz, Teresa Ganzel, Wilfrid Hyde-White, Tony King
'Tasteless in implication, flavourless in execution.' – *Sight and Sound*

The Toy Maker
US 1991 Foto-Kem
Still Silent (Brian Yuzna, Richard N. Gladstein)
The son of a sweet old alcoholic toy-maker creates toys with a difference: they kill.
A nasty little gory horror movie.
w Martin Kitrosser, Brian Yuzna *d* Martin Kitrosser *ph* James Mathers *m* Matthew Morse *pd* W. Brooke Wheeler *ed* Norman Buckley *sp* Screaming Mad George, Ken Tarallo
☆ Jane Higginson, Tracy Fraim, Brian Bremer, William Thorne, Neith Hunter, Mickey Rooney

Toy Soldiers
US 1991 112m Continental Color
Columbia TriStar/Island World (Jack E. Freedman, Wayne S. Williams, Patricia Herskovic)
Wealthy teenage American schoolkids turn the tables on a group of mercenaries, hired by a South American drug dealer, who take them hostage.
Silly, violent action movie presumably aimed at a teen audience that likes plenty of blood and gore.
w Daniel Petrie Jnr, David Koepp *novel* William P. Kennedy *d* Daniel Petrie Jnr *ph* Thomas Burstyn *m* Robert Folk *pd* Chester Kaczenski *ed* Michael Kahn
☆ Sean Astin, Wil Wheaton, Keith Coogan, Andrew Divoff, R. Lee Ermey, Mason Adams, Denholm Elliott, Louis Gossett Jnr, George Perez
'Incompetent botch-up of a potentially good if unlikely story.' – *Derek Malcolm, Guardian*

Toy Story ****
US 1995 80m Technicolor
Buena Vista/Walt Disney/Pixar (Ralph Guggenheim, Bonnie Arnold)
A toy cowboy, the long-time favourite of a small boy, is jealous of a new arrival, an astronaut figure who refuses to believe that he is a toy and replaces him in the boy's affections.
A brilliant animated feature, the first to be entirely computer-generated, and notable for its energy and considerable wit; it is darker in tone than most recent Disney movies, but none the worse for that. With its hyper-realism, glossy textures, its dazzling use of perspective and movement, it makes conventional animations look old-fashioned.
w Joss Whedon, Andrew Stanton, Joel Cohen, Alec Sokolow story Joe Ranft, John Lasseter, Pete Docter, d John Lasseter m Randy Newman *ad* Ralph Eggleston *ed* Robert Gordon, Lee Unkrich
☆ Featuring the voices of: *Tom Hanks, Tim Allen,* Don Rickles, Jim Varney, Wallace Shawn, John Ratzenberger, Annie Potts
Academy Award: John Lasseter (special achievement)
Academy Award nomination: Randy Newman; song 'You've Got a Friend' (m/ly Randy Newman); screenplay

Toy Story 2 ***
US 1999 92m Technicolor
Buena Vista/Walt Disney/Pixar (Helene Plotkin, Karen Robert Jackson)
A wicked toyshop owner steals the cowboy Woody so that he can complete a set of toys, based on a 50s TV show, and sell them to a Japanese museum.
Witty, brilliantly realised comedy of celebrity and obsolescence; it shows an advance in technique over the original, but its narrative, lacking the darker impulses of the first film, is not as resonant.
w Andrew Stanton, Rita Hsiao, Doug Chamberlin, Chris Webb, John Lasseter, Pete Docter, Ash Brannon *d* John Lasseter, Lee Unkrich, Ash Brannon *ph* Sharon Calahan

m Randy Newman *pd* William Cone, Jim Pearson *ed* Edie Bleiman, David Ian Salter, Lee Unkrich
☆ Featuring voices of: Tom Hanks, Tim Allen, Joan Cusack, Kelsey Grammer, Don Rickles, Jim Varney, Wallace Shawn, John Ratzenberger, Wayne Knight, John Morris, Laurie Metcalf

'It is not a sequel. It is an upgrade. It is a manufacturer's improvement of staggering ingenuity. It is a software refinement. It is a species leap, a higher order of being.' – *Peter Bradshaw, Guardian*

'A movie that is dazzlingly inventive in its graphic detail, tells an exciting, sophisticated story and raises complex ideas with clarity and wit.' – *Philip French, Observer*

song 'When She Loved Me' (m/l Randy Newman)

Toy Tiger
US 1956 88m Technicolor Cinemascope
U-I (Howard Christie)
The imaginative small son of a widow 'adopts' her business friend as his father.
Flat sentimental comedy off the studio's conveyor belt, a remake of Mad about Music.
w Ted Sherdeman *d* Jerry Hopper *ph* George Robinson *md* Joseph Gershenson *ad* Alexander Golitzen, Richard H. Riedel *ed* Milton Carruth
☆ Jeff Chandler, Laraine Day, Tim Hovey, Cecil Kellaway, Richard Haydn, David Janssen

The Toy Wife *
US 1938 95m bw
MGM (Merian C. Cooper)
GB title: *Frou Frou*
In the early 19th century in Louisiana, a flirtatious girl causes jealousy and tragedy.
Another bid in the Jezebel/Gone with the Wind *stakes, this handsome production proved a commercial misfire and hastened the end of its star's career.*
w Zoe Akins *d* Richard Thorpe *ph* Oliver T. Marsh *m* Edward Ward
☆ Luise Rainer, Melvyn Douglas, Robert Young, Barbara O'Neil, H. B. Warner, Alma Kruger, Walter Kingsford

'Old-fashioned melodrama, beautifully produced but creaky.' – *Variety*

'Laughter Is A State of Mind.'
Toys
US 1992 121m CFI color
TCF (Mark Johnson, Barry Levinson)
An uptight army officer inherits a toy factory and switches production from cuddly toys to increasingly aggressive ones.
Visually splendid but otherwise totally incoherent movie.
w Valerie Curtin, Barry Levinson *d* Barry Levinson *ph* Adam Greenberg *m* Hans Zimmer, Trevor Horn *pd Ferdinando Scarfiotti ed* Stu Linder
☆ Robin Williams, Michael Gambon, Joan Cusack, Robin Wright, LL Cool J, Donald O'Connor, Jack Warden

'Only a filmmaker with Barry Levinson's clout would have been so indulged to create such a sprawling, seemingly unsupervised mess … It will be hard to top as the season's major clunker.' – *Variety*

'A disaster … It is quite unlike anything Levinson has done before, and it is sincerely to be hoped that he never does anything like it again.' – *Derek Malcolm, Guardian*

Ferdinando Scarfiotti; Albert Wolsky (costume design)

Toys in the Attic *
US 1963 90m bw Panavision
UA/Claude/Mirisch
In a shabby New Orleans home, two ageing spinsters struggle to look after their ne'er-do-well brother.
Play into film doesn't go in this case, but the script and acting are interesting.
w James Poe play Lillian Hellman d George Roy Hill *ph* Joseph Biroc *m* George Duning *ad* Cary Odell
☆ *Geraldine Page, Wendy Hiller,* Dean Martin, Yvette Mimieux, Gene Tierney, Larry Gates

Traces of Red
US 1992 105m colour
Entertainment/Samuel Goldwyn Company (Mark Gordon)
A cop attempts to solve a series of killings of women with whom he has been involved and for which he is chief suspect.
Deadly dull thriller, of no interest whatsoever.
w Jim Piddock *d* Andy Wolk *ph* Tim Suhrstedt *m* Graeme Revel *pd* Dan Bishop, Dianna Freas *ed* Trudy Ship
☆ James Belushi, Lorraine Bracco, Tony Goldwyn, William Russ, Faye Grant, Michelle Joyner, Joe Lisi, Victoria Bass, Jim Piddock

'What could have been, and perhaps was intended to be, a fetching latterday film noir, is constantly stymied by a wooden script, a cast that is at a loss to deal with it, and direction that gives nobody any help.' – *Derek Malcolm, Guardian*

'A dramatic failure but an entertaining exercise in camp.' – *Variety*

Track 29
GB 1988 91m colour
Recorded Releasing/Handmade (Rick McCullum)
A sensual woman, whose husband prefers playing with his electric train-set, is attracted to a mysterious stranger who claims to be her long-lost son.
Offbeat but unsatisfactory psychological drama that loses its way in thickets of sexuality.
w Dennis Potter *d* Nicolas Roeg *ph* Alex Thomson *m* Stanley Myers *ad* David Brockhurst *ed* Tony Lawson
☆ Theresa Russell, Gary Oldman, Christopher Lloyd, Sarah Bernhard, Colleen Camp, Seymour Cassel

'A story of how men and women act when they think nobody is looking!'
Track of the Cat *
US 1954 102m Warnercolor Cinemascope
Warner/Wayne-Fellows/Batjac (Robert Fellows)
In the northern California backwoods one winter in the 1880s a farming family is menaced by a marauding mountain lion.
With the lion a symbol of evil, this is real Cold Comfort Farm *country and despite good intentions all round becomes irresistibly funny before the end, largely because everyone moves and speaks so s-l-o-w-l-y. The bleached colour is interesting but would suit only snowy settings.*
w A. I. Bezzerides *novel* Walter Van Tilburg Clark *d William A. Wellman ph William H. Clothier* *m* Roy Webb
☆ Robert Mitchum, Diana Lynn, Beulah Bondi, Teresa Wright, Tab Hunter, Philip Tonge, William Hopper, Carl Switzer

'Cinemascope's first genuine weirdie … the script is redolent of Eugene O'Neill, and to its presentation the director brings a touch of Poe … Despair hangs in the air like a curse … unfortunately ambition overreaches itself, and the film topples over into barnstorming melodrama.' – *MFB*

'Bill Wellman had the idea: he wanted to make a colour picture with very little colour.' – *William Clothier*

Trackdown
US 1976 98m DeLuxe
UA/Essaness (Bernard Schwarz)
A Montana rancher follows his sister to Los Angeles and avenges her ill-treatment there by gangsters.
Routine action thriller with fashionable realism and violence.
w Paul Edwards *d* Richard T. Heffron *ph* Gene Polito *m* Charles Bernstein
☆ Jim Mitchum, Karen Lamm, Anne Archer, Erik Estrada, Cathy Lee Crosby, Vince Cannon

Tracks
US 1976 90m colour
Rainbow Pictures (Howard Zuker)
A Vietnam veteran begins to lose his reason as he makes a train journey to take back home the coffin of his friend, killed in action.
A movie with an improvised feel, consisting of a series of desultory meetings and conversations between travellers which never quite reach any destination.
wd Henry Jaglom *ph* Paul Glickman *ed* George Folsey Jnr
☆ Dennis Hopper, Taryn Power, Dean Stockwell, Topo Swope, Alfred Ryder, Zack Norman, Michael Emil

Trade Winds
US 1938 93m bw
Walter Wanger
A girl who thinks she has committed murder flees to the Far East, and a cynical detective is sent to bring her back. Guess what happens.
Smartly written mixture of comedy, drama, mystery and travelogue which comes off only in spots; it needed a firmer hand.
w Dorothy Parker, Alan Campbell, Frank R. Adams *d* Tay Garnett *ph* Rudolph Maté *m* Alfred Newman
☆ Fredric March, Joan Bennett, Ralph Bellamy, Ann Sothern, Sidney Blackmer, Thomas Mitchell, Robert Elliott

'All the elements that provide broad entertainment are present in this picture, and it should reap healthy grosses.' – *Variety*

Trader Horn *
US 1930 120m bw
MGM (Irving Thalberg)
An experienced African trader overcomes tribal hostility.
Primitive talkie for which second units were sent to Africa amid much publicity hoo-ha. After fifty years, nothing of interest remains to be seen.
w Richard Schayer, Dale Van Every, Thomas Neville *novel* Alfred Aloysius Horn, Ethelreda Lewis *d* W. S. Van Dyke *ph* Clyde de Vinna
☆ Harry Carey, Edwina Booth, Duncan Renaldo, Mutia Omoolu, C. Aubrey Smith

'Sure money-getter. Outstanding animal stuff, great sound effects, and thin story, which has good-looking white girl romping around scantily clad.' – *Variety*

'A movie that contains all the best features of a zoo, a cannibal dance, and a big yarn by Rider Haggard.' – *National Board of Review*

best picture

Trader Horn
US 1973 105m Metrocolor
MGM (Lewis J. Rachmil)
Pitiful remake patched together largely from stock footage.
w William Norton, Edward Harper *d* Reza Badiyi *ph* Ronald W. Browne *m* Shelly Manne
☆ Rod Taylor, Anne Heywood, Jean Sorel

'Laughably inept … it cannot face word of mouth for long.' – *Variety*

'No More Vegetables, No More Homework, No More Cleaning Your Room…'
Trading Mom
US 1994 83m colour
Trimark (Raffaella De Laurentiis)
aka: *The Mommy Market*
Tired of their nagging mother, three children use a spell to wish her away and audition three new mothers, who turn out to be much worse.
A broadly-acted movie intended for a family audience, but only likely to be appreciated by mothers who enjoy saying 'I told you so.'
wd Tia Brelis *novel The Mommy Market* by Nancy Brelis *ph* Buzz Feitshans IV *m* David Kitay *pd* Cynthia Charette *ed* Isaac Sehayek
☆ Sissy Spacek (Mommy/Mama/Mom/Natasha), Anna Chlumsky (Elizabeth), Aaron Michael Metchik (Jeremy), Asher Metchik (Harry), Maureen Stapleton (Mrs Cavour)

'An amicable if undistinguished film for the whole family.' – *Variety*

Trading Places **
US 1983 116m Technicolor
Paramount/Landis-Folsey (Aaron Russo)
Two rich men arrange a wager on the effects of environment over heredity, and arrange for a con man and a stockbroker to change places.
Surprisingly witty comedy, which while not aspiring to great heights, and marred by a few excesses, brought a refreshing breath of air to a declining genre.
w Timothy Harris, Herschel Weingrod *d John Landis ph* Robert Paynter *m* Elmer Bernstein *pd* Gene Rudolf
☆ Dan Aykroyd, Eddie Murphy, *Ralph Bellamy, Don Ameche, Denholm Elliott*, Jamie Lee Curtis, Kristin Holby

'Proof positive that the genuine American populist comedy can still attract attention.' – *John Pym, MFB*

Elmer Bernstein

Jamie Lee Curtis, Denholm Elliott

Traffic *
France/Italy 1970 96m Eastmancolor
Corona/Gibe/Selenia (Robert Dorfman)
The designer of a camping car has various little accidents on the way from the works to a show.
Rambling comedy with understated jokes and an almost invisible star.
w Jacques Tati, Jacques Lagrange *d* Jacques Tati (with Bert Haanstra) *ph* Edouard Van Den Enden, Marcel Weiss *m* Charles Dumont
☆ Jacques Tati

'No One Gets Away Clean'
Traffic **
US 2000 147m CFI
Entertainment/USA Films/Initial/Bedford Falls (Edward Zwick, Marshall Herskovitz, Laura Bickford)
A new American drugs czar gets a close-up view of the problems when his daughter becomes an addict; while in Mexico DEA agents and Tijuana cops struggle against millionaire dealers and corrupt officials.
Inside this fat, complex colour-coded saga, all pale yellows and moody blues, is a lean thriller struggling to get out, but it becomes bogged down by lengthy exposition and awkward moralising; it is centrally flawed by Douglas's implausible official, who, however much he clenches his jaw, is never more than a narrative device.
w Stephen Gaghan *TV series Traffik* by Simon Moore *d* Steven Soderbergh *ph* Peter Andrews *m* Cliff Martinez *pd* Philip Messina *ed* Stephen Mirrione *cos* Louise Frogley
☆ Michael Douglas (Robert Wakefield), Don Cheadle (Montel Gordon), *Benicio Del Toro* (Javier Rodriguez), Luiz Guzman (Ray Castro), Dennis Quaid (Arnie Metzger), Catherine Zeta-Jones (Helena Ayala), Steven Bauer (Carlos Ayala), Benjamin Bratt (Juan Obregon), James Brolin (General Ralph Landry), Erika Christensen (Caroline Wakefield), Clifton Collins Jnr (Francisco Flores), Miguel Ferrer (Eduardo Ruiz), Albert Finney (Chief of Staff), Topher Grace (Seth Abrahms), Amy Irving (Barbara Wakefield) and also Tomas Milian, D.W. Moffett, Peter Riegert

'A flashy entertainment that can only offer frustrating glimpses of the currents of psychology and desire far beneath the surface.' – *Andrew O'Hehir, Sight and Sound*

Steven Soderbergh; Benicio Del Toro; Stephen Gaghan; Stephen Mirrione

picture

Stephen Gaghan; Benicio Del Toro

The Tragedy of a Ridiculous Man ***
Italy 1981 116m Technicolor
Warner/Ladd Company (Giovanni Bertolucci)
original title: *La Tragedia Di Un Uomo Ridicolo*
A dairy farmer is faced with losing his livelihood in order to pay a ransom demanded by terrorists who have kidnapped his son.
Engrossing study of contemporary terrorism and individual responsibility, though its refusal to explain everything alienated many audiences.
wd Bernardo Bertolucci *ph* Carlo Di Palma *m* Ennio Morricone *pd* Gianni Silvestri *ed* Gabriella Cristiani
☆ Ugo Tognazzi, Anouk Aimee, Laura Morante, Victor Cavallo, Olympia Carlisi, Riccardo Tognazzi, Vittorio Caprioli

The Tragedy of a Switchboard Operator:
see *The Switchboard Operator*

The Trail Beyond
US 1934 57m bw
Monogram/Lone Star (Paul Malvern)
A cowboy goes to Canada to find missing relatives of his father's best friend and helps an old college friend along the way.

A routine Western, with rather more plot and less action than usual.
w Lindsley Parsons *story* *The Wolf Hunters* by James Oliver Curwood *d* Robert N. Bradbury *ph* Archie Stout *ad* E. R. Hickson *ed* Charles Hunt
☆ John Wayne, Verna Hillie, Noah Beery Snr, Noah Beery Jnr, Robert Frazer, Iris Lancaster, James Marcus

The Trail of '98 *
US 1928 90m (24 fps) bw silent
MGM
San Franciscans leave their homes for the Klondike gold rush.
Impressive spectacular while it stays outdoors; not so good when the plot takes over.
w Waldemar Young, Ben Glazer *novel* Robert W. Service *d* Clarence Brown
☆ Dolores Del Rio, Ralph Forbes, Harry Carey, Karl Dane, Tully Marshall

'The surging drama of love in the Kentucky hills springs to thrilling life as the first outdoor action romance filmed in colour!'
The Trail of the Lonesome Pine *
US 1936 102m Technicolor
Paramount (Walter Wanger)
A hillbilly girl goes back home when her brother is killed in a family feud.
Antediluvian Ozarkian melodrama, notable as the first outdoor film to be shot in three-colour Technicolor.
w Grover Jones, Horace McCoy, Harvey Thew *novel* John Fox Jnr *d* Henry Hathaway *ph* *Howard Greene* *m* Hugo Friedhofer, Gerard Carbonara
☆ Sylvia Sidney, Fred MacMurray, Henry Fonda, Fred Stone, Nigel Bruce, Beulah Bondi, Robert Barrat, Spanky McFarland, Fuzzy Knight
'A good show saleable for big grosses, a flicker the ballyhoo boys can and will do tricks with.' – *Variety*
'Unnatural as it is, the colour does no serious damage to the picture. This moldy bit of hokum ... takes movies back to the days of their childhood.' – *Newsweek*
† The story was first filmed in 1915 by Cecil B. de Mille.
song 'A Melody from the Sky' (*m*Louis Alter, *ly*Sidney Mitchell)

Trail of the Pink Panther
GB 1982 97m Technicolor Panavision
MGM-UA/Titan (Blake Edwards, Tony Adams)
Inspector Clouseau is reported missing at sea and a television reporter interviews those who had known him.
Flimsy, necrophiliac excuse for a movie, with a star cast clearly failing to make bricks without straw two years after the nominal star's death.
w Frank and Tom Waldman, Blake Edwards, Geoffrey Edwards *d* Blake Edwards *ph* Dick Bush *m* Henry Mancini *pd* Peter Mullins *ed* Alan Jones
☆ Peter Sellers, Joanna Lumley, Herbert Lom, David Niven, Richard Mulligan, Capucine, Robert Loggia, Harvey Korman, Burt Kwouk, Graham Stark, Leonard Rossiter, Peter Arne, Ronald Fraser

Trail of the Vigilantes *
US 1940 78m bw
Universal
In the old west, a reporter sets out to break up a band of outlaws.
A mild Western which at the time had some reputation as a wild comedy; the fact was that it turned out badly and the editors did the best they could.
w Harold Shumate *d* Allan Dwan
☆ Franchot Tone, Warren William, Broderick Crawford, Andy Devine, Mischa Auer, Porter Hall, Peggy Moran
'As light amusement it does all right, but it is amusement in confusion.' – *Otis Ferguson*

Trail Street
US 1947 84m bw
RKO (Nat Holt)
US Marshall Bat Masterson cleans up the Kansas town of Liberal, where pioneering farmers are driven off their land and their crops destroyed by ruthless trail riders and their herds of cattle.
Pretty good, unpretentious Western in which cowboys are the villains.
w Norman Houston, Gene Lewis *novel* William Corcoran *d* Ray Enright *ph* J. Roy Hunt *m* Paul Sawtell *md* C. Bakaleinikoff *ad* Albert D'Agostino, Ralph Berger *ed* Lyle Boyer
☆ Randolph Scott (Bat Masterson), Robert Ryan, Anne Jeffreys, Billy House, George 'Gabby' Hayes, Steve Brodie, Madge Meredith

'It carried their hopes, their nation's honour!'
The Train **
US 1965 140m bw
UA/Ariane/Dear (Jules Bricken)
In 1944, the French resistance tries to prevent the Nazis from taking art treasures back to Germany on a special train.
Proficient but longwinded suspense actioner with spectacular sequences; a safe bet for train enthusiasts.
w Franklin Coen, Frank Davis, Walter Bernstein *d* *John Frankenheimer* *ph* Jean Tournier, Walter Wottiz *m* Maurice Jarre
☆ Burt Lancaster, *Paul Scofield*, Jeanne Moreau, Michel Simon, Wolfgang Preiss, Suzanne Flon
'Extraordinarily good in many of its parts but rather disappointing as a whole ... its greatest virtue is an almost overpowering physical realism.' – *Moira Walsh, America*
script

Train of Dreams
Canada 1987 89m colour
NFBC (Sam Grana)
An arrogant teenage mugger is sent to a correctional centre for two years.
Earnest but inconsequential social tract, with flashbacks to the protagonist's violent past.
w John N. Smith, Sally Bochner, Sam Grana *d* John N. Smith *ph* David de Volpi *m* Malcolm MacKenzie Jnr *ed* John N. Smith
☆ Jason St Amour, Marcella Santa Maria, Fred Ward, Christopher Neil, David Linetsky, Milton Hartman

Train of Events
GB 1949 89m bw
Ealing (Michael Relph)
Portmanteau of stories à la *Friday the 13th* or *Dead of Night*, linked by a train disaster.
A rather mechanical entertainment, proficiently made.
w Basil Dearden, T. E. B. Clarke, Ronald Millar, Angus MacPhail *d* Basil Dearden, Charles Crichton, Sidney Cole *ph* Lionel Banes, Gordon Dines *m* Leslie Bridgewater
☆ Valerie Hobson, John Clements, Jack Warner, Gladys Henson, Peter Finch, Irina Baronova, Susan Shaw, Patric Doonan, Joan Dowling, Laurence Payne, Mary Morris

The Train Robbers
US 1973 92m Technicolor Panavision
Warner/Batjac (Michael Wayne)
A widow asks three gunmen to help her clear her husband's name by retrieving gold he had stolen.
Shaggy-dog Western, sadly lacking in comic situation and detail.
wd Burt Kennedy *ph* William Clothier *m* Dominic Frontière
☆ John Wayne, Ann-Margret, Rod Taylor, Ben Johnson, Bobby Vinton, Christopher George

'The only thing more dangerous than the line being crossed, is the cop who will cross it.'
Training Day **
US 2001 122m Technicolor Panavision
Warner/Village Roadshow/NPV/Outlaw (Jeffrey Silver, Bobby Newmyer)
On his first day as a member of an elite narcotics unit, a rookie cop discovers that his commander is corrupt.
Tense, violent, urban thriller notable for the opportunity it provides for Washington to strut his stuff as a harsh, charismatic, psychopathic cop.
w David Ayer *d* Antoine Fuqua *ph* Mauro Fiore *m* Mark Mancina *pd* Naomi Shohan *ed* Conrad Buff
☆ *Denzel Washington* (Alonzo Harris), Ethan Hawke (Jake Hoyt), Scott Glenn (Roger), Tom Berenger (Stan Gursky), Harris Yulin (Doug Rosselli), Raymond J. Barry (Lou Jacobs), Cliff Curtis (Smiley), Dr Dre (Paul), Snoop Dogg (Blue), Macy Gray (Sandman's Wife), Charlotte Ayanna (Lisa)
'Grotesquely, continuously violent, injecting its adrenaline rush into the bloodstream with a non-stop series of confrontational showdowns.' – *Alexander Walker, London Evening Standard*
'Moves rapidly, is extremely violent and not entirely plausible.' – *Philip French, Observer*
Denzel Washington
Ethan Hawke

Trainspotting ***
GB 1996 94m colour
Polygram/Channel 4/Figment/Noel Gay (*Andrew Macdonald*)
Four Scottish friends enjoy the highs, and suffer the lows, of heroin addiction, while indulging in petty theft, sex, booze and violence whenever they are capable of it.
A dark and ironic take on young junkies at their antisocial worst, directed with terrific energy and style, a witty subversion of the usual documentary approach to such subjects, and excellently acted by its ensemble cast.
w *John Hodge* *novel* Irvine Welsh *d* *Danny Boyle* *ph* Brian Tufano *pd* Kave Quinn *ed* Masahiro Hirakubo
☆ *Ewan McGregor*, Ewen Bremner, Jonny Lee Miller, Kevin McKidd, *Robert Carlyle*, Kelly Macdonald, Peter Mullan, Irvine Welsh
'Spends far too much time with its nose pressed up against the glass of American cinema, desperate for a piece of the action, but merely fogging up the screen with longing. Until British cinema kicks this habit, it will continue to churn out films such as this, which bear the same relation to real film-making that drugs do to real pleasure. It's utterly empty: a cold turkey, despite the fancy trimmings' – *Tom Shone, Sunday Times*
'An extraordinary achievement and a breakthrough British film.' – *Derek Malcolm, Guardian*
'For all its brilliance, the film finally feels sour and hollow.' – *Sheila Johnston*
'Scabrous, brutal and hip, *Trainspotting* is a *Clockwork Orange* for the 90s.' – *Variety*
† The film cost $3m and grossed more than $64 worldwide.
John Hodge
John Hodge

The Traitor *
GB 1957 88m bw
Fantur (E. J. Fancey)
US title: *The Accused*
At the annual reunion of a resistance group, the host announces that one of their number was a traitor.
Heavy-handed theatrical melodrama, helped by a stout plot and some directional flair.
wd *Michael McCarthy* *ph* Bert Mason *m* Jackie Brown
☆ Donald Wolfit, Robert Bray, Jane Griffiths, Carl Jaffe, Anton Diffring, Oscar Quitak, Rupert Davies, John Van Eyssen

The Traitors *
GB 1962 69m bw
Ello (Jim O'Connolly)
A top scientist is killed and MI5 springs into action.
Commendable second feature with narrative virtues absent in most big films.
w *Jim O'Connolly* *d* *Robert Tronson* *ph* Michael Reed *m* Johnny Douglas
☆ Patrick Allen, James Maxwell, Ewan Roberts, Zena Walker

Traitor's Gate
GB 1965 80m bw
Columbia/Summit (Ted Lloyd)
A London businessman organizes a gang to steal the Crown Jewels.
Modest caper melodrama, routine but watchable.
w John Sansom *novel* Edgar Wallace *d* Freddie Francis *ph* Denys Coop
☆ Albert Lieven, Gary Raymond, Margot Trooger, Klaus Kinski, Catherina von Schell, Edward Underdown

The Tramp *
US 1915 20m approx (24 fps) bw silent
Mutual
A tramp saves a girl from crooks, is wounded and cared for by her, deliriously happy – until her lover arrives.
Fairly funny star comedy, the first with sentimental touches and the origin of the into-the-sunset fade-out.
wd Charles Chaplin *ph* Rollie Totheroh
☆ Charles Chaplin, Edna Purviance, Bud Jamison, Leo White, Lloyd Bacon

Tramp Tramp Tramp *
US 1926 65m approx (24 fps) bw silent
Harry Langdon
Harry enters a cross-country walking contest in order to impress his girl.
Well-staged peripatetic comedy, the star's first feature.
w Frank Capra, Tim Whelan, Hal Conklin, Gerald Duffy, Murray Roth, J. Frank Holliday *d* Harry Edwards
☆ *Harry Langdon*, Joan Crawford, Alec B. Francis

'Jack Deth is back ... and he's never been here before!'
Trancers *
US 1985 85m DeLuxe
Empire Pictures (Charles Band)
aka: *Future Cop*
A tough policeman, Jack Deth, is sent from the future into the present day to hunt down a villain who wants to take over the world by creating Trancers, weak-willed and violent individuals under his psychic influence.
Engaging and occasionally witty low-budget science-fiction action movie, featuring a hero with the manner of a world-weary private eye of the 1930s.
w Paul de Meo, Danny Bilson *d* Charles Band *ph* Mac Ahlberg *m* Mark Ryder, Phil Davies *pd* Jeff Staggs *ed* Ted Nicolaou *sp* John Buechler
☆ *Tim Thomerson*, Helen Hunt, Michael Stefani, Art La Fleur, Telma Hopkins, Richard Herd, Anne Seymour, Miguel Fernandez, Biff Manard

Trancers II
US 1991 87m colour
Full Moon (Charles Band)
aka: *Trancers II: The Return of Jack Deth*
Jack Deth protects the father of a future high official against attacks from Trancers.
Abysmal sequel in which little happens and nothing matters, made, by the look of it, on an even more infinitesimal budget.
w Jackson Barr *story* Jackson Barr, Charles Band *d* Charles Band *ph* Adolfo Bartoli *m* Mark Ryder, Phil Davies *pd* Kathleen Coates *ed* Ted Nicolaou, Andy Hornitch *sp* Palah Sandling, Kevin McCarthy
☆ Tim Thomerson, Helen Hunt, Megan Ward, Biff Manard, Richard Lynch, Martine Beswick, Jeffrey Combs, Telma Hopkins
'Some unintentional humor doesn't save this unnecessary sequel, a quickie that's all talk and no action.' – *Variety*

Trancers III
US 1992 83m Foto-Kem
Paramount/Full Moon (Albert Band)
aka: *Trancers III: Deth Lives*
While working as a detective in Los Angeles in 1992, Jack Deth is transported to 2352, when the Trancers are destroying the world, to be ordered back to 2005 to kill their creator.
A low-budget variation on the familiar theme of one man single-handedly overcoming a highly trained army; it is also low on skill and imagination.
wd C. Courtney Joyner *ph* Adolfo Bartoli *m* Mark Ryder, Phil Davies, Richard Band *pd* Milo *ed* Lauren Schaffer, Margaret-Anne Smith *sp* Kurtzman, Nicotero, Berger EFX Group
☆ Tim Thomerson, Melanie Smith, Andrew Robinson, Tony Pierce, Ed Beechner, Dawn Ann Billings, Helen Hunt, Megan Ward, Stephen Macht, Telma Hopkins
'This has some funny lines, smart science fiction riffs, hateworthy villains and, most valuable of all, Thomerson's hard-bitten but hilarious leading performance, to make it worth checking out.' – *Empire*

† The film was cut to 72m on its British video release.

Trans-Europe Express *
France 1966 90m bw
Como Film (Samy Halfon)
Film-makers on a train invent a violent plot and then find life aping it.
A theme beloved of Hollywood is treated intellectually, and almost succeeds in attracting all classes.
wd Alain Robbe-Grillet *ph* Willy Kurant
m Verdi
☆ Jean-Louis Trintignant, Marie-France Pisier, Nadine Verdier, Christian Barbier, Charles Millot, Alain Robbe-Grillet

Transatlantic *
US 1931 74m bw
Fox
Various personal stories come to a climax aboard a transatlantic liner.
Early attempt at what has now become a very worn format; quite lively it must have seemed then.
w Guy Bolton, Lynn Starling *d* William K. Howard *ad* Gordon Wiles
☆ Edmund Lowe, Lois Moran, John Halliday, Greta Nissen, Jean Hersholt, Myrna Loy, Earle Foxe, Billy Bevan
'An aquatic Grand Hotel; should prosper.' – *Variety*
Gordon Wiles

Transatlantic Merry Go Round
US 1934 92m bw
Reliance
Romantic misunderstandings on an ocean liner.
Patchy comedy with some good scenes.
w Joseph Moncure March, Harry W. Conn, Leon Gordon *d* Ben Stoloff *ph* Ted Tetzlaff *md* Alfred Newman
☆ Jack Benny, Nancy Carroll, Gene Raymond, Sydney Howard
'Good, popular screen entertainment; certain box office fodder.' – *Variety*

Transatlantic Tunnel: see *The Tunnel*

Transgression
US 1931 70m bw
RKO
During a Paris vacation, a man forgives his wife for her affair with a Spanish gigolo.
Very routine, matinée drama.
w Elizabeth Meehan *novel* Kate Jordan
d Herbert Brenon
☆ Kay Francis, Ricardo Cortez, Paul Cavanagh, Nance O'Neil
'Doubtful de luxe subject, principally because its story lacks conviction.' – *Variety*

'Rules are made to be broken,'
The Transporter
France/US 2002 92m colour 'Scope
TCF/Europacorp/TF1/Current Entertainment/Canal+ (Luc Besson, Steven Chasman)
A driver who will transport anything for money takes his revenge when his latest client, a gangster, tries to kill him.
Routine action movie that delivers the expected car chases and punch ups with commendable slickness but not much else.
w Luc Besson, Robert Mark Kamen *d* Cory Yuen *ph* Pierre Morel *m* Stanley Clarke
pd HuguesTissandier *ed* Nicolas Trembasiewicz
☆ Jason Statham (Frank Martin), Shu Qi (Lai), François Berleand (Tarconi), Matt Schulze (Wall Street), Ric Young (Mr Kwai)
'What a yawn this truly abysmal film is: a sub-Hong Kong actioner set on the Eurotrash Cote d'Azur.' – *Peter Bradshaw, Guardian*
'Simultaneously the best (the fight scenes) and worst (everything else) action movie of the year. Destined for drunken Friday night rental heaven.' – *Empire*

The Transvestite: see *Glen or Glenda*

The Trap *
US 1958 84m Technicolor
Paramount/Parkwood-Heath (Melvin Frank, Norman Panama)
GB title: *The Baited Trap*
A lawyer helps a vicious killer to escape into Mexico, but the plan backfires.
Reasonably tense action thriller with desert backgrounds.
w Richard Alan Simmons, Norman Panama
d Norman Panama *ph* Daniel L. Fapp *m* Irvin Talbot
☆ Richard Widmark, Lee J. Cobb, Earl Holliman, Tina Louise, Carl Benton Reid, Lorne Greene

The Trap
GB/Canada 1966 106m Eastmancolor Panavision
Parallel (George H. Brown)
In 19th-century British Columbia a rough trapper takes a wife, who at first is terrified of him but nurses him when he is hurt …
Primitive open air melodrama with good action sequences; well made but hardly endearing.
w David Osborn *d* Sidney Hayers *ph* Robert Krasker *m* Ron Goodwin
☆ Oliver Reed, Rita Tushingham, Rex Sevenoaks, Barbara Chilcott

'The Wonder Show Of The World!'
Trapeze **
US 1956 105m DeLuxe Cinemascope
UA/Hecht-Lancaster (James Hill)
A circus partnership almost breaks up when a voluptuous third member is engaged.
Concentrated, intense melodrama filmed almost entirely within a French winter circus and giving a very effective feel, almost a smell, of the life therein. Despite great skill in the making, however, the length is too great for a wisp of plot that goes back to The Three Maxims *and doubtless beyond.*
w James R. Webb *d Carol Reed ph Robert Krasker*
m Malcolm Arnold
☆ *Burt Lancaster, Tony Curtis, Gina Lollobrigida,* Thomas Gomez, Johnny Puleo, Katy Jurado, Sidney James
† This version was supposedly adapted from a Max Catto novel, *The Killing Frost*, but in 1932 Harmonie of Germany issued a film with the title *Trapeze* and a remarkably similar story. It had a scenario by Alfred Machard and was directed by E. A. Dupont. The Anna Neagle film *The Three Maxims* (qv) was also very similar, but that was supposedly an original by Herman Mankiewicz.

Trapped in Paradise
US 1994 112m DeLuxe
TCF (Jon Davison, George Gallo)
Three brothers rob a small-town bank on Christmas Eve and try to return the money when the locals show them kindness.
A comedy that just about gets by on seasonal goodwill, though it might have worked better at half its length.
wd George Gallo *ph* Jack N. Green *m* Robert Folk *pd* Bob Ziembicki *ed* Terry Rawlings
☆ Nicolas Cage, Jon Lovitz, Dana Carvey, John Ashton, Mädchen Amick, Donald Moffat, Richard Jenkins, Jack Heller
'This is a comedy which depends entirely on its playing and certainly not on its script, which is fairly witless.' – *Derek Malcolm, Guardian*

Trash *
US 1970 103m colour
Vaughn/Andy Warhol
aka: *Andy's Warhol's Trash*
A drug addict finds that the women he knows are anxious to cure him of his impotence.
Casually filmed and acted, with casual sexual encounters and moments of comedy along the way.
wd Paul Morrissey
☆ Joe Dallesandro, Geri Miller, Holly Woodlawn, Bruce Pecheur, Jane Forth, Michael Sklar

Trauma
US 1993 105m Technicolor
Overseas Filmgroup/ADC (Dario Argento)
A couple track down a serial killer who is decapitating his victims.
Argento's first American film has little of the visual flair of the best of his Italian shockers; its predictability soon becomes wearing.
w Dario Argento, T. E. D. Klein, Franco Ferrini, Giovanni Romoli *d* Dario Argento *ph* Raffaele Mertes *m* Pino Donaggio *pd* Billy Jett
ed Conrad Gonzalez *sp* Tom Savini
☆ Christopher Rydell, Asia Argento, Piper Laurie, Frederic Forrest, James Russo, Brad Dourif, Laura Johnson
'A by-the-numbers stalker thriller for undemanding genre fans only.' – *Variety*

The Traveling Executioner *
US 1970 95m Metrocolor Panavision
MGM (Jack Smight)
In 1918 an ex-carnival showman travels the American South with his portable electric chair and charges a hundred dollars per execution, but falls for one of his proposed victims.
Oddball fable without apparent moral; neither fantastic nor funny enough.
w Garrie Bateson *d* Jack Smight *ph* Philip Lathrop *m* Jerry Goldsmith
☆ Stacy Keach, Marianna Hill, Bud Cort, Graham Jarvis

Traveling Saleslady
US 1935 75m bw
Warner
A toothpaste manufacturer's daughter shows her father the value of advertising.
Warner stock company comedy which hits no heights but provided reliable entertainment.
w Hugh Herbert, Manuel Seff, Benny Rubin, Frank Howard Clark *d* Ray Enright
☆ Joan Blondell, Hugh Herbert, Glenda Farrell, William Gargan, Al Shean, Grant Mitchell, Ruth Donnelly, Bert Roach
'It will please and should do all right at the wicket.' – *Variety*

Traveller
US 1997 100m CFI color
First Independent/MDP/October/Banner (Bill Paxton, Brian Swardstrom, Mickey Liddell, David Blocker)
A con man, who is part of an inward-looking group of travellers, teaches a young hopeful the tricks of his trade.
A tiresome buddy-buddy movie set in an enclosed community, where to be a buddy is to rat on everyone in the wider world.
w Jim McGlynn *d* Jack Green *ph* Jack Green (uncredited) *m* Andy Paley *pd* Michael Helmy
ed Michael Ruscio
☆ Bill Paxton, Mark Wahlberg, Julianna Margulies, James Gammon, Luke Askew, Nikki Deloach
'With muddled characterisation, a slight script and an over-the-top ending, it emerges as an ill-conceived attempt to make a thriller out of almost nothing.' – *Jessica Mellor, Empire*

Traveller's Joy
GB 1949 78m bw
Gainsborough/Rank
A divorced couple, stranded in Sweden by lack of funds, have to take joint action.
Mild topical comedy from a popular play.
w Allan MacKinnon, Bernard Quayle
play Arthur Macrae *d* Ralph Thomas *ph* Jack Cox *m* Arthur Wilkinson
☆ Googie Withers, John McCallum, Yolande Donlan, Maurice Denham, Geoffrey Sumner, Colin Gordon, Dora Bryan

Travelling North *
Australia 1986 96m Eastmancolor
View Pictures/CEL (Ben Gannon)
A vigorous 70-year-old leaves Melbourne for sub-tropical Queensland, but his health gives out.
Moving Australian mirror image of On Golden Pond, *with good acting and direction.*
w David Williamson *play* David Williamson
d Carl Schultz ph Julian Penney *md* Alan John
pd Owen Paterson *ed* Henry Dangar
☆ *Leo McKern*, Julia Blake, Graham Kennedy, Henri Szeps

Travels with My Aunt *
US 1972 109m Metrocolor Panavision
MGM (Robert Fryer, James Cresson)
A staid bank accountant is landed in a series of continental adventures by his eccentric life-loving aunt.
Busy but fairly disastrous adaptation of a delightful novel, ruined by ceaseless chatter, lack of characterization, shapeless incident and an absurdly caricatured central performance.
w Jay Presson Allen, Hugh Wheeler
novel Graham Greene *d* George Cukor
ph Douglas Slocombe *m* Tony Hatch *pd* John Box
☆ Maggie Smith, *Alec McCowen*, Lou Gossett, Robert Stephens, Cindy Williams
'It seems to run down before it gets started.' – *New Yorker, 1977*
Douglas Slocombe; Maggie Smith

La Traviata **
Italy 1982 109m colour
Accent Films/RAI (Tarak Ben Ammar)
A much-acclaimed version of an opera which had previously defied transcription to the screen.
w Francesco Maria Piave, Franco Zeffirelli
opera Verdi *d Franco Zeffirelli ph* Ennio Guarnieri
pd Franco Zeffirelli, Gianni Quaranta *ed* Peter Taylor, Franca Sylvi
☆ Placido Domingo, Teresa Stratas, Cornell MacNeil, Allan Monk, Axell Gall
'Décors so opulent as on occasion to resemble a three-ring circus.' – *Sight and Sound*
costume design; art direction
production design

Tread Softly Stranger *
GB 1958 91m bw
Alderdale (George Minter)
In a north country town, two brothers in love with the same girl rob a safe.
Hilarious murky melodrama full of glum faces, with a well-worn trick ending; rather well photographed.
w George Minter, Denis O'Dell *play* Jack Popplewell *d* Gordon Parry *ph Douglas Slocombe*
m Tristram Cary
☆ George Baker, Terence Morgan, Diana Dors, Wilfrid Lawson, Patrick Allen, Jane Griffiths, Joseph Tomelty, Norman MacOwan

Treasure Hunt
GB 1952 79m bw
Romulus (Anatole de Grunwald)
The eccentric middle-aged members of an Irish family find their father's fortune is missing.
Theatrical comedy with some charm and humour, but very much a photographed play.
w Anatole de Grunwald *play* M. J. Perry *d* John Paddy Carstairs *ph* C. Pennington-Richards
m Mischa Spoliansky
☆ Jimmy Edwards, *Martita Hunt, Athene Seyler*, Naunton Wayne, June Clyde, Susan Stephen, Brian Worth

Treasure Island **
US 1934 105m bw
MGM (Hunt Stromberg)
An old pirate map leads to a long sea voyage, a mutiny, and buried treasure.
Nicely mounted Hollywood version of a classic adventure story, a little slow in development but meticulously produced.
w John Lee Mahin novel Robert Louis Stevenson
d Victor Fleming *ph* Ray June, Clyde de Vinna, Harold Rosson *m* Herbert Stothart
☆ *Wallace Beery*, Jackie Cooper, Lewis Stone, *Lionel Barrymore*, Otto Kruger, Douglass Dumbrille, Nigel Bruce, Chic Sale
'While much of it entrances, the whole is somewhat tiring.' – *Variety*
'The first three-quarters is so lively and well established in its mood as to make the whole quite worth going to.' – *Otis Ferguson*

Treasure Island *

GB 1950 96m Technicolor
RKO/Walt Disney (Perce Pearce)

Cheerful Disney remake, poor on detail but transfixed by a swaggeringly overplayed and unforgettable leading performance.

w Lawrence Edward Watkin *d* Byron Haskin *ph* F. A. Young *m* Clifton Parker *pd* Thomas Morahan *ed* Alan Jaggs

☆ *Robert Newton*, Bobby Driscoll, Walter Fitzgerald, Basil Sydney, Denis O'Dea, Geoffrey Wilkinson, Ralph Truman

'Serviceable rather than imaginative.' – *Lindsay Anderson*

'The result is an absolutely super party, but not "the world's greatest adventure story". Walt Disney may have, as Synopsis suggests, "much in common with Stevenson". But not this; shiver my timbers, not *Treasure Island*.' – *C. A. Lejeune*.

'The Long John Silver of Robert Newton … is the finest I ever saw … as succulent as peach-fed ham, as sweet as a spoonful of sugar held high over the porridge plate, as darkly oily as a car sump, as tricky as an ageing jockey.' – *Paul Holt*

Treasure Island

GB/France/Germany/Spain 1971 95m colour
Massfilms/FDL/CCC/Eguiluz (Harry Alan Towers)

Spiritless and characterless international remake with poor acting, production and dubbing.

w Wolf Mankowitz, O. W. Jeeves (Welles) *d* John Hough *ph* Cicilio Paniagua *m* Natal Massara

☆ Orson Welles, Kim Burfield, Lionel Stander, Walter Slezak, Rik Battaglia

'Sail the high seas. Battle the pirates. Live the adventure.'

Treasure Island

US 1990 132m colour
Warner/Agamemnon/British Lion (Fraser C. Heston)

Faithful to the original, but a version lacking in panache, and plodding when it should be exciting.

wd Fraser C. Heston *novel* Robert Louis Stevenson *ph* Robert Steadman *m* Paddy Maloney *pd* Tony Woollard *ed* Eric Boyd-Perkins, Bill Parnell, Gregory Gontz

☆ Charlton Heston, Christian Bale, Oliver Reed, Christopher Lee, Richard Johnson, Julian Glover, Clive Wood, John Benfield, Isla Blair

Treasure Island

France/USA 1991 115m colour
BFI/Les Films du Passage/Cannon (Paolo Branco)
French title: *L'Ile au trésor*

A boy dreams, or perhaps lives, a series of events that bear some resemblance to Stevenson's tale of pirates and buried treasure.

A delirious modern-day version, in which events are repeated with variations from different viewpoints, and nothing is what it seems. And nothing is what it amounts to.

wd Raúl Ruiz *novel* *Treasure Island* by Robert Louis Stevenson *ph* Acacio de Almeida *m* Georges Arriagada *ad* Maria-José Branco *ed* Rodolfo Wedeles

☆ Melvil Poupaud, Martin Landau, Vic Tayback, Lou Castel, Jeffrey Kime, Anna Karina, Jean-Pierre Léaud

'One of Ruiz's most seductive films because it so evidently falls short of the grandiose completeness to which it aspires. A richly messy narrative bricolage, it is finally revealed as a game that the viewer is invited to play. It may finally be about very little of serious substance – or indeed about something as trivial as the "future of Western Civilisation", to which the dying Captain portentously alludes – but that in itself makes it all the more worth playing.' – *Jonathan Romney, Sight and Sound*

The Treasure of Lost Canyon

US 1952 82m Technicolor
U-I (Leonard Goldstein)

A small boy robbed of his inheritance finds it with the help of a country doctor who turns out to be his uncle.

Modest juvenile adventure, rather boringly narrated.

w Brainerd Duffield, Emerson Crocker *story* Robert Louis Stevenson *d* Ted Tetzlaff *ph* Russell Metty *m* Joseph Gershenson *ad* Alexander Golitzen, Bernard Herzbrun *ed* Milton Carruth

☆ William Powell, Julia Adams, Charles Drake, Rosemary de Camp, Henry Hull, Tommy Ivo

Treasure of Matecumbe

US 1976 116m Technicolor
Walt Disney (Bill Anderson)

Two boys seek buried gold in the Florida keys.

Cheerful adventure tale with a few nods to Treasure Island; *all very competent in the Disney fashion*.

w Don Tait *d* Vincent McEveety *ph* Frank Phillips *m* Buddy Baker

☆ Robert Foxworth, Joan Hackett, Peter Ustinov, Vic Morrow, Jane Wyatt, Johnny Duran, Billy Attmore

Treasure of Monte Cristo

US 1949 76m bw
Lippert/Screen Guild

In modern San Francisco, a descendant of Monte Cristo is framed for murder.

Mildly amusing but slackly made variant on a familiar theme.

w Aubrey Wisberg, Jack Pollexfen *d* William Berke *ph* Benjamin Kline *m* Albert Glasser

☆ Glenn Langan, Adele Jergens, Steve Brodie, Robert Jordan, Michael Whalen

The Treasure of Pancho Villa

US 1955 96m Technicolor Superscope
RKO/Edmund Grainger

Mexico 1915: an American adventurer becomes involved with the revolutionary Pancho Villa; both seek a gold consignment but it is buried in an avalanche.

Modestly well made, routine action drama.

w Niven Busch *story* J. Robert Glen, Gladys Atwater *d* George Sherman *ph* William Snyder *m* Leith Stevens

☆ Rory Calhoun, Shelley Winters, *Gilbert Roland*, Joseph Calleia

Treasure of San Teresa

GB 1959 81m bw
Orbit (John Nasht, Patrick Filmer-Sankey)

An American secret service agent finds Nazi loot in a Czech convent.

Roughly-made, watchable actioner.

w Jack Andrews, Jeffrey Dell *d* Alvin Rakoff *ph* Wilkie Cooper *m* Philip Martell

☆ Eddie Constantine, Dawn Addams, Marius Goring, Christopher Lee, Walter Gotell

Treasure of the Golden Condor

US 1952 93m Technicolor
TCF (Jules Buck)

A young Frenchman flees to the South Seas but returns to discredit his wicked uncle.

Ineffectual remake of Son of Fury *(qv) with Guatemalan backgrounds and no punch at all.*

wd Delmer Daves *ph* Edward Cronjager *m* Sol Kaplan

☆ Cornel Wilde, Finlay Currie, Constance Smith, George Macready, Walter Hampden, Anne Bancroft, Fay Wray, Leo G. Carroll

'Greed, gold and gunplay on a Mexican mountain of malice!'

'The nearer they got to their treasure the further they got from the law!'

The Treasure of the Sierra Madre **

US 1948 126m bw
Warner (Henry Blanke)

Three gold prospectors come to grief through greed.

Well-acted but partly miscast action fable on the oldest theme in the world; rather tedious and studio-bound for a film with such a high reputation.

wd John Huston *novel* B. Traven *ph* Ted McCord *m* Max Steiner *md* Leo F. Forbstein

☆ Humphrey Bogart, *Walter Huston*, Tim Holt, Alfonso Bedoya, John Huston, Bruce Bennett, Barton MacLane

'This bitter fable is told with cinematic integrity and considerable skill.' – *Henry Hart*

'The faces of the men, in close-up or in a group, achieve a kind of formal pattern and always dominate the screen.' – *Peter Ericsson*

'One of the very few movies made since 1927 which I am sure will stand up in the memory and esteem of qualified people alongside the best of the silent movies.' – *James Agee*

John Huston (as writer and director); Walter Huston

best picture

Treasure Planet *

US 2002 95m Technicolor
Buena Vista/Walt Disney (Roy Conli, John Musker, Ron Clements)

On a distant planet in another universe, a sulky teenager goes in search of a space pirate's treasure.

This space age version of Stevenson's oft-filmed story still keeps a period look, with spaceships resembling galleons. But its visual flair does not compensate for its uninvolving script.

w John Musker, Ron Clements, Rob Edwards *novel* *Treasure Island* by Robert Louis Stevenson *d* John Musker, Ron Clements *m* James Newton Howard *m/ly* John Rzeznik *pd* Steven Olds, Frank Nissen *ed* Michael Kelly

☆ voices of: Joseph Gordon-Levitt (Jim Hawkins), Brian Murray (John Silver), David Hyde Pierce (Doctor Doppler), Emma Thompson (Captain Amelia), Michael Wincott (Scroop), Martin Short (B.E.N.), Laurie Metcalf (Sarah), Patrick McGoohan (Billy Bones), Dane A. Davis (Morph), Roscoe Lee Browne (Mr Arrow), Corey Burton (Onus), Michael McShane (Hands), Austin Majors (Young Jim), Tony Jay (Narrator)

'The listlessness of the script, particularly during the final half hour, leaves only visual invention to keep the aud's eyes on the screen.' – *Andy Klein, Variety*

'Disney is still much better at musicals aimed at young children than it is at post-Star Wars fantasy adventures aimed at teenagers.' – *Nicholas Barber, Independent*

† The film, which cost more than $100m to make, flopped at the US box-office, taking around $38m.

animated feature

The Treasure Seekers

US 1977 88m colour
Halart (Sam Manners)

Two old friends search for Henry Morgan's pirate treasure on Jamaica.

Dull thriller, in which very little happens and nothing to catch one's interest or attention.

w Rod Taylor *story* Walter Brough *d* Henry Levin *ph* Richard Kelly, Joe Jackman *m* Byron Lee *ed* Keith Stafford

☆ Rod Taylor, Stuart Whitman, Elke Sommer, Jeremy Kemp, Keenan Wynn, Bob Phillips, Jennie Sherman

A Tree Grows in Brooklyn ***

US 1945 128m bw
TCF (Louis D. Lighton)

Life for an Irish family with a drunken father in New York's teeming slums at the turn of the century.

A superbly-detailed studio production of the type they don't make any more: a family drama with interest for everybody.

w Tess Slesinger, Frank Davis novel Betty Smith d Elia Kazan ph Leon Shamroy *m* Alfred Newman

☆ *Peggy Ann Garner, James Dunn, Dorothy McGuire, Joan Blondell, Lloyd Nolan*, Ted Donaldson, James Gleason, Ruth Nelson, John Alexander, Adeline de Walt Reynolds, Charles Halton

'He tells a maximum amount of story with a minimum of film. Little touches of humour and human understanding crop up throughout.' – *Frank Ward, NBR*

'An artistically satisfying and emotionally quickening tearjerker.' – *Kine Weekly*

'Its drabness is softened by a glow of love and hope.' – *Picture Show*

James Dunn; Peggy Ann Garner (Special Award as outstanding child actress)

script

Tree of Hands

GB 1988 89m Eastmancolor
Pathé/Granada/British Screen/Film Four International/Greenpoint (Ann Scott)

After her young son dies, an American writer gives a home to an abused boy kidnapped by her mother.

Turgid and downbeat thriller that offers few pleasures.

w Gordon Williams *novel* Ruth Rendell *d* Giles Foster *ph* Kenneth MacMillan *m* Richard Hartley *pd* Adrian Smith *ed* David Martin

☆ Helen Shaver, Lauren Bacall, Malcolm Stoddard, Peter Firth, Paul McGann, Kate Hardie, Tony Haygarth, Phyllida Law

'The film remains essentially comic-strip in its description of the various milieux and its treatment of the theme of who, in this chaotic selfish world, is best suited to care for the innocent.' – *Louise Sweet, MFB*

The Tree of Liberty: see *The Howards of Virginia*

The Tree of Wooden Clogs *

Italy 1978 186m Gevacolor
Curzon Films/RAI/GPC (Giulio Mandelli)

In 19th-century Lombardy the lives of four peasant families are interwined.

Sensitive, novel-like investigation of times gone by; never very exciting but certainly never dull, despite the limits of 16mm and a non-professional cast.

wd Ermanno Olmi *ph* Carlo Petriocioli *m* Bach *md* Fernando Germani *pd* Franco Gambarana

'One man's search for … who knows what.'

Trees Lounge *

US 1996 95m DuArt
Electric/Live Film/Mediaworks (Brad Wyman, Chris Hanley)

An unemployed motor mechanic drinks too much and has problems with women.

A slice of bar-room life, as desultory and apparently aimless as the real thing, but also managing to suggest a few home truths along the way.

wd Steve Buscemi *ph* Lisa Rinzler *m* Evan Lurie *pd* Steve Rosenzweig *ed* Kate Williams

☆ Steve Buscemi, Chloe Sevigny, Michael Buscemi, Anthony LaPaglia, Elizabeth Bracco, Mark Boone Jnr, Danny Baldwin, Seymour Cassel, Carol Kane, Bronson Dudley, Samuel L. Jackson, Mimi Rogers

'A surprisingly tart and astute chronicle.' – *Movieline*

Trelawny of the Wells: see *The Actress*

Tremors **

US 1989 96m DeLuxe
UIP/Universal/No Frills/Brent Maddock, S. S. Wilson

Giant man-eating worms threaten a small Western town.

Enjoyable monster movie in the style of 50s films, which manages to be both funny and suspenseful.

w S. S. Wilson, Brent Maddock, Ron Underwood *d Ron Underwood ph* Alexander Gruszynski *m* Ernest Troost *pd* Ivo Cristante *ed* O. Nicholas Brown

☆ Kevin Bacon, Fred Ward, Finn Carter, Michael Gross, Reba McEntire, Bobby Jacoby, Charlotte Stewart, Tony Genaro

'Shrewdly, unpretentiously written, energetically directed and played with high comic conviction, Tremors is bound to become a cult classic.' – *Richard Schickel, Time*

Tremors II: Aftershocks *

US 1995 90m Foto-Kem
Universal/MCA TV/Stampede (Nancy Roberts, Christopher deFaria)

An ostrich farmer is hired to destroy 'graboids', giant man-eating worms that ravage Mexico's biggest oilfield.

Enjoyable sequel, maintaining some of the humour and suspense of the original, though not as polished; it does contain interesting new monsters.

w Brent Maddock, S. S. Wilson *d* S. S. Wilson *ph* Virgil Harper *m* Jay Ferguson *pd* Ivo Cristante *ed* Bob Ducsay *sp* Alec Gillis, Tom Woodruff Jnr; Tippett Studio

☆ Fred Ward, Christopher Gartin, Helen Shaver, Michael Gross, Marcello Tubert, Marco Hernandez

'For some it will be shelter. For others a prison...No-one will ever forget.'
'It Is A Place 8FT Wide, 600 Miles Long, Man-Made and God-Forsaken.'

The Trench
GB/France 1999 99m Technicolor
Entertainment/Blue PM/Skyline/Galatée (Steve Clark-Hall)

A platoon of British soldiers prepare to leave their trench and advance on the enemy at the start of the Somme offensive in 1916.
This is Journey's End *revisited, as a small group of men reveal their own fears and insecurities in the face of death; there are many better war movies than this low-budget effort.*
wd William Boyd *ph* Tony Pierce-Roberts *m* Evelyn Glennie, Greg Malcangi *pd* Jim Clay *ed* Jim Clark, Laurence Méry-Clark
☆ Paul Nicholls (Billy Macfarlane), Daniel Craig (Sgt Telford Winter), Julian Rhind-Tutt (Ellis Hart), Danny Dyer (Victor Dell), James D'Arcy (Colin Daventry), Tam Williams (Eddie Macfarlane), Antony Strachan (Horace Beckwith), Michael Moreland (George Hogg)
'The sort of small, compact, unambitious play you'd have expected to find on TV 20 years ago.' – *Alexander Walker, London Evening Standard*

Trenchcoat
US 1983 91m Technicolor
Buena Vista/Walt Disney (Jerry Leider)
A would-be thriller writer becomes accidentally involved with real-life skulduggery in Malta.
Lacklustre comedy-drama that never finds a satisfactory tone; its style is one of anonymous blandness.
w Jeffrey Price, Peter Seaman *d* Michael Tuchner *ph* Tonino delli Colli *m* Charles Fox *pd* Rodger Maus *ed* Frank J. Urioste
☆ Margot Kidder, Robert Hays, David Suchet, Gila von Weitershausen, Ronald Lacey, Daniel Faraldo, John Justin

Trent's Last Case
GB 1952 90m bw
Wilcox-Neagle (Herbert Wilcox)

A journalist suspects that the death of a tycoon was murder.
Desultory version of a famous novel, with none of the original style and a few naïveties of its own.
w Pamela Bower *novel* E. C. Bentley *d* Herbert Wilcox *ph* Max Greene *m* Anthony Collins
☆ Michael Wilding, Margaret Lockwood, Orson Welles, John McCallum, Miles Malleson

Trespass **
US 1993 101m DeLuxe
Universal (Neil Canton)

Two firemen go on a treasure hunt for a gold cross, which turns out to be hidden in a deserted factory, used as a headquarters by a heavily armed black gang.
Tense and violent thriller, like a modernized, interior, technological version of The Treasure of the Sierra Madre.
w Bob Gale, Robert Zemeckis *d* Walter Hill *ph* Lloyd Ahern *m* Ry Cooder *pd* Jon Hutman *ed* Freeman Davies
☆ Bill Paxton, Ice T, William Sadler, Ice Cube, Art Evans, De'Voreaux White, Bruce A. Young, Glenn Plummer
'Fizzles like a Molotov cocktail with a soggy fuse.' – *Kim Newman, Empire*

Trial *
US 1955 109m bw
MGM (Charles Schnee)
A young lawyer defends a Mexican boy accused of rape and murder.
Stereotyped but pacy and watchable racial drama with political overtones, Our Hero having to resist bigots, Commies and McCarthyites.
w Don M. Mankiewicz *novel* Don M. Mankiewicz *d* Mark Robson *ph* Robert Surtees *m* Daniele Amfitheatrof
☆ Glenn Ford, Dorothy McGuire, Arthur Kennedy, John Hodiak, Katy Jurado, Rafael Campos, Juano Hernandez, Robert Middleton, John Hoyt
Arthur Kennedy

The Trial *
France/Italy/West Germany 1962 120m bw
Paris Europe/Ficit/Hisa (Alexander Salkind)

original title: *Le Procès*
Joseph K is tried and condemned for an unspecified crime.
Kafka's nightmares tend to go on too long, and this film of one of them is no exception, despite its pin-screen prologue by Alexeieff and its inventive setting in the old Gare d'Orsay. Once again Welles the magician badly needs a Hollywood studio behind him.
wd Orson Welles *ph* Edmond Richard *m* Jean Ledrut *pd* Jean Mandarut *ed* Orson Welles
☆ Orson Welles, Jeanne Moreau, Anthony Perkins, Madeleine Robinson, Elsa Martinelli, Suzanne Flon, Akim Tamiroff, Romy Schneider
'The elaboration of scale and decor is as boring as in any biblical spectacular and for the same reason: because it is used without mind or feeling, not to bring out meaning but to distract us from asking for it.' – *Dwight MacDonald*

The Trial
GB 1992 120m colour
BBC/Europanda (Louis Marks)

In Prague, Joseph K is arrested, tried and condemned without being able to discover his crime.
Plodding and uninteresting version, with a vacuous central performance and listless direction.
w Harold Pinter *novel* Franz Kafka *d* David Jones *ph* Phil Meheux *m* Carl Davis *pd* Don Taylor *ed* John Stothart
☆ Kyle MacLachlan, Anthony Hopkins, Jason Robards, Juliet Stevenson, Polly Walker, Alfred Molina, Michael Kitchen
'Dull, lifeless and strictly TV-bound in its aesthetics.' – *Variety*
'The result is like a translation of a translation of a translation; it has zero vitality.' – *Michael Sragow, New Yorker*

Trial and Error: see *The Dock Brief (1962)*

Trial and Error
US 1997 98m CFI color Panavision
Entertainment/New Line/Larger Than Life (Gary Ross, Jonathan Lynn)

An incapacitated lawyer gets his friend, an unemployed actor, to impersonate him in court.
Disappointingly heavy-handed and predictable comedy, often sentimental and never funny.
w Sarah Bernstein, Gregory Bernstein *d* Jonathan Lynn *ph* Gabriel Beristain *m* Phil Marshall *pd* Victoria Paul *ed* Tony Lombardo
☆ Michael Richards (Richard Rietti), Jeff Daniels (Charles Tuttle), Charlize Theron (Billie Tyler), Jessica Steen (Elizabeth), Austin Pendleton (Judge Paul Z. Graff), Rip Torn (Benny Gibbs), Alexandra Wentworth (Tiffany), Jennifer Coolidge (Jacqueline)
'Pleasant, amusing and periodically inspired.' – *Variety*

Trial by Combat
GB 1976 90m Technicolor
Warner/Combat (Fred Weintraub, Paul Heller)

aka: *Choice of Weapons*
An apparently harmless secret society of 'medieval knights' rededicates itself to the ritual execution of criminals who have escaped the law.
A rare specimen of comic macabre apparently inspired by the TV series The Avengers. *Sadly, not much of it really works.*
w Julian Bond, Steven Rossen, Mitchell Smith *d* Kevin Conner *ph* Alan Hume *m* Frank Cordell *pd* Edward Marshall
☆ John Mills, Donald Pleasence, Peter Cushing, Barbara Hershey, David Birney, Margaret Leighton, Brian Glover

Trial by Jury
US 1994 107m colour
Warner/Morgan Creek (James G. Robinson, Chris Meledandri, Mark Gordon)

A member of the jury trying a gangland boss is threatened with her son being hurt if she finds him guilty.
Ridiculous courtroom drama, in which a ham-fisted script gets the performances it deserves before toppling over into absurdity.
w Jordan Katz, Heywood Gould *d* Heywood Gould *ph* Frederick Elmes *m* Terence Blanchard *pd* David Chapman *ed* Joel Goodman
☆ Joanne Whalley-Kilmer, Armand Assante, Gabriel Byrne, William Hurt, Ed Lauter, Margaret Whitton, Kathleen Quinlan, Stuart Whitman
'Enough laughable dialogue to fill a camp film festival.' – *Variety*

The Trial of Joan of Arc: see *Procès de Jeanne d'Arc*

The Trial of Mary Dugan
US 1929 120m bw
MGM
Prosecution and defence counsel both change their feelings towards the girl on trial for murder.
A cast-iron audience pleaser, this adapted stage play was the studio's first all-talking picture. It wouldn't stand the test of time.
w Bayard Veiller, Becky Gardner *play* Bayard Veiller *d* Bayard Veiller
☆ Norma Shearer, H. B. Warner, Raymond Hackett, Lewis Stone, Lilyan Tashman
† A 1940 remake directed by Norman Z. McLeod starred Laraine Day, Tom Conway, Robert Young, John Litel and Frieda Inescort, but was not a particular success.

The Trial of Vivienne Ware
US 1932 56m bw
Fox
An attempt is made to kill a woman witness during a murder trial.
Fast, complex courtroom murder mystery which even finds time for frequent bouts of comic relief.
w Philip Klein, Barry Connors *novel* Kenneth M. Ellis *d* William K. Howard
☆ Joan Bennett, Donald Cook, Skeets Gallagher, ZaSu Pitts, Lillian Bond, Alan Dinehart, Herbert Mundin, Noel Madison
'A skilful bit of claptrap melodrama.' – *Variety*

Trial on the Road **
Russia 1985 98m bw
Lenfilm
original title: *Proverka Na Dorogakh*
A former Red Army sergeant fighting for the Germans in Russia deserts to join the partisans.
Banned for 14 years, a stark, unheroic account of war and its effect on the human spirit, set in a bleak winter landscape.
w Eduard Volodarsky *story* Yuri Gherman *d* Alexei Gherman *ph* L. Kolganov, B. Alexsandrovsky, V. Mironov *m* I. Shvarts *ad* V. Yurkevich
☆ Rolan Bykov, Anatoly Solonitsin, Vladimir Zamansky, Oleg Borisov, Fedor Odinokov, Gennady Dindoyev
† Produced in 1971.

Trial Run
New Zealand 1984 89m colour
Cinema and Television/Double Feature (Don Reynolds)
An amateur photographer finds her metier photographing penguins, but in her remote retreat finds herself terrorized by a mysterious prowler.
Suspenseful but overlong thriller with a weak ending and too much psychological probing.
wd Melanie Read *ph* Allen Guilford *m* Jan Preston, Blair Greenberg *pd* Judith Crozier *ed* Finola Dwyer
☆ Annie Whittle, Judith Gibson, Christopher Broun, Philippa Mayne, Stephen Tozer

The Trials of Oscar Wilde **
GB 1960 123m Super Technirama 70
Warwick/Viceroy (Harold Huth)
US title: *The Man with the Green Carnation*
Oscar Wilde fatally sues the Marquis of Queensberry for libel, and loses; he is then prosecuted for sodomy.
Plush account of a fascinating event; narrative drive is unfortunately lacking, but one is left with interesting performances.
wd Ken Hughes *ph* Ted Moore *m* Ron Goodwin *ad* Ken Adam, Bill Constable
☆ *Peter Finch*, Yvonne Mitchell, *John Fraser*, Lionel Jeffries, *Nigel Patrick*, James Mason, Emrys Jones, Maxine Audley, Paul Rogers, James Booth
Peter Finch

Tribute *
Canada 1980 122m colour
TCF/Joel B. Michaels, Garth B. Drabinsky

A Broadway press agent comes to know his son by his divorced wife just as he comes to know of his own fatal illness.
Satisfactory screen treatment of a play which is really a vehicle for a charismatic star.
w Bernard Slade *play* Bernard Slade *d* Bob Clark *ph* Reginald H. Morris *m* various
☆ *Jack Lemmon*, Lee Remick, Robby Benson, Colleen Dewhurst, Kim Cattrall, John Marley
Jack Lemmon

Tribute to a Bad Man
US 1956 95m Eastmancolor Cinemascope
MGM (Sam Zimbalist)

A Wyoming horse breeder is callous in his treatment of rustlers, and wins the woman he wants when he becomes more understanding.
Somewhere behind an unsympathetic story and hesitant development lies a convincing picture of life in the old west.
w Michael Blankfort *story* Jack Schaefer *d* Robert Wise *ph* Robert Surtees *m* Miklos Rozsa
☆ James Cagney, Irene Papas, Don Dubbins, Stephen McNally, Vic Morrow, Royal Dano, Lee Van Cleef

'A story about two guys trying to make it in the big city.'

Trick
US 1999 89m colour
Millivres/Roadside Attractions/Good Machine (Eric d'Arbeloff, Jim Fall, Ross Katz)

A would-be songwriter in New York spends a night trying to find a place to be alone with a go-go dancer.
A gay romantic comedy, pleasant in an unassuming way.
w Jason Schafer *d* Jim Fall *ph* Terry Stacey *m* David Friedman *pd* Jody Asnes *ed* Brian A. Kates
☆ Christian Campbell (Gabriel), John Paul Pitoc (Mark), Tori Spelling (Katherine), Steve Hayes (Perry), Kevin Chamberlin (Perry's Ex), Brad Beyer (Rich), Lorri Bagley (Judy)
'The most appealing and most erotic gay date movie ever made.' – *Emanuel Levy, Variety*

Trigger Happy
US 1996 93m DeLuxe
MGM/UA/Skylight/Dreyfus/James (Judith Rutherford James)

aka: *Mad Dog Time*
Returning from a stay in a lunatic asylum, a gang boss demands that his old rivals are eliminated; they also want him out of the way.
An attempt at an ultra-cool gangster movie, in which everyone wisecracks as the gunplay plays; the ever-present attitudinizing quickly wears out its welcome.
wd Larry Bishop *ph* Frank Byers *m* Earl Rose *pd* Dina Lipton *ed* Norman Hollyn
☆ Ellen Barkin, Gabriel Byrne, Richard Dreyfuss, Jeff Goldblum, Diane Lane, Larry Bishop, Gregory Hines, Kyle MacLachlan, Burt Reynolds, Christopher Jones, Henry Silva
'The problem is, the film doesn't seem to be about anything except ironic detachment. With guns pointed at them, characters simply arch their eyebrows or mutter a throwaway joke, as if genuine emotions were strictly squaresville. If the characters don't seem to care about what's going on, imagine what it's like for the audience.' – *Timothy M. Gray, Variety*
† The director's father, Joey Bishop, Paul Anka, Richard Pryor, Rob Reiner, Michael J. Pollard and Billy Idol appear in cameo roles.

Trinity Is Still My Name (dubbed)
Italy 1971 90m DeLuxe Scope
Avco Embassy/West Film (Italo Zingarelli)

original title: *Continuavamo a Chiamarlo Trinity*
Two brothers set out for a life of crime but are sidetracked in rescuing some monks from a gun-runner.
Amiable parody of spaghetti Westerns, high-spirited rather than funny.

wd E. B. Clucher (Enzo Barboni) *ph* Aldo Giordani *m* Guido de Angelis, Maurizio de Angelis, Enzo Bulgarelli *ed* Antonio Siciliano
☆ Terence Hill (Mario Girotti), Bud Spencer (Carlo Pedersoli), Harry Carey Jnr, Jessica Dublin, Yanti Somer, Enzo Tarascio
† The film was originally released in Italy at 121m.

Trio *
GB 1950 91m bw
Rank/Gainsborough (Antony Darnborough)

Following *Quartet* (qv), three more stories from Somerset Maugham: 'The Verger', 'Mr Knowall', and 'Sanatorium'.
An enjoyable package, unpretentiously handled but with full weight to the content.
w W. Somerset Maugham, R. C. Sherriff, Noel Langley *stories* W. Somerset Maugham *d* Ken Annakin, Harold French *ph* Reg Wyer, Geoffrey Unsworth *m* John Greenwood *ad* Maurice Carter *ed* Alfred Roome
☆ *James Hayter*, Kathleen Harrison, Michael Hordern, Felix Aylmer; Nigel Patrick, Anne Crawford, Naunton Wayne, Wilfrid Hyde-White; Michael Rennie, Jean Simmons, *John Laurie, Finlay Currie*, Roland Culver, Betty Ann Davies, Raymond Huntley, André Morell
'The casting of all three films with stars and near stars is equally happy. Excellent entertainment.' – *Joan Lester*

'Listen to the sound of love! Feel people! Taste green!'
The Trip *
US 1967 85m Pathécolor
AIP (Roger Corman)
A director of TV commercials tries LSD and has hallucinations.
Much-banned plotless wallow, the ultimate opt-out movie; well done for those who can take it.
w Jack Nicholson *d* Roger Corman *ph* Arch Dalzell *psychedelic effects* Peter Gardiner *montage* Dennis Jakob
☆ Peter Fonda, Susan Strasberg, Bruce Dern, Salli Sachse, Dennis Hopper

The Trip to Bountiful *
US 1985 106m Allied and WBS colour
Island/Film Dallas/Bountiful Film Partners (Sterling Vanwagenen, Horton Foote)

An old woman leaves her tiresome family to return by bus to the town where she was raised.
A relic of the fifties, when writers were mystical about mid-America, this oddity survives as an acting tour de force.
w Horton Foote *play* Horton Foote *d* Peter Masterson *ph* Fred Murphy *m* J. A. C. Redford
☆ Geraldine Page, John Heard, Carlin Glynn, Richard Bradford, Rebecca de Mornay
'A wistful tale made for people old enough to appreciate that there is no going back – that the present, however wretched, is all we have.' – *Quentin Crisp*
Geraldine Page
adapted screenplay

Triple Bogey on a Par 5 Hole
US 1991 85m colour/bw
ICA/Poe/Island World (Amos Poe)
A researcher questions three rich and spoiled children about the violent deaths of their parents on a golf course 13 years earlier.
Introspective navel-gazing movie that combines many of the least attractive aspects of underground cinema.
wd Amos Poe *ph* Joe Desalvo *m* Anna Domino, Michel Delory, Mader, Chic Streetman *pd* Jocelyne Beaudoin *ed* Dana Congdon
☆ Eric Mitchell, Daisy Hall, Angela Goethals, Jesse McBride, Alba Clemente, Robbie Coltrane, Olga Bagnasco
'Deeply minimalist, deeply minimal.' – *Nigel Andrews, Financial Times*
'Deliberately repetitious, funny and slightly threatening at the same time.' – *Derek Malcolm, Guardian*

Triple Cross
GB 1967 140m colour
Warner/Cineurop (Fred Feldkamp)

A small-time crook imprisoned on Jersey at the start of World War II offers to spy for the Nazis but reports to the English.
Ho-hum biopic of double agent Eddie Chapman; effective scenes merely interrupt the general incoherence.
w René Hardy *book* *The Eddie Chapman Story* by Frank Owen *d* Terence Young *ph* Henri Alekan *m* Georges Garvarentz
☆ Christopher Plummer, Yul Brynner, Trevor Howard, Romy Schneider, Gert Frobe, Claudine Auger

Triple Cross
Hong Kong 1991 81m colour
Rapi Films (Gope T. Samtani)

Rival gangs trying to steal a computer in a suitcase are outwitted by a female security chief.
Car and boat chases, gun and fist fights, and martial arts action with an occasional spectacular stunt take most of the running time so that viewers will have little time to attend to the silly, confused narrative and unsubtle acting, or wonder why so many would kill, or die, for a portable computer.
w Christopher Mitchum *story* Deddy Armand *d* Ackyl Anwary *ph* H. Asmawi *m* Embie C. Noor *ad* Hendro Tangkilisan *ed* Amin Kertaraharia
☆ Cynthia Rothrock, Chris Barnes, Peter O'Brian, Jurek Kylne, Roy Marten, Tanaka, Agust Melasz, Fei Lung, Jack Maland

Triple Echo *
GB 1972 94m colour
Hemdale/Senta (Graham Cottle)

In 1942, a soldier's wife welcomes another soldier to her farm for tea; he deserts and poses as her sister.
Foolish story which would possibly have worked as a TV play but hardly justifies a film despite the talent on hand.
w Robin Chapman *novel* H. E. Bates *d* Michael Apted *ph* John Coquillon *m* Marc Wilkinson
☆ Glenda Jackson, Brian Deacon, Oliver Reed

Triple Trouble: see *Kentucky Kernels*

Tripoli
US 1950 95m Technicolor
Paramount/Pine-Thomas
In 1805 the United States sends marines to rout the Barbary pirates.
Not a superior actioner, but it passed the time.
w Winston Miller *d* Will Price *ph* James Wong Howe *m* David Chudnow
☆ John Payne, Maureen O'Hara, Howard Da Silva, Philip Reed, Grant Withers, Lowell Gilmore

Tristana ****
Spain/Italy/France 1970 105m Eastmancolor
Academy/Connoisseur/Epoca/Talia/Selenia/Les Films Corona (Juan Estelrich)

An impoverished, womanizing aristocrat seduces his young ward and pays the price for his action.
Complex black comedy of obsessive behaviour which also mocks religion and other forms of consolation.
w Luis Buñuel, Julio Alejandro *novel* Benito Pérez Galdós *d* Luis Buñuel *ph* José F. Aguayo *ad* Enrique Alarcón *ed* Pedro Del Rey
☆ Catherine Deneuve, Fernando Rey, Franco Nero, Lola Gaos, Antonio Casas, Jesús Fernández
'It is Buñuel at his most majestic.' – *Tom Milne, MFB*

The Triumph of Sherlock Holmes *
GB 1935 84m bw
Real Art

Sherlock Holmes solves a murder stemming from enmity between Pennsylvania coal miners.
Solidly satisfying adaptation of Conan Doyle's The Valley of Fear, *with more of Moriarty added.*
w H. Fowler Mear, Cyril Twyford *d* Leslie Hiscott
☆ Arthur Wontner, Ian Fleming, Lyn Harding, Jane Carr, Leslie Perrins, Michael Shepley

Triumph of the Spirit *
US 1989 120m Eastmancolor
Guild/Nova International (Arnold Kopelson, Shimon Arama)

A Jewish boxer is forced by the Nazis to fight for his life in a series of boxing matches in Auschwitz.
Tough, sincere but not always convincing drama, based on fact.
w Andrzej Krakowski, Laurence Heath *story* Shimon Arama, Zion Haen *d* Robert M. Young *ph* Curtis Clark *m* Cliff Eidelman *pd* Jerzy Maslowska *ed* Arthur Coburn, Norman Buckley
☆ Willem Dafoe, Edward James Olmos, Robert Loggia, Wendy Gazelle, Kelly Wolf, Costas Mandylor, Kario Salem, Edward Zentara, Hartmut Becker

Triumph of the Will ****
Germany 1936 120m bw
Leni Riefenstahl/Nazi Party

The official record of the Nazi party congress held at Nuremberg in 1934.
A devastatingly brilliant piece of filmmaking – right from the opening sequence of Hitler descending from the skies, his plane shadowed against the clouds. The rally scenes are a terrifying example of the camera's power of propaganda. After World War II it was banned for many years because of general fears that it might inspire a new Nazi party.
ph Sepp Allgeier and 36 assistants *m* Herbert Windt *d/ed* Leni Riefenstahl
'Its length and lack of variety scream incompetence... Interminable, self-indulgent, repetitive – in a word, turgid.' – *Brian Winston, Sight and Sound, 2002*

Triumphs of a Man Called Horse
Spain 1982 89m CFI color
Sandy Howard/Redwing/Transpacific/Hesperia

Third in a dispensable series (*A Man Called Horse, Return of a Man Called Horse*) of dour Westerns.
In this scrappy item the man dies early on, but his son upholds the tradition.
w Ken Blackwell, Carlos Aured, Jack de Witt *d* John Hough *ph* John Alcott *m* Georges Garvarentz
☆ Richard Harris, Michael Beck, Ana de Sade, Vaughn Armstrong, Buck Taylor

Trmavomodry Svet: see *Dark Blue World*

'From a million years back – horror explodes into today!'
Trog
GB 1970 91m Technicolor
Warner/Herman Cohen
A man-ape is discovered in a pothole and trained by a lady scientist.
Ridiculous semi-horror film which degrades its star.
w Aben Kandel *d* Freddie Francis *ph* Desmond Dickinson *m* John Scott
☆ Joan Crawford, Michael Gough, Bernard Kay, David Griffin

Trois Couleurs: Bleu: see *Three Colours: Blue*

Trois Hommes et un Couffin: see *Three Men and a Cradle*

Trois Huit **
France 2001 97m colour
Metro Tartan/Lazennec/StudioCanal/France 3 (Alain Rocca)

aka: *Nightshift*
A mild-mannered worker in a glassworks transfers to the night shift, where he encounters the hostility of a swaggering bully.
Clever, disturbing psychological drama that emphasizes the complicity between victim and bully, each seeking out the other.
w Philippe Le Guay, Regis Franc, Olivier Dazat *d* Philippe Le Guay *ph* Jean-Marc Favre *m* Yann Tiersen *ad* Jimmy Vansteenkiste *ed* Emmanuelle Castro
☆ Gerald Laroche (Pierre), Marc Barbe (Fred), Bernard Ballet (Franck), Alexandre Carriere (Danny), Jean-Francois Lapalus (Mickey), Sabri Lahmer (Farid), Luce Mouchel (Carole), Bastien Le Roy (Victor)
'A movie of intense psychological and physical pain. A real treat.' – *Alexander Walker*

Trojan Eddie *
GB/Ireland 1997 105m Metrocolor
Film Four/Channel 4/IFB/Initial/Irish Screen (Emma Burge)

Trapped between his sluttish wife and impatient girlfriend, despised by his thuggish boss, who rules the small community with a gang of travellers, a hangdog salesman finally triumphs.
An intriguing variation on the meek inheriting the earth, set on the fringe of Irish society, in a temporary, shifting world, where nothing seems settled; but the tension of the tale is dissipated by its too-leisurely approach.
w Billy Roche *d* Gillies MacKinnon *ph* John de Borman *m* John Keane *pd* Frank Conway *ed* Scott Thomas
☆ Richard Harris, Stephen Rea, Brendan Gleeson, Sean McGinley, Angeline Ball, Brid Brennan, Stuart Townsend, Aislin McGuckin
'This blatant bit of blarney is a joy from start to finish.' – *Film Review*
'Resembling a slow-moving travelogue for the Irish Lake and Fields Promotions Board.' – *Neon*

The Trojan Horse: see *The Trojan War*

The Trojan War
Italy/France 1961 105m Technicolor Techniscope
Europa Cinematografica/CICC/Les Films Modernes (Gian Paolo Bigazzi)
original title: *La Guerra di Troia*
aka: *The Wooden Horse of Troy; The Trojan Horse*
Aeneas performs heroic deeds before fleeing from his doomed city with his new-born son.
Good-looking, if stolid, epic which is one of the better efforts of its muscular star.
w Ugo Liberatore, Giorgio Stegani, Federico Zardi, Giorgio Ferroni *d* Giorgio Ferroni *ph* Rino Filippini *m* Giovanni Fusco *pd* Pier Vittorio Marchi *ed* Antonietta Zita
☆ Steve Reeves, John Drew Barrymore, Juliette Mayniel, Hedy Vessel, Lydia Alfonsi

'The strength of mankind has always been its women'
The Trojan Women *
US 1971 111m Eastmancolor
Josef Shaftel (Michael Cacoyannis, Anis Nohra)

Troy has fallen to the Greeks and its women bemoan their fate.
And oh, how they bemoan! Even with this cast, Greek tragedy does not fill the big screen.
w Michael Cacoyannis *play* Euripides *d* Michael Cacoyannis *ph* Alfio Contini *m* Mikis Theodorakis
☆ Katharine Hepburn, Vanessa Redgrave, Geneviève Bujold, Irene Papas, Patrick Magee, Brian Blessed, Pauline Letts

'Waiting! Watching! Wanton!'
'None can escape this slithering terror spawned from a nuclear hell lusting for another taste of human blood ... Maybe Yours!'
The Trollenberg Terror
GB 1958 84m bw
Tempean
US title: *The Crawling Eye*
Extraterrestrials invade Switzerland.
Tolerable low-budget sci-fi from a BBC serial.
w Jimmy Sangster *story* Peter Key *d* Quentin Lawrence *ph* Monty Berman *m* Stanley Black
☆ Forrest Tucker, Laurence Payne, Janet Munro, Jennifer Jayne, Warren Mitchell

Trolösa: see *Faithless (2000)*

Tromeo & Juliet
US 1996 107m colour
Starlight/Troma (Michael Herz, Lloyd Kaufman)

In Manhattan, a youth falls in love with the daughter of his father's greatest enemy, his former partner in an exploitation film company.
Coarse and crude version that horribly mangles what remains of Shakespeare's verse; the acting is bad and the direction perfunctory, but that seems to be the point of Troma's output.
w James Gunn, Lloyd Kaufman *play* *Romeo and Juliet* by William Shakespeare *d* Lloyd Kaufman *ph* Brendan Flynt *m* Willie Wisely *pd* Roshelle Berliner *ed* Frank Reynolds
☆ Jane Jensen, Will Keenan, Valentine Miele, Maximilian Shaun, Steve Gibbons, Sean Gunn, Debbie Rochon, Lemmy
'Shakespeare as you never want to see it.' – *Film Review*

Tron *
US 1982 96m Technicolor Super Panavision 70mm
Walt Disney/Lisberger-Kushner
A computer games designer gets his revenge on an enemy by fighting things out in the computer world he has created.
Complicated science fantasy chiefly interesting for its computerized blend of live action and animation, which isn't always successful.
wd Steven Lisberger *ph* Bruce Logan *m* Michael Femer *pd* Dean Edward Mitzner *associate producer (animation)* Harrison Ellenshaw
☆ Bruce Boxleitner, Jeff Bridges, David Warner, Barnard Hughes
'Loaded with the expected visual delights, but falls way short of the mark in story and viewer involvement.' – *Variety*
costume design; sound

Troop Beverly Hills
US 1989 106m Metrocolor
Columbia TriStar/Weintraub Entertainment/Fries Entertainment (Ava Ostern Fries, Martin Mickelson, Peter MacGregor-Scott)
A wealthy mother transforms her daughter's disintegrating Girl Scout troop by giving them badges in shopping and other consumer activities.
A broad and far from sparkling comedy which emphasizes that it is best to be born rich.
w Pamela Norris, Margaret Grieco Oberman *story* Ava Ostern Fries *d* Jeff Kanew *ph* Donald E. Thorin *m* Randy Edelman, Lou Hemsey *pd* Robert F. Boyle *ed* Mark Melnick
☆ Shelley Long, Craig T. Nelson, Betty Thomas, Mary Gross, Stephanie Beacham, David Gautreaux, Karen Kopins, Dinah Lacey, Shelley Morrison

Trooper Hook
US 1957 92m bw
UA/Sol Baer Fielding
A woman prisoner of the Indians has a half-breed son and becomes an outcast when returned to her people.
Peculiar Western with good moments, but generally very slow and downbeat.
w Charles Marquis Warren, David Victor, Herbert Little Jnr *story* Jack Schaefer *d* Charles Marquis Warren *ph* Ellsworth Fredericks *m* Gerald Fried
☆ Barbara Stanwyck, Joel McCrea, Earl Holliman, Edward Andrews, John Dehner, Susan Kohner, Royal Dano

Troopship: see *Farewell Again*

Trop Belle pour Toi! *
France 1989 91m colour
Artificial Eye/Cine Valse/DD Productions/Orly Films/SEDIF/TF1 (Bernard Marescot)
aka: *Too Beautiful for You*
A successful car salesman with a beautiful wife begins an affair with his homely secretary.
Mildly amusing romantic comedy, for all that it seems no more than a heterosexual variation on Blier's Tenue de Soirée.
wd Bertrand Blier *ph* Philippe Rousselot *m* Schubert *ad* Theobald Meurisse *ed* Claudine Merlin
☆ Gérard Depardieu, Josiane Balasko, Carole Bouquet, Roland Blanche, François Cluzet, Didier Benureau, Philippe Loffredo

'Estupendo! Magnifico! Esplendido!'
Tropic Holiday
US 1938 78m bw
Paramount
A Hollywood scriptwriter finds romance in Mexico.
Musical time-filler with a bit of everything and not much of anything.
w Don Hartman, Frank Butler, John C. Moffett and Duke Atterbery *d* Theodore Reed
☆ Ray Milland, Dorothy Lamour, Bob Burns, Martha Raye, Binnie Barnes, Tito Guizar
'Will need strong selling to top average business.' – *Variety*
Boris Morros (music direction)

Tropic of Cancer
US 1970 88m Eastmancolor
Paramount/Tropic (Joseph Strick)
The sexual exploits of an American writer in Paris.
An adaptation that fails to capture the raw energy of the original, despite, or possibly owing to, quoting from it at great length.
w Joseph Strick, Betty Botley *novel* Henry Miller *d* Joseph Strick *ph* Alain Derobe *m* Stanley Myers
☆ Rip Torn, James Callahan, Ellen Burstyn, David Bauer, Laurence Ligneres, Phil Brown
'The cinema here pays unfortunate tribute to literary achievement – by erecting a blank and ugly monument with the work itself firmly interred beneath.' – *Richard Combs, MFB*
'A trivial but entertaining sex comedy.' – *Pauline Kael*

Tropic Zone
US 1953 94m Technicolor
Paramount/Pine-Thomas
In a banana port a man wanted by the police saves a plantation from being taken over by crooks.
Tropical thick ear, not entirely unendurable.
wd Lewis R. Foster *novel* Tom Gill *ph* Lionel Linden *m* Lucien Cailliet
☆ Ronald Reagan, Rhonda Fleming, Noah Beery Jnr, Estelita, Grant Withers, John Wengraf

Tropicana: see *The Heat's On*

Trottie True *
GB 1949 98m Technicolor
GFD/Two Cities (Hugh Stewart)
US title: *The Gay Lady*
Adventures of a Gaiety girl who married a lord.
Self-conscious period comedy which could have been highly diverting but manages only to be sporadically charming in a whimsically amateurish way.
w C. Denis Freeman *novel* Caryl Brahms, S. J. Simon *d* Brian Desmond Hurst *ph* Harry Waxman *m* Benjamin Frankel *ad* Ralph Brinton
☆ Jean Kent, James Donald, Hugh Sinclair, Bill Owen, Andrew Crawford, Lana Morris

Le Trou: see *The Hole*

Trouble along the Way
US 1953 110m bw
Warner (Melville Shavelson)
A famous football coach is co-opted to help a bankrupt college but some of his methods are not quite above board.
American college comedy with dollops of religiosity – a double threat.
w Melville Shavelson, Jack Rose *d* Michael Curtiz *ph* Archie Stout *m* Max Steiner
☆ John Wayne, Donna Reed, Charles Coburn, Tom Tully, Sherry Jackson, Marie Windsor
'No opportunities for a laugh or a tear are missed by the entire cast.' – *MFB*

Trouble at Midnight
US 1937 69m bw
Universal (Barney A. Sarecky)
A dairy farmer loses his stock in a series of midnight raids, but gets the girl.
A trivial gangster movie in a western setting, with Beery ill-at-ease as a romantic hero.
w Maurice Geraghty, Ford Beebe *d* Ford Beebe *ph* Jerome Ash *ed* John Rawlins
☆ Noah Beery Jnr (Kirk Cameron), Catherine Hughes (Catherine Benson), Larry Blake (Tony Michaels), Barnadene Hayes (Marion), Louis Mason (Elmer), Earl Dwire (Goff), Charles Halton (Everett Benson), Frank Melton (Frank Gordeen)

Trouble Bound
US 1993 89m CFI color
ITC (Tom Kuhn, Fred Weintraub)
A gullible small-time crook finds himself in the middle of a gang war after he picks up a girl on the run from her Mafia family.
Routine road movie that takes the fast lane to clichéville.
w Darrell Fetty, Francis Delia *d* Jeffrey Reiner *ph* Janusz Kaminski *m* Vinny Golia *pd* Richard Sherman *ed* Neil Grieve
☆ Michael Madsen, Patricia Arquette, Florence Stanley, Seymour Cassel, Sal Jenco, Paul Ben-Victor
'A likeable road movie with a couple of decent central performances but few original ideas.' – *Empire*

Trouble Brewing *
GB 1939 87m bw
ATP
A newspaper printer catches counterfeiters.
Lively star comedy.
w Anthony Kimmins, Angus MacPhail, Michael Hogan *d* Anthony Kimmins *ph* Ronald Neame
☆ George Formby, Googie Withers, Gus MacNaughton, Joss Ambler, Martita Hunt, Garry Marsh, Ronald Shiner, C. Denier Warren, Basil Radford

'The ability to love. The inability to love... The hunger to love.'
Trouble Every Day
France 2001 102m colour
Messaoud/a/Rezo/Arte France/Dacia/Kinetique (Georges Benayoun, Jean-Michel Rey, Philippe Liegeois)
An American scientist goes to Paris for his honeymoon – and to search for his fellow doctor whose experiments have turned him and others into sexual cannibals.
Bloody, risible, emetic movie with an emaciated narrative that has Vincent Gallo looking moody while Béatrice Dalle literally consumes her lovers.
w Jean-Pol Fargeau, Claire Denis *d* Claire Denis *ph* Agnes Godard *m* Tindersticks *pd* Arnaud de Moleron *ed* Nelly Quettier
☆ Vincent Gallo (Shane Brown), Tricia Vessey (June Brown), Béatrice Dalle (Core), Alex Descas (Leo Semeneau), Florence Loiret-Caille (Christelle), Nicolas Duvauchelle (Erwan), José Garcia (Choart), Hélène Lapiower (Malecot)
'Resolutely silly movie... Over-long, under-written and needlessly obscure.' – *Derek Elley, Variety*
'Dracula with pretensions.' – *New York Times*

Trouble for Two *
US 1936 75m bw
MGM (Louis D. Lighton)
GB title: *The Suicide Club*
A European prince in London for an arranged wedding gets involved with an ingenious organization for murder.
Light-hearted, black-edged Victorian literary spoof which starts nicely but can't quite keep up the pace.
w Manuel Seff, Edward Paramore Jnr *stories* New Arabian Nights by Robert Louis Stevenson *d* J. Walter Rubin *ph* Charles G. Clarke *m* Franz Waxman
☆ *Robert Montgomery*, Rosalind Russell, *Reginald Owen*, Frank Morgan, *Louis Hayward*, E. E. Clive, Walter Kingsford

Trouble in Mind
US 1985 111m colour
Island Alive/Terry Glinwood (Carolyn Pfeiffer, David Blocker)
In some seedy future, the lives of an ex-cop, just out of prison, a petty crook, his innocent girlfriend and their baby interwine in a run-down diner.
Moody, blue-tinged, blues-tinged melodrama, too preoccupied with creating atmosphere, attitudinizing and indulging in windy philosophizing to appeal to any but cultists.
wd Alan Rudolph *ph* Toyomichi Kurita *m* Mark Isham *pd* Stephen Legler *ed* Tom Walls
☆ Kris Kristofferson, Keith Carradine, Lori Singer, Geneviève Bujold, Joe Morton, George Kirby, Divine, John Considine
'At once gritty and weirdly exotic, Rudolph's self-reflective *noir* thriller takes genre commonplaces and pushes them to the limits.' – *Sight and Sound*

Trouble in Paradise ****
US 1932 86m bw
Paramount (Ernst Lubitsch)
Jewel thieves insinuate themselves into the household of a rich Parisienne, and one falls in love with her.
A masterpiece of light comedy, with sparkling dialogue, innuendo, great performances and masterly cinematic narrative. For connoisseurs, it can't be faulted, and is the masterpiece of American sophisticated cinema.
w Samson Raphaelson, Grover Jones play The Honest Finder by Laszlo Aladar *d Ernst Lubitsch* *ph* Victor Milner *m* W. Franke Harling
☆ *Herbert Marshall, Miriam Hopkins, Kay Francis, Edward Everett Horton, Charles Ruggles*, C. Aubrey Smith, Robert Greig, Leonid Kinskey
'Swell title, poor picture. Better for the class houses than the subsequents.' – *Variety*
'One of the gossamer creations of Lubitsch's narrative art ... it would be impossible in this brief notice to describe the innumerable touches of wit and of narrative skill with which it is unfolded.' – *Alexander Bakshy*
'A shimmering, engaging piece of work ... in virtually every scene a lively imagination shines forth.' – *New York Times*
'An almost continuous musical background pointed up and commented on the action. The settings were the last word in modernistic design.' – *Theodor Huff, 1948*

Trouble in Store *
GB 1953 85m bw
GFD/Two Cities (Maurice Cowan)
A stock assistant causes chaos in a department store.
First, simplest and best of the Wisdom farces.
w John Paddy Carstairs, Maurice Cowan, Ted Willis *d* John Paddy Carstairs *ph* Ernest Steward *m* Mischa Spoliansky
☆ *Norman Wisdom*, Jerry Desmonde, Margaret Rutherford, Moira Lister, Derek Bond, Lana Morris, Megs Jenkins, Joan Sims
Norman Wisdom (newcomer)

Trouble in the Glen
GB 1954 91m Trucolor
Republic/Wilcox-Neagle (Stuart Robertson)
An Argentinian laird in a Scottish glen causes ill-feeling.
Heavy-handed Celtic comedy whose predictability and sentimentality could have been forgiven were it not for the most garish colour ever seen.
w Frank S. Nugent *novel* Maurice Walsh *d* Herbert Wilcox *ph* Max Greene *m* Victor Young
☆ Margaret Lockwood, Orson Welles, Forrest Tucker, Victor McLaglen, John McCallum, Eddie Byrne, Archie Duncan, Moultrie Kelsall

Trouble in the Sky: see *Cone of Silence*

The Trouble Shooter: see *The Man with the Gun*

The Trouble with Angels
US 1966 112m Pathécolor
Columbia/William Frye
Two mischievous new pupils cause trouble at a convent school.
Fun with the nuns, for addicts only.
w Blanche Hanalis *novel* Life with Mother Superior by Jane Trahey *d* Ida Lupino *ph* Lionel Lindon *m* Jerry Goldsmith
☆ Rosalind Russell, Hayley Mills, June Harding, Marge Redmond, Binnie Barnes, Gypsy Rose Lee, Camilla Sparv, Mary Wickes, Margalo Gillmore
'A relentless series of prankish escapades.' – *MFB*

Trouble With Eve
GB 1959 64m bw
Mancunian/Butcher/Blakeley's
A widow who runs a teashop in a small village finds that her reputation for propriety is endangerd when her beatnik daughter comes to stay.
Minor comedy of middle-clsass scandal among the teacups that seemed very dated within a year or so of its release.
w Brock Williams *play* Widows are Dangerous by June Garland *d* Francis Searle *ph* James Harvey *ad* John Earl *ed* Eric Boyd Perkins
☆ Robert Urquhart, Hy Hazel, Garry Marsh, Vera Day, Sally Smith, Tony Quinn, Brenda Hogan, Denis Shaw, Grace Denbeigh-Russell, Bruce Seton

The Trouble with Girls
US 1969 105m Metrocolor Panavision
MGM (Lester Welch)

In the twenties the manager of a travelling chautauqua (educational medicine show) gets involved in a small-town murder.
Curious vehicle for a very bored singing star, with some interesting background detail.
w Arnold and Lois Peyser *novel* The Chautauqua by Day Keene, Dwight Babcock *d* Peter Tewkesbury *ph* Jacques Marquette *m* Billy Strange
☆ Elvis Presley, Marlyn Mason, Nicole Jaffe, Sheree North, Edward Andrews, John Carradine, Vincent Price, Joyce Van Patten

The Trouble with Harry **
US 1955 99m Technicolor Vistavision
Paramount (Alfred Hitchcock)

In the New England woods, various reasons cause various people to find and bury the same body.
Black comedy which never quite, despite bright moments, catches the style of the book; however, it is finely performed and the autumnal backgrounds are splendid.
w John Michael Hayes *novel* Jack Trevor Story *d* Alfred Hitchcock *ph* Robert Burks *m* Bernard Herrmann
☆ Edmund Gwenn, Mildred Natwick, John Forsythe, Shirley MacLaine, Mildred Dunnock
'Has, I fear, neither the desperation which makes the predicament of its characters wryly enjoyable nor the urbanity which would make their actions sympathetic.' – *Dilys Powell*

The Troublemaker
US 1964 80m bw
Ozymandias/Seneca/Janus (Robert Gaffney)
Arriving in New York to open a coffee house, a gullible chicken farmer learns the hard way that corruption is the way to success.
Amiable, though not often amusing, comedy, performed in an easy-going, easily satisfied manner.
w Buck Henry, Theodore J. Flicker *d* Theodore J. Flicker *ph* Gayne Rescher *m* Cy Coleman *ad* David Moon *ed* John McManus
☆ Tom Aldredge, Joan Darling, James Frawley, Theodore J. Flicker, Buck Henry, Charles White, Godfrey Cambridge

Truck Turner
US 1974 91m Movielab
Focus/AIP/Sequoia (Paul M. Heller, Fred Weintraub)

Hired to find a thuggish criminal, a bounty hunter finds he has offended a big-time gangster.
Crude blaxploitation thriller, packed with violent action.
w Oscar Williams, Michael Allin, Leigh Chapman *story* Jerry Wilkes *d* Jonathan Kaplan *ph* Charles F. Wheeler *m* Isaac Hayes *ed* Michael Kahn
☆ Isaac Hayes, Yaphet Kotto, Alan Weeks, Nichelle Nichols, Sam Laws, Paul Harris, Scatman Crothers, Dick Miller
'Exceedingly tame even by the genre's current standards.' – *Tony Raynes, MFB*
† It was cut to 83m for its British release.

True as a Turtle
GB 1956 96m Eastmancolor
Rank (Peter de Sarigny)
Honeymooners join a variety of friends on a yacht crossing the Channel, and get involved in smuggling.
Artless, undemanding comedy for those who like messing about in boats.
w Jack Davies, John Coates, Nicholas Phipps *d* Wendy Toye *ph* Reg Wyer *m* Robert Farnon
☆ John Gregson, June Thorburn, Cecil Parker, *Elvi Hale*, Keith Michell, Avice Landone

True Believer *
US 1989 103m DeLuxe
Columbia (Walter F. Parkes, Lawrence Lasker)

aka: *Fighting Justice*
A tough, once idealistic lawyer is persuaded to take on the case of an Asian-American who may have been wrongfully imprisoned.
Entertaining thriller, though it would have been as effective on television and, indeed, led to a TV series, Eddie Dodd, based on its central character.
w Wesley Strick *d* Joseph Ruben *ph* John W. Lindley *m* Brad Fiedel *pd* Lawrence Miller *ed* George Bowers
☆ James Woods, Robert Downey Jnr, Margaret Colin, Yuji Okumoto, Kurtwood Smith, Tom Bower, Miguel Fernandes, Charles Hallahan

True Blue
GB 1996 118m colour
Film Four/Channel 4/Arts Council/Booker/Film and General/Rafford (Clive Parsons, Davina Belling)

As the day of the annual Boat Race between Oxford and Cambridge universities approaches, the Oxford coach faces a crisis when American members of the crew refuse to row.
A true story, based on Oxford's unexpected win in the 1987 Boat Race, makes for a doggedly dull film.
w Rupert Walters *book* Daniel Topolski, Patrick Robinson *d* Ferdinand Fairfax *ph* Brian Tufano *m* Stanislas Syrewicz *pd* Alison Riva *ed* Les Healy
☆ Johan Leysen, Dominic West, Dylan Baker, Geraldine Somerville, Josh Lucas, Brian McGovern, Ryan Bollman, Andrew Tees, Robert Bogue
'An air of ripe ridiculousness hangs over the whole thing.' – *Sunday Times*

True Blue
US 2001 97m colour
Sandstorm (Scott Einbinder, Carol Kottenbrook)

A New York cop finds himself in trouble when he begins an affair with a murder witness.
Dreary compendium of every cliché of every maverick cop movie ever made, with a cast that does no more than go through the over-familiar motions.
wd J. S. Cardone *ph* Darko Suvak *m* Tim Jones *pd* Oleg Savytski *ed* Matthew Ramsey
☆ Tom Berenger (Rem Macy), Lori Heuring (Nikki), Pamela Gidley (Beck), Barry Newman (Monty), Soon-Tek Oh (Tiger), Leo Lee (Benny Lee), Richard Chevolleau (Toots)
'Insultingly banal.' – *Sight and Sound*

True Colors
US 1991 111m Technicolor
Paramount (Herbert Ross, Laurence Mark)

A principled lawyer watches the rise and fall of his former classmate, who is prepared to use any method to succeed in politics.
Unengrossing story of corruption that never grips, despite its slick presentation.
w Kevin Wade *d* Herbert Ross *ph* Dante Spinotti *m* Trevor Jones *pd* Edward Pisoni *ed* Robert Reitano, Stephen A. Rotter
☆ John Cusack, James Spader, Imogen Stubbs, Mandy Patinkin, Richard Widmark, Dina Merrill, Philip Bosco, Paul Guilfoyle, Brad Sullivan

True Confession **
US 1937 85m bw
Paramount (Albert Lewin)

A fantasy-prone girl confesses to a murder she didn't commit, and her upright lawyer husband defends her.
Archetypal crazy comedy with fine moments despite longueurs and a lack of cinematic inventiveness.
Remade as Cross My Heart *(qv).*
w Claude Binyon *play* Mon Crime by Louis Verneuil, George Berr *d* Wesley Ruggles *ph* Ted Tetzlaff *m* Frederick Hollander
☆ *Carole Lombard*, Fred MacMurray, *John Barrymore*, Una Merkel, Porter Hall, Edgar Kennedy, Lynne Overman, Fritz Feld, *Irving Bacon*
'Not a big bet but a favourable enough one … it just falls short of being a smash.' – *Variety*
'The best comedy of the year.' – *Graham Greene*

True Confessions *
US 1981 108m colour
United Artists/Chartoff-Winkler (James D. Brubaker)

A policeman working on a murder case finds that his brother, a priest, is involved.
Unnecessary fictional elaboration on a real Los Angeles murder case of the forties (the 'Black Dahlia'); chiefly notable for performances.
w John Gregory Dunne, Joan Didion *novel* John Gregory Dunne *d* Ulu Grosbard *ph* Owen Roizman *m* Georges Delerue *pd* Stephen S. Grimes *ed* Lynzee Klingman *cos* Joe I. Tompkins
☆ *Robert Duvall, Robert DeNiro*, Charles Durning, Kenneth McMillan, Ed Flanders, Cyril Cusack, Burgess Meredith, Rose Gregorio, Jeanette Nolan, Dan Hedaya, Pat Corley, Jorge Cervera Jnr
'Carries hardboiled detective fiction to a virtually abstract level.' – *Pauline Kael, New Yorker*

True Crime *
US 1999 127m Technicolor
Warner/Zanuck/Malpaso (Clint Eastwood, Richard D. Zanuck, Lili Fini Zanuck)

An elderly investigative reporter has 24 hours to prove that a man about to be hanged for murder is innocent.
A predictable against-the-clock thriller is enlivened with a few deft touches of character, but not enough to lift it out of the ordinary.
w Larry Gross, Paul Brickman, Stephen Schiff *novel* Andrew Klavan *d* Clint Eastwood *ph* Jack N. Green *m* Lennie Niehaus *pd* Henry Bumstead *ed* Joel Cox
☆ Clint Eastwood (Steve Everett), Isaiah Washington (Frank Louis Beechum), Denis Leary (Bob Findley), Lisa Gay Hamilton (Bonnie Beechum), James Woods (Alan Mann), Bernard Hill (Warden Luther Plunkitt), Diane Venora (Barbara Everett), Michael McKean (Rev Shillerman), Michael Jeter (Dale Porterhouse), Mary McCormack (Michelle Ziegler), Hattie Winston
'A wickedly effective thriller.' – *Roger Ebert, Chicago Sun-Times*
'An awkward, if intermittently gripping affair.' – *The Times*

'The Victory You Helped To Make … Now on the screen in all its glory!'
The True Glory ****
GB/US 1945 90m bw
Ministry of Information/Office of War Information

The last year of the war, retold by edited newsreels: D-Day to the Fall of Berlin.
A magnificent piece of reportage, worth a dozen fiction films in its exhilarating Shakespearean fervour, though the poetic commentary does occasionally go over the top. One of the finest of all compilations.
w Eric Maschwitz, Arthur Macrae, Jenny Nicholson, Gerald Kersh, Guy Trosper d Carol Reed, Garson Kanin m William Alwyn research Peter Cusick
'Dwarfs all the fiction pictures of the year.' – *Richard Mallett, Punch*
'Bold, welcome but inadequate use of blank verse; much more successful use of many bits of individualized vernacular narration, unusually free of falseness. Very jab-paced, energetic cutting; intelligent selection of shots, of which several hundred are magnificent.' – *James Agee*
'An inspiring recital of human endeavour which all the world will want to see.' – *The Cinema*
best documentary

True Grit *
US 1969 128m Technicolor
Paramount/Hal B. Wallis (Paul Nathan)

In the Old West, a young girl wanting to avenge her murdered father seeks the aid of a hard-drinking old marshal.
Disappointingly slow-moving and uninventive semi-spoof Western with a roistering performance from a veteran star, who won a sentimental Oscar for daring to look fat and old.
w Marguerite Roberts *novel* Charles Portis *d* Henry Hathaway *ph* Lucien Ballard *m* Elmer Bernstein
☆ *John Wayne*, Kim Darby, Glen Campbell, Dennis Hopper, Jeremy Slate, Robert Duvall, Strother Martin, Jeff Corey
'Readers may remember it as a book about a girl, but it's a film about John Wayne.' – *Stanley Kauffmann*
'There is a slight consistent heightening or lowering into absurdity, but there is also a strong feeling for the unvarnished preposterousness of everyday existence.' – *John Simon*
† *Rooster Cogburn* featured more adventures of the Wayne character, who also showed up on TV in 1978 in the guise of Warren Oates.
John Wayne
title song (*m*Elmer Bernstein, *ly*Don Black)

True Heart Susie *
US 1919 62m approx (24 fps) bw silent
D. W. Griffith/Artcraft
A country girl sells her cow to send her boyfriend to college, but he is ungrateful.
Lavender-flavoured rustic romance, with the director at his most sentimental. But of its kind it is carefully done.
wd D. W. Griffith *story* Marion Fremont *ph* Billy Bitzer
☆ Lillian Gish, Robert Harron, Clarine Seymour

True Identity
USA 1991 93m Technicolor
Warner/Touchstone/Silver Screen Partners IV/ Sandollar (Carol Baum, Teri Schwartz)

On the run from the Mafia, a black actor disguises himself as a white man.
A star vehicle that, despite an engaging central performance, failed, due to a weak script.
w Andy Breckman *d* Charles Lane *ph* Tom Ackerman *m* Marc Marder *pd* John DeCuir Jnr *ed* Kent Beyda
☆ Lenny Henry, Frank Langella, Charles Lane, J. T. Walsh, Anne-Marie Johnson, Andreas Katsulas, Michael McKean, Peggy Lipton
'Mild comedy that works best as a showcase for Lenny Henry.' – *New York Times*

'When he said I do, he never said what he did.'
True Lies
US 1994 141m CFI color
TCF/Lightstorm (James Cameron, Stephanie Austin)

An American secret agent combating Arab terrorism pretends to his wife that he is a very boring computer salesman.
Either a romantic comedy with violent sequences or a Bond-like thriller that ignores the rule that women shouldn't get in the way of action; either way, it long overstays its welcome, though the destruction is on an extremely lavish scale.
wd James Cameron *screenplay* Claude Zidi, Simon Michael, Didier Kaminka *ph* Russell Carpenter *m* Brad Fiedel *pd* Peter Lamont *ed* Conrad Buff, Mark Goldblatt, Richard A. Harris *sp* Digital Domain
☆ Arnold Schwarzenegger, Jamie Lee Curtis, Tom Arnold, Bill Paxton, Art Malik, Tia Carrere, Eliza Dushku, Grant Heslov, Charlton Heston
'Every now and then there comes a film with the power to bring criticism to its knees, whimpering. Such a film is the opposite of a masterpiece, nothing so humble as a failure but an astounding condensation of everything that can go wrong with a project. *True Lies* is just such a reverse classic or anti-paragon.' – *Adam Mars-Jones, Independent*
'Will breed content and contempt in equal measure. With half-an-hour cut, I would certainly have been less inclined to drop an eyelid occasionally.' – *Derek Malcolm, Guardian*
'A loud misfire. It rarely brings its potent themes to life.' – *Richard Corliss, Time*
† The film, which cost around $120m, was based on Claude Zidi's domestic comedy *La Totale*, made in 1992.
†† The version released on video in Britain runs for 135m and has been 'edited for censorship purposes' to remove some moments of violence so that it could receive a 15 video certificate. The cuts were supervised by the director.
visual effects

'If All You Want To Do Is Have A Good Time … Why Get Married?'
True Love **
US 1989 100m DuArt
Oasis/UA (Richard Guay, Shelley Houis)

A young Italian-American couple in the Bronx prepare for their marriage, she with determination, he with reluctance.
Well-observed, low-budget comedy with a ring of truth about it.
w Nancy Savoca, Richard Guay *d* Nancy Savoca *ph* Lisa Rinzler *pd* Lester W. Cohen *ed* John Tintori
☆ Annabella Sciorra, Ron Eldard, Aida Turturro, Roger Rignack, Star Jasper, Michael J. Wolfe, Kelly Cinnante, Rick Shapiro

'...Stealing ... Cheating ... Killing ... who says romance is dead?'

True Romance **

US 1993 119m colour Panvision
Warner/Morgan Creek/Davis (Bill Unger, Steve Perry, Samuel Hadida)

A shop assistant and a callgirl go on the run with a suitcase full of cocaine, chased by gangsters.
A clever, very violent, high-energy thriller, providing opportunity for striking cameos by a variety of actors as well as narrative twists that owe much to farce; the conclusion, a three-way stand-off, brings to mind a minor 30s screwball comedy, The Housekeeper's Daughter, *but then the film is stuffed with references to other movies.*
w *Quentin Tarantino* d Tony Scott ph Jeffrey L. Kimball m Hans Zimmer pd Benjamin Fernandez ed Michael Tronick, Christian Wagner
☆ Christian Slater, Patricia Arquette, *Dennis Hopper*, Val Kilmer, *Gary Oldman*, Brad Pitt, *Christopher Walken*

CLIFF (DENNIS HOPPER): 'I don't know whether you know this or not, Sicilians were spawned by niggers.'

COCCOTTI (CHRISTOPHER WALKEN): 'Come again?'

CLIFF: 'It's a fact. Sicilians have nigger blood pumpin' through their hearts. If you don't believe me, look it up. You see, hundreds and hundreds of years ago the Moors conquered Sicily. And Moors are niggers. Way back then, Sicilians were like the wops in northern Italy. Blond hair. Blue eyes. But, once the Moors moved in there, they changed the whole country. They did so much fuckin' with the Sicilian women, they changed the blood-line for ever, from blond hair and blue eyes to black hair and dark skin. I find it absolutely amazing to think that to this day, hundreds of years later, Sicilians still carry that nigger gene. I'm just quotin' history. It's a fact. It's written. Your ancestors were niggers. Your great, great, great, great, great-grandmother was fucked by a nigger, and had a half-nigger kid. That is a fact. Now tell me, am I lying?'

'Creates a new genre: screwball violence.' – *Tom Hutchinson*

'Provides some amazing encounters, bravura acting turns and gruesome carnage. But it doesn't add up to enough, as preposterous plotting and graphic violence ultimately prove an audience turnoff.' – *Variety*

'Looks like a piece of designer chic searching but unable to find any kind of holding centre.' – *Derek Malcolm, Guardian*

True Stories *

US 1986 89m DuArt
Warner/Edward R. Pressman/Gary Kurfirst

A narrator introduces people from the town of Virgil, Texas.
A curious entertainment which plays like a whimsical update of Thornton Wilder's Our Town, *though without the subtlety.*
w Stephen Tobolowsky, Beth Henley, David Byrne d David Byrne ph Ed Lachman m David Byrne
☆ David Byrne, John Goodman, Annie McEnroe, Jo Harvey Allen, Spalding Gray, Alix Elias, Swoosie Kurtz

'The story is just a trick to get your attention. It opens the door and lets the real movie in.' – *David Byrne*

The True Story of Jesse James

US 1956 92m Eastmancolor Cinemascope
TCF (Herbert Swope Jnr)
GB title: *The James Brothers*

After the Civil War, Jesse and Frank James become outlaws and train robbers.
Fairly slavish remake of Jesse James, *without the style.*
w Walter Newman d Nicholas Ray ph Joe MacDonald m Leigh Harline
☆ Robert Wagner, Jeffrey Hunter, Hope Lange, Agnes Moorehead, John Carradine, Alan Hale Jnr, Alan Baxter

True to Life *

US 1943 93m Technicolor
Paramount (Paul Jones)

The writer of a radio soap opera moves in with an average family to get the right atmosphere.
Quite a percipient comedy of its day, though it does not forgo the customary romantic entanglements.
w Don Hartman, Harry Tugend d George Marshall ph Charles Lang m Victor Young
☆ Mary Martin, Dick Powell, Franchot Tone, Victor Moore, Mabel Paige, William Demarest, Clarence Kolb, Ernest Truex

True to the Navy

US 1930 70m bw
Paramount

A drug store girl has too many sailor sweethearts for comfort.
Very ordinary star vehicle, with little about it worth remembering next day.
w Keene Thompson, Doris Anderson, Herman Mankiewicz d Frank Tuttle
☆ Clara Bow, Fredric March, Harry Green, Rex Bell, Eddie Fetherston

'Hardly better than fair. Slow in tempo, sappy in story, and bearing the stamp of perfunctory production.' – *Variety*

Truly, Madly, Deeply **

GB 1990 106m colour
Samuel Goldwyn Company/Winston/BBC/Lionheart (Robert Cooper)

A woman grieving for the death of her husband is visited by his ghost.
Unusual story of coming to terms with loss, combining wit, insight and excellent acting.
wd Anthony Minghella ph Remi Adefarasin m Barrington Pheloung pd Barbara Gasnold ed John Stothart
☆ Juliet Stevenson, Alan Rickman, Bill Paterson, Michael Maloney, Jenny Howe, Carolyn Choa, Christopher Rozycki, Keith Bartlett, David Ryall

'Intelligent, charming, ironic and exceptionally well played.' – *Derek Malcolm, Guardian*

best original screenplay

The Truman Show ***

US 1998 102m DeLuxe
Paramount (Scott Rudin, Andrew Niccol, Edward S. Feldman, Adam Schroeder)

A man who lives happily in an island community discovers that he is the star of an all-day TV soap opera, and that his wife, friends and neighbours are all acting their parts.
A clever (if implausible) conceit that can be taken several ways: as a satire on our all-controlling media, as a comment on television's pervasiveness, and the way everyone wants to appear on it, or as an instance of situationists' desire to disrupt the spectacle, to tear away the false tinsel of everyday life, and reveal the real tinsel beneath. Whichever way, it's a pleasure to watch.
w *Andrew Niccol* d *Peter Weir* ph Peter Biziou m Burkhard Dallwitz pd Dennis Gassner ed William Anderson
☆ Jim Carrey, Laura Linney, Noah Emmerich, Natascha McElhone, Holland Taylor, Ed Harris

'An emerging genre of cheerfully subversive movies finds its first near-masterpiece.' – *David Thomson, Esquire*

Peter Weir; Andrew Niccol; Ed Harris
Peter Weir; Andrew Niccol; Dennis Gassner

The Trumpet Blows

US 1934 68m bw
Paramount

A matador comes home to Mexico and quarrels with his bandit brother.
Tedious melodrama with bullring scenes.
w Bartlett Cormack, Wallace Smith, Porter Emerson Browne, J. Parker Read Jnr d Stephen Roberts
☆ George Raft, Adolphe Menjou, Frances Drake, Sidney Toler, Edward Ellis, Nydia Westman

'Story weak, dialogue bad, casting hopeless.' – *Variety*

Trunk Crime

GB 1939 51m bw
Charter (John Boulting)

A student goes mad and tries to bury his enemy alive.
Now dated, but at the time a smart little programme-filler by an enterprising young producer-director team.
w Francis Miller play Edward Percy, Reginald Denham d Roy Boulting
☆ Manning Whiley, Barbara Everest, Hay Petrie, Thorley Walters

The Trunk Mystery: see *One New York Night*

'A slightly twisted comedy.'

Trust **

GB/USA 1990 106m colour
Palace/Zenith/True Fiction/Film Four (Bruce Weiss)

A pregnant teenager meets a moody, grenade-carrying electronics expert and takes him home with her.
Off-beat film that examines motherhood and marriage with a beady eye.
wd Hal Hartley ph Michael Spiller m Phillip Reed pd Dan Ouellette ed Nick Gomez
☆ Adrienne Shelly, Martin Donovan, Marritt Nelson, John MacKay, Edie Falco, Gary Sauer, Matt Malloy

'An existentialist comedy of manners. It comes from the nowhere that its maker grew up in.' – *Terrence Rafferty, New Yorker*

'Brian's About To Discover The Woman He Loves Isn't The Woman He Loves.'

The Truth about Cats & Dogs **

US 1996 97m DeLuxe
TCF/Noon Attack (Cari-Esta Albert)

A radio vet, who thinks of herself as unattractive, gets her beautiful friend to impersonate her on a date with a handsome photographer and his dog.
Charming comic variation on the theme of Cyrano de Bergerac *which is witty about the value of good looks and the dangers of self-hatred while delivering a nicely paced romance.*
w Audrey Wells d Michael Lehmann ph Robert Brinkmann m Howard Shore pd Sharon Seymour ed Stephen Semel
☆ Uma Thurman, *Janeane Garofalo*, Ben Chaplin, Jamie Foxx, James McCaffrey, Richard Coca, Stanley DeSantis

'Cleverly hints at the penalties which women have to pay for achieving feminist success without conforming to a feminine ideal.' – *Alexander Walker*

'everybody has a secret'

The Truth About Charlie *

US 2002 104m DeLuxe Panavision
Universal/Mediastream/Clinica Estetico (Jonathan Demme, Peter Saraf)

In Paris, a mysterious man comes to the aid of a widow, who discovers that her husband may have hidden a fortune that others are determined to get.
A remake of the 1963 thriller Charade, *with Wahlberg no substitute for the original's Cary Grant; no doubt to conceal his inadequacies Demme directs in the style of a French New Wave movie, as if Godard were still in fashion.*
w Jonathan Demme, Steve Schmidt, Peter Joshua, Jessica Bendinger *screenplay* Charade by Peter Stone d Jonathan Demme ph Tak Fujimoto m Rachel Portman pd Hugo Luczyc-Wyhowski ed Carol Littleton
☆ Mark Wahlberg (Joshua Peters), Thandie Newton (Regina Lambert), Tim Robbins (Mr Bartholomew), Joong-Hoon Park (Il-Sang Lee), Ted Levine (Emil Zadapec), Lisa Gay Hamilton (Lola Jansco), Stephen Dillane (Charlie), Charles Aznavour (Himself), Anna Karina (Karina), Agnès Varda (The Widow Hyppolite)

'A work of virtuoso filmmaking in a vain search for substance.' – *Todd McCarthy, Variety*

'At once listless and overheated, giddy and utterly zipless, the current incarnation lacks not just the savoir-faire of its stylish predecessor but also the sex appeal.' – *Ann Hornaday, Washington Post*

The Truth About Demons: see *The Irrefutable Truth About Demons*

The Truth about Spring *

GB 1964 102m Technicolor
U-I /Quota Rentals (Alan Brown)

The bored nephew of a millionaire cruising in the Caribbean jumps at the chance to join friends on a scruffy yacht, but they all get involved with pirates.
Pleasing family film with good scenery and a friendly cast.
w James Lee Barrett novel H. de Vere Stacpoole d Richard Thorpe ph Ted Scaife m Robert Farnon
☆ Hayley Mills, James MacArthur, David Tomlinson, Lionel Jeffries, John Mills, Harry Andrews, Niall MacGinnis

The Truth about Women

GB 1957 107m Eastmancolor
British Lion/Beaconsfield (Sydney Box)

An old roué recounts to his son-in-law his early amorous adventures.
Tedious charade with neither wit nor grace.
w Muriel and Sydney Box d Muriel Box ph Otto Heller m Bruce Montgomery
☆ Laurence Harvey, Julie Harris, Diane Cilento, Mai Zetterling, Eva Gabor, Michael Denison, Derek Farr, Roland Culver, Wilfrid Hyde-White, Christopher Lee, Marius Goring, Thorley Walters, Ernest Thesiger, Griffith Jones

'It's amazing that with all those talented people nothing happens on the screen.' – *Pauline Kael, 70s*

'When You're Running On Fear, Don't Stop For Gas.'

Truth or Consequences, N.M.

US 1997 106m Technicolor
(J. Paul Higgins, Kevin J. Messick)

A couple are kidnapped by four psychopathic robbers on the run after stealing drugs from the mob.
Violent, unoriginal thriller peopled by unsympathetic characters and reliant on stock situations and dialogue.
w Brad Mirman d Kiefer Sutherland ph Ric Waite m Jude Cole pd Anne Stuhler ed Lawrence Jordan
☆ Vincent Gallo (Raymond Lembecke), Mykelti Williamson (Marcus Weans), Kiefer Sutherland (Curtis Freley), Kevin Pollak (Gordon Jacobson), Kim Dickens (Addy Monroe), Grace Phillips (Donna Moreland), James McDaniel (Frank Thompson), Rick Rossovich (Robert Boylan), John C. McGinley (Eddie Grillo), Rod Steiger (Tony Vago), Martin Sheen (Sir), Max Perlich (Wayne)

'A crime caper so hackneyed it might have been written by a computer following a program labeled "sub-Tarantino."' – *Godfrey Cheshire, Variety*

Truth or Dare *

US 1991 119m colour/bw
Rank/Propaganda/Boy Toy (Tim Clawson, Jay Roewe)
GB title: *In Bed with Madonna*

Documentary of Madonna's international concert tour of 1990.
Fascinating, if manipulative, look at a current phenomenon, made under the control of Madonna and carefully projecting an image of wild sexuality.
d Alek Keshishian ph Robert Leacock md Jai Winding ad Christopher Ciccone ed Barry Alexander Brown, Anne B. Erikson, John Murray

'An ace manipulator's self-portrait, unmediated by interviewers or pundits. Raw, raunchy and epically entertaining, this is pure, unadulterated Madonna.' – *Richard Corliss, Time*

Try and Find It: see *Hi Diddle Diddle*

Try and Get Me *

US 1951 92m bw
(UA)
GB title: *The Sound of Fury*

Two men are arrested for kidnapping and murder, and a journalist stirs the small town to lynch fury.
Harrowing, relentless melodrama, possibly the best on this subject.
w *Joe Pagano novel* The Condemned by Joe Pagano d Cy Endfield ph Guy Roe m Hugo Friedhofer
☆ Frank Lovejoy, Lloyd Bridges, Kathleen Ryan, Richard Carlson, Katherine Locke, Adele Jergens, Art Smith

'The characterization and the handling of the drama are remarkable, at times reaching a complexity rare in films of this type.' – *Gavin Lambert*

'A strange, uncomfortable, sometimes brutal and depressing picture.' – *Richard Mallett, Punch*

The Trygon Factor *

GB 1966 88m Technicolor
Rank/Rialto Film/Preben Phillipsen (Ian Warren)

Bogus nuns plan a million pound bank raid.
When you get used to its mixture of styles, this Anglo-German production is pretty good imitation Edgar Wallace, with bags of mystery and melodramatic goings-on involving larger than life characters most of whom come to sticky ends.

w Derry Quinn, Stanley Munro, Kingsley Amis d Cyril Frankel ph Harry Waxman m Peter Thomas
☆ Stewart Granger, Susan Hampshire, Cathleen Nesbitt, Robert Morley, James Culliford, Brigitte Horney, Sophie Hardy, James Robertson Justice

Tsareubiitsa: see *Assassin of the Tsar*

Tsubaki Sanjuro: see *Sanjuro*

Tsvet Granata: see *The Colour of Pomegranates*

Tucker: The Man and His Dream **
US 1988 115m colour
UIP/Lucasfilm (Fred Roos, Fred Fuchs)
A designer is put out of business after he creates a revolutionary new car.
Slick, engaging, well-crafted story, based on fact.
w Arnold Schulman, David Seidler d Francis Ford Coppola ph Vittorio Storaro m Joe Jackson pd Dean Tavoularis ad Armin Ganz ed Priscilla Nedd
☆ Jeff Bridges, Joan Allen, Martin Landau, Frederic Forrest, Mako, Elias Koteas, Christian Slater, Lloyd Bridges, Dean Stockwell
Martin Landau; Dean Tavoularis, Armin Ganz; best costume design
Dean Tavoularis

Tudor Rose *
GB 1936 78m bw
GFD/Gainsborough (Michael Balcon)
US title: *Nine Days a Queen*
The brief life and reign of Lady Jane Grey.
Modestly well made historical textbook.
w Robert Stevenson, Miles Malleson d Robert Stevenson ph Max Greene m Louis Levy
☆ Cedric Hardwicke, Nova Pilbeam, John Mills, Felix Aylmer, Leslie Perrins, Frank Cellier, Desmond Tester, Gwen Ffrangcon Davies, Sybil Thorndike, Martita Hunt, Miles Malleson, John Laurie
'There is not a character, not an incident in which history has not been altered for the cheapest of reasons.' – *Graham Greene*

Tuff Turf
US 1985 112m CFI color
Blue Dolphin/New World (Donald P. Borchers)
A street rebel and his moll have trouble understanding themselves and their world.
Audiences had trouble getting interested.
w Jette Rinck story Greg Collins O'Neill, Murray Michaels d Fritz Kiersch ph Willy Kurant m Jonathan Elias ad Craig Stearns ed Marc Grossman
☆ James Spader, Kim Richards, Paul Mones, Robert Downey, Matt Clark

Tugboat Annie **
US 1933 88m bw
MGM (Harry Rapf)
An elderly waterfront lady and her boozy friend smooth out the path of young love.
Hilarious and well-loved comedy vehicle for two great stars of the period.
w Zelda Sears, Eve Greene stories Norman Reilly Raine d Mervyn Le Roy ph Gregg Toland
☆ *Marie Dressler, Wallace Beery*, Robert Young, Maureen O'Sullivan, Willard Robertson, Paul Hurst
'One of those rare naturals in the picture business – a flicker that sells itself immediately the stars' names go into the lights.' – *Variety*
'A bare outline of the story cannot convey the note of mother love that runs through it, the laughs, the pathos.' – *Picturegoer*

Tugboat Annie Sails Again
US 1940 75m bw
Warner (Edmund Grainger)
The river lady defeats all comers in her efforts to whip up trade.
Badly developed sequel which isn't badly acted but gets nowhere.
w Walter DeLeon d Lewis Seiler
☆ Marjorie Rambeau, Alan Hale, Jane Wyman, Ronald Reagan, Clarence Kolb, Charles Halton, Victor Kilian

Tulitikkutehtaan Tytto: see *The Match Factory Girl*

'Meet Cherokee Lansing ... half wildcat ... half angel ... all woman!'
Tulsa *
US 1949 88m Technicolor
Eagle-Lion (Walter Wanger)
The daughter of a cattle owner builds an oil empire.
Splendid Hollywood hokum of the second grade, very predictable but well-oiled.
w Frank Nugent, Curtis Kenyon d Stuart Heisler ph Winton Hoch m Frank Skinner
☆ Susan Hayward, Robert Preston, Pedro Armendariz, Lloyd Gough, Chill Wills, Ed Begley
'Like a damp fuse, it produces a loud bang at the end of a long splutter.' – *Time*

Tumbleweed
US 1953 79m Technicolor
Universal (Ross Hunter)
A cowboy is accused of helping Indians raid the wagon-train he was guarding.
Unpretentious, action-packed minor Western; the horse who plays the title-role takes the acting honours.
d Nathan Juran ph Russell Metty m Henry Mancini
☆ Audie Murphy (Jim Harvey), Lori Nelson (Laura), Chill Wills (Sheriff Murchoree), K. T. Stevens (Louella Buckley), Russell Johnson (Lam), Madge Meredith (Sarah), Roy Roberts (Nick Buckley), Lee Van Cleef (Marv)

Tumbleweeds **
US 1925 80m (24 fps) bw silent
United Artists/William S. Hart
A wandering cowboy helps a family of settlers.
The same plot as Shane works wonders in the last film of William S. Hart, which has the apparently authentic flavour of the old west.
w C. Gardner Sullivan story Hal G. Evarts d King Baggott ph Joseph August
☆ *William S. Hart*, Barbara Bedford, Lucien Littlefield, Monte Collins
† Reissued in 1939 with an added eight-minute introduction by Hart, showing how the west has changed.

'They ran away from everything...but each other'
Tumbleweeds *
US 1999 103m Foto-Kem
Entertainmeny/ALH/Spanky/Solaris/River One (Greg O'Connor)
A 12-year-old girl rebels against her mother's footloose approach to life.
Slight, well-acted domestic drama of role-reversal, with a feckless adult learning lessons in life from a maturer child.
w Gavin O'Connor, Angela Shelton d Gavin O'Connor ph Dan Stoloff m David Mansfield pd Bruce Eric Holtshousen ed John Gilroy
☆ *Janet McTeer* (Mary Jo Walker), Kimberly J. Brown (Ava Walker), Gavin O'Connor (Jack Ranson), Jay O'Sanders (Dan Miller), Lois Smith (Ginger), Lolloman (Laurie Pendleton), Michael J. Pollard (Mr Cummings), Noah Emmerich (Vertis Dewey), Ashley Buccille (Zoe Broussard), Cody McMains (Adam Riley)
'As cute and charming as a mum-and-daughter buddy-picture can be.' – *Cosmo Landesman, Sunday Times*
† A similar movie of a mother-daughter conflict, released around the same time, was *Anywhere But Here* (qv).
Janet McTeer

The Tune **
US 1992 72m colour
A songwriter has problems writing a new song against the clock.
Clever, episodic animated feature, where the wit lies in the surreal visual imagination of its creator, reaching its height in a duel where two men commit ever more bizarre acts of violence upon one another; the musical pastiches also contribute.
wd Bill Plympton m Maureen McElheron ed Merril Stern
☆ Featuring the voices of: Daniel Neiden, Maureen McElheron, Marty Nelson, Emily Bindinger, Chris Hoffman

'They're having a secret love affair. Only fifty thousand listeners know about it.'
Tune In Tomorrow *
US 1990 104m colour
Hobo/Polar/Odyssey/Cinecom (John Fielder, Mark Tarlov)
GB title: *Aunt Julia and The Scriptwriter*
A writer of a daily radio serial manipulates an affair between a young journalist and his older aunt to provide material for his scripts.
A comedy at the expense of soap operas and the original novel.
w William Boyd novel *Aunt Julia and The Scriptwriter* by Mario Vargas Llosa d Jon Amiel ph Robert Stevens m Wynton Marsalis pd Jim Clay, James L. Schoppe ed Peter Boyle
☆ Barbara Hershey, Keanu Reeves, Peter Falk, Bill McCutcheon, Patricia Clarkson, Richard Portnow, Jerome Dempsey
'A sharp-fanged novel has been turned into an ingratiating puppy walking on its hind legs.' – *Philip French, Observer*

Tunes of Glory ***
GB 1960 107m Technicolor
UA/Knightsbridge (Albert Fennell)
The new disciplinarian CO of a highland regiment crosses swords with his lax, hard drinking predecessor.
Wintry barracks melodrama, finely acted and well made with memorable confrontation scenes compensating for a somewhat underdeveloped script.
w James Kennaway novel James Kennaway d *Ronald Neame* ph *Arthur Ibbetson*
☆ *Alec Guinness, John Mills*, Susannah York, Dennis Price, Kay Walsh, *Duncan Macrae*, Gordon Jackson, John Fraser, Allan Cuthbertson
'The picture is persuasive. But I daresay one does it wrong by looking too hard for social reflections. Lucky enough to find a film which has life in it.' – *Dilys Powell*
James Kennaway

Tung-Tung-te chia-ch'i: see *A Summer at Grandpa's*

The Tunnel *
GB 1935 94m bw
Gaumont (Michael Balcon)
US title: *Transatlantic Tunnel*
Crooked finances mar the completion of an undersea tunnel to America.
A rare example of British science fiction from this period, though the film was in fact first made in German and French versions, the latter with Jean Gabin.
w Curt Siodmak, L. DuGarde Peach, Clemence Dane novel Bernard Kellerman d Maurice Elvey ph Gunther Krampf m Louis Levy
☆ Richard Dix, Leslie Banks, Madge Evans, Helen Vinson, C. Aubrey Smith, George Arliss, Walter Huston, Basil Sydney, Jimmy Hanley
'I was quite unable to sit this film through, though by leaving I missed the "courtesy appearance" of Mr George Arliss as the Prime Minister of Great Britain, an actor from whose Athenaeum manner I sometimes derive a rather humble pleasure.' – *Graham Greene*

Tunnel 28: see *Escape from East Berlin*

The Tunnel of Love
US 1958 98m bw Cinemascope
MGM/Joseph Fields
A husband applying to adopt an orphan thinks he may, while drunk, have seduced the glamorous orphan agency official.
Tasteless and not very funny comedy, somewhat miscast.
w Joseph Fields, Jerome Chodorov play Joseph Fields, Jerome Chodorov, Peter de Vries novel Peter de Vries d Gene Kelly ph Robert Bronner
☆ Richard Widmark, Doris Day, Gig Young, Gia Scala, Elisabeth Fraser, Elizabeth Wilson
† Jerome Chodorov's name was omitted from the film's credits at the time because he was blacklisted.

Tunnel Vision
Australia 1994 92m colour
Beyond/Pro (Phillip Avalon)
A maverick detective is having a hard time: his marriage is in trouble, his boss hates him, his female partner is behaving oddly, his investigation of a serial killer is going badly, and he is suspected of having killed his wife's business associate.
Risible thriller that gets sillier, and less interesting, by the minute.
wd Clive Fleury ph Paul Murphy m David Hirschfelder, Ric Formosa pd Phil Warner ed John Scott
☆ Patsy Kensit, Robert Reynolds, Rebecca Rigg, Gary Day, Shane Briant

'Fear is in the air'
Turbulence
US 1997 100m colour Panavision
Entertainment/Rysher (Martin Ransohoff, David Valdes)
A psychopathic killer, who is being flown from New York to Los Angeles, takes over a 747 just as the plane is heading into a major storm.
Ridiculous thriller that adds violence and special-effects mayhem to the plot of Airport 1975; it may put you off going to the cinema again.
w Jonathan Brett d Robert Butler ph Lloyd Ahern II m Shirley Walker pd Mayling Cheng ed John Duffy
☆ Ray Liotta (Ryan Weaver), Lauren Holly (Teri Holloran), Brendan Gleeson (Stubbs), Hector Elizondo (Detective Aldo Hines), Ben Cross (Captain Sam Bowen), Rachel Ticotin (Rachel Taper), Jeffrey DeMunn (Brooks), John Finn (Sinclair), Catherine Hicks (Maggie)
'There's the usual pert air hostess being frightfully brave. This should be straight-to-video stuff.' – *Derek Malcolm, Guardian*

Turk 182 *
US 1985 98m TVC Color
TCF (Ted Field, Rene DuPont)
A mystery do-gooder embarrasses the city bureaucracy into doing right by citizens with a grievance.
Interesting urban drama with a non-violent vigilante.
w James Gregory Kingston, Denis and John Hamill d Bob Clark ph Reginald H. Morris m Paul Zaza pd Harry Pottle ed Stan Cole
☆ Timothy Hutton, Robert Urich, Kim Cattrall, Robert Culp, Darren McGavin, Steven Keats, Peter Boyle, Paul Sorvino

Turkey Time
GB 1933 73m bw
Gaumont
Family indiscretions come out at Christmas time.
Vehicle for fruity characterizations by the popular Aldwych team, but not very strong as a farce.
w Ben Travers play Ben Travers d Tom Walls ph Charles Van Enger
☆ Tom Walls, Ralph Lynn, Robertson Hare, Dorothy Hyson, Mary Brough, Norma Varden

The Turkish Bath: see *Hamam*

Turkish Delight *
Netherlands 1973 106m colour
Columbia-Warner/Rob Houwer (Mia van't Hof)
original title: *Turks Fruit*
A promiscuous young sculptor marries unhappily but falls in love with his wife again during her terminal illness.
Scabrous satire on Dutch middle-class attitudes combined with shock tactics and as much sex as the director could get past the censor; undeniably displaying talent of a not very likeable kind, it was a box-office success in Holland.
w Gerard Soeteman novel Jan Wolkers d Paul Verhoeven ph Jan de Bont m Rogier van Otterloo ad Ralf van der Elst ed Jan Bosdriess
☆ Monique van de Ven, Rutger Hauer, Tonny Huurdeman, Wim van den Brink, Dolf de Vries
'Repulsive and meaningless' – *Clyde Jeavons, MFB*
'Underscored by a romanticism which slowly accumulates as time goes by. The difficulties of combining scatology and tenderness are neatly handled.' – *Derek Elley, Films and Filming*

Turks Fruit: see *Turkish Delight*

Turksib *
USSR 1929 60m approx (24 fps) bw silent
Vostok Kino
The making of the Turkestan–Siberia railway.
A highly fluent and pictorial documentary with an especially famous climax as the men struggle to lay the last rails and meet a deadline.
w Victor Turin and others *d* Victor Turin
ph Yevgeni Slavinsky, Boris Frantzisson

Turn Back the Clock *
US 1933 80m bw
MGM
A man dreams of changing places with his rich friend.
Unusual, quite pleasing comedy-drama.
w Edgar Selwyn, Ben Hecht *d* Edgar Selwyn
☆ Lee Tracy, Otto Kruger, Mae Clarke, C. Henry Gordon, George Barbier
'Neatly turned domestic comedy with a dramatic touch that will please all round.' – *Variety*

The Turn of the Screw
GB/France 1992 95m colour/bw
Electric Pictures/Michael White/Lakedell/Cinemax (Staffan Ahrenberg, Nicole Seguin)
A woman in group therapy tells what happened to her and her brother when, as small children, their new governess was haunted by the evil ghosts of a predecessor and her lover.
Updated for no apparent reason to the 60s, this is a heavy-handed version, treated as a melodramatic horror story, and so overburdened with the trappings of the genre – spooky house, spookier music, sudden shocks, grinning masks, mechanical toys and disturbing dolls – that it stifles the subtlety of the original. Despite his star billing, Sands appears only for a few languid minutes.
wd Rusty Lemorande *story* Henry James
ph Witold Stok *m* Simon Boswell *pd* Max Gottlieb *ed* John Victor Smith
☆ Patsy Kensit, Stephane Audran, Julian Sands, Marianne Faithfull, Olivier Debray, Bryony Brand, Joseph England, Claire Szekeres
'This is one screw that needed no further turning, especially when it's done in such a clumsy, pedestrian manner.' – *Variety*

Turn of the Tide *
GB 1935 80m bw
British National (John Corfield)
A feud between two fishing families ends in marriage.
Low-key, location-set action drama with a moral. The film which brought J. Arthur Rank into the business, which he saw had religious possibilities.
w L. DuGarde Peach, J. O. C. Orton *novel Three Fevers* by Leo Walmsley *d* Norman Walker
ph Franz Planer *m* Arthur Benjamin
☆ Geraldine Fitzgerald, John Garrick, Niall MacGinnis, J. Fisher White, Joan Maude, Sam Livesey, Wilfrid Lawson, Moore Marriott
'Cut to an hour, it should make an acceptable second feature.' – *Variety*
'An unpretentious and truthful film.' – *Graham Greene*
† The film has been released on video together with *The Man at the Gate*.

Turn Off the Moon
US 1937 79m bw
Paramount/Fanchon
The proprietor of a department store is persuaded by an astrologer to stage a big show in celebration of his 25th anniversary.
Thinly structured musical with some acceptable gags and turns.
w Marguerite Roberts, Harlan Ware, Paul Gerard Smith, Mildred Harrington *d* Lewis Seiler
☆ Charles Ruggles, Eleanore Whitney, Johnny Downs, Kenny Baker, Phil Harris and his Orchestra, Ben Blue, Andrew Tombes, Marjorie Gateson, Grady Sutton, Franklin Pangborn
'B from title to climax.' – *Variety*

Turn the Key Softly
GB 1953 81m bw
GFD/Chiltern (Maurice Cowan)
The problems of three women released from prison.
Soppy formula multi-drama with contrived and uninteresting plots and characters.
w Jack Lee, Maurice Cowan *novel* John Brophy *d* Jack Lee *ph* Geoffrey Unsworth *m* Mischa Spoliansky
☆ Yvonne Mitchell, Terence Morgan, Joan Collins, Kathleen Harrison, Thora Hird, Dorothy Alison, Glyn Houston, Geoffrey Keen, Clive Morton

'Pardon my error, the stork meekly smiled, I've overlooked wifey, gave hubby the child!'
Turnabout *
US 1940 83m bw
Hal Roach
A benevolent god enables a quarrelsome couple to change bodies and see how they like it.
'The man's had a baby instead of the lady', said the ads. Well, not quite, but it did seem pretty daring at the time, and it still provides a hilarious moment or two.
w Mickell Novak, Berne Giler, John McLain *novel* Thorne Smith *d* Hal Roach *ph* Norbert Brodine *m* Arthur Morton
☆ Adolphe Menjou, John Hubbard, Carole Landis, Mary Astor, Verree Teasdale, Donald Meek, William Gargan, Joyce Compton

Turned Out Nice Again
GB 1941 81m bw
ATP
An employee teaches an underwear firm to move with the times.
Tolerable star comedy from his late period.
w Austin Melford, John Dighton, Basil Dearden *play As You Are* by Hugh Mills, Wells Root *d* Marcel Varnel
☆ George Formby, Peggy Bryan, Edward Chapman, Elliot Mason, Mackenzie Ward, O. B. Clarence

Turner & Hooch
US 1989 99m Metrocolor
Warner/Touchstone/Silver Screen Partners IV (Raymond Wagner)
In order to solve a murder, a cop teams up with the only witness, a large dog.
The cycle of police buddy-buddy movies reaches its nadir in this strenuously unfunny release.
w Dennis Shryack, Michael Blodgett, Daniel Petrie Jnr, Jim Cash, Jack Epps Jnr *d* Roger Spottiswoode *ph* Adam Greenberg *m* Charles Gross *pd* John DeCuir Jnr *ed* Paul Seydor, Mark Conte, Kenneth Morrisey, Lois Freeman-Fox
☆ Tom Hanks, Mare Winningham, Craig T. Nelson, Reginald VelJohnson, Scott Paulin, J. C. Quinn, John McIntire

The Turners of Prospect Road
GB 1947 88m bw
Grand National (Victor Katona)
A taxi driver's family greyhound wins a big race.
Uneasily cast domestic comedy drama.
w Victor Katona, Patrick Kirwan *d* Maurice J. Wilson *ph* Freddie Ford *m* Nicholas Brodszky *md* Philip Green *ad* George Ward *ed* Ken Hume
☆ Wilfrid Lawson, Jeanne de Casalis, Maureen Glynne, Helena Pickard, Leslie Perrins, Peter Bull, Amy Veness, Shamus Locke

The Turning
US 1992 87m Technicolor
White Deer/L. A. Puopolo
Returning home after four years away, a 22-year-old fascist discovers that his parents are divorcing and decides that they should stay together.
Overwrought melodrama that attempts to deal with the rise of right-wing fundamentalism within the context of a family breaking apart; it fails to convince as a study either of politics or of a dysfunctional family.
w L. A. Puopolo, Chris Cesaro *play Home Fires Burning* by Chris Cesaro *d* L. A. Puopolo *ph* J. Michael McClary *m* Herb Pilhofer *pd* Mike Moran *ed* Lesley Topping
☆ Karen Allen, Raymond J. Barry, Michael Dolan, Tess Harper, Gillian Anderson
'Though it packs an undeniable emotional punch, pic comes across as overwritten and contrived as a cinema experience.' – *David Stratton, Variety*
† Under the title *Home Fires Burning*, it was shown at the 1992 Cannes Film Festival in a version running for 103m.

The Turning Point *
US 1952 85m bw
Paramount (Irving Asher)
original title: *This is Dynamite!*
A young lawyer is appointed by the state governor to smash a crime syndicate.
Familiar exposé drama of its time, quite crisply done.
w Warren Duff *d* William Dieterle *ph* Lionel Lindon *md* Irwin Talbot
☆ William Holden, Alexis Smith, Edmond O'Brien, Tom Tully, Ray Teal

'A story of envy, hatred, friendship, triumph and love!'
The Turning Point *
US 1977 119m DeLuxe
TCF/Hera (Nora Kaye)
The American Ballet Theatre visits Oklahoma City, and its ageing star revisits an ex-colleague, now a housewife.
Posh person's soap opera, rather boringly made and interesting only for its performances, which are certainly vivid.
w Arthur Laurents *d* Herbert Ross *ph* Robert Surtees *m* John Lanchbery *pd* Albert Brenner *ed* William Reynolds
☆ *Anne Bancroft, Shirley MacLaine*, Mikhail Baryshnikov, Leslie Browne, Tom Skerritt, Martha Scott, Marshall Thompson
'A backstage musical dressed up with smart cultural trimmings.' – *Alan Brien*
'We get a glimpse of something great in the movie – Mikhail Baryshnikov dancing – and these two harpies out of the soaps block the view.' – *New Yorker, 1978*
best picture; Herbert Ross; Robert Surtees; Anne Bancroft; Shirley MacLaine; Mikhail Baryshnikov; Leslie Browne; Arthur Laurents; art direction; editing

Turtle Beach
Australia 1992 88m colour
Warner/Roadshow/Coote & Carroll
A reporter leaves her husband and children to go to Malaysia to cover the story of the problems of Vietnamese boat people and witnesses a massacre.
An apparent attempt to expose racism and corruption in Malaysia and Australia, but too muddled to make much sense.
w Ann Turner *novel* Blanche d'Alpuget *d* Stephen Wallace *ph* Russell Boyd *m* Chris Neal *pd* Brian Thomson *ed* Lee Smith, Louise Innes
☆ Greta Scacchi, Joan Chen, Jack Thompson, Art Malik, Norman Kaye, Victoria Longley, Martin Jacobs, William McInnes, George Whaley
'Rarely has such an interesting story resulted in such drab fare.' – *Variety*

Turtle Diary *
GB 1985 97m Technicolor
CBS/United British Artists/Britannic (Richard Johnson)
Two self-admitted eccentrics take it upon themselves to release turtles from captivity in the London Zoo.
Mainly ineffective character comedy, memorable only for fragments of dialogue and acting.
w Harold Pinter *novel* Russell Hoban *d* John Irvin *ph* Peter Hannan *m* Geoffrey Burgon *pd* Leo Austin *ed* Peter Tanner
☆ *Glenda Jackson, Ben Kingsley*, Richard Johnson, Michael Gambon, Rosemary Leach, Eleanor Bron, Harriet Walter, Nigel Hawthorne, Michael Aldridge

The Tuttles of Tahiti
US 1942 91m bw
RKO (Sol Lesser)
The Tuttles have one ambition: to do no work.
A negative prospect even for a light comedy, and this one rapidly sinks under a welter of flat dialogue.
w S. Lewis Meltzer, Robert Carson, James Hilton *novel No More Gas* by Charles Nordhoff, James Norman Hall *d* Charles Vidor *ph* Nicholas Musuraca *m* Roy Webb
☆ Charles Laughton, Jon Hall, Victor Francen, Peggy Drake, Florence Bates

'He's Not Looking For Trouble… He's Wearing It.'
The Tuxedo
US 2002 99m Technicolor
DreamWorks/Vanguard/Parkes/MacDonald (Adam Schroeder, John H. Williams)
The chauffeur of a secret agent replaces his injured master with the aid of a gadget-filled tuxedo so that he can prevent a villain from poisoning the world's water.
Ludicrous comedy thriller that wastes Jackie Chan's talents and an audience's time.
w Michael J. Wilson, Michael Leeson *d* Kevin Donovan *ph* Stephen F. Windon *m* John Debney, Christophe Beck *pd* Paul Denham Austerberry, Monte Fay Hallis *ed* Craig P. Herring
☆ Jackie Chan (Jimmy Tong), Jennifer Love Hewitt (Del Blaine), Jason Isaacs (Clark Devlin), Debi Mazar (Steena), Ritchie Coster (Diedrich Banning), Peter Stormare (Dr Simms), Mia Cottet (Cheryl), Romany Malco (Mitch)
'The movie is silly beyond comprehension, and even if it weren't silly, it would still be beyond comprehension.' – *Roger Ebert, Chicago Sun-Times*

Tv Killar Och en Tjej: see *Happy We*

Twelfth Night *
US 1996 133m Technicolor
Entertainment/Fine Line/Twelfth Night/Renaissance (Stephen Evans, David Parfitt)
In Illyria, shipwrecked twins become involved in the romantic misunderstandings of a duke and the woman he thinks he loves.
An updated version of Shakespeare's comedy of sexual confusions, set in some unspecified, presumably Edwardian period, in which the farcical elements fare badly and the play's melancholy undercurrent is stressed; it never comes fully to life.
wd Trevor Nunn *play* William Shakespeare
ph Clive Tickner *m* Shaun Davey *pd* Sophie Becher *ed* Peter Boyle
☆ Helena Bonham Carter, Richard E. Grant, Nigel Hawthorne, Ben Kingsley, Mel Smith, Imelda Staunton, Toby Stephens, Imogen Stubbs, Steven MacKintosh, Nicholas Farrell, Sid Livingstone
'Works best not as a commentary on gender confusion but simply as an old-fashioned actors' showcase. There isn't a weak performance in the ensemble.' – *Stephen Farber, Movieline*
† The American trailer for the film emphasized its cross-dressing aspects, featuring Imogen Stubbs in male attire, accompanied by the song 'Macho Man'. The voice-over began: 'In the tradition of *Some Like It Hot*, *Tootsie* and *The Adventures of Priscilla, Queen of the Desert* comes the classic romantic comedy that proves sometimes clothes really do make the man…'

12 Angry Men ****
US 1957 95m bw
(UA) Orion-Nova (Henry Fonda, Reginald Rose)
A murder case jury about to vote guilty is convinced otherwise by one doubting member.
Though unconvincing in detail, this is a brilliantly tight character melodrama which is never less than absorbing to experience. Acting and direction are superlatively right, and the film was important in helping to establish television talents in Hollywood.
w Reginald Rose play Reginald Rose *d Sidney Lumet ph Boris Kaufman m* Kenyon Hopkins
☆ *Henry Fonda, Lee J. Cobb, E. G. Marshall, Jack Warden, Ed Begley, Martin Balsam, John Fiedler, Jack Klugman, George Voskovec, Robert Webber, Edward Binns, Joseph Sweeney*
'Holds the attention unquestioning. It is one of the most exciting films for months.' – *Dilys Powell*
'Generates more suspense than most thrillers.' – *New Yorker*
picture; Reginald Rose; Sidney Lumet
Henry Fonda

The Twelve Chairs: see *Twelve Plus One*

The Twelve Chairs
US 1970 93m Movielab
UMC/Crossbow (Michael Hertzberg)
A Russian bureaucrat chases twelve dining chairs, in one of which is hidden the family jewels.

Tedious Mel Brooks romp with not too many laughs, from a yarn better handled in Keep Your Seats Please *and* It's in the Bag, *from both of which he might have learned something about comedy timing.*
w Mel Brooks *novel* Ilya Ilf, Evgeny Petrov
d Mel Brooks *ph* Dorde Nikolic *m* John Morris
☆ *Ron Moody*, Frank Langella, Dom DeLuise, Bridget Brice, Diana Coupland, Mel Brooks

'In the end it runs out of both steam and jokes.' – *Michael Billington, Illustrated London News*

Twelve Good Men
GB 1936 64m bw
Warner
A convict escapes to murder the jury who convicted him.
Solidly carpentered suspenser.
w Sidney Gilliat, Frank Launder novel Murders in Praed Street *by John Rhode d* Ralph Ince *ph* Basil Emmott
☆ Henry Kendall, Nancy O'Neil, Percy Parsons, Morland Graham, Bernard Miles

'The Future Is History.'
Twelve Monkeys
US 1995 129m colour
Polygram/Universal/Atlas/Classico (Charles Roven)
In 2035, when the few remaining people live underground to escape the effects of a deadly virus, a convict is sent back to 1996 to discover more about the disease – or perhaps a psychotic is having a bad dream.
A bleak and confused conundrum, which often seems designed for no other purpose than to allow Willis to suffer stoically; despite its visual exuberance, the effect is deadening.
w David Peoples, Janet Peoples *inspired by* La Jetée by Chris Marker *d* Terry Gilliam *ph* Roger Pratt *m* Paul Buckmaster *pd* Jeffrey Beecroft *ed* Mick Audsley
☆ Bruce Willis, Brad Pitt, Madeleine Stowe, Christopher Plummer, Joseph Melito, Jon Seda, Michael Chance, Vernon Campbell

'It's confused, overwrought, illogical and derivative. Far too much is going on inside Gilliam's head, little of it original.' – *Alexander Walker*

'A spectacular mess ... long on sensibility, short on sense.' – *Variety*

† The film took more than $60m at the US box-office and more than $120m worldwide.
Brad Pitt; costume design (Julie Weiss)

'A story of twelve men as their women never knew them!'
Twelve O'Clock High **
US 1949 132m bw
TCF (Darryl F. Zanuck)
During World War II, the commander of a US bomber unit in Britain begins to crack under the strain.
Absorbing character drama, justifiably a big box-office success of its day, later revived as a TV series. All production values are excellent.
w Sy Bartlett, Beirne Lay Jnr d Henry King ph Leon Shamroy m Alfred Newman
☆ *Gregory Peck*, Hugh Marlowe, Gary Merrill, Millard Mitchell, Dean Jagger, Robert Arthur, Paul Stewart, John Kellogg

'The best war film since the fighting stopped.' – *Daily Mirror*

'Integrity all the way down the line.' – *New York Times*

Dean Jagger
best picture; Gregory Peck

Twelve Plus One
Italy/France 1969 108m Technicolor
CEF/COFCI (Claude Giroux, Edward J. Pope)
original title: *Una su 13*
aka: *The Twelve Chairs*
After he sells some chairs inherited from his aunt, a barber discovers that one of them contains a fortune and sets out to retrieve it.
Broad farce that wastes the talents of its cast, though it contains a bizarrely enjoyable moment by Welles as a barnstorming actor giving a ham performance of Dr Jekyll and Mr Hyde.
w Marc Behm, Dennis Norden, Nicolas Gessner *novel* Twelve Chairs by Ilf and Petrov *d* Nicolas Gessner *ph* Giuseppe Ruzzolini *m* Stelvio Cipriani *ed* Giancarlo Cappelli
☆ Sharon Tate, Vittorio Gassman, Orson Welles, Vittorio de Sica, Terry-Thomas, Mylene Demongeot, Grégoire Aslan, Tim Brooke-Taylor, Lionel Jeffries

Twentieth Century **
US 1934 91m bw
Columbia (Howard Hawks)
A temperamental Broadway producer trains an untutored actress, but when a star she proves a match for him.
Though slightly lacking in pace, this is a marvellously sharp and memorable theatrical burlesque, and the second half, set on the train of the title, reaches highly agreeable peaks of insanity.
w Ben Hecht, Charles MacArthur play Napoleon of Broadway by Charles Bruce Millholland *d Howard Hawks ph* Joseph August
☆ *John Barrymore, Carole Lombard*, Roscoe Karns, Walter Connolly, Ralph Forbes, *Etienne Girardot*, Charles Lane, Edgar Kennedy

'Probably too smart for general consumption ... a long shot for grosses outside the large cities that boast a cosmopolitan clientele.' – *Variety*

'Notable as the first comedy in which sexually attractive, sophisticated stars indulged in their own slapstick instead of delegating it to their inferiors.' – *Andrew Sarris, 1963*

'In the role of Jaffe John Barrymore fits as wholly and smoothly as a banana in a skin.' – *Otis Ferguson*

'When you pass the buck, the last thing you expect is change.'
Twenty Bucks *
US 1993 91m DeLuxe
Triton/Big Tomorrow (Karen Murphy)
The lives of various people are touched by a 20-dollar bill as it passes from one to another.
An old-fashioned notion for a movie which adds up to little more than a succession of slight and not very rewarding anecdotes, though Lloyd provides some interest as a robber who believes in order and discipline.
w Leslie and Endre Bohem *d* Keva Rosenfeld *ph* Emmanuel Lubezki *m* David Robbins *pd* Joseph T. Garrity *ed* Michael Ruscio
☆ Linda Hunt, Christopher Lloyd, Brendan Fraser, Elisabeth Shue, Steve Buscemi, Spalding Gray, Matt Frewer, Gladys Knight

'Delightful if patchy comedy.' – *Film Review*

† Endre Bohem, a Hungarian-born producer and writer, wrote the unproduced script in 1935; it was revised and updated by his son Leslie.

'The Life of the Party... before she got a life.'
28 Days
US 2000 104m DeLuxe
Columbia/Tail Trees (Jenno Topping)
An alcoholic young woman is sent to a rehabilitation centre.
Predictable movie of redemption that is enough to drive anyone to drink.
w Susannah Grant *d* Betty Thomas *ph* Declan Quinn *m* Richard Gibbs *pd* Marcia Hinds-Johnson *ed* Peter Teschner *cos* Ellen Lutter
☆ Sandra Bullock (Gwen Cummings), Viggo Mortensen (Eddie Boone), Dominic West (Jasper), Diane Ladd (Bobbie Jean), Elizabeth Perkins (Lily), Steve Buscemi (Cornell), Alan Tudyk (Gerhardt), Michael O'Malley (Oliver), Azura Skye (Andrea), Reni Santoni (Daniel), Marianne Jean-Baptiste (Roshanda), Margo Martindale (Betty)

'Isn't a particularly bad film, just a seen-it-all-before jaunt through the world of instituions and inner demons.' – *Caroline Westbrook, Empire*

'The Days Are Numbered.'
28 Days Later...
GB 2002 113m Technicolor
TCF/DNA/Film Council (Andrew Macdonald)
A man wakes up in a deserted hospital to discover that a virus has wiped out most of the inhabitants of London and turned others into zombies.
A zombie movie with a little twist – these ones are athletic – and a certain tension; nothing original otherwise, but very watchable.
w Alex Garland *d* Danny Boyle *ph* Anthony Dod Mantle *m* John Murphy *pd* Mark Tildesley *ed* Chris Gill *sp* Cliff Wallace
☆ Cillian Murphy (Jim), Noah Huntley (Mark), Naomie Harris (Selena), Brendan Gleeson (Frank), Megan Burns (Hannah), Christopher Eccleston (Major West)

'Shows a rather arrogant disdain for its audience in between occasional flashes of flair.' – *Derek Elley, Variety*

'The best purely British horror/science-fiction film in decades. And the first great apocalypse movie of the new millennium.' – *Empire*

'Can you change your whole life in a day?'
25th Hour *
US 2002 135m Technicolor 'Scope
Buena Vista/Touchstone/40Acres and a Mule Filmworks/Industry Entertainment/Gamut (Spike Lee, Jon Kilik, Tobey Maguire, Julia Chasman)
A New York drug-dealer has one last day of freedom, which he spends with friends, lover and his father, before beginning a seven-year prison sentence.
A sometimes turgid, very occasionally striking, drama of a man regretting his choices in life, and what awaits him in prison; setting it in the aftermath of 9/11 and the destruction of the World Trade Center only diminishes the movie's impact.
w David Benioff *novel* David Benioff *d* Spike Lee *ph* Rodrigo Prieto *m* Terence Blanchard *pd* James Chinlund *ed* Barry Alexander Brown
☆ Edward Norton (Monty Brogan), Philip Seymour Hoffman (Jacob Elinsky), Barry Pepper (Francis Xavier Slaughtery), Rosario Dawson (Naturelle Riviera), Anna Paquin (Mary D'Annunzio), Brian Cox (James Brogan), Tony Siragusa (Kostya Novotny)

'For all the trauma of 9/11, the atmosphere isn't markedly different from that of any other Spike Lee joint... Perhaps the tone is slightly chastened, and the conciliatory spirit of its ending is untypically earnest, but for the rest, it's another square yard of New York attitude.' – *Anthony Quinn, Independent*

'A turgid, bombastic and outrageously self-satisfied movie.' – *Peter Bradshaw, Guardian*

'Genius. Poet. Twat.'
24 Hour Party People *
GB 2002 117m DeLuxe
Pathé/Film Consortium/United Artists/Film Council/FilmFour/Wave/Revolution (Andrew Eaton)
In the mid-'70s, a Manchester TV presenter opens a night club and forms Factory Records, which for a time releases hit records by local bands.
A true story, of drugs and rock, of pop success and business failure, that is treated as low comedy; it will be enjoyed by those who can relate to the music and the brief years when Manchester bands were significant.
w Frank Cottrell Boyce *d* Michael Winterbottom *ph* Robby Mulle *pd* Mark Tildesley *ed* Michael Winterbottom
☆ Steve Coogan (Tony Wilson), Lennie James (Alan Erasmus), Shirley Henderson (Lindsay Wilson), Paddy Considine (Rob Gretton), Andy Serkis (Martin Hannett), Sean Harris (Ian Curtis), John Simm (Bernard Sumner), Ralf Little (Peter Hook), Keith Allen (Roger Ames)

'Reasonably entertaining stuff – but haven't we seen and heard it all before? It makes no serious attempt to find convincing or compelling human stories behind the legends.' – *Peter Bradshaw, Guardian*

24 Hours
US 1931 65m bw
Paramount
A day in the life of an ultra-rich couple whose marriage has gone sour.
Fairly slick matrimonial drama with an attempt at filmic treatment.
w Louis Weitzenkorn *novel* Louis Bromfield *d* Marion Gering
☆ Clive Brook, Kay Francis, Miriam Hopkins, Regis Toomey, George Barbier, Adrienne Ames

'An absorbing bit of fiction that should engage the attention of the fan regulars and register abundantly at the box office.' – *Variety*

24 Hours in London
GB 2000 90m DeLuxe
Blue Dolphin/One World (Fergal McGrath)
In 2009, a London gangster attempts to kill a murder witness before organising a deal with an American outfit.
A cheap rip off of The Long Good Friday *without that film's feeling of reality; here there is only a vague, futuristic thriller rooted in past movies.*
wd Alexander Finbow *ph* Chris Plevin *m* Edmund Butt *pd* Matthew Davies *ed* Ian Farr
☆ Gary Olsen (Christian), Anjela Lauren-Smith (Martha), John Benfield (Inspector Duggan), Amita Dhiri (Helen Lucas), James Oliver (Paul Cameron), Sara Stockbridge (Simone), Richard Graham (Novell), James Hicks (Tom Wall), David Sonnethal (Bubbles Healy)

'Dismal from start to finish.' – *Empire*

20 Million Miles to Earth
US 1957 82m bw
Columbia/Morningside (Charles Schneer)
An American rocket ship returning from Venus breaks open and a scaly monster escapes into the Mediterranean and is cornered in the Roman coliseum.
Cheeseparing monster fiction which doesn't wake up till the last five minutes, and looks pretty silly even then.
w Bob Williams, Chris Knopf *d* Nathan Juran *ph* Irving Lippmann *m* Mischa Bakaleinikoff *sp* Ray Harryhausen
☆ William Hopper, Joan Taylor, Frank Puglia, John Zaremba

Twenty Million Sweethearts
US 1934 89m bw
Warner
Singing radio sweethearts are kept apart because of their images.
Thin musical with moderate numbers, remade as My Dream Is Yours.
w Warren Duff, Harry Sauber *story* Hot Air by Paul Finder Moss, Jerry Wald *d* Ray Enright *ph* Sid Hickox *m/ly* Harry Warren, Al Dubin *ad* Esdras Hartley *ed* Clarence Kolster
☆ Dick Powell, Ginger Rogers, Pat O'Brien, the Mills Brothers, Ted Fio Rito and his band, the Radio Rogues, Allen Jenkins, Grant Mitchell

'An entry the theatre boys won't have to worry about.' – *Variety*

Twenty Mule Team *
US 1940 84m bw
MGM (J. Walter Ruben)
Rivalry among the borax miners in Death Valley.
Adequate semi-Western with an unusual theme and setting.
w Robert C. DuSoe, Owen Atkinson *d* Richard Thorpe *ph* Clyde de Vinna *m* David Snell
☆ Wallace Beery, Leo Carrillo, Marjorie Rambeau, Anne Baxter, Douglas Fowley, Berton Churchill, Noah Beery Jnr, Arthur Hohl, Clem Bevans, Charles Halton, Minor Watson

29 Acacia Avenue
GB 1945 83m bw
Boca/Columbia (Sydney Box)
Young people are having a good time when their parents return unexpectedly from holiday.
Popular domestic comedy of its day.
w Muriel and Sydney Box *play* Mabel and Denis Constanduros *d* Henry Cass *ph* Ernest Palmer, Nigel Huke *m* Clifton Parker
☆ Gordon Harker, Betty Balfour, Carla Lehmann, Jimmy Hanley, Jill Evans, Hubert Gregg, Dinah Sheridan, Henry Kendall, Guy Middleton

The Twenty Questions Murder Mystery
GB 1949 95m bw
Pax-Pendennis
A killer taunts the police with clues sent to a radio quiz show.
Somewhat heavy comedy mystery with interest arising from the broadcasting background.
w Patrick Kirwan, Victor Katona *d* Paul Stein *ph* Ernest Palmer *m* Hans May
☆ Robert Beatty, Rona Anderson, Clifford Evans, Edward Lexy, Olga Lindo, Richard Dimbleby, Jack Train, Stewart MacPherson, Daphne Padel, Norman Hackforth, Jeanne de Casalis

Twenty Thousand Leagues under the Sea **
US 1954 122m Technicolor
Cinemascope
Walt Disney
Victorian scientists at sea are wrecked and captured by the mysterious captain of a futuristic submarine.

Pretty full-blooded adaptation of a famous yarn, with strong performances and convincing art and trick work.
w Earl Felton *novel Jules Verne d Richard Fleischer ph* Franz Planer, Franz Lehy, Ralph Hammeras, Till Gabbani *m* Paul Smith *ad John Meehan ed* Elmo Williams
☆ *Kirk Douglas, James Mason,* Paul Lukas, Peter Lorre, Robert J. Wilke, Carleton Young, Ted de Corsia
art direction; special effects
editing

Twenty Thousand Men a Year
US 1939 83m bw
Cosmopolitan/TCF (Sol M. Wurtzel)
Experiences of recruits to college student aviation training.
Very threadbare flagwaver.
w Lou Breslow, Owen Francis, Frank Wead
d Alfred E. Green
☆ Randolph Scott, Preston Foster, Margaret Lindsay, Robert Shaw, Mary Healy, Kane Richmond, Maxie Rosenbloom, Sen Yung
'Needs exploitation as upper-bracket attraction.' – *Variety*

Twenty Thousand Years in Sing Sing **
US 1933 77m bw
Warner (Robert Lord)
A tough criminal escapes from prison but his girl kills a man during the attempt, and he takes the blame.
Dated but fast-moving and still-powerful crime melodrama, remade to less effect as Castle on the Hudson *(qv).*
w Wilson Mizner, Brown Holmes *book* Lewis E. Lawes *d Michael Curtiz ph* Barney McGill
m Bernhard Kaun
☆ Spencer Tracy, Bette Davis, Arthur Byron, Lyle Talbot, Louis Calhern, Warren Hymer, Sheila Terry, Edward McNamara
'Good entertainment and good box office with that inside prison routine touch … Finally, it begins to appear Sing Sing wouldn't be a bad place at all to spend a vacation during the depression.' – *Variety*

23:58
France 1993 85m colour
BFI/MW/Canal
A cop and film buff hunts two former motorbike racers who steal six million francs, the takings of the 24-hour Le Mans motorcycle race, basing their plan on the one in Stanley Kubrick's film *The Killing*.
An odd little act of homage to Kubrick's thriller, although this one has a happier ending; but its effect is to send you back to watch the original again and note how much more interesting it is.
w Pierre William-Glen, Edith Vergne, Frédéric Leroy *d* Pierre William-Glen *ph* Jean-Claude Vicquery *m* Laurent Cugny *pd* Jacques Voizet
ed Anita Perez
☆ Jean-François Stevenin, Jean-Pierre Malo, Gérald Garnier, Yan Epstein, Amelie Glenn, Kader Boukanef
'A superior thriller in all departments, unravelling into an accomplished feature spiked with wry humour.' – *Empire*

The Twenty-Fifth Hour
France/Italy/Yugoslavia 1967 133m
Eastmancolor Franscope
Concordia/CCC/Avala/Carlo Ponti
When the Nazis deport Rumanian Jews, a simple-minded farmer is sent with them because the officer desires his wife.
Peripatetic adventure with the storm-tossed hero flitting from one symbolic situation to another. All a bit much.
w Henri Verneuil, Wolf Mankowitz, François Boyer *novel* C. Virgil Gheorghiu *d* Henri Verneuil *ph* Andreas Winding *m* Georges Delerue
☆ Anthony Quinn, Virna Lisi, Grégoire Aslan, Michael Redgrave, Serge Reggiani, Marcel Dalio, Marius Goring, Alexander Knox, Liam Redmond, Meier Tzelniker, John Le Mesurier, Françoise Rosay

Twenty-Four Hours of a Woman's Life
GB 1952 90m Technicolor
ABPC (Ivan Foxwell)
US title: *Affair in Monte Carlo*
A young widow tries to reform an inveterate gambler, but he kills himself.
Stilted, over-literary romantic melodrama with philosophical dialogue, flashback framing and Riviera settings.
w Warren Chetham Strode *novel* Stefan Zweig
d Victor Saville *ph* Christopher Challis
m Robert Gill, Philip Green
☆ Merle Oberon, Leo Genn, Richard Todd, Stephen Murray, Peter Illing, Isabel Dean

'Old enough to know better, young enough not to care.'
Twenty-One
GB 1991 101m colour
Entertainment/Anglo International (Morgan Mason, John Hardy)
A 21-year-old English girl living in New York recalls her past lovers.
Tedious semi-comedy, full of unconvincing monologues delivered direct to the camera.
w Zoe Heller, Don Boyd *d* Don Boyd *ph* Keith Goddard *m* Michael Berkeley *ed* David Spiers
☆ Patsy Kensit, Jack Shepherd, Patrick Ryecart, Maynard Eziashi, Rufus Sewell, Sophie Thompson, Susan Wooldridge
'A movie that is vulgarly flawed, often made like it was improvised fast on the spot but still managing to contain not only a holding central performance but a certain honesty you can't ignore.' – *Derek Malcolm, Guardian*

Twenty-One Days *
GB 1937 75m bw
London Films (Alexander Korda)
aka: *The First and the Last*
A barrister's brother accidentally kills a man and lets an old eccentric take the blame.
Watchable but very stilted melodrama with interesting early performances by Olivier and Leigh and a few good moments.
w Graham Greene *play The First and the Last* by John Galsworthy *d* Basil Dean *ph* Jan Stallich
m John Greenwood
☆ Laurence Olivier, Vivien Leigh, Leslie Banks, Hay Petrie, Francis L. Sullivan, Esmé Percy, Robert Newton, Victor Rietti
'I wish I could tell the extraordinary story that lies behind this shelved and resurrected picture, a story involving a theme song, and a bottle of whisky, and camels in Wales. Meanwhile let one guilty man, at any rate, stand in the dock, swearing never to do it again…' – *Graham Greene*
† The film was not shown until 1940.

'Somewhere in the fog there is a voice, a perfume, a glove, a knife – and a victim!'
Twenty-Three Paces to Baker Street *
US 1956 103m Eastmancolor
Cinemascope
TCF (Henry Ephron)
A blind playwright in a pub overhears a murder plot and follows the trail to the bitter end despite attacks on his life.
Sufficiently engrossing murder mystery with a weird idea of London's geography: the hero's Portman Square apartment has a balcony overlooking the Thames two miles away. Perhaps this is part of the script's light touch.
w Nigel Balchin *novel* Philip MacDonald
d Henry Hathaway *ph* Milton Krasner *m* Leigh Harline
☆ *Van Johnson,* Vera Miles, *Cecil Parker,* Patricia Laffan, Maurice Denham, *Estelle Winwood,* Liam Redmond

TwentyFourSeven **
GB 1997 96m bw
Pathé/BBC/Scala (Imogen West)
aka: *24 07*
A one-time amateur boxer remembers the man who started a boxing club for the local youths, and how the enterprise came unstuck.
A throwback in style to the British working-class films of the 60s, and none the worse for that, though the tone is bleaker, and less defiantly rebellious.
w Shane Meadows, Paul Fraser *d* Shane Meadows *ph* Ashley Rowe *m* Neill MacColl, Boo Hewerdine *pd* John-Paul Kelly *ed* Bill Diver
☆ Bob Hoskins, Mat Hand, Sun Hand, Sarah Thom, Sammy Pasha, Gina Aris, James Corden, Frank Harper, Anthony Clarke
'Best described as Ken Loach with a smile.' – *Film Review*
† The title refers to twenty-four hours a day, seven days a week, or, as one character says, 'the people in this town have been living the same day their whole lives'.

Twice Blessed
US 1945 76m bw
MGM (Arthur L. Field)
Twin daughters of a divorced couple deliberately confuse their parents into a reconciliation.
Paper-thin comedy without much wit.
w Ethel Hill *d* Harry Beaumont
☆ Preston Foster, Gail Patrick, Lee and Lyn Wilde, Richard Gaines, Jean Porter, Ethel Smith at the organ

Twice in a Lifetime
US 1985 117m colour
Yorkin Company/Bud Yorkin
A man turns fifty and decides to make a clean break with his family.
Comedy drama of the mid-life crisis: nothing new.
w Colin Welland *play Kisses at 50* by Colin Welland *d* Bud Yorkin *ph* Nick McLean *m* Pat Metheny, Paul McCartney *pd* William Creber
ed Robert Jones
☆ Gene Hackman, Ellen Burstyn, Ann-Margret, Amy Madigan, Ally Sheedy
Amy Madigan (supporting actress)

Twice round the Daffodils
GB 1962 89m bw
Anglo Amalgamated/GHW (Peter Rogers)
Comic and serious episodes in the lives of male patients at a TB sanatorium.
Acceptable broadening, almost in Carry On *style, of a modestly successful play.*
w Norman Hudis *play Ring for Catty* by Patrick Cargill, Jack Beale *d* Gerald Thomas *ph* Alan Hume *m* Bruce Montgomery
☆ Juliet Mills, Donald Sinden, Donald Houston, Kenneth Williams, Ronald Lewis, Joan Sims, Andrew Ray, Lance Percival, Jill Ireland, Sheila Hancock, Nanette Newman

Twice Two
US 1933 20m bw
Hal Roach
Stan and Ollie have each married the other's twin sister …
Strained and laboured trick comedy in which neither the double exposures nor the gags quite come off.
w Stan Laurel *d* James Parrott *ph* Art Lloyd
ed Bert Jordan
☆ Stan Laurel, Oliver Hardy, Baldwin Cooke, Charlie Hall

'Some people can buy their way out of anything. Except the past.'
Twilight *
US 1998 94m DeLuxe
Paramount/Cinehaus (Arlene Donovan, Scott Rudin)
Living off the charity of a married film-star couple, an elderly, alcoholic ex-cop finds himself investigating the death of the wife's first husband twenty years before.
A downbeat thriller, tinged with melancholy and an awareness of time running out for its participants; the narrative is a familiar one, but the performances give it a little grace.
w Robert Benton, Richard Russo *d* Robert Benton *ph* Piotr Sobocinski *m* Elmer Bernstein
pd David Gropman *ed* Carol Littleton
☆ Paul Newman (Harry Ross), Susan Sarandon (Catherine Ames), Gene Hackman (Jack Ames), Reese Witherspoon (Mel Ames), Stockard Channing (Verna), James Garner (Raymond Hope), Giancarlo Esposito (Reuben), Liev Schreiber (Jeff Willis), Margo Martindale (Gloria Lamar), John Spencer (Captain Phil Egan), M. Emmet Walsh (Lester Ivar)
'Younger audiences are unlikely to connect with the old-fashioned format and aging thesps, but enough traditionally minded fans should turn out for this beautifully crafted effort.' – *Todd McCarthy, Variety*

The Twilight Avengers (dubbed)
Italy 1970 89m Eastmancolor
PAC/Caravel
original title: *I Vendicatori dell'Ave Maria*
In California, a travelling circus thwarts the ambitions of a ruthless landowner who murders the sheriff and takes over the town.
Dull spaghetti Western, with the emphasis on slapstick humour.
wd Al Albert (Adalberto Albertini) *ph* Antonio Modica *m* Piero Umiliani *ad* Franco Fontana
☆ Tony Kendall, Alberto Dell'Acqua, Peter Thorrys, Ida Meda, Albert Farley, Spartaco Conversi

Twilight for the Gods
US 1958 120m Eastmancolor
U-I (Gordon Kay)
The captain of an old sailing ship takes her for a last voyage from Mexico to Tahiti.
Dull and miscast adventure story lacking the spark of the original novel; watchable only for the travelogue elements.
w Ernest K. Gann *novel* Ernest K. Gann
d Joseph Pevney *ph* Irving Glassberg *m* David Raksin *md* Joseph Gershenson
☆ Rock Hudson, Cyd Charisse, Arthur Kennedy, Leif Erickson, Charles McGraw, Ernest Truex, Richard Haydn, Wallace Ford, Celia Lovsky, Vladimir Sokoloff
'Rock Hudson has difficulty in suggesting a dedicated seaman who has served under sail for thirty years.' – *MFB*

The Twilight Hour
GB 1944 85m bw
British National
A nobleman's gardener turns out to be the amnesiac father of the girl about to marry into the family.
Plodding and very predictable drama with popular cast.
w Jack Whittingham *novel* Arthur Valentine
d Paul Stein *ph* James Wilson *m* Hans May
☆ Mervyn Johns, Basil Radford, Marie Lohr, A. E. Matthews, Lesley Brook, Grey Blake

Twilight of Honor
US 1963 115m bw Panavision
MGM/Perlsea
GB title: *The Charge Is Murder*
A young small-town lawyer defends a neurotic no-good on a murder charge.
Modest courtroom melodrama in which the detail is better than the main plot.
w Henry Denker *novel* Al Dewlen *d* Boris Sagal
ph Philip Lathrop *m* John Green
☆ Richard Chamberlain, *Claude Rains,* Joey Heatherton, Nick Adams, Joan Blackman, James Gregory, Pat Buttram, Jeanette Nolan
Nick Adams

Twilight of The Dead: see *City of The Living Dead*

Twilight on the Prairie
US 1944 62m bw
Universal (Warren Wilson)
A cowboy band from New York are forced to find work on a Texas ranch when they become stranded on the way to Hollywood.
Enjoyable low-budget comedy; jazz aficionados will enjoy the bizarre spectacle of trombonist Teagarden, dressed in Stetson and woolly chaps, singing and playing 'The Blues'.
w Clyde Bruckman *story* Warren Wilson *d* Jean Yarbrough *ph* Jerome Ash *m* Hans J. Salter
ad John B. Goodman, Abraham Grossman
ed Fred Feitshans Jnr
☆ Johnny Downs (Bucky), Vivian Austin (Sally), Leon Errol (Cactus), Connie Haines (Ginger), Eddie Quillan (Phil), Jack Teagarden (Jackson), Milburn Stone (Gainsworth), Jimmie Dodd (Chuck), Olin Howlin (Jed), Foy Willing and the Riders of the Purple Sage

'You're travelling through another dimension into a wondrous land whose only boundaries are those of the imagination'
Twilight Zone: The Movie *
US 1983 101m Technicolor
Warner (Steven Spielberg, John Landis)
Four supernatural stories in the tradition of Rod Serling's long-running TV series of the fifties.

A disappointing collection on the whole, though with these talents what's on the screen is never quite boring.
w John Landis, George Clayton Johnson, Richard Matheson, Josh Rogan, Rod Serling *d* John Landis, Steven Spielberg, Joe Dante, George Miller *ph* Stevan Larner, Allen Daviau, John Hora *m* Jerry Goldsmith
☆ Dan Aykroyd, Vic Morrow, Scatman Crothers, Bill Quinn, Kathleen Quinlan, Kevin McCarthy, John Lithgow

'If there is an overriding irony to this catalogue of misfortunes, it is that the desire of four up-and-coming directors to honour TV as an imaginative source should have rebounded so disastrously on their cinematic reputations.' – *Richard Combs, MFB*

Twilight's Last Gleaming
US/West Germany 1977 146m Technicolor
Lorimar/Bavaria Studios (Helmut Jedele)

An ex-general commandeers an atomic missile plant and blackmails the president into telling some political truths.
Suspense thriller, fairly incompetent on its level and with ideas above its station. A distinctly overlong and unlikeable entertainment.
w Ronald M. Cohen, Edward Huebsch *novel* Viper Three by Walter Wager *d* Robert Aldrich *ph* Robert Hauser *m* Jerry Goldsmith
☆ Burt Lancaster, Richard Widmark, Charles Durning, Melvyn Douglas, Paul Winfield, Burt Young, Joseph Cotten, Roscoe Lee Browne, Gerald S. O'Loughlin, Charles Aidman

'It suggests an overextended episode of a TV series, and the attempts at wit are pathetically gross.' – *New Yorker*

Twin Beds *
US 1942 84m bw
Edward Small
A married couple are embarrassed by the antics of a drunken neighbour.
Slight pretext for a pretty funny old-fashioned farce.
w Curtis Kenyon, Kenneth Earl, E. Edwin Moran *play* Margaret Mayo, Edward Salisbury Field *d Tim Whelan* *ph* Hal Mohr *m* Dimitri Tiomkin
☆ George Brent, Joan Bennett, *Mischa Auer*, Una Merkel, Glenda Farrell, Ernest Truex, Margaret Hamilton, Charles Coleman

Twin Dragons (dubbed)
Hong Kong 1992 89m DeLuxe 'Scope
Dimension/Distant Horizon/Media Asia/HK FDG (Teddy Robin)

original title: *Shuanglong Hui*
Twin brothers are separated at birth, one to become a martial arts expert, the other a concert pianist.
A broad comedy with moments of violent action, this is a likable time-waster, but in no way memorable.
w Barry Wong, Hark, Cheung Tung Jo, Wong Yik *d* Tsui Hark, Ringo Lam *ph* Wong Wing Hang, Wong Ngor Tai *m* Michael Wandmacher, Phe Loung *ad* Lun Chon Hung, Lam Chun Fai *ed* Mak Che Sin *English adaptation* Rod Lean, Val Kuklowsky
☆ Jackie Chan, Maggie Cheung, Nina Li Chi, Anthony Chan, Philip Chan, Sylvia Chang, James Wong, Lai Ying Chow, Kirk Wong, Ringo Lam, John Woo, Tsui Hark

'Sad to say, there's less fighting than mugging: broad Hong Kong comedy is an acquired taste.' – *Guardian*

† The film was originally made in 1992 and then re-edited in 1998 and dubbed into English to take advantage of Chan's growing US popularity.

'Bound by birth. Liberated by love.'
'A tale of three hearts.'

Twin Falls Idaho *
US 1999 110m DeLuxe
Seattle Pacific Investments/Fresh Produce (Marshall Persinger, Rena Ronson, Stephen J. Wolfe)

Siamese twins fall out when the healthier one of the pair is attracted to a prostitute.
A curious and affecting film, made by, and starring, identical (though not conjoined) twins and making the point, understated though it is, that seemingly ordinary people are frequently the real freaks.
w Mark and Michael Polish *d* Michael Polish *ph* M. David Mullen *m* Stuart Matthewman *pd* Warren Alan Young *ed* Leo Trombetta *cos* Bic Owen
☆ Michael Polish (Francis Falls), Mark Polish (Blake Falls), Michele Hicks (Penny), Jon Gries (Jay), Patrick Bauchau (Miles), Garrett Morris (Jesus), William Katt (Surgeon), Lesley Ann Warren (Francine), Teresa Hill (Sissy), Ant (Tre), Holly Woodlawn (Flamboyant at Party)

'An offbeat, atmospheric drama that casts a minor but distinctive spell.' – *Todd McCarthy, Variety*

Twin Peaks *
US 1989 113m colour Panavision
Lynch-Frost Productions/Propaganda Films (David J. Latt)

An FBI agent is sent to a small town to investigate the murder of a young girl.
The pilot for what became a controversial and cult TV series was released on video in Europe as a surrealist parody of soap opera, full of deliberately over-the-top performances.
w Mark Frost, David Lynch *d* David Lynch *ph* Ron Garcia *m* Angelo Badalamenti *pd* Patricia Norris *ed* Duwayne R. Dunham
☆ Kyle MacLachlan, Michael Ontkean, Mädchen Amick, Dana Ashbrook, Richard Beymer, Lara Flynn Boyle, Sherilyn Fenn, Warren Frost, Joan Chen, Piper Laurie

'In a town like Twin Peaks, no one is innocent.'
'These are the last seven days of Laura Palmer.'

Twin Peaks: Fire Walk with Me
US 1992 134m CFI color Panavision
Guild/Twin Peaks (Gregg Fienberg)

Events leading up to the murder of the teenage Laura Palmer.
Mystifyingly obscure and dull prequel to the TV series Twin Peaks *which tries one's patience with its visions and precognitions.*
w David Lynch, Robert Engels *d* David Lynch *ph* Ron Garcia *m* Angelo Badalamenti *pd* Patricia Norris *ed* Mark Sweeney
☆ Sheryl Lee, Ray Wise, Mädchen Amick, Dana Ashbrook, Phoebe Augustine, David Bowie, Eric DaRe, Miguel Ferrer, Chris Isaak, Kyle MacLachlan, James Marshall, Jürgen Prochnow, Harry Dean Stanton, Kiefer Sutherland, David Lynch

'Pic will inevitably attract die-hard fans but is too weird and not very meaningful for general audiences.' – *Variety*

'It looks, in fact, like a very bad movie made by a very good director, tired of fooling around for a television audience.' – *Derek Malcolm, Guardian*

'Rugby. Tom Jones. Male Voice Choirs. Shirley Bassey. Llanfairpwllgwyngyllgogerychwyrndrobwyllllantisilio gogogoch. Snowdonia. Prince of Wales. Anthony Hopkins. Daffodils. Sheep. Sheep Lovers. Coal. Slate Quarries. The Blaenau Ffestiniog Dinkey-Doo Miniature Railway. Now If That's Your Idea Of Thousands Of Years Of Welsh Culture, You Can't Blame Us For Trying To Liven The Place Up A Little Bit Can You?'

Twin Town **
GB 1997 99m Technicolor
Polygram/Figment/Agenda/Aimimage (Peter McAleese)

Two delinquent brothers take revenge on the local businessman and crooked cop responsible for the deaths of their parents and sister.
The name of Dylan Thomas is invoked, and his cosy Welsh culture rejected, at the beginning of this exuberantly nihilistic demolition of its traditions, where joyriders, karaoke and corruption rule, the police deal drugs and only the old sing. Its bleak, black-comic tone may shock, but is fuelled by a genuine anger.
w Kevin Allen, Paul Durden *d* Kevin Allen *ph* John Mathieson *m* Mark Thomas *pd* Pat Campbell *ed* Oral Norrie Ottey
☆ Llyr Evans, Rhys Ifans, Dorien Thomas, Dougray Scott, Brian Hibbard, William Thomas, Jenny Evans, Biddug Williams, Ronnie Williams, Huw Ceredig, Rachel Scorgie, Di Botcher, Keith Allen

'Where the film scores is with its group portrait of a sour but not meaningless Welsh reality – a world that at least has the merit of being trapped in the present rather than the past.' – *Adam Mars-Jones, Independent*

'The most depressing thing about *Twin Town* is that it seems to mark the almost instant decay of a new and exciting cinematic language in British films.' – *Ben Thompson, Sight and Sound*

Twin Warriors *
Hong Kong 1994 97m colour
Dimension/Golden Harvest/Eastern (Jet Li)

original title: *Tai Ji Zhang San Feng*
aka: *Tai Chi Master*
Two childhood friends, expelled from a Shaolin temple, go their separate ways and eventually find themselves on opposing sides, one supporting the rebels, the other a ruthless governor.
Effective martial arts drama with many spectacular fights.
w Ip Kwong Kim *d* Yuen Wo-Ping *ph* Tom Lau *m* Steve Edwards *pd* Raymond Li *ed* Angie Lam
☆ Jet Li (Jun Bo), Michelle Yeoh (Siu Lin), Chin Siu Ho (Chin Bo), Fannie Yuen (Miss Li), Yuen Cheung Yan (Rev Ling), Lau Shun (Master), Yue Hoi (Head Master)

The Twinkle in God's Eye
US 1955 73m bw
Republic (Mickey Rooney)
A parson rebuilds a church in a Western town where his father was killed by Indians.
Amiable if unlikely Western drama with the star more convincing than one might expect.
w P. J. Wolfson *d* George Blair *ph* Bud Thackery *m* Van Alexander
☆ *Mickey Rooney*, Hugh O'Brian, Colleen Gray, Michael Connors, Don Barry

Twinkle Twinkle Lucky Stars (dubbed)
Hong Kong 1985 90m colour
Golden Harvest/Paragon (Eric Tsang)

Cops protect an actress from assassination.
Comic martial arts, more under the influence of the Three Stooges than of Bruce Lee. There are, however, some splendidly choreographed fight sequences to compensate for the laborious slapstick.
w Barry Wong *story* Barry Wong, Szeto Cheuk Hon, Lo Kin *d* Samo Hung *ph* Arthur Wong, Johnny Koo *m* Anders Nelson *ad* Eddie Ma *ed* Peter Cheung
☆ Jackie Chan, Samo Hung, Yuen Biao, Richard Ng, Eric Tsang, Fung Shui Fan, Miu Kiu Wai, John Shum, Sibelle Hu, Rosamund Kwan, Richard Norton

Twinky
GB 1969 98m Technicolor
Rank/World Film Services (Clive Sharp)
US title: *Lola*
A 16-year-old London schoolgirl marries a dissolute 40-year-old American author.
Dreary sex comedy drama, the fag end of London's swinging sixties.
w Norman Thaddeus Vane *d* Richard Donner *ph* Walter Lassally *m* John Scott
☆ Charles Bronson, Susan George, Trevor Howard, Michael Craig, Honor Blackman, Robert Morley, Jack Hawkins

Twins *
US 1988 107m DeLuxe
UIP/Universal (Ivan Reitman)

A 36-year-old man, bred in a genetic experiment as the perfect man, discovers that he has a less-than-perfect twin brother.
Amusing, if sometimes ponderous, comedy with the joke depending on the physical disparity of its two protagonists.
w William Davies, William Osborne, Timothy Harris, Herschel Weingrod *d* Ivan Reitman *ph* Andrzej Bartkowiak *m* Georges Delerue, Randy Edelman *pd* James D. Bissel *ed* Sheldon Kahn, Donn Cambern
☆ Arnold Schwarzenegger, Danny DeVito, Kelly Preston, Chloe Webb, Bonnie Bartlett, Marshall Bell, Trey Wilson, David Caruso, Hugh O'Brian

'They use the satanic power of their bodies to turn men and women into their blood slaves!'
'Torture. Terror. Sacrifice. Times Two.'

Twins of Evil
GB 1971 87m Eastmancolor
Rank/Hammer (Harry Fine, Michael Style)

Identical Austrian twins become devotees of a vampire cult.
Vampire-chasing Puritans add a little flavour to a routine Hammer horror.
w Tudor Gates *d* John Hough *ph* Dick Bush *m* Harry Robinson *ad* Roy Stannard *ed* Spencer Reeve
☆ Madeleine Collinson, Mary Collinson, Peter Cushing, Kathleen Byron, Dennis Price, Isobel Black

Twist around the Clock
US 1961 83m bw
Columbia/Sam Katzman

An astute manager discovers a small-town dance called the twist and promotes it nationally.
Rock around the Clock *revisited, with an even lower budget and fewer shreds of talent.*
w James B. Gordon *d* Oscar Rudolph *ph* Gordon Avil *md* Fred Karger
☆ Chubby Checker, the Marcels, Dion, John Cronin, Mary Mitchell

Twist of Fate: see *Beautiful Stranger*

A Twist of Sand
GB 1968 91m DeLuxe
UA/Christina (Fred Engel)
An ill-matched set of criminals seek hidden diamonds on Africa's skeleton coast.
Pattern melodrama of thieves falling out, quite nicely put together but with performances too high pitched.
w Marvin H. Albert *novel* Geoffrey Jenkins *d Don Chaffey* *ph* John Wilcox *m* Tristram Cary
☆ Richard Johnson, Honor Blackman, Roy Dotrice, Peter Vaughan, Jeremy Kemp

'Enough to make even Hitchcock jump!'

Twisted Nerve
GB 1968 118m Eastmancolor
British Lion/Charter (John Boulting)
A rich, disturbed young man disguises himself as a retarded teenager in order to kill his hated stepfather.
Absurd, unpleasant, longwinded and naïvely scripted shocker, rightly attacked because it asserted that brothers of mongoloids are apt to become murderers. A long way behind the worst Hitchcock.
w Leo Marks, Roy Boulting *d* Roy Boulting *ph* Harry Waxman *m* Bernard Herrmann
☆ Hayley Mills, Hywel Bennett, Phyllis Calvert, Billie Whitelaw, Frank Finlay, *Barry Foster*, Salmaan Peer

'Curious and in some respects disagreeable … never thrilling enough to reach the Hitchcock level and without sufficient medical credibility to be taken seriously as a case history.' – *Michael Billington, Illustrated London News*

Billie Whitelaw

Twister *
US 1996 113m Technicolor Panavision
Warner/Universal/Amblin (Kathleen Kennedy, Ian Bryce, Michael Crichton)

Rival meteorologists chase tornadoes and rediscover romance.
Sensation for its own sake, with all the anarchic destruction an audience could hope for, done with a terrifying hyper-realism; those wanting an equally engaging narrative will be disappointed.
w Michael Crichton, Anne-Marie Martin *d* Jan de Bont *ph* Jack N. Green *m* Mark Mancina *pd* Joseph Nemec III *ed* Michael Kahn *sp* Industrial Light and Magic
☆ Helen Hunt, Bill Paxton, Jami Gertz, Cary Elwes, Lois Smith, Philip Seymour Hoffman, Alan Ruck

'Another theme park ride of a movie without an ounce of emotional credibility to it.' – *Todd McCarthy, Variety*

'It's the world's first thriller about thin air. No stars, precious little plot to speak of and zero content to hold it back. It's a blast.' – *Tom Shone, Sunday Times*

† It was among the box-office successes of 1996, grossing more than $493m around the world.

†† Giving evidence in a case involving alleged plagiarism of the idea for *Twister*, Steven Spielberg told a court that the script accounted for only 5 per cent of the film's success. The action and special effects accounted for 60 per cent, Helen Hunt for 20 per cent, and sound effects for 10 per cent.
🏆 visual effects; sound

Twitch of the Death Nerve: see *A Bay of Blood*

Two a Penny
GB 1967 98m Eastmancolor
World Wide (Frank R. Jacobson)
An idle art student becomes involved in the drug racket but finally sees the light.
Naive religious propaganda sponsored by the Billy Graham movement and featuring the evangelist in a cameo. A curiosity.
w Stella Linden *d* James F. Collier *ph* Michael Reed *m* Mike Leander
☆ Cliff Richard, Dora Bryan, Ann Holloway, Avril Angers, Geoffrey Bayldon, Peter Barkworth

Two against the World
US 1936 64m bw
Warner (Bryan Foy)
GB title: *The Case of Mrs Pembroke*
A gutter newspaper unnecessarily digs up a sordid murder case and causes the suicide of two people involved.
Remake of Five Star Final *with the interest boringly shifted to the do-gooders who don't want to publish the story.*
w Michel Jacoby *play* Louis Weitzenkorn *d* William McGann *ph* Sid Hickox *m* Heinz Roemheld
☆ Humphrey Bogart, Beverly Roberts, Helen MacKellar, Henry O'Neill, Linda Perry, Virginia Brissac

Two Alone
US 1934 72m bw
RKO
The orphanage drudge on a remote farm gets herself pregnant.
Heavy-going Cold Comfort Farm *melodrama, with virtually no light relief in sight.*
w Josephine Lovett, Joseph Moncure March *play* Wild Birds by Dan Totheroh *d* Elliott Nugent *ph* Lucien Andriot *md* Max Steiner
☆ Jean Parker, Tom Brown, Arthur Byron, ZaSu Pitts, Beulah Bondi, Nydia Westman

Two Bright Boys
US 1939 69m bw
Universal (Burt Kelly)
A British boy and his father help an American boy save his oil ranch from a foreclosing villain.
Traditional action stuff, quite pleasantly done for undemanding audiences.
w Val Burton, Edmund L. Hartmann *d* Joseph Santley
☆ Jackie Cooper, Freddie Bartholomew, Melville Cooper, Dorothy Peterson, Alan Dinehart, Willard Robertson
'Adequate support for the duals.' – *Variety*

Two Can Play That Game
US 2001 91m DeLuxe
Columbia-TriStar/Screen Gems/C4 (Doug McHenry, Mark Brown, Paddy Cullen)
In Los Angeles, a female advertising executive plays hard-to-get with her boyfriend.
Unlovely and clumsy romantic comedy, in which two manipulative characters play mind games with one another.
wd Mark Brown *ph* Alexander Gruszynski *m* Marcus Miller *pd* Amy Ancona *ed* Earl Watson
☆ Vivica A. Fox (Shante Smith), Morris Chestnut (Keith Fenton), Anthony Anderson (Tony), Gabrielle Union (Conny), Wendy Raquel Robinson (Karen), Tamala Jones (Trayce), Diedre (Mo'Nique), Ray Wise (Bill)
'Charmless, unfunny and displaying the most boorishly reactionary sexual politics, it is uphill work from beginning to end.' – *Peter Bradsahw, Guardian*

2 Days in the Valley
US 1996 105m DeLuxe Panavision
Entertainment/Rysher/Redemption (Jeff Wald, Herb Nanas)
The lives of two hitmen, a couple of cops, a suicidal director, a wealthy art dealer, an angry woman and an Olympic skier collide, leaving death and destruction behind.
An excessively violent comedy about people behaving badly in Los Angeles; it suffers from overkill.
wd John Herzfeld *ph* Oliver Wood *m* Anthony Marinelli *pd* Catherine Hardwicke *ed* Jim Miller, Wayne Wahrman
☆ Danny Aiello, Greg Cruttwell, Jeff Daniels, Teri Hatcher, Glenne Headly, Peter Horton, Marsha Mason, Paul Mazursky, James Spader, Eric Stoltz, Keith Carradine, Louise Fletcher, Austin Pendleton, Lawrence Tierney
'Marked by a wearying amount of hostile and antisocial behavior by its criminal and civilian characters alike ... Pic does offer some entertainment value for mainstream audiences.' – *Todd McCarthy, Variety*

Two Deaths *
GB 1995 96m colour
BBC/British Screen (Luc Roeg, Carolyn Montagu)
As revolution rages on the streets of Bucharest, three old friends gather at the house of a successful surgeon for a reunion dinner, which ends in confessions of sexual obsessions, pathological behaviour and requited passion.
A well-acted, complex narrative of corruption, of the facing up to unpleasant truths at a moment of national crisis, but the conjunction of political and personal revelations is too contrived to be entirely engaging.
w Allan Scott *novel* The Two Deaths of Señora Puccini by Stephen Dobyns *d* Nicolas Roeg *ph* Witold Stok *m* Hans Zimmer *pd* Don Taylor *ed* Tony Lawson
☆ Michael Gambon, Sonia Braga, Patrick Malahide, Nickolas Grace, Ion Caramitru
'Will connect with filmgoers who relish a stern mix of psychology and politics.' – *Variety*

Two English Girls: see *Anne And Muriel*

The Two Faces of Dr Jekyll
GB 1960 88m Technicolor Megascope
Hammer (Michael Carreras, Anthony Nelson-Keys)
US title: *House of Fright*
A variation on the much-filmed story: the schizo's evil half is the more handsome.
Surprisingly flat and tedious remake.
w Wolf Mankowitz *novel* Robert Louis Stevenson *d* Terence Fisher *ph* Jack Asher *m* David Heneker, Monty Norman *ad* Bernard Robinson *ed* Jim Needs, Eric Boyd-Perkins
☆ Paul Massie, Dawn Addams, Christopher Lee, David Kossoff, Francis de Wolff

Two Fisted
US 1935 60m bw
Paramount (Harold Hurley)
A prizefighter and his manager join a socialite's household as bodyguards.
Flat comedy which doesn't get very far in any direction; a remake of the silent Is Zat So?
w Sam Hellman, Francis Martin, Eddie Moran *play* James Gleason, Richard Taber *d* James Cruze
☆ Lee Tracy, Roscoe Karns, Grace Bradley, Kent Taylor, Gail Patrick
'Some periods of hilarity.' – *Variety*

Two Flags West *
US 1950 92m bw
TCF (Casey Robinson)
Sixty Confederate prisoners of war are granted an amnesty and go west to fight the Indians.
Laboured but good-looking Civil War Western.
w Casey Robinson *d* Robert Wise *ph* Leon Shamroy *m* Hugo Friedhofer
☆ Joseph Cotten, Jeff Chandler, Linda Darnell, Cornel Wilde, Dale Robertson, Jay C. Flippen, Noah Beery Jnr, Harry von Zell
'Its period reconstruction is remarkable.' – *Gavin Lambert*

Two for the Road *
GB 1966 113m DeLuxe Panavision
TCF/Stanley Donen
An architect and his wife motoring through France recall the first twelve years of their relationship.
Fractured, fashionable light romantic comedy dressed up to seem of more significance than the gossamer thing it really is; and some of the gossamer has a Woolworth look.
w Frederic Raphael *d* Stanley Donen *ph* Christopher Challis *m* Henry Mancini
☆ *Albert Finney, Audrey Hepburn*, Eleanor Bron, William Daniels, Claude Dauphin
'The facile, comic bits set off audience expectations which are then betrayed, and the clever, bitter stuff just seems sour.' – *Pauline Kael, New Yorker*
🏆 Frederic Raphael

Two for the Seesaw
US 1962 120m bw Panavision
UA/Seesaw/Mirisch/Argyle/Talbot (Robert Wise)
A New York dance instructress has a tempestuous affair with an Omaha attorney on the verge of divorce.
Serious comedy or light drama, meticulously detailed but immensely long for its content and too revealing of its stage origins.
w Isobel Lennart *play* William Gibson *d* Robert Wise *ph* Ted McCord *m* André Previn *ad* Boris Leven
☆ Robert Mitchum, Shirley MacLaine
🏆 Ted McCord; song 'Second Chance' (*m* André Previn, *ly* Dory Langdon)

Two for Tonight
US 1935 60m bw
Paramount (Douglas MacLean)
Three half-brothers write a play for a temperamental star.
Much ado about nothing, but not an unpleasant way of passing an hour.
w George Marion Jnr, Jane Storm *play* Max and J. O. Lief *d* Frank Tuttle *ph* Karl Struss
☆ Bing Crosby, Joan Bennett, Mary Boland, Lynne Overman, Thelma Todd, Ernest Cossart
'No wow ... the songs, the fetching title, the competent cast and mostly Crosby will have to offset the other deficiencies.' – *Variety*
'A very amusing and well-written entertainment.' – *Graham Greene*

'Thanks to his two girlfriends, Blake's about to learn a new sexual position. Honesty.'
Two Girls and a Guy
US 1997 84m Technicolor
Fox Searchlight/Muse Prods (Edward R. Pressman, Chris Hanley)
Two women discover that they are dating the same actor, and confront him about his duplicity.
An unstructured account of a compulsive womanizer trying to charm his way out of a tight corner that feels as if it is semi-improvised. It is interesting for as long as it lasts, without saying anything new about relationships.
wd James Toback *ph* Barry Markowitz *pd* Kevin Thompson *ed* Alan Oxman
☆ Robert Downey Jnr, Heather Graham, Natasha Gregson Wagner, Angel David, Frederique Van Der Wal
'A work that is as bracingly entertaining at times as it is unfulfilled at others.' – *Todd McCarthy, Variety*
† The film was shot in 11 days.

Two Girls and a Sailor **
US 1944 124m bw
MGM (Joe Pasternak)
The title says it all.
Loosely-linked wartime musical jamboree with first-class talent; a lively entertainment of its type.
w Richard Connell, Gladys Lehman *d* Richard Thorpe *ph* Robert Surtees *m* George Stoll *songs* various
☆ *June Allyson*, Gloria de Haven, Van Johnson, Xavier Cugat and his Orchestra, *Jimmy Durante*, Tom Drake, Lena Horne, Carlos Ramirez, Harry James and his Orchestra, Jose Iturbi, *Gracie Allen*, Virginia O'Brien, Albert Coates
🏆 script

Two Girls on Broadway
US 1940 73m bw
MGM
GB title: *Choose Your Partner*
A song and dance man breaks up a sister act.
Acceptable lower-case vaudeville musical which rewrites the already wispy plot of Broadway Melody.
w Joseph Fields, Jerome Chodorov *d* S. Sylvan Simon
☆ George Murphy, Joan Blondell, Lana Turner, Kent Taylor, Wallace Ford, Lloyd Corrigan

Two Guys from Milwaukee
US 1946 90m bw
Warner
GB title: *Royal Flush*
A young Balkan prince goes incognito in Brooklyn and befriends a cab driver.
Rumbustious comedy with an amiable cast and gag guest appearances.
w I. A. L. Diamond, Charles Hoffman *d* David Butler
☆ Dennis Morgan, Jack Carson, Joan Leslie, Janis Paige, S. Z. Sakall, Franklin Pangborn

Two Guys from Texas
US 1948 86m Technicolor
Warner
GB title: *Two Texas Knights*
Two vaudevillians find themselves on the run from crooks.
Little more than a peg on which to hang some clowning and a few musical numbers.
w I. A. L. Diamond, Allen Boretz *d* David Butler *ph* Arthur Edeson, William V. Skal *m* Jule Styne
☆ Dennis Morgan, Jack Carson, Dorothy Malone, Penny Edwards, Fred Clark, Gerald Mohr, Forrest Tucker

'It seemed simple. Just deliver the cash.'
Two Hands **
Australia 1998 103m colour
AFFC/CML/Meridian (Marian Macgowan)
A naive young bouncer is threatened with death after he loses £10,000 belonging to a local gangster.
Slick, violent thriller, set among denizens of the low-life, that has a bracingly black humorous tone, though having the narrative told by a dead man adds little to the proceedings.
wd Gregor Jordan *ph* Malcolm McCulloch *m* Cezary Skubiszewski *pd* Steven Jones-Evans *ed* Lee Smith *cos* Emily Seresin
☆ Heath Ledger (Jimmy), Bryan Brown (Pando), Rose Byrne (Alex), Susie Porter (Deirdre), Steven Vidler (The Man), David Field (Acko), Tom Long (Wally), Tony Forrow (Eddie)

'It's 11:59 on New Year's Eve. Do you know where your date is?'
200 Cigarettes
US 1999 101m DeLuxe
Paramount/Lakeshore/MTV/Dogstar (Betsy Beers, David Gale, Van Toffler)
In New York in 1981, various people, all bent on pleasure and sexual gratification, celebrate New Year's Eve.
An uninvolving ensemble piece; some irony or genuine humour might have added a little spice to this stew of the self-absorbed hipsters.
w Shana Larsen *d* Risa Bramon Garcia *ph* Frank Prinzi *m* Bob and Mark Mothersbaugh *pd* Ina Mayhew *ed* Lisa Zeno Churgin
☆ Ben Affleck (Bartender), Casey Affleck (Tom), David Chappelle (Disco Cabbie), Guillermo Diaz (Dave), Angela Featherstone (Caitlyn), Janeane Garofalo (Ellie), Gaby Hoffmann (Stephie), Kate Hudson (Cindy), Catherine Kellner (Hilary), Courtney Love (Lucy), Brian McCardie (Eric), Christina Ricci (Val), Martha Plimpton (Monica), Paul Rudd (Kevin), Jay Mohr (Jack) and also Elvis Costello
'A dismally unfunny farce.' – *Todd McCarthy*
'Wry ensemble comedy throws up moments of genuine inspiration... the overall effect is charming in an understated way.' – *Sight and Sound*

200 Motels *
US 1971 98m Technicolor
United Artists/Murakami Wolf/Bizarre (Jerry Good, Herb Cohen)
Concert footage of Zappa and The Mothers of Invention is intercut with jokes, sketches and animation, derived from the life of a band on the road – 'touring can make you crazy', as Zappa comments.
A minor cult movie, an often inventive and witty surrealist montage and a notable influence on later rock videos.
wd Frank Zappa, Tony Palmer *m* Frank Zappa *ch* Gillian Lynne *pd* Cal Schenkel *ed* Rich Harrison
☆ The Mothers of Invention (Mark Volman, Howard Kaylan, Ian Underwood, Aynsley Dunbar, George Duke), Theodore Bikel, Keith Moon, Ringo Starr
† The film was shot on videotape in England at Pinewood Studios. Zappa had intended it as a live concert, but turned to video after it was cancelled on the grounds that the libretto was obscene.

Two If by Sea
US 1996 96m DeLuxe
Warner/Morgan Creek (James G. Robinson)
GB title: *Stolen Hearts*
An incompetent small-time thief steals a valuable painting and goes off on holiday with his girlfriend, closely followed by the FBI.
Dire mix of romantic comedy and chase movie, poorly plotted and lacking in laughs.
w Denis Leary, Mike Armstrong *d* Bill Bennett *ph* Andrew Lesnie *m* Nick Glennie-Smith, Paddy Moloney *pd* David Chapman *ed* Bruce Green
☆ Denis Leary, Sandra Bullock, Stephen Dillane, Yaphet Kotto, Wayne Robson, Jonathan Tucker, Mike Starr
'The dialogue has the crispness of aging lettuce, and the situations rely on coincidence, disbelief and a singular disregard for character.' – *Leonard Klady, Variety*

Two in the Dark
US 1936 72m bw
RKO
An amnesiac tries to find out whether he was involved in the murder of a theatrical producer.
Mildly intriguing mystery.
w Seton I. Miller *novel* Gelett Burgess *d* Ben Stoloff
☆ Walter Abel, Margot Grahame, Wallace Ford, Gail Patrick, Alan Hale, Leslie Fenton, Eric Blore
'A programmer that'll suit both audiences and b.o. outside of larger first runs.' – *Variety*

The Two Jakes *
US 1990 138m Technicolor
Blue Dolphin/Paramount (Robert Evans, Harold Schneider)
A private eye, hired by a real-estate developer to investigate his wife's adultery, tape-records a murder that is part of a complex conspiracy.
Convoluted thriller of small-scale corruption that overstays its welcome.
w Robert Towne *d* Jack Nicholson *ph* Vilmos Zsigmond *m* Van Dyke Parks *pd* Jeremy Railton, Richard Sawyer *ed* Anne Goursaud
☆ Jack Nicholson, Harvey Keitel, Meg Tilly, Madeleine Stowe, Eli Wallach, Ruben Blades, Frederic Forrest, David Keith, Richard Farnsworth
'A jumbled, obtuse yet not entirely unsatisfying follow-up.' – *Variety*
† A sequel to *Chinatown* (qv), it was originally to have been made in 1985 with Robert Towne directing and producer Robert Evans in the role played by Harvey Keitel.

Two Lane Blacktop
US 1971 103m Technicolor scope
Universal/Michael S. Laughlin
In the American southwest, the aimless owners of two souped-up cars have an interminable race.
Occasionally arresting, generally boring eccentricity by a big studio looking for another Easy Rider.
w Rudolph Wurlitzer, Will Corry *d* Monte Hellman *ph* Jack Deerson *m* Billy James
☆ James Taylor, Warren Oates, Laurie Bird, Dennis Wilson

Two Left Feet
GB 1963 93m bw
British Lion/Roy Baker (Leslie Gilliat)
A callow 19-year-old has girl trouble.
Ponderous sex comedy with no apparent purpose but some well observed scenes.
w Roy Baker, John Hopkins *novel In My Solitude* by David Stuart Leslie *d* Roy Baker *ph* Wilkie Cooper *m* Philip Green
☆ Michael Crawford, Nyree Dawn Porter, Julia Foster, David Hemmings, Dilys Watling, David Lodge, Bernard Lee

The Two Lives of Mattia Pascal **
Italy/West Germany 1985 118m colour
RAI/Excelsior Cinematografica/Cinecitta/Antenne 2/ Telemunchen/RTVE/RTS1/Channel 4 (Silvia D'Amico Bendico, Carlo Cucci)
original title: *Le Due Vite di Mattia Pascal*
Cheated out of his inheritance and humiliated by his wife, a man adopts a new identity.
Witty, dark comedy of a personality crisis.
w Suso Cecchi D'Amico, Ennio de Concini, Amanzo Todini, Mario Monicelli *novel Il Fu Mattia Pascal* by Luigi Pirandello *d* Mario Monicelli *ph* Camillo Bazzoni *m* Nicola Piovani *ad* Lorenzo Baraldi *ed* Ruggero Mastroianni
☆ Marcello Mastroianni, Flavio Bucci, Laura Morante, Laura Del Sol, Nestor Garay, Alessandro Haber, Carlo Bagno, Rosalia Maggio, Senta Berger, Bernard Blier

Two Loves
US 1961 100m Metrocolor Cinemascope
MGM/Julian Blaustein
GB title: *Spinster*
An American teacher in New Zealand teaches Maoris and whites and falls for two men.
Pretentious romantic drama with unspeakable dialogue and eccentric characters.
w Ben Maddow *novel* Sylvia Ashton Warner *d* Charles Walters *ph* Joseph Ruttenberg *m* Bronislau Kaper
☆ Shirley MacLaine, Jack Hawkins, Laurence Harvey, Nobu McCarthy

Two Men and a Girl: see *Honeymoon*

'England expects every dentist to do his duty.'
Two Men Went to War
GB 2002 109m DeLuxe
Guerilla/Little Wing/Ira Trattner
Tiring of waiting to go to war in 1942, a sergeant and a trainee in the Dental Corps desert and go to France to fight the Germans.
Gently amusing comedy of well-meaning blunderers in the stiff-upper-lip tradition; it has an old-fashioned charm and is apparently based on a true story.
w Richard Everett, Christopher Villiers *book Amateur Commandos* by Raymond Foxall *d* John Henderson *ph* John Ignatius *m* Richard Harvey *pd* Sophie Becher, Steve Carter *ed* David Yardley
☆ Kenneth Cranham (Sgt Peter King), Leo Bill (Pvt. Leslie Cuthbertson), Derek Jacobi (Major Desmond Merton), Rosanna Lavelle (Emma Fraser), Phyllida Law (Faith), James Fleet (Major Bates), Julian Glover (Col Hatchard), Anthony Valentine (Sgt Major Dudley), David Ryall (Winston Churchill)
'A harmless slice of nostalgia.' – *Anthony Quinn, Independent*

Two Minds for Murder: see *Someone Behind the Door*

'91,000 people ... 33 exit gates ... one sniper!'
Two Minute Warning
US 1976 115m Technicolor Panavision
Universal/Filmways (Edward S. Feldman)
A sniper terrifies the crowd at a championship football game.
Smartly directed but weakly plotted and scripted disaster movie: the mystery gunman remains a mystery at the end.
w Edward Hume *novel* George LaFountaine *d* Larry Peerce *ph* Gerald Hirschfeld *m* Charles Fox
☆ Charlton Heston, John Cassavetes, Martin Balsam, Beau Bridges, David Janssen, Marilyn Hassett, Jack Klugman, Gena Rowlands, Walter Pidgeon, Brock Peters, Mitch Ryan
'Even by the standards of exploitation movies, this film is an unusually dehumanizing experience. Not only does it exist solely for its gore, but it reduces the victims to the dimensions of plastic ducks at a shooting gallery.' – *Frank Rich, New York Post*

Two Moon Junction
US 1988 105m CFI color
Recorded Releasing/DDM/Samuel Goldwyn Company (Donald P. Borchers)
Despite her approaching marriage, a rich Southern woman begins an affair with a handsome carnival worker.
Ludicrously overwrought romantic melodrama.
wd Zalman King *story* Zalman King, MacGregor Douglas *ph* Mark Plummer *m* Jonathan Elias *pd* Michelle Minch *ed* Marc Grossman
☆ Sherilyn Fenn, Richard Tyson, Louise Fletcher, Burl Ives, Kristy McNichol, Martin Hewitt, Juanita Moore, Don Galloway, Millie Perkins

Two Mothers or The Comedy of Innocence: see *Comédie de L'Innocence*

The Two Mrs Carrolls
US 1947 99m bw
Warner (Mark Hellinger)
A psychopathic artist paints his wives as the Angel of Death, then murders them with poisoned milk.
Stilted film of an old warhorse of a play, unhappily cast but working up some last-minute tension.
w Thomas Job *play* Martin Vale *d* Peter Godfrey *ph* Peverell Marley *m* Franz Waxman
☆ Barbara Stanwyck, Humphrey Bogart, Alexis Smith, Nigel Bruce, Isobel Elsom, Pat O'Moore, Peter Godfrey
'Most of the show is a clutter of entrance and exit, about as dramatically arresting as a game in and out of the window. Miss Stanwyck, who does well enough with a tough worldly kind of part, is baffled by the sleight of hand required for this one. Humphrey Bogart also appears uncomfortable.' – *Time*
† Made in 1945.

Two Much
Spain/US 1996 118m Technicolor Panavision
Polygram/Sogetel/Lola/Occidental Media/Fernando Trueba
A conniving art dealer, who is engaged to a wealthy woman, invents a twin brother so that he can marry her sister.
A would-be screwball romantic comedy; it might have worked had it been cast with actors capable of comedy acting, or exhibited some wit in the writing.
w Fernando Trueba, David Trueba *novel* Donald E. Westlake *d* Fernando Trueba *ph* José Luis Alcaine *m* Michel Camilo *pd* Juan Botella *ed* Nena Bernard
☆ Antonio Banderas, Melanie Griffith, Daryl Hannah, Danny Aiello, Joan Cusack, Eli Wallach, Gabino Diego, Austin Pendleton
'The comedy is almost entirely misjudged, mistimed and often visually infantile, and while Miami looks appealing, it serves merely as window dressing for a plot that is, frankly, abysmal.' – *Deborah Brown, Empire*

Two Mules for Sister Sara
US 1969 116m Technicolor Panavision
Universal/Malpaso (Martin Rackin)
A wandering cowboy kills three men trying to rape a nun, but she is not what she seems.
Vaguely unsatisfactory Western with patches of nasty brutality leading to an action-packed climax.
w Albert Maltz, Budd Boetticher *d* Don Siegel *ph* Gabriel Figueroa, Gabriel Torres *m* Ennio Morricone
☆ Clint Eastwood, Shirley MacLaine, Manolo Fabregas, Alberto Morin

Two of a Kind
US 1951 75m bw
Columbia (William Dozier)
A man is picked up by a glamorous girl who involves him in an elaborate scheme to defraud an elderly couple.
Modest suspenser.
w Lawrence Kimble, James Grunn *d* Henry Levin *ph* Burnett Guffey *m* George Duning
☆ Edmond O'Brien, Lizabeth Scott, Terry Moore, Alexander Knox, Griff Barnett, Virginia Brissac

Two of a Kind
US 1983 87m DeLuxe
TCF (Roger M. Rothstein, Joe Wizan)
Four angels propose that Earth be spared from a second flood if two arbitrarily chosen human beings can be seen to perform a great sacrifice for each other.
Curious reversion to angelic comedies of the thirties and forties. Lacking the right measures of wit and whimsy, it is totally unsuccessful.
wd John Herzfeld *ph* Fred Koenekamp, Warren Rothenberger *md* Patrick Williams *pd* Albert Brenner
☆ John Travolta, Olivia Newton-John, Charles Durning, Oliver Reed, Beatrice Straight, Scatman Crothers
'It feels as if it must be a remake of something...' – *Sheila Johnston, MFB*

The Two of Us: see *A Nous Deux*

Two on a Guillotine *
US 1965 107m bw Panavision
Warner (William Conrad)
An illusionist arranges to be chained into his coffin at his funeral but promises to return from the dead.
Longwinded and unconvincing shocker with some effectively scary sequences.
w Henry Slesar, John Kneubuhl *d* William Conrad *ph* Sam Leavitt *m* Max Steiner
☆ Connie Stevens, Dean Jones, Cesar Romero, Parley Baer, Virginia Gregg, Connie Gilchrist, John Hoyt

Two or Three Things I Know about Her **
France 1967 95m Eastmancolor Techniscope
Contemporary/Anouchka/Argos/Les Films du Carrosse/Parc Film (Philippe Senné)
original title: *Deux ou trois choses que je sais d'elle*
A mother of two spends her day window-shopping and working as a prostitute to maintain her middle-class way of life.
An episodic and critical look at city life – the title refers to Paris, not the central character – and the constraints it puts upon individuals. Godard at his most polemic, by turns infuriating and fascinating.
wd Jean-Luc Godard *ph* Raoul Coutard *m* Beethoven *ed* Françoise Collin, Chantal Delattre
☆ Jean-Luc Godard (narrator), Marina Vlady, Anny Duperey, Roger Montsoret, Jean Narboni, Christophe Bourseiller, Marie Bourseiller
'A bit of pontifical journalism, a column and a half, interviews and all, about housing estates, the cost of living and the decay of family life.' – *Dilys Powell*

Two Pennyworth of Hope: see *Due Soldi de Speranza*

'They had just 36 hours to share the love of a lifetime!'
Two People
US 1973 100m Technicolor
Universal (Robert Wise)
An army deserter returns home and falls for a fashion photographer.
Solemn, inconsequential topical drama which made no impact whatever.
w Richard de Roy *d* Robert Wise *ph* Gerald Hirschfeld *m* David Shire
☆ Peter Fonda, Lindsay Wagner, Estelle Parsons, Alan Fudge
'Sluggish pacing, lifeless looping and terminally ludicrous dialogue eventually turn the film into a travesty of its own form.' – *Variety*

Two Rode Together
US 1961 109m Technicolor
Columbia/John Ford/Shpetner
An army commander and a tough marshal negotiate with Comanches for the return of prisoners.
Substandard Ford, moderately good-looking but uninteresting of plot and dreary of development.

w Frank Nugent *novel* Will Cook *d* John Ford *ph* Charles Lawton Jnr *m* George Duning
☆ James Stewart (Guthrie McCabe), Richard Widmark (Lt Jim Gray), Shirley Jones (Marty Purcell), Linda Cristal (Elena), Andy Devine (Sgt Darius Posey), John McIntire (Major Fraser), Paul Birch (Edward Purcell)

Two Seconds *
US 1932 68m bw
Warner
In the last two seconds of his life a criminal reviews the events leading up to his execution.
Competent, pacy crime melodrama.
w Harvey Thew *play* Elliott Lester *d* *Mervyn Le Roy* *ph* Sol Polito *m* W. Franke Harling
☆ Edward G. Robinson, Preston Foster, Vivienne Osborne, J. Carrol Naish, Guy Kibbee, Adrienne Dare
'General slowness and stodgy overdramatics won't draw the flaps, nor will a tragic finale help.' – *Variety*
'A film that compels attention.' – *Mordaunt Hall, New York Times*

Two Sinners
US 1935 71m bw
Republic
A man jailed for shooting his wife's lover makes a fresh start.
Curious but tedious romantic drama.
w Jefferson Parker *story* *Two Black Sheep* by Warwick Deeping *d* Arthur Lubin
☆ Otto Kruger, Martha Sleeper, Minna Gombell, Cora Sue Collins

Two Sisters from Boston *
US 1946 112m bw
MGM (Joe Pasternak)
Two girls visiting New York find work in a Bowery saloon.
Nicely-detailed turn-of-the-century musical with pleasant talent.
w Myles Connolly *d* Henry Koster *ph* Robert Surtees *md* Charles Previn *songs* Sammy Fain, Ralph Freed
☆ June Allyson, Kathryn Grayson, Lauritz Melchior, Jimmy Durante, Peter Lawford, Ben Blue
'If MGM think they have disguised the tiredest old musical bore of them all by putting it in period costume they're wrong.' – *Richard Winnington*

Two Smart People
US 1946 93m bw
MGM (Ralph Wheelwright)
A con man on parole in New Orleans is chased by a lady crook in search of his hidden loot.
Dog-eared comedy drama.
w Ethel Hill, Leslie Charteris *d* Jules Dassin *ph* Karl Freund *m* George Bassman
☆ Lucille Ball, John Hodiak, Lloyd Nolan, Hugo Haas, Lenore Ulric, Elisha Cook Jnr, Lloyd Corrigan, Vladimir Sokoloff

Two Tars ****
US 1928 20m bw silent
Hal Roach
Two sailors in an old banger cause a traffic jam and a consequent escalation of violence.
Marvellous elaboration of a tit-for-tat situation, with the stars already at their technical best.
w Leo McCarey, H. M. Walker *d* James Parrott *ph* George Stevens *ed* Richard Currier
☆ Stan Laurel, Oliver Hardy, Edgar Kennedy, Charley Rogers, Thelma Hill, Ruby Blaine, Charlie Hall

Two Texas Knights: see *Two Guys from Texas*

'An Entire Town Bathed In Pulsing Human Blood!' 'Madmen Crazed For Carnage!'
Two Thousand Maniacs
US 1964 84m Eastmancolor
Box Office Spectaculars (David F. Friedman)
Holidaying couples are lured to a small Southern town and slaughtered as part of the centennial celebrations.
Exuberantly incompetent film-making from a cult director.
wd Herschell Gordon Lewis *ph* Herschell Gordon Lewis *m* Herschell Gordon Lewis *md* Chuck Scott *pd* David F. Friedman *ed* Robert Sinise
☆ Connie Mason (Terry Adams), Thomas Wood (Tom White), Jeffrey Allen (Mayor Buckman), Ben Moore (Lester), Shelby Livingston (Bea Miller), Gary Bakeman (Rufe), Jerome Eden (John Miller)

2001: A Space Odyssey ****
GB 1968 141m Metrocolor Panavision
MGM/Stanley Kubrick (Victor Lyndon)
From ape to modern space scientist, mankind has striven to reach the unattainable.
A lengthy montage of brilliant model work and obscure symbolism, this curiosity slowly gathered commercial momentum and came to be cherished by those who used it as a trip without LSD.
w Stanley Kubrick, Arthur C. Clarke *story* *The Sentinel* by Arthur C. Clarke *d* *Stanley Kubrick* *ph* *Geoffrey Unsworth, John Alcott* *m* various classics *pd* *Tony Masters, Harry Lange, Ernie Archer* *ad* John Hoesli
☆ Gary Lockwood (Frank Poole), Keir Dullea (David Bowman), William Sylvester (Dr Heywood Floyd), Leonard Rossiter (Smyslov), Robert Beatty (Halvorsen), Daniel Richter (Moon-watcher), Douglas Rain (voice of HAL), Margaret Tyzack (Elena)
'Somewhere between hypnotic and immensely boring.' – *Renata Adler*
'Morally pretentious, intellectually obscure and inordinately long ... intensely exciting visually, with that peculiar artistic power which comes from obsession ... a film out of control, an infuriating combination of exactitude on small points and incoherence on large ones.' – *Arthur Schlesinger Jnr*
'The satire throughout is tepid and half-hearted, and tends to look like unintended stupidity.' – *John Simon*
† Alex North's rejected score for the film has also been released on compact disc.
special effects
script; Stanley Kubrick; art direction
cinematography; production design

2010
US 1984 114m Metrocolor Panavision
MGM-UA (Peter Hyams)
With Earth on the brink of war, scientists return to Jupiter to decide on the fate of *Discovery* and the meaning of the black monolith.
Tame, almost flatfooted sequel to 2001: A Space Odyssey, *with none of the supposed significance and not much else to offer.*
wd Peter Hyams *novel* Arthur C. Clarke *m* David Shire *pd* Albert Brenner *ed* James Mitchell
☆ Roy Scheider, John Lithgow, Helen Mirren, Bob Balaban, Keir Dullea, Dana Elcar, Madolyn Smith
art direction

Two Thousand Women
GB 1944 97m bw
GFD/Gainsborough (Edward Black)
Two pilots try to rescue British women from a French concentration camp.
Routine mix of laughter and tears; hardly an outstanding film of its time, but mildly entertaining.
wd Frank Launder *ph* Jack Cox *md* Louis Levy
☆ Phyllis Calvert, Flora Robson, Patricia Roc, Renée Houston, Anne Crawford, Jean Kent, James McKechnie, Reginald Purdell, Robert Arden, Thora Hird, Dulcie Gray, Carl Jaffe, Muriel Aked

Two Tickets to Broadway
US 1951 106m Technicolor
RKO (Jerry Wald)
Small-town college girl finds romance and success in the big city.
Very mild musical with TV studio backdrop.
w Sid Silvers, Hal Kanter *d* James V. Kern *ph* Edward Cronjager, Harry J. Wild *m* Walter Scharf
☆ Janet Leigh, Eddie Bracken, Gloria de Haven, Tony Martin, Barbara Lawrence, *Joe Smith, Charlie Dale*

Two Way Stretch **
GB 1960 87m bw
British Lion/Shepperton (M. Smedley Aston)
Three convicts break jail to rob a maharajah.
Amusing comedy with good performances and situations, unofficially borrowed in part from Convict 99.
w John Warren, Len Heath d Robert Day *ph* Geoffrey Faithfull *m* Ken Jones
☆ Peter Sellers, *Lionel Jeffries*, Wilfrid Hyde-White, Bernard Cribbins, David Lodge, Maurice Denham, Beryl Reid, Liz Fraser, Irene Handl, George Woodbridge

Two Weeks in Another Town *
US 1962 107m Metrocolor Cinemascope
MGM (John Houseman)
An ex-alcoholic film director gets his comeback chance in Rome but is plagued by old memories.
Self-indulgent melodrama with entertaining patches for cinéastes, especially those who saw The Bad and the Beautiful.
w *Charles Schnee* *novel* Irwin Shaw *d* Vincente Minnelli *ph* Milton Krasner *m* David Raksin
☆ Kirk Douglas, Edward G. Robinson, Cyd Charisse, Daliah Lavi, George Hamilton, Claire Trevor, Rosanna Schiaffino, James Gregory, George Macready
'The result may be a fantasy world, but it is a fantasy which this director understands and makes his own and into which he can breathe an intense, feverish life.' – *Dilys Powell*

'Over. Done. Finished. A comedy about love at last glance.'
Two Weeks Notice
US/Australia 2002 101m Technicolor
Warner/Castle Rock/Village Roadshow/NPV/Fortis (Sandra Bullock)
A property tycoon hires an idealistic lawyer, with whom he improbably falls in love.
Both leads coast along in roles that they have played often before – the floppy-haired charmer and the lovable klutz – and never convince that two such opposites would attract.
d Marc Lawrence *ph* Laszlo Kovacs *m* John Powell *pd* Peter Larkin *ed* Susan E. Morse
☆ Sandra Bullock (Lucy Kelson), Hugh Grant (George Wade), Alicia Witt (June Carter), Dana Ivey (Ruth Kelson), Robert Klein (Larry Kelson), Heather Burns (Meryl), David Haig (Howard Wade), Dorian Missick (Tony)
'Not the worst film I've seen this year; it is not even the worst film I have seen in the last two weeks. That gives you a pretty good idea of how bad things have gotten recently.' – *Joe Queenan*
'The spark isn't there and the soufflé doesn't rise.' – *Peter Bradsahw, Guardian*

Two Weeks with Love *
US 1950 92m Technicolor
MGM (Jack Cummings)
Adventures on a family summer holiday at the turn of the century.
Pleasant family musical.
w John Larkin, Dorothy Kingsley *d* Roy Rowland *ph* Al Gilks *m* Georgie Stoll
☆ Jane Powell, Ricardo Montalban, Louis Calhern, Ann Harding, Phyllis Kirk, Debbie Reynolds, Carleton Carpenter, Clinton Sundberg

Two Who Dared: see *A Woman Alone*

Two Women *
Italy/France 1960 110m bw
Champion/Marceau/Cocinor/SGC (Carlo Ponti)
original title: *La Ciociara*
During the Allied bombing of Rome a woman and her daughter travel arduously south and have a hard time at the hands of invading soldiers.
Rather hysterical character drama allowing for a splendid top-note performance from its star.
w Cesare Zavattini, Vittorio de Sica *novel* Alberto Moravia *d* Vittorio de Sica *ph* Gabor Pogany *m* Armando Trovaioli
☆ *Sophia Loren*, Eleonora Brown, Jean-Paul Belmondo, Raf Vallone
Sophia Loren
Sophia Loren

Two Yanks in Trinidad
US 1942 82m bw
Samuel Bischoff/Columbia
Minor racketeers join the army and capture a German agent.
One of the many variations on the Flagg and Quirt formula, and not a bad one.
w Sy Bartlett, Richard Carroll, Harry Segall *d* Gregory Ratoff
☆ Pat O'Brien, Brian Donlevy, Janet Blair, Roger Clark, Donald MacBride, John Emery

Two Years before the Mast *
US 1946 98m bw
Paramount (Seton I. Miller)
In the mid-19th century, a writer becomes a sailor to expose bad conditions.
Well-made but unconvincing-looking picturization of a famous book.
w Seton I. Miller, George Bruce *book* Richard Henry Dana *d* John Farrow *ph* Ernest Laszlo *m* Victor Young
☆ Alan Ladd, Brian Donlevy, William Bendix, Barry Fitzgerald, Howard da Silva, Albert Dekker, Luis Van Rooten, Darryl Hickman

Two-Faced Woman *
US 1941 90m bw
MGM (Gottfried Reinhardt)
A ski instructress, who fears she may be losing her publisher husband to another woman, poses as her own more vivacious twin sister.
The failure of this scatterbrained comedy is alleged to be the reason for Garbo's premature retirement. Looked at half a century later, it is no great shakes but harmless and eager to please; what sabotages it is a shoddy production and flagging pace.
w S. N. Behrman, Salka Viertel, George Oppenheimer *play* Ludwig Fulda *d* George Cukor *ph* Joseph Ruttenberg *m* Bronislau Kaper
☆ Greta Garbo, Melvyn Douglas, *Constance Bennett*, Roland Young, Robert Sterling, Ruth Gordon, George Cleveland
'It is almost as shocking as seeing your mother drunk.' – *Time*

The Two-Headed Spy *
GB 1958 93m bw
Columbia (Hal E. Chester)
A bogus Nazi worms his way into the Gestapo hierarchy.
Adequate, not too exciting biopic of Colonel Alex Schottland; standard production values.
w James O'Donnell *d* André de Toth *ph* Ted Scaife *m* Gerard Schurmann
☆ Jack Hawkins, Gia Scala, Alexander Knox, Erik Schumann, Felix Aylmer, Laurence Naismith, Donald Pleasence, Kenneth Griffith

Two's Company
GB 1936 74m bw
B and D/Paul Soskin
An earl's son loves the daughter of an American millionaire.
Not particularly successful hands-across-the-sea comedy.
w Tom Geraghty, Roland Pertwee, J. B. Morton, John Paddy Carstairs, Tim Whelan *novel* *Romeo and Julia* by Sidney Horler *d* Tim Whelan
☆ Gordon Harker, Ned Sparks, Mary Brian, Patric Knowles, Robb Wilton, Morton Selten

Tycoon
US 1947 129m Technicolor
RKO
An engineer is hired to drive a tunnel through the Andes, and starts a feud with his boss when he falls in love with his daughter.
Boring, studio-set action saga with too many stops for romance.
w Borden Chase, John Twist *d* Richard Wallace *ph* Harry J. Wild *m* Leigh Harline
☆ John Wayne, Cedric Hardwicke, Laraine Day, James Gleason, Judith Anderson, Anthony Quinn, Grant Withers

Typhoon
US 1940 70m Technicolor
Paramount (Anthony Veiller)
On a Dutch Guianan island, two sailors find a girl who has been a castaway since childhood.
One of Lamour's several sarongers, quite entertaining in its way and commendably brisk.

w Allen Rivkin *d* Louis King *ph* William Mellor *m* Frederick Hollander
☆ Dorothy Lamour, Robert Preston, Lynne Overman, J. Carrol Naish, Frank Reicher
'One of the most emphatically silly pictures I ever saw in my life.' – *Richard Mallet, Punch*
'The gem of pure, pellucid silliness.' – *James*

Tystnaden: see *The Silence*

U2 Rattle and Hum *
US 1988 99m colour/bw
Paramount/Midnight (Michael Hamlyn)

Documentary on the Irish rock group recording a new album and performing at home and in the States, described by its participants as 'a musical journey'. Blues guitarist and singer B. B. King joins them for one number.
Fans will enjoy this celebration of one of the most successful groups of the period, which alternates between coarse-toned black and white and colour photography for no apparent reason; those looking for some deeper insight into the business and art of rock will need to go elsewhere.
d Phil Joanou *ph* Jordan Cronenweth (colour), Robert Brinkman (bw) *ed* Phil Joanou

U Boat 29: see *The Spy in Black*

U.F.O.
GB 1993 79m colour
Feature Film/Polygram/George Foster (Simon Wright)

Feminists from outer space kidnap comedian Roy 'Chubby' Brown so that they can try him for telling offensive jokes.
Witless, cheap and nasty movie, starring the self-styled 'rudest, crudest, filthiest comedian in the world'; it is certainly crudely made and performed.
w Richard Hall, Simon Wright, Roy 'Chubby' Brown *d* Tony Dow *ph* Paul Wheeler *m* Clever Music *pd* David McHenry *ed* Geoff Hogg
☆ Roy 'Chubby' Brown, Sara Stockbridge, Amanda Symonds, Roger Lloyd Pack, Shirley Anne Field, Sue Lloyd, Kenny Baker
'Wildly uneven, often offensive, but with a cheerful inanity which goes some way to compensate for its grosser shortcomings.' – *Sight and Sound*

'The cop who won't stop is back. But this time he's chasing a lot more than a fugitive.'
US Marshals *
US 1998 133m Technicolor Panavision
Warner (Arnold and Anne Kopelson)

A US marshal tracks down a man accused of killing two FBI agents.
Not only a sequel to The Fugitive*, but one that attempts to copy its narrative with only slight variations: a plane crash substituting for a train derailment and so on; but, this time around, they left out human interest.*
w John Pogue *d* Stuart Baird *ph* Andrzej Bartkowiak *m* Jerry Goldsmith *pd* Maher Ahmad *ed* Terry Rawlings
☆ Tommy Lee Jones, Wesley Snipes, Robert Downey Jnr, Kate Nelligan, Joe Pantoliano, Irene Jacob, Daniel Robuck
'The plot, like nearly every one you see nowadays, defies sense and resists explication.' – *Alexander Walker, London Evening Standard*

USS Teakettle: see *You're in the Navy Now*

'Sex. Murder. Betrayal. Everything That Makes Life Worth Living.'
'A stranger in a strange town ... A wife with murder on her mind ... A husband who wants her dead ... They think their troubles are over ... But they've only just begun.'
U Turn *
US 1997 125m Technicolor
TriStar/Phoenix/Illusion/Clyde is Hungry (Dan Halsted, Clayton Townsend)

A gambler is having a bad day: his car breaks down in a dreary small town, inhabited by nymphomaniacs and thugs, the money to pay off his debts is lost, and one of the locals wants to hire him as a hitman.
Overblown, overwrought film noir, as seen through a drug-induced haze, in which character and incident are heightened to the point of hysteria.
w John Ridley *novel Stray Dogs* by John Ridley *d* Oliver Stone *ph* Robert Richardson *m* Ennio Morricone *pd* Victor Kempster *ed* Hank Corwin, Thomas J. Nordberg
☆ Sean Penn, Nick Nolte, Jennifer Lopez, Powers Boothe, Claire Danes, Joaquin Phoenix, Billy Bob Thornton, Jon Voight, Julie Haggerty, Bo Hopkins, Liv Tyler
'Exceedingly raw, imaginative, daring and energized ... loaded with twisted motives, brazen amorality, double dealing, incestuous relationships, subversive intent and hilarious asides.' – *Todd McCarthy*
'Oddly watchable, in the way the ever-circling buzzards find interest in the goings-on beneath them.' – *Alexander Walker, London Evening Standard*

'Heroes are ordinary men who do extraordinary things in extraordinary times.'
U-571
US 2000 116m DeLuxe
Universal/Canal+ (Dino De Laurentiis, Martha De Laurentiis)

In 1942, in the Atlantic, American submariners seize a German submarine and its secret Enigma code-machine and attempt to fight their way to freedom.
Apart from the addition of Enigma, this is a standard submarine drama, no better than the many average productions of the 40s and 50s.
w Jonathan Mostow, Sam Montgomery, David Ayer *d* Jonathan Mostow *ph* Oliver Wood *m* Richard Marvin *pd* Wm Ladd Skinner, Gotz Weidner *ed* Wayne Wahrman
☆ Matthew McConaughey (Lt Andrew Tyler), Bill Paxton (Lt Commander Mike Dahlgren), Harvey Keitel (Chief Klough), Jon Bon Jovi (Lt Pete Emmett), Jake Weber (Lt Hirsch), David Keith (Marine Maj Coonan), T.C. Carson (Eddie), Jack Noseworthy (Wentz), Thomas Guiry (Trigger), Thomas Kretschmann (Wassner), Matthew Settle (Larson), Erik Palladino (Mazzola), Dave Power (Tank), Will Estes (Rabbit), Derk Cheetwood (Griggs)
'While it may rewrite history, it leaves the handbook of submarine movie clichés pretty much in pristine condition.' – *Birmingham Post*
† In reality, the Nazi's Enigma code machine was recovered from the U-110 by a British boarding party, an event that took place before America entered the Second World War. Paul Truswell, MP for the constituency that helped pay for *HMS Aubretia*, one of the British ships involved in the conflict, tabled a motion in the House of Commons protesting at the film's 'gross distortion of history'.
sound editing (Jon Johnson)
sound (Steve Maslow, Gregg Landaker, Rick Kline, Ivan Sharrock)

Uccellacci e Uccellini: see *Hawks and Sparrows*

Ucho: see *The Ear*

Ugetsu Monogatari *
Japan 1953 94m bw
Daiei (Masaichi Nagata)

During a 16th-century civil war two potters find a way of profiteering, but their ambitions bring disaster on their families.
Unique mixture of action, comedy and the supernatural, with strong, believable characters participating and a delightfully delicate touch in script and direction. On its first release it began to figure in many best ten lists, but quickly seemed to fade from public approbation.
w Matsutaro Kawaguchi, *from 17th-century collection by Akinara Ueda, Tales of a Pale and Mysterious Moon after the Rain d Kenji Mizoguchi ph Kazuo Miyagawa m* Fumio Hayasaka
☆ Masayuki Mori, Machiko Kyo, Sakae Ozawa, Mitsuko Mito
'Heavy going in spots, but with marvellous passages that are worth a bit of patience.' – *New Yorker*

'You Can Run. But You Can't Hide.'
The Ugly *
New Zealand 1996 94m colour
Metrodome/NZFC/Essential (Jonathan Dowling)

A psychiatrist examines an apparently insane serial killer, who claims that he is forced to murder by the ghosts of his victims.
Unsettling horror movie with a surrealist tinge.
wd Scott Reynolds *ph* Simon Raby *m* Victoria Kelly *pd* Grant Major *ed* Wayne Cook
☆ Paolo Rotondo, Rebecca Hobbs, Roy Ward, Vanessa Burns, Sam Wallace, Paul Glover, Chris Graham, Jennifer Ward-Lealand
'There is a lot to admire and be disturbed by here.' – *Kim Newman*

The Ugly American
US 1962 120m Eastmancolor
U-I/George Englund

A publisher is made ambassador to a southeast Asian state.
Self-dating anti-communist drama which was muddled and boring when new.
w Stewart Stern *novel* William J. Lederer, Eugene Burdick *d* George Englund *ph* Clifford Stine *m* Frank Skinner *ad* Alexander Golitzen, Alfred Sweeney *ed* Ted J. Kent
☆ Marlon Brando, Eiji Okada, Sandra Church, Pat Hingle, Arthur Hill, Jocelyn Brando, *Kukrit Pramoj*

The Ugly Dachshund *
US 1965 93m Technicolor
Walt Disney (Winston Hibler)

A dachshund bitch fosters among its puppies an orphan Great Dane.
Cheerful, fast-moving animal farce.
w Albert Aley *novel* G. B. Stern *d* Norman Tokar *ph* Edward Colman *m* George Bruns
☆ Dean Jones, Suzanne Pleshette, Charles Ruggles, Kelly Thordsen, Parley Baer, Mako, Charles Lane

'The story of a family on the edge, and a man who brought them back.'
Ulee's Gold ***
US 1997 111m DuArt
Orion/Jonathan Demme/Nunez/Gowan/Clinica Estetico

A bee-keeper, a middle-aged widower with family problems, is threatened by two hoodlums, associates of his jailed son and his drug-addicted wife.
A slow-moving drama that builds inexorably to its compelling, emotionally satisfying peak.
wd Victor Nuñez *ph* Virgil Marcus Mirano *m* Charles Engstrom *pd* Robert 'Pat' Garner *ed* Victor Nunez
☆ *Peter Fonda*, Patricia Richardson, Jessica Biel, J. Kenneth Campbell, Christine Dunford, Steven Flynn, Dewey Weber
'Nunez achieves a rare, and rarely earned, emotional depth that rewards the moderate demands he makes on contemporary viewers' short attention spans.' – *Todd McCarthy, Variety*
Peter Fonda

Ulisse contro Ercole: see *Ulysses versus the Sons of Hercules*

'In his world, brute force isn't enough.'
Ulterior Motives
US 1991 92m DeLuxe
Den Music/Elk/Ian Page (J. Max Kirishima, Thomas Ian Griffith)

A *New York Times* journalist hires a high-kicking private eye to help her expose a Japanese research scientist in America who is selling classified information.
Unpleasant paranoid thriller with unsympathetic characters and a little martial arts action thrown in for bad measure.
wd James Becket *story* James Becket, Thomas Ian Griffith *ph* Stephen M. Katz *m* Parmer Fuller *pd* Michael Helmy *ed* Virginia Katz
☆ Thomas Ian Griffith, Mary Page Keller, Joe Yamanaka, Ellen Crawford, Tyra Ferrell, M. C. Gainey, Ken Howard
'Spoilt only by the weak ending which negates our hero's most despicable act of violence.' – *Sight and Sound*
'The fight sequences are fair only.' – *Empire*

La Ultima Cena: see *The Last Supper*

La Ultima Siembra: see *The Last Harvest*

Ultimas Imagenes del Naufragio: see *Last Images of the Shipwreck*

Ultimate Revenge: see *Sioux City*

The Ultimate Solution of Grace Quigley: see *Grace Quigley*

The Ultimate Warrior
US 1975 94m Technicolor
Warner (Fred Weintraub, Paul Heller)

In AD 2012 New York is ruled by a gangster, the atmosphere is poisoned, and the only hope is a new community on an island off North Carolina.
Curious pretentious fantasy without the courage of its convictions or much entertainment value.
wd Robert Clouse *ph* Gerald Hirschfeld *m* Gil Melle
☆ Yul Brynner, Max von Sydow, Joanna Miles, William Smith, Richard Kelton, Stephen McHattie
'Less a prophetic vision than a kind of thick-ear West Side Story.' – *Richard Combs*

Ultra *
Italy 1991 90m Telecolor
Sacis/Numero Uno/RAI (Claudio Bonivento)

aka: *Hooligans*
A football-obsessed thief comes out of prison in Rome to reassume leadership of a gang of football fans and travels to Turin for a pitched battle with rivals.
A well-observed drama of the rougher passions that football excites, and of a group of fans defined by their exclusion – from the club management and the official supporters, from jobs, family and home.
w Simona Izzo, Graziano Diana, Giuseppe Manfridi, Ricky Tognazzi *d* Ricky Tognazzi *ph* Alessio Gelsini *m* Antonella Venditti *ed* Carla Simoncelli
☆ Claudio Amendola, Ricky Memphis, Gianmarco Tognazzi, Giuppy Izzo, Alessandro Tiberi, Fabrizio Vidale

'Actually filmed along the route he travelled 3000 years ago!'

Ulysses *
Italy 1954 103m Technicolor
Lux Film/Ponti-de Laurentiis (Fernando Cinquini)

Ulysses and his crew sail under the curse of Cassandra, and encounter Circe, the sirens and the cyclops.
Peripatetic adventure yarn not too far after Homer; narrative style uncertain but highlights good.
w Franco Brusati, Mario Camerini, Ennio de Concini, Hugh Gray, Ben Hecht, Ivo Perelli, Irwin Shaw *poem* *The Odyssey* by Homer *d* Mario Camerini *ph* *Harold Rosson* *m* Alessandro Cicognini
☆ Kirk Douglas, Silvana Mangano, Anthony Quinn, Rossana Podesta

Ulysses *
GB 1967 132m bw Panavision
Walter Reade (Joseph Strick)

Twenty-four hours in Dublin with a young poet and a Jewish newspaper man.
A pleasant enough literary exercise, a decent précis of an unmanageably prolix classic novel, this specialized offering would have passed unnoticed were it not for its language, which got it banned in many places but now seems mild indeed.
w Joseph Strick, Fred Haines *novel* James Joyce *d Joseph Strick ph Wolfgang Suschitsky m* Stanley Myers
☆ Maurice Roeves, Milo O'Shea, Barbara Jefford, T. P. McKenna, Anna Manahan, Maureen Potter
'No amount of pious invoking of Joyce's name can disguise the fact that a cheaply produced film is being sold at exorbitant prices so that someone can make his boodle off "culture".' – *John Simon*
'An act of homage in the form of readings from the book plus illustrated slides.' – *Pauline Kael*
'A facile and ludicrous reduction.' – *Stanley Kauffmann*
script

Ulysses' Gaze *
Greece/France/Italy 1995 177m colour
Theo Angelopoulos/GFC/Paradis/La Generale d'Images/La Sept/Basic/RAI

original title: *To Vlemma Tou Odyssea*
A Greek-American director returns to his homeland after a gap of 35 years to make a documentary about pioneer film-makers and to search for their lost film.
A brooding, melancholy meditation on the past, rewarding if you can surrender to its slow pace and introspection.
w Theo Angelopoulos, Tonino Guerra, Petros Markaris *d* Theo Angelopoulos *ph* Yorgos Arvanitis *m* Eleni Karaindrou *pd* Yorgos Patsas, Mile Nicolic *ed* Giannis Tsitsopoulos
☆ Harvey Keitel, Maia Morgenstern, Erland Josephson, Thanassis Vengos, Yorgos Michalokopoulos, Dora Volonaki
'A tremendously challenging and demanding work that will leave audiences who latch onto its style and mood satisfied but utterly drained.' – *David Stratton, Variety*

Ulysses versus the Sons of Hercules
Italy/France 1961 82m Eastmancolor
Fidès/CCM (G. Pasquale, A. Fantechi)

original title: *Ulisse contro Ercole*
The sons of Hercules are told to capture Ulysses so that he can be punished by the Cyclops.
Minor sword-and-sandal epic with a great deal of muscle-flexing.
w Mario Caiano, André Tabet *d* Mario Caiano *ph* Alvaro Mancori *m* Angelo Francesco Lavagnino *pd* Piero Filippone *ed* Renato Cinquini *sp* Galliano Ricci
☆ Georges Marchal, Michael Lane, Alessandro Panaro, Gianni Santuccio, Yvette Lebon, Eleonora Bianchi, Gabrielle Tinti

'Only one man understood the savagery of the early American west!'

Ulzana's Raid
US 1972 103m Technicolor
Universal/Carter de Haven/Robert Aldrich

An ageing Indian fighter and a tenderfoot officer lead a platoon sent out to counter a murderous Apache attack.
Bloodthirsty, reactionary Western with unpleasant shock moments.
w Alan Sharp *d* Robert Aldrich *ph* Joseph Biroc *m* Frank de Vol
☆ Burt Lancaster, Bruce Davison, Jorge Luke, Richard Jaeckel, Lloyd Bochner

Umberto D **
Italy 1952 89m bw
Dear Films

A retired civil servant can barely afford his rent but won't part with his dog.
Downbeat, immensely moving study of old age in a society which fails to provide for it.
w Cesare Zavattini, Vittorio de Sica *d Vittorio de Sica ph* G. R. Aldo *m* Alessandro Cicognini
☆ *Carlo Battista*, Maria Pia Casilio, Lina Gennari
'There isn't a minute of banality in this simple, direct film.' – *New Yorker*
Cesare Zavattini (original story)

The Umbrellas of Cherbourg: see *Les Parapluies de Cherbourg*

Una su 13: see *Twelve Plus One*

Unaccustomed as We Are
US 1929 20m bw silent
Hal Roach

Ollie takes a friend home to dinner, but his wife walks out, leaving him to get into all kinds of trouble.
The team's first sound comedy, rather hesitant in its use of the new medium. The story was later reworked as the last half hour of Blockheads.
w Leo McCarey, H. M. Walker *d* Lewis R. Foster *ph* George Stevens, Len Powers *ed* Richard Currier
☆ Stan Laurel, Oliver Hardy, Edgar Kennedy, Mae Busch, Thelma Todd

The Unbearable Lightness of Being **
US 1987 172m Technicolor/DeLuxe
Saul Zaentz

A womanizing brain surgeon and his two lovers painfully achieve maturity after the putting down of the Prague Spring by Soviet troops.
Brave and largely successful attempt to transfer a complex, ironic Czech novel to the screen.
w Jean-Claude Carrière, Philip Kaufman *novel* Milan Kundera *d Philip Kaufman ph* Sven Nykvist *m* Leos Janáček *pd* Pierre Guffroy
☆ Daniel Day-Lewis, Juliette Binoche, Lena Olin, Erland Josephson, Daniel Olbrychski
'It's a prankish sex comedy that treats modern political events with a delicate – yet almost sly – sense of tragedy. It's touching in sophisticated ways that you don't expect from an American director.' – *Pauline Kael, New Yorker*
Sven Nykvist; best adapted screenplay
adapted screenplay

Unbelievable Truth *
US 1989 90m colour
Electric/Contemporary/Action (Bruce Weiss, Hal Hartley)

A convicted murderer returns to his home town and attracts the intellectual daughter of his employer, a garage owner.
Clever low-budget first feature of an unlikely romance.
wd Hal Hartley *ph* Michael Spiller *m* Jim Coleman *pd* Carla Gerona *ed* Hal Hartley
☆ Adrienne Shelly, Robert Burke, Christopher Cooke, Julia McNeal, Mark Bailey, Gary Sauer, Katherine Mayfield

'Some things are only revealed by accident.'

Unbreakable **
US 2000 107m Technicolor Panavision
Buena Vista/Touchstone/Blinding Edge (M. Night Shyamalan, Barry Mendel, Sam Mercer)

A crippled dealer in comics persuades a security guard that he is a real-life superhero.
Clever thriller which manages to convince its audience to take seriously what is essentially hokum; its elegant and painstaking framing of every shot adds to its moody, comic book feel.
wd M. Night Shyamalan *ph* Eduardo Serra *m* James Newton Howard *pd* Larry Fulton *ed* Dylan Tichenor *cos* Joanna Johnston
☆ Bruce Willis (David Dunn), Samuel L. Jackson (Elijah Price), Robin Wright Penn (Audrey Dunn), Charlayne Woodard (Elijah's Mother), Spencer Treat Clark (Joseph Dunn), James Handy (Priest), Eamonn Walker (Dr Mathison), Elizabeth Lawrence (School Nurse), Leslie Stefanson (Kelly)
'Great performances, moments and ideas.' – *Empire*

'A trilogy of feline terror!'

The Uncanny
Canada/GB 1977 85m colour
Rank/Cinevideo/Tor (Claude Héroux, Milton Subotsky)

An author tells his publisher three stories about evil cats.
Below-par horror compendium with crude effects failing to bolster a sagging script.
w Michel Parry *d* Denis Héroux *ph* Harry Waxman, James Bawden *m* Wilfred Josephs
☆ Peter Cushing, Ray Milland, Susan Penhaligon, Joan Greenwood, Simon Williams, Roland Culver, Alexandra Stewart, Donald Pleasence, Samantha Eggar, John Vernon

Uncensored
GB 1942 108m bw
GFD/Gainsborough (Edward Black)
In Brussels during the Nazi occupation, the leader of a toe-the-line paper secretly leads the patriots.
Unconvincing underground melodrama with stilted presentation and performances.
w Wolfgang Wilhelm, Terence Rattigan, Rodney Ackland *novel* Oscar Millard *d* Anthony Asquith *ph* Arthur Crabtree *m* Hans May
☆ Eric Portman, Phyllis Calvert, Griffith Jones, Raymond Lovell, Peter Glenville, Irene Handl, Carl Jaffe, Felix Aylmer

Uncertain Glory
US 1944 102m bw
Warner (Robert Buckner)

During World War II, a French playboy sacrifices himself for his country.
Tame star vehicle needing more action and less philosophy.
w Laszlo Vadnay, Max Brand *d* Raoul Walsh *ph* Sid Hickox *m* Adolph Deutsch
☆ Errol Flynn, Paul Lukas, Jean Sullivan, Lucile Watson, Faye Emerson, James Flavin, Douglass Dumbrille, Dennis Hoey

Uncertain Lady
US 1934 63m bw
Universal
An executive wife recovers her husband from the clutches of another woman.
Transparent comedy with the principals ill cast.
w Daniel Evena, Martin Brown *play* Harry Segal *d* Karl Freund
☆ Edward Everett Horton, Genevieve Tobin, Renee Gadd, Paul Cavanagh, Mary Nash

Uncle Benjamin
France 1969 90m Eastmancolor
Gaumont International (Robert Sussfeld, Roger Debelmas)
original title: *Mon Oncle Benjamin*
A rakish country doctor tries to seduce the virginal daughter of the local innkeeper.
A Gallic attempt at the bawdy zest of Tom Jones, *often coarse in tone and closer to the Carry On films in style.*
w André Couteaux, Jean-François Hauduro, Edouard Molinaro *d* Edouard Molinaro *ph* Alain Levent *m* Jacques Brel, François Rauber *ed* Robert and Monique Isnardon
☆ Jacques Brel, Claude Jade, Rosy Varte, Bernard Alane, Paul Frankeur, Alfred Adam, Bernard Blier

Uncle Buck *
US 1989 100m DeLuxe
UIP/Universal (John Hughes, Tom Jacobson)

A good-natured but slobbish layabout straightens out his sister's warring children and learns to love domesticity.
Rambling, moderately enjoyable comedy, although it is not far removed from a television sit-com.
wd John Hughes *ph* Ralf D. Bode *m* Ira Newborn *pd* John W. Corso *ed* Lou Lombardo, Tom Lombardo, Peck Prior
☆ John Candy, Jean Louisa Kelly, Gaby Hoffman, Macaulay Culkin, Amy Madigan, Elaine Bromka, Garrett M. Brown

Uncle Harry: see *The Strange Affair of Uncle Harry*

Uncle Silas *
GB 1947 103m bw
GFD/Two Cities (Josef Somlo, Laurence Irving)

US title: *The Inheritance*
A young Victorian heiress finds herself menaced by her uncle and his housekeeper.
Slow-starting but superbly made period suspenser; unfortunately the characters are all sticks.
w Ben Travers *novel* Sheridan Le Fanu *d* Charles Frank *ph* Robert Krasker *m* Alan Rawsthorne *pd* Laurence Irving *ed* Ralph Kemplen
☆ Jean Simmons (Caroline Ruthyn), Derrick de Marney (Uncle Silas), Katina Paxinou (Madame de la Rougierre), Derek Bond (Lord Ilbury), Esmond Knight (Dr Bryerly), Sophie Stewart (Lady Monica Waring), Manning Whiley (Dudley), Reginald Tate (Austin Ruthyn), Marjorie Rhodes (Mrs Rusk), John Laurie (Giles)

Uncommon Valor
US 1983 105m Movielab
Paramount/Ted Kotcheff (John Milius, Buzz Feitshans)

A retired colonel goes looking for his son, declared missing in action in Vietnam, and is helped by a similarly placed industrialist who backs a rescue raid.
Slam-bang action piece with the customary patriotic and personal sentiment.
w Joe Gayton *d* Ted Kotcheff *ph* Stephen H. Burum *m* James Horner *pd* James L. Schoppe
☆ Gene Hackman, Robert Stack, Fred Ward, Reb Brown, Randall Cobb, Patrick Swayze

'Plunging over the falls – lashed at the stake – trapped by savages in the mightiest love-spectacle de Mille ever filmed!'
'I bought this woman for my own ... and I'll kill the man who touches her!"

Unconquered
US 1947 146m Technicolor
Paramount/Cecil B. de Mille

An 18th-century English convict girl is deported to the American colonies and suffers various adventures before marrying a Virginia militiaman.
Cardboard epic, expensive and noisy but totally unpersuasive despite cannon, arrows, fire and dynamite.
w Charles Bennett, Fredric M. Frank, Jesse Lasky Jnr *novel* Neil H. Swanson *d* Cecil B. de Mille *ph* Ray Rennahan *m* Victor Young
☆ *Paulette Goddard*, Gary Cooper, Boris Karloff, Howard da Silva, Cecil Kellaway, Ward Bond, Katherine de Mille, Henry Wilcoxon, C. Aubrey Smith, Victor Varconi, Virginia Grey, Porter Hall, Mike Mazurki
'De Mille bangs the drum as loudly as ever but his sideshow has gone cold on us.' – *Richard Winnington*
'A five-million dollar celebration of Gary Cooper's virility, Paulette Goddard's femininity, and the American frontier spirit.' – *Time*

Unconventional Linda: see *Holiday (1938)*

The Undead
US 1956 75m bw
Balboa Productions (Roger Corman)

A psychic researcher hypnotizes a prostitute, sending her back to a past life in a medieval world of witchcraft and magic.

A tale told by the devil, but signifying no more than the usual ineptly acted fantasy.
w Charles Griffith, Mark Hanna *d* Roger Corman *ph* William Sickner *m* Ronald Stein *ed* Frank Sullivan
☆ Pamela Duncan, Richard Garland, Allison Hayes, Val Dufour, Mel Welles, Dorothy Neumann, Billy Barty

The Undefeated
US 1969 119m DeLuxe Panavision
TCF (Robert L. Jacks)
After the Civil War, two colonels from opposite sides meet on the Rio Grande.
Sprawling, lethargic star Western with moments of glory.
w James Lee Barrett *d* Andrew V. McLaglen *ph* William H. Clothier *m* Hugo Montenegro
☆ John Wayne, Rock Hudson, Lee Meriwether, Tony Aguilar, Roman Gabriel

Under a Texas Moon
US 1930 70m Technicolor
Warner
A rancher of the Don Juan type makes hay with the ladies but also rounds up cattle rustlers.
Lightweight early talkie outdoor spectacle with music, not at all memorable.
w Gordon Rigby, Stewart Edward White
d Michael Curtiz *ph* Bill Rees *song* Ray Perkins
☆ *Frank Fay*, Myrna Loy, Raquel Torres, Armida, Noah Beery, George E. Stone, Fred Kohler
'Unusually pleasing western ... de luxe programmer of its kind.' – *Variety*

Under California Stars
US 1948 70m Trucolor
Republic (Edward J. White)
After celebrating his 10th anniversary as a film star, Roy Rogers rides out to deal with the crooks who have kidnapped Trigger, 'the smartest horse in the West', an activity that does not prevent him singing songs at the drop of a stetson.
Amiably daft Western in Rogers' usual mode of music, comedy and occasional mayhem.
w Sloan Nibley, Paul Gangelin *d* William Witney *ph* Jack Marta *m* Morton Scott *ad* Frank Hotaling *ed* Tony Martinelli
☆ Roy Rogers, Jane Frazee, Andy Devine, Bob Nolan and the Sons of the Pioneers.

Under Capricorn
GB 1949 117m Technicolor
Transatlantic (Sidney Bernstein, Alfred Hitchcock)
In Australia in 1830 an English immigrant stays with his cousin Henrietta, who has become a dipsomaniac because of her husband's cruelty.
Cardboard 'woman's picture' with elements of Rebecca, *shot with vestiges of Hitch's ten-minute take. A pretty fair disaster.*
w James Bridie *novel* Helen Simpson *d* Alfred Hitchcock *ph* Jack Cardiff, Paul Beeson, Ian Craig *m* Richard Addinsell
☆ Ingrid Bergman, Joseph Cotten, Michael Wilding, Margaret Leighton, Jack Watling, Cecil Parker, Denis O'Dea
'A lengthy, unhurried, and generally quiet picture, directed by Hitchcock with the dreamy contemplation of one embarked on a long sea voyage ... I can't feel that the choice of subject is a very happy one, for either Hitchcock or his actors.' – C. A. Lejeune

Under Cover of Night
US 1937 70m bw
MGM (Lucien Hubbard)
A city detective and his wife nab a murderer.
One of many to which this plot might be applied in the wake of The Thin Man, *and not a good example.*
w Bertram Millhauser *d* George B. Seitz
☆ Edmund Lowe, Florence Rice, Henry Daniell, Nat Pendleton, Sara Haden, Dean Jagger, Frank Reicher

Under Fire *
US 1983 127m Technicolor
Orion/Lion's Gate/Greenberg Brothers (Jonathan Taplin)
War correspondents in Nicaragua become involved in the dirty politics on both sides.
A thinking man's action piece, but no help to anybody in finding the true facts.
w Ron Shelton, Clayton Frohman *d* Roger Spottiswoode *ph* John Alcott *m* Jerry Goldsmith
☆ Gene Hackman, Nick Nolte, Joanna Cassidy, Jean-Louis Trintignant, Ed Harris, Richard Masur, Rene Enriquez
'A complex, genuinely thrilling drama of commitment, the mercenary mentality and the tortuous ironies of history.' – *Sight and Sound*
Jerry Goldsmith

Under Milk Wood *
GB 1971 88m Technicolor
Timon (Hugo French, Jules Buck)
Life in the Welsh village of Llareggub, as seen by the poet's eye.
Attractive but vaguely unsatisfactory screen rendering of an essentially theatrical event (originally a radio play); everything is much too literal, a real place instead of a fantasy.
wd Andrew Sinclair *play* Dylan Thomas *ph* Bob Huke *m* Brian Gascoigne
☆ Richard Burton, Elizabeth Taylor, Peter O'Toole, Glynis Johns, Vivien Merchant, Sian Phillips, Victor Spinetti, Rachel Thomas, Angharad Rees, Ann Beach

Under Satan's Sun *
France 1987 98m colour
Cannon/Erato films/A2/Action Films (Daniel Toscan du Plantier)
original title: *Sous le Soleil du Satan*
A rural priest begins to believe that Satan is controlling mankind.
Austere examination of the nature of religious belief that won the Palme d'Or for best film at the 1987 Cannes Film Festival.
w Sylvie Danton *novel* Georges Bernanos *d* Maurice Pialat *ph* Willy Kurant *m* Henri Dutilleux *ad* Katia Vischkof *ed* Yann Dedet
☆ Gérard Depardieu, Sandrine Bonnaire, Maurice Pialat, Alain Artur, Yann Dedet, Brigitte Legendre

'1992 ... Stop ... Battleship Besieged By Terrorists ... Stop ... Nuclear Warheads Stolen ... Stop ... Crew Helpless ... Stop ... Lone Man Fighting To Save Ship...'
Under Siege
US 1992 102m Technicolor
Warner (Arnon Milchan, Steven Seagal, Steven Reuther)
A ship's cook, aided by a stripper, saves the day after a battleship is hijacked by a force of highly trained killers intent on stealing its nuclear weapons.
Often risible, always predictable action movie in which one man conquers all, and consisting of a succession of slickly done martial arts combats and gun battles. For diehard fans of the star, or fans of Die Hard.
w J. F. Lawton *d* Andrew Davis *ph* Frank Tidy *m* Gary Chang *pd* Bill Kenney *ed* Robert A. Ferretti
☆ Steven Seagal, Tommy Lee Jones, Gary Busey, Erika Eleniak, Patrick O'Neal, Damian Chapa, Troy Evans, David McKnight, Lee Hinton
'An immensely slick, if also old-fashioned and formulaic, entertainment. Steven Seagal fans and action buffs should eat this up.' – *Variety*
'This delivers lean, suspenseful, he-man heroics with all the whizz-bang aplomb you could wish for.' – *Matt Mueller, Empire*
Sound; sound effects editing

Under Siege 2: Dark Territory
US 1995 99m Technicolor
Warner/Regency (Steven Seagal, Steve Perry, Arnon Milchan)
A former CIA agent finds himself on a train hijacked by a mad military genius who plans to blow up the world if his ransom demands are not met.
Idiotic action film with a dull and doltish hero, enlivened by a few spectacular stunts; rather as vaudeville theatres used to end with a bad act in order to get audiences to leave quickly, Seagal sings a song he wrote himself over the final credits.
w Richard Hatem, Matt Reeves *d* Geoff Murphy *ph* Robbie Greenberg, Alexander Witt, Rick Bota *m* Basil Poledouris *pd* Albert Brenner *ed* Michael Tronick
☆ Steven Seagal, Eric Bogosian, Everett McGill, Katherine Heigl, Morris Chestnut, Brenda Bakke, Nick Mancuso
'Muscle-bending, mind-numbing action at high-decibel levels for the lowest and least discriminating common denominator.' – *Leonard Klady, Variety*
'Nothing one says can possibly affect the money-spinning capacity of so routine a corporate product, which does without style, characterisation or even basic coherence in order to give the undemanding audience worldwide what it presumably paid for: a spiralling body count and explosions.' – *Peter Matthews, Sight and Sound*

Under Suspicion *
GB 1991 100m colour
Rank/Carnival/Columbia/LWT (Brian Eastman)
In the 1950s, a private detective specializing in divorce is accused of murdering his client and his wife when they are found dead in a hotel room.
Moody attempt at a film noir that looks clumsy when set against the classics of the genre.
wd Simon Moore *ph* Vernon Layton, Ivan Strasberg *m* Christopher Gunning *pd* Tim Hutchinson *ed* Tariq Anwar
☆ Liam Neeson, Kenneth Cranham, Laura San Giacomo, Maggie O'Neill, Alan Talbot, Malcolm Storry, Martin Grace, Kevin Moore
'Displays most of the virtues of a well-constructed seaside roller-coaster. Twists, switchbacks, lots of flashing lights and gaudy paintwork: no great emotional significance but a thoroughly exhilarating ride.' – *Philip Kemp, Sight and Sound*
'A taut and entertaining mystery melodrama.' – *Vincent Canby, New York Times*

'A Hidden Past. A Secret Life. Witness Or Suspect, Guilty Or Innocent?'
'Everyone has secrets. Some of them are crimes.'
Under Suspicion
US 2000 Technicolor
Revelations/TF1
In Puerto Rico, a cop interrogates a rich lawyer about the murder of a young girl.
Disappointing duel between two fine actors, who are not helped by the hyperkinetic style of the director. The result is much less compelling then the French original The Inquisitor/Garde à Vue *(qv).*
w Tom Provost, W. Peter Iliff *screenplay* Garde à Vue by Claude Miller, Jean Herman, Michel Audiard *book* Brainwash by John Wainwright *d* Stephen Hopkins *ph* Peter Levy *m* BT *pd* Cecilia Montiel *ed* John Smith *cos* Francine Jamison-Tanchuck
☆ Morgan Freeman (Henry Hearst), Gene Hackman (Captain Victor Benezet), Thomas Jane (Detective Felix Owens), Monica Bellucci (Chantal Hearst), Nydia Caro (Isabella), Miguel Angel Suarez (Superintendent), Pablo Cunqueiro (Detective Castillo), Isabel Algaz (Camille Rodriguez), Jackeline Duprey (Maria Rodriguez), Luis Caballero (Paco Rodriguez), Patricia Beato (Darlita)
'A sleazy police procedural with wobbly philosophical pretensions.' – *Dennis Lim, Village Voice*

Under Ten Flags
US 1960 92m bw
Paramount/Dino de Laurentiis
In World War II, a German surface raider in disguise menaces British shipping.
Muddled naval epic with too many allegiances.
w Vittorio Petrilli, Duilio Coletti, Ulrich Mohr, Leonardo Bercovici, William Douglas Home *diaries* Bernhard Rogge *d* Duilio Coletti, Silvio Narizzano *ph* Aldo Tonti *m* Nino Rota
☆ Van Heflin, Charles Laughton, John Ericson, Mylène Demongeot, Cecil Parker, Folco Lulli, Alex Nicol, Liam Redmond
† Leonardo Bercovici's name was omitted from the film's original credits because he was blacklisted.

Under the Clock: see *The Clock*

Under the Gun
US 1950 83m bw
Universal-International
A racketeer is jailed and tries to escape.
Lower-case prison adventure without much conviction.
w George Zuckerman *d* Ted Tetzlaff *ph* Henry Freulich *m* Joseph Gershenson
☆ Richard Conte, Audrey Totter, John McIntire, Sam Jaffe, Shepperd Strudwick

Under the Pampas Moon
US 1935 78m bw
Fox
A gaucho leader recovers his stolen horse.
Amiable modern adventure set in Argentina.
w Ernest Pascal, Bradley King *d* James Tinling
☆ Warner Baxter, Ketti Gallian, Rita Hayworth, Jack La Rue, J. Carrol Naish

Under the Rainbow
US 1981 95m colour
Orion/Warner
Nazis and midgets mingle backstage while *The Wizard of Oz* is being filmed.
Zany fantasy which someone must have thought was a good idea. Wrong.
w Pat McCormick, Harry Hurwitz, Martin Smith, Pat Bradley, Fred Bauer *d* Steve Rash
☆ Chevy Chase, Carrie Fisher, Billy Barty, Eve Arden, Joseph Maher
† The film allegedly cost 20 million dollars and took eight.

Under the Red Robe *
GB 1937 82m bw
New World (Robert T. Kane)
A hell-raising nobleman is persuaded by Cardinal Richelieu to unmask the ringleader of an anti-monarchist conspiracy.
Smart, unusual swashbuckler on the lines of The Prisoner of Zenda, *modestly but quite effectively made.*
w Lajos Biro, Philip Lindsay, J. L. Hodson *novel* Stanley J. Weyman *d Victor Sjostrom* *ph* Georges Périnal
☆ *Conrad Veidt*, *Raymond Massey*, Annabella, Romney Brent, Sophie Stewart, Wyndham Goldie, Lawrence Grant
'Gripping meller of swashbuckling era ... surprisingly fine entertainment.' – *Variety*

Under the Roofs of Paris: see *Sous les Toits de Paris*

Under the Sand: see *Sous Le Sable*

Under the Skin **
GB 1997 83m colour
BFI/Channel 4/Strange Dog/Rouge/MFP (Kate Ogborn)
After their mother dies from a brain tumour, two sisters deal with their grief in different ways, one taking refuge in casual sex.
A gritty film about sibling rivalry and reconciliation, powered by excellent acting and observant direction.
wd Carine Adler *ph* Barry Ackroyd *m* Ilona Sekacz *pd* John-Paul Kelly *ed* Ewa J. Lind
☆ *Samantha Morton*, Claire Rushbrook, Rita Tushingham, Mark Womack, Matthew Delamere, Christine Tremarco, Stuart Townsend
'Its levels of integrity and accomplishment place it among the most impressive and affecting British films of the year.' – *Richard Williams, Guardian*
† It won the Michael Powell Award for the best British feature at the 1997 Edinburgh Film Festival.

Under the Volcano *
US 1984 111m Technicolor
TCF/Ithaca/Michael and Kathy Fitzgerald (Moritz Borman, Wieland Schulz-Keil)
Mexico 1938: the ex-British consul, drinking himself to death, is surprised by a visit from his ex-wife.
A subtle novel has on film become a drunken monologue, fascinating as a tour de force but scarcely tolerable after the first half-hour.
w Guy Gallo *novel* Malcolm Lowry *d* John Huston *ph* Gabriel Figueroa *m* Alex North *pd* Gunther Gerzso
☆ *Albert Finney*, Jacqueline Bisset, Anthony Andrews, Katy Jurado, James Villiers
'Ultimately one is left not, as in the novel, with a man destroyed by the apocalypse of his own imagination, but with little more than another

world-weary cuckold following in the wake of Greene's whisky priest and all those other drunkards who have mooned in Mexico.' – *Tom Milne, MFB*
Albert Finney; music

'Here Comes Jack And Those Yum-Yum Girls – With "Yes-Yes" On Their Lips And Yum-Yum In Their Eyes!'
Under the Yum Yum Tree
US 1963 110m Eastmancolor
Columbia/Sonnis/Swift (Frederick Brisson)
Two college students have a trial marriage in an apartment block with a lecherous landlord.
Coy, non-erotic and extremely tedious comedy which runs out of jokes after reel one.
w Lawrence Roman, David Swift *d* David Swift *ph* Joseph Biroc *m* Frank de Vol
☆ Jack Lemmon, Carol Lynley, Dean Jones, Imogene Coca, Edie Adams, Paul Lynde, Robert Lansing
'A disgusting comedy in which we're supposed to be titillated to hear young people speak of sleeping together and then to be reassured when they carry on and on and on about not quite doing so.' – *Brendan Gill, New Yorker*

'Love as burning as Sahara's sands!'
Under Two Flags *
US 1936 111m bw
TCF (Raymond Griffith)
A dashing French Foreign Legionnaire is helped by a café girl.
Despite a highly predictable plot (of Destry Rides Again) *this was a solidly-produced epic with a nice deployment of star talent.*
w W. P. Lipscomb, Walter Ferris *novel* 'Ouida' *d Frank Lloyd ph* Ernest Palmer *m* Louis Silvers
☆ *Ronald Colman,* Claudette Colbert, Rosalind Russell, Victor McLaglen, J. Edward Bromberg, Nigel Bruce, Herbert Mundin, Gregory Ratoff, C. Henry Gordon, John Carradine, Onslow Stevens
'How Ouida would have loved the abandon of this picture, the thirty-two thousand rounds of ammunition shot off into the Arizona desert, the cast of more than ten thousand, the five thousand pounds which insured the stars against camel bites ... and, in the words of the programme, a fort two hundred feet square, an Arabian oasis with eight full-sized buildings, a forest of transplanted date palms, two Arabian cities, a horse market and a smaller fort.' – *Graham Greene*

Under Western Skies
US 1945 83m bw
Universal (Warren Wilson)
A small-town schoolmaster falls in love with the singer from a travelling vaudeville show that is down on its luck.
Comic Western with a few indifferent songs and dances; neither cast nor director displays any interest in the creaking narrative.
w Stanley Roberts, Clyde Bruckman *d* Jean Yarbrough *ph* Charles Van Enger *m/ly* Milton Rosen/Everett Carter *md* H. J. Salter *ad* John B. Goodman *ed* Arthur Hilton
☆ Martha O'Driscoll, Noah Beery Jnr, Leo Carrillo, Leon Errol, Ian Keith, Jennifer Holt, Frank Lackteen

Under Your Hat *
GB 1940 79m bw
Grand National (Jack Hulbert)
Film stars chase spies and recover a stolen carburettor.
Light-hearted adaptation of a stage musical, showing the stars in their best film form.
w Rodney Ackland, Anthony Kimmins *play* Jack Hulbert, Archie Menzies, Geoffrey Kerr, Arthur Macrae *d* Maurice Elvey *ph* Mutz Greenbaum (Max Greene)
☆ *Jack Hulbert, Cicely Courtneidge,* Austin Trevor, Leonora Corbett, Cecil Parker, H. F. Maltby, Glynis Johns, Charles Oliver

Undercover: see *Maisie (Undercover Maisie) (1939)*

Undercover
GB 1943 80m bw
Ealing (Michael Balcon)
Yugoslavian partisans fight the Nazis.
A rather obviously English cast doesn't help to make this flagwaver convincing.
w John Dighton, Monja Danischewsky *story* George Slocombe *d* Sergei Nolbandov *ph* W. Cooper *m* Frederic Austin *ad* Duncan Sutherland *ed* Sidney Cole, Eily Boland
☆ Tom Walls, Michael Wilding, Mary Morris, John Clements, Godfrey Tearle, Robert Harris, Rachel Thomas, Stephen Murray, Charles Victor
'I just didn't believe a word of it.' – *James Agate*

Undercover Blues
US 1993 90m DuArt
MGM (Mike Lobell)
A married couple who are also FBI agents have trouble with a vengeful mugger while trying to capture an arms dealer.
A comedy that desperately strains for laughs without delivering any; it is almost a throwback to the spy spoofs of the 60s.
w Ian Abrams *d* Herbert Ross *ph* Donald E. Thorin *m* David Newman *pd* Ken Adam *ed* Patricia Nedd-Friendly, Gregg London
☆ Kathleen Turner, Dennis Quaid, Fiona Shaw, Stanley Tucci, Larry Miller, Obba Babatunde, Tom Arnold, Park Overall
'Plays like a big-screen, big-budget pilot for a TV series.' – *Variety*
'Virtually incomprehensible and unfunny to boot. A waste of two good talents.' – *Derek Malcolm*

'He's All Action'
Undercover Brother
US 2002 86m DeLuxe
Winchester/Imagine (Brian Grazer, Michael Jenkinson, Damon Lee)
An undercover agent foils Operation Whitewash, an attempt to drug the black population.
This late-coming spoof of blaxploitation lets fly a barrage of jokes that might havce sounded funnier 30 years ago.
w John Ridley, Michael McCullers *d* Malcolm D. Lee *ph* Tom Priestley *m* Stanley Clarke *pd* William Elliott *ed* William Kerr
☆ Eddie Griffin (Undercover Brother), Chris Kattan (Mr Feather), Denise Richards (White She Devil), Aunjanue Ellis (Sistah Girl), Dave Chappelle (Conspiracy Brother), Chi McBride (The Chief), Neil Patrick Harris (Lance), Gary Anthony Williams (Smart Brother), Billy Dee Williams (General Boutwell), James Brown (Himself)
'Traffics in the kind of prechewed racial clichés that have already been through the corporate stand-up-comedy mill.' – *Owen Gleiberman, Entertainment Weekly*
'A frequently inspired hit-and-miss burlesque that definitely hits more than it misses.' – *Joe Leydon, Variety*

Undercover Girl
GB 1958 67m bw
Butcher's/Bill & Michael Luckwell (Kay Luckwell)
A journalist investigates the murder of his brother-in-law, a crime reporter.
Dull, by-the-numbers thriller, remarkable only for the poverty of imagination shown by all those involved.
w Bernard Lewis, Bill Luckwell *d* Francis Searle *ph* Geoffrey Faithfull *md* Bill Trytel *ad* Dennis Pavitt *ed* Douglas Myers
☆ Paul Carpenter, Kay Callard, Bruce Seton, Monica Grey, Jackie Collins, Maya Koumani

Undercover Man
US 1932 74m bw
Paramount
A man avenges his father's death by going undercover for the FBI and nabbing a bond-stealing gang.
Routine gangster thriller with situations well worn even in 1932.
w Garrett Fort, Francis Faragoh *d* James Flood
☆ George Raft, Nancy Carroll, Roscoe Karns, Gregory Ratoff, Lew Cody

Undercover Man *
US 1949 89m bw
Columbia (Robert Rossen)
US treasury agents indict a gang leader for tax evasion.
Good semi-documentary crime melodrama based on the Al Capone case.
w Sydney Boehm, Malvin Wald *d Joseph H. Lewis ph* Burnett Guffey *m* George Duning
☆ Glenn Ford, Nina Foch, Barry Kelley, James Whitmore, David Wolf, Esther Minciotti

Undercovers Hero: see *Soft Beds, Hard Battles*

Undercurrent *
US 1946 116m bw
MGM (Pandro S. Berman)
A professor's daughter marries an industrialist and is frightened and finally endangered by the mystery surrounding his brother.
Overlong suspenser with solid performances and production values; a variation on Gaslight.
w Edward Chodorov *story* Thelma Strabel *d* Vincente Minnelli *ph* Karl Freund *m* Herbert Stothart
☆ *Katharine Hepburn,* Robert Taylor, Robert Mitchum, Edmund Gwenn, Marjorie Main, Jayne Meadows, Clinton Sundberg, Dan Tobin
'The indigestible plot, full of false leads and unkept promises, is like a woman's magazine serial consumed at one gulp.' – *Time*

Underground
US 1970 100m DeLuxe
UA/Levy-Gardner-Laven
An American paratrooper joins a French resistance group to kidnap a Nazi general.
Routine war actioner.
w Ron Bishop, Andy Lewis *d* Arthur H. Nadel *ph* Ken Talbot *m* Stanley Myers
☆ Robert Goulet, Danièle Gaubert, Lawrence Dobkin, Carl Duering

Underground *
France/Germany/Hungary 1995 170m colour
Artificial Eye/Mayfair/CiBy 2000/Pandora/Novo (Pierre Spengler)
original title: *Il était une fois un pays*
Two petty crooks in Belgrade survive changing times, from the Second World War to the break-up of Yugoslavia in the 90s.
A long and involved drama on Yugoslavian identity, which it takes to be a myth created for his own purposes by Tito; ranging in time from the 40s to the 90s, it depends on a sort of magic realism, with ghosts from the past still inhabiting the present.
w Dusan Kovacevic, Emir Kusturica *play* Dusan Kovacevic *d* Emir Kusturica *ph* Vilko Filac *m* Goran Bregovic *pd* Miljan Kljakovic *ed* Branka Ceperac
☆ Miki Manojlovic, Lazar Ristovski, Mirjana Jokovic, Slavko Stimac, Ernst Stotzner
'A steamroller circus that leaves the viewer dazed and exhausted, but mightily impressed.' – *Deborah Young, Variety*
† Originally shown at 192m, it won the Palme d'Or at the Cannes Film Festival in 1995.

The Underneath *
US 1995 100m colour
UIP/Gramercy (John Hardy)
A security guard who rekindles his affair with a former girlfriend plans a way to get rid of her husband, a vicious bank robber.
A movie that takes the heat out of its story of a manipulative woman and a double-crossing man, substituting instead a cool character study of irresponsible individuals.
w Sam Lowry, Daniel Fuchs *d* Steven Soderbergh *ph* Elliot Davis *m* Cliff Martinez *pd* Howard Cummings *ed* Stan Salfas
☆ Peter Gallagher, Alison Elliott, William Fichtner, Adam Trese, Joe Don Baker, Paul Dooley, Elisabeth Shue, Anjanette Comer
'It plays more like an art film than as a suspense melodrama, but effort will linger resonantly in the minds of those who tune into its rather rarefied wavelength.' – *Todd McCarthy, Variety*
† A remake of *Criss Cross* (qv), directed by Robert Siodmak in 1948 and starring Burt Lancaster, Yvonne de Carlo and Dan Duryea.

Underneath the Arches
GB 1937 71m bw
Julius Hagen/Twickenham
Ship stowaways help to prevent a peace gas from getting into the wrong hands.
Moderate star comedy with music.
w H. Fowler Mear *story* Alison Booth *d* Redd Davis *ph* Sydney Blythe
☆ Flanagan and Allen, Stella Moya, Enid Stamp Taylor, Lyn Harding, Edmund Willard, Edward Ashley

The Underpup
US 1939 81m bw
Joe Pasternak/Universal
A slum girl wins a country holiday among rich folk who ignore her.
Light comedy-drama with music which seemed about to launch a rival to Deanna Durbin.
w Grover Jones *d* Richard Wallace
☆ Gloria Jean, Robert Cummings, Nan Grey, C. Aubrey Smith, Beulah Bondi, Virginia Weidler, Raymond Walburn, Margaret Lindsay

Undersea Kingdom
US 1936 bw
Republic
At the bottom of the ocean lies Atlantis, where the White Robes are in constant battle with the Black Robes.
Slightly hilarious chapter play.
d B. Reeves Eason, Joseph Kane
☆ Ray 'Crash' Corrigan, Lois Wilde, Monte Blue, William Farnum, Smiley Burnette, Lon Chaney Jnr, Raymond Hatton
† Serial in 12 episodes.

Underwater!
US 1955 99m Technicolor SuperScope
RKO/Howard Hughes
Treasure hunters dive in the Caribbean for sunken pirate treasure.
Flabby adventure yarn, badly designed for the purpose of showing off its star in a variety of dress and undress.
w Walter Newman, Hugh King, Robert B. Bailey *d* John Sturges *ph* Harry J. Wild, Lamar Boren *m* Roy Webb
☆ Jane Russell, Gilbert Roland, Richard Egan, Lori Nelson, Robert Keith, Joseph Calleia
'This presentation of Miss Russell is like one of those fountain pens guaranteed to write under water – novel, but impractical.' – *Bosley Crowther, New York Times*

Underwater Warrior
US 1958 91m bw Cinemascope
MGM (Ivan Tors)
A naval reserve commander trains frogmen.
Dry semi-documentary drama, unlikely to win any recruits.
w Gene Levitt *d* Andrew Marton
☆ Dan Dailey, Ross Martin, James Gregory, Claire Kelly

'Revolvers bark! Figures steal slowly among the shadows of the night! Then all is still ... That's just a bit of the underworld!'
'It takes you to the haunts of the human birds of prey, to the refuge of the hunted!'
Underworld
US 1927 82m (24 fps) bw silent
Paramount (Hector Turnbull)
GB title: *Paying the Penalty*
A gangster is rescued from prison by his moll and his lieutenant, and when he realizes they are in love he allows them to escape when the law closes in.
An innovative film in its time, this melodrama was the first to look at crime from the gangsters' point of view. Its main appeal now lies in its lush direction.
w Ben Hecht, Robert N. Lee, Josef von Sternberg *d* Josef von Sternberg *ph* Bert Glennon *ad* Hans Dreier
☆ George Bancroft, Evelyn Brent, Clive Brook, Larry Semon
† The film was a great international success and had an influence on the pessimistic French school of the thirties.
Ben Hecht

Underworld
GB 1985 100m colour
Limehouse/Green Man
A mad doctor keeps his mutants underground.
H. G. Wells up to date, but none the better for it.
w Clive Barker, James Caplin *d* George Pavlou
☆ Denholm Elliott, Steven Berkoff, Larry Lamb, Miranda Richardson, Art Malik, Ingrid Pitt

Underworld Informers: see *The Informers*

The Underworld Story **
US 1950 90m bw
UA (Hal E. Chester)

An unscrupulous reporter buys a half-share in a small-town newspaper and brings his slick city methods with him when he covers a murder.
Very effective, moodily atmospheric and unpretentious thriller.
w Henry Blankfort, Cy Endfield *story* Craig Rice *d* Cy Endfield *ph* Stanley Cortez *m* David Rose *ad* Gordon Wiles *ed* Richard Heermance
☆ Dan Duryea, Herbert Marshall, Gale Storm, Howard Da Silva, Michael O'Shea, Mary Anderson, Gar Moore, Melville Cooper, Frieda Inescort, Art Baker

'A sensational film that puts the finger on today's biggest business – crime.'
Underworld USA *
US 1961 99m bw
Columbia/Globe (Samuel Fuller)

A young gangster takes elaborate revenge for the killing of his father.
Violent syndicate melodrama with a semi-documentary veneer and some brutal scenes. Well done but heavy going.
wd Samuel Fuller *ph* Hal Mohr *m* Harry Sukman *ad* Robert Peterson *ed* Jerome Thoms
☆ Cliff Robertson, Beatrice Kay, Larry Gates, Dolores Dorn, *Robert Emhardt*, Paul Dubov, Richard Rust

'One's Fighting For Freedom. One's Fighting For Greed. It's Going To Be War.'
Undisputed **
US 2002 94m DeLuxe Panavision
MiramaxM/illennium/Hollywood Partners/Amen Ra/MPC (David Giler, Walter Hill, Brad Krevoy, Andrew Sugerman)

When the world heavyweight champion is jailed for rape, he challenges the prison's top fighter to a contest that can end only with a knockout.
Tough no-holds barred boxing drama, a very masculine movie that has no room for sentiment but delivers a lethal punch.
w David Giler, Walter Hill *d* Walter Hill *ph* Lloyd Ahern *m* Stanley Clarke *pd* Maria Caso *ed* Freeman Davies *fight choreographer* Cole McKay
☆ Wesley Snipes (Monroe Hutchens), Ving Rhames (Iceman Chambers), Peter Falk (Mendy Ripstein), Michael Rooker (A. J. Mercker), Jon Seda (Jesus 'Chuy' Campos), Wes Studi (Mingo Pace), Fisher Stevens (Ratbag Dolan)
'At times, the picture seems to have been edited with a blowtorch. But it gets the job done efficiently and swiftly.' – *Elvis Mitchell, New York Times*

'Savage! Sinister! Supernatural! The black fury of a werewolf – sacrificing life and love to the maddening evil that drove him to the most monstrous murders man ever committed!'
The Undying Monster *
US 1943 63m bw
TCF

GB title: *The Hammond Mystery*
A curse hangs over the English ancestral home of the Hammonds.
Silly but well-photographed and directed minor horror on wolf man lines.
w Lillie Hayward, Michel Jacoby *novel* Jessie D. Kerruish *d John Brahm ph Lucien Ballard m* Emil Newman, David Raksin
☆ James Ellison, John Howard, Heather Angel, Bramwell Fletcher, Heather Thatcher, Eily Malyon, Halliwell Hobbes, Aubrey Mather

Une Hirondelle A Fait Le Printemps: see *The Girl from Paris*

Unearthly Stranger *
GB 1963 75m bw
Independent Artists (Julian Wintle, Leslie Parkyn, Albert Fennell)
Scientists working on a time-space formula find that the bride of one of them is an alien in search of their secret.
Surprisingly effective minor science fiction, in some ways all the better for its modest, TV-style production values.
w Rex Carlton d John Krish ph Reg Wyer *m* Edward Williams
☆ John Neville, Gabriella Licudi, Philip Stone, Jean Marsh, Patrick Newell, Warren Mitchell

Uneasy Riders *
France 2000 95m colour
Blue Light/La Sept/Arte/Télécip (Jacques Fansten)
original title: *Nationale 7*
In a home for the physically disabled, a terminally-ill, bad-tempered, middle-aged man is determined to have sex before he dies.
Witty social comedy, examing the frustrated lives of patients and staff; it is filmed in a semi-documentary style using a handheld camera.
w Jean-Pierre Sinapi, Anne-Marie Catois *d* Jean-Pierre Sinapi *ph* Jean-Paul Meurisse *ad* Ermina Sinapi, Jean-Noel Borecek *ed* Catherine Schwartz
☆ Nadia Kaci (Julie), Olivier Gourmet (René), Lionel Abelanski (Roland), Chantal Neuwirth (Sandrine), Julien Boisselier (Jacques), Nadine Marcovici (Florele), Said Taghmaoui (Rabah)
'A stirring, highly original film.' – *James Christopher, Times*
'A highly satisfying, suspenseful and entertaining endeavor whose lingering aura of emotional uplift is organic and earned.' – *Lisa Nesselson, Variety*
† The film was made as a digital video feature that was shown on French television before getting a cinema release.

Uneasy Terms
GB 1948 91m bw
British National
Detective Slim Callaghan proves that a blackmail victim is not a murderer.
The film which proved that the British simply can't make crime movies on the American model.
w Peter Cheyney *novel* Peter Cheyney *d* Vernon Sewell *ph* Ernest Palmer *m* Hans May
☆ Michael Rennie, Moira Lister, Faith Brook, Joy Shelton, Nigel Patrick, Paul Carpenter, Barry Jones

Unexpected Father
US 1939 78m bw
Universal
GB title: *Sandy Takes a Bow*
A dancer looks after his late partner's baby.
Genial comedy introducing a baby star who was popular until she got out of diapers.
w Leonard Spigelgass, Charles Grayson *d* Charles Lamont *ph* George Robinson *md* Charles Previn *ad* Jack Otterson *ed* Ted J. Kent
☆ Baby Sandy, Mischa Auer, Dennis O'Keefe, Shirley Ross, Mayo Methot

Unexpected Uncle
US 1941 67m bw
RKO
An elderly steel tycoon gives everything up to become a tramp and play Cupid.
Money-is-not-everything fable, entirely dependent on amiable performances.
w Delmer Daves, Noel Langley *novel* Eric Hatch *d* Peter Godfrey
☆ Charles Coburn, Anne Shirley, James Craig, Ernest Truex, Russell Gleason, Jed Prouty

'If she were yours, would you forgive?'
The Unfaithful *
US 1947 109m bw
Warner (Jerry Wald)
A wife gets involved in a murder while her husband is out of town.
Glossy romantic melodrama, an unofficial remake of The Letter.
w David Goodis, James Gunn *d* Vincent Sherman *ph* Ernest Haller *m* Max Steiner
☆ Ann Sheridan, Zachary Scott, Lew Ayres, Eve Arden, Steve Geray, Jerome Cowan, John Hoyt

Unfaithful *
US 2002 124m DeLuxe
TCF/Fox 2000/Regency (Adrian Lyne, G. Mac Brown)

In New York, a suburban housewife risks her marriage when she impulsively begins an affair with a visiting Frenchman.
Effective drama, though it falls short of Chabrol's original film; it is notable for Diane Lane's performance as the adulterous wife.
w Alvin Sargent, William Broyles Jnr *film La Femme Infidèle* by Claude Chabrol *d* Adrian Lyne *ph* Peter Biziou *m* Jan A. P. Kaczmarek *pd* Brian Morris *ed* Anne V. Coates *cos* Ellen Mirojnick
☆ Richard Gere (Edward Sumner), *Diane Lane* (Connie Sumner), Olivier Martinez (Paul Martel), Erik Per Sullivan (Charlie Sumner), Zeljko Ivanek (Detective Dean), Dominic Chianese (Frank Wilson), Kate Burton (Tracy), Chad Lowe (Bill Stone)
'This seductive tease of a thriller gets the job done. It's a scorcher.' – *Peter Travers, Rolling Stone*
'It's wrong-edge-of-the-seat stuff: You'll be tipping backwards with torpor.' – *Peter Bradshaw, Guardian*
† It is based on *La Femme Infidèle* (qv), which was written and directed by Claude Chabrol in 1968.
Diane Lane

The Unfaithful Wife: see *La Femme Infidèle*

Unfaithfully Yours **
US 1948 105m bw
TCF (Preston Sturges)

An orchestral conductor believes his wife is unfaithful, and while conducting a concert thinks of three different ways of dealing with the situation.
A not entirely happy mixture of romance, farce, melodrama and wit, but in general a pretty entertaining concoction and the last major film of its talented writer-director.
wd Preston Sturges ph Victor Milner *m* Alfred Newman
☆ *Rex Harrison*, Linda Darnell, Barbara Lawrence, Rudy Vallee, Kurt Kreuger, Lionel Stander, *Edgar Kennedy, Al Bridge*, Julius Tannen, Torben Meyer, Robert Greig
'Harrison discovers more ways of tripping over a telephone cable than one can count, and his efforts to falsify evidence through a recalcitrant tape recorder are as funny as anything thought up by Clair in *A Nous La Liberté* or by Chaplin in *Modern Times*.' – *Basil Wright, 1972*
† The Rex Harrison character is named Sir Alfred de Carter and is meant to be Sir Thomas Beecham. (In America the equivalent of Beecham's Pills is Carter's Little Liver Pills.)
♫ The pieces of music played are as follows:
For murder: the *Semiramide Overture* by Rossini
For surrender: the *Venusberg* music from *Tannhäuser*, by Wagner
For Russian roulette: *Francesca da Rimini* by Tchaikovsky

Unfaithfully Yours
US 1983 96m DeLuxe
TCF (Marvin Worth, Joe Wizan)

Modernized and simplified version of the above, with only one plot instead of three.
This proves to be an advantage, and the film does deliver some laughs.
w Valerie Curtin, Barry Levinson, Robert Klane *d* Howard Zieff *ph* David M. Walsh *m* Bill Conti *pd* Albert Brenner
☆ Dudley Moore, Nastassja Kinski, Armand Assante, Albert Brooks, Cassie Yates, Richard Libertini, Richard B. Shull

Unfinished Business
US 1941 95m bw
Universal (Gregory La Cava)
A wife has thoughts that she should have married her husband's brother.
Smooth but disappointing romantic comedy; the detail is good enough, but it sadly lacks drive.
w Eugene Thackery *d* Gregory La Cava *ph* Joseph Valentine *m* Franz Waxman
☆ Irene Dunne, Robert Montgomery, Eugene Pallette, Preston Foster, Walter Catlett, June Clyde, Phyllis Barry, Esther Dale, Samuel S. Hinds
'Once sentiment gets the upper hand, reach for the exit.' – *Otis Ferguson*

The Unfinished Dance
US 1947 101m Technicolor
MGM (Joe Pasternak)
The young star of a ballet school becomes jealous of a talented newcomer, and causes her injury in an accident.
The delicacies of the French original, La Mort du Cygne, *give way to standard Hollywood hokum and produce an accomplished but totally uninteresting film.*
w Myles Connolly *story* Paul Morand *d* Henry Koster *ph* Robert Surtees *md* Herbert Stothart
☆ Margaret O'Brien, Cyd Charisse, Karin Booth, Danny Thomas, Esther Dale
'The same old story, with pathos, humour and ballet substituted for pathos, humour and chorus girls.' – *MFB*

Unforgettable
US 1996 117m DeLuxe
MGM/Spelling (Dino de Laurentiis, Martha de Laurentiis)

A doctor, who is suspected of killing his wife, makes use of a dangerous experimental technique to experience other people's memories in order to discover the real killer.
Daft thriller from a director and cast worthy of better things, but here seeming, understandably, uninterested in events.
w Bill Geddie *d* John Dahl *ph* Jeffrey Jur *m* Christopher Young *pd* Rob Pearson *ed* Eric L. Beason, Scott Chestnut
☆ Ray Liotta, Linda Fiorentino, Peter Coyote, Christopher McDonald, Kim Cattrall, Duncan Fraser, Garwin Sanford, David Paymer
'A curious hybrid, a suspense film with a scientific theme, but one that is equally unsatisfactory in both disciplines.' – *Anwar Brett, Film Review*

The Unforgiven *
US 1960 125m Technicolor Panavision
UA/James Productions/Hecht-Hill-Lancaster (James Hill)

A rancher's daughter is suspected of being an Indian orphan, and violence results.
Good-looking, expensive but muddled racist Western, hard to enjoy.
w Ben Maddow *novel* Alan le May *d* John Huston *ph Franz* Planer *m* Dimitri Tiomkin
☆ Burt Lancaster, Audrey Hepburn, Audie Murphy, Lillian Gish, Charles Bickford, Doug McClure, John Saxon, Joseph Wiseman, Albert Salmi
'How much strain can a director's reputation take? Of late, John Huston seems to have been trying to find out. I think he has carried the experiment too far with *The Unforgiven* … a work of profound phoniness, part adult western, part that *Oklahoma!* kind of folksy Americana.' – *Dwight MacDonald*
'Ludicrous … a hodgepodge of crudely stitched sententiousness and lame story-conference inspirations.' – *Stanley Kauffmann*

Unforgiven ****
US 1992 131m Technicolor Panavision
Warner (Clint Eastwood)

A former hired killer turned unsuccessful farmer, together with a young would-be gunfighter and an old friend, set out to collect a thousand-dollar reward for killing the cowboys who slashed the face of a prostitute.
Harsh Western of revenge and needless slaughter that re-invents and revives the genre to spectacular effect.
w David Webb Peoples d Clint Eastwood ph Jack N. Green *m* Lennie Niehaus *pd* Henry Bumstead *ed* Joel Cox
☆ *Clint Eastwood, Gene Hackman, Morgan Freeman, Richard Harris*, Jaimz Woolvett, Saul Rubinek, Frances Fisher, Anna Thomson, David Mucci, Rob Campbell, Anthony James
'The movie's grizzled male ensemble, its gradual build, and its juxtaposition of brutality and sardonic humor testify to its disdain for box-office conventions.' – *Michael Sragow, New Yorker*
'Eastwood climbs back into the saddle to make a classic western.' – *Ian Johnstone, Sunday Times*
'A tense, hard-edged, superbly dramatic yarn that is also an exceedingly intelligent meditation on the West, its myths and its heroes.' – *Variety*
best picture; Clint Eastwood (as director); Gene Hackman; Joel Cox
Clint Eastwood (as actor); Henry Bumstead; Jack N. Green; David Webb Peoples; best sound
Gene Hackman

The Unguarded Hour *
US 1936 87m bw
MGM
A blackmailed woman has evidence to free a man accused of murder, but dare not reveal it.
Twisty suspense thriller with a rather splendid cast.
w Howard Emmett Rogers, Leon Gordon *play* Ladislas Fodor, Bernard Merivale *d* Sam Wood
☆ Franchot Tone, Loretta Young, Roland Young, Henry Daniell, Jessie Ralph, Lewis Stone, Dudley Digges, E. E. Clive, Robert Greig, Aileen Pringle

The Unguarded Moment
US 1956 85m Technicolor
U-I (Gordon Kay)
A schoolmistress who receives anonymous love notes from a psychotic pupil is discredited by his even more unbalanced father.
Well-meaning but boring melodrama with the star attractively out of her usual element.
w Herb Meadow, Larry Marcus *story* Rosalind Russell *d* Harry Keller *ph* William Daniels *m* Herman Stein
☆ *Esther Williams*, George Nader, John Saxon, *Edward Andrews*, Jack Albertson

'You Haven't Got A Prayer.'
The Unholy
US 1987 102m CFI color
Vestron/Limelight Studios/Team Effort (Matthew Hayden)
A new priest is sent to a demon-haunted church.
Routine horror, in which evil seems to be equated with sexual desire.
w Philip Yordan, Fernando Fonseca *d* Camilo Vilo *ph* Henry Vargas *m* Roger Bellon, Fernando Fonseca *pd* Fernando Fonseca, Jim Darfus, Cathy Carlisle *ed* Mark Melnick
☆ Ben Cross, Ned Beatty, William Russ, Jill Carroll, Hal Holbrook, Trevor Howard, Peter Frechette, Claudia Robinson
'A particularly routine effort in an already overcrowded horror sub-genre.' – *Julian Petley, MFB*

The Unholy Four: see *The Stranger Came Home*

The Unholy Garden
US 1931 75m bw
Samuel Goldwyn
A gentleman thief hides out in a North African den of misfits.
Would-be romantic nonsense, much less interesting than its credits.
w Ben Hecht, Charles MacArthur *d* George Fitzmaurice *ph* Gregg Toland, George Barnes *m* Alfred Newman
☆ Ronald Colman, Fay Wray, Estelle Taylor, Tully Marshall, Warren Hymer, Mischa Auer, Henry Armetta, Lawrence Grant
'Splendid presentation of an ordinary story.' – *Variety*

The Unholy Night
US 1929 94m bw
MGM
A strangler is caught in the London fog.
Clumsy and talkative early talkie, chiefly interesting for its cast.
w Ben Hecht *d* Lionel Barrymore
☆ Lionel Barrymore, Roland Young, Boris Karloff, John Loder, Natalie Moorhead, Ernest Torrence, Polly Moran, John Miljan

Unholy Partners *
US 1941 95m bw
MGM (Samuel Marx)
The editor of a sensational newspaper has to accept finance from a gangster, but friction results when the newspaper exposes some of the gangster's activities.
Agreeable twenties melodrama with two solid stars battling it out.
w Earl Baldwin, Lesser Samuels, Bartlett Cormack *d* Mervyn Le Roy *ph* George Barnes *m* David Snell
☆ *Edward G. Robinson, Edward Arnold*, Laraine Day, Marsha Hunt, William T. Orr, Don Beddoe, Charles Dingle, Walter Kingsford, Marcel Dalio

The Unholy Three *
US 1925 76m approx (24 fps) bw silent
MGM
A ventriloquist, a dwarf and a strong man carry out a series of crimes which end in murder.
Curious melodrama which set its star and director off on a series of seven more and even weirder eccentricities.
w Waldemar Young *story* Clarence Robbins *d* Tod Browning *ph* David Kesson
☆ Lon Chaney, Harry Earles, Victor McLaglen, Mae Busch, Matt Moore

The Unholy Three *
US 1930 74m bw
MGM
Remake of the above.
The star's only talkie – he died before it was released – is less effective than the silent version.
w J. C. and Elliott Nugent *novel* Clarence Robbins *d* Jack Conway *ph* Percy Hilburn
☆ *Lon Chaney*, Lila Lee, Harry Earles, Ivan Linow, Elliott Nugent, John Miljan

'Half-Angel ... Half-Devil. She Made Him Half-A-Man!'
'All A Guy Had To Do Was Whistle! Frank! Outspoken!'
The Unholy Wife
US 1957 94m Technicolor RKOscope
RKO/Treasure
A bored wife shoots a friend in mistake for her husband but is sentenced for the accidental death of her mother-in-law.
Totally uninteresting melodrama in the Double Indemnity *style, professionally made but turgid.*
w Jonathan Latimer *d* John Farrow *ph* Lucien Ballard *m* Daniele Amfitheatrof
☆ Diana Dors, Rod Steiger, Tom Tryon, Beulah Bondi, Marie Windsor, Arthur Franz, Luis Van Rooten

Unhook the Stars
US 1996 103m Foto-Kem
Miramax/Hachette Première/Gérard Depardieu (René Cleitman)
A widow befriends a bedraggled young mother and her six-year-old son.
Glossy emotional wallow for the most part, convincingly acted but never seeming in touch with any observable reality.
w Nick Cassavetes, Helen Caldwell *d* Nick Cassavetes *ph* Phedon Papamichael *m* Steven Hufsteter *pd* Phedon Papamichael Snr *ed* Petra von Oelffen
☆ Gena Rowlands, Marisa Tomei, Gérard Depardieu, Jake Lloyd, Moira Kelly, David Sherrill, David Thornton, Bridgette Wilson, Bobby Cooper, Clint Howard
'If the film is a love-letter from a director to his mother, it's close to being a rejection-slip sent to his dad. Anything less like the American independent tradition would be hard to imagine.' – *Adam Mars-Jones*

Unidentified Flying Oddball: see *The Spaceman and King Arthur*

'A love haunted by nameless evil which fought to live in their hearts!'
The Uninvited **
US 1944 98m bw
Paramount (Charles Brackett)
A girl returns to her family house and is haunted by her mother's spirit, which seems to be evil.
One of the cinema's few genuine ghost stories, and a good one, though encased in a rather stiff production; it works up to a fine pitch of frenzy.
w Dodie Smith novel Uneasy Freehold by Dorothy Macardle *d Lewis Allen ph* Charles Lang *m* Victor Young
☆ Ray Milland, Ruth Hussey, *Gail Russell*, Donald Crisp, Cornelia Otis Skinner, Dorothy Stickney, Barbara Everest, Alan Napier
'It will hold audiences glued to their seats.' – *Variety*
'It sets out to give you the shivers – and will do so, if you're readily disposed.' – *New York Times*
'I experienced thirty-five first class jolts, not to mention a well calculated texture of minor frissons.' – *Nation*
'Still manages to ice the blood with its implied horrors ... you can almost smell the ghostly mimosa.' – *Peter John Dyer, 1966*
'A superior and satisfying shocker.' – *Newsweek*
† British critics of the time congratulated the director on not showing the ghosts: in fact the visible manifestations had been cut by the British censor.
Academy Award nomination: Charles Lang

Union Depot
US 1932 68m bw
Warner
GB title: *Gentleman for a Day*
The fortunes of several people clash in a railway station.
Pale but moderately interesting imitation of Grand Hotel.
w Kenyon Nicholson, Walter de Leon *play* Gene Fowler, Douglas Durkin, Joe Laurie *d* Alfred E. Green
☆ Douglas Fairbanks Jnr, Joan Blondell, Alan Hale, Frank McHugh, George Rosener, Guy Kibbee, David Landau

Union Pacific **
US 1939 133m bw
Paramount/Cecil B. de Mille
Indians and others cause problems for the railroad builders.
Standard big-scale Western climaxing in a spectacular wreck; not exactly exciting, but very watchable.
w Walter de Leon, C. Gardner Sullivan, Jesse Lasky Jnr *d Cecil B. de Mille ph* Victor Milner, Dewey Wrigley *m* John Leipold, Sigmund Krumgold *ad* Hans Dreier, Roland Anderson
☆ Barbara Stanwyck, Joel McCrea, Akim Tamiroff, Robert Preston, Lynne Overman, Brian Donlevy, Robert Barrat, Anthony Quinn, Stanley Ridges, Henry Kolker, Evelyn Keyes, Regis Toomey
'A socko spectacular, surefire for big grosses right down the line.' – *Variety*
'This latest de Mille epic contains all the excelsior qualities we expect of his work – that sense of a Salvationist drum beating round the next corner – but it is never as funny as *The Crusades* and he has lost his touch with crowds.' – *Graham Greene*
'Excitement is the dominant emotion, with swift succession of contrasting materials and episodes, grim and gay, often furious, sometimes funny. The narrative and action take hold at the start and never let go.' – *Motion Picture Herald*
'The largest conglomeration of thrills and cold-blooded murder since Pauline was in peril.' – *Brooklyn Daily Eagle*
'A movie in the old tradition, melodramatic and breathtaking and altogether wonderful.' – *Photoplay*
† De Mille's last picture in black and white.

L'Union Sacrée: see *Brothers in Arms (1989)*

Union Station **
US 1950 80m bw
Paramount (Jules Schermer)
Kidnappers nominate a crowded railroad station as their ransom collection point.
Compelling little thriller modelled after Naked City, *with real locations and plenty of excitement.*
w Sydney Boehm *novel* Thomas Walsh *d Rudolph Maté ph* Daniel L. Fapp *m* David Buttolph, Heinz Roemheld *md* Irvin Talbot
☆ William Holden, *Barry Fitzgerald*, Nancy Olson, *Lyle Bettger*, Jan Sterling, Allene Roberts

Universal Soldier
GB 1971 96m colour
Appaloosa/Ionian (Frank J. Schwarz, Donald L. Factor)
A mercenary returns to London but can't escape his past.
Solemnly meaningful melodrama on a tight budget.
wd Cy Endfield *ph* Tony Imi *m* Philip Goodhand-Tait
☆ George Lazenby, Edward Judd, Benito Carruthers, Germaine Greer, Rudolph Walker

'The future has a bad attitude.'
Universal Soldier
US 1992 103m Technicolor Panavision
Guild/Carolco (Allen Shapiro, Craig Baumgarten, Joel B. Michaels)
Two soldiers who killed each other in Vietnam are resurrected as androids to form part of an élite group of soldiers for special missions; but one of them goes out of control.
Science-fiction hokum intended to boost the appeal of its two action stars, done with enough energy and containing more than enough mayhem to appeal to fans of action movies.
w Richard Rothstein, Christopher Leitch, Dean Devlin *d* Roland Emmerich *ph* Karl Walter Lindenlaub *m* Christopher Franke *md* Brynmor Jones *pd* Holger Gross *ed* Michael J. Duthie
☆ Jean-Claude Van Damme, Dolph Lundgren, Ally Walker, Ed O'Ross, Jerry Orbach, Leon Rippy, Tico Wells
'To get through the garish mayhem, you need a high vicarious-pain threshold.' – *Michael Sragow, New Yorker*
'A classy rollercoaster ride through the clichés of modern fantasy cinema.' – *Mark Kermode, Sight and Sound*

'Prepare to become obsolete.'
Universal Soldier: The Return
US 1999 83m DeLuxe
Columbia TriStar/IndieProd/Long Road (Craig Baumgarten, Allen Shapiro, Jean-Claude Van Damme)
Only one man, a bionic commando, can save the world when rogue cyborgs, controlled by a super-intelligent computer, go on the rampage.
Extremely dull action movie, with no sense of urgency about it, despite its loud explosions, thumping soundtrack, and endlessly repetitive fights.
w William Malone, John Fasano *ph* Michael A. Benson *m* Don Davis *pd* David Chapman *ed* Peck Prior
☆ Jean-Claude Van Damme (Luc Deveraux), Michael Jai White (SETH), Heidi Schanz (Erin), Xander Berkeley (Dylan Cotner), Justin Lazard (Capt Blackburn), Kiana Tom (Maggie), Daniel Von Bargen (Gen Radford), James Black (Sgt Morrow), Karis Paige Bryant (Hillary), Bill Goldberg (Romeo)
'Rot from start to finish.' – *Edward Porter, Sunday Times*

The Unknown
US 1927 65m bw silent
MGM
A fake armless wonder has his arms amputated to please a girl who can't stand the touch of a man's hand. (She then changes her mind.)
Weird melodrama which even this contortionist star can't save.
w Waldemar Young *d* Tod Browning
☆ Lon Chaney, Joan Crawford, Norman Kerry

The Unknown
US 1946 70m bw
Columbia
An amnesiac heiress returns to her family mansion.
Twisty creeper in the I Love a Mystery *series; not bad for a second feature.*
w Malcolm Stuart Boylan, Julian Harmon *d* Henry Levin
☆ Karen Morley, Jeff Donnell, Jim Bannon

Unknown Chaplin ***
GB 1986 157m colour/bw
Thames Television
A three-part documentary on Chaplin's early years including excerpts from films, out-takes and on-camera rehearsals never seen in public before, much of it taken from Chaplin's own archives, which he had ordered to be destroyed.
First shown as three television programmes, this is by far the finest examination available of Chaplin's genius, which is shown to be due to constant hard work as well as to improvisation.
wd Kevin Brownlow, David Gill *ph* Ted Adcock *m* Carl Davis *ed* Trevor Waite
☆ James Mason (narrator)

The Unknown Guest
US 1943 61m bw
Monogram (Maurice King)
A supposedly no-good young man is suspected of murdering his aunt and uncle.
Rather tedious and silly mystery with little happening.
w Philip Yordan *d* Kurt Neumann
☆ Victor Jory, Pamela Blake, Harry Hayden, Veda Ann Borg, Nora Cecil

The Unknown Man
US 1951 86m bw
MGM (Robert Thomsen)
A civil court lawyer of high principles successfully undertakes a criminal case, finds his client was really guilty, and sets matters straight.
Contrived but entertaining morality with standard production and performances.
w Ronald Millar, George Froeschel *d* Richard Thorpe *ph* William Mellor *m* Conrad Salinger
☆ Walter Pidgeon, Ann Harding, Lewis Stone, Barry Sullivan, Keefe Brasselle, Eduard Franz, Richard Anderson, Dawn Addams

Unknown World
US 1951 74m bw
Lippert/J. R. Rabin, I. A. Block
Scientists burrow down 1,640 miles below the Earth's surface to find a geological shelter in which to preserve civilization from the H-bomb.
Dull, cheap science fiction with a hectoring tone; it raises the question of whether a civilization capable of producing such tedium is worth saving.
w Millard Kaufman *d* Terry Morse (as Terrell O. Morse) *ph* Allen G. Siegler, Henry Freulich *m* Ernest Gold *pd* I. A. Block, J. R. Rabin *ed* Terry Morse (as Terrell O. Morse)
☆ Bruce Kellogg, Marilyn Nash, Otto Waldis, Jim Bannon, Tom Handley, Dick Cogan, George Baxter

Unlawful Entry *
US 1992 111m DeLuxe
TCF/Largo/JVC (Charles Gordon)
A Los Angeles policeman who befriends a young couple turns out to be a psychopath.
Moderate thriller of a now very familiar kind that deals with a flatmate, tenant, nanny, and, in this instance, a cop from hell.
w Lewis Colick *story* George D. Putnam, John Katchmer, Lewis Colick *d* Jonathan Kaplan *ph* Jamie Anderson *m* James Horner *pd* Lawrence G. Paull *ed* Curtiss Clayton
☆ Kurt Russell, Ray Liotta, Madeleine Stowe, Roger E. Mosley, Ken Lerner, Deborah Offner, Carmen Argenziano, Andy Romano, Johnny Ray McGhee
'The film's main achievement is to fit its trenchant social critique into conventional thriller form … The film catches the fear and paranoia of the couple "home alone".' – *Geoffrey Macnab, Sight and Sound*

Unman, Wittering and Zigo
GB 1971 102m colour
Paramount/Mediarts (Gareth Wigan)
A nervous schoolmaster discovers that his predecessor was murdered by the boys.
Macabre school story which overreaches itself and peters out.
w Simon Raven *TV play* Giles Cooper *d* John Mackenzie *ph* Geoffrey Unsworth *m* Michael J. Lewis
☆ David Hemmings, Douglas Wilmer, Hamilton Dyce, Carolyn Seymour

Unmarried
US 1939 66m bw
Paramount
GB title: *Night Club Hostess*
An ex-boxer, shy of marriage, raises an orphan boy.
Modest domestic drama notable as one of the rare non-Western appearances of its star.
w Lillie Hayward, Brian Marlow, Grover Jones *d* Kurt Neumann
☆ Buck Jones, Donald O'Connor, Helen Twelvetrees

An Unmarried Woman *
US 1978 124m Movielab
TCF (Paul Mazursky, Tony Ray)
A sophisticated New York woman is deserted by her husband, fights with her daughter, and takes up with two men.
Frank, well-observed depiction of one woman in New York's new society; as modern as all get out but not very attractive.
wd Paul Mazursky *ph* Arthur J. Ornitz *m* Bill Conti *pd* Pato Guzman
☆ *Jill Clayburgh*, Alan Bates, Michael Murphy, Cliff Gorman, Pat Quinn, Kelly Bishop
'The motions of the story are not what cripple it – it's the low level of insight and the pervasive sense of exploitation … It's what once would have been called woman's-magazine fiction.' – *Stanley Kauffmann*
best picture; script; Jill Clayburgh

The Unnamable
Canada 1988 87m Foto-Kem
Yankee Classic/KP (Dean Ramser, Jean-Paul Ouellette)
Students explore a deserted house and discover a monster that has been imprisoned there for 200 years.
Unexceptional, low-budget, gory rendition of Lovecraft's short stories, padded out with a great deal of irrelevance.
wd Jean-Paul Ouellette *story* *The Statement of Randolph Carter and The Unnamable* by H. P. Lovecraft *ph* Tom Fraser *m* David Bergeaud *pd* Gene Abel *ed* Wendy J. Plump *sp* R. Christopher Biggs
☆ Charles King, Mark Kinsey Stephenson, Alexandra Durrell, Laura Albert, Katrin Alexandre, Eben Ham, Blane Wheatley, Mark Parra

The Unnamable Returns
Canada 1992 92m Foto-Kem
Yankee Classic/AM East/Prism/New Age (Jean-Paul Ouellette)
aka: *H. P. Lovecraft's The Unnamable Returns*
Students dabbling in black magic unleash a murderous demon on the Miskatonic university campus in Arkham.
Supernatural variation on the usual low-budget slasher movie, featuring a cut-price monster.
wd Jean-Paul Ouellette *story* *The Statement of Randolph Carter and The Unnamable* by H. P. Lovecraft *ph* Greg Gardener, Roger Olkowski *m* David Bergeaud *pd* Tim Keating *ed* William C. Williams *sp* R. Christopher Biggs
☆ John Rhys-Davies, Mark Kinsey Stephenson, Charles Klausmeyer, Maria Ford, Julie Strain, Peter Breck, David Warner

Unpublished Story
GB 1942 91m bw
Columbia/Two Cities (Anthony Havelock-Allan)
A reporter exposes the Nazis behind a pacifist organization.
Ho-hum formula flagwaver with generally stilted production.
w Anatole de Grunwald, Patrick Kirwan *d* Harold French *ph* Bernard Knowles *m* Nicholas Brodzky
☆ Valerie Hobson, Richard Greene, Basil Radford, Roland Culver, Brefni O'Rorke, Miles Malleson, George Carney, André Morell

Unsane: see *Tenebrae*

The Unseen
US 1945 82m bw
Paramount
A London governess comes to suspect that dark deeds have taken place in the empty house next door.
Period suspenser with good atmosphere but an insubstantial plot.
w Hagar Wilde, Raymond Chandler *d* Lewis Allen *ph* John Seitz *m* Ernst Toch
☆ Joel McCrea, Gail Russell, Herbert Marshall, Richard Lyon, Nona Griffith
† The film seems to have been a hurried attempt to repeat and combine the previous year's successes, *Gaslight* and *The Uninvited.*

Unseen Heroes: see *The Battle of the V1*

Unsichtbare Gegner: see *Invisible Adversaries*

The Unsinkable Molly Brown *
US 1964 128m Metrocolor Panavision
MGM/Marten (Lawrence Weingarten)
Western orphan Molly Brown grows up determined to become a member of Denver society.
Semi-Western comedy-musical about a real lady who wound up surviving the Titanic. *Bouncy and likeable but not at all memorable.*
w Helen Deutsch *musical play* Richard Morris *d* Charles Walters *ph* Daniel L. Fapp *md* Robert Armbruster *ad* George W. Davis, Preston Ames
☆ *Debbie Reynolds*, Harve Presnell, *Ed Begley*, Jack Kruschen, Hermione Baddeley, Martita Hunt
Daniel L. Fapp; Robert Armbruster; Debbie Reynolds

'Sometimes you find your heroes in the most unlikely places.'
Unstrung Heroes *
US 1995 94m Technicolor
Buena Vista/Hollywood (Susan Arnold, Donna Roth, Bill Badalato)
A 12-year-old, unhappy at home, goes to live with his two eccentric uncles.
Oddball drama of a dysfunctional family; it takes the once-fashionable view that it is the mad who are truly sane and builds on that shaky foundation an affecting domestic drama of people's various strategies for survival.
w Richard LaGravenese *book* Franz Lidz *d* Diane Keaton *ph* Phedon Papamichael *m* Thomas Newman *pd* Garreth Stover *ed* Lisa Churgin
☆ Andie MacDowell, John Turturro, Michael Richards, Maury Chaykin, Nathan Watt, Kendra Krull
'A funny and fond piece of film-making, with a remarkably well-sustained tone – somewhere between an Anne Tyler novel and a Marx Brothers film, if you can imagine that. Keaton has.' – *Tom Shone, Sunday Times*
Thomas Newman

An Unsuitable Job for a Woman
GB 1982 90m Gevacolor
Gold Crest/NFFC/Boyd's Co (Michael Relph, Peter McKay)
A young woman, hired to discover why the son of a wealthy businessman killed himself, becomes obsessed by the dead youth.
Tepid and murky thriller that irons out the ambiguities of a convoluted plot.
w Elizabeth McKay, Brian Scobie, Christopher Petit *novel* P. D. James *d* Christopher Petit *ph* Martin Schäfer *m* Chaz Jankel, Philip Bagenal, Pete Van-Hooke *pd* Anton Furst *ed* Mick Audsley
☆ Billie Whitelaw, Paul Freeman, Pippa Guard, Dominic Guard, Elizabeth Spriggs, David Horovitch, Dawn Archibald

The Unsuspected *
US 1947 103m bw
Warner (Charles Hoffman)
A writer-producer of radio crime shows commits a murder and is forced to follow the clues on air.
Sleek, new look mystery thriller with a disappointing plot which gives its interesting cast little to do, and allows itself to peter out in chases.
w Ranald MacDougall *novel* Charlotte Armstrong *d* *Michael Curtiz* *ph* *Woody Bredell* *m* Franz Waxman *ad* Anton Grot
☆ Claude Rains, Joan Caulfield, Audrey Totter, Constance Bennett, Michael North, Hurd Hatfield, Fred Clark

The Untamed: see *Return to Snowy River*

Untamed
US 1940 83m Technicolor
Paramount (Paul Jones)
A doctor in the frozen north is beset by an epidemic as well as natural hazards.
Old-fashioned melodrama which found an eager audience.
w Frederick Hazlitt Brennan, Frank Butler *novel* *Mantrap* by Sinclair Lewis *d* George Archainbaud *ph* Leo Tover, W. Howard Greene *m* Victor Young
☆ Ray Milland, Patricia Morison, Akim Tamiroff, William Frawley, Jane Darwell, Esther Dale, J. M. Kerrigan, Eily Malyon
† A remake of Clara Bow's 1926 film *Mantrap.*

Untamed
US 1955 109m Technicolor Cinemascope
TCF (Bert E. Friedlob, William A. Bacher)
A Dutchman and an Irish girl meet again on a Boer trek to South Africa, and survive Zulu attacks.
A long and involved epic-style plot provides standard excitements and predictable romantic complications.
w Talbot Jennings, Michael Blankfort, Frank Fenton *novel* Helga Moray *d* Henry King *ph* Leo Tover *m* Franz Waxman
☆ Tyrone Power, Susan Hayward, Richard Egan, John Justin, Agnes Moorehead, Rita Moreno, Hope Emerson, Brad Dexter, Henry O'Neill
'A not unenjoyable essay in hokum.' – *MFB*

Untamed Frontier
US 1952 78m Technicolor
U-I (Leonard Goldstein)
The son of an unpopular Texan landowner commits murder.
Stolid minor Western.
w Gerald Drayson Adams, Gwen and John Bagni *d* Hugo Fregonese *ph* Charles P. Boyle *m* Hans Salter
☆ Joseph Cotten, Shelley Winters, Scott Brady, Suzan Ball, Minor Watson

'He doesn't make sense. She doesn't make sense. Together they make sense.'
Untamed Heart
US 1993 102m DeLuxe
MGM (Tony Bill, Helen Buck Bartlett)
A young man with a heart condition begins a tentative love affair with a waitress.
Sickly romantic sob-story, a teenage fantasy of idealized passion which is remote from real life.
w Tom Sierchio *d* Tony Bill *ph* Jost Vacano *m* Cliff Eidelman *pd* Steven Jordan *ed* Mia Goldman
☆ Christian Slater, Marisa Tomei, Rosie Perez, Kyle Secor, Willie Carson
'The movie largely works on its own terms, particularly for those looking for a traditional "good cry".' – *Variety*
'Has the kind of sympathetic handling that isn't totally destroyed by the American propensity for weepie but upbeat endings, and slurpy music to enable even people as silly as ourselves to pinpoint its more dramatic moments.' – *Derek Malcolm, Guardian*

Until September
US 1985 95m Metrocolor
UA (Michael Gruskoff)
An American woman unexpectedly stuck in Paris begins an affair with a married French banker.
Dull, lightweight romantic comedy of two chauvinistic people divided by their cultures; it is extremely bland and rarely interesting.
w Janice Lee Graham *d* Richard Marquand *ph* Philippe Welt *m* John Barry *pd* Hilton McConnico *ed* Sean Barton
☆ Karen Allen, Thierry L'hermitte, Christopher Cazenove, Marie-Catherine Conti, Hutton Cobb, Michael Mellinger, Nitza Saul

Until the End of the World *
Germany/France/Australia 1991 158m colour
Warner/Road Movies/Argos/Village Roadshow (Anatole Dauman, Jonathan Taplin)
original title: *Bis ans Ende der Welt*
As a rogue nuclear satellite threatens to explode, a woman tracks a man with multiple identities across Europe to Japan, China and Australia, where she meets his blind mother and his father, who has invented a camera enabling the blind to see.
Rambling, often confusing, sometimes boring road movie with moments of brilliance.
w Peter Carey, Wim Wenders *d* Wim Wenders *ph* Robby Müller *m* Graeme Revell *pd* Thierry Flamand, Sally Campbell *ed* Peter Przygodda
☆ William Hurt, Solveig Dommartin, Sam Neill, Max von Sydow, Rüdiger Vogler, Ernie Dingo, Jeanne Moreau, Chick Ortega, David Gulpilil, Ryu Chishu

'A dream still partly realised and partly still in the head of the director.' – *Variety*

'Comes across as heavy-handed, chaotic and immensely cluttered, finally leaving one with an overwhelming sense of bewilderment.' – *Julia Knight, Sight and Sound*

† Wenders has announced his intention of releasing a five-hour version of the film on video.

Until They Sail
US 1957 95m bw Cinemascope
MGM (Charles Schnee)

Four New Zealand sisters have wartime romances.
Solid 'woman's picture', well enough presented.
w Robert Anderson *novel* James A. Michener *d* Robert Wise *ph* Joseph Ruttenberg *m* David Raksin
☆ Jean Simmons, Joan Fontaine, Paul Newman, Piper Laurie, Charles Drake, Wally Cassell, Sandra Dee

The Untouchables **
US 1987 119m Technicolor
Paramount/Art Linson

Law enforcers in 20s Chicago go after Al Capone and other mobsters.
The long-running TV show is given a new polish in this showy, violent gangster picture, which seemed to please all classes.
w David Mamet *d* *Brian de Palma* *ph* Stephen H. Burum *m* Ennio Morricone *pd* Patrizia von Brandenstein *ad* Hal Gausman *ed* Jerry Greenberg, Bill Pankow
☆ *Kevin Costner, Sean Connery, Robert DeNiro,* Charles Martin Smith, Andy Garcia, Richard Bradford

'Time honoured mayhem in the windy city.' – *Time Out*

'The picture is more like an attempt to visualize the public's collective dream of Chicago gangsters; our movie-fed imagination of the past is enlarged and given new vividness.' – *Pauline Kael, New Yorker*

Sean Connery
Ennio Morricone; art direction; costume design (Marilyn Vance-Straker)
Ennio Morricone

The Unvanquished: see *Aparajito*

'Unhooked. Undressed. Unhinged.'
'A behind-the-seams look at the world of high fashion.'
Unzipped **
US 1995 73m Technicolor/bw
Buena Vista/Hachette Filipacchi (Michael Alden)

A documentary about fashion designer Isaac Mizrahi who, after his 1994 fashion show is poorly received, returns in triumph with a new collection, inspired by Robert Flaherty's *Nanook of the North*.
An enjoyable insider's account of the often bizarre world of high fashion and its exotic denizens.
d Douglas Keeve *ph* Ellen Kuras *ed* Paula Heredia

'Keeve unzips the false chic to show the real chic beneath. Divine!' – *Alexander Walker*

Up at the Villa
US 2000 114m Technicolor
UIP/Universal/Intermedia/Mirage/Stanley Buchthal (Geoff Stier)

In Florence in the 1930s, a widow, courted by an English diplomat and an American playboy, finds herself in a compromising situation.
Photogenic, glossy romantic drama that seems extremely dated; it requires an effort of will to summon up any interest in the affairs of this expatriate society just before the beginning of the Second World War.
w Belinda Haas *novella* W. Somerset Maugham *d* Philip Haas *ph* Maurizio Calvesi *m* Pino Donaggio *pd* Paul Brown *ed* Belinda Haas
☆ Kristin Scott Thomas (Mary Panton), Sean Penn (Rowley Flint), Anne Bancroft (Princess San Ferdinando), James Fox (Sir Edgar Swift), Jeremy Davies (Karl Richter), Derek Jacobi (Lucky Leadbetter), Massimo Ghini (Beppino Leopardi)

'A decent period drama that occasionally rises above the reliable.' – *Derek Elley, Variety*

'Every Day We Have Is One More Than We Deserve.'
Up Close and Personal
US 1996 124m Technicolor
Entertainment/Touchstone/Cinergi (Jon Avnet, David Nicksay, Jordan Kerner)

Under the romantic guidance of an experienced executive, a waitress becomes a star TV newscaster.
Very much a 'so what?' movie, a sentimental weepie about what are presumably intended as glamorous and powerful lives; outside its home territory, it looks and sounds ridiculous.
w Joan Didion, John Gregory Dunne *book* Golden Girl by Alanna Nash *d* Jon Avnet *ph* Karl Walter Lindenlaub *m* Thomas Newman *pd* Jeremy Conway *ed* Debra Neil-Fisher
☆ Robert Redford, Michelle Pfeiffer, Stockard Channing, Joe Mantegna, Kate Nelligan, Glenn Plummer, James Rebhorn

'A Sunday afternoon time-filling movie.' – *Empire*

song 'Because You Loved Me' (*m/ly* Diane Warren)

Up for the Cup
GB 1931 76m bw
B & D (Herbert Wilcox)
A Yorkshireman gets into trouble when he comes to London for the Cup Final.
Slap-happy star farce which pleased the public.
w Con West, R. P. Weston, Bert Lee *d* Jack Raymond
☆ Sydney Howard, Joan Wyndham, Stanley Kirk, Sam Livesey, Moore Marriott
† The same star appeared in *Up for the Derby* in the following year; and in 1950 the original, with much the same script, was refashioned for Albert Modley; it was also directed by Jack Raymond.

'A lone American sergeant on the most impossible mission of the war!'
Up from the Beach *
US 1965 98m bw Cinemascope
TCF/Panoramic (Christian Ferry)
Just after D-Day, GIs have trouble in a Normandy village.
A kind of subdued sequel to The Longest Day, *well made for war action addicts, but barely memorable.*
w Stanley Mann, Claude Brule *novel Epitaph for an Enemy* by George Barr *d* *Robert Parrish* *ph* *Walter Wottitz* *m* Edgar Cosma
☆ Cliff Robertson, Red Buttons, Françoise Rosay, Marius Goring, Irina Demick, Broderick Crawford, James Robertson Justice, Slim Pickens

Up Goes Maisie
US 1946 89m bw
MGM (George Haight)
Maisie becomes a secretary and outwits a crooked industrialist trying to steal her boss's invention of an easy-to-fly helicopter.
Lively little programmer.
w Thelma Robinson *d* Harry Beaumont *ph* Robert Planck *m* David Snell *ad* Cedric Gibbons, Richard Duce *ed* Irvine Warburton
☆ Ann Sothern, George Murphy, Hillary Brooke, Horace McNally, Ray Collins, Jeff York, Murray Alper, Lewis Howard, Jack Davis, Gloria Grafton, John Eldredge

Up in Arms **
US 1944 106m Technicolor
Samuel Goldwyn

A hypochondriac joins the army.
Loose, generally pleasant introductory vehicle for Danny Kaye.
w Don Hartman, Robert Pirosh, Allen Boretz *d* Elliott Nugent *ph* Ray Rennahan *md* Ray Heindorf, Louis Forbes
☆ Danny Kaye, Dinah Shore, Constance Dowling, Dana Andrews, Louis Calhern, Lyle Talbot

'Not since Greta Garbo made her bow has there been anything so terrific as the inimitable Danny, one of the most exhilarating and spontaneous personalities in film history.' – *New York Daily Mirror*

'Dreadful beyond words.' – *James Agate*

song 'Now I Know' (*m* Harold Arlen, *ly* Ted Koehler); Ray Heindorf, Louis Forbes

Up in Central Park
US 1948 88m bw
U-I (Karl Tunberg)
In turn-of-the-century New York, an Irish girl becomes involved in a crooked political set up.
Stiff and unyielding star musical.
w Karl Tunberg *d* William A. Seiter *ph* Milton Krasner *md* John Green *songs* Sigmund Romberg, Dorothy Fields
☆ Deanna Durbin, Vincent Price, Dick Haymes, Albert Sharpe, Tom Powers

'A misery.' – *New Yorker*

Up in Mabel's Room
US 1944 77m bw
Edward Small
A flustered professor has to retrieve incriminating evidence from an old flame's room.
Antediluvian bedroom farce which keeps several ardent practitioners working happily.
w Tom Reed *play* Wilson Collison, Otto Harbach *d* Allan Dwan *m* Edward Paul
☆ Dennis O'Keefe, Mischa Auer, Marjorie Reynolds, Gail Patrick

'As horrible, and wonderful, as watching a Gopher Prairie dramatic club play a mail order farce (6m, 6f).' – *James Agee*

Edward Paul

Up in Smoke
US 1978 86m colour
Paramount (Lou Adler, Lou Lombardo)

Two dopeheads from a rock band go in search of pot so that they can play.
Direly unamusing; the slapstick is badly timed and the humour infantile. Stoned or sober, Cheech and Chong are the least funny comedy team since The Three Stooges.
w Thomas Chong, Cheech Marin *d* Lou Adler *ph* Gene Polito *ad* Leon Ericksen *ed* Scott Conrad, Lou Lombardo
☆ Cheech Marin, Thomas Chong, Strother Martin, Edie Adams, Stacy Keach, Tom Skerritt

'The humor is like dogface underclass humor – but without the resentment of the officers. And Cheech and Chong are so gracefully dumb-assed that if you're in a relaxed mood you can't help laughing at them.' – *Pauline Kael, New Yorker*

Up in the Cellar
US 1970 94m Movielab
AIP (William J. Immerman)

A dejected freshman tries various schemes to revenge himself on the college president.
Youth satire aimed at a number of targets which quickly became obsolete; mildly interesting sociologically.
wd Theodore J. Flicker *novel The Late Boy Wonder* by Angus Hall *ph* Earl Roth *m* Don Randi
☆ Wes Stern, Joan Collins, Larry Hagman, Judy Pace

Up in the World
GB 1956 91m bw
Rank (Hugh Stewart)
A window cleaner becomes friendly with a boy millionaire.
Slow and unattractive comedy star vehicle.
w Jack Davies, Henry Blyth, Peter Blackmore *d* John Paddy Carstairs *ph* Jack Cox *m* Philip Green
☆ Norman Wisdom, Martin Caridia, Jerry Desmonde, Maureen Swanson, Ambrosine Philpotts, Colin Gordon

Up 'n' Under
GB 1998 100m Rank Colour
Entertainment/Touchdown/Lluniau Lliw (Mark Thomas)

A former rugby league player takes a bet that he can train any team in eight weeks to beat the local champions.
Broad, quite likable comedy, cosy and insular.
wd John Godber *play* John Godber *ph* Alan M. Trow *m* Mark Thomas *pd* Hayden Pearce *ed* Chris Lawrence
☆ Gary Olsen, Richard Ridings, Samantha Janus, Ralph Brown, Neil Morrissey, Adrian Hood, David MacCreedy, Tony Slattery, Brian Glover, Griff Rhys-Jones

'A game try that still ends up in the second division.' – *Variety*

'Friends are for life.'
Up on the Roof *
GB 1997 101m Rank Colour 'Scope
Rank/Castle Rock/Turner/Carnival/Production Line (Jane Prowse, Pippa Cross, Brian Eastman)

Five people, who shared a house and formed a student vocal group, get together for reunion six, and fifteen, years after their first meeting.
Slight but pleasant drama verging on the bland, with moments of music, which would look better on the television screen.
w Jane Prowse, Simon Moore *d* Simon Moore *ph* Nic Morris *m* Alan Parker *pd* Tim Hutchinson *ed* Peter Hollywood
☆ Billy Carter, Clare Cathcart, Adrian Lester, Amy Robbins, Daniel Ryan, Lavinia Bertram, Robin Herford

'The most unfunny, fatuous, irritating and insipid little British "comedy" I have ever had the misfortune to sit and suffer through.' – *Cosmo Landesman, Sunday Times*

Up Periscope
US 1959 111m Technicolor Warnerscope
Warner/Lakeside (Aubrey Schenck)

During World War II a submarine frogman is landed on a Pacific island to steal a Japanese code book.
Stock adventure story given stock presentation.
w Richard Landau *novel* Robb White *d* Gordon Douglas *ph* Carl Guthrie *m* Ray Heindorf
☆ James Garner, Edmond O'Brien, Alan Hale Jnr, Carleton Carpenter

Up Pompeii
GB 1971 90m Technicolor
EMI/Associated London Films (Ned Sherrin)

A wily slave outwits Nero and escapes the eruption of Vesuvius.
Yawnmaking spinoff of a lively TV comedy series: the jokes just lie there, and die there.
w Sid Colin *d* Bob Kellett *ph* Ian Wilson *m* Carl Davis
☆ Frankie Howerd, Patrick Cargill, Michael Hordern, Barbara Murray, Lance Percival, Bill Fraser, Adrienne Posta
† Sequels: *Up the Front, Up the Chastity Belt* (qv).

Up Pops the Devil
US 1931 74m bw
Paramount
A wife supports her husband so that he can write novels.
Odd little comedy-drama which struck most people as rather half-hearted.
w Arthur Kober, Eve Unsell *play* Frances Goodrich, Albert Hackett *d* A. Edward Sutherland
☆ Carole Lombard, Norman Foster, Skeets Gallagher, Stuart Erwin, Lilyan Tashman

'Here's a plenty satisfying strip of celluloid but it won't do any drawing unless it's by word-of-mouth advertising.' – *Variety*

Up She Goes: see *Maisie (Up Goes Maisie)*

Up the Chastity Belt *
GB 1971 94m Technicolor
EMI/Associated London Films (Ned Sherrin)

Medieval adventures of the serf Lurkalot and his master Sir Coward de Custard.
Patchy pantomime which doesn't always have the courage of its own slapdash vulgarity.
w Sid Colin, Ray Galton, Alan Simpson *d* Bob Kellett *ph* Ian Wilson *m* Carl Davis
☆ Frankie Howerd, Graham Crowden, Bill Fraser, Roy Hudd, Hugh Paddick, Anna Quayle, Eartha Kitt, Dave King, Fred Emney

Up the Creek *
GB 1958 83m bw HammerScope
Byron (Henry Halsted)

A none-too-bright naval lieutenant is assigned command of a broken-down shore establishment.
Cheeky remake of Oh Mr Porter. *Jokes fair, atmosphere cheerful and easy-going.*
wd Val Guest *ph* Arthur Grant
☆ David Tomlinson, Peter Sellers, Wilfrid Hyde-White, Vera Day, Tom Gill, Michael Goodliffe, Reginald Beckwith, Lionel Jeffries
† Sequel: *Further Up the Creek.*

Up the Down Staircase *
US 1967 124m Technicolor
Warner/Pakula-Mulligan

Problems of a schoolteacher in one of New York's tough sections.
Earnest, well-acted, not very likeable melodrama.
w Tad Mosel *novel* Bel Kaufman *d* Robert Mulligan *ph* Joseph Coffey *m* Fred Karlin
☆ Sandy Dennis, Patrick Bedford, Eileen Heckart, Ruth White, Jean Stapleton, Sorrell Booke, Roy Poole
'Sandy Dennis, blinking as if she'd taken pills and been awakened in the middle of the night ... She reacts confusedly before the situations even develop, but the audience is ahead of her anyway.' – *Pauline Kael, New Yorker*

Up the Front
GB 1972 89m Technicolor
EMI/Associated London Films (Ned Sherrin)

A footman is hypnotized into enlisting in World War I and has an enemy 'plan' tattooed on his buttocks.
Threadbare end-of-the-pier romp.
w Sid Colin, Eddie Braben *d* Bob Kellett *ph* Tony Spratling *m* Peter Greenwell *ad* Seamus Flannery
☆ Frankie Howerd, Bill Fraser, Zsa Zsa Gabor, Stanley Holloway, Hermione Baddeley, Robert Coote, Lance Percival, Dora Bryan

'Don't get caught is what she wasn't taught!'
Up the Junction
GB 1967 119m Techniscope
Paramount/BHE (Anthony Havelock-Allan, John Brabourne)
A well-off girl crosses London's river to live among the workers of Clapham.
Socially obsolete sensationalism based on a television semi-documentary. An irritating heroine moves hygienically among motorbikes.
w Roger Smith *book* Nell Dunn *d* Peter Collinson *ph* Arthur Lavis *m* Mike Hugg, Manfred Mann
☆ Suzy Kendall, Dennis Waterman, Adrienne Posta, Maureen Lipman, Michael Gothard, Liz Fraser, Hylda Baker, Alfie Bass

Up the River
US 1930 80m bw
Fox
An ex-convict is threatened with exposure, but his two pals escape to help him.
Very minor comedy with interesting credits.
w Maurine Watkins *d* John Ford *ph* Joseph August
☆ Spencer Tracy, Warren Hymer, Claire Luce, Humphrey Bogart, William Collier Snr
'No cast names to draw, but if the exploitation can make 'em attend, the film will meet its entertainment obligations.' – *Variety*
† In 1938 TCF released a remake directed by Alfred Werker, with Preston Foster, Tony Martin, Slim Summerville and Arthur Treacher.

Up the Sandbox
US 1972 98m Technicolor
Barwood/First Artists (Robert Chartoff, Irwin Winkler)

A professor's wife finds she is pregnant again and fantasizes about her future life.
Muddled comedy-drama with little point and less entertainment value.
w Paul Zindel *novel* Anne Richardson Roiphe *d* Irvin Kershner *ph* Gordon Willis, Andy Marton *m* Billy Goldenberg *ad* Harry Horner
☆ Barbra Streisand, David Selby, Ariane Heller, Jane Hoffman
'A magical mystery tour through the picture book mind of one Manhattan housewife.' – *Richard Combs*

Up Tight
US 1968 104m Technicolor
Paramount/Marlukin (Jules Dassin)
A black street cleaner betrays his criminal pals for money and is hunted down by them.
Ponderous black remake of The Informer, *too schematic to make any dramatic or human impression.*
w Jules Dassin, Ruby Dee, Julian Mayfield *d* Jules Dassin *ph* Boris Kaufman *m* Booker T. Jones *pd* Alexander Trauner
☆ Raymond St Jacques, Ruby Dee, Julian Mayfield, Frank Silvera, Roscoe Lee Browne, Juanita Moore

Uphill All the Way
US 1985 86m colour
Melroy/Guardian (Burr Smidt, David L. Ford)

In the early 1900s, two down-and-out confidence tricksters are mistaken for bank robbers and chased across Texas.
Raucous and depressingly unamusing comedy, dependent on heavy-handed slapstick; its two country-singing stars fail to transfer their hit-making abilities to the screen.
wd Frank Q. Dobbs *ph* Roland 'Ozzie' Smith *m* Dennis M. Pratt *pd* Hal Matheny *ed* Chuck Weiss
☆ Roy Clark, Mel Tillis, Burl Ives, Glen Campbell, Trish Van Devere, Elaine Joyce, Jacque Lynn Colton, Frank Gorshin, Sheb Wooley, Richard Paul
† Burt Reynolds appears uncredited.

Upperworld
US 1934 75m bw
Warner
A society-conscious wife drives her husband into the arms of a girl from the Bronx.
Smooth romantic melodrama with a murder angle; dated but enjoyable.
w Ben Markson *story* Ben Hecht *d* Roy del Ruth
☆ Warren William, Mary Astor, Ginger Rogers, Andy Devine, J. Carrol Naish, Henry O'Neill

The Ups and Downs of a Handyman
GB 1975 90m colour
KFR/Nigel A. Marsh (Kenneth F. Rowles)
aka: *Confessions of an Odd-Job Man*
A newly-wed couple move to the country, where the husband finds work servicing the bored wives and daiughters of the locals.
Trivial sex farce, of the kind that brought the British film industry to its nadir in the mid-70s.
w Derrick Slater, John Sealey *d* John Sealey *ph* Doug Hill *m* Vic Elms *ed* Jim Atkinson, John Carr
☆ Barry Stokes, Gay Soper, Sue Lloyd, Bob Todd, Chic Murray, Robert Dorning, Valerie Leon, Penny Meredith, Helli Louise, John Blythe
'Repressive, sniggeringly unfunny soft-core farce.' – *MFB*

Upstairs and Downstairs
GB 1959 101m Eastmancolor
Rank (Betty E. Box)
Newlyweds have trouble with maids and au pair girls.
Glossy, cheerful, empty-headed domestic comedy.
w Frank Harvey *novel* Ronald Scott Thorn *d* Ralph Thomas *ph* Ernest Steward *m* Philip Green
☆ Michael Craig, Anne Heywood, Mylène Demongeot, James Robertson Justice, Sidney James, Daniel Massey, Claudia Cardinale, Joan Hickson, Joan Sims

'Evil Lives Closer Than You Think.'
The Upstairs Neighbor
US 1994 91m colour
Brandon Foley/Matt Devlen

A novelist begins to believe that the man who lives above him is tapping his phone and involved in occult practices.
A low-budget venture into paranoia and madness, which transverses familiar territory, leaving no trace as it goes.
wd James Merendino *ph* Greg Littlewood *m* Bruce Langhorne *ad* Charlotte Malmlof *ed* Esther P. Russell
☆ Sebastian Gutierrez, Rustam Branaman, Christina Fulton, Kane Picoy
'An effective, if derivative, slice of mood-driven entertainment.' – *Variety*

Uptown Saturday Night *
US 1974 104m Technicolor
Warner/Verdon/First Artists (Melville Tucker)

Three friends pursue crooks who have inadvertently stolen a winning lottery ticket.
Witless but high-spirited star comedy for blacks, with a variety of sordid backgrounds.
w Richard Wesley *d* Sidney Poitier *ph* Fred J. Koenekamp *m* Tom Scott
☆ Sidney Poitier, Bill Cosby, Harry Belafonte, Flip Wilson, Roscoe Lee Browne, Richard Pryor, Rosalind Cash, Paula Kelly
'If it had been filmed with a white cast this collection of atrophied comedy routines would have been indistinguishable from a Monogram farce of the forties.' – *David McGillivray*

The Upturned Glass *
GB 1947 86m bw
GFD/Triton (Sydney Box, James Mason)
A Harley Street surgeon murders the woman responsible for the death of the girl he loved.
Rather pointless psychopathology with an ill-explained title; an interesting example of a top star not knowing what's best for him.
w Jon P. Monaghan, Pamela Kellino *d* Lawrence Huntington *ph* Reg Wyer *m* Bernard Stevens *md* Muir Mathieson *ad* Andrew Mazzei *ed* Alan Osbiston
☆ James Mason, Pamela Kellino, Rosamund John, Ann Stephens, Henry Oscar, Morland Graham, Brefni O'Rorke
'The psychology is genuine; so too is the tension; the camera plays some good quiet tricks.' – *William Whitebait*

Upworld
US 1990 88m DeLuxe
Lightning/Interscope/Trilogy (Robert W. Cort, Scott Kroopf, Pen Densham, Richard Lewis)
An undercover cop uncovers corruption and crime with the aid of a gnome called Gnorm from an underground world.
An unsuccessful oddity, with its combination of a paranoid thriller, full of guns and explosions, and an underdeveloped fantasy about a diminutive creature; it is too violent for small children, and too silly for older ones.
w Pen Densham, John Watson *d* Stan Winston *ph* Bojan Bazelli *m* Richard Gibbs *pd* Marcia Hinds *ed* Marcus Manton *sp* Stan Winston
☆ Anthony Michael Hall, Jerry Orbach, Claudia Christian, Eli Danker, Mark Harelik, Robert Z'Dar

Uranus **
France 1990 99m colour
Artificial Eye/Renn/DD/Sofica (Patrick Bordier)

In the aftermath of the Second World War, political rivalries between Communists and Fascists, Resistance fighters and collaborators, tear apart the inhabitants of a small French town.
Excellently acted and engaging, though wordy, account of postwar witch hunts.
w Claude Berri, Arlette Langmann *novel* Marcel Aymé *d* Claude Berri *ph* Renato Berta *m* Jean-Claude Petit *ad* Bernard Vezat *ed* Hervé de Luze
☆ Philippe Noiret, Gérard Depardieu, Jean-Pierre Marielle, Michel Blanc, Gérard Desarthe, Michel Galabru, Fabrice Luchini
'The intrinsic interest of the subject matter holds us for a while, which is just as well, because this dull, talkative film is dramatically barren.' – *Philip French, Observer*
'The film makes the case against the totalitarian intolerance of empowered Stalinism – in French practice it often amounted to a settling of personal scores – with persuasive force.' – *Richard Schickel, Time*

Urban Cowboy
US 1980 135m Movielab Panavision
Paramount (Robert Evans, Irving Azoff)

A rural Texan finds it difficult to succeed in the big city.
Unpleasant and uninteresting star melodrama with a plot vaguely reminiscent of the first part of An American Tragedy.
w James Bridges *novel* Aaron Latham *d* James Bridges *ph* Ray Villalobos *m* various songs *pd* Stephen Grimes
☆ John Travolta, Debra Winger, Scott Glenn, Madolyn Smith
'A fatuous vehicle for John Travolta, requiring him to stride (stiffly and expressionlessly) through various macho torments ... the two-hour-plus running time, incorporating a wealth of cliché characters, is excruciatingly protracted.' – *Tom Milne, MFB*

Urban Ghost Story *
GB 1998 88m Soho Images
Visual Entertainment/Ratpack/Living Spirit (Chris Jones)
After a 12-year-old Glaswegian girl has a near-death experience during a car crash, a poltergeist haunts the tower-block flat where she lives with her mother and brother.
Effective small-scale drama, set in a run down council estate that contributes to the sense of something unpleasant lurking around the corner.
w Geneviève Jolliffe, Chris Jones *d* Geneviève Jolliffe *ph* Jon Walker *m* Rupert Gregson-Williams *pd* Simon Pickup *ed* Eddie Hamilton
☆ Jason Connery (John Fox), Stephanie Buttle (Kate Fisher), Heather Ann Foster (Lizzie Fisher), Nicola Stapleton (Kerrie), James Cosmo (Minister), Elizabeth Berrington (Mrs Ash)
'One of the most credible studies of spectral obsession on film.' – *James Cameron-Wilson*

'It Happened To Someone Who Knows Someone You Know ... You're Next.'
Urban Legend
US 1998 100m colour Super 35
Columbia TriStar/Phoenix (Neil H. Moritz, Gina Matthews, Michael McDonnell)

A serial killer acts out urban legends, such as a driver ignoring a stuttering informant who was trying to tell him that there was someone with an axe hiding in the back of his car.
A horror movie that begins with a clever concept, though otherwise it offers the usual mix of multiple murders and shocks.
w Silvio Horta *d* Jamie Blanks *ph* James Chressanthis *m* Christopher Young *pd* Charles Breen *ed* Jay Cassidy
☆ Jared Leto, Alicia Witt, Rebecca Gayheart, Joshua Jackson, Loretta Devine, Tara Reid, Michael Rosenbaum, Robert Englund
'A silly but not unlikeable formula horror picture.' – *Kim Newman, Empire*

'Legends Never die.'
Urban Legends: Final Cut
US 2000 98m DeLuxe Panavision
Columbia/Phoenix (Neal H. Moritz, Gina Matthews, Richard Luke Rothschild)

A student filmmaker begins a film about urban legends while the cast of another student movie die one by one.
Feeble slasher movie, derivative of a dozen or more other horrors.
w Paul Harris Boardman, Scott Derrickson *d* John Ottman *ph* Brian Pearson *m* John Ottman *pd* Mark Zuelzke *ed* John Ottman, Rob Kobrin *sp* Gajdecki Visual Effects *cos* Marie-Sylvie Deveau, Trysha Bakker
☆ Jennifer Morrison (Amy Mayfield), Matthew Davis (Travis/Trevor), Hart Bochner (Professor Solomon), Loretta Devine (Reese), Joseph Lawrence (Graham), Anson Mount (Toby), Eva Mendez (Vanessa), Jessica Cauffiel (Sandra), Anthony Anderson (Stan), Michael Bacall (Dirk), Marco Hofschneider (Simon), Chas Lawther (Dean Patterson)
'It takes a special talent to make a film quite as bad as this.' – *James Christopher, Times*

'It's Judgement Day'
Urban Menace
US 1999 76m colour
Filmwerks/Ice-T (Tom Karnowski, Gary Schmoeller)

A minister takes revenge on those who burned his church and killed his family.
Cheap, shoddy, violent and incoherent movie that ranks among the worst ever made.
w Hannah Blue, Andrew Markell *d* Albert Pyun *ph* Philip Alan Waters *m* Ice-T, Tony Riparetti *pd* Nenad Pecur *ed* Errin Vasquez
☆ Ice-T, Snoop Dogg, Fat Joe, Big Pun, T J Storm, Karen Dyer, Ernie Hudson Jnr, Rob Ladesich, Tahitia

Urga **

France/USSR 1991 120m colour
Hachette Première/Studio Trite (Michel Seydoux)

US title: *Close to Eden*

A Mongolian herdsman rescues a Russian lorry-driver who crashes into a river and takes him home to his family.

Delightful and exuberant fable of a clash between urban and rural ways of life.

w Nikita Mikhalkov, Roustam Ibraguimbekov *d* Nikita Mikhalkov *ph* Villenn Kaluta *m* Eduard Artemiev *pd* Alexei Levchenko *ed* Joelle Hache

☆ Bayaertu, Badema, Vlodimir Gostukhin, Babuskha

'It hardly advances cinematic art, but story and characters resonate with life.' – *Geoff Brown, The Times*

foreign language film

Urotsukidō: see *Legend of the Overfiend*

Urotsukidōji II: see *Legend of the Demon Womb*

Urotsukidoxji III: see *Legend of the Demon Womb*

Ursus (dubbed)

Italy/Spain 1961 95m Eastmancolor
Totalscope
UA/Ciné Italia/Atenea (Italo Zingarelli)

aka: *Mighty Ursus*

Ursus returns from the wars to discover that the woman he loves has been kidnapped.

Mundane muscle-man epic, with a dreary narrative and very little action.

w Giuseppe Mangione, Sergio Sollima, Giuliano Carnimeo *d* Carlo Campogalliani *ph* Eloy Mella *m* Roman Vlad *ad* Romoloa Girolami *ed* Jolanda Benvenuti, Julia Pena

☆ Ed Fury, Cristina Gajoni, Moira Orfei, Mary Marlon, Mario Scaccia

'The stiff performances and excruciating dialogue come as no surprise, but even the spectacle is gracelessly mounted.' – *David McGillivray*

Ursus and the Tartar Princess (dubbed)

France/Italy 1961 80m Technicolor
Techniscope
Explorer Film '58/CFFP (Nino Battiferri)

In 17th-century Poland, a captured nobleman falls in love with the daughter of the leader of an invading Tartar army.

A romantic epic, with strongman Ursus's role reduced to a walk-on; it is a little different from the usual Italian spectacles in preaching a gospel of peace between scenes of swordplay and bloodshed.

w Remigio del Grosso (English dialogue John Hart) *d* (English-language version) Richard McNamara *ph* Anchise Brizzi *m* A. F. Lavagnino *ad* Antonio Visone *ed* Antonietta Zita

☆ Yoko Tani, Ettore Manni, Joe Robinson, Akim Tamiroff, Roland Lesaffre, Maria Grazia Spina

Used Cars *

US 1980 111m Metrocolor
Columbia (Bob Gale)

For the love of his boss's daughter, a fast-talking car salesman saves a used-car lot from being taken over by a mean-spirited rival.

Vigorous broad comedy, amusing enough if you're feeling indulgent.

w Robert Zemeckis, Bob Gale *d* Robert Zemeckis *ph* Donald M. Morgan *m* Patrick Williams *pd* Peter M. Jamison *ed* Michael Kahn

☆ Kurt Russell, Gerrit Graham, Frank McRae, Deborah Harmon, Jack Russell

'A classic screwball fantasy – a neglected modern comedy that's like a more restless and visually high-spirited version of the W. C. Fields pictures.' – *Pauline Kael, New Yorker*

'A story about love, family and other embarrassments.'

Used People *

US 1992 116m DeLuxe
TCF/Largo (Peggy Rajski)

An Italian widower courts a Jewish widow whom he has loved from a distance for more than 20 years.

A romantic comedy for the middle-aged, leisurely in pace, giving its cast room to display their skills.

w Todd Graff *play* *The Grandma Plays* by Todd Graff *d* Beeban Kidron *ph* David Watkin *m* Rachel Portman *pd* Stuart Wurtzel *ed* John Tintori

☆ Shirley MacLaine, Marcello Mastroianni, Bob Dishy, Kathy Bates, Jessica Tandy, Marcia Gay Harden, Lee Wallace, Louis Guss

'An actors' showcase, with heightened performances by the ensemble eschewing the naturalism favored by mainstream fare.' – *Variety*

'Funny, touching and very well-observed ... But it finally exposes itself as clichéd, a little shapeless and too long.' – *Derek Malcolm, Guardian*

'Five Criminals. One Line Up. No Coincidence.'

The Usual Suspects ***

US 1995 105m Technicolor Panavision
Polygram/Spelling/Blue Parrot/Bad Hat Harry/Rosco (Bryan Singer, Michael McDonnell)

Five crooks, who meet in a police line-up and decide to work together on a couple of robberies, come to believe that they are being manipulated by a mysterious master criminal.

Excellent, gripping thriller that plays tricks with its audience, leading it down one blind alley after another, dealing in deliberate confusion and double-cross. Its refusal to come clean until its final revelation may infuriate some, but it is part of its appeal, aided by some nicely edgy performances from the actors.

w Christopher McQuarrie *d* Bryan Singer *ph* Newton Thomas Sigel *m* John Ottman *pd* Howard Cummings *ed* John Ottman

☆ Gabriel Byrne, Stephen Baldwin, Chazz Palminteri, Kevin Pollak, Pete Postlethwaite, Kevin Spacey, Suzy Amis, Giancarlo Esposito, Dan Hedaya, Benicio del Toro, Paul Bartel

'What is most rewarding about *The Usual Suspects* is not method acting or directorial flair, but its vivid, audacious, relentless intelligence.' – *Stephen Amidon, Sunday Times*

'An ironic, bang-up thriller about the wages of crime. A terrific cast of exciting actors socks over this absorbing complicated yarn.' – *Todd McCarthy, Variety*

Kevin Spacey; Christopher McQuarrie
Christopher McQuarrie

Utomlennye Solntsem: see *Burnt by the Sun*

Utopia: see *Robinson Crusoeland*

Utu ***

New Zealand 1983 118m Fujicolour
Glitteron (Geoff Murphy, Don Blakeney)

In New Zealand in the 1870s, a Maori, whose family is massacred by the army, and a farmer, whose wife is killed by the Maoris, are both obsessed by revenge.

Powerful and absorbing drama of imperialistic and colonial attitudes, set against wild, open spaces.

w Geoff Murphy, Keith Aberdein *d* Geoff Murphy *ph* Graeme Cowley *m* John Charles *pd* Ron Highfield *ed* Michael Horton, Ian John

☆ Anzac Wallace, Bruno Lawrence, Wi Kuki Kaa, Kelly Johnson, Tim Elliott, Tanya Bristowe, Ilona Rodgers, Merata Mita, Tom Polan

Utvandrarna: see *The Emigrants*

Utz *

GB/Germany/Italy 1992 colour
BBC/NDR/Academy/Cine Electric/Viva (John Goldschmidt)

An American art dealer tries to discover what has happened to a priceless collection of porcelain figures.

Gently civilized entertainment on acquisitive and obsessive pleasures, although one lacking much popular appeal.

w Hugh Whitemore *novel* Bruce Chatwin *d* George Sluizer *ph* Gerard Vandenberg *m* Nicola Piovani *pd* Karel Vacek *ed* Lin Friedman

☆ Armin Mueller-Stahl, Brenda Fricker, Peter Riegert, Paul Scofield, Gaye Brown, Miriam Karlin, Pauline Melville, Vera Soukupova

'The polyglot cast and crew can't provide a cohesive basis on which to pin a frustratingly fragmented screenplay.' – *Variety*

V. I. Warshawski
US 1991 89m Technicolor
Warner/Hollywood Pictures/Silver Screen Partners IV/ Chestnut Hill (Jeffrey Lurie)

A female private eye is hired to investigate the murder of a businessman.
Exceedingly dull thriller intended to introduce to film a tough feminist detective from fiction. Its failure to find an audience is likely to mean that the planned sequels will not appear.
w Edward Taylor, David Aaron Cohen, Nick Thiel *novel* Indemnity Only by Sara Paretsky *d* Jeff Kanew *ph* Jan Kiesser *m* Randy Edelman *pd* Barbara Ling *ed* C. Timothy O'Meara, Debra Neil
☆ Kathleen Turner, Jay O. Sanders, Charles Durning, Angela Goethals, Nancy Paul, Frederick Coffin, Charles McCaughan, Stephen Meadows, Wayne Knight
'The feebly-plotted movie comes over as a padded-out 90-minute episode of a routine private eye series, or more accurately the black box from a TV pilot that crashed shortly after take-off. It could be shown in film schools as an example of how not to adapt a novel for the screen.' – *Philip French, Observer*

Va Savoir **
France/Italy/Germany 2001 154m colour
Artificial Eye/France 2/VM/MikadoFilms/Kinowelt

aka: *Who Knows?*
In Paris, six characters in search of love change partners during a production of Pirandello's play *As You Desire Me*.
Witty, sophisticated, feather-light comedy of relationships based on illusion as much as truth, in the style of the French New Wave that Rivette helped to create in the 1960s.
w Christine Laurent, Pascal Bonitzer, Jacques Rivette *d* Jacques Rivette *ph* William Lubtchansky *ad* Manu de Chauvigny *ed* Nicole Lubtchansky
☆ Jeanne Balibar (Camille), Sergio Castellitto (Ugo), Jacques Bonnaffe (Pierre), Marianne Basler (Sonia), Helene de Fougerolles (Do), Bruno Todeschini (Arthur), Catherine Rouvel (Mother)
'A very cute title for a very cute piece of cinema. Don't miss it.' – *Peter Bradshaw, Guardian*
'An entrancing ensemble piece, directed with calm assurance, acted by a fine ensemble, and structured and scripted with wit and precision.' – *David Stratton, Variety*

Les Vacances de Monsieur Hulot: see *Monsieur Hulot's Holiday*

'A tale of violence, romance and madness.'
Vacas *
Spain 1992 96m colour
ICA/Sogetel (Ricardo Garcia Arrojos)

Rivalry and love between two families, linked by children, continue over three generations.
An intricate, enjoyable story of family feuds and affairs, agreeably tinged with fantasy.
w Julio Medem, Michael Gaztambide *d* Julio Medem *ph* Carles Gusi *m* Alberto Iglesias *ed* Maria Elena Sainz de Rozas
☆ Emma Suárez, Carmelo Gómez, Ana Torrent, Karra Elejalde, Klara Badiola, Txema Blasco
'With lush cinematography, energetic performances and a strong sense of the mystery and terror to be found in the Great Outdoors, pic lingers in the memory as impressive and unusual.' – *Variety*
'A poetic, boldly directed first film that serves notice of a promising talent.' – *Sheila Johnston, Independent*

Vacation from Marriage: see *Perfect Strangers (GB)*

La Vache et le Prisonnier: see *The Cow and I*

The Vagabond King
US 1956 88m Technicolor Vistavision
Paramount (Pat Duggan)
The life and loves of French medieval poet and rebel François Villon.
Shiny, antiseptic studio-set remake of an old musical warhorse.
w Ken Englund, Noel Langley *operetta* Rudolf Friml *d* Michael Curtiz *ph* Robert Burks *m/ly* Rudolf Friml, Brian Hooker, Johnny Burke *md* Victor Young *ad* Hans Dreier
☆ Oreste, Kathryn Grayson, Rita Moreno, Walter Hampden, Leslie Nielsen, Cedric Hardwicke, William Prince
† A 1930 version with Dennis King is lost. Non-musical versions of the story include *If I Were King*, in 1920 with William Farnum, 1928's *The Beloved Rogue* with John Barrymore, and in 1938 with Ronald Colman.
Hans Dreier

Vagabonde ***
France 1985 104m colour
Cine-Tamaris/A2/Ministère de la Culture

French title: *Sans Toit ni Loi*
aka: *Vagabond*
After a young woman is found frozen to death in a ditch, people tell of their experiences of her in the last weeks of her life, and of how she abandoned conventional living to become a tramp.
Disturbingly chill movie of the accidental collisions of people's lives, and the changes they cause, with an enigma at its centre.
wd Agnès Varda *ph* Patrick Blossier *m* Joanna Bruzdowicz *ed* Agnès Varda, Patricia Mazuy
☆ Sandrine Bonnaire, Macha Meril, Stéphane Freiss, Laurence Cortadellas, Marthe Jarnais, Yolande Moreau, Joel Fosse
† It won the Golden Lion award for best film at the Venice Film Festival in 1985.

'He's *not* home alone.'
The Vagrant
US/France 1992 91m DeLuxe
TCF/MGM/Pathé Communications/Brooksfilms/Canal+ (Gillian Richardson)

A paranoid office worker is persecuted by a murderous, evil-smelling tramp.
Mind-numbingly dreadful horror comedy, inane from start to finish.
w Richard Jefferies *d* Chris Walas *ph* Jack Wallner, John J. Connor *m* Christopher Young *pd* Michael Bolton *ed* Jay Ignaszewski *sp* Chris Walas
☆ Bill Paxton, Michael Ironside, Marshall Bell, Mitzi Kapture, Colleen Camp, Patrika Darbo

The Valachi Papers
France/Italy 1972 127m Technicolor
Euro France/de Laurentiis Intermarco (Dino de Laurentiis)

A convicted gangster talks to an FBI agent about his life in the Mafia.
Rough, violent gangster melodrama, none the better for being based on actual events.
w Stephen Geller *book* Peter Maas *d* Terence Young *ph* Aldo Tonti *m* Riz Ortolani
☆ Charles Bronson, Fred Valleca, Gerald S. O'Loughlin, Lino Ventura, Walter Chiari, Amedeo Nazzari, Joseph Wiseman
'One of the worst films ever made.' – *Peter Maas*

Valborgsmässoafton: see *Walpurgis Night*

The Valdez Horses
Italy/France/Spain 1973 97m Technicolor
De Laurentiis/Coral/Universal (Duilio Coletti)

aka: *Valdez, the Halfbreed*
US title: *Chino*
A loner who runs a stud farm in New Mexico is faced with the death of his horses when he falls in love with the sister of a wealthy rancher.
Odd little Western that denies its audience the expected denoument: Bronson plays against his usual role as a reluctant but vengeful killer, though otherwise he remains his taciturn self.
w Dino Maiuri, Massimo De Rita, Clair Huffaker *novel* The Valdez Horses by Lee Hoffman *d* John Sturges *ph* Armando Nannuzzi *m* Guido De Angelis, Maurizio De Angelis *ad* Mario Garbuglia *ed* Vanio Amici, Peter Zinner
☆ Charles Bronson (Chino Valdez), Jill Ireland (Louise), Vincent Van Patten (Jamie Wagner), Marcel Bozzuffi (Maral), Melissa Chimenti (Indian Girl), Fausto Tozzi (Cruz), Ettore Manni (Sheriff), Adolfo Thous (Cayate), Florencio Amarilla (Little Bear), Corrado Gaipa (Indian), Diana Lorys (Indian)

Valdez Is Coming
US 1970 90m DeLuxe
UA/Norlan/Ira Steiner

A Mexican confronts a rancher who has double-crossed him.
Simply conceived Western which doesn't quite manage to be the classic intended.
w Roland Kibbee, David Rayfiel *novel* Elmore Leonard *d* Edwin Sherin *ph* Gabor Pogany *m* Charles Gross
☆ Burt Lancaster, Susan Clark, Jon Cypher, Barton Heyman, Frank Silvera

Valdez, the Halfbreed: see *The Valdez Horses*

Vale Abraao: see *Abraham Valley*

'Fall In Love with Terror!'
'Love hurts.'
Valentine
US/Australia 2001 96m Technicolor Panavision
Warner/Village Roadshow/NPV (Dylan Sellars)

13 years after being humiliated at school, a killer in a Cupid mask begins murdering former classmates.
Run-of-the-mill slasher movie that occasionally works up a little suspense, though it owes too much to Carrie, *and many other masked killer efforts, to surprise.*
w Donna Powers, Wayne Powers, Gretchen J. Berg, Aaron Harberts *novel* Tom Savage *d* Jamie Blanks *ph* Rick Bota *m* Don Davis *pd* Stephen Geaghan *ed* Steve Mirkovich
☆ David Boreanaz (Adam Carr), Denise Richards (Paige Prescott), Marley Shelton (Kate Davies), Jessica Capshaw (Dorothy Wheeler), Jessica Cauffiel (Lily), Katherine Heigl (Shelley), Fulvio Cecere (Det Vaughn), Daniel Cosgrove (Campbell), Johnny Whitworth (Max Ives), Hedy Burress (Ruthie)
'A straightforward slasher pic that's acceptably scary until a weak finale.' – *Dennis Harvey, Variety*

Valentino
US 1951 105m Technicolor
Columbia (Edward Small)
An Italian immigrant to the US becomes a world-famous romantic film star but dies young.
Disastrously flat attempt to recapture the feel of Hollywood in the twenties as a background to a flatulent romance.
w George Bruce *d* Lewis Allen *ph* Harry Stradling *m* Heinz Roemheld
☆ Anthony Dexter, Eleanor Parker, Richard Carlson, Patricia Medina, Joseph Calleia, Dona Drake, Lloyd Gough, Otto Kruger
'One can almost see the decorated border round the words ... it mixes fact, speculation, needless inaccuracy and bathos.' – *Gavin Lambert*
'The dialogue is unbelievably ham, the "entirely imaginary" story commonplace; the players deserve sympathy.' – *Richard Mallett, Punch*

Valentino *
GB 1977 127m DeLuxe
UA/Aperture/Chartoff-Winkler (Harry Benn)

Reporters quiz celebrities at a star's funeral, and his eccentric life unfolds.
Sensationalist 'exposé' of Valentino's rise to fame, with excellent period detail but no sympathy for its subject.
w Ken Russell, Mardik Martin *book* Brad Steiger, Chaw Mank *d* Ken Russell *ph* Peter Suschitzky *m* Ferde Grofe, Stanley Black *ad* Philip Harrison
☆ Rudolf Nureyev, Leslie Caron, Michelle Phillips, Carol Kane, Felicity Kendal, Huntz Hall, David de Keyser, Alfred Marks, Anton Diffring, Jennie Linden, John Justin
'By attaching the names of actual people to his sadomasochistic fantasies, the director, Ken Russell, gives the picture a nasty inside-joke appeal.' – *Pauline Kael*

Valentino Returns
US 1989 90m Alpha Cine
Owl/Vidmark (Peter Hoffman, David Wisnievitz)

The adolescent son of a mismatched couple buys a pink Cadillac in order to impress his girlfriend.
Low-key, lacklustre drama stuck in a familiar groove.
w Leonard Gardner *story* Christ Has Returned to Earth and Preaches Here Nightly by Leonard Gardner *d* Peter Hoffman *ph* Jerzy Zielinski *ad* Woody Romine *ed* Denine Rowan
☆ Barry Tubb, Frederic Forrest, Veronica Cartwright, Jenny Wright, Macon McCalman, Kit McDonough, Seth Isler, Miguel Ferrer, Leonard Gardner

Valerie A Týden Divu: see *Valerie and Her Week of Wonders*

Valerie and Her Week of Wonders **
Czechoslovakia 1970 77m Eastmancolor
Contemporary/Ceskoslovensky/Barrandov

original title: *Valerie A Týden Divu*
A young girl on the verge of puberty dreams of vampires and her own death, burned as a witch by a priest who tried to rape her.
A surrealist vision of the awakening of sexuality, full of startling images drawn from myth and religious ritual, somewhat like a more explicity Freudian version of Alice in Wonderland.
w Jaromil Jires, Ester Krumbachová *story* Vitezlav Nezval *d* Jaromil Jires *ph* Jan Curik *m* Jan Klusák *ad* Jan Oliva *ed* Josef Valusiak
☆ Jaroslava Schallerová, Helena Anýzová, Petr Kopriva, Jüiri Prymek, Jan Klusák, Libuse Komancová, Karel Engel, Alena Stojáková
'The real and the unreal are disturbingly fused, while the images are continually eloquent.' – *Gordon Gow, Films and Filming*

The Valley of Decision *
US 1945 119m bw
MGM (Edwin H. Knopf)

In old Pittsburgh, an Irish housemaid marries the master's son.
Trouble at t' mill epic romance, American style; starrily cast but not excitingly made.

w John Meehan, Sonya Levien *novel* Marcia Davenport *d* Tay Garnett *ph* Joseph Ruttenberg *m* Herbert Stothart
☆ Greer Garson, Gregory Peck, Lionel Barrymore, Donald Crisp, Preston Foster, Gladys Cooper, Marsha Hunt, Reginald Owen, Dan Duryea, Jessica Tandy, Barbara Everest, Marshall Thompson
Herbert Stothart, Greer Garson

Valley of Fury: see *Chief Crazy Horse*

'Cowboys Battle Monsters In The Strangest Roundup Of All!'

The Valley of Gwangi
US 1968 95m Technicolor
Warner/Morningside (Charles H. Schneer)
Cowboys and scientists discover prehistoric monsters in a 'forbidden' Mexican Valley.
Tedious adventure yarn enhanced by good special effects.
w William E. Best *d* Jim O'Connolly *ph* Erwin Hillier *m* Jerome Moross *sp Ray Harryhausen*
☆ Richard Carlson, Laurence Naismith, James Franciscus, Gila Golan, Freda Jackson

Valley of the Dolls *
US 1967 123m DeLuxe Panavision
TCF/Red Lion (David Weisbart)
An innocent young actress is corrupted by Broadway and Hollywood, and takes to drugs.
Cliché-ridden but good-looking road-to-ruin melodrama from a bitchy bestseller; production values high, but the whole thing goes over the top at the end.
w Helen Deutsch, Dorothy Kingsley *novel* Jacqueline Susann *d* Mark Robson *ph William H. Daniels* *m* André Previn *md* John Williams *ad* Jack Martin Smith, Richard Day
☆ Barbara Parkins, Patty Duke, Susan Hayward, Paul Burke, Sharon Tate, Martin Milner, Tony Scotti, Charles Drake, Alex Davion, Lee Grant, Robert H. Harris

'What kind of pills do you take to sit through a film like this?' – *The Golden Turkey Awards*

'A skilfully deceptive imitation of a real drama … on a closer look the characters turn out to be images that have almost nothing to do with people.' – *Christian Science Monitor*

'One of the most stupefyingly clumsy films ever made by alleged professionals.' – *Joseph Morgenstern, Newsweek*

† Judy Garland was originally slated to play the Susan Hayward part.
John Williams

Valley of the Giants
US 1938 79m Technicolor
Warner
A lumberman fights pirates to preserve his beloved redwoods.
Routine outdoor thick ear to which colour lent the semblance of freshness.
w Seton I. Miller, Michael Fessier *novel* Peter B. Kyne *d* William Keighley
☆ Wayne Morris, Claire Trevor, Frank McHugh, Alan Hale, Donald Crisp, Charles Bickford

'A yarn which contains nearly all the proven surefire elements of the successful outdoor picture.' – *Variety*

† This was the third version of the story; the first, in 1919, starred Wallace Reid; the second, in 1927, starred Milton Sills. The 1952 movie *The Big Trees*, with Kirk Douglas, had a suspiciously similar storyline.

Valley of the Kings
US 1954 86m Eastmancolor
MGM
Archaeologists fight looters in the tomb of a Pharaoh.
Thin as drama, with little action or suspense and dispirited acting, this hokum piece nevertheless benefits from splendid locations.
w Robert Pirosh, Karl Tunberg *d* Robert Pirosh *ph* Robert Surtees *m* Miklos Rozsa
☆ Robert Taylor, Eleanor Parker, Carlos Thompson, Kurt Kasznar, Victor Jory

Valley of the Sun
US 1942 79m bw
RKO (Graham Baker)
A government spy in old Arizona outwits a crooked Indian agent.
Cheapjack Western with nothing to commend it.
w Horace McCoy *story* Clarence Budington Kelland *d* George Marshall *ph* Harry J. Wild *m* Paul Sawtell
☆ James Craig, Lucille Ball, Dean Jagger, Billy Gilbert, Cedric Hardwicke, Peter Whitney, Tom Tyler, Antonio Moreno, George Cleveland

Valley of the Zombies
US 1946 56m bw
Republic
A big city zombie goes on a murder spree.
Entirely unpersuasive hokum which wouldn't chill a baby. No valley is apparent.
w The McGowans *d* Philip Ford
☆ Ian Keith, Robert Livingston, Adrian Booth, Thomas Jackson, Charles Trowbridge

Valmont
France/GB 1989 137m colour
Orion/Claude Berri/Renn (Paul Rassam, Michael Hausman)
In the 1780s, two aristocrats conspire in the seduction of a young and virginal bride-to-be.
A playful adaptation and one that suggests a fancy dress party rather than a period film, with the tragic ending of the original being altered into something more upbeat and cynical.
w Jean-Claude Carrière *novel Les Liaisons Dangereuses* by Choderlos de Laclos *d* Milos Forman *ph* Miroslav Ondricek *m* Christopher Palmer *pd* Pierre Guffroy *ed* Alan Heim, Nena Danevic
☆ Colin Firth, Annette Bening, Meg Tilly, Fairuza Balk, Sian Phillips, Jeffrey Jones, Henry Thomas, Fabia Drake, T. P. McKenna, Isla Blair, Ronald Lacey
† A rival, and better, version of the novel was filmed almost simultaneously as *Dangerous Liaisons* (qv).

Les Valseuses **
France 1974 118m Eastmancolor
CAPAC/UPF/SN (Paul Claudon)
aka: *Making It; Getting It Up*
US title: *Going Places*
The adventures of two high-spirited layabouts and petty thieves in their wanderings among easy money and willing women.
Enjoyable, though amoral, comedy of two incompetents on the make, lightened by the engaging interplay between its two leads; as it's a French buddy-buddy movie, the male bonding extends to sex.
w Bertrand Blier, Philippe Dumarçay *novel* Bertrand Blier *d* Bertrand Blier *ph* Bruno Nuytten *m* Stéphane Grappelli *ad* Jean-Jacques Caziot *ed* Kénout Peltier
☆ *Gérard Depardieu, Patrick Dewaere, Miou-Miou,* Jeanne Moreau, Christian Alers, Brigitte Fossey, Michel Peyrelon, Gérard Boucaron, Jacques Chailleux, Éva Damien, Isabelle Huppert

'An explosively funny erotic farce – both a celebration and a satire of men's daydreams – and some people find its gusto revolting in much the same way that the bursting comic force of the sexual hyperbole in Henry Miller's *Tropic of Cancer* was thought revolting.' – *Pauline Kael*

'This dispiriting romp.' – *Sight and Sound*

† The French title is slang for 'testicles'.

Value for Money
GB 1955 93m Technicolor Vistavision
Rank/Group Films (Sergei Nolbandov)
A Yorkshire businessman determines to broaden his outlook, and falls in love with a London showgirl.
Highly undistinguished north country romantic farce which wastes a good production and cast.
w R. F. Delderfield, William Fairchild *novel* Derick Boothroyd *d* Ken Annakin *ph* Geoffrey Unsworth *m* Malcolm Arnold
☆ John Gregson, Diana Dors, Susan Stephen, Derek Farr, Frank Pettingell, Jill Adams, *Ernest Thesiger*, Charles Victor, Joan Hickson

Vamos a Matar, Compañeros!: see *Compañeros*

Vamp
US 1986 94m Metrocolor
New World/Balcor (Donald P. Borchers)
Three college boys in search of a stripper find themselves in a den of vampires.
A cheap and gory horror flick, luridly photographed, and most likely to be enjoyed by colour-blind teenagers.
wd Richard Wenk *story* Donald P. Borchers, Richard Wenk *ph* Elliot Davis *m* Jonathan Elias *pd* Alan Roderick-Jones *ed* Marc Grossman *sp* Greg Cannom
☆ Grace Jones, Chris Makepeace, Sandy Baron, Robert Rusler, Dedee Pfeiffer, Gedde Watanabe, Billy Drago

Vampira
GB 1974 88m colour
Columbia/World Film Services (Jack H. Wiener)
US title: *Old Dracula*
A vampire count lures beauty-contest winners to his castle and uses their blood to revive his dead wife.
Would-be spoof which falls flat on its fangs.
w Jeremy Lloyd *d* Clive Donner *ph* Tony Richmond *m* David Whitaker
☆ David Niven, Teresa Graves, Peter Bayliss, Jennie Linden, Linda Hayden, Nicky Henson, Bernard Bresslaw, Veronica Carlson

The Vampire
US 1957 74m bw
UA/Gardner-Levy
A research scientist takes bat essence and becomes a vampire.
Silly attempt to turn a legend into science fiction: more risible than sinister.
w Pat Fielder *d* Paul Landres *ph* Jack Mackenzie *m* Gerald Fried
☆ John Beal, Coleen Gray, Kenneth Tobey, Lydia Reed

'Mad? I, who have solved the secret of life, you call me mad?'

The Vampire Bat
US 1932 71m bw
Majestic (Phil Goldstone)
A mad doctor kills townsfolk in search of 'blood substitute'.
Primitive but vigorous low budget chiller.
w Edward T. Lowe *d* Frank Strayer *ph* Ira Morgan
☆ Lionel Atwill, Fay Wray, Melvyn Douglas, Maude Eburne, George E. Stone, Dwight Frye, Lionel Belmore

'Shiver picture, well enough done but coming too late in the cycle to take any money.' – *Variety*

'The Greatest Blood Show On Earth!'

Vampire Circus
GB 1971 87m colour
Rank/Hammer (Wilbur Stark)
In 1825 a plague-ridden village is visited by a circus of animal vampires.
Silly but quite inventive horror thriller.
w Judson Kinberg *d* Robert Young *ph* Moray Grant *m* David Whittaker *ad* Scott MacGregor *ed* Peter Musgrave
☆ Adrienne Corri, Laurence Payne, Thorley Walters, John Moulder Brown, Elizabeth Seal, Lynne Frederick, Robin Hunter

Vampire Cop
US 1993 81m colour
Overseas (Manette Rosen, Marion Zola)
A female cop, bitten by a vampire serial killer, begins to crave blood while trying to track down the monster.
Nasty little shocker, flatly acted apart from its over-the-top vampire.
w John Weidner, Ken Lamplugh *d* Joel Bender *ph* Alan Caso *m* Emilio Kauderer *pd* Don Day *ed* Mark Helfrich, Joel Bender *sp* S.O.T.A. F/X
☆ Michelle Owens, Michael McMillen, Robert Miano, B. J. Gates, Michael Shawn, Gregory A. Greer

'Some smart one-liners and a tough heroine are the plus points in an otherwise average vampire yarn.' – *Sight and Sound*

Vampire in Brooklyn
US 1995 101m DeLuxe
Paramount (Eddie Murphy, Mark Lipsky)
The last surviving Caribbean vampire goes to Brooklyn in search of a mate.
A dire attempt to combine Murphy's cocksure humour and the mechanics of a horror movie; the result is an unlovely and unfunny mess.
w Charles Murphy, Michael Lucker, Chris Parker *story* Eddie Murphy, Vernon Lynch Jnr, Charles Murphy *d* Wes Craven *ph* Mark Irwin *m* J. Peter Robinson *ad* Gary Diamond, Cynthia Charette *ed* Patrick Lussier *sp* Kurtzman, Nicotero, Berger EFX; Fantasy II
☆ Eddie Murphy, Angela Bassett, Allen Payne, Kadeem Hardison, John Witherspoon, Zakes Mokae, Joanna Cassidy, Simbi Khali

'Mixes lame blood-pellet effects with lame gags. Its one lingering image is that of Eddie Murphy trying, and failing, to rise from the dead.' – *Owen Gleiberman, Entertainment Weekly*

'Even the dead can love.'

The Vampire Lovers
GB 1970 91m Technicolor
MGM-EMI/Hammer/AIP (Harry Fine, Michael Style)
A lady vampire worms her way into several noble households.
Reasonably close retelling of Sheridan Le Fanu's Carmilla, complete with lesbian love scenes. Adequate production but not much spirit.
w Tudor Gates, Harry Fine, Michael Styles *story Carmilla* by Sheridan Le Fanu *d* Roy Ward Baker *ph* Moray Grant *m* Harry Robinson *ad* Scott MacGregor *ed* James Needs
☆ Ingrid Pitt, Peter Cushing, Pippa Steele, Madeleine Smith, George Cole, Dawn Addams, Douglas Wilmer, Kate O'Mara

La Vampire Nue (dubbed)
France 1969 90m colour
Tigon/Films ABC (Jean Lavie)
aka: *The Naked Vampire*
A son discovers that his father is a member of a private club given over to investigations of ritual suicide, sex and vampirism.
A perversely unconventional horror movie, more concerned with surrealist ornament, nudity and fetishistic costumes than narrative; the director's interest rarely strays beyond striking images and interior decor, but you may be amused by his pretension.
wd Jean Rollin *ph* Jean-Jacques Renon *m* Yvon Serault *ad* Jio Berk
☆ Christine François, Olivier Martin, Maurice Lemaître, Bernard Musson, Jean Aron, Ursule Pauly, Michel Delahaye

'The essential thinness of the script is reinforced by Rollin's tendency to strive for a sustained mood of mystery by holding shots for several seconds after the action has been completed. Unfortunately, the cumulative effect of these delays is a deadeningly slow pace which appears more contrived than supernatural.' – *David McGillivray, MFB*

'One of Rollin's most enjoyable films.' – *Peter Tombs and Cathal Tohill, NFT*

† The British video release runs for 82m. The film was cut to 79m on its British cinema release in 1973.

Vampire of Venice: see *Vampires in Venice*

Vampire Thrills: see *Le Frisson des Vampires*

Vampire Woman: see *Crypt of the Living Dead*

Vampires: see *John Carpenter's Vampires*

Vampires in Venice
Italy 1988 90m colour
Scena/Reteitalia (Augusto Caminito)
original title: *Nosferatu a Venezia*
aka: *Vampire of Venice*
In Venice, where Nosferatu was last seen 200 years earlier, a princess summons the vampire during a seance.
Despite an atmospheric opening, a muddled and unenticing addition to the endless round of vampire movies, with Kinski reprising his role without visible enthusiasm.

wd Augusto Caminito *story Alberto Alfieri, Leandro Luchetti ph* Antonio Nardi *m* Luigi Ceccarelli, Vangelis *pd* Joseph Teichner, Luca Antonucci *ed* Claudio Cutry
☆ Klaus Kinski, Donald Pleasence, Christopher Plummer, Barbara de Rossi, Yorgo Voyagis, Anne Knecht

'Seduction. Romance. Murder. The things one does for love.'
Vampire's Kiss
US 1989 103m colour
Hemdale/Magellan Pictures (Barry Shils, Barbara Zitwer)
A literary agent begins to fantasize that he is a vampire and behaves accordingly.
Over-heated film of urban disquiet, too tame for die-hard horror fans and too incoherent to interest any other audience.
w Joseph Minion *d* Robert Bierman *ph* Stefan Czapsky *m* Colin Towns *pd* Christopher Nowak *ed* Angus Newton
☆ Nicolas Cage, Maria Conchita Alonso, Jennifer Beals, Elizabeth Ashley, Kasi Lemmons, Bob Lujan, Jessica Lundy, John Walker

Vampires: Los Muertos
US 2002 103m colour
Screen Gems/Storm King (Ricardo Del Río)
A vampire hunter and a priest set out to prevent a vampire getting the means to survive in sunlight.
Anaemic follow-up to John Carpenter's Vampires, with the bland Bon Jovi as the hunter. It recyles the same plot to much lesser effect.
wd Tommy Lee Wallace *ph* Henner Hofmann *m* Brian Tyler *pd* Marcelo Del Rio *ed* Charles Bornstein
☆ Jon Bon Jovi (Derek Bliss), Cristian de la Fuente (Father Rodrigo), Natasha Gregson Wagner (Zoey), Arly Jover (Una), Ray Collins (Darius McCrary), Sancho (Diego Luna)

Vampyr **
Germany/France 1932 83m bw
Tobis Klangfilm/Carl Dreyer
US title: *Castle of Doom*
aka: *The Strange Adventure of David Gray*
A young man staying in a remote inn suspects that he is surrounded by vampires and has a dream of his own death.
Vague, misty, virtually plotless but occasionally frightening and always interesting to look at, this semi-professional film long since joined the list of minor classics for two scenes: the hero dreaming of his own death and the villain finally buried by flour in a mill.
w Christen Jul, Carl Dreyer *story Carmilla* by Sheridan Le Fanu *d Carl Dreyer ph Rudolph Maté, Louis Née m* Wolfgang Zeller
☆ Julian West, Sybille Schmitz, Maurice Schutz, Jan Hieronimko
'It makes our contemporary, explicit Draculas look like advertisements for false teeth.' – *Sunday Times, 1976*
'It is intensely a film of hints, of eerie non sequiturs, of barely perceivable yet striking images ... evil wafts off the screen like a smell of bad breath.' – *New Statesman, 1976*
'Imagine we are sitting in an ordinary room. Suddenly we are told there is a corpse behind the door. In an instant, the room is completely altered; everything in it has taken another look; the light, the atmosphere have changed, though they are physically the same. This is because we have changed, and the objects are as we perceive them. That is the effect I meant to get in my film.' – *Carl Dreyer*
† 'Julian West' was really Baron Nicholas de Gunsberg, who financed the project.

Vampyres *
GB 1974 84m Eastmancolor
Fox-Rank/Essay (Brian Smedley-Aston)
Two murdered lesbian lovers become vampires after their deaths and lure men to a deserted mansion so that they can suck their blood.
Cheaply made, single-minded horror that manages to generate a relentless tension.
w D. Daubeney *d* Joseph Larraz (José Ramón Larraz) *ph* Harry Waxman *m* James Clarke *ad* Ken Bridgeman *ed* Geoff R. Brown
☆ Marianne Morris, Anulka, Murray Brown, Brian Deacon, Sally Faulkner, Michael Byrne, Karl Lanchbury, Bessie Love
'A sex-horror film about lesbian vampires for which the budget and schedule were insignificant, even by British exploitation standards.' – *David Pirie, MFB*
'A minor masterpiece of erotic fantasy.' – *Peter Tombs and Cathal Tohill, NFT*

Vampyros Lesbos
West Germany/Spain 1971 87m colour
Tele-Cine/Fenix (Karl Heinz Mannchen)
aka: *Erbin des Dracula*
aka: *Lesbian Vampires*
Countess Carody, a man-hating vampire who performs in a lesbian cabaret act in Istanbul, decides to initiate a German woman who comes to the city.
A dull and inept horror movie made worse by Franco's penchant for meaningless zooms, abrupt transitions and inappropriate soundtrack music; the pace is leaden, the cast act as though they're zombies, and the director resorts to scenes of lesbian lovemaking at frequent intervals.
wd Franco Manera (Jesús Franco) *ph* Manuel Merino *m* Mannfred Hubler, Siegfried Schwab *ed* Clarissa Ambach
☆ Susann Korda (Soledad Miranda), Dennis Price, Paul Muller, Ewa Stroemberg, Heidrun Kussin, Michael Berling, Viktor Feldmann
† A different version of the film was released in Spain in 1974. The video release includes the original West German trailer, which describes it as 'a daring film version of the story of Dracula, whose legacy brings fear and terror'.

'A large portion of life...'
The Van
Eire/GB 1996 100m Technicolor
TCF/Deadly/BBC Films/Beacon (Lynda Myles)
In Dublin, a baker uses his redundancy payment to buy a dilapidated van and goes into the mobile fish-and-chip business with a friend.
A flat, small-scale kitchen-sink drama of tensions between friends and family, as experienced by middle-aged men, in which all end battered by life.
w Roddy Doyle *novel* Roddy Doyle *d* Stephen Frears *ph* Oliver Stapleton *m* Eric Clapton, Richard Hartley *pd* Mark Geraghty *ed* Mick Audsley
☆ Colm Meaney, Donal O'Kelly, Ger Ryan, Caroline Rothwell, Neili Conroy, Ruaidhri Conroy, Brendan O'Carroll
'As television drama, this is fine. As a theatrical release, it is sadly a bit flat.' – *Leslie Felperin, Sight and Sound*

'Some stones are best left unturned.'
The Van Boys
GB 1999 90m DeLuxe
Double Life (John McCormack, John Alexander Wilson)
A group of petty criminals who steal paving stones become involved with more violent crooks.
Dull and unimaginative low-life thriller, never escaping from cliché and too slow-paced to disguise the holes in its narrative; it resorts to a voice-over to fill in the gaps.
wd John McCormack *ph* Paul Englefield *ad* Deborah Morley *ed* Ian Bowden, Paul Rowbottom, J. Simon Walton
☆ Scot Williams (Chris McColl), Paul Usher (Stuart McColl), Malcolm Pitt (Gary), Liam Fox (Dave), Stuart Wolfenden (Daniel), Mark Jephcott (Paul), Julie Brown (Angie), Gillian Jephcott, Sandra Couch

Van Gogh *
France 1991 158m colour
Artificial Eye/Erato/Canal/A2/Livradois (Daniel Toscan du Plantier)
In the final three months of his life, Vincent Van Gogh goes to live in Auvers, where he begins an affair with the young daughter of the local doctor, a collector of paintings, quarrels with his brother and kills himself.
Fictionalized biopic that adds little to an understanding of the artist, even if it sets him in an everyday context as one man among many.
wd Maurice Pialat *ph* Gilles Henry *m* A. Bernot, J. M. Bourget, J. Dutronc, P. Revedy
☆ Jacques Dutronc, Alexandra London, Bernard Le Coq, Gerard Sety, Corinne Bourdon, Elsa Zylberstein, Leslie Azoulai, Jacques Vidal, Chantal Barbarit
'The punitive running time and unlovely hero mean that this will hardly be embraced by all cinemagoers, but *Van Gogh* is certainly the best of the Van Gogh movies to date.' – *Kim Newman, Empire*

Van Wilder Party Liaison: see *National Lampoon's Van Wilder*

Vanessa, Her Love Story
US 1935 76m bw
MGM (David O. Selznick)
When her husband becomes insane, a Victorian lady falls for a gypsy.
Very dated romance which finished Helen Hayes's star career, for thirty years at least.
w Lenore Coffee, Hugh Walpole *novel* Hugh Walpole *d* William K. Howard *ph* Ray June *m* Herbert Stothart
☆ Helen Hayes, Robert Montgomery, May Robson, Otto Kruger, Lewis Stone, Henry Stephenson, Violet Kemble-Cooper, Jessie Ralph
'It drips with agony and dullness.' – *Variety*

Il Vangelo Secondo Matteo: see *The Gospel According to St Matthew*

'Love Hate Dreams Life Work Play Friendship Sex'
Vanilla Sky
US 2001 134m DeLuxe
Paramount (Tom Cruise, Paula Wagner, Cameron Crowe)
Accused of murder, a publishing tycoon explains to a prison psychiatrist how his life fell apart.
A glossy remake of a superior Spanish thriller; the grittiness of the original has been given a high fashion makeover which, coupled with Cruise's self-regarding performance, fails to convince, even on the level of a bad dream.
wd Cameron Crowe *film Abre los ojos* by Alejandro Amenábar, Mateo Gil *ph* John Toll *m* Nancy Wilson *pd* Catherine Hardwicke *ed* Joe Hutshing, Mark Livolsi *cos* Betsy Heimann
☆ Tom Cruise (David Aames), Penelope Cruz (Sofia Serrano), Cameron Diaz (Julie Gianni), Kurt Russell (McCabe), Jason Lee (Brian Shelby), Noah Taylor (Edmund Ventura), Timothy Spall (Thomas Tipp), Tilda Swinton (Rebecca Dearborn)
'A good example of what self-destructive cinematic havoc can be wrought by handing over millions of dollars to movie stars to produce their own ego trips.' – *Rex Reed, New York Observer*
'We're left with a cracked hall of mirrors taped together by a preposterous what-is-reality? cryogenics plot and scored to Cameron Crowe's record collection.' – *Owen Gleiberman, Entertainment Weekly*
'A non-commercial, self-consciously arty mess.' – *Joe Queenan*
song 'Vanilla Sky' (m/l Paul McCartney)

The Vanishing *
Netherlands/France 1988 106m colour
Metro/Golden Egg Film/Ingrid Productions/MGS Film (Anne Lordo, George Sluizer)
original title: *Spoorloos*
After spending three years searching for his girlfriend who suddenly disappeared while they were on holiday, a man is approached by her kidnapper.
Black thriller with a shock ending.
w Tim Krabbé *novel The Golden Egg* by Tim Krabbé *d* George Sluizer *ph* Toni Kuhn *m* Henry Vrienten *ad* Santiago Isidro Pin, Cor Spijk *ed* George Sluizer, Lin Friedman
☆ Bernard-Pierre Donnadieu, Gene Bervoets, Johanna Ter Steege, Gwen Eckhaus, Bernadette Le Sache, Tania Latarjet
'A consistently bewildering and surprising thriller, chillingly unsentimental and expertly constructed.' – *Kim Newman, MFB*

'Obsession is the Ultimate Weapon.'
The Vanishing
US 1993 110m DeLuxe
TCF/Morra, Brezner, Steinberg and Tenenbaum (Larry Brezner, Paul Schiff)
A teacher searches for his kidnapped girlfriend for three years without success; then he gets a call from the kidnapper.
A disastrous remake of a chilling original, so softened and given such a happy Hollywood ending that the narrative loses all point.
w Todd Graff *novel The Golden Egg* by Tim Krabbé *d* George Sluizer *ph* Peter Suschitzky *m* Jerry Goldsmith *pd* Jeannine C. Oppewall *ed* Bruce Green
☆ Jeff Bridges, Kiefer Sutherland, Nancy Travis, Sandra Bullock, Park Overall, Lisa Eichhorn, Maggie Linderman
'This is one remake that sacrifices much of what made the original work so well.' – *Variety*
'Has been systematically and often laughably divested of its subtler moments.' – *Derek Malcolm, Guardian*

The Vanishing American
US 1925 110m (24 fps) bw silent
Paramount
A history of the American Indian.
Solid Western epic, now of historical interest only.
story Zane Grey *d* George B. Seitz
☆ Richard Dix, Lois Wilson, Noah Beery, Malcolm McGregor, Charles Stevens

The Vanishing Corporal *
France 1962 106m bw
Films du Cyclope (J. W. Beyer)
original title: *Le Caporal Epinglé*
After several attempts, three Frenchmen succeed in escaping from a detention camp.
Symbolic World War II drama told in mainly comic terms. Not one of its director's great films, but a warm and assured one.
w Jean Renoir, Guy Lefranc *d* Jean Renoir *ph* Georges Leclerc *m* Joseph Kosma
☆ Jean-Pierre Cassel, Claude Brasseur, Claude Rich, O. E. Hasse
'A comedy which shades sometimes into farce and once into tragedy ... The mood, except in two or three scenes, is deliberately light.' – *Dilys Powell*

'The Ultimate Car Chase Movie!'
Vanishing Point *
US 1971 107m DeLuxe
TCF/ Cupid (Norman Spencer)
An ex-racing driver who delivers cars for a living becomes hepped up on benzedrine and leads police a rare chase through the Nevada desert.
Strange, fashionable action suspenser which is better to look at than to understand.
w Guillermo Cain *d Richard Sarafian ph John A. Alonzo md* Jimmy Brown
☆ Barry Newman, Cleavon Little, Dean Jagger, Victoria Medlin, Paul Koslo, Bob Donner
'Uncomfortably reminiscent of Easy Rider as an odyssey through an unknown America in its discovery of strange alliances and unpredictable hostilities.' – *Tom Milne*

The Vanishing Virginian
US 1941 97m bw
MGM (Edwin H. Knopf)
A conservative Virginian finds that he harbours suffragettes in his household.
Life with Father *in another setting; rather yawn-provoking.*
w Jan Fortune *novel* Rebecca Yancey Williams *d* Frank Borzage *ph* Charles Lawton Jnr *m* David Snell
☆ Frank Morgan, Spring Byington, Kathryn Grayson, Elizabeth Patterson, Louise Beavers

The Vanquished
US 1953 84m Technicolor
Paramount/Pine-Thomas
After the Civil War, a returning Confederate officer finds corruption in his home town.
Uninspiring semi-Western.
w Winston Miller, Frank Moss, Lewis R. Foster *novel* Karl Brown *d* Edward Ludwig *ph* Lionel Lindon *m* Lucien Cailliet

☆ John Payne, Jan Sterling, Coleen Gray, Lyle Bettger, Willard Parker, Roy Gordon

Vanya on 42nd Street **
US 1994 119m DuArt
Artificial Eye/Laura Pels/Mayfair (Fred Berner)
Actors and a small audience gather in a derelict New York theatre for a rehearsal of *Uncle Vanya*, directed by André Gregory.
A film, part documentary, part recreation, of a theatrical event, performed by a cast that had worked on the play at various times over four years. It works both as a version of the play and as cinema.
w David Mamet *play* Uncle Vanya by Anton Chekhov *d* Louis Malle *ph* Declan Quinn *m* Joshua Redman *pd* Eugene Lee *ed* Nancy Baker
☆ Wallace Shawn, Julianne Moore, Brooke Smith, Larry Pine, George Gaynes, Phoebe Brand, Madhur Jaffrey, André Gregory (himself), Lynn Cohen, Jeffrey Mayer

'A splendid demonstration of how great art seduces us, has its way with us. The movie is designed to give the audience the experience of total surrender to theatrical illusion.' – *Terrence Rafferty, New Yorker*

Vargtimmen: see *The Hour of the Wolf*

Variety **
Germany 1925 104m (24 fps) bw silent
UFA
aka: *Vaudeville*
An ageing acrobat seduces a young girl and later kills another man who is interested in her.
Crude, vivid backstage story, inventively presented to overcome the dullness and tawdriness of the plot.
w E. A. Dupont, Leo Birinsky *novel* Frederick Hollander *d* E. A. Dupont *ph* Karl Freund
☆ Emil Jannings, Lya de Putti, Maly Delschaft, Warwick Ward

'A continually roving lens seizes the best angle for every detail, expression and scene.' – *Leon Moussinac*

'The enduring power of the movie is not in its far from original story but in the restless, subjective camera and the fast editing which make it an almost voluptuous experience.' – *Pauline Kael, 70s*

'It was my aim to show a single childish grown-up, devoted, lovable, and his reaction to betrayal and duplicity.' – *E. A. Dupont*

Variety Girl
US 1947 83m bw
Paramount (Daniel Dare)
Of all the young hopefuls arriving in Hollywood, one girl becomes a star.
The slightest of excuses for a tour of the Paramount studios, with all the contract stars doing bits. It doesn't add up to much.
w Edmund Hartmann, Frank Tashlin, Monte Brice, Robert Welch *d* George Marshall *ph* Lionel Lindon, Stuart Thompson *md* Joseph J. Lilley, Troy Saunders
☆ Mary Hatcher, Olga San Juan, DeForest Kelley, Glenn Tryon, Bob Hope, Bing Crosby, Gary Cooper, Ray Milland, Alan Ladd, Barbara Stanwyck, Paulette Goddard, Dorothy Lamour, Veronica Lake, Sonny Tufts, Joan Caulfield and also William Holden, Lizabeth Scott, Burt Lancaster, Gail Russell, Diana Lynn, Sterling Hayden, Robert Preston, William Bendix, Barry Fitzgerald, Billy de Wolfe, George Pal Puppetoons, Cecil B. de Mille, Mitchell Leisen, George Marshall, Spike Jones and his City Slickers, etc

Variety Jubilee
GB 1942 92m bw
Butcher's
Two generations in the life of a music hall.
Naïve romance with fascinating appearances by some famous names of variety.
w Kathleen Butler *d* Maclean Rogers *ph* Geoffrey Faithfull *md* Percival Mackey
☆ Lesley Brook, Ellis Irving, Reginald Purdell, George Robey, Charles Coborn, Ella Retford, Wilson Keppel and Betty, The Ganjou Brothers and Juanita, Slim Rhyder, Betty Warren (Florrie Forde), Marie Lloyd Jnr, Tom Finglass, John Rorke (Gus Elen)

Variety Lights: see *Lights of Variety*

Variety Time
US 1948 90m bw
RKO (George Bilson)
The film's subtitle puts it, somewhat optimistically, 'a revue of specialities and highlights from RKO film hits'.
It turns out to be a succession of indifferent moments, including two overlong comedy sketches and some ill-advised mockery of silent films, linked by some feeble stand-up comedy from Jack Paar. Little of it retains any interest, other than archaeological.
w Hal Law, Hal Yates, Leo Solomon, Joseph Quillan *d* Hal Yates (of Edgar Kennedy and Leon Errol's sketches) *md* C. Bakaleinikoff *ad* Charles Pyke *ed* Les Millbrook, Edward W. Williams
☆ Jack Paar, Edgar Kennedy, Leon Errol, Frankie Carle and his orchestra, Pat Rooney, Miguelito Valdes, Harold & Lola, Jesse & James, Lynn, Royce & Vanya

'Make your own rules.'
Varsity Blues
US 1999 104m DeLuxe
Paramount/MTV (Tova Laiter, Mike Tollin, Brian Robbins)
A Texas high-school student is treated as a local celebrity when he replaces the football team's injured quarterback.
Tiresome teenage drama of small-town worship of athletes that looks merely quaint to audiences not involved in such rituals.
w W. Peter Iliff *d* Brian Robbins *ph* Charles Cohen *m* Mark Isham *pd* Jaymes Hinkle *ed* Ned Bastille
☆ James Van Der Beek, Jon Voight, Paul Walker, Ron Lester, Scott Caan, Richard Lineback, Tiffany C. Love, Amy Smart, Eliel Swinton

'An unappetizing mix of raucously vulgar comedy and teen-angst melodrama.' – *Joe Leydon, Variety*

Varsity Show
US 1937 120m bw
Warner (Louis F. Edelman)
Collegians stage a revue.
Mild musical.
w Warren Duff, Richard Macaulay, Jerry Wald, Sig Herzig *d* William Keighley *ph* Sol Polito, George Barnes *m/ly* Richard Whiting, Johnny Mercer *ch* Busby Berkeley
☆ Dick Powell, Priscilla Lane, Rosemary Lane, Fred Waring and his Pennsylvanians, Buck and Bubbles, Johnny 'Scat' Davis, Ted Healy, Walter Catlett

'A rah-rah musical entertainment made to order for early autumn business when college boys start pegging out the pigskin.' – *Variety*

Busby Berkeley

Vaudeville: see *Variety*

'Everything that makes life worth leaving!'
Vault of Horror *
GB 1973 86m Eastmancolor
Metromedia/Amicus (Milton Subotsky)
Five men trapped in the basement of a skyscraper tell of their recurring dreams.
All-star horror omnibus, plainly but well staged.
w Milton Subotsky *stories* William Gaines *d* Roy Ward Baker *ph* Denys Coop *m* Douglas Gamley
☆ Daniel Massey, Anna Massey, Terry-Thomas, Glynis Johns, Curt Jurgens, Dawn Addams, Michael Craig, Edward Judd, Tom Baker, Denholm Elliott

'Crime At The Speed Of Light.'
Velocity Trap
US 1998 90m colour
UFO (Christian McIntire, Ken Olandt, Phillip Roth, Elizabeth Weintraub)
In 2150, only a disgraced security officer can prevent space pirates from stealing forty billion dollars from a freighter on a six month journey to Earth.
Familiar, cynical action fare in which men with guns run around shooting at one another; it is set in a future world that resembles yesterday (and what a dull day that was).
w Phillip Roth, Patrick Phillips *d* Phillip Roth *ph* Philip Schwartz *m* Richard McHugh, Mike Slamer *pd* David Huang *sp* Andrew Hofman
☆ Olivier Gruner (Ray Stokes), Alicia Coppola (Beth Sheffield), Ken Olandt (Nick), Jorja Fox (Pallas), Bruce Weitz (Captain Fenner), Ray Oriel (Cruz), Jaason Simmons (Simms), Victor Love (Fallout), Yannock Bisson (Robinson), Craig Wasson (Dawson)

'Leave your expectations at the door.'
Velvet Goldmine **
US 1998 123m Rank Colour
Film Four/Zenith/Killer/Single Cell/Newmarket Capital/Goldwyn/Miramax/Channel 4 (Christine Vachon)
In Britain in the 80s, a journalist sets out to discover what happened to a glam-rock star of the 70s, who faked his death and disappeared from view.
A camp account of a camp phenomenon, flamboyantly revelling in the fakery and the androgynous appeal of it all.
wd Todd Haynes *ph* Maryse Alberti *m* Carter Burwell *pd* Christopher Hobbs *ed* James Lyons *cos* Sandy Powell
☆ Ewan McGregor (Curt Wild), Jonathan Rhys Meyers (Brian Slade), Toni Collette (Mandy Slade), Christian Bale (Arthur Stuart), Eddie Izzard (Jerry Devine), Emily Woof (Shannon), Michael Feast (Cecil)

'Tells a story the way operas do: blazing with exquisite yet abstract passions, and with quite a lot to look at on the side.' – *Janet Maslin, New York Times*

Sandy Powell (costumes)
Sandy Powell (costumes)

The Velvet Touch *
US 1948 97m bw
RKO/Independent Artists (Frederick Brisson)
A famous actress murders her producer and is struck by conscience but allows a detective to find his own way to the truth.
Solid murder melodrama with an excellent theatrical atmosphere.
w Leo Rosten *d* John Gage *ph* Joseph Walker *m* Leigh Harline
☆ Rosalind Russell, Leo Genn, Sydney Greenstreet, Claire Trevor, Leon Ames, Frank McHugh

'Child of the devil, she lives by a secret code!'
Vendetta
US 1950 84m bw
RKO/Howard Hughes
The daughter of an esteemed Corsican family takes vengeance on her father's enemies.
Outmoded ethnic melodrama with nothing to recommend it.
w W. R. Burnett *novel* Columba by Prosper Mérimée *d* Mel Ferrer *ph* Franz Planer, Al Gilks *m* Roy Webb *md* Constantin Bakaleinikoff
☆ Faith Domergue, George Dolenz, Donald Buka, Hillary Brooke, Nigel Bruce, Joseph Calleia, Hugo Haas

Vendetta
Italy 1990 120m Fujicolour
Reteitalia/Titanus (Ciro Ippolito)
An Irish hit-man working for the Mafia falls in love with the daughter of a man he shot by mistake.
Interminable and predictable movie, with too little action to work as a thriller and too shallow and stereotypical to be a character study. It also requires the viewer to be sympathetic to the problems of hoodlums and murderers.
w Ennio de Concini, Stuart Margolin, Alan Di Fiore *novel* Woman of Honor by Svena Casati Modignani *d* Stuart Margolin *ph* Ennio Guarnieri *m* Bruce Ruddel, Stuart Margolin, Riz Ortolani *pd* Danilo Donati *ed* Mario Morra
☆ Eric Roberts, Carol Alt, Burt Young, Nick Mancuso, Thomas Calabro, Marcie Leeds, Serena Grandi, Billy Barty, Stuart Margolin, Eli Wallach
† There is also a version, made for TV, that lasts 200m.

La vendetta di Ursus: see *The Vengeance of Ursus*

I Vendicatori dell'Ave Maria: see *The Twilight Avengers*

The Venetian Affair
US 1966 92m Metrocolor Panavision
MGM/Jerry Thorpe
A reporter investigates the death in Venice of an American diplomat.
Uninteresting and complicated spy thriller with pleasant locations.
w E. Jack Neuman *novel* Helen MacInnes *d* Jerry Thorpe *ph* Milton Krasner, Enzo Serafin *m* Lalo Schifrin
☆ Robert Vaughn, Karl Boehm, Elke Sommer, Ed Asner, Boris Karloff, Felicia Farr, Roger C. Carmel, Luciana Paluzzi, Joe de Santis

Venetian Bird *
GB 1952 95m bw
Rank/British Film Makers (Betty E. Box)
US title: *The Assassin*
A private detective goes to Venice to reward a wartime partisan, who turns out to have become a notorious criminal.
Standard action fare with a nod to The Third Man *but not much excitement or sense of place.*
w Victor Canning *novel* Victor Canning *d* Ralph Thomas *ph* Ernest Steward *m* Nino Rota
☆ Richard Todd, Eva Bartok, John Gregson, George Coulouris, Margot Grahame, Walter Rilla, Sidney James

La Venganza Del Sexo (dubbed)
Argentina 1967 87m bw
Forbes/Unistar (Orestes Trucco)
aka: *The Curious Doctor Humpp*
A mad scientist kidnaps couples and drugs them to engage in sexual activity so that he can create eternal life and dominate the world.
Risible, crudely-made, extremely low-budget mix of horror and soft-core porn, some of which was added by its American distributor.
wd Emilio Vieyra *story* Raul Zorrilla *ph* Anibal Paz *m* Victor Buchino *ed* Jacinto Cascales
☆ Richard Bauleo, Gloria Prat, Aldo Barbero, Susan Beltran, Justin Martin, Michel Angel, Mary Albano, Al Bigatti

Vengeance
GB/Germany 1962 83m bw
CCC/Raymond Stross
aka: *The Brain*
After a fatal accident, the brain of a tycoon is kept alive and persuades a doctor to find his murderer.
Twisty remake of Donovan's Brain *(qv), not too badly done.*
w Robert Stewart, Philip Mackie *d* Freddie Francis *ph* Bob Hulke *m* Ken Jones
☆ Anne Heywood, Peter Van Eyck, Cecil Parker, Bernard Lee, Maxine Audley, Jeremy Spenser, Miles Malleson

Vengeance (dubbed) *
Italy/West Germany 1968 100m Eastmancolor Cromoscope
MGM-EMI/Super International/Top (Renato Savino)
original title: *Joko, Invoca Dio ... e Muori*
An outlaw takes revenge on the five men who tortured and killed his friend after a bungled bullion robbery.
A bravura and baroque, if violent, spaghetti Western, in which style triumphs over substance.
w Renato Savino, Antonio Margheriti *d* Anthony Dawson (Antonio Margheriti) *ph* Riccardo Pallottini *m* Carlo Savina *ed* Otello Colangeli
☆ Richard Harrison, Claudio Camaso, Werner Pochath, Paolo Gozlino

'An immensely enjoyable mix of Gothic horror, thriller and Western motifs, the deaths in particular are unusually imaginative.' – *Sight and Sound*

† The British release was cut to 81m.

The Vengeance of Fu Manchu
GB 1967 92m Eastmancolor
Anglo Amalgamated/Harry Alan Towers
The Yellow Peril plans a crime syndicate to counter Interpol, and creates a double for Nayland Smith...
Limp addition to a series which started well, but was subsequently robbed of period flavour.
w Harry Alan Towers *novel* Sax Rohmer *d* Jeremy Summers *ph* John von Kotze *m* Malcolm Lockyer

☆ Christopher Lee, Douglas Wilmer, Tony Ferrer, Tsai Chin, Howard Marion Crawford, Wolfgang Kieling

The Vengeance of She
GB 1968 101m Technicolor
Warner-Pathé/Hammer (Aida Young)

A girl is possessed by the spirit of long-dead Queen Ayesha.
Grotesquely unpersuasive reincarnation melodrama, a long long way from its inspiration.
w Peter O'Donnell *d* Cliff Owen *ph* Wolfgang Suschitsky *m* Mario Nascimbene *pd* Lionel Couch *ed* Raymond Poulton
☆ John Richardson, Olinka Berova, Edward Judd, Colin Blakely, Derek Godfrey, Noel Willman, André Morell, Jill Melford

The Vengeance of Ursus (dubbed)
Italy 1962 90m Eastmancolor Techniscope
Jonia/Splendor
original title: *La vendetta di Ursus*
aka: *The Mighty Warrior*
Ursus overthrows a tyrant who plans to marry the princess he loves.
Standard Italian muscleman stuff, following a familiar narrative and with little to distinguish it from similar movies featuring Hercules and Maciste.
w Marcello Ciorciolini, Nino Scolaro, Roberto Gianviti *d* Luigi Capuano *ph* Oberdan Troiani *m* Carlo Innocenzi *ad* Alfredo Montiori *ed* Antonietta Zita *d (English language)* Richard McNamara *English dialogue* John Hart
☆ Samson Burke, Wandisa Guida, Livio Lorenzon, Nadine Sanders, Nerio Bernardi, Gianni Rizzo, Franco Fantasia, Roberto Chevalier, Gina Rovere

Vengeance: The Demon: see *Pumpkinhead*

Vengeance Valley
US 1951 82m Technicolor
MGM (Nicholas Nayfack)

A Western rancher keeps his foster-brother's misdeeds from their father.
Well-made character Western, a little short on action.
w Irving Ravetch *novel* Luke Short *d* Richard Thorpe *ph* George Folsey *m* Rudolph G. Kopp
☆ Burt Lancaster, Robert Walker, Ray Collins, Joanne Dru, Sally Forrest, John Ireland, Carleton Carpenter, Ted de Corsia

Venom
GB 1981 92m Technicolor
Aribage/Morison (Martin Bregman)

A kidnap plan goes awry when a deadly snake is let loose in a besieged house.
Hoary melodrama which veers between dullness, artificial suspense and unpleasant detail.
w Robert Carrington *novel* Alan Scholefield *d* Piers Haggard *ph* Gilbert Taylor *m* Michael Kamen
☆ Sterling Hayden (Howard Anderson), Klaus Kinski (Jacmel), Oliver Reed (Dave), Sarah Miles (Dr Marion Stowe), Cornelia Sharpe, Nicol Williamson (Commander William Bulloch), Susan George (Louise)
'Woefully archaic in its British B-picture reliance on very cheap thrills, and without any self-parodic saving grace.' – *Time Out*

Vénus Beauté (institut) **
France 1999 105m colour
Agat/Arte France/Tabo Tabo/Canal+/Sofica

GB title: *Venus Beauty (salon)*
A middle-aged beautician who does not believe in love is wooed by a passionate sculptor.
Slight but enjoyable romantic comedy that makes gentle fun of the beauty business.
w Tonie Marshall, Marion Vernoux, Jacques Audiard *d* Tonie Marshall *ph* Gérard De Battista *m* Khalie Chahine *pd* Michel Vandestien *ed* Jacques Comets
☆ Nathalie Baye (Angèle), Bulle Ogier (Madame Nadine), Samuel LeBihan (Antoine), Jacques Bonnaffé (Jacques), Mathilde Seigner (Samantha), Audrey Tautou (Marie), Robert Hossein (Pilot), Edith Scob (Customer with spots on her hands), Marie Rivière (Customer), Hélène Fillières (Antoine's fiancée), Brigitte Roüan (Madame Marianne), Claire Nebout (Asthmatic customer), Elli Medeiros (Mlle Evelyne), Micheline Presle (Tante Maryse), Emmanuelle Riva (Tante Lyda)
'A rueful examination of the comedy, the pain, the unexpectedness of love, this adult fairy tale may sound familiar, but the way it plays is not like that at all.' – *Kenneth Turan, Los Angeles Times*

Venus in Furs (dubbed)
Italy 1970 81m colour
VIP/Roxy

While on holiday, a writer falls in love with, and marries, a woman staying in the next room, believing that she can satisfy his masochistic and voyeuristic sexual fantasies.
Trite, poorly dubbed would-be erotic thriller, updating the original to the swinging 60s and transforming the unreadable into the unwatchable.
w Fabio Massimo *novel* Leopold Sacher-Masoch *d* Massimo Dallamano *ph* Sergio D'Offizi *m* Gian Franco Reverberi *ad* Alida Cappellini
☆ Laura Antonelli, Régis Vallée, Ewing Loren, Renate Kasche

Venus Peter **
GB 1989 94m Fujicolour
Recorded Releasing/BFI/Channel 4/British Screen (Christopher Young)
A young boy grows up in a Scottish fishing village in the 1950s.
Nostalgic and enjoyable account of a community on the point of disintegration.
w Ian Sellar, Christopher Rush *book A Twelve-month and a Day* by Christopher Rush *d* Ian Sellar *ph* Gabriel Beristain *m* Jonathan Dove *pd* Andy Harris *ed* David Spiers
☆ Ray McAnally, David Hayman, Sinead Cusack, Gordon R. Strachan, Sam Hayman, Caroline Paterson, Alex McAvoy

Vera Cruz **
US 1953 94m Technicolor Superscope
UA/Hecht-Lancaster (James Hill)

Adventurers in 1860 Mexico become involved in a plot against Emperor Maximilian.
Terse, lively Western melodrama with unusual locations and comedy and suspense touches. Great outdoor entertainment.
w Roland Kibbee, James R. Webb, Borden Chase d Robert Aldrich ph Ernest Laszlo m Hugo Friedhofer
☆ *Gary Cooper, Burt Lancaster*, Denise Darcel, Cesar Romero, George Macready, Sarita Montiel, Ernest Borgnine, Morris Ankrum, Charles Bronson

'A Mad Generation Spawned In Lust ... Consumed By Hate. Where Everything Decent Is...'
Verboten! *
US 1959 93m bw
Columbia/Globe (Samuel Fuller)

In Germany at the end of the Second World War, an American soldier marries a German girl and faces trouble from people of both nationalities and a secret Nazi organization.
An effective mix of thriller and romance which gives some sense of the messy aftermath and confusions of war.
wd Samuel Fuller *ph* Joseph Biroc *m* Harry Sukman, Wagner, Beethoven *ad* John Mansbridge *ed* Philip Cahn
☆ James Best, Susan Cummings, Tom Pittman, Paul Dubov, Harold Daye, Dick Kallman, Stuart Randall

Verbrechen am Seelenleben eines Menschens: see *Kaspar Hauser*

The Verdict *
US 1946 86m bw
Warner (William Jacobs)
A retired Scotland Yard inspector continues to work on a case which vexes him.
Victorian murder mystery with very unconvincing Hollywood sets and curious casting, but rather nicely detailed.
w Peter Milne *novel The Big Bow Mystery* by Israel Zangwill *d Don Siegel ph* Ernest Haller *m* Frederick Hollander
☆ Sydney Greenstreet, Peter Lorre, Joan Lorring, George Coulouris, Rosalind Ivan, Paul Cavanagh, Arthur Shields

Verdict *
France/Italy 1974 97m Eastmancolor
Concordia/CCC (Carlo Ponti)
A gangster's widow kidnaps the judge who is trying her son for rape and murder.
Tortuous but watchable melodrama with star performances and the director's usual eagerness to exploit legal morality.
w Andre Cayatte, Henri Coupon *novel* Henri Coupon *d André Cayatte ph* Jean Badal *m* Louiguy
☆ *Sophia Loren, Jean Gabin*, Henri Garcin, Julien Bertheau
'Not exciting enough to qualify as a thriller nor penetrating enough to make you support Gallic penal reform.' – *Michael Billington, Illustrated London News*

'Frank Galvin has one last chance to do something right'
The Verdict *
US 1982 128m Technicolor
TCF/Zanuck-Brown (Richard D. Zanuck, David Brown)

An ageing and failed attorney is unexpectedly handed a case of medical malpractice and successfully sues a hospital.
Complex and interesting but rather sombrely handled exposé of legal and medical ethics.
w David Mamet *novel* Barry Reed *d* Sidney Lumet *ph* Andrzej Bartkowiak *m* Johnny Mandel *pd* Edward Pisoni
☆ *Paul Newman, James Mason*, Charlotte Rampling, Jack Warden, Milo O'Shea, Lindsay Crouse, Edward Binns, Wesley Addy
'When Sidney Lumet gets serious, his energetic, fast-moving style falls apart. The camera sits like Death on the dark, angled images of this anguished movie.' – *New Yorker*
best picture; Paul Newman; James Mason; Sidney Lumet; screenplay (adaptation)

Verführung: die Grausame Frau: see *Seduction: The Cruel Woman*

Vérités et Mensonges: see *F for Fake*

Veronika Voss **
West Germany 1982 104m bw
Maura/Tango/Rialto/Trio/Maran (Thomas Schühly)

In the fifties, a distraught star of the previous decade flees from her own image, but finds that her psychiatrist is her own worst enemy.
Fascinatingly convoluted puzzle play with enough to say for a year of late-night discussions; but the bleached-out black and white photography is an unnecessary strain.
w Peter Märthesheimer, Pea Fröhlich, Rainer Werner Fassbinder *d* Rainer Werner Fassbinder *ph* Xaver Schwarzenberger *m* Peer Raben
☆ Rosel Zech, Hilmar Thate, Annemarie Düringer, Doris Schade, Cornelia Froboess
'A dazzling parable of all cinema, of the penalties of living out one another's fantasies.' – *Sight and Sound*

Das Versprechen: see *The Promise*

'Hold Your Breath.'
Vertical Limit *
US/Germany 2000 126m DeLuxe
Columbia/Global/Movie KG (Lloyd Phillips, Robert King, Martin Campbell)

A photographer sets out to rescue his sister and two others, trapped in a crevasse on K2 – he takes some volunteers and lots of nitro-glycerine along for the trip.
Saturday morning matinee stuff, with one cliff-hanger after another: it's pulp fiction at its most unoriginal, but entertaining enough for the moment.
w Robert King, Terry Hayes *d* Martin Campbell *ph* David Tattersall *m* James Newton Howard *pd* Jon Bunker *ed* Thom Noble *cos* Graciela Mazon
☆ Chris O'Donnell (Peter Garrett), Bill Paxton (Elliot Vaughn), Robin Tunney (Annie Garrett), Scott Glenn (Montgomery Wick), Izabella Scorupco (Monique Aubertine), Temuera Morrison (Major Rasul), Stuart Wilson (Royce Garrett), Nicholas Lea (Tom McLaren), Alexander Siddig (Kareem Nazir), Robert Taylor (Skip Taylor), Roshan Seth (Col Amir Salim), David Hayman (Frank 'Chainsaw' Williams), Ben Mendelsohn (Malcolm Bench), Steve Le Marquand (Cyril Bench)
'This brawny suspenser features typically one-dimensional characters but more than fills the bill as roller-coaster-ride entertainment.' – *Todd McCarthy, Variety*
'Not so much a sincere movie about the dangers and codes of mountain climbing as a thriller with lots of snow.' – *Roger Ebert, Chicago Sun-Times*

The Vertical Rays of the Sun: see *Mua He Chieu Thang Dung*

Vertigo ****
US 1958 128m Technicolor Vistavision
Paramount (Alfred Hitchcock)

A detective with a fear of heights is drawn into a complex plot in which a girl he loves apparently falls to her death. Then he meets her double ...
Double identity thriller which has many sequences in Hitchcock's best style. A film as unsettling as the phobia it deals with, keeping its audience dizzy and off balance throughout.
w Alec Coppel, Samuel Taylor *novel D'entre les Morts* by Pierre Boileau, Thomas Narcejac *d Alfred Hitchcock ph Robert Burks m Bernard Herrmann ad* Hal Pereira, Henry Bumstead *ed* George Tomasini *cos* Edith Head
☆ James Stewart (John Ferguson), Kim Novak (Madeleine Elster/Judy Barton), Barbara Bel Geddes (Midge), Tom Helmore (Gavin Elster), Henry Jones (Coroner)
art direction; sound (George Dutton)

'About to be very big in a very small town.'
Very Annie-Mary
GB/France 2001 104m DeLuxe
FilmFour/Canal+/Dragon (Graham Broadbent, Damian Jones)

In a small Welsh town, a gawky woman gradually comes into her own when her strict, domineering, widowed father suffers a stroke.
An awkward, uneasy mix of whimsy, slapstick and grotesque comedy, set in a community of eccentrics; the cast give more than the script and direction deserve.
wd Sara Sugerman *ph* Barry Ackroyd *m* Stephen Warbeck *pd* Alice Normington *ed* Robin Sales
☆ Rachel Griffiths (Annie-Mary), Jonathan Pryce (Jack Pugh), Ioan Gruffudd (Hob), Matthew Rhys (Nob), Kenneth Griffiths (Minister), Ruth Madoc (Mrs Ifans), Joanna Page (Bethan Bevan), Rhys Miles Thomas (Colin Thomas)
'As sorry a mess as its director's diabolical debut, *Mad Cows.*' – *Empire*
'Hilarious, utterly charming comedy.' – *Film Review*

'They've Been Bad. Very Bad.'
Very Bad Things
US 1998 100m CFI color
Polygram/Initial Entertainment/Interscope/BallPark (Michael Schiffer, Diane Nabatoff, Cindy Cowan)

Five friends try to cover up the accidental killing of a prostitute on their stag night in Las Vegas.
Gruesome black comedy, of homicidal mania let loose, that escalates into a very sick joke; it will be enjoyed by those who find dead people funny.
wd Peter Berg *ph* David Hennings *m* Stewart Copeland *pd* Dina Lipton *ed* Dan Lebental
☆ Christian Slater, Cameron Diaz, Daniel Stern, Jeanne Tripplehorn, Jon Favreau, Jeremy Piven, Leland Orser, Joey Zimmerman, Tyler Malinger, Carla Scott
'The film has a real sense of a situation slipping out of control, with marvellous displays of hysteria matched by movie trickery that spreads the edginess to the audience.' – *Kim Newman, Empire*

Very Important Person **
GB 1961 98m bw
Rank/Independent Artists (Julian Wintle, Leslie Parkyn)
US title: *A Coming-Out Party*
A senior British scientist is caught by the Nazis and has to be rescued.
Very satisfactory British comedy with a few suspense scenes; POW fare with a difference.

w Jack Davies, Henry Blyth *d* Ken Annakin *ph* Ernest Steward *m* Reg Owen *ad* Harry Potter *ed* Ralph Sheldon
☆ *James Robertson Justice* (Sir Ernest Pease), *Stanley Baxter* (Jock Everett/Kommondant Stamfel), Leslie Phillips (Jimmy Cooper), Eric Sykes (Willoughby), Richard Wattis (Woodcock), Colin Gordon (Briggs), John Le Mesurier (Piggott), Jeremy Lloyd ('Bonzo' Baines), Norman Bird (Travers), Godfrey Winn (Himself)

A Very Private Affair: see *Vie Privée*

A Very Special Favor *
US 1965 105m Technicolor
Universal/Lankershim (Robert Arthur)
A Frenchman with a spinster daughter asks an American lawyer to 'initiate' her.
Tasteless, smirking comedy with several funny scenes, glossily photographed in the lap of luxury and interesting in its early use of homosexuality as a comedy subject.
w Nate Monaster, Stanley Shapiro *d* Michael Gordon *ph Leo Tover m* Vic Mizzy
☆ Rock Hudson, Charles Boyer, Leslie Caron, *Nita Talbot*, Dick Shawn, *Walter Slezak*, Larry Storch

The Very Thought of You
US 1944 99m bw
Warner (Jerry Wald)
◉
Problems of a wartime marriage.
Tepid romantic potboiler.
w Alvah Bessie, Delmer Daves *d* Delmer Daves *ph* Bert Glennon *m* Franz Waxman
☆ Dennis Morgan, Eleanor Parker, Dane Clark, Faye Emerson, Beulah Bondi, Henry Travers, William Prince, Andrea King

A Very Young Lady
US 1941 80m bw
TCF (Robert T. Kane)
A tomboy develops a crush on her headmaster.
Remake of Girls' Dormitory, *used as a vehicle for an ageing child star. Predictable comedy, neatly made.*
w Ladislas Fodor, Elaine Ryan *play* Ladislas Fodor *d* Harold Schuster
☆ Jane Withers, John Sutton, Nancy Kelly, Janet Beecher, Cecil Kellaway

Vesnicko Ma Strediskova: see *My Sweet Little Village*

Vesolye Rebyata: see *Jazz Comedy*

Vessel of Wrath **
GB 1938 93m bw
Mayflower (Erich Pommer)
US title: *The Beachcomber*
In the Dutch East Indies, the missionary's spinster sister falls for a drunken beachcomber.
First-rate character comedy, remade as The Beachcomber *(qv).*
w Bartlett Cormack, B. Van Thal *story W. Somerset Maugham d* Erich Pommer *ph* Jules Kruger *m* Richard Addinsell
☆ *Charles Laughton, Elsa Lanchester*, Robert Newton, Tyrone Guthrie, Dolly Mollinger, Eliot Makeham
'The moment this film starts you recognize the master touch.' – *Variety*

La Veuve de Saint-Pierre *
France/Canada 2000 112m colour
FilmFour/Epithète/France3/France2/Cinémaginaire (Frédéric Brillion, Gilles Legrand)
In the mid-19th century, on a small island off the Canadian coast, a condemned murderer ingratiates himself with residents and the wife of the man deputed to guard him while they await the arrival of the necessary guillotine.
Period drama of justice, morality, retribution and repressed emotions; enjoyable but unmemorable.
w Claude Faraldo *d* Patrice Leconte *ph* Eduardo Serra *m* Pascal Estève *ad* Ivan Maussion *ed* Joelle Hache *cos* Christian Gasc
☆ Juliette Binoche (Pauline, Madame La), Daniel Auteuil (Jean, the captain), Emir Kusturica (Ariel Neel Auguste), Michel Duchaussoy (Governor), Philippe Magnan (President Venot), Christian Charmetant (Officer), Philippe Du Janerand (Customs Officer), Reynald Bouchard (Louis Ollivier), Ghyslain Tremblay (Chevassus), Marc Béland (Soldier), Yves Jacques (Rear Admiral)
'The lack of palpable emotion stalls the drama short of engrossing.' – *Patrick Peters, Empire*
† Leconte replaced the original director Alain Corneau, who quit before filming began.

Viaggio in Italia: see *Voyage to Italy*

El Viaje: see *The Voyage*

Vibes
US 1988 99m DeLuxe
Imagine (Deborah Blum, Tony Ganz)
🇺🇸
A psychic couple go to Ecuador to find a lost city of gold.
Dim comedy that had no future at the box-office.
w Lowell Ganz, Babaloo Mandel *d* Ken Kwapis *ph* John Bailey *m* James Horner *pd* Richard Sawyer *ed* Carol Littleton
☆ Cyndi Lauper, Jeff Goldblum, Julian Sands, Peter Falk, Karen Akers, Michael Lerner, Ramon Bieri, Elizabeth Pena

The Vicar of Bray
GB 1937 68m bw
Twickenham (Julius Hagen)
A clergyman manages to hold on to his living through the reigns of Charles I, Cromwell and Charles II.
Stilted historical comedy, although Stanley Holloway seizes what chances he has to inject a little life and song into the dull pageant.
w H. Fowler Mear *story* Anson Dyer *d* Henry Edwards *ph* William Luff *md* M. de Wolfe *ad* James A. Carter *ed* R. T. Verrall
☆ Stanley Holloway (the Vicar of Bray), Felix Aylmer, Hugh Miller (King Charles I), K. Hamilton Price, Margaret Vines, Garry Marsh, Esmond Knight, Martin Walker

The Vice Squad *
US 1931 78m bw
Paramount
Stool pigeons account for many arrests of supposed prostitutes.
Rather draggy exposé of police methods, allegedly torn from the headlines.
w Oliver H. P. Garrett *d* John Cromwell
☆ Kay Francis, Paul Lukas, Judith Wood, William B. Davidson, Rockcliffe Fellowes, Esther Howard
'Should draw adult attention in the large cities.' – *Variety*

Vice Squad
US 1953 88m bw
UA/Jules Levy, Arthur Gardner
GB title: *The Girl in Room 17*
A police captain tracks down two bank robbers who have killed a cop.
A day in the life of a police captain, quite watchable but scarcely engrossing.
w Lawrence Roman *novel Harness Bull* by Leslie T. White *d* Arnold Laven *ph* Joseph C. Biroc *m* Herschel Burke Gilbert
☆ Edward G. Robinson, Paulette Goddard, K. T. Stevens, Porter Hall, Adam Williams, Edward Binns, Lee Van Cleef

Vice Versa *
GB 1947 111m bw
Rank/Two Cities (Peter Ustinov, George H. Brown)
A magic stone enables an unhappy Victorian boy to change places with his pompous father.
Funny moments can't disguise the fact that this overlong comedy is a bit of a fizzle, its talented creator not being a film-maker. A pity, as British films have so rarely entered the realms of fancy.
wd Peter Ustinov *novel* F. Anstey *ph* Jack Hildyard *m* Antony Hopkins *ad* Carmen Dillon *ed* John Guthridge
☆ Roger Livesey, Kay Walsh, Anthony Newley, *James Robertson Justice*, David Hutcheson, Petula Clark, Joan Young
'A repository of English oddities.' – *John Russell Taylor*

Vice Versa
US 1988 98m colour
Columbia (Dick Clement, Ian La Frenais)
A father and his 11-year-old son find their minds transplanted into the other's body by a magic skull.
One of the last and certainly the least of the mid-1980s cycle of role swapping movies.
w Dick Clement, Ian La Frenais *d* Brian Gilbert *ph* King Baggot *m* David Shire *pd* Jim Schoppe *ed* David Garfield
☆ Judge Reinhold, Fred Savage, Corinne Bohrer, Swoosie Kurtz, David Proval, Jane Kaczmarek, William Prince

The Vicious Circle
US 1948 77m bw
United Artist (W. Lee Wilder)
GB title: *The Woman in Brown*
Five Jewish farmers in Hungary are framed for murder.
Well-meaning but tedious and very static melodrama.
w Heinz Herald, Guy Endore *play The Burning Bush* by Heinz Herald, Geza Herczeg *d* W. Lee Wilder *ph* George Robinson *m* Paul Dessau
☆ Conrad Nagel, Fritz Kortner, Reinhold Schunzel, Philip Van Zandt, Edwin Maxwell, Lyle Talbot

The Vicious Circle *
GB 1957 84m bw
Romulus (Peter Rogers)
US title: *The Circle*
An actress is found dead in Dr Latimer's flat and the weapon turns up in the boot of his car …
Entertaining whodunnit from a TV serial.
w Francis Durbridge serial The Brass Candlestick by *Francis Durbridge d* Gerald Thomas *ph* Otto Heller *m* Stanley Black
☆ *John Mills*, Derek Farr, Noelle Middleton, Roland Culver, Wilfrid Hyde-White, Mervyn Johns, René Ray, Lionel Jeffries, Lisa Daniely

Vicki *
US 1953 85m bw
TCF (Leonard Goldstein)
A girl model is murdered, and her sister proves that her boyfriend is innocent, despite the efforts of a brutal detective.
Very competent if uninspired remake of I Wake Up Screaming *(qv).*
w Dwight Taylor *d* Harry Horner *ph* Milton Krasner *m* Leigh Harline
☆ Jeanne Crain, Jean Peters, Richard Boone, Elliott Reid, Casey Adams, Alex D'Arcy, Carl Betz, Aaron Spelling

Le Vicomte Règle Ses Comptes: see *The Investigator*

'Fear is the oxygen of blackmail. If Barrett was paying, others are. Find me one!'
Victim ***
GB 1961 100m bw
Rank/Allied Filmmakers/Parkway (Michael Relph)
🇺🇸
A barrister with homosexual inclinations tracks down a blackmailer despite the risk to his own reputation.
A plea for a change in the law is very smartly wrapped up as a murder mystery which allows all aspects to be aired, and the London locations are vivid.
w Janet Green, John McCormick d Basil Dearden ph Otto Heller m Philip Green
☆ *Dirk Bogarde*, Sylvia Syms, John Barrie, Norman Bird, Peter McEnery, Anthony Nicholls, Dennis Price, *Charles Lloyd Pack*, Derren Nesbitt, John Cairney, Hilton Edwards, Peter Copley, Donald Churchill, Nigel Stock
'Ingenious, moralistic, and moderately amusing.' – *Pauline Kael, 70s*

La Victoire en Chantant: see *Black and White in Colour*

Victor/Victoria *
GB 1982 134m Technicolor Panavision
MGM/Peerford/Ladbroke Entertainments/Blake Edwards
In 1934 Paris, a girl singer becomes successful when she poses as a female impersonator, but it causes complications in her love life.
The story was previously filmed more innocuously as a Jessie Matthews vehicle, First a Girl; *Edwards makes it a sexually harping, grotesque low comedy, but there are pleasurable moments.*
wd Blake Edwards, from the German film of 1933 Viktor und Viktoria (wd Reinhold Schünzel) ph Dick Bush *m* Henry Mancini *pd* Rodger Maus
☆ Julie Andrews, James Garner, *Robert Preston*, Lesley Ann Warren, Alex Karras, John Rhys-Davies, Graham Stark
'An audience pleaser in the worst sense.' – *New Yorker*
'Edwards' idea of European sophistication and Gallic naughtiness is seen throughout to be depressingly crude, parochial and second-hand, based on old American farces and reprises of his own Clouseau routines.' – *Sunday Times*
original song score (Henry Mancini, Leslie Bricusse)
Julie Andrews; Robert Preston; Lesley Ann Warren; screenplay (adaptation); costume design; art direction

Victoria the Great ***
GB 1937 112m bw (Technicolor sequence)
British Lion/Imperator/Herbert Wilcox
Episodes in the life of Queen Victoria.
A decent film with all the British virtues, and a milestone in the cinema of its time. Script and performances are excellent; production sometimes falters a little.
w Robert Vansittart, Miles Malleson play Victoria Regina by Laurence Housman *d* Herbert Wilcox *ph* F. A. Young, William V. Skall *m* Anthony Collins
☆ *Anna Neagle, Anton Walbrook, H. B. Warner*, Walter Rilla, Mary Morris, C. V. France, Charles Carson, Felix Aylmer, Derrick de Marney
'The effect of the final colour reel is to make the picture look like something enamelled on pottery and labelled "A Present from Blackpool".' – *James Agate*

'The six most exciting women in the world – in the most expensive entertainment you have ever seen!'
The Victors *
GB 1963 175m bw Panavision
Columbia/Open Road (Carl Foreman)
World War II adventures of an American infantry platoon.
Patchy compendium with moral too heavily stressed but plenty of impressive scenes and performances along the way. The mixture of realism and irony, though, doesn't really mix.
w Carl Foreman *novel The Human Kind* by Alexander Baron *d* Carl Foreman *ph* Christopher Challis *m* Sol Kaplan
☆ *George Peppard*, George Hamilton, Albert Finney, Melina Mercouri, Eli Wallach, Vince Edwards, Rosanna Schiaffino, James Mitchum, *Jeanne Moreau*, Elke Sommer, Senta Berger, Peter Fonda, Michael Callan
'Doggerel epic.' – *John Coleman*
'War has revealed Mr Foreman as a pompous bore.' – *John Simon*
'Having made a point through an image it continually feels the need to state it all over again by way of dialogue.' – *Penelope Houston*

Victory *
US 1940 77m bw
Paramount (Anthony Veiller)
A Dutch East Indies recluse rescues a girl and is menaced by three villains who think he is wealthy.
Curious, ineffective but occasionally compelling attempt to translate the untranslatable to the screen.
w John L. Balderston *novel* Joseph Conrad *d* John Cromwell *ph* Leo Tover *m* Frederick Hollander
☆ *Fredric March*, Betty Field, *Cedric Hardwicke*, Sig Rumann, Margaret Wycherly, Jerome Cowan, Fritz Feld, Rafaela Ottiano
'There is achieved a combination of amateur theatricals and earnest emptiness of motive and motion that will throw a blanket of reminiscent affection around this solemn, unusual and exotic buffoonery.' – *Otis Ferguson*
'A mood of impending doom and horror more than makes up for its slow and deliberate action … a fine and penetrating motion picture melodrama.' – *New York World Telegram*
'This is an unusual film at almost every level, yet it's unusual and disturbing, too.' – *Pauline Kael, 70s*
'Not a film of flamboyant hues … but it has quality, weight, and above all, compelling drama.' – *Philadelphia Record*
† The story was previously filmed in 1919 by Maurice Tourneur (with Jack Holt) and in 1930 by William Wellman (with Richard Arlen).

Victory
US 1981 117m Metrocolor Panavision
Lorimar/Victory Company/Tom Stern (Freddie Fields)
alternative and GB release title: *Escape to Victory*
A German POW camp in 1943 houses many international football stars. A Nazi officer sees propaganda in a game against a German side, but the allies make it an opportunity for escape.
Flabby and unconvincing POW story with agreeably old-fashioned values sacrificed to trendy casting and a silly ending.
w Evan Jones, Yabo Yablonsky *d* John Huston *ph* Gerry Fisher *m* Bill Conti *pd* J. Dennis Washington
☆ Sylvester Stallone, Michael Caine, Pele, Bobby Moore, Max von Sydow, George Mikell, Daniel Massey
'Even readers of the Boy's Own Paper might have blenched … ludicrous beyond belief.' – *Tom Milne, MFB*

Victory through Air Power **
US 1943 65m Technicolor
Walt Disney
The history of aviation and the theories of Major Alexander de Seversky.
What was thought by many to be propaganda was in fact a demonstration of Disney's own fascination with the theories of a controversial figure. The cartoon segments are put together with the studio's accustomed brilliance.
w various *d* H. C. Potter (live action), various *m* Edward H. Plumb, Paul J. Smith, Oliver G. Wallace
Edward H. Plumb, Paul J. Smith, Oliver G. Wallace

Videodrome
Canada 1982 89m colour
Filmplan International
A videodrome TV channel induces pornographic hallucinations in the viewer.
Dangerous when it is not visible, this thoroughly tawdry concept is made worse by being slickly done.
wd David Cronenberg *ph* Mark Irwin *m* Howard Shore *sp* Michael Lennick
☆ James Woods, Sonja Smits, Deborah Harry, Peter Dvorsky
'Almost as incoherent as it is speculative.' – *Sight and Sound*

La Vie à l'Envers: see *Life Upside Down*

La Vie de Château **
France 1965 93m bw
Ancinex/Cobela/Guéville (Nicole Stéphane)
aka: *A Matter of Resistance*
aka: *Gracious Living*
In a Normandy château just before the D-Day landings, a husband discovers that his wife is being courted by a Nazi officer and a hero of the Resistance.
A delightful, broad comedy of conflicting desires, marked by slick timing and resourceful performances.
w Jean-Paul Rappeneau, Claude Sautet, Alain Cavalier, Daniel Boulanger *d* Jean-Paul Rappeneau *ph* Pierre Lhomme *m* Michel Legrand *ad* Jacques Saulnier *ed* Jacques Gillette
☆ Catherine Deneuve, Pierre Brasseur, Philippe Noiret, Henri Garcin, Carlos Thompson, Mary Marquet, Donald O'Brien

La Vie Devant Soi: see *Madame Rosa*

La Vie Est un Long Fleuve Tranquille
France 1988 91m colour
Electric/Contemporary/Téléma/MK2/FR3 (Charles Gassot)
GB title: *Life is a Long Quiet River*
Wealthy and respectable parents discover that their child was switched at its birth twelve years before with the baby of a poor and feckless family.
Glossy comedy at the expense of class, demonstrating that environment is more important than breeding in creating character.
w Florence Quentin, Etienne Chatiliez *d* Etienne Chatiliez *ph* Pascal Lebegue *m* Gérard Kawczynski *pd* Geoffroy Larcher *ed* Chantal Delattre
☆ Benoît Magimel, Valerie Lalande, Tara Romer, Jérôme Floc'h, Sylvie Cubertafon, Emmanuel Cendrier

La Vie Est Un Roman: see *Life Is a Bed of Roses*

La Vie et Rien D'Autre: see *Life and Nothing But*

Vie Privée *
France 1961 103m Eastmancolor
Progefi/Cipra/CCM (Christine Gouze-Rénal)
aka: *A Very Private Affair*
A promiscuous movie star who retreats from fame to her home town of Geneva falls again for the theatre director who was her first love.
An unsatisfactory movie given to melodrama, but interesting for its insights into the universe of an actress much like Bardot herself in her strong-willed refusal to conform.
w Jean-Paul Rappeneau, Louis Malle, Jean Ferry *d* Louis Malle *ph* Henri Decaë *m* Fiorenzo Carpi *ad* Bernard Evein *ed* Kenout Peltier
☆ Brigitte Bardot, Marcello Mastroianni, Eleonore Hirt, Grégoire von Rezzori, Dirk Sanders
† The production was troubled, with Bardot and Mastroianni, who played lovers, not hiding their dislike for one another. A dubbed version was cut to 94m by MGM for its American release, despite Malle's protests.

La Vie Rêvée des Anges: see *The Dreamlife of Angels*

La vieille qui marchait dans la mer: see *The Old Lady Who Walked in the Sea*

De Vierde Man: see *The Fourth Man*

Une Vierge chez les Morts Vivants: see *Virgin among the Living Dead*

The View from Pompey's Head *
US 1955 97m Eastmancolor Cinemascope
TCF (Philip Dunne)
GB title: *Secret Interlude*
A New York lawyer returns on a case to the small town of his youth, and falls in love again with his old sweetheart.
Routine Marquand-type novelette, long on atmosphere and short on plot.
wd Philip Dunne *novel* Hamilton Basso *ph* Joe MacDonald *m* Elmer Bernstein
☆ Richard Egan, Dana Wynter, Cameron Mitchell, *Sidney Blackmer, Marjorie Rambeau*

A View from the Bridge
France 1961 117m bw
Transcontinental (Paul Graetz)
original title: *Vu du Pont*
A longshoreman on the New York waterfront has passionate feelings for his wife's niece, and these erupt when she announces her engagement.
Solemn, self-examining melodrama, poorly adapted from the stage.
w Norman Rosten *play* Arthur Miller *d* Sidney Lumet *ph* Michel Kelber *m* Maurice Leroux
☆ Raf Vallone, Maureen Stapleton, Carol Lawrence, Jean Sorel, Raymond Pellégrin, Morris Carnovsky, Harvey Lembeck, Vincent Gardenia
† The film was shot in several languages.

A View to a Kill
GB 1985 121m Metrocolor Panavision
MGM-UA/Albert R. Broccoli
James Bond tangles with a ruthless international industrialist.
A tedious Bond adventure in which even the expensive highlights are unmemorable.
w Richard Maibaum, Michael G. Wilson *d* John Glen *ph* Alan Hume *m* John Barry *pd* Peter Lamont *ed* Peter Davies
☆ Roger Moore, Christopher Walken, Grace Jones, Tanya Roberts, Patrick Macnee, David Yip, Fiona Fullerton

Vigil *
New Zealand 1984 90m Eastmancolor
First Blood/Last Rites/John Maynard
On a remote farm, a teenage girl learns about life after her father is killed.
Austere but vaguely impressive drama; one is pleased however when it ends.
w Vincent Ward, Graeme Tetley *d* Vincent Ward *ph* Alun Bollinger *m* Jack Body *pd* Kai Hawkins *ed* Simon Reece
☆ Bill Kerr, Fiona Kay, Gordon Shields, Penelope Stewart, Frank Whitten

Vigil in the Night
US 1940 96m bw
RKO (George Stevens)
Two nurses are attracted to the same doctor; one dies during an epidemic.
Dull, downbeat romantic melodrama with a miscast lead.
w Fred Guiol, P. J. Wolfson, Rowland Leigh *novel* A. J. Cronin *d* George Stevens *ph* Robert de Grasse *m* Alfred Newman
☆ Carole Lombard, Anne Shirley, Brian Aherne, Julien Mitchell, Robert Coote, Peter Cushing, Ethel Griffies

Vigilante Force
US 1976 89m DeLuxe
United Artists/Corman Company (Gene Corman)
A Vietnam veteran goes too far in using his wartime skills to crush lawlessness in a small town.
Standard action movie, full of mindless mayhem.
wd George Armitage *ph* William Cronjager *m* Gerald Fried *ad* Jack Fisk *ed* Morton Tubor
☆ Kris Kristofferson, Jan-Michael Vincent, Victoria Principal, Bernadette Peters, Brad Dexter, Judson Pratt
'Sharp, bright, and not averse to exploitation band-wagons.' – *Tom Milne, MFB*

The Vigilantes Return
US 1947 67m bw
Universal (Howard Welsch)
A US marshal is framed for murder by the outlaw gang he infiltrates.
Routine minor Western with more plot than action.
w Roy Chanslor *d* Ray Taylor *ph* Virgil Miller *md* Paul Sawtell *ad* Jack Otterson, Frank A. Richards *ed* Paul Landres
☆ Jon Hall, Margaret Lindsay, Andy Devine, Paula Drew, Robert Wilcox, Jonathan Hale, Arthur Hohl

Vigo: Passion for Life *
GB/France/Japan/Spain 1997 106m colour
Channel Four/Little Magic/Impact/Nitrate/MACT (Amanda Temple, Jeremy Bolt)
Biopic of influential French director Jean Vigo, who died at the age of 29 after completing three films.
The passion, heightened by sickness, that marked the life of the tubercular Vigo is nowhere evident in this trudge through his life, which unfortunately reduces him to a conventional portrait of an artist at odds with the world.
w Peter Ettedgui, Anne Devlin, Julien Temple *play* Love's a Revolution by Chris Ward *biography* Jean Vigo by Paulo Emilio Salles *d* Julien Temple *ph* John Mathieson *m* Bingen Mendizabal *pd* Caroline Greville-Morris *ed* Marie-Thérèse Boiché
☆ Romane Bohringer (Lydu), James Frain (Jean Vigo), Jim Carter (Bonaventure), Diana Quick (Emily), William Scott-Masson (Marcel), James Faulkner (Dr Gerard), Francine Bergé (Mama Lozinska), Vernon Dobtcheff (Papa Lozinska), Adolfo Fernandez (Almereyda)
'Absolutely dreadful.' – *Sight and Sound*
'Fans of Vigo's slender output will find the works illuminated in fresh and interesting ways. Not incidentally, then, this is Temple's best film to date.' – *Kim Newman, Empire*

The Viking Queen
GB 1967 91m Technicolor
Warner/Hammer (John Temple-Smith)
During the first century AD, the queen of the Iceni tries to keep peace with the occupying Romans but has trouble with hot-headed Druids.
Stuff and nonsense from the Dark Ages; light should not have been shed upon it.
w Clarke Reynolds *story* John Temple-Smith *d* Don Chaffey *ph* Stephen Dade *m* Gary Hughes *pd* George Provis *ed* James Needs, Peter Boita
☆ Don Murray, Carita, Donald Houston, Andrew Keir, Patrick Troughton, Adrienne Corri, Niall MacGinnis, Wilfrid Lawson, Nicola Pagett

Viking Women
US 1957 66m bw
AIP (Roger Corman)
A group of Viking women set sail in search of their men, who went on an expedition three years before.
This claims to be 'The Saga of the Viking Women and Their Voyage to the Waters of the Great Sea Serpent'. Viking women, it turns out, are all leggy, slim blondes who wear skin-tight leather and plenty of eyeliner, and look incapable of even fixing their own make-up.
w Lawrence Louis Goldman *story* Irving Block *d* Roger Corman *ph* Monroe P. Askins *m* Albert Glasser *ch* Wilda Taylor *ad* Bob Kinoshita *ed* Ronald Sinclair
☆ Abby Dalton, Susan Cabot, Brad Jackson, June Kenney, Richard Devon, Betsy Jones-Moreland, Jonathan Haze, Jay Sayer

'Mightiest Of Men … Mightiest Of Spectacles … Mightiest Of Motion Pictures!'
The Vikings ***
US 1958 116m Technirama
UA/KD Productions (Jerry Bresler)
Two Viking half-brothers quarrel over the throne of Northumbria.
Slightly unpleasant and brutal but extremely well-staged and good-looking epic in which you can almost feel the harsh climate. Fine colour, strong performances, natural settings, vivid action, and all production values as they should be.
w Calder Willingham, Dale Wasserman *novel The Viking* by Edison Marshall *d Richard Fleischer* *ph Jack Cardiff* *m Mario Nascimbene* *md* Franco Ferrara *pd* Harper Goff *ed* Elmo Williams *sp* credit titles United Productions of America
☆ *Orson Welles* (narrator), *Kirk Douglas, Tony Curtis*, Ernest Borgnine, Janet Leigh, Alexander Knox, Frank Thring, James Donald, Maxine Audley, Eileen Way

Villa des Roses
GB/Belgium/Netherlands/Luxembourg 2002 119m colour
Miracle/Favorite/Dan/Isabella/Samsa/Eurimages (Dirk Impens, Rudy Verzyck)
In 1913, a French widow goes to Paris to work as a maid in a boarding house and begins an anguished affair with a German artist.
Based on a classic Flemish novel about a love at a time of catastrophic change, this is a visually interesting but dramatically inert work.
w Christophe Dirickx *novel* Willem Elsschot *d* Frank Van Passel
☆ Julie Delpy, Shaun Dingwall, Harriet Walter, Shirley Henderson, Timothy West, Frank Vercruyssen
'Yet another complicated, mostly English-lingo international coproduction rich in high-priced production values, but devoid of substance.' – *Scott Foundas, Variety*

Villa Rides!
US 1968 125m Technicolor Panavision
Paramount (Ted Richmond)
1912 Mexico: an American pilot who has been gun-running for the rebels is pressed into more active service.
Bang-bang actioner which pauses too often for reflection and local colour.
w Robert Towne, Sam Peckinpah *d* Buzz Kulik *ph* Jack Hildyard *m* Maurice Jarre *ad* Ted Howarth
☆ Yul Brynner, Robert Mitchum, Charles Bronson, Grazia Bucetta, Herbert Lom, Alexander Knox, Fernando Rey, Jill Ireland
'A textbook on How Not To Make a Movie.' – *Robert Towne*

Village of Daughters
GB 1961 86m bw
MGM (George H. Brown)
An unemployed commercial traveller in an Italian village finds himself choosing a bride for a successful émigré.
Voluble, gesticulating minor comedy.
w David Pursall, Jack Seddon *d* George Pollock *ph* Geoffrey Faithfull *m* Ron Goodwin
☆ Eric Sykes, Warren Mitchell, Scilla Gabel, Carol White, Grégoire Aslan, John Le Mesurier

Village of the Damned **
GB 1960 78m bw
MGM (Ronald Kinnoch)
Children born simultaneously in an English village prove to be super-intelligent and deadly beings from another planet.
Modestly made but absorbing and logical science fiction, cleanly presented.
w Stirling Silliphant, Wolf Rilla, Geoffrey Barclay novel The Midwich Cuckoos by *John Wyndham d Wolf Rilla ph* Geoffrey Faithfull *m* Ron Goodwin
☆ George Sanders, Barbara Shelley, Michael Gwynn, Martin Stephens, Laurence Naismith
† Sequel: *Children of the Damned* (qv).

Village of the Damned
US 1995 98m Foto-Kem Panavision
Universal/Alphaville (Michael Preger, Sandy King)
In a small Californian town, ten women give simultaneous birth to fair-haired children with strange powers.
A drear remake with a somewhat larger budget, but a decrease in skill and interest; there seems no reason to reproduce an old film, unless it is to exhibit the makers' lack of imagination and originality.
w David Himmelstein *novel The Midwich Cuckoos* by John Wyndham *d* John Carpenter *ph* Gary B. Kibbe *m* John Carpenter, Dave Davies *pd* Rodger Maus *ed* Edward A. Warschilka
☆ Christopher Reeve, Kirstie Alley, Linda Kozlowski, Michael Pare, Meredith Salenger, Mark Hamill, Pippa Pearthree
'A risible remake.' – *Variety*

A Village Tale *
US 1935 79m bw
RKO (David Hempstead)
Envy leads to a clash between two rural landowners.
Unusual but very interesting attempt by Hollywood to film with integrity an old-fashioned country novel. Very dated, but pleasant to watch.
w Allan Scott *novel* Phil Stong *d* John Cromwell *ph* Nicholas Musuraca *m* Alberto Columbo
☆ Randolph Scott, Robert Barrat, Kay Johnson, Arthur Hohl, Janet Beecher, Edward Ellis, Donald Meek, Dorothy Burgess, Andy Clyde, Guinn Williams
'Depressing story without marquee strength. Restricted in appeal.' – *Variety*

Villain
GB 1971 98m Technicolor Panavision
EMI/Kastner/Ladd/Kanter
The come-uppance of a cowardly, sadistic, homosexual East End gang boss with a mother fixation.
Very unpleasant and unentertaining British low life shocker, plainly inspired by White Heat.
w Dick Clement, Ian La Frenais *novel The Burden of Proof* by James Barlow *d* Michael Tuchner *ph* Christopher Challis *m* Jonathan Hodge
☆ Richard Burton, Ian MacShane, Nigel Davenport, Joss Ackland, Cathleen Nesbitt, Donald Sinden, T. P. McKenna, Fiona Lewis

The Villain
US 1979 89m Metrocolor
Columbia/Rastar (Paul Maslansky, Mort Engelberg)
GB title: *Cactus Jack*
An incompetent outlaw rides from one disaster to another.
No doubt amusing in conception, this attempt to put the cartoon character Wile E. Coyote into human form lamentably misfires, six minutes being an ideal length for that kind of comedy.
w Robert G. Kane *d* Hal Needham *ph* Bobby Byrne *m* Bill Justis
☆ Kirk Douglas, Arnold Schwarzenegger, Ann-Margret, Paul Lynde, Ruth Buzzi, Jack Elam, Strother Martin
'Timing is entirely absent from this limp, laughless fiasco, as is any evidence of imagination ... desperation is the keynote.' – *Paul Taylor, MFB*

The Villain Still Pursued Her *
US 1940 66m bw
RKO (Harold B. Franklin)
An innocent family suffers at the hands of a villainous landlord.
Clumsy burlesque of old time melodrama, interesting that it was done at all and with this cast.
w Elbert Franklin *d* Edward F. Cline *ph* Lucien Ballard *m* Frank Tours
☆ Buster Keaton, Alan Mowbray, Anita Louise, Hugh Herbert, Joyce Compton, Margaret Hamilton, Billy Gilbert

La Ville Est Tranquille *
France 2000 133m colour
Artificial Eye/Agat/Cie-Diaphana/Canal+ (Gilles Sandoz, Michel Saint-John, Robert Guediguian)
US title: *The Town is Quiet*
The lives of various people cohere around a hard-working woman, who turns prostitute in an attempt to support her alcoholic husband, drug-addicted daughter, and grandchild.
An ironic title for a impassioned panoramic movie about Marseille and its suffering inhabitants: only at the end, after a catalogue of disasters and deaths, is there a ray of hope.
w Robert Guédiguian, Jean-Louis Milesi *d* Robert Guédiguian *ph* Bernard Cavalie *pd* Michel Vandestien *ed* Bernard Sasia
☆ Ariane Ascaride (Michele), Jean-Pierre Darroussin (Paul), Gerard Meylan (Gerard), Alexandre Ogou (Abderramane), Pierre Banderet (Claude), Jacques Boudet (Paul's Father), Pascale Roberts (Paul's Mother), Julie-Marie Parmentier (Viviane), Christine Brucher (Fiona)
'A film that combines an allegorical structure with an operatic style that pushes every dramatic situation to the extreme.' – *Stephen Holden, New York Times*

Vincent and Theo *
France/GB 1990 140m colour
Blue Dolphin/Belbo Films/Central Films (Ludi Boeken, David Conroy, Emma Hayter)
original title: *Vincent et Theo*
Biopic of Van Gogh and his supportive, but equally tortured, brother.
Interesting, unsensational account of the brothers' lives, though not particularly illuminating.
w Julian Mitchell *d* Robert Altman *ph* Jean Lepine *m* Gabriel Yared *pd* Stephen Altman *ed* Françoise Coispeau, Geraldine Peroni
☆ Tim Roth, Paul Rhys, Johanna Ter Steege, Wladimir Yordanoff, Jip Wijngaarden, Anne Canovas

Vincent: The Life and Death of Vincent van Gogh **
Australia 1987 99m colour
Illumination/Look/Daska (Tony Llewellyn-Jones)
The life and suicide of the artist is recalled in his letters to his brother Theo.
Intriguing documentary, beautifully filmed and much helped by the passion and urgency of John Hurt's readings.
d Paul Cox
☆ John Hurt (narrator)

The Vintage
US 1957 92m Metrocolor Cinemascope
MGM (Edwin H. Knopf)
Two fugitives from justice cause trouble when they become grape pickers.
Steamy drama with an unconvincing French setting; a Hollywood aberration.
w Michael Blankfort *novel* Ursula Keir *d* Jeffrey Hayden *ph* Joseph Ruttenberg *m* David Raksin
☆ Mel Ferrer, John Kerr, Michèle Morgan, Pier Angeli, Theodore Bikel, Leif Erickson

Vintage Wine
GB 1935 90m bw
Gaumont-British/Real Art (Julius Hagen)
A 62-year-old widower upsets his family by marrying a young girl.
Amiable boulevard comedy transferred to the screen in a stagey fashion but providing a vehicle for the well-honed comic skills of Seymour Hicks.
w H. Fowler Mear, Seymour Hicks, Ashley Dukes *play Der Ewige Jüngling* by Alexander Engel *d* Henry Edwards *ph* Sydney Blyth *md* W. L. Trytel *ad* James A. Carter *ed* Ralph Kemplen
☆ Seymour Hicks, Claire Luce, Eva Moore, Judy Gunn, Miles Malleson, Kynaston Reeves, A. Bromley Davenport, Michael Shepley

Violent City
Italy/France 1970 100m Technicolor Techniscope
Rank/Fono Roma/Unidis/Universal France (Harry Colombo, George Papi)
original title: *Città Violenta*
aka: *The Family*
Released from prison, a hitman goes after the man who betrayed him and stole his girlfriend.
Fast-moving, body-strewn melodrama that rarely strays from the obvious.
wd Sauro Scavolini, Gianfranco Calligarich, Lina Wertmüller, Sergio Sollima *story* Dino Maiuri, Massimo de Rita *ph* Aldo Tonti *m* Ennio Morricone *ad* Francesco Bronzi *ed* Nino Baragli
☆ Charles Bronson, Jill Ireland, Michel Constantin, Telly Savalas, Umberto Orsini, George Savalas
† The film was cut to 91m for its British release.

Violent Cop *
Japan 1989 103m colour
ICA/Bandai/Shochiku-Fuji (Hisao Nabeshima, Takio Yoshida, Shozo Ichoyama)
original title: *Sono Otoko Kyobo ni Tsuki*
aka: *Warning, This Man Is Wild*
A maverick homicide cop, while teaching his new partner the tricks of the trade, discovers that his crooked colleagues are involved in drug dealing.
A violent story of revenge and casual brutality, which resembles Dirty Harry translated to Tokyo.
w Hisashi Nozawa *d* Takeshi Kitano *ph* Yasushi Sakakibara *m* Daisaku, Kume, Eric Satie *ad* Masuteru Mochizuki *ed* Nobutake Kamiya
☆ 'Beat' Takeshi (Takeshi Kitano), Maiko Kawakami, Makoto Ashigawa, Haku Ryu, Ken Yoshizawa, Shiro Sano, Ittoku Kishibe, Shigeru Hiraizumi
'Slow tempo and arty look suits it for film festival dates.' – *Variety*

The Violent Enemy
GB 1968 98m Eastmancolor
Trio/Group W. (Wilfrid Eades)
An IRA explosives expert escapes from a British jail but quarrels with his leaders.
Dullish political melodrama needlessly rubbing salt in old wounds.
w Edmund Ward *novel A Candle for the Dead* by Hugh Marlowe *d* Don Sharp *ph* Alan Hume *m* John Scott
☆ Tom Bell, Ed Begley, Susan Hampshire, Noel Purcell, Michael Standing

The Violent Men *
US 1955 96m Technicolor Cinemascope
Columbia (Lewis J. Rachmil)
GB title: *Rough Company*
A crippled cattle baron drives small landowners from his valley, while his wife has an affair with his younger brother.
So much snarling goes on that this seems like a gangster film in fancy dress, but it does hold the attention.
w Harry Kleiner *novel* Donald Hamilton *d* Rudolph Maté *ph* Burnett Guffey, W. Howard Greene *m* Max Steiner
☆ Edward G. Robinson, Barbara Stanwyck, Glenn Ford, Brian Keith, Dianne Foster, May Wynn, Warner Anderson, Basil Ruysdael

The Violent Ones *
US 1967 90m Eastmancolor
Madison/Harold Goldman
In a small Mexican town, three American hobos are interrogated after the rape and murder of a local girl.
Rather well-shot murder mystery with emphasis on character, leading to a desert chase climax.
w Doug Wilson, Charles Davis *d Fernando Lamas ph Fleet Southcott m* Marlin Skiles
☆ Fernando Lamas, Aldo Ray, David Carradine, Tommy Sands

Violent Playground
GB 1958 108m bw
Rank (Michael Relph)
A junior liaison officer in the Liverpool slums falls in love with the sister of a fire-raiser.
'Realistic' melodrama sabotaged by an entirely schematic and predictable plot; enervatingly dull until the siege climax.
w James Kennaway *d* Basil Dearden *ph* Reg Wyer *m* Philip Green
☆ Stanley Baker, Anne Heywood, David McCallum, Peter Cushing, John Slater, Clifford Evans

'The bank robbers that caught a town with its morals down!'
Violent Saturday *
US 1955 90m DeLuxe Cinemascope
TCF (Buddy Adler)
Crooks move quietly into a small town with the intention of robbing the bank.
Interesting little melodrama which the wide screen robs of its proper tension. Adequate presentation and performance.
w Sydney Boehm *d* Richard Fleischer *ph* Charles G. Clarke *m* Hugo Friedhofer
☆ Richard Egan, Victor Mature, Stephen McNally, Sylvia Sidney, Virginia Leith, Tommy Noonan, Lee Marvin, Margaret Hayes, J. Carrol Naish, Ernest Borgnine

Violent Streets: see *The Thief*

Violent Tradition: see *John Woo's Once a Thief*

Violette Nozière *
France/Canada 1977 122m Eastmancolor
Filmel/Cinevideo (Roger Morand)
In 1933 Paris, an eighteen-year-old girl leads a double life, gets syphilis, poisons her parents and is convicted of murder.
Oddly erratic but interesting recapitulation of a famous French murder case, not quite typical of its director.
w Odile Barski, Herve Bromberger, Frederic Grendel *d* Claude Chabrol *ph* Jean Rabier *m* Pierre Jansen *pd* Jacques Brizzio
☆ Isabelle Huppert, Jean Carmier, Stephane Audran, Bernadette Lafont

The VIPs **
GB 1963 119m Metrocolor Panavision
MGM (Anatole de Grunwald)
Passengers at London Airport are delayed by fog and spend the night at a hotel.
Multi-story compendium cunningly designed to exploit the real-life Burton-Taylor romance. In itself, competent rather than stimulating.
w Terence Rattigan *d* Anthony Asquith *ph* Jack Hildyard *m* Miklos Rozsa
☆ Richard Burton, Elizabeth Taylor, Maggie Smith, Rod Taylor, *Margaret Rutherford*, Louis Jourdan, Elsa Martinelli, Orson Welles, Linda Christian, Dennis Price, Richard Wattis, David Frost, Robert Coote, Joan Benham, Michael Hordern and also Lance Percival, Martin Miller
'If Mr Rattigan's Aunt Edna still goes to the pictures she should like his latest offering, especially if she has a good lunch first.' – *Brenda Davies*
Margaret Rutherford

Virgin among the Living Dead
France 1971 85m Eastmancolor
J.K. Films/Prodif (K. H. Mannchen)
original title: *Une Vierge chez les Morts Vivants*
aka: *Christina; Princesse de l'Erotisme*
A young woman visits an isolated chateau for the reading of her father's will and is haunted by erotic dreams of death.
Bizarre but dull attempt at an atmospheric ghost story coupled with some exploitative nudity; it is shot in the director's usual clumsy style, with much use of pointless zooms to uninteresting images.
wd Jess (Jesús) Franco *ph* J. Climent *ed* P. Belair *m/sp* Bruno Nicolai

☆ Cristine von Blanc, Howard Vernon, Britt Nichols, Rosa Palomar, Anne Libert, Jesus Manera, Paul Muller

'A rambling, self-indulgent mess that is low on scares and high on skin content. Watch at your peril.' – *The Dark Side*

The Virgin and the Gypsy *

GB 1970 95m colour
Kenwood/Dimitri de Grunwald (Kenneth Harper)

A Midlands clergyman's daughter falls in love with a gypsy fortune teller.

Slow, sensitive, stylish picturization of a Lawrence novella, with generally good performances.

w *Alan Plater* *story* *D. H. Lawrence* *d* *Christopher Miles* *ph* Robert Huke *m* Patrick Gowers *pd* Terence Knight

☆ Joanna Shimkus, Franco Nero, Honor Blackman, Mark Burns, Maurice Denham, Fay Compton, Kay Walsh, Norman Bird

'A minor but lively pleasure.' – *John Simon*

Virgin Island

GB 1958 94m Eastmancolor
British Lion/Countryman (Leon Clore, Graham Tharp)
US title: *Our Virgin Island*

A young couple set up house on a tiny Caribbean island.

Pleasant comedy slowed down by lack of plot and too much conversation.

w Philip Rush, Pat Jackson *book* *Our Virgin Island* by Robb White *d* Pat Jackson *ph* Freddie Francis *m* Clifton Parker

☆ Virginia Maskell, John Cassavetes, Sidney Poitier, Isabel Dean, Colin Gordon

'Twentieth Century Fox spectacularly spreads before you the violent age and velvet cape of Sir Walter Raleigh!'

The Virgin Queen *

US 1955 92m DeLuxe Cinemascope
TCF (Charles Brackett)

The relationship of Queen Elizabeth I and Sir Walter Raleigh.

Unhistorical charade, quite pleasantly made and worth noting for its star performance.

w Harry Brown, Mindret Lord *d* Henry Koster *ph* Charles G. Clarke *m* Franz Waxman

☆ *Bette Davis*, Richard Todd, Joan Collins, Herbert Marshall, Jay Robinson, Dan O'Herlihy, Robert Douglas, Romney Brent

'Sooner or later they're going to get it!'

The Virgin Soldiers **

GB 1969 96m Technicolor
Columbia/Carl Foreman (Leslie Gilliat, Ned Sherrin)

Serio-comic adventures of recruits in the British army in 1960 Singapore.

Autobiographical fragments, mostly from below the belt, sharply observed and often very funny.

w *John Hopkins* *novel* *Leslie Thomas* *d* *John Dexter* *ph* *Ken Higgins* *m* Peter Greenwell

☆ *Hywel Bennett*, Nigel Patrick, *Lynn Redgrave*, Nigel Davenport, *Rachel Kempson*, Michael Gwynn, Tsai Chin

'A kind of monstrous mating of *Private's Progress* and *The Family Way*, with bits of *The Long and the Short and the Tall* thrown in for good measure.' – *David Pirie*

† Sequel 1977: *Stand Up Virgin Soldiers.*

The Virgin Spring *

Sweden 1959 87m bw
Svensk Filmindustri (Allan Ekelund)

original title: *Jungfrukällan*

When her murderers are killed, a spring bubbles up from the spot where a young maiden met her death.

Stark and rather lovely filming of a medieval legend, with heavy symbolism and a strong pictorial sense.

w Ulla Isaakson *d* Ingmar Bergman *ph* Sven Nykvist *m* Erik Nordgren

☆ Max von Sydow, Birgitta Valberg, Gunnel Lindblom, Brigitta Pettersson

'When I first saw the film I thought it merely nauseous. At a second view I find it generally tedious, occasionally absurd, and always retrograde.' – *Dilys Powell*

best foreign film

'Love. Sex. Passion. Fear. Obsession.'

Virgin Suicides *

US 1999 97m CFI
American Zoetrope (Francis Ford Coppola, Julie Costanzo, Chris Hanley, Dan Halsted)

A man recalls how, 25 years earlier, he and his friends could not prevent five teenage daughters of repressive parents killing themselves.

A tale of suburban America in the 70s that approaches its subject with sympathy and subtlety, but leaves the deaths as a puzzle that it does not attempt to explain.

wd Sofia Coppola *novel* Jeffrey Eugenides *ph* Edward Lachman *m* Air *pd* Jasna Stefanovic *ed* James Lyon, Melissa Kent *cos* Nancy Steiner

☆ James Woods (Mr Lisbon), Kathleen Turner (Mrs Lisbon), Kirsten Dunst (Lux), John Hartnett (Trip Fontaine), Hannah Hall (Cecilia), Chelse Swain (Bonnie), A.J. Cook (Mary), Leslie Hayman (Theres), Danny DeVito (Dr Hornicker), Scott Glenn (Father Moody), Jonathan Tucker (Tim), Anthony DeSimone (Chase), Giovanni Ribisi (Narrator)

'Catches both the triviality and the grandeur of youth, its prosaic details and its mythopoetic flights.' – *A. O. Scott, New York Times*

'Lays the table beautifully, but then serves only snacks.' – *Adam Mars-Jones, Times*

Virgin Witch

GB 1971 89m colour
Univista (Ralph Solomons)

Two sisters run away to London and become involved with the lesbian head of a modelling agency who persuades them to take part in satanic rituals.

Cheaply and ineptly shot horror movie, with script and acting to match, in which the cast shed their clothes at the slightest opportunity.

w Klaus Vogel *d* Ray Austin *ph* Gerald Moss *m* Ted Dicks *ed* Philip Barnikel

☆ Patricia Haines, Neil Hallett, Keith Buckley, James Chase, Vicki Michelle, Ann Michelle

Virginia

US 1940 107m Technicolor
Paramount (Edward H. Griffith)

A showgirl goes home to claim her inheritance, but thinks of marrying a rich Yankee.

Languid post-Civil War romantic melodrama, only memorable for its colour.

w Virginia Van Upp *d* Edward H. Griffith *ph* Bert Glennon, William V. Skall

☆ Madeleine Carroll, Fred MacMurray, Sterling Hayden, Helen Broderick, Paul Hurst, Marie Wilson, Carolyn Lee, Louise Beavers

Virginia City *

US 1940 121m bw
Warner (Robert Fellows)

A dance hall girl is really a Southern spy helping a rebel colonel to steal a gold shipment from her Yankee boyfriend.

Lumpy Western in Warner's best budget but worst manner: the stars look unhappy and the plot progresses in fits and starts.

w Robert Buckner *d* Michael Curtiz *ph* Sol Polito *m* Max Steiner

☆ Errol Flynn, Randolph Scott, Miriam Hopkins, Humphrey Bogart, Frank McHugh, Alan Hale, Guinn Williams, John Litel, Moroni Olsen, Russell Hicks, Douglass Dumbrille

The Virginia Judge

US 1935 70m bw
Paramount (Charles R. Rogers)

A Southern judge's ne'er-do-well son gets deeper into trouble.

Homely vehicle for a star whose 'judge' was for many years the centre of a vaudeville monologue.

w Henry Johnson, Frank Adams, Inez Lopez *d* Edward Sedgwick

☆ Walter C. Kelly, Marsha Hunt, Stepin Fetchit, Johnny Downs, Robert Cummings

The Virginian *

US 1929 95m bw
Paramount (Louis D. Lighton)

A stalwart ranch foreman has to see his best friend hanged for rustling, and defeats the local bad man.

Standard Western with famous clichés, e.g. 'Smile when you say that…'

w Edward E. Paramore Jnr, Howard Estabrook *novel* Owen Wister *d* Victor Fleming *ph* J. Roy Hunt

☆ *Gary Cooper*, *Walter Huston*, Richard Arlen, Mary Brian, Chester Conklin, Eugene Pallette

The Virginian

US 1946 90m Technicolor
Paramount (Paul Jones)

A cowboy discovers that his best friend has become a cattle-rustler.

Vapid remake of the classic story.

w Frances Goodrich, Albert Hackett *d* Stuart Gilmore *ph* Harry Hallenberger *m* Daniele Amfitheatrof

☆ Joel McCrea, Brian Donlevy, Sonny Tufts, Barbara Britton, William Frawley, Henry O'Neill, Fay Bainter

Virgins and Vampires: see *Requiem for a Vampire*

Viridiana ****

Spain/Mexico 1961 91m bw
Uninci/Films 59/Gustavo Alatriste (Munoz Suay)

A novice about to take her vows is corrupted by her wicked uncle and installs a load of beggars in his house.

Often hilarious surrealist melodrama packed with shades of meaning, most of them sacrilegious. A fascinating film to watch.

w Luis Buñuel, Julio Alajandro *d* *Luis Buñuel* *ph* José F. Agayo

☆ Silvia Pinal, Francisco Rabal, Fernando Rey

'One of the cinema's few major philosophical works.' – *Robert Vas*

'An extraordinary film, a superb film.' – *Dilys Powell*

Virtual Assassin: see *Cyberjack*

'The world's last virgin!'

Virtual Sexuality

GB 1999 92m DeLuxe
Columbia TriStar/The Bridge/Noel Gay (Christopher Figg)

When a computer experiment goes wrong, a teenage schoolgirl is transformed into two people, herself and a teenage youth with her mind, with whom she falls in love.

A British attempt a a highschool movie with a gender-changing gimmick and the usual smutty jokes.

w Nick Fisher *novel* Chloe Rayban *d* Nick Hurran *ph* Brian Tufano *m* Rupert Gregson-Williams *pd* Chris Edwards *ed* John Richards

☆ Laura Fraser (Justine), Rupert Penry-Jones (Jake), Luke De Lacey (Chas), Kieran O'Brien (Alex), Marcelle Duprey (Fran), Natasha Bell (Hoover), Steve John Shepherd (Jason), Laura Macauley (Monica)

'Vulgar, tacky and creepy.' – *Peter Bradshaw, Guardian*

Virtue

US 1932 68m bw
Columbia

A woman of the streets is regenerated through marriage.

Routine matinée programmer.

w Robert Riskin *story* Ethel Hill *d* Edward Buzzell

☆ Carole Lombard, Pat O'Brien, Mayo Methot, Jack La Rue, Ward Bond

'A lot of plot is squeezed into the running time … the picture will be liked.' – *Variety*

Virtuosity

US 1995 105m DeLuxe
Paramount (Gary Lucchesi)

In 1999, a computer-created psychopathic killer enters the real world, where he is hunted by a former cop.

Frenetic action movie, all show, no substance and not much sense amid the noise.

w Eric Bernt *d* Brett Leonard *ph* Gale Tattersall *m* Christopher Young *pd* Nilo Rodis *ed* B. J. Sears, Rob Kobrin *sp* L2 Communications

☆ Denzel Washington, Kelly Lynch, Russell Crowe, Stephen Spinella, William Forsythe, Louise Fletcher, William Fichtner

'Offers only the evanescent thrills of a videogame, despite a profusion of flashy effects and high-velocity pacing.' – *Variety*

The Virtuous Bigamist: see *Four Steps in the Clouds*

The Virtuous Sin

US 1930 81m bw
Paramount
GB title: *Cast Iron*

A girl tries to help her student husband when war takes him away from bacteriology.

Stilted romantic drama.

w Martin Brown, Louise Long *novel* Lajos Zilahy *d* George Cukor, Louis Gasnier *ph* David Abel

☆ Walter Huston, Kay Francis, Kenneth MacKenna, Paul Cavanagh

'Average programme flicker … cast names all from legit … nor is there much excuse for the picture running 80 minutes when 70 would have been better.' – *Variety*

'Earth is in for a shock.'

Virus

US 1999 100m DeLuxe
Universal/Mutual/Dark Horse/Valhalla (Gale Anne Hurd)

The crew of a salvage tug boards an apparently abandoned Russian ship, but it has been taken over by an extra-terrestrial force that regards humans as a virus to be eradicated.

Frenetic, simple-minded science-fiction that follows an obvious course with few surprises along the way.

w Chuck Pfarrer, Dennis Feldman *comic books* Chuck Pfarrer *d* John Bruno *ph* David Eggby *m* Joel McNeely *pd* Mayling Cheng *ed* Scott Smith *sp* Chuck Gaspar; robotic fx: Steve Johnson, Eric Allard

☆ Jamie Lee Curtis (Kit Foster), William Baldwin (Steve Baker), Donald Sutherland (Captain Everton), Joanna Pacula (Nadia), Marshall Bell (J.W. Woods Jnr), Julio Oscar Mechoso (Squeaky), Sherman Augustus (Richie), Cliff Curtis (Hiko), Yuri Chervotkin (Colonel Kominski), Keith Flippen (Captain Lonya Rostov)

'Derivative sci-fi shocker that isn't likely to spark much interest beyond its target audience of undemanding genre fans.' – *Joe Leydon, Variety*

The Viscount: see *The Investigator*

Visions of Light ***

US/Japan 1992 92m bw/colour
City Screen/American Film Institute/NHK (Stuart Samuels)

Documentary tracing the development of cinematography from *The Birth of a Nation* in 1915 through to the present day.

An engrossing look at the contribution to film of the often unsung cinematographers, with excerpts from 125 feature films and interviews with 27 practitioners, from Nestor Almendros to Vilmos Zsigmond.

w Todd McCarthy *d* Arnold Glassman, Todd McCarthy, Stuart Samuels *ph* Nancy Schreiber *ed* Arnold Glassman

☆ Todd McCarthy (interviewer)

The Visit

West Germany/France/Italy/US 1964 100m bw Cinemascope
TCF/Deutschefox/Cinecittà/Dear Film/Films du Siècle/PECF (Julien Derode, Anthony Quinn)

A millionairess offers a fortune to her home town, providing someone will kill her ex-lover.

A realistic production ill befits an essentially theatrical play, and all the effort goes for nothing.

w Ben Barzman *play* Friedrich Durrenmatt *d* Bernhard Wicki *ph* Armando Nannuzzi *m* Richard Arnell, Hans-Martin Majewski

☆ Ingrid Bergman, Anthony Quinn, Paolo Stoppa, Hans-Christian Blech, Valentina Cortesa, Irina Demick, Claude Dauphin, Eduardo Ciannelli

† The film's score was written by Richard Arnell with the exception of one sequence retained from Hans-Martin Majewski's otherwise rejected music.

Visit to a Chief's Son

US 1974 92m DeLuxe Panavision
UA/Robert Halmi

An American anthropologist and his son hope to film the rituals of an African tribe.

Minor adventure film with a happy resolution, based on a photomontage by the producer, a Life photographer.
w Albert Ruben *d* *Lamont Johnson* *ph* Ernest Day *m* Francis Lai
☆ Robert Mulligan, Johnny Sekka, John Philip Hodgdon

Visit to a Small Planet
US 1960 101m bw
Paramount/Wallis-Hazen
A young man from outer space takes a look at Earth and falls in love.
A satirical play disastrously adapted for the moronic comedy of an unsuitable star.
w Edmund Beloin, Henry Garson *play* Gore Vidal *d* Norman Taurog *ph* Loyal Griggs *m* Leigh Harline
☆ Jerry Lewis, Joan Blackman, Earl Holliman, Fred Clark, John Williams, Jerome Cowan, Gavin Gordon, Lee Patrick
ad Hal Pereira, Walter Tyler

'They Weren't Born Yesterday!'
Les Visiteurs *
France 1993 107m colour
Arrow/Gaumont/France 3/Alpilles/Amigo (Alain Terzian)
A knight and his servant are transported from the 12th century to the modern day.
Broad farce that will appeal to lovers of Carry On *films.*
w Christian Claiver, Jean-Marie Poiré *d* Jean-Marie Poiré *ph* Jean-Yves Le Mener *m* Eric Lévi *pd* Hugues Tissandier *ed* Catherine Kelber
☆ Christian Clavier, Jean Reno, Valérie Lemercier, Marie-Anne Chazel, Christian Bujeau, Isabelle Nanty, Didier Pain

'The French tradition doesn't always recognise the distinction between high and low comedy, and there is certainly a boisterousness about the proceedings which some viewers will find wearing.' – *Adam Mars-Jones*

'People fall over a lot, or hit each other, or shout very loud.' – *Sight and Sound*

† The film was the biggest box-office success of 1993 in France, taking twice as much at the box-office as the No. 2 film, *Jurassic Park*.

Les Visiteurs du Soir *
France 1942 110m bw
André Paulvé
aka: *The Devil's Envoys*
The devil sends messengers to Earth to corrupt two lovers, but he fails: even though he turns them to stone, their hearts still beat.
Made during the Occupation, this stately medieval fable was intended to be significant: the devil was Hitler, and the heartbeat that of France. Perhaps because it is so conscious of hidden meanings, it moves rather stiffly but is often beautiful to behold.
w Jacques Prévert, Pierre Laroche *d* *Marcel Carné* *ph* Roger Hubert *m* Joseph Kosma, Maurice Thiriet *ad* Alexandre Trauner, Georges Wakhevitch
☆ Arletty, *Jules Berry*, Marie Déa, Alain Cuny, Fernand Ledoux, Marcel Herrand

'There are wonderful images, but the movie is heavy on the allegorical and becomes rather slow and stylized.' – *Pauline Kael, 70s*

Visiting Hours
Canada 1981 105m colour Panavision
Filmplan International (Claude Héroux)
A homicidal maniac is at large in a hospital.
Tedious shocker wasting a reliable idea.
w Brian Taggert *d* Jean Claude Lord *ph* René Verzier *m* Jonathan Goldsmith
☆ Michael Ironside, Lee Grant, Linda Purl, William Shatner, Lenore Zann, Harvey Atkin

The Visitor
Italy 1979 90m colour
Ovidio Assonitis
Creatures from another world come to Earth to deal with a child who is the offspring of an evil mutant alien.
Fussy direction, minimal acting and a plot that makes little sense combine to create an incoherent movie.
w Lou Comici, Robert Mundy *story* Michael J. Paradise, Ovidio Assonitis *d* Michael J. Paradise (Giulio Paradisi) *ph* Ennio Guarnieri *m* Franco Micalizzi *ad* Frank Vanorio *ed* Robert Curi
☆ Mel Ferrer, Glenn Ford, Lance Henriksen, John Huston, Joanne Nail, Sam Peckinpah, Shelley Winters, Paige Conner

Viskingar och Rop: see *Cries and Whispers*

Visckningar och Rop ****
Sweden 1972 91m Eastmancolor
Cinematograph (Ingmar Bergman)
aka: *Cries and Whispers*
A young woman dying of cancer in her family home is tended by her two sisters.
Quiet, chilling, classical chapter of doom which variously reminds one of Chekhov, Tolstoy and Dostoievsky but is also essential Bergman. Tough but important viewing, it lingers afterwards in the mind like a picture vividly painted in shades of red.
wd Ingmar Bergman ph Sven Nykvist m Chopin and Bach
☆ *Harriet Andersson, Kari Sylwan, Ingrid Thulin, Liv Ullmann*

'Harrowing, spare and perceptive, but lacking the humour that helps to put life and death into perspective.' – *Michael Billington, Illustrated London News*

Sven Nykvist
best picture; Ingmar Bergman (as writer); Ingmar Bergman (as director)

Visszaesök: see *Forbidden Relations*

La Vita è Bella: see *Life Is Beautiful*

I Vitelloni
Italy/France 1953 109m bw
Peg/Cité (Lorenzo Pegoraro)
aka: *Spivs*
In a small Italian resort, aimless young people get into various kinds of trouble.
Interesting in its realistic detail, this sharply observed slice of life is long enough for its basic purposelessness to become apparent.
w Federico Fellini, Ennio Flaiano, Tullio Pinelli *d* Federico Fellini *ph* Otello Martelli, Tasatti, Carlini *m* Nino Rota
☆ Franco Fabrizi, Franco Interlenghi, Eleonora Ruffo, Alberto Sordi
script

Viva Knievel!
US 1977 106m Technicolor Panavision
Warner/Metropolitan (Stan Hough)
Gangsters plan to kill motorcycle stunt rider Evel Knievel in order to use his trailer as a means of smuggling cocaine from Mexico into the United States.
Dreary hagiography, an uneasy mix of fact and fiction that preaches an anti-drug message, while using drugs and gangsters to provide its spurious excitement. In between his stunts, Evel makes the lame walk, causes women to go weak at the knees, cures junkies, reconciles an estranged father and son, and bores cinema audiences.
w Antonio Santillan, Norman Katkov *d* Gordon Douglas *ph* Fred Jackman *m* Charles Bernstein *pd* Ward Preston *ed* Harold Kress
☆ Evel Knievel, Gene Kelly, Lauren Hutton, Marjoe Gortner, Red Buttons, Eric Shea, Leslie Nielsen, Cameron Mitchell, Dabney Coleman

Viva Las Vegas!: see *Meet Me in Las Vegas (1956)*

Viva Las Vegas
US 1964 85m Metrocolor Panavision
MGM (Jack Cummings, George Sidney)
GB title: *Love in Las Vegas*
A sports car racer has fun in the gambling city.
Tolerable star musical.
w Sally Benson *d* George Sidney *ph* Joseph Biroc *md* George Stoll
☆ Elvis Presley, Ann-Margret, Cesare Danova, William Demarest, Nicky Blair, Jack Carter

Viva Maria!
France/Italy 1965 120m Eastmancolor Panavision
Nouvelles Editions/Artistes Associés/Vides (Oscar Dancigers, Louis Malle)
An Irish anarchist girl arrives in Central America and joins a group of strolling players.
All show and no substance, this is a colour supplement of a film, neither fish, flesh nor good red herring.
w Louis Malle, Jean-Claude Carrière *d* Louis Malle *ph* Henri Decaë *m* Georges Delerue *ad* Bernard Evein
☆ Jeanne Moreau, Brigitte Bardot, George Hamilton, Paulette Dubost, Claudio Brook
Jeanne Moreau

Viva Max
US 1969 93m Eastmancolor
Commonwealth United/Mark Carliner
A Mexican general marches his troops into Texas and seizes the Alamo.
Flat comedy with mildly amusing passages but too much noise, bluster and sentiment.
w Elliott Baker *novel* James Lehrer *d* Jerry Paris *ph* Jack Richards *m* Hugo Montenegro
☆ Peter Ustinov, *John Astin*, Pamela Tiffin, Jonathan Winters, Keenan Wynn, Henry Morgan, Alice Ghostley

'1001 nights of glorious romantic adventure!'
Viva Villa! **
US 1934 110m bw
MGM (David O. Selznick)
The career of a Mexican rebel.
Gutsy action drama with some smoothing over of fact in the name of entertainment. A big, highly competent production of its year.
w Ben Hecht d Jack Conway ph James Wong Howe, Charles G. Clarke m Herbert Stothart
☆ *Wallace Beery*, Fay Wray, Leo Carrillo, Donald Cook, Stuart Erwin, George E. Stone, Joseph Schildkraut, Henry B. Walthall, Katherine de Mille

'Glorified western ... strong b.o. fodder, handicapped a bit perhaps by its abnormal masculine appeal.' – *Variety*

'A strange poem of violence.' – *John Baxter, 1968*

'A glorified horse opera ... the spectator's excitement is incited by the purely physical impact of the furious riding and war sequences, by the frequent sadism, and by the lively musical score.' – *Irving Lerner*

† Howard Hawks directed some sequences, uncredited.
best picture; script

Viva Zapata **
US 1952 113m bw
TCF (Darryl F. Zanuck)
A Mexican revolutionary is finally betrayed by a friend.
Moody, good-looking star vehicle taking a romanticized but glum view of history.
w John Steinbeck *d Elia Kazan ph Joe MacDonald* *m* Alex North *md* Alfred Newman *ad* Lyle Wheeler, Leland Fuller
☆ Marlon Brando, Jean Peters, Joseph Wiseman, Anthony Quinn, Arnold Moss, Margo, *Frank Silvera*
Anthony Quinn
John Steinbeck; Alex North; Marlon Brando; art direction
Marlon Brando

Vivacious Lady *
US 1938 90m bw
RKO (George Stevens)
A night-club singer marries a botany professor and has trouble with his parents.
Pleasant romantic comedy for two popular stars.
w P. J. Wolfson, Ernest Pagano *d* George Stevens *ph* Robert de Grasse *m* Roy Webb
☆ *Ginger Rogers, James Stewart*, Charles Coburn, Beulah Bondi, James Ellison, Frances Mercer, Franklin Pangborn, Grady Sutton, Jack Carson

'A good-natured, unpretentiously entertaining comedy.' – *New Yorker*

Robert de Grasse

Vivement Dimanche!: see *Finally, Sunday*

Vivre pour Vivre: see *Live for Life*

Vixen
US 1968 71m Eastmancolor
Cinecenta/Eve/Coldstream (Russ Meyer)
A nymphomaniac seduces every passing stranger of either sex.
Comic exploitation film in which the cast, at least, appear to be enjoying themselves.
w Robert Rudelson *story* Russ Meyer, Anthony James Ryan *d* Russ Meyer *ph* Russ Meyer *ad* Wilfred Kues *ed* Russ Meyer, Richard Brummer
☆ Erica Gavin, Harrison Page, Garth Pillsbury, Michael Donovan O'Donnell, Vincene Wallace
† The film was cut to 47m for its British release.

I Vizi Morbosi di una Governante: see *Crazy Desires of a Murderer*

Vogues of 1938 *
US 1937 108m Technicolor
Walter Wanger
reissue title: *All This and Glamour Too*
Rival fashion houses compete at the Seven Arts Ball.
A fashion show with threads of plot, interesting for clothes and cast, all working hard.
w Bella and Samuel Spewack *d* Irving Cummings *ph* Ray Rennahan *m* Victor Young *md* Boris Morros *ch* Seymour Felix *ad* Alexander Toluboff
☆ Joan Bennett, Warner Baxter, Helen Vinson, Mischa Auer, Alan Mowbray, Jerome Cowan, Alma Kruger, Marjorie Gateson, Penny Singleton, Hedda Hopper
song 'That Old Feeling' (*m*Sammy Fain, *ly*Lew Brown); Alexander Toluboff

The Voice in the Mirror
US 1958 102m bw Cinemascope
Universal-International
A reformed alcoholic thinks back on his past life.
Glum case history of no particular point or persuasiveness.
w Larry Marcus *d* Harry Keller *ph* William H. Daniels *m* Henry Mancini
☆ Richard Egan, Julie London, Walter Matthau, Arthur O'Connell, Troy Donahue, Mae Clarke, Ann Doran

A Voice in the Wind
US 1944 85m bw
UA/Arthur Ripley
Two refugees from the Nazis meet again and die on a remote island.
Pretentious romantic claptrap, fascinating only for a few of the impressionist effects it contrives on the lowest of budgets.
w Frederick Torberg *d Arthur Ripley* *m* Michel Michelet
☆ Francis Lederer, Sigrid Gurie, J. Carrol Naish

'Like a mid-thirties French melodrama drenched in the Rembrandt-and-molasses manner of German films of the early to middle twenties. Even within those terms it is much less good than it might be, solemn, unimaginative, thinly detailed; but it is also richly nostalgic if you have any feeling for bad period art.' – *James Agee*

Michel Michelet

The Voice of Bugle Ann *
US 1936 70m bw
MGM (John Considine Jnr)
When a dog is killed its embittered owner seeks revenge.
Old-fashioned country tale, rather heavy-going but emotionally strong.
w Harvey Gates, Samuel Hoffenstein *novel* Mackinlay Kantor *d* Richard Thorpe *ph* Ernest Haller
☆ Lionel Barrymore, Maureen O'Sullivan, Eric Linden, Dudley Digges, Spring Byington, Charley Grapewin

'A very fine movie indeed.' – *Pare Lorentz*

The Voice of Merrill
GB 1952 84m bw
Tempean (Robert Baker, Monty Berman)
US title: *Murder Will Out*
Three men are suspected of murder but one becomes a potential victim.
Complicated murder thriller which intrigues but hardly satisfies.

wd John Gilling *ph* Monty Berman *m* Frank Cordell
☆ Valerie Hobson, James Robertson Justice, Edward Underdown, Henry Kendall, Garry Marsh, Sam Kydd

The Voice of the Turtle **
US 1948 103m bw
Warner (Charles Hoffman)
aka: *One for the Book*
A girl shares her apartment with a soldier on leave.
A three-character play is smoothly filmed, slightly broadened, and burnished till its pale wit glows nicely.
w John Van Druten play John Van Druten
d Irving Rapper ph Sol Polito *m* Max Steiner
☆ *Eleanor Parker*, Ronald Reagan, *Eve Arden*, Wayne Morris, Kent Smith
'A light and lovely comedy.' – *People*

Voices
GB 1973 91m Technicolor
Hemdale/Warden (Robert Enders)
A young couple in an old country house are haunted by the voice of their dead son.
Twisty little ghost story which would have been more effective at one third of its length.
w George Kirgo, Robert Enders *play* Richard Lortz *d* Kevin Billington *ph* Geoffrey Unsworth *m* Richard Rodney Bennett
☆ Gayle Hunnicutt, David Hemmings

La Voie Lactée: see *The Milky Way*

Volcano: see *Les Rendezvous du Diable (1958)*

'The Coast Is Toast.'
Volcano *
US 1997 102m DeLuxe
TCF/Shuler Donner/Donner (Neal H. Moritz, Andrew Z. Davis)
A tunnel being constructed under Los Angeles causes a volcanic eruption that wipes out much of the city.
Hectic disaster flick, played with a straight face by its cast; it's silly enough to be enjoyable.
w Jerome Armstrong, Billy Ray *d* Mick Jackson *ph* Theo van de Sande *m* Alan Silvestri *pd* Jackson DeGovia *ed* Michael Tronick, Don Brochu
☆ Tommy Lee Jones, Anne Heche, Gaby Hoffman, Don Cheadle, Jacqueline Kim, Keith David, John Corbett
'It's all total hokum, and if you don't quake with terror, you can always laugh.' – *The Times*

Volere Volare *
Italy 1991 92m colour
Metro/Italtoons (Ernesto di Sarro, Mario Cecchi Gori, Vittorio Cecchi Gori)
A sound engineer who dubs animated films finds himself changing into a cartoon character as he becomes involved with a psycho-sexual prostitute.
Witty and inventive comedy that mixes live action and animation to amusing effect.
wd Maurizio Nichetti, Guido Manuli *ph* Mario Battistoni *ad* Maria Pio Angelini *ed* Rita Rossi
☆ Maurizio Nichetti, Angela Finocchiaro, Mariella Valentina, Patrizio Roversi
'An offbeat fable for adults. Pic's expensive technical bravura is more impressive than the comedy.' – *Variety*

Les Voleurs
France 1996 116m colour
Metro Tartan/TF1/Rhône-Alpes/DA/Alain Sarde
aka: *Thieves*
A world-weary cop, the brother of a crook, becomes the lover of a petty thief, who is in love with her female philosophy teacher.
A downbeat, tangled tale of dysfunctional families and awkward relationships.
w André Téchiné, Gilles Taurand *d* André Téchiné *ph* Jeanne Lapoirie *m* Philippe Sarde *ad* Ze Branco *ed* Martine Giordano
☆ Catherine Deneuve, Daniel Auteuil, Laurence Côte, Benoite Magimel, Fabienne Babe, Didier Bezace, Julien Riviere, Ivan Desny
'A dense, dark film, filled with pessimism and solitude, but also with a passion for film-making.' – *Ginette Vincendeau, Sight and Sound*

Voltaire *
US 1933 72m bw
Warner (Ray Griffith)
The life and times of the 18th-century French wit.
One of the better Arliss charades, because the film is as stagey as his performance.
w Paul Green, Maude T. Howell *novel* George Gibbs, E. Laurence Dudley *d* John Adolfi *ph* Tony Gaudio
☆ *George Arliss*, Doris Kenyon, Margaret Lindsay, Reginald Owen, Alan Mowbray, David Torrence, Douglass Dumbrille, Theodore Newton
'Sumptuously staged and photographed ... sufficiently modern story to get interest.' – *Variety*

Volunteers
US 1985 106m Metrocolor
EMI/HBO/Tri-Star/Silver Screen (Richard Shepherd, Walter F. Parkes)
High jinks in the 1962 Peace Corps.
Tawdry comedy about the exploits of a young Home Guard.
w Ken Levine, David Isaacs *story* Keith Critchlow *d* Nicholas Meyer *ph* Ric Waite *m* James Horner *pd* James Schoppe, Delia Castaneda *ed* Ronald Roose, Steven Polivka
☆ Tom Hanks, John Candy, Rita Wilson, Tim Thomerson

Von Richthofen and Brown
US 1971 97m DeLuxe
UA/Roger Corman (Gene Corman)
GB title: *The Red Baron*
During World War I, a Canadian pilot takes on Germany's air ace.
The airplanes are nice, but the film is grounded by plot and dialogue.
w John and Joyce Corrington *d* Roger Corman *ph* Michael Reed *m* Hugo Friedhofer
☆ John Phillip Law, Don Stroud, Barry Primus, Karen Huston, Corin Redgrave, Hurd Hatfield

Von Ryan's Express **
US 1965 117m DeLuxe Cinemascope
TCF (Saul David)
In an Italian POW camp during World War II, an unpopular American captain leads English prisoners in a train escape.
Exhilarating action thriller with slow spots atoned for by nail-biting finale, though the downbeat curtain mars the general effect.
w Wendell Mayes, Joseph Landon *novel* Davis Westheimer *d Mark Robson ph* William H. Daniels, Harold Lipstein *m* Jerry Goldsmith
☆ *Frank Sinatra, Trevor Howard, Sergio Fantoni*, Edward Mulhare, Brad Dexter, John Leyton, Wolfgang Preiss, James Brolin, Adolfo Celi, Rafaela Cara

Voodoo
US 1995 89m CFI color
First Independent/Image/A-pix (Donald P. Borchers)
A student discovers that a university is the headquarters of a voodoo cult practising black magic.
Plodding, unpleasantly nasty little horror, perfunctorily done.
w Brian DiMuccio, Dino Vindeni *d* Rene Eram *ph* Dan Gillham *m* Keith Bilderbeck *pd* Jodi Ginnever *ed* Paolo Mazzucato
☆ Corey Feldman, Joel J. Edwards, Diana Nadeau, Ron Melendez, Sarah Douglas, Maury Ginsberg, Amy Raasch, Jack Nance

Voodoo Man
US 1944 62m bw
Monogram (Sam Katzman)
A mad scientist kidnaps young girls and reduces them to zombies.
Hopeless chiller wasting three stars.
w Robert Charles *d* William Beaudine
☆ Bela Lugosi, John Carradine, George Zucco, Michael Ames, Wanda McKay

Voodoo Woman
US 1956 77m bw
AIP/Carmel (Alex Gordon)
A domineering woman and her weak boyfriend go in search of treasure in the jungle, where a mad scientist in a silly hat has created an indestructible beastlike woman with the aid of voodoo rituals.
Ridiculous horror, with clichéd dialogue and situations; the monster looks like Mighty Joe Young in drag.
w Russell Bender, V. I. Voss *d* Edward L. Cahn *ph* Frederick E. West *m* Darrell Calker *ad* Don Ament *ed* Ronald Sinclair *sp* Harry Thomas
☆ Marla English, Tom Conway, Touch Connors, Lance Fuller, Mary Ellen Kaye
WIFE: 'You're insane.'
HUSBAND: 'Never say that! Never say that to me again!'

Vou Para Casa: see *I'm Going Home*

The Voyage **
Argentina/France 1991 150m colour
Metro/Cinesur/Du Sud (Fernando E. Solanas)
An isolated and unhappy student sets out on a long journey to find his father, a comic-book artist last heard of in Buenos Aires.
An acerbic, always engaging trip through South American consciousness, part fantasy but never far from being real, as an innocent gains experience of the world.
wd Fernando E. Solanas *ph* Felix Monti *m* Egberto Gismonti, Astor Piazzolla, Fernando E. Solanas *pd* Fernando E. Solanas *ed* Alberto Borello, Jacqueline Meppiel, Jacques Gaillard
☆ Walter Quiroz, Soledad Alfaro, Ricardo Bartis, Cristina Becerra, Marc Berman, Chiquinho Brandao, Franklin Caicedo
'A smooth mixture of stunningly beautiful camerawork and bitter two-fingers-to-them-all political satire.' – *Marcus Trower, Empire*
† Solanas survived an attempt to assassinate him during his post-production work on the film.

Voyage of the Damned *
GB 1976 155m Eastmancolor
ITC/Associated General (Robert Fryer)
In 1939, a ship leaves Hamburg for Cuba with Jewish refugees; but Cuba won't take them.
High-minded, expensive, but poorly devised rehash of Ship of Fools, *with too many stars in cameos and not enough central plot.*
w Steve Shagan, David Butler *book* Gordon Thomas, Max Morgan-Witts *d* Stuart Rosenberg *ph* Billy Williams *m* Lalo Schifrin
☆ Faye Dunaway, Max von Sydow, Oskar Werner, Malcolm McDowell, James Mason, Orson Welles, Katharine Ross, Ben Gazzara, Lee Grant, Sam Wanamaker, Julie Harris, Helmut Griem, Luther Adler, Wendy Hiller, Nehemiah Persoff and also Maria Schell, Fernando Rey, Donald Houston, José Ferrer, Denholm Elliott, Janet Suzman
'Not a single moment carries any conviction.' – *New Yorker*
'The movie stays surprisingly distanced and impersonal, like a panning shot that moves too quickly for all the details to register.' – *Charles Champlin, Los Angeles Times*
'With a story that is true (or thereabouts), tragic in its detail and implications, and about which it is impossible to take a neutral attitude, you feel an absolute bounder unless you give it the thumbs up.' – *Barry Took, Punch*
script; Lalo Schifrin; Lee Grant

Voyage to Italy **
Italy/France 1953 100m bw
Titanus/Sveva/Junior/Italiafilm (Mario Del Papa, Marcello D'Amico)
original title: *Viaggio in Italia*
aka: *Journey to Italy; The Lonely Woman; Strangers (US)*
During a trip to Italy to sell a property they have inherited, an English couple realize that their marriage is empty and sterile.
Understated narrative of two repressed Northerners failing to respond to the warmth and fecundity of Italians and their landscape. As a portrait of an unhappy marriage it has its moments, but they do not include the film's unsatisfactory resolution.
Undervalued on its first release, it later featured in lists of the top ten films compiled by Italian and French critics.
w Vitaliano Brancati, Roberto Rossellini *d* Roberto Rossellini *ph* Enzo Serafin *m* Renzo Rossellini *ad* Piero Filippone *ed* Jolanda Benvenuti
☆ Ingrid Bergman, George Sanders, Maria Mauban, Anna Proclemer, Paul Muller, Leslie Daniels, Natalia Rai, Jackie Frost
'It seems impossible to me to see *Viaggio in Italia* without experiencing, like a whip, the fact that this film opens a breach that the entire cinema must pass through under the pain of death.' – *Jacques Rivette, Cahiers du Cinema*
'An influential film ... marred by banality and clumsiness.' – *Pauline Kael*
† The film was cut to 80m in its English-language version, which is the one released on video. The filming itself was fraught, with both the leads unhappy. Sanders was sometimes in tears over Rossellini's habit of giving him his lines at the last moment.

Voyage to the Bottom of the Sea *
US 1961 105m DeLuxe
Cinemascope
TCF/Windsor (Irwin Allen)
USN Admiral Nelson takes scientists in his futuristic atomic submarine to explode a belt of radiation.
Childish but sometimes entertaining science fiction which spawned a long-running TV series.
w Irwin Allen, Charles Bennett *d* Irwin Allen *ph* Winton Hoch, John Lamb *m* Paul Sawtell, Bert Shefter *ad J. M. Smith, Herman A. Blumenthal*
☆ Walter Pidgeon, Robert Sterling, Joan Fontaine, Peter Lorre, Barbara Eden, Michael Ansara, Henry Daniell, Regis Toomey, Frankie Avalon

Voyager
Germany/France 1991 117m colour
Palace/Bioskop/Action/Stefi 2/Hellas (Eberhard Junkersdorf)
A middle-aged engineer begins an affair with a teenage girl, only to discover that she is the daughter of his former mistress.
Involved drama, depending upon a series of coincidences, that never fully engages its audience.
w Rudy Wurlitzer *novel Homo Faber* by Max Frisch *d* Volker Schlöndorff *ph* Yorgos Arvanitis, Pierre L'homme *m* Stanley Myers *pd* Nicos Perakis *ed* Dagmar Hirtz
☆ Sam Shepard, Julie Delpy, Barbara Sukowa, Dieter Kirchlechner, Traci Lind, Deborah Lee-Furness, August Zirner, Thomas Heinze
'The film's knowing slickness, especially in an array of visually stunning locations and masterfully choreographed crowd scenes, may leave cinema-goers feeling strangely dissatisfied with the whole enterprise.' – *Screen International*

Le Voyou **
France/Italy 1970 120m Eastmancolor
UA/Les Films Ariane/Les Films 13/Artistes Associés/P.E.A. (Alexandre Mnouchkine)
aka: *Simon the Swiss*
US title: *The Crook*
A crooked lawyer escapes from prison so that he can see his daughter, implicate the accomplice who put him behind bars and flee the country with his swag.
Entertaining, light-hearted thriller, done with great style.
w Claude Lelouch, Pierre Uytterhoeven, Claude Pinoteau *d* Claude Lelouch *ph* Claude Lelouch *m* Francis Lai *ad* Albert Volper *ed* Marie-Claude Lacambre
☆ Jean-Louis Trintignant, Christine Lelouch, Charles Gérard, Danièle Delorme, Yves Robert, Amidou, Sacha Distel
'It is all much too good-tempered to be taken seriously. It is strictly for fun, and on that level it works very well.' – *Brenda Davies, MFB*

Vredens Dag: see *Day of Wrath*

Vrema Cuda: see *Time of Miracles*

Vssichni Dobrsri Rodáci: see *All My Good Countrymen*

Vu du Pont: see *A View from the Bridge*

The Vulture
GB 1967 92m bw
Lawrence Huntington Productions
A family curse transforms a scientist into a giant vulture.

Incredible nonsense – incredible that anyone should try to get away with it. Fun for those who like to watch actors in trouble.
wd Lawrence Huntington *ph* Stephen Dade
m Eric Spear
☆ Robert Hutton, Akim Tamiroff, Broderick Crawford, Diane Clare

Vzlomshchik: see *The Burglar*

W

W
US 1973 95m DeLuxe
Bing Crosby Productions (Mel Ferrer)

A young wife is threatened by her psychotic first husband.
Tedious rehash of several frightened lady themes, all rather sick.
w Gerald di Pego, James Kelly *d* Richard Quine *ph* Gerry Hirschfeld *m* Johnny Mandell
☆ Twiggy, Michael Witney, Eugene Roche, Dirk Benedict, John Vernon

'On screen he played the child-hating, dog-hating, acid-tongued old swindler. It was no act!'
W. C. Fields and Me
US 1976 112m Technicolor Panavision
Universal (Jay Weston)
The rise to Hollywood fame of alcoholic comedian W. C. Fields.
Untruthful and rather boring biopic, with minor compensations.
w Bob Merrill *book* Carlotta Monti *d* Arthur Hiller *ph* David M. Walsh *m* Henry Mancini *pd* Robert Boyle
☆ Rod Steiger (W.C. Fields), Valerie Perrine (Carlotta Monti), John Marley, Jack Cassidy (John Barrymore), Paul Stewart (Florenz Ziegfeld), Billy Barty, Bernadette Peters
'Steiger's impersonation largely keeps pace with the overriding vulgarity of the enterprise.' – *Sight and Sound*
'A stupid and pointless slander.' – *Judith Crist*
'Just the sort of memorial Fields might have wished for Baby Leroy.' – *Les Keyser, Hollywood in the Seventies*

The W Plan *
GB 1930 105m bw
BIP/Burlington (Victor Saville)
A British spy helps destroy Germany's secret tunnels.
Slightly fantasticated spy/war action which was a big popular success at the time.
w Victor Saville, Miles Malleson, Frank Launder *novel* Graham Seton *d* Victor Saville *ph* F. A. Young, Werner Brandes
☆ Brian Aherne, Madeleine Carroll, Gordon Harker, Gibb McLaughlin, George Merritt, Mary Jerrold
'One of the best pictures yet from England, but unconvincing b.o. for the US. Lacks punch.' – *Variety*
'Fast, spectacular action, fine acting and notably realistic war scenes.' – *NFT, 1971*

WR – Mysteries of the Organism ***
Yugoslavia 1971 86m colour
Neoplanta

original title: *WR Misterije Organizma*
A free-wheeling exploration of the life and teachings of Wilhelm Reich, which resulted in his imprisonment in the United States and the burning of his books, and on the sexual attitudes in the USA and Yugoslavia in the late 60s and early 70s.
A witty, iconoclastic examination of sex and politics and their interaction, using documentary techniques, newsreel footage and fiction; it brought Makavejev an international reputation.
wd Dusan Makavejev ph Pega Popovic, Aleksandar Petkovic *ad* Dragoljub Ivkov *ed* Ivanka Vukasovic
☆ *Milena Dravic*, Ivica Vidovic, Jagoda Kaloper, Tuli Kupferberg, Zoran Radmilovic, Jackie Curtis, Miodrag Andric
'The point of view is so unstable that it seems to be more sophomoric than anything else.' – *Pauline Kael, New Yorker*
† The version released on video in Britain is the TV version 'improved by the author for Channel 4', which mainly meant that the scenes showing an erect penis – the first time an erection had been passed by the British Board of Film Censors for exhibition on the screen of a public cinema – were obscured by digital effects.

WUSA *
US 1970 117m Technicolor Panavision
Paramount/Mirror/Coleytown/Stuart Rosenberg (Paul Newman, John Foreman)
A penniless wanderer causes chaos when he becomes the announcer for a right-wing radio station.
A farcical melodrama for the intelligentsia, and for the most part a thoroughgoing bore. The last part offers a compensation or two.
w Robert Stone *novel Hall of Mirrors* by Robert Stone *d* Stuart Rosenberg *ph* Richard Moore *m* Lalo Schifrin
☆ Paul Newman, Joanne Woodward, Laurence Harvey, Anthony Perkins, Pat Hingle, Cloris Leachman, Don Gordon, Robert Quarry, Bruce Cabot, Moses Gunn, Wayne Rogers
'The most significant film I've ever made and the best.' – *Paul Newman*

WW and the Dixie Dancekings
US 1975 94m TVC Color
TCF (Stanley S. Canter)
In a Southern state in the 1950s, a crook uses a travelling band as an alibi and stays to promote them.
Combination of American Graffiti *and* Easy Rider, *either tiresome or tolerable according to one's mood. Very flashy, anyway.*
w Thomas Rickman *d* John G. Avildsen *ph* Jim Crabe *m* Dave Grusin
☆ Burt Reynolds, Art Carney, Conny Van Dyke, Jerry Reed, Ned Beatty

Waati
Mali/France/Burkina Faso 1995 143m colour
Les Films Cissé/Sisé/Erato/La Sept/Kenn/Carthago (Souleymane Cissé)
In South Africa, a young black girl shoots a white policeman after he has murdered her father and brother and escapes to West Africa and a better life.
Sprawling, overlong account of endemic racism and brutality, one that is both too simple and contrived in its narrative to be effective.
wd Souleymane Cissé *ph* Vincenzo Marano, Gheorghy Rerberg, Alexei Rodionov, Jean-Jacques Bouhon *m* Bruno Coulais, Dave Pollecutt, Group Ki-Yi, Kaloury Sory *pd* Joseph Kpobly, Angela Halle *ed* Andrée Davanture
☆ Linéo Tsolo, Sidi Yaya Cissé, Eric Miyeni, Nakedi Ribane, Vusi Kunen, Mary Twala, Martin Le Maitre, Michelle Burger, Balla Moussa Keita

Wabash Avenue *
US 1950 92m Technicolor
TCF (William Perlberg)
During the Chicago World's Fair of 1892, a shimmy dancer is pursued by two men.
Bright rehash of Coney Island *(qv), with solid tunes and performances.*
w Harry Tugend, Charles Lederer *d* Henry Koster *ph* Arthur E. Arling *md* Lionel Newman
☆ Betty Grable, Victor Mature, Phil Harris, Reginald Gardiner, Margaret Hamilton, James Barton, Barry Kelley
song 'Wilhelmina' (*m*Josef Myrow, *ly*Mack Gordon)

Das Wachsfigurenkabinett: see *Waxworks*

'The Ocean Roars And So Will You.'
The Wackiest Ship in the Army
US 1960 99m Technicolor Cinemascope
Columbia/Fred Kohlmar

In the South Pacific during World War II a decrepit sailing ship with an inexperienced crew manages to confuse Japanese patrols and land a scout behind enemy lines.
Slapstick war comedy with fragments of action; effect rather muddled.
wd Richard Murphy *story* Herbert Carlson *ph* Charles Lawton *m* George Duning
☆ Jack Lemmon, Ricky Nelson, John Lund, Chips Rafferty, Tom Tully, Joby Baker, Warren Berlinger, Richard Anderson
'A zany and occasionally amusing farce. Yachtsmen should find it good fun.' – *Bosley Crowther*

Wacko
US 1981 90m Movielab
OSM (Greydon Clark)

A slobbish cop tracks down a Halloween killer armed with a lawn mower.
Dire parody of slasher and horror movies, lacking anything resembling a joke.
w Dana Olsen, Michael Spound, M. James Kouf Jnr, David Greenwalt *d* Greydon Clark *ph* Nicholas J. von Sternberg *m* Arthur Kempel *ad* Chester Kaczenski *ed* Earl Watson, Curtis Burch
☆ Joe Don Baker, Stella Stevens, George Kennedy, Julia Duffy, Scott McGinnis, Andrew Clay

'A comedy about truth, justice and other special effects.'
'A Hollywood producer. A Washington spin-doctor. When they get together, they can make you believe anything.'
Wag the Dog **
US 1997 97m Technicolor
Entertainment/New Line/Tribeca/Baltimore/Punch (Jane Rosenthal, Robert de Niro, Barry Levinson)

In order to divert public attention away from a sexual scandal involving the President, his aides hire a Hollywood producer to create the impression of an international crisis.
Enjoyable comedy that skates over the surface of political life with some elegance, but never cuts quite deep enough.
w Hilary Henkin, David Mamet *novel American Hero* by Larry Beinhart *d* Barry Levinson *ph* Robert Richardson *m* Mark Knopfler *pd* Wynn Thomas *ed* Stu Linder
☆ Dustin Hoffman, Robert de Niro, Anne Heche, Woody Harrelson, Denis Leary, Willie Nelson, Andrea Martin, Kirsten Dunst, William H. Macy
'Satirizes media culture in a way that hardly delivers real insight or pungency, but shrewdly flatters the educated viewer's knowingness.' – *Godfrey Cheshire, Variety*
Dustin Hoffman; Hilary Henkin, David Mamet

Waga Jinsei Saiaku No Toki *
Japan 1993 92m bw
Film Detective Office/For Life Records/Shutter (Kaizo Hayashi, Shunsuke Koga, Yu Wei Yen)
aka: *The Most Terrible Time of My Life*
Hired by an immigrant waiter to track down his missing brother, a cinema projectionist who doubles as a private eye is plunged into the midst of a struggle between Japanese and Taiwanese crooks.
An odd and quirky movie that begins as a tongue-in-cheek thriller – its posturing would-be tough hero is named Maiku Hama after Spillane's Mike Hammer – and becomes less original and more violent as it continues.
w Kaizo Hayashi, Daisuke Tengan *d* Kaizo Hayashi *ph* Yuichi Nagat *m* Meina Co, Kazuharu Urata *pd* Takeo Kimura *ed* Nobuko Tomita
☆ Masatoshi Nagase (Maiku Hama), Shiro Sano (Kanno), Kiyotaka Nanbara (Hoshino), Yang Haitin (Yang Haitin), Hou De Jian (Hou De Jian), Akaji Maro (Lt Nakayama), Shinya Tsukamoto, Jo Shishido
'For all its rampant cine-snob knowingness, this is, at heart, a work of infectious, unironic affection.' – *Dennis Lim, Village Voice*

The Wages of Fear ***
France/Italy 1953 140m bw
Filmsonor/CICC/Vera

original title: *Le Salaire de la Peur*
The manager of a Central American oilfield offers big money to drivers who will take nitro-glycerine into the jungle to put out an oil well fire.
After too extended an introduction to the less than admirable characters, this fascinating film resolves itself into a suspense shocker with one craftily managed bad moment after another.
wd Henri-Georges Clouzot novel Georges Arnaud *ph Armand Thirard m* Georges Auric
☆ *Yves Montand*, Folco Lulli, Peter Van Eyck, *Charles Vanel*, Vera Clouzot, William Tubbs
'As skilful as, in its preoccupation with violence and its unrelieved pessimism, it is unlikeable.' – *Penelope Houston, Sight and Sound*
'It has some claim to be the greatest suspense thriller of all time; it is the suspense not of mystery but of Damocles' sword.' – *Basil Wright, 1972*
† See *Sorcerer*, a lamentable remake.
picture

Wages of Fear: see *Sorcerer (1977)*

Wagonmaster **
US 1950 86m bw
RKO/Argosy (John Ford, Merian C. Cooper)

Adventures of a Mormon wagon train journeying towards Utah in 1879.
Low-key Ford Western, essentially a collection of incidents, fondly and enjoyably presented.
w Frank Nugent, Patrick Ford *d John Ford* *ph* Bert Glennon *m* Richard Hageman
☆ Ben Johnson, Joanne Dru, Harry Carey Jnr, Ward Bond, Charles Kemper, Alan Mowbray, Jane Darwell, Russell Simpson
'The feel of the period, the poetry of space and of endeavour, is splendidly communicated.' – *Lindsay Anderson*
'What emerges at the end is nothing less than a view of life itself, the view of a poet.' – *Patrick Gibbs, 1965*

Wagons East!
US 1994 106m Technicolor
Guild/Outlaw (Gary Goodman, Barry Rosen, Robert Newmyer, Jeffrey Silver)

Disgruntled citizens of a Western town hire an alcoholic wagonmaster to take them back to the east.
Lacklustre comedy, recycling old gags in a listless fashion.
w Matthew Carlson *story* Jerry Abrahamson *d* Peter Markle *ph* Frank Tidy *m* Michael Small *pd* Vince J. Cresciman *ed* Scott Conrad
☆ John Candy, Richard Lewis, John C. McGinley, Ellen Greene, Robert Picardo, Ed Lauter, William Sanderson, Rodney A. Grant
'It offers an ideal night out for anyone who's spent the past two decades pining for a remake of *Blazing Saddles*.' – *Kevin Jackson, Independent*
† John Candy died while making the movie.

The Wagons Roll at Night
US 1941 83m bw
Warner (Harlan Thompson)
The sweetheart of a circus owner makes a pass at the new young lion-tamer.
Dull remake of Kid Galahad *(qv), whose plot was borrowed from* Tiger Shark *(qv). Warner were good at this kind of retreading, but gradually poor quality began to show.*
w Fred Niblo Jnr, Barry Trivers *d* Ray Enright *ph* Sid Hickox *m* Heinz Roemheld
☆ Humphrey Bogart, Sylvia Sidney, Eddie Albert, Joan Leslie, Sig Rumann, Cliff Clark, Frank Wilcox

Waikiki Wedding *
US 1937 89m bw
Paramount (Arthur Hornblow Jnr)
A press agent in Hawaii promotes a Pineapple Queen contest.
Light-hearted, empty-headed musical very typical of this studio ... except that this one is quite good.
w Frank Butler, Walter de Leon, Don Hartman, Francis Martin *d* Frank Tuttle *ph* Karl Struss *m* Leo Shukin *md* Boris Morros *ch* Leroy Prinz
☆ Bing Crosby, Shirley Ross, Bob Burns, Martha Raye, George Barbier, Leif Erickson, Grady Sutton, Granville Bates, Anthony Quinn
'Shouldn't have any trouble getting by ... it's saccharine celluloid, sugar-coated.' – *Variety*
song 'Sweet Leilani' (m/ly Harry Owens)
Leroy Prinz

Wait 'Til the Sun Shines, Nellie *
US 1952 108m Technicolor
TCF (George Jessel)
The life of a small-town barber, from marriage through tragedy to retirement.
Amiable, leisurely family drama with pleasant settings; small beer, but oddly compulsive.
w Allan Scott *novel* Ferdinand Reyher *d* Henry King *ph* Leon Shamroy *m* Alfred Newman
☆ David Wayne, Jean Peters, Hugh Marlowe, Albert Dekker, Alan Hale Jnr, Helene Stanley

Wait until Dark **
US 1967 108m Technicolor
Warner Seven Arts (Mel Ferrer)
A photographer unwittingly smuggles a drug-filled doll into New York, and his blind wife, alone in their flat, is terrorized by murderous crooks in search of it.
Sharp suspenser with shock moments, from a successful play; in this case the claustrophobic atmosphere helps, though a lack of light relief makes itself felt.
w Robert and Jane Howard-Carrington *play* Frederick Knott *d* Terence Young *ph* Charles Lang *m* Henry Mancini *ad* George Jenkins
☆ *Audrey Hepburn, Alan Arkin*, Richard Crenna, Efrem Zimbalist Jnr, Jack Weston
Audrey Hepburn

Waiting *
Australia 1990 94m colour
Contemporary/Filmside/ABC/Film Four (Ross Matthews)
A group of friends gather in a remote farmhouse as one of their number, an artist who has agreed to bear a baby for a friend, goes into labour.
Interesting and ironic film about surrogate motherhood and doctors' attitudes to childbirth.
wd Jackie McKimmie *ph* Steve Mason *m* Martin Arminger *pd* Murray Picknett *ed* Michael Honey
☆ Noni Hazelhurst, Deborra-Lee Furness, Frank Whitten, Helen Jones, Denis Moore, Fiona Press, Ray Barrett

Waiting for the Light *
US 1989 94m DeLuxe
Entertainment/Epic Productions/Sarlui/Diamant (Caledecot Chubb, Ron Bozman)
Business at a rundown diner is boosted by fake religious visions.
Ramshackle comedy of character that yields a succession of small pleasures.
wd Christopher Monger *ph* Gabriel Beristain *m* Michael Storey *pd* Phil Peters *ed* Eva Gardos
☆ Colin Baumgartner, Clancy Brown, Vincent Schiavelli, John Bedford Lloyd, Jeff McCracken, Jack McGee, Louis Guzzo, William Dore
'A wholly appealing confection that crumbles at the first critical touch.' – *Philip Strick, MFB*

Waiting to Exhale *
US 1995 121m DeLuxe
TCF (Ezra Swerdlow, Deborah Schindler)
Four successful black women friends complain about the men in their lives.
Opulent melodrama of female bonding which settles into an entertaining soap opera rather than a serious examination of relationships.
w Terry McMillan, Ron Bass *novel* Terry McMillan *d* Forest Whitaker *ph* Toyomichi Kurita *m* Kenneth 'Babyface' Edmonds *pd* David Gropman *ed* Richard Chew
☆ Whitney Houston, Angela Bassett, Loretta Devine, Lela Rochon, Gregory Hines, Dennis Haysbert, Mykelti Williamson
'Smoothly combines the elan and emotional luxuriance of old-fashioned woman's mellers with a modern black-pop sensibility.' – *Godfrey Cheshire, Variety*

Waiting Women *
Sweden 1952 107m bw
Svensk Filmindustri
original title: *Kvinnors Väntan*
aka: *Secrets of Women*
While waiting for their husbands to arrive, three wives share secrets about their marriages.
Deft drama, with occasional comic touches, about relationships between strong women and weak men, and about freedom and responsibility.
wd Ingmar Bergman *ph* Gunnar Fischer *m* Erik Nordgren *ad* Nils Svenwall *ed* Oscar Rosander
☆ Anita Björk, Eva Dahlbeck, Maj-Britt Nilsson, Birger Malmsten, Gunnar Björnstrand, Jarl Kulle, Karl-Arne Holmsten

Wake in Fright: see *Outback*

'It thrills the women!'
'To the last gun – to the last plane – to the last man!'
Wake Island *
US 1942 78m bw
Paramount (Joseph Sistrom)
During World War II, marines fight to hold an American base on a small Pacific island.
Terse, violent flagwaver, well done within its limits.
w W. R. Burnett, Frank Butler *d* John Farrow *ph* Theodor Sparkuhl, William C. Mellor *m* David Buttolph
☆ Brian Donlevy (Maj Geoffrey Caton), Macdonald Carey (Lt Cameron), Robert Preston (Joe Doyle), William Bendix (Smacksie Randall), Albert Dekker (Shad McClosky), Walter Abel (Cdr Roberts), Mikhail Rasumny (Probenzky), Rod Cameron, Barbara Britton, Don Castle (Private Cunkel)
'Hollywood's first intelligent, honest and completely successful attempt to dramatize the deeds of an American force on a fighting front.' – *Newsweek*
best picture; script; John Farrow; William Bendix

Wake Me When It's Over
US 1960 126m DeLuxe Cinemascope
TCF/Mervyn Le Roy
Soldiers holding a Pacific island build a de luxe hotel from surplus war material.
Aptly-titled army farce on the lines of The Teahouse of the August Moon *but constructed from inferior material. Yawningly tedious.*
w Richard Breen *novel* Howard Singer *d* Mervyn Le Roy *ph* Leon Shamroy *m* Cyril Mockridge
☆ Ernie Kovacs, Dick Shawn, Jack Warden, Margo Moore, Nobu McCarthy, Don Knotts, Robert Emhardt

Wake of the Red Witch **
US 1948 106m bw
Republic (Edmund Grainger)
The owner and captain of a ship settle their differences to seek treasure on an East Indian island.
Rattling good action yarn told in flashback, with adequate production and performances.
w Harry Brown, Kenneth Gamet novel Garland Roark *d* Edward Ludwig *ph* Reggie Lanning *m* Nathan Scott
☆ John Wayne, *Luther Adler*, Gail Russell, Gig Young, Adele Mara, Eduard Franz, Grant Withers, Henry Daniell, Paul Fix, Dennis Hoey

Wake Up and Dream
US 1946 92m Technicolor
TCF (Walter Morosco)
A little girl is determined to find her brother who is missing in action in World War II.
Ambitious but unappealing whimsy which descends into sentimentality; either way it bewildered audiences and critics.
w Elick Moll *novel The Enchanted Voyage* by Robert Nathan *d* Lloyd Bacon *ph* Harry Jackson *m* Cyril Mockridge *md* Emil Newman
☆ June Haver, John Payne, Connie Marshall, Charlotte Greenwood, John Ireland, Clem Bevans, Lee Patrick

'The Sho-wow of Shows! The Hotcha-Topsa Of Them All!'
Wake Up and Live *
US 1937 91m bw
TCF (Kenneth MacGowan)
Success and failure in the radio world as a commentator and a bandleader fight a verbal duel in public.
Fast-moving spoof in which something is always happening, and usually something funny.
w Harry Tugend, Jack Yellen *book* Dorothea Brande *d* Sidney Lanfield *ph* Edward Cronjager *m* Louis Silvers *songs* Mack Gordon, Harry Revel
☆ *Walter Winchell, Ben Bernie and his band*, Alice Faye, Jack Haley, Patsy Kelly, Ned Sparks, Grace Bradley, Walter Catlett, Joan Davis, Douglas Fowley, Miles Mander, Etienne Girardot
'Thoroughly satisfying film entertainment.' – *Variety*

Waking Life **
US 2001 100m DeLuxe
TCF/IFC/Thousand Words/Line Research/Detour (Anne Walker-McBay, Tommy Pallotta, Palmer West, Jonah Smith)
After being run over, a man dreams dreams in which he meets varied and various people discussing the meaning of life and the difference between a waking life and a dream one.
Shot on digital video with live actors and rotoscoped to create a tremulous, brightly coloured animated movie, this looks better than it sometimes sounds, with much undergraduate philosophizing to little effect.
wd Richard Linklater *ph* Richard Linklater, Tommy Pallotta *m* Glover Gill, Tosca Tango Orchestra *ed* Sandra Adair *animation director* Bob Sabiston
☆ Wiley Wiggins, Trevor Jack Brooks, Lorelei Linklater, Glover Gill, Lara Hicks, Ames Asbell, Leigh Mahoney, Sara Nelson
'A wildly invigorating, unexpectedly thrilling and even moving film.' – *Peter Bradshaw, Guardian*
'So verbally dexterous and visually innovative that you can't absorb it unless you have all your wits about you. And even then, you may want to see it again to enjoy its subtle humor and warm humanity.' – *Stephen Holden, New York Times*

Waking Ned *
GB/France/US 1998 91m Technicolor Panavision
TCF/Fox Searchlight/Tomboy (Glynis Murray, Richard Holmes)
US title: *Waking Ned Devine*
In Ireland, villagers conspire in a local's impersonation of a multimillion-pound lottery winner, who died of shock before he could collect his winnings.
Rumbustious, folksy comedy that rather overdoes the Irish whimsy.
wd Kirk Jones *ph* Henry Braham *m* Shaun Davey *pd* John Ebden *ed* Alan Strachan
☆ Ian Bannen, David Kelly, Fionnula Flanagan, Susan Lynch, James Nesbitt, Maura O'Malley, Robert Hickey, Paddy Ward, James Ryland, Fintan McKeown, Matthew Devitt
'Warm-heartedness just short of sentimentality ... Keeps a steady laugh count rolling.' – *Empire*
† The film was not shot in Ireland, but on the Isle of Man.

Walk a Crooked Mile
US 1948 91m bw
Columbia (Edward Small)
British and American agents investigate the leakage of atomic secrets.
Moderate semi-documentary spy thriller.
w George Bruce *d* Gordon Douglas *ph* George Robinson *m* Paul Sawtell
☆ Louis Hayward, Dennis O'Keefe, Louise Allbritton, Carl Esmond, Raymond Burr, Onslow Stevens

Walk a Crooked Path
GB 1969 88m Eastmancolor
Hanover (John Brason)
A housemaster at a boys' school is accused of homosexuality.
Po-faced melodrama in a minor key; reasonably effective but not exciting.
w Barry Perowne *d* John Brason *ph* John Taylor *m* Leslie Bridgewater
☆ Tenniel Evans, Faith Brook, Christopher Coll, Patricia Haines, Pat Endersby, Margery Mason, Peter Copley

Walk, Don't Run *
US 1966 114m Technicolor Panavision
Columbia/Granley (Sol C. Siegel)
In Tokyo during the Olympics accommodation is hard to find, and two men move in with a girl.
Witless reprise of The More the Merrier, *notable only for the Tokyo backgrounds and for Cary Grant's farewell appearance.*
w Sol Saks *d* Charles Walters *ph* Harry Stradling *m* Quincy Jones
☆ *Cary Grant*, Samantha Eggar, Jim Hutton, *John Standing*, Miiko Taka
'Too long as are most comedies today, it seems to take its title far too literally; but there are several very funny sequences, a jaunty score, and the unflawed elegance of Mr Grant.' – *Arthur Knight*

Walk East on Beacon *
US 1952 98m bw
Columbia (Louis de Rochemont)
GB title: *The Crime of the Century*
The FBI exposes communist spies in the US.
Fast-moving semi-documentary spy thriller modelled on the same producer's The House on 92nd Street.
w Leo Rosten *d* Alfred Werker *ph* Joseph Brun *m* Louis Applebaum
☆ George Murphy, Finlay Currie, Virginia Gilmore, Karel Stepanek, Louisa Horton

'A man in search. A woman in need. A story of fate.'
A Walk in the Clouds
US 1995 103m DeLuxe
TCF (Gil Netter, David Zucker, Jerry Zucker)
A travelling chocolate salesman agrees to pretend to be the husband of a pregnant woman returning home to her parents' vineyard.
An over-sweet confection, so resolutely old-fashioned that in the 40s it would have been described as 'a woman's picture'; it is unlikely to find an appreciative audience of any sex these days.
w Robert Mark Kamen, Mark Miller, Harvey Weitzman *d* Alfonso Arau *ph* Emmanuel Lubezki *m* Maurice Jarre *pd* David Gropman *ed* Don Zimmerman
☆ Keanu Reeves, Aitana Sanchez-Gijon, Anthony Quinn, Giancarlo Giannini, Angelica Aragon, Evangelina Elizondo, Freddy Rodriguez
'The filmmaking, so sold on its own fruitiness, is cheap, sickly, sodden. It's cinematic liebfraumilch.' – *Tom Shone, Sunday Times*
† The film is a remake of Italian director Alessandro Blasetti's *Four Steps in the Clouds*, made in 1942.

'There weren't supposed to be any more surprises in their lives. And then they met each other!'
A Walk in the Spring Rain
US 1969 98m Technicolor Panavision
Columbia/Pingee (Stirling Silliphant)
A college lecturer's wife, on holiday in the mountains, falls in love with a local man.
Romance for the middle-aged, nicely done if lacking in surprise.
w Stirling Silliphant *novel* Rachel Maddox *d* Guy Green *ph* Charles B. Lang *m* Elmer Bernstein
☆ Ingrid Bergman, Anthony Quinn, Fritz Weaver, Katherine Crawford
'Not one line or scene is believably written or acted and the direction is so lazy it appears to have been mailed in during the postal strike.' – *Richard Roud*

A Walk in the Sun ***
US 1946 117m bw
Lewis Milestone Productions

The exploits of a single army patrol during the Salerno landings of 1943, on one vital morning.
Vivid war film in a minor key, superbly disciplined and keenly acted.
w *Robert Rossen* *novel* Harry Brown *d* *Lewis Milestone* *ph* *Russell Harlan* *m* Fredric Efrem Rich
☆ Dana Andrews, Richard Conte, Sterling Holloway, John Ireland, George Tyne, Herbert Rudley, Richard Benedict, Norman Lloyd, Lloyd Bridges, Huntz Hall
'Concerned with the individual rather than the battlefield, the film is finely perceptive, exciting, and very moving.' – *Penelope Houston*
'A swiftly overpowering piece of work.' – *Bosley Crowther*
'A notable war film, if not the most notable war film to come from America.' – *Richard Winnington*
'After nearly two hours one is sorry when it ends.' – *Richard Mallett, Punch*

Walk like a Dragon
US 1960 95m bw
Paramount/James Clavell
In 1870 San Francisco, a cowboy sets free a Chinese slave girl but incurs racial intolerance when he takes her home.
Curious 'liberated' Western which gets itself in a muddle and doesn't come off at all.
w James Clavell, Dan Mainwaring *d* James Clavell *ph* Loyal Griggs *m* Paul Dunlap
☆ Jack Lord, James Shigeta, Nobu McCarthy, Mel Tormé, Josephine Hutchinson, Rodolfo Acosta

'It was the summer of Woodstock... when she became the woman she always wanted to be.'
A Walk on the Moon *
US 1998 107m Technicolor
Miracle/Punch/Village Roadshow/Groucho (Dustin Hoffman, Tony Goldwyn, Jay Cohen, Neil Koenigsberg, Lee Gottsegan, Murray Schisgal)

Taking advantage of her husband's absence and an atmosphere of sexual liberation, a woman begins an affair, to the distress of her teenage daughter, and goes to Woodstock with her lover.
Small scale domestic drama set against a background of the moon landings and the shifting sensibilities of the late 60s, centring on a wife who married too young and feels that she has somehow missed out on life.
w Pamela Gray *d* Tony Goldwyn *ph* Anthony Richmond *m* Mason Daring *pd* Dan Leigh *ed* Dana Congdon
☆ Diane Lane (Pearl Kantrowitz), Liev Schreiber (Marty Kantrowitz), Anna Paquin (Alison Kantrowitz), Viggo Mortensen (Walker Jerome), Tovah Feldshuh (Lilian Kantrowitz), Bobby Boriello (Daniel Kantrowitz), Stewart Bick (Neil Leiberman), Jess Platt (Herb Fogler)
'A quietly satisfying piece of work.' – *Adam Mars-Jones, Times*

'A side of life you never expected to see on the screen!'
Walk on the Wild Side
US 1962 114m bw
Columbia/Famous Artists (Charles K. Feldman)

In the thirties, a penniless farmer finds the girl he once loved working in a New Orleans brothel.
A brilliant title sequence heralds the dreariest and most verbose of self-conscious melodramas, quite missing the sensational effect promised by the advertising.
w John Fante, Edmund Morris *novel* Nelson Algren *d* Edward Dmytryk *ph* Joe MacDonald *m* Elmer Bernstein *credits* Saul Bass
☆ Jane Fonda, Capucine, Barbara Stanwyck, Laurence Harvey, Anne Baxter, Richard Rust
'Since the film prides itself in calling a spade a spade, it is surprising to find all concerned reacting to their material as though they were up to their waists in a quagmire.' – *MFB*
'I was raped.' – *Nelson Algren*
title song (*m* Elmer Bernstein, *ly* Mack David)

Walk Softly Stranger
US 1950 81m bw
RKO (Robert Sparks)

A crook on the run falls for a crippled girl, who promises to wait for him.
Dismal love-conquers-all melodrama.
w Frank Fenton *d* Robert Stevenson *ph* Harry J. Wild *m* Frederick Hollander
☆ Alida Valli, Joseph Cotten, Spring Byington, Paul Stewart, Jack Paar, Jeff Donnell, John McIntire

Walk the Proud Land
US 1956 88m Technicolor Cinemascope
U-I (Aaron Rosenberg)
An Indian agent persuades the army to use less violent methods.
Fair standard Western with a thoughtful and sympathetic attitude.
w Gil Doud, Jack Sher *d* Jesse Hibbs *ph* Harold Lipstein *m* Hans Salter
☆ Audie Murphy, Anne Bancroft, Pat Crowley, Robert Warwick, Charles Drake, Tommy Rall, Jay Silverheels

'There's more to attraction than meets the eye.'
A Walk to Remember
US 2002 101m Technicolor
Warner/Di Novi/Pandora

A delinquent highschool student mends his ways when he falls in love with the drab daughter of the local pastor.
Gruesomely sentimental teen variation on Love Story *that failed to launch a movie career for singer Mandy Morore.*
w Karen Janszen *novel* Nicholas Sparks *d* Adam Shankman *ph* Julio Macat *m* Mervyn Warren *pd* Doug Hall *ed* Emma E. Hickox
☆ Shane West (Landon Carter), Mandy Moore (Jamie Sullivan), Peter Coyote (Reverend Sullivan), Daryl Hannah (Cynthia Carter), Lauren German (Belinda), Clayne Crawford (Dean), Al Thompson (Eric), Paz De La Huerta (Tracie)
'Best watched from between your fingers, or from under your seat, or perhaps standing outside the cinema looking in the opposite direction.' – *Peter Bradshaw, Guardian*

'In a strange and horrifying playground the innocents act out their game of life and death...'
Walkabout ****
Australia 1970 100m DeLuxe
Max L. Raab/Si Litvinoff

A man kills himself in the desert and his small children trek among the aborigines to safety.
Eerily effective contrast of city with native life, a director's and photographer's experimental success.
w Edward Bond *novel* James Vance Marshall *m* John Barry *d/ph* *Nicolas Roeg*
☆ Jenny Agutter, Lucien John, David Gulpilil
'The film is rich enough, especially at a second look, to make you forget the flaws. You are left with the impression of a fresh, powerful and humane imagination.' – *Dilys Powell*

Walker
US 1987 94m colour
Recorded Releasing/Walker Film/Incine (Lorenzo O'Brien, Angel Flores Marini)

In the 1850s, an American adventurer invades Nicaragua and sets himself up as the country's dictator.
Based on fact, it fails to develop its fascinating theme in a satisfactory way, relying on anachronistic details such as helicopters to point its message.
w Rudy Wurlitzer *d* Alex Cox *ph* David Bridges *m* Joe Strummer *pd* Bruno Rubeo, J. Rae Fox *ed* Carlos Puente, Alex Cox
☆ Ed Harris, Richard Masur, Rene Auberjonois, Keith Szarabajka, Sy Richardson, Xander Berkeley, John Diehl, Peter Boyle

'Eating & sleeping, fighting & joking, dating & cheating...'
Walking & Talking *
GB/US 1996 86m DuArt
Electric/Zenith (Ted Hope, James Schamus)

Two young professional women, friends from childhood, find that their love affairs are changing their relationship with one another.
Light-hearted gloss on emotional traumas, one that is likely to find its most responsive audience among young, professional women.
wd Nicole Holofcener *ph* Michael Spiller *m* Billy Bragg *pd* Anne Stuhler *ed* Alisa Lepselter
☆ Catherine Keener, Anne Heche, Todd Field, Liev Schreiber, Kevin Corrigan, Randall Batinkoff
'A glibly observant comedy about the anxieties of romance and the evolution of a female friendship.' – *Todd McCarthy, Variety*

The Walking Dead *
US 1936 66m bw
Warner (Louis F. Edelman)
A man is revived after electrocution and takes revenge on his enemies.
Dour but well-mounted horror thriller in a shadowy style very typical of its director.
w Ewart Adamson, Peter Milne, Robert Andrews, Lillie Hayward *d* *Michael Curtiz* *ph* *Hal Mohr*
☆ Boris Karloff, Edmund Gwenn, Marguerite Churchill, Ricardo Cortez, Barton MacLane, Warren Hull, Henry O'Neill
'Weak story and haphazardly interpolated assortment of scientific abadaba prevent Karloff from making much of a shocker out of this one.' – *Variety*

Walking Down Broadway: see *Hello Sister*

The Walking Hills *
US 1949 78m bw
Columbia (Harry Joe Brown)
Various interests combine to locate gold bullion hidden in Death Valley ... then thieves fall out.
Elementary but fairly satisfying Western.
w Alan LeMay *d* John Sturges
☆ Randolph Scott, Ella Raines, William Bishop, Edgar Buchanan, Arthur Kennedy, John Ireland, Jerome Courtland, Josh White

Walking My Baby Back Home *
US 1953 95m Technicolor
U-I (Ted Richmond)
Ex-army musicians hit on a combination of symphonic and dixieland jazz.
The lightest of light musicals, this highly polished offering remains mildly pleasing though thinly written throughout.
w Don McGuire, Oscar Brodney *d* Lloyd Bacon *ph* Irving Glassberg *md* Joseph Gershenson *ad* Bernard Herzbrun, Emrich Nicholson *ed* Ted J. Kent
☆ Donald O'Connor, Janet Leigh, Buddy Hackett, Lori Nelson, Scatman Crothers, Kathleen Lockhart, George Cleveland, John Hubbard

The Walking Stick *
GB 1970 101m Metrocolor Panavision
MGM/Winkast (Alan Ladd Jnr)
A repressed girl polio victim falls reluctantly in love with a painter who involves her in his criminal schemes.
Slow moving character romance which has its heart in the right place but too often promises suspense which never comes, and is made in a chintzy cigarette commercial style.
w George Bluestone *novel* Winston Graham *d* Eric Till *ph* Arthur Ibbetson *m* Stanley Myers
☆ *David Hemmings, Samantha Eggar*, Phyllis Calvert, Ferdy Mayne, Emlyn Williams, Francesca Annis, Dudley Sutton

Walking Tall *
US 1973 125m DeLuxe
Bing Crosby Productions (Mort Briskin)

A Tennessee farmer-sheriff meets violence with violence and becomes a local hero.
True story of an American vigilante, made with modest competence; its great commercial success may have been due to the support of the righteous, or of those who revel in violence.
w Mort Briskin *d* Phil Karlson *ph* Jack Marta *m* Walter Scharf
☆ Joe Don Baker, Elizabeth Hartman, Gene Evans, Noah Beery Jnr
'A terrifying image of Nixon's silent majority at work.' – *Gareth Jones*
'It generates a primitive, atavistic sort of power: it awakens more apprehension and dredges up more complicated and contradictory emotions than one anticipates.' – *Gary Arnold*
† Sequel 1976: *Part Two Walking Tall*. (GB title: *Legend of the Lawman*.) 1977: *Walking Tall: Final Chapter*.

The Wall *
France 1983 117m Fujicolour
Contemporary/Guney Productions/MK2 Productions/TFI Films (Marin Karmitz)
original title: *Le Mur*
aka: *Guney's The Wall*
Boys in a Turkish prison revolt against their persecutors.
Powerfully filmed indictment of brutality, based on a true incident and made a year before the director's death.
wd Yilmaz Guney *ph* Izzet Akay *m* Ozan Garip Sahin, Setrak Bakirel, Ali Dede Altuntas, Robert Kempler *ed* Sabine Mamou
☆ Tuncel Kurtiz, Ayse Emel Mesci, Saban, Sisko, Ziya, Garip, Zapata, Mankafa, Malik Berrichi, Nicolas Hossein, Habes Bounabi

The Wall of Death: see *There is Another Sun*

Wall of Noise
US 1963 112m bw
Warner (Joseph Landon)
A racehorse trainer falls for the boss's wife.
Complex but predictable melodrama of the old school, adequately presented and performed.
w Joseph Landon *novel* Daniel Michael Stein *d* Richard Wilson *ph* Lucien Ballard *m* William Lava
☆ Suzanne Pleshette, Ty Hardin, Dorothy Provine, Ralph Meeker, Simon Oakland, Murray Matheson, Robert F. Simon

A Wall of Silence: see *Black Flowers*

Wall Street **
US 1987 124m DeLuxe
Edward R. Pressman/American Entertainment

An ambitious young financial broker is forced to choose between the values of his Wall Street hero and his own father, an aircraft mechanic.
Almost documentary in its detailed account of financial skulduggery but slipping ultimately into sentimentality, the film is marked by a brilliant performance from Michael Douglas as the scheming megalomaniac Gordon Gekko.
w Stanley Weiser, Oliver Stone *d* Oliver Stone *ph* Robert Richardson *m* Stewart Copeland *pd* Stephen Hendrickson *ed* Claire Simpson
☆ Charlie Sheen (Bud Fox), *Michael Douglas (Gordon Gekko)*, Martin Sheen (Carl Fox), Daryl Hannah (Darien Taylor), Terence Stamp (Sir Larry Wildman), Sean Young (Kate Gekko), Sylvia Miles (Realtor), James Spader (Roger Barnes), Hal Holbrook (Lou Mannheim), Saul Rubinek (Harold Salt)
Michael Douglas

The Walls Came Tumbling Down *
US 1946 81m bw
Columbia (Albert J. Cohen)
A Broadway columnist tracks down the murderer of a priest.
Very acceptable whodunnit with familiar cast.
w Wilfrid H. Pettitt *novel* Jo Eisinger *d* Lothar Mendes
☆ Lee Bowman, Marguerite Chapman, George Macready, Edgar Buchanan, Lee Patrick, Jonathan Hale, J. Edward Bromberg, Elizabeth Risdon, Miles Mander, Moroni Olsen, Robert Ryan

Walls of Glass *
US 1985 86m colour
Tenth Muse (Scott Goldstein, Mark Slater)
A Shakespeare-loving taxi-driver tries to cope with his life's frustrations and return to his first love, the stage.
An engaging character study with a strong central performance.
w Edmond Collins, Scott Goldstein *d* Scott Goldstein *ph* Ivan Strasburg *m* Scott Goldstein *pd* Ruth Ammon *ed* Scott Vickrey
☆ Philip Bosco, Geraldine Page, Olympia Dukakis, Brian Bloom, Steven Weber, Louis Zorich, Linda Thorsen

The Walls of Jericho
US 1948 106m bw
TCF (Lamar Trotti)
An influential small-town newspaperman is undermined by his vindictive wife.
Filmed novel of standard competence but minimum interest, ending in a courtroom scene.
w Lamar Trotti *novel* Paul Wellman *d* John M. Stahl *ph* Arthur Miller *m* Cyril Mockridge
☆ Cornel Wilde, Linda Darnell, Anne Baxter, Kirk Douglas, Ann Dvorak, Marjorie Rambeau, Henry Hull, Colleen Townsend

Walpurgis Night
Sweden 1935 80m bw
Svensk Filmindustri
original title: *Valborgsmässoafton*
A secretary falls in love with her unhappily married boss, whose situation is compromised when his wife has an abortion without his knowledge.
Effective, though sometimes heavy-handed, domestic melodrama of love, birth and death, though its happy ending seems contrived.
w Oscar Rydquist *d* Gustav Edgren *ph* Martin Bodin *m* Eric Bengtson
☆ Ingrid Bergman, Lars Hanson, Karin Kavli, Victor Sjöström, Erik Berglund

Waltz across Texas
US 1982 99m colour
Aster (Martin Jurow)
Love blossoms when an uptight female geologist agrees to help a laid-back Texan search for oil.
Folksy, sentimental, romantic drama, pleasant without being in any way memorable.
w Bill Svanoe *d* Ernest Day *ph* Robert Elswit *m* Steve Dorff *ed* Jay Lash Cassidy
☆ Anne Archer, Terry Jastrow, Noah Beery, Richard Farnsworth, Mary Kay Place, Josh Taylor, Ben Piazza

The Waltz King
US 1963 95m Technicolor
Walt Disney (Peter V. Herald)
The life of young Johann Strauss in 1850s Vienna.
Medium-budget international family musical, tolerably well done.
w Maurice Tombragel *d* Steve Previn *ph* Gunther Anders *md* Helmuth Froschauer
☆ Kerwin Mathews, Brian Aherne, Senta Berger, Peter Kraus, Fritz Eckhardt

The Waltz of the Toreadors *
GB 1962 105m Technicolor
Rank Wintle-Parkyn (Peter de Sarigny)
A lecherous retired general finds his past creeping up on him and loses his young mistress to his son.
Lukewarm adaptation of a semi-classic comedy, disastrously translated to English setting and characters.
w Wolf Mankowitz *play* Jean Anouilh *d* John Guillermin *ph* John Wilcox *m* Richard Addinsell *pd* Wilfrid Shingleton
☆ Peter Sellers, Margaret Leighton, Dany Robin, John Fraser, Cyril Cusack, Prunella Scales

Waltz Time
GB 1933 82m bw
Gaumont
Things are not what they seem to be at a Viennese masked ball.
Pleasant but slight musical comedy vaguely derived from Die Fledermaus.
w A. P. Herbert *d* William Thiele
☆ Evelyn Laye, Fritz Schultz, Gina Malo, Jay Laurier, Frank Titterton

Waltz Time
GB 1945 100m bw
British National
At a Viennese ball, an Empress poses as her masked friend to win a philandering count.
Rather plodding operetta which also has an unattributed allegiance to Die Fledermaus.
w Montgomery Tully, Jack Whittingham, Henry C. James, Karl Rossier *d* Paul Stein *ph* Ernest Palmer *m* Hans May
☆ Carol Raye, Peter Graves, Patricia Medina, Thorley Walters, Richard Tauber, Harry Welchman, George Robey, Anne Ziegler, Webster Booth

Waltzes from Vienna
GB 1933 80m bw
Gaumont (Tom Arnold)
US title: *Strauss's Great Waltz*
A romance of the Strausses.
There is very little music and very little Hitchcock in this extremely mild romantic comedy.
w Alma Reville, Guy Bolton *play* Guy Bolton *d* Alfred Hitchcock *ph* Glen MacWilliams
☆ Jessie Matthews, Esmond Knight, Frank Vosper, Fay Compton, Edmund Gwenn, Robert Hale, Hindle Edgar
'I hate this sort of thing. Melodrama is the only thing I can do.' – *Alfred Hitchcock*

Wanda *
US 1971 105m colour
Foundations for Filmakers/F.F. (Harry Shuster)
Divorced by her husband for neglecting him and the children, a woman drifts into a disastrous relationship with a bad-tempered, incompetent robber.
An impressive, if depressing, account of a loveless life, notable for its unflinching, yet sympathetic, approach.
wd Barbara Loden *ph* Nicholas T. Proferes *ed* Nicholas T. Proferes
☆ Barbara Loden, Michael Higgins, Dorothy Shupenes, Peter Shupenes, Jerome Thier
'The director never falls back on coy tricks or clichés and the performances are admirable, but the movie is such an extremely drab and limited piece of realism that it makes Zola seem like musical comedy.' – *Pauline Kael*

Wanda Nevada
US 1979 105m Technicolor Panavision
UA/Pando (Neil Dobrofsky, Dennis Hackin)
A gambler wins a 13-year-old girl in a poker game and they go looking for gold in the Grand Canyon.
A casual road movie, easy-going but never getting anywhere very interesting.
w Dennis Hackin *d* Peter Fonda *ph* Michael Butler *m* Ken Lauber *ad* Lynda Paradise *ed* Scott Conrad
☆ Peter Fonda, Brooke Shields, Fiona Lewis, Luke Askew, Ted Markland, Severn Darden, Paul Fix, Henry Fonda

Wandafuru Raifu: see *After Life*

The Wanderers
US/Netherlands 1979 117m Technicolor
GTO/PSO/Poly International (Martin Ransohoff)
In 1963, teenage street gangs fight in the Bronx.
A bad boys' American Graffiti, *all violence and unpleasantness.*
w Rose and Philip Kaufman *novel* Richard Price *d* Philip Kaufman *ph* Michael Chapman *ad* Jay Moore *ed* Ronald Roose, Stuart H. Pappe
☆ Ken Wahl, John Friedrich, Karen Allen, Toni Kalem, Linda Manz

The Wandering Jew *
GB 1933 111m bw
Gaumont/Twickenham (Julius Hagen)
A Jew is condemned to live forever, but dies in the Spanish Inquisition.
Ambitious fantasy which comes off pretty well for those in the mood, but was a curious choice for a British studio at the time.
w H. Fowler Mear *play* E. Temple Thurston *d* Maurice Elvey *ph* Sydney Blythe
☆ *Conrad Veidt*, Marie Ney, Basil Gill, Anne Grey, Dennis Hoey, John Stuart, Peggy Ashcroft, Francis L. Sullivan, Felix Aylmer, Abraham Sofaer
'A beautiful production, a historic triumph – and most likely a commercial error.' – *Variety*

The Wannsee Conference *
Germany/Austria 1987 87m colour
Infafilm/Austrian TV/ORF/Bavarian Broadcasting (Manfred Korytowski)
original title: *Die Wannseekonferenz*
A group of Nazi officials gather for a conference to discuss Hitler's 'final solution' to exterminate the Jewish people.
Careful re-creation of an historic event, which lasted for 85 minutes, demonstrating the banality of evil. It was originally made for television, to which medium it is better suited.
w Paul Mommertz *d* Heinz Schirk *ph* Horst Schier *ad* Robert Hofer-Ach, Barbara Siebner *ed* Ursula Mollinger
☆ Robert Artzorn, Friedrich Beckhaus, Gerd Bochmann, Jochen Busse, Hans W. Bussinger, Harald Dietl, Peter Fitz, Reinhard Glemnitz, Dieter Groest, Martin Luttge

Wanted for Murder *
GB 1946 103m bw
Marcel Hellman
A man, obsessed with the fact that his father was the public hangman, becomes a murderer himself.
Curiously stagey melodrama with intermittent use of London backgrounds; an interesting curiosity.
w Emeric Pressburger, Rodney Ackland, Maurice Cowan *d* Lawrence Huntington *ph* Max Greene *m* Mischa Spoliansky
☆ *Eric Portman*, Dulcie Gray, Derek Farr, Roland Culver, Stanley Holloway, Barbara Everest, Bonar Colleano, Kathleen Harrison
'A pleasant and unpretentious thriller of the second or third grade.' – *James Agee*

Wanted: Jane Turner
US 1936 64m bw
Cliff Reid/RKO
The postal service tracks down mail van crooks.
Familiar but lively action support.
w John Twist *d* Edward Killy
☆ Lee Tracy, Gloria Stuart, Judith Blake, John McGuire, Frank M. Thomas

The Wanton: see *Manèges*

The Wanton Countess: see *Senso*

'What's worth fighting for?'
The War
US 1994 125m DeLuxe
UIP/Universal/Island World (Jon Avnet, Jordan Kerner)
In 1970, an unemployed Vietnam veteran tries to teach his son and daughter a non-violent approach to life as they battle with neighbouring children for control of a tree-house.
An earnest and didactic drama that settles for an easy uplift and provides the message that love will conquer all.
w Kathy McWorter *d* Jon Avnet *ph* Geoffrey Simpson *m* Thomas Newman *pd* Kristi Zea *ed* Debra Neil
☆ Kevin Costner, Elijah Wood, Mare Winningham, Lexi Randall, Christine Baranski, Raynor Scheine, Bruce A. Young, LaToya Chisholm, Charlette Julius, Gary Basaraba, Nick Searcy
'For those in quest of severe moral uplift only.' – *Sheila Johnston, Independent*
'Has neither the edge to attract adult tastes nor the action to please youngsters.' – *Denis Seguin, Screen International*

The War against Mrs Hadley *
US 1942 86m bw
MGM (Irving Asher)
A Washington matron tries to ignore the war and preserve her social life.
Efficient little propaganda piece with a middle-aged heroine.
w George Oppenheimer *d* Harold S. Bucquet *ph* Karl Freund *m* David Snell
☆ Fay Bainter, Edward Arnold, Richard Ney, Jean Rogers, Sara Allgood, Spring Byington, Van Johnson, Isobel Elsom, Halliwell Hobbes, Miles Mander, Frances Rafferty, Connie Gilchrist
'If this film is, as some have labelled it, the American Mrs Miniver, then some of us must have grave illusions about our own (or the English) way of life.' – *Bosley Crowther*
George Oppenheimer

War and Peace **
US/Italy 1956 208m Technicolor Vistavision
Carlo Ponti/Dino de Laurentiis
A Russian family's adventures at the time of Napoleon's invasion.
Despite miscasting and heavy dubbing, the pictorial parts of this précis of a gargantuan novel are powerful and exciting enough; the human side drags a little.
w Bridget Boland, Robert Westerby, King Vidor, Mario Camerini, Ennio de Concini, Ivo Perelli *novel* Leo Tolstoy *d* King Vidor, *(battle scenes)* Mario Soldati *ph* Jack Cardiff, *(battle scenes)* Aldo Tonti *m* Nino Rota *ad* Mario Chiari
☆ *Audrey Hepburn*, Henry Fonda, Mel Ferrer, *Herbert Lom*, John Mills, Oscar Homolka, Wilfrid Lawson, Vittorio Gassman, Anita Ekberg, Helmut Dantine, Milly Vitale, Barry Jones
'The film has no more warmth than pictures in an art gallery.' – *Philip T. Hartung*
'When I first agreed to do it the screenplay by Irwin Shaw was fine, but what happened? King Vidor used to go home nights with his wife and rewrite it. All the genius of Tolstoy went out the window.' – *Henry Fonda*
King Vidor; Jack Cardiff

War and Peace ***
USSR 1967 507m Sovcolor 'Scope 70mm
Mosfilm
An immensely long Russian version with some of the most magnificently spectacular battle scenes ever filmed.
A treat for the eyes throughout, and perhaps less taxing than reading the novel, which it follows punctiliously.
w Sergei Bondarchuk, Vasili Solovyov *d* *Sergei Bondarchuk* *ph* *Anatoli Petritsky* *m* Vyacheslav Ovchinnikov
☆ Lyudmila Savelyeva, Sergei Bondarchuk, Vyacheslav Tikhonov
† The film was five years in production and cost between 50 and 70 million dollars.
best foreign film

War Arrow
US 1953 78m Technicolor
Universal-International (John W. Rogers)
A cavalry officer has to overcome prejudice when he decides to recruit Seminole Indians to fight against the warlike Kiowa tribe.
Routine Western, recycling some familiar elements: an Indian-loving officer at odds with his superiors, a villainous fellow-officer, and a misunderstanding woman, who provides romantic interest, ingredients that also featured in the similar Tomahawk, made two years earlier.
w John Michael Hayes *d* George Sherman *ph* William Daniels *md* Joseph Gershenson *ad* Bernard Herzbrun, Alexander Golitzen *ed* Frank Gross
☆ Jeff Chandler (Major Howell Brady), Maureen O'Hara (Elaine Corwin), John McIntire (Col.Jackson Meade), Suzan Ball (Avis), Noah Beery Jnr (Sgt Augustus Wilks), Charles Drake (Sgt Luke Schermerhorn), Henry Brandon (Maygro), Dennis Weaver (Pino), Jay Silverheels (Satanta)

The War at Home
US 1996 119m Foto-Kem
Buena Vista/Touchstone/Motion Picture Corp/Avatar (Emilio Estevez, Brad Krevoy, Steve Stabler, James Duff)
In Texas in the early 70s, a young soldier returns to his family from Vietnam, traumatized by his experience.
Domestic melodrama that begins over the top and just gets louder.
w James Duff *play* *Homefront* by James Duff *d* Emilio Estevez *ph* Peter Levy *m* Basil Poledouris *pd* Eve Cauley *ed* Craig Bassett
☆ Kathy Bates, Martin Sheen, Kimberly Williams, Emilio Estevez, Carla Gugino, Geoffrey Blake, Corin Nemec, Ann Hearn
'There's a fuzziness of dramatic tone and lack of accruing tension that makes this "War" more a series of skirmishes than a deeply felt analysis.' – *Variety*

The War between Men and Women
US 1972 105m Technicolor Panavision
National General/Jalem/Llenroc/4D (Danny Arnold)
A half-blind cartoonist marries a divorcee and is troubled by her ex-husband.
Semi-serious comedy vaguely based on Thurber, but not so that you'd notice, apart from the blind hero; generally neither funny nor affecting.
w Mel Shavelson, Danny Arnold, based on the writings of James Thurber *d* Melville Shavelson *ph* Charles F. Wheeler *m* Marvin Hamlisch *pd* Stan Jolley
☆ Jack Lemmon, Barbara Harris, Jason Robards Jnr, Herb Edelman, Lisa Gerritsen

'Muddle-minded, sloppy and the sappy antithesis of everything the tough-minded Thurber held dear.' – *Paul D. Zimmerman, Newsweek*

The War Bride
GB/Canada 2001 107m colour
Miracle/Random Harvest/DB (Alistair MacLean-Clark, Doug Berquist)
A Cockney girl marries a Canadian soldier; when she joins him in Canada she discovers that life is harsher than she expected.
Muted domestic drama about the gap between dreams and reality that is too humdrum to remain interesting for long.
w Angela Workman *d* Lyndon Chubbuck *ph* Ron Orieux *m* John Sereda *pd* Ken Rempel *ed* Alan Strachan
☆ Anna Friel (Lily), Brenda Fricker (Betty), Aden Young (Charlie Travis), Loren Dean (Joe Clark), Julie Cox (Sophie), Molly Parker (Sylvia), Caroline Cave (Peggy)
'Lacks the creative imagination to make up for its limited budget' – *Philip French, Observer*

War Correspondent: see *The Story of GI Joe*

War Games *
US 1983 113m Metrocolor
MGM-UA/Sherwood (Leonard Goldberg, Harold Schneider)
A teenager unwittingly taps his home computer into the Pentagon and pretends to be Russia on the point of launching missiles.
Mildly intriguing science fantasy which becomes uncomfortable and finally boring because of the excess of jargon and flashing lights.
w Lawrence Lasker, Walter F. Parkes *d* John Badham *ph* William A. Fraker *m* Arthur B. Rubinstein *pd* Angelo P. Graham
☆ Matthew Broderick, Dabney Coleman, John Wood, Ally Sheedy, Barry Corbin, Kent Williams
'All the film's adventure and suspense is inevitably at odds with its ostensible sentiments … [but] the result has a kind of seamless efficiency.' – *Steve Jenkins, MFB*
screenplay; cinematography

War Gods of the Deep: see *City under the Sea*

'It Happened On A Raging Battlefield, But He Could Have Been A Murderer Stalking A City's Street!'
War Hunt
US 1961 83m bw
TD Enterprises (Terry Sanders)
Korea 1953: a kill-crazy private is befriended by a war orphan but finally has to be shot.
Vaguely commendable but not very expert indictment of the realities of war.
w Stanford Whitmore *d* Denis Sanders *ph* Ted McCord *m* Bud Shank
☆ John Saxon, Robert Redford, Sydney Pollack, Charles Aidman, Tommy Matsuda

The War Is Over: see *La Guerre Est Finie*

The War Lord **
US 1965 121m Technicolor Panavision
Universal/Court (Walter Seltzer)
An officer of the Duke of Normandy has trouble with Druids and the law of *droit de seigneur*.
Complex medieval melodrama with an air of fantasy about it; generally likeably strange, but the production should have been more stylized and fanciful.
w John Collier, Millard Kaufman *play The Lovers* by Leslie Stevens *d Franklin Schaffner ph Russell Metty m* Jerome Moross *ad* Alexander Golitzen, Henry Bumstead
☆ Charlton Heston, Richard Boone, Rosemary Forsyth, Maurice Evans, Guy Stockwell, Niall MacGinnis, Henry Wilcoxon, James Farentino

The War Lover
GB 1962 105m bw
Columbia/Arthur Hornblow Jnr
In 1943, a Flying Fortress commander based in East Anglia has the wrong ideas about women and war.
Solemn character drama punctuated by aerial battles.
w Howard Koch *novel* John Hersey *d* Philip Leacock *ph* Bob Huke *m* Richard Addinsell
☆ Steve McQueen, Shirley Anne Field, Robert Wagner, Gary Cockrell, Michael Crawford

War Nurse
US 1930 79m bw
MGM
Problems of a nurse behind the lines in World War I.
Ambitious but unsuccessful attempt to do another Big Parade; *a lack of style and story kills it.*
w Becky Gardner, Joe Farnham, from an anonymous autobiography *d* Edgar Selwyn
☆ Robert Montgomery, Anita Page, June Walker, Robert Ames, ZaSu Pitts, Marie Prevost, Helen Jerome Eddy, Hedda Hopper
'Won't get anywhere in the major houses; too filled with audible suffering to class as entertainment.' – *Variety*

'Most wars last years. This one had to be over by dinner.'
War of the Buttons *
GB/France 1994 90m colour
Warner/Enigma/De La Guéville (David Puttnam)
In rural Ireland the down-at-heel boys from one village indulge in gang warfare with the posher children from the next village.
A pleasant, light-hearted comedy of a civil war with only a hint of violence.
w Colin Welland *novel* Louis Pergaud *d* John Roberts *ph* Bruno de Keyzer *m* Rachel Portman *pd* Jim Clay *ed* David Freeman
☆ Liam Cunningham, Gregg Fitzgerald, Colm Meaney, John Coffey, Paul Batt, Eveanna Ryan, Dervla Kirwan, Thomas Kavanagh
'Engaging, funny and good-looking dramatic comedy that should appeal to both children and adults.' – *James Cameron-Wilson, Film Review*
† It is a remake of the French film *La Guerre des Boutons*, directed by Yves Robert in 1962.

War of the Colossal Beast
US 1958 68m bw/colour
AIP (Bert I. Gordon)
A 60-foot-tall man, turned bestial by exposure to nuclear radiation and mutilated in a bazooka attack, escapes from his captors and runs amok in Los Angeles.
Dull science fiction movie that runs out of ideas within the first five minutes, after which it tediously repeats not only itself but the movie to which it is a sequel. Originally, the last few minutes were in colour, though surviving prints appear to be monochrome.
w George Worthing Yates *story* Bert I. Gordon *d* Bert I. Gordon *ph* Jack Marta *m* Albert Glasser *ad* Walter Keller *ed* Ronald Sinclair *sp* Bert I. Gordon
☆ Sally Fraser, Roger Pace, Dean Parkin, Russ Bender, John McNamara, Loretta Nicholson, George Navarro
† It was a sequel to *The Amazing Colossal Man* (qv).

'Once in a lifetime comes a motion picture that makes you feel like falling in love all over again. This is not that movie.'
The War of the Roses *
US 1989 116m DeLuxe
Fox/Gracie Films (James L. Brooks, Arnon Milchan)
A couple who decide to divorce fight to the death over who gets the house.
Rancorous comedy, sometimes amusing but too mean-spirited for many laughs.
w Michael Leeson *novel* Warren Adler *d* Danny DeVito *ph* Stephen H. Burum *m* David Newman *pd* Ida Random *ed* Lynzee Klingman
☆ Michael Douglas, Kathleen Turner, Danny DeVito, Marianne Sägebrecht, Sean Astin, Heather Fairfield, G. D. Spradlin, Trenton Teigen, Bethany McKinney

War of the Wildcats
US 1943 102m bw
Republic (Robert North)
aka: *In Old Oklahoma*
A lady writer causes friction between an oil operator and a cowboy.
Action potboiler which once passed an hour and three-quarters quite painlessly.
w Ethel Hill, Eleanore Griffith, Thomson Burtis *d* Albert S. Rogell *ph* Jack Marta *m* Walter Scharf
☆ John Wayne, Martha Scott, Albert Dekker, George 'Gabby' Hayes, Marjorie Rambeau, Dale Evans, Grant Withers, Sidney Blackmer
Walter Scharf

The War of the Worlds *
US 1953 85m Technicolor
Paramount/George Pal
Terrifying aliens invade Earth via the American midwest.
Spectacular battle scenes are the mainstay of this violent fantasy, which goes to pieces once the cardboard characters open their mouths.
w Barre Lyndon *novel* H. G. Wells *d* Byron Haskin *ph* George Barnes *m* Leith Stevens *ad* Hal Pereira, Albert Nozaki *ed* Everett Douglas
☆ Gene Barry, Ann Robinson, Les Tremayne, Robert Cornthwaite, Sandro Giglio, Cedric Hardwicke (narrator)
special effects
editing

War Party
US 1989 97m CFI color
Hemdale (John Daly, Derek Gibson)
The centennial re-enactment of a massacre by the US Cavalry of the local Blackfoot Indians leads to a real battle after a white youth murders one of the Indians.
A mundane excuse for a not very interesting modern-day Western.
w Spencer Eastman *d* Franc Roddam *ph* Brian Tufano *m* Chaz Jankel *pd* Michael Bingham *ed* Sean Barton
☆ Billy Wirth, Kevin Dillon, Tim Sampson, Jimmie Ray Weeks, Kevyn Major Howard, M. Emmet Walsh, Jerry Hardin, Bill McKinney
'Its message is that it takes danger and excitement to release the pent-up, dulled emotions of both the Indians on the reservation and the white men in town. The result is a straightforward celebration of action-movie clichés.' – *Julian Stringer, MFB*

War Requiem *
GB 1988 93m bw/colour
Anglo International/BBC (Don Boyd)
Images of war, and of the poet Wilfred Owen in the trenches, accompany the music of Benjamin Britten's *War Requiem*.
A series of tableaux, some savagely comic but most tragic, intensify the experience of the music.
d Derek Jarman *ph* Richard Greatrex *m* Benjamin Britten *pd* Lucy Morahan *ed* Rick Elgood
☆ Nathaniel Parker, Tilda Swinton, Laurence Olivier, Patricia Hayes, Rohan McCillough, Nigel Terry, Owen Teale, Sean Bean, Alex Jennings

The War Wagon **
US 1967 99m Technicolor Panavision
Universal/Batjac (Marvin Schwartz)
Two cowboys and an Indian plan to ambush the gold wagon of a crooked mining contractor.
Exhilarating but simply-plotted action Western with strong comedy elements and a cast of old reliables.
w Clair Huffaker novel Badman by Clair Huffaker *d Burt Kennedy ph* William H. Clothier *m* Dimitri Tiomkin
☆ *John Wayne, Kirk Douglas*, Howard Keel, Robert Walker, Keenan Wynn, Bruce Cabot, Gene Evans, Bruce Dern
'It all works splendidly.' – *MFB*

The War Zone *
GB/Italy 1998 99m colour Panavision
Film Four/Portobello/Fandango/Mikado (Sarah Radclyffe, Dixie Linder)
A teenage boy discovers that his father is having an incestuous relationship with his sister.
Downbeat domestic drama, filmed in bleak colours, that works best in its portrait of traumatised adolescence; its adults are less convincing.
w Alexander Stuart *novel* Alexander Stuart *d* Tim Roth *ph* Seamus McGarvey *m* Simon Boswell *pd* Michael Carlin *ed* Trevor Waite
☆ Ray Winstone (Dad), Lara Belmont (Jessie), Freddie Cunliffe (Tom), Tilda Swinton (Mum), Annabel Apsion (Nurse), Kate Ashfield (Lucy), Colin J. Farrell (Nick)
'It is dismaying that this film misfires so catastrophically, ending up as what can only be described as a soft-core child abuse drama, reeking of good intentions and middlebrow art-house good taste.' – *Peter Bradshaw, Guardian*

Wara Mandel: see *Dance of the Wind*

The Ware Case *
GB 1938 79m bw
Ealing/Capad (S. C. Balcon)
A nobleman is suspected of murdering his wife's rich brother.
Courtroom melodrama twice filmed as a silent; stagey but reasonably compelling in its way.
w Robert Stevenson, Roland Pertwee, E. V. H. Emmett *play* G. P. Bancroft *d* Robert Stevenson *ph* Ronald Neame *m* Ernest Irving
☆ Clive Brook, Jane Baxter, Barry K. Barnes, C. V. France, Francis L. Sullivan, Frank Cellier, Edward Rigby, Peter Bull, Athene Seyler, Ernest Thesiger
† Previous versions had been made in 1917 (with Matheson Lang) and 1930 (with Stewart Rome).

Warlock *
US 1959 123m DeLuxe Cinemascope
TCF (Edward Dmytryk)
The cowardly citizens of a small Western town hire a gunman as their unofficial marshal.
Overlong, talkative and somewhat pretentious star Western with good sequences.
w Robert Alan Aurthur *novel* Oakley Hall *d* Edward Dmytryk *ph* Joe MacDonald *m* Leigh Harline
☆ Henry Fonda, Richard Widmark, Anthony Quinn, Dorothy Malone, Dolores Michaels, Wallace Ford, Tom Drake, Richard Arlen, Regis Toomey, Don Beddoe, DeForest Kelley

Warlock
US 1988 102m DeLuxe
Medusa/New World (Steve Miner)
A witchfinder and the warlock he is hunting are translated from the 17th century to modern-day Los Angeles.
Enjoyable chase film, energetically performed.
w David T. Twohy *d* Steve Miner *ph* David Eggby *m* Jerry Goldsmith *pd* Roy Forge Smith *ed* David Finfer
☆ Richard E. Grant, Julian Sands, Lori Singer, Kevin O'Brien, Mary Woronov, Richard Kuss, Juli Burkhart, Harry Johnson, David Carpenter

Warlock – The Armageddon
US 1993 98m Image Transform colour
Trimark/Tapestry (Peter Abrams, Robert L. Levy)
With only two teenage druids to oppose him, the son of Satan has six days to search for five missing runestones that will bring an end to the world.
Moderately effective sequel, with moments of sardonic wit, though dependent on special effects for its shock value; the real horror lies in the opening moments of Shakespeare.
w Kevin Rock, Sam Bernard *d* Anthony Hickox *ph* Gerry Lively *m* Mark McKenzie *pd* Steve Hardie *ed* Christopher Cibelli, James D. R. Hickox *sp* visual effects: BB&J Visual Effects; make-up: Bob Keen
☆ Julian Sands, Chris Young, Paula Marshall, Steve Kahan, Joanna Pacula, Charles Hallahan, R. G. Armstrong, Zach Galligan
'Intriguing, despite the plot's many weaknesses.' – *Sight and Sound*
† The film was released direct to video in Britain.

Warlords of Atlantis
GB 1978 96m Technicolor
EMI/John Dark, Kevin Connor
Victorian sea scientists discover a lost land under the Mediterranean.
Predictable compote of monsters and unwearable costumes, without a trace of wit in the script. For infants only.
w Brian Hayles *d* Kevin Connor *ph* Alan Hume *m* Mike Vickers *pd* Elliot Scott
☆ Doug McClure, Peter Gilmore, Shane Rimmer, Lea Brodie, Michael Gothard

A Warm December
GB/US 1972 101m Technicolor
First Artists/Verdon (Melville Tucker)
A widowed American doctor in London falls for a mysterious African girl who turns out to be the dying niece of a diplomat.
Weird mishmash of Love Story, Brief Encounter *and* Dark Victory, *getting the worst of all worlds.*
w Lawrence Roman *d* Sidney Poitier *ph* Paul Beeson *m* Coleridge-Taylor Parkinson
☆ Sidney Poitier, Esther Anderson, George Baker, Johnny Sekka, Earl Cameron

Warm Nights on a Slow Moving Train *
Australia 1988 91m colour
Western Pacific/Ross Dimsey
An art teacher at a Catholic school, who moonlights as a prostitute on an overnight express at weekends, becomes involved with a shady customer.
An efficient psychological thriller, an account of love and betrayal that is less interested in suspense than in the study of character.
w Bob Ellis, Denny Lawrence *d* Bob Ellis *ph* Yuri Sokol *m* Peter Sullivan *pd* Tracy Watt *ed* Tim Lewis
☆ *Wendy Hughes*, Colin Friels, Norman Kaye, John Clayton, Lewis Fitz-Gerald, Rod Zuanic, Peter Sullivan

Warm Water Under The Red Bridge: see *Akai Hashi Noshitano Nurui Mizu*

Warn London
GB 1934 74m bw
British Lion
A London policeman who is the double of a well-known burglar replaces him and infiltrates an international gang.
Exuberant minor thriller which made a good novelty booking at the time.
w Charles Bennett, Billie Bristow *novel* Denison Clift *d* T. Hayes Hunter *ph* Alex Bryce *ad* Norman Arnold
☆ Edmund Gwenn, John Loder, Leonora Corbett, D. A. Clarke-Smith

Warn That Man
GB 1943 82m bw
ABPC
German spies pose as an English nobleman and his staff but are routed by an unexpected guest.
On the stage this must have been an effective comedy-thriller, but the film is stymied by stiff handling.
w Vernon Sylvaine, Lawrence Huntington *play* Vernon Sylvaine *d* Lawrence Huntington
☆ Gordon Harker, Raymond Lovell, Jean Kent, Finlay Currie, Philip Friend, Frederick Cooper
'Slick drama, mounting success, and spectacular military enterprise.' – *The Cinema*

'What's a little bullet between friends?'
Warning Shot *
US 1966 100m Technicolor
Paramount/Bob Banner (Buzz Kulik)
While looking for a psychopathic killer, a cop shoots dead a man who draws a gun on him. But the dead man's gun cannot be found, and the officer is suspended ...
Watchable mystery decked out with guest stars; possibly intended as a TV movie.
w Mann Rubin *novel 711–Officer Needs Help* by Whit Masterson *d* Buzz Kulik *ph* Joseph Biroc *m* Jerry Goldsmith
☆ David Janssen, Lillian Gish, Ed Begley, Keenan Wynn, Sam Wanamaker, Eleanor Parker, Stefanie Powers, Walter Pidgeon, George Sanders, George Grizzard, Steve Allen, Carroll O'Connor, Joan Collins

Warning Sign
US 1985 100m DeLuxe
TCF/Barwood-Robbins (Jim Bloom)
A solitary cop combats scientists who may unwittingly unleash a deadly plague.
Unimpressive as propaganda and tedious as suspense.
w Hal Barwood, Matthew Robbins *d* Hal Barwood *ph* Dean Cundey *m* Craig Safan *pd* Henry Bumstead *ed* Robert Lawrence
☆ Sam Waterston, Kathleen Quinlan, Yaphet Kotto, Richard Dysart, Jeffrey de Munn

Warning, This Man Is Wild: see *Violent Cop*

Warning to Wantons
GB 1948 104m bw
Aquila/GFD
A nobleman takes in a flirtatious girl and finds she causes trouble for him and his family.
Interminable comedy-drama made even duller by the Independent Frame production method, which cut costs but restricted movement.
w Donald B. Wilson, James Laver *novel* Mary Mitchell *d* Donald B. Wilson
☆ Harold Warrender, Anne Vernon, David Tomlinson, Sonia Holm, Marie Burke, Judy Kelly

Warpath
US 1951 93m Technicolor
Paramount (Nat Holt)
An ex-army captain tracks down the outlaws who murdered his girl.
Goodish standard Western.
w Frank Gruber *d* Byron Haskin *ph* Ray Rennahan *m* Paul Sawtell
☆ Edmond O'Brien, Dean Jagger, Forrest Tucker, Harry Carey Jnr, Wallace Ford, Polly Bergen

The Warrior *
GB/France/Germany 2001 86m colour Panavision
FilmFour/SenatorBritish ScreenBureauLazennec (Bertrand Faivre)
Sickened by constant killing at the orders of his master, a warrior flees and is hunted down.
Good-looking, elemental adventure, told with an engaging simplicity and played out against unforgiving landscapes.
w Asif Kapadia, Tim Miller *d* Asif Kapadia *ph* Roman Osin *m* Dario Marianelli *pd* Adrian Smith *ed* Ewa J. Lind
☆ Irfan Khan (Lafcadia), Puru Chhibber (Katiba, His Son), Mandakini Goswami (Shawl Seller), Sunita Sharma (The Girl), Noor Mani (Riaz the Thief), Damayanti Marfatia (Blind Woman), Firoz Khan (Biswas), Anupam Shyam (The Lord)
'It is as accessible as any Hollywood Western; but redemption, not revenge is at its core.' – *Alexander Walker, London Evening Standard*
British film; Asif Kapadia (most promising newcomer)

Warrior Queen
US 1986 79m colour
Lightning (Harry Alan Towers)
Berenice, mistress of the Roman Caesar Titus, visits Pompeii and becomes involved with a charioteer and slaves who have been sold to a local brothel.
A movie with no discernible narrative; its director is content to set up scenes involving female nudity and uninmaginative decadence before reaching a climax with the eruption of Vesuvius which uses footage taken from a 60s Italian film, The Last Days of Pompeii, *which is a measure of its penny-pinching unoriginality.*
w Rick Marx *story* Peter Welbeck (Harry Alan Towers) *d* Chuck Vincent *ph* Lorenzo Battaglia *m* Ian Shaw, Kai Joffe *pd* Lucio Parese *ed* Anthony Delcampo, Chuck Vincent
☆ Sybil Danning, Donald Pleasence, Richard Hill, Josephine Jacqueline Jones, Tally Chanel, Stasia Micula (Samantha Fox), Suzanna Smith
† The US cinema release ran for 69 minutes, after some orgy scenes were cut.

The Warriors: see *The Dark Avenger (1955)*

'These are the armies of the night...'
The Warriors *
US 1979 94m Movielab
Paramount (Lawrence Gordon)
A New York street gang is forced to fight its way through hostile territory from the Bronx back to its home turf of Coney Island.
Slick exploitation movie, a retelling, in urban teenage terms, of Xenophon's epic retreat with his Ten Thousand following the death of Cyrus; the pace is fast, and the action violent, though stylised.
w David Shaber, Walter Hill *novel* Sol Yurick *d* Walter Hill *ph* Andrew Laszlo *m* Barry de Vorzon *ad* Don Swanagan, Bob Wightman *ed* David Holden *cos* Bobbie Mannix
☆ Michael Beck (Swan), James Remar (Ajax), Deborah Van Valkenburgh (Mercy), Marcelino Sanchez (Rembrandt), Brian Tyler (Snow), David Harris (Cochise), Tom McKitterick (Cowboy), Dorsey Wright (Cleon), Terry Michos (Vermin), David Patrick Kelly (Luther), Roger Hill (Cyrus), Edward Sewer (Gramercy Riff), Thomas Waites (Fox), Lynne Thigpen (DJ), Mercedes Ruehl (Policewoman)

The Warrior's Husband
US 1933 75m bw
Fox (Jesse L. Lasky)
The Greeks break into Amazonia and conquer the women, provoking a worm to turn.
A weird attempt by Hollywood to film a whimsical comedy which belonged only on Broadway, where the Greeks no doubt have a word for it.
w Sonya Levien *play* Julian Thompson *d* Walter Lang
☆ Elissa Landi, Marjorie Rambeau, Ernest Truex, David Manners, Helen Ware, Maude Eburne
'Novel farce will need astute exploitation aid.' – *Variety*

Warriors of Virtue
US 1997 101m colour Panavision
MGM (Dennis Law, Ronald Law, Christopher Law, Jeremy Law, Patricia Ruben)
A lonely boy is transported into a fantastic world and joins villagers in a battle against an evil dictator.
Kung fu kangaroos, the warriors of the title, turn out to be not much fun in this childish fantasy which mixes a little preaching with a great deal of fighting.
w Michael Vickerman, Hugh Kelley *d* Ronny Yu *ph* Peter Pau *m* Don Davis *pd* Eugenio Zanetti *ed* David Wu
☆ Angus MacFadyen, Mario Yedidia, Marley Shelton, Chao-Li Chi, Dennis Dun, Jack Tate, Doug Jones
'A slack-jawed kids' adventure in which genre conventions chafe against cutting-edge martial arts.' – *Variety*

Warui Yatsu Yoku Nemuru: see *The Bad Sleep Well*

The Wash
US 2001 96m colour
Metrodome/Lions Gate/Lithium (DJ Pooh, Phillip Atwell, Kip Konwiser)
Flatmates working at a Los Angeles car wash are given three days by their landlord to pay the rent.
Shamefully shoddy comedy, lazily acted, written and directed; well worth avoiding.
wd DJ Pooh *ph* Keith Smith *m* Camara Kambon *pd* Albert Cueller *ed* Jack Hofstra
☆ Dr Dre (Sean), Snoop Dogg (Dee Loc), George Wallace (Mr Washington), Angell Conwell (Antoinette), Tommy "Tiny" Lister Jnr (Bear), Bruce Bruce (DeWayne)
'An appallingly inept comedy.' – *Philip French, Observer*
'Clearly demonstrates the right of black American film-makers to make movies every bit as appalling as everyone else's.' – *Steve Grant, Sunday Times*

Washington Masquerade
US 1932 92m bw
MGM
GB title: *Mad Masquerade*
A high-minded senator is corrupted by a worthless girl.
Solid star melodrama.
w John Meehan, Samuel Blythe *play* The Claw by Henri Bernstein *d* Charles Brabin
☆ Lionel Barrymore, Karen Morley, Nils Asther, C. Henry Gordon, William Collier Snr

Washington Merry-go-round *
US 1932 75m bw
Columbia
A crusading young congressman attacks the crooks in the government.
Naïve comedy-drama with a miscast star.
w Jo Swerling from an original by Maxwell Anderson *d* James Cruze
☆ Lee Tracy, Constance Cummings, Alan Dinehart, Walter Connolly, Clarence Muse, Arthur Vinton
'Lots of flagwaving and political timeliness the chief appeal.' – *Variety*

'He was beautiful, passionate and penniless. For a lonely young heiress, the promise of his love was worth any price.'
Washington Square
US 1997 115m Technicolor
Buena Vista/Hollywood/Caravan/Alchemy (Roger Birnbaum, Julie Bergman Sender)
An ungainly heiress, the daughter of a domineering man, falls for a fortune hunter.
Clumsily routine adaptation, with generally unconvincing performances, and given a feminist slant that confuses the point of James's work.
w Carol Doyle *novel* Henry James *d* Agnieszka Holland *ph* Jerzy Zielinski *m* Jan A. P. Kaczmarek *pd* Allan Starski *ed* David Siegel
☆ Jennifer Jason Leigh, Albert Finney, Ben Chaplin, Maggie Smith, Judith Ivey, Betsy Brantley, Jennifer Garner
'Emerges with only a portion of its force and complexity intact.' – *Todd McCarthy, Variety*
† The novel was first filmed in 1949 as *The Heiress* (qv).

Washington Story
US 1952 82m bw
MGM (Dore Schary)
GB title: *Target for Scandal*
A lady reporter goes to Washington to expose corruption, but falls for an honest congressman.
Standard flagwaver which takes itself a shade too seriously.
wd Robert Pirosh *ph* John Alton *m* Conrad Salinger
☆ Van Johnson, Patricia Neal, Louis Calhern, Sidney Blackmer, Philip Ober, Patricia Collinge, Elizabeth Patterson, Moroni Olsen

Watch It, Sailor
GB 1961 81m bw
Columbia/Cormorant/Hammer (Maurice Cowan)
A sailor about to be married receives a paternity accusation.
Glum farce with wasted talent.
w Falkland Cary, Philip King *play* Falkland Cary, Philip King *d* Wolf Rilla *ph* Arthur Grant *m* Douglas Gamley *ad* Bernard Robinson, Don Mingaye *ed* James Needs, Alfred Cox
☆ Dennis Price, Marjorie Rhodes, Irene Handl, Liz Fraser, Vera Day, John Meillon, Cyril Smith

Watch Me When I Kill: see *The Cat's Victims*

Watch on the Rhine **
US 1943 114m bw
Warner (Hal B. Wallis)
A German refugee and his family are pursued by Nazi agents in Washington.
Talky play doesn't make much of a film, though the talk is good talk and the performances outstanding; but it made a prestige point or two for Hollywood.
w Dashiell Hammett *play* Lillian Hellman *d* Herman Shumlin *ph* Merritt Gerstad, Hal Mohr *m* Max Steiner
☆ *Paul Lukas*, Bette Davis, Lucile Watson, *George Coulouris*, Donald Woods, Geraldine Fitzgerald, Beulah Bondi, Henry Daniell
Paul Lukas
best picture; script; Lucile Watson

Watch the Birdie
US 1950 71m bw
MGM (Harry Ruskin)
A photographer meets a rich girl and saves her from a crook.
Unhappy remake of Buster Keaton's The Cameraman, *enlivened by a chase finale, but not helped by the star playing three members of the same family.*
w Ivan Tors, Devery Freeman, Harry Ruskin *d* Jack Donohue *ph* Paul C. Vogel *m* George Stoll
☆ Red Skelton, Arlene Dahl, Ann Miller, Leon Ames, Pamela Britton, Richard Rober

Watch Your Stern
GB 1960 88m bw
Allied Artists/GHW (Peter Rogers)
A ship's steward pretends to be the inventor of a homing torpedo.

Routine farce, well handled by its crew of expert comic actors, but too much driven by its narrative to do more than intermittently amuse.
w Alan Hackney, Vivian A. Cox *play Something about a Sailor* by Earle Couttie *d* Gerald Thomas *ph* Ted Scaife *m* Bruce Montgomery *ad* Carmen Dillon *ed* John Shirley
☆ Kenneth Connor, Eric Barker, Leslie Phillips, Joan Sims, Hattie Jacques, Spike Milligan, Eric Sykes, Sidney James, Ed Devereaux, David Lodge, Noel Purcell

The Watcher
US 2000 97m DeLuxe
Universal/Interlight (Christopher Eberts, Elliot Lewitt, Jeff Rice, Nile Niami)
A stressed FBI agent finds that he cannot escape the taunting of a serial killer who murders young women.
Miscast and shallow thriller in which visual tricks are used in an attempt to disguise its lack of suspense and insight.
w David Elliott, Clay Ayers *d* Joe Charbanic *ph* Michael Chapman *m* Marco Beltrami *pd* Brian Eatwell, Maria Caso *ed* Richard Nord
☆ James Spader (Joel Campbell), Marisa Tomei (Polly), Keanu Reeves (David Allen Griffin), Ernie Hudson (Ibby), Chris Ellis (Hollis), Robert Cicchini (Mitch), Yvonne Niami (Lisa), Jennifer McShane (Diana), Gina Alexander (Sharon), Rebakah Louise Smith (Ellie), Joe Sikora (Skater)
'Emerges as a formulaic thriller that plays more like direct-to-video fare than a megaplex-worthy feature.' – *Joe Leydon, Variety*
'A damp, morose bit of gristle.' – *A. O. Scott, New York Times*

The Watcher in the Woods
US 1980 100m Technicolor
Walt Disney (Tom Leetch)
The teenage daughter of an American composer has strange and apparently supernatural experiences in the British countryside.
Unsatisfactory attempt by the Disney people to aim at a wider audience than is expected of them. The mixture of cuteness, menace and the supernatural simply doesn't gel, and the film was much re-edited between its two appearances.
w Brian Clemens, Harry Spaulding, Rosemary Anne Sisson *novel* Florence Engel Randall *d* John Hough (and Vincent McEveety) *ph* Alan Hume *m* Stanley Myers
☆ Bette Davis, Carroll Baker, David McCallum, Lynn-Holly Johnson, Kyle Richards, Ian Bannen, Richard Pasco

Watchers
Canada 1988 91m colour
Guild/Concorde/Centaur/Carolco (Damian Lee, David Mitchell)
Two experimental animals, an intelligent dog and an ape-like killer, escape from a top secret government research laboratory.
Dogged horror movie, with plentiful gore but little suspense.
w Bill Freed, Damian Lee *novel* Dean R. Koontz *d* Jon Hess *ph* Richard Leiterman *m* Joel Goldsmith *pd* Richard Wilcox *ed* Bill Freda, Carolle Alain, Rick Fields
☆ Michael Ironside, Christopher Carey, Graeme Campbell, Dan O'Dowd, Lala, Corey Haim, Dale Wilson, Blu Mankuma, Colleen Winton

The Watchmaker of St Paul ***
France 1973 105m Eastmancolor
Lira (Raymond Danon)
original title: *L'Horloger de St Paul*
A watchmaker's tranquil life is shattered when he learns that his son is wanted for murder.
Solid character drama with careful writing and acting.
w Jean Aurenche, Pierre Bost, Bertrand Tavernier *novel L'Horloger d'Everton* by Georges Simenon *d* Bertrand Tavernier *ph* Pierre William Glenn *m* Philippe Sarde
☆ Philippe Noiret, Jean Rochefort, Sylvain Rougerie, Christine Pascal

Water *
GB 1985 95m colour
HandMade (Ian La Frenais)
Chaos comes to a Caribbean island when industrialists check it for mineral springs.
Hysterical comedy which never develops a single line for long, and quickly wears out its welcome.
w Dick Clement, Ian La Frenais, Bill Bersky *d* Dick Clement *ph* Douglas Slocombe *m* Mike Moran
☆ Michael Caine, Valerie Perrine, Brenda Vaccaro, Leonard Rossiter, Billy Connolly, Fred Gwynne, Maureen Lipman

The Water Babies
GB/Poland 1978 92m colour
Ariadne/Studio Miniatur Filmowych (Peter Shaw)
An 1850 chimney sweep evades his pursuers by jumping into a pool, where he becomes involved in an underwater adventure.
The live action bookends are strangely subdued, the animated middle totally characterless and seeming to bear little relation to the rest. A considerable disappointment.
w Michael Robson *novel* Charles Kingsley *d* Lionel Jeffries *ph* Ted Scaife *m* Phil Coulter
☆ James Mason, Billie Whitelaw, Bernard Cribbins, Joan Greenwood, David Tomlinson, Tommy Pender

Water Birds: see *The Living Desert*

Water Drops On Burning Rocks *
France/Japan 1999 85m colour
Artificial Eye/Fidélité/Les Films Alain Sarde/Euro Space (Olivier Delbosc, Marc Missonnier)
original title: *Gouttes D'eau Sur Pierres Brulantes*
In Germany, a 50 year-old insurance salesman begins an affair with a 19 year-old student, who has been having girlfriend problems.
Intriguing drama of sexual power games and shifting relationships.
wd François Ozon *play Tropfen auf heisse Steine* by Rainer Werner Fassbinder *ph* Jeanne Lapoirie *pd* Arnaud de Moléron *ed* Laurence Bawedin
☆ Bernard Giraudeau (Léopold Blum), Malik Zidi (Franz Meister), Ludivine Sagnier (Anna), Anna Thomson (Véra)
'An elegant, mischevious chamber piece about the mystery of erotic submission and the mortality of desire.' – *Peter Bradshaw, Guardian*
'I'd rather cultivate piles than have to sit through it again.' – *James Christopher, Times*

The Water Gypsies
GB 1932 80m bw
ATP
Adventures of two girls who live on a Thames barge.
Rather naïve and ordinary version of a successful book which many years later emerged as a stage musical; the film production has a stagey look throughout.
w Basil Dean, Miles Malleson, Alma Reville, John Paddy Carstairs *novel* A. P. Herbert *d* Maurice Elvey
☆ Ann Todd, Sari Maritza, Richard Bird, Frances Doble, Ian Hunter, Anthony Ireland
'Should do business in the best type of places.' – *Variety*

The Waterboy
US 1998 91m Technicolor
Buena Vista/Touchstone (Robert Simonds, Jack Giarraputo)
A simple-minded hick becomes a star football player when he learns to channel all the humiliation he has suffered into aggression.
An unattractive comedy about stupidity that was a surprising box-office hit in the United States.
w Tim Herlihy, Adam Sandler *d* Frank Coraci *ph* Steven Bernstein *m* Alan Pasqua *pd* Perry Andelin Blake *ed* Tom Lewis
☆ Adam Sandler, Kathy Bates, Henry Winkler, Fairuza Balk, Jerry Reed, Larry Gilliard Jnr, Blake Clark, Rob Schneider, Robert Kokol, Clint Howard, Al Whiting
'This escapist comedy is so cheerfully outlandish that it's hard to resist, and so good-hearted that it's genuinely endearing.' – *Janet Maslin, New York Times*
'The formulaic mix of mirth and mayhem is aimed way down the MTV food chain.' – *Glenn Lovell, Variety*

The Waterdance **
US 1991 107m colour
Samuel Goldwyn/No Frills (Gale Anne Hurd)
Three paraplegics in a rehabilitation centre attempt to come to terms with their condition and each other.
Graceful, perceptive, quietly effective movie on the pain of adjustment and the pleasures of friendship.
w Neal Jimenez *d* Neal Jimenez, Michael Steinberg *ph* Mark Plummer *m* Michael Convertino *pd* Robert Ziembicki *ed* Jeff Freeman
☆ Eric Stoltz, Wesley Snipes, William Forsythe, Helen Hunt, Elizabeth Pena, William Allen Young, Henry Harris, Tony Genaro, Eva Rodriguez, Grace Zabriskie
'An honest, unsentimental, deeply moving, often extremely funny account of an adjustment to a new way of living, of confronting overnight the deprivations that time will visit on us should we live into old age, of facing up to the injustices and misfortunes of life.' – *Philip French, Observer*
'A smashing success if great performances and a deftly told, thoroughly absorbing tale mean anything.' – *Variety*

'The desires and loneliness of seafaring men and their women!'
Waterfront
GB 1950 80m bw
GFD/Conqueror/Paul Soskin
US title: *Waterfront Women*
A drunken ship's fireman comes back to Liverpool after many years and causes trouble.
Unintentionally funny melodrama which gives the actors a lot of trouble.
w John Brophy, Paul Soskin *novel* John Brophy *d* Michael Anderson *ph* Harry Waxman *md* Muir Mathieson
☆ Robert Newton, Richard Burton, Kathleen Harrison, Susan Shaw, Avis Scott, Kenneth Griffith

Waterfront Women: see *Waterfront*

Waterhole Three
US 1967 100m Techniscope
Paramount
Sheriff, crooks and a gambler seek buried loot.
Rather irritatingly immoral Western with a hero who defines rape as assault with a friendly weapon; in between it tries hard for the ballad style.
w Joseph Steck, Robert R. Young *d* William Graham *ph* Robert Burks *m* Dave Grusin
☆ James Coburn, Carroll O'Connor, Margaret Blye, Claude Akins, Joan Blondell, Timothy Carey

Waterland
GB 1992 95m colour Scope
Mayfair/Palace/Pandora/Channel 4 Films/British Screen (Katy McGuinness, Patrick Cassavetti)
In the 1970s an English history teacher working in Pittsburgh tells his class of his own difficult past growing up in East Anglia.
A domestic saga of marital difficulties, incest and murder that soon slides into glum melodrama.
w Peter Prince *novel* Graham Swift *d* Stephen Gyllenhaal *ph* Robert Elswit *m* Carter Burwell *pd* Hugo Luczyc-Wyhowski *ed* Lesley Walker
☆ Jeremy Irons, Sinead Cusack, Ethan Hawke, Grant Warnock, Lena Headey, David Morrissey, John Heard
'A talented but terminably parched piece of literary cinema. Decorous, academic treatment of bizarre and traumatic material makes for a merely unpleasant film rather than an insightful or genuinely disturbing one.' – *Variety*

'The men, the battle, the glory the world will remember forever!'
Waterloo *
Italy/USSR 1970 132m Technicolor Panavision
Columbia/DDL/Mosfilm (Dino de Laurentiis)
Historical events leading up to the 1815 battle.
The battle forms the last hour of this historical charade, and looks both exciting and splendid, though confusion is not avoided. The rest is a mixed blessing.
w H. A. L. Craig, Sergei Bondarchuk *d Sergei Bondarchuk ph Armando Nannuzzi m* Nino Rota *pd* Mario Garbuglia
☆ Rod Steiger, Christopher Plummer, Orson Welles, Jack Hawkins, Virginia McKenna, Dan O'Herlihy, Rupert Davies, Ian Ogilvy, Michael Wilding
Mario Garbuglia

Waterloo Bridge *
US 1931 72m bw
Universal (Carl Laemmle Jnr)
An army officer marries a ballerina; when he is reported missing his family ignore her and she sinks into prostitution.
One for the ladies, who lapped it up.
w Tom Reed, Benn W. Levy *play* Robert E. Sherwood *d* James Whale *ph* Arthur Edeson
☆ Mae Clarke, Kent Douglass, Doris Lloyd, Ethel Griffies, Enid Bennett, Frederick Kerr, Bette Davis
'Just fair programme fodder, and it ought to be better. Not helped by an uninspiring sad ending.' – *Variety*

Waterloo Bridge **
US 1940 103m bw
MGM (Sidney Franklin)
Lush, all-stops-out remake of the above; for yet another version see *Gaby*.
w S. N. Behrman, Hans Rameau, George Froeschel *d* Mervyn Le Roy *ph Joseph Ruttenberg m* Herbert Stothart
☆ Vivien Leigh, Robert Taylor, Lucile Watson, Virginia Field, Maria Ouspenskaya, C. Aubrey Smith, Steffi Duna
'The director uses candlelight and rain more effectively than he does the actors.' – *New Yorker, 1977*
Joseph Ruttenberg; Herbert Stothart

The Waterloo Bridge Handicap *
GB 1978 21m colour
Paramount/Fetter
Commuters enjoy a daily race across Westminster Bridge.
Amusing trifle, well shot and edited.
wd Ross Cramer ed Sean Barton
☆ Leonard Rossiter, Lynda Bellingham, John Quentin, Gordon Laye

Waterloo Road
GB 1944 76m bw
GFD/Gainsborough (Edward Black)
A soldier whose wife is enamoured of a petty crook absents himself to settle matters.
What at the time seemed cheerful realism now seems chronically forced, but amusing moments can still be found.
wd Sidney Gilliat *story* Val Valentine *ph* Arthur Crabtree *md* Louis Levy
☆ *John Mills*, Stewart Granger, Joy Shelton, Alastair Sim, Beatrice Varley, Alison Leggatt, *Jean Kent*
'The harsh rattle of trains over a viaduct, the clamour of the street market, the wailing of sirens and the crash of bombs are the accompaniment of this wartime love story.' – *Richard Winnington*
'Unpretentious, credible, continuously entertaining and just the right length.' – *Richard Mallett, Punch*

Watermelon Man
US 1970 100m Technicolor
Columbia/Johanna (John B. Bennett)
A bigoted insurance salesman wakes up one morning to find he has turned into a black man.
Spasmodically funny racial comedy, compromised by the impossibility of a black man playing white even with heavy make-up.
w Herman Raucher *d* Melvin Van Peebles *ph* W. Wallace Kelley *m* Melvin Van Peebles
☆ Godfrey Cambridge, Estelle Parsons, Howard Caine, Mantan Moreland

Watermelon Woman
US 1997 105m DuArt
Dangerous To Know/Dancing Girl/Cheryl Dunye (Barry Swimar, Alexandra Juhasz)

A lesbian video-shop worker, who wants to be a film-maker, researches the life of an actress who is credited as the Watermelon Woman in films of the 30s and 40s.
A fake documentary, shot in a rough-and-ready manner, that will interest only some of those who share the sexual preferences of its maker.
wd Cheryl Dunye *ph* Michelle Crenshaw *m* Paul Shapiro *pd* Robert 'Ratface' Holtzman *ed* Annie Taylor
☆ Cheryl Dunye, Guinevere Turner, Valerie Walker, Lisa Marie Bronson, Irene Dunye, Brian Freeman, Camille Paglia
'It is very unlikely that it will be seen by anyone who wouldn't otherwise go and see an art movie by a black lesbian film-maker. I wish I could say that this is a shame.' – *Andrea Turner, Sight and Sound*

Waters of Time *
GB 1951 37m bw
Port of London Authority
A poetic impression of the Port of London, from the mouth of the Thames to Kingston.
Notably stylish documentary, made to coincide with the Festival of Britain.
wd Basil Wright, Bill Launder ed Basil Wright, Bill Launder

Watership Down
GB 1978 92m Technicolor
Nepenthe (Martin Rosen)

A colony of rabbits seek a new home following a vision of the destruction of their warren.
A brilliantly written if somewhat pretentious parable becomes a rather flatly made cartoon in which it is difficult to distinguish one rabbit from another; the whole thing becomes a bit doomladen for family audiences, while adults will presumably prefer to re-read the novel.
wd Martin Rosen *novel* Richard Adams
m Angela Morley *animation director* Tony Guy
☆ Featuring the voices of John Hurt, Richard Briers, Ralph Richardson, Zero Mostel, Roy Kinnear, Denholm Elliott, John Bennett, Simon Cadell

'Beyond The Horizon Lies A Secret To A New Beginning'
Waterworld *
US 1995 135m DeLuxe
UIP/Universal (Charles Gordon, John Davis, Kevin Costner)

The adventures in the future, when the ice caps have melted and the world is flooded, of a mutant human, who searches across the oceans for land, with the aid of a woman and her adopted daughter.
Overblown action movie with a leaky narrative, relying on stunts to retain an audience's attention; it looks good, though, and is energized by Dennis Hopper as a psychotic villain.
w Peter Rader, David Twohy *d* Kevin Reynolds *ph* Dean Semler *m* James Newton Howard *pd* Dennis Gassner *ed* Peter Boyle *sp* Michael J. McAlister
☆ Kevin Costner, Dennis Hopper, Jeanne Tripplehorn, Tina Majorino, Michael Jeter, Gerard Murphy, Zakes Mokae
'Splashes enough spectacular mayhem up on the screen to divert thrill-seeking audiences through most of its running time.' – *Todd McCarthy, Variety.*
'*Waterworld* doesn't suck, but neither will it blow you away, and it spends most of its two hours with no propulsion whatsoever, save memories of other movies and large, gusty gales of superstar ego.' – *Tom Shone, Sunday Times*
'More like a couple of hours in a flotation tank than a white-knuckle roller coaster ride.' – *Adam Mars-Jones, Independent*
† The film was the most expensive yet made in Hollywood, at a reported cost of $175m (or $1.3m a minute of screen-time). It had its genesis in a script commissioned from Rader as a low-budget variation on *Mad Max*, which was rejected by its original producers when it was estimated that the resulting movie would cost at least $5m. Reynolds left the film during post-production after a disagreement with Costner. It took around $88m at the US box-office and a further $166m elsewhere in the world.
sound

Watusi
US 1959 85m Technicolor
MGM (Al Zimbalist)
Harry Quartermain retraces his father's footsteps to King Solomon's Mines.
Skilful re-use of King Solomon's Mines *footage; acceptable* Boy's Own Paper *stuff.*
w James Clavell *d* Kurt Neumann *ph* Harold E. Wellman
☆ George Montgomery, Taina Elg, David Farrar, Rex Ingram, Dan Seymour

The Wax Mask (dubbed) *
Italy/France 1995 95m colour
Cine 2000/Mediaset/FFI (Giuseppe Colombo)

In Milan, the proprietor of a wax museum is a homicidal maniac.
Stylish, though excessively gory and gruesome, variation on House of Wax *with touches of* The Terminator *thrown in for good measure.*
w Lucio Fulci, Daniele Stroppa, Dario Argento *d* Sergio Stivaletti *ph* Sergio Salvati *m* Maurizio Abeni *ad* Antonello Geleng *ed* Paolo Benassi *sp* Sergio Stivaletti; make-up: Benoit Lestang
☆ Robert Hossein, Romina Mondello, Riccardo Serventi Longhi, Gabriella Giorgelli, Umberto Balli, Valery Valmond, Aldo Massasso

Waxwork
US 1988 96m colour
Vestron/Palla Pictures/Filmrullen (Staffen Ahrenberg)

Students visit a waxworks' chamber of horrors in an old dark house, where the figures come to life.
Direly unimaginative, hammily acted horror movie.
wd Anthony Hickox *ph* Gerry Lively *m* Roger Bellon *pd* Gianni Quaranta *ed* Christopher Cibelli
☆ Zach Galligan, Deborah Freeman, Michelle Johnson, Dana Ashbrook, Miles O'Keeffe, Charles McCaughan, J. Kenneth Campbell, John Rhys-Davies, Patrick Macnee, David Warner
'Film-making by numbers.' – *MFB*

'An eye popping, teeth chattering, mind blowing movie!!!'
Waxwork II: Lost in Time
US 1991 100m Foto-Kem
Electric Pictures (Nancy Paloian)

aka: *Lost in Time*
Having destroyed a wax museum where monsters came to life, a couple travel into a parallel universe of 'God's Nintendo game' where the battle between good and evil is fought as scenarios from horror movies.
From Nosferatu *to* Godzilla *and* Alien, *taking in* Frankenstein, Jekyll and Hyde, *Edgar Allen Poe and* The Haunting *along the way, classic horrors are parodied in a clever low-budget style with cut-rate wit, ham acting and a lot of blood-letting. The result may entertain fans of the genre in an indulgent mood.*
wd Anthony Hickox *ph* Gerry Lively *m* Steve Schiff *pd* Steve Hardie *ed* Christopher Cibelli *sp* Bob Keen
☆ Zach Galligan, Monika Schnarre, Martin Kemp, Bruce Campbell, Michael Des Barres, Jim Metzler, Sophie Ward, Bill Kane, Juliet Mills, John Ireland, Patrick Macnee, David Carradine, Alexander Godunov
'A loopy gags-and-gore fest striving a mite too self-consciously for cult status.' – *Variety*
'A profound lack of style that confirms just because Hickox loves good horror movies doesn't necessarily mean he knows how to make them.' – *Shivers*

Waxworks *
Germany 1924 62m approx (24 fps) bw silent
Neptun-Film
original title: *Das Wachsfigurenkabinett*
A young poet in a fairground waxwork museum concocts stories about Haroun al Raschid, Ivan the Terrible and Jack the Ripper.
The form later became familiar in such horror films as Torture Garden *and* Tales from the Crypt, *but here the emphasis is not on horror but on grotesquerie, and indeed the idea is somewhat more entertaining than the rather plodding execution.*
w Henrik Galeen *d Paul Leni ph* Helmar Lerski *ad* Paul Leni, Ernst Stern, Alfred Junge
☆ William Dieterle, Emil Jannings, Conrad Veidt, Werner Krauss

The Way: see *Yol*

The Way Ahead ***
GB 1944 115m bw
GFD/Two Cities (John Sutro, Norman Walker)

US title: *Immortal Battalion*
Adventures of a platoon of raw recruits during World War II.
Memorable semi-documentary originally intended as a training film; the warm humour of the early scenes, however, never leads quite naturally into the final action and tragedy.
w Eric Ambler, Peter Ustinov *d Carol Reed ph* Guy Green *m* William Alwyn
☆ *David Niven, Stanley Holloway,* Raymond Huntley, *William Hartnell,* James Donald, John Laurie, Leslie Dwyer, Hugh Burden, Jimmy Hanley, Renée Asherson, Penelope Dudley Ward, Reginald Tate, Leo Genn, Mary Jerrold, Peter Ustinov
'Is to be admired and recommended for its direction, its writing and its playing.' – *Dilys Powell*

Way Back Home
US 1932 81m bw
RKO
Problems of a Maine preacher.
Unintentionally hilarious farrago of dark deeds in a small town, from a radio serial.
w Jane Murfin *d* William A. Seiter
☆ Phillips Lord, Bette Davis, Effie Palmer, Bennett Kilpack, Frank Albertson, Mrs Phillips Lord

Way Down East **
US 1920 110m approx (24 fps) bw (colour sequence) silent
D. W. Griffith

A country girl is seduced; her baby dies; her shame is revealed; but a kindly farmer rescues her from drowning and marries her.
Old-fashioned tearjerker impeccably mounted and very typical of its director in its sentimental mood. The ice floe sequence is famous for its excitement and realism.
w Anthony Paul Kelly, Joseph R. Grismer, D. W. Griffith *play* Lottie Blair Parker *d D. W. Griffith ph* Billy Bitzer, Henrik Sortov
☆ *Lillian Gish,* Richard Barthelmess, Lowell Sherman, Creighton Hale
'Griffith took a creaking, dated stage melodrama and turned it into a melodramatic epic.' – *Pauline Kael, 70s*

Way Down East
US 1935 85m bw
TCF (Winfield Sheehan)
Tedious and unwise remake.
w Howard Estabrook, William Hurlbut *d* Henry King
☆ Rochelle Hudson, Henry Fonda, Slim Summerville, Edward Trevor, Margaret Hamilton, Andy Devine, Spring Byington, Russell Simpson, Sara Haden

Way for a Sailor
US 1930 83m bw
MGM
Adventures of a tough seafarer and a pet seal.
Thin vehicle for a declining star whose talkie voice was at odds with his image.
w Laurence Stallings, W. L. River *novel* Albert Richard Wetjen *d* Sam Wood *ph* Percy Hilburn
☆ John Gilbert, Wallace Beery, Leila Hyams, Jim Tully, Polly Moran, Doris Lloyd
'It throws John Gilbert for a loss, and it's not his fault. His voice is okay.' – *Variety*

The Way I Killed My Father: see *Comment J'Ai Tué Mon Pére*

Way of a Gaucho
US 1952 91m Technicolor
TCF (Philip Dunne)
An Argentine gaucho joins the militia and fights Indians.
Mildly interesting Western-in-disguise.
w Philip Dunne *novel* Herbert Childs *d* Jacques Tourneur *ph* Harry Jackson *m* Sol Kaplan
☆ Rory Calhoun, Gene Tierney, Richard Boone, Hugh Marlowe, Everett Sloane, Enrique Chaico

The Way of All Flesh *
US 1928 94m (24 fps) bw silent
Paramount (Adolph Zukor, Jesse L. Lasky)
A respectable man leaves his wife, goes to the dogs, and is too ashamed to come back.
Star character drama, most watchable now when it goes over the top.
d Victor Fleming
☆ Emil Jannings, Belle Bennett, Phyllis Haver
Emil Jannings
best picture

'He left his heart behind when he took it!'
The Way of All Flesh
US 1940 82m bw
Paramount (Eugene Zukor)
Remake of the above, well enough done but clearly outmoded.
w Lenore Coffee *story* Jules Furthman, Lajos Biro *novel Perley Poore Sheehan d* Louis King *ph* Theodor Sparkuhl
☆ Akim Tamiroff, Gladys George, Muriel Angelus, Berton Churchill, Fritz Leiber

The Way of the Dragon (dubbed)
Hong Kong 1973 99m Cineart Scope
Cathay/Concord/Golden Harvest (Raymond Chow)

aka: *Return of the Dragon*
A martial arts expert goes to Rome to help a friend save her restaurant which is threatened by gangsters.
A kung fu movie incongruously shifted from the East to Italy, where it seems silly, although the fight sequences are well done.
wd Bruce Lee *ph* Ho Lan Shan *m* Joseph Koo *ad* Chien Hsin *ed* Chang Yao Ching
☆ Bruce Lee, Nora Miao, Chuck Norris, Wei Ping Ao, Wang Chung Hsin
'At once deeply flawed and the most personal film to have come out of Hong Kong.' – *Tony Rayns, MFB*
† The film was cut to 91m on its British release.

The Way of the Gun *
US 2000 119m DeLuxe
Momentum/Artisan (Kenneth Kokin)

Two petty criminals kidnap a surrogate mother, who is carrying a child for a wealthy gangster.
Convoluted thriller that gains little from its complexity; underneath the plotting, it's a film about unpleasant people doing very bad things.
wd Christopher McQuarrie *ph* Dick Pope *m* Joe Kraemer *pd* Maia Javan *ed* Stephen Semel *cos* Genevieve Tyrrell, Heather Neely McQuarrie
☆ Ryan Phillippe (Parker), Benicio Del Toro (Longbaugh), James Caan (Joe Sarno), Juliette Lewis (Robin), Taye Diggs (Jeffers), Nicky Katt (Obecks), Dylan Kussman (Dr Allen Painter), Scott Wilson (Hale Chidduck), Kristin Lehman (Francesca Chidduck), Geoffrey Lewis (Abner)
'A striking attempt to rethink the action movie.' – *Adam Mars-Jones, Times*
'A lethargically paced yarn that overextends its welcome by at least 25 minutes.' – *Emanuel Levy, Variety*
† Parker and Longbaugh, the names of the crooks played by Ryan Phillippe and Benicio De Toro, are the actual surnames of outlaws Butch Cassidy and The Sundance Kid.

Way Out West ****
US 1937 66m bw
Hal Roach (Stan Laurel)

Laurel and Hardy come to Brushwood Gulch to deliver the deed to a gold mine.
Seven reels of perfect joy, with the comedians at their very best in brilliantly-timed routines, plus two song numbers as a bonus.
w Jack Jevne, Charles Rogers, James Parrott, Felix Adler d James Horne ph Art Lloyd, Walter Lundin *m* Marvin Hatley
☆ *Stan Laurel, Oliver Hardy, James Finlayson, Sharon Lynne,* Rosina Lawrence
'Thin returns indicated ... for added feature on duallers.' – *Variety*

'Not only one of their most perfect films, it ranks with the best screen comedy anywhere.' – *David Robinson, 1962*

'The film is leisurely in the best sense; you adjust to a different rhythm and come out feeling relaxed as if you'd had a vacation.' – *New Yorker, 1980*

Marvin Hatley

'Of course he's naughty! But that's the way you love him best!'

The Way to Love

US 1933 80m bw

Paramount (Benjamin Glazer)

A would-be Paris tourist guide works as a pavement hawker and helps a showgirl evade her knife-thrower partner.

Thin star vehicle with a few pleasant moments.

w Gene Fowler, Benjamin Glazer *d* Norman Taurog *ph* Charles Lang *m/ly* Ralph Rainger, Leo Robin

☆ *Maurice Chevalier*, Edward Everett Horton, Ann Dvorak, Arthur Pierson, Minna Gombell, Blanche Frederici, Douglass Dumbrille, John Miljan

'The poorest of the Chevaliers but poor entertainment which will get by on the strength of the star.' – *Variety*

The Way to the Gold

US 1957 94m bw

TCF (David Weisbart)

An ex-convict seeks hidden loot but is pursued by competitors.

Gloomy, self-pitying melodrama.

w Wendell Mayes *novel* Wilber Steele *d* Robert D. Webb *ph* Leo Tover *m* Lionel Newman

☆ Jeffrey Hunter, Sheree North, Barry Sullivan, Walter Brennan, Ruth Donnelly, Neville Brand

The Way to the Stars ****

GB 1945 109m bw

Two Cities (Anatole de Grunwald)

US title: *Johnny in the Clouds*

World War II as seen by the guests at a small hotel near an airfield.

Generally delightful comedy drama suffused with tragic atmosphere but with very few flying shots, one of the few films which instantly bring back the atmosphere of the war in Britain for anyone who was involved.

w Terence Rattigan, Anatole de Grunwald poem John Pudney d Anthony Asquith ph Derick Williams *m Nicholas Brodszky*

☆ *John Mills, Rosamund John, Michael Redgrave, Douglass Montgomery*, Basil Radford, Stanley Holloway, Joyce Carey, Renée Asherson, Felix Aylmer, Bonar Colleano, Trevor Howard, Jean Simmons

'Not for a long time have I seen a film so satisfying, so memorable, or so successful in evoking the precise mood and atmosphere of the recent past.' – *Richard Mallett, Punch*

'Humour, humanity, and not a sign of mawkishness ... a classic opening sequence, with the camera wandering through an abandoned air base, peering in at each detail in the nissen huts, the sleeping quarters, the canteens, noting all the time a procession of objects each of which will have its own special significance in the action of the film.' – *Basil Wright, 1972*

Way Way Out

US 1966 105m DeLuxe Cinemascope

TCF/Coldwater/Jerry Lewis (Malcolm Stuart)

In 1994 a weather expert on the moon has woman trouble.

Dismal sex farce with an unusual backdrop; painful to sit through.

w William Bowers, Laslo Vadnay *d* Gordon Douglas *ph* William H. Clothier *m* Lalo Schifrin

☆ Jerry Lewis, Connie Stevens, Robert Morley, Dick Shawn, Anita Ekberg, Dennis Weaver, Howard Morris, Brian Keith

'Everything seemed so important then – even love!'

The Way We Were **

US 1973 118m Eastmancolor Panavision

Columbia/Rastar (Ray Stark)

The romance and marriage of an upper-crust young novelist and a Jewish bluestocking girl, from college to Hollywood in the thirties, forties and fifties.

Instant nostalgia for Americans, some fun and a lot of boredom for everybody is provided by this very patchy star vehicle which makes a particular mess of the McCarthy witch hunt sequence but has undeniable moments of vitality.

w Arthur Laurents *novel* Arthur Laurents *d* Sydney Pollack *ph* Harry Stradling Jnr *m* Marvin Hamlisch

☆ *Barbra Streisand, Robert Redford*, Patrick O'Neal, Viveca Lindfors, Bradford Dillman, Lois Chiles, Allyn Ann McLerie, Herb Edelman, Murray Hamilton

'Not one moment of the picture is anything but garbage under the gravy of false honesty.' – *Stanley Kauffmann*

'A real curate's egg of a movie, composed of so many disparate parts as to put you in mind of Leacock's knight, who got on his horse and rode off furiously in all directions.' – *Benny Green, Punch*

Marvin Hamlisch; title song (*m* Marvin Hamlisch, *ly* Alan and Marilyn Bergman)

Harry Stradling Jnr; Barbra Streisand

The Way West *

US 1967 122m DeLuxe Panavision

UA/Harold Hecht

Hazards of a wagon train between Missouri and Oregon in 1843.

Semi-spectacular Western which looks good but falls apart dramatically, especially in its insistence on a sub-plot about a most unlikely nymphet.

w Ben Maddow, Mitch Lindemann *novel* A. B. Guthrie Jnr *d* Andrew V. McLaglen *ph* William H. Clothier *m* Bronislau Kaper *md* André Previn *ad* Edward S. Hayworth *ed* Otho Lovering

☆ Kirk Douglas (Tadlock), Robert Mitchum (Dick Summers), Richard Widmark (Lije Evans), Lola Albright (Rebecca Evans), Michael Witney (Johnnie Mack), Sally Field (Mercy McBee), Stubby Kaye (Sam Fairman), Jack Elam (Weatherby), Harry Carey Jnr (McBee), Katherine Justice (Amanda Mack)

'A jerk's idea of an epic; big stars, big landscapes, bad jokes, folksy-heroic music to plug up the holes, and messy hang-ups.' – *Pauline Kael*

'You'll laugh. You'll cry. You'll hurl.'

Wayne's World

US 1992 95m Technicolor

UIP/Paramount (Lorne Michaels)

A ramshackle cable TV show, put together by two girl- and rock-obsessed teenagers, is given big-time exposure by a sleazy TV executive.

Tedious teen comedy, based on characters developed for the Saturday Night Live *TV show, which long outstays its welcome. It was, though, one of 1992's surprise hits, ranking sixth at the US box-office and doing well in Europe.*

w Mike Myers, Bonnie Turner, Terry Turner *d* Penelope Spheeris *ph* Theo Van de Sande *m* J. Peter Robinson *pd* Gregg Fonseca *ed* Malcolm Campbell

☆ Mike Myers, Dana Carvey, Rob Lowe, Tia Carrere, Brian Doyle-Murray, Lara Flynn Boyle, Michael DeLuise, Dan Bell

'Aggressively pitched at a young white male audience, feature is unlikely to appeal to mainstream moviegoers ... Even for fans of the TV comics, the laugh-to-running-time ratio is extremely low.' – *Variety*

Wayne's World 2 *

US 1993 95m DeLuxe

Paramount (Lorne Michaels)

In a dream, Wayne is told to organize Waynestock, the ultimate rock concert.

The mixture is much the same as the first film, but this time around the jokes are slightly better.

w Mike Myers, Bonnie Turner, Terry Turner *d* Stephen Surjik *ph* Francis Kenny *m* Carter Burwell *pd* Gregg Fonseca *ed* Malcolm Campbell

☆ Mike Myers, Dana Carvey, Christopher Walken, Tia Carrere, Ralph Brown, Kim Basinger, Drew Barrymore, Michael Nickles (Jim Morrison), Aerosmith

'A puerile, misguided and loathsome effort ... NOT!' – *Variety*

'Something of a disappointment, though that is not to say that a lot of people won't enjoy it – especially if drunk or on drugs.' – *Ben Thompson, Sight and Sound*

The Wayward Bus

US 1957 89m bw Cinemascope

TCF (Charles Brackett)

A landslide strands an assortment of bus passengers in a lonely farmhouse ...

...but not the old dark house, unfortunately: this lot does nothing but talk, and the plot never really forms.

w Ivan Moffat *novel* John Steinbeck *d* Victor Vicas *ph* Charles G. Clarke *m* Leigh Harline

☆ Dan Dailey, Jayne Mansfield, Joan Collins, Rick Jason, Dolores Michaels, Larry Keating, Betty Lou Keim

We Are Not Alone *

US 1939 112m bw

Warner (Henry Blanke)

A man having an innocent affair is accused of murdering his wife.

Gloomy, well-acted drama with a rather uneasy English setting.

w James Hilton, Milton Krims *novel* James Hilton *d* Edmund Goulding *ph* Tony Gaudio *m* Max Steiner

☆ *Paul Muni*, Jane Bryan, Flora Robson, Raymond Severn, Una O'Connor, Henry Daniell, Montagu Love, James Stephenson, Cecil Kellaway

'It has dignity and warmth and is genuinely moving ... handsomely produced, skilfully directed, and eloquently played.' – *Variety*

'An extraordinarily moving story, beautifully told and perfectly acted.' – *MFB*

We Dive at Dawn

GB 1943 98m bw

GFD/Gainsborough (Edward Black)

World War II adventures of a British submarine disabled in the Baltic.

Fairly routine war suspenser.

w J. B. Williams, Val Valentine, Frank Launder *d* Anthony Asquith *ph* Jack Cox *md* Louis Levy

☆ John Mills, Eric Portman, Reginald Purdell, Niall MacGinnis, Joan Hopkins, Josephine Wilson, Jack Watling

We Don't Want to Talk about It **

Argentina/Italy 1993 105m colour

Artificial Eye/Aura/Oscar Kramer

original title: *De Eso No Se Habla*

A widow makes sure her daughter, a dwarf, is unaware that there are others like her; the girl marries a sophisticated stranger, but then the circus comes to town.

An oddly enchanting bitter-sweet fable, a satire of conventional life and political correctness, a celebration of growing up, assuming responsibility for oneself and following one's own destiny.

w Maria Luisa Bemberg, Jorge Goldenberg *story* Julio Llinás *d Maria Luisa Bemberg ph* Felix Monti *m* Nicola Piovani *pd* Jorge Sarudiansky *ed* Juan Carlos Macias

☆ Marcello Mastroianni, Luisina Brando, Alejandra Podesta, Betiana Blum, Alberto Segado, Roberto Carnaghi, Jorge Luz

'It is a rare feat of enchanted cinema that what could so easily have been grotesque achieves a fairy-tale quality ... one of the year's strangest, most mesmeric movies.' – *Tom Hutchinson, Film Review*

We Faw Down

US 1928 20m bw silent

Hal Roach

Stan and Ollie have an evening out, but their lies to their wives become apparent.

Moderate star comedy, later elaborated in Sons of the Desert.

w H. M. Walker *d* Leo McCarey *ed* Richard Currier

☆ Stan Laurel, Oliver Hardy, Bess Flowers, Vivien Oakland, Kay Deslys

We Have Our Moments

US 1937 63m bw

Edmund Grainger/Universal

Gangsters hide their loot in the trunk of a schoolteacher going to Europe on a vacation.

Rather slackly handled comedy with amusing bits.

w Bruce Manning, Charles Grayson, David Belden, Frederick Stephani *d* Alfred Werker

☆ James Dunn, Sally Eilers, Mischa Auer, David Niven, Warren Hymer, Marjorie Gateson, Thurston Hall

'As the number two feature on doubles it will manage to get by.' – *Variety*

We Humans: see *Young America*

We Joined the Navy

GB 1962 105m Eastmancolor Cinemascope

Dial/Daniel M. Angel

A carefree naval commander and three cadets get involved in the affairs of a small Mediterranean country.

Desperate naval farce which sinks from script malnutrition in reel two.

w Howard Dimsdale *novel* John Winton *d* Wendy Toye *ph* Otto Heller *m* Ron Grainer

☆ Kenneth More, Lloyd Nolan, Mischa Auer, Joan O'Brien, Jeremy Lloyd, Dinsdale Landen, Derek Fowlds

† The film originally credited Arthur Dales as the screenwriter because Howard Dimsdale was blacklisted.

We Live Again *

US 1934 85m bw

Samuel Goldwyn

A Russian prince is brought up in the country and falls in love with a servant girl whose life later takes a downward path.

Beautifully made but dramatically uninteresting version of a Russian classic.

w Preston Sturges, Maxwell Anderson, Leonard Praskins *novel Resurrection* by Leo Tolstoy *d Rouben Mamoulian ph Gregg Toland m* Alfred Newman

☆ Fredric March, Anna Sten, Jane Baxter, C. Aubrey Smith, Ethel Griffies, Jessie Ralph, Sam Jaffe

'It's a class picture basically. That limits its mass b.o. appeal.' – *Variety*

We of the Never Never *

Australia 1982 134m Eastmancolor Technovision

Adams Packer/Film Corporation of Western Australia/GTC (Greg Tepper)

Around 1900, a city girl marries the owner of an isolated cattle station.

Longwinded but attractively photographed recollections of another time and another place. Not really very memorable despite a plethora of incident.

w Peter Schreck *book* Mrs Aeneas Gunn *d* Igor Auzins *ph Gary Hansen m* Peter Best

☆ Angela Punch-McGregor, Arthur Dignam, Tony Barry, Martin Vaughan

'Tasteful period re-creation, choked-back emotionalism, a *Men of Two Worlds* attempt at assuaging colonial guilt, and the kind of tidily suffering heroine Deborah Kerr used to play.' – *Kim Newman, MFB*

We Think the World of You *

GB 1988 94m Technicolor

Recorded Releasing/Gold Screen/Film Four International/British Screen (Tommaso Jandelli)

A middle-aged homosexual becomes devoted to his lover's dog.

Understated and reticent drama, enjoyable mainly for its acting.

w Hugh Stoddart *novel* J. R. Ackerley *d* Colin Gregg *ph* Mike Garfath *m* Julian Jacobson *pd* Jamie Leonard *ed* Peter Delfgou

☆ Alan Bates, Max Wall, Liz Smith, Frances Barber, Gary Oldman, Ryan Batt, Kerry Wise, Sheila Ballantine

We Were Dancing

US 1942 93m bw

MGM (Robert Z. Leonard, Orville Dull)

A Polish princess elopes from her engagement party with a gigolo.

Leaden romantic comedy produced in high style.

w Claudine West, Hans Rameau, George Froeschel *play Tonight at 8.30* by Noël Coward *d* Robert Z. Leonard *ph* Robert Planck *m* Bronislau Kaper

☆ Norma Shearer, Melvyn Douglas, Gail Patrick, Lee Bowman, Marjorie Main, Reginald Owen, Alan Mowbray, Florence Bates, Sig Rumann, Dennis Hoey, Heather Thatcher, Connie Gilchrist

'Fathers, Brothers, Husbands & Sons.'

We Were Soldiers *

US 2002 137m DeLuxe Panavision
Paramount/Icon/Wheelhouse (Bruce Davey, Stephen McEveety, Randall Wallace)

In 1965, an outnumbered battalion of American soldiers fights heroically in the first major battle of the Vietnam war.

A movie of old-fashioned gung-ho heroics, with Gibson in long-shot looking remarkably like John Wayne; it's convincing on the thud and blunder of battle, though otherwise seems advance propaganda for the next World War.

wd Randall Wallace *book* *We Were Soldiers Once...and Young* by Lt Gen. Harold G. Moore, Joseph L. Galloway *ph* Dean Semler *m* Nick Glennie-Smith *pd* Tom Sanders *ed* William Hoy

☆ Mel Gibson (Lt Col Hal Moore), Madeleine Stowe (Julie Moore), Greg Kinnear (Major Bruce Crandall), Sam Elliott (Sgt Major Basil Plumley), Chris Klein (2nd Lt Jack Geoghegan), Keri Russell (Barbara Geoghegan), Barry Pepper (Joe Galloway), Don Duong (Lt Col Nguyen Huu An)

'While responsive to the themes of bravery, innocence and its loss, the film has an inherited, second-hand feel when it comes to the profound ramifications of the actions it shows.' – *Todd McCarthy, Variety*

'The real point of the picture is pronounced: it assures us that military service, though it may cost our lives, can fulfill our lives in ways otherwise unavailable' – *Stanley Kaufmann, New Republic*

'We cannot forget what this film prefers to avoid knowing, that bravery and self-sacrifice without a reason are not cause for celebration but rather one of the saddest, one of the most regrettable of human activities.' – *Kenneth Turan, Los Angeles Times*

† The Vietnamese National Film Censorship Council denounced Don Duong for his role in the film. He was called a "national traitor" and told that he would be banned from making films for five years. Mel Gibson and others organised a campaign for his rehabilitation.

We Were Strangers *

US 1949 105m bw
Columbia/Horizon (Sam Spiegel)

Cuban rebels in the thirties plan to assassinate a politician and have to build a tunnel through a cemetery.

Well-made but very downbeat adventure story, too cheerless to be exciting.

w Peter Viertel, John Huston *novel* *Rough Sketch* by Robert Sylvester *d* John Huston *ph* Russell Metty *m* Georges Antheil

☆ John Garfield, Jennifer Jones, Pedro Armendariz, Gilbert Roland, Wally Cassell, Ramon Novarro, David Bond, Jose Perez

'There is so much about this film I cannot swallow – the implausibilities of detail, the convention of broken accents, the literary conversaziones, the naïve doctrines of revolution ... [but] it continues to haunt the mind and has therefore had its say.' – *Richard Winnington*

We Who Are About to Die

US 1937 82m bw
RKO

Life on Death Row.

Modest prison melodrama with a lot of opportunity for character actors to display hysteria.

w John Twist, David Lamson *d* Christy Cabanne

☆ Preston Foster, Ann Dvorak, John Beal, Ray Mayer, Gordon Jones, Russell Hopton, J. Carrol Naish, Willie Fung, Paul Hurst, Frank Jenks, Barnett Parker, John Wray, John Carroll

'An action drama of considerable tension that should please the general run of fans with plenty of special charm for the kids and the menfolk.' – *Variety*

The Weak and the Wicked

GB 1953 88m bw
ABPC/Marble Arch (Victor Skutezky)

Flashbacks show how various women came to find themselves in prison.

Predictable portmanteau drama with stalwart performances.

w J. Lee-Thompson, Anne Burnaby *book* *Who Lie in Gaol* by Joan Henry *d* J. Lee-Thompson *ph* Gilbert Taylor *m* Leighton Lucas

☆ Glynis Johns, John Gregson, Diana Dors, Jane Hylton, Sidney James, Olive Sloane, Eliot Makeham, A. E. Matthews, Athene Seyler, Sybil Thorndike, Anthony Nicholls, Joan Haythorne

Weak at Denise

GB 2000 87m DeLuxe
Blakeman & Hopper/Peninsula (Julian Nott)

A middle-aged bachelor marries his childhood sweetheart, who has unpleasant plans in store for him.

Feeble attempt at a black comedy; it is merely very grey.

w Graham Williams, Julian Nott *novel* Graham Williams *d* Julian Nott *ph* Marco Wyndham *m* Julian Nott *ad* Kate Woodman *ed* Melanie Adams, Simon Beeley

☆ Bill Thomas (Colin), Chrissie Cotterill (Denise), Craig Fairbrass (Roy), Tilly Blackwood (Wendy), Claudine Spiteri (Sharon), Edna Doré (Iris), Indira Joshi (Mrs Kumar)

'It's as bad as the title sounds.' – *Alexander Walker*

The Weaker Sex

GB 1948 84m bw
Two Cities (Paul Soskin)

Day-to-day problems of a well-to-do war widow.

Mild suburban comedy which sparkled more on stage, with such curtain lines as: 'Quick, the fishmonger's got fish!'

w Esther McCracken, Paul Soskin *play* *No Medals* by Esther McCracken *d* Roy Baker *ph* Erwin Hillier *m* Arthur Wilkinson

☆ Ursula Jeans, Cecil Parker, Joan Hopkins, Derek Bond, Lana Morris, Thora Hird, John Stone

The Weapon

GB 1956 81m bw Superscope 235
Periclean (Frank Bevis)

A boy finds a loaded revolver on a bomb site and mistakenly thinks he has killed someone with it.

Standard suspenser with a cast worthy of something more interesting.

w Fred Freiberger *d* Val Guest *ph* Reg Wyer *m* James Stevens

☆ Lizabeth Scott, Steve Cochran, George Cole, Herbert Marshall, Nicole Maurey, Jon Whiteley, Laurence Naismith

Weather Girl: see *A Weatherwoman*

'The Forecast Is Really Heating Up!'

A Weatherwoman

Japan 1995 84m colour
Bandai/Tohokushinsha/Office Border (Atsuhito Kaji)

original title: *Otenki Onesan*
aka: *Weather Girl*

A substitute TV weather girl antagonises her rivals when she causes a sensation by flashing her underwear on air, which sends the network's ratings soaring.

Absurdist comic-book fantasy that makes fun of celebrity-obsessed television, but, like its heroine, is too self-indulgent to make much sense, or have any purpose other than to amuse and, occasionally, shock.

wd Tomoaki Hosoyama *manga* Tetsu Adachi *ph* Yoichi Shiga *m* Kunihiko Ida *ad* Kazuro Toyama *ed* Naoki Kaneko *cos* Keiko Kusakabe

☆ Kei Mizutani (Keiko Nakadai), Takashi Sumida (Minoru Yamagishi), Yasuyo Shirashima (Kaori Shimamori), Saori Taira (Michiko Kawai), Satoru Saito, Kunihiko Ida, Ren Osugi, Hirosi Okouchi

The Web *

US 1947 87m bw
Universal (Jerry Bresler)

A financier hires a young lawyer as his bodyguard and lures him into committing murder.

Modestly well staged and glossy thriller.

w William Bowers, Bertram Millhauser *d* Michael Gordon *ph* Irving Glassberg *m* Hans Salter

☆ Edmond O'Brien, Vincent Price, Ella Raines, William Bendix

Web of Evidence: see *Beyond This Place*

Web of Passion: see *à Double Tour*

A Wedding *

US 1978 125m DeLuxe
TCF/Lion's Gate (Thommy Thompson, Robert Altman)

Two families converge for a fashionable wedding, but the day is beset by calamities.

Wide-ranging satirical comedy which despite excellent moments goes on far too long, is rather too black, and is sabotaged by the director's penchant for having fourteen people talking at the same time. An exhausting experience.

w John Considine, Patricia Resnick, Allan Nicholls, Robert Altman *d* Robert Altman *ph* Charles Rosher *md* Tom Walls

☆ Carol Burnett, Paul Dooley, Amy Stryker, Mia Farrow, Peggy Ann Garner, Lillian Gish, Nina Van Pallandt, Vittorio Gassman, Howard Duff, Desi Arnaz Jnr, Dina Merrill, Geraldine Chaplin, Viveca Lindfors, Lauren Hutton, John Cromwell

'Altman has become our leading silky utilizer of film styles. This time it's quick-sale ugliness. Just because he is so technically accomplished, so vacuously smooth and smart, he is depressing: he seems a kind of walking death sentence on the prospects of American film, much more menacing than clumsy or arrantly sentimental film-makers.' – *Stanley Kauffmann*

'Everyone Wants To Kiss The Bride ... Except The Groom.'

The Wedding Banquet ***

Taiwan/US 1993 108m DuArt
Mainline/Central Motion Picture/Good Machine (Ang Lee, Ted Hope, James Schamus)

original title: *Xiyan*

A homosexual American-Taiwanese businessman has to conceal his sexual preferences and his lover when his staid mother and father arrive in New York to celebrate his arranged marriage to a Chinese woman.

A delightful comedy of culture clashes, racial and generational differences and the problems of living up to your parents' expectations; it makes light of situations without concealing their truth and occasional pain.

w Ang Lee, Neil Peng, James Schamus *d* Ang Lee *ph* Jong Lin *m* Mader *pd* Steve Rosenzweig *ed* Tim Squyres

☆ Mitchell Lichtenstein, Winston Chao, May Chin, Sihung Lung, Ah-Leh Gua, Dion Birney, Jeanne Kuo Chang

'Canny mix of feelgood elements and ethnic color.' – *Variety*

'A wish-fulfilment fantasy on a par with the equally crowd-pleasing *Strictly Ballroom*.' – *Tony Rayns, Sight and Sound*

best foreign-language film

Wedding Bells: see *Royal Wedding*

Wedding Breakfast: see *The Catered Affair*

The Wedding March **

US 1928 196m approx (24 fps) bw silent
Paramount/Celebrity

A Habsburg prince loves a poor girl but is forced to marry a crippled princess, who dies; he is then murdered by the poor girl's enraged defender.

A marathon dose of Stroheim's favourite subject, sex, with some violence and a few fetishes thrown in. Full of fascinating touches, but desperately overlong, it was originally released in two parts, but failed to draw.

w Harry Carr, Erich von Stroheim *d* Erich von Stroheim *ph* Hal Mohr, Ben Reynolds *ad* Erich von Stroheim, Richard Day

☆ Erich von Stroheim, Fay Wray, ZaSu Pitts, Matthew Betz, Maude George, Cesare Gravina, George Fawcett

'A pitilessly authentic portrait of decadent Imperialist Austria.' – *Georges Sadoul*

'The slowness, heaviness, mindlessness of this temple of unnaturalness through which man passes as through a forest of clichés defied description.' – *John Simon, 1967*

† In 1975 there was published a pictorial record, *The Complete Wedding March*, by Herman G. Weinberg

The Wedding Night *

US 1935 83m bw
Samuel Goldwyn

A Connecticut author causes tragedy when he takes an interest in the local Polish immigrant farmers and especially in the daughter of one of them.

Interesting and unusual but slightly tediously told drama.

w Edith Fitzgerald *d* King Vidor *ph* Gregg Toland *md* Alfred Newman

☆ Gary Cooper, Anna Sten, Sig Rumann, Helen Vinson, Ralph Bellamy, Esther Dale

'Fine artistic film, possibly too artistic.' – *Variety*

'Convincing and curiously powerful.' – *New York Herald Tribune*

The Wedding of Lilli Marlene

GB 1953 87m bw
Monarch

The heroine of World War II becomes a success in show business.

Poorly confected programme filler, an unnecessary sequel if ever there was one.

w John Baines *d* Arthur Crabtree *ph* Arthur Grant *m* Eric Rogers

☆ Lisa Daniely, Hugh McDermott, Sid James, Gabrielle Brune, Robert Ayres

'His Big Day Is Her Big Problem.'

The Wedding Planner

US/Germany/GB 2001 102m DeLuxe Panavision
Pathé/Columbia/Intermedia/Tapestry/Dee Gee/IMF/Prufrock (Peter Abrams, Robert L. Levy, Jennifer Gibgot, Gigi Pritzker, Deborah Del Prete)

A tough professional wedding planner falls for a doctor, who is about to marry her rich client.

This would-be sophisticated romantic quickly loses its way after requiring the hero to behave badly; its stars strike no sparks off each other and become mired in the contrivances of a feeble script.

w Pamela Falk, Michael Ellis *d* Adam Shankman *ph* Julio Macat *m* Mervyn Warren *pd* Bob Ziembicki *ed* Lisa Zeno Churgin *cos* Pamela Withers

☆ Jennifer Lopez (Mary Fiore), Matthew McConaughey (Steve Edison), Bridgette Wilson-Sampras (Fran Donolly), Justin Chambers (Massimo), Judy Greer (Penny), Alex Rocco (Salvatore), Joanna Gleason (Mrs Donolly), Charles Kimbroug (Mr Donolly), Kevin Pollak (Dr John Dojny)

'Begins with considerable charm but eventually loses its winning ways with an excess of ridiculous elements.' – *Robert Koehler, Variety*

'The movie cannot abide common sense, and recycles decades of cliches about the wrong people getting married and the right ones making stupid decisions.' – *Roger Ebert, Chicago Sun-Times*

'He gave her something to remember him by!'

Wedding Present *

US 1936 81m bw
Paramount (B. P. Schulberg)

A pair of crack newspaper reporters take their jobs and themselves lightly.

Whimsical star comedy with some funny scenes.

w Joseph Anthony *story* Paul Gallico *d* Richard Wallace *ph* Leon Shamroy

☆ Cary Grant, Joan Bennett, George Bancroft, Conrad Nagel, Gene Lockhart, William Demarest, Edward Brophy

'Grant and Bennett try hard, but the combination of story, direction and whatnot is pretty much against them.' – *Variety*

Wedding Rehearsal

GB 1932 84m bw
Ideal/London Films/Alexander Korda

A Guards officer foils his grandmother's plans to get him married by finding suitors for all the young ladies offered.

Frail comedy with unsure technique.

w Helen Gardom *story* Lajos Biro, George Grossmith *d* Alexander Korda *ph* Leslie Rowson *m* Kurt Schroeder *ad* O. F. Werndorff, Vincent Korda *ed* Harold Young

☆ Roland Young, George Grossmith, John Loder, Lady Tree, Wendy Barrie, Maurice Evans, Joan Gardner, Merle Oberon, Kate Cutler, Edmund Breon

'If I were Korda, I would get up in the night, steal the negative, and quietly drop it in the Thames.' – *Marcel Ermans, World Film News*

The Wedding Singer *
US 1998 96m CFI color
Entertainment/New Line (Robert Simonds, Jack Giarraputo)
A singer and a waitress, both involved in unhappy relationships, fall in love.
Broad comedy that succeeds by energy and its delight in the tackier fashions of the 80s.
w Tim Herlihy *d* Frank Coraci *ph* Tim Suhrstedt *m* Teddy Castellucci *pd* Perry Andelin Blake *ed* Tom Lewis
☆ Adam Sandler, Drew Barrymore, Christine Taylor, Allen Covert, Matthew Glave, Ellen Albertini Dow, Angela Featherstone, Alexis Arquette, Christina Pickles, Jon Lovitz (uncredited), Steve Buscemi (uncredited)
'A good-natured romp, a pantomime for grown-ups that has more charm and more laughs in its 97 minutes than some other comedies can muster in a whole series of sequels.' – *Anwar Brett, Film Review*

'To stop a marriage made in Heaven....a stag night made in Hell!'
The Wedding Tackle
GB 2000 93m DeLuxe
Ratpack/Viking (Nigel Horne)
An engaged couple who do not trust one another find their fears realised during a revelatory stag night.
Drear and inept comedy that would not pass muster as a half-hour TV sitcom.
w Nigel Horne *d* Rami Dvir *ph* Shelley Hirst *m* Charles Hodgkinson *pd* Sarah Beauman *ed* Matthew Tabern, Mike Latham *cos* Jane Spicer
☆ Adrian Dunbar (Mr Mac), James Purefoy (Hal), Tony Slattery (Little Ted), Neil Stuke (Salty), Leslie Grantham (George), Victoria Smurfit (Clodagh), Susan Vidler (Vinni), Amanda Redman (Petula), Sara Stockbridge (Felicity), Martin Armstrong (Trev)
'Yet another misconceived and ill-written flail through the romantic complications of a bunch of urban thirtysomethings.' – *Anthony Quinn, Independent*

Wedlock
US 1991 98m CFI color
Spectacor (Branko Lustig)
aka: *Deadlock*
Two convicts go on the run linked by electronic collars that will explode if they are more than a hundred yards apart.
Plodding, violent thriller which reaches the conclusion that it's acceptable to steal providing you can get away with it.
w Broderick Miller *d* Lewis Teague *ph* Dietrich Lohmann *m* Richard Gibbs *pd* Veronica Hadfield *ed* Carl Kress
☆ Rutger Hauer, Mimi Rogers, Joan Chen, James Remar
'Nice idea, unsatisfying results.' – *Sight and Sound*

Wee Geordie: see *Geordie*

'From Rudyard Kipling's Heroic Pen!'
Wee Willie Winkie **
US 1937 99m bw
TCF (Gene Markey)
A small girl becomes the mascot of a British regiment in India.
Vaguely based on a Kipling tale, this was the most expensive Temple vehicle and a first-rate family action picture with sentimental asides.
w Ernest Pascal, Julien Josephson *story* Rudyard Kipling *d* *John Ford* *ph* Arthur Miller *m* Alfred Newman *ad* William S. Darling, David Hall
☆ Shirley Temple, Victor McLaglen, C. Aubrey Smith, June Lang, Michael Whalen, Cesar Romero, Constance Collier, Gavin Muir
'Will add another clean-up to her cycle, but those knees are losing their contour ... a pretentiously produced melodrama which launches the leading feminine box office star into a distinctly new phase of her career and story material.' – *Variety*
art direction

Weeds
US 1987 115m Technicolor
DEG/Kingsgate (Bill Badalato)
A prisoner serving a life sentence turns playwright and writes himself out of jail.
Intriguing claustrophobic drama of prison life and release, notable for some excellent performances.
w John Hancock, Dorothy Tristan *d* John Hancock *ph* Jan Weincke *m* Angelo Badalamenti *pd* Joseph T. Garrity *ed* Dennis M. O'Connor
☆ *Nick Nolte*, William Forsythe, Lane Smith, John Toles-Bey, Joe Mantegna, Ernie Hudson, Mark Rolston, Rita Taggart
† The film is loosely based on Rick Cluchey, who wrote a play while serving life in San Quentin prison and was paroled, forming a theatre group with other former convicts.

Week of the Killer: see *Cannibal Man*

Weekend ****
France/Italy 1968 103m Eastmancolor
Comacico/Copernic/Lira/Ascot
A bourgeois couple leave Paris for the weekend and are caught in an endless traffic jam, where cars crash, tempers fray and savagery takes over.
A brilliant black satire at the expense of consumerism and conventional values.
wd Jean-Luc Godard *ph* Raoul Coutard *m* Antoine Duhamel, Mozart *ed* Agnes Guillemot
☆ Mireille Darc, Jean Yanne, Jean-Pierre Kalfon, Valerie Lagrange, Jean-Pierre Léaud, Yves Beneyton, Paul Gegauff
'Though deeply flawed, this film has more depth than any of Godard's earlier work. It's his vision of Hell and it ranks with the greatest.' – *Pauline Kael, New Yorker*

Weekend at Bernie's
US 1989 99m DuArt
Fox/Gladden (Victor Drai)
Two minor executives, fearing that they will be blamed when they discover the murdered body of their boss on a weekend visit to his beach house, pretend that he is still alive.
Black farce that manages occasionally to amuse.
w Robert Klane *d* Ted Kotcheff *ph* François Protat *m* Andy Summers *pd* Peter Jamison *ed* Joan E. Chapman
☆ Andrew McCarthy, Jonathan Silverman, Catherine Mary Stewart, Terry Kiser, Don Calfa, Catherine Parks, Eloise Broady, Ted Kotcheff

Weekend at Bernie's II
US 1993 97m DeLuxe
Warner/Artimm/Victor Drai
Two former employees of a murdered boss, as well as crooks and an insurance investigator, try to get their hands on the dead man's money, an attempt complicated by the fact that his corpse has been semi-revived in a voodoo ceremony.
Witless comedy which even the most frantic efforts at resuscitation by its cast cannot bring back to life.
wd Robert Klane *ph* Edward Morey III *m* Peter Wolf *pd* Michael Bolton *ed* Peck Prior
☆ Andrew McCarthy, Jonathan Silverman, Terry Kiser, Troy Beyer, Barry Bostwick, Tom Wright, Steve James

Weekend at the Waldorf *
US 1945 130m bw
MGM (Arthur Hornblow Jnr)
Four stories about guests at New York's largest hotel.
Disguised version of Grand Hotel, *with the same stories twisted; the talent at hand, however, is serviceable rather than inspiring.*
w Sam and Bella Spewack *d* Robert Z. Leonard *ph* Robert Planck *md* Johnny Green
☆ Ginger Rogers, Walter Pidgeon, Van Johnson, Lana Turner, Robert Benchley, Edward Arnold, Constance Collier, Leon Ames, Warner Anderson, Phyllis Thaxter, Keenan Wynn, Porter Hall, Samuel S. Hinds, George Zucco, Xavier Cugat

Weekend in Havana
US 1941 80m Technicolor
TCF (William Le Baron)
A shopgirl in Havana falls for a shipping executive.
Routine Fox musical showcasing familiar talents: adequate wartime escapist fare.
w Karl Tunberg, Darrell Ware *d* Walter Lang *ph* Ernest Palmer *md* Alfred Newman
☆ Alice Faye, John Payne, Carmen Miranda, Cesar Romero, Cobina Wright Jnr, George Barbier, Sheldon Leonard, Leonid Kinskey

Weekend Marriage
US 1932 64m bw
First National
GB title: *Weekend Lives*
A wife wants to remain independent.
Comedy drama with nothing new to say about a familiar subject.
w Sheridan Gibney *novel* *Part-Time Wives* by Faith Baldwin *d* Thornton Freeland
☆ Loretta Young, Norman Foster, George Brent, Aline MacMahon, Vivienne Osborne
'Unimportant rewrite on familiar theme minus necessary key strength.' – *Variety*

Weekend of Shadows
Australia 1977 95m Eastmancolor
Samson (Tom Jeffrey, Matt Carroll)
After a farmer's wife is found murdered, townspeople form a posse and search for the obvious suspect, a Polish worker who has gone missing.
A competent but uninspired drama exposing a small town's pettiness and intolerance.
w Peter Yeldham *novel* *The Reckoning* by Hugh Atkinson *d* Tom Jeffrey *ph* Richard Wallace *m* Charles Marawood *ad* Christopher Webster *ed* Rod Adamson
☆ John Waters, Graeme Blundell, Wyn Roberts, Graham Rouse, Melissa Jaffer, Keith Lee, Bill Hunter, Barbara West, Kit Taylor, Les Foxcroft, Bryan Brown

Weekend with Father
US 1951 83m bw
U-I (Ted Richmond)
A widow and a widower fall in love when taking their respective children to a summer camp.
Mechanical comedy of upsets and embarrassments.
w Joseph Hoffman *d* Douglas Sirk *ph* Clifford Stine *m* Frank Skinner
☆ *Van Heflin*, Patricia Neal, Gigi Perreau, Virginia Field, Richard Denning

Weird Science
US 1985 94m Technicolor
Universal (Joel Silver)
Teenage science students create a woman from a computer.
Sex-obsessed frolics which go nowhere.
wd John Hughes *ph* Matthew F. Leonetti, Joseph Calloway *m* Ira Newborn *pd* John W. Corso *ed* Mark Warner, Christopher Lebenzon, Scott Wallace
☆ Anthony Michael Hall, Kelly Le Brock, Ilan Mitchell-Smith, Bill Paxton, Robert Downey Jnr

'She strikes with the curse of voodoo!'
Weird Woman
US 1944 64m bw
Universal
A professor brings home from the South Seas a wife who seems to bring murder in her wake.
Stiff and stilted thriller from an interesting original; one of the disappointing Inner Sanctum series.
w Brenda Weisberg *novel* *Conjure Wife* by Fritz Leiber *d* Reginald Le Borg *ph* Virgil Miller *md* Paul Sawtell *ad* John B. Goodman, Richard H. Riedel *ed* Milton Carruth
☆ Lon Chaney, Evelyn Ankers, Anne Gwynne, Ralph Morgan, Elizabeth Risdon

Welcome Danger *
US 1929 110m bw
Harold Lloyd
The meek son of a police chief gets involved in a tong war.
Moderate early talkie comedy showing the star in some trouble with pace and dialogue.
w Clyde Bruckman, Lex Neal, Felix Adler, Paul Gerard Smith *d* Clyde Bruckman *ph* Walter Lundin, Henry Kohler
☆ Harold Lloyd, Barbara Kent, Noah Young, Charles Middleton

Welcome Home: see *SNAFU*

Welcome Home
US 1989 92m Eastmancolor
Rank (Martin Ransohoff)
Presumed dead in the Vietnamese war, a pilot who has acquired a Cambodian wife and two children returns after a 17-year absence to his American wife, who has remarried, and their teenage son.
Mundane, slow-moving drama that raises more questions than it answers.
w Maggie Kleinman *d* Franklin J. Schaffner *ph* Fred J. Koenekamp *pd* Dan Yarhi, Dennis Davenport *ed* Bob Swink
☆ Kris Kristofferson, JoBeth Williams, Brian Keith, Sam Waterston, Trey Wilson

Welcome Home Roxy Carmichael
US 1991 96m Technicolor
Castle Premier/ITC (Penney Finkelman Cox)
An adopted teenage girl, who is unhappy at home, convinces herself that she is the illegitimate daughter of her small town's only celebrity.
Limp and unconvincing drama of fame and teenage angst.
w Karen Leigh Hopkins *d* Jim Abrahams *ph* Paul Elliott *m* Thomas Newman *pd* Dena Roth *ed* Bruce Green
☆ Winona Ryder, Jeff Daniels, Laila Robins, Thomas Wilson Brown, Joan McMurtrey, Graham Beckel, Frances Fisher, Robby Kiger
'Just another tale about a girl who discovers she's pretty in pink.' – *Sight and Sound*

Welcome Home Soldier Boys
US 1972 92m DeLuxe
TCF
Four war veterans go home and start a wave of violence.
Clumsily brutal anti-war tract which merely repels.
w Guerdon Trueblood *d* Richard Crompton
☆ Joe Don Baker, Paul Koslo, Alan Vint, Billy Green Bush

Welcome II The Terrordome
GB 1994 90m Technicolor
Metro Tartan/Non Aligned/Channel 4 (Simon Onwurah)
An African family who walk into the sea to escape slavery in the 1650s are reincarnated in an apocalyptic future ghetto, where black gangs fight to control the drug trade before they unite against a common enemy.
An angry film about black suffering at the hands of whites, but couched in such second-hand terms with so unoriginal a scenario that it loses all meaning.
wd Ngozi Onwurah *ph* Alwin H. Kuchler *m* John Murphy, David A. Hughes, Black Radical Mk II *pd* Lindi Pankiv, Miraphora Mina *ed* Liz Webber
☆ Suzette Llewellyn, Saffron Burrows, Felix Joseph, Valentine Nonyela, Ben Wynter, Sian Martin, Jason Traynor
'Fails on all fronts. It's too ham-fisted to impress in purely cinematic terms, too pleasureless for the multiplexes, and too confused to stir any real debate.' – *Jonathan Romney, Guardian*
'Characters are one-dimensional mouthpieces, the dialogue seemingly pasted together from hip, US-influenced clichés, and Onwurah's visual language largely conservative and immobile. Performances border on the amateur.' – *Derek Elley, Variety*

Welcome Mr Washington
GB 1944 90m bw
British National/Shaftesbury
A US sergeant in an English village falls for a local lady.
Mild plea for harmony between allies; rather embarrassing to watch even at the time.
w Jack Whittingham *novel* Noel Streatfeild *d* Leslie Hiscott
☆ Barbara Mullen, Donald Stewart, Peggy Cummins, Graham Moffatt, Martita Hunt

Welcome Stranger
US 1947 107m bw
Paramount (Sol C. Siegel)
A genial young doctor fills in for a crusty old one on vacation in a small town.
Formula sentimental comedy, one of several reuniting the stars of Going My Way.

w Arthur Sheekman story Frank Butler d Elliott Nugent ph Lionel Lindon m Robert Emmett Dolan
☆ Bing Crosby, Barry Fitzgerald, Joan Caulfield, Wanda Hendrix, Frank Faylen, Elizabeth Patterson, Robert Shayne, Percy Kilbride

Welcome to Arrow Beach
US 1973 99m colour
Brut (Jack Cushingham)
aka: *Tender Flesh*
A photographer living in a California beach community has become a cannibal after his experiences in the Korean War.
Abysmal horror movie with insufficient plot.
w Wallace C. Bennett, Jack Gross Jnr d Laurence Harvey ph Gerald Perry Finnerman m Tony Camillo
☆ Laurence Harvey, Joanna Pettet, Stuart Whitman, John Ireland, Meg Foster

Welcome to Blood City
GB/Canada 1977 96m colour Panavision
EMI/Ben Herberman (Marilyn Stonehouse)
A scientist in a totalitarian state becomes emotionally involved in an experiment to find killers by involving them in a fantasy life in a tough western town where murder is encouraged.
Risible science fiction, with a narrative that makes little sense, additionally hampered by mediocre performances.
w Stephen Schenck, Michael Winder d Peter Sasdy ph Reginald H. Morris m Roy Budd pd Jack McAdam ed Keith Palmer
☆ Jack Palance, Keir Dullea, Samantha Eggar, Hollis McLaren, Chris Wiggins, Barry Morse, Allan Royale, Henry Ramer, Ken James, John Evans
'Swiss-cheese script strains coherence and interest with each development.' – *Variety*

Welcome to Hard Times *
US 1967 103m Metrocolor
MGM/Max E. Youngstein, David Carr
GB title: *Killer on a Horse*
A small Western town arms itself against a mysterious bandit.
Curiously likeable, almost symbolic suspense Western which has a good start and middle but not much idea how to end.
wd Burt Kennedy novel E. L. Doctorow ph Harry Stradling Jnr m Harry Sukman
☆ Henry Fonda, Janice Rule, Keenan Wynn, Janis Paige, John Anderson, Warren Oates, Fay Spain, Edgar Buchanan, Aldo Ray, Lon Chaney Jnr, Elisha Cook Jnr

Welcome to LA *
US 1976 106m DeLuxe
Lion's Gate/Robert Altman
A young composer in Los Angeles has a varied sex life.
Fragmentary, vaguely mystical, momentarily interesting, frequently confusing slice of life as seen through misty glasses.
wd Alan Rudolph ph Dave Myers m Richard Baskin
☆ Keith Carradine, Sally Kellerman, Geraldine Chaplin, Harvey Keitel, Lauren Hutton, Viveca Lindfors, Sissy Spacek, Denver Pyle
'The supposedly free-form, improvisational dynamics of an Altman movie have here become a strictly choreographed ballet.' – *Richard Combs, MFB*

'For this celebrated, outrageous, adrenaline-loving bunch of reporters, home is the latest war zone. Now, one of them is about to do the unthinkable – get emotionally involved.'
'The true story of an extraordinary act of courage.'
Welcome to Sarajevo **
GB/US 1997 101m colour 'Scope
Film Four/Channel 4/Miramax (Graham Broadbent, Damian Jones)
Reporting the siege of Sarajevo by the Bosnian Serbs in 1992, a television journalist smuggles a young girl out to live in Britain with his family.
A fierce, polemical drama of the horrors of a civil war and a lack of politicial will among the Western powers that suddenly goes soft and manipulative; it is uneven, but very watchable.
w Frank Cottrell Boyce book *Natasha's Story* by Michael Nicholson d Michael Winterbottom ph Daf Hobson m Adrian Johnston pd Mark Geraghty ed Trevor Waite
☆ Stephen Dillane, Woody Harrelson, Marisa Tomei, Emira Nusevic, Kerry Fox, Goran Visnjic, James Nesbitt, Emily Lloyd, Juliet Aubrey
'A film of extremes, then, by turns brash and simplistic and utterly powerful. See it. Then argue.' – *Ian Nathan, Empire*

Welcome to the Club
GB 1970 88m bw
Welcome (Sam Lomberg)
Hiroshima 1945; an American Quaker sergeant upsets military protocol.
Pale satirical comedy shot in Copenhagen.
w Clement Biddle Wood novel Clement Biddle Wood d Walter Shenson ph Mikael Salomon m Ken Thorne
☆ Brian Foley, Jack Warden, Lee Meredith, Andy Jarrell

Welcome to the Dollhouse *
US 1995 88m DuArt
Artificial Eye/Suburban (Ted Skillman, Todd Solondz)
An unattractive 11-year-old girl is ridiculed and ostracized at school and at home.
A tartly observant account of the damage that people can knowingly do to one another.
wd Todd Solondz ph Randy Drummond m Jill Wisoff pd Susan Block ed Alan Oxman
☆ Heather Matarazzo, Victoria Davis, Christina Brucato, Christina Vidal, Siri Howard, Brendan Sexton Jnr, Dana Kalinia, Matthew Faber
'A canny black comedy with plenty of adult appeal even though any school pupil will relate to each and every scene with a nasty chill of recognition.' – *Marianne Gray, Film Review*

'There's No Place Like Hell...'
Welcome to Woop Woop
Australia/GB 1997 102m colour
MGM/Goldwyn/AFFC/Scala/Unthank (Finola Dwyer)
An American finds himself trapped in a small outback community, and married to the daughter of its tyrannical, boozy boss.
Bizarre comedy that attempts to satirise macho attitudes, but is rarely more than a irritating, slackly scripted muddle.
w Michael Thomas book *The Dead Heart* by Douglas Kennedy d Stephan Elliott ph Mike Molloy m Guy Gross pd Owen Paterson ed Martin Walsh
☆ Johnathon Schaech, Rod Taylor, Susie Porter, Dee Smart, Richard Moir, Maggie Kirkpatrick, Paul Mercurio, Rachel Griffiths, Barry Humphries, Tina Louise
'Desperately unfunny...An incoherent mess of thrown-together scenes heaping scorn and ridicule on the Australian equivalent of Dogpatch, USA.' – *Stephen Holden, New York Times*

The Well *
US 1951 85m bw
Cardinal/Harry M. Popkin (Clarence Greene, Leo Popkin)
A black child falls down a well, and the town unites to save her.
Forceful high-pitched melodrama, cut to a do-gooder pattern which became very familiar.
w Russel Rouse, Clarence Greene d Leo Popkin, Russel Rouse ph Ernest Laszlo m Dimitri Tiomkin ed Chester Schaeffer
☆ Richard Rober, Henry Morgan, Barry Kelley, Christine Larson
script; editing

The Well Groomed Bride *
US 1946 75m bw
Paramount (Fred Kohlmar)
A naval officer searches San Francisco for a magnum of champagne with which to launch a ship.
Thin but cheerful star comedy.
w Claude Binyon, Robert Russell d Sidney Lanfield ph John F. Seitz m Roy Webb
☆ Ray Milland, Olivia de Havilland, Sonny Tufts, James Gleason, Constance Dowling, Percy Kilbride, Jean Heather

We'll Meet Again
GB 1942 84m bw
Columbia
A girl singer suffers while her boyfriend loves another.
Unassuming star vehicle for the Forces' Sweetheart.
w James Seymour, Howard Thomas d Phil Brandon
☆ Vera Lynn, Geraldo, Patricia Roc, Ronald Ward, Donald Gray, Frederick Leister

The Well-Digger's Daughter: see *La Fille du Puisatier*

'Paramount's thundering romance of the winning of the west!'
Wells Fargo *
US 1937 115m bw
Paramount (Frank Lloyd)
How the express delivery service was built up.
Large-scale, entertaining Western with overmuch emphasis on domestic issues.
w Paul Schofield, Gerald Geraghty, John Boland story Stuart N. Lake d Frank Lloyd ph Theodor Sparkuhl m Victor Young
☆ Joel McCrea, Bob Burns, Frances Dee, Lloyd Nolan, Henry O'Neill, Mary Nash, Ralph Morgan, John Mack Brown, Porter Hall, Clarence Kolb
'Big b.o. right across the playdate board.' – *Variety*

Wendy Cracked a Walnut
Australia 1990 87m colour
Rosen, Harper, Mortlock/ABC/Rough Diamond (John Edwards)
US video title: *Almost*
An office worker, bored by her marriage to an accident-prone salesman, takes refuge in romantic fantasies.
Turgid comedy, devoid of wit or imagination; it does not work on any level.
w Suzanne Hawley d Michael Pattinson ph Jeffrey Malouf m Bruce Smeaton pd Leigh Tierney ed Michael Honey
☆ Rosanna Arquette, Bruce Spence, Hugo Weaving, Kerry Walker, Doreen Warburton, Desiree Smith
'A listless, laughless affair which suffers from dire miscasting and awkward direction.' – *Variety*

Went the Day Well? ***
GB 1942 92m bw
Ealing (S. C. Balcon)
US title: *Forty-eight Hours*
Villagers resist when German paratroopers invade an English village and the squire proves to be a quisling.
Could-it-happen melodrama which made excellent wartime propaganda; generally well staged.
w Angus MacPhail, John Dighton, Diana Morgan story Graham Greene d *Alberto Cavalcanti* ph Wilkie Cooper m William Walton
☆ Leslie Banks, Elizabeth Allan, Frank Lawton, Basil Sydney, Valerie Taylor, Mervyn Johns, Edward Rigby, Marie Lohr, C. V. France, David Farrar
'At last, it seems, we are learning to make films with our own native material.' – *Sunday Times*
'It has the sinister, freezing beauty of an Auden prophecy come true.' – *James Agee*
'A refreshing, an exciting and an excellent film.' – *Documentary News Letter*

We're Going to Be Rich
GB 1938 80m bw
TCF
In the South African goldfields in 1880, a singer leaves her worthless husband for a publican.
First American attempt to take over Our Gracie; it didn't work, but the damage was done.
w Monty Banks, James Edward Grant, Rohama Siegel, Sam Hellman d Monty Banks
☆ Gracie Fields, Victor McLaglen, Brian Donlevy, Coral Browne, Gus McNaughton
'Will do well in England. In the States, will slide into the duals.' – *Variety*

We're in the Army Now: see *Pack Up Your Troubles*

We're in the Money
US 1935 65m bw
Warner
Adventures of female process servers working for a dizzy lawyer.
Minor comedy using up contract artistes.
w F. Hugh Herbert, Brown Holmes, Erwin Gelsey, George Bilson d Ray Enright
☆ Joan Blondell, Glenda Farrell, Hugh Herbert, Ross Alexander, Hobart Cavanaugh
'Only those exhibitors whose clients get hysterical on short notice will profit from it.' – *Variety*

We're No Angels *
US 1954 106m Technicolor Vistavision
Paramount (Pat Duggan)
Three escaped Devil's Island convicts help a downtrodden storekeeper and his family to outwit a scheming relative.
Whimsical, overstretched period comedy suffering from miscasting but with some pleasantries along the way.
w Ranald MacDougall play *La Cuisine des Anges* by Albert Husson d Michael Curtiz ph Loyal Griggs m Frederick Hollander
☆ Humphrey Bogart, *Peter Ustinov*, Aldo Ray, Joan Bennett, Basil Rathbone, Leo G. Carroll, John Smith

We're No Angels
US 1989 106m Technicolor Panavision
UIP/Paramount (Art Linson)
Convicts on the run disguise themselves as priests and take refuge in a monastery.
Dismal remake that suggests its stars have little talent for comedy.
w David Mamet play *La Cuisine des Anges* by Albert Husson d Neil Jordan ph Philippe Rousselot m George Fenton pd Wolf Kroeger ed Mick Audsley, Joke Van Wijk
☆ Robert DeNiro, Sean Penn, Demi Moore, Hoyt Axton, Bruno Kirby, Ray McAnally, James Russo, Wallace Shawn, John C. Reilly, Jay Brazeau

'It's a circus! Something doing every minute!'
We're Not Dressing *
US 1934 77m bw
Paramount (Benjamin Glazer)
A spoiled heiress shipwrecked on a Pacific island is tamed by an easy-going sailor.
Pleasant, madly dated, light-hearted variation on a much-filmed play, resolving itself into a series of comic turns.
w Horace Jackson, Francis Martin, George Marion Jnr play *The Admirable Crichton* by J. M. Barrie d Norman Taurog ph Charles Lang songs Harry Revel, Mack Gordon
☆ Bing Crosby, Carole Lombard, George Burns, Gracie Allen, Leon Errol, Ethel Merman, Jay Henry, Ray Milland
'Tiptop audience appeal musical.' – *Variety*

We're Not Married *
US 1952 85m bw
TCF (Nunnally Johnson)
Six couples find that they were never legally married.
Amiable, smartly-played compendium of sketches on a familiar theme.
w Nunnally Johnson d Edmund Goulding ph Leo Tover m Cyril Mockridge
☆ Ginger Rogers, Fred Allen, Victor Moore, Paul Douglas, Eve Arden, Marilyn Monroe, David Wayne, Louis Calhern, Zsa Zsa Gabor, Mitzi Gaynor, Eddie Bracken, James Gleason, Jane Darwell

We're on the Jury
US 1937 71m bw
RKO
Disagreements break out in the jury room after a murder trial.
More comedy than drama, a modest remake of Ladies of the Jury *(qv).*
w Franklin Coen play John Frederick Ballard d Ben Holmes
☆ Helen Broderick, Victor Moore, Philip Huston, Louise Latimer, Robert McWade
'Good secondary b.o. value.' – *Variety*

We're Only Human
US 1936 67m bw
RKO (Edward Kaufman)
A police sergeant loses a convicted prisoner and catches him again.
Routine bang-bang melodrama with unconvincing dialogue.
w Rian James *story* Thomas Walsh *d* James Flood *ph* J. Roy Hunt *ad* Van Nest Polglase
☆ Preston Foster, Jane Wyatt, James Gleason, Arthur Hohl, Jane Darwell, Christian Rub, Moroni Olsen, Mischa Auer
'Nothing which will raise it above double-feature standards.' – *Variety*

The Werewolf
US 1956 80m bw
Columbia/Clover (Sam Katzman)
In a small mountain town, a victim of radiation exposure periodically becomes a werewolf and is hounded down.
Absurd and tedious thriller which wastes an interesting background.
w Robert E. Kent, James B. Gordon *d* Fred F. Sears *ph* Edwin Linden *m* Mischa Bakaleinikoff
☆ Steven Ritch, Don McGowan, Joyce Holden

Werewolf of London *
US 1935 75m bw
Universal (Stanley Bergerman)
Werewolves fight for a rare Tibetan flower with curative properties.
Patchy horror film which lurches from excellent suspense scenes to tedious chunks of superfluous dialogue. In many ways a milestone in the history of its kind.
w Robert Harris *d* Stuart Walker *ph* Charles Stumar *m* Karl Hajos
☆ Henry Hull, Warner Oland, Valerie Hobson, Spring Byington, Lester Matthews, Zeffie Tilbury, Ethel Griffies
'Horror attempt that doesn't horrify sufficiently. Requires a build-up and may disappoint.' – *Variety*

The Werewolf of Washington
US 1973 90m colour
Millco (Nina Schulman)
The US President attempts to cover up the fact that a White House press secretary has turned werewolf and is running amok.
A political satire in the aftermath of Watergate that lacks bite and fails as a horror spoof.
wd Milton Moses Ginsberg *ph* Bob Baldwin *m* Arnold Freed *ad* Nancy Miller-Corwin *sp* Bob Obradovich
☆ Dean Stockwell, Biff McGuire, Clifton James, Michael Dunn, Beeson Carroll, Thayer David

Werewolf Woman (dubbed)
Italy 1976 100m colour
Agora/Dialchi (Diego Alchimede)
original title: *La Lupa Mannara*
US title: *Legend of the Wolf Woman*
A woman becomes a werewolf to satisfy her sexual and murderous appetites.
Trivial mix of sex and horror, directed without style.
wd Rino Di Silvestro *ph* Mario Capriotti *m* Coriolano Gori *ed* Angelo Curi
☆ Annik Borel, Frederick Stafford, Dagmar Lassander, Tino Carraro, Elio Zamuto, Osvaldo Ruggieri, Andrea Scotti, Howard Ross (Renato Rossini)
† According to the credits, the English language version was written and directed by Tony La Penna.

Wes Craven Presents: They: see *They*

'Freddy's Back in the Best "Nightmare" Ever!'
'...Missed me?'
Wes Craven's New Nightmare
US 1994 112m Foto-Kem
Rank/New Line (Marianne Maddalena)
Wes Craven explains that he is making a new film in a series that concluded with *Freddy's Dead: The Final Nightmare* because it is the only way to prevent the evil represented by Freddy becoming manifest in the real world.
A strange mixture of fantasy and what passes for reality in Hollywood, with Heather Langenkamp playing herself as the star of the first Elm Street film but being given a fictional life as a wife and mother threatened by Freddy. The result is likely to appeal to the diminishing audience for the series, but to few others.
wd Wes Craven *ph* Mark Irwin *m* J. Peter Robinson *pd* Cynthia Charette *ed* Patrick Lussier *sp* visual effects: Flash Film Works; Digital Filmworks; make-up effects: Kurtzman, Nicotero & Berger
☆ Robert Englund, Miko Hughes, David Newsome, Tracy Middendorf, Heather Langenkamp, John Saxon, Wes Craven
'Craven is still one of the horror cinema's most imaginative creators of purely frightening moments.' – *Kim Newman, Sight and Sound*
† The film is a self-referential sequel to the *Nightmare on Elm Street* series (qv).

West Beirut: see *West Beyrouth*

West Beyrouth **
France/Lebanon/Belgium/Norway 1998 109m colour 'Scope
Metrodome/La Sept/Arte/Douri/Ciné Libre/Exposed/Bjorn Eivind Aarskog (Rachid Bouchareb, Jean Brehat)
aka: *West Beirut*
In 1975, an adolescent Muslim youth experiences the outbreak of a civil war that divided his city.
Energetic, free-wheeling drama of war as seen through the eyes of teenagers, who find freedom and excitement in the situation.
wd Ziad Doueiri *ph* Ricardo Jacques Gale *m* Stewart Copeland *ad* Hamzé Nasrallah *ed* Dominique Marcombe
☆ Rami Doueiri (Tarek), Mohamad Chamas (Omar), Rola Al Amin (May), Carmen Lebbos (Hala Noueiri), Joseph Bou Nassar (Riad Noueiri), Liliane Nemry (Nahida), Leila Karam (Oum Walid), Hassan Frahat (Milicien Zeytouni)
'A technically polished, frequently funny and emotionally affecting work.' – *Lisa Nesselson, Variety*

West Eleven
GB 1963 93m bw
ABP/Daniel M. Angel (Vivian Cox)
A young London drifter is offered £10,000 to commit murder.
Dingy but not very convincing 'realist' melodrama with a jazzy style which induces weariness.
w Keith Waterhouse, Willis Hall *novel The Furnished Room* by Laura del Rivo *d* Michael Winner *ph* Otto Heller *m* Stanley Black, Acker Bilk
☆ Alfred Lynch, Eric Portman, Kathleen Harrison, Diana Dors, Kathleen Breck, Freda Jackson, Finlay Currie, Harold Lang

West of Broadway
US 1932 68m bw
MGM
A millionaire gets married while drunk and regrets it the next day.
Unappetizing light drama which did no good to anyone concerned with it.
w Gene Markey, J. K. McGuinness, Ralph Graves, Bess Meredyth *d* Harry Beaumont
☆ John Gilbert, El Brendel, Lois Moran, Madge Evans, Ralph Bellamy, Frank Conroy, Hedda Hopper
'Rates neighbourhood and grind spotting only.' – *Variety*

West of Montana: see *Mail Order Bride*

West of Shanghai
US 1937 64m bw
Warner
Fugitives in the Far East are saved by the self-sacrifice of a Chinese war lord.
Unpersuasive melodrama remade from The Bad Man *(1930), heavily depending on a star performance.*
w Crane Wilbur *d* John Farrow
☆ Boris Karloff, Beverly Roberts, Ricardo Cortez, Gordon Oliver, Vladimir Sokoloff
† First released as *Warlord*.

West of the Divide
US 1933 54m bw
Monogram/Lone Star (Paul Malvern)
A cowboy who is searching for his long-lost brother impersonates a killer in order to expose a crooked rancher.
John Wayne gets the girl, the boy and a ranch in this otherwise routine Western.
wd Robert N. Bradbury *ph* Archie Stout *ed* Carl Pierson
☆ John Wayne, Virginia Faire Brown, George Hayes, Lloyd Whitlock, Yakima Canutt, Lafe McKee, Billie O'Brien

West of the Pecos
US 1934 70m bw
RKO
In Texas after the Civil War a girl masquerades as a boy in order to get things done.
Moderate Western.
w Milton Krims, John Twist *novel* Zane Grey *d* Phil Rosen
☆ Richard Dix, Martha Sleeper, Samuel S. Hinds, Fred Kohler, Louise Beavers, Willie Best ('Sleep 'n Eat')
'Superior entertainment of the horse opera type.' – *Variety*
† It was remade in 1945, directed by Edward Killy and starring Robert Mitchum and Barbara Hale.

West of Zanzibar
US 1928 70m (24 fps) bw silent
MGM
A paralysed magician turned ivory trader settles an old score.
Corny star vehicle remade in 1932 as Kongo, *with Walter Huston.*
w Waldemar Young, Elliott Clawson *d* Tod Browning
☆ Lon Chaney, Lionel Barrymore, Jacqueline Gadsden, Mary Nolan

West of Zanzibar
GB 1954 94m Technicolor
Ealing (Leslie Norman)
Native tribesmen move towards Mombasa and are drawn into ivory smuggling.
Fairly feeble follow-up to Where No Vultures Fly; *quite good to look at but clearly not an original.*
w Max Catto, Jack Whittingham *d* Harry Watt *ph* Paul Beeson *m* Alan Rawsthorne
☆ Anthony Steel, Sheila Sim, William Simons, Orlando Martins, Martin Benson, Edric Connor, Howard Marion Crawford

West Point of the Air
US 1935 90m bw
MGM (Monta Bell)
The army sergeant father of an air cadet has great hopes for him.
Routine sentimental flagwaver.
w James K. McGuinness, John Monk Saunders, Frank Wead, Arthur J. Beckhard *d* Richard Rosson *ph* Clyde de Vinna, Charles A. Marshall, Elmer Dyer *m* Charles Maxwell
☆ Wallace Beery, Robert Young, Maureen O'Sullivan, Lewis Stone, James Gleason, Rosalind Russell, Russell Hardie, Henry Wadsworth, Robert Taylor
'Trite story holds it down to just moderate entertainment rating.' – *Variety*

West Point Story *
US 1950 107m bw
Warner (Louis F. Edelman)
GB title: *Fine and Dandy*
A Broadway producer stages a show at the military academy.
Thin and rather tedious musical saved by its irrepressible star.
w John Monks Jnr, Charles Hoffman, Irving Wallace *d* Roy del Ruth *ph* Sid Hickox *md* Ray Heindorf *songs* Sammy Cahn, Jule Styne
☆ *James Cagney*, Virginia Mayo, Doris Day, Gordon MacRae, Gene Nelson, Alan Hale Jnr, Roland Winters, Jerome Cowan
Ray Heindorf

West Side Story ****
US 1961 155m Technicolor Panavision 70
(UA) Mirisch/Seven Arts (Robert Wise)
The Romeo and Juliet story in a New York dockland setting.
The essentially theatrical conception of this entertainment is nullified by determinedly realistic settings, but production values are fine and the song numbers electrifying.
w Ernest Lehman *play* Arthur Laurents, after William Shakespeare *d Robert Wise, Jerome Robbins ph Daniel L. Fapp m/ly Leonard Bernstein, Stephen Sondheim ch Jerome Robbins pd Boris Leven ed Thomas Stanford cos Irene Sharaff*
☆ Natalie Wood (sung by Marni Nixon) (Maria), Richard Beymer (sung by Jimmy Bryant) (Tony), Russ Tamblyn (Riff), *Rita Moreno (sung by Betty Wand)* (Anita), George Chakiris (Bernardo), Simon Oakland (Lt Schrank), Bill Bramley (Officer Krupke), Tucker Smith (Ice), Tony Mordente, Tony Winters, Eliot Feld
† Jerome Robbins also received an honorary Oscar for 'his brilliant achievements in the art of choregraphy on film.'
best picture; Robert Wise, Jerome Robbins; Daniel L. Fapp; Rita Moreno; George Chakiris; Thomas Stanford; Irene Sharaff; musical direction (Saul Chaplin, Johnny Green, Sid Ramin, Irwin Kostal); art direction; sound
Ernest Lehman

Westbound
US 1959 69m Warnercolor
Warner
A stagecoach manager is entrusted with Californian gold, which attracts assorted villains.
Stalwart star Western which served its purpose.
w Berne Giler *d* Budd Boetticher *ph* J. Peverell Marley *m* David Buttolph
☆ Randolph Scott, Virginia Mayo, Karen Steele, Andrew Duggan, Michael Pate

Westbound Limited
US 1937 76m bw
Universal (Henry MacRae, Ben Koenig)
A railway employee becomes a fugitive when he is wrongly convicted of causing a train crash that killed 27 passengers.
Conventional melodrama of redemption through love, though the rail system seems more than somewhat accident-prone.
w Maurice Geraghty *story* Ford Beebe *d* Ford Beebe *ph* Elwood Bredell *md* Charles Previn *ad* Ralph DeLacy *ed* Philip Cahn
☆ Lyle Talbot (Dave Tolliver), Polly Rowles (Janet Martin), Frank Reicher (Pop Martin), Henry Brandon (Joe Forbes), Henry Hunter (Howard), William Lundigan (Dispatcher)

Western *
France 1997 134m colour Panavision
Artificial Eye/Salomé-Diaphana (Maurice Bernart, Michel Saint-Jean)
A travelling salesman loses his car, his job and his girlfriend but finds friendship on the road with the Russian hitch-hiker who robbed him.
Amiable road movie of contrasting masculinities, marked by a gently observant humour.
w Manuel Poirier, Jean-François Goyet *d* Manuel Poirier *ph* Nara Keo Kosal *m* Bernardo Sandoval *ad* Roland Mabille *ed* Yann Dedet
☆ Sergi Lopez, Sacha Bourdo, Elisabeth Vitali, Marie Matheron

Western Approaches ***
GB 1944 83m Technicolor
Crown Film Unit
US title: *The Raider*
Torpedoed merchantmen in the Atlantic are used by a U-boat as a decoy.
A fictional story is played to great documentary effect by men of the allied navies. One of the outstanding 'factual' films of the war years.
wd Pat Jackson ph Jack Cardiff m Clifton Parker
'Without a doubt the best sea film in existence.' – *Daily Mail*

Western Union **
US 1941 94m Technicolor
TCF (Harry Joe Brown)
Politicians and crooks hamper the laying of cross-country cables.
First-rate Western with familiar excitements.
w Robert Carson *novel* Zane Grey *d* Fritz Lang *ph* Edward Cronjager *m* David Buttolph
☆ Randolph Scott, Robert Young, Dean Jagger, Virginia Gilmore, Slim Summerville, John Carradine, Chill Wills, Barton MacLane

'Two women helped him overthrow the most ruthless power in the west!'
The Westerner **
US 1940 99m bw
Samuel Goldwyn
Judge Roy Bean comes to grief through his love for Lily Langtry.
Moody, melodramatic Western with comedy touches; generally entertaining, the villain more so than the hero.
w Jo Swerling, Niven Busch *story* Stuart N. Lake *d William Wyler ph* Gregg Toland *m* Dimitri Tiomkin *ad* James Basevi
☆ Gary Cooper, *Walter Brennan*, Doris Davenport, Fred Stone, Paul Hurst, Chill Wills, Charles Halton, Forrest Tucker, Dana Andrews, Lillian Bond, Tom Tyler
Walter Brennan
Stuart N. Lake; James Basevi

Westward Ho the Wagons
US 1956 85m Technicolor
Cinemascope
Walt Disney (Bill Walsh)
A wagon train defends itself against Indians.
Slow and simple-minded family Western.
w Tom Blackburn *d* William Beaudine *ph* Charles Boyle *m* Paul Smith
☆ Fess Parker, Kathleen Crowley, Jeff York, David Stollery, Sebastian Cabot, George Reeves

Westward Passage
US 1932 73m bw
RKO (David O. Selznick)
A wealthy girl weds a poor novelist but wants the rich full life for their children.
Dogged romantic drama with only the casting of interest.
w Bradley King, Humphrey Pearson *novel* Margaret Ayer Barnes *d* Robert Milton *ph* Lucien Andriot *m* Max Steiner
☆ Ann Harding, Laurence Olivier, ZaSu Pitts, Irving Pichel, Juliette Compton, Florence Roberts
'Slow, prone to be dull, and hardly warm weather theatre inducement.' – *Variety*

Westward the Women *
US 1951 118m bw
MGM (Dore Schary)
In the 1850s an Indian scout leads 150 Chicago women to meet husbands in California.
Good-looking episodic Western, apparently intended mainly to amuse but seldom rising to the occasion.
w Charles Schnee *d* William Wellman *ph William Mellor m* Jeff Alexander
☆ Robert Taylor, Denise Darcel, John McIntire, Marilyn Erskine, Hope Emerson, Lenore Lonergan, Julie Bishop

'Where nothing can possibly go worng...'
Westworld **
US 1973 89m Metrocolor Panavision
MGM (Paul N. Lazarus III)
In a millionaire holiday resort which recreates the past, a Western badman robot goes berserk and relentlessly attacks two visitors.
Unusual and amusing but under-produced melodrama with slipshod story development and continuity, atoned for by memorable moments and underlying excitement.
wd Michael Crichton *ph* Gene Polito *m* Fred Karlin *ad* Herman Blumenthal
☆ Yul Brynner, Richard Benjamin, James Brolin, Norman Bartold, Alan Oppenheimer
† It was followed by a sequel, *Futureworld* (q.v.)

The Wet Parade *
US 1932 122m bw
MGM (Hunt Stromberg)
A politician points to the corruption caused by prohibition.
Sociologically interesting melodrama.
w John Lee Mahin *novel* Upton Sinclair *d* Victor Fleming *ph* George Barnes *m* William Axt
☆ Walter Huston, Myrna Loy, Neil Hamilton, Lewis Stone, Jimmy Durante, Wallace Ford, Dorothy Jordan, John Miljan, Robert Young
'Final impression strongly anti-liquor, but outside of reaction that may bring, picture hasn't much chance. What it lacks as entertainment isn't covered by propaganda possibilities.' – *Variety*

Wetherby *
GB 1985 97m Technicolor
Greenpoint/Film Four/Zenith (Simon Relph)
After a party at the home of a lonely and frustrated woman, a young man shoots himself.
Interesting if rather irritating drama which leaves as many puzzles as it solves.
wd David Hare *ph* Stuart Harris *m* Nick Bicat *pd* Hayden Griffin
☆ Vanessa Redgrave, Ian Holm, Judi Dench, Tim McInnerny, Stuart Wilson

We've Never Been Licked
US 1943 103m bw
Universal (Walter Wanger)
GB title: *Texas to Tokyo*
A young American raised in Japan finds himself on the wrong side after Pearl Harbor.
Shoddy flagwaver, low on talent and inspiration.
w Norman Reilly Raine, Nick Grinde *d* John Rawlins
☆ Richard Quine, Anne Gwynne, Noah Beery Jnr, Harry Davenport, Martha O'Driscoll, William Frawley, Robert Mitchum

Whale Music *
Canada 1994 112m Alpha Cine
Alliance/Cape Scott (Raymond Massey, Steven DeNure)
The decaying mansion of an ageing, overweight, reclusive rock musician, who is tormented by the past, is invaded by a teenage girl on the run from the law.
Gently offbeat drama of an unlikely relationship which gains interest from its leading performance and its literate script, though the music is less convincing as the work of a pop genius.
w Paul Quarrington, Richard J. Lewis *novel* Paul Quarrington *d* Richard J. Lewis *ph* Vic Sarin *m* George Blondheim, Rheostatics *pd* Rex Raglan *ed* Richard Martin
☆ *Maury Chaykin*, Cyndy Preston, Jennifer Dale, Paul Gross, Blu Mankuma, Alan Jordan, Kenneth Welsh
'Has decided artistic assets, but doesn't connect on an emotional level.' – *Leonard Klady, Variety*

The Whales of August *
US 1987 90m TVC Color
Circle/Nelson (Carolyn Pfeiffer, Mike Kaplan)
Two elderly sisters live on the Maine coast and think of the past.
Edgy, sympathetic talk-piece in which old ladies prove that they are still stars.
w David Berry *novel* David Berry *d* Lindsay Anderson *ph* Mike Fash *m* Alan Price *pd* Joselyn Herbert
☆ Bette Davis, Lillian Gish, Vincent Price, Ann Sothern, Harry Carey Jnr, Mary Steenburgen, Tisha Sterling
'Lovely on all counts.' – *Daily Variety*
Ann Sothern

'He had a price on his head ... she had a price on her heart!'
Wharf Angel
US 1934 65m bw
Paramount
To quote *Variety*, prostie goes softie for sailor with murder rap hanging over his head.
Dim little fogbound melodrama.
w Sam Hoffenstein, Frank Partos, Steve Avery, Frederick Schlick *d* William Cameron Menzies, George Somnes
☆ Victor McLaglen, Dorothy Dell, Preston Foster, Alison Skipworth
'Poor stuff for de luxe audiences: old-fashioned, drab, lacking in box office draw.' – *Variety*

What?
Italy/France/West Germany 1972 113m
Eastmancolor Todd-AO 35
Gala/C.C. Champion/Concordia/Dieter Geissler (Carlo Ponti)
original title: *Che?*
An American hitch-hiker, who is forever losing her clothes, seeks refuge in the home of an Italian millionaire full of curious and lecherous guests.
Eccentric comedy of innocence and experience that works only fitfully.
w Gerard Brach, Roman Polanski *d* Roman Polanski *ph* Marcello Gatti, Giuseppe Ruzzolini *m* Schubert, Mozart, Beethoven *md* Claudio Gizzi *pd* Aurelio Crugnola *ed* Alastair McIntyre
☆ Sydne Rome, Marcello Mastroianni, Hugh Griffith, Romolo Valli, Guido Alberti, Roman Polanski
'Despite its erratic moments of brilliance, the overall impression left by the film is of a rather puerile graffito scrawled in the margins of its literary antecedants.' – *Jan Dawson, MFB*
'Far from being a masterpiece and several notches below being even a good film, but it does stand in danger of being seriously underrated – not to say dismissed – by virtue of its gaudy wrapping.' – *Derek Elley, Films and Filming*

What a Carve Up
GB 1961 88m bw
New World/Baker-Berman
A madman fakes his own death in order to murder his relatives.
Spooky house farce, allegedly a remake of The Ghoul *but bearing little resemblance to it.*
w Ray Cooney, Tony Hilton *novel The Ghoul* by Frank King *d* Pat Jackson *ph* Monty Berman *m* Muir Mathieson
☆ Sid James, Kenneth Connor, Shirley Eaton, Dennis Price, Donald Pleasence, Michael Gough, Valerie Taylor

What a Chassis: see *La Belle Américaine*

What a Crazy World
GB 1963 88m bw
Capricorn/AB Pathé (Michael Carreras)
A working-class London boy sets out to be a rock-and-roller.
Unsurprising star musical, quite lively of its kind.
w Alan Klein *play* Alan Klein *d* Michael Carreras
☆ Joe Brown, Susan Maughan, Marty Wilde, Harry H. Corbett, Avis Bunnage

What a Life
US 1939 75m bw
Paramount
Henry Aldrich has difficulties in high school.
First of the domestic comedy series (see under Henry) which became more farcical and had a different cast; this episode closely followed the Broadway success.
w Charles Brackett, Billy Wilder *play* Clifford Goldsmith *d* Theodore Reed
☆ Jackie Cooper, Betty Field, John Howard, Janice Logan, Lionel Stander, Hedda Hopper, Dorothy Stickney
'A fine comedy drama, excellent for family trade.' – *Variety*

What a Man: see *Never Give a Sucker an Even Break*

What a Way to Go *
US 1964 111m DeLuxe Cinemascope
TCF/APJAC/Orchard (Arthur P. Jacobs)
An immensely rich girl tells her psychiatrist how all her husbands proved not only successful but accident-prone.
Wild, mainly agreeable, star-and-gag-laden black comedy which starts on too high a note and fails to sustain.
w Betty Comden, Adolph Green *d* J. Lee-Thompson *ph* Leon Shamroy *md* Nelson Riddle *ly* Betty Comden, Adolph Green *songs* Jule Styne
☆ Shirley MacLaine, Bob Cummings, Dick Van Dyke, Robert Mitchum, Gene Kelly, Dean Martin, Paul Newman, Reginald Gardiner, Margaret Dumont

What a Whopper
GB 1969 89m bw
Regal/Viscount (Teddy Joseph)
A writer fakes a photograph of the Loch Ness monster in the hope of selling his book on the subject.
Feeble farce built around a pop singer of limited acting ability; its supporting cast of accomplished character actors struggle with the inept script and their Scottish accents.
w Terry Nation *story* Trevor Peacock, Jeremy Lloyd *d* Gilbert Gunn *ph* Reginald Wyer *m* Laurie Johnson *ad* Lionel Couch *ed* Bernard Gribble
☆ Adam Faith (Tony Blake), Sidney James (Harry), Carole Lesley (Charlie Pinner), Terence Longdon (Vernon), Clive Dunn (Mr Slate), Freddie Frinton (Gilbert Pinner), Marie France (Marie), Charles Hawtrey (Arnold), Spike Milligan (Tramp), Wilfrid Brambell (Postie), Fabia Drake (Mrs Pinner), Harold Berens (Sammy), Terry Scott (Sergeant), Fyfe Robertson (Commentator)

What a Woman
US 1943 90m bw
Columbia
aka: *The Beautiful Cheat*
An author's agent gets into romantic escapades with her writers.
Ho-hum romantic comedy, quickly forgotten.
w Therese Lewis, Barry Trivers *d* Irving Cummings
☆ Rosalind Russell, Brian Aherne, Willard Parker, Ann Savage, Alan Dinehart

What about Bob? *
US 1991 99m Technicolor
Warner/Touchstone/Touchwood Pacific Partners I (Laura Ziskin)
A disturbed patient moves in on holidaying psychiatrist and his equally disturbed family.
Intermittently amusing black comedy.
w Tom Schulman *story* Alvin Sargent, Laura Ziskin *d* Frank Oz *ph* Michael Ballhaus *m* Miles Goodman *pd* Les Dilley *ed* Anne V. Coates
☆ Bill Murray, Richard Dreyfuss, Julie Hagerty, Charlie Korsmo, Kathryn Erbe, Tom Aldredge, Susan Willis
'Frank Oz proves that he's a director with just the mean sense of humor these bland times desperately need.' – *Richard Schickel, Time*

'Off to grandmother's house they go, For love in the attic and death down below!'
What Became of Jack and Jill?
GB 1971 90m DeLuxe
Palomar/Amicus (Milton Subotsky)
A young man tries to hasten his grandmother's death but she has the last laugh.
Feeble suspenser with a dim ending.
w Roger Marshall *novel The Ruthless Ones* by Laurence Moody *d* Bill Bain *ph* Gerry Turpin *m* Carl Davis
☆ Vanessa Howard, Paul Nicholas, Mona Washbourne, Peter Copley, Peter Jeffrey

What Becomes of the Broken-Hearted? *
New Zealand 1999 108m colour
NZFC/South Pacific/Polygram (Bill Gavin)
After his son is killed in a gang fight, a hot-tempered father attempts to get on better terms with the family he has neglected.
Tough, raw-edged sequel that eschews the family dynamics of Once Were Warriors *(qv) in favour of an action drama closer to Mad Max in its emphasis on gang warfare.*
w Alan Duff *novel* Alan Duff *d* Ian Mune *ph* Allen Guilford *m* David Hirschfelder *pd* Brett Schwieters *ed* Mike Horton *cos* Pauline Bowkett
☆ Temuera Morrison (Jake Heke), Clint Eruera (Sonny Heke), Nancy Brunning (Tania Rogers), Pete Smith (Apeman), Lawrence Makaore (Grunt), Rawiri Paratene (Mulla Rota), Julian Arahanga (Nig Heke), Rena Owen (Beth Heke), Edna Stirling (Rita), Tammy Davis (Mookie),

Anaru Grant (Kohl Douglas), Warwick Morehu (Gary Douglas)

What Changed Charley Farthing
GB 1975 101m Eastmancolor
Patina-Hidalgo (Tristam Cones)
US title: *The Bananas Boat*
A philandering sailor has adventures in Cuba.
Weirdly ineffective comedy actioner which never gets started and should never have been thought of.
w David Pursall, Jack Seddon *novel* Mark Hebdon *d* Sidney Hayers *ph* Graham Edgar *m* Angela Arteaga
☆ Doug McClure, Lionel Jeffries, Warren Mitchell, Hayley Mills, Dilys Hamlett, Fernando Sancho

What Did You Do in the War, Daddy?
US 1966 115m DeLuxe Panavision
UA/Mirisch/Geoffrey (Owen Crump, Blake Edwards)
In 1943, an Italian town surrenders readily to the Americans providing its wine festival and football match can take place.
Silly war comedy with insufficient jokes for its wearisome length. The performances are bright enough.
w William Peter Blatty *d* Blake Edwards *ph* Philip Lathrop *m* Henry Mancini
☆ James Coburn, Dick Shawn, Sergio Fantoni, Giovanna Ralli, Aldo Ray, Harry Morgan, Carroll O'Connor, Leon Askin

'Where One World Ends, Another Begins.'
'After Life There Is More.'
What Dreams May Come
US 1998 113m Monaco Film Lab Panavision
Polygram/Interscope/Metafilmics (Stephen Simon, Barnet Bain)
A doctor, whose two children die in a car crash, is himself later killed in another crash; they all meet in the afterlife and, when his widow commits suicide, he sets out to rescue her from hell.
Hollywood's brand of warm, huggy theology gets ever stranger: heaven here is a gooey oil painting, psychobabble is the angelic language, there's no deity in view, and the occupants can't wait to leave the place and get back to Earth. The mind boggles.
w Ron Bass *novel* Richard Matheson *d* Vincent Ward *ph* Eduardo Serra *m* Michael Kamen *pd* Eugenio Zanetti *ed* David Brenner, Maysie Hoy *sp* visual fx: Joel Hynek, Nicholas Brooks, Stuart Robertson, Kevin Mack
☆ Robin Williams, Cuba Gooding Jnr, Annabella Sciorra, Max von Sydow, Jessica Brooks Grant, Josh Paddock, Rosalind Chao
'All the weeping and hugging the characters do can't make up for the film's fatal lack of texture and psychological nuance.' – *Stephen Holden, New York Times*
visual effects
Eugenio Zanetti

What Every Woman Knows *
US 1934 90m bw
MGM
A quiet little wife encourages her husband into parliament.
Adequate version of the sentimental play, very pleasantly acted.
w Monckton Hoffe, John Meehan, James Kevin McGuinness *play* J. M. Barrie *d* Gregory La Cava
☆ *Helen Hayes, Brian Aherne*, Madge Evans, Lucile Watson, Dudley Digges, Henry Stephenson, Donald Crisp, David Torrence
'Cinch b.o., a swell woman's picture.' – *Variety*

What Happened to Santiago *
Puerto Rico 1989 100m colour
Dios Los Cria (Pedro Muñiz)
original title: *Lo que le pasó de Santiago*
An accountant retires and falls for a woman with a mysterious past.
A gently charming domestic drama, most likely to appeal to the over-50s.
wd Jacobo Morales *ph* Augustin Cubano *m* Pedro Rivera Toledo *ad* Ivonne Torres *ed* Alfonso Borrell
☆ Tommy Muñiz, Gladys Rodriguez, Johanna Rosaly, René Monclova, Pedro Javier Muñiz, Jacobo Morales
Best foreign language film

What Have I Done to Deserve This? *
Spain 1984 101m colour
Metro/Tesauro/Kaktus (Tadeo Villabla)
original title: *Que He Hecho Yo Para Merecer Esto?*
A slum family falls apart, to the indifference of the busy mother, who takes drugs to keep her awake as she works hard as a cleaner.
Fast-paced inconsequential black comedy, lacking any internal coherence as it rushes from one tasteless joke to another.
wd Pedro Almodóvar *ph* Angel Luis Fernandez *m* Bernardo Bonezzi *ed* Jose Solcedo
☆ Carmen Maura, Luis Hostalot, Angel de Andres-Lopez, Gonzalo Suarez, Veronica Forque, Juan Martinez, Miguel Angel Harranz
'Almodóvar is an underground theatre clown. He may not know how to make anything stay with you – he may not even care to. He just likes to put on a show. Some of the vignettes might be comedy classics if their timing weren't so sloppy.' – *Pauline Kael, New Yorker*

'He was the perfect husband until his one mistake followed them home.'
What Lies Beneath *
US 2000 130m Technicolor Panavision
TCF/Imagemover (Steve Starkey, Robert Zemeckis, Jack Rapke)
A scientist's wife investigates odd happenings at her home that include glimpses of the ghost of a young woman.
Slick sub-Hitchcockian drama, which can't quite decide whether to settle for being a thriller or a supernatural chiller.
w Clark Gregg *d* Robert Zemeckis *ph* Don Burgess *m* Alan Silvestri *pd* Rick Carter, Jim Teegarden *ed* Arthur Schmidt *cos* Susie DeSanto
☆ Harrison Ford (Norman Spencer), Michelle Pfeiffer (Claire Spencer), Diana Scarwid (Jody), Miranda Otto (Mary Feur), James Remar (Warren Feur), Joe Morton (Dr Drayton), Amber Valletta (Madison Elizabeth Frank), Victoria Birdwell (Beatrice), Katharine Towne (Caitlin Spencer)
'Sufficiently frightening that its virtues far outweight its shortcomings.' – *Joe Queenan*
'A convoluted thriller bogged down by a familiar plot and middle-aged protagonists.' – *Emanuel Levy, Variety*

What Lola Wants: see *Damn Yankees*

What, No Beer?
US 1933 65m bw
MGM
A barber rushes to be first on the market with beer after its legalization, but finds himself premature and at odds with gangsters.
Topical farce ending in a slapstick mêlée.
w Carey Wilson, Jack Cluett, Robert E. Hopkins *d* Edward Sedgwick
☆ Buster Keaton, Jimmy Durante, Roscoe Ates, Phyllis Barry, John Miljan, Henry Armetta
'A commercial little laugh picture.' – *Variety*

What Planet Are You From?
US 2000 104m DeLuxe
Columbia/Brad Grey/Bernie Brillstein (Mike Nichols, Garry Shandling, Neil Machlis)
An emotion-free alien with a mechanical penis comes to Earth to artificially impregnate a woman so that his race can take over the planet.
The question should be: what made them make this? Presumably Shandling, as producer, could hire himself as writer and star, but it's difficult to understand why talented people should have got involved in this witless, sniggering silliness.
w Garry Shandling, Michael Leeson, Ed Solomon, Peter Toland *d* Mike Nichols *ph* Michael Ballhaus *m* Carter Burwell *pd* Bo Welch *ed* Richard Marks *sp* Sony Pictures Imageworks
☆ Garry Shandling (Harold Anderson), Annette Bening (Susan), Greg Kinnear (Perry Gordon), Ben Kingsley (Graydon), Linda Fiorentino (Helen Gordon), John Goodman (Roland Jones), Richard Jenkins (Don Fisk), Caroline Aaron (Nadine), Judy Greer (Rebecca), Nora Dunn (Madeline), Ann Cusack (Liz), Camryn Manheim (Alison)
'A dirty-middle-aged-man's comedy.' – *Variety*
'The most uncomfortable movie of the new year, an exercise in feel-good smut.' – *Roger Ebert, Chicago Sun-Times*

What Price Glory? *
US 1952 111m Technicolor
TCF (Sol C. Siegel)
In 1917 France Captain Flagg and Sergeant Quirt spar for the same girl.
Stagey remake of the celebrated silent film and play; watchable if not exactly inspired.
w Phoebe and Henry Ephron *play* Maxwell Anderson, Laurence Stallings *d* John Ford *ph* Joe MacDonald *m* Alfred Newman
☆ James Cagney, Dan Dailey, Corinne Calvet, William Demarest, Robert Wagner, Marisa Pavan, James Gleason

'A heart-touching drama of the world, the flesh and the movies!'
What Price Hollywood? *
US 1932 87m bw
RKO (Pandro S. Berman)
A waitress becomes a film star with the help of a drunken director who later commits suicide.
Fairly trenchant early study of the mores of the film city, later revamped as A Star Is Born.
w Ben Markson, Gene Fowler, Rowland Brown, Jane Murfin *story* Adela Rogers St John *d* George Cukor *ph* Charles Rosher *m* Max Steiner *montage* Slavko Vorkapich
☆ Constance Bennett, Lowell Sherman, Neil Hamilton, Gregory Ratoff, Brooks Benedict, Louise Beavers, Eddie Anderson
'Many of the scenes are like sketches for the later versions, but this film has its own interest, especially because of its glimpses into the studio life of the time.' – *New Yorker, 1977*
Adela Rogers St John, Jane Murfin

What Shall It Profit: see *Hard Steel*

What Time Is It There?
France/Taiwan 2001 116m colour
ICA/Arena/Homegreen (Bruno Pesery)
original title: *Ni Neibian Jidian*
Mourning the death of his father and concerned for his mother's well-being, a street trader becomes obsessed with a woman who buys his watch on her way to Paris.
A movie about isolation and loneliness on two continents, mixing melancholia and deadpan humour, and enjoyable once you adjust to its languorous pace.
w Tsai Ming-liang, Yang Pi-ying *d* Tsai Ming-liang *ph* Benoit Delhomme *pd* Yip Kam-tim *ed* Chen Sheng-chang
☆ Lee Kang-sheng (Hsiao-kang), Chen Shiang-chyi (Shiang-chyi), Lu Yi-ching (Mother), Miao Tien (Father), Cecilia Yip (Hong Kong girl), Jean-Pierre Leaud (Man)
'It haunts you, you can't forget it, you admire its conception and are able to resolve some of the confusions you had while watching it.' – *Roger Ebert, Chicago Sun-Times*
'A film of surprise and wonder, lyrically attuned to the ticking intensity of romance.' – *Peter Travers, Rolling Stone*

What Waits Below: see *Secrets of the Phantom Caverns*

'He has the power to hear everything women are thinking. Finally... a man is listening.'
What Women Want *
US 2000 126m DeLuxe
Paramount/Icon/Wind Dancer (Nancy Meyers, Bruce Davey, Matt Williams, Susan Cartsonis, Gina Matthews)
After an accident with a hair-dryer in the bath, a failing, womanising advertising executive discovers that he can hear the secret thoughts of women.
Lightweight romantic comedy, though its central conceit is hardly developed – all women apparently, will settle for even an unreconstructed Mel Gibson – as subplots of office intrigue and family disharmony proliferate.
w Josh Goldsmith, Cathy Yuspa *d* Nancy Meyers *ph* Dean Cundey *m* Alan Silvestri *pd* Jon Hutman *ed* Stephen A. Rotter, Thomas J. Nordberg *cos* Ellen Mirojnick
☆ Mel Gibson (Nick Marshall), Helen Hunt (Darcy Maguire), Marisa Tomei (Lola), Mark Feuerstein (Morgan Farwell), Lauren Holly (Gigi), Ashley Johnson (Alex Marshall), Judy Greer (Erin), Alan Alda (Dan Wanamaker), Delta Burke (Eve), Valerie Perrine (Margo), Lisa Edelstein (Dina), Sarah Paulson (Annie)
'The movie has none of the giddy wit we associate with classic romantic comedy. It just runs on and on — like a slightly stupid story you wish you hadn't overheard in a singles bar.' – *Richard Schickel, Time*
'Has sheer energy and audience allure to burn, even if numerous speed bumps cause many of the comic possibilities to go tumbling overboard.' – *Todd McCarthy, Variety*

Whatever *
France 1999 121m colour
Artificial Eye/Lazzenec/Canal+ (Adeline Lécallier)
original title: *Extension du Domaine de la Lutte*
A lonely, depressed middle-aged middle manager who has withdrawn into a celibate and boring existence wonders how he is going to get through his life.
Quietly witty study of a man in terminal despair over the modern world ('I know life. I've been there.'), expressed in images of dull and dreay hotels, car parks, offices and clubs.
w Philippe Harel, Michel Houellebecq *novel* Michel Houellebecq *d* Philippe Harel *ph* Gilles Henry *pd* Louise Marzaroli *ed* Bénédicte Teiger *cos* Anne Schotte
☆ Philippe Harel (Our Hero), José Garcia (Raphael Tisserand), Catherine Mouchet (Psychologist), Cécile Reigher (Catherine Lechardey), Marie Charlotte Leclaire (Secretary), Philippe Agael (Henri La Brette), Alain Guillo (Buvet), Philippe Bianco (Narrator)

'What makes her garden grow... wouldn't you like to know!'
Whatever Happened to Aunt Alice? *
US 1969 101m Metrocolor
Palomar/Associates and Aldrich (Robert Aldrich)
A genteel widow murders her housekeepers for their private incomes.
Ladylike shocker with some black humour and good performances.
w Theodore Apstein *novel* The Forbidden Garden by Ursula Curtiss *d* Lee H. Katzin *ph* Joseph Biroc *m* Gerald Fried *ad* William Glasgow *ed* Frank J. Urioste
☆ Geraldine Page (Claire Marrable), Ruth Gordon (Alice Dimmock), Rosemary Forsyth (Harriet Vaughn), Robert Fuller (Mike Darrah), Mildred Dunnock (Edna Tinsley), Joan Huntington (Julia Lawson)

'Sister, sister, oh so fair, why is there blood all over your hair?'
Whatever Happened to Baby Jane? *
US 1962 132m bw
Warner Seven Arts/Associates and Aldrich (Robert Aldrich)
In middle age, a demented ex-child star lives in an old Hollywood mansion with her invalid sister, and tension leads to murder.
Famous for marking the first time Hollywood's ageing first ladies stooped to horror, and followed by Hush Hush Sweet Charlotte *and the other* Whatevers, *this dreary looking melodrama only occasionally grabs the attention and has enough plot for about half its length. The performances, however, are striking.*
w Lukas Heller *novel* Henry Farrell *d* Robert Aldrich *ph* Ernest Haller *m* Frank de Vol
☆ *Bette Davis, Joan Crawford, Victor Buono*, Anna Lee
'It goes on and on, in a light much dimmer than necessary, and the climax, when it belatedly arrives, is a bungled, languid mingling of pursuers and pursued...' – *New Yorker*
Ernest Haller; Bette Davis; Victor Buono

'In 1977, disco wasn't the only magic in town.'
Whatever Happened To Harold Smith? *
GB 1998 94m DeLuxe
UIP/Intermedia/October/Arts Council/West Eleven (Ruth Jackson, David Brown)
In Sheffield in the mid-70s, a working class father develops telekinetic powers, while his son tries to pluck up courage to date a middle-class girl.

Lively, inconsequential domestic comedy of misplaced aspirations, set against a background of punk rock and disco.
w Ben Steiner *d* Peter Hewitt *ph* David Tattersall *m* Rupert Gregson-Williams *ch* Litza Bixler *pd* Gemma Jackson *ed* Martin Walsh *cos* Marie France
☆ Tom Courtenay (Harold Smith), Stephen Fry (Dr Peter Robinson), Michael Legge (Vince Smith), Laura Fraser (Joanna Robinson), Lulu (Irene Smith), David Thewlis (Nesbit), Rosemary Leach (Harold's mother), Amanda Root (Margaret Robinson), Matthew Rhys (Ray Smith), James Corden (Walter), Charlie Hunnam (Daz), Charlotte Roberts (Lucy Robinson)
'Busy direction and bright performances partly compensate for a script that goes in too many directions at the same time.' – *Derek Elley, Variety*

What's a Nice Girl Like You Doing in a Place Like This? *
US 1963 10m bw 16mm
Contemporary/New York University Department of Television, Motion Picture and Radio Presentation Summer Motion Picture Workshop
A would-be writer tries various ways to overcome his hang-ups.
An exuberant and amusing short, much influenced by the style of the French New Wave.
wd Martin Scorsese *ph* James Newman *m* Richard H. Cole *ed* Robert Hunsicker
☆ Zeph Michaelis, Mimi Stark, Sarah Braveman, Fred Sica, Robert Uricola
† It was released on video with three other shorts under the title *Scorsese x 4*.

What's Buzzin', Cousin?
US 1943 75m bw
Columbia (Jack Fier)
An attorney turns band singer and helps revive a droopy hotel.
Listless musical with a few good numbers.
w Harry Sauber *d* Charles Barton
☆ Ann Miller, John Hubbard, Eddie Anderson, Leslie Brooks, Jeff Donnell

'A Delicious Comedy Of Table Manners.'
'A celebration of food, tradition & relative insanity.'
What's Cooking? *
US/GB 2000 109m Foto-Kem
Redbus/Flashpoint/Stagescreen/Hope and Glory (Jeffrey Taylor)
In Los Angeles, the Thanksgiving celebrations overlap of four differing American families: African American, Jewish, Latino and Vietnamese.
A broad comedy of culture, culinary and generation clashes in a multi-ethnic mix.
w Gurinder Chadha, Paul Mayeda Berges *d* Gurinder Chadha *ph* Jong Lin *m* Craig Pruess *pd* Stuart Blatt *ed* Janice Hampton *cos* Eduardo Castro
☆ Alfre Woodard (Audrey Williams), Dennis Haysbert (Ronald Williams), Ann Weldon (Grace Williams), Mercedes Ruehl (Elizabeth Avila), Victor Rivers (Javier Avila), Douglas Spain (Anthony Avila), A. Martinez (Daniel), Lainie Kazan (Ruth Seeling), Maury Chaykin (Herb Seeling), Kyra Sedgwick (Rachel Seeling), Julianna Margulies (Carla), Estelle Harris (Aunt Bea), Joan Chen (Trinh Nguyen)
'There are so many characters, so vividly drawn, with such humor and life, that a synopsis is impossible. What's strange is the spell the movie weaves. By its end, there is actually a sort of tingle of pleasure in seeing how this Thanksgiving ends.' – *Roger Ebert, Chicago Sun-Times*

'A film about the love you find ... in the last place you look.'
What's Eating Gilbert Grape?
US 1993 118m DeLuxe
Paramount (Meir Teper, Bertil Ohlsson, David Matalon)
A small-town grocery clerk is the main support of his family: obese, stay-at-home mother, two disturbed sisters and a brain-damaged brother.
Gentle, unsentimental drama, but so low-key that it does not always engage the interest.
w Peter Hedges *novel* Peter Hedges *d* Lasse Hallström *ph* Sven Nykvist *m* Alan Parker *pd* Bernt Capra *ed* Andrew Monshein
☆ Johnny Depp, Juliette Lewis, Mary Steenburgen, Leonardo DiCaprio, Darlene Cates, Laura Harrington, Mary Kate Schellhardt, Crispin Glover, Kevin Tighe
'An offbeat middleweight charmer that is lent a measure of substance by its astute performances and observational insight.' – *Variety*
'The film is still implicitly condescending since almost all the characters (including the afflicted ones) function as tests of Gilbert's patience.' – *Michael Sragow, New Yorker*
Leonardo DiCaprio

What's Good for the Goose
GB 1969 104m Eastmancolor
Tigon (Tony Tenser, Norman Wisdom)
An assistant bank manager falls for a girl hitch-hiker and tries to recover his youth.
Embarrassing attempt to build a sexy vehicle for a star whose sentimental mugging always appealed mainly to children.
w Norman Wisdom *d* Menahem Golan *ph* William Brayne *m* Reg Tilsley
☆ Norman Wisdom, Sally Geeson, Sally Bazely, Derek Francis, Terence Alexander

'Who needs a heart when a heart can be broken?'
What's Love Got to Do with It *
US 1993 118m Technicolor
Buena Vista/Touchstone (Doug Chapin, Barry Krost)
aka: *Tina: What's Love Got to Do with It*
Biopic of the rock singer Tina Turner, from her violent relationship with, and marriage to, Ike Turner to her successful emergence as a solo artist.
Excellent performances by the two leads, some well-staged musical numbers and marital rows and lusty singing by Tina Turner herself make this a better than average picture of its kind.
w Kate Lanier *book* I, *Tina* by Tina Turner, Kurt Loder *d* Brian Gibson *ph* Jamie Anderson *m* Stanley Clarke *pd* Stephen Altman *ed* Stuart Pappé
☆ *Angela Bassett, Laurence Fishburne*, Vanessa Bell Calloway, Jenifer Lewis, Phyllis Yvonne Stickney, Khandi Alexander, Rae'ven Kelly
'A passionate personal and professional drama that hits both the high and low notes of an extraordinary life and career. An immensely enjoyable saga.' – *Variety*
Laurence Fishburne; Angela Bassett

What's New Pussycat?
US/France 1965 108m Technicolor
UA/Famous Artists (Charles K. Feldman)
A fashion editor is distracted by beautiful girls.
Zany sex comedy with many more misses than hits, a product of the wildly swinging sixties when it was thought that a big budget and stars making fools of themselves would automatically ensure a success.
w Woody Allen *d* Clive Donner *ph* Jean Badal *m* *Burt Bacharach*
☆ Peter O'Toole, Peter Sellers, Woody Allen, Ursula Andress, Romy Schneider, Capucine, Paula Prentiss
'Unfortunately for all concerned, to make something enjoyably dirty a lot of taste is required.' – *John Simon*
title song (*m* Burt Bacharach, *ly* Hal David)

What's So Bad about Feeling Good?
US 1965 94m Technicolor
Universal (George Seaton)
A 'happy virus' is carried into New York by a toucan, and affects the lives of various people.
Flimsy pretext for a comedy, further hampered by a less than sparkling script. The actors have their moments.
w George Seaton, Robert Pirosh *d* George Seaton *ph* Ernesto Caparros *m* Frank de Vol
☆ George Peppard, Mary Tyler Moore, Dom DeLuise, John McMartin, Susan St James, Don Stroud, Charles Lane

What's the Matter with Helen? *
US 1971 101m DeLuxe
Filmways/Raymax (George Edwards, James C. Pratt)
In 1934 Hollywood, two women run a dancing school for child stars; one of them is a killer.
More Baby Jane melodramatics, quite lively and with interesting period detail.
w Henry Farrell *d* Curtis Harrington *ph* Lucien Ballard *m* David Raksin *pd* *Eugene Lourié*
☆ *Debbie Reynolds, Shelley Winters, Michael MacLiammoir*, Dennis Weaver, Agnes Moorehead
'A cast of seasoned troupers cannot quite alter the impression that they are all working to revive a stiff.' – *Bruce Williamson*

'It takes a thief to nail a crook.'
What's the Worst That Could Happen?
US 2001 97m DeLuxe
MGM/Turman-Morrissey/Hyde Park (Lawrence Turman, David Hoberman, Ashok Amritraj, Wendy Dytman)
A thief plans revenge on the tycoon who stole his lucky ring..
Anyone who sits through this tedious comedy will realise that the worst has indeed just happened, with a miscast Lawrence floundering through an inept script.
w Matthew Chapman *novel* Donald E. Westlake *ph* Anastas Michos *m* Tyler Bates, Marc Shaiman *pd* Howard Cummings *ed* Garth Craven, Nick Moore
☆ Martin Lawrence (Kevin Caffery), Danny DeVito (Max Fairbanks), John Leguizamo (Berger), Glenne Headly (Gloria), Carmen Ejogo (Amber Belhaven), Bernie Mac (Uncle Jack), Larry Miller (Earl Radburn), Nora Dunn (Lutetia Fairbanks)
'I have questions of my own. Where's the exit?' – *Tim Nagle, Sunday Times*
'The title cries out for countless punchlines in response, of which I shall select 'a sequel' as the best' – *Jason Solomons, Observer*

What's Up, Doc? **
US 1972 94m Technicolor
Warner/Saticoy (Peter Bogdanovich)
In San Francisco, an absent-minded young musicologist is troubled by the attentions of a dotty girl who gets him involved with crooks and a series of accidents.
Madcap comedy, a pastiche of several thirties originals. Spectacular slapstick and willing players are somewhat let down by exhausted patches and a tame final reel.
w Buck Henry, David Newman, Robert Benton *d* *Peter Bogdanovich* *ph* Laszlo Kovacs *m* Artie Butler *pd* Polly Platt
☆ Barbra Streisand, Ryan O'Neal, Kenneth Mars, Austin Pendleton, Madeline Kahn, Mabel Albertson, Sorrell Booke
'A comedy made by a man who has seen a lot of movies, knows all the mechanics, and has absolutely no sense of humour. Seeing it is like shaking hands with a joker holding a joy buzzer: the effect is both presumptuous and unpleasant.' – *Jay Cocks*
'It's all rather like a 19th-century imitation of Elizabethan blank verse drama.' – *Stanley Kauffmann*
'It freely borrows from the best screen comedy down the ages but has no discernible style of its own.' – *Michael Billington, Illustrated London News*

What's Up, Tiger Lily? *
US 1966 80m Eastmancolor Tohoscope
Benedict/Toho (Woody Allen)
A Japanese agent searches for the world's greatest egg salad recipe.
Woody Allen and his American cast re-dub a Japanese spy film to create an off-beat comedy that is amusing in fits and starts.
w Kazuo Yamada, Woody Allen and others *d* Senkichi Taniguchi *m* Jack Lewis, The Lovin' Spoonful *ed* Richard Krown
☆ Tatsuya Mihashi, Mie Hama, Akiko Wakabayashi, Tadeo Nakamaru, Susumu Kurobe, Woody Allen, Frank Buxton, Len Maxwell, Louise Lasser, Mickey Rose
'The jokes get rather desperate, but there are enough wildly sophomoric ones to keep this pop stunt fairly amusing until about midway.' – *Pauline Kael, New Yorker*

The Wheeler Dealers
US 1963 106m Metrocolor Panavision
MGM/Filmways (Martin Ransohoff)
GB title: *Separate Beds*
A Texas tycoon with a flair for the stock market sets Wall Street agog by manipulating a mysterious and non-existent new product.
Fun for financiers, but barely worth following for the rest. A slick, loud, hollow show.
w G. J. W. Goodman, Ira Wallach *d* Arthur Hiller *ph* Charles Lang Jnr *m* Frank de Vol
☆ James Garner, Lee Remick, Phil Harris, Chill Wills, Jim Backus, Louis Nye, John Astin

Wheels on Meals
Hong Kong 1984 102m colour
Paragon Films (Leonard K. C. Ho)
Two Chinese fast-food operatives working in Spain bring fortune to a local girl.
Bizarre kung-fu comedy with a little romance on the side. Too slow and with not enough action to interest fans of the genre, even if it does include a parody of The Three Musketeers.
d Samo Hung
☆ Jackie Chan, Benny Urquidez, Keith Vitali, Herb Edelman, Samo Hung

When a Man Loves
US 1927 83m (24 fps) bw silent with synchronized music
Warner
A hero escapes from a prison ship and gives his all for love of a worthless woman.
Freely adapted version of Manon Lescaut, *successful because of the real-life romance of the stars.*
w Bess Meredyth *d* Alan Crosland
☆ John Barrymore, Dolores Costello, Warner Oland, Stuart Holmes, Holmes Herbert

'Through the good times. Through the bad times.'
'It's for all times.'
When a Man Loves a Woman
US 1994 124m Technicolor
Buena Vista/Touchstone (Jordan Kerner, Jon Avnet)
A husband finds that his wife's alcoholism is a problem and her sobriety even worse.
A domestic drama that evades the realities of the situation it shows in its determination to reach a happy ending.
w Ronald Bass, Al Franken *d* Luis Mandoki *ph* Lajos Koltai *m* Zbigniew Preisner *pd* Stuart Wurtzel *ed* Garth Craven
☆ Andy Garcia, Meg Ryan, Philip Seymour Hoffman, Lauren Tom, Tina Majorino, Mae Whitman, Ellen Burstyn
'Nothing resonates in this tale of a romance with drink.' – *Time*
'With a little patience, audiences should find themselves emotionally polarized by this adult, intelligent drama that exhumes the detritus of male–female relationships with painful precision.' – *James Cameron-Wilson, Film Review*
'Little more than emotional pornography.' – *Sight and Sound*

'Every baby sitter's nightmare becomes real!'
When a Stranger Calls
US 1979 97m colour
UA/Melvin Simon (Doug Chapin, Steve Feke)
A policeman determinedly chases a baby-murdering maniac.
Middling screamer extended from a short, The Sitter; *a passive midsection separates a suspenseful start and finish.*
w Steve Feke, Fred Walton *d* Fred Walton *ph* Don Peterman *m* Dana Kaproff *pd* Elayne Barbara Ceder *ed* Sam Vitale
☆ Charles Durning, Tony Beckley, Carol Kane, Colleen Dewhurst, Rachel Roberts

When Boys Leave Home: see *Downhill*

When Brendan Met Trudy
Ireland/GB 2000 95m colour
Momentum/Collins Avenue/Deadly Films 2 (Lynda Myles)
In Dublin, a shy schoolteacher loses his inhibitions when he begins an affair with a high-spirited, secretive woman.

Gently amusing romantic comedy that is more interested in cramming in references to other movies than in developing its characters.
w Roddy Doyle *d* Kieron J. Walsh *ph* Ashley Rowe *m* Richard Hartley *pd* Fiona Daly *ed* Scott Thomas *cos* Consolata Boyle
☆ Peter McDonald (Brendan), Flora Montgomery (Trudy), Marie Mullen (Mother), Pauline McLynn (Nuala), Don Wycherley (Niall), Maynard Eziashi (Edgar), Eileen Walsh (Siobhan), Barry Cassin (Headmaster)

'A gleeful comic anthology of cinematic jokes and references, which it trots out with a cocky exuberance that would be annoying if most of the choices weren't so witty.' – *Stephen Holden, New York Times*

When Comedy Was King ***
US 1959 84m bw
Robert Youngson Productions
Valuable compilation of silent comedy sequences, with the high print quality and poor commentary to be expected from this source. Extracts include Buster Keaton in *Cops*, Laurel and Hardy in *Big Business*, and a Fatty Arbuckle comedy.
ed Robert Youngson

When Dinosaurs Ruled the Earth
GB 1969 100m Technicolor
Warner/Hammer (Aida Young)
In prehistoric times, a girl is swept out to sea by a cyclone and adopted by a dinosaur.
Sequel to One Million Years BC, *all very silly but tolerably well done.*
wd Val Guest, from a treatment by J. G. Ballard *ph* Dick Bush *m* Mario Nascimbene *ad* John Blezard *ed* Peter Curran *sp* Jim Danforth
☆ Victoria Vetri, Patrick Allen, Robin Hawdon, Patrick Holt, Imogen Hassall

'I'm very proud that my first screen credit was for what is, without doubt, the worst film ever made.' – *J. G. Ballard*

special visual effects (Jim Danforth, Roger Dicken)

When Eight Bells Toll *
GB 1971 94m Eastmancolor Panavision
Winkast (Elliott Kastner)
A naval secret service agent investigates the pirating of gold bullion ships off the Scottish coast.
Acceptable kill-happy thriller: humourless James Bondery graced by splendid Scottish landscapes.
w Alistair MacLean *novel* Alistair Maclean *d* Etienne Perier *ph* Arthur Ibbetson *m* Wally Stott
☆ *Anthony Hopkins, Robert Morley*, Corin Redgrave, Jack Hawkins, Ferdy Mayne, Derek Bond, Nathalie Delon

When Father Was Away on Business **
Yugoslavia 1985 136m colour
Cannon/Forum/Sarajevo Film (Vera Mihic-Jolic)
original title: *Otac Na Sluašbenom Putu*
Family life in Yugoslavia in the 1950s, as seen through the eyes of a young boy whose father is sent to the mines after being betrayed by his mistress and brother-in-law.
Well-observed study of politics seen from a child's perspective, which adds charm and humour. It won the Palme d'Or for best film at the Cannes Film Festival in 1985.
w Abdulah Sidran *d* Emir Kusturica *ph* Vilko Filač *m* Zoran Simjanović *pd* Predrag Lukovac *ed* Andrija Zafranovic
☆ Moreno de Bartoli, Miki Manojlović, Mirjana Karanović, Mustafa Nadarević, Mira Furlan, Zoran Radmilovic, Jelena Covic, Tomislav Gelić, Davor Dujmović, Amir Kapetanović

When Harry Met Sally ****
US 1989 95m DuArt
Palace/Castle Rock/Nelson Entertainment (Rob Reiner, Andrew Scheinman)
Over a period of 12 years, a couple meet occasionally to debate whether there can be friendship without sex between a man and a woman.
Deft, witty romantic comedy, as good of its kind as we're likely to get these days.
w Nora Ephron d Rob Reiner *ph* Barry Sonnenfeld *m* Harry Connick Jnr and others *pd* Jane Musky *ed* Robert Leighton
☆ Billy Crystal, *Meg Ryan*, Carrie Fisher, Bruno Kirby, Steven Ford, Lisa Jane Persky, Michelle Nicastro
Nora Ephron
Nora Ephron

When I Fall in Love
US 1988 127m Technicolor
Warner/New Visions (Taylor Hackford, Laura Ziskin, Ian Sander)
US title: *Everybody's All-American*
A star football player and his beauty queen wife survive 25 years of married life.
A lengthy soap opera, sentimentally indulging in an emotional switchback as its protagonists go from happiness to grief and back.
w Tom Rickman *novel* Frank Deford *d* Taylor Hackford *ph* Stephen Goldblatt *m* James Newton Howard *pd* Joe Alves *ed* Don Zimmerman
☆ Dennis Quaid, Jessica Lange, Timothy Hutton, John Goodman, Carl Lumbly, Raymond Baker, Savannah Smith Boucher, Patricia Clarkson

When I Grow Up *
US 1951 90m bw
Horizon (S. P. Eagle)
A boy about to run away changes his mind after reading his grandfather's diaries.
Pleasant, sentimental family film with an unusual approach.
wd Michael Kanin *ph* Ernest Laszlo *m* Jerome Moross
☆ Bobby Driscoll, Robert Preston, Charley Grapewin, Martha Scott, Ralph Dumke

When in Rome
US 1952 78m bw
MGM (Clarence Brown)
A gangster in Rome steals a priest's clothes and is accepted in his place.
Typically American religious comedy, nicely made but straying somewhat over the top when the gangster reforms and becomes a monk.
w Charles Schnee, Dorothy Kingsley, Robert Buckner *d* Clarence Brown *ph* William Daniels *m* Carmen Dragon
☆ Van Johnson, Paul Douglas, Joseph Calleia, Carlo Rizzo, Tudor Owen, Aldo Silvani, Dono Nardi

When Johnny Comes Marching Home
US 1942 73m bw
Universal (Bernard W. Burton)
A war hero on leave escapes formalities and returns to the theatrical boarding house he remembers.
And so to the puttin'-on-a-show finale: not bad of its kind.
w Oscar Brodney, Dorothy Bennett *d* Charles Lamont
☆ Allan Jones, Jane Frazee, Gloria Jean, Donald O'Connor, Peggy Ryan, Phil Spitalny and his all-girl orchestra

When Knights Were Bold
GB 1929 80m (24 fps) bw silent
Herbert Wilcox
An incompetent heir dreams that he lives in medieval times.
Naïve romp which pleased at the time.
w Tim Whelan, Herbert Wilcox *play* Charles Marlow *d* Tim Whelan
☆ Nelson Keys, Miriam Seegar, Eric Bransby Williams
† Remade in 1936 with Jack Buchanan, Fay Wray and Garry Marsh; directed by Jack Raymond; for Max Schach.

When Ladies Meet *
US 1933 73m bw
MGM
A successful lady novelist falls in love with her married publisher.
Smartish comedy of manners which still has a sting.
w John Meehan, Leon Gordon *play* Rachel Crothers *d* Harry Beaumont *ph* Ray June *ad* Cedric Gibbons
☆ *Ann Harding*, Robert Montgomery, *Myrna Loy, Alice Brady*, Frank Morgan, Martin Burton, Luis Alberni

'Nice production. Well-spaced comedy helps, and picture should be an outstander.' – *Variety*

Cedric Gibbons

When Ladies Meet
US 1941 108m bw
MGM (Robert Z. Leonard, Orville O. Dull)
Over-produced and very talkative remake of the above.
w S. K. Lauren, Anita Loos *d* Robert Z. Leonard *ph* Robert Planck *m* Bronislau Kaper *ad* Cedric Gibbons, Randall Duell
☆ Joan Crawford, Robert Taylor, Greer Garson, Spring Byington, Herbert Marshall, Rafael Storm, Olaf Hytten
Cedric Gibbons, Randall Duell

When London Sleeps
GB 1932 78m bw
APD/Twickenham (Julius Hagen)
An unscrupulous Hampstead gambler kidnaps the adopted daughter of a travelling showman, who is heiress to a fortune.
Stilted melodrama, with direction to match.
w H. Fowler Mear, Bernard Merivale *play* Charles Darrel *d* Leslie S. Hiscott *ph* Basil Emmott *md* W. L. Trytel *ad* James Carter *ed* Jack Harris
☆ Harold French, Francis L. Sullivan, Rene Ray, Alexander Field, Ben Field, A. Bromley Davenport, Herbert Lomas, Barbara Everest

'Let the journey take you there.'
When Love Comes
New Zealand 1998 94m colour
Millivres/MF (Michele Fantl, Jonathan Dowling)
With her career in the doldrums, a middle-aged singer leaves her lover in the US to return to New Zealand, where she meets an old friend whose own love affair is going badly.
Drama set in a pop world of drugs and gay sex, in which its superficial characters endlessly examine the minutiae of their mundane lives.
w Garth Maxwell, Rex Pelgrim, Peter Wells *d* Garth Maxwell *ph* Darryl Ward *m* Chris Anderton *pd* Grace Mok *ed* Cushla Dillon
☆ Rena Owen (Katie), Dean O'Gorman (Mark), Simon Prast (Stephen), Sophia Hawthorne (Sally), Nancy Brunning (Fig), Simon Westaway (Eddie)

'The film depends fatally on us finding other people's self-pity interesting.' – *Philip French, Observer*

When Love Is Young
US 1937 75m bw
Universal (Robert Presnell)
A Broadway stage star returns to her home town in hopes of marrying her old beau, but he is found wanting.
Very moderate comedy to fill a programme.
w Eve Greene, Joseph Fields *story Class Prophecy* by Eleanore Griffin *d* Hal Mohr
☆ Virginia Bruce, Kent Taylor, Walter Brennan, Greta Meyer, Christian Rub, Sterling Holloway, Nydia Westman

'Will provide average filmgoers with averagely good amusement.' – *Variety*

When My Baby Smiles at Me
US 1948 98m Technicolor
TCF (George Jessel)
A vaudevillian goes on the skids but is saved by his wife.
Routine musical handling of a dreary drama previously filmed as Dance of Life *(1929) and* Swing High Swing Low *(qv).*
w Lamar Trotti *play Burlesque* by George Manker Walters, Arthur Hopkins *d* Walter Lang *ph* Harry Jackson *md* Alfred Newman
☆ Betty Grable, Dan Dailey, Jack Oakie, June Havoc, Richard Arlen, James Gleason, Jean Wallace
Alfred Newman; Dan Dailey

When New York Sleeps: see *Now I'll Tell*

When Night Is Falling
Canada 1995 96m colour
Alliance/Crucial (Barbara Tranter)
A teacher of mythology unexpectedly falls in love with a seductive female circus performer, which changes her attitude to the values of the Christian college where she works, and to the theologian she planned to marry.
Good-looking, intense, serious drama of sexual confusions that founders on overwrought dialogue and its failure to explore the issues of morality and individual choice it raises; its attempt at magic realism, reinterpreting the myth of Cupid and Psyche, is even less successful.
wd Patricia Rozema *ph* Douglas Koch *m* Lesley Barber *pd* John Dondertman *ed* Susan Shipton
☆ Pascale Bussières, Rachael Crawford, David Fox, Tracy Wright, Don McKellar, Henry Czerny

'Ultimate proof that ravishing photography, crisp cutting and a finely wrought score can't paper over a feeble script.' – *Derek Elley, Variety*

When Saturday Comes
GB 1996 97m colour
Guild/Capitol/A Pint O' Bitter (James Daly, Christopher Lambert)
In Sheffield, a brewery worker's ambitions to be a professional footballer are fulfilled.
Risible drama that lacks all credibility, though those who dream of scoring a hat-trick on their debut may enjoy it.
wd Maria Giese *story* James Daly *ph* Gerry Fisher *m* Anne Dudley *pd* Hugo Luczyc-Wyhowski *ed* George Akers
☆ Sean Bean, Emily Lloyd, Pete Postlethwaite, John McEnery, Ann Bell, Melanie Hill, Craig Kelly, David Leland

'You can't believe any of this tosh for an instant: it's like *Rocky* Blu-tacked to Northern England and washed down with Tennents Extra.' – *James Cameron-Wilson, Film Review*

When Strangers Marry *
US 1944 67m bw
Monogram (Maurice King)
aka: *Betrayed*
A young bride in New York discovers that she may have married a murderer.
Much-praised second feature: a bit stodgy now, but still entertaining.
w Philip Yordan, Dennis Cooper *d William Castle* *ph* Ira Morgan *m* Dimitri Tiomkin
☆ Dean Jagger, Kim Hunter, Robert Mitchum, Neil Hamilton, Lou Lubin, Milt Kibbee, Dewey Robinson

'The obviousness of the low budget is completely overcome by the solid craftsmanship of the direction, script, music, editing and performances.' – *Don Miller*

'Taking it as a whole I have seldom for years now seen one hour so energetically and sensibly used in a film.' – *James Agee*

When the Bough Breaks
GB 1947 81m bw
GFD/Gainsborough (Betty Box)
The bewildered wife of a bigamist allows her child to be adopted and then regrets it.
Peg's Paper *stuff in the then-accepted Gainsborough tradition.*
w Peter Rogers *story* Moie Charles, Herbert Victor *d* Lawrence Huntington *ph* Bryan Langley *m* Clifton Parker *ad* John Elphick *ed* Gordon Hales
☆ Patricia Roc, Rosamund John, Bill Owen, Patrick Holt, Brenda Bruce, Leslie Dwyer, Jane Hylton

When the Cat's Away **
France 1996 91m colour
Artificial Eye/Vertigo/France 2 (Aïssa Djabri, Farid Lahoussa, Manuel Munz)
original title: *Chacun cherche son chat*
The adventures, amorous and otherwise, of a woman searching for her missing cat.
Slight but enjoyable drama of life among fashionable young Parisians.
wd Cédric Klapisch *ph* Benoît Delhomme *ad* Françoise Emmanuelli
☆ Garance Clavel, Zinedine Soualem, Renée Lecalm, Olivier Py, Joël Brisse, Arapimou, Rambo

'The type of film that several viewings later will still give something new to the audience.' – *Marianne Gray, Film Review*

When the Daltons Rode *
US 1940 80m bw
Universal
Adventures of the Dalton Gang.
Good standard Western with whitewashed bad men for heroes.
w Harold Shumate, Stuart Anthony, Lester Cole *d* George Marshall *ph* Hal Mohr *m* Frank Skinner
☆ Randolph Scott, Kay Francis, Brian Donlevy, Andy Devine, George Bancroft, Stuart Erwin

When the Door Opened: see *Escape (1940)*

When the Legends Die **
US 1972 105m DeLuxe
Fox-Rank/Sagaponack (Stuart Miller)
An ageing rodeo rider befriends a young Indian and teaches him the tricks of the trade.
Downbeat tale of the souring of the American dream, with fine performances from the two leads.
w Robert Dozier *novel* Hal Borland *d* Stuart Miller *ph* Richard H. Kline *m* Glenn Paxton *md* Lionel Newman *ad* Angelo Graham *ed* Louis San Andres
☆ Richard Widmark, Frederic Forrest, Luana Anders, Vito Scotti, Herbert Nelson, John War Eagle

When the Lights go on Again
US 1944 70m bw
PRC (Leon Fromkess)
An ex-marine comes home with shell shock.
One of the first films to deal with the problems of war veterans: a modest effort, but sincere.
w Milton Lazarus *story* Frank Craven *d* William K. Howard
☆ James Lydon, Barbara Belden, Grant Mitchell, Dorothy Peterson, Regis Toomey

'In 1996 one investigative reporter uncovered the truth and changed a nation.'
'When the truth is hidden. when the witness is silenced.'
When the Sky Falls
Ireland/GB 1999 107m colour
TCF/Icon/Irish Screen/Sky/IFB/Redeemable (Nigel Warren-Green, Michael Wearing)
A Dublin journalist undertakes a dangerous investigation into the gangster who controls the city's drug trade.
A thriller based on fact, though it plays like a standard gangster movie, which may add to its immediate appeal but is a serious limitation to its wider purpose.
w Michael Sheridan, Ronan Gallagher, Colum McCann *additional dialogue* Guy Andrews *d* John Mackenzie *ph* Seamus Deasy *m* Pol Brennan *pd* Mark Geraghty *ed* Graham Walker
☆ Joan Allen (Sinead Hamilton), Mackey (Patrick Bergin), Liam Cunningham (John Cosgrave), Kevin McNally (Tom Hamilton), Jimmy Smallhorne (Mickey O'Fagan), Jason Barry (Dempsey), Gerard Flynn (Dave Hackett), Pete Postlethwaite (Martin Shaughnessy), Des McAleer (Jimmy Keaveney), Ruaidhri Conroy (Jamie Thornton)
† It is based on the life of Dublin crime reporter Veronica Guerin who was shot dead while sitting in her in car at traffic lights in 1996, probably on the orders of drug dealers whom she had exposed.

When the Whales Came
GB 1989 100m Fujicolour
Fox/Golden Swan/Central Television (Simon Channing Williams)
In 1914, fishermen on one of the Scilly Isles are persuaded by a recluse and a boy to save a beached whale, an act which brings them luck.
Ecologically sound, dramatically dull story, not helped by its insistently soft focus photography.
w Michael Morpurgo *novel* Why the Whales Came by Michael Morpurgo *d* Clive Rees *ph* Robert Paynter *m* Christopher Gunning *pd* Bruce Grimes *ed* Andrew Boulton
☆ Helen Mirren, Paul Scofield, David Suchet, Barbara Jefford, David Threlfall, Barbara Ewing, John Hallam, Jeremy Kemp, Max Rennie, Helen Pearce

When the Wind Blows *
GB 1987 85m TVC Color
Film Four/Penguin/TVC/NFFC (John Coates)
An elderly man and wife fail to cope with nuclear destruction.
Cartoon picturization of a popular book; the film was less likely, despite its merits, to find an audience.
w Raymond Briggs *book* Raymond Briggs *d* Jimmy Murakami *m* Roger Waters *ed* John Cary
☆ Featuring the voices of John Mills, Peggy Ashcroft

When Thief Meets Thief: see *Jump for Glory*

When Time Ran Out
US 1980 109m Technicolor Panavision
Warner/Irwin Allen
Inhabitants of a South Sea island are threatened by a volcano.
Incredibly inept disaster movie, with all clichés on hand in the characters of some downcast actors.
w Carl Foreman, Stirling Silliphant *novel The Day the World Ended* by Max Morgan Witts and Gordon Thomas *d* James Goldstone *ph* Fred J. Koenekamp *m* Lalo Schifrin *pd* Philip M. Jefferies *ed* Edward Biery, Freeman A. Davies
☆ Paul Newman, Jacqueline Bisset, William Holden, Edward Albert, Burgess Meredith, Valentina Cortesa, Red Buttons, Alex Karras, Ernest Borgnine, James Franciscus
'Disaster movies don't come any more disastrous than this.' – *Tom Milne, MFB*
† Said to have cost 22 million dollars and taken less than two.
costumes (Paul Zastupnevich)

When Tomorrow Comes **
US 1939 82m bw
Universal (John M. Stahl)
A waitress falls for a concert pianist with a mad wife.
Fascinating star romantic drama, a successful follow-up to Love Affair*; full of clichés, but impeccably set and acted. The stuff that Hollywood dreams were made of.*
w Dwight Taylor *story* James M. Cain *d John M. Stahl ph* John Mescall *m* Charles Previn *ed* Milton Carruth
☆ *Charles Boyer, Irene Dunne, Barbara O'Neil,* Nydia Westman, Onslow Stevens
'A persuasive love story ... a director's achievement.' – *Variety*
† The same story was remade twice in 1956, as *Serenade* and *Interlude*, and in 1968 as *Interlude* (all qv).

When We Are Married *
GB 1942 98m bw
British National (John Baxter)
In 1890s Yorkshire, three couples celebrating their silver wedding are told they were never legally married.
A very funny play smartly filmed with a superb cast of character actors.
w Austin Melford, Barbara K. Emery *play J. B. Priestley d* Lance Comfort *ph* James Wilson
☆ Raymond Huntley, Marian Spencer, Lloyd Pearson, Olga Lindo, Ernest Butcher, Ethel Coleridge, Sydney Howard, Barry Morse, Lesley Brook, Marjorie Rhodes, Charles Victor, Cyril Smith, George Carney

'The True Story Of The Rumble In The Jungle.'
When We Were Kings **
US 1996 88m Technicolor
Polygram/DAS (David Sonenberg, Leon Gast)
Documentary of the world heavyweight fight between the challenger Muhammad Ali and champion George Foreman, which was staged in Zaire in 1974 and marked the emergence of promoter Don King as a not-always-benign influence on the sport.
Enjoyable celebration of a great athlete, even if it is released so long after the event as to lose some of its significance.
d Leon Gast *ph* Maryse Alberti, Paul Goldsmith, Kevin Keating, Albert Maysles, Roderick Young. *ed* Leon Gast, Taylor Hackford, Jeffrey Levy-Hinte, Keith Robinson
☆ Muhammad Ali, George Foreman, Don King, President Mobutu Sese Seko, Spike Lee, Norman Mailer
'A genuinely inspiring film about a real twentieth-century hero.' – *Sight and Sound*
† The director originally planned a film about the concert, featuring James Brown, B. B. King, Miriam Makeba and others, that accompanied the fight; problems of finance and copyright held up that material for many years, and the footage was then fashioned into a documentary about the fight itself.
documentary

When Willie Comes Marching Home *
US 1950 82m bw
TCF (Fred Kohlmar)
During World War II, events suddenly transform a small-town air training instructor into a war hero.
Awkwardly paced comedy which could have been much funnier but does amuse in fits and starts.
w Mary Loos, Richard Sale *d* John Ford *ph* Leo Tover *m* Alfred Newman
☆ *Dan Dailey*, Colleen Townshend, Corinne Calvet, William Demarest, Evelyn Varden, James Lydon, Mae Marsh, Lloyd Corrigan
original story (Sy Gomberg)

When Worlds Collide
US 1951 82m Technicolor
Paramount (George Pal)
Another planet is found to be rushing inevitably towards Earth, but before the collision a few people escape in a space ship.
Stolid science fiction with a spectacular but not marvellous climax following seventy minutes of inept talk.
w Sydney Boehm *novel* Philip Wylie, Edwin Balmer *d* Rudolph Maté *ph* John Seitz, W. Howard Greene *m* Leith Stevens
☆ Richard Derr, Barbara Rush, Larry Keating, Peter Hanson, John Hoyt
special effects
John Seitz, W. Howard Greene

When You're in Love *
US 1937 110m bw
Columbia (Everett Riskin)
GB title: *For You Alone*
A European opera singer takes on a husband in order to get into the United States.
Pleasing musical star vehicle with comedy touches.
wd Robert Riskin *ph* Joseph Walker *md* Alfred Newman
☆ *Grace Moore*, Cary Grant, Aline MacMahon, Henry Stephenson, Thomas Mitchell, Catherine Doucet, Luis Alberni, Emma Dunn
'Nice musical with fair quota of giggles ... should do nice biz.' – *Variety*

'Two lovers caught between convention and passion...'
Where Angels Fear to Tread
GB 1991 112m Eastmancolor
Rank/Sovereign/LWT/Stagescreen/Compact (Derek Granger)
A brother and sister travel to Italy to bring back the baby of their sister-in-law who defied family opposition to marry a young Italian and died in childbirth.
Vapid and disjointed adaptation, glossily made but not helped by mannered performances.
w Tim Sullivan, Derek Granger, Charles Sturridge *d* Charles Sturridge *ph* Michael Coulter *m* Rachel Portman *pd* Simon Holland *ed* Peter Coulson
☆ Helena Bonham Carter, Judy Davis, Rupert Graves, Giovanni Guidelli, Barbara Jefford, Helen Mirren, Thomas Wheatley, Sophie Kullman
'A story about fine ironies and "fine" behaviour becomes a genre exercise in fine acting and even finer linen.' – *MFB*

Where Angels Go, Trouble Follows
US 1968 95m Eastmancolor
Columbia/William Frye
Nuns from a convent school take pupils to a California youth rally, and learn a thing or two.
Peripatetic comedy, rather frantically assembled; a sequel to The Trouble with Angels.
w Blanche Hanalis *d* James Neilson *ph* Sam Leavitt *m* Lalo Schifrin
☆ Rosalind Russell, Stella Stevens, Binnie Barnes, Mary Wickes, Milton Berle, Arthur Godfrey, Robert Taylor, Van Johnson, Susan St James

Where Are Your Children?
US 1943 78m bw
Monogram (Jeffrey Bernerd)
A wandering rich boy takes up with a hash slinger, and they wind up suspected of murder ...
An 'awful warning' melodrama, risible now.
w Hilary Lynn, George W. Sayre *d* William Nigh
☆ Jackie Cooper, Gale Storm, Patricia Morison, John Litel, Gertrude Michael, Addison Richards, Betty Blythe

Where Danger Lives
US 1950 84m bw
RKO (Irving Cummings Jnr)
A doctor falls in love with a murderous patient and is drawn into her schemes.
Standard film noir of its time, competent enough in its depressing way.
w Charles Bennett *story* Leo Rosten *d* John Farrow *ph* Nicholas Musuraca *m* Roy Webb
☆ Faith Domergue, Robert Mitchum, Claude Rains, Maureen O'Sullivan, Charles Kemper

Where Do We Go from Here? *
US 1945 77m Technicolor
TCF (William Perlberg)
A writer stumbles on a genie who takes him through periods of American history, including a voyage with Christopher Columbus.
Well-staged and rather funny charade with at least one memorable song.
w Morrie Ryskind *d* Gregory Ratoff *ph* Leon Shamroy *m* David Raksin *songs* Kurt Weill, Ira Gershwin
☆ Fred MacMurray, June Haver, Joan Leslie, Gene Sheldon, Anthony Quinn, Carlos Ramirez, Fortunio Bonanova, Alan Mowbray, Herman Bing, Otto Preminger
'Nine parts heavy facetiousness to one part very good fun.' – *James Agee*

'Don't tell your doctor about this film – it could give him ideas!'
Where Does it Hurt?
US 1971 88m colour
Josef Shaftel (Rod Amateau, William Schwarz)
Adventures of a profiteering hospital administrator.
Dislikeable, plodding smut in the form of black comedy.
wd Rod Amateau *novel The Operator* by Budd Robinson, Rod Amateau *ph* Brick Marquard *m* Keith Allison
☆ Peter Sellers, Jo Ann Pflug, Rick Lenz, Eve Bruce

Where Eagles Dare **
GB 1969 155m Metrocolor Panavision 70
MGM/Winkast (Elliott Kastner)
During World War II, seven British paratroopers land in the Bavarian Alps to rescue a high-ranking officer from an impregnable castle.
Archetypal schoolboy adventure, rather unattractively photographed but containing a sufficient variety of excitements.
w Alistair MacLean *novel* Alistair MacLean *d* Brian G. Hutton *ph* Arthur Ibbetson, H. A. R. Thompson *m* Ron Goodwin
☆ Richard Burton, Clint Eastwood, Mary Ure, Patrick Wymark, Michael Hordern, Donald Houston, Peter Barkworth, Robert Beatty

Where It's At
US 1969 106m DeLuxe
UA/Frank Ross
The owner of a Las Vegas gambling hotel tries to make his son take an interest in the business.
Flaccid comedy drama which belies its credits.
wd Garson Kanin *ph* Burnett Guffey *m* Benny Olsen
☆ David Janssen, Rosemary Forsyth, Robert Drivas, Brenda Vaccaro

Where Love Has Gone *
US 1964 114m Techniscope
Paramount/Embassy (Joseph E. Levine)
A middle-aged man is appalled to hear that his teenage daughter has killed her mother's lover.

Squalid, glossy pulp fiction lightly based on the Lana Turner case, distinguished only by the game performances of its leading ladies.
w John Michael Hayes *novel* Harold Robbins *d* Edward Dmytryk *ph* Joe MacDonald *m* Walter Scharf
☆ Susan Hayward, Bette Davis, Mike Connors, Joey Heatherton, Jane Greer, George Macready
'A typical Robbins pastiche of newspaper clippings liberally shellacked with sentiment and glued with sex.' – *Newsweek*
title song (*m*James Van Heusen, *ly*Sammy Cahn)

Where No Vultures Fly *
GB 1951 107m Technicolor
Ealing (Leslie Norman)
US title: *Ivory Hunter*
Adventures of an East African game warden.
Pleasantly improving family film, nicely shot on location; a sequel, West of Zanzibar, *was less impressive.*
w W. P. Lipscomb, Ralph Smart, Leslie Norman *d* Harry Watt *ph* Geoffrey Unsworth *m* Alan Rawsthorne
☆ Anthony Steel, Dinah Sheridan, Harold Warrender, Meredith Edwards
'These expeditionary films are really journalistic jobs. You get sent out to a country by the studio, stay as long as you can without getting fired, and a story generally crops up.' – *Harry Watt*
'No one will wonder why it was chosen for this year's royal film show. It is not sordid, as so many new films are; it has a theme that almost everyone will find appealing; and the corner of the Empire where it is set is fresh, beautiful and exciting to look at.' – *Daily Telegraph*

Where Sinners Meet
US 1934 68m bw
RKO
GB title: *The Dover Road*
A millionaire eccentric kidnaps eloping couples to find out whether they are making a mistake.
Stagebound whimsy saddled with an absurd American title.
w H. W. Hanemann *play* The Dover Road by A. A. Milne *d* J. Walter Ruben
☆ Diana Wynyard, Clive Brook, Billie Burke, Reginald Owen, Alan Mowbray, Gilbert Emery, Phyllis Barry
'Despite fine performances and good production, very dubious.' – *Variety*

Where Sleeping Dogs Lie
US 1991 91m colour
Columbia TriStar/August (Mario Sotela)
A writer moves into a house where a family was slaughtered and discovers that his new tenant is the murderer.
A dreary thriller that contains a great deal of posturing but not much sense; it is best left alone.
w Charles Finch, Yolande Turner *d* Charles Finch *ph* Miles Cooke *m* Hans Zimmer, Mark Mancina *pd* Eve Cauley *ed* B. J. Sears, Gene M. Gamache
☆ Dylan McDermott, Tom Sizemore, Sharon Stone, Charles Finch, Mary Woronov, Ron Karabatsos

Where the Boys Are
US 1960 99m Metrocolor Cinemascope
MGM/Euterpe (Joe Pasternak)
Four college girls spend the Easter vacation near a Florida military post in search of conquests.
Mindless, frothy youth musical, quite smoothly done.
w George Wells *novel* Glendon Swarthout *d* Henry Levin *ph* Robert Bronner *m* George Stoll
☆ George Hamilton, Dolores Hart, Paula Prentiss, Jim Hutton, Yvette Mimieux, Connie Francis, Frank Gorshin, Chill Wills, Barbara Nichols

Where the Boys Are
US 1984 94m colour
ITC/TriStar (Allan Carr)
The 1960 musical becomes a teenage sex movie.
Neither version has much to do with the original novel.
w Stu Krieger, Jeff Burkhart *d* Hy Averback *ph* James A. Contner *m* Sylvester Levay *ed* Melvin Shapiro, Bobbie Shapiro
☆ Lisa Hartman, Lorna Luft, Wendy Schaal, Lynn-Holly Johnson, Russell Todd, Howard McGillin
'A travesty … insufferably coy.' – *Tom Milne, MFB*

Where the Buffalo Roam
US 1980 98m Technicolor Panavision
Universal (Art Linson)
A drug-crazed journalist takes a trip through Nixon's America.
Frenetic, rarely funny comedy, based on the work of self-styled 'gonzo journalist' Hunter S. Thompson.
w John Kaye *d* Art Linson *ph* Tak Fujimoto *m* Mal Young *pd* Richard Sawyer *ed* Christopher Greenburg
☆ Peter Boyle, Bill Murray, Bruno Kirby, Rene Auberjonois, R. G. Armstrong, Rafael Campos, Leonard Frey

Where the Day Takes You
US 1992 103m Foto-Kem
New Line/Cinetel (Paul Hertzberg)
A youth on parole tries to keep the homeless gang of delinquents he leads out of trouble.
Desultory 'teen drama of an unsympathetic, attudinizing group.
w Michael Hitchcock, Kurt Voss, Marc Rocco *d* Marc Rocco *ph* King Baggot *m* Mark Morgan *pd* Kirk Petrucelli *ed* Russell Livingstone
☆ Dermot Mulroney, Lara Flynn Boyle, Balthazar Getty, Sean Astin, James LeGros, Ricki Lake, Kyle MacLachlan, Stephen Tobolowsky, Will Smith, Christian Slater (uncredited)
'Inevitably winds up giving the runaway's life the kind of romantic-tragic scope that appeals to troubled teens.' – *Variety*

Where the Green Ants Dream
West Germany 1984 100m colour
Werner Herzog Filmproduktion/ZDF (Lucki Stipetić)
original title: *Wo die grünen Ameisen träumen*
Aborigines object to a mining company developing one of their sacred sites.
Dull drama that engages its subject matter only in a desultory way.
w Werner Herzog, Bob Ellis *d* Werner Herzog *ph* Jörg Schmidt-Reitwein *m* Fauré, Wagner and others *pd* Ulrich Bergfelder *ed* Beate Mainka-Jellinghaus
☆ Bruce Spence, Wandjuk Marika, Roy Marika, Ray Barrett, Norman Kaye, Colleen Clifford

Where the Heart Is *
US 1990 94m Technicolor
Buena Vista/Touchstone (John Boorman)
A tycoon orders his children to leave their life of luxury and live in a slum tenement.
Domestic comedy with some heavy-handed humour that is never funny enough to be entertaining.
w John Boorman, Telsche Boorman *d* John Boorman *ph* Peter Suschitzky *m* Peter Martin *pd* Carol Spier *ed* Ian Crafford
☆ Dabney Coleman, Uma Thurman, Joanna Cassidy, Crispin Glover, Suzy Amis, Christopher Plummer

'Laughter is harder… Friendship is stronger… Trust is deeper… When it comes from the heart.'
Where the Heart Is
US 2000 120m DeLuxe
TCF/Wind Dancer (Susan Cartsonis, David McFadzean, Patricia Whitcher, Matt Williams)
Abandoned by her boyfriend, a pregnant teenage girl moves into a Wal-Mart, has her baby and becomes a minor celebrity.
Melodramatic soap opera, so full of hapless accidents, from killer tornados to legless alcoholics, as to be unintentionally funny; it attempts to convince audience of the joys of single motherhood.
w Lowell Ganz, Babaloo Mandel *novel* Billie Letts *d* Matt Williams *ph* Richard Greatrex *m* Mason Daring *pd* Paul Peters *ed* Ian Crafford
☆ Natalie Portman (Novalee Nation), Ashley Judd (Lexie Çoop), Stockard Channing (Sister Husband), Joan Cusack (Ruth Meyers), James Frain (Forney Hall), Dylan Bruno (Willy Jack Pickens), Keith David (Moses Whitecotten), Sally Field (Mama Lil), Richard Jones (Mr Sprock)
'An epic of unwed motherhood that is almost stunning in its sustained superficiality. Banal and trite where it could have been insightful and emotionally truthful.' – *Todd McCarthy, Variety*

Where the Hot Wind Blows
France/Italy 1958 125m bw
MGM/Cité Films/Groupe des Quatre/Titanus (Jacques Bar)
original title: *La Loi*
In an Adriatic port, a voluptuous young girl is pursued by the aged local squire, a racketeer, her brother-in-law and a young agriculturist. Guess who wins her.
Hoary melodrama with the emphasis on virility and illicit passion. Long and tiresome, it failed to justify the pretensions with which it announced itself at the time.
w Jules Dassin, Diego Fabbri *novel* Roger Vailland *d* Jules Dassin *ph* Otello Martelli *m* Roman Vlad
☆ Gina Lollobrigida, Yves Montand, Marcello Mastroianni, Pierre Brasseur, Melina Mercouri, Paolo Stoppa
† An English version was generally available.

Where the Lilies Bloom
US 1974 96m DeLuxe
Radnitz/Mattel Productions (Robert B. Radnitz)
Fearful of being sent to an institution, four children living in the Appalachians keep secret the death of their father and fend for themselves.
Slight but charming domestic drama which keeps sentimentality at bay for the most part.
w Earl Hamner Jnr *book* Vera and Bill Cleaver *d* William A. Graham *ph* Urs Furrer *m* Earl Scruggs *ad* Tambi Larsen *ed* O. Nicholas Brown
☆ Julie Gholson, Harry Dean Stanton, Jan Smithers, Matthew Burril, Helen Harmon, Sudie Bond, Rance Howard, Tom Spratley, Alice Beardsley, Helen Bragdon

'Another con. Another sting. Another day.'
Where The Money Is *
US 2000 90m DeLuxe
Gramercy/Intermedia/Pacific Film/Scott Free/IMF (Ridley Scott, Charles Weinstock, Chris Zarpas, Christopher Dorr)
An elderly robber is persuaded by a nurse in an old people's home to help her rob a bank.
Enjoyable small-scale caper with Newman having fun with his impersonation of senility.
w E. Max Frye, Topper Lilien, Carroll Cartwright *d* Marek Kanievska *ph* Thomas Burstyn *m* Mark Isham *pd* Andre Chamberland *ed* Sam Craven, Garth Craven, Dan Lebental *cos* Francesca Chamberland
☆ Paul Newman (Henry Manning), Linda Fiorentino (Carol), Dermot Mulroney (Wayne), Susan Barnes (Mrs Foster), Anne Pioniak (Mrs Tetlow), Bruce MacVittie (Karl), Irma St Paul (Mrs. Galer), Michel Perron (Guard), Dorothy Gordon (Mrs Norton)
'A formulaic caper-and-heist story with a bit of high concept thrown in.' – *John Sutherland*

Where the River Bends: see *Bend of the River*

Where the River Runs Black
US 1986 92m colour
MGM/IPI (Joe Roth, Harry Ufland)
In Brazil a Catholic priest tries to care for the wild, orphaned son of an Indian woman and a priest working in the rain forest.
Slight, sentimental, ecological fable, given over to lyrical nature photography rather than to story-telling.
w Peter Silverman, Neal Jimenez *book* David Kendall *d* Christopher Cain *ph* Juan-Ruiz Anchia *m* James Horner *pd* Marcos Flaksman *ed* Richard Chew
☆ Charles Durning, Peter Horton, Ajay Naidu, Conchata Ferrell, Castulo Guerra, Alessandro Rabelo

'A sweeping tale of one man's mission to preserve himself and his way of life.'
Where the Rivers Flow North *
US 1993 106m colour
Ulysse/Caledonia (Bess O'Brien, Jay Craven)
In Vermont in the 20s, a woodsman refuses to give up his land so that a new dam can be built.
Intermittently effective backwoods drama, with a deeply flawed protagonist who veers between violent protection of his environment and wilful destruction of it; Cardinal's performance, as a woman fighting to make space for her own life, keeps you watching until the end.
w Don Bredes, Jay Craven *novel* Howard Frank Mosher *d* Jay Craven *ph* Paul Ryan *pd* David Wasco
☆ Rip Torn, *Tantoo Cardinal*, Treat Williams, Michael J. Fox, Bill Raymond, John Griesemer, Mark Margolis, Dennis Mientka, Amy Wright

Where the Sidewalk Ends
US 1950 95m bw
TCF (Otto Preminger)
A tough policeman accidentally kills a suspect and tries to implicate a gang leader.
Gloomy policier with curious moral values.
w Rex Connor (Ben Hecht) *novel* William L. Stuart *d* Otto Preminger *ph* Joseph LaShelle *m* Cyril Mockridge
☆ Dana Andrews, Gene Tierney, Gary Merrill, Bert Freed, Tom Tully, Karl Malden, Ruth Donnelly, Craig Stevens, Robert Simon
'A pretty beefy affair, not calculated to the taste of customers who shrink from the sight of the male fist contacting with the male or female jawbone.' – *C. A. Lejeune*

Where the Spies Are
GB 1965 113m Metrocolor Panavision
MGM/Val Guest
A country doctor is bribed to become a spy by the promise of a car he greatly covets.
Patchy spy adventure which never settles into a comfortable style but provides occasional entertainment along its bumpy way.
w Wolf Mankowitz, Val Guest *novel* Passport to Oblivion by James Leasor *d* Val Guest *ph* Arthur Grant *m* Mario Nascimbene
☆ David Niven, Françoise Dorleac, Nigel Davenport, John Le Mesurier, Ronald Radd, Cyril Cusack, Eric Pohlmann

Where There's a Will *
GB 1936 81m bw
Gainsborough (Edward Black, Sidney Gilliat)
A seedy education expert sponges on his rich relations but redeems himself by rounding up gangsters at a Christmas party.
Rather slapdash star comedy with very good scenes along the way.
w Will Hay, Robert Edmunds, Ralph Spence *story* Leslie Arliss, Sidney Gilliat *d* William Beaudine *ph* Charles Van Enger *md* Louis Levy
☆ *Will Hay*, Hartley Power, Gibb McLaughlin, Graham Moffatt, Norma Varden, Gina Malo

Where There's a Will
GB 1955 79m bw
Film Locations/Eros
A London family inherits a dilapidated Devon farm and makes a go of it.
Slight comedy with pleasant players.
w R. F. Delderfield *play* R. F. Delderfield *d* Vernon Sewell *ph* Basil Emmott *m* Robert Sharples
☆ Kathleen Harrison, George Cole, Leslie Dwyer, Dandy Nichols, Ann Hanslip, Michael Shepley

'If you laugh yourself sick at this picture – sue Bob Hope!'
Where There's Life
US 1947 75m bw
Paramount (Paul Jones)
A timid New Yorker turns out to be heir to the throne of a Ruritanian country, and is harassed by spies of both sides.
Mild star comedy with slow patches.
w Allen Boretz, Melville Shavelson *d* Sidney Lanfield *ph* Charles Lang Jnr *md* Irvin Talbot
☆ Bob Hope, Signe Hasso, William Bendix, George Coulouris

Where Were You When the Lights Went Out? *
US 1968 94m Metrocolor Panavision
MGM (Everett Freeman, Martin Melcher)
New York's famous electrical blackout in 1965 has its effect on the life of a musical comedy star.
Cheerful sex farce with intriguing beginnings; the later confinement to one set is just a bit harmful.

w Everett Freeman, Karl Tunberg *play* Claude Magnier *d* Hy Averback *ph* Ellsworth Fredericks *m* Dave Grusin
☆ Doris Day, Terry-Thomas, Patrick O'Neal, Robert Morse, Lola Albright, Jim Backus, Ben Blue

Where's Charley? ★
GB 1952 97m Technicolor
Warner
An Oxford undergraduate impersonates the rich aunt of his best friend.
Slow and rather stately musical version of the famous farce Charley's Aunt, *unsatisfactorily shot on a mixture of poor sets and sunlit Oxford locations; worth cherishing for the ebullient performance of its over-age star.*
w John Monks Jnr *play* Brandon Thomas (via stage musical) *book* George Abbott *d* David Butler *ph* Erwin Hillier *m* Frank Loesser *ch* Michael Kidd
☆ *Ray Bolger*, Robert Shackleton, Mary Germaine, Allyn McLerie, Margaretta Scott, Horace Cooper

Where's Jack? ★
GB 1969 119m Eastmancolor
Paramount/Oakhurst (Stanley Baker)
In 18th-century London Jack Sheppard becomes a romantic highwayman at the behest of underworld leader Jonathan Wild.
Deliberately unromantic, squalid and 'realistic' period piece which takes no hold on the fancy despite the considerable care which was obviously taken in all departments.
w Rafe and David Newhouse *d* James Clavell *ph John Wilcox* *m* Elmer Bernstein *pd Cedric Dawe*
☆ Tommy Steele, Stanley Baker, Fiona Lewis, Alan Badel, Dudley Foster, Sue Lloyd, Noel Purcell

Where's Poppa? ★
US 1970 82m DeLuxe
Jerry Tokovsky/Marvin Worth
A Jewish lawyer's aged mother constantly harms his love life, and he considers various means of getting rid of her.
Much-censored black comedy which might have been funnier in a complete form. Even so, it has its moments.
w Robert Klane *novel* Robert Klane *d* Carl Reiner *ph* Jack Priestly *m* Jack Elliott
☆ George Segal, Ruth Gordon, Trish Van Devere, Ron Leibman

Where's That Fire? ★
GB 1939 73m bw
TCF (Edward Black)
An incompetent village fire brigade accidentally saves the crown jewels from thieves.
Routine but not despicable star comedy, long thought lost; flat patches are well separated by hilarious sequences.
w Marriott Edgar, Val Guest, J. O. C. Orton *d* Marcel Varnel *ph* Arthur Crabtree
☆ Will Hay, Moore Marriott, Graham Moffatt, Peter Gawthorne, Eric Clavering, Charles Hawtrey
'A superb sequence when they try to fix a pole in the station, otherwise not so funny.' – *Graham Greene*

Which Way to the Front?
US 1970 96m Technicolor
Warner/Jerry Lewis
In 1943, rejected as unfit for military service, the richest man in the world forms his own commando unit with other misfits and decides to kidnap Field Marshal Kesselring to sabotage the Nazis in Italy.
Wretchedly unfunny comedy, the cinematic equivalent of vanity publishing, providing its star with the opportunity to play two frenetic roles: a billionaire who resorts to mouthing gibberish when thwarted and a German commander who does much the same.
w Gerald Gardner, Dee Caruso, Richard Miller *d* Jerry Lewis *ph* W. Wallace Kelley *m* Louis Y. Brown *pd* John Beckman *ed* Russell Wiles
☆ Jerry Lewis, Jan Murray, John Wood, Steve Franken, Dack Rambo, Robert Middleton, Willie Davis, Kaye Ballard, Harold J. Stone, Paul Winchell, Sidney Miller (as Hitler)

W.H.I.F.F.S.
US 1975 92m Technicolor Panavision
Brut (C. O. Erickson)
GB title: *C.A.S.H.*
An impotent army veteran finds that a criminal career, helped by stolen army gas, helps his sex life.
Over-the-top comedy with vaguely anti-war and anti-pollution leanings.
w Malcolm Marmorstein *d* Ted Post *ph* David M. Walsh *m* John Cameron
☆ Elliott Gould, Eddie Albert, Harry Guardino, Godfrey Cambridge, Jennifer O'Neill
† Rather typical of the film was its ambiguous catch line: 'The biggest bang in history!'
song 'Now That We're in Love' (*m* George Barrie, *ly* Sammy Cahn)

While I Live
GB 1947 85m bw
Edward Dryhurst
reissue title: *The Dream of Olwen*
A Cornishwoman believes an amnesiac girl to be the reincarnation of her dead sister.
Silly melodrama which achieved phenomenal popularity, despite poor production, because of its haunting theme tune The Dream of Olwen *by Charles Williams.*
w John Harlow, Doreen Montgomery *play This Same Garden* by Robert Bell *d* John Harlow *ph* F. A. Young *m Charles Williams* *ad* Bernard Robinson *ed* Ray Poulton
☆ Tom Walls, Sonia Dresdel, Carol Raye, Clifford Evans, Patricia Burke, John Warwick, Edward Lexy
'What cannot be conveyed is the flatulence of the production, the haplessness of the players as they stray heavy-eyed through the sets like lost sheep with Tom Walls yapping around them like a knowing old collie dog.' – *Richard Winnington*

'A Girl leaves her door open ... A Stranger tiptoes in ... A big city newspaper blazes with murder headlines! Then the chase as newsmen and women feud with each other ... to be the first to find the killer!'
While the City Sleeps
US 1956 100m bw Superscope
RKO (Bert Friedlob)
Three chief executives of a newspaper empire are pitted against each other in a search for a murder scoop.
Star-packed but leaden-paced news bureau melodrama; a major disappointment considering the talent.
w Casey Robinson *novel The Bloody Spur* by Charles Einstein *d* Fritz Lang *ph* Ernest Laszlo *m* Herschel Burke Gilbert
☆ Dana Andrews, George Sanders, Ida Lupino, Sally Forrest, Thomas Mitchell, Rhonda Fleming, Vincent Price, Howard Duff, James Craig, Robert Warwick, John Barrymore Jnr

While the Patient Slept
US 1935 65m bw
First National
A nurse hired to look after a stricken millionaire finds herself in the middle of a murder case.
Announced as the first of a series of Clue Club Mysteries, this was derived from a source similar to, or possibly the same as, Miss Pinkerton *(qv). It sufficed.*
w Robert N. Lee *novel* Mignon G. Eberhart *d* Ray Enright
☆ Aline MacMahon, Guy Kibbee, Lyle Talbot, Patricia Ellis, Allen Jenkins, Gene Solow, Brown Holmes, Robert Barrat, Hobart Cavanaugh
'Seems probable that it will please wherever mysteries are liked.' – *Variety*

While the Sun Shines
GB 1946 81m bw
ABPC/International Screenplays (Anatole de Grunwald)
An American soldier and a young Frenchman seek to woo Lady Elizabeth away from her intended.
Mild wartime comedy, rather stagey and considerably undercast.
w Anatole de Grunwald, Terence Rattigan *play* Terence Rattigan *d* Anthony Asquith *ph* Jack Hildyard *m* Nicholas Brodszky *ad* Tom Morahan *ed* F. Wilson
☆ Brenda Bruce, Ronald Howard, Bonar Colleano, Ronald Squire, Barbara White, Margaret Rutherford, Miles Malleson, Joyce Grenfell

'A story about love at second sight.'
While You Were Sleeping ★
US 1995 103m Technicolor
Buena Vista/Hollywood/Caravan (Joe Roth, Roger Birnbaum)
After a lawyer is mugged and lies in hospital in a coma, his parents mistakenly believe that the woman who saved his life is his fiancée and welcome her into the family.
A pleasing romantic time-waster, with a leading performance that may charm, but it is not a film that will linger long in the memory.
w Daniel G. Sullivan, Frederic Lebow *d* Jon Turteltaub *ph* Phedon Papamichael *m* Randy Edelman *pd* Garreth Stover *ed* Bruce Green
☆ Sandra Bullock, Bill Pullman, Peter Gallagher, Peter Boyle, Jack Warden, Glynis Johns, Ally Walker
'There is really nothing exceptional in the film – no stand-out scenes, no real tension about the ending and the usual wallpaper film music that tells us what to feel. But Bullock, the real find of the movie, and Pullman pull it off neatly.' – *Derek Malcolm, Guardian*

The Whip Hand
US 1951 82m bw
RKO (Lewis J. Rachmil)
A fisherman finds himself unwelcome in a lonely town run by ex-Nazi, now communist, bacteriologists.
Preposterous, pretentious anti-communist low-budgeter, mildly enjoyable for its sheer gall.
w George Bricker, Frank L. Moss *ph* Nicholas Musuraca *m* Paul Sawtell *d/pd* William Cameron Menzies
☆ Elliott Reid, Carla Balenda, Edgar Barrier, Raymond Burr

Whiplash
US 1948 90m bw
Warner (William Jacobs)
A painter becomes a prizefighter.
Hokey, unpersuasive romantic melodrama.
w Maurice Geraghty, Harriet Frank Jnr *d* Lewis Seiler *ph* Peverell Marley *m* Franz Waxman
☆ Dane Clark, Alexis Smith, Zachary Scott, Eve Arden, Jeffrey Lynn, S. Z. Sakall, Alan Hale, Douglas Kennedy

'Never underestimate the power of a woman.'
Whipped
US 2000 82m Technicolor
Pathé/Hi-Rez (Peter M. Cohen)
Three compulsive seducers get their come-uppance when they all date the same woman.
Slender, foul-mouthed, misogynistic comedy that is no fun.
d Peter M. Cohen *ph* Peter B. Kowalski *m* Michael Montes *pd* Katherine M. Szilagyi *ed* Tom McArdle
☆ Amanda Peet (Mia), Brian Van Holt (Brad), Judah Domke (Eric), Zorie Barber (Zeke), Jonathan Abrahams (Jonathan), Callie Thorne (Liz)
'Grotesquely smutty and obnoxiously overbearing, this is a pitiful excuse for a comedy.' – *Joe Leydon, Variety*

Whipsaw ★
US 1935 88m bw
MGM (Harry Rapf)
A G-man infiltrates a gang by wooing its girl member.
Fairly snappy romantic drama which further established both its stars.
w Howard Emmett Rogers *d* Sam Wood *ph* James Wong Howe *m* William Axt
☆ Spencer Tracy, Myrna Loy, Harvey Stephens, Clay Clement, William Harrigan
'Should do okay biz ... romance and sex angles mingling with the light touch of sophistication so popular nowadays carries events along at a speedy pace that is unabated until the fadeout.' – *Variety*

Whirlpool
US 1934 69m bw
Columbia
A convict is released and makes contact with the daughter who never knew him.
Heavily plotted melodrama with an unhappy ending; technically quite proficient.
w Dorothy Howell, Ethel Hill, Howard Emmett Rogers *d* Roy William Neill
☆ Jack Holt, Jean Arthur, Allen Jenkins, Donald Cook, Lila Lee, John Miljan, Ward Bond
'One of the most surefire father and daughter stories ever screened, with heart interest running high throughout ... well above fair in entertainment appeal.' – *Variety*

Whirlpool ★
US 1950 98m bw
TCF (Otto Preminger)
A girl is accused of a murder committed by her hypnotist, who has willed himself out of a hospital bed.
Silly murder melodrama; glossy production makes it entertaining.
w Lester Barstow, Andrew Solt *novel* Guy Endore *d* Otto Preminger *ph* Arthur Miller *m* David Raksin
☆ Gene Tierney, *José Ferrer*, Richard Conte, Charles Bickford, Barbara O'Neil, Eduard Franz, Fortunio Bonanova
'It is sometimes difficult to discover from Miss Tierney's playing whether she is or is not under hypnosis.' – *MFB*
† Lester Barstow = Ben Hecht.

Whirlpool
GB 1959 95m Eastmancolor
Rank (George Pitcher)
A killer escapes in Cologne; his girlfriend separates from him and gets a lift down the Rhine in a barge; the trip reforms her and she betrays her lover.
Modestly attractive travelogue with the burden of a very boring melodrama.
w Lawrence P. Bachmann *novel The Lorelei* by Lawrence P. Bachmann *d* Lewis Allen *ph* Geoffrey Unsworth *m* Ron Goodwin
☆ Juliette Greco, O. W. Fischer, William Sylvester, Marius Goring, Muriel Pavlow

Whisky Galore ★★★★
GB 1948 82m bw
Ealing (Monja Danischewsky)
US title: *Tight Little Island*
During World War II, a ship full of whisky is wrecked on a small Hebridean island, and the local customs and excise man has his hands full.
Marvellously detailed, fast-moving, well-played and attractively photographed comedy which firmly established the richest Ealing vein.
w Compton Mackenzie, Angus MacPhail *novel* Compton Mackenzie *d Alexander Mackendrick* *ph Gerald Gibbs* *m Ernest Irving*
☆ Basil Radford, Joan Greenwood, Jean Cadell, Gordon Jackson, James Robertson Justice, Wylie Watson, John Gregson, Morland Graham, Duncan Macrae, Catherine Lacey, Bruce Seton, Henry Mollinson, Compton Mackenzie, A. E. Matthews
'Brilliantly witty and fantastic, but wholly plausible.' – *Sunday Chronicle*
† Fourteen whisky bottles, said to be the last surviving from the wreck of the SS *Politician*, the real-life shipwreck that inspired the film, were sold in 1993 at a Glasgow auction for £12,012, with a bottle of Haig Dimple fetching £1,210.

The Whisperers
GB 1966 106m bw
UA/Seven Pines (Michael S. Laughlin, Ronald Shedlo)
An old lady hears voices and is put upon by her son, her wandering husband, and various others.
Interesting but cold and finally unsatisfactory character melodrama; even the acting, though in a sense admirable, is too genteel.
w Bryan Forbes *novel* Robert Nicolson *d* Bryan Forbes *ph* Gerry Turpin *m* John Barry
☆ *Edith Evans*, Eric Portman, Avis Bunnage, Nanette Newman, Gerald Sim, Ronald Fraser
Edith Evans
Gerry Turpin; Edith Evans

Whispering City
Canada 1947 95m bw
Quebec/Eagle Lion
A girl reporter has dangerous information.
Fairly watchable mystery, all Canadian apart from the three leads.
w Rian James, Leonard Lee *d* Fedor Ozep
☆ Paul Lukas, Mary Anderson, Helmut Dantine, John Pratt, George Alexander

Whispering Ghosts
US 1942 75m bw
TCF (Sol M. Wurtzel)
A radio detective tackles the unsolved murder of an old sea captain.
No ghosts are evident, and not much plot, in this slow mystery comedy which failed to do for Berle what The Cat and the Canary *did for Hope.*
w Lou Breslow *d* Alfred Werker
☆ Milton Berle, Brenda Joyce, John Carradine, John Shelton, Willie Best

'The epic spectacle of America's most flaming era!'
Whispering Smith
US 1948 88m Technicolor
Paramount (Mel Epstein)
A government agent investigating robberies finds his friend is implicated.
Fairly entertaining detective Western.
w Frank Butler, Karl Lamb *novel* Frank H. Spearman *d* Leslie Fenton *ph* Ray Rennahan *m* Adolph Deutsch
☆ Alan Ladd, Robert Preston, Brenda Marshall, Donald Crisp, William Demarest, Fay Holden, Murvyn Vye, Frank Faylen

Whispering Smith Hits London
GB 1951 82m bw
Exclusive/Hammer (Anthony Hinds)
US title: *Whispering Smith vs. Scotland Yard*
An American detective in London investigates the case of a suicide which may be murder.
Tolerable programmer of its time: competence without inspiration.
w John Gilling *story* Frank H. Spearman *d* Francis Searle *ph* Walter Harvey *m* Frank Spencer *ed* James Needs
☆ Richard Carlson, Greta Gynt, Herbert Lom, Rona Anderson, Alan Wheatley, Dora Bryan, Reginald Beckwith

Whispers in the Dark
US 1992 98m DeLuxe
Paramount (Martin Bregman, Michael S. Bregman)
A New York psychiatrist is disturbed to discover that her new and apparently gentle boyfriend seems also to be the sadistic lover who acts out dangerous fantasies with one of her patients.
Mindlessly entertaining thriller that makes few demands on its audience and concludes that psychiatrists need their heads examined.
wd Christopher Crowe *ph* Michael Chapman *m* Thomas Newman *pd* John Jay Moore *ed* Bill Pankow
☆ Annabella Sciorra, Jamey Sheridan, Anthony LaPaglia, Jill Clayburgh, John Leguizamo, Deborah Unger, Alan Alda, Anthony Heald
'An entertaining pot-boiler, this bypassed the cinemas, but is certainly better value for your rental money than many another upmarket sex slasher.' – *Kim Newman, Empire*

The Whistle at Eaton Falls *
US 1951 96m bw
Columbia (Louis de Rochemont)
GB title: *Richer than the Earth*
The story of a strike at a small-town plastics factory.
Reasonably absorbing semi-documentary with a final 'solution' which rather evades the issues.
w Lemist Esler, Virginia Shaler *d* Robert Siodmak *ph* Joseph Brun *m* Louis Applebaum
☆ Lloyd Bridges, Dorothy Gish, Carleton Carpenter, Murray Hamilton, James Westerfield, Lenore Lonergan

Whistle Down the Wind *
GB 1961 99m bw
Rank/Allied Film Makers/Beaver (Richard Attenborough)
Three north country children think a murderer on the run is Jesus Christ.
Charming allegorical study of childhood innocence, extremely well made, amusing, and avoiding sentimentality.
w Keith Waterhouse, Willis Hall novel Mary Hayley Bell *d Bryan Forbes ph* Arthur Ibbetson *m* Malcolm Arnold
☆ Hayley Mills, Bernard Lee, Alan Bates, Norman Bird, Elsie Wagstaff, Alan Barnes

Whistle Stop
US 1946 84m bw
United Artists/Nero/Seymour Nebenzal
A city girl returns to her small-town home and finds herself torn between a night-club proprietor and an indolent charmer.
Would-be film noir, miscast and rather glum when it isn't unintentionally funny.
w Philip Yordan *novel* Maritta M. Wolff *d* Leonide Moguy *ph* Russell Metty *m* Dimitri Tiomkin
☆ George Raft, Ava Gardner, Tom Conway, Victor McLaglen

The Whistler
Originally a radio series of suspense stories introduced by someone whistling the theme tune, this was turned by Columbia into a fairly workmanlike series of second features quite unrelated to each other except for the leading actor, Richard Dix, who alternated as hero and villain, and William Castle, who directed or produced most of them.
1944 The Whistler, The Mark of the Whistler
1945 The Power of the Whistler
1946 The Voice of the Whistler
1947 Mysterious Intruder, The Secret of the Whistler, The 12th Hour
1948 The Return of the Whistler

Whistling in Brooklyn
US 1943 87m bw
MGM (George Haight)
An actor who plays 'The Fox', a radio detective, is suspected of murder and chased by cops and robbers.
Amusing, lightweight comedy thriller.
w Nat Perrin, Wilkie Mahoney *d* S. Sylvan Simon *ph* Lester White *m* George Bassman *ad* Cedric Gibbons *ed* Ben Lewis
☆ Red Skelton, Ann Rutherford, Jean Rogers, 'Rags' Ragland, Ray Collins, Henry O'Neill, William Frawley, Sam Levene, The Brooklyn Dodgers
† It was a sequel to *Whistling in the Dark* (qv).

Whistling in Dixie
US 1942 87m bw
MGM (George Haight)
A radio detective known as 'The Fox' solves a murder while waiting to get married in Georgia.
Mildly entertaining comedy thriller, though it overplays the joke of its cowardly hero.
w Nat Perrin, Wilkie Mahoney *d* S. Sylvan Simon *ph* Clyde DeVinna *m* Lennie Hayton *ad* Cedric Gibbons *ed* Frank Sullivan
☆ Red Skelton, Ann Rutherford, George Bancroft, Guy Kibbee, Diana Lewis, Peter Whitney
† It was a sequel to *Whistling in Brooklyn* (qv).

Whistling in the Dark *
US 1941 77m bw
MGM (George Haight)
A radio detective is kidnapped by a criminal who wants him to devise a perfect murder which will then be pinned on him.
Scatty comedy-thriller which, though it now seems slow to start, was popular enough to warrant two sequels (Whistling in Brooklyn, Whistling in Dixie).
w Robert MacGunigle, Harry Clork, Albert Mannheimer *play* Laurence Gross, Edward Childs Carpenter *d* S. Sylvan Simon *ph* Sidney Wagner *m* Bronislau Kaper
☆ *Red Skelton*, Conrad Veidt, Ann Rutherford, Virginia Grey, Eve Arden, Rags Ragland, Don Douglas, Lloyd Corrigan
† The play was previously filmed in 1933 with Ernest Truex, and this version is now shown on TV as *Scared*.

The White Angel *
US 1936 91m bw
Warner (Henry Blanke)
The life of Florence Nightingale.
Starchy biopic; the Victorian atmosphere is never quite caught.
w Mordaunt Shairp, Michel Jacoby *d* William Dieterle *ph* Tony Gaudio
☆ Kay Francis, Ian Hunter, Donald Woods, Nigel Bruce, Donald Crisp, Henry O'Neill, Billy Mauch, Halliwell Hobbes
'Miss Kay Francis, handicapped by her beauty, does her best to sober down this sentimental version of Florence Nightingale's character, but she is defeated by the scenario-writers.' – *Graham Greene*

White Angel
GB 1993 95m colour
Pilgrim/Living Spirit (Genevieve Joliffe)
aka: *Interview with a Serial Killer*
A crime writer is blackmailed by her lodger, a dentist and serial killer, when he discovers that she murdered her violent husband.
Dull and derivative thriller, no more than another indication of the current fascination with mass murderers.
w Chris Jones, Genevieve Joliffe *d* Chris Jones *ph* Jon Walker *m* Harry Gregson-Williams *ed* John Holland
☆ Peter Firth, Harriet Robinson, Don Henderson, Anne Catherine Arton
'This amateurish thriller wants to plumb some *Silence of the Lambs* depths, but silly plot and lame thesping will soon send it straight to video prison.' – *Variety*

The White Balloon **
Iran 1995 85m colour
Electric/CMI/Farabi/Fredos (Kurosh Mozkouri)
original title: *Badkonake Sefid*
A seven-year-old girl drops her money on the way to buy a goldfish and sets out to get it back.
Pleasant, well-observed, rambling tale of street life in Teheran.
w Abbas Kiarostami *idea* Parviz Shahbazi *d* Jafar Panahi *ph* Farzad Jowdat *pd* Jafar Panahi *ed* Jafar Panahi
☆ Aida Mohammadkhani, Mohsen Kalifi, Fereshteh Sadr Orfani, Anna Bourkowska
'By turns suspenseful and amusing, deceptively slight tale is a charmer with lots of local color.' – *Variety*
† The film won the Camera D'Or at the 1995 Cannes Film Festival.

White Banners *
US 1938 88m bw
Warner (Henry Blanke)
A social worker tries to solve the problems of a troubled family among whom is her own son, a fact unknown to him.
Moderate middle-class drama.
w Lenore Coffee, Cameron Rogers, Abem Finkel *novel* Lloyd C. Douglas *d* Edmund Goulding *ph* Charles Rosher *m* Max Steiner
☆ Fay Bainter, Claude Rains, Jackie Cooper, Bonita Granville, Henry O'Neill, James Stephenson, Kay Johnson
'Emotional drama, okay for the family trade … there is something fine and tender about it.' – *Variety*
Fay Bainter

White Blood: see *The Planter's Wife*

The White Buffalo
US 1977 97m Technicolor
Dino de Laurentiis (Pancho Kohner)
Wild Bill Hickok and Chief Crazy Horse join forces to kill a marauding white buffalo.
Ridiculous symbolic Western, not helped by the very artificial looking beast of the title.
w Richard Sale *novel* Richard Sale *d* J. Lee-Thompson *ph* Paul Lohmann *m* John Barry
☆ Charles Bronson, Jack Warden, Will Sampson, Kim Novak, Clint Walker, Stuart Whitman, John Carradine, Slim Pickens, Cara Williams, Douglas Fowley
'The dried husk of a *Moby Dick* allegory seems to be rattling around here amidst all the other dead wood.' – *Jonathan Rosenbaum, MFB*

White Captive: see *White Savage*

White Cargo *
US 1942 90m bw
MGM (Victor Saville)
White rubber planters are driven mad with desire for a scheming native girl.
Antediluvian melodrama previously filmed in 1930. Good for laughing at, and the star looked great as Tondelayo.
w Leon Gordon *play* Leon Gordon *novel Hell's Playground* by *Vera Simonton d* Richard Thorpe *m* Bronislau Kaper
☆ Hedy Lamarr, Walter Pidgeon, Richard Carlson, Frank Morgan, Bramwell Fletcher, Richard Ainley, Reginald Owen
† There was also a British version in 1929 (silent) with Leslie Faber and Gypsy Rhouma; and a few months later it emerged with added dialogue.

White Cargo
GB 1973 62m Eastmancolor
Border/Negus-Fancey (Mervyn Collard)
A dim-witted civil servant becomes involved in rescuing some Soho strippers who are being sold to an Arab harem.
Limp comedy that mixes poor slapstick and coy sex to no effect.
w Ray Selfe, David McGillivray *d* Ray Selfe *ph* John Barnard *m* David Lindup *ad* Jack Shampan *ed* Peter Austen-Hunt
☆ David Jason, Hugh Lloyd, Imogen Hassall, Tim Barrett, Dave Prowse, Raymond Cross, John Barber
'Mercifully, there is every sign that the film has been heavily cut.' – *Tony Rayns, MFB*

White Christmas *
US 1954 120m Technicolor Vistavision
Paramount (Robert Emmett Dolan)
Two entertainers boost the popularity of a winter resort run by an old army buddy.
Humdrum musical lifted only by its stars; a revamp of Holiday Inn, *which was much better.*
w Norman Krasna, Norman Panama, Melvin Frank *d* Michael Curtiz *ph* Loyal Griggs *songs* Irving Berlin
☆ Bing Crosby, Danny Kaye, Rosemary Clooney, Vera-Ellen, Dean Jagger, Mary Wickes, Sig Rumann, Grady Sutton
'Count Your Blessings Instead of Sheep'

The White Cliffs of Dover *
US 1944 126m bw
MGM (Sidney Franklin)
An American girl who marries into the British aristocracy loses a husband in World War I and a son in World War II.
Tearful flagwaver with some entertaining scenes in the first half and the general sense of an all-stops-out production.
w Claudine West, Jan Lustig, George Froeschel *poem* Alice Duer Miller *d* Clarence Brown *ph* George Folsey *m* Herbert Stothart
☆ *Irene Dunne*, Alan Marshal, Frank Morgan, May Whitty, Roddy McDowall, C. Aubrey Smith, Gladys Cooper, Peter Lawford, Van Johnson
'A long, earnest, well-intentioned, over-emotionalized cliché.' – *Richard Mallett, Punch*
'This sterling silver picture … is such a tribute to English gentility as only an American studio would dare to make.' – *New York Times*
'Sentimental patriotism … a truly monstrous cultural artifact.' – *Pauline Kael, 70s*
George Folsey

The White Cockatoo
US 1935 72m bw
Warner
Male and female heirs to a will suffer death threats.
Bland transcription of a popular mystery book.
w Ben Markson, Lillie Hayward *novel* Mignon G. Eberhart *d* Alan Crosland *ph* Tony Gaudio *ad* John Hughes *ed* Clarence Kolster
☆ Ricardo Cortez, Jean Muir, Ruth Donnelly, Minna Gombell, Walter Kingsford, John Eldredge

White Comanche
Spain/US 1968 92m Eastmancolor
Rank/International Producers/Cinematográficas A.B. (Sam White)
aka: *Comancho Blanco*
A renegade Comanche is challenged to a duel to the death by his law-abiding twin brother.
Uninteresting, unconvincing and unoriginal Western.
w José Briz, Manuel G. Rivera *story* Robert I. Holt, Frank Gruber *d* Gilbert Lee Kay (José Briz) *ph* Francisco Fraile *m* Jean Ledut
☆ William Shatner, Joseph Cotten, Rossana Yani, Perla Cristal
'The story rambles through stock routines accommodating stock characters.' – *MFB*
† The film was cut to 83m on its British release.

White Corridors *

GB 1951 102m bw
GFD/Vic (Joseph Janni, John Croydon)
Life in a small Midlands hospital.
Competent multi-drama which found a big audience.
w Jan Read, Pat Jackson *novel* *Yeoman's Hospital* by Helen Ashton *d* Pat Jackson *ph* C. Pennington-Richards
☆ James Donald, Googie Withers, Godfrey Tearle, Petula Clark, Jack Watling, Moira Lister, Barry Jones, Megs Jenkins, Basil Radford
'This quality of professionalism is comparatively rare in British films.' – *Gavin Lambert*

White Cradle Inn

GB 1947 83m bw
British Lion/Peak (Ivor McLaren, A. G. Hardman)
US title: *High Fury*
A Swiss hotel owner adopts a refugee boy and is menaced by her ne'er-do-well husband, who finally sacrifices himself for the boy.
Unimpressive little drama which wastes its cast, but provides beautiful scenery.
w Harold French, Lesley Storm *d* Harold French *ph* Derick Williams, Irvin Hillier *m* Bernard Grun *ad* Carmen Dillon *ed* Bert Bates
☆ Madeleine Carroll, Michael Rennie, Ian Hunter, Anne Marie Blanc, Michael McKeag

The White Dawn

US 1976 110m Movielab
Paramount/American Film Properties (Martin Ransohoff)
In 1900, survivors from a whaling ship are cared for by Eskimos, who turn on them when nature proves unkind.
Unpleasant fable with lots of bitter weather and subtitled Eskimos. Scarcely an entertainment, and its message is mumbled.
w James Houston, Tom Rickman *d* Philip Kaufman *ph* Michael Chapman *m* Henry Mancini
☆ Warren Oates, Timothy Bottoms, Lou Gossett, Eskimo cast
'Chief among the pleasures the film offers us is the sensation of having gained insight into a distant, primitive culture.' – *Wall Street Journal*

White Dog *

US 1982 90m Metrocolor
Paramount/Edgar J. Scherick
An actress unknowingly acquires a dog that has been trained to attack blacks only.
Oddball thriller that attracted unjustified criticism as a racist work, which prevented it from obtaining a proper release.
w Samuel Fuller, Curtis Hanson *book* Romain Gary *d* Samuel Fuller *ph* Bruce Surtees *m* Ennio Morricone
☆ Kristy McNichol, Paul Winfield, Burl Ives, Jameson Parker, Lynne Moody, Marshall Thompson

White Fang

US 1990 109m Eastmancolor
Warner/Hybrid/Disney/Silver Screen Partners IV (Marykay Powell)
A youth, who goes to the Klondike to take over his dead father's gold-mining claim, befriends a dog that is half-wolf.
Tame, youth-oriented version, far closer to Lassie than to Jack London's original.
w Jeanne Rosenberg, Nick Thiel, David Fallon *novel* Jack London *d* Randal Kleiser *ph* Tony Pierce-Roberts *m* Basil Poledouris *pd* Michael Bolton *ed* Lisa Day
☆ Klaus Maria Brandauer, Ethan Hawke, Seymour Cassel, Susan Hogan, James Remar, Bill Moseley, Clint B. Youngreen

White Fang II: The Myth of the White Wolf

US 1994 106m Technicolor
Buena Vista/Walt Disney (Preston Fischer)
White Fang's new master helps save from starvation an Indian tribe who regard him as the incarnation of a wolf.
Unsophisticated entertainment for the under-teens, full of noble savages, nobler dogs and the great outdoors.
w David Fallon *d* Ken Olin *ph* Hiro Narita *m* John Debney *pd* Cary White *ed* Elba Sanchez-Short
☆ Scott Bairstow, Charmaine Craig, Al Harrington, Victoria Racimo, Alfred Molina, Geoffrey Lewis, Ethan Hawke (uncredited)
'Corny but entertaining outdoor adventure in the manner of yesteryear's Saturday matinees.' – *Variety*

White Feather *

US 1955 100m Technicolor Cinemascope
TCF/Panoramic (Robert L. Jacks)
A cavalry colonel tries to hold back gold prospectors until the Cheyenne have moved on to their new reservations.
Old-fashioned cowboys and (sympathetic) Indians, very efficiently done.
w Delmer Daves, Leo Townsend *d* Robert Webb *ph* Lucien Ballard *m* Hugo Friedhofer
☆ Robert Wagner, John Lund, Jeffrey Hunter, Debra Paget, Eduard Franz, Noah Beery Jnr, Hugh O'Brian, Virginia Leith, Emile Meyer

'Pick up the pieces, folks, Jimmy's in action again!'
White Heat ***

US 1949 114m bw
Warner (Louis F. Edelman)
A violent, mother-fixated gangster gets his comeuppance when a government agent is infiltrated into his gang.
This searing melodrama reintroduced the old Cagney and then some: spellbinding suspense sequences complemented his vivid and hypnotic portrayal.
w Ivan Goff, Ben Roberts *story* Virginia Kellogg *d* *Raoul Walsh* *ph* Sid Hickox *m* Max Steiner
☆ *James Cagney*, Edmond O'Brien, *Margaret Wycherly*, Virginia Mayo, Steve Cochran, John Archer
'The most gruesome aggregation of brutalities ever presented under the guise of entertainment.' – *Cue*
'In the hurtling tabloid traditions of the gangster movies of the thirties, but its matter-of-fact violence is a new post-war style.' – *Time*
'A wild and exciting picture of mayhem and madness.' – *Life*
Virginia Kellogg

The White Hell of Pitz Palu *

Germany 1929 90m approx bw
UFA
Mountaineers have a difficult ascent of Pitz Palu.
Classic semi-documentary, noted for its pictorial compositions more than its dramatic qualities.
wd G. W. Pabst, Dr Arnold Fank
'An astonishing and, to me, wildly terrifying film.' – *James Agate*

White Hunter

US 1936 65m bw
TCF/Darryl F. Zanuck
An African hunter is hired by an old enemy.
Extremely predictable melodrama with poor technical work.
w Sam Duncan, Kenneth Earl, Gene Markey *d* Irving Cummings
☆ Warner Baxter, Wilfrid Lawson, June Lang, Gail Patrick, Alison Skipworth

'An adventure in obsession...'
White Hunter Black Heart **

US 1990 112m Technicolor
Warner/Malpaso/Rastar (Clint Eastwood)
A film director goes to Africa ostensibly to make a film but primarily to shoot an elephant.
Based on a novel about John Huston making The African Queen, *by a writer involved in that film, it emerges as an entertaining account of Hollywood egotism.*
w Peter Viertel, James Bridges, Burt Kennedy *novel* Peter Viertel *d* Clint Eastwood *ph* Jack N. Green *m* Lennie Niehaus *pd* John Graysmark *ed* Joel Cox
☆ Clint Eastwood (John Wilson), Jeff Fahey (Pete Verrill), Charlotte Cornwell (Miss Wilding), Norman Lumsden (Butler George), George Dzundza (Paul Landers), Edward Tudor Pole (Reissar), Roddy Maude-Roxby (Thompson), Richard Warwick (Basil Fields)
'Its chief strength is that it is one of those increasingly rare Hollywood entertainments that treats its audience as adults.' – *Derek Malcolm, Guardian*
'Trapped unhappily between fact and fiction, the film builds up not to a bang but a whimper, leaving one wondering bemusedly what it is trying to say, and about whom.' – *Tom Milne, MFB*

White Lightning

US 1973 101m DeLuxe
United Artists/Levy-Gardner-Laven
A convict escapes to wreak vengeance on the corrupt sheriff who had killed his brother.
Heavy-going Southern melodrama which comes to life only during its occasional fits of violence. Gator *was a kind of sequel.*
w William Norton *d* Joseph Sargent *ph* Edward Rosson *m* Charles Bernstein
☆ Burt Reynolds, Jennifer Billingsley, Ned Beatty, Matt Clark, Bo Hopkins, Louise Latham, Diane Ladd

White Line Fever

US/Canada 1975 89m Metrocolor
Columbia-Warner/White Line Fever Syndicate/International Cinemedia (John Kemeny)
A poor but honest trucker riles the powerful by refusing to haul stolen goods.
A predictably violent action thriller with little to recommend it.
w Ken Friedman, Jonathan Kaplan *d* Jonathan Kaplan *ph* Fred Koenekamp *m* David Nichtern *ad* Sydney Litwak *ed* O. Nicholas Brown
☆ Jan-Michael Vincent, Kay Lenz, Slim Pickens, L. Q. Jones, Don Porter, Sam Laws, Dick Miller

The White Man: see *The Squaw Man*

White Man's Burden

US/France 1995 89m Technicolor
TCF/UGC/Band Apart (Lawrence Bender)
In an America where the black race holds the power, a white worker kidnaps his boss after he is unfairly sacked.
Feeble and heavy-handed satire that deals unilluminatingly in stereotypical characters and situations.
wd Desmond Nakano *ph* Willy Kurant *m* Howard Shore *pd* Naomi Shohan *ed* Nancy Richardson
☆ John Travolta, Harry Belafonte, Kelly Lynch, Margaret Avery, Tom Bower, Andrew Lawrence, Bumper Robinson, Tom Wright, Sheryl Lee Ralph
'A noble but dumb idea decimated by uninspired execution and a disastrously misplaced focus.' – *Film Review*

'It Ain't Easy Being This Good.'
White Men Can't Jump **

US 1992 112m DeLuxe
TCF (Don Miller, David Lester)
Two basketball hustlers – one white, one black – team up to part the unwary from their money.
Crisply performed, enjoyable caper with something to say about relationships between races.
wd Ron Shelton *ph* Russell Boyd *m* Bennie Wallace *pd* Dennis Washington *ed* Paul Seydor
☆ Wesley Snipes, Woody Harrelson, Rosie Perez, Tyra Ferrell, Cylk Cozart, Kadeem Hardison, Ernest Harden Jnr
'As fast, buoyant and full of feinting rubato as basketball itself.' – *Nigel Andrews, Financial Times*
'With a remarkable lack of soap-box oratory, Shelton's film manages to catch the prevailing tone of American race relations, to show us what urban America really looks like, and to depict the moral quandaries that poverty inevitably forces on its victims.' – *Henry Sheehan, Sight and Sound*

White Mischief

GB 1987 107m Agfacolor
Umbrella (Michael White)
Real-life unsolved murder of Lord Erroll in Kenya's Happy Valley.
Starry cast and slick direction fail to engage interest in the sybaritic lifestyle of white settlers in colonial Africa.
w Michael Radford, Jonathan Gems *book* James Fox *d* Michael Radford *ph* Roger Deakins *m* George Fenton *pd* Roger Hall
☆ Charles Dance, Greta Scacchi, Joss Ackland, Sarah Miles, John Hurt, Trevor Howard

White Nights

US 1985 135m Metrocolor
Columbia/New Visions/Delphi V (Taylor Hackford, William S. Gilmore)
After a plane crash, a Russian emigré ballet star finds himself a prisoner in Leningrad.
Basically an escape story with silly details, this tries also to be a dance film about relationships. Despite the star's powerful presence, it fails on most counts.
w James Goldman, Eric Hughes *d* Taylor Hackford *ph* David Watkin *m* Michel Colombier *pd* Philip Harrison *ed* Fredric and William Steinkamp
☆ *Mikhail Baryshnikov*, Gregory Hines, Jerzy Skolimowski, Helen Mirren, Geraldine Page, Isabella Rossellini
'Good looks but no style ... neither fish nor fowl, good nor bad, box office gold nor poison.' – *Variety*
song 'Say You, Say Me' (Lionel Richie)
song 'Separate Lives' (m/ly Stephen Bishop)

White of the Eye

GB 1986 111m colour
Elliott Kastner (Cassian Elwes, Brad Wyman)
A loving father and husband is also a serial killer.
Conventional material is made slightly more interesting by some slick camerawork and editing; but surface gloss it all that it offers.
w China and Donald Cammell *novel* *Mrs White* by Margaret Tracy *d* Donald Cammell *ph* Alan Jones *m* Nick Mason, Rick Fenn *pd* Philip Thomas *ed* Terry Rawlings
☆ David Keith, Cathy Moriarty, Art Evans, Alan Rosenberg, Mark Hayashi, William Schilling, David Chow, Alberta Watson

'Love is the last thing on their minds.'
White Palace

US 1990 103m colour
UIP/Universal/Mirage/Double Play (Mark Rosenberg, Amy Robinson, Griffin Dunne)
A successful young advertising executive begins an affair with a fortyish waitress in a hamburger joint.
Soft-centred romance in which love conquers social differences and aspirations.
w Ted Tally, Alvin Sargent *novel* Glenn Savan *d* Luis Mondoki *ph* Lajos Koltai *m* George Fenton *pd* Jeannine C. Oppewall *ed* Carol Fischer
☆ Susan Sarandon, James Spader, Jason Alexander, Kathy Bates, Eileen Brennan, Steven Hill, Rachel Levin
'One of the best films of its kind since *The Graduate*. Rave word-of-mouth should help warm up the box-office grill.' – *Variety*

The White Parade

US 1934 80m bw
TCF (Jesse L. Lasky)
Incidents at the nurses' training school of a midwestern hospital.
Smooth but very predictable semi-documentary.
w Sonya Levien, Ernest Pascal *novel* Rian James *d* Irving Cummings
☆ Loretta Young, John Boles, Dorothy Wilson, Muriel Kirkland, Sara Haden, Astrid Allwyn, Jane Darwell, Frank Conroy
'Sympathetic comedy drama with strong *femme* draw value.' – *Variety*
best picture

White Room

Canada 1990 91m colour
Vos Productions (Alexandra Raffé)
A voyeuristic youth, upset by witnessing the murder of a famous singer, begins a relationship with a mysterious woman he meets at the funeral.
A modern fairy story, a fantasy on themes of feminism and obsessive voyeurism, but lacking in any magic.
wd Patricia Rozema *ph* Paul Sarossy *m* Mark Korven *pd* Valanne Ridgeway *ed* Patricia Rozema
☆ Kate Nelligan, Maurice Godin, Margot Kidder, Sheila McCarthy

'The most dangerous way to solve a murder ... become the victim.'
White Sands
US 1992 101m colour
Warner/Morgan Creek (William Sackheim, Scott Rudin)

Investigating a murder in New Mexico, a deputy sheriff finds himself involved with the FBI, the CIA and arms dealers.
Confusing thriller of cross and double-cross that fails to sustain an interest in its many twists and turns.
w Daniel Pyne *d* Roger Donaldson *ph* Peter Menzies Jnr *m* Patrick O'Hearn *pd* John Graysmark *ed* Nicholas Beauman, Sue Blainey
☆ Willem Dafoe, Mary Elizabeth Mastrantonio, Mickey Rourke, M. Emmet Walsh, Mimi Rogers, James Rebhorn, Maura Tierney
'An absorbing, tightly coiled thriller not always easy to follow.' – *Variety*
'Initially intriguing, ultimately disappointing, but fun for much of the way.' – *Philip French, Observer*

White Savage: see *South of Tahiti (1941)*

White Savage
US 1943 75m Technicolor
Universal (George Waggner)
GB title: *White Captive*
The queen of a beautiful South Sea island has trouble with shark hunters and crooks after her mineral deposits.
Self-admitted hokum strung loosely and colourfully around its star: big box-office in the middle of the war.
w Richard Brooks *d* Arthur Lubin *ph* Lester White, William Snyder *m* Frank Skinner
☆ Maria Montez, Jon Hall, Sabu, Thomas Gomez, Sidney Toler, Paul Guilfoyle, Turhan Bey, Don Terry
'It may be that these semi-burlesques were more fun to make than to watch.' – *Pauline Kael, 70s*

White Shadows in the South Seas *
US 1928 88m bw
MGM
An alcoholic doctor in Tahiti finds happiness with a native girl until he is killed by white colonials.
Rather boring melodrama illuminated by superb photography.
w John Colton, Jack Cunningham *book* Frederick J. O'Brien *d* W. S. Van Dyke (and Robert Flaherty) *ph* Clyde DeVinna and others (including Flaherty)
☆ Monte Blue, Raquel Torres
Clyde DeVinna

The White Sheik **
Italy 1952 88m bw
PDC/OFI (Luigi Rovere)

original title: *Lo Sceicco Bianco*
A provincial couple come to Rome on their honeymoon, where the wife is infatuated with a common actor who portrays a dashing, aristocratic lover in a photo-novel.
A gently comic, ironic drama of illusion and reality, based on an idea of Michelangelo Antonioni's.
w Federico Fellini, Tullio Pinelli, Ennio Flaiano *d* Federico Fellini *ph* Arturo Gallea *m* Nino Rota *ad* Raffaello Tolfo *ed* Rolando Bebedetti
☆ Brunella Bovo, Leopoldo Trieste, *Alberto Sordi*, Giulietta Masina
'This affectionate satire on glamour and delusion is probably the most gentle and naturalistic of Fellini's films, but it was not a success, maybe because it is a little flat in places.' – *Pauline Kael*

The White Sister
US 1933 110m bw
MGM (Hunt Stromberg)

When her lover is reported killed in the war, an Italian noblewoman takes the veil ... but he comes back.
Tiresome romantic drama from another age, a big prestige production of its time.
w Donald Ogden Stewart *novel* F. Marion Crawford, Walter Hackett *d* Victor Fleming *ph* William Daniels *m* Herbert Stothart
☆ Helen Hayes, Clark Gable, Lewis Stone, Louise Closser Hale, May Robson, Edward Arnold
'An eloquent yoking of marquee names ... certain money maker for general release.' – *Variety*
† The silent version of 1923 starred Lillian Gish and Ronald Colman, and bore the tagline: 'A love that outlived passion!'

'The Strongest Force In Nature Is The Will To Survive.'
White Squall *
US 1996 127m Technicolor
Buena Vista/Hollywood/Largo/Scott Free (Mimi Polk Gitlin, Rocky Lang)

The competence of a captain is questioned after his boat, crewed by teenagers spending a year sailing in the Caribbean, runs into trouble in a sudden storm.
Based on a true story, this is no more than an average rites-of-passage drama, with excitement and interest limited to the storm scenes, which are a long time coming.
w Todd Robinson *d* Ridley Scott *ph* Hugh Johnson *m* Jeff Rona *pd* Peter J. Hampton *ed* Gerry Hambling
☆ Jeff Bridges, Caroline Goodall, John Savage, Scott Wolf, Jeremy Sisto, Ryan Phillippe, David Lascher, Eric Michael Cole, Jason Marsden
'Lavish production isn't totally satisfying, coasting aimlessly at times before suddenly leaping into a more intense dramatic plane.' – *Brian Lowry, Variety*

White Tie and Tails
US 1946 81m bw
Universal
A butler left in charge of the house gets ideas above his station.
Modest comedy which lacks the required high style.
w Bertram Millhauser *novel* *The Victoria Docks at Eight* by Rufus King, Charles Leakon *d* Charles Barton
☆ Dan Duryea, Ella Raines, William Bendix, Richard Gaines, Clarence Kolb, Frank Jenks

'Revenge knows no limits.'
White Tiger
US 1995 93m colour
Keystone/Evergreen/Gail Force (Robert Vince, William Vince)

A DEA agent goes after the ruthless Chinese gangster and drug dealer who murdered his partner.
Violent martial arts movie with the usual revenge narrative and usual high-kicking fight scenes; it is likely to interest only the most fervent fans of the genre.
w Gordon Melbourne, Roy Sallows, Don Woodman *story* Bey Logan *d* Richard Martin *ph* Gregory Middleton *m* Graeme Coleman *ad* Don Macaulay *ed* Kerry Uchida
☆ Gary Daniels (Mike Ryan), Matt Craven (John Grogan), Cary-Hiroyuki Tagawa (Victor Chow), Lisa Langlois (Joanne Grogan), Ron Winston Yuan (Severin), Dana Lee (Zhou), George Cheung (Detective Fong), Julia Nickson (Jade)

The White Tower
US 1950 98m Technicolor
RKO (Sid Rogell)

Various people have personal reasons for climbing an Alpine mountain.
Pretentiously symbolic melodrama with some good action sequences and curiously stilted performances.
w Paul Jarrico *novel* James Ramsay Ullman *d* Ted Tetzlaff *ph* Ray Rennahan *m* Roy Webb
☆ Glenn Ford, Claude Rains, Alida Valli, Oscar Homolka, Cedric Hardwicke, Lloyd Bridges, June Clayworth
'The main interest is a curiosity as to who will fall over which precipice when.' – *Penelope Houston*

The White Unicorn
GB 1947 97m bw
GFD/John Corfield (Harold Huth)
US title: *Bad Sister*
In a home for delinquent girls, the worst offender exchanges reminiscences with the warden.
Peg's Paper *melodrama in complex flashback form.*
w Robert Westerby, A. R. Rawlinson, Moie Charles *novel* Flora Sandstrom *d* Bernard Knowles *ph* Reginald Wyer *m* Bretton Byrd *ad* Norman Arnold *ed* R. Johnson
☆ Margaret Lockwood, Joan Greenwood, Ian Hunter, Dennis Price, Guy Middleton, Catherine Lacey, Mabel Constanduros, Paul Dupuis

White Witch Doctor
US 1953 96m Technicolor
TCF (Otto Lang)
A nurse in the Congo converts a gold-seeking adventurer.
Stale hokum in which the animals are the most interesting feature.
w Ivan Goff, Ben Roberts *novel* Louise A. Stinetorf *d* Henry Hathaway *ph* Leon Shamroy *m* Bernard Herrmann
☆ Susan Hayward, Robert Mitchum, Walter Slezak, Timothy Carey

'Alone among outcasts who hadn't seen a white woman in ten years!'
White Woman
US 1933 68m bw
Paramount
A Cockney overseer in the Malaysian jungle takes back a cabaret singer as his bride.
Risible melodrama with an obvious outcome.
w Samuel Hoffenstein, Gladys Lehman *story* Norman Reilly Raine, Frank Butler *d* Stuart Walker *ph* Harry Fischbeck
☆ Charles Laughton, Carole Lombard, Kent Taylor, Charles Bickford, Percy Kilbride, Charles Middleton, James Bell
'Bromidic South Sea stuff ... seems best for dual bills.' – *Variety*
† Remade as *Island of Lost Men.*

White Zombie **
US 1932 74m bw
American Securities Corporation (Edward Halperin)

Haitian zombies work a sugar mill for a white schemer.
Genuinely eerie horror film with a slow, stagey, out-of-this world quality coupled with an interesting sense of composition.
w Garnett Weston *d* Victor Halperin *ph* Arthur Martinelli *md* Abe Meyer
☆ Bela Lugosi, Madge Bellamy, John Harron, Joseph Cawthorn
'Fine work of Lugosi is backed by good cast and bizarre staging ... not quite up to Broadway.' – *Variety*
'A Gothic fairy tale filled with dreamlike imagery, traditional symbols, echoes of Romanticism, and (probably unintentional) psychosexual overtones.' – *Carlos Clarens*
'For those absolutely dedicated to gothic silliness.' – *New Yorker, 1977*

Whither Germany?: see *Kühle Wampe*

Who?
GB 1974 93m Eastmancolor
British Lion/Hemisphere/Maclean

An American scientist is captured by the Russians after a car crash and returned six months later as a somewhat suspect android.
So-what mixture of character drama and James Bondery; aiming clearly at no particular audience, it failed to get a release.
w John Gould *novel* Algis Budrys *d* Jack Gold *ph* Petrus Schloemp *m* John Cameron
☆ Elliott Gould, Trevor Howard, Joseph Bova, Ed Grover, James Noble, Lyndon Brook

Who Am I?
Hong Kong 1998 108m colour Panavision
Columbia TriStar/Golden Harvest (Barbie Tung)
original title: *Wo Shi Shui*
In South Africa. the only surviving commando on a special mission suffers amnesia after a deliberately arranged plane crash, and faces death from his corrupt boss.
What begins as a broad comedy in a remote African village gradually segues into a familiar espionage drama, rather in the manner of a cut-price Bond movie; the climax is action-packed, but it's a long wait.
w Jackie Chan, Susan Chan, Lee Reynolds *d* Jackie Chan, Benny Chan *ph* Poon Hang Sang *m* Nathan Wang *ad* Oliver Wong *ed* Peter Cheung, Yau Chi Wai
☆ Jackie Chan (Jackie), Michelle Ferre (Christine), Mirai Yamamoto (Yuki), Ron Smerczak (Morgan), Ed Nelson (Gen Sherman), Tom Pompert (CIA Chairman), Yannick Mbali (Baba), Washington Sixolo (Village Chief)
'A tired, disjointed effort that neither momentary thrills nor Chan's winning personality can enliven.' – *Leonard Klady, Variety*
† The Hong Kong version, and the film originally shown in the US, ran for 120m.

'The Closest You'll Ever Get To Knowing The Secrets Of The Legendary S.A.S.'
Who Dares Wins
GB 1982 125m colour
Rank/Richmond Light Horse/Euan Lloyd (Raymond Menmuir)

US title: *The Final Option*
An SAS captain infiltrates a ruthless antinuclear group which finally holds the American Secretary of State to ransom.
Crude exploitation of the SAS's successful relief of the Iranian Embassy. The entertainment is thick ear at best, and some of the dialogue and performances have to be seen to be believed.
w Reginald Rose *d* Ian Sharp *ph* Phil Meheux *m* Roy Budd, Jerry and Marc Donahue *pd* Syd Cain
☆ Lewis Collins, Judy Davis, Ingrid Pitt, Richard Widmark, Edward Woodward, Robert Webber, Kenneth Griffith, Norman Rodway
'It should manage to offend anybody – punk, pacifist or policeman – inclined to take seriously the subject of global security.' – *Philip Strick, MFB*
'Cinematically antiquated and with hawkish politics poking unappealingly through the thin cloak of fiction.' – *Sight and Sound*

Who Done It?
US 1942 77m bw
Universal (Alex Gottlieb)

Soda jerks in a New York radio station catch a murderer.
So-so comedy thriller, fatally lacking atmosphere (and good jokes).
w Stanley Roberts, Edmund Joseph, John Grant *d* Erle C. Kenton *ph* Charles Van Enger *m* Frank Skinner
☆ Bud Abbott, Lou Costello, William Gargan, Louise Allbritton, Patric Knowles, Don Porter, Jerome Cowan, William Bendix, Mary Wickes, Thomas Gomez

Who Done It?
GB 1956 85m bw
Ealing (Michael Relph, Basil Dearden)

An ice-rink sweeper sets up as a private eye and captures a ring of spies.
Lively but disappointing film debut for a star comic whose screen personality proved too bland.
w T. E. B. Clarke *d* Basil Dearden *ph* Otto Heller *m* Philip Green
☆ Benny Hill, Belinda Lee, David Kossoff, Garry Marsh, Ernest Thesiger, Thorley Walters

Who Framed Roger Rabbit ****
US 1988 103m Rank Colour/Metrocolor/DeLuxe
Warner/Touchstone/Amblin (Robert Watts, Frank Marshall)

Cartoon characters become involved in Dashiel Hammett-style whodunnit.
Criticisms of thin plotting are irrelevant: the seamless integration of animation and live-action enchanted audiences.
w Jeffrey Price, Peter S. Seaman *book* *Who Censored Roger Rabbit?* by Gary K. Wold *d* Robert Zemeckis *ph* Dean Cundey *m* Alan Silvestri *pd* Elliot Scott *ed* Arthur Schmidt *animation* Richard Williams
☆ Bob Hoskins, Christopher Lloyd, Joanna Cassidy, Stubby Kaye and also the voices of Charles Fleischer, Kathleen Turner, Amy Irving, Lou Hirsch, Mel Blanc
'A deplorable development in the possibilities of animation – and a melancholy waste of the gifts of one of our most gifted actors.' – *Dilys Powell*
Arthur Schmidt; visual effects
Dean Cundey; art direction

Who Goes There?
GB 1952 85m bw
British Lion/London Films (Anthony Kimmins)
US title: *The Passionate Sentry*
In a Grace and Favour house near St James's Palace, a guardsman is involved in a trail of romantic intrigue.

film suitable for family viewing | VHS video-cassette for the British PAL system | VHS video-cassette for the British PAL system in wide screen-format | Video cassette in a computer-colourised version | American NTSC video-cassette | Laser disc

Very British romantic farce, dully and quickly filmed from a West End success.
w John Dighton play John Dighton d Anthony Kimmins ph John Wilcox, Ted Scaife m Muir Mathieson
☆ Peggy Cummins, Valerie Hobson, George Cole, Nigel Patrick, A. E. Matthews, Anthony Bushell

Who Is Harry Kellerman and Why Is He Saying Those Terrible Things About Me?
US 1971 108m DeLuxe
Cinema Center (Ulu Grosbard, Herb Gardner)
A New York composer is persecuted by a mysterious figure who turns out to be himself.
Wild, shapeless, satirical psycho-comedy-melodrama. Not very good.
w Herb Gardner d Ulu Grosbard ph Victor Kemper pd Harry Horner
☆ Dustin Hoffman, Barbara Harris, Jack Warden, David Burns, Gabriel Dell, Dom DeLuise
Barbara Harris

Who Is Killing the Great Chefs of Europe? *
US 1978 112m Metrocolor
Warner/Aldrich/Lorimar (Merv Adelson, Lee Rich, William Aldrich)
GB title: *Too Many Chefs*
A fast food entrepreneur in London finds himself at the centre of a series of grisly murders.
Unusual and lighthearted black comedy against the background of international gastronomy.
w Peter Stone novel Nan and Ivan Lyons d Ted Kotcheff ph John Alcott m Henry Mancini
☆ George Segal, Jacqueline Bisset, *Robert Morley*, Jean-Pierre Cassel, Philippe Noiret, Jean Rochefort, Madge Ryan

Who Killed Doc Robbin?
US 1948 55m Cinecolor
Hal Roach
Local kids prowl a supposedly haunted mansion.
Hesitant revival of the Our Gang comedy style in a semi-feature format; it had only mild success.
w Maurice Geraghty, Dorothy Reid d Bernard Carr ph John Boyle m Heinz Roemheld
☆ George Zucco, Virginia Grey, Don Castle

Who Killed Mary What's Her Name?
US 1971 90m DeLuxe
Cannon (George Manasse)
An ex-boxer determines to solve the murder of a prostitute.
Old-fashioned whodunnit with something to say grafted on every five minutes: an unsatisfactory mix.
w John O'Toole d Ernest Pintoff ph Greg Sandor m Gary McFarland
☆ Red Buttons, Alice Playten, Sylvia Miles, Sam Waterston

Who Knows: see *Va Savoir*

Who Saw Her Die? (dubbed)
Italy/Germany 1972 84m Technicolor Techniscope
Doria/Roas/Geissler (Enzio Doria, Dieter Geissler)
original title: *Chi L'ha Vista Morire?*
In Venice, a sculptor investigates the murder of his young daughter.
Slick thriller of no particular distinction, though its setting gives it a sense of style, and Morricone's score adds emphasis to its moments of suspense.
w Massimo D'Avak, Aldo Lado, Francesco Barilli, Rudiger von Spiess d Aldo Lado ph Franco di Giacomo m Ennio Morricone ad Gisella Longo, Alessandro Parenzo ed Angelo Curi, Jutta Brandstaedter
☆ George Lazenby, Anita Strindberg, Peter Chatel, Adolfo Celi, Dominique Boschero, Rosemarie Lindt, Georg Willing
† Aficionados of non-sequiturs may enjoy one line of dialogue: 'If you can't play ping-pong, don't get mixed up in politics.'

Who Shot Patakango?
US 1990 102m colour
Patakango United Partnership (Halle Brooks)
aka: *Who Shot Pat?*
In the 50s, a group of tough Brooklyn boys fight and play through their final days at high school.
Pleasant, nostalgic rite-of-passage drama to a rock 'n' roll soundtrack.
w Robert and Halle Brooks d Robert Brooks ph Robert Brooks ed Robert and Halle Brooks
☆ David Knight, Sandra Bullock, Kevin Otto, Aaron Ingram, Brad Randall, Chris Cardona, Michael Puzzo, Christopher Creon, Gregg Marc Miller

Who Was That Lady? *
US 1960 115m bw
Columbia/Ansark/George Sidney (Norman Krasna)
A professor seen kissing a student persuades a friend to tell his wife that they are both FBI agents on duty. Foreign spies believe them ...
Agreeably wacky comedy with a strained and prolonged middle section leading to a totally zany climax.
w Norman Krasna play Norman Krasna d George Sidney ph Harry Stradling m André Previn
☆ *Tony Curtis, Dean Martin*, Janet Leigh, James Whitmore, John McIntire, Barbara Nichols, Larry Keating

Whoever Says the Truth Shall Die *
Holland 1984 52m bw/colour
Vara
A documentary on the life, and especially death, of director Pier Paolo Pasolini which suggests that he was murdered not by a homosexual pick-up but as the victim of a right-wing conspiracy.
Interesting though somewhat inconsequential examination of what made Pasolini a vital and feared figure in modern Italian culture.
wd Philo Bregstein ph Michel Pensato, Alan Jones, Ali Movahed, Richard Laurent ed Mario Steenbergen
☆ Bernardo Bertolucci, Laura Betti, Maria Antonietta Macciochi, Alberto Moravia

'The hand that rocks the cradle has no flesh on it!'
Whoever Slew Auntie Roo?
GB 1972 91m Movielab
EMI-MGM/AIP/Hemdale (Louis M. Heyward)
US title: *Who Slew Auntie Roo?*
A madwoman menaces two orphan children.
Pointless and slenderly plotted adaptation of Hansel and Gretel, *crude in all departments.*
w Robert Blees, Jimmy Sangster d Curtis Harrington ph Desmond Dickinson m Ken Jones
☆ Shelley Winters, Ralph Richardson, Mark Lester, Lionel Jeffries, Chloe Franks, Hugh Griffith, Rosalie Crutchley, Pat Heywood
'Not content with being a delicate fantasy of childish nightmare, it tries to add a totally inappropriate seasoning of Grand Guignol.' – *Tom Milne*

'In a nice quiet suburb, a hitman with a heart has just moved in.'
'Life's a comedy. It's all in the execution.'
The Whole Nine Yards
US 2000 101m DeLuxe
Warner/Morgan Creek/Franchise/Rational Packaging/Lansdown (David Willis, Allan Kaufman)
A Montreal dentist realises that his new next-door neighbour is a notorious hitman being hunted by the mob for turning informant.
Crude farce, in which Willis does his familiar tough-guy act, Arquette and Pollak use the oddest accents ever heard, and Perry provides the physical comedy; it somehow misses its target.
w Mitchell Kapner d Jonathan Lynn ph David Franco m Randy Edelman pd David L. Snyder ed Tom Lewis
☆ Bruce Willis (Jimmy Tudeski), Matthew Perry ('Oz' Oseransky), Rosanna Arquette (Sophie), Michael Clarke Duncan (Frankie Figs), Natasha Henstridge (Cynthia), Amanda Peet (Jill), Kevin Pollak (Janni)
'A crudely funny farce that covers no new ground but sees its talented players running some surefire plays.' – *Todd McCarthy, Variety*
'Passable pap.' – *Empire*

The Whole Town's Talking *
US 1935 86m bw
Columbia (Lester Cowan)
GB title: *Passport to Fame*
A gangster finds it convenient occasionally to pose as his double, a meek little clerk.
Pleasingly neat comedy, well staged and acted.
w Jo Swerling, Robert Riskin novel W. R. Burnett d John Ford ph Joseph August
☆ *Edward G. Robinson*, Jean Arthur, Arthur Hohl, Wallace Ford, Arthur Byron, Donald Meek, Edward Brophy, Etienne Girardot
'Wow comedy-melodrama ... swell entertainment.' – *Variety*
'A lively and satisfactory combination of farce and melodrama.' – *Richard Watts Jnr*

The Whole Truth *
GB 1958 84m bw
Columbia/Romulus (Jack Clayton)
A jealous husband poses as a detective in order to murder his wife and incriminate a film producer.
A filmed play, but quite a solidly carpentered murder thriller with a couple of neat twists.
w Jonathan Latimer play Philip Mackie d John Guillermin ph Wilkie Cooper m Mischa Spoliansky
☆ Stewart Granger, George Sanders, Donna Reed, Gianna Maria Canale

The Whole Wide World *
US 1996 111m DeLuxe
Kushner-Locke/Cineville/Eventide (Carl-Jan Colpaert, Vincent D'Onofrio, Dan Ireland, Kevin Reidy)
In a small Texas town in the 1930s, a tentative romance develops between a local schoolmistress and the introverted, mother-dominated pulp writer Robert E. Howard, creator of Conan the Barbarian.
Pleasant, nostalgic, low key drama of a hesitant relationship, given affecting performances by the two leads, though D'Onofrio plays down Howard's peculiarities.
w Michael Scott Myers book *One Who Walked Alone* by Novalyne Price Ellis ph Claudio Rocha m Harry Gregson-Williams, Hans Zimmer pd John Frick ed Luis Colina cos Gail McMullen
☆ Renee Zellweger (Novalyne Price), Vincent D'Onofrio (Robert E. Howard), Ann Wedgeworth (Mrs Howard), Harve Presnell (Dr Howard), Benjamin Mouton (Clyde Smith), Michael Corbett (Booth Adams), Helen Cates (Enid)
'Invest some patience and you'll be richly rewarded with rolling frontier vistas, butterscotch sunsets and a sweet, melancholy romance that will sneak up on you and grab your heart.' – *Susan Wloszczyna, USA Today*

Who'll Stop the Rain? *
US 1978 125m colour
UA/Gabriel Katzka, Herb Jaffe
GB title: *Dog Soldiers*
A Vietnam veteran takes to smuggling heroin into the US, but gets his wife and friend involved with gangsters.
Heavy-going, downbeat character drama with action sequences.
w Judith Roscoe novel *Dog Soldiers* by Robert Stone d Karel Reisz ph Richard H. Kline m Laurence Rosenthal
☆ Nick Nolte, Tuesday Weld, Michael Moriarty, Anthony Zerbe, Richard Masur, David Opatoshu, Ray Sharkey, Gail Strickland
'Just another ambition-downer, a wasted effort to make something meaningful out of wasted lives.' – *Richard Schickel, Time*

Wholly Moses
US 1980 109m Metrocolor Panavision
Columbia/David Begelman
A shepherd hears God talking to Moses, and thinks he himself has been ordained to set his people free.
Inept and tasteless biblical spoof which must set back by about ten years the reputations of all connected with it.
w Guy Thomas d Gary Weis ph Frank Stanley m Patrick Williams
☆ Dudley Moore, James Coco, Paul Sand, Jack Gilford, Dom DeLuise, John Houseman, Madeline Kahn
'Deadly dullness of both writing and execution render pointless any attempt to single out blame for misfire, which leaves many talented performers flailing about in desperate attempts to generate laughs.' – *Variety*

Whoopee *
US 1930 94m Technicolor
Samuel Goldwyn, Florenz Ziegfeld
A timid young man is catapulted into various adventures.
Early sound musical from a popular Broadway show, later remade as Up in Arms *(qv).*
w William Conselman musical play William Anthony McGuire play *The Nervous Wreck* by *Owen Davis* d Thornton Freeland ph Lee Garmes, Ray Rennahan, Gregg Toland ch Busby Berkeley ad Richard Day songs Walter Donaldson, Gus Kahn
☆ *Eddie Cantor*, Eleanor Hunt, Paul Gregory, Jack Rutherford, Ethel Shutta
'Dandiest of screen musicals and okay dough-getter.' – *Variety*
Richard Day

Whoops Apocalypse
GB 1986 91m Eastmancolor
ITC (Brian Eastman)
First woman president of the US tries to avert nuclear attack.
Frenetic but pathetic attempt at Dr Strangelove *for the 80s.*
w Andrew Marshall, David Renwick d Tom Bussmann ph Ron Robson m Patrick Gowers pd Tony Noble ed Peter Boyle
☆ Loretta Swit, Peter Cook, Rik Mayall, Ian Richardson, Alexei Sayle, Herbert Lom

Whore
US 1991 85m colour
Palace/Trimark (Dan Ireland, Ronaldo Vasconcellos)
A prostitute, hiding from her vicious pimp, recalls good customers and bad.
Dispiriting account of sexual exploitation, not helped by transferring the original's specifically London setting to the United States.
w Ken Russell, Deborah Dalton play *Bondage* by David Hines d Ken Russell ph Amir Mokri m Michael Gibbs pd Richard Lewis ed Brian Tagg
☆ Theresa Russell, Benjamin Mouton, Antonio Fargas, Sanjay, Elizabeth Moorehead, Michael Crabtree

'You are cordially invited to George and Martha's for an evening of fun and games!'
Who's Afraid of Virginia Woolf? ****
US 1966 129m bw
Warner (Ernest Lehman)
A college professor and his wife have an all-night shouting match and embarrass their guests.
As a film of a play, fair to middling; as a milestone in cinematic permissiveness, very important; as an entertainment, sensational for those in the mood.
w Ernest Lehman play *Edward Albee* d *Mike Nichols* ph Haskell Wexler m Alex North
☆ *Richard Burton, Elizabeth Taylor, George Segal, Sandy Dennis*
'A magnificent triumph of determined audacity.' – *Bosley Crowther*
'One of the most scathingly honest American films ever made.' – *Stanley Kauffmann*
Haskell Wexler; Elizabeth Taylor; Sandy Dennis
best picture; Ernest Lehman; Mike Nichols; Alex North; Richard Burton; George Segal
best picture; Richard Burton; Elizabeth Taylor

Who's Been Sleeping in My Bed?
US 1963 103m Technicolor Panavision
Paramount/Amro (Jack Rose)
A TV matinee idol finds he is a sex symbol also in his private life.
Coy bedroom farce with no real action but a smattering of jokes.
w Jack Rose d Daniel Mann ph Joseph Ruttenberg m George Duning
☆ Dean Martin, Elizabeth Montgomery, Martin Balsam, Jill St John, Richard Conte, Carol Burnett, Louis Nye, Yoko Tani, Elisabeth Fraser

'The most riotous bedtime story ever!'
Who's Got the Action?
US 1962 93m Technicolor Panavision
Paramount/Amro (Jack Rose)
A bored wife and her law partner husband have remarkable success betting on horses.

Badly cast and rather slow comedy with flashes of wit.
w Jack Rose *novel* Four Horse Players Are Missing by Alexander Rose *d* Daniel Mann *ph* Joseph Ruttenberg *m* George Duning
☆ Dean Martin, Lana Turner, Eddie Albert, Walter Matthau, Nita Talbot, Margo, Paul Ford, John McGiver

Who's Harry Crumb?
US 1989 90m Technicolor
Columbia TriStar/NBC (Arnon Milchan)
An incompetent, accident-prone private detective investigates the kidnapping of a millionaire's daughter.
Broad, slapstick comedy that offers occasional pleasures.
w Robert Conte, Peter Martin Wortmann *d* Paul Flaherty *ph* Stephen M. Katz *m* Michel Colombier *pd* Trevor Williams *ed* Danford B. Greene, Scott Conrad
☆ John Candy, Jeffrey Jones, Annie Potts, Tim Thomerson, Barry Corbin, Shawnee Smith, Valri Bromfield, Doug Steckler, Renee Coleman

Who's Minding the Mint? *
US 1967 97m Technicolor
Columbia/Norman Maurer
An employee of the US mint and his friends find a means of printing bills at night.
Smartly-made action comedy with good performances.
w R. S. Allen, Harvey Bullock *d* Howard Morris *ph* Joseph Biroc *m* Lalo Schifrin
☆ Jim Hutton, Dorothy Provine, Milton Berle, Joey Bishop, Bob Denver, Walter Brennan, Victor Buono, Jack Gilford

Who's Minding the Store? *
US 1963 90m Technicolor
Paramount/York/Jerry Lewis (Paul Jones)
An accident-prone young man gets a job in a department store.
Better-than-average star comedy, slapstick being allowed precedence over sentimentality.
w Frank Tashlin, Harry Tugend *d* Frank Tashlin *ph* W. Wallace Kelley *m* Joseph J. Lilley
☆ Jerry Lewis, Jill St John, Agnes Moorehead, John McGiver, Ray Walston, Nancy Kulp

Who's That Girl?
US 1987 94m Technicolor
Warner/Peter Guber, Jon Peters, Roger Birnbaum
A mild lawyer finds an ex-jailbird starlet his hardest client to handle.
Muddled 'realistic' comedy which starts at screaming pitch and stays there.
w Andrew Smith, Ken Finkleman *d* James Foley *ph* Jan DeBont *ed* Pembroke J. Herring
☆ Madonna, Griffin Dunne, Haviland Morris, John McMartin, Robert Swan, Drew Pillsbury
'What's lacking is pure and simple good humour.' – *Variety*

Who's That Knocking at My Door *
US 1968 90m bw
Cinegate/Tri-Mod (Joseph Weill, Haig Manoogian, Betzi Manoogian)
aka: *I Call First*
aka: *J. R.*
An Italian-American's relationship with a more sophisticated woman is ruined by his working-class Catholic upbringing.
Scorsese's first and an intriguing film, a groping towards the subject-matter that found assured expression in Mean Streets.
wd Martin Scorsese *ph* Michael Wadleigh, Richard Coll *ad* Vic Magnotta *ed* Thelma Schoonmaker
☆ Harvey Keitel, Zina Bethune, Lennard Kuras, Ann Collette, Michael Scala, Harry Northup, Catherine Scorsese, Phil Carlson
† The film was first shown under the title *I Call First* at the Chicago Film Festival in 1967. It was later released under its present title with the addition of a nude scene.

Who's the Man?
US 1993 87m Technicolor
Metro Tartan/New Line/Tin Pan Apple/De Passe/Thomas (Charles Stettler, Maynell Thomas)
Two Harlem barbers become policemen and save the neighbourhood from a wicked developer.
Rappers tread where only Police Academy *has trod before in a crudely slapstick comedy that also attempts, and fails, to make a serious point; the reason for it all seems to be the music, which is also an acquired taste.*
w Seth Greenland *d* Ted Demme *ph* Adam Kimmel *m* Michael Wolff, Nic ten-Broek *pd* Ruth Ammon *ed* Jeffrey Wolf
☆ Ed Lover, Doctor Dre, Badja Djola, Richard Bright, Ice-T
'An enjoyable, kinetic mess of music, low comedy and social drama.' – *Variety*

Whose Life Is It Anyway?
US 1981 118m Metrocolor
MGM/Martin C. Schute, Ray Cooney (Lawrence P. Bachmann)
Totally paralysed after a car crash, a young sculptor lies in hospital wanting to die.
Ill-advised film of a very static play which was a freak success on account of various very good leading performances. It makes a very uneasy movie.
w Brian Clark, Reginald Rose *play* Brian Clark *d* John Badham *ph* Mario Tosi *m* Arthur B. Rubinstein
☆ Richard Dreyfuss, John Cassavetes, Christine Lahti, Bob Balaban, Kenneth McMillan

Why Bother to Knock: see *Don't Bother to Knock*

Why Did Bodhi-Dharma Leave for the East? *
South Korea 1989 135m colour
ICA/Bae Yong-Kyun
original title: *Dharmaga Tongjoguro Kan Kkadalgun?*
In a remote monastery an old monk prepares for his death, a younger one feels guilt about abandoning his family and his blind mother, and an orphaned child grieves for a moment over a bird he kills accidentally.
A leisurely Zen Buddhist meditation on death and enlightenment that offers few of the usual pleasures of movies, such as narrative and character development.
wd Bae Yong-Kyun *ph* Bae Yong-Kyun *m* Chin Kyn-Yong *ed* Bae Yong-Kyun
☆ Yi Pan-Yong, Sin Won-Sop, Huang Hae-Jin, Ko Su Myoung
† The film won the Golden Leopard award at the 1990 Locarno Film Festival.

Why Me?
US 1989 87m colour
Entertainment/Epic Productions/Sarlui/Diamant (Marjorie Israel)
Two jewel thieves, who inadvertently steal a famous ruby ring, double-cross the authorities who demand its return.
Weakly acted, limp comedy-thriller that fails to sparkle.
w Donald E. Westlake, Leonard Maas Jnr *novel* Donald E. Westlake *d* Gene Quintano *ph* Peter Deming *m* Phil Marshall *pd* Woody Crocker *ed* Alan Balsam
☆ Christopher Lambert, Kim Greist, Christopher Lloyd, J. T. Walsh, Gregory Millar, Wendel Meldrum, Michael J. Pollard, John Plana, Tony Plana

Why Shoot the Teacher?
Canada 1976 99m colour
WSTT/Fraser Films (Lawrence Hertzog)
In 1935 a school teacher finds a chilly reception when he settles in a Saskatchewan village.
Unsatisfactory but occasionally quite entertaining comedy-drama which hovers around the Cold Comfort Farm *mark.*
w James Defelice *novel* Max Braithwaite *d* Silvio Narizzano *ph* Marc Champion *m* Ricky Hyslop
☆ Bud Cort, Samantha Eggar, Chris Wiggins, Gary Reineke

Why We Fight ****
US 1942 bw
Frank Capra
A series of feature-length compilations released during 1942–5, primarily for showing to the armed forces, these were superbly vigorous documentaries which later fascinated the public at large. Editing, music and diagrams were all used to punch home the message. Individual titles were:
Prelude to War (53m):
w Eric Knight, Anthony Veiller d Frank Capra
The Nazis Strike (42m):
w and *d* as above
Divide and Conquer (58m):
w Anthony Veiller, Robert Heller d Frank Capra, Anatole Litvak
The Battle of Britain (54m):
wd Anthony Veiller
The Battle of Russia (80m):
w Anthony Veiller, Robert Heller, Anatole Litvak d Anatole Litvak oscar best documentary
The Battle of China (60m):
w Eric Knight, Anthony Veiller d Frank Capra, Anatole Litvak
War Comes to America (70m)
w Anthony Veiller d Anatole Litvak
All had editing by *William Hornbeck*, music by *Dimitri Tiomkin* and commentary by *Walter Huston*.
best documentary (Prelude to War)

Why Worry? *
US 1923 60m approx (24 fps) bw silent
Hal Roach-Harold Lloyd
A hypochondriac is cured when he gets mixed up in a South American revolution.
Moderate star comedy with highlights well spaced out.
d Sam Taylor, Fred Newmeyer
☆ Harold Lloyd, Jobyna Ralston, Leo White

Wichita
US 1955 81m Technicolor Cinemascope
Walter Mirisch/AA
Wyatt Earp is hired to bring law and order to a wide-open cow town.
Standard, i.e. romanticized, version of Earp's exploits: quite entertaining to watch.
w Daniel Ullman *d* Jacques Tourneur *ph* Harold Lipstein *m* Hans J. Salter
☆ Joel McCrea, Vera Miles, Lloyd Bridges, Wallace Ford, Edgar Buchanan, Peter Graves, Keith Larsen, Carl Benton Reid

Wicked
US 1931 57m bw
Fox
A woman is innocently sent to prison and when she comes out sets about finding the child she had to sign away.
Woman's picture, packed with predictable incident.
w anonymous hands *d* Allan Dwan
☆ Elissa Landi, Victor McLaglen, Theodore von Eltz, Alan Dinehart, Una Merkel, Oscar Apfel, Irene Rich
'Old-fashioned tearjerker now too old to jerk tears or grosses.' – *Variety*

'If every woman has her price ... there's a reason!'
Wicked As They Come
GB 1956 94m bw
Columbia/Film Locations (Maxwell Setton)
US title: *Portrait in Smoke*
A beauty contest winner from the slums makes money and luxury her goal.
Busy melodrama which interests without edifying.
wd Ken Hughes *ph* Basil Emmott *m* Malcolm Arnold *co-w* Robert Westerby, Sigmund Miller
☆ Arlene Dahl, Herbert Marshall, Phil Carey, Michael Goodliffe, David Kossoff, Sidney James, Ralph Truman, Faith Brook

Wicked City (dubbed)
Japan 1993 81m colour
Hideyuki Kikuchi/Tokuma Shoten/Video Art/Japan Home Video/Manga (Kenji Kurada, Makoto Sedani)
A human bodyguard and a woman from the dark world of monsters are assigned to guard from assassins a doctor essential to the signing of a peace treaty between the two worlds.
A well-animated saga of exotic sex, violence and sentimentality.
w Maretoshi Naga *novel* Hideyuki Kikuchi *d* Yoshiaki Kawajiri *ph* Kinichi Ishikawa *m* Yoshimasa Tokai *ad* Kazuo Oga *ed* Nobuyuki Ogata
☆ Featuring the voices of Stuart Miller, Tammy Holloway, George Littlewood, Bill Richards, Ronald Baker, Lisa Robinson, Philip Gough

The Wicked Lady *
GB 1945 104m bw
GFD/Gainsborough (R. J. Minney)
In the days of Charles II, Lady Skelton befriends a highwayman and takes to crime.
The most commercially successful of the Gainsborough costume charades because of its atmosphere of gloomy sin. Dramatically turgid and surprisingly poorly acted and directed, but with good period detail. It had to be reshot for America because of the ladies' décolletage.
wd Leslie Arliss *novel* The Life and Death of the Wicked Lady Skelton by Magdalen King-Hall *ph* Jack Cox *m* Hans May *md* Louis Levy
☆ Margaret Lockwood, James Mason, Griffith Jones, Patricia Roc, Michael Rennie, Enid Stamp-Taylor, Felix Aylmer, Martita Hunt, David Horne
'A mixture of hot passion and cold suet pudding.' – *Manchester Guardian*
'Rather dull and juvenile in its determination to be daring.' – *Richard Mallett, Punch*

The Wicked Lady
GB 1983 99m colour
Columbia/Cannon (Menahem Golan, Yoram Globus)
A remake with colour, sex and violence.
Pictorially quite attractive, but that's about all. It caused controversy when the British censor tried to cut a scene showing Faye Dunaway lashing another woman with a horse-whip but retracted after Winner protested. (The fight owed much to a similar scene in Idol of Paris *[qv], directed by Leslie Arliss in 1948.)*
w Leslie Arliss, Michael Winner *d* Michael Winner *ph* Jack Cardiff *m* Tony Banks *ad* John Blezard *ed* Arnold Crust
☆ Faye Dunaway, Alan Bates, John Gielgud, Denholm Elliott, Prunella Scales, Oliver Tobias, Glynis Barber, Joan Hickson
'The images look as cheap as expensive greetings cards.' – *Sunday Times*
'A first-class piece of popular entertainment.' – *Lindsay Anderson*

Wicked Stepmother
US 1989 92m DeLuxe
MGM/Larco (Robert Littman)
A wife returns from holiday with her husband to discover that in their absence her father has married a strange old woman.
A bizarre oddity: a psychological horror movie that turned into a broad, occult comedy when its star left in the early stages. It has a few amusing moments amid the chaos, but would probably have been no better had the production gone smoothly.
wd Larry Cohen *ph* Bryan England *m* Robert Folk *ad* Gene Abel *ed* David Kern
☆ Bette Davis, Colleen Camp, Lionel Stander, David Rasche, Tom Bosley, Barbara Carrera, Richard Moll, Seymour Cassel, Evelyn Keyes
† Bette Davis (who, at 80, looked shrivelled and ill) quit the production after she saw herself in early, unedited scenes, necessitating some swift rewriting in order to try to incorporate her work in a new narrative in which she is transformed into Barbara Carrera. Problems with her false teeth made it difficult for her to say her lines, which she also had difficulty remembering. It was her last, and least, screen appearance.

The Wicked Wife: see *Grand National Night*

A Wicked Woman
US 1934 71m bw
MGM (Harry Rapf)
A woman kills her drunken husband to protect her children, later confesses and is exonerated.
The tail end of the mother love saga, better made than most.
w Florence Ryerson, Zelda Sears *novel* Anne Austin *d* Charles Brabin *ph* Lester White *m* William Axt
☆ Mady Christians, Charles Bickford, Betty Furness, William Henry, Jackie Searl, Robert Taylor, Paul Harvey

'Flesh to touch...Flesh to burn! Don't keep the Wicker Man waiting!'
The Wicker Man **
GB 1973 86m Eastmancolor
British Lion (Peter Snell)
A policeman flies to a remote Scottish isle to investigate the death of a child, and finds himself in the hands of diabolists.
Old-fashioned but remarkably well made scare story, with effective shock moments.
w Anthony Shaffer d Robin Hardy ph Harry Waxman *m* Paul Giovanni *ad* Seamus Flannery *ed* Eric Boyd-Perkins

☆ Edward Woodward (Sgt Howie), Britt Ekland (Willow), Christopher Lee (Lord Summersisle), Ingrid Pitt (Librarian), Diane Cilento (Miss Rose), Lindsay Kemp (Alder MacGregor), Russell Waters (Harbour Master)

'An encouraging achievement for those who had begun to despair of the British cinema.' – *David McGillivray*

† The film also exists in other versions, the longest running for 102m. It was also released on DVD in a director's cut running for 117m.

Wide Open Faces

US 1938 67m bw
Columbia (David L. Loew)

Public enemies congregate in a wayside inn where missing loot is supposedly buried.

Moderately amusing slapstick farce.

w Earle Snell, Clarence Marks, Joe Bigelow, Richard Flournoy *d* Kurt Neumann

☆ Joe E. Brown, Jane Wyman, Alison Skipworth, Lyda Roberti, Alan Baxter, Lucien Littlefield, Sidney Toler, Berton Churchill

'On the corny side, strictly for dual bills.' – *Variety*

'An erotic tale of beauty and bewitchment.'

Wide Sargasso Sea

Australia 1992 98m colour
Rank/Sargasso/New Line/Laughing Kookaburra (Jan Sharp)

In Jamaica in the mid-1800s, as her marriage to an English gentleman disintegrates, a plantation owner fears that, like her mother, she may go mad.

A prequel to Jane Eyre, *concentrating on the fate of the mad Mrs Rochester, this is a lush and overblown saga of sex and revenge, bordering on the risible.*

w Jan Sharp, Carole Angier, John Duigan *novel* Jean Rhys *d* John Duigan *ph* Geoff Burton *m* Stewart Copeland *pd* Franckie D *ed* Anne Goursaud

☆ Karina Lombard, Nathaniel Parker, Claudia Robinson, Michael York, Rachel Ward, Martine Beswick, Huw Christie Williams

'A faintly absurd erotic melodrama whose protagonists must have been cast for their looks and their eagerness to sweat through copious bed scenes rather than for acting ability.' – *Sheila Johnston, Independent*

† The same theme was explored in an earlier film, *I Walked with a Zombie* (qv).

The Widow from Chicago

US 1930 63m bw
First National

A woman mixes with a gang to avenge her brother's murder.

Bottom-of-the-barrel gangster drama, presented with little flair.

w Earl Baldwin *d* Edward F. Cline

☆ Alice White, Edward G. Robinson, Neil Hamilton, Frank McHugh, E. H. Calvert

'Barely makes programme grade ... will have to struggle to break even.' – *Variety*

Widow from Monte Carlo

US 1935 60m bw
Warner

The theft of an indiscreet letter causes much embarrassment in an English country house.

Society comedy-drama with curious farcical asides: not an obvious success.

w F. Hugh Herbert, Charles Belden *play* Ian Hunter, A. E. W. Mason *d* Arthur G. Collins

☆ Warren William, Dolores del Rio, Louise Fazenda, Colin Clive, Herbert Mundin, Warren Hymer

'Behind the eight ball where big-time dates are concerned.' – *Variety*

Widow's Peak

GB 1993 101m Eastmancolor
Rank/Jo Manuel

An overbearing widow who dominates life in a small Irish town gets her come-uppance.

A revenge comedy that begins in a broad and lively manner and then loses its way.

w Hugh Leonard *d* John Irvin *ph* Ashley Rowe *m* Carl Davis *pd* Leo Austin *ed* Peter Tanner

☆ Mia Farrow, Joan Plowright, Natasha Richardson, Jim Broadbent, Adrian Dunbar, John Kavanagh, Anne Kent

'A forgettable saga worth seeing if only to immerse yourself in Ireland without seeing it rain for an hour.' – *Neville Judd, Film Review*

Wife, Doctor and Nurse *

US 1937 84m bw
TCF (Raymond Griffith)

A romantic triangle as the title suggests.

Agreeable fluff with a mildly surprising end (for 1937) suggesting a ménage à trois.

w Kathryn Scola, Darrell Ware, Lamar Trotti *d* Walter Lang *ph* Edward Cronjager *m* Arthur Lange

☆ Loretta Young, Warner Baxter, Virginia Bruce, Jane Darwell, Sidney Blackmer, Maurice Cass, Minna Gombell, Elisha Cook Jnr, Lon Chaney Jnr

'A smart comedy that will please all.' – *Variety*

Wife, Husband and Friend *

US 1939 80m bw
TCF (Nunnally Johnson)

A man sabotages his wife's efforts to become a professional singer.

Modestly agreeable romantic comedy later remade as Everybody Does It *(qv).*

w Nunnally Johnson *story* James M. Cain *d* Gregory Ratoff *ph* Ernest Palmer *m* David Buttolph

☆ Loretta Young, Warner Baxter, Binnie Barnes, Cesar Romero, George Barbier, J. Edward Bromberg, Eugene Pallette, Helen Westley

'Diverting farce comedy with appeal pointed to class audiences.' – *Variety*

The Wife of General Ling

GB 1937 72m bw
John Stafford/Premier

In China, a merchant's white wife unmasks him as a criminal.

Stilted melodrama.

w Akos Tolnay, Reginald Long, Peter Cheyney, Dorothy Hope *d* Ladislas Vajda

☆ Griffith Jones, Inkijinoff, Adrianne Renn, Alan Napier, Anthony Eustrel, Hugh McDermott, Gibson Gowland

'Hardly up to West End level.' – *Variety*

Wife of Monte Cristo

US 1946 83m bw
PRC (Leon Fromkess)

In 1832 Paris, the Count leads an underground movement against racketeers.

And the film plays like a Brooklyn melodrama in fancy dress; as such, not too bad.

w Dorcas Cochran *d* Edgar G. Ulmer

☆ John Loder, Lenore Aubert, Charles Dingle, Fritz Kortner, Martin Kosleck, Eduardo Ciannelli, Fritz Feld, Eva Gabor

The Wife Takes a Flyer

US 1942 86m bw
Columbia (B. P. Schulberg)
GB title: *A Yank in Dutch*

A Dutchwoman whose husband is in the asylum takes in a fugitive USAF pilot in his place although a Nazi officer is billeted on the household.

Downright peculiar World War II comedy which at the time seemed the height of bad taste – and no laughs.

w Gina Kaus, Jay Dratler *d* Richard Wallace *ph* Franz Planer *m* Werner Heyman

☆ Joan Bennett, Franchot Tone, Allyn Joslyn, Cecil Cunningham, Lloyd Corrigan, Georgia Caine

'Kicks in the pants, belching, and exaggerated face-making are lifted from burlesque to decorate this feeble attempt.' – *New York Post*

Wife versus Secretary *

US 1936 88m bw
MGM (Hunt Stromberg)

A publisher's wife starts to believe rumours about his attention to his secretary.

Practised star comedy drama which provided thoroughly satisfactory entertainment of a kind the cinema seems to have forgotten.

w Norman Krasna, Alice Duer Miller, John Lee Mahin *novel* Faith Baldwin *d* Clarence Brown *ph* Ray June *m* Herbert Stothart, Edward Ward

☆ Clark Gable, Myrna Loy, Jean Harlow, May Robson, George Barbier, James Stewart, Hobart Cavanaugh

'A real box office picture for the sticks and the stems.' – *Variety*

'See this picture if you enjoy the spectacle of three clever stars shining for all they are worth.' – *Film Weekly*

The Wilby Conspiracy *

GB 1975 105m DeLuxe
UA/Optimus/Baum-Dantine (Stanley Sopel)

A British mining engineer is persuaded to help a black revolutionary in his flight from Cape Town to Johannesburg.

Reasonably exciting political chase thriller with a sufficiency of twists and action sequences; philosophy is present but secondary.

w Rod Amateau, Harold Nebenzal *novel* Peter Driscoll *d* Ralph Nelson *ph* John Coquillon *m* Stanley Myers *ad* Harold Pottle *ed* Ernest Walter

☆ Sidney Poitier, Michael Caine, Nicol Williamson, Prunella Gee, Saeed Jaffrey, Persis Khambatta

Wild

Hong Kong 1996 87m colour
(Suen Ging On)
original title: *Kuang Ye San Qian Jing*
aka: *Invitation to Die*

After a car crash ends in murder, a woman finds herself on the run with a ruthless killer and his gang.

Senseless sex and violence is presented with the minimum of narrative or characterisation; it is simply a chase movie with a high body count, big explosions and an apparent admiration for gangsters.

w Ng Man Fai *d* 'Billy' Tang Hin Shing *ph* Zhang Wenbao *m* Simon Lui Yu Yeung, Jin Peida *ed* Cai Xiong

☆ Francoise Yip (Wai), Bowie Lam Bo Yi (Shing), Qiming Chen, Simon Lui Yu Yeung, Leung Yat-Ho

'Harry can't remember... what he's forgotten!'

Wild About Harry

GB 2000 90m colour
BBC/Scala/Winchester (Robert Cooper, Laurie Borg)

A philandering, alcoholic, middle-aged TV cook, on the point of being divorced, loses his memory of what happened after he was 18.

A slight comedy of redemption.

w Colin Bateman *d* Declan Lowney *ph* Ron Fortunato *m* Murray Gold *pd* Claire Kenny *ed* Tim Waddell

☆ Brendan Gleeson (Harry McKee), Amanda Donohoe (Ruth McKee), Adrian Dunbar (J. J. MacMahon), James Nesbitt (Walter Adair), George Wendt (Frankie), Henry Deazley (Billy McKee), Bronagh Gallagher (Miss Boyle)

'A grave disappointment from which nobody emerges happily.' – *Philip French, Observer*

The Wild Affair *

GB 1965 87m bw
Seven Arts (Richard Patterson)

An office Christmas party nearly turns into an orgy.

Curious little comedy drama which plays almost like the Road to Ruin *and has an attractive but miscast leading lady. Interesting elements.*

wd John Krish *novel* *The Last Hours of Sandra Lee* by William Sansom *ph* Arthur Ibbetson *m* Martin Slavin

☆ Nancy Kwan, Terry-Thomas, Jimmy Logan, Bud Flanagan, Betty Marsden, Gladys Morgan, Paul Whitsun-Jones, Donald Churchill, Victor Spinetti

'Take a ride on the wild side.'

Wild America

US 1997 106m DuArt Panavision
Warner/Morgan Creek/Steve Tisch (James G. Robinson, Irby Smith, Mark Stouffer)

In the 60s, three brothers in Arkansas set out with a dream to make a documentary on wildlife in America.

Pleasant, rambling family film of scrapes and escapes with animals.

w David Michael Wieger *d* William Dear *ph* David Burr *m* Joel McNeely *pd* Steve Jordan *ed* O. Nicholas Brown, Stuart Pappe

☆ Jonathan Taylor Thomas, Devon Sawa, Scott Bairstow, Frances Fisher, Jamie Sheridan, Tracey Walter, Don Stroud

'An abundance of humor, excitement, heart and soul.' – *Michael Medved, New York Post*

'The stuff of second rate children's fiction.' – *Sight and Sound*

† The film is based on a true story of the Stouffer brothers, who became documentary film-makers.

The Wild and the Innocent

US 1959 85m Eastmancolor Cinemascope
Universal-International

A trapper is torn between a mountain girl and a city tart.

Oddly old-fashioned Western, like The Gold Rush *without laughs.*

w Sy Gomberg, Jack Sher *d* Jack Sher *ph* Harold Lipstein *m* Hans J. Salter

☆ Audie Murphy, Joanne Dru, Gilbert Roland, Sandra Dee, Jim Backus, Peter Breck

The Wild and the Willing

GB 1962 112m bw
Rank/Box-Thomas (Betty E. Box)
US title: *Young and Willing*

A troublesome student at a provincial university seduces the wife of his professor.

Watchable sex melodrama with an interesting background on which no one seems to have quite enough grip; 'realism' is simply there to be exploited.

w Nicholas Phipps, Mordecai Richler *play* *The Tinker* by Laurence Dobie, Robert Sloman *d* Ralph Thomas *ph* Ernest Steward *m* Norrie Paramor

☆ Virginia Maskell, Paul Rogers, Ian McShane, Samantha Eggar, John Hurt, Catherine Woodville, John Standing, Jeremy Brett

Wild and Wonderful

US 1963 88m Eastmancolor
U-I/Harold Hecht

A French film star poodle makes friends with an American gambler.

Amiable zany comedy in a set-bound Gay Paree.

w Larry Markes, Michael Morris, Waldo Salt *d* Michael Anderson *ph* Joseph LaShelle *m* Morton Stevens

☆ Tony Curtis, Christine Kaufmann, Larry Storch, Marty Ingels, Jacques Aubuchon, Jules Munshin

Wild and Woolly

US 1937 90m bw
TCF (John Stone)

During a small-town frontier celebration an attempt to rob the bank is thwarted.

Pleasant family Western with music.

w Lynn Root, Frank Fenton *d* Alfred Werker

☆ Jane Withers, Walter Brennan, Pauline Moore, Alfalfa Switzer, Jackie Searl, Berton Churchill, Lon Chaney Jnr

'Whatever its companion feature happens to be, this is the one the audience talks about on the way home.' – *Variety*

The Wild Angels *

US 1966 85m Pathécolor Panavision
AIP (Roger Corman)

A Californian motorcycle gang is run on semi-religious, ritualistic, Nazi lines.

Much-banned melodrama, cheaply made but vigorously handled and of some interest on social and historical levels.

w Charles B. Griffith *d* Roger Corman *ph* Richard Moore *m* Mike Curb *ad* Leon Ericksen *ed* Monte Hellman

☆ Peter Fonda, Nancy Sinatra, Bruce Dern, Michael J. Pollard, Gayle Hunnicutt

'Roger Corman's color-film account of the orgiastic raping, looting, brawling, pot-smoking, corpse-desecrating, church-wrecking, parson-torturing, swastika-swaddled activities of a gang of motorcyclists. After we've feasted our eyes on the detailing thereof by, incidentally, a thoroughly inept cast, without even the context of good cycling sequences, we're given a one-line moral by the suddenly regenerate gang leader: "There's no place to go," he mumbles. Yes, indeed, there's still room at the bottom.' – *Judith Crist*

Wild at Heart **

US 1990 127m

Palace/Polygram/Propaganda (Monty Montgomery, Steve Golin, Joni Sighvatsson)

A petty criminal is redeemed by the love of a histrionic woman.

Over-ripe acting, violent action, and a melodramatic plot combine to produce the cinematic equivalent of Grand Guignol. *It won the Palme d'Or at the Cannes Film Festival in 1990.*

wd David Lynch *novel* Barry Gifford *ph* Fred Elmes *m* Angelo Badalamenti *ed* Duwayne Dunham

☆ Nicolas Cage, Laura Dern, Diane Ladd, Willem Dafoe, Isabella Rossellini, Harry Dean Stanton, Crispin Glover, J. E. Freeman, W. Morgan Sheppard

'Joltingly violent, wickedly funny and rivetingly erotic.' – *Variety*

'The picture is packed with so much deranged energy, so many bravura images, that it's hard not to be seduced by the sick wonder of it all.' – *Richard Corliss, Time*

Diane Ladd

Wild Beauty

US 1946 61m bw

Universal (Wallace W. Fox)

An Indian boy protects his wild horse from men who want to to kill the herd he leads for shoe leather.

Amiable minor Western for horse and dog lovers, though it is given to some complacent, if well-meaning, pontification on the plight of Native Americans; the sermon might have been more convincing if the leading role had not been played by an obviously white youth.

w Adele Buffington *d* Wallace W. Fox *ph* Maury Gertsman *m* Paul Sawtell *ad* Jack Otterson, Abraham Grossman *ed* D. Patrick Kelley

☆ Don Porter, Lois Collier, Robert 'Buzzy' Henry, Jacqueline de Wit, Robert Wilcox, George Cleveland, Dick Curtis

Wild Bill *

US 1995 97m DeLuxe/bw

MGM/UA/Zanuck Co. (Richard D. Zanuck, Lili Fini Zanuck)

A Western gunfighter takes to drugs as he examines his life and legend.

A complex, fragmentary look at the life of Wild Bill Hickok that strips away the heroics to present a confused and unhappy killer; spasmodically interesting, if rather too glum.

wd Walter Hill *play Fathers and Sons* by Thomas Babe *novel Deadwood* by *Pete Dexter ph* Lloyd Ahern *pd* Joseph Nemec III *ed* Freeman Davies

☆ Jeff Bridges, Ellen Barkin (Calamity Jane), John Hurt, Diane Lane, David Arquette, Christina Applegate, Bruce Dern, James Gammon, Marjoe Gortner, James Remar, Keith Carradine (as Buffalo Bill)

'An art Western that manages to shoot itself in both feet.' – *Variety*

† The film cost $30m and took $2.2m at the US box-office.

Wild Bill Hickok Rides

US 1941 81m bw

Warner

Wild Bill helps a homesteader keep his land.

Oddly cast, rather naïve little Western.

w Charles Grayson, Paul Gerard Smith and Raymond Schrock *d* Ray Enright *ph* Ted McCord *m* Howard Jackson *ed* Clarence Kolster

☆ Constance Bennett, Bruce Cabot, Warren William, Ward Bond, Howard da Silva

The Wild Blue Yonder

US 1952 98m bw

Republic (Herbert J. Yates)

GB title: *Thunder Across the Pacific*

Incidents in the lives of bomber pilots in the Pacific during World War II.

Routine action flagwaver.

w Richard Tregaskis *d* Allan Dwan *ph* Reggie Lanning *m* Victor Young

☆ Wendell Corey, Vera Hruba Ralston, Forrest Tucker, Phil Harris, Walter Brennan, Ruth Donnelly

Wild Boys of the Road *

US 1933 88m bw

Warner (Robert Presnell)

GB title: *Dangerous Days*

Boys of poor families take to the road in gangs.

Vivid social melodrama of its day, now rather overstated.

w Earl Baldwin *d* William Wellman *ph* Arthur Todd

☆ Frankie Darro, Rochelle Hudson, Edwin Philips, Arthur Hohl

'A depressing evening in the theatre, one which the general fan public will gladly avoid.' – *Variety*

Wild Brian Kent

US 1936 57m bw

TCF (Sol Lesser)

An amiable Western con man helps a town to rid itself of a villain.

Mild comedy drama.

w Earle Snell, Don Swift *novel The Recreation of Brian Kent* by Harold Bell Wright *d* Howard Bretherton

☆ Ralph Bellamy, Mae Clarke, Helen Lowell, Stanley Andrews, Lew Kelly

'Little to commend it.' – *Variety*

'Nine men who came too late and stayed too long!' 'The land had changed. They hadn't. The earth had changed. They couldn't!'

The Wild Bunch ****

US 1969 145m Technicolor Panavision

Warner Seven Arts/Phil Feldman

In 1914, Texas bandits are ambushed by an old enemy and die bloodily in defence of one of their number against a ruthless Mexican revolutionary.

Arguably the director's best film, and one which set a fashion for blood-spurting violence in Westerns. Undeniably stylish, thoughtful, and in places very exciting.

w Walon Green, Sam Peckinpah *d Sam Peckinpah ph Lucien Ballard m* Jerry Fielding *ad* Edward Carrere

☆ William Holden, Ernest Borgnine, Robert Ryan, Edmond O'Brien, Warren Oates, Jaime Sanchez, Ben Johnson, Strother Martin, L. Q. Jones, Albert Dekker

'A western that enlarged the form aesthetically, thematically, demonically.' – *Stanley Kauffmann, 1972*

'We watch endless violence to assure us that violence is not good.' – *Judith Crist, 1976*

'The bloody deaths are voluptuous, frightening, beautiful. Pouring new wine into the bottle of the western, Peckinpah explodes the bottle; his story is too simple for this imagist epic.' – *Pauline Kael, New Yorker*

'One of the most moving elegies for a vanished age ever created within the genre.' – *Time Out, 1984*

script; Jerry Fielding

The Wild Child: see *L'Enfant Sauvage*

The Wild Country

US 1970 100m Technicolor

Walt Disney (Ron Miller)

In the late 1880s a farmer buys a dilapidated Wyoming ranch and falls foul of a local rancher who controls the water supply.

Predictable family Western in the familiar Disney style.

w Calvin Clements Jnr, Paul Savage *novel Little Britches* by Ralph Moody *d* Robert Totten *ph* Frank Phillips *m* Robert Brunner

☆ Steve Forrest, Vera Miles, Jack Elam, Ronny Howard, Morgan Woodward

'The best ******* mercenaries in the business!'

The Wild Geese

GB 1978 134m Eastmancolor Panavision

Rank/Richmond (Euan Lloyd)

Adventures of four British mercenaries in a central African state.

All-star blood and guts with a few breezy touches in the script.

w Reginald Rose *novel* Daniel Carney *d* Andrew V. McLaglen *ph* Jack Hildyard *m* Roy Budd

☆ Roger Moore, Richard Burton, Richard Harris, Hardy Kruger, Stewart Granger, Jack Watson, Frank Finlay, Kenneth Griffith, Barry Foster, Jeff Corey, Ronald Fraser, Percy Herbert, Patrick Allen, Jane Hylton

Wild Geese Calling

US 1941 77m bw

TCF (Harry Joe Brown)

A young adventurer in Oregon weds the girlfriend of a conniving gambler.

Minor semi-Western which never really finds a style.

w Horace McCoy *novel* Stewart Edward White *d* John Brahm *ph* Lucien Ballard *m* Alfred Newman

☆ Joan Bennett, Henry Fonda, Warren William, Ona Munson, Barton MacLane, Russell Simpson, Iris Adrian

Wild Geese II

GB 1985 125m Technicolor

Thorn EMI/Frontier/Euan Lloyd

A mercenary is commissioned by an American TV station to kidnap Rudolf Hess from Spandau jail.

Ingenious if unlikely premise for another tough adventure; it largely fails because of silly plotting.

w Reginald Rose *novel The Square Circle* by Daniel Carney *d* Peter Hunt *ph* Michael Reed *m* Roy Budd *pd* Syd Cain *ed* Keith Palmer

☆ Scott Glenn, Barbara Carrera, Edward Fox, Laurence Olivier, Robert Webber, Kenneth Haigh, Stratford Johns

Wild Harvest

US 1947 92m bw

Paramount (Robert Fellows)

A romantic triangle develops among wheat harvesters on the Western plains.

Standard star hokum.

w John Monks Jnr *d* Tay Garnett *ph* John F. Seitz *m* Hugo Friedhofer

☆ Alan Ladd, Dorothy Lamour, Robert Preston, Lloyd Nolan, Dick Erdman, Allen Jenkins, Will Wright

The Wild Heart: see *Gone to Earth*

Wild Hearts Can't Be Broken *

US 1991 88m colour

Buena Vista/Disney/Silver Screen Partners IV (Matt Williams)

In the early 30s, a young girl struggles to make her way in the world as a horse-riding high diver in a fairground show.

Soft-centred romantic drama, based on a true story, that effectively captures the flavour of its times.

w Matt Williams, Oley Sassone *d* Steve Miner *ph* Daryn Okada *m* Mason Daring *pd* Randy Ser *ed* Jon Poll

☆ Gabrielle Anwar, Michael Schoeffling, Kathleen York, Dylan Kussman, Cliff Robertson

Wild Heritage

US 1958 78m Eastmancolor Cinemascope

Universal (John E. Horton)

Two pioneer families settling in the west find the going tough, and the bullets flying.

Dull and verbose Western, in which the characters stagger cheerfully through crises that include death, fever, cattle rustling, gunfights and men doing what men have gotta do.

w Paul King, Joseph Stone *story* Steve Frazee *d* Charles Haas *ph* Philip Lathrop *md* Joseph Gershenson *ad* Alexander Golitzen, Robert Boyle *ed* Edward Mann

☆ Will Rogers Jnr, Maureen O'Sullivan, Rod McKuen, Casey Tibbs, Judy Meredith, Troy Donahue, Gigi Perreau, Jeanette Nolan

Wild in the Country

US 1961 114m DeLuxe Cinemascope

TCF/Company of Artists (Jerry Wald)

A rebellious hillbilly is involved with three women.

Weird confection designed to show the star in all his facets.

w Clifford Odets *novel The Lost Country* by J. R. Salamanca *d* Philip Dunne *ph* William C. Mellor *m* Kenyon Hopkins

☆ Elvis Presley, Hope Lange, Tuesday Weld, Millie Perkins, John Ireland, Gary Lockwood

'One can't help feeling he was better off prior to this misguided bid for class.' – *MFB*

Wild in the Sky

US 1971 83m colour

AIP/Bald Eagle (William T. Naud, Dick Gautier)

Three young offenders skyjack a B52 jet bomber.

Black comedy melodrama, uncontrolled but with some engaging absurdities.

w William T. Naud, Dick Gautier *d* William T. Naud *ph* Thomas E. Spalding *m* Jerry Styner

☆ Brandon de Wilde, Keenan Wynn, Dick Gautier, Tim O'Connor, James Daly, Robert Lansing

Wild in the Streets *

US 1968 97m Perfectcolor

AIP (Jack Cash)

In the imminent future, a pop singer becomes president and launches a campaign for teenage emancipation.

Satirical melodrama with a profusion of wild gags, some of which hit the target.

w Robert Thom *d* Barry Shear *ph* Richard Moore *m* Les Baxter *ed* Fred Feitshans, Eve Newman

☆ Shelley Winters, Chris Jones, Diane Varsi, Hal Holbrook, Millie Perkins

'Blatant, insensitive, crummy-looking … enjoyable at a pop, comic-strip level.' – *New Yorker, 1977*

'It is no less timely a parable today than Orwell's *1984* was 20 years ago.' – *Daily Telegraph*

editing

Wild Is the Wind

US 1957 114m bw Vistavision

Paramount/Hal B. Wallis

A widowed Italian sheep rancher in Nevada marries his wife's sister from Italy, but she falls for his adopted son.

Intense Cold Comfort Farm *melodrama with a strong similarity to* They Knew What They Wanted; *the strain shows, and the performances are tiresomely noisy.*

w Arnold Schulman *d* George Cukor *ph* Charles Lang Jnr *m* Dimitri Tiomkin

☆ Anna Magnani, Anthony Quinn, Tony Franciosa, Dolores Hart, Joseph Calleia

title song (mDimitri Tiomkin, lyNed Washington); Anna Magnani; Anthony Quinn

Wild Man Blues *

US 1997 105m DuArt

Film Four/Magnolia/Sweetland (Jean Doumanian, Barbara Kopple)

Documentary of a European tour by Woody Allen and his jazz band, playing music in the New Orleans style.

Enjoyable account of Allen in a different performing context, concentrating not only on the music, but on Allen's relationship with Soon-Yi Previn, and with his unimpressed parents. What is surprising is his clarinet sound: you might have expected him to emulate the piping, everything's-coming-up-neuroses style of Pee Wee Russell; instead he plays in the heart-on-the-sleeve manner of George Lewis.

d Barbara Kopple *ph* Tom Hurwitz *ed* Lawrence Silk

'A hilarious pendant-piece to *Deconstructing Harry*.' – *Alexander Walker*

The Wild Man of Borneo

US 1941 78m bw

MGM (Joseph L. Mankiewicz)

An unsuccessful braggart comes to live with his daughter in a Manhattan boarding house.

Mildly likeable though very predictable sentimental comedy from an old Broadway warhorse.

w Waldo Scott, John McClain *play* Herman J. Mankiewicz, Marc Connelly *d* Robert B. Sinclair *ph* Oliver T. Marsh *m* David Snell

☆ Frank Morgan, Mary Howard, Dan Dailey, Billie Burke, Donald Meek, Bonita Granville, Marjorie Main, Connie Gilchrist, Walter Catlett, Andrew Tombes, Phil Silvers, Joe Yule

The Wild North

US 1951 97m Anscocolor

MGM (Stephen Ames)

A mountie gets his man but needs his help getting back to base.

Standard adventure story with avalanche and wolf attacks.

w Frank Fenton *d* Andrew Marton *ph* Robert Surtees *m* Bronislau Kaper
☆ Stewart Granger, Wendell Corey, Cyd Charisse

'That streetcar man has a new desire!'
The Wild One **
US 1954 79m bw
Columbia/Stanley Kramer

Hoodlum motorcyclists terrorize a small town.
Brooding, compulsive, well-made little melodrama which was much banned because there was no retribution. As a narrative it does somewhat lack dramatic point.
w John Paxton *story* The Cyclists' Raid by Frank Rooney *d* Laslo Benedek *ph* Hal Mohr *m* Leith Stevens
☆ Marlon Brando, Lee Marvin, Mary Murphy, Robert Keith, Jay C. Flippen
'A picture that tries to grasp an idea, even though the reach falls short.' – *New York Times*
† 'What are you rebelling against?' 'What've you got?' – *sample dialogue*.
†† Sharpness of photography was achieved by the Garutso lens.

Wild Orchid
US 1989 111m DeLuxe
Entertainment/Vision (Mark Damon, Tony Anthony)

An American businessman in Rio plays sexual games with two female lawyers in a struggle over the ownership of an hotel.
Voyeuristic thriller that is less than watchable.
w Patricia Louisianna Knop, Zalman King *d* Zalman King *ph* Gale Tattersall *m* Geoff MacCormack, Simon Goldenberg *pd* Carlos Conti *ed* Marc Grossman, Glenn A. Morgan
☆ Mickey Rourke, Jacqueline Bisset, Carre Otis, Assumpta Serna, Bruce Greenwood, Jens Peter, Oleg Vidov

The Wild Party
US 1956 81m bw
UA/Security (Sidney Harmon)
An ex-football player and some Los Angeles layabouts plot a kidnap.
Unpleasant melodrama laced with sex, violence and loud music.
w John McPartland *d* Harry Horner *ph* Sam Leavitt *m* Buddy Bregman
☆ Anthony Quinn, Carol Ohmart, Jay Robinson, Arthur Franz, Nehemiah Persoff, Kathryn Grant, Paul Stewart

The Wild Party
US 1974 91m Movielab
AIP/Edgar Lansbury, Joseph Beruh (Ismail Merchant)

In 1929, a silent film comedian on the skids throws a party to show his latest movie.
Evocative of its period but virtually confined to a single set which becomes boring, this collection of unlikely events and tedious people has only obvious points to make and its final descent into tragedy is not compelling.
w Walter Marks *poem* Joseph Moncure March *d* James Ivory *ph* Walter Lassally *m* Larry Rosenthal
☆ James Coco, Raquel Welch, Perry King, Tiffany Bolling, Royal Dano, David Dukes, Dena Dietrich
'Seems to promise a pointillist precision about its characters and milieu which it never quite delivers.' – *Jonathan Rosenbaum*

The Wild Reeds: see *Les Roseaux Sauvages*

Wild River *
US 1960 115m DeLuxe Cinemascope
TCF (Elia Kazan)
In 1933 a Tennessee Valley Authority inspector incurs the wrath of a local matriarch who will not leave her valley even though it is to be flooded.
Interesting liberal-minded sociological drama marred by an added love story, as the similar Last Days of Dolwyn *was marred by melodrama. Well made but somehow unmemorable.*
w Paul Osborn *novels Borden Deal, William Bradford Huie* *d* Elia Kazan *ph* Ellsworth Fredericks *m* Kenyon Hopkins
☆ Montgomery Clift, *Jo Van Fleet*, Lee Remick, Albert Salmi, Jay C. Flippen, James Westerfield, Bruce Dern

Wild Rovers
US 1971 132m Metrocolor Panavision 70
MGM/Geoffrey (Blake Edwards, Ken Wales)

A middle-aged cowboy, depressed with the state of his life, joins with a younger man to become a bank robber.
Fashionable, derivative, quite unsuccessful Western tragi-comedy mixing in shades of every director from Ford to Peckinpah.
wd Blake Edwards *ph* Philip Lathrop *m* Jerry Goldsmith
☆ William Holden, Ryan O'Neal, Karl Malden, Lynn Carlin, Tom Skerritt, Joe Don Baker, Rachel Roberts, Leora Dana, Moses Gunn
'An existentialist western which will not do much for existentialism, the western, or the box office.' – *Charles Champlin, Los Angeles Times*

Wild Search
Hong Kong 1989 90m colour
Silver Medal/Born Top (Ringo Lam)
Investigating arms smuggling, a maverick cop falls for the sister of a murdered crook.
Engaging thriller, low-key by the frenetic standards of Hong Kong, with a little romance and comedy on the side.
w Nam Yin *d* Ringo Lam *ph* Lau Wai Keung *m* Lowell Lo *ad* Luk Tse Fung
☆ Chow Yun-at, Cherie Chung, Elaine Kam, Paul Chin, Chan Cheuk-Yan, Lau Kong

Wild Seed: see *Fargo*

The Wild Side: see *Suburbia (1983)*

Wild Stallion: see *Crin Blanc*

Wild Strawberries ****
Sweden 1957 93m bw
Svensk Filmindustri (Allan Ekelund)

original title: *Smultronstället*
An elderly professor has a nightmare and thinks back over his long life.
A beautifully paced and acted, but somewhat obscure piece of probing symbolism.
wd Ingmar Bergman *ph* Gunnar Fischer *m* Erik Nordgren
☆ *Victor Sjostrom*, Ingrid Thulin, Gunnar Bjornstrand, Bibi Andersson, Naima Wifstrand, Jullan Kindahl
'The work of a man obsessed by cruelty, especially spiritual cruelty, trying to find some resolution.' – *Kenneth Cavander, MFB*
script

Wild Target *
France 1993 88m colour
Gala/Pelléas/Locofilms/France 2/M6 Films (Philippe Martin)

original title: *Cible Émouvante*
A hitman and his apprentice are hired to kill a woman who has swindled a gangster, but decide to protect her instead.
Amusing blackish comedy, mainly notable for Rochefort's expert comic playing as a prissy killer who finds his precisely ordered life going awry.
wd Pierre Salvadori *ph* Gilles Henry *m* Philippe Eidel *ad* Yan Arlaud *ed* Hélène Viard
☆ *Jean Rochefort*, Marie Trintignant, Guillaume Depardieu, Patachou, Wladimir Yordanoff, Serge Riaboukine, Charlie Nelson
'Though limited in its ambitions, this is a convincingly quirky experience.' – *Empire*

Wild Things
US 1998 108m Technicolor Panavision
Columbia/Mandalay (Rodney Liber, Steven A. Jones)

A teacher faces ruin when a wealthy young girl accuses him of attempted rape.
Convoluted courtroom thriller that plays games with an audience's expectations, but not well enough to capture its interest.
w Stephen Peters *d* John McNaughton *ph* Jeffrey L. Kimball *m* George S. Clinton *pd* Edward T. McAvoy *ed* Elena Maganini
☆ Kevin Bacon, Matt Dillon, Neve Campbell, Theresa Russell, Denise Richards, Robert Wagner, Bill Murray, Carrie Snodgress, Daphne Rubin-Vega
'Sly, torrid and original.' – *Variety*

'This Could Be The Beginning Of A Beautiful Adventure.'
The Wild Thornberrys Movie *
US 2002 85m DeLuxe
Paramount/Nickelodeon (Arlene Klasky, Gabor Csupo)

An Anglo-American family involved in wildlife documentaries foil poacher's attempts to kill cheetahs and elephants.
A popular TV cartoon series moves to the big screen, where it provides pleasant entertainment (if you can pardon the caricature English) of the sort that can be watched more easily on television.
w Kate Boutilier *characters created by* Arlene Klasky, Gabor Csupo, Steve Pepoon, David Silverman, Stephen Sustarsic *d* Jeff McGrath, Cathy Malkasian *m* Drew Neumann *pd* Dima Malanitshev *ed* John Bryant
☆ voices of: Lacey Chabert (Eliza Thornberry), Tom Kane (Darwin), Tim Curry (Nigel Thornberry/Colonel Thornberry), Lynn Redgrave (Cordelia Thornberry), Jodi Carlisle (Marianne Thornberry), Danielle Harris (Debbie Thornberry), Flea (Donnie Thornberry), Rupert Everett (Sloan Blackburn), Marisa Tomei (Bree Blackburn), Obba Babatunde (Boko), Alfre Woodard (Akela), Brock Peters (Jomo), Brenda Blethyn (Mrs Fairgood)
'The film's draughtsmanship is more than adequate, the voicing of the characters excellent, and the songs are way above average for such fare.' – *Philip French, Observer*
song 'Father and Daughter' (*m/l* Paul Simon)

Wild West *
GB 1992 100m Metrocolor
Initial/Channel 4/British Screen (Eric Fellner)

Young Asians, living in London and dreaming of stardom, form a country and western band.
Engagingly energetic comedy of cultural misunderstandings and fantasies.
w Harwant Bains *d* David Attwood *ph* Nic Knowland *m* Dominic Miller *pd* Caroline Hanania *ed* Martin Walsh
☆ Naveen Andrews, Sarita Choudhury, Ronny Jhutti, Ravi Kapoor, Ameet Chana, Bhasker, Lalita Ahmed, Shaun Scott
'Mangy and artless, this boisterous low-budgeter generates plenty of good laughs and gets lots of mileage from its comic, knowing observations about a vibrant British sub-culture.' – *Variety*

Wild Wild West
US 1999 106m Technicolor
Warner (Jon Peters, Barry Sonnenfeld)

In the 1860s, two ill-matched government agents are dispatched by the President to deal with a Confederate general, who is creating a powerful new weapon with the aid of a wheelchair-bound mad scientist.
Asinine would-be comedy that wastes a great many talents on an ill-thought-out, unfunny narrative and irrelevant special effects.
w S.S. Wilson, Brent Maddock, Jeffrey Price, Peter S. Seaman *story* Jim Thomas, John Thomas *d* Barry Sonnenfeld *ph* Michael Ballhaus *m* Elmer Bernstein *pd* Bo Welch *ed* Jim Miller *sp* ILM; Cinesite
☆ Will Smith (James West), Kevin Kline (Artemus Gordon/ President Grant), Kenneth Branagh (Dr Arliss Loveless), Salma Hayek (Rita Escobar), Ted Levine (General McGrath), M. Emmet Walsh (Coleman), Bai Ling (Miss East), Rodney A. Grant (Hudson), Garcelle Beauvais (Girl in Water Tower), Musetta Vander (Munitia), Sofia Eng (Miss Lippenreider), Frederique van der Wal (Amazonia)
'A would-be blockbuster that figures out how to go thud more often than anything since *Hudson Hawk*.' – *Owen Gleiberman, Entertainment Weekly*
'An extended, incoherent Tourette's-style yelping of design-ideas, soundtrack-styles, FX flourishes, rewrites and mismatched performances.' – *Peter Bradshaw, Guardian*
† The movie was based on the TV series that ran from 1965-1970, starring Robert Conrad as West, Ross Martin as Gordon, and Michael Dunn as the diminutive villain Dr Miguelito Loveless.
†† It grossed more than $113m at the US box-office and a total of $218m around the world.

Wildcat: see *The Great Scout and Cathouse Thursday*

Wildcats
US 1986 107m Technicolor
Warner (Anthea Sylbert)

A girl is appointed football coach at a ghetto school, and of course works wonders.
Silly comedy with few laughs and not much plot development.
w Ezra Sacks *d* Michael Ritchie *ph* Donald E. Thorin *m* Hawk Wolinski, James Newton Howard *pd* Boris Leven *ed* Richard A. Harris
☆ Goldie Hawn, Swoosie Kurtz, Robyn Lively, Brandy Gold, James Keach, Bruce McGill, M. Emmet Walsh

The Wildcats of St Trinian's
GB 1980 91m Technicolor
Wildcat (E. M. Smedley-Aston)
The awful schoolgirls get unionized, and kidnap an Arab's daughter to gain attention.
Crude and belated tailpiece to a series which was never very satisfactory. (See The Belles of ..., Blue Murder at ..., The Pure Hell of ..., The Great St Trinian's Train Robbery.*)*
wd Frank Launder *ph* Ernest Steward *m* James Kenelm Clarke
☆ Sheila Hancock, Michael Hordern, Joe Melia, Thorley Walters, Rodney Bewes, Maureen Lipman, Ambrosine Philpotts

'We are all in the gutter, but some of us are looking at the stars.'
Wilde **
GB 1997 115m Metrocolor 'Scope
Polygram/Samuelson/Dove/NDF/Pony Canyon/ Pandora/BBC (Mark Samuelson, Peter Samuelson)

Oscar Wilde's love for Lord Alfred Douglas brings about his disgrace and exile from Britain.
A handsome, well-acted, slightly stately biopic that, despite its declared intent to celebrate Wilde's homosexuality, seems determined to reclaim him as a heterosexual and father.
w Julian Mitchell *biography Oscar Wilde by Richard Ellmann* *d* Brian Gilbert *ph* Martin Fuhrer *m* Debbie Wiseman *pd* Maria Djurkovic *ed* Michael Bradsell
☆ *Stephen Fry* (Oscar Wilde), *Jude Law* (Bosie), Vanessa Redgrave, Jennifer Ehle, Gemma Jones, Michael Sheen, Zoe Wanamaker, Tom Wilkinson (Marquess of Queensberry)
'A well-made film in the brass-bound tradition of British heritage cinema.' – *Richard Williams, Guardian*
'A curious mixture of haste and complacency.' – *Tom Shone, Sunday Times*
'In the end *Wilde* triumphs because it manages to do what Wilde himself achieved. In the famous plays he portrayed an English society dominated by the vice of hypocrisy. A hundred years later people are still being destroyed and pilloried in this country for publicly stating that the emperor is wearing a spandex jock strap. *Wilde* gives us a vivid take on this eternal and hateful row.' – *Will Self, New Statesman*

Wilder Napalm
US 1993 110m Technicolor
TriStar/Baltimore (Mark Johnson, Stuart Cornfeld)

Two feuding brothers, who can start fires with the power of thought, quarrel when one makes love to the wife of the other.
Plotless, witless confection about three very uninteresting people.
w Vince Gilligan *d* Glenn Gordon Caron *ph* Jerry Hartleben *m* Michael Kamen *pd* John Muto *ed* Artie Mandelberg
☆ Debra Winger, Dennis Quaid, Arliss Howard, M. Emmet Walsh, Jim Varney, Mimi Lieber, Marvin J. McIntyre
'There's little to recommend in the slow-moving, fuzzy-minded yarn.' – *Variety*

Will Any Gentleman?
GB 1953 84m Technicolor
ABPC

A meek bank clerk is hypnotized and becomes a ladies' man.
Efficient comedy from a stage success.

w Vernon Sylvaine *play* Vernon Sylvaine *d* Michael Anderson *ph* Erwin Hillier *m* Wally Stott

☆ George Cole, Veronica Hurst, Jon Pertwee, Heather Thatcher, James Hayter, William Hartnell, Diana Decker, Joan Sims, Alan Badel

Will It Snow for Christmas? ***

France 1996 91m colour

Artificial Eye/Ognon (Danny Lebigot)

original title: *Y'Aura T'il de la Neige à Noël?*

In rural France, a married farmer's lover and their seven children scratch a bare living from the land.

Bleak, minimalist drama of poverty and maternal love that, with its slow rhythms, is hypnotically unforgettable.

wd Sandrine Veysset *ph* Hélène Louvart *m* Henri Ancillotti *ad* Jacques Dubus *ed* Nelly Quettier

☆ Dominique Reymond, Daniel Duval, Jessica Martinez, Alexandre Roger, Xavier Colonna, Fanny Rochetin

'If it does happen to snow for Christmas, make a snowman, slide down Ben Nevis on a tea tray, teach your grandma to ski, anything – just don't seek shelter in a cinema showing this miserable tale.' – *Giala Murray, Empire*

'Will heats up slow, but when he gets there, he's hell with the hide off!'

Will Penny *

US 1967 109m Technicolor

Paramount/Fred Engel/Walter Seltzer/Tom Gries

A middle-aged cowpuncher falls foul of a family of maniacal cut-throats.

Realistically spare, laconic, uncomforting Western with a curiously melodramatic set of villains.

wd Tom Gries *ph* Lucien Ballard *m* David Raksin

☆ *Charlton Heston*, Joan Hackett, Donald Pleasence, Lee Majors, Bruce Dern, Anthony Zerbe, Clifton James, Ben Johnson

Will Success Spoil Rock Hunter?

US 1957 95m Eastmancolor Cinemascope

TCF (Frank Tashlin)

GB title: *Oh! For a Man!*

A timid advertising executive is touted for a publicity stunt as the world's greatest lover.

A too-wild satire on TV commercials: less frenzied direction and gag-writing would have prised more humour from the situations.

w Frank Tashlin *play* George Axelrod *d* Frank Tashlin *ph* Joe MacDonald *m* Cyril Mockridge

☆ Jayne Mansfield, Tony Randall, Betsy Drake, Joan Blondell, John Williams, Henry Jones, Mickey Hargitay

Will Tomorrow Ever Come?: see *That's My Man*

Will-O'-The-Wisp: see *Le Feu Follet*

'The one film you should not see alone! Where your nightmare ends, Willard *begins!*'

Willard *

US 1971 95m DeLuxe

Cinerama/Bing Crosby (Mort Briskin)

A shy, withdrawn young man breeds and trains rats to kill his enemies.

Modest, rather unusual suspenser which builds well after a slow start; only horrifying to people who can't stand rats. A sequel, Ben *(qv), later appeared.*

w Gilbert Ralston *novel Ratman's Notebooks* by Stephen Gilbert *d* Daniel Mann *ph* Robert B. Hauser *m* Alex North *rat trainer* Moe de Sesso

☆ *Bruce Davison*, Elsa Lanchester, Ernest Borgnine, Sondra Locke, Michael Dante, J. Pat O'Malley

William at the Circus

GB 1948 89m bw

A. A. Shipman & David Coplan (John R. Sloan)

aka: *William Comes to Town*

William achieves national notoriety and overcomes parental obstacles in his determination to see a circus.

Tired and miscast comedy, with much documentary footage of fun-fair and circus to pad out its trite narrative.

wd Val Guest *novel* Richmal Crompton *ph* Bert Mason *m* Robert Farnon *ad* Harry Moore *ed* Carmen Beliaeff

☆ William Graham, Garry Marsh, Jane Walsh, Hugh Cross, Kathleen Stuart, Muriel Aked, A. E. Matthews, Michael Medwin, Michael Balfour, Jon Pertwee

† It was a sequel to *Just William's Luck* (qv).

William Comes to Town: see *William at the Circus*

'Love makes fools of us all.'

William Shakespeare's A Midsummer Night's Dream **

US/Germany 1999 116m DeLuxe

TCF/Fox Searchlight/Regency (Leslie Urdang, Michael Hoffman)

aka: *A Midsummer Night's Dream*

The course of true love does not run smooth for three couples.

Set for no particular reason in an Italian village at the turn of the 19th century, this is a patchy version, with some awkward clashes in acting styles, and much of the verse-speaking disappointing; but the play gradually works its charm and the finale is well-managed.

play William Shakespeare *d* Michael Hoffman *ph* Oliver Stapleton *m* Simon Boswell *pd* Luciana Arrighi *ed* Garth Craven *cos* Gabriella Pescucci

☆ Michelle Pfeiffer (Titania), Rupert Everett (Oberon), Kevin Kline (Bottom), Stanley Tucci (Puck), Calista Flockhart (Helena), Anna Friel (Hermia), Christian Bale (Demetrius), Dominic West (Lysander), David Strathairn (Theseus), Sophie Marceau (Hippolyta), Roger Rees (Peter Quince), Bernard Hill (Egeus), Bill Irwin (Tom Snout), Sam Rockwell (Francis Flute)

'Whimsical, intermittently enjoyable but decidedly unmagical.' – *Variety*

'A parade of incongruities with performances ranging from the sublime to the you-know-what.' – *Janet Maslin, New York Times*

'Hope & vengeance. Tragedy & love.'

'The greatest love story the world has ever known.'

William Shakespeare's Romeo and Juliet ***

US 1996 120m DeLuxe Panavision

TCF/Bazmark (Gabriella Martinelli, Baz Luhrmann)

In modern-day Verona Beach, two young lovers suffer from family opposition to their affair.

Exuberantly witty version of Shakespeare, where for once the language and the present-day setting match: the weapons toted by its hoodlum cast may be guns, but they bear trademarks such as 'Sword' and 'Dagger'. The poetry of the play tends to get lost in the ethnic mix and loud rock accompaniment, and it dazzles the eye, with its vivid, kitsch settings, rather than the ear, but the updating has been thought through with an invigorating invention that sweeps objections aside.

w Craig Pearce, Baz Luhrmann *play* William Shakespeare *d Baz Luhrmann ph Donald McAlpine m* Nellee Hooper, Craig Armstrong, Marius de Vries *pd Catherine Martin ed* Jill Bilcock

☆ Leonardo DiCaprio (Romeo), Claire Danes (Juliet), Brian Dennehy, John Leguizamo, Pete Postlethwaite, Paul Sorvino, Diane Venora

'This acid-house rendition … is something to behold.' – *Sight and Sound*

'Will undoubtedly do for Shakespeare what *Strictly Ballroom* did for ballroom dancing and make it fresh, vibrant and hot, hot, hot for a whole generation new to the Bard.' – *Marianne Gray, Film Review*

'Luhrmann has produced a splendid rock video.' – *Mark Steyn, Spectator*

† Leonardo DiCaprio won the best actor award at the Berlin Film Festival in 1997.

Catherine Martin

Baz Luhrmann; Catherine Martin; Nellee Hooper; screenplay

Willie and Phil

US 1980 116m DeLuxe

TCF (Paul Mazursky, Tony Ray)

Two men and a woman enjoy a variable *ménage à trois* throughout the seventies.

Curious attempt at an American Jules et Jim; not badly done if you have to do it, but why do it?

wd Paul Mazursky *ph* Sven Nykvist *m* Claude Bolling

☆ Michael Ontkean, Margot Kidder, Ray Sharkey

'Truffaut's film existed both in the real world and in a world of the imagination. Mazursky's has no imagination and doesn't even touch a passable form of reality.' – *Sunday Times*

Willow *

US 1988 126m colour

UIP/MGM (Nigel Wooll)

In a time of magic, two heroes set out to bring a baby to safety and fulfil a prophecy that will overthrow an evil empire.

Spectacular jaunt around familiar material, plundered from mythology, fairy-tales and old movies, that relies on special effects to maintain interest.

w Bob Dolman *story* George Lucas *d* Ron Howard *ph* Adrian Biddle *m* James Horner *pd* Allan Cameron *ed* Daniel Hanley, Michael Hill *sp* John Richardson

☆ Val Kilmer, Joanne Whalley, Warwick Davies, Jean Marsh, Patricia Hayes, Billy Barty, Pat Roach, Gavan O'Herlihy, David Steinberg

'It's doubtful if any action-adventure director has a strong enough style to give this script a tone and a shape, and Ron Howard, who's got the job, is lost.' – *Pauline Kael, New Yorker*

Willy Wonka and the Chocolate Factory *

US 1971 100m Technicolor

David Wolper

A boy wins a tour of the local chocolate factory and finds himself in the power of a magician.

Semi-satiric Grimms Fairy Tale pastiche which looks good but never seems quite happy with itself.

w Roald Dahl *novel* Roald Dahl *d* Mel Stuart *ph* Arthur Ibbetson *md* Walter Scharf *ad Harper Goff songs* Leslie Bricusse, Anthony Newley

☆ Gene Wilder, Jack Albertson, Peter Ostrum, Roy Kinnear, Aubrey Woods

Walter Scharf

Wilson **

US 1944 154m Technicolor

TCF (Darryl F. Zanuck)

The rise and fall of an American president.

Admirably careful biopic which raises no particular excitement but entertains and instructs on various levels.

w Lamar Trotti d Henry King ph Leon Shamroy m Alfred Newman ad James Basevi, Wiard Ihnen ed Barbara McLean

☆ *Alexander Knox*, Charles Coburn, Cedric Hardwicke, Geraldine Fitzgerald, Thomas Mitchell, Ruth Nelson, William Eythe, Vincent Price, Mary Anderson, Ruth Ford, Sidney Blackmer, Stanley Ridges, Eddie Foy Jnr, Charles Halton, Thurston Hall and also J. M. Kerrigan, Francis X. Bushman

'Not without tedium, but worth seeing as an enormous expensive curiosity.' – *Richard Mallett, Punch*

'Rich with the sense of movement and multitude.' – *Daily Sketch*

'Absorbing, significant and entertaining.' – *Time*

† Alexander Knox had 1194 lines in 294 scenes.

Lamar Trotti; Leon Shamroy; art direction; editing

best picture; Henry King; Alfred Newman; Alexander Knox

Wilt

GB 1989 93m Eastmancolor

Rank/LWT/Picture Partnership (Brian Eastman)

A polytechnic lecturer is suspected of having murdered his wife by an inept police inspector.

A low farce which, briskly directed, affords moderate amusement.

w Andrew Marshall, David Renwick *novel* Tom Sharpe *d* Michael Tuchner *ph* Norman Langley *m* Anne Dudley *pd* Leo Austin *ed* Chris Blunden

☆ Griff Rhys Jones, Mel Smith, Alison Steadman, Diana Quick, Jeremy Clyde, Roger Allam, David Ryall, Roger Lloyd Pack, Dermot Crowley, John Normington

Winchester 73 **

US 1950 92m bw

U-I (Aaron Rosenberg)

Long-time enemies settle an old grudge and vie for the possession of a rare gun.

Entertaining, popular, hard-riding, hard-shooting Western of the old school.

w Robert L. Richards, Borden Chase *story* Stuart N. Lake *d Anthony Mann ph William Daniels m* Frank Skinner *md* Joseph Gershenson *ad* Bernard Herzbrun, Nathan Juran *ed* Edward Curtiss *cos* Yvonne Wood

☆ James Stewart (Lin McAdam), Shelley Winters (Lola Manners), Dan Duryea (Waco Johnny Dean), Stephen McNally (Dutch Henry Brown), Millard Mitchell (High Spade), Charles Drake (Steve Miller), John McIntire (Joe Lamont), Will Geer (Wyatt Earp), Jay C. Flippen (Sgt Wilkes), Rock Hudson (Young Bull), Tony Curtis (Doan), John Alexander (Jack Riker), Steve Brodie (Wesley)

The Wind ***

US 1928 75m bw

MGM

A sheltered Virginia girl goes to live on the rough and windy Texas prairie, marries a man she doesn't love and kills a would-be rapist.

Heavy melodrama with a strong visual sense.

w Frances Marion *novel* Dorothy Scarborough *d Victor Sjostrom ph* John Arnold

☆ *Lillian Gish*, Lars Hanson, Montagu Love, Dorothy Cummings

'So penetrating is the atmosphere that one can almost feel the wind itself and taste the endless dust.' – *Georges Sadoul*

'Unrelieved by the ghost of a smile … but its relentlessness is gripping … a fine and dignified achievement.' – *Pictureplay*

† New version by Thames Silents 1984.

The Wind

Mali 1982 100m colour

Les Films Cissé

original title: *Finyé*

The daughter of a military governor becomes involved in political demonstrations against army rule after falling in love with a poor student.

Episodic account of romance and repression in Africa.

wd Souleymane Cissé *ph* Etienne Carton de Grammont *m* Pierre Gorse

☆ Fousseyni Sossoko, Guondo Guisse, Balla Moussa Keita, Ismaila Sarr, Oumou Diarra, Ismaila Cissé, Massitan Ballo, Dioncounda Kone

Wind

US 1992 125m Technicolor

Filmlink International/American Zoetrope (Mata Yamamoto, Tom Luddy)

A young sailor, who loses the America's Cup to the Australians, persuades a designer to create a new yacht to win back the title.

Uninteresting and water-logged drama.

w Rudy Wurlitzer, Mac Gudgeon *story* Jeff Benjamin, Roger Vaughan, Kimball Livingston *d* Carroll Ballard *ph* John Toll *m* Basil Poledouris *pd* Laurence Eastwood *ed* Michael Chandler

☆ Matthew Modine, Jennifer Grey, Stellan Skarsgard, Rebecca Miller, Ned Vaughn, Cliff Robertson, Jack Thompson

'Despite the sometimes striking images of expert crews guiding their beautiful boats through challenging waters, predictable story trajectory and bland human element will keep this physically ambitious picture in a b.o. stall.' – *Variety*

Wind across the Everglades *

US 1958 93m Technicolor

(Warner) Schulberg Productions (Stuart Schulberg)

Florida 1900: a young schoolteacher tracks down those responsible for hunting rare birds for their feathers, and becomes a game warden.

Meandering adventure story with a purpose, relying heavily on violence and eccentric characters.

w Budd Schulberg *d* Nicholas Ray *ph* Joseph Brun *ad* Richard Sylbert *ed* Georges Klotz, Joseph Sigman

☆ Christopher Plummer (Walt Murdock), Burl Ives (Cottonmouth), Gypsy Rose Lee (Mrs

Bradford), Emmett Kelly (Bigamy Bob), George Voskovec (Aaron Nathanson), Tony Galento (Beef), MacKinlay Kantor (Judge Harris), Peter Falk (Writer), Chana Eden (Naomi)
† The film was marked by disagreements between Nicholas Ray and Budd Schulberg. Ray was absent for the final two or so weeks, and scenes were shot by Schulberg and Charles Maguire, the assistant director. After seeing the film at a preview, Ray said that he wanted his name removed from the film because 'I cannot allow it to be associated with the style of acting employed by Burl in the death scene'. The scene remained (though Ives wanted to have it shot again), as did Ray's name.
†† The music score used existing music owned by Warner because of a musicians' strike in California.

The Wind and the Lion

US 1975 119m Metrocolor Panavision
Columbia/MGM (Herb Jaffe, Phil Rawlins)

In 1904 Tangier, an American widow and her children are kidnapped by a Riffian chief, and the eyes of the world are focused on the incident.
Basing itself very lightly on an actual event, this adventure story is both confused as a narrative and unexciting as an action piece: the camera stops too often to look at sunsets, the plot stops too often for philosophizing, and there are too many underexplained characters and incidents fitting into the international jigsaw.
wd John Milius *ph* Billy Williams *m* Jerry Goldsmith
☆ Sean Connery, Candice Bergen, Brian Keith, John Huston, Geoffrey Lewis, Steve Kanaly, Vladek Sheybal
'When the actors begin to talk (which they do incessantly) the flat-footed dialogue and the amateurish acting take one back to the low-budget buffoonery of Maria Montez and Turhan Bey.' – *Pauline Kael, New Yorker*
Jerry Goldsmith

The Wind Cannot Read

GB 1958 115m Eastmancolor
Rank (Betty E. Box)

In India and Burma during World War II, a flying officer falls in love with a Japanese language instructor suffering from a brain disease.
Or, love is a many-splendoured dark victory. Old-fashioned romance for addicts, well enough produced.
w Richard Mason *novel* Richard Mason *d* Ralph Thomas *ph* Ernest Steward *m* Angelo Lavagnino
☆ Dirk Bogarde, Yoko Tani, Ronald Lewis, John Fraser, Anthony Bushell, Michael Medwin
† David Lean was to have directed the film, starring Japanese actress Kishi Keiko; but producer Alexander Korda, who was unhappy about Lean's approach to the subject, died before production began and the project was sold to Rank. Lean signed to make *The Bridge over the River Kwai* instead.

Wind in the Willows: see *Ichabod and Mr Toad (1949)*

The Wind in the Willows

GB 1996 88m Technicolor
Guild/Allied Filmmakers (John Goldstone, Jake Eberts)

Weasel property developers threaten the homes of a mole and a toad.
Disappointing adaptation of Kenneth Grahame's classic novel of a threatened idyll, given a broad pantomime treatment.
wd Terry Jones *novel* Kenneth Grahame *ph* David Tattersall *m* John Du Prez *m/ly* John Du Prez, André Jacquemin, Terry Jones, Dave Howman *pd* James Acheson *ed* Julian Doyle
☆ Eric Idle, Steve Coogan, Terry Jones, John Cleese, Anthony Sher, Nicol Williamson, Stephen Fry, Bernard Hill, Nigel Planer, Julia Sawalha, Victoria Wood
'The comedy and the songs have a forced desperate quality, as if the filmmakers aren't quite sure whether they're pitching at an adult or child audience, and think that making a lot of noise is the best way of grabbing the attention of both.' – *Geoffrey Macnab, Sight and Sound*

The Wind Will Carry Us **

France/Iran 1999 118m colour
ICA/MK2/Abbas Kiarostami

Visitors arrive at a village and, using a young boy as a guide, express interest in an old lady who is dying.
This is film making refined to a point where only metaphors remain, which can be read in the landscape, particularly the road to the cemetery along which the leader of the mysterious visitors races so that he can use his mobile phone: the message is that the journey towards death should be savoured slowly.
wd Abbas Kiarostami *idea* Mahmoud Ayedin *ph* Mahmoud Kalari *m* Peyman Yazdanian *ed* Abbas Kiarostami
☆ Behzad Dourani (Engineer), Farzad Sohrabi, Shahpour Ghobadi, Masood Mansouri, Masoameh Salimi, Bahman Ghobadi, Noghre Asadi, Ali Reza Naderi
'You feel you've been on a remarkable odyssey while standing still. This form of realism offers no easy answers, it just points to the unfathomable mystery of life.' – *Philip French, Observer*
'Baffling, and mildly amusing.' – *James Christopher, Times*

Windbag the Sailor

GB 1936 85m bw
Gainsborough (Edward Black)
An incompetent seaman is washed away on an old ketch and lands on a South Sea isle.
Rather uninventive star comedy with inevitable pleasing moments.
w Marriott Edgar, Stafford Dickens, Will Hay *d* William Beaudine *ph* Jack Cox *md* Louis Levy
☆ Will Hay, Moore Marriott, Graham Moffatt, Norma Varden

Windom's Way *

GB 1957 108m Technicolor
Rank (John Bryan)

A doctor on a Far Eastern island tries to quell a native uprising.
Tolerably well intentioned action melodrama, topical because of Malaya; dramatically rather sober and predictable.
w Jill Craigie *novel* James Ramsay Ullman *d* Ronald Neame *ph* Christopher Challis *m* James Bernard
☆ Peter Finch, Mary Ure, Natasha Parry, Robert Flemyng, Michael Hordern

The Window ***

US 1949 73m bw
RKO (Frederick Ullman)

A New York slum boy is always telling tall tales, so no one believes him when he actually witnesses a murder … except the murderer.
Classic little second feature, entertaining and suspenseful; unfortunately it had few successful imitators.
w Mel Dinelli *d* Ted Tetzlaff *ph* William Steiner *m* Roy Webb *ed* Frederic Knudtson
☆ *Bobby Driscoll*, Barbara Hale, Arthur Kennedy, Paul Stewart, Ruth Roman
'Logical, well-shaped, cohesive, admirably acted, beautifully photographed and cut to a nicety.' – *Richard Winnington*
editing

A Window in London *

GB 1939 77m bw
G and S/GFD

US title: *Lady in Distress*
A *crime passionel* is witnessed from a passing train.
Modest Anglo-Saxon remake of the French film Metropolitan.
w Ian Dalrymple, Brigid Cooper *d* Herbert Mason
☆ Michael Redgrave, Sally Gray, Paul Lukas, Hartley Power, Patricia Roc

A Window to the Sky: see *The Other Side of the Mountain*

Windprints

GB 1989 99m colour
Virgin/Apex Motion Pictures/United British Artists (Michael L. Games, Raymond Day)

A British journalist and a South African cameraman go in search of a black poet and murderer in Namibia.
Confusing thriller that deals ineffectually with apartheid and its aftermath.
w David Wicht, Johann Potgieter, Heinrich Dahms *d* David Wicht *ph* Brian Tufano *m* John Keane *pd* Michael Phillips *ed* Robin Sales
☆ John Hurt, Sean Bean, Marius Weyers, Eric Nobbs, Lesley Fong, Kurt Egelhof, Dana Niehaus, Trudie Taljaard, Goliath Davids

Windrider

Australia 1986 83m colour
Barron/Bush Christmas (Paul D. Barron)

A rich, spoilt young man, whose passion is windsurfing, finds his life coming apart when he falls for a rock singer.
A tedious romantic comedy, in which uninteresting people behave in unlikely ways.
w Everett DeRoche, Bonnie Harris *d* Vincent Monton *ph* Joseph Pickering *m* Kevin Peek *ad* Phil Peters *ed* John Scott
☆ Tom Burlinson, Nicole Kidman, Charles Tingwell, Jill Perryman, Simon Chilvers, Kim Bullard

'Honor Was Their Code.'

Windtalkers

US 2002 134m colour Panavision
TCF/Lion Rock (John Woo, Terence Chang, Tracie Graham)

During the Second World War in the Pacific, Navaho marines use their language as a radio code that the Japanese cannopt crack.
Cliché-ridden war movie that ignores its interesting story in favour of one seen too many times, about a brave, self-sacrificng soldier traumatized by the deaths of men who died following his orders.
w John Rice, Joe Batteer *d* John Woo *ph* Jeffrey Kimball *m* James Horner *pd* Holger Gross *ed* Steven Kemper, Jeff Gullo, Tom Rolf
☆ Nicolas Cage (Joe Enders), Adam Beach (Ben Yahzee), Peter Stormare (Hjelmstad), Noah Emmerich (Chick), Mark Ruffalo (Pappas), Brian Van Holt (Harrigan), Martin Henderson (Nellie), Charlie Whitehorse (Roger Willie), Frances O'Connor (Rita), Christian Slater (Ox Henderson), Jason Isaacs (Major Mellitz)
'A powerful premise turned into a stubbornly flat, derivative war movie.' – *Robert Koehler, Variety*
'Cage is the only reason to check out an otherwise mediocre movie.' – *Peter Rainer, New York*

Wing and a Prayer *

US 1944 97m bw
TCF (William Becker, William Morosco)

Life aboard an aircraft carrier.
Standard action flagwaver.
w Jerome Cady *d* Henry Hathaway *ph* Glen MacWilliams *m* Hugo Friedhofer
☆ Don Ameche, Cedric Hardwicke, Dana Andrews, Charles Bickford, Richard Jaeckel, Henry Morgan
Jerome Cady

'At The Edge Of Our Universe, All Hell Is About To Break Loose.'

Wing Commander

US 1999 100m Technicolor
TCF/No Prisoners/Digital Anvil/Origin/Carousel (Todd Moyer)

In the 21st century, a young pilot joins the battle against the evil alien Kilrathi.
A routine war film set in outer space, but otherwise staying close to all the clichés of the genre; the video game that inspired it is a great deal more enjoyable than anything on offer here.
w Kevin Droney *story* Chris Roberts *d* Chris Roberts *ph* Thierry Arbogast *m* Kevin Kiner, David Arnold *pd* Peter Lamont *ed* Peter Davies *sp* Chris Brown
☆ Freddie Prinze Jnr, Saffron Burrows, Matthew Lillard, Tcheky Karyo, Jurgen Prochnow, David Suchet, David Warner
'Based on a video game and has roughly the same degree of character development. That is all most moviegoers will need to know … painfully boring and funny in the wrong places.' – *Anita Gates, New York Times*

The Winged Serpent: see *Q, The Winged Serpent*

Winged Victory **

US 1944 130m bw
TCF (Darryl F. Zanuck)
During World War II, pilots are inducted, trained and sent on dangerous missions.
Solid, competent, best-foot-forward flagwaver of the highest inspirational intention.
w Moss Hart *play* Moss Hart *d* George Cukor *ph* Glen MacWilliams *m* David Rose
☆ Lon McCallister, Jeanne Crain, Edmond O'Brien, Jane Ball, Mark Daniels, Don Taylor, Lee J. Cobb, Judy Holliday, Peter Lind Hayes, Alan Baxter, Red Buttons, Barry Nelson, Gary Merrill, Karl Malden, Martin Ritt and also Jo-Carroll Dennison
'I suppose it is all right, but I don't enjoy having anyone tell me, so cheerfully and energetically, that the Air Force personnel is without exception composed of boy scouts old enough to shave.' – *James Agee*
'There is no question that Mr Hart captured much of the gallantry and pathos of youth rushing towards dangerous adventures with surface enthusiasm and inner dread.' – *Bosley Crowther, New York Times*

Wings *

US 1927 136m (24 fps) bw silent
Paramount (B. P. Schulberg)

Two young men join the Air Service during World War I, and one eventually shoots down the other by accident.
An epic of early aviation, still stirring in its action sequences.
w Hope Loring, Louis D. Lighton *d* *William Wellman* *ph* *Harry Perry*
☆ Clara Bow, Charles Buddy Rogers, Richard Arlen, Gary Cooper, Jobyna Ralston, El Brendel
'Air battles are photographed from every conceivable angle, producing many bold cinematic effects … so much in fact happens in the air that it is impossible to take it all in.' – *National Board of Review*
best picture; best engineering effects (Roy Pomeroy)

Wings and the Woman: see *They Flew Alone*

Wings for the Eagle

US 1942 85m bw
Warner (Robert Lord)
Aircraft workers do their bit during World War II.
Home Front propaganda, well enough produced.
w Byron Morgan, Harrison Orkow *d* Lloyd Bacon *ph* Tony Gaudio *m* Frederick Hollander
☆ Ann Sheridan, Dennis Morgan, Jack Carson, George Tobias, Don Defore

Wings in the Dark *

US 1935 75m bw
Paramount (Arthur Hornblow Jnr)
Embittered after being blinded in an accident, a research flyer finally leaps into action when his stranded girlfriend needs help.
Satisfactory romantic melodrama.
w Jack Kirkland, Frank Partos *d* James Flood *ph* William C. Mellor
☆ Cary Grant, Myrna Loy, Roscoe Karns, Hobart Cavanaugh, Dean Jagger, Bert Hanlon, Samuel S. Hinds
'Unconvincing and improbable story, but handled so deftly that it may nose through to moderate grosses.' – *Variety*

Wings of Desire ****
France/West Germany 1987 127m bw/colour
Road Movies/Argos films
original title: *Der Himmel über Berlin*
One of a pair of angels, visiting Berlin, decides he wants to be human after falling in love with a circus performer.
Marvellously photographed encounter with humanity and recent German history, full of a quiet joy.
w Wim Wenders, Peter Handke *d* Wim Wenders *ph* Henri Alekan *m* Jürgen Knieper *ad* Heidi Ludi *ed* Peter Przygodda
☆ Bruno Ganz, Solveig Dommartin, Otto Sander, Curt Bois, Peter Falk
'A friend of mine says that he loved every second of this movie and he couldn't wait to leave. To put it simply, *Wings of Desire* has a visual fascination but no animating force – that's part of why it's being acclaimed as art.' – *Pauline Kael, New Yorker*

The Wings of Eagles *
US 1957 110m Metrocolor
MGM (Charles Schnee)
A navy flyer breaks his neck in an accident and on recovery becomes a Hollywood writer.
Sentimental biopic of Frank 'Spig' Wead, a routine, easy-going assignment for its director (who is caricatured by Ward Bond as John Dodge).
w Frank Fenton, William Wister Haines *d* John Ford *ph* Paul C. Vogel *m* Jeff Alexander
☆ John Wayne, Maureen O'Hara, Ward Bond, Dan Dailey, Ken Curtis, Edmund Lowe, Kenneth Tobey, Sig Rumann, Henry O'Neill

Wings of Fame
Netherlands 1990 109m Agfacolor
Gala/First Floor Features (Laurens Geels, Dick Maas)
After a writer kills a film star, both find themselves in a luxury hotel for the famous dead where they can stay for as long as they are remembered.
Unsuccessful entry in the current cycle of revenant movies.
w Otakar Votocěk, Herman Koch *d* Otakar Votocěk *ph* Alex Thomson *m* Paul van Brugge *pd* Dick Schillemans *ed* Hans van Dongen
☆ Peter O'Toole, Colin Firth, Marie Trintignant, Ellen Umlauf, Andréa Ferréol, Maria Becker, Gottfried John

The Wings of Honneamise (dubbed) *
Japan 1994 120m colour
Bandai/Gainax (Hirohiko Sueyoshi, Hiroaki Inoue)
A space cadet volunteers to be the first astronaut, while politicians use the occasion to plot war and revolution.
One of the better examples of Japanese animation: a straightforward science-fiction drama well told and with some spectacular moments.
wd Hiroyuki Yamaga *ph* Hiroshi Isagawa *md* Ryuichi Sakamoto *ad* Hiromasa Ogura *ed* Harutoshi Ogata
☆ Featuring the voices of Robert Matthews, Melody Lee, Lee Stone, Steve Blum
'Anime's own *The Right Stuff* blasts onto the small screen with superb direction and design, sharply realised characters and a fine sound track.' – *Manga Mania*
'One of the greatest animated films in the world.' – *John Gosling, Movie Collector*

Wings of the Apache
US 1990 85m
Medusa/Inter-Ocean Films (William Badalato)
US title: *Fire Birds*
US pilots go into action against drug barons.
Top Gun with helicopters, but even less interesting.
w Nick Thiel, Paul F. Edwards *story* Step Tyner, John K. Swensson, Dale Dye *d* David Green *ph* Tony Imi *m* David Newman *pd* Joseph T. Garrity *ed* Jon Poll, Norman Buckley, Dennis O'Connor
☆ Nicolas Cage, Tommy Lee Jones, Sean Young, Bryan Kestner, Dale Dye, Mary Ellen Trainor, J. A. Preston, Peter Onorati, Charles Lanyer, Bert Rhine
'Enjoyable, old-fashioned aerial adventure pic.' – *Variety*

'A couple with everything but money. An heiress with everything but love. A temptation no one could resist.'
The Wings of the Dove **
GB/US 1997 101m Rank Colour 'Scope
Miramax/Renaissance Dove (David Parfitt, Stephen Evans)
A poor journalist is persuaded by the woman he loves to seduce a wealthy heiress, who is dying.
An updated version of Henry James that takes the basic narrative but little else from the original novel; despite its faltering period sense, it succeeds on its own account as a modest drama of a triangular love affair.
w Hossein Amini *novel* Henry James *d* Iain Softley *ph* Eduardo Serra *m* Edward Shearmur *pd* John Beard *ed* Tariq Anwar
☆ Helena Bonham Carter, Linus Roache, Alison Elliott, Elizabeth McGovern, Charlotte Rampling, Alex Jennings, Michael Gambon
'One of those rare movies that evokes not just the essence of a great novel but the experience of it. We are enveloped, at every turn, in the hidden pulse of the characters' motivating passions.' – *Owen Gleiberman, Entertainment Weekly*
Helena Bonham Carter; Hossein Amini; Eduardo Serra; Sandy Powell (costumes)
Eduardo Serra

'For A Nation's Richest Prize He Fought Its Wildest Revolt!'
'...and tamed a fiery Bandit Queen for his own!'
Wings of the Hawk
US 1953 81m Technicolor 3-D
U-I (Aaron Rosenberg)
Mexico 1911: a gold miner falls into the hands of revolutionaries.
Routine bang-bang, rather sloppily produced.
w James E. Moser *d* Budd Boetticher *ph* Clifford Stine *m* Frank Skinner
☆ Van Heflin, Julie Adams, George Dolenz, Pedro Gonzales-Gonzales, Rodolfo Acosta, Antonio Moreno, Abbe Lane

Wings of the Morning *
GB 1937 89m Technicolor
New World (Robert T. Kane)
In 1899, a gypsy princess marries an Irish nobleman; in 1937, romance again blooms between their descendants.
Britain's first Technicolor film was great to look at and quite charming, though slight; its major attractions being horse races, songs from John McCormack, and a heroine dressed for plot purposes as a boy.
w Tom Geraghty *story* Donn Byrne *d* Harold Schuster *ph* Ray Rennahan, Jack Cardiff *m* Arthur Benjamin
☆ Henry Fonda, *Annabella*, Stewart Rome, John McCormack, Leslie Banks, Irene Vanbrugh, Harry Tate, Edward Underdown, Helen Haye
'A wholesome, refreshing and altogether likeable little romance.' – *Frank S. Nugent*

Wings of the Navy
US 1938 89m bw
Warner (Lou Edelman)
The loves and careers of navy pilots.
Competent animated recruiting poster.
w Michael Fessier *d* Lloyd Bacon *ph* Arthur Edeson, Elmer Dyer
☆ George Brent, Olivia de Havilland, John Payne, Frank McHugh, John Litel, Victor Jory, Henry O'Neill, John Ridgely
'A convincer to mould public opinion and support in favour of current government plans for wide expansion of American air defence forces.' – *Variety*

Wings over Honolulu
US 1937 78m bw
Universal
A young naval airman is posted to Hawaii and followed by his bride.
Lightweight flagwaver, all smiles at the end.
w Isabel Dawn, Boyce DeGaw, Mildred Cram *d* H. C. Potter *ph* Joseph Valentine
☆ Ray Milland, Wendy Barrie, William Gargan, Kent Taylor, Polly Knowles, Samuel S. Hinds
Joseph Valentine

The Winner
US/Australia 1996 89m colour
Feature/Mark Damon/Village Roadshow-Clipsal (Ken Schwenker)
Gangsters and low life gather to fleece a gambler who cannot stop winning at the casinos.
A muddled thriller that was recut by its producers; its director has disowned it as 'incomprehensible' and attempted, unsuccessfully, to have his name removed from the credits.
w Wendy Riss *play* *A Darker Purpose* by Wendy Riss *d* Alex Cox *ph* Denis Maloney *m* Pray for Rain, Zander Schloss *pd* Cecilia Montiel *ed* Carlos Puente
☆ Vincent D'Onofrio, Rebecca DeMornay, Delroy Lindo, Frank Whaley, Michael Madsen, Billy Bob Thornton, Richard Edson, Saverio Guerra
'A film that's meant to be quirkily comic but ultimately is more annoying than thrilling.' – *Emanuel Levy, Variety*
'It's not my film. It was completely re-edited and the music they put on it was just appalling ... I don't want anyone to see it.' – *Alex Cox*

'He never knew a knockout until he met her!'
Winner Take All *
US 1932 76m bw
Warner
A prizefighter rises to fame and helps a sick girl and her child.
Slightly-plotted comedy-drama allowing its star full rein.
w Wilson Mizner, Robert Lord, Gerald Beaumont *d* Roy del Ruth
☆ *James Cagney*, Marian Nixon, Guy Kibbee, Clarence Muse, Virginia Bruce, Dickie Moore
'Enjoyable prizefight talker: sprightly gags and bits bolster conventional story.' – *Variety*

Winning *
US 1969 123m Technicolor Panavision 70
Universal/Newman-Foreman (John Foreman)
A racing driver's professional problems strain his relationship with his wife.
Cliché track melodrama with pretensions, well but needlessly made.
w Howard Rodman *d* James Goldstone *ph* *Richard Moore* *m* Dave Grusin
☆ Paul Newman, Joanne Woodward, Richard Thomas, Robert Wagner, David Sheiner, Clu Gulager

The Winning of Barbara Worth *
US 1926 97m (24 fps) bw silent
Samuel Goldwyn
Desert engineers vie for the daughter of a landowner.
Forgettable action romance, a big hit in its day because of the climactic flood sequence, which still thrills.
w Frances Marion *novel* Harold Bell Wright *d* Henry King *ph* *George Barnes* *m* Ted Henkel
☆ Ronald Colman, Vilma Banky, Charles Lane, Gary Cooper, Paul McAllister

Winning of the West
US 1953 60m bw
Columbia/Gene Autry (Armand Schaefer)
A cowboy protects a newspaper proprietor from bandits and renegade Indians and redeems his crooked brother.
Better-than-usual Autry Western, with a reasonable narrative and stock footage borrowed from bigger-budget movies between the usual songs and fist fights.
w Norman S. Hall *d* George Archainbaud *ph* William Bradford *md* Ross DiMaggio *ad* George Brooks *ed* James Sweeney
☆ Gene Autry, Smiley Burnette, Gail Davis, Richard Crane, Robert Livingston, House Peters Jnr, Gregg Barton, William Forrest

The Winning Team
US 1952 98m bw
Warner (Bryan Foy)
A telephone linesman becomes a great baseball player despite trouble with his vision after an accident.
Standard biopic of Grover Cleveland Alexander; all very pleasant but no surprises.
w Ted Sherdeman, Seeleg Lester, Merwin Gerard *d* Lewis Seiler *ph* Sid Hickox *m* David Buttolph
☆ Doris Day, Ronald Reagan, Frank Lovejoy, Eve Miller, James Millican, Russ Tamblyn

The Winning Ticket
US 1935 69m bw
MGM
An Italian barber wins a sweepstake but can't find his ticket.
Modest, lively comedy which pleased at the time.
w Ralph Spence, Richard Shayer, Robert Pirosh, George Seaton *d* Charles F. Reisner
☆ Leo Carrillo, Louise Fazenda, Ted Healy, Irene Hervey, James Ellison, Luis Alberni, Akim Tamiroff

The Winning Way: see *The All-American*

The Winslow Boy ***
GB 1948 117m bw
British Lion/London Films (Anatole de Grunwald)
A naval cadet is expelled for stealing a postal order; his father spends all he has on proving his innocence.
Highly enjoyable middle-class British entertainment based on an actual case; performances and period settings are alike excellent, though the film is a trifle overlong.
w *Terence Rattigan, Anatole de Grunwald* *play* Terence Rattigan *d* *Anthony Asquith* *ph* Frederick Young *m* William Alwyn
☆ *Robert Donat, Cedric Hardwicke, Margaret Leighton, Frank Lawton*, Jack Watling, Basil Radford, Kathleen Harrison, Francis L. Sullivan, Marie Lohr, Neil North, Wilfrid Hyde-White, Ernest Thesiger
'Only a clod could see this film without excitement, laughter and some slight moisture about the eyes.' – *Daily Telegraph*

'In 1910 A Court Case Concerning A Cadet Accused Of Stealing A Five Shilling Postal Order Brought Down The British Empire.'
The Winslow Boy **
US 1998 104m Technicolor
Columbia TriStar/Sony Pictures Classics (Sarah Green)
In Edwardian England, a father fights to clear his son's name when he is expelled from naval college for stealing a postal order.
Mannered, buttoned-up version of a successful play that gains emotional power from its repression of feelings.
wd David Mamet *play* Terence Rattigan *ph* Benoit Delhomme *m* Alaric Jans *pd* Gemma Jackson *ed* Barbara Tulliver
☆ Nigel Hawthorne (Arthur Winslow), Jeremy Northam (Sir Robert Morton), Rebecca Pidgeon (Catherine Winslow), Gemma Jones (Grace Winslow), Guy Edwards (Ronnie Winslow), Colin Stinton (Desmond Curry), Sarah Flind (Violet), Neil North (First Lord of the Admiralty), Sara Stewart (Miss Barnes), Perry Fenwick (Fred), Alan Polanski (Mr Michaels)
'Little more than dusty museum piece.' – *Guardian*

Winsor McCay: Animation Legend **
US bw
Milestone/Lumivision (Albert M. Miller)
A collection, released on video, of animated films from La Cinémathèque Québécoise by the pioneering Winsor McCay: *Little Nemo*, made in 1911, *How a Mosquito Operates*, 1912, *Gertie the Dinosaur*, 1914, *The Sinking of the Lusitania*, 1918, *Bug Vaudeville*, c. 1921, *The Pet*, 1921, *The Flying House*, 1921, and fragments of *The Centaurs*, 1918–21, *Gertie on Tour*, 1918–21, and *Flip's Circus*, 1918–21.
Fascinating collection of McCay's early animation that reveals him as far more sophisticated, and much better at portraying people, than his rivals; it also includes glimpses of him at work and play.
m R. J. Miller

Winstanley *
GB 1978 96m colour
Other Cinema/BFI (Andrew Mollo, Kevin Brownlow)
In 1649, after the English Civil War, the Diggers, a millenarian group who espoused social equality, meet hostility when they form a farming commune in Surrey.

Intense, low-budget ideological drama of the collision of class and greed, distinguished by its cinematography.
w uncredited *novel* *Comrade Jacob* by David Caute *d* Kevin Brownlow, Andrew Mollo
ph Ernest Vincze *m* Sergei Prokoviev *ad* Andrew Mollo *ed* Sarah Ellis
☆ Miles Halliwell, Jerome Willis, Terry Higgins, Phil Oliver, David Bramley, Alison Halliwell, Sid Rawle, Dawson France, Barry Shaw

Winter Carnival
US 1939 89m bw
UA (Walter Wanger)
College romances over a holiday weekend.
Nondescript romantic comedy.
w Lester Cole, Budd Schulberg *d* Charles Riesner *ph* Merritt Gerstad *m* Werner Janssen
☆ Ann Sheridan, Richard Carlson, Helen Parrish, Virginia Gilmore, Robert Walker
'Slick production of an undistinguished yarn about the annual Dartmouth winter sports.' – *Variety*

'No matter where you hide, life will always find you.'
The Winter Guest *
GB/US 1996 110m Technicolor
Film Four/Fine Line/Channel 4/Capitol/Scottish Arts Council/Lottery Fund (Ken Lipper, Edward R. Pressman)
A mother attempts to re-establish a happy relationship with her recently widowed daughter.
A melancholy drama of family life, over which hangs the shadow of death; it is enlivened by a mordant humour.
w Sharman MacDonald, Alan Rickman *d* Alan Rickman *ph* Seamus McGarvey *m* Michael Kamen *pd* Robin Cameron Don *ed* Scott Thomas
☆ Phyllida Law, Emma Thompson, Sheila Reid, Sandra Voe, Arlene Cockburn, Gary Hollywood, Sean Biggerstaff, Douglas Murphy
'Solemn, lengthy and pretentious.' – *Lucy Maycock, New Statesman*

Winter Kills
US 1979 97m colour Panavision
Avco Embassy/Winter Gold (Fred Caruso)
The brother of an assassinated president tracks down the killers, but finds that his tycoon father is involved.
Heavy-going and confusing melodrama with much flashy editing. Despite its cast, it was never satisfactorily released.
wd William Richert *novel* Richard Condon
ph Vilmos Zsigmond *pd* Robert Boyle *ed* David Bretherton
☆ Jeff Bridges, John Huston, Anthony Perkins, Elizabeth Taylor, Sterling Hayden, Eli Wallach, Dorothy Malone, Tomas Milian, Richard Boone, Toshiro Mifune

Winter Light *
Sweden 1962 80m bw
Svensk Filmindustri (Allan Ekelund)
original title: *Nattvardsgästerna*
A widowed village pastor loses his vocation.
In a sense almost parody Bergman; in another, one of his clearest statements of despair. The middle section of a pessimistic trilogy which also included Through a Glass Darkly *and* The Silence.
wd Ingmar Bergman *ph* Sven Nykvist *m* none
☆ Max von Sydow, Ingrid Thulin, Gunnar Bjornstrand, Gunnel Lindblom
'The film-maker's mastery alone does not guarantee a great film. *Winter Light* is scarcely even a good one.' – *John Simon, 1967*

Winter Meeting
US 1948 104m bw
Warner (Henry Blanke)
A repressed spinster falls for a naval hero intent on becoming a priest.
Dreary talk marathon which did its star's career no good at all.
w Catherine Turney *novel* Ethel Vance
d Bretaigne Windust *ph* Ernest Haller *m* Max Steiner
☆ Bette Davis, James Davis, Janis Paige, John Hoyt, Florence Bates, Walter Baldwin

Winter of Our Dreams *
Australia 1981 90m Eastmancolor
Vega Films (Richard Mason)
A bookseller investigates the suicide of an old girlfriend, and becomes involved with an unhappy prostitute.
Intriguing character drama with a tendency to haunt the mind, though its effectiveness depends largely on its acting.
wd John Duigan *ph* Tom Cowan *m* Sharyn Calcraft
☆ *Judy Davis, Bryan Brown*, Cathy Downes, Baz Luhrmann

Winter People
US 1988 111m DeLuxe
Rank/Nelson Entertainment/Castle Rock (Robert H. Solo)
In the 1930s, a wandering clockmaker becomes involved in a feud between two families in a backwoods community.
Frenzied old-fashioned melodrama guaranteed to chill the interest of its audience.
w Carol Sobieski *novel* John Ehle *d* Ted Kotcheff *ph* François Protat *m* John Scott
pd Ron Foreman *ed* Thom Noble
☆ Kurt Russell, Kelly McGillis, Lloyd Bridges, Mitchell Ryan, Amelia Burnette, Eileen Ryan, Lanny Flaherty

'You Can't Run Away From Destiny.'
Winter Sleepers *
Germany/France 1997 123m colour
original title: *Winterschlafer*
A hit-and-run accident on a snowbound road links the lives of four self-obsessed young people with that of a farmer, seeking the driver who killed his daughter.
An ambitious, slightly ponderous drama that aspires to be a portrait of a disconsolate generation. It is almost worth seeing for one extraordinary sequence of a skier in free-fall.
w Tom Tykwer, Anne-Françoise Pyszora
novel *Expense of the Spirit* by Anne-Françoise Pyszora *d* Tom Tykwer *ph* Frank Griebe
m Rheinhold Hell, Johnny Klimek, Tom Tykwer
ed Katya Dringenberg
☆ Floriane Daniel, Heino Ferch, Ulrich Mattes, Marie-Lou Sellem, Laura Tonke, Sebastian Schipper, Agathe Taffertshofer, Sofia Dirscheri
'At once scary, erotic and desperately sad.' – *Peter Bradshaw, Guardian*

A Winter's Tale: see *Conte d'hiver*

Winterschlafer: see *Winter Sleepers*

'Like a thunderbolt of naked light it struck Broadway – now it tears at your heart on the screen!'
Winterset **
US 1936 78m bw
RKO
On the New York waterfront, a drifter determines to avenge his father's death.
Very dated poetic melodrama, here given a talky, artificial production which at the time impressed many critics but is now fairly difficult to endure.
w Anthony Veiller *play* Maxwell Anderson
d Alfred Santell *ph* Peverell Marley *m* Nathaniel Shilkret *ad* Perry Ferguson
☆ *Burgess Meredith, Eduardo Ciannelli*, Margo, Paul Guilfoyle, John Carradine, Edward Ellis, Stanley Ridges, Maurice Moscovich, Myron McCormick, Mischa Auer
'Not big box office … in certain locales they may even wonder what it's all about.' – *Variety*
'Still in a grand manner that just won't do on the screen … but there are fine moments in the performances, and there's something childishly touching in the florid dramatic effects.' – *New Yorker, 1978*
Nathaniel Shilkret; Perry Ferguson

Wintertime
US 1943 82m bw
TCF (William Le Baron)
A Norwegian skating star comes to Canada where her uncle's winter resort is on its uppers.
The last of the star's Fox musicals is pure routine.
w Edward Moran, Jack Jevne, Lynn Starling
d John Brahm *ph* Glen MacWilliams *m* Alfred Newman *md* Charles Henderson
☆ Sonja Henie, Jack Oakie, Cesar Romero, S. Z. Sakall, Carole Landis, Cornel Wilde, Woody Herman and his Band

Wired
US 1989 109m colour
Entertainment/Lion Screen Entertainment (Edward A. Feldman, Charles R. Meeker)
The ghost of comedian John Belushi, dead from a drug overdose, relives his life, while a journalist interviews his friends.
Fantasy substitutes for the harder, documented facts in a frenetic film that fails to capture Belushi's comic talents.
w Earl MacRauch *book* *Wired: The Short Life and Fast Times of John Belushi* by Bob Woodward
d Larry Peerce *ph* Tony Imi *m* Michael Ruff
pd Brian Eatwell *ed* Eric Sears
☆ Michael Chiklis, Patti D'Arbanville, J. T. Walsh, Lucinda Jenney, Gary Groomes, Ray Sharkey, Alex Rocco, Jere Burns

'No one is entirely human.'
The Wisdom of Crocodiles
GB 1998 98m DeLuxe
Entertainment/Zenith/Goldwyn//Film Foundry Partners (David Lascelles, Carolyn Choa)
A vampire can survive only by drinking the blood of women who love him.
Risible would-be horror, bland and bloodless, and lumbered with a script that makes no sense at all.
w Paul Hoffman *d* Po Chih Leong *ph* Oliver Curtis *m* John Lunn, Orlando Gough *pd* Andy Harris *ed* Robin Sales
☆ Jude Law, Elina Lowensohn, Timothy Spall, Kerry Fox, Jack Davenport, Colin Salmon, Rick Lamont, Ashley Artus
'Starts intriguingly but ends up thrashing around as a toothless wonder.' – *Derek Elley, Variety*
'Might have got away with being laughable; the fact that it's funded by an Arts Council grant makes it deplorable too.' – *Anthony Quinn, Independent*

Wise Blood ***
US/Germany 1979 108m colour
Artificial Eye/Anthea/Ithaca (Michael Fitzgerald, Kathy Fitzgerald)
In the deep South, a war veteran with no beliefs becomes a travelling preacher.
Odd story, not easy to like but with many impressive moments.
w Benedict Fitzgerald *novel* Flannery O'Connor
d John Huston *ph* Gerry Fisher *m* Alex North
ad Sarah Fitzgerald *ed* Roberto Silver
☆ Brad Dourif, Ned Beatty, Harry Dean Stanton, Daniel Shor, Amy Wright, John Huston

Wise Girl
US 1937 70m bw
RKO (Edward Kaufman)
A rich girl goes bohemian in Greenwich village.
Pretty absurd romantic comedy which strains the patience.
w Allan Scott, Charles Norman *d* Leigh Jason
☆ Miriam Hopkins, Ray Milland, Walter Abel, Henry Stephenson, Alec Craig, Guinn Williams, Margaret Dumont
'Slow-moving narrative, considerable silliness, lack of convincing plot.' – *Variety*

Wise Guys
US 1986 91m Technicolor
MGM-UA (Aaron Russo)
Two small-time hoods unwittingly heist Mafia funds.
Haven't we seen this somewhere before? And done better?
w George Gallo *d* Brian de Palma *ph* Fred Schuler *m* Ira Newborn *pd* Edward Pisoni
ed Jerry Greenberg
☆ Danny DeVito, Joe Piscopo, Harvey Keitel, Ray Sharkey, Patti LuPone

The Wiser Sex
US 1932 72m bw
Paramount
A society girl goes undercover to save her public prosecutor boyfriend from smears.
Unattractive comedy-melodrama which never seems to get going.
w Harry Hervey, Caroline Franke *play* *Her Confessions* by Clyde Fitch *d* Berthold Viertel
☆ Claudette Colbert, Melvyn Douglas, Lilyan Tashman, William Boyd, Ross Alexander, Douglass Dumbrille
'Story a handicap: picture suffers accordingly.' – *Variety*

Wish You Were Here **
GB 1987 92m colour
Zenith/Film Four (Sarah Radclyffe)
The growing pains of a teenage girl in a seaside town.
Noted chiefly for its central performance, this is a film full of telling detail and compassion, despite its apparently defiant mood.
wd David Leland *ph* Ian Wilson *m* Stanley Myers
pd Caroline Amies *ed* George Akers
☆ *Emily Lloyd*, Tom Bell, Clare Clifford, Barbara Durkin, Geoffrey Hutchings
'What is as depressing as the film itself is the fact that no one has thought even to comment on its one binding quality – the perception of sex, class and history entirely in terms of grotesque appearances.' – *Judith Williamson, New Statesman*
original screenplay

Wishmaster
US 1997 90m colour
First Independent/Live/Mediaworks (Pierre David, Clark Peterson, Noel A. Zanitsch)
An evil spirit, imprisoned for 800 years, is released in modern-day Los Angeles and grants wishes with an unpleasant twist to them.
A violent and nasty horror that numbingly repeats, with diminishing results, its one small idea.
w Peter Atkins *d* Robert Kurtzman *ph* Jacques Haitkin *m* Harry Manfredini *pd* Dorian Vernaccio, Deborah Raymond *ed* Dorian Vernaccio
☆ Tammy Lauren, Andrew Divoff, Robert Englund, Tony Todd, Wendy Benson, Tony Crane, Chris Lemmon, Jenny O'Hara, Kane Hodder
'A washout in its painfully obvious attempt to launch a new horror franchise. Unconscionably sadistic, even by genre standards, and mind-numbingly formulaic.' – *Joe Leydon, Variety*
† The cast includes three actors from other horror series: Robert Englund (Freddy Kruger from the *Nightmare on Elm Street* series), Tony Todd (Candyman in the series of the same name), and Kane Hodder (Jason from the *Friday the 13th* series).

The Wistful Widow of Wagon Gap *
US 1947 78m bw
U-I (Robert Arthur)
In old Montana, an accident-prone wayfarer accidentally kills a man and has to look after his family.
Tame and disappointing comedy vehicle.
w Robert Lees, Frederic I. Rinaldo, John Grant
story D. D. Beauchamp, William Bowers
d Charles T. Barton *ph* Charles Van Enger
m Walter Shumann
☆ Bud Abbott, Lou Costello, Marjorie Main, Audrey Young, George Cleveland

Witch Doctor: see *Men of Two Worlds*

Witch Hunt *
US 1994 98m CFI color
HBO/Pacific Western (Michael R. Joyce)
Working in a world where magic is real and a witch conjures up Shakespeare to write additional dialogue for movies, Hollywood private eye H. Phillip Lovecraft investigates the death of a film producer, who is turned into an incredible shrinking man and torn apart by his dogs; at the same time, a Congressman investigates magic itself and burns witches at the stake.
An odd and witty mix of cod-Chandler and satirical fantasy, making an oblique comment on McCarthyism

and the Hollywood blacklisting of the 50s and including even more film references than Tarantino manages.
w Joseph Dougherty d Paul Schrader ph Jean Yves Escoffier m Angelo Badalamenti pd Curtis A. Schnell ed Kristina Boden
☆ Dennis Hopper, Penelope Ann Miller, Eric Bogosian, Sheryl Lee Ralph, Julian Sands, Valerie Mahaffey, Lypsinka
'Weird, wonderful and quite unlike anything you've ever seen before. Highly recommended.' – *Film Review*
† The film, made for cable TV, was released direct to video in Britain.

Witchcraft *
GB 1964 79m bw
TCF/Lippert (Robert Lippert, Jack Parsons)
A family of witches take revenge on their longtime enemies.
Spasmodically arresting horror film spoiled by too complex a plot line and some variable acting.
w Harry Spaulding d *Don Sharp* ph Arthur Lavis m Carlo Martelli
☆ Jack Hedley, Lon Chaney Jnr, Marie Ney, Jill Dixon, David Weston
'Unpretentious and uncommonly gripping.' – *MFB*

Witchcraft through the Ages **
Sweden 1922 83m approx (24 fps) bw silent
Svensk Filmindustri
original title: *Häxan*
A 'documentary' investigation of the history of witchcraft, with acted examples.
Fascinating reconstruction of ancient rituals, still maintaining its power to frighten.
wd Benjamin Christensen ph Johan Ankarstjerne
☆ Oscar Stribolt, Clara Pontoppidan, Karen Winther

The Witches
GB 1966 91m Technicolor
Warner/Hammer (Anthony Nelson-Keys)
US title: *The Devil's Own*
A schoolmistress finds witchcraft in an English village.
Chintzy horror with predictable development and visible climax.
w Nigel Kneale novel *The Devil's Own* by Peter Curtis d Cyril Frankel ph Arthur Grant m Richard Rodney Bennett pd Bernard Robinson ed James Needs, Chris Barnes
☆ Joan Fontaine, Kay Walsh, Alec McCowen, Gwen Ffrangcon Davies, Ingrid Brett, John Collin, Michèle Dotrice, Leonard Rossiter, Martin Stephens, Carmel McSharry

The Witches **
US 1990 91m Eastmancolor
Warner/Lorimar (Mark Shivas)
A small boy, who has been turned into a mouse, schemes with his granny to thwart witches' plans to poison all the children in Britain.
Superior entertainment, intended for children, but as likely to be enjoyed by adults.
w Allan Scott novel Roald Dahl d Nicolas Roeg ph Harvey Harrison m Stanley Myers pd Voytek, Andrew Sanders ed Tony Lawson
☆ Anjelica Huston, Mai Zetterling, Jasen Fisher, Rowan Atkinson, Bill Paterson, Brenda Blethyn, Charlie Potter, Anne Lambton, Jane Horrocks
'A controlled and suitably dark piece of filmmaking.' – *Variety*

The Witches of Eastwick **
US 1987 118m Technicolor
Warner/Guber-Peters/Kennedy Miller
Three divorcees on the make are seduced by the devil.
Horny fantasy, impeccably played, though it could have been shorter.
w Michael Cristofer novel John Updike d George Miller ph Vilmos Zsigmond m John Williams pd Polly Platt
☆ Jack Nicholson, Cher, Susan Sarandon, Michelle Pfeiffer, Veronica Cartwright, Richard Jenkins
John Williams

The Witches of Salem *
France/East Germany 1957 143m bw
Borderie/CICC/DEFA/Pathé (Raymond Borderie)
original title: *Les Sorcières de Salem*
In 1692 Massachusetts, jealousies lead to accusations of witchcraft and multiple trials and executions.
An account of a horrifying historical fact which was also intended to reflect on the McCarthy witch hunts of the fifties; but the film, despite splendid acting, is too literal and slow-moving.
w Jean-Paul Sartre play *The Crucible* by Arthur Miller d Raymond Rouleau ph Claude Renoir m Georges Auric
☆ Simone Signoret, Yves Montand, Mylène Demongeot, Jean Debucourt
Simone Signoret

'Keep the children home! And if you're squeamish, stay home with them!'
'The Depraved Must Die... Beware The Witchfinder!'
Witchfinder General *
GB 1968 87m Eastmancolor
Tigon/American International (Arnold Miller, Philip Waddilove, Louis M. Heyward)
US title: *The Conqueror Worm*
In 1645 a villainous lawyer finds it profitable to travel the country instigating witch hunts.
Savage, stylish minor horror melodrama with a growing reputation as the best work of its young director. Not for the squeamish despite its pleasing countryside photography.
w Michael Reeves, Tom Baker novel Ronald Bassett d *Michael Reeves* ph *John Coquillon* m Paul Ferris, Jim Morahan ad Jim Morahan ed Howard Lanning
☆ Vincent Price (Matthew Hopkins), Rupert Davies (John Lowes), Ian Ogilvy (Richard Marshall), Patrick Wymark (Oliver Cromwell), Hilary Dwyer (Sara), Wilfrid Brambell (Master Loach), Robert Russell (John Stearne), Nicky Henson (Trooper Swallow)

'He made a murderer of the boy who was to marry his own daughter!'
The Witching Hour
US 1934 65m bw
Paramount (Bayard Veiller)
A gambler hypnotizes a young man into taking the blame for a murder.
Stalwart melodrama, reasonably well done.
w Anthony Veiller, Salisbury Field play Augustus Thomas d Henry Hathaway
☆ John Halliday, Guy Standing, Judith Allen, Tom Brown, William Frawley
† There was a previous (silent) version in 1921.

With a Friend Like Harry...: see *Harry, He's Here To Help*

With a Song in My Heart *
US 1952 117m Technicolor
TCF (Lamar Trotti)
Singer Jane Froman is crippled in a plane crash but finally makes a comeback.
Romanticized showbiz biopic with the singer providing voice only. Adequate production and plenty of familiar tunes made this a successful mass appeal sob story.
w Lamar Trotti d Walter Lang ph Leon Shamroy md Alfred Newman
☆ Susan Hayward, David Wayne, Rory Calhoun, Thelma Ritter, Una Merkel, Robert Wagner, Helen Westcott
♫ 'Blue Moon'; 'With a Song in My Heart'; 'Embraceable You'; 'Tea for Two'; 'It's a Good Day'; 'I'll Walk Alone'; 'Indiana'; 'Deep in the Heart of Texas'.
Alfred Newman
Susan Hayward; Thelma Ritter

With Honors
US 1994 100m Technicolor
Warner/Spring Creek (Paula Weinstein, Amy Robinson)
A homeless man persuades a Harvard student to take him home with him in return for giving back, a page at a time, the student's lost thesis.
Saccharine and preachy drama, far removed from any reality and providing little in the way of escapist pleasures.
w William Mastrosimone d Alek Keshishian ph Sven Nykvist m Patrick Leonard pd Barbara Long ed Michael R. Miller
☆ Joe Pesci, Brendan Fraser, Moira Kelly, Patrick Dempsey, John Hamilton, Gore Vidal
'An incredibly mawkish comedy drama.' – *Sight and Sound*

With or Without You
GB 1999 90m colour
Miramax/Film4/Revolution (Andrew Eaton)
In Belfast, the marriage of a former policeman and his wife is complicated by the arrival of the wife's French pen pal.
Small-scale romantic drama, a TV play masquerading as a movie.
w John Forte d Michael Winterbottom ph Benoit Delhomme m Adrian Johnson pd Mark Tildesley ed Trevor Waite
☆ Christopher Eccleston (Vincent Boyd), Dervla Kirwan (Rosie Boyd), Yvan Attal (Benoit), Julie Graham (Cathy), Alun Armstrong (Sammy), Lloyd Hutchinson (Neil), Michael Liebmann (Brian), Doon MacKichan (Deidre), Gordon Kennedy (Ormonde), Fionnula Flanagan (Irene)
'Handles the material with freshness and vitality, keeping the viewer attracted even when the screenplay is developing along familiar lines.' – *David Stratton, Variety*

With Six You Get Egg Roll
US 1968 99m DeLuxe Panavision
Cinema Center/Arwin (Martin Melcher)
A widow with three sons marries a widower with one daughter.
Quite a bright and inventive family comedy.
w Gwen Bagni, Paul Dubov d Howard Morris ph Ellsworth Fredericks, Harry Stradling Jnr m Robert Mersey
☆ Doris Day, Brian Keith, Pat Carroll, Barbara Hershey

Within a Cloister: see *Behind Convent Walls*

Within the Law: see *Paid (1930)*

Within the Law
US 1939 66m bw
MGM
A girl wrongly convicted studies law in prison and later takes her revenge on the real culprit.
Reasonably interesting melodrama, filmed several times previously: in 1912, 1917, 1923 and in 1930 as Paid.
w Charles Lederer, Edith Fitzgerald play Bayard Veiller d Gustav Machaty
☆ Ruth Hussey, Tom Neal, Paul Kelly, William Gargan, Paul Cavanagh, Samuel S. Hinds, Rita Johnson, Sidney Blackmer
'Certain of appeal where cops and robbers click.' – *Variety*

'If you can't remember the 60's, ...don't worry. Neither can they.'
Withnail and I **
GB 1987 108m colour
Recorded Releasing/HandMade Films (Paul M. Heller)
In the 60s in Britain two out-of-work actors settle in a dilapidated country cottage.
Deliberately seedy comedy which settles down as a study of character and contrives to be hard to forget.
wd Bruce Robinson ph Peter Hannan m David Dundas pd Michael Pickwoad ed Alan Strachan
☆ Richard E. Grant, Paul McGann, Richard Griffiths, Ralph Brown, Michael Elphick

Without a Clue
US 1988 107m CFI color
Rank/ITC (Marc Stirdivant)
Dr Watson hires a failed actor to impersonate Sherlock Holmes, a fictional character he has invented to hide his own abilities as a detective.
The mystery is that anyone should have released this witless spoof.
w Gary Murphy, Larry Strawther d Thom Eberhardt ph Alan Hume m Henry Mancini pd Brian Ackland-Snow, Martyn Hebert ed Peter Tanner cos Judy Moorcroft
☆ Michael Caine (Sherlock Holmes/Reginald Kincaid), Ben Kingsley (Dr Watson), Jeffrey Jones (Inspector Lestrade), Lysette Anthony (Fake Leslie), Paul Freeman (Moriarty), Nigel Davenport (Lord Smithwick), Pat Keen (Mrs Hudson), Peter Cook (Norman Greenhough), Tim Killick (Sebastian), Matthew Savage (Wiggins), Harold Innocent (Mayor Johnson)

Without a Trace
US 1983 120m DeLuxe
TCF (Stanley R. Jaffe)
A mother solves the mystery of her missing child.
Fairly interesting modern melodrama with emphasis on character rather than the somewhat arbitrarily resolved plot.
w Beth Gutcheon novel *Still Missing* by Beth Gutcheon d Stanley R. Jaffe ph John Bailey m Jack Nitzsche pd Paul Sylbert
☆ Kate Nelligan, Judd Hirsch, David Dukes, Stockard Channing, Jacqueline Brookes, Keith McDermott, Kathleen Widdoes
'Dignified understatement is the keynote.' – *Tom Milne, MFB*

'Pre. His spirit set a pace only his heart could follow.'
Without Limits
US 1998 118m Technicolor
Warner (Paula Wagner, Tom Cruise)
After clashing with his coach at the University of Oregon over the best way to win his races, athlete Steve Prefontaine runs poorly in the 1972 Olympics, then tries, too late, to change his approach.
A biopic of a charismatic American long distance runner who died young and failed to win the glittering prizes; at its heart is a sometimes affecting drama of Prefontaine's relationship with his coach.
w Robert Towne, Kenny Moore d Robert Towne ph Conrad L. Hall m Randy Miller pd William Creber ed Claire Simpson
☆ Billy Crudup (Steve Prefontaine), Donald Sutherland (William Bowerman), Monica Potter (Mary Marckx), Jeremy Sisto (Frank Shorter), Gabriel Olds (Don Kardong), Judith Ivey (Barbara Bowerman), Dean Norris (Bill Dellinger), Billy Burke (Kenny Moore), Adam Setliff (Mac Wilkins), Nicholas Oleson (Russ Francis), William Mapother (Bob Peters), Matthew Lillard (Roscoe Devine)
'Saddled with a strident soundtrack, the film feels at times like an over-earnest made-for-television feature.' – *Edward Lawrenson, Sight and Sound*
† Prefontaine was also the subject of another biopic *Prefontaine* (qv), made in 1997.

Without Love *
US 1945 111m bw
MGM (Lawrence Weingarten)
The housing shortage in wartime Washington causes a widow to allow a scientist to move in with her, quite platonically.
Altered version of a popular play; rather long-drawn-out and disappointing considering the talent on hand.
w Donald Ogden Stewart play Philip Barry d Harold S. Bucquet ph Karl Freund m Bronislau Kaper
☆ Spencer Tracy, Katharine Hepburn, Lucille Ball, Keenan Wynn, Carl Esmond, Patricia Morison, Felix Bressart, Gloria Grahame
'One of those glossy conversation pieces that MGM does up so handsomely.' – *Rose Pelswick*

Without Reservations
US 1946 101m bw
RKO/Jesse L. Lasky
A famous woman writer heads for Hollywood by train and meets a marine who seems ideal for her male lead.
Would-be zany romantic comedy à la It Happened One Night; *doesn't quite come off.*
w Andrew Solt d Mervyn Le Roy ph Milton Krasner m Roy Webb
☆ Claudette Colbert, John Wayne, Don Defore, Phil Brown, Frank Puglia

Without Witnesses: see *A Private Conversation*

Without You I'm Nothing

US 1990 89m Technicolor
Electric/MCEG (Jonathan D. Krane)

Stand-up comedian Sandra Bernhard performs her one-woman show.

A self-indulgent ramble through the performer's past, interspersed with a few deft but uninteresting recreations of popular musical styles.

w Sandra Bernhard, John Boscovich *d* John Boscovich *ph* Joseph Yacoe *m* Patrice Rushen *pd* Kevin Rupnik *ed* Pamela Malouf-Cundy

☆ Sandra Bernhard, John Doe, Steve Antin, Lu Leonard, Ken Foree, Cynthia Bailey

'It aims for the spin-off thrills of a transgressive act in which much is suggested but nothing really is said.' – *Cynthia Rose, Sight and Sound*

'One of the sharpest and original comic talents of the past decade.' – *Empire*

'A big city cop who knows too much. His only witness – a small boy who's seen too much!'

Witness ****

US 1985 112m Technicolor
Paramount/Edward S. Feldman

A young Amish boy witnesses a murder, and a big-city detective hides out in the community to protect him.

As much about the meeting of cultures as about cops and robbers, this is one of those lucky movies which works out well on all counts and shows that there are still craftsmen lurking in Hollywood.

w Earl W. Wallace, William Kelley d Peter Weir ph John Seale *m* Maurice Jarre *pd* Stan Jolley *ed* Thom Noble

☆ *Harrison Ford,* Kelly McGillis, Josef Sommer, Lukas Haas, Jan Rubes, Alexander Godunov

editing; original screenplay

best picture; direction; Harrison Ford; photography; music; art direction

music

The Witness Chair

US 1936 64m bw
RKO

A secretary accidentally kills her nasty employer and almost allows an associate to take the blame.

Stiff, old-fashioned melodrama that served its purpose.

w Rian James, Gertrude Purcell *story* Rita Weiman *d* George Nicholls Jnr

☆ Ann Harding, Walter Abel, Douglass Dumbrille, Frances Sage, Moroni Olsen, Margaret Hamilton

Witness for the Prosecution ***

US 1957 114m bw
UA/Theme/Edward Small (Arthur Hornblow Jnr)

A convalescent QC takes on a murder defence and finds himself in a web of trickery.

Thoroughly likeable though relentlessly over-expanded movie version of a clever stage thriller. Some miscasting and artificiality is condoned by smart dialogue and handling, one celebrated performance, and a handful of surprises.

w Billy Wilder, Harry Kurnitz play Agatha Christie d Billy Wilder ph Russell Harlan *m* Matty Melneck *ed* Daniel Mandell

☆ *Charles Laughton,* Tyrone Power, Marlene Dietrich, John Williams, Henry Daniell, Elsa Lanchester, Norma Varden, Una O'Connor, Ian Wolfe

best picture; Billy Wilder; Charles Laughton; Elsa Lanchester; Daniel Mandell

Witness to Murder *

US 1954 81m bw
UA (Chester Erskine)

A lonely woman sees a strangling in the flat across the street; the police don't believe her but the murderer does.

Predictable but quite effective screamer with a nick-of-time dénouement.

w Chester Erskine *d* Roy Rowland *ph* John Alton *m* Herschel Burke Gilbert

☆ Barbara Stanwyck, George Sanders, Gary Merrill, Jesse White, Harry Shannon, Claire Carleton

Wittgenstein **

GB 1993 75m colour
BFI/Channel 4/Uplink/Bandung (Tariq Ali)

Biopic of the linguistic philosopher Ludwig Wittgenstein, from his birth in Austria to his death in Cambridge in 1951.

Made on a tiny budget and shot as a series of scenes, using a minimum of props, against a black background, this is nevertheless a colourful and intriguing work, interested both in Wittgenstein as a person and in what he had to say; inevitably, its appeal will be limited to those interested in philosophy and in the inventive use of film

w Derek Jarman, Terry Eagleton, Ken Butler *d* Derek Jarman *ph* James Welland *m* Jan Latham-Koenig *ad* Annie Lapaz *ed* Budge Tremlett

☆ Karl Johnson, Michael Gough, Tilda Swinton, John Quentin, Kevin Collins, Clancy Chassay, Jill Balcon

'Wonderfully theatrical in its execution, this is Jarman pared down to basics – actors, stage, lighting – allowing the script, the real strength of the film, with its equal measures of wit and weight (and surprisingly little pretension) to take centre stage.' – *Philippa Bloom, Empire*

'You can't tell them apart without a scorecard!'

Wives and Lovers

US 1963 103m bw
Paramount/Hal B. Wallis

A successful author moves his family into Connecticut, where sex rears its ugly head.

Would-be sophisticated comedy with insufficient bubbles.

w Edward Anhalt *play The First Wife* by Jay Presson Allen *d* John Rich *ph* Lucien Ballard *m* Lyn Murray

☆ Van Johnson, Janet Leigh, Ray Walston, Shelley Winters, Martha Hyer, Jeremy Slate

Wives under Suspicion

US 1938 68m bw
Universal

A district attorney involved in a love-triangle murder discovers a similar situation developing in his own life.

Flat remake of the same director's The Kiss Before the Mirror; *of little interest.*

w Myles Connolly *d* James Whale

☆ Warren William, Gail Patrick, Ralph Morgan, William Lundigan, Constance Moore

The Wiz *

US 1978 134m Technicolor
Universal/Motown (Robert Cohen)

A black version of *The Wizard of Oz*, set in New York.

Glossy version of the Broadway musical hit; it offers some rewards, but on the whole the first is the best.

w Joel Schumacher *play* Charlie Smalls *(m/ly) book* William Brown *d* Sidney Lumet *ph* Oswald Morris *m* Quincy Jones *md* Quincy Jones *pd* Tony Walton *songs* Charlie Smalls

☆ Diana Ross, Michael Jackson, Nipsey Russell, Ted Ross, Lena Horne, Richard Pryor, Mabel King, Theresa Merritt

Oswald Morris; Quincy Jones

The Wizard

US 1989 97m DeLuxe
UIP/Universal (David Chisholm, Ken Topolsky)

A young boy runs away with his almost-mute even younger brother in order to compete in a video-game championship.

Uninteresting pre-teen road movie, which has no other purpose than to sell video games.

w David Chisholm *d* Todd Holland *ph* Robert Yeoman *m* J. Peter Robinson *pd* Michael Mayer *ed* Tom Finan

☆ Fred Savage, Luke Edwards, Christian Slater, Beau Bridges, Vincent Leahr, Wendy Phillips, Dea McAllister, Sam McMurray, Will Seltzer

'The Maniac Magician Whose Tricks Actually Work!'

Wizard of Gore

US 1970 96m colour
Mayflower (Herschell Gordon Lewis)

A stage conjuror hypnotises his audience into thinking his sawing women in half or driving swords or spikes through them are tricks when he is really killing his victims.

The emphasis is on gory deaths here – unusually for this director there are no women with outsize breasts on view – combined with amatuerish acting, script and direction.

w Allen Kahn *d* Herschell Gordon Lewis *ph* Alex Ameri, Daniel Krogh *m* Larry Wellington *ed* Eskandor Ameripoor *sp* Herschell Gordon Lewis

☆ Ray Sager (Montag the Magnificent), Sherry Carson (Judy Cler), Wayne Ratay (Jack), Phil Laurenson (Greg), Don Alexander (Det. Kramer), John Elliot (Det. Harlan)

The Wizard of Loneliness

US 1988 110m DuArt
American Playhouse

During the Second World War, a lonely boy goes to stay with his grandparents and observes the complex lives of those around him, centring on his widowed aunt and her former lover, a disturbed soldier on the run.

A good central performance from Haas cannot hold together a rambling narrative.

w Nancy Larsen *novel* John Nichols *d* Jenny Bowen *ph* Richard Bowen *m* Michel Colombier

☆ Lukas Haas, Lea Thompson, John Randolph, Anne Pitoniak, Dylan Baker, Lance Guest, Jeremiah Warner, Steve Hendrikson

The Wizard of Oz

US 1925 70m bw silent
Larry Semon

On her 18th birthday a girl abandoned as a small baby at a Kansas farm discovers that she is the Queen of Oz and, after deposing its dictator, lives there happily ever after.

The emphasis is on farmyard slapstick comedy, mainly executed with a heavy hand, which makes it hard to appreciate why Semon was once almost as popular as Chaplin and Keaton, but it has its moments – particularly a chase sequence in wooden boxes.

w L. Frank Baum Jnr, Leon Lee, Larry Semon *novel* L. Frank Baum *d* Larry Semon *ph* H. F. Koenenkamp, Frank Good, Leonard Smith *ad* Robert Stevens *ed* Sam Zimbalist

☆ Larry Semon (The Scarecrow), Oliver N. Hardy (The Tin Woodsman), Dorothy Dwan, Mary Carr, Virginia Pearson, Bryant Washburn, Josef Swickard, Otto Lederer, Charles Murray

† The film is available on video with a musical accompaniment.

The Wizard of Oz ***

US 1939 102m Technicolor
MGM (Mervyn Le Roy)

Unhappy Dorothy runs away from home, has adventures in a fantasy land, but finally decides that happiness was in her own back yard all the time.

Classic fairy tale given vigorous straightforward treatment, made memorable by performances, art direction and hummable tunes.

w Noel Langley, Florence Ryerson, Edgar Allan Woolf *book* L. Frank Baum *d Victor Fleming ph* Harold Rosson *md* Herbert Stothart *ad Cedric Gibbons, William A. Horning songs E. Y. Harburg, Harold Arlen*

☆ *Judy Garland, Frank Morgan, Ray Bolger, Jack Haley, Bert Lahr, Margaret Hamilton, Billie Burke,* Charley Grapewin, Clara Blandick

SCARECROW (RAY BOLGER): 'I could while away the hours
Conversin' with the flowers
Consultin' with the rain.
And perhaps I'd deserve you
And be even worthy erv you
If I only had a brain…'

COWARDLY LION (BERT LAHR): 'Oh, it's sad to be admittin'
I'm as vicious as a kitten
Widout de vim and voive;
I could show off my prowess
Be a lion, not a mowess
If I only had de noive.'

GLINDA, THE GOOD WITCH (BILLIE BURKE): 'Close your eyes and tap your heels together three times. And think to yourself, there's no place like home.'

DOROTHY (JUDY GARLAND): 'If I ever go looking for my heart's desire again, I won't look any further than my own back yard, because if it isn't there, I never really lost it to begin with.'

DOROTHY, LION, SCARECROW, TIN MAN: 'We're off to see the Wizard
The wonderful Wizard of Oz.
We hear he is a whiz of a wiz
If ever a wiz there was.
If ever a wever a wiz there was
The Wizard of Oz is one because
Because of the wonderful things he does…'

'There's an audience for it wherever there's a projection machine and a screen.' – *Variety*

'I don't see why children shouldn't like it, but for adults there isn't very much except Bert Lahr.' – *Richard Mallett, Punch*

'As for the light touch of fantasy, it weighs like a pound of fruitcake soaking wet.' – *Otis Ferguson*

† Ray Bolger was originally cast as the tin man but swapped roles with Buddy Ebsen who was to have been the scarecrow. Ebsen then got sick from the aluminium dust and was replaced by Jack Haley. Edna May Oliver was originally cast as the wicked witch. For Dorothy MGM wanted Shirley Temple, but Twentieth Century Fox wouldn't loan her. Richard Thorpe was the original director. He was fired after 12 days. George Cukor did some costume and make-up tests while a new director was found, removing the blonde wig that Judy Garland had been given for her role.

†† The sepia scenes at beginning and end were directed by King Vidor.

††† Aljean Harmetz's book *The Making of the Wizard of Oz* (Pavilion, 1989) is an entertaining account of the story behind the film.

♫ 'Over the Rainbow'; 'Ding Dong the Witch is Dead'; 'We're Off to See the Wizard'; 'Follow the Yellow Brick Road'; 'If I Only Had a Brain'; 'The Merry Old Land of Oz'; 'If I Were King of the Forest'

song 'Over the Rainbow'; Herbert Stothart; Judy Garland (special award)

best picture; art direction

Wizards of the Lost Kingdom

US/Argentina 1985 75m colour
Concorde (Frank Isaac, Alex Sessa)

A young magician, accompanied by a swordsman and what appears to be a giant two-legged poodle, saves his kingdom from an evil sorceror.

Cheapskate sword and sorcery, presumably intended for a young audience, and certainly only watchable by an undemanding one; a pity no one was able to conjure up a less banal script.

w Tom Edwards *d* Hector Olivera *ph* Leonard Solis *m* James Horner, Chris Young *pd* Mary Bertram *ed* Silvia Roberts *sp* Richard Lennox

☆ Bo Svenson, Vidal Peterson, Thom Christopher, Barbara Stock, Maria Socas, Dolores Michaels, Rick Gallo

Wo Ai Chufang: see *Kitchen*

Wo De Fu Qin Mu Qin: see *The Road Home*

Wo die Grünen Ameisen Träumen: see *Where the Green Ants Dream*

Wo Hu Zang Long: see *Crouching Tiger, Hidden Dragon*

Wo Shi Shui: see *Who Am I?*

'The Animal Is Out.'

Wolf *

US 1994 125m Technicolor
Columbia (Douglas Wick)

Bitten by a wolf, a mild-mannered publishing executive who is demoted in a takeover finds that he is developing the characteristics of the animal, with keener senses but also with a tendency to grow hair and go around on all fours at the time of the full moon.

A werewolf movie for people who don't like werewolf movies: sometimes witty and clever, particularly in its scenes of office politics, but finally relying on some dated narrative devices and succumbing to all the usual clichés of the genre.

w Jim Harrison, Wesley Strick *d* Mike Nichols *ph* Giuseppe Rotunno *m* Ennio Morricone *pd* Bo Welch *ed* Sam O'Steen *sp* make-up: Rick Baker
☆ Jack Nicholson, Michelle Pfeiffer, James Spader, Kate Nelligan, Christopher Plummer, Richard Jenkins, Eileen Atkins, David Hyde Pierce, Prunella Scales

'A genre movie for grownups.' – *Richard Schickel, Time*

'It's simply too ridiculous for a mainstream audience and too familiar for horror fans.' – *Kim Newman, Empire*

'Less than entirely convincing, an intriguing thriller more enjoyable for its humor and sophistication than for its scare quotient.' – *Todd McCarthy, Variety*

The Wolf at the Door **

France/Denmark 1986 90m colour
Dagmar/Famous French/TF1 (Henning Carlsen)

In Paris in 1893, Paul Gaugin returns penniless from Tahiti to show his paintings, expecting acclaim; but he sells few, his friends and lovers desert him, and he has trouble raising the money to go back.

Engrossing, low-key portrait of an artist at odds with conventional society.

w Christopher Hampton *original scenario* Henning Carlsen, Jean-Claude Carriere *d* Henning Carlsen *ph* Mikael Salomon *m* Roger Bourland *ad* Andre Guerin, Karl-Otto Hedal *ed* Janus Billeskov Jansen
☆ Donald Sutherland, Max von Sydow (Strindberg), Jean Yanne, Sofie Gråbol, Valerie Glandut, Fanny Bastien, Ghita Norbye, Merete Voldstedlund

Wolf Larsen

US 1958 83m bw
AA (Lindsley Parsons)

Serviceable remake of *The Sea Wolf* (qv) without the Nietzschean overtones.

w Jack de Witt, Turnley Walker *d* Harmon Jones *ph* Floyd Crosby *m* Paul Dunlap
☆ Barry Sullivan, Peter Graves, Thayer David, Gita Hall

'His hideous howl a dirge of death!'
'Night monster with the blood lust of a savage beast!'

The Wolf Man *

US 1941 70m bw
Universal (George Waggner)

The son of an English squire comes home, is bitten by a gypsy werewolf, and becomes one himself.

Dazzlingly cast, moderately well staged, but dramatically very disappointing horror piece which established a new Universal monster who later met Frankenstein, Abbott and Costello, and several other eccentrics.

w Curt Siodmak *d* George Waggner *ph* Joseph Valentine *m* Hans Salter, Frank Skinner *md* Charles Previn *ad* Jack Otterson *ed* Ted J. Kent *sp* make-up: Jack Pierce
☆ Lon Chaney Jnr, Claude Rains, Warren William, Ralph Bellamy, Bela Lugosi, *Maria Ouspenskaya*, Patric Knowles, Evelyn Ankers, Fay Helm

MALEVA (MARIA OUSPENSKAYA): 'Even the man who is pure in heart
And says his prayers by night
May become a wolf when the wolf bane blooms
And the moon is pure and bright…'

'It will tear the scream from your throat!'

Wolfen

US 1981 115m Technicolor Panavision
Warner/Orion (Rupert Hitzig)

Mutilation murders in New York turn out to be the work of savage beasts descended from Indian hunters who went underground in despair at the future of mankind.

Nuthatch horror movie with a message, though providing little of either commodity. Clearly a waste of money.

w David Eyre, Michael Wadleigh *novel* Whitley Strieber *d* Michael Wadleigh *ph* Gerry Fisher, Fred Abeles *m* James Horner *pd* Paul Sylbert
☆ Albert Finney, Diane Venora, Edward James Olmos, Gregory Hines, Tom Noonan

'A thriller so slow, complicated and frankly rather dull that one's sympathy is all on the side of the predators.' – *Daily Mail*

The Wolves of Willoughby Chase

GB 1988 93m colour
Entertainment/Subatomnic/Zenith (Mark Forstater)

Two girls discover that their wicked governess is attempting to steal the family estate.

Lively children's film with relishable villains.

w William M. Akers *novel* Joan Aiken *d* Stuart Orme *ph* Paul Beeson *m* Colin Towns *pd* Christopher Hobbs *ed* Martin Walsh
☆ Stephanie Beacham, Mel Smith, Geraldine James, Richard O'Brien, Emily Hudson, Aleks Darowska, Jane Horrocks, Eleanor David, Jonathan Coy

Woman Accused *

US 1933 73m bw
Paramount

A woman kills her ex-lover in a struggle and goes on the run.

Intriguing rigmarole written as a magazine serial by ten well-known authors contributing a chapter each. The result confirms the method.

w Bayard Veiller *serial* Rupert Hughes, Vicki Baum, Zane Grey, Vina Delmar, Irvin S. Cobb, Gertrude Atherton, J. P. McEvoy, Ursula Parrott, Polan Banks, Sophie Kerr *d* Paul Sloane *ph* Karl Struss
☆ Nancy Carroll, Cary Grant, John Halliday, Irving Pichel, Louis Calhern, Jack La Rue, John Lodge

'It may convince producers and exhibitors that new writing talent should be encouraged … business possibilities anything but bright on so-so cast names.' – *Variety*

A Woman Alone

GB 1936 78m bw
Garrett-Klement
US title: *Two Who Dared*

In 19th-century Russia, a captain falls for a peasant girl.

Uninteresting melodrama with stilted actors.

w Leo Lania, Warren Chetham Strode *novel* Fedor Ozep *d* Eugene Frenke
☆ Anna Sten, Henry Wilcoxon, Viola Keats, John Garrick, Romilly Lunge

A Woman Alone: see *Sabotage (1936)*

The Woman Between: see *The Woman I Love*

A Woman Called Abé Sada *

Japan 1975 77m colour
Nikkatsu (Yoshiteru Yuuki)

original title: *Jitsuroku Abe Sada*

A maid and former prostitute recalls how, involved in a sado-masochistic affair with her married employer, she strangled and castrated him in an excess of passion.

Chilling drama of love and death that also encompasses the theme of a woman rebelling against her sexually subservient role. It suffers from the fact that Nagisa Oshima made the superior Ai No Corrida *(qv) a year later, based on the same true incident that took place in the mid-30s.*

w Akio Ido *d Noboru Tanaka ph* Masaru Mori *ad* Gunji Kawasaki
☆ Junko Miyashi, Hideaki Azumi, Nagatoshi Sakamoto, Genshu Hanayagi, Ikunosuke Koizumi

Woman Chases Man

US 1937 71m bw
Samuel Goldwyn

A lady architect persuades a millionaire to help his land developer father.

Thin, lame comedy which constantly amazes by its lack of success.

w Joseph Anthony, Manny Seff, David Hertz *story* Lynn Root, Frank Fenton *d* John G. Blystone *ph* Gregg Toland *m* Alfred Newman
☆ Miriam Hopkins, Joel McCrea, Charles Winninger, Erik Rhodes, Broderick Crawford, Leona Maricle, Ella Logan, Charles Halton

'Laughs stopped at the Music Hall when the action on the screen became so insanely illogical, and dull, that the amazed disappointment of the house expressed itself in chilly silence.' – *Variety*

'A pleasant warm weather fabrication – lightweight, attractively tailored and not meant to withstand the rigours of wear or the chill blasts of the critics.' – *Frank S. Nugent*

† The unhappy production began as a vehicle for Miss Hopkins. Writers who worked on it include Ben Hecht, Sam and Bella Spewack, and Dorothy Parker. Directors involved were Edward Ludwig, William Wyler and Gregory La Cava.

A Woman Commands

US 1932 85m bw
RKO Pathé

A cabaret entertainer rejects her lover for a king, but regains him when the king is murdered.

Romantic melodrama of the silent school, quite unrevivable.

w Thilde Forster *d* Paul Stein
☆ Pola Negri, Basil Rathbone, Roland Young, H. B. Warner, Anthony Bushell, Reginald Owen

A Woman Destroyed: see *Smash-Up, The Story of a Woman*

A Woman Disappeared, Portrait of a Woman: see *Une Femme Disparait*

Woman Doctor

US 1939 65m bw
Republic (Sol C. Siegel)

Her career prospers, her marriage suffers.

Old hat domestic drama, tolerably put over.

w Joseph Moncure March *d* Sidney Salkow
☆ Frieda Inescort, Henry Wilcoxon, Claire Dodd, Sybil Jason, Cora Witherspoon

The Woman for Joe

GB 1955 91m Technicolor VistaVision
Rank/Group

A circus midget falls in love with a singer who falls in love with the circus's owner.

Sentimental little tragedy of misplaced affection, hardly worth a second glance.

w Neil Paterson *d* George More O'Ferrall *ph* Georges Perinal *m* Malcolm Arnold *ad* Maurice Carter *ed* Alfred Roome
☆ Diane Cilento, George Baker, Jimmy Karoubi, David Kossoff, Sydney Tafler, Violet Farebrother, Earl Cameron, Derek Sydney

The Woman from Monte Carlo

US 1931 68m bw
Warner

The wife of a naval officer is suspected of adultery.

Stiff marital melodrama based on a silent film The Night Watch; *it worked no wonders for its German star.*

w Harvey Thew *d* Michael Curtiz
☆ Lil Dagover, Walter Huston, Warren William, Robert Warwick, John Wray

'Looks a light draw at best.' – *Variety*

The Woman from Nowhere: see *La Femme de Nulle Part*

Woman Hater

GB 1948 105m bw
GFD/Two Cities (William Sistrom)

An English nobleman tries to disprove a film star's statement that she hates men and loves solitude.

Incredibly slight material is interminably stretched out, well beyond an excellent cast's ability to help.

w Robert Westerby, Nicholas Phipps *d* Terence Young *ph* André Thomas *m* Lambert Williamson
☆ Stewart Granger, Edwige Feuillère, Ronald Squire, Mary Jerrold, Jeanne de Casalis

Woman Hunt: see *Au Royaume des Cieux*

'Gloriously lifting two great stars to new greatness!'

The Woman I Love *

US 1937 85m bw
RKO (Albert Lewis)
GB title: *The Woman Between*

In World War I France, a pilot loves his superior officer's wife.

Well-made romantic action melodrama from a well-praised original.

w Mary Borden *novel L'Equipage* by Joseph Kessel *d Anatole Litvak ph* Charles Rosher *m* Arthur Honegger, Maurice Thiriet
☆ Paul Muni, Miriam Hopkins, Louis Hayward, Colin Clive, Minor Watson, Elizabeth Risdon, Paul Guilfoyle, Mady Christians

'Needs all the marquee help it can get … spotty business indicated.' – *Variety*

Woman in a Dressing Gown *

GB 1957 94m bw
Godwin/Willis/J. Lee-Thompson

After twenty years of marriage, a wife's slatternly ways alienate her once devoted husband, and he asks for a divorce.

Classic British TV play adequately filmed but now rather dated and irritating.

w Ted Willis *play* Ted Willis *d* J. Lee-Thompson *ph* Gilbert Taylor *m* Louis Levy
☆ Yvonne Mitchell, Anthony Quayle, Sylvia Syms, Andrew Ray, Carole Lesley

The Woman in Green

US 1945 68m bw
Universal (Roy William Neill)

Sherlock Holmes is called in after the police are baffled by a serial killer who murders women and cuts off their right forefingers as souvenirs.

Deft little thriller that owes little to Conan Doyle but nevertheless manages to entertain.

w Bertram Millhauser *d* Roy William Neill *ph* Virgil Miller *md* Mark Levant *ad* John B. Goodman, Martin Obzina *ed* Edward Curtiss
☆ Basil Rathbone, Nigel Bruce, Hillary Brooke, Henry Daniell, Paul Cavanagh, Matthew Boulton, Eve Amber

Woman in Hiding

US 1949 92m bw
U-I (Michael Kraike)

After escaping her husband's attempts to murder her, a woman goes into hiding while evidence is being accumulated against him.

Modest suspenser with too many near escapes and not much else.

w Oscar Saul *d* Michael Gordon *ph* William Daniels *m* Frank Skinner *ad* Robert Clatworthy, Bernard Herzbrun *ed* Milton Carruth
☆ Ida Lupino, Howard Duff, Stephen McNally, John Litel, Taylor Holmes, Irving Bacon, Peggy Dow, Joe Besser, Don Beddoe

'The detail is full of things interesting and amusing at the time and pleasant to remember afterwards.' – *Richard Mallett, Punch*

The Woman in His House: see *The Animal Kingdom*

The Woman in Question *

GB 1949 88m bw
GFD/Javelin (Teddy Baird)
US title: *Five Angles on Murder*

Police investigating a woman's death build up several different impressions of her.

Multi-flashback melodrama which somehow doesn't quite come off despite effort all round.

w John Cresswell *d* Anthony Asquith *ph* Desmond Dickinson *m* John Wooldridge
☆ Jean Kent, Dirk Bogarde, Susan Shaw, John McCallum, Hermione Baddeley, Charles Victor, Duncan Macrae, Lana Morris, Vida Hope

The Woman in Red

US 1935 68m bw
Warner

A professional horsewoman marries into society and is ill received.

Stiff class melodrama partly redeemed by its star.

w Mary McCall Jnr, Peter Milne *novel North Shore* by Wallace Irwin *d* Robert Florey
☆ Barbara Stanwyck, Genevieve Tobin, John Eldredge, Gene Raymond, Philip Reed

The Woman in Red *

US 1984 86m DeLuxe
Orion (Victor Drai)

A middle-aged married man has fantasies of infidelity.

Moderately successful transfer to America of a French comedy success.

wd Gene Wilder, *from the film* Un Eléphant ça Trompe Enormement *by Jean-Loup Dabadie, Yves Robert ph* Fred Schuler *m* John Morris *pd* David L. Snyder *ed* Christopher Greenbury
☆ Gene Wilder, Kelly Le Brock, Charles Grodin, Joseph Bologna, Judith Ivey, Gilda Radner
song 'I Just Called to Say I Love You' (Stevie Wonder)

The Woman in Room 13
US 1932 58m bw
Fox
The wife of an innocent convict tricks the real culprit into a confession.
Stagey melodrama which just about fills an hour.
w Guy Bolton *play* Sam Shipman, Max Marcin, Percival Wilde *d* Henry King
☆ Elissa Landi, Ralph Bellamy, Neil Hamilton, Myrna Loy, Gilbert Roland
'Just another factory-made release.' – *Variety*

Woman in the Dark
US 1935 68m bw
Select/RKO
A man convicted of manslaughter gets himself on his release into another awkward situation.
Moderate semi-crime melodrama.
w Sada Cowan *story* Dashiell Hammett *d* Phil Rosen
☆ Fay Wray, Melvyn Douglas, Ralph Bellamy, Roscoe Ates
'Marquee weakness only thing that may keep it out of single-feature houses … murder mystery fare of sufficient relish to keep 'em from leaving the table.' – *Variety*

Woman in the Dunes: see *Woman of the Dunes*

The Woman in the Hall
GB 1947 93m bw
GFD/IP/Wessex (Ian Dalrymple)
A well-intentioned woman takes to begging and becomes a bad influence on her daughter.
Finger-wagging novelette makes an unrewarding film.
w G. B. Stern, Ian Dalrymple, Jack Lee *novel* G. B. Stern *d* Jack Lee *ph* C. Pennington-Richards, H. E. Fowle *m* Temple Abady *pd* Peter Proud *ed* John Krish
☆ Ursula Jeans, Cecil Parker, Jean Simmons, Jill Raymond, Edward Underdown, Joan Miller, Susan Hampshire

The Woman in the Moon *
Germany 1929 125m (24 fps) bw silent
UFA
original title: *Frau im Mond*
Two scientists are forced to journey to the moon by criminals anxious to mine its gold deposits.
Heavy-handed fantasy which is not among its director's best work.
w Thea von Harbou *d* Fritz Lang
☆ Willy Fritsch, Gerda Maurus, Gusti Stark-Gatettenbaur
'Half of it could be removed; as it is, it winds ponderously on.' – *Variety*

'It was the look in her eyes that did it. How could he resist? How could he know it meant murder?'
The Woman in the Window ***
US 1944 95m bw
International (Nunnally Johnson)
A grass widow professor befriends a girl who gets him involved with murder.
A refreshingly intelligent little thriller which was criticized at the time for a cop-out ending; this can now be seen as a decorative extra to a story which had already ended satisfactorily. Good middlebrow entertainment.
w Nunnally Johnson novel Once Off Guard by J. H. Wallis *d Fritz Lang ph Milton Krasner m* Arthur Lange, Hugo Friedhofer
☆ *Edward G. Robinson*, Joan Bennett, *Raymond* Massey, Dan Duryea, Edmund Breon, Thomas Jackson, Dorothy Peterson, Arthur Loft
'A perfect example of its kind, and a very good kind too.' – *James Shelley Hamilton*
'The accumulation of tiny details enlarged as though under a district attorney's magnifying glass gives reality a fantastic and anguishing appearance.' – *Jacques Bourgeois*
'In its rather artificial, club library style an effective and well made piece, absorbing, diverting and full of often painful suspense.' – *Richard Mallett, Punch*
'Art and Mammon, it seems to me, have been very prettily served.' – *Spectator*
🏅 Arthur Lange, Hugo Friedhofer

'Born in shame – living in mystery – what is her sinister secret?'
The Woman in White *
US 1948 109m bw
Warner (Henry Blanke)
The new tutor of a strange household finds himself among eccentrics, villains and ill-used ladies.
A Victorian thriller which is long on atmosphere but not so hot on suspense or plot development. The cast helps a lot.
w Stephen Morehouse Avery *novel* Wilkie Collins *d* Peter Godfrey *ph Carl Guthrie m* Max Steiner *ad* Stanley Fleischer *ed* Clarence Kolster
☆ Gig Young, Eleanor Parker, *Sydney Greenstreet*, Alexis Smith, Agnes Moorehead, John Emery, *John Abbott*, Curt Bois
'The Wilkie Collins novel is given the studious, stolid treatment ordinarily reserved for the ritual assassination of a great classic. This is not intended as a recommendation.' – *James Agee*
'Greenstreet and others move through the murky passages of the story like visitors in some massive Gothic museum, and they move, on the whole, with stately discretion, and do not scribble on the objects or show anything but the greatest veneration for them.' – *C. A. Lejeune*

A Woman Is a Woman **
France 1961 85m Eastmancolor Scope
original title: *Une Femme est une Femme*
A stripper quarrels with her boyfriend because she wants to have a baby and he doesn't.
Exuberantly playful tribute to the high spirits of MGM's classic musicals, even though there is little actual singing and dancing. It has a lovers' bicycle ride that was imitated much later in Butch Cassidy and The Sundance Kid.
wd Jean-Luc Godard *ph* Raoul Coutard *m* Michel Legrand
☆ Jean-Paul Belmondo, Jean-Claude Brialy, Anna Karina, Marie Dubois, Jeanne Moreau
'As bad a film as anyone is ever likely to see.' – *John Simon*

The Woman Next Door
France 1981 106m Fujicolour
Les Films du Carrosse/TF1
An engineer is embarrassed when an old flame, now married, comes to live next door; their love rekindles but ends in tragedy.
Rather uninteresting melodrama with a failure to communicate its apparent personal importance for the director.
w François Truffaut, Suzanne Schiffman, Jean Aurel *d* François Truffaut *ph* William Lubtchansky *m* Georges Delerue
☆ Gérard Depardieu, Fanny Ardant, Henri Garcin, Michele Baumgarner

Woman Obsessed
US 1959 102m DeLuxe Cinemascope
TCF (Sydney Boehm)
In the Canadian Rockies, a pioneer woman's small son does not take to his new stepfather.
Antediluvian pulp fiction with quicksand and a forest fire for highlights. Shades of D. W. Griffith, and badly done into the bargain.
w Sydney Boehm *novel* John Mantley *d* Henry Hathaway *ph* William C. Mellor *m* Hugo Friedhofer
☆ Susan Hayward, Stephen Boyd, Dennis Holmes, Theodore Bikel, Barbara Nichols, Ken Scott, Arthur Franz

A Woman of Affairs
US 1928 90m (24 fps) bw silent
MGM
A wild rich girl goes from man to man and finally kills herself in a car crash.
Romantic star tosh from a fashionable novel of the time.
w Bess Meredyth *novel The Green Hat* by Michael Arlen *d* Clarence Brown *ph* William Daniels
☆ Greta Garbo, Lewis Stone, John Gilbert, John Mack Brown, Douglas Fairbanks Jnr, Hobart Bosworth
🏅 Bess Meredyth

Woman of Antwerp: see *Dédée d'Anvers*

A Woman of Distinction
US 1950 85m bw
Columbia (Buddy Adler)
The lady dean of a New England school falls for a British astronomer.
Pratfall farce for ageing stars. No go.
w Charles Hoffman *d* Edward Buzzell *ph* Joseph Walker *m* Werner Heymann *md* Morris Stoloff
☆ Rosalind Russell, Ray Milland, Edmund Gwenn, Janis Carter, Mary Jane Saunders, Francis Lederer, Jerome Courtland

Woman of Dolwyn: see *The Last Days of Dolwyn*

A Woman of Paris **
US 1923 85m (24 fps) bw silent (music track added 1976)
Charles Chaplin
A country girl goes to the city, becomes a demi-mondaine, and inadvertently causes the death of the one man she loves.
Remarkably simply-handled 'road to ruin' melodrama; its subtleties of treatment make it still very watchable for those so inclined.
wd Charles Chaplin ph Rollie Totheroh, Jack Wilson
☆ *Edna Purviance, Adolphe Menjou*, Carl Miller, Lydia Knott
'A thoroughly workmanlike entertainment and a candidate for honours and dollars entirely independent of the drawing power built up by Chaplin in other fields.' – *Variety*
'After five minutes of watching the sparkling new print, the spell begins to work. Chaplin is neatly turning the clichés inside out, like a glove.' – *Alan Brien, Sunday Times, 1980*
'Mr Chaplin as writer and director has not done anything radical or anything esoteric; he has merely used his intelligence to the highest degree, an act which for many years has ceased to be expected of motion picture people.' – *Robert E. Sherwood*
'The plot is desperately simple, but played with a control, a complete absence of histrionic vehemence, rare in the early twenties.' – *Dilys Powell, Punch, 1980*
† Chaplin appeared unbilled as a railway porter. The film was not a commercial success and he withdrew it for fifty years.

Woman of Straw *
GB 1964 114m Eastmancolor
UA/Novus (Michael Relph)
A rich old man's nurse conspires with his nephew in a murder plot.
Rather half-hearted but good-looking star melodrama which ventures into Hitchcock territory.
w Robert Muller, Stanley Mann, Michael Relph *novel* Catherine Arley *d* Basil Dearden *ph* Otto Heller *m* Muir Mathieson *pd* Ken Adam
☆ Gina Lollobrigida, Sean Connery, *Ralph Richardson*, Johnny Sekka, Laurence Hardy, Alexander Knox

Woman of Summer: see *The Stripper*

Woman of the Dunes *
Japan 1964 127m bw
Teshigahara (Kiichi Ichikawa)
original title: *Suna no Onna*
US title: *Woman in the Dunes*
An entomologist on a deserted beach finds an attractive young widow living in a shack at the bottom of a huge sand pit, spends the night with her, can't escape, and finally doesn't want to.
Unique sex melodrama, all shifting sand and picturesque angles, with a clear meaning; but far too long.
w Kobo Abe *d* Hiroshi Teshigahara *ph* Hiroshi Segawa *m* Toru Takemitsu *ed* F. Susui
☆ Eiji Okada (The man), Kyoko Kishoda (The woman)
'Teasingly opaque, broodingly erotic.' – *MFB*
🏅 Hiroshi Teshigahara; best foreign film

Woman of the North Country
US 1952 90m Trucolor
Republic (Joseph Kane)
Minnesota 1890: rivalry over an iron ore mine erupts between a young engineer and an ambitious woman.
Standard Western.
w Norman Reilly Raine *d* Joseph Kane *ph* Jack Marta *m* R. Dale Butts
☆ Ruth Hussey, Rod Cameron, John Agar, Gale Storm, Jim Davis, J. Carrol Naish

Woman of the River *
Italy/France 1955 95m Technicolor
Ponti/de Laurentiis/Films du Centaure
original title: *La Donna del Fiume*
A peasant girl has nothing but trouble after falling for a handsome smuggler.
Lively melodrama whose primary purpose was to demonstrate the physical charms of its new star. It succeeded well enough in the Bitter Rice tradition.
w Basilio Franchina, Giorgio Bassani, Pier Paolo Pasolini, Florestano Vancini, Antonio Antoviti, Mario Soldati *story* Alberto Moravia, Ennio Flaiano *d* Mario Soldati *ph* Otello Martelli *m* Angelo Lavagnini, Armando Trovaioli
☆ Sophia Loren, Gerard Oury, Rik Battaglia, Lise Bourdin

The Woman of the Town *
US 1943 87m bw
United Artists (Harry Sherman)
Bat Masterson becomes marshal of Dodge and falls for a saloon singer.
Busy, old-fashioned urban Western with good entertainment values.
w Aeneas Mackenzie *d* George Archainbaud *m* Miklos Rozsa
☆ Albert Dekker, Claire Trevor, Barry Sullivan, Henry Hull, Marion Martin, Porter Hall, Percy Kilbride
🏅 Miklos Rozsa

A Woman of the World: see *Outcast Lady*

Woman of the Year ***
US 1942 114m bw
MGM (Joseph L. Mankiewicz)
A sports columnist marries a lady politician; they have nothing in common but love.
Simple, effective, mildly sophisticated comedy which allows two splendid stars, in harness for the first time, to do their thing to the general benefit.
w Ring Lardner Jnr, Michael Kanin d George Stevens ph Joseph Ruttenberg *m* Franz Waxman
☆ *Spencer Tracy, Katharine Hepburn*, Fay Bainter, Reginald Owen, William Bendix, Dan Tobin, Minor Watson, Roscoe Karns
'Between them they have enough charm to keep any ball rolling.' – *William Whitebait*
🏆 script
🏅 Katharine Hepburn

The Woman on Pier 13
US 1949 73m bw
RKO (Jack J. Gross)
aka: *I Married a Communist*
A shipping executive is blackmailed by communists, who know of a youthful crime, into helping them spy.
Laboured witch-hunt melodrama.
w Charles Grayson, Robert Hardy Andrews *d* Robert Stevenson *ph* Nicholas Musuraca *m* Leigh Harline
☆ Laraine Day, Robert Ryan, John Agar, Thomas Gomez, Janis Carter, Richard Rober, William Talman

Woman on the Run
US 1950 77m bw
Universal-International/Fidelity (Howard Welsch)
A man runs away after witnessing a murder; his wife is menaced by the killer.
Slightly unusual thriller which alas fails to thrill.
w Norman Foster, Alan Campbell *d* Norman Foster *ph* Hal Mohr *m* Emil Newman
☆ Ann Sheridan, Dennis O'Keefe, Robert Keith, Ross Elliott

Woman on Top
US 2000 92m DeLuxe Super 35
TCF/Fox Searchlight (Alan Poul)
Discovering her husband's adultery, a Brazilian woman moves to San Francisco to begin a new life as a chef; but he is determined to win her back.
Exuberant fable of love and cooking that serves up all the familiar Latin American stereotypes.

w Vera Blasi *d* Fina Torres *ph* Thierry Arbogast *m* Luis Bacalov *pd* Philippe Chiffre *ed* Leslie Jones
☆ Penélope Cruz (Isabella Oliveira), Murilo Benício (Toninho Oliveira), Harold Perrineau Jnr (Monica Jones), Mark Feuerstein (Cliff Lloyd), John de Lancie (Alex Reeves), Anne Ramsay (TV Director), Ana Gasteyer (TV Director), Eliane Guttman (Isabella's Mother), Eduardo Mattedi (Isabella's Father)
'A fantastical romp with a buoyant pace, exotic locations, a finger-popping score, appealing leads and spicy cooking demonstrations.' – *Lisa Nesselson, Variety*

A Woman or Two: see *Une Femme ou Deux*

A Woman Rebels *
US 1936 88m bw
RKO (Pandro S. Berman)
A Victorian miss fights for women's rights and has an illegitimate baby.
Interesting, half-forgotten star drama.
w Anthony Veiller, Ernest Vajda *novel Portrait of a Rebel* by Netta Syrett *d* Mark Sandrich *ph* Robert de Grasse *m* Roy Webb *ad* Van Nest Polglase
☆ Katharine Hepburn, Herbert Marshall, Elizabeth Allan, Donald Crisp, Doris Dudley, David Manners, Van Heflin, Lucile Watson, Eily Malyon
'Delving into the fascinating ugliness of Victorian England, RKO Radio have found material that is picturesque, humorous and tragic.' – *Frank Nugent, New York Times*

The Woman They Almost Lynched
US 1952 90m bw
Republic
An innocent girl out west is blamed for a crime wave and almost executed as a spy.
Incredible, random-plotted Western with a few entertaining moments.
w Steve Fisher *story* Michael Fessier *d* Allan Dwan *ph* Reggie Lanning *m* Stanley Wilson
☆ Joan Leslie, Audrey Totter, John Lund, Brian Donlevy, Ben Cooper

'As naughty as a black lace nightgown!'
Woman Times Seven
US/France 1967 99m DeLuxe
TCF/Embassy (Arthur Cohn)
Seven sketches, in each of which a woman behaves typically of her sex.
Humourless after-dinner entertainment.
w Cesare Zavattini *d* Vittorio de Sica *ph* Christian Matras *m* Riz Ortolani
☆ Shirley MacLaine, Peter Sellers, Rossano Brazzi, Vittorio Gassman, Lex Barker, Elsa Martinelli, Robert Morley, Adrienne Corri, Patrick Wymark, Alan Arkin, Michael Caine, Anita Ekberg, Philippe Noiret

Woman to Woman
GB 1923 83m (24 fps) bw silent
Balcon, Freedman and Saville
A shell-shocked officer marries into society and later adopts his son by a French ballerina.
Far-fetched melodrama in what later became the Random Harvest *style; a great box-office hit of its time.*
w Alfred Hitchcock *play* Michael Morton *d* Graham Cutts
☆ Betty Compson, Clive Brook, Josephine Earle, Marie Ault
† Victor Saville directed a sound remake in 1929, with Betty Compson and George Barraud; and in 1946 Maclean Rogers had another shot with Adele Dixon and Douglass Montgomery.

A Woman under the Influence *
US 1974 155m colour
Faces International (Sam Shaw)
A Los Angeles housewife and mother suffers a mental breakdown as she increasingly feels at odds with society.
Fine acting from Rowlands and Falk lifts an otherwise overlong domestic drama.
wd John Cassavetes *ph* Mitch Breit, Caleb Deschanel *m* Bo Harwood *ad* Phedon Papamichael *ed* Tom Cornwell
☆ *Peter Falk, Gena Rowlands*, Matthew Cassel, Matthew Laborteaux, Christina Grisanti, Katherine Cassavetes
'Though some in the audience will once again accept what is going on as raw, anguishing truth, most people will – rightly, I think – take their embarrassment as evidence of Cassavetes' self-righteous ineptitude.' – *Pauline Kael, New Yorker*
John Cassavetes (as director); Gena Rowlands

Woman Wanted
US 1935 65m bw
MGM
A girl accused of murder is helped by an attorney.
Initially appealing comedy-thriller which moves fast enough but has a very muddled plotline.
w Leonard Fields, Dave Silverstein, Wilson Collison *d* George B. Seitz
☆ Maureen O'Sullivan, Joel McCrea, Lewis Stone, Louis Calhern, Edgar Kennedy, Adrienne Ames, Robert Greig, Noel Madison

The Woman Who Came Back *
US 1945 68m bw
Republic (Walter Colmes)
A girl returning to her home village in New England is made to think she is a witch.
Quite an agreeably spooky second feature.
w Dennis Cooper, Lee Willis *d* Walter Colmes
☆ Nancy Kelly, John Loder, Otto Kruger, Ruth Ford, Harry Tyler

The Woman with No Name
GB 1950 83m bw
IFP/ABP
US title: *Her Panelled Door*
An amnesiac wife finds herself threatened from all sides.
Hoary melodrama with some unintentional laughs.
w Ladislas Vajda, Guy Morgan *novel Happy Now I Go* by Theresa Charles *d* Ladislas Vajda, George More O'Ferrall *ph* Otto Heller *m* Allan Gray
☆ Phyllis Calvert, Edward Underdown, Helen Cherry, Richard Burton, Anthony Nicholls, James Hayter, Betty Ann Davies

Woman without a Face: see *Mister Buddwing*

The Woman's Angle
GB 1952 86m bw
ABP/Leslie Arliss/Bow Belles (Walter Mycroft)
In a divorce court three flashbacks tell of the life of a composer.
Damp little formula drama for matinée audiences, refashioned from a successful silent film.
wd Leslie Arliss *novel Three Cups of Coffee* by Ruth Feiner *ph* Erwin Hillier *m* Robert Gill; the Mansell Concerto by Kenneth Leslie Smith
☆ Edward Underdown, Cathy O'Donnell, Lois Maxwell, Claude Farrell, Peter Reynolds, Marjorie Fielding

'Whatever I am, men made me!'
A Woman's Face **
US 1941 105m bw
MGM (Victor Saville)
A scarred and embittered woman turns to crime but jibs at murder.
Curious, unexpected but very entertaining melodrama with a courtroom frame, Swedish settings, an excellent cast and some bravura sequences.
w Donald Ogden Stewart, Elliot Paul *play Il Était une Fois* by François de Croisset *d George Cukor* *ph Robert Planck* *m* Bronislau Kaper
☆ Joan Crawford, Melvyn Douglas, *Conrad Veidt*, Osa Massen, Reginald Owen, Albert Basserman, Marjorie Main, Donald Meek, Connie Gilchrist
† Also involved in the script were Elliott Paul and Christopher Isherwood.

A Woman's Secret
US 1949 85m bw
RKO (Herman J. Mankiewicz)
An ex-singer grooms a girl as her successor but lives to regret it.
Downright peculiar little film noir by the co-author of Citizen Kane *(though not so that you'd notice).*
w Herman J. Mankiewicz *novel Mortgage on Life* by Vicki Baum *d* Nicholas Ray *ph* George Diskant *m* Frederick Hollander *md* Constantin Bakaleinikoff
☆ Maureen O'Hara, Gloria Grahame, Melvyn Douglas, Bill Williams, Victor Jory, Mary Philips

A Woman's Tale *
Australia 1991 93m colour
Beyond/Illumination (Paul Cox, Santhana Naidu)
An old woman prepares for death.
A low-key drama about a person who insists on how much she loves life, while disliking, or snubbing, most of the people she meets; the result is not as life-enhancing as it might have been.
w Paul Cox, Barry Dickins *d* Paul Cox *ph* Nino Martinetti *m* Paul Grabowsky *pd* Neil Angwin *ed* Russell Hurley
☆ *Sheila Florance*, Gosia Dobrowolska, Norman Kaye, Chris Haywood, Ernest Gray, Myrtle Woods
† Like the elderly woman she plays, Sheila Florance was also suffering from cancer, dying a few days after receiving a best actress award for her performance.

A Woman's Vengeance *
US 1948 96m bw
Universal-International (Zoltan Korda)
A man is convicted for the murder of his invalid wife, actually committed by a jealous woman in love with him but later spurned.
Interesting but very stagey melodrama from one of its author's more commercial ventures.
w Aldous Huxley *story and play The Gioconda Smile* by *Aldous Huxley* *d* Zoltan Korda *ph* Russell Metty *m* Miklos Rozsa
☆ Charles Boyer, Jessica Tandy, Ann Blyth, Cedric Hardwicke, Mildred Natwick
'A rather literary movie, but most movies aren't even that; much less are they real movies.' – *James Agee*

'It's a great big wonderful woman's world because men are in it!'
Woman's World **
US 1954 94m Technicolor Cinemascope
TCF (Charles Brackett)
Three top salesmen and their wives are summoned to New York by the boss, who seeks to choose a new general manager.
Amusing, superficial pattern comedy-drama for an all-star cast, backed by all-round technical competence.
w Claude Binyon, Mary Loos, Richard Sale *d Jean Negulesco* *ph* Joe MacDonald *m* Cyril Mockridge
☆ *Clifton Webb, Lauren Bacall, Van Heflin*, June Allyson, Fred MacMurray, Arlene Dahl, Cornel Wilde, Elliott Reid, Margalo Gillmore

Wombling Free
GB 1977 96m Eastmancolor
Rank/Ian Shand
The furry creatures who live under Wimbledon Common at last make contact with humans.
Disastrous attempt to film a popular TV series for children. The series came in five-minute chunks; this elephantine transcription leaves several talents high and dry.
wd Lionel Jeffries, from characters created by Elizabeth Beresford *ph* Alan Hume *m* Mike Batt
☆ David Tomlinson, Frances de la Tour, Bonnie Langford, Bernard Spear
'A fiasco. If you really must take your kids, it would be less of a pain to go shopping at the same time.' – *Derek Malcolm, Guardian*

'135 women with men on their minds!'
The Women ***
US 1939 132m bw (Technicolor sequence)
MGM (Hunt Stromberg)
A New York socialite gets a divorce but later thinks better of it.
Bitchy comedy drama distinguished by an all-girl cast ('135 women with men on their minds'). An over-generous slice of real theatre, skilfully adapted, with rich sets, plenty of laughs, and some memorable scenes between the fighting ladies.
w Anita Loos, Jane Murfin *play Clare Boothe* *d George Cukor* *ph* Oliver T. Marsh, Joseph Ruttenberg *m* Edward Ward, David Snell
☆ *Norma Shearer*, Joan Crawford, *Rosalind Russell*, Mary Boland, Paulette Goddard, Joan Fontaine, Lucile Watson, Phyllis Povah, Virginia Weidler, Ruth Hussey, Margaret Dumont, Marjorie Main, Hedda Hopper
'Smash hit of solid proportions for extended runs and heavy profits ... a strong woman entry but still has plenty of spicy lines and situations for the men.' – *Variety*
'A mordant, mature description of the social decay of one corner of the American middle class.' – *Time*
'So marvellous that we believe every Hollywood studio should make at least one thoroughly nasty picture a year.' – *New York Times*
'Whether you go or not depends on whether you can stand Miss Shearer with tears flowing steadily in all directions at once, and such an endless damn back fence of cats.' – *Otis Ferguson*

Women Are Like That
US 1938 78m bw
Warner
A separated couple meet again years later and find each other changed.
Witless elaboration of a good idea: far too slow and talky.
w Horace Jackson, Albert Z. Carr *d* Stanley Logan
☆ Kay Francis, Pat O'Brien, Ralph Forbes, Melville Cooper, Thurston Hall, Grant Mitchell
'Terribly tiresome, slow and talky.' – *Variety*

Women in Bondage
US 1943 72m bw
Monogram (Herman Millakowsky)
How the Nazis treat their women.
Cheap but vigorous exploitation piece, not quite so sensational as it now sounds.
w Houston Branch, Frank Wisbar *d* Steve Sekely
☆ Gail Patrick, Nancy Kelly, Gertrude Michael, Anne Nagel, Tala Birell, Maris Wrixon, William Henry, H. B. Warner, Alan Baxter

Women in Love ***
GB 1969 130m DeLuxe
UA/Brandywine (Larry Kramer)
Two girls have their first sexual encounters in the Midlands during the twenties.
Satisfactory rendering of a celebrated novel, with excellent period detail atoning for rather irritating characters. The nude wrestling scene was a famous first.
w Larry Kramer *novel D. H. Lawrence* *d Ken Russell* *ph Billy Williams* *m* Georges Delerue
☆ *Glenda Jackson*, Jennie Linden, Alan Bates, Oliver Reed, Michael Gough, Alan Webb
'They should take all the pretentious dialogue off the soundtrack and call it Women in Heat.' – *Rex Reed*
'Two-thirds success, one-third ambitious failure.' – *Michael Billington, Illustrated London News*
Glenda Jackson
Larry Kramer; Ken Russell; Billy Williams

Women in the Wind
US 1939 63m bw
Warner (Mark Hellinger)
Conflict arises between contestants in the Women's Air Derby.
Formula multi-character picture, only moderately watchable.
w Lee Katz, Albert DeMond *novel* Francis Walton *d* John Farrow
☆ Kay Francis, William Gargan, Victor Jory, Maxie Rosenbloom, Eddie Foy Jnr, Eve Arden
'Good programmer for duals and cinch for action spots.' – *Variety*

Women of All Nations
US 1931 72m bw
Fox
Flagg and Quirt, back in the Marines, have amorous adventures in Sweden, Nicaragua and Egypt.
Routine fun and games with the heroes of What Price Glory *(qv).*
w Barry Connors *d* Raoul Walsh *ph* Lucien Andriot *m* Reginald H. Bassett
☆ Edmund Lowe, Victor McLaglen, Greta Nissen, El Brendel, Fifi D'Orsay, Bela Lugosi, Humphrey Bogart

Women of Glamour
US 1937 65m bw
Columbia
A man is loved by a society flower and a gold-digger, and chooses the latter.
Minor woman's picture.
w Lynn Starling, Mary McCall Jnr *story* Milton Herbert Gropper *d* Gordon Wiles

☆ Melvyn Douglas, Virginia Bruce, Reginald Denny, Leona Maricle, Pert Kelton

'Featherweight triangle headed for the dual round-up.' – *Variety*

Women of Twilight

GB 1953 89m bw

Romulus/Daniel M. Angel

US title: *Twilight Women*

The pregnant lover of a murderer finds lodgings in a boarding house for unmarried mothers run by a money-grasping harridan.

Effective but downbeat domestic melodrama.

w Anatole de Grunwald *play* Sylvia Rayman *d* Gordon Parry *ph* Jack Asher *m* Allan Gray *md* Philip Martell *ad* William Kellner *ed* Ralph Kemplen

☆ Freda Jackson, Rene Ray, Lois Maxwell, Laurence Harvey, Joan Dowling, Dora Bryan, Vida Hope, Mary Germaine, Ingeborg Wells, Dorothy Gordon

Women on the Verge of a Nervous Breakdown **

Spain 1988 89m Eastmancolor

Rank/El Deseo/Lauren Film/Orion (Agustin Almodóvar)

original title: *Mujeres al borde de un ataque de nervios*

Three women approach crack-up as their lives entangle: a demented wife whose husband has abandoned her, her husband's estranged mistress, a temperamental actress, and the actress's friend, who has fallen in love with a terrorist.

Frenetic, fashionable farce that manages to amuse most of the time.

wd Pedro Almodóvar *ph* Jose Luis Alcaine *m* Bernardo Bonezzi *ed* Jose Salcedo

☆ Carmen Maura, Antonio Banderas, Julieta Serrano, Maria Barranco, Rossy de Palma, Guillermo Montesinos, Kiti Manver

'The best to be said for *Women on the Verge* is that Almodóvar makes a good interior decorator.' – *Mark Finch, MFB*

best foreign film

Women Talking Dirty

US/GB 1999 97m DeLuxe

UIP/Jean Doumanian/Rocket (David Furnish, Polly Steele)

In Edinburgh, an outgoing, pregnant university dropout and an inhibited graphic artist become friends.

Minor feminist buddy movie about two women who bond through the unsaisfactory men that love and leave them.

w Isla Dewar *novel* Isla Dewar *d* Coky Giedroyc *ph* Brian Tufano *m* Elton John *pd* Lynne Whiteread *ed* Budge Tremlett

☆ Helena Bonham Carter (Cora), Gina McKee (Ellen), Richard Wilson (Ronald), Eileen Atkins (Emily Boyle), Kenneth Cranham (George), James Nesbitt (Stanley), James Purefoy (Daniel)

'The plotting is as chaotic as the film's handling of Edinburgh's geography, but the performances keep it afloat.' – *Philip French, Observer*

Women's Prison *

US 1955 80m bw

Columbia (Bryan Foy)

A prison doctor attempts to protect female inmates against the harsh and unjust regime of the warden.

Enjoyable, fast-moving 'B' movie that races through most of the clichés of the genre, including pregnancy and a full-scale riot.

w Crane Wilbur, Jack DeWitt *d* Lewis Seiler *ph* Lester H. White *md* Mischa Bakaleinikoff *ad* Cary Odell *ed* Henry Batista

☆ Ida Lupino, Jan Sterling, Cleo Moore, Audrey Totter, Phyllis Thaxter, Howard Duff, Mae Clarke, Juanita Moore

Won Ton Ton, the Dog Who Saved Hollywood

US 1976 92m colour

Paramount/David V. Picker, Arnold Schulman, Michael Winner

In twenties Hollywood, a lost Alsatian dog becomes a movie star but later suffers some ups and downs before being reunited with his mistress.

Scatty, unlikeable comedy with too frantic a pace, apparently in desperation at the dearth of funny lines and situations. The sixty 'guest stars' barely get a look in; the director seems to think (erroneously) that their appearance makes some kind of point even though they have nothing to do. Altogether, an embarrassment.

w Arnold Schulman, Cy Howard *d* Michael Winner *ph* Richard H. Kline *m* Neal Hefti

☆ Madeline Kahn, Art Carney, Bruce Dern, Ron Leibman; and Dennis Morgan, William Demarest, Virginia Mayo, Rory Calhoun, Henry Wilcoxon, Ricardo Montalban, Jackie Coogan, Johnny Weissmuller, Aldo Ray, Ethel Merman, Joan Blondell, Yvonne de Carlo and also Andy Devine, Broderick Crawford, Richard Arlen, Jack La Rue, Dorothy Lamour, Phil Silvers, Gloria de Haven, Stepin Fetchit, Rudy Vallee, George Jessel, Ann Miller, Janet Blair, the Ritz Brothers, Victor Mature, Fernando Lamas, Cyd Charisse, Huntz Hall, Edgar Bergen, Peter Lawford, Regis Toomey, Alice Faye, Milton Berle, John Carradine, Walter Pidgeon, etc

'The film tries to conceal its deficiencies in comic ideas and comic skill by doing everything at the pace of a clockwork toy with a too-tight spring.' – *Dave Robinson, Times*

Wonder Bar **

US 1934 84m bw

Warner (Robert Lord)

Love and hate backstage at a Paris night-club.

Curious musical drama with an interesting cast and fairly stunning numbers.

w Earl Baldwin *play* Geza Herczeg, Karl Farkas, Robert Katscher *d* Lloyd Bacon *ph* Sol Polito *ch* Busby Berkeley *ad* Jack Okey *songs* Harry Warren, Al Dubin

☆ *Al Jolson*, Kay Francis, Dolores del Rio, Ricardo Cortez, Dick Powell, Guy Kibbee, Ruth Donnelly, Hugh Herbert, Louise Fazenda, Fifi D'Orsay

'Romance, flash, dash, colour, songs, star-studded talent, and almost every known requisite to ensure sturdy attention and attendance.' – *Variety*

'A tip-top musical.' – *Variety*

'A Weekend From Hell Became The Time Of His Life.'

Wonder Boys **

US/Germany/GB/Japan 2000 112m DeLuxe Super 35

Paramount/Mutual (Scott Rudin, Curtis Hanson)

The life and loves of an academic novelist with a writer's block begin to unravel as he spends time with his most talented and eccentric student.

Engaging comedy of a mid-life crisis, complicated by a series of disasters, that rings true for most of its length; in the end too much is left unsaid and underdeveloped.

w Steve Kloves *novel* Michael Chabon *d* Curtis Hanson *ph* Dante Spinotti *m* Christopher Young *pd* Jeannine Oppewall *ed* Dede Allen

☆ Michael Douglas (Grady Tripp), Tobey Maguire (James Leer), Frances McDormand (Sara Gaskell), Robert Downey Jnr (Terry Grabtree), Katie Holmes (Hannah Green), Richard Thomas (Walter Gaskell), Rip Torn (Q), Philip Bosco (Hank Winters), Jane Adams (Oola), Richard Knox (Vernon Hardapple), Michael Cavaias (Miss Sloviak/Tony)

'Superbly mounted screwball comedy.' – *Variety*

'A rich, complex broth which steams slowly into your senses and leaves you with a warm, lasting glow.' – *Empire*

Bob Dylan (song 'Things Have Changed')

Steve Kloves; Roger Deakins; Dede Allen

Wonder Man **

US 1945 97m Technicolor

Samuel Goldwyn

A mild-mannered student is persuaded by the ghost of his dead twin to avenge his murder.

Smooth, successful mixture of Topper, *a night-club musical, a gangster drama and the star's own brand of fooling; this is possibly his best vehicle after* The Court Jester.

w Don Hartman, Melville Shavelson, Philip Rapp story Arthur Sheekman *d H. Bruce Humberstone ph* Victor Milner, William Snyder *md* Louis Forbes, Ray Heindorf *sp* John Fulton

☆ *Danny Kaye*, Vera-Ellen, Virginia Mayo, Steve Cochran, S. Z. Sakall, Allen Jenkins, Ed Brophy, Donald Woods, Otto Kruger, Richard Lane, Natalie Schafer

Louis Forbes, Ray Heindorf; song 'So in Love' (*m* David Rose, *ly* Leo Robin)

The Wonderful Country

US 1959 96m Technicolor

UA/DRM (Chester Erskine)

A wandering gunman is offered a job by the Texas Rangers.

Complexly plotted Western offering a range of familiar exploits.

w Robert Ardrey *novel* Tom Lea *d* Robert Parrish *ph* Floyd Crosby, Alex Phillips *m* Alex North

☆ Robert Mitchum, Julie London, Pedro Armendariz, Gary Merrill, Jack Oakie, Albert Dekker, Charles McGraw, John Banner, Jay Novello

Wonderful Day: see *I've Gotta Horse*

Wonderful Life *

GB 1964 113m Techniscope

EMI/Elstree Distributors/Ivy (Kenneth Harper)

Four entertainers on a luxury liner are hired by a film crew in Africa.

Slight but zestful youth musical with highly illogical detail; the highlight is a ten-minute spoof history of the movies.

w Peter Myers, Ronald Cass *d* Sidney J. Furie *ph* Ken Higgins *pd* Stanley Dorfman

☆ Cliff Richard, Walter Slezak, Susan Hampshire, Melvyn Hayes, Richard O'Sullivan, Una Stubbs, Derek Bond, Gerald Harper, the Shadows

Wonderful Life: see *After Life (1998)*

Wonderful to Be Young: see *The Young Ones*

The Wonderful World of Dogs

Australia 1990 60m colour

Radio Pictures/Australian Film Commission/ABC/ Channel 4 (Mark Lewis)

A documentary on dogs and their effect on people's lives in an Australian suburb.

Witty and bizarre account of man's best, or worst, friend, one that even cat-lovers should enjoy.

wd Mark Lewis *ph* Tony Wilson, Steve Windon *m* Martin Armiger *ed* Lindsay Frazer

The Wonderful World of the Brothers Grimm *

US 1962 134m Technicolor Cinerama

MGM/Cinerama/George Pal

An account of the lives of the German fairy tale writers is supplemented by three of their stories, *The Dancing Princess, The Cobbler and the Elves* and *The Singing Bone.*

Saccharine, heavy-handed pantomime with insufficient comedy, menace or spectacle.

w David P. Harmon, Charles Beaumont, William Roberts *d* Henry Levin, George Pal *ph* Paul C. Vogel *m* Leigh Harline *ad* George W. Davis, Edward Carfagno *songs* Bob Merrill

☆ Laurence Harvey, Karl Boehm, Claire Bloom, Barbara Eden, Walter Slezak, Oscar Homolka, *Martita Hunt*, Russ Tamblyn, Yvette Mimieux, *Jim Backus*, Beulah Bondi, Terry-Thomas, Buddy Hackett, Otto Kruger

Paul C. Vogel; Leigh Harline

'Everbody's looking for something.'

Wonderland *

GB 1999 108m colour

Universal/BBC/Kismet/Revolution

In London, three sisters have problems with men: they can't get the ones they want, and want to get rid of the ones they have.

Gritty, downbeat, working-class drama in which London features as a harsh and soulless place where lives goes awry without anyone caring very much.

w Laurence Coriat *d* Michael Winterbottom *ph* Sean Bobbitt *m* Michael Nyman *pd* Mark Tildesley *ed* Trevor Waite *cos* Natalie Ward

☆ Shirley Henderson (Debbie), Gina McKee (Nadia), Molly Parker (Molly), Ian Hart (Dan), John Simm (Eddie), Stuart Townsend (Tim), Kika Markham (Eileen), Jack Shepherd (Bill), Enzo Cilenti (Darren), Sarah-Jane Potts (Melanie), David Fahm (Franklyn)

'The performances of an ensemble cast are flawless, but it's all so similar to the bleak lives that the telly shows us several times a week.' – *Alexander Walker, London Evening Standard*

The Wonders of Aladdin

Italy 1961 92m Technicolor Cinemascope

Embassy/Lux

With the help of a genie, Aladdin defeats a usurper and wins the princess's hand.

Flat and disappointing pantomime with virtually no charm.

w Luther Davis *d* Henry Levin, Mario Bava *ph* Tonino Delli Colli *m* Angelo Lavagnino

☆ Donald O'Connor, Vittorio de Sica, Aldo Fabrizi, Michèle Mercier

Wonderwall

GB 1968 92m Eastmancolor

Cinecenta/Alan Clore-Compton (Andrew Braunsberg)

An absent-minded scientist fantasizes about the girl who lives next door after he discovers a hole in the wall of his flat which enables him to spy on her.

One of the last gasps of the 'swinging London' cycle of films, complete with psychedelic settings, mini-skirts, discreet nudity and George Harrison's Indian-style music; it is also vapid and witless.

w G. Cain *story* Gerard Brach *d* Joe Massot *ph* Harry Wayman *m* George Harrison *ad* Assheton Garton

☆ Jack MacGowran, Jane Birkin, Richard Wattis, Irene Handl, Iain Quarrier, Beatrix Lehmann, Brian Walsh, Sean Lynch

'It's her world... we're just living in it.'

Woo

US 1998 84m DeLuxe

Entertainment/New Line/New Deal/Gotham (Beth Hubbard, Michael Hubbard)

In New York, encouraged by her fortune-teller, an excessively extroverted woman goes on a blind date with a timid man.

With its unsympathetic, self-obsessed protagonist, this would-be comedy is never less than irritating and more often insufferable.

w David C. Johnson *d* Daisy V. S. Mayer *ph* Jean Lepine *m* Michel Colombier *pd* Ina Mayhew *ed* Nicholas Eliopoulos, Janice Hampton

☆ Jada Pinkett Smith (Woo), Tommy Davidson (Tim), Duane Martin (Frankie), Michael Ralph (Romaine), Darrel M. Heath (Hop), Dave Chappelle (Lenny), Paula Jai Parker (Claudette), LL Cool J (Darry), Aida Turturro (Tookie)

'A graceless and gratingly unfunny comedy that brings out the worst in just about everybody involved.' – *Joe Leydon, Variety*

The Woo Woo Kid *

US 1987 100m CFI color

Guild/Lorimar/Kings Road Entertainment (Gary Adelson, Karen Mack)

US title: *In the Mood*

A 15-year-old boy marries an older woman and, after the marriage is annulled, runs away with a soldier's wife.

Based on a true story from the 1940s, the comedy has a bizarre period charm.

wd Phil Alden Robinson *story* Bob Kosberg, David Simon, Phil Alden Robinson *ph* John Lindley *m* Ralph Burns *pd* Dennis Gassner *ed* Patrick Kennedy

☆ Patrick Dempsey, Talia Balsam, Beverly D'Angelo, Michael Constantine, Betty Jinnette, Kathleen Freeman, Peter Hobbs, Tony Longo, Douglas Rowe

'From boyhood to manhood, you can always count on your best friends.'

The Wood

US 1999 107m DeLuxe

Paramount/MTV/Bona Fide (Albert Berger, Ron Yerxa, David Gale)

On the day he is to marry, a man gathers his childhood friends around him to give him confidence.

A nostalgic movie about growing up and accepting responsibility, with a likeable cast doing their best with shallow material.

d Rick Famuyiwa *ph* Steven Bernstein *m* Robert Hurst *pd* Roger Fortune, Maxine Shepard *ed* John Carter

☆ Taye Diggs (Roland), Omar Epps (Mike), Richard T. Jones (Slim), Sean Nelson (Young Mike), Trent Cameron (Young Roland), Duane

Finley (Young Sam), Malinda Williams (Young Alicia), De'Aundre Bonds (Stacey), Sanaa Lathan (Alicia), LisaRaye (Lisa)

'A functional feel-good movie, occasionally sweet but predominantly bland.' – *Edward Porter, Sunday Times*

The Wooden Horse **

GB 1950 101m bw

British Lion/Wessex/London Films (Ian Dalrymple)

During World War II, British prisoners escape from Stalag Luft III by tunnelling under a vaulting horse.

Standard, solid POW drama with predictable but exciting and occasionally moving developments.

w Eric Williams *novel* Eric Williams *d* Jack Lee *ph* C. Pennington-Richards *m* Clifton Parker

☆ *Leo Genn, David Tomlinson*, Anthony Steel, David Greene, Michael Goodliffe, Bryan Forbes, Jacques Brunius

'All the suspense I care to take.' – *Sunday Chronicle*

The Wooden Horse of Troy: see *The Trojan War*

Wooden Soldiers: see *Babes in Toyland (1934)*

The Woodlanders *

GB 1997 96m Technicolor Panavision

Pathé/Channel 4/Arts Council/River (Barney Reisz, Phil Agland)

In a rural village in Victorian England, a social-climbing timber merchant marries his daughter to a new doctor, despite his promise that she would marry a local woodsman.

A stolid, painstaking version of Hardy's tale of misplaced love, but one that only occasionally flares into felt life.

w David Rudkin *novel* Thomas Hardy *d* Phil Agland *ph* Ashley Rowe *m* George Fenton *pd* Andy Harris *ed* David Dickie

☆ Rufus Sewell, Emily Woof, Cal MacAninch, Tony Haygarth, Jodhi May, Polly Walker, Walter Sparrow, Sheila Burrell

'A classy and emotionally involving costumer whose only fault is lack of breadth.' – *Variety*

'This time the whole world is watching...'

Woodstock ****

US 1970 184m Technicolor

Warner/Wadleigh-Maurice (Bob Maurice)

A documentary on the three-day festival ('of peace, music ... and love') that attracted an audience of around 500,000 young people.

A definitive moment of the 60s, with the mood and music brilliantly captured on film. To do it took a team of 20 cameramen, who shot 120 hours of film, as well as eight camera assistants, 20 sound-men and engineers, six still photographers and 30 production assistants.

d Michael Wadleigh ph Michael Wadleigh and others *ed Thelma Schoonmaker, Martin Scorsese*

☆ Joan Baez, Canned Heat, Joe Cocker, Country Joe and The Fish, Crosby, Stills, Nash & Young, Arlo Guthrie, Richie Havens, Jimi Hendrix, Santana, John Sebastian, Sha-Na-Na, Sly & The Family Stone, Ten Years After and also The Who

'A joyous, volcanic new film that will make those who missed the festival feel as if they were there. But *Woodstock* is far more than a sound-and-light souvenir of a long weekend concert. Purely as a piece of cinema, it is one of the finest documentaries ever made in the U.S.' – *Time*

'What is distressing about most of the performers at this mammoth mud-in, apart from their obvious lack of musical talent, is, in most cases, their equally obvious hostility. I mean not just laudable hostility to the war, but also profound neurotic hostility.' – *John Simon*

† A 'director's cut' lasting 220m was released in cinemas and on video in 1994.

best documentary

Words and Music **

US 1948 121m Technicolor

MGM (*Arthur Freed*)

The songwriting collaboration of Richard Rodgers and Lorenz Hart.

Musical biopic which packs in a lot of good numbers and manages a script which is neither too offensive nor too prominent.

w Guy Bolton, Jean Holloway, Fred Finklehoffe d Norman Taurog *ph* Charles Rosher, Harry Stradling *md* Lennie Hayton *ch* Robert Alton, Gene Kelly

☆ *Tom Drake, Mickey Rooney*, Perry Como, *Mel Tormé*, Betty Garrett, *June Allyson*, Lena Horne, Ann Sothern, Allyn McLerie, *Gene Kelly*, Vera-Ellen, Cyd Charisse, Janet Leigh, Marshall Thompson

Work Is a Four-Letter Word

GB 1968 93m Technicolor

Universal/Cavalcade (Thomas Clyde)

A power station attendant is interested only in growing mushrooms, which have a chaotic effect on his private life.

Weakly futuristic industrial fantasy which the author would probably claim to be about lack of communication. Bored audiences might have a similar view.

w Jeremy Brooks *play Eh?* by Henry Livings *d* Peter Hall *ph* Gilbert Taylor *m* Guy Woolfenden

☆ David Warner, Cilla Black, Elizabeth Spriggs, Zia Mohyeddin, Joe Gladwin

Working Girl **

US 1988 113m DuArt

Fox (Douglas Wick)

A secretary outsmarts her female boss in business and love.

Glossy comedy that owes much to the performances of its leading actors.

w Kevin Wade *d* Mike Nichols *ph* Michael Ballhaus *m* Carly Simon *pd* Patrizia von Brandenstein *ed* Sam O'Steen, Richard Nord

☆ Harrison Ford, Sigourney Weaver, Melanie Griffith, Alec Baldwin, Joan Cusack, Philip Bosco, Nora Dunn, Oliver Platt, James Lally, Olympia Dukakis

best song

best picture; Mike Nicholls; Melanie Griffith; Joan Cusack; Sigourney Weaver

Working Girls **

US 1986 90m colour

Lizzie Borden/Alternate Current (Lizzie Borden, Andi Gladstone)

After a hard day's work and overtime, a prostitute decides to quit working in a New York brothel.

A near-documentary style enlivens an account of workaday prostitutes, an upwardly mobile madame, and their rather sad male clients.

w Lizzie Borden, Sandra Kay *d* Lizzie Borden *ph* Judy Irola *m* David Van Tieghen *pd* Kurt Ossenfort *ed* Lizzie Borden

☆ Louise Smith, Ellen McElduff, Amanda Goodwin, Marusia Zach, Janne Peters, Helen Nicholas

The Working Man

US 1933 78m bw

Warner

A wealthy shoe manufacturer hands over his business, goes on holiday, and finds himself helping his bitterest rival.

Palatable star parable.

w Maude T. Howell, Charles Kenyon *novel* Edgar Franklin *d* John Adolfi

☆ George Arliss, Bette Davis, Theodore Newton, J. Farrell MacDonald

The World According to Garp *

US 1982 136m Technicolor

Warner/Pan Arts (George Roy Hill, Robert L. Crawford)

A young man grows up with a determination to become a writer.

Unlikely and uneasy film version of a somewhat cerebral novel; any drama there might have been in the original got lost in the transition, but at least the intention is to be applauded.

w Steve Tesich *novel* John Irving *d* George Roy Hill *ph* Miroslav Ondricek *m* David Shire *pd* Henry Bumstead *ed* Stephen A. Rotter

☆ Robin Williams, Mary Beth Hurt, Glenn Close, John Lithgow, Hume Cronyn, Jessica Tandy, Swoosie Kurtz

'Rather like watching a puppy chasing its own tail: engaging, touching, but pointless.' – *Margaret Hinxman, Daily Mail*

'When the movie was over, all I could find to ask myself was: What the hell was all that about?' – *Roger Ebert*

John Lithgow; Glenn Close (supporting actress)

The World and His Wife: see *State of the Union*

A World Apart **

GB 1987 110m colour

Palace/British Screen/Atlantic/Working Title (Sarah Radclyffe)

Anti-apartheid struggles in the 1960s seen through the eyes of a 13-year-old South African girl whose mother is imprisoned for her support of the African National Congress.

Excellently acted and moving mix of political and domestic drama.

w Shawn Slovo *d* Chris Menges *ph* Peter Biziou *m* Hans Zimmer *pd* Brian Morris *ed* Nicolas Gaster

☆ Jodhi May, Jeroen Krabbé, Barbara Hershey, Linda Mvusi, David Suchet, Paul Freeman, Tim Roth, Yvonne Bryceland, Albee Lesotho, Rosalie Crutchley

† Shawn Slovo is the daughter of Ruth First, on whose life the story is based.

Shawn Slovo

The World Changes *

US 1933 91m bw

Warner (Robert Lord)

A simple farmer becomes a powerful executive, and success goes to his head.

Adequate moral drama of its time, well staged and acted.

w Edward Chodorov *story* Sheridan Gibney *d* Mervyn Le Roy *ph* Tony Gaudio

☆ *Paul Muni*, Aline MacMahon, Mary Astor, Donald Cook, Patricia Ellis, Jean Muir, Margaret Lindsay, Guy Kibbee, Alan Dinehart

'It won't appeal to the hotsy-totsy type of fan, but the parents will bring the youngsters, which should sort of balance things.' – *Variety*

World Gone Wild

US 1987 90m colour

Apollo Pictures (Robert L. Rosen)

In 2087, a small desert community seeks help against an attack from a messianic killer and his disciples.

Inept combination of The Magnificent Seven *and* Mad Max, *lacking in style and substance.*

w Jorge Zamacona *d* Lee H. Katzin *ph* Don Burgess *m* Laurence Juber *pd* Donald L. Harris *ed* Gary A. Griffin

☆ Bruce Dern, Michael Pare, Catherine Mary Stewart, Anthony James, Rick Podell, Julius J. Carry III, Alan Autry, Mindy McEnnan, Adam Ant

World in Flames *

US 1940 62m bw

Paramount (Albert J. Richard)

A newsreel account of the rise to power of dictators during the thirties.

Effective propaganda at the time, and a neat editing job.

The World in His Arms *

US 1952 104m Technicolor

Universal (Aaron Rosenberg)

In old San Francisco, a seal-poaching sea captain meets a Russian countess.

Romantic melodrama with plushy period backgrounds and a fair measure of action, climaxing in a boat race.

w Borden Chase, Horace McCoy *novel* Rex Beach *d* Raoul Walsh *ph* Russell Metty *m* Frank Skinner

☆ Gregory Peck, Ann Blyth, Anthony Quinn, John McIntire, Andrea King, Carl Esmond, Eugenie Leontovich

World in My Corner *

US 1955 85m bw

U-I (Aaron Rosenberg)

A penniless would-be prizefighter becomes the protégé of a millionaire and wins his daughter but not the crucial fight.

Well-done minor melodrama.

w Jack Sher *d* Jesse Hibbs *ph* Maury Gertsman *md* Joseph Gershenson *ad* Alexander Golitzen, Bill Newberry *ed* Milton Carruth

☆ Audie Murphy, Barbara Rush, Jeff Morrow, John McIntire, Tommy Rall, Howard St John

The World in My Pocket: see *On Friday at Eleven*

The World Is Full of Married Men

GB 1979 106m Eastmancolor

New Realm/Married Men Productions (Adrienne Fancey)

The wife of an advertising executive tries to pay him out in kind for his infidelity.

Tedious jet-setting morality play which shows in great detail all the vices it wags a finger at.

w Jackie Collins *novel* Jackie Collins *d* Robert Young *ph* Ray Parslow *m* Frank Musker, Dominic Bugatti

☆ Carroll Baker, Anthony Franciosa, Sherrie Cronn, Paul Nicholas, Gareth Hunt, Georgina Hale, Anthony Steel

The World Is Not Enough **

US 1999 125m DeLuxe Panavision

MGM/Eon (Michael G. Wilson, Barbara Broccoli)

James Bond saves the world from a villain who can feel no pain.

A spectacular opening sequence provides most of the thrills, after which Brosnan's charm smooths over the bumpy narrative and second-rate bad guys on offer here; Denise Richards in a wet T-shirt will no doubt do wonders for the image of nuclear scientists everywhere.

w Neal Purvis, Robert Wade, Bruce Feirstein *d* Michael Apted *ph* Adrian Biddle *m* David Arnold *pd* Peter Lamont *ed* Jim Clark *sp* Mara Bryan; Chris Corbould

☆ Pierce Brosnan (James Bond), Sophie Marceau (Elektra), Robert Carlyle (Renard), Denise Richards (Christmas Jones), Robbie Coltrane (Valentin Zukovsky), Judi Dench (M), Desmond Llewelyn (Q), John Cleese (R), Maria Grazia Cucinotta (Cigar Girl), Samantha Bond (Moneypenny), Michael Kitchen (Tanner), Colin Salmon (Robinson), Goldie (Bull), David Calder (Sir Robert King), Serena Scott Thomas (Dr Molly Warmflash)

'Formula film-making, but at least it's Formula One.' – *Adam Mars-Jones, Times*

'19th assignment of Bond's 37-year screen career sees 007 undone by villainous scripting and misguided casting and acting in a couple of key secondary roles.' – *Todd McCarthy, Variety*

The World Moves On *

US 1934 104m bw

Fox (Winfield Sheehan)

The saga of a Louisiana family up to World War I.

Careful, good-looking general entertainment.

w Reginald C. Berkeley *d* John Ford *ph* George Schneiderman *m* Louis de Francesco

☆ Madeleine Carroll, Franchot Tone, Reginald Denny, Stepin Fetchit, Lumsden Hare, Louise Dresser, Sig Rumann

'Pacifistic picture inviting endorsement from all bodies. Big on production and cast with six minutes of superb war stuff.' – *Variety*

The World of Apu ****

India 1959 106m bw

Satyajit Ray Productions

original title: *Apur Sansar*

An impoverished writer, working as a clerk, who agrees to an arranged marriage, is devastated by the death of his wife in childbirth and rejects his son.

An emotional and satisfyingly moving conclusion to a great artistic experience.

wd Satyajit Ray novel Aparajita by Bibhutibhusan Banerjee *ph* Subrata Mitra *m* Ravi Shankar *ad* Bansi Chandragupta *ed* Dulal Dutta

☆ Soumitra Chatterjee, Sarmila Tagore, Alok Chakravarti, Swapan Mukherjee, Dhiresh Majumdar, Sefalika Devi, Dhires Ghosh

'Rich and contemplative, and a great, convincing affirmation.' – *Pauline Kael, New Yorker*

† The film is the final part of a trilogy that began with *Pather Panchali* and continued with *Aparajito* (qqv).

The World of Henry Orient **
US 1964 106m DeLuxe Panavision
UA/Pan Arts (Jerome Hellman)

Two rich 14-year-old New York girls build fantasies around a concert pianist.
Charming, immaculately mounted, refreshingly unusual but overlong comedy.
w *Nora and Nunnally Johnson* *novel* Nora Johnson *d* *George Roy Hill* *ph* Boris Kaufman, Arthur J. Ornitz *m* Elmer Bernstein *pd* *James Sullivan*
☆ *Tippy Walker*, *Merri Spaeth*, Peter Sellers, Angela Lansbury, Paula Prentiss, Phyllis Thaxter, Tom Bosley, Bibi Osterwald

World of Plenty ***
GB 1943 45m bw
The Ministry of Information
How the distribution of food should be handled after the war.
Classic documentary with many new film-making insights, including the use of statistical diagrams.
w Paul Rotha, Eric Knight, Miles Malleson *d* *Paul Rotha*
'Any theatre audience will be grateful for seeing it. It is the epitome of educational picture-making.' – *Variety*

The World of Suzie Wong
GB 1960 129m Technicolor
Paramount/Ray Stark (Hugh Perceval)

A Hong Kong prostitute falls in love with the artist for whom she poses.
Dull, set-bound romantic melodrama without much gusto.
w John Patrick *play* Paul Osborn *novel* *Richard Mason* *d* Richard Quine *ph* Geoffrey Unsworth *m* George Duning
☆ William Holden, Nancy Kwan, Sylvia Syms, Michael Wilding, Laurence Naismith, Jackie Chan
'Maybe one day it will all make the grade as a musical.' – *MFB*

The World Owes Me a Living
GB 1944 91m bw
British National
A man gets his memory back and recalls his air force career.
Pointless flagwaving farrago.
w Vernon Sewell, Erwin Reiner *novel* John Llewellyn Rhys *d* Vernon Sewell
☆ David Farrar, Judy Campbell, Sonia Dresdel, Jack Livesey, John Laurie, Wylie Watson

World Premiere *
US 1940 70m bw
Paramount (Sol C. Siegel)
A zany film producer thinks up some wild publicity schemes for his new film and accidentally traps some Nazi spies.
Occasionally amusing farce mainly notable for its star.
w Earl Felton *d* Ted Tetzlaff *ph* Daniel Fapp
☆ John Barrymore, Ricardo Cortez, Frances Farmer, Sig Rumann, Fritz Feld, Eugene Pallette, Luis Alberni, Virginia Dale, Don Castle

The World Ten Times Over
GB 1963 93m bw
Cyclops (Michael Luke)
US title: *Pussycat Alley*
Two semi-prostitutes try to improve their lot.
Dreary, derivative low-life drama with flashy technique.
wd Wolf Rilla *ph* Larry Pizer *m* Edwin Astley
☆ Sylvia Syms, June Ritchie, Edward Judd, William Hartnell, Francis de Wolff

The World, the Flesh and the Devil *
US 1959 95m bw Cinemascope
MGM/Sol C. Siegel/Harbel
Trapped for five days in a mine cave-in, a man struggles to the surface to find a dead world devastated by atomic war; but still alive are the elements of an eternal triangle …
Enterprising but rather disappointing fantasy which tends to become merely glum and rather self-consciously carries a panic button message.
wd Ranald MacDougall *ph* Harold J. Marzorati *m* Miklos Rozsa *ad* William A. Horning, Paul Groesse
☆ Harry Belafonte, Inger Stevens, Mel Ferrer

World without End
US 1956 80m Technicolor Cinemascope
AA (Richard Heermance)
A space ship breaks the time barrier and returns to Earth in 2508, to find that intelligent humans have been driven underground by mutants.
Reasonably lively sci-fi with horror elements, and a plot borrowed from H. G. Wells.
wd Edward Bernds *ph* Ellsworth Fredericks *m* Leith Stevens
☆ Hugh Marlowe, Nancy Gates, Rod Taylor

A World without Pity
France 1989 88m colour
Artificial Eye/Les Productions Lazennec (Alain Rocca)

A poker-playing youth, living with his young drug-dealing brother, falls in love with a clever student.
A thin romance, whose appeal will depend on how much sympathy can be summoned up for its shiftless, egocentric central character.
wd Eric Rochant *ph* Pierre Novion *m* Gerard Torikian *ad* Thierry François *ed* Michele Darmon
☆ Hippolyte Girardot, Mireille Perrier, Yvan Attal, Jean-Marie Rollin, Cecile Mazan, Aline Still, Paul Pavel

The World's Greatest Athlete
US 1973 92m Technicolor
Walt Disney (Bill Walsh)

An American sports coach on an African holiday finds a young Tarzan with amazing powers.
Simple-minded comedy with lame tomfoolery and trickwork.
w Gerald Gardiner, Dee Caruso *d* Robert Scheerer *ph* Frank Phillips *m* Marvin Hamlisch
☆ Tim Conway, Jan-Michael Vincent, John Amos, Roscoe Lee Browne

The World's Greatest Lover
US 1977 89m DeLuxe
TCF (Gene Wilder)

In the twenties, a rival studio starts a search for a man to surpass Valentino.
Imitative slapstick extravaganza in which anything goes but hardly anything pleases.
wd Gene Wilder *ph* Gerald Hirschfeld *m* John Morris
☆ Gene Wilder, Carol Kane, Dom DeLuise, Fritz Feld
'Infantile humour for young, slow kids who want everything pounded at them.' – *Pauline Kael, New Yorker*
† The film carries a credit to Federico Fellini, 'for encouragement at the right time'.

Worm's Eye View
GB 1951 77m bw
ABFD/Byron (Henry Halsted)
Incidents in the lives of a group of RAF billetees.
Plotless comedy from a highly successful stage romp; plainly made and empty-headed but not disagreeable.
w R. F. Delderfield *play* R. F. Delderfield *d* Jack Raymond *ph* James Wilson *m* Tony Lowry, Tony Fones
☆ Ronald Shiner, Garry Marsh, Diana Dors, Eric Davis, John Blythe

The Worst Woman in Paris
US 1933 75m bw
Jesse L. Lasky/Fox
An American girl unfairly gets a bad reputation in Paris and on her way home becomes a heroine in Kansas.
Silly, pointless story on which good production values are wasted.
w Marion Dix, Monta Bell, Martin Brown *d* Monta Bell
☆ Benita Hume, Adolphe Menjou, Harvey Stephens, Helen Chandler, Margaret Seddon
'Does not give promise of scoring in any placement.' – *Variety*

'A hunter never leaves his prey wounded.'
Wounded
US 1996 94m colour
Keystone/Republic/Wounded
An animal conservationist battles for her survival against a poacher who is killing grizzly bears and anyone who attempts to stop him.
Dull and implausible revenge drama.
w Lindsay Bourne, Harry S. Longstreet *d* Richard Martin *ph* Gregory Middleton *m* Ross Vannelli *pd* Al Benjamin *ed* Kerry Uchida
☆ Madchen Amick (Julie Clayton), Adrian Pasdar (Hanaghan), Graham Greene (Rollins), Richard Joseph Paul (Don Powell), Daniel Kash (David Boyd), Jim Beaver (Eric Ashton), Francois Chau (Mr Lee)
'For the most part this is an interesting new take on a familiar formula.' – *Sight and Sound*

Woyzeck **
Germany 1979 81m Eastmancolor
Contemporary/ZDF/Werner Herzog

In a small garrison town, a fearful army private grows jealous of his lover's flirtation with a drum major.
Deft, swift tragedy of a fragmented play, with a powerful performance from Kinski as a man trying to exist in a world he cannot comprehend.
wd Werner Herzo *play* Georg Büchner *ph* Jörg Schmidt-Reitwein *m* Vivaldi et al *ad* Henning von Gierke *ed* Beate Mainka-Jellinghaus
☆ *Klaus Kinski* (Woyzeck), Eva Mattes (Marie), Wolfgang Reichmann (Captain), Willy Semmelrogge (Doctor), Josef Bierbichler (Drum Major), Paul Burian (Andres), Volker Prechtel (Journeyman)
'Brilliantly acted, staged with claustrophobic discretion, it builds to a peak of intensity.' – *Tom Milne, MFB*

The Wrath of God
US 1972 111m Metrocolor Panavision
MGM/Rainbow/Cineman (William S. Gilmore Jnr)
During a twenties Central American revolution, a bootlegger joins forces with a defrocked priest.
Noisy, violent adventure yarn which works up to a gory climax but does not take itself too seriously.
wd Ralph Nelson *novel* James Graham *ph* Alex Phillips Jnr *m* Lalo Schifrin
☆ Robert Mitchum, Frank Langella, Rita Hayworth, Victor Buono, John Colicos

The Wreck of the Mary Deare *
US 1959 108m Metrocolor Cinemascope
MGM/Blaustein-Baroda (Julian Blaustein)

An insurance fraud comes to light when a salvage boat is rescued from high seas.
Curious, star-studded amalgam of seafaring action and courtroom melodrama, originally intended for Hitchcock.
w Eric Ambler *novel* Hammond Innes *d* Michael Anderson *ph* Joseph Ruttenberg, F. A. Young *m* George Duning
☆ Charlton Heston, Gary Cooper, Michael Redgrave, Emlyn Williams, Cecil Parker, Alexander Knox, Virginia McKenna, Richard Harris

The Wrecking Crew
US 1968 104m Technicolor
Columbia/Meadway/Claude (Irving Allen)

Special agent Matt Helm recovers bullion stolen from a Danish train.
Camped-up spy buffoonery with the usual nubile ladies and a production which seeks to be flashy but succeeds only in being tatty.
w William McGivern *novel* Donald Hamilton *d* Phil Karlson *ph* Sam Leavitt *m* Hugo Montenegro
☆ Dean Martin (Matt Helm), Elke Sommer (Linka Karensky), Sharon Tate (Freya Carlson), Nancy Kwan (Yu-Rang), Nigel Green (Count Contini), Tina Louise (Lola Medina), John Larch (MacDonald), John Brascia (Karl)

'Time To Clean House'
The Wrecking Crew
US 1999 80m colour
Filmwerks/Ice-T/Scanbox/Detonator (Tom Karnowski, Gary Schmoeller)

In Detroit, a team of violent agents wipe out the three street gangs that control the city's drug trade.
Cynical and repellent exploitation movie that should have been quietly buried for its multiple inadequacies; it displays only contempt for its audience.
w Hannah Blue *d* Albert Pyun *ph* Philip Alan Waters *m* Ice-T, Tony Riparetti *pd* Nenad Pecur *ed* Errin Vasquez
☆ Ice-T (Menace), Snoop Dogg (Dra-Man), Ernie Hudson Jnr (Hakiem), T. J. Storm (Josef), David Askew (Sly), Miss Jones (Reporter), Vince Klyn (Judah), Rob Ladesich (Captain)
† It was one of three films – the others being *Urban Menace* and *Corrupt* – that used the same crew and cast and were made back-to-back, or, possibly, shot in the same afternoon.
†† Although Snoop Dogg is billed above the title, he appears only in a short, pre-credits sequence.

Wrestling Ernest Hemingway *
US 1993 122m Technicolor
Warner (Joe Wizan, Todd Black)

Two lonely old men – a repressed and fastidious retired barber and an exuberant alcoholic sailor – find consolation in each other's company.
Two accomplished performances by its stars, playing off each other with skill, give some resonance to this otherwise predictable story of the bonding of an odd couple.
w Steve Conrad *d* Randa Haines *ph* Lajos Koltai *m* Michael Convertino *pd* Waldermar Kalinowski *ed* Paul Hirsch
☆ Robert Duvall, Richard Harris, Shirley MacLaine, Sandra Bullock, Micole Mercurio, Piper Laurie, Marty Belafsky
'A poignant tale of intimate friendship between two elderly, eccentric men.' – *Variety*

'The story of a family's ugly secret and the stark moment that thrust their private lives into public view!'
Written on the Wind **
US 1956 99m Technicolor
U-I (Albert Zugsmith)

A secretary marries her oil tycoon boss and finds herself the steadying force in a very rocky family.
The sheerest Hollywood moonshine: high-flying melodramatic hokum which moves fast enough to be very entertaining.
w George Zuckerman *novel* Robert Wilder *d* *Douglas Sirk* *ph* *Russell Metty* *m* Frank Skinner
☆ Lauren Bacall, *Robert Stack*, *Dorothy Malone*, Rock Hudson, Robert Keith, Grant Williams
Academy Award: Dorothy Malone
Academy Award nomination: title song (*m*Victor Young, *ly*Sammy Cahn); Robert Stack

Wrong Again
US 1929 20m bw silent
Hal Roach
A horse instead of a painting is delivered to a rich man's house.
Pleasing but not very inventive star comedy.
w Lewis R. Foster, Leo McCarey, H. M. Walker *d* Leo McCarey *ph* George Stevens *ed* Richard Currier
☆ Stan Laurel, Oliver Hardy, Del Henderson, Josephine Crowell

The Wrong Arm of the Law *
GB 1962 94m bw
Romulus/Robert Verlaise (Aubrey Baring, E. M. Smedley Aston)

London gangsters plan retaliation against Australian interlopers, and offer Scotland Yard a temporary truce.
Forgettable but pretty funny crook comedy in the British vein, with pacy script and excellent comedy timing.
w Ray Galton, Alan Simpson, John Antrobus *screenplay* Len Heath, John Warren *d* *Cliff Owen* *ph* Ernest Steward *m* Richard Rodney Bennett
☆ Peter Sellers, Lionel Jeffries, Bernard Cribbins, Davy Kaye, Nanette Newman, Bill Kerr, John Le Mesurier

Wrong Bet: see *A.W.O.L.*

The Wrong Box *
GB 1966 110m Technicolor
Columbia/Salamander (Bryan Forbes)

Two elderly Victorian brothers are the last survivors of a tontine (an involved form of lottery) and try to murder each other.
Well-intentioned and star-studded black farce in which the excellent period trappings and stray jokes completely overwhelm the plot.

w Larry Gelbart, Burt Shevelove *novel* Robert Louis Stevenson, Lloyd Osbourne *d* Bryan Forbes *ph Gerry Turpin m* John Barry *ad Ray Simm*
☆ *Ralph Richardson*, John Mills, Michael Caine, *Wilfrid Lawson*, Nanette Newman, Peter Cook, Dudley Moore, Peter Sellers, Tony Hancock, Thorley Walters, Cicely Courtneidge, Irene Handl, John Le Mesurier, Gerald Sim, Norman Bird and also Tutte Lemkow

'A slapdash affair in which anything goes, irrespective of whether or not it fits.' – *Tom Milne*

The Wrong Guy
Canada 1998 87m colour
Hollywood/Paragon/HandMade (Jon Slan)
Mistakenly believing that he is wanted for murdering his boss, an incompetent business executive goes on the run.
Sub-Hitchcockian parody that began life as a TV sketch and has been stretched beyond breaking point, although there are a couple of laughs along the way.
w Dave Foley, David Higgins, Jay Kogen *d* David Steinberg *ph* David A. Makin *m* Lawrence Shragge *pd* Gregory P. Keen *ed* Christopher Cooper
☆ Dave Foley (Nelson Hibbert), David Higgins (Detective Arlen), Jennifer Tilly (Lynn Holden), Colm Feore (The Killer), Joe Flaherty (Fred Holden), Dan Redican (Ken Daly), Alan Scarfe (Farmer Brown)

'Keeps the emphasis on goofy gags, making for quite a funny first half. But pic bogs down big-time in the home stretch.' – *Brendan Kelly, Variety*

† The film was made in 1996.

'Only Patrick Hale Can Prevent A Desperate President, The Head Of The CIA, A Trigger-Happy General, Terrorists, An Arms Dealer, And Religious Fanatics From Destroying The World. But He Has Other Things On His Mind.'
Wrong Is Right
US 1982 117m Metrocolor
Columbia/Richard Brooks
GB title: *The Man with the Deadly Lens*
An international TV commentator discovers that the world is being manipulated by the CIA.
Wild satiric melodrama which takes potshots at everything and usually misses.
wd Richard Brooks *novel The Deadly Angels* by Charles McCarry *ph* Fred J. Koenekamp *m* Artie Kane *pd* Edward Carfagno *ed* George Grenville
☆ Sean Connery, George Grizzard, Katharine Ross, Robert Conrad, G. D. Spradlin, John Saxon, Henry Silva, Leslie Nielsen, Robert Webber, Rosalind Cash, Hardy Kruger, Dean Stockwell, Ron Moody

'Intended as a sharply cynical overview of the current political scene, it emerges as a drearily murky thriller.' – *Sight and Sound*

The Wrong Kind of Girl: see *Bus Stop*

The Wrong Man *
US 1957 105m bw
Warner (Herbert Coleman)
A New York musician is mistaken by police for an armed bandit, and both witnesses and circumstances prevent the truth from emerging.
True but downbeat story from the headlines, filmed with remarkably little persuasion; not its director's métier despite evidence of his usual thoroughness.
w Maxwell Anderson, Angus MacPhail *d* Alfred Hitchcock *ph Robert Burks m* Bernard Herrmann
☆ Henry Fonda, Vera Miles, Anthony Quayle, Harold J. Stone, Esther Minciotti

Wrongfully Accused
US 1998 85m Technicolor
Warner/Morgan Creek/Constantin (James G.Robinson, Bernd Eichinger, Pat Proft)
Framed on a murder charge, a violinist escapes on his way to prison and goes in search of the real killer, a one-armed, one-legged, one-eyed killer.
A send up of The Fugitive, *but so clumsily done that it can raise only the slightest of smiles.*
wd Pat Proft *characters created by* Roy Huggins *ph* Glen MacPerson *m* Bill Conti *pd* Michael Bolton *ed* James R. Symons
☆ Leslie Nielsen (Ryan Harrison), Richard Crenna (Lt Fergus Falls), Kelly Le Brock (Lauren Goodhue), Melinda McGraw (Cass Lake), Michael York (Hibbing Goodhue), Sandra Bernhard (Dr Fridley), Aaron Pearl (Sean Laughrea), Leslie Jones (Sgt Tina Bagley), Ben Ratner (Sgt Orono)

'The broad comedy misses its target except by accident, creating more mess than mirth in its pie-flinging approach.' – *Leonard Klady, Variety*

'Torn with desire ... twisted with hate!'
Wuthering Heights ***
US 1939 104m bw
Samuel Goldwyn
The daughter of an unhappy middle-class Yorkshire family falls passionately in love with a gypsy who has been brought up with her.
Despite American script and settings, this wildly romantic film makes a pretty fair stab at capturing the power of at least the first half of a classic Victorian novel, and in all respects it's a superb Hollywood production of its day and a typical one, complete with ghostly finale and a first-rate cast.
w Ben Hecht, Charles MacArthur *novel* Emily *Brontë d William Wyler ph* Gregg Toland *m Alfred Newman ad James Basevi*
☆ *Laurence Olivier, Merle Oberon*, David Niven, Hugh Williams, Flora Robson, Geraldine Fitzgerald, Donald Crisp, Leo G. Carroll, Cecil Kellaway, *Miles Mander*

CATHY (MERLE OBERON): 'I don't think I belong in heaven, Ellen. I dreamt once I was there. I dreamt I went to heaven and that heaven didn't seem to be my home and I broke my heart with weeping to come back to earth and the angels were so angry they flung me out in the middle of the heath on top of Wuthering Heights and I woke up sobbing with joy.'

HEATHCLIFF (LAURENCE OLIVIER): 'What do they know of heaven or hell, Cathy, who know nothing of life? Oh, they're praying for you, Cathy. I'll pray one prayer with them. I'll repeat till my tongue stiffens: Catherine Earnshaw, may you not rest while I live on. I killed you. Haunt me, then! Haunt your murderer! I know that ghosts have wandered on the earth. Be with me always – take any form – drive me mad! Only do not leave me in this dark alone where I cannot find you. I cannot live without my life! I cannot die without my soul…'

'Sombre dramatic tragedy, productionally fine, but with limited appeal.' – *Variety*

'Unquestionably one of the most distinguished pictures of the year.' – *Frank S. Nugent, New York Times*

'A pattern of constant forward motion, with overtones maintained throughout the rise of interest and suspense.' – *Otis Ferguson*

'A strong and sombre film, poetically written as the novel not always was, sinister and wild as it was meant to be, far more compact dramatically than Miss Brontë had made it.' – *Richard Mallett, Punch*

Gregg Toland
best picture; script; William Wyler; Alfred Newman; Laurence Olivier; Geraldine Fitzgerald; art direction

'The power, the passion, the terror!'
Wuthering Heights *
GB 1970 105m Movielab
AIP (John Pellatt)
Somewhat rewritten and overkeen to find a 1970 mood and interpretation for what can only be a period piece, this disappointing version marks a Z-film company's first determined effort to enter the big-time.
w Patrick Tilley *d* Robert Fuest *ph John Coquillon m* Michel Legrand
☆ Anna Calder-Marshall, Timothy Dalton, Harry Andrews, Pamela Brown, Judy Cornwell, James Cossins, Rosalie Crutchley, Julian Glover, Hugh Griffith, Ian Ogilvy, Aubrey Woods

Wuthering Heights
US 1992 106m colour
UIP/Paramount (Mary Selway)
Heathcliff, an orphaned gypsy, seeks revenge on those who humiliated him despite his passionate love for the girl with whom he was brought up.
Unimaginative version, hampered by Binoche's unconvincing English and the lack of any spark between her and Fiennes.
w Anne Devlin *novel* Emily Brontë *d* Peter Kosminsky *ph* Mike Southon *m* Ryuichi Sakamoto *pd* Brian Morris *ed* Tony Lawson
☆ Juliette Binoche, Ralph Fiennes, Janet McTeer, Sophie Ward, Simon Shepherd, Jeremy Northam, Jason Riddington, Simon Ward, John Woodvine

Wuya Yu Maque: see *Crows and Sparrows*

'The Epic Story Of Love And Adventure In A Lawless Land.'
Wyatt Earp **
US 1994 189m Technicolor
Warner/Tig/Kasdan (Jim Wilson, Kevin Costner, Lawrence Kasdan)
The life of Wyatt Earp, from his youth to his later life as horse thief, buffalo hunter and successful lawman.
Over-solemn retelling of a story familiar from many other Westerns, though never before at this length or detail. Moments of tedium are inevitable, and after a revisionist beginning the film finally settles for a celebration of a mythic hero, with Costner playing Wyatt Earp as a legend rather than a flesh-and-blood person; but it often works on an epic scale.
w Dan Gordon, Lawrence Kasdan *d* Lawrence Kasdan *ph* Owen Roizman *m* James Newton Howard *pd* Ida Random *ed* Carol Littleton
☆ Kevin Costner, Dennis Quaid, Gene Hackman, Jeff Fahey, Mark Harmon, Michael Madsen, Catherine O'Hara, Bill Pullman, Isabella Rossellini, Tom Sizemore, JoBeth Williams, Mare Winningham, Joanna Going, David Andrews, Linden Ashby

'A stately, handsome, grandiose gentleman's Western that evenhandedly but too doggedly tries to tell more about the famous Tombstone lawman than has ever before been put onscreen.' – *Todd McCarthy, Variety*

† The film was originally intended as an eight-hour TV mini-series.
Owen Roizman

Wyoming
US 1940 88m bw
MGM
GB title: *Bad Man of Wyoming*
A Missouri badman is persuaded to try an honest life.
Well-liked minor Western responsible for the first teaming of its inelegant stars.
w Jack Jevne, Hugo Butler *d* Richard Thorpe
☆ Wallace Beery, Marjorie Main, Leo Carrillo, Ann Rutherford, Joseph Calleia, Lee Bowman, Henry Travers

Wyoming
US 1947 84m bw
Republic
Early settlers in the west meet trouble from government squatters.
Minor Western for undemanding audiences.
w Lawrence Hazard, Gerald Geraghty *d* Joseph Kane *ph* John Alton *m* Ernest Gold
☆ Bill Elliott, Vera Ralston, John Carroll, George 'Gabby' Hayes, Albert Dekker

The Wyoming Kid: see *Cheyenne*

Wyoming Mail
US 1950 87m Technicolor
Universal (Aubrey Schenck)
A government agent pretends to be a bank robber in order to infiltrate a gang robbing mail trains.
Trite, glossy Western, focusing more on romance than action.
w Harry Essex, Leonard Lee *story* Robert Hardy Andrew *d* Reginald LeBorg *ph* Russell Metty *md* Joseph Gershenson *ad* Bernard Herzbrun, Hilyard Brown *ed* Edward Curtiss
☆ Stephen McNally, Alexis Smith, Howard da Silva, Ed Begley, Whit Bissell, Richard Egan, James Arness, Richard Jaeckel, Gene Evans

'The time has come for those who are different to stand united.'

X2 ★

US 2002 134m Technicolor Panavision

TCF/Marvel/Donners' Co./Bad Hat Harry (Lauren Shuler Donner, Ralph Winter)

aka: *X-Men 2*

Mutant rivals combine forces to prevent their destruction by a fanatical military man who has the President's confidence.

Formulaic action movie that relies on special effects rather than an engaging narrative or characters – the mutants are single dimensional, no more than the sum of their peculiar capabilities.

w Michael Dougherty, Dan Harris *story* Bryan Singer, David Hayter, Zak Penn *d* Bryan Singer *ph* Newton Thomas Sigel *m* Ottman *pd* Guy Hendrix Dyas *ed* John Ottman, Elliot Graham *sp* Michael Fink; makeup: Gordon Smith

☆ Patrick Stewart (Professor Charles Xavier), Hugh Jackman (Logan/Wolverine), Ian McKellen (Eric Lensherr/Magneto), Halle Berry (Storm), Famke Janssen (Jean Grey), James Marsden (Scott Summers/Cyclops), Rebecca Romijn-Stamos (Mystique), Brian Cox (William Stryker), Alan Cumming (Kurt Wagner/Nightcrawler), Bruce Davison (Senator Kelly), Shawn Ashmore (Bobby Drake/Iceman), Anna Paquin (Rogue)

'There are simply too many characters to get a handle on, and the sheer proliferation of special effects offers Singer a license so unfettered that most of the mutants act not according to their natures but purely on the ground of what, at that juncture, looks most groovy.' – *Anthony Lane, New Yorker*

'The new picture is about twice as good as the original.' – *Todd McCathy, Variety*

'I wish I could say it wasn't so, but for most of us, this "X" marks a splat.' – *Stephen Hunter, Washington Post*

'If thine eye offends thee, pluck it out!'

X – the Man with X-Ray Eyes

US 1963 80m Pathécolor 'Spectarama'

AIP (Roger Corman)

GB title: *The Man with the X-Ray Eyes*

A scientist gives himself X-ray vision and goes mad.

Interesting but rather unpleasant horror story with moments of cleverness but a general air of disappointment.

w Robert Dillon, Ray Russell *d* Roger Corman *ph* Floyd Crosby *m* Les Baxter *pd* Daniel Haller *ed* Anthony Carras

☆ Ray Milland, Diana Van Der Vlis, Harold J. Stone, John Hoyt, Don Rickles, John Dierkes

'When the dialogue suggests that Xavier is being driven insane by strange and satanic visions, what one actually sees is rather a comedown.' – *MFB*

'Concise, confident, and not an ounce overweight.' – *NFT, 1967*

X the Unknown ★

GB 1956 78m bw

Exclusive/Hammer (Anthony Hinds)

A mysterious force feeds on radiation from a research station on a Scottish moor, and becomes a seeping mass.

Minor sci-fi horror with a monster-like liquid lino, rushed into release to cash in on The Quatermass Experiment.

w Jimmy Sangster *d* Leslie Norman *ph* Gerald Gibbs *m* James Bernard *ed* James Needs

☆ Dean Jagger, Edward Chapman, Leo McKern, William Lucas, John Harvey, Peter Hammond, Michael Ripper, Anthony Newley

'A New Breed Of Secret Agent.'

XXX

US 2002 124m DeLuxe Panavision

Columbia-TriStar/Revolution (Neal H. Moritz)

An extreme-sports practitioner is recruited by a US government agent to infiltrate a renegade Russian organization that threatens the world.

Not so much a movie as a probably successful attempt to create a new franchise to rival James Bond, substituting a thuggish hero in keeping with the times but otherwise adhering to the same formula of beautiful, disposable women, mad scientists and spectacular stunts.

w Rich Wilkes *d* Rob Cohen *ph* Dean Semler *m* Randy Edelman *pd* Gavin Bocquet *ed* Chris Lebenzon, Paul Rubell, Joel Negron *sp* Digital Domain

☆ Vin Diesel (Xander Cage), Asia Argento (Yelena), Marton Csokas (Yorgi), Samuel L. Jackson (Agent Gibbons), Danny Trejo (El Jefe), Michael Roof (Toby Lee Shavers), Tom Everett (Senator Dick Hotchkiss)

'Even as a work of mindless popcorn entertainment, it fails to deliver.' – *Cosmo Landesman, Sunday Times*

'An even faster and more furious example of enjoyably no-brain entertainment.' – *Sunday Mirror*

† The film took more than $141.5m at the US box-office.

X, Y and Zee: see *Zee and Co*

'Fight The Future.'

The X-Files

US 1998 120m DeLuxe Panavision

TCF/Ten Thirteen (Chris Carter, Daniel Sackheim)

FBI agents, who are blamed for a bomb blast in Dallas, discover that there is an alien conspiracy responsible for the event.

Plodding big-screen version of the TV series that will appeal only to fans of the programme and its two glum leads and/or paranoid theorists.

w Chris Carter *d* Rob Bowman *ph* Ward Russell *m* Mark Snow *pd* Christopher Nowak *ed* Stephen Mark *sp* Mat Beck; make-up fx: Alec Gillis, Tom Woodruff Jnr

☆ David Duchovny, Gillian Anderson, Martin Landau, Armin Mueller-Stahl, Blythe Danner, William B. Davis, John Neville, Mitch Pileggi, Jeffrey DeMunn, Terry O'Quinn, Glenne Headly, Lucas Black

'More a grand marketing exercise for its hugely popular TV series than a real movie.' – *Screen International*

'File under unexceptional.' – *Variety*

'Trust a few. Fear the rest.'

X-Men

US 2000 104m DeLuxe Panavision

TCF/Marvel/Donners' Co./Bad Hat Harry (Lauren Shuler Donner, Ralph Winter)

Two groups of mutants with special powers struggle for supremacy, one attempting to save humanity, the other to change it.

Stylish comicbook action movie that is one of the few to suggest that some intelligence is involved, though its attempt to find a connection between its mutants and the Jewish victims of the concentration camps is ill-judged.

w David Hayter *story* Tom DeSanto, Bryan Singer *based on Marvel Comics' series* by Stan Lee *d* Bryan Singer *ph* Newton Thomas Sigel *m* Michael Kamen *pd* John Myhre *ed* Steven Rosenblum, Kevin Stitt, John Wright *sp* Digital Domain; Cinesite; Hammerhead *cos* Louise Mingenbach

☆ Hugh Jackman (Wolverine), Patrick Stewart (Xavier), Ian McKellen (Magneto), Famke Janssen (Jean Grey), James Marsden (Cyclops), Halle Berry (Storm), Anna Paquin (Rogue), Tyler Mane (Sabretooth), Ray Park (Toad), Rebecca Romijn-Stamos (Mystique), Bruce Davison (Sen Kelly), Matthew Sharp (Henry Guyrich), Brett Morris (Young Magneto)

'It is preposterous and sinister and enjoyable.' – *Peter Bradshaw, Guardian*

'Though fast paced and reasonably entertaining, pic never exhilarates or finds a distinctive style.' – *Dennis Harvey, Variety*

† The film cost $75m to make and took $294.3m at the international box office.

X-Men 2: see *X2*

Xala ★

Senegal 1974 123m colour

Filmi Domireew/Société Nationale Cinématographique (Paulin Soumanou Vieyra)

GB title: *The Curse*

A leading businessman is humiliated when he finds that he is unable to consummate his marriage to his third wife.

Exuberant satire on corruption and a clash of cultures: tribal and urban, African and European, revolutionary and colonial, feminine and masculine, rich and poor.

wd Ousmane Sembène *novel* Ousmane Sembène *ph* Georges Caristan, Orlando R. Lopez, Seydina D. Gaye, Farba Seck *m* Samba Diabare Samb *ed* Florence Eymon

☆ Thierno Lege, Miriam Niang, Seune Samb, Fatim Diagne, Younouss Seye, Moustapha Toure, Dieynaba Niang

Xanadu

US 1980 93m Technicolor

Universal/Lawrence Gordon

The muse Terpsichore comes to Earth and becomes involved in the opening of a roller-derby disco.

Misguided attempt at a clean nostalgic musical, apparently conceived in a nightmare after somebody saw Down to Earth *on the late show.*

w Richard Christian Danus, Marc Reid Rubel *d* Robert Greenwald *ph* Victor J. Kemper *m* Barry de Vorzon *pd* John W. Corso *songs* Jeff Lynne, John Farrar

☆ Olivia Newton-John, Gene Kelly, Michael Beck

'Truly a stupendously bad film whose only salvage is the music.' – *Variety*

'A forties musical submerged by contemporary tat.' – *Guardian*

'Mushy and limp, so insubstantial it evaporates before our eyes.' – *Roger Ebert*

† Gene Kelly uses the same character name, Danny McGuire, as he did in *Cover Girl*.

Xia Dao Gao Fei: see *Full Contact*

Xianggang Zhizao: see *Made in Hong Kong*

Xich Lo: see *Cyclo*

Xingfu Shiguang: see *Happy Times*

Xiyan: see *The Wedding Banquet*

Xizao ★

China 1999 94m colour

Momentum/Xi'an Film Studio/Zhang Peimin/Imar (Peter Loehr)

aka: *Shower*

A businessman returns home to the decaying, public bathhouse run by his elderly father and retarded brother.

Gentle, nostalgic, humane, but predictable comedy, in praise of traditional values that are losing out to a more impersonal way of life.

w Zhang Yang, Liu Fendou, Huo Xin, Diao Yinan, Cai Xiangjun *d* Zhang Yang *ph* Zhang Jian, Bi'er *m* Ye Xiaogang *ad* Tian Meng *ed* Yang Hongyu

☆ Zhu Xu (Liu), Pu Cunxin (Daming), Jiang Wu (Erming), Li Ding (Lin), Feng Shun (Wu), He Bing (He Zheng), Du Peng (Miao Zhuang)

'I found the movie slick and facile, despite its good intentions.' – *Andrew Sarris, New York Observer*

Xtro

GB 1982 86m colour

New Realm/Ashley/Amalgamated Film Enterprises (Mark Forstater)

An alien on the rampage rapes a woman who gives birth to a man – the clone of one who was abducted by a flying saucer three years earlier.

Weird but not wonderful low-budget horror that is a succession of odd moments rather than a conventional narrative.

w Iain Cassie, Robert Smith, Jo Ann Kaplan, Michel Parry, Harry Bromley Davenport *d* Harry Bromley Davenport *ph* John Metcalfe *m* Harry Bromley Davenport *ad* Andrew Mollo *ed* Nicolas Gaster

☆ Bernice Stegers, Philip Sayer, Danny Brainin, Simon Nash, Maryam D'Abo, David Cardy, Anna Wing, Peter Mandell

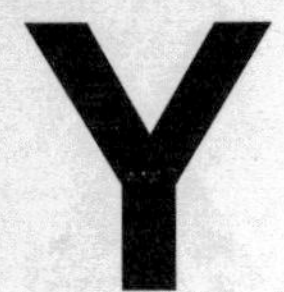

Y Tu Mamá También ***
Mexico 2001 105m colour
Icon/Anhelo (Jorge Vergara)
GB and US title: *And Your Mother Too*
Two Mexican youths learn about life and love from an older woman while on a road trip to find the perfect beach.
Joyous, sexy odyssey through Mexico that glances lightly at the country's political corruption and social divisions, and also uses an omniscient narrator to add a little gravity to the high-spirited proceedings.
w Alfonso and Carlos Cuaron *d* Alfonso Cuaron *ph* Emmanuel Lubezki *ad* Miguel Alvarez *ed* Alfonso Cuaron, Alex Rodriguez
☆ Maribel Verdu (Luisa Cortes), Gael Garcia Bernal (Julio Zapata), Diego Luna (Tenoch Iturbide), Diana Bracho, Emilio Echevarria, Ana Lopez Mercado, Maria Aura, Andres Almeida
'Outrageous without being offensive, provocatively and unapologetically sexual, alive to the possibilities of life and cinema.' – *Kenneth Turan, Los Angeles Times*
'The movie is fast, funny, unafraid of sexuality and finally devastating.' – *Elvis Mitchell, New York Times*
Carlos Cuarón; Alfonso Cuarón

Yaaba **
Burkina Faso/France/Switzerland 1989 90m colour
Oasis/Les Films de l'Avenir/Thelma Film/Arcadia Films (Pierre Alain Meier, Freddy Denaês, Idrissa Ouedraogo)
A young boy befriends an old woman, ostracized by the villagers and regarded as a witch.
Riveting account of African village life and a child's growing to maturity, told with directness and humour.
wd Idrissa Ouédraogo *ph* Matthias Kalin *m* Francis Bebey *ed* Loredana Cristelli
☆ Fatima Sanga, Noufou Ouedraogo, Barry Roukietou, Adama Ouedraogo, Amade Toure, Sibidou Ouedraogo, Adame Sidibe

Yacula: see *Female Vampire*

The Yakuza
US 1975 112m Technicolor Panavision
Warner (Sydney Pollack, Michael Hamilburg)
Japanese gangsters kidnap the daughter of a Los Angeles shipping magnate.
Violent thriller roughly exploiting an ancient Japanese genre.
w Paul Schrader, Robert Towne *d* Sydney Pollack *ph* Okazaki Kozo, Duke Callaghan *m* Dave Grusin
☆ Robert Mitchum, Takakura Ken, Brian Keith, Kishi Keiko, Okada Eiji
'No more than a curious footnote to the western exploitation of oriental action movies.' – *Tony Rayns*

Yam Daabo: see *The Choice*

Yangtse Incident *
GB 1957 113m bw
British Lion/Wilcox/Neagle (Herbert Wilcox)
US title: *Battle Hell*
aka: *Escape of the Amethyst*
In 1949 a British frigate is shelled and held captive by communist shore batteries in the Yangtse.
Stalwart but not very exciting British war heroics.
w Eric Ambler *book* Franklin Gollings *d* Michael Anderson *ph* Gordon Dines *m* Leighton Lucas
☆ Richard Todd, William Hartnell, Akim Tamiroff, Donald Houston, Keye Luke, Sophie Stewart, Robert Urquhart, James Kenney, Barry Foster

A Yank at Eton
US 1942 88m bw
MGM (John Considine Jnr)
A rich, wild American boy is sent to Eton to cool down.
Tame, tasteless imitation of A Yank at Oxford *with younger participants.*
w George Oppenheimer, Lionel Houser, Thomas Phipps *d* Norman Taurog *ph* Karl Freund, Charles Lawton *m* Bronislau Kaper
☆ Mickey Rooney, Freddie Bartholomew, Ian Hunter, Edmund Gwenn, Alan Mowbray, Tina Thayer, Marta Linden, Alan Napier, Terry Kilburn

A Yank at Oxford **
GB 1937 105m bw
MGM (Michael Balcon)
A cocky young American student comes to Oxford and meets all kinds of trouble.
A huge pre-war success which now seems naïve, this was the first big Anglo-American production from a team which went on to make The Citadel *and* Goodbye Mr Chips *before war stymied them.*
w Malcolm Stuart Boylan, Walter Ferris, George Oppenheimer, Leon Gordon, Roland Pertwee, Sidney Gilliat, Michael Hogan from an idea by John Monk Saunders *d* Jack Conway *ph* Harold Rosson *m* Edward Ward
☆ *Robert Taylor*, Vivien Leigh, Maureen O'Sullivan, Lionel Barrymore, Robert Coote, Edmund Gwenn, C. V. France, Griffith Jones, Morton Selten
'A draw picture for Taylor at a critical moment in his meteoric bid for fame.' – *Variety*
† A total of 31 writers are alleged to have worked without credit.

A Yank in Dutch: see *The Wife Takes a Flyer*

A Yank in Ermine
GB 1955 85m colour
Monarch
An American finds that he is really an English earl.
Thin comedy, thinly developed.
w John Paddy Carstairs *novel* Solid Said the Earl by John Paddy Carstairs *d* Gordon Parry *ph* Arthur Grant *m* Stanley Black
☆ Peter Thompson, Noelle Middleton, Harold Lloyd Jnr, Diana Decker, Jon Pertwee, Reginald Beckwith, Edward Chapman, Richard Wattis

A Yank in London: see *I Live in Grosvenor Square*

A Yank in the RAF *
US 1941 98m bw
TCF (Lou Edelman)
An American chorine stranded in London falls for the titular gentleman.
Silly but entertaining wartime flagwaver.
w Karl Tunberg, Darrell Ware *story* Melville Crossman (Zanuck) *d* Henry King *ph* Leon Shamroy *m* Alfred Newman
☆ Tyrone Power, Betty Grable, John Sutton, Reginald Gardiner, Donald Stuart, Morton Lowry, Richard Fraser, Bruce Lester

Yankee Doodle Dandy ***
US 1942 126m bw
Warner (Hal B. Wallis, William Cagney)
The life story of dancing vaudevillian George M. Cohan.
Outstanding showbiz biopic, with unassuming but effective production, deft patriotic backdrops and a marvellous, strutting, magnetic star performance.
w Robert Buckner, Edmund Joseph *d Michael Curtiz ph James Wong Howe m* Heinz Roemheld *md* Heinz Roemheld, Ray Heindorf *ed* George Amy *songs George M. Cohan*
☆ *James Cagney*, Joan Leslie, *Walter Huston*, Rosemary de Camp, Richard Whorf, George Tobias, Jeanne Cagney, Irene Manning, S. Z. Sakall, George Barbier, Frances Langford, Walter Catlett, Eddie Foy Jnr
COHAN (JAMES CAGNEY) AT END OF VAUDEVILLE ACT: 'My mother thanks you. My father thanks you. My sister thanks you. And I thank you.'
COHAN: 'Where else in the world could a plain guy like me sit down and talk things over with the head man?'
ROOSEVELT (CAPTAIN JACK YOUNG): 'Well now, you know, Mr Cohan, that's as good a description of America as I've ever heard.'
'Possibly the most genial screen biography ever made.' – *Time*
♫ 'Harrigan'; 'The Yankee Doodle Boy'; 'Give My Regards to Broadway'; 'Oh, You Wonderful Girl'; 'Mary's a Grand Old Name'; 'So Long, Mary'; 'You're a Grand Old Flag'; 'Over There'.
music direction; James Cagney
best picture; original story (Robert Buckner); Michael Curtiz; Walter Huston; George Amy

A Yankee in King Arthur's Court: see *A Connecticut Yankee in King Arthur's Court*

Yankee Pasha
US 1954 84m Technicolor
Universal-International (Howard Christie)
An American adventurer in 19th-century Marseilles saves his girlfriend from pirates.
Studio-bound hokum for double-featuring.
w Joseph Hoffman *novel* Edison Marshall *d* Joseph Pevney *ph* Carl Guthrie *m* Joseph Gershenson
☆ Jeff Chandler, Rhonda Fleming, Mamie Van Doren, Lee J. Cobb, Bart Roberts, Hal March

Yanks **
GB 1979 141m Technicolor
United Artists/CIP/Joe Janni-Lester Persky
Romances of American GIs billeted on a Lancashire town during World War II.
Not an entirely promising subject, this overlong piece maintains its interest by sheer skill of dramaturgy and cinematic narrative.
w Colin Welland, Walter Bernstein *d John Schlesinger ph* Dick Bush *m* Richard Rodney Bennett *pd* Brian Morris
☆ Vanessa Redgrave, Richard Gere, William Devane, Lisa Eichhorn, Rachel Roberts, Chick Vennera
Rachel Roberts

Yanzhi Kou: see *Rouge*

Yao a Yao Yao dao Waipo Qiao: see *Shanghai Triad*

'There's nothing more dangerous than an innocent man.'
The Yards **
US 2000 116m DeLuxe Panavision
Film4/Miramax (Nick Wecksler, Paul Webster, Kerry Orent)
Working for his uncle's subway company, an ex-convict finds himself framed for murder by his uncle's associates.
Tense thriller of double-dealing, corruption and family strife.
w James Gray, Matt Reeves *d* James Gray *ph* Harris Savides *m* Howard Shore *pd* Kevin Thompson *ed* Jeffrey Ford
☆ Mark Wahlberg (Leo Handler), Joaquin Phoenix (Willie Gutierrez), Charlize Theron (Erica Stoltz), James Caan (Frank Olchin), Ellen Burstyn (Val Handler), Faye Dunaway (Kitty Olchin), Chad Aaron (Bernard Stoltz), Andrew Davoli (Raymond Price), Steve Lawrence (Arthur Mydanick), Tony Musante (Seymour Korman), Victor Argo (Paul Lazarides), Tomas Milian (Manuel Sequiera), Robert Montano (Hector Gallardo), Victor Arnold (Albert Granada)
'An "On the Waterfront" wannabe, directed with a heavy portentousness that smothers the drama in a thick sauce of self-importance.' – *Todd McCarthy, Variety*

Y'Aura T'il de la Neige à Noël?: see *Will it Snow for Christmas?*

The Year My Voice Broke *
Australia 1987 105m colour
Palace/Kennedy Miller Productions (Terry Hayes, Doug Mitchell, George Miller)
A 15-year-old boy, who is having a troubled relationship with an orphaned girl, discovers the shameful secret behind a haunted house in his small town.
An engaging account of growing up that avoids nostalgia and easy sentiment.
wd John Duigan *ph* Geoff Burton *pd* Roger Ford *ed* Neil Thumpston
☆ Noah Taylor, Loene Carmen, Ben Mendelsohn, Graeme Blundell, Lynette Curran, Malcolm Robertson, Judi Farr

'Risking it was all part of the job!'
The Year of Living Dangerously *
Australia 1982 114m Eastmancolor
MGM/McElroy and McElroy (Jim McElroy)
A young Australian journalist takes his first international assignment in Indonesia.
Freshly observed but ultimately pointless political parable which undoubtedly means more to its maker than it will to audiences.
w David Williamson, Peter Weir, A. J. Koch *novel* C. J. Koch *d Peter Weir ph* Russell Boyd *m* Maurice Jarre *ed* Bill Anderson
☆ Mel Gibson, Sigourney Weaver, Linda Hunt, Michael Murphy, Bill Kerr, Noel Ferrier
'I was held by it and had a very good time, though I didn't believe any of it. And I was held despite my aversion to its gusts of wind about destiny, truth versus appearance and so on.' – *Pauline Kael*
Linda Hunt

Year of the Comet
US 1992 89m colour
Columbia/Castle Rock/New Line (Peter Yates, Nigel Wooll)
Various people scramble to obtain a 150-year-old bottle of wine, found in a Scottish castle.
A disappointing romantic comedy, given the talents involved, which fails to sparkle.
w William Goldman *d* Peter Yates *ph* Roger Pratt *m* Hummie Mann *pd* Anthony Pratt *ed* Ray Lovejoy
☆ Penelope Ann Miller, Tim Daly, Louis Jourdan, Art Malik, Ian Richardson, Ian McNeice, Timothy Bentinck, Julia McCarthy, Jacques Mathou
'This wine-soaked comedy-adventure never really ferments, in part due to a lack of chemistry between its romantic leads.' – *Variety*

'It's Chinatown – and it's about to explode!'
The Year of the Dragon
US 1985 136m Technicolor Panavision
MGM-UA/Dino de Laurentiis
A tough cop clears Chinatown of a group of murderous youth gangs.
Extremely violent and convoluted thriller with an unpleasant hero.
w Oliver Stone, Michael Cimino *novel* Robert Daley *d* Michael Cimino *ph* Alex Thomson

m David Mansfield *pd* Wolf Kroeger *ed* Noelle Boisson
☆ Mickey Rourke, John Lone, Ariane, Leonard Termo, Ray Barry
'Never as important as the director thinks it is ... nothing is clearly resolved beyond the last dead body.' – *Variety*

'In A City Bathed In Blood ... Who Can You Trust?'
Year of the Gun
US 1991 111m DeLuxe
First Independent/J & M Entertainment/Initial (Edward R. Pressman)
In the 1970s an American journalist working in Rome becomes a target for the terrorist Red Brigades.
Dull political thriller with a bland and uninteresting hero.
w David Ambrose *novel* Michael Mewshaw *d* John Frankenheimer *ph* Blasco Giurato *m* Bill Conti *pd* Aurelio Crugnola *ed* Lee Percy
☆ Andrew McCarthy, Valeria Golino, Sharon Stone, John Pankow, George Murcell, Mattia Sbragia, Roberto Posse
'How can a thriller so stacked with gunfire, chases, twists and red herrings send one to sleep?' – *Geoff Brown, The Times*

Year of the Horse **
US 1997 106m colour/bw
October/Shakey Pictures (L. A. Johnson)
A documentary on rock singer-songwriter and guitarist Neil Young and Crazy Horse, covering episodes from their 30-odd years on the road.
Revealing glimpse into the dynamics and development of a rock group, one that also celebrates the group's music, with plenty of footage of concert performances.
d Jim Jarmusch *ph* L. A. Johnson, Jim Jarmusch *m* Crazy Horse *ed* Jay Rabinowitz
☆ Neil Young, Frank 'Poncho' Sempedro, Billy Talbot, Ralph Molina

'They tamed a tropic wilderness!'
The Yearling **
US 1946 134m Technicolor
MGM (Sidney Franklin)
The son of an old-time country farmer is attached to a stray deer.
Excellent family film for four-handkerchief patrons.
w Paul Osborn *novel* Marjorie Kinnan Rawlings *d* Clarence Brown *ph* Charles Rosher, Leonard Smith *m* Herbert Stothart *ad* Cedric Gibbons, Paul Groesse *ed* Harold Kress
☆ Gregory Peck, Jane Wyman, Claude Jarman Jnr, Chill Wills, Clem Bevans, Margaret Wycherly, Henry Travers, Forrest Tucker
'An unspoilt and simple story of human dignity, patience, struggle, and love, and its appeal should be universal.' – *Fred Majdalany, Daily Mail*
Claude Jarman Jnr (Special Award as outstanding child actor); Charles Rosher, Leonard Smith (and Arthur Arling); art direction
best picture; Clarence Brown; Gregory Peck; Jane Wyman; editing

The Years Between
GB 1946 100m bw
GFD/Sydney Box
An MP returns after being presumed dead in the war and finds his wife has been elected in his place.
Stilted variation on the Enoch Arden theme; plot and performances alike unpersuasive.
w Muriel and Sydney Box *play* Daphne du Maurier *d* Compton Bennett *ph* Reg Wyer
☆ Michael Redgrave, Valerie Hobson, Flora Robson, Felix Aylmer, James McKechnie, Dulcie Gray, Edward Rigby

Years without Days: see *Castle on the Hudson*

Yeelen *
Mali 1987 105m colour
Artificial Eye/Les Films Cissé/Souleymane Cissé
US title: *Brightness*
A son struggles to destroy his father, a black magician.
Engrossing and lively mythic tale that holds the attention even when the significance of certain rituals is hard to grasp.
wd Souleymane Cissé *ph* Jean-Noel Ferragut, Jean-Michel Humeau *m* Michel Portal, Salif Keita *ad* Kossa Mody Keita *ed* Dounamba Coulibaly, Andree Davanture, Marie-Catherine Mique
☆ Issiaka Kane, Niamanto Sanogo, Aoua Sangare, Balla Moussa Keita, Soumba Traore, Ismaila Sarr, Youssouf Cissé, Koke Sangare

The Yellow Balloon
GB 1952 80m bw
ABP (Victor Skutezky)
A small boy who thinks he has killed his friend is terrorized by a murderer.
Tense but not especially rewarding suspenser, clearly borrowed from The Window.
w Anne Burnaby, J. Lee-Thompson *d* J. Lee-Thompson *ph* Gilbert Taylor *m* Philip Green
☆ Kenneth More, William Sylvester, Kathleen Ryan, Andrew Ray, Bernard Lee, Veronica Hurst

The Yellow Cab Man
US 1950 84m bw
MGM (Richard Goldstone)
A taxi-driving inventor is pursued by crooks after his secret formula.
Moderate star comedy.
w Devery Freeman, Albert Beich *d* Jack Donohue *ph* Harry Stradling *m* Scott Bradley
☆ Red Skelton, Gloria de Haven, Walter Slezak, Edward Arnold, James Gleason, Paul Harvey, Jay C. Flippen

Yellow Canary *
GB 1943 98m bw
RKO/Imperator (Herbert Wilcox)
A socialite suspected of being a Nazi sympathizer is really a British spy.
Mild wartime melodrama chiefly notable for allotting an apparently unsympathetic part to the beloved Miss Neagle.
w De Witt Bodeen, Miles Malleson *story* Pamela Bower *d* Herbert Wilcox *ph* Max Greene
☆ Anna Neagle, Richard Greene, Nova Pilbeam, Lucie Mannheim, Cyril Fletcher, Albert Lieven, Margaret Rutherford, Marjorie Fielding

Yellow Canary
US 1963 93m bw Cinemascope
TCF/Cooga Mooga (Maury Dexter)
The baby son of a singing idol is kidnapped.
Rather dreary suspenser with too much dialogue.
w Rod Serling *novel* *Evil Come, Evil Go* by Whit Masterson *d* Buzz Kulik *ph* Floyd Crosby *m* Kenyon Hopkins
☆ Pat Boone, Barbara Eden, Steve Forrest, Jack Klugman, Jesse White, John Banner, Jeff Corey

Yellow Dog
GB 1973 101m Eastmancolor
Scotia-Barber/Akari (Terence Donovan)
A Japanese agent in London keeps watch on a mysterious scientist.
Incoherent spy thriller with a few hybrid oddities.
w Shinobu Hashimoto *d* Terence Donovan *ph* David Watkin *m* Ron Grainer
☆ Jiro Tamiya, Robert Hardy, Carolyn Seymour, Joseph O'Conor

Yellow Earth **
China 1984 89m colour
Guangxi Film Studio
aka: *Huang Tudi*
In 1939, a communist soldier collecting folk songs tries to persuade a peasant family to abandon their traditional ways.
Lyrically photographed against a vast and barren landscape, it celebrates folk traditions in a modern and colourful way.
w Zhang Ziliang *novel* *Echo in the Deep Valley* by Ke Lan *d* Chen Kaige *ph* Zhang Yimou *m* Zhao Jiping *ad* He Qun *ed* Wan Liu, Pei Xiaonan
☆ Xue Bai, Wang Xueqi, Tan Tuo, Liu Qiang

Yellow Jack *
US 1938 83m bw
MGM (Jack Cummings)
In 1899 Cuba a marine offers himself as a guinea pig to combat yellow fever.
Solid, unsurprising, period medical melodrama with conventional romantic sidelights.
w Edward Chodorov *play* Sidney Howard, Paul de Kruif *d* George B. Seitz *ph* Lester White *m* William Axt
☆ Robert Montgomery, Virginia Bruce, Lewis Stone, Andy Devine, Henry Hull, Charles Coburn, Buddy Ebsen, Henry O'Neill, Janet Beecher
'Okay for single billing, but no wow.' – *Variety*

The Yellow Mountain
US 1954 77m Technicolor
Universal (Ross Hunter)
Two old friends fall out over a gold mine and a girl.
Lethargic drama that , after a promising beginning, substitutes talk for action.
w George Zuckerman, Russell Hughes, Robert Blees *Story* Harold Channing Wire *d* Jesse Hibbs *ph* George Robinson *md* Joseph Gershenson *ad* Alexander Golitzen, Alfred Sweeney *ed* Edward Curtis
☆ Lex Barker (Andy Martin), Mala Powers (Nevada Wray), Howard Duff (Pete Menlo), William Demarest (Jackpot Wray), John McIntire (Bannon), Leo Gordon (Drake), Dayton Lummis (Geraghty), Hal K. Dawson (Sam Torrence), William Fawcett (Old Prospector), James Parnell (Joe)

Yellow Pages
GB 1988 88m Technicolor
Miramax/Norfolk International (John D. Schofield, Jefferson Colegate-Stone)
US title: *Going Undercover*
An incompetent private eye is hired to look after a wild young woman by her wicked stepmother.
Dreary slapstick comedy, directed with a very heavy hand.
d James Kenelm Clarke *ph* John Coquillon *m* Alan Hawkshaw *ad* Jim Dultz *ed* Eric Boyd Perkins, Danny Retz
☆ Jean Simmons, Lea Thompson, Chris Lemmon, Viveca Lindfors, Mills Watson, Nancy Cartwright, Joe Michael Terry, Jewell Sheppard

The Yellow Passport: see *The Yellow Ticket*

The Yellow Rolls Royce *
GB 1964 122m Metrocolor Panavision
MGM (Anatole de Grunwald)
Three stories about the owners of an expensive car: an aristocrat, a gangster, and a wandering millionairess.
Lukewarm all-star concoction lacking either good stories or a connecting thread.
w Terence Rattigan *d* Anthony Asquith *ph* Jack Hildyard *m* Riz Ortolani *pd* Vincent Korda
☆ Rex Harrison, Jeanne Moreau, Edmund Purdom, Moira Lister, Roland Culver, Shirley MacLaine, George C. Scott, Alain Delon, Art Carney, Ingrid Bergman, Omar Sharif, Joyce Grenfell
'Tame, bloodless, smothered in elegance and the worst kind of discreetly daring good taste.' – *Peter John Dyer*

Yellow Sands
GB 1938 68m bw
ABPC (Walter C. Mycroft)
A Cornish family sets to bickering over a will.
Reliable comedy from a popular stage original.
w Michael Barringer, Rodney Ackland *play* Eden and Adelaide Phillpotts *d* Herbert Brenon *ph* Walter J. Harvey *m* Hubert Bath
☆ Marie Tempest, Wilfrid Lawson, Belle Chrystal, Robert Newton, Patrick Barr, Edward Rigby

'It was a moment for being a woman ... for only a woman's revenge could keep her alive – now!'
Yellow Sky **
US 1948 98m bw
TCF (Lamar Trotti)
Outlaws on the run take over a desert ghost town.
Gleaming, stylish Western melodrama which benefits from its unusual and confined setting.
w Lamar Trotti *story* W. R. Burnett *d* *William Wellman* *ph* *Joe MacDonald* *m* Alfred Newman
☆ Gregory Peck, Anne Baxter, Richard Widmark, Robert Arthur, John Russell, Henry Morgan, James Barton

Yellow Submarine *
GB 1968 87m DeLuxe
King Features/Apple (Al Brodax)
The happy kingdom of Pepperland is attacked by the Blue Meanies.
Way-out cartoon fantasia influenced by Beatlemania and the swinging sixties; hard to watch for non-addicts.
w Lee Minoff, Al Brodax, Jack Mendelsohn, Erich Segal *d* George Duning *ph* John Williams *m* George Martin *m/ly* John Lennon, Paul McCartney, George Harrison *ad* Heinz Edelmann *ed* Brian J. Bishop
☆ John Lennon, Paul McCartney, George Harrison, Ringo Starr and also voices of: John Clive (John), Geoffrey Hughes (Paul), Peter Batten (George), Paul Angelis (Ringo/Chief Blue Meanie), Dick Emery (Nowhere Man/Lord Mayor/Max), Lance Perceval (Old Fred)
'The film is fun, and an animated feature that holds the interest of adults of all ages (I don't think there are children of any age left) is not to be sneezed at.' – *John Simon*
♫ Yellow Submarine; Eleanor Rigby; All Together Now; When I'm 64; Only a Northern Song; With a Little Help from My Friends; Sgt Pepper's Lonely Hearts Club Band; Lucy in the Sky with Diamonds; Nowhere Man; All You Need Is Love; It's All Too Much; Toy Bulldog

'What they learned isn't on any report card!'
The Yellow Teddybears
GB 1964 88m bw
(Robert Hartford-Davis)
Sixth-form girls run the risk of pregnancy because of the lack of sex education in schools.
One of the first British sex films, cashing in on a tabloid report that schoolgirls showed that they were no longer virgins by wearing brooches that were being given away as a sales gimmick by a jam manufacturer; at the time it caused a minor sensation, but now seems merely risible.
w Derek Ford, Donald Ford *d* Robert Hartford-Davis *ph* Peter Newbrook *m* Malcolm Mitchell *ad* Bernard Sarron *ed* Teddy Darvas
☆ Jacqueline Ellis, Annette Whiteley, Iain Gregory, Doug Sheldon, Georgina Patterson, Victor Brooks, John Bonney, Anne Kettle, Jill Adams, Raymond Huntley, Harriette Johns, John Glyn Jones

The Yellow Ticket *
US 1931 76m bw
Fox
GB title: *The Yellow Passport*
In Russia during the pogroms, a Jewish girl pretends to be a prostitute in order to get a travel permit to see her dying father.
Curious anti-Russian melodrama deriving its plot from La Tosca.
w *Jules Furthman, Guy Bolton* *play* Michael Morton *d* Raoul Walsh *ph* James Wong Howe
☆ Elissa Landi, Laurence Olivier, Lionel Barrymore, Walter Byron, Sarah Padden, Mischa Auer, Boris Karloff

'A picture filled with swashbucklers, privateers, public floggings, saucy tarts, looney lords, beggars, queens, and even a very jolly Roger!'
Yellowbeard
US 1983 96m DeLuxe
Orion/Seagoat (Carter de Haven Jnr)
Farcical adventures of a 17th-century pirate captain.
A spoofy saga in deliberately bad taste, this ragbag of old gags and new unpleasantness sank rapidly to the bottom of the box-office barrel.
w Graham Chapman, Peter Cook, Bernard McKenna *d* Mel Damski *ph* Gerry Fisher *m* John Morris *pd* Joseph R. Jennings
☆ Graham Chapman, Peter Boyle, Cheech and Chong, Peter Cook, Marty Feldman, Michael Hordern, Eric Idle, Madeline Kahn, James Mason, John Cleese, Kenneth Mars, Spike Milligan, Susannah York, Beryl Reid, Ferdy Mayne and also Peter Bull
'The atrocious script and haphazard direction elicit generally embarrassing performances from all concerned.' – *Kim Newman, MFB*

Yellowstone Kelly
US 1959 91m Technicolor
Warner
A fur trapper prevents war between Indians and whites.
Standard Western with routine excitements and a cast of TV faces.
w Burt Kennedy *d* Gordon Douglas *ph* Carl Guthrie *m* Howard Jackson
☆ Clint Walker, Edd Byrnes, John Russell, Ray Danton, Claude Akins

Yentl *
GB 1983 133m Technicolor
MGM-UA/Barwood/Ladbroke (Barbra Streisand, Rusty Lemorande)

Many years ago in Poland, a Jewish girl tries to get on in the world by dressing as a boy.
A personal and some would say megalomaniac extravagance by its producer-director-writer-star, who before embarking should have learned the value of brevity. Nevertheless there is about the enterprise a certain heavy style which may appeal strongly to Jews while precluding the interest and understanding of others.
w Jack Rosenthal, Barbra Streisand *story* Isaac Bashevis Singer *d* Barbra Streisand *ph* David Watkin *m* Michel Legrand *pd* Roy Walker *ed* Terry Rawlings
☆ Barbra Streisand, Mandy Patinkin, Amy Irving, Nehemiah Persoff, Steven Hill, David de Keyser, Bernard Spear
music
Amy Irving; songs 'Papa, Can You Hear Me?', 'The Way He Makes Me Feel' (*m* Michel Legrand, *ly* Alan Bergman, Marilyn Bergman); art director

'A glorious uproarious love story!'
Yes, Giorgio *
US 1982 110m Metrocolor
MGM-UA/Peter Fetterman

A top international tenor falls for the lady throat specialist who cures his ailment.
Nostalgic musical romance, fine in its way but out of key with the modern film business. A treat for television viewers.
w Norman Steinberg *novel* Anne Piper
d Franklin J. Schaffner *ph* Fred J. Koenekamp
m John Williams *pd* William J. Creber
☆ Luciano Pavarotti, Kathryn Harrold, Eddie Albert, Paola Borboni
† The film allegedly cost 19 million and took only one.
original song 'If We Were In Love' (*m* John Williams, *ly* Alan and Marilyn Bergman)

Yes, Madam?
GB 1938 77m bw
ABPC
Heirs to a fortune are obliged to act as servants for three months.
Agreeable minor comedy.
w Clifford Grey, Bert Lee and William Freshman *novel* K. R. G. Browne *d* Norman Lee *ph* Walter J. Harvey *m* Jack Waller
☆ Bobby Howes, Diana Churchill, Billy Milton, Fred Emney, Bertha Belmore, Wylie Watson, Vera Pearce
† Previously filmed in 1933 with Frank Pettingell and Kay Hammond.

Yes Mr Brown *
GB 1933 90m bw
British and Dominions/Herbert Wilcox
A businessman's secretary pretends to be his wife after the latter has walked out on him.
One of its star's most fondly remembered musical farces, a thin thing but his own.
w Douglas Furber *play* *Business with America* by Paul Frank, Ludwig Hershfield *d* Herbert Wilcox, Jack Buchanan *ph* F. A. Young *m/ly* Paul Abraham, Douglas Furber
☆ Jack Buchanan, Elsie Randolph, Hartley Power, Clifford Heatherley, Vera Pearce

Yes My Darling Daughter
US 1939 86m bw
Warner (Ben Glazer)
Lovers elope and are pursued by her family.
Mildly amusing domestic comedy.
w Casey Robinson *play* Mark Reed *d* William Keighley *ph* Charles Rosher
☆ Priscilla Lane, Jeffrey Lynn, Roland Young, Fay Bainter, May Robson, Genevieve Tobin, Ian Hunter

Yeshou Xingling: see *Beastcops*

Yesterday Girl: see *Abschied von Gestern*

Yesterday, Today and Tomorrow
Italy/France 1963 119m Techniscope
CCC/Concordia/Joseph E. Levine (Carlo Ponti)

Three stories of naughty ladies.
A relentlessly boring compendium with everybody shouting at once.
w Eduardo de Filippo, Cesare Zavattini, others
d Vittorio de Sica *ph* Giuseppe Rotunno
m Armando Trovajoli
☆ Marcello Mastroianni, Sophia Loren
'A sad intimation of the sort of rainy day the Italian cinema is currently having.' – *MFB*
'One begins to see, amid the sunsets and sunrises and Roman rooftops, the sheer venality of the creation, the cynical circus thrust upon us on the assumption that breasts and bodies and fornication are all that these leading lights of the Italian cinema need provide to keep us from baying at the moon.' – *Judith Crist*
best foreign film
Marcello Mastroianni

Yesterday's Enemy
GB 1959 95m bw Megascope
Columbia/Hammer (T. S. Lyndon-Haynes)
In 1942 Burma, a British unit violently takes over a village and finds an unsolved puzzle.
Would-be ironic war suspenser, economically made but quite effective in putting its message across.
w Peter R. Newman *TV play* Peter R. Newman
d Val Guest *ph* Arthur Grant *m* none
ad Bernard Robinson *ed* James Needs, Alfred Cox
☆ Stanley Baker, Guy Rolfe, Leo McKern, Philip Ahn, Gordon Jackson, David Oxley, Richard Pasco, Russell Waters, Bryan Forbes, David Lodge, Percy Herbert

Yesterday's Hero
GB 1979 95m colour
Columbia/CinemaSeven (Elliott Kastner)
A successful footballer goes to the bad but redeems himself.
Totally uninteresting sporting version of the Road to Ruin.
w Jackie Collins *d* Neil Leifer *ph* Brian West
md Stanley Myers *pd* Keith Wilson
☆ Ian McShane, Suzanne Somers, Adam Faith, Paul Nicholas, Sam Kydd

Les Yeux sans Visage: see *Eyes without a Face*

Yi Ge Dou Bu Neng Shao: see *Not One Less*

Yi Yi: see *A One and a Two…*

Yield to the Night *
GB 1956 99m bw
ABP (Kenneth Harper)
US title: *Blonde Sinner*
A condemned murderess relives the events which led to her arrest.
Gloomy prison melodrama vaguely based on the Ruth Ellis case and making an emotional plea against capital punishment.
w John Cresswell, Joan Henry *novel* Joan Henry
d J. Lee-Thompson *ph* Gilbert Taylor *m* Ray Martin
☆ *Diana Dors*, Yvonne Mitchell, Michael Craig, Marie Ney, Athene Seyler, Geoffrey Keen

Yinshi Nan Nu: see *Eat Drink Man Woman*

Yo, la peor de todas: see *I, The Worst of All*

Yoidore Tenshi: see *Drunken Angel*

Yojimbo ****
Japan 1961 110m bw
Toho

A wandering samurai tricks two rival gangs of cutthroats into destroying one other.
Masterful, beautifully composed, witty movie that inspired the 'spaghetti Western' cycle when it was remade by Sergio Leone as A Fistful Of Dollars.
w Ryuzo Kikushima, Akira Kurosawa *d* *Akira Kurosawa* *ph* *Kazuo Miyagawa* *m* Masuru Sato
☆ *Toshiro Mifune*, Eijiro Tono, Kamatari Fujiwara, Takashi Shimura, Seizaburo Kawazu, Isuzu Yamada, Hiroshi Tachikawa
'One of the rare Japanese movies that is both great and funny to American audiences.' – *New Yorker*

Yokel Boy
US 1942 69m bw
Republic (Robert North)
GB title: *Hitting the Headlines*
A film buff from the sticks comes to Hollywood and gets involved with production.
Spoofy comedy which doesn't come off despite the talent around.
w Isabel Dawn *story* Russel Rouse (the legit musical by Lew Brown was thrown away, together with the songs) *d* Joseph Santley *ph* Ernest Miller *md* Cy Feuer
☆ Eddie Foy Jnr, Joan Davis, Albert Dekker, Alan Mowbray, Roscoe Karns, Mikhail Rasumny, Marc Lawrence, Tom Dugan

Yol ***
Switzerland 1982 114m Fujicolour
Cactus/Maran/Antenne 2/Swiss Television/Güney (Edi Hubschmid, K. L. Puldi)

Five convicts are released on a week's leave, and their various circumstances lead them to tragedy.
Rewarding if heavy-going Turkish saga which exhausts the spectator almost as much as its long-suffering characters. It feels and looks like an epic.
w Yilmaz Güney *d* Serif Gören *ph* Erdogan Engin *m* Sebastian Argol *ed* Yilmaz Güney, Elisabeth Waelchli
☆ Tarik Akan, Halil Ergün, Necmettin Cobanoglu, Serif Sezer

Yolanda and the Thief *
US 1945 108m Technicolor
MGM (Arthur Freed)

A con man poses as the guardian angel of a naïve heiress.
Laboured musical fantasy with arty Mexican settings; not a success in any way, but with a few effective moments.
w Irving Brecher *story* Ludwig Bemelmans, Jacques Théry *d* Vincente Minnelli *ph* Charles Rosher *m* Lennie Hayton *songs* Harry Warren, Arthur Freed
☆ Fred Astaire, Lucille Bremer, Frank Morgan, Leon Ames, Mildred Natwick
'The most extreme of the big musical mistakes.' – *New Yorker, 1979*
'It perhaps needs to be seen by anyone who wants to know what killed the MGM musicals.' – *New Yorker*

'Every time she says I love you, she breaks the law!'
You and Me
US 1938 90m bw
Paramount (Fritz Lang)
A department store owner employs ex-convicts, one of whom has not quite reformed.
Curious comedy drama which never has a hope of coming off.
w Virginia Van Upp *story* Norman Krasna
d Fritz Lang *ph* Charles Lang Jnr *m* Kurt Weill
☆ Sylvia Sidney, George Raft, Harry Carey, Barton MacLane, Warren Hymer, Roscoe Karns, George E. Stone, Adrian Morris
'Lang's individual touch is visible everywhere … but for the ordinary George Raft fan it will not only be unappreciated, it will be actually confusing.' – *National Board of Review*
'Given proper control over story and scenario, Lang couldn't have made so bad a film as *You and Me*; the whole picture is like an elegant and expensive gesture of despair.' – *Graham Greene*

You Belong to Me
US 1934 67m bw
Paramount (Louis D. Lighton)
An alcoholic vaudeville comic plays father to an orphan.
Muddled backstage melodrama which would be enjoyed by fans of the star.
w Walter DeLeon, Elizabeth Alexander *d* Alfred Werker
☆ Lee Tracy, Helen Mack, Helen Morgan, Lynne Overman, David Holt
'Should gain attention in the nabe spots.' – *Variety*

You Belong to Me *
US 1941 94m bw
Columbia (Wesley Ruggles)
GB title: *Good Morning, Doctor*
A playboy becomes jealous of the male patients of his doctor wife.
Mild comedy for two stars who are well capable of keeping it afloat.
w Claude Binyon, Dalton Trumbo *d* Wesley Ruggles *ph* Joseph Walker *m* Frederick Hollander
☆ Barbara Stanwyck, Henry Fonda, Edgar Buchanan, Roger Clark, Ruth Donnelly, Melville Cooper, Maude Eburne

You Belong to My Heart: see *Mr Imperium*

You Came Along
US 1945 103m bw
Paramount (Hal B. Wallis)
A girl from the treasury department falls in love with one of three GIs she takes on a war bond tour, but he dies of leukaemia.
Weird mishmash of farce and sentimentality; quite watchable in its way, but an odd showcase for a new female star.
w Robert Smith, Ayn Rand *d* John Farrow
ph Daniel L. Fapp *m* Victor Young
☆ Lizabeth Scott, Robert Cummings, Don Defore, Charles Drake, Julie Bishop, Kim Hunter, Rhys Williams, Franklin Pangborn, Minor Watson

You Can Count On Me **
US 2000 109m DeLuxe
Shooting Gallery (John Hart, Jeff Sharp, Larry Meistrich, Barbara De Fina)

In a small town, a hard-working single mother with a young son has trouble with her new boss and her aimless brother, who visits her to borrow money after being released from prison.
Affecting well-acted drama of a family relationship between two people whose shared experience has given them contrasting outlooks on life.
wd Kenneth Lonergan *ph* Stephen Kazmierski
m Lesley Barber *pd* Michael Shaw *ed* Anne McCabe
☆ *Laura Linney* (Sammy Prescott), Mark Ruffalo (Terry Prescott), Rory Culkin (Rudy), Matthew Broderick (Brian), Jon Tenney (Bob), V. Smith-Cameron (Mabel), Kenneth Lonergan (Priest)
'A family drama that wins your heart – and respect.' – *Time*
'Curiosity should take you to see *You Can Count On Me*. After a bit you realise, for a change, you're watching real people.' – *Alexander Walker, London Evening Standard*
Kenneth Lonergan (script); Laura Linney

You Can't Buy Everything *
US 1934 72m bw
MGM
A woman obsessed by her mounting bank balance almost ruins the lives of her family.
Unusual and rather well-acted period melodrama with a pleasing cast.
w Dudley Nichols, Lamar Trotti *d* Charles F. Reisner
☆ *May Robson*, Jean Parker, Lewis Stone, Mary Forbes, Reginald Mason

You Can't Cheat an Honest Man *
US 1939 79m bw
Universal (Lester Cowan)
Trials and tribulations of a circus owner.
Flat, desultory and generally disappointing comedy vehicle for an irresistible star combination.
w George Marion Jnr, Richard Mack, Everett Freeman *story* Charles Bogle (W. C. Fields)
d George Marshall *ph* Milton Krasner *m* Charles Previn
☆ W. C. Fields, Edgar Bergen (with Charlie McCarthy and Mortimer Snerd), Constance Moore, Mary Forbes, Thurston Hall, Charles Coleman, Edward Brophy
'Fairly amusing but lacks sustained overall interest.' – *Variety*

You Can't Do That to Me: see *Maisie (Maisie Goes to Reno)*

You Can't Escape Forever
US 1942 77m bw
Warner (Mark Hellinger)
A girl reporter demoted to the lovelorn column exposes a racket boss.
Untidy remake of Hi Nellie; *tolerable on a double bill, but not for close criticism.*
w Fred Niblo Jnr, Hector Chevigny *story* Roy Chanslor *d* Jo Graham

☆ George Brent, Brenda Marshall, Gene Lockhart, Roscoe Karns, Eduardo Ciannelli, Paul Harvey

You Can't Get Away with Murder
US 1939 78m bw
Warner (Sam Bischoff)
A juvenile delinquent teams up with a gangster and takes a prison rap for him.
Standard post-Dead End crime melodrama with no surprises.
w Robert Buckner, Don Ryan, Kenneth Gamet *play* Chalked Out by Lewis Lawes, Jonathan Finn *d* Lewis Seiler *ph* Sol Polito *m* Heinz Roemheld
☆ Humphrey Bogart, Billy Halop, Gale Page, John Litel, Henry Travers, Harvey Stephens, Harold Huber

'Strictly a filler for the duals ... ponderous and slow moving.' – *Variety*

You Can't Have Everything *
US 1937 99m bw
TCF (Lawrence Schwab)
A failed play is turned into a musical.
Lively backstage comedy with good moments.
w Harry Tugend, Jack Yellen, Karl Tunberg *story* Gregory Ratoff *d* Norman Taurog *ph* Lucien Andriot *md* David Buttolph *songs* Mack Gordon, Harry Revel
☆ Alice Faye, *the Ritz Brothers*, Don Ameche, Charles Winninger, Gypsy Rose Lee, Tony Martin, Arthur Treacher, Louis Prima, Tip Tap and Toe, Wally Vernon

'An expert piecing together of story, melody, blackouts, night club specialties and production numbers.' – *Variety*

You Can't Have Everything
US 1970 90m Eastmancolor
Koala (Lou Brandt)
aka: *Cactus in the Snow*
An 18-year-old virgin GI is about to leave for Vietnam when he picks up a girl and spends a happy but platonic twenty-four hours.
An agreeably understated little love story for those absorbed by teenage sex problems.
wd Martin Zweiback *ph* David M. Walsh *m* Joe Parnello
☆ Richard Thomas, Mary Layne, Lucille Benson, Oscar Beregi

You Can't Ration Love
US 1944 78m bw
Michel Kraike/Paramount
It's wartime at college, and dates are rationed.
Silly idea for a forgettable musical.
w Val Burton, Hal Fimberg, Muriel Roy Bolton *d* Lester Fuller
☆ Betty Jane Rhodes, Johnnie Johnston, Bill Edwards, Marjorie Weaver, Marie Wilson, Mabel Paige

You Can't Run Away from It
US 1956 96m Technicolor Cinemascope
Columbia (Dick Powell)
An heiress runs away from a marriage arranged by her father, and falls for an amiable reporter.
Flat remake of It Happened One Night, *with practically no comic sense or talent.*
w Claude Binyon, Robert Riskin *d* Dick Powell *ph* Charles Lawton Jnr *m* George Duning *md* Morris Stoloff
☆ June Allyson, Jack Lemmon, Charles Bickford, Jim Backus, Stubby Kaye, Paul Gilbert, Allyn Joslyn

You Can't Sleep Here: see *I Was a Male War Bride*

You Can't Take It with You **
US 1938 127m bw
Columbia (Frank Capra)
The daughter of a highly eccentric New York family falls for a rich man's son.
A hilarious, warm and witty play is largely changed into a tirade against big business, but the Capra expertise is here in good measure and the stars all pull their weight.
w Robert Riskin *play* George S. Kaufman, Moss Hart *d Frank Capra ph* Joseph Walker *m* Dimitri Tiomkin *ed* Gene Havlik
☆ Jean Arthur, Lionel Barrymore, James Stewart, Edward Arnold, Spring Byington, Mischa Auer, Ann Miller, Samuel S. Hinds, Donald Meek, H. B. Warner, Halliwell Hobbes, Mary Forbes, Dub Taylor, Lillian Yarbo, Eddie Anderson and also *Harry Davenport*

GRANDPA VANDERHOF (LIONEL BARRYMORE) OFFERING A PRAYER: 'Well, sir, here we are again. We had a little trouble, but that's not your fault. You spread the milk of human kindness, and if some of it gets curdled, that's our look-out. Anyway, things have turned out fine. Alice is going to marry Tony. The Kirbys are going to live with us for a while. And everybody on the block is happy. We've all got our health – and as far as anything else is concerned, we'll leave it up to you. Thank you.'

'The comedy is wholly American, wholesome, homespun, human, appealing, and touching in turn.' – *Variety*

'Shangri-La in a frame house.' – *Otis Ferguson*

best picture; Frank Capra

Robert Riskin; Joseph Walker; Spring Byington; Gene Havlik

You Can't Take Money: see *Internes Can't Take Money*

'It's bedlam in Islam!'
You Can't Win 'em All
GB 1970 99m Technicolor Panavision
Columbia/SRO (Gene Corman)
In 1922, two rival American mercenaries have adventures in the Mediterranean.
Hectic, overplotted comedy actioner.
w Leo V. Gordon *d* Peter Collinson *ph* Ken Higgins *m* Bert Kaempfert
☆ Tony Curtis, Charles Bronson, Michèle Mercier, Grégoire Aslan, Patrick Magee

You Don't Need Pajamas at Rosie's: see *The First Time*

You Gotta Stay Happy
US 1948 100m bw
Universal (Karl Tunberg)
A runaway heiress joins cargo pilots on a transcontinental hop with some very queer passengers.
Ho-hum imitation of a Capra comedy; the effort shows.
w Karl Tunberg *story* Robert Carson *d* H. C. Potter *ph* Russell Metty *m* Daniele Amfitheatrof
☆ Joan Fontaine, James Stewart, Eddie Albert, Roland Young, Willard Parker, Percy Kilbride, Porter Hall, Paul Cavanagh, Halliwell Hobbes

You Light Up My Life
US 1977 90m Technicolor
Columbia/Mondial International (Joseph Brooks)
A comedian's daughter tries for success as a composer and singer.
Commonplace showbiz schmaltz, ineptly presented.
wd Joseph Brooks *ph* Eric Saarinen *m* Joseph Brooks *m/ly* Joseph Brooks *pd* Tom Rasmussen *ed* Lynzee Klingman
☆ Didi Conn, Joe Silver, Michael Zaslow, Stephen Nathan, Melanie Mayron, Amy Letterman, Jerry Keller

'The movie is both amateurish and slick – it oozes heart. The scenes go on too long and there isn't enough in them.' – *Pauline Kael*

song 'You Light Up My Life' (*m/ly* Joseph Brooks)

You Live and Learn
GB 1937 80m bw
Warner
American night-club dancers are stranded in Paris and helped by a nitwit Englishman who turns out to be not what he seems.
Rather flat comedy which gets flatter as it goes along.
w Brock Williams, Tom Phipps *story* Norma Petterson *d* Arthur Woods
☆ Glenda Farrell, Claude Hulbert, Glen Alyn, John Carol, James Stephenson, George Galleon

You Made Me Love You
GB 1934 69m bw
British International
A temperamental heiress is tamed by an amorous songwriter.
Flimsy comedy with amusing moments.
w Frank Launder *story* Stanley Lupino *d* Monty Banks *ph* John Cox *md* Harry Acres *songs* Stanley Lupino, Noel Gay, Clifford Grey
☆ Thelma Todd, Stanley Lupino, John Loder, James Carew, Gerald Rawlinson

You, Me & Marley **
GB 1992 90m colour
BBC
Three friends on a West Belfast estate persist in joy-riding in stolen cars to the annoyance of residents and the IRA.
Excellent drama, tough and authentic in feeling, which deals on a small scale with the complexities of the Irish situation.
w Graham Reid *story* Richard Spence *d* Graham Veevers *m* Stephen Warbeck *pd* David Wilson *ed* Greg Miller
☆ Marc O'Shea, Bronagh Gallagher, Michael Liebmann, Michael Gregory, Emma Moylan, Marie Jones, Frank Grimes
† The film was made for TV, but was shown at the 1992 Edinburgh Film Festival, where it won an award.

You Must Be Joking *
GB 1965 100m bw
Columbia/Ameran (Charles H. Schneer)
Assorted army personnel vie in an extended initiative test.
Slam-bang location comedy with more hits than misses: cheerful entertainment.
w Alan Hackney *d* Michael Winner *ph* Geoffrey Unsworth *m* Laurie Johnson
☆ Terry-Thomas, Lionel Jeffries, Michael Callan, Gabriella Licudi, *Denholm Elliott*, Lee Montague, Bernard Cribbins, Wilfrid Hyde-White, James Robertson Justice, Richard Wattis, James Villiers

You Never Can Tell *
US 1951 78m bw
U-I (Leonard Goldstein)
GB title: *You Never Know*
An Alsatian dog is murdered and is sent back from heaven in the guise of a private detective to expose his killer.
Self-confidently outrageous comedy fantasy in the wake of Here Comes Mr Jordan; *not badly done if you accept the premise.*
w Lou Breslow, David Chandler *d* Lou Breslow *ph* Maury Gertsman *m* Hans Salter
☆ Dick Powell, Peggy Dow, Charles Drake, Joyce Holden, Albert Sharpe, Sara Taft

You Never Know: see *You Never Can Tell*

'Living, loving – as though any moment a vengeful world might tear her from his arms!'
You Only Live Once **
US 1937 85m bw
Walter Wanger
A petty crook framed for murder breaks out of prison and tries to escape to Canada with his wife.
Gloomy melodrama partly based on Bonnie and Clyde and incorporating a plea for justice; very well made and acted.
w Graham Baker *story* Gene Towne *d Fritz Lang ph* Leon Shamroy *m* Alfred Newman
☆ Sylvia Sidney, Henry Fonda, Barton MacLane, Jean Dixon, William Gargan, Jerome Cowan, Chic Sale, Margaret Hamilton, Warren Hymer

'Crack blend of spectacular drama and romance ... good direction, strong scripting and an arresting production.' – *Variety*

'Again and again in this film we find what can only be described as camera style, the use of the pictorial image to narrate with the maximum of emotional impact.' – *Dilys Powell*

You Only Live Twice **
GB 1967 117m Technicolor Panavision
UA/Eon (Harry Saltzman, Albert R. Broccoli)
James Bond goes to Japan.
The Bond saga at its most expensive and expansive, full of local colour and in-jokes, with an enormously impressive set for the climactic action.
w Roald Dahl *novel* Ian Fleming *d Lewis Gilbert ph* Freddie Young, Bob Huke *m* John Barry *pd Ken Adam*
☆ Sean Connery, Tetsuro Tamba, Akiko Wakabayashi, Mie Hama, Karin Dor, Bernard Lee, Lois Maxwell, Desmond Llewelyn, *Charles Gray, Donald Pleasence*

You Pay Your Money
GB 1957 67m bw
Butcher's (W. G. Chalmers)
Investigating the shady girlfriend of his boss, a man and his wife uncover an Arab plot to dominate the world.
Mundane low-budget thriller with a narrative that is a little different, but hampered by routine direction and acting.
w Michael Cronin *novel* Michael Cronin *d* MacLean Rogers *ph* James Harvey *md* Wilfred Burns *ad* Bill Bennison *ed* Ben Hipkins
☆ Hugh McDermott, Jane Hylton, Honor Blackman, Hugh Moxey, Ivan Samson, Ferdy Mayne, Shirley Deane, Gerard Heinz

You Said a Mouthful
US 1932 75m bw
Warner
The inventor of an unsinkable bathing suit is mistaken for a champion swimmer.
Tepid star comedy.
w Robert Lord and Bolton Mallory *d* Lloyd Bacon
☆ Joe E. Brown, Ginger Rogers, Sheila Terry, Guinn Williams, Oscar Apfel

'You Talkin' to Me?'
US 1987 97m colour
UA/Second Generation (Michael Polaire)
A New York actor, obsessed with De Niro's performance in *Taxi Driver*, goes to Hollywood in search of fame and finds it working for a producer of right-wing and fundamentalist films.
An attempt to combine a semi-satirical drama about ambition and the laid-back ways of California with an attack on racism; it is moderately engaging but lacks coherence.
wd Charles Winkler *ph* Paul Ryan *m* Joel McNeely *ad* Alexandra Kicenik *ed* David Handman
☆ Jim Youngs, Faith Ford, Mykel T. Williamson, Bess Motta, Alan King, James Noble

You Were Meant for Me
US 1948 92m bw
TCF (Fred Kohlmar)
A small-town girl marries a bandleader.
Mildly pleasing, muted, musical romance, with good twenties atmosphere.
w Elick Moll, Valentine Davies *d* Lloyd Bacon *ph* Victor Milner *m/ly* various *md* Lionel Newman
☆ Jeanne Crain, Dan Dailey, Oscar Levant, Barbara Lawrence, Selena Royle, Percy Kilbride, Herbert Anderson

You Were Never Lovelier *
US 1942 97m bw
Columbia (Louis F. Edelman)
An Argentinian hotel tycoon tries to interest his daughter in marriage by creating a mysterious admirer.
Pleasing musical, a follow-up for the stars of You'll Never Get Rich.
w Michael Fessier, Ernest Pagano, Delmer Daves *d* William A. Seiter *ph* Ted Tetzlaff *m* Leigh Harline *m/ly* Jerome Kern, Johnny Mercer
☆ Fred Astaire, Rita Hayworth, Adolphe Menjou, Leslie Brooks, Adele Mara, Isobel Elsom, Gus Schilling, Xavier Cugat and his Orchestra, Larry Parks
† Rita Hayworth's singing was dubbed by Nan Wynn.

Leigh Harline; song 'Dearly Beloved'

You Will Remember
GB 1940 86m bw
Jack Raymond Productions
The life of the late Victorian songwriter Leslie Stuart.
Pleasant, rather surprising, minor British biopic.
w Lydia Hayward *d* Jack Raymond *ph* Henry Harris *md* Percival Mackay
☆ Robert Morley, Emlyn Williams, Dorothy Hyson, Tom E. Finglass, Nicholas Phipps, Allan Jeayes

You'll Find Out *
US 1940 97m bw
RKO (David Butler)

Kay Kyser's band is hired to play for a 21st birthday party at a gloomy mansion; they help save the life of the girl concerned.
Cheerful if slow-starting spooky house send-up with a splendid trio of villains.
w James V. Kern, David Butler *d* David Butler *ph* Frank Redman *m* Roy Webb *m/ly* Jimmy McHugh, Johnny Mercer
☆ Kay Kyser, Boris Karloff, Peter Lorre, Bela Lugosi, Dennis O'Keefe, Ginny Simms, Helen Parrish, Alma Kruger, Ish Kabibble
'Generates a fast pace that carries proceedings along in zestful tempo through a maze of humorous and chiller complications.' – *Variety*
song 'I'd Know You Anywhere'

You'll Like My Mother
US 1972 92m Technicolor
Universal/Bing Crosby Productions (Mort Briskin)
Pregnant widow visits neurotic mother-in-law in a snowbound mansion.
Predictable frightened lady shocker aiming somewhere between Psycho *and* Fanatic; *of strictly routine interest.*
w Jo Heims *novel* Naomi Hintze *d* Lamont Johnson *ph* Jack Marta *m* Gil Melle
☆ Rosemary Murphy, Patty Duke, Richard Thomas, Sian Barbara Allen

You'll Never Get Rich *
US 1941 88m bw
Columbia (Sam Bischoff)

A Broadway dance director helps his philandering producer by taking a romantically-inclined showgirl off his hands.
Smart comedy-musical which set its female lead as a top star.
w Michael Fessier, Ernest Pagano *d* Sidney Lanfield *ph* Philip Tannura *m* Morris Stoloff *m/ly* Cole Porter *ch* Robert Alton
☆ *Fred Astaire, Rita Hayworth*, Robert Benchley, John Hubbard, Osa Massen, Frieda Inescort, Guinn Williams, Donald MacBride
Morris Stoloff; song 'Since I Kissed My Baby Goodbye'

Young America
US 1932 74m bw
Fox
GB title: *We Humans*
Two young boys get into trouble with the law.
Dog-eared domestic flagwaver.
w William Conselman *play* John Frederick Ballard *d* Frank Borzage *ph* George Schneiderman *md* George Lipschultz
☆ Spencer Tracy, Doris Kenyon, Tommy Conlon, Ralph Bellamy, Beryl Mercer, Sarah Padden
'Hokey propaganda for juvenile courts. Not for smart houses and doubtful elsewhere unless there is a preponderance of mothers.' – *Variety*

'American Drug Wars Come To Britain ... And It Takes A Special Cop To Infiltrate Their World Of Violence.'
The Young Americans *
GB 1993 103m Rank Colour Panavision
Rank/Polygram/Live Entertainment (Paul Trijbits)

An American cop comes to London to help local police investigate drug-related killings.
Loud, frenetic attempt to make an English imitation of an American gangster movie; it is partially successful, though the more it resembles an American film, the more it becomes a lurid fantasy.
wd Danny Cannon, David Hilton *d* Danny Cannon *ph* Vernon Layton *m* David Arnold *pd* Laurence Dorman *ed* Alex Mackie
☆ Harvey Keitel, Iain Glen, John Wood, Terence Rigby, Keith Allen, Craig Kelly, Thandie Newton, Viggo Mortensen
'A high-octane, in-your-face cop thriller that's got everything going for it except a well-rounded script.' – *Variety*

Young and Eager: see *Claudelle Inglish*

Young and Innocent ***
GB 1937 80m bw
GFD/Gainsborough (Edward Black)

US title: *A Girl Was Young*
A girl goes on the run with her boyfriend when he is suspected of murder.
Pleasant, unassuming chase melodrama with a rather weak cast but plenty of its director's touches.
w Charles Bennett, Alma Reville *novel A Shilling for Candles* by Josephine Tey *d Alfred Hitchcock* *ph* Bernard Knowles *m* Louis Levy
☆ Nova Pilbeam, Derrick de Marney, Mary Clare, Edward Rigby, Basil Radford, George Curzon, Percy Marmont, John Longden
'I like it best of all his pictures. It may not be, academically speaking, the cleverest. The adepts who go to a Hitchcock film to grub out bits of montage may be disappointed.' – C. A. Lejeune

The Young and the Damned: see *Los Olvidados*

Young and Willing
US 1942 83m bw
UA (made by Paramount) (Edward H. Griffith)

Impecunious actors in a New York boarding house hit on a great play.
Very mild, innocuous comedy which passed quickly from the public memory.
w Virginia Van Upp *play* Francis Swann *d* Edward H. Griffith *ph* Leo Tover *m* Victor Young
☆ William Holden, Susan Hayward, Eddie Bracken, Robert Benchley, Martha O'Driscoll, Barbara Britton, James Brown, Mabel Paige

Young and Willing: see *The Wild and the Willing (1962)*

Young as You Feel *
US 1931 78m bw
Fox
In order to reform his family a father pretends to be as irresponsible as they are.
Medium star vehicle.
w Edwin Burke *play Father and the Boys* by George Ade *d* Frank Borzage
☆ Will Rogers, Fifi D'Orsay, Lucien Littlefield, Donald Dillaway
'Looks fair b.o. due to star.' – *Variety*

Young at Heart **
US 1954 117m Warnercolor
Warner/Arwin (Henry Blanke)

The daughters of a small-town music teacher have romantic problems.
Softened, musicalized remake of Four Daughters *(qv), an old-fashioned treat with roses round the door and a high standard of proficiency in all departments.*
w Julius J. Epstein, Lenore Coffee *novel* Fannie Hurst *d* Gordon Douglas *ph* Ted McCord *md* Ray Heindorf
☆ *Doris Day, Frank Sinatra, Ethel Barrymore*, Gig Young, Dorothy Malone, Robert Keith, Elisabeth Fraser, Alan Hale Jnr

Young Bess *
US 1953 112m Technicolor
MGM (Sidney Franklin)
The early years of Elizabeth I and her romance with Tom Seymour.
Historical fiction, wildly unreliable as to fact and dramatically not very rewarding. The character actors have the best of it.
w Arthur Wimperis, Jan Lustig *novel* Margaret Irwin *d* George Sidney *ph* Charles Rosher *m* Miklos Rozsa *ad* Cedric Gibbons, Urie McCleary
☆ Jean Simmons, Stewart Granger, Charles Laughton (Henry VIII), Kay Walsh, Deborah Kerr, Guy Rolfe, Kathleen Byron, Cecil Kellaway, Robert Arthur, Leo G. Carroll, Elaine Stewart, Dawn Addams, Rex Thompson
art direction

Young Billy Young
US 1969 89m DeLuxe
UA/Talbot-Youngstein (Max Youngstein)

A young Western gunman is helped out of scrapes by a mysterious stranger bent on revenge.
Good-looking but rather ineffective Western which throws away good production values.
wd Burt Kennedy *novel Who Rides with Wyatt* by Will Henry *ph* Harry Stradling Jnr *m* Shelly Manne
☆ Robert Mitchum, Angie Dickinson, Robert Walker Jnr, David Carradine, John Anderson, Paul Fix

Young Cassidy *
GB 1964 110m Technicolor
MGM/Sextant (Robert D. Graff, Robert Emmett Ginna)
A romantic view of the early Dublin life of writer Sean O'Casey.
Ambling, unconvincing but generally interesting picture of a past time.
w John Whiting, from the writings of Sean O'Casey *d* Jack Cardiff, John Ford *ph* Ted Scaife *m* Sean O'Riada
☆ Rod Taylor, Maggie Smith, Edith Evans, Flora Robson, Michael Redgrave, Julie Christie, Jack MacGowran, Sian Phillips, T. P. McKenna

Young Dillinger
US 1964 102m bw
Alfred Zimbalist

An embittered young convict becomes Public Enemy Number One.
Fantasized forgettable biopic with violent moments.
w Arthur Hoerl, Don Zimbalist *d* Terry Morse *ph* Stanley Cortez *m* Shorty Rogers
☆ Nick Adams, John Ashley, Robert Conrad, Mary Ann Mobley, Victor Buono, John Hoyt, Reed Hadley

The Young Doctors *
US 1961 102m bw
UA/Drexel/Stuart Millar/Laurence Turman
Old Dr Pearson resents his modern young assistant and almost causes a tragedy.
Routine medical melo of the Kildare/Gillespie kind, given a Grade A production and cast.
w Joseph Hayes *novel The Final Diagnosis* by Arthur Hailey *d* Phil Karlson *ph* Arthur J. Ornitz *m* Elmer Bernstein
☆ *Fredric March*, Ben Gazzara, Dick Clark, Eddie Albert, Ina Balin, Aline MacMahon, Edward Andrews, Arthur Hill, George Segal, Rosemary Murphy

Young Doctors in Love
US 1982 95m Metrocolor
TCF/ABC (Jerry Bruckheimer)

Goings-on in a modern hospital.
Spoof soap opera in the wake of Airplane *but seeming more like a flat edition of* Carry On.
w Michael Elias, Rich Eustis *d* Garry Marshall *ph* Don Peterman *m* Maurice Jarre
☆ Michael McKean, Sean Young, Harry Dean Stanton, Patrick Macnee, Hector Elizondo, Dabney Coleman

Young Eagles *
US 1930 71m bw
Paramount
The adventures of American aviators in World War I.
Spirited early sound actioner.
w William McNutt, Grover Jones *d* William Wellman *ph* Archie Stout
☆ Charles Rogers, Jean Arthur, Paul Lukas, Stuart Erwin, Virginia Bruce, James Finlayson
'Pint-sized version of *Wings*. Comedy and production almost square silly plot.' – *Variety*

Young Einstein
Australia 1988 91m colour
Warner/Serious Productions (Yahoo Serious, Warwick Ross, David Roach)

Einstein discovers the theory of relativity, falls in love with Marie Curie, and then invents the surfboard, the electric guitar and rock 'n' roll.
A smash-hit in its native land, it is a ramshackle, slapstick comedy that, relatively speaking, does not travel well.
w Yahoo Serious, David Roach *d* Yahoo Serious *ph* Jeff Darling *m* William Motzing, Martin Armiger, Tommy Tycho *ad* Steve Marr, Laurie Faen, Colin Gibson, Ron Highfield *ed* Yahoo Serious
☆ Yahoo Serious, Odile Le Clezio, John Howard, Peewee Wilson, Su Cruikshank
'A film which manages to be innocuous and appalling at the same time.' – *MFB*

Young Frankenstein ***
US 1974 108m bw
TCF/Gruskoff/Venture/Jouer/Crossbow (Michael Gruskoff)

Young Frederick Frankenstein, a brain surgeon, goes back to Transylvania and pores over his grandfather's notebooks.
The most successful of Mel Brooks's parodies, Mad Magazine *style; the gleamingly reminiscent photography is the best of it, the script being far from consistently funny, but there are splendid moments.*
w Gene Wilder, Mel Brooks *d* Mel Brooks *ph Gerald Hirschfeld* *m* John Morris *ad Dale Hennesy*
☆ Gene Wilder, Marty Feldman, Madeline Kahn, *Peter Boyle*, Cloris Leachman, Kenneth Mars, Gene Hackman, Richard Haydn, Teri Garr
'Like a sketch from the old Sid Caesar show, for which Brooks wrote, spun out ten times as long. Ten times too long. Brooks is a sprinter, and there aren't enough good sprints here.' – *Stanley Kauffmann*
script

Young Giants
US 1983 97m DeLuxe Panavision
Entertainment Enterprises (Tom Moyer, Megan Moyer)
A San Diego priest helps a boys' home by re-organizing a football team so that an old priest can die happy.
Shades of Going My Way, *but somewhat ineptly done, with a guest appearance from Pele as* deus ex machina.
w Tom Moyer, Terrill Tannen, Mike Lammers *d* Terrill Tannen *ph* Raoul Lomas *m* Rick Patterson *ad* Daniel R. Webster *ed* Denine Rowan, Marion W. Cronin, Daniel Gross
☆ Peter Fox, John Huston, Lisa Wills, F. William Parker, Severn Darden
'At least it has the courage of its throwback convictions.' – *Kim Newman, MFB*

The Young Girls of Rochefort
France 1967 126m Eastmancolor
Franscope
Parc Film//Madeleine/Seven Arts (Mag Bodard, Gilbert de Goldschmidt)

original title: *Les Demoiselles de Rochefort*
Two country girls join a travelling dancing troupe, and find love on the day of the fair.
Flat, empty tribute to the Hollywood musical, which never inspires despite the presence of one of its greatest stars.
wd Jacques Demy *ph* Ghislain Cloquet *m* Michel Legrand
☆ Catherine Deneuve, Françoise Dorléac, George Chakiris, Gene Kelly, Danielle Darrieux, Grover Dale, Michel Piccoli
Michel Legrand

Young Guns
US 1988 107m DeLuxe
Vestron/Morgan Creek Productions (Joe Roth, Christopher Cain)

Billy Bonney joins a group of young ranch hands and they are quickly transformed into Billy the Kid and a gang of outlaws.
Teenage Western, with a background authenticity that does not extend to the characterization.
w John Fusco *d* Christopher Cain *ph* Dean Semler *m* Anthony Marinelli, Brian Banks *pd* Jane Musky *ed* Jack Hofstra
☆ Emilio Estevez, Kiefer Sutherland, Lou Diamond Phillips, Charlie Sheen, Dermot Mulroney, Casey Siemaszko, Terence Stamp, Jack Palance, Patrick Wayne

Young Guns II
US 1990 103m DeLuxe
Fox/Morgan Creek (Paul Schiff, Irby Smith)

Billy the Kid and his gang, on the run from justice, face death as they begin to squabble among themselves.

Continuing from where the first film ended, it provides a similar modern treatment of its youthful anti-heroes.
w John Fusco *d* Geoff Murphy *ph* Dean Semler *m* Alan Silvestri *m/ly* Jon Bon Jovi *pd* Gene Rudolph *ad* Christa Munro *ed* Bruce Green
☆ Emilio Estevez, Kiefer Sutherland, Lou Diamond Phillips, Christian Slater, William Petersen, Alan Ruck, R. D. Call, James Coburn, Balthazar Getty, Jack Kehoe
song 'Blaze of Glory' (m/l Jon Bon Jovi)

Young Guns of Texas
US 1962 78m DeLuxe Cinemascope
TCF (Maury Dexter)
An Easterner, accompanied by two cowboys and a runaway heiress, rides into Indian territory in search of stolen gold.
Dull, routine Western featuring the untalented offspring of the famous.
w Henry Cross *d* Maury Dexter *ph* John Nickolaus Jnr *m* Paul Sawtell, Bert Shefter *ed* Jodie Copelan, Richard Einfeld
☆ James Mitchum, Alana Ladd, Jody McCrea, Chill Wills, Gary Conway, Barbara Mansell, Robert Lowery

Young Ideas
US 1943 75m bw
MGM (Robert Sisk)
The proposed marriage of two academics is interrupted by the protests of their children.
Predictable light concoction with practised players.
w Ian McLellan Hunter, Bill Noble *d* Jules Dassin
☆ Mary Astor, Herbert Marshall, Susan Peters, Elliott Reid, Richard Carlson, Allyn Joslyn

The Young in Heart ***
US 1938 91m bw
David O. Selznick
A family of charming confidence tricksters move in on a rich old lady but she brings out the best in them.
Delightful, roguish romantic comedy, perfectly cast and pacily handled.
w Paul Osborn, Charles Bennett novel The Gay Banditti by I. A. R. Wylie *d Richard Wallace* *ph* Leon Shamroy *m* Franz Waxman
☆ *Douglas Fairbanks Jnr, Janet Gaynor, Roland Young, Billie Burke, Minnie Dupree*, Paulette Goddard, Richard Carlson, Henry Stephenson
'Sentimental drama, vastly touching and entertaining ... has everything to ensure box office success.' – *Variety*
'It comes as a gentle breeze in the hurricane of hurly burly comedies that have hurtled across the screen of late.' – *Motion Picture Herald*
Leon Shamroy; Franz Waxman

The Young Invaders: see *Darby's Rangers*

The Young Land
US 1957 89m Technicolor
Columbia/C. V. Whitney (Patrick Ford)
A young sheriff arrests a gunman and after the trial has to save him from lynching.
Rather stiff attempt at a youth Western.
w Norman Shannon Hall *d* Ted Tetzlaff *ph* Winton C. Hoch, Henry Sharp *m* Dimitri Tiomkin
☆ Dan O'Herlihy, Patrick Wayne, Yvonne Craig, Dennis Hopper
song 'Strange Are the Ways of Love' (mDimitri Tiomkin, lyNed Washington)

The Young Lions **
US 1958 167m bw Cinemascope
TCF (Al Lichtman)
World War II adventures of two Americans and a German skiing instructor.
Three strands are loosely interwoven into a would-be modern epic; the result is well mounted and generally absorbing but uneven and decidedly overlong.
w Edward Anhalt *novel* Irwin Shaw *d* Edward Dmytryk *ph* Joe MacDonald *m* Hugo Friedhofer
☆ Marlon Brando, Montgomery Clift, Dean Martin, Hope Lange, Barbara Rush, May Britt, Maximilian Schell, Lee Van Cleef
'Episodic and overproduced, like a wartime Grand Hotel.' – *Pauline Kael, 70s*
Joe MacDonald; Hugo Friedhofer

The Young Lovers *
GB 1954 96m bw
GFD/Group Films (Anthony Havelock-Allan)
US title: *Chance Meeting*
A US Embassy man in London falls in love with the daughter of an Iron Curtain minister.
Romeo and Juliet, cold war style, quite nicely put together with a thriller climax.
w Robin Estridge *story* George Tabori *d* Anthony Asquith *ph* Jack Asher *m* Tchaikovsky
☆ Odile Versois, David Knight, David Kossoff, Joseph Tomelty, Paul Carpenter, Theodore Bikel, Jill Adams
David Kossoff (newcomer); Robin Estridge, George Tabori

Young Man of Music: see *Young Man with a Horn*

'Put down your trumpet, jazz man – I'm in the mood for love'
Young Man with a Horn *
US 1950 112m bw
Warner (Jerry Wald)
GB title: *Young Man of Music*
The professional and romantic tribulations of a trumpet player.
Overwrought character melodrama based on the life of Bix Beiderbecke; quite absorbing though occasionally risible.
w Carl Foreman, Edmund H. North *novel* Dorothy Baker *d* Michael Curtiz *ph* Ted McCord *md* Ray Heindorf (trumpet dubbed by Harry James)
☆ *Kirk Douglas, Lauren Bacall*, Doris Day, Hoagy Carmichael, Juano Hernandez, Jerome Cowan, Mary Beth Hughes, Nestor Paiva

Young Man with Ideas *
US 1952 84m bw
MGM (Gottfried Reinhardt, William H. Wright)
A small-town lawyer tries to better himself in Los Angeles.
Modestly likeable comedy which doesn't add up to much.
w Arthur Sheekman *d* Mitchell Leisen *ph* Joseph Ruttenberg *m* David Rose
☆ Glenn Ford, Ruth Roman, Nina Foch, Denise Darcel, Donna Corcoran, Mary Wickes, Sheldon Leonard

Young Man's Fancy
GB 1939 77m bw
Ealing
A young Victorian lord avoids an unsuitable match by eloping to Paris.
Rather pallid romantic comedy with likeable period detail.
w Roland Pertwee, Rodney Ackland, E. V. H. Emmett *d* Robert Stevenson
☆ Griffith Jones, Anna Lee, Seymour Hicks, Billy Bennett, Edward Rigby, Francis L. Sullivan

The Young Master
Hong Kong 1980 101m colour
Golden Harvest (Leonard Ho)
original title: *Shidi Chuma*
The adventures of a student in a school for martial arts, searching for a friend who betrayed their master.
An episodic movie with the emphasis on comedy, one of Chan's earliest movies as actor-director in which he is still developing his screen persona.
w Lau Tin Chee, Tung Lu, Edward Tang *d* Jackie Chan *ph* Cheng Hui-Jan, Tsai Hua *m* Ryudo Uzaki, Akira Inoue, Gustav Holst *ed* Peter Cheung
☆ Jackie Chan (Dragon), Yuen Biao (Sang Kung's son), Wei Pai (Tiger), Lily Li (Sang Kung's daughter), Whong In Sik (Kam), Shek Kin (aka Shieh Kien) (Sang Kung), Tiang Feng (Master)

'The Story Of Abraham Lincoln That Has Never Been Told!'
'His thrilling, exciting, romantic youth ... wrestling, fighting, telling funny stories, falling in love! A picture stirring with its drama, romance, action, emotion!'
Young Mr Lincoln ***
US 1939 100m bw
TCF (Kenneth MacGowan)
Abraham Lincoln as a young country lawyer stops a lynching and proves a young man innocent of murder.
Splendid performances and period atmosphere are rather nipped in the bud by second-feature courtroom twists, but this is a marvellous old-fashioned entertainment with its heart in the right place.
w Lamar Trotti *d* John Ford *ph* Bert Glennon *m* Alfred Newman
☆ *Henry Fonda, Alice Brady, Marjorie Weaver*, Arleen Whelan, Eddie Collins, Richard Cromwell, Donald Meek, Eddie Quillan, Spencer Charters
'A dignified saga of early Lincolniana, paced rather slowly ... lack of romance interest is one of the prime factors which deter the film from interpreting itself into big box office.' – *Variety*
'Its simple good faith and understanding are an expression of the country's best life that says as much as forty epics.' – *Otis Ferguson*
'Period details are lovingly sketched in – a log splitting contest, a tug of war, a tar barrel rolling match...' – *Charles Higham*
'Its source is a womb of popular and national spirit. This could account for its unity, its artistry, its genuine beauty.' – *Sergei Eisenstein*
'A film which indisputably has the right to be called Americana.' – *New York Times*
'In spite of the excitements of a murder, a near-lynching and a crackerjack trial, it remains a character study.' – *New York Sun*
'One of John Ford's most memorable films.' – *Pauline Kael, 70s*
Lamar Trotti

The Young Mr Pitt *
GB 1942 118m bw
TCF (Edward Black)
Britain's youngest prime minister quells the threat of invasion by Napoleon.
Shapeless and overlong but generally diverting historical pastiche timed as wartime propaganda against Hitler.
w Frank Launder, Sidney Gilliat *d* Carol Reed *ph* Frederick A. Young *m* Charles Williams *ad* Vetchinsky
☆ *Robert Donat*, Robert Morley, Phyllis Calvert, John Mills, Raymond Lovell, Max Adrian, Felix Aylmer, Albert Lieven

The Young Ones *
GB 1961 108m Technicolor Cinemascope
ABP (Kenneth Harper)
US title: *Wonderful to be Young*
The son of a tycoon starts a youth club and puts on a musical to raise funds.
A shopworn idea is the springboard for a brave try in a field where Britain was presumed to have failed; despite the enthusiasm with which it was greeted at the time, it has dated badly.
w Peter Myers, Ronald Cass *d* Sidney J. Furie *ph* Douglas Slocombe *m* Stanley Black
☆ *Cliff Richard*, Robert Morley, Carole Grey, Richard O'Sullivan, Melvyn Hayes, Gerald Harper, Robertson Hare

Young People
US 1940 78m bw
TCF (Harry Joe Brown)
Vaudevillians retire to give their daughter a proper upbringing, but find that showbiz is in her blood.
Pleasant but unremarkable comedy-drama with music, marking the end of its star's association with the studio.
w Edwin Blum, Don Ettlinger *d* Allan Dwan *ph* Edward Cronjager *md* Alfred Newman
☆ Shirley Temple, Jack Oakie, Charlotte Greenwood, Arleen Whelan, George Montgomery, Kathleen Howard, Mae Marsh

The Young Philadelphians *
US 1959 136m bw
Warner (producer not credited)
GB title: *The City Jungle*
A forceful young lawyer pushes his way to the top of the snobbish Philadelphia heap despite threats to expose his illegitimacy.
Novel on film, gleamingly done and acted with assurance.
w James Gunn *novel* The Philadelphian by Richard Powell *d* Vincent Sherman *ph* Harry Stradling *m* Ernest Gold
☆ Paul Newman, Barbara Rush, Alexis Smith, Brian Keith, Billie Burke, John Williams, Otto Kruger, Diane Brewster, Robert Vaughn, Paul Picerni, Robert Douglas
Harry Stradling; Robert Vaughn

'Nothing's More Deadly Than A Poisoned Mind'
The Young Poisoner's Handbook *
GB/Germany 1995 106m Metrocolor
Electric/Mass/Kinowelt/Haut et Court (Sam Taylor)
A boy obsessed with the power of poisons tries them out on his stepmother and uncle, and is sent to a hospital for the criminally insane, where he is eventually declared cured and released, whereupon he begins poisoning people once more.
A gruesome little tale, approached in a style of black comedy peopled by caricatures; like its hero's concoctions, the result is not always palatable, despite the considerable skills on show.
w Jeff Rawle, Benjamin Ross *d* Benjamin Ross *ph* Herbert Taczanowski *m* Robert Lane, Frankie Strobel *pd* Maria Djorkovic *ed* Anne Sopel
☆ Hugh O'Conor, Anthony Sher, Ruth Sheen, Roger Lloyd Pack, Charlotte Coleman, Paul Stacey, Samantha Edmonds
'Will appeal to younger audiences internationally who like their entertainment rude and impudent.' – *Variety*
† The film was based on the life of Graham Young, known as 'The St Albans Poisoner', who was sent to Broadmoor in 1962 at the age of 14 for giving poison to his father, sister and a friend. He was released as 'no longer a danger' in 1971, when he killed two people with poison and damaged six more. He died in prison in 1990.

The Young Rebel: see *Cervantes*

The Young Savages *
US 1961 103m bw
UA/Contemporary (Pat Duggan)
An assistant DA prosecutes three hoodlums for murder but begins to feel that one is not guilty.
Tough, realistic melodrama of the New York slums, with roughhouse climaxes and a political conscience.
w Edward Anhalt, J. P. Miller *novel* A Matter of Conviction by Evan Hunter *d John Frankenheimer* *ph* Lionel Lindon *m* David Amram
☆ Burt Lancaster, Shelley Winters, John Davis Chandler, Dina Merrill, Edward Andrews, Telly Savalas

Young Scarface: see *Brighton Rock*

Young Sherlock Holmes
US 1985 109m Technicolor
Paramount/Amblin (Mark Johnson)
GB title: *Young Sherlock Holmes and the Pyramid of Fear*
Holmes and Watson meet as teenage students, and trace some mysterious murders to an eastern cult.
More expensive gimmickry with acres of tedium in between the technical highlights. Nothing for Holmes buffs.
w Chris Columbus *d* Barry Levinson *ph* Stephen Goldblatt *m* Bruce Broughton *pd* Norman Reynolds *ed* Stu Linder
☆ Nicholas Rowe, Alan Cox, Sophie Ward, Anthony Higgins, Freddie Jones, Nigel Stock
'Another Steven Spielberg version of those lamps made from driftwood and coffee tables from redwood burl. It's not art but they all serve their purpose and sell by millions.' – *Variety*
(This one was a box-office disappointment.)
visual effects

Young Soul Rebels ☆
GB 1991 105m colour
BFI/Film Four/Sankofa/La Sept/Kinowelt/Iberoamericana (Nadine Marsh-Edwards)
In the mid-1970s, two pirate radio disc jockeys specializing in soul music solve the murder of a friend.
Examining black and gay culture in Britain, the movie tries to pack in too much, losing focus as a result.
w Paul Hallam, Derrick Saldaan McClintock, Isaac Julien *d* Isaac Julien *ph* Nina Kellgren *m* Simon Boswell *pd* Derek Brown *ed* John Wilson
☆ Valentine Nonyela, Mo Sesay, Dorian Healy, Frances Barber, Sophie Okonedo, Jason Durr, Gary McDonald, Debra Gillet
'It ultimately suffers from trying to say too many things too fast to too many people, the penalty, one suspects, from working in a British film industry where your first film so easily doubles up as your last.' – *Empire*

'Seventeen Isn't An Age... It's An Eternity.'
The Young Stranger ☆
US 1957 84m bw
RKO (Stuart Millar)
The 16-year-old son of a film executive gets into trouble with the police.
Reasonably stimulating film of a TV play about the kind of causeless rebel who quickly became a cliché.
w Robert Dozier *d* John Frankenheimer *ph* Robert Planck *m* Leonard Rosenman
☆ James MacArthur, Kim Hunter, James Daly, James Gregory, Whit Bissell

Young Tom Edison ☆
US 1940 82m bw
MGM (John Considine Jnr)
First of a two-parter (see *Edison the Man*) tracing Edison's first experiments.
Reasonably factual and absorbing junior biopic.
w Bradbury Foote, Dore Schary, Hugo Butler *d* Norman Taurog *ph* Sidney Wagner *m* Edward Ward
☆ Mickey Rooney, Eugene Pallette, George Bancroft, Fay Bainter, Virginia Weidler, Victor Kilian, Lloyd Corrigan
'A picture for all of the people in all of the places.' – *Motion Picture Herald*

The Young Warriors
US 1967 93m Technicolor Panavision
Universal (Gordon Kay)
In the Second World War, a sergeant takes a fatherly interest in the young squad he leads into action.
Low budget, backlot shot, by the numbers B picture, featuring as the new recruits a cast of unknowns (most of whom were hardly heard of again).
w Richard Matheson *novel The Beardless Warriors* by Richard Matheson *d* John Peyser *ph* Loyal Griggs *ad* Alexander Golitzen, Alfred Ybarra *ed* Russell Schoengarth
☆ James Drury (Sgt Cooley), Steve Carlson (Hacker), Jonathan Daly (Guthrie), Robert Pine (Foley), Jeff Scott (Lippincott), Michael Stanwood (Riley), Johnny Alladin (Harris), Hank Jones (Fairchild), Tom Nolan (Tremont), Norman Fell (Sgt Wadley)

Young Warriors
US 1983 103m colour
Cannon
After the sister of one of them dies after being raped, high-school graduates set themselves up as vigilantes.
Dangerous rubbish.
w Lawrence D. Foldes, Russell W. Colgin *d* Lawrence D. Foldes *ph* Mac Ahlberg *m* Rob Walsh
☆ Ernest Borgnine, Richard Roundtree, Lynda Day George, James Van Patten, Anne Lockhart, Tom Reilly, Dick Shawn
'A lurid mishmash.' – *Jo Imeson, MFB*

Young Werther: see *Le Jeune Werther*

The Young Widow
US 1946 100m bw
UA/Hunt Stromberg
The widow of a World War II flyer returns to the Virginia farm where they had spent happy hours.
Glum sudser with talent all at sea.
w Richard Macaulay, Margaret Buell Wilder *novel* Clarissa Fairchild Cushman *d* Edwin L. Marin *ph* Lee Garmes *m* Carmen Dragon *pd* Nicolai Remisoff
☆ Jane Russell, Louis Hayward, Faith Domergue, Marie Wilson, Kent Taylor, Penny Singleton, Connie Gilchrist, Cora Witherspoon

Young, Willing and Eager: see *Rag Doll*

Young Winston ☆☆
GB 1972 157m Eastmancolor Panavision
Columbia/Open Road/Hugh French (Carl Foreman)
The adventurous life of Winston Churchill up to his becoming an MP.
Generally engaging if lumpy film which switches too frequently from action to family drama to politics to character study and is not helped by irritating directorial tricks.
w Carl Foreman *book My Early Life* by Winston Churchill *d* Richard Attenborough *ph* Gerry Turpin *m* Alfred Ralston *pd* Don Ashton, Geoffrey Drake
☆ *Simon Ward*, Robert Shaw, Anne Bancroft, Jack Hawkins, Ian Holm, *Anthony Hopkins*, John Mills, Patrick Magee, Edward Woodward
Carl Foreman

Young Wives' Tale
GB 1951 79m bw
ABPC
A playwright and his slaphappy wife share a house with a super-efficient couple.
Very mild but palatable comedy set 'at the wrong end of St John's Wood'.
w Anne Burnaby *play* Ronald Jeans *d* Henry Cass
☆ Joan Greenwood, Nigel Patrick, Derek Farr, Guy Middleton, Athene Seyler, Helen Cherry, Audrey Hepburn, Irene Handl

Young Woodley
GB 1929 79m bw
BIP
A schoolboy falls in love with his teacher's wife.
Modest early talkie version of a play thought mildly shocking at the time.
w John Van Druten, Victor Kendall *play* John Van Druten *d* Thomas Bentley *ph* Claude Friese-Greene
☆ Madeleine Carroll, Frank Lawton, Sam Livesey, Gerald Rawlinson, Billy Milton
† A silent version made earlier in the same year, with Marjorie Hume and Robin Irvine, was never released.

Youngblood
US 1986 109m Metrocolor
United Artists/Guber-Peters (Peter Bart, Patrick Wells)
Romances of a young hockey star, for those interested; it turned out that there weren't many.
wd Peter Markle *story* Peter Markle, Patrick Wells *ph* Mark Irwin *m* William Orbit *ad* Alicia Keywan *ed* Stephen E. Rivkin, Jack Hofstra
☆ Rob Lowe (Dean Youngblood), Cynthia Gibb (Jessie Chadwick), Patrick Swayze (Derek Sutton), Ed Lauter (Murray Chadwick), Eric Nesterenko (Blane Youngblood), Jim Youngs (Kelly Youngblood)
'It is doomed by its plot, which is yet another example of what I like to call the Climb from Despair to Victory (CLIDVIC, rhymes with Kid Pic).' – *Roger Ebert, Chicago Sun-Times*

Youngblood Hawke
US 1964 137m bw
Warner (Delmer Daves)
A Kentucky truck driver becomes a successful novelist and is spoiled by New York success.
Absurdly archetypal soap opera from a bestseller, spilling over with every imaginable cliché; some of its excesses are glossily entertaining.
wd Delmer Daves *novel* Herman Wouk *ph* Charles Lawton *m* Max Steiner
☆ James Franciscus, Genevieve Page, Suzanne Pleshette, Eva Gabor, *Mary Astor*, Lee Bowman, Edward Andrews, John Emery, Don Porter

Younger & Younger ☆
Germany/France/Canada 1994 99m colour
PelemeleKushner-LockeYounger (Eleanore Adlon)
A German immigrant, who runs a failing business in Hollywood, is haunted by the memory of his much more capable wife, who died as a result of his infidelity.
A middling comedy of a hapless man forced out of his fantasy world by guilt.
w Percy Adlon, Felix O. Adlon *d* Percy Adlon *ph* Bernd Heinl *m* Hans Zimmer *pd* Steven Legler *ed* Suzanne Fenn
☆ Donald Sutherland (Jonathan Younger), Lolita Davidovich (Penelope Younger), Brendan Fraser (Winston Younger), Sally Kellerman (Zig Zag Lilian), Julie Delpy (Melodie), Linda Hunt (Frances)

The Younger Brothers
US 1949 76m Technicolor
Warner (Saul Elkins)
A whitewashed version of the career of the legendary outlaws, who wind up expecting pardons; otherwise routine sagebrush stuff.
w Edna Anhalt *d* Edwin L. Marin *ph* William Snyder
☆ Wayne Morris, Janis Paige, Bruce Bennett, Geraldine Brooks, Robert Hutton, Alan Hale, Fred Clark

The Youngest Profession
US 1943 82m bw
MGM (B. F. Ziedman)
Teenage autograph hounds cause trouble at the MGM studio.
Innocuous comedy with guest stars.
w George Oppenheimer, Charles Lederer, Leonard Spigelgass *book* Lillian Day *d* Edward Buzzell *ph* Charles Lawton *m* David Snell
☆ Virginia Weidler, Jean Porter, Edward Arnold, John Carroll, Agnes Moorehead, Greer Garson, William Powell, Lana Turner, Walter Pidgeon, Robert Taylor

Your Beating Heart
France 1991 100m colour
Artifical Eye/Hachette Première/FR3/UGC/Avril (René Cleitman)
A middle-aged married actress begins an affair with a man she meets on the Paris Métro.
Glum story of an adulterous relationship that no one seems to enjoy, least of all an audience.
wd François Dupeyron *ph* Yves Angelo *ad* Carlos Conti *ed* Françoise Collin
☆ Dominique Faysse, Thierry Fortineau, Jean-Marie Winling, Steve Kalfa, Daniel Laloux, Christophe Pichon
'The miasma of doom lies over this gloomy film, remarkable for the unattractiveness of its main characters.' – *George Perry, Sunday Times*

'A Modern Immorality Tale.'
Your Friends & Neighbors ☆
US 1998 99m DeLuxe
Polygram/Propaganda/Fleece (Steve Golin, Jason Patric)
Three couples, whose love lives are unsatisfactory, seek partners elsewhere.
A misogynistic comedy of sexual manners, with smart dialogue compensating for the somewhat theatrical situations.
wd Neil LaBute *ph* Nancy Schreiber *m* Metallica, Apocalyptica *pd* Charles Breen *ed* Joel Plotch
☆ Amy Brenneman, Aaron Eckhart, Catherine Keener, Nastassja Kinski, Jason Patric, Ben Stiller
'Callow, nasty-minded movie.' – *Peter Matthews, Sight and Sound*

Your Money Or Your Wife
GB 1960 91m bw
Rank/Alliance (Norman Williams)
A couple with financial problems resort to letting rooms to lodgers, who turn out to be penniless.
Creaking farce, done without subtlety and resorting to crude slapstick in an attempt to amuse.
w Ronald Jeans *d* Anthony Simmons *ph* Brendan J. Stafford *m* Philip Green *ad* Tony Inglis *ed* Bernard Gribble
☆ Donald Sinden (Pelham Butterworth), Peggy Cummins (Gay Butterworth), Richard Wattis (Hubert Fry), Peter Reynolds (Theodore Malek), Georgina Cookson (Thelma Cressingdon), Gladys Boot (Mrs Compton-Chamberlain), Barbara Steele (Juliet Frost), Betty Baskcomb (Janet Fry), Olive Sloane (Mrs Withers), Ian Fleming (Judge)

Your Past Is Showing: see *The Naked Truth*

Your Three Minutes Are Up
US 1973 92m DeLuxe
Jerry Gershwin
An irresponsible, smooth-talking, penniless con man takes his respectable friend out on one last spree.
Dispiriting comedy of contrasting attitudes to life which plunges into bathos at the end.
w James Dixon *d* Douglas N. Schwartz *ph* Stephen M. Katz *m* Perry Botkin Jnr *ed* Aaron Stell
☆ Beau Bridges, Ron Leibman, Janet Margolin, Kathleen Freeman, David Ketchum, Stu Nisbet, Read Morgan

Your Witness ☆
GB 1950 100m bw
Warner/Coronado (Joan Harrison)
US title: *Eye Witness*
An American lawyer comes to an English village to defend a war buddy on a murder charge.
Interesting but ineffective blend of comedy and courtroom procedure intended to contrast English and American ways.
w Hugo Butler, Ian Hunter, William Douglas Home *d* Robert Montgomery *ph* Gerald Gibbs *m* Malcolm Arnold
☆ Robert Montgomery, Leslie Banks, Patricia Cutts, Felix Aylmer, Andrew Cruickshank, Harcourt Williams, Jenny Laird, Michael Ripper

You're a Big Boy Now ☆
US 1967 96m Eastmancolor
Warner Seven Arts (William Fadiman)
A young assistant librarian discovers girls.
Freewheeling semi-surrealist comedy with exhilarating moments and the inevitable letdowns associated with this kind of campy high style.
wd Francis Ford Coppola *novel* David Benedictus *ph* Andy Laszlo *m* Bob Prince
☆ Peter Kastner, Elizabeth Hartman, Geraldine Page, Julie Harris, Rip Torn, Tony Bill, Karen Black, Michael Dunn
'A half-kooky, half-sweetly-innocent comedy … which is wonderfully photogenic from a young director's point of view.' – *Judith Crist*
Geraldine Page

You're a Lucky Fellow, Mr Smith
US 1943 63m bw
Edward Lilley/Universal
A girl must marry quickly in order to secure her inheritance.
Very light musical support.
w Lawrence Riley, Ben Barzman, Louis Lantz *d* Felix Feist
☆ Allan Jones, Evelyn Ankers, Billie Burke, David Bruce, Patsy O'Connor, Stanley Clements

You're a Sweetheart
US 1937 96m bw
Universal (B. G. de Sylva)
A Broadway star suffers from her press agent's bright ideas.
Muffed musical with all concerned ill at ease with below par material.
w Monte Brice, Charles Grayson *d* David Butler *ph* George Robinson *md* Charles Previn *ad* Jack Otterson *songs* various
☆ Alice Faye, George Murphy, Ken Murray, William Gargan, Frances Hunt, Frank Jenks, Andy Devine, Charles Winninger, Donald Meek
'Just what the doctor ordered for the holiday first runs … enough entertainers for two shows.' – *Variety*

You're Darn Tootin' ☆☆☆
US 1929 20m bw silent
Hal Roach
Two musicians get into trouble at work, in their digs and in the street.

Star comedy which though early in their teaming shows Stan and Ollie at their best in a salt shaker routine and in a surreal pants-ripping contest.
w H. M. Walker *d* Edgar Kennedy *ph* Floyd Jackman *ed* Richard Currier
☆ Stan Laurel, Oliver Hardy, Agnes Steele, Otto Lederer

You're Dead...
US/Germany 1999 97m colour
Entertainment/Atlantic Streamkine (Marco Weber)
An undercover policewoman explains why she is the only survivor of a nine-day siege that resulted after a London bank robbery went wrong.
Frenetic crime caper notable for hammy acting and fussy direction.
wd Andy Hurst *ph* Wedigo von Schultzendorff *m* Robert Folk *pd* Frank Bollinger *ed* Andrew Starke
☆ John Hurt (Maitland), Claire Skinner (Jo), Rhys Ifans (Eddie), David Schneider (Ian), Barbara Flynn (Professor Corner), John Benfield (Insp Dick Badger), Roger Ashton-Griffiths (Cliff Sefton), Patrick Field (Det Insp Guiffin), Badi Uzzaman (Dr Chandra)
'A thoroughly stupid piece of work, slightly redeemed by a maniacal devotion to plot twists.' – *Edward Porter, Sunday Times*

You're in the Army Now: see *O.H.M.S. (1936)*

You're in the Army Now **
US 1941 79m bw
Warner (Ben Stoloff)
Two incompetent vacuum cleaner salesmen accidentally join the army.
An excellent vehicle for two star comedians who have often suffered from poor material, with a silent-comedy-style climax involving a house on wheels.
w Paul Gerard Smith, George Beatty *d* Lewis Seiler *ph* James Van Trees *m* Howard Jackson
☆ *Jimmy Durante, Phil Silvers, Donald MacBride,* Jane Wyman, Regis Toomey

You're in the Navy Now *
US 1951 93m bw
TCF (Fred Kohlmar)
aka: *USS Teakettle*
Trouble results when the navy instals steam turbines in an experimental patrol craft.
Amusing service comedy with good script touches and capable performances.
w Richard Murphy *d* Henry Hathaway *ph* Joe MacDonald *m* Cyril Mockridge
☆ Gary Cooper, Millard Mitchell, Jane Greer, Eddie Albert, John McIntire, Ray Collins, Harry von Zell, Jack Webb, Richard Erdman

You're My Everything *
US 1949 94m Technicolor
TCF (Lamar Trotti)
A Boston socialite marries a hoofer and becomes a movie star.
Pleasant twenties comedy with good period detail and lively performances.
w Lamar Trotti, Will Hays Jnr *d* Walter Lang *ph* Arthur E. Arling *m* Alfred Newman
☆ Anne Baxter, Dan Dailey, Anne Revere, Stanley Ridges, Shari Robinson, Henry O'Neill, Selena Royle, Alan Mowbray, Buster Keaton

You're Never Too Young
US 1955 103m Technicolor Vistavision
Paramount/Hal B. Wallis (Paul Jones)
An apprentice barber on the run from a murderer poses as a 12-year-old child to travel half fare.
Unattractive revamping of The Major and the Minor *(qv), with the star team trying too obviously to make bricks with inferior straw.*
w Sidney Sheldon *d* Norman Taurog *ph* Daniel L. Fapp *m* Arthur Schwartz
☆ Dean Martin, Jerry Lewis, Diana Lynn, Nina Foch, Raymond Burr, Veda Ann Borg

You're Only Young Once: see *The Hardy Family*

You're Only Young Twice
GB 1952 81m bw
Group Three (Terry Bishop)
The puritanical head of a Scottish university is laid low by circumstance and his own folly.
Misfire eccentric comedy which deserves marks for trying but fails to amuse.
w Reginald Beckwith, Lindsay Galloway, Terry Bishop *play What Say They* by James Bridie *d* Terry Bishop *ph* Jo Jago
☆ *Duncan Macrae, Charles Hawtrey,* Joseph Tomelty, Patrick Barr, Diane Hart, Robert Urquhart

You're Telling Me *
US 1934 66m bw
Paramount
A small-town inventor meets a princess and makes the social grade.
Meaninglessly-titled star vehicle which is often defiantly unamusing but does include the famous golf routine.
w Walter de Leon, Paul M. Jones *story* Julian Street *d* Erle C. Kenton *ph* Alfred Gilks *m* Arthur Johnston
☆ *W. C. Fields,* Larry 'Buster' Crabbe, Joan Marsh, Adrienne Ames, Louise Carter
'The kind of comedy that Chaplin used to do in two reels, but stretched out like Carnera's suspenders to run an even six.' – *Variety*

Yours Mine and Ours *
US 1968 111m Technicolor
UA/Desilu/Walden (Robert F. Blumofe)
A widower with nine children marries a widow with eight, and they settle in an old San Francisco house.
Generally appealing comedy, based on fact and well suited to its stars.
w Melville Shavelson, Mort Lachman *d* Melville Shavelson *ph* Charles Wheeler *m* Fred Karlin
☆ Lucille Ball, Henry Fonda, Van Johnson

Youth Runs Wild
US 1944 67m bw
RKO (Val Lewton)
Indifferent parents are responsible for the problems of teenagers.
Dreary little sermon from the unit which produced semi-classic horrors.
w John Fante, Herbert Kline *d* Mark Robson
☆ Bonita Granville, Kent Smith, Jean Brooks, Glenn Vernon, Arthur Shields

Youth Takes a Fling
US 1938 77m bw
Universal (Joe Pasternak)
A reluctant truck driver is chased by a department store salesgirl.
Mildly scatty comedy which failed to ring the bell.
w Myles Connolly *d* Archie Mayo
☆ Joel McCrea, Andrea Leeds, Frank Jenks, Dorothea Kent, Isabel Jeans, Virginia Grey, Grant Mitchell, Willie Best
'Good standard entertainment with many light and diverting passages.' – *Variety*

You've Got Mail *
US 1998 119m Technicolor
Warner (Nora Ephron, Lauren Shuler Donner)
The owner of a small New York bookshop unknowingly conducts a love affair by e-mail with the heir to a large bookshop chain that is putting her out of business.
Almost a sequel to Sleepless in Seattle*, this provides the same stars and much the same pleasures, for those sweet on romance.*
w Nora Ephron, Delia Ephron *play Parfumerie* by Miklos Laszlo *screenplay The Shop around the Corner* by Samson Raphaelson *d* Nora Ephron *ph* John Lindley *m* George Fenton *pd* Dan Davis *ed* Richard Marks
☆ Tom Hanks, Meg Ryan, Parker Posey, Greg Kinnear, Jean Stapleton, Steve Zahn, David Chappelle, Dabney Coleman, John Randolph, Heather Burns
'This winning romantic comedy and great date movie will be propelled to hefty B.O. by its alluring, high-powered stars.' – *Lael Loewenstein, Variety*
† This is the third version of the story, which, after Ernst Lubitsch's 1940 film *The Shop around the Corner* (qv), was also used as the basis of the musical *In the Good Old Summertime* (qv) in 1949.

You've Got to Live Dangerously: see *Il Faut Vivre Dangereusement*

Yukinojo Henge: see *An Actor's Revenge*

Yvonne's Perfume: see *Le Parfum d'Yvonne*

Z

Z ****

France/Algeria 1968 125m Eastmancolor
Reggane/ONCIC/Jacques Pérrin

A leading opposition MP is murdered at a rally. The police are anxious to establish the event as an accident, but the examining magistrate proves otherwise.

An exciting police suspense drama which also recalls events under the Greek colonels and was therefore highly fashionable for a while both as entertainment and as a political roman à clef.

w Costa-Gavras, Jorge Semprun *novel* Vassili Vassilikos *d* Costa-Gavras *ph* Raoul Coutard *m* Mikis Theodorakis

☆ Jean-Louis Trintignant, Jacques Pérrin, Yves Montand, François Périer, Irene Papas, Charles Denner

best foreign film

best picture; director; script

Mikis Theodorakis

'It will blow your mind!'

Zabriskie Point

US 1969 112m Metrocolor Panavision
MGM/Carlo Ponti

A rebellious Los Angeles student steals a private airplane, meets an aimless girl, and finds a revelation in Death Valley …

Highly self-indulgent and unattractive fantasy about escape from the crudities of our over-civilized world. An expensive failure and an awful warning of what happens if you give an arty director carte blanche.

w Michelangelo Antonioni, Fred Gardner, Sam Shepard, Tonino Guerra, Clare Peploe *d* Michelangelo Antonioni *ph* Alfio Contini *m* pop songs

☆ Mark Frechette, Daria Halprin, Rod Taylor, Paul Fix

'Not even a good tourist's notebook … from the choice of Death Valley as a symbol of American civilization to the inclusion of gag signs on bar-room walls to the shots of garish billboards, this film sticks to the surface, stranded.' – *Stanley Kauffman*

'A huge, jerry-built, crumbling ruin of a movie.' – *Pauline Kael, New Yorker*

'A small, sad shambles of a film that has obviously been salvaged from a larger shambles. Bad enough to give anti-Americanism a bad name.' – *Joseph Morgenstern, Newsweek*

'He has tried to make a serious movie and hasn't even achieved a beach party level of insight.' – *Roger Ebert*

'The First Electric Western.'

Zachariah

US 1971 93m Metrocolor
Cinerama/ABC (George Englund)

A youth leaves home to become a gunfighter but learns that pacificism is best.

Bizarre rock Western that is never sure whether it's satirical or serious; an audience is likely to be as confused. It was not only the first of its kind, but also the last.

w Joe Massot, The Firesign Theatre (Philip Austin, Peter Bergman, David Ossman, Philip Proctor) *d* George Englund *ph* Jorge Shahl *m* Jimmie Haskell *pd* Assheton Gorton *ed* Gary Griffen

☆ John Rubinstein, Pat Quinn, Don Johnson, Country Joe and the Fish, Elvin Jones, Doug Kershaw, William Challee, Dick Van Patten, The James Gang

'Nothing quite works, yet it's a relaxed and generally inoffensive movie.' – *Pauline Kael*

Zamani Baraye Masti Asbha **

Iran 2000 80m colour
Porter Frith/B.H. (Bahman Ghobadi)

GB title: *A Time for Drunken Horses*

A young Kurdish orphan joins a group of smugglers in order to raise money for treatment for his dying and disabled brother.

A harsh, moving documentary-style feature of life lived at the extreme of hardship and poverty – the title refers to the alcohol-laced water given to the mules in order that they can cope with the snow-bound journeys – told without sentimentality and using non-professional actors.

wd Bahman Ghobadi *ph* Saed Nikzat *m* Hossein Alizadeh *ed* Samad Tavazoi

☆ Amaneh Ekhtiar-Dini, Madi Ekhtiar-Dini, Ayoub Ahmadi, Rouvin Younessi, Nezhad Ekhtiar-Dini

'The film carries a searing emotional charge.' – *Geoffrey Macnab, Sight and Sound*

Zamri, Umri, Voskresni! **

USSR 1989 103m bw
Artificial Eye/Lenfilm/Trinity Bridge/First Film Creative Studio (Valentina Tarasova)

aka: *Don't Move, Die and Rise Again!*

In the 1940s in a grim Soviet town, the 12-year-old son of a prostitute is befriended by a girl of his own age.

Supposedly autobiographical film of a depressingly violent semi-criminal childhood marked by tragedy.

wd Vitaly Kanevsky *ph* Vladimir Bryliakov *m* Sergei Banevich *pd* Yury Pashigorev *ed* G. Kornilova

☆ Dinara Drukarova, Pavel Nazarov, Elena Popova

'It makes a compulsive, unpredictable, unreliable, contradictory, and often remarkably beautiful autobiographical memoir from a powerful and refreshingly undisciplined voice.' – *Philip Strick, Sight and Sound*

'One of those autobiographical first features which suddenly arrives out of nowhere and surprises us with its freshness, power and rough-hewn skill.' – *Derek Malcolm, Guardian*

† The film won the Camera d'Or for best first feature at the Cannes Film Festival in 1990.

'One woman … two men … one driven by desire. The other driven to the edge.'

Zandalee

US 1990 104m colour
Rank/Electric (William Blaycock, Eyal Rimmon)

A hard-drinking artist makes love to the wife of his increasingly unhappy childhood friend.

Appalling dialogue and a ludicrous narrative are combined with lubricious sexual encounters to create a wholly unlovely experience.

w Mari Kornhauser *d* Sam Pillsbury *ph* Walt Lloyd *m* Pray For Rain *pd* Michael Corenblith *ed* Michael Horton

☆ Nicolas Cage, Judge Reinhold, Erika Anderson, Viveca Lindfors, Aaron Neville, Joe Pantoliano, Steve Buscemi

'Ill-written, pretentious trash.' – *Philip French, Observer*

Zandy's Bride

US 1974 116m Technicolor Panavision
Warner (Harry Matofsky)

aka: *For Better, For Worse*

Life for a frontier family.

Dour semi-Western.

w Marc Norman *novel* The Stranger by Lillian Bos Ross *d* Jan Troell *ph* Jordan Cronenweth *m* Michael Franks

☆ Gene Hackman, Liv Ullmann, Eileen Heckart, Harry Dean Stanton, Joe Santos, Frank Cady

Zapped!

US 1982 98m CFI color
Thunder Associates

A high-school boffin discovers his own telekinetic powers, by which he is able to tear everyone's clothes off at the senior prom.

Mild adolescent smut, half-way between Porky's and the unbearable Disney comedies of the sixties.

w Bruce Rubin, Robert J. Rosenthal *d* Robert J. Rosenthal *ph* Daniel Pearl *m* Charles Fox

☆ Scott Baio, Willie Aames, Robert Mandan, Scatman Crothers

Zarak *

GB 1956 99m Technicolor Cinemascope
Columbia/Warwick (Phil C. Samuel)

An Afghan outlaw finally saves a British officer at the cost of his own life.

Box-office actioner, shot in Morocco with a weird cast and the help of old movie clips.

w Richard Maibaum *d* Terence Young *ph* John Wilcox, Ted Moore, Cyril Knowles *m* William Alwyn *ad* John Box *second unit* Yakima Canutt

☆ Victor Mature, Michael Wilding, Anita Ekberg, Bonar Colleano, Finlay Currie, Bernard Miles, Eunice Gayson, Peter Illing, Frederick Valk, André Morell

Zardoz

GB 1974 105m DeLuxe Panavision
TCF/John Boorman

Life in 2293, when the Earth has become wasteland and a mass of Brutals are ruled by a few Exterminators who have both memory and intelligence.

Pompous, boring fantasy for the so-called intelligentsia.

wd John Boorman *ph* Geoffrey Unsworth *m* David Munrow *pd* Anthony Pratt

☆ Sean Connery, Charlotte Rampling, John Alderton

'A glittering cultural trash pile … the most gloriously fatuous movie since *The Oscar*.' – *New Yorker*

Zärtlichkeit der Wölfe: see *Tenderness of Wolves*

Zateriannyi v Sibiri: see *Lost in Siberia*

Zaza

US 1938 83m bw
Paramount (Albert Lewin)

A 1904 French chanteuse is in love with a married aristocrat.

Rather flat period romantic drama with interesting credits.

w Zoe Atkins *play* Pierre Berton, Charles Simon *d* George Cukor *ph* Charles Lang *songs* Frank Loesser, Frederick Hollander

☆ Claudette Colbert, Herbert Marshall, Bert Lahr, Constance Collier, Helen Westley, Genevieve Tobin, Walter Catlett, Rex O'Malley

'Fine production with hefty woman-appeal.' – *Variety*

† The original David Belasco stage production made Mrs Leslie Carter famous. Silent film versions starred Pauline Frederick in 1915 and Gloria Swanson in 1923.

Zazie dans le Métro ***

France 1960 88m Eastmancolor
Nouvelles Editions (Irène Leriche)

A naughty little girl has a day in Paris and causes chaos.

Inventive little comedy which almost turns into a French Hellzapoppin, with everybody chasing or fighting everybody else.

wd Louis Malle *novel* Raymond Queneau *ph* Henri Raichi *m* Fiorenzo Capri

☆ Catherine Demongeot, Philippe Noiret, Vittorio Caprioli

'There is something not quite innocent or healthy about this film.' – *Bosley Crowther*

Zebra in the Kitchen

US 1965 93m Metrocolor
MGM/Ivan Tors

A young boy tries to improve the lot of zoo animals.

Pleasing family film.

w Art Arthur *d* Ivan Tors *ph* Lamar Boren

☆ Jay North, Martin Milner, Andy Devine, Joyce Meadows, Jim Davis

'Live Together Or Die.'

Zebrahead *

US 1992 98m colour
Triumph/Ixtlan (Jeff Dowd, Charles Mitchell, William F. Willett)

GB title: *The Colour of Love*

In Detroit, racial and family tensions come to a head when a white boy begins a relationship with a black girl.

Intense, well-meaning drama of teenage emotional turmoil, but one without a satisfactory ending.

wd Anthony Drazan *ph* Maryse Alberti *m* Taj Mahal *pd* Naomi Shohan *ed* Elizabeth Kling

☆ Michael Rapaport (Zack), N'Bushe Wright (Nikki), Paul Butler (Otis), DeShonn Castle (Dee), Candy Ann Brown (Marlene), Luke Reilly (Mr Modell), Dan Ziskie (Mr Cimino), Ray Sharkey (Richard)

'Not so much a movie as notes toward a movie – a good one, judging by what's on the screen.' – *Roger Ebert, Chicago Sun-Times*

A Zed and Two Noughts **

GB 1985 115m colour
Artificial Eye/BFI/Allarts Enterprises/Film Four International (Peter Sainsbury, Kees Kasander)

An assemblage of images of loss and decay decorate a slim narrative about twin husbands, whose wives are killed in a car crash with a swan, and their relationship with the survivor, a woman whose leg is amputated.

Intriguing, visually compelling and witty, although it may not appeal to those expecting a traditional narrative.

wd Peter Greenaway *ph* Sacha Vierny *m* Michael Nyman *pd* Ben Van Os, Jan Roelfs *ed* John Wilson

☆ Andrea Ferreol, Eric Deacon, Brian Deacon, Frances Barber, Joss Ackland

Zee and Co *

GB 1971 109m colour
Columbia/Zee Films (Kastner-Ladd-Kanter)

US title: *X, Y and Zee*

A successful architect battles with his termagant wife and seeks an affair.

Overwritten but entertaining sexual melodrama about an absolute bitch. The flow of bad language was new at the time.

w Edna O'Brien *d* Brian G. Hutton *ph* Billy Williams *m* Stanley Myers *ad* Peter Mullins

☆ Elizabeth Taylor, Michael Caine, Susannah York, Margaret Leighton, John Standing

'Miss Taylor is rapidly turning into a latterday Marie Dressler.' – *Tom Milne*

'A slice-of-jet-set-life nightmare far beyond the dreams of the piggiest male chauvinist … the distinction of this film is that its characters are repulsive, its style vulgar, its situations beyond belief and its dialogue moronic.' – *Judith Crist*

Zelig ***
US 1983 79m bw/colour
Orion/Rollins-Joffe (Robert Greenhut)

A parody documentary tracing a chameleon-like nonentity who contrives to have been associated with all the major events of the 20th century.
The central idea is more elusive than appealing, and the mid-section of psychiatric consultation is downright dull, but considerable amusement derives from the technical trickery which puts Woody Allen in pictorial association with Hitler, Roosevelt and Eugene O'Neill. In all, an after-dinner treat for the intellectuals.
wd Woody Allen *ph* Gordon Willis *m* Dick Hyman *pd* Mel Bourne *ed* Susan E. Morse
☆ Woody Allen (Leonard Zelig), Mia Farrow (Dr Eudora Fletcher), John Buckwater (Dr Sindell), Marvin Chatinover, Stanley Swerdlow, Paul Nevens, Howard Erskine
'We can all admire the brilliance and economy with which it is made. But is it funny enough? I take leave to doubt it.' – *Derek Malcolm, Guardian*
'*Citizen Kane* miraculously transformed into side-splitting comedy.' – *New York Times*
'The movie is a technical masterpiece, but in artistic and comic terms, only pretty good.' – *Roger Ebert*
cinematography; costume design

Zelly and Me *
US 1988 87m Technicolor
Columbia/Cypress Films/Tony Mark/Sue Jett

A poor little rich girl, who lives with a grandmother greedy for love, is comforted by her governess.
Unusual in its depiction of the psychological damage an adult can inflict on a child, it handles sympathetically its themes of the failure of love and the need to develop individual strength.
wd Tina Rathbone *ph* Mikael Salomon *m* Pino Donaggio *pd* David Morong *ed* Cindy Kaplan Rooney
☆ *Isabella Rossellini, Glynis Johns,* Kaiulani Lee, David Lynch, Joe Morton, Alexandra Johnes

Zemlya: see *Earth*

Zenobia
US 1939 83m bw
Hal Roach

GB title: *Elephants Never Forget*
A small-town doctor finds himself looking after a performing elephant.
Very mild small-town comedy made during a break-up in the Laurel and Hardy contract.
w Corey Ford, Arnold Belgard, Walter de Leon *d* Gordon Douglas *ph* Karl Struss *m* Marvin Hatley
☆ Oliver Hardy, Harry Langdon, Jean Parker, Billie Burke, Alice Brady, James Ellison, Stepin Fetchit, Hattie McDaniel

Zentropa: see *Europa, Europa*

Zeppelin *
GB 1971 97m Technicolor Panavision
Warner/Getty and Fromkess (Owen Crump)

In 1915, the British need to steal secrets from the zeppelin works at Friedrichshafen.
Undistinguished but entertaining period actioner with adequate spectacle but wooden performances.
w Arthur Rowe, Donald Churchill *d* Etienne Périer *ph* Alan Hume *m* Roy Budd *sp* Wally Veevers
☆ Michael York, Elke Sommer, Peter Carsten, Marius Goring, Anton Diffring, Andrew Keir, Rupert Davies

Zéro de Conduite **
France 1933 45m approx bw
Gaumont/Franco Film/Aubert

Boys return from the holiday to a nasty little boarding school, where the headmaster is an unpleasant dwarf and all the staff are hateful. A revolution breaks out …
A clear forerunner of If … *and one of the most famous of surrealist films, though it pales beside Buñuel and is chiefly valuable for being funny.*
wd Jean Vigo *ph* Boris Kaufman *m* Maurice Jaubert *ed* Jean Vigo
☆ Jean Dasté, Louis Lefébvre, Gilbert Pruchon, le nain Delphin
'One of the most poetic films ever made and one of the most influential.' – *New Yorker, 1978*

'The World's Most Private Detective.'
Zero Effect *
US 1998 115m Technicolor
Warner/Castle Rock/Manifest (Lisa Henson, Janet Yang, Jake Kasdan)

A reclusive private eye investigates a case of blackmail.
Quirky mix of comedy, romance and thriller that offers intermittent amusement.
wd Jake Kasdan *ph* Bill Pope *m* The Greyboy Allstars *pd* Gary Frutkoff *ed* Tara Timpone
☆ Bill Pullman, Ben Stiller, Kim Dickens, Angela Featherstone, Ryan O'Neal, Hugh Ross, Matt O'Toole
'Top heavy with artifice but punctuated with enough off-beat inspiration to make the experience worthwhile.' – *Sight and Sound*

Zero Hour!
US 1957 83m bw
Paramount/Bartlett/Champion (John Champion)
Half the passengers and all the crew of a jet plane are stricken with food poisoning and a shell-shocked ex-fighter pilot has to land the plane.
Adequate air melodrama with a premise which later served for Terror in the Sky *(TV) and* Airport 75.
w Arthur Hailey, John Champion, Hall Bartlett *teleplay Flight into Danger by Arthur Hailey d* Hall Bartlett *ph* John F. Warren *m* Ted Dale
☆ Dana Andrews, Linda Darnell, Sterling Hayden, Elroy Hirsch, Jerry Paris

Zero Patience
Canada 1993 88m colour
Dangerous To Know/Zero Patience/Telefilm Canada/OFDC/Channel 4 (Louise Garfield, Anna Stratton)

English explorer Sir Richard Burton, working at the Natural History Museum in Toronto, is visited by the ghost of the first man to bring AIDS to North America as he plans an exhibition on the disease.
Bizarre gay musical satirizing homophobia in the style of a rock video.
wd John Greyson *ph* Miroslaw Baszak *m/ly* Glenn Schellenberg, John Greyson *pd* Sandra Kybartas *ed* Miume Jan
☆ John Robinson, Normand Fauteux, Dianne Heatherington, Richardo Keens-Douglas, Maria Lukofsky, Bernard Behrens, Michael Callen
'While one may agree with almost everything it says, the little matter of the way it says it renders the film almost unwatchable.' – *Derek Malcolm, Guardian*
'Enormously entertaining, and perfectly cast … This is an angry film, a powerful indictment of a society that seems more concerned with finding a scapegoat rather than a cure for one of the biggest killers today.' – *Nigel Robinson, Film Review*

Zero Population Growth
US 1971 96m Eastmancolor
Sagittarius (Thomas F. Madigan)
In the 21st century there is a death penalty for having children, but a young couple defy the authorities.
Good sci-fi quickly develops into sticky sentimentality.
w Max Ehrlich, Frank de Felitta *d* Michael Campus *ph* Michael Reed *m* Jonathan Hodge *pd* Tony Masters
☆ Oliver Reed, Geraldine Chaplin, Diane Cilento, Don Gordon, Bill Nagy, Aubrey Woods

Zero Tolerance
US 1994 92m Foto-Kem
PM Entertainment (Richard Pepin, Joseph Merhi)

An FBI agent takes revenge on the drug-runners who murder his wife and children and force him to smuggle liquid heroin.
Frenetic, melodramatic, violent, repetitious and senseless action movie, a concussive sequence of car crashes, gunshots and explosions, mixed with a little sentimentality.
w Jacobsen Hart *d* Joseph Merhi *ph* Ken Blakey *m* John Gonzalez *pd* Steve Ramos *ed* Chris Worland, Chris Maybach
☆ Robert Patrick, Titus Welliver, Kristen Meadows, Mick Fleetwood, Barbara Patrick, Billy Hufsey, Miles O'Keeffe

Zert: see *The Joke*

Zeta One
GB 1969 84m Eastmancolor
Tigon (George Maynard)

A spy plays strip poker as he explains how he saved the world from being taken over by women wearing orange mini-dresses and white thigh boots.
Based on a comic-strip, an incompetent James Bond spoof with cruder double entendres and more irrelevant sexual activity; tedium sets in very quickly.
w Michael Cort, Alistair McKenzie *d* Michael Cort *ph* Jack Atchelor *m* Johnny Hawksworth *ad* Martin Gascoigne *ed* Jack T. Knight, Dennis Lanning
☆ James Robertson Justice, Charles Hawtrey, Robin Hawdon, Anna Gael, Brigitte Skay, Valerie Leon, Yutte Stensgaard, Lionel Murton, Dawn Addams, Rita Webb

Zeus and Roxanne
US 1997 98m DeLuxe
MGM/Rysher (Frank Price, Gene Rosow, Ludi Boeken)

When a woman's friendly dolphin bonds with her neighbour's dog, their children know that romance is in the offing.
Pleasant family film with some scene-stealing animals and not too much sentimentality.
w Tom Benedek *d* George Miller *ph* David Connell *m* Bruce Rowland *pd* Bernt Capra *ed* Harry Hitner
☆ Steve Guttenberg, Kathleen Quinlan, Arnold Vosloo, Dawn McMillan, Miko Hughes, Majandra Delfino, Jessica Howard
'Simple-minded but efficient piece of filmmaking clearly aimed at small fry.' – *Variety*
† The role of Zeus was played by three dogs.

Zhanta: see *Platform*

Zhantai: see *Platform*

Zhivoi Trup: see *The Living Corpse*

Ziegfeld Follies **
US 1946 110m Technicolor
MGM (Arthur Freed)

In heaven, Florenz Ziegfeld dreams up one last spectacular revue.
A rather airless all-star entertainment in which the comedy suffers from the lack of an audience but some of the production numbers are magnificently stylish.
w various *d Vincente Minnelli ph George Folsey, Charles Rosher m* various *md* Lennie Hayton *ch* Robert Alton *ad* Cedric Gibbons, Merrill Pye, Jack Martin Smith *ed* Albert Akst *cos* Florence Bunin, Irene, Helen Rose
☆ *Fred Astaire,* Lucille Ball, Bunin's Puppets, William Powell (Florenz Ziegfeld), Jimmy Durante, Edward Arnold, *Fanny Brice,* Lena Horne, Lucille Bremer, Esther Williams, Judy Garland, *Red Skelton, Gene Kelly,* James Melton, Hume Cronyn and also Victor Moore, Marion Bell
'Between opening and closing is packed a prodigious amount of material, some of which is frankly not deserving of the lavish treatment accorded it.' – *Film Daily*
'The fastidious are advised to head for the lobby while Kathryn Grayson sings "There's Beauty Everywhere" against magenta foam skies.' – *Pauline Kael, 70s*
† Made in 1944, but not released until later.
♫ 'Here's to the Girls'; 'This Heart of Mine'; 'Love'; 'Limehouse Blues'

Ziegfeld Girl *
US 1941 131m bw
MGM (Pandro S. Berman)

The professional and romantic problems of Ziegfeld chorus girls.
Adequate big-budget drama with music.
w Marguerite Roberts, Sonya Levien *d* Robert Z. Leonard *ph* Ray June *m* Herbert Stothart *ch* Busby Berkeley *songs* various
☆ James Stewart, Judy Garland, Hedy Lamarr, Lana Turner, Tony Martin, Jackie Cooper, Ian Hunter, *Charles Winninger, Al Shean,* Edward Everett Horton, Philip Dorn, Paul Kelly, Eve Arden, Dan Dailey, Fay Holden and also Felix Bressart
'Heaping portions of show life in the opulent days of Flo Ziegfeld, the man who wanted bigger and better staircases.' – *C. A. Lejeune*
♫ 'You Stepped Out of a Dream'; 'I'm Always Chasing Rainbows'; 'Mr Gallagher and Mr Shean'; 'You Never Looked So Beautiful'.

Zigzag *
US 1970 104m Metrocolor Panavision
MGM/Freeman-Enders
GB title: *False Witness*
A dying man frames himself for an unsolved murder so that the reward money, claimed under another name, will go to his wife.
Complex thriller which sustains itself pretty well most of the way, but lacks humour and character.
w John T. Kelley *d* Richard A. Colla *ph* James A. Crabe *m* Oliver Nelson
☆ George Kennedy, Anne Jackson, Eli Wallach, Steve Ihnat, William Marshall, Joe Maross

Zoltan, Hound of Dracula: see *Dracula's Dog*

Zombi 2: see *Zombie Flesh Eaters*

Zombie: see *Zombie Flesh Eaters*

'When The Earth Spits Out The Dead.'
Zombie Flesh Eaters
Italy 1979 93m Technicolor
Variety Film (Ugo Tucci, Fabrizio de Angelis)

original title: *Zombi 2*
aka: *Zombie; Island of The Living Dead*
After a yacht with a zombie aboard is found floating off New York, a journalist discovers that it originated on a small Caribbean island where a mad scientist's experiments result in the dead, including Spanish conquistadores, rising from their graves.
Visceral, gore-filled horror movie, owing much to the example of George Romero but made by a director who does not understand that less can be more.
w Elisa Briganti *d* Lucio Fulci *ph* Sergio Salvati *m* Fabio Frizzi, Giorgio Tucci *pd* Walter Patriarca
☆ Ian McCulloch, Tisa Farrow, Richard Johnson, Al Cliver, Auretta Gay
† The film was cut to 85m for its British video release.

Zombie Island Massacre
US 1984 95m colour
Troma/Broadnax

Tourists who travel to the Caribbean for a voodoo ritual are killed one by one by an apparent zombie.
Dull horror, seemingly designed as a showcase to display the body of former Playboy *model Jenrette; its plot owes much to Agatha Christie's* Ten Little Indians.
w William Stoddard, Logan O'Neill *d* John N. Carter *m* Harry Manfredini *ed* John N. Carter *sp* Dennis Eger
☆ David Broadnax, Rita Jenrette, Tom Cantrell, Diane Clayre Holub, Ian MacMillan, George Peters, Dennis Stephenson, Debbie Ewing

The Zombies of Mora Tau
US 1957 71m bw
Columbia (Sam Katzman)

GB title: *The Dead that Walk*
A diver plans to salvage a subterranean West African treasure: but it is guarded by zombies.
Modest addition to the walking dead cycle.
w Raymond T. Marcus *d* Edward Cahn *ph* Benjamin Kline *m* Mischa Bakaleinikoff
☆ Gregg Palmer, Allison Hayes, Autumn Russell, Morris Ankrum

Zombies on Broadway
US 1945 70m bw
RKO (Ben Stoloff)

Press agents seek a real zombie for the opening of a new night-club … and a mad professor provides one.

Knockabout comedy-thriller, just tolerable for addicts of the genre.
w Lawrence Kimble *d* Gordon Douglas
☆ Wally Brown, Alan Carney, Bela Lugosi, Anne Jeffreys, Sheldon Leonard

Zongheng Sihai: see *Once a Thief (1991)*

Zoo in Budapest *
US 1933 83m bw
Fox (Jesse Lasky)
An orphan waif runs away to live with a zookeeper.
Curious little romance remembered for its luminescent photography.
w Dan Totheroh, Louise Long, Rowland V. Lee *d* Rowland V. Lee *ph* Lee Garmes
☆ Loretta Young, Gene Raymond, O. P. Heggie, Wally Albright, Paul Fix
'Appeal for all classes … a subject of great photographic and pictorial beauty.' – *Variety*
'Richly composed impressionistic images, assisted by highly imaginative use of sound and background music, create a poem that Murnau himself would have envied.' – *NFT, 1971*

Un Zoo La Nuit: see *Night Zoo*

Zoolander *
US 2001 89m DeLuxe Panavision
Paramount/Village Roadshow/VH1/NPV (Scott Rudin, Ben Stiller, Stuart Cornfeld)
A dim-witted fashion model is brainwashed by a gang of designers to kill the Prime Minister of Malaysia.
Energetic farce that aims to be a satire on pop culture, but is too toothless for the task.
w Drake Sather, Ben Stiller, John Hamburg *d* Ben Stiller *ph* Barry Peterson *m* David Arnold *pd* Robin Standefer *ed* Greg Hayden *cos* David C. Robinson
☆ Ben Stiller (Derek Zoolander), Owen Wilson (Hansel), Will Ferrell (Mugatu), Christine Taylor (Matilda Jeffries), Milla Jovovich (Katinka), Jerry Stiller (Maury Ballstein), Jon Voight (Larry Zoolander), David Duchovny (J. P. Prewitt), Judah Friedlander (Scrappy Zoolander)
'Gleefully goofy and consistently funny.' – *Claudia Puig, USA Today*
'A freakishly potent farce – stuffed with throwaway non sequiturs, fueled by absurdist counterintuition, premised on fearless repetition.' – *Dennis Lim, Village Voice*

Zorba the Greek **
GB 1964 142m bw
TCF/Rockley/Cacoyannis (Michael Cacoyannis)
A young English writer in Crete is befriended by a huge gregarious Greek who comes to dominate his life.
A mainly enjoyable character study of a larger-than-life character, this film made famous by its music does not really hang together dramatically and has several melodramatic excrescences.
wd Michael Cacoyannis novel Nikos Kazantzakis *ph Walter Lassally m Mikis Theodorakis ad* Vasseli Fotopoulos *ed* Alex Archamboult, Michael Cacoyannis
☆ *Anthony Quinn* (Alexis Zorba), *Alan Bates* (Basil), *Lila Kedrova* (Mme Hortense), Irene Papas (The Widow), George Foundas (Mavrandoni), Eleni Anousaki (Lola)
'For all its immense length, the film never gets down to a clear statement of its theme, or comes within measuring distance of its vast pretensions.' – *Brenda Davies*
† Lila Kedrova replaced Simone Signoret after a week's filming, as Signoret was unable to portray a weak woman.
Walter Lassally; Lila Kedrova
best picture; Michael Cacoyannis (as writer and director); Anthony Quinn

Zorro (dubbed)
Italy/France 1975 100m colour
Mondial/Artistes Associés (Vittorio Galiano)
After his friend is assassinated, Zorro takes his place as governor of a Spanish colony where a corrupt colonel and his friends are terrorizing and exploiting the locals.
Swashbuckling, tongue-in-cheek adventure done with some style and very little bloodshed.
w Giorgio Arlorio *d* Duccio Tessari *ph* Giulio Albonico *m* Guido and Maurizio de Angelis *ad* Enzo Bulgarelli *ed* Mario Morra
☆ Alain Delon, Stanley Baker, Ottavia Piccolo, Enzo Cerusico, Moustache, Adriana Asti, Giacomo Rossi Stuart, Gianpiero Albertini, Marino Mase, Rajka Jurcec

'Zany! Zexy! Zensational!'
Zorro the Gay Blade
US 1981 93m DeLuxe
Melvin Simon (George Hamilton, C. O. Erickson)
Zorro, the masked avenger, not only pretends to be a fop but is one. Luckily he has a twin brother.
Abysmal attempt to do for Zorro what Love at First Bite *did for Dracula.*
w Hal Dresner *d* Peter Medak *ph* John A. Alonzo *m* Max Steiner themes
☆ George Hamilton, Lauren Hutton, Brenda Vaccaro, Ron Leibman, James Booth
'A wonderful giddy farce.' – *Pauline Kael*

Zotz!
US 1962 87m bw
Columbia/William Castle
A professor finds a rare coin with occult powers.
Footling farce patterned after The Absent-Minded Professor. *Poor, to say the least.*
w Ray Russell *novel* Walter Karig *d* William Castle *ph* Gordon Avil *m* Bernard Green
☆ Tom Poston, Fred Clark, Jim Backus, Cecil Kellaway, Margaret Dumont

Zuckerbaby: see *Sugarbaby*

Zulu *
GB 1964 135m Technirama
Paramount/Diamond (Stanley Baker, Cyril Endfield)
In 1879 British soldiers stand fast against the Zulus at Rorke's Drift.
Standard period heroics, well presented and acted.
w John Prebble, Cy Endfield *d* Cy Endfield *ph* Stephen Dade *m* John Barry
☆ Stanley Baker, Jack Hawkins, *Michael Caine*, Ulla Jacobsson, James Booth, Nigel Green, Ivor Emmanuel, Paul Daneman

Zulu Dawn
US/Netherlands 1979 117m
Technicolor Panavision
Samarkand/Zulu Dawn NV (Barrie Saint Clair)
In January 1879, 24,000 Zulus overwhelm and kill 1,300 British and African troops at Isandhlwana.
Confusing historical action adventure, very similar to Zulu *but failing in its cross-cut attempt to show both sides.*
w Cy Endfield, Anthony Storey *d* Douglas Hickox *ph* Ousama Rawi *m* Elmer Bernstein *pd* John Rosewarne
☆ Burt Lancaster, Denholm Elliott, Peter O'Toole, John Mills, Simon Ward, Nigel Davenport, Michael Jayston, Ronald Lacey, Freddie Jones, Christopher Cazenove, Ronald Pickup, Anna Calder-Marshall

Academy Award Winners

1927/28
Picture: *Wings*
Unique and Artistic Picture: *Sunrise* (F. W. Murnau)
Director: Frank Borzage (*Seventh Heaven*)
Comedy Director: Lewis Milestone (*Two Arabian Knights*)
Actor: Emil Jannings (*The Last Command, The Way of All Flesh*)
Actress: Janet Gaynor (*Seventh Heaven, Street Angel, Sunrise*)
Original Screenplay: Ben Hecht (*Underworld*)
Adapted Screenplay: Benjamin Glazer (*Seventh Heaven*)
Title Writing: Joseph Farnham (*Telling the World*)

1928/29
Picture: *Broadway Melody*
Director: Frank Lloyd (*The Divine Lady, Weary River, Drag*)
Actor: Warner Baxter (*Old Arizona*)
Actress: Mary Pickford (*Coquette*)
Writing Achievement: Hans Kraly (*The Patriot*)

1929/30
Picture: *All Quiet on the Western Front*
Director: Lewis Milestone (*All Quiet on the Western Front*)
Actor: George Arliss (*Disraeli*)
Actress: Norma Shearer (*The Divorcee*)
Writing Achievement: Frances Marion (*The Big House*)

1930/31
Picture: *Cimarron*
Director: Norman Taurog (*Skippy*)
Actor: Lionel Barrymore (*A Free Soul*)
Actress: Marie Dressler (*Min and Bill*)
Original Screenplay: John Monk Saunders (*The Dawn Patrol*)
Adapted Screenplay: Howard Eastabrook (*Cimarron*)

1931/32
Picture: *Grand Hotel*
Director: Frank Borzage (*Bad Girl*)
Actor: Wallace Beery (*The Champ*), Fredric March (*Dr Jekyll and Mr Hyde*)
Actress: Helen Hayes (*The Sin of Madelon Claudet*)
Original Screenplay: Francis Marion (*The Champ*)
Adapted Screenplay: Edwin Burke (*Bad Girl*)

1932/33
Picture: *Cavalcade*
Director: Frank Lloyd (*Cavalcade*)
Actor: Charles Laughton (*The Private Life of Henry VIII*)
Actress: Katharine Hepburn (*Morning Glory*)
Original Screenplay: Robert Lord (*One Way Passage*)
Adapted Screenplay: Victor Heerman, Sarah Y. Mason (*Little Women*)

1934
Picture: *It Happened One Night*
Director: Frank Capra (*It Happened One Night*)
Actor: Clark Gable (*It Happened One Night*)
Actress: Claudette Colbert (*It Happened One Night*)
Original Screenplay: Arthur Caesar (*Manhattan Melodrama*)
Adapted Screenplay: Robert Riskin (*It Happened One Night*)

1935
Picture: *Mutiny on the Bounty*
Director: John Ford (*The Informer*)
Actor: Victor McLaglen (*The Informer*)
Actress: Bette Davis (*Dangerous*)
Original Screenplay: Ben Hecht, Charles MacArthur (*The Scoundrel*)
Adapted Screenplay: Dudley Nichols (*The Informer*)

1936
Picture: *The Great Ziegfeld*
Director: Frank Capra (*Mr Deeds Goes to Town*)
Actor: Paul Muni (*The Story of Louis Pasteur*)
Actress: Luise Rainer (*The Great Ziegfeld*)
Supporting Actor: Walter Brennan (*Come and Get It*)
Supporting Actress: Gale Sondergaard (*Anthony Adverse*)
Original Screenplay: Pierre Collings, Sheridan Gibney (*The Story of Louis Pasteur*)

1937
Picture: *The Life of Emile Zola*
Director: Leo McCarey (*The Awful Truth*)
Actor: Spencer Tracy (*Captains Courageous*)
Actress: Luise Rainer (*The Good Earth*)
Supporting Actor: Joseph Schildkraut (*The Life of Emile Zola*)
Supporting Actress: Alice Brady (*In Old Chicago*)
Original Story: William A. Wellman, Robert Carson (*A Star Is Born*)
Original Screenplay: Heinz Herald, Geza Herczeg, Norman Reilly Raine (*The Life of Emile Zola*)

1938
Picture: *You Can't Take It with You*
Director: Frank Capra (*You Can't Take It with You*)
Actor: Spencer Tracy (*Boys' Town*)
Actress: Bette Davis (*Jezebel*)
Supporting Actor: Walter Brennan (*Kentucky*)
Supporting Actress: Fay Bainter (*Jezebel*)
Original Story: Eleanore Griffin, Dore Schary (*Boys' Town*)
Screenplay: George Bernard Shaw, adapted by Ian Dalrymple, Cecil Lewis, W. P. Liscomb (*Pygmalion*)

1939
Picture: *Gone with the Wind*
Director: Victor Fleming (*Gone with the Wind*)
Actor: Robert Donat (*Goodbye Mr Chips*)
Actress: Vivien Leigh (*Gone with the Wind*)
Supporting Actor: Thomas Mitchell (*Stagecoach*)
Supporting Actress: Hattie McDaniel (*Gone with the Wind*)
Original Story: Lewis R. Foster (*Mr Deeds Goes to Washington*)
Screenplay: Sidney Howard (*Gone with the Wind*)

1940
Picture: *Rebecca*
Director: John Ford (*The Grapes of Wrath*)
Actor: James Stewart (*The Philadelphia Story*)
Actress: Ginger Rogers (*Kitty Foyle*)
Supporting Actor: Walter Brennan (*The Westerner*)
Supporting Actress: Jane Darwell (*The Grapes of Wrath*)
Original Story: Benjamin Glazer, John S. Toldy (*Arise My Love*)
Original Screenplay: Preston Sturges (*The Great McGinty*)
Screenplay: Donald Ogden Stewart (*The Philadelphia Story*)

1941
Picture: *How Green Was My Valley*
Director: John Ford (*How Green Was My Valley*)
Actor: Gary Cooper (*Sergeant York*)
Actress: Joan Fontaine (*Suspicion*)
Supporting Actor: Donald Crisp (*How Green Was My Valley*)
Supporting Actress: Mary Astor (*The Great Lie*)
Original Story: Harry Segall (*Here Comes Mr Jordan*)
Original Screenplay: Herman J. Mankiewicz, Orson Welles (*Citizen Kane*)
Screenplay: Sidney Buchman, Seton I. Miller (*Here Comes Mr Jordan*)

1942
Picture: *Mrs Miniver*
Director: William Wyler (*Mrs Miniver*)
Actor: James Cagney (*Yankee Doodle Dandy*)
Actress: Greer Garson (*Mrs Miniver*)
Supporting Actor: Van Heflin (*Johnny Eager*)
Supporting Actress: Teresa Wright (*Mrs Miniver*)
Original Story: Emeric Pressburger (*The Invaders*)
Original Screenplay: Michael Kanin, Ring Lardner Jnr (*Woman of the Year*)
Screenplay: George Froeschel, James Hilton, Claudine West, Arthur Wimperis (*Mrs Miniver*)

1943
Picture: *Casablanca*
Director: Michael Curtiz (*Casablanca*)
Actor: Paul Lukas (*Watch on the Rhine*)
Actress: Jennifer Jones (*Song of Bernadette*)
Supporting Actor: Charles Coburn (*The More the Merrier*)
Supporting Actress: Katina Paxinou (*For Whom the Bell Tolls*)
Original Story: William Saroyan (*The Human Comedy*)
Original Screenplay: Norman Krasna (*Princess O'Rourke*)
Screenplay: Julius J. Epstein, Philip G. Epstein, Howard Koch (*Casablanca*)

1944
Picture: *Going My Way*
Director: Leo McCarey (*Going My Way*)
Actor: Bing Crosby (*Going My Way*)
Actress: Ingrid Bergman (*Gaslight*)
Supporting Actor: Barry Fitzgerald (*Going My Way*)
Supporting Actress: Ethel Barrymore (*None but the Lonely Heart*)
Original Story: Leo McCarey (*Going My Way*)
Original Screenplay: Lamar Trotti (*Wilson*)
Screenplay: Frank Butler, Frank Cavett (*Going My Way*)

1945
Picture: *The Lost Weekend*
Director: Billy Wilder (*The Lost Weekend*)
Actor: Ray Milland (*The Lost Weekend*)
Actress: Joan Crawford (*Mildred Pierce*)
Supporting Actor: James Dunn (*A Tree Grows in Brooklyn*)
Supporting Actress: Anne Revere (*National Velvet*)
Original Story: Charles G. Booth (*The House on 92nd Street*)
Original Screenplay: Richard Schweizer (*Marie-Louise*)
Screenplay: Charles Brackett, Billy Wilder (*The Lost Weekend*)

1946
Picture: *The Best Years of Our Lives*
Director: William Wyler (*The Best Years of Our Lives*)
Actor: Fredric March (*The Best Years of Our Lives*)
Actress: Olivia de Havilland (*To Each His Own*)
Supporting Actor: Harold Russell (*The Best Years of Our Lives*)
Supporting Actress: Anne Baxter (*The Razor's Edge*)
Original Story: Clemence Dane (*Vacation from Marriage*)
Original Screenplay: Muriel Box, Sydney Box (*The Seventh Veil*)
Screenplay: Robert E. Sherwood (*The Best Years of Our Lives*)

1947
Picture: *Gentleman's Agreement*
Director: Elia Kazan (*Gentleman's Agreement*)
Actor: Ronald Colman (*A Double Life*)
Actress: Loretta Young (*The Farmer's Daughter*)
Supporting Actor: Edmund Gwenn (*Miracle on 34th Street*)
Supporting Actress: Celeste Holm (*Gentleman's Agreement*)
Original Story: Valentine Davies (*Miracle on 34th Street*)
Original Screenplay: Sidney Sheldon (*The Bachelor and the Bobby-Soxer*)
Screenplay: George Seaton (*Miracle on 34th Street*)

1948
Picture: *Hamlet*
Director: John Huston (*The Treasure of the Sierra Madre*)
Actor: Laurence Olivier (*Hamlet*)
Actress: Jane Wyman (*Johnny Belinda*)
Supporting Actor: Walter Huston (*The Treasure of the Sierra Madre*)
Supporting Actress: Claire Trevor (*Key Largo*)
Motion Picture Story: Richard Sweizer, David Wechsler (*The Search*)
Screenplay: John Huston (*The Treasure of the Sierra Madre*)

1949
Picture: *All the King's Men*
Director: Joseph L. Mankiewicz (*A Letter to Three Wives*)
Actor: Broderick Crawford (*All the King's Men*)
Actress: Olivia de Havilland (*The Heiress*)
Supporting Actor: Dean Jagger (*Twelve O'Clock High*)
Supporting Actress: Mercedes McCambridge (*All the King's Men*)
Motion Picture Story: Douglas Morrow (*The Stratton Story*)
Screenplay: Joseph L. Mankiewicz (*A Letter to Three Wives*)
Story & Screenplay: Robert Pirosh (*Battleground*)

1950
Picture: *All About Eve*
Director: Joseph L. Mankiewicz (*All About Eve*)
Actor: José Ferrer (*Cyrano de Bergerac*)
Actress; Judy Holliday (*Born Yesterday*)
Supporting Actor: George Sanders (*All About Eve*)
Supporting Actress: Josephine Hull (*Harvey*)
Motion Picture Story: Edna Anhalt, Edward Anhalt (*Panic in the Streets*)
Screenplay: Joseph L. Mankiewicz (*All About Eve*)
Story & Screenplay: Charles Brackett, Billy Wilder, D. M. Marshman Jnr (*Sunset Boulevard*)

1951
Picture: *An American in Paris*
Director: George Stevens (*A Place in the Sun*)
Actor: Humphrey Bogart (*The African Queen*)
Actress: Vivien Leigh (*A Streetcar Named Desire*)
Supporting Actor: Karl Malden (*A Streetcar Named Desire*)
Supporting Actress: Kim Hunter (*A Streetcar Named Desire*)
Motion Picture Story: Paul Dehn, James Bernard (*Seven Days to Noon*)
Screenplay: Michael Wilson, Harry Brown (*A Place in the Sun*)
Story & Screenplay: Alan Jay Lerner (*An American in Paris*)

1952
Picture: *The Greatest Show on Earth*
Director: John Ford (*The Quiet Man*)
Actor: Gary Cooper (*High Noon*)
Actress: Shirley Booth (*Come Back Little Sheba*)
Supporting Actor: Anthony Quinn (*Viva Zapata!*)
Supporting Actress: Gloria Grahame (*The Bad and the Beautiful*)
Motion Picture Story: Frederic M. Frank, Theodore St John, Frank Cavett (*The Greatest Show on Earth*)
Screenplay: Charles Schnee (*The Bad and the Beautiful*)
Story & Screenplay: T. E. B. Clarke (*The Lavender Hill Mob*)

1953
Picture: *From Here to Eternity*
Director: Fred Zinnemann (*From Here to Eternity*)

Actor: William Holden (*Stalag 17*)
Actress: Audrey Hepburn (*Roman Holiday*)
Supporting Actor: Frank Sinatra (*From Here to Eternity*)
Supporting Actress: Donna Reed (*From Here to Eternity*)
Motion Picture Story: Ian McLellan Hunter, fronting for the blacklisted Dalton Trumbo (*Roman Holiday*)
Screenplay: Daniel Taradash (*From Here to Eternity*)
Story & Screenplay: Charles Brackett, Walter Reisch, Richard Breen (*Titanic*)

1954
Picture: *On the Waterfront*
Director: Elia Kazan (*On the Waterfront*)
Actor: Marlon Brando (*On the Waterfront*)
Actress: Grace Kelly (*The Country Girl*)
Supporting Actor: Edmond O'Brien (*The Barefoot Contessa*)
Supporting Actress: Eva Marie Saint (*On the Waterfront*)
Motion Picture Story: Philip Yordan (*Broken Lance*)
Screenplay: George Seaton (*The Country Girl*)
Story & Screenplay: Budd Schulberg (*On the Waterfront*)

1955
Picture: *Marty*
Director: Delbert Mann (*Marty*)
Actor: Ernest Borgnine (*Marty*)
Actress: Anna Magnani (*The Rose Tattoo*)
Supporting Actor: Jack Lemmon (*Mister Roberts*)
Supporting Actress: Jo Van Fleet (*East of Eden*)
Motion Picture Story: Daniel Fuchs (*Love Me or Leave Me*)
Screenplay: Paddy Chayevsky (*Marty*)
Story & Screenplay: William Ludwig, Sonya Levien (*Interrupted Melody*)

1956
Picture: *Around the World in Eighty Days*
Director: George Stevens (*Giant*)
Actor: Yul Brynner (*The King and I*)
Actress: Ingrid Bergman (*Anastasia*)
Supporting Actor: Anthony Quinn (*Lust for Life*)
Supporting Actress: Dorothy Malone (*Written on the Wind*)
Motion Picture Story: Dalton Trumbo (as Robert Rich) (*The Brave One*)
Original Screenplay: Albert Lamorisse (*The Red Balloon*)
Adapted Screenplay: James Poe, John Farrow, S. J. Perelman (*Around the World in Eighty Days*)

1957
Picture: *The Bridge on the River Kwai*
Director: David Lean (*The Bridge on the River Kwai*)
Actor: Alec Guinness (*The Bridge on the River Kwai*)
Actress: Joanne Woodward (*The Three Faces of Eve*)
Supporting Actor: Red Buttons (*Sayonara*)
Supporting Actress: Miyoshi Umeki (*Sayonara*)
Original Story & Screenplay: George Wells (*Designing Woman*)
Adapted Screenplay: Pierre Boulle, Michael Wilson, Carl Foreman (*The Bridge on the River Kwai*)

1958
Picture: *Gigi*
Director: Vincente Minnelli (*Gigi*)
Actor: David Niven (*Separate Tables*)
Actress: Susan Hayward (*I Want to Live*)
Supporting Actor: Burl Ives (*The Big Country*)
Supporting Actress: Wendy Hiller (*Separate Tables*)
Original Story & Screenplay: Nathan E. Douglas (the blacklisted Ned Young), Harold Jacob Smith (*The Defiant Ones*)
Adapted Screenplay: Alan Jay Lerner (*Gigi*)

1959
Picture: *Ben-Hur*
Director: William Wyler (*Ben-Hur*)
Actor: Charlton Heston (*Ben-Hur*)
Actress: Simone Signoret (*Room at the Top*)
Supporting Actor: Hugh Griffith (*Ben-Hur*)
Supporting Actress: Shelley Winters (*The Diary of Anne Frank*)
Original Story & Screenplay: Russell Rouse, Clarence Greene, Stanley Shapiro, Maurice Richlin (*Pillow Talk*)
Adapted Screenplay: Neil Paterson (*Room at the Top*)

1960
Picture: *The Apartment*
Director: Billy Wilder (*The Apartment*)
Actor: Burt Lancaster (*Elmer Gantry*)
Actress: Elizabeth Taylor (*Butterfield 8*)
Supporting Actor: Peter Ustinov (*Spartacus*)
Supporting Actress: Shirley Jones (*Elmer Gantry*)
Original Story & Screenplay: Billy Wilder, I. A. L. Diamond (*The Apartment*)
Adapted Screenplay: Richard Brooks (*Elmer Gantry*)

1961
Picture: *West Side Story*
Director: Jerome Robbins, Robert Wise (*West Side Story*)
Actor: Maximilian Schell (*Judgment at Nuremberg*)
Actress: Sophia Loren (*Two Women*)
Supporting Actor: George Chakiris (*West Side Story*)
Supporting Actress: Rita Moreno (*West Side Story*)
Original Story & Screenplay: William Inge (*Splendor in the Grass*)
Adapted Screenplay: Abby Mann (*Judgment at Nuremberg*)

1962
Picture: *Lawrence of Arabia*
Director: David Lean (*Lawrence of Arabia*)
Actor: Gregory Peck (*To Kill a Mockingbird*)
Actress: Anne Bancroft (*The Miracle Worker*)
Supporting Actor: Ed Begley (*Sweet Bird of Youth*)
Supporting Actress: Patty Duke (*The Miracle Worker*)
Original Story & Screenplay: Ennio de Concini, Alfredo Gianetti, Pietro Germi (*Divorce Italian Style*)
Adapted Screenplay: Horton Foote (*To Kill a Mockingbird*)

1963
Picture: *Tom Jones*
Director: Tony Richardson (*Tom Jones*)
Actor: Sidney Poitier (*Lilies of the Field*)
Actress: Patricia Neal (*Hud*)
Supporting Actor: Melvyn Douglas (*Hud*)
Supporting Actress: Margaret Rutherford (*The VIPs*)
Original Story & Screenplay: James R. Webb (*How the West Was Won*)
Adapted Screenplay: John Osborne (*Tom Jones*)

1964
Picture: *My Fair Lady*
Director: George Cukor (*My Fair Lady*)
Actor: Rex Harrison (*My Fair Lady*)
Actress: Julie Andrews (*Mary Poppins*)
Supporting Actor: Peter Ustinov (*Topkapi*)
Supporting Actress: Lila Kedrova (*Zorba the Greek*)
Original Story & Screenplay: S. H. Barnett, Peter Stone, Frank Tarloff (*Father Goose*)
Adapted Screenplay: Edward Anhalt (*Becket*)

1965
Picture: *The Sound of Music*
Director: Robert Wise (*The Sound of Music*)
Actor: Lee Marvin (*Cat Ballou*)
Actress: Julie Christie (*Darling*)
Supporting Actor: Martin Balsam (*A Thousand Clowns*)
Supporting Actress: Shelley Winters (*A Patch of Blue*)
Original Story & Screenplay: Frederic Raphael (*Darling*)
Adapted Screenplay: Robert Bolt (*Dr Zhivago*)

1966
Picture: *A Man for All Seasons*
Director: Fred Zinnemann (*A Man for All Seasons*)
Actor: Paul Scofield (*A Man for All Seasons*)
Actress: Elizabeth Taylor (*Who's Afraid of Virginia Woolf?*)
Supporting Actor: Walter Matthau (*The Fortune Cookie*)
Supporting Actress: Sandy Dennis (*Who's Afraid of Virginia Woolf?*)
Original Story & Screenplay: Claude Lelouch, Pierre Uytterhoeven (*A Man and a Woman*)
Adapted Screenplay: Robert Bolt (*A Man for All Seasons*)

1967
Picture: *In the Heat of the Night*
Director: Mike Nichols (*The Graduate*)
Actor: Rod Steiger (*In the Heat of the Night*)
Actress: Katharine Hepburn (*Guess Who's Coming to Dinner*)
Supporting Actor: George Kennedy (*Cool Hand Luke*)
Supporting Actress: Estelle Parsons (*Bonnie and Clyde*)
Original Story & Screenplay: William Rose (*Guess Who's Coming to Dinner*)
Adapted Screenplay: Sterling Silliphant (*In the Heat of the Night*)

1968
Picture: *Oliver!*
Director: Carol Reed (*Oliver!*)
Actor: Cliff Robertson (*Charly*)
Actress: Katharine Hepburn (*The Lion in Winter*), Barbra Streisand (*Funny Girl*)
Supporting Actor: Jack Albertson (*The Subject Was Roses*)
Supporting Actress: Ruth Gordon (*Rosemary's Baby*)
Original Story & Screenplay: Mel Brooks (*The Producers*)
Adapted Screenplay: James Goldman (*The Lion in Winter*)

1969
Picture: *Midnight Cowboy*
Director: John Schlesinger (*Midnight Cowboy*)
Actor: John Wayne (*True Grit*)
Actress: Maggie Smith (*The Prime of Miss Jean Brodie*)
Supporting Actor: Gig Young (*They Shoot Horses, Don't They?*)
Supporting Actress: Goldie Hawn (*Cactus Flower*)
Original Story & Screenplay: William Goldman (*Butch Cassidy and the Sundance Kid*)
Adapted Screenplay: Waldo Salt (*Midnight Cowboy*)

1970
Picture: *Patton*
Director: Franklin J. Schaffner (*Patton*)
Actor: George C. Scott (*Patton*)
Actress: Glenda Jackson (*Women in Love*)
Supporting Actor: John Mills (*Ryan's Daughter*)
Supporting Actress: Helen Hayes (*Airport*)
Original Story & Screenplay: Francis Ford Coppola, Edmund H. North (*Patton*)
Adapted Screenplay: Ring Lardner Jnr (*M*A*S*H*)

1971
Picture: *The French Connection*
Director: William Friedkin (*The French Connection*)
Actor: Gene Hackman (*The French Connection*)
Actress: Jane Fonda (*Klute*)
Supporting Actor: Ben Johnson (*The Last Picture Show*)
Supporting Actress: Cloris Leachman (*The Last Picture Show*)
Original Story & Screenplay: Paddy Chayevsky (*The Hospital*)
Adapted Screenplay: Ernest Tidyman (*The French Connection*)

1972
Picture: *The Godfather*
Director: Bob Fosse (*Cabaret*)
Actor: Marlon Brando (*The Godfather*)
Actress: Liza Minnelli (*Cabaret*)
Supporting Actor: Joel Grey (*Cabaret*)
Supporting Actress: Eileen Heckart (*Butterflies Are Free*)
Original Story & Screenplay: Jeremy Larner (*The Candidate*)
Adapted Screenplay: Mario Puzo, Francis Ford Coppola (*The Godfather*)

1973
Picture: *The Sting*
Director: George Roy Hill (*The Sting*)
Actor: Jack Lemmon (*Save the Tiger*)
Actress: Glenda Jackson (*A Touch of Class*)
Supporting Actor: John Houseman (*The Paper Chase*)
Supporting Actress: Tatum O'Neal (*Paper Moon*)
Original Story & Screenplay: David S. Ward (*The Sting*)
Adapted Screenplay: William Peter Blatty (*The Exorcist*)

1974
Picture: *The Godfather Part II*
Director: Francis Ford Coppola (*The Godfather Part II*)
Actor: Art Carney (*Harry and Tonto*)
Actress: Ellen Burstyn (*Alice Doesn't Live Here Any More*)
Supporting Actor: Robert de Niro (*The Godfather Part II*)
Supporting Actress: Ingrid Bergman (*Murder on the Orient Express*)
Original Story & Screenplay: Robert Towne (*Chinatown*)
Adapted Screenplay: Francis Ford Coppola, Mario Puzo (*The Godfather Part II*)

1975
Picture: *One Flew over the Cuckoo's Nest*
Director: Milos Forman (*One Flew over the Cuckoo's Nest*)
Actor: Jack Nicholson (*One Flew over the Cuckoo's Nest*)
Actress: Louise Fletcher (*One Flew over the Cuckoo's Nest*)
Supporting Actor: George Burns (*The Sunshine Boys*)
Supporting Actress: Lee Grant (*Shampoo*)
Original Screenplay: Frank Pierson (*Dog Day Afternoon*)
Adapted Screenplay: Lawrence Hauben, Bo Goldman (*One Flew over the Cuckoo's Nest*)

1976
Picture: *Rocky*
Director: John G. Avildsen (*Rocky*)
Actor: Peter Finch (*Network*)
Actress: Faye Dunaway (*Network*)
Supporting Actor: Jason Robards (*All the President's Men*)
Supporting Actress: Beatrice Straight (*Network*)
Original Screenplay: Paddy Chayevsky (*Network*)
Adapted Screenplay: William Goldman (*All the President's Men*)

1977
Picture: *Annie Hall*
Director: Woody Allen (*Annie Hall*)
Actor: Richard Dreyfuss (*The Goodbye Girl*)
Actress: Diane Keaton (*Annie Hall*)
Supporting Actor: Jason Robards (*Julia*)
Supporting Actress: Vanessa Redgrave (*Julia*)
Original Screenplay: Woody Allen, Marshall Brickman (*Annie Hall*)
Adapted Screenplay: Alvin Sargent (*Julia*)

1978
Picture: *The Deer Hunter*
Director: Michael Cimino (*The Deer Hunter*)
Actor: Jon Voight (*Coming Home*)
Actress: Jane Fonda (*Coming Home*)
Supporting Actor: Christopher Walken (*The Deer Hunter*)
Supporting Actress: Maggie Smith (*California Suite*)
Original Screenplay: Nancy Dowd, Waldo Salt, Robert C. Jones (*Coming Home*)
Adapted Screenplay: Oliver Stone (*Midnight Express*)

1979
Picture: *Kramer versus Kramer*
Director: Robert Benton (*Kramer versus Kramer*)
Actor: Dustin Hoffman (*Kramer versus Kramer*)
Actress: Sally Field (*Norma Rae*)
Supporting Actor: Melvyn Douglas (*Being There*)
Supporting Actress: Meryl Streep (*Kramer versus Kramer*)
Original Screenplay: Steve Tesich (*Breaking Away*)
Adapted Screenplay: Robert Benton (*Kramer versus Kramer*)

1980
Picture: *Ordinary People*
Director: Robert Redford (*Ordinary People*)
Actor: Robert de Niro (*Raging Bull*)
Actress: Sissy Spacek (*Coal Miner's Daughter*)
Supporting Actor: Timothy Hutton (*Ordinary People*)
Supporting Actress: Mary Steenburgen (*Melvin and Howard*)
Original Screenplay: Bo Goldman (*Melvin and Howard*)
Adapted Screenplay: Alvin Sargent (*Ordinary People*)

1981
Picture: *Chariots of Fire*
Director: Warren Beatty (*Reds*)
Actor: Henry Fonda (*On Golden Pond*)

Actress: Katharine Hepburn (*On Golden Pond*)
Supporting Actor: John Gielgud (*Arthur*)
Supporting Actress: Maureen Stapleton (*Reds*)
Original Screenplay: Colin Welland (*Chariots of Fire*)
Adapted Screenplay: Ernest Thompson (*On Golden Pond*)

1982
Picture: *Gandhi*
Director: Richard Attenborough (*Gandhi*)
Actor: Ben Kingsley (*Gandhi*)
Actress: Meryl Streep (*Sophie's Choice*)
Supporting Actor: Louis Gossett Jnr (*An Officer and a Gentleman*)
Supporting Actress: Jessica Lange (*Tootsie*)
Original Screenplay: John Briley (*Gandhi*)
Adapted Screenplay: Costa-Gavras, Donald Stewart (*Missing*)

1983
Picture: *Terms of Endearment*
Director: James L. Brooks (*Terms of Endearment*)
Actor: Robert Duvall (*Tender Mercies*)
Actress: Shirley Maclaine (*Terms of Endearment*)
Supporting Actor: Jack Nicholson (*Terms of Endearment*)
Supporting Actress: Linda Hunt (*The Year of Living Dangerously*)
Original Screenplay: Horton Foote (*Tender Mercies*)
Adapted Screenplay: James L. Brooks (*Terms of Endearment*)

1984
Picture: *Amadeus*
Director: Milos Forman (*Amadeus*)
Actor: F. Murray Abraham (*Amadeus*)
Actress: Sally Field (*Places in the Heart*)
Supporting Actor: Haing S. Ngor (*The Killing Fields*)
Supporting Actress: Peggy Ashcroft (*A Passage to India*)
Original Screenplay: Robert Benton (*Places in the Heart*)
Adapted Screenplay: Peter Shaffer (*Amadeus*)

1985
Picture: *Out of Africa*
Director: Sydney Pollack (*Out of Africa*)
Actor: William Hurt (*Kiss of the Spider Woman*)
Actress: Geraldine Page (*The Trip to Bountiful*)
Supporting Actor: Don Ameche (*Cocoon*)
Supporting Actress: Anjelica Huston (*Prizzi's Honor*)
Original Screenplay: William Kelley, Pamela Wallace, Earl W. Wallace (*Witness*)
Adapted Screenplay: Kurt Luedtke (*Out of Africa*)

1986
Picture: *Platoon*
Director: Oliver Stone (*Platoon*)
Actor: Paul Newman (*The Color of Money*)
Actress: Marlee Matlin (*Children of a Lesser God*)
Supporting Actor: Michael Caine (*Hannah and Her Sisters*)
Supporting Actress: Dianne Wiest (*Hannah and Her Sisters*)
Original Screenplay: Woody Allen (*Hannah and Her Sisters*)
Adapted Screenplay: Ruth Prawer Jhabvala (*A Room with a View*)

1987
Picture: *The Last Emperor*
Director: Bernardo Bertolucci (*The Last Emperor*)
Actor: Michael Douglas (*Wall Street*)
Actress: Cher (*Moonstruck*)
Supporting Actor: Sean Connery (*The Untouchables*)
Supporting Actress: Olympia Dukakis (*Moonstruck*)
Original Screenplay: John Patrick Shanley (*Moonstruck*)
Adapted Screenplay: Mark Peploe, Bernardo Bertolucci (*The Last Emperor*)

1988
Picture: *Rain Man*
Director: Barry Levinson (*Rain Man*)
Actor: Dustin Hoffman (*Rain Man*)
Actress: Jodie Foster (*The Accused*)
Supporting Actor: Kevin Kline (*A Fish Called Wanda*)
Supporting Actress: Geena Davis (*The Accidental Tourist*)
Original Screenplay: Ronald Bass, Barry Morrow (*Rain Man*)
Adapted Screenplay: Christopher Hampton (*Dangerous Liaisons*)

1989
Picture: *Driving Miss Daisy*
Director: Oliver Stone (*Born on the Fourth of July*)
Actor: Daniel Day-Lewis (*My Left Foot*)
Actress: Jessica Tandy (*Driving Miss Daisy*)
Supporting Actor: Denzel Washington (*Glory*)
Supporting Actress: Brenda Fricker (*My Left Foot*)
Original Screenplay: Tom Schulman (*Dead Poets Society*)
Adapted Screenplay: Alfred Uhry (*Driving Miss Daisy*)

1990
Picture: *Dances with Wolves*
Director: Kevin Costner (*Dances with Wolves*)
Actor: Jeremy Irons (*Reversal of Fortune*)
Actress: Kathy Bates (*Misery*)
Supporting Actor: Joe Pesci (*GoodFellas*)
Supporting Actress: Whoopi Goldberg (*Ghost*)
Original Screenplay: Bruce Joel Rubin (*Ghost*)
Adapted Screenplay: Michael Blake (*Dances with Wolves*)

1991
Picture: *Silence of the Lambs*
Director: Jonathan Demme (*Silence of the Lambs*)
Actor: Anthony Hopkins (*Silence of the Lambs*)
Actress: Jodie Foster (*Silence of the Lambs*)
Supporting Actor: Jack Palance (*City Slickers*)
Supporting Actress: Mercedes Ruehl (*The Fisher King*)
Original Screenplay: Callie Khouri (*Thelma and Louise*)
Adapted Screenplay: Ted Tally (*Silence of the Lambs*)

1992
Picture: *Unforgiven*
Director: Clint Eastwood (*Unforgiven*)
Actor: Al Pacino (*Scent of a Woman*)
Actress: Emma Thompson (*Howards End*)
Supporting Actor: Gene Hackman (*Unforgiven*)
Supporting Actress: Marisa Tomei (*My Cousin Vinny*)
Original Screenplay: Neil Jordan (*The Crying Game*)
Adapted Screenplay: Ruth Prawer Jhabvala (*Howards End*)

1993
Picture: *Schindler's List*
Director: Steven Spielberg (*Schindler's List*)
Actor: Tom Hanks (*Philadelphia*)
Actress: Holly Hunter (*The Piano*)
Supporting Actor: Tommy Lee Jones (*The Fugitive*)
Supporting Actress: Anna Paquin (*The Piano*)
Original Screenplay: Jane Campion (*The Piano*)
Adapted Screenplay: Steven Zaillian (*Schindler's List*)

1994
Picture: *Forrest Gump*
Director: Robert Zemeckis (*Forrest Gump*)
Actor: Tom Hanks (*Forrest Gump*)
Actress: Jessica Lange (*Blue Sky*)
Supporting Actor: Martin Landau (*Ed Wood*)
Supporting Actress: Dianne Wiest (*Bullets over Broadway*)
Original Screenplay: Quentin Tarantino, Roger Avary (*Pulp Fiction*)
Adapted Screenplay: Eric Roth (*Forrest Gump*)

1995
Picture: *Braveheart*
Director: Mel Gibson (*Braveheart*)
Actor: Nicolas Cage (*Leaving Las Vegas*)
Actress: Susan Sarandon (*Dead Man Walking*)
Supporting Actor: Kevin Spacey (*The Usual Suspects*)
Supporting Actress: Mira Sorvino (*Mighty Aphrodite*)
Original Screenplay: Christopher McQuarrie (*The Usual Suspects*)
Adapted Screenplay: Emma Thompson (*Sense and Sensibility*)

1996
Picture: *The English Patient*
Director: Anthony Minghella (*The English Patient*)
Actor: Geoffrey Rush (*Shine*)
Actress: Frances McDormand (*Fargo*)
Supporting Actor: Cuba Gooding Jr (*Jerry Maguire*)
Supporting Actress: Juliette Binoche (*The English Patient*)
Original Screenplay: Ethan Coen, Joel Coen (*Fargo*)
Adapted Screenplay: Billy Bob Thornton (*Slingblade*)

1997
Picture: *Titanic*
Director: James Cameron (*Titanic*)
Actor: Jack Nicholson (*As Good As It Gets*)
Actress: Helen Hunt (*As Good As It Gets*)
Supporting Actor: Robin Williams (*Good Will Hunting*)
Supporting Actress: Kim Basinger (*LA Confidential*)
Original Screenplay: Matt Damon, Ben Affleck (*Good Will Hunting*)
Adapted Screenplay: Curtis Hanson, Brian Helgeland (*LA Confidential*)

1998
Picture: *Shakespeare in Love*
Director: Steven Spielberg (*Saving Private Ryan*)
Actor: Roberto Begnini (*Life is Beautiful*)
Actress: Gwyneth Paltrow (*Shakespeare in Love*)
Supporting Actor: James Coburn (*Affliction*)
Supporting Actress: Judi Dench (*Shakespeare in Love*)
Original Screenplay: Marc Norman, Tom Stoppard (*Shakespeare in Love*)
Adapted Screenplay: Bill Condon (*Gods and Monsters*)

1999
Picture: *American Beauty*
Director: Sam Mendes (*American Beauty*)
Actor: Kevin Spacey (*American Beauty*)
Actress: Hilary Swank (*Boys Don't Cry*)
Supporting Actor: Michael Caine (*The Cider House Rules*)
Supporting Actress: Angelina Jolie (*Girl, Interrupted*)
Original Screenplay: Alan Ball (*American Beauty*)
Adapted Screenplay: John Irving (*The Cider House Rules*)

2000
Picture: *Gladiator*
Director: Stephen Soderbergh (*Traffic*)
Actor: Russell Crowe (*Gladiator*)
Actress: Julia Roberts (*Erin Brockovich*)
Supporting Actor: Benicio Del Toro (*Traffic*)
Supporting Actress: Marcia Gay Harden (*Pollock*)
Original Screenplay: Cameron Crowe (*Almost Famous*)
Adapted Screenplay: Stephen Gaghan (*Traffic*)

2001
Picture: *A Beautiful Mind*
Director: Ron Howard (*A Beautiful Mind*)
Actor: Denzel Washington (*Training Day*)
Actress: Halle Berry (*Monster's Ball*)
Supporting Actor: Jim Broadbent (*Iris*)
Supporting Actress: Jennifer Connelly (*A Beautiful Mind*)
Original Screenplay: Julian Fellowes (*Gosford Park*)
Adapted Screenplay: Akiva Goldsman (*A Beautiful Mind*)
Animated Feature: *Shrek*

2002
Picture: Chicago
Director: Roman Polanski (*The Pianist*)
Actor: Adrien Brody (*The Pianist*)
Actress: Nicole Kidman (*The Hours*)
Supporting Actor: Chris Cooper (*Adaptation*)
Supporting Actress: Catherine Zeta-Jones (*Chicago*)
Original Screenplay: Pedro Almodovar (*Talk to Her/Hable con Ella*)
Adapted Screenplay: Ronald Harwood (*The Pianist*)
Animated Feature: Spirited Away/Sen Yo Chihiro No Kamikakushi

Four-Star Films – by Title

A Bout de Souffle
A Nous la Liberté
The Adventures of Robin Hood
After Life
Aguirre, Wrath of God
Aladdin
Alexander Nevsky
Alien
All Quiet on the Western Front
All that Money Can Buy
All the President's Men
American Beauty
An American in Paris
And Then There Were None
Andrei Rublev
Angels with Dirty Faces
Annie Hall
Aparajito
Ashes and Diamonds
Au Revoir Les Enfants
Bad Day at Black Rock
Badlands
Bambi
The Band Wagon
The Battle of Algiers
The Battleship Potemkin
Begone Dull Care
Belle de Jour
The Best Years of Our Lives
Big Business
The Birth of a Nation
The Blue Angel
Bonnie and Clyde
Breaking the Waves
The Bride of Frankenstein
The Bridge on the River Kwai
Brief Encounter
Butch Cassidy and the Sundance Kid
Cabaret
The Cabinet of Dr Caligari
Casablanca
The Chant of Jimmie Blacksmith
Chinatown
Cinema Paradiso
Citizen Kane
Crossfire
The Cure
David Copperfield
A Day at the Races
Day for Night
Days of Heaven
The Dead
Dead of Night
Deliverance
Destry Rides Again
The Discreet Charm of the Bourgeoisie
Doctor Jekyll and Mr Hyde
Dr Strangelove; or, How I Learned to Stop Worrying and Love the Bomb
La Dolce Vita
Don't Look Now
Double Indemnity
The Driver
Duck Soup
Dumbo
E.T. The Extra-Terrestrial
Easy Rider
Easy Street
Eight and a Half
Les Enfants du Paradis
The Enigma of Kaspar Hauser
Face to Face
Fanny and Alexander
Fantasia
Fargo
Fitzcarraldo
Foreign Correspondent
The Four Feathers
Frankenstein
The French Connection
Gaslight
The Gay Divorcee
The General
Genevieve
The Godfather
The Godfather Part II
The Golden Age of Comedy
Gone with the Wind
GoodFellas
Gosford Park
The Graduate
The Grapes of Wrath
Great Expectations
A Hard Day's Night
Harold Lloyd's World of Comedy
Henry V
High Noon
His Girl Friday
Hud
The Hunchback of Notre Dame
The Hustler
I Am a Fugitive from a Chain Gang
If…
In the Heat of the Night
In Which We Serve
Intolerance
Invasion of the Body Snatchers
The Invisible Man
It's a Wonderful Life
The Jazz Singer
The Jolson Story
Jules et Jim
Kes
The Kid Brother
A Kind of Loving
King Kong
King of Comedy
Kings Row
The Knack
Kwaidan
LA Confidential
Lacombe, Lucien
The Lady Vanishes
The Last Metro
The Last Picture Show
The Lavender Hill Mob
Lawrence of Arabia
The Leopard
The Letter
Listen to Britain
Little Caesar
London Can Take It
Lost Horizon
The Lost Weekend
Love Me Tonight
The Magnificent Ambersons
The Maltese Falcon
A Man for All Seasons
The Man in the White Suit
The Manchurian Candidate
Manhattan
Marty
M*A*S*H
A Matter of Life and Death
Mean Streets
Mephisto
Midnight Cowboy
Le Million
Les Misérables
Mr Smith Goes to Washington
Monsieur Hulot's Holiday
The Music Box
The Naked City
Napoleon
Network
A Night at the Opera
North by Northwest
October
Oh Mr Porter
The Old Dark House
Oliver Twist
On the Town
On the Waterfront
Once Upon a Time in America
One Flew over the Cuckoo's Nest
The Passion of Joan of Arc
Passport to Pimlico
Pather Panchali
Paths of Glory
Pelle the Conqueror
Persona
The Philadelphia Story
The Piano
Picnic at Hanging Rock
Pinocchio
The Player
The Prisoner of Zenda
Psycho
Pygmalion
Raging Bull
Ran
Rashomon
Rear Window
Rebecca
The Red Balloon
The Red Shoes
Rembrandt
San Francisco
Saturday Night and Sunday Morning
Scarface
Schindler's List
The Searchers
The Seven Samurai
The Seventh Seal
A Short Film about Killing
Singin' in the Rain
Snow White and the Seven Dwarfs
Some Like It Hot
Sons of the Desert
Southern Comfort
Stagecoach
Star Wars
Sullivan's Travels
Sweet Smell of Success
Target for Tonight
Taxi Driver
The Thief of Baghdad
Things to Come
The Third Man
The 39 Steps
This Is Spinal Tap
Throne of Blood
The Tin Drum
To Be or Not to Be
Tokyo Story
Tom Jones
Tootsie
Top Hat
Touch of Evil
Toy Story
Tristana
Triumph of the Will
Trouble in Paradise
The True Glory
12 Angry Men
Two Tars
2001: A Space Odyssey
Unforgiven
Vertigo
Viridiana
Viskningar och Rop
Walkabout
Way Out West
The Way to the Stars
Weekend
West Side Story
When Harry Met Sally
Whisky Galore
Who Framed Roger Rabbit
Who's Afraid of Virginia Woolf?
Why We Fight
The Wild Bunch
Wild Strawberries
Wings of Desire
Witness
Woodstock
The World of Apu
Yojimbo
Z

Four-Star Films – Year by Year

1915
The Birth of a Nation

1916
Intolerance

1917
The Cure
Easy Street

1919
The Cabinet of Dr Caligari

1925
The Battleship Potemkin

1926
The General

1927
The Jazz Singer
The Kid Brother
Napoleon
October

1928
The Passion of Joan of Arc
Two Tars

1929
Big Business

1930
All Quiet on the Western Front
The Blue Angel

1931
A Nous la Liberté
Doctor Jekyll and Mr Hyde
Frankenstein
Little Caesar
Le Million

1932
I Am a Fugitive from a Chain Gang
Love Me Tonight
The Music Box
The Old Dark House
Scarface
Trouble in Paradise

1933
Duck Soup
The Invisible Man
King Kong

1934
David Copperfield
The Gay Divorcee
Sons of the Desert

1935
The Bride of Frankenstein
Les Misérables
A Night at the Opera
The 39 Steps
Top Hat

1936
Rembrandt
San Francisco
Things to Come
Triumph of the Will

1937
A Day at the Races
Lost Horizon
Oh Mr Porter
The Prisoner of Zenda
Snow White and the Seven Dwarfs
Way Out West

1938
The Adventures of Robin Hood
Alexander Nevsky
Angels with Dirty Faces
The Lady Vanishes
Pygmalion

1939
Destry Rides Again
The Four Feathers
Gone with the Wind
The Hunchback of Notre Dame
Mr Smith Goes to Washington
Stagecoach

1940
Fantasia
Foreign Correspondent
Gaslight
The Grapes of Wrath
His Girl Friday
The Letter
London Can Take It
The Philadelphia Story
Pinocchio
Rebecca
The Thief of Baghdad

1941
All that Money Can Buy
Citizen Kane
Dumbo
Listen to Britain
The Maltese Falcon
Sullivan's Travels
Target for Tonight

1942
Bambi
Casablanca
In Which We Serve
Kings Row
The Magnificent Ambersons
To Be or Not to Be
Why We Fight

1944
Double Indemnity
Henry V

1945
And Then There Were None
Brief Encounter
Dead of Night
Les Enfants du Paradis
The Lost Weekend
The True Glory
The Way to the Stars

1946
The Best Years of Our Lives
Great Expectations
It's a Wonderful Life
The Jolson Story
A Matter of Life and Death

1947
Crossfire

1948
The Naked City
Oliver Twist
The Red Shoes
Whisky Galore

1949
On the Town
Passport to Pimlico
The Third Man

1951
An American in Paris
The Lavender Hill Mob
The Man in the White Suit
Rashomon

1952
High Noon
Singin' in the Rain

1953
The Band Wagon
Begone Dull Care
Genevieve
Monsieur Hulot's Holiday
Tokyo Story

1954
On the Waterfront
Rear Window
The Seven Samurai

1955
Bad Day at Black Rock
Invasion of the Body Snatchers
Marty
Pather Panchali
The Red Balloon

1956
Aparajito
The Searchers

1957
The Bridge on the River Kwai
The Golden Age of Comedy
Paths of Glory
The Seventh Seal
Sweet Smell of Success
Throne of Blood
12 Angry Men
Wild Strawberries

1958
Ashes and Diamonds
Touch of Evil
Vertigo

1959
North by Northwest
Some Like It Hot
The World of Apu

1960
A Bout de Souffle
La Dolce Vita
Psycho
Saturday Night and Sunday Morning

1961
The Hustler
Viridiana
West Side Story
Yojimbo

1962
Harold Lloyd's World of Comedy
Jules et Jim
A Kind of Loving
Lawrence of Arabia
The Manchurian Candidate

1963
Dr Strangelove; or, How I Learned to Stop
Worrying and Love the Bomb
Eight and a Half
Hud
The Leopard
Tom Jones

1964
A Hard Day's Night
Kwaidan

1965
The Battle of Algiers
The Knack

1966
Andrei Rublev
A Man for All Seasons
Persona
Who's Afraid of Virginia Woolf?

1967
Belle de Jour
Bonnie and Clyde
The Graduate
In the Heat of the Night

1968
If…
2001: A Space Odyssey
Weekend
Z

1969
Butch Cassidy and the Sundance Kid
Easy Rider
Kes
Midnight Cowboy
The Wild Bunch

1970
M*A*S*H
Tristana
Walkabout
Woodstock

1971
The French Connection
The Last Picture Show

1972
Aguirre, Wrath of God
Cabaret
Deliverance
The Discreet Charm of the Bourgeoisie
The Godfather
Visknin gar och Rop

1973
Badlands
Day for Night
Don't Look Now
Mean Streets

1974
Chinatown
The Enigma of Kaspar Hauser
The Godfather Part II
Lacombe, Lucien

1975
One Flew over the Cuckoo's Nest
Picnic at Hanging Rock

1976
All the President's Men
Face to Face
Network
Taxi Driver

1977
Annie Hall
Star Wars

1978
The Chant of Jimmie Blacksmith
Days of Heaven
The Driver

1979
Alien
Manhattan
The Tin Drum

1980
The Last Metro
Raging Bull

1981
Mephisto
Southern Comfort

1982
E.T. The Extra-Terrestrial
Fanny and Alexander
Fitzcarraldo
Tootsie

1983
King of Comedy

1984
Once Upon a Time in America
This Is Spinal Tap

1985
Ran
Witness

1987
The Dead
Pelle the Conqueror
Wings of Desire

1988
Au Revoir Les Enfants
A Short Film about Killing
Who Framed Roger Rabbit

1989
Cinema Paradiso
When Harry Met Sally

1990
GoodFellas

1992
Aladdin
The Player
Unforgiven

1993
The Piano
Schindler's List

1995
Toy Story

1996
Breaking the Waves
Fargo

1997
LA Confidential

1998
After Life

1999
American Beauty

2001
Gosford Park

Three-Star Films – by Title

About Schmidt
The Accidental Tourist
Ace in the Hole
Across 110th Street
Across the Pacific
Adaptation
The Adventurer
The Adventures of Robinson Crusoe
The Adventures of Tom Sawyer
The African Queen
Airport
Alexander's Ragtime Band
Alias Nick Beal
Alice
Alice Doesn't Live Here Any More
All About Eve
All That Jazz
All the King's Men
Amadeus
American Graffiti
An American Werewolf in London
Amores Perros
Angi Vera
Animal Crackers
Anne and Muriel
Antonia's Line
Aranyer Din Ratri
Arise My Love
The Army in the Shadows
Around the World in Eighty Days
Arsenic and Old Lace
As Good as It Gets
The Asphalt Jungle
The Assault
Assault on Precinct 13
The Asthenic Syndrome
Atlantic City
Autobus
An Autumn Afternoon
The Awful Truth
Babe
The Bachelor and the Bobbysoxer
Bachelor Mother
The Bachelor Party
Back to the Future
Bad Company
Bagdad Café
La Balance
The Bank Dick
Barefaced Flatfoot
Barton Fink
Battle for Russia
Battle of Britain
La Beauté du Diable
Beauty and the Beast
The Bedford Incident
Before the Rain
Being John Malkovich
La Belle Noiseuse
Ben-Hur
Berlin, Symphony of a Great City
Best Boy
The Best Intentions
The Best Man
Bicycle Thieves
The Big Country
The Big Parade
The Big Sleep
Billy Elliot
Billy Liar
The Birds
Black Narcissus
The Black Pirate
Black Robe
The Black Swan
Blackmail
The Blair Witch Project
Blithe Spirit
Blockheads
The Blue Bird
Blue Collar
The Blue Lamp
The Body Snatcher
Bombshell
Boomerang!
Le Boucher
Boudu Sauvé des Eaux
The Bowery
Bowling for Columbine
Boys Don't Cry
Braveheart
Breaker Morant
A Brighter Summer Day
Brighton Rock
Bringing Out the Dead
Bringing Up Baby
Buena Vista Social Club
The Burmese Harp
Burnt by the Sun
Buster Keaton: A Hard Act to Follow
Butcher Boy
The Butterfly Murders
Cabaret Balkan
Cabiria
Call Me Madam
The Cameraman
The Candidate
Cape Fear
Carry On up the Khyber
Casino
Casque d'Or
The Cat and the Canary
The Cat and the Canary
Central Station
César
The Charge of the Light Brigade
Chariots of Fire
Charley Varrick
Charlie Bubbles
Chicken Run
The Childhood of Maxim Gorky
The China Syndrome
La Chinoise
Christ Stopped at Eboli
City Lights
City of Hope
City Slickers
Civilization
Claire's Knee
Coal Miner's Daughter
The Colour of Pomegranates
Comrades
Confessions of a Nazi Spy
The Conformist
The Conversation
Cops
The Count of Monte Cristo
The Court Jester
Cousin, Cousine
Creature Comforts
Crimes and Misdemeanors
The Crowd
Crumb
The Crying Game
Cyrano de Bergerac
Dark Star
A Day in the Death of Joe Egg
The Day of the Jackal
Day of Wrath
Dayereh
Days of Thrills and Laughter
Dead End
Dear Diary
Death by Hanging
Death in Venice
Death of a Salesman
Decline of the American Empire
Delicatessen
Desert Victory
Les Diaboliques
Diary for My Children
A Diary for Timothy
The Diary of a Country Priest
Dinner at Eight
Dirty Harry
Dirty Work
Distant Thunder
Do the Right Thing
Dr Ehrlich's Magic Bullet
Doctor Mabuse the Gambler
Doctor No
Doctor Zhivago
Dodge City
Dodsworth
Dog Day Afternoon
Donnie Brasco
Donnie Darko
Dracula
Dracula
The Dreamlife of Angels
The Dresser
Early Summer
Earth
East is East
Eight Men Out
Election
The Elephant Man
Elizabeth
Empire of the Sun
The Empire Strikes Back
Les Enfants du Marais
The Enforcer
England Made Me
Erin Brockovich
Ermo
The Exterminating Angel
The Face
A Face in the Crowd
Fail Safe
The Fallen Idol
Family Life
Fanny
Farewell My Concubine
Farewell My Lovely
Farewell, My Lovely
Father Brown
Felicia's Journey
The Fencing Master
Festen
Le Feu Follet
Field of Dreams
Fire over England
A Fistful of Dollars
Five Graves to Cairo
Fog over Frisco
Folies Bergère
Footlight Parade
For Me and My Gal
49th Parallel
42nd Street
Four Daughters
Four Weddings and a Funeral
Fourteen Hours
Friday the Thirteenth
From Here to Eternity
From Russia with Love
From This Day Forward
The Front Page
The Fugitive
The Full Monty
The Further Perils of Laurel and Hardy
Fury
'G' Men
The Game
Gandhi
The General
Gerald McBoing Boing
Germinal
The Ghost Breakers
Ghost Dog: The Way of the Samurai
The Ghost Goes West
Ghost World
Gigi
Gilda
Gimme Shelter
Ginger and Fred
Gladiator
The Go-Between
Gold Diggers of 1933
The Gold Rush
Goldfinger
The Golem
The Good Earth
The Good, the Bad and the Ugly
Goodbye Mr Chips
La Grande Illusion
The Great Lie
The Great Race
The Great Train Robbery
The Great Waltz
Greed
Green for Danger
The Green Pastures
Gregory's Girl
The Grifters
Groundhog Day
The Group
Gunga Din
Hail the Conquering Hero
Hannah and Her Sisters
The Happiest Days of Your Life
Happiness
The Happy Time
Hardcore
Harold Lloyd's Funny Side of Life
Harvey
Heaven Can Wait
Heavenly Creatures
Heimat
Hell's Angels
Hellzapoppin
Helpmates
Henry V
Here Comes Mr Jordan
Hobson's Choice
Hog Wild
Holiday
Hoop Dreams
Horse Feathers
The Hospital
The Hot Rock
The Hours
House of Games
The House on 92nd Street
How Green Was My Valley
Howards End
Hue and Cry
Husbands and Wives
I Married a Witch
I'm All Right Jack
I'm No Angel
In Cold Blood
In Old Chicago
In Search of the Castaways
In the Mood for Love
The Informer
The Innocent
Innocents with Dirty Hands
The Insider
Intermezzo
Interrogation
Intruder in the Dust
L'Invitation
The Iron Giant
It Always Rains on Sunday
It Happened One Night
It Happened Tomorrow
An Italian Straw Hat
Ivan's Childhood
Jane Eyre
Jason and the Argonauts
Jazz on a Summer's Day
Jesus of Montreal
Jeux Interdits
Jezebel
Johann Mouse
Jour de Fête
Le Jour Se Lève

Journey into Fear
Journey to the Center of the Earth
Julia
Kagemusha
Key Largo
The Kid
The Killers
The Killers
The Killing Fields
Kind Hearts and Coronets
King of Jazz
Kipps
Kiss Me Deadly
Kitty
Klute
Kolya
Kramer versus Kramer
Kühle Wampe
The Lady Eve
Lady for a Day
Lady Killer
The Ladykillers
Laissez-Passer
Lamerica
Lancelot du Lac
Land and Freedom
Lantana
Last Exit to Brooklyn
The Last Flight
The Last Laugh
Last Orders
The Last Seduction
The Last Waltz
Last Year at Marienbad
Laughing Gravy
Laura
Le Fils
The League of Gentlemen
Lenny
Letter from an Unknown Woman
The Life and Death of Colonel Blimp
Life Is Beautiful
The Life of Emile Zola
The Life of Oharu
Lights of New York
Limelight
The Lion King
The Little Foxes
Little Women
The Living Desert
The Lodger
The Loneliness of the Long Distance Runner
The Long Day Closes
The Lord of the Rings: The Fellowship Of The Ring
The Lord of the Rings: The Two Towers
Love Affair
Love on the Dole
Lovers and Other Strangers
Lovers of the Arctic Circle
M
The Madness of King George
Major Barbara
The Man Who Came to Dinner
The Man Who Could Work Miracles
The Man Who Knew Too Much
The Man Who Shot Liberty Valance
The Man Who Wasn't There
Mandy
Manon des Sources
Marathon Man
Margie
The Mark of Zorro
Mary Poppins
The Matrix
Meet John Doe
Meet Me in St Louis
Melvin and Howard
Memento
The Men
Metropolis
Metropolitan
Mickey's Christmas Carol
Midnight
A Midsummer Night's Dream
Milou in May
Mine Own Executioner
The Miracle of Morgan's Creek
Miracle on 34th Street
Les Misérables
Mrs Brown
Mr Blandings Builds His Dream House
Mr Deeds Goes to Town
Mr Skeffington
Modern Times
Monkey Business
Monty Python and the Holy Grail
The Moon and Sixpence
Moonlighting
The More the Merrier
Morgan – A Suitable Case for Treatment
Morocco
The Most Dangerous Game
Mother
Mother and Son
The Music Man
Mutiny on the Bounty
My Ain Folk
My American Uncle
My Brilliant Career
My Childhood
My Darling Clementine
My Fair Lady
My Favorite Blonde
My Favorite Wife
My Favorite Year
My Girl Tisa
My Learned Friend
My Man Godfrey
My Name Is Joe
Mystery of the Wax Museum
Nada
The Narrow Margin
Nashville
The Nasty Girl
The Navigator
Newsfront
The Next of Kin
Niagara
The Niebelungen
Night Mail
Night of the Demon
The Night of the Hunter
The Night of the Iguana
The Night of The Living Dead
A Night to Remember
Night Train to Munich
The Nightmare before Christmas
Ninotchka
Nixon
Northwest Frontier
Northwest Passage (Part One, Rogers' Rangers)
Nosferatu
Nothing Sacred
Notorious
Now Voyager
The Nun's Story
O Brother, Where Art Thou?
O Lucky Man!
Occupe-Toi d'Amélie
Odd Man Out
Of Mice and Men
Oliver!
Olympische Spiele
On Approval
On Golden Pond
Once Upon a Time in the West
Once Were Warriors
A One and a Two...
One False Move
One Hour with You
One Hundred and One Dalmatians
One Hundred Men and a Girl
Only Two Can Play
The Opposite of Sex
Ordinary People
Orphée
Our Hospitality
Our Relations
Out of Sight
Padre Padrone
The Pajama Game
The Paleface
The Palm Beach Story
Panic in the Streets
The Parallax View
Une Partie de Campagne
Patterns
Patton
The People vs. Larry Flynt
Performance
Peter Pan
The Phantom of Liberty
Phantom of the Opera
The Pianist
Picnic
The Picture of Dorian Gray
Planet of the Apes
The Ploughman's Lunch
Poil de Carotte
Portrait of Jennie
Prelude to War
Pretty Village Pretty Flame
Pride and Prejudice
A Private Conversation
A Private Function
The Private Life of Henry VIII
The Private Life of Sherlock Holmes
Private's Progress
The Prize
Public Enemy
Pulp Fiction
The Pumpkin Eater
Quai des Brumes
Quartet
Que la Bête Meure
Queen Christina
The Quiet American
The Quiet Man
Quiet Wedding
Rabbit-Proof Fence
Raiders of the Lost Ark
The Railway Children
The Rains Came
Random Harvest
Red Dust
Red Sorghum
Reds
La Règle du Jeu
Repentance
Reservoir Dogs
Richard III
Richard III
The Roaring Twenties
Robocop
Rocky
The Rocky Horror Picture Show
Rome Express
La Ronde
Room at the Top
A Room with a View
Rosetta
Run Lola Run
Sabotage
Saboteur
Safety Last
The Samurai
Sanger Fran Andra Vaningen
Sansho the Bailiff
Saturday Night Fever
Saving Private Ryan
The Scarlet Empress
The Scarlet Pimpernel
Scenes from a Marriage
Scrooge
The Sea Hawk
Secrets and Lies
A Self-Made Hero
Sense and Sensibility
The Set Up
Seven
Seven Days in May
Shadow of a Doubt
Shadowlands
Shakespeare in Love
Shane
Shanghai Express
She Done Him Wrong
Shine
Ship of Fools
Shoah
The Shootist
Short Cuts
Show Business
Showboat
Shrek
The Sign of the Cross
Silence of the Lambs
A Simple Plan
Since You Went Away
Sing As We Go
Sitting Pretty
The Sixth Sense
A Slight Case of Murder
Smile
Smiles of a Summer Night
Solaris
Son of Frankenstein
Sons and Lovers
Le Souffle au Coeur
The Sound of Music
The Southerner
Speed
The Spiral Staircase
Stage Door
Stanley and Livingstone
La Stanza del Figlio
A Star Is Born
Star Spangled Rhythm
State of the Union
The Sting
Stormy Weather
The Story of Louis Pasteur
The Story of Qiu Ju
La Strada
The Straight Story
Strangers on a Train
Strictly Ballroom
Strike
Summertime
Sunday, Bloody Sunday
Sunset Boulevard
Sunshine State
Sur Mes Lèvres
The Sweet Hereafter
Taking Off
The Tale of the Fox
The Talk of the Town
Tango
Tarzan
A Taste of Honey
10
Terminus
Thank Your Lucky Stars
Thelma and Louise
They Shoot Horses, Don't They?
They Won't Forget
The Thief
The Thief of Bagdad
The Thin Man
The Thin Red Line
This Gun for Hire
This Sporting Life
Those Who Love Me Can Take The Train
Those Wonderful Movie Cranks
The Three Caballeros
Three Colours: Blue
Three Colours: Red
Three Colours: White
Three Kings
The Three Musketeers
Thunder Rock
Tillsammans
Time in the Sun
Tin Pan Alley
The Titfield Thunderbolt
Tobacco Road
Todo Sobre Mi Madre
Topsy-Turvy
A Touch of Zen
Towed in a Hole
The Towering Inferno
Toy Story 2
The Tragedy of a Ridiculous Man
Trainspotting
A Tree Grows in Brooklyn
The Truman Show
Tunes of Glory
Ulee's Gold
Unknown Chaplin
The Usual Suspects
Utu
Vagabonde
Victim
Victoria the Great
The Vikings
Visions of Light
WR – Mysteries of the Organism
The Wages of Fear
A Walk in the Sun
War and Peace
The Watchmaker of St Paul
The Way Ahead
The Wedding Banquet
Went the Day Well?
Western Approaches
When Comedy Was King
White Heat
Will It Snow for Christmas?
William Shakespeare's Romeo and Juliet
The Wind
The Window
The Winslow Boy
Wise Blood
Witness for the Prosecution
The Wizard of Oz
The Woman in the Window
Woman of the Year
The Women
Women in Love

World of Plenty
Wuthering Heights
Y Tu Mamá También
Yankee Doodle Dandy
Yol
Young and Innocent
Young Frankenstein
The Young in Heart
Young Mr Lincoln
You're Darn Tootin'
Zazie dans le Métro
Zelig

Three-Star Films – Year by Year

1903
The Great Train Robbery

1916
Civilization

1917
The Adventurer

1920
The Golem

1921
The Kid
Nosferatu

1922
Cops
Doctor Mabuse the Gambler

1923
Our Hospitality
Safety Last

1924
Greed
The Last Laugh
The Navigator
The Niebelungen
Strike
The Thief of Bagdad

1925
Ben-Hur
The Big Parade
The Gold Rush
Phantom of the Opera

1926
The Black Pirate
The Lodger
Metropolis
Mother

1927
Berlin, Symphony of a Great City
The Cat and the Canary
An Italian Straw Hat

1928
The Cameraman
The Crowd
Lights of New York
The Wind

1929
Blackmail
You're Darn Tootin'

1930
Animal Crackers
Earth
Hell's Angels
Hog Wild
King of Jazz
Morocco

1931
City Lights
Dracula
The Front Page
The Last Flight
Laughing Gravy
M
Monkey Business
Public Enemy
The Tale of the Fox

1932
Boudu Sauvé des Eaux
Fanny
Helpmates
Horse Feathers
Kühle Wampe
The Most Dangerous Game
One Hour with You
Poil de Carotte
Red Dust
Rome Express
Shanghai Express
The Sign of the Cross
Towed in a Hole

1933
Bombshell
The Bowery
Dinner at Eight
Dirty Work
Footlight Parade
42nd Street
Friday the Thirteenth
Gold Diggers of 1933
I'm No Angel
Lady for a Day
Lady Killer
Little Women
Mystery of the Wax Museum
The Private Life of Henry VIII
Queen Christina
She Done Him Wrong
Time in the Sun

1934
The Count of Monte Cristo
Fog over Frisco
It Happened One Night
The Man Who Knew Too Much
The Scarlet Empress
The Scarlet Pimpernel
Sing As We Go
The Thin Man

1935
Folies Bergère
'G' Men
The Ghost Goes West
The Informer
A Midsummer Night's Dream
Mutiny on the Bounty

1936
César
The Charge of the Light Brigade
Dodsworth
Fury
The Green Pastures
The Man Who Could Work Miracles
Mr Deeds Goes to Town
Modern Times
My Man Godfrey
Night Mail
Olympische Spiele
Our Relations
Une Partie de Campagne
Sabotage
Showboat
The Story of Louis Pasteur

1937
The Awful Truth
Dead End
Fire over England
The Good Earth
La Grande Illusion
In Old Chicago
The Life of Emile Zola
Nothing Sacred
One Hundred Men and a Girl
Stage Door
A Star Is Born
They Won't Forget
Victoria the Great
Young and Innocent

1938
The Adventures of Tom Sawyer
Alexander's Ragtime Band
Blockheads
Bringing Up Baby
The Childhood of Maxim Gorky
Four Daughters
The Great Waltz
Holiday
Jezebel
Quai des Brumes
A Slight Case of Murder
The Young in Heart

1939
Bachelor Mother
The Cat and the Canary
Confessions of a Nazi Spy
Dodge City
Goodbye Mr Chips
Gunga Din
Intermezzo
Le Jour Se Lève
Love Affair
Midnight
Ninotchka
Of Mice and Men
The Rains Came
La Règle du Jeu
The Roaring Twenties
Son of Frankenstein
Stanley and Livingstone
The Wizard of Oz
The Women
Wuthering Heights
Young Mr Lincoln

1940
Arise My Love
The Bank Dick
The Blue Bird
Dr Ehrlich's Magic Bullet
The Ghost Breakers
The Mark of Zorro
My Favorite Wife
Night Train to Munich
Northwest Passage (Part One, Rogers' Rangers)
Pride and Prejudice
Quiet Wedding
The Sea Hawk
Tin Pan Alley

1941
49th Parallel
The Great Lie
Here Comes Mr Jordan
How Green Was My Valley
Kipps
The Lady Eve
The Little Foxes
Love on the Dole
Major Barbara
The Man Who Came to Dinner
Meet John Doe
Tobacco Road

1942
Across the Pacific
The Black Swan
For Me and My Gal
Hellzapoppin
I Married a Witch
Journey into Fear
My Favorite Blonde
The Next of Kin
Now Voyager
The Palm Beach Story
Random Harvest
Saboteur
Star Spangled Rhythm
The Talk of the Town
This Gun for Hire
Thunder Rock
Went the Day Well?
Woman of the Year
Yankee Doodle Dandy

1943
Battle for Russia
Battle of Britain
Day of Wrath
Desert Victory
Five Graves to Cairo
Heaven Can Wait
Jane Eyre
The Life and Death of Colonel Blimp
The Miracle of Morgan's Creek
The Moon and Sixpence
The More the Merrier
My Learned Friend
On Approval
Prelude to War
Shadow of a Doubt
Stormy Weather
Thank Your Lucky Stars
World of Plenty

1944
Arsenic and Old Lace
Farewell My Lovely
Hail the Conquering Hero
It Happened Tomorrow
Laura
Meet Me in St Louis
Mr Skeffington
Show Business
Since You Went Away
The Way Ahead
Western Approaches
The Woman in the Window

1945
Blithe Spirit
The Body Snatcher
A Diary for Timothy
The House on 92nd Street
Kitty
The Picture of Dorian Gray
The Southerner
The Spiral Staircase
The Three Caballeros
A Tree Grows in Brooklyn

1946
The Big Sleep
From This Day Forward
Gilda
Green for Danger
Hue and Cry
The Killers
Margie
My Darling Clementine
Notorious
Odd Man Out
A Walk in the Sun

1947
The Bachelor and the Bobbysoxer
Black Narcissus
Boomerang!
Brighton Rock
It Always Rains on Sunday
Mine Own Executioner
Miracle on 34th Street

1948
Bicycle Thieves
The Fallen Idol
Jour de Fête
Key Largo
Letter from an Unknown Woman
Mr Blandings Builds His Dream House
My Girl Tisa
The Paleface

Portrait of Jennie
Quartet
Sitting Pretty
State of the Union
The Three Musketeers
The Winslow Boy

1949
Alias Nick Beal
All the King's Men
La Beauté du Diable
The Blue Lamp
Intruder in the Dust
Kind Hearts and Coronets
Occupe-Toi d'Amélie
Orphée
The Set Up
White Heat
The Window

1950
All About Eve
The Asphalt Jungle
The Diary of a Country Priest
The Enforcer
The Happiest Days of Your Life
Harvey
The Men
Panic in the Streets
La Ronde
Sunset Boulevard

1951
Ace in the Hole
The African Queen
Death of a Salesman
Early Summer
Fourteen Hours
Gerald McBoing Boing
Scrooge
Strangers on a Train

1952
Barefaced Flatfoot
Casque d'Or
The Happy Time
Jeux Interdits
Johann Mouse
The Life of Oharu
Limelight
Mandy
The Narrow Margin
Niagara
The Quiet Man
The Titfield Thunderbolt

1953
The Adventures of Robinson Crusoe
Call Me Madam
From Here to Eternity
Hobson's Choice
The Living Desert
Peter Pan
Shane
The Wages of Fear

1954
Les Diaboliques
Father Brown
Sansho the Bailiff
La Strada

1955
The Court Jester
Kiss Me Deadly
The Ladykillers
The Night of the Hunter
Picnic
Richard III
Smiles of a Summer Night
Summertime

1956
Around the World in Eighty Days
The Burmese Harp
Patterns
Private's Progress

1957
The Bachelor Party
Cabiria
A Face in the Crowd
Night of the Demon
The Pajama Game
Witness for the Prosecution

1958
The Big Country
Dracula
The Face
Gigi
A Night to Remember
Room at the Top
The Vikings

1959
I'm All Right Jack
Jazz on a Summer's Day
Journey to the Center of the Earth
Northwest Frontier
The Nun's Story
When Comedy Was King

1960
The League of Gentlemen
Sons and Lovers
Tunes of Glory
Zazie dans le Métro

1961
Days of Thrills and Laughter
In Search of the Castaways
Last Year at Marienbad
One Hundred and One Dalmatians
A Taste of Honey
Terminus
Victim

1962
An Autumn Afternoon
Doctor No
The Exterminating Angel
Ivan's Childhood
The Loneliness of the Long Distance Runner
The Man Who Shot Liberty Valance
The Music Man
Only Two Can Play

1963
Billy Liar
The Birds
Le Feu Follet
From Russia with Love
Harold Lloyd's Funny Side of Life
Jason and the Argonauts
The Prize
This Sporting Life

1964
The Best Man
Fail Safe
A Fistful of Dollars
Goldfinger
The Killers
Mary Poppins
My Fair Lady
The Night of the Iguana
The Pumpkin Eater
Seven Days in May

1965
The Bedford Incident
Doctor Zhivago
The Great Race
Ship of Fools
The Sound of Music

1966
The Good, the Bad and the Ugly
The Group
Morgan – A Suitable Case for Treatment

1967
La Chinoise
The Further Perils of Laurel and Hardy
In Cold Blood
The Samurai
War and Peace

1968
Carry On up the Khyber
Charlie Bubbles
Death by Hanging
The Night of The Living Dead
Oliver!
Planet of the Apes

1969
Aranyer Din Ratri
The Army in the Shadows
Le Boucher
The Colour of Pomegranates
The Conformist
Once Upon a Time in the West
Patton
Que la Bête Meure
They Shoot Horses, Don't They?
A Touch of Zen
Women in Love

1970
Airport
Claire's Knee
Gimme Shelter
The Go-Between
Lovers and Other Strangers
Performance
The Private Life of Sherlock Holmes
The Railway Children

1971
Anne and Muriel
A Day in the Death of Joe Egg
Death in Venice
Dirty Harry
Family Life
The Hospital
Klute
Le Souffle au Coeur
Sunday, Bloody Sunday
Taking Off
WR – Mysteries of the Organism

1972
Across 110th Street
Bad Company
The Candidate
England Made Me
The Hot Rock
My Childhood
Solaris

1973
American Graffiti
Charley Varrick
The Day of the Jackal
Distant Thunder
L'Invitation
My Ain Folk
O Lucky Man!
Scenes from a Marriage
The Sting
The Watchmaker of St Paul

1974
Alice Doesn't Live Here Any More
The Conversation
Dark Star
Lancelot du Lac
Lenny
Nada
The Parallax View
The Phantom of Liberty
The Towering Inferno
Young Frankenstein

1975
Cousin, Cousine
Dog Day Afternoon
Farewell, My Lovely
Innocents with Dirty Hands
Monty Python and the Holy Grail
Nashville
The Rocky Horror Picture Show
Smile

1976
Assault on Precinct 13
The Innocent
Marathon Man
Rocky
The Shootist

1977
Julia
Padre Padrone
Saturday Night Fever

1978
Angi Vera
Blue Collar
The Last Waltz
Newsfront
Those Wonderful Movie Cranks

1979
All That Jazz
Best Boy
The Butterfly Murders
The China Syndrome
Christ Stopped at Eboli
Hardcore
Kramer versus Kramer
My Brilliant Career
Wise Blood

1980
Breaker Morant
Coal Miner's Daughter
The Elephant Man
The Empire Strikes Back
Gregory's Girl
Kagemusha
Melvin and Howard
My American Uncle
Ordinary People

1981
An American Werewolf in London
Atlantic City
Chariots of Fire
On Golden Pond
Raiders of the Lost Ark
Reds
The Tragedy of a Ridiculous Man

1982
La Balance
Diary for My Children
Gandhi
Interrogation
Moonlighting
My Favorite Year
Yol

1983
The Dresser
Mickey's Christmas Carol
The Ploughman's Lunch
A Private Conversation
Utu
Zelig

1984
Amadeus
Heimat
The Killing Fields
A Private Function
Repentance

1985
Back to the Future
A Room with a View
Shoah
Vagabonde

1986
The Assault
Decline of the American Empire
Ginger and Fred
Hannah and Her Sisters
Manon des Sources
Unknown Chaplin

1987
Buster Keaton: A Hard Act to Follow
Comrades
Empire of the Sun
House of Games
Red Sorghum
Robocop

1988
The Accidental Tourist
Alice
Bagdad Café
Eight Men Out

1989
The Asthenic Syndrome
Creature Comforts
Crimes and Misdemeanors
Do the Right Thing
Field of Dreams
Henry V
Jesus of Montreal
Last Exit to Brooklyn
Metropolitan
Milou in May

1990
Cyrano de Bergerac
Delicatessen
The Grifters
The Nasty Girl
Silence of the Lambs

1991
Autobus
Barton Fink
Beauty and the Beast
La Belle Noiseuse
Black Robe
A Brighter Summer Day
Cape Fear
City of Hope
City Slickers
Reservoir Dogs
Thelma and Louise

1992
The Best Intentions
The Crying Game
The Fencing Master
Howards End
Husbands and Wives
The Long Day Closes
One False Move
The Story of Qiu Ju
Strictly Ballroom
Visions of Light

1993
Farewell My Concubine
The Fugitive
Germinal
Groundhog Day
The Nightmare before Christmas
Shadowlands
Short Cuts
Tango
Three Colours: Blue
Three Colours: White
The Wedding Banquet

1994
Before the Rain
Burnt by the Sun
Crumb
Dear Diary
Ermo
Four Weddings and a Funeral
Heavenly Creatures
Hoop Dreams
Lamerica
The Last Seduction
The Lion King
The Madness of King George
Once Were Warriors
Pulp Fiction
Speed
Three Colours: Red

1995
Antonia's Line
Babe
Braveheart
Casino
Land and Freedom
Les Misérables
Nixon
Richard III
Secrets and Lies
A Self-Made Hero
Sense and Sensibility
Seven
The Usual Suspects

1996
Kolya
The People vs. Larry Flynt
Pretty Village Pretty Flame
Shine
Trainspotting
Will It Snow for Christmas?
William Shakespeare's Romeo and Juliet

1997
As Good as It Gets
Butcher Boy
Donnie Brasco
The Full Monty
The Game
Life Is Beautiful
Mrs Brown
Mother and Son
The Sweet Hereafter
The Thief
Ulee's Gold

1998
The Blair Witch Project
Buena Vista Social Club
Cabaret Balkan
Central Station
The Dreamlife of Angels
Elizabeth
Les Enfants du Marais
Festen
The General
Happiness
Lovers of the Arctic Circle
My Name Is Joe
The Opposite of Sex
Out of Sight
Run Lola Run
Saving Private Ryan
Shakespeare in Love
A Simple Plan
The Thin Red Line
Those Who Love Me Can Take The Train
The Truman Show

1999
Being John Malkovich
Boys Don't Cry
Bringing Out the Dead
East is East
Election
Felicia's Journey
Ghost Dog: The Way of the Samurai
The Insider
The Iron Giant
The Matrix
Rosetta
The Sixth Sense
The Straight Story
Tarzan
Three Kings
Todo Sobre Mi Madre
Topsy-Turvy
Toy Story 2

2000
Amores Perros
Billy Elliot
Chicken Run
Dayereh
Erin Brockovich
Gladiator
In the Mood for Love
Memento
O Brother, Where Art Thou?
A One and a Two...
Sanger Fran Andra Vaningen
Tillsammans

2001
Donnie Darko
Ghost World
Laissez-Passer
Lantana
Last Orders
The Lord of the Rings: The Fellowship Of The Ring
The Man Who Wasn't There
Shrek
La Stanza del Figlio
Sur Mes Lèvres
Y Tu Mamá También

2002
About Schmidt
Adaptation
Bowling for Columbine
The Hours
Le Fils
The Lord of the Rings: The Two Towers
The Pianist
The Quiet American
Rabbit-Proof Fence
Sunshine State
10

Index of Leading Directors

George Abbott My Sin 31. Secrets of a Secretary 31. Stolen Heaven 31. Too Many Girls 40. Damn Yankees 58.

Jim Abrahams Airplane 80. Top Secret! 84. Ruthless People 86. Big Business 88. Hot Shots! 91. Welcome Home Roxy Carmichael 91. Hot Shots!: Part Deux 93. Mafia! 98.

Percy Adlon Céleste 81. The Swing 83. Sugarbaby 84. Bagdad Café 88. Rosalie Goes Shopping 89. Salmonberries 91. Younger & Younger 94.

John Adolfi Show of Shows 29. Sinner's Holiday 30. A Successful Calamity 31. Alexander Hamilton 31. The Millionaire 31. Central Park 32. The Man Who Played God 32. The King's Vacation 33. The Working Man 33. Voltaire 33.

Franklin Adreon Canadian Mounties vs Atomic Invaders 53. The Man with the Steel Whip 54. Trader Tom of the China Seas 54. King of the Carnival 55. Panther Girl of the Congo 55. The Nun and the Sergeant 62. Dimension 5 66.

Robert Aldrich Big Leaguer 53. Vera Cruz 53. Apache 54. Kiss Me Deadly 55. The Big Knife 55. Attack! 56. Autumn Leaves 56. The Garment Jungle 57. Ten Seconds to Hell 59. The Angry Hills 59. The Last Sunset 61. Whatever Happened to Baby Jane? 62. Four for Texas 63. Sodom and Gomorrah 63. Hush Hush Sweet Charlotte 64. The Flight of the Phoenix 65. The Dirty Dozen 67. The Legend of Lylah Clare 68. The Killing of Sister George 69. Too Late the Hero 69. The Grissom Gang 71. Ulzana's Raid 72. Emperor of the North Pole 73. The Longest Yard 74. Hustle 75. Twilight's Last Gleaming 77. The Choirboys 78. The Frisco Kid 79. All the Marbles… 81.

Marc Allégret Fanny 32. Entrée des Artistes 38. Blanche Fury 48. Blackmailed 50. Lady Chatterley's Lover 55. Plucking the Daisy 56.

Yves Allégret Dédée d'Anvers 48. Une Si Jolie Petite Plage 48. Manèges 50. The Seven Deadly Sins 52. The Proud and the Beautiful 53. Oasis 56.

Irwin Allen The Animal World 56. The Story of Mankind 57. The Lost World 60. Voyage to the Bottom of the Sea 61. Five Weeks in a Balloon 62. City beneath the Sea 70. The Towering Inferno 74. The Swarm 78. Beyond the Poseidon Adventure 79.

Lewis Allen Our Hearts Were Young and Gay 44. The Uninvited 44. The Unseen 45. Those Endearing Young Charms 45. The Imperfect Lady 46. The Perfect Marriage 46. Desert Fury 47. Sealed Verdict 48. So Evil My Love 48. Appointment with Danger 49. Chicago Deadline 49. Valentino 51. At Sword's Point 52. Suddenly 54. A Bullet for Joey 55. Illegal 55. Another Time, Another Place 58. Whirlpool 59.

Woody Allen Take the Money and Run 68. Bananas 71. Everything You Always Wanted to Know about Sex 72. Sleeper 73. Love and Death 75. Annie Hall 77. Interiors 78. Manhattan 79. Stardust Memories 80. A Midsummer Night's Sex Comedy 82. Zelig 83. Broadway Danny Rose 84. The Purple Rose of Cairo 84. Hannah and Her Sisters 86. Radio Days 87. September 87. Another Woman 88. Crimes and Misdemeanors 89. New York Stories 89. Alice 90. Shadows and Fog 91. Husbands and Wives 92. Manhattan Murder Mystery 93. Bullets over Broadway 94. Mighty Aphrodite 95. Everyone Says I Love You 96. Deconstructing Harry 97. Celebrity 98. Sweet and Lowdown 99. Small Time Crooks 00. The Curse of the Jade Scorpion 01.

Pedro Almodóvar Pepi, Luci, Bom 80. Labyrinth of Passion 82. Dark Habits 83. What Have I Done to Deserve This? 84. Law of Desire 87. Matador 88. Women on the Verge of a Nervous Breakdown 88. Tie Me Up! Tie Me Down! 89. High Heels 91. Kika 93. The Flower of My Secret 95. Live Flesh 97. Todo Sobre Mi Madre 99.

Robert Altman Countdown 67. That Cold Day in the Park 69. Brewster McCloud 70. M*A*S*H 70. McCabe and Mrs Miller 71. Images 72. The Long Goodbye 73. California Split 74. Thieves Like Us 74. Nashville 75. Buffalo Bill and the Indians, or Sitting Bull's History Lesson 76. Three Women 77. A Wedding 78. A Perfect Couple 79. Health 79. Quintet 79. Popeye 80. Come Back to the Five and Dime, Jimmy Dean, Jimmy Dean 83. Streamers 83. Fool for Love 85. Beyond Therapy 86. O. C. and Stiggs 87. Aria 88. Vincent and Theo 90. The Player 92. Short Cuts 93. Prêt-à-Porter 94. Kansas City 96. The Gingerbread Man 97. Cookie's Fortune 99. Dr T and the Women 00. Gosford Park 01. Dr T and the Women 00.

Rod Amateau Pussycat, Pussycat, I Love You 70. The Statue 70. Where Does it Hurt? 71. Drive-in 76. The Seniors 77.

Jon Amiel Queen of Hearts 89. Tune In Tomorrow 90. Sommersby 93. Copycat 95. The Man Who Knew Too Little 97. Entrapment 99.

Lindsay Anderson This Sporting Life 63. If… 68. O Lucky Man! 73. In Celebration 74. Britannia Hospital 82. The Whales of August 87.

Michael Anderson Waterfront 50. Hell Is Sold Out 51. Night Was Our Friend 51. Will Any Gentleman? 53. The Dam Busters 54. 1984 55. Around the World in Eighty Days 56. Chase a Crooked Shadow 57. Yangtse Incident 57. Shake Hands with the Devil 59. The Wreck of the Mary Deare 59. All the Fine Young Cannibals 60. The Naked Edge 61. Flight from Ashiya 63. Wild and Wonderful 63. Operation Crossbow 65. The Quiller Memorandum 66. The Shoes of the Fisherman 68. Pope Joan 72. Conduct Unbecoming 75. Doc Savage, Man of Bronze 75. Logan's Run 76. Orca – Killer Whale 77. Dominique 78. Millennium 89.

Paul W.S. Anderson Shopping 94. Mortal Kombat 95. Event Horizon 97. Soldier 98. Resident Evil 02.

Ken Annakin Holiday Camp 47. Miranda 47. Broken Journey 48. Here Come the Huggetts 48. Landfall 49. Double Confession 50. Trio 50. Hotel Sahara 51. The Planter's Wife 52. The Story of Robin Hood and his Merrie Men 52. The Sword and the Rose 52. The Seekers 54. Value for Money 55. Loser Takes All 56. Three Men in a Boat 56. Across the Bridge 57. Nor the Moon By Night 58. Third Man on the Mountain 59. The Swiss Family Robinson 60. The Hellions 61. Very Important Person 61. Crooks Anonymous 62. The Fast Lady 62. The Longest Day 62. The Informers 63. Battle of the Bulge 65. Those Magnificent Men in Their Flying Machines, or How I Flew from London to Paris in 25 hours and 11 Minutes 65. The Biggest Bundle of Them All 67. The Long Duel 67. Those Daring Young Men in Their Jaunty Jalopies 69. Call of the Wild 72. Paper Tiger 75. The Fifth Musketeer 78. The Pirate Movie 82. The New Adventures of Pippi Longstocking 88.

Jean-Jacques Annaud Black and White in Colour 76. Quest for Fire 81. The Name of the Rose 86. The Bear 89. L'Amant 92. Seven Years in Tibet 97. Enemy at the Gates 01.

Joseph Anthony The Rainmaker 56. The Matchmaker 58. Career 59. All in a Night's Work 61. The Captive City 63.

Michelangelo Antonioni Le Amiche 55. Il Grido 57. L'Avventura 60. La Notte 60. The Eclipse 62. The Red Desert 64. Blow-Up 66. Zabriskie Point 69. The Passenger 75. The Oberwald Mystery 80. Identification of a Woman 82. Beyond the Clouds 95.

Michael Apted Triple Echo 72. Stardust 74. The Squeeze 77. Agatha 79. Coal Miner's Daughter 80. Continental Divide 81. Gorky Park 83. Firstborn 84. Critical Condition 86. Gorillas in the Mist 88. Class Action 90. Thunderheart 92. Blink 94. Nell 94. Extreme Measures 96. The World Is Not Enough 99. Enigma 01. Enough 02.

George Archainbaud Penguin Pool Murder 32. State's Attorney 32. The Lost Squadron 32. Thirteen Women 32. After Tonight 33. Alias French Gertie 34. Murder on the Blackboard 34. Thunder in the Night 35. Hideaway Girl 36. My Marriage 36. Hotel Haywire 37. Thrill of a Lifetime 37. Her Jungle Love 38. Thanks for the Memory 38. Boy Trouble 39. Some Like It Hot 39. Untamed 40. The Kansan 43. The Woman of the Town 43. The Devil's Playground 46. The Dead Don't Dream 47. Blue Canadian Rockies 52. On Top of Old Smoky 53. Winning of the West 53.

Dario Argento The Bird with the Crystal Plumage 69. Cat o' Nine Tails 71. Deep Red 75. Suspiria 76. Inferno 80. Tenebrae 82. Creepers 84. Trauma 93. The Stendhal Syndrome 96.

Leslie Arliss The Farmer's Wife 40. The Night Has Eyes 42. The Man in Grey 43. Love Story 44. The Wicked Lady 45. A Man about the House 47. Idol of Paris 48. Saints and Sinners 48. The Woman's Angle 52. See How They Run 55. Danger List 57.

Gillian Armstrong My Brilliant Career 79. Starstruck 82. Mrs Soffel 84. High Tide 87. Fires Within 91. Last Days of Chez Nous 92. Little Women 94. Oscar and Lucinda 97. Charlotte Gray 01.

Jack Arnold Girls in the Night 53. It Came from Outer Space 53. The Glass Web 53. The Creature from the Black Lagoon 54. Tarantula 55. The Man from Bitter Ridge 55. Red Sundown 56. Man in the Shadow 57. The Incredible Shrinking Man 57. The Tattered Dress 57. High School Confidential! 58. Monster on the Campus 58. No Name on the Bullet 58. The Lady Takes a Flyer 58. The Space Children 58. The Mouse that Roared 59. Bachelor in Paradise 61. A Global Affair 63. Hello Down There 69. The Swiss Conspiracy 75.

Dorothy Arzner Anybody's Woman 30. Paramount on Parade 30. Sarah and Son 30. Honor Among Lovers 31. Merrily We Go to Hell 32. Christopher Strong 33. Nana 34. Craig's Wife 36. The Bride Wore Red 37. Dance, Girl, Dance 40. First Comes Courage 43.

Hal Ashby The Landlord 70. Harold and Maude 71. The Last Detail 73. Shampoo 75. Bound for Glory 76. Coming Home 78. Being There 79. Let's Spend the Night Together 82. Lookin' to Get Out 82. 8 Million Ways to Die 86.

Robert Asher Follow a Star 59. Make Mine Mink 60. The Bulldog Breed 60. On the Beat 62. She'll Have to Go 62. A Stitch in Time 63. The Early Bird 65. The Intelligence Men 65. Press for Time 66.

William Asher The Shadow on the Window 57. Beach Party 63. Johnny Cool 63. Bikini Beach 64. Muscle Beach Party 64. Beach Blanket Bingo 65. How to Stuff a Wild Bikini 65. Movers and Shakers 85.

Anthony Asquith Shooting Stars 28. Cottage on Dartmoor 29. Escape from Dartmoor 30. Tell England 31. Dance Pretty Lady 32. Moscow Nights 36. Pygmalion 38. French without Tears 39. Quiet Wedding 40. Cottage to Let 41. Freedom Radio 41. Uncensored 42. The Demi-Paradise 43. We Dive at Dawn 43. Fanny by Gaslight 44. The Way to the Stars 45. While the Sun Shines 46. The Winslow Boy 48. The Woman in Question 49. The Browning Version 51. The Importance of Being Earnest 52. The Final Test 53. The Net 53. Carrington VC 54. The Young Lovers 54. On Such a Night 55. Orders to Kill 58. The Doctor's Dilemma 58. Libel 59. The Millionairess 60. Guns of Darkness 62. The VIPs 63. The Yellow Rolls Royce 64.

Richard Attenborough Oh What a Lovely War 69. Young Winston 72. A Bridge Too Far 77. Magic 78. Gandhi 82. A Chorus Line 85. Cry Freedom 87. Chaplin 92. Shadowlands 93. In Love and War 96. Grey Owl 98.

John H. Auer The Crime of Dr Crespi 35. Hit Parade of 1941 40. A Man Betrayed 41. Women in War 42. Gangway for Tomorrow 43. Johnny Doughboy 43. Music in Manhattan 44. Pan-Americana 45. The Flame 47. Angel on the Amazon 48. I, Jane Doe 48. Thunderbirds 52. City that Never Sleeps 53. Hell's Half Acre 53. The Eternal Sea 55. Johnny Trouble 56.

Bille August Pelle the Conqueror 87. The Best Intentions 92. The House of the Spirits 93. Smilla's Feeling for Snow 97. Les Misérables 98.

Claude Autant-Lara Douce 43. Sylvia and the Ghost 44. Le Diable au Corps 46. Occupe-Toi d'Amélie 49. The Red Inn 51. The Seven Deadly Sins 52. Le Rouge et le Noir 54. Marguerite de la Nuit 55. En Cas de Malheur 58. The Oldest Profession 67.

Hy Averback Chamber of Horrors 66. I Love You, Alice B. Toklas 68. Where Were You When the Lights Went Out? 68. Suppose They Gave a War and Nobody Came 69. The Great Bank Robbery 69. Where the Boys Are 84.

John G. Avildsen Save the Tiger 73. WW and the Dixie Dancekings 75. Rocky 76. Slow Dancing in the Big City 78. The Formula 80. Neighbors 81. The Karate Kid 84. The Karate Kid Part II 86. Happy New Year 87. Maybe Baby 88. Karate Kid III 89. Lean on Me 89. Rocky V 90. The Power of One 91. 8 Seconds 94.

Lloyd Bacon Private Izzy Murphy 26. The Singing Fool 28. Honky Tonk 29. Say It with Songs 29. Moby Dick 30. Fifty Million Frenchmen 31. Gold Dust Gertie 31. Honor of the Family 31. Manhattan Parade 31. Alias the Doctor 32. Crooner 32. Fireman Save My Child 32. Miss Pinkerton 32. The Famous Ferguson Case 32. You Said a Mouthful 32. 42nd Street 33. Footlight Parade 33. Mary Stevens M.D. 33. The Picture Snatcher 33. He Was Her Man 34. Here Comes the Navy 34. Six Day Bike Rider 34. Wonder Bar 34. Broadway Gondolier 35. Devil Dogs of the Air 35. In Caliente 35. The Frisco Kid 35. The Irish in Us 35. Cain and Mabel 36. Gold Diggers of 1937 36. Sons o' Guns 36. Ever Since Eve 37. Marked Woman 37. San Quentin 37. Submarine D1 37. A Slight Case of Murder 38. Boy Meets Girl 38. Cowboy from Brooklyn 38. Racket Busters 38. Wings of the Navy 38. A Child Is Born 39. Espionage Agent 39. Indianapolis Speedway 39. Invisible Stripes 39. The Oklahoma Kid 39.

Brother Orchid 40. Knute Rockne, All American 40. Three Cheers for the Irish 40. Affectionately Yours 41. Footsteps in the Dark 41. Honeymoon for Three 41. Navy Blues 41. Larceny, Inc 42. Silver Queen 42. Wings for the Eagle 42. Action in the North Atlantic 43. Sunday Dinner for a Soldier 44. The Sullivans 44. Captain Eddie 45. Home Sweet Homicide 46. Wake Up and Dream 46. I Wonder Who's Kissing Her Now 47. Don't Trust Your Husband 48. Give My Regards to Broadway 48. Mother Is a Freshman 48. You Were Meant for Me 48. It Happens Every Spring 49. Miss Grant Takes Richmond 49. Kill the Umpire 50. The Fuller Brush Girl 50. Call Me Mister 51. Golden Girl 51. The Frogmen 51. She Couldn't Say No 52. The French Line 53. The Great Sioux Uprising 53. The I Don't Care Girl 53. Walking My Baby Back Home 53.

John Badham The Bingo Long Traveling All-Stars and Motor Kings 76. Saturday Night Fever 77. Dracula 79. Whose Life Is It Anyway? 81. Blue Thunder 83. War Games 83. American Flyers 85. Short Circuit 86. Stakeout 87. Bird on a Wire 90. The Hard Way 91. Another Stakeout 93. Point of No Return 93. Drop Zone 94. Nick of Time 95. Incognito 97.

Graham Baker The Final Conflict 81. Impulse 84. Alien Nation 88. Born to Ride 91. Beowulf 98.

Roy Ward Baker The October Man 47. The Weaker Sex 48. Paper Orchid 49. Highly Dangerous 50. Morning Departure 50. The House in the Square 51. Don't Bother to Knock 52. Night without Sleep 52. Inferno 53. Passage Home 55. Jacqueline 56. Tiger in the Smoke 56. The One that Got Away 57. A Night to Remember 58. The Singer Not the Song 60. Flame in the Streets 61. The Valiant 61. Two Left Feet 63. Quatermass and the Pit 67. The Anniversary 68. Moon Zero Two 69. Scars of Dracula 70. The Vampire Lovers 70. Dr Jekyll and Sister Hyde 71. Asylum 72. And Now The Screaming Starts 73. Vault of Horror 73. The Legend of the Seven Golden Vampires 74. The Monster Club 80.

Carroll Ballard The Black Stallion 80. Never Cry Wolf 83. Nutcracker – The Motion Picture 86. Wind 92. Fly Away Home 96.

Charles Band Crash! 77. The Alchemist 81. Parasite 82. Trancers 85. Trancers II 91.

Monty Banks My Wife's Family 31. You Made Me Love You 34. Man of the Moment 35. No Limit 35. Keep Your Seats Please 36. Queen of Hearts 36. Keep Smiling 38. We're Going to Be Rich 38. Shipyard Sally 39. Great Guns 41.

Richard Bare Flaxy Martin 48. Smart Girls Don't Talk 48. The House across the Street 49. Return of the Frontiersman 50. Prisoners of the Casbah 53. Shootout at Medicine Bend 57.

Steve Barron Electric Dreams 84. Teenage Mutant Ninja Turtles 90. Coneheads 93. The Adventures of Pinocchio 96. Mike Bassett: England Manager 01.

Lionel Barrymore His Glorious Night 29. Madame X 29. The Unholy Night 29. The Rogue Song 30. Ten Cents a Dance 31.

Paul Bartel Death Race 2000 75. Cannonball 76. Eating Raoul 82. Lust in the Dust 84. The Longshot 86. Scenes from the Class Struggle in Beverly Hills 89.

Hall Bartlett Unchained 55. Drango 57. Zero Hour! 57. All the Young Men 60. The Caretakers 63. Jonathan Livingston Seagull 73. The Children of Sanchez 78.

Charles Barton Car 99 35. Rocky Mountain Mystery 35. The Last Outpost 35. And Sudden Death 36. Behind Prison Gates 39. Five Little Peppers and How They Grew 39. The Richest Man in Town 41. Is Everybody Happy? 43. Laugh Your Blues Away 43. Reveille With Beverly 43. She Has What It Takes 43. What's Buzzin', Cousin? 43. Beautiful but Broke 44. Hey Rookie 44. Men in Her Diary 45. Buck Privates Come Home 46. Smooth as Silk 46. The Time of Their Lives 46. White Tie and Tails 46. The Wistful Widow of Wagon Gap 47. Abbott and Costello Meet Frankenstein 48. Abbott and Costello Meet the Killer, Boris Karloff 48. Mexican Hayride 48. The Noose Hangs High 48. Africa Screams 49. Free for All 49. Double Crossbones 50. The Milkman 50. The Shaggy Dog 59. Toby Tyler 59.

Mario Bava Black Sunday 60. Mask of Satan 60. The Wonders of Aladdin 61. Black Sabbath 63. Blood and Black Lace 64. Dr Goldfoot and the Girl Bombs 66. Danger: Diabolik 67. Five Dolls for an August Moon 70. A Bay of Blood 71. Baron Blood 72. Quante Volte… Quella Notte 72. Lisa and the Devil 74.

John Baxter Dosshouse 33. Say It with Flowers (A Human Story) 34. Men of Yesterday 36. Song of the Road 37. Crooks' Tour 40. Love on the Dole 41. The Common Touch 41. Let the People Sing 42. Shipbuilders 43. Theatre Royal 43. Dreaming 44. Here Comes the Sun 46. Judgment Deferred 51.

William Beaudine Little Annie Rooney 25. The Mad Parade 31. Make Me a Star 32. Three Wise Girls 32. Crime of the Century 33. The Old-Fashioned Way 34. Boys Will Be Boys 35. Dandy Dick 35. Get Off My Foot 35. Educated Evans 36. Where There's a Will 36. Windbag the Sailor 36. Feather Your Nest 37. Said O'Reilly to McNab 37. Phantom Killer 42. The Panther's Claw 42. Clancy Street Boys 43. The Ape Man 43. The Mystery of the 13th Guest 43. Adventures of Kitty O'Day 44. Follow the Leader 44. Voodoo Man 44. Come Out Fighting 45. Black Market Babies 46. The Face of Marble 46. Bela Lugosi Meets a Brooklyn Gorilla 52. Westward Ho the Wagons 56. Ten Who Dared 60. Billy the Kid vs Dracula 65. Jesse James Meets Frankenstein's Daughter 65.

Harry Beaumont Beau Brummell 24. Our Dancing Daughters 28. The Broadway Melody 29. The Florodora Girl 30. Dance Fools Dance 31. Laughing Sinners 31. The Great Lover 31. Are You Listening? 32. Faithless 32. West of Broadway 32. Made on Broadway 33. Should Ladies Behave? 33. When Ladies Meet 33. Murder in the Private Car 34. Enchanted April 35. The Girl on the Front Page 36. Maisie Goes to Reno 44. Twice Blessed 45. Up Goes Maisie 46. Alias a Gentleman 47.

Harold Becker The Ragman's Daughter 72. The Onion Field 79. The Black Marble 80. Taps 81. The Boost 88. Sea of Love 89. Malice 93. City Hall 96. Mercury Rising 98. Domestic Disturbance 01.

Jacques Becker Goupi Mains Rouges 43. Antoine et Antoinette 47. Rendezvous de Juillet 49. Edouard et Caroline 51. Casque d'Or 52. Rue de l'Estrapade 53. Touchez pas au Grisbi 53. Ali Baba and the Forty Thieves 54. The Adventures of Arsène Lupin 56. Lovers of Montparnasse 58. The Hole 59.

Ford Beebe The Shadow of the Eagle 32. Adventures of Rex and Rinty 35. Ace Drummond 36. Jungle Jim 37. Radio Patrol 37. Secret Agent X9 37. Tim Tyler's Luck 37. Trouble at Midnight 37. Westbound Limited 37. Wild West Days 37. Red Barry 38. Buck Rogers 39. The Oregon Trail 39. The Phantom Creeps 39. Junior G-Men 40. The Green Hornet 40. The Green Hornet Strikes Again 40. Winners of the West 40. Riders of Death Valley 41. Sky Raiders 41. Don Winslow of the Navy 42. Night Monster 42. Overland Mail 42. Enter Arsène Lupin 44. The Invisible Man's Revenge 44. Bomba the Jungle Boy 49. Indian Scout 49.

Jean-Jacques Beineix Diva 81. The Moon in the Gutter 83. Betty Blue 86. Roselyne and the Lions 89. IP5 92.

Monta Bell Lights of Old Broadway 25. Pretty Ladies 25. The Torrent 25. Man, Woman and Sin 27. East Is West 30. Downstairs 32. The Worst Woman in Paris 33.

Earl Bellamy Blackjack Ketchum, Desperado 56. Stagecoach to Dancer's Rock 58. Fluffy 64. Gunpoint 65. Incident at Phantom Hill 66. Against a Crooked Sky 75.

Laslo Benedek The Kissing Bandit 48. Port of New York 49. Death of a Salesman 51. Bengal Brigade 54. The Wild One 54. Moment of Danger 60. Namu the Killer Whale 66. The Daring Game 67. The Night Visitor 71.

Richard Benjamin My Favorite Year 82. City Heat 84. Racing with the Moon 84. The Money Pit 86. Little Nikita 88. My Stepmother Is an Alien 88. Downtown 90. Mermaids 90. Made in America 93. Milk Money 94. Mrs Winterbourne 96.

Spencer G. Bennet The Last Frontier 32. The Mysterious Pilot 37. The Secret Code 42. The Valley of Vanishing Men 42. Secret Service in Darkest Africa 43. The Masked Marvel 43. Haunted Harbor 44. The Tiger Woman 44. Zorro's Black Whip 44. Federal Operator 99 45. Manhunt of Mystery Island 45. The Purple Monster Strikes 45. King of the Forest Rangers 46. The Phantom Rider 46. Brick Bradford 47. Son of Zorro 47. The Black Widow 47. Congo Bill 48. Superman 48. Adventures of Sir Galahad 49. Bruce Gentry – Daredevil of the Skies 49. Atom Man vs Superman 50. Cody of the Pony Express 50. Pirates of the High Seas 50. Mysterious Island 51. Roar of the Iron Horse 51. Blackhawk 52. Blazing the Overland Trail 52. King of the Congo 52. Son of Geronimo 52. The Lost Planet 53. Gunfighters of the Northwest 54. Riding with Buffalo Bill 54. Adventures of Captain Africa 55. Perils of the Wilderness 56. Atomic Submarine 59. Jungle Jim .

Compton Bennett The Seventh Veil 45. The Years Between 46. Daybreak 48. My Own True Love 48. That Forsyte Woman 49. King Solomon's Mines 50. It Started in Paradise 52. So Little Time 52. The Gift Horse 52. Desperate Moment 53. After the Ball 57. That Woman Opposite 57. Beyond the Curtain 60.

Thomas Bentley Young Woodley 29. Harmony Heaven 30. Keepers of Youth 31. After Office Hours 32. The Old Curiosity Shop 34. Those Were the Days 34. Music Hath Charms 35. Royal Cavalcade 35. Silver Blaze 37. Dead Man's Shoes 39.

Robert Benton Bad Company 72. The Late Show 77. Kramer versus Kramer 79. Still of the Night 82. Places in the Heart 84. Nadine 87. Billy Bathgate 91. Nobody's Fool 94. Twilight 98.

Bruce Beresford The Adventures of Barry Mackenzie 72. Barry McKenzie Holds His Own 74. Side by Side 75. Don's Party 76. The Getting of Wisdom 77. Money Movers 78. Breaker Morant 80. The Club 80. Puberty Blues 82. Tender Mercies 82. King David 85. Crimes of the Heart 86. Fringe Dwellers 86. Aria 88. Driving Miss Daisy 89. Her Alibi 89. Mr Johnson 90. Black Robe 91. Rich in Love 92. A Good Man in Africa 94. Silent Fall 94. Last Dance 96. Paradise Road 97. Double Jeopardy 99. Evelyn 02.

Andrew Bergman So Fine 81. The Freshman 90. Honeymoon in Vegas 92. It Could Happen to You 94. Striptease 96. Isn't She Great 00.

Ingmar Bergman It Rains on Our Love 46. A Ship to India 47. Music Is My Future 48. Port of Call 48. The Devil's Wanton 49. Three Strange Loves 49. Summer Interlude 50. To Joy 50. Summer with Monika 52. Waiting Women 52. Sawdust and Tinsel 53. A Lesson in Love 54. Journey into Autumn 54. Smiles of a Summer Night 55. The Seventh Seal 57. Wild Strawberries 57. So Close to Life 58. The Face 58. The Virgin Spring 59. The Devil's Eye 60. Through a Glass Darkly 61. Winter Light 62. The Silence 63. Now About These Women … 64. Persona 66. The Hour of the Wolf 68. The Touch 70. Viskningar och Rop 72. Scenes from a Marriage 73. Face to Face 76. The Serpent's Egg 77. Autumn Sonata 78. Aus Dem Leben Der Marionetten 80. Fanny and Alexander 82. After the Rehearsal 84.

William Berke The Falcon in Mexico 44. Betrayal from the East 45. Dick Tracy 45. Skyliner 49. Treasure of Monte Cristo 49. The Bandit Queen 50. Jungle Jim .

Busby Berkeley Bright Lights 35. The Go-Getter 37. Comet over Broadway 38. Garden of the Moon 38. Hollywood Hotel 38. Men Are Such Fools 38. They Made Me a Criminal 39. Forty Little Mothers 40. For Me and My Gal 42. Cinderella Jones 46. Take Me Out to the Ball Game 49.

Edward Bernds Gasoline Alley 51. Harem Girl 52. Navy Wife 56. World without End 56. Quantrill's Raiders 58. Queen of Outer Space 58. Space Master X-7 58. Return of the Fly 59.

Curtis Bernhardt The Beloved Vagabond 36. Carrefour 38. Lady with Red Hair 40. My Love Came Back 40. Million Dollar Baby 41. Happy Go Lucky 42. Juke Girl 42. Conflict 45. A Stolen Life 46. Devotion 46. My Reputation 46. High Wall 47. Possessed 47. The Doctor and the Girl 49. Payment on Demand 51. Sirocco 51. The Blue Veil 51. The Merry Widow 52. Miss Sadie Thompson 53. Beau Brummell 54. Interrupted Melody 55. Gaby 56. Kisses for My President 64.

Claude Berri A Summer Affair 77. Je Vous Aime 81. Jean de Florette 86. Manon des Sources 86. Uranus 90. Germinal 93. Lucie Aubrac 97.

John Berry Cross My Heart 45. From This Day Forward 46. Miss Susie Slagle's 46. Casbah 48. Robinson Crusoeland 50. Tension 50. He Ran All the Way 51. Maya 66. Claudine 74. Thieves 77. The Bad News Bears Go to Japan 78. Boesman & Lena 99.

Bernardo Bertolucci The Grim Reaper 62. Before the Revolution 64. The Conformist 69. The Spider's Stratagem 70. Last Tango in Paris 72. 1900 76. La Luna 79. The Tragedy of a Ridiculous Man 81. The Last Emperor 87. The Sheltering Sky 90. Little Buddha 93. Stealing Beauty 95. Besieged 98.

Luc Besson The Last Battle 83. Subway 85. The Big Blue 88. Nikita 90. Atlantis 91. Leon 94. The Fifth Element 97. The Messenger: The Story Of Joan Of Arc 99.

Abner Biberman The Golden Mistress 54. The Looters 55. Behind the High Wall 56. Gun for a Coward 56. The Price of Fear 56. Flood Tide 58.

Kathryn Bigelow The Loveless 83. Near Dark 87. Blue Steel 90. Point Break 91. Strange Days 95. K-19: The Widowmaker.

Tony Bill My Bodyguard 80. Six Weeks 82. Five Corners 88. Crazy People 90. A Home of Our Own 93. Untamed Heart 93.

Claude Binyon Family Honeymoon 48. The Saxon Charm 48. Mother Didn't Tell Me 50. Aaron Slick from Punkin Crick 52. Dreamboat 52. Here Come the Girls 53.

Daniel Birt No Room at the Inn 48. The Three Weird Sisters 48. The Interrupted Journey 49. She Shall Have Murder 50. Background 53.

George Blair Secrets of Scotland Yard 44. Gangs of the Waterfront 45. Scotland Yard Investigator 45. The Twinkle in God's Eye 55. The Hypnotic Eye 60.

John E. Blakeley Somewhere in England 40. Somewhere on Leave 42. Demobbed 44. Home Sweet Home 45. It's a Grand Life 53.

Bertrand Blier Les Valseuses 74. Get Out Your Handkerchiefs 78. Buffet Froid 79. Beau-Père 81. My Best Friend's Girl 83. Our Story 84. Tenue de Soirée 86. Trop Belle pour Toi! 89. Merci La Vie 91. Mon Homme 96.

Don Bluth The Secret of Nimh 82. An American Tail 86. The Land before Time 88. Rock-a-Doodle 90. Thumbelina 94. The Pebble and the Penguin 95. Anastasia 97. Titan A.E. 00.

John G. Blystone Captain Lash 29. Amateur Daddy 32. Painted Woman 32. She Wanted a Millionaire 32. Too Busy to Work 32. Hot Pepper 33. Shanghai Madness 33. Change of Heart 34. Hell in the Heavens 34. The County Chairman 34. Great Guy 36. The Magnificent Brute 36. Music for Madame 37. Woman Chases Man 37. Blockheads 38. Swiss Miss 38.

Budd Boetticher The Missing Juror 44. Escape in the Fog 45. The Bullfighter and the Lady 51.

The Cimarron Kid 51. Bronco Buster 52. Horizons West 52. Red Ball Express 52. City beneath the Sea 53. East of Sumatra 53. Seminole 53. The Man from the Alamo 53. Wings of the Hawk 53. The Magnificent Matador 55. Seven Men from Now 56. The Killer Is Loose 56. Decision at Sundown 57. The Tall T 57. Buchanan Rides Alone 58. Ride Lonesome 59. Westbound 59. Comanche Station 60. The Rise and Fall of Legs Diamond 60.

Paul Bogart Halls of Anger 69. Marlowe 69. The Skin Game 71. Cancel My Reservation 72. Class of '44 73. Mr Ricco 75. Oh God, You Devil 84. Torch Song Trilogy 88. Broadway Bound 91.

Peter Bogdanovich Targets 67. The Last Picture Show 71. What's Up, Doc? 72. Paper Moon 73. Daisy Miller 74. At Long Last Love 75. Nickelodeon 76. Saint Jack 79. They All Laughed 82. Mask 85. Illegally Yours 88. Texasville 90. Noises Off 92. The Thing Called Love 93.

Richard Boleslawski The Gay Diplomat 31. Rasputin and the Empress 32. Storm at Daybreak 32. Beauty for Sale 33. Clive of India 34. Fugitive Lovers 34. Hollywood Party 34. Men in White 34. Operator 13 34. The Painted Veil 34. Les Misérables 35. Metropolitan 35. O'Shaughnessy's Boy 35. The Garden of Allah 36. Theodora Goes Wild 36. The Last of Mrs Cheyney 37.

Mauro Bolognini The Oldest Profession 67. Arabella 69. The Inheritance 76. The Lady of the Camelias 81. In Excess 91.

John Boorman Catch Us If You Can 65. Point Blank 67. Hell in the Pacific 69. Leo the Last 69. Deliverance 72. Zardoz 74. Exorcist II: The Heretic 77. Excalibur 81. The Emerald Forest 85. Hope and Glory 87. Where the Heart Is 90. Beyond Rangoon 95. The General 98. The Tailor of Panama 01.

Reginald Le Borg Calling Doctor Death 43. Destiny 44. San Diego I Love You 44. Weird Woman 44. Joe Palooka, Champ 46. The Great Jesse James Raid 53. The Black Sleep 56. The Flight that Disappeared 61. Diary of a Madman 62.

Walerian Borowczyk Blanche 71. Immoral Tales 74. La Marge 76. Behind Convent Walls 77. The Art of Love 83.

Frank Borzage Seventh Heaven 27. Street Angel 28. Liliom 30. Song o' My Heart 30. Bad Girl 31. Young as You Feel 31. A Farewell to Arms 32. After Tomorrow 32. Young America 32. Man's Castle 33. Secrets 33. Flirtation Walk 34. Little Man, What Now? 34. No Greater Glory 34. Living on Velvet 35. Shipmates Forever 35. Stranded 35. Desire 36. Green Light 36. Hearts Divided 36. History Is Made at Night 37. Mannequin 37. The Big City 37. The Shining Hour 38. Three Comrades 38. Disputed Passage 39. Flight Command 40. Strange Cargo 40. The Mortal Storm 40. Smilin' Through 41. The Vanishing Virginian 41. Seven Sweethearts 42. His Butler's Sister 43. Stage Door Canteen 43. Till We Meet Again 44. The Spanish Main 45. I've Always Loved You 46. Magnificent Doll 46. That's My Man 46. Moonrise 48. China Doll 58. The Big Fisherman 59.

John Boulting Journey Together 44. Brighton Rock 47. Seven Days to Noon 50. The Magic Box 51. Private's Progress 56. Lucky Jim 57. I'm All Right Jack 59. Suspect 60. Heavens Above 63. Rotten to the Core 65.

Roy Boulting Consider Your Verdict 38. Inquest 39. Trunk Crime 39. Pastor Hall 40. Thunder Rock 42. Fame Is the Spur 47. The Guinea Pig 48. High Treason 51. Single-Handed 53. Seagulls over Sorrento 54. Josephine and Men 55. Run for the Sun 56. Brothers in Law 57. Happy Is the Bride 57. Carlton-Browne of the FO 58. A French Mistress 60. Suspect 60. The Family Way 66. Twisted Nerve 68. There's a Girl in My Soup 70. Mr Forbush and the Penguins 71. Soft Beds, Hard Battles 73. The Last Word 79.

Muriel Box The Happy Family 52. Street Corner 53. The Beachcomber 54. Simon and Laura 55. Eye Witness 56. The Passionate Stranger 56. The Truth about Women 57. Subway in the Sky 58. Too Young to Love 59. This Other Eden 60. Rattle of a Simple Man 64.

Charles Brabin Call of the Flesh 30. Sporting Blood 31. The Great Meadow 31. Beast of the City 32. New Morals for Old 32. The Mask of Fu Manchu 32. Washington Masquerade 32. Stage Mother 33. The Secret of Madame Blanche 33. A Wicked Woman 34.

Robert N. Bradbury Riders of Destiny 33. The Lucky Texan 33. West of the Divide 33. Blue Steel 34. The Lawless Frontier 34. The Man from Utah 34. The Star Packer 34. The Trail Beyond 34. Texas Terror 35. The Dawn Rider 35.

John Brahm Broken Blossoms 36. Counsel for Crime 37. Let Us Live 37. Penitentiary 38. Rio 39. Escape to Glory 40. Wild Geese Calling 41. The Undying Monster 43. Tonight We Raid Calais 43. Wintertime 43. Guest in the House 44. The Lodger 44. Hangover Square 45. The Brasher Doubloon 46. The Locket 46. Singapore 47. Face to Face 52. The Miracle of Our Lady of Fatima 52. The Diamond Queen 53. The Mad Magician 54. Bengazi 55.

Kenneth Branagh Henry V 89. Dead Again 91. Peter's Friends 92. Much Ado about Nothing 93. Mary Shelley's Frankenstein 94. In the Bleak Midwinter 95. Hamlet 96. Love's Labours Lost 00.

Fred C. Brannon The Purple Monster Strikes 45. King of the Forest Rangers 46. The Crimson Ghost 46. The Phantom Rider 46. Jesse James Rides Again 47. Son of Zorro 47. The Black Widow 47. Adventures of Frank and Jesse James 48. Dangers of the Canadian Mounted 48. G-Men Never Forget 48. Federal Agents vs Underworld Inc 49. Ghost of Zorro 49. King of the Rocket Men 49. Desperadoes of the West 50. Radar Patrol vs Spy King 50. The Invisible Monster 50. The James Brothers of Missouri 50. Don Daredevil Rides Again 51. Flying Disc Men from Mars 51. Government Agents vs The Phantom Legion 51. Radar Men from the Moon 52. Zombies of the Stratosphere 52. Jungle Drums of Africa 53.

Herbert Brenon The Alaskan 24. Beau Geste 26. The Case of Sergeant Grischa 30. Beau Ideal 31. Transgression 31. Royal Cavalcade 35. Someone at the Door 36. The Dominant Sex 37. Housemaster 38. Yellow Sands 38. Black Eyes 39.

Robert Bresson Les Anges du Péché 43. Les Dames du Bois de Boulogne 46. The Diary of a Country Priest 50. Pickpocket 59. Procès de Jeanne d'Arc 62. Balthazar 66. Mouchette 66. Une Femme Douce 69. Lancelot du Lac 74. The Devil, Probably 77. L'Argent 83.

Martin Brest Going in Style 79. Beverly Hills Cop 84. Midnight Run 88. Scent of a Woman 92. Meet Joe Black 98.

Howard Bretherton The Match King 32. Ladies They Talk About 33. The Return of the Terror 34. Dinky 35. Wild Brian Kent 36. Who's Guilty? 45. The Monster and the Ape 46. Prince of Thieves 48.

Alan Bridges Act of Murder 64. Invasion 66. The Hireling 73. Out of Season 75. Age of Innocence 77. The Return of the Soldier 82. The Shooting Party 84.

James Bridges The Baby Maker 70. The Paper Chase 73. 9/30/55 77. The China Syndrome 79. Urban Cowboy 80. Mike's Murder 84. Perfect 85. Bright Lights, Big City 88.

Peter Brook The Beggar's Opera 52. Lord of the Flies 63. The Marat/Sade 66. King Lear 70. The Mahabharata 89.

Albert Brooks Real Life 79. Modern Romance 81. Lost in America 85. Defending Your Life 91. The Muse 99.

Mel Brooks The Producers 68. The Twelve Chairs 70. Blazing Saddles 74. Young Frankenstein 74. Silent Movie 76. High Anxiety 77. History of the World Part One 81. Spaceballs 87. Life Stinks 91. Robin Hood: Men in Tights 93. Dracula: Dead and Loving It 95.

Richard Brooks Crisis 50. The Light Touch 51. Battle Circus 52. Deadline USA 52. Take the High Ground 53. The Flame and the Flesh 54. The Last Time I Saw Paris 54. The Blackboard Jungle 55. The Catered Affair 56. The Last Hunt 56. Something of Value 57. Cat on a Hot Tin Roof 58. The Brothers Karamazov 58. Elmer Gantry 60. Sweet Bird of Youth 62. Lord Jim 64. The Professionals 66. In Cold Blood 67. The Happy Ending 69. Dollars 71. Bite the Bullet 75. Looking for Mr Goodbar 77. Wrong Is Right 82. Fever Pitch 85.

Otto Brower Paramount on Parade 30. Fighting Caravans 31. Devil Horse 32. Mystery Mountain 34. The Girl from Avenue A 40. Little Tokyo USA 42. Dixie Dugan 43. Behind Green Lights 45.

Clarence Brown The Eagle 25. The Goose Woman 25. Flesh and the Devil 26. A Woman of Affairs 28. The Trail of '98 28. Anna Christie 30. Inspiration 30. Romance 30. A Free Soul 31. Possessed 31. Emma 32. Letty Lynton 32. The Son-Daughter 32. Looking Forward 33. Night Flight 33. Chained 34. Sadie McKee 34. Ah, Wilderness 35. Anna Karenina 35. The Gorgeous Hussy 36. Wife versus Secretary 36. Conquest 37. Of Human Hearts 38. Idiot's Delight 39. The Rains Came 39. Edison the Man 40. Come Live with Me 41. They Met in Bombay 41. The Human Comedy 43. The White Cliffs of Dover 44. National Velvet 45. The Yearling 46. Song of Love 47. Intruder in the Dust 49. To Please a Lady 50. Angels in the Outfield 52. It's a Big Country 52. Plymouth Adventure 52. When in Rome 52.

Tod Browning The Blackbird 25. The Unholy Three 25. Road to Mandalay 26. London after Midnight 27. The Big City 27. The Unknown 27. West of Zanzibar 28. The Thirteenth Chair 29. Outside the Law 30. Dracula 31. The Iron Man 31. Freaks 32. Fast Workers 33. Mark of the Vampire 35. Devil-Doll 36. Miracles for Sale 39.

Clyde Bruckman The General 26. Putting Pants on Philip 27. The Battle of the Century 27. Leave 'Em Laughing 28. The Finishing Touch 28. Welcome Danger 29. Feet First 30. Movie Crazy 32. The Fatal Glass of Beer 33. The Man on the Flying Trapeze 35.

Adrian Brunel Blighty 26. The Crooked Billet 29. Elstree Calling 30. The City of Beautiful Nonsense 35. The Lion Has Wings 39. The Rebel Son 39.

Harold S. Bucquet Calling Dr Kildare 39. On Borrowed Time 39. Dr Kildare Goes Home 40. Dr Kildare's Crisis 40. Dr Kildare's Strange Case 40. Dr Kildare's Wedding Day 41. Kathleen 41. The Penalty 41. Calling Dr Gillespie 42. The War against Mrs Hadley 42. The Adventures of Tartu 43. Dragon Seed 44. Without Love 45.

Luis Buñuel The Fall of the House of Usher 28. Un Chien Andalou 28. L'Age d'Or 30. Los Olvidados 51. Él 52. The Brute 52. The Adventures of Robinson Crusoe 53. Cela s'appelle l'Aurore 55. The Criminal Life of Archibaldo de la Cruz 55. Nazarin 58. Viridiana 61. The Exterminating Angel 62. The Diary of a Chambermaid 64. Simon of the Desert 65. Belle de Jour 67. The Milky Way 68. Tristana 70. The Discreet Charm of the Bourgeoisie 72. The Phantom of Liberty 74. That Obscure Object of Desire 77.

Tim Burstall Alvin Purple 73. Eliza Fraser 76. Attack Force Z 81. The Naked Country 85. Kangaroo 87.

David Burton The Bishop Murder Case 30. Fighting Caravans 31. Dancers in the Dark 32. Let's Fall in Love 33. Lady By Choice 34. Sisters under the Skin 34. Princess O'Hara 35. The Melody Lingers On 35. Make Way for a Lady 36. Manhattan Heartbeat 40. The Man Who Wouldn't Talk 40.

Tim Burton Pee-wee's Big Adventure 85. Beetlejuice 88. Batman 89. Edward Scissorhands 90. Batman Returns 92. Ed Wood 94. Mars Attacks! 96. Sleepy Hollow 99. Planet of the Apes 01.

David Butler Fox Movietone Follies of 1929 29. Sunny Side Up 29. High Society Blues 30. Just Imagine 30. A Connecticut Yankee 31. Business and Pleasure 31. Delicious 31. Down to Earth 32. My Weakness 33. Bottoms Up 34. Bright Eyes 34. Handy Andy 34. Have a Heart 34. Doubting Thomas 35. The Little Colonel 35. The Littlest Rebel 35. Captain January 36. Pigskin Parade 36. Ali Baba Goes to Town 37. You're a Sweetheart 37. Kentucky 38. Kentucky Moonshine 38. Straight, Place and Show 38. East Side of Heaven 39. That's Right, You're Wrong 39. If I Had My Way 40. You'll Find Out 40. Caught in the Draft 41. Playmates 41. Road to Morocco 42. Thank Your Lucky Stars 43. They Got Me Covered 43. Shine on Harvest Moon 44. The Princess and the Pirate 44. San Antonio 45. The Time, the Place and the Girl 46. Two Guys from Milwaukee 46. My Wild Irish Rose 47. John Loves Mary 48. Two Guys from Texas 48. It's a Great Feeling 49. Look for the Silver Lining 49. The Story of Seabiscuit 49. Tea for Two 50. The Daughter of Rosie O'Grady 50. Lullaby of Broadway 51. Painting the Clouds with Sunshine 51. April in Paris 52. Where's Charley? 52. By the Light of the Silvery Moon 53. Calamity Jane 53. King Richard and the Crusaders 54. The Command 54. Glory 55. Jump into Hell 55. The Girl He Left Behind 56. The Right Approach 61.

Robert Butler Guns in the Heather 68. The Barefoot Executive 70. The Computer Wore Tennis Shoes 70. Scandalous John 71. Now You See Him Now You Don't 72. Hot Lead and Cold Feet 78. Night of the Juggler 80. Turbulence 97.

Edward Buzzell Hollywood Speaks 32. Virtue 32. Child of Manhattan 33. The Human Side 34. The Girl Friend 35. The Luckiest Girl in the World 36. Paradise for Three 37. Fast Company 38. Honolulu 38. At the Circus 39. Go West 40. The Getaway 41. Ship Ahoy 42. The Omaha Trail 42. Best Foot Forward 43. The Youngest Profession 43. Keep Your Powder Dry 45. Easy to Wed 46. Three Wise Fools 46. Neptune's Daughter 49. A Woman of Distinction 50. Confidentially Connie 53. Ain't Misbehavin' 55.

Christy Cabanne Girl of the Limberlost 34. Jane Eyre 34. Another Face 35. Keeper of the Bees 35. One Frightened Night 35. Rendezvous at Midnight 35. Storm over the Andes 35. Criminal Lawyer 37. The Outcasts of Poker Flat 37. We Who Are About to Die 37. Alias the Deacon 40. The Mummy's Hand 40. Scattergood Baines 41. Scared to Death 47.

Michael Cacoyannis The Girl in Black 55. A Matter of Dignity 57. Zorba the Greek 64. The Day the Fish Came Out 67. The Trojan Women 71.

Edward L. Cahn Law and Order 32. Confidential 35. Main Street After Dark 44. Dangerous Partners 45. I Cheated the Law 48. The Checkered Coat 48. Destination Murder 50. The Creature with the Atom Brain 55. Shake, Rattle & Rock! 56. The She Creature 56. Voodoo Woman 56. Dragstrip Girl 57. Invasion of the Saucermen 57. Motorcycle Gang 57. The Zombies of Mora Tau 57. Curse of the Faceless Man 58. It! The Terror from Beyond Space 58. The Four Skulls of Jonathan Drake 59.

Christopher Cain That Was Then … This Is Now 85. Where the River Runs Black 86. Young Guns 88. Pure Country 92. The Next Karate Kid 94. The Amazing Panda Adventure 95. Gone Fishin' 97.

James Cameron Piranha II: The Spawning 82. The Terminator 84. Aliens 86. The Abyss 89. Terminator 2: Judgment Day 91. True Lies 94. Titanic 97.

Joe Camp Benji 74. Hawmps 76. For the Love of Benji 77. The Double McGuffin 79. Oh Heavenly Dog 80. Benji the Hunted 87.

Martin Campbell The Sex Thief 73. Criminal Law 89. Defenceless 91. No Escape 94. GoldenEye 95. The Mask of Zorro 98. Vertical Limit 00.

Jane Campion Sweetie 89. An Angel at My Table 90. The Piano 93. The Portrait of a Lady 96. Holy Smoke 99.

Men 95. The Odd Couple II 98. The Replacements 00.

Michel Déville Benjamin, or The Diary of an Innocent Young Man 66. La Petite Bande 83. Death in a French Garden 85. Paltoquet 86. La Lectrice 88.

Philippe de Broca Cartouche 61. That Man from Rio 64. King of Hearts 66. The Oldest Profession 67. Dear Inspector 77. Le Bossu 97.

Frederick de Cordova Her Kind of Man 46. Always Together 47. Love and Learn 47. That Way with Women 47. Countess of Monte Cristo 48. For the Love of Mary 48. Wallflower 48. Buccaneer's Girl 49. Illegal Entry 49. The Gal Who Took the West 49. The Desert Hawk 50. Bedtime for Bonzo 51. Here Come the Nelsons 51. Katie Did It 51. Little Egypt 51. Column South 52. I'll Take Sweden 65. Frankie and Johnny 66.

Albert de Courville The Midshipmaid 32. Charing Cross Road 35. Things Are Looking Up 35. Seven Sinners 36. Crackerjack 38. An Englishman's Home 39. The Lambeth Walk 39.

Cecil B. de Mille The Cheat 15. Joan the Woman 16. The Affairs of Anatol 21. Adam's Rib 22. Manslaughter 22. The Ten Commandments 23. King of Kings 27. Dynamite 29. Madam Satan 30. The Squaw Man 31. The Sign of the Cross 32. This Day and Age 33. Cleopatra 34. Four Frightened People 34. The Crusades 35. The Plainsman 36. The Buccaneer 38. Union Pacific 39. Northwest Mounted Police 40. Reap the Wild Wind 42. The Story of Dr Wassell 44. Unconquered 47. Samson and Delilah 49. The Greatest Show on Earth 52. The Ten Commandments 56.

Brian De Palma Greetings 68. Hi, Mom! 69. Get to Know Your Rabbit 72. Sisters 73. Phantom of the Paradise 74. Carrie 76. Obsession 76. The Fury 78. Dressed to Kill 80. Blow Out 81. Scarface 83. Body Double 84. Wise Guys 86. The Untouchables 87. Casualties of War 89. The Bonfire of the Vanities 90. Raising Cain 92. Carlito's Way 93. Mission: Impossible 96. Snake Eyes 98. Mission to Mars 00.

Vittorio de Siça Shoeshine 46. Bicycle Thieves 48. Miracle in Milan 51. Umberto D 52. Indiscretion of an American Wife 54. Gold of Naples 55. Two Women 60. The Condemned of Altona 62. Yesterday, Today and Tomorrow 63. After the Fox 66. Woman Times Seven 67. A Place for Lovers 69. Sunflower 70. The Garden of the Finzi-Continis 70.

André de Toth The Jungle Book 42. Passport to Suez 43. Dark Waters 44. None Shall Escape 44. Ramrod 47. The Other Love 47. Pitfall 48. Slattery's Hurricane 49. Man in the Saddle 51. Carson City 52. Springfield Rifle 52. House of Wax 53. The Last of the Comanches 53. The Stranger Wore a Gun 53. Thunder over the Plains 53. Crime Wave 54. Riding Shotgun 54. Tanganyika 54. The Bounty Hunter 54. The Indian Fighter 55. Hidden Fear 57. Monkey on My Back 57. The Day of the Outlaw 58. The Two-Headed Spy 58. Man on a String 60. Play Dirty 69.

Thorold Dickinson The High Command 36. The Arsenal Stadium Mystery 39. Gaslight 40. The Prime Minister 41. The Next of Kin 42. Men of Two Worlds 46. The Queen of Spades 48. The Secret People 51. Hill 24 Doesn't Answer 54.

William Dieterle Her Majesty Love 31. The Last Flight 31. Jewel Robbery 32. Lawyer Man 32. Man Wanted 32. Scarlet Dawn 32. Six Hours to Live 32. The Crash 32. Adorable 33. Female 33. From Headquarters 33. Grand Slam 33. The Devil's in Love 33. Fashions of 1934 34. Fog over Frisco 34. Madame Dubarry 34. The Firebird 34. A Midsummer Night's Dream 35. Dr Socrates 35. The Secret Bride 35. Satan Met a Lady 36. The Story of Louis Pasteur 36. The White Angel 36. Another Dawn 37. The Great O'Malley 37. The Life of Emile Zola 37. Blockade 38. Juarez 39. The Hunchback of Notre Dame 39. A Dispatch from Reuters 40. Dr Ehrlich's Magic Bullet 40. All that Money Can Buy 41. Syncopation 42. Tennessee Johnson 43. I'll Be Seeing You 44. Kismet 44. Love Letters 45. This Love of Ours 45. The Searching Wind 46. Portrait of Jennie 48. The Accused 48. Paid in Full 49. Rope of Sand 49. Dark City 50. September Affair 50. Peking Express 51. Red Mountain 51. Boots Malone 52. The Turning Point 52. Salome 53. Elephant Walk 54. Magic Fire 54. Omar Khayyam 56. Quick Let's Get Married 65.

John Francis Dillon Bride of the Regiment 30. Kismet 30. Sally 30. The Girl of the Golden West 30. Pagan Lady 31. The Finger Points 31. Behind the Mask 32. Call Her Savage 32. Man about Town 32. The Big Shakedown 34.

Edward Dmytryk Golden Gloves 39. Television Spy 39. Mystery Sea Raider 40. Sweetheart of the Campus 41. The Devil Commands 41. Seven Miles from Alcatraz 42. Behind the Rising Sun 43. Captive Wild Woman 43. Hitler's Children 43. Tender Comrade 43. The Falcon Strikes Back 43. Farewell My Lovely 44. Back to Bataan 45. Cornered 45. Till the End of Time 46. Crossfire 47. So Well Remembered 47. Obsession 48. Give Us This Day 49. Eight Iron Men 52. Mutiny 52. The Sniper 52. The Juggler 53. Broken Lance 54. The Caine Mutiny 54. The End of the Affair 54. Soldier of Fortune 55. The Left Hand of God 55. The Mountain 56. Raintree County 57. The Young Lions 58. The Blue Angel 59. Warlock 59. Walk on the Wild Side 62. The Carpetbaggers 64. Where Love Has Gone 64. Mirage 65. Alvarez Kelly 66. Anzio 68. Shalako 68. Bluebeard 72. The Human Factor 75.

Roger Donaldson Smash Palace 81. The Bounty 84. Marie 85. No Way Out 87. Cocktail 88. Cadillac Man 90. White Sands 92. The Getaway 94. Species 95. Dante's Peak 97. Thirteen Days 00. The Recruit 03.

Stanley Donen Love Is Better Than Ever 51. Royal Wedding 51. Fearless Fagan 52. Give a Girl a Break 53. Deep in My Heart 54. Seven Brides for Seven Brothers 54. It's Always Fair Weather 55. Funny Face 56. Kiss Them for Me 57. The Pajama Game 57. Damn Yankees 58. Indiscreet 58. Once More with Feeling 60. Surprise Package 60. The Grass Is Greener 60. Charade 63. Arabesque 66. Two for the Road 66. Bedazzled 67. Staircase 69. The Little Prince 74. Lucky Lady 75. Movie Movie 78. Saturn 3 80. Blame It on Rio 83.

Clive Donner The Sinister Man 61. Some People 62. Nothing but the Best 64. The Caretaker 64. What's New Pussycat? 65. Here We Go Round the Mulberry Bush 67. Luv 67. Alfred the Great 69. Vampira 74. The Thief of Baghdad 78. Charlie Chan and the Curse of the Dragon Queen 80. The Nude Bomb 80. Stealing Heaven 88.

Richard Donner Salt and Pepper 68. Twinky 69. The Omen 76. Superman 78. Inside Moves 80. The Toy 83. Ladyhawke 85. The Goonies 85. Lethal Weapon 87. Scrooged 88. Lethal Weapon 2 89. Lethal Weapon 3 92. Radio Flyer 92. Maverick 94. Assassins 95. Conspiracy Theory 97. Lethal Weapon 4 98.

Jack Donohue The Yellow Cab Man 50. Watch the Birdie 50. Lucky Me 54. Babes in Toyland 61. Marriage on the Rocks 65. Assault on a Queen 66.

Gordon Douglas General Spanky 36. Zenobia 39. Saps at Sea 40. Broadway Limited 41. Niagara Falls 41. Road Show 41. The Devil with Hitler 42. The Great Gildersleeve 42. The Falcon in Hollywood 44. First Yank into Tokyo 45. Zombies on Broadway 45. Dick Tracy vs Cueball 46. San Quentin 46. If You Knew Susie 48. The Black Arrow 48. Walk a Crooked Mile 48. Mr Soft Touch 49. The Doolins of Oklahoma 49. Between Midnight and Dawn 50. Fortunes of Captain Blood 50. Kiss Tomorrow Goodbye 50. Only the Valiant 50. Rogues of Sherwood Forest 50. The Great Missouri Raid 50. The Nevadan 50. Come Fill the Cup 51. I Was a Communist for the FBI 51. Mara Maru 52. The Iron Mistress 52. So This Is Love 53. The Charge at Feather River 53. Them! 54. Young at Heart 54. Sincerely Yours 55. The McConnell Story 55. Santiago 56. Bombers B-52 57. Fort Dobbs 57. The Big Land 57. The Fiend Who Walked the West 58. Up Periscope 59. Yellowstone Kelly 59. Claudelle Inglish 61. Gold of the Seven Saints 61. The Sins of Rachel Cade 61. Call Me Bwana 62. Follow That Dream 62. Rio Conchos 64. Robin and the Seven Hoods 64. Sylvia 64. Harlow 65. Stagecoach 66. Way Way Out 66. Chuka 67. In Like Flint 67. Tony Rome 67. Lady in Cement 68. The Detective 68. Skullduggery 69. Barquero! 70. They Call Me Mister Tibbs! 70. Slaughter's Big Rip-Off 73. Viva Knievel! 77.

Stan Dragoti Dirty Little Billy 72. Love at First Bite 79. Mr Mom 83. The Man with One Red Shoe 85. She's Out of Control 89. Necessary Roughness 91.

Arthur Dreifuss Baby Face Morgan 42. The Payoff 43. Ever Since Venus 44. Eadie was a Lady 45. There's a Girl in my Heart 49. The Last Blitzkrieg 59. The Quare Fellow 62.

Carl Theodor Dreyer Leaves from Satan's Book 19. Master of the House 25. The Passion of Joan of Arc 28. Vampyr 32. Day of Wrath 43. Ordet 57. Gertrud 66.

Dennis Dugan Problem Child 90. Brain Donors 92. Happy Gilmore 96. Beverly Hills Ninja 97. Big Daddy 99. Saving Silverman 01. National Security 03.

Christian Duguay Scanners II: The New Order 91. Scanners III: The Takeover 92. Screamers 96. The Assignment 97. The Art of War 00.

John Duigan Mouth to Mouth 78. Winter of Our Dreams 81. Far East 82. The Year My Voice Broke 87. Flirting 89. Romero 89. Wide Sargasso Sea 92. Sirens 94. The Journey of August King 95. The Leading Man 96. Lawn Dogs 97. The Parole Officer 01.

Philip Dunne Prince of Players 55. The View from Pompey's Head 55. Hilda Crane 56. Three Brave Men 56. In Love and War 58. Ten North Frederick 58. Blue Denim 59. The Inspector 61. Wild in the Country 61. Blindfold 65.

E. A. Dupont Variety 25. Atlantic 29. Piccadilly 29. The Bishop Misbehaves 35. Forgotten Faces 36. On Such a Night 37. Hell's Kitchen 39. The Scarf 51. The Neanderthal Man 53.

Julien Duvivier Poil de Carotte 32. Maria Chapdelaine 34. Golgotha 35. La Belle Equipe 36. Pépé le Moko 36. The Golem 36. Un Carnet de Bal 37. The Great Waltz 38. La Fin du Jour 39. Heart of a Nation 40. Lydia 41. Tales of Manhattan 42. Flesh and Fantasy 43. The Impostor 44. Panique 46. Anna Karenina 48. Au Royaume des Cieux 49. Sous le Ciel de Paris Coule la Seine 51. Captain Blackjack 52. La Fête à Henriette 52. The Little World of Don Camillo 52. Marie Octobre 58.

Allan Dwan Robin Hood 22. The Iron Mask 29. Chances 31. Wicked 31. Counsel's Opinion 33. Hollywood Party 34. Black Sheep 35. Navy Wife 35. High Tension 36. The Song and Dance Man 36. Heidi 37. One Mile from Heaven 37. Josette 38. Rebecca of Sunnybrook Farm 38. Suez 38. Frontier Marshal 39. The Gorilla 39. The Three Musketeers 39. Trail of the Vigilantes 40. Young People 40. Look Who's Laughing 41. Rise and Shine 41. Here We Go Again 42. Around the World 43. Abroad with Two Yanks 44. Up in Mabel's Room 44. Brewster's Millions 45. Getting Gertie's Garter 45. Rendezvous with Annie 46. Calendar Girl 47. Driftwood 47. Northwest Outpost 47. Angel in Exile 48. Sands of Iwo Jima 49. Belle le Grand 51. I Dream of Jeannie 52. Montana Belle 52. The Wild Blue Yonder 52. The Woman They Almost Lynched 52. Flight Nurse 53. Cattle Queen of Montana 54. Passion 54. Silver Lode 54. Escape to Burma 55. Tennessee's Partner 55. Hold Back the Night 56. Slightly Scarlet 56. The River's Edge 56. The Restless Breed 57. Enchanted Island 58.

B. Reeves Eason The Galloping Ghost 31. The Vanishing Legion 31. Mystery Mountain 34. The Law of the Wild 34. Adventures of Rex and Rinty 35. Fighting Marines 35. Phantom Empire 35. The Miracle Rider 35. Darkest Africa 36. Undersea Kingdom 36. The Kid Comes Back 37. Murder in the Big House 42. The Phantom 43. Black Arrow 44. The Desert Hawk 44.

Clint Eastwood Play Misty for Me 71. High Plains Drifter 72. Breezy 73. The Eiger Sanction 75. The Outlaw Josey Wales 76. The Gauntlet 77. Bronco Billy 80. Firefox 82. Honkytonk Man 82. Sudden Impact 83. Pale Rider 85. Heartbreak Ridge 86. Bird 88. The Rookie 90. White Hunter Black Heart 90. Unforgiven 92. A Perfect World 93. The Bridges of Madison County 95. Absolute Power 97. Midnight in the Garden of Good and Evil 97. True Crime 99. Space Cowboys 00. Blood Work 02.

Blake Edwards Bring Your Smile Along 55. He Laughed Last 56. Mister Cory 57. The Perfect Furlough 58. This Happy Feeling 58. Operation Petticoat 59. High Time 60. Breakfast at Tiffany's 61. Days of Wine and Roses 62. Experiment in Terror 62. The Pink Panther 63. A Shot in the Dark 64. The Great Race 65. What Did You Do in the War, Daddy? 66. Gunn 67. The Party 68. Darling Lili 70. Wild Rovers 71. The Carey Treatment 72. The Return of the Pink Panther 74. The Tamarind Seed 74. The Pink Panther Strikes Again 76. Revenge of the Pink Panther 78. '10' 79. S.O.B. 81. Trail of the Pink Panther 82. Victor/Victoria 82. Curse of the Pink Panther 83. The Man Who Loved Women 83. Micki and Maude 84. A Fine Mess 85. That's Life! 86. Blind Date 87. Sunset 88. Skin Deep 89. Switch 91. Son of the Pink Panther 93.

Henry Edwards The Flag Lieutenant 33. Are You a Mason? 34. Lord Edgware Dies 34. The Man Who Changed His Name 34. D'Ye Ken John Peel? 35. Scrooge 35. Squibs 35. The Lad 35. The Private Secretary 35. Vintage Wine 35. In the Soup 36. Juggernaut 37. The Vicar of Bray 37.

Christine Edzard Stories from a Flying Trunk 79. Little Dorrit 87. The Fool 90. As You Like It 92. The Children's Midsummer Night's Dream 01.

Atom Egoyan Family Viewing 88. Speaking Parts 89. The Adjuster 91. Calendar 93. Exotica 94. The Sweet Hereafter 97. Felicia's Journey 99.

Sergei Eisenstein Strike 24. The Battleship Potemkin 25. October 27. The General Line 29. Time in the Sun 33. Bezhin Meadow 37. Alexander Nevsky 38.

Maurice Elvey Comradeship 19. High Treason 29. The School for Scandal 30. Sally in Our Alley 31. The Lodger 32. The Water Gypsies 32. I Lived with You 33. Soldiers of the King 33. The Wandering Jew 33. This Week of Grace 33. Love, Life and Laughter 34. My Song for You 34. Princess Charming 34. Road House 34. The Clairvoyant 34. The Tunnel 35. Spy of Napoleon 36. The Man in the Mirror 36. Romance in Flanders 37. Sons of the Sea 39. The Spider 39. For Freedom 40. Under Your Hat 40. Salute John Citizen 42. The Gentle Sex 43. The Lamp Still Burns 43. Medal for the General 44. Strawberry Roan 45. Beware of Pity 46. The Late Edwina Black 51. The Great Game 52. The Gay Dog 54. The Happiness of Three Women 54. Dry Rot 56.

Roland Emmerich Ghost Chase 87. Moon 44 89. Universal Soldier 92. Stargate 94. Independence Day 96. Godzilla 98. The Patriot 00.

Cy Endfield Stork Bites Man 48. The Underworld Story 50. Try and Get Me 51. Tarzan's Savage Fury 52. The Master Plan 54. Child in the House 56. Hell Drivers 57. Sea Fury 58. Jet Storm 59. Mysterious Island 61. Hide and Seek 63. Zulu 64. Sands of the Kalahari 65. De Sade 69. Universal Soldier 71.

John English Zorro Rides Again 37. Dick Tracy Returns 38. Fighting Devil Dogs 38. Hawk of the Wilderness 38. The Lone Ranger 38. Daredevils of the Red Circle 39. Dick Tracy's G-Men 39. The Lone Ranger Rides Again 39. Zorro's Fighting Legion 39. Adventures of Red Ryder 40. Drums of Fu Manchu 40. King of the Royal Mounted 40. The Mysterious Dr Satan 40. Adventures of Captain Marvel 41. Dick Tracy vs Crime Inc 41. Jungle Girl 41. King of the Texas Rangers 41. Daredevils of the West 43. Captain America 44. Grissly's Millions 45. Murder in the Music Hall 46. Riders in the Sky 49. Mule Train 50. Valley of Fire 51.

Ray Enright Golden Dawn 30. The Tenderfoot 31. Blondie Johnson 33. Havana Widows 33. Dames 34. I've Got Your Number 34. The St Louis Kid 34. Twenty Million Sweethearts 34. Alibi Ike 35. Miss Pacific Fleet 35. Traveling Saleslady 35. We're in the Money 35. While the Patient Slept 35. China Clipper 36. Earthworm Tractors 36. Sing Me a Love Song 36. Back in Circulation 37. Ready Willing and Able 37. Slim 37. Swing Your Lady 37. The Singing Marine 37. Going Places 38. Gold Diggers in Paris 38. Hard to Get 38. Brother Rat and a Baby 39. Naughty but Nice 39. On Your Toes 39. The Angels Wash Their Faces 39. An Angel from Texas 40. Bad Men of Missouri 41. Law of the Tropics 41. The Wagons Roll at Night 41. Thieves Fall Out 41. Wild Bill Hickok Rides 41. Men of Texas 42. Sin Town 42. The Spoilers 42. Gung Ho! 43. The Iron Major 43. China Sky 45. Man Alive 45. One Way to Love 45. Albuquerque 47. Trail Street 47. Coroner Creek 48. South of St Louis 48. The Return of the Bad Men 48. Montana 50. Flaming Feather 51. Kansas Raiders 51.

Nora Ephron This Is My Life 92. Sleepless in Seattle 93. Mixed Nuts 95. Michael 96. You've Got Mail 98.

Chester Erskine Midnight 34. The Egg and I 47. Take One False Step 49. A Girl in Every Port 51. Androcles and the Lion 52.

James Fargo The Enforcer 76. Caravans 78. Every Which Way but Loose 78. A Game for Vultures 79. Forced Vengeance 82.

Bobby Farrelly Kingpin 96. There's Something about Mary 98. Me, Myself and Irene 00. Osmosis Jones 01. Shallow Hal 01.

Peter Farrelly Dumb & Dumber 94. Kingpin 96. There's Something about Mary 98. Me, Myself and Irene 00. Osmosis Jones 01. Shallow Hal 01.

John Farrow West of Shanghai 37. Broadway Musketeers 38. The Invisible Menace 38. Five Came Back 39. Full Confession 39. Reno 39. The Saint Strikes Back 39. Women in the Wind 39. A Bill of Divorcement 40. The Commandos Strike at Dawn 42. Wake Island 42. China 43. The Hitler Gang 44. You Came Along 45. Calcutta 46. California 46. Two Years before the Mast 46. Blaze of Noon 47. Easy Come, Easy Go 47. The Big Clock 47. Beyond Glory 48. Night Has a Thousand Eyes 48. Alias Nick Beal 49. Copper Canyon 49. Where Danger Lives 50. His Kind of Woman 51. Submarine Command 51. Botany Bay 52. Hondo 53. Plunder of the Sun 53. Ride, Vaquero 53. A Bullet Is Waiting 54. The Sea Chase 55. Back from Eternity 56. The Unholy Wife 57. John Paul Jones 59.

Rainer Werner Fassbinder The Bitter Tears of Petra von Kant 72. Effi Briest 74. Fear Eats the Soul 74. Fox 75. Chinese Roulette 76. I Only Want You to Love Me 76. Despair 78. In a Year with 13 Moons 78. The Marriage of Maria Braun 78. The Third Generation 79. Lili Marleen 80. Lola 82. Querelle 82. Veronika Voss 82.

Felix Feist You're a Lucky Fellow, Mr Smith 43. Pardon My Rhythm 44. This Is the Life 44. George White's Scandals 45. The Devil Thumbs a Ride 47. Guilty of Treason 50. The Man Who Cheated Himself 50. Tomorrow Is Another Day 51. The Big Trees 52. The Man Behind the Gun 52. This Woman Is Dangerous 52. Battles of Chief Pontiac 53. Donovan's Brain 53. Pirates of Tripoli 55.

Federico Fellini The White Sheik 52. I Vitelloni 53. La Strada 54. Il Bidone 55. Cabiria 57. La Dolce Vita 60. Eight and a Half 63. Juliet of the Spirits 65. Histoires Extraordinaires 68. Satyricon 69. Fellini's Roma 72. Amarcord 73. Casanova 76. City of Women 80. And the Ship Sails On 83. Ginger and Fred 86. Intervista 87.

Leslie Fenton Stronger than Desire 39. Tell No Tales 39. The Golden Fleecing 40. The Man from Dakota 40. The Saint's Vacation 41. Tomorrow the World 44. Pardon My Past 45. Saigon 47. Lulu Belle 48. On Our Merry Way 48. Whispering Smith 48. Streets of Laredo 49.

Abel Ferrara The Driller Killer 79. Fear City 85. China Girl 87. Cat Chaser 88. King of New York 90. Bad Lieutenant 92. Body Snatchers 93. Snake Eyes 93. The Addiction 95. The Funeral 96. The Blackout 97.

José Ferrer Cockleshell Heroes 55. The Shrike 55. The Great Man 56. I Accuse 57. The High Cost of Loving 58. Return to Peyton Place 61. State Fair 62.

Jacques Feyder L'Atlantide 21. Crainquebille 22. Les Nouveaux Messieurs 28. The Kiss 29. Daybreak 31. Le Grand Jeu 34. La Kermesse Héroïque 35. Knight without Armour 37. Les Gens du Voyage 38. Une Femme Disparait 44.

Mike Figgis Stormy Monday 87. Internal Affairs 90. Liebestraum 91. Mr Jones 93. The Browning Version 94. Leaving Las Vegas 95. One Night Stand 97. The Loss of Sexual Innocence 98. Miss Julie 99. Timecode 00.

David Fincher Alien³ 92. Seven 95. The Game 97. Fight Club 99. Panic Room 02.

Sam Firstenberg Breakin' 2: Electric Boogaloo 84. American Ninja 86. American Ninja 2: The Confrontation 87. Delta Force 3: The Killing Game 91. American Samurai 92. Cyborg Cop 93. Cyborg Cop II 94. Operation Delta Force 97.

Terence Fisher Portrait from Life 48. Marry Me 49. The Astonished Heart 49. So Long at the Fair 50. Home to Danger 51. Stolen Face 52. The Last Page 52. Wings of Danger 52. Four Sided Triangle 53. Spaceways 53. Face the Music 54. Final Appointment 54. The Stranger Came Home 54. The Last Man to Hang? 56. Kill Me Tomorrow 57. The Curse of Frankenstein 57. Dracula 58. The Revenge of Frankenstein 58. The Hound of the Baskervilles 59. The Man Who Could Cheat Death 59. The Mummy 59. Sword of Sherwood Forest 60. The Brides of Dracula 60. The Stranglers of Bombay 60. The Two Faces of Dr Jekyll 60. The Curse of the Werewolf 61. Phantom of the Opera 62. The Gorgon 64. Dracula Prince of Darkness 66. Frankenstein Created Woman 66. Island of Terror 66. Night of the Big Heat 67. The Devil Rides Out 68. Frankenstein Must Be Destroyed 69. Frankenstein and the Monster from Hell 73.

George Fitzmaurice The Dark Angel 25. The Son of the Sheik 26. The Locked Door 29. One Heavenly Night 30. Raffles 30. The Bad One 30. The Devil to Pay 30. As You Desire Me 31. Mata Hari 31. Strangers May Kiss 31. The Unholy Garden 31. All Men Are Enemies 34. Petticoat Fever 36. Suzy 36. Live, Love and Learn 37. The Emperor's Candlesticks 37. Arsène Lupin Returns 38. Adventure in Diamonds 40.

Robert Flaherty White Shadows in the South Seas 28. Tabu 31. Man of Aran 34. Elephant Boy 37. Louisiana Story 48.

Richard Fleischer So This Is New York 48. Follow Me Quietly 49. The Clay Pigeon 49. Armored Car Robbery 50. The Happy Time 52. The Narrow Margin 52. Arena 53. Twenty Thousand Leagues under the Sea 54. The Girl in the Red Velvet Swing 55. Violent Saturday 55. Bandido 56. Between Heaven and Hell 56. The Vikings 58. These Thousand Hills 58. Compulsion 59. Crack in the Mirror 60. The Big Gamble 60. Barabbas 62. Fantastic Voyage 66. Dr Dolittle 67. The Boston Strangler 68. Che! 69. Tora! Tora! Tora! 70. Blind Terror 71. Ten Rillington Place 71. The Last Run 71. The New Centurions 72. Soylent Green 73. The Don Is Dead 73. Mr Majestyk 74. The Spikes Gang 74. Mandingo 75. The Incredible Sarah 76. The Prince and the Pauper 77. Ashanti 79. The Jazz Singer 80. Tough Enough 83. Amityville 3-D 84. Conan the Destroyer 84. Red Sonja 85. Money Mania 87.

Victor Fleming The Way of All Flesh 28. The Virginian 29. Common Clay 30. Renegades 30. Around the World in Eighty Minutes 31. Red Dust 32. The Wet Parade 32. Bombshell 33. The White Sister 33. Treasure Island 34. Reckless 35. The Farmer Takes a Wife 35. Captains Courageous 37. Test Pilot 38. Gone with the Wind 39. The Wizard of Oz 39. Dr Jekyll and Mr Hyde 41. Tortilla Flat 42. A Guy Named Joe 44. Adventure 45. Joan of Arc 48.

James Flood The She-Wolf 31. Life Begins 32. The Mouthpiece 32. Undercover Man 32. All of Me 34. Such Women Are Dangerous 34. Shanghai 35. Wings in the Dark 35. We're Only Human 36. Midnight Madonna 37. Off the Record 39.

Robert Florey The Life and Death of a Hollywood Extra 27. The Battle of Paris 29. The Cocoanuts 29. The Hole in the Wall 29. Murders in the Rue Morgue 32. Ex-Lady 33. I Am a Thief 34. Going Highbrow 35. I Sell Anything 35. Ship Café 35. The Florentine Dagger 35. The Woman in Red 35. Hollywood Boulevard 36. Till We Meet Again 36. Daughter of Shanghai 37. King of Gamblers 37. Mountain Music 37. This Way Please 37. Dangerous to Know 38. Disbarred 38. King of Alcatraz 38. Death of a Champion 39. Hotel Imperial 39. The Magnificent Fraud 39. Women without Names 40. Dangerously They Live 41. The Face behind the Mask 41. The Desert Song 43. Roger Touhy, Gangster 44. Danger Signal 45. God Is My Co-Pilot 45. The Beast with Five Fingers 46. Rogues' Regiment 48. Tarzan and the Mermaids 48. Outpost in Morocco 49. The Crooked Way 49. Johnny One-Eye 50.

John Flynn The Sergeant 68. The Jerusalem File 71. The Outfit 74. Rolling Thunder 77. Defiance 80. Best Seller 87. Lock Up 89. Out for Justice 91. Brainscan 94.

James Foley At Close Range 86. Can't Buy Me Love 87. Who's That Girl? 87. After Dark, My Sweet 90. Glengarry Glen Ross 92. Fear 96. The Chamber 96. The Corruptor 99.

Bryan Forbes Whistle Down the Wind 61. The L-Shaped Room 62. Seance on a Wet Afternoon 64. King Rat 65. The Whisperers 66. The Wrong Box 66. Deadfall 68. The Madwoman of Chaillot 69. The Raging Moon 70. The Stepford Wives 74. The Slipper and the Rose 76. International Velvet 78. Better Late Than Never 83. The Naked Face 84.

John Ford The Iron Horse 24. Hangman's House 28. Born Reckless 30. Men without Women 30. Up the River 30. Arrowsmith 31. Air Mail 32. Flesh 32. Dr Bull 33. Pilgrimage 33. Judge Priest 34. The Lost Patrol 34. The World Moves On 34. Steamboat Round the Bend 35. The Informer 35. The Whole Town's Talking 35. Mary of Scotland 36. The Plough and the Stars 36. The Prisoner of Shark Island 36. The Hurricane 37. Wee Willie Winkie 37. Four Men and a Prayer 38. Submarine Patrol 38. Drums Along the Mohawk 39. Stagecoach 39. Young Mr Lincoln 39. The Grapes of Wrath 40. The Long Voyage Home 40. How Green Was My Valley 41. Tobacco Road 41. They Were Expendable 45. My Darling Clementine 46. The Fugitive 47. Fort Apache 48. Three Godfathers 48. She Wore a Yellow Ribbon 49. Rio Grande 50. Wagonmaster 50. When Willie Comes Marching Home 50. The Quiet Man 52. What Price Glory? 52. Mogambo 53. The Sun Shines Bright 53. Mister Roberts 55. The Long Gray Line 55. The Searchers 56. The Rising of the Moon 57. The Wings of Eagles 57. Gideon's Day 58. The Last Hurrah 58. The Horse Soldiers 59. Sergeant Rutledge 60. Two Rode Together 61. How the West Was Won 62. The Man Who Shot Liberty Valance 62. Donovan's Reef 63. Cheyenne Autumn 64. Young Cassidy 64. Seven Women 66.

Eugene Forde Mystery Woman 34. The Great Hotel Murder 34. Midnight Taxi 36. Step Lively, Jeeves 37. Inspector Hornleigh 38. International Settlement 38. One Wild Night 38. Buy Me That Town 41. Berlin Correspondent 42.

Walter Forde The Ghost Train 31. Condemned to Death 32. Jack's the Boy 32. Rome Express 32. Orders Is Orders 33. Bulldog Jack 34. Chu Chin Chow 34. Jack Ahoy! 34. Brown on Resolution 35. King of the Damned 35. Land without Music 36. Kicking the Moon Around 38. The Gaunt Stranger 38. Cheer Boys Cheer 39. Inspector Hornleigh on Holiday 39. Let's Be Famous 39. The Four Just Men 39. Charley's Big-Hearted Aunt 40. Inspector Hornleigh Goes to It 40. Sailors Three 40. Saloon Bar 40. Atlantic Ferry 41. The Ghost Train 41. Flying Fortress 42. It's That Man Again 42. The Peterville Diamond 42. One Exciting Night 44. Time Flies 44. Master of Bankdam 47. Cardboard Cavalier 49.

Milos Forman Loves of a Blonde 65. The Firemen's Ball 67. Taking Off 71. One Flew over the Cuckoo's Nest 75. Hair 79. Ragtime 81. Amadeus 84. Valmont 89. The People vs. Larry Flynt 96. Man on the Moon 99.

Bill Forsyth Gregory's Girl 80. Local Hero 83. Comfort and Joy 84. Housekeeping 87. Breaking In 89. Being Human 94. Gregory's Two Girls 99.

Lewis R. Foster Double Whoopee 28. Angora Love 29. Berth Marks 29. Men o' War 29. The Bacon Grabbers 29. Unaccustomed as We Are 29. Love Letters of a Star 36. The Man Who Cried Wolf 37. Captain China 49. El Paso 49. Manhandled 49. The Eagle and the Hawk 49. The Lucky Stiff 49. Crosswinds 51. Hong Kong 51. Passage West 51. The Last Outpost 51. Jamaica Run 53. Tropic Zone 53. Crashout 55. Dakota Incident 56. The Bold and the Brave 56. Tonka 58.

Norman Foster Fair Warning 37. Think Fast, Mr Moto 37. Mr Moto Takes a Chance 38. Mysterious Mr Moto 38. Thank You, Mr Moto 38. Mr Moto's Last Warning 39. Scotland Yard 41. Journey into Fear 42. Kiss the Blood Off My Hands 48. Rachel and the Stranger 48. Tell It to the Judge 49. Father Is a Bachelor 50. Woman on the Run 50. Sky Full of Moon 52. Sombrero 53. Davy Crockett 55.

Wallace Fox Bowery at Midnight 42. The Corpse Vanishes 42. Block Busters 44. Brenda Starr, Reporter 45. Docks of New York 45. Mr Muggs Rides Again 45. Pillow of Death 45. Wild Beauty 46. Jack Armstrong 47. The Vigilante 47.

Freddie Francis Two and Two Make Six 61. Vengeance 62. Paranoiac 63. Nightmare 64. The Evil of Frankenstein 64. Dr Terror's House of Horrors 65. Hysteria 65. The Skull 65. Traitor's Gate 65. The Deadly Bees 66. The Psychopath 66. They Came from Beyond Space 67. Torture Garden 67. Dracula Has Risen from the Grave 68. Mumsy, Nanny, Sonny and Girly 69. Trog 70. Tales from the Crypt 72. The Creeping Flesh 72. Craze 73. Tales That Witness Madness 73. Legend of the Werewolf 74. The Ghoul 75. The Doctor and the Devils 85.

Jesús Franco The Awful Dr Orloff 62. Sadisterotica 67. Succubus 67. Castle of Fu Manchu 68. Sax Rohmer's The Blood of Fu Manchu 69. Bram Stoker's Count Dracula 70. She Killed in Ecstasy 70. The Devil Came from Akasava 70. Vampyros Lesbos 71. Virgin among the Living Dead 71. Dracula – Prisoner of Frankenstein 72. The Demons 72. Female Vampire 73. Tender and Perverse Emanuelle 73.

Melvin Frank The Reformer and the Redhead 50. Callaway Went Thataway 51. Strictly Dishonourable 51. Above and Beyond 52. Knock on Wood 54. The Court Jester 55. That Certain Feeling 56. Li'l Abner 59. The Jayhawkers 59. The Facts of Life 60. Strange Bedfellows 65. Buona Sera Mrs Campbell 68. A Touch of Class 73. The Prisoner of Second Avenue 75. The Duchess and the Dirtwater Fox 76. Lost and Found 79.

Cyril Frankel Devil on Horseback 54. Make Me an Offer 54. It's Great to Be Young 56. No Time for Tears 57. Alive and Kicking 58. She Didn't Say No! 58. Never Take Sweets from a Stranger 60. Don't Bother to Knock 61. On the Fiddle 61. The Very Edge 62. The Trygon Factor 66. The Witches 66. Permission to Kill 75.

John Frankenheimer The Young Stranger 57. The Young Savages 61. All Fall Down 62. Birdman of Alcatraz 62. The Manchurian Candidate 62. Seven Days in May 64. The Train 65. Grand Prix 66. Seconds 66. The Extraordinary Seaman 68. The Fixer 68. The Gypsy Moths 69. I Walk the Line 70. The Horsemen 70. Story of a Love Story 73. 99 and 44/100 Per Cent Dead 74. French Connection II 75. Black Sunday 77. Prophecy 79. The Pursuit of D. B. Cooper 81. The Challenge 82. The Holcroft Covenant 85. 52 Pick-up 86. Dead-Bang 89. The Fourth War 90. Year of the Gun 91. The Island of Dr Moreau 96. Ronin 98. Reindeer Games 00.

Richard Franklin Patrick 78. Road Games 81. Psycho 2 83. Link 86. F/X2: The Deadly Art of Illusion 91. Hotel Sorrento 94.

Sidney Franklin Beverly of Graustark 26. The Actress 28. The Last of Mrs Cheyney 29. A Lady's

Morals 30. Lady of Scandal 30. Private Lives 31. The Guardsman 31. Smilin' Through 32. Reunion in Vienna 33. The Barretts of Wimpole Street 34. The Dark Angel 35. The Good Earth 37. The Barretts of Wimpole Street 56.

Harry Fraser The Wolf Dog 33. 'Neath the Arizona Skies 34. Randy Rides Alone 34. Jungle Menace 37. Chained for Life 50.

Stephen Frears Gumshoe 71. The Hit 84. My Beautiful Laundrette 85. Prick up Your Ears 87. Sammy and Rosie Get Laid 87. Dangerous Liaisons 88. The Grifters 90. Hero 92. Mary Reilly 96. The Van 96. The Hi-Lo Country 99. High Fidelity 00. Liam 00. Dirty Pretty Things 02.

Thornton Freeland Whoopee 30. Love Affair 32. They Call It Sin 32. Weekend Marriage 32. Flying Down to Rio 33. George White's Scandals 34. Brewster's Millions 35. Accused 36. The Amateur Gentleman 36. Jericho 37. Paradise for Two 37. Hold My Hand 38. So This Is London 39. The Gang's All Here 39. Over the Moon 40. Meet Me at Dawn 46. The Brass Monkey 48. Dear Mr Prohack 49.

Hugo Fregonese One Way Street 50. Saddle Tramp 50. Apache Drums 51. Mark of the Renegade 51. Decameron Nights 52. My Six Convicts 52. Untamed Frontier 52. Blowing Wild 53. The Man in the Attic 53. Black Tuesday 54. The Raid 54. Seven Thunders 57. Harry Black 58. Savage Pampas 67.

Harold French Dead Men Are Dangerous 38. The House of the Arrow 40. Jeannie 41. Major Barbara 41. Secret Mission 42. Talk About Jacqueline 42. The Day Will Dawn 42. Unpublished Story 42. Dear Octopus 43. English without Tears 44. Mr Emmanuel 44. Quiet Weekend 46. My Brother Jonathan 47. The Blind Goddess 47. White Cradle Inn 47. Adam and Evelyne 49. The Dancing Years 49. Trio 50. Encore 51. Isn't Life Wonderful? 52. The Hour of Thirteen 52. The Man Who Watched Trains Go By 52. Rob Roy the Highland Rogue 53. Forbidden Cargo 54. The Man Who Loved Redheads 54.

Lloyd French That's My Wife 29. Busy Bodies 33. Dirty Work 33. Me and My Pal 33. Midnight Patrol 33. Oliver the Eighth 33.

Charles Frend The Big Blockade 41. The Foreman Went to France 41. San Demetrio London 43. Johnny Frenchman 45. The Loves of Joanna Godden 47. Scott of the Antarctic 48. A Run for Your Money 49. The Magnet 50. The Cruel Sea 53. Lease of Life 54. The Long Arm 56. Barnacle Bill 57. Cone of Silence 60. Girl on Approval 62.

Karl Freund The Mummy 32. The Countess of Monte Cristo 33. I Give My Love 34. Madame Spy 34. The Gift of Gab 34. Uncertain Lady 34. Mad Love 35.

William Friedkin Good Times 67. The Birthday Party 68. The Night They Raided Minsky's 68. The Boys in the Band 70. The French Connection 71. The Exorcist 73. Sorcerer 77. The Brinks Job 78. Cruising 80. Deal of the Century 83. To Live and Die in L.A. 85. The Guardian 90. Blue Chips 94. Jade 95. Rules of Engagement 00.

Seymour Friedman Chinatown at Midnight 49. Her First Romance 51. Son of Dr Jekyll 51. Escape Route 52. Loan Shark 52. Flame of Calcutta 53. The Saint's Return 54.

Robert Fuest Just Like a Woman 66. And Soon the Darkness 70. Wuthering Heights 70. The Abominable Dr Phibes 71. Dr Phibes Rises Again 72. The Final Programme 73. The Devil's Rain 75.

Jun Fukuda Ebirah, Horror of the Deep 66. Son of Godzilla 67. Godzilla versus Gigan 72. Godzilla versus Mechagodzilla 74. Godzilla versus Megalon 76.

Samuel Fuller I Shot Jesse James 48. The Baron of Arizona 50. Fixed Bayonets! 51. Park Row 52. Pickup on South Street 53. Hell and High Water 54. House of Bamboo 55. China Gate 57. Forty Guns 57. Run of the Arrow 57. The Crimson Kimono 59. Verboten! 59. Underworld USA 61. Merrill's Marauders 62. Shock Corridor 63. The Naked Kiss 64. Shark 69. Dead Pigeon on Beethoven Street 72. The Big Red One 80. White Dog 82.

Sidney J. Furie Doctor Blood's Coffin 60. During One Night 61. The Young Ones 61. The Boys 62. The Leather Boys 63. Wonderful Life 64. The Ipcress File 65. The Appaloosa 66. The Naked Runner 67. Little Fauss and Big Halsy 70. The Lawyer 70. Lady Sings the Blues 72. Hit! 73. Gable and Lombard 76. The Boys in Company C 77. The Entity 81. Purple Hearts 84. Iron Eagle 86. Superman IV: The Quest for Peace 87. Iron Eagle II 88. Ladybugs 92. Iron Eagle IV 95. Top of the World 97. Hide and Seek 00.

Tay Garnett Her Man 30. Okay America 32. One Way Passage 32. Prestige 32. Destination Unknown 33. SOS Iceberg 33. China Seas 35. She Couldn't Take It 35. Professional Soldier 36. Love Is News 37. Slave Ship 37. Stand In 37. Joy of Living 38. Trade Winds 38. Eternally Yours 39. Seven Sinners 40. Slightly Honorable 40. Cheers for Miss Bishop 41. My Favorite Spy 42. Bataan 43. Mrs Parkington 44. The Cross of Lorraine 44. The Valley of Decision 45. The Postman Always Rings Twice 46. Wild Harvest 47. A Connecticut Yankee in King Arthur's Court 49. The Fireball 50. Cause for Alarm 51. Soldiers Three 51. One Minute to Zero 52. Main Street to Broadway 53. The Black Knight 54. A Terrible Beauty 60. Cattle King 63.

Louis Gasnier The Exploits of Elaine 14. Slightly Scarlet 30. The Virtuous Sin 30. Forgotten Commandments 32. The Strange Case of Clara Deane 32. The Last Outpost 35. Reefer Madness 36.

Marion Gering 24 Hours 31. I Take This Woman 31. Ladies of the Big House 31. Devil and the Deep 32. Madame Butterfly 32. Jennie Gerhardt 33. Pick Up 33. Good Dame 34. Thirty Day Princess 34. Rose of the Rancho 35. Rumba 35. Lady of Secrets 36. Thunder in the City 37. She Married an Artist 38.

Pietro Germi Il Cammino della Speranza 50. La Città Si Difende 51. Divorce Italian Style 61. The Birds, the Bees and the Italians 65. Alfredo Alfredo 71.

Clyde Geronimi Ichabod and Mr Toad 49. Cinderella 50. Alice in Wonderland 51. Peter Pan 53. Lady and the Tramp 55. The Sleeping Beauty 59. One Hundred and One Dalmatians 61.

Nicolas Gessner The Blonde from Peking 68. Twelve Plus One 69. Someone Behind the Door 71. The Little Girl Who Lives Down the Lane 76. Quicker than the Eye 89.

Alan Gibson Crescendo 70. Goodbye Gemini 70. Dracula AD 1972 72. The Satanic Rites of Dracula 73. Martin's Day 85.

Brian Gibson Breaking Glass 80. Poltergeist II 86. What's Love Got to Do with It 93. The Juror 96. Still Crazy 98.

Brian Gilbert The Frog Prince 84. Vice Versa 88. Not without My Daughter 91. Tom and Viv 94. Wilde 97.

Lewis Gilbert Once a Sinner 50. The Scarlet Thread 50. There Is Another Sun 51. Cosh Boy 52. Emergency Call 52. Time Gentlemen Please 52. Albert RN 53. The Good Die Young 54. The Sea Shall Not Have Them 54. Cast a Dark Shadow 55. Reach for the Sky 56. The Admirable Crichton 57. A Cry from the Streets 58. Carve Her Name with Pride 58. Ferry to Hong Kong 58. Light Up the Sky 60. Sink the Bismarck! 60. The Greengage Summer 61. HMS Defiant 62. The Seventh Dawn 64. Alfie 66. You Only Live Twice 67. The Adventurers 70. Friends 71. Operation Daybreak 75. Seven Nights in Japan 76. The Spy Who Loved Me 77. Moonraker 79. Educating Rita 83. Not Quite Jerusalem 85. Shirley Valentine 89. Stepping Out 91. Haunted 95. Before You Go 02.

Terry Gilliam Monty Python and the Holy Grail 75. Jabberwocky 77. Time Bandits 81. Brazil 85. Adventures of Baron Munchausen 89. The Fisher King 91. Twelve Monkeys 95. Fear and Loathing in Las Vegas 98.

Sidney Gilliat Millions like Us 43. Waterloo Road 44. The Rake's Progress 45. Green for Danger 46. London Belongs to Me 48. State Secret 50. The Story of Gilbert and Sullivan 53. The Constant Husband 55. Fortune Is a Woman 57. Left Right and Centre 59. Only Two Can Play 62. The Great St Trinian's Train Robbery 66. Endless Night 71.

John Gilling No Trace 50. Mother Riley Meets the Vampire 52. The Frightened Man 52. The Voice of Merrill 52. Escape by Night 53. Recoil 53. The Gamma People 55. The Gilded Cage 55. Tiger by the Tail 55. Odongo 56. High Flight 57. Interpol 57. The Man Inside 58. The Bandit of Zhobe 59. The Flesh and the Fiends 59. Fury at Smugglers' Bay 60. The Challenge 60. Pirates of Blood River 61. Shadow of the Cat 61. The Scarlet Blade 63. The Brigand of Kandahar 65. The Night Caller 65. The Plague of the Zombies 65. The Mummy's Shroud 66. The Reptile 66.

John Glen For Your Eyes Only 81. Octopussy 83. A View to a Kill 85. The Living Daylights 87. Licence to Kill 89. Aces: Iron Eagle III 92. Christopher Columbus: The Discovery 92.

Peter Glenville The Prisoner 55. Me and the Colonel 58. Summer and Smoke 61. Term of Trial 62. Becket 64. Hotel Paradiso 66. The Comedians 67.

Jean-Luc Godard A Bout de Souffle 60. A Woman Is a Woman 61. Contempt 63. A Married Woman 64. Bande à Part 64. Alphaville 65. Paris Vu Par… 65. Masculin Féminin 66. La Chinoise 67. The Oldest Profession 67. Two or Three Things I Know about Her 67. One Plus One 68. Pierrot Le Fou 68. Weekend 68. Sauve Qui Peut (La Vie) 80. Passion 82. First Name Carmen 83. Detective 85. King Lear 87. Aria 88. Éloge De L'amour 01.

Peter Godfrey Unexpected Uncle 41. Highways by Night 42. Make Your Own Bed 44. Christmas in Connecticut 45. Hotel Berlin 45. One More Tomorrow 46. Cry Wolf 47. Escape Me Never 47. That Hagen Girl 47. The Two Mrs Carrolls 47. The Decision of Christopher Blake 48. The Woman in White 48. Barricade 49. The Girl from Jones Beach 49. He's a Cockeyed Wonder 50. The Great Jewel Robber 50. Please Murder Me 56.

Menahem Golan What's Good for the Goose 69. Lepke 74. Diamonds 75. Operation Thunderbolt 77. The Magician of Lublin 79. Over the Brooklyn Bridge 83. Delta Force 86. Over the Top 87. Hanna's War 88.

Jack Gold The Bofors Gun 68. The Reckoning 69. The National Health 73. Who? 74. Man Friday 75. Aces High 76. The Medusa Touch 78. The Sailor's Return 78. The Chain 84.

Willis Goldbeck Dr Gillespie's New Assistant 42. Dr Gillespie's Criminal Case 43. Rationing 43. Dark Delusion 47. Johnny Holiday 49. Ten Tall Men 51.

James Goldstone A Man Called Gannon 69. Winning 69. Brother John 70. Red Sky at Morning 70. The Gang That Couldn't Shoot Straight 71. They Only Kill Their Masters 72. Swashbuckler 76. Rollercoaster 77. When Time Ran Out 80.

Leslie Goodwins Let's Make Music 40. Men Against the Sky 40. Pop Always Pays 40. Parachute Battalion 41. They Met in Argentina 41. Silver Skates 42. Adventures of a Rookie 43. Ladies' Day 43. Casanova in Burlesque 44. Murder in the Blue Room 44. The Singing Sheriff 44. I'll Tell the World 45. Radio Stars on Parade 45. The Mummy's Curse 45. Genius at Work 46. Riverboat Rhythm 46. Fireman Save My Child 54. Tammy and the Millionaire 67.

Bert I. Gordon The Cyclops 56. Attack of the Puppet People 57. The Amazing Colossal Man 57. The Beginning of the End 57. Earth vs The Spider 58. War of the Colossal Beast 58. The Boy and the Pirates 60. The Magic Sword 62. Picture Mommy Dead 66. The Mad Bomber 72. Necromancy 73. The Food of the Gods 76. Empire of the Ants 77.

Michael Gordon Crime Doctor 43. One Dangerous Night 43. The Web 47. An Act of Murder 48. Another Part of the Forest 48. The Lady Gambles 49. Woman in Hiding 49. Cyrano de Bergerac 50. I Can Get It for You Wholesale 51. The Secret of Convict Lake 51. Pillow Talk 59. Portrait in Black 60. Boys' Night Out 62. For Love or Money 63. Move Over Darling 63. A Very Special Favor 65. Texas across the River 66. The Impossible Years 68. How Do I Love Thee 70.

Stuart Gordon Re-Animator 85. Dolls 86. From Beyond 86. Fortress 93. Castle Freak 94. Space Truckers 96. Dagon, Sect of the Sea 01.

Marleen Gorris A Question of Silence 82. Broken Mirrors 84. The Last Island 90. Antonia's Line 95. Mrs Dalloway 97. The Luzhin Defence 00.

Edmund Goulding Love 27. Devil's Holiday 30. Paramount on Parade 30. Reaching for the Moon 31. The Night Angel 31. Blondie of the Follies 32. Grand Hotel 32. Riptide 34. The Flame Within 35. That Certain Woman 37. The Dawn Patrol 38. White Banners 38. Dark Victory 39. The Old Maid 39. We Are Not Alone 39. 'Til We Meet Again 40. The Great Lie 41. Claudia 43. Forever and a Day 43. The Constant Nymph 43. Of Human Bondage 46. The Razor's Edge 46. Nightmare Alley 47. Everybody Does It 49. Mister 880 50. Down among the Sheltering Palms 52. We're Not Married 52. Teenage Rebel 56. Mardi Gras 58.

William A. Graham Submarine X-1 67. Waterhole Three 67. Change of Habit 69. Where the Lilies Bloom 74. Return to the Blue Lagoon 91.

Walter Grauman The Disembodied 57. 633 Squadron 64. Lady in a Cage 64. A Rage to Live 65. The Last Escape 70.

Godfrey Grayson Meet Simon Cherry 49. What the Butler Saw 50. The Fake 53. An Honourable Murder 59. The Spider's Web 60.

Alfred E. Green Little Lord Fauntleroy 21. Ella Cinders 26. Disraeli 29. Old English 30. Sweet Kitty Bellairs 30. The Green Goddess 30. The Man from Blankley's 30. Road to Singapore 31. Smart Money 31. It's Tough to be Famous 32. Parachute Jumper 32. Silver Dollar 32. The Dark Horse 32. The Rich Are Always with Us 32. Union Depot 32. Baby Face 33. I Loved a Woman 33. The Narrow Corner 33. A Lost Lady 34. As the Earth Turns 34. Dark Hazard 34. Gentlemen Are Born 34. Housewife 34. Side Streets 34. Sweet Music 34. The Merry Frinks 34. Dangerous 35. Here's To Romance 35. The Girl from Tenth Avenue 35. The Goose and the Gander 35. Colleen 36. Golden Arrow 36. More than a Secretary 36. League of Frightened Men 37. Let's Get Married 37. Mr Dodd Takes the Air 37. Thoroughbreds Don't Cry 37. Ride a Crooked Mile 38. The Duke of West Point 38. The Gracie Allen Murder Case 39. Twenty Thousand Men a Year 39. East of the River 40. Flowing Gold 40. South of Pago Pago 40. Adventure in Washington 41. Badlands of Dakota 41. Meet the Stewarts 42. The Mayor of 44th Street 42. Appointment in Berlin 43. There's Something about a Soldier 43. Mr Winkle Goes to War 44. A Thousand and One Nights 45. Tars and Spars 45. The Jolson Story 46. Copacabana 47. The Fabulous Dorseys 47. Cover Up 48. Four Faces West 48. The Girl from Manhattan 48. Sierra 50. Invasion USA 52. Paris Model 53. The Eddie Cantor Story 53. Top Banana 53.

Guy Green Lost 55. Portrait of Alison 55. House of Secrets 56. Sea of Sand 58. The Snorkel 58. SOS Pacific 59. The Angry Silence 60. The Mark 61. Diamond Head 62. The Light in the Piazza 62. A Patch of Blue 65. Pretty Polly 67. The Magus 68. A Walk in the Spring Rain 69. Luther 73. Once Is Not Enough 75. The Devil's Advocate 77.

Peter Greenaway The Draughtsman's Contract 82. A Zed and Two Noughts 85. The Belly of an Architect 87. Drowning by Numbers 88. The Cook, the Thief, His Wife & Her Lover 89. Prospero's Books 91. The Baby of Macon 93. The Pillow Book 95. Eight and a Half Women 99.

David Greene The Shuttered Room 67. Sebastian 68. The Strange Affair 68. I Start Counting 69. The People Next Door 70. Godspell 73. Gray Lady Down 78. Hard Country 81.

Edmond T. Gréville Mademoiselle Docteur 37. Noose 48. The Romantic Age 49. Guilty? 56. 'Beat' Girl 60. The Hands of Orlac 60.

Love Story 70. The Out of Towners 70. Plaza Suite 71. The Hospital 71. Man of La Mancha 72. The Crazy World of Julius Vrooder 74. Silver Streak 76. W. C. Fields and Me 76. Nightwing 79. The In-Laws 79. Author, Author! 82. Making Love 82. Romantic Comedy 83. Teachers 84. The Lonely Guy 84. Outrageous Fortune 87. See No Evil, Hear No Evil 89. Taking Care of Business 90. The Babe 92. Married to It 93. Carpool 96. An Alan Smithee Film: Burn, Hollywood, Burn! 97.

Lambert Hillyer Once to Every Woman 34. The Most Precious Thing 34. The Invisible Ray 35. Dracula's Daughter 36. Batman 43.

Leslie Hiscott Alibi 31. The Sleeping Cardinal 31. The Missing Rembrandt 32. When London Sleeps 32. A Fire Has Been Arranged 35. She Shall Have Music 35. The Triumph of Sherlock Holmes 35. Millions 36. Tilly of Bloomsbury 40. The Seventh Survivor 41. Lady from Lisbon 42. The Butler's Dilemma 43. Welcome Mr Washington 44. The Time of His Life 55.

Alfred Hitchcock The Pleasure Garden 25. The Lodger 26. The Mountain Eagle 26. Downhill 27. Easy Virtue 27. The Ring 27. Champagne 28. The Farmer's Wife 28. Blackmail 29. The Manxman 29. Elstree Calling 30. Juno and the Paycock 30. Murder 30. Rich and Strange 31. Number Seventeen 32. The Skin Game 32. Waltzes from Vienna 33. The Man Who Knew Too Much 34. The 39 Steps 35. Sabotage 36. The Secret Agent 36. Young and Innocent 37. The Lady Vanishes 38. Jamaica Inn 39. Foreign Correspondent 40. Rebecca 40. Mr and Mrs Smith 41. Suspicion 41. Saboteur 42. Shadow of a Doubt 43. Lifeboat 44. Spellbound 45. Notorious 46. The Paradine Case 47. Rope 48. Under Capricorn 49. Stage Fright 50. Strangers on a Train 51. I Confess 53. Dial M For Murder 54. Rear Window 54. The Trouble with Harry 55. To Catch a Thief 55. The Man Who Knew Too Much 56. The Wrong Man 57. Vertigo 58. North by Northwest 59. Psycho 60. The Birds 63. Marnie 64. Torn Curtain 66. Topaz 69. Frenzy 72. Family Plot 76.

Jack Hively The Spellbinder 39. Anne of Windy Poplars 40. The Saint Takes Over 40. The Saint's Double Trouble 40. Father Takes a Wife 41. Four Jacks and a Jill 41. The Saint in Palm Springs 41. They Met in Argentina 41. Street of Chance 42. Are You With It? 48.

Mike Hodges Get Carter 71. Pulp 72. The Terminal Man 74. A Prayer for the Dying 87. Black Rainbow 89. Croupier 97.

Michael Hoffman Privileged 82. Restless Natives 85. Promised Land 88. Sisters 88. Soapdish 91. One Fine Day 96. Restoration 96. William Shakespeare's A Midsummer Night's Dream 99.

James Hogan Ebb Tide 37. The Last Train from Madrid 37. Scandal Street 38. The Texans 38. Queen of the Mob 40. Texas Rangers Ride Again 40. The Farmer's Daughter 40. Enemy Agents Meet Ellery Queen 42. The Mad Ghoul 43. The Strange Death of Adolf Hitler 43.

Agnieszka Holland Bittere Ernte 85. To Kill a Priest 88. Europa Europa 91. Olivier, Olivier 92. The Secret Garden 93. Total Eclipse 95. Washington Square 97.

Tom Holland Fright Night 85. Fatal Beauty 87. Child's Play 88. The Temp 93. Stephen King's Thinner 96.

Seth Holt Nowhere to Go 58. Taste of Fear 61. Station Six Sahara 62. The Nanny 65. Danger Route 67. Blood from the Mummy's Tomb 71.

Tobe Hooper The Texas Chainsaw Massacre 74. Death Trap 76. Salem's Lot: The Movie 79. The Funhouse 81. Poltergeist 82. Life Force 85. Lifeforce 85. Invaders from Mars 86. The Texas Chainsaw Massacre Part 2 86. Spontaneous Combustion 90. Tobe Hooper's Night Terrors 93. The Mangler 95.

Stephen Hopkins A Nightmare on Elm Street: The Dream Child 89. Predator 2 90. Judgment Night 93. Blown Away 94. The Ghost and the Darkness 96. Lost in Space 98. Under Suspicion 00.

Dennis Hopper Easy Rider 69. The Last Movie 71. Out of the Blue 80. Colors 88. Catchfire 89. The Hot Spot 90. Chasers 94.

Jerry Hopper Hurricane Smith 52. The Atomic City 52. Alaska Seas 53. Pony Express 53. Naked Alibi 54. The Secret of the Incas 54. Never Say Goodbye 55. One Desire 55. Smoke Signal 55. The Private War of Major Benson 55. The Square Jungle 55. Everything But the Truth 56. The Sharkfighters 56. Toy Tiger 56. Blueprint for Robbery 60. Madron 70.

James W. Horne College 27. Big Business 29. Beau Hunks 31. Chickens Come Home 31. Come Clean 31. Laughing Gravy 31. One Good Turn 31. Our Wife 31. Any Old Port 32. Bonnie Scotland 35. Thicker than Water 35. The Bohemian Girl 36. All Over Town 37. Way Out West 37. The Spider's Web 38. Flying G-Men 39. Deadwood Dick 40. Terry and the Pirates 40. The Green Archer 40. The Shadow 40. Holt of the Secret Service 41. Iron Claw 41. The Spider Returns 41. White Eagle 41. Captain Midnight 42. Perils of the Royal Mounted 42.

Harry Horner Beware My Lovely 52. Red Planet Mars 52. Vicki 53. A Life in the Balance 54. New Faces 54. Man from Del Rio 56. The Wild Party 56.

John Hough Eyewitness 70. Treasure Island 71. Twins of Evil 71. The Legend of Hell House 73. Dirty Mary, Crazy Larry 74. Escape to Witch Mountain 74. Brass Target 78. Return from Witch Mountain 78. The Watcher in the Woods 80. Incubus 81. Triumphs of a Man Called Horse 82. Biggles 86. American Gothic 88. Howling IV: The Original Nightmare 88. Something to Believe In 97.

Ron Howard Night Shift 82. Splash! 84. Cocoon 85. Gung Ho 86. Willow 88. Parenthood 89. Backdraft 91. Far and Away 92. The Paper 94. Apollo 13 95. Ransom 96. EdTV 99. Dr Seuss' How the Grinch Stole Christmas 00. A Beautiful Mind 01.

William K. Howard Surrender 31. Transatlantic 31. Sherlock Holmes 32. The First Year 32. The Trial of Vivienne Ware 32. The Cat and the Fiddle 33. The Power and the Glory 33. Evelyn Prentice 34. This Side of Heaven 34. Mary Burns Fugitive 35. Rendezvous 35. Vanessa, Her Love Story 35. The Princess Comes Across 36. Fire over England 37. The Squeaker 37. Back Door to Heaven 39. Money and the Woman 40. Bullets for O'Hara 41. Johnny Come Lately 43. When the Lights go on Again 44.

Hou Hsiao-Hsien The Boys from Fengkuei 83. A Summer at Grandpa's 84. The Time to Live and the Time to Die 85. Dust in the Wind 87. Daughter of the Nile 88. Beiqing Chengshi 89. The Puppetmaster 93.

Hugh Hudson Chariots of Fire 81. Greystoke: The Legend of Tarzan, Lord of the Apes 84. Revolution 85. The Road Home 89. I Dreamed of Africa 00.

John Hughes Sixteen Candles 85. The Breakfast Club 85. Weird Science 85. Ferris Bueller's Day Off 86. Planes, Trains and Automobiles 87. Uncle Buck 89. Curly Sue 91.

Ken Hughes Little Red Monkey 54. The Brain Machine 54. Confession 55. Joe Macbeth 55. Wicked As They Come 56. Jazzboat 59. The Trials of Oscar Wilde 60. The Small World of Sammy Lee 62. Of Human Bondage 64. Drop Dead Darling 66. Casino Royale 67. Chitty Chitty Bang Bang 68. Cromwell 70. The Internecine Project 74. Alfie Darling 75. Sextette 78.

H. Bruce Humberstone If I Had a Million 32. King of the Jungle 33. The Merry Wives of Reno 34. Ladies Love Danger 35. The Silk Hat Kid 35. Checkers 37. Rascals 38. Pack Up Your Troubles 39. I Wake Up Screaming 41. Sun Valley Serenade 41. Tall, Dark and Handsome 41. Iceland 42. To the Shores of Tripoli 42. Hello Frisco Hello 43. Pin Up Girl 44. Within These Walls 45. Wonder Man 45. Three Little Girls in Blue 46. The Homestretch 47. Fury at Furnace Creek 48. South Sea Sinner 49. Happy Go Lovely 50. She's Working Her Way through College 52. The Desert Song 53. Ten Wanted Men 55. The Purple Mask 55. Tarzan and the Lost Safari 57. Tarzan and the Trappers 58. Tarzan's Fight for Life 58. Madison Avenue 61.

Samo Hung The Prodigal Son 81. Wheels on Meals 84. Twinkle Twinkle Lucky Stars 85. Dragons Forever 88. Moon Warriors 92. Mr Nice Guy 97.

Peter Hunt On Her Majesty's Secret Service 69. 1776 72. Gold 74. Gulliver's Travels 76. Shout at the Devil 76. Death Hunt 81. Wild Geese II 85. Assassination 86.

Lawrence Huntington The Tower of Terror 41. This Man Is Dangerous 41. Suspected Person 43. Warn That Man 43. Night Boat to Dublin 45. Wanted for Murder 46. The Upturned Glass 47. When the Bough Breaks 47. Mr Perrin and Mr Traill 48. Man on the Run 49. The Franchise Affair 50. Contraband Spain 55. Death Drums along the River 63. The Vulture 67.

Brian Desmond Hurst Ourselves Alone 36. Sensation 36. The Tenth Man 36. Glamorous Night 37. Prison without Bars 38. On the Night of the Fire 39. The Lion Has Wings 39. Dangerous Moonlight 41. Alibi 42. The Hundred Pound Window 43. Hungry Hill 46. The Mark of Cain 47. Trottie True 49. Scrooge 51. The Malta Story 53. Simba 55. The Black Tent 56. Dangerous Exile 57. Behind the Mask 58. His and Hers 60.

Waris Hussein A Touch of Love 69. Quackser Fortune Has a Cousin in the Bronx 70. Melody 71. The Possession of Joel Delaney 71. Henry VIII and His Six Wives 72. Sixth Happiness 97.

John Huston The Maltese Falcon 41. Across the Pacific 42. In This Our Life 42. Report from the Aleutians 43. Key Largo 48. On Our Merry Way 48. The Treasure of the Sierra Madre 48. We Were Strangers 49. The Asphalt Jungle 50. The African Queen 51. The Red Badge of Courage 51. Moulin Rouge 52. Beat the Devil 53. Moby Dick 56. Heaven Knows Mr Allison 57. The Barbarian and the Geisha 58. The Roots of Heaven 58. The Unforgiven 60. The Misfits 61. Freud 62. The List of Adrian Messenger 63. The Night of the Iguana 64. The Bible 66. Casino Royale 67. Reflections in a Golden Eye 67. Sinful Davey 68. The Kremlin Letter 70. Fat City 72. The Life and Times of Judge Roy Bean 72. The Mackintosh Man 73. The Man Who Would Be King 75. Wise Blood 79. Phobia 80. Victory 81. Annie 82. Under the Volcano 84. Prizzi's Honor 85. The Dead 87.

Harold Huth East of Piccadilly 40. Breach of Promise 41. Look Before You Love 48. Night Beat 48. The Hostage 56.

Brian G. Hutton Fargo 64. The Pad, and How to Use It 66. Sol Madrid 68. Where Eagles Dare 69. Kelly's Heroes 70. Zee and Co 71. Night Watch 73. The First Deadly Sin 80. High Road to China 83.

Peter Hyams Busting 73. Peeper 75. Capricorn One 78. Hanover Street 79. Outland 81. The Star Chamber 83. 2010 84. Running Scared 86. The Presidio 88. Stay Tuned 92. Timecop 94. Sudden Death 95. The Relic 97. End of Days 99. Musketeer 01.

John Irvin The Dogs of War 80. Ghost Story 81. Champions 83. Turtle Diary 85. Raw Deal 86. Hamburger Hill 87. Next of Kin 89. Robin Hood 91. Widow's Peak 93. A Month by the Lake 94. City of Industry 96. Shiner 00.

James Ivory Shakespeare Wallah 65. The Guru 69. Bombay Talkie 70. Savages 72. The Wild Party 74. Autobiography of a Princess 75. Roseland 77. The Europeans 79. Quartet 81. Heat and Dust 82. The Bostonians 84. A Room with a View 85. Maurice 87. Slaves of New York 89. Mr & Mrs Bridge 90. Howards End 92. The Remains of the Day 93. Jefferson in Paris 95. Surviving Picasso 96. A Soldier's Daughter Never Cries 98. The Golden Bowl 00.

Mick Jackson Chattahoochee 89. L.A. Story 91. The Bodyguard 92. Clean Slate 94. Volcano 97.

Pat Jackson Western Approaches 44. Shadow on the Wall 49. Encore 51. White Corridors 51. Something Money Can't Buy 52. The Feminine Touch 56. The Birthday Present 57. Virgin Island 58. What a Carve Up 61. Don't Talk to Strange Men 62.

Peter Jackson Meet the Feebles 89. Braindead 92. Heavenly Creatures 94. The Frighteners 96. The Lord of the Rings: The Fellowship Of The Ring 01. The Lord of the Rings: The Two Towers 02.

Wilfred Jackson Song of the South 46. Cinderella 50. Alice in Wonderland 51. Peter Pan 53. Lady and the Tramp 55.

Henry Jaglom Tracks 76. Sitting Ducks 78. National Lampoon's Movie Madness 81. Can She Bake a Cherry Pie? 83. Someone to Love 87. New Year's Day 89. Last Summer in the Hamptons 95. Déjà Vu 97.

Alan James Dick Tracy 37. SOS Coast Guard 37. Flaming Frontiers 38. Red Barry 38. Scouts to the Rescue 39.

Derek Jarman Sebastiane 76. Jubilee 78. The Tempest 80. The Angelic Conversation 85. Caravaggio 86. The Last of England 87. Aria 88. War Requiem 88. The Garden 90. Edward II 91. Blue 93. Wittgenstein 93.

Jim Jarmusch Stranger than Paradise 84. Down by Law 86. Mystery Train 89. Night on Earth 92. Dead Man 96. Year of the Horse 97. Ghost Dog: The Way of the Samurai 99.

Charles Jarrott Anne of the Thousand Days 69. Mary Queen of Scots 71. Lost Horizon 73. The Dove 74. Escape from the Dark 76. The Other Side of Midnight 77. The Last Flight of Noah's Ark 80. Condorman 81. The Amateur 81. The Boy in Blue 86.

Leigh Jason That Girl from Paris 36. The Bride Walks Out 36. New Faces of 1937 37. Wise Girl 37. The Mad Miss Manton 38. Career 39. Model Wife 41. Lady for a Night 42. Three Girls about Town 42. Dangerous Blondes 43. Carolina Blues 44. Nine Girls 44. Meet Me on Broadway 46. Lost Honeymoon 47. Out of the Blue 47. Okinawa 52.

Vadim Jean Leon the Pig Farmer 92. Beyond Bedlam 94. Clockwork Mice 95. The Real Howard Spitz 97. One More Kiss 99.

Lionel Jeffries The Railway Children 70. Baxter 72. The Amazing Mr Blunden 72. Wombling Free 77. The Water Babies 78.

Norman Jewison Forty Pounds of Trouble 63. The Thrill of It All 63. Send Me No Flowers 64. The Art of Love 65. The Cincinnati Kid 65. The Russians Are Coming, The Russians Are Coming 66. In the Heat of the Night 67. The Thomas Crown Affair 68. Gaily, Gaily 69. Fiddler on the Roof 71. Jesus Christ Superstar 73. Rollerball 75. F.I.S.T. 78. And Justice for All 79. Best Friends 82. A Soldier's Story 84. Agnes of God 85. Moonstruck 87. In Country 89. Other People's Money 91. Only You 94. Bogus 96. The Hurricane 99.

Phil Joanou Three O'Clock High 87. U2 Rattle and Hum 88. State of Grace 90. Final Analysis 92. Heaven's Prisoners 96.

Roland Joffé The Killing Fields 84. The Mission 86. Shadow Makers 89. City of Joy 92. The Scarlet Letter 95. Goodbye, Lover 98.

Lamont Johnson A Covenant with Death 66. A Gunfight 70. The McKenzie Break 70. The Groundstar Conspiracy 72. You'll Like My Mother 72. The Last American Hero 73. Visit to a Chief's Son 74. Lipstick 76. One on One 77. Somebody Killed Her Husband 78. Cattle Annie and Little Britches 80. Spacehunter: Adventures in the Forbidden Zone 83.

Nunnally Johnson Black Widow 54. Night People 54. How to Be Very Very Popular 55. The Man in the Gray Flannel Suit 56. Oh Men! Oh Women! 57. The Three Faces of Eve 57. The Man Who Understood Women 59. The Angel Wore Red 60.

Joe Johnston Honey, I Shrunk the Kids 89. The

Rocketeer 91. The Pagemaster 94. Jumanji 95. October Sky 99. Jurassic Park III 01.

Harmon Jones As Young as You Feel 51. Bloodhounds of Broadway 52. The Pride of St Louis 52. City of Bad Men 53. The Kid from Left Field 53. Gorilla at Large 54. Princess of the Nile 54. Target Zero 55. A Day of Fury 56. Wolf Larsen 58.

Terry Jones Monty Python and the Holy Grail 75. Monty Python's Life of Brian 79. Monty Python's The Meaning of Life 83. Personal Services 87. Erik the Viking 89. The Wind in the Willows 96.

Neil Jordan Angel 82. The Company of Wolves 84. Mona Lisa 86. High Spirits 88. We're No Angels 89. The Miracle 90. The Crying Game 92. Interview with the Vampire: The Vampire Chronicles 94. Michael Collins 96. Butcher Boy 97. In Dreams 99. The End of the Affair 99. Good Thief 02.

Nathan Juran The Black Castle 52. Gunsmoke 53. Law and Order 53. The Golden Blade 53. Tumbleweed 53. Drums Across the River 54. Highway Dragnet 54. The Crooked Web 55. 20 Million Miles to Earth 57. Hellcats of the Navy 57. The Brain from Planet Arous 57. The Deadly Mantis 57. The Attack of the 50-Foot Woman 58. The Seventh Voyage of Sinbad 58. Good Day for a Hanging 59. Jack the Giant Killer 61. The Mark of Zorro 63. The Siege of the Saxons 63. East of Sudan 64. First Men in the Moon 64. The Boy Who Cried Werewolf 73.

Jeremy Kagan Heroes 77. The Big Fix 78. The Chosen 81. The Sting 2 83. The Journey of Natty Gann 85.

Chen Kaige Yellow Earth 84. The Big Parade 86. King of the Children 88. Life on a String 91. Farewell My Concubine 93. Temptress Moon 96. The Emperor and the Assassin 99. Killing Me Softly 02.

Joseph Kane Fighting Marines 35. Darkest Africa 36. Undersea Kingdom 36. Dakota 45. Flame of the Barbary Coast 45. The Cheaters 45. The Plainsman and the Lady 46. Wyoming 47. The Gallant Legion 48. The Plunderers 48. Brimstone 49. Fair Wind to Java 52. Hoodlum Empire 52. Ride the Man Down 52. San Antone 52. Woman of the North Country 52. Sea of Lost Ships 53. Jubilee Trail 54. Timberjack 54. The Maverick Queen 55. The Road to Denver 55. Accused of Murder 56. Thunder over Arizona 56.

Jeff Kanew Eddie Macon's Run 83. Revenge of the Nerds 84. Tough Guys 86. Troop Beverly Hills 89. V. I. Warshawski 91.

Garson Kanin A Man to Remember 38. The Great Man Votes 38. The Next Time I Marry 38. Bachelor Mother 39. My Favorite Wife 40. They Knew What They Wanted 40. Tom, Dick and Harry 41. The True Glory 45. Some Kind of a Nut 69. Where It's At 69.

Jonathan Kaplan Truck Turner 74. White Line Fever 75. Mr Billion 77. Over the Edge 79. Heart Like a Wheel 83. Project X 87. The Accused 88. Immediate Family 89. Love Field 92. Unlawful Entry 92. Bad Girls 94. Brokedown Palace 99.

Wong Kar-wai As Tears Go By 88. Days of Being Wild 91. Chungking Express 94. Fallen Angels 95. Happy Together 97. In the Mood for Love 00.

Phil Karlson Black Gold 47. Kilroy Was Here 47. Louisiana 47. Ladies of the Chorus 48. Down Memory Lane 49. The Big Cat 49. Lorna Doone 51. Mask of the Avenger 51. Kansas City Confidential 52. Scandal Sheet 52. The Brigand 52. 99 River Street 53. They Rode West 54. Five Against the House 55. Hell's Island 55. The Phenix City Story 55. Tight Spot 55. The Brothers Rico 57. Gunman's Walk 58. The Scarface Mob 58. Hell to Eternity 60. The Secret Ways 61. The Young Doctors 61. Kid Galahad 62. Rampage 63. The Silencers 66. A Time for Killing 67. The Wrecking Crew 68. Hornet's Nest 69. Ben 72. Walking Tall 73. Framed 74.

Lawrence Kasdan Body Heat 81. The Big Chill 83. Silverado 85. The Accidental Tourist 88. I Love You to Death 90. Grand Canyon 91. Wyatt Earp 94. French Kiss 95. Mumford 99.

Lee H. Katzin Heaven with a Gun 69. Whatever Happened to Aunt Alice? 69. Le Mans 71. The Salzburg Connection 72. World Gone Wild 87.

Philip Kaufman The Great Northfield Minnesota Raid 71. The White Dawn 76. Invasion of the Body Snatchers 78. The Wanderers 79. The Right Stuff 83. The Unbearable Lightness of Being 87. Henry and June 90. Rising Sun 93. Quills 00.

Aki Kaurismäki Hamlet Goes Business 87. Ariel 88. Leningrad Cowboys Go America 89. I Hired a Contract Killer 90. The Match Factory Girl 90. Take Care of Your Scarf, Tatjana 94. Drifting Clouds 96.

Helmut Kautner Der Apfel ist ab 49. The Last Bridge 53. The Devil's General 55. A Stranger in My Arms 58. The Restless Years 59.

Elia Kazan A Tree Grows in Brooklyn 45. Boomerang! 47. Gentleman's Agreement 47. The Sea of Grass 47. Pinky 49. Panic in the Streets 50. A Streetcar Named Desire 51. Viva Zapata 52. Man on a Tightrope 53. On the Waterfront 54. East of Eden 55. Baby Doll 56. A Face in the Crowd 57. Wild River 60. Splendor in the Grass 61. America, America 63. The Arrangement 69. The Last Tycoon 76.

Buster Keaton Cops 22. Our Hospitality 23. The Love Nest 23. The Three Ages 23. The Navigator 24. Go West 25. Seven Chances 25. Battling Butler 26. The General 26.

William Keighley Easy to Love 33. Ladies They Talk About 33. Babbitt 34. Big Hearted Herbert 34. Dr Monica 34. Journal of a Crime 34. Kansas City Princess 34. 'G' Men 35. Mary Jane's Pa 35. Special Agent 35. Stars over Broadway 35. The Right to Live 35. Bullets or Ballots 36. God's Country and the Woman 36. The Green Pastures 36. The Singing Kid 36. The Prince and the Pauper 37. Varsity Show 37. Brother Rat 38. Secrets of an Actress 38. The Adventures of Robin Hood 38. Valley of the Giants 38. Each Dawn I Die 39. Yes My Darling Daughter 39. Four Mothers 40. No Time for Comedy 40. The Fighting 69th 40. Torrid Zone 40. The Bride Came C.O.D. 41. The Man Who Came to Dinner 41. George Washington Slept Here 42. Honeymoon 47. The Street with No Name 48. Rocky Mountain 50. Close to My Heart 51. The Master of Ballantrae 53.

Harry Keller Rose of Cimarron 52. The Unguarded Moment 56. Day of the Badman 57. Man Afraid 57. Quantez 57. The Female Animal 57. The Voice in the Mirror 58. Step Down to Terror 59. Seven Ways from Sundown 60. Tammy Tell Me True 61. Six Black Horses 62. Tammy and the Doctor 63. The Brass Bottle 64. In Enemy Country 68.

Bob Kellett A Home of Your Own 65. Futtock's End 69. Girl Stroke Boy 71. Up Pompeii 71. Up the Chastity Belt 71. Our Miss Fred 72. The Alf Garnett Saga 72. Up the Front 72. Don't Just Lie There, Say Something! 73. Spanish Fly 75. Are You Being Served? 77.

Roy Kellino Catch As Catch Can 37. The Last Adventurers 37. I Met a Murderer 39. Guilt Is My Shadow 50. Charade 52. Lady Possessed 52. The Silken Affair 56.

Gene Kelly It's Always Fair Weather 55. The Happy Road 56. The Tunnel of Love 58. Gigot 62. A Guide for the Married Man 67. Hello Dolly 69. The Cheyenne Social Club 70. That's Entertainment Part Two 76.

Burt Kennedy The Canadians 61. Mail Order Bride 63. The Rounders 65. Return of the Seven 66. The Money Trap 66. The War Wagon 67. Welcome to Hard Times 67. Support Your Local Sheriff 68. The Good Guys and the Bad Guys 69. Young Billy Young 69. Dirty Dingus Magee 70. The Deserter 70. Hannie Caulder 71. Support Your Local Gunfighter 71. The Train Robbers 73. The Killer Inside Me 76. Suburban Commando 91.

Erle C. Kenton The Last Parade 31. Guilty as Hell 32. Island of Lost Souls 32. Big Executive 33. From Hell to Heaven 33. Search for Beauty 34. The Best Man Wins 34. You're Telling Me 34. Grand Exit 35. Party Wire 35. Little Tough Guys in Society 38. North to the Klondike 41. Frisco Lil 42. The Ghost of Frankenstein 42. Who Done It? 42. It Ain't Hay 43. House of Frankenstein 44. House of Dracula 45. She Gets Her Man 45. The Cat Creeps 46.

James V. Kern The Doughgirls 44. Never Say Goodbye 46. Stallion Road 47. April Showers 48. The Second Woman 50. Two Tickets to Broadway 51.

Irvin Kershner Stakeout on Dope Street 58. The Hoodlum Priest 61. A Face in the Rain 63. The Luck of Ginger Coffey 64. A Fine Madness 66. The Flim Flam Man 67. Loving 70. Up the Sandbox 72. S*P*Y*S 74. The Return of a Man Called Horse 76. Eyes of Laura Mars 78. The Empire Strikes Back 80. Never Say Never Again 83. Robocop 2 90.

Krzysztof Kieslowski Camera Buff 79. No End 84. A Short Film about Killing 88. A Short Film about Love 88. The Double Life of Véronique 91. Three Colours: Blue 93. Three Colours: White 93. Three Colours: Red 94.

Edward Killy Freckles 35. Seven Keys to Baldpate 35. Bunker Bean 36. Wanted: Jane Turner 36. Along the Rio Grande 41.

Anthony Kimmins Keep Fit 37. I See Ice 38. It's in the Air 38. Come on George 39. Trouble Brewing 39. Mine Own Executioner 47. Bonnie Prince Charlie 48. Flesh and Blood 51. Mr Denning Drives North 51. Who Goes There? 52. The Captain's Paradise 53. Aunt Clara 54. Smiley 56. Smiley Gets a Gun 58. The Amorous Prawn 62.

George King Sweeney Todd, the Demon Barber of Fleet Street 36. The Crimes of Stephen Hawke 36. Merry Comes to Town 37. Ticket of Leave Man 37. Sexton Blake and the Hooded Terror 38. Crimes at the Dark House 39. The Chinese Bungalow 39. The Face at the Window 39. George and Margaret 40. The Case of the Frightened Lady 40. Tomorrow We Live 42. Candlelight in Algeria 43. Gaiety George 46. The Shop at Sly Corner 46. Forbidden 49.

Henry King Tol'able David 21. Stella Dallas 25. The Winning of Barbara Worth 26. Hell Harbor 30. Lightnin' 30. Merely Mary Ann 31. Over the Hill 31. The Woman in Room 13 32. I Loved You Wednesday 33. State Fair 33. Carolina 34. Marie Galante 34. One More Spring 35. Way Down East 35. Lloyd's of London 36. Ramona 36. The Country Doctor 36. In Old Chicago 37. Seventh Heaven 37. Alexander's Ragtime Band 38. Jesse James 39. Stanley and Livingstone 39. Chad Hanna 40. Little Old New York 40. Maryland 40. A Yank in the RAF 41. Remember the Day 41. The Black Swan 42. The Song of Bernadette 43. Wilson 44. A Bell for Adano 45. Margie 46. Captain from Castile 47. Deep Waters 48. Prince of Foxes 49. Twelve O'Clock High 49. The Gunfighter 50. David and Bathsheba 51. I'd Climb the Highest Mountain 51. The Snows of Kilimanjaro 52. Wait 'Til the Sun Shines, Nellie 52. King of the Khyber Rifles 53. Love Is a Many Splendored Thing 55. Untamed 55. Carousel 56. The Sun Also Rises 57. The Bravados 58. Beloved Infidel 59. This Earth Is Mine 59. Tender Is the Night 61.

Louis King Murder in Trinidad 34. Road Gang 36. Draegerman Courage 37. Melody for Two 37. Hunted Men 38. Illegal Traffic 38. Prison Farm 38. Tip-off Girls 38. Persons in Hiding 39. Moon over Burma 40. Seventeen 40. The Way of All Flesh 40. Typhoon 40. Chetniks – The Fighting Guerrillas 42. Thunderhead, Son of Flicka 45. Smoky 46. Bob, Son of Battle 47. Green Grass of Wyoming 48. Mrs Mike 49. Frenchie 50. Powder River 53. Sabre Jet 53. Dangerous Mission 54.

Takeshi Kitano Violent Cop 89. Boiling Point 90. A Scene at the Sea 91. Sonatine 93. Kids Return 96. Hana-Bi 97. Kikujiro 99. Brother 00.

Randal Kleiser Grease 78. The Blue Lagoon 80. Summer Lovers 82. Flight of the Navigator 86. Getting It Right 89. White Fang 90. Honey, I Blew Up the Kid 92. It's My Party 96.

Bernard Knowles A Place of One's Own 44. The Magic Bow 46. Jassy 47. The Man Within 47. The White Unicorn 47. Easy Money 48. The Lost People 49. The Perfect Woman 49. The Reluctant Widow 50.

Howard W. Koch Big House USA 54. The Girl in Black Stockings 57. Andy Hardy Comes Home 58. Frankenstein '70 58. The Last Mile 59. Badge 373 73.

Andrei Konchalovsky Asya's Happiness 67. Maria's Lovers 84. Runaway Train 85. Duet for One 87. Shy People 87. Tango & Cash 89. The Inner Circle 91.

Alexander Korda The Squall 29. Lilies of the Field 30. Marius 31. Service for Ladies 32. Wedding Rehearsal 32. The Girl from Maxim's 33. The Private Life of Henry VIII 33. The Private Life of Don Juan 34. Rembrandt 36. That Hamilton Woman 41. Perfect Strangers 45. An Ideal Husband 47.

Zoltan Korda Men of Tomorrow 32. Cash 33. Sanders of the River 35. Forget Me Not 36. Elephant Boy 37. The Drum 38. The Four Feathers 39. Conquest of the Air 40. The Jungle Book 42. Sahara 43. Counterattack 45. The Macomber Affair 46. A Woman's Vengeance 48. Cry the Beloved Country 51.

Henry Koster Three Smart Girls 36. One Hundred Men and a Girl 37. The Rage of Paris 38. First Love 39. Three Smart Girls Grow Up 39. Spring Parade 40. It Started with Eve 41. Between Us Girls 42. Music for Millions 44. Two Sisters from Boston 46. The Bishop's Wife 47. The Unfinished Dance 47. The Luck of the Irish 48. Come to the Stable 49. The Inspector General 49. Harvey 50. My Blue Heaven 50. Wabash Avenue 50. Elopement 51. Mr Belvedere Rings the Bell 51. No Highway 51. My Cousin Rachel 52. Stars and Stripes Forever 52. The Robe 53. Desirée 54. A Man Called Peter 55. Good Morning, Miss Dove 55. The Virgin Queen 55. D-Day the Sixth of June 56. The Power and the Prize 56. My Man Godfrey 57. Fräulein 58. The Naked Maja 59. The Story of Ruth 60. Flower Drum Song 61. Mr Hobbs Takes a Vacation 62. Take Her, She's Mine 63. Dear Brigitte 65. The Singing Nun 66.

Ted Kotcheff Life at the Top 65. Outback 70. Billy Two Hats 73. The Apprenticeship of Duddy Kravitz 74. Fun with Dick and Jane 76. Who Is Killing the Great Chefs of Europe? 78. North Dallas Forty 79. First Blood 82. Split Image 82. Uncommon Valor 83. Switching Channels 88. Winter People 88. Weekend at Bernie's 89. Folks! 92. The Shooter 94.

Stanley Kramer Not as a Stranger 55. The Pride and the Passion 57. The Defiant Ones 58. On the Beach 59. Inherit the Wind 60. Judgment at Nuremberg 61. It's a Mad Mad Mad Mad World 63. Ship of Fools 65. Guess Who's Coming to Dinner 67. The Secret of Santa Vittoria 69. RPM (Revolutions Per Minute) 70. Bless the Beasts and Children 71. Oklahoma Crude 73. The Domino Principle 77. The Runner Stumbles 79.

Stanley Kubrick The Killing 56. Paths of Glory 57. Spartacus 60. Lolita 62. Dr Strangelove; or, How I Learned to Stop Worrying and Love the Bomb 63. 2001: A Space Odyssey 68. A Clockwork Orange 71. Barry Lyndon 75. The Shining 80. Full Metal Jacket 87. Eyes Wide Shut 99.

Buzz Kulik Yellow Canary 63. Warning Shot 66. Riot 68. Villa Rides! 68. To Find a Man 71. Shamus 72. The Hunter 80. The Pursuit of D. B. Cooper 81.

Akira Kurosawa No Regrets for Our Youth 46. Drunken Angel 48. Rashomon 51. Ikiru 52. The Seven Samurai 54. Ikimono No Kiroku 55. The Lower Depths 57. Throne of Blood 57. The Hidden Fortress 58. The Bad Sleep Well 60. Yojimbo 61. Sanjuro 62. High and Low 63. Redbeard 65. Dodes'ka-den 70. Dersu Uzala 75. Kagemusha 80. Ran 85. Akira Kurosawa's Dreams 90. Rhapsody in August 90.

Diane Kurys Coup de Foudre 83. Man in Love 87. C'est la Vie 90. Après l'Amour 92. Six Days, Six Nights 94.

Emir Kusturica When Father Was Away on Business 85. Time of the Gypsies 89. Arizona Dream 91. Underground 95. Black Cat, White Cat 98.

Harry Lachman The Outsider 31. Aren't We All? 32. Face in the Sky 33. Paddy the Next Best Thing 33. Baby Take a Bow 34. George White's Scandals 34. Dante's Inferno 35. Our Relations 36. The Man Who Lived Twice 36. It Happened in Hollywood 37. The Devil Is Driving 37. They Came by Night 39. Castle in the Desert 42. Dr Renault's Secret 42. The Loves of Edgar Allan Poe 42.

Ringo Lam Esprit d'Amour 83. City on Fire 87. Wild Search 89. Full Contact 92. Twin Dragons 92. Maximum Risk 96.

Charles Lamont Little Accident 39. Unexpected Father 39. Sandy Is a Lady 40. Give Us Wings 41. Road Agent 41. Get Hep to Love 42. It Comes Up Love 42. When Johnny Comes Marching Home 42. Fired Wife 43. Mr Big 43. Top Man 43. Bowery to Broadway 44. Chip off the Old Block 44. Her Primitive Man 44. The Merry Monahans 44. Frontier Gal 45. Salome Where She Danced 45. That's the Spirit 45. She Wrote the Book 46. The Runaround 46. Slave Girl 47. Baghdad 49. Curtain Call at Cactus Creek 49. Ma and Pa Kettle 49. Abbott and Costello in the Foreign Legion 50. Abbott and Costello Meet the Invisible Man 51. Flame of Araby 51. Abbott and Costello Meet Captain Kidd 52. Abbott and Costello Go to Mars 53. Abbott and Costello Meet Dr Jekyll and Mr Hyde 53. Abbott and Costello Meet the Keystone Kops 54. Ricochet Romance 54. Abbott and Costello Meet the Mummy 55.

Lew Landers Tailspin Tommy 34. The Red Rider 34. The Vanishing Shadow 34. Rustlers of Red Dog 35. Stormy 35. The Call of the Savage 35. The Raven 35. Crashing Hollywood 37. Danger Patrol 37. Flight from Glory 37. The Man Who Found Himself 37. Condemned Women 38. Pacific Liner 38. Smashing the Rackets 38. Annabel Takes a Tour 39. Enemy Agent 40. Honeymoon Deferred 40. La Conga Nights 40. I Was a Prisoner on Devil's Island 41. Submarine Raider 42. Junior Army 43. Murder in Times Square 43. Power of the Press 43. The Ghost that Walks Alone 43. The Return of the Vampire 43. The Black Parachute 44. The Boogie Man Will Get You 44. The Enchanted Forest 45. The Mask of Dijon 46. The Adventures of Gallant Bess 48. The Stagecoach Kid 49. The Last of the Buccaneers 50. Hurricane Island 51. The Magic Carpet 51. California Conquest 52. Man in the Dark 53. Captain Kidd and the Slave Girl 54.

John Landis The Kentucky Fried Movie 77. National Lampoon's Animal House 78. The Blues Brothers 80. An American Werewolf in London 81. Trading Places 83. Twilight Zone: The Movie 83. Into the Night 85. Spies Like Us 85. Three Amigos! 86. Amazon Women on the Moon 87. Coming to America 88. Oscar 91. Innocent Blood 92. Beverly Hills Cop 3 94. The Stupids 95. Blues Brothers 2000 98. Susan's Plan 98.

Paul Landres Last of the Bad Men 57. The Vampire 57. Go, Johnny Go! 58. Johnny Rocco 58. The Return of Dracula 58. Son of a Gunfighter 64.

Sidney Lanfield Dance Team 31. Hush Money 31. Society Girl 32. Broadway Bad 33. Moulin Rouge 34. The Last Gentleman 34. Hold 'em Yale 35. King of Burlesque 35. Red Salute 35. One in a Million 36. Sing Baby Sing 36. Love and Hisses 37. Thin Ice 37. Wake Up and Live 37. Always Goodbye 38. Second Fiddle 39. Swanee River 39. The Hound of the Baskervilles 39. You'll Never Get Rich 41. My Favorite Blonde 42. The Lady Has Plans 42. Let's Face It 43. The Meanest Man in the World 43. Standing Room Only 44. Bring On the Girls 45. The Well Groomed Bride 46. The Trouble with Women 47. Where There's Life 47. Station West 48. Sorrowful Jones 49. Follow the Sun 51. The Lemon Drop Kid 51. Skirts Ahoy 52.

Fritz Lang Destiny 21. Doctor Mabuse the Gambler 22. The Niebelungen 24. Metropolis 26. The Woman in the Moon 29. M 31. The Testament of Dr Mabuse 33. Fury 36. You Only Live Once 37. You and Me 38. The Return of Frank James 40. Man Hunt 41. Western Union 41. Hangmen Also Die! 43. Ministry of Fear 44. The Woman in the Window 44. Scarlet Street 45. Cloak and Dagger 46. Secret Beyond the Door 48. An American Guerilla in the Philippines 50. House by the River 50. Clash by Night 52. Rancho Notorious 52. The Big Heat 53. The Blue Gardenia 53. Human Desire 54. Moonfleet 55. Beyond a Reasonable Doubt 56. While the City Sleeps 56. The Thousand Eyes of Dr Mabuse 60.

Walter Lang Meet the Baron 33. The Warrior's Husband 33. Carnival 34. The Mighty Barnum 34. Hooray for Love 35. Love before Breakfast 36. Second Honeymoon 37. Wife, Doctor and Nurse 37. I'll Give a Million 38. The Baroness and the Butler 38. The Little Princess 39. Star Dust 40. The Blue Bird 40. The Great Profile 40. Tin Pan Alley 40. Moon over Miami 41. Weekend in Havana 41. Song of the Islands 42. The Magnificent Dope 42. Coney Island 43. Greenwich Village 44. State Fair 45. Claudia and David 46. Sentimental Journey 46. Mother Wore Tights 47. Sitting Pretty 48. When My Baby Smiles at Me 48. You're My Everything 49. Cheaper by the Dozen 50. The Jackpot 50. On the Riviera 51. With a Song in My Heart 52. Call Me Madam 53. There's No Business like Show Business 54. The King and I 56. Desk Set 57. But Not for Me 59. Can Can 60. Snow White and the Three Stooges 61. The Marriage Go Round 61.

Frank Launder Millions like Us 43. Two Thousand Women 44. I See a Dark Stranger 45. Captain Boycott 47. The Blue Lagoon 49. The Happiest Days of Your Life 50. Lady Godiva Rides Again 51. Folly to be Wise 52. The Belles of St Trinian's 54. Geordie 55. Blue Murder at St Trinians 57. The Bridal Path 59. The Pure Hell of St Trinian's 60. Joey Boy 65. The Great St Trinian's Train Robbery 66. The Wildcats of St Trinian's 80.

Arnold Laven Without Warning 52. Vice Squad 53. Down Three Dark Streets 54. The Rack 56. Slaughter on Tenth Avenue 57. The Monster that Challenged the World 57. Anna Lucasta 58. Geronimo 62. The Glory Guys 65. Rough Night in Jericho 67. Sam Whiskey 69.

Philip Leacock Appointment in London 52. The Brave Don't Cry 52. The Kidnappers 53. Escapade 55. The Spanish Gardener 56. High Tide at Noon 57. Innocent Sinners 57. Take a Giant Step 58. The Rabbit Trap 59. Hand in Hand 60. Let No Man Write My Epitaph 60. 13 West Street 62. Reach for Glory 62. Tamahine 62. The War Lover 62. Adam's Woman 70.

David Lean Major Barbara 41. In Which We Serve 42. This Happy Breed 44. Blithe Spirit 45. Brief Encounter 45. Great Expectations 46. Oliver Twist 48. The Passionate Friends 48. Madeleine 49. The Sound Barrier 52. Hobson's Choice 53. Summertime 55. The Bridge on the River Kwai 57. Lawrence of Arabia 62. Doctor Zhivago 65. Ryan's Daughter 70.

Reginald LeBorg Dead Man's Eyes 44. Jungle Woman 44. The Mummy's Ghost 44. Wyoming Mail 50. The Flanagan Boy 53.

Patrice Leconte Monsieur Hire 89. The Hairdresser's Husband 90. Tango 93. Le Parfum d'Yvonne 94. Ridicule 96. The Girl on the Bridge 98. La Veuve de Saint-Pierre 00. The Man on the Train 02.

D. Ross Lederman The Phantom of the West 31. Dinky 35. The Body Disappears 41. Bullet Scars 42. Busses Roar 42. The Gorilla Man 42. Adventure in Iraq 43. Find the Blackmailer 43. The Tanks Are Coming 51.

Ang Lee The Wedding Banquet 93. Eat Drink Man Woman 94. Sense and Sensibility 95. The Ice Storm 97. Ride With The Devil 99. Crouching Tiger, Hidden Dragon 00.

Jack Lee The Woman in the Hall 47. Once a Jolly Swagman 48. The Wooden Horse 50. South of Algiers 52. Turn the Key Softly 53. A Town like Alice 56. Robbery under Arms 57. The Captain's Table 58. Circle of Deception 60.

Norman Lee Doctor's Orders 34. Royal Cavalcade 35. No Escape 36. Bulldog Drummond at Bay 37. Yes, Madam? 38. The Door with Seven Locks 40. The Farmer's Wife 40. The Case of Charles Peace 49. The Girl Who Couldn't Quite 50.

Rowland V. Lee Barbed Wire 27. The Mysterious Dr Fu Manchu 29. A Man from Wyoming 30. Derelict 30. Ladies Love Brutes 30. Paramount on Parade 30. The Guilty Generation 31. I Am Suzanne 33. That Night in London 33. Zoo in Budapest 33. Gambling 34. The Count of Monte Cristo 34. Cardinal Richelieu 35. One Rainy Afternoon 35. The Three Musketeers 35. Love from a Stranger 36. The Toast of New York 37. Mother Carey's Chickens 38. Service De Luxe 38. Son of Frankenstein 39. The Sun Never Sets 39. Tower of London 39. Son of Monte Cristo 40. Powder Town 42. The Bridge of San Luis Rey 44. Captain Kidd 45.

Spike Lee She's Gotta Have It 86. Do the Right Thing 89. Mo' Better Blues 90. Jungle Fever 91. Malcolm X 92. Crooklyn 94. Clockers 95. Get On the Bus 96. Girl 6 96. He Got Game 98. Summer of Sam 99. Bamboozled 00. 25th Hour 02.

J. Lee-Thompson Murder without Crime 50. The Yellow Balloon 52. The Weak and the Wicked 53. For Better For Worse 54. An Alligator Named Daisy 55. As Long as They're Happy 55. The Good Companions 56. Yield to the Night 56. Woman in a Dressing Gown 57. Ice Cold in Alex 58. No Trees in the Street 58. Northwest Frontier 59. Tiger Bay 59. I Aim at the Stars 60. Cape Fear 61. The Guns of Navarone 61. Taras Bulba 62. What a Way to Go 64. John Goldfarb, Please Come Home 65. Return from the Ashes 65. Eye of the Devil 67. Before Winter Comes 68. Country Dance 69. MacKenna's Gold 69. The Most Dangerous Man in the World 69. Battle for the Planet of the Apes 73. Huckleberry Finn 74. The Reincarnation of Peter Proud 74. The White Buffalo 77. The Greek Tycoon 78. Happy Birthday to Me 80. 10 to Midnight 83. The Evil that Men Do 84. King Solomon's Mines 85. Firewalker 86. Death Wish 4: The Crackdown 87. Kinjite: Forbidden Subjects 89.

Herbert Leeds Five of a Kind 38. Keep Smiling 38. Cisco Kid and The Lady 39. Mr Moto in Danger Island 39. The Chicken Wagon Family 39. The Return of the Cisco Kid 39. Just Off Broadway 42. Manila Calling 42. It Shouldn't Happen to a Dog 46. Bunco Squad 50.

Michael Lehmann Heathers 88. Meet the Applegates 90. Hudson Hawk 91. Airheads 94. The Truth about Cats & Dogs 96. 40 Days and 40 Nights 02.

Mike Leigh Bleak Moments 71. High Hopes 88. Life Is Sweet 90. Naked 93. Secrets and Lies 95. Career Girls 97. Topsy-Turvy 99. All or Nothing 02.

Mitchell Leisen Cradle Song 33. Behold My Wife 34. Death Takes a Holiday 34. Murder at the Vanities 34. Four Hours to Kill 35. Hands across the Table 35. The Big Broadcast of 1937 36. Thirteen Hours by Air 36. Easy Living 37. Swing High Swing Low 37. The Big Broadcast of 1938 37. Artists and Models Abroad 38. Midnight 39. Arise My Love 40. Remember the Night 40. Hold Back the Dawn 41. I Wanted Wings 41. Take a Letter, Darling 42. The Lady Is Willing 42. No Time for Love 43. Frenchman's Creek 44. Lady in the Dark 44. Practically Yours 44. Kitty 45. Masquerade in Mexico 45. To Each His Own 46. Dream Girl 47. Golden Earrings 47. Suddenly It's Spring 47. Bride of Vengeance 48. Song of Surrender 49. Captain Carey USA 50. No Man of Her Own 50. The Mating Season 50. Darling How Could You 51. Young Man with Ideas 52. Tonight We Sing 53. Bedevilled 55. The Girl Most Likely 58.

Claude Lelouch A Man and a Woman 66. Le Voyou 70. And Now My Love 74. Another Man, Another Chance 77. A Nous Deux 79. Edith and Marcel 84. Long Live Life 84. A Man and a Woman: Twenty Years Later 86. Les Misérables 95. Men Women: A User's Manual 96. Chance or Coincidence 98.

Robert Z. Leonard In Gay Madrid 30. Let Us Be Gay 30. The Divorcee 30. Bachelor Father 31. Five and Ten 31. It's a Wise Child 31. Susan Lenox, Her Fall and Rise 31. Lovers Courageous 32. Strange Interlude 32. Dancing Lady 33. Peg o' My Heart 33. Outcast Lady 34. After Office Hours 35. Escapade 35. Piccadilly Jim 36. The Great Ziegfeld 36. Maytime 37. The Firefly 37. The Girl of the Golden West 38. Broadway Serenade 39. New Moon 40. Pride and Prejudice 40. Third Finger Left Hand 40. When Ladies Meet 41. Ziegfeld Girl 41. We Were Dancing 42. Stand by for Action 43. The Man from Down Under 43. Marriage Is a Private Affair 44. Weekend at the Waldorf 45. The Secret Heart 46. Cynthia 47. B.F.'s Daughter 48. In the Good Old Summertime 49. The Bribe 49. Grounds for Marriage 50. Nancy Goes to Rio 50. The Duchess of Idaho 50. Too Young to Kiss 51. Everything I Have Is Yours 52. The Clown 52. The Great Diamond Robbery 53. Her Twelve Men 54. Beautiful but Dangerous 55. The King's Thief 55. Kelly and Me 56.

Sergio Leone The Colossus of Rhodes 61. A Fistful of Dollars 64. For a Few Dollars More 65. The Good, the Bad and the Ugly 66. Once Upon a Time in the West 69. A Fistful of Dynamite 71. Once Upon a Time in America 84.

Mark L. Lester Stunts 77. Roller Boogie 79. Class of 84 81. Firestarter 84. Armed and Dangerous 85. Commando 85. Class of 1999 89. Showdown in Little Tokyo 91. Extreme Justice 93. Night of the Running Man 94.

Richard Lester The Mouse on the Moon 63. A Hard Day's Night 64. Help! 65. The Knack 65. A Funny Thing Happened on the Way to the Forum 66. How I Won the War 67. Petulia 68. The Bed Sitting Room 69. The Three Musketeers (The Queen's Diamonds) 73. Juggernaut 74. The Four Musketeers (The Revenge of Milady) 74. Royal Flash 75. Robin and Marian 76. The Ritz 76. Butch and Sundance: The Early Days 79. Cuba 79. Superman II 80. Superman III 83. Finders Keepers 84. The Return of the Musketeers 89. Get Back 91.

Brian Levant Problem Child 2 91. Beethoven 92. The Flintstones 94. Jingle All the Way 96. The Flintstones in Viva Rock Vegas 00. Snow Dogs 02.

Henry Levin I Love a Mystery 45. The Fighting Guardsman 45. The Bandit of Sherwood Forest 46. The Devil's Mask 46. The Return of Monte Cristo 46. The Unknown 46. The Corpse Came COD 47. The Guilt of Janet Ames 47. The Gallant Blade 48. The Man from Colorado 48. The Mating of Millie 48. Jolson Sings Again 49. Mr Soft Touch 49. And Baby Makes Three 50. Convicted 50. The Flying Missile 50. The Petty Girl 50. The Family Secret 51. Two of a Kind 51. Belles on Their Toes 52. Mr Scoutmaster 53. The Farmer Takes a Wife 53. The President's Lady 53. Gambler from Natchez 54. The Dark Avenger 55. April Love 57. Bernardine 57. Let's Be Happy 57. The Lonely Man 57. A Nice Little Bank That Should Be Robbed 58. The Remarkable Mr Pennypacker 58. Holiday for Lovers 59. Journey to the Center of the Earth 59. Where the Boys Are 60. The Wonders of Aladdin 61. Come Fly with Me 62. If a Man Answers 62. The Wonderful World of the Brothers Grimm 62. Genghis Khan 64. Honeymoon Hotel 64. Kiss the Girls and Make Them Die 66. Murderer's Row 66. The Ambushers 67. The Desperados 68. That Man Bolt 73. The Treasure Seekers 77.

Barry Levinson Diner 82. The Natural 84. Young Sherlock Holmes 85. Good Morning, Vietnam 87. Tin Men 87. Rain Man 88. Avalon 90. Bugsy 91. Toys 92. Disclosure 94. Jimmy Hollywood 94. Sleepers 96. Wag the Dog 97. Sphere 98. Liberty Heights 99. An Everlasting Piece 00. Bandits 01.

Albert Lewin The Moon and Sixpence 43. The Picture of Dorian Gray 45. The Private Affairs of Bel Ami 46. Pandora and the Flying Dutchman 50. Saadia 53. The Living Idol 56.

Jerry Lewis The Bellboy 60. The Errand Boy 61. The Ladies Man 61. The Nutty Professor 63. The Patsy 64. The Family Jewels 65. Three on a Couch 66. The Big Mouth 67. One More Time 69. Which Way to the Front? 70.

Joseph H. Lewis Pride of the Bowery 41. The Invisible Ghost 41. Bombs Over Burma 42. The Mad Doctor of Market Street 42. Minstrel Man 44.

My Name Is Julia Ross 45. The Falcon in San Francisco 45. So Dark the Night 46. The Jolson Story 46. The Swordsman 47. The Return of October 48. Gun Crazy 49. Undercover Man 49. A Lady without Passport 50. Desperate Search 52. Retreat, Hell! 52. A Lawless Street 55. The Big Combo 55. Seventh Cavalry 56. The Halliday Brand 56. Terror in a Texas Town 58.

Richard Linklater Slacker 91. Dazed and Confused 93. Before Sunrise 95. SubUrbia 96. The Newton Boys 98. Waking Life 01. Tape 01.

Dwight Little Halloween Four: The Return of Michael Myers 88. Phantom of the Opera 89. Marked for Death 90. Rapid Fire 92. Free Willy 2: The Adventure Home 95. Murder at 1600 97.

Anatole Litvak Tell Me Tonight 32. Sleeping Car 33. L'Equipage 35. Mayerling 35. The Woman I Love 37. Tovarich 37. The Amazing Dr Clitterhouse 38. The Sisters 38. Confessions of a Nazi Spy 39. The Roaring Twenties 39. All This and Heaven Too 40. Castle on the Hudson 40. City for Conquest 40. Blues in the Night 41. Out of the Fog 41. This Above All 42. The Long Night 47. Sorry, Wrong Number 48. The Snake Pit 48. Decision before Dawn 51. Act of Love 54. The Deep Blue Sea 55. Anastasia 56. The Journey 59. Goodbye Again 61. Five Miles to Midnight 62. The Night of the Generals 67. The Lady in the Car with Glasses and a Gun 69.

Frank Lloyd The Divine Lady 29. Son of the Gods 30. The Lash 30. East Lynne 31. The Age for Love 31. Passport to Hell 32. Berkeley Square 33. Cavalcade 33. Hoopla 33. Servants' Entrance 34. Mutiny on the Bounty 35. Under Two Flags 36. Maid of Salem 37. Wells Fargo 37. If I Were King 38. Rulers of the Sea 39. The Howards of Virginia 40. The Lady from Cheyenne 41. This Woman Is Mine 41. Forever and a Day 43. Blood on the Sun 45. The Last Command 55.

Ken Loach Poor Cow 67. Kes 69. Family Life 71. Black Jack 79. Hidden Agenda 90. Riff-Raff 90. Raining Stones 93. Ladybird Ladybird 94. Land and Freedom 95. Carla's Song 96. My Name Is Joe 98. Bread and Roses 00. The Navigators 01. Sweet Sixteen 02.

Joshua Logan I Met My Love Again 37. Picnic 55. Bus Stop 56. Sayonara 57. South Pacific 58. Tall Story 60. Fanny 61. Ensign Pulver 64. Camelot 67. Paint Your Wagon 69.

Richard Loncraine Full Circle 76. Brimstone and Treacle 82. The Missionary 83. Bellman and True 87. Richard III 95.

Joseph Losey The Boy with Green Hair 48. The Lawless 49. The Prowler 50. M 51. The Big Night 51. Stranger on the Prowl 52. The Sleeping Tiger 54. A Man on the Beach 56. The Intimate Stranger 56. The Gypsy and the Gentleman 57. Time without Pity 57. Blind Date 59. The Criminal 60. Eva 62. The Damned 63. The Servant 63. King and Country 64. Modesty Blaise 66. Accident 67. Boom! 68. Secret Ceremony 69. Figures in a Landscape 70. The Go-Between 70. The Assassination of Trotsky 72. A Doll's House 73. Galileo 75. The Romantic Englishwoman 75. Mr Klein 76. Don Giovanni 79. Steaming 85.

Arthur Lubin Two Sinners 35. The House of a Thousand Candles 36. California Straight Ahead 37. Call a Messenger 39. Risky Business 39. The Big Guy 39. Black Friday 40. San Francisco Docks 40. Buck Privates 41. Hold That Ghost 41. In the Navy 41. Keep 'Em Flying 41. Ride 'Em Cowboy 41. Eagle Squadron 42. The Phantom of the Opera 43. White Savage 43. Ali Baba and the Forty Thieves 44. Delightfully Dangerous 45. A Night in Paradise 46. The Spider Woman Strikes Back 46. New Orleans 47. Francis 49. Impact 49. Rhubarb 51. It Grows on Trees 52. South Sea Woman 53. Footsteps in the Fog 55. Lady Godiva 55. The First Traveling Saleslady 56. Escapade in Japan 57. The Thief of Baghdad 60. The Incredible Mr Limpet 64.

Ernst Lubitsch Madame Dubarry 19. Forbidden Paradise 24. The Marriage Circle 24. Three Women 24. Kiss Me Again 25. Lady Windermere's Fan 25. The Patriot 28. Eternal Love 29. The Love Parade 29. Monte Carlo 30. Paramount on Parade 30. Broken Lullaby 31. The Smiling Lieutenant 31. If I Had a Million 32. One Hour with You 32. Trouble in Paradise 32. Design for Living 33. The Merry Widow 34. Angel 37. Bluebeard's Eighth Wife 38. Ninotchka 39. The Shop around the Corner 40. That Uncertain Feeling 41. To Be or Not to Be 42. Heaven Can Wait 43. Cluny Brown 46. That Lady in Ermine 48.

George Lucas THX 1138 70. American Graffiti 73. Star Wars 77. Star Wars Episode I: The Phantom Menace 99. Star Wars: Episode II - Attack of the Clones .

Edward Ludwig They Just Had to Get Married 33. Friends of Mr Sweeney 34. The Man Who Reclaimed His Head 34. Age of Indiscretion 35. Old Man Rhythm 35. Three Kids and a Queen 35. Adventure in Manhattan 36. Fatal Lady 36. Her Husband Lies 37. The Last Gangster 37. That Certain Age 38. The Swiss Family Robinson 40. Born to Sing 41. The Man Who Lost Himself 41. Bomber's Moon 43. They Came to Blow Up America 43. The Fighting Seabees 44. Three Is a Family 44. The Fabulous Texan 47. Wake of the Red Witch 48. The Big Wheel 49. Big Jim McLain 52. Caribbean 52. The Blazing Forest 52. Jivaro 53. Sangaree 53. The Vanquished 53. Flame of the Islands 55. The Black Scorpion 57.

Sidney Lumet 12 Angry Men 57. Stage Struck 57. That Kind of Woman 59. The Fugitive Kind 60. A View from the Bridge 61. Long Day's Journey into Night 62. Fail Safe 64. The Hill 65. The Pawnbroker 65. The Deadly Affair 66. The Group 66. Bye Bye Braverman 68. The Sea Gull 68. The Appointment 69. The Anderson Tapes 71. Child's Play 72. The Offence 72. Lovin' Molly 73. Serpico 73. Murder on the Orient Express 74. Dog Day Afternoon 75. Network 76. Equus 77. The Wiz 78. Just Tell Me What You Want 80. Prince of the City 81. Deathtrap 82. The Verdict 82. Daniel 83. Garbo Talks 84. Power 86. The Morning After 86. Running on Empty 88. Family Business 89. Q & A 90. Close to Eden 92. Guilty as Sin 93. Critical Care 97. Night Falls on Manhattan 97. Gloria 98.

Hamilton S. Luske Cinderella 50. Alice in Wonderland 51. Peter Pan 53. Lady and the Tramp 55. One Hundred and One Dalmatians 61.

William Lustig Street Gang 82. Maniac Cop 88. Relentless 89. Maniac Cop 2 90. Maniac Cop 3: Badge of Silence 92.

David Lynch Eraserhead 76. The Elephant Man 80. Dune 84. Blue Velvet 86. Twin Peaks 89. Wild at Heart 90. Twin Peaks: Fire Walk with Me 92. Lost Highway 96. The Straight Story 99. Mulholland Dr. 01.

Adrian Lyne Foxes 80. Flashdance 83. Nine and a Half Weeks 86. Fatal Attraction 87. Jacob's Ladder 90. Indecent Proposal 93. Lolita 97. Unfaithful 02.

Jonathan Lynn Clue 85. Nuns on the Run 90. My Cousin Vinny 92. The Distinguished Gentleman 92. Greedy 94. Sgt Bilko 96. Trial and Error 97. The Whole Nine Yards 00.

Francis D. Lyon The Bob Mathias Story 54. Cult of the Cobra 55. The Great Locomotive Chase 56. The Oklahoman 56. Bail Out at 43,000 57. Escort West 58. Castle of Evil 66.

David MacDonald It's Never Too Late to Mend 37. Dead Men Tell No Tales 38. Meet Mr Penny 38. This Man Is News 38. Spies of the Air 39. This Man in Paris 39. Law and Disorder 40. This England 41. Desert Victory 43. The Brothers 47. Good Time Girl 48. Snowbound 48. Christopher Columbus 49. Diamond City 49. The Bad Lord Byron 49. Cairo Road 50. The Adventurers 50. The Lost Hours 52. Devil Girl from Mars 54. Alias John Preston 56. Small Hotel 57. The Moonraker 57. Petticoat Pirates 61.

Ranald MacDougall Queen Bee 55. Man on Fire 57. The World, the Flesh and the Devil 59. Go Naked in the World 60. The Subterraneans 60.

Alexander Mackendrick Whisky Galore 48. The Man in the White Suit 51. Mandy 52. The Maggie 53. The Ladykillers 55. Sweet Smell of Success 57. Sammy Going South 63. A High Wind in Jamaica 65. Don't Make Waves 67.

John Mackenzie One Brief Summer 69. Unman, Wittering and Zigo 71. The Long Good Friday 80. The Honorary Consul 83. The Fourth Protocol 87. Blue Heat 90. Ruby 92. When the Sky Falls 99.

Gillies MacKinnon Conquest of the South Pole 89. The Playboys 92. A Simple Twist of Fate 94. Small Faces 95. Regeneration 97. Trojan Eddie 97. Hideous Kinky 98.

John Madden Ethan Frome 93. Golden Gate 93. Mrs Brown 97. Shakespeare in Love 98. Captain Corelli's Mandolin 01.

Dusan Makavejev Innocence Unprotected 68. The Switchboard Operator 69. WR – Mysteries of the Organism 71. Montenegro 81. The Coca-Cola Kid 85. Manifesto 88.

Louis Malle Lift to the Scaffold 57. Les Amants 58. Zazie dans le Métro 60. Vie Privée 61. Le Feu Follet 63. Viva Maria! 65. Histoires Extraordinaires 68. Le Souffle au Coeur 71. Lacombe, Lucien 74. Pretty Baby 78. Atlantic City 81. My Dinner with André 81. Crackers 84. Alamo Bay 85. Au Revoir Les Enfants 88. Milou in May 89. Damage 92. Vanya on 42nd Street 94.

David Mamet House of Games 87. Things Change 88. Homicide 91. Oleanna 94. The Spanish Prisoner 97. The Winslow Boy 98. State and Main 00. Heist 01.

Rouben Mamoulian Applause 29. City Streets 31. Doctor Jekyll and Mr Hyde 31. Love Me Tonight 32. Queen Christina 33. Song of Songs 33. We Live Again 34. Becky Sharp 35. The Gay Desperado 36. High, Wide and Handsome 37. Golden Boy 39. The Mark of Zorro 40. Blood and Sand 41. Rings on Her Fingers 42. Summer Holiday 48. Silk Stockings 57.

Luis Mandoki Gaby – A True Story 87. Born Yesterday 93. When a Man Loves a Woman 94. Message in a Bottle 99. Angel Eyes 01.

Joseph L. Mankiewicz Dragonwyck 46. Somewhere in the Night 46. The Late George Apley 46. The Ghost and Mrs Muir 47. Escape 48. A Letter to Three Wives 49. House of Strangers 49. All About Eve 50. No Way Out 50. People Will Talk 51. Five Fingers 52. Julius Caesar 53. The Barefoot Contessa 54. Guys and Dolls 55. The Quiet American 57. Suddenly Last Summer 59. Cleopatra 63. The Honey Pot 66. There Was a Crooked Man 70. Sleuth 72.

Anthony Mann Dr Broadway 42. Moonlight in Havana 42. The Great Flamarion 45. Two O'Clock Courage 45. The Bamboo Blonde 46. Desperate 47. Railroaded 47. T-Men 47. Raw Deal 48. Border Incident 49. The Black Book 49. Devil's Doorway 50. Side Street 50. The Furies 50. Winchester 73 50. The Tall Target 51. Bend of the River 52. The Naked Spur 52. The Glenn Miller Story 53. Thunder Bay 53. The Far Country 54. Strategic Air Command 55. The Man from Laramie 55. Savage Wilderness 56. Serenade 56. Men in War 57. The Tin Star 57. God's Little Acre 58. Man of the West 58. Cimarron 60. El Cid 61. The Fall of the Roman Empire 64. The Heroes of Telemark 65. A Dandy in Aspic 68.

Daniel Mann Come Back Little Sheba 52. About Mrs Leslie 54. I'll Cry Tomorrow 55. The Rose Tattoo 55. The Teahouse of the August Moon 56. Hot Spell 58. The Last Angry Man 59. Butterfield Eight 60. The Mountain Road 60. Ada 61. Five Finger Exercise 62. Who's Got the Action? 62. Who's Been Sleeping in My Bed? 63. Judith 65. Our Man Flint 65. For Love of Ivy 68. A Dream of Kings 69. Willard 71. The Revengers 72. Lost in the Stars 74. Matilda 78.

Delbert Mann Marty 55. The Bachelor Party 57. Desire under the Elms 58. Separate Tables 58. Middle of the Night 59. The Dark at the Top of the Stairs 60. Lover Come Back 61. The Outsider 61. That Touch of Mink 62. A Gathering of Eagles 63. Dear Heart 64. Quick Before It Melts 64. Mister Buddwing 66. Fitzwilly 67. The Pink Jungle 68. Jane Eyre 70. Kidnapped 71. Birch Interval 76. Night Crossing 82.

Michael Mann Thief 81. The Keep 83. L.A. Takedown 89. The Last of the Mohicans 92. Heat 95. The Insider 99. Ali 01.

Edwin L. Marin The Death Kiss 32. A Study in Scarlet 33. Bombay Mail 33. Affairs of a Gentleman 34. Paris Interlude 34. Pursuit 35. The Casino Murder Case 35. Everybody Sing 37. Man of the People 37. Married Before Breakfast 37. A Christmas Carol 38. Hold That Kiss 38. Listen Darling 38. The Chaser 38. Fast and Loose 39. Maisie 39. Society Lawyer 39. Florian 40. Hullabaloo 40. Paris Calling 41. Ringside Maisie 41. A Gentleman after Dark 42. Invisible Agent 42. Miss Annie Rooney 42. Two Tickets to London 43. Show Business 44. Tall in the Saddle 44. Johnny Angel 45. Abilene Town 46. Lady Luck 46. Mr Ace 46. Nocturne 46. The Young Widow 46. Christmas Eve 47. Intrigue 47. Race Street 48. Canadian Pacific 49. Fighting Man of the Plains 49. The Younger Brothers 49. Colt 45 50. The Cariboo Trail 50. Fort Worth 51. Raton Pass 51. Sugarfoot 51.

Richard Marquand The Legacy 78. Eye of the Needle 81. Return of the Jedi 83. Jagged Edge 85. Until September 85. Hearts of Fire 87.

Garry Marshall Young Doctors in Love 82. The Flamingo Kid 84. Nothing in Common 86. Overboard 87. Beaches 88. Pretty Woman 90. Frankie and Johnny 91. Exit to Eden 94. Dear God 96. Runaway Bride 99. The Other Sister 99. The Princess Diaries 01.

George Marshall Pack Up Your Troubles 31. Their First Mistake 32. Towed in a Hole 32. 365 Nights in Hollywood 34. She Learned about Sailors 34. In Old Kentucky 35. Life Begins at 40 35. Music Is Magic 35. Show Them No Mercy 35. A Message to Garcia 36. Can This Be Dixie? 36. The Crime of Dr Forbes 36. Love under Fire 37. Nancy Steele is Missing 37. Battle of Broadway 38. Hold That Co-Ed 38. The Goldwyn Follies 38. Destry Rides Again 39. You Can't Cheat an Honest Man 39. The Ghost Breakers 40. When the Daltons Rode 40. Pot o' Gold 41. Texas 41. Star Spangled Rhythm 42. The Forest Rangers 42. Valley of the Sun 42. And the Angels Sing 43. Riding High 43. True to Life 43. Hold That Blonde 45. Incendiary Blonde 45. Murder He Says 45. Monsieur Beaucaire 46. The Blue Dahlia 46. The Perils of Pauline 47. Variety Girl 47. Hazard 48. Tap Roots 48. My Friend Irma 49. Fancy Pants 50. Never a Dull Moment 50. A Millionaire for Christy 51. The Savage 52. Houdini 53. Off Limits 53. Scared Stiff 53. Destry 54. Duel in the Jungle 54. Money from Home 54. Red Garters 54. Beyond Mombasa 55. The Second Greatest Sex 55. Pillars of the Sky 56. The Guns of Fort Petticoat 57. The Sad Sack 57. Imitation General 58. The Mating Game 58. The Sheepman 58. It Started with a Kiss 59. The Gazebo 59. Cry for Happy 61. How the West Was Won 62. The Happy Thieves 62. Papa's Delicate Condition 63. Advance to the Rear 64. Boy, Did I Get a Wrong Number 66. Eight on the Lam 66. Hook, Line and Sinker 68.

Penny Marshall Jumpin' Jack Flash 86. Big 88. Awakenings 90. A League of Their Own 92. Renaissance Man 94. The Preacher's Wife 96. Riding In Cars With Boys 01.

Leslie H. Martinson The Atomic Kid 54. Black Gold 63. PT 109 63. FBI Code 98 64. For Those Who Think Young 64. Batman 66. Fathom 67. Mrs Pollifax – Spy 70. …and millions will die! 73. Cruise Missile 78.

Andrew Marton The Secret of Stamboul 36. School for Husbands 37. A Little Bit of Heaven 40. Gentle Annie 44. Gallant Bess 46. Storm over Tibet 51. The Wild North 51. The Devil Makes Three 52. Green Fire 54. Gypsy Colt 54. Men of the Fighting Lady 54. Prisoner of War 54. Underwater Warrior 58. Ben-Hur 59. It Happened in Athens 61. The Longest Day 62. 55 Days at Peking 63. The Thin Red Line 64. Clarence the Cross-Eyed Lion 65. Crack in the World 65. Around the World under the Sea 66. Birds Do It 66. Africa Texas Style 67.

Herbert Mason East Meets West 36. His Lordship 36. Man of Affairs 37. Take My Tip 37. Strange Boarders 38. A Window in London 39. The Silent Battle 39. Dr O'Dowd 40. Once a Crook 41. Back Room Boy 42. The Night Invader 43. Flight from Folly 44.

Rudolph Maté Aren't We All? 32. It Had to Be You 47. The Dark Past 48. Branded 50. D.O.A. 50. No Sad Songs for Me 50. Union Station 50. The Prince Who Was a Thief 51. When Worlds Collide 51. Paula 52. Sally and St Anne 52. The Green Glove 52. Forbidden 53. Mississippi Gambler 53. Second Chance 53. The Black Shield of Falworth 54. The Siege at Red River 54. Miracle in the Rain 55. The Far Horizons 55. The Violent Men 55. Port Afrique 56. The Rawhide Years 56. Three Violent People 56. The Deep Six 58. For the First Time 59. Seven Seas to Calais 62. The 300 Spartans 62.

Joe May Asphalt 29. Music in the Air 34. Confession 37. The House of Fear 39. The House of Seven Gables 40. The Invisible Man Returns 40. Johnny Doesn't Live Here Any More 44.

Gerald Mayer Dial 1119 50. Inside Straight 51. The Sellout 51. Holiday for Sinners 52. Bright Road 53. The Marauders 55.

Les Mayfield Encino Man 92. Miracle on 34th Street 94. Flubber 97. Blue Streak 99. American Outlaws 01.

Archie Mayo My Man 28. Is Everybody Happy? 29. Courage 30. Doorway to Hell 30. Bought 31. Illicit 31. Svengali 31. Night after Night 32. Street of Women 32. Convention City 33. Ever in My Heart 33. The Life of Jimmy Dolan 33. The Mayor of Hell 33. Bordertown 34. Desirable 34. Gambling Lady 34. The Man with Two Faces 34. Go Into Your Dance 35. The Case of the Lucky Legs 35. Give Me Your Heart 36. I Married a Doctor 36. The Petrified Forest 36. Black Legion 37. Call It a Day 37. It's Love I'm After 37. The Adventures of Marco Polo 38. Youth Takes a Fling 38. They Shall Have Music 39. Four Sons 40. The House across the Bay 40. Charley's Aunt 41. Confirm or Deny 41. The Great American Broadcast 41. Moontide 42. Orchestra Wives 42. Crash Dive 43. A Night in Casablanca 46. Angel on My Shoulder 46.

Paul Mazursky Bob & Carol & Ted & Alice 69. Alex in Wonderland 70. Blume in Love 73. Harry and Tonto 74. Next Stop Greenwich Village 75. An Unmarried Woman 78. Willie and Phil 80. Tempest 82. Moscow on the Hudson 84. Down and Out in Beverly Hills 85. Moon over Parador 88. Enemies, a Love Story 89. Scenes from a Mall 90. The Pickle 93. Faithful 96.

Leo McCarey We Faw Down 28. Liberty 29. Wrong Again 29. Let's Go Native 30. Indiscreet 31. The Kid from Spain 32. Duck Soup 33. Belle of the Nineties 34. Six of a Kind 34. Ruggles of Red Gap 35. The Milky Way 36. Make Way for Tomorrow 37. The Awful Truth 37. Love Affair 39. Once Upon a Honeymoon 42. Going My Way 44. The Bells of St Mary's 45. Good Sam 48. My Son John 52. An Affair to Remember 57. Rally Round the Flag Boys 58. Satan Never Sleeps 62.

Ray McCarey Pack Up Your Troubles 31. Scram! 32. Millions in the Air 35. Accent on Love 41. Murder among Friends 41. The Perfect Snob 41. A Gentleman at Heart 42. Passport to Destiny 43. Atlantic City 44. The Falcon's Alibi 46. The Gay Intruders 48.

Michael McCarthy Assassin for Hire 51. Mystery Junction 51. Shadow of a Man 54. It's Never Too Late 56. The Traitor 57. Operation Amsterdam 58.

Frank McDonald Broadway Hostess 35. The Murder of Dr Harrigan 35. Boulder Dam 36. Isle of Fury 36. Smart Blonde 36. Flirting with Fate 38. No Hands on the Clock 41. Alaska Highway 43. One Body Too Many 44. Scared Stiff 45. Tell It to a Star 45. My Pal Trigger 46. Hit Parade of 1947 47. The Purple Gang 60. Gunfight at Comanche Creek 63.

Bernard McEveety Ride beyond Vengeance 66. The Brotherhood of Satan 70. Napoleon and Samantha 72. One Little Indian 73. The Bears and I 74.

Vincent McEveety Firecreek 67. Million Dollar Duck 71. Charley and the Angel 74. Superdad 74. The Castaway Cowboy 74. Gus 76. The Strongest Man in the World 76. Treasure of Matecumbe 76. Herbie Goes to Monte Carlo 77. The Apple Dumpling Gang Rides Again 79. Herbie Goes Bananas 80. The Watcher in the Woods 80. Amy 81.

Hamilton McFadden Riders of the Purple Sage 31. The Black Camel 31. The Man Who Dared 33. As Husbands Go 34. Stand Up and Cheer 34. Elinor Norton 35.

William McGann I Like Your Nerve 31. Man of Iron 35. The Case of the Black Cat 36. Two against the World 36. Alcatraz Island 37. Marry the Girl 37. Penrod and Sam 37. Sh! The Octopus 37. Girls on Probation 38. Blackwell's Island 39. The Parson of Panamint 41. American Empire 42. In Old California 42. Tombstone (The Town Too Tough to Die) 42. Frontier Badmen 43.

Joe McGrath Casino Royale 67. Thirty Is a Dangerous Age, Cynthia 67. The Bliss of Mrs Blossom 68. The Magic Christian 69. Digby: the Biggest Dog in the World 73. The Great McGonagall 74. Rising Damp 80.

Andrew V. McLaglen The Abductors 57. McLintock 63. Shenandoah 65. Monkeys Go Home 66. The Rare Breed 66. The Ballad of Josie 67. The Way West 67. Bandolero! 68. Hellfighters 68. The Devil's Brigade 68. The Undefeated 69. Chisum 70. Fools Parade 71. One More Train to Rob 71. Something Big 71. Cahill, US Marshal 73. The Last Hard Men 76. The Wild Geese 78. North Sea Hijack 79. Sergeant Steiner 79. The Sea Wolves 80. Sahara 84. Return from the River Kwai 88.

Norman Z. McLeod Finn and Hattie 30. Monkey Business 31. Horse Feathers 32. If I Had a Million 32. The Miracle Man 32. A Lady's Profession 33. Alice in Wonderland 33. Mama Loves Papa 33. It's a Gift 34. Many Happy Returns 34. Melody in Spring 34. Coronado 35. Here Comes Cookie 35. Pennies from Heaven 36. Mind Your Own Business 37. Topper 37. Merrily We Live 38. There Goes My Heart 38. Remember? 39. Topper Takes a Trip 39. Lady Be Good 41. Jackass Mail 42. Panama Hattie 42. The Powers Girl 42. The Kid from Brooklyn 46. Road to Rio 47. The Secret Life of Walter Mitty 47. Isn't It Romantic 48. The Paleface 48. Let's Dance 50. My Favorite Spy 51. Never Wave at a WAC 52. Casanova's Big Night 54. Alias Jesse James 59.

John McNaughton The Borrower 89. Henry: Portrait of a Serial Killer 90. Mad Dog and Glory 92. Normal Life 96. Wild Things 98.

Henry McRae Tarzan the Tiger 29. Terry of the Times 30. The Indians Are Coming 30. The Lightning Express 30. Detective Lloyd 32. The Lost Special 32.

John McTiernan Nomads 85. Predator 87. Die Hard 88. The Hunt for Red October 90. Medicine Man 92. Last Action Hero 93. Die Hard with a Vengeance 95. The 13th Warrior 99. The Thomas Crown Affair 99. Rollerball 02.

Peter Medak Negatives 68. A Day in the Death of Joe Egg 71. The Ruling Class 72. The Odd Job 78. The Changeling 79. Zorro the Gay Blade 81. The Men's Club 86. The Krays 90. Let Him Have It 91. Romeo Is Bleeding 93. Pontiac Moon 94. Species II 98.

Jean-Pierre Melville Les Enfants Terribles 50. Léon Morin, Priest 61. The Samurai 67. The Army in the Shadows 69. The Red Circle 70. Dirty Money 72.

Lothar Mendes Dangerous Curves 29. Interference 29. The Four Feathers 29. The Marriage Playground 29. Paramount on Parade 30. Ladies' Man 31. Payment Deferred 32. Strangers in Love 32. Luxury Liner 33. Jew Suss 34. The Man Who Could Work Miracles 36. Moonlight Sonata 37. International Squadron 41. Flight for Freedom 43. Tampico 44. The Walls Came Tumbling Down 46.

Jiri Menzel Closely Observed Trains 66. Capricious Summer 68. Larks on a String 69. Those Wonderful Movie Cranks 78. My Sweet Little Village 85. The Life and Extraordinary Adventures of Private Ivan Chonkin 94.

William Cameron Menzies Always Goodbye 31. The Spider 31. Almost Married 32. Chandu the Magician 32. I Loved You Wednesday 33. Wharf Angel 34. The Green Cockatoo 40. Address Unknown 44. Drums in the Deep South 51. The Maze 53.

Alan Metter Girls Just Want to Have Fun 85. Back to School 86. Moving 88. Cold Dog Soup 89. Police Academy 7: Mission to Moscow 94.

Nicholas Meyer Time after Time 80. Star Trek: The Wrath of Khan 82. Volunteers 85. The Deceivers 88. Company Business 91. Star Trek VI: The Undiscovered Country 91.

Russ Meyer Fanny Hill 65. Faster, Pussycat! Kill! Kill! 66. Common-Law Cabin 67. Finders Keepers, Lovers Weepers! 68. Vixen 68. Cherry, Harry and Raquel! 69. Beyond the Valley of the Dolls 70. The Seven Minutes 71. Supervixens 75.

Nikita Mikhalkov A Private Conversation 83. Black Eyes 87. Urga 91. Burnt by the Sun 94. The Barber of Siberia 99.

Christopher Miles The Virgin and the Gypsy 70. A Time for Loving 71. The Maids 74. That Lucky Touch 75. Priest of Love 81. The Clandestine Marriage 99.

Lewis Milestone The Cave Man 26. The Kid Brother 27. New York Nights 29. All Quiet on the Western Front 30. The Front Page 31. Rain 32. Hallelujah, I'm a Bum 33. The Captain Hates the Sea 34. Paris in Spring 35. Anything Goes 36. The General Died at Dawn 36. Of Mice and Men 39. The Night of Nights 39. Lucky Partners 40. My Life with Caroline 41. Edge of Darkness 43. North Star 43. The Purple Heart 44. A Walk in the Sun 46. The Strange Love of Martha Ivers 46. Arch of Triumph 48. No Minor Vices 48. The Red Pony 49. Halls of Montezuma 50. Kangaroo 52. Les Misérables 52. Melba 53. They Who Dare 53. Pork Chop Hill 59. Ocean's Eleven 60. Mutiny on the Bounty 62.

John Milius Dillinger 73. The Wind and the Lion 75. Big Wednesday 78. Conan the Barbarian 81. Red Dawn 84. Farewell to the King 88. Flight of the Intruder 91.

Ray Milland A Man Alone 55. Lisbon 56. The Safecracker 58. Panic in Year Zero 62. Hostile Witness 68.

Claude Miller The Inquisitor 81. An Impudent Girl 85. La Petite Voleuse 88. The Accompanist 92. Class Trip 98. Betty Fisher et Autres Histoires 01.

David Miller Billy the Kid 41. Flying Tigers 42. Love Happy 49. Top o' the Morning 49. Our Very Own 50. Saturday's Hero 51. Sudden Fear 52. Beautiful Stranger 54. Diane 56. The Opposite Sex 56. The Story of Esther Costello 57. Happy Anniversary 59. Midnight Lace 60. Back Street 61. Lonely Are the Brave 62. Captain Newman MD 63. Hammerhead 68. Executive Action 73. Bittersweet Love 76.

George Miller The Man from Snowy River 82. The Aviator 85. Les Patterson Saves the World 87. The Neverending Story II: The Next Chapter 90. Frozen Assets 92. Over the Hill 93. Andre 94. Zeus and Roxanne 97.

George Miller Mad Max 79. Mad Max 2 81. Twilight Zone: The Movie 83. Mad Max Beyond Thunderdome 85. The Witches of Eastwick 87. Lorenzo's Oil 92. Babe: Pig in the City 98.

Robert Ellis Miller Any Wednesday 66. Sweet November 68. The Heart Is a Lonely Hunter 68. The Buttercup Chain 70. The Girl from Petrovka 74. The Baltimore Bullet 80. Reuben, Reuben 82. Hawks 88. Bed and Breakfast 92. Brenda Starr 92.

Robert Milton Charming Sinners 29. Behind the Make-up 30. Outward Bound 30. Devotion 31. Husband's Holiday 31. Strange Evidence 32. Westward Passage 32. Belladonna 34.

Steve Miner Friday the 13th Part II 81. Friday the 13th Part III 82. House 86. Soul Man 86. Warlock 88. Wild Hearts Can't Be Broken 91. Forever Young 92. My Father, the Hero 94. Big Bully 96. Halloween H20 98. Lake Placid 99.

Vincente Minnelli Cabin in the Sky 43. I Dood It! 43. Meet Me in St Louis 44. The Clock 45. Yolanda and the Thief 45. Undercurrent 46. Ziegfeld Follies 46. The Pirate 48. Madame Bovary 49. Father of the Bride 50. An American in Paris 51. Father's Little Dividend 51. The Bad and the Beautiful 52. The Band Wagon 53. The Story of Three Loves 53. Brigadoon 54. The Long Long Trailer 54. Kismet 55. The Cobweb 55. Lust for Life 56. Tea and Sympathy 56. Designing Woman 57. Gigi 58. Some Came Running 58. The Reluctant Débutante 58. Bells Are Ringing 60. Home from the Hill 60. The Four Horsemen of the Apocalypse 61. The Courtship of Eddie's Father 62. Two Weeks in Another Town 62. Goodbye Charlie 64. The Sandpiper 65. On a Clear Day You Can See Forever 70. A Matter of Time 76.

Kenji Mizoguchi The Life of Oharu 52. Ugetsu Monogatari 53. Sansho the Bailiff 54. Tales of the Taira Clan 55. Street of Shame 56.

Edouard Molinaro To Commit a Murder 67. Uncle Benjamin 69. L'Emmerdeur 73. The Pink Telephone 75. La Cage aux Folles 78. La Cage aux Folles II 80. Just the Way You Are 84. Beaumarchais 96.

Robert Montgomery The Lady in the Lake 46. Ride the Pink Horse 47. Once More My Darling 49. Your Witness 50. The Gallant Hours 59.

Philippe Mora Brother Can You Spare a Dime? 75. The Return of Captain Invincible 82. A Breed Apart 84. Howling II … Your Sister Is a Werewolf 85. Death of a Soldier 86. The Howling III 87. Communion 90.

Paul Morrissey The Chelsea Girls 66. Flesh 68. Lonesome Cowboys 68. Trash 70. Heat 72. Dracula 74. The Hound of the Baskervilles 77.

Terry Morse On Trial 39. Smashing the Money Ring 39. British Intelligence 40. Fog Island 45. Unknown World 51. Young Dillinger 64.

Russell Mulcahy Razorback 84. Highlander 86. Highlander II – The Quickening 90. Ricochet 91. Blue Ice 92. The Real McCoy 93. The Shadow 94. Resurrection 99.

Robert Mulligan Fear Strikes Out 57. The Rat Race 60. Come September 61. The Great Imposter 61. The Spiral Road 62. To Kill a Mockingbird 62. Baby, the Rain Must Fall 64. Love with the Proper Stranger 64. Inside Daisy Clover 65. Up the Down Staircase 67. The Stalking Moon 68. The Pursuit of Happiness 70. Summer of '42 71. The Other 72. The Nickel Ride 75. Bloodbrothers 78. Same Time, Next Year 78. Kiss Me Goodbye 82. The Man in the Moon 91.

F. W. Murnau Nosferatu 21. The Last Laugh 24. Faust 26. Sunrise 27. City Girl 30. Tabu 31.

Geoff Murphy Goodbye Pork Pie 80. Utu 83. The Quiet Earth 85. Young Guns II 90. Freejack 92. Blind Side 93. Under Siege 2: Dark Territory 95. Fortress 2: Re-entry 00.

Ralph Murphy 70,000 Witnesses 32. Song of the Eagle 33. Menace 34. The Great Flirtation 34. The Notorious Sophie Lang 34. Collegiate 35. McFadden's Flats 35. Men without Names 35. Night Club Scandal 37. Partners in Crime 37. Top of the Town 37. Our Neighbours the Carters 39. I Want a Divorce 40. Glamour Boy 41. Mrs Wiggs of the Cabbage Patch 42. Night Plane from Chungking 42. Pacific Blackout 42. Salute for Three 43. Rainbow Island 44. The Man in Half Moon Street 44. Sunbonnet Sue 45. The Town Went Wild 45. The Lady and the Bandit 51. Captain Pirate 52. Lady in the Iron Mask 52.

Mira Nair Salaam Bombay! 88. Mississippi Masala

91. The Perez Family 95. Kama Sutra 96. Monsoon Wedding 01.

Silvio Narizzano Under Ten Flags 60. Fanatic 65. Georgy Girl 66. Blue 68. Loot 70. Redneck 72. Why Shoot the Teacher? 76. The Class of Miss McMichael 78.

Ronald Neame Take My Life 47. The Golden Salamander 49. The Card 52. The Million Pound Note 53. The Man Who Never Was 55. The Seventh Sin 57. Windom's Way 57. The Horse's Mouth 58. Tunes of Glory 60. Escape from Zahrain 61. I Could Go on Singing 63. The Chalk Garden 64. Mister Moses 65. A Man Could Get Killed 66. Gambit 66. The Prime of Miss Jean Brodie 69. Scrooge 70. The Poseidon Adventure 72. The Odessa File 74. Meteor 79. Hopscotch 80. First Monday in October 81.

Hal Needham Smokey and the Bandit 77. Hooper 78. The Villain 79. Smokey and the Bandit II 80. The Cannonball Run 80. Cannonball Run II 83. Stroker Ace 83. Body Slam 87.

Jean Negulesco Singapore Woman 41. The Conspirators 44. The Mask of Dimitrios 44. Humoresque 46. Nobody Lives Forever 46. Three Strangers 46. Deep Valley 47. Britannia Mews 48. Johnny Belinda 48. Road House 48. Under My Skin 49. The Mudlark 50. Three Came Home 50. Take Care of My Little Girl 51. Lure of the Wilderness 52. Lydia Bailey 52. Phone Call from a Stranger 52. How to Marry a Millionaire 53. Scandal at Scourie 53. Titanic 53. Three Coins in the Fountain 54. Woman's World 54. Daddy Longlegs 55. The Rains of Ranchipur 55. Boy on a Dolphin 57. A Certain Smile 58. The Gift of Love 58. Count Your Blessings 59. The Best of Everything 59. Jessica 62. The Pleasure Seekers 64. Hello Goodbye 70.

Roy William Neill The Menace 32. The Circus Queen Murder 33. Blind Date 34. Jealousy 34. Mills of the Gods 34. The Ninth Guest 34. Whirlpool 34. The Black Room 35. Gypsy 36. Dr Syn 37. A Gentleman's Gentleman 39. Hoots Mon 39. The Good Old Days 39. Eyes of the Underworld 42. Madame Spy 42. Sherlock Holmes and the Secret Weapon 42. Frankenstein Meets the Wolf Man 43. Rhythm of the Islands 43. Sherlock Holmes Faces Death 43. Sherlock Holmes in Washington 43. Gypsy Wildcat 44. Spider Woman 44. The House of Fear 44. The Pearl of Death 44. The Scarlet Claw 44. Pursuit to Algiers 45. The Woman in Green 45. Black Angel 46. Dressed to Kill 46. Terror by Night 46.

James Neilson Night Passage 57. Moon Pilot 61. Bon Voyage 62. Dr Syn Alias the Scarecrow 63. Summer Magic 63. The Moon Spinners 64. The Adventures of Bullwhip Griffin 65. The Gentle Giant 67. Where Angels Go, Trouble Follows 68. Flare Up 69.

Gary Nelson Santee 72. Freaky Friday 76. The Black Hole 79. Jimmy the Kid 82. Allan Quatermain and the Lost City of Gold 87.

Ralph Nelson Requiem for a Heavyweight 62. Lilies of the Field 63. Soldier in the Rain 63. Fate Is the Hunter 64. Father Goose 64. Once a Thief 65. Duel at Diablo 66. Counterpoint 67. Charly 68. Tick, Tick, Tick… 69. Soldier Blue 70. Flight of the Doves 71. The Wrath of God 72. The Wilby Conspiracy 75. Embryo 76. A Hero Ain't Nothing but a Sandwich 77.

Kurt Neumann King for a Night 33. The Big Cage 33. The Secret of the Blue Room 33. Half a Sinner 34. Alias Mary Dow 35. Rainbow on the River 36. Espionage 37. Make a Wish 37. Ambush 38. Wide Open Faces 38. Island of Lost Men 39. Unmarried 39. A Night at Earl Carroll's 40. Ellery Queen, Master Detective 40. Fall In 43. The Unknown Guest 43. Tarzan and the Amazons 45. Tarzan and the Huntress 47. Bad Men of Tombstone 49. Rocketship X-M 50. The Kid from Texas 50. Cattle Drive 51. Hiawatha 52. Son of Ali Baba 52. The Ring 52. Tarzan and the She-Devil 53. Carnival Story 54. Mohawk 56. The Fly 58. Watusi 59.

Mike Newell The Awakening 80. Bad Blood 81. Dance with a Stranger 85. The Good Father 86. Amazing Grace and Chuck 87. Soursweet 88. Enchanted April 91. Into the West 92. An Awfully Big Adventure 94. Four Weddings and a Funeral 94. Donnie Brasco 97. Pushing Tin 99.

Sam Newfield Knight of the Plains 38. The Lone Rider Ambushed 41. The Lone Rider Fights Back 41. The Lone Rider in Ghost Town 41. The Mad Monster 42. Dead Men Walk 43. The Monster Maker 44. The Flying Serpent 45. Gas House Kids 46. Adventure Island 47. The Counterfeiters 48.

Joseph M. Newman Abandoned 49. The Great Dan Patch 49. 711 Ocean Drive 50. I'll Get You for This 50. Love Nest 51. The Guy Who Came Back 51. Pony Soldier 52. Red Skies of Montana 52. The Outcasts of Poker Flat 52. Dangerous Crossing 53. The Human Jungle 54. Kiss of Fire 55. This Island Earth 55. Flight to Hong Kong 56. Fort Massacre 58. Gunfight at Dodge City 58. Tarzan the Ape Man 59. The Big Circus 59. A Thunder of Drums 61. King of the Roaring Twenties 61. The George Raft Story 61.

Paul Newman Rachel, Rachel 68. Sometimes a Great Notion 71. The Effect of Gamma Rays on Man-in-the-Moon Marigolds 72. Harry and Son 84. The Glass Menagerie 87.

Fred Newmeyer Doctor Jack 22. Grandma's Boy 22. Safety Last 23. Why Worry? 23. Girl Shy 24. Hot Water 24. The Freshman 25. Fast and Loose 30. General Spanky 36.

Fred Niblo The Mark of Zorro 20. Blood and Sand 22. Ben-Hur 25. The Temptress 27. The Mysterious Lady 28. Redemption 30.

George Nicholls Jnr Anne of Green Gables 34. Finishing School 34. Chasing Yesterday 35. Chatterbox 35. The Return of Peter Grimm 35. M'liss 36. The Witness Chair 36. Portia on Trial 37. The Soldier and the Lady 37. Army Girl 38. Man of Conquest 39. The Marines Fly High 40.

Mike Nichols Who's Afraid of Virginia Woolf? 66. The Graduate 67. Catch 22 70. Carnal Knowledge 71. The Day of the Dolphin 73. The Fortune 75. Silkwood 83. Heartburn 86. Biloxi Blues 88. Working Girl 88. Postcards from the Edge 90. Regarding Henry 91. Wolf 94. The Birdcage 96. Primary Colors 98. What Planet Are You From? 00.

William Nigh Mr Wu 27. Thunder 29. Mystery Liner 34. His Night Out 35. Mysterious Mr Wong 35. Boy of the Streets 37. Hoosier Schoolboy 37. Mutiny in the Big House 39. Streets of New York 39. The Ape 40. Mob Town 41. City of Silent Men 42. The Strange Case of Doctor RX 42. Corregidor 43. The Ghost and the Guest 43. Where Are Your Children? 43. Are These Our Parents? 44. Divorce 45.

Leonard Nimoy Star Trek III: The Search for Spock 84. Star Trek IV: The Voyage Home 86. Three Men and a Baby 87. The Good Mother 88. Funny about Love 90. Holy Matrimony 94.

Leslie Norman The Night My Number Came Up 54. X the Unknown 56. The Shiralee 57. Dunkirk 58. Summer of the Seventeenth Doll 59. The Long and the Short and the Tall 60. Mix Me a Person 61. Spare the Rod 61.

Phillip Noyce Newsfront 78. Heatwave 82. Shadows of the Peacock 87. Dead Calm 88. Blind Fury 89. Patriot Games 92. Sliver 93. Clear and Present Danger 94. The Saint 97. The Bone Collector 99. Rabbit-Proof Fence 02. The Quiet American 02.

Elliott Nugent The Mouthpiece 32. If I Were Free 33. Three Cornered Moon 33. Enter Madame 34. Love in Bloom 34. She Loves Me Not 34. Two Alone 34. And So They Were Married 35. College Scandal 35. Splendor 35. It's All Yours 37. Give Me a Sailor 38. Professor Beware 38. Never Say Die 39. The Cat and the Canary 39. Nothing but the Truth 41. The Male Animal 42. The Crystal Ball 43. Up in Arms 44. My Favorite Brunette 47. Welcome Stranger 47. My Girl Tisa 48. Mr Belvedere Goes to College 49. The Great Gatsby 49. My Outlaw Brother 51. Just for You 52.

Jim O'Connolly The Hi-Jackers 63. Smokescreen 64. Berserk! 67. The Valley of Gwangi 68. Crooks and Coronets 69. Tower of Evil 72.

Pat O'Connor Cal 84. A Month in the Country 87. Stars and Bars 88. The January Man 89. Fools of Fortune 90. Circle of Friends 95. Inventing the Abbots 97. Dancing at Lughnasa 98.

George More O'Ferrall The Woman with No Name 50. Angels One Five 52. The Holly and the Ivy 52. The Heart of the Matter 53. The Green Scarf 54. Three Cases of Murder 54. The Woman for Joe 55.

Gerry O'Hara The Pleasure Girls 65. Maroc 7 67. Amsterdam Affair 68. All the Right Noises 69. The Brute 75. Leopard in the Snow 77. The Bitch 79.

Arch Oboler Bewitched 45. Strange Holiday 45. The Arnelo Affair 46. Five 51. Bwana Devil 52. The Bubble 66.

Laurence Olivier Henry V 44. Hamlet 48. Richard III 55. The Prince and the Showgirl 57. The Three Sisters 70.

Max Ophüls Liebelei 32. Tendre Ennemie 38. Sans Lendemain 40. Caught 48. Letter from an Unknown Woman 48. The Exile 48. The Reckless Moment 49. La Ronde 50. Le Plaisir 52. Madame De… 53. Lola Montes 55.

Nagisa Oshima Death by Hanging 68. Diary of a Shinjuku Thief 69. Ai No Corrida 76. Ai No Borei 78. Merry Christmas, Mr Lawrence 82. Max Mon Amour 86. Gohatto 99.

Gerd Oswald A Kiss before Dying 56. Crime of Passion 56. The Brass Legend 56. Paris Holiday 57. Valerie 57. Screaming Mimi 58. Agent for Harm 66. Bunny O'Hare 71.

Idrissa Ouédraogo The Choice 87. Yaaba 89. Tilai 90. Samba Traoré 92. Le Cri du Coeur 94. Kini and Adams 97.

Cliff Owen Offbeat 60. A Prize of Arms 61. The Wrong Arm of the Law 62. A Man Could Get Killed 66. That Riviera Touch 66. The Magnificent Two 67. The Vengeance of She 68. Ooh, You Are Awful 72. Steptoe and Son 72. No Sex Please, We're British 73. The Bawdy Adventures of Tom Jones 76.

Frank Oz The Dark Crystal 82. The Muppets Take Manhattan 84. Little Shop of Horrors 86. Dirty Rotten Scoundrels 88. What about Bob? 91. Housesitter 92. The Indian in the Cupboard 95. In & Out 97. Bowfinger 98. The Score 01.

G. W. Pabst Joyless Street 25. Secrets of a Soul 26. The Love of Jeanne Ney 27. Diary of a Lost Girl 29. Pandora's Box 29. The White Hell of Pitz Palu 29. Die Dreigroschenoper 31. Kameradschaft 31. Don Quixote 33. A Modern Hero 34. Jackboot Mutiny 55.

Marcel Pagnol César 36. Harvest 37. La Femme du Boulanger 38. La Fille du Puisatier 46. Manon des Sources 52.

Alan J. Pakula The Sterile Cuckoo 69. Klute 71. Love and Pain and the Whole Damn Thing 72. The Parallax View 74. All the President's Men 76. Comes a Horseman 78. Starting Over 79. Rollover 81. Sophie's Choice 82. Dream Lover 86. Orphans 87. See You in the Morning 88. Presumed Innocent 90. Consenting Adults 92. The Pelican Brief 93. The Devil's Own 97.

George Pal Tom Thumb 58. The Time Machine 60. Atlantis, the Lost Continent 61. The Wonderful World of the Brothers Grimm 62. Seven Faces of Dr Lao 64.

Norman Panama The Reformer and the Redhead 50. Callaway Went Thataway 51. Strictly Dishonourable 51. Above and Beyond 52. Knock on Wood 54. The Court Jester 55. That Certain Feeling 56. The Trap 58. Li'l Abner 59. Road to Hong Kong 62. Not with My Wife, You Don't! 66. How to Commit Marriage 69. The Maltese Bippy 69. I Will … I Will … for Now 75. Barnaby and Me 77.

Jerry Paris Don't Raise the Bridge, Lower the River 67. Never a Dull Moment 67. How Sweet It Is 68. The Grasshopper 69. Viva Max 69. The Star Spangled Girl 71. Police Academy 2: Their First Assignment 85. Police Academy 3: Back in Training 86.

Alan Parker Bugsy Malone 76. Midnight Express 78. Fame 80. Shoot the Moon 81. Pink Floyd The Wall 82. Birdy 84. Angel Heart 87. Mississippi Burning 88. Come See the Paradise 90. The Commitments 91. The Road to Wellville 94. Evita 96. Angela's Ashes 99. The Life of David Gale 02.

Gordon Parks The Learning Tree 69. Shaft 71. Shaft's Big Score! 72. The Super Cops 74. Leadbelly 76.

Gianfranco Parolini Sartana 68. Sabata 69. The Bounty Hunters 70. Return of Sabata 71. God's Gun 76.

Robert Parrish Cry Danger 51. The Mob 51. Assignment Paris 52. My Pal Gus 52. Rough Shoot 52. The San Francisco Story 52. The Purple Plain 54. Lucy Gallant 55. Fire Down Below 57. Saddle the Wind 58. The Wonderful Country 59. In the French Style 62. Up from the Beach 65. Casino Royale 67. The Bobo 67. Duffy 68. Journey to the Far Side of the Sun 69. A Town Called Bastard 71. The Marseille Contract 74.

James Parrott Habeas Corpus 28. Should Married Men Go Home? 28. Their Purple Moment 28. Two Tars 28. Perfect Day 29. The Hoosegow 29. They Go Boom 29. Another Fine Mess 30. Below Zero 30. Blotto 30. Brats 30. Hog Wild 30. Night Owls 30. The Laurel and Hardy Murder Case 30. Be Big 31. Pardon Us 31. County Hospital 32. Helpmates 32. The Chimp 32. The Music Box 32. Twice Two 33.

Gordon Parry Bond Street 48. Third Time Lucky 48. Now Barabbas… 49. Midnight Episode 50. Tom Brown's Schooldays 51. Golden Arrow 52. Front Page Story 53. Innocents in Paris 53. Women of Twilight 53. Fast and Loose 54. A Yank in Ermine 55. A Touch of the Sun 56. Sailor Beware! 56. Tread Softly Stranger 58.

Pier Paolo Pasolini Accattone 61. Mamma Roma 62. The Gospel According to St Matthew 64. Hawks and Sparrows 66. Oedipus Rex 67. Theorem 68. Medea 70. The Canterbury Tales 71. The Decameron 71. Il Fiore delle Mille e una Notte 74. 120 Days of Sodom 75.

Ivan Passer Born to Win 71. Law and Disorder 74. Silver Bears 77. Cutter and Bone 81. Creator 85. Haunted Summer 88.

Richard Pearce Heartland 79. Country 84. No Mercy 86. Leap of Faith 92. A Family Thing 96.

Sam Peckinpah The Deadly Companions 61. Ride the High Country 62. Major Dundee 64. The Wild Bunch 69. The Ballad of Cable Hogue 70. Straw Dogs 71. Junior Bonner 72. The Getaway 72. Pat Garrett and Billy the Kid 73. Bring Me the Head of Alfredo Garcia 74. The Killer Elite 75. Cross of Iron 77. Convoy 78. The Osterman Weekend 83.

Larry Peerce Goodbye Columbus 69. Ash Wednesday 73. The Other Side of the Mountain 75. Two Minute Warning 76. The Other Side of the Mountain Part Two 77. The Bell Jar 79. Wired 89.

Anthony Pelissier The History of Mr Polly 48. The Rocking Horse Winner 49. Encore 51. Night without Stars 51. Meet Me Tonight 52. Meet Mr Lucifer 53. Personal Affair 53.

Arthur Penn The Left Handed Gun 58. The Miracle Worker 62. Mickey One 65. The Chase 66. Bonnie and Clyde 67. Alice's Restaurant 69. Little Big Man 70. Night Moves 75. The Missouri Breaks 76. Four Friends 81. Target 85. Dead of Winter 86.

C. Pennington-Richards The Oracle 52. The Hour of Decision 57. Double Bunk 60. Inn for Trouble 60. Dentist on the Job 61. Mystery Submarine 62. Ladies Who Do 63. A Challenge for Robin Hood 67.

Frank Perry David and Lisa 62. The Swimmer 68. Last Summer 69. Diary of a Mad Housewife 70. Doc 71. Play It as It Lays 72. Rancho De Luxe 74. Man on a Swing 75. Mommie Dearest 81. Monsignor 82. Compromising Positions 85. Hello Again 87.

Wolfgang Petersen The Boat 81. The Neverending Story 84. Enemy Mine 85. Shattered 91. In the Line of Fire 93. Outbreak 95. Air Force One 97. The Perfect Storm 00.

Daniel Petrie The Bramble Bush 60. A Raisin in the Sun 61. The Main Attraction 62. Stolen Hours 63. The Idol 66. The Spy with a Cold Nose 66. The Neptune Factor 72. Buster and Billie 73. Lifeguard 76. The Betsy 77. Fort Apache, the Bronx 80. Resurrection 80. Six Pack 82. The Bay Boy 84. Square Dance 86. Cocoon: The Return 88. Lassie 94.

Donald Petrie Mystic Pizza 88. Grumpy Old Men 93. Richie Rich 94. The Favor 94. The Associate 96. My Favorite Martian 99. Miss Congeniality 00.

Joseph Pevney Shakedown 50. Undercover Girl 50. Air Cadet 51. Iron Man 51. Meet Danny Wilson 51. The Lady from Texas 51. The Strange Door 51. Because of You 52. Flesh and Fury 52. Just Across the Street 52. Back to God's Country 53. Desert Legion 53. It Happens Every Thursday 53. 3 Ring Circus 54. Playgirl 54. Yankee Pasha 54. Foxfire 55. Six Bridges to Cross 55. The Female on the Beach 55. Away All Boats 56. Congo Crossing 56. Istanbul 56. Man of a Thousand Faces 57. Tammy and the Bachelor 57. Torpedo Run 58. Twilight for the Gods 58. Cash McCall 60. The Crowded Sky 60. The Plunderers 60. Portrait of a Mobster 61. The Night of the Grizzly 66.

Maurice Pialat L'Enfance Nue 68. Loulou 80. To Our Loves 83. Police 85. Under Satan's Sun 87. Van Gogh 91.

Irving Pichel The Most Dangerous Game 32. Before Dawn 33. She 35. The Sheik Steps Out 37. Earthbound 40. Hudson's Bay 40. The Great Commandment 40. The Man I Married 40. Dance Hall 41. Life Begins at Eight-Thirty 42. Secret Agent of Japan 42. The Pied Piper 42. Happy Land 43. The Moon Is Down 43. And Now Tomorrow 44. A Medal for Benny 45. Tomorrow Is Forever 45. Colonel Effingham's Raid 46. O.S.S. 46. Temptation 46. The Bride Wore Boots 46. Something in the Wind 47. They Won't Believe Me 47. Mr Peabody and the Mermaid 48. The Miracle of the Bells 48. Destination Moon 50. Quicksand 50. The Great Rupert 50. Santa Fe 51. Martin Luther 53.

Robert Pirosh Go for Broke 51. Washington Story 52. Valley of the Kings 54. The Girl Rush 55. Spring Reunion 56.

Sidney Poitier Buck and the Preacher 71. A Warm December 72. Uptown Saturday Night 74. Let's Do It Again 75. A Piece of the Action 77. Stir Crazy 80. Hanky Panky 82. Ghost Dad 90.

Roman Polanski Knife in the Water 62. Repulsion 65. Cul de Sac 66. The Fearless Vampire Killers, or Pardon Me, Your Teeth Are in My Neck 67. Rosemary's Baby 68. Macbeth 72. What? 72. Chinatown 74. The Tenant 76. Tess 79. Pirates 86. Frantic 88. Bitter Moon 92. Death and the Maiden 95. The Ninth Gate 99. The Pianist 02.

Sydney Pollack The Slender Thread 65. This Property Is Condemned 66. The Scalphunters 68. The Swimmer 68. Castle Keep 69. They Shoot Horses, Don't They? 69. Jeremiah Johnson 72. The Way We Were 73. The Yakuza 75. Three Days of the Condor 75. Bobby Deerfield 77. The Electric Horseman 79. Absence of Malice 81. Tootsie 82. Out of Africa 85. Havana 90. The Firm 93. Sabrina 95. Random Hearts 99.

George Pollock Broth of a Boy 58. Rooney 58. Don't Panic, Chaps! 59. And the Same To You 60. Murder She Said 61. Village of Daughters 61. Kill or Cure 62. Murder at the Gallop 63. Murder Ahoy 64. Murder Most Foul 64. Ten Little Indians 66.

Ted Post The Legend of Tom Dooley 59. Hang 'em High 67. Beneath the Planet of the Apes 69. Magnum Force 73. The Baby 73. The Harrad Experiment 73. W.H.I.F.F.S. 75. Good Guys Wear Black 77. Go Tell the Spartans 78.

H. C. Potter Beloved Enemy 36. Wings over Honolulu 37. Romance in the Dark 38. Shopworn Angel 38. The Cowboy and the Lady 38. Blackmail 39. The Story of Vernon and Irene Castle 39. Second Chorus 40. Hellzapoppin 42. Mr Lucky 43. Victory through Air Power 43. A Likely Story 47. The Farmer's Daughter 47. Mr Blandings Builds His Dream House 48. The Time of Your Life 48. You Gotta Stay Happy 48. The Miniver Story 50. Three for the Show 55. Top Secret Affair 56.

Dick Powell Split Second 53. The Conqueror 55. You Can't Run Away from It 56. The Enemy Below 57. The Hunters 58.

Michael Powell The Night of the Party 34. The Love Test 35. The Phantom Light 35. The Man Behind the Mask 36. Edge of the World 37. The Lion Has Wings 39. The Spy in Black 39. Contraband 40. The Thief of Baghdad 40. 49th Parallel 41. One of Our Aircraft Is Missing 41. The Life and Death of Colonel Blimp 43. A Canterbury Tale 44. I Know Where I'm Going 45. A Matter of Life and Death 46. Black Narcissus 47. The Red Shoes 48. The Small Back Room 49. Gone to Earth 50. The Elusive Pimpernel 50. The Tales of Hoffman 51. Oh Rosalinda! 55. Ill Met by Moonlight 56. The Battle of the River Plate 56. Honeymoon 59. Peeping Tom 59. The Queen's Guards 60. They're a Weird Mob 66. Age of Consent 69.

Otto Preminger Danger, Love at Work 37. Margin for Error 43. In the Meantime, Darling 44. Laura 44. A Royal Scandal 45. Fallen Angel 45. Centennial Summer 46. Daisy Kenyon 47. Forever Amber 47. That Lady in Ermine 48. The Fan 49. Where the Sidewalk Ends 50. Whirlpool 50. The Thirteenth Letter 51. Angel Face 52. The Moon Is Blue 53. Carmen Jones 54. River of No Return 54. The Court Martial of Billy Mitchell 55. The Man with the Golden Arm 56. Bonjour Tristesse 57. Saint Joan 57. Anatomy of a Murder 59. Porgy and Bess 59. Exodus 60. Advise and Consent 62. The Cardinal 63. Bunny Lake Is Missing 65. In Harm's Way 65. Hurry Sundown 67. Skidoo 68. Tell Me That You Love Me, Junie Moon 69. Such Good Friends 71. Rosebud 75. The Human Factor 79.

Emeric Pressburger One of Our Aircraft Is Missing 41. The Life and Death of Colonel Blimp 43. A Canterbury Tale 44. I Know Where I'm Going 45. A Matter of Life and Death 46. Black Narcissus 47. The Red Shoes 48. The Small Back Room 49. Gone to Earth 50. The Elusive Pimpernel 50. The Tales of Hoffman 51. Oh Rosalinda! 55. Ill Met by Moonlight 56. The Battle of the River Plate 56.

Albert Pyun The Sword and the Sorcerer 82. Captain America 89. Cyborg 89. Kickboxer II: The Road Back 90. Nemesis 93. Omega Doom 95. Adrenalin: Fear the Rush 96. Mean Guns 96. Postmortem 97. Corrupt 99. The Wrecking Crew 99. Urban Menace 99.

Richard Quine Purple Heart Diary 51. All Ashore 52. Rainbow round My Shoulder 52. Sound Off 52. Cruisin' Down the River 53. Siren of Bagdad 53. Drive a Crooked Road 54. Pushover 54. So This Is Paris 54. My Sister Eileen 55. Full of Life 56. The Solid Gold Cadillac 56. Operation Mad Ball 57. Bell, Book and Candle 58. It Happened to Jane 59. Strangers When We Meet 60. The World of Suzie Wong 60. The Notorious Landlady 62. Paris When It Sizzles 63. How to Murder Your Wife 64. Sex and the Single Girl 64. Synanon 65. Oh Dad, Poor Dad, Mamma's Hung You in the Closet and I'm Feelin' So Sad 66. Hotel 67. A Talent for Loving 69. The Moonshine War 70. W 73. The Prisoner of Zenda 79.

Michael Radford Another Time, Another Place 83. 1984 84. White Mischief 87. Il Postino 94. B. Monkey 98. Dancing at the Blue Iguana 00.

Bob Rafelson Head 68. Five Easy Pieces 70. The King of Marvin Gardens 72. Stay Hungry 76. The Postman Always Rings Twice 81. Black Widow 87. Mountains of the Moon 89. Man Trouble 92. Blood & Wine 96.

Stewart Raffill Adventures of the Wilderness Family 75. High Risk 81. The Ice Pirates 84. The Philadelphia Experiment 84. Mac and Me 88. Mannequin Two: On the Move 91.

Alan Rafkin The Ghost and Mr Chicken 65. The Ride to Hangman's Tree 67. The Shakiest Gun in the West 67. Nobody's Perfect 68. Angel in My Pocket 69.

Sam Raimi The Evil Dead 83. Crimewave 86. Evil Dead 2: Dead by Dawn 87. Darkman 90. Army of Darkness 92. The Quick and the Dead 95. A Simple Plan 98. For Love of the Game 99. The Gift 00. Spider-Man 02.

Alvin Rakoff Passport to Shame 59. Treasure of San Teresa 59. On Friday at Eleven 60. The Comedy Man 64. Crossplot 69. Hoffman 70. Say Hello to Yesterday 70. City on Fire 79. Death Ship 80.

Harold Ramis Caddyshack 80. National Lampoon's Vacation 83. Club Paradise 86. Groundhog Day 93. Stuart Saves His Family 95. Multiplicity 96. Analyze This 99. Analyze That 02.

Jean-Paul Rappeneau La Vie de Château 65. The Scoundrel 71. Call Him Savage 75. Le Sauvage 78. Cyrano de Bergerac 90. The Horseman on the Roof 95.

Irving Rapper One Foot in Heaven 41. Shining Victory 41. Now Voyager 42. The Gay Sisters 42. The Adventures of Mark Twain 44. Rhapsody in Blue 45. The Corn Is Green 45. Deception 47. The Voice of the Turtle 48. Anna Lucasta 49. The Glass Menagerie 50. Another Man's Poison 51. Forever Female 53. Bad for Each Other 54. The Brave One 56. Strange Intruder 57. Marjorie Morningstar 58. The Miracle 59. Pontius Pilate 61. Born Again 78.

Steve Rash The Buddy Holly Story 78. Under the Rainbow 81. Queens Logic 91. Son-in-Law 93. Eddie 96.

Gregory Ratoff Lancer Spy 37. Barricade 39. Daytime Wife 39. Hotel for Women 39. Intermezzo 39. Rose of Washington Square 39. Wife, Husband and Friend 39. I Was an Adventuress 40. Public Deb Number One 40. Adam Had Four Sons 41. The Corsican Brothers 41. The Men in Her Life 41. Footlight Serenade 42. Two Yanks in Trinidad 42. Something to Shout About 43. The Heat's On 43. Irish Eyes Are Smiling 44. Song of Russia 44. Paris Underground 45. Where Do We Go from Here? 45. Do You Love Me? 46. Carnival in Costa Rica 47. Moss Rose 47. Black Magic 49. That Dangerous Age 49. My Daughter Joy 50. Taxi 52. Abdulla the Great 54. Oscar Wilde 59.

John Rawlins Junior G-Men 40. The Green Hornet Strikes Again 40. A Dangerous Game 41. Bombay Clipper 41. Six Lessons from Madame La Zonga 41. Arabian Nights 42. Half Way to Shanghai 42. Overland Mail 42. Sherlock Holmes and the Voice of Terror 42. The Great Impersonation 42. We've Never Been Licked 43. Ladies Courageous 44. Her Adventurous Night 46. Dick Tracy Meets Gruesome 47. Dick Tracy's Dilemma 47. Fort Defiance 51.

Nicholas Ray They Live by Night 48. A Woman's Secret 49. Knock on Any Door 49. Born to Be Bad 50. In a Lonely Place 50. Flying Leathernecks 51. On Dangerous Ground 51. Macao 52. The Lusty Men 52. Johnny Guitar 53. Hot Blood 55. Rebel without a Cause 55. Run for Cover 55. Bigger than Life 56. The True Story of Jesse James 56. Bitter Victory 57. Party Girl 58. Wind across the Everglades 58. The Savage Innocents 60. King of Kings 61. 55 Days at Peking 63. Lightning over Water 80.

Satyajit Ray Pather Panchali 55. Aparajito 56. The Music Room 58. The World of Apu 59. Devi 60. Kanchenjungha 62. The Big City 63. Charulata 64. Aranyer Din Ratri 69. Company Limited 71. Distant Thunder 73. The Middle Man 75. The Chess Players 77. Home and the World 84. An Enemy of the People 89. The Branches of the Tree 90. Agantuk 91.

Jack Raymond Splinters 29. French Leave 30. The Speckled Band 31. Up for the Cup 31. Night of the Garter 33. Sorrell and Son 33. Come Out of the Pantry 35. King of Paris 35. The Frog 37. The Rat 37. A Royal Divorce 38. Blondes for Danger 38. No Parking 38. The Mind of Mr Reeder 39. You Will Remember 40. Reluctant Heroes 51. Worm's Eye View 51.

Robert Redford Ordinary People 80. The Milagro Beanfield War 88. A River Runs through It 92. Quiz Show 94. The Horse Whisperer 98. The Legend of Bagger Vance 00.

Carol Reed Midshipman Easy 35. Laburnum Grove 36. Talk of the Devil 36. Bank Holiday 38. Climbing High 38. Penny Paradise 38. A Girl Must Live 39. The Stars Look Down 39. Night Train to Munich 40. The Girl in the News 40. Kipps 41. The Young Mr Pitt 42. The Way Ahead 44. The True Glory 45. Odd Man Out 46. The Fallen Idol 48. The Third Man 49. Outcast of the Islands 51. The Man Between 53. A Kid for Two Farthings 55. Trapeze 56. The Key 58. Our Man in Havana 59. The Running Man 63. The Agony and the Ecstasy 65. Oliver! 68. Flap 70. Follow Me 71.

Theodore Reed Double or Nothing 37. Tropic Holiday 38. I'm from Missouri 39. What a Life 39. Her First Beau 41.

Carl Reiner Enter Laughing 66. The Comic 69. Where's Poppa? 70. Oh, God 77. The One and Only 78. The Jerk 79. Dead Men Don't Wear Plaid 82. The Man with Two Brains 83. All of Me 84. Summer Rental 85. Summer School 87. Bert Rigby, You're a Fool 89. Sibling Rivalry 90. Fatal Instinct 93. That Old Feeling 97.

Rob Reiner This Is Spinal Tap 84. The Sure Thing 85. Stand by Me 86. The Princess Bride 87. When Harry Met Sally 89. Misery 90. A Few Good Men 92. North 94. The American President 95. Ghosts of Mississippi 96. The Story of Us 99.

Gottfried Reinhardt Invitation 52. The Story of Three Loves 53. Betrayed 54. Town without Pity 61. Situation Hopeless But Not Serious 65.

Irving Reis A Date with the Falcon 41. Weekend for Three 41. The Big Street 42. Crack Up 46. The Bachelor and the Bobbysoxer 47. All My Sons 48. Enchantment 48. Dancing in the Dark 49. Roseanna McCoy 49. Three Husbands 50. New Mexico 52. The Four-Poster 52.

Charles Reisner The Better 'Ole 26. The Hollywood Revue of 1929 29. Caught Short 30. Politics 31. Reducing 31. A Divorce in the Family 32. Student Tour 34. You Can't Buy Everything 34. The Winning Ticket 35. Manhattan Merry-go-round 37. Murder Goes to College 37. The Big Store 41. Lost in a Harem 44. Meet the People 44.

Karel Reisz Saturday Night and Sunday Morning 60. Night Must Fall 64. Morgan – A Suitable Case for Treatment 66. Isadora 68. The Gambler 75. Who'll Stop the Rain? 78. The French Lieutenant's Woman 81. Sweet Dreams 85. Everybody Wins 90.

Wolfgang Reitherman One Hundred and One Dalmatians 61. The Sword in the Stone 63. Jungle Book 67. The Aristocats 70. Robin Hood 73. The Rescuers 77.

Ivan Reitman Cannibal Girls 72. Meatballs 79. Stripes 81. Ghostbusters 84. Legal Eagles 86. Twins 88. Ghostbusters II 89. Kindergarten Cop 90. Dave 93. Junior 94. Fathers' Day 97. Six Days, Seven Nights 98. Evolution 01.

Michael Relph Saraband for Dead Lovers 48. Out of the Clouds 54. Davy 57. Rockets Galore 58. Desert Mice 59.

Jean Renoir La Chienne 31. Boudu Sauvé des Eaux 32. Madame Bovary 33. Les Bas-fonds 36. The Crime of Monsieur Lange 36. Une Partie de Campagne 36. La Grande Illusion 37. La Bête Humaine 38. La Marseillaise 38. La Règle du Jeu 39. Swamp Water 41. This Land Is Mine 43. The Southerner 45. The Diary of a Chambermaid 46. The Woman on the Beach 47. The River 51. The Golden Coach 53. French Can-Can 55. Lunch on the Grass 59. The Vanishing Corporal 62.

Alain Resnais Hiroshima Mon Amour 59. Last

Year at Marienbad 61. Muriel 63. La Guerre Est Finie 66. Je T'Aime, Je T'Aime 67. Providence 77. My American Uncle 80. Life Is a Bed of Roses 83. L'Amour à Mort 84. Mélo 86. Smoking/No Smoking 93. Same Old Song 97.

Kevin Reynolds Fandango 84. The Beast 88. Robin Hood: Prince of Thieves 91. Rapa Nui 94. Waterworld 95. 187 97. The Count of Monte Cristo 02.

David Lowell Rich Madame X 65. Rosie 67. A Lovely Way to Die 68. Eye of the Cat 69. That Man Bolt 73. The Concorde: Airport '79 79. Chu Chu and the Philly Flash 81.

John Rich Wives and Lovers 63. Roustabout 64. The New Interns 64. Boeing-Boeing 65. Easy Come, Easy Go 66.

Dick Richards The Culpeper Cattle Company 72. Farewell, My Lovely 75. Rafferty and the Gold Dust Twins 75. March or Die 77. Death Valley 81. Man, Woman and Child 82.

Tony Richardson Look Back in Anger 59. Sanctuary 60. The Entertainer 60. A Taste of Honey 61. The Loneliness of the Long Distance Runner 62. Tom Jones 63. The Loved One 65. The Sailor from Gibraltar 67. The Charge of the Light Brigade 68. Hamlet 69. Laughter in the Dark 69. Ned Kelly 70. Dead Cert 74. A Delicate Balance 75. Joseph Andrews 77. The Border 82. The Hotel New Hampshire 84. Blue Sky 94.

Charles Riesner Steamboat Bill Jnr 28. Chasing Rainbows 29. Flying High 31. The Chief 33. The Show-Off 34. Everybody Dance 36. Winter Carnival 39.

Wolf Rilla The Black Rider 54. The End of the Road 54. The Blue Peter 55. Pacific Destiny 56. The Scamp 57. Bachelor of Hearts 58. Piccadilly Third Stop 60. Village of the Damned 60. Watch It, Sailor 61. Cairo 63. The World Ten Times Over 63.

Michael Ritchie Downhill Racer 69. Prime Cut 72. The Candidate 72. Smile 75. The Bad News Bears 76. Semi-Tough 77. An Almost Perfect Affair 79. Divine Madness 80. The Island 80. The Survivors 83. Fletch 85. The Golden Child 86. Wildcats 86. The Couch Trip 88. Fletch Lives 89. Diggstown 92. Cops and Robbersons 94. A Simple Wish 97.

Martin Ritt Edge of the City 57. No Down Payment 57. The Black Orchid 58. The Long Hot Summer 58. The Sound and the Fury 59. Five Branded Women 60. Paris Blues 61. Hemingway's Adventures of a Young Man 62. Hud 63. The Outrage 64. The Spy Who Came in from the Cold 65. Hombre 67. The Brotherhood 68. The Great White Hope 70. The Molly Maguires 70. Pete 'n Tillie 72. Sounder 72. Conrack 74. The Front 76. Casey's Shadow 78. Norma Rae 79. Back Roads 81. Cross Creek 83. Murphy's Romance 85. Nuts 87. Stanley & Iris 89.

Jacques Rivette Paris Belongs to Us 61. Celine and Julie Go Boating 74. La Belle Noiseuse 91. Jeanne la Pucelle: Part I, Les Batailles; Part II, Les Prisons 94. Secret Défense 97. Va Savoir 01.

Hal Roach The Rogue Song 30. Fra Diavolo 33. Kelly the Second 36. Captain Fury 39. The Housekeeper's Daughter 39. One Million BC 40. Turnabout 40.

Matthew Robbins Corvette Summer 79. Dragonslayer 81. The Legend of Billie Jean 85. Batteries Not Included 87. Bingo 91.

Yves Robert Le Grand Blond avec une Chaussure Noire 72. Salut l'Artiste 73. Return of the Tall Blond 74. Pardon Mon Affaire 77. Courage Fuyons 79. La Gloire de Mon Père 90. Le Château de Ma Mère 90.

Stephen Roberts If I Had a Million 32. Sky Bride 32. The Night of June 13th 32. One Sunday Afternoon 33. The Story of Temple Drake 33. Romance in Manhattan 34. The Trumpet Blows 34. Star of Midnight 35. The Man Who Broke the Bank at Monte Carlo 35. The Ex-Mrs Bradford 36. The Lady Consents 36.

John Robertson Dr Jekyll and Mr Hyde 21. Captain of the Guard 30. Phantom of Paris 31. Little Orphan Annie 32. One Man's Journey 33. Crime Doctor 34. Our Little Girl 35.

Mark Robson The Ghost Ship 43. The Seventh Victim 43. Youth Runs Wild 44. Isle of the Dead 45. Bedlam 46. Champion 49. Home of the Brave 49. My Foolish Heart 49. Roughshod 49. Edge of Doom 50. Bright Victory 51. I Want You 51. Return to Paradise 53. Hell below Zero 54. Phffft 54. The Bridges at Toko-Ri 54. A Prize of Gold 55. Trial 55. The Harder They Fall 56. Peyton Place 57. The Little Hut 57. The Inn of the Sixth Happiness 58. From the Terrace 60. Nine Hours to Rama 62. The Prize 63. Von Ryan's Express 65. Lost Command 66. Valley of the Dolls 67. Daddy's Gone A-Hunting 69. Happy Birthday Wanda June 71. Limbo 72. Earthquake 74. Avalanche Express 79.

Franc Roddam Quadrophenia 79. The Lords of Discipline 82. The Bride 85. Aria 88. War Party 89. K2 91.

Robert Rodriguez El Mariachi 92. Desperado 95. From Dusk till Dawn 95. The Faculty 98. Spy Kids 01. Spy Kids 2: Island of Lost Dreams 02.

Nicolas Roeg Performance 70. Don't Look Now 73. The Man Who Fell to Earth 76. Bad Timing 80. Eureka 82. Insignificance 85. Castaway 86. Aria 88. Track 29 88. The Witches 90. Cold Heaven 92. Two Deaths 95.

Albert S. Rogell Mamba 30. Fog 33. No More Women 34. Air Hawks 35. Atlantic Adventure 35. Start Cheering 38. The Last Warning 38. Argentine Nights 40. Private Affairs 40. The Black Cat 41. Tight Shoes 41. Priorities on Parade 42. Hit Parade of 1943 43. War of the Wildcats 43. Earl Carroll Sketchbook 46. Heaven Only Knows 47. Northwest Stampede 48. Song of India 49. The Admiral Was a Lady 50.

Charles Rogers Fra Diavolo 33. Me and My Pal 33. Babes in Toyland 34. Going Bye Bye 34. The Live Ghost 34. Them Thar Hills 34. The Fixer Uppers 35. Tit for Tat 35. The Bohemian Girl 36.

Maclean Rogers Gert and Daisy's Weekend 41. Variety Jubilee 42. Heaven Is Round the Corner 43. Give Me the Stars 44. The Story of Shirley Yorke 48. Down among the Z Men 52. Assignment Redhead 56. Not Wanted on Voyage 57. You Pay Your Money 57. Mark of the Phoenix 59.

Eric Rohmer Le Signe du Lion 59. Paris Vu Par… 65. Ma Nuit Chez Maud 69. Claire's Knee 70. L'Amour, L'Après-midi 72. The Marquise of O 76. Perceval Le Gallois 78. The Aviator's Wife 80. Le Beau Mariage 81. Pauline at the Beach 83. Four Adventures of Reinette and Mirabelle 86. The Green Ray 86. My Girlfriend's Boyfriend 87. Conte de Printemps 90. Conte d'hiver 92. Rendez-vous in Paris 95. Conte d'été 96. Conte D'Automne 98. L'Anglaise et Le Duc 01.

George A. Romero Season of the Witch 73. The Crazies 73. Martin 78. Dawn of the Dead 79. Knightriders 81. Creepshow 82. Day of the Dead 85. Monkey Shines 88. The Dark Half 91.

Darrell Roodt Jobman 90. To the Death 91. Sarafina! 92. Father Hood 93. Dangerous Ground 96.

Bernard Rose Paperhouse 88. Chicago Joe and the Showgirl 89. Candyman 92. Immortal Beloved 94. Leo Tolstoy's Anna Karenina 97. Ivansxtc 00.

Phil Rosen The Exquisite Sinner 26. The Vanishing Frontier 32. The Sphinx 33. Beggars in Ermine 34. Dangerous Corner 34. West of the Pecos 34. Little Men 35. Woman in the Dark 35. Ex-Champ 39. Forgotten Girls 40. Paper Bullets 41. Spooks Run Wild 41. The Mystery of Marie Roget 42. Captain Tugboat Annie 45. The Strange Mr Gregory 45. Step by Step 46. The Secret of St Ives 49.

Stuart Rosenberg Murder, Incorporated 60. Cool Hand Luke 67. The April Fools 69. Move 70. WUSA 70. Pocket Money 72. The Laughing Policeman 73. The Drowning Pool 75. Voyage of the Damned 76. Love and Bullets 78. The Amityville Horror 79. Brubaker 80. The Pope of Greenwich Village 84. My Heroes Have Always Been Cowboys 91.

Rick Rosenthal Halloween Two 81. Bad Boys 83. American Dreamer 84. Distant Thunder 88. Devlin 92. Halloween Resurrection 02.

Francesco Rosi Salvatore Giuliano 61. Hands over the City 63. Illustrious Corpses 75. Christ Stopped at Eboli 79. Carmen 84. Chronicle of a Death Foretold 87.

Milton Rosmer Dreyfus 31. Channel Crossing 33. The Secret of the Loch 34. Maria Marten, or The Murder in the Red Barn 35. The Guv'nor 35. Everything Is Thunder 36. The Great Barrier 37. The Challenge 38.

Herbert Ross Goodbye Mr Chips 69. The Owl and the Pussycat 70. T. R. Baskin 71. Play It Again Sam 72. The Last of Sheila 73. Funny Lady 75. The Sunshine Boys 75. The Seven Per Cent Solution 76. The Goodbye Girl 77. The Turning Point 77. California Suite 78. Nijinsky 80. Pennies from Heaven 81. I Ought to Be in Pictures 82. Max Dugan Returns 83. Footloose 84. Protocol 84. Dancers 87. The Secret of My Success 87. Steel Magnolias 89. My Blue Heaven 90. True Colors 91. Undercover Blues 93. Boys on the Side 95.

Roberto Rossellini Open City 45. Paisà 46. Germany Year Zero 47. L'Amore 48. The Miracle 48. Stromboli 49. Francis, God's Jester 50. Europa 51 52. The Seven Deadly Sins 52. Voyage to Italy 53. General Della Rovere 59. The Rise of Louis XIV 66.

Robert Rossen Johnny O'Clock 46. Body and Soul 47. All the King's Men 49. The Brave Bulls 51. Mambo 54. Alexander the Great 56. Island in the Sun 57. They Came to Cordura 59. The Hustler 61. Lilith 64.

Russel Rouse The Well 51. The Thief 52. New York Confidential 55. The Fastest Gun Alive 56. House of Numbers 57. Thunder in the Sun 59. A House Is Not a Home 64. The Caper of the Golden Bulls 66. The Oscar 66.

Roy Rowland Hollywood Party 34. A Stranger in Town 43. Lost Angel 43. Our Vines Have Tender Grapes 45. Boys' Ranch 46. Killer McCoy 47. The Romance of Rosy Ridge 47. Tenth Avenue Angel 48. The Outriders 50. Two Weeks with Love 50. Excuse My Dust 51. Bugles in the Afternoon 52. Affair with a Stranger 53. The 5000 Fingers of Doctor T 53. The Moonlighter 53. Rogue Cop 54. Witness to Murder 54. Hit the Deck 55. Many Rivers to Cross 55. Meet Me in Las Vegas 56. Slander 56. These Wilder Years 56. Gun Glory 57. Seven Hills of Rome 57. The Girl Hunters 63.

Mervyn Le Roy Little Johnny Jones 29. Show Girl in Hollywood 30. Broadminded 31. Five Star Final 31. Gentleman's Fate 31. Little Caesar 31. Tonight or Never 31. Big City Blues 32. Heart of New York 32. High Pressure 32. I Am a Fugitive from a Chain Gang 32. Three on a Match 32. Two Seconds 32. Elmer the Great 33. Gold Diggers of 1933 33. Hard to Handle 33. The World Changes 33. Tugboat Annie 33. Happiness Ahead 34. Heat Lightning 34. Hi Nellie 34. Sweet Adeline 34. I Found Stella Parish 35. Oil for the Lamps of China 35. Page Miss Glory 35. Anthony Adverse 36. Three Men on a Horse 36. The King and the Chorus Girl 37. They Won't Forget 37. Fools for Scandal 38. Escape 40. Waterloo Bridge 40. Blossoms in the Dust 41. Unholy Partners 41. Johnny Eager 42. Random Harvest 42. Madame Curie 43. Thirty Seconds over Tokyo 44. Without Reservations 46. Desire Me 47. Homecoming 48. Any Number Can Play 49. East Side West Side 49. Little Women 49. Quo Vadis 51. Lovely to Look At 52. Million Dollar Mermaid 52. Latin Lovers 53. Rose Marie 54. Mister Roberts 55. Strange Lady in Town 55. The Bad Seed 56. Toward the Unknown 56. Home before Dark 58. No Time for Sergeants 58. The FBI Story 59. Wake Me When It's Over 60. A Majority of One 61. The Devil at Four o'Clock 61. Gypsy 62. Mary Mary 63. Moment to Moment 66.

J. Walter Ruben Secret Service 31. Phantom of Crestwood 32. Ace of Aces 33. The Great Jasper 33. Java Head 34. Man of Two Worlds 34. Success at Any Price 34. Where Sinners Meet 34. Public Hero Number One 35. Riff Raff 35. Old Hutch 36. Bad Man of Brimstone 37. Good Old Soak 37.

Joseph Ruben Dreamscape 84. The Stepfather 86. True Believer 89. Sleeping with the Enemy 90. The Good Son 93. Money Train 95. Return to Paradise 98.

Alan Rudolph Welcome to LA 76. Remember My Name 78. Endangered Species 82. Choose Me 84. Songwriter 84. Trouble in Mind 85. Made in Heaven 87. The Moderns 88. Love at Large 90. Mortal Thoughts 91. Equinox 92. Mrs Parker and the Vicious Circle 94. Afterglow 97. Breakfast of Champions 99.

Wesley Ruggles Condemned 29. Cimarron 30. Honey 30. The Sea Bat 30. Are These Our Children? 31. Roar of the Dragon 32. College Humor 33. I'm No Angel 33. No Man of Her Own 33. Bolero 34. Shoot the Works 34. Accent on Youth 35. The Bride Comes Home 35. The Gilded Lily 35. Valiant Is the Word for Carrie 36. I Met Him in Paris 37. True Confession 37. Sing You Sinners 38. Invitation to Happiness 39. Arizona 40. Too Many Husbands 40. You Belong to Me 41. Somewhere I'll Find You 42. Slightly Dangerous 43. See Here Private Hargrove 44. London Town 46.

Richard Rush Of Love and Desire 63. Hells Angels on Wheels 67. Getting Straight 70. Freebie and the Bean 74. The Stunt Man 80. Color of Night 94.

Chuck Russell A Nightmare on Elm Street Part Three: Dream Warriors 87. The Blob 88. The Mask 94. Eraser 96. Bless the Child 00. The Scorpion King 02.

Ken Russell French Dressing 63. Billion Dollar Brain 67. Women in Love 69. The Devils 70. The Music Lovers 70. The Boy Friend 71. Savage Messiah 72. Mahler 74. Lisztomania 75. Tommy 75. Valentino 77. Altered States 80. Crimes of Passion 84. Gothic 86. Salome's Last Dance 87. Aria 88. The Lair of the White Worm 88. The Rainbow 88. Whore 91.

William D. Russell Our Hearts Were Growing Up 46. Dear Ruth 47. Ladies' Man 47. The Sainted Sisters 48. Bride for Sale 49. Green Promise 49. Best of the Badmen 51.

Roy del Ruth Ham and Eggs at the Front 27. The Terror 28. Gold Diggers of Broadway 29. The Desert Song 29. The Hottentot 29. Hold Everything 30. Life of the Party 30. The Aviator 30. The Second-Floor Mystery 30. Three Faces East 30. Blonde Crazy 31. Taxi! 31. The Maltese Falcon 31. Beauty and the Boss 32. Blessed Event 32. Winner Take All 32. Bureau of Missing Persons 33. Captured 33. Employees' Entrance 33. Lady Killer 33. The Little Giant 33. The Mind Reader 33. Bulldog Drummond Strikes Back 34. Kid Millions 34. Upperworld 34. Broadway Melody of 1936 35. Folies Bergère 35. Thanks a Million 35. Born to Dance 36. It Had to Happen 36. Private Number 36. Broadway Melody of 1938 37. On the Avenue 37. Happy Landing 38. My Lucky Star 38. Tail Spin 38. Here I Am a Stranger 39. The Star Maker 39. He Married His Wife 40. The Chocolate Soldier 41. Topper Returns 41. Broadway Rhythm 43. Dubarry Was a Lady 43. Barbary Coast Gent 44. It Happened on Fifth Avenue 47. The Babe Ruth Story 48. Always Leave Them Laughing 49. The Red Light 49. West Point Story 50. On Moonlight Bay 51. Starlift 51. About Face 52. Stop You're Killing Me 53. Three Sailors and a Girl 53. Phantom of the Rue Morgue 54. The Alligator People 59.

Frank Ryan Call Out the Marines 42. Hers to Hold 43. Can't Help Singing 44. Patrick the Great 44. So Goes My Love 46.

Mark Rydell The Fox 68. The Reivers 69. The Cowboys 72. Cinderella Liberty 74. Harry and Walter Go to New York 76. The Rose 79. On Golden Pond 81. The River 84. For the Boys 91. Intersection 94.

Boris Sagal Twilight of Honor 63. Girl Happy 65. The Helicopter Spies 67. Mosquito Squadron 68.

The One Thousand Plane Raid 69. The Omega Man 71.

Gene Saks Barefoot in the Park 67. The Odd Couple 68. Cactus Flower 69. Last of the Red Hot Lovers 72. Mame 74. Brighton Beach Memoirs 86.

Richard Sale A Ticket to Tomahawk 50. I'll Get By 50. Half Angel 51. Let's Make It Legal 51. Meet Me after the Show 51. My Wife's Best Friend 52. The Girl Next Door 53. Malaga 54. Gentlemen Marry Brunettes 55. Seven Waves Away 56.

Sidney Salkow Woman Doctor 39. The Lone Wolf Strikes 40. The Lone Wolf Keeps a Date 41. The Lone Wolf Meets a Lady 41. The Lone Wolf Takes a Chance 41. Flight Lieutenant 42. The Adventures of Martin Eden 42. City without Men 43. Faithful in My Fashion 46. Shadow of the Eagle 50. Jack McCall Desperado 52. Scarlet Angel 52. The Golden Hawk 52. Prince of Pirates 53. Sitting Bull 54. Robbers' Roost 55. Chicago Confidential 57. Blood on the Arrow 64. The Quick Gun 64. The Great Sioux Massacre 65.

Denis Sanders A Time out of War 54. Crime and Punishment USA 58. War Hunt 61. One Man's Way 64. Shock Treatment 64.

Mark Sandrich Aggie Appleby Maker of Men 33. Melody Cruise 33. Cockeyed Cavaliers 34. Hips Hips Hooray 34. The Gay Divorcee 34. Top Hat 35. A Woman Rebels 36. Follow the Fleet 36. Shall We Dance? 37. Carefree 38. Man about Town 39. Buck Benny Rides Again 40. Skylark 41. Holiday Inn 42. So Proudly We Hail 43. Here Come the Waves 44. I Love a Soldier 44.

Alfred Santell Bluebeard's Seven Wives 26. The Arizona Kid 30. Body and Soul 31. Daddy Longlegs 31. Polly of the Circus 32. Rebecca of Sunnybrook Farm 32. Tess of the Storm Country 32. The Life of Vergie Winters 34. A Feather in Her Hat 35. People Will Talk 35. The Dictator 35. Winterset 36. Breakfast for Two 37. Internes Can't Take Money 37. Cocoanut Grove 38. Having Wonderful Time 38. The Arkansas Traveller 38. Our Leading Citizen 39. Aloma of the South Seas 41. Beyond the Blue Horizon 42. Jack London 43. The Hairy Ape 44. Mexicana 45. That Brennan Girl 46.

Joseph Santley The Cocoanuts 29. Harmony Lane 35. Her Master's Voice 36. Meet the Missus 37. She's Got Everything 37. There Goes the Groom 37. Spirit of Culver 39. Two Bright Boys 39. Music in My Heart 40. Ice-Capades 41. Joan of Ozark 42. Yokel Boy 42. Chatterbox 43. Thumbs Up 43. Brazil 44. Rosie the Riveter 44. Earl Carroll Vanities 45. Shadow of a Woman 46.

Deran Sarafian Death Warrant 90. Back in the USSR 91. Gunmen 92. Roadflower 93. Terminal Velocity 94.

Richard Sarafian Run Wild, Run Free 69. Fragment of Fear 70. Man in the Wilderness 71. Vanishing Point 71. Lolly Madonna XXX 73. The Man Who Loved Cat Dancing 73. The Next Man 76. Sunburn 79. Eye of the Tiger 86. Solar Crisis 92.

Joseph Sargent One Spy Too Many 66. The Hell with Heroes 68. The Forbin Project 69. White Lightning 73. The Taking of Pelham 123 74. MacArthur the Rebel General 77. Goldengirl 79. Coast to Coast 80. Jaws: The Revenge 87.

Peter Sasdy Taste the Blood of Dracula 70. Countess Dracula 71. Hands of the Ripper 71. Doomwatch 72. Nothing but the Night 72. I Don't Want to Be Born 75. Welcome to Blood City 77. The Lonely Lady 82.

Charles Saunders Tawny Pipit 44. One Wild Oat 51. Meet Mr Callaghan 54. The Narrowing Circle 55. The Man without a Body 57. Kill Her Gently 58. Naked Fury 59. The Gentle Trap 60. Dangerous Afternoon 61. Danger by My Side 62.

Carlos Saura Raise Ravens 75. Blood Wedding 81. Carmen 83. A Love Bewitched 85. El Dorado 88. Ay, Carmela! 90. Tango 98. Goya in Bordeaux 99.

Philip Saville The Best House in London 68. Shadey 85. The Fruit Machine 88. Fellow Traveller 89. Metroland 97.

Victor Saville Kitty 28. The W Plan 30. Michael and Mary 31. Sunshine Susie 31. The Sport of Kings 31. Love on Wheels 32. Friday the Thirteenth 33. I Was a Spy 33. The Good Companions 33. Evensong 34. Evergreen 34. The Iron Duke 34. First a Girl 35. Me and Marlborough 35. The Dictator 35. It's Love Again 36. Dark Journey 37. South Riding 37. Storm in a Teacup 37. Forever and a Day 43. Tonight and Every Night 45. The Green Years 46. Green Dolphin Street 47. If Winter Comes 48. Conspirator 49. Kim 50. Calling Bulldog Drummond 51. Twenty-Four Hours of a Woman's Life 52. The Long Wait 54. The Silver Chalice 54.

John Sayles Baby It's You 82. The Brother from Another Planet 84. Matewan 87. Eight Men Out 88. City of Hope 91. Passion Fish 92. The Secret of Roan Inish 93. Lone Star 96. Men with Guns 97. Limbo 99. Sunshine State 02.

Armand Schaefer The Lightning Warrior 31. Fighting with Kit Carson 33. Sagebrush Trail 33. The Three Musketeers 33. Burn 'Em Up Barnes 34. The Law of the Wild 34. The Lost Jungle 34. The Miracle Rider 35.

Franklin J. Schaffner The Stripper 63. The Best Man 64. The War Lord 65. The Double Man 67. Planet of the Apes 68. Patton 69. Nicholas and Alexandra 71. Papillon 73. Islands in the Stream 77. The Boys from Brazil 78. Sphinx 80. Yes, Giorgio 82. Lionheart 87. Welcome Home 89.

Jerry Schatzberg Puzzle of a Downfall Child 70. The Panic in Needle Park 71. Scarecrow 73. Dandy the All-American Girl 76. The Seduction of Joe Tynan 79. Honeysuckle Rose 80. Street Smart 87. Reunion 89.

Fred Schepisi The Devil's Playground 76. The Chant of Jimmie Blacksmith 78. Barbarosa 81. Iceman 84. Plenty 85. Roxanne 87. A Cry in the Dark 88. The Russia House 90. Mr Baseball 92. Six Degrees of Separation 93. I.Q. 94. Fierce Creatures 97. Last Orders 01.

Victor Schertzinger Heads Up 30. Paramount on Parade 30. Friends and Lovers 31. Beloved 33. One Night of Love 34. Let's Live Tonight 35. Love Me Forever 35. The Mikado 39. Rhythm on the River 40. Road to Singapore 40. Kiss the Boys Goodbye 41. Road to Zanzibar 41. The Birth of the Blues 41. The Fleet's In 42.

John Schlesinger Terminus 61. A Kind of Loving 62. Billy Liar 63. Darling 65. Far from the Madding Crowd 67. Midnight Cowboy 69. Sunday, Bloody Sunday 71. The Day of the Locust 74. Marathon Man 76. Yanks 79. Honky Tonk Freeway 81. The Falcon and the Snowman 84. The Believers 87. Madame Sousatzka 88. Pacific Heights 90. The Innocent 93. Cold Comfort Farm 95. Eye for an Eye 96. The Next Best Thing 00.

Volker Schlöndorff The Tin Drum 79. Circle of Deceit 81. Swann in Love 83. The Handmaid's Tale 90. Voyager 91. Palmetto 98.

Ernest Schoedsack The Four Feathers 29. Rango 31. The Most Dangerous Game 32. Blind Adventure 33. King Kong 33. Son of Kong 33. Long Lost Father 34. The Last Days of Pompeii 35. Dr Cyclops 40. Mighty Joe Young 49.

Paul Schrader Blue Collar 78. Hardcore 79. American Gigolo 80. Cat People 82. Mishima 85. Light of Day 87. Patty Hearst 88. The Comfort of Strangers 90. Light Sleeper 91. Witch Hunt 94. Touch 96. Affliction 97. Auto Focus 02.

Barbet Schroeder Maitresse 76. Barfly 87. Reversal of Fortune 90. Single White Female 92. Kiss of Death 95. Before and After 96. Desperate Measures 98. Murder by Numbers 02.

Michael Schultz Cooley High 75. Car Wash 76. Greased Lightning 77. Sgt Pepper's Lonely Hearts Club Band 78. Scavenger Hunt 79. Carbon Copy 81. The Last Dragon 85.

Joel Schumacher The Incredible Shrinking Woman 81. D. C. Cab 83. St Elmo's Fire 85. The Lost Boys 87. Cousins 89. Flatliners 90. Dying Young 91. Falling Down 92. The Client 94. Batman Forever 95. A Time to Kill 96. Batman & Robin 97. 8mm 99. Flawless 99. Tigerland 00. Bad Company 02. Phone Booth 02.

Harold Schuster Dinner at the Ritz 37. Wings of the Morning 37. Diamond Frontier 40. Zanzibar 40. A Very Young Lady 41. Girl Trouble 42. Bomber's Moon 43. My Friend Flicka 43. Marine Raiders 44. Breakfast in Hollywood 45. The Tender Years 47. So Dear to My Heart 48. Jack Slade 53. Tarzan's Hidden Jungle 55. Dragoon Wells Massacre 57.

Ettore Scola Jealousy Italian Style 70. La Nuit de Varennes 82. Le Bal 82. Passione d'Amore 82. Macaroni 85. The Family 87. Splendor 88.

Martin Scorsese What's a Nice Girl Like You Doing in a Place Like This? 63. It's Not Just You Murray! 64. The Big Shave 67. Who's That Knocking at My Door 68. Boxcar Bertha 72. Mean Streets 73. Alice Doesn't Live Here Any More 74. ItalianAmerican 74. Taxi Driver 76. New York, New York 77. The Last Waltz 78. Raging Bull 80. King of Comedy 83. After Hours 85. The Color of Money 86. The Last Temptation of Christ 88. New York Stories 89. GoodFellas 90. Cape Fear 91. The Age of Innocence 93. Casino 95. Kundun 97. Bringing Out the Dead 99. Gangs of New York 02.

Peter Graham Scott Escape Route 52. Account Rendered 57. Devil's Bait 59. Captain Clegg 62. The Pot Carriers 62. Bitter Harvest 63. Father Came Too 63. The Cracksman 63. Mister Ten Per Cent 67. Subterfuge 68.

Ridley Scott The Duellists 77. Alien 79. Blade Runner 82. Legend 85. Someone to Watch Over Me 87. Black Rain 89. Thelma and Louise 91. 1492: Conquest of Paradise 92. White Squall 96. G.I. Jane 97. Gladiator 00. Black Hawk Down 01. Hannibal 01.

Tony Scott The Hunger 83. Top Gun 86. Beverly Hills Cop 2 87. Revenge 89. Days of Thunder 90. The Last Boy Scout 91. True Romance 93. Crimson Tide 95. The Fan 96. Enemy of the State 98. Spy Game 01.

Francis Searle A Girl in a Million 46. Celia 49. A Case for P.C. 49 50. Cloudburst 51. Whispering Smith Hits London 51. Never Look Back 52. One Way Out 55. Undercover Girl 58. Trouble With Eve 59. Emergency 62. Gaolbreak 62. Night of the Prowler 62. Dead Man's Evidence 67.

Fred F. Sears Last Train from Bombay 52. Ambush at Tomahawk Gap 53. The Forty-Ninth Man 53. The Nebraskan 53. The Miami Story 54. Cell 2455 Death Row 55. Chicago Syndicate 55. Inside Detroit 55. Don't Knock the Rock 56. Earth Versus the Flying Saucers 56. Miami Exposé 56. Rock around the Clock 56. The Werewolf 56. The Giant Claw 57. Badman's Country 58.

George Seaton Diamond Horseshoe 45. Junior Miss 45. The Shocking Miss Pilgrim 46. Miracle on 34th Street 47. Apartment for Peggy 48. Chicken Every Sunday 49. For Heaven's Sake 50. The Big Lift 50. Anything Can Happen 52. Little Boy Lost 53. The Country Girl 54. The Proud and Profane 56. Teacher's Pet 58. The Pleasure of His Company 61. The Counterfeit Traitor 62. The Hook 62. Thirty-Six Hours 64. What's So Bad about Feeling Good? 65. Airport 70. Showdown 72.

Edward Sedgwick The Cameraman 28. Spite Marriage 29. Doughboys 30. Free and Easy 30. Parlor, Bedroom and Bath 31. Speak Easily 32. The Passionate Plumber 32. What, No Beer? 33. Death on the Diamond 34. Father Brown Detective 34. Murder in the Fleet 35. The Virginia Judge 35. Mister Cinderella 36. Fit for a King 37. Pick a Star 37. Burn 'Em Up O'Connor 38. The Gladiator 38. Beware Spooks! 39. Air Raid Wardens 43. A Southern Yankee 48.

Susan Seidelman Smithereens 82. Desperately Seeking Susan 85. Making Mr Right 87. Cookie 89. She-Devil 89.

Lewis Seiler Frontier Marshal 33. Paddy O'Day 35. Career Woman 36. Turn Off the Moon 37. Crime School 38. Heart of the North 38. King of the Underworld 38. Dust Be My Destiny 39. Hell's Kitchen 39. The Kid from Kokomo 39. You Can't Get Away with Murder 39. Flight Angels 40. It All Came True 40. South of Suez 40. Tugboat Annie Sails Again 40. Kisses for Breakfast 41. The Smiling Ghost 41. You're in the Army Now 41. Pittsburgh 42. The Big Shot 42. Guadalcanal Diary 43. Something for the Boys 44. Doll Face 45. If I'm Lucky 45. Molly and Me 45. Whiplash 48. Breakthrough 50. The Tanks Are Coming 51. Operation Secret 52. The Winning Team 52. The System 53. The Bamboo Prison 55. Women's Prison 55. Battle Stations 56.

William A. Seiter Sunny 30. The Flirting Widow 30. Caught Plastered 31. Kiss Me Again 31. Peach O'Reno 31. Girl Crazy 32. Hello Everybody 32. Hot Saturday 32. If I Had a Million 32. Way Back Home 32. Diplomaniacs 33. Professional Sweetheart 33. Sons of the Desert 34. The Richest Girl in the World 34. If You Could Only Cook 35. In Person 35. Orchids to You 35. Roberta 35. Dimples 36. Stowaway 36. The Case against Mrs Ames 36. The Moon's Our Home 36. Life Begins in College 37. Life of the Party 37. This Is My Affair 37. Room Service 38. Sally, Irene and Mary 38. Thanks for Everything 38. Three Blind Mice 38. Allegheny Uprising 39. Susannah of the Mounties 39. Hired Wife 40. It's a Date 40. Appointment for Love 41. Nice Girl? 41. Broadway 42. You Were Never Lovelier 42. A Lady Takes a Chance 43. Destroyer 43. Four Jills in a Jeep 44. Belle of the Yukon 45. It's a Pleasure 45. That Night with You 45. The Affairs of Susan 45. Little Giant 46. Lover Come Back 46. I'll Be Yours 47. One Touch of Venus 48. Up in Central Park 48. The Lady Wants Mink 53. Make Haste to Live 54.

George B. Seitz The Exploits of Elaine 14. The Vanishing American 25. Danger Lights 30. Exclusive Story 34. Lazy River 34. Calm Yourself 35. Kind Lady 35. Shadow of Doubt 35. Society Doctor 35. Times Square Lady 35. Woman Wanted 35. Absolute Quiet 36. Mad Holiday 36. The Last of the Mohicans 36. A Family Affair 37. Between Two Women 37. My Dear Miss Aldrich 37. Under Cover of Night 37. Yellow Jack 38. 6,000 Enemies 39. Thunder Afloat 39. Gallant Sons 40. Kit Carson 40. A Yank on the Burma Road 41. Pierre of the Plains 42.

Steve Sekely Miracle on Main Street 40. Behind Prison Walls 43. Revenge of the Zombies 43. Women in Bondage 43. Lake Placid Serenade 44. My Buddy 44. The Scar 48. Cartouche 54. The Day of the Triffids 62.

Lesley Selander The Barrier 37. Cherokee Strip 40. Bandit Ranger 42. Buckskin Frontier 43. Jungle Raiders 45. The Vampire's Ghost 45. Catman of Paris 46. Belle Starr's Daughter 47. Panhandle 48. Rider from Tucson 50. Storm over Wyoming 50. Flight to Mars 51. I Was an American Spy 51. The Highwayman 51. Battle Zone 52. Desert Passage 52. Riders of Vengeance 52. Fighter Attack 53. Fort Algiers 53. Fort Vengeance 53. Arrow in the Dust 54. Royal African Rifles 54. Shotgun 54. Fort Yuma 55. Tall Man Riding 55. The Lone Ranger and the Lost City of Gold 58. Fort Utah 67. Arizona Bushwhackers 68.

Edgar Selwyn War Nurse 30. The Sin of Madelon Claudet 31. Skyscraper Souls 32. Men Must Fight 33. Turn Back the Clock 33. The Mystery of Mr X 34.

Vernon Sewell The Silver Fleet 43. The World Owes Me a Living 44. Latin Quarter 45. The Ghosts of Berkeley Square 47. Uneasy Terms 48. The Black Widow 51. The Dark Light 51. Ghost Ship 52. Where There's a Will 55. The Battle of the V1 58. House of Mystery 61. Strongroom 61. The Man in the Back Seat 61. A Matter of Choice 63. The Blood Beast Terror 67. Curse of the Crimson Altar 68. Burke and Hare 71.

Tom Shadyac Ace Ventura, Pet Detective 94. The Nutty Professor 96. Liar, Liar 97. Patch Adams 98. Dragonfly 02.

Don Sharp The Golden Disc 58. Linda 60. It's All Happening 63. Devil Ship Pirates 64. Kiss of the Vampire 64. Witchcraft 64. The Face of Fu Manchu 65. Our Man in Marrakesh 66. Rasputin

Frank Strayer Let's Go Places 30. The Monster Walks 32. The Vampire Bat 32. Fugitive Road 34. The Ghost Walks 34. Death from a Distance 36. Laughing at Trouble 37. Blondie 38. Go West Young Lady 40.

Herbert L. Strock Battle Taxi 54. Gog 54. Blood of Dracula 57. I Was a Teenage Frankenstein 57. How to Make a Monster 58. Rider on a Dead Horse 62.

Erich von Stroheim Blind Husbands 19. Foolish Wives 21. Greed 24. The Merry Widow 25. Queen Kelly 28. The Wedding March 28. Hello Sister 33.

John Sturges The Sign of the Ram 48. The Walking Hills 49. Mystery Street 50. Right Cross 50. The Capture 50. The Magnificent Yankee 50. Kind Lady 51. The People against O'Hara 51. It's a Big Country 52. Jeopardy 52. The Girl in White 52. Escape from Fort Bravo 53. Fast Company 53. Bad Day at Black Rock 55. The Scarlet Coat 55. Underwater! 55. Backlash 56. Gunfight at the OK Corral 57. The Law and Jake Wade 58. The Old Man and the Sea 58. Last Train from Gun Hill 59. Never So Few 59. The Magnificent Seven 60. By Love Possessed 61. Sergeants Three 61. A Girl Named Tamiko 62. The Great Escape 63. The Hallelujah Trail 65. The Satan Bug 65. Hour of the Gun 67. Ice Station Zebra 68. Marooned 69. Joe Kidd 72. Chino 73. The Valdez Horses 73. McQ 74. The Eagle Has Landed 76.

Preston Sturges Christmas in July 40. The Great McGinty 40. Sullivan's Travels 41. The Lady Eve 41. The Palm Beach Story 42. The Miracle of Morgan's Creek 43. Hail the Conquering Hero 44. The Great Moment 44. Unfaithfully Yours 48. The Beautiful Blonde from Bashful Bend 49. The Diary of Major Thompson 55.

Charles Sturridge Runners 83. A Handful of Dust 88. Aria 88. Where Angels Fear to Tread 91. Fairytale – A True Story 97.

Walter Summers Raise the Roof 30. The Return of Bulldog Drummond 34. Music Hath Charms 35. Royal Cavalcade 35. Ourselves Alone 36. Premiere 38. Dark Eyes of London 39.

A. Edward Sutherland Pointed Heels 29. Paramount on Parade 30. Gang Buster 31. Sky Devils 31. Up Pops the Devil 31. Mr Robinson Crusoe 32. Palmy Days 32. Secrets of the French Police 32. International House 33. Murders in the Zoo 33. Too Much Harmony 33. Diamond Jim 35. Mississippi 35. Poppy 36. Champagne Waltz 37. Every Day's a Holiday 37. The Flying Deuces 39. Beyond Tomorrow 40. One Night in the Tropics 40. The Boys from Syracuse 40. Nine Lives Are Not Enough 41. Sing Your Worries Away 41. The Invisible Woman 41. The Navy Comes Through 42. Dixie 43. Follow the Boys 44. Secret Command 44. Having Wonderful Crime 45. Abie's Irish Rose 46. Bermuda Affair 56.

David Swift Pollyanna 60. The Parent Trap 61. Love Is a Ball 62. The Interns 62. Under the Yum Yum Tree 63. Good Neighbour Sam 64. How to Succeed in Business without Really Trying 67.

István Szabó Mephisto 81. Colonel Redl 84. Hanussen 88. Meeting Venus 90. Sweet Emma, Dear Böbe 92. Sunshine 99.

Jeannot Szwarc The Bug 75. Jaws 2 78. Somewhere in Time 80. Enigma 82. Supergirl 84. Santa Claus 85. Honor Bound 89.

Tibor Takacs The Gate 87. I, Madman 89. Gate II 92. Sabotage 96. Armageddon 97.

Andrei Tarkovsky Ivan's Childhood 62. Andrei Rublev 66. Solaris 72. Mirror 74. Nostalgia 83. The Sacrifice 86.

Frank Tashlin Son of Paleface 52. Marry Me Again 53. Susan Slept Here 54. Artists and Models 55. The Lieutenant Wore Skirts 55. Hollywood or Bust 56. The Girl Can't Help It 56. Will Success Spoil Rock Hunter? 57. Rock a Bye Baby 58. The Geisha Boy 58. Say One for Me 59. Cinderfella 60. Bachelor Flat 61. It's Only Money 62. The Man from the Diners' Club 63. Who's Minding the Store? 63. The Disorderly Orderly 64. The Alphabet Murders 65. The Glass Bottom Boat 66. Caprice 67. The Private Navy of Sergeant O'Farrell 68.

Nadia Tass Malcolm 86. Rikky and Pete 88. The Big Steal 90. Pure Luck 91. Mr Reliable (A True Story) 96.

Jacques Tati L'école des Facteurs 47. Jour de Fête 48. Monsieur Hulot's Holiday 53. Mon Oncle 56. Playtime 68. Traffic 70. Parade 74.

Norman Taurog Lucky Boy 29. Finn and Hattie 30. Follow the Leader 30. Huckleberry Finn 31. Skippy 31. If I Had a Million 32. The Phantom President 32. A Bedtime Story 33. The Way to Love 33. College Rhythm 34. Mrs Wiggs of the Cabbage Patch 34. We're Not Dressing 34. Strike Me Pink 35. The Big Broadcast of 1936 35. Reunion 36. Rhythm on the Range 36. Fifty Roads to Town 37. You Can't Have Everything 37. Boys Town 38. Mad about Music 38. The Adventures of Tom Sawyer 38. The Girl Downstairs 38. Broadway Melody of 1940 39. Lucky Night 39. Little Nellie Kelly 40. Young Tom Edison 40. Design for Scandal 41. Men of Boys' Town 41. A Yank at Eton 42. Are Husbands Necessary? 42. Girl Crazy 43. Presenting Lily Mars 43. The Hoodlum Saint 46. The Beginning or the End 47. Big City 48. The Bride Goes Wild 48. Words and Music 48. That Midnight Kiss 49. Mrs O'Malley and Mr Malone 50. Please Believe Me 50. The Toast of New Orleans 50. Rich, Young and Pretty 51. Jumping Jacks 52. Room for One More 52. The Stars Are Singing 52. The Stooge 52. The Caddy 53. Living It Up 54. You're Never Too Young 55. Bundle of Joy 56. Pardners 56. The Birds and the Bees 56. The Fuzzy Pink Nightgown 57. Onionhead 58. Don't Give Up the Ship 59. GI Blues 60. Visit to a Small Planet 60. All Hands on Deck 61. Blue Hawaii 61. Girls! Girls! Girls! 62. It Happened at the World's Fair 62. Palm Springs Weekend 63. Dr Goldfoot and the Bikini Machine 65. Sergeant Deadhead 65. Tickle Me 65. Spinout 66.

Bertrand Tavernier The Watchmaker of St Paul 73. The Judge and the Assassin 76. Deathwatch 80. Coup de Torchon 81. Sunday in the Country 84. Round Midnight 86. Life and Nothing But 89. Daddy Nostalgie 90. L.627 92. D'Artagnan's Daughter 94. The Bait 95. It All Starts Today 99. Laissez-Passer 01.

Paolo Taviani Padre Padrone 77. The Night of San Lorenzo 81. Kaos 84. Good Morning Babylon 87. Night Sun 90. Fiorile 93.

Vittorio Taviani Padre Padrone 77. The Night of San Lorenzo 81. Kaos 84. Good Morning Babylon 87. Night Sun 90. Fiorile 93.

Don Taylor Everything's Ducky 61. Ride the Wild Surf 64. Jack of Diamonds 67. Escape from the Planet of the Apes 71. Tom Sawyer 73. Echoes of a Summer 75. The Great Scout and Cathouse Thursday 76. The Island of Dr Moreau 77. Damien: Omen Two 78. The Final Countdown 80.

Ray Taylor The Ace of Scotland Yard 29. The Jade Box 30. Battling with Buffalo Bill 31. Danger Island 31. Fingerprints 31. Heroes of the West 32. The Airmail Mystery 32. The Jungle Mystery 32. Clancy of the Mounted 33. Gordon of Ghost City 33. The Phantom of the Air 33. Pirate Treasure 34. The Perils of Pauline 34. The Return of Chandu 34. Tailspin Tommy in the Great Air Mystery 35. The Roaring West 35. Robinson Crusoe of Clipper Island 36. The Phantom Rider 36. The Vigilantes are Coming 36. Dick Tracy 37. The Painted Stallion 37. Flaming Frontiers 38. The Spider's Web 38. Flying G-Men 39. Scouts to the Rescue 39. The Green Hornet 40. Winners of the West 40. Riders of Death Valley 41. Sky Raiders 41. Don Winslow of the Navy 42. Gang Busters 42. Junior G-Men of the Air 42. Mug Town 42. Adventures of Smilin' Jack 43. Adventures of the Flying Cadets 43. Mystery of the River Boat 44. Raiders of Ghost City 44. The Great Alaskan Mystery 44. Jungle Queen 45. Secret Agent X9 45. The Daltons Ride Again 45. The Master Key 45. The Royal Mounted Rides Again 45. Lost City of the Jungle 46. The Scarlet Horseman 46. The Michigan Kid 47. The Vigilantes Return 47.

Sam Taylor Safety Last 23. Why Worry? 23. Girl Shy 24. Hot Water 24. The Freshman 25. Exit Smiling 26. My Best Girl 27. Coquette 29. The Taming of the Shrew 29. Du Barry, Woman of Passion 30. Ambassador Bill 31. Kiki 31. Vagabond Lady 35. The Cat's Paw 36. Nothing but Trouble 44. The Monte Carlo Story 56.

Lewis Teague The Lady in Red 79. Alligator 80. Fighting Back 82. Cujo 83. Cat's Eye 85. Jewel of the Nile 85. Navy SEALS 90. Wedlock 91.

André Téchiné Barocco 76. Rendez-Vous 85. J'Embrasse Pas 91. Ma Saison Préferée 93. Les Voleurs 96. Alice et Martin 98.

Julien Temple Absolute Beginners 86. Aria 88. Earth Girls Are Easy 88. Bullet 95. Vigo: Passion for Life 97. Pandaemonium 00. The Filth and the Fury 00.

Duccio Tessari A Pistol for Ringo 65. The Return of Ringo 65. The Heroes 72. Zorro 75. Tex and The Lord of the Deep 85. Desert Law 90.

Ted Tetzlaff World Premiere 40. Riff Raff 47. Fighting Father Dunne 48. A Dangerous Profession 49. Johnny Allegro 49. The Window 49. Gambling House 50. The White Tower 50. Under the Gun 50. The Treasure of Lost Canyon 52. Time Bomb 52. Son of Sinbad 55. The Young Land 57.

William Thiele Drei von der Tankstelle 30. Waltz Time 33. Lottery Lover 35. The Jungle Princess 36. Beg, Borrow or Steal 37. London by Night 37. Bad Little Angel 39. Bridal Suite 39. The Ghost Comes Home 40. Tarzan Triumphs 43. Tarzan's Desert Mystery 43. The Madonna's Secret 46.

Gerald Thomas The Vicious Circle 57. Time Lock 57. Carry On Sergeant 58. The Duke Wore Jeans 58. Carry On Nurse 59. Carry On Teacher 59. Please Turn Over 59. Carry On Constable 60. No Kidding 60. Watch Your Stern 60. Carry On Regardless 61. Raising the Wind 61. Carry On Cruising 62. The Iron Maiden 62. Twice round the Daffodils 62. Carry On Cabby 63. Nurse on Wheels 63. Carry On Cleo 64. Carry On Jack 64. Carry On Spying 64. Carry On Cowboy 65. The Big Job 65. Carry On Screaming 66. Carry On – Don't Lose Your Head 66. Carry On – Follow That Camel 66. Carry On Doctor 68. Carry On up the Khyber 68. Carry On Again Doctor 69. Carry On Camping 69. Carry On Loving 70. Carry On up the Jungle 70. Carry On at Your Convenience 71. Carry On Henry 71. Bless This House 72. Carry On Abroad 72. Carry On Matron 72. Carry On Girls 73. Carry On Dick 74. Carry On Behind 75. Carry On England 76. Carry On Emmannuelle 78. The Second Victory 86. Carry On Columbus 92.

Ralph Thomas Once Upon a Dream 48. Helter Skelter 49. Traveller's Joy 49. The Clouded Yellow 50. Appointment with Venus 51. Venetian Bird 52. A Day to Remember 53. Doctor in the House 54. Mad about Men 54. Above Us the Waves 55. Doctor at Sea 55. Checkpoint 56. The Iron Petticoat 56. Campbell's Kingdom 57. Doctor at Large 57. A Tale of Two Cities 58. The Wind Cannot Read 58. The Thirty-Nine Steps 59. Upstairs and Downstairs 59. Conspiracy of Hearts 60. Doctor in Love 60. No Love for Johnnie 60. A Pair of Briefs 61. No, My Darling Daughter 61. The Wild and the Willing 62. Doctor in Distress 63. Hot Enough for June 63. The High Bright Sun 65. Deadlier than the Male 66. Doctor in Clover 66. Nobody Runs Forever 68. Some Girls Do 69. Doctor in Trouble 70. Percy 71. Quest for Love 71. It's a 2'6" above the Ground World 72. Percy's Progress 74.

J. Lee Thompson Conquest of the Planet of the Apes 72. St Ives 76. The Passage 78. Caboblanco 81. The Ambassador 84. Murphy's Law 86.

Richard Thorpe The Lone Defender 30. King of the Wild 31. Cheating Cheaters 34. Tarzan Escapes 36. The Voice of Bugle Ann 36. Dangerous Number 37. Double Wedding 37. Man Proof 37. Night Must Fall 37. Love Is a Headache 38. The Crowd Roars 38. The First Hundred Years 38. The Toy Wife 38. Three Loves Has Nancy 38. Huckleberry Finn 39. Tarzan Finds a Son! 39. The Earl of Chicago 39. The Bad Man 40. Twenty Mule Team 40. Wyoming 40. Barnacle Bill 41. Tarzan's Secret Treasure 41. Apache Trail 42. Joe Smith American 42. Tarzan's New York Adventure 42. White Cargo 42. Above Suspicion 43. Cry Havoc 43. Three Hearts for Julia 43. Two Girls and a Sailor 44. Her Highness and the Bellboy 45. Thrill of a Romance 45. Fiesta 47. This Time for Keeps 47. A Date with Judy 48. On an Island with You 48. Big Jack 49. Black Hand 49. Challenge to Lassie 49. Malaya 49. Three Little Words 50. The Great Caruso 51. The Unknown Man 51. Vengeance Valley 51. Carbine Williams 52. It's a Big Country 52. Ivanhoe 52. The Prisoner of Zenda 52. All the Brothers Were Valiant 53. Knights of the Round Table 53. The Girl Who Had Everything 53. Athena 54. The Student Prince 54. Quentin Durward 55. The Prodigal 55. Ten Thousand Bedrooms 56. Jailhouse Rock 57. Tip on a Dead Jockey 57. House of the Seven Hawks 59. The Killers of Kilimanjaro 59. The Tartars 60. The Honeymoon Machine 61. The Horizontal Lieutenant 62. Follow the Boys 63. Fun in Acapulco 63. The Golden Head 64. The Truth about Spring 64. That Funny Feeling 65.

Eric Till Hot Millions 68. The Walking Stick 70. It Shouldn't Happen to a Vet 76. Improper Channels 79. Oh, What a Night 92.

James Tinling Arizona to Broadway 33. Love Time 34. Under the Pampas Moon 35. Champagne Charlie 36. Angel's Holiday 37. Change of Heart 37. Forty-Five Fathers 37. Sing and Be Happy 37. The Great Hospital Mystery 37. The Holy Terror 37. Mr Moto's Gamble 38. Sharpshooters 38. Dangerous Millions 46. Deadline for Murder 46. Rendezvous 24 46.

James Toback Fingers 77. Love and Money 80. Exposed 83. The Pick-Up Artist 87. The Big Bang 89. Two Girls and a Guy 97. Black and White 99.

Norman Tokar Big Red 62. Savage Sam 62. A Tiger Walks 63. Those Calloways 64. The Ugly Dachshund 65. Follow Me Boys 66. The Happiest Millionaire 67. The Horse in the Grey Flannel Suit 69. The Boatniks 70. Snowball Express 72. The Apple Dumpling Gang 74. No Deposit, No Return 76. Candleshoe 77. The Cat from Outer Space 78.

Giuseppe Tornatore Cinema Paradiso 89. Stanno Tutti Bene 90. The Starmaker 94. The Legend of 1900 98. Malèna 00.

Jacques Tourneur Nick Carter, Master Detective 39. Cat People 42. I Walked with a Zombie 43. The Leopard Man 43. Days of Glory 44. Experiment Perilous 44. Canyon Passage 46. Out of the Past 47. Berlin Express 48. Easy Living 49. Circle of Danger 50. Stars in My Crown 50. The Flame and the Arrow 50. Anne of the Indies 51. Way of a Gaucho 52. Appointment in Honduras 53. Great Day in the Morning 55. Wichita 55. Nightfall 56. Night of the Demon 57. The Fearmakers 58. Timbuktu 58. The Giant of Marathon 60. The Comedy of Terrors 63. City under the Sea 65.

Wendy Toye The Stranger Left No Card 52. The Teckman Mystery 54. Three Cases of Murder 54. All for Mary 55. Raising a Riot 55. On the Twelfth Day 56. True as a Turtle 56. We Joined the Navy 62.

John Trent Homer 70. Sunday in the Country 75. Find the Lady 76. Middle Age Crazy 80. Best Revenge 83.

Margarethe von Trotta Sisters or The Balance of Happiness 79. The German Sisters 81. Friends and Husbands 82. Rosa Luxemburg 86. Three Sisters 87. The Promise 94.

François Truffaut The Four Hundred Blows 59. Shoot the Pianist 60. Jules et Jim 62. Silken Skin 64. Fahrenheit 451 66. Stolen Kisses 68. The Bride Wore Black 68. The Mississippi Mermaid 69. Bed and Board 70. L'Enfant Sauvage 70. Anne and Muriel 71. Une Belle Fille Comme Moi 72. Day for Night 73. The Story of Adèle H 75. Small Change 76. The Man Who Loved Women 77. Love on the Run 79. The Last Metro 80. The Woman Next Door 81. Finally, Sunday 83.

Michael Tuchner Villain 71. Fear Is the Key 72. Mister Quilp 75. The Likely Lads 76. Trenchcoat 83. Wilt 89.

Montgomery Tully Murder in Reverse 45. Mrs Fitzherbert 47. Boys in Brown 49. A Tale of Five Cities 51. The Diamond 54. The Glass Cage 54. Escapement 57. No Road Back 57. The Diplomatic Corpse 58. The Third Alibi 61. Master Spy 63. Battle Beneath the Earth 67.

Jon Turteltaub 3 Ninjas 92. Cool Runnings 93. While You Were Sleeping 95. Phenomenon 96. Instinct 99. Disney's The Kid 00.

Frank Tuttle The Studio Murder Mystery 29. Her Wedding Night 30. Love among the Millionaires 30. Paramount on Parade 30. True to the Navy 30. It Pays to Advertise 31. The Big Broadcast 32. This Is the Night 32. Dangerously Yours 33. Roman Scandals 33. Here Is My Heart 34. Ladies Should Listen 34. All the King's Horses 35. Springtime for Henry 35. The Glass Key 35. Two for Tonight 35. College Holiday 36. Waikiki Wedding 37. Dr Rhythm 38. Paris Honeymoon 38. Charlie McCarthy, Detective 39. I Stole a Million 39. Lucky Jordan 42. This Gun for Hire 42. Hostages 43. The Hour before the Dawn 44. Don Juan Quilligan 45. The Great John L. 45. Suspense 46. Swell Guy 46. The Magic Face 51. Hell on Frisco Bay 55. A Cry in the Night 56. Island of Lost Women 58.

Derek Twist The End of the River 47. All Over the Town 49. Green Grow the Rushes 51. Police Dog 55. RX Murder 58.

Edgar G. Ulmer People on Sunday 29. The Black Cat 34. Damaged Lives 37. Isle of Forgotten Sins 43. Bluebeard 44. Detour 45. Club Havana 46. Her Sister's Secret 46. The Strange Woman 46. Wife of Monte Cristo 46. Carnegie Hall 47. Ruthless 48. St Benny the Dip 51. The Man from Planet X 51. Babes in Baghdad 52. The Naked Dawn 56. Daughter of Dr Jekyll 57. Beyond the Time Barrier 59. Hannibal 59. Journey Beneath the Desert 61. The Cavern 66.

Ron Underwood Tremors 89. City Slickers 91. Heart and Souls 93. Speechless 94. Mighty Joe Young 98. The Adventuires of Pluto Nash 02.

Peter Ustinov School for Secrets 46. Vice Versa 47. Private Angelo 49. Romanoff and Juliet 61. Billy Budd 62. Lady L 65. Hammersmith Is Out 72. Memed My Hawk 84.

Roger Vadim And God Created Woman 57. Heaven Fell That Night 58. Les Liaisons Dangereuses 59. Blood and Roses 60. La Ronde 64. Barbarella 67. Histoires Extraordinaires 68. Pretty Maids All in a Row 71. Charlotte 74. Night Games 80. And God Created Woman 87.

W. S. Van Dyke White Shadows in the South Seas 28. The Pagan 29. Trader Horn 30. Cuban Love Song 31. Guilty Hands 31. Never the Twain Shall Meet 31. Night Court 32. Tarzan the Ape Man 32. Eskimo 33. Penthouse 33. The Prizefighter and the Lady 33. Forsaking All Others 34. Hide-out 34. Laughing Boy 34. Manhattan Melodrama 34. The Thin Man 34. I Live My Life 35. Naughty Marietta 35. After the Thin Man 36. His Brother's Wife 36. Love on the Run 36. Rose Marie 36. San Francisco 36. The Devil Is a Sissy 36. Personal Property 37. Rosalie 37. They Gave Him a Gun 37. Marie Antoinette 38. Stand Up and Fight 38. Sweethearts 38. Another Thin Man 39. I Take This Woman 39. It's a Wonderful World 39. Bitter Sweet 40. I Love You Again 40. Rage in Heaven 41. The Feminine Touch 41. Cairo 42. Dr Kildare's Victory 42. I Married an Angel 42. Journey for Margaret 42.

Gus Van Sant Mala Noche 88. Drugstore Cowboy 89. My Own Private Idaho 91. Even Cowgirls Get the Blues 93. To Die For 95. Good Will Hunting 97. Psycho 98. Finding Forrester 00.

Marcel Varnel Chandu the Magician 32. The Silent Witness 32. Dance Band 35. Royal Cavalcade 35. All In 36. Good Morning Boys 37. O-Kay for Sound 37. Oh Mr Porter 37. Alf's Button Afloat 38. Ask a Policeman 38. Convict 99 38. Hey! Hey! USA! 38. Old Bones of the River 38. Band Waggon 39. The Frozen Limits 39. Where's That Fire? 39. Gasbags 40. Let George Do It 40. Neutral Port 40. Hi Gang 41. I Thank You 41. South American George 41. The Ghost of St Michael's 41. Turned Out Nice Again 41. Get Cracking 42. King Arthur Was a Gentleman 42. Much Too Shy 42. Bell Bottom George 43. He Snoops to Conquer 44. I Didn't Do It 45. George in Civvy Street 46. This Man Is Mine 46.

Paul Verhoeven Turkish Delight 73. Keetje Tippel 75. Spetters 80. The Fourth Man 83. Flesh & Blood 85. Robocop 87. Total Recall 90. Basic Instinct 91. Showgirls 95. Starship Troopers 97. Hollow Man 00.

Henri Verneuil Forbidden Fruit 52. The Lovers of Lisbon 54. The Sheep Has Five Legs 54. The Cow and I 59. A Monkey in Winter 62. Guns for San Sebastian 67. The Twenty-Fifth Hour 67. The Burglars 71. The Serpent 74. Night Caller 75.

Charles Vidor The Mask of Fu Manchu 32. Double Door 34. His Family Tree 35. Strangers All 35. The Arizonian 35. Muss 'em Up 36. A Doctor's Diary 37. The Great Gambini 37. Blind Alley 39. Those High Grey Walls 39. My Son, My Son 40. The Lady in Question 40. Ladies in Retirement 41. New York Town 41. The Tuttles of Tahiti 42. Desperadoes 43. A Song to Remember 44. Cover Girl 44. Together Again 44. Gilda 46. The Loves of Carmen 48. Thunder in the East 51. Hans Christian Andersen 52. It's a Big Country 52. Rhapsody 54. Love Me or Leave Me 55. The Swan 56. A Farewell to Arms 57. The Joker Is Wild 57. Song without End 60.

King Vidor The Big Parade 25. Bardelys the Magnificent 26. La Bohème 26. Show People 28. The Crowd 28. The Patsy 28. Hallelujah! 29. Not So Dumb 29. Billy the Kid 30. Street Scene 31. The Champ 31. Bird of Paradise 32. Cynara 32. The Stranger's Return 33. Our Daily Bread 34. So Red the Rose 35. The Wedding Night 35. The Texas Rangers 36. Stella Dallas 37. The Citadel 38. Comrade X 40. H.M. Pulham Esquire 40. Northwest Passage (Part One, Rogers' Rangers) 40. An American Romance 44. Duel in the Sun 46. On Our Merry Way 48. Beyond the Forest 49. The Fountainhead 49. Lightning Strikes Twice 51. Japanese War Bride 52. Ruby Gentry 52. Man without a Star 55. War and Peace 56. Solomon and Sheba 59.

Berthold Viertel The Man from Yesterday 32. The Wiser Sex 32. Little Friend 34. The Passing of the Third Floor Back 35. Rhodes of Africa 36.

Luchino Visconti Ossessione 42. La Terra Trema 48. Bellissima 51. Senso 53. Rocco and His Brothers 60. The Leopard 63. The Damned 69. Death in Venice 71. Ludwig 72. Conversation Piece 74. The Innocent 76.

Bernard Vorhaus The Ghost Camera 33. The Last Journey 35. Cotton Queen 37. Dusty Ermine 38. Fisherman's Wharf 39. Meet Dr Christian 39. Three Faces West 40. Lady from Louisiana 41. Ice-Capades Revue 42. Bury Me Dead 47. The Amazing Dr X 48.

George Waggner Man Made Monster 40. Horror Island 41. South of Tahiti 41. The Wolf Man 41. The Climax 44. Frisco Sal 45. Shady Lady 45. Tangier 46. Gunfighters 47. The Fighting Kentuckian 49. Operation Pacific 50.

Andrzej Wajda Generation 54. Kanal 56. Ashes and Diamonds 58. Man of Marble 78. The Conductor 79. Man of Iron 81. Danton 82. A Love in Germany 83. Korczak 90.

Hal Walker Duffy's Tavern 45. Out of this World 45. Road to Utopia 45. The Stork Club 45. My Friend Irma Goes West 50. At War with the Army 51. That's My Boy 51. Road to Bali 52. Sailor Beware 52.

Norman Walker The Middle Watch 30. Turn of the Tide 35. Our Fighting Navy 37. Sunset in Vienna 37. The Man at the Gate 41. Hard Steel 42. The Great Mr Handel 42. They Knew Mr Knight 45.

Peter Walker The Flesh and Blood Show 72. The Four Dimensions of Greta 72. Tiffany Jones 73. Frightmare 74. House of Whipcord 74. House of Mortal Sin 75. Schizo 76. The Comeback 78. House of the Long Shadows 83.

Stuart Walker Evenings for Sale 32. The Misleading Lady 32. Tonight Is Ours 32. The Eagle and the Hawk 33. White Woman 33. Great Expectations 34. Romance in the Rain 34. The Mystery of Edwin Drood 35. Werewolf of London 35.

Richard Wallace Shopworn Angel 28. Innocents of Paris 29. Seven Days Leave 29. The Right to Love 30. Man of the World 31. Thunder Below 32. Tomorrow and Tomorrow 32. The Masquerader 33. The Little Minister 34. Wedding Present 36. Blossoms on Broadway 37. John Meade's Woman 37. The Young in Heart 38. The Underpup 39. Captain Caution 40. A Girl, a Guy and a Gob 41. She Knew All the Answers 41. The Obliging Young Lady 41. The Wife Takes a Flyer 42. A Night to Remember 43. Bombardier 43. My Kingdom for a Cook 43. The Fallen Sparrow 43. Bride by Mistake 44. Because of Him 45. It's in the Bag 45. Kiss and Tell 45. Framed 47. Sinbad the Sailor 47. Tycoon 47. Let's Live a Little 48. A Kiss for Corliss 49. Adventure in Baltimore 49.

Tom Walls Canaries Sometimes Sing 30. Plunder 30. Rookery Nook 30. Tons of Money 30. A Night Like This 32. Thark 32. A Cuckoo in the Nest 33. Turkey Time 33. A Cup of Kindness 34. Dirty Work 34. Fighting Stock 35. Foreign Affaires 35. Stormy Weather 35. Dishonour Bright 36. Pot Luck 36. For Valour 37. Old Iron 38. Second Best Bed 38.

Raoul Walsh The Thief of Bagdad 24. Sadie Thompson 28. In Old Arizona 29. The Cockeyed World 29. The Big Trail 30. The Man Who Came Back 30. The Yellow Ticket 31. Women of All Nations 31. Me and My Gal 32. Going Hollywood 33. The Bowery 33. Baby Face Harrington 35. Every Night at Eight 35. Big Brown Eyes 36. Klondike Annie 36. O.H.M.S. 36. Spendthrift 36. Artists and Models 37. Jump for Glory 37. College Swing 38. St Louis Blues 39. The Roaring Twenties 39. Dark Command 40. They Drive by Night 40. High Sierra 41. Manpower 41. The Strawberry Blonde 41. They Died with Their Boots On 41. Desperate Journey 42. Gentleman Jim 42. Background to Danger 43. Northern Pursuit 43. Uncertain Glory 44. Objective Burma! 45. Salty O'Rourke 45. The Horn Blows at Midnight 45. Cheyenne 47. Pursued 47. The Man I Love 47. Fighter Squadron 48. One Sunday Afternoon 48. Silver River 48. Colorado Territory 49. White Heat 49. Along the Great Divide 50. Captain Horatio Hornblower RN 51. Distant Drums 51. Blackbeard the Pirate 52. Glory Alley 52. The Lawless Breed 52. The World in His Arms 52. A Lion Is in the Streets 53. Gun Fury 53. Sea Devils 53. Saskatchewan 54. Battle Cry 55. The Tall Men 55. The King and Four Queens 56. The Revolt of Mamie Stover 56. Band of Angels 57. The Naked and the Dead 58. The Sheriff of Fractured Jaw 58. A Private's Affair 59. Esther and the King 60. Marines Let's Go 61. A Distant Trumpet 64.

Charles Walters Good News 47. Easter Parade 48. The Barkleys of Broadway 49. Summer Stock 50. Texas Carnival 51. Three Guys Named Mike 51. The Belle of New York 52. Dangerous When Wet 53. Easy to Love 53. Torch Song 53. The Glass Slipper 54. The Tender Trap 55. High Society 56. Don't Go Near the Water 57. Ask Any Girl 59. Please Don't Eat the Daisies 60. Two Loves 61. Jumbo 62. The Unsinkable Molly Brown 64. Walk, Don't Run 66.

Wayne Wang Chan Is Missing 81. Dim Sum: a Little Bit of Heart 85. Slamdance 87. Eat a Bowl of Tea 89. Life Is Cheap … But Toilet Paper Is Expensive 90. The Joy Luck Club 93. Blue in the Face 95. Smoke 95. Chinese Box 97. Anywhere But Here 99. The Center of the World 01. Maid in Manhattan 02.

David S. Ward Cannery Row 82. Major League 89. King Ralph 91. The Program 93. Major League II 94. Down Periscope 96.

Charles Marquis Warren Little Big Horn 51. Hellgate 52. Arrowhead 53. Flight to Tangier 53. Seven Angry Men 54. Tension at Table Rock 56. Back from the Dead 57. Trooper Hook 57. Cattle Empire 58. Charro 69.

John Waters Beau Sabreur 28. The Mighty McGurk 46. Desperate Living 77. Polyester 81. Hairspray 88. Cry-Baby 90. Serial Mom 94. Pecker 98. Cecil B. Demented 00.

Harry Watt Night Mail 36. London Can Take It 40. Target for Tonight 41. Nine Men 43. Fiddlers Three 44. The Overlanders 46. Eureka Stockade 48. Where No Vultures Fly 51. West of Zanzibar 54. The Siege of Pinchgut 59.

Jack Webb Dragnet 54. Pete Kelly's Blues 55. The DI 57. –30– 59. The Last Time I Saw Archie 61.

Robert D. Webb The Caribbean Mystery 45. Beneath the Twelve Mile Reef 53. The Glory Brigade 53. Seven Cities of Gold 55. White Feather 55. Love Me Tender 56. On the Threshold of Space 56. The Proud Ones 56. The Way to the Gold 57. Guns of the Timberland 60. Pirates of Tortuga 61. Capetown Affair 67.

Peter Weir The Cars that Ate Paris 74. Picnic at Hanging Rock 75. The Last Wave 77. Gallipoli 81. The Year of Living Dangerously 82. Witness 85. The Mosquito Coast 86. Dead Poets Society 89. Green Card 90. Fearless 93. The Truman Show 98.

Don Weis Bannerline 51. A Slight Case of Larceny 52. It's a Big Country 52. You for Me 52. Half a Hero 53. I Love Melvin 53. Remains to Be Seen 53. The Affairs of Dobie Gillis 53. The Adventures of Hajji Baba 54. Ride the High Iron 57. The Gene Krupa Story 59. Critic's Choice 63. Looking for Love 64. Pajama Party 64. Billie 65. The Ghost in the Invisible Bikini 66. Did You Hear the One about the Traveling Saleslady? 67. The King's Pirate 67.

Orson Welles Citizen Kane 41. Journey into Fear 42. The Magnificent Ambersons 42. The Stranger 46. Macbeth 48. The Lady from Shanghai 48. Othello 51. Confidential Report 55. Touch of Evil 58. The Trial 62. Chimes at Midnight 66. The Immortal Story 68. F for Fake 73.

William A. Wellman Wings 27. Beggars of Life 28. Young Eagles 30. Night Nurse 31. Other Men's Women 31. Public Enemy 31. The Star Witness 31. Love Is a Racket 32. So Big 32. The Conquerors 32. The Hatchet Man 32. Central Airport 33. College Coach 33. Frisco Jenny 33. Heroes for Sale 33. Lilly Turner 33. Midnight Mary 33. Wild Boys of the Road 33. Looking for Trouble 34. Stingaree 34. The President Vanishes 34. Call of the Wild 35. Robin Hood of El Dorado 36. Small Town Girl 36. A Star Is Born 37. Nothing Sacred 37. Men with Wings 38. Beau Geste 39. The Light that Failed 39. Reaching for the Sun 41. The Great Man's Lady 41. Roxie Hart 42. Thunderbirds 42. Lady of Burlesque 43. The Ox-Bow Incident 43. Buffalo Bill 44. The Story of GI Joe 45. This Man's Navy 45. Gallant Journey 46. Magic Town 47. The Iron Curtain 48. Yellow Sky 48. Battleground 49. The Happy Years 50. The Next Voice You Hear 50. Across the Wide Missouri 51. Westward the Women 51. It's a Big Country 52. My Man and I 52. Island in the Sky 53. The High and the Mighty 54. Track of the Cat 54. Blood Alley 55. Goodbye My Lady 56. Darby's Rangers 57. Lafayette Escadrille 57.

Wim Wenders The Goalkeeper's Fear of the Penalty Kick 71. Alice in the Cities 74. Kings of the Road 75. The American Friend 77. Lightning over Water 80. Hammett 82. The State of Things 82. Paris, Texas 84. Wings of Desire 87. Notebook on Cities and Clothes 89. Until the End of the World 91. Faraway, So Close 93. Beyond the Clouds 95. The End of Violence 97. Buena Vista Social Club 98. The Million Dollar Hotel 99.

Paul Wendkos The Case against Brooklyn 58. Battle of the Coral Sea 59. Face of a Fugitive 59. Gidget 59. Angel Baby 60. Because They're Young 60. Johnny Tiger 66. Attack on the Iron Coast 67. Guns of the Magnificent Seven 69. Cannon for Cordoba 70. Hell Boats 70. The Mephisto Waltz 71. Special Delivery 76.

Alfred Werker Annabelle's Affairs 31. Bachelor's Affairs 31. Rackety Rax 32. Advice to the Lovelorn 33. Hello Sister 33. The House of Rothschild 34. You Belong to Me 34. Stolen Harmony 35. Love in Exile 36. Big Town Girl 37. City Girl 37. We Have Our Moments 37. Wild and Woolly 37. Gateway

38. Kidnapped 38. It Could Happen to You 39. News Is Made at Night 39. The Adventures of Sherlock Holmes 39. The Reluctant Dragon 41. A-Haunting We Will Go 42. The Mad Martindales 42. Whispering Ghosts 42. Shock 46. Pirates of Monterey 47. Repeat Performance 47. He Walked by Night 48. Lost Boundaries 49. Sealed Cargo 51. Walk East on Beacon 52. Devil's Canyon 53. The Last Posse 53. Canyon Crossroads 54. At Gunpoint 55. Rebel in Town 56.

Lina Wertmüller Violent City 70. Seven Beauties 75. The End of the World (in our usual bed in a night full of rain) 78. Blood Feud 79. Camorra: the Naples Connection 85.

James Whale Journey's End 30. Frankenstein 31. Waterloo Bridge 31. The Impatient Maiden 32. The Old Dark House 32. By Candlelight 33. The Invisible Man 33. The Kiss before the Mirror 33. One More River 34. The Bride of Frankenstein 35. Remember Last Night? 36. Showboat 36. The Great Garrick 37. The Road Back 37. Port of Seven Seas 38. Sinners in Paradise 38. Wives under Suspicion 38. The Man in the Iron Mask 39. Green Hell 40. They Dare Not Love 41.

Claude Whatham That'll Be the Day 73. All Creatures Great and Small 74. Swallows and Amazons 74. Sweet William 80. Buddy's Song 90.

Tim Whelan When Knights Were Bold 29. Aunt Sally 33. It's a Boy 33. The Camels are Coming 34. The Murder Man 35. The Perfect Gentleman 35. Two's Company 36. Action for Slander 37. Farewell Again 37. Smash and Grab 37. The Mill on the Floss 37. St Martin's Lane 38. The Divorce of Lady X 38. Q Planes 39. Ten Days in Paris 39. The Thief of Baghdad 40. International Lady 41. The Mad Doctor 41. Nightmare 42. Seven Days Leave 42. Twin Beds 42. Higher and Higher 43. Swing Fever 43. Step Lively 44. Badman's Territory 46. This Was a Woman 48. Rage at Dawn 55. Texas Lady 55.

Richard Whorf Blonde Fever 44. The Hidden Eye 45. The Sailor Takes a Wife 45. Till the Clouds Roll By 46. It Happened in Brooklyn 47. Love from a Stranger 47. Luxury Liner 48. Champagne for Caesar 50. The Groom Wore Spurs 51.

Bo Widerberg Adalen 31 69. The Ballad of Joe Hill 71. The Man on the Roof 76. The Man from Majorca 84. Love Lessons 95.

Crane Wilbur I Am Not Afraid 39. Canon City 48. The Story of Molly X 49. Inside the Walls of Folsom Prison 51. The Bat 59.

Fred M. Wilcox Lassie Come Home 43. The Hills of Home 48. Three Daring Daughters 48. The Secret Garden 49. Shadow in the Sky 51. Code Two 53. Tennessee Champ 54. Forbidden Planet 56. I Passed for White 60.

Herbert Wilcox Dawn 28. Goodnight Vienna 32. Bitter Sweet 33. The Little Damozel 33. Yes Mr Brown 33. Nell Gwyn 34. Limelight 35. Peg of Old Drury 35. This'll Make You Whistle 36. London Melody 37. The Three Maxims 37. Victoria the Great 37. Sixty Glorious Years 38. Nurse Edith Cavell 39. Irene 40. No No Nanette 40. Sunny 41. They Flew Alone 41. Forever and a Day 43. Yellow Canary 43. I Live in Grosvenor Square 45. Piccadilly Incident 46. The Courtneys of Curzon Street 47. Elizabeth of Ladymead 48. Spring in Park Lane 48. Maytime in Mayfair 49. Into the Blue 50. Odette 50. The Lady with a Lamp 51. Derby Day 52. Trent's Last Case 52. Laughing Anne 53. Lilacs in the Spring 54. Trouble in the Glen 54. King's Rhapsody 55. My Teenage Daughter 56. The Man Who Wouldn't Talk 57. These Dangerous Years 57. The Lady Is a Square 58. The Heart of a Man 59.

Cornel Wilde Storm Fear 55. The Devil's Hairpin 57. Maracaibo 58. Lancelot and Guinevere 62. The Naked Prey 66. Beach Red 67. No Blade of Grass 70. Shark's Treasure 74.

Billy Wilder The Major and the Minor 42. Five Graves to Cairo 43. Double Indemnity 44. The Lost Weekend 45. A Foreign Affair 48. The Emperor Waltz 48. Sunset Boulevard 50. Ace in the Hole 51. Stalag 17 53. Sabrina 54. The Seven Year Itch 55. Love in the Afternoon 57. The Spirit of St Louis 57. Witness for the Prosecution 57. Some Like It Hot 59. The Apartment 60. One, Two, Three 61. Irma La Douce 63. Kiss Me Stupid 64. The Fortune Cookie 66. The Private Life of Sherlock Holmes 70. Avanti! 72. The Front Page 74. Fedora 78. Buddy Buddy 81.

Hugh Wilson Police Academy 84. Rustler's Rhapsody 85. Burglar 87. Guarding Tess 94. The First Wives Club 96. Blast from the Past 99. Dudley Do-Right 99.

Richard Wilson Man with the Gun 55. The Big Boodle 57. Raw Wind in Eden 58. Al Capone 59. Pay or Die! 60. Wall of Noise 63. Invitation to a Gunfighter 64. Three in the Attic 68.

Simon Wincer Harlequin 80. Phar Lap 83. D.A.R.Y.L. 85. The Lighthorsemen 88. Quigley Down Under 90. Harley Davidson and the Marlboro Man 91. Free Willy 93. Lightning Jack 94. Operation Dumbo Drop 95. The Phantom 96. Crocodile Dundee in Los Angeles 01.

Bretaigne Windust June Bride 48. Winter Meeting 48. Perfect Strangers 50. Pretty Baby 50. The Enforcer 50. Face to Face 52.

Michael Winner Play It Cool 62. Cool Mikado 63. West Eleven 63. The System 64. You Must Be Joking 65. I'll Never Forget Whatshisname 67. The Jokers 67. Hannibal Brooks 68. Lawman 70. The Games 70. Chato's Land 71. The Nightcomers 71. Scorpio 72. The Mechanic 72. The Stone Killer 73. Death Wish 74. The Sentinel 76. Won Ton Ton, the Dog Who Saved Hollywood 76. The Big Sleep 77. Firepower 79. Death Wish 2 81. The Wicked Lady 83. Scream for Help 84. Death Wish 3 85. A Chorus of Disapproval 88. Appointment with Death 88. Bullseye! 90. Dirty Weekend 93. Parting Shots 98.

Michael Winterbottom Butterfly Kiss 95. Jude 96. Welcome to Sarajevo 97. I Want You 98. With or Without You 99. Wonderland 99. The Claim 00. 24 Hour Party People 02. In This World 02.

Robert Wise Mademoiselle Fifi 44. The Curse of the Cat People 44. A Game of Death 45. The Body Snatcher 45. Criminal Court 46. Born to Kill 47. Blood on the Moon 48. Mystery in Mexico 48. The Set Up 49. Three Secrets 50. Two Flags West 50. The Captive City 51. The Day the Earth Stood Still 51. The House on Telegraph Hill 51. Something for the Birds 52. Destination Gobi 53. So Big 53. The Desert Rats 53. Executive Suite 54. Helen of Troy 55. Somebody Up There Likes Me 56. Tribute to a Bad Man 56. This Could Be the Night 57. Until They Sail 57. I Want to Live! 58. Run Silent Run Deep 58. Odds against Tomorrow 59. West Side Story 61. Two for the Seesaw 62. The Haunting 63. The Sound of Music 65. The Sand Pebbles 66. Star! 68. The Andromeda Strain 70. Two People 73. The Hindenburg 75. Audrey Rose 77. Star Trek: The Motion Picture 79. Rooftops 89.

William Witney SOS Coast Guard 37. The Painted Stallion 37. Zorro Rides Again 37. Dick Tracy Returns 38. Fighting Devil Dogs 38. Hawk of the Wilderness 38. The Lone Ranger 38. Daredevils of the Red Circle 39. Dick Tracy's G-Men 39. The Lone Ranger Rides Again 39. Zorro's Fighting Legion 39. Adventures of Red Ryder 40. Drums of Fu Manchu 40. King of the Royal Mounted 40. The Mysterious Dr Satan 40. Adventures of Captain Marvel 41. Dick Tracy vs Crime Inc 41. Jungle Girl 41. King of the Texas Rangers 41. King of the Mounties 42. Perils of Nyoka 42. Spy Smasher 42. G-Men vs The Black Dragon 43. The Crimson Ghost 46. Bells of St Angelo 47. Under California Stars 48. The Outcast 54. Santa Fe Passage 55. Stranger at My Door 56. The Bonnie Parker Story 58. The Cool and the Crazy 58. Master of the World 61. Apache Rifles 64. Arizona Raiders 65. Forty Guns to Apache Pass 66. I Escaped from Devil's Island 73.

John Woo A Better Tomorrow 87. A Better Tomorrow II 87. Just Heroes 89. The Killer 89. Bullet in the Head 90. Once a Thief 91. Hard Boiled 92. Hard Target 93. John Woo's Once a Thief 95. Broken Arrow 96. Face/Off 97. Mission: Impossible 2 00. Windtalkers 02.

Sam Wood Rookies 27. Paid 30. Way for a Sailor 30. The Man in Possession 31. The New Adventures of Get-Rich-Quick Wallingford 31. Huddle 32. Prosperity 32. Christopher Bean 33. Hold Your Man 33. The Barbarian 33. Stamboul Quest 34. A Night at the Opera 35. Let 'Em Have It 35. Whipsaw 35. The Unguarded Hour 36. A Day at the Races 37. Madame X 37. Navy Blue and Gold 37. Lord Jeff 38. Stablemates 38. Gone with the Wind 39. Goodbye Mr Chips 39. Raffles 39. Kitty Foyle 40. Our Town 40. Rangers of Fortune 40. The Devil and Miss Jones 41. Kings Row 42. The Pride of the Yankees 42. For Whom the Bell Tolls 43. Saratoga Trunk 43. Casanova Brown 44. Guest Wife 45. Heartbeat 46. Ivy 47. Ambush 49. Command Decision 49. The Stratton Story 49.

Arthur Woods Give Her a Ring 34. Radio Parade of 1935 34. Drake of England 35. Music Hath Charms 35. You Live and Learn 37. They Drive by Night 38. The Nursemaid Who Disappeared 39. Busman's Honeymoon 40.

Mack Wright Haunted Gold 32. Somewhere in Sonora 33. The Man from Monterey 33. Robinson Crusoe of Clipper Island 36. The Vigilantes are Coming 36. The Great Adventures of Wild Bill Hickok 38. The Sea Hound 47.

William Wyler Hell's Heroes 30. The Storm 30. A House Divided 31. Tom Brown of Culver 32. Counsellor at Law 33. Glamour 34. The Gay Deception 35. The Good Fairy 35. Come and Get It 36. Dodsworth 36. These Three 36. Dead End 37. Jezebel 38. Wuthering Heights 39. The Letter 40. The Westerner 40. The Little Foxes 41. Mrs Miniver 42. The Memphis Belle 44. The Best Years of Our Lives 46. The Heiress 49. Detective Story 51. Carrie 52. Roman Holiday 53. The Desperate Hours 55. Friendly Persuasion 56. The Big Country 58. Ben-Hur 59. The Children's Hour 62. The Collector 65. How to Steal a Million 66. Funny Girl 68. The Liberation of L. B. Jones 70.

Jean Yarbrough The Devil Bat 41. Follow the Band 43. Good Morning, Judge 43. In Society 44. Twilight on the Prairie 44. Here Come the Coeds 45. On Stage Everybody 45. The Naughty Nineties 45. Under Western Skies 45. Cuban Pete 46. House of Horrors 46. She Wolf of London 46. The Brute Man 46. Henry the Rainmaker 48. The Challenge 48. The Creeper 48. According to Mrs Hoyle 51. Abbott and Costello Lost in Alaska 52. Jack and the Beanstalk 52.

Peter Yates Summer Holiday 62. One Way Pendulum 64. Robbery 67. Bullitt 68. John and Mary 69. Murphy's War 71. The Hot Rock 72. The Friends of Eddie Coyle 73. For Pete's Sake 74. Mother, Jugs and Speed 76. The Deep 77. Breaking Away 79. Eyewitness 81. Krull 83. The Dresser 83. Eleni 85. Suspect 87. The House on Carroll Street 88. An Innocent Man 89. Year of the Comet 92. Roommates 95. The Run of the Country 95.

Zhang Yimou Red Sorghum 87. Ju Dou 90. Raise the Red Lantern 91. The Story of Qiu Ju 92. To Live 94. Shanghai Triad 95. Not One Less 99. The Road Home 00. Happy Times 00.

Bud Yorkin Come Blow Your Horn 63. Never Too Late 65. Divorce American Style 67. Inspector Clouseau 68. Start the Revolution without Me 69. The Thief Who Came to Dinner 73. Twice in a Lifetime 85. Arthur 2: On the Rocks 88. Love Hurts 90.

Harold Young The Scarlet Pimpernel 34. 52nd Street 37. Let Them Live 37. Little Tough Guy 38. The Storm 38. Forgotten Woman 39. Newsboys' Home 39. Bachelor Daddy 41. The Mummy's Tomb 42. Hi Buddy 43. Hi Ya Chum 43. I Escaped from the Gestapo 43. Jungle Captive 45. The Frozen Ghost 45.

Robert Young Vampire Circus 71. Keep It Up Downstairs 76. The World Is Full of Married Men 79. Splitting Heirs 93. Fierce Creatures 97. Captain Jack 98.

Robert M. Young Rich Kids 79. One-Trick Pony 80. Extremities 86. Saving Grace 86. Nicky and Gino 88. Triumph of the Spirit 89. Talent for the Game 91. Caught 95.

Terence Young Corridor of Mirrors 48. One Night with You 48. Woman Hater 48. They Were Not Divided 50. Valley of Eagles 51. The Tall Headlines 52. The Red Beret 53. Storm over the Nile 55. That Lady 55. Safari 56. Zarak 56. Action of the Tiger 57. Serious Charge 59. Too Hot to Handle 60. Doctor No 62. From Russia with Love 63. The Amorous Adventures of Moll Flanders 65. Thunderball 65. Triple Cross 67. Wait until Dark 67. Mayerling 68. The Christmas Tree 69. Cold Sweat 70. Red Sun 71. The Valachi Papers 72. The Klansman 74. Bloodline 79. Inchon 81. The Jigsaw Man 85.

Brian Yuzna Re-Animator 2 89. Society 89. Necronomicon 93. Return of The Living Dead III 93. The Dentist 96. Progeny 98. The Dentist 2 98.

Mario Zampi Spy for a Day 39. The Fatal Night 48. Laughter in Paradise 51. Top Secret 52. Happy Ever After 54. Now and Forever 55. The Naked Truth 57. Too Many Crooks 58. Bottoms Up 59. Five Golden Hours 60.

Franco Zeffirelli The Taming of the Shrew 67. Romeo and Juliet 68. Brother Sun, Sister Moon 72. The Champ 79. Endless Love 81. La Traviata 82. Otello 86. Hamlet 91. Sparrow 93. Jane Eyre 96. Tea with Mussolini 99.

Robert Zemeckis I Wanna Hold Your Hand 78. Used Cars 80. Romancing the Stone 84. Back to the Future 85. Who Framed Roger Rabbit 88. Back to the Future II 89. Back to the Future III 90. Death Becomes Her 92. Forrest Gump 94. Contact 97. Cast Away 00. What Lies Beneath 00.

Howard Zieff Slither 72. Hearts of the West 75. House Calls 78. The Main Event 79. Private Benjamin 80. Unfaithfully Yours 83. The Dream Team 89. My Girl 91. My Girl II 94.

Fred Zinnemann People on Sunday 29. Eyes in the Night 42. Kid Glove Killer 42. The Seventh Cross 44. Little Mr Jim 46. My Brother Talks to Horses 46. Act of Violence 48. The Search 48. Teresa 50. The Men 50. High Noon 52. The Member of the Wedding 52. From Here to Eternity 53. Oklahoma! 55. A Hatful of Rain 57. The Nun's Story 59. The Sundowners 60. Behold a Pale Horse 64. A Man for All Seasons 66. The Day of the Jackal 73. Julia 77. Five Days One Summer 82.

David Zucker Airplane 80. Top Secret! 84. Ruthless People 86. The Naked Gun: From the Files of Police Squad 88. Naked Gun 2½;: The Smell of Fear 91. BASEketball 98.

Jerry Zucker Airplane 80. Top Secret! 84. Ruthless People 86. Ghost 90. First Knight 95. Rat Race 01.

Edward Zwick About Last Night 86. Glory 89. Leaving Normal 92. Legends of the Fall 94. Courage Under Fire 96. The Siege 98.

HALLIWELL'S WHO'S WHO IN THE MOVIES

THIRD EDITION

EDITED BY JOHN WALKER

'A filmic fountain of knowledge'
The Guardian

The 3rd edition of *Halliwell's Who's Who in the Movies* is the comprehensive guide to the Who, Why, What and How of cinema. Everything you ever wanted to know, explained with wit and concision:

The People:
Biographies and filmographies of stars, moguls, directors, writers and other key players. Plus fictional characters from Ali Baba to Zorro.

The Prizes:
Full year-by-year listings of the Oscars. Plus winners of the world's leading festivals and critics' awards.

The History:
The chronology of cinema from its beginnings to today. Plus a country-by-country breakdown of national film industries.

The Background:
Details of the studios, the genres, the technology and trends. Plus listings of the best film books and magazines.

Halliwell's Who's Who in the Movies is the essential companion to *Halliwell's Film and Video Guide*.

0 00 715085 7

£17.99